inwards ['ɪn·wərds] *adv* hacia adentro, para
dentro
I/O COMPUT *abbr of* **input/output** E/S
IOC *n abbr of* **International Olympic Committee** COI *m*
iodine ['aɪ·ə·daɪn] *n* yodo *m*
bring [brɪŋ] <brought, brought> *vt* **1.** ...
◆**bring about** *vt* **1.** (*cause to happen*) provocar ...
incense[1] ['ɪn·sents] *n* incienso *m*
incense[2] [ɪn·'sents] *vt* indignar
flexibility [ˌflek·sə·'bɪl·ə·t̬i] *n* **1.** (*of material*)
...
flexible ['flek·sə·bəl] *adj* **1.** (*pliable: material,*
...
flexitarian [flek·sɪ·'te·ri·ən] *n v* ...

child [tʃaɪld] <children> ...
be [bi] <was, been>
uncanny [ʌn·'kæn·i] *adj* <-ier, -iest> ...

abrupt [ə·'brʌpt] *adj* **1.** (*sudden*) repentino, -a;
(*change*) brusco, -a; ...
instructor [ɪn·'strʌk·tər] *n* **1.** (*teacher*) instruc-
tor(a) *m(f)*; **driving ~** profesor(a) *m(f)* de
autoescuela; ...
mute [mjut] **I.** *n* **1.** (*person*) mudo, -a *m, f*
2. MUS sordina *f* **II.** *vt* MUS poner sordina a
III. *adj* mudo, -a; ...
horse [hɔrs] *n* **1.** ZOOL caballo *m;* **to ride a ~**
montar a caballo; ►**to change ~s (in)
midstream** cambiar de parecer a mitad de
camino; **to get sth straight from the ~'s
mouth** saber algo de buena tinta; **don't look
a gift ~ in the mouth** *prov* a caballo regalado,
no le mires el dentado *prov;* ...

horn [hɔrn] *n* **1.** ZOOL cuerno *m* **2.** MUS trompa *f*
3. AUTO bocina *f* ...
wild [waɪld] **I.** *adj* **1.** (*not domesticated: animal, man*) salvaje; (*flower*) silvestre; (*horse*)
no domesticado, -a ...
celery ['sel·ə·ri] *n* apio *m,* panul *m CSur*

juice [dʒus] *n* **1.** (*drink*) zumo *m* **2.** (*of meat*)
jugo *m* **3.** *sl* (*electricity*) luz *f;* (*fuel*) sopa *f* ...

ego surfing *n* COMPUT *introducir en un buscador de Internet el propio nombre*
Sunday school *n* REL ≈ catequesis *f inv*
gallon ['gæl·ən] *n* galón *m* (*3,79 l*)

March [martʃ] *n* marzo *m; s.a.* **April**
tenth [tenθ] **I.** *adj* décimo, -a **II.** *n* **1.** (*order*)
décimo, -a *m, f* **2.** (*date*) diez *m* **3.** (*fraction*)
décimo *m;* (*part*) décima parte *f; s.a.* **eighth**

How to use the dictionary

All **entries** (including words, abbreviations, compounds,
variant spellings and cross-references) appear in alphabetical order and are printed in bold type.

English phrasal verbs come directly after the base verb
and are marked with a diamond (◆).

Superscript or raised numbers indicate identically spelled
words with different meanings (so-called **homographs**).
The International Phonetic Alphabet is used for all **phonetic transcriptions.** In Spanish, the common Latin-
American pronunciation is given first. Centered dots are
used for syllable division. Please note that this does not
always correspond with the orthographic division into syl-
lables.
Angle brackets are used to show **irregular plural forms**
and **forms of irregular verbs and adjectives.** Model
conjugations for Spanish (e.g. e→ie, z→c, etc.) can be
found in the appendix.

Feminine forms of nouns and adjectives are shown unless
they are identical to the masculine form. Spanish nouns
are followed by their gender.

Roman numerals are used for the **parts of speech** of a
word, and Arabic numerals for **sense divisions.**

The **swung dash** represents the entry word in examples
and idioms. The ► sign introduces **a block of set
expressions, idioms and proverbs.** Key words are
underlined as a guide.

Various kinds of **meaning indicators** are used to guide
you to the required translation:

• **Subject labels** (which indicate areas of specialization)

• **Definitions** or **synonyms,** typical **context partners,
subjects** or **objects** of the entry .

• **Regional vocabulary and variants** are shown both
as headwords and translations
• **Usage Labels** (which indicate restriction to a particular level or style of usage)

When a word or expression has no direct translation, an
explanation or **approximate equivalent** is given (≈).
Where a translation may be ambiguous, it is followed by
an explanation in brackets.

s. a. (see also) and *v.t.* (*véase también*) invite the reader
to consult a model en~~~~ ~~~ ~~~~~~~ ~~~~~~~~~~~

With the aid of the alphabetical thumb index overleaf (at the edge of the page) you can quickly locate the letter you need to find in the Spanish-English and English-Spanish dictionary. Once you have located the letter you need on the thumb index, simply flip to the correspondingly marked part of the dictionary. If you are left-handed, you can use the thumb index at the end of this book.

Gracias al índice alfabético del borde derecho (véase al dorso), puede ir directamente a la letra que necesite del diccionario Español-Inglés e Inglés-Español. Una vez localizada en el índice la letra que busca, puede pasar directamente a la parte correspondiente del diccionario. Si usted es zurdo/a puede utilizar el índice alfabético que hay al final del diccionario.

SPANISH– ENGLISH Dictionary

Diccionario ESPAÑOL–INGLÉS

BARRON'S Foreign Language Guides
Spanish-English Dictionary
Diccionario Español-Inglés

First edition for the United States and Canada © Copyright 2006 by Barron's Educational Series, Inc.
Original edition © Copyright 2006 by Ernst Klett Sprachen GmbH, Stuttgart, Federal Republic of Germany.

Editorial management: Dr. Meg Cop

Contributors: Jeremy Berg, Lucía Borrero, Almudena García Hernández, María Teresa González Núñez, Glenn C. Johnston, Yolanda Mateos Ortega, Eugenio Presno Ruiz, Josep Ràfols i Ventosa, Andrea A. Salusso, Eva Schellert, Dr. Eric Steinbaugh, William Steinmetz, Daniel A. Valencia Becker, Caroline Wilcox Reul

Typesetting: Dörr + Schiller, Stuttgart
Data Processing: Andreas Lang, conTEXT AG für Informatik und Kommunikation, Zürich

All inquiries should be addressed to:
Barron's Educational Series, Inc.
250 Wireless Boulevard
Hauppauge, NY 11788
http://www.barronseduc.com

ISBN-10: 0-7641-3329-2
ISBN-13: 978-0-7641-3329-9
Library of Congress Control Number: 2006925697

Printed in China
9 8 7 6 5 4 3 2

Índice

Contents

Introduction

This is a new bilingual dictionary designed to meet the needs of people in a time of ever-expanding communication among English and Spanish speakers. It has been written and edited by a large team of native speakers of both languages so that it constitutes an updated, comprehensive, and most useful linguistic tool.

This dictionary provides accurate coverage of current vocabulary in English and Spanish, as well as abundant examples of words used in context to illustrate idiomatic usage. To facilitate self-expression, pronunciation is provided in both languages, so that the users may express themselves correctly and idiomatically – both orally and in writing.

A unique characteristic is the possibility of downloading this dictionary into your home computer, laptop, and nearly all PDAs and smartphones. In addition, attention is given to small but meaningful features that include alphabet tabs for ease of use, maps and cultural boxes to enrich the process of language acquisition, and useful explanatory sections.

Introducción

Este nuevo diccionario bilingüe ha sido concebido para satisfacer la creciente necesidad de comunicación entre gente de habla española e inglesa. Escrito y editado por un grupo numeroso de especialistas en ambos idiomas, este diccionario constituye un auxiliar lingüístico actualizado, detallado y de enorme utilidad.

El vocabulario español e inglés aquí abarcado es moderno, preciso y dinámico, e incluye abundantes ejemplos de palabras empleadas en contexto para ilustrar su uso idiomático. Para facilitar la expresión oral, todos los términos en uno y otro idioma vienen provistos de indicaciones fonéticas. El lector puede así expresarse de una forma correcta e idiomática, tanto en forma oral como escrita.

Una característica exclusiva de este diccionario es la posibilidad de transferirlo a su computadora de escritorio o portátil, y prácticamente a cualquier tipo de dispositivo digital personal, incluyendo teléfonos multiactivos. Otras propiedades que revelan su carácter práctico incluyen indicadores alfabéticos para facilitar la búsqueda, útiles secciones explicativas, como también notas culturales y mapas concebidos para enriquecer el proceso de adquisición lingüística.

La pronunciación del español –
Spanish pronunciation

Remarkable variations are evident in Spanish pronunciation, both within the regions of the Iberian Peninsula and amongst the individual countries in which Spanish is spoken. Surprisingly, these variations are stronger within Spain itself than between the various Spanish-speaking countries in America. In the bilingual regions of the Iberian Peninsula – Catalonia, Valencia, the Balearic Islands, the Basque Provinces, and Galicia – pronunciation of Spanish is strongly influenced by the native languages of these areas. In other regions, it is the phonetic features of a range of dialects that have been mixed into spoken Spanish. Particularly characteristic of Andalusia, for example, is this dialect's particular variant of so-called *ceceo* pronunciation, in which not only the usual *z* and *c*, but also *s* is pronounced θ (as in *think*). So, in Andalusia, the words *la casa* ('the house') and *la caza* ('the hunt') are pronounced in exactly the same way.

In the vernacular pronunciation of some areas of Spain and Spanish America, one encounters aspiration of *s* at the end of a word. In the case of *las casas*, for example, the pronunciation would be **lah kása**, instead of **las kásas**. The *s* can even disappear altogether as is the case in the pronunciation **mímo**, instead of **mísmo** for the word *mismo*. Both phenomena are considered nonstandard and should therefore be avoided.

Ceceo (θe·'θeo)

This refers to the pronunciation of *z* in all positions and of *c* before *e* or *i* as θ, e.g., paθ for *paz*, θínko for *cinco* or aθeptáble for *aceptable*. Generally speaking, *ceceo* is associated with Spain.

Pronunciation in Spanish America

Spanish-American pronunciation bears the closest similarity to that of the Andalusian region. Among the phonetic characteristics of Spanish America, the following are the most characteristic:

Seseo (se·'seo)

Seseo refers to the pronunciation of *z* and *c* as *s* (e.g., **pas** instead of paθ for *paz* or **sínko**, instead of θínko for *cinco*). Though this is a characteristic mainly of Spanish America, it also occurs in subregions of Andalusia and on the Canary Islands.

In this dictionary, *seseo* pronunciation is given first and c*eceo* pronunciation is given as a second variant.

Yeísmo

Yeísmo is common not only in Spanish-speaking areas of America but also in various regions of Spain such as Andalusia, the Canary Islands, Extremadura, Madrid, and Castilian subregions. It refers to the pronunciation of *ll* as *y* (e.g., **yovér**, instead of **llovér** for *llover*). However, it would be incorrect to assume that **yeísmo** is a practiced all over Spanish America. As a matter of fact, the standard pronunciation of *ll* is used in the subregions of Chile, Peru, Columbia, and Ecuador.

In this dictionary, *yeísmo* pronunciation is given first and ʎ pronunciation is provided as a second variant.

Also characteristic of Spanish America is the pronunciation of of *y* as dʒ (e.g., adʒér, instead of ajér for *ayer*) in Argentina, Uruguay, and subregions of Ecuador and Mexico.

Símbolos fonéticos del español – Spanish phonetic symbols

Vowels/Vocales

Symbol/ Símbolo	Graphic representation/ Representación gráfica	Examples/Ejemplos
[a]	a	san, acción
[e]	e	pez, saber
[i]	i	sí, mirar
[o]	o	con
[u]	u	tú, dibujo

Diphthongs/Diptongos

Symbol/ Símbolo	Graphic representation/ Representación gráfica	Examples/ Ejemplos	Notes/Notas
[ai]	ai, ay	baile, hay	Pronounced like *i* in *write*
[au]	au	auto, causa	Pronounced like *ow* in *how*
[ei]	ei, ey	aceite, ley	Pronounced like *a* in *rate*
[eu]	eu	deuda	Pronounced similarly to *ay* in *hay*
[oi]	oi, oy	boicoteo, hoy	Pronounced like *oi* in *foil*
[ja]	ia, ya	envidia, adyacente	Pronounced like *ya* in *yard*
[je]	ie, ye	abierto, ayer	Pronounced like *ye* in *yellow*
[jo]	io, yo	aleatorio, apoyo	Pronounced like *Yo* in *York*
[ju]	iu, yu	ciudad, ayuda	Pronounced like *u* in *fuse*
[wa]	ua	adecuado	Pronounced like *wa* in *water*
[we]	ue	bueno, cuerda	Pronounced like *wa* in *wake*
[wi]	ui	ruido	Pronounced like *wee* in *week*
[wo]	uo	arduo	Pronounced like *uo* in *quote*

Triphthongs/Triptongos

Symbol/ Símbolo	Graphic representation/ Representación gráfica	Examples/ Ejemplos	Notes/Notas
[jai]	iái	apreciáis	Pronounced like *yi* in *yikes!*
[jei]	iéi	despreciéis	Pronounced like the cheer *yay!*
[wai]	uay	Paraguay	Pronounced like *why*
[wie]	uey	buey	Pronounced like *way*

Consonants/Consonantes

Symbol/ Símbolo	Graphic representation/ Representación gráfica	Examples/ Ejemplos	Notes/Notas
[p]	p	pato	
[b]	b, v	vacío, bola, hombre	*Used for b and v at the beginning of a word and for b following m.*
[β]	b, v	objeto, pueblo, vivir	*Used for all positions except b and v at the beginning of a word and for b following m; pronounced like v in never and with both lips touching.*
[m]	m, n	mamá	
[n]	n	nadie, entre	
[ɲ]	ñ	viña, ñácara	*Pronounced like ny in canyon.*
[f]	f	fabuloso, café	
[k]	c, q, k	casa, cosa, Cuba, actual, que, quinta, kilo	*Used in the combinations c + a, o, u, c before a consonant and qu + e, i. Also used in a number of words of foreign origin beginning with k.*
[g]	g, gu	garra, gobierno, gubernamental, guerra, guija, mango	*Used at the beginning of a word or in the combinations g + a, o, u and gu + e, i. Also used in the middle of a word, preceded by n.*
[x]	j, g	justo, rojo, girar, gente, agitar, México	*Used for j and for the combinations g + e, i except at the end of a word; sometimes also used for x.*
[ɣ]	g, gu	paga, agosto, agua, alegre, estigma, alargar,	*Used in the combinations g + a, o, u and gu + e, i in the middle of a word and when not preceded by n.*
[t]	t	letra, tío	
[d]	d	dedo, conde, caldo	
[θ]	c, z	cero, cita, zarza, cruz	*Occurs in the combinations c + e,i as well as in z in all positions in ceceo pronunciation characteristic of Spain.*
[l]	l	libro, bloque, sal	
[ʎ]	ll	llueve, pollo	*Pronounced similarly to lli in million. Used for ll in all positions.*
[s]	s, c	sábado, así, coser, afueras, cebra, cierto, zarza, cruz	*Used for s in all positions; in seseo pronunciation characteristic of Spanish America: for c+e, i and for z in all positions.*
[r]	r	caro, prisa, vivir	*Used in the middle or at the end of a word when not preceded by n, l, s.*

Symbol/ Símbolo	Graphic representation/ Representación gráfica	Examples/ Ejemplos	Notes/Notas
[rr]	r, rr	roca, honrado	*Used for **r** when it occurs at the beginning of a word; also used for **-rr-** and **-r-** at the beginning of a syllable after **n, l, s.***
[tʃ]	ch	chino, mucho	
[j]	y, ll	cónyuge, inyección, yunque, llueve, pollo	*Used when **y** occurs at the beginning of a syllable. Also used for **ll** in yeismo.*
[ʃ]	sh	shock	*Like English **sh**ock, **sh**ow.*
[w]	u, w	adecuado, bueno, ruido, arduo, windsurf, whisky	*Used as the first element of the diphthongs wa, we, wi, wo; also in w or wh in some words of foreign origin.*

English phonetic symbols –
Símbolos fonéticos del inglés

Vowels/Vocales

[a]	farm, not
[æ]	man, sad
[e]	bed, get, hair, dare
[ə]	ago, better, actor, anonymous, antivirus
[ɜ]	bird, her
[i]	beat, bee, me, belief, hobby
[ɪ]	it, wish, near
[ɔ]	all, law, long, sauce, floor
[u]	do, you, soon
[ʊ]	look, push, sure, tour
[ʌ]	but, son
[ɑ̃]	genre

Diphthongs/Diptongos

[aɪ]	life, buy, by
[aʊ]	house, now
[eɪ]	lame, name
[ɔɪ]	boy, oil
[oʊ]	rope, piano, road, toe, show, plateau
[ju]	accuse, beauty

Consonants/Consonantes

[b]	been, blind
[d]	do, had
[ð]	father, this
[dʒ]	cartridge, garbage, jam, object
[f]	father, wolf
[g]	beg, go
[h]	house
[j]	youth
[ʒ]	pleasure
[k]	keep, milk
[l]	ill, lamp, oil
[m]	am, man
[n]	manner, no
[ŋ]	long, sing, prank
[p]	happy, paper
[r]	dry, red, current, player, part
[s]	sand, stand, yes, cent, capacity
[ʃ]	ship, station, fish
[t]	fat, tell
[t̬]	butter, water
[θ]	death, thank
[tʃ]	catch, church
[v]	live, voice
[w]	water, we, which, will, wore
[z]	gaze, these, zeal

Signs/Otros símbolos

[']	primary stress
[,]	secondary stress
[·]	syllable division

A

A, a [a] *f* A, a; ~ **de Antonio** A as in Alpha
a [a] *prep* **1.** (*dirección*) to; **ir** ~ **Caracas/
China** to go to Caracas/China; **llegar** ~ **Santiago** to arrive in Santiago; **ir** ~ **casa de alguien** to go to sb's house; **ir** ~ **la escuela/**~**l
cine** to go to school/to the movies **2.** (*posición*) at; **estar sentado** ~ **la mesa** to be sitting at the table; **esperar** ~ **la puerta de la
casa** to wait at the front door; ~ **la derecha** on
the right; ~**l sur** (**de**) to the south (of); ~**l sol**
in the sun **3.** (*distancia*) ~ **10 kilómetros
de aquí** 10 kilometers (away) from here
4. (*tiempo*) at; (*hasta*) until; ~ **las tres** at three
o'clock; ~ **mediodía** at noon; ~ **los veinte
años** at (the age of) twenty; ~**l poco rato**
shortly after; ¿~ **cuántos estamos?** what's the
date? **5.** (*modo*) ~ **pie** on foot; **ir** ~ **pie** to
walk; ~ **mano** by hand; ~ **oscuras** in the dark;
tortilla a la española Spanish omelet **6.** (*precio*) ¿~ **cómo está?** how much is it?; ~ **2
pesos el kilo** (at) 2 pesos a [*o* per] kilo **7.** (*relación*) **el partido terminó dos** ~ **dos** the
game ended two all **8.** (*complemento* (*in*)*directo, con infinitivo*) to; **dio su fortuna** ~ **los
pobres** he/she gave his/her fortune to the
poor; **he visto** ~ **tu hermano** I've seen your
brother; **empezó** ~ **correr** he/she began to
run **9.** (*con verbo, expresiones*) **oler** ~ **gas** to
smell of gas; **jugar** ~ **los dados** to play dice;
¡~ **que llueve mañana!** I bet it'll rain tomorrow!; ~ **Pedro le gusta mucho nadar,**
¿~ **que sí, Pedro?** Pedro likes swimming a lot.
Don't you, Pedro?
abacado [a·βa·'ka·do] *m AmL* BOT avocado, alligator pear
abacorar [a·βa·ko·'rar] *vt AmL* to hound
abad(esa) [a·'βad, a·βa·'de·sa] *m(f)* abbot *m*,
abbess *f*
abadía [a·βa·'di·a] *f* abbey
abajeño, -a [a·βa·'xe·ɲo, -a] *adj AmL* coastal
abajo [a·'βa·xo] **I.** *adv* **1.** (*movimiento*) down;
calle ~ down the street; **cuesta** ~ downhill;
de arriba ~ from top to bottom **2.** (*estado*)
down (below); (*en casa*) downstairs; **boca** ~
face down; **hacia** ~ down, downward; **el** ~
firmante the undersigned; **de veinte para** ~
twenty or under; **véase más** ~ see below
II. *interj* ¡~ **el dictador!** down with the dictator!
abalanzarse <z→c> [a·βa·lan·'sar·se, -'θar·
se] *vr* ~ **a la ventana** to dash (over) to the window; ~ **sobre** [*o* contra] **algo** to pounce on
sth
abalear [a·βa·le·'ar] *vt Col* to shoot
abandonado, -a [a·βan·do·'na·do, -a] *adj ser*
neglected; (*desaseado*) slovenly
abandonar [a·βan·do·'nar] **I.** *vt* **1.** (*dejar*) to
leave; (*desamparar*) to abandon; **niño abandonado** abandoned baby; **le** ~ **on sus fuerzas**

his/her strength deserted him/her; **estar
abandonado a sí mismo** to be left to one's
own devices **2.** (*renunciar*) to give up **II.** *vr:*
~**se 1.** (*entregarse*) to give oneself over **2.** (*ir
desaliñado*) to let oneself go
abandono [a·βan·'do·no] *m* **1.** (*abando-
namiento*) abandonment; ~ **de servicio** giving-
up work; ~ **de la víctima** denial of assistance
2. (*renuncia*) renunciation; (*de una empresa,
idea*) giving-up **3.** (*descuido*) neglect; **en un
momento de** ~ in a moment of weakness
abanicar(se) <c→qu> [a·βa·ni·'kar·(se)] *vt,*
(*vr*) to fan (oneself)
abanico [a·βa·'ni·ko] *m* fan; **en** (**forma de**) ~
fan-shaped; **un** ~ **de posibilidades** a range of
possibilities
abaratar [a·βa·ra·'tar] **I.** *vt* to make cheaper;
(*precios*) to lower; ~ **costes** to cut costs **II.** *vr:*
~**se** to get cheaper
abarcar <c→qu> [a·βar·'kar] *vt* (*comprender*) to include; (*contener*) to contain;
~ **con la vista** to take in; ~ **muchas cosas a
la vez** to have one's work cut out; **quien
mucho abarca poco aprieta** *prov* don't bite
off more than you can chew
abarrotar [a·βa·rro·'tar] *vt* ~ **algo de algo** to
pack sth with sth
abarrote [a·βa·'rro·te] *m Cuba, Méx* grocery
store
abarrotería [a·βa·rro·te·'ri·a] *f* **1.** *AmL* (*ferretería*) hardware store **2.** *Guat* (*abacería*) retail grocery
abastecer(se) [a·βas·te·'ser·(se), -'θer·(se)]
irr como crecer vt, (*vr*) ~(**se**) **de** [*o* con] **algo**
to provide (oneself) with sth; COM to supply
(oneself) with sth
abastero [a·βas·'te·ro] *m Chile* (*de carne*)
wholesale livestock dealer; *Méx* (*de artículos*)
purveyor
abasto [a·'βas·to] *m* **1.** (*abastecimiento*) supply **2.** (*provisiones*) provisions *pl*; **no dar** ~
con algo to be unable to cope with sth
abatí [a·βa·'ti] *m Arg, Par* (*maíz*) corn;
(*bebida*) corn whisky
abatible [a·βa·'ti·βle] *adj* **asiento** ~ folding
chair
abatido, -a [a·βa·'ti·do, -a] *adj* dejected
abatimiento [a·βa·ti·'mjen·to] *m* **1.** (*desánimo*) dejection **2.** (*derribo*) demolition
abatir [a·βa·'tir] **I.** *vt* **1.** (*muro, casa*) to demolish; (*árbol*) to fell, to chop down; (*velas*) to
lower; (*avión*) to shoot down; ~ **el respaldo**
to recline the back-rest **2.** (*desmontar*) to dismantle **3.** (*debilitar*) to lay low **II.** *vr:* ~**se** to
become dejected; ~**se sobre algo** (*precipi-
tarse*) to pounce on sth
abdicación [aβ·di·ka·'sjon, -'θjon] *f* abdication; ~ **al trono** abdication from the throne
abdicar <c→qu> [aβ·di·'kar] *vt* (*monarca*) to
abdicate; (*ideales*) to renounce; **la reina
abdicó la corona en su hija** the queen abdi-
cated in favor of her daughter; ~ **la presidencia** to resign from the presidency

abdomen [aβ·'do·men] *m* abdomen

abdominal [aβ·do·mi·'nal] **I.** *adj* abdominal **II.** *m* DEP sit-up

abdominoplastia [aβ·do·mi·no·'plast·ja] *f* MED abdominoplasty, tummy tuck

abecé [a·βe·'se, -'θe] *m* ABC, alphabet; **el ~ de la matemática** the fundamentals of mathematics; **no saber el ~** to have no clue; **ser el ~ de algo** to be the basis of sth

abecedario [a·βe·se·'da·rjo, a·βe·θe-] *m* alphabet

abedul [a·βe·'dul] *m* BOT birch

abeja [a·βe·'xa] *f* bee; **~ reina** queen bee; **~ obrera** worker (bee) ▶ **estar como ~ en flor** to be in top form; **ser como una ~** to be a hard worker

abejorro [a·βe·'xo·rro] *m* bumblebee; **ser un ~** to be a pain (in the neck)

aberración [a·βe·rra·'sjon, -'θjon] *f* **1.** (*desviación*) aberration; **~ mental** mental aberration **2.** (*disparate*) absurdity **3.** *AmL* (*error*) mistake

aberrante [a·βe·'rran·te] *adj* aberrant

abertura [a·βer·'tu·ra] *f* **1.** (*acción*) opening **2.** (*hueco*) hole

abeto [a·'βe·to] *m* BOT fir; **~ rojo** spruce

abiertamente [a·βjer·ta·'men·te] *adv* **1.** (*francamente*) openly **2.** (*patentemente*) clearly

abierto [a·'βjer·to] *m* DEP **~ de tenis** tennis open championship

abierto, -a [a·'βjer·to, -a] **I.** *pp de* **abrir II.** *adj* open; **~ a nuevas ideas** open to new ideas; **en campo ~** in the open country; **un libro ~** an open book; **la gente aquí es muy abierta** people here are very open-minded

abismado, -a [a·βis·'ma·do, -a] *adj* (*absorto*) engrossed; (*sorprendido*) amazed

abismal [a·βis·'mal] *adj* enormous; (*odio*) profound

abismar [a·βis·'mar] **I.** *vt* to cast down; **~ a alguien en la desesperación** to plunge sb into despair **II.** *vr:* **~se 1.** (*hundirse*) to sink **2.** *AmL* (*asombrarse*) to be amazed

abismo [a·'βis·mo] *m* GEO abyss; **entre tus opiniones y las mías hay un ~** there's a world of difference between our opinions

abjurar [aβ·xu·'rar] *vi, vt* **~ (de) algo** to renounce sth

ablandar [a·βlan·'dar] **I.** *vt* **1.** (*poner blando*) to soften **2.** (*calmar*) to soothe **II.** *vr:* **~se** to soften; (*persona*) to relent

abnegación [aβ·ne·ɣa·'sjon, -'θjon] *f* self-denial; **con ~** selflessly

abnegado, -a [aβ·ne·'ɣa·do, -a] *adj* selfless

abocado, -a [a·βo·'ka·do, -a] *adj* (*vino*) smooth

abocetar [a·βo·se·'tar, -θe·'tar] *vt* to sketch

abochornar [a·βo·tʃor·'nar] **I.** *vt* **1.** (*calor*) to oppress; **este calor me abochorna** I'm suffocated by this heat; **estoy abochornado** I'm stifled **2.** (*avergonzar*) to embarrass **II.** *vr:* **~se de** [*o por*] **algo** to be embarrassed by sth

abofetear [a·βo·fe·te·'ar] *vt* to slap

abogacía [a·βo·ɣa·'si·a, -'θi·a] *f* legal profession; **ejercer la ~** to practice law

abogado, -a [a·βo·'ɣa·do, -a] *m, f* **1.** JUR lawyer; (*notario*) lawyer; (*en tribunal*) attorney; **~ defensor** defense lawyer; **~ divorcista** divorce lawyer; **~ de oficio** court-appointed counsel **2.** (*defensor*) advocate ▶ **ser un ~ de las causas perdidas** to be a champion of lost causes

abogar <g→gu> [a·βo·'ɣar] *vi* **~ por** [*o* **en favor de**] **algo** to advocate sth

abolengo [a·βo·'len·go] *m* ancestry; **de rancio ~** of noble descent

abolición [a·βo·li·'sjon, -'θjon] *f* abolition

abolir [a·βo·'lir] *irr vt* to abolish

abolladura [a·βo·ja·'du·ra, a·βo·ʎa-] *f* dent

abollar [a·βo·'jar, -'ʎar] *vt* to dent

abombar [a·βom·'bar] **I.** *vt* to make convex **II.** *vr:* **~se 1.** (*abultarse*) to bulge **2.** *CSur, Ecua, Nic* (*alimentos*) to go bad

abominable [a·βo·mi·'na·βle] *adj* abominable

abominación [a·βo·mi·na·'sjon, -'θjon] *f* abomination

abominar [a·βo·mi·'nar] *vi, vt* **1.** (*aborrecer*) to loathe **2.** (*renegar*) **~ de alguien** to condemn sb

abonado, -a [a·βo·'na·do, -a] *m, f* (*a revistas*) subscriber; (*al gas*) customer

abonar [a·βo·'nar] **I.** *vt* **1.** (*garantizar*) to guarantee **2.** (*pagar*) to pay; **~ en cuenta** to credit to an account; **para ~ en cuenta** A/C payee only **3.** (*terreno*) to fertilize **4.** PREN to subscribe to; **~ a alguien a una revista** (*convencer*) to persuade sb to subscribe to a magazine **II.** *vr:* **~se** to subscribe; **~se a la temporada de ópera** to buy a season ticket to the opera

abono [a·'βo·no] *m* **1.** *t.* TEAT (*para el tren*) season ticket; **~ mensual** monthly ticket; **~ de 10 viajes** 10-trip ticket; **sacar un ~** to buy a season ticket **2.** PREN subscription **3.** (*pago*) payment; **~ en cuenta** credit **4.** (*fertilizante*) fertilizer, manure; **~ químico** chemical fertilizer

abordable [a·βor·'da·βle] *adj* (*persona*) approachable; (*tema*) broachable; **no ~** taboo

abordaje [a·βor·'da·xe] *m* boarding; **tomar al ~** to board

abordar [a·βor·'dar] *vt* **1.** (*barco*) to board (*in attack*); (*chocar*) to ram **2.** (*persona*) to approach **3.** (*tema*) to discuss; (*problema*) to tackle

aborigen [a·βo·'ri·xen] **I.** *adj* aboriginal **II.** *mf* aborigine

aborrecer [a·βo·rre·'ser, -'θer] *irr como crecer vt* **1.** (*sentir aversión*) to loathe; **~ a alguien de muerte** not to be able to abide sb **2.** (*exasperar*) to infuriate

aborrecible [a·βo·rre·'si·βle, -'θi·βle] *adj* detestable

aborrecimiento [a·βo·rre·si·'mjen·to, -θi·'mjen·to] *m* **1.** (*aversión*) loathing **2.** (*antipatía*) dislike

abortar [a·βor·'tar] I. *vi* (*provocado*) to have an abortion; (*espontáneo*) to have a miscarriage II. *vt* to abort; (*hacer fracasar*) to cause to fail

aborto [a·'βor·to] *m* (*provocado*) abortion; (*espontáneo*) miscarriage

abota(r)garse <g→gu> [a·βo·ta·'γar·se/a·βo·tar·'γar·se] *vr* to become bloated

abotonar [a·βo·to·'nar] *vt* to button up

abr. *abr de* **abril** Apr.

abra ['a·βra] *f AmL* (*desmonte*) clearing

abrasar [a·βra·'sar] I. *vi* (*sol*) to scorch; (*comida*) to be burning hot II. *vt* 1. (*quemar, dolor*) to burn; (*ácidos*) to corrode; (*plantas*) to dry up; ¡**cuidado!, este café abrasa la lengua** take care not to burn your tongue on the coffee! 2. (*odio*) to consume; **la sed me abrasa (la garganta)** I'm dying of thirst III. *vr:* ~ **se** to burn (up); ~ **se en deseos de algo** *fig* to be desperate for sth; ~ **se de impaciencia por algo** *fig* to be desperately impatient to do sth

abrasivo [a·βra·'si·βo] *m* abrasive

abrasivo, -a [a·βra·'si·βo, -a] *adj* abrasive; **líquido** ~ abrasive liquid

abrazar <z→c> [a·βra·'sar, -'θar] I. *vt* 1. (*persona*) to embrace 2. (*contener*) to include; (*abarcar*) to take in 3. (*doctrina*) to embrace; (*religión*) to adopt II. *vr:* ~ **se** to embrace (each other)

abrazo [a·'βra·so, -θo] *m* embrace; **dar un** ~ **a alguien** to give sb a hug; **un** (**fuerte**) ~ (*en cartas*) best regards

abrebotellas [a·βre·βo·'te·jas, -ʎas] *m inv* bottle opener

abrecartas [a·βre·'kar·tas] *m inv* letter opener

abrelatas [a·βre·'la·tas] *m inv* can opener

abrevadero [a·βre·βa·'de·ro] *m* 1. (*pila*) water trough 2. (*lugar*) watering place

abrevar [a·βre·'βar] *vt* (*ganado*) to water

abreviación [a·βre·βja·'sjon, -'θjon] *f* 1. *t.* LING (*abreviatura*) abbreviation 2. (*de un texto*) abridgement

abreviado, -a [a·βre·'βja·do, -a] *adj* abridged; (*corto*) short

abreviar [a·βre·'βjar] I. *vt* 1. (*acortar*) to shorten 2. (*palabras*) to abbreviate 3. (*texto*) to abridge II. *vi* to hurry

abreviatura [a·βre·βja·'tu·ra] *f* abbreviation

abridor [a·βri·'dor] *m* opener

abrigado, -a [a·βri·'γa·do, -a] *adj* (*con ropa*) **estar** (*o* **ir**) ~ to be wrapped up warm

abrigar <g→gu> [a·βri·'γar] I. *vt* 1. (*cubrir*) to cover 2. (*tener*) to hold; ~ **esperanzas** to cherish hopes; ~ **proyectos** to harbor plans II. *vr:* ~ **se** to wrap up (warm)

abrigo [a·'βri·γo] *m* 1. (*prenda*) coat; ~ **de pieles** fur coat; **de** ~ warm 2. (*refugio*) shelter; **al** ~ **de** protected by ▶ **ser** ~ to be tough

abril [a·'βril] *m* April; *v.t.* **marzo** ▶ **tener trece** ~ **es** *inf* to be thirteen (years old)

abrillantado, -a [a·βri·jan·'ta·do, -a; a·βri·ʎan-] *adj AmL* shining; **fruta abrillantada** *Arg* glazed fruit

abrillantar [a·βri·jan·'tar, a·βri·ʎan-] *vt* to polish; (*piedras*) to cut and polish

abrir [a·'βrir] *irr* I. *vt* 1. (*algo cerrado*) to open; (*paraguas*) to put up; (*grifo*) to turn on; (*con la llave*) to unlock; (*luz*) to turn on; ~ **la cabeza a alguien** to split sb's head open; ~ **una calle al tráfico** to open a street to traffic; ~ **a golpes** to knock open; ~ **de par en par** to open wide; **a medio** ~ (*puerta*) half-open 2. (*túnel*) to dig; (*agujero*) to bore 3. (*inaugurar*) to open; (*curso*) to begin; **en un** ~ **y cerrar de ojos** in the blink of an eye II. *vr:* ~ **se** 1. (*puerta*) to open; **la ventana se abre al jardín** the window opens (out) onto the garden 2. (*confiar*) to confide 3. (*perspectivas*) to open up 4. *inf* (*irse*) to beat it

abrochar [a·βro·'tʃar] *vt* (*con broches*) to fasten; (*con botones*) to button (up); **abróchense los cinturones (de seguridad)** fasten your seat belts

abrojo [a·'βro·xo] *m Ven* (*urticaria*) rash

abrumador(a) [a·βru·ma·'dor, -·'do·ra] *adj* (*agobiador*) overwhelming; (*apabullante*) crushing

abrumar [a·βru·'mar] *vt* to overwhelm; (*con trabajo*) to wear out

abrupto, -a [a·'βrup·to, -a] *adj* (*camino*) steep; (*carácter*) abrupt

absceso [aβ·'se·so, -aβs·'θe·so] *m* abscess

absentismo [aβ·sen·'tis·mo] *m* absenteeism; ~ **laboral** absenteeism from work

absolución [aβ·so·lu·'sjon, -'θjon] *f* 1. JUR acquittal; ~ **por falta de pruebas** acquittal owing to lack of evidence 2. REL absolution; **dar la** ~ **a alguien** to give absolution to sb

absolutamente [aβ·so·lu·ta·'men·te] *adv* absolutely, completely; **está** ~ **de acuerdo con nosotros** he/she completely agrees with us; ~ **nada** nothing at all; **es** ~ **posible** it's quite possible

absoluto, -a [aβ·so·'lu·to, -a] *adj* absolute ▶ **nada en** ~ nothing at all; **en** ~ not at all

absolver [aβ·sol·'βer] *irr como volver vt* 1. JUR to acquit 2. REL to absolve

absorber [aβ·sor·'βer] *vt* 1. (*tierra*) *t.* Fís to absorb; (*aspiradora*) to suck (up) 2. (*cautivar*) to engross 3. (*empresa*) to take over

absorción [aβ·sor·'sjon, -'θjon] *f* 1. (*de líquidos*) *t.* Fís absorption 2. ECON takeover

absorto, -a [aβ·'sor·to, -a] *adj* 1. (*pasmado*) amazed 2. (*entregado*) absorbed

abstemio, -a [aβs·'te·mjo, -a] I. *adj* abstemious; (*completamente*) teetotal II. *m, f* teetotaler, non-drinker

abstención [aβs·ten·'sjon, -'θjon] *f t.* POL abstention

abstenerse [aβs·te·'ner·se] *irr como tener vr* (*privarse de*) *t.* POL to abstain; ~ **de votar** to abstain; ~ **del tabaco** to refrain from smoking; **rogamos que se abstengan de realizar visitas** we request you to refrain from visiting

abstinencia [aβs·ti·'nen·sja, -θja] *f* abstinence; (*de alcohol*) abstemiousness; (*completa*) teetotalism; ~ **de consumo** cutting down on consumption; **síndrome de** ~ withdrawal symptoms

abstinente [aβs·ti·'nen·te] *adj* abstinent; (*de alcohol*) abstemious; (*completamente*) teetotal

abstracción [aβs·trak·'sjon, -'θjon] *f* abstraction

abstracto, -a [aβs·'trak·to, -a] *adj* abstract; **en** ~ in the abstract

abstraer [aβs·tra·'er] *irr como traer* I. *vt* to abstract II. *vr* ~ **se en algo** to be absorbed in sth; ~ **se de algo** to detach oneself from sth; **consiguió** ~ **se de los gritos en la calle** he/she managed not to be distracted by the shouting in the street

abstraído, -a [aβs·tra·'i·do, -a] *adj* lost in thought; **estar** ~ **en algo** to be preoccupied by sth

absurdo [aβ·'sur·do] *m* absurdity; **reducir algo al** ~ to reduce sth to absurdity [*o* absurdum]

absurdo, -a [aβ·'sur·do, -a] *adj* absurd

abuchear [a·βu·tʃe·'ar] *vt* to boo; (*silbando*) to hiss

abucheo [a·βu·'tʃeo] *m* booing; (*silbidos*) hissing

abuelo, -a [a·'βwe·lo] *m, f* grandfather *m*, grandmother *f*; **los** ~**s** the grandparents; **éramos pocos y parió la abuela** *inf* that was all we needed

abulia [a·'βu·lja] *f* apathy

abultado, -a [a·βul·'ta·do, -a] *adj* bulky; (*labios*) thick

abultar [a·βul·'tar] I. *vi* to take up a lot of room II. *vt* to increase; *fig* (*exagerar*) to exaggerate

abundancia [a·βun·'dan·sja, -θja] *f* abundance; (*de bienes*) plenty; **en** ~ in abundance; **nadar en la** ~ to be loaded *sl*; **vivir en la** ~ to be affluent

abundante [a·βun·'dan·te] *adj* abundant; ~ **en algo** abounding in sth; ~**s lluvias** heavy rains; **una cosecha muy** ~ a plentiful harvest

abundar [a·βun·'dar] *vi* to abound; ~ **en algo** to be rich in sth

aburrido, -a [a·βu·'rri·do, -a] *adj* 1. *estar* (*harto*) bored; **estar** ~ **de algo** to be bored with sth; **tus chistes me tienen** ~ I'm tired of your jokes 2. *ser* (*pesado*) boring

aburrimiento [a·βu·rri·'mjen·to] *m* 1. (*tedio*) boredom 2. (*fastidio*) bore

aburrir [a·βu·'rrir] I. *vt* 1. (*hastiar*) to bore 2. (*fastidiar*) to tire II. *vr:* ~ **se** to be [*o* to get] bored; ~ **se de algo** to tire of sth

abusar [a·βu·'sar] *vi* 1. (*usar mal*) ~ **de algo** to misuse sth; ~ **de su salud** to abuse one's health 2. (*aprovecharse*) ~ **de alguien** to take advantage of sb 3. (*sexualmente*) ~ **de alguien** to sexually abuse sb

abusivo, -a [a·βu·'si·βo, -a] *adj* improper; (*precios*) outrageous

abuso [a·'βu·so] *m* misuse; ~ **de autoridad** abuse of authority; ~ **deshonesto** indecent assault; **este precio es un** ~ this is an outrageous price

abyección [aβ·jek·'sjon, -'θjon] *f* wretchedness

acá [a·'ka] *adv* here; ~ **y allá** here and there; **para** ~ over here; **¡ven** ~**!** come here!

acabado [a·ka·'βa·do] *m* TÉC finish

acabado, -a [a·ka·'βa·do, -a] *adj* (*completo, sin futuro*) finished

acabar [a·ka·'βar] I. *vi* 1. (*terminar*) to end; ~ **bien/mal** to turn out well/badly; ~ **en punta** to end in a point; ~ **de hacer algo** to have just done sth; **ella acaba de llegar** she's just arrived; **el libro acaba de publicarse** the book has just been published; ~ **con algo** to finish sth off; ~ **con alguien** to settle with sb; **este niño** ~**á conmigo** this child will be the death of me 2. (*finalmente*) ~ **ás por comprenderlo** you'll understand it in the end; ~ **ás por volverme loco** you'll end up driving me mad II. *vt* to finish; (*consumir*) to finish off; ~ **todas las galletas** to eat up all the biscuits III. *vr:* ~ **se** to come to an end; **la mantequilla se ha acabado** there's no butter left; **todo se acabó** it's all over; **¡se acabó!** and that's that!

acacia [a·'ka·sja, -θja] *f* acacia

academia [a·ka·'de·mja] *f* 1. (*corporación*) academy 2. (*colegio*) (private) school; ~ **militar** military academy

académico, -a [a·ka·'de·mi·ko, -a] *adj* academic

acaecer [a·kae·'ser, -'θer] *irr como crecer vi* to happen

acaecimiento [a·kae·si·'mjen·to, a·kae·θi-] *m* happening, occurrence

acahual [a·ka·'wal] *m Méx* sunflower

acalambrarse [a·ka·lam·'brar·se] *vr AmL* to get a cramp

acallar [a·ka·'jar, -'ʎar] *vt* 1. (*hacer callar*) to silence 2. (*apaciguar*) to pacify

acalorado, -a [a·ka·lo·'ra·do, -a] *adj* heated

acalorar [a·ka·lo·'rar] I. *vt* 1. (*dar calor*) to heat 2. (*enfadar*) to inflame II. *vr:* ~ **se** 1. (*sofocarse*) **se acaloró al correr** he/she got hot (while) running 2. (*apasionarse*) ~ **se con algo** to get worked up over sth 3. (*enfadarse*) ~ **se por algo** to get angry about sth; **se acalora por nada** he/she gets all worked up about nothing *inf*

acampar [a·kam·'par] *vi* to camp

acanalar [a·ka·na·'lar] *vt* to furrow; TÉC to groove

acantilado [a·kan·ti·'la·do] *m* cliff

acantilado, -a [a·kan·ti·'la·do, -a] *adj* steep

acaparar [a·ka·pa·'rar] *vt* to hoard; ~ **se de algo** to lay claim to sth; ~ **todas las miradas** to captivate everyone's attention

acapillar [a·ka·pi·'jar, -'ʎar] *vt Méx* (*atrapar*) to seize

acaramelar [a·ka·ra·me·'lar] I. *vt* to coat with caramel II. *vr:* ~ **se** to be all over each other

acariciar [a·ka·ri·'sjar, -'θjar] *vt* **1.** (*persona*) to caress **2.** (*plan*) to toy with

acarrear [a·ka·rre·'ar] *vt* **1.** (*transportar*) to transport **2.** (*ocasionar*) to cause

acaso [a·'ka·so] **I.** *m* chance; **el ~ hizo que...** +*subj* as chance would have it... **II.** *adv* maybe; **¿está ~ enfermo?** is he/she sick by any chance? ▶ **por si ~** (*en caso de*) in case; (*en todo caso*) just in case

acatar [a·ka·'tar] *vt* **1.** (*respetar*) to respect **2.** (*obedecer*) to obey **3.** *Col, Guat, PRico* (*caer en cuenta*) to realize

acatarrarse [a·ka·ta·'rrar·se] *vr* to catch a cold

acaudalado, -a [a·kau·da·'la·do, -a] *adj* well-off

acceder [ak·se·'der, ak·θe·-] *vi* **1.** (*consentir*) to agree; **~ a una petición** to agree to a request **2.** (*tener acceso*) to gain access **3.** (*ascender*) to accede; **~ a la presidencia** to assume the presidency; **~ a un cargo** to take office; **~ al trono** to succeed to the throne

accesible [ak·se·'si·βle, ak·θe·-] *adj* **1.** (*persona*) approachable **2.** (*lugar*) accessible

accésit [ak·'se·sit, aɣ·'θe·-] *m inv* consolation prize

acceso [ak·'se·so, aɣ·'θe·so] *m* **1.** (*a un lugar*) *t.* COMPUT access; **de fácil ~** (easily) accessible; **libre ~** open access **2.** (*ataque*) attack

accesorio [ak·se·'so·rjo, aɣ·θe·-] *m* **1.** (*utensilio*) implement **2.** *pl* (*de máquinas*) spare parts *pl*

accesorio, -a [ak·se·'so·rjo, -a; aɣ·θe·-] *adj* accessory

accidentado, -a [ak·si·den·'ta·do, -a; aɣ·θi·-] **I.** *adj* rugged; *fig* difficult **II.** *m, f* accident victim

accidental [ak·si·den·'tal, aɣ·θi·-] *adj* **1.** (*no esencial*) incidental **2.** (*casual*) casual

accidentarse [ak·si·den·'tar·se, aɣ·θi·-] *vr* to have an accident

accidente [ak·si·'den·te, aɣ·θi·-] *m* **1.** (*suceso*) accident; **~ en cadena** pile-up; **~ de circulación** traffic [*o* road] accident; **por ~** by accident; **sufrir un ~** to have an accident **2.** (*desnivel*) unevenness; **~s geográficos** geographical features

accidentógeno, -a [ak·si·den·'to·xe·no, -a; aɣ·θi·-] *adj* accident-prone

acción [ak·'sjon, aɣ·'θjon] *f* **1.** (*acto*) act; **¡~!** CINE action!; **un hombre de ~** a man of action; **entrar en ~** to go into action; **poner en ~** to put into action **2.** (*influencia*) *t.* MIL, JUR action; **~ recíproca** interaction; **de rápida ~** rapid-action; **de ~ retardada** (*bomba*) delayed-action; **~ por daños y perjuicios** action for damages; **~ popular** incidental action **3.** FIN share; **~ común** common share; **~ preferente** preferred share

accionar [ak·sjo·'nar, aɣ·θjo·-] *vt* TÉC to operate; **~ un cohete** to fire a rocket

accionista [ak·sjo·'nis·ta, aɣ·θjo·-] *mf* shareholder, stockholder

acebo [a·'se·βo, a·'θe·-] *m* holly

acechar [a·se·'tʃar, a·θe·-] *vt* **1.** (*espiar*) to spy on **2.** (*esperar*) to lie in wait for

acecho [a·'se·tʃo, a·θe·-] *m* spying; **estar al ~** to lie in wait

aceitada [a·sei·'ta·da, a·θei·-] *f AmL* oiling; *inf* (*soborno*) kickback

aceitar [a·sei·'tar, a·θei·-] *vt* (*motor*) to oil; (*ensalada*) to dress

aceite [a·'sei·te, a·'θei·-] *m* oil; **~ bruto** crude oil; **~ comestible** cooking oil; **~ esencial** essential oil; **~ lubrificante** lubricating oil ▶ **echar ~ al fuego** to add fuel to the flames

aceitera [a·sei·'te·ra, a·θei·-] *f* **1.** (*recipiente*) oil-can **2.** *pl* (*vinagreras*) cruet

aceitoso, -a [a·sei·'to·so, -a; a·θei·-] *adj* oily

aceituna [a·sei·'tu·na, a·θei·-] *f* olive ▶ **llegar a las ~s** to arrive late

aceitunado, -a [a·sei·tu·'na·do, -a; a·θei·-] *adj* olive(-green)

aceleración [a·se·le·ra·'sjon, a·θe·le·ra·'θjon] *f* acceleration

acelerador [a·se·le·ra·'dor, a·θe·-] *m* gas pedal; **pisar el ~** to step on the gas; **~ de partículas** FÍS particle accelerator

acelerar [a·se·le·'rar, a·θe·-] *vt, vi* to accelerate; **¡no aceleres tanto!** don't go so fast!; **~ el paso** to walk faster

acelga [a·'sel·ɣa, a·'θel·-] *f* chard

acento [a·'sen·to, -'θen·to] *m* **1.** (*prosódico*) stress; **el ~ cae en la primera sílaba** the stress falls on the first syllable **2.** (*signo*) accent; **hablar inglés sin ~** to speak English without any accent; **esta palabra se escribe sin ~** this word is written without an accent **3.** (*énfasis*) emphasis; **poner especial ~ en algo** to put special emphasis on sth

acentuación [a·sen·twa·'sjon, a·θen·twa·'θjon] *f* (*prosódica*) stress; (*ortográfica*) accentuation

acentuado, -a [a·sen·tu·'a·do, -a; a·θen·-] *adj* **1.** (*al pronunciar*) stressed; (*al escribir*) with an accent; **no ~** unstressed; (*sin tilde*) unaccented **2.** (*marcado*) marked

acentuar <*1. pres:* acentúo> [a·sen·tu·'ar, a·θen·-] **I.** *vt* **1.** (*al pronunciar*) to stress; (*al escribir*) to write with an accent **2.** (*resaltar*) to highlight **II.** *vr:* **~se** *AmL* to worsen

acepción [a·sep·'sjon, a·θep·'θjon] *f* sense, meaning

aceptable [a·sep·'ta·βle, a·θep·-] *adj* acceptable

aceptación [a·sep·ta·'sjon, a·θep·ta·'θjon] *f* **1.** (*aprobación*) approval; **tener ~** to be popular [*o* successful] **2.** COM, JUR acceptance

aceptado [a·sep·'ta·do, a·θep·-] *interj AmL* (*vale*) OK

aceptar [a·sep·'tar, a·θep·-] *vt* **1.** (*recibir*) to accept **2.** (*aprobar*) to approve; **~ un compromiso** to accept an agreement; **~ hacer algo** to agree to do sth

acequia [a·'se·kja, a·'θe·-] *f* **1.** (*canal de riego*) irrigation ditch **2.** *Méx* (*albañal*) gutter

acera [a·'se·ra, -'θe·ra] *f* sidewalk ▶ **es de la ~**

de enfrente *inf* (*homosexual*) (s)he is an invert [*o* is gay]

acerca [a·'ser·ka, a·'θer-] *prep* **~ de** (*sobre*) about; (*en relación a*) concerning

acercamiento [a·ser·ka·'mjen·to, a·θer-] *m* approach

acercar <c→qu> [a·ser·'kar, a·θer-] **I.** *vt* **1.** (*poner cerca*) to bring nearer; **acerca la silla a la mesa** draw the chair up to the table; (*traer*) to bring over **2.** *inf* (*llevar*) to take, to bring **II.** *vr:* **~ se a alguien/algo** to approach sb/sth; **~ se a la tienda a por patatas** to go to the store for potatoes

acero [a·'se·ro, -'θe·ro] *m* steel

acérrimo, -a [a·'se·rri·mo, -a; a·'θe-] **I.** *superl de* **acre II.** *adj* (*partidario*) staunch

acertado, -a [a·ser·'ta·do, -a; a·θer-] *adj* **1.** (*atinado*) accurate **2.** (*conveniente*) apt

acertar <e→ie> [a·ser·'tar, a·θer-] **I.** *vi* **1.** (*dar*) to hit; **~ al blanco** to hit the mark **2.** (*hacer con acierto*) to be right; **acertaste en protestar** you were right to protest; **no acerté a encontrar la respuesta** I didn't manage to find the answer **3.** (*por casualidad*) **~ a hacer algo** to happen to do sth; **~ con algo** to come across sth **II.** *vt* **1.** (*dar en el blanco*) to hit **2.** (*adivinar*) to get right

acertijo [a·ser·'ti·xo, a·θer-] *m* riddle

acervo [a·'ser·βo, a·'θer-] *m* store; **~ cultural** cultural heritage; **~ genético** BIOL gene pool

acetona [a·se·'to·na, a·θe-] *f* acetone

achacar <c→qu> [a·tʃa·'kar] *vt* to attribute

achachay [a·tʃa·'tʃai] *interj Col, Ecua* brr

achacoso, -a [a·tʃa·'ko·so, -a] *adj* sickly; **estar ~** to be ailing

achalay [a·tʃa·'lai] *interj Arg, Perú* wow

achaque [a·'tʃa·ke] *m* ailment

achatado, -a [a·tʃa·'ta·do, -a] *adj* flattened; **nariz achatada** snub nose

achicar <c→qu> [a·tʃi·'kar] **I.** *vt* **1.** (*empequeñecer*) to make smaller; (*persona*) to intimidate **2.** (*agua*) to bale out **II.** *vr:* **~ se 1.** (*empequeñecerse*) to become smaller **2.** (*persona*) to take fright; (*no atreverse*) not to dare **3.** *AmL* (*humillarse*) to demean oneself

achicharrar [a·tʃi·tʃa·'rrar] **I.** *vt* **1.** (*calor*) to scorch; **estoy achicharrado** I'm burning up **2.** (*comida*) to burn **II.** *vr:* **~ se 1.** (*comida*) to get burnt **2.** (*persona*) to be sweltering; (*planta*) to be wilting (in the heat)

achichiguar [a·tʃi·tʃi·'ɣwar] *vt Méx* **1.** (*servir de niñera*) to baby-it **2.** (*malcriar*) to spoil

achichinque [a·tʃi·'tʃin·ke] *m Méx* (*adulador*) groupie

achicoria [a·tʃi·'ko·rja] *f* chicory

achinado, -a [a·tʃi·'na·do, -a] *adj* **1.** (*rasgos*) oriental; **ojos ~s** slant-eyed **2.** *CSur* (*aplebeyado*) coarse

achiote [a·'tʃjo·te] *m AmC, Bol, Méx* **1.** BOT annatto tree **2.** (*pigmento*) annatto

achipolarse [a·tʃi·po·'lar·se] *vr Méx* **1.** (*personas*) to grow sad **2.** (*plantas*) to wither

achiquillado, -a [a·tʃi·ki·'ja·do, -a; 'ʎa·do, -a]

adj **1.** *Méx* (*infantil*) childish **2.** *Chile* (*aniñado*) boyish

achira [a·'tʃi·ra] *f AmS* BOT canna

achís [a·'tʃis] *interj* atchoo

achispar [a·tʃis·'par] **I.** *vt* to cheer up **II.** *vr:* **~ se** to become tipsy

acholado, -a [a·tʃo·'la·do, -a] *adj CSur, Perú, Bol* **1.** (*mestizo*) mestizo (*of mixed Spanish American and American Indian descent*) **2.** (*acobardado*) intimidated

acholar [a·tʃo·'lar] **I.** *vt Chile, Perú, Bol* **1.** (*avergonzar*) to embarrass **2.** (*amilanar*) to scare **II.** *vr:* **~ se** *CSur, Perú, Bol* to become intimidated

achuchado, -a [a·tʃu·'tʃa·do, -a] *adj inf* **1.** (*duro*) tough **2.** (*débil*) feverish

achuchar [a·tʃu·'tʃar] *vt* **1.** *inf* (*persona*) to stir up; **~ a un perro contra alguien** to set a dog on sb **2.** *inf* (*estrujar*) to crush **3.** (*atosigar*) to harass **4.** *inf* (*acariciar*) to caress

achucutado, -a [a·tʃu·ku·'ta·do, -a] *adj* **1.** *AmL* (*abatido*) depressed **2.** *Ven, Hond, Guat* (*triste*) sad

achucutarse [a·tʃu·ku·'tar·se] *vr Col, Ecua,*
achucuyarse [a·tʃu·ku·'jar·se] *vr AmC* **1.** (*humillarse*) to shame **2.** (*acobardarse*) to chicken out *inf*

achumado, -a [a·tʃu·'ma·do, -a] *adj Ecua* drunk

achumarse [a·tʃu·'mar·se] *vr Ecua* to get drunk

achunchar [a·tʃun·'tʃar] *vt AmL* to humiliate

achura [a·'tʃu·ra] *f AmS* offal

achurar [a·tʃu·'rar] *vt CSur* (*res*) to gut; (*persona*) to stab to death

achuras [a·'tʃu·ras] *fpl Arg* offal

aciago, -a [a·'sja·ɣo, -a; a·'θja-] *adj* ill-fated; **un día ~** a fateful day

acicalarse [a·si·ka·'lar·se, a·θi-] *vr* to get dressed up

acicate [a·si·'ka·te, a·θi-] *m* spur; *fig* stimulus

acidez [a·si·'des, a·θi·'deθ] *f* acidity; **~ de estómago** MED heartburn, acid indigestion

ácido ['a·si·do, 'a·θi-] *m t.* QUÍM acid; **~ cianhídrico** hydrocyanic acid; **~ clorhídrico** hydrochloric acid; **~ s grasos insaturados** unsaturated fatty acids

ácido, -a ['a·si·do, -a; 'a·θi-] *adj* **1.** (*agrio*) sour; QUÍM acidic **2.** (*mordaz*) sharp

acierto [a·'sjer·to, a'θjer-] *m* **1.** (*en el tiro*) accuracy **2.** (*éxito*) success; **el casarte ha sido un ~** you did well to get married; **hacer algo con ~** to do sth skillfully

acitrón [a·si·'tron, a·θi-] *m Méx* CULIN candied citron

aclamación [a·kla·ma·'sjon, -'θjon] *f* applause; **por ~** POL by acclamation [*o* acclaim]

aclamar [a·kla·'mar] *vt* to cheer; POL to acclaim

aclaración [a·kla·ra·'sjon, -'θjon] *f* **1.** (*clarificación*) clarification **2.** (*explicación*) explanation **3.** (*de un crimen*) solution

aclarar [a·kla·'rar] **I.** *vt* **1.** (*hacer más claro*) to lighten; (*un líquido*) to thin (down); (*la ropa*) to rinse; ~ **el bosque** to clear [*o* thin out] the forest; ~ **la voz** to clear one's throat **2.** (*explicar*) to explain **3.** (*crimen*) to solve **II.** *vr:* ~ **se** to be clarified; *inf* (*entender*) to catch on; **no te aclaras contigo mismo** you don't know what you want **III.** *vimpers* **está aclarando** it's clearing up

aclaratorio, -a [a·kla·ra·'to·rjo, -a] *adj* explanatory

aclimatación [a·kli·ma·ta·'sjon, -'θjon] *f* acclimation

aclimatar [a·kli·ma·'tar] **I.** *vt* to acclimate **II.** *vr:* ~ **se** to get acclimated

acné [ay·'ne] *m o f* acne

acobardar [a·ko·βar·'dar] **I.** *vt* to frighten; **le acobarda el fuego** he/she is afraid of fire **II.** *vr:* ~ **se 1.** (*desanimarse*) ~ **se ante** [*o* **frente a**] **algo** to flinch from sth **2.** (*intimidarse*) to be frightened; **se acobarda de sí mismo** he is afraid of his own shadow

acogedor(a) [a·ko·xe·'dor, -·'do·ra] *adj* welcoming, inviting

acoger <g→j> [a·ko·'xer] **I.** *vt* to welcome; (*recibir*) to receive **II.** *vr:* ~ **se 1.** (*ampararse*) to shelter **2.** (*basarse*) to resort; ~ **se a algo** to avail oneself of sth

acogida [a·ko·'xi·da] *f* welcome; (*recibimiento*) reception; **encontrar una buena** ~ to be well received; **el cantante tuvo una buena** ~ the singer was received with applause; **el proyecto no tuvo una buena** ~ the project didn't meet with approval

acojonado, -a [a·ko·xo·'na·do, -a] *adj vulg* (*asustado*) scared shitless [*o* stiff]; (*acobardado*) intimidated; **ahora está** ~ he/she is scared now

acojonante [a·ko·xo·'nan·te] *adj vulg* (*fantástico, impresionante*) nasty *sl*

acojonar [a·ko·xo·'nar] **I.** *vt vulg* **1.** (*asustar*) to scare (sb) stiff, to scare the shit out of (sb) **2.** (*impresionar*) to impress **II.** *vr:* ~ **se** *vulg* (*asustarse*) to be scared shitless; (*acobardarse*) to back down; **no** ~ **se** not to be scared

acometer [a·ko·me·'ter] **I.** *vi* to attack **II.** *vt* **1.** (*embestir*) to attack; (*risa*) to overcome; **lo acometió la risa** he was overcome by laughter **2.** (*emprender*) to undertake

acometida [a·ko·me·'ti·da] *f* **1.** (*embestida*) attack **2.** TÉC connection

acomodado, -a [a·ko·mo·'da·do, -a] *adj* well-off; **tener una vida acomodada** to live comfortably

acomodador(a) [a·ko·mo·da·'dor, -·'do·ra] *m(f)* CINE usher

acomodar [a·ko·mo·'dar] **I.** *vt* **1.** (*adaptar*) to adapt **2.** (*colocar*) to place **3.** (*albergar*) to accommodate **II.** *vr:* ~ **se 1.** (*adaptarse*) to adapt oneself; ~ **se con todo** to put up with everything **2.** (*ponerse cómodo*) to make oneself comfortable

acomodo [a·ko·'mo·do] *m* **1.** (*arreglo*) arrangement **2.** (*acuerdo*) agreement **3.** *AmL* (*soborno*) bribe

acompañado, -a [a·kom·pa·'ɲa·do, -a] *adj* accompanied; **bien/mal** ~ in good/bad company; **iba acompañada por su padre** she was accompanied by her father

acompañante [a·kom·pa·'ɲan·te] *mf* (*de una dama*) escort; (*en el coche*) passenger

acompañar [a·kom·pa·'ɲar] *vt* **1.** (*ir con*) *t.* MÚS to accompany; ~ **a alguien a casa** to see sb home; ~ **a alguien en un viaje** to go with sb on a journey; ~ **a alguien de compras** to go shopping with sb; ~ **a alguien con la guitarra/al piano** to accompany sb on the guitar/on the piano; ~ **el pollo con arroz y verduras** to serve the chicken with rice and vegetables **2.** (*hacer compañía*) ~ **a alguien** to keep sb company **3.** (*adjuntar*) to enclose; **el informe acompaña a la carta** the report is enclosed with the letter

acompasado, -a [a·kom·pa·'sa·do, -a] *adj* MÚS rhythmic

acomplejado, -a [a·kom·ple·'xa·do, -a] *adj* full of complexes

acomplejar [a·kom·ple·'xar] **I.** *vt* to give (sb) a complex **II.** *vr:* ~ **se** to get a complex

aconchar [a·kon·'tʃar] *vt Méx* to tell (sb) off **II.** *vr:* ~ **se 1.** *Chile, Perú* (*sedimentarse*) to settle; ~ **a alguien los meados** *inf* to chicken out **2.** *Chile, Perú* (*serenarse*) to calm down

acondicionado, -a [a·kon·di·sjo·'na·do, -a; -θjo·'na·do, -a] *adj* **bien/mal** ~ in good/bad condition

acondicionador [a·kon·di·sjo·na·'dor, -θjo·na·'dor] *m* (*de aire*) air-conditioner; (*para el pelo*) conditioner

acondicionar [a·kon·di·sjo·'nar, -θjo·'nar] *vt* **1.** (*preparar*) to prepare **2.** (*climatizar*) to air-condition

acongojar [a·kon·go·'xar] *vt* to distress

aconsejable [a·kon·se·'xa·βle] *adj* advisable

aconsejar [a·kon·se·'xar] *vt* to advise; ~ **algo a alguien** to recommend sth to sb; **esto aconseja prudencia** this calls for caution

acontecer [a·kon·te·'ser, -'θer] *irr como crecer vi* to happen

acontecimiento [a·kon·te·si·'mjen·to, a·kon·te·θi-] *m* event

acopiar [a·ko·'pjar] *vt* to gather together

acopio [a·'ko·pjo] *m* store; **hacer** ~ **de algo** to stock up on sth; **hacer** ~ **de paciencia** to draw on all one's reserves of patience; **hacer** ~ **de valor** to muster one's courage

acoplado [a·ko·'pla·do] *m RíoPl* trailer

acoplar [a·ko·'plar] **I.** *vt* **1.** (*ajustar*) to adjust; (*juntar*) to join **2.** (*piezas*) to fit together **3.** ELEC to connect **II.** *vr:* ~ **se** to adapt

acoquinar [a·ko·ki·'nar] **I.** *vt* to intimidate **II.** *vr:* ~ **se** to allow oneself to be intimidated, to chicken out *inf*

acorazar <z→c> [a·ko·ra·'sar, -'θar] **I.** *vt* to armor-plate **II.** *vr:* ~ **se** to arm oneself

acordar <o→ue> [a·kor·'dar] **I.** *vt* **1.** (*convenir*) to agree **2.** (*decidir*) to decide **II.** *vr* ~ **se de algo/alguien** to remember sth/sb; **si mal**

no me acuerdo if my memory serves me right; ¡acuérdate de decírselo! remember to tell him/her!

acorde [aˈkorˌde] I. *adj* agreed; **estar ~ con alguien** to be in agreement with sb; **~ con el medio ambiente** in keeping with the environment II. *m* MÚS chord; **~ mayor/menor** major/minor chord; **a los ~s de un vals** to the strains of a waltz

acordeón [aˌkorˌdeˈon] *m* accordion

acordonar [aˌkorˌdoˈnar] *vt* (*botas*) to lace up; (*lugar*) to cordon off

acorralar [aˌkoˌrraˈlar] *vt* **1.** (*ganado*) to round up; (*lugar*) to fence in **2.** (*intimidar*) to intimidate; (*con preguntas*) to corner

acortar [aˌkorˈtar] I. *vt* to shorten; (*duración*) to cut down; (*distancia*) to reduce; **~ camino** to take a short cut; **~ un pantalón unos centímetros** to take up a pair of pants by a few centimeters II. *vr:* **~se** to get shorter

acosar [aˌkoˈsar] *vt* **1.** (*perseguir*) to hound **2.** (*asediar*) to harass; **~ a alguien a** [*o* con] **preguntas** to pester sb with questions

acosijar [aˌkoˌsiˈxar] *vt Méx* (*acosar*) to hound

acoso [aˈkoˌso] *m* relentless pursuit; *fig* harassment; **~ sexual** sexual harassment

acostar <o→ue> [aˌkosˈtar] I. *vt* to put to bed II. *vr:* **~se** **1.** (*descansar*) to lie down; **estar acostado** to be lying down **2.** (*ir a la cama*) to go to bed; **~se con alguien** to go to bed with sb **3.** *AmC, Méx, Col* (*dar a luz*) to give birth

acostumbrado, -a [aˌkosˌtumˈbraˌdo, -a] *adj* accustomed; **mal ~** spoiled

acostumbrar [aˌkosˌtumˈbrar] I. *vi* **~ a hacer algo** to be used to doing sth; **como se acostumbra a decir** as they say II. *vt* **~ a alguien a hacer algo** to get sb used to doing sth III. *vr:* **~se a algo** to get accustomed [*o* used] to sth

acotación [aˌkoˌtaˈsjon, -ˈθjon] *f* **1.** (*nota*) margin note, annotation; TEAT stage direction **2.** (*cota*) elevation mark

acotamiento [aˌkoˌtaˈmjenˌto] *m Méx* (*arcén*) shoulder

acotar [aˌkoˈtar] *vt* **1.** (*delimitar*) to delimit; **terreno acotado** private property **2.** (*plano*) **~ algo** to mark elevations on sth **3.** (*texto*) to annotate

ácrata [ˈaˌkraˌta] I. *adj* (*anárquico*) anarchic; (*anarquista*) anarchistic II. *mf* anarchist

acre¹ [ˈaˌkre] *adj* <acérrimo> bitter; (*ácido*) sour; *fig* scathing

acre² [ˈaˌkre] *m* acre

acreditado, -a [aˌkreˌdiˈtaˌdo, -a] *adj* reputable

acreditar [aˌkreˌdiˈtar] I. *vt* **1.** (*atestiguar*) to vouch for; **~ como embajador** to accredit as ambassador **2.** (*autorizar*) to authorize **3.** (*dar reputación*) to do credit **4.** FIN to credit II. *vr:* **~se** (*reputación*) to get a reputation; (*crédito*) to prove one's worth

acreedor(a) [aˌkreˈdor/aˌkreˈeˌdor, -ˈdoˌra]

I. *adj* **hacerse ~ a** [*o* **de**] **algo** to be worthy of sth II. *m(f)* FIN creditor

acribillar [aˌkriˌβiˈjar, -ˈʎar] *vt* to riddle; **acribillado a balazos** riddled with bullets; **anoche me acribillaron los mosquitos** last night I was eaten alive by the mosquitoes; **~ a alguien a preguntas** *fig* to pester sb with questions

acrílico, -a [aˈkriliˌko, -a] *adj* acrylic; **fibra acrílica** acrylic fiber

acriollarse [aˌkrjoˈjarˌse, -ˈʎarˌse] *vr AmL* to go native

acrobacia [aˌkroˈβaˌsja, -θja] *f* acrobatics *pl*; **~ aérea** aerobatics *pl*, stunt flying

acróbata [aˈkroˌβaˌta] *mf* acrobat

acrobático, -a [aˌkroˈβatiˌko, -a] *adj* acrobatic

acrónimo [aˈkroniˌmo] *m* acronym

acta [ˈakˌta] *f* **1.** (*de una reunión*) minutes *pl*; **levantar ~ de algo** to draw up a document of sth; **hacer constar en ~** to record in the minutes **2.** JUR act; **~ de acusación** bill of indictment

actitud [akˌtiˈtud] *f* **1.** (*corporal*) posture; **~ de ataque** threatening stance; **~ de extrema cautela en cuanto a algo** policy of extreme caution with regard to sth **2.** (*disposición*) attitude; **adoptar una ~ reservada** to adopt a reserved attitude **3.** (*comportamiento*) behavior; **adoptar una ~ incomprensible** to behave strangely

activamente [akˌtiˌβaˈmenˌte] *adv* actively

activar [akˌtiˈβar] *vt* **1.** (*avivar*) to stimulate; **~ la digestión** to aid digestion **2.** QUÍM, COMPUT to activate; **~ una bomba** to detonate a bomb

actividad [akˌtiˌβiˈdad] *f* activity; (*ocupación*) occupation; **~ profesional** profession; **las ~es artísticas de un país** the cultural activities of a country; **en ~** active; **volcán en ~** active volcano; **entrar en ~** to become active

activo [akˈtiˌβo] *m* FIN assets *pl*; **~ circulante** current assets; **~ fijo** fixed assets

activo, -a [akˈtiˌβo, -a] *adj* active; (*medicamento*) effective

acto [ˈakˌto] *m* **1.** (*acción*) action; **~ de cortesía** act of courtesy; **~ jurídico** (*válido*) legal act; (*negocio*) legal transaction; **~ penal** criminal act; **~ sexual** sexual act; **~ de violencia** act of violence; **~ de voluntad** professed intention; **cometer ~s de gamberrismo** to commit acts of vandalism; **hacer ~ de presencia** to put in an appearance **2.** (*ceremonia*) ceremony; **~ conmemorativo** commemoration; **~ estatal** state occasion; **~ necrológico** funeral service **3.** TEAT act ▶ **~ seguido...** immediately after...; **en el ~** immediately, on the spot

actor, actriz [akˈtor, akˈtris, -ˈtriθ] *m, f* actor *m*, actress *f*; **~ de cine** film actor; **~ suplente** understudy; **primer ~** principal actor, leading man

actor(a) [akˈtor, -ˈtoˌra] *m(f)* plaintiff

actuación [ak·twa·'sjon, -'θjon] *f* **1.** (*conducta*) conduct; **la ~ de la policía** the police action **2.** (*actividad*) activity **3.** TEAT performance; **~ en directo** live performance **4.** *pl* JUR legal proceedings *pl*

actual [ak·tu·'al] *adj* (*de ahora*) present; (*corriente*) current

actualidad [ak·twa·li·dad] *f* present; **en la ~** at present; **de ~** topical; **ser de gran ~** to be topical

actualizar <z→c> [ak·twa·li·'sar, -'θar] *vt* to update

actualmente [ak·twal·'men·te] *adv* at the moment, currently

actuar <*1.pres:* actúo> [ak·tu·'ar] *vi* **1.** (*hacer*) to work; **~ contra alguien** JUR to take legal action against sb **2.** (*tener efecto*) **~ sobre algo** to have an effect on sth **3.** TEAT to act; **~ en directo** to perform live; **~ de Don Juan** to play Don Juan; **ella no actúa en esta función** she doesn't appear in this performance

acuache [a·'kwa·tʃe] *m Méx* (*compinche*) pal

acuarela [a·kwa·'re·la] *f* watercolor

acuario [a·'kwa·rjo] *m* aquarium

Acuario [a·'kwa·rjo] *m* Aquarius

acuático, -a [a·'kwa·ti·ko, -a] *adj* aquatic; **parque ~** water park

acuchamarse [a·ku·tʃa·'mar·se] *vr Ven* (*entristecerse*) to get depressed

acuchillar [a·ku·tʃi·'jar, -'ʎar] *vt* **1.** (*herir*) to knife; (*matar*) to stab to death **2.** (*parqué*) to sand down

acuclillarse [a·ku·kli·'jar·se, -'ʎar·se] *vr* to squat

acudiente [a·ku·'djen·te] *m Col* (*tutor*) tutor

acudir [a·ku·'dir] *vi* to go; **~ a una cita** to keep an appointment; **~ al trabajo/a la puerta** to go to work/to the door; **~ a las urnas** to go to the polls; **~ a la memoria de alguien** to come to sb's mind; **~ a alguien** to go to help sb; **~ en socorro de alguien** to come to sb's aid; **~ a** (*recurrir*) to turn to

acueducto [a·kwe·'duk·to] *m* aqueduct

acuerdo [a·'kwer·do] *m* **1.** (*convenio*) *t.* POL agreement; **Acuerdo General sobre Aranceles y Comercio** General Agreement on Tariffs and Trade; **llegar a un ~** to reach an agreement; **estar de ~ con alguien** to agree with sb; **ponerse de ~** to come to an agreement; **sin ponerse de ~** without reaching (an) agreement; **de común ~** by mutual consent **2.** (*decisión*) decision; **tomar un ~** to pass a resolution ▸ **¡de ~!** I agree!, OK!; **de ~ con** in accordance with

acuerpado, -a [a·kwer·'pa·do, -a] *adj Bol* (*corpulento*) hefty

acullicar [a·ku·ji·'kar, -ʎi·'kar] *vi Arg, Bol, Chile, Perú* to chew coca leaves

acullico [a·ku·'ji·ko, -'ʎi·ko] *m Arg, Bol, Perú* small ball of coca

acumuchar [a·ku·mu·'tʃar] *vt Chile* to pile up

acumulación [a·ku·mu·la·'sjon, -'θjon] *f* accumulation; (*de cosas reunidas*) collection

acumular [a·ku·mu·'lar] *vt* **1.** (*reunir*) to collect **2.** (*amontonar*) to accumulate

acunar [a·ku·'nar] *vt* to rock (to sleep)

acuñar [a·ku·'ɲar] *vt* (*monedas*) to mint; (*palabras*) to coin

acupuntura [a·ku·pun·'tu·ra] *f* acupuncture

acurí [a·ku·'ri] *m Col, Ven* ZOOL agouti, guinea pig

acurrucarse <c→qu> [a·ku·rru·'kar·se] *vr* to curl up; (*por el frío*) to huddle up; **~ en un sillón** to curl up in an armchair

acusación [a·ku·sa·'sjon, -'θjon] *f* **1.** (*inculpación*) accusation; **~ de corrupción** charge of corruption **2.** JUR (*en juicio*) charge; (*escrito*) indictment; **~ constitucional** *charge involving a violation of the constitution*; **~ particular** private prosecution

acusado, -a [a·ku·'sa·do, -a] **I.** *adj* (*claro*) pronounced; (*marcado*) marked **II.** *m, f* accused

acusador(a) [a·ku·sa·'dor, -'do·ra] *m(f)* accuser

acusar [a·ku·'sar] *vt* **1.** (*culpar*) to accuse; **lo acusan de asesinato** he is accused of murder **2.** (*en juicio*) to charge **3.** ECON to confirm; **~ recibo de un pedido** to acknowledge receipt of an order

acusativo [a·ku·sa·'ti·βo] *m* LING accusative

acuse [a·'ku·se] *m* **~ de recibo** acknowledgement of receipt

acústica [a·'kus·ti·ka] *f* **1.** (*ciencia*) acoustics *sing* **2.** (*de un sitio*) acoustics *pl*

acústico, -a [a·'kus·ti·ko, -a] *adj* acoustic

acutí [a·ku·'ti] *m Arg, Par, Urug* ZOOL agouti

adagio [a·'da·xjo] *m* **1.** (*proverbio*) adage **2.** MÚS adagio

adaptable [a·dap·'ta·βle] *adj* adaptable

adaptación [a·dap·ta·'sjon, -'θjon] *f* adaptation; **la ~ de una obra de teatro al cine** the film version of a play

adaptador [a·dap·ta·'dor] *m* TÉC adapter

adaptar [a·dap·'tar] **I.** *vt* **1.** (*acomodar*) to adapt; *t.* LIT; **bien adaptado al grupo** well adapted to the group; **~ un piso para oficina** to convert an apartment into an office; **~ una novela a la pantalla** to adapt a novel for the screen **2.** (*ajustar*) to adjust; **~ algo a algo** to adapt sth to sth **II.** *vr:* **~se** to adapt; **se han adaptado muy bien el uno al otro** they have adjusted very well to each other

adecentar(se) [a·de·sen·'tar·(se), a·de·θen-] *vt, (vr)* to tidy (oneself) up

adecuado, -a [a·de·'kwa·do, -a] *adj* **1.** (*apto*) appropriate **2.** (*palabras*) fitting; **la decoración de tu casa es muy adecuada** your house is very well decorated

adecuar [a·de·'kwar] *vt, vr:* **~se** to adapt

adefesio [a·de·'fe·sjo] *m* (*prenda*) rag, ridiculous costume; (*persona*) scarecrow; **estar hecho un ~** to look a sight

a. de (J)C. ['an·tes de (xe·su)·'kris·to] *abr de* **antes de (Jesu)cristo** BC

adelantado, -a [a·de·lan·'ta·do, -a] *adj* (*avan-*

zado) advanced; **estar muy ~** to be very advanced ▶ **por ~** in advance
adelantamiento [a·de·lan·ta·'mjen·to] *m* **1.** (*avance*) advance **2.** (*del coche*) passing; **realizar un ~** to pass
adelantar [a·de·lan·'tar] **I.** *vi* **1.** (*reloj*) to be fast **2.** (*progresar*) to progress; **no adelanto nada en francés** I'm not making any progress in French **3.** (*coche*) to pass **II.** *vt* **1.** (*reloj*) to put forward **2.** (*avanzar*) to move forward; **~ unos pasos** to go forward a few steps **3.** (*coche*) to pass **4.** (*viaje*) to bring forward **5.** (*paga*) to advance **6.** (*ganar*) to gain; **¿qué adelantas con esto?** where does that get you? **III.** *vr:* **~ se 1.** (*reloj*) to be fast **2.** (*avanzarse*) to go forward; **te has adelantado a mis deseos** you've anticipated my wishes
adelante [a·de·'lan·te] *adv* forward, ahead; **llevar un plan ~** to carry forward a plan, to go ahead with a plan; **sacar una familia ~** to provide for a family; **¡~!** come in!; **seguir ~** to go (straight) ahead; **véase más ~** see below
adelanto [a·de·'lan·to] *m* progress; (*anticipo*) advance; **~s técnicos** technical innovations
adelgazar <z→c> [a·del·ya·'sar, -'θar] **I.** *vi, vr:* **~se** to lose weight **II.** *vt* to make thin; (*peso*) to reduce
ademán [a·de·'man] *m* gesture; **hacer ~ de salir** to make as if to leave; **en ~ de** getting ready to
además [a·de·'mas] *adv* besides, moreover
adentrarse [a·den·'trar·se] *vr* (*tema*) to study thoroughly; **~ en algo** to go into sth; (*penetrar*) to penetrate into sth
adentro [a·'den·tro] *adv* inside; **mar ~** out to sea; **tierra ~** inland; **el grito le salió de muy ~** his/her cry came from deep within
adentros [a·'den·tros] *mpl* innermost being; **para sus ~** inwardly; **guardar algo para sus ~** to keep sth to oneself
adepto, -a [a·'dep·to, -a] *m, f* supporter
aderezar <z→c> [a·de·re·'sar, -'θar] *vt* **1.** (*preparar*) to prepare **2.** (*condimentar*) to season; (*ensalada*) to dress
aderezo [a·de·'re·so, -θo] *m* preparation; (*condimentación*) seasoning; (*de ensalada*) dressing
adeudar [a·deu·'dar] **I.** *vt* **1.** (*deber*) to owe **2.** (*cargar*) to charge; **~ una cantidad en cuenta** to debit an account for a sum **II.** *vr:* **~se** to run into debt; **~se mucho** to get deep into debt
adherir [a·de·'rir] *irr como sentir* **I.** *vt* to stick **II.** *vr:* **~se 1.** (*pegarse*) to adhere **2.** (*a una opinión*) to adhere, to support; **~se a un partido** to join a party
adhesión [a·de·'sjon] *f* **1.** (*adherencia*) adhesion **2.** (*a una opinión*) adherence, support; **~ a alguien** support of sb; **~ a algo** membership in sth
adhesivo [a·de·'si·βo] *m* **1.** (*sustancia*) adhesive; **~ multiuso** all-purpose adhesive **2.** (*pegatina*) sticker

adhesivo, -a [a·de·'si·βo, -a] *adj* adhesive
adicción [a·dik·'sjon, -a·diy·'θjon] *f* addiction; **~ a las drogas** drug addiction
adición [a·di·'sjon, -'θjon] *f t.* MAT addition
adicional [a·di·sjo·'nal, -θjo·'nal] *adj* additional
adicionar [a·di·sjo·'nar, -θjo·'nar] *vt* to add
adicto, -a [a·'dik·to, -a] **I.** *adj* addicted; **~ a las drogas** addicted to drugs; **~ a la televisión** *inf* addicted to television **II.** *m, f* addict; *CSur* (*partidario*); **~ a alguien** supporter of sb
adiestrar [a·djes·'trar] *vt* to train
adifés [a·di·'fes] **I.** *adj Guat* (*difícil*) difficult **II.** *adv Ven* (*adrede*) on purpose
adinerado, -a [a·di·ne·'ra·do, -a] *adj* wealthy
adiós [a·'djos] **I.** *interj* (*despedida*) goodbye, bye; (*al pasar*) hello, hi **II.** *m* farewell; **decir ~ a alguien** to say goodbye to sb
aditamento [a·di·ta·'men·to] *m* addition
aditivo [a·di·'ti·βo] *m* additive
aditivo, -a [a·di·'ti·βo, -a] *adj* additional
adivinanza [a·di·βi·'nan·sa, -θa] *f* riddle
adivinar [a·di·βi·'nar] *vt* **1.** (*el futuro*) to foretell **2.** (*conjeturar*) to guess; **¡adivina cuántos años tengo!** guess how old I am!
adjetivo [ad·xe·'ti·βo] *m* adjective; **~ numeral** numeral
adjudicación [ad·xu·di·ka·'sjon, -'θjon] *f* **1.** (*de un premio*) award(ing) **2.** (*en una subasta*) sale
adjudicar <c→qu> [ad·xu·di·'kar] **I.** *vt* **1.** (*premio*) to award **2.** (*en subasta*) to sell at auction **II.** *vr:* **~se** to appropriate; (*premio*) to win
adjuntar [ad·xun·'tar] *vt* to enclose
adjunto, -a [ad·'xun·to, -a] *adj* **1.** (*junto*) enclosed **2.** (*auxiliar*) assistant; **profesor(a) ~** UNIV associate professor
administración [ad·mi·nis·tra·'sjon, -'θjon] *f* **1.** (*gestión*) administration; **la ~ española** the Spanish authorities; **la ~ de correos** the postal service; **~ de una cuenta** managing of an account; **~ de fincas** property management; **~ municipal** town/city council **2.** (*de medicamentos*) administering **3.** *Arg* (*gobierno*) government
administrador(a) [ad·mi·nis·tra·'dor] *m(f)* administrator; (*gerente*) manager
administrar [ad·mi·nis·'trar] *vt* **1.** (*dirigir*) administer; **~ justicia** to dispense justice **2.** (*racionar*) to ration **3.** (*medicamentos*) to administer
administrativo, -a [ad·mi·nis·tra·'ti·βo, -a] **I.** *adj* administrative **II.** *m, f* clerk
admirable [ad·mi·'ra·βle] *adj* admirable
admiración [ad·mi·ra·'sjon, -'θjon] *f* **1.** (*respeto*) admiration **2.** (*asombro*) amazement **3.** (*signo*) exclamation point
admirado, -a [ad·mi·'ra·do, -a] *adj* amazed; **me quedé admirada de tus conocimientos** I was amazed at your knowledge
admirador(a) [ad·mi·ra·'dor, -·'do·ra] *m(f)* admirer

admirar [ad·mi·'rar] *vt* **1.** (*adorar*) to admire **2.** (*asombrar*) to amaze

admisible [ad·mi·'si·βle] *adj* admissible

admisión [ad·mi·'sjon] *f* ~ **en algo** admission [*o* acceptance] to sth

admitir [ad·mi·'tir] *vt* **1.** (*en una universidad*) ~ **en algo** to accept into sth **2.** (*aceptar*) to accept **3.** (*reconocer*) to recognize **4.** (*permitir*) to permit; ~ **una queja** JUR to accept a complaint; **el asunto no admite dilación** the matter allows no delay; **es cosa admitida que... it** is generally admitted that...

ADN [a·de·'e·ne] *m abr de* **ácido desoxirribonucleico** DNA

adobar [a·do·'βar] *vt* **1.** (*con salsa*) to marinade; (*carne*) to pickle **2.** (*piel*) to tan

adobe [a·'do·βe] *m* adobe

adobo [a·'do·βo] *m* **1.** (*salsa*) marinade **2.** (*de pieles*) tanning

adoctrinar [a·dok·tri·'nar] *vt* to indoctrinate; ~ **a alguien sobre algo** to instruct sb about sth

adolecer [a·do·le·'ser, -'θer] *irr como crecer vi* (*enfermar*) to get sick; (*padecer*) to suffer; **este chico adolece de falta de imaginación** this boy suffers from a lack of imagination

adolescencia [a·do·les·'sen·sja, -'θen·θja] *f* adolescence

adolescente [a·do·les·'sen·te, -'θen·te] **I.** *adj* adolescent **II.** *mf* teenager

adonde [a·'don·de] *adv* where; **el pueblo ~ iremos es muy bonito** the village we'll go to is very pretty

adónde [a·'don·de] *adv* (*interrogativo*) where

adondequiera [a·don·de·'kje·ra] *adv* ~ **que** +*subj* wherever

adopción [a·dop·'sjon, -'θjon] *f* adoption

adoptar [a·dop·'tar] *vt* to adopt

adoptivo, -a [a·dop·'ti·βo, -a] *adj* (*personas*) foster; (*cosas*) adopted, foster

adoquín [a·do·'kin] *m* cobblestone

adoquinado [a·do·ki·'na·do] *m* cobbles *pl*

adoquinar [a·do·ki·'nar] *vt* to cobble

adorable [a·do·'ra·βle] *adj* adorable

adorar [a·do·'rar] *vt* to adore

adormecer [a·dor·me·'ser, -'θer] *irr como crecer* **I.** *vt* to make sleepy; (*dolor*) to numb **II.** *vr:* ~**se** to fall asleep

adormecido, -a [a·dor·me·'si·do, -a; -'θi·do, -a] *adj*, **adormilado, -a** [a·dor·mi·'la·do, -a] *adj* sleepy

adormilarse [a·dor·mi·'lar·se] *vr* to doze

adornar [a·dor·'nar] **I.** *vt* to adorn; (*con ornamentos*) to decorate **II.** *vr:* ~**se** to adorn oneself

adorno [a·'dor·no] *m* adornment; **árbol de ~** ornamental tree; **la lámpara sólo está de ~** the lamp is just for decoration; **estar de ~** *fig* to be for show

adosado, -a [a·do·'sa·do, -a] *adj* **casa adosada** duplex, two-family house

adquirir [ad·ki·'rir] *irr vt* **1.** (*conseguir*) to acquire; ~ **un hábito** to acquire a habit **2.** (*com-*

prar) to purchase

adquisición [ad·ki·si·'sjon, -'θjon] *f* acquisition; ~ **de lenguas** acquisition of languages; **este coche es una buena ~** this car is a good buy

adquisitivo, -a [ad·ki·si·'ti·βo, -a] *adj* acquisitive; **poder ~** purchasing power

adrede [a·'dre·de] *adv* on purpose

adrenalina [a·dre·na·'li·na] *f* adrenalin

Adriático [a·'drja·ti·ko] *m* Adriatic

adscribir [ads·kri·'βir] *irr como escribir vt* to appoint

aduana [a·'dwa·na] *f* **1.** (*tasa*) customs duty; **declaración de ~s** customs declaration; **despacho de ~** customs clearance; **sin ~** duty-free **2.** (*oficina*) customs office; **pase por la ~, por favor** go through customs, please

aduanero, -a [a·dwa·'ne·ro, -a] **I.** *adj* customs; **exento de derechos ~s** duty-free; **sujeto a derechos ~s** dutiable **II.** *m, f* customs officer

aducir [a·du·'sir, -'θir] *irr como traducir vt* (*razón*) to put forward; (*prueba*) to provide

adueñarse [a·dwe·'ɲar·se] *vr* to take possession; ~ **del poder** to take over; **el pánico se adueñó de él** panic got the better of him

adulación [a·du·la·'sjon, -'θjon] *f* flattery

adulador(a) [a·du·la·'dor, -'do·ra] *adj* flattering

adular [a·du·'lar] *vt* to flatter

adulterar [a·dul·te·'rar] *vt* to falsify; (*alimentos*) to adulterate

adulterio [a·dul·'te·rjo] *m* adultery

adúltero, -a [a·'dul·te·ro, -a] **I.** *adj* adulterous **II.** *m, f* adulterer

adulto, -a [a·'dul·to, -a] *adj, m, f* adult

advenedizo, -a [ad·βe·ne·'di·so, -a; -'di·θo, -a] **I.** *adj* foreign; *pey* (*arribista*) upstart **II.** *m, f* newcomer; *pey* (*arribista*) upstart

adverbial [ad·βer·'βjal] *adj* adverbial

adverbio [ad·'βer·βjo] *m* adverb; ~ **de modo/ de lugar/de tiempo** adverb of manner/of place/of time

adversario, -a [ad·βer·'sa·rjo, -a] *m, f* opponent

adversidad [ad·βer·si·'dad] *f* **1.** (*contrariedad*) adversity **2.** (*desgracia*) setback

adverso, -a [ad·'βer·so, -a] *adj* adverse; (*clima*) harsh

advertencia [ad·βer·'ten·sja, -θja] *f* **1.** (*amonestación*) warning **2.** (*indicación*) advice

advertir [ad·βer·'tir] *irr como sentir vt* **1.** (*reparar*) to notice; **advirtió mis intenciones** he/she guessed my intentions **2.** (*indicar*) to point out **3.** (*avisar*) to warn; ~ **algo** to draw attention to sth

advocar <c→qu> [ad·βo·'kar] *vt AmL* JUR to advocate

adyacencia [ad·ja·'sen·sja, -'θen·θja] *f RíoPl* (*proximidad*) proximity; **en las ~s** in the vicinity

adyacente [ad·ja·'sen·te, -'θen·te] *adj* adjacent

aéreo, -a [a·'e·reo, -a] *adj* aerial; **base aérea**

MIL airbase; **compañía aérea** airline (company); **por vía aérea** (by) airmail

aeróbic [ae·'ro·βik] *m* aerobics

aerodinámico, -a [ae·ro·di·'na·mi·ko, -a] *adj* aerodynamic; (*vehículo*) streamlined

aeródromo [ae·'ro·dro·mo] *m* aerodrome

aeroespacial [ae·ro·es·pa·'sjal, -'θjal] *adj* aerospace

aerolínea [ae·ro·'li·nea] *f* airline

aeromoza [ae·ro·'mo·sa, -θa] *f Méx, AmS* (*azafata*) stewardess, flight attendant

aeronauta [ae·ro·'nau·ta] *mf* aeronaut

aeronáutica [ae·ro·'nau·ti·ka] *f* aeronautics

aeronave [ae·ro·'na·βe] *f* airship; **~ espacial** spaceship

aeroplano [ae·ro·'pla·no] *m* airplane

aeropuerto [ae·ro·'pwer·to] *m* airport

aerosol [ae·ro·'sol] *m* aerosol; (*espray*) spray; (*recipiente*) spray can

afable [a·'fa·βle] *adj* affable

afamado, -a [a·fa·'ma·do, -a] *adj* famous

afán [a·'fan] *m* 1. (*ahínco*) eagerness; **~ de algo** urge for sth; **~ de lucro** profit motive; **con ~** eagerly; **poner mucho ~ en algo** to put a lot of effort into sth 2. (*anhelo*) **~ de algo** longing for sth; **~ de notoriedad** hunger for publicity

afanador(a) [a·fa·na·'dor, -'do·ra] *m(f)* 1. *Arg* (*carterista*) pickpocket; (*descuidero*) sneak thief 2. *Méx* (*para la limpieza*) cleaner

afanar [a·fa·'nar] I. *vi* to work hard II. *vt CSur, inf* to steal, to pinch III. *vr:* **~ se** (*esforzarse*) to toil (away)

afano [a·'fa·no] *m Arg, inf* job

afanoso, -a [a·fa·'no·so, -a] *adj* laborious; (*persona*) industrious

afarolarse [a·fa·ro·'lar·se] *vr Chile, Perú, inf* to get worked up

afear [a·fe·'ar] *vt* to disfigure; (*censurar*) to censure

afección [a·fek·'sjon, a·feɣ·'θjon] *f* 1. MED condition 2. (*inclinación*) inclination

afeccionarse [a·fek·sjo·'nar·se, a·feɣ·θjo-] *vr CSur* **~ de algo/alguien** to take a liking to sth/sb

afectación [a·fek·ta·'sjon, -'θjon] *f* affectation; **comportarse con ~** to behave affectedly

afectado, -a [a·fek·'ta·do, -a] *adj* affected

afectar [a·fek·'tar] I. *vt* 1. (*influir*) to concern 2. (*dañar*) to harm 3. (*impresionar*) to affect 4. (*aparentar*) to feign 5. *AmL* (*girar*) to transfer 6. *AmL* (*destinar dinero*) **~ a algo** to set aside for sth II. *vr:* **~ se** *AmL* to get sick

afectivo, -a [a·fek·'ti·βo, -a] *adj* 1. (*de afecto*) affective 2. (*cariñoso*) affectionate

afecto [a·'fek·to] *m* emotion; **~ a algo/alguien** affection for sth/sb

afecto, -a [a·'fek·to, -a] *adj* **~ a algo/alguien** inclined towards sth/sb; **estar ~ al pago de impuestos** *fig* to be taxable

afectuoso, -a [a·fek·tu·'o·so, -a] *adj* affectionate; (*cordial*) kind; **afectuosamente** yours affectionately

afeitada [a·fei·'ta·da] *f Arg*, **afeitado** [a·fei·'ta·do] *m* shave; **afeitado húmedo** wet shave

afeitar [a·fei·'tar] I. *vt* to shave; **máquina de ~** (safety) razor II. *vr:* **~ se** to shave

afeminado [a·fe·mi·'na·do] *m* effeminate man

afeminado, -a [a·fe·mi·'na·do, -a] *adj* effeminate

aferrar [a·fe·'rrar] I. *vt* to grasp II. *vr:* **~ se** to stand by; **~ a algo** to cling to sth

afgano, -a [af·'ɣa·no, -a] *adj, m, f* Afghan

afianzamiento [a·fjan·sa·'mjen·to, a·fjan·θa-] *m* 1. (*sujeción*) fastening 2. (*firmeza*) strength

afianzar <z→c> [a·fjan·'sar, -'θar] I. *vt* 1. (*sujetar*) to fasten 2. (*dar firmeza*) to strengthen II. *vr:* **~ se** 1. (*apoyarse*) to lean 2. (*afirmarse*) to become established

afiche [a·'fi·ʧe] *m AmL* poster

afición [a·fi·'sjon, -'θjon] *f* 1. (*inclinación*) liking; **cobrar** [*o* **tomar**] **una ~ por** [*o* **a**] **algo** to develop [*o* take] a liking for [*o* to] sth; **tener** [*o* **sentir**] **una ~ hacia** [*o* **a**] **algo** to be fond of sth 2. (*pasatiempo*) hobby; **de ~** as a hobby; **hacer algo por ~** to do sth as a hobby 3. (*hinchada*) fans *pl*

aficionado, -a [a·fi·sjo·'na·do, -a; a·fi·θjo-] I. *adj* amateur; **ser ~ a la arquitectura** to be an architecture enthusiast; **ser ~ a tocar la flauta** to be fond of playing the flute II. *m, f* 1. (*entusiasta*) lover; DEP fan; **~ a la ópera** opera lover 2. (*no profesional*) amateur

aficionar [a·fi·sjo·'nar, a·fi·θjo-] I. *vt* **~ a alguien a algo** to get sb interested in sth II. *vr* **~ se a algo** (*acostumbrarse*) to take a liking to sth; **~ se a alguien** to become fond of sb

afilado, -a [a·fi·'la·do, -a] *adj* (*nariz*) pointed; (*cara*) thin; **tener uñas afiladas** *inf* to be light-fingered; **lengua afilada** *fig* sharp tongue

afilalápices [a·fi·la·'la·pi·ses, -θes] *m inv* pencil sharpener

afilar [a·fi·'lar] I. *vt* to sharpen II. *vr:* **~ se** to get sharp; (*cara*) to grow thin

afiliación [a·fi·lja·'sjon, -'θjon] *f* affiliation; **~ política** political affiliation

afiliado, -a [a·fi·'lja·do, -a] *m, f* member; **~ a un sindicato** trade union member

afiliar [a·fi·'ljar] I. *vt* **~ a algo** to admit into sth II. *vr:* **~ se a algo** to join sth

afín [a·'fin] *adj* related

afinar [a·fi·'nar] I. *vi* (*cantando*) to sing in tune; (*tocando*) to play in tune II. *vt* 1. (*hacer más fino*) to refine; (*metales*) to purify; (*lápiz*) to sharpen; **~ la puntería** to sharpen one's aim 2. MÚS to tune

afinidad [a·fi·ni·'dad] *f* similarity; **~ de caracteres** relatedness of character; **son parientes por ~** they are related by marriage

afirmación [a·fir·ma·'sjon, -'θjon] *f* 1. (*confirmación*) confirmation; **contestar algo con afirmaciones** to answer in the affirmative 2. (*aseveración*) assertion

afirmar [a·fir·'mar] I. *vt* 1. (*decir sí*) to affirm; (*dar por cierto*) to confirm; **~ con la cabeza** to nod in agreement 2. (*aseverar*) to state

II. *vr:* ~**se** to be confirmed; ~**se en algo** to reaffirm sth

afirmativo, -a [a·fir·ma·'ti·βo, -a] *adj* affirmative; **en caso** ~ if so; **respuesta afirmativa** positive answer

aflicción [a·flik·'sjon, -ɣ'θjon] *f* ~ **por algo/alguien** grief for sth/sb; **dar** ~ **a alguien** to cause sb worry

afligir <g→j> [a·fli·'xir] **I.** *vt* **1.** (*apenar*) to upset **2.** (*atormentar*) to afflict **II.** *vr:* ~**se por** [*o* **de**] **algo** to get upset about [*o* over] sth

aflojar [a·flo·'xar] **I.** *vi* to slacken **II.** *vt* **1.** (*nudo*) to loosen; (*cuerda*) to slacken (off) **2.** (*velocidad*) to reduce; ~ **el paso** to slacken one's pace; **un tira y afloja** a tug-of-war **III.** *vr:* ~**se** to slacken

aflorar [a·flo·'rar] *vi* **1.** (*salir*) to come to the surface **2.** (*apuntar*) to appear

afluencia [a·'flwen·θja, -sja] *f* abundance; (*gente*) crowd; ~ **de votantes** turnout (at the polls)

afluente [a·'flwen·te] *m* tributary

afluir [a·flu·'ir] *irr como huir vi* ~ **a algo** (*río*) to flow into sth; (*calle*) to lead into sth; (*gente*); ~ **a un concierto/a Madrid** to flock to a concert/to Madrid

afluxionarse [a·fluk·sjo·'nar·se] *vr* **1.** *AmC* (*hincharse*) to swell **2.** *Col, Cuba* (*acatarrarse*) to catch cold

afonía [a·fo·'ni·a] *f* hoarseness; **tener** ~ to be hoarse

afónico, -a [a·'fo·ni·ko, -a] *adj* hoarse

aforismo [a·fo·'ris·mo] *m* aphorism

aforo [a·'fo·ro] *m* **1.** (*en teatro*) capacity; **la sala tiene un** ~ **de 300 personas** the hall can seat 300 people **2.** TÉC gauging

afortunado, -a [a·for·tu·'na·do, -a] *adj* fortunate; **¡qué afortunada eres!** how lucky you are!

afrenta [a·'fren·ta] *f* affront, insult; **hacer una** ~ **a alguien** to insult sb

afrentar [a·fren·'tar] **I.** *vt* to insult **II.** *vr:* ~**se** to take offense

África ['a·fri·ka] *f* Africa

africano, -a [a·fri·'ka·no, -a] *adj, m, f* African

afrodisiaco [a·fro·di·'sja·ko] *m*, **afrodisíaco** [a·fro·di·'si·a·ko] *m* aphrodisiac

afrontar [a·fron·'tar] *vt* to face; ~ **un problema** to tackle a problem

afrutado, -a [a·fru·'ta·do, -a] *adj* fruity

afuera [a·'fwe·ra] *adv* outside; **la parte de** ~ the outside; **¡~!** *inf* get out of here!

afueras [a·'fwe·ras] *fpl* outskirts *pl;* ~ **de la ciudad** outskirts of the city

agachar [a·ɣa·'tʃar] **I.** *vt* to lower **II.** *vr:* ~**se** **1.** (*encogerse*) to crouch **2.** *AmL* (*ceder*) to give in

agache [a·'ɣa·tʃe] *m* **1.** *Col* (*mentira*) fib **2.** *Cuba* **andar de** ~ to be on the run **3.** *Ecua* (*de tapadillo*) **de** ~ on the sly

agalla [a·'ɣa·ja, -ʎa] *f* gill; **tener** ~**s** *fig* to have guts

agarrada [a·ɣa·'rra·da] *f inf* fight; **tener una** ~

to have a fight

agarradera [a·ɣa·rra·'de·ra] *f AmL*, **agarradero** [a·ɣa·rra·'de·ro] *m* influence

agarrado, -a [a·ɣa·'rra·do] *adj* stingy

agarrador [a·ɣa·rra·'dor] *m* pot holder

agarrar [a·ɣa·'rrar] **I.** *vi* **1.** (*comida*) to stick **2.** (*coche*) to grip the road; **agarró y salió** *inf* he/she upped and left **II.** *vt* **1.** (*tomar*) to take **2.** (*asir*) to grasp; (*delincuente*) to seize **3.** (*enfermedad*) to catch; ~ **una borrachera** to get drunk; ~ **una pulmonía** to catch pneumonia **III.** *vr:* ~**se** **1.** (*asirse*) to hold on; **agárrate, que te voy a contar qué me pasó ayer** *inf* just hold on! Wait till you hear what happened to me yesterday **2.** (*reñir*) to have a fight **3.** (*comida*) to stick; ~**se al retraso del tren para justificarse** *inf* to use the train's late arrival as an excuse **4.** *AmL* (*coger*) to catch; (*frutas*) to pluck

agarrotar [a·ɣa·rro·'tar] **I.** *vt* **1.** (*entumecer*) to stiffen up **2.** (*oprimir*) to squeeze tight **II.** *vr:* ~**se** **1.** (*entumecerse*) to go numb; (*por el miedo*) to stiffen with fear **2.** TÉC to seize up

agasajar [a·ɣa·sa·'xar] *vt* to receive in great style; **el embajador fue agasajado con un banquete** a banquet was given in the ambassador's honor

agatas [a·'ɣa·tas] *adv Par, RíoPl* **1.** (*con dificultad*) with great difficulty **2.** (*casi no*) hardly; ~ **sabe leer** he/she can barely read **3.** (*tan sólo*) barely; ~ **hace una hora** barely an hour ago

agaucharse [a·ɣau·'tʃar·se] *vr AmS* to imitate or dress like a gaucho; **tras tantos años de vida en el campo se agauchó mucho** after so many years in the country he/she had become very gaucho-like

agencia [a·'xen·sja, -θja] *f* **1.** (*empresa*) agency; ~ **de colocaciones** employment agency; ~ **inmobiliaria** real estate agency; ~ **de noticias** news agency [*o* service]; ~ **de publicidad** advertising agency; ~ **de transportes** carriers; **Agencia Tributaria** tax office; ~ **de viajes** travel agency **2.** (*sucursal*) branch

agenciarse [a·xen·'sjar·se, -'θjar·se] *vr* to get hold of; **agenciárselas** to manage; **agénciatelas como puedas** try to get by as best you can

agenciero [a·xen·'sje·ro, -a; a·xen·'θje-] *m*, *f* **1.** *Arg* (*de negocios*) representative; (*de lotería*) lottery vendor **2.** *Chile* (*prestamista*) pawnbroker

agenda [a·'xen·da] *f* **1.** (*calendario*) engagement [*o* date] book; ~ **de bolsillo** pocket diary; **tener una** ~ **apretada** to have a tight schedule **2.** (*orden del día*) agenda

agente[1] [a·'xen·te] *mf* **1.** (*representante*) representative; (*de un artista*) agent; ~ **autorizado** authorized agent; ~ **de bolsa** stockbroker; ~ **exclusivo** exclusive agent; ~ **de la propiedad inmobiliaria** realtor; ~ **de transportes** carrier **2.** (*funcionario*) ~ **de aduanas** customs officer; ~ **judicial** bailiff; ~ **de policía** police officer

agente² [a·'xen·te] *m t.* MED agent

ágil ['a·xil] *adj* (*de movimiento*) agile; (*mental*) alert, quick-witted

agilidad [a·xi·li·'dad] *f* (*física*) agility; ~ **de dedos** dexterity; (*mental*) acumen

agilizar <z→c> [a·xi·li·'sar, -'θar] *vt* to speed up

agitación [a·xi·ta·'sjon, -'θjon] *f* movement; *t.* POL agitation; (*excitación*) excitement

agitado, -a [a·xi·'ta·do, -a] *adj* hectic

agitar [a·xi·'tar] **I.** *vt* **1.** (*mover*) to move; (*bandera*) to wave; **agítese antes de usar** shake well before use **2.** (*intranquilizar*) to worry **3.** (*sublevar*) to rouse **II.** *vr:* ~**se 1.** (*moverse*) to move about; (*bandera*) to wave; (*mar*) to get rough **2.** (*excitarse*) to get excited

aglomeración [a·ɣlo·me·ra·'sjon, -'θjon] *f* agglomeration; ~ **de gente** crowd of people; ~ **urbana** urban sprawl

aglomerar [a·ɣlo·me·'rar] **I.** *vt* to gather (together); (*amontonar*) to pile up **II.** *vr:* ~**se** to crowd (together)

aglutinar [a·ɣlu·ti·'nar] *vt* to agglutinate; (*unir*) to unite; *fig* to bring together

ago. *abr de* **agosto** Aug.

agobiado, -a [a·ɣo·'βja·do, -a] *adj* exhausted; ~ **por los años** weighed down by the years; **estar ~ de trabajo** to be overloaded with work; **estoy ~ de deudas** I'm burdened with debts

agobiante [a·ɣo·'βjan·te] *adj* overwhelming; (*persona*) tiresome

agobiar [a·ɣo·'βjar] **I.** *vt* **1.** (*abrumar*) to overwhelm; ~ **a alguien con alabanzas** to overwhelm sb with praise; **¡no me agobies!** *inf* don't keep going on at me! **2.** (*calor*) to suffocate **II.** *vr:* ~**se 1.** (*angustiarse*) ~**se por algo** to be weighed down with sth **2.** (*sentirse abatido*) to feel overwhelmed

agobio [a·'ɣo·βjo] *m* **1.** (*carga*) burden **2.** (*cansancio*) exhaustion **3.** (*opresión*) oppression

agolparse [a·ɣol·'par·se] *vr* (*personas*) to crowd (together); (*líquido*) to stream; **se agolparon las lágrimas en sus ojos** tears welled up in his/her eyes

agonía [a·ɣo·'ni·a] *f* **1.** (*del moribundo*) death throes *pl;* (*de un pueblo*) decline **2.** (*angustia*) anguish

agónico, -a [a·'ɣo·ni·ko, -a] *adj* **período ~** hour of death; **estar ~** to be dying

agonizar <z→c> [a·ɣo·ni·'sar, -'θar] *vi* to be dying; (*terminar*) to come to an end

agosto [a·'ɣos·to] *m* August; **hacer su ~** to make a killing; *v.t.* **marzo**

agotado, -a [a·ɣo·'ta·do, -a] *adj* (*producto*) out of stock; (*persona*) exhausted

agotador(a) [a·ɣo·ta·'dor, -·'do·ra] *adj* exhausting; **hace un calor ~** the heat is unbearable

agotamiento [a·ɣo·ta·'mjen·to] *m* exhaustion

agotar [a·ɣo·'tar] **I.** *vt* **1.** (*existencias*) to use

up; (*mercancía*) to deplete; (*paciencia*) to exhaust **2.** (*cansar*) to tire (out) **II.** *vr:* ~**se 1.** (*mercancía*) to run out; (*pilas*) to run down [*o* out]; (*fuerzas*) to give out; **esta edición se agotó enseguida** this edition sold out immediately **2.** (*cansarse*) to wear oneself out

agraciado, -a [a·ɣra·'sja·do, -a; -'θja·do, -a] *adj* **1.** (*gracioso*) graceful **2.** (*bien parecido*) attractive **3.** (*afortunado*) lucky; **salir ~ en la lotería** to win in the lottery

agraciar [a·ɣra·'sjar, -'θjar] *vt* **1.** (*conceder*) to award; **fue agraciado con un premio** he/she was awarded a prize **2.** (*vestido*) to enhance; **este traje le agracia la figura** this dress flatters her figure

agradable [a·ɣra·'da·βle] *adj* pleasant; ~ **al paladar** tasty; **es ~ a la vista** it is pleasing to the eye; ~ **con alguien** pleasant to sb

agradar [a·ɣra·'dar] *vi* to please; **me agrada oír música** I like listening to music; **me agrada esta gente** I like these people; **quieres ~ a todos** you want to please everyone

agradecer [a·ɣra·de·'ser, -'θer] *irr como* **crecer** *vt* to thank; **te agradezco la invitación** thanks for the invitation; **les agradezco que me lo hayan dicho** I'm grateful to you for having told me; **le ~ía mucho que** +*subj* I'd be very grateful if; **no sabes ~ mi trabajo** you don't appreciate my work; **el campo ha agradecido la lluvia** the rain has been good for the fields

agradecido, -a [a·ɣra·de·'si·do, -a; -'θi·do, -a] *adj* **1.** (*que agradece*) ~ **por algo** grateful for sth; **le estaría muy ~ que** [*o* **si**] **me contestara lo antes posible** I would appreciate it very much if you could reply as soon as possible; **le estoy sumamente ~** I am extremely grateful (to you); **le quedamos muy ~s** we are very grateful (to you) **2.** (*que compensa*) worthwhile

agradecimiento [a·ɣra·de·si·'mjen·to, -θi·'mjen·to] *m* gratitude

agrado [a·'ɣra·do] *m* **1.** (*afabilidad*) affability; **tratar a alguien con ~** to treat sb kindly **2.** (*complacencia*) willingness; **decidir según su ~** to decide as one likes; **he recibido con ~ su carta** I was very pleased to receive your letter; **esto no es de mi ~** this isn't to my liking

agrandar [a·ɣran·'dar] **I.** *vt* to make bigger; ~ **la importancia de algo** to exaggerate the importance of sth **II.** *vr:* ~**se** to get bigger

agrario, -a [a·'ɣra·rjo, -a] *adj* agrarian; **crédito ~** agrarian credit; **población agraria** rural population

agravamiento [a·ɣra·βa·'mjen·to] *m* aggravation; *t.* MED worsening

agravante [a·ɣra·'βan·te] *m o f* aggravating factor

agravar [a·ɣra·'βar] **I.** *vt* to make worse, to aggravate **II.** *vr:* ~**se** to worsen

agraviar [a·ɣra·'βjar] **I.** *vt* to offend; JUR to harm **II.** *vr:* ~**se** to be offended

agravio [aˈɣra·βjo] *m* offense; JUR grievance; ~ **material** material damage; **sufrir** ~**s** to suffer injustice

agredir [a·yreˈdir] *vt* to attack; ~ **a alguien de palabra** to attack sb verbally

agregado [a·yre·ˈɣa·do] *m* 1.(*conglomerado*) aggregate 2.(*aditamento*) addition

agregado, -a [a·yre·ˈɣa·do, -a] *m*, *f* 1.(*diplomático*) attaché; ~ **comercial** commercial attaché; ~ **militar** military attaché 2. UNIV associate professor

agregar <g→gu> [a·yre·ˈɣar] I. *vt* to add II. *vr*: ~ **se** to join; ~ **se a alguien** to join sb

agremiar [a·yre·ˈmjar] I. *vt* to unionize II. *vr*: ~ **se** to form a union

agresión [a·yre·ˈsjon] *f* aggression

agresividad [a·yre·si·βi·ˈdad] *f* aggressiveness

agresivo, -a [a·yre·ˈsi·βo, -a] *adj* aggressive

agresor(a) [a·yre·ˈsor] I. *adj* aggressor II. *m(f)* aggressor, assailant

agreste [a·ˈyres·te] *adj* 1.(*campestre*) country 2.(*terreno*) rough, wild 3.(*persona*) uncouth

agriar [a·ˈyrjar] I. *vt* (*alimentos*) to sour; (*persona*) to make bitter II. *vr*: ~ **se** (*alimentos*) to turn sour; (*persona*) to become embittered [*o* bitter]

agrícola [a·ˈyri·ko·la] *adj* agricultural; **cooperativa** ~ agricultural cooperative

agricultor(a) [a·yri·kul·ˈtor, -·ˈto·ra] *m(f)* farmer

agricultura [a·yri·kul·ˈtu·ra] *f* agriculture

agridulce [a·yri·ˈdul·se, -θe] *adj* bittersweet; CULIN sweet-and-sour

agrietar [a·yrje·ˈtar] I. *vt* to crack II. *vr*: ~ **se** to crack; (*pared*) to become cracked; (*piel*) to become chapped

agringarse <g→gu> [a·yrin·ˈgar·se] *vr* AmL: to imitate or adopt the customs of a foreigner

agrio, -a [ˈa·yrjo, -a] *adj* 1.(*sabor*) sour 2.(*crítica*) sharp 3.(*carácter*) bitter

agripado, -a [a·yri·ˈpa·do, -a] *adj* Col, inf(*griposo*) **estar** ~ to have the flu

agronomía [a·yro·no·ˈmi·a] *f* agronomy

agrónomo, -a [a·ˈyro·no·mo, -a] *m*, *f* agronomist

agropecuario, -a [a·yro·pe·ˈkwa·rjo, -a] *adj* agricultural, farming

agroturismo [a·yro·tu·ˈris·mo] *m* agrotourism

agrupación [a·yru·pa·ˈsjon, -ˈθjon] *f* 1.(*agrupamiento*) grouping 2.(*conjunto*) group; ~ **de municipios** municipal association 3.(*asociación*) society

agrupar [a·yru·ˈpar] I. *vt* to group (together); ~ **algo por temas** to group sth by subject II. *vr*: ~ **se** to form a group

agua [ˈa·ywa] *f* 1.(*líquido*) water; ~ **de colonia** eau de cologne; ~**s depuradas** purified water; ~ **con gas** sparkling water; ~ **del grifo** tap water; ~ **de mar** seawater; ~ **de nieve** meltwater; ~ **nieve** sleet; ~ **potable** drinking water; ¡**hombre al** ~! man overboard!; **claro como el** ~ crystal clear; **esta noche ha caído mucha** ~ it rained a lot last night 2. *pl* (*mares*)

waters *pl*; ~**s interiores** inland waters; ~**s jurisdiccionales** territorial waters; ~**s residuales** sewage; ~**s termales** hot baths [*o* springs]; ~**s abajo/arriba** downstream/upstream 3. *pl* (*orina*) urine; ~**s menores** urine; **hacer** ~**s** to urinate ▶ **quedar en** ~ **de borrajas** to come to nothing; **volver las** ~**s a su cauce** to go back to normal; **estoy con el** ~ **hasta el cuello** I'm up to my neck in it; **como** ~ **de mayo** very welcome; **no hallar** ~ **en el mar** to act stupid; **llevar el** ~ **a su molino** to turn things to one's advantage; ~ **pasada no mueve molino** *prov* it's no use crying over spilled milk; **sacar** ~ **a las piedras** to make something out of nothing; **no llegará el** ~ **al río** it won't go that far; **estar entre dos** ~**s** to be sitting on the fence; **es** ~ **pasada** that's water under the bridge; **hacer** ~ (*buque*) to take in water; (*negocio*) to founder; **tomar las** ~**s** to take the waters

aguacate [a·ywa·ˈka·te] *m* avocado

aguacero [a·ywa·ˈse·ro, -ˈθe·ro] *m* downpour; **cayó un** ~ there was a cloudburst

aguachento, -a [a·ywa·ˈtʃen·to, -a] *adj* AmL v. **aguado**

aguachirle [a·ywa·ˈtʃir·le] *f* pey dishwater

aguacil [a·ywa·ˈsil, -ˈθil] *m* CSur ZOOL dragonfly

aguado, -a [a·ˈywa·do, -a] *adj* watered-down; (*fruta*) tasteless

aguafiestas [a·ywa·ˈfjes·tas] *mf inv, inf* spoilsport, party pooper

aguafuerte [a·ywa·ˈfwer·te] *m* etching; **grabar al** ~ to etch

aguaitar [a·ywai·ˈtar] *vt* 1. Arg, Cuba (*acechar*) to lie in wait for 2. Col (*esperar*) to wait; ~ **unos días** to wait a few days; ~ **algo/a alguien** to wait for sth/sb

aguamiel [a·ywa·ˈmjel] *f* AmL (*jugo del maguey*) maguey juice

aguanieve [a·ywa·ˈnje·βe] *f* sleet

aguantable [a·ywan·ˈta·βle] *adj* bearable

aguantadero [a·ywan·ta·ˈde·ro] *m* Arg, Urug hide-out

aguantar [a·ywan·ˈtar] I. *vt* 1.(*sostener*) to hold; (*sujetar*) to hold tight; ~ **la risa** to hold back one's laughter 2.(*soportar*) to bear; **no aguanto más** I can't bear it any more; **no poder** ~ **a alguien** not to be able to stand sb; **esta película no se aguanta** this film is unbearable; ~ **la mirada de alguien** to hold sb's stare 3.(*durar*) to last; **este abrigo** ~**á mucho** this coat will last for a long time II. *vr*: ~**se** 1.(*contenerse*) to restrain oneself 2.(*soportar*) to put up with it 3.(*conformarse*) to resign oneself 4.(*sostenerse*) to support oneself; ~**se de pie** to stay standing

aguante [a·ˈywan·te] *m* 1.(*paciencia*) patience; **tener mucho** ~ to be very patient 2.(*resistencia*) stamina

aguar <gu→gü> [a·ˈywar] I. *vt* 1.(*mezclar*) to water (down) 2.(*frustrar*) to spoil II. *vr*: ~ **se** 1.(*con agua*) to fill with water; **no pude evitar que se me** ~**an los ojos** I couldn't stop my eyes from watering; **nuestras vacaciones se ~on** our vacation was spoiled by rain **2.** (*estropearse*) to be spoiled

aguardar [a·ɣwar·'dar] **I.** *vt* to wait for; **~ unos días** to wait a few days; **~ algo/a alguien** to await sth/sb **II.** *vr:* **~se** to be awaited

aguardiente [a·ɣwar·'djen·te] *m* brandy

aguarrás [a·ɣwa·'rras] *m* turpentine

agudeza [a·ɣu·'de·sa, -θa] *f* **1.** (*del cuchillo*) sharpness; **~ visual** keenness of sight **2.** (*ingenio*) wittiness

agudizar <z→c> [a·ɣu·di·'sar, -'θar] **I.** *vt* **1.** (*hacer agudo*) to sharpen **2.** (*agravar*) to make worse **II.** *vr:* **~se** to worsen

agudo, -a [a·'ɣu·do, -a] *adj* **1.** (*afilado*) sharp; **vista aguda** keen sight **2.** (*ingenioso*) witty; (*mordaz*) scathing **3.** (*dolor*) acute; (*olor*) pungent **4.** (*sonido*) piercing **5.** (*grave*) severe

agüero [a·'ɣwe·ro] *m* omen; **de mal ~** ill-fated; **ser de buen ~** to augur well

aguerrido, -a [a·ɣe·'rri·do, -a] *adj* (*fuerte*) hardened

aguijón [a·ɣi·'xon] *m* **1.** (*punta*) goad; ZOOL sting, stinger **2.** (*estímulo*) stimulus

aguijonear [a·ɣi·xo·ne·'ar] *vt* **1.** (*animales*) to goad **2.** (*estimular*) to spur on

águila ['a·ɣi·la] *f* eagle; **~ real** golden eagle; **ser un ~ para los negocios** *fig* to be sharp in business

aguileño, -a [a·ɣi·'le·ɲo, -a] *adj* aquiline; **rostro ~** angular face

aguinaldo [a·ɣi·'nal·do] *m* tip (*given at Christmas*)

agüita [a·'ɣwi·ta] *f Perú, inf* dough

agüitado, -a [a·ɣwi·'ta·do, -a] *adj Méx, inf* gloomy

aguja [a·'ɣu·xa] *f* **1.** (*general*) needle; (*de una jeringa*) hypodermic needle; **~ de gancho** crochet hook; **~ de punto** knitting needle; **~ de la iglesia** church steeple; **buscar una ~ en un pajar** to look for a needle in a haystack; **las torres de esa catedral terminan en ~s** the towers of that cathedral are topped with spires **2.** (*del reloj*) hand; (*de un instrumento*) pointer; **~** (**de marear**) NÁUT ship's compass **3.** FERRO point **4.** CULIN **carne de ~** rib roast

agujerear [a·ɣu·xe·re·'ar] *vt* to make holes in; (*orejas*) to pierce

agujero [a·ɣu·'xe·ro] *m* hole; **~** (**en la capa**) **de ozono** hole in the ozone layer; **tapar un ~** to fill a hole

agujetas [a·ɣu·'xe·tas] *fpl* stiffness

aguzado, -a [a·ɣu·'sa·do, -a; -'θa·do, -a] *adj* sharp

aguzar <z→c> [a·ɣu·'sar, -'θar] *vt* **1.** (*afilar*) to sharpen **2.** (*avivar*) **~ la atención** to heighten one's attention; **~ los sentidos** to sharpen one's senses; **~ la vista** to look more carefully

ahí [a·'i] **I.** *adv* (*lugar*) there; **~ está** there he/she/it is; **~ viene** there he/she/it comes; **llámame de ~** call me from there; **~ está el problema** that's the problem; **me voy por ~** I'm going that way ▶ **¡~ es nada!** not bad!;

~ me las den todas *inf* I couldn't care less; **por ~, por ~** something like that **II.** *conj* **de ~ que...** that is why...

ahijado, -a [a·i·'xa·do, -a] *m, f* godchild; *fig* protégé *m*, protégée *f*

ahínco [a·'in·ko] *m* **1.** (*empeño*) effort **2.** (*insistencia*) insistence

ahogado, -a [a·o·'ɣa·do, -a] *adj* drowned; **estar ~ de trabajo** *fig* to be snowed under with work

ahogar <g→gu> [a·o·'ɣar] **I.** *vt* **1.** (*en el agua*) to drown **2.** (*estrangular*) to strangle **3.** (*asfixiar*) to suffocate **II.** *vr:* **~se 1.** (*en el agua*) to drown **2.** (*asfixiarse*) to suffocate; **~se de calor** to be sweltering (in the heat) **3.** (*motor*) to flood ▶ **~se en un vaso de agua** to make mountains out of molehills

ahogo [a·'o·ɣo] *m* **1.** (*sofocación*) breathlessness **2.** (*asfixia*) asphyxiation **3.** (*apuro*) hardship; **~s económicos** financial difficulties

ahondar [a·on·'dar] **I.** *vi* to put down roots; **~ en algo** (*tema*) to go deeply into sth **II.** *vt* **1.** (*profundizar*) to deepen **2.** (*introducir*) to introduce **III.** *vr:* **~se** to go in more deeply

ahora [a·'o·ra] *adv* now; (*muy pronto*) very soon; **~ bien** now then; **de ~ en adelante** from now on; **hasta ~** up to now; **por ~** for the present; **~ ríe, ~ llora** laughing one minute, crying the next; **¡~** (**lo entiendo**)! now I've got it!; **¡~ sí que hemos tenido suerte!** we were really lucky there!; **~ mismo vengo** I'm just coming; **acaba de salir ~ mismo** he/she has just gone out; **¡ven ~ mismo!** come right now!; **¿y ~ qué?** what now?

ahorcado, -a [a·or·'ka·do, -a] *m, f* hanged person

ahorcar <c→qu> [a·or·'kar] **I.** *vt* to hang; **~ los libros** to give up one's studies **II.** *vr:* **~se** to hang oneself

ahorita [a·o·'ri·ta] *adv AmL* right away

ahorrador(a) [a·o·rra·'dor, -·'do·ra] **I.** *adj* thrifty **II.** *m(f)* saver

ahorrar [a·o·'rrar] **I.** *vt* to save; **~ fuerzas** to save [*o* conserve] one's energy; **~ esfuerzos a alguien** to save sb the trouble; **ahórrame explicaciones** spare me your explanation **II.** *vr:* **~se** (*evitar*) to save oneself

ahorrativo, -a [a·o·rra·'ti·βo, -a] *adj* thrifty

ahorrista [a·o·'rris·ta] *mf AmL* FIN savings account holder

ahorro [a·'o·rro] *m* (*cantidad*) saving

ahuecar <c→qu> [a·we·'kar] **I.** *vt* **1.** (*vaciar*) to hollow out **2.** (*tierra*) to break up; (*colchón*) to plump up **II.** *vr:* **~se 1.** (*ave*) to ruffle (up) its feathers **2.** (*envanecerse*) to put on airs

ahuevarse [a·we·'βar·se] *vr Col, vulg* (*acobardarse*) to chicken out

ahulado [a·u·'la·do] *m* **1.** *AmC, Méx* (*mantel*) (oilcloth) table cover; **pon el ~ en la mesa** put the tablecloth on the table **2.** *pl, AmC* (*zapatos*) rubbers *pl*

ahumado, -a [a·u·'ma·do, -a] *adj* **1.** (*cristal*) tinted **2.** (*salmón*) smoked

ahumar [a·u'·mar] I. *vi* to smoke II. *vt* CULIN to smoke; (*una colmena*) to smoke out III. *vr:* ~**se** 1.(*pared*) to become blackened 2.(*guiso*) to acquire a burnt taste

ahuyentar [a·u·jen·'tar] *vt* 1.(*espantar*) to frighten off [*o away*] 2.(*dudas*) to dispel

aimara, aimará [ai·ma·ra] I. *adj* Aymara II. *mf* Aymara

aindiado, -a [a·in·'dja·do, -a] *adj AmL* Indian-looking

airar [ai·'rar] *irr* I. *vt* to anger II. *vr:* ~**se** to get angry

airbag ['er·βaɣ] *m* airbag

aire ['ai·re] *m* 1.(*atmósfera*) air; ~ **acondicionado** air conditioning; **Ejército del Aire** air force; **al** ~ **libre** in the open air; **echar una moneda al** ~ to toss a coin (into the air); **tomar el** ~ to go for a stroll; **dejar una pregunta en el** ~ to leave a question open; **cambiar de** ~**s** to have a change of air; **¡**~**!** *inf* beat it! 2.(*viento*) wind; **corriente de** ~ draft; **corre** ~ it's drafty; **hoy hace** ~ it's windy today 3.(*aspecto*) appearance; **no me gusta el** ~ **de este hombre** I don't like the look of this man; **tener** ~ **de despistado** to look absent-minded; **darse** ~**s de grandeza** to have pretensions of grandeur; **darse** ~**s de intelectual** to put on an intellectual air; **¡tiene unos** ~**s!** he/she is always putting on airs! 4.(*garbo*) elegance 5.*Arg, Par* (*cuello*) stiff neck

aireado, -a [ai·re·'a·do, -a] *adj* ventilated

airear [ai·re·'ar] I. *vt* to air II. *vr:* ~**se** 1.(*ventilarse*) to air 2.(*coger aire*) to get some fresh air

airoso, -a [ai·'ro·so, -a] *adj* graceful; **salir** ~ **de algo** to acquit oneself well in sth

aislado, -a [ais·'la·do, -a] *adj* isolated

aislamiento [ais·la·'mjen·to] *m* 1.(*retiro*) isolation 2. *t.* TÉC insulation; ~ **acústico** soundproofing

aislante [ais·'lan·te] I. *adj* insulating; **cinta** ~ electrical tape II. *m* insulator

aislar [ais·'lar] I. *vt* to isolate; TÉC to insulate; **aislado contra el ruido** soundproof II. *vr:* ~**se** to isolate oneself

ajardinado, -a [a·xar·di·'na·do, -a] *adj* landscaped

ajedrecista [a·xe·dre·'sis·ta, -'θista] *mf* chess player

ajedrez [a·xe·'dres, -'dreθ] *m* 1.DEP chess 2.(*tablero*) chess set

ajenjo [a·'xen·xo] *m* 1.BOT wormwood 2.(*bebida*) absinthe

ajeno, -a [a·'xe·no, -a] *adj* 1.(*de otro*) somebody else's; **la felicidad ajena** other people's happiness 2. *ser* (*impropio*) inappropriate; **esto es** ~ **a su carácter** this is alien to his/her character 3. *estar* (*ignorante*) ignorant; **ser** ~ **a** [*o de*] **algo** to be unaware of sth; **vivía** ~ **a todo lo que pasaba en el mundo** he/she lived unaware of what was happening in the world 4.(*exento de*) ~ **a** [*o de*] lacking; ~ **de piedad** pitiless; ~ **de preocupaciones** care-

free; **él es** ~ **a todo eso** he is not involved in that

ajetrear [a·xe·tre·'ar] I. *vt* to overwork II. *vr:* ~**se** to tire oneself out; (*darse prisa*) to rush around

ajetreo [a·xe·'treo] *m* (*de personas*) drudgery; (*en un sitio*) bustle

ají [a·'xi] *m AmS, Ant* 1.(*arbusto*) pepper (plant) 2.(*pimentón*) chili; (*de las Indias*) cayenne (pepper)

ajilimoje [a·xi·li·'mo·xe] *m*, **ajilimójili** [a·xi·li·'mo·xi·li] *m* CULIN garlic and pepper sauce; **con todos sus** ~**s** with all the trimmings

ajillo [a·'xi·jo, -ʎo] *m* CULIN **al** ~ with garlic

ajo ['a·xo] *m* BOT garlic; (*diente*) clove of garlic ▸ **andar** tieso **como un** ~ *inf* to be stuck-up; andar (**metido**) **en el** ~ *inf,* estar **en el** ~ *inf* to be mixed up in it

ajotar [a·xo·'tar] *vt* 1.*AmC, Ant* (*azuzar*) to incite 2. *Cuba* (*desdeñar*) to scorn

ajuar [a·'xwar] *m* 1.(*de novia*) trousseau 2.(*de casa*) furnishings *pl*

ajumarse [a·xu·'mar·se] *vr Col, Cuba, PRico, inf* to get drunk

ajustable [a·xus·'ta·βle] *adj* adjustable; **sábanas** ~**s** fitted sheets

ajustado, -a [a·xus·'ta·do, -a] *adj* 1.(*ropa*) tight 2.(*adecuado*) fitting

ajustar [a·xus·'tar] I. *vi* to fit II. *vt* 1.(*adaptar*) *t.* TÉC to adjust; ~ **un vestido** to take in a dress; ~ **una correa** to adjust a strap 2.(*dos piezas*) to fit III. *vr:* ~**se** 1.(*ponerse de acuerdo*) to come to an agreement 2.(*adaptarse*) to adapt; **no** ~**se al tema** not to keep to the subject; ~**se a la verdad** to stick to the truth

ajuste [a·'xus·te] *m* 1.(*adaptación*) adjustment; ~ **financiero** financial adjustment 2.(*graduación*) graduation; ~ **de brillo** brightness control 3.(*encaje*) fitting 4.(*acuerdo*) compromise; ~ **de cuentas** settling of scores

ajusticiar [a·xus·ti·'sjar, -'θjar] *vt* to execute

al [al] = **a + el** *v.* **a**

ala ['a·la] *f* wing; (*de hélice*) propeller blade; (*de sombrero*) brim; (*del tejado*) eaves *pl* ▸ **tener** demasiadas ~**s** to be overconfident; **estar** tocado **del** ~ *inf* to be crazy; ahuecar **el** ~ to get going; cortar **las** ~**s a alguien** to clip sb's wings; dar ~**s a alguien** to encourage sb; **le** faltan ~**s para...** he/she lacks the courage to...

Alá [a·'la] *m* Allah

alabanza [a·la·'βan·sa, -θa] *f* praise; **deshacerse en** ~**s para con alguien** to shower praises on sb; **hacer una** ~ **de alguien** to sing sb's praises

alabar [a·la·'βar] I. *vt* ~ **a alguien por algo** to praise sb for sth; **alabado sea el Señor** praise be to God II. *vr:* ~**se** to boast

alabastro [a·la·'βas·tro] *m* alabaster

alabear(se) [a·la·βe·'ar·(se)] *vt,* (*vr*) to warp

alacena [a·la·'se·na, -'θe·na] *f* pantry

alacrán [a·la·'kran] *m* ZOOL scorpion; **ser un** ~ *pey* to be a gossiper

alado, -a [a·'la·do, -a] *adj* winged

ALALC [a·'lalk] *abr de* **Asociación Latinoamericana de Libre Comercio** LAFTA

alambique [a·lam·'bi·ke] *m* distillery

alambrada [a·lam·'bra·da] *f* wire fence; (*de espinas*) barbed wire fence; ~ **eléctrica** electric fence

alambrar [a·lam·'brar] *vt* to wire

alambre [a·'lam·bre] *m* wire; ~ **de espinas** barbed wire

alambrista [a·lam·'bris·ta] *mf* tightrope walker

alameda [a·la·'me·da] *f* **1.** (*lugar*) poplar grove **2.** (*paseo*) tree-lined avenue

álamo ['a·la·mo] *m* BOT poplar; ~ **temblón** aspen

alarde [a·'lar·de] *m* show; **hacer** ~ **de algo** to make a show of sth

alardear [a·lar·de·'ar] *vi* ~ **de algo** to boast about sth

alardeo [a·lar·'deo] *m Méx* (*alarde*) showing off

alargado, -a [a·lar·'ya·do, -a] *adj* elongated

alargar <g→gu> [a·lar·'yar] **I.** *vt* **1.** (*extensión*) to lengthen; ~ **la pierna** to stretch one's leg; ~ **el cuello** to crane one's neck; ~ **la mano** to hold out one's hand **2.** (*duración*) to prolong **3.** (*retardar*) to delay **II.** *vr:* ~**se 1.** (*en la extensión*) to lengthen; **no te alargues** be brief; ~**se en cumplidos** to be full of compliments **2.** (*retardarse*) to be delayed

alarido [a·la·'ri·do] *m* shriek

alarife [a·la·'ri·fe] *m Arg* (*listo*) smart customer *inf*

alarma [a·'lar·ma] *f* **1.** (*general*) alarm; ~ **por ozono** ozone warning; **falsa** ~ false alarm; **dar la** ~ to raise the alarm; **ha saltado la** ~ **del banco** the alarm in the bank has gone off **2.** (*susto*) scare; ~ **social** social unrest

alarmar [a·lar·'mar] **I.** *vt* **1.** (*dar la alarma*) to alarm **2.** (*asustar*) to frighten; **noticia alarmante** terrible news **II.** *vr:* ~**se** (*inquietarse*) to get worried; (*asustarse*) to be alarmed

alarmista [a·lar·'mis·ta] *mf* alarmist

alba ['al·βa] *f* dawn; **al rayar** [*o* **romper**] **el** ~ at daybreak

albacea [al·βa·'sea, -'θea] *mf* executor

albacora [al·βa·'ko·ra] *f Chile, Perú, Méx* swordfish

albahaca [al·'βa·ka/al·βa·'a·ka] *f* basil

albanés, -esa [al·βa·'nes, -·'ne·sa] *adj, m, f* Albanian

Albania [al·'βa·nja] *f* Albania

albañil [al·βa·'ɲil] *mf* **1.** (*constructor*) builder **2.** (*artesano*) bricklayer

albañilería [al·βa·ɲi·le·'ri·a] *f* **1.** (*profesión*) masonry **2.** (*obra*) brickwork; **obra de** ~ masonry

albarán [al·βa·'ran] *m* delivery note, invoice

albaricoque [al·βa·ri·'ko·ke] *m* apricot

albatros [al·'βa·tros] *m inv* albatross

albazo [al·'βa·so, -θo] *m Perú* morning serenade

albear [al·βe·'ar] *vi Arg* to get up very early

albedrío [al·βe·'dri·o] *m* whim; **libre** ~ free will; **a** [*o* **según**] **mi** ~ just as I like

alberca [al·'βer·ka] *f* cistern, reservoir

albergar <g→gu> [al·βer·'yar] **I.** *vt* to house **II.** *vr:* ~**se** to lodge

albergue [al·'βer·ɣe] *m* refuge; ~ **juvenil** youth hostel; ~ **de montaña** mountain hut

albino, -a [al·'βi·no, -a] *adj, m, f* albino

albóndiga [al·'βon·di·ɣa] *f* (*de carne*) meatball; (*de pescado*) fish rissole

alborada [al·βo·'ra·da] *f* MIL reveille

albornoz [al·βor·'nos -'noθ,] *m* bathrobe

alborotado, -a [al·βo·ro·'ta·do, -a] *adj* **1.** (*excitado*) excited **2.** (*irreflexivo*) rash

alborotar [al·βo·ro·'tar] **I.** *vi* to make a racket; (*niños*) to roughhouse **II.** *vt* **1.** (*excitar*) to excite **2.** (*desordenar*) to agitate **3.** (*sublevar*) to stir up **III.** *vr:* ~**se 1.** (*excitarse*) to get excited **2.** (*sublevarse*) to riot

alboroto [al·βo·'ro·to] *m* **1.** (*vocerío*) racket; (*ruido*) noise **2.** (*bulla*) uproar; (*disturbio*) disturbance

alborozo [al·βo·'ro·so, -θo] *m* joy

albricias [al·'βri·sjas, -θjas] *fpl inf* ¡~! good news!, congratulations

albufera [al·βu·'fe·ra] *f* lagoon

álbum ['al·βun] *m* <álbum(e)s> album; ~ **infantil** picture book

albur [al·'βur] *m* ZOOL bleak ► **correr un** ~ to run a risk; **al** ~ at random

alburear [al·βu·re·'ar] **I.** *vt CRi* to disturb **II.** *vi* **1.** *Col* (*dinero*) to get money **2.** *Cuba* (*engañar*) to deceive **3.** *Méx* (*juegos de palabras*) to play on words

alcachofa [al·ka·'tʃo·fa] *f* **1.** BOT artichoke **2.** (*de ducha*) shower head; (*de regadera*) sprinkler

alcahuete, -a [al·ka·'we·te, -a] *m, f* pimp

alcalde(sa) [al·'kal·de, al·kal·'de·sa] *m(f)* mayor

alcaldía [al·kal·'di·a] *f* (*oficio, oficina*) mayor's office

álcali ['al·ka·li] *m* alkali

alcalino, -a [al·ka·'li·no, -a] *adj* alkaline

alcamonero, -a [al·ka·mo·'ne·ro, -a] *adj Ven* (*entrometido*) nosy; (*de novedades*) newsy

alcance [al·'kan·se, -θe] *m* **1.** (*distancia*) range; **misil de corto** ~ short-range missile; **de** ~ **limitado** short-range; **al** ~ **de la mano** within reach; **al** ~ **de todos los bolsillos** within everybody's means; **tener la victoria a su** ~ to have victory within one's grasp **2.** (*importancia*) importance; **de mucho/poco** ~ of great/little importance ► **la noticia de último** ~ the latest news; **ser persona de pocos** ~**s** to be a person of limited talents; **dar** ~ **a alguien** to catch up with sb

alcancía [al·kan·'si·a, -'θi·a] *f* piggy bank

alcanfor [al·kan·'for] *m* camphor

alcanforarse [al·kan·fo·'rar·se] *vr* **1.** *Col, Ven* (*evaporarse*) to vaporize **2.** *Hond* (*perderse*) to make oneself scarce *inf*

alcantarilla [al·kan·ta·'ri·ja, -ʎa] *f* **1.**(*cloaca*) sewer **2.**(*sumidero*) drain

alcantarillado [al·kan·ta·ri·'ja·do, -'ʎa·do] *m* sewer system, drains *pl*

alcanzar <z→c> [al·kan·'sar, -'θar] **I.** *vi* to reach; **este cañón alcanza 10 kilómetros** this gun has a range of 10 kilometers; **el dinero no alcanza para pagar la comida** the money's not enough to pay for the food; **no alcanzo a todo el trabajo** I can't manage to do all the work **II.** *vt* **1.**(*dar alcance*) to catch up (with); **el ladrón fue alcanzado** the thief was caught; **ve tirando, ya te ~é** keep going, I'll catch up with you **2.**(*llegar*) to reach; **~ un acuerdo** to reach an agreement; **el disparo le alcanzó en la pierna** he was shot in the leg; **~ fama** to become famous **3.**(*entender*) to grasp **III.** *vr:* **~se no se me alcanza qué intentas con ello** I can't figure out what you mean by that

alcaparra [al·ka·'pa·rra] *f* caper

alcatraz [al·ka·'tras, -'traθ] *m* **1.**ZOOL gannet **2.**BOT arum

alcaucil [al·kau·'sil, -'θil] *m Arg* (*trotaconventos*) pimp

alcázar [al·'ka·sar, -θar] *m* MIL fortress

alce ['al·se, -θe] *m* elk, moose

alcista [al·'sis·ta, -'θis·ta] **I.** *adj* **mercado ~ de la bolsa** bull [*o* bullish] market; **movimiento ~ de los precios** upward trend in prices **II.** *mf* speculator, bull

alcoba [al·'ko·βa] *f* bedroom

alcohol [al·'kol/al·ko·'ol] *m* alcohol; **~ de quemar** methanol, methyl alcohol; **bebida sin ~** non-alcoholic drink; **no tomo ~** I don't drink alcohol; **estar bajo los efectos del ~** to be under the influence of alcohol

alcohólico, -a [al·'ko·li·ko/al·ko·'o·li·ko, -a] *adj, m, f* alcoholic

alcoholímetro [al·ko·'li·me·tro/al·ko·o'li·me·tro] *m* Breathalyzer®

alcoholismo [al·ko·'lis·mo/al·ko·o·'lis·mo] *m* alcoholism

alcoholista [al·ko·'lis·ta/al·ko·o·'lis·ta] **I.** *adj Arg* drunk **II.** *mf Arg* drunkard

alcoholizado, -a [al·ko·li·'sa·do, -a/al·ko·o·li·'sa·do, -a; 'θa·do, -a] *adj* alcoholic

alcoholizar <z→c> [al·ko·li·'sar/al·ko·o·li·'sar, -'θar] **I.** *vt* to get (sb) drunk **II.** *vr:* **~se** to become an alcoholic

alcornoque [al·kor·'no·ke] *m* BOT cork oak; (*pedazo de*) **~** idiot

alcurnia [al·'kur·nja] *f* ancestry; **de ~** of noble birth

aldaba [al·'da·βa] *f* **1.**(*picaporte*) doorknocker **2.**(*para puertas*) bolt ▶ **tener buenas ~s** *inf* to have influence

aldea [al·'dea] *f* small village

aldeano, -a [al·de·'a·no, -a] **I.** *adj* **1.**(*de la aldea*) village **2.**(*ignorante*) rustic **II.** *m, f* **1.**(*de la aldea*) villager **2.**(*inculto*) country bumpkin

aleación [a·lea·'sjon, -'θjon] *f* alloy; **~ ligera**

light alloy

aleatorio, -a [a·lea·'to·rjo, -a] *adj* random, fortuitous

aleatorización [a·le·a·to·ri·sa·'sjon, -θa·'θjon] *f* (*en estadística*) randomization *no pl*

alebrestarse [a·le·βes·'trar·se] *vr Col, inf* to become agitated

aleccionar [a·lek·sjo·'nar, a·ley·θjo-] *vt* to instruct; **esto te ~á para no volver a hacer lo mismo** this will teach you not to do the same thing again

aledaño, -a [a·le·'da·ɲo, -a] *adj* adjoining

alegación [a·le·ɣa·'sjon, -'θjon] *f* **1.**JUR (*declaración*) declaration; (*escrito*) statement; **~ de culpabilidad** plea of guilty **2.** *pl* (*objeciones*) objections *pl*

alegar <g→gu> [a·le·'ɣar] **I.** *vt* to cite; (*pruebas*) to produce; **~ dolor de cabeza** to claim to have a headache **II.** *vi AmL* (*discutir*) to argue

alegato [a·le·'ɣa·to] *m* **1.**(*escrito*) bill of indictment; (*oral*) plea **2.**AmL (*disputa*) argument

alegoría [a·le·ɣo·'ri·a] *f* allegory

alegrar [a·le·'ɣrar] **I.** *vt* **1.**(*a personas*) to make happy **2.**(*cosas*) to brighten up **II.** *vr:* **~se de** [*o* con] **algo** to be glad about sth; **me alegro de verle de nuevo** I'm pleased to see you again; **nos alegramos de que haya aceptado la invitación** we're glad that he/she has accepted the invitation; **me alegro (por ti)** I'm so happy for you

alegre [a·'le·ɣre] *adj* **1.**(*contento*) happy; (*divertido*) merry; (*color*) bright; **un espíritu/una cara ~** a cheerful nature/face; **estoy ~ de que** +*subj* I'm pleased that; **estar más ~ que unas pascuas** to be pleased as Punch **2.**(*frívolo*) frivolous; **llevar una vida ~** to lead a free-and-easy life **3.** *inf* (*achispado*) merry; **estar ~** to be tipsy

alegría [a·le·'ɣri·a] *f* **1.**(*gozo*) happiness; (*buen humor*) cheerfulness; **llevarse una gran ~** to be very happy **2.**BOT (*ajonjolí*) sesame

alegrón, -ona [a·le·'ɣron, --'ɣro·na] *adj Arg* tipsy

alejamiento [a·le·xa·'mjen·to] *m* removal; *fig* aloofness

alejar [a·le·'xar] **I.** *vt* **1.**(*distanciar*) to remove **2.**(*ahuyentar*) to drive away; **aleja estos pensamientos de tu cabeza** banish these thoughts from your mind **II.** *vr:* **~se** to move away; (*retirarse*) to withdraw; **todos se alejan de él** everyone avoids him

alelar [a·le·'lar] **I.** *vt* to stupefy **II.** *vr:* **~se** to be stupefied

aleluya [a·le·'lu·ja] *interj, m o f* REL hallelujah; **estar de ~** to rejoice

alemán [a·le·'man] *m* German; **alto ~** High German, standard German; **decir algo en ~** to say sth in German

alemán, -ana [a·le·'man, --'ma·na] *adj, m, f* German

Alemania [a·le·'ma·nja] *f* Germany; **República Federal de** ~ Federal Republic of Germany
alentar <e→ie> [a·len·'tar] I. *vi* to be alive II. *vt* to encourage III. *vr:* ~ **se 1.** (*animarse*) to take heart **2.** *Hond, Méx, Col, Ecua* (*restablecerse*) to get well
alerce [a·'ler·se, -θe] *m* larch
alergia [a·'ler·xia] *f* allergy; ~ **a la primavera** hay fever; ~ **alimentaria** food allergy; ~ **al polen** pollen allergy; **esto me da** ~ I'm allergic to this
alérgico, -a [a·'ler·xi·ko, -a] *adj* allergic; **es** ~ **a estos temas** *fig inf* he/she really isn't keen on these subjects
alergólogo, -a [a·ler·'yo·lo·yo, -a] *m, f* allergist
alerta [a·'ler·ta] I. *adj* alert; **estar** ~ **de algo** to be alert to sth II. *f* alert; ~ **por vibración** TEL vibration [*o* vibrate] alert; **dar la** ~ to give the alarm; **poner en** ~ **a alguien** to put sb on the alert III. *interj* watch out
aleta [a·'le·ta] *f* wing; (*de un buzo*) flipper; (*de un pez*) fin
aletargar <g→gu> [a·le·tar·'yar] I. *vt* to become drowsy II. *vr:* ~ **se** to get drowsy
aletear [a·le·te·'ar] *vi* **1.** (*ave*) to flutter; (*pez*) to wriggle **2.** *inf* (*cobrar fuerza*) to regain one's strength
alevosía [a·le·βo·'si·a] *f* treachery; **con** ~ treacherously
alevoso, -a [a·le·'βo·so, -a] *adj* treacherous
alfa [´al·fa] *f* alpha; ~ **y omega** *fig* the beginning and the end, Alpha and Omega
alfabético, -a [al·fa·'βe·ti·ko, -a] *adj* alphabetic(al); **estar por orden** ~ to be in alphabetical order
alfabetizar <z→c> [al·fa·βe·ti·'sar, -'θar] *vt* to teach to read and write
alfabeto [al·fa·'βe·to] *m* alphabet
alfalfa [al·'fal·fa] *f* alfalfa
alfarería [al·fa·re·'ri·a] *f* pottery
alfarero, -a [al·fa·'re·ro, -a] *m, f* potter
alféizar [al·'fei·sar, -θar] *m* windowsill
alférez [al·'fe·res, -reθ] *m* MIL second lieutenant
alfil [al·'fil] *m* (*ajedrez*) bishop
alfiler [al·fi·'ler] *m* **1.** (*aguja*) pin **2.** (*broche*) brooch; ~ **de corbata** tiepin; ~ **de gancho** *CSur, Ecua, Perú* safety pin ▸ **llevo la lección prendida con** ~ **es** I'm hardly prepared for the exam; **ir de veinticinco** ~ **es** to be all dressed up; **no caber un** ~ to be bursting at the seams
alfombra [al·'fom·bra] *f* carpet; ~ **persa** Persian carpet
alfombrado [al·fom·'bra·do] *m AmL* carpeting
alfombrar [al·fom·'brar] *vt* to carpet
alfombrilla [al·fom·'bri·ja, -ʎa] *f* **1.** (*estera*) mat; ~ **de baño** bath mat **2.** MED German measles **3.** COMPUT mousepad
alforja [al·'for·xa] *f* bag; (*de caballería*) saddlebag ▸ **sacar los pies de las** ~ **s** to come out of one's shell

alga [´al·ya] *f* alga
algarabía [al·ya·ra·'βi·a] *f* **1.** (*griterío*) uproar **2.** (*lengua*) Arabic
algarada [al·ya·'ra·da] *f* outcry
algarrobo [al·ya·'rro·βo] *m* carob tree
algazara [al·ya·'sa·ra, -'θa·ra] *f* clamor; (*de alegría*) jubilation
álgebra [´al·xe·βra] *f* MAT algebra
álgido, -a [´al·xi·do, -a] *adj* **1.** (*culminante*) **el período** ~ **del Barroco** the high point of the Baroque period; **la crisis está en su momento más** ~ the crisis has reached a climax **2.** (*muy frío*) freezing; **fiebre álgida** MED shivering fit
algo [´al·yo] I. *pron indef* (*en frases afirmativas*) something; (*en neg., int. y condicionales*) anything; ~ **es** ~ it's better than nothing; **¿quieres** ~**?** do you want anything?; **¿apostamos** ~**?** do you want to bet?; **esta película es** ~ **aparte** this film is something special; **me suena de** ~ it seems familiar to me; **se cree** ~ he/she thinks he/she is something; **por** ~ **lo habrá dicho** he/she must have had a reason for saying it II. *adv* a little; **aún falta** ~ **hasta llegar** there's still a bit to go; ~ **así como** something like
algodón [al·yo·'don] *m* **1.** (*tejido*) cotton; **una camisa de** ~ a cotton shirt; ~ **en rama** raw cotton **2.** (*cosmético*) cotton ▸ **criado entre algodones** pampered
algodonero, -a [al·yo·do·'ne·ro, -a] I. *adj* cotton II. *m, f* **1.** (*comerciante*) cotton dealer **2.** (*cultivador*) cotton grower
alguacil [al·ywa·'sil, -'θil] *mf* bailiff
alguien [´al·yjen] *pron indef* (*en frases afirmativas*) somebody, someone; (*en int. y condicionales*) anybody, anyone; **¿hay** ~ **aquí?** is anybody [*o* anyone] there?; ~ **me lo ha contado** somebody [*o* someone] told me; **se cree** ~ he/she thinks he/she is somebody [*o* someone]
algún [al·'yun] *adj v.* **alguno**[1]
alguno, -a[1] [al·'yu·no, -a] *adj* <algún> **1.** (*antepuesto*) some; (*en frases neg. e int.*) any; **¿alguna pregunta?** any questions?; **de alguna manera** somehow; **en algún sitio** somewhere; **alguna vez** sometimes; **algún día** some day **2.** (*postpuesto: ninguno*) no, not any; **en sitio** ~ nowhere; **persona alguna** no one
alguno, -a[2] [al·'yu·no, -a] *pron indef* somebody, someone; ~ **s de los presentes** some of those present; ~ **s ya se han ido** some have already gone; **¿tienes caramelos?** — **sí, me quedan** ~ **s** do you have any candy? — yes, I still have some left; **los niños han vuelto a hacer alguna de las suyas** the children have been up to their tricks again
alhaja [a·'la·xa] *f* **1.** (*de piedras preciosas*) piece of jewelry; (*de bisutería*) costume jewelry **2.** *inf* (*persona*) **¡esta chica es una** ~**!** this girl's a real gem; **¡menuda** ~, **este niño!** *irón* this boy's a fine one!

alhajado, -a [a·la·'xa·do, -a] *adj Col* (*rico*) wealth

alhajera [a·la·'xe·ra] *f Arg, Chile* jewel box

alharaca [a·la·'ra·ka] *f* fuss

alhelí [a·le·'li] *m* <alhelíes> wallflower

aliado, -a [a·li·'a·do, -a] I. *adj* allied II. *m, f* ally; los ~s POL the Allies

alianza [a·li·'an·sa, -θa] *f* 1.(*pacto*) alliance; Alianza Atlántica Atlantic Alliance, NATO 2.(*anillo*) wedding ring

aliar(se) <l. pres: alío> [a·li·'ar·(se)] *vt, (vr)* to ally (oneself)

alias ['a·ljas] *adv, m inv* alias

alicaído, -a [a·li·ka·'i·do, -a] *adj* weak; (*deprimido*) dejected

alicates [a·li·'ka·tes] *mpl* pliers *pl;* ~ universales combination pliers

aliciente [a·li·'sjen·te, -'θjen·te] *m* incentive

aliento [a·'ljen·to] *m* 1.(*respiración*) breath; mal ~ bad breath; sin ~ out of breath; cobrar ~ to get one's breath back; esto me quita el ~ this takes my breath away; tomar ~ to take a breath 2.(*ánimo*) courage; dar ~ a alguien to encourage sb

aligátor [a·li·'ya·tor] *m* alligator

aligerar [a·li·xe·'rar] I. *vi* to hurry (up) II. *vt* 1.(*cargas*) to lighten 2.(*aliviar*) to alleviate 3.(*acelerar*) to quicken; ~ el paso to go faster

alimaña [a·li·'ma·na] *f* 1.(*animal*) pest; ~s vermin 2.(*persona*) animal, brute

alimentación [a·li·men·ta·'sjon, -'θjon] *f* 1.(*nutrición*) food; industria de la ~ food industry 2.(*de animales*) feeding 3.(*de un horno*) stoking; (*de una máquina*) feeding; ~ de energía energy supply; ~ de papel COMPUT sheet feeder

alimentador(a) [a·li·men·ta·'dor, -'do·ra] *adj* TÉC feeder

alimentar [a·li·men·'tar] I. *vi* to be nourishing II. *vt* 1.(*nutrir*) to feed; ~ el odio to fuel hatred 2.(*horno*) to stoke; (*máquina*) to feed; ~ la máquina con energía to supply the machine with energy 3.COMPUT ~ un ordenador con datos to feed data into a computer III. *vr* ~se de algo to live on sth

alimenticio, -a [a·li·men·'ti·sjo, -a; -θjo, -a] *adj* 1.(*nutritivo*) nourishing 2.(*alimentario*) food; industria alimenticia food industry; pensión alimenticia alimony; productos ~s foodstuffs *pl*

alimento [a·li·'men·to] *m* 1.(*sustancia*) food; los ~s foodstuffs *pl;* ~s congelados frozen food; ~s genéticamente modificados genetically modified foods 2.(*alimentación*) nourishment; de mucho/poco ~ full of/lacking nutritional value 3.*pl* JUR (*asistencia financiera*) alimony

alineación [a·li·nea·'sjon, -'θjon] *f*, alineamiento [a·li·nea·'mjen·to] *m* 1.(*general*) alignment; no ~ POL non-alignment 2.DEP line-up

alinear [a·li·ne·'ar] I. *vt* 1.(*poner en línea*) to line up 2.DEP to select; (*para un partido*) to

field; país no alineado POL non-aligned country II. *vr:* ~se to line up

aliñar [a·li·'nar] *vt* to season; (*ensalada*) to dress

aliño [a·'li·no] *m* seasoning; (*para ensalada*) dressing

alioli [a·li·'o·li] *m sauce of garlic and olive oil*

alisar [a·li·'sar] *vt* (*superficie*) to smooth down; (*un terreno*) to level (off); (*el pelo*) to smooth

aliso [a·'li·so] *m t.* BOT alder

alistamiento [a·lis·ta·'mjen·to] *m* 1.(*inscripción*) enrollment 2.MIL enlistment

alistar [a·lis·'tar] I. *vt* 1.(*inscribir*) to enroll 2.(*enumerar*) to list 3.MIL to recruit; (*en la marina*) to enlist II. *vr:* ~se 1.(*inscribirse*) to enroll 2.MIL to enlist

aliteración [a·li·te·ra·'sjon, -'θjon] *f* alliteration

aliviar [a·li·'βjar] I. *vi* to go faster II. *vt* 1.(*carga*) to lighten; tienes que ~ la maleta you'll have to reduce the weight of the suitcase 2.(*de una preocupación*) to relieve 3.(*dolor*) to alleviate; ~ un bloqueo económico to relax an economic blockade III. *vr:* ~se 1.(*dolor*) to ease off [*o* up] 2.(*de una enfermedad*) to recover

alivio [a·'li·βjo] *m* 1.(*aligeramiento*) relief 2.(*de una enfermedad*) recovery; (*mejoría*) improvement ► ser de ~ *inf* to be horrible; pescar un catarro de ~ *inf* to get an awful cold; vestir de ~ to be in mourning

aljibe [al·'xi·βe] *m* 1.(*cisterna*) cistern 2.(*tanque*) tank

allá [a·'ja, a·'ʎa] *adv* 1.(*lugar, dirección*) there; el más ~ REL the hereafter; ¿cuánto se tarda de aquí ~? how long does it take to go there?; ponte más ~ move further over 2.(*tiempo*) back; ~ por el año 1964 around 1964; ~ en tiempos de Maricastaña in the olden days ► ¡~ tú! *inf* that's your problem!

allanamiento [a·ja·na·'mjen·to, a·ʎa-] *m* 1.(*de un terreno*) leveling 2.JUR ~ de morada breaking and entering

allanar [a·ja·'nar, a·ʎa-] I. *vt* 1.(*terreno*) to level (out); (*construcción*) to demolish 2.(*dificultades*) to remove 3.JUR ~ una casa to break into a house II. *vr:* ~se to agree; no se allana nunca he/she never gives in

allegado, -a [a·je·'ya·do, -a; a·ʎe-] I. *adj* close II. *m, f* relative

allegar <g→gu> [a·je·'yar, a·ʎe-] *vt* (*recursos*) to gather together; (*pruebas*) to collect

allende [a·'jen·de, a·'ʎen-] *elev* I. *adv* beyond; ~ de ser guapa, es agradable besides being pretty, she's pleasant as well II. *prep* beyond; ~ las montañas beyond the mountains

allí [a·'ji, a·'ʎi] *adv* (*lugar, dirección*) there; ~ cerca, por ~ over there; ¡~ viene! he's/she's just coming!; hasta ~ as far as that

alma ['al·ma] *f* 1.(*espíritu*) soul; agradecer con el ~ to thank with all one's heart; me arranca el ~ it's heartbreaking; me llega al ~

I'm deeply touched; **lo siento en el ~** I'm terribly sorry; **no tener ~** to be heartless; **fue el ~ de la fiesta** he/she was the life and soul of the party **2.** (*ánimo*) spirit **3.** TÉC core ▸ **~ de cántaro** simpleton; **como ~ que lleva el diablo** *inf* like a bat out of hell; **un ~ de Dios** a good soul; **estar con el ~ en un hilo** *inf* to have one's heart in one's mouth; **~ en pena** lost soul; **¡~ mía!** my darling!; **se le cayó el ~ a los pies** *inf* his/her heart sank

almacén [al·ma·'sen, -'θen] *m* **1.** (*depósito*) warehouse; **~ al por mayor** wholesale warehouse; **franco en ~** ex-works; **tener en ~** to have in stock **2.** (*tienda*) **grandes almacenes** department store

almacenaje [al·ma·se·'na·xe, al·ma·θe-] *m*, **almacenamiento** [al·ma·se·na·'mjen·to, al·ma·θe-] *m* **1.** (*de mercancías*) *t.* COMPUT storage; **~ definitivo** permanent storage **2.** (*tasa*) storage charge

almacenar [al·ma·se·'nar, al·ma·θe-] *vt t.* COMPUT to store; **~ en disco duro** to store on the hard disk

almacenero, -a [al·ma·se·'ne·ro, -a; al·ma·θe-] *m, f* CSur (*dueño*) grocer

almacenista [al·ma·se·'nis·ta, al·ma·θe-] *mf* wholesaler

almanaque [al·ma·'na·ke] *m* almanac

almeja [al·'me·xa] *f* **1.** ZOOL clam **2.** *vulg* (*vagina*) cunt

almena [al·'me·na] *f* merlon

almendra [al·'men·dra] *f* **1.** (*fruta*) almond; **~s garapiñadas** sugar almonds **2.** (*semilla*) kernel

almendro [al·'men·dro] *m* almond tree

almiar [al·'mjar] *m* haystack

almíbar [al·'mi·βar] *m* syrup; **melocotón en ~** peach in syrup

almidón [al·mi·'don] *m* starch; (*cola*) paste

almidonado, -a [al·mi·do·'na·do, -a] *adj* (*acicalado*) spruced up

almidonar [al·mi·do·'nar] *vt* to starch

almirante [al·mi·'ran·te] *mf* admiral

almirez [al·mi·'res, -'reθ] *m* mortar

almizcle [al·'mis·kle, al·'miθ-] *m* musk

almohada [al·mo·'a·da] *f* **1.** (*cojín*) cushion; (*de la cama*) pillow **2.** (*funda*) pillowcase ▸ **consultar** algo con la ~ *inf* to sleep on sth

almohadilla [al·moa·'di·ja, -'di·ʎa] *f* (*cojín*) small cushion; (*acerico*) pin cushion; **~ de tinta** inkpad

almohadón [al·moa·'don] *m* cushion

almorranas [al·mo·'rra·nas] *fpl* piles *pl*

almorzar [al·mor·'sar, -'θar] *irr como forzar* **I.** *vi* **1.** (*a mediodía*) to have lunch **2.** *reg* (*desayunar*) to have breakfast **II.** *vt* **1.** (*a mediodía*) to have for lunch **2.** *reg* (*desayunar*) to have for breakfast

almuerzo [al·'mwer·so, -θo] *m* **1.** (*al mediodía*) lunch; **~ de negocios** business lunch; **¿qué hay de ~?** what's for lunch? **2.** *reg* (*desayuno*) breakfast

aló [a·'lo] *interj* AmC, AmS TEL hello; **~,**

¿quién es? hello, who's speaking?

alocado, -a [a·lo·'ka·do, -a] *adj* **1.** (*loco*) crazy **2.** (*imprudente*) reckless

alocución [a·lo·ku·'sjon, -'θjon] *f* speech

alojamiento [a·lo·xa·'mjen·to] *m* **1.** (*lugar*) accommodation **2.** (*acción*) housing; MIL billeting

alojar [a·lo·'xar] **I.** *vt* **1.** (*albergar*) to accommodate **2.** (*procurar alojamiento*) to house; (*tropa*) to billet **3.** (*cosa*) to lodge **II.** *vr:* **~se** to stay

alondra [a·'lon·dra] *f* lark

alopecia [a·lo·'pe·sja, -θja] *f* alopecia

alpaca [al·'pa·ka] *f* **1.** (*tela*) *t.* ZOOL alpaca **2.** (*aleación*) nickel silver, German silver

alpargata [al·par·'ɣa·ta] *f* espadrille ▸ **no tener ni para ~s** not to have a penny to one's name

Alpes ['al·pes] *mpl* **los ~** the Alps + *pl vb*, Alps

alpinismo [al·pi·'nis·mo] *m* mountaineering, mountain climbing

alpinista [al·pi·'nis·ta] *mf* mountaineer, mountain climber

alpino, -a [al·'pi·no, -a] *adj* Alpine; **refugio ~** mountain refuge

alpiste [al·'pis·te] *m* **1.** BOT canary grass **2.** (*para pájaros*) birdseed **3.** *inf* (*alcohol*) **le gusta mucho el ~** he's/she's a boozer ▸ **no tener para ~** *inf* to be dirt poor

alquilado, -a [al·ki·'la·do, -a] *m, f* PRico (*sirviente*) hireling

alquilar [al·ki·'lar] **I.** *vt* **1.** (*dejar*) to rent (out), to let **2.** (*tomar en alquiler*) to rent **II.** *vr:* **~se** to be let; **se alquila** for rent

alquiler [al·ki·'ler] *m* **1.** (*acción*) renting, letting; **~ de coches** car-rental; **~ con opción de compra** leasing **2.** (*precio*) rent, rental

alquimia [al·'ki·mja] *f* alchemy

alquimista [al·ki·'mis·ta] *mf* alchemist

alquitrán [al·ki·'tran] *m* tar

alrededor [al·rre·de·'dor] *adv* **1.** (*local*) around; **~ de la plaza** around the square; **un viaje ~ de la tierra** a trip around the world **2.** (*aproximadamente*) **~ de** around

alrededores [al·rre·de·'do·res] *mpl* surroundings *pl*; (*de una ciudad*) outskirts *pl*

alta ['al·ta] *f* **1.** (*documento*) (certificate of) discharge; **dar el ~** to discharge; **dar de ~ del hospital** to discharge from hospital **2.** (*inscripción*) registration; (*ingreso*) membership; **darse de ~ en** (el registro de) **una ciudad** to register as being resident in a city; **darse de ~ en una asociación** to become a member of an association; **dar de ~ a alguien en un partido** to admit sb as a member to a party

altamente [al·ta·'men·te] *adv* highly; **~ contaminado** highly contaminated; **~ cualificado** highly qualified

altanería [al·ta·ne·'ri·a] *f* arrogance, haughtiness

altanero, -a [al·ta·'ne·ro, -a] *adj* arrogant, haughty

altar [al·'tar] *m* altar; **~ mayor** high altar ▸ **quedarse para adornar ~es** to be left on the shelf; **poner a alguien en los ~es** to put sb on a pedestal; **tener a alguien en los ~es** to be full of admiration for sb

altavoz [al·ta·'βoθ, -'βos] *m* loudspeaker

alteración [al·te·ra·'sjon, -'θjon] *f* **1.**(*de planes*) alteration, change; FIN fluctuation; **~ del horario** change [*o* alteration] to the timetable **2.**(*perturbación*) disturbance **3.**(*turbación*) unrest **4.**(*irritación*) irritation **5.**(*adulteración*) adulteration

alterado, -a [al·te·'ra·do, -a] *adj* upset

alterar [al·te·'rar] **I.** *vt* **1.**(*cambiar*) to alter **2.**(*perturbar*) to disturb **3.**(*turbar*) to upset **4.**(*adulterar*) to adulterate **II.** *vr:* **~se 1.~se por algo** (*aturdirse*) to get upset over sth; (*irritarse*) to be irritated by sth **2.**(*cambiar*) to alter **3.**(*alimentos*) to go off [*o* bad]; (*leche*) to go sour

altercado [al·ter·'ka·do] *m* argument, altercation *form*

alternar [al·ter·'nar] **I.** *vi* **1.**(*turnarse*) to alternate; **los veranos cálidos han alternado con los lluviosos** warm summers have alternated with rainy ones; **~ en el volante** to take turns at the wheel **2.**(*tratar*) **~ con alguien** to associate with sb; **es persona que alterna** he/she is a good mixer **3.**(*en un club*) to go clubbing **II.** *vt* to alternate; **~ el trabajo con la diversión** to alternate between periods of work and leisure **III.** *vr* **~se en algo** to take turns at sth

alternativa [al·ter·na·'ti·βa] *f* alternative; **no le queda otra ~ que...** he/she has no other alternative than...; **dar la ~ a alguien para algo** *fig* to consider sb mature enough to do sth

alternativamente [al·ter·na·ti·βa·'men·te] *adv* alternatively

alternativo, -a [al·ter·na·'ti·βo, -a] *adj* **1.**(*opcional*) alternative **2.**(*con alternación*) alternating

alterne [al·'ter·ne] *m* **chica de ~** hostess; **bar de ~** singles bar

alterno, -a [al·'ter·no, -a] *adj* alternate; **cultivo ~** AGR crop rotation; **en días ~s** every other day

alteza [al·'te·sa, -θa] *f* **1.**(*tratamiento*) nobleness; **Su Alteza Real** His/Her/Your Royal Highness **2.**(*calidad*) eminence

altibajos [al·ti·'βa·xos] *mpl* **1.**(*de un terreno*) undulations *pl* **2.**(*cambios*) ups *pl* and downs; **es una persona con muchos ~ en su estado de ánimo** he's/she's very moody

altiplanicie [al·ti·pla·'ni·sje, -θje] *f*, **altiplano** [al·ti·'pla·no] *m* high plateau

altisonante [al·ti·so·'nan·te] *adj* high-flown

altitud [al·ti·'tud] *f* height, altitude; **a una ~ de 1500 metros** at a height of 1,500 meters

altivez [al·ti·'βeθ, -'βes] *f* arrogance, haughtiness

altivo, -a [al·'ti·βo, -a] *adj* (*soberbio*) arrogant, haughty

alto ['al·to] **I.** *interj* halt!; **¡~ el fuego!** cease fire! **II.** *m* **1.**(*descanso*) stop; **~ el fuego** ceasefire;

dar el ~ to order to halt **2.**(*altura*) height; **medir 8 metros de ~** to be 8 meters high **3.**(*collado*) hill **III.** *adv* (*en un lugar elevado*) high (up); **ponlo en lo más ~** put it as high up as possible; **de ~ abajo** from top to bottom ▶ **pasar por ~** to ignore; **pasar una pregunta por ~** to overlook a question; **pasar un saludo por ~** to ignore a greeting; **por todo lo ~** splendidly

alto, -a ['al·to, -a] *adj* <más alto *o* superior, altísimo> **1.**(*en general*) high; **un ~ cargo** a high-ranking position; **la alta Edad Media** the high Middle Ages; **notas altas** MÚS high notes; **artículos de cuero de alta calidad** high-quality leather goods; **~s funcionarios** high officials; **tener un ~ concepto de alguien** to have a high opinion of sb **2.**(*persona*) tall; (*edificio*) high, tall **3.**(*en la parte superior*) upper; **clase alta** upper class **4.** GEO (*río*) upper; **la alta montaña** the high mountains; **el ~ Orinoco** the Upper Orinoco **5.**(*época*) high **6.**(*tiempo*) late; **a altas horas de la noche** late at night **7.**(*río*) torrential; (*mar*) rough; **el río está ~** the river is rough **8.**(*sonido*) loud; **hablar en voz alta** to speak loudly

altoparlante [al·to·par·'lan·te] *m AmL* loudspeaker

altozano [al·to·'sa·no, -'θa·no] *m* small hill

altramuz [al·tra·'mus, -'muθ] *m* lupine

altruismo [al·tru·'is·mo] *m* altruism

altruista [al·tru·'is·ta] **I.** *adj* altruistic **II.** *mf* altruist

altura [al·'tu·ra] *f* **1.**(*altitud*) height; **de gran ~** high; **de poca ~** low; **a gran ~** at a great height; **una montaña de 2000 metros de ~** a 2,000-meter-high mountain; **el avión pierde ~** the plane is losing altitude **2.**(*estatura*) height **3.**(*de un sonido*) pitch **4.** *pl* (*cielo*) heaven ▶ **estar a la ~ del betún** *inf* to look really stupid; **estar a la ~ de las circunstancias** to rise to the occasion; **estar a la ~ de Valencia** to be in the vicinity of Valencia; **a estas ~s** at this point

alubia [a·'lu·βja] *f* bean

alucinación [a·lu·si·na·'sjon, -θi·na·'θjon] *f* hallucination

alucinado, -a [a·lu·si·'na·do, -a; a·lu·θi-] *adj inf* (*asombrado*) **miraba ~ a la chica** he looked at the girl in amazement; **me quedé ~ al leerlo en el periódico** I was stunned on reading it in the newspaper

alucinante [a·lu·si·'nan·te, a·lu·θi-] *adj inf* **1.**(*estupendo*) fantastic **2.**(*increíble*) incredible

alucinar [a·lu·si·'nar, a·lu·θi-] **I.** *vi inf* **1.**(*hablando*) to hallucinate; **¡tú alucinas!** *fig* you're crazy! **2.**(*quedar fascinado*) to be fascinated; **aluciné con sus conocimientos de chino** I was amazed by his/her knowledge of Chinese **II.** *vt inf* **1.**(*pasmar*) to amaze **2.**(*fascinar*) to fascinate

alud [a·'lud] *m* avalanche; **un ~ de gente** *fig* a throng of people

aludir [a·lu·'dir] *vi* (*referirse*) to allude; (*mencionar*) to mention; **darse por aludido** (*ofenderse*) to take it personally; **no darse por aludido** not to take the hint

alumbrado [a·lum·'bra·do] *m* lighting; ~ **público** street lighting

alumbramiento [a·lum·bra·'mjen·to] *m* **1.**(*iluminación*) lighting **2.**(*parto*) childbirth

alumbrar [a·lum·'brar] I. *vi* **1.**(*iluminar*) to give off light; **la lámpara alumbra poco** the lamp doesn't give off much light **2.**(*parir*) to give birth II. *vt* **1.**(*iluminar*) to light (up); (*a alguien*) to shine a light on **2.**(*parir*) to give birth to III. *vr:* ~**se** *inf* to get tipsy

aluminio [a·lu·'mi·njo] *m* aluminum

alumnado [a·lum·'na·do] *m* (*de escuela*) pupils *pl;* (*de universidad*) students *pl*

alumno, -a [a·'lum·no, -a] *m, f* (*de escuela*) pupil; (*de universidad*) student

alunizaje [a·lu·ni·'sa·xe, -'θa·xe] *m* moon landing

alusión [a·lu·'sjon] *f* **1.**(*mención*) ~ **a algo** mention of sth **2.**(*insinuación*) allusion; **hacer una** ~ **a algo** to allude to sth

alusivo, -a [a·lu·'si·βo, -a] *adj* ~ **a algo** regarding sth; **dijo una frase alusiva a la situación** he/she said a few words about the situation

aluvión [a·lu·'βjon] *m* **1.**(*inundación*) *t. fig* flood **2.** GEO alluvium; **tierra de** ~ alluvial soil

álveo ['al·βeo] *m* riverbed

alveolo [al·βe'o·lo] *m,* **alvéolo** [al·'βeo·lo] *m* **1.** ANAT alveolus **2.**(*del panal*) cell

alza ['al·sa, -θa] *f* **1.**(*elevación*) rise; ~ **abusiva de los precios** extortionate price rise; **ir** [*o* **estar**] **en** ~ (*precios*) to be rising; (*persona*) to be up-and-coming **2.**(*de un zapato*) raised insole

alzado, -a [al·'sa·do, -a; al·θa-] *adj* **1.**(*fijado*) fixed **2.** *AmL* (*montaraz*) wild; (*en celo*) on heat

alzamiento [al·sa·'mjento, al·θa-] *m* uprising

alzar <z→c> [al·'sar, -'θar] I. *vt* **1.**(*levantar*) to lift (up); (*precio*) to raise **2.**(*poner vertical*) to put up **3.**(*quitar*) to remove; (*mantel*) to take off; (*mesa*) to put away; (*campamento*) to break **4.**(*construir*) to erect II. *vr:* ~**se** **1.**(*levantarse*) to rise (up); **allí se alza la universidad** the university buildings rise up over there **2.** JUR to appeal **3.** *AmL* (*animales*) to become wild **4.** *AmL* (*sublevarse*) to revolt **5.** *AmL* (*robar*) to steal; ~**se con la pasta** *inf* to make off with the money [*o* dough]

ama ['a·ma] *f* (*dueña*) mistress; (*propietaria*) owner; ~ **de casa** housewife; ~ **de cría** wet nurse; ~ **de llaves** housekeeper

amabilidad [a·ma·βi·li·'dad] *f* kindness; **tuvo la** ~ **de avisarme** he/she was kind enough to warn me; **le agradezco su** ~ thank you for your kindness

amable [a·'ma·βle] *adj* kind; **ser** ~ (**para**) **con alguien** to be kind to sb; **¿sería Ud. tan** ~ **de explicármelo?** would you be so kind as to explain it to me?

amadrinar [a·ma·dri·'nar] *vt* ~ **algo** to act as sponsor to sth; ~ **a alguien** to be godmother to sb

amaestrar [a·maes·'trar] *vt* to train; (*caballos*) to break in

amagar <g→gu> [a·ma·'ɣar] I. *vi* **1.**(*amenazar*) to threaten; **estaba amagando la guerra cuando...** war was threatening to break out when... **2.**(*enfermedad*) to show the first symptoms II. *vt* **1.**(*indicar*) **amagó un golpe** he/she made as if to strike **2.**(*amenazar*) to threaten; ~ **a alguien con algo** to threaten sb with sth

amago [a·'ma·ɣo] *m* **1.**(*amenaza*) threat **2.**(*indicio*) hint **3.** DEP feint

amainar [a·mai·'nar] I. *vi* to abate II. *vt* NÁUT to shorten

amalaya [a·ma·'la·ja] *interj AmL* I wish

amalgama [a·mal·'ɣa·ma] *f* **1.** QUÍM amalgam **2.**(*mezcla*) mixture

amalgamar [a·mal·ɣa·'mar] I. *vt* **1.** TÉC to amalgamate **2.**(*mezclar*) to mix II. *vr:* ~**se** to amalgamate

amamantar [a·ma·man·'tar] *vt* (*bebé*) to breastfeed; (*cachorro*) to suckle

amanecer [a·ma·ne·'ser, -'θer] I. *vimpers* to dawn; **está amaneciendo** it's getting light II. *irr como crecer vi* to wake up III. *m* dawn; **al** ~ at dawn

amanecida [a·ma·ne·'si·da, -'θi·da] *f AmL* dawn

amanerado, -a [a·ma·ne·'ra·do, -a] *adj* **1.**(*persona*) affected **2.**(*estilo*) mannered

amanerarse [a·ma·ne·'rar·se] *vr* (*persona*) to become affected

amanezquera [a·ma·nes·'ke·ra, a·ma·neθ-] *f Méx, PRico* (*alba*) dawn; **en la** [*o* **de**] ~ at daybreak

amansador [a·man·sa·'dor] *m Méx* (*domador*) horse breaker

amansar [a·man·'sar] I. *vt* **1.**(*animal*) to tame **2.**(*persona*) to subdue; (*sosegar*) to calm down II. *vr:* ~**se** to become tame

amante [a·'man·te] I. *adj* **soy poco** ~ **de hablar en público** I don't like speaking in public II. *mf* lover; **un** ~ **de la naturaleza** a nature-lover

amanuense [a·ma·'nwen·se] *mf* **1.**(*secretario*) secretary **2.**(*copista*) copyist

amañar [a·ma·'ɲar] I. *vt* **1.**(*asunto*) to fix; ~ **una solución** to cook up a solution **2.**(*resultado*) to fake II. *vr* ~**se con alguien** to get along well with sb; **amañárselas** (**para todo**) to manage to get by (in everything)

amapola [a·ma·'po·la] *f* poppy ▶ **ponerse como una** ~ to turn beet red

amar [a·'mar] *vt* to love

amargar <g→gu> [a·mar·'ɣar] I. *vt* to make bitter; ~ **la vida a alguien** to make life difficult for sb II. *vi* to be bitter; **la verdad amarga** the painful truth III. *vr:* ~**se** to become bitter

amargo, -a [a·'mar·ɣo] *adj* bitter

amargor [a·mar·'ɣor] *m,* **amargura** [a·mar·

'yu·ra] *f* bitterness; **llorar con** ~ to weep bitterly

amarillear [a·ma·ri·je·'ar, -ʎe·'ar] *vi* to turn [*o* go] yellow

amarillento, -a [a·ma·ri·'jen·to, -a; -'ʎen·to, -a] *adj* yellowish; (*papel*) yellowed

amarillismo [a·ma·ri·'jis·mo, -'ʎis·mo] *m* sensationalism

amarillo, -a [a·ma·'ri·jo, -ʎo] *adj* **1.** (*color*) yellow **2.** (*pálido*) pale

amarra [a·'ma·rra] *f* **1.** NÁUT hawser **2.** *pl* (*apoyo*) connections *pl*

amarradero [a·ma·rra·'de·ro] *m* **1.** (*poste*) post, bollard **2.** NÁUT berth

amarrado, -a [a·ma·'rra·do, -a] **I.** *pp de* **amarrar II.** *adj Arg, Par, PRico, Urug* (*tacaño*) stingy; (*innoble*) low

amarrar [a·ma·'rrar] **I.** *vt* **1.** (*atar*) to tie up **2.** NÁUT to moor **3.** *inf* (*empollar*) to cram; **estar** [*o* **ir**] **amarrado** (*haber empollado*) to have crammed; (*tener enchufe*) to have good connections ▶ **tener a alguien muy amarrado** *inf* to keep sb under tight control **II.** *vr:* ~**se** *AmL* to get married

amartillar [a·mar·ti·'jar, -'ʎar] *vt* **1.** (*arma*) to cock **2.** *inf* (*negocio*) to secure

amasandería [a·ma·san·de·'ri·a] *f Chile* bakery

amasar [a·ma·'sar] *vt* **1.** (*masa*) to knead **2.** (*fortuna*) to amass

amasiato [a·ma·'sja·to] *m Méx, CRi, Perú* concubinage

amasijar [a·ma·si·'xar] *vt AmL, inf* (*dar paliza*) to give a beating; (*pegar brutalmente*) to beat to a pulp

amasijo [a·ma·'si·xo] *m* **1.** (*para pan*) dough **2.** (*acción*) kneading **3.** (*argamasa*) mortar **4.** *inf* (*mezcla*) mixture

amateur [a·ma·'ter] **I.** *adj* amateur **II.** *mf* <amateurs> amateur

amatista [a·ma·'tis·ta] *f* amethyst

amatorio, -a [a·ma·'to·rjo, -a] *adj* amatory

amauta [a·'mau·ta] *m Bol, Perú* **1.** (*de los incas*) Incan sage **2.** (*autoridad*) village elder

amazona [a·ma·'so·na, -'θo·na] *f* **1.** (*mujer*) Amazon **2.** DEP rider **3.** (*traje*) riding habit

ámbar ['am·bar] *adj, m inv* amber

Amberes [am·'be·res] *m* Antwerp

ambición [am·bi·'sjon, -'θjon] *f* ambition; ~ **de poder** hunger for power; **sin ambiciones** unambitious; **mi** ~ **en la vida es...** my ambition in life is...

ambicionar [am·bi·sjo·'nar, -θjo·'nar] *vt* to aspire to; **sólo ambiciono salud** I only want to be healthy

ambicioso, -a [am·bi·'sjo·so, -a; am·bi·'θjo-] *adj* ambitious

ambientación [am·bjen·ta·'sjon, -'θjon] *f* **1.** CINE, LIT setting **2.** (*ambiente*) atmosphere

ambientador [am·bjen·ta·'dor] *m* air freshener

ambientar [am·bjen·'tar] **I.** *vt* **1.** (*novela*) to set; ~ **la acción de una novela en el siglo** pasado to set a novel in the last century; **la novela está ambientada en Lima** the novel is set in Lima **2.** (*fiesta*) to enliven **II.** *vr:* ~**se** **1.** (*aclimatarse*) to adjust **2.** (*en una fiesta*) to get into the mood

ambiente [am·'bjen·te] *m* **1.** (*aire*) air **2.** (*medio*) surroundings *pl;* **medio** ~ environment; **nocivo para el medio** ~ harmful to the environment **3.** (*social*) milieu **4.** (*atmósfera*) atmosphere; **dar** ~ to create a favorable atmosphere; **no había** ~ **en la calle** there wasn't much happening in the street; **el** ~ **en la reunión estaba caldeado** the atmosphere at the meeting was very tense **5.** *CSur, Perú* (*habitación*) room; **un departamento de cuatro** ~**s** a four-room flat

ambigüedad [am·bi·ɣwe·'dad] *f* ambiguity; **sin** ~ **es** unambiguous

ambiguo, -a [am·'bi·ɣwo, -a] *adj* **1.** (*de doble significado*) ambiguous **2.** LING *having two genders*

ámbito ['am·bi·to] *m* **1.** (*contorno*) surroundings *pl* **2.** (*espacio*) area; **en el** ~ **nacional** on a national level

ambivalente [am·bi·βa·'len·te] *adj* ambivalent

ambo ['am·bo] *m Arg* two-piece suit

ambos, -as ['am·bos, -as] *adj* both

ambulancia [am·bu·'lan·sja, -θja] *f* **1.** (*vehículo*) ambulance **2.** MIL field hospital **3.** FERRO ~ **de correos** mail truck

ambulante [am·bu·'lan·te] *adj* walking; **circo** ~ traveling circus; **vendedor** ~ peddler; **venta** ~ peddling

ambulatorio [am·bu·la·'to·rjo] *m* outpatient department

ambulatorio, -a [am·bu·la·'to·rjo, -a] *adj* outpatient

ameba [a·'me·βa] *f* ameba

amedrentar [a·me·dren·'tar] **I.** *vt* **1.** (*asustar*) to scare **2.** (*intimidar*) to intimidate **II.** *vr:* ~**se** **1.** (*asustarse*) to get scared **2.** (*intimidarse*) to be intimidated

amelcochar [a·mel·ko·'tʃar] **I.** *vt Arg, Méx, Par* (*almíbar*) to thicken **II.** *vi* **1.** *Cuba* (*enamorarse*) to fall in love **2.** *Méx* (*reblandecerse*) to soften

amén [a·'men] **I.** *m* amen; **decir** ~ **a todo** to agree to everything; **no decir ni** ~ not to say a word; **en un decir** ~ *inf* in a flash **II.** *prep* ~ **de** except for

amenaza [a·me·'na·sa, -θa] *f* **1.** (*intimidación*) threat; **bajo la** ~ **de violencia** under the threat of violence **2.** (*peligro*) menace

amenazador(a) [a·me·na·sa·'dor, -'do·ra; a·me·na·θa-] *adj* **1.** (*tono*) threatening; **gesto** ~ threatening gesture **2.** (*que anuncia peligro*) menacing

amenazar <z→c> [a·me·na·'sar, -'θar] **I.** *vt* (*intimidar*) to threaten; **el jefe lo ha amenazado con despedirle** the boss has threatened him with dismissal **II.** *vi, vt* (*presagiar*) to threaten; **amenaza tormenta** there's a storm

ahead; **está amenazando lluvia** it looks like rain
amenidad [a·me·ni·'dad] *f* **1.** (*lo agradable*) pleasantness **2.** (*entretenimiento*) entertainment **3.** (*distracción*) enjoyment
amenizar <z→c> [a·me·ni·'sar, -'θar] *vt* **1.** (*hacer agradable*) to make pleasant **2.** (*entretener*) to entertain **3.** (*conversación*) to liven up
ameno, -a [a·'me·no, -a] *adj* **1.** (*agradable*) pleasant **2.** (*entretenido*) entertaining
América [a·'me·ri·ka] *f* America; **~ Central** Central America; **~ Latina** Latin America; **~ del Norte/del Sur** North/South America

i Many Spaniards emigrated to Latin America in the 19th and 20th centuries. The expression "**hacer las Américas**" refers directly to this fact and essentially means "to make one's fortune in the Americas."

americana [a·me·ri·'ka·na] *f* jacket
americanismo [a·me·ri·ka·'nis·mo] *m* LING Americanism
americanista [a·me·ri·ka·'nis·ta] *mf* Americanist
americano, -a [a·me·ri·'ka·no] **I.** *adj* (*de América del Sur*) South American; (*estadounidense*) American; **el estilo de vida ~** the American way of life **II.** *m, f* (*de América del Sur*) South American; (*estadounidense*) American
amerindio, -a [a·me·'rin·djo, -a] **I.** *adj* American Indian, Amerindian **II.** *m, f* American Indian, Amerindian
ametralladora [a·me·tra·ja·'do·ra, a·me·tra·ʎa-] *f* machine gun
ametrallar [a·me·tra·'jar, -'ʎar] *vt* to machine-gun
amigable [a·mi·'ɣa·βle] *adj* friendly
amígdala [a·'miɣ·da·la] *f* tonsil
amigdalitis [a·miɣ·da·'li·tis] *f inv* tonsillitis
amigo, -a [a·'mi·ɣo, -a] **I.** *adj* **1.** (*amistoso*) friendly; **es muy amiga mía** she's a good friend of mine; **somos (muy) ~s desde la infancia** we've been close friends since our childhood **2.** (*aficionado*) **ser ~ de algo** to be fond of sth; **soy más ~ de veranear en el campo que en la costa** I prefer spending the summer in the country rather than at the seaside; **soy ~ de decir las cosas claras** I'm all for calling a spade a spade; **este tipo es muy ~ de lucir** this guy is a great one for showing off ▸ **¡y tan ~s!** and that's that! **II.** *m, f* **1.** (*general*) friend; **~ de lo ajeno** thief; **~ por correspondencia** pen pal; **hacerse ~ de alguien** to make friends with sb; **poner a alguien cara de pocos ~s** to look grimly at sb **2.** (*amante*) lover **3.** (*adepto*) supporter
amiguete [a·mi·'ɣe·te] *m inf* pal, buddy
amilanar [a·mi·la·'nar] **I.** *vt* **1.** (*intimidar*) to intimidate **2.** (*desanimar*) to discourage **II.** *vr:*

~se 1. (*acobardarse*) to become frightened **2.** (*abatirse*) to become discouraged
aminoácido [a·mi·no·'a·si·do, -'a·θi·do] *m* amino acid
aminorar [a·mi·no·'rar] **I.** *vi* to diminish **II.** *vt* to reduce; **~ el paso** to slow down
amistad [a·mis·'tad] *f* **1.** (*entre amigos*) friendship; **tener ~ con alguien** to be friendly with sb; **trabar ~ con alguien** to become friends with sb; **hacer las ~es con alguien** to make it up with sb **2.** *pl* (*amigos*) friends *pl*
amistar [a·mis·'tar] **I.** *vi Méx* to befriend **II.** *vr:* **~se** *CSur* to become friends
amistoso, -a [a·mis·'to·so, -a] *adj* friendly, amicable; **partido ~** friendly match; **llegar a un acuerdo ~** to come to an amicable agreement
amnesia [am·'ne·sja] *f* amnesia
amnistía [am·nis·'ti·a] *f* amnesty; **Amnistía Internacional** Amnesty International; **conceder ~ a alguien** to grant amnesty to sb
amnistiar <1. pres: amnistío> [am·nis·'tjar] *vt* to grant amnesty
amo ['a·mo] *m* **1.** (*de la casa*) head of the household **2.** (*propietario*) owner **3.** (*patrón*) boss; **ser el ~ en algo** to be the boss in sth ▸ **ser el ~ del cotarro** *inf* to be the top dog; **hacerse el ~** (*de una asociación*) to become the leader (of an association)
amodorrarse [a·mo·do·'rrar·se] *vr* to become drowsy [*o* sleepy]
amoldar [a·mol·'dar] **I.** *vt* **1.** (*ajustar*) to adjust **2.** (*moldear*) to mold **3.** (*acomodar*) to adapt **II.** *vr:* **~se** to adapt oneself
amonestación [a·mo·nes·ta·'sjon, -'θjon] *f* **1.** (*advertencia*) warning; **tarjeta de ~** DEP yellow card **2.** (*de los novios*) marriage banns *pl;* **correr las amonestaciones** to publish the banns
amonestar [a·mo·nes·'tar] **I.** *vt* **1.** (*advertir*) to warn; (*reprender*) to reprimand **2.** (*los novios*) to publish the banns of **II.** *vr:* **~se** to have banns published
amoníaco [a·mo·'ni·a·ko] *m* ammonia
amontonar [a·mon·to·'nar] **I.** *vt* **1.** (*tierra*) to pile up **2.** (*conocimientos*) to accumulate; **los refugiados estaban amontonados en el transbordador** the refugees were crowded together on the ferry **II.** *vr:* **~se** to pile up; (*personas*) to crowd together; (*noticias*) to accumulate
amor [a·'mor] *m* love; **~ al prójimo** love for one's neighbor; **~ propio** self-esteem; **~ a primera vista** love at first sight; **¡~ mío!** my love!; **mi gran ~ es el cine** my great passion is the cinema; **hacer el ~ con alguien** *inf* to make love with sb; **hacer algo con ~** to do sth lovingly ▸ **por ~ al arte** for nothing; **en ~ y compaña** in peace and harmony; **¡por ~ de Dios!** for God's sake!; **con [*o* de] mil ~es** with the greatest of pleasure; **~ con ~ se paga** *prov* one good turn deserves another
amoratado, -a [a·mo·ra·'ta·do, -a] *adj* purple;

un ojo ~ a black eye; **tengo los labios** ~**s de frío** my lips are blue with cold; **tengo el brazo** ~ **de la caída** my arm is bruised from the fall

amordazar <z→c> [a·mor·da·'sar, -'θar] *vt* to gag; *fig* to silence, to gag

amorfo, -a [a·'mor·fo, -a] *adj* shapeless, amorphous

amorío(s) [a·mo·'ri·o(s)] *m(pl) pey* love affair

amoroso, -a [a·mo·'ro·so, -a] *adj* **1.** (*de amor*) loving **2.** (*cariñoso*) ~ **con/para con alguien** affectionate to/towards sb **3.** (*tierra*) soft **4.** (*tiempo*) mild

amortiguador [a·mor·ti·ɣwa·'dor] *m* AUTO shock absorber

amortiguar <gu→gü> [a·mor·ti·'ɣwar] *vt* (*sonido*) to muffle; (*golpe*) to cushion; (*dolor*) to soothe; ~ **los faros** AUTO to dim one's headlights

amortización [a·mor·ti·sa·'sjon, -θa·'θjon] *f* **1.** (*de una deuda*) repayment **2.** (*fiscal*) depreciation

amortizar <z→c> [a·mor·ti·'sar, -'θar] *vt* **1.** (*deuda*) to pay off **2.** (*fiscalmente*) to write off **3.** (*inversión*) to recover

amotinar [a·mo·ti·'nar] **I.** *vt* to stir up **II.** *vr:* ~**se** to rebel

amparar [am·pa·'rar] **I.** *vt* to protect; ~ **a alguien** to shelter sb; **la constitución ampara la libertad de religión** the constitution guarantees religious freedom **II.** *vr:* ~ **se** to seek protection; ~**se bajo algo** to shelter behind sth; **se ampara en una ley antigua** he/she has recourse to an old law; **el espía se amparó en la oscuridad para escapar** the spy escaped under cover of darkness

amparo [am·'pa·ro] *m* **1.** (*protección*) protection; **estar al** ~ **de alguien** to be under sb's protection; **al** ~ **de la oscuridad** under cover of darkness **2.** (*refugio*) shelter

amperio [am·'pe·rjo] *m* amp

ampliación [am·plja·'sjon, -'θjon] *f* **1.** (*engrandecimiento*) enlargement; (*de capital*) increase; (*de un territorio*) expansion; (*de una carretera*) extension; ~ **del surtido** stock enlargement **2.** (*de conocimientos*) broadening **3.** (*de un sonido*) amplification; ~ **de RAM** COMPUT RAM expansion

ampliar <1. *pres:* amplío> [am·pli·'ar] *vt* **1.** (*hacer más grande*) to enlarge; (*capital*) to increase; (*territorio*) to expand; **edición ampliada** extended edition **2.** (*conocimientos*) to broaden **3.** (*sonido*) to amplify

amplificador [am·pli·fi·ka·'dor] *m* amplifier

amplificar <c→qu> [am·pli·fi·'kar] *vt* to amplify

amplio, -a ['am·pljo, -a] *adj* **1.** (*casa*) spacious; (*parque*) extensive **2.** (*vestido*) loose-fitting **3.** (*informe*) detailed; (*experiencia*) wide-ranging; (*red*) extensive; (*interés*) broad; **una derrota amplia** a serious defeat; **amplias partes de la población** large sections of the population; **en un sentido más** ~ in a wider sense

amplitud [am·pli·'tud] *f* **1.** (*extensión*) extent;

(*de conocimientos*) range; ~ **de miras** broad-mindedness; ~ **del surtido** ECON range of stock; **de gran** ~ wide-ranging **2.** (*de una casa*) roominess; (*de un parque*) extensiveness **3.** FÍS amplitude

ampolla [am·'po·ja, -ʎa] *f* **1.** (*burbuja*) blister; **tener** ~**s en los pies** to have blisters on one's feet **2.** (*garrafa*) flask **3.** (*para inyecciones*) ampoule ▶ **levantar** ~**s** to get people's backs up

ampolleta [am·po·'je·ta, -'ʎe·ta] *f Arg* light bulb

amputar [am·pu·'tar] *vt* to amputate

amuchar [a·mu·'tʃar] *vt Arg, Bol, Chile* to multiply

amueblar [a·mwe·'βlar] *vt* to furnish

amuermado, -a [a·mwer·'ma·do, -a] *adj inf* **1.** *ser* boring **2.** *estar* bored

amuermar [a·mwer·'mar] **I.** *vt inf* **1.** (*aburrir*) to bore **2.** (*calor*) to make drowsy **II.** *vr:* ~**se** *inf* to get bored

amularse [a·mu·'lar·se] *vr Méx* (*mercancía*) to become unsalable; (*persona*) to get stubborn

amuleto [a·mu·'le·to] *m* amulet

amurallar [a·mu·ra·'jar, -'ʎar] *vt* to wall

anabolizante [a·na·βo·li·'san·te, -'θan·te] *m* anabolic steroid

anacardo [a·na·'kar·do] *m* **1.** BOT cashew tree **2.** (*fruto*) cashew (nut)

anaconda [a·na·'kon·da] *f* anaconda

anagrama [a·na·'ɣra·ma] *m* anagram

anal [a·'nal] *adj* anal

anales [a·'na·les] *mpl* **1.** HIST annals *pl* **2.** (*de una sociedad*) records *pl*

analfa [a·'nal·fa] *mf inf* illiterate (person)

analfabetismo [a·nal·fa·βe·'tis·mo] *m* illiteracy

analfabeto, -a [a·nal·fa·'βe·to, -a] *m, f* illiterate (person)

analgésico [a·nal·'xe·si·ko] *m* painkiller

análisis [a·'na·li·sis] *m inv* **1.** (*general*) *t.* MAT analysis; ~ **de sistemas** COMPUT systems analysis; ~ **de la situación económica** analysis of the economic situation; **¿qué** ~ **haces de la situación?** what's your analysis of the situation? **2.** MED test; ~ **del grupo sanguíneo** blood test (*to determine blood group*)

analista [a·na·'lis·ta] *mf* **1.** (*de anales*) chronicler **2.** (*que analiza*) analyst; ~ **político** political analyst; ~ **de sistemas** COMPUT systems analyst; **el médico mandó las pruebas al** ~ the doctor sent the samples to the laboratory

analítico, -a [a·na·'li·ti·ko, -a] *adj* analytic(al)

analizar <z→c> [a·na·li·'sar, -'θar] *vt* **1.** (*examinar*) *t.* MED to analyze **2.** LING to parse

analogía [a·na·lo·'xi·a] *f* analogy; **por** ~ **con algo** on the analogy of sth

análogo, -a [a·'na·lo·ɣo, -a] *adj* analogous

ananá(s) [a·na·'na(s)] *m CSur* pineapple

anaquel [a·na·'kel] *m* shelf

anaranjado, -a [a·na·ran·'xa·do, -a] *adj* orange

anarquía [a·nar·'ki·a] *f* anarchy

anárquico, -a [a·'nar·ki·ko, -a] *adj* anarchic

anarquismo [a·nar·'kis·mo] *m* anarchism

anarquista [a·nar·'kis·ta] *adj, mf* anarchist

anatema [a·na·'te·ma] *m o f* **1.** (*maldición*) curse; **lanzar ~s contra alguien** to hurl abuse at sb **2.** (*excomunión*) anathema

anatomía [a·na·to·'mi·a] *f* anatomy

anatómico, -a [a·na·'to·mi·ko, -a] *adj* **1.** MED anatomical **2.** (*adaptado al cuerpo*) anatomically designed

anca ['an·ka] *f* **1.** (*de animal*) haunch; **~s de rana** frogs' legs **2.** (*cadera*) hip **3.** *pl, inf* (*nalgas*) backside ▶ **montar a las ~s** to sit behind

ancestral [an·ses·'tral, an·θes-] *adj* **1.** (*de los antepasados*) ancestral **2.** (*antiguo*) ancient

ancho ['an·tʃo] *m* width; **~ de vía** FERRO gauge [*o* gage]; **tener** [*o* **medir**] **cinco metros de ~** to be five meters wide

ancho, -a ['an·tʃo, -a] *adj* wide; (*vestidos*) loose-fitting; **~ de espaldas** broad-shouldered; **a lo ~** widthwise; **un árbol tumbado a lo ~ de la calle** a tree lying across the street ▶ **estar a sus anchas** to feel at ease; **en este pueblo estoy a mis anchas** I feel at home in this village; **se queda tan ~ cuando dice tonterías** he doesn't turn a hair when he talks nonsense; **venir a alguien muy ~** to be too much for sb

anchoa [an·'tʃoa] *f* anchovy

anchura [an·'tʃu·ra] *f* width; (*de un vestido*) looseness

ancianidad [an·sja·ni·'dad, an·θja-] *f* old age

anciano, -a [an·'sja·no, -a; an·'θja-] **I.** *adj* old **II.** *m, f* old man *m*, old woman *f*

ancla ['an·kla] *f* anchor; **echar ~s** to drop anchor; **levar ~s** to weigh anchor

anclar [an·'klar] *vi, vt* to anchor; **estar anclado** to be anchored

ancuviña [an·ku·'βi·ɲa] *f Chile* **1.** (*sepelio*) burial **2.** (*tumba*) grave

andadas [an·'da·das] *fpl* **volver a las ~** to revert to [*o* to fall back into] old habits

ándale ['an·da·le] *interj Méx* (*adiós*) bye; (*deprisa*) come on

Andalucía [an·da·lu·'si·a, -'θi·a] *f* Andalusia

andaluz(a) [an·da·'lus, -·'lu·sa; -'luθ, -·'lu·θa] *adj, m(f)* Andalusian

andamiaje [an·da·'mja·xe] *m*, **andamio** [an·'da·mjo] *m* scaffolding

andanada [an·da·'na·da] *f* **por ~s** *Arg* in excess

andante [an·'dan·te] *adj* errant; **parecer un cadáver ~** to look like a walking corpse

andanza [an·'dan·sa, -θa] *f* **1.** (*aventura*) adventure **2.** (*suerte*) **buena ~** good fortune; **mala ~** misfortune

andar [an·'dar] *irr* **I.** *vi* **1.** (*caminar*) to walk; **~ a caballo** to ride (a horse); **~ a gatas** to go on all fours; (*bebés*) to crawl; **~ con paso majestuoso** to strut; **~ de prisa** to go quickly; **~ detrás de algo** to be after sth; **desde la estación hay 10 minutos andando** it's 10 minutes walk from the station; **esta niña andaba ya a los ocho meses** this girl was al-

ready walking at the age of eight months **2.** (*coche*) to run; (*máquina*) to work **3.** (*tiempo*) to pass **4.** (*estar*) **¿dónde está el periódico? — ~á por ahí** where's the newspaper? — it'll be around here somewhere; **~ atareado** to be busy; **~ metido en un asunto** to be involved in a matter; **~ haciendo algo** to be doing sth; **anda mucha gente buscando empleo** there are a lot of people looking for a job; **te ando llamando desde hace una hora** I've been trying to call you for an hour; **~ con gente de bien** to mix with respectable people; **los precios andan por las nubes** prices are sky-high; **~ mal de dinero** to be short of money; **~ mal de inglés** to be poor in English; **~emos por los 30 grados** it must be about 30 degrees; **~ por los 30** to be about 30; **no andes en mi escritorio** don't go rummaging in my desk ▶ **dime con quien andas y te diré quien eres** *prov* your friends are a guide to your character; **~ a la que salta** to seize the opportunity; **¡anda!** good heavens! **II.** *vt* **he andado toda la casa para encontrarte** I've looked all over the house for you **III.** *m* walk, gait

andén [an·'den] *m* **1.** FERRO platform **2.** (*de muelle*) quayside

Andes ['an·des] *mpl* **los ~** the Andes + *pl vb*

> ⓘ The **Andes**, whose peaks rise higher than 6,000 meters (19,685 ft.), run down the entire length of South America, stretching more than 5,000 miles from Venezuela to Tierra del Fuego. In the South, the foothills gradually give way to islands and fjords. Many volcanoes can be found in the Andes, which were formed by the collision of two tectonic plates. The **ñandú**, a flightless bird, and the **guanaco**, a wild llama, are two of the many animal species that call the Andes home.

andinismo [an·di·'nis·mo] *m AmL* mountaineering, mountain climbing

andinista [an·di·'nis·ta] *mf AmL* mountaineer, mountain climber

andino, -a [an·'di·no, -a] *adj* Andean

Andorra [an·'do·rra] *f* Andorra

andrajo [an·'dra·xo] *m* rag

andrajoso, -a [an·dra·'xo·so, -a] *adj* ragged

andurrial [an·du·'rrjal] *m Arg, Ecua, Perú* muddy road

anécdota [a·'ney·do·ta] *f* anecdote

anegar <g→gu> [a·ne·'yar] **I.** *vt* to flood; **~ una sublevación en sangre** *fig* to suppress a revolt with violence **II.** *vr:* **~se** to flood; **~se en lágrimas** to dissolve into tears

anejo [a·'ne·xo] *m* **1.** (*edificio*) annex **2.** (*carta*) enclosure; COMPUT attachment **3.** (*de diario*) supplement **4.** (*en un libro*) appendix

anejo, -a [a·'ne·xo, -a] *adj* joined; (*a cartas*)

enclosed
anemia [a·'ne·mja] *f* anemia
anémona [a·'ne·mo·na] *f* anemone
anestesia [a·nes·'te·sja] *f* anesthesia
anestesiar [a·nes·te·'sjar] *vt* to anesthetize
anestésico [a·nes·'te·si·ko] *m* anesthetic
anestesista [a·nes·te·'sis·ta] *mf* anesthetist
anexión [a·nek·'sjon] *f* annexation
anexionar [a·nek·sjo·'nar] *vt* to annex
anexo [a·'nek·so] *m v.* **anejo**
anexo, -a [a·'nek·so, -a] *adj v.* **anejo, -a**
anfibio [an·'fi·βjo] *m* amphibian
anfibio, -a [an·'fi·βjo, -a] *adj* amphibious; **animal** ~ amphibious animal; **vehículo** ~ amphibious vehicle
anfiteatro [an·fi·te·'a·tro] *m* **1.** (*local*) amphitheater **2.** (*en la universidad*) lecture hall
anfitrión, -ona [an·fi·'trjon] *m*, *f* host *m*, hostess *f*
ánfora ['an·fo·ra] *f* **1.** (*cántaro*) amphora **2.** *Méx* (*electoral*) ballot box
ángel ['an·xel] *m* angel; ~ **de la guarda** guardian angel; **tener mucho** ~ to be very charming
angelical [an·xe·li·'kal] *adj* angelic(al); **rostro** ~ angelic face
angina [an·'xi·na] *f* ~ **de pecho** angina (pectoris); ~**s** sore throat
anglicismo [an·gli·'sis·mo, -'θis·mo] *m* Anglicism
angoleño, -a [an·go·'le·ɲo, -a] *adj, m, f* Angolan
angosto, -a [an·'gos·to, -a] *adj* narrow
angostura [an·gos·'tu·ra] *f* narrowness
anguila [an·'gi·la] *f* ZOOL eel
angula [an·'gu·la] *f* glass eel, elver
angular [an·gu·'lar] **I.** *adj* angular; **piedra** ~ cornerstone **II.** *m* **gran** ~ FOTO wide-angle lens
ángulo ['an·gu·lo] *m* **1.** MAT angle; ~ **recto** right angle; **en** ~ angled; ~ **de tiro** DEP angle of fire **2.** (*rincón*) corner **3.** (*arista*) edge **4.** (*de vista*) angle of vision
anguloso, -a [an·gu·'lo·so, -a] *adj* full of twists and turns; (*cara*) angular
angurria [an·'gu·rrja] *f AmL, inf* **1.** (*ganas*) craving; (*hambre*) ravenous hunger; *pey* (*glotonería*) gluttony **2.** (*codicia*) greed
angurriento, -a [an·gu·'rrjen·to, -a] *adj AmL* **1.** *pey* (*glotón*) gluttonous; (*hambriento*) greedy; *t. fig* (*devorador*) voracious **2.** (*codicioso*) avaricious
angustia [an·'gus·tja] *f* **1.** (*temor*) anguish; ~ **vital** angst **2.** (*aflicción*) anxiety; **dar** ~ to make anxious
angustiar [an·gus·'tjar] **I.** *vt* **1.** (*acongojar*) to distress **2.** (*causar temor*) to frighten **3.** (*afligir*) to worry **II.** *vr:* ~**se 1.** (*afligirse*) to get worried **2.** (*atemorizarse*) to get scared
angustioso, -a [an·gus·'tjo·so, -a] *adj* **1.** (*lleno de angustia*) anguished **2.** (*inquietante*) worrying
anhelante [a·ne·'lan·te] *adj* longing; **estar** ~ **por algo** to be longing for sth
anhelar [a·ne·'lar] **I.** *vi* to pant **II.** *vt* to long for

anhelo [a·'ne·lo] *m* ~ **de algo** longing for sth
anidar [a·ni·'dar] **I.** *vi* **1.** (*hacer nido*) to nest **2.** (*morar*) to live **II.** *vt* to take in
anilla [a·'ni·ja, -ʎa] *f* **1.** (*aro*) ring **2.** *pl* DEP rings *pl*
anillo [a·'ni·jo, -ʎo] *m* ring; ~ **de boda** wedding ring; ~ (**de crecimiento**) BOT growth ring ▶**venir como** ~ **al dedo** to be just right; **ese vestido te viene como** ~ **al dedo** this dress suits you perfectly; **no se me caen los** ~**s por...** it's not beneath me to...
ánima ['a·ni·ma] *f* soul ▶**a las** ~**s** in the evening
animación [a·ni·ma·'sjon, -'θjon] *f* **1.** (*acción*) animation; **dar** ~ to animate **2.** (*viveza*) liveliness **3.** (*actividad*) activity; **había mucha** ~ **en la calle** the street was very busy
animado, -a [a·ni·'ma·do, -a] *adj* **1.** (*persona*) in high spirits; **no estar muy** ~ not to be very cheerful **2.** (*lugar*) busy **3.** (*actividad*) lively **4. estar** ~ **a hacer algo** to be keen on doing sth; ~ **por ordenador** COMPUT computer-animated
animador(a) [a·ni·ma·'dor, -'do·ra] **I.** *adj* encouraging **II.** *m(f)* **1.** (*artista*) entertainer **2.** (*presentador*) presenter **3.** DEP cheerleader
animal [a·ni·'mal] **I.** *adj* **1.** (*de los animales*) animal; **comportamiento** ~ animal behavior **2.** (*grosero*) rude; **el aspecto** ~ **del hombre** the animal side of man **II.** *m* **1.** ZOOL animal; ~**es de caza** game; ~ **de compañía** pet; ~ **de presa** predator; **comer como un** ~ *inf* to eat like a horse **2.** *pey* (*persona ignorante*) fool; (*bruta*) brute
animalada [a·ni·ma·'la·da] *f inf* **1.** (*disparate*) (piece of) nonsense **2.** (*barbaridad*) disgrace; **¡qué** ~**!** how outrageous! **3.** (*cantidad*) massive amount
animar [a·ni·'mar] **I.** *vt* **1.** (*dinamizar*) to liven up **2.** (*alentar*) to encourage **3.** (*persona*) to cheer up **4.** (*economía*) to stimulate **II.** *vr:* ~**se 1.** (*cobrar vida*) to liven up **2.** (*atreverse*) to dare; **¡por fin te has animado a escribir** (**una carta**)**!** so you've finally decided to write (a letter)!; **¿te animas?** are you up for it? **3.** (*alegrarse*) to cheer up
ánimo ['a·ni·mo] *m* **1.** (*espíritu*) spirit; **no estoy con** ~**s de...** I don't feel like... **2.** (*energía*) energy; (*valor*) courage; **cobrar** ~ to take heart; **dar** ~ to encourage; **¡**~**!** cheer up! **3.** (*intención*) intention; **con** ~ **de...** with the intention of...; **sin** ~ **de lucro** non-profit-making; **sin** ~ **de ofender a nadie** without wishing to offend anyone
animoso, -a [a·ni·'mo·so, -a] *adj* brave
aniñado, -a [a·ni·'ɲa·do, -a] *adj* childlike; *pey* childish
aniquilar [a·ni·ki·'lar] **I.** *vt* **1.** (*destruir*) to annihilate; ~ **todas las esperanzas** to destroy all hope **2.** (*salud*) to ruin **3.** (*desanimar*) to shatter **II.** *vr:* ~**se 1.** (*desaparecer*) to be annihilated **2.** (*deteriorarse*) to deteriorate
anís <anises> [a·'nis] *m* **1.** (*planta*) anise;

(*semilla*) aniseed 2.(*licor*) anisette
aniversario [a·ni·βer·'sa·rjo] *m* anniversary; **~ de bodas** wedding anniversary; **~ de muerte de alguien** anniversary of sb's death
ano ['a·no] *m* ANAT anus; **~ artificial** colostomy
anoche [a·'no·tʃe] *adv* last night; **antes de ~** the night before last; **~ no pude dormir** I couldn't sleep last night
anochecer [a·no·tʃe·'ser, -'θer] I. *irr como crecer vimpers* **anochece** it's getting dark II. *irr como crecer vi* **anochecimos en Quito** we arrived in Quito at dusk III. *m* nightfall; **al ~** at dusk
anodino, -a [a·no·'di·no, -a] *adj* (*cosa*) insipid; (*persona*) bland
ánodo ['a·no·do] *m* anode
anomalía [a·no·ma·'lia] *f* anomaly
anonadar [a·no·na·'dar] I. *vt* to astound; (*maravillar*) to overwhelm; **la noticia me dejó anonadado** I was astonished by the news II. *vr:* **~se** 1.(*descorazonarse*) to be discouraged 2.(*aniquilarse*) to be destroyed
anonimato [a·no·ni·'ma·to] *m* anonymity; **mantener el ~** to remain anonymous
anónimo [a·'no·ni·mo] *m* (*autor*) anonymous author; (*escrito*) anonymous work; **guardar el ~** to preserve one's anonymity
anónimo, -a [a·'no·ni·mo, -a] *adj* anonymous; **sociedad anónima** ECON stock corporation
anorak <anoraks> [a·no·'rak] *m* anorak
anorexia [a·no·'rek·sja] *f* anorexia
anormal [a·nor·'mal] *adj* abnormal; **~ (físico)** physically handicapped; **~ (síquico)** mentally handicapped
anotación [a·no·ta·'sjon, -'θjon] *f* 1.(*acción*) annotation; (*en un registro*) record; **~ de intereses** credit (entry) 2.(*nota*) note
anotar [a·no·'tar] *vt* to note (down); (*en un registro*) to record
anquilosar [an·ki·lo·'sar] I. *vt* to paralyze II. *vr:* **~se** 1.(*articulaciones*) to get stiff 2.(*paralizarse*) to become paralyzed
ansia ['an·sja] *f* 1.(*angustia*) anguish 2.(*intranquilidad*) anxiety 3.(*afán*) longing; **~ de poder** craving for power 4. *pl* (*náusea*) nausea
ansiar <1. *pres:* ansío> [an·'sjar] *vt* to long for; **el momento ansiado** the long-awaited moment; **lograr la tan ansiada copa** to win the much-longed-for cup; **~ el regreso de alguien** to long for sb's return
ansiedad [an·sje·'dad] *f* anxiety
ansioso, -a [an·'sjo·so, -a] *adj* 1.(*intranquilo*) anxious 2.(*anheloso*) eager 3.(*impaciente*) impatient
antagónico, -a [an·ta·'yo·ni·ko, -a] *adj* 1.(*opuesto*) opposed 2.(*rival*) antagonistic
antagonismo [an·ta·yo·'nis·mo] *m* (*oposición*) opposition; (*rivalidad*) antagonism
antagonista [an·ta·yo·'nis·ta] *mf* antagonist
antaño [an·'ta·ɲo] *adv* long ago
antártico, -a [an·'tar·ti·ko, -a] *adj* Antarctic; **el polo ~** the South Pole; **Océano Glacial**

Antártico Antarctic Ocean
Antártida [an·'tar·ti·da] *f* Antarctica
ante ['an·te] I. *m* 1.ZOOL elk 2.(*piel*) suede II. *prep* 1.(*posición*) before 2.(*en vista de*) in view of 3.(*adversario*) faced with
anteanoche [an·te·a·'no·tʃe] *adv* the night before last
anteayer [an·te·a·'jer] *adv* the day before yesterday
antebrazo [an·te·'βra·so, -θo] *m* ANAT forearm
antecámara [an·te·'ka·ma·ra] *f* anteroom
antecedente [an·te·se·'den·te, an·te·θe-] *m* 1.LING antecedent 2. *pl* history; (*de una persona*) background; **~s penales** criminal record; **estar en ~s de algo** to be well informed about sth; **poner a alguien en ~s de algo** to fill sb in about sth
anteceder [an·te·se·'der, an·te·θe-] *vt* to precede
antecesor(a) [an·te·se·'sor, -·'so·ra; anteθe-] *m(f)* 1.(*en un cargo*) predecessor 2.(*antepasado*) ancestor
antedicho, -a [an·te·'di·tʃo, -a] *adj* aforementioned, above-mentioned
antelación [an·te·la·'sjon, -'θjon] *f* **con ~** in advance; **con la debida ~** in good time
antemano [an·te·'ma·no] *adv* **de ~** in advance; **calcular de ~** to calculate in advance
antena [an·'te·na] *f* 1.ZOOL antenna 2.(*de televisor*) antenna; **~ colectiva** community antenna; **~ interior** indoor antenna; **estar en ~** to be on the air; **el programa lleva un año en ~** the program has been running for a year; **estar con las ~s puestas** *irón* to be all ears
anteojo [an·te·'o·xo] *m* 1.(*catalejo*) telescope 2. *pl* (*gemelos*) opera glasses *pl;* (*prismáticos*) binoculars *pl;* (*lentes*) glasses *pl*
antepasado, -a [an·te·pa·'sa·do, -a] *m, f* ancestor
antepecho [an·te·'pe·tʃo] *m* 1.(*barandilla*) handrail 2.(*pretil*) parapet
antepenúltimo, -a [an·te·pe·'nul·ti·mo, -a] *adj* antepenultimate, third from the end
anteponer [an·te·po·'ner] *irr como poner* I. *vt* 1.(*poner delante*) **~ algo a algo** to place sth in front of sth 2.(*dar preferencia*) to give priority to II. *vr:* **~se** 1.(*ponerse delante*) **~se a alguien** to stand in front of sb 2.(*tener preferencia*) to be preferred
anteproyecto [an·te·pro·'jek·to] *m* draft
anterior [an·te·'rjor] I. *adj* previous; **la noche ~ había llovido** the night before it had rained; **en la página ~** on the preceding [o previous] page; **el presidente ~** the previous president II. *prep* **~ a** prior to
anterioridad [an·te·rjo·ri·'dad] *f* anteriority; **con ~ a** prior to, before
anteriormente [an·te·rjor·'men·te] *adv* before, previously
antes ['an·tes] I. *adv* 1.(*de tiempo*) before; (*hace un rato*) just now; (*antiguamente*) formerly; (*primero*) first; **poco ~** shortly before; **piénsate ~ lo que dices** think before you

speak; **ahora como** ~ still; ~ **con** ~, **cuanto** ~ as soon as possible; ~ **de nada** first of all; ~ **que nada** above all; **los cardenales van** ~ **que los obispos** cardinals come before bishops **2.** (*comparativo*) rather **II.** *prep* ~ **de** before **III.** *conj* **1.** (*temporal*) before; ~ (**de**) **que llegues** before you arrive **2.** (*adversativo*) **no estoy satisfecho con el examen,** ~ **bien decepcionado** I'm not happy with the examination, on the contrary, I'm disappointed **IV.** *adj* **el día** ~ the previous day

antesala [an·te·'sa·la] *f* anteroom; **hacer** ~ to wait (to be received)

antiaéreo, -a [an·tja·'e·reo, -a] *adj* MIL anti-air-craft

antialcohólico, -a [an·tjal·'ko·li·ko, -a/an·tjal·ko·'o·li·ko, -a] *adj* teetotal

antiatómico, -a [an·tja·'to·mi·ko, -a] *adj* **refugio** ~ fall-out shelter

antibalas [an·ti·'βa·las] *adj inv* bullet-proof

antibiótico [an·ti·'βjo·ti·ko] *m* antibiotic

anticiclón [an·ti·si·'klon, -θi·'klon] *m* anticyclone

anticipación [an·ti·si·pa·'sjon, -θi·pa·'θjon] *f* **1.** (*de fecha, de suceso*) anticipation **2.** COM advance; **con** ~ (*pago*) in advance

anticipadamente [an·ti·si·pa·da·'men·te, an·ti·θi-] *adv* in advance; **jubilar** ~ **a alguien** to retire sb early

anticipado, -a [an·ti·si·'pa·do, -a; an·ti·θi-] *adj* early; **pagar por** ~ to pay in advance

anticipar [an·ti·si·'par, an·ti·θi-] **I.** *vt* **1.** (*fecha*) to move up **2.** (*suceso*) to anticipate; **no anticipemos los acontecimientos** let's not anticipate events **3.** (*dinero*) to advance; ~ **una paga sobre el sueldo** to give an advance on a salary **II.** *vr* ~ **se a alguien** to beat sb to it; **el verano se ha anticipado este año** summer is early this year; **los invitados se han anticipado** the guests have arrived early

anticipo [an·ti·'si·po, -'θi·po] *m* **1.** (*del sueldo*) advance; ~ **sobre el sueldo** advance on a salary **2.** (*de un pago*) advance payment

anticonceptivo [an·ti·kon·sep·'ti·βo, -θep·'ti·βo] *m* contraceptive, birth control method

anticonceptivo, -a [an·ti·kon·sep·'ti·βo, -a; -θep·'ti·βo, -a] *adj* contraceptive, birth-control; **píldora anticonceptiva** contraceptive pill

anticongelante [an·ti·kon·xe·'lan·te] *m* anti-freeze

anticonstitucional [an·ti·kons·ti·tu·sjo·'nal, -θjo·'nal] *adj* unconstitutional

anticorrosivo [an·ti·ko·rro·'si·βo] *m* anticorrosive

anticuado, -a [an·ti·'kwa·do, -a] *adj* old-fashioned

anticuario, -a [an·ti·'kwa·rjo, -a] *m, f* antique dealer

anticucho [an·ti·'ku·tʃo] *m Perú* kebob

anticuerpo [an·ti·'kwer·po] *m* antibody

antideportivo, -a [an·ti·de·por·'ti·βo, -a] *adj* unsporting

antideslizante [an·ti·des·li·'san·te, -'θan·te] *adj* non-slip; (*neumático*) non-skid

antidoping [an·ti·'do·piŋ] *adj inv* **control** ~ drugs test

antídoto [an·'ti·do·to] *m* antidote

antieconómico, -a [an·tje·ko·'no·mi·ko, -a] *adj* uneconomic(al)

antier [an·'tjer] *adv AmL, inf* the day before yesterday

antiestético, -a [an·tjes·'te·ti·ko, -a] *adj* unattractive

antifaz [an·ti·'fas, -'faθ] *m* mask

antifris [an·ti·'fris] *m inv, AmL* anti-freeze

antigás [an·ti·'ɣas] *adj inv* **máscara** ~ gasmask

antigualla [an·ti·'ɣwa·ja, -ʎa] *f pey* **1.** (*objeto*) piece of junk **2.** (*costumbre*) relic

antiguamente [an·ti·ɣwa·'men·te] *adv* once, long ago

antigüedad [an·ti·ɣwe·'dad] *f* **1.** (*edad antigua*) antiquity; **la** ~ **clásica** classical antiquity **2.** (*objeto*) antique; **tener una** ~ **de 100 años** to be 100 years old **3.** (*en una empresa*) seniority; **tengo 5 años de** ~ (**en el trabajo**) I've been working for 5 years (in the job)

antiguo, -a [an·'ti·ɣwo, -a] *adj* <antiquísimo> **1.** (*viejo*) old; (*relación*) long-standing **2.** (*anticuado*) antiquated; (*muy anticuado*) ancient; **a la antigua** in the old-fashioned way; **está chapado a la antigua** he is old-fashioned **3.** (*de la antigüedad*) ancient **4.** (*anterior*) former **5.** (*en un cargo*) **es el más** ~ **en esta empresa** he's the most senior member of staff in this firm

antihigiénico, -a [an·ti·'xje·ni·ko, -a/an·ti·i·'xje·ni·ko, -a] *adj* unhygienic

antiinflamatorio, -a [an·tin·fla·ma·'to·rjo/an·ti·in·fla·ma·'to·rjo] *adj* anti-inflammatory

antílope [an·'ti·lo·pe] *m* antelope

antinatural [an·ti·na·tu·'ral] *adj* unnatural

antinomia [an·ti·'no·mja] *f* antinomy

antiparras [an·ti·'pa·rras] *fpl inf* specs *pl*

antipatía [an·ti·pa·'ti·a] *f* antipathy; ~ **a** [*o* **contra**] **alguien** antipathy for sb

antipático, -a [an·ti·'pa·ti·ko, -a] *adj* unpleasant

antipirina [an·ti·pi·'ri·na] *f AmL* MED antipyretic, antifebrile

antiquísimo, -a [an·ti·'ki·si·mo, -a] *adj superl de* **antiguo**

antirreglamentario, -a [an·ti·rre·ɣla·men·'ta·rjo, -a] *adj* unlawful; **entrada antirreglamentaria** DEP foul

antirrobo [an·ti·'rro·βo] *m* anti-theft device

antisemita [an·ti·se·'mi·ta] **I.** *adj* anti-Semitic **II.** *mf* anti-Semite

antisemitismo [an·ti·se·mi·'tis·mo] *m* anti-Semitism

antiséptico, -a [an·ti·'sep·ti·ko] *adj* antiseptic

antisísmico, -a [an·ti·'sis·mi·ko, -a] *adj* earthquake-proof

antisocial [an·ti·so·'sjal, -'θjal] *adj* antisocial

antiterrorista [an·ti·te·rro·'ris·ta] *adj* antiterrorist; **lucha** ~ fight against terrorism

antítesis [an·'ti·te·sis] *f inv* antithesis

antojadizo, -a [an·to·xa·'di·so, -a; -'di·θo, -a] *adj* capricious

antojarse [an·to·'xar·se] *vimpers* 1.(*encapricharse*) **se le antojó comprarse un coche nuevo** he/she took it into his/her head to buy a new car; **se me antojó un helado** I fancied an ice cream; **hace siempre lo que se le antoja** he/she always does as he/she pleases 2.(*tener la sensación*) **se me antoja que no vas a venir** I've a feeling that you're not going to come; **se me antoja que va a nevar** I think it's going to snow

antojitos [an·to·'xi·tos] *mpl Méx* CULIN appetizers *pl*

antojo [an·'to·xo] *m* 1.(*capricho*) whim; **a mi ~ as** I please 2.(*de una embarazada*) craving; **tener ~s** (*ganas*) to have cravings; *CSur* (*estar embarazada*) to be pregnant 3. *Méx* (*apetito*) appetite

antología [an·to·lo·'xi·a] *f* anthology ▶ **de ~** (*memorable*) excellent

antonomasia [an·to·no·'ma·sja] *f* **por ~ par** excellence

antorcha [an·'tor·ʧa] *f* torch

antro ['an·tro] *m pey* dive; **un ~ de corrupción** a den of iniquity

antropófago, -a [an·tro·'po·fa·ɣo, -a] *m, f* cannibal

antropología [an·tro·po·lo·'xi·a] *f* anthropology

antropólogo, -a [an·tro·'po·lo·ɣo, -a] *m, f* anthropologist

anual [a·nu·'al] *adj* annual, yearly; **informe ~** annual report

anualidad [a·nwa·li·'dad] *f* annuity; **~ vitalicia** life annuity

anualmente [a·nwal·'men·te] *adv* annually, yearly

anuario [a·nu·'a·rjo] *m* yearbook

anubarrado, -a [a·nu·βa·'rra·do, -a] *adj* cloudy

anudar [a·nu·'dar] I. *vt* to knot II. *vr:* **~se** to become knotted; **~se la voz** to get a lump in one's throat

anulación [a·nu·la·'sjon, -'θjon] *f* (*de una ley*) repeal; (*de una sentencia*) overturning; (*de un matrimonio*) annulment; (*de un contrato*) cancellation; (*de una decisión*) revocation

anular [a·nu·'lar] I. *vt* 1.(*ley*) to repeal; (*sentencia*) to overturn; (*matrimonio*) to annul; (*contrato*) to cancel; (*decisión*) to revoke; (*tren*) to cancel; (*gol*) to disallow 2.(*persona*) to subjugate II. *vr:* **~se** (*persona*) to limit oneself III. *adj* 1.(*del anillo*) annular 2.(*como el anillo*) ring-shaped

anunciación [a·nun·sja·'sjon, -θja·'θjon] *f* announcement

anunciar [a·nun·'sjar, -'θjar] I. *vt* 1.(*comunicar*) to announce; **acaban de ~ la llegada del vuelo** they've just announced the arrival of the flight 2.(*dar publicidad*) to advertise 3.(*presagiar*) to herald II. *vr:* **~se** 1.(*hacer publicidad*)

to be advertised 2.(*aparecer*) to be heralded

anuncio [a·'nun·sjo, -θjo] *m* 1.(*de una noticia*) announcement 2.(*en la TV*) commercial; (*en un periódico*) advertisement, ad *inf;* **~ en internet** banner; **~ por palabras** classified advertisement

anverso [am·'ber·so] *m* obverse

anzuelo [an·'swe·lo, -'θwe·lo] *m* 1.(*para pescar*) (fish-)hook 2. *inf* (*aliciente*) bait, lure; **echar el ~** to offer an inducement; **echar el ~ a alguien** to lure sb; **morder** [*o* **picar en**] [*o* **tragar**] **el ~** to swallow the bait

añadidura [a·ɲa·di·'du·ra] *f* addition; **por ~** in addition

añadir [a·ɲa·'dir] *vt* to add; **a esto hay que ~ que...** there's also the fact that...; **~ dos centímetros a las mangas** to lengthen the sleeves by two centimeters

añares [a·'ɲa·res] *mpl Arg* ages *pl*

añejo, -a [a·'ɲe·xo, -a] *adj* old; (*vino*) mature

añicos [a·'ɲi·kos] *mpl* fragments *pl;* **hacer algo ~** to smash sth up; **estoy hecho ~** *inf* I'm shattered

añil [a·'ɲil] *m* 1. BOT indigo 2.(*color*) indigo blue

año ['a·ɲo] *m* year; **~ bisiesto** leap year; **~ civil** calendar year; **~ luz** light year; **~ natural** calendar year; **~ nuevo** New Year; **la víspera de ~ nuevo** New Year's Eve; **~ de servicio** year of service; **los ~s 60** the sixties; **por los ~s 60** in the sixties; **en el ~ 1960** in 1960; **el ~ de la pera** the year one; **cumplir ~s** to have a birthday; **cumplir 60 ~s** to turn sixty; **necesitar ~s** to take years; **¿cuántos ~s tienes?** how old are you?; **Juan le saca cinco ~s a Pepe** Juan is five years older than Pepe; **los ~s no pasan en balde** the years take their toll; **los ~s corren que vuelan** the years fly by ▶ **estar de buen ~** (*saludable*) to look well; (*gordo*) to be plump; **un hombre entrado en ~s** an elderly man; **por él no pasan los ~s** he doesn't seem to get any older; **quitarse ~s** to be older than one admits; **a mis ~s** at my age

añoranza [a·ɲo·'ran·sa, -θa] *f* yearning; (*morriña*) homesickness

añorar [a·ɲo·'rar] *vt* to yearn for; (*tener morriña*) to be homesick for; **~ los viejos tiempos** to long for the old days

aojada [ao·'xa·da] *f Col* (*grande*) skylight; (*pequeña*) bull's eye

aorta [a·'or·ta] *f* aorta

aovar [ao·'βar] *vi* to lay eggs

apabullar [a·pa·βu·'jar, -'ʎar] *vt* to intimidate; (*confundir*) to confuse; **me quedé apabullado cuando oí la noticia** I was devastated when I heard the news

apacible [a·pa·'si·βle, -'θi·βle] *adj* 1.(*persona*) placid; (*temperamento*) even 2.(*tiempo*) mild; (*viento*) gentle

apaciguar <gu→gü> [a·pa·si·'ɣwar, a·pa·θi-] I. *vt* 1.(*persona*) to pacify 2.(*calmar*) to calm down; (*dolor*) to ease II. *vr:* **~se** to calm down

apadrinar [a·pa·dri·'nar] *vt* 1.(*ser padrino*) ~

A

a alguien (*en un bautizo*) to be sb's godfather; (*en una boda*) to be sb's best man **2.** (*patrocinar*) to sponsor

apagado, -a [a·pa·'ɣa·do, -a] *adj* (*volcán*) extinct; (*sonido*) muffled; (*persona*) lifeless; (*color*) dull

apagar <g→gu> [a·pa·'ɣar] **I.** *vt* (*luz*) to put out; **~ el fuego con una manta** to put out [*o* to extinguish] the fire with a blanket; (*sed*) to quench; (*hambre*) to satisfy; (*protesta*) to suppress; (*radio*) to switch off; (*vela*) to snuff; (*color*) to tone down ▸ **estar apagado** to not be in form; **¡apaga y vámonos!** that's enough! **II.** *vr:* **~se** (*fuego*) to go out; (*sonido*) to die out; (*color*) to fade

apagón [a·pa·'ɣon] *m* blackout; ELEC power cut

apaisado, -a [a·pai·'sa·do, -a] *adj* landscape; **formato ~** landscape format

apalabrar [a·pa·la·'βrar] *vt* to arrange

apalancar <c→qu> [a·pa·lan·'kar] **I.** *vt* to jack up **II.** *vr:* **~se** *inf* to install oneself

apaleada [a·pa·le·'a·da] *f Arg, Méx,* **apaleamiento** [a·pa·lea·'mjen·to] *m* **1.** (*zurra*) drubbing **2.** (*de una alfombra*) beating

apalear [a·pa·le·'ar] *vt* to thrash, to beat; **~ un árbol** to shake the branches of a tree; **~ un manzano** to knock fruit from an apple tree

apancle [a·'pan·kle] *m Méx* irrigation ditch

apandorgarse [a·pan·dor·'ɣar·se] *vr Perú* **1.** (*emperezarse*) to become lazy **2.** (*repantingarse*) to fill out **3.** (*vaguear*) to be indolent

apantallado, -a [a·pan·ta·'ja·do, -a; -'ʎa·do, -a] *adj Méx* overwhelmed

apañado, -a [a·pa·'ɲa·do, -a] *adj* **1.** (*hábil*) skillful **2.** (*adecuado*) suitable; **estás ~ si crees que te voy a ayudar** *inf* you're quite mistaken if you think I'm going to help you

apañar [a·pa·'ɲar] **I.** *vt* (*remendar*) to mend ▸ **¡ya te ~é yo!** I'll give you what for! **II.** *vr:* **~se 1.** (*darse maña*) to contrive to **2.** (*arreglárselas*) to manage; **no sé cómo te las apañas** I don't know how you manage; **¡apáñatelas como puedas!** get by as best you can!

apaño [a·'pa·ɲo] *m* **1.** (*remiendo*) patch; **encontrar un ~** to find a solution **2.** (*chanchullo*) scam **3.** (*amorío*) affair

aparador [a·pa·ra·'dor] *m* sideboard

aparato [a·pa·ra·'to] *m* **1.** (*utensilio*) *t.* DEP apparatus; **~ indicador** meter; **~ de precisión** precision instrument; **~ de televisión** television set; **~ para la ventilación** ventilation system; **gimnasia de ~s** apparatus gymnastics **2.** TEL receiver; **ponerse al ~** to come to the phone; **el señor X está al ~** Mr. X is on the phone **3.** (*avión*) plane **4.** ANAT system; **~ digestivo** digestive system **5.** (*ostentación*) pomp **6.** POL (*de un partido*) machine

aparatoso, -a [a·pa·ra·'to·so, -a] *adj* **1.** (*ostentoso*) ostentatious **2.** (*desmedido*) excessive; **un accidente ~** a spectacular accident

aparcamiento [a·par·ka·'mjen·to] *m* **1.** (*acción*) parking **2.** (*lugar*) parking lot

aparcar <c→qu> [a·par·'kar] *vt* **1.** (*coche*) to park **2.** (*decisión*) to put off

aparear [a·pa·re·'ar] **I.** *vt* **1.** (*animales*) to mate **2.** (*formar un par*) to pair; **~ personas** to pair people off **II.** *vr:* **~se 1.** (*animales*) to mate **2.** (*formar un par*) to form a pair

aparecer [a·pa·re·'ser, -'θer] *irr como crecer* **I.** *vi* to appear; (*algo inesperado*) to turn up; **~ ante la opinión pública** to appear in public; **han aparecido casos de difteria** some cases of diphtheria have appeared **II.** *vr:* **~se** to appear

aparejador(a) [a·pa·re·xa·'dor, -'do·ra] *m(f)* foreman builder *m,* forewoman builder *f*

aparentar [a·pa·ren·'tar] *vt* to feign; **trata de ~ que es rico** he tries to make out that he's rich; **~ estar enfermo** to pretend to be ill; **no aparentas la edad que tienes** you don't look your age

aparente [a·pa·'ren·te] *adj* **1.** (*que parece*) apparent **2.** (*visible*) visible **3.** (*de buen aspecto*) attractive

aparentemente [a·pa·ren·te·'men·te] *adv* apparently, seemingly

aparición [a·pa·ri·'sjon, -'θjon] *f* **1.** (*acción*) appearance **2.** (*visión*) apparition

apariencia [a·pa·'rjen·sja, -θja] *f* appearance; **en ~** apparently; **guardar las ~s** to keep up appearances ▸ **las ~s engañan** appearances can be deceptive

aparragarse [a·pa·rra·'ɣar·se] *vr* **1.** *Chile, Hond, Méx, Par* (*achaparrarse*) to remain stunted **2.** *Chile* (*agazaparse*) to crouch

apartado [a·par·'ta·do] *m* **1.** (*párrafo*) paragraph **2.** ADMIN **~ de Correos** post office box

apartado, -a [a·par·'ta·do, -a] *adj* (*lugar*) isolated; (*persona*) unsociable

apartamento [a·par·ta·'men·to] *m* apartment

apartar [a·par·'tar] **I.** *vt* **1.** (*separar*) to separate; (*la vista*) to avert; (*la atención*) to divert **2.** (*a un lado*) to put aside; **~ a alguien para decirle algo** to take sb aside to tell him/her sth; **~ el plato** to push the plate aside; **¡aparta la mano del taladro!** take your hand off the drill! **3.** (*de un cargo*) to remove **II.** *vr:* **~se 1.** (*separarse*) to separate; (*del tema*) to deviate **2.** (*de un camino*) to turn off; **¡apártate!** get out of the way!

aparte [a·'par·te] **I.** *adv* apart; **por correo ~** under separate cover; **he sumado los euros y, ~, los dólares** I've added up the euros and the dollars separately; **esta cuestión debe tratarse ~** this question must be dealt with on its own **II.** *prep* **1.** (*separado*) **él estaba ~ del grupo** he was separated from the group **2.** (*además de*) **~ de** apart from; **esta sopa ~ de mala está fría** besides tasting bad, this soup is cold as well; **~ de esto, perdí las llaves** apart from that, I lost the keys **III.** *m* paragraph; **punto y ~** new paragraph **IV.** *adj inv* **1.** (*singular*) special **2.** (*separado*) separate; **en un plato ~** on a separate plate

apasionado, -a [a·pa·sjo·'na·do, -a] **I.** *adj*

1. (*con pasión*) passionate **2.** (*entusiasta*) enthusiastic **II.** *m, f* enthusiast

apasionante [a·pa·sjo·'nan·te] *adj* exciting

apasionar [a·pa·sjo·'nar] **I.** *vt* to fill with enthusiasm **II.** *vr:* ~**se por algo** to become enthusiastic about sth; ~**se por alguien** to fall passionately in love with sb

apatía [a·pa·'ti·a] *f* apathy

apático, -a [a·'pa·ti·ko, -a] *adj* apathetic

apátrida [a·'pa·tri·da] *adj* stateless

apatusco [a·pa·'tus·ko] *m Ven* **1.** (*intriga*) intrigue **2.** (*fingimiento*) pretense

apeadero [a·pea·'de·ro] *m* **1.** (*poyo*) mounting block **2.** FERRO halt

apear [a·pe·'ar] **I.** *vt inf* to dissuade **II.** *vr:* ~**se** (*de un vehículo*) to get out; (*de un caballo*) to dismount

apechugar <g→gu> [a·pe·ʧu·'ɣar] *vi* ~ **con** to put up with stoically; ~ **con las consecuencias** to suffer the consequences; ~ **con una tarea complicada** to take on a difficult task

apedrear [a·pe·dre·'ar] **I.** *vimpers* to hail **II.** *vt* to throw stones at; (*lapidar*) to stone (to death)

apegado, -a [a·pe·'ɣa·do, -a] *adj* **estar** ~ **a alguien** to be attached to sb

apegarse <g→gu> [a·pe·'ɣar·se] *vr* to become attached

apego [a·'pe·ɣo] *m* attachment; **tener un gran** ~ **a algo** to be very attached to sth

apelación [a·pe·la·'sjon, -'θjon] *f* JUR appeal; **esto no tiene** ~ *fig* there's nothing to be done

apelar [a·pe·'lar] *vi* **1.** (*invocar*) to appeal; (*referirse*) to refer **2.** (*recurrir*) to turn; (*a algo*) to resort; ~ **a todos los medios** to try everything **3.** JUR (*recurrir*) to appeal; **la sentencia ha sido apelada** an appeal has been filed against [*o* from] the judgment

apelativo [a·pe·la·'ti·βo] *m* **1.** (*apellido*) name **2.** (*sobrenombre*) nickname; ~ **cariñoso** pet name

apellidar [a·pe·ʎi·'dar, -ʎi·'dar] **I.** *vt* to name **II.** *vr:* ~**se** to be called; **se apellida Martínez** his/her surname is Martínez

apellido [a·pe·'ji·do, -'ʎi·do] *m* surname; ~ **de soltera** maiden name; **primer** ~ father's surname; **por el** ~ **no caigo** the name doesn't mean anything to me

---

i Spanish-speaking people have two **apellidos** (surnames). The first is the father's name and the second is the mother's name. If, for example, Señora Iglesias Vieira and Señor González Blanco were to become parents, the child's surname would be González Iglesias.

---

apelmazar <z→c> [a·pel·ma·'sar, -'θar] **I.** *vt* to compress **II.** *vr:* ~**se** (*colchón*) to become hard; (*nieve*) to crust; (*harina*) to become lumpy; (*lana*) to become matted

apelotonar [a·pe·lo·to·'nar] **I.** *vt* (*cosas*) to roll into a ball; (*personas*) to crowd together

II. *vr:* ~**se** **1.** (*cosas*) to mass, to crowd together; ~**se en la entrada** to throng at the entrance; **en esta calle se apelotonan los coches** the traffic gets snarled up in this street **2.** (*masa*) to become lumpy

apenar [a·pe·'nar] **I.** *vt* to sadden **II.** *vr:* ~**se** **1.** (*afligirse*) ~**se por algo** to grieve over [*o* at] sth **2.** *AmC* (*sentir vergüenza*) ~**se por algo** to feel embarrassed about sth

apenas [a·'pe·nas] **I.** *adv* **1.** (*casi no*) hardly; ~ **había nadie** there was hardly anybody [*o* anyone] there **2.** (*tan solo*) just; (*escasamente*) barely; ~ **hace un mes que estudio alemán** I've been learning German for just a month; ~ **hace una hora** barely an hour ago; **tengo** ~ **10 dólares en el bolsillo** I have just 10 dollars in my pocket **II.** *conj* (*tan pronto como*) as soon as; ~ **salí a la calle, se puso a llover** as soon as I went out into the street it began to rain

apéndice [a·'pen·di·se, -θe] *m* **1.** (*de un libro*) appendix; (*tomo separado*) supplement **2.** (*complemento*) appendage **3.** ANAT appendix; ~ **vermiforme** (vermiform) appendix

apendicitis [a·pen·di·'si·tis, -'θi·tis] *f inv* appendicitis

apensionarse [a·pen·sjo·'nar·se] *vr* **1.** *Arg, Chile, Méx* (*entristecerse*) to become sad **2.** *Col* (*inquietarse*) to become distressed

apercibir [a·per·si·'βir, -θi·'βir] **I.** *vt* **1.** (*avisar*) *t.* JUR to warn; **lo han apercibido con el despido** they threatened him with dismissal **2.** (*amonestar*) ~ **a alguien por algo** to rebuke sb for sth **II.** *vr:* ~**se de algo** to notice sth; **me he apercibido de lo importante que es el examen** I've become aware of how important the examination is

aperitivo [a·pe·ri·'ti·βo] *m* **1.** (*bebida*) aperitif **2.** (*comida*) appetizer ▶ **¡y ésto es tan solo el** ~**!** and that's only the beginning!

apertura [a·per·'tu·ra] *f* opening; (*de testamento*) reading; ~ **de un crédito** opening of a credit

apesadumbrar [a·pe·sa·dum·'brar] **I.** *vt* to sadden **II.** *vr* ~**se por algo** to grieve over [*o* at] sth

apestar [a·pes·'tar] **I.** *vi* ~ **a algo** to stink of sth **II.** *vt* **1.** (*contagiar*) to infect (with the plague) **2.** (*dar mal olor a*) ~ **algo** (*cuarto, casa*) to smell sth up **III.** *vr:* ~**se** (*contagiarse*) to become infected; *AmL* to catch a cold

apestoso, -a [a·pes·'to·so, -a] *adj* **1.** (*que apesta*) stinking, stinky *inf* **2.** (*fastidioso*) annoying

apetecer [a·pe·te·'ser, -'θer] *irr como crecer vi* **1.** (*tener ganas de*) to feel like; **¿qué te apetece?** what would you like?; **¿un viaje?** — **sí, me apetece la idea** a trip? yes — the idea appeals to me; **me apetece un helado** I feel like an ice cream **2.** (*gustar*) **una copa de vino siempre apetece** a glass of wine is always welcome; **este libro me apetece más** this book appeals to me more

apetecible [a·pe·te·'si·βle, -'θi·βle] *adj* attractive; (*objetivo*) desirable

apetito [a·pe·'ti·to] *m* **1.**(*de comida*) ~ **de algo** appetite for sth; **abrir el** ~ to whet one's appetite **2.**(*deseo*) ~ **de algo** desire for sth; ~ **sexual** sexual appetite

apetitoso, -a [a·pe·ti·'to·so, -a] *adj* **1.**(*que da apetito*) appetizing **2.**(*sabroso*) tasty **3.**(*deseable*) desirable

apiadar [a·pja·'dar] **I.** *vt* to move to pity; **su mala suerte apiadó a sus vecinos** his/her misfortune moved his/her neighbors to pity **II.** *vr* ~ **se de** to take pity on; **¡Dios, apiádate de nosotros!** God have mercy on us!

ápice ['a·pi·se, -θe] *m* apex; **no ceder un** ~ *fig* not to yield an inch; **no entender un** ~ *fig* not to understand the slightest thing

apicultor(a) [a·pi·kul·'tor, --'to·ra] *m(f)* beekeeper

apicultura [a·pi·kul·'tu·ra] *f* beekeeping, apiculture

apilar(se) [a·pi·'lar·(se)] *vt, (vr)* to pile up

apiñar [a·pi·'ɲar] **I.** *vt* **1.**(*cosas*) to cram; **apiñó las cosas en el coche** he/she crammed the things into the car **2.**(*personas*) to crowd together; (*animales*) to herd together **II.** *vr:* ~ **se** to crowd together

apio ['a·pjo] *m* celery

apirularse [a·pi·ru·'lar·se] *vr Chile* to dress up

apisonadora [a·pi·so·na·'do·ra] *f* steamroller

apisonar [a·pi·so·'nar] *vt* to roll flat

aplacar <c→qu> [a·pla·'kar] **I.** *vt* **1.**(*persona*) to calm down **2.**(*dolor*) to soothe; (*hambre*) to satisfy; (*sed*) to quench **II.** *vr:* ~ **se** to calm down

aplanamiento [a·pla·na·'mjen·to] *m* **1.**(*allanamiento*) leveling **2.**(*desánimo*) dejection

aplanar [a·pla·'nar] **I.** *vt* **1.**(*allanar*) to level **2.**(*aplastar*) to flatten **3.**(*desanimar*) to discourage **II.** *vr:* ~ **se** to get discouraged

aplastante [a·plas·'tan·te] *adj* overwhelming; (*derrota*) crushing; (*prueba*) devastating

aplastar [a·plas·'tar] *vt* **1.**(*chafar*) to flatten; (*con la mano*) to squash; (*con el pie*) to crush; ~ **un cigarrillo** to stub out a cigarette; **el desprendimiento de piedras aplastó a dos personas** the rockfall crushed two people **2.**(*derrotar*) to overwhelm **3.**(*persona*) to devastate

aplatanarse [a·pla·ta·'nar·se] *vr Cuba, PRico* (*adoptar las costumbres*) to go native

aplaudir [a·plau·'dir] **I.** *vi* to applaud, to clap; **el publico rompió a** ~ the audience burst into applause **II.** *vt* **1.**(*palmear*) to applaud **2.**(*aprobar*) to approve

aplauso [a·'plau·so] *m* applause; **salva de ~s** storm of applause; **digno de** ~ *fig* worthy of applause

aplazamiento [a·pla·sa·'mjen·to, a·pla·θa-] *m* **1.**(*de fecha*) postponement; (*de reunión*) postponement, adjournment **2.**(*de decisión*) deferment

aplazar <z→c> [a·pla·'sar, -'θar] *vt* **1.**(*fecha*) to postpone; (*reunión*) to postpone, to adjourn (*after having begun*); ~ **el viaje una semana** to postpone the trip by one week; **la reunión se aplaza hasta nueva orden** the meeting is adjourned until further notice **2.**(*decisión*) to defer **3.** *AmL* (*suspender*) to fail

aplicación [a·pli·ka·'sjon, -'θjon] *f* **1.**(*de pintura*) application **2.**(*utilización*) use; **las múltiples aplicaciones del plástico** the various applications [*o* uses] of plastic

aplicacioncita [ap·li·ka·sjon·'si·ta, -θjon·'θi·ta] *f* COMPUT *inf* applet

aplicado, -a [a·pli·'ka·do, -a] *adj* (*trabajador*) hardworking

aplicar <c→qu> [a·pli·'kar] **I.** *vt* **1.**(*poner sobre*) to apply; ~ **dando un ligero masaje** apply, massaging lightly; ~ **un lazo a un vestido** to sew a bow onto a dress; ~ **el oído a la puerta** to put one's ear to the door; **aplicado con regularidad...** applied regularly... **2.**(*utilizar*) to use; ~ **una máquina para un trabajo** to use a machine for a job; ~ **el freno** to apply the brake; ~ **un tipo de interés** to apply a rate of interest **3.** JUR ~ **una sanción** to impose; **la ley no se puede** ~ **en este caso** the law is not applicable in this case **II.** *vr:* ~ **se 1.**(*esforzarse*) to apply oneself; ~ **se al estudio** to apply [*o* to devote] oneself to one's studies **2.**(*emplearse*) to be used

aplique [a·'pli·ke] *m* **1.** wall lamp, sconce **2.** COMPUT applet

aplomo [a·'plo·mo] *m* self-confidence, composure; **perder el** ~ to lose one's composure

apocar <c→qu> [a·po·'kar] **I.** *vt* to intimidate **II.** *vr:* ~ **se** to lose heart

apodar [a·po·'dar] **I.** *vt* to call; (*un apodo*) to nickname **II.** *vr* ~ **se...** (*tener el sobrenombre*) to be called ...; (*el apodo*) to be nicknamed...

apoderado, -a [a·po·de·'ra·do, -a] *m, f* **1.** JUR proxy **2.** COM agent

apoderar [a·po·de·'rar] **I.** *vt* to authorize; JUR to grant power of attorney to **II.** *vr:* ~ **se** to take possession; **el espía se apoderó del maletín** the spy seized the briefcase; ~ **se de los clientes de la competencia** to woo customers away from competitors; ~ **se del liderato** to take the lead

apodo [a·'po·do] *m* nickname

apogeo [a·po·'xeo] *m* **1.** ASTR apogee **2.**(*cumbre*) summit; **estar en el** ~ **de su carrera** to be at the peak of one's career; **el** ~ **del Barroco** the height of the baroque period

apolillado, -a [a·po·li·'ja·do, -a; -'ʎa·do, -a] *adj* **1.**(*de polilla*) moth-eaten **2.**(*anticuado*) antiquated

apolillar [a·po·li·'jar, -'ʎar] **I.** *vt* to eat away **II.** *vr:* ~ **se** to get moth-eaten

apolismado, -a [a·po·lis·'ma·do, -a] *adj* **1.** *AmL* (*magullado*) damaged **2.** *Col, Méx, PRico* (*raquítico*) sickly **3.** *CRi* (*holgazán*) lazy **4.** *Méx, Ven* (*deprimido*) depressed **5.** *PRico* (*tonto*) stupid; (*simple*) simple

apolítico, -a [a·po·'li·ti·ko, -a] *adj* apolitical

apología [a·po·lo·'xi·a] *f* defense

apoltronarse [a·pol·tro·'nar·se] *vr* **1.** (*emperezarse*) to get lazy **2.** (*repantigarse*) to lounge

apoplejía [a·po·ple·'xi·a] *f* stroke

apoquinar [a·po·ki·'nar] *vt inf* to fork out; **apoquina lo que me debes** pay up what you owe me

aporrear [a·po·rre·'ar] **I.** *vt* **1.** (*dar golpes*) to beat; ~ **el piano** to bang on the piano; ~ **la máquina de escribir** to hammer away on the typewriter; ~ **la puerta** to bang [*o* hammer] on the door **2.** (*molestar*) to bother; **esta música me aporrea los oídos** (*por estar muy alta*) this music is deafening; (*por ser mala*) this music is unbearable **II.** *vr:* ~**se** to toil

aportación [a·por·ta·'sjon, -'θjon] *f* **1.** (*contribución*) contribution; ~ **dineraria** cash contribution; ~ **en especie** contribution in kind; **hacer una** ~ **a un trabajo** to make a contribution to a job **2.** (*donación*) donation

aportar [a·por·'tar] *vt* **1.** (*contribuir*) to contribute; **he aportado algo a la fiesta** I've made a contribution to the party; **no aporta nada ir a esa conferencia** it's not worth going to that conference **2.** (*información*) to provide **3.** (*traer*) to bring; ~ **al matrimonio** to bring to the marriage

aposentar [a·po·sen·'tar] **I.** *vt* to lodge, to put up **II.** *vr* ~**se en algo** to lodge [*o* put up] at sth; MIL to be billeted in sth

aposento [a·po·'sen·to] *m* **1.** (*hospedaje*) lodging; **nos dieron** ~ they put us up **2.** (*cuarto*) room

aposición [a·po·si·'sjon, -'θjon] *f* apposition

apósito [a·'po·si·to] *m* (*vendaje*) dressing; (*adhesivo*) adhesive tape

aposta [a·'pos·ta] *adv* on purpose

apostar <o→ue> [a·pos·'tar] **I.** *vi* ~ **por algo/alguien** to back sth/sb; ~**las a** [*o* con] **alguien** to compete with sb **II.** *vt, vr:* ~**se** to bet; **¿qué/cuánto apostamos?** what/how much should we bet?; **¿qué te apuestas a que no lo hace?** I bet you he/she won't do it; ~ **doble contra sencillo que...** I bet you two to one that...; **puedes** ~ **la cabeza que...** you can bet your life that...

apóstata [a·'pos·ta·ta] *mf* apostate

a posteriori [a pos·te·'rjo·ri] *adv* with hindsight

apostilla [a·pos·'ti·ja, -ʎa] *f* marginal note

apóstol [a·'pos·tol] *m* apostle; **Hechos de los Apóstoles** Acts of the Apostles; **ser un buen** ~ *fig* to be a good disciple

apostrofar [a·pos·tro·'far] *vt* to apostrophize

apóstrofo [a·'pos·tro·fo] *m* LING apostrophe

apostura [a·pos·'tu·ra] *f* good looks *pl*

apoteósico, -a [a·po·te·'o·si·ko, -a] *adj* tremendous; **éxito** ~ tremendous success

apoteosis [a·po·te·'o·sis] *f inv* **1.** (*de un héroe*) apotheosis **2.** (*de un espectáculo*) climax

apoyar [a·po·'jar] **I.** *vt* **1.** (*colocar sobre*) to rest; (*contra*) to lean **2.** (*fundar*) to base; ~

(**con pruebas**) to support **3.** (*confirmar*) to confirm **4.** (*patrocinar*) to back; ~ **una moción/un ascenso** to support a motion/a promotion; ~ **una reforma** to back a reform **II.** *vi* ARQUIT to rest **III.** *vr:* ~ **se 1.** (*descansar*) to rest; ~ **se en** [*o* contra] **algo** to lean on sth; ~ **se con los brazos** to prop oneself up with one's arms; ~ **se con la mano** to support oneself with one's hand **2.** (*fundarse*) to be based

apoyo [a·'po·jo] *m* **1.** (*sostén*) support **2.** (*respaldo*) backing, support; (*ayuda*) help; **prestar** ~ **a un plan** to support [*o* back] a plan; **tener un** ~ **en alguien** to have sb's support [*o* backing]; **cuenta con mi** ~ you can rely on me; **en** ~ **de** in support of

apreciable [a·pre·'sja·βle, -'θja·βle] *adj* **1.** (*observable*) noticeable; ~ **al oído** audible **2.** (*considerable*) considerable **3.** (*digno de estima*) worthy

apreciación [a·pre·sja·'sjon, -θja·'θjon] *f* **1.** (*juicio*) assessment **2.** (*de una moneda*) appreciation **3.** (*de una casa*) valuation; (*del tamaño*) estimation

apreciado, -a [a·pre·'sja·do, -a; -'θja·do, -a] *adj* (*en cartas*) ~**s Sres** Dear Sirs

apreciar [a·pre·'sjar, -'θjar] *vt* **1.** (*estimar*) to appreciate; **aprecio los perros** I like dogs; **si aprecias tu vida, ¡desaparece de aquí!** if you value your life, get out of here!; **aprecio la libertad** I value my liberty **2.** (*una moneda*) to appreciate **3.** (*una casa*) to value; (*tamaño*) to estimate **4.** (*captar*) to detect; **de lejos no se aprecia ningún sonido** no sound can be heard from afar; **este cronómetro aprecia centésimas de un segundo** this chronometer indicates hundredths of a second; **el médico apreció una contusión en el pecho** the doctor detected bruising in the chest **5.** (*valorar*) to assess

aprecio [a·'pre·sjo, -θjo] *m* **1.** (*afecto*) affection; **te tengo un gran** ~ I'm very fond of you **2.** (*estima*) esteem; **gran** ~ high opinion; **tengo un gran** ~ **por este político** I hold this politician in high regard **3.** FIN valuation

aprehender [a·pren·'der/a·pre·en·'der] *vt* **1.** (*coger*) to apprehend; (*contrabando*) to seize **2.** (*percibir*) to perceive

aprehensión [a·pren·'sjon/a·pre·en·'sjon] *f* **1.** (*acción de coger*) apprehension; (*del botín*) seizure **2.** (*percepción*) perception

apremiante [a·pre·'mjan·te] *adj* pressing

apremiar [a·pre·'mjar] **I.** *vt* **1.** (*acuciar*) to urge (on) **2.** (*compeler*) to compel **II.** *vi* to be urgent; **el tiempo apremia** time is pressing

apremio [a·'pre·mjo] *m* **1.** (*prisa*) urgent situation; **por** ~ **de tiempo** because time is short **2.** JUR legal proceedings *pl*

aprender [a·pren·'der] *vt* to learn; **fácil de** ~ easy to learn; ~ **a leer** to learn to read; ~ **de la historia** to learn from history; ~ **de memoria** to learn by heart; **¿dónde has aprendido estos malos modales?** where did you learn such bad manners?; **siempre se aprende**

algo nuevo you live and learn

aprendiz(a) [a·pren·'dis, -·'di·sa, -·'diθ, -·'di·θa] *m/f* apprentice; **entrar de** ~ to become an apprentice; **trabajar de** ~ to work as an apprentice ▶**ser** ~ **de mucho, maestro de nada** *prov* to be jack of all trades and master of none *prov*

aprendizaje [a·pren·di·'sa·xe, -'θa·xe] *m* **1.**(*acción*) learning; ~ **en línea** internet-based learning **2.**(*formación*) apprenticeship; **contrato de** ~ contract of apprenticeship; **puesto** [*o* **tiempo**] **de** ~ apprenticeship

aprensión [a·pren·'sjon] *f* **1.**(*recelo*) apprehension; **me da** ~ **decírtelo** I daren't tell you **2.**(*asco*) disgust; **he cogido** ~ **a la leche** I've taken a strong dislike to milk; **me da** ~ **beber de este vaso** I find it disgusting to drink from this glass **3.**(*temor*) fear; (*impresión*) impression; **tener la** ~ **de que...** +*subj* (*temer*) to be afraid that...; (*creer*) to have the impression that...; **son aprensiones suyas** (*figuración*) those are just his/her strange ideas

aprensivo, -a [a·pren·'si·βo, -a] *adj* overanxious; (*hipocondríaco*) hypochondriac

apresar [a·pre·'sar] *vt* to seize; (*delincuente*) to capture

aprestar [a·pres·'tar] I. *vt* **1.**(*preparar*) to prepare **2.**(*telas*) to size II. *vr:* ~ **se** to prepare

apresurado, -a [a·pre·su·'ra·do, -a] *adj* hurried; (*con excesiva prisa*) hasty; **andar con paso** ~ to walk quickly

apresuramiento [a·pre·su·ra·'mjen·to] *m* hurry, haste

apresurar [a·pre·su·'rar] I. *vt* **1.**(*dar prisa*) to hurry **2.**(*acelerar*) to speed up; ~ **el paso** to quicken one's step; ~ **la salida del viaje** to depart hastily II. *vr:* ~ **se** to hurry; **¡no te apresures!** take your time!

apretado, -a [a·pre·'ta·do, -a] *adj* **1.**(*oprimido*) oppressed **2.**(*tornillo*) tight; (*vestido*) close-fitting, tight; (*cuerda*) taut; (*personas*) tight-fisted **3.**(*difícil*) **un caso** ~ an awkward case; **verse** [*o* **estar**] **muy** ~ to be in a very difficult situation **4.**(*apurado*) **estar** ~ **de dinero** to be short of money; **estar** ~ **de tiempo** to be short of time

apretar <e→ie> [a·pre·'tar] I. *vi* **1.**(*calor*) to become oppressive; (*lluvia*) to become heavier **2.**(*vestido*) to be too tight; **la americana me aprieta por detrás** the jacket is too tight around the back **3.**(*deudas*) ~ **a alguien** to weigh heavily on sb **4.**(*esforzarse*) **tenemos que** ~ **si queremos aprobar** we'll have to make more of an effort if we want to pass; **si aprietas un poco puedes ganar el partido** if you put more effort into it, you can win the game **5.**(*exigir*) **este profesor aprieta mucho en los exámenes** this professor demands a lot in the examinations II. *vt* **1.**(*hacer presión*) to press; ~ **un botón** to press a button; ~ **algo contra el pecho** to press sth against one's chest; ~ **el tubo de la pasta de dientes** to squeeze the toothpaste

tube; ~ **el acelerador** to step on the accelerator; ~ **la ropa en la maleta** to pack clothes into the suitcase **2.**(*estrechar*) ~ **las cuerdas de la guitarra** to tighten the strings of the guitar; ~ **los dientes** to grit one's teeth; ~ **filas** to close ranks; ~ **las letras** to squeeze letters together; ~ **las manos** to clasp one's hands; ~ **el puño** to clench one's fist; ~ **un nudo/un tornillo** to tighten a knot/a screw III. *vr:* ~ **se** **1.**(*estrecharse*) to become narrower **2.**(*agolparse*) to crowd together **3.**(*ceñirse*) ~ **se el cinturón** to tighten one's belt

apretón [a·pre·'ton] *m* **1.**(*presión*) squeeze **2.**(*aprieto*) jam *inf* **3.**(*apretura*) crush

apretujar [a·pre·tu·'xar] I. *vt inf* to squeeze II. *vr:* ~ **se** to squeeze together

aprieto [a·'prje·to] *m* jam, fix; ~ **económico** financial difficulties; **estar en un** ~ to be in a jam; **poner a alguien en un** ~ **con una pregunta** to embarrass sb with a question; **sacar a alguien de un** ~ to get sb out of a fix

a priori [a pri·'o·ri] *adv* a priori

aprisa [a·'pri·sa] *adv* quickly

aprisionar [a·pri·sjo·'nar] *vt* **1.**(*atar*) to bind **2.**(*inmovilizar*) to immobilize; (*pillar*) to catch; **quedarse aprisionado en el barro** to be trapped in the mud

aprobación [a·pro·βa·'sjon, -'θjon] *f* (*de decisión*) approval; (*de una ley*) passing; **murmullo de** ~ murmur of approval; **encontrar la** ~ **de alguien** to meet with sb's approval

aprobado [a·pro·'βa·do] *m* ENS pass; **he sacado un** ~ **en historia** I've passed history

aprobar <o→ue> [a·pro·'βar] I. *vt* **1.**(*decisión*) to approve; (*ley*) to pass; ~ **las condiciones** to agree to the conditions; **la censura no aprobaba muchas películas** the board of censors didn't pass many films; **la solicitud fue aprobada** the application was approved **2.**(*examen*) to pass II. *vi* ENS to pass

aproches [a·'pro·tʃes] *mpl AmL* **1.**(*proximidad*) surrounding districts *pl* **2.**(*parentesco*) relation **3.**(*vía de acceso*) approaches *pl*

apronte [a·'pron·te] *m AmL* preparation

apropiación [a·pro·pja·'sjon, -'θjon] *f* appropriation; ~ **indebida** misappropriation

apropiado, -a [a·pro·'pja·do, -a] *adj* **1.**(*adecuado*) ~ **a** [*o* **para**] **algo** suitable for sth **2.**(*oportuno*) appropriate; (*precio*) reasonable

apropiar [a·pro·'pjar] I. *vt AmL* (*premio*) to award; (*encargo*) to assign II. *vr* ~ **se de algo** to appropriate sth

aprovechable [a·pro·βe·'tʃa·βle] *adj* usable

aprovechado, -a [a·pro·βe·'tʃa·do, -a] *adj* **1.**(*alumno*) hardworking **2.**(*calculador*) opportunistic

aprovechamiento [a·pro·βe·tʃa·'mjen·to] *m* exploitation; ~ **del tiempo libre** use of one's leisure time

aprovechar [a·pro·βe·'tʃar] I. *vi* **1.**(*valer*) to be of use **2.**(*progresar*) **mi hijo no aprovecha en los estudios** my son isn't making progress in his studies ▶ **¡que aproveche!** enjoy your meal! **II.** *vt* to make good use of; (*abusar*) to exploit; ~ **una idea** to exploit an idea; ~ **un invento** to capitalize on an invention; ~ **el máximo de algo** to get the most out of sth **III.** *vr:* ~ **se 1.** (*sacar provecho*) ~ **se de algo** to profit by [*o* from] sth; **ellos hacen el trabajo sucio y luego los otros se aprovechan** they do the dirty work and then others get the benefit **2.** (*abusar*) to take advantage; ~ **se de una mujer** to take advantage of a woman **3.** (*explotar*) ~ **se de alguien** to exploit sb

aprovisionar [a·pro·βi·sjo·'nar] *vt* ~ **de** [*o* con] **algo** to supply with sth

aproximación [a·prok·si·ma·'sjon] *f* **1.** (*acercamiento*) approach **2.** (*en una lotería*) consolation prize

aproximado, -a [a·prok·si·'ma·do, -a] *adj* approximate

aproximar [a·prok·si·'mar] **I.** *vt* to bring nearer; **aproxima la silla a la mesa** draw your chair up to the table; ~ **opiniones** to bring opinions closer together **II.** *vr:* ~ **se** to approach; ~ **se con la silla a la ventana** to move one's chair over to the window; ~ **se a los 50** to be getting on to 50; **se aproxima a la realidad** it comes close to the truth; **se aproxima agosto** August is approaching; **las tropas se aproximan** the troops are getting closer

aptitud [ap·ti·'tud] *f* **1.** (*talento*) aptitude; ~ **para algo** aptitude for sth **2.** (*conveniencia*) suitability; ~ **para algo** fitness for sth; ~ **para el servicio militar** fitness for military service; **tener** ~ **es físicas para la natación** to have the physical requirements for swimming

apto, -a ['ap·to, -a] *adj* suitable; ~ **para algo** fit for sth; ~ **para el servicio militar** fit for military service; **la película no es apta para menores** the film is not suitable for minors

apuesta [a·'pwes·ta] *f* **1.** (*juego*) bet; **corredor de** ~ **s** bookmaker **2.** (*cantidad*) bid

apuesto, -a [a·'pwes·to, -a] *adj* handsome

apuntador(a) [a·pun·ta·'dor, -'do·ra] *m(f)* TEAT prompter; **en esta película no se salva ni el** ~ *fig* nobody is spared in this film

apuntalar [a·pun·ta·'lar] *vt* to prop up

apuntar [a·pun·'tar] **I.** *vi* to appear; (*día*) to break; **apunta la primavera** spring is coming; **la recuperación económica empieza a** ~ economic recovery is starting **II.** *vt* **1.** (*con un arma*) ~ **a algo** to aim at sth; **¡apunten!** take aim! **2.** (*con el dedo*) ~ **a algo** to point at sth **3.** (*anotar*) to note (down) **4.** (*inscribir*) to enroll; (*en una lista*) to enter **5.** (*dictar*) to dictate; TEAT to prompt **6.** (*insinuar*) to hint at; ~ **algo y no dar** to make a promise and fail to keep it **7.** (*indicar*) to point out; ~ **que...** to point out that...; **todo apunta en esta dirección** everything points in this direction **III.** *vr:* ~ **se 1.** (*inscribirse*) ~ **se a algo** to enroll in sth; (*en una lista*) to enter one's name in sth; ~ **se a un club** to join a club **2.** (*tanto*) to score; (*victoria*) to achieve

apunte [a·'pun·te] *m* **1.** (*escrito*) note; **tomar** ~ **s** to take notes; **¿me dejas los** ~ **s de física?** can you lend me your physics notes? **2.** (*bosquejo*) sketch

apuñalar [a·pu·ɲa·'lar] *vt* to stab

apurado, -a [a·pu·'ra·do, -a] *adj* **1.** (*falto*) ~ **de dinero** hard up; ~ **de tiempo** short of time **2.** (*dificultoso*) difficult; **verse** ~ to be in trouble **3.** *AmL* (*apresurado*) hurried; **estar** ~ to be in a hurry; **hacer un trabajo a las apuradas** to do a job hurriedly

apurar [a·pu·'rar] **I.** *vt* **1.** (*vaso*) to drain; (*plato*) to finish off **2.** (*paciencia*) to exhaust; ~ **todos los medios** to try everything **3.** (*atosigar*) to harass; **¡no me apures, mi paciencia tiene un límite!** don't hassle me, my patience is limited!; **ya vendrás cuando te apure el hambre** you'll come when you're hungry **4.** (*avergonzar*) to embarrass; **me apura decirle que no tengo dinero** I'm embarrassed to tell him/her that I don't have any money **5.** *AmL* (*dar prisa*) to hurry **II.** *vr:* ~ **se 1.** (*preocuparse*) to worry; **¡no te apures por eso!** don't worry about that! **2.** *AmL* (*darse prisa*) to hurry up; **¡no te apures!** there's no hurry

apuro [a·'pu·ro] *m* **1.** (*aprieto*) fix; (*dificultad*) difficulty; **estar en un** ~ to be in a fix; **sacar a alguien de un** ~ to get sb out of a fix; **poner en** ~ to put in an awkward position **2.** (*estrechez*) financial need; **sufrir grandes** ~ **s** to be in financial difficulties **3.** (*vergüenza*) embarrassment; **me da** ~ **pedirle el dinero** it's embarrassing for me to ask him/her for money **4.** *AmL* (*prisa*) hurry

aquejar [a·ke·'xar] *vt* to afflict; **lo aquejaba una enfermedad grave** he suffered from a serious disease

aquel, -ella [a·'kel, -'ke·ja, -'ke·ʎa] **I.** *adj dem* <aquellos, -as> that, those *pl*; **aquella casa es nuestra** that house is ours; **¿qué fue del hombre** ~? what became of that man?; **¿estabais de acuerdo en** ~ **punto?** did you agree on that point?; **en aquellos tiempos** in those days **II.** *pron dem v.* **aquél, aquélla, aquello**

aquí [a·'ki] *adv* **1.** (*lugar*) here; (*por*) ~ **cerca** around here; ~ **dentro** in here; **éste de** ~ this guy here; **¡ah,** ~ **estás!** oh, there you are!; **andar de** ~ **para allá** to walk up and down; **mira** ~ **dentro** look in here; **de** ~ **hasta allí hay 10 minutos a pie** it's a 10-minute walk from here; **mejor ir por** ~ it's better to go this way **2.** (*de tiempo*) **de** ~ **en adelante** from now on; **de** ~ **a una semana** a week from now; **hasta** ~ up until now

ara¹ ['a·ra] *f* altar ▶ **dar la vida en** ~ **s de una idea** to sacrifice one's life for an idea; **en** ~ **s de la paz** in the interests of peace; **acogerse a las** ~ **s de alguien** to take refuge with sb

ara² ['a·ra] *m AmL* parrot

árabe ['a·ra·βe] **I.** *adj* **1.** (*país*) Arab **2.** (*palabra*) Arabic **3.** (*península*) Arabian **4.** (*de los moros*) Moorish **II.** *mf* (*persona*) Arab **III.** *m*

A

(*lengua*) Arabic
Arabia [a·'ra·βja] *f* Arabia; ~ **Saudita** Saudi Arabia
arábigo, -a [a·'ra·βi·ɣo] *adj* Arab; (*número*) Arabic
arado [a·'ra·do] *m* plow
Aragón [a·ra·'ɣon] *m* Aragon
aragonés, -esa [a·ra·ɣo·'nes, --'ne·sa] *adj, m, f* Aragonese
arancel [a·ran·'sel, -'θel] *m* tariff; (*impuesto*) duty
arancelario, -a [a·ran·se·'la·rjo, -a; a·ran·θe-] *adj* tariff, customs
arándano [a·'ran·da·no] *m* blueberry
araña [a·'ra·ɲa] *f* 1.ZOOL spider; **tela de ~** spider web 2.(*candelabro*) chandelier
arañar [a·ra·'ɲar] I. *vt* 1.(*rasguñar*) to scratch 2. *inf*(*reunir*) to scrape together; **con un poco de suerte ~é un aprobado** with a little luck I'll manage to pass II. *vi* to scratch III. *vr:* **~se** to scratch oneself
arañazo [a·ra·'ɲa·so, -θo] *m* scratch; **dar un ~ a alguien** to scratch sb; **defenderse a ~ limpio** to defend oneself stubbornly
arar [a·'rar] *vt* to plow
arbitraje [ar·βi·'tra·xe] *m* 1.(*juicio*) arbitration 2.(*en fútbol*) refereeing; (*en tenis*) umpiring
arbitral [ar·βi·'tral] *adj* arbitral; **jurisdicción ~** arbitral jurisdiction
arbitrar [ar·βi·'trar] I. *vt* 1.(*disputa*) ~ **algo** to arbitrate in sth 2.(*medios*) to provide 3.DEP (*en fútbol*) to referee; (*en tenis*) to umpire II. *vi* to adjudge
arbitrariedad [ar·βi·tra·rje·'dad] *f* 1.(*cualidad*) arbitrariness 2.(*acción*) arbitrary act
arbitrario, -a [ar·βi·'tra·rjo, -a] *adj* arbitrary
arbitrio [ar·'βi·trjo] *m* 1.(*voluntad*) free will; **estar al ~ de alguien** to be at sb's discretion; **dejar algo al ~ de alguien** to leave sth to sb's discretion 2.(*salida*) way out 3. *pl* (*impuesto*) **~s municipales** local taxes
árbitro, -a ['ar·βi·tro, -a] *m, f* 1.(*mediador*) arbitrator 2.(*fútbol*) referee; (*tenis*) umpire
árbol ['ar·βol] *m* 1.BOT tree; **~ de Navidad** Christmas tree; **~ de la ciencia** tree of knowledge; **~ genealógico** family tree 2.TÉC (*eje*) shaft 3.NÁUT mast ▶ **los ~es no le dejan ver el bosque** he can't see the wood for the trees; **del ~ caído todos hacen leña** *prov* there are always those who will seek to benefit from another's misfortune
arbolado [ar·βo·'la·do] *m*, **arboleda** [ar·βo·'le·da] *f* woods + *sing or pl vb*
arbusto [ar·'βus·to] *m* shrub, bush
arca ['ar·ka] *f* chest; (*para dinero*) safe; **las ~s del estado** the treasury ▶ **~ de la alianza** REL Ark of the Covenant; **~ de Noé** Noah's Ark; **~ del pan** *inf* stomach, breadbasket *inf*; **ser un ~ cerrada** to be very reserved
arcada [ar·'ka·da] *f* 1.ARQUIT arcade 2.*pl* (*náusea*) heaving
arcaico, -a [ar·'kai·ko, -a] *adj* archaic
arcángel [ar·'kan·xel] *m* archangel

arcano [ar·'ka·no] *m* mystery
arcano, -a [ar·'ka·no, -a] *adj* arcane
arce ['ar·se, -θe] *m* maple
arcén [ar·'sen, -'θen] *m* edge; (*de carretera*) shoulder
archipiélago [ar·tʃi·'pje·la·ɣo] *m* archipelago; **el ~ canario** the Canary Islands
archisabido, -a [ar·tʃi·sa·'βi·do, -a] *adj inf* very well-known; **esto está ya ~** this is a well-known fact
archivador [ar·tʃi·βa·'dor] *m* 1.(*mueble*) filing cabinet 2.(*carpeta*) file
archivador(a) [ar·tʃi·βa·'dor, --'do·ra] *m(f)* archivist
archivar [ar·tʃi·'βar] *vt* to file; COMPUT to store; (*asunto: por un tiempo*) to put on file; (*para siempre*) to close the file on
archivero, -a [ar·tʃi·'βe·ro, -a] *m, f* archivist
archivo [ar·'tʃi·βo] *m* 1.(*lugar*) archive(s); **~ fotográfico** picture library; **constar en los ~s** to be on record 2.*pl* (*documentos*) archives *pl* 3.COMPUT file
arcilla [ar·'si·ja, -'θi·ʎa] *f* clay
arcilloso, -a [ar·si·'jo·so, -a; ar·θi·'ʎo-] *adj* clayey
arco ['ar·ko] *m* 1.ARQUIT, MAT arc; **~ de medio punto** round arch; **~ iris** rainbow; **~ parlamentario** political spectrum; **~ voltaico** arc lamp 2.(*arma*) *t.* MÚS bow 3.AmL DEP goal
arcón [ar·'kon] *m* large chest
arder [ar·'der] *vi* 1.(*quemar*) to burn; **~ con fuerza** to blaze; **~ sin llama** to smolder; **~ por los cuatro costados** to be ablaze; **~ de fiebre** to have a very high temperature; **~ de pasión** to be inflamed with passion; **~ de rabia** to be mad with rage; **me arde la garganta** my throat is burning; **la reunión está que arde** things are getting heated at the meeting; **estoy que ardo** (*enfadado*) I'm furious 2. + *en, fig* **ardo en deseos de conocerte** I'm dying to get to know you; **Buenos Aires arde en fiestas** the festivities in Buenos Aires are at their height; **el país arde en guerra** war is raging in the country
ardid [ar·'did] *m* ruse
ardiente [ar·'djen·te] *adj* 1.(*pasión*) burning 2.(*sed*) raging 3.(*persona*) passionate
ardilla [ar·'di·ʎa, -ʎa] *f* squirrel
ardor [ar·'dor] *m* 1.(*calor*) heat; **~ de estómago** heartburn 2.(*fervor*) ardor; **el ~ de su mirada** the ardor of his/her look; **en el ~ del combate** in the heat of battle
ardoroso, -a [ar·do·'ro·so, -a] *adj* 1.(*apasionado*) ardent 2.(*caliente*) hot; (*calor*) burning
arduo, -a ['ar·dwo, -a] *adj* arduous
área ['a·rea] *f t.* MAT area; **un ~ de 200 metros cuadrados** an area of 200 square meters; **~ de descanso** AUTO rest stop; **~ de castigo** DEP penalty area; **~ metropolitana** metropolitan area; **~ de no fumar** no-smoking area
arena [a·'re·na] *f* 1.(*materia*) sand; **~s movedizas** quicksand 2.(*escenario*) arena ▶ **edificar sobre ~** to build on sandy ground;

sembrar en ~ to labor in vain

arenal [a·re·'nal] *m* sandy area

arenga [a·'ren·ga] *f* **1.** *inf* (*discurso*) harangue **2.** *Chile* (*disputa*) argument

arenoso, -a [a·re·'no·so, -a] *adj* sandy

arenque [a·'ren·ke] *m* herring; **~s ahumados** kippers *pl*

arepa [a·'re·pa] *f AmL: cornmeal griddlecake*

arequipa [a·re·'ki·pa] *f Col, Méx* rice pudding

arete [a·'re·te] *m* earring

argamasa [ar·ɣa·'ma·sa] *f* mortar

Argel [ar·'xel] *m* Algiers

Argelia [ar·'xe·lja] *f* Algeria

argelino, -a [ar·xe·'li·no, -a] *adj, m, f* Algerian

Argentina [ar·xen·'ti·na] *f* Argentina

> **i** **Argentina** (formally named **República Argentina**) is located in the southern part of South America. It is the continent's second largest country, after Brazil. The capital of Argentina is **Buenos Aires**. The country's official language is Spanish and the official currency is the **peso argentino**.

argentino, -a [ar·xen·'ti·no, -a] *adj, m, f* Argentine

argolla [ar·'ɣo·ja, -ʎa] *f* **1.** (*anilla*) ring **2.** *Chile, Col, Hond, Méx* (*alianza*) wedding ring

argot <argots> [ar·'ɣo(t)] *m* (*marginal*) slang; (*profesional*) jargon

argucia [ar·'ɣu·sja, -θja] *f* **1.** (*argumento*) fallacy **2.** (*truco*) trick

argüende [ar·'ɣwen·de] *m Méx* (*chisme*) gossip

argüir [ar·ɣu·'ir] *irr como huir* **I.** *vt* **1.** (*alegar*) to argue **2.** (*deducir*) to deduce **II.** *vi* to argue

argumentación [ar·ɣu·men·ta·'sjon, -'θjon] *f* line of argument

argumentar [ar·ɣu·men·'tar] *vi, vt* to argue

argumento [ar·ɣu·'men·to] *m* **1.** (*razón*) argument; (*razonamiento*) reasoning **2.** CINE plot **3.** *AmL* (*discusión*) discussion; (*alegato*) argument

aria ['a·rja] *f* aria

aridez [a·ri·'des, -'deθ] *f* aridity

árido, -a ['a·ri·do, -a] *adj* (*terreno*) arid, dry; (*tema*) dry

Aries ['a·rjes] *m inv* Aries

ariete [a·'rje·te] *m* MIL battering ram; DEP striker

ario, -a ['a·rjo, -a] *adj, m, f* Aryan

arisco, -a [a·'ris·ko, -a] *adj* (*persona*) surly, unfriendly; (*animal*) skittish

arista [a·'ris·ta] *f* edge

aristocracia [a·ris·to·'kra·sja, -θja] *f* aristocracy

aristócrata [a·ris·'to·kra·ta] *mf* aristocrat

aristocrático, -a [a·ris·to·'kra·ti·ko, -a] *adj* aristocratic

aritmética [a·rit·'me·ti·ka] *f* arithmetic

aritmético, -a [a·rit·'me·ti·ko, -a] *adj* arithmetical

arlequín [ar·le·'kin] *m* harlequin

arma ['ar·ma] *f* **1.** (*instrumento*) weapon, arm; **~s de destrucción masiva** weapons of mass destruction; **un ~ homicida** a murder weapon; **~ blanca** knife; **~ de fuego** firearm; **~ reglamentaria** regulation weapon; **llegar a las ~s** to become violent; **pasar a alguien por las ~s** to shoot sb; **rendir las ~s** to surrender [o to lay down] one's arms; **tomar las ~s** to take up arms; **¡apunten ~s!** take aim!; **¡descansen ~s!** order arms! **2.** *pl* (*blasón*) arms *pl* ▸ **ser un ~ de doble filo** to be a double-edged sword; **ser de ~s tomar** to be bold

armada [ar·'ma·da] *f* **1.** (*fuerzas navales*) navy; **un oficial de la ~** a naval officer **2.** (*escuadra*) fleet; HIST armada

armadillo [ar·ma·'di·jo, -ʎo] *m* armadillo

armado, -a [ar·'ma·do] *adj* armed; **~ de algo** armed with sth

armador(a) [ar·ma·'dor, -'do·ra] *m(f)* shipowner

armadura [ar·ma·'du·ra] *f* **1.** (*de caballero*) armor; **una ~** a suit of armor **2.** (*de edificio*) framework

armamento [ar·ma·'men·to] *m* arms *pl*; (*de un país*) armaments *pl*

armar [ar·'mar] **I.** *vt* **1.** (*ejército*) to arm; **~ a alguien de** [*o* con]**...** to arm sb with... **2.** TÉC to assemble; (*tienda de campaña*) to pitch **3.** *inf* (*jaleo*) to stir up; (*ruido*) to raise; **~ la** to start a row ▸ **~ a alguien caballero** to knight sb; **~ un Cristo** *inf* to make a stink (about sth) **II.** *vr* **~se** [*o* con] **algo** to arm oneself with sth ▸ **~se de paciencia** to muster one's patience; **~se de valor** to find courage

armario [ar·'ma·rjo] *m* cupboard; **~ empotrado** built-in cupboard; **~ (ropero)** wardrobe

armatoste [ar·ma·'tos·te] *m* monstrosity (*huge useless object*)

armazón [ar·ma·'son, -'θon] *m o f* (*armadura*) frame; (*de edificio*) skeleton

Armenia [ar·'me·nja] *f* Armenia

armenio, -a [ar·'me·njo, -a] *adj, m, f* Armenian

armería [ar·me·'ri·a] *f* **1.** (*tienda*) gunsmith's (shop) **2.** (*museo*) armory

armiño [ar·'mi·ɲo] *m* **1.** (*animal*) stoat **2.** (*piel*) ermine

armisticio [ar·mis·'ti·sjo, -θjo] *m* armistice

armonía [ar·mo·'ni·a] *f* harmony; **falta de ~** (*entre personas*) discord; **su comportamiento no estuvo en ~ con la solemnidad del acto** his/her behavior wasn't in keeping with the solemnity of the ceremony

armónica [ar·'mo·ni·ka] *f* harmonica, mouth organ

armónico, -a [ar·'mo·ni·ko] *adj* harmonic

armonio [ar·'mo·njo] *m* harmonium

armonioso, -a [ar·mo·'njo·so, -a] *adj* harmonious

armonizar <z→c> [ar·mo·ni·'sar, -'θar] **I.** *vi* to harmonize; **~ con** (*colores*) to blend with; **estos dos objetos armonizan** these two objects go together **II.** *vt* to harmonize; ~ **colores** to harmonize colors; ~ **ideas** to reconcile ideas

árnica [ˈar·ni·ka] *f* arnica

aro [ˈa·ro] *m* **1.** (*argolla*) ring; (*para jugar*) hoop **2.** *Arg* (*arete*) earring **3.** *AmL* (*anillo de boda*) wedding ring ▸ **entrar** [*o* **pasar**] **por el** ~ to give in

aroma [a·ˈro·ma] *m* (*olor*) scent; (*de café*) aroma

aromático, -a [a·ro·ˈma·ti·ko, -a] *adj* aromatic

aromatizar <z→c> [a·ro·ma·ti·ˈsar, -ˈθar] *vt* **1.** (*perfumar*) to scent **2.** CULIN to flavor

arpa [ˈar·pa] *f* harp

arpón [ar·ˈpon] *m* harpoon

arquear [ar·ke·ˈar] **I.** *vt* **1.** (*doblar*) to bend; (*espalda*) to arch; **el gato arqueó el lomo** the cat arched its back **2.** (*cejas*) to raise **II.** *vr:* ~ **se** to bend

arqueología [ar·keo·lo·ˈxi·a] *f* archeology

arqueológico, -a [ar·keo·ˈlo·xi·ko, -a] *adj* archeological

arqueólogo, -a [ar·ke·ˈo·lo·ɣo, -a] *m, f* archaeologist

arquero, -a [ar·ˈke·ro, -a] *m, f* **1.** archer **2.** *Arg* DEP goalkeeper

arquetipo [ar·ke·ˈti·po] *m* archetype

arquitecto, -a [ar·ki·ˈtek·to, -a] *m, f* architect; ~ **interiorista** interior designer; ~ **técnico** quantity surveyor

arquitectónico, -a [ar·ki·tek·ˈto·ni·ko] *adj* architectural

arquitectura [ar·ki·tek·ˈtu·ra] *f* architecture

arrabal [a·rra·ˈβal] *m* (*periferia*) suburb; (*barrio bajo*) slum area; **vivir en los ~es** to live on the outskirts

arrabalero, -a [a·rra·βa·ˈle·ro, -a] **I.** *adj* suburban; *pey* (*grosero*) vulgar **II.** *m, f* slumdweller; *pey* vulgar person

arracachada [a·rra·ka·ˈʧa·da] *f Col* silliness; **no dijeron más que ~s** they said nothing but nonsense

arraigar <g→gu> [a·rrai·ˈɣar] *vi, vr:* ~ **se** *t. fig* to take root

arraigo [a·ˈrrai·ɣo] *m t. fig* rooting; **de mucho** ~ deep-rooted

arrancar <c→qu> [a·rran·ˈkar] **I.** *vt* **1.** (*planta*) to pull up; **el viento arrancó el árbol** the wind uprooted the tree **2.** (*pegatina*) to tear off; (*página*) to tear out **3.** (*muela*) to extract, to pull (out); **le ~on el arma** they wrenched the weapon from him/her; **el ladrón le arrancó el bolso de la mano** the thief snatched her handbag from her hand; **la granada le arrancó un brazo** the grenade blew off his/her arm; **la corriente arrancó el puente** the current swept away the bridge **4.** (*vehículo, motor*) to start **5.** (*conseguir*) ~ **aplausos al público** to draw applause from the audience; ~ **una promesa a alguien** to force a promise out of sb; ~ **un secreto a alguien** to worm a secret out of sb; ~ **una victoria** to snatch (a) victory **II.** *vi* **1.** (*vehículo*) to

start **2.** (*empezar*) ~ **a hacer algo** to start doing sth; ~ **a correr** to start running; ~ **a cantar** to burst out singing **3.** (*provenir*) to stem; **esto arranca del siglo XV** this goes back to the 15th century

arranque [a·ˈrran·ke] *m* **1.** (*comienzo*) start; **en el** ~ **de la temporada** at the start of the season **2.** AUTO starting; ~ **automático** self-starter **3.** (*arrebato*) outburst; **un** ~ **de cólera/celos** a fit of anger/jealousy; **en un** ~ impulsively **4.** (*prontitud*) promptness; (*decisión*) initiative; **tener** ~ **para hacer algo** to have initiative to do sth **5.** COMPUT boot (up)

arrasar [a·rra·ˈsar] **I.** *vt* (*edificios*) to demolish; (*región*) to devastate **II.** *vi* to triumph; POL to sweep the board **III.** *vr:* ~ **se** (*ojos*) to fill with tears

arrastrado, -a [a·rras·ˈtra·do, -a] *adj* poor, miserable; **traer una vida arrastrada** to have a miserable life

arrastrar [a·rras·ˈtrar] **I.** *vt* **1.** (*tirar de*) to pull; (*algo pesado*) to drag; ~ **on la caja montaña arriba** they dragged the box up the mountain; **el agua arrastra las piedras** the water sweeps the stones along; **el viento arrastra las hojas** the wind sweeps away the leaves; ~ **los pies** (*al caminar*) to drag one's feet **2.** (*impulsar*) ~ **a alguien a hacer algo** to lead sb to do sth; **lo pude** ~ **al cine** I was able to drag him to the cinema; **no te dejes** ~ **por ese problema** don't get carried away by that problem **3.** (*producir*) to cause; **eso le arrastró dolores de cabeza** that caused him/her to have headaches **II.** *vi* to drag **III.** *vr:* ~ **se 1.** (*reptar*) to crawl; ~ **se por el suelo** to crawl along; **se arrastró hasta la habitación** he/she dragged himself/herself to the room **2.** (*humillarse*) to grovel

arrastre [a·ˈrras·tre] *m* dragging; (*en pesca*) trawling ▸ **estar para el** ~ *inf* (*cosa*) to be ruined; (*persona*) to be a wreck

arre [ˈa·rre] *interj* giddy-up, giddap

arreada [a·rre·ˈa·da] *f Arg, Chile, Méx* rustling

arrear [a·rre·ˈar] **I.** *vt* (*ganado*) to drive; *inf* (*golpe*) to give **II.** *vi inf* to hurry along; **¡arrea!** (*rápido*) get a move on!; (*atiza*) heavens!

arrebatado, -a [a·rre·βa·ˈta·do, -a] *adj* **1.** (*alocado*) hasty, violent **2.** (*impetuoso*) rash **3.** (*rostro*) flushed

arrebatar [a·rre·βa·ˈtar] **I.** *vt* **1.** (*arrancar*) to snatch (away); **el viento le arrebató el sombrero** the wind blew off his/her hat; **fue arrebatado por la corriente** he was swept away by the current; ~ **la vida a alguien** to take sb's life; ~ **la victoria a alguien** to snatch victory from sb **2.** (*extasiar*) to captivate **II.** *vr:* ~ **se** to get carried away

arrebato [a·rre·ˈβa·to] *m* **1.** (*arranque*) outburst; **un** ~ **de cólera** a fit of anger **2.** (*éxtasis*) ecstasy

arrecho, -a [a·ˈrre·ʧo, -a] *adj Col, inf* **1.** (*vigoroso*) vigorous **2.** (*cachondo*) horny, randy **3.** (*enfadado*) angry

arrechucho [a·rre·'ʧu·ʧo] *m inf* indisposition; **le dio un ~** he/she had a bad turn

arreciar [a·rre·'sjar, -'θjar] *vi* (*viento*) to get stronger; (*lluvia*) to get heavier; (*críticas*) to intensify

arrecife [a·rre·'si·fe, -'θi·fe] *m* reef

arreglado, -a [a·rre·'ɣla·do, -a] *adj* **1.** (*ordenado*) tidy; (*cuidado*) neat **2.** (*elegante*) smart ▶ **¡estamos ~s!** now we're in trouble!; **estás arreglado si crees que te ayudaré** you're very much mistaken if you think I'm going to help you; **¡vas ~ si piensas que...!** you're in for a big surprise if you think ...!

arreglar [a·rre·'ɣlar] **I.** *vt* **1.** (*reparar*) to repair; (*ropa*) to mend; **esta sopa te ~á el estómago** this soup will do your stomach good **2.** (*ordenar*) to tidy up; **~ la habitación** to tidy up the room; **~ la habitación para los invitados** to get the room ready for the guests; **~ una mesa con flores** to adorn a table with flowers; **~ a los niños para salir** to get the children ready for going out **3.** (*pelo*) to do **4.** (*resolver*) to sort out, to arrange; **~ las cuentas con alguien** to get even with sb **5.** MÚS to arrange ▶ **¡ya te ~é yo!** *inf* I'll sort you out! **II.** *vr:* **~se 1.** (*vestirse*) to get ready **2.** (*componérselas*) to manage; **no sé cómo te las arreglas** I don't know how you manage; **¿cómo te has arreglado para convencerlo?** how did you manage to convince him? **3.** (*ponerse de acuerdo*) to come to an agreement; **al final todo se arregló** everything worked out all right in the end **4.** (*mejorar*) to get better; **el tiempo se está arreglando** the weather is getting better

arreglo [a·'rre·ɣlo] *m* **1.** (*reparación*) repair **2.** (*solución*) solution; **no tienes ~** you're a hopeless case; **este trabajo ya no tiene ~** this job is completely botched **3.** (*acuerdo*) agreement; **llegar a un ~** to reach a settlement; **con ~ a lo convenido** as agreed; **obré con ~ a las normas** I worked in accordance with the regulations **4.** MÚS arrangement

arremangar <g→gu> [a·rre·man·'gar] *vt, vr:* **~se** to roll up; **arremángate** roll up your sleeves

arremeter [a·rre·me·'ter] *vi* **1.** (*criticar*) to attack; **~ contra alguien** to attack sb **2.** (*embestir*) to charge

arremetida [a·rre·me·'ti·da] *f* attack

arremolinarse [a·rre·mo·li·'nar·se] *vr* (*hojas*) to swirl around; (*gente*) to mill around

arrendador(a) [a·rren·da·'dor, -'do·ra] *m(f)* (*de casa*) landlord *m*, landlady *f*; (*de terreno*) *t.* JUR lessor

arrendamiento [a·rren·da·'mjen·to] *m* **1.** (*alquiler*) rent; (*de terreno*) lease; **~ financiero** leasing **2.** (*contrato*) contract

arrendar <e→ie> [a·rren·'dar] *vt* (*propietario*) to rent, to let; (*inquilino*) to rent, to lease

arrendatario, -a [a·rren·da·'ta·rjo, -a] *m, f* (*de una casa*) tenant; (*de un terreno*) *t.* JUR lessee, leaseholder

arrepentido, -a [a·rre·pen·'ti·do, -a] *adj* sorry; REL repentant; **estar ~ de algo** to be sorry about sth, to regret sth; **un terrorista ~** a reformed terrorist

arrepentimiento [a·rre·pen·ti·'mjen·to] *m* (*lamento*) regret; REL repentance

arrepentirse [a·rre·pen·'tir·se] *irr como sentir vr* (*lamentar*) to regret; REL to repent; **~ de algo** to regret sth, REL to repent of sth

arrestar [a·rres·'tar] *vt* to arrest; MIL to confine to barracks

arresto [a·'rres·to] *m* **1.** (*detención*) arrest; (*reclusión*) imprisonment; MIL detention; **estar bajo ~** to be under arrest; **~ domiciliario** house arrest **2.** *pl* (*arrojo*) daring; **tener ~s** to be bold

arria ['a·rrja] *f AmL* train of pack animals

arriar <1. *pres:* arrío> [a·rri·'ar] *vt* **1.** (*bandera*) to lower **2.** (*cabo*) to loosen **3.** (*inundar*) to flood

arriba [a·'rri·βa] *adv* **1.** (*posición*) above; (*en una casa*) upstairs; **más ~** higher up; **te espero ~** I'll wait for you upstairs; **lo ~ mencionado** the foregoing *form;* **la habitación de ~** (*de encima*) the room above; **el piso de ~** (*el último*) the top floor; **de ~ abajo** from top to bottom; (*persona*) from head to foot; **ensuciarse de ~ abajo** to get dirty from head to foot [*o* toe]; **leer un libro de ~ abajo** to read a book from cover to cover; **¡manos ~!** hands up! **2.** (*dirección*) up, upwards; **río ~** upstream; **¡~!** get up! **3.** (*cantidad*) **tener de 60 años para ~** to be over 60; **precios de 100 pesos para ~** prices from 100 pesos upwards **4.** *CSur* **de ~** (*gratis*) free (of charge); (*sin merecerlo*) for no reason

arribar [a·rri·'βar] *vi* **1.** NÁUT to reach port **2.** *AmL* (*llegar*) to arrive

arribista [a·rri·'βis·ta] *mf* arriviste; (*en sociedad*) social climber

arriendo [a·'rrjen·do] *m v.* **arrendamiento**

arriesgado, -a [a·rrjes·'ɣa·do, -a] *adj* **1.** (*peligroso*) risky, dangerous **2.** (*atrevido*) daring

arriesgar <g→gu> [a·rrjes·'ɣar] **I.** *vt* **1.** (*vida*) to risk **2.** (*en el juego*) to stake **3.** (*hipótesis*) to venture **II.** *vr:* **~se** to take a risk; **~se a hacer algo** to risk doing sth

arrimar [a·rri·'mar] **I.** *vt* **1.** (*acercar*) to bring closer **2.** (*apoyar*) ~ **algo a** to lean sth against **II.** *vr:* **~se 1.** (*acercarse*) to come close(r); **~se a algo** to move closer to sth; **~se al poder** to seek the protection of the authorities **2.** (*apoyarse*) **~se a algo** to lean against sth; **el niño se arrimó a su madre** the child snuggled up to his mother

arrinconado, -a [a·rrin·ko·'na·do, -a] *adj* **1.** (*apartado*) remote **2.** (*desatendido*) neglected

arrinconar [a·rrin·ko·'nar] **I.** *vt* **1.** (*objeto*) to put in a corner **2.** (*enemigo*) to corner **3.** (*rehuir*) to ignore **II.** *vr:* **~se** to withdraw from the world

arroba [a·'rro·βa] *f* **1.** COMPUT at **2.** *AmL* (*uni-*

dad de peso) arroba, ≈ *25 lbs. av.* (*9.5 kg*)
arrodillarse [a·rro·di·'jar·se, -'ʎar·se] *vr* to kneel (down)
arrogancia [a·rro·'ɣan·sja, -θja] *f* arrogance
arrogante [a·rro·'ɣan·te] *adj* arrogant
arrogarse <g→gu> [a·rro·'ɣar·se] *vr* to assume; ~ **la facultad de juzgar a los demás** to presume to judge other people
arrojado, -a [a·rro·'xa·do, -a] *adj* daring
arrojar [a·rro·'xar] I. *vt* 1. (*lanzar*) to throw; **el caballo arrojó al jinete** the horse threw the rider 2. (*emitir*) to emit, to give off [*o* out]; **la chimenea arroja humo** the chimney is giving off smoke; ~ **un mal olor** to give off a bad smell 3. (*expulsar*) to throw out 4. *AmL, inf* (*vomitar*) to throw up 5. (*un resultado*) to produce; ~ **beneficios** to yield profits; ~ **fallos** to contain errors; **mi cuenta arroja un saldo de 800 pesos** my account shows a balance of 800 pesos II. *vr:* ~**se** to throw oneself; ~**se al agua** to jump into the water
arrojo [a·'rro·xo] *m* daring; **con** ~ boldly
arrollador(a) [a·rro·ja·'dor, -·'do·ra, a·rro·ʎa-] *adj* 1. (*mayoría*) overwhelming; (*fuerza*) devastating 2. (*carácter*) irresistible
arrollar [a·rro·'jar, -'ʎar] *vt* 1. (*enrollar*) to roll up 2. (*atropellar*) to run over 3. DEP (*derrotar*) to crush
arropar [a·rro·'par] I. *vt* 1. (*abrigar*) to wrap up; (*en la cama*) to tuck in 2. (*proteger*) to protect II. *vr:* ~**se** to wrap oneself up; **¡arrópate bien!** wrap up warm!
arrorró [a·rro·'rro] *m AmS* lullaby
arroyo [a·'rro·jo] *m* stream; **salir del** ~ to climb out of the gutter
arroz [a·'rros, -roθ] *m* rice; ~ **con leche** rice pudding
arrozal [a·rro·'sal, -'θal] *m* rice field
arruga [a·'rru·ɣa] *f* (*en la piel*) wrinkle; (*en papel*) crease; **este vestido hace** ~**s** this dress creases
arrugar <g→gu> [a·rru·'ɣar] I. *vt* (*piel*) to wrinkle; (*papel*) to crease II. *vr:* ~**se** 1. (*piel*) to wrinkle, to get wrinkled; (*papel*) to crease, to get creased 2. (*achicarse*) to get scared
arruinar [a·rrwi·'nar] I. *vt* 1. (*causar ruina*) to ruin 2. (*fiesta*) to spoil; (*plan*) to wreck II. *vr:* ~**se** to be ruined
arrullar [a·rru·'jar, -'ʎar] I. *vt* to lull to sleep II. *vi* (*paloma*) to coo III. *vr:* ~**se** to bill and coo
arrullo [a·'rru·jo, -ʎo] *m* 1. (*para niños*) lullaby 2. (*de paloma*) cooing
arrumbar [a·rrum·'bar] *vt* 1. (*cosa*) to discard 2. (*persona*) to ignore
arsenal [ar·se·'nal] *m* arsenal
arsénico [ar·'se·ni·ko] *m* arsenic
arte ['ar·te] *m o f* (*m en sing, f en pl*) 1. (*disciplina*) art; ~ **culinario** culinary art; ~ **dramático** drama; ~ **narrativo** narrative art; ~**s plásticas** visual arts; ~**s y oficios** arts and crafts; **bellas** ~**s** fine arts; **el séptimo** ~ the movies 2. (*habilidad*) skill; **tiene mucho** ~

para la pintura he's quite a skilled painter 3. (*maña*) trick; **conseguir algo por malas** ~**s** to obtain sth by trickery; **desplegó todas sus** ~**s para convencerlo** she used all her wiles to convince him ▶**como por** ~ **de magia** as if by magic; **no tener** ~ **ni parte en algo** to have nothing whatsoever to do with sth; ~**s de pesca** fishing tackle
artefacto [ar·te·'fak·to] *m* appliance; (*mecanismo*) device; ~ **explosivo** explosive device
arteria [ar·'te·rja] *f* 1. ANAT artery 2. (*de tráfico*) thoroughfare
arterio(e)sclerosis [ar·te·rjos·kle·'ro·sis/ar·te·rjo·es·kle·'ro·sis] *f inv* arteriosclerosis
artesa [ar·'te·sa] *f* trough
artesanal [ar·te·sa·'nal] *adj* craft; **industria** ~ craft industry
artesanía [ar·te·sa·'ni·a] *f* 1. (*arte*) craftsmanship; **jarrón de** ~ handmade vase 2. (*obras*) handicrafts *pl*
artesano, -a [ar·te·'sa·no, -a] *m, f* artisan, craftsman *m*, craftswoman *f*
ártico ['ar·ti·ko, -a] *m* 1. (*océano*) Arctic Ocean 2. (*región*) Arctic
ártico, -a ['ar·ti·ko, -a] *adj* Arctic
articulación [ar·ti·ku·la·'sjon, -'θjon] *f* 1. ANAT joint 2. LING articulation
articulado, -a [ar·ti·ku·'la·do] *adj* articulated; **camión** ~ tractor-trailer truck
articular [ar·ti·ku·'lar] *vt* 1. TÉC to join together 2. LING to articulate
artículo [ar·'ti·ku·lo] *m* 1. (*objeto*) *t.* PREN article; COM commodity; ~**s de consumo** consumer goods; ~**s de lujo** luxury goods; ~**s de primera necesidad** basic commodities; ~**s de tocador** toiletries 2. (*en un diccionario*) entry
artífice [ar·'ti·fi·se, -θe] *mf* artist; *fig* architect
artificial [ar·ti·fi·'sjal, -'θjal] *adj* artificial
artificio [ar·ti·'fi·sjo, -θjo] *m* 1. (*mecanismo*) device 2. (*habilidad*) skill; (*truco*) trick; **un** ~ **técnico** a technical contrivance; **hablar con** ~ pey to speak affectedly
artillería [ar·ti·je·'ri·a, ar·ti·ʎe-] *f* artillery
artillero [ar·ti·'je·ro, -'ʎe·ro] *m* gunner
artimaña [ar·ti·'ma·ɲa] *f* (sly) trick
artista [ar·'tis·ta] *mf* (*de bellas artes*) artist; (*de circo*) artist(e) *m(f)*; **es un** ~ **en su especialidad** he's an expert in his field
artístico, -a [ar·'tis·ti·ko, -a] *adj* artistic
artritis [ar·'tri·tis] *f inv* arthritis
artrosis [ar·'tro·sis] *f inv* arthrosis
arzobispo [ar·so·'βis·po, ar·θo-] *m* archbishop
as [as] *m t. fig* ace; **un** ~ **del volante** an ace at the wheel
asa ['a·sa] *f* handle
asado [a·'sa·do] *m* 1. CULIN roast 2. *Arg* (*comida*) barbecue
asador [a·sa·'dor] *m* 1. (*pincho*) spit 2. (*aparato*) spit roaster 3. (*restaurante*) rotisserie
asalariado, -a [a·sa·la·'rja·do, -a] *m, f* wage earner

asaltante [a·sal·'tan·te] *mf* attacker; (*de banco*) raider

asaltar [a·sal·'tar] *vt* **1.** (*fortaleza*) to storm; (*banco*) to break into, to raid **2.** (*persona*) to attack, to assault; ~ **a alguien con preguntas** to bombard sb with questions **3.** (*duda*) to assail; **me asaltó una idea** I was struck by an idea; **me asaltó el pánico** I got into a panic

asalto [a·'sal·to] *m* **1.** (*a una fortaleza*) storming; ~ **a algo** storming of sth; **tomar por** [*o* al] ~ to take by storm **2.** (*a un banco*) raid; ~ **a un banco/a alguien** raid on a bank/of sb **3.** (*a una persona*) attack, assault **4.** DEP (*en boxeo*) round

asamblea [a·sam·'blea] *f* assembly; ~ **general** general assembly; ~ **plenaria** plenary meeting; ~ **de trabajadores** workers' meeting

asar [a·'sar] **I.** *vt* CULIN to roast; ~ **a la parrilla** to grill **II.** *vr:* ~**se** to roast; **en esta casa se asa uno vivo** *inf* it's absolutely roasting in this house

asbesto [as·'βes·to] *m* asbestos

ascendencia [a·sen·'den·sja, as·θen·'den·θja] *f* **1.** (*linaje*) ancestry, descent; **de** ~ **escocesa** of Scottish descent **2.** (*antepasados*) ancestors *pl*

ascendente [a·sen·'den·te, as·θen-] **I.** *adj* ascending; **en orden** ~ in ascending order; **la carrera** ~ **de un pistón** the up-stroke of a piston **II.** *m* ascendant

ascender <e→ie> [a·sen·'der, as·θen-] **I.** *vi* **1.** (*subir*) to rise; DEP to go up; **el equipo asciende a primera** (**división**) the team goes up to the first division **2.** (*escalar*) to climb **3.** (*de empleo*) to be promoted **4.** COM ~ **a** (*cuenta*) to come to; (*cantidad*) to amount to **II.** *vt* to promote

ascendiente¹ [a·sen·'djen·te, as·θen-] *mf* (*antepasado*) ancestor

ascendiente² [a·sen·'djen·te, as·θen-] *m* (*influencia*) influence

ascensión [a·sen·'sjon, as·θen-] *f* ascent; REL Ascension

ascenso [a·'sen·so, as·'θen-] *m* **1.** (*de precio*) rise **2.** (*a una montaña*) ascent; **el** ~ **a primera** (**división**) the promotion to the first division

ascensor [a·sen·'sor, as·θen-] *m* elevator; **tomar el** ~ to take the elevator

ascético, -a [a·'se·ti·ko, -a; as·'θe-] *adj* ascetic

asco ['as·ko] *m* **1.** (*sensación*) disgust, loathing; **tomar** ~ **a algo** to get sick of sth; **este olor me da** ~ this smell makes me feel sick; **las espinacas me dan** ~ I hate spinach; **este hombre me da** ~ I really detest this man; **hacer** ~**s a algo** to turn up one's nose at sth; **¡qué** ~ **de gente!** *inf* what dreadful people!; **¡qué** ~**!** how awful! **2.** (*situación*) **estar hecho un** ~ (*lugar*) to be a mess; (*persona*) to feel low; **estar muerto de** ~ to be bored stiff; **ser un** ~ to be disgusting

ascua ['as·kwa] *f* ember ▶ **arrimar el** ~ **a su sardina** to feather one's nest; **estar en** [*o*

sobre] ~**s** to be on tenterhooks; **pasar algo sobre** ~**s** to deal with sth superficially; **tener a alguien en** ~**s** to keep sb on tenterhooks

aseado, -a [a·se·'a·do, -a] *adj* clean, tidy; (*arreglado*) smart

asear [a·se·'ar] **I.** *vt* to clean up **II.** *vr:* ~**se** to wash (up)

asechanza [a·se·'tʃan·sa, -θa] *f* **1.** (*trampa*) trap **2.** *pl* (*intrigas*) intrigues *pl*

asediar [a·se·'djar] *vt* **1.** MIL to besiege **2.** (*importunar*) to bother

asedio [a·'se·djo] *m* **1.** MIL siege **2.** (*fastidio*) harassment

asegurado, -a [a·se·ɣu·'ra·do, -a] *adj, m, f* insured

asegurador(a) [a·se·ɣu·ra·'dor, -'do·ra] *m(f)* insurance agent

asegurar [a·se·ɣu·'rar] **I.** *vt* **1.** (*fijar*) to secure; ~ **una puerta** to secure a door **2.** (*afirmar*) to affirm; **asegura no haber dicho nada** she maintains that she did not say anything **3.** (*prometer*) to assure; **se lo aseguro** I assure you; **aseguró que no lo sabía** he/she declared that he/she didn't know **4.** (*con un seguro*) to insure **II.** *vr:* ~**se 1.** (*comprobar*) to make sure; ~**se de que funciona** to make sure that it works **2.** (*hacerse un seguro*) to insure oneself

asemejarse [a·se·me·'xar·se] *vr* to be alike; ~ **a algo** to resemble sth, to be like sth

asentado, -a [a·sen·'ta·do, -a] *adj* **1.** (*juicioso*) sensible **2.** (*estable*) settled

asentar <e→ie> [a·sen·'tar] **I.** *vt* **1.** (*poner*) to place; (*campamento*) to pitch; ~ **los cimientos** to lay the foundations; **la lluvia ha asentado el polvo** the rain has caused the dust to settle **2.** (*sentar*) to seat; ~ **en el trono** to seat on the throne **3.** (*población*) to found **4.** (*estómago*) to settle **5.** (*golpe*) to fetch **II.** *vr:* ~**se** to settle

asentimiento [a·sen·ti·'mjen·to] *m* assent

asentir [a·sen·'tir] *irr como sentir vi* to agree; ~ **a algo** to agree to sth; ~ **con la cabeza** to nod in agreement

aseo [a·'seo] *m* **1.** (*acción*) cleaning; (*cuarto de*) ~ bathroom; ~ **personal** personal hygiene **2.** *pl* (*servicios públicos*) restrooms *pl*

aséptico, -a [a·'sep·ti·ko, -a] *adj* MED aseptic; *fig* (*desapasionado*) dispassionate

asequible [a·se·'ki·βle] *adj* **1.** (*precio*) reasonable; **esta casa no es** ~ **para nosotros** this house is beyond our means **2.** (*objetivo*) attainable; (*plan*) feasible **3.** (*persona*) approachable

aserradero [a·se·rra·'de·ro] *m* sawmill

asesinar [a·se·si·'nar] *vt* to murder; (*personaje público*) to assassinate

asesinato [a·se·si·'na·to] *m* murder; (*de personaje público*) assassination; **robo con** ~ robbery with murder

asesino, -a [a·se·'si·no, -a] **I.** *adj f, fig* murderous; **ballena asesina** killer whale **II.** *m, f* murderer; (*de personaje público*) assassin; ~ (**a sueldo**) hit man

asesor(a) [a·se·'sor, -'so·ra] **I.** *adj* advisory

II. *m(f)* adviser, consultant; ~ **legal** legal adviser

asesorar [a·se·so·'rar] **I.** *vt* to advise **II.** *vr* ~ **se en algo** to take advice about sth; ~ **se con un médico/abogado** to take medical/legal advice

asesoría [a·se·so·'ri·a] *f* **1.** (*oficio*) consultancy **2.** (*oficina*) consultant's office

asestar [a·ses·'tar] *vt* to deal; ~ **una puñalada a alguien** to stab sb; ~ **un tiro a alguien** to fire a shot at sb

aseveración [a·se·βe·ra·'sjon, -'θjon] *f* assertion

aseverar [a·se·βe·'rar] *vt* to affirm; (*asegurar*) to assure; (*con energía*) to assert

asfaltado [as·fal·'ta·do] *m* **1.** (*acción*) asphalting **2.** (*capa*) asphalt

asfaltar [as·fal·'tar] *vt* to asphalt

asfalto [as·'fal·to] *m* asphalt

asfixia [as·'fik·sja] *f* suffocation, asphyxia

asfixiante [as·fik·'sjan·te] *adj* suffocating; **una atmósfera** ~ a stifling atmosphere; **hace un calor** ~ the heat is suffocating

asfixiar [as·fik·'sjar] **I.** *vt* (*persona*) to suffocate; (*humo*) to asphyxiate **II.** *vr:* ~ **se** to suffocate

así [a·'si] **I.** *adv* **1.** (*de este modo*) accordingly; **lo hizo** ~ he/she did it like this; ~ **es como lo hizo** that's how he/she did it; **yo soy** ~ that's the way I am; **no puedes decir esto** ~ **como** ~ you just can't say that; **no puedes tomar esta decisión** ~ **como** ~ you can't take [*o* make] this decision just like that; **¡**~ **es!** that's right!; **¡**~ **es la vida!** that's life; **¿no es** ~**?** isn't it?; **por** ~ **decirlo** so to speak **2.** (*ojalá*) **¡**~ **revientes!** I hope you die! **3.** (*de extrañeza*) **¿**~ **que me dejas?** so you're leaving me? **4.** (*de esta medida*) ~ **de grande** this big; **era** ~ **de feo** he was that ugly ▶ ~ **y todo** even so; ~ **o asá** *inf* one way or another; **¿**~ **qué?** what now?; ~ ~ so-so **II.** *conj* **1.** (*concesiva*) ~ **se esté muriendo de frío...** even though he's/she's freezing...; ~ **lo ahorques no dará su brazo a torcer** no matter what you say to him, he won't back down **2.** (*consecutiva*) **empezó a llover,** ~ **que nos quedamos en casa** it began to rain, so we stayed indoors; **sólo hay una plaza libre,** ~ (**es**) **que decídete pronto** there's only one free seat, so make up your mind; **te esperaré en la calle;** ~ **pues, no te retrases** I'll wait for you in the street, so don't be late **3.** (*comparativa*) ~ **el uno como el otro** both one and the other; ~ **en la tierra como en el cielo** on earth as in heaven **III.** *adj inv* like this, like that; **un sueldo** ~ a salary of that amount; **una cosa** ~ something like that

Asia ['a·sja] *f* Asia; ~ **menor** Asia Minor

asiático, -a [a·'sja·ti·ko, -a] *adj, m, f* Asian, Asiatic

asidero [a·si·'de·ro] *m* handle; *fig* pretext

asiduo, -a [a·'si·dwo, -a] *adj* frequent; **un** ~ **cliente de este local** a regular in this bar

asiento [a·'sjen·to] *m* **1.** (*silla*) seat; ~ **delantero** front seat; ~ **trasero** [*o* **de atrás**] rear seat; **tomar** ~ to take a seat **2.** (*sitio*) site **3.** (*de botella*) bottom **4.** (*poso*) sediment **5.** (*en una cuenta*) entry; ~ **de cierre** closing entry

asignación [a·siɣ·na·'sjon, -'θjon] *f* **1.** *t.* COMPUT assignment; (*de recursos*) allocation; ~ **de una tecla** assignment of a key **2.** FIN allowance

asignar [a·siɣ·'nar] *vt t.* COMPUT to assign; (*recursos*) to allocate; (*subvención*) to award

asignatura [a·siɣ·na·'tu·ra] *f* subject; ~ **pendiente** subject which has to be repeated

asilado, -a [a·si·'la·do, -a] *m, f* POL political refugee

asilar [a·si·'lar] **I.** *vt* POL to grant political asylum **II.** *vr:* ~ **se** to seek political asylum

asilo [a·'si·lo] *m* **1.** POL asylum; **pedir/conceder** ~ to seek/to grant political asylum **2.** (*de ancianos*) (old people's) home **3.** (*de huérfanos*) orphanage

asimetría [a·si·me·'tri·a] *f* asymmetry

asimétrico, -a [a·si·'me·tri·ko, -a] *adj* asymmetric(al)

asimilación [a·si·mi·la·'sjon, -'θjon] *f* assimilation

asimilar [a·si·mi·'lar] *vt* to assimilate

asimismo [a·si·'mis·mo] *adv* likewise, also

asir [a·'sir] *irr* **I.** *vt* to seize **II.** *vr* ~ **se a algo** to seize sth

asistencia [a·sis·'ten·sja, -θja] *f* **1.** (*presencia*) attendance, presence; **sin la** ~ **del presidente** in the president's absence **2.** (*ayuda*) assistance, help; ~ **financiera** financial assistance; ~ **letrada** JUR legal aid; ~ **médica** medical care; ~ **social** social work

asistenta [a·sis·'ten·ta] *f* **1.** (*ayudante*) assistant **2.** (*para limpiar*) cleaning woman

asistente[1] [a·sis·'ten·te] *mf* **1.** (*ayudante*) assistant **2.** (*presentes*) **los** ~ **s** those present ▶ ~ **social** social worker

asistente[2] [a·sis·'ten·te] *m* COMPUT ~ **personal digital** PDA, personal digital assistant

asistido, -a [a·sis·'ti·do, -a] *adj* assisted; ~ **por ordenador** computer-assisted; **dirección asistida** power(-assisted) steering; **fecundación/respiración asistida** artificial insemination/respiration

asistir [a·sis·'tir] **I.** *vi* **1.** (*ir*) ~ **a algo** to attend sth; **no voy a** ~ I won't go **2.** (*estar presente*) to be present; **asistieron unas 50 personas** some 50 people were present **3.** (*presenciar*) ~ **a algo** to witness sth **II.** *vt* **1.** (*estar presente en*) to attend **2.** (*ayudar*) to help, assist; ~ **a un enfermo** to care for a patient

asma ['as·ma] *f* asthma

asmático, -a [as·'ma·ti·ko, -a] *adj, m, f* asthmatic

asno ['as·no] *m* ZOOL donkey, ass; *inf* (*persona*) ass

asociación [a·so·sja·'sjon, -θja·'θjon] *f* association; **siempre pienso en él en** ~ **con...** I always think of him in connection with...; **Asociación Europea de Libre Cambio**

European Free Trade Area; **Asociación de Padres de Alumnos** parent-teacher association; ~ **de vecinos** residents' association

asociado, -a [a·so·'sja·ðo, -a; -'θja·ðo, -a] I. *adj* associated; (*miembro*) associate II. *m, f* **1.** (*socio*) associate; (*miembro*) member **2.** COM (*de una empresa*) partner

asociar [a·so·'sjar, -'θjar] I. *vt* **1.** *t.* POL to associate; **la asocio con alguien** I associate her with sb **2.** (*juntar*) to join **3.** COM to take into partnership II. *vr:* ~**se** to associate; COM to become partners, to form a partnership; ~**se con alguien** (*hacer compañía*) to join sb

asolar <o→ue> [a·so·'lar] *vt* to devastate

asoleada [a·so·le·'a·ða] *f Col, Chile, Guat* (*insolación*) sunstroke

asomar [a·so·'mar] I. *vt* **1.** (*mostrar*) to show **2.** (*destacar*) to stick out; ~ **la cabeza por la ventana** to put one's head out of the window II. *vi* (*verse*) to show; (*aparecer*) to appear; **asoma el día** day is breaking III. *vr:* ~ **se 1.** (*mostrarse*) to show up; ~**se al balcón** to come out onto the balcony; **¡asómate!** stick your head out! **2.** (*acercarse*) to pop in; **¿por qué no te asomas un rato?** why don't you pop in for a bit?

asombrar [a·som·'brar] I. *vt* to amaze II. *vr* ~**se de algo** to be amazed at sth

asombro [a·'som·bro] *m* amazement; **poner cara de** ~ to look amazed; **no salir de su** ~ not to get over one's amazement

asombroso, -a [a·som·'bro·so, -a] *adj* amazing

asomo [a·'so·mo] *m* hint; **hay** ~**s de recuperación económica** there are signs of economic recovery; **no pienso en ello ni por** ~ I don't give it the slightest thought; **¿tienes miedo? — ni por** ~ are you afraid? — not in the slightest; **sin el menor** ~ **de...** without the slightest trace of...

asonancia [a·so·'nan·sja, -θja] *f* assonance

asorocharse [a·so·ro·'tʃar·se] *vr AmS* to get altitude sickness

aspa ['as·pa] *f* cross; (*de molino*) sail; **marcar con un** ~ to mark with a cross; **en forma de** ~ cross-shaped

aspamento [as·pa·'men·to] *m Arg,* **aspaviento** [as·pa·'βjen·to] *m* fuss; **hacer** ~**s to** make a fuss

aspecto [as·'pek·to] *m* **1.** (*apariencia*) appearance; **tener buen/mal** ~ to look/not to look well **2.** (*punto de vista*) aspect; **bajo ese** ~ from that point of view

áspero, -a ['as·pe·ro, -a] *adj* **1.** (*superficie*) rough **2.** (*terreno*) rugged **3.** (*persona*) harsh; **tener un carácter** ~ to be bad-tempered **4.** (*clima*) tough

aspersión [as·per·'sjon] *f* sprinkling; **riego por** ~ watering by sprinkler

aspiración [as·pi·ra·'sjon, -'θjon] *f* **1.** (*inspiración*) breathing in **2.** (*pretensión*) aspiration; **tener grandes aspiraciones** to have great aspirations

aspiradora [as·pi·ra·'ðo·ra] *f* vacuum cleaner; **pasar la** ~ to vacuum

aspirante [as·pi·'ran·te] *mf* aspirant; (*a un empleo*) applicant; POL candidate

aspirar [as·pi·'rar] I. *vt* **1.** (*inspirar*) to breathe in, inhale; **salir a** ~ **aire fresco** to go out to get a breath of fresh air **2.** (*aspirador*) to suck in II. *vi* **1.** (*inspirar*) to breathe in **2.** (*pretender*) to aspire; ~ **a mucho en la vida** to have high aims in life

aspirina® [as·pi·'ri·na] *f* aspirin®

asquear [as·ke·'ar] I. *vt* **1.** (*dar asco*) to disgust **2.** (*fastidiar*) to bother II. *vr:* ~**se** to feel disgusted

asquerosidad [as·ke·ro·si·'dad] *f* disgusting mess; **esta casa está hecha una** ~ this house is filthy

asqueroso, -a [as·ke·'ro·so, -a] *adj* disgusting; (*sucio*) filthy

asta ['as·ta] *f* **1.** (*de bandera*) flagpole; **a media** ~ at half mast **2.** (*cuerno*) horn

asterisco [as·te·'ris·ko] *m* asterisk

asteroide [as·te·'roi·ðe] *m* asteroid

astilla [as·'ti·ja, -ʎa] *f* splinter; **clavarse una** ~ to get a splinter

astillar [as·ti·'jar, -'ʎar] *vt, vr:* ~(**se**) to splinter

astillero [as·ti·'je·ro, -'ʎe·ro] *m* shipyard

astro ['as·tro] *m t. fig* star; ~ **de la pantalla** film star

astrología [as·tro·lo·'xi·a] *f* astrology

astrólogo, -a [as·'tro·lo·ɣo, -a] *m, f* astrologer

astronauta [as·tro·'nau·ta] *mf* astronaut

astronáutica [as·tro·'nau·ti·ka] *f* astronautics

astronomía [as·tro·no·'mi·a] *f* astronomy

astronómico, -a [as·tro·'no·mi·ko, -a] *adj t. fig* astronomical

astrónomo, -a [as·'tro·no·mo, -a] *m, f* astronomer

astucia [as·'tu·sja, -θja] *f* astuteness, shrewdness; **actuar con** ~ to be crafty

astuto, -a [as·'tu·to, -a] *adj* astute, shrewd; (*con malicia*) crafty

asueto [a·'swe·to] *m* (*descanso*) time off; (**día de**) ~ day off; **un rato de** ~ a break

asumir [a·su·'mir] *vt* **1.** (*responsabilidad*) to assume, to take on; (*cargo*) to take over; (*gastos*) to agree to pay **2.** (*suponer*) to assume; **la catástrofe está asumiendo proporciones espantosas** the catastrophe is assuming frightening proportions

Asunción [a·sun·'sjon, -'θjon] *f* REL Assumption

asunto [a·'sun·to] *m* **1.** (*cuestión*) matter; **ir al** ~ to get to the point; **el** ~ **es que...** the thing is (that)...; **¡**~ **concluido!** that's the end of it!; **ocúpate de tus** ~**s** mind your own business **2.** (*negocio*) business; **tener** ~ **s en el extranjero** to have business dealings abroad; **el ministro está envuelto en un** ~ **sucio** the minister is mixed up in a dubious affair **3.** LIT (*tema*) theme **4.** (*amorío*) affair **5.** POL **Ministerio de Asuntos Exteriores** State Department; **Ministro de Asuntos Exteriores** Secretary of State

asustadizo, -a [a·sus·ta·'di·so, -a; -'di·θo, -a] *adj* jumpy; (*animal*) easily startled

asustar [a·sus·'tar] **I.** *vt* to scare, to frighten; **la responsabilidad no me asusta** I'm not afraid of the responsibility **II.** *vr:* ~**se** to be scared, to be frightened; ~**se de algo** to be frightened at sth; **no te asustes** don't be frightened

atacar <c→qu> [a·ta·'kar] **I.** *vt* **1.** (*embestir*) to attack; ~ **por la espalda** to attack from behind **2.** (*sueño*) to overcome **3.** (*problema*) to tackle **II.** *vi t.* DEP to attack; ~ **por las bandas** to attack from the wings

ataché [a·ta·'tʃe] *m AmC, PRico* paper clip

atadura [a·ta·'du·ra] *f* **1.** (*acción*) tying **2.** (*cuerda*) rope, string **3.** (*entre personas*) tie, bond

atajar [a·ta·'xar] **I.** *vi* to take a short cut; **por este camino atajamos mucho** this road shortens our trip considerably **II.** *vt* **1.** (*detener*) to stop; (*agua*) to stem **2.** (*cortar el paso*) to head off

atajo [a·'ta·xo] *m* short cut; **ir por un** ~ to take a short cut ▶**echar por el** ~ *inf* to take the easy way out

atalaya [a·ta·'la·ja] *f* **1.** (*torre*) watchtower **2.** (*lugar*) vantage point

atañer <3. *pret:* atañó> [a·ta·'ɲer] *vimpers* **eso no te atañe** that doesn't concern you; **por lo que atañe a tu empleo** as far as your job is concerned

ataque [a·'ta·ke] *m* **1.** (*embestida*) attack; ~ **bioterrorista** bioterrorist attack; ~ **químico** chemical attack; ~ **por sorpresa** surprise attack; **pasar al** ~ to go on the offensive **2.** *t.* MED attack, fit; ~ **al** [*o* **de**] **corazón** heart attack; ~ **de nervios** nervous breakdown; ~ **de tos** fit of coughing

atar [a·'tar] **I.** *vt* **1.** (*sujetar*) to tie; (*cerrar*) to tie up; (*cautivo*) to bind; ~ **a alguien las manos a la espalda** to tie sb's hands behind his/her back; ~ **al perro** to tie up the dog **2.** (*comprometer*) **esta profesión te ata mucho** this profession ties you down a lot ▶**dejar algo atado y bien atado** to finish sth off completely; ~ **corto a alguien** to keep a tight rein on sb; **estar de** ~ to be in a rage **II.** *vr:* ~**se** to do up; ~**se los zapatos** to tie one's shoes

atardecer [a·tar·de·'ser, -'θer] **I.** *irr como crecer vimpers* **atardece** it's getting dark **II.** *m* dusk; **al** ~ at dusk

atarear [a·ta·re·'ar] **I.** *vt* to give a job to **II.** *vr:* ~**se** to work hard

atascar <c→qu> [a·tas·'kar] **I.** *vt* to block **II.** *vr:* ~**se 1.** (*cañería*) to get blocked (up); **el desagüe se ha atascado** the drain is blocked (up) **2.** (*coche*) to get stuck; (*mecanismo*) to jam **3.** (*en un discurso*) to get stuck, to dry up *inf*

atasco [a·'tas·ko] *m* **1.** (*de una cañería*) blockage **2.** (*de un mecanismo*) blocking; ~ **de papel** COMPUT paper jam **3.** (*de tráfico*) traffic jam

ataúd [a·ta·'ud] *m* coffin

ataviar <1. *pres:* me atavío> [a·ta·βi·'ar] *vt, vr:* ~**se** to dress up

atavío [a·ta·'βi·o] *m* attire

ate ['a·te] *m Méx* CULIN *fruit paste*

ateísmo [a·te·'is·mo] *m* atheism

atejonarse [a·te·xo·'nar·se] *vr Méx* **1.** (*agacharse*) to crouch; (*esconderse*) to hole up *inf* **2.** (*volverse astuto*) to sharpen (up)

atemorizar <z→c> [a·te·mo·ri·'sar, -'θar] **I.** *vt* to scare, to frighten **II.** *vr* ~**se** (**de algo**) to get scared (at sth)

atemperar [a·tem·pe·'rar] *vt* (*crítica*) to temper; (*cólera*) to curb

Atenas [a·'te·nas] *f* Athens

atenazar <z→c> [a·te·na·'sar, -'θar] *vt* (*miedo*) to grip; (*duda*) to torment

atención [a·ten·'sjon, -'θjon] *f* **1.** (*interés*) attention; **falta de** ~ inattentiveness; **digno de** ~ noteworthy; **¡~, por favor!** your attention please!; **estamos llamando la** ~ we're attracting attention; **los coches no me llaman la** ~ I'm not very interested in cars; **llamar la** ~ **de alguien sobre** [*o* **a**] **algo** to draw sb's attention to sth; **mantener la** ~ **de alguien** to hold sb's attention; **prestar** ~ **a algo** to pay attention to sth; (*escuchar*) to listen to sth; **absorber la** ~ **de alguien** to command sb's attention; **en** ~ **a este hecho** in view of this fact; **a la** ~ **de...** for the attention of... **2.** (*cuidado*) attention, care; ~ **médica** medical care **3.** (*cortesía*) kindness; **colmar a alguien de atenciones** to make a real fuss over sb; **tener muchas atenciones con alguien** to be very nice to sb ▶**llamar la** ~ **a alguien** to rebuke sb

atender <e→ie> [a·ten·'der] **I.** *vt* **1.** (*prestar atención a*) to pay attention to; (*escuchar*) to listen to **2.** (*consejo*) to heed; (*petición*) to comply with; ~ **una solicitud** to grant a request **3.** (*cuidar*) ~ **a alguien** to care for sb **4.** (*tratar*) to treat **5.** (*despachar*) to wait on, to help; **¿lo atienden?** are you being helped? **6.** (*llamada*) to answer; ~ **el teléfono** to answer the telephone **II.** *vi* **1.** (*prestar atención*) to pay attention; (*escuchar*) to listen **2.** (*tener en cuenta*) ~ **a algo** to take sth into account; **atendiendo a las circunstancias actuales** bearing in mind present circumstances

atenerse [a·te·'ner·se] *irr como tener vr* ~ **a** (*reglas*) to abide by; (*lo dicho*) to stand by, to keep to; ~ **a lo seguro** to play (it) safe; **me atengo a lo que dije antes** I'm sticking to what I said before; **saber a qué** ~ to know where one stands; (*en un futuro*) to know what to expect; **si no lo haces, atente a las consecuencias** if you don't do it, you'll bear the consequences

atentado [a·ten·'ta·do] *m* attack, assault; (*crimen*) crime; ~ **contra alguien** assassination attempt on sb; ~ **suicida** suicide attack; ~ **terrorista** terrorist attack; **ser víctima de un** ~ to be the victim of an assassination attempt; **esta ley es un ~ contra la libertad de expresión** this law is a threat to freedom of speech

atentamente [a·ten·ta·'men·te] *adv* (*carta*) (**muy**) ~ (*si la carta empieza "Dear Sir"*) yours truly; (*si la carta empieza "Dear Mr. X"*) sincerely yours

atentar [a·ten·'tar] *vi* ~ **contra alguien** to make an attempt on sb's life; ~ **contra la ley** to break the law

atento, -a [a·'ten·to, -a] *adj* **1.** (*observador*) attentive; **estar ~ a la conversación** to follow the conversation closely; **estar ~ al peligro** to be aware of the danger **2.** (*cortés*) kind; **es muy ~ de su parte** it's most kind of you; **estuvo muy ~ con nosotros** he was very considerate towards us; **es muy ~ con las mujeres** he's very attentive to women

atenuante [a·te·nu·'an·te] *f* **1.** *pl* JUR extenuating circumstances *pl* **2.** *AmL* (*perdón*) excuse

atenuar <*1. pres:* atenúo> [a·te·nu·'ar] **I.** *vt* **1.** to attenuate; (*dolor*) to ease **2.** JUR to extenuate **II.** *vr:* ~ **se** to ease

ateo, -a [a·'teo, -a] **I.** *adj* atheistic **II.** *m, f* atheist; **ser ~** to be an atheist

aterciopelado, -a [a·ter·sjo·pe·'la·do, -a; a·ter·θjo-] *adj* velvety

aterirse [a·te·'rir·se] *irr como abolir vr* to become numb; **quedarse aterido** to be cold stiff

aterrador(a) [a·te·rra·'dor, -·'do·ra] *adj* terrifying; **noticias ~as** terrible news

aterrar [a·te·'rrar] **I.** *vt* to terrify **II.** *vr:* ~ **se** (*sobresaltarse*) to be startled; (*tener miedo*) to be afraid

aterrizaje [a·te·rri·'sa·xe, -'θa·xe] *m* landing; ~ **con daños** (**para el avión**) crash-landing; ~ **forzoso** forced landing; ~ **movido/suave** bumpy/soft landing

aterrizar <z→c> [a·te·rri·'sar, -'θar] *vi* to land

aterrorizar <z→c> [a·te·rro·ri·'sar, -'θar] **I.** *vt* **1.** POL, MIL to terrorize **2.** (*causar terror*) to terrify; **me aterroriza volar** I'm terrified of flying **II.** *vr:* ~ **se** to be afraid

atesorar [a·te·so·'rar] *vt* **1.** (*tesoros*) to store up; ECON to hoard; **este museo atesora pinturas de gran valor** this museum has a collection of very valuable paintings **2.** (*virtudes*) to possess

atestado [a·tes·'ta·do] *m* ~ (**policial**) statement

atestar [a·tes·'tar] *vt* **1.** JUR to attest **2.** (*llenar*) ~ **de algo** to pack with sth; **la maleta está atestada** the suitcase is packed full; **atestado de gente** crammed with people

atestiguar <gu→gü> [a·tes·ti·'ywar] *vt* to testify to

atiborrar [a·ti·βo·'rrar] **I.** *vt* to stuff **II.** *vr* ~ **se de algo** to stuff oneself with sth

ático ['a·ti·ko] *m* attic; (*de lujo*) penthouse

atinar [a·ti·'nar] *vi* **1.** (*acertar*) ~ **con algo** to hit on sth; **no atiné con la respuesta** I didn't come up with the answer **2.** (*encontrar*) ~ **con algo** to find sth **3.** (*ser capaz*) ~ **a hacer algo**

to manage to do sth

atípico, -a [a·'ti·pi·ko, -a] *adj* atypical

atisbar [a·tis·'βar] **I.** *vt* to spy on **II.** *vr:* ~ **se** to be discerned

atisbo [a·'tis·βo] *m* **un ~ de esperanza** a glimmer of hope; **en Marte hay ~s de vida** there are signs of life on Mars

atizar <z→c> [a·ti·'sar, -'θar] **I.** *vt* **1.** (*fuego*) to poke; (*pasión*) to rouse **2.** (*bofetada*) to give **II.** *vr* (*trago*) to take **III.** *vi* ¡**atiza!** good heavens!

atlántico, -a [at·'lan·ti·ko, -a] *adj* Atlantic

Atlántico [at·'lan·ti·ko] *m* **el ~** the Atlantic

atlas ['at·las] *m inv* atlas

atleta [at·'le·ta] *mf* athlete

atlético, -a [at·'le·ti·ko, -a] *adj* athletic

atletismo [at·le·'tis·mo] *m* athletics

atmósfera [at·'mos·fe·ra] *f* atmosphere

atole [a·'to·le] *m AmC: drink prepared with cornmeal gruel*

atolladero [a·to·ja·'de·ro, a·to·ʎa-] *m* **1.** (*lugar*) mire **2.** (*apuro*) jam; **estar en un ~** to be in a fix; **sacar a alguien de un ~** to get sb out of a jam

atolón [a·to·'lon] *m* atoll

atolondrado, -a [a·to·lon·'dra·do, -a] *adj* bewildered

atolondrar [a·to·lon·'drar] **I.** *vt* to stun **II.** *vr:* ~ **se** to be stunned

atomía [a·to·'mi·a] *f AmL* evil act; **decir ~s** (*decir tonterías*) to talk nonsense; (*injuriar*) to mouth off *inf*

atómico, -a [a·'to·mi·ko, -a] *adj* atomic; **refugio ~** fallout shelter

átomo ['a·to·mo] *m* atom

atónito, -a [a·'to·ni·to, -a] *adj* amazed

átono, -a ['a·to·no, -a] *adj* unstressed

atontado, -a [a·ton·'ta·do, -a] *adj* **1.** (*tonto*) stupid **2.** (*distraído*) inattentive

atontar [a·ton·'tar] **I.** *vt* **1.** (*aturdir*) to stun **2.** (*entontecer*) to bewilder **II.** *vr:* ~ **se** to be stunned

atorar [a·to·'rar] **I.** *vt* to stop up **II.** *vr:* ~ **se** (*atascarse*) to get clogged [*o* stopped] up; (*al hablar*) to falter

atormentar [a·tor·men·'tar] **I.** *vt* (*molestar*) to harass; (*mortificar*) to torment **II.** *vr:* ~ **se** to torment oneself

atornillador [a·tor·ni·ja·'dor, -ʎa·'dor] *m* screwdriver

atornillar [a·tor·ni·'jar, -'ʎar] *vt* to screw down; (*fijar*) to screw on; ~ **en la pared** to screw into the wall; ~ **fuertemente** to screw tight

atorozarse [a·to·ro·'sar·se, -'θar·se] *vr AmC* **1.** (*atascarse*) to block up **2.** (*al hablar*) to choke up

atorrante [a·to·'rran·te] *mf CSur, inf* tramp

atosigar <g→gu> [a·to·si·'yar] **I.** *vt* to harass; (*importunar*) to pester **II.** *vr:* ~ **se** to be harassed; **no te atosigues** don't get worked up

atracadero [a·tra·ka·'de·ro] *m* mooring

atracador(a) [a·tra·ka·'dor, -·'do·ra] *m(f)* bank robber

atracar <c→qu> [a·tra·'kar] I. *vi* NÁUT to berth II. *vt* 1. NÁUT to moor 2. (*asaltar*) to hold up III. *vr inf* ~ se de algo to stuff oneself with sth
atracción [a·trak·'sjon, -'θjon] *f t.* FÍS attraction; ~ universal gravity; parque de atracciones amusement park
atraco [a·'tra·ko] *m* hold-up; ~ a un banco bank robbery; ~ a mano armada armed robbery
atracón [a·tra·'kon] *m inf* blowout; darse un ~ de dulces to stuff oneself with sweets; darse un ~ de televisión to watch too much television
atractivo [a·trak·'ti·βo] *m* attraction; ~ sexual sex appeal
atractivo, -a [a·trak·'ti·βo, -a] *adj* attractive
atraer [a·tra·'er] *irr como traer* I. *vt* to attract; ~ a los inversores to attract investors; ~ a alguien a su bando to get sb on one's side; el cebo atrae a los peces the bait lures the fish; sentirse atraído hacia alguien to feel drawn towards sb II. *vr* (*ganarse*) to win; ~ se las simpatías de alguien to win sb's affections; ~ se las iras del público to incite public anger
atrancar <c→qu> [a·tran·'kar] I. *vt* (*puerta*) to bolt II. *vr:* ~ se (*tubo*) to become blocked; (*al hablar*) to get stuck
atrapar [a·tra·'par] *vt* to trap; (*ladrón*) to catch; (*animal*) to capture; el portero atrapó la pelota the goalkeeper caught the ball; ~ on al ladrón en plena faena they caught the thief red-handed; ~ un empleo to land a job; ~ una novia *inf* to get oneself a girlfriend
atrás [a·'tras] *adv* 1. (*hacia detrás*) back, backwards; contar ~ to count down; dar un paso ~ to take a step backwards [*o* back]; ir marcha ~ (con el coche) to go in reverse, to back up; quedar ~ to fall behind; volver ~ to go back; ¡~! get back! 2. (*detrás*) back, behind; rueda de ~ rear wheel; dejar ~ a los perseguidores to leave one's pursuers behind; quedarse ~ to remain behind; sentarse ~ to sit at the back 3. (*de tiempo*) años ~ years ago; la amistad venía de ~ we/they had been friends for a long time ▶ echarse ~ de un acuerdo to back out of an agreement; volverse ~ to back down
atrasado, -a [a·tra·'sa·do, -a] *adj* 1. (*en el desarrollo*) behind; (*país*) backward; viven 20 años ~ s they're 20 years behind the times 2. (*pago*) overdue 3. (*tarde*) late; llegué ~ a la reunión I arrived late for the meeting; el reloj va ~ the watch is slow
atrasar [a·tra·'sar] I. *vt* 1. (*aplazar*) to postpone; la historia atrasa unos años esta batalla history pushes the date of this battle back a few years 2. (*reloj*) to put back II. *vr:* ~ se 1. (*quedarse atrás*) to remain behind 2. (*retrasarse*) to be late; el tren se ha atrasado the train is late; ~ se en los plazos to be behind in one's installments
atraso [a·'tra·so] *m* 1. (*de un tren*) delay 2. (*de un país*) backwardness 3. FIN arrears *pl*

atravesar <e→ie> [a·tra·βe·'sar] I. *vt* 1. (*persona*) ~ la calle to cross the street; ~ un río nadando to swim across a river; hemos atravesado Francia (con el coche) we drove across France; ~ un momento difícil to go through a difficult time 2. (*cuerpo*) ~ algo con una aguja to pierce sth with a needle; ~ algo taladrando to bore through sth; la bala le atravesó el corazón the bullet went through his/her heart; el avión atraviesa las nubes the plane breaks through the clouds; la lluvia atravesó el abrigo the rain penetrated the coat; una cicatriz le atraviesa el pecho a scar runs across his/her chest 3. (*poner de través*) to lay across; ~ un coche en medio de la calle to park a car diagonally across the road II. *vr:* ~ se 1. (*ponerse*) no te atravieses en mi camino don't get in my way; se me ha atravesado una miga en la garganta a crumb has got stuck in my throat; cuando estoy nervioso se me atraviesan las palabras when I'm worked up, I get tongue-tied 2. (*en una conversación*) ~ se en algo to butt into sth 3. (*no soportar*) se me atraviesa ese tipo I can't stand that fellow
atrayente [a·tra·'jen·te] *adj* attractive
atreverse [a·tre·'βer·se] *vr* to dare; ~ a hacer algo to dare to do sth; ~ a afrontar un problema to venture to tackle a problem; ¿cómo te atreves a hablarme así? how dare you speak to me like that?; ¡no te atreverás! you wouldn't dare!
atrevido, -a [a·tre·'βi·do, -a] *adj* 1. (*persona*) daring 2. (*insolente*) insolent
atrevimiento [a·tre·βi·'mjen·to] *m* 1. (*audacia*) boldness 2. (*descaro*) nerve *fig*
atribución [a·tri·βu·'sjon, -'θjon] *f* 1. (*de un hecho*) attribution 2. (*competencia*) authority; atribuciones de un empleado an employee's area of responsibility; tiene atribuciones mías para llevar las negociaciones I've authorized him/her to conduct the negotiations
atribuible [a·tri·βu·'i·βle] *adj* attributable
atribuir [a·tri·βu·'ir] *irr como huir* I. *vt* 1. (*hechos*) to attribute; ~ la culpa de algo a alguien to blame sth on sb; ~ a alguien grandes facultades to attribute great capabilities to sb; atribuye el accidente a un defecto de los frenos he/she puts the accident down to brake failure 2. (*funciones*) to confer II. *vr:* ~ se 1. (*hechos*) to claim for oneself 2. (*facultades*) ~ se todo el poder to assume absolute power
atributo [a·tri·'βu·to] *m t.* LING attribute
atril [a·'tril] *m* MÚS music stand; (*de mesa*) lectern
atrincherar [a·trin·tʃe·'rar] *vt, vr:* ~ se to entrench (oneself)
atrio ['a·trjo] *m* atrium
atrocidad [a·tro·si·'dad, a·tro·θi-] *f* 1. (*cosa*) atrocity 2. (*disparate*) foolish remark; ¡no digas ~ es! don't talk nonsense!; este artículo

está lleno de ~es this article is full of outrageous comments; **tener una ~ de dinero** to be rolling in money

atronador(a) [a·tro·na·'dor, -'do·ra] *adj* deafening; (*aplauso*) thunderous

atropellar [a·tro·pe·'jar, -'ʎar] I. *vt* 1.(*vehículo*) to run over; **por poco me atropellan** I was almost run over 2.(*empujar*) to push past 3.(*agraviar*) to insult 4.(*leyes*) to violate; **~ la lengua** to murder the language II. *vr:* **~se** to rush

atropello [a·tro·'pe·jo, -'pe·ʎo] *m* 1.(*colisión*) collision; (*accidente*) accident 2.(*empujón*) push 3.(*insulto*) insult; **¡esto es un ~!** this is preposterous! 4.(*prisa*) **tomar una decisión sin prisas ni ~s** not to rush a decision

atroz [a·'tros, -'troθ] *adj* 1.(*horroroso*) atrocious 2.(*cruel*) cruel 3.(*enorme*) huge

atuendo [a·'twen·do] *m* outfit

atufar [a·tu·'far] I. *vt* to make feel sick II. *vr:* **~se** to feel sick

atún [a·'tun] *m* tuna (fish)

aturdido, -a [a·tur·'di·do, -a] *adj* 1.(*pasmado*) stunned 2.(*irreflexivo*) thoughtless

aturdimiento [a·tur·di·'mjen·to] *m* 1.(*por un golpe*) daze 2.(*irreflexión*) thoughtlessness

aturdir [a·tur·'dir] I. *vt* 1.(*los sentidos*) to stupefy 2.(*pasmar*) to stun II. *vr:* **~se** *t. fig* to be stunned

atusar [a·tu·'sar] I. *vt* (*el peinado*) to smooth; (*la barba*) to trim II. *vr:* **~se** to do oneself up

audacia [au·'da·sja, -θja] *f* boldness, audacity

audaz [au·'das, -'daθ] *adj* bold, audacious

audible [au·'di·βle] *adj* audible

audición [au·di·'sjon, -'θjon] *f* 1.(*acción*) hearing 2.(*concierto*) concert 3. TEAT audition

audiencia [au·'djen·sja, -θja] *f* 1. TEL audience; **nivel de ~** viewing figures *pl* 2.JUR (*sesión*) hearing; (*sala*) courtroom; (*tribunal*) court

audífono [au·'di·fo·no] *m* 1.(*para sordos*) hearing aid 2. *AmL* (*auricular*) receiver

auditivo [au·di·'ti·βo] *m* TEL earpiece

auditivo, -a [au·di·'ti·βo, -a] *adj* ANAT hearing

auditor(a) [au·di·'tor] *m(f)* auditor

auditorio [au·di·'to·rjo] *m* 1.(*público*) audience 2.(*sala*) auditorium

auge ['au·xe] *m* 1.(*cumbre*) peak; **en el ~ de su belleza** at the height of her beauty 2.(*mejora*) improvement

augurar [au·yu·'rar] *vt* to predict

augurio [au·'yu·rjo] *m* prediction

aula ['au·la] *f* classroom; (*de universidad*) lecture hall; **~ magna** main lecture hall

aullar [au·'jar, -'ʎar] *irr vi* to howl

aullido [au·'ji·do, -'ʎi·do] *m* howl

aumentar [au·men·'tar] I. *vi, vt* 1.(*subir*) to increase; (*precios*) to rise, to increase; **~ de volumen** to increase in volume; **~ de velocidad** to speed up; **~ de altura** to become taller; **~ de peso** to get heavier; **los disturbios aumentan** the disturbances are spreading 2.(*extender*) to extend; **~ mucho** to extend

greatly II. *vt* to increase; (*precios*) to raise, to increase; **~ el poder/el dominio** to extend the power/the authority III. *vr:* **~se** to increase; (*en extensión*) to extend

aumentativo [au·men·ta·'ti·βo] *m* LING augmentative

aumento [au·'men·to] *m* increase; (*de la temperatura*) rise; (*de valor*) appreciation; (*en la extensión*) expansion; **~ de precio** price rise

aun [aun] I. *adv* even; **~ así** even so; **ni ~** not even II. *conj* **~ cuando** even though; **~ no comprando nada, no me llega el dinero** even when I don't buy anything, I don't have enough money

aún [a'un] *adv* still; **~ más** even more; **~ no** yet; **¿~ no ha llegado?** hasn't he/she arrived yet?

aunar [au·'nar] *irr como aullar* I. *vt* 1.(*unir*) to unite; **~ esfuerzos** to join forces 2.(*unificar*) to unify II. *vr:* **~se** to unite

aunque ['aun·ke] *conj* 1.(*concesivo*) even though; **~ es viejo, aún puede trabajar** although he's old, he can still work; **la casa, ~ pequeña, está bien** the house is nice, even if it's small; **tengo que conseguirte ~ me cueste la vida** I must have you, even if it costs me my life; **~ parezca extraño** however strange it may seem; **tengo que regalarle ~ sea un boli** I must give him/her a present, even if it's only a ballpoint 2.(*adversativa*) but

aúpa [a·'u·pa] *interj* up!, get up! ▶ **de ~** *inf* tremendous

au pair [o·'per] *mf* au pair

aupar [au·'par] *irr como aullar vt* to lift up; **~ a alguien a la presidencia** to help sb become president

aura ['au·ra] *f* aura; **tiene un ~ misteriosa** he/she has a mysterious aura

áureo, -a ['au·reo, -a] *adj* golden

aureola [au·re·'o·la] *f* halo

auricular [au·ri·ku·'lar] I. *adj* aural; **testigo ~** ear-witness II. *m* 1.TEL receiver; **coger/colgar el ~** to pick up/put down the receiver 2. *pl* (*de música*) headphones *pl*

aurora [au·'ro·ra] *f* dawn

auscultar [aus·kul·'tar] *vt* MED **el médico lo auscultó** the doctor sounded his chest

ausencia [au·'sen·sja, -θja] *f* 1.(*estado*) absence 2.(*falta*) lack; **~ de interés** lack of interest; **en ~ de algo mejor** for want of something better 3.PSICO mental blackouts ▶ **en ~ del gato bailan los ratones** *prov* when the cat's away the mice will play *prov*; **brillar por su ~** to be conspicuous by one's absence

ausentarse [au·sen·'tar·se] *vr* to go away; **~ de la ciudad** to leave town

ausente [au·'sen·te] *adj* 1.(*no presente*) absent; **estar ~** to be absent; **estar ~ del trabajo** to be off work 2.(*distraído*) distracted

auspiciar [aus·pi·'sjar, -'θjar] *vt* 1.(*presagiar*) to predict 2.(*patrocinar*) to back

austeridad [aus·te·ri·'dad] *f* austerity

austero, -a [aus·'te·ro, -a] *adj* austere

austral [aus·'tral] *adj* southern

Australia [aus·'tra·lja] *f* Australia
australiano, -a [aus·tra·'lja·no, -a] *adj, m, f* Australian
Austria ['aus·trja] *f* Austria
austriaco, -a [aus·'trja·ko, -a], **austríaco, -a** [aus·'tri·a·ko, -a] *adj, m, f* Austrian
autenticidad [au·ten·ti·si·'dad, -θi·'dad] *f* authenticity; **sobre la ~ de tus palabras tengo mis dudas** I have my doubts about the truth of your words; **no creo en la ~ de esta información** I don't believe that this information is reliable
auténtico, -a [au·'ten·ti·ko, -a] *adj* authentic; **un ~ fracaso** an absolute failure; **hacía un calor ~** it was really hot; **es un ~ maestro en su especialidad** he's an absolute expert in his field
autista [au·'tis·ta] *adj* autistic
auto ['au·to] *m* **1.** (*resolución*) decision **2.** *pl* (*actas*) proceedings *pl* ▶ **constar en ~s** to be proven; **estar en ~s** to be in the picture; **poner en ~s** to put in the picture
autobiografía [au·to·βjo·ɣra·'fi·a] *f* autobiography
autobiográfico, -a [au·to·βjo·'ɣra·fi·ko, -a] *adj* autobiographic(al)
autobús [au·to·'βus] *m* bus
autocar <autocares> [au·to·'kar] *m* bus
autocarril [au·to·ka·'rril] *m Bol, Chile, Nic* divided highway
autocensura [au·to·sen·'su·ra, -θen·'su·ra] *f* self-censorship
autochoque [au·to·'ʧo·ke] *m* bumper car
autocine [au·to·'si·ne, -'θi·ne] *m* drive-in cinema
autóctono, -a [au·'tok·to·no, -a] *adj* indigenous
autodefensa [au·to·de·'fen·sa] *f* self-defense
autodeterminación [au·to·de·ter·mi·na·'sjon, -'θjon] *f* self-determination
autodominio [au·to·do·'mi·njo] *m* self-control
autoescuela [au·to·es·'kwe·la] *f* driving school
autogestión [au·to·xes·'tjon] *f* self-management
autógrafo [au·'to·ɣra·fo] *m* autograph
autolavado [au·to·la·'βa·do] *m* car wash
autómata [au·'to·ma·ta] *m* **1.** (*aparato*) automatic device **2.** (*robot*) robot **3.** *pey* (*persona*) automaton
automático [au·to·'ma·ti·ko] *m* snap fastener
automático, -a [au·to·'ma·ti·ko, -a] *adj* automatic; **dispositivo ~** automatic mechanism; **fusil ~** automatic rifle; **la puerta se cierra de modo ~** the door snaps shut; (*en un metro*) the door closes automatically; **su despido fue ~** he/she was dismissed without notice
automatizar <z→c> [au·to·ma·ti·'sar, -'θar] *vt* to automate
automóvil [au·to·'mo·βil] *m* car; **~ de carreras** racing car; **~ eléctrico** electrically powered car; **~ todo terreno** all-terrain vehicle; **Salón del Automóvil** motor show

automovilista [au·to·mo·βi·'lis·ta] *mf* motorist, driver
automovilístico, -a [au·to·mo·βi·'lis·ti·ko, -a] *adj* car; **parque ~** fleet of vehicles
autonomía [au·to·no·'mi·a] *f* **1.** (*personal*) autonomy; **~ colectiva** free collective bargaining; **~ municipal** municipal self-administration; **en esta empresa no tengo ~ para tomar decisiones** in this company I've no scope for making my own decisions **2.** (*territorio*) autonomous region
autonómico, -a [au·to·'no·mi·ko, -a] *adj* autonomous; **proceso ~** process leading to autonomy; **política autonómica** regional policy; **elecciones autonómicas** regional elections
autónomo, -a [au·'to·no·mo, -a] *adj* **1.** POL autonomous **2.** (*trabajador*) self-employed; **trabajar de ~** to be self-employed; **¿cuánto pagas de ~s?** how much do you pay for your private health insurance?
autopista [au·to·'pis·ta] *f* highway, freeway; **~ de datos** COMPUT data highway; **~ de la información** COMPUT information highway; **~ de peaje** turnpike
autopsia [au·'toβ·sja] *f* MED autopsy
autor(a) [au·'tor, -·'to·ra] *m(f)* **1.** LIT author; **derechos de ~** royalties; **una novela de ~ desconocido** a novel by an anonymous author **2.** (*de un acto*) originator; (*de un crimen*) perpetrator
autoridad [au·to·ri·'dad] *f* **1.** (*en general*) authority; **~ del estado** state official; **~ judicial** jurisdiction; **~ de los padres** parental authority; **estar bajo la ~ de alguien** to be under sb's control; **¡aquí soy yo la ~!** I make the decisions here! **2.** (*pl*) (*policía*) authorities *pl*; **desacato a la ~** contempt (of court) **3.** (*experto*) authority
autoritario, -a [au·to·ri·'ta·rjo, -a] *adj* authoritarian
autorización [au·to·ri·sa·'sjon, -θa·'θjon] *f* authorization; (*para vender alcohol*) license; **~ de acceso** COMPUT access privileges
autorizado, -a [au·to·ri·'sa·do, -a; -'θa·do, -a] *adj* **1.** (*facultado*) authorized; **persona no autorizada** unauthorized person; **~ para firmar** authorized to sign; **de fuentes autorizadas** from approved sources **2.** (*oficial*) official
autorizar <z→c> [au·to·ri·'sar, -'θar] *vt* **1.** (*consentir*) to approve; **mi jefe me ha autorizado para ausentarme** my boss has given me permission to be off **2.** (*facultar*) to authorize **3.** (*dar derecho*) to entitle; **que sea mi jefe no le autoriza para insultarme** even though you're my boss, it doesn't give you the right to insult me; **este hecho nos autoriza a pensar que...** this fact gives us reason to believe that...
autorretrato [au·to·rre·'tra·to] *m* self-portrait
autoservicio [au·to·ser·'βi·sjo, -θjo] *m* self-service

autostopista [au·tos·to·'pis·ta] *mf* hitchhiker
autosuficiente [au·to·su·fi·'sjen·te, -'θjen·te] *adj* self-sufficient; *pey* smug
autovía [au·to·'βi·a] *f* divided highway
auxiliar¹ [auk·si·'ljar] I. *adj* assistant; **profesor** ~ UNIV assistant professor; (*en la escuela*) supply teacher II. *mf* assistant; ~ **administrativo** administrative assistant; ~ **técnico sanitario** medical technician; ~ **de vuelo** flight attendant III. *vt* to help
auxiliar² [auk·si·'ljar] *m* LING auxiliary verb
auxilio [auk·'si·ljo] *m* help; ~**s espirituales** REL last rites; **primeros** ~**s** first aid; **pedir** ~ to ask for help; **pedir** ~ **a alguien** to ask for sb's help
avalancha [a·βa·'lan·tʃa] *f* avalanche
avance [a·'βan·se, -θe] *m* 1. *t.* MIL advance; ~ **de los precios** price rise; ~ **de algo** CINE trailer for sth; ~ **informativo** TV news summary 2. (*presupuesto*) estimate
avanzado, -a [a·βan·'sa·do, -a; a·βan·'θa-] *adj* advanced
avanzar <z→c> [a·βan·'sar, -'θar] I. *vi* 1. (*seguir adelante*) *t.* MIL to advance; ~ **por una calle** to go along a street; ~ **hacia alguien** to go towards sb; **a medida que el tiempo avanzaba** as time went by 2. (*progresar*) to progress; **no** ~ **nada** not to make any headway; **esta tendencia está avanzando** this trend is gaining ground II. *vt* to advance; ~ **un pie** to put a foot forward
avaricia [a·βa·'ri·sja, -θja] *f* 1. (*codicia*) greed 2. (*tacañería*) avarice
avaricioso, -a [a·βa·ri·'sjo·so, -a; a·βa·ri·'θjo-] *adj*, **avariento, -a** [a·βa·'rjen·to, -a] *adj* 1. (*codicioso*) greedy 2. (*tacaño*) avaricious
avaro, -a [a·'βa·ro, -a] I. *adj* miserly; **ser muy** ~ **de algo** to be very mean with sth II. *m, f* miser
avasallar [a·βa·sa·'jar, -'ʎar] *vt* 1. (*subyugar*) to subjugate 2. (*atropellar*) to steamroller
avatares [a·βa·'ta·res] *mpl* **los** ~**es de la vida** life's ups and downs; **los** ~**es de la suerte** the vagaries of fortune
ave ['a·βe] *f* bird; ~**s de corral** poultry; ~ **de paso** migratory bird; ~ **rapaz** [*o* **de rapiña**] bird of prey
AVE ['a·βe] *m abr de* **Alta Velocidad Española** Spanish high-speed train
avecinarse [a·βe·si·'nar·se, -θi·'nar·se] *vr* to approach
avellana [a·βe·'ʎa·na] *f* hazelnut
avemaría [a·βe·ma·'ri·a] *f* Hail Mary
avena [a·'βe·na] *f* oats *pl*
avenencia [a·βe·'nen·sja, -θja] *f* agreement; **en buena** ~ in harmony
avenida [a·βe·'ni·da] *f* 1. (*de un río*) flood 2. (*calle*) avenue
avenido, -a [a·βe·'ni·do, -a] *adj* **dos personas bien avenidas** two good friends; **una pareja mal avenida** an ill-matched couple
avenir [a·βe·'nir] *irr como venir* I. *vt* to reconcile II. *vr:* ~**se** 1. (*entenderse*) to get on

2. (*ponerse de acuerdo*) ~**se en algo** to agree on sth; **no** ~**se a...** not to agree to...; ~**se a dialogar** to agree to hold talks
aventajado, -a [a·βen·ta·'xa·do, -a] *adj* outstanding; **de estatura aventajada** extremely tall
aventajar [a·βen·ta·'xar] *vt* 1. (*ser mejor*) to surpass; (*en una carrera*) to pass; ~ **a todos** to get ahead of everyone 2. (*anteponer*) to prefer
aventar <e→ie> [a·βen·'tar] *vt* to blow away; (*el grano*) to winnow
aventón [a·βen·'ton] *m Méx, inf* push; **dar un** ~ to give a lift; **ir de** ~ to ride free
aventura [a·βen·'tu·ra] *f* adventure; (*arriesgada*) venture; (*amorosa*) affair; **espíritu de** ~ spirit of adventure
aventurado, -a [a·βen·tu·'ra·do, -a] *adj* risky
aventurar [a·βen·tu·'rar] I. *vt* to venture; (*algo atrevido*) to dare II. *vr:* ~**se** to dare; **perdieron dinero al** ~**se en el mundo editorial** they lost money when they went into publishing
aventurero, -a [a·βen·tu·'re·ro, -a] I. *adj* adventurous; **espíritu** ~ thirst for adventure II. *m, f* adventurer
avergonzado, -a [a·βer·yon·'sa·do, -a; -'θa·do, -a] *adj* embarrassed; **sentirse** ~ to be ashamed
avergonzar [a·βer·yon·'sar, -'θar] *irr* I. *vt* to shame II. *vr:* ~**se de** [*o* **por**] **algo/alguien** to be ashamed of sth/sb
avería [a·βe·'ri·a] *f* 1. AUTO breakdown 2. (*de mercancía*) damage 3. TÉC fault; ~ **gruesa/simple** NÁUT general/petty average
averiar <1. *pres:* averío> [a·βe·ri·'ar] I. *vt* to damage II. *vr:* ~**se** AUTO to break down; TÉC to fail
averiguación [a·βe·ri·ɣwa·'sjon, -'θjon] *f* inquiry
averiguar <gu→gü> [a·βe·ri·'ɣwar] *vt* to inquire into; **averigua a qué hora sale el tren** find out (at) what time the train leaves
averigüetas [a·βe·ri·'ɣwe·tas] *m inv, Méx* busybody
aversión [a·βer·'sjon] *f* aversion
avestruz [a·βes·'trus, -'truθ] *m* ostrich
aviación [a·βja·'sjon, -'θjon] *f* 1. AVIAT aviation; **compañía de** ~ airline (company) 2. MIL air force
aviador(a) [a·βja·'dor, -·'do·ra] *m(f)* aviator
aviar <1. *pres:* avío> [a·βi·'ar] I. *vt* (*maleta*) to pack; (*mesa*) to set II. *vi* 1. (*apresurar*) ~ **a alguien** to hurry sb up; **diles que vayan aviando** tell them to get a move on; **estar aviado** (*en un apuro*) to be in a tight spot 2. *AmS* (*prestar*) to lend III. *vr:* ~**se** 1. (*arreglarse*) to get ready 2. (*espabilarse*) to get by
avícola [a·'βi·ko·la] *adj* poultry
avicultura [a·βi·kul·'tu·ra] *f* poultry farming
avidez [a·βi·'des, -'deθ] *f* eagerness; ~ **de algo** eagerness for sth
ávido, -a ['a·βi·do, -a] *adj* eager; ~ **de algo** eager for sth

avinagrarse [a·βi·na·'γrar·se] *vr* (*vino*) to turn sour; (*persona*) to become bitter

avío [a·'βi·o] *m* 1. (*apresto*) preparation 2. *AmS* (*de dinero, de utensilios*) loan 3. *pl* (*utensilios*) ~s de coser sewing things; ~s de escribir stationery

avión [a·βi·'on] *m* 1. AVIAT airplane; ~ a reacción jet (plane); por ~ (*correos*) by airmail; ir en ~ a La Paz to fly to La Paz 2. ZOOL martin

avioneta [a·βjo·'ne·ta] *f* light aircraft

avisado, -a [a·βi·'sa·do, -a] *adj* sensible; mal ~ ill-advised

avisador [a·βi·sa·'dor] *m* ~ de movimientos movement sensor

avisar [a·βi·'sar] *vt* 1. (*dar noticia*) to notify; avísame cuando estés de vuelta let me know when you're back; nos avisó que venía a cenar he/she told us that he/she was coming to dinner; llegar sin ~ to arrive unannounced 2. (*poner sobre aviso*) to warn 3. (*llamar*) to call

aviso [a·'βi·so] *m* 1. (*notificación*) notification; (*nota*) notice; (*por altavoz*) announcement; ~ de llegada COM (acknowledgement of) receipt; ~ de salida FERRO departure announcement; ~ de siniestro accident report; hasta nuevo ~ until further notice; sin previo ~ without notice 2. (*advertencia*) warning; ~ de bomba bomb warning; estar sobre ~ to be warned; poner sobre ~ to warn; servir a alguien de ~ to be a lesson to sb 3. *AmL* (*en el periódico*) ad(vertisement)

avispa [a·'βis·pa] *f* wasp

avispado, -a [a·βis·'pa·do, -a] *adj* sharp

avispero [a·βis·'pe·ro] *m* 1. (*nido*) wasps' nest 2. (*avispas*) swarm of wasps ▶ meterse en un ~ to get oneself into a mess

avistar [a·βis·'tar] *vt* to sight

avivar [a·βi·'βar] *vt* to enliven; (*fuego*) to stoke; (*pasión*) to arouse; (*sentidos*) to sharpen; ~ el paso to increase one's pace

avizor [a·βi·'sor, -'θor] *adj* estar ojo ~ to be alert

avizorar [a·βi·so·'rar, -θo·'rar] *vt* to spy on

axila [ak·'si·la] *f* 1. ANAT armpit 2. BOT axil

axioma [ak·'sjo·ma] *m* axiom

ay [ai] *interj* 1. (*de dolor*) ouch 2. (*de sorpresa*) oh; ¡~, qué divertido! oh, how funny! 3. (*de miedo*) oh, my 4. (*de amenaza*) ¡~ si vienes tarde! you'll regret it if you come late!; ~ del que... +*subj* Heaven help anyone who...

ayer [a·'jer] *adv* yesterday; ~ (por la) noche last night; ~ hace una semana a week ago yesterday; de ~ acá overnight; ¡parece que fue ~! it seems like only yesterday!; no he nacido ~ I wasn't born yesterday

ayo, -a ['a·jo, -a] *m, f* tutor

ayuda¹ [a·'ju·da] *f* 1. (*auxilio*) help; ~ en línea COMPUT online help; perro de ~ watchdog; eso no me sirve de ninguna ~ that doesn't help me 2. (*lavativa*) enema

ayuda² [a·'ju·da] *m* helper

ayudado, -a [a·ju·'da·do, -a] *m, f Col*

1. (*brujo*) witchdoctor; (*de tribu*) medicine man 2. (*endemoniado*) possessed person

ayudante [a·ju·'dan·te] *mf* helper; (*cargo*) assistant; (*en una escuela*) substitute teacher

ayudar [a·ju·'dar] I. *vt* to help; ~ a alguien en el trabajo to help sb with his/her work; ~ a alguien a levantarse to help sb up; ~ a alguien a salir del coche to help sb to get out of the car; ~ a pasar la calle to help across the road; ~ a misa to serve at mass; ¡Dios me ayude! God help me!; ¿le puedo ~ en algo? can I help you with anything?; ~ a conseguir un trabajo to help to get a job II. *vr:* ~se 1. (*mutuamente*) to help each other 2. (*valerse de*) to help oneself

ayunar [a·ju·'nar] *vi* to fast

ayunas [a·'ju·nas] *adv* estar en ~ to have an empty stomach; (*ignorante*) never to understand anything

ayuno [a·'ju·no] *m* fast

ayuntamiento [a·jun·ta·'mjen·to] *m* 1. (*corporación*) district council; (*de una ciudad*) town/city council 2. (*edificio*) town/city hall

azabache [a·sa·'βa·tʃe, a·θa-] *m* jet; ojos de ~ jet-black eyes

azada [a·'θa·da, a·'θa-] *f* hoe

azafata [a·sa·'fa·ta, a·θa-] *f* 1. AVIAT air hostess; ~ de congresos conference hostess 2. *Chile, Col* (*bandeja*) tray

azafrán [a·sa·'fran, a·θa-] *m* saffron

azahar [a·'sar, a·sa·'ar; a·'θar, a·θa·'ar] *m* orange blossom

azalea [a·sa·'lea, a·θa-] *f* azalea

azar [a·'sar, -'θar] *m* 1. (*casualidad*) chance; juegos de ~ games of chance; al ~ at random; por ~ by chance 2. (*imprevisto*) misfortune; los ~es de la vida life's ups and downs

azarar [a·sa·'rar, a·θa-] I. *vt* to shame II. *vr:* ~se 1. (*ruborizarse*) to blush 2. (*turbarse*) to get confused

Azerbaiyán [a·ser·βa·'jan, a·θer-] *m* Azerbaiján

azorar [a·so·'rar, a·θo-] I. *vt* to confuse II. *vr:* ~se to get flustered; (*ante un acto público*) to get stage fright

Azores [a·'so·res, -θo·res] *fpl* las ~ the Azores + *pl vb*

azoro [a·'so·ro, -θo·ro] *m* 1. *AmC* (*fantasma*) ghost 2. *AmC* (*aparición*) apparition 3. *Méx, Perú, PRico* (*azoramiento*) bewilderment

azotaina [a·so·'tai·na, a·θo-] *f* spanking; dar una ~ to spank

azotar [a·so·'tar, a·θo-] *vt* 1. (*con un látigo*) to whip; (*con la mano*) to thrash, to spank; el viento me azota (en) la cara the wind is hitting my face 2. (*producir daños*) to devastate; una epidemia azota la región an epidemic is causing havoc in the region

azote [a·'so·te, -'θo·te] *m* 1. (*látigo*) whip 2. (*golpe*) lash; (*en las nalgas*) spank

azotea [a·so·'tea, a·θo-] *f* terrace roof ▶ estar mal de la ~ *inf* to be off one's rocker

azteca [as·'te·ka, aθ-] I. *adj* Aztec; el equipo

~ (*en fútbol*) Mexico **II.** *mf* Aztec

> **i** The **aztecas** were an indigenous people who built up a vast and powerful empire between the 14th and 16th centuries in the southern and central parts of Mexico. They were conquered by the Spanish in 1521. The language of the **aztecas** was **náhuatl**.

azúcar [a·'su·kar, a·'θu-] *m* sugar; ~ **de corta-dillo** rock candy; ~ **en polvo** icing sugar; **tener el ~ muy alto** MED to have a very high blood-sugar level

azucarar [a·su·ka·'rar, a·'θu-] *vt* to sugar

azucarero [a·su·ka·'re·ro, a·'θu-] *m* sugar bowl

azucena [a·su·'se·na, a·θu·'θe·na] *f* Madonna lily

azufre [a·'su·fre, a·'θu-] *m* sulfur

azul [a·'sul, a'θul] *adj* blue; ~ **celeste** sky blue; ~ **marino** navy blue; ~ **verdoso** greenish-blue

azulado, -a [a·su·'la·do, -a; a·θu-] *adj* bluish

azulejo [a·su·'le·xo, a·θu-] *m* **1.** (*para pared*) (glazed) tile **2.** ZOOL blue wrasse **3.** (*aciano*) cornflower

azulgrana [a·sul·'yra·na, a·θul-] *adj* blue and scarlet; **el equipo ~** DEP Barcelona Football Club

azuzar <z→c> [a·su·'sar, a·θu·'θar] *vt* to incite

B

B, b [be] *f* B, b; ~ **de Barcelona** B as in Bravo

baba ['ba·βa] *f* spittle; (*del caracol*) slime; **caerse a alguien la ~ por alguien** *inf* to dote on sb

babasfrías [ba·βas·'fri·as] *m inv*, Col, *inf* fool

babastibias [ba·βas·'ti·βjas] *m inv*, Ecua fool

babear [ba·βe·'ar] *vi* to dribble, to drool

babel [ba·'βel] *m o f* confusion; (*sitio*) bedlam

babero [ba·'βe·ro] *m* bib

babor [ba·'βor] *m* NÁUT port; **a ~** on the port side

babosa [ba·'βo·sa] *f* **1.** ZOOL slug **2.** AmL (*tontería*) stupid thing

babosada [ba·βo·'sa·da] *f* AmC, Méx (*bobería*) silliness

babosear [ba·βo·se·'ar] *vi inf* to drool, to dribble

baboso, -a [ba·'βo·so, -a] **I.** *adj* **1.** (*con babas*) slimy **2.** *inf* (*zalamero*) fawning **3.** AmL (*tonto*) silly **II.** *m, f* fawning individual

baca ['ba·ka] *f* roof rack, luggage rack

bacalao [ba·ka·'lao] *m* **1.** (*pez*) cod; (*salado*) salt cod **2.** MÚS techno music ► **cortar el ~** to run the show

bacán [ba·'kan] **I.** *m* AmL (*rico*) rich guy, sugar daddy **II.** *adj* Perú (*estupendo*) great

bacanal [ba·ka·'nal] *f* bacchanalia; (*orgía*) orgy

bachata [ba·'tʃa·ta] *f* RDom, PRico party

bachatear [ba·tʃa·te·'ar] *vi* AmL to go out on the town

bache ['ba·tʃe] *m* **1.** (*en la calle*) pothole; AVIAT air pocket **2.** (*económico, psíquico*) slump

bachicha [ba·'tʃi·tʃa] *mf* CSur, Perú, pey (*italiano*) dago *offensive sl*, wop *offensive sl*

bachiller [ba·tʃi·'jer, -'ʎer] *mf* school-leaver; **título de ~** ≈ high school graduate

bachillerato [ba·tʃi·je·'ra·to, -ʎe·'ra·to] *m* (*título*) certificate of secondary education; (*estudios*) high school education for 14-17-year-olds

bacía [ba·'si·a, -'θi·a] *f* basin; (*para animales*) feeding trough

bacilo [ba·'si·lo, -'θi·lo] *m* bacillus

backup [ba·'kap] *m* <backups> COMPUT backup

bacteria [bak·'te·rja] *f* bacteria

bactericida [bak·te·ri·'si·da, -'θi·da] *m* bactericide

bacteriológico, -a [bak·te·rjo'lo·xi·ko, -a] *adj* bacteriological

báculo ['ba·ku·lo] *m* crosier; *fig* (*apoyo*) support

badén [ba·'den] *m* dip; (*en carreteras*) drainage channel

bádminton ['bad·min·ton] *m* DEP badminton

badulaquear [ba·du·la·ke·'ar] *vi* Arg, Col, Chile, Perú (*engañar*) to swindle

bafle ['ba·fle] *m* (loud)speaker

bagaje [ba·'ɣa·xe] *m* MIL baggage; ~ **cultural** cultural knowledge

bagatela [ba·ɣa·'te·la] *f* trifle

bagayo [ba·'ɣa·jo] *m* **1.** Arg, *inf* (*equipaje*) baggage **2.** Arg, *inf* (*objetos robados*) stolen goods *pl* **3.** Arg, *inf* (*prostituta*) whore

bagre [ba·ɣre] **I.** *adj* **1.** Bol, Col (*cursi*) coarse **2.** Guat, Hond, ElSal (*inteligente*) clever **II.** *m* **1.** AmL ZOOL catfish **2.** And (*antipático*) unpleasant person **3.** And (*mujer fea*) old bag **4.** CRi (*prostituta*) slut

bah [ba] *interj* **1.** (*incredulidad*) never **2.** (*desprecio*) that's nothing

bahía [ba·'ia] *f* bay

bailador(a) [bai·la·'dor, -'do·ra] **I.** *adj* dancing **II.** *m(f)* dancer (of flamenco)

bailar [bai·'lar] **I.** *vi* **1.** (*danzar*) to dance **2.** (*objetos*) to move; **hacer ~ una peonza** to spin a top ► ~ **con la más fea** to get the short end of the stick; **¡que me quiten lo bailado!** *inf* nobody can take away the good times I've had!; **otro que tal ~** he/she is just as bad **II.** *vt* to dance

bailarín, -ina [bai·la·'rin, -'ri·na] **I.** *adj* dancing **II.** *m, f* dancer; (*de ballet*) ballet dancer

baile ['bai·le] *m* **1.** (*acto*) dancing **2.** (*danza*) dance **3.** (*fiesta*) dance party; (*de etiqueta*) ball; ~ **de San Vito** MED Saint Vitus' dance

B

baja ['ba·xa] *f* **1.**(*disminución*) decrease; (*de precio*) drop **2.**(*de trabajo*) vacancy; ~ **por maternidad** maternity leave; **darse de** ~ (*temporalmente*) to take time off; (*por enfermedad*) to be on sick leave; (*definitivamente*) to give up one's job; **estar de** ~ (**por enfermedad**) to be off sick **3.**(*en una asociación*) resignation; **dar de** ~ **a alguien** to expel sb **4.**(*documento*) discharge certificate; (*del médico*) doctor's note **5.** MIL casualty
bajada [ba·'xa·da] *f* **1.**(*descenso*) descent; ~ **de tipos de interés** ECON fall in interest rates; ~ **de bandera** minimum fare **2.**(*camino*) way down; (*pendiente*) slope
bajamar [ba·xa·'mar] *f* low tide
bajar [ba·'xar] **I.** *vi* **1.**(*ir hacia abajo*) to go down; (*venir hacia abajo*) to come down; ~ **en ascensor** to go/come down in the lift; ~ **las escaleras** to go/come down the stairs **2.**(*apearse*) ~ **de** (*de un caballo*) to dismount, to get down from; (*de un coche*) to get out of **3.**(*disminuir*) to decrease; (*temperatura*) to drop; (*las aguas*) to fall **II.** *vt* **1.**(*transportar*) to bring down; (*coger*) to take down; ~ **las persianas** to lower the blinds **2.**(*precios*) to lower **3.**(*voz*) to lower; (*radio*) to turn down **4.** COMPUT to download **5.** *Cuba, inf* (*pagar*) pay **III.** *vr:* ~ **se** **1.**(*descender*) ~ **se de** (*de un caballo*) to dismount; (*de un coche*) to get out of **2.**(*humillarse*) to lower oneself
bajativo [ba·xa·'ti·βo] *m AmL* digestive
bajeza [ba·'xe·sa, -θa] *f* **1.**(*humillación*) mean act; (*vileza*) vile act **2.**(*carácter*) baseness
bajista [ba·'xis·ta] **I.** *adj* FIN bearish; **tendencia** ~ bearish tendency **II.** *mf* **1.** MÚS bass player **2.** FIN bear
bajo ['ba·xo] **I.** *m* **1.**(*instrumento*) bass **2.**(*persona*) bass player **3.** *pl* (*piso*) first floor *Am* **4.** *pl* (*parte inferior*) underneath; (*de una prenda*) hemline **II.** *adv* **1.**(*posición*) below **2.**(*voz*) quietly **III.** *prep* **1.**(*debajo*) below **2.**(*por debajo de*) underneath; ~ **llave** under lock and key; ~ **la lluvia** in the rain; ~ **fianza** on bail; ~ **la condición de que** +*subj* on condition that
bajo, -a <más bajo *o* inferior, bajísimo> ['ba·xo, -a] *adj* **1.** estar (*posición*) low **2.** ser (*de temperatura*) low; (*de estatura*) short; **baja tensión** ELEC low tension; **con la cabeza baja/los ojos** ~**s** with head/eyes lowered; **tener la moral baja** to be in poor spirits **3.**(*voz*) low; (*sonido*) soft **4.**(*metal*) base **5.**(*comportamiento*) mean **6.**(*clase social*) humble **7.**(*calidad*) poor
bajón [ba·'xon] *m* **1.**(*descenso*) decline; (*de precios*) drop **2.**(*de la salud*) worsening
bakalao [ba·ka·'lao] *m* MÚS techno music
bala ['ba·la] *f* **1.**(*proyectil*) bullet; ~ **de fogueo** blank cartridge; **como una** ~ like a flash **2.**(*fardo*) bale
balacear [ba·la·se·'ar, ba·la·θe·'ar] *vt AmL* (*herir o matar*) to shoot; (*disparar contra*) to shoot at
balada [ba·'la·da] *f* ballad

balance [ba·'lan·se, -θe] *m* **1.** COM (*resultado*) balance; **hacer un** ~ to draw up a balance **2.**(*comparación*) comparison; **hacer (el)** ~ to take stock of the situation
balancear [ba·lan·se·'ar, ba·lan·θe·-] **I.** *vt* **1.**(*mecer*) to sway; (*acunar*) to rock **2.**(*equilibrar*) to balance **II.** *vr:* ~ **se** **1.**(*columpiarse*) to swing **2.** NÁUT to roll
balanceo [ba·lan·'seo, -'θeo] *m* swaying; NÁUT rocking
balanza [ba·'lan·sa, -θa] *f* **1.**(*pesa*) scales *pl;* **inclinar el fiel de la** ~ *fig* to tip the scales **2.** COM balance; ~ **de pagos** balance of payments
balar [ba·'lar] *vi* to bleat
balaustrada [ba·laus·'tra·da] *f* balustrade
balazo [ba·'la·so, -θo] *m* **1.**(*tiro*) shot **2.**(*herida*) bullet wound
balbucear [bal·βu·se·'ar, -θe·'ar] *vi, vt v.* **balbucir**
balbuceo [bal·βu·'seo, -'θeo] *m* stammering; (*de niños*) babbling
balbucir [bal·βu·'sir, -'θir] *vi, vt* to stammer; (*niño*) to babble
Balcanes [bal·'ka·nes] *mpl* **los** ~ the Balkans
balcón [bal·'kon] *m* balcony
balda ['bal·da] *f* shelf
baldado, -a [bal·'da·do, -a] *adj* crippled; *inf* (*muy cansado*) exhausted
baldaquín [bal·da·'kin] *m* canopy
balde ['bal·de] *m* bucket ▶ **obtener algo de** ~ to get sth for nothing; **en** ~ in vain
baldío [bal·'di·o] *m* AGR wasteland, uncultivated land
baldío, -a [bal·'di·o, -a] *adj* **1.**(*terreno*) uncultivated **2.**(*inútil*) useless; (*en balde*) vain
baldosa [bal·'do·sa] *f* paving stone, floor tile
baldosado [bal·do·'sa·do] *m Col, Chile* (*suelo*) tiled floor
baldosín [bal·do·'sin] *m* tile
balear [ba·le·'ar] **I.** *vt AmL* ~ **a alguien** (*disparar contra*) to shoot at sb; (*herir, matar*) to shoot sb **II.** *vr:* ~ **se** *AmL* **1.**(*disparar*) to exchange shots **2.**(*disputar*) to argue **III.** *adj* Balearic **IV.** *mf* native/inhabitant of the Balearic Islands
Baleares [ba·le·'a·res] *fpl* **las (islas)** ~ the Balearic Islands
baleo [ba·'leo] *m AmL* (*disparo*) shot
balero [ba·'le·ro] *m AmL* (*juego*) cup and ball
ball [bal] *f AmL* **1.**(*balón*) ball **2.**(*proyectil*) shell
ballena [ba·'je·na, -'ʎe·na] *f* whale
ballesta [ba·'jes·ta, -'ʎes·ta] *f* **1.** TÉC spring **2.** HIST crossbow
ballet <ballets> [ba·'le] *m* ballet
balneario [bal·ne·'a·rjo] *m* **1.**(*baños*) spa **2.**(*estación*) health resort
balompié [ba·lom·'pje] *m* soccer
balón [ba·'lon] *m* **1.** DEP ball **2.**(*para gases*) bag **3.**(*en tebeos*) speech balloon ▶ **echar balones fuera** to evade the question
baloncesto [ba·lon·'ses·to, -'θes·to] *m* basket-

ball

balonmano [ba·lon·'ma·no, ba·lom·'ma·no] *m* handball

balonvolea [ba·lom·bo·'lea] *m* volleyball

balotaje [ba·lo·'ta·xe] *m Méx* voting

balsa ['bal·sa] *f* **1.** (*charca*) pool **2.** NÁUT (*barca*) ferry; (*plataforma*) raft; ~ **neumática** rubber dinghy ▶ **ser una ~ de** <u>aceite</u> (*mar*) to be as calm as a millpond

balsámico, -a [bal·'sa·mi·ko, -a] *adj* balsamic; *fig* soothing

bálsamo ['bal·sa·mo] *m* balm

báltico, -a ['bal·ti·ko, -a] *adj* Baltic; **el mar ~** the Baltic Sea; **los países ~s** the Baltic countries

baluarte [ba·'lwar·te] *m* bastion; **un ~ de la libertad** a bulwark of freedom

balumba [ba·'lum·ba] *f AmS* (*barullo*) racket

bambalina [bam·ba·'li·na] *f* TEAT drop(-scene); **entre ~s** backstage

bambolear [bam·bo·le·'ar] *vt, vr:* ~(**se**) to swing, to sway

bambú [bam·'bu] *m* bamboo

banal [ba·'nal] *adj* banal

banalidad [ba·na·li·'dad] *f* banality

banalizar <z→c> [ba·na·li·'sar, -'θar] *vt* to trivialize

banana [ba·'na·na] *f AmL* banana

banano [ba·'na·no] *m AmL* banana tree

banca ['ban·ka] *f* **1.** (*en el mercado*) stall **2.** *AmL* (*asiento*) bench **3.** FIN banking; ~ **electrónica** electronic banking **4.** (*en juegos*) bank **5.** *AmS* (*influencia*) influence; **tener ~** to have pull

bancario, -a [ban·'ka·rjo, -a] *adj* bank(ing); **cuenta bancaria** bank account

bancarrota [ban·ka·'rro·ta] *f* bankruptcy

banco ['ban·ko] *m* **1.** (*asiento*) bench **2.** FIN bank; ~ **en casa** home banking; **Banco Interamericano de Desarrollo** Inter-American Development Bank; **Banco Central** Central Bank; ~ **emisor** issuing bank; **Banco Mundial** World Bank **3.** TÉC bench, work table; ~ **de pruebas** test bed; *fig* testing ground **4.** (*de peces*) shoal ▶ ~ **de** <u>datos</u> COMPUT databank; ~ **de medicamentos** medication [*o* medicine] bank; ~ **de** <u>sangre</u> blood bank

banda ['ban·da] *f* **1.** (*cinta*) band; (*insignia*) sash; ~ **de frecuencia** RADIO frequency band; ~ **sonora** CINE soundtrack; **estar fuera de ~** DEP to be out **2.** (*pandilla*) gang; ~ **terrorista** terrorist group **3.** (*de música*) band; (*música moderna*) group **4.** FIN ~ **de fluctuación** fluctuation range

bandada [ban·'da·da] *f* **1.** (*de pájaros*) flock; (*de peces*) shoal **2.** (*de personas*) gang

bandear [ban·de·'ar] I. *vt* **1.** *AmC* (*perseguir a alguien*) to chase; (*herir de gravedad*) to seriously wound **2.** *Arg, Par, Urug* (*taladrar*) to drill **3.** *Arg, Par, Urug* (*un río*) to cross **4.** *Guat* (*pretender*) to court **5.** *Urug* (*herir con palabras*) to hurt; (*inculpar*) to charge II. *vr:* ~ **se** (*en la vida*) to shift for oneself

bandeja [ban·'de·xa] *f* tray; ~ **de entrada** intray; ~ **de salida** out-tray; **pasar la ~** to pass the hat around; **servir en ~** to hand on a plate

bandera [ban·'de·ra] *f* flag ▶ **estar hasta la ~** *inf* to be packed full

banderilla [ban·de·'ri·ja, -ʎa] *f* TAUR banderilla (*short decorated dart*)

banderola [ban·de·'ro·la] *f* CSur (*ventana*) transom

bandido, -a [ban·'di·do, -a] *m, f* **1.** (*criminal*) bandit **2.** (*persona pilla*) rogue

bando ['ban·do] *m* **1.** (*edicto*) edict **2.** (*partido*) faction

bandolero, -a [ban·do·'le·ro] *m, f* bandit

bandolina [ban·do·'li·na] *f* MÚS mandolin

---

i The **bandoneón**, a concertina-like instrument that produces a moaning sound, is an integral and characteristic component of **tango** music. Heinrich Band, an accordion maker from Germany, developed the instrument in the middle of the 19th century for use in churches which had no organ. At the end of the century, tango musicians began to play the **bandoneón**, which is the soul of the tango even today.

---

bangladesí [ban·gla·de·'si] *adj, mf* Bangladeshi

banquero, -a [ban·'ke·ro, -a] *m, f* banker

banqueta [ban·'ke·ta] *f* **1.** (*taburete*) stool; (*para los pies*) footstool **2.** *AmC* (*acera*) sidewalk

banquete [ban·'ke·te] *m* banquet

banquillo [ban·'ki·jo, -ʎo] *m* bench; (*para los pies*) footstool; JUR dock

bañada [ba·'ɲa·da] *f AmL* (*baño*) swim; (*de pintura*) coat

bañadera [ba·ɲa·'de·ra] *f AmL* bathtub

bañado [ba·'ɲa·do] *m Arg, Bol, Par* marshland

bañador [ba·ɲa·'dor] *m* (*de mujer*) swimsuit; (*de hombre*) swimming trunks

bañar [ba·'ɲar] I. *vt* **1.** (*lavar*) to bathe **2.** (*sumergir*) to immerse **3.** (*mar*) to bathe **4.** (*recubrir*) to coat; **bañado en sudor** in a bath of sweat II. *vr:* ~ **se** **1.** (*lavarse*) to take a bath, to bathe **2.** (*en el mar*) to take a swim

bañera [ba·'ɲe·ra] *f* bathtub

bañista [ba·'ɲis·ta] *mf* (*en playa*) swimmer; (*en balneario*) guest at a spa

baño ['ba·ɲo] *m* **1.** (*acto*) bathing; ~ **energizante** energizing bath; ~ **de fijación** FOTO fixation; ~ **(de) María** CULIN double boiler; ~ **de sangre** bloodbath **2.** (*cuarto*) bathroom; **ir al ~** to go to the bathroom **3.** (*de pintura*) coat; (*de chocolate*) coating **4.** *pl* (*balneario*) spa; ~**s termales** hot springs; **ir a los ~s** to go to the spa

baptisterio [bap·tis·'te·rjo] *m* baptistery

bar [bar] *m* **1.** (*café*) café; (*tasca*) bar **2.** FÍS bar

baraja [ba·'ra·xa] *f* deck of cards; **una ~ de**

B

posibilidades *fig* a range of possibilities
barajar [ba·ra·'xar] *vt* **1.**(*naipes*) to shuffle **2.**(*mezclar*) to mix up **3.**(*posibilidades*) to consider; **se barajan varios nombres** several names are being bandied about **4.** *CSur* (*detener*) to catch
barandilla [ba·ran·'di·ja, -ʎa] *f* (*de balcón*) handrail; (*pasamanos*) banister
barato [ba·'ra·to] *adv* cheap(ly)
barato, -a [ba·'ra·to, -a] *adj* cheap
barba ['bar·βa] *f* **1.**(*mentón*) chin **2.**(*pelos*) beard; **dejarse** ~ to grow a beard; **por** ~ per head **3.** *pl* (*de peces*) barbels *pl* **4.** *pl* (*de papel*) ragged edges *pl* ▶ **subirse a las ~s de alguien** to be disrespectful to sb
barbacoa [bar·βa·'koa] *f* barbecue
barbaridad [bar·βa·ri·'dad] *f* **1.**(*crueldad*) barbarity; **¡qué ~!** how terrible! **2.**(*temeridad*) rash act **3.**(*disparate*) nonsense
barbarie [bar·'βa·rje] *f* savagery
bárbaro, -a ['bar·βa·ro] **I.** *adj* **1.**(*cruel*) savage **2.** *inf* (*estupendo*) tremendous **II.** *m, f* **1.**(*grosero*) brute **2.** HIST barbarian
barbear [bar·βe·'ar] *vt* **1.** *AmC, Par* (*afeitar*) to shave **2.** *AmC, Méx* (*adular*) to flatter
barbería [bar·βe·'ri·a] *f* barber's (shop)
barbero [bar·'βe·ro] *m* barber
barbilla [bar·'βi·ja, -ʎa] *f* chin
barbitúrico [bar·βi·'tu·ri·ko] *m* barbiturate
barbo ['bar·βo] *m* ZOOL barbel
barbudo, -a [bar·'βu·do, -a] *adj* bearded
barca ['bar·ka] *f* (small) boat; **dar un paseo en** ~ to take a boat ride
barchilón, -ona [bar·tʃi·'lon, -·'lo·na] *m, f AmL* (*curandero*) healer
barco ['bar·ko] *m* ship; ~ **cisterna** tanker; ~ **de pasajeros** passenger ship; ~ **de vapor** steamer; ~ **de vela** sailing ship
baremo [ba·'re·mo] *m* range of values
barítono [ba·'ri·to·no] *m* MÚS baritone
barniz [bar·'nis, -'niθ] *m* polish; (*para madera*) varnish
barnizar <z→c> [bar·ni·'sar, -'θar] *vt* to put a gloss on; (*madera*) to varnish
barómetro [ba·'ro·me·tro] *m* barometer
barón, -onesa [ba·'ron, ba·ro·'ne·sa] *m, f* baron *m*, baroness *f*
barquero, -a [bar·'ke·ro, -a] *m, f* (*en un bote*) boatman *m*, boatwoman *f*
barquillo [bar·'ki·jo, -ʎo] *m* wafer
barra ['ba·rra] *f* **1.**(*pieza*) bar; (*de pan*) loaf; (*de chocolate*) bar; ~**s asimétricas** DEP asymmetric bars; ~ **de ejercicios** DEP exercise bar; ~ **de labios** lipstick; **desodorante en** ~ deodorant stick **2.**(*en un bar*) bar; ~ **americana** singles bar **3.**(*raya*) dash; (*signo gráfico*) slash; MÚS bar **4.** COMPUT ~ **de comandos** taskbar; ~ **de desplazamiento** scroll bar; ~ **espaciadora** space bar; ~ **de inversa** backslash; ~ **de navegación** navigation bar **5.** *AmL* (*pandilla*) gang **6.** *AmS* (*público*) public
barraca [ba·'rra·ka] *f* **1.**(*casa*) cabin **2.**(*choza*) hut **3.** *AmL* MIL barracks **4.** *AmL*

(*almacén*) storage shed
barranco [ba·'rran·ko] *m* **1.**(*despeñadero*) cliff **2.**(*cauce*) ravine
barrena [ba·'rre·na] *f* **1.**(*taladrador*) drill **2.** AVIAT spin
barrenar [ba·rre·'nar] *vt* to drill
barrendero, -a [ba·rren·'de·ro, -a] *m, f* sweeper
barreño [ba·'rre·ɲo] *m* washbasin
barrer [ba·'rrer] *vt* **1.**(*habitación*) to sweep; *fig* (*obstáculo*) to sweep aside **2.** *inf* (*derrotar*) to defeat ▶ ~ **para** [*o* **hacia**] **dentro** to look after number one
barrera [ba·'rre·ra] *f* **1.**(*barra*) barrier; ~ **lingüística** language barrier; ~ **del sonido** sound barrier **2.** DEP wall **3.** TAUR barrier
barriada [ba·'rrja·da] *f* **1.**(*barrio*) district **2.** *AmL* (*barrio pobre*) shanty town
barricada [ba·rri·'ka·da] *f* barricade
barriga [ba·'rri·ya] *f* **1.**(*vientre*) belly **2.**(*de una vasija*) rounded part ▶ **rascarse la** ~ to laze about, to twiddle one's thumbs
barrigón [ba·rri·'yon] *m* big belly
barrigón, -ona [ba·rri·'yon, -·'yo·na] *adj* pot-bellied
barril [ba·'rril] *m* **1.**(*cuba*) barrel; **cerveza de** ~ draught beer **2.** *AmL* (*cometa*) hexagonal kite
barrilete [ba·rri·'le·te] *m* **1.**(*barril*) small keg **2.**(*de carpintero*) clamp **3.**(*en un revólver*) cylinder **4.** *AmL* (*cometa*) hexagonal kite
barrio ['ba·rrjo] *m* **1.**(*de ciudad*) district, neighborhood; ~ **chino** red-light district; ~ **comercial** business quarter **2.**(*arrabal*) suburb ▶ **irse al otro** ~ *inf* to snuff it
barrizal [ba·rri·'sal, -'θal] *m* mire
barro ['ba·rro] *m* **1.**(*lodo*) mud **2.**(*arcilla*) clay; **de** ~ earthenware
barroco [ba·'rro·ko] **I.** *m* baroque **II.** *adj* baroque; *fig* overly elaborate, gaudy *pej*
barrote [ba·'rro·te] *m* (heavy) bar; **entre ~s** *fig, inf* behind bars
barruntar(se) [ba·rrun·'tar·(se)] *vt, vr* to conjecture
bártulos ['bar·tu·los] *mpl* belongings *pl*
barullo [ba·'ru·jo, -ʎo] *m inf* **1.**(*ruido*) din **2.**(*desorden*) confusion
basalto [ba·'sal·to] *m* basalt
basar [ba·'sar] **I.** *vt* to ground **II.** *vr* ~**se en algo** (*teoría*) to be based on sth; (*persona*) to base oneself on sth
basca ['bas·ka] *f* **1.** MED (*espasmo*) nausea; **tener ~s** to feel sick **2.** *inf* (*arrebato*) fit of rage **3.** *inf* (*gentío*) gang
bascosidad [bas·ko·si·'dad] *f Ecua* (*insulto*) obscenity
bascoso, -a [bas·'ko·so, -a] *adj* **1.** *Col, Ecua* (*nauseabundo*) nauseating **2.** *Col, Ecua* (*indigno*) contemptible, vile **3.** *Col, Ecua* (*obsceno*) obscene
báscula ['bas·ku·la] *f* scales *pl*
bascular [bas·ku·'lar] *vi* **1.**(*inclinarse*) to tilt **2.**(*oscilar*) to seesaw

base ['ba·se] *f* **1.**(*fundamento*) basis; ~ **de datos** COMPUT database; **elaborado a ~ de algo** drawn up on the basis of sth; **partir de la ~ de que...** to start with the idea that... **2.** ARQUIT, MAT base; (*superficie*) area ▶ **a ~ de bien** *inf* really well

básico, -a ['ba·si·ko, -a] *adj* (*t. quím*) basic

Basilea [ba·si·'lea] *f* Basle, Basel

basílica [ba·'si·li·ka] *f* basilica

basta ['bas·ta] *f* **1.**(*hilván*) basting **2.** AmL (*bastilla*) hem

bastante [bas·'tan·te] **I.** *adj* enough; **tengo ~ frío** I'm very cold **II.** *adv* (*suficientemente*) sufficiently; (*considerablemente*) rather; **con esto tengo ~** this is enough for me

bastar [bas·'tar] **I.** *vi* to be enough; **¡basta!** that's enough! **II.** *vr* ~**se** (**uno**) **solo** to be self-sufficient

bastardo, -a [bas·'tar·do, -a] **I.** *adj* **1.**(*hijo*) bastard **2.**(*vil*) wicked **II.** *m, f* bastard

bastedad [bas·te·'dad] *f* coarseness

bastidor [bas·ti·'dor] *m* **1.** TÉC frame(work); (*de coche*) chassis *inv*; (*de ventana*) frame **2.** TEAT wing; **entre ~es** behind the scenes

bastión [bas·'tjon] *m* bastion

basto, -a ['bas·to, -a] *adj* **1.**(*grosero*) rude; (*vulgar*) coarse **2.**(*superficie*) rough

bastón [bas·'ton] *m* **1.**(*para andar*) stick; (*para esquiar*) ski pole **2.**(*de mando*) baton; **empuñar el ~** to take command

bastoncillo [bas·ton·'si·jo, -'θi·ʎo] *m* *diminutivo de* **bastón** small stick; ~ **de algodón** cotton swab, Q-tip®

bastos ['bas·tos] *mpl* clubs *pl* (*in Spanish deck of cards*) ▶ **pintan ~** things are getting difficult

basura [ba·'su·ra] *f* **1.**(*desperdicios*) garbage; ~ **del hogar** domestic garbage; **echar algo a la ~** to throw sth away **2.**(*lo despreciable*) trash

basural [ba·su·'ral] *m* AmL garbage dump

basurear [ba·su·re·'ar] *vt* Arg, Urug **1.** *vulg* (*tratar*) to treat like shit **2.**(*vencer*) to defeat

basurero [ba·su·'re·ro] *m* **1.**(*vertedero*) garbage dump **2.**(*recipiente*) trashcan

basurero, -a [ba·su·'re·ro, -a] *m, f* garbage [*o* trash] collector, garbage man

bata ['ba·ta] *f* (*albornoz*) dressing gown; (*guardapolvos*) coverall; (*de laboratorio*) lab coat; (*de hospital*) white coat

batacazo [ba·ta·'ka·so, -θo] *m* **1.**(*golpe*) thump **2.**(*caída*) heavy fall; **se pegó un ~** *inf* he/she came a cropper **3.** CSur, PRico (*de suerte*) stroke of luck

bataclán [ba·ta·'klan] *m* AmL striptease show

batalla [ba·'ta·ja, -ʎa] *f* **1.** MIL battle; ~ **campal** pitched battle; *fig* bitter dispute **2.**(*interior*) struggle

batallar [ba·ta·'jar, -'ʎar] *vi* **1.**(*con armas*) to fight; ~ **por algo** to battle over sth **2.**(*disputar*) to quarrel

batallita [ba·ta·'ji·ta, -'ʎi·ta] *f* story

batallón [ba·ta·'jon, -'ʎon] *m* **1.** MIL battalion

2. *inf* (*grupo*) group

batán [ba·'tan] *m* **1.** AmL (*piedra lisa*) millstone **2.** Chile (*tintorería*) dry cleaner's

batata [ba·'ta·ta] **I.** *adj* CSur (*tímido*) shy **II.** *f* **1.**(*planta*) sweet potato plant **2.**(*tubérculo*) sweet potato **3.** CSur (*susto*) shock **4.** CSur (*vergüenza*) embarrassment **5.** AmL ~ **de la pierna** calf

bate ['ba·te] *m* DEP bat; ~ **de béisbol** baseball bat

batear [ba·te·'ar] *vt* DEP to bat

batería¹ [ba·te·'ri·a] *f* **1.** *t.* TÉC battery; ~ **de cocina** pots and pans; ~ **solar** solar panel; **aparcar en ~** to parallel park **2.** TEAT footlights **3.** MÚS drums *pl*

batería² [ba·te·'ri·a] *mf*, **baterista** [ba·te·'ris·ta] *mf* drummer

batida [ba·'ti·da] *f* **1.**(*de cazadores*) beat **2.**(*de policía*) raid **3.** AmL (*paliza*) beating, thrashing

batido [ba·'ti·do] *m* (*bebida*) milk shake; (*de huevos*) batter; ~ **de fresa** strawberry milk shake

batidor [ba·ti·'dor] *m* **1.**(*instrumento*) whisk **2.**(*en la caza*) beater **3.**(*explorador*) scout

batidora [ba·ti·'do·ra] *f* (*de mano*) whisk; (*eléctrica*) mixer, blender

batifondo [ba·ti·'fon·do] *m* CSur, *inf* (*alboroto*) uproar; (*disturbio*) commotion; (*zozobra*) uneasiness

batín [ba·'tin] *m* (man's) dressing gown

batir [ba·'tir] **I.** *vt* **1.**(*golpear, metal*) to beat; (*toldo*) to flap; (*las olas*) to crash against; ~ **palmas** to clap **2.**(*moneda*) to mint **3.**(*enemigo*) to defeat; MIL to beat; ~ **un récord** to beat a record **4.**(*un terreno*) to comb **5.** CSur (*denunciar*) to inform on **II.** *vr:* ~**se 1.**(*combatir*) to fight **2.**(*en duelo*) to fight a duel

batuta [ba·'tu·ta] *f* MÚS baton ▶ **llevar la ~** to be in charge

baúl [ba·'ul] *m* **1.**(*mueble*) trunk **2.** AmL (*portamaletas*) trunk

bausán, -ana [bau·'san, -'sa·na] *adj* AmL (*perezoso*) lazy

bautismal [bau·tis·'mal] *adj* baptismal; **pila ~** font

bautismo [bau·'tis·mo] *m* baptism; ~ **de sangre** first combat

bautista [bau·'tis·ta] *mf* Baptist; **San Juan Bautista** St John the Baptist

bautizar [bau·ti·'sar, -'θar] *vt* REL to baptize; (*nombrar*) to christen; ~ **el vino** *inf* to water down the wine

bautizo [bau·'ti·so, -θo] *m* baptism; (*ceremonia*) christening; (*fiesta*) christening party

baya ['ba·ja] *f* berry

bayeta [ba·'je·ta] *f* rag, dishcloth

bayoneta [ba·jo·'ne·ta] *f* bayonet

bayoya [ba·'jo·ja] *m* PRico, RDom uproar

baza ['ba·sa, -θa] *f* **1.**(*naipes*) trick; **meter ~ en algo** *inf* to butt in on sth **2.**(*provecho*) benefit; **sacar ~ de algo** to profit from sth

bazar [ba·'sar, -'θar] *m* (*mercado*) bazaar;

(*gran almacén*) large shop

bazo ['ba·so, -θo] *m* ANAT spleen

bazofia [ba·'so·fja, ba·'θo-] *f* **1.** *pey* (*comida*) scraps *pl* **2.** (*cosa*) filthy thing

be [be] *f letter B*

beatería [bea·te·'ri·a] *f* (*exagerada*) sanctimoniousness; (*falsa*) affected piety

beatificar <c→qu> [bea·ti·fi·'kar] *vt* to beatify

beatitud [bea·ti·'tud] *f* beatitude

beato, -a [be·'a·to, -a] I. *adj* **1.** (*piadoso*) devout **2.** (*beatificado*) beatified II. *m, f* REL beatified person; (*devoto*) devout person

bebe, -a ['be·βe, -a] *m, f AmL* baby

bebé [be·'βe] *m* baby

bebedera [be·βe·'de·ra] *f Méx* drinking spree

bebedero [be·βe·'de·ro] *m* **1.** (*para animales*) waterhole; (*para animales domésticos*) drinking trough **2.** (*de jarro*) spout

bebedizo [be·βe·'di·so, -θo] *m* **1.** (*medicinal*) potion **2.** (*enamoradizo*) love potion

bebedor(a) [be·βe·'dor, --'do·ra] *m(f)* drinker

bebendurria [be·βen·'du·rrja] *f AmL, inf* drinking binge

bebé-probeta [be·'βe-pro·'βe·ta] *m* <bebés-probeta> test-tube baby

beber [be·'βer] I. *vi, vt* **1.** (*líquido*) to drink; ~ **de la botella** to drink from the bottle; ~ **a sorbos** to sip; ~ **de un trago** to gulp **2.** (*información*) to absorb II. *vr:* ~ **se** to drink up; **bebérselo todo** to drink it all up

bebida [be·'βi·da] *f* drink, beverage *form;* ~ **alcohólica** alcoholic drink; ~ **energética** energy drink; **darse a la** ~ to take to drink

bebido, -a [be·'βi·do, -a] *adj* (*borracho*) drunk

beca ['be·ka] *f* (*de estudios*) grant; (*por méritos*) scholarship; **conceder una** ~ **a alguien** to award a grant to sb

becar <c→qu> [be·'kar] *vt* to award a grant to

becario, -a [be·'ka·rjo, -a] *m, f* grant holder; (*por méritos*) scholarship holder

becerro [be·'se·rro, be·'θe-] *m* HIST register

becerro, -a [be·'se·rro, -a; be·'θe-] *m, f* yearling calf; **el** ~ **de oro** the golden calf

bechamel [be·tʃa·'mel] *f* white sauce

bedel(a) [be·'del, --'de·la] *m(f)* beadle, proctor

beduino, -a [be·'dwi·no, -a] *adj, m, f* Bedouin

befo ['be·fo] *m* lip (of horse)

begonia [be·'yo·nja] *f* begonia

beicon ['bei·kon] *m* bacon

beige [beis] *adj* beige

béisbol ['beis·βol] *m* DEP baseball

bejuco [be·'xu·ko] *m* liana

belduque [bel·'du·ke] *m AmL* pointed sword

belén [be·'len] *m* **1.** (*nacimiento*) crib, Nativity scene **2.** *inf* (*confusión*) confusion

Belén [be·'len] *m* Bethlehem

belga ['bel·ya] *adj, mf* Belgian

Bélgica ['bel·xi·ka] *f* Belgium

Belgrado [bel·'yra·do] *m* Belgrade

belicista [be·li·'sis·ta, -'θis·ta] I. *adj* belligerent II. *mf* warmonger

bélico, -a ['be·li·ko, -a] *adj* warlike

belicoso, -a [be·li·'ko·so, -a] *adj* (*población*)

warlike; (*persona*) aggressive

beligerancia [be·li·xe·'ran·sja, -θja] *f* belligerency

beligerante [be·li·xe·'ran·te] *adj* belligerent

bellaco, -a [be·'ja·ko, -a; be·'ʎa-] I. *adj* cunning II. *m, f* rascal

bellaquear [be·ja·ke·'ar, be·'ʎa-] *vi* **1.** (*persona*) to cheat **2.** *AmL* (*caballo*) to shy

belleza [be·'je·sa, -'ʎe·θa] *f* beauty

bello, -a ['be·jo, -a; -ʎo, -a] *adj* beautiful

bellota [be·'jo·ta, -'ʎo·ta] *f* acorn

bemba ['bem·ba] *f AmL, pey* lip

bembo, -a ['bem·bo, -a] *adj AmL* thick-lipped

bembudo, -a [bem·'bu·do, -a] *adj AmL* thick-lipped

bemol [be·'mol] *m* MÚS flat ► **tener** ~**es** to be difficult

benceno [ben·'se·no, -'θe·no] *m* benzene

bencina [ben·'si·na, -'θi·na] *f* benzine

bendecir [ben·de·'sir, -'θir] *irr como decir vt* **1.** (*sacerdote*) to bless; ~ **la mesa** to say grace **2.** (*alabar*) to praise **3.** (*consagrar*) to consecrate

bendición [ben·di·'sjon, -'θjon] *f* **1.** (*acto*) blessing **2.** (*cosa magnífica*) marvel

bendito, -a [ben·'di·to, -a] I. *adj* **1.** REL blessed; (*agua*) holy; (*santo*) saintly; **¡~ sea!** *inf* thank God! **2.** (*dichoso*) lucky II. *m, f* kind soul

benedictino, -a [be·ne·dik·'ti·no, -a] *adj, m, f* REL Benedictine

benefactor(a) [be·ne·fak·'tor, --'to·ra] I. *adj* beneficent II. *m(f)* benefactor

beneficencia [be·ne·fi·'sen·sja, -'θen·θja] *f* charity

beneficiado, -a [be·ne·fi·'sja·do, -'θja·do] *adj, m, f* beneficiary

beneficiar [be·ne·fi·'sjar, -'θjar] I. *vt* **1.** (*favorecer*) to benefit **2.** (*mina*) to work; (*mineral*) to refine **3.** *AmL* (*animal*) to slaughter II. *vr:* ~ **se 1.** (*sacar provecho*) ~ **se de algo** to benefit from sth **2.** *pey* (*enriquecerse*) ~ **se de algo** to take advantage of sth

beneficiario, -a [be·ne·fi·'sja·rjo, -a; be·ne·fi·'θja-] *m, f* beneficiary; (*de una letra de crédito*) assignee; ~ **de la pensión** receiver of the pension

beneficio [be·ne·'fi·sjo, -θjo] *m* **1.** (*bien*) good **2.** (*provecho*) *t.* FIN profit; **a** ~ **de** for the benefit of **3.** *AmL* (*matanza*) slaughter

beneficioso, -a [be·ne·fi·'sjo·so, -a; be·ne·fi·'θjo-] *adj* **1.** (*favorable*) beneficial **2.** (*útil*) useful **3.** (*productivo*) profitable

benéfico, -a [be·'ne·fi·ko, -a] *adj* **1.** (*que hace bien*) beneficial **2.** (*caritativo*) charitable

beneplácito [be·ne·'pla·si·to, -θi·to] *m* **1.** (*permiso*) approval **2.** (*consentimiento*) consent

benévolo, -a [be·'ne·βo·lo, -a] *adj* **1.** (*favorable*) benevolent **2.** (*clemente*) indulgent

bengala [ben·'ga·la] *f* flare; (*pequeña*) sparkler

benigno, -a [be·'niɣ·no, -a] *adj* **1.** (*persona*) kind; **ser** ~ **con alguien** to be kind to sb

2. (*clima*) mild **3.** MED benign
benjamín, -ina [ben·xa·'min] *m*, *f* **1.** (*hijo menor*) youngest child **2.** (*de un grupo*) youngest member
beodo, -a [be·'o·do, -a] **I.** *adj* drunk **II.** *m*, *f* drunkard
berbén [ber·'βen] *m Méx* (*escorbuto*) scurvy
berberecho [ber·βe·'re·ʧo] *m* cockle
bereber [be·re·'βer], **beréber** [be·'re·βer] *adj*, *mf* Berber
berenjena [be·ren·'xe·na] *f* eggplant
Berlín [ber·'lin] *m* Berlin
berlina [ber·'li·na] *f* **1.** (*vehículo*) sedan **2.** AmL (*pastel*) jelly donut
berlinés, -esa [ber·li·'nes, -·'ne·sa] **I.** *adj* Berlin **II.** *m*, *f* Berliner
bermejo, -a [ber·'me·xo, -a] *adj* red
bermudas [ber·'mu·das] *mpl* Bermuda shorts *pl*
Berna ['ber·na] *f* Berne
berrear [be·rre·'ar] *vi* **1.** (*animal*) to bellow **2.** (*llorar*) to howl **3.** (*chillar*) to screech
berrinche [be·'rrin·ʧe] *m* *inf* **1.** (*llorera*) tantrum **2.** (*enfado*) rage
berrinchudo, -a [be·rrin·'ʧu·do, -a] *adj AmL* on heat
berro ['be·rro] *m* watercress
berza ['ber·sa, -θa] *f* cabbage
berzotas [ber·'so·tas, ber·'θo-] *mf* *inv, inf* chump
besar [be·'sar] **I.** *vt* to kiss; *inf* (*objetos*) to touch **II.** *vr:* ~**se** to kiss each other; (*dos objetos*) to touch
beso ['be·so] *m* kiss; **comerse a alguien a ~s** to smother sb with kisses
bestia¹ ['bes·tja] **I.** *adj* stupid **II.** *mf* **1.** (*bruto*) brute; (*grosero*) boor **2.** (*ignorante*) ignoramus
bestia² ['bes·tja] *f* animal; (*salvaje*) (wild) beast
bestial [bes·'tjal] *adj* **1.** (*de una bestia*) bestial **2.** (*muy brutal*) brutal **3.** *inf* (*muy intenso*) tremendous; (*muy grande*) huge; (*muy bueno*) marvelous
bestialidad [bes·tja·li·'dad] *f* **1.** (*cualidad*) bestiality **2.** (*crueldad*) brutality **3.** *inf* (*gran cantidad*) huge amount
besugo [be·'su·ɣo] *m* **1.** ZOOL bream; **ojos de ~** *inf* bulging eyes **2.** *inf* (*persona*) idiot; **¡no seas ~!** don't be an idiot!
besuquear [be·su·ke·'ar] *vt* to cover with kisses
betabel [be·ta·'βel] *f Méx* (*remolacha*) beet; ~ **forrajera** fodder beet
betarraga [be·ta·'rra·ya] *f AmL* beet
betún [be·'tun] *m* **1.** QUÍM bitumen **2.** (*para el calzado*) shoe polish; **negro como el ~** as black as pitch
biaba ['bja·βa] *f Arg, Urug* (*cachetada*) slap; (*paliza*) beating; **dar la ~** (*pegar*) to beat up; (*derrotar*) to defeat
bianual [bi·a·nu·'al] *adj* biannual; BOT biennial
biberón [bi·βe·'ron] *m* feeding bottle
Biblia ['bi·βlja] *f* Bible

bíblico, -a ['bi·βli·ko, -a] *adj* biblical
bibliobús [bi·βljo·'bus] *m* mobile library
bibliófilo, -a [bi·'βljo·fi·lo, -a] *m*, *f* bibliophile, book lover
bibliografía [bi·βljo·ɣra·'fi·a] *f* bibliography
bibliográfico, -a [bi·βljo·'ɣra·fi·ko, -a] *adj* bibliographic(al)
biblioteca [bi·βljo·'te·ka] *f* **1.** (*local*) library; ~ **de consulta** reference library **2.** (*mueble*) bookcase **3.** (*estantería*) bookshelves *pl*
bibliotecario, -a [bi·βljo·te·'ka·rjo, -a] *m*, *f* librarian
bicarbonato [bi·kar·βo·'na·to] *m* bicarbonate; ~ **sódico** bicarbonate of soda, baking soda, sodium bicarbonate
bicéfalo, -a [bi·'se·fa·lo, -a; bi·'θe-] *adj* two-headed
bicentenario [bi·sen·te·'na·rjo, bi·θen-] *m* bicentennial
bíceps ['bi·seps, -θeps] *m* *inv* ANAT biceps *inv*
bicho ['bi·ʧo] *m* **1.** (*animal*) (small) animal; (*insecto*) bug **2.** TAUR bull **3.** *inf* (*persona*) ~ **raro** weirdo; **mal** ~ rogue
bici ['bi·si, -θi] *f inf abr de* **bicicleta** bike
bicicleta [bi·si·'kle·ta, bi·θi-] *f* bicycle; ~ **de carreras** racing bike; ~ **estática** exercise bike; ~ **de montaña** mountain bike
bicisenda [bi·si·'sen·da, bi·θi-] *f Arg* bicycle [*o* bike] path
bicoca [bi·'ko·ka] *f* **1.** *inf* (*ganga*) bargain **2.** *inf* (*pequeñez*) trifle **3.** *AmL* (*de eclesiásticos*) skull cap
bicolor [bi·ko·'lor] *adj* two-color
bidireccional [bi·di·rek·sjo·'nal, -rey·θjo·'nal] *adj* two-way; COMPUT bidirectional
bidón [bi·'don] *m* steel drum
biela [bi·'e·la] *f* TÉC connecting rod; (*de bicicleta*) crank
bieldo ['bjel·do] *m* winnowing fork
Bielorrusia [bje·lo·'rru·sja] *f* Byelorussia
bielorruso, -a [bje·lo·'rru·so, -a] *adj*, *m*, *f* Byelorussian
bien ['bjen] **I.** *m* **1.** (*bienestar*) well-being **2.** (*bondad*) good **3.** (*provecho*) benefit **4.** *pl* ECON goods *pl* **5.** *pl* (*posesiones*) property; (*riqueza*) wealth; ~**es inmuebles** real estate; ~**es de la tierra** agricultural produce **II.** *adv* **1.** (*convenientemente*) properly; (*correctamente*) well; ~ **mirado** well thought of; **estar** ~ **de salud** to be in good health; **estar (a)** ~ **con alguien** to get on well with sb; **hacer algo** ~ to do sth well; **hacer** ~ **en** +*infin* to do well to +*infin*; **¡pórtate** ~**!** behave yourself!; **tener a** ~ +*infin* to see fit to +*infin;* **te está** ~ that serves you right **2.** (*con gusto*) willingly **3.** (*seguramente*) surely **4.** (*muy*) very; (*bastante*) quite; **es** ~ **fácil** it's very simple **5.** (*asentimiento*) all right; **¡está** ~**!** OK! ▸ **ahora** ~ however; ~ **que mal** one way or another **III.** *adj* well-off **IV.** *conj* **1.** (*aunque*) ~ **que** although; **si** ~ even though **2.** (*o...o*) ~ **...** ~ **...** either... or ... **V.** *interj* well done
bienal [bje·'nal] **I.** *adj* biennial **II.** *f* biennial

show

bienaventuranza [bje·na·βen·tu·'ran·sa, -θa] *f* **1.** REL (*gloria*) bliss; **las ~s** the Beatitudes **2.** (*felicidad*) happiness

bienestar [bje·nes·'tar] *m* **1.** (*estado*) well-being **2.** (*riqueza*) prosperity; **estado del ~** welfare state

bienhechor(a) [bje·ne·'tʃor, -'tʃo·ra] **I.** *adj* beneficent **II.** *m(f)* benefactor

bienintencionado, -a [bjen·in·ten·sjo·'na·do, -a; bjen·in·ten·θjo-] *adj* well-meaning

bienio [bi·'e·njo] *m* two-year period

bienvenida [bjem·be·'ni·da] *f* welcome; **dar la ~ a alguien** to welcome sb

bienvenido, -a [bjem·be·'ni·do, -a] *adj, interj* welcome; **¡~ a casa!** welcome home!; **¡~ a España!** welcome to Spain!

bife ['bi·fe] *m CSur* **1.** (*carne*) steak **2.** *inf* (*sopapo*) slap

bifocal [bi·fo·'kal] *adj* bifocal

bifurcación [bi·fur·ka·'sjon, -'θjon] *f* fork

bifurcarse <c→qu> [bi·fur·'kar·se] *vr* to fork

bigamia [bi·'ɣa·mja] *f* bigamy

bígamo, -a ['bi·ɣa·mo, -a] **I.** *adj* bigamous **II.** *m, f* bigamist

bigote [bi·'ɣo·te] *m* **1.** (*de hombre*) moustache, mustache; **estar de ~(s)** *inf* to be terrific **2.** *pl* (*de animal*) whiskers *pl* **3.** *AmL* (*croqueta*) croquette

bigotudo, -a [bi·ɣo·'tu·do, -a] *adj* with a big moustache

bigudí [bi·ɣu·'di] *m* curler

bikini [bi·'ki·ni] *m* bikini

bilateral [bi·la·te·'ral] *adj* bilateral

bilingüe [bi·'lin·gwe] *adj* bilingual

bilingüismo [bi·lin·'gwis·mo] *m* bilingualism

bilis ['bi·lis] *f inv* **1.** ANAT bile **2.** (*cólera*) spleen; **no tuve más remedio que tragar ~** I had no choice but to put up with it

billar [bi·'jar, -'ʎar] *m* **1.** (*juego*) billiards; **~ americano** pool **2.** (*mesa*) billiard table

billete [bi·'je·te, -'ʎe·te] *m* **1.** (*pasaje*) ticket; **~ de ida y vuelta** roundtrip ticket; **sacar un ~** to get a ticket **2.** FIN bill **3.** (*de lotería*) ticket; **~ premiado** winning ticket

billetera [bi·je·'te·ra, bi·ʎe-] *f*, **billetero** [bi·je·'te·ro, bi·ʎe-] *m* billfold

billón [bi·'jon, -'ʎon] *m* **1.** (10^{12}) trillion **2.** (10^9) billion

billonario, -a [bi·ʎo·'na·rjo, -a; bi·ʎo-] *m, f* billionaire

bimba ['bim·ba] *f AmL* (*embriaguez*) **pegarse una ~** to get drunk

bimensual [bi·men·'swal] *adj* semimonthly

bimotor [bi·mo·'tor] *m* twin-engine plane

binario, -a [bi·'na·rjo, -a] *adj* binary

bingo ['bin·go] *m* (*juego*) bingo; (*sala*) bingo hall

binoculares [bi·no·ku·'la·res] *mpl* binoculars *pl*

binóculo [bi·'no·ku·lo] *m* pince-nez

bioactivo, -a [bio·ak·'ti·βo, -a] *adj* bioactive

biodegradable [bio·de·ɣra·'da·βle] *adj* biodegradable

biodiversidad [bio·di·βer·si·'dad] *f* biodiversity

biofísica [bio·'fi·si·ka] *f* biophysics

biogenética [bio·xe·'ne·ti·ka] *f* biogenetics

biografía [bjo·ɣra·'fi·a] *f* biography

biógrafo [bi'o·ɣra·fo] *m CSur* (*cine*) cinema

biógrafo, -a [bi'o·ɣra·fo, -a] *m, f* (*persona*) biographer

biología [bio·lo·'xi·a] *f* biology

biólogo, -a [bi'o·lo·ɣo, -a] *m, f* biologist

biombo [bi·'om·bo] *m* (folding) screen, bionic

i **Biopiratería** (biopiracy) refers, for example, to the act of individuals or institutions from outside the country of origin illegally patenting biological resources such as grains and medicinal herbs. If local farmers plant the patented grains or if the medicinal herbs are used in traditional, natural medicine, the farmers or healers are then subjected to paying licensing fees.

biopsia [bi·'oβ·sja] *f* biopsy

bioquímica [bio·'ki·mi·ka] *f* biochemistry

biorritmo [bio·'rrit·mo] *m* biorhythm

biosfera [bios·'fe·ra] *f* biosphere

bipartidismo [bi·par·ti·'dis·mo] *m* POL two-party system

bípedo, -a ['bi·pe·do, -a] *adj, m, f* biped

biplano [bi·'pla·no] *m* biplane

bipolaridad [bi·po·la·ri·'dad] *f* FÍS bipolarity

biquini [bi·'ki·ni] *m* bikini

birlar [bir·'lar] *vt inf* (*hurtar*) to swipe; **Carlos me birló el lápiz** Carlos swiped my pencil

birmano, -a [bir·'ma·no, -a] *adj, m, f* Burmese

birome [bi·'ro·me] *m o f CSur* ballpoint (pen)

birra ['bi·rra] *f inf* beer

birria ['bi·rrja] *f* **1.** (*persona*) drip; **el delantero centro es una ~** the center forward is useless; **va hecho una ~** he looks really scruffy **2.** (*objeto*) rubbish, trash; **la película es una ~** the film is rubbish

birriondo, -a [bi·'rrjon·do, -a] *adj Méx* **1.** (*callejero*) street; (*animales*) jumpy; **perro ~** mutt **2.** (*enamoradizo*) easily infatuated **3.** (*cachondo*) randy *inf*

biruje [bi·'ru·xe] *m AmL*, **biruji** [bi·'ru·xi] *m* cold wind

bis [bis] **I.** *interj, m* MÚS encore **II.** *adv* **1.** MÚS bis **2.** (*piso*) **7 ~ 7A**

bisabuelo, -a [bi·sa·'βwe·lo, -a] *m, f* great-grandfather *m*, great-grandmother *f*

bisagra [bi·'sa·ɣra] *f* hinge

bisbis(e)ar [bis·βi·'sar/bis·βi·se·'ar] *vt inf* to whisper

biscote [bis·'ko·te] *m* rusk

bisexual [bi·sek·'swal] *adj* bisexual

bisexualidad [bi·sek·swa·li·'dad] *f* bisexuality

bisiesto [bi·'sjes·to] *adj* **año ~** leap year

bisílabo, -a [bi·'si·la·βo, -a] *adj* two-syllable

bisnieto, -a [bis·'nje·to, -a] *m, f* great-grandson *m,* great-granddaughter *f*

bisonte [bi·'son·te] *m* (*americano*) buffalo; (*europeo*) bison

bisoñé [bi·so·'ɲe] *m* toupee

bisté [bis·'te] *m* <bistés>, **bistec** [bis·'te] *m* <bistecs> steak

bisturí [bis·tu·'ri] *m* scalpel

bisutería [bi·su·te·'ri·a] *f* costume jewelry

bit [bit] *m* <bits> COMPUT bit; ~ **de parada** stop bit

bitoque [bi·'to·ke] *m* **1.** *AmC* (*cloaca*) sewer **2.** *AmL* (*cánula de jeringa*) cannula **3.** *Méx, RíoPl* (*grifo*) faucet

bizarro, -a [bi·'sa·rro, -a; bi·'θa-] *adj* **1.** (*valiente*) brave **2.** (*apuesto*) dashing

bizco, -a ['bis·ko, -a; 'biθ-] *adj* cross-eyed; **dejar a alguien** ~ *fig* to leave sb speechless

bizcocho [biθ·'ko·tʃo, biθ-] **I.** *adj Méx* (*cobarde*) cowardly **II.** *m* CULIN sponge cake

biznieto, -a [bis·'nje·to, -a; biθ-] *m, f v.* **bisnieto**

bizquera [bis·'ke·ra, biθ-] *f* (*estrabismo*) squint; **tener** ~ to be cross-eyed

blanca ['blan·ka] *f* **1.** MÚS half note **2.** (*de dominó*) double-blank ▸ **estar sin** ~ *inf* to be broke

Blancanieves [blan·ka·'nje·βes] *f* Snow White

blanco ['blan·ko] *m* **1.** (*color*) white; **película en** ~ **y negro** black and white film **2.** (*en un escrito*) blank space; **cheque en** ~ blank check **3.** (*diana*) target; **dar en el** ~ *fig* to hit the mark ▸ **se me quedó la mente en** ~ my mind went blank; **pasar la noche en** ~ to have a sleepless night; ~ **del ojo** white of the eye; **quedarse en** ~ to go blank

blanco, -a ['blan·ko, -a] **I.** *adj* white; (*tez*) pale **II.** *m, f* white man *m,* white woman *f*

blando, -a ['blan·do] *adj* **1.** (*objeto*) soft; **créditos** ~**s** ECON soft credits **2.** (*carácter*) mild; (*blandengue*) soft; (*cobarde*) cowardly; ~ **de corazón** soft-hearted

blanquear [blan·ke·'ar] **I.** *vi* to whiten **II.** *vt* **1.** (*poner blanco*) to whiten; (*pared*) to whitewash; (*tejido*) to bleach **2.** (*dinero*) to launder

blasfemar [blas·fe·'mar] *vi* **1.** REL to blaspheme **2.** (*maldecir*) ~ **de algo** to swear about sth

blasfemia [blas·'fe·mja] *f* **1.** REL blasphemy **2.** (*injuria*) insult

blasfemo, -a [blas·'fe·mo, -a] **I.** *adj* blasphemous **II.** *m, f* blasphemer

blasón [bla·'son] *m* **1.** (*de armas*) coat of arms **2.** (*honor*) honor; (*gloria*) glory

bledo ['ble·do] *m* goosefoot ▸ **(no) me importa un** ~ I couldn't care less

blindado, -a [blin·'da·do] *adj* MIL armor-plated; **puerta blindada** reinforced door

blindaje [blin·'da·xe] *m* (*armor*) plating

blindar [blin·'dar] *vt* to plate

bloc [blok] *m* <blocs> **1.** (*cuaderno*) notepad **2.** (*calendario*) calendar pad

blofear [blo·fe·'ar] *vi AmL* (*engañar*) to bluff

blofero, -a [blo·'fe·ro, -a] *m, f,* **blofista** [blo-**'fis·ta**] *mf AmC, PRico* braggart, bluffer

bloque ['blo·ke] *m* **1.** block; ~ **de viviendas** block of flats **2.** POL bloc ▸ **en** ~ en bloc

bloquear [blo·ke·'ar] **I.** *vt* **1.** (*el paso*) *t.* DEP to block; MIL to blockade **2.** (*aislar*) to cut off **3.** TÉC to jam **4.** FIN to freeze **5.** (*obstaculizar*) to obstruct **II.** *vr:* ~**se** (*cosa*) to jam; (*persona*) to have a mental block

bloqueo [blo·'keo] *m* **1.** (*de paso*) *t.* DEP blocking; MIL blockade; ~ **comercial** COM trade embargo **2.** TÉC (*de un mecanismo*) jamming **3.** (*de un proceso*) deadlock **4.** (*mental*) block

bluff [bluf] *m* <bluffs> *AmL* (*fanfarronería*) bluff

blusa ['blu·sa] *f* blouse

blusón [blu·'son] *m* smock

bluyin [blu·'jin] <bluyines> *m* blue jeans *pl*

boa ['boa] *f* boa

bobada [bo·'βa·da] *f* silly thing; **decir** ~**s** to talk nonsense

bobalicón, -ona [bo·βa·li·'kon, -·'ko·na] *adj, m, f v.* **bobo**

bobina [bo·'βi·na] *f* ELEC coil; (*de película*) reel

bobo, -a ['bo·βo] **I.** *adj* **1.** (*tonto*) silly **2.** (*simple*) simple **II.** *m, f* **1.** (*tonto*) fool **2.** (*simplón*) simpleton

boca ['bo·ka] *f* **1.** ANAT mouth; ~ **abajo** face down(ward); ~ **arriba** face up(ward); **estaba tumbada** ~ **abajo/arriba** she was lying on her stomach/on her back; **andar de** ~ **en** ~ to be the subject of gossip **2.** (*abertura*) opening; ~ **de metro** subway entrance; ~ **de riego** hydrant **3.** (*agujero*) hole; (*de cañón*) muzzle; (*de volcán*) mouth **4.** (*del vino*) taste **5.** MÚS mouthpiece **6.** COMPUT slot ▸ **echar por la** ~ **sapos y culebras** to rant and rave; **quedarse con la** ~ **abierta** to be dumbfounded; **a pedir de** ~ perfectly

bocacalle [bo·ka·'ka·je, -ʎe] *f* (*de una calle*) street entrance; (*calle secundaria*) side street

bocadillo [bo·ka·'di·jo, -ʎo] *m* **1.** (*sándwich*) sandwich **2.** (*refrigerio*) snack **3.** (*tira cómica*) balloon, bubble

bocadito [bo·ka·'di·to] *m* **1.** *Cuba* (*cigarrillo*) cigarette (*wrapped in tobacco leaf*) **2.** *Cuba, RíoPl:* coconut or sweet potato dessert

bocado [bo·'ka·do] *m* **1.** (*mordisco*) mouthful; ~ **de Adán** Adam's apple **2.** (*freno*) bit

bocajarro [bo·ka·'xa·rro] *adv* **a** ~ (*tirar*) point-blank; **decir algo a** ~ to say sth straight out

bocanada [bo·ka·'na·da] *f* puff; **echar** ~**s** *fig* to boast

bocatero, -a [bo·ka·'te·ro, -a] *m, f Ven, Hond, Cuba,* **bocaza(s)** [bo·'ka·sa(s), -'θa(s)] *mf* (*inv*) loudmouth; (*fanfarrón*) boaster

bocera [bo·'se·ra, bo·'θe-] *f* **1.** (*de comida*) crumbs *pl* on the mouth; (*de bebida*) smears *pl* on the mouth **2.** (*pupa*) cold sore

boceto [bo·'se·to, bo·'θe-] *m* sketch

bocha ['bo·tʃa] *f* **1.** (*bola*) bowl; (*juego de*) **las** ~**s** bowling **2.** *AmL, inf* (*cabeza*) nut

bochar [bo·'tʃar] *vt inf* **1.** *AmL* (*rechazar*) to reject **2.** *Arg* (*fracasar*) to fail

boche ['bo·tʃe] *m* **1.** *Arg* (*alemán*) German **2.** *CSur, inf* (*bronca*) telling-off **3.** *AmL, inf* (*repulsa*) snub

bochinche [bo·'tʃin·tʃe] *m AmL* piece of gossip

bochorno [bo·'tʃor·no] *m* **1.** METEO sultry weather **2.** (*sofocación*) stifling atmosphere **3.** (*vergüenza*) shame; **me da ~ que esté mirando** it embarrasses me that he/she is looking

bochornoso, -a [bo·tʃor·'no·so, -a] *adj* **1.** METEO sultry **2.** (*vergonzoso*) shameful

bocina [bo·'si·na, bo·'θi-] *f* **1.** (*de coche*) horn; **tocar la ~** to blow the horn **2.** MÚS trumpet **3.** (*megáfono*) megaphone

bocio ['bo·sjo, 'bo·θjo] *m* goiter

boda ['bo·da] *f* **1.** (*ceremonia*) wedding **2.** (*fiesta*) wedding reception; **noche de ~s** wedding night

bodega [bo·'de·ɣa] *f* **1.** (*habitación*) wine cellar **2.** (*tienda*) wine shop; (*taberna*) bar **3.** NÁUT (*en un puerto*) storeroom; (*en un buque*) hold

bodegón [bo·de·'ɣon] *m* **1.** (*taberna*) bar **2.** ARTE still life

bodeguero, -a [bo·de·'ɣe·ro, -a] *m, f* **1.** (*en una bodega*) owner of a wine cellar **2.** *Cuba* (*en una abacería*) grocer

bodoque [bo·'do·ke] *m* **1.** *Méx* (*chichón*) bump **2.** *Méx* (*pelota de papel*) lump; (*de lodo*) gob **3.** *Méx* (*cosa mal hecha*) badly made thing, sloppy job *inf*

bodrio ['bo·drjo] *m* **1.** *inf*(*cosa*) rubbish, trash; **esta película es un ~** this film is rubbish **2.** *inf* (*comida*) hotchpotch; **la comida fue un ~** the meal was terrible **3.** *AmL* (*confusión*) mess

body ['bo·di] *m* <bodies> body

BOE ['boe] *m abr de* **Boletín Oficial del Estado** ≈ The Congressional Record

bofe ['bo·fe] *m* lung; **echar los ~s** (**por algo**) *inf*to work like heck (for sth)

bofetada [bo·fe·'ta·da] *f* smack; **dar una ~ a alguien** to slap sb

bofia ['bo·fja] *f inf*cops *pl*

boga ['bo·ɣa] *f* **1.** NÁUT rowing **2.** (*moda*) vogue; **estar en ~** to be in vogue

bogavante [bo·ɣa·'βan·te] *m* lobster

bogotano, -a [bo·ɣo·'ta·no, -a] **I.** *adj* of/from Bogotá **II.** *m, f* native/inhabitant of Bogotá

Bohemia [bo·'e·mja] *f* Bohemia

bohemio, -a [bo·'e·mjo, -a] *adj, m, f* bohemian

bohío [bo·'i·o] *m AmL* rustic hut (*made of wood and branches, cane or straw*)

boicot <boicots> [boi·'ko(t)] *m* boycott

boicotear [boi·ko·te·'ar] *vt* to boycott

boicoteo [boi·ko·'teo] *m* boycott

boina ['boi·na] *f* beret

bol [bol] *m* **1.** (*tazón*) bowl **2.** (*red*) dragnet

bola ['bo·la] *f* **1.** (*cuerpo*) ball; **~ del mundo** globe; **~ de nieve** snowball **2.** (*canica*) marble; **jugar a las ~s** to play marbles **3.** *inf* (*mentira*) fib; (*rumor*) rumor **4.** *pl, vulg* (*testículos*) balls *pl*, nuts *pl*; **en ~s** *inf*naked, in the buff *inf* ▸ **no dar pie con ~** to be unable to do anything right; **ir a su ~** to go one's own way

bolado [bo·'la·do] *m AmL* (*asunto*) matter

bolazo [bo·'la·so, -θo] *m CSur, inf* **1.** (*disparate*) bunk *inf***2.** (*mentira*) bull *sl*

bolchevique [bol·tʃe·'βi·ke] *adj, mf* Bolshevik

boleadoras [bo·lea·'do·ras] *fpl CSur* bolas *pl*

bolear [bo·le·'ar] *vt* **1.** *CSur* (*cazar*) to hunt; (*atrapar*) to catch with a lasso **2.** *Méx* (*zapatos*) to polish **3.** (*alumno*) to fail

bolera [bo·'le·ra] *f* bowling alley

bolero [bo·'le·ro] *m* MÚS bolero

boleta [bo·'le·ta] *f AmL* **1.** (*entrada*) ticket **2.** (*documento*) permit **3.** (*para votar*) ballot (paper)

boletería [bo·le·te·'ri·a] *f AmL* (*taquilla*) ticket agency [*o* office]; TEAT box office

boletero, -a [bo·le·'te·ro, -a] *m, f AmL* (*taquillero*) ticket clerk

boletín [bo·le·'tin] *m* **1.** (*publicación*) bulletin; **~ informativo** news bulletin **2.** (*informe*) report; **~ de noticias** news report **3.** (*cédula*) form

boleto [bo·'le·to] *m* **1.** *AmL* (*entrada*) ticket **2.** (*de quiniela*) coupon **3.** *Arg* (*mentira*) lie

boliche [bo·'li·tʃe] *m* **1.** (*bola*) jack **2.** (*bochas*) bowls; (*bolos*) skittles **3.** *AmL* (*establecimiento*) grocery shop **4.** *Arg, inf* (*bar*) bar

bólido ['bo·li·do] *m* **1.** ASTR meteorite **2.** AUTO racing car

bolígrafo [bo·'li·ɣra·fo] *m* (ballpoint) pen, biro®

bolillo [bo·'li·jo, -ʎo] *m* **1.** (*de encajes*) bobbin; **trabajar al ~** to make lace by hand **2.** *Col* (*de tambor*) drumstick **3.** *Méx* (*panecillo*) bread roll

bolita [bo·'li·ta] *f* **1.** *CSur* (*canica*) marble **2.** *Chile* (*balota*) ballot

bolívar [bo·'li·βar] *m* bolivar

Bolivia [bo·'li·βja] *f* Bolivia

> **i** **Bolivia** is the fifth largest country in South America. Although **Sucre** is the capital, the seat of government is in **La Paz**, the country's largest city. In addition to Spanish, the official languages of Bolivia are **quechua** and **aimara** (also known as **aimará**). The official currency is the **boliviano**.

boliviano [bo·li·'βja·no] *m* (*moneda*) boliviano

boliviano, -a [bo·li·'βja·no, -a] *adj, m, f* Bolivian

bollería [bo·je·'ri·a, bo·ʎe-] *f* (*tienda*) baker's; (*bollos*) buns *pl*, baked goods *pl*

bollo ['bo·jo, -ʎo] *m* **1.** (*panecillo*) bun; (*pastelillo*) cake **2.** (*abolladura*) dent; (*chichón*) lump **3.** (*confusión*) mix-up **4.** *CSur, inf*(*puñetazo*) punch

bolo ['bo·lo] *m* **1.** DEP skittle; (**juego de**) **~s** skittles **2.** TEAT (*compañía*) traveling [*o* road] company; (*papel*) guest star; **el grupo hizo muchos ~s en verano** the company put on a lot of shows in the summer

bolsa ['bol·sa] *f* **1.** (*saco*) bag; ~ **de agua caliente** hot-water bottle **2.** (*bolso*) handbag, purse; ~ **de plástico** plastic bag; ~ **de la compra** shopping bag; ~**s de los ojos** bags under the eyes **3.** (*pliegue*) crease **4.** FIN stock exchange; ~ **de estudios** educational grant; ~ **de trabajo** employment bureau; ~ **negra** *AmL* black market; ~ **de valores** stock exchange **5.** *AmL* (*bolsillo*) pocket

bolsear [bol·se·'ar] *vt AmC, Méx, inf* ~ **a alguien** to pick sb's pocket; ~ **algo a alguien** to sponge sth off sb

bolsillo [bol·'si·jo, -ʎo] *m* **1.** (*en una prenda*) pocket; **edición de** ~ pocket edition **2.** (*monedero*) purse; **rascarse el** ~ *inf* to fork out

bolsista [bol·'sis·ta] *mf AmC* (*carterista*) pickpocket

bolso ['bol·so] *m* bag; (*pequeño*) handbag, purse; (*en una vela*) bulge; **hacer** ~ to belly out

boludo, -a [bo·'lu·do, -a] *inf* **I.** *adj Arg, Urug* (*imbécil*) dummy **II.** *m, f Arg, Urug* (*imbécil*) jerk

bomba ['bom·ba] **I.** *f t.* MIL bomb; ~ **de fragmentación** frag(mentation) bomb; ~ **de mano** hand grenade; ~ **de racimo** cluster bomb; ~ **de relojería** time bomb **2.** TÉC pump; ~ **neumática** air pump; **dar a la** ~ to pump **3.** *AmL* (*bola*) ball **4.** *AmL* (*pompa*) bubble **5.** *AmL, inf* (*borrachera*) **pegarse una** ~ to get drunk ▶ **a prueba de** ~**s** bomb-proof; **estar** ~ *inf* (*mujer*) to be gorgeous; (*comida*) to be great **II.** *adj inf* astounding; **éxito** ~ great success; **pasarlo** ~ to have a great time

bombacha [bom·'ba·tʃa] *f CSur* (*ropa interior*) panties *pl*

bombardear [bom·bar·de·'ar] *vt* **1.** MIL to bomb **2.** *inf* (*abrumar*) to overwhelm **3.** FÍS to bombard

bombardeo [bom·bar·'deo] *m* **1.** MIL bombing; ~ **aéreo** air raid **2.** FÍS bombardment

bombazo [bom·'ba·so, -θo] *m* bomb explosion; *inf* (*sensación*) bombshell

bombeador(a) [bom·bea·'dor, -'do·ra] *m(f) Arg* bomber

bombear [bom·be·'ar] *vt* **1.** (*un líquido*) to pump **2.** (*un balón*) to lob **3.** *CSur* (*explorar*) to survey

bombero [bom·'be·ro] *m* **1.** (*oficio*) fireman **2.** *pl* (*cuerpo*) fire brigade; **coche de** ~**s** fire engine

bombilla [bom·'bi·ja, -ʎa] *f* **1.** ELEC (light) bulb **2.** *AmS* (*caña*) drinking straw

bombín [bom·'bin] *m* bowler hat

bombita [bom·'bi·ta] *f Arg* (*bombilla*) bulb

bombo ['bom·bo] *m* **1.** MÚS (*tambor*) bass drum; (*en un sorteo*) drum **2.** (*elogio*) exaggerated praise ▶ **tener la cabeza hecha un** ~ to have a splitting headache; **anunciar algo a** ~ **y platillo** to announce sth with a lot of hype

bombón [bom·'bon] *m* **1.** (*golosina*) chocolate **2.** *inf* (*mujer*) **es un** ~ she's gorgeous

bombona [bom·'bo·na] *f* (*vasija*) carboy; (*de gas*) cylinder

bombonera [bom·bo·'ne·ra] *f* **1.** (*caja*) chocolate box **2.** *inf* (*vivienda*) cozy little place

bómper ['bom·per] *m AmC* (*parachoques*) bumper

bonachón, -ona [bo·na·'tʃon, -'tʃo·na] *adj* **1.** (*buenazo*) kindly **2.** (*crédulo*) naive **3.** (*cándido*) simple

bonaerense [bo·nae·'ren·se] **I.** *adj* of/from Buenos Aires province **II.** *mf* native/inhabitant of Buenos Aires province

bonanza [bo·'nan·sa, -θa] *f* **1.** NÁUT calm conditions *pl* **2.** (*prosperidad*) prosperity

bondad [bon·'dad] *f* **1.** (*de bueno*) goodness **2.** (*de amable*) kindness; **tenga la** ~ **de seguirme** be so kind as to follow me

bondadoso, -a [bon·da·'do·so, -a] *adj* good-natured, kind

bondi ['bon·di] *m Arg, inf* (*bus*) bus

bonete [bo·'ne·te] *m* cap

bonetería [bo·ne·te·'ri·a] *f Méx* (*mercería*) draper's shop

bóngalo ['bon·ga·lo] *m AmL* (*casa pequeña*) bungalow

bongo ['bon·go] *m AmL* (*canoa*) small canoe; (*balsa*) small raft

bonificación [bo·ni·fi·ka·'sjon, -'θjon] *f* **1.** (*gratificación*) bonus **2.** (*rebaja*) discount

bonificar <c→qu> [bo·ni·fi·'kar] *vt* **1.** (*abonar*) to improve **2.** (*gratificar*) to discount

bonito [bo·'ni·to] **I.** *m* ZOOL bonito **II.** *adv AmL* nicely

bonito, -a [bo·'ni·to, -a] *adj* pretty

bonitura [bo·ni·'tu·ra] *f AmL* (*hermosura*) beauty

bono ['bo·no] *m* voucher; COM bond

bonsái [bon·'sai] *m* <bonsais> bonsai

boquera [bo·'ke·ra] *f* cold sore

boquerón [bo·ke·'ron] *m* ZOOL (fresh) anchovy

boquete [bo·'ke·te] *m* opening; (*en pared*) hole

boquiabierto, -a [bo·kja·'βjer·to, -a] *adj* open-mouthed; **dejar a alguien** ~ *fig* to astonish sb

boquilla [bo·'ki·ja, -ʎa] *f* **1.** MÚS mouthpiece **2.** (*de cigarrillos*) cigarette holder; ~ **de filtro** filter tip **3.** TÉC nozzle ▶ **decir algo de** ~ to say sth without meaning it

borboll(e)ar [bor·βo·'jar, -'ʎar; bor·βo·je·'ar, -ʎe·'ar] *vi* to bubble

borbollón [bor·βo·'jon, -'ʎon] *m v.* **borbotón**

Borbón [bor·'βon] *m* HIST Bourbon

borbónico, -a [bor·'βo·ni·ko, -a] *adj* Bourbon

borbotón [bor·βo·'ton] *m* bubbling; **hablar a borbotones** to talk ten to the dozen; **salir a borbotones** (*agua*) to gush out

borda ['bor·da] *f* **1.** NÁUT (*borde*) gunwale; **motor fuera (de)** ~ outboard motor; **echar algo por la** ~ *t. fig* to throw sth overboard **2.** NÁUT (*vela*) mainsail

bordado [bor·'da·do] *m* embroidery

bordado, -a [bor·'da·do, -a] *adj inf* superbly executed

bordar [bor·'dar] *vt* to embroider; *inf* to do superbly

borde ['bor·de] I. *adj inf* (*persona*) difficult, hostile II. *m* (*de camino*) verge; (*de mesa*) edge; (*de río*) bank; (*de sombrero*) brim

bordear [bor·de·'ar] *vt* 1. (*ir por*) to skirt; (*en coche*) to drive along 2. (*estar*) to border on 3. (*aproximarse*) to verge on; **su comportamiento bordea la locura** his/her behavior borders on madness

bordillo [bor·'di·jo, -ʎo] *m* curb

bordo ['bor·do] *m* 1. NÁUT board; **ir a ~** to go on board 2. *Méx* (*presa*) dam

boreal [bo·re·'al] *adj* northern; **hemisferio ~** northern hemisphere

borgoña [bor·'ɣo·na] *m* burgundy

borona [bo·'ro·na] *f AmL* corn bread

borra ['bo·rra] *f* 1. (*relleno*) stuffing 2. (*pelusa*) fluff

borrachera [bo·rra·'tʃe·ra] *f* 1. (*ebriedad*) drunkenness; **agarrar una ~** to get drunk 2. (*juerga*) drinking binge

borracho, -a [bo·'rra·tʃo, -a] I. *adj* 1. *ser* (*alcohólico*) hard drinking; (*pastel*) soaked in liqueur 2. *estar* (*ebrio*) drunk; **estar ~ como una cuba** *inf* to be as drunk as a lord; **~ de algo** *fig* elated with sth II. *m, f* drunk

borrador [bo·rra·'dor] *m* 1. (*escrito*) rough draft 2. (*cuaderno*) scribbling pad 3. (*utensilio*) duster; (*esponja*) board rubber, board eraser

borrar [bo·'rrar] I. *vt* 1. (*con goma*) to rub out, to erase; (*con esponja*) to wipe off 2. (*tachar*) to cross out; COMPUT to delete 3. (*huellas*) to remove II. *vr*: **~se** to blur; **~se de algo** to resign from sth

borrasca [bo·'rras·ka] *f* 1. METEO squall; (*tempestad*) storm 2. (*orgía*) spree

borrascoso, -a [bo·rras·'ko·so, -a] *adj* 1. METEO stormy; **Cumbres Borrascosas** Wuthering Heights 2. (*desenfrenado*) tempestuous

borrego, -a [bo·'rre·ɣo, -a] *m, f* 1. (*cordero*) lamb 2. (*persona*) meek person 3. *AmL* (*noticia falsa*) hoax

borrico [bo·'rri·ko] *m* TÉC sawhorse

borrico, -a [bo·'rri·ko, -a] *m, f* donkey

borrón [bo·'rron] *m* 1. (*mancha*) stain 2. (*defecto*) blemish ▸ **hacer ~ y cuenta nueva** to wipe the slate clean

borroso, -a [bo·'rro·so, -a] *adj* (*escritura*) unclear; (*foto*) blurred

boruquear [bo·ru·ke·'ar] *vt Méx* to be rowdy

boscoso, -a [bos·'ko·so, -a] *adj* wooded

Bósforo ['bos·fo·ro] *m* Bosporus

bosnio, -a ['bos·njo, -a] *adj, m, f* Bosnian

bosorola [bo·so·'ro·la] *f CRi, Méx* sediment

bosque ['bos·ke] *m* wood; **~ de coníferas** coniferous woodland; **~ frondoso** broad-leaved woodland; **~ pluvial** rainforest

bosquejar [bos·ke·'xar] *vt* to sketch

bosquejo [bos·'ke·xo] *m* sketch

bostezar <z→c> [bos·te·'sar, -'θar] *vi* to yawn

bostezo [bos·'te·so, -θo] *m* yawn

bota ['bo·ta] I. *adj Méx* 1. (*torpe*) dim 2. (*borracho*) drunk II. *f* 1. (*calzado*) boot; **estar con las ~s puestas** *fig* to be ready to go; **ponerse las ~s** *inf* to strike it rich 2. (*cuba*) large barrel

botado, -a [bo·'ta·do, -a] I. *adj* 1. *AmC* (*malgastador*) spendthrift 2. *Ecua* (*resignado*) resigned; (*resuelto*) resolute 3. *Guat* (*tímido*) shy 4. *Méx* (*barato*) dirt cheap II. *m, f Méx* foundling

botador(a) [bo·ta·'dor] *adj AmL* spendthrift

botánica [bo·'ta·ni·ka] *f* botany

botánico, -a [bo·'ta·ni·ko, -a] I. *adj* botanical II. *m, f* botanist

botar [bo·'tar] I. *vi* (*pelota*) to bounce; (*persona*) to jump; (*caballo*) to rear (up) ▸ **estar (uno) que bota** to be hopping mad II. *vt* 1. (*lanzar*) to throw; (*pelota*) to bounce 2. NÁUT (*barco*) to launch 3. *AmL* (*tirar*) to throw away 4. *AmL* (*expulsar*) to fire; **lo ~on del colegio** he was expelled from school 5. *AmL* (*derrochar*) to squander 6. *AmL* (*extraviar*) to lose

botarate [bo·ta·'ra·te] *m* 1. (*informal*) madcap 2. *AmL* (*derrochador*) spendthrift

bote ['bo·te] *m* 1. (*golpe*) blow 2. (*salto*) jump; **pegar un ~** to jump 3. (*de pelota*) bounce; **la pelota dio cuatro ~s** the ball bounced four times 4. (*vasija*) jar; **~ de cuestación** collecting tin 5. (*en la lotería*) jackpot 6. NÁUT boat; **~ salvavidas** lifeboat ▸ **a ~ pronto** (*adj*) sudden; (*adv*) suddenly; **chupar del ~** *inf* to feather one's nest; **darse el ~** *inf* to beat it; **estar de ~ en ~** to be packed; **la tiene en el ~** *inf* he has her in his pocket

botella [bo·'te·ja, -ʎa] *f* bottle; **~ de cerveza** bottle of beer; **cerveza de ~** bottled beer

botica [bo·'ti·ka] *f* pharmacy, drugstore

botija [bo·'ti·xa] *f* 1. (*vasija*) earthenware jug 2. *AmL* (*tesoro*) buried treasure

botín [bo·'tin] *m* 1. (*calzado*) high shoe 2. MIL booty

botiquín [bo·ti·'kin] *m* medicine chest; (*de emergencia*) first-aid kit

botón [bo·'ton] *m* 1. (*en vestidos*) button 2. ELEC knob; **~ de muestra** sample; *fig* illustration; **~ de opciones** COMPUT option button 3. MÚS key 4. BIO bud; **~ de oro** buttercup 5. *CSur, pey* (*policía*) cop

botones [bo·'to·nes] *m inv* errand boy; (*de hotel*) bellboy

boutique [bu·'tik] *f* boutique

bóveda ['bo·βe·da] *f* ARQUIT vault; **~ celeste** firmament

bovino, -a [bo·'βi·no, -a] *adj* bovine

box [boks] *m* 1. (*para caballos*) stall 2. *AmL* (*boxeo*) boxing 3. *AmC* (*postal*) mailbox 4. *pl* AUTO pits *pl*; **entrar en ~es** to make a pit-stop

boxeador(a) [bok·sea·'dor, -'do·ra] *m(f)* boxer

boxear [bok·se·'ar] *vi* to box

boxeo [bok·'seo] *m* boxing
boya ['bo·ja] *f* buoy; (*en una red*) float
boyante [bo·'jan·te] *adj* prosperous; **el nego-cio va** ~ business is booming
boyero [bo·'je·ro] *m Col* goad
boy scout <boy scouts> ['boi es·'kaut] *mf* boy scout
bozal [bo·'sal, -'θal] *m* **1.** (*de perro*) muzzle **2.** *AmL* (*cabestro*) halter; (*cuerda*) headstall
bozo ['bo·so, -θo] *m* down
bracear [bra·se·'ar, bra·θe·] *vi* **1.** (*los brazos*) to swing one's arms **2.** (*nadar*) to swim
bracero [bra·'se·ro, -'θe·ro] *m AmL* farmhand; (*peón*) laborer
braga ['bra·ya] *f* **1.** (*de bebé*) diaper **2.** *pl* (*de mujer*) panties *pl* ▶ **dejar** a alguien en ~s *inf* to leave sb penniless; **estar en** ~s *inf* to be broke
bragapañal [bra·ya·pa·'ɲal] *m* disposable diaper
bragueta [bra·'ye·ta] *f* fly
braille ['brai·le] *m* Braille
bramar [bra·'mar] *vi* (*animal*) to roar; (*persona*) to bluster; (*viento*) to howl; **está que brama** he/she is furious
bramido [bra·'mi·do] *m* (*animales*) roar; (*persona*) blustering; (*viento*) howling
brandy ['bran·di] *m* brandy
branquia ['bran·kja] *f* gill
brasa ['bra·sa] *f* ember; **a la** ~ grilled
brasero [bra·'se·ro] *m* **1.** (*estufa*) brazier **2.** *AmL* (*fuego*) fireplace; (*hogar*) hearth
Brasil [bra·'sil] *m* (**el**) ~ Brazil
brasileño, -a [bra·si·'le·ɲo, -a] *adj, m, f* Brazilian
brava ['bra·βa] *f Cuba* (*golpe*) punch; **dar una** ~ to intimidate; **a la** ~, **por las** ~s *Arg, Cuba, Méx, PRico* by force
bravío [bra·'βi·o] *m* fierceness
bravío, -a [bra·'βi·o, -a] *adj* **1.** (*animal*) wild; (*sin domar*) untamed **2.** (*persona*) impetuous
bravo, -a ['bra·βo, -a] *adj* **1.** (*valiente*) brave **2.** (*salvaje*) wild; (*mar*) stormy **3.** *AmL* (*picante*) hot
bravucón, -ona [bra·βu·'kon, -·'ko·na] **I.** *adj* boastful **II.** *m, f* braggart
bravura [bra·'βu·ra] *f* (*de animales*) ferocity; (*de personas*) bravery
brazada [bra·'θa·da, -'θa·da] *f* stroke
brazalete [bra·sa·'le·te, bra·θa-] *m* (*pulsera*) bracelet; (*banda*) armband
brazo ['bra·so, -θo] *m* **1.** ANAT arm; ~ **derecho** *fig* right-hand man; **cruzarse de** ~s to fold one's arms; *fig* to stand by and do nothing; **dar el** ~ **a torcer** to give in; **ir cogidos del** ~ to walk arm-in-arm; **recibir a alguien con los** ~s **abiertos** to welcome sb with open arms **2.** (*de una silla*) arm **3.** GEO (*del río*) branch; (*del mar*) sound **4.** (*poder*) power
brea ['brea] *f* tar
brebaje [bre·'βa·xe] *m* (*bebida*) brew; (*medicina*) potion

brecha ['bre·tʃa] *f* **1.** MIL breach **2.** (*abertura*) opening; (*en una pared*) gap **3.** (*herida*) gash ▶ **estar** en la ~ to be in the thick of things
brécol(es) ['bre·kol, -·ko·l(es)] *m(pl)* broccoli
bregar <g→gu> [bre·'yar] *vi* **1.** (*reñir*) to quarrel **2.** (*luchar*) to struggle **3.** (*trabajar*) to slave away
Bretaña [bre·'taɲa] *f* Brittany; **Gran** ~ Great Britain
brete ['bre·te] *m* fetters *pl*; **estar en un** ~ to be in a jam; **poner en un** ~ to put on the spot
breva ['bre·βa] *f* **1.** (*higo*) early fig **2.** (*cigarro*) flat cigar **3.** *AmL* (*tabaco*) chewing tobacco; **¡no caerá esa** ~**!** *inf* no such luck!
breve ['bre·βe] **I.** *adj* (*de duración*) brief; (*de extensión*) short; **en** ~ shortly **II.** *m* PREN short news item
brevedad [bre·βe·'dad] *f* (*duración*) brevity; (*extensión*) shortness; **a la mayor** ~ **posible** as soon as possible
breviario [bre·'βja·rjo] *m* prayer book
briago, -a ['brja·yo, -a] *adj Méx, inf* drunk
bribón, -ona [bri·'βon, -·'bo·na] *adj* **1.** (*pícaro*) rascally **2.** (*vago*) idle
bricolaje [bri·ko·'la·xe] *m* do-it-yourself
brida [bri·'da] *f* **1.** (*de caballo*) bridle **2.** TÉC flange **3.** *pl* MED adhesion
brigada¹ [bri·'ya·da] *f* **1.** MIL brigade **2.** (*de obreros*) gang; (*de policía*) squad
brigada² [bri·'ya·da] *m* MIL sergeant-major
brillante [bri·'jan·te, -'ʎan·te] **I.** *m* diamond **II.** *adj* **1.** (*luz*) bright; (*joya*) sparkling **2.** (*compañía*) brilliant
brillantez [bri·jan·'tes, bri·ʎan·'teθ] *f t. fig* brilliance
brillantina [bri·jan·'ti·na, bri·ʎan-] *f* brilliantine, hair cream
brillar [bri·'jar, -'ʎar] *vi* to shine; ~ **por su ausencia** *irón* to be conspicuous by one's absence
brillo ['bri·jo, -ʎo] *m* **1.** (*cualidad*) shine; (*reflejo*) glow; **dar** ~ **a algo** to polish sth **2.** (*gloria*) splendor
brincar <c→qu> [brin·'kar] *vi* to hop; (*hacia arriba*) to jump; ~ **de alegría** *fig* to jump for joy; ~ **de rabia** *fig* to dance with rage
brinco ['brin·ko] *m* hop; **dar** ~s to hop; **de un** ~ in one bound
brindar [brin·'dar] **I.** *vi* to drink a toast; ~ **por alguien** to drink to sb **II.** *vt* to offer; TAUR to dedicate **III.** *vr* ~**se a hacer algo** to offer to do sth
brindis ['brin·dis] *m inv* toast; **echar un** ~ to drink a toast
brío ['bri·o] *m* **1.** (*energía*) spirit **2.** (*pujanza*) drive
brioso, -a [bri·'o·so, -a] *adj* **1.** (*con energía*) spirited **2.** (*con pujanza*) vigorous
brisa ['bri·sa] *f* breeze
británico, -a [bri·'ta·ni·ko, -a] **I.** *adj* British; **inglés** ~ British English **II.** *m, f* Briton
brit-pop [brit·'pop] *m* MÚS Brit-pop
brizna ['bris·na, 'briθ-] *f* **1.** (*hebra*) strand; BOT

blade 2.(*porción*) scrap; **no tiene ni una ~ de humor** he/she has no sense of humor at all 3. *AmL* (*llovizna*) drizzle

brocado [bro·'ka·do] *m* brocade

brocha ['bro·tʃa] *f* brush; (*de afeitar*) shaving brush; **de ~ gorda** crudely painted; *fig* slap-dash; **pintor de ~ gorda** house painter

broche ['bro·tʃe] *m* 1.(*en la ropa*) clasp; (*de adorno*) brooch; **~ de oro** *fig* finishing touch 2. *AmL* (*sujetapapeles*) paper clip 3. *pl, AmL* (*gemelos*) cufflinks *pl*

brocheta [bro·'tʃe·ta] *f* skewer

broma ['bro·ma] *f* 1.(*gracia*) fun, kidding 2.(*tontería*) joke; **~ pesada** practical joke; **decir algo en ~** to be kidding; **gastar ~s a alguien** to play jokes on sb; **~s aparte...** joking apart...; **estoy de ~** I'm not serious; **no estoy para ~s** I'm in no mood for jokes; **no hay que andar con ~s con él** he doesn't put up with any nonsense; **¡ni en ~!** no way!

bromear [bro·me·'ar] *vi* to joke, to kid; **¿bromeas?** are you kidding?

bromista [bro·'mis·ta] I. *adj* fond of jokes II. *mf* joker

bromo ['bro·mo] *m* bromine

bronca ['bron·ka] *f* 1.(*riña*) argument 2.(*reprimenda*) earful 3.(*tumulto*) uproar 4. *AmL* (*enfado*) anger; **me da ~** it makes me mad

bronce ['bron·se, -θe] *m* bronze

bronceado [bron·se·'a·do, bron·θe-] *m* (*de un objeto*) bronze finish; (*de la piel*) tan

bronceado, -a [bron·se·'a·do, -a; bron·θe-] *adj* (*objeto*) bronze; (*piel*) tanned

bronceador [bron·sea·'dor, bron·θe-] *m* sun-tan lotion

broncear [bron·se·'ar, bron·θe-] I. *vt* (*un objeto*) to bronze; (*la piel*) to tan II. *vr:* **~se** to get a (sun)tan

bronco, -a ['bron·ko, -a] *adj* 1.(*voz*) gruff 2.(*genio*) surly 3. *AmL* (*caballo*) untamed

bronquio ['bron·kjo] *m* ANAT bronchial tube

bronquitis [bron·'ki·tis] *f inv* MED bronchitis

broquel [bro·'kel] *m t. fig* shield

broqueta [bro·'ke·ta] *f* skewer

brotar [bro·'tar] *vi* 1. BOT to sprout; (*semilla*) to germinate 2.(*agua*) to flow 3.(*enfermedad*) to break out

brote ['bro·te] *m* 1. BOT shoot; **~s de soja** bean sprouts 2.(*erupción*) outbreak

bruces ['bru·ses, 'bru·θes] *adv* **caer de ~** to fall headlong; **darse de ~ con alguien** (*chocar*) to crash into sb; (*hallar casualmente*) to run into sb

bruja ['bru·xa] *f* witch

Brujas ['bru·xas] *f* Bruges

brujería [bru·xe·'ri·a] *f* witchcraft

brujo ['bru·xo] *m* 1.(*hechicero*) wizard 2. *AmL* (*curandero*) medicine man

brújula [bru·xu·la] *f* compass; **perder la ~** *fig* to lose one's bearings

brulote [bru·'lo·te] *m AmS* (*taco*) swear word

bruma ['bru·ma] *f* mist

brumoso, -a [bru·'mo·so, -a] *adj* misty

bruñir <3. *pret:* bruñó> [bru·'ɲir] *vt* 1.(*dar brillo*) to polish 2. *AmL* (*molestar*) to pester

brusco, -a ['brus·ko, -a] *adj* 1.(*repentino*) sudden; **un ~ aumento** a sharp increase 2.(*persona*) abrupt

Bruselas [bru·'se·las] *f* Brussels

brutal [bru·'tal] *adj* 1.(*violento*) brutal 2. *inf* (*enorme*) huge 3. *inf* (*estupendo*) tremendous

brutalidad [bru·ta·li·'dad] *f* 1.(*calidad*) brutality 2.(*acción*) brutal act 3.(*cantidad*) huge amount

bruto ['bru·to] *adj* 1.(*tosco*) uncut; **diamante en ~** rough diamond 2.(*peso*) gross

bruto, -a ['bru·to, -a] I. *adj* 1.(*brutal*) brutal 2.(*rudo*) uncouth II. *m, f* brute

buceador(a) [bu·sea·'dor, -'do·ra; bu·θea-] *m(f)* diver

bucear [bu·se·'ar, bu·θe-] *vi* to dive; **~ en algo** *fig* to delve into sth

buceo [bu·'seo, -'θeo] *m* diving

buche ['bu·tʃe] *m* 1.(*en las aves*) crop 2. *inf* (*estómago*) belly; **guardar algo en el ~** to keep sth hidden

bucle ['bu·kle] *m* 1.(*de cabello*) curl 2.(*onda*) *t.* COMPUT loop

bucólico, -a [bu·'ko·li·ko, -a] *adj* LIT bucolic

buda ['bu·da] *m* Buddha

budín [bu·'din] *m* pudding

budismo [bu·'dis·mo] *m* Buddhism

budista [bu·'dis·ta] *adj, mf* Buddhist

buen [bwen] *adj v.* **bueno**

buenamente [bwe·na·'men·te] *adv* 1.(*fácilmente*) easily 2.(*voluntariamente*) voluntarily

buenaventura [bwe·na·βen·'tu·ra] *f* 1.(*suerte*) good luck 2.(*adivinación*) fortune; **echar la ~ a alguien** to tell sb's fortune

buenazo, -a [bwe·'na·so, -a; -θo, -a] *m, f* good-natured person

bueno ['bwe·no] *interj* OK

bueno, -a ['bwe·no, -a] *adj* <mejor *o* más bueno, el mejor *o* bonísimo *o* buenísimo> *ante substantivo masc. sing.:* buen 1.(*calidad*) good; (*tiempo*) fine; (*constitución*) sound; (*decisión*) right; **~s días** good morning; **buenas tardes/noches** good afternoon/evening; **buen viaje** have a good journey; **hace ~** it's nice weather; **dar algo por ~** to accept sth; **estar de buenas** to be in a good mood; **lo que tiene de ~ es que...** the good thing about it is that...; **por las buenas o por las malas** by fair means or foul 2.(*apropiado*) suitable 3.(*honesto*) honest; (*bondadoso*) kindly; (*niño*) well-behaved; **es buena gente** he/she is a nice person 4.(*sano*) healthy 5. *inf* (*atractivo*) attractive; **está buenísima** she's hot stuff 6.(*bonito*) fine; **¡buena la has hecho!** *irón* you've done it now!; **¡estaría ~!** *fig* I should think not!

buey [bwei] *m* 1. ZOOL ox 2. *AmC* (*cornudo*) cuckold

búfalo ['bu·fa·lo] *m* buffalo

bufanda [bu·'fan·da] *f* scarf

bufar [bu·'far] *vi* **1.**(*resoplar*) to snort; **está que bufa** he/she is really furious **2.** *AmL* (*oler mal*) to stink

bufeo [bu·'feo] *m Ant, Hond, Méx* (*delfín*) dolphin; (*atún*) tuna

bufete [bu·'fe·te] *m* **1.**(*escritorio*) desk **2.**(*de abogado*) lawyer's office; **abrir ~** to set up in practice **3.**(*aparador*) sideboard

bufido [bu·'fi·do] *m* **1.**(*resoplido*) snort **2.**(*exabrupto*) sharp remark

bufón, -ona [bu·'fon, -·'fo·na] *m, f* **1.**(*bromista*) joker **2.** TEAT buffoon

buganvilla [bu·yam·'bi·ja, -ʎa] *f* bougainvillea

buhardilla [bwar·'di·ja, -ʎa] *f* **1.**(*ventana*) dormer window **2.**(*vivienda*) garret

búho ['buo] *m* ZOOL owl

buitre ['bwi·tre] *m* **1.** ZOOL vulture, buzzard **2.** *inf*(*persona*) sponger

buitrear [bwi·tre·'ar] *vi* **1.** *AmL* (*cazar*) to kill **2.** *CSur*(*vomitar*) to throw up

bujía [bu·'xi·a] *f* **1.**(*vela*) candle **2.** AUTO spark plug

bula ['bu·la] *f* (papal) bull

bulbo ['bul·βo] *m* bulb

bule ['bu·le] *m Méx* BOT gourd

bulevar [bu·le·'βar] *m* boulevard

Bulgaria [bul·'ya·rja] *f* Bulgaria

búlgaro, -a ['bul·ya·ro] *adj, m, f* Bulgarian

bulimia [bu·'li·mja] *f* MED bulimia

bulla ['bu·ja, -ʎa] *f* **1.**(*ruido*) racket **2.**(*aglomeración*) mob **3.** *AmL* (*pelea*) brawl

bullicio [bu·'jis·jo, -ʎi·θjo] *m* uproar

bullicioso, -a [bu·ji·'sjo·so, -a; bu·ʎi·'θjo-] *adj* noisy

bullir <3. *pret:* bulló> [bu·'jir, -'ʎir] *vi* **1.**(*hervir*) to boil; (*borbotar*) to bubble; **le bulle la sangre (en las venas)** *fig* he/she is a bundle of energy **2.**(*moverse*) to stir **3.**(*pulular*) to swarm, to budge

bulo [bu·'lo] *m* false rumor

bulto ['bul·to] *m* **1.**(*tamaño*) size; **a ~** roughly; **de ~** bulky; **escurrir el ~** *inf* to pass the buck **2.**(*importancia*) importance; **un error de ~** a major error **3.**(*objeto*) mass **4.**(*paquete*) piece of luggage **5.** MED swelling

búnker ['bun·ker] *m* MIL bunker

buñuelo [bu·'ɲwe·lo] *m* doughnut, donut; *inf* botched job

buque ['bu·ke] *m* (*barco*) ship; **~ de pasajeros** passenger ship; **~ de carga** freighter; **~ de guerra** warship; **~ insignia** flagship; **~ de vapor** steamer

buqué [bu·'ke] *m* (*de vino*) bouquet

buraco [bu·'ra·ko] *m Arg, Par, Urug* hole

burata [bu·'ra·ta] *f Ven, inf* cash, dough *inf*

burbuja [bur·'βu·xa] *f* bubble

burbujear [bur·βu·xe·'ar] *vi* to bubble

burdel [bur·'del] *m* brothel

Burdeos [bur·'deos] *m* Bordeaux

burdo, -a ['bur·do, -a] *adj* coarse; (*excusa*) clumsy

bureo [bu·'reo] *m* amusement; **ir de ~** to have a good time

burgués, -esa [bur·'yes, -·'ye·sa] I. *adj t. pey* bourgeois, middle-class II. *m, f t. pey* bourgeois *m*, bourgeoise *f*

burguesía [bur·ye·'si·a] *f* bourgeoisie

burla ['bur·la] *f* **1.**(*mofa*) taunt; **hacer ~ de alguien** to make fun of sb **2.**(*engaño*) hoax

burlador(a) [bur·la·'dor, -·'do·ra] *m(f)* seducer

burlar [bur·'lar] I. *vt* to cheat II. *vr:* **~se** to joke

burlón, -ona [bur·'lon, -·'lo·na] I. *adj* mocking II. *m, f* **1.**(*mofador*) mocker **2.**(*guasón*) joker

buró [bu·'ro] *m* **1.**(*escritorio*) bureau **2.** *AmL* (*mesilla*) bedside table

burocracia [bu·ro·'kra·sja, -θja] *f* bureaucracy

burócrata [bu·'ro·kra·ta] *mf* bureaucrat

burocrático, -a [bu·ro·'kra·ti·ko, -a] *adj* bureaucratic

burocratizar <z→c> [bu·ro·kra·ti·'sar, -'θar] *vt* to bureaucratize

burrada [bu·'rra·da] *f inf* silly thing; **decir ~s** to talk nonsense

burro ['bu·rro] *m* **1.** *AmC* (*escalera*) step ladder **2.** *AmC* (*columpio*) swing

burro, -a ['bu·rro, -a] I. *adj* **1.**(*tonto*) stupid **2.**(*obstinado*) obstinate II. *m, f* **1.** ZOOL donkey; **~ de carga** *t. fig* beast of burden **2.**(*trabajador*) hard worker ▶ **esto es un ~ con dos albardas** that's saying the same thing twice over; **apearse del ~** to recognize one's mistake; **no ver tres en un ~** to be as blind as a bat

bursátil [bur·'sa·til] *adj* stock exchange

bus [bus] *m t.* COMPUT bus

busaca [bu·'sa·ka] *f* **1.** *Col, Ven* (*bolsa*) bag **2.** *Ven* (*cartera*) satchel

busca¹ ['bus·ka] *f* search; **en ~ de alguien** in search of sb

busca² ['bus·ka] *m* beeper

buscapleitos [bus·ka·'plei·tos] *mf inv, AmL* troublemaker

buscar <c→qu> [bus·'kar] *vi, vt* to look for; **enviar a alguien a ~ algo** to send sb to fetch sth; **ir a ~ algo** to go and look for sth; **me viene a ~ a las 7** he/she is picking me up at 7; **él se lo ha buscado** he brought it on himself; **~ tres pies al gato** to complicate matters; **'se busca'** 'wanted'

buscatesoros [bus·ka·te·'so·ros] *mf inv* treasure-seeker

buscavidas [bus·ka·'βi·das] *mf inv* go-getter

buscona [bus·'ko·na] *f* whore

buseta [bu·'se·ta] *f Col, Ven* (*pequeño autobús*) minibus

búsqueda ['bus·ke·da] *f t.* COMPUT search

busto ['bus·to] *m* bust

butaca [bu·'ta·ka] *f* armchair; (*de cine*) seat

butano [bu·'ta·no] I. *adj* orange II. *m* **1.** QUÍM butane (gas) **2.**(*color*) orange

buzo ['bu·so, -θo] *m* diver

buzón [bu·'son, -'θon] *m* (*de correos*) mailbox; **~ (electrónico)** COMPUT mailbox

byte [bait] *m* COMPUT byte; **~ de control** control byte

C

C, c [se, θe] *f* C, c; **~ de Carmen** C as in Charlie

C/ ['ka·je, -ʎe] *abr de* **calle** St

cabal [ka·'βal] *adj* **1.** (*completo*) complete **2.** (*persona*) honest; **no estar en sus ~es** *inf* not to be in one's right mind

cabalgar <g→gu> [ka·βal·'ɣar] **I.** *vi* to ride horseback **II.** *vt* to ride

cabalgata [ka·βal·'ɣa·ta] *f* procession, cavalcade

caballa [ka·'βa·ja, -ʎa] *f* mackerel

caballerango [ka·βa·je·'ran·go, ka·βa·ʎe-] *m Méx* groom

caballeresco, -a [ka·βa·je·'res·ko, -a; ka·βa·ʎe-] *adj* **1.** HIST knightly **2.** (*galante*) chivalrous

caballería [ka·βa·je·'ri·a, -ʎe·'ri·a] *f* **1.** (*montura*) mount **2.** MIL cavalry

caballero [ka·βa·'je·ro, -'ʎe·ro] *m* **1.** (*galán*) gentleman **2.** HIST knight

caballerosidad [ka·βa·je·ro·si·'dad, ka·βa·ʎe-] *f* gentlemanliness

caballete [ka·βa·'je·te, -'ʎe·te] *m* **1.** (*de mesa*) trestle **2.** (*de cuadro*) easel

caballo [ka·'βa·jo, -ʎo] *m* **1.** (*animal*) horse; **a ~ on horseback**; **ir a ~** to ride; **~ de batalla** *fig* hobby horse **2.** (*ajedrez*) knight **3.** DEP **~ (de saltos)** jumper **4.** AUTO horsepower **5.** (*naipes*) queen **6.** *inf* (*heroína*) smack

cabaña [ka·'βa·ɲa] *f* cabin

cabecear [ka·βe·se·'ar, -θe·'ar] **I.** *vi* **1.** (*mover la cabeza*) to shake one's head **2.** (*dormitar*) to nod off **II.** *vt* DEP to head

cabecera [ka·βe·'se·ra, -'θe·ra] *f* **1.** (*de cama*) head **2.** (*del periódico*) masthead; **médico de ~** general practitioner

cabecilla [ka·βe·'si·ja, -'θi·ʎa] *mf* ringleader

cabellera [ka·βe·'je·ra, -'ʎe·ra] *f* **1.** (*de la cabeza*) mane **2.** ASTR tail (of a comet)

cabello [ka·'βe·jo, -ʎo] *m* hair; **se le pusieron los ~s de punta** his/her hair stood on end; **traído por los ~s** far-fetched

caber [ka·'βer] *irr vi* **1.** (*tener espacio*) **~ en algo** to fit in [*o* into] sth; **no ~ en sí de...** to be beside oneself with...; **esta falda no me cabe** this skirt doesn't fit me **2.** (*ser posible*) to be possible

cabestrillo [ka·βes·'tri·jo, -ʎo] *m* MED sling

cabeza¹ [ka·'βe·sa, -θa] *f* **1.** *t.* ANAT, TÉC head; **~ de ajo** bulb of garlic; **~ atómica** atomic warhead; **~ de lectura** COMPUT read head; **~ de partido** headquarters; **~ abajo** upside down; **~ arriba** upright; **de ~** headfirst; **por ~** a head; **abrirse la ~** to split one's head open; **asentir con la ~** to nod (one's head); **negar con la ~** to shake one's head; **se me va la ~** I feel dizzy; **de la ~ a los pies** from head to toe; **estar mal de la ~** *inf* to be out of one's mind; **jugarse la ~** to risk one's life; **levantar ~** to pull through; **métetelo en la ~** get it into your head; **algo**

se le pasa a alguien por la ~ sth crosses sb's mind; **quitarse algo de la ~** to put sth out of one's mind; **sentar (la) ~** to settle down; **tener la ~ dura** to be stubborn; **traer a alguien de ~** to drive sb crazy; **este chico tiene ~** this boy is clever; **tener ~ para los negocios** to be business-minded **2.** (*extremo*) top; **ir en ~** DEP to be in the lead **3.** AGR (*res*) head

cabeza² [ka·'βe·sa, -θa] *m* head; **~ de familia** head of the family; **~ rapada** skinhead

cabezada [ka·βe·'sa·da, -'θa·da] *f* blow on the head; **dar** [*o* **echar**] **una ~** *inf* to take a nap

cabezazo [ka·βe·'sa·so, -θa·θo] *m* blow on the head; DEP header; **darse un ~** to bang one's head

cabezón, -ona [ka·βe·'son, -'θon] *adj* **1.** (*de cabeza grande*) with a big head **2.** *inf* (*obstinado*) pigheaded

cabida [ka·'βi·da] *f* space

cabina [ka·'βi·na] *f* cabin; **~ de control** TÉC control room; **~ del piloto** cockpit; **~ de proyección** projection room; **~ de teléfonos** phone booth

cabinera [ka·βi·'ne·ra] *f Col* air hostess, stewardess

cabizbajo, -a [ka·βis·'βa·xo, -a; ka·βiθ-] *adj* dejected

cable ['ka·βle] *m t.* ELEC (*telegrama*) cable; **se le cruzaron los ~s** *inf* he/she lost control; **echar un ~ a alguien** *inf* to help sb out

cabo ['ka·βo] *m* **1.** (*extremo*) end; **al fin y al ~** in the end; **de ~ a rabo** from beginning to end; **llevar a ~** to carry out; **no dejar ningún ~ suelto** to leave no loose ends **2.** GEO cape; **Ciudad del Cabo** Cape Town **3.** MIL corporal **4.** NÁUT rope ► **al ~ de** after

cabotaje [ka·βo·'ta·xe] *m* coastal shipping

cabra ['ka·βra] *f* goat; **~ montés** wild goat; **estar como una ~** *inf* to be off one's head

cabrear [ka·βre·'ar] **I.** *vt inf* to infuriate; **estar cabreado** to be furious **II.** *vr:* **~se** *inf* to get angry

cabriola [ka·'βrjo·la] *f* caper; **hacer ~s** to caper about

cabro ['ka·βro] *m AmS* male goat, billy goat *inf*

cabrón [ka·'βron] *m* billy goat

cabrón, -ona [ka·'βron, -·'βro·na] *m, f vulg* bastard, bugger

cábula ['ka·βu·la] *f* **1.** *Arg, Par* (*amuleto*) amulet **2.** *Arg* (*cábala*) cabal **3.** *Chile, Méx, Perú, PRico* (*ardid*) ruse

caca ['ka·ka] *f inf* **1.** (*excremento*) poop **2.** (*chapuza*) rubbish

cacahuate [ka·ka·'wa·te] *m Méx* (*cacahuete*) peanut

cacahuete [ka·ka·'we·te] *m* peanut

cacalote [ka·ka·'lo·te] *m AmC* **1.** CULIN popcorn **2.** *inf* (*disparate*) silly thing

cacao [ka·'kao] *m* **1.** (*planta*) cacao **2.** *inf* (*jaleo*) to-do; **pedir ~** *AmL* to give in

---

i The **Moctezuma**, Aztec rulers in Mexico, drank **cocoatl** (a bitter beverage made of cocoa beans) from golden mugs. **Cacao** (cocoa) was considered a food of the gods and was worshipped as a holy drink. Cocoa beans even served as currency. As a result of the conquest, cocoa was introduced to the New World, where the first chocolate factories were built in the 17th century.

cacarear [ka·ka·re·'ar] I. *vi* **1.** (*gallinas*) to cackle **2.** *inf* (*presumir*) to brag II. *vt inf* to brag about

cacarizo, -a [ka·ka·'ri·so, -a; -'ri·θo, -a] *adj Méx* pitted

cacastle [ka·'kas·tle] *m AmC, Méx* **1.** (*esqueleto*) skeleton **2.** (*armazón*) pack frame

cacatúa [ka·ka·'tua] *f* **1.** ZOOL cockatoo **2.** *inf* (*mujer*) old bag

cacería [ka·se·'ri·a, ka·θe-] *f* **1.** (*partida*) hunting **2.** (*piezas*) bag

cacerola [ka·se·'ro·la, ka·θe-] *f* saucepan

cachafaz [ka·tʃa·'fas, -'faθ] *adj AmS* roguish

cachar [ka·'tʃar] *vt* **1.** *AmC, Col, Chile* (*cornear*) to gore **2.** *Arg, Nic, Urug* (*asir*) to seize **3.** *AmC* (*hurtar*) to steal **4.** *Arg, Chile* (*agarrar*) to grab **5.** *AmL* (*al vuelo*) to catch in mid-air **6.** *Chile* (*sospechar*) to suspect **7.** *AmS, inf* (*burlarse*) to make fun of

cacharpas [ka·'tʃar·pas] *fpl AmS* odds mpl and ends

cacharro [ka·'tʃa·rro] *m* **1.** (*recipiente*) pot **2.** *pey, inf* (*aparato*) gadget **3.** *pey, inf* (*trasto*) piece of junk; **¡quita ese ~ de ahí!** get rid of that junk!

cachas[1] ['ka·tʃas] I. *adj inv* **1.** *inf* (*fuerte*) strong **2.** *vulg* (*sexy*) sexy II. *fpl inf* bottom

cachas[2] ['ka·tʃas] *mf inv, inf* (*hombre*) hunk; (*mujer*) muscular woman

cachear [ka·tʃe·'ar] *vt* to frisk

cachemir [ka·tʃe·'mir] *m* cashmere

cachete [ka·'tʃe·te] *m* **1.** (*golpe*) slap **2.** (*carrillo*) (fat) cheek

cachetear [ka·tʃe·te·'ar] *vt AmL* to slap

cachetón, -ona [ka·tʃe·'ton, -'to·na] *adj AmL* chubby-cheeked

cachimba [ka·'tʃim·ba] *f AmL* **1.** (*pipa*) pipe **2.** (*cartucho*) cartridge

cachondear [ka·tʃon·de·'ar] *vr:* ~**se de uno** *inf* to make fun of sb

cachondeo [ka·tʃon·'deo] *m* **1.** *inf* (*broma*) joke; **tomar algo a** ~ to take sth as a joke; **esto es un** ~ this is a joke **2.** *vulg* (*burla*) farce

cachondo, -a [ka·'tʃon·do, -a] I. *adj* **1.** *vulg* (*sexual*) sexy, horny; (*perra*) on heat; **poner a alguien** ~ to turn sb on **2.** *inf* (*gracioso*) funny II. *m, f* *vulg* (*juerguista*) reveler **2.** *inf* (*gracioso*) joker; **es un** ~ he's a real laugh

cachorro, -a [ka·'tʃo·rro, -a] I. *adj AmL* despicable II. *m, f* (*de tigre*) cub; (*de perro*) pup(py)

cachudo, -a [ka·'tʃu·do, -a] *adj* **1.** *AmL* (*animal*) horned **2.** *Méx* (*persona*) long-faced

cacique [ka·'si·ke, -'θi·ke] *m* **1.** (*indio*) chief **2.** (*tirano*) tyrant

caciquismo [ka·si·'kis·mo, ka·θi-] *m pey: system of petty tyranny run by the local political boss*

caco ['ka·ko] *m inf* burglar

cacto ['kak·to] *m* cactus

cada ['ka·da] *adj* each; ~ **uno/una** each one; **libros a 5 pesos** ~ **uno** books at 5 pesos each; ~ **hora** hourly; ~ **día** daily; ~ **vez más/peor** more and more/worse and worse; **¿~ cuánto?** how often?

cadalso [ka·'dal·so] *m* scaffold

cadáver [ka·'da·βer] *m* corpse; (*de animales*) carcass

cadavérico, -a [ka·da·'βe·ri·ko, -a] *adj* (*muerto*) cadaverous; (*pálido*) deathly pale

cadena [ka·'de·na] *f* **1.** *t. fig* chain; ~ **alimentaria** BIO food chain; ~ (**antideslizante**) AUTO snow chain; ~ **hotelera** hotel chain; ~ **humana** human chain; ~ **perpetua** JUR life imprisonment; ~ **de reciclaje** ECOL recycling chain; **trabajo en** ~ assembly-line work; **atar un perro con** ~ to chain up a dog; **choque en** ~ pile-up; **reacción en** ~ chain reaction **2.** GEO mountain chain **3.** RADIO, TV network; ~ **de sonido** sound system

cadencia [ka·'den·sja, -θja] *f* rhythm; MÚS cadence

cadera [ka·'de·ra] *f* hip

cadmio ['kad·mjo] *m* cadmium

caducar <c→qu> [ka·du·'kar] *vi* **1.** (*documento*) to expire; **este pasaporte está caducado** this passport has expired **2.** (*producto*) **la leche está caducada** the milk is past its sell-by date

caducidad [ka·du·si·'dad, ka·du·θi-] *f* **fecha de** ~ (*de documento*) date of expiry; (*de productos*) use-by date

caduco, -a [ka·'du·ko, -a] *adj* senile

caer [ka·'er] *irr* I. *vi* **1.** (*objeto*) to fall (down); (*precio*) to fall; ~ **al suelo** to fall to the ground; ~ **en manos de alguien** to fall into sb's hands; **dejarse** ~ *inf* to show up; **tu amigo me cae bien/mal** *fig* I like/I don't like your friend; **estar al** ~ *inf* to be about to happen **2.** (*presidente*) to fall from power **3.** (*comida*) ~ **bien a** to agree with **4.** (*vestidos*) to suit **5.** *inf* (*encontrarse*) to be (located); **¿por dónde cae Jerez?** whereabouts is Jerez? **6.** (*atacar*) **sobre algo/alguien** to fall on sth/sb II. *vr:* ~**se** to collapse; (*un avión*) to crash; (*pelo*) to fall out; (*casa*) to fall down; ~**se de culo** *inf* to fall on one's backside; **se me ha caído el pañuelo** I dropped my handkerchief; ~**se de sueño** to be ready to drop

café [ka·'fe] *m* **1.** (*bebida*) coffee; ~ **con leche** coffee with milk; ~ **solo** black coffee; **tomar un** ~ to have a coffee **2.** (*local*) café **3.** (*planta*) coffee tree; (*semilla*) coffee bean

cafeína [ka·fe·'i·na] *f* caffeine

cafetal [ka·fe·'tal] *m* coffee plantation

cafetera [ka·fe·'te·ra] *f* **1.** (*jarra*) coffee pot;

~ eléctrica coffeemaker **2.** *inf* (*vehículo*) old banger
cafetería [ka·fe·te·'ri·a] *f* café
cagar <g→gu> [ka·'ɣar] **I.** *vi vulg* to take a shit **II.** *vt vulg* to mess up; **¡ya la hemos cagado!** now we're really in the shit! **III.** *vr:* **~se** *vulg* (*de miedo*) to shit oneself; **¡me cago en diez!** shit!
caída [ka·'i·da] *f* **1.** (*acción*) fall; (*de aviones*) crash; **~ del cabello** hair loss; **~ de gobierno** fall of the government; **~ del sistema** COMPUT system crash; **la ~ del muro de Berlín** the fall of the Berlin wall **2.** (*de agua*) waterfall **3.** (*puesta*) **a la ~ del sol** at sunset
caimán [kai·'man] *m* caiman
Cairo ['kai·ro] *m* **El ~** Cairo
caja ['ka·xa] *f* **1.** (*recipiente*) box; **~ fuerte** safe; **~ de herramientas** *t.* COMPUT tool box; **~ de música** musical box; **~ negra** AVIAT black box **2.** (*carcasa*) case; **~ de cambios** AUTO gearbox; **~ torácica** ANAT thoracic cavity **3.** FIN fund; **Caja** (**Postal**) **de Ahorros** (Post Office) savings bank
cajero, -a [ka·'xe·ro, -a] *m, f* cashier; **~ automático** cash dispenser
cajeta [ka·'xe·ta] *f* **1.** *Arg* (*cepo*) trap **2.** *AmC* CULIN toffee-like sweet
cajetilla [ka·xe·'ti·ja, -ʎa] *f* small box; (*de cigarrillos*) pack of cigarettes
cajón [ka·'xon] *m* drawer; (*de embalaje*) crate; **~ de salida** DEP starting gate; **eso es de ~** *inf* that goes without saying
cajuela [ka·'xwe·la] *f Méx* AUTO trunk
cake [keik] *m AmL* cake
cal [kal] *f* lime; **cerrar a ~ y canto** to shut firmly
cala ['ka·la] *f* **1.** (*bahía*) cove **2.** NÁUT hold **3.** (*prueba*) probe
calabacín [ka·la·βa·'sin, -'θin] *m* zucchini
calabaza [ka·la·'βa·sa, -θa] *f* BOT pumpkin
▶ **dar ~ s a alguien** (*un suspenso*) to fail sb; (*una negativa*) to brush sb off
calabozo [ka·la·'βo·so, -θo] *m* **1.** (*mazmorra*) dungeon **2.** (*celda*) (prison) cell
calada [ka·'la·da] *f inf* puff; **¿me das una ~?** give me a drag, will you?
calado [ka·'la·do] *m* **1.** (*bordado*) open work **2.** NÁUT draught
calaguasca [ka·la·'ɣwas·ka] *f Col* CULIN raw brandy
calamar [ka·la·'mar] *m* squid
calambre [ka·'lam·bre] *m* (*eléctrico*) electric shock; (*muscular*) cramp; **~ de estómago** stomach cramp
calamidad [ka·la·mi·'dad] *f* calamity; *inf* (*persona*) disaster
calandria [ka·'lan·drja] *f* **1.** ZOOL calandra lark **2.** (*máquina*) calender; (*para ropa*) mangle
calaña [ka·'la·ɲa] *f* **ser de mala ~** to be bad
calar [ka·'lar] **I.** *vi* to soak in **II.** *vt* **1.** (*líquido*) to soak; **el chaparrón me ha calado la chaqueta** the downpour has drenched my jacket **2.** (*afectar*) **~ a alguien** to make an im-

pression on sb **3.** (*una prenda*) to do openwork on **4.** (*cortar*) to cut a piece out of **5.** *inf* (*desenmascarar*) to see through **6.** (*motor*) to stall **III.** *vr:* **~se 1.** (*mojarse*) to get soaked **2.** (*motor*) to stall **3.** (*gorra*) to pull down
calato, -a ['ka·la·to, -a] *adj Perú* naked
calavera [ka·la·'βe·ra] *f* skull
calcañar [kal·ka·'ɲar] *m* ANAT heel
calcar <c→qu> [kal·'kar] *vt* **1.** (*dibujar*) to trace **2.** (*imitar*) to copy; **es calcado a su padre** he's the spitting image of his father
calceta [kal·'se·ta, kal·'θe-] *f* knitting
calcetín [kal·se·'tin, kal·θe-] *m* sock
calcificar(se) <c→qu> [kal·si·fi·'kar·(se), kal·θi-] *vt,* (*vr*) to calcify
calcinar(se) [kal·si·'nar·(se), kal·θi-] *vt,* (*vr*) to burn
calcio ['kal·sjo, -θjo] *m* calcium
calco ['kal·ko] *m* **1.** (*de dibujos*) tracing **2.** (*imitación*) imitation
calcomanía [kal·ko·ma·'ni·a] *f* transfer
calculador(a) [kal·ku·la·'dor, -·'do·ra] *adj* calculating
calculadora [kal·ku·la·'do·ra] *f* calculator; **~ de bolsillo** pocket calculator
calcular [kal·ku·'lar] *vt* **1.** (*computar*) to calculate **2.** (*aproximadamente*) to estimate; **calculo que llegaré sobre las diez** I reckon that I'll arrive around ten
cálculo ['kal·ku·lo] *m* **1.** *t.* ECON calculation; **~ diferencial** differential calculus; **~ mental** mental arithmetic; **~ de probabilidades** theory of probability; **hacer un ~ de algo** to calculate sth **2.** (*suposición*) conjecture **3.** MED stone
caldear [kal·de·'ar] **I.** *vt* **1.** (*calentar*) to heat (up) **2.** (*acalorar*) to inflame **II.** *vr:* **~se 1.** (*calentarse*) to heat up **2.** (*acalorarse*) to get heated
caldera [kal·'de·ra] *f* TÉC boiler
calderilla [kal·de·'ri·ja, -ʎa] *f* small change
caldero [kal·'de·ro] *m* caldron
calefacción [ka·le·fak·'sjon, -faɣ·'θjon] *f* heating
calefactor [ka·le·fak·'tor] *m* heater
calefón [ka·le·'fon] *m Arg* gas water heater
caleidoscopio [ka·lei·dos·'ko·pjo] *m* kaleidoscope
calendario [ka·len·'da·rjo] *m* calendar; **~ de taco** tear-off calendar; **~ de trabajo** schedule

---

i Calendars are an essential component of farming culture, since farmers have to plan the cycle of planting and harvesting crops according to the dry and rainy periods. The highly developed understanding of astronomy that the Mayans possessed allowed them to develop the elaborate and extremely accurate **calendario maya** (Mayan calendar) that uses the vigesimal (base 20) system. According to that system, the cycle of dates repeats itself only once every 52 years. The calendar served as the basis for calculating the occurrence of astronomical events such as eclipses of the sun and moon and for scheduling important events.

calentador [ka·len·ta·'dor] *m* heater; (*para la cama*) bed-warmer

calentamiento [ka·len·ta·'mjen·to] *m* warming; DEP warm-up

calentar <e→ie> [ka·len·'tar] **I.** *vi* to be warm **II.** *vt* **1.** (*caldear*) to heat (up); (*con calefacción*) to warm (up); ~ **al rojo vivo** to make red-hot **2.** *vulg* (*sexualmente*) to turn on **3.** *inf* (*pegar*) to give a good hiding to **III.** *vr:* ~ **se 1.** (*caldearse*) to heat up; DEP to warm up **2.** (*enfadarse*) to get angry

calentura [ka·len·'tu·ra] *f* cold sore

calesita [ka·le·'si·ta] *f Arg, Par* merry-go-round

caleta [ka·'le·ta] *f AmL* (*barco*) coaster

calibrar [ka·li·'βrar] *vt* **1.** TÉC (*medir*) to gauge, to gage **2.** (*graduar*) to calibrate

calibre [ka·'li·βre] *m* **1.** (*diámetro*) caliber; **eso es una mentira de** ~ *inf* that's a huge lie **2.** (*instrumento*) gauge, gage

calidad [ka·li·'dad] *f* quality; **de alta** ~ high-quality; **de primera** ~ top-quality; **en** ~ **de** as

cálido, -a ['ka·li·do, -a] *adj* (*país*) hot; *fig* warm

caliente [ka·'ljen·te] *adj* **1.** (*cálido*) warm; (*ardiente*) hot **2.** (*acalorado*) heated; **poner(se)** ~ *vulg* to get randy

califa [ka·'li·fa] *m* caliph

calificación [ka·li·fi·ka·'sjon, -'θjon] *f* **1.** (*denominación*) description; (*evaluación*) assessment; ~ **profesional** professional qualification **2.** (*nota*) mark, grade

calificado, -a [ka·li·fi·'ka·do, -a] *adj* qualified; (*reconocido*) well-known

calificar <c→qu> [ka·li·fi·'kar] *vt* **1.** (*definir*) ~ **de algo** to describe as sth **2.** (*evaluar*) to assess; ENS to mark, to grade

calificativo [ka·li·fi·ka·'ti·βo] *m* description, qualifier

California [ka·li·'for·nja] *f* California

caligrafía [ka·li·γra·'fi·a] *f* calligraphy

cáliz ['ka·lis, -liθ] *m* **1.** REL chalice **2.** BOT calyx

callado, -a [ka·'ja·do, -a; ka·'ʎa-] *adj* **1.** *estar* (*sin hablar*) silent; (*silencioso*) quiet **2.** *ser* (*reservado*) quiet

callampa [ka·'jam·pa, ka·'ʎam-] *f* **1.** *Col, Chile, Perú* (*seta*) mushroom **2.** *Chile* (*sombrero*) felt hat

callana [ka·'ja·na, -'ʎa·na] *f* **1.** *AmS* (*vasija*) earthenware pan **2.** *Chile* (*reloj*) large pocket watch **3.** *Perú* (*tiesto*) flowerpot

callar [ka·'jar, -'ʎar] **I.** *vi, vr* ~ **se de** [*o* **por**] **algo** (*no hablar*) to keep quiet because of sth; (*enmudecer*) to fall silent due to sth; **¡cállate de una vez!** just shut up! **II.** *vt* to keep quiet about; **hacer** ~ **a alguien** to make sb keep quiet

calle ['ka·je, -ʎe] *f* street; (*de autopista*) *t.* DEP lane; ~ **comercial** shopping street; ~ **de dirección única** one-way street; ~ **peatonal** pedestrian street; ~ **sin salida** cul-de-sac; ~ **arriba/abajo** up/down the street; **hacer la** ~ *inf* to be a streetwalker; **quedarse en la** ~ *inf* to be out of a job

callejero [ka·je·'xe·ro, ka·ʎe-] *m* street directory

callejón [ka·je·'xon, ka·ʎe-] *m* alley; ~ **sin salida** cul-de-sac

callista [ka·'jis·ta, -'ʎis·ta] *mf* chiropodist

callo ['ka·jo, -ʎo] *m* **1.** (*callosidad*) callus; (*ojo de gallo*) corn; **dar el** ~ *inf* to slave away **2.** *pl* CULIN tripe

calma ['kal·ma] *f* **1.** (*silencio*) calm; ~ **chicha** NÁUT dead calm; **¡(con)** ~**!** calm down! **2.** *inf* (*indolencia*) indolence

calmante [kal·'man·te] *m* painkiller

calmar [kal·'mar] **I.** *vt* **1.** (*tranquilizar*) to calm (down) **2.** (*dolor*) to relieve **II.** *vr:* ~ **se** to calm down; (*dolor*) to ease off

caló [ka·'lo] *m* gypsy slang

calor [ka·'lor] *m* **1.** (*de un cuerpo*) warmth **2.** (*clima*) heat; ~ **sofocante** stifling heat; **hace mucho** ~ it's very hot **3.** (*entusiasmo*) passion

caloría [ka·lo·'ri·a] *f* calorie; **bajo en** ~**s** low-calorie

calote [ka·'lo·te] *m RíoPl* swindle

caluma [ka·'lu·ma] *f Perú* Andean gorge

calumnia [ka·'lum·nja] *f* slander

calumniar [ka·lum·'njar] *vt* to slander

caluroso, -a [ka·lu·'ro·so, -a] *adj* hot; *fig* warm; **un recibimiento** ~ a warm reception

calva ['kal·βa] *f* bald patch

calvario [kal·'βa·rjo] *m* REL Stations *pl* of the Cross; **pasar un** ~ to suffer agonies

calvicie [kal·'βi·sje, -θje] *f* baldness

calvo, -a ['kal·βo, -a] *adj* bald; **estar** ~ to be bald

calzada [kal·'sa·da, -'θa·da] *f* (*carretera*) (paved) road; (*carril*) lane

calzado [kal·'sa·do, -'θa·do] *m* footwear

calzador [kal·sa·'dor, kal·θa-] *m* shoehorn

calzar <z→c> [kal·'sar, -'θar] **I.** *vt* **1.** (*zapatos*) to put on; (*esquís*) to clip on; (*cuña*) to wedge **2.** (*llevar puesto*) to wear **II.** *vr:* ~ **se** to put one's shoes on

calzón [kal·'son, -'θon] *m AmL* (*pantalón*) trousers *pl*, pants *pl*

calzoncillo(s) [kal·son·'si·jo(s), kal·θon·'θi·ʎo(s)] *m(pl)* men's underpants *pl*

calzoneras [kal·so·'ne·ras, kal·θo-] *fpl Méx* (*pantalón de montar*) riding pants *pl*

cama ['ka·ma] *f* bed; ~ **elástica** trampoline; **caer en** ~ to fall ill

camada [ka·'ma·da] *f* litter

camaleón [ka·ma·le·'on] *m t. fig* chameleon

cámara[1] ['ka·ma·ra] *f* **1.** FOTO camera; ~ **de vídeo** video camera; **a** ~ **lenta** in slow motion **2.** (*consejo*) house; **Cámara Alta** POL upper house; **Cámara Baja** POL lower house **3.** (*recinto*) chamber; ~ **frigorífica** cold-stor-

age room
cámara² ['ka·ma·ra] *mf* CINE cameraman *m*, camerawoman *f*
camarada [ka·ma·'ra·da] *mf* **1.** POL comrade **2.** (*amigo*) companion
camaradería [ka·ma·ra·de·'ri·a] *f* comradeship
camarero, -a [ka·ma·'re·ro, -a] *m*, *f* **1.** (*en restaurantes*) waiter *m*, waitress *f*; ¡~! waiter! **2.** (*en la barra*) barman *m*, barmaid *f*
camarilla [ka·ma·'ri·ja, -ʎa] *f t. pey* clique
camarón [ka·ma·'ron] *m* prawn, shrimp
camarote [ka·ma·'ro·te] *m* NÁUT cabin, berth
camarotero [ka·ma·ro·'te·ro] *m AmL* steward
camastro [ka·'mas·tro] *m* hard old bed
cambiador [kam·bja·'dor] *m Chile* switchman
cambiante [kam·'bjan·te] *adj* changeable; *pey* (*veleidoso*) moody
cambiar [kam·'bjar] **I.** *vi* to change; **~ de casa** to move (house); **~ de coche** to buy a new car; **~ de marcha** AUTO to change gear **II.** *vt* **1.** (*algo comprado*) to (ex)change; **~ dinero** to change money; **~ unas palabras con alguien** to exchange a few words with sb **2.** (*variar*) to change; **~ algo de lugar** to move sth **III.** *vr* **1.** (*transformarse*) **~ en algo** to change [*o* turn] into sth **2.** (*de ropa*) to change; (*de casa*) to move; **~ se a otra ciudad** to move to another town
cambiavía [kam·bja·'βi·a] *m AmL* switchman
cambio ['kam·bjo] *m* **1.** (*transformación*) change; **~ de aceite** AUTO oil change; **~ climático** climatic change; **~ de domicilio** change of address; **~ de marchas** shift lever, gearshift; **~ de tendencia** new trend; **hay un ~ en el horario** there's a change in the timetable; **a las primeras de ~** at the first opportunity; **¿tiene ~ de 100 dólares?** can you change 100 dollars?; **en ~** however **2.** (*intercambio*) exchange; **libre ~** COM free trade; **a ~ de algo** in exchange for sth; **~ de impresiones** exchange of views **3.** FIN exchange rate; **~ de divisa** [*o* **de moneda**] foreign exchange; **al ~ del día** at the current exchange rate **4.** TÉC gearshift; **~ de marchas** gearbox, transmission **5.** DEP substitution
Camboya [kam·'bo·ja] *f* Cambodia
cambuto, -a [kam·'bu·to] *adj Perú* small and chubby
camelar [ka·me·'lar] *vt inf* **1.** (*engañar*) to cajole **2.** (*seducir*) to seduce
camelia [ka·'me·lja] *f* camellia
camello, -a [ka·'me·jo, -ʎo] *m*, *f* **1.** ZOOL camel **2.** *inf* (*persona*) drug dealer
camerino [ka·me·'ri·no] *m* TEAT dressing room
Camerún [ka·me·'run] *m* Cameroon
camilla [ka·'mi·ja, -ʎa] *f* stretcher
camillero, -a [ka·mi·'je·ro, -a; ka·mi·'ʎe-] *m*, *f* stretcher-bearer
camilucho, -a [ka·mi·'lu·tʃo, -a] *m*, *f AmL* Indian day laborer
caminar [ka·mi·'nar] **I.** *vi* **1.** (*ir*) to go; (*a pie*) to walk **2.** (*astro*) to move **3.** *AmL* (*funcionar*) to work **II.** *vt* (*distancia*) to cover

caminata [ka·mi·'na·ta] *f* long walk
camino [ka·'mi·no] *m* **1.** (*senda*) path; (*estrecho*) track; (*calle*) road; **a medio ~** halfway (there); **de ~ a Londres** on the road to London; **abrirse ~** to make one's way; **ponerse en ~** to set out [*o* off]; **ir por buen/mal ~** *fig* to be on the right/wrong track **2.** (*distancia*) way; **está a dos horas de ~** it's two hours away **3.** (*manera*) way; **todos los ~s llevan a Roma** *prov* all roads lead to Rome; **~ de rosas** bed of roses; **su vida no ha sido ningún ~ de rosas** his/her life has been no bed of roses

i Santiago de Compostela, the capital of Galicia, has been an important place of pilgrimage for the Roman Catholic Church since the 9th century. The **Camino de Santiago**, which leads to Santiago de Compostela, is a route that thousands of pilgrims from all over the world travel along every year.

camión [ka·'mjon] *m* AUTO truck; **~ de la basura** garbage truck; **~ volquete** dump truck
camionero, -a [ka·mjo·'ne·ro, -a] *m*, *f* truck driver
camioneta [ka·mjo·'ne·ta] *f* **1.** (*furgoneta*) van; **~ de reparto** delivery van **2.** *AmL* (*autobús*) bus
camisa [ka·'mi·sa] *f* **1.** (*prenda*) shirt; **~ de fuerza** straitjacket; **cambiar de ~** to change sides; **no me llegaba la ~ al cuerpo** *inf* I was scared stiff **2.** (*funda*) case **3.** (*de reptil*) slough ▶ **meterse en ~ de once varas** to bite off more than one can chew
camiseta [ka·mi·'se·ta] *f* (*exterior*) T-shirt; (*interior*) undershirt; DEP shirt
camisón [ka·mi·'son] *m* nightgown
camote [ka·'mo·te] *m AmL* **1.** (*batata*) sweet potato **2.** (*molestia*) nuisance **3.** (*amante*) lover
camotear [ka·mo·te·'ar] *vi Méx* (*vagabundear*) to roam
campamento [kam·pa·'men·to] *m* camp; **~ de veraneo** summer camp
campana [kam·'pa·na] *f* bell; **~ extractora de humos** extractor hood; **el coche dio tres vueltas de ~** the car turned over three times; **echar las ~s a vuelo** *inf* to let everybody know
campanada [kam·pa·'na·da] *f* chime; **dar la ~** *fig* to cause a stir
campanario [kam·pa·'na·rjo] *m* bell tower
campanilla [kam·pa·'ni·ja, -ʎa] *f* **1.** (*campana*) small bell **2.** ANAT uvula **3.** BOT bellflower
campante [kam·'pan·te] *adj inf* **1.** (*tranquilo*) calm; **quedarse tan ~** not to bat an eyelid **2.** (*satisfecho*) (self-)satisfied
campaña [kam·'pa·ɲa] *f* **1.** (*campo*) countryside; **tienda de ~** tent **2.** POL campaign; AGR season; **~ de acoso y derribo** smear cam-

paign; ~ **antitabaco** anti-smoking campaign; ~ **electoral** electoral [o election] campaign **3.** COM sales drive

campar [kam·'par] *vi* to camp

campear [kam·pe·'ar] *vi* **1.** *AmL* (*ir de acampada*) to camp **2.** *inf* (*arreglárselas*) **ir campeando** to get by **3.** (*sobresalir*) to abound

campechana [kam·pe·'tʃa·na] *f Méx, Cuba* (*bebida*) cocktail

campechano, -a [kam·pe·'tʃa·no, -a] *adj* **1.** (*llano*) straightforward **2.** (*cordial*) cheerful

campeón, -ona [kam·pe·'on, -'o·na] *m, f* champion

campeonato [kam·peo·'na·to] *m* championship; **de ~** *inf* terrific

campera [kam·'pe·ra] *f CSur* Windbreaker®

campesino, -a [kam·pe·'si·no, -a] **I.** *adj* rural; *t. pey* (*de un labrador*) peasant **II.** *m, f* countryman *m*, countrywoman *f*; **los ~s** country people; *t. pey* (*labrador*) peasant

camping ['kam·piŋ] *m* **1.** (*campamento*) camping site **2.** (*actividad*) camping; **hacer ~** to go camping

campirano, -a [kam·pi·'ra·no, -a] *adj* **1.** *AmL* (*patán, rural*) rustic **2.** *Méx* (*campesino*) peasant **3.** *Méx* (*entendido en el campo*) good at farming **4.** *Méx* (*que maneja bien caballos*) skilled at handling horses

campista [kam·'pis·ta] *mf* **1.** (*de camping*) camper **2.** *Méx* MIN mine leaseholder

campo ['kam·po] *m* **1.** (*terreno*) countryside; (*de cultivo*) field; *t.* DEP; **~ de tiro** firing range; **gente del ~** country people; **ir al ~** to go into the country; **tener ~ libre para hacer algo** *fig* to be free to do sth **2.** *t.* POL, MIL camp; **~ de concentración** HIST concentration camp; **~ de trabajo** work camp **3.** *t.* FÍS, COMPUT field; **~ de actuación** field of activity; **~ para entradas** COMPUT input field; **~ de opción** COMPUT option field; **~ visual** field of vision

camposanto [kam·po·'san·to] *m* cemetery

campus ['kam·pus] *m inv* campus

camuflaje [ka·mu·'fla·xe] *m* camouflage

camuflar [ka·mu·'flar] *vt t. fig* to camouflage

cana ['ka·na] *f* **1.** (*pelo*) white hair; **echar una ~ al aire** *fig* to let one's hair down **2.** *Arg, inf* (*policía*) police **3.** *Arg, inf* (*prisión*) jail

Canadá [ka·na·'da] *m* (**el**) ~ Canada

canal [ka·'nal] *m* **1.** *t.* ANAT canal **2.** GEO, TV channel; **el Canal de la Mancha** the English Channel; **el Canal de Panamá** the Panama Canal

canalización [ka·na·li·sa'sjon, -θa·'θjon] *f* **1.** (*de un río*) canalization **2.** (*alcantarillado*) sewerage system

canalizar <z→c> [ka·na·li·'sar, -'θar] *vt* to canalize; *fig* to channel

canalla [ka·'na·ja, -ʎa] *mf pey* swine

canalón [ka·na·'lon] *m* gutter

canana [ka·'na·na] *f* **1.** (*cinturón*) cartridge belt **2.** *AmL, inf* (*canallada*) dirty trick

Canarias [ka·'na·rjas] *fpl* **las Islas ~** the Canary Islands

canario [ka·'na·rjo] *m* canary

canasta [ka·'nas·ta] *f* basket

canastero, -a [ka·nas·'te·ro, -a] *m, f Chile* (*panadería*) baker's helper

canastilla [ka·nas·'ti·ja, -ʎa] *f Arg, PRico* (*de la novia*) hope chest

cancanear [kan·ka·ne·'ar] *vi* **1.** *inf* (*vagar*) to wander about **2.** *AmL* (*tartamudear*) to stutter; (*hablar entrecortadamente*) to speak haltingly

cancel [kan·'sel, -'θel] *m* inner door

cancelar [kan·se·'lar, kan·θe·-] *vt* **1.** (*anular*) to cancel; **~ una cita** to cancel an appointment **2.** FIN (*una cuenta*) to close; (*una deuda*) to pay (off)

cáncer ['kan·ser, -θer] *m* **1.** *t. fig* MED cancer **2.** ASTR Cancer

cancerígeno, -a [kan·se·'ri·xe·no, -a; kan·θe·-] *adj* carcinogenic

canceroso, -a [kan·se·'ro·so, -a; kan·θe·-] *adj* cancerous; **tumor ~** cancerous tumor

cancha ['kan·tʃa] *f* **1.** DEP (*de deporte*) sports field; (*de tenis*) court **2.** *AmL* (*hipódromo*) racetrack **3.** *AmL* (*de un río*) broad part of a river **4.** *AmL* (*espacio*) space

canchero, -a [kan·'tʃe·ro, -a] *m, f Arg* ground(s)keeper

canciller [kan·si·'jer, -θi·'ʎer] *mf* **1.** POL chancellor **2.** *AmL* (*de Asuntos Exteriores*) foreign minister

cancillería [kan·si·je·'ri·a, kan·θi·ʎe-] *f* **1.** POL chancellery **2.** *AmL* (*Asuntos Exteriores*) foreign ministry

canción [kan·'sjon, -'θjon] *f* song; **~ de moda** pop song; **~ popular** folk song; (**es**) **siempre la misma ~** (it's) always the same old story

cancionero [kan·sjo·'ne·ro, kan·θjo-] *m* MÚS songbook

canco ['kan·ko] *m* **1.** *Bol* (*nalga*) buttock **2.** *Chile* (*olla*) earthenware casserole **3.** *Chile* (*tiesto*) flowerpot

cancona [kan·'ko·na] *adj Chile* broad-hipped

candado [kan·'da·do] *m* padlock

candelabro [kan·de·'la·βro] *m* candelabra

candelejón, -ona [kan·de·le·'xon, -'xo·na] *adj Chile, Col, Perú* naïve

candelero [kan·de·'le·ro] *m* candlestick; **estar en el ~** *fig* to be in the limelight

candelilla [kan·de·'li·ja, -ʎa] *f* **1.** *CRi, Chile, Hond* (*luciérnaga*) glow-worm **2.** *Cuba* (*hilván*) overstitch

candente [kan·'den·te] *adj* **1.** (*al rojo*) red-hot **2.** (*palpitante*) burning

candidato, -a [kan·di·'da·to, -a] *m, f* applicant; POL candidate; **~ al título** DEP contender for the title

candidatura [kan·di·da·'tu·ra] *f* **1.** (*presentación*) application; POL candidature **2.** (*papeleta*) ballot paper

candidez [kan·di·'des, -'deθ] *f v.* candor

candil [kan·'dil] *m* **1.** (*lámpara*) oil lamp **2.** *AmL* (*candelabro*) candelabra

candinga [kan·'din·ga] *f* **1.** *Chile* (*necedad*) absurdity **2.** *Hond* (*maraña*) mess

candonga [kan·'don·ga] *f Col* (*pendiente*) earring

candor [kan·'dor] *m* **1.** (*inocencia*) innocence **2.** (*ingenuidad*) naiveté

caneca [ka·'ne·ka] *f* **1.** *Col* (*basurero*) trash can **2.** *Cuba* (*de agua caliente*) hot-water bottle **3.** *AmL* (*barril*) drum; (*balde*) bucket

caneco, -a [ka·'ne·ko, -a] *adj Bol* (*embriagado*) tipsy

canela [ka·'ne·la] *f* cinnamon; **¡esto es ~ fina!** *fig* this is exquisite!

canelones [ka·ne·'lo·nes] *mpl* CULIN cannelloni

canesú [ka·ne·'su] *m* **1.** (*en una prenda*) bodice **2.** *AmS* (*escote*) yoke

canfín [kan·'fin] *m AmC* (*petróleo*) gasoline

cangrejo [kan·'gre·xo] *m* crab; **~ de río** crayfish

cangrina [kan·'gri·na] *f Col* discomfort

cangro ['kan·gro] *m Col, Guat* MED (*cáncer*) cancer

canguro[1] [kan·'gu·ro] *m* ZOOL kangaroo

canguro[2] [kan·'gu·ro] *mf inf* baby-sitter

caníbal [ka·'ni·βal] *adj, mf* cannibal

canica [ka·'ni·ka] *f* marble

canijo, -a [ka·'ni·xo, -a] *adj AmL* (*malvado*) sly

canilla [ka·'ni·ja, -ʎa] *f Arg, Par, Urug* (*grifo*) tap

canillera [ka·ni·'je·ra, -'ʎe·ra] *f AmL* **1.** (*espinillera*) shin guard **2.** (*temblor*) trembling

canillita [ka·ni·'ji·ta, -'ʎi·ta] *m AmS* newspaper vendor

canino [ka·'ni·no] *m* canine (tooth)

canjear [kan·xe·'ar] *vt* to exchange

canoa [ka·'noa] *f* **1.** *t.* DEP (*bote a remo*) canoe; **~ canadiense** Canadian canoe **2.** *AmL* (*artesa*) feeding trough

canon ['ka·non] *m* **1.** (*precepto*) rule **2.** ARTE canon **3.** ECON levy

canónico, -a [ka·'no·ni·ko, -a] *adj* canonical

canoso, -a [ka·'no·so, -a] *adj* grizzled

cansado, -a [kan·'sa·do, -a] *adj* **1.** *estar* (*fatigado*) tired; (*harto*) tired **2.** *ser* (*fatigoso*) tiring; (*aburrido*) boring; (*molesto*) tiresome **3.** *AmL* **a las cansadas** at long last

cansador(a) [kan·sa·'dor, -·'do·ra] *adj Arg* **1.** *ser* (*fatigoso*) tiring **2.** *ser* (*aburrido*) boring **3.** *ser* (*molesto*) tiresome

cansancio [kan·'san·sjo, -θjo] *m* **1.** (*fatiga*) tiredness; **estoy muerto de ~** I'm dead tired **2.** (*hastío*) boredom

cansar [kan·'sar] **I.** *vi* **1.** (*fatigar*) to tire **2.** (*hastiar*) to be tiresome **II.** *vt* **1.** (*fatigar*) to tire (out) **2.** (*hastiar*) to bore **III.** *vr:* **~se 1.** (*fatigarse*) to tire oneself out **2.** (*hartarse*) **~se de algo** to get tired of sth

cansera [kan·'se·ra] *f Col* (*tiempo malgastado*) wasted effort

cantábrico, -a [kan·'ta·βri·ko, -a] *adj* Cantabrian; **el Mar Cantábrico** the Bay of Biscay

cantaletear [kan·ta·le·te·'ar] *vt AmL* to harp on

cantante [kan·'tan·te] **I.** *adj* singing; **llevar la voz ~** *fig* to call the tune **II.** *mf* singer

cantar [kan·'tar] *vi, vt* **1.** (*personas*) to sing; (*gallo*) to crow; (*grillo*) to chirp; (*ranas*) to croak; **en menos que canta un gallo** *inf* in no time at all **2.** *inf* (*confesar*) to talk **3.** *inf* (*oler mal*) to stink

cántaro ['kan·ta·ro] *m* pitcher; **llover a ~s** to rain cats and dogs

cantautor(a) [kan·tau·'tor, -'to·ra] *m(f)* singer-songwriter

cantera [kan·'te·ra] *f* quarry; DEP young local club players

cantero [kan·'te·ro] *m* **1.** (*picapedrero*) stonemason **2.** *AmL* (*sembradío*) flowerbed

cántico ['kan·ti·ko] *m* REL canticle

cantidad [kan·ti·'dad] **I.** *f* quantity; (*número*) number; (*dinero*) sum; **una gran ~ de** lots of; **¿qué ~ necesitas?** how much do you need? **II.** *adv inf* a lot

cantimplora [kan·tim·'plo·ra] *f* water bottle, canteen

cantina [kan·'ti·na] *f* (*en estaciones*) buffet; (*en cuarteles*) canteen

canto ['kan·to] *m* **1.** (*acción*) singing; (*canción*) song; **~ gregoriano** Gregorian chant; **~ de los pájaros** birdsong; **estudia ~** he's/she's studying singing **2.** (*alabanza*) song of praise **3.** (*esquina*) corner; (*arista*) edge **4.** (*de cuchillo*) back; (*de libro*) fore-edge; **poner de ~** to put on end **5.** (*guijarro*) pebble

cantón [kan·'ton] *m* ADMIN canton; MIL cantonment

cantor(a) [kan·'tor, -'to·ra] *adj* singing; **los canarios son muy ~es** canaries sing a lot

canuto [ka·'nu·to] *m* tube; *inf* (*porro*) joint

caña ['ka·ɲa] *f* **1.** AGR reed; (*tallo*) stalk; **~ de azúcar** sugar cane **2.** (*de la pierna*) shinbone **3.** (*de pescar*) (fishing) rod **4.** (*de cerveza*) glass

cañada [ka·'ɲa·da] *f* GEO gully, gulch; (*de ganado*) cattle track

cáñamo ['ka·ɲa·mo] *m* **1.** (*planta*) hemp **2.** (*tejido*) canvas; **de ~** hempen

cañería [ka·ɲe·'ri·a] *f* pipe; **~ del agua** plumbing

cañizal [ka·ɲi·'sal, -'θal] *m* reed bed

caño ['ka·ɲo] *m* tube; (*de la fuente*) spout; (*chorro*) jet

cañón [ka·'ɲon] *m* **1.** (*tubo*) tube; **~ de escopeta** barrel; **de dos cañones** double-barreled **2.** MIL cannon; **~ de nieve** snow cannon; **carne de ~** cannon fodder **3.** (*de pluma*) quill **4.** GEO canyon; **el Cañón del Colorado** the Grand Canyon

cañonazo [ka·ɲo·'na·so, -θo] *m* cannon shot; *inf* (*en fútbol*) powerful shot

cañonera [ka·ɲo·'ne·ra] *f AmL* (*pistolera*) holster

caoba [ka·'o·βa] *f* **1.** (*madera, color*) mahogany **2.** (*árbol*) mahogany tree

caos ['ka·os] *m inv* chaos

caótico, -a [ka·'o·ti·ko, -a] *adj* chaotic

capa ['ka·pa] *f* **1.** *t.* TAUR (*prenda*) cape

2. (*cobertura*) covering; (*recubrimiento*) layer; (*baño*) coating; **~ aislante** insulating layer; **~ de nieve** covering of snow; **~ de ozono** ozone layer **3.** GEO, MIN stratum ▸ **defender a ~ y espada** to defend with all one's might; **hacer de su ~ un sayo** to do as one pleases; **andar** [*o* **estar**] **de ~ caída** *inf* to be down in the mouth

capacho [ka·'pa·tʃo] *m* (large) basket, hamper

capacidad [ka·pa·si·'dad, ka·pa·θi-] *f* **1.** *t.* FÍS (*cabida*) capacity **2.** (*aptitud*) aptitude; **~ adquisitiva** purchasing power; **~ negociadora** negotiating skills *pl*; **~ de persuasión** persuasiveness **3.** *AmL* (*persona dotada*) talented person

capacitación [ka·pa·si·ta·'sjon, -θi·ta·'θjon] *f* capacity; (*formación*) training

capacitado, -a [ka·pa·si·'ta·do, -a; ka·pa·θi-] *adj* **~ para algo** qualified for [*o* to do] sth

capacitar [ka·pa·si·'tar, ka·pa·θi-] **I.** *vt* **1.** (*formar*) to train; (*preparar*) to prepare **2.** *AmL* JUR (*habilitar*) to capacitate **II.** *vr:* **~ se** to qualify

capar [ka·'par] *vt* to castrate; (*pollo*) to caponize

caparazón [ka·pa·ra·'son, -'θon] *m t. fig* shell

capataz [ka·pa·'tas, -'taθ] *m* foreman

capaz [ka·'pas, -'paθ] *adj* **1.** (*con cabida*) capacious **2.** (*en condiciones*) capable **3.** *AmL* (*tal vez*) perhaps

capcioso, -a [kap·'sjo·so, -a; kaβ·'θjo-] *adj* deceitful

capellán [ka·pe·'jan, -'ʎan] *m* chaplain

capelo [ka·'pe·lo] *m Cuba, PRico, Ven* (*de doctor*) academic cap, mortarboard

caperuza [ka·pe·'ru·sa, -θa] *f* (pointed) hood

capi ['ka·pi] *m* **1.** *AmS* (*maíz*) corn **2.** *Bol* (*harina*) white corn flour

capicúa [ka·pi·'kua] *m* symmetrical [*o* reversible] number

capilla [ka·'pi·ja, -ʎa] *f* REL chapel; **~ ardiente** funeral chapel

capisayo [ka·pi·'sa·jo] *m Col* (*camiseta*) undershirt

capital¹ [ka·pi·'tal] **I.** *adj* essential; **letra ~** *AmL* capital letter(s); **pena ~** capital punishment; **de ~ importancia** of prime importance **II.** *m* capital; **~ fijo** fixed capital; **~ a plazo** fixed-term deposit; **bienes de ~** capital goods

capital² [ka·pi·'tal] *f* capital (city)

capitalismo [ka·pi·ta·'lis·mo] *m* capitalism

capitalista [ka·pi·ta·'lis·ta] **I.** *adj* capitalist(ic) **II.** *mf* capitalist

capitán [ka·pi·'tan] *m* MIL, DEP, AVIAT captain; **~ general** MIL commander-in-chief

capitel [ka·pi·'tel] *m* capital

capitolio [ka·pi·'to·ljo] *m* **el Capitolio** the Capitol

capitulación [ka·pi·tu·la·'sjon, -'θjon] *f* MIL surrender

capitular [ka·pi·tu·'lar] *vi* **1.** (*acordar*) to agree to [*o* on] **2.** MIL to surrender

capítulo [ka·'pi·tu·lo] *m t.* REL chapter

capota [ka·'po·ta] *f* AUTO convertible top

capote [ka·'po·te] *m* cloak; **~ de monte** *AmL* poncho; **echar un ~ a alguien** *fig* to give sb a helping hand

capotera [ka·po·'te·ra] *f Hond* (*percha*) clothes peg; (*perchero*) coat rack

capricho [ka·'pri·tʃo] *m* whim; **a ~** as you/he/she like(s); **darse un ~** to allow oneself sth

caprichoso, -a [ka·pri·'tʃo·so, -a] *adj* capricious; *pey* (*inconstante*) moody

Capricornio [ka·pri·'kor·njo] *m* Capricorn

cápsula ['kaβ·su·la] *f* capsule; **~ espacial** AVIAT space capsule

captar [kap·'tar] **I.** *vt* **1.** (*recoger*) to collect; (*capital*) to raise **2.** (*percibir*) to make out; (*comprender*) to grasp **3.** COMPUT to capture **II.** *vr:* **~ se** to be obtained

captura [kap·'tu·ra] *f* **1.** (*apresamiento*) capture **2.** (*detención*) arrest **3.** NÁUT seizure **4.** (*piezas cobradas*) catch

capturar [kap·tu·'rar] *vt* **1.** (*apresar*) to capture **2.** (*detener*) to arrest **3.** NÁUT to seize **4.** (*cazar*) to catch

capucha [ka·'pu·tʃa] *f* hood

capujar [ka·pu·'xar] *vt Arg, inf* (*captar al vuelo*) to catch in mid-air

capullo [ka·'pu·jo, -ʎo] *m* **1.** BOT (*de flor*) bud **2.** ZOOL cocoon; **salir del ~** to hatch out **3.** *inf* (*prepucio*) foreskin **4.** *vulg* (*canalla*) bastard

caqui ['ka·ki] *m* **1.** (*color*) khaki **2.** BOT persimmon

cara ['ka·ra] **I.** *f* **1.** (*rostro*) face; **~ a ~** face to face; **a ~ descubierta** openly; **(no) dar la ~ por alguien** (not) to come to sb's defense; **echar en ~** to reproach; **hacer** [*o* **plantar**] **~ a** to face up to; **partir** [*o* **romper**] **la ~ a alguien** *inf* to smash sb's face in; **~ de póker** *inf* poker face; **una ~ larga** a long face; **una ~ de pocos amigos** *inf* a long face; **salvar la ~** to save face; **tener buena/mala ~** to look good/bad **2.** (*lado*) side; (*de una moneda*) face; **~ o cruz** heads or tails **3.** *inf* (*osadía*) nerve; **¡qué ~!** what cheek!; **tener mucha ~** to have some nerve **II.** *prep* (**de**) **~ a** facing; **de ~ al futuro** with an eye to the future **III.** *conj* **de ~ a +** *infin* in order to **+** *infin*

carabela [ka·ra·'βe·la] *f* NÁUT caravel

carabina [ka·ra·'βi·na] *f* carbine

caracol [ka·ra·'kol] *m* **1.** ZOOL snail **2.** (*concha*) conch (shell)

caracola [ka·ra·'ko·la] *f* conch

caracolillo [ka·ra·ko·'li·jo, -ʎo] *m AmL: high quality small-bean coffee*

carácter <caracteres> [ka·'rak·ter] *m* **1.** (*en general*) character; **(no) tiene ~** he/she has (no) character; **sin ~** characterless; **~ de separación** hyphen **2.** (*índole*) nature; **con ~ de** as **3.** *AmL* (*personaje*) character

característica [ka·rak·te·'ris·ti·ka] *f* characteristic

característico, -a [ka·rak·te·'ris·ti·ko, -a] *adj* characteristic; **rasgo ~** characteristic

caracterizar <z→c> [ka·rak·te·ri·'sar, -'θar]

I. *vt* 1. (*marcar*) to characterize 2. TEAT to play
II. *vr:* ~se to be characterized
caracú [ka·ra·'ku] *m CSur* CULIN marrow
caradura [ka·ra·'du·ra] *mf inf* shameless person
caramanchel [ka·ra·man·'ʧel] *m* 1. *Perú*
(*cobertizo*) shed 2. *Chile* (*taberna*) canteen
caramba [ka·'ram·ba] *interj inf* ¡(**qué**) ~!
(*enfado*) damn!; (*extrañeza*) good heavens!
carámbano [ka·'ram·ba·no] *m* icicle
carambola [ka·ram·'bo·la] *f* cannon; *inf*
(*trampa*) trick; **de** [*o* **por**] ~ *inf* by pure chance
caramelo [ka·ra·'me·lo] *m* (*golosina*) candy;
(*azúcar*) caramel; (**de**) **color** ~ caramel-colored
caraota [ka·ra·'o·ta] *f Ven* (*haba*) kidney bean
carapacho [ka·ra·'pa·ʧo] *m* 1. ZOOL carapace,
shell 2. *Cuba* CULIN *shellfish cooked in the shell*
caraqueño, -a [ka·ra·'ke·ɲo, -a] *adj* of/from
Caracas
carátula [ka·'ra·tu·la] *f* 1. (*careta*) mask 2. (*de
un disco*) album [*o* CD] cover
caravana [ka·ra·'βa·na] *f* 1. (*remolque*) trailer
2. (*embotellamiento*) tailback
carbón [kar·'βon] *m* coal; ~ **de leña** [*o* **vegetal**] charcoal; **dibujo al** ~ ARTE charcoal
drawing; **papel** ~ carbon paper
carbonato [kar·βo·'na·to] *m* carbonate
carbonilla [kar·βo·'ni·ja, -ʎa] *f AmL* charcoal
carbonizar <z→c> [kar·βo·ni·'sar, -'θar] I. *vt*
to char; QUÍM to carbonize II. *vr:* ~se to carbonize
carbono [kar·'βo·no] *m* carbon; **dióxido de** ~
carbon dioxide
carburador [kar·βu·ra·'dor] *m* TÉC carburetor
carburante [kar·βu·'ran·te] *m* fuel
carburo [kar·'βu·ro] *m* carbide
carcajada [kar·ka·'xa·da] *f* guffaw; **reírse a**
~**s** to roar with laughter; **soltar una** ~ to burst
out laughing
carcajear [kar·ka·xe·'ar] *vi, vr:* ~se to roar
with laughter; ~**se de algo/alguien** *inf* to
have a good laugh at sth/sb
carcasa [kar·'ka·sa] *f* TÉC casing
cárcel ['kar·sel, -θel] *f* prison; ~ **de régimen
abierto** open prison; **tres años de** ~ three
years imprisonment; **estar en la** ~ to be in
prison; **ir a parar a la** ~ to end up in prison
carcelero, -a [kar·se·'le·ro, -a; kar·θe-] *m, f*
prison officer, jailer
carcinoma [kar·si·'no·ma, kar·θi-] *m* MED carcinoma
carcoma [kar·'ko·ma] *f* 1. ZOOL woodworm
2. (*polvillo*) wood dust (*left by woodworm*)
carcomer [kar·ko·'mer] *vt* 1. (*corroer*) to eat
away [*o* into] 2. (*minar*) to undermine
cardar [kar·'dar] *vt* 1. (*textil*) to card 2. (*pelo*)
to backcomb
cardenal [kar·de·'nal] *m* 1. REL cardinal
2. (*hematoma*) bruise
cardiaco, -a [kar·'dja·ko, -a] *adj*, **cardíaco, -a**
[kar·'di·a·ko, -a] *adj* heart; MED cardiac;

ataque ~ heart attack; **paro** ~ cardiac arrest
cardinal [kar·di·'nal] *adj* cardinal; **los cuatro
puntos** ~**es** the four cardinal points
cardiología [kar·djo·lo·'xi·a] *f* MED cardiology
cardiólogo, -a [kar·'djo·lo·yo, -a] *m, f* MED
cardiologist
cardiovascular [kar·djo·βas·ku·'lar] *adj* MED
cardiovascular
cardo ['kar·do] *m* 1. BOT thistle 2. *pey, inf* (*desabrido*) prickly character
cardume(n) [kar·'du·me(n)] *m CSur, inf*
(*abundancia*) great quantity
carear [ka·re·'ar] I. *vt* to bring face to face II. *vr:*
~se to confront
carecer [ka·re·'ser, -'θer] *irr como crecer vi* ~
de algo to lack sth; **carece de importancia/
de sentido** it's not important/it doesn't make
sense; **tu afirmación carece de lógica** your
assertion is illogical
carencia [ka·'ren·sja, -θja] *f* lack; (*escasez*)
shortage, scarcity; ~ **de algo** MED deficiency in
sth
carente [ka·'ren·te] *adj* ~ **de algo** lacking in
sth, devoid of sth; ~ **de escrúpulos** unscrupulous; ~ **de interés** uninteresting
careo [ka'reo] *m* confrontation
carestía [ka·res·'ti·a] *f* ECON (*encarecimiento*)
high cost; **la** ~ **de la vida** the high cost of living
careta [ka·'re·ta] *f* mask; **quitar la** ~ **a alguien**
t. fig to unmask sb
carga ['kar·ya] *f* 1. (*acto*) loading; **permitida**
~ **y descarga** loading and unloading 2. (*cargamento*) load; **animal de** ~ pack animal;
buque de ~ freighter 3. (*obligación*) obligation; **ser una** ~ **para alguien** to be a burden
on sb 4. MIL charge; ~ **explosiva** explosive
charge; ~ **policial** baton charge; **¡a la** ~! MIL
charge!; ~ **fiscal** [*o* **impositiva**] tax burden
cargado, -a [kar·'ya·do, -a] *adj* 1. (*lleno*) ~
con [*o* **de**] **algo** loaded with sth; ~ **de problemas** laden with problems; **la batería está
cargada** the battery is charged; **un café muy**
~ very strong coffee; **un ambiente** ~ *fig* a
tense atmosphere 2. *inf* (*borracho*) drunk
cargamento [kar·ya·'men·to] *m* (*acto*) loading; (*carga*) load, cargo
cargar <g→gu> [kar·'yar] I. *vi* 1. (*llevar*) ~
con algo to carry sth 2. (*atacar*) ~ **contra** [*o*
sobre] **alguien** to charge at sb 3. FIN ~ **en
cuenta a uno** to charge to sb's account II. *vt*
1. *t.* MIL to load; ~ **las tintas** *fig* to lay it on
thick 2. (*achacar*) to attribute; ~ **las culpas en**
to put the blame on 3. FIN (*en una cuenta*) to
charge 4. *inf* **a Paco le han cargado las
mates** Paco failed Math; **este tipo me carga**
this guy is getting on my nerves 5. COMPUT to
load 6. *AmL* (*llevar*) to have; **¿cargas dinero?**
do you have any money on you? III. *vr:* ~se
1. (*llenarse*) ~se **de algo** to fill up with sth
2. *inf* (*romper*) to smash up; **¡te la vas a** ~! *fig*
you're in for it! 3. *inf* (*matar*) to do in
cargo ['kar·yo] *m* 1. FIN charge; ~ **a cuenta**

debit; **con ~ a nosotros** at our expense
2. (*puesto*) post; **desempeñar un ~** to hold a
position **3.** (*cuidado*) **estoy a ~ de las correcciones** I'm responsible for the corrections;
~ de conciencia feeling of guilt

cariar <*l. pres:* carío> [ka·ri·'ar] **I.** *vt* MED to
cause to decay **II.** *vr:* **~se** MED to decay

caribe [ka·'ri·βe] **I.** *adj* **1.** *AmL* (*caribeño*) Caribbean **2.** *AmL* (*antropófago*) cannibalistic
3. *AmL* (*cruel*) cruel **4.** *Ant* (*furioso*) furious
II. *m* **1.** (*indígena*) Carib **2.** *AmL* (*cruel*) savage

Caribe [ka·'ri·βe] *m* **el** (**Mar**) **~** the Caribbean
(Sea)

caribeño, -a [ka·ri·'βe·ɲo, -a] *adj* Caribbean

caricatura [ka·ri·ka·'tu·ra] *f* caricature, cartoon

caricaturista [ka·ri·ka·tu·'ris·ta] *mf* caricaturist, cartoonist

caricia [ka·'ri·sja, -θja] *f* caress; **hacer ~s a alguien** to caress sb

caridad [ka·ri·'dad] *f* charity; (*limosna*) alms
pl; **hacer obras de ~** to do works of charity;
¡una limosna, por ~! alms!

caries ['ka·rjes] *f inv* tooth decay, caries

carillón [ka·ri·'jon, -'ʎon] *m* carillon

carimbo [ka·'rim·bo] *m Bol* branding iron

cariño [ka·'ri·ɲo] *m* affection; (*amor*) love;
hacer algo con ~ to do sth lovingly; **sentir ~
por alguien** to be fond of sb; **¡~ (mío)!** (my)
dear!; **hacer ~s** *inf* to caress

cariñoso, -a [ka·ri·'ɲo·so, -a] *adj* **~ con alguien** affectionate [*o* tender] towards sb

carioca [ka·'rjo·ka] *adj* of/from Rio de Janeiro;
(*brasileño*) Brazilian

carisma [ka·'ris·ma] *m* charisma

caritativo, -a [ka·ri·ta·'ti·βo, -a] *adj* charitable

cariz [ka·'ris, -'riθ] *m* look; **esto toma buen ~**
this is looking good

carmelito, -a [kar·me·'li·to, -a] *adj AmL*
(*color*) light brown

carmesí [kar·me·'si] *adj* crimson

carmín [kar·'min] *m* **1.** (*color*) carmine **2.** BOT
dog rose **3.** (*pintalabios*) (**barra de**) **~** lipstick

carnal [kar·'nal] *adj* carnal; **trato ~** sexual
intercourse; **somos primos ~es** we're first
cousins

carnaval [kar·na·'βal] *m* carnival; REL Shrovetide

carnaza [kar·'na·sa, -θa] *f* bait

carne ['kar·ne] *f* **1.** (*del cuerpo*) flesh; **echar
~s** to put on weight; **ser uña y ~** to be inseparable; **los placeres de la ~** the pleasures of
the flesh **2.** (*alimento*) meat; **~ asada** roast
meat; **~ de cerdo/vacuna** pork/beef;
~ picada ground meat ▶ **poner toda la ~ en
el asador** to risk all; **~ de gallina** gooseflesh;
ser de ~ y hueso (*auténtico*) to be real;
(*humano*) to be quite human

carné [kar·'ne] *m* <carnés> identity card;
~ de de identidad identity card; **~ de conducir** driver's license

carneada [kar·ne·'a·da] *f AmL* **1.** (*matanza*)

slaughter **2.** (*matadero*) slaughterhouse

carnear [kar·ne·'ar] *vt* **1.** *CSur* (*matar: un animal*) to slaughter; (*una persona*) to murder
brutally **2.** *Chile* (*engañar*) to cheat **3.** *Méx*
(*apuñalar*) to stab (to death)

carnero [kar·'ne·ro] *m* **1.** ZOOL ram **2.** *CSur*
(*débil*) weakling; (*desertor de huelga*) blackleg

carnet [kar·'ne] *m* <carnets> *v.* **carné**

carnicería [kar·ni·se·'ri·a, kar·ni·θe·] *f* butcher's (shop); *fig* (*masacre*) massacre

carnicero, -a [kar·ni·'se·ro, -a; kar·ni·θe·]
I. *adj* carnivorous; *fig* (*sanguinario*) bloodthirsty **II.** *m, f* butcher

carnitas [kar·'ni·tas] *fpl AmC* CULIN barbecued
pork

carnívoro, -a [kar·'ni·βo·ro, -a] *adj* carnivorous; **animal ~** carnivore

caro ['ka·ro] *adv* dear(ly); **esto nos costará ~**
fig this'll cost us dear

caro, -a ['ka·ro, -a] *adj* expensive

carozo [ka·'ro·so, -θo] *m CSur* stone (*of fruit*)

carpa ['kar·pa] *f* **1.** ZOOL carp **2.** (*entoldado*)
marquee; **~ del circo** big top **3.** *AmL* (*tienda
de campaña*) tent **4.** *AmL* (*puesto de mercado*) market stall

Cárpatos ['kar·pa·tos] *mpl* **los** (**Montes**) **~**
the Carpathians

carpeta [kar·'pe·ta] *f* folder; **~ de anillas** ring
binder

carpincho [kar·'pin·tʃo] *m AmL* ZOOL capybara

carpintería [kar·pin·te·'ri·a] *f* carpentry

carpintero, -a [kar·pin·'te·ro, -a] *m, f* carpenter; **pájaro ~** woodpecker

carpir [kar·'pir] *vt AmL* to hoe

carraspear [ka·rras·pe·'ar] *vi* to clear one's
throat

carrasposo, -a [ka·rras·'po·so, -a] *adj Col,
Ecua, Ven* (*áspero*) rough

carrera [ka·'rre·ra] *f* **1.** (*movimiento*) run
2. (*recorrido*) journey; (*de un astro*) course
3. DEP (*competición*) race; **~ de armamento**
(**nuclear**) (nuclear) arms race; **~ de relevos**
relay race; **coche de ~s** racing car **4.** (*profesión*) profession; **~ profesional** career
5. (*estudios*) degree course; **persona de ~**
graduate; **hacer una ~** to study **6.** (*calle*)
street; *AmL* (*avenida*) avenue; **hacer la ~** *inf*
to be on the game **7.** (*en medias*) ladder

carreta [ka·'rre·ta] *f* wagon

carrete [ka·'rre·te] *m t.* FOTO spool, reel; **~ de
película** roll of film

carretera [ka·rre·'te·ra] *f* (main) road; **~ de
circunvalación** bypass, beltway

carretilla [ka·rre·'ti·ja, -ʎa] *f* wheelbarrow

carriel [ka·rri·'el] *m Col, inf* (*bolso*) shoulder-bag

carril [ka·'rril] *m* **1.** (*en la carretera*) lane;
~ de adelantamiento/lento fast/slow lane
2. (*raíl*) rail

carrilano, -a [ka·rri·'la·no, -a] *m, f Chile*
1. (*ferroviario*) railway worker **2.** (*bandolero*)
bandit

carrillo [ka·'rri·jo, -ʎo] *m inf* cheek
carro ['ka·rro] *m* **1.** (*vehículo*) cart; ~ **acorazado** [*o* **blindado**] armored car; **el Carro Mayor/Menor** ASTR the Big/Little Dipper; **¡para el ~!** *inf* hold your horses! **2.** *AmL* (*coche*) car **3.** (*de una máquina*) carriage
carrocería [ka·rro·se·'ri·a, ka·rro·θe-] *f* bodywork
carroña [ka·'rro·ɲa] *f* carrion
carroza [ka·'rro·sa, -θa] *f* carriage
carruaje [ka·'rrwa·xe] *m* carriage; (*de caballos*) coach
carrusel [ka·rru·'sel] *m* **1.** (*tiovivo*) merry-go-round, carousel **2.** (*ecuestre*) cavalcade
carta ['kar·ta] *f* **1.** (*escrito*) letter; ~ **certificada** registered letter; **~s al director** letters to the editor; ~ **de porte** bill of lading; ~ **de presentación** [*o* **de recomendación**] letter of introduction; **echar una** ~ to mail a letter; ~ **credencial** letter of credence; **Carta Magna** Magna Carta; **tomar ~s en un asunto** to intervene in a matter **2.** (*naipes*) card; **jugar a las ~s** to play (at) cards; **echar las ~s a alguien** to tell sb's fortune **3.** GEO (*mapa*) map; ~ **astral** ASTR astral chart **4.** (*menú*) menu
cartel [kar·'tel] *m* poster; (*rótulo*) sign; TEAT bill; **prohibido fijar ~es** bill posters will be prosecuted; **tener buen** ~ *fig* to be well-known
cártel ['kar·tel] *m* ECON cartel
cartelera [kar·te·'le·ra] *f* notice board; TEAT publicity board; **estar en** ~ to be on
cartera [kar·'te·ra] *f* (*de bolsillo*) wallet; (*de mano*) handbag, purse; (*escolar*) schoolbag; **ministro sin** ~ POL minister without portfolio; ~ **de valores** FIN securities portfolio; ~ **de pedidos** ECON order book
carterista [kar·te·'ris·ta] *mf* pickpocket
cartero, -a [kar·'te·ro, -a] *m, f* mailman *m*, mailwoman *f*
cartílago [kar·'ti·la·ɣo] *m* cartilage
cartilla [kar·'ti·ja, -ʎa] *f* **1.** (*catón*) first reader **2.** (*cuaderno*) notebook; ~ **de ahorros** savings book; ~ **sanitaria** health services card **3.** *AmL* (*carnet*) identity card
cartografía [kar·to·ɣra·'fi·a] *f* cartography
cartón [kar·'ton] *m* **1.** (*material*) cardboard; **caja de** ~ cardboard box **2.** (*envase*) carton; ~ **de leche** carton of milk; **un** ~ **de tabaco a** carton of cigarettes **3.** ARTE cartoon **4.** *AmL* (*en periódicos*) cartoon
cartucho [kar·'tu·tʃo] *m* **1.** *t.* MIL cartridge; ~ **de tinta** ink cartridge; ~ **de fogueo** blank cartridge **2.** (*cucurucho*) cone
cartulina [kar·tu·'li·na] *f* thin cardboard; ~ **amarilla** DEP yellow card
casa ['ka·sa] *f* **1.** (*edificio*) house; ~ **adosada** semi-detached house; ~ **de campo** country house; ~ **de citas** brothel; **venta de** ~ **en** ~ door-to-door selling **2.** (*vivienda*) flat **3.** (*hogar*) home; **ir a** ~ to go home; **¿vienes a mi** ~**?** will you come (over) to my place?; **vengo de** ~ I'm coming from home; **en** ~ at home; **estoy en** ~

de Paco I'm at Paco's (place); **llevar la** ~ to run the house; **no parar en** ~ to be always on the go; **todo queda en** ~ it'll stay in the family; ~ **real** royal family **4.** ECON (*empresa*) firm; ~ **discográfica** record company; ~ **editorial** publishing house ▶ **echar** [*o* **tirar**] **la** ~ **por la ventana** *inf* to spare no expense
casabe [ka·'sa·βe] *m AmL* CULIN cassava bread
casal [ka·'sal] *m AmS* couple; **un** ~ **de águilas** a pair of eagles
casamiento [ka·sa·'mjen·to] *m* marriage
casar [ka·'sar] I. *vi* to match II. *vt* **1.** (*novios*) to marry; **estar** [*o* **ser**] **casado** to be married; **los recién casados** the newlyweds **2.** (*combinar*) to combine; (*piezas*) to join together III. *vr* **-se con alguien** to get married to sb; **~se en** [*o* **por**] **la Iglesia** to get married in church; **~se por lo civil** to get married in a registry office
cascabel [kas·ka·'βel] *m* (little) bell; **serpiente de** ~ rattlesnake ▶ **poner el** ~ **al gato** to bell the cat
cascada [kas·'ka·da] *f* waterfall; (*artificial*) cascade
cascado, -a [kas·'ka·do, -a] *adj* **1.** (*roto*) broken (down) **2.** (*voz*) hoarse
cascanueces [kas·ka·'nwe·ses, -θes] *m inv* nutcracker
cascar <c→qu> [kas·'kar] I. *vi* **1.** *inf* (*charlar*) to chatter **2.** *vulg* (*morir*) to kick the bucket II. *vt* **1.** (*romper*) to crack; ~ **un huevo** to crack an egg **2.** *inf* (*pegar*) to clout III. *vr:* **~se** to crack; (*estropearse*) to break
cáscara [kas·ka·ra] *f* shell; ~ **de huevo** eggshell; ~ **de limón** lemon peel; **¡~s!** *inf* wow!
cascarón [kas·ka·'ron] *m* shell
cascarrabias [kas·ka·'rra·βjas] *mf inv, inf* cantankerous person, grouch
cascarudo [kas·ka·'ru·do] *m Arg* beetle
casco ['kas·ko] *m* **1.** (*para cabeza*) helmet; **los ~s azules** the blue helmets (*members of the U.N. peacekeeping force*) **2.** *inf* (*cabeza*) head; **ligero de ~s** featherbrained; **calentarse la ~s** to agonize over **3.** (*pezuña*) hoof **4.** (*de barco*) hull **5.** (*botella*) (empty) bottle **6.** (*de ciudad*) center city, downtown; **el ~ antiguo** the old city **7.** (*cascote*) piece of rubble **8.** *pl* (*auriculares*) headphones *pl*
cascote [kas·'ko·te] *m* piece of rubble; **~s** rubble
caserío [ka·se·'ri·o] *m* farmhouse
casero, -a [ka·'se·ro, -a] I. *adj* **1.** (*de casa*) homemade; **cocina casera** plain [*o* homestyle] cooking; **remedio** ~ household remedy **2.** (*hogareño*) home-loving II. *m, f* (*propietario*) landlord *m*, landlady *f*
caseta [ka·'se·ta] *f* hut; (*de feria*) booth; (*de muestras*) stand; ~ **del perro** doghouse; ~ **de tiro** shooting gallery
casete¹ [ka·'se·te] *m o f* (*cinta*) cassette; ~ **de vídeo** video cassette
casete² [ka·'se·te] *m* **1.** (*aparato*) cassette recorder **2.** (*pletina*) cassette deck

casi ['ka·si] *adv* almost; ~ ~ very nearly

casilla [ka·'si·ja, -ʎa] *f (en cuadrícula)* box; *(en tablero)* square; *(en casillero)* pigeonhole; **sacar a alguien de sus ~s** *fig* to drive sb mad

casillero [ka·si·'je·ro, -'ʎe·ro] *m* set of pigeonholes

casimba [ka·'sim·ba] *f AmL (hoyo)* well; *(manantial)* spring; *(barril)* bucket

casino [ka·'si·no] *m* casino

caso ['ka·so] *m* **1.** *(hecho)* case; ~ **aislado** isolated case; ~ **de fuerza mayor** case of force majeure; **¡eres un ~!** *inf* you're a right one!; **yo, en tu ~…** if I were you…; **en ~ de +***infin* in the event of; **dado** [*o* **llegado**] **el ~** if it comes to it; **dado el ~ de que +***subj* supposing (that); **en ~ contrario** otherwise; **en cualquier ~** in any case; **en ningún ~** on no account; **en último ~** as a last resort; **en tal ~** in such a case; **en todo ~** in any case **2.** *(atención)* notice; **hacer ~ a alguien** *(considerar)* to pay attention to sb; *(obedecer)* to obey sb; *(creer)* to believe sb

caspa ['kas·pa] *f* dandruff

Caspio ['kas·pjo] *m* **(el) Mar ~** (the) Caspian Sea

caspiroleta [kas·pi·ro·'le·ta] *f AmL* CULIN eggnog

casquete [kas·'ke·te] *m* cap; ~ **polar** polar cap

casta ['kas·ta] *f* **1.** *(raza)* race; **de ~ le viene al galgo** *fig* it runs in the family **2.** *(clase social)* caste

castaña [kas·'ta·ɲa] *f* **1.** *(fruto)* chestnut; ~**s asadas** roast chestnuts **2.** *inf (golpe)* blow; **darse una ~** to give oneself a knock **3.** *inf (bofetada)* slap; *(puñetazo)* thump **4.** *inf (borrachera)* drunkenness; **coger una ~** to get tight **5.** *inf (rápido)* **a toda ~** flat out

castañetear [kas·ta·ɲe·te·'ar] *vi (dedos)* to snap; **me castañeteaban los dientes de frío** my teeth were chattering with cold

castaño [kas·'ta·ɲo] *m* chestnut tree

castaño, -a [kas·'ta·ɲo, -a] *adj* brown

castañuela [kas·ta·'ɲwe·la] *f* castanet

castellano [kas·te·'ja·no, -'ʎa·no] *m (español)* Spanish; *(variedad)* Castilian

castellano, -a [kas·te·'ja·no, -a; -'ʎa·no, -a] *adj, m, f* Castilian; **la lengua castellana** the Spanish language

castellanohablante [kas·te·ja·no·a·'βlan·te, kas·te·ʎa-] *adj* Spanish-speaking

castidad [kas·ti·'dad] *f* chastity; **cinturón de ~** chastity belt

castigar <g→gu> [kas·ti·'ɣar] *vt* **1.** *(punir)* ~ **por algo** to punish for sth; **¡castigado sin postre!** as a punishment you'll go without dessert! **2.** *(físicamente)* to beat; *fig* to castigate

castigo [kas·'ti·ɣo] *m* **1.** *(punición)* punishment **2.** *(aflicción)* affliction

Castilla [kas·'ti·ja, -ʎa] *f* Castile

castillo [kas·'ti·jo, -ʎo] *m t.* NÁUT (fore)castle; ~ **de arena** sandcastle; ~ **de naipes** house of cards; **hacer ~s en el aire** *fig* to build castles in the air

castizo, -a [kas·'ti·so, -a; -θo, -a] *adj (típico)* typical; *(auténtico)* authentic

casto, -a ['kas·to, -a] *adj* chaste

castor [kas·'tor] *m* beaver

castración [kas·tra·'sjon, -'θjon] *f t.* MED castration

castrar [kas·'trar] *vt t.* MED to castrate

casual [ka·'swal] *adj* chance; **por un ~** *inf* by chance

casualidad [ka·swa·li·'dad] *f* chance; **de** [*o* **por**] ~ by chance; **¡qué ~!** what a coincidence!; **da la ~ que conozco a tu mujer** it so happens that I know your wife

casualmente [ka·swal·'men·te] *adv* by chance

cata ['ka·ta] *f* sampling; ~ **de vinos** wine-tasting

cataclismo [ka·ta·'klis·mo] *m* cataclysm

catacumbas [ka·ta·'kum·bas] *fpl* catacombs *pl*

catador(a) [ka·ta·'dor, -·'do·ra] *m(f)* taster

catalán [ka·ta·'lan] *m (lengua)* Catalan

catalán, -ana [ka·ta·'lan, -·'la·na] *adj, m, f* Catalan, Catalonian

catalejo [ka·ta·'le·xo] *m* telescope

catalizador [ka·ta·li·sa·'dor, ka·ta·li·θa-] *m* catalyst; AUTO catalytic converter

catalogar <g→gu> [ka·ta·lo·'ɣar] *vt* to catalog(ue); ~ **a alguien de algo** to classify sb as sth

catálogo [ka·'ta·lo·ɣo] *m* catalog(ue); ~ **por autores** author index; **casa de ventas por ~** mail-order company; **en ~** available

Cataluña [ka·ta·'lu·ɲa] *f* Catalonia

catamarán [ka·ta·ma·'ran] *m* DEP catamaran

cataplasma [ka·ta·'plas·ma] *f* MED poultice; *inf (pesado)* bore

catapultar [ka·ta·pul·'tar] *vt* to catapult

catar [ka·'tar] *vt* to taste

catarata [ka·ta·'ra·ta] *f* **1.** GEO waterfall; **las ~s del Niágara** the Niagara Falls **2.** MED cataract

catarro [ka·'ta·rro] *m* cold; MED catarrh; ~ **de nariz** head cold

catarsis [ka·'tar·sis] *f inv* catharsis

catastro [ka·'tas·tro] *m* cadastre; **oficina del ~** land register

catástrofe [ka·'tas·tro·fe] *f* catastrophe

catastrófico, -a [ka·tas·'tro·fi·ko, -a] *adj* catastrophic; **zona catastrófica** disaster area

catchup ['ke·tʃup] *m* <catchups> ketchup

cate ['ka·te] *m inf* **1.** *(suspenso)* **me han dado dos ~s** I've failed two subjects **2.** *(bofetada)* whack

catear [ka·te·'ar] *vt inf* to fail, to flunk

catecismo [ka·te·'sis·mo, -'θis·mo] *m* REL catechism

cátedra ['ka·te·dra] *f* ENS chair; **sentar ~** to lay down the law; *irón* to pontificate

catedral [ka·te·'dral] *f* cathedral; **como una ~** *fig* massive

catedrático, -a [ka·te·'dra·ti·ko, -a] *m, f* ENS professor; ~ **de instituto** ≈ secondary-school teacher

categoría [ka·te·γo·'ri·a] *f* **1.** (*clase*) category; ~ **fiscal** tax bracket **2.** (*calidad*) quality; **de primera** ~ first-class; **dar** ~ to lend prestige; **tener mucha/poca** ~ to be important/unimportant

catequesis [ka·te·'ke·sis] *f inv* REL catechesis

catete [ka·'te·te] *m Chile* **1.** CULIN pork-broth porridge **2.** (*diablo*) devil

catéter [ka·'te·ter] *m* MED catheter

cateto, -a [ka·'te·to] *m, f* yokel

catolicismo [ka·to·li·'sis·mo, -'θis·mo] *m* REL (Roman) Catholicism

católico, -a [ka·'to·li·ko, -a] *adj, m, f* (Roman) Catholic

catorce [ka·'tor·se, -θe] *adj inv, m* fourteen; *v.t.* **ocho**

catre ['ka·tre] *m t. pey* plank bed; *inf* (*cama*) bed, sack *inf;* **llevar a alquien al** ~ to lay sb *vulg*

Cáucaso ['kau·ka·so] *m* **el** ~ the Caucasus

cauce ['kau·se, -θe] *m* **1.** GEO (*lecho*) river bed **2.** (*camino*) channel, course; ~ **jurídico** [*o* **legal**] JUR legal action; ~ **reglamentario** official channel

cauchal [kau·'tʃal] *m AmL* rubber plantation

caucho ['kau·tʃo] *m* **1.** (*sustancia*) rubber; **árbol del** ~ rubber tree **2.** *AmL* (*neumático*) tire

caución [kau·'sjon, -'θjon] *f* JUR security

caudal [kau·'dal] **I.** *adj* tail **II.** *m* **1.** (*de agua*) volume **2.** (*dinero*) fortune; **caja de ~ es** safe **3.** (*abundancia*) abundance; **un ~ de conocimientos** a wealth of knowledge

caudaloso, -a [kau·da·'lo·so, -a] *adj* (*río*) large

caudillaje [kau·di·'ja·xe, -'ʎa·xe] *m Arg, Chile, Perú, pey* (*caciquismo*) bossism

caudillo [kau·'di·jo, -ʎo] *m* MIL, POL leader; **el Caudillo** *Franco's nickname during his dictatorship*

caula ['kau·la] *f AmL* (*estratagema*) trick

causa ['kau·sa] *f* **1.** *t.* POL (*ideal*) cause; (*motivo*) reason; **a** [*o* **por**] ~ **de** on account of; **la ~ de su despido** the reason for his/her dismissal; **morir por la** ~ to die for the cause **2.** JUR lawsuit; (*proceso*) trial; **entender en una** ~ to handle a case; **instruir una** ~ to initiate legal proceedings *pl*

causante [kau·'san·te] **I.** *adj* causing **II.** *mf* originator; (*culpable*) person responsible

causar [kau·'sar] *vt* to cause; ~ **alegría** to make happy; ~ **daño** to cause damage; ~ **efecto** to have an effect; ~ **problemas** to cause problems; ~ **risa a alguien** to make sb laugh; ~ **trabajo** to make work

causeo [kau·'seo] *m Chile* CULIN snack

cautela [kau·'te·la] *f* caution

cauteloso, -a [kau·te·'lo·so, -a] *adj* cautious

cauterizar <z→c> [kau·te·ri·'sar, -'θar] *vt* MED to cauterize

cautivador(a) [kau·ti·βa·'dor, --'do·ra] *adj* captivating

cautivar [kau·ti·'βar] *vt* **1.** (*apresar*) to capture

2. (*fascinar*) to captivate

cautiverio [kau·ti·'βe·rjo] *m,* **cautividad** [kau·ti·βi·'dad] *f* captivity

cautivo, -a [kau·'ti·βo, -a] *adj, m, f* captive

cauto, -a ['kau·to, -a] *adj* cautious

cava ['ka·βa] *m* cava

> **i Cava** is referred to as the Spanish champagne. This quality sparkling white wine is produced in champagne cellars in the northeast of Spain.

cavar [ka·'βar] *vi, vt* to dig

caverna [ka·'βer·na] *f* cave; (*gruta*) *t.* MED cavern; **los hombres de las ~ s** cavemen

cavernícola [ka·βer·'ni·ko·la] *mf* cave dweller; *inf* (*retrógrado*) reactionary

caviar [ka·'βjar] *m* caviar

cavidad [ka·βi·'dad] *f t.* MED cavity

cavilar [ka·βi·'lar] *vt* ~ **algo** to ponder (on) sth

cayado [ka·'ja·do] *m* crook

caza¹ ['ka·sa, -θa] *f* **1.** (*montería*) hunting; **ir de** [*o* **a la**] ~ to go hunting **2.** (*animales*) game; ~ **mayor** big game; **carne de** ~ game

caza² ['ka·sa, -θa] *m* MIL fighter plane

cazabombardero [ka·sa·βom·bar·'de·ro, ka·θa-] *m* MIL fighter-bomber

cazador(a) [ka·sa·'dor, ka·θa-] **I.** *adj* hunting **II.** *m(f)* hunter *m,* huntress *f;* ~ **furtivo** poacher

cazadora [ka·sa·'do·ra, ka·θa-] *f* bomber jacket; ~ **de piel** leather jacket

cazar <z→c> [ka·'sar, -'θar] *vt* **1.** (*atrapar*) to hunt; (*perseguir*) to pursue **2.** (*coger*) to catch; (*conseguir*) to get **3.** (*probar la culpabilidad*) to catch sb in error; (*sorprender*) to surprise **4.** *inf* (*engañar*) to take in

cazo ['ka·so, -θo] *m* **1.** (*puchero*) saucepan **2.** (*cucharón*) ladle

cazuela [ka·'swe·la, -'θwe·la] *f* casserole

cazurro, -a [ka·'su·rro, -a; ka·'θu-] **I.** *adj* **1.** (*hosco*) sullen **2.** (*obstinado*) stubborn **3.** (*torpe*) slow-witted **II.** *m, f* **1.** (*hosco*) sullen person **2.** (*obstinado*) stubborn person **3.** (*patán*) boor

CE [se·'e, θe·'e] *f* HIST *abr de* **Comunidad Europea** EC

cebada [se·'βa·da, θe-] *f* barley

cebar [se·'βar, θe-] **I.** *vt* **1.** (*engordar*) to fatten (up) **2.** (*horno*) to stoke (up) **3.** (*un arma*) to prime **4.** (*el anzuelo*) to bait **5.** (*máquina*) to start **6.** (*cólera*) to inflame **II.** *vr:* ~ **se 1.** (*ira*) to vent one's anger; **se cebó en él** he/she vented his/her anger on him **2.** (*alimentarse*) to feed

cebiche [se·'bi·tʃe, θe-] *m AmS* CULIN ceviche (*dish of raw fish marinated in lemon juice*)

cebo ['se·βo, θe-] *m* **1.** (*de anzuelo*) bait; *t. fig* lure **2.** (*en un arma*) primer **3.** (*en un horno*) fuel

cebolla [se·'βo·ja, θe·'βo·ʎa] *f* **1.** BOT (*comestible*) onion **2.** BOT (*bulbo*) bulb

cebolleta [se·βo·'je·ta, θe·βo·'ʎe·ta] *f* **1.** BOT

(*cebolla tierna*) scallion **2.** BOT chive

cebra ['se·bra, 'θe-] *f* zebra; **paso de ~** AUTO crosswalk

cebú [se·'βu, θe-] *m* zebu

cecear [se·se·'ar, θe·θe-] *vi to pronounce Spanish 'z' and 'c' before 'e' or 'i' as* [θ]

ceceo [se·'seo, θe·'θeo] *m* **1.** (*en algunas regiones*) *pronunciation of Spanish 'z' in all occurrences and of 'c' before 'e' or 'i' as* [θ] **2.** (*defecto*) lisp

cedazo [se·'da·so, θe·'da·θo] *m* (*para cribar*) sieve; (*para pescar*) large net

ceder [se·'der, θe-] I. *vi* **1.** (*renunciar*) to renounce; (*de una pretensión*) to give up **2.** (*disminuir*) to diminish; **cedió la fiebre** the fever went down; **cedió la lluvia** the rain eased off **3.** (*capitular*) **~ a algo** to give in to sth **4.** (*cuerda*) to give way II. *vt* **1.** (*dar*) to hand over; (*balón*) to pass **2.** (*transferir*) to transfer **3.** AUTO **"ceda el paso" "yield"**

cedro ['se·dro, 'θe-] *m* cedar

cedrón [se·'dron, θe-] *m AmS* BOT lemon verbena

cédula ['se·du·la, 'θe-] *f* certificate; **~ de ahorro** savings certificate; **~ de cambio** bill of exchange; **~ de citación** summons; **~ personal** identity card; **~ real** royal charter

CEE [se·e·'e, θe·e·'e] *f* HIST *abr de* **Comunidad Económica Europea** EEC

cegar [se·'γar, θe-] *irr como fregar* I. *vi* to go [*o* become] blind II. *vt* **1.** (*quitar la vista*) to blind; **le ciega la ira** he/she is blinded by rage **2.** (*ventana*) to wall up; (*pozo*) to fill up III. *vr:* **~se** to be blinded; **~se de ira** to be blinded by rage

ceguera [se·'γe·ra, θe-] *f t. fig* blindness

Ceilán [sei·'lan, θei-] *m* Ceylon

ceja ['se·xa, 'θe-] *f* **1.** (*entrecejo*) eyebrow; **fruncir las ~s** to knit one's eyebrows; **tener a alguien entre ~ y ~** *inf* to have it in for sb **2.** (*borde*) rim **3.** MÚS (*instrumento de cuerda*) nut; (*instrumento de teclado*) pressure bar

cejar [se·'xar, θe-] *vi* to give up; (*en discusiones*) to climb down; **sin ~** unceasingly

celador(a) [se·la·'dor, -·'do·ra; θe-] *m(f)* watchman *m*, watchwoman *f*; (*de cárcel*) prison guard; (*de escuela*) monitor

celaje [se·'la·xe, θe-] *m AmL* (*fantasma*) ghost

celar [se·'lar, θe-] *vt* to keep a watchful eye on

celda ['sel·da, 'θel-] *f* (*celdilla*) cell; (*en prisión*) prison cell; **~ de castigo** solitary confinement; **~ acolchada** padded cell

celebración [se·le·βra·'sjon, θe·le·βra·'θjon] *f* **1.** (*acto*) celebration; **la ~ de una misa** the celebration of a Mass **2.** (*aplausos*) applause **3.** (*organización*) holding

celebrar [se·le·'βrar, θe-] I. *vt* **1.** (*mérito*) to celebrate **2.** (*reuniones*) to hold; **~ una subasta** to hold an auction **3.** (*alegrarse*) to be delighted; (*aplaudir*) to applaud **4.** (*llegada*) to welcome **5.** (*ventajas*) to dwell on **6.** (*tratado*) to conclude II. *vi* REL to celebrate [*o* to say] Mass III. *vr:* **~se** (*fiesta*) to be celebrated; (*reu-*

nión) to be held

célebre <celebérrimo> ['se·le·βre, 'θe-] *adj* **~ por algo** famous for sth

celebridad [se·le·βri·'dad, θe-] *f* **1.** (*personaje*) celebrity **2.** (*renombre*) fame

celeridad [se·le·ri·'dad, θe-] *f* swiftness

celeste [se·'les·te, θe-] *adj* **1.** (*célico*) celestial; **cuerpos ~s** heavenly bodies **2.** (*color*) sky blue

celestial [se·les·'tjal, θe-] *adj* (*del cielo*) celestial, heavenly; (*delicioso*) heavenly

celibato [se·li·'βa·to, θe-] *m* REL celibacy

célibe ['se·li·βe, 'θe-] I. *adj* single; REL celibate II. *mf* unmarried person

celo ['se·lo, 'θe-] *m* **1.** (*afán*) zeal **2.** *pl* (*por amor*) jealousy; **tener ~s** to be jealous **3.** *pl* (*envidia*) envy **4.** ZOOL (*macho*) rut; (*hembra*) heat; **estar en ~** (*macho*) to be in rut; (*hembra*) to be on heat **5.** (*cinta*) adhesive [*o* Scotch®] tape

celosía [se·lo·'si·a, θe-] *f* **1.** (*rejilla*) lattice **2.** (*contraventanas*) slatted shutter; (*persianas*) (Venetian) blinds *pl*

celoso, -a [se·'lo·so, -a; θe-] *adj* **1.** (*con fervor*) **~ en algo** zealous in sth **2.** (*exigente*) **~ de algo** conscientious about sth **3.** (*con celos*) jealous **4.** (*con envidia*) envious

celta ['sel·ta, 'θel-] I. *adj* Celtic II. *mf* Celt

célula ['se·lu·la, 'θe-] *f* BIO, POL cell; **~ fotoeléctrica** photoelectric cell

celulitis [se·lu·'li·tis, θe-] *f inv* MED cellulitis

cementar [se·men·'tar, θe-] *vt* TÉC to cement

cementerio [se·men·'te·rjo, θe-] *m* **1.** (*camposanto*) cemetery; **~ de coches** used-car junkyard **2.** (*depósito*) dump; **~ nuclear** nuclear waste dump

cemento [se·'men·to, θe-] *m* ARQUIT, ANAT cement; **~ armado** reinforced concrete

cena ['se·na, 'θe-] *f* supper; **la Última Cena** the Last Supper

cenáculo [se·'na·ku·lo, θe-] *m* **1.** (*tertulia*) group; (*reunión*) meeting **2.** REL cenacle

cenador [se·na·'dor, θe-] *m* dining room; (*en el jardín*) arbor

cenaduría [se·na·du·'ri·a, θe-] *f Méx* eating house (*serving only at night*)

cenagal [se·na·'γal, θe-] *m* bog; (*problema*); **estar en un ~** *inf* to be in a fix

cenar [se·'nar, θe-] I. *vi* to have dinner; **hoy hemos cenado lentejas** we had lentils for dinner today II. *vt* to have for dinner

cenicero [se·ni·'θe·ro, θe-] *m* ashtray

cenicienta [se·ni·'sjen·ta, θe·ni·'θjen-] *f*, **Cenicienta** *f t. fig* Cinderella

ceniciento, -a [se·ni·'sjen·to, -a; θe·ni·'θjen-] *adj* ash-colored

cenit [se·'nit, θe-] *m* zenith

ceniza [se·'ni·sa, θe·'ni·θa] *f* **1.** (*residuo*) ash; **Miércoles de Ceniza** Ash Wednesday; **reducir algo a ~s** to reduce sth to ashes **2.** *pl* (*restos mortales*) ashes *pl*

cenizo [se·'ni·so, θe·'ni·θo] *m* **1.** BOT goosefoot **2.** (*que trae mala suerte*) jinx

censar [sen·'sar, θen-] I. *vi* to carry out a census II. *vt* to take a census of

censo ['sen·so, 'θen-] *m* census; ~ **electoral** POL electoral roll

censor(a) [sen·'sor, -·'so·ra; θen-] *m(f)* censor

censura [sen·'su·ra, θen-] *f* 1. (*crítica*) censorship; ~ **cinematográfica** film censorship; **someter a la** ~ to censor 2. (*entidad*) censor's office 3. FIN ~ **de cuentas** auditing 4. POL **moción de** ~ motion of censure

censurar [sen·su·'rar, θen-] *vt* to censure; ~ **on todas las escenas violentas** all the violent scenes were taken out

centauro [sen·'tau·ro, θen-] *m* centaur

centavo [sen·'ta·βo, θen-] *m* 1. (*centésima parte*) hundredth (part) 2. (*de dólar*) cent, penny 3. *AmC, CSur* FIN (*moneda*) centavo

centavo, -a [sen·'ta·βo, -a; θen-] *adj* hundredth; *v.t.* **octavo**

centella [sen·'te·ja, θen·'te·ʎa] *f* 1. (*rayo*) flash of lightning 2. (*chispa*) spark 3. (*destello*) sparkle

centell(e)ar [sen·te·je·'ar, θen·te·ʎe·'ar; sen·te·'jar, θen·te·'ʎar] *vi* 1. (*relámpago*) to flash 2. (*fuego*) to spark 3. (*estrella*) to twinkle 4. (*ojos*) to glitter

centena [sen·'te·na, θen-] *f* hundred

centenar [sen·te·'nar, θen-] *m* hundred

centenario [sen·te·'na·rjo, θen-] *m* centennial

centenario, -a [sen·te·'na·rjo, -a; θen-] *adj, m, f* centenarian

centeno [sen·'te·no, θen-] *m* rye

centésimo [sen·'te·si·mo, θen-] *m* Chile, Pan, Urug FIN (*moneda*) centesimo

centésimo, -a [sen·'te·si·mo, -a; θen-] I. *adj* (*parte*) hundredth; **la centésima parte de...** a hundredth of... II. *m, f* hundredth (part)

centígrado [sen·'ti·yra·ðo, θen-] *m* centigrade; **grado** ~ degree centigrade

centigramo [sen·ti·'yra·mo, θen-] *m* centigram

centilitro [sen·ti'li·tro, θen-] *m* centiliter

centímetro [sen·'ti·me·tro, θen-] *m* centimeter

céntimo ['sen·ti·mo, -a; 'θen-] I. *adj* hundredth II. *m* 1. (*parte*) hundredth part 2. FIN (*moneda*) hundredth part of a peseta; *CRi, Par, Ven* centimo; ~ **de euro** eurocent; **estar sin un** ~ to be broke

centinela [sen·ti·'ne·la; θen-] *mf* (*de museo*) guard; MIL sentry

centollo [sen·'to·jo, -a; θen·'to·ʎo, -a] *m* spider crab

centrado, -a [sen·'tra·ðo, -a; θen-] *adj* 1. (*en el centro*) centered 2. (*forma de ser*) stable

central [sen·'tral, θen-] I. *adj* central; **Europa Central** Central Europe; **comité** ~ central committee; **estación** ~ main station II. *f* 1. (*oficina*) head office; ~ **de Correos** general [*o* main] post office; ~ **telefónica** TEL telephone exchange; (*de una empresa*) (telephone) switchboard 2. TÉC plant; ~ **depuradora** waterworks; ~ **eléctrica** electric power

station; ~ **hidroeléctrica** hydroelectric power station; ~ **nuclear** nuclear power station; ~ **térmica** oil-fired power station

centralismo [sen·tra·'lis·mo, θen-] *m* POL centralism

centralista [sen·tra·'lis·ta, θen-] *mf AmC, Ant* sugar-mill owner

centralita [sen·tra·'li·ta, θen-] *f* TEL switchboard

centralización [sen·tra·li·sa·'sjon, θen·tra·li·θa·'θjon] *f* centralization

centralizar <z→c> [sen·tra·li·'sar, θen·tra·li·'θar] *vt* to centralize

centrar [sen·'trar, θen-] I. *vt* 1. TÉC (*colocar*) to center 2. (*concentrar*) to concentrate 3. (*interés*) to focus II. *vi, vt* DEP (*fútbol*) to center III. *vr:* ~**se** 1. (*basarse*) to center 2. (*familiarizarse*) ~**se en algo** to get to know sth; (*en un trabajo*) to settle (down) to sth 3. (*interés*) to focus

céntrico, -a ['sen·tri·ko, -a; 'θen-] *adj t.* TÉC central; **punto** ~ focal point; **piso** ~ an apartment in the center of town

centrifugar <g→gu> [sen·tri·fu·'yar, θen-] *vt* to spin-dry; TÉC to centrifuge

centrífugo, -a [sen·'tri·fu·yo, -a; θen-] *adj* centrifugal; **fuerza centrífuga** centrifugal force

centrista [sen·'tris·ta, θen-] I. *adj* POL centrist; **partido** ~ centrist party II. *mf* POL centrist

centro ['sen·tro, 'θen-] *m* 1. *t.* POL, DEP (*el medio*) center; (*de la ciudad*) center city, downtown; ~ **de gravedad** center of gravity; ~ **industrial** industrial center 2. (*institución*) center; ~ **de atención de llamadas** call center; ~ **de computación** computer center; ~ **de desintoxicación** detox(ification) center [*o* clinic]; ~ **de enseñanza** teaching institution; ~ **comercial** shopping center, mall 3. ANAT ~ **nervioso** nerve center

centroafricano, -a [sen·tro·a·fri·'ka·no, -a; θen-] *adj, m, f* Central African

Centroamérica [sen·tro·a·'me·ri·ka, θen-] *f* Central America

centroamericano, -a [sen·tro·a·me·ri·'ka·no, -a; θen-] *adj, m, f* Central American

Centroeuropa [sen·tro·eu·'ro·pa, θen-] *f* Central Europe

centuplicar <c→qu> [sen·tu·pli·'kar, θen-] *vt* to increase a hundredfold

céntuplo ['sen·tu·plo, 'θen-] *m* hundredfold

centuria [sen·'tu·rja, θen-] *f elev* century

centurión [sen·tu·'rjon, θen-] *m* HIST centurion

ceñido, -a [se·'ɲi·ðo, -a; θen-] *adj* tight-fitting, figure-hugging

ceñir [se·'ɲir, θe-] *irr* I. *vt* 1. *t.* MIL (*rodear*) to surround 2. (*ponerse*) to put on; (*cinturón*) to buckle on II. *vr:* ~**se** 1. (*ajustarse*) to limit oneself; (*al hablar*) to be brief; ~ **se al presupuesto** to keep to the budget 2. (*vestido*) to be close-fitting 3. (*ponerse*) to put on; **se ciñó el cinturón** he/she buckled on his/her belt

ceño ['se·ɲo, 'θe-] *m* frown; **fruncir** [*o* **arrugar**] **el** ~, **mirar con** ~ to frown

cepa ['se·pa, 'θe-] *f t.* BOT (*tronco*) stump; (*en la vid*) stock; **de pura ~** real

cepillar [se·pi·'jar, θe·pi·'ʎar] **I.** *vt* **1.** (*traje*) to brush; TÉC (*madera*) to plane **2.** *inf* (*robar*) to rip off **3.** *AmL, inf* (*adular*) to butter up **4.** *inf* (*ganar*) to win **5.** (*suspender*) to fail, to flunk **II.** *vr:* **~ se 1.** *inf* (*robar*) to rip off **2.** *inf* (*devorar*) to polish off **3.** *inf* (*dinero*) to squander **4.** *inf* (*matar*) to bump off **5.** *vulg* (*seducir*) to make it with; **~ se a una chica** to screw a girl

cepillo [se·'pi·jo, θe·'pi·ʎo] *m* **1.** (*para traje*) brush; TÉC (*para madera*) plane; (*de limpiar*) scrubbing brush; **~ de barrer** broom; **~ de dientes** toothbrush; **pasar el ~** to brush **2.** (*en misa*) collection box

cepo ['se·po, 'θe-] *m* **1.** (*caza*) trap; **caer en el ~** to fall into the trap **2.** (*grilletes*) stocks *pl* **3.** *pl* AUTO wheel clamp

ceporro, -a [se·'po·rro, θe-] **I.** *adj inf* (*ignorante*) dim-witted **II.** *m, f inf* dimwit; **dormir como un ~** to sleep like a log

cera ['se·ra, 'θe-] *f* wax; **~ de los oídos** earwax; **~ para suelos** wax polish; **museo de ~** wax museum; **blanco como la ~** white as a sheet

cerámica [se·'ra·mi·ka, θe-] *f* ceramics *pl*

cerca ['ser·ka, 'θer-] **I.** *adv* **1.** (*en el espacio*) near; **aquí ~** near here; **mirar de ~** to look closely at **2.** (*en el tiempo*) close **II.** *prep* **1.** (*lugar*) **~ de** near **2.** (*cantidad*) about **III.** *f* fence

cercanía [ser·ka·'ni·a, θer-] *f* **1.** (*proximidad*) closeness; (*vecindad*) neighborhood **2.** *pl* (*alrededores*) outskirts *pl*

cercano, -a [ser·'ka·no, -a; θer-] *adj* near

cercar <c→qu> [ser·'kar, θer-] *vt* **1.** (*vallar*) to fence in **2.** (*rodear*) to surround **3.** MIL (*sitiar*) to besiege

cercenar [ser·se·'nar, θer·θe-] *vt* to cut off; MED to amputate; (*sueldo*) to cut (back)

cerciorarse [ser·sjo·'rar·se, θer·θjo-] *vr* to make sure

cerco ['ser·ko, 'θer-] *m* **1.** (*círculo*) circle; (*borde*) rim **2.** (*valla*) fence **3.** ASTR halo **4.** MIL siege

cerda ['ser·da, 'θer-] *f* **1.** ZOOL sow **2.** (*pelo*) bristle; **~ de cerdo** pigs bristle

Cerdeña [ser·'de·ɲa, θer-] *f* Sardinia

cerdo, -a ['ser·do, -a; 'θer-] **I.** *adj* (*sucio*) dirty **II.** *m, f* **1.** ZOOL pig; **carne de ~** pork **2.** (*insulto*) swine

cereales [se·re·'a·les, θe-] *mpl* cereals *pl*, grain

cerebelo [se·re·'βe·lo, θe-] *m* ANAT cerebellum

cerebro [se·'re·βro, θe-] *m* **1.** ANAT brain **2.** (*inteligencia*) brains *pl*

ceremonia [se·re·'mo·nja, θe-] *f* **1.** (*acto*) ceremony **2.** (*cortesía*) formality; **sin ~s** without any fuss

ceremonial [se·re·mo·'njal, θe-] *adj, m* ceremonial

ceremonioso, -a [se·re·mo·'njo·so, -a; θe-] *adj* **1.** (*solemne*) ceremonious **2.** (*persona*) stiff

cereza [se·'re·sa, θe·'re·θa] *f* cherry

cerezo [se·'re·so, θe·'re·θo] *m* (*árbol*) cherry tree; (*madera*) cherry wood

cerilla [se·'ri·ja, θe·'ri·ʎa] *f* **1.** (*fósforo*) match **2.** (*cerumen*) earwax

cerillero [se·ri·'je·ro, θe·ri·'ʎe·ro] *m AmL* (*cajita*) matchbox

cerillo [se·'ri·jo, θe·'ri·ʎo] *m Méx* (*fósforo*) match

cerner [ser·'ner, θer-] *irr vt* **1.** (*cribar*) to sieve, to sift **2.** (*observar*) to observe; (*cielo*) to scan

cero ['se·ro, 'θe-] *m t.* MAT zero; **ocho (grados) bajo/sobre ~** eight below/above zero; **partir de ~** to start from scratch

cerote [se·'ro·te, θe-] *m AmC, Méx, inf* (*excremento*) stool; **estar hecho un ~** to look a mess

cerrado, -a [se·'rra·do, -a; θe-] *adj* **1.** *estar* (*no abierto*) closed; (*con llave*) locked; (*cielo*) overcast; **la puerta está cerrada** the door is closed; **a puerta cerrada** behind closed doors; **aquí huele a ~** it smells stuffy in here **2.** *ser* (*actitud*) reserved **3.** *ser* (*espeso*) thick; (*denso*) dense; **noche cerrada** dark night **4.** *ser* (*acento*) broad **5.** *ser* (*curva*) sharp **6.** *ser* (*lerdo*) thick; **~ de mollera** *inf* very dense

cerradura [se·rra·'du·ra, θe-] *f* **1.** (*dispositivo*) lock; **~ antirrobo** steering(-wheel) lock **2.** (*acción*) closing; (*con llave*) locking

cerrajería [se·rra·xe·'ri·a, θe-] *f* **1.** (*taller*) locksmith's (shop) **2.** (*oficio*) locksmith's craft

cerrajero, -a [se·rra·'xe·ro, -a; θe-] *m, f* locksmith

cerrar <e→ie> [se·'rrar, θe-] **I.** *vt* **1.** (*puerta*) to close; (*con llave*) to lock; (*carta*) to seal; **~ los oídos** to turn a deaf ear; **~ el pico** *inf* to keep one's trap shut; **~ archivo** COMPUT to close a file; **~ el paso a alguien** to block sb's way **2.** (*agujero*) to block (up); (*agua*) to turn off **3.** (*terreno*) to close off; (*con un cerco*) to enclose **4.** (*negociación*) to conclude **II.** *vi* **1.** (*puerta*) to close **2.** (*acabar*) to end **III.** *vr:* **~ se 1.** (*puerta*) **la puerta se cerró sola** the door closed by itself **2.** (*herida*) to heal (up) **3.** (*obstinarse*) to persist **4.** (*el cielo*) to become overcast **5.** (*ser intransigente*) to close one's mind **6.** (*agruparse*) to crowd together

cerrazón [se·rra·'son, θe·rra·'θon] *f* **1.** (*torpeza*) dimness **2.** (*obstinación*) stubbornness **3.** METEO storm clouds

cerril [se·'rril, θe-] *adj* **1.** (*obstinado*) obstinate **2.** (*torpe*) dense **3.** (*tosco*) uncouth **4.** (*caballerías*) wild

cerro ['se·rro, 'θe-] *m* hill; (*peñasco*) crag; **irse por los ~s de Úbeda** *inf* to go off on a tangent; (*decir tonterías*) to talk (a lot of) rubbish

cerrojo [se·'rro·xo, θe-] *m* bolt; **echar el ~ a la puerta** to bolt the door

certamen [ser·'ta·men, θer-] *m* competition

certero, -a [ser·'te·ro, -a; θer-] *adj* **1.** (*acertado*) accurate **2.** (*tirador*) crack **3.** (*informado*) well-informed

certeza [ser·'te·sa, θer·'te·θa] *f* certainty
certidumbre [ser·ti·'dum·bre, θer-] *f* certainty
certificación [ser·ti·fi·ka·'sjon, θer·ti·fi·ka·'θjon] *f* **1.**(*documento*) certification **2.**JUR (*atestado*) attestation
certificado [ser·ti·fi·'ka·do, θer-] *m* certificate; **~ de aptitud** testimonial; **~ de asistencia** certificate of attendance; **~ escolar** school report; **~ médico** medical certificate
certificado, -a [ser·ti·fi·'ka·do, -a; θer-] *adj* JUR certified; **carta certificada** (*correos*) registered letter
certificar <c→qu> [ser·ti·fi·'kar, θer-] *vt* **1.** *t.* JUR (*afirmar*) to certify **2.**(*correos*) to register
cerumen [se·'ru·men, θe-] *m* earwax
cervecería [ser·βe·se·'ri·a, θer·βe·θe-] *f* **1.**(*bar*) bar **2.**(*fábrica*) brewery
cervecero, -a [ser·βe·'se·ro, -a; θer·βe·'θe-] *adj* beer; (*industria*) brewing
cerveza [ser·'βe·sa, θer·'βe·θa] *f* beer; **~ de barril** draft beer; **~ negra** dark beer, stout; **~ rubia** lager beer
cervical [ser·βi·'kal, θer-] *adj* **1.**ANAT neck **2.**MED cervical
cerviz [ser·'βis, θer·'βiθ] *f* ANAT nape of the neck
cesación [se·sa·'sjon, θe·sa·'θjon] *f*, **cesamiento** [se·sa·'mjen·to, θe-] *m* cessation; **~ del fuego** ceasefire
cesante [se·'san·te, θe-] **I.** *adj* suspended **II.** *mf* laid-off civil servants
cesar [se·'sar, θe-] **I.** *vi* **1.**(*parar*) to stop; **sin ~** ceaselessly **2.**(*en una profesión*) **~ en algo** to leave sth **II.** *vt* **1.**(*pagos*) to stop **2.**(*despedir*) to dismiss
cesárea [se·'sa·rea, θe-] *f* Cesarean, C-section
cese ['se·se, 'θe-] *m* **1.**(*que termina*) cessation; (*interrupción*) suspension; **~ de pagos** suspension of payments **2.**(*de obrero*) sacking; (*de funcionario*) dismissal; **~ en el cargo** to retire from office
cesio ['se·sjo, 'θe-] *m* cesium
cesión [se·'sjon, 'θe-] *f* **1.**(*entrega*) transfer **2.**JUR cession
césped ['ses·ped, 'θes-] *m* grass; **'prohibido pisar el ~'** 'keep off the grass'
cesta ['ses·ta, 'θes-] *f* basket
cesto ['ses·to, 'θes-] *m t.* DEP basket; **~ de los papeles** wastebasket
cesura [se·'su·ra, θe-] *f* caesura
ceta ['se·ta, 'θe-] *f* Z
cetáceo [se·'ta·θeo, θe-] *m* cetacean
cetrería [se·tre·'ri·a, θe-] *f* falconry
cetro ['se·tro, 'θe-] *m* **1.**(*vara*) scepter; **empuñar el ~** *elev* to ascend the throne **2.** DEP championship; **ostentar el ~** to reign supreme
cf. *abr de* **compárese** cf.
chabacanería [tʃa·βa·ka·ne·'ri·a] *f* vulgarity
chabacano, -a [tʃa·βa·'ka·no, -a] *adj* vulgar
chabola [tʃa·'βo·la] *f* **1.**(*casucha*) shack **2.** *pl* (*barrio*) shanty town
chabolismo [tʃa·βo·'lis·mo] *m* shanty-town conditions *pl*, slums *pl*

chacal [tʃa·'kal] *m* jackal
chacalín [tʃa·ka·'lin] *m AmC* ZOOL shrimp
chacanear [tʃa·ka·ne·'ar] *vt Chile* (*montura*) to spur on
chácara ['tʃa·ka·ra] *f Par, Nic, Bol* **1.**(*granja*) small farm **2.** MED ulcer
chacarero, -a [tʃa·ka·'re·ro] *m, f AmL* farmer; (*trabajador*) farm laborer
chacha ['tʃa·tʃa] *f inf* (*niñera*) nursemaid; (*criada*) maid; (*de limpieza*) cleaning lady
cháchara ['tʃa·tʃa·ra] *f inf* (*charla*) chatter; **andar** [*o* **estar**] **de ~** to have a chat
chacho, -a ['tʃa·tʃo, -a] *m, f inf* (*muchacho*) boy *m*; (*muchacha*) girl *f*
chacolotear [tʃa·ko·lo·te·'ar] *vi* to clatter
chacra ['tʃa·kra] *f AmL* (*granja*) small farm; (*finca*) country estate
Chad [tʃad] *m* Chad
chafar [tʃa·'far] **I.** *vt* **1.**(*aplastar*) to flatten *fig*, to squelch; (*arrugar*) to crease; (*deshacer*) to mess up **2.**(*confundir*) to confuse; **quedar(se) chafado** to be speechless **3.**(*estropear*) to spoil; **le ~on sus proyectos** they spoiled his/her plans **II.** *vr:* **~se** (*aplastarse*) to be flattened; (*deshacerse*) to be messed up; (*arrugarse*) to be creased
chaflán [tʃa·'flan] *m* **1.**(*bisel*) bevel (edge) **2.**(*en una calle*) street corner; (*en un edificio*) house corner
chagra ['tʃa·ɣra] *mf Ecua* (*labriego*) peasant
cháguar ['tʃa·ɣwar] *m AmS* BOT Paraguayan sisal
chal [tʃal] *m* shawl
chalado, -a [tʃa·'la·do, -a] **I.** *adj inf* crazy; **estar ~ por alguien** to be crazy about sb **II.** *m, f inf* nutcase
chalanear [tʃa·la·ne·'ar] *vt AmL* (*un caballo*) to break in; (*adiestrar*) to train
chalar [tʃa·'lar] **I.** *vt inf* to drive crazy **II.** *vr:* **~se** *inf* to go crazy; **~se por alguien** to be crazy about sb
chalé [tʃa·'le] *m* (*casa unifamiliar*) detached family home; (*de campo*) country house; (*villa*) chalet
chaleco [tʃa·'le·ko] *m* vest; **~ salvavidas** life jacket
chalina [tʃa·'li·na] *f Arg, Col, CRi* (*chal*) narrow shawl
chalupa [tʃa·'lu·pa] *f* NÁUT launch
chamaco, -a [tʃa·'ma·ko, -a] *m, f Cuba, Méx* **1.**(*muchacho*) boy; (*muchacha*) girl **2.**(*novio*) boyfriend; (*novia*) girlfriend
chamagoso, -a [tʃa·ma·'ɣo·so, -a] *adj Méx* (*mugriento*) filthy
chamborote [tʃam·bo·'ro·te] *adj Ecua* **1.**(*de nariz larga*) long-nosed **2.**(*blanco*) **pimiento ~** long white pepper
chamico [tʃa·'mi·ko] *m AmL* BOT thorn apple
champán [tʃam·'pan] *m*, **champaña** [tʃam·'pa·ɲa] *m* champagne
Champaña [tʃam·'pa·ɲa] *f* Champagne
champiñón [tʃam·'pi·ɲon] *m* mushroom
champú [tʃam·'pu] *m* shampoo; **~ anticaspa**

anti-dandruff shampoo

chamuscado, -a [tʃa·mus·'ka·do, -a] *adj* **1.**(*quemado*) scorched **2.** *inf*(*receloso*) suspicious

chamuscar <c→qu> [tʃa·mus·'kar] **I.** *vt* (*quemar*) to scorch; (*aves*) to singe **II.** *vr:* **~se 1.**(*quemarse*) to get scorched **2.** *inf* (*ponerse receloso*) to become suspicious

chamusquina [tʃa·mus·'ki·na] *f* (*quemadura*) scorching; (*de aves*) singeing; **esto huele a ~** *inf*(*sospechoso*) this smells fishy; (*peligroso*) there's trouble in store

chance ['tʃan·se, -θe] *m o f AmC* (*oportunidad*) chance

chanchería [tʃan·tʃe·'ri·a] *f AmL* pork butcher's shop

chancho ['tʃan·tʃo] *m AmL* pig

chancho, -a ['tʃan·tʃo, -a] *adj AmL* **1.**(*marrano*) dirty **2.**(*desaseado*) slovenly

chanchullo [tʃan·'tʃu·jo, -ʎo] *m inf* swindle, fiddle

chancla ['tʃan·kla] *f* **1.**(*zapato viejo*) old shoe **2.**(*zapatilla*) slipper **3.**(*de playa*) flip flop

chancleta [tʃan·'kle·ta] *f* **1.**(*chinela*) slipper **2.** *AmL* (*bebé*) baby girl **3.** *inf*(*persona inepta*) fool **4.** *AmL, pey* (*mujer*) slut

chanclo ['tʃan·klo] *m* **1.**(*zueco*) clog **2.**(*de goma*) (rubber) overshoe, galosh

chándal ['tʃan·dal] *m* <chándals> tracksuit

changa ['tʃan·ga] *f* **1.** *Arg* (*ocupación*) trade **2.** *AmS* (*transporte*) porterage **3.** *AmS, Cuba* (*broma*) joke

changador [tʃan·ga·'dor] *m* **1.** *AmS* (*cargador*) carrier **2.** *Arg* (*temporero*) casual worker

chanta ['tʃan·ta] *mf Arg, inf* (*impostor*) fraud

chantaje [tʃan·'ta·xe] *m* blackmail

chantajear [tʃan·ta·xe·'ar] *vt* to blackmail

chantajista [tʃan·ta·'xis·ta] *mf* blackmailer

chantar [tʃan·'tar] *vt Chile* (*golpe*) to deal

chanza ['tʃan·sa, -θa] *f* joke; **estar de ~** to be joking

chapa ['tʃa·pa] *f* **1.**(*metal*) sheet **2.**(*lámina*) plate **3.**(*contrachapado*) plywood **4.**(*tapón*) (bottle)cap **5.**(*chapeta*) flush (in the cheeks) **6.**(*placa*) badge **7.** *AmL* (*cerradura*) lock **8.** *pl* (*juego*) game played with bottle caps

chapar [tʃa·'par] *vt* to plate; (*con oro*) to gold-plate; **chapado a la antigua** *fig* old-fashioned

chaparreras [tʃa·pa·'rre·ras] *fpl Méx* (*pantalones para montar a caballo*) chaps *pl*

chaparro [tʃa·'pa·rro] *m* dwarf oak

chaparro, -a [tʃa·'pa·rro, -a] **I.** *adj inf* squat **II.** *m, f inf* shorty

chaparrón [tʃa·pa·'rron] *m* **1.**(*lluvia*) downpour; (*chubasco*) cloudburst **2.** *inf* (*cantidad grande*) barrage

chapear [tʃa·pe·'ar] *vt* **1.**(*con un metal*) to plate; (*con oro*) to gold-plate **2.** *AmL* (*la tierra*) to weed

chapero [tʃa·'pe·ro] *m inf* **1.**(*prostituto*) male prostitute, rent boy *inf* **2.**(*homosexual*) queer

chapetón, -ona [tʃa·pe·'ton] **I.** *adj AmL* newly arrived **II.** *m, f AmL* Spaniard in America

chapisca [tʃa·'pis·ka] *f AmC* AGR (*cosecha de maíz*) corn harvest

chapopote [tʃa·po·'po·te] *m Ant, Méx* (*asfalto*) asphalt

chapotear [tʃa·po·te·'ar] *vi* (*persona*) to paddle; (*agua*) to splash (around)

chapucear [tʃa·pu·se·'ar, -θe·'ar] *vt* to botch

chapucero, -a [tʃa·pu·'se·ro, -a; -'θe·ro, -a] **I.** *adj* **1.**(*trabajando*) shoddy **2.**(*embustero*) deceitful **II.** *m, f* **1.**(*chambón*) bungler **2.**(*embustero*) cheat

chapulín [tʃa·pu·'lin] *m* **1.** *AmL* (*langosta*) large cicada **2.** *AmC* (*niño*) child

chapurr(e)ar [tʃa·pu·rre·'ar/tʃa·pu·'rrar] *vt* to speak badly

chapuza [tʃa·'pu·sa, -θa] *f* **1.**(*chapucería*) shoddy job **2.**(*trabajo*) odd job

chapuzón [tʃa·pu·'son, -'θon] *m* dip; **darse un ~** to go for a dip

chaqué [tʃa·'ke] *m* morning coat

chaqueta [tʃa·'ke·ta] *f* jacket; **cambiar de** [*o* **la**] **~** *fig* to change sides

chaquetón [tʃa·ke·'ton] *m* long jacket; (*cazadora*) windbreaker

charada [tʃa·'ra·da] *f* charade

charanga [tʃa·'ran·ga] *f* **1.**(*banda*) brass band **2.** *AmL* (*baile*) dance

ⓘ The **charango**, found throughout South America, is originally from **Bolivia**. This small guitar-like instrument has five pairs of strings and a sound box traditionally made out of armadillo shells. Today, charangos are more commonly made out of wood.

charca ['tʃar·ka] *f* pond

charco ['tʃar·ko] *m* puddle, pool

charcón, -ona [tʃar·'kon, -·'ko·na] *adj Arg, Bol, Urug* (*flaco*) skinny

charcutería [tʃar·ku·te·'ri·a] *f* **1.**(*productos*) cooked or cured pork products *pl* **2.**(*tienda*) ≈ delicatessen

charla ['tʃar·la] *f* **1.**(*conversación*) chat; **estar de ~** to have a chat **2.**(*conferencia*) talk

charlar [tʃar·'lar] *vi* **1.**(*conversar*) to chat **2.**(*parlotear*) to chatter

charlatán, -ana [tʃar·la·'tan, -·'ta·na] **I.** *adj* talkative **II.** *m, f* **1.**(*hablador*) chatterbox **2.**(*chismoso*) gossip **3.**(*vendedor*) hawker **4.**(*curandero*) charlatan

charlatanería [tʃar·la·ta·ne·'ri·a] *f* **1.**(*locuacidad*) talkativeness **2.**(*palabrería*) sales talk **3.**(*curanderismo*) charlatanism

charol [tʃa·'rol] *m* **1.**(*barniz*) varnish **2.**(*cuero*) patent leather **3.** *AmL* (*bandeja*) tray

charqui ['tʃar·ki] *m AmS* (*charque*) beef jerky

charro, -a ['tʃa·rro] *adj* in bad taste; (*chillón*) flashy

chárter ['tʃar·ter] *adj inv* charter; **vuelo ~** charter flight

chasca ['tʃas·ka] *f* **1.**(*ramaje*) brushwood **2.** *CSur* (*pelo*) mop of hair

chascar <c→qu> [ʧas·'kar] I. *vi* 1.(*con la lengua*) to click; (*con el látigo*) to crack; (*con los dedos*) to snap 2.(*madera*) to creak; (*fuego*) to crackle II. *vt* (*comida*) to gulp down

chascarrillo [ʧas·ka·'rri·jo, -ʎo] *m* funny story

chasco ['ʧas·ko] *m* 1.(*burla*) joke 2.(*decepción*) disappointment

chasco, -a ['ʧas·ko, -a] *adj CSur* crinkly

chasis ['ʧa·sis] *m inv* 1.AUTO chassis 2.FOTO plate holder

chasque ['ʧas·ke] *m AmS* (*mensajero*) Indian messenger

chasquear [ʧas·ke·'ar] I. *vt* to play a trick on II. *vi* 1.(*con la lengua*) to click; (*con el látigo*) to crack; (*con los dedos*) to snap 2.(*madera*) to creak; (*fuego*) to crackle

chasqui ['ʧas·ki] *m AmS* (*chasque*) messenger

chasquido [ʧas·'ki·do] *m* 1.(*de lengua*) click; (*de látigo*) crack 2.(*de la madera*) creak

chatarra [ʧa·'ta·rra] *f* 1.(*metal viejo*) scrap (metal) 2.(*trastos*) junk 3. *inf* (*dinero*) change

chatarrería [ʧa·ta·rre·'ri·a] *f* junkyard

chatarrero, -a [ʧa·ta·'rre·ro, -a] *m, f* junkman *m; * junkwoman *f*

chato, -a ['ʧa·to] I. *adj* 1.(*nariz*) snub 2.(*persona*) snub-nosed 3.(*objeto*) blunt; (*aplastado*) flattened II. *m, f inf* (*tratamiento*) kid

chatre ['ʧa·tre] *adj Chile, Ecua* (*elegante*) elegantly dressed

chaucha ['ʧau·ʧa] *f AmS* 1.(*judía verde*) green bean 2.(*patata*) new potato 3. *pl* (*calderilla*) small change

chauchera [ʧau·'ʧe·ra] *f Chile, Ecua* (*monedero*) purse

chauvinista [ʧo·βi·'nis·ta] I. *adj* chauvinist(ic) II. *mf* chauvinist

chaval(a) [ʧa·'βal, -'βa·la] *m(f) inf* (*chico*) kid; (*joven*) young man *m*, young woman *f*

che [ʧe] *interj AmS* hey

chécheres ['ʧe·ʧe·res] *mpl Col, CRi* things *pl*

checo, -a ['ʧe·ko, -a] I. *adj* Czech; **República Checa** Czech Republic II. *m, f* Czech

checo(e)slovaco, -a [ʧe·kos·lo·'βa·ko, -a/ʧe·ko·es·lo·'βa·ko, -a] HIST I. *adj* Czechoslovak(ian) II. *m, f* Czechoslovakian

chelín [ʧe·'lin] *m* (*moneda*) shilling

chelista [ʧe·'lis·ta] *mf* cellist

chelo ['ʧe·lo] *m* cello

chepa ['ʧe·pa] *f inf* hump ▶ **subirse a la ~ de alguien** to be disrespectful to sb

cheque ['ʧe·ke] *m* check; **~ bancario** bank check; **~ en blanco** blank check; **~ cruzado** check crossed for deposit only; **~ sin fondo** bounced check; **~ de viaje** traveler's check; **cobrar un ~** to cash a check; **librar** [*o* **extender| un ~** to write a check

chequear [ʧe·ke·'ar] I. *vt AmL* (*comprobar*) to check II. *vr:* **~se** to get a checkup

chequeo [ʧe·'keo] *m* (*de la salud*) checkup; (*de un mecanismo*) service

chequera [ʧe·'ke·ra] *f AmL* checkbook

Chequia ['ʧe·kja] *f* Czech Republic

chévere ['ʧe·βe·re] I. *adj Ven, inf* terrific II. *mf*

Cuba, PRico, Ven braggart

chica ['ʧi·ka] I. *adj* (*pequeña*) small; (*joven*) young II. *f* 1.(*niña*) girl; (*joven*) young woman 2.(*criada*) maid

chicano, -a [ʧi·'ka·no, -a] *m, f* Chicano (*person of Mexican origin living in the USA*)

chicarrón, -ona [ʧi·ka·'rron, -·'rro·na] I. *adj* sturdy II. *m, f* sturdy kid

chicha ['ʧi·ʧa] I. *f* 1. *inf* (*carne*) meat; **tener pocas ~s** (*delgado*) to be slim 2. *AmL* CULIN chicha (*a type of corn-based beer*) ▶ **ni ~ ni limonada** neither fish nor fowl II. *adj* NÁUT **calma ~** dead calm

i **Chicha** is a slightly sour corn-based beer that is frequently drunk in the **Andes** region. Chicha is produced by the natives themselves and can be purchased in **chicherías**. To make **chicha**, corn is mixed with water and left until it germinates. Then, it is ground and cooked in water. After filtration, the liquid is fermented in earthenware jugs. **Chicha** is usually only allowed to ferment over night to prevent the alcohol content from getting too high.

chicharrón [ʧi·ʧa·'rron] *m* 1.(*carne*) piece of burnt meat 2.CULIN crackling (of pork)

chichi ['ʧi·ʧi] *adj AmC* (*fácil*) easy

chichón [ʧi·'ʧon] *m* bump

chicle ['ʧi·kle] *m* chewing gum

chico ['ʧi·ko] I. *adj* 1.(*pequeño*) small 2.(*joven*) young II. *m* 1.(*niño*) boy; (*joven*) young man 2.(*de los recados*) errand boy

chicote [ʧi·'ko·te] *m AmL* (*látigo*) whip

chiflado, -a [ʧi·'fla·do, -a] I. *adj inf* crazy; **estar ~ por alguien** to be crazy about sb II. *m, f inf* nutcase

chifladura [ʧi·fla·'du·ra] *f* 1.(*locura*) craziness; (*empeño*) keenness 2.(*antojo*) whim

chiflar [ʧi·'flar] I. *vt inf* (*gustar*) to be crazy about; **me chiflan las aceitunas** I love olives II. *vr:* **~se** *inf* 1.(*pirrarse*) **~se por alguien** to be crazy about sb 2.(*volverse loco*) to go crazy

chiflón [ʧi·'flon] *m AmL* (*viento*) gale; (*corriente*) draft; **un ~ de aire** a blast of air

chigüín [ʧi·'ɣwin] *m AmC* (*chavalín*) kid

chiíta [ʧi·'i·ta] *adj, mf* Shiite

chile ['ʧi·le] *m* (*especia*) chili

Chile ['ʧi·le] *m* Chile

i The capital of **Chile** (formally named **República de Chile**) is **Santiago (de Chile)**. Although the country stretches for over 4,000 km (2,500 miles) from north to south, Chile is only 180 km (112 miles) wide on average. The country's official language is Spanish and the official currency is the **peso chileno**.

chileno, -a [tʃi·'le·no, -a] *adj, m, f* Chilean
chillar [tʃi·'jar, -'ʎar] *vi* 1. (*persona*) to yell; **¡no me chilles!** don't shout at me! 2. (*animal*) to howl; (*frenos*) to screech; (*puerta*) to creak 3. (*colores*) to clash 4. *AmL* (*sollozar*) to sob
chillido [tʃi·'ji·do, -'ʎi·do] *m* 1. (*de persona*) yell 2. (*de animal*) howl; (*de frenos*) screech; (*de puerta*) creak 3. *AmL* (*sollozo*) sob
chilote [tʃi·'lo·te] *m Méx*: drink made of chili and pulque (*beverage made of agave*)
chilpayate [tʃil·pa·'ja·te] *m Méx, inf* kid
chimenea [tʃi·me·'nea] *f* 1. *t.* GEO (*de un edificio*) chimney 2. (*hogar*) fireplace
chimpancé [tʃim·pan·'se, -'θe] *mf* chimpanzee
china ['tʃi·na] *f* 1. (*piedra*) pebble 2. *AmL* (*india*) Indian woman; (*mestiza*) half-caste woman 3. *AmL* (*amante*) mistress
China ['tʃi·na] *f* (**la**) ~ China
chinchar [tʃin·'tʃar] I. *vt inf* to pester II. *vr:* ~ **se** *inf* to get upset; **¡chínchate!** so there!, tough luck!
chinche¹ ['tʃin·tʃe] *m o f* ZOOL bedbug
chinche² ['tʃin·tʃe] *mf inf* (*pelmazo*) pain
chincheta [tʃin·'tʃe·ta] *f* thumbtack
chinchudo, -a [tʃin·'tʃu·do, -a] *adj Arg, inf* **estar** ~ to be angry
chincol [tʃin·'kol] *f AmS* ZOOL crown sparrow
chinela [tʃi·'ne·la] *f* slipper
chingado, -a [tʃin·'ga·do, -a] *adj Méx, inf* 1. (*frustrado*) annoyed 2. (*estropeado*) lousy
chingar <g→gu> [tʃin·'gar] I. *vt* 1. *inf* (*molestar*) to annoy 2. *inf* (*bebidas*) to drink 3. *vulg* (*joder*) to fuck II. *vr:* ~ **se** *inf* 1. (*emborracharse*) to get plastered 2. *AmL* (*frustrarse*) to be a washout 3. *AmL* (*fallar*) to fail
chingo, -a ['tʃin·go, -a] *adj* 1. *AmC* (*animal*) with a cropped tail 2. *AmC, Ven* (*chato*) flat-nosed 3. *AmC* (*corto*) short 4. *CRi* (*desnudo*) naked 5. *Ven* (*ansioso*) anxious 6. *Col, Cuba* (*pequeño*) tiny 7. *Nic* (*bajo*) short
chingue ['tʃin·ge] *m Chile* ZOOL skunk
chinita [tʃi·'ni·ta] *f Chile* (*insecto*) ladybug
chino ['tʃi·no] *m AmL* (*indio*) Indian; (*mestizo*) mestizo
chino, -a ['tʃi·no, -a] I. *adj* Chinese II. *m, f* Chinese man *m*, Chinese woman *f* ▸ **engañar a alguien como a un** ~ *inf* to take sb for a ride
chip [tʃip] *m* COMPUT chip
chipichipi [tʃi·pi·'tʃi·pi] *m Méx* (*llovizna*) drizzle
Chipre ['tʃi·pre] *f* Cyprus
chipriota [tʃi·'prjo·ta] *adj, mf* Cypriot
chiqueo [tʃi·'keo] *m* 1. *Cuba, Méx* (*mimo*) pampering 2. *AmC* (*contoneo*) swagger
chiquillada [tʃi·ki·'ja·da, -'ʎa·da] *f* 1. (*niñería*) childishness 2. (*travesura*) childish prank
chiquillo, -a [tʃi·'ki·jo, -a; -'ki·ʎo, -a] I. *adj* young II. *m, f* (*niño*) (small) child; (*chico*) (little) boy; (*chica*) (little) girl
chirigota [tʃi·ri·'ɣo·ta] *f* joke
chirimbolo [tʃi·rim·'bo·lo] *m inf* 1. (*chisme*) gadget 2. *pl* things *pl*
chirimoya [tʃi·ri·'mo·ja] *f* custard apple

chiringuito [tʃi·rin·'gi·to] *m* kiosk (*selling snacks and drinks*)
chiripa [tʃi·'ri·pa] *f inf* stroke of luck; (*en el juego*) lucky break; (*casualidad*) fluke
chirola [tʃi·'ro·la] *f* 1. *Arg* (*moneda*) old coin made of nickel 2. *Chile* (*moneda*) silver 20 centavo coin 3. *pl, Arg* (*calderilla*) small change
chirona [tʃi·'ro·na] *f inf* jail, clink *inf*
chirriar <1. pres: chirrío> [tʃi·rri·'ar] *vi* 1. (*metal*) to squeak; (*madera*) to creak 2. (*pájaros*) to chirp
chisme ['tʃis·me] *m* 1. (*habladuría*) piece of gossip; **andar** [*o* **ir**] **con** ~**s** to gossip 2. (*objeto*) thingamajig; **recoge esos** ~**s** put away those things
chismorrear [tʃis·mo·rre·'ar] *vi* to gossip
chismoso, -a [tʃis·'mo·so, -a] I. *adj* gossiping II. *m, f* gossip
chispa ['tʃis·pa] *f* 1. *t.* ELEC spark; **echar** ~**s** to give off sparks; *fig* to be hopping mad 2. (*ingenio*) wit; **ser una** ~ to be (very) lively 3. *inf* (*borrachera*) drunkenness 4. (*una pizca*) **una** ~ **de...** a bit of...
chispear [tʃis·pe·'ar] I. *vi* 1. (*centellear*) to spark 2. (*brillar*) to sparkle II. *vimpers* (*lloviznar*) to drizzle
chistar [tʃis·'tar] *vi* to speak; **no** ~ not to say a word
chiste ['tʃis·te] *m* 1. (*cuento*) funny story; (*broma*) joke; ~ **verde** dirty joke; **no tiene** ~ **la cosa** that's not at all funny 2. (*gracia*) point
chistoso, -a [tʃis·'to·so, -a] I. *adj* funny II. *m, f* joker
chita ['tʃi·ta] *f* ANAT anklebone; **a la** ~ **callando** *fig* on the sly
chitón [tʃi·'ton] *interj* hush!
chiva ['tʃi·βa] *f Col, inf* (*noticia*) (piece of) news
chivarse [tʃi·'βar·se] *vr inf* 1. (*hablar*) to grass 2. *AmL* (*enojarse*) to get annoyed
chivatazo [tʃi·βa·'ta·so, -θo] *m inf* tip-off; **dar el** ~ to give a tip-off
chivatear [tʃi·βa·te·'ar] *vi* 1. *Arg, Chile* (*chillar*) to shout 2. *AmS* (*alborotar*) to make a ruckus
chivato, -a [tʃi·'βa·to, -a] *m, f inf* (*informador*) stool pigeon; (*en la escuela*) tell-tale
chivo ['tʃi·βo, -a] *m, f* kid; ~ **expiatorio** scapegoat
choapino [tʃoa·'pi·no] *m Chile* potato-beetle larva
chocante [tʃo·'kan·te] *adj* 1. (*raro*) strange; (*sorprendente*) startling 2. *AmL* (*fastidioso*) annoying; (*repugnante*) disgusting
chocar <c→qu> [tʃo·'kar] I. *vi* 1. (*vehículos*) ~ **contra algo** to collide with sth; (*dar*) to crash into sth; (*coches*) to run into sth 2. (*encontrarse*) ~ **con alguien** to come across sb; (*personas*) to run into sb; (*discutir*) to have words with sb; **chocó con su jefe** he/she clashed with his/her boss II. *vt* 1. (*entrechocar*) ~ **las copas** to clink glasses 2. (*perturbar*) to startle 3. *AmL* (*repugnar*) to disgust;

me chocan sus opiniones I can't stand his/her opinions

chochear [ʧo·ʧe·'ar] *vi* 1.(*por vejez*) to dodder (around); *inf* (*atontar*) to become stupid 2.(*sentir cariño*) to dote

chocho, -a ['ʧo·ʧo] I. *adj* doddering; *inf* (*lelo*) stupid II. *m, f* 1.(*dulce*) sweet 2. *vulg* (*coño*) cunt

choclo ['ʧo·klo] *m* 1.*AmS* (*maíz*) corn; (*mazorca tierna*) ear of corn 2.*AmS* CULIN sweet tamale

choclón [ʧo·'klon] *m Chile* POL rally

chocolate [ʧo·ko·'la·te] *m* chocolate; *inf* (*hachís*) hash *inf*

chocolatería [ʧo·ko·la·te·'ri·a] *f* (*establecimiento*) café specializing in hot chocolate drinks; (*fábrica*) chocolate factory

chocolatina [ʧo·ko·la·'ti·na] *f* chocolate bar

chofer [ʧo·'fer] *m*, **chófer** ['ʧo·fer] *m* chauffeur

chollo ['ʧo·jo, -ʎo] *m inf* 1.(*suerte*) luck 2.(*ganga*) bargain 3.(*trabajo*) cushy job

cholo, -a ['ʧo·lo, -a] *m, f AmL* 1.(*indio*) Indian integrated into Creole society 2.(*mestizo*) mestizo

chomba ['ʧom·ba] *f Arg* (*polo*) polo shirt

chongo ['ʧon·go] *m* 1.*Méx, inf* (*trenza*) braid; (*moño*) knot, bun 2.*Chile* (*cuchillo*) blunt knife

chopo ['ʧo·po] *m* black poplar

choque ['ʧo·ke] *m* 1.(*impacto*) impact; (*colisión*) crash; ~ **de frente** head-on collision 2.(*encuentro*) clash 3. MED shock

choricear [ʧo·ri·se·'ar, -θe·'ar] *vt inf* to swipe

chorizo [ʧo·'ri·so, -θo] *m* chorizo (*hard pork sausage*)

chorizo, -a [ʧo·'ri·so, -a; -θo, -a] *m, f inf* petty thief; (*carterista*) pickpocket

chorlito [ʧor·'li·to] *m* plover; **cabeza de ~** *fig* scatterbrain

choro ['ʧo·ro] *m* 1. *Chile* (*mejillón*) large mussel 2.*AmS, inf* (*ladrón*) thief

chorote [ʧo·'ro·te] *m Méx, Ven* (*chocolate*) chocolate drink

chorrada [ʧo·'rra·da] *f* 1. *inf* (*tontería*) stupid remark 2. *inf* (*cosa superflua*) trivial thing

chorrear [ʧo·rre·'ar] *vi* 1.(*fluir*) to gush (out) 2.(*gotear*) to drip

chorro ['ʧo·rro] *m* 1.(*hilo*) trickle; (*de ingrediente*) drop 2.(*torrente*) stream; *t.* TÉC jet; **avión a ~** jet plane; **llover a ~s** to pour 3. *Arg, inf* (*ladrón*) thief

choteo [ʧo·'teo] *m* joke

choza ['ʧo·sa, -θa] *f* hut

chubasco [ʧu·'βas·ko] *m* (heavy) shower

chubasquero [ʧu·βas·'ke·ro] *m* raincoat

chúcaro, -a ['ʧu·ka·ro, -a] *adj Arg, inf* 1.(*poco amable*) awkward 2.(*huraño*) shy

chuchería [ʧu·ʧe·'ri·a] *f* 1.(*dulce*) sweet 2.(*menudencia*) trinket

chucho ['ʧu·ʧo] *m* 1. *inf* (*perro*) mutt 2.*AmL* (*escalofrío*) shivers *pl*; (*fiebre*) fever

chucrut [ʧu·'kru] *m* sauerkraut

chueco, -a ['ʧwe·ko, -a] *adj AmL* 1.(*pies*) bow-legged 2. *inf* (*torcido*) crooked

chufa ['ʧu·fa] *f* tiger nut

chufla ['ʧu·fla] *f* joke

chulada [ʧu·'la·da] *f* 1.(*insolencia*) impudence 2. *inf* (*cosa estupenda*) cool thing

chulear [ʧu·le·'ar] *vi, vr:* ~ **se** (*jactarse*) to brag

chulería [ʧu·le·'ri·a] *f* bragging

chuleta [ʧu·'le·ta] I. *f* 1.(*costilla*) chop 2. *inf* (*apunte*) crib (sheet) II. *adj inf* cheeky; **ponerse ~** to get fresh

chuletón [ʧu·le·'ton] *m* T-bone steak

chulo ['ʧu·lo] *m* 1.(*mal educado*) boor 2. *inf* (*proxeneta*) pimp

chulo, -a ['ʧu·lo, -a] I. *adj* 1.(*jactancioso*) boastful; (*presumido*) conceited; **ponerse ~** to get cocky 2. *inf* (*elegante*) smart II. *m, f* flashy type

chumbera [ʧum·'be·ra] *f* prickly pear cactus

chumbo ['ʧum·bo] *m* (*fruto*) prickly pear

chunga ['ʧun·ga] *f inf* joke; **estar de ~** to be in high spirits

chungo, -a ['ʧun·go, -a] *adj inf* 1.(*malo*) bad; (*comida*) spoiled 2.(*raro*) odd; (*enfermiza*) poorly

chuño ['ʧu·ɲo] *m AmS* (*fécula*) potato flour

chupa ['ʧu·pa] *f AmC* drunkenness

chupa-chups® [ʧu·pa·'ʧups] *m inv* lollipop

chupada [ʧu·'pa·da] *f* (*paja*) suck; (*cigarrillo*) puff

chupado, -a [ʧu·'pa·do, -a] *adj* 1.(*flaco*) skinny; (*consumido*) emaciated 2. *inf* (*fácil*) a cinch 3.*AmL* (*borracho*) drunk

chupaflor [ʧu·pa·'flor] *m AmC* ZOOL hummingbird

chupamirto [ʧu·pa·'mir·to] *m Méx* ZOOL hummingbird

chupar [ʧu·'par] I. *vt* 1.(*extraer*) to suck out; (*aspirar*) to suck in; (*absorber*) to absorb 2.(*caramelo*) to suck; (*helado*) to lick 3.(*cigarrillo*) to smoke, to puff on II. *vi* 1. *inf* (*mamar*) to suckle; ~ **del bote** to line one's pocket 2.*AmL, inf* (*beber*) to booze; (*fumar*) to smoke III. *vr:* ~ **se** 1.(*secarse*) to get very thin 2. *inf* (*aguantar*) to sit out, to put up with

chupatintas [ʧu·pa·'tin·tas] *m inv, pey* clerk

chupe ['ʧu·pe] *m CSur, Ecua, Perú* CULIN spicy chowder

chupete [ʧu·'pe·te] *m* 1.(*del bebé*) pacifier; (*del biberón*) nipple 2.*AmL* (*pirulí*) lollipop

chupetear [ʧu·pe·te·'ar] *vi, vt* to lick

chupetón [ʧu·pe·'ton] *m* (*acción*) suck; (*efecto*) hickey *sl*

chupo ['ʧu·po] *m Col* teat

chupón, -ona [ʧu·'pon] I. *adj* 1.(*chupador*) sucking 2.(*parásito*) scrounging II. *m, f* scrounger

churrasco [ʧu·'rras·ko] *m* steak

churrete [ʧu·'rre·te] *m* spot

churro ['ʧu·rro] *m* 1.(*fritura*) ≈ fritter; **¡vete a freír ~s!** go fly a kite! 2.(*chapuza*) (piece of) shoddy work 3.(*suerte*) piece of luck 4. *Col* (*persona atractiva*) good-looker

[i] A very typical Spanish breakfast consists of **chocolate** (hot chocolate) **con churros,** which are deep-fried strips of dough. **Churros** can be bought in a **churrería,** in a **cafetería,** or at a special kiosk in the street (**un puesto de churros**).

churro, -a ['ʧu·rro, -a] *adj* (*cordero*) one-year old
churumbel [ʧu·rum·'bel] *m* (*voz gitana*) kid
chusco ['ʧus·ko] *m* crust (of bread)
chusma ['ʧus·ma] *f* rabble, riffraff
chutar [ʧu·'tar] I. *vt* to shoot; **esto va que chuta** *inf* it's going well II. *vr:* **~se** *inf* to shoot up
chute ['ʧu·te] *m inf* shot; (*droga*) fix
chuza ['ʧu·sa, -θa] *f* 1. *Arg, Urug* (*lanza*) pike 2. *Arg* (*gallo*) cock's spur 3. *Méx* (*juego: bolos*) strike 4. *pl, Arg* (*pelo*) rats' tails
chuzar <z→c> [ʧu·'sar, -'θar] *vt Col* to prick
Cía ['si·a, 'θi·a] *abr de* **compañía** Co.
cianuro [sja·'nu·ro, θja-] *m* cyanide
ciberadicción [si·ber·a·dik·'sjon, θi·ber·a·diy·'θjon] *f* Internet addiction
ciberdelincuencia [si·βer·de·liŋ·'kwen·sja, θi·βer·de·liŋ·'kwen·θja] *f* cyber crime
ciberespacio [si·βer·es·'pa·sjo, θi·βer·es·'pa·θjo] *m* cyberspace
cibernauta [si·βer·'nau·ta, θi-] *mf* websurfer, cybernaut
cibernética [si·βer·'ne·ti·ka, θi-] *f* cybernetics *pl*
ciberspanglish [si·βer·es·'paŋ·lis, θi-] *m* COMPUT CyberSpanglish *no pl*
cicatería [si·ka·te·'ri·a, θi-] *f* stinginess
cicatriz [si·ka·'tris, θi·ka·'triθ] *f* scar
cicatrizar <z→c> [si·ka·tri·'sar, θi·ka·tri·'θar] *vt, vi, vr:* **~se** to heal
ciclamen [si·'kla·men, θi-] *m* cyclamen
ciclismo [si·'klis·mo, θi-] *m* DEP cycling
ciclista [si·'klis·ta, θi-] I. *adj* cycle II. *mf* cyclist
ciclo ['si·klo, 'θi-] *m* cycle; **~ económico** economic cycle
ciclomotor [si·klo·mo·'tor, θi-] *m* moped, motorbike
ciclón [si·'klon, θi-] *m* cyclone
cicuta [si·'ku·ta, θi-] *f* hemlock
ciego, -a ['sje·yo, 'θje-] I. *adj* 1. (*persona*) blind; **quedarse ~** to go blind 2. (*taponado*) blocked II. *m, f* blind man *m,* blind woman *f* III. *adv* **a ciegas** blindly; **obrar a ciegas** to act thoughtlessly
cielo ['sje·lo, 'θje-] I. *m* 1. (*atmósfera*) sky; **a ~ raso** in the open air; **el reino de los ~s** the Kingdom of Heaven; **como caído del ~** out of the blue 2. (*apelativo*) darling II. *interj* ¡**~s!** good heavens!
ciempiés [sjem·'pjes, θjem-] *m inv* centipede
cien [sjen, θjen] *adj inv* a [*o* one] hundred; **al ~ por ~** one hundred per cent; *v.t.* **ochocientos**
ciénaga ['sje·na·ya, 'θje-] *f* swamp

ciencia ['sjen·sja, 'θjen·θja] *f* 1. (*saber*) knowledge; **a** [*o* **de**] **~ cierta** for sure 2. (*disciplina*) science; **~s ambientales** environmental sciences; **~ cognitiva** cognitive science; **~s físicas** physical science; **~s políticas** political science; **~s** (**naturales**) natural science(s)
ciencia-ficción ['sjen·sja-fik·'sjon, 'θjen·θja-fiy·'θjon] *f* science fiction
cienciología [sjen·sjo·lo·'xi·a, θjen·θjo-] *f* Scientology
cienciólogo, -a [sjen·'sjo·lo·yo, -a; θjen·'θjo-] *m, f* Scientologist
cieno ['sje·no, 'θje-] *m* mud
científico, -a [sjen·'ti·fi·ko, -a; θjen-] I. *adj* scientific II. *m, f* scientist
ciento ['sjen·to, 'θjen-] *adj* <cien> *inv* a [*o* one] hundred; **~s de huevos** hundreds of eggs; **el cinco por ~** five per cent; *v.t.* **ochenta**
cierre ['sje·rre, 'θje-] *m* 1. (*conclusión*) closing; (*clausura*) closure; PREN time of going to press; **~ del ejercicio** close of the financial year; **~ patronal** lockout; **hora de ~** closing time; **~ centralizado** AUTO central locking 2. *Arg* (*cremallera*) zipper
cierro ['sje·rro, 'θje-] *m Chile* (*sobre*) envelope
ciertamente [sjer·ta·'men·te, θjer-] *adv* certainly
cierto ['sjer·to, 'θjer-] *adv* certainly; **por ~** by the way
cierto, -a ['sjer·to, -a; 'θjer-] *adj* <certísimo> 1. (*verdadero*) true; (*seguro*) sure; **una información cierta** a correct piece of information; **estar en lo ~** to be right; **lo ~ es que...** the fact is that... 2. (*alguno*) a certain; **~ día** one day
ciervo, -a ['sjer·βo, -a; 'θjer-] *m, f* deer
cifra ['si·fra, 'θi-] *f* 1. (*guarismo*) figure; **~ de negocios** ECON turnover; **~ de ventas** ECON sales figures 2. (*clave*) code; **en ~** in code 3. (*resumen*) summary
cifrar [si·'frar, θi-] *vt* 1. (*codificar*) to code 2. (*calcular*) to reckon 3. (*esperanza*) to place
cigala [si·'ya·la, θi-] *f* crayfish
cigarra [si·'ya·rra, θi-] *f* cicada
cigarrera [si·ya·'rre·ra, θi-] *f* 1. (*caja*) cigar box 2. (*petaca*) cigar case
cigarrillo [si·ya·'rri·jo, θi·ya·'rri·ʎo] *m* cigarette
cigarro [si·'ya·rro, θi-] *m* cigar
cigüeña [si·'ywe·na, θi-] *f* stork
cilindrada [si·lin·'dra·da, θi-] *f* AUTO cubic capacity
cilindro [si·'lin·dro, θi-] *m* cylinder
cima ['si·ma, 'θi-] *f t. fig* summit; **~ del árbol** tree top; **~ del monte** mountain peak
cimarrón, -ona [si·ma·'rron, -·'rro·na; θi-] *adj AmL* wild
cimbrar [sim·'brar, θim-], **cimbrear** [sim·bre·'ar, θim-] I. *vt* 1. (*agitar*) to shake 2. (*doblar*) to bend II. *vr:* **~se** 1. (*agitarse*) to sway 2. (*doblarse*) to bend
cimbreo [sim·'breo, θim-] *m* swaying
cimbronazo [sim·bro·'na·so, θim·bro·'na·θo]

m AmL **1.**(*temblor*) jolt; (*de tierra*) earthquake **2.**(*tirón*) yank

cimentar <e→ie> [si·men·'tar, θi-] *vt* **1.**(*fundamentar*) to lay the foundations of **2.**(*consolidar*) to strengthen

cimiento [si·'mjen·to, θi-] *m* foundation

cimpa ['sim·pa, θim-] *f Perú* braid

cinc [siŋ, θiŋ] *m* zinc

cincel [sin·'sel, θin·'θel] *m* chisel

cincelar [sin·se·'lar, θin·θe-] *vt* to chisel

cinco ['sin·ko, 'θin-] **I.** *adj inv* five ▸ **estar sin ~** to be broke **II.** *m* five; ¡**choca esos ~**! give me five!; *v.t.* **ocho**

cincuenta [sin·'kwen·ta, θin-] *adj inv, m* fifty; *v.t.* **ochenta**

cincuentenario [sin·kwen·te·'na·rjo, θin-] *m* fiftieth anniversary

cine ['si·ne, 'θi-] *m* **1.**(*arte*) cinema, movies *pl*; **~ mudo/sonoro** silent/talking films; **~ negro** film noir; **me gusta el ~** I like films **2.**(*sala*) cinema, movie theater; **~ de barrio** local cinema, local movie theater; **ir al ~** to go to the movies

cineasta [si·ne·'as·ta, θi-] *mf* filmmaker

cinemateca [si·ne·ma·'te·ka, θi-] *f* film library

cinematografía [si·ne·ma·to·γra·'fi·a, θi-] *f* cinematography

cinematógrafo [si·ne·ma·'to·γra·fo, θi-] *m* **1.**(*proyector*) projector **2.**(*cine*) cinema

cingalés, -esa [sin·ga·'les, -·'le·sa; θin-] *adj, m, f* Singhalese

cíngaro, -a ['sin·ga·ro, -a; θin-] *adj, m, f* gypsy

cínico, -a ['si·ni·ko, -a; 'θi-] **I.** *adj* cynical **II.** *m, f t.* FILOS cynic

cinismo [si·'nis·mo, θi-] *m* cynicism

cinta ['sin·ta, 'θin-] *f* band; **~ adhesiva** adhesive tape; **~ aislante** insulating tape; **~ métrica** tape measure; **~ del pelo** hair ribbon; **~ de vídeo** videotape; **~ virgen** blank tape; **~ transportadora** conveyor belt

cinto ['sin·to, 'θin-] *m* belt

cintura [sin·'tu·ra, θin-] *f* waist; **~ de avispa** wasp waist

cinturón [sin·tu·'ron, θin-] *m* belt; **~ salvavidas** lifebelt; **ponerse el ~** to fasten one's seatbelt; **apretarse el ~** *fig* to tighten one' belt

cipe ['si·pe, 'θi-] *adj AmC* sickly, runty

ciprés [si·'pres, θi-] *m* cypress

circense [sir·'sen·se, θir·'θen·se] *adj* circus

circo ['sir·ko, 'θir-] *m* **1.**(*arena*) circus; **~ ambulante** traveling circus **2.** GEO cirque

circuito [sir·ku·'i·to, θir-] *m* **1.** *t.* ELEC circuit; **~ integrado** integrated circuit; **corto ~** short circuit **2.** DEP circuit, track

circulación [sir·ku·la·'sjon, θir·ku·la·'θjon] *f* **1.** *t.* ECON circulation; **~ sanguínea** (blood) circulation; **retirar de la ~** to withdraw from circulation **2.**(*tránsito*) traffic

circular [sir·ku·'lar, θir-] **I.** *adj* circular **II.** *vi* **1.**(*recorrer*) to circulate **2.**(*personas*) to walk (around); (*vehículos*) to drive (around); ¡**circulen!** move along! **III.** *f* circular

circulatorio, -a [θir·ku·la·'to·rjo, -a; θir-] *adj*

MED circulatory

círculo ['θir·ku·lo, 'θir-] *m* circle; **~ de amistades** circle of friends; **~ vicioso** vicious circle

circuncidar [sir·kun·si·'dar, θir·kun·θi-] *vt* to circumcise

circuncisión [sir·kun·si·'sjon, θir·kun·θi-] *f* circumcision

circundar [sir·kun·'dar, θir-] *vt* to surround

circunferencia [sir·kun·fe·'ren·sja, θir·kun·fe·'ren·θja] *f t.* MAT circumference

circunlocución [sir·kun·lo·ku·'sjon, θir·kun·lo·ku'θjon] *f* circumlocution

circunnavegar <g→gu> [sir·kun·na·βe·'γar, θir-] *vt* to circumnavigate

circunscribir [sir·kuns·kri·'βir, θir-] *irr como* **escribir I.** *vt* to circumscribe **II.** *vr:* **~se** to limit oneself

circunscripción [sir·kuns·krip·'sjon, θir·kuns·kriβ·'θjon] *f* electoral district

circunscrito, -a [sir·kuns·'kri·to, -a; θir-] *pp de* **circunscribir**

circunstancia [sir·kuns·'tan·sja, θir·kuns·'tan·θja] *f* circumstance; **en estas ~s** in these circumstances

circunstancial [sir·kuns·tan·'sjal, θir·kuns·tan·'θjal] *adj* circumstantial

circunvalación [sir·kum·ba·la·'sjon, θir·kum·ba·la·'θjon] *f* **carretera de ~** bypass

cirio ['si·rjo, 'θir-] *m* candle; *inf* (*jaleo*) fight

cirro ['si·rro, 'θir-] *m* cirrus

cirrosis [si·'rro·sis, θi-] *f inv* MED cirrhosis

ciruela [si·'rwe·la, θi-] *f* plum; **~ pasa** prune

ciruelo [si·'rwe·lo, θi-] *m* BOT plum tree

cirugía [si·ru·'xi·a, θi-] *f* MED surgery; **~ estética** cosmetic surgery

cirujano, -a [si·ru·'xa·no, -a; θi-] *m, f* MED surgeon

ciscar <c→qu> [sis·'kar, θis-] **I.** *vt inf* to dirty, to soil **II.** *vr:* **~se** *inf* to do one's business

cisco ['sis·ko, θis-] *m* **1.**(*carbón*) coal dust; **estar hecho un ~** *inf* to be a wreck **2.**(*jaleo*) fight

Cisjordania [sis·xor·'da·nja, θis-] *f* (the) West Bank

cisma ['sis·ma, θis-] *m* REL schism

cisne ['sis·ne, θis-] *m* swan

císter ['sis·ter, θis-] *m* REL Cistercian Order

cisterna [sis·'ter·na, θis-] **I.** *adj* tank; **barco ~** tanker **II.** *f* tank

cisura [si·'su·ra, θi-] *f* crack

cita ['si·ta, θi-] *f* **1.**(*convocatoria*) appointment **2.**(*encuentro*) meeting; (*romántico*) date; **~ anual** annual meeting; **~ a ciegas** blind date; **tener una ~ con alguien** to be meeting sb; (*romántica*) to have a date with sb **3.**(*mención*) quotation

citación [si·ta·'sjon, θi·ta·'θjon] *f* **1.** JUR summons **2.**(*mención*) quotation

citar [si·'tar, θi-] **I.** *vt* **1.**(*convocar*) to arrange to meet **2.**(*mencionar*) to quote **3.** JUR to summon **II.** *vr:* **~se** to arrange to meet

cítara ['si·ta·ra, 'θi-] *f* MÚS zither

cítrico, -a ['si·tri·ko, -a; 'θi-] *adj* citric

cítricos ['si·tri·kos, 'θi-] *mpl* citrus fruits *pl*
ciudad [sju·'dad, θju-] *f* town; (*más grande*) city; ~ **hermanada** twin town; ~ **industrial** industrial town [*o* city]; ~ **de origen** home town; ~ **universitaria** university campus; ~ **dormitorio** dormitory town
ciudadanía [sju·da·da·'ni·a, θju-] *f* 1.(*nacionalidad*) citizenship 2.(*ciudadanos*) citizenry, citizens *pl* 3.(*civismo*) civic responsibility
ciudadanización [sju·da·da·ni·sa·'sjon, θju·da·da·ni·θa·'θjon] *f* POL civic participation *no pl*
ciudadano, -a [sju·da·'da·no, -a; θju-] I. *adj* 1.(*de la ciudad*) city 2.(*del ciudadano*) civic II. *m, f* 1.(*residente*) resident 2.(*súbdito*) citizen
cívico, -a ['si·βi·ko, -a; 'θi-] *adj* 1.(*del ciudadano*) civic 2.(*del civismo*) public-spirited
civil [si·'βil, θi-] *adj* civil; **derecho** ~ civil law; **guerra** ~ civil war
civilización [si·βi·li·sa·'sjon, θi·βi·li·θa·'θjon] *f* civilization
civilizar <z→c> [si·βi·li·'sar, θi·βi·li·'θar] *vt* to civilize
civismo [si·'βis·mo, θi-] *m* community spirit, civic-mindedness
cizaña [si·'sa·ɲa, θi·'θa-] *f* 1.BOT darnel 2.(*enemistad*) discord
clamar [kla·'mar] I. *vi* to cry out II. *vt* to demand
clamor [kla·'mor] *m* lament
clamoroso, -a [kla·mo·'ro·so, -a] *adj* resounding; **acogida clamorosa** rousing reception
clan [klan] *m* clan
clandestinidad [klan·des·ti·ni·'dad] *f* secrecy; POL underground
clandestino, -a [klan·des·'ti·no, -a] *adj* secret; **reunión clandestina** secret meeting; **movimiento** ~ underground movement
claqué [kla·'ke] *f* tap dancing
claqueta [kla·'ke·ta] *f* CINE clapperboard
clara ['kla·ra] *f* (*del huevo*) white
claraboya [kla·ra·'βo·ja] *f* skylight
claramente [kla·ra·'men·te] *adv* clearly
clarear [kla·re·'ar] I. *vi* 1.(*amanecer*) to grow light; **al** ~ **el día** at dawn 2.(*despejarse*) to clear up II. *vt* to brighten III. *vr:* ~ **se** to be transparent
clarete [kla·'re·te] *m* rosé (wine)
claridad [kla·ri·'dad] *f* 1.(*luminosidad*) brightness 2.(*lucidez*) clarity
clarificación [kla·ri·fi·ka·'sjon, -'θjon] *f* 1.(*iluminación*) illumination 2.(*aclaración*) clarification
clarificar <c→qu> [kla·ri·fi·'kar] *vt* 1.(*iluminar*) to illuminate 2.(*aclarar*) to clarify
clarín [kla·'rin] *m* (*instrumento*) bugle; (*músico*) bugler
clarinete [kla·ri·'ne·te] *m* (*instrumento*) clarinet; (*músico*) clarinet(t)ist
clarividencia [kla·ri·βi·'den·sja, -θja] *f* 1.(*perspicacia*) discernment 2.(*percepción*) clair-

voyance
clarividente [kla·ri·βi·'den·te] *adj* 1.(*perspicaz*) discerning 2.(*que percibe*) clairvoyant
claro ['kla·ro] I. *interj* of course II. *m* 1.(*hueco*) gap 2.(*calvero*) clearing III. *adv* clearly
claro, -a ['kla·ro, -a] *adj* 1.(*iluminado*) bright; **azul** ~ light blue 2.(*evidente*) clear; **poner** [*o* **sacar**] **en** ~ to clarify 3.(*fino*) thin
claroscuro [kla·ros·'ku·ro] *m* chiaroscuro
clase ['kla·se] *f* 1.(*tipo*) kind; **trabajos de toda** ~ all kinds of jobs 2.(*categoría*) class; ~ **turista** tourist class; ~ **media** middle class 3.ENS class; (*aula*) classroom; **dar** ~**s** to teach
clasicismo [kla·si·'sis·mo, -'θis·mo] *m* classicism
clásico, -a ['kla·si·ko, -a] I. *adj* classical; *fig* classic II. *m, f* classic
clasificación [kla·si·fi·ka·'sjon, -'θjon] *f* 1.(*ordenación*) sorting; ~ **en grupos** sorting into groups 2. *t.* BIO classification
clasificar <c→qu> [kla·si·fi·'kar] I. *vt* ~ **por algo** (*ordenar*) to sort according to sth; BIO to classify under sth II. *vr:* ~**se** to qualify
clasismo [kla·'sis·mo] *m* class-consciousness
claudicación [klau·di·ka·'sjon, -'θjon] *f* 1.(*de principios*) abandonment 2.(*cesión*) giving in
claudicar <c→qu> [klau·di·'kar] *vi* 1.(*principios*) ~ **de algo** to abandon sth 2.(*ceder*) to give in
claustro ['klaus·tro] *m* 1.ARTE cloister 2.ENS senate; (*reunión*) senate meeting
claustrofobia [klaus·tro·'fo·βja] *f* claustrophobia
cláusula ['klau·su·la] *f* clause; (*ley*) article
clausura [klau·'su·ra] *f* 1.(*cierre*) closure; **sesión de** ~ closing session 2.REL cloister
clausurar [klau·su·'rar] *vt* to close
clavado, -a [kla·'βa·do, -a] *adj* 1.(*semejante*) very similar 2.(*exacto*) **a las dos clavadas** (at) two sharp
clavar [kla·'βar] I. *vt* 1.(*hincar*) to knock in; (*enclavar*) to nail 2.(*fijar*) to fix; **tener la vista clavada en algo** to have one's eyes set on sth 3. *inf* (*dar*) to give 4. *inf* (*cobrar*) to rip off II. *vr* ~**se una astilla en el dedo** to get a splinter in one's finger
clave ['kla·βe] I. *adj inv* key II. *f* 1.(*secreto*) ~ **de algo** key to sth 2.(*código*) code; ~ **de acceso** password; **en** ~ coded 3.ARQUIT keystone 4.MÚS clef
clavel [kla·'βel] *m* carnation
clavicémbalo [kla·βi·'sem·ba·lo, -'θem·ba·lo] *m* harpsichord
clavicordio [kla·βi·'kor·djo] *m* clavichord
clavícula [kla·'βi·ku·la] *f* collar bone
clavija [kla·'βi·xa] *f* 1.TÉC pin; (*enchufe*) plug 2.MÚS peg ▶ **apretar las** ~**s a alguien** to put the screws on sb
clavo ['kla·βo] *m* 1.(*punta*) nail; **dar en el** ~ to hit the nail on the head 2.(*especia*) clove 3.(*callo*) corn
claxon ['klak·son] *m* horn

clemencia [kle·'men·sja, -θja] *f* mercy

clemente [kle·'men·te] *adj* merciful

clementina [kle·men·'ti·na] *f* tangerine

cleptómano, -a [klep·'to·ma·no, -a] *adj, m, f* PSICO kleptomaniac

clerical [kle·ri·'kal] *adj* clerical

clérigo ['kle·ri·ɣo] *m* clergyman; (*católico*) priest

clero ['kle·ro] *m* clergy

clic [klik] *m* click

cliché [kli·'tʃe] *m* 1.(*tópico*) cliché 2. FOTO negative

cliente, -a ['kljen·te] *m, f* customer; (*de un abogado*) client; ~ **fijo** regular customer

clientela [kljen·'te·la] *f* customers *pl*; (*de un abogado*) clients *pl*

clima ['kli·ma] *m* 1.(*atmósfera*) atmosphere 2. GEO climate

climatizar <z→c> [kli·ma·ti·'sar, -'θar] *vt* to air-condition

climatología [kli·ma·to·lo·'xi·a] *f* climatology

clímax ['kli·maks] *m inv* climax

clínica ['kli·ni·ka] *f* clinic

clínico ['kli·ni·ko] *m* clinical

clip [klip] *m* 1.(*pinza*) clip 2. TV video (clip)

clítoris ['kli·to·ris] *m inv* clitoris

cloaca [klo·'a·ka] *f* sewer; ZOOL cloaca

clon [klon] *m* BIO clone

clonar [klo·'nar] *vt* to clone

cloro ['klo·ro] *m* chlorine

clorofila [klo·ro·'fi·lja] *f* chlorophyl(l)

cloruro [klo·'ru·ro] *m* chloride

club <clubs *o* clubes> [kluβ] *m* club; ~ **de alterne** hostess bar; ~ **deportivo** sports club

cm [sen·'ti·me·tro, θen-] *abr de* **centímetro** cm.

coacción [ko·ak·'sjon, -aɣ·'θjon] *f* coercion

coaccionar [ko·ak·sjo·'nar, ko·aɣ·'θjo-] *vt* to coerce

coagulación [ko·a·ɣu·la·'sjon, -'θjon] *f* coagulation, clotting

coagular(se) [ko·a·ɣu·'lar·(se)] *vt, (vr)* to coagulate

coágulo [ko·'a·ɣu·lo] *m* clot

coalición [koa·li·'sjon, -'θjon] *f* coalition

coaligarse <g→gu> [koa·li·'ɣar·se] *vr* to form an alliance

coartada [koar·'ta·da] *f* alibi

coartar [koar·'tar] *vt* (*libertad*) to restrict; (*persona*) to inhibit

coautor(a) [ko·au·'tor, -'to·ra] *m(f)* co-author

coba ['ko·βa] *f* lie; **dar ~ a alguien** to suck up to sb

cobalto [ko·'βal·to] *m* cobalt

cobarde [ko·'βar·de] **I.** *adj* cowardly **II.** *m* coward

cobardía [ko·βar·'di·a] *f* cowardice

cobaya [ko·'βa·ja] *m o f* guinea pig

cobertizo [ko·βer·'ti·so, -θo] *m* 1.(*tejado*) canopy 2.(*cabaña*) shed

cobertura [ko·βer·'tu·ra] *f* COM (*acción*) coverage

cobija [ko·'βi·xa] *f* 1. AmL (*manta*) blanket

2. *pl, AmL* (*ropa de cama*) bedclothes *pl;* **pegarse a alguien las ~ s** to oversleep

cobijar [ko·'βi·xar] **I.** *vt* 1.(*proteger*) to shelter 2.(*acoger*) to give shelter to **II.** *vr:* ~ **se** to take shelter

cobijo [ko·'βi·xo] *m* shelter

cobo ['ko·βo] *m AmC, Ant* 1. ZOOL giant sea snail 2.(*persona*) unsociable person; **ser un ~** to be shy

cobra ['ko·βra] *f* cobra

cobrador(a) [ko·βra·'dor] *m(f)* COM collector; (*de tranvía*) conductor

cobrar [ko·'βrar] **I.** *vt* 1.(*recibir*) to receive; (*suma*) to collect; (*cheque*) to cash; (*sueldo*) to earn; **¿me cobra, por favor?** can I pay, please? 2.(*intereses*) to charge; (*deudas*) to recover 3.(*conseguir*) ~ **ánimos** to gather courage; ~ **fama** to become famous 4.(*cuerda*) to haul in **II.** *vi* 1.(*sueldo*) to get one's wages 2. *inf* (*una paliza*) to get a beating; **¡que vas a ~!** you're going to get it! **III.** *vr:* ~ **se** to cash up; *fig* to claim

cobre ['ko·βre] *m* 1. QUÍM copper 2. *AmL* (*moneda*) copper coin

cobro ['ko·βro] *m* 1.(*acto*) recovery 2. FIN (*impuestos*) collection; (*pago*) payment; ~ **por adelantado** advance payment; ~ **pendiente** outstanding payment; **llamar a ~ revertido** to reverse the charges 3. *pl* COM arrears *pl*

coca ['ko·ka] *f* 1. BOT coca 2.(*droga*) cocaine 3.(*de pelo*) coil, bun

cocaína [ko·ka·'i·na] *f* cocaine

cocainómano, -a [ko·kai·'no·ma·no, -a] *m, f* cocaine addict

cocción [kok·'sjon, koɣ·'θjon] *f* cooking; (*duración*) cooking time

cocear [ko·se·'ar, -θe·'ar] *vi* to kick

cocer [ko·'ser, -'θer] *irr* **I.** *vt* 1.(*cocinar*) to cook; (*hervir*) to boil 2.(*cerámica*) to fire **II.** *vi* 1.(*cocinar*) to cook 2.(*hervir*) to boil **III.** *vr:* ~ **se** 1.(*cocinarse*) to be cooked 2.(*tramarse*) to be going on 3. *inf* (*pasar calor*) to be sweltering

cocha ['ko·tʃa] *f AmS* (*laguna*) lagoon; (*charco*) puddle

cochambroso, -a [ko·tʃam·'bro·so, -a] *adj inf* (*sucio*) filthy; (*asqueroso*) disgusting

cochayuyo [ko·tʃa·'ju·jo] *m AmS* BOT rockweed

coche ['ko·tʃe] *m* 1.(*automóvil*) car; ~ **de bomberos** fire engine; ~ **de carreras** DEP racing car; ~ **de línea** coach, bus; **ir en ~** to go by car 2.(*de caballos*) coach, carriage; ~ **de equipajes** baggage car

coche-bomba <coches-bomba> ['ko·tʃe·'βom·ba] *m* car bomb

coche-cama <coches-cama> ['ko·tʃe-'ka·ma] *m* FERRO sleeping car

cochecito [ko·tʃe·'si·to, -'θi·to] *m* baby carriage

coche-patrulla <coches-patrulla> ['ko·tʃe·pa·'tru·ja, -ʎa] *m* patrol car

cochera [ko·'tʃe·ra] *f* garage; ~ **de tranvías** tram depot

coche-restaurante <coches-restaurante> ['ko·tʃe-rres·tau·'ran·te] *m* FERRO dining car

cochinada [ko·tʃi·'na·da] *f*, **cochinería** [ko·tʃi·ne·'ri·a] *f inf* filthy thing

cochinillo [ko·tʃi·'ni·jo, -ʎo] *m* piglet; ~ **asado** roast suckling pig

cochino, -a [ko·'tʃi·no, -a] **I.** *adj inf* filthy **II.** *m, f* **1.** ZOOL (*macho*) pig; (*hembra*) sow **2.** *inf* (*guarro*) swine

cocho ['ko·tʃo] *m* Chile **1.** (*bebida*) hot corn drink **2.** CULIN pudding made with toasted flour

cocido [ko·'si·do, ko·'θi-] *m* stew (*made with chickpeas and meat*)

cociente [ko·'sjen·te, ko·'θjen-] *m* MAT quotient; ~ **intelectual** IQ

cocina [ko·'si·na, ko·'θi-] *f* **1.** (*habitación*) kitchen **2.** (*aparato*) stove **3.** (*arte*) cookery, cooking; **la ~ francesa** French cooking [*o* cuisine]; **libro de ~** cookbook

cocinar [ko·si·'nar, ko·'θi-] *vt, vi* to cook

cocinero, -a [ko·si·'ne·ro, -a; ko·'θi-] *m, f* cook

coco ['ko·ko] *m* **1.** BOT (*fruto*) coconut; (*árbol*) coconut palm **2.** *inf* (*cabeza*) head; **comerse el ~** to worry **3.** *inf* (*ogro*) bogeyman

cocodrilo [ko·ko·'dri·lo] *m* crocodile

cocoliche [ko·ko·'li·tʃe] *m* Arg, Urug LING *pidgin Spanish of Italian immigrants*

cocotero [ko·ko·'te·ro] *m* coconut palm

coctel <coctels> [kok·'tel] *m*, **cóctel** <cócteles> ['kok·tel] *m* cocktail

coctelera [kok·te·'le·ra] *f* cocktail shaker

cocuy [ko·'kuj] *m* AmL **1.** BOT agave **2.** (*bebida alcohólica*) corn whiskey **3.** ZOOL firefly

cocuyo [ko·'ku·jo] *m* AmL **1.** ZOOL firefly **2.** AUTO rear light

codazo [ko·'da·so, -θo] *m* nudge (with one's elbow)

codear [ko·de·'ar] **I.** *vi* to nudge **II.** *vr:* ~ **se** to rub shoulders [*o* elbows]

códice ['ko·di·se, -θe] *m* codex

codicia [ko·'di·sja, -θja] *f* greed; (*algo ajeno*) covetousness; ~ **de algo** greed for sth

codiciar [ko·di·'sjar, -'θjar] *vt* to covet

codicioso, -a [ko·di·'sjo·so, -a; ko·di·'θjo-] *adj* covetous

codificación [ko·di·fi·ka·'sjon, -'θjon] *f* coding; *t.* COMPUT encoding; JUR codification

codificar <c→qu> [ko·di·fi·'kar] *vt* to code; *t.* COMPUT to encode; JUR to codify

código ['ko·di·ɣo] *m* code; ~ **de circulación** highway code; **Código Civil** civil code; ~ **de barras** bar code; ~ **bancario** bank sorting code; ~ **genético** genetic code; ~ **postal** postal code, zip code; **mensaje en** ~ coded message

codillo [ko·'di·jo, -ʎo] *m* **1.** ZOOL elbow **2.** CULIN knuckle **3.** (*de rama*) stump **4.** TÉC elbow joint

codo ['ko·do] *m* **1.** ANAT elbow; ~ **de tenis** tennis elbow; **empinar el** ~ *inf* to go on the booze; **trabajar** ~ **a** ~ to work side by side; **hablar por los** ~**s** *inf* to talk nonstop **2.** TÉC

(*doblez*) elbow joint **3.** (*de camino*) bend

codorniz [ko·dor·'nis, -'niθ] *f* quail

coeficiente [ko·e·fi·'sjen·te, -'θjen·te] *m* MAT coefficient

coetáneo, -a [koe·'ta·neo, -a] *adj, m, f* contemporary

coexistencia [ko·ek·sis·'ten·sja, -θja] *f* coexistence

coexistir [ko·ek·sis·'tir] *vi* to coexist

cofia ['ko·fja] *f* cap

cofradía [ko·fra·'di·a] *f* **1.** (*hermandad*) brotherhood **2.** (*gremio*) guild

cofre ['ko·fre] *m* chest; (*baúl*) trunk; (*de joyas*) jewel case

cofundador(a) [ko·fun·da·'dor, -'do·ra] *m(f)* co-founder

cogedor [ko·xe·'dor] *m* dustpan

coger <g→j> [ko·'xer] **I.** *vt* **1.** (*agarrar*) to take hold, to seize; (*del suelo*) to pick up; (*flores*) to pick; ~ **la cosecha** to harvest; **le cogió del brazo** he/she took him by the arm; **le cogió en brazos** he/she picked him up in his arms **2.** (*quitar*) to take away; (*en la aduana*) to confiscate **3.** (*atrapar*) to catch; (*apresar*) to capture **4.** AUTO (*atropellar*) to knock down **5.** (*trabajo*) to take (up) **6.** (*hábito*) to acquire; ~ **cariño a alguien** to get fond of sb; ~ **el hábito de fumar** to start smoking **7.** (*enfermedad*) to catch; ~ **frío** to catch a cold; **ha cogido una gripe** he's/she's caught the flu **8.** (*sorprender*) to find **9.** (*obtener*) to get; **¿vas a** ~ **el piso?** are you going to take the apartment? **10.** (*tomar*) to take; ~ **el tren/autobús** to take the train/bus **11.** AmL, *vulg* (*copular*) to screw **II.** *vi* **1.** (*planta*) to take **2.** (*tener sitio*) to fit **3.** AmL, *vulg* (*copular*) to screw **III.** *vr* catch; ~ **se los dedos** to catch one's fingers

cogida [ko·'xi·da] *f* **1.** TAUR goring **2.** AmL, *vulg* (*cópula*) screw

cognición [koɣ·ni·'sjon, -'θjon] *f* cognition

cognitivo, -a [koɣ·ni·'ti·βo, -a] *adj* cognitive

cogollo [ko·'ɣo·jo, -ʎo] *m* **1.** (*de col*) heart **2.** *inf* (*núcleo*) core

cogote [ko·'ɣo·te] *m inf* scruff; **estar hasta el** ~ *inf* to have had enough

cogotudo, -a [ko·ɣo·'tu·do, -a] *m, f AmL* self-made man *m*, self-made woman *f*

cohabitar [ko·a·βi·'tar] *vi* to live together; *pey* (*amancebarse*) to cohabit

cohecho [ko·'e·tʃo] *m* bribery

coherencia [ko·e·'ren·sja, -θja] *f* coherence

coherente [ko·e·'ren·te] *adj* coherent

cohesión [ko·e·'sjon] *f* cohesion

cohesionar [ko·e·sjo·'nar] *vt* to unite

cohete [ko·'e·te] *m* rocket

cohibido, -a [koi·'βi·do, -a] *adj* **1.** (*intimidado*) intimidated **2.** (*inhibido*) inhibited

cohibir [koi·'βir] *irr como prohibir* **I.** *vt* **1.** (*intimidar*) to intimidate **2.** (*incomodar*) to inhibit **II.** *vr:* ~ **se** to feel inhibited

coima ['koi·ma] *f And, CSur* (*soborno*) bribe; (*dinero*) rake-off

coimear [koi·me·'ar] *vt AmS* to bribe

coincidencia [koin·si·'den·sja, koin·θi·'den·θja] *f* **1.** (*simultaneidad*) coincidence; **¡qué ~!** what a coincidence! **2.** (*acuerdo*) agreement

coincidente [koin·si·'den·te, koin·θi-] *adj* **1.** (*simultáneo*) coincidental **2.** (*concordante*) concordant

coincidir [koin·si·'dir, koin·θi-] *vi* **1.** (*sucesos*) to coincide **2.** (*toparse*) to meet; **~ con alguien** to meet sb **3.** (*concordar*) to agree; **~ con alguien** to agree with sb

coipo ['koi·po] *m Arg, Chile* ZOOL coypu

coito ['koi·to] *m* coitus, (sexual) intercourse

cojear [ko·xe·'ar] *vi* (*persona*) to limp; (*mueble*) to wobble; *fig* (*tener defecto*) to have a weak point; **saber de qué pie cojea alguien** to know sb's weaknesses

cojín [ko·'xin] *m* cushion

cojo, -a ['ko·xo, -a] *adj* (*persona*) lame; (*mueble*) wobbly; **a la pata coja** on one leg

cojón [ko·'xon] *m vulg* **1.** *pl* (*testículos*) balls *pl* **2.** *pl* (*interjecciones*) **¡cojones!** damn it!; **es una música de cojones** it's really cool music

cojonudo, -a [ko·xo·'nu·do, -a] *adj vulg* fantastic, fucking great *vulg*

cojudo, -a [ko·'xu·do, -a] *adj AmL* stupid

col [kol] *f* cabbage; **~es de Bruselas** Brussels sprouts

cola ['ko·la] *f* **1.** (*de cometa*) *t.* ANAT tail; (*de conejo*) scut **2.** (*de vestido*) train; **llevar la ~** to wear a train **3.** (*al esperar*) line; **hacer ~** to line up; **ponerse a la ~** to get in line **4.** (*pegamento*) glue **5.** *AmL, inf* **pedir ~** to ask for a lift

colaboración [ko·la·βo·ra·'sjon, -'θjon] *f* collaboration; (*periódico*) contribution

colaboracionismo [ko·la·βo·ra·sjo·'nis·mo, -θjo·'nis·mo] *m* POL collaboration

colaborador(a) [ko·la·βo·ra·'dor, -·'do·ra] **I.** *adj* collaborating **II.** *m(f)* collaborator; LIT contributor

colaborar [ko·la·βo·'rar] *vi* **1.** (*cooperar*) to collaborate **2.** LIT to contribute

colación [ko·la·'sjon, -'θjon] *f* **sacar algo a ~** to bring sth up

colada [ko·'la·da] *f* **1.** (*de ropa*) washing **2.** QUÍM lye

coladera [ko·la·'de·ra] *f Méx* (*alcantarilla*) sewer

colado, -a [ko·'la·do, -a] *adj inf* (*enamorado*) **~ por alguien** crazy about sb

colador [ko·la·'dor] *m* sieve, strainer

colapsar [ko·lap·'sar] **I.** *vt* to bring to a standstill; **~ la red** COMPUT to bring down [*o* to collapse] the net **II.** *vi, vr:* **~se 1.** (*tráfico*) to come to a standstill **2.** MED to collapse

colapso [ko·'lap·so] *m* **1.** MED collapse **2.** (*paralización*) standstill

colar <o→ue> [ko·'lar] **I.** *vt* **1.** (*filtrar*) to filter; (*metal*) to cast **2.** *inf* (*en la aduana*) to slip through **II.** *vi* **1.** (*líquido*) to seep (through); (*aire*) to get in **2.** *inf* (*información*) to be cred-

ible; **a ver si cuela** let's see if it comes off **III.** *vr:* **~se 1.** *inf* (*entrar*) to slip in **2.** (*en una cola*) to jump in line [*o* line] **3.** *inf* (*equivocarse*) to be wrong; **¡te colaste!** you're way off!

colcha ['kol·tʃa] *f* bedspread

colchón [kol·'tʃon] *m* mattress; **~ de agua** water bed

colchonería [kol·tʃo·ne·'ri·a] *f* mattress store

colchoneta [kol·tʃo·'ne·ta] *f* (*neumática*) airbed; (*isoterma*) foam mattress; (*de gimnasia*) mat

colear [ko·le·'ar] *vi* **1.** (*la cola*) to wag **2.** (*durar*) to last

colección [ko·lek·'sjon, -leɣ·'θjon] *f* collection

coleccionar [ko·lek·sjo·'nar, ko·leɣ·θjo-] *vt* to collect

coleccionista [ko·lek·sjo·'nis·ta, ko·leɣ·θjo-] *mf* collector

colecta [ko·'lek·ta] *f* collection (for charity); REL collect

colectividad [ko·lek·ti·βi·'dad] *f* group

colectivo [ko·lek·'ti·βo] *m* **1.** POL collective, group **2.** *Méx* (*microbús*) minibus

i In Latin America, **colectivos** are one of the forms of public transportation. In Mexico, for instance, colectivos are large cars and minivans that drive along fixed routes like regular buses. Colectivos also stop to pick up passengers who flag them down the way taxis do. They are safer than buses and cheaper than taxis and are therefore the preferred means of transportation.

colectivo, -a [ko·lek·'ti·βo, -a] *adj* collective; **acción colectiva** joint action

colega [ko·'le·ɣa] *mf* **1.** (*compañero*) colleague **2.** (*homólogo*) counterpart **3.** *inf* (*amigo*) pal, buddy

colegiado, -a [ko·le·'xja·do, -a] **I.** *adj* collegiate **II.** *m, f* member; DEP referee

colegial(a) [ko·le·'xjal, -'xja·la] **I.** *adj* school **II.** *m(f)* schoolboy *m*, schoolgirl *f*

colegio [ko·'le·xjo] *m* **1.** ENS school; **ir al ~** to go to school **2.** *AmL* (*universidad*) college; **~ mayor** hall of residence **3.** (*profesional*) association; **~ de abogados** bar association

cólera[1] ['ko·le·ra] *m* MED cholera

cólera[2] ['ko·le·ra] *f* (*ira*) anger; **acceso de ~** fit of anger

colérico, -a [ko·'le·ri·ko, -a] *adj* **1.** (*de temperamento*) bad-tempered **2.** (*furioso*) furious

colesterol [ko·les·te·'rol] *m* cholesterol

coletilla [ko·le·'ti·ja, -ʎa] *f* **1.** (*de un escrito*) postscript **2.** (*palabra*) tag

colgado, -a [ko·'ya·do, -a] *adj* **1.** (*cuadro*) hung up **2.** (*bandera*) hung out **2.** (*suspendido*) failed

colgador [kol·ya·'dor] *m* hanger; (*gancho*) (coat)hook; (*percha*) coat-hanger

colgante [kol·'yan·te] I. *adj* hanging; **puente ~** (*entre dos lados*) suspension bridge; (*de castillo*) drawbridge II. *m* pendant
colgar [kol·'yar] *irr* I. *vt* 1.(*pender*) **~ algo** to hang sth; (*decorar*) to decorate with sth; **~ el teléfono** to put down the phone 2.(*dejar*) **~ los libros** to abandon one's studies 3. *inf* (*suspender*) to fail 4.(*atribuir*) to attribute II. *vi* 1.(*pender*) to hang; (*lengua*) to droop 2. TEL (*auricular*) to hang up III. *vr:* **~se** to hang oneself
colibrí [ko·li·'βri] *m* hummingbird
cólico ['ko·li·ko] *m* MED colic
coliflor [ko·li·'flor] *f* cauliflower
colilla [ko·'li·ja, -ʎa] *f* cigarette end, fag end, butt
colín [ko·'lin] *m* AmC, Ant ZOOL American bobwhite
colina [ko·'li·na] *f* hill
colindar [ko·lin·'dar] *vi* **~ con algo** to adjoin sth
colirio [ko·'li·rjo] *m* eye drops *pl*
colisión [ko·li·'sjon] *f* collision
colisionar [ko·li·sjo·'nar] *vi* **~ con** [*o* **contra**] **algo** to collide with sth; *fig* to conflict with sth
collado [ko·'ja·do, -'ʎa·do] *m* 1.(*colina*) hill 2.(*puerto*) pass
collage [ko·'laʃ] *m* ARTE collage
collar [ko·'jar, -'ʎar] *m* 1.(*adorno*) necklace; **~ de perlas** string of pearls; **~ de perro** dog collar 2.(*insignia*) chain (of office)
colmado [kol·'ma·do] *m* grocer's shop, grocery
colmado, -a [kol·'ma·do, -a] *adj* full; **un año ~ de felicidad** a very happy year
colmar [kol·'mar] I. *vt* 1.(*vaso*) **~ de algo** to fill to the brim with sth 2.(*alabanzas*) **~ de algo** to heap on sth II. *vr:* **~se** to be fulfilled
colmena [kol·'me·na] *f* beehive
colmenar [kol·me·'nar] *m* apiary
colmillo [kol·'mi·jo, -ʎo] *m* eyetooth; (*de elefante*) tusk; (*de perro*) fang; **enseñar los ~s** *fig* to show one's teeth
colmo ['kol·mo] *m* height; **el ~ de la elegancia** the height of elegance ▶ **¡esto es el ~!** this is the last straw!; **para ~** on top of everything
colocado, -a [ko·lo·'ka·do, -a] *adj inf* (*bebido*) plastered; (*drogado*) high, stoned
colocar <c→qu> [ko·lo·'kar] I. *vt* 1.(*emplazar*) to place; (*ordenar*) to arrange; (*poner*) to put 2. DEP (*balón*) to kick; (*flecha*) to shoot 3. COM (*invertir*) to invest; (*mercancías*) to sell 4.(*empleo*) to find a job for II. *vr:* **~se** 1.(*empleo*) to get a steady job 2.(*sombrero*) to put on 3.(*posicionarse*) to place oneself; (*sentarse*) to sit (down) 4. *inf* (*alcohol*) to get plastered; (*drogas*) to get high; (*heroína*) to shoot up
Colombia [ko·'lom·bja] *f* Colombia

i **Colombia** (formally named **República de Colombia**) is located in the northwestern part of South America, between the Caribbean Sea and the Pacific Ocean. The capital, (**Santa Fe de**) **Bogotá**, is also the country's largest city. The official language of **Colombia** is Spanish and the official currency is the **peso**.

colombiano, -a [ko·lom·'bja·no, -a] *adj, m, f* Colombian
colombino, -a [ko·lom·'bi·no, -a] *adj* of Columbus
colon [ko·'lon] *m* ANAT colon
Colón [ko·'lon] *m* 1.(*Cristóbal*) Columbus 2.(*moneda*) colon
colonia [ko·'lo·nja] *f* 1.(*grupo*) colony 2. *pl* (*para niños*) holiday camp 3.(*barrio*) suburb 4.(*perfume*) cologne
Colonia [ko·'lo·nja] *f* Cologne; **agua de ~** eau de cologne
coloniaje [ko·lo·'nja·xe] *m* AmL 1.(*período*) colonial period 2.(*sistema*) system of colonial government 3. *pey* (*esclavitud*) slavery
colonialismo [ko·lo·nja·'lis·mo] *m* colonialism
colonialista [ko·lo·nja·'lis·ta] *adj, mf* colonialist
colonización [ko·lo·ni·sa·'sjon, -θa·'θjon] *f* 1.(*conquista*) colonization 2.(*población*) settling
colonizador(a) [ko·lo·ni·sa·'dor, -'do·ra; ko·lo·ni·θa-] I. *adj* colonizing II. *m(f)* 1.(*conquistador*) colonizer 2.(*poblador*) settler
colonizar <z→c> [ko·lo·ni·'sar, -'θar] *vt* 1.(*conquistar*) to colonize 2.(*poblar*) to settle
colono [ko·'lo·no, -a] *m* settler; (*labrador*) tenant farmer
coloquial [ko·lo·'kjal] *adj* LING colloquial
coloquio [ko·'lokjo] *m* conversation; (*científico*) colloquium
color [ko·'lor] *m* 1.(*en general*) color; **película en ~** color film; **un hombre de ~** a dark-skinned man; **huevos de ~** AmL brown eggs; **nuestros ~es** DEP our team; **mudar de ~** (*palidecer*) to turn pale; (*ruborizarse*) to blush; **subido de ~** risqué; **sacar los ~es a alguien** to embarrass sb 2.(*sustancia*) dye 3. POL (*ideología*) hue ▶ **verlo todo de ~ de rosa** to see everything through rose-tinted glasses
colorado, -a [ko·lo·'ra·do] *adj* 1.(*rojo*) red; **ponerse ~** to blush 2.(*coloreado*) colored
colorante [ko·lo·'ran·te] *adj, m* coloring
colorar [ko·lo·'rar] *vt* to color
colorear [ko·lo·re·'ar] *vt* to color; (*pintar*) to paint
colorido [ko·lo·'ri·do] *m* color(ing)
colosal [ko·lo·'sal] *adj* colossal
coloso [ko·'lo·so] *m* 1.(*estatua*) colossus 2.(*persona*) giant
columna [ko·'lum·na] *f* column; *fig* pillar; **~ vertebral** ANAT spinal column
columnista [ko·lum·'nis·ta] *mf* columnist
columpiar [ko·lum·'pjar] I. *vt* 1.(*balancear*)

C

to swing (to and fro) **2.** (*mecer*) to push on a swing **II.** *vr:* ~ **se** to swing

columpio [ko·'lum·pjo] *m* **1.** (*para niños*) swing **2.** *AmL* (*mecedora*) rocking chair

colza ['kol·sa, -θa] *f* BOT rape

coma[1] ['ko·ma] *m* MED coma

coma[2] ['ko·ma] *f* LING comma

comadre [ko·'ma·dre] *f* **1.** *inf* (*comadrona*) midwife **2.** (*madrina*) godmother **3.** *inf* (*amiga íntima*) bosom friend **4.** *inf* (*chismosa*) gossip **5.** *inf* (*celestina*) go-between

comadrona [ko·ma·'dro·na] *f* midwife

comandancia [ko·man·'dan·sja, -θja] *f* **1.** (*mando*) command **2.** (*cuartel*) command headquarters

comandante [ko·man·'dan·te] *m* **1.** MIL commander; (*grado*) commanding officer **2.** NÁUT captain

comando [ko·'man·do] *m* MIL command; ~ **de arranque** COMPUT start command

comarca [ko·'mar·ka] *f* (*zona*) area; (*región*) region

comba ['kom·ba] *f* **1.** (*curvatura*) bend; (*de madera*) warp **2.** (*cuerda*) skipping rope; (*juego*) skipping; **saltar a la** ~ to skip

combar [kom·'bar] *vt, vr:* ~ **se** to bend; (*madera*) to warp

combate [kom·'ba·te] *m* **1.** (*lucha*) combat; (*batalla*) battle **2.** DEP match; ~ **de boxeo** boxing match; **fuera de** ~ out of action

combatiente [kom·ba·'tjen·te] *adj, mf* combatant

combatir [kom·ba·'tir] *vt, vi* to fight

combinación [kom·bi·na·'sjon, -'θjon] *f* **1.** (*composición*) combination; ~ **ganadora** winning combination **2.** (*de transportes*) connection **3.** (*lencería*) slip

combinado [kom·bi·'na·do] *m* cocktail

combinar [kom·bi·'nar] *vt* **1.** (*componer*) to combine **2.** (*unir*) to unite; ~ **ideas** to link ideas **3.** (*coordinar*) to coordinate; MAT to permute **II.** *vr:* ~ **se** to combine

combustible [kom·bus·'ti·βle] **I.** *adj* combustible **II.** *m* fuel

combustión [kom·bus·'tjon] *f* combustion

comecocos [ko·me·'ko·kos] *m inv* **1.** *inf* (*obsesión*) obsession **2.** (*juego*) Pac-Man

comedia [ko·'me·dja] *f* **1.** TEAT (*obra*) play; (*divertida*) comedy **2.** CINE comedy **3.** *inf* (*farsa*) farce; **hacer** ~ to pretend

comediante, -a [ko·me·'djan·te, -a] *m, f* **1.** CINE actor **2.** (*farsante*) fraud

comedido, -a [ko·me·'di·do, -a] *adj* **1.** (*moderado*) moderate; (*contenido*) restrained **2.** *AmL* (*servicial*) obliging

comedimiento [ko·me·di·'mjen·to] *m AmL* willingness

comedirse [ko·me·'dir·se] *irr como pedir vr* **1.** (*moderarse*) to behave moderately; (*contenerse*) to show restraint **2.** *AmL* (*ofrecerse*) to offer

comedor [ko·me·'dor] *m* **1.** (*sala*) dining room; (*en una empresa*) canteen; ~ **universi-**

tario refectory **2.** (*mobiliario*) dining-room furniture

comején [ko·me·'xen] *m AmL* **1.** (*termita*) termite **2.** (*zozobra*) nagging uneasiness

comensal [ko·men·'sal] *mf* fellow diner

comentador(a) [ko·men·ta·'dor, -'do·ra] *m(f)* commentator

comentar [ko·men·'tar] *vt* **1.** (*hablar*) to talk about; (*hacer comentarios*) to comment on; (*explicar*) to explain; ~ **algo** *pey* to gossip about sth **2.** (*una obra*) to discuss, to review

comentario [ko·men·'ta·rjo] *m* **1.** (*general*) comment **2.** *pl* (*murmuraciones*) gossip

comentarista [ko·men·ta·'ris·ta] *mf* commentator

comenzar [ko·men·'sar, -'θar] *irr como empezar vt, vi* to begin, to commence; ~ **por hacer algo** to begin by doing sth; ~ **a trabajar** to begin to work; **para** ~ to begin with

comer [ko·'mer] **I.** *vi* **1.** (*alimentarse*) to eat; **dar de** ~ **a un animal** to feed an animal; ~ **caliente** to have a warm meal **2.** (*almorzar*) to have lunch; **antes/después de** ~ before/after lunch ▸ ~ **por siete** to eat like a horse **II.** *vt* **1.** (*ingerir*) to eat **2.** *fig* (*consumir*) to consume **3.** (*corroer*) to eat away **4.** (*colores*) to fade **5.** (*en juegos*) to take ▸ **sin** ~**lo ni beberlo** without asking for it; **me echaron la culpa a mí sin** ~**lo ni beberlo** I got blamed although I had nothing to do with it **III.** *vr:* ~ **se 1.** (*ingerir*) to eat up; ~ **se a alguien a besos** to smother sb with kisses; **está para comérsela** she looks a treat **2.** (*corroer*) to eat away **3.** (*colores*) to fade **4.** (*palabras*) to skip; (*al pronunciar*) to slur

comercial[1] [ko·mer·'sjal, -'θjal] **I.** *adj* commercial **II.** *mf* sales representative

comercial[2] [ko·mer·'sjal, 'θjal] *m AmL* (*anuncio*) commercial

comercialización [ko·mer·sja·li·sa·'sjon, -θja·li·θa·'θjon] *f* (*de un producto*) marketing; (*de un acontecimiento*) commercialization

comercializar <z→c> [ko·mer·sja·li·'sar, -θja·li·'θar] *vt* (*producto*) to market; (*acontecimiento*) to commercialize

comerciante, -a [ko·mer·'sjan·te, -a; -'θjan·te, -a] *m, f* shopkeeper; (*negociante*) dealer

comerciar [ko·mer·'sjar, -'θjar] *vi* **1.** (*tener trato con*) ~ **con un país** to trade with a country **2.** (*traficar en*) ~ **en algo** to deal in sth

comercio [ko·'mer·sjo, -θjo] *m* **1.** (*actividad*) trade; ~ **exterior** foreign trade; ~ **justo** fair trade; ~ **al por mayor** wholesale trade; ~ **sexual** sex trade **2.** (*tienda*) shop

comestibles [ko·mes·'ti·βles] *mpl* foods; **tienda de** ~ grocer's (shop), grocery

cometa[1] [ko·'me·ta] *m* ASTR comet

cometa[2] [ko·'me·ta] *f* (*de papel*) kite

cometer [ko·me·'ter] *vt t.* JUR to commit; (*error*) to make

cometido [ko·me·'ti·do] *m* (*encargo*) assignment; (*tarea*) task; (*obligación*) commitment

comezón [ko·me·'son, -'θon] *f* **1.** (*picor*) itch

2. (*malestar*) uneasiness
cómic ['ko·mik] *m* <cómics> comic
comicios [ko·'mi·sjos, -θjos] *mpl* elections *pl*
cómico, -a ['ko·mi·ko, -a] I. *adj* comedy; (*divertido*) comical II. *m, f* comedian
comida [ko·'mi·da] *f* **1.**(*alimento*) food; (*plato*) meal; ~ **de** [*o* **para**] **animales** pet food; ~ **basura** junk food; ~ **casera** homestyle cooking; ~ **francesa** French cuisine; ~ **rápida** fast food; **cama y** ~ bed and board **2.**(*horario*) ~ **principal** main meal (of the day) **3.**(*almuerzo*) lunch; ~ **de negocios** business lunch **4.** *Col, Perú, Chile* (*cena*) supper
comidilla [ko·mi·'di·ja, -ʎa] *f inf* special interest; **ser la** ~ **del pueblo** to be the talk of the town
comienzo [ko·'mjen·so, -θo] *m* beginning; **al** ~ at first; **a** ~**s de mes** at the beginning of the month
comilona [ko·mi·'lo·na] *f inf* feast, blowout *inf*
comino [ko·'mi·no] *m* cumin; **no valer un** ~ *inf* not to be worth anything
comisaría [ko·mi·sa·'ri·a] *f* **1.**(*edificio*) ~ **de policía** police station [*o* precinct] **2.**(*cargo*) commissionership
comisariato [ko·mi·sa·'rja·to] *m AmL* company store; (*almacén*) warehouse
comisario, -a [ko·mi·'sa·rjo, -a] *m, f* **1.**(*delegado*) commissioner **2.**(*de policía*) superintendent, chief of police
comisión [ko·mi·'sjon] *f* **1.**(*delegación*) commission; (*comité*) committee; **Comisión Europea** European Commission; ~ **permanente** standing committee **2.** COM commission; **a** ~ on a commission basis **3.** ADMIN ~ **de servicios** temporary duty
comisionar [ko·mi·sjo·'nar] *vt* to commission
comisura [ko·mi·'su·ra] *f* ANAT commissure; ~ **de los labios** corner of the mouth
comité [ko·mi·'te] *m* committee; ~ **de empresa** works committee
comitiva [ko·mi·'ti·βa] *f* procession; ~ **fúnebre** cortège
como ['ko·mo] I. *adv* **1.**(*del modo que*) as, like; **hazlo** ~ **quieras** do it any way you like; ~ **quien** [*o* **aquel que**] **dice** so to speak; **blanco** ~ **la nieve** white as snow; **vivía** ~ **un hermitaño** he lived like a hermit **2.**(*comparativo*) as; **es tan alto** ~ **su hermano** he's as tall as his brother **3.**(*aproximadamente*) about; **hace** ~ **un año** about a year ago **4.**(*y también*) as well as **5.**(*en calidad de*) as; **trabaja** ~ **camarero** he works as a waiter II. *conj* **1.**(*causal*) as, since; ~ **no tengo tiempo, no voy** I'm not going because I don't have time; **lo sé,** ~ **que lo vi** I know because I saw it **2.**(*condicional*) if **3.**(*con "si"* +*subj o con "que"*) as if **4.**(*final*) ~ **para** + *infin* in order to **5.**(*temporal*) as soon as
cómo ['ko·mo] I. *adv* **1.**(*modal, exclamativo*) how; ¿~ **estás?** how are you?; ¿~ (**dice**)? sorry?, pardon?; **según y** ~ it all depends **2.**(*por qué*) why; ¿~ (**no**)? why not?; **¡**~ **no!** certain-

ly! II. *m* **el** ~ the how
cómoda ['ko·mo·da] *f* chest (of drawers), dresser
comodidad [ko·mo·di·'dad] *f* **1.**(*confort*) comfort **2.**(*conveniencia*) convenience
comodín [ko·mo·'din] *m* **1.**(*en juegos*) joker **2.**(*palabra*) all-purpose word **3.** COMPUT wild card
cómodo, -a ['ko·mo·do, -a] *adj* **1.** *ser* (*cosa*) comfortable; (*conveniente*) convenient **2.** *ser* (*perezoso*) lazy **3.** *estar* (*a gusto*) comfortable; **¡ponte** ~**!** make yourself comfortable!
comoquiera [ko·mo·'kje·ra] *conj* **1.**(*causal*) ~ **que** +*subj* since **2.**(*concesiva*) ~ **que** +*subj* in whatever way; ~ **que sea eso** however that may be
compact (**disc**) ['kom·pak (disk)] *m* compact disc
compacto [kom·'pak·to] *m* **1.**(*disco*) compact disc **2.**(*reproductor*) compact disc player
compacto, -a [kom·'pak·to, -a] *adj* compact; (*denso*) dense; (*firme*) firm; (*escritura*) close; **disco** ~ compact disc
compadecer [kom·pa·de·'ser, -'θer] *irr como crecer* I. *vt* to feel sorry for II. *vr* ~**se de alguien/algo** to (take) pity (on) sb/sth
compadre [kom·'pa·dre] *m* **1.**(*padrino*) godfather **2.**(*amigo*) friend, buddy
compadrear [kom·pa·dre·'ar] *vi CSur* (*presumir*) to show off
compadrito [kom·pa·'dri·to] *m AmS* braggart
compaginación [kom·pa·xi·na·'sjon, -'θjon] *f* **1.**(*combinación*) combining **2.**(*paginación*) page makeup
compaginar [kom·pa·xi·'nar] I. *vt* **1.**(*combinar*) to combine **2.**(*paginar*) to page up II. *vr:* ~**se 1.**(*combinar*) to combine **2.**(*armonizar*) to go together
compañerismo [kom·pa·ɲe·'ris·mo] *m* companionship; (*camaradería*) comradeship; DEP team spirit
compañero, -a [kom·pa·'ɲe·ro, -a] *m, f* **1.**(*persona*) companion; (*amigo*) friend; (*pareja*) partner; *t.* POL comrade; ~ **de clase** schoolmate; UNIV fellow student; ~ **de piso** roommate; ~ **de trabajo** fellow worker **2.**(*cosa*) other one (of a pair)
compañía [kom·pa·'ɲi·a] *f* company; **animal de** ~ pet; **hacer** ~ **a alguien** to keep sb company
comparación [kom·pa·ra·'sjon, -'θjon] *f* comparison; **no hay ni punto de** ~ there's no comparison
comparar [kom·pa·'rar] I. *vt* to compare II. *vr:* ~**se** to be compared
comparativo [kom·pa·ra·'ti·βo] *m* comparative
comparecencia [kom·pa·re·'sen·sja, -'θen·θja] *f t.* JUR appearance (in court); **no** ~ failure to appear
comparecer [kom·pa·re·'ser, -'θer] *irr como crecer vi t.* JUR to appear (in court)
comparsa [kom·'par·sa] *mf* **1.** TEAT extra

2. (*desfile de carnaval*) group of people with float

compartim(i)ento [kom·par·ti·'m(j)en·to] *m* compartment

compartir [kom·par·'tir] *vt* **1.** (*tener en común*) to share **2.** (*repartirse*) to share (out)

compás [kom·'pas] *m* **1.** (*en dibujo*) compass **2.** (*ritmo*) beat; MÚS time **3.** NÁUT compass

compasión [kom·pa·'sjon] *f* ~ **de alguien** pity on sb, compassion [*o* sympathy] with sb; **sin** ~ pitiless(ly)

compasivo, -a [kom·pa·'si·βo, -a] *adj* compassionate, sympathetic

compatibilidad [kom·pa·ti·βi·li·'dad] *f* compatibility

compatibilizar <z→c> [kom·pa·ti·βi·li·'sar, -'θar] *vt* to reconcile

compatible [kom·pa·'ti·βle] *adj* compatible

compatriota [kom·pa·'trjo·ta] *mf* compatriot, fellow citizen

compeler [kom·pe·'ler] *vt* to compel

compendiar [kom·pen·'djar] *vt* to summarize

compendio [kom·'pen·djo] *m* **1.** (*resumen*) summary; (*manual*) textbook **2.** (*epítome*) epitome

compenetración [kom·pe·ne·tra·'sjon, -'θjon] *f* (mutual) understanding

compenetrarse [kom·pe·ne·'trar·se] *vr* **1.** (*identificarse*) to reach an understanding **2.** QUÍM to interpenetrate

compensación [kom·pen·sa·'sjon, -'θjon] *f* compensation

compensar [kom·pen·'sar] *vt* ~ **de algo** to compensate for sth

competencia [kom·pe·'ten·sja, -θja] *f* **1.** *t.* COM competition; (*rivalidad*) rivalry; ~ **desleal** unfair competition **2.** *t.* LING competence **3.** (*responsabilidad*) responsibility; **esto** (**no**) **es de mi** ~ I'm not responsible for this

competente [kom·pe·'ten·te] *adj* competent

competer [kom·pe·'ter] *vi* ~ **a alguien** to be the responsibility of sb

competición [kom·pe·ti·'sjon, -'θjon] *f* competition

competidor(a) [kom·pe·ti·'dor, --'do·ra] **I.** *adj* competing **II.** *m(f) t.* ECON competitor

competir [kom·pe·'tir] *irr como pedir vi* **1.** (*enfrentarse*) ~ **por algo** to compete for sth **2.** (*igualarse*) to rival each other

competitividad [kom·pe·ti·ti·βi·'dad] *f* competitiveness

competitivo, -a [kom·pe·ti·'ti·βo, -a] *adj* competitive

compilar [kom·pi·'lar] *vt t.* COMPUT to compile

compinche [kom·'pin·tʃe] *mf pey, inf* buddy

complacencia [kom·pla·'sen·sja, -'θen·θja] *f* **1.** (*agrado*) willingness; (*satisfacción*) satisfaction **2.** (*indulgencia*) indulgence

complacer [kom·pla·'ser, -'θer] *irr como crecer* **I.** *vt* to please; ~ **una petición** to grant a request **II.** *vr:* ~ **se en algo** to be pleased to sth

complaciente [kom·pla·'sjen·te, -'θjen·te] *adj*

1. (*servicial*) obliging **2.** (*indulgente*) ~ **para** [*o* **con**] **alguien** indulgent towards sb

complejidad [kom·ple·xi·'dad] *f* complexity

complejo [kom·'ple·xo] *m* complex

complejo, -a [kom·'ple·xo, -a] *adj* complex

complemento [kom·ple·'men·to] *m* **1.** *t.* LING complement **2.** (*paga*) supplementary payment, bonus **3.** *pl* (*accesorio*) accessory

completamente [kom·ple·ta·'men·te] *adv* completely

completar [kom·ple·'tar] *vt* to complete

completo, -a [kom·'ple·to, -a] *adj* (*íntegro*) complete; (*total*) total; (*lleno*) full; (*espectáculo*) sold out; **pensión completa** full board; **la obra completa de Lorca** the complete works of Lorca

complexión [kom·plek·'sjon] *f* **1.** (*constitución*) constitution, build **2.** AmL (*tez*) complexion

complicación [kom·pli·ka·'sjon, -'θjon] *f* **1.** *t.* MED (*problema*) complication **2.** (*complejidad*) complexity

complicar <c→qu> [kom·pli·'kar] **I.** *vt* **1.** (*dificultar*) to complicate **2.** (*implicar*) to involve **II.** *vr:* ~ **se 1.** (*dificultarse*) to get complicated **2.** (*embrollarse*) to get involved

cómplice ['kom·pli·se, -θe] *mf t.* JUR accomplice; **hacerse** ~ **de alguien** to become sb's accomplice

complicidad [kom·pli·θi·'dad, kom·pli·θi-] *f* complicity

componente [kom·po·'nen·te] *m* **1.** *t.* TÉC component; ~**s lógicos** COMPUT software **2.** (*miembro*) member

componer [kom·po·'ner] *irr como poner* **I.** *vt* **1.** (*formar*) to put together; (*organizar*) to organize **2.** (*constituir*) to make up **3.** *t.* MÚS to compose **4.** TIPO to set (up) **5.** (*asear*) to arrange **6.** AmL (*castrar*) to castrate **7.** AmL (*hueso*) to set **II.** *vr:* ~ **se 1.** (*constituirse*) to consist **2.** (*arreglarse*) to tidy oneself up **3.** AmL (*mejorarse*) to get better

comportamiento [kom·por·ta·'mjen·to] *m* conduct, behavior; *t.* TÉC performance

comportar [kom·por·'tar] **I.** *vt* to involve; **esto** (**no**) **comporta que** +*subj* this (doesn't) mean(s) that **II.** *vr:* ~ **se** to behave

composición [kom·po·si·'sjon, -'θjon] *f* **1.** *t.* MÚS composition **2.** TIPO typesetting; **taller de** ~ composing room

compositor(a) [kom·po·si·'tor, --'to·ra] *m(f)* composer

compostura [kom·pos·'tu·ra] *f* **1.** (*realización*) composition **2.** (*aspecto*) tidiness **3.** (*comedimiento*) composure

compota [kom·'po·ta] *f* compote

compra ['kom·pra] *f* purchase; ~**s** shopping; **ir de** ~**s** to go shopping

comprador(a) [kom·pra·'dor, --'do·ra] *m(f)* buyer; (*cliente*) customer

comprar [kom·'prar] *vt* **1.** (*adquirir*) to buy; ~ **al contado** to pay cash; ~ **a plazos** to buy on hire-purchase, to buy on an installment plan

2. (*corromper*) to buy off

comprender [kom·pren·'der] *vt* **1.** (*entender*) to understand; **hacerse** ~ to make oneself understood; ~ **mal** to misunderstand **2.** (*contener*) to comprise; (*abarcar*) to take in

comprensible [kom·pren·'si·βle] *adj* understandable, comprehensible

comprensión [kom·pren·'sjon] *f* **1.** (*capacidad*) understanding; (*entendimiento*) comprehension **2.** (*inclusión*) inclusion

comprensivo, -a [kom·pren·'si·βo, -a] *adj* **1.** (*benévolo*) understanding **2.** (*tolerante*) tolerant

compresa [kom·'pre·sa] *f* **1.** *t.* MED (*apósito*) compress **2.** (*higiénica*) sanitary napkin [*o* pad]

compresión [kom·pre·'sjon] *f* compression

comprimido [kom·pri·'mi·do] *m* pill

comprimir [kom·pri·'mir] **I.** *vt t.* FÍS, TÉC to compress **II.** *vr:* ~**se** to control oneself

comprobación [kom·pro·βa·'sjon, -'θjon] *f* **1.** (*control*) checking **2.** (*verificación*) verification; (*prueba*) proof

comprobante [kom·pro·'βan·te] *m* voucher, proof

comprobar <o→ue> [kom·pro·'βar] *vt* **1.** (*controlar*) to check **2.** (*verificar*) to verify; (*probar*) to prove

comprometedor(a) [kom·pro·me·'te·dor, -'do·ra] *adj* compromising

comprometer [kom·pro·me·'ter] **I.** *vt* **1.** (*implicar*) to involve **2.** (*exponer*) to endanger **3.** (*arriesgar*) to put at risk **4.** (*obligar*) to commit **II.** *vr:* ~**se 1.** (*implicarse*) to compromise oneself **2.** (*obligarse*) to commit oneself; ~**se** (**en matrimonio**) to get engaged

compromiso [kom·pro·'mi·so] *m* **1.** (*vinculación*) commitment; (*obligación*) obligation; **visita de** ~ formal visit; **sin** ~ without obligation; (**soltero y**) **sin** ~ free and single **2.** (*promesa*) promise; ~ **matrimonial** engagement **3.** (*acuerdo*) agreement **4.** (*aprieto*) awkward situation **5.** (*cita*) engagement

compuerta [kom·'pwer·ta] *f* sluice gate

compuesto [kom·'pwes·to] *m t.* QUÍM compound

compulsa [kom·'pul·sa] *f* certified copy

compulsar [kom·pul·'sar] *vt* to compare; JUR to certify

compulsivo, -a [kom·pul·'si·βo, -a] *adj* compulsive

compungido, -a [kom·pun·'xi·do, -a] *adj* (*contrito*) remorseful; (*triste*) sad

compungir <g→j> [kom·pun·'xir] **I.** *vt* to make remorseful **II.** *vr:* ~**se** to feel remorseful

computación [kom·pu·ta·'sjon, -'θjon] *f* calculation; COMPUT computing

computador [kom·pu·ta·'dor] *m AmL* computer

computador(a) [kom·pu·ta·'dor, -'do·ra] *adj* computer

computadora [kom·pu·ta·'do·ra] *f AmL* computer

computar [kom·pu·'tar] *vt* **1.** (*calcular*) to calculate **2.** (*considerar*) to count

computerizar <z→c> [kom·pu·te·ri·'sar, -'θar] *vt* to computerize

cómputo ['kom·pu·to] *m* calculation; ~ **de votos** count of votes

comulgar <g→gu> [ko·mul·'ɣar] *vi* REL to take communion; *fig* (*estar de acuerdo*) to agree

común [ko·'mun] **I.** *adj* common; **de** ~ **acuerdo** by common consent; **sentido** ~ common sense; **fuera de lo** ~ out of the ordinary; **poco** ~ unusual; **por lo** ~ usually **II.** *m* POL **los Comunes** the (House of) Commons

comuna [ko·'mu·na] *f* **1.** *t.* HIST commune **2.** *AmL* (*municipio*) municipality

comunal [ko·mu·'nal] *adj* communal; **elecciones** ~**es** municipal elections

comunicación [ko·mu·ni·ka·'sjon, -'θjon] *f* **1.** (*en general*) communication; **ponerse en** ~ **con alguien** to get in touch with sb **2.** (*comunicado*) message; (*ponencia*) paper **3.** (*conexión*) connection; ~ **telefónica** telephone call **4.** (*de transporte*) link **5.** *pl t.* TEL communications *pl*

comunicado [ko·mu·ni·'ka·do] *m* communiqué; ~ **de prensa** press release

comunicar <c→qu> [ko·mu·ni·'kar] **I.** *vi* **1.** (*estar unido*) to be joined; (*estar en contacto*) to be connected **2.** (*conectar*) to connect **3.** (*teléfono*) to be busy **II.** *vt* **1.** (*informar*) to inform **2.** (*transmitir*) to communicate **3.** (*unir*) to connect; (*contactar*) to contact **4.** (*al teléfono*) to put through **III.** *vr:* ~**se 1.** (*entenderse*) to communicate **2.** (*relacionarse*) to be connected

comunicativo, -a [ko·mu·ni·ka·'ti·βo, -a] *adj* communicative

comunidad [ko·mu·ni·'dad] *f* community; ~ **de vecinos** residents' association

comunión [ko·mu·'njon] *f* communion

comunismo [ko·mu·'nis·mo] *m* POL communism

comunista [ko·mu·'nis·ta] **I.** *adj* POL communist **II.** *mf* POL communist

comunitario, -a [ko·mu·ni·'ta·rjo, -a] *adj* **1.** (*colectivo*) communal **2.** (*municipal*) community **3.** POL (*Comunidad Europea*) Community

con [kon] **I.** *prep* **1.** (*compañía, modo*) with; **estar** ~ **la gripe** to have the flu; ~ **el tiempo...** with time... **2.** MAT **3** ~ **5** 3 point 5 **3.** (*actitud*) (**para**) ~ to, towards **4.** (*circunstancia*) ~ **este tiempo...** in this weather... **5.** (*a pesar de*) in spite of **II.** *conj* + *infin* if; ~ **que** +*subj* as long as; ~ **sólo que** +*subj* if only

concatenar [kon·ka·te·'nar] *vt* to link together

cóncavo, -a ['kon·ka·βo, -a] *adj* concave

concebir [kon·se·'βir, kon·θe-] *irr como pedir vt, vi* to conceive; ~ **esperanzas** to have hopes

conceder [kon·se·'der, kon·θe-] *vt* **1.** (*otorgar*) to grant; (*asignar*) to give; ~ **la palabra a alguien** to give sb the floor; ~ **un premio** to award a prize **2.** (*admitir*) to concede

concejal(a) [kon·se·'xal, -·'xa·la, kon·θe-] *m(f)* councilman *m*, councilwoman *f*

concejo [kon·'se·xo, -·'θe·xo] *m* council

concentración [kon·sen·tra·'sjon, -θen·tra·'θjon] *f* concentration; ~ **pacífica** peaceful demonstration

concentrado [kon·sen·'tra·do, kon·θen-] *m* concentrate

concentrar [kon·sen·'trar, kon·θen-] **I.** *vt* to concentrate **II.** *vr*: ~ **se 1.** (*reunirse*) to assemble; (*agruparse*) to gather together **2.** (*centrarse*) to concentrate

concepción [kon·sep·'sjon, -θeβ·'θjon] *f* conception

concepto [kon·'sep·to, kon·'θep-] *m* **1.** (*noción*) notion; (*plan*) concept **2.** (*opinión*) opinion **3.** (*motivo*) **bajo** [*o* por] **ningún** ~ on no account **4.** (*calidad*) **en** ~ **de** by way of

conceptualizar <z→c> [kon·sep·twa·li·'sar, -θep·twa·li·'θar] *vt* to conceptualize

concernir [kon·ser·'nir, kon·θer-] *irr como cernir vi* to concern; **en** [*o* por] **lo que concierne a alguien...** as far as sb is concerned...

concertar <e→ie> [kon·ser·'tar, kon·θer-] **I.** *vi t.* LING to agree **II.** *vt* **1.** (*arreglar*) to arrange **2.** MÚS (*afinar*) to tune **3.** (*armonizar*) to harmonize

concertista [kon·ser·'tis·ta, kon·θer-] *mf* MÚS soloist

concesión [kon·se·'sjon, kon·θe-] *f t.* COM concession; (*de un premio*) awarding

concesionario, -a [kon·θe·sjo·'na·rjo, -a; kon·θe-] *m, f* dealer

concha ['kon·tʃa] *f* **1.** (*del molusco*) shell; (*de tortuga*) tortoiseshell **2.** TEAT prompt box **3.** *AmL* (*descaro*) nerve **4.** *AmL*, *vulg* (*vulva*) pussy ▶ **tener más ~s que un galápago** *inf* to be a slippery customer

conchabar [kon·tʃa·'βar] *vt AmL* to hire

conchudo, -a [kon·'tʃu·do, -a] *adj* **1.** *AmL*, *inf* (*sinvergüenza*) shameless **2.** *Méx, Col, inf* (*indolente*) sluggish

conciencia [kon·'sjen·sja, -·'θjen·θja] *f* **1.** (*conocimiento*) awareness; **tomar ~ de algo** to become aware of sth **2.** (*moral*) conscience; **a ~** conscientiously; **libertad de ~** freedom of worship; (**sin**) **cargo de ~** (without) remorse; **me remuerde la ~** my conscience is pricking me

concienciar [kon·sjen·'sjar, -θjen·'θjar] **I.** *vt* to make aware **II.** *vr*: ~ **se 1.** (*convencerse*) to convince oneself **2.** (*sensibilizarse*) to become aware

concienzudo, -a [kon·sjen·'su·do, -a; -θjen·'θu·do, -a] *adj* conscientious

concierto [kon·'sjer·to, kon·'θjer-] *m* **1.** MÚS (*función*) concert; (*obra*) concerto **2.** (*orden*) order **3.** *t.* ECON (*acuerdo*) agreement

conciliación [kon·si·lja·'sjon, -θi·lja·'θjon] *f* conciliation; (*reconciliación*) reconciliation; ~ **laboral** arbitration

conciliador(a) [kon·si·lja·'dor, -·'do·ra, kon·θi-] *adj* conciliatory

conciliar [kon·si·'ljar, kon·θi-] **I.** *vt* to reconcile; (*armonizar*) to harmonize; ~ **el sueño** *fig* to get to sleep **II.** *vr*: ~ **se** to be reconciled

concilio [kon·'si·ljo, -·'θi·ljo] *m t.* REL council

conciso, -a [kon·'si·so, -a; kon·'θi-] *adj* concise

conciudadano, -a [kon·sju·da·'da·no, -a; kon·θju-] *m, f* fellow citizen

concluir [kon·klu·'ir] *irr como huir* **I.** *vt* **1.** (*terminar*) to complete **2.** (*deducir*) ~ **de algo** to conclude from sth **II.** *vi, vr*: ~ **se** to end; **¡asunto concluido!** that's settled!

conclusión [kon·klu·'sjon] *f* conclusion; **en** ~ (*en suma*) in short; (*por último*) in conclusion; **llegar a la ~ de que...** to come to the conclusion that...

concluyente [kon·klu·'jen·te] *adj* conclusive; (*determinante*) decisive, unequivocal

concordancia [kon·kor·'dan·sja, -θja] *f* concordance; LING agreement

concordar <o→ue> [kon·kor·'dar] **I.** *vi* to coincide; LING to agree **II.** *vt* to reconcile; LING to make agree

concordia [kon·'kor·dja] *f* harmony

concretar [kon·kre·'tar] **I.** *vt* **1.** (*precisar*) to put in concrete form **2.** (*limitar*) to limit **II.** *vr*: ~ **se** to limit oneself

concretizar <z→c> [kon·kre·ti·'sar, -'θar] *vt v.* **concretar**

concreto, -a [kon·'kre·to] *adj* concrete; **en** ~ specifically

concubina [kon·ku·'βi·na] *f* concubine

concurrencia [kon·ku·'rren·sja, -θja] *f* **1.** (*coincidencia*) coincidence **2.** (*asistencia*) attendance **3.** (*competencia*) competition

concurrido, -a [kon·ku·'rri·do, -a] *adj* crowded

concurrir [kon·ku·'rrir] *vi* **1.** (*en un lugar*) to come together; (*en el tiempo*) to coincide **2.** (*concursar*) ~ **por algo** to compete for sth **3.** (*participar*) to take part

concursante [kon·kur·'san·te] *mf* **1.** (*aspirante*) candidate **2.** (*participante*) competitor, contestant

concursar [kon·kur·'sar] *vi* to compete

concurso [kon·'kur·so] *m* **1.** *t.* DEP competition **2.** (*oposición*) (public) competition **3.** (*coincidencia*) coincidence **4.** (*ayuda*) help

conde(sa) ['kon·de, kon·'de·sa] *m(f)* count *m*, countess *f*

condecoración [kon·de·ko·ra·'sjon, -'θjon] *f* MIL decoration

condecorar [kon·de·ko·'rar] *vt* MIL to decorate

condena [kon·'de·na] *f* sentence, conviction; **cumplir una** ~ to serve a sentence

condenado, -a [kon·de·'na·do, -a] **I.** *adj inf* condemned **II.** *m, f* **1.** (*reo*) convicted person, convict **2.** REL **los ~s** the damned **3.** *inf* (*endemoniado*) wretch

condenar [kon·de·'nar] **I.** *vt* **1.** (*sentenciar*) to condemn **2.** REL to damn **II.** *vr*: ~ **se 1.** REL to be

damned **2.** (*acusarse*) to confess
condensar [kon·den·'sar] *vt, vr:* ~ **se** to condense
condesa [kon·'de·sa] *f v.* **conde**
condescendencia [kon·de·sen·'den·sja, -des·θen·'den·θja] *f* **1.** (*dignación*) condescension **2.** (*transigencia*) ~ **con algo/alguien** acquiescence to [*o* in] sth/sb
condescender <e→ie> [kon·de·sen·'der, kon·des·θen-] *vi* **1.** (*avenirse*) ~ **con algo/alguien** to agree to sth/with sb **2.** (*rebajarse*) to condescend
condescendiente [kon·de·sen·'djen·te, kon·des·θen-] *adj* **1.** (*benévolo*) kind **2.** (*complaciente*) obliging
condición [kon·di·'sjon, -'θjon] *f* **1.** (*índole*) nature **2.** (*estado*) condition; **a ~ de que** +*subj* on condition that, providing **3.** (*situación*) position **4.** (*clase*) social class
condicional [kon·di·sjo·'nal, kon·di·θjo-] *adj, m* LING conditional
condicionar [kon·di·sjo·'nar, kon·di·θjo-] *vt* (*supeditar*) ~ **a algo** to make conditional on sth
condimentar [kon·di·men·'tar] *vt* to season, to flavor
condimento [kon·di·'men·to] *m* seasoning, flavoring
condolencia [kon·do·'len·sja, -θja] *f* condolence, sympathy
condolerse <o→ue> [kon·do·'ler·se] *vr* ~ **se de algo** to sympathize with sth
condón [kon·'don] *m* condom
condonar [kon·do·'nar] *vt* (*deuda*) to write off
cóndor ['kon·dor] *m* condor
conducción [kon·duk·'sjon, --duɣ'θjon] *f* **1.** (*transporte*) transport(ation) **2.** (*coche*) driving; ~ **temeraria** reckless driving **3.** (*gestión*) management
conducir [kon·du·'sir, -'θir] *irr como traducir* **I.** *vt* **1.** (*llevar*) to take; (*transportar*) to transport **2.** (*guiar*) to guide **3.** (*arrastrar*) to lead **4.** (*pilotar*) to drive **II.** *vi* **1.** (*dirigir*) to lead **2.** (*pilotar*) to drive **III.** *vr:* ~ **se** to behave
conducta [kon·'duk·ta] *f* conduct, behavior
conductismo [kon·duk·'tis·mo] *m* PSICO behaviorism
conducto [kon·'duk·to] *m* **1.** (*tubo*) pipe **2.** MED canal; ~ **auditivo** ear canal **3.** (*mediación*) channels *pl*
conductor [kon·duk·'tor] *m* FÍS conductor
conductor(a) [kon·duk·'tor, --'to·ra] **I.** *adj* conductive; **hilo** ~ conductor wire **II.** *m(f)* driver
conectar [ko·nek·'tar] **I.** *vt* **1.** (*enlazar*) to connect **2.** (*enchufar*) to plug in **II.** *vi* to communicate
conejo, -a [ko·'ne·xo] *m, f* rabbit
conexión [ko·nek·'sjon] *f* **1.** *t.* TEL connection **2.** *pl* (*amistades*) connections *pl*
confabularse [kon·fa·βu·'lar·se] *vr* to plot
confección [kon·fek·'sjon, -feɣ'θjon] *f* making; (*de vestidos*) dressmaking

confeccionar [kon·fek·sjo·'nar, kon·fey·θjo-] *vt* to make; (*plan*) to draw up
confederación [kon·fe·de·ra·'sjon, -'θjon] *f* confederation
conferencia [kon·fe·'ren·sja, -θja] *f* **1.** (*charla*) lecture **2.** (*encuentro*) conference **3.** (*telefónica*) call
conferenciante [kon·fe·ren·'sjan·te, -'θjan·te] *mf*, **conferencista** [kon·fe·ren·'sis·ta, -'θis·ta] *mf AmL* lecturer
conferir [kon·fe·'rir] *irr como sentir vt* to confer
confesar <e→ie> [kon·fe·'sar] **I.** *vt* **1.** (*admitir*) to confess **2.** REL (*declarar*) to confess; ~ **a alguien** to confess, to hear sb's confession **II.** *vr:* ~ **se** to confess; ~ **se culpable** to admit one's guilt
confesión [kon·fe·'sjon] *f* confession
confes(i)onario [kon·fe·s(j)o·'na·rjo] *m* confessional (box)
confesor [kon·fe·'sor] *m* confessor
confiado, -a [kon·fi·'a·do, -a] *adj* **1.** *ser* (*crédulo*) trusting **2.** *estar* (*presumido*) vain; (*de sí mismo*) self-confident
confianza [kon·fi·'an·sa, -θa] *f* **1.** (*crédito*) trust; **amiga de** ~ close friend **2.** (*esperanza*) confidence **3.** (*en uno mismo*) self-confidence **4.** (*familiaridad*) familiarity
confiar <1. *pres:* confío> [kon·fi·'ar] **I.** *vi* ~ **en algo/alguien** to trust in sth/sb **II.** *vt* to entrust **III.** *vr* ~ **se a alguien** to confide in sb
confidencia [kon·fi·'den·sja, -θja] *f* secret
confidencial [kon·fi·den·'sjal, -'θjal] *adj* confidential
confidente [kon·fi·'den·te] *mf* **1.** (*cómplice*) confidant *m*, confidante *f* **2.** (*espía*) informer
configuración [kon·fi·ɣu·ra·'sjon, -'θjon] *f* **1.** (*formación*) shaping **2.** (*forma*) shape; COMPUT configuration
configurar [kon·fi·ɣu·'rar] **I.** *vt* to shape; COMPUT to configure **II.** *vr:* ~ **se** to take shape
confín [kon·'fin] **I.** *adj* bordering **II.** *m* **1.** (*frontera*) border **2.** (*final*) limit
confinar [kon·fi·'nar] *vt* to confine
confirmación [kon·fir·ma·'sjon, -'θjon] *f t.* REL confirmation
confirmar [kon·fir·'mar] **I.** *vt t.* REL to confirm **II.** *vr:* ~ **se** to be confirmed
confiscar <c→qu> [kon·fis·'kar] *vt* to confiscate
confitar [kon·fi·'tar] *vt* (*en almíbar*) to preserve in syrup; (*con azúcar*) to candy
confitería [kon·fi·te·'ri·a] *f* cake [*o* pastry] shop, candy shop
conflictividad [kon·flik·ti·βi·'dad] *f* disputes *pl*
conflicto [kon·'flik·to] *m* conflict
confluencia [kon·flu·'en·sja, -θja] *f* confluence
confluir [kon·flu·'ir] *irr como huir vi* (*calles*) to meet
conformar [kon·for·'mar] **I.** *vt* **1.** (*dar forma*) to shape **2.** (*ajustar*) to adjust **II.** *vr:* ~ **se**

1. (*contentarse*) to be satisfied **2.** (*ajustarse*) to adjust
conforme [kon·'for·me] **I.** *adj* (*adecuado*) **estar ~ con algo** to be satisfied with sth **II.** *prep* according to **III.** *conj* (*como*) as
conformidad [kon·for·mi·'dad] *f* **1.** (*afinidad*) similarity **2.** (*aprobación*) approval
confort [kon·'fort] *m* comfort
confortable [kon·for·'ta·βle] *adj* comfortable
confortar [kon·for·'tar] **I.** *vt* **1.** (*vivificar*) to strengthen **2.** (*alentar*) to encourage; (*consolar*) to comfort **II.** *vr:* **~ se 1.** (*reanimarse*) to regain one's strength **2.** (*consolarse*) to take comfort
confrontación [kon·fron·ta·'sjon, -'θjon] *f* **1.** (*comparación*) comparison **2.** (*enfrentamiento*) confrontation
confrontar [kon·fron·'tar] **I.** *vt* **1.** (*comparar*) to compare **2.** (*enfrentar*) to confront **II.** *vr* **~ se con alguien** to face up to sb
confundir [kon·fun·'dir] **I.** *vt* **1.** (*trastocar*) to mistake **2.** (*mezclar*) to mix up **3.** (*embrollar*) to confuse **II.** *vr:* **~ se 1.** (*mezclarse*) to mix **2.** (*embrollarse*) to get confused
confusión [kon·fu·'sjon] *f* confusion
confuso, -a [kon·'fu·so, -a] *adj* confused
congelación [kon·xe·la·'sjon, -'θjon] *f* **1.** (*solidificación*) freezing; **~ salarial** pay freeze **2.** frostbite; MED
congelador [kon·xe·la·'dor] *m* **1.** (*electrodoméstico*) freezer **2.** (*de un frigorífico*) ice [*o* freezer] compartment
congelar [kon·xe·'lar] **I.** *vt t. fig* to freeze **II.** *vr:* **~ se 1.** (*solidificarse*) to freeze **2.** (*helarse*) to get frostbitten
congeniar [kon·xe·'njar] *vi* **~ con** to get on [*o* along] with
congénito, -a [kon·'xe·ni·to, -a] *adj* congenital
congestión [kon·xes·'tjon] *f t.* MED congestion
congestionar [kon·xes·tjo·'nar] **I.** *vt t.* MED to congest **II.** *vr:* **~ se** *t.* MED to become congested
conglomerar [kon·glo·me·'rar] *vt, vr:* **~ se** to conglomerate
Congo ['kon·go] *m* **el ~** the Congo
congoja [kon·'go·xa] *f* **1.** (*pena*) sorrow **2.** (*desconsuelo*) anguish
congola [kon·'go·la] *f Col* (*pipa de fumar*) pipe
congoleño, -a [kon·go·'le·ɲo, -a], **congolés, -esa** [kon·go·'les, -·'le·sa] *adj, m, f* Congolese
congraciar [kon·gra·'sjar, -'θjar] **I.** *vt* to win over **II.** *vr:* **~ se** to ingratiate oneself
congratular [kon·gra·tu·'lar] **I.** *vt* to congratulate **II.** *vr* **~ se de** [*o* **por**] **algo** to congratulate oneself on sth
congregación [kon·gre·ɣa·'sjon, -'θjon] *f* **1.** (*reunión*) meeting **2.** REL congregation
congregar <g→gu> [kon·gre·'ɣar] **I.** *vt* to bring together **II.** *vr:* **~ se** to gather
congresal [kon·gre·'sal] *mf AmL* member of a congress
congresista [kon·gre·'sis·ta] *mf* **1.** POL delegate, congressman *m*, congresswoman *f*

2. (*en un congreso*) congress member
congreso [kon·'gre·so] *m* **1.** POL congress **2.** (*reunión*) congress, convention
congrio ['kon·grjo] *m* conger eel
congruencia [kon·'grwen·sja, -θja] *f* coherence; MAT congruence
cónico, -a ['ko·ni·ko, -a] *adj* conical
conífera [ko·'ni·fe·ra] *f* conifer
conjetura [kon·xe·'tu·ra] *f* conjecture
conjeturar [kon·xe·tu·'rar] *vt* to speculate
conjugación [kon·xu·ɣa·'sjon, -'θjon] *f* conjugation
conjugar <g→gu> [kon·xu·'ɣar] *vt* **1.** (*combinar*) to combine **2.** LING to conjugate
conjunción [kon·xun·'sjon, -'θjon] *f* conjunction
conjuntamente [kon·xun·ta·'men·te] *adv* jointly; **~ con** together with
conjuntar [kon·xun·'tar] **I.** *vi* to match; **~ con** to go with **II.** *vt* to harmonize **III.** *vr:* **~ se** to come together
conjuntivitis [kon·xun·ti·'βi·tis] *f inv* conjunctivitis
conjunto [kon·'xun·to] *m* **1.** (*totalidad*) whole; **en ~** as a whole **2.** TEAT ensemble **3.** (*ropa*) outfit **4.** MAT set
conjura [kon·'xu·ra] *f*, **conjuración** [kon·xu·ra·'sjon, -'θjon] *f* conspiracy
conjurar [kon·xu·'rar] **I.** *vi* to conspire **II.** *vt* **1.** (*invocar*) to beseech **2.** (*alejar*) to ward off **III.** *vr:* **~ se** to conspire
conllevar [kon·je·'βar, kon·ʎe·-] *vt* **1.** (*implicar*) to involve **2.** (*soportar*) to bear
conmemoración [kon·me·mo·ra·'sjon, kom·me·-, -'θjon] *f* commemoration
conmemorar [kon·me·mo·'rar, kom·me·mo·'rar] *vt* to commemorate
conmemorativo, -a [kon·me·mo·ra·'ti·βo, -a; kom·me·-] *adj* commemorative
conmigo [kon·'mi·ɣo, kom·'mi·ɣo] *pron pers* with me
conmiseración [kon·mi·se·ra·'sjon, kom·mi·-, -'θjon] *f* commiseration
conmoción [kon·mo·'sjon, kom·mo·-, -'θjon] *f* **1.** MED concussion **2.** *fig* shock
conmocionar [kon·mo·sjo·'nar, kom·mo·-, -θjo·'nar] *vt* **1.** MED to concuss **2.** *fig* to shake
conmovedor(a) [kon·mo·βe·'dor, -·'do·ra; kom·mo·-] *adj* **1.** (*conmocionando*) stirring **2.** (*sentimental*) moving
conmover <o→ue> [kon·mo·'βer, kom·mo·-] **I.** *vt* **1.** (*emocionar*) to move **2.** (*sacudir*) to shake **II.** *vr:* **~ se 1.** (*emocionarse*) to be moved **2.** (*sacudirse*) to be shaken
conmutación [kon·mu·ta·'sjon, kom·mu·-, -'θjon] *f t.* LING commutation
conmutador [kon·mu·ta·'dor, kom·mu·-] *m* ELEC switch
conmutar [kon·mu·'tar, kom·mu·-] *vt* **1.** (*cambiar*) to exchange; **~ por algo** to commute to sth **2.** ELEC to switch
cono ['ko·no] *m* cone; **Cono Sur** GEO Southern Cone (*Argentina, Chile, Paraguay and Uru-*

guay)

conocedor(a) [ko·no·se·'dor, -·'do·ra, ko·no·θe-] I. *adj* ~ **de algo** knowledgeable about sth II. *m(f)* expert

conocer [ko·no·'ser, -'θer] *irr como crecer* I. *vt* 1. (*saber, tratar*) to know; ~ **de vista** to know by sight; **dar a** ~ to make known 2. (*reconocer*) to recognize 3. (*descubrir*) to get to know 4. (*por primera vez*) to meet; **les conocí en una fiesta** I met them at a party II. *vi* ~ **de algo** to know about sth III. *vr:* ~ **se** 1. (*tener trato*) to know each other 2. (*a sí mismo*) to know oneself

conocido, -a [ko·no·'si·do, -a; ko·no·'θi-] I. *adj* (well-)known II. *m, f* acquaintance

conocimiento [ko·no·θi·'mjen·to, ko·no·θi-] *m* 1. (*saber*) knowledge 2. (*entendimiento*) understanding 3. (*consciencia*) consciousness 4. *pl* (*nociones*) knowledge

conque ['kon·ke] *conj inf* so

conquista [kon·'kis·ta] *f* conquest

conquistador(a) [kon·kis·ta·'dor, -·'do·ra] I. *adj* conquering II. *m(f)* 1. conqueror 2. *pl* (*de América*) conquistadores

conquistar [kon·kis·'tar] *vt* to conquer

consagración [kon·sa·ɣra·'sjon, -'θjon] *f* 1. REL consecration 2. (*dedicación*) dedication

consagrar [kon·sa·'ɣrar] I. *vt* 1. REL to consecrate 2. (*dedicar*) to dedicate II. *vr:* ~ **se** 1. (*dedicarse*) to devote oneself 2. (*acreditarse*) to distinguish oneself

consanguíneo, -a [kon·san·'gi·neo, -a] I. *adj* related by blood II. *m, f* blood relation

consciencia [kon·'sjen·sja, -'θjen·θja] *f* consciousness

consciente [kon·'sjen·te, kons·'θjen·te] *adj* conscious; **estar** ~ MED to be conscious; **ser** ~ **de algo** to be aware of sth

conscripción [kons·krip·'sjon, -'θjon] *f* Arg (*servicio militar*) conscription

conscripto [kons·'krip·to] *m AmS* (*quinto*) recruit, conscript

consecución [kon·se·ku·'sjon, -'θjon] *f* attainment

consecuencia [kon·se·'kwen·sja, -θja] *f* 1. (*efecto*) consequence; **a** ~ **de** as a result of 2. (*coherencia*) consistency

consecuente [kon·se·'kwen·te] *adj* consistent

consecuentemente [kon·se·kwen·te·'men·te] *adv* 1. (*por consiguiente*) consequently 2. (*con consistencia*) consistently

consecutivo, -a [kon·se·ku·'ti·βo, -a] *adj* consecutive

conseguir [kon·se·'ɣir] *irr como seguir vt* to get; ~ **obtener algo** to succeed in obtaining sth

consejero, -a [kon·se·'xe·ro, -a] *m, f* 1. (*guía*) adviser, counselor, consultant 2. (*miembro de un consejo*) member; ~ **delegado** managing director 3. (*de una autonomía española*) minister

consejo [kon·'se·xo] *m* 1. (*recomendación*) piece of advice 2. (*organismo*) council 3. (*reunión*) meeting

consenso [kon·'sen·so] *m* consensus

consentido, -a [kon·sen·'ti·do, -a] *adj* spoiled

consentimiento [kon·sen·ti·'mjen·to] *m* ~ **para algo** consent to sth

consentir [kon·sen·'tir] *irr como sentir* I. *vi* (*admitir*) ~ **en algo** to agree to sth II. *vt* 1. (*autorizar*) to allow; (*tolerar*) to tolerate 2. (*mimar*) to spoil 3. (*aguantar*) to put up with

conserje [kon·'ser·xe] *mf* 1. (*encargado*) janitor 2. (*hotel*) concierge, receptionist 3. (*portero*) (hall) porter

conserjería [kon·ser·xe·'ri·a] *f* 1. (*cargo*) job of caretaker 2. (*oficina*) caretaker's office 3. (*hotel*) reception (desk)

conserva [kon'serβa] *f* canned food

conservación [kon·ser·βa·'sjon, -'θjon] *f* 1. (*mantenimiento*) maintenance 2. (*guarda*) conservation 3. (*conserva*) preserving

conservador(a) [kon·ser·'·βa·dor] I. *adj* conservative II. *m(f)* 1. (*guardador*) curator 2. POL conservative

conservar [kon·ser·'βar] I. *vt* 1. (*mantener*) to maintain 2. (*guardar*) to conserve 3. (*hacer conservas*) to can 4. (*práctica*) to preserve II. *vr:* ~ **se** to survive; (*mantenerse*) to keep

conservatorio [kon·ser·βa·'to·rjo] *m* conservatory

considerable [kon·si·de·'ra·βle] *adj* considerable

consideración [kon·si·de·ra·'sjon, -'θjon] *f* 1. (*reflexión*) consideration; **en** ~ **a** in consideration of 2. (*respeto*) respect

considerado, -a [kon·si·de·'ra·do, -a] *adj* 1. (*tenido en cuenta*) considered 2. (*apreciado*) respected 3. (*atento*) considerate

considerar [kon·si·de·'rar] *vt, (vr):* ~ **se** to consider (oneself)

consigna [kon·'siɣ·na] *f* 1. MIL motto 2. POL instruction 3. (*de equipajes*) checkroom

consignar [kon·siɣ·'nar] *vt* 1. (*asignar*) to assign 2. (*protocolar*) to record 3. (*en depósito*) to check 4. COM to dispatch

consignatario, -a [kon·siɣ·na·'ta·rjo, -a] *m, f* 1. (*destinatario*) addressee 2. COM consignee

consigo [kon·'si·ɣo] *pron pers* **tiene el libro** ~ he/she has the book with him/her; **lléveselo** ~ take it with you

consiguiente [kon·si·'ɣjen·te] *adj* resulting; **por** ~ consequently

consistencia [kon·sis·'ten·sja, -θja] *f* consistency

consistir [kon·sis·'tir] *vi* 1. (*componerse*) ~ **en algo** to consist of sth 2. (*radicar*) ~ **en algo** to lie in sth

consola [kon·'so·la] *f* (*mesa*) console table; ELEC console; (*de videojuegos*) video console

consolar <o→ue> [kon·so·'lar] *vt, vr:* ~ **se** to console (oneself)

consolidación [kon·so·li·da·'sjon, -'θjon] *f* consolidation

consolidar [kon·so·li·'dar] I. *vt* to consolidate

II. *vr:* ~ **se** to be consolidated

consomé [kon·so·'me] *m* consommé

consonancia [kon·so·'nan·sja, -θja] *f* harmony; LIT rhyme; **en ~ con** in keeping with

consonante [kon·so·'nan·te] *f* LING consonant

consorcio [kon·'sor·sjo, -θjo] *m* consortium

consorte [kon·'sor·te] *mf* **1.** (*cónyuge*) spouse **2.** *pl* JUR accomplices *pl*, co-litigants *pl*

conspiración [kons·pi·ra·'sjon, -'θjon] *f* conspiracy

conspirar [kons·pi·'rar] *vi* to conspire

constancia [kons·'tan·sja, -θja] *f* **1.** (*firmeza*) constancy **2.** (*perseverancia*) perseverance **3.** (*certeza*) certainty **4.** (*prueba*) proof; **dejar ~ de algo** to show evidence of sth

constante [kons·'tan·te] *adj* constant

constar [kons·'tar] *vi* **1.** (*ser cierto*) to be clear **2.** (*figurar*) to be on record; **hacer ~ algo** to put sth on record **3.** (*componerse*) to consist

constatar [kons·ta·'tar] *vt* to confirm

constelación [kons·te·la·'sjon, -'θjon] *f* constellation

consternación [kons·ter·na·'sjon, -'θjon] *f* consternation

consternar [kons·ter·'nar] **I.** *vt* to dismay **II.** *vr:* ~ **se** to be dismayed

constipado [kons·ti·'pa·do] *m* cold

constipado, -a [kons·ti·'pa·do, -a] *adj* **estar ~** to have a cold

constipar [kons·ti·'par] *vr:* ~ **se** to catch a cold

constitución [kons·ti·tu·'sjon, -'θjon] *f* **1.** *t.* POL constitution **2.** (*establecimiento*) setting-up **3.** (*composición*) make-up

constitucional [kons·ti·tu·sjo'nal, -θjo·'nal] *adj* constitutional

constituir [kons·ti·tu·'ir, kons·ti·'twir] *irr como huir* **I.** *vt* **1.** (*formar*) to constitute **2.** (*ser*) to be **3.** (*establecer*) to establish **4.** (*designar*) ~ **en algo** to designate as sth **II.** *vr:* ~ **se en algo** to become sth

constricción [kons·trik·'sjon, -triɣ·'θjon] *f* constriction

construcción [kons·truk·'sjon, -truɣ·'θjon] *f* **1.** (*acción*) construction **2.** (*edificio*) building; **~ aneja** annex

constructivo, -a [kons·truk·'ti·βo, -a] *adj* constructive

constructor(a) [kons·truk·'tor, -·'to·ra] *m(f)* builder

construir [kons·tru·'ir/kons·'trwir] *irr como huir vt* **1.** (*casa*) to build; (*erigir*) to erect **2.** LING to construe

consuelo [kon·'swe·lo] *m* consolation

cónsul ['kon·sul] *mf* consul

consulado [kon·su·'la·do] *m* **1.** (*lugar*) consulate **2.** (*cargo*) consulship

consulta [kon·'sul·ta] *f* **1.** (*acción*) consultation; **~ popular** POL referendum **2.** (*de un médico*) surgery; **horas de ~** surgery hours

consultar [kon·sul·'tar] *vt* to consult

consultoría [kon·sul·to·'ri·a] *f* consultancy; (*empresa*) consultancy (firm)

consultorio [kon·sul·'to·rjo] *m* **1.** (*estableci-*

miento) consultancy; (*de un médico*) surgery **2.** (*en la radio*) phone-in

consumar [kon·su·'mar] *vt* to carry out; **~ el matrimonio** JUR to consummate the marriage

consumición [kon·su·mi·'sjon, -'θjon] *f* **1.** (*bar*) drink; **~ mínima** minimum charge **2.** (*agotamiento*) consumption

consumidor(a) [kon·su·mi·'dor, -·'do·ra] *m(f)* consumer

consumir [kon·su·'mir] **I.** *vt* **1.** (*gastar*) to consume **2.** (*acabar*) to use **3.** (*comer*) to eat **II.** *vr:* ~ **se 1.** (*persona*) to waste away **2.** (*gastarse*) to be consumed

consumo [kon·'su·mo] *m* consumption; **bienes de ~** consumer goods; **sociedad de ~** consumer society

contabilidad [kon·ta·βi·li·'dad] *f* **1.** (*sistema*) accounting **2.** (*profesión*) accountancy

contabilizar <z→c> [kon·ta·βi·li·'sar, -'θar] *vt* to enter

contable [kon·'ta·βle] **I.** *adj* countable **II.** *mf* accountant

contactar [kon·tak·'tar] *vi, vt* ~ **con alguien** to contact sb

contacto [kon·'tak·to] *m* **1.** (*tacto*) contact **2.** AUTO ignition

contado [kon·'ta·do] *m* **pagar al ~** to pay (in) cash

contador [kon·ta·'dor] *m* meter

contagiar [kon·ta·'xjar] **I.** *vt* to transmit, to infect **II.** *vr:* ~ **se de algo** to become infected with sth

contagio [kon·'ta·xjo] *m* contagion

contagioso, -a [kon·ta·'xjo·so, -a] *adj* contagious; **risa contagiosa** contagious laugh

contaminación [kon·ta·mi·na·'sjon, -'θjon] *f* pollution; **~ acústica** noise pollution; **~ ambiental** environmental pollution

contaminante [kon·ta·mi·'nan·te] **I.** *adj* polluting **II.** *m* pollutant

contaminar [kon·ta·mi·'nar] **I.** *vt* **1.** (*infestar*) to pollute **2.** (*contagiar*) to infect **II.** *vr:* ~ **se 1.** (*infectarse*) to become contaminated **2.** (*contagiarse*) to become infected

contar <o→ue> [kon·'tar] **I.** *vi* **1.** (*calcular*) to count **2.** (+ *con: confiar*) ~ **con alguien/algo** to rely on sb/sth **3.** (+ *con: tener en cuenta*) ~ **con algo** to expect sth **II.** *vt* **1.** (*numerar*) to count; **sin ~ con** without taking into account **2.** (*narrar*) to tell; **¿qué (te) cuentas?** (*saludo*) how's it going? **III.** *vr:* ~ **se** to be counted

contemplación [kon·tem·pla·'sjon, -'θjon] *f* **1.** (*observación*) contemplation; REL meditation **2.** *pl* (*miramientos*) indulgence

contemplar [kon·tem·'plar] *vt* **1.** (*mirar*) to look at **2.** (*considerar*) to consider **3.** REL to meditate

contemplativo, -a [kon·tem·pla·'ti·βo, -a] *adj* contemplative

contemporáneo, -a [kon·tem·po·'ra·neo, -a] *adj, m, f* contemporary

contender <e→ie> [kon·ten·'der] *vi* ~ **por algo** to contend for sth

contendiente [kon·ten·'djen·te] *mf* contender

contenedor [kon·te·ne·'dor] *m* (*recipiente*) container; (*basura*) dumpster

contener [kon·te·'ner] *irr como tener* **I.** *vt* **1.** (*encerrar*) to contain **2.** (*refrenar*) to hold back; (*respiración*) to hold **II.** *vr:* ~**se** to contain oneself

contenido [kon·te·'ni·do] *m* **1.** (*lo incluido*) contents *pl* **2.** (*concentración*) content

contentar [kon·ten·'tar] **I.** *vt* to satisfy **II.** *vr:* ~**se** to be contented

contento, -a [kon·'ten·to] *adj* (*alegre*) happy; (*satisfecho*) content

contestación [kon·tes·ta·'sjon, -'θjon] *f* answer

contestador [kon·tes·ta·'dor] *m* answering machine

contestar [kon·tes·'tar] **I.** *vt* to answer **II.** *vi* to answer; (*replicar*) to answer back

contexto [kon·'tes·to] *m* context

contienda [kon·'tjen·da] *f* dispute

contigo [kon·'ti·ɣo] *pron pers* with you; **me siento** ~ I'll sit beside you

contiguo, -a [kon·'ti·ɣwo, -a] *adj* adjoining

continencia [kon·ti·'nen·sja, -θja] *f* continence

continental [kon·ti·nen·'tal] *adj* continental

continente [kon·ti·'nen·te] *m* **1.** GEO continent **2.** (*cosa*) container

contingencia [kon·tin·'xen·sja, -θja] *f* eventuality; *t.* FILOS contingency

continuación [kon·ti·nwa·'sjon, -'θjon] *f* continuation; **a** ~ (*después*) next; (*en un escrito*) as follows

continuar <*1. pres:* continúo> [kon·ti·nu·'ar] *vt, vi* to continue; ~**á** to be continued

continuidad [kon·ti·nwi·'dad] *f* continuity

continuo, -a [kon·'ti·nwo] *adj* continuous; **movimiento** ~ perpetual motion

contonearse [kon·to·ne·'ar·se] *vr* to swing one's hips, to wiggle

contorno [kon·'tor·no] *m* **1.** (*de una figura*) outline **2.** (*pl*) (*territorio*) surrounding area

contra[1] ['kon·tra] **I.** *prep* against; **tener algo en** ~ to object **II.** *m* **los pros y los** ~**s** the pros and the cons

contra[2] ['kon·tra] *f* **1.** (*dificultad*) snag **2.** (*oposición*) **llevar la** ~ **a alguien** to contradict sb **3.** (*guerrilla*) contra

contraataque [kon·tra·'ta·ke/kon·tra·a·'ta·ke] *m* MIL counterattack

contrabajo [kon·tra·'βa·xo] *m* **1.** (*instrumento*) double bass **2.** (*músico*) double-bass player

contrabandista [kon·tra·βan·'dis·ta] *mf* smuggler; ~ **de armas** gunrunner

contrabando [kon·tra·'βan·do] *m* **1.** (*comercio*) smuggling; **pasar algo de** ~ to smuggle sth in **2.** (*mercancía*) contraband

contracción [kon·trak·'sjon, -tray'θjon] *f* **1.** *t.* LING contraction **2.** (*pl*) MED contractions *pl*

contracorriente [kon·tra·ko·'rrjen·te] *f* cross-current

contractual [kon·trak·tu·'al] *adj* contractual

contradecir [kon·tra·de·'sir, -'θir] *irr como decir vt,* (*vr*): ~**se** to contradict (oneself)

contradicción [kon·tra·dik·'sjon, -diy·'θjon] *f* contradiction

contradictorio, -a [kon·tra·dik·'to·rjo, -a] *adj* contradictory

contraer [kon·tra·'er] *irr como traer* **I.** *vt* **1.** (*encoger*) to contract **2.** (*deudas*) to contract; (*enfermedad*) to catch, to contract *form* **3.** (*limitar*) to limit **II.** *vr:* ~**se** to contract

contraespionaje [kon·tra·es·pjo·'na·xe] *m* counterespionage

contrafuerte [kon·tra·'fwer·te] *m* **1.** ARQUIT buttress **2.** (*zapato*) heel stiffener **3.** GEO spur

contraindicación [kon·tra·in·di·ka·'sjon, -'θjon] *f* MED contraindication

contralor [kon·tra·'lor] *m AmL* FIN tax inspector

contraloría [kon·tra·lo·'ri·a] *f AmL* tax inspector's office

contraluz [kon·tra·'lus, -'luθ] *m o f* back light(ing)

contramedida [kon·tra·me·'di·da] *f* countermeasure

contraofensiva [kon·tra·o·fen·'si·βa] *f* counteroffensive

contraoferta [kon·tra·o·'fer·ta] *f* counteroffer

contraorden [kon·tra·'or·den] *f* countermand *form*

contrapartida [kon·tra·par·'ti·da] *f* compensation

contrapeso [kon·tra·'pe·so] *m* counterweight

contraportada [kon·tra·por·'ta·da] *f* back cover [*o* page]

contraposición [kon·tra·po·si·'sjon, -'θjon] *f* comparison

contraproducente [kon·tra·pro·du·'sen·te, -'θen·te] *adj* counterproductive

contrapunto [kon·tra·'pun·to] *m* MÚS counterpoint

contrariar <*1. pres:* contrarío> [kon·tra·ri·'ar] *vt* **1.** (*oponerse*) to oppose **2.** (*disgustar*) to upset

contrariedad [kon·tra·rje·'dad] *f* **1.** (*inconveniente*) obstacle **2.** (*disgusto*) annoyance

contrario, -a [kon·'tra·rjo, -a] **I.** *adj* (*opuesto*) contrary; (*perjudicial*) harmful; **al** ~ on the contrary; **en caso** ~ otherwise; **de lo** ~ or else; **llevar la contraria a alguien** to oppose [*o* contradict] sb **II.** *m, f* opponent

contrarrestar [kon·tra·rres·'tar] *vt* to counteract

contrasentido [kon·tra·sen·'ti·do] *m* contradiction

contraseña [kon·tra·'se·na] *f* password

contrastar [kon·tras·'tar] **I.** *vi* to contrast **II.** *vt* (*oro*) to hallmark; (*peso*) to verify

contraste [kon·'tras·te] *m* **1.** *t.* FOTO contrast **2.** MED contrast medium **3.** (*señal*) hallmark

contratación [kon·tra·ta·'sjon, -'θjon] *f* contracting; ~ **bursátil** FIN trading (*on the stock* *exchange*)

contratar [kon·tra·'tar] *vt* **1.**(*trabajador*) to hire; (*artista*) to sign up **2.**(*encargar*) to contract

contratiempo [kon·tra·'tjem·po] *m* setback

contratista [kon·tra·'tis·ta] *mf* contractor

contrato [kon·'tra·to] *m* contract; ~ **de alquiler** lease; ~ **colectivo** wage agreement

contravenir [kon·tra·βe·'nir] *irr como venir vt* to contravene

contraventana [kon·tra·βen·'ta·na] *f* shutter

contrayente [kon·tra·'jen·te] *mf* contracting party; (*de un matrimonio*) bridegroom *m*, bride *f*

contribución [kon·tri·βu·'sjon, -'θjon] *f* **1.**(*aportación*) contribution; **aportar una ~ a algo** to make a contribution to sth **2.**(*impuesto*) tax; ~ **municipal** local tax

contribuir [kon·tri·βu·'ir] *irr como huir vt, vi* **1.**(*ayudar*) to contribute **2.**(*tributar*) to pay (taxes)

contribuyente [kon·tri·βu·'jen·te] *mf* taxpayer

contrición [kon·trik·'sjon, -triɣ·'θjon] *f* contrition

contrincante [kon·trin·'kan·te] *mf* opponent

control [kon·'trol] *m* control; (*inspección*) inspection; ~ **al azar** spot check; ~ **a distancia** TÉC remote control

controlador [kon·tro·la·'dor] *m* COMPUT driver; ~ **de la impresora** printer driver

controlador(a) [kon·tro·la·'dor, -'do·ra] *m(f)* controller; ~ **de vuelo** [*o* **de tráfico aéreo**] air traffic controller

controlar [kon·tro·'lar] **I.** *vt* (*revisar*) to check; (*gobernar*) to control **II.** *vr:* ~ **se** to control oneself

controversia [kon·tro·'βer·sja] *f* controversy

controvertido, -a [kon·tro·βer·'ti·do, -a] *adj* controversial

controvertir [kon·tro·βer·'tir] *irr como sentir* **I.** *vi* to argue **II.** *vt* to discuss

contundencia [kon·tun·'den·sja, -θja] *f* force

contundente [kon·tun·'den·te] *adj* contusive; *fig* convincing; **prueba ~** conclusive proof

contusión [kon·tu·'sjon] *f* MED bruise

convalecencia [kom·ba·le·'sen·sja, -'θen·θja] *f* convalescence

convaleciente [kom·ba·le·'sjen·te, -'θjen·te] *mf* convalescent

convalidación [kom·ba·li·da·'sjon, -'θjon] *f* **1.**(*de un título*) (re)validation **2.**(*confirmación*) confirmation, recognition

convalidar [kom·ba·li·'dar] *vt* **1.**(*título*) to (re)validate **2.**(*confirmar*) to confirm, to recognize

convencer <c→z> [kom·ben·'ser, -'θer] **I.** *vt* **1.**(*persuadir*) to persuade **2.**(*satisfacer*) **no me convence ese piso** I'm not at all sure about that flat **II.** *vr:* ~ **se** to be convinced

convencido, -a [kom·ben·'si·do, -a; -'θi·do, -a] *adj* sure

convencimiento [kom·ben·si·'mjen·to, kom·

ben·θi-] *m* conviction; **tengo el ~ de que...** I'm convinced that...

convención [kom·ben·'sjon, -'θjon] *f* convention

convencional [kom·ben·sjo·'nal, kom·ben·θjo-] *adj* conventional

conveniencia [kom·be·'njen·sja, -θja] *f* usefulness; **matrimonio de ~** marriage of convenience

conveniente [kom·be·'njen·te] *adj* **1.**(*adecuado*) suitable **2.**(*provechoso*) advisable; (*útil*) useful

convenio [kom·'be·njo] *m* agreement

convenir [kom·be·'nir] *irr como venir vi* **1.**(*acordar*) to agree **2.**(*ser oportuno*) to be advisable

convento [kom·'ben·to] *m* (*de monjes*) monastery; (*de monjas*) convent

convergencia [kom·ber·'xen·sja, -θja] *f* convergence

convergente [kom·ber·'xen·te] *adj* convergent

converger <g→j> [kom·ber·'xer] *vi*, **convergir** <g→j> [kom·ber·'xir] *vi* **1.**(*líneas*) to converge **2.**(*coincidir*) to coincide

conversación [kom·ber·sa·'sjon, -'θjon] *f* conversation

conversar [kom·ber·'sar] *vi* to talk

conversión [kom·ber·'sjon] *f* conversion

converso, -a [kom·'ber·so, -a] *m, f* convert

convertir [kom·ber·'tir] *irr como sentir* **I.** *vt* **1.**(*transformar*) ~ **en algo** to turn into sth **2.** COM, TÉC to convert **II.** *vr:* ~ **se 1.**(*transformarse*) ~ **se en algo** to turn into sth **2.** REL to convert

convexo, -a [kom·'bek·so, -a] *adj* convex

convicción [kom·bik·'sjon, -biɣ·'θjon] *f* conviction

convicto, -a [kom·'bik·to, -a] *adj* convicted

convidar [kom·bi·'dar] *vt, (vr):* ~ **se** to invite (oneself)

convincente [kom·bin·'sen·te, -'θen·te] *adj* convincing

convite [kom·'bi·te] *m* banquet

convivencia [kom·bi·'βen·sja, -θja] *f* living together; *fig* co-existence

convivir [kom·bi·'βir] *vi* to live together; *fig* to coexist

convocar <c→qu> [kom·bo·'kar] *vt* **1.**(*citar*) to summon; **me ~ on al examen** I was called for the examination **2.**(*concurso*) to announce **3.**(*reunión*) to call

convocatoria [kom·bo·ka·'to·rja] *f* **1.**(*citación*) summons **2.**(*de un concurso*) official announcement **3.**(*de una conferencia*) notification

convoy [kom·'boi] *m* **1.** MIL convoy **2.** *inf*(*vinagreras*) cruet

convulsión [kom·bul·'sjon] *f* **1.** MED convulsion **2.** POL upheaval **3.** GEO tremor

convulsionar [kom·bul·sjo·'nar] *vt t.* GEO, POL to convulse; MED to produce convulsions in

conyugal [kon·ju·'ɣal] *adj* marital

cónyuge ['kon·ju·xe] *mf* spouse; **los ~s** the married couple

coña ['ko·ɲa] *f vulg* **1.**(*broma*) joking; **tomar algo a ~** to take sth as a joke; **¡ni de ~!** no way! **2.**(*lata*) annoyance; **eres la ~** you're a pain in the neck [*o ass*]

coñac [ko·'ɲak] *m* <coñacs> cognac

coñazo [ko·'ɲa·so, -θo] *m vulg* pain in the ass; **¡esto es un ~!** this is a drag!

coñete [ko·'ɲe·te] *adj Chile, Perú, inf*(*tacaño*) stingy, tight *inf*

coño ['ko·ɲo] **I.** *interj vulg* shit! **II.** *m vulg* cunt, pussy; **vive en el quinto ~** he/she lives out in the sticks; **¿qué ~ te importa?** why the hell does it matter to you? **III.** *adj Chile, vulg: pejorative term for a Spaniard*

cooperación [ko·pe·ra·'sjon/ko·o·pe·ra·'sjon, -'θjon] *f* cooperation

cooperador(a) [ko·pe·ra·'dor/ko·o·pe·ra·'dor, -·'do·ra] *m(f)* collaborator

cooperar [ko·pe·'rar/ko·o·pe·'rar] *vi* to co-operate

cooperativa [ko·pe·ra·'ti·βa/ko·o·pe·ra·'ti·βa] *f* cooperative, co-op

cooperativo, -a [ko·pe·ra·'ti·βo, -a/ko·o·pe·ra·'ti·βo, -a] *adj* cooperative

coordenada [kor·de·'na·da/ko·or·de·'na·da] *f* MAT coordinate

coordinación [kor·di·na·'sjon/ko·or·di·na·'sjon, -'θjon] *f* coordination

coordinador(a) [kor·di·na·'dor/ko·or·di·na·'dor, -·'do·ra] *m(f)* coordinator

coordinar [kor·di·'nar/ko·or·di·'nar] *vt* to co-ordinate

copa ['ko·pa] *f* **1.**(*vaso*) glass; **una ~ de vino** a glass of wine; **una ~ para el vino** a wine glass; **ir de ~s** to go out for a drink; **tener una ~ de más** to have had one too many **2.**(*de árbol*) top **3.** *t.* DEP (*de sujetador*) cup **4.**(*de sombrero*) crown; **sombrero de ~** top hat

copar [ko·'par] *vt* **1.**(*acorralar*) to corner; MIL to cut off; **estar copado** to be stuck; (*negociaciones*) to be bogged down **2.**(*premios*) to win; **~ la banca** (*en un juego*) to sweep the board

copartícipe [ko·par·'ti·si·pe, -θi·pe] *mf* (*codueño*) joint owner; (*socio*) partner

Copenhague [ko·pe·'na·ɣe] *m* Copenhagen

copete [ko·'pe·te] *m* **1.**(*de pelo*) tuft **2.**(*de ave*) crest; (*de caballo*) forelock **3.**(*linaje*) **ser de alto ~** to be aristocratic

copetín [ko·pe·'tin] *m* **1.** *Méx* (*copa de licor*) glass of liquor; (*aperitivo*) aperitif **2.** *Arg* (*cóctel*) cocktail

copetón, -ona [ko·pe·'ton, -·'to·na] *adj Col* tipsy; **estar ~** to be slightly drunk

copia ['ko·pja] *f* copy; (*al carbón*) carbon copy; FOTO print; **~ en limpio** fair copy; **~ de seguridad** COMPUT back-up copy

copiar [ko·'pjar] *vt* **1.**(*general*) to copy **2.**(*fotocopiar*) to photocopy, to xerox

copiloto, -a [ko·pi·'lo·to, -a] *m, f* AVIAT copilot; AUTO co-driver

copioso, -a [ko·'pjo·so, -a] *adj* copious; (*abundante*) abundant

copista [ko·'pis·ta] *mf* copyist

copo ['ko·po] *m* flake; **~ de nieve** snowflake; **~s de maíz** cornflakes

copón [ko·'pon] *m* REL ciborium; **del ~** *inf* tremendous

copropietario, -a [ko·pro·pje·'ta·rjo, -a] *m, f* co-owner

copucha [ko·'pu·tʃa] *f Chile* **1.**(*mentira*) lie **2.**(*vejiga de animal*) bladder

cópula ['ko·pu·la] *f* **1.** BIO copulation **2.** LING copula

copular [ko·pu·'lar] *vi* to copulate

coqueta [ko·'ke·ta] *f* (*mueble*) dressing table

coquetear [ko·ke·te·'ar] *vi* to flirt

coqueto, -a [ko·'ke·to, -a] *adj* **1.**(*que coquetea*) flirtatious **2.**(*vanidoso*) vain **3.**(*objeto*) pretty

coracha [ko·'ra·tʃa] *f AmL* leather bag

coraje [ko·'ra·xe] *m* **1.**(*valor*) courage; **tener ~** to be courageous **2.**(*ira*) anger; **dar ~ a** to make angry

coral [ko·'ral] **I.** *adj* **1.**(*color*) coral **2.** MÚS choral **II.** *m t.* ZOOL coral **III.** *f* (*coro*) choir

Corán [ko·'ran] *m* REL Koran

coraza [ko·'ra·sa, -θa] *f* **1.** MIL cuirass **2.** NÁUT armor-plating **3.** ZOOL shell **4.** *fig* shield

corazón [ko·ra·'son, -'θon] *m* **1.** *t. fig* ANAT heart; **blando de ~** soft-hearted; **duro de ~** hard-hearted; **de todo ~** with all one's heart; **con el ~ en la mano** with one's heart on one's sleeve; **hacer algo de ~** to do sth willingly; **tener un ~ de oro** to have a heart of gold; **hacer de tripas ~** to gather courage; **~ (mío)** darling, to be heartless **2.** BOT core

corazonada [ko·ra·so·'na·da, ko·ra·θo-] *f* **1.**(*presentimiento*) hunch **2.**(*impulso*) sudden impulse

corbata [kor·'βa·ta] *f* tie

Córcega ['kor·se·ɣa, 'kor·θe-] *f* Corsica

corcel [kor·'sel, -'θel] *m* LIT steed

corchea [kor·'tʃe·a] *f* quaver

corchete [kor·'tʃe·te] *m* **1.**(*broche*) hook and eye; (*pieza*) hook **2.** TIPO square bracket

corcho ['kor·tʃo] **I.** *m* cork; (*en la pesca*) float **II.** *interj* for heaven's sake

cordel [kor·'del] *m* cord

cordero [kor·'de·ro] *m* **1.**(*carne*) mutton, lamb **2.**(*piel*) lambskin

cordero, -a [kor·'de·ro, -a] *m, f* lamb

cordial [kor·'djal] *adj, m* cordial

cordialidad [kor·dja·li·'dad] *f* cordiality

cordillera [kor·di·'je·ra, -'ʎe·ra] *f* mountain range

cordillerano, -a [kor·di·je·'ra·no, -a; kor·di·ʎe-] *adj AmL* GEO Andean

córdoba ['kor·do·βa] *m Nic* (*moneda*) cordoba

cordobés, -esa [kor·do·'βes, -·'βe·sa] *adj, m, f* Cordovan

cordón [kor·'don] *m* **1.**(*cordel*) cord; (*de zapatos*) shoelace; **~ umbilical** ANAT umbilical

cord **2.** ELEC cord **3.** MIL cordon **4.** *CSur* (*de la acera*) curb
cordura [kor·'du·ra] *f* **1.** (*razón*) good sense **2.** (*juicio*) wisdom
Corea [ko·'rea] *f* Korea
coreano, -a [ko·re·'a·no] *adj, m, f* Korean
corear [ko·re·'ar] *vt* to chant; *fig* (*aclamar*) to applaud
coreografía [ko·reo·γra·'fi·a] *f* choreography
coreógrafo, -a [ko·re·'o·γra·fo, -a] *m, f* choreographer
corintio, -a [ko·'rin·tjo, -a] *adj, m, f* Corinthian
corinto [ko·'rin·to] *adj inv* maroon
corista¹ [ko·'ris·ta] *mf* MÚS chorister
corista² [ko·'ris·ta] *f* TEAT chorus girl
cornada [kor·'na·da] *f* (*golpe*) butt; (*herida*) goring
cornamenta [kor·na·'men·ta] *f* horns *pl;* (*de ciervos*) antlers *pl*
córnea ['kor·nea] *f* cornea
cornear [kor·ne·'ar] *vt* (*golpear*) to butt; (*herir*) to gore
corneja [kor·'ne·xa] *f* crow
córner ['kor·ner] *m* DEP corner
corneta [kor·'ne·ta] *f* cornet; (*en el ejército*) bugle; **hacer algo a toque de ~** *fig* to do sth on command
corneta [kor·'ne·ta] *m* cornet player; MIL bugler
cornudo [kor·'nu·do, -a] **I.** *adj inf* cuckolded **II.** *m inf* cuckold
cornudo, -a [kor·'nu·do, -a] *adj* (*animal*) horned
coro ['ko·ro] *m* choir; **a ~** in unison; **hacer ~ a alguien** to back sb up
corola [ko·'ro·la] *f* corolla
corolario [ko·ro·'la·rjo] *m* corollary
corona [ko·'ro·na] *f* **1.** (*real*) crown; (*de flores*) garland, wreath **2.** (*de eclesiásticos*) tonsure **3.** (*de santos*) halo **4.** (*de los dientes*) crown **5.** ASTR corona
coronación [ko·ro·na·'sjon, -'θjon] *f* **1.** (*de un rey*) coronation **2.** (*de una acción*) culmination
coronar [ko·ro·'nar] *vt* to crown; **para ~lo...** *fig* to crown it all...
coronel(a) [ko·ro·'nel, -·'ne·la] *m(f)* colonel
coronilla [ko·ro·'ni·ja, -ʎa] *f* crown (of the head); **estar hasta la ~ de algo** *inf* to be fed up to the back teeth with sth
corotos [ko·'ro·tos] *mpl AmL* (*bártulos*) things *pl*
corpiño [kor·'pi·ɲo] *m* bodice; *CSur* (*sujetador*) bra
corporación [kor·po·ra·'sjon, -'θjon] *f t.* COM corporation; **~ de estudiantes** students' society
corporal [kor·po·'ral] *adj* physical
corporativo, -a [kor·po·ra·'ti·βo, -a] *adj* corporate
corpóreo, -a [kor·'po·reo , -a] *adj* bodily
corpulencia [kor·pu·'len·sja, -θja] *f* (*de alguien*) heftiness; (*de algo*) massiveness
corpulento, -a [kor·pu·'len·to, -a] *adj* (*per-*

sona) hefty; (*cosa*) massive
corpúsculo [kor·'pus·ku·lo] *m* corpuscle
corral [ko·'rral] *m* **1.** (*cercado*) yard; (*redil*) stockyard; (*para gallinas*) chicken run **2.** (*lugar sucio*) pigsty **3.** (*para niños*) playpen
corralón [ko·rra·'lon] *m CSur* (*maderería*) lumberyard
correa [ko·'rrea] *f* **1.** (*tira*) strap **2.** (*cinturón*) belt; **~ de transmisión** TÉC driving belt, drive **3.** *inf* (*aguante*) **tener ~** to be long-suffering
corrección [ko·rrek·'sjon, -reγ·'θjon] *f* **1.** TIPO proofreading **2.** (*represión*) rebuke **3.** (*cualidad*) correctness; (*comportamiento*) courtesy, (good) manners *pl*
correccional [ko·rrek·sjo·'nal, ko·rreγ·θjo-] *m* reformatory
correcto, -a [ko·'rrek·to, -a] *adj* correct
corrector(a) [ko·rrek·'tor] **I.** *adj* correcting **II.** *m(f)* TIPO proofreader
corredor [ko·rre·'dor] *m* corridor
corredor(a) [ko·rre·'dor, -·'do·ra] *m(f)* **1.** DEP runner; **~ de coches** racing driver; **~ de fondo** long-distance runner **2.** COM agent, broker; **~ de fincas** real estate agent
correduría [ko·rre·du·'ri·a] *f* **1.** (*oficio*) brokerage **2.** (*comisión*) commission
corregir [ko·rre·'xir] *irr como elegir* **I.** *vt* **1.** *t.* TIPO to correct **2.** (*reprender*) to rebuke **II.** *vr:* **~ se** (*en la conducta*) to change one's ways; (*al expresarse*) to correct oneself
correlación [ko·rre·la·'sjon, -'θjon] *f* correlation
correlacionar [ko·rre·la·sjo·'nar, -θjo·'nar] *vi, vt* to correlate
correlativo, -a [ko·rre·la·'ti·βo, -a] *adj form* correlative
correligionario, -a [ko·rre·li·xjo·'na·rjo, -a] *m, f* POL fellow supporter
correntada [ko·rren·'ta·da] *f AmL* (*rápido*) rapids *pl*
correo [ko·'rreo] *m* **1.** (*correspondencia*) mail; **~ aéreo** airmail; **~ basura** COMPUT spam; **~ caracol** COMPUT snail mail, s-mail; **~ certificado** certified mail; **~ electrónico** e-mail; **~ urgente** special delivery; **a vuelta de ~** by return mail; **echar al ~** to mail **2.** (*persona*) courier
Correos [ko·'rreos] *mpl* post office; **ir a ~** to go to the post office
correoso, -a [ko·rre·'o·so, -a] *adj* tough
correr [ko·'rrer] **I.** *vi* **1.** (*caminar*) to run; **echarse a ~** (*partir*) to start to run; (*escaparse*) to run off; **salir corriendo** to run out; **a todo ~** at top speed **2.** (*conducir*) to go fast **3.** (*tiempo*) to pass (quickly); **el mes que corre** this month; **en los tiempos que corremos...** at the present time... **4.** (*líquido*) to flow **5.** (*viento*) to blow **6.** (*camino*) to run **7.** (*moneda*) to be valid **8.** (*rumor*) to circulate **9.** (*estar a cargo de*) **eso corre de** [*o* **por**] **mi cuenta** (*gastos*) I'm paying for that; (*un asunto*) I'm responsible for that ▶**el que no corre, <u>vuela</u>** ≈ opportunity knocks but once

prov **II.** *vt* **1.**(*un mueble*) to move; (*una cortina*) to draw; (*un cerrojo*) to slide **2.**(*un lugar*) to travel over; ~ **mundo** to travel widely **3.** MIL to overrun **4.**(*un caballo*) to race **5.**(*la caza*) to chase **6.**(*tener*) ~ **la misma suerte** to suffer the same fate; **corre prisa** it's urgent ▶ **dejar** ~ **algo** not to worry about sth; ~**la** to make a night of it **III.** *vr:* ~**se 1.**(*moverse*) to move **2.** *vulg*(*eyacular*) to come **3.**(*colores*) to run

correspondencia [ko·rres·pon·'den·sja, -θja] *f* **1.**(*correo, cartas*) mail; **correo por** ~ correspondence course; **llevar la** ~ to attend to the correspondence **2.**(*equivalente*) correspondence **3.**(*entre trenes*) connection

corresponder [ko·rres·pon·'der] **I.** *vi* **1.**(*equivaler*) to correspond **2.**(*armonizar*) to match **3.**(*convenir*) to tally **4.**(*contestar*) to respond **5.**(*incumbir*) to concern; **no me corresponde criticarlo** it's not for me to criticize him **6.**(*trenes*) to connect **II.** *vr:* ~**se 1.**(*equivaler, escribir*) to correspond; (*armonizar*) to match **2.**(*comunicarse*) to communicate with each other

correspondiente [ko·rres·pon·'djen·te] *adj* **1.**(*oportuno*) corresponding **2.**(*apropiado*) appropriate **3.**(*respectivo*) respective

corresponsable [ko·rres·pon·'sa·βle] *adj* jointly responsible

corresponsal [ko·rres·pon·'sal] *mf* correspondent

corretear [ko·rre·te·'ar] *vi* **1.**(*vagar*) to stroll around **2.**(*niños*) to run about

corrida [ko·'rri·da] *f* **1.** TAUR bullfight **2.**(*carrera*) run; **decir algo de** ~ to reel off sth from memory **3.** *vulg*(*orgasmo*) orgasm

corrido, -a [ko·'rri·do] *adj* **1.** *t.* ARQUIT continuous **2.**(*cantidad*) large; **un quilo** ~ a good kilo **3.** *ser*(*astuto*) astute

corriente [ko·'rrjen·te] **I.** *adj* **1.**(*fluente*) running **2.**(*actual*) current; (*moneda*) valid; **estar al** ~ **de algo** to be aware of sth; **ponerse al** ~ **de algo** to get to know about sth **3.**(*ordinario*) ordinary **4.**(*normal*) normal **II.** *f* **1.**(*de fluido*) current; ~ **de aire** draft; ~ **alterna** alternating current; **hace** ~ there's a draft; **ir contra la** ~ to swim against the tide; **seguir** [*o* **llevar**] **la** ~ **a alguien** to play along with sb **2.**(*tendencia*) tendency

corrimiento [ko·rri·'mjen·to] *m* **1.**(*movimiento*) movement **2.** GEO slipping; ~ **de tierras** landslide

corro ['ko·rro] *m* **1.**(*círculo*) circle; **hacer** ~ (*hacer un círculo*) to form a circle; (*hacer sitio*) to make room **2.**(*juego*) ring-around-the-rosy

corroborar [ko·rro·βo·'rar] *vt* to corroborate

corroer [ko·rro·'er] *irr como roer* **I.** *vt* **1.**(*un material*) to corrode **2.**(*una persona*) consume; **el remordimiento lo corroe** he's consumed by remorse **II.** *vr:* ~**se** to corrode

corromper [ko·rrom·'per] **I.** *vt* **1.**(*descomponer*) to rot **2.**(*sobornar*) to bribe **3.**(*enviciar*) to debauch; (*pervertir*) to corrupt **II.** *vr:* ~**se 1.**(*descomponerse*) to rot; (*alimentos*) to go bad **2.**(*degenerar*) to become corrupted

corronchoso, -a [ko·rron·'tʃo·so, -a] *adj AmL* (*basto*) coarse

corrosca [ko·'rros·ka] *f Col* broad-brimmed straw hat

corrosión [ko·rro·'sjon] *f* corrosion

corrosivo, -a [ko·rro·'si·βo, -a] *adj* **1.**(*sustancia*) corrosive **2.**(*estilo*) caustic

corrupción [ko·rrup·'sjon, -rruβ·'θjon] *f* **1.**(*descomposición*) decay **2.**(*moral*) corruption **3.**(*soborno*) bribery, graft

corrupto, -a [ko·'rrup·to, -a] *adj* corrupt

corsé [kor·'se] *m* corset

cortacésped [kor·ta·'ses·ped, -'θes·ped] *m* lawnmower

cortada [kor·'ta·da] *f AmL* (*herida*) cut

cortado [kor·'ta·do] *m* CULIN *coffee with only a little milk*

cortado, -a [kor·'ta·do, -a] *adj* **1.**(*leche*) sour **2.**(*tímido*) shy; (*avergonzado*) self-conscious, embarrassed

cortafuegos [kor·ta·'fwe·γos] *m inv* **1.** AGR firebreak, fire lane **2.** COMPUT firewall

cortapisa [kor·ta·'pi·sa] *f* **1.**(*restricción*) restriction **2.**(*obstáculo*) obstacle; **hablar sin** ~**s** to talk freely; **poner** ~**s a alguien** to put obstacles in sb's path

cortar [kor·'tar] **I.** *vt* **1.**(*tajar*) *t.* COMPUT to cut; (*por el medio*) to cut through; (*en pedazos*) to cut up; (*un traje*) to cut out; (*un árbol*) to cut down; (*leña*) to chop; (*el césped*) to mow; (*pelo*) to trim; ~ **al rape** to cut close; **¡corta el rollo!** that's enough! **2.** DEP (*la pelota*) to slice **3.**(*el agua*) to cut off; (*la corriente*) to switch off; (*carretera*) to cut; (*comunicación*) to cut off **II.** *vt* cut; **ha cortado con su novio** *inf* she has split up with her boyfriend **III.** *vr:* ~**se 1.**(*persona*) to cut oneself **2.**(*turbarse*) to become embarrassed; **no se cortó ni un pelo** he/she wasn't embarrassed in the least **3.**(*leche*) to turn **4.**(*piel*) to get chapped **5.** TEL to get cut off

cortaúñas [kor·ta·'u·ɲas] *m inv* nail clippers *pl*

corte[1] ['kor·te] *m* **1.**(*herida*) cut **2.**(*de pelo*) haircut **3.** TÉC section; ~ **transversal** cross section **4.** ELEC ~ **de corriente** power cut ▶ **hacer a alguien un** ~ **de mangas** ≈ to give sb the V-sign; **dar** ~ to embarrass; **¡qué** ~! how embarrassing!

corte[2] ['kor·te] *f* court

cortejar [kor·te·'xar] *vt* to court

cortejo [kor·'te·xo] *m* **1.**(*séquito*) retinue **2.**(*desfile*) procession

Cortes ['kor·tes] *fpl* POL Spanish parliament

cortés [kor·'tes] *adj* polite

cortesano [kor·te·'sa·no] *m* courtier

cortesía [kor·te·'si·a] *f* courtesy; (*gentileza*) politeness; **fórmula de** ~ polite expression

corteza [kor·'te·sa, -θa] *f* **1.**(*de un tronco*) bark; (*del pan*) crust; **la** ~ **terrestre** GEO the earth's crust **2.**(*exterioridad*) outward appearance

cortijo [kor·'ti·xo] *m* (*finca*) country estate; (*casa*) country house

cortina [kor·'ti·na] *f* curtain; ~ **de humo** MIL smokescreen; **correr/descorrer la** ~ to draw/to draw back the curtain

corto, -a ['kor·to] *adj* 1.(*pequeño*) short; ~ **de oído** hard of hearing; ~ **de vista** short-sighted; **se ha casado de** ~ she got married in a short dress; **a la corta o a la larga...** sooner or later... 2.(*breve*) brief 3.(*poco listo*) slow

cortocircuito [kor·to·sir·'kwi·to/kor·to·sir·ku·'i·to, kor·to·θir-] *m* ELEC short circuit

cortometraje [kor·to·me·'tra·xe] *m* CINE short

corzo, -a ['kor·so, -a; -θo, -a] *m*, *f* roe deer

cosa ['ko·sa] *f* 1.(*en general*) thing; **la trata como una** ~ he treats her like an object; **eso es** ~ **tuya/mía** that's your/my affair; **¿sabes una** ~**?** do you know what?; **no me queda otra** ~ **que...** I have no alternative but...; **ser una** ~ **nunca vista** to be unique; **no valer gran** ~ not to be worth much; **tal como están las** ~**s...** as things stand...; **como si tal** ~ as if nothing had happened; **esas son** ~**s de Inés** that's typical of Inés 2. *pl* (*pertenencias*) things *pl*

coscacho [kos·'ka·ʧo] *m AmS*, *inf*(*capón*) rap on the head

coscorrón [kos·ko·'rron] *m* 1.(*golpe*) bump 2. *inf*(*contratiempo*) setback

cosecha [ko·'se·ʧa] *f* 1.AGR harvest 2.(*conjunto de frutos*) crop; **de** ~ **propia** homegrown

cosechadora [ko·se·ʧa·'do·ra] *f* combine harvester

cosechar [ko·se·'ʧar] *vi*, *vt* to harvest

coser [ko·'ser] I. *vt* 1.(*un vestido*) to sew; (*un botón*) to sew on; (*un roto*) to sew up; ~ **a alguien a balazos** to riddle sb with bullets 2. MED to stitch (up) II. *vi* to sew; **esto es** ~ **y cantar** this is child's play

cosmética [kos·'me·ti·ka] *f* cosmetics *pl*

cosmético, -a [kos·'me·ti·ko] *adj* cosmetic

cósmico, -a ['kos·mi·ko, -a] *adj* cosmic

cosmografía [kos·mo·ɣra·'fi·a] *f* ASTR cosmography

cosmología [kos·mo·lo·'xi·a] *f* ASTR cosmology

cosmonauta [kos·mo·'nau·ta] *mf* cosmonaut

cosmopolita [kos·mo·po·'li·ta] *adj*, *mf* cosmopolitan

cosmos ['kos·mos] *m inv* cosmos

cosquillas [kos·'ki·jas, -ʎas] *fpl* **hacer** ~ to tickle; **tener** ~ to be ticklish; **buscar las** ~ **a alguien** *fig* to try to stir sb up

cosquilleo [kos·ki·'jeo, -'ʎeo] *m* tickling

costa ['kos·ta] *f* 1.GEO coast; **Costa Azul** Côte d'Azur; **Costa de Marfil** Ivory Coast 2.FIN cost; **a toda** ~ at any price 3. *pl* JUR costs *pl*

costado [kos·'ta·do] *m* 1.(*lado*) side; **por los cuatro** ~**s** through and through 2.MIL flank; **entrar de** ~ to come in sideways

costal [kos·'tal] *m* sack; **eso es harina de otro** ~ *fig* that's something quite different

costalearse [kos·ta·le·'ar·se] *vr Chile* 1.(*recibir un costalazo*) to fall heavily 2. *fig* (*sufrir una decepción*) to be disappointed

costanera [kos·ta·'ne·ra] *f Arg* (*paseo marítimo*) jetty

costar <o→ue> [kos·'tar] *vi*, *vt* 1.(*valer*) to cost; ~ **caro** to be expensive; **esto te va a** ~ **caro** this is going to cost you dear; **cueste lo que cueste** cost what it may 2.(*ser difícil*) **me cuesta convencerlo** I find it difficult to persuade him

Costa Rica [kos·ta·'rri·ka] *f* Costa Rica

---

i **Costa Rica** is located in Central America and borders on Nicaragua and Panama, as well as the Pacific Ocean and the Caribbean Sea. The capital of Costa Rica is **San José**. Spanish is the country's official language and the official currency is the **colón**.

---

costarriqueño, -a [kos·ta·rri·'ke·ɲo, -a] *adj*, *m*, *f* Costa Rican

coste ['kos·te] *m* 1.(*costo*) cost; ~ **de la vida** cost of living 2.(*precio*) price

costear [kos·te·'ar] I. *vt* to pay for II. *vi* NÁUT to sail along the coast of III. *vr*: ~ **se** to cover the expenses

costero, -a [kos·'te·ro] *adj* coastal

costilla [kos·'ti·ja, -ʎa] *f* 1.ANAT rib 2.CULIN chop 3. *irón* (*mujer*) better half

costillar [kos·ti·'jar, -'ʎar] *m* 1.(*costillas*) ribs *pl* 2. *inf*(*tórax*) ribcage

costo ['kos·to] *m* 1.(*coste*) cost 2.*AmL* (*esfuerzo*) effort

costoso, -a [kos·'to·so, -a] *adj* 1.(*en dinero*) expensive 2.(*en esfuerzo*) difficult

costra ['kos·tra] *f* 1.MED scab 2.(*corteza*) crust

costumbre [kos·'tum·bre] *f* 1.(*hábito*) habit; **de** ~ **se levanta bastante tarde** he/she usually gets up rather late; **como de** ~ as usual 2.(*tradición*) custom

costura [kos·'tu·ra] *f* 1.(*efecto*) seam 2.(*acción*) sewing, needlework 3.(*confección*) dressmaking; **alta** ~ haute couture

costurero [kos·tu·'re·ro] *m* sewing box

cota ['ko·ta] *f* 1.(*armadura*) doublet 2.GEO height above sea level

cotejar [ko·te·'xar] *vt* to compare

cotidiano, -a [ko·ti·'dja·no, -a] *adj* daily

cotilla [ko·'ti·ja, -ʎa] *mf inf* gossip

cotillear [ko·ti·je·'ar, ko·ti·ʎe-] *vi inf* to gossip

cotilleo [ko·ti·'jeo, -'ʎeo] *m inf* gossip

cotización [ko·ti·sa·'sjon, -θa·'θjon] *f* 1.(*de acciones*) price 2.(*pago*) contribution

cotizar <z→c> [ko·ti·'sar, -'θar] I. *vt* 1.FIN ~ **algo** to stand at sth 2.(*estimar*) to value II. *vi* to pay contributions III. *vr*: ~ **se** 1.FIN ~ **algo** to sell at sth 2.(*ser popular*) to be valued

coto ['ko·to] *m* 1.(*vedado*) ~ **de caza** game [*o* hunting] preserve 2.(*límite*) limit

cotorra [ko·'to·rra] *f* 1.(*papagayo*) parrot 2. *inf*(*persona habladora*) chatterbox

cotorrear [ko·to·rre·'ar] *vi inf* to chatter
cototo [ko·'to·to] *m AmL, inf* (*chichón*) bump
coxis ['kok·sis] *m inv* ANAT coccyx
coyote [ko·'jo·te] *m* coyote
coyuntura [ko·jun·'tu·ra] *f* **1.** (*situación*) situation, circumstances *pl;* ECON current economic situation **2.** ANAT joint
coyuntural [ko·jun·tu·'ral] *adj* ECON current
coz [kos, koθ] *f* **1.** (*patada*) kick; **dar coces** to kick **2.** (*grosería*) rude remark
crack [krak] *m* **1.** ECON crash **2.** (*droga*) crack
cráneo ['kra·neo] *m* ANAT skull
cráter ['kra·ter] *m* crater
creación [krea·'sjon, -'θjon] *f* creation; *fig* the world
creador(a) [krea·'dor,-·'do·ra] **I.** *adj* creative **II.** *m(f)* creator; **Dios** ~ God, the Creator
crear [kre·'ar] **I.** *vt* **1.** (*hacer*) to create; ~ **archivo** COMPUT to make a new file **2.** (*fundar*) to establish **II.** *vr:* ~ **se** to be created
creatividad [krea·ti·βi·'dad] *f* creativity
creativo, -a [krea·'ti·βo, -a] *adj* creative
crecer [kre·'ser, -'θer] *irr* **I.** *vi* **1.** (*aumentar*) to grow, to increase **2.** (*luna*) to wax **3.** (*agua*) to rise **II.** *vr:* ~ **se** (*persona*) to grow more confident
creces ['kre·ses, -θes] *fpl* **con** ~ fully
crecida [kre·'si·da, -'θi·da] *f* flood
crecimiento [kre·si·'mjen·to, kre·θi-] *m* **1.** *t.* ECON growth **2.** (*moneda*) appreciation
credencial [kre·den·'sjal, -'θjal] **I.** *adj* accrediting **II.** *fpl* credentials
credibilidad [kre·di·βi·li·'dad] *f* credibility
crédito ['kre·di·to] *m* **1.** FIN (*préstamo*) credit; ~ **puente** bridging loan; **dar a** ~ to loan; **pedir un** ~ to ask for a loan **2.** (*fama*) reputation **3.** (*confianza*) **dar** ~ **a algo/alguien** to believe in sth/sb
credo ['kre·do] *m* **1.** (*creencias*) beliefs *pl* **2.** (*oración*) creed
credulidad [kre·du·li·'dad] *f* credulity
crédulo, -a ['kre·du·lo, -a] *adj* credulous
creencia [kre·'en·sja, -θja] *f* belief; REL faith
creer [kre·'er] *irr como leer* **I.** *vi* ~ **en Dios/alguien** to believe in God/sb **II.** *vt* **1.** (*dar por cierto*) to believe; **¡quién iba a ~lo!** who would have believed it!; **no te creo** I don't believe you; **hacer** ~ **algo a alguien** to make sb believe sth **2.** (*pensar*) **¡ya lo creo!** I should think so! **III.** *vr:* ~ **se 1.** (*tener por probable*) to believe **2.** (*considerarse*) to believe oneself to be; **¡qué te has creído!** what do you take me for?
creíble [kre·'i·βle] *adj* credible, believable
creído, -a [kre·'i·do, -a] *adj* **1.** *ser inf* (*vanidoso*) conceited **2.** *estar* (*seguro*) sure
crema ['kre·ma] **I.** *adj* cream **II.** *f* **1.** cream; ~ **antiarrugas** anti-wrinkle cream **2.** (*natillas*) custard; **la** ~ **y la nata** *fig* the crème de la crème **3.** LING dieresis
cremación [kre·ma·'sjon, -'θjon] *f* **1.** (*incineración*) cremation **2.** (*de desechos*) incineration

cremallera [kre·ma·'je·ra, -'ʎe·ra] *f* **1.** (*cierre*) zipper **2.** TÉC rack; **tren de** ~ rack [*o* cog] railway
crematorio [kre·ma·'to·rjo] *m* crematorium
crematorio, -a [kre·ma·'to·rjo, -a] *adj* **horno** ~ crematorium
cremoso, -a [kre·'mo·so, -a] *adj* creamy
crepé [kre·'pe] *m* **1.** (*tejido*) crepe **2.** (*postizo*) hairpiece
crepitar [kre·pi·'tar] *vi* to crackle
crepuscular [kre·pus·ku·'lar] *adj* twilight
crepúsculo [kre·'pus·ku·lo] *m* twilight, dusk; ~ **matutino** dawn
crespón [kres·'pon] *m* crepe
cresta ['kres·ta] *f* **1.** (*del gallo*) (cocks)comb **2.** (*de ola, montaña*) crest **3.** (*plumas*) crest **4.** (*cabello*) tuft
Creta ['kre·ta] *f* Crete
cretense [kre·'ten·se] *adj, mf* Cretan
cretino, -a [kre·'ti·no, -a] *m, f t. fig* cretin
creyente [kre·'jen·te] *mf* believer
cría ['kri·a] *f* **1.** (*acción*) rearing, raising **2.** (*cachorro*) baby animal **3.** (*camada*) litter
criadero [krja·'de·ro] *m* **1.** (*plantel*) nursery **2.** (*vivero*) breeding ground
criadero, -a [krja·'de·ro, -a] *adj* fertile
criado, -a [kri·'a·do, -a] *m, f* servant
criandera [krjan·'de·ra] *f AmL* wet nurse
crianza [kri·'an·sa, -θa] *f* **1.** (*lactancia*) lactation **2.** (*educación*) upbringing **3.** (*vinos*) maturing
criar < *1. pres:* crío> [kri·'ar] **I.** *vt* **1.** (*alimentar*) to feed; (*mamíferos*) to suckle **2.** (*reproducir*) to breed **3.** (*educar*) to bring up **4.** (*el vino*) to mature **II.** *vi* to have young **III.** *vr:* ~ **se** to grow up
criatura [krja·'tu·ra] *f t. fig* creature; (*niño*) child
criba ['kri·βa] *f* sieve; *fig* selection process
cribar [kri·'βar] *vt* to sieve
Crimea [kri·'mea] *f* Crimea
crimen ['kri·men] *m* crime
criminal [kri·mi·'nal] *adj, mf* criminal
criminalidad [kri·mi·na·li·'dad] *f* criminality
criminalista [kri·mi·na·'lis·ta] *mf* criminal lawyer
criminología [kri·mi·no·lo·'xi·a] *f* criminology
crío, -a ['kri·o, -a] *m, f inf* kid
criollo, -a [kri·'o·jo, -a; -·'o·ʎo, -a] *adj, m, f* Creole
cripta ['krip·ta] *f* crypt
críptico, -a ['krip·ti·ko, -a] *adj* cryptic
criptografía [krip·to·ɣra·'fi·a] *f* cryptography
crisálida [kri·'sa·li·da] *f* chrysalis
crisantemo [kri·san·'te·mo] *m* chrysanthemum
crisis ['kri·sis] *f inv* crisis; ~ **nerviosa** nervous breakdown
crisma¹ ['kris·ma] *m* REL chrism
crisma² ['kris·ma] *f inf* (*cabeza*) head
crisol [kri·'sol] *m* crucible; *fig* melting pot
crispación [kris·pa·'sjon, -'θjon] *f* **1.** (*irritación*) tension **2.** (*contracción*) contraction

crispar [kris·'par] I. *vt* **1.** (*exasperar*) to exasperate **2.** (*contraer*) to contract II. *vr:* ~**se** **1.** (*exasperarse*) to become exasperated **2.** (*contraerse*) to contract

cristal [kris·'tal] *m* **1.** (*cuerpo*) crystal **2.** (*vidrio*) glass

cristalera [kris·ta·'le·ra] *f* **1.** (*aparador*) glass cabinet **2.** (*puertas*) French windows *pl*

cristalino [kris·ta·'li·no] *m* MED crystalline lens

cristalino, -a [kris·ta·'li·no, -a] *adj* crystalline; (*transparente*) crystal-clear

cristalizar <z→c> [kris·ta·li·'sar, -'θar] *vt, vi, vr:* ~**se** to crystallize

cristiandad [kris·tjan·'dad] *f* Christendom

cristianismo [kris·tja·'nis·mo] *m* Christianity

cristiano [kris·'tja·no, -a] *m inf* **1.** (*persona*) person **2.** (*castellano*) Spanish; **hablar en ~** *fig* to speak plainly

cristiano, -a [kris·'tja·no, -a] *adj, m, f* Christian

cristo ['kris·to] *m* crucifix; **todo ~** *inf* everyone

Cristo ['kris·to] *m* Christ ▶ **donde ~ perdió el gorro** *inf* in the middle of nowhere; **donde ~ dio las tres voces** *inf* in the back of beyond

criterio [kri·'te·rjo] *m* **1.** (*norma*) criterion **2.** (*discernimiento*) judgment **3.** (*opinión*) opinion

crítica ['kri·ti·ka] *f* **1.** (*juicio*) criticism **2.** (*prensa*) review, write-up; **tener buenas ~s** to get good reviews

criticar <c→qu> [kri·ti·'kar] I. *vt* to criticize II. *vi* to gossip

crítico, -a ['kri·ti·ko, -a] I. *adj* critical II. *m, f* critic

criticón, -ona [kri·ti·'kon, -·'ko·na] *m, f* fault-finder

Croacia [kro·'a·sja, -θja] *f* Croatia

croar [kro·'ar] *vi* to croak

croata [kro·'a·ta] *adj, mf* Croat(ian)

cromar [kro·'mar] *vt* to chromium-plate

cromo ['kro·mo] *m* **1.** QUÍM chromium **2.** (*estampa*) (picture) card; **~s de béisbol** baseball cards; **estar** [*o* **ir**] **hecho un ~** to look wonderful *iron*

cromosoma [kro·mo·'so·ma] *m* chromosome

crónica ['kro·ni·ka] *f* **1.** HIST chronicle **2.** (*prensa*) (feature) article; (*reportaje*) report

crónico, -a ['kro·ni·ko, -a] *adj t.* MED chronic

cronista [kro·'nis·ta] *mf* **1.** HIST chronicler **2.** (*periodista*) journalist

cronología [kro·no·lo·'xi·a] *f* chronology, sequence of events

cronológico, -a [kro·no·'lo·xi·ko, -a] *adj* chronological

cronometraje [kro·no·me·'tra·xe] *m* DEP time-keeping

cronometrar [kro·no·me·'trar] *vt* to time

cronómetro [kro·'no·me·tro] *m* chronometer; DEP stopwatch

croquet ['kro·ket] *m* croquet

croqueta [kro·'ke·ta] *f* ≈ croquette

croquis ['kro·kis] *m inv* sketch, outline

cruasán [krwa·'san/kru·'san] *m* croissant

cruce ['kru·se, -θe] *m* **1.** (*acción*) crossing **2.** (*intersección*) crossing, intersection **3.** (*mezcla*) crossing, cross; **~ de peatones** pedestrian crossing **4.** (*interferencia*) interference **5.** BIO cross

crucero [kru·'se·ro, -'θe·ro] *m* **1.** ARQUIT transept **2.** (*buque*) cruiser **3.** (*viaje*) cruise

crucial [kru·'θjal, -'sjal] *adj* crucial

crucificado, -a [kru·si·fi·'ka·do, kru·θi-] *m* el Crucificado Christ

crucificar <c→qu> [kru·si·fi·'kar, kru·θi-] *vt* to crucify

crucifijo [kru·si·'fi·xo, kru·θi-] *m* crucifix

crucifixión [kru·si·fik·'sjon, kru·θi-] *f* crucifixion

crucigrama [kru·si·'γra·ma, kru·θi-] *m* crossword (puzzle)

crudeza [kru·'de·sa, -θa] *f* **1.** (*rigor*) harshness **2.** (*crueldad*) cruelty

crudo ['kru·do] *m* crude oil

crudo, -a ['kru·do, -a] *adj* **1.** (*sin cocer*) raw **2.** (*tiempo*) harsh **3.** (*color*) yellowish-white **4.** (*despiadado*) cruel

cruel [kru·'el] *adj* <crudelísimo> **~ con alguien** cruel to sb

crueldad [krwel·'dad] *f* **~ con alguien** cruelty to sb

cruento, -a [kru·'en·to, -a] *adj* bloody

crujido [kru·'xi·do] *m* (*de papel*) rustling; (*de madera*) creaking

crujiente [kru·'xjen·te] *adj* (*pan*) crunchy

crujir [kru·'xir] *vi* (*papel*) to rustle; (*madera*) creak

crupier [kru·'pjer] *m* croupier

crustáceo [krus·'ta·seo, -θeo] *m* crustacean

cruz [krus, kruθ] *f* **1.** (*figura*) cross; **~ gamada** swastika; **Cruz Roja** Red Cross **2.** (*de moneda*) reverse; **¿cara o ~?** heads or tails? **3.** (*de árbol*) top of trunk where branches begin; (*de animal*) withers *pl* **4.** (*suplicio*) burden; **llevar una ~** to have a cross to bear

cruzada [kru·'sa·da, -'θa·da] *f* crusade

cruzado, -a [kru·'sa·do, -a; -'θa·do, -a] *adj* **animal ~** BIO crossbred animal; **chaqueta cruzada** double-breasted jacket

cruzar <z→c> [kru·'sar, -'θar] I. *vt, vi* to cross; **~ los brazos** to cross one's arms; **~ algo con una raya** to cross out sth II. *vr:* ~**se 1.** (*caminos*) to cross **2.** (*encontrarse*) to meet; ~**se con alguien** to pass sb **3.** *t.* MAT to intersect

cu [ku] *f* (name of the letter) q

cuácara ['kwa·ka·ra] *f* **1.** *Col, Ven* (*levita*) frock coat **2.** *Chile* (*camisa ordinaria*) workman's blouse; (*chaqueta*) jacket

cuaderno [kwa·'der·no] *m* notebook; **~ de bitácora** NÁUT logbook

cuadra ['kwa·dra] *f* **1.** (*establo*) stable **2.** (*caballos*) stables *pl* **3.** (*lugar*) pigsty **4.** *AmL* (*manzana de casas*) block (of houses)

cuadrado [kwa·'dra·do] *m t.* ASTR square; **elevar al ~** to square

cuadrado, -a [kwa·'dra·do, -a] *adj* **1.** (*forma*) square; **tener la cabeza cuadrada** to be pigheaded; **tenerlos ~s** *inf* to have balls *vulg* **2.** (*corpulento*) hefty

cuadrángulo [kwa·'dran·gu·lo] *m* quadrangle

cuadrar [kwa·'drar] **I.** *vi* **1.** (*convenir*) to fit in **2.** (*coincidir*) to tally **II.** *vt t.* MAT to square **III.** *vr:* **~se 1.** MIL to stand to attention **2.** *inf* (*plantarse*) to dig one's heels in

cuadratura [kwa·dra·'tu·ra] *f* ASTR quadrature

cuadrícula [kwa·'dri·ku·la] *f* grid squares *pl;* **papel de ~** squared paper

cuadrilátero [kwa·dri·'la·te·ro] *m* quadrilateral; DEP ring

cuadrilla [kwa·'dri·ja, -ʎa] *f* (*de amigos*) group; (*de trabajo*) work team; (*de maleantes*) gang

cuadro ['kwa·dro] *m* **1.** (*cuadrado*) square; **a ~s** plaid, check(er)ed **2.** (*pintura*) painting **3.** (*marco*) frame **4.** (*escena*) scene **5.** (*descripción*) description; **~ sinóptico** synoptic chart **6.** MIL officers *pl* **7.** TÉC panel

cuadrúpedo [kwa·'dru·pe·do] *m* quadruped

cuadruplicar <c→qu> [kwa·dru·pli·'kar] *vt, vr:* **~se** to quadruple

cuádruplo, -a ['kwa·dru·plo, -a] *adj* quadruple

cuajada [kwa·'xa·da] *f* curd

cuajar [kwa·'xar] **I.** *vi* **1.** (*espesarse*) to thicken; (*nieve*) to lie **2.** *inf* (*realizarse*) to come off **II.** *vt* **1.** (*leche*) to curdle **2.** (*cubrir*) to cover **III.** *vr:* **~se** to coagulate; (*leche*) to curdle; **~se de algo** to fill (up) with sth **IV.** *m* fourth stomach

cuajo ['kwa·xo] *m* **1.** (*sustancia*) rennet **2.** *fig* phlegm ▸ **de ~** completely

cual [kwal] *pron rel* **1.** (*explicativo*) **el/la ~** (*persona*) who, whom; (*cosa*) which; **lo ~** which; **los/las ~es** (*personas*) who, whom; (*cosas*) which; **cada ~** everyone **2.** (*correlativo*) **hazlo tal ~ te lo digo** do it just as I tell you (to); **sea ~ sea su intención** whatever his/her intention may be

cuál [kwal] **I.** *pron interrog* which (one); **¿~ es el tuyo?** which is yours? **II.** *pron indef* **1.** (*distributivo*) **~ más ~ menos** some more, some less **2.** (*ponderativo*) **tengo tres hermanas a ~ más bella** I have three sisters, each more beautiful than the other

cualesquier(a) [kwa·les·'kje·ra] *pron indef pl de* cualquiera

cualidad [kwa·li·'dad] *f* quality

cualificación [kwa·li·fi·ka·'sjon, -'θjon] *f* qualification

cualificar <c→qu> [kwa·li·fi·'kar] *vt* to qualify

cualitativo, -a [kwa·li·ta·'ti·βo, -a] *adj* qualitative

cualquiera [kwal·'kje·ra] **I.** *pron indef* (*ante sustantivo: cualquier*) anyone; **en un lugar ~** anywhere; **a cualquier hora** at any time; **cualquier cosa** anything; **de cualquier modo** whichever way; (*de todas maneras*) anyway; **¡~ lo puede hacer!** anybody can do it! **II.** *mf* **ser una ~** *pey* to be a whore

cuan [kwan] *adv* how; **cayó ~ largo era** he/she fell his/her whole length

cuando ['kwan·do] *conj* **1.** (*presente, pasado*) when; **de ~ en ~** from time to time **2.** (*futuro; +subj*) when; **~ quieras** when(ever) you want **3.** (*relativo*) **el lunes es ~ no trabajo** I don't work on Mondays **4.** (*condicional*) if; **~ más** [*o* **mucho**] at (the) most; **~ menos** at least **5.** (*aunque*) **aun ~** even if

cuándo ['kwan·do] *adv* when

cuantía [kwan·'ti·a] *f* amount

cuantificar <c→qu> [kwan·ti·fi·'kar] *vt* to quantify

cuantioso, -a [kwan·'tjo·so, -a] *adj* substantial

cuantitativo, -a [kwan·ti·ta·'ti·βo, -a] *adj* quantitative

cuanto ['kwan·to] **I.** *adv* **~ antes** as soon as possible; **~ antes mejor** the sooner the better; **~ más que...** all the more that...; **~ más lo pienso, menos me gusta** the more I think about it, the less I like it **II.** *prep* **en ~ a** as regards **III.** *conj* **1.** (*temporal*) **en ~ (que)** as soon as **2.** (*puesto que*) **por ~ que** inasmuch as **IV.** *m* FÍS quantum

cuanto, -a ['kwan·to, -a] **I.** *pron rel* **1.** (*neutro*) all that (which); **tanto...~** as much... as; **dije (todo) ~ sé** I said all that I know **2.** *pl* all those that; **la más hermosa de cuantas conozco** the most beautiful of those I know **II.** *pron indef* **unos ~s/unas cuantas** some, several

cuánto ['kwan·to] *adv* **1.** (*interrogativo*) how much **2.** (*exclamativo*) how; **¡~ llueve!** how hard it's raining!

cuánto, -a ['kwan·to, -a] **I.** *adj* **¿~ vino?** how much wine?; **¿~s libros?** how many books?; **¿~ tiempo?** how long?; **¿cuántas veces?** how often? **II.** *pron interrog* how much [*o* many]; **¿~ hay de aquí a Veracruz?** how far is it from here to Veracruz?

cuarenta [kwa·'ren·ta] **I.** *adj inv* forty **II.** *m* forty; *v.t.* **ochenta** ▸ **cantar las ~ a alguien** to give sb a piece of one's mind

cuarentena [kwa·ren·'te·na] *f* **1.** (*aislamiento*) quarantine **2.** (*conjunto*) **una ~ de veces** about forty times

cuaresma [kwa·'res·ma] *f* REL Lent

cuartear [kwar·te·'ar] **I.** *vt* to quarter **II.** *vr:* **~se** to crack

cuartel [kwar·'tel] *m* **1.** MIL (*acuartelamiento*) encampment; **~ general** headquarters *pl* **2.** MIL (*edificio*) barracks *pl*

cuartelillo [kwar·te·'li·jo, -ʎo] *m* police station

cuarteto [kwar·'te·to] *m* MÚS quartet

cuartilla [kwar·'ti·ja, -ʎa] *f* (*hoja*) sheet of paper

cuarto ['kwar·to] *m* **1.** (*habitación*) room; **~ de aseo** lavatory; **~ de baño** bathroom; **~ de estar** living room; **~ trastero** lumber room **2.** (*pl*), *inf* (*dinero*) money, dough *inf;* **tener cuatro ~s** to have to watch every penny **3.** (*de un caballo*) **~s delanteros** forequarters *pl;* **~s traseros** hindquarters *pl*

cuarto, -a ['kwar·to, -a] **I.** *adj* fourth **II.** *m, f*

quarter; ~ **creciente/menguante** first/last quarter; **~s de final** DEP quarterfinal; **un ~ de hora** a quarter of an hour; **es la una y/menos ~** it's a quarter past/to one; *v.t.* **octavo**
cuarzo ['kwar·so, -θo] *m* quartz
cuate, -a ['kwa·te, -a] *m, f* 1. *Méx* (*gemelo*) twin 2. *Guat, Méx* (*amigo*) buddy
cuatrero, -a [kwa·'tre·ro, -a] *m, f* rustler
cuatrillizo, -a [kwa·tri·'ʝi·so, -a; -'ʎi·θo, -a] *m, f* quadruplet
cuatrimestre [kwa·tri·'mes·tre] *m* four-month period
cuatro ['kwa·tro] *adj inv, m* four; *v.t.* **ocho**
cuatrocientos, -as [kwa·tro·'sjen·tos, -as; kwa·tro·'θjen-] *adj* four hundred; *v.t.* **ochocientos**
cuatrojos [kwa·'tro·xos] *mf inv, inf* four-eyes
cuba ['ku·βa] *f* (*tonel*) barrel; **estar como una ~** *inf* (*borracho*) to be plastered
Cuba ['ku·βa] *f* Cuba

> ℹ️ **Cuba** (formally named **República de Cuba**) is the largest of the West Indian Islands. The capital, **La Habana**, is also the largest city in Cuba. The country's official language is Spanish and the official currency is the **peso cubano**.

cubano, -a [ku·'βa·no, -a] *adj, m, f* Cuban
cubertería [ku·βer·te·'ri·a] *f* cutlery, silverware
cubeta [ku·'βe·ta] *f* 1. (*cubo*) pail; FOTO tray 2. (*de un termómetro*) bulb
cúbico, -a ['ku·βi·ko, -a] *adj t.* MAT cubic
cubículo [ku·'βi·ku·lo] *m* cubicle
cubierta [ku·'βjer·ta] *f* 1. (*cobertura*) cover; (*de libro*) jacket; (*de rueda*) tire; **~ de cama** bedspread 2. NÁUT deck 3. ARQUIT roof
cubierto [ku·'βjer·to] *m* 1. *t.* CULIN place setting; **poner un ~** to set a place; **los ~s** the cutlery, the silverware 2. (*techumbre*) **ponerse a ~** to take cover
cubierto, -a [ku·'βjer·to, -a] I. *pp de* **cubrir** II. *adj* (*cielo*) overcast; **cheque no ~** FIN bounced check
cubilete [ku·βi·'le·te] *m* 1. (*en juegos*) cup 2. (*molde*) mold
cubismo [ku·'βis·mo] *m* ARTE cubism
cubitera [ku·βi·'te·ra] *f* ice tray
cubito [ku·'βi·to] *m* **~ de hielo** ice cube
cubo ['ku·βo] *m* 1. (*recipiente*) bucket; **~ de basura** trashcan 2. *t.* MAT cube
cubrir [ku·'βrir] *irr como* **abrir** I. *vt* 1. (*tapar*) cover 2. (*vacante*) to fill II. *vr:* **~se** 1. (*taparse*) to cover oneself; (*con sombrero*) to put on one's hat 2. (*cielo*) to become overcast 3. (*protegerse*) to cover oneself; MIL to take cover
cucaracha [ku·ka·'ra·tʃa] *f* cockroach
cuchara [ku·'tʃa·ra] *f* spoon; **~ de palo** wooden spoon; **~ sopera** soup spoon; **meter (su) ~** to meddle

cucharada [ku·'tʃa·ra·da] *f* (*porción*) spoonful; **una ~ grande/pequeña** a tablespoonful/teaspoonful; **a ~s** in spoonfuls; **meter su ~** *fig* to meddle
cucharilla [ku·'tʃa·ri·ja, -ʎa] *f* teaspoon
cucharón [ku·'tʃa·'ron] *m* ladle
cuchichear [ku·'tʃi·'tʃe·'ar] *vi* to whisper
cuchicheo [ku·'tʃi·'tʃeo] *m* whispering
cuchilla [ku·'tʃi·ja, -ʎa] *f* 1. (*hoja*) blade; (*de afeitar*) 2. (*de carnicero*) cleaver, razor blade
cuchillada [ku·'tʃi·'ja·da, -'ʎa·da] *f* slash; **andar a ~s con alguien** *fig* to be bitterly hostile to sb
cuchillo [ku·'tʃi·jo, -ʎo] *m* 1. (*para cortar*) knife; **~ de bolsillo** pocket knife; **~ de cocina** kitchen knife; **~ de monte** hunting knife; **pasar a ~** to put to the sword 2. (*de la ropa*) gore 3. ARQUIT support
cuchitril [ku·'tʃi·'tril] *m* pigsty; *fig* (*habitación*) hole
cuchuco [ku·'tʃu·ko] *m Col* CULIN pork and barley soup
cuclillas [ku·'kli·jas, -ʎas] *fpl* **estar en ~** to be squatting
cuclillo [ku·'kli·jo, -ʎo] *m* cuckoo
cuco ['ku·ko] *m* cuckoo
cuco, -a ['ku·ko, -a] *adj* 1. (*astuto*) crafty 2. (*bonito*) pretty
cucufato, -a [ku·ku·'fa·to, -a] I. *adj Bol, Perú* sanctimonious II. *m, f Bol, Perú* hypocrite
cucurucho [ku·ku·'ru·tʃo] *m* 1. (*de papel*) cone; (*de helado*) ice-cream cone 2. (*gorro*) pointed hat
cuello ['kwe·jo, -ʎo] *m* 1. ANAT neck; **~ de botella** *fig* bottleneck; **~ uterino** cervix; **alargar el ~** to crane one's neck; **estar con el agua al ~** to be in a tight spot 2. (*de una prenda*) collar; **~ alto** turtleneck; **~ de pico** V-neck; **~ redondo** crew neck
cuenca ['kwen·ka] *f* 1. GEO basin; **~ del río** river basin 2. (*región*) valley 3. (*de los ojos*) socket
cuenco ['kwen·ko] *m* 1. (*vasija*) bowl 2. (*concavidad*) hollow
cuenta ['kwen·ta] *f* 1. (*cálculo*) counting; **~ atrás** countdown; **~s atrasadas** outstanding debts *pl;* **rendición de ~s** balance; **Tribunal de Cuentas** National Audit Office; **por ~ del Estado** at the public expense; **pagar la ~** to pay the bill; **trabajar por ~ propia** to be self-employed; **establecerse por su ~** to set up one's own business; **a ~ de alguien** on sb's account; **echar ~s** to reflect; **dar ~ de algo** to report on sth; **ajustar las ~s a alguien** to get even with sb; **ajuste de ~s** act of revenge; **caer en la ~** to catch on; **hablar más de la ~** to talk too much; **a fin de ~s** after all; **en resumidas ~s** in short; **perder la ~** to lose count 2. (*en el banco*) account; **~ corriente** [*o de giros*] current account; **~ de crédito** loan account; **abonar en ~** to credit; **abrir una ~** to open an account; **girar a una ~** to transfer to an account 3. (*consideración*)

tener en ~ to bear in mind; **tomar en** ~ to take into consideration; **darse ~ de algo** to realize sth **4.** (*de un collar*) bead ▶ **hacer la ~ de la vieja** to count on one's fingers

cuentagotas [kwen·ta·'yo·tas] *m inv* dropper; **con** [*o* **a**] ~ *fig* bit by bit

cuentista [kwen·'tis·ta] *mf* **1.** (*chismoso*) gossip **2.** (*fanfarrón*) braggart

cuento ['kwen·to] *m* LIT (*historieta*) story; ~ **chino** *inf* tall story; ~ **de hadas** fairy tale [*o* story]; ~ **de nunca acabar** never-ending story; **tener mucho** ~ *inf* (*presumir*) to boast a lot; (*exagerar*) to exaggerate everything; **dejarse de ~s** to stop beating about the bush ▶ **eso es como el ~ de la lechera** don't count your chickens before they're hatched; **venir a** ~ to matter; **no venir a** ~ to be beside the point

cuerda ['kwer·da] *f* **1.** (*gruesa*) rope; (*delgada*) string; ~ **floja** tightrope; **andar en la ~ floja** *fig* to be in an unstable position; **ser de la misma** ~ *fig* to be cast in the same mold; **bajo** ~ secretly **2.** (*del reloj*) spring; **dar** ~ **al reloj** to wind up one's watch; **dar** ~ **a alguien** to encourage sb **3.** ANAT ~**s vocales** vocal chords **4.** (*de instrumentos*) string; ~ **metálica** steel string; ~ **de tripa** gut string; **juego de ~s** set of strings; **apretar las ~s** *fig* to tighten up

cuerdo, -a ['kwer·do, -a] *adj* sensible; **estar ~** to be sane

cueriza [kwe·'ri·sa, -θa] *f AmL* (*zurra*) beating

cuerno ['kwer·no] *m* **1.** ZOOL horn; ~ **de la abundancia** horn of plenty, cornucopia; **poner a alguien los ~s** *inf* to be unfaithful to sb **2.** *inf* (*exclamativo*) **¡y un ~!** my foot!; **irse al** ~ to be ruined; (*plan*) to fall through; **¡que se vaya al ~!** he/she can go to hell!

cuero ['kwe·ro] *m* leather; ~ **cabelludo** scalp; ~ **curtido** tanned hide; **estar en ~s** *inf* to be stark naked; **dejar a alguien en ~s** *inf* to fleece sb

cuerpear [kwer·pe·'ar] *vi Arg, Urug, inf* to dodge

cuerpo ['kwer·po] *m* **1.** (*organismo*) body; (*tronco*) trunk; (*figura*) figure; (*cadáver*) corpse, cadaver; **a ~ descubierto** unarmed; **una foto de ~ entero** a full-length photo(graph); **luchar ~ a ~** to fight hand-to-hand; **dar con el ~ en tierra** to fall down; **tomar ~** to take shape; **estar de ~ presente** to lie in state; **hacer de(l) ~** to relieve oneself; **haz lo que te pida el ~** do what you feel like doing **2.** (*objeto, corporación*) body; ~ **de bomberos** fire department; ~ **diplomático** diplomatic corps; ~ **docente** teaching staff **3.** (*grosor*) thickness; ~ **de letra** TIPO point size; **tener poco** ~ to be thin **4.** (*de iglesia*) nave ▶ **vivir a ~ de rey** to live like a king

cuervo ['kwer·βo] *m* raven, crow; **cría ~s y te sacarán los ojos** *prov* a dog bites the hand that feeds it *prov*

cuesta ['kwes·ta] *f* slope; ~ **abajo/arriba** downhill/uphill; **un camino en** ~ an uphill road; **llevar algo a ~s** to carry sth on one's

back; **la ~ de enero** January (*when, following Christmas spending, people are often short of money*)

cuestación [kwes·ta·'sjon, -'θjon] *f* charity collection

cuestión [kwes·'tjon] *f* question, matter; ~ **de confianza** POL vote of confidence; ~ **de gustos** question of taste; ~ **secundaria** minor matter; **eso es otra** ~ that's another matter; **la ~ es pasarlo bien** the main thing is to enjoy oneself

cuestionable [kwes·tjo·'na·βle] *adj* questionable

cuestionar [kwes·tjo·'nar] *vt* to question

cuestionario [kwes·tjo·'na·rjo] *m* questionnaire

cuete ['kwe·te] *m Méx* **1.** (*loncha de carne*) slice of meat **2.** (*borrachera*) drunken spree; **traer un** ~ to be plastered

cueva ['kwe·βa] *f* cave; ~ **de ladrones** *fig* den of thieves

cuidado [kwi·'da·do] *m* care; **¡~!** careful!; **¡~ con el escalón!** mind the step!; **¡anda con ~!** watch your step!; **de** ~ serious; **eso me tiene sin** ~ I couldn't care less about that

cuidador(a) [kwi·da·'dor] *m(f)* caregiver; *Arg* nurse

cuidadora [kwi·da·'do·ra] *f Méx* nanny

cuidadoso, -a [kwi·da·'do·so, -a] *adj* careful

cuidar [kwi·'dar] **I.** *vi* to take care **II.** *vt* to look after **III.** *vr:* ~**se** to look after oneself; ~**se mucho de (no) hacer algo** to take good care not to do sth; **¡cuídate!** take care!

culata [ku·'la·ta] *f* butt; **salir el tiro por la** ~ to backfire

culebrón [ku·le·'βron] *m* TV soap opera

culinario, -a [ku·li·'na·rjo, -a] *adj* culinary

culminación [kul·mi·na·'sjon, -'θjon] *f* culmination

culminante [kul·mi·'nan·te] *adj* **punto** ~ high point

culminar [kul·mi·'nar] *vi* to culminate

culo ['ku·lo] *m* bottom; (*de vaso*) bottom; **caer de** ~ to fall on one's backside; *fig* to be amazed; **lamer el ~ a alguien** *vulg* to kiss sb's ass; **ser ~ de mal asiento** *inf* to be restless; **tonto del** ~ idiot; **¡vete a tomar por el ~!** *vulg* fuck off!

culpa ['kul·pa] *f* fault; JUR guilt; **echar la ~ a alguien** to blame sb; **y ¿qué ~ tengo yo?** and how am I to blame (for that)?

culpabilidad [kul·pa·βi·li·'dad] *f* guilt

culpabilizar <z→c> [kul·pa·βi·li·'sar, -'θar] *vt* to blame

culpable [kul·'pa·βle] **I.** *adj* guilty; **declarar ~** to find guilty **II.** *mf* culprit

culpar [kul·'par] **I.** *vt* ~ **de** [*o* **por**] **algo** to blame for sth **II.** *vr* ~**se de** [*o* **por**] **algo** to be to blame for sth

cultismo [kul·'tis·mo] *m* learned word

cultivar [kul·ti·'βar] *vt t. fig* AGR to cultivate; (*bacterias*) to culture; ~ **la tierra** to farm the land

cultivo [kul·'ti·βo] *m* AGR (*acto*) cultivation;

(*resultado*) crop; (*de bacterias*) culture; ~ **de regadío** irrigated crop

culto ['kul·to] *m* worship; ~ **divino** REL divine service; ~ **de la personalidad** personality cult

culto, -a ['kul·to, -a] *adj* educated, cultured

cultura [kul·'tu·ra] *f* culture; ~ **ambiental** environmental conservation; ~ **general** general knowledge

cultural [kul·tu·'ral] *adj* cultural

culturismo [kul·tu·'ris·mo] *m* body-building

cuma ['ku·ma] *f* **1.** *AmC* (*machete*) long knife **2.** *Perú* (*comadre*) godmother

cumbre ['kum·bre] *f* **1.** (*cima*) summit **2.** (*reunión*) summit meeting **3.** (*culminación*) height

cumiche [ku·'mi·tʃe] *m AmC* baby of the family

cumpleaños [kum·ple·'a·ɲos] *m inv* birthday

cumplido [kum·'pli·do] *m* compliment; **visita de** ~ formal [*o* courtesy] visit; **hacer algo por** ~ to do sth out of courtesy

cumplido, -a [kum·'pli·do, -a] *adj* **1.** (*acabado*) completed; **¡misión cumplida!** mission accomplished! **2.** (*abundante*) plentiful **3.** (*cortés*) courteous

cumplimentar [kum·pli·men·'tar] *vt* **1.** (*felicitar*) to congratulate **2.** (*visitar*) to pay one's respects to **3.** (*una orden*) to carry out **4.** (*un impreso*) to complete

cumplimiento [kum·pli·'mjen·to] *m* **1.** (*observación*) fulfillment; ~ **de un deber** performance of a duty; **no** ~ nonfulfillment **2.** (*cumplido*) compliment

cumplir [kum·'plir] I. *vi* **1.** (*satisfacer*) ~ **con su deber/su promesa** to do one's duty/to keep one's promise; **hacer algo sólo por** ~ to do sth as a matter of form; ~ **é por ti** I'll act on your behalf **2.** (*soldado*) to finish one's military service **3.** (*plazo*) to end II. *vt* **1.** (*orden*) to carry out **2.** (*promesa*) to keep **3.** (*plazo*) to keep to **4.** (*servicio militar*) to do **5.** (*una pena*) to serve **6.** (*las leyes*) to observe **7.** (*años*) **en mayo cumplo treinta años** I'm thirty years old in May III. *vr:* ~ **se** to be fulfilled

cúmulo ['ku·mu·lo] *m* **1.** (*amontonamiento*) heap **2.** METEO cumulus

cuna ['ku·na] *f* cradle; **canción de** ~ lullaby

cundir [kun·'dir] *vi* **1.** (*dar de sí*) to be productive; **esta comida cunde mucho** this food is very nourishing **2.** (*trabajo*) to go well **3.** (*rumor*) to spread

cuneco, -a [ku·'ne·ko, -a] *m, f Ven* baby of the family

cuneta [ku·'ne·ta] *f* ditch

cuña ['ku·ɲa] *f* **1.** (*traba*) wedge **2.** *fig* (*enchufe*) influence **3.** MED bedpan

cuñado, -a [ku·'ɲa·do, -a] *m, f* brother-in-law *m,* sister-in-law *f*

cuño ['ku·ɲo] *m* die stamp; **de nuevo** ~ (*palabra*) newly-coined

cuota ['kwo·ta] *f* **1.** (*porción*) quota; ~ **de crecimiento** rate of increase; ~ **de mercado** market share **2.** (*contribución*) fee; ~ **de socio** membership fee

cupé [ku·'pe] *m* AUTO coupé, coupe

cupido [ku·'pi·do] *m* HIST Cupid

cupo ['ku·po] I. *3. pret de* **caber** II. *m* **1.** ECON quota **2.** MIL draft

cupón [ku·'pon] *m* coupon; (*de lotería*) lottery ticket; ~ **de descuento** discount coupon

cúpula ['ku·pu·la] *f* ARQUIT dome; ~ **dirigente** POL top management

cura[1] ['ku·ra] *m* priest

cura[2] ['ku·ra] *f* **1.** (*curación*) cure **2.** (*tratamiento*) treatment; ~ **para adelgazar** diet; ~ **de deshabituación** cure for drug addiction [*o* alcoholism]; **primera** ~ first aid

curable [ku·'ra·βle] *adj* curable

curación [ku·ra·'sjon, -'θjon] *f* treatment

curado, -a [ku·'ra·do, -a] *adj* **1.** (*alimento*) cured **2.** *AmL* (*borracho*) drunk

curandero, -a [ku·ran·'der·o, -a] *m, f* healer

---

i **Curanderos** are prevalent throughout Latin America. These primarily indigenous healers use many different techniques, including traditional methods of healing that have been passed down from generation to generation, natural remedies such as herbs and minerals, and spiritual rituals and ceremonies.

---

curar [ku·'rar] I. *vi* to recover II. *vt* **1.** (*tratar*) to treat; (*sanar*) to cure **2.** (*alimentos*) to cure; (*pieles*) to tan; (*madera*) to season III. *vr:* ~ **se** to recover; ~ **se en salud** to take precautions

curativo, -a [ku·ra·'ti·βo, -a] *adj* curative

curcuncho, -a [kur·'kun·tʃo, -a] *adj AmL* (*corcovado*) hunchbacked

curdo, -a ['kur·do, -a] I. *adj* Kurdish II. *m, f* Kurd

curia ['ku·rja] *f* **1.** REL Curia **2.** (*tribunal*) bar

curiosear [ku·rjo·se·'ar] *vi* to look round; (*fisgar*) to snoop

curiosidad [ku·rjo·si·'dad] *f* curiosity; **despertar la** ~ **de alguien** to arouse sb's curiosity

curioso, -a [ku·'rjo·so, -a] I. *adj* curious; **estar** ~ **por saber algo** to be curious to know sth; **¡qué** ~! how curious! II. *m, f* **1.** (*indiscreto*) busybody, snoop **2.** (*mirón*) onlooker, bystander **3.** *AmL* (*curandero*) quack doctor

currante [ku·'rran·te] *mf inf* worker

currar [ku·'rrar] *vi inf* to work

currículo [ku·'rri·ku·lo] *m* curriculum

curro ['ku·rro] *m inf* job

curry ['ku·rri] *m* curry

cursar [kur·'sar] *vt* **1.** (*cursos*) to take **2.** (*orden*) to issue; (*telegrama*) to send; (*solicitud*) to pass on

cursi ['kur·si] I. *adj inf* affected II. *mf inf* affected person

cursilada [kur·si·'la·da] *f inf*, **cursilería** [kur·si·le·'ri·a] *f inf* **1.** (*cosa*) pretentious act **2.** (*acción*) affectation

cursillo [kur·'si·jo, -ʎo] *m* short course; ~ **de**

socorrismo life-saving classes
cursiva [kur·'si·βa] *f* italics *pl*
cursivo, -a [kur·'si·βo, -a] *adj* cursive
curso ['kur·so] *m* 1. (*transcurso*) course; ~ **de agua** watercourse; **estar en** ~ to be going on; FIN to be in circulation; **en el** ~ **del año** in the course of the year; **tomar un** ~ **favorable** to go favorably; **dar** ~ **a una solicitud** to deal with an application 2. ENS course; ~ **acelerado** crash course; **asistir a un** ~ to take part in a course; **perder el** ~ to fail a subject
cursor [kur·'sor] *m* 1. COMPUT cursor 2. TÉC slide
curtido [kur·'ti·do] *m* tanned hide
curtido, -a [kur·'ti·do, -a] *adj* 1. *fig* hardened 2. (*cuero*) tanned
curtiduría [kur·ti·du·'ri·a] *f* tannery
curtiembre [kur·'tjem·bre] *f AmL* 1. (*taller*) tannery 2. (*acción*) tanning
curtir [kur·'tir] I. *vt* to tan; *fig* to harden II. *vr:* ~**se** 1. (*piel*) to become tanned 2. (*a la vida dura*) to become inured
curva ['kur·βa] *f* curve
curvatura [kur·βa·'tu·ra] *f* curvature
curvilíneo, -a [kur·βi·'li·neo, -a] *adj* MAT curvilinear
cusca ['kus·ka] *f* 1. *Méx* (*prostituta*) whore 2. *Col* (*embriaguez*) drunkenness 3. *Col* (*colilla de cigarro*) butt ▶ **hacer la** ~ **a alguien** *inf* to play a dirty trick on sb
cusma ['kus·ma] *f AmS* coarse woolen Indian shirt
cúspide ['kus·pi·de] *f* 1. MAT apex 2. *fig* pinnacle
custodia [kus·'to·dja] *f* 1. (*guarda*) custody; **bajo** ~ in custody; **estar bajo la** ~ **de alguien** to be in sb's care 2. REL monstrance
custodiar [kus·to·'djar] *vt* to guard
custodio, -a [kus·'to·djo, -a] *m, f* guardian
cususa [ku·'su·sa] *f AmC* uncured rum
cutáneo, -a [ku·'ta·neo] *adj* skin
cutis ['ku·tis] *m inv* skin, complexion
cuyo, -a ['ku·jo, -a] *pron rel* whose; **por cuya causa** for which reason

D

D, d [de] *f* D, d; ~ **de Dolores** D as in Delta
D. [don] *abr de* **Don** Mr.
Dª ['do·ɲa] *abr de* **Doña** Mrs.
dactilar [dak·ti·'lar] *adj* **huellas** ~**es** fingerprints *pl*
dadivoso, -a [da·di·'βo·so, -a] *adj* generous
dado¹ ['da·do] *m* 1. (*cubo*) die; ~**s** dice *pl*; **tirar los** ~**s** to throw the dice 2. *pl* (*juego*) dice; **jugar a los** ~**s** to play dice
dado² ['da·do] *conj* 1. (*ya que*) ~ **que llueve...** given that it's raining... 2. (*supuesto que*) ~

que sea demasiado difícil... supposing it's too difficult...
dado, -a ['da·do, -a] *adj* (*supuesto, determinado*) given; **dada la coyuntura actual...** given the current situation...; **en el caso** ~ in this particular case ▶ **no ser** ~ *Méx* to be brave
daga ['da·ɣa] *f* dagger; *PRico* (*machete*) machete
daiquiri [dai·'ki·ri] *m* CULIN daiquiri
dalia ['da·lja] *f* dahlia
dálmata ['dal·ma·ta] *m* ZOOL dalmatian
daltónico, -a [dal·'to·ni·ko, -a] *adj* color-blind
dama ['da·ma] *f* 1. (*señora*) lady; ~ **de honor** (*de la reina*) lady-in-waiting; (*de la novia*) bridesmaid; **primera** ~ POL first lady 2. *pl* (*juego*) (**juego de**) ~**s** checkers *pl*
damnificar [<c→qu>] [dam·ni·fi·'kar] *vt* (*persona*) to injure; (*cosa*) to damage
danés [da·'nes] *m* **gran** ~ Great Dane
danés, -esa [da·'nes, --'ne·sa] I. *adj* Danish II. *m, f* Dane
danta ['dan·ta] *f Ven, Col* ZOOL tapir
Danubio [da·'nu·βjo] *m* Danube
danza ['dan·sa, -θa] *f* dance
danzar [<z→c>] [dan·'sar, -'θar] I. *vi* 1. (*bailar, girar*) to dance 2. (*moverse*) to run around II. *vt* to dance
danzarín, -ina [dan·sa·'rin, --'ri·na; dan·θa-] *m, f* dancer
dañar [da·'ɲar] I. *vi* to harm II. *vt* (*cosa*) to damage; (*persona*) to injure; ~ **la imagen** to ruin the image III. *vr:* ~**se** to get damaged; (*fruta, cosecha*) to go bad
dañero, -a [da·'ɲe·ro, -a] *adj Ven* (*embaucador*) misleading
dañino, -a [da·'ɲi·no, -a] *adj* harmful
daño ['da·ɲo] *m* 1. (*perjuicio*) damage; ~ **material** physical damage; ~**s ecológicos** environmental harm; ~**s y perjuicios** JUR damages 2. (*dolor*) hurt; **hacer** ~ **a alguien** to hurt sb; **hacerse** ~ to hurt oneself; **no hace** ~ it doesn't hurt
dar [dar] *irr* I. *vt* 1. (*entregar*) to give; ~ **una patada a alguien** to kick sb; ~ **un abrazo a alguien** to hug sb; **¿a quién le toca** ~ **(las cartas)?** whose turn is it to deal?; ~ **forma a algo** to shape sth; ~ **permiso** to give permission; ~ **importancia a algo** to consider sth important 2. (*producir*) **la vaca da leche** cow yields milk; **este árbol da naranjas** this tree bears oranges 3. (*celebrar*) to give; ~ **clases** to teach; ~ **una conferencia** to give a talk 4. (*causar*) ~ **gusto** to please; ~ **miedo** to be frightening; **me das pena** I feel sorry for you 5. (*presentar*) ~ **una película** to show a film; **¿dónde dan la película?** where's the film showing? 6. (*expresar*) ~ **las buenas noches** to say goodnight; ~ **la enhorabuena a alguien** to congratulate sb; ~ **el pésame a alguien** to give one's condolences to sb; ~ **recuerdos** to send one's regards 7. (*comunicar: una noticia, un mensaje*) to give 8. (*hacer*) ~ **un paseo** to take a walk

9. (*encender*) to turn on; ~ **el agua** to turn the water on **10.** (*sonar*) **el reloj ha dado las dos** the clock has struck two o'clock **11.** (*aplicar: crema*) to apply **12.** (+ *'de'*) ~ **a alguien de alta** MED to discharge sb; ~ **a alguien de baja** MED to put sb on sick leave; (*miembro*) to expel sb **13.** (+ *'a'*) ~ **a conocer algo** to let sth be known; ~ **a entender algo a alguien** to let sb know sth **II.** *vi* **1.** (+ *'a'*) **el balcón da a la calle** the balcony faces the street; **la ventana da al patio** the window opens onto the courtyard **2.** (+ *'con'*) ~ **con alguien en la calle** to run into sb in the street; ~ **con la solución** to find the solution **3.** (+ *'contra'*) ~ **contra algo** to hit sth; **la piedra ha dado contra el cristal** the stone hit the glass **4.** (*caer*) ~ **de espaldas/de narices en el suelo** to land on one's back/on one's face on the ground **5.** (*acertar*) ~ **en el blanco** *fig* to hit the target; ~ **en el clavo** *fig* to hit the nail on the head **6.** (+ *'para'*) **da para vivir** it's enough to live on **7.** (+ *'por'* + *adjetivo*) ~ **a alguien por inocente** to assume sb is innocent; ~ **a alguien por muerto** to take sb for dead; ~ **por concluido algo** to treat sth as concluded; ~ **el libro por leído** to assume that the book has been read **8.** (+ *'por'* + *verbo*) **le ha dado por dejarse el pelo largo** he/she has decided to grow his/her hair long **9.** (+ *'que'* + *verbo*) ~ **que decir** to give cause for comment; ~ **que hablar** to be the topic of conversation; ~ **que hacer** to be a lot of work; ~ **que pensar** to give cause for thought ▶ **¡qué más da!** *inf* what does it matter? **III.** *vr:* ~ **se 1.** (*suceder*) to happen **2.** (*frutos*) to grow **3.** (+ *'a': consagrarse*) to devote oneself; (*entregarse*) to surrender; ~ **se a la bebida** to abandon oneself to drink **4.** (+ *'contra'*) ~ **se contra algo** to hit sth **5.** (+ *'por'* + *adjetivo: creerse*) ~ **se por algo** to believe oneself to be sth; ~ **se por aludido** to take the hint; ~ **se por vencido** to give up; ~ **se por enterado** to show that one has understood **6.** (+ *'a'* + *verbo*) ~ **se a conocer** (*persona*) to make oneself known; (*noticia*) to become known; ~ **se a entender** to hint **7.** (+ *'de'*) ~ **se de baja** to sign off; ~ **se de alta** to sign up; ~ **se de alta en Hacienda** to register with the Inland Revenue; **dárselas de valiente** *inf* to pretend to be brave **8.** (+ *sustantivo*) ~ **se un baño** to take a bath; ~ **se cuenta de algo** to realize sth; ~ **se prisa** to hurry up; ~ **se un susto** to get scared
dardo ['dar·do] *m* (*del juego*) dart; **jugar a los** ~ **s** to play darts
datar [da·'tar] *vi, vt* to date
dátil ['da·til] *m* date
dativo [da·'ti·βo] *m* dative
dato ['da·to] *m* **1.** (*circunstancia*) fact; ~ **s personales** personal details **2.** (*cantidad*) figure **3.** *pl* COMPUT data *pl;* ~ **s de entrada/de salida** input/output data; ~ **s fijos** fixed data; **elaborar** ~ **s** to compile data
dcha. [de·'re·tʃa] *abr de* **derecha** rt.

d. de J.C. [des·'pwes de xe·su·'kris·to] *abr de* **después de Jesucristo** AD
de [de] *prep* **1.** (*posesión*) **el reloj** ~ **mi padre** my father's watch **2.** (*origen*) from; **ser** ~ **Italia/**~ **Lisboa** to come from Italy/from Lisbon; ~ **Caracas a Bogotá** from Caracas to Bogotá; **el avión procedente** ~ **Lima** the plane from Lima; **un libro** ~ **Allende** a book by Allende; ~ **ti a mí** from you to me **3.** (*material, cualidad*) of; ~ **oro** of gold, gold; ~ **madera** of wood, wooden; **un hombre** ~ **buen corazón** a good-hearted man **4.** (*temporal*) from; ~ **niño** as a child **5.** (*finalidad*) **máquina** ~ **escribir** typewriter; **hora** ~ **comer** mealtime **6.** (*causa*) of, from **7.** (*condición*) ~ **haberlo sabido no habríamos ido** if we had known we wouldn't have gone **8.** (*partitivo*) **dos platos** ~ **sopa** two bowls of soup **9.** (+ *nombre propio*) **la ciudad** ~ **Cuzco** the city of Cuzco; **el tonto** ~ **Luis lo ha roto** that idiot Luis broke it; **pobre** ~ **mí** poor me
deambular [de·am·bu·'lar] *vi* to wander around
debajo [de·'βa·xo] **I.** *adv* underneath **II.** *prep* ~ **de** (*local*) below, under; (*con movimiento*) under; **pasar por** ~ **del puente** to go under the bridge
debate [de·'βa·te] *m* **1.** POL debate **2.** (*charla*) discussion
debatir [de·βa·'tir] **I.** *vt* **1.** POL to debate **2.** (*considerar*) to discuss **II.** *vr:* ~ **se** to struggle; ~ **se entre la vida y la muerte** to hover between life and death
debe ['de·βe] *m* debit
deber [de·'βer] **I.** *vi* (*suposición*) **debe de estar al llegar** he/she should arrive soon; **deben de ser las nueve** it must be nine o'clock **II.** *vt* **1.** (*estar obligado*) to have to; **no** ~ **ías haberlo dicho** you shouldn't have said it **2.** (*tener que dar*) to owe **III.** *vr:* ~ **se 1.** (*tener por causa*) ~ **se a algo** to be due to sth; (*agradeciendo algo*) to be thanks to sth **2.** (*estar obligado*) to have a duty; **se debe a su profesión** his/her job is his/her vocation **IV.** *m* **1.** (*obligación*) duty; ~ **de conciencia** moral duty **2.** *pl* (*tareas*) homework; **tener muchos** ~ **es** to have a lot of homework
debido [de·'βi·do] *prep* ~ **a** due to
debido, -a [de·'βi·do, -a] *adj* (*conveniente, necesario*) proper; **como es** ~ as is proper
débil ['de·βil] *adj* weak; (*sonido*) faint; (*luz*) dim
debilidad [de·βi·li·'dad] *f* ~ **por algo** weakness for sth
debilitar [de·βi·li·'tar] *vt* to weaken
debitar [de·βi·'tar] *vt AmL* to debit
débito ['de·βi·to] *m* debt; (*debe*) debit; ~ **conyugal** marital duty
debocar <c→qu> [de·βo·'kar] *vi Arg, Bol* to vomit
debut <debuts> [de·'βu(t)] *m* debut; **hacer su** ~ to make one's debut; (*teatro*) opening, first performance

debutar [de·βu·'tar] *vi* to make one's debut

década ['de·ka·da] *f* decade; **la ~ de los 40** the 40s

decadencia [de·ka·'den·sja, -θja] *f* **1.** (*decaimiento*) decay; **~ moral** decadence **2.** (*de un imperio*) decline

decadente [de·ka·'den·te] *adj* (*en declive*) declining; (*moralmente*) decadent

decaer [de·ka·'er] *irr como caer vi* to decline; **~ en fuerza** to lose strength; **~ el ánimo** to get discouraged; **decae de ánimo** he/she is losing heart

decaído, -a [de·ka·'i·do, -a] *adj* **1.** (*abatido*) downhearted **2.** (*débil*) weak

decaimiento [de·kai·'mjen·to] *m* **1.** (*afligimiento*) dejection **2.** (*debilidad*) weakness

decálogo [de·'ka·lo·yo] *m* REL Decalogue

decano, -a [de·'ka·no, -a] *m, f* UNIV dean

decapitar [de·ka·pi·'tar] *vt* to decapitate

decatlón [de·kad·'lon] *m* decathlon

decena [de·'se·na, -'θe·na] *f* ten; **~s** MAT tens; **~s de miles** tens of thousands; **una ~ de huevos** ten eggs

decencia [de·'sen·sja, -'θen·θja] *f* decency

decenio [de·'se·njo, -'θe·njo] *m* decade

decente [de·'sen·te, -'θen·te] *adj* **1.** (*decoroso*) decent **2.** (*honesto*) upright **3.** (*respetable*) respectable

decepción [de·sep·'sjon, -θeβ·'θjon] *f* disappointment; **llevarse una ~** to be disappointed

decepcionar [de·sep·sjo·'nar, -θeβ·θjo·'nar] *vt* to disappoint

deceso [de·'se·so, -'θe·so] *m* death, passing

decibel(io) [de·si·'βel, -·'βe·ljo, de·θi·] *m* decibel

decididamente [de·si·di·da·'men·te, de·θi·] *adv* **1.** (*resueltamente*) resolutely **2.** (*definitivamente*) decidedly

decidido, -a [de·θi·'di·do, -a; de·θi·] *adj* determined

decidir [de·si·'dir, de·θi·] **I.** *vi* to decide **II.** *vt* **1.** (*determinar, acordar*) to decide **2.** (*mover a*) to persuade **III.** *vr* **~se por/en contra de algo** to decide in favor of/against sth

décima ['de·si·ma, de·θi·] *f* tenth ▶ **tener ~s** to have a slight temperature

decimal [de·si·'mal, de·θi·] *adj* decimal; **número ~** decimal number

décimo ['de·si·mo, -a; de·θi·] *m* (*de lotería*) tenth share of a lottery ticket

décimo, -a ['de·si·mo, -a; de·θi·] **I.** *adj* tenth **II.** *m, f* tenth; (*de lotería*) tenth share of a lottery ticket; *v.t.* **octavo**

decimonono [de·si·mo·'no·no, -a; de·θi·] *adj*, **decimonoveno, -a** [de·si·mo·no·'βe·no, -a; de·θi·] *adj* nineteenth; *v.t.* **octavo**

decimotercero, -a [de·si·mo·ter·'se·ro, -a; de·θi·mo·ter·'θe·] *adj*, **decimotercio, -a** [de·si·mo·'ter·sjo, -a; de·θi·mo·'ter·θjo, -a] *adj* thirteenth; *v.t.* **octavo**

decir [de·'sir, -θir] *irr* **I.** *vi* **1.** (*expresar*) **~ algo de alguien** to say sth about sb; **~ que sí** to say yes; **diga** [*o* **dígame**] TEL hello; **es** [*o* **quiere**] **~** in other words; **¡no me digas!** *inf* really!; **~ por ~** to talk for the sake of talking; **por ~ lo así** to put it like that; **el qué dirán** what people will say; **¡quién lo diría!** who would have thought it!; **y que lo digas** you can say that again; **y no digamos** not to mention; **dicen de él que es un buen profesor** they say he is a good teacher **2.** (*contener*) to say; **la regla dice lo siguiente:...** the rule says the following: ... **3.** (*armonizar*) to suit; **~ con algo** to go with sth **II.** *vt* **1.** (*expresar*) to say; (*comunicar*) to tell; **~ algo para sí** to say sth to oneself; **¡no digas tonterías!** *inf* don't talk rubbish!; **dicho y hecho** no sooner said than done; **como se ha dicho** as has been said **2.** (*mostrar*) to show; **su cara dice alegría** he/she has a happy face **III.** *vr* **¿cómo se dice en inglés?** how do you say it in English? **IV.** *m* saying ▶ **ser un ~** to be a manner of speaking

decisión [de·si·'sjon, de·θi·] *f* **1.** (*resolución*) resolution; (*acuerdo*) decision; **tomar una ~** to make a decision **2.** (*firmeza*) determination; **tener ~** to be determined

decisivo, -a [de·si·'si·βo, -a; de·θi·] *adj* decisive

declamar [de·kla·'mar] *vt* to declaim; (*versos*) to recite

declaración [de·kla·ra·'sjon, -'θjon] *f* **1.** (*a la prensa*) declaration; **hacer declaraciones** to make a statement **2.** JUR statement; **~ final** closing statement; **prestar ~** to give evidence; **tomar ~ a alguien** to take sb's statement **3.** (*de bienes, impuestos*) **~ de la renta** income-tax return; **hacer una ~ de valor de algo** to declare the value of sth

declarar [de·kla·'rar] **I.** *vi* **1.** (*testigo*) to testify, to give evidence **2.** (*a la prensa*) to make a statement **II.** *vt* **1.** (*manifestar*) to declare; **~ abierta la reunión** to declare the meeting open; **~ a alguien culpable/inocente** to convict/acquit sb **2.** (*ingresos, a aduanas*) to declare **III.** *vr:* **~se** (*manifestarse*) to declare oneself; **~se en huelga** to go on strike; **~se inocente** to plead innocent; **~se en quiebra** to declare oneself bankrupt

declinación [de·kli·na·'sjon, -'θjon] *f* **1.** (*disminución*) decline **2.** LING declension

declinar [de·kli·'nar] **I.** *vi* **1.** (*disminuir*) to decline **2.** (*extinguirse*) to come to an end **II.** *vt* (*rechazar*) *t. fig* to decline

declive [de·'kli·βe] *m* **1.** (*del terreno*) slope; **en ~** sloping; **en fuerte ~** steeply sloping **2.** (*decadencia*) decline; **en ~** in decline

decolaje [de·ko·'la·xe] *m AmL* take-off

decolar [de·ko·'lar] *vi AmL* to take off

decolorar [de·ko·lo·'rar] **I.** *vt* **1.** QUÍM to discolor **2.** (*el sol*) to bleach **II.** *vr:* **~se** to fade

decomisar [de·ko·mi·'sar] *vt* to confiscate

decoración [de·ko·ra·'sjon, -'θjon] *f* **1.** (*adorno*) decoration **2.** (*con muebles*) furnishing **3.** TEAT scenery

decorado [de·ko·'ra·do] *m* TEAT set

decorador(a) [de·ko·ra·'dor, -·'do·ra] *m(f)*

decorator; TEAT set designer; ~ **de interiores** interior designer [*o* decorator]; ~ **de escaparates** window-dresser

decorar [de·ko·'rar] *vt* **1.** (*adornar*) to decorate **2.** (*con muebles*) to furnish; ~ **con moqueta** to carpet

decorativo, -a [de·ko·ra·'ti·βo, -a] *adj* decorative

decoro [de·'ko·ro] *m* **1.** (*dignidad*) dignity; **con** ~ with dignity **2.** (*respeto*) respect; **guardar el** ~ to show respect **3.** (*pudor*) decency; **con** ~ decently

decoroso, -a [de·ko·'ro·so, -a] *adj* **1.** (*decente*) decent **2.** (*digno*) dignified

decrecer [de·kre·'ser, -'θer] *irr como crecer vi* to decrease; (*nivel, fiebre*) to fall; ~ **en intensidad** to diminish in intensity

decrépito, -a [de·'kre·pi·to, -a] *adj* **1.** (*persona*) decrepit **2.** (*sociedad*) declining

decretar [de·kre·'tar] *vt* to decree

decreto [de·'kre·to] *m* decree; ~ **gubernamental** government decree

dedal [de·'dal] *m* thimble

dédalo ['de·da·lo] *m* **1.** (*laberinto*) labyrinth **2.** (*lío*) mess

dedear [de·de·'ar] *vt Méx* to finger

dedicación [de·di·ka·'sjon, -'θjon] *f* **1.** (*consagración*) consecration **2.** (*entrega*) dedication, commitment; ~ **plena** (*en el trabajo*) full-time

dedicar <c→qu> [de·di·'kar] **I.** *vt* **1.** (*destinar*) to dedicate **2.** (*consagrar*) to consecrate **II.** *vr:* ~**se** to devote oneself; ~**se a algo** (*profesionalmente*) to work as sth; ~**se a la enseñanza** to be a teacher; **¿a qué se dedica Ud.?** what do you do?

dedicatoria [de·di·ka·'to·rja] *f* dedication

dedillo [de·'di·jo, -ʎo] *m inf* **saberse algo al** ~ to know sth inside out

dedo ['de·do] *m* (*de mano*) finger; (*de pie*) toe; ~ **anular** ring finger; ~ **corazón** middle finger; ~ **gordo** big toe; ~ **índice** index finger, forefinger; ~ **meñique** little [*o* pinkie] finger; ~ **pulgar** thumb; **chuparse el** ~ *inf* to suck one's thumb; **señalar a alguien con el** ~ to point sb out ▶ **hacer** [*o* **ir a**] ~ to hitch-hike; **no mover un** ~ to not lift a finger; **nombrar a** ~ to hand-pick

deducción [de·duk·'sjon, -duɣ·'θjon] *f* **1.** (*derivación*) deduction **2.** ECON deduction; (*fiscal*) allowance, deduction; ~ **estándar** basic allowance; ~ **por hijo** child tax allowance

deducir [de·du·'sir, -'θir] *irr como traducir vt* **1.** (*derivar*) to deduce **2.** (*descontar*) to deduct

defecar <c→qu> [de·fe·'kar] *vi* to defecate

defecto [de·'fek·to] *m* **1.** (*carencia*) lack; **en** ~ **de** in the absence of; **en su** ~ (*cosa*) if it is unavailable; (*persona*) in his/her absence **2.** (*falta*) defect; ~ **físico** physical defect; ~ **genético** genetic defect

defectuoso, -a [de·fek·tu·'o·so, -a] *adj* faulty, defective

defender <e→ie> [de·fen·'der] **I.** *vt* **1.** (*ideas, contra ataques*) *t.* JUR to defend **2.** (*proteger*)

to protect **II.** *vr:* ~**se 1.** (*contra ataques*) to defend oneself **2.** (*arreglárselas*) to get by; **¿hablas francés? — me defiendo** do you speak French? — I can get by

defensa¹ [de·'fen·sa] *f* **1.** (*contra ataques*) *t.* JUR, DEP defense; **en legítima** ~ JUR in self-defense; **acudir en** ~ **de alguien** to come to sb's defense **2.** *pl t.* BIO defenses *pl;* **tener** ~**s** to have resistance **3.** *Méx* (*paragolpes*) bumper, fender

defensa² [de·'fen·sa] *mf* DEP defender

defensiva [de·fen·'si·βa] *f* defensive; **a la** ~ on the defensive

defensivo, -a [de·fen·'si·βo, -a] *adj* defensive

defensor(a) [de·fen·'sor, -·'so·ra] **I.** *adj* defending **II.** *m(f)* defender; ~ **de la naturaleza** environmental campaigner

deferencia [de·fe·'ren·sja, -θja] *f* (*consideración*) deference; (*cortesía*) courtesy; **por** ~ **a algo** in deference to sth; **tener la** ~ **de...** + *infin* to be so kind as to...

deficiencia [de·fi·'sjen·sja, -θja] *f* **1.** (*insuficiencia*) lack **2.** (*defecto*) deficiency

deficiente [de·fi·'sjen·te, -'θjen·te] **I.** *adj* **1.** (*insuficiente*) lacking **2.** (*defectuoso*) deficient **II.** *mf* ~ **mental** mentally handicapped person

déficit ['de·fi·sit, -θit] *m inv* **1.** FIN deficit; ~ **presupuestario** budget deficit **2.** (*escasez*) shortage

deficitario, -a [de·fi·si·'ta·rjo, -a; de·fi·θi-] *adj* (*empresa*) loss-making; (*cuenta*) in deficit

definición [de·fi·ni·'sjon, -'θjon] *f* (*aclaración*) *t.* TV definition; **por** ~ by definition

definido, -a [de·fi·'ni·do] *adj* (*claro*) definite

definir [de·fi·'nir] **I.** *vt* to define **II.** *vr:* ~**se** to take a stand

definitivo, -a [de·fi·ni·'ti·βo, -a] *adj* **1.** (*irrevocable*) final **2.** (*decisivo*) decisive ▶ **en definitiva** in short

deforestación [de·fo·res·ta·'sjon, -'θjon] *f* deforestation

deformación [de·for·ma·'sjon, -'θjon] *f* **1.** (*alteración*) distortion **2.** (*desfiguración*) deformation; ~ **física** physical deformity

deformar [de·for·'mar] **I.** *vt* **1.** (*alterar*) to distort **2.** (*desfigurar*) to deform **II.** *vr:* ~**se** to become deformed; (*jersey*) to lose its shape

deforme [de·'for·me] *adj* **1.** (*imagen*) distorted **2.** (*cuerpo*) deformed

deformidad [de·for·mi·'dad] *f* MED deformity

defraudar [de·frau·'dar] *vt* **1.** (*estafar*) to cheat; ~ **a Hacienda** to evade one's taxes **2.** (*decepcionar*) to disappoint

defunción [de·fun·'sjon, -'θjon] *f* death; **certificado de** ~ death certificate

degeneración [de·xe·ne·ra·'sjon, -'θjon] *f* (*proceso*) degeneration

degenerar [de·xe·ne·'rar] *vi* to degenerate

deglutir [de·ɣlu·'tir] *vt* to swallow

degollar <o→ue> [de·ɣo·'jar, -'ʎar] *vt* (*matar*) ~ **un animal** to slit an animal's throat; ~ **a alguien** (*decapitar*) to behead sb; (*cortar* *la garganta*) to slit sb's throat

degradación [de·γra·da·'sjon, -'θjon] *f* (*humillación*) humiliation

degradante [de·γra·'dan·te] *adj* demeaning

degradar [de·γra·'dar] I. *vt* 1.(*en el cargo*) to demote 2.(*calidad*) to worsen; ~ **el medio ambiente** to damage the environment 3.(*humillar*) to humiliate 4.(*color*) to tone down II. *vr* to degrade [*o* demean] oneself

degustación [de·γus·ta·'sjon, -'θjon] *f* tasting; ~ **de vinos** wine tasting

degustar [de·γus·'tar] *vt* to taste

dehesa [de·'e·sa] *f* pasture

deidad [dei·'dad] *f* (*dios*) deity

deificar <c→qu> [dei·fi·'kar] *vt* 1.(*divinizar*) to deify 2.(*ensalzar*) to idolize

dejadez [de·xa·'des, -'deθ] *f* 1.(*falta de aseo*) slovenliness 2.(*pereza*) laziness 3.(*negligencia*) neglect

dejado, -a [de·'xa·do, -a] *adj* 1. *ser* (*descuidado*) slovenly 2. *estar* (*abatido*) dejected

dejar [de·'xar] I. *vi* ~ **de hacer algo** to stop doing sth; **no dejes de escribirles** don't fail to write them; **¡no deje de venir!** make sure you come! II. *vt* 1.(*en general*) to leave; ~ **el libro sobre la mesa** to leave the book on the table; ~ **acabado** to finish; ~ **caer** to drop; ~ **claro** to make clear; ~ **constancia de algo** to put sth on record; ~ **a deber** to owe; ~ **en libertad** to set free; ~ **algo para mañana** to leave sth for tomorrow; ~ **a alguien en paz** to leave sb in peace; **¡déjanos en paz!** leave us alone!; ~ **mucho que desear** to leave a lot to be desired; ~ **algo sin lavar** to leave sth dirty; ~ **triste** to sadden 2.(*abandonar*) to leave; ~ **la carrera** to drop out of university 3.(*ganancia*) to give 4.(*permitir: algo*) to allow, to let; **no me dejan salir** they won't let me go out 5.(*entregar*) to give; (*prestar*) to lend; (*en herencia*) to leave; ~ **un recado** to leave a message; ~ **algo en manos de alguien** to leave sth in sb's hands III. *vr:* ~ **se** 1.(*descuidarse*) to neglect oneself 2.(*olvidar*) to forget ▶ ~ **se caer** to hint; ~ **se llevar** to let oneself get carried away; ~ **se querer** to let oneself be loved

deje ['de·xe] *m* lilt; **se te nota un ~ argentino** you have a slight Argentine accent

dejo ['de·xo] *m* 1.(*entonación*) lilt; (*acento*) accent 2.(*regusto*) *t. fig* aftertaste

del [del] *v.* = **de** + **el** *v.* **de**

delantal [de·lan·'tal] *m* apron

delante [de·'lan·te] I. *adv* 1.(*ante, en la parte delantera*) in front; **de** ~ from the front; **abierto por** ~ open at the front 2.(*enfrente*) opposite II. *prep* ~ **de** in front of; ~ **mío** [*o* **de mí**] in front of me

delantera [de·lan·'te·ra] *f* 1.(*parte anterior*) front (part) 2.(*primera fila*) front row 3.(*distancia*) lead; **coger la ~ a alguien** to gain a lead on sb; **llevar la ~ a alguien** to have a lead over sb 4. DEP forward line

delantero [de·lan·'te·ro] *m* 1.(*parte anterior*) front (part) 2. DEP forward; ~ **centro** center forward

delantero, -a [de·lan·'te·ro, -a] *adj* front

delatar [de·la·'tar] I. *vt* 1.(*denunciar*) to inform on 2.(*manifestar*) to reveal II. *vr:* ~ **se** to give oneself away

delegación [de·le·γa·'sjon, -'θjon] *f* 1.(*atribución, comisión*) delegation; ~ **de poderes** delegation; **actuar por ~ de alguien** to act on behalf of sb 2.(*oficina*) local office; (*filial*) branch; **Delegación de Hacienda** (local) tax office 3. *Méx* (*comisaría*) police station; (*ayuntamiento*) council

delegado, -a [de·le·'γa·do, -a] *m, f* delegate; ~ **gubernamental** government representative

delegar <g→gu> [de·le·'γar] *vt* 1.(*encargar*) ~ **algo en alguien** to delegate sth to sb 2.(*transferir*) to transfer

deleitar [de·lei·'tar] I. *vt* to delight II. *vr* ~ **se con** [*o* **en**] **algo** to delight in sth

deleite [de·'lei·te] *m* delight; **con** ~ with pleasure

deletrear [de·le·tre·'ar] *vt* to spell

deleznable [de·les·'na·βle, de·leθ-] *adj* 1.(*frágil*) fragile 2.(*inconsistente*) weak; (*despreciable*) contemptible

delfín [del·'fin] *m* dolphin

delgado, -a [del·'γa·do, -a] *adj* thin; (*esbelto*) slender

deliberado, -a [de·li·βe·'ra·do, -a] *adj* 1.(*tratado*) considered 2.(*intencionado*) deliberate

deliberar [de·li·βe·'rar] *vi, vt* 1.(*reflexionar*) to deliberate 2.(*discutir*) ~ **sobre** [*o* **acerca de**] **algo** to discuss sth

delicadeza [de·li·ka·'de·sa, -θa] *f* 1.(*finura*) delicacy; **con** ~ delicately 2.(*debilidad*) weakness 3.(*miramiento*) attentiveness; **tener la ~ de...** to be thoughtful enough to...

delicado, -a [de·li·'ka·do, -a] *adj* 1.(*fino, frágil*) delicate 2.(*exquisito*) fine 3.(*atento*) thoughtful 4.(*enfermizo*) frail; **ser ~ de salud** to suffer from poor health 5.(*asunto*) delicate 6.(*exigente*) demanding

delicia [de·'li·sja, -θja] *f* delight

delicioso, -a [de·li·'sjo·so, -a; -'θjo·so, -a] *adj* (*persona, cosa*) delightful; (*comida*) delicious

delictivo, -a [de·lik·'ti·βo, -a] *adj* criminal; **acto** ~ criminal act

delimitar [de·li·mi·'tar] *vt* 1.(*terreno*) to mark out 2.(*definir*) to define

delincuencia [de·lin·'kwen·sja, -θja] *f* crime, delinquency; ~ **juvenil** juvenile delinquency

delincuente [de·lin·'kwen·te] I. *adj* criminal II. *mf* criminal; ~ **reincidente** persistent offender

delinear [de·li·ne·'ar] *vt* to draw

delinquir <qu→c> [de·lin·'kir] *vi* to commit an offense

delirar [de·li·'rar] *vi* 1.(*desvariar*) to be delirious 2.(*disparatar*) to talk nonsense

delirio [de·'li·rjo] *m* 1.(*enfermedad*) delirium 2.(*ilusión*) delusion; ~ **s de grandeza** delusions of grandeur

delito [de·'li·to] *m* crime; ~ **contra los derechos humanos** human rights violation; ~ **de guerra** war crime; **cuerpo del** ~ corpus delicti; ~ **común** common offence

delta ['del·ta] *m* **1.** GEO delta **2.** DEP **ala** ~ (*aparato*) hang-glider; (*actividad*) hang-gliding

demacrarse [de·ma·'krar·se] *vr* to become haggard

demagogia [de·ma·'ɣo·xja] *f* demagoguery

demanda [de·'man·da] *f* **1.** (*petición*) request; ~ **de empleo** job application; ~ **de extradición** JUR extradition request; **en** ~ **de algo** in search of sth **2.** COM ~ **de algo** demand for sth; ~ **adicional** surplus demand; ~ **agregada** total demand; ~ **energética** energy demands *pl*; **tener mucha** ~ to be in great demand **3.** JUR action, lawsuit; **presentar una** ~ **contra alguien** to bring an action against sb

demandado, -a [de·man·'da·do, -a] **I.** *adj* (*solicitado*) requested **II.** *m, f* JUR defendant

demandante [de·man·'dan·te] **I.** *adj* JUR **parte** ~ plaintiff **II.** *mf* claimant; JUR plaintiff

demandar [de·man·'dar] *vt* **1.** (*pedir*) to ask for; (*solicitar*) to request **2.** JUR ~ **por algo** to sue for sth

demarcación [de·mar·ka·'sjon, -'θjon] *f* (*delimitación*) demarcation

demás [de·'mas] **I.** *adj* other; ...**y** ~ ... (*y otros*) ...and other...; **y** ~ (*etcétera*) and so on; **por lo** ~ otherwise **II.** *adv* besides, moreover; **por** ~ more; **está por** ~ **que** +*subj* there is no point (in)

demasía [de·ma·'si·a] *f* **1.** (*exceso*) excess; **en** ~ in excess **2.** (*insolencia*) insolence

demasiado [de·ma·'sja·do] *adv* (+ *adj*) too; (+ *verbo*) too much; **comió** ~ he/she ate too much

demasiado, -a [de·ma·'sja·do] *adj* (*singular*) too much; (*plural*) too many; **hace** ~ **calor** it's too hot; **demasiado vino** too much wine; **demasiados libros** too many books

demencia [de·'men·sja, -θja] *f* **1.** MED dementia; ~ **senil** senile dementia **2.** (*locura*) madness, insanity

demencial [de·men·'sjal, -'θjal] *adj*, **demente** [de·'men·te] *adj* insane

demérito [de·'me·ri·to] *m* **1.** (*falta de mérito*) fault **2.** (*perjuicio*) disadvantage; **obrar en** ~ **de alguien** to count against sb

democracia [de·mo·'kra·sja, -θja] *f* democracy

demócrata [de·'mo·kra·ta] **I.** *adj* democratic **II.** *mf* democrat

democrático, -a [de·mo·'kra·ti·ko, -a] *adj* democratic

democratizar <z→c> [de·mo·kra·ti·'sar, -'θar] **I.** *vt* to democratize **II.** *vr:* ~**se** to become democratic

demográfico, -a [de·mo·'ɣra·fi·ko, -a] *adj* demographic; **explosión demográfica** population explosion; **estadísticas demográficas** vital statistics

demoler <o→ue> [de·mo·'ler] *vt* **1.** (*edificio*)

to demolish **2.** *fig* (*destruir*) to destroy

demonio [de·'mo·njo] *m* **1.** (*espíritu*) demon **2.** (*diablo*) devil; **ser el mismísimo** ~ to be a real devil ▸ **de mil** ~**s** dreadful; **saber a** ~**s** to taste awful; **tentar al** ~ to tempt fate; **¡véte al** ~! go to hell!; **cómo/dónde/qué** ~**s**... how/where/what the hell...; **como un** ~ like a madman; **¡~(s)!** damn!

demora [de·'mo·ra] *f* delay

demorar [de·mo·'rar] **I.** *vt* to delay **II.** *vr:* ~**se 1.** (*retrasarse*) ~**se en hacer algo** to delay in doing sth **2.** (*detenerse*) to be held up

demostración [de·mos·tra·'sjon, -'θjon] *f* **1.** (*prueba*) test **2.** (*argumentación*) proof **3.** (*explicación*) explanation **4.** (*exteriorización*) display **5.** (*exhibición*) exhibition, demonstration

demostrar <o→ue> [de·mos·'trar] *vt* **1.** (*probar*) to demonstrate **2.** (*mostrar, exhibir*) to show **3.** (*explicar*) to explain

demostrativo, -a [de·mos·tra·'ti·βo, -a] *adj* (*probatorio*) evidential; **documento** ~ **del pago** document showing proof of payment

demudado, -a [de·mu·'da·do, -a] *adj* (*pálido*) pale

demudar [de·mu·'dar] **I.** *vt* **1.** (*variar*) to alter; **la mala noticia le demudó el rostro** he/she was visibly distressed by the bad news **2.** (*desfigurar*) to distort **II.** *vr:* ~**se 1.** (*de color*) to go pale **2.** (*desfigurarse*) to change

denegar [de·ne·'ɣar] *irr como fregar vt* **1.** (*negar*) to deny; ~ **un derecho a alguien** to deny sb a right **2.** (*rechazar*) to refuse; ~ **una solicitud** to reject a request

denigrar [de·ni·'ɣrar] *vt* **1.** (*humillar*) to denigrate **2.** (*calumniar*) to vilify **3.** (*injuriar*) to insult

denominación [de·no·mi·na·'sjon, -'θjon] *f* **1.** (*nombre*) name **2.** (*acción*) naming; **Denominación de Origen** guarantee of region of origin of wine or food **3.** FIN denomination

denominador [de·no·mi·na·'dor] *m* MAT denominator; **reducir a un común** ~ *t. fig* to reduce to a common denominator

denominar [de·no·mi·'nar] **I.** *vt* (*llamar*) to name **II.** *vr:* ~**se** to be called

denotar [de·no·'tar] *vt* (*significar*) to denote

densidad [den·si·'dad] *f* density

denso, -a ['den·so, -a] *adj* **1.** (*compacto*) dense **2.** (*espeso*) thick **3.** (*pesado*) heavy

dentadura [den·ta·'du·ra] *f* teeth *pl*; ~ **postiza** false teeth

dental [den·'tal] *adj* dental

dentellada [den·te·'ja·da, -'ʎa·da] *f* **1.** (*mordisco*) bite; **comer algo a** ~**s** to wolf sth down; **matar a alguien a** ~**s** (*fiera*) to tear sb to bits; **pelearse a** ~**s** to fight tooth and nail **2.** (*herida*) bite

dentera [den·'te·ra] *f* **dar** ~ **a alguien** (*dar grima*) to set sb's teeth on edge; *inf* (*dar envidia*) to make sb jealous

dentífrico [den·'ti·fri·ko] *m* toothpaste

dentífrico, -a [den·'ti·fri·ko, -a] *adj* **pasta dentífrica** toothpaste
dentista [den·'tis·ta] I. *adj* dental II. *mf* dentist
dentro ['den·tro] I. *adv* inside; **a** ~ inside; **desde** ~ from within; **por** ~ inside II. *prep* 1. (*local*) ~ **de** inside 2. (*con movimiento*) ~ **de** into; **mirar** ~ **de la habitación** to look into the room 3. (*temporal*) ~ **de** within; ~ **de poco** soon ▶ ~ **de lo posible** as far as possible
denuncia [de·'nun·sja, -θja] *f* 1. (*acusación*) accusation; **hacer una** ~ **ante alguien por algo** to make [*o* file] a complaint to sb about sth; **hacer una** ~ **por falta de pago** to make an official complaint of nonpayment 2. (*de una injusticia*) denunciation; **ser una** ~ **de algo** to expose sth 3. (*tratado*) cancellation
denunciar [de·nun·'sjar, -'θjar] *vt* 1. (*acusar*) ~ **a alguien por algo** to accuse sb of sth 2. (*delatar*) to betray 3. (*hacer público*) to expose; **oficial, quiero** ~ **un robo** officer, I want to report a robbery 4. (*tratado*) to cancel
deparar [de·pa·'rar] *vt* to bring
departamento [de·par·ta·'men·to] *m* 1. (*de un establecimiento*) *t.* UNIV department; ~ **de contabilidad** accounts department 2. (*de un objeto*) compartment 3. (*distrito*) district 4. *AmL* (*apartamento*) apartment
departir [de·par·'tir] *vi* to converse
dependencia [de·pen·'den·sja, -θja] *f* 1. (*sujeción*) dependency; **vivir en** ~ **de alguien** to be dependent on sb 2. (*sección*) section 3. *pl* (*habitaciones*) rooms *pl*
depender [de·pen·'der] *vi* **depender de algo/alguien** to depend on sth/sb; **¡depende!** it depends!; **depende de ti** it's up to you
dependiente [de·pen·'djen·te] *adj* ~ **de algo/alguien** dependent on sth/sb
dependiente, -a [de·pen·'djen·te, -a] *m, f* dependent; (*de una tienda*) shop assistant
depilación [de·pi·la·'sjon, -'θjon] *f* hair removal
depilar [de·pi·'lar] I. *vt* to remove hair from II. *vr* ~**se las cejas** to pluck one's eyebrows; ~**se las piernas** (*con cera*) to wax one's legs; (*con maquinilla*) to shave one's legs
deplorable [de·plo·'ra·βle] *adj* deplorable; **espectáculo** ~ dreadful scene
deplorar [de·plo·'rar] *vt* 1. (*lamentar*) to regret deeply 2. (*condenar*) to deplore
deponer [de·po·'ner] *irr como poner* I. *vt* 1. (*destituir*) to remove; (*monarca*) to depose; ~ **de un cargo** to remove from a position 2. (*deshacerse de*) to set aside; ~ **las armas** to lay down one's weapons II. *vi* to give evidence, to testify
deportación [de·por·ta·'sjon, -'θjon] *f* deportation
deportar [de·por·'tar] *vt* to deport
deporte [de·'por·te] *m* sport; ~ **de** (**alta**) **competición** competitive sport; ~ **hípico** equestrian sport; ~**s de invierno** winter sports; **hacer** ~ to practice sports

deportista [de·por·'tis·ta] I. *adj* sporty II. *mf* sportsman *m*, sportswoman *f*; ~ **aficionado** amateur sportsman *m*, amateur sportswoman *f*; ~ **profesional** professional sportsman *m*, professional sportswoman *f*
deportivo [de·por·'ti·βo] *m* 1. (*club*) sports club 2. (*automóvil*) sports car
deportivo, -a [de·por·'ti·βo, -a] *adj* sporting; **noticias deportivas** sports news; (*zapatillas*) **deportivas** sneakers
depositar [de·po·si·'tar] I. *vt* to deposit; (*cadáver*) to lay out; ~ **su confianza en alguien** to place one's trust in sb II. *vr:* ~**se** to settle
depósito [de·'po·si·to] *m* 1. (*acción de guardar*) keeping; **en** ~ bonded 2. (*acción de poner al cuidado*) depositing 3. (*almacén*) warehouse; ~ **de armas** weapons store; ~ **de cadáveres** morgue, mortuary; ~ **de objetos perdidos** lost-and-found 4. AUTO gas tank 5. *t.* FIN deposit; **hacer un** ~ to make a deposit
depravar [de·pra·'βar] I. *vt* to corrupt II. *vr:* ~**se** to become depraved
depre ['de·pre] *f inf* **estar con la** ~ to be feeling down
depreciación [de·pre·sja·'sjon, -θja·'θjon] *f* (*desvalorización*) depreciation; ~ **monetaria** devaluation
depreciar [de·pre·'sjar, -'θjar] I. *vt* (*desvalorizar*) to depreciate; (*moneda*) to devalue II. *vr:* ~**se** to depreciate
depredación [de·pre·da·'sjon, -'θjon] *f* (*saqueo*) pillage
depredador(a) [de·pre·da·'dor, -·'do·ra] *adj* ZOOL predatory
depredar [de·pre·'dar] *vt* (*saquear*) to pillage
depresión [de·pre·'sjon] *f* 1. (*tristeza*) depression 2. ECON, METEO depression; ~ **cíclica** cyclical depression; ~ **económica** recession, slump
depresivo, -a [de·pre·'si·βo, -a] *adj* 1. (*que deprime*) depressing 2. (*propenso a*) depressive
deprimir [de·pri·'mir] I. *vt* (*abatir*) to depress II. *vr:* ~**se** (*abatirse*) to become depressed
deprisa [de·'pri·sa] *adv* fast, quickly; ~ **y corriendo** in a rush
depuración [de·pu·ra·'sjon, -'θjon] *f* purification; POL purge
depurado, -a [de·pu·'ra·do, -a] *adj* (*estilo*) polished
depuradora [de·pu·ra·'do·ra] *f* (*de agua*) water-treatment plant; ~ **de aguas residuales** sewage plant
depurar [de·pu·'rar] *vt* 1. (*purificar*) to purify; ~ **el estilo** to polish one's style 2. POL to purge
derecha [de·'re·tʃa] *f* 1. (*lado*) right-hand side; **a la** ~ (*estar*) on the right; (*ir*) to the right; **doblar a la** ~ to turn right; **tengo a mi madre a la** ~ my mother is on my right; **rebasar por la** ~ to go down to the right 2. POL right (wing); **de** ~(**s**) right-wing
derechista [de·re·'tʃis·ta] I. *adj* POL right-wing II. *mf* POL right-winger

D

derecho [de·'re·ʧo] **I.** *adv* straight **II.** *m* **1.** (*legitimidad*) right; ~ **de asociación** freedom of association; ~**s de pago de indemnización** right to receive compensation; ~**s de propiedad intelectual** intellectual property rights; ~ **de sufragio** right to vote; **con** ~ **a** with the right to; **miembro de pleno** ~ full member; **estar en su** (**perfecto**) ~ to be within one's rights; **hacer uso de un** ~ to exercise one's right; **por** ~ **propio** in one's own right; **tener** ~ **a** to have the right to **2.** (*jurisprudencia, ciencia*) law; ~ **criminal** criminal law; ~ **político** political law; **estudiar** ~ to study law; **conforme a** ~ lawful; **de** ~ by right **3.** (*de un papel, una tela*) right side **4.** *pl* (*impuestos*) duties *pl;* ~**s de exportación** export duties; **libre de** ~**s** duty-free; **sujeto a** ~**s** subject to duty **5.** *pl* (*honorarios*) fee(s); ~**s de mediación** intermediary fee; ~**s de autor** royalties, copyright

derecho, -a [de·'re·ʧo, -a] *adj* **1.** (*diestro*) right; **lado** ~ right-hand side **2.** (*recto*) straight **3.** (*erguido*) upright; **ponerse** ~ to stand up straight **4.** (*justo*) honest; **a derechas** fairly **5.** (*directo*) direct

derivación [de·ri·βa·'sjon, -'θjon] *f* **1.** MAT derivative; ~ **a tierra** ELEC earth connection **2.** (*de agua*) channel

derivado [de·ri·'βa·do] *m* derivative

derivar [de·ri·'βar] **I.** *vi* **1.** (*proceder*) to derive **2.** (*tornar*) ~ **hacia algo** to turn towards sth **II.** *vt* **1.** *t.* MAT, LING (*deducir*) to derive **2.** (*desviar*) to divert; ~ **una conversación hacia otro tema** to move on to another topic **3.** ELEC to shunt **III.** *vr* ~**se de algo** to come from sth

dermatólogo, -a [der·ma·'to·lo·ɣo, -a] *m, f* dermatologist

dérmico, -a ['der·mi·ko, -a] *adj* skin, dermal

derogación [de·ro·ɣa·'sjon, -'θjon] *f* (*de una ley*) repeal

derogar <g→gu> [de·ro·'ɣar] *vt* (*una ley*) to repeal

derramamiento [de·rra·ma·'mjen·to] *m* spilling; (*de sangre, lágrimas*) shedding

derramar [de·rra·'mar] **I.** *vt* **1.** (*verter*) to pour; (*sin querer*) to spill; (*lágrimas, sangre*) to shed **2.** (*repartir*) ~ **un gasto** to share out an expense **II.** *vr:* ~**se 1.** (*esparcirse: líquidos*) to spill; (*otros*) to scatter **2.** (*desaguar*) ~ **en algo** to leak onto sth **3.** (*diseminarse*) to spread

derrame [de·'rra·me] *m* **1.** *v.* **derramamiento 2.** MED hemorrhage

derrapar [de·rra·'par] *vi* to skid

derredor [de·rre·'dor] *m* surroundings; **en** ~ around

derrengado, -a [de·rren·'ga·do, -a] *adj* (*exhausto*) exhausted

derretir [de·rre·'tir] *irr como pedir* **I.** *vt* **1.** (*deshacer*) to melt **2.** (*derrochar*) to squander **II.** *vr:* ~**se 1.** (*deshacerse*) to melt **2.** *inf* (*consumirse*) ~**se de calor** to be boiling hot

derribar [de·rri·'βar] *vt* **1.** (*edificio*) to demolish, to knock down, to tear down; (*puerta*) to

batter down; (*árbol*) to fell; (*avión*) to shoot down **2.** (*jinete*) to knock off; (*boxeador*) to knock down **3.** (*del cargo, poder*) to remove; (*gobierno*) to overthrow

derrocar <c→qu> [de·rro·'kar] *vt* **1.** (*despeñar: persona*) to knock over; (*edificio*) to knock down, to tear down **2.** (*destituir*) to remove

derrochador(a) [de·rro·ʧa·'dor, -·'do·ra] *adj, m(f)* spendthrift

derrochar [de·rro·'ʧar] *vt* **1.** (*despilfarrar*) to squander **2.** *inf* (*tener en abundancia*) to be brimming with

derroche [de·'rro·ʧe] *m* **1.** (*despilfarro*) waste **2.** (*exceso*) profusion

derrota [de·'rro·ta] *f* **1.** (*fracaso*) defeat **2.** NÁUT course

derrotar [de·rro·'tar] *vt* **1.** (*vencer*) to defeat **2.** (*desmoralizar*) to demoralize

derrotero [de·rro·'te·ro] *m* (*rumbo*) course; **ir por nuevos** ~**s** *fig* to follow a new course

derruir [de·rru·'ir] *irr como huir* *vt* **1.** (*derribar*) to knock [o tear] down **2.** (*destruir*) to destroy

derrumbamiento [de·rrum·ba·'mjen·to] *m* (*de un edificio*) demolition

derrumbar [de·rrum·'bar] **I.** *vt* **1.** (*despeñar, derruir*) to knock [o tear] down **2.** (*moralmente*) to devastate **II.** *vr:* ~**se 1.** (*edificio*) to fall down **2.** (*esperanzas*) to collapse

desabotonar [de·sa·βo·to·'nar] *vt, vr:* ~**se** to unbutton

desabrido, -a [de·sa·'βri·do, -a] *adj* **1.** (*comida*) insipid **2.** (*tiempo*) bad **3.** (*persona*) disagreeable

desabrigado, -a [de·sa·βri·'ɣa·do, -a] *adj* unprotected; **estar** ~ (*persona*) to be too lightly dressed

desabrochar [de·sa·βro·'ʧar] *vt, vr:* ~**se** (*botones, hebillas, ganchos*) to undo, to unfasten; (*cordones*) to untie

desacatar [de·sa·ka·'tar] *vt* to disobey

desacato [de·sa·'ka·to] *m* ~ **a algo** disrespect for sth; JUR contempt (of court)

desacertado, -a [de·sa·ser·'ta·do, -a; de·sa·θer-] *adj* **1.** (*equivocado*) mistaken **2.** (*inapropiado*) unfortunate

desacierto [de·sa·'sjer·to, -'θjer·to] *m* mistake

desaconsejar [de·sa·kon·se·'xar] *vt* to advise against; ~ **algo a alguien** to advise sb against sth

desacorde [de·sa·'kor·de] *adj* (*opinión*) conflicting; **estar** ~ **con algo/alguien** to not agree with sth/sb

desacostumbrado, -a [de·sa·kos·tum·'bra·do, -a] *adj* (*fuera de la rutina*) unaccustomed; (*no común*) unusual

desacostumbrar [de·sa·kos·tum·'brar] **I.** *vt* ~ **a alguien de algo** to break sb of the habit of sth **II.** *vr* ~**se a** [o de] **hacer algo** (*perder el hábito*) to get out of the habit of doing sth; (*perder la rutina*) to become unused to sth

desacreditar [de·sa·kre·di·'tar] **I.** *vt* to discredit **II.** *vr:* ~**se** to become discredited

desactivar [des·ak·ti·'βar] *vt* (*explosivos*) to defuse

desacuerdo [de·sa·'kwer·do] *m* (*discrepancia*) disagreement; **estar en ~** to disagree

desafiar <*l. pres:* desafío> [de·sa·fi·'ar] I. *vt* 1. (*retar*) to challenge 2. (*hacer frente a*) to defy II. *vr:* ~**se** to challenge each other

desafinado, -a [de·sa·fi·'na·do, -a] *adj* (*tono*) out of tune

desafinar [de·sa·fi·'nar] *vi* MÚS (*al cantar*) to sing out of tune; (*al tocar*) to play out of tune; (*instrumento*) to be out of tune

desafío [de·sa·'fi·o] *m* 1. (*reto, prueba*) challenge 2. (*duelo*) duel

desaforado, -a [de·sa·fo·'ra·do, -a] *adj* 1. (*fuera de la ley*) lawless 2. (*desmedido*) excessive

desafortunado, -a [de·sa·for·tu·'na·do, -a] *adj* unlucky

desafuero [de·sa·'fwe·ro] *m* outrage

desagradable [de·sa·ɣra·'da·βle] *adj* unpleasant; **ser ~ al tacto/gusto** to feel/taste unpleasant

desagradar [de·sa·ɣra·'dar] *vi* to displease; **me desagrada...** I don't like...

desagradecido, -a [de·sa·ɣra·de·'si·do, -a; -'θi·do, -a] *adj* ungrateful

desagrado [de·sa·'ɣra·do] *m* displeasure

desagraviar [de·sa·ɣra·'βjar] I. *vt* 1. (*excusarse*) to apologize 2. (*compensar*) to compensate II. *vr* ~ **se de algo** to make amends for sth

desaguar <gu→gü> [de·sa·'ɣwar] I. *vi* 1. (*desembocar*) to flow 2. (*verterse*) to spill II. *vt* (*desecar*) to drain; ~ **el sótano** to pump water out of the cellar III. *vr:* ~**se** (*verterse*) to spill

desagüe [de·'sa·ɣwe] *m* drain

desaguisado [de·sa·ɣi·'sa·do] *m* 1. (*agravio*) offense 2. *inf* (*lío*) mess

desaguisado, -a [de·sa·ɣi·'sa·do, -a] *adj* 1. (*ilegal*) illegal 2. (*escandaloso*) outrageous

desahogado, -a [de·sa·o·'ɣa·do, -a] *adj* 1. (*lugar*) spacious; (*prenda*) loose 2. (*adinerado*) well-off 3. (*descarado*) shameless

desahogar <g→gu> [de·sa·o·'ɣar] I. *vt* 1. (*aliviar*) to relieve 2. (*consolar*) to console II. *vr:* ~**se** 1. (*desfogarse*) to let off steam 2. (*confiarse*) ~**se con alguien** to tell one's troubles to sb 3. (*recuperarse*) to recover

desahogo [de·sa·'o·ɣo] *m* 1. (*alivio*) relief 2. (*reposo*) rest 3. (*holgura económica*) comfort

desahuciado, -a [de·sau·'sja·do, -a; -'θja·do, -a] *adj* 1. (*enfermo*) hopeless 2. (*inquilino*) dispossessed

desahuciar [de·sau·'sjar, -'θjar] I. *vt* 1. (*enfermo*) to declare past saving 2. (*inquilino*) to evict 3. (*quitar la esperanza*) to deprive of hope II. *vr:* ~**se** to lose all hope

desairar [de·sai·'rar] *irr como airar vt* 1. (*humillar*) to insult 2. (*desestimar*) to slight 3. (*rechazar*) to snub

desaire [de·'sai·re] *m* 1. (*humillación*) insult 2. (*desprecio*) disdain 3. (*desatención*) discourtesy

desajustar [de·sa·xus·'tar] I. *vt* 1. (*desordenar*) to put out of balance; (*aparato*) to put out of order 2. (*aflojar*) to loosen II. *vr:* ~**se** 1. (*desavenir*) to break down 2. (*aflojarse*) to come loose

desajuste [de·sa·'xus·te] *m* 1. (*desorden*) imbalance 2. (*desconcierto*) confusion 3. (*de aparatos*) breakdown

desalentador(a) [de·sa·len·ta·'dor, -'do·ra] *adj* discouraging

desalentar <e→ie> [de·sa·len·'tar] I. *vt* (*desesperanzar*) to discourage II. *vr:* ~**se** to lose heart

desaliento [de·sa·'ljen·to] *m* 1. (*falta de valor*) dismay 2. (*de fuerzas*) weakness

desaliñado, -a [de·sa·li·'na·do, -a] *adj* shabby

desalmado, -a [de·sal·'ma·do, -a] I. *adj* heartless II. *m, f* swine

desalojar [de·sa·lo·'xar] I. *vi* to move out II. *vt* (*abandonar: casa*) to vacate; (*puesto*) to leave; (*persona*) to eject; (*cosa*) to dislodge

desamor [de·sa·'mor] *m* 1. (*falta de amor*) indifference 2. (*aborrecimiento*) dislike

desamparado, -a [des·am·pa·'ra·do, -a] *adj* (*persona*) defenseless

desamparar [des·am·pa·'rar] *vt* 1. (*dejar*) to abandon 2. (*desasistir*) to fail to help

desamparo [des·am·'pa·ro] *m* 1. (*falta de protección*) defenselessness 2. (*abandono*) abandonment

desamueblado, -a [de·sa·mwe·'βla·do, -a] *adj* unfurnished

desamueblar [de·sa·mwe·'βlar] *vt* ~ **algo** to remove the furniture from sth

desandar [des·an·'dar] *irr como andar vt* ~ **lo andado** to retrace one's steps; *fig* to go back to square one; **no se puede ~ lo andado** *prov* it's no use crying over spilled milk *prov*

desangrar [de·san·'grar] I. *vt* 1. (*animales*) to bleed 2. (*arruinar*) to bleed dry II. *vr:* ~**se** 1. (*perder mucha sangre*) to bleed heavily 2. (*morirse*) to bleed to death

desanimado, -a [de·sa·ni·'ma·do, -a] *adj* 1. (*persona*) downhearted 2. (*lugar*) lifeless

desanimar [de·sa·ni·'mar] I. *vt* to discourage II. *vr:* ~**se** to lose heart

desánimo [de·'sa·ni·mo] *m* dejection

desanudar [de·sa·nu·'dar] *vt* (*nudo*) to untie

desapacible [de·sa·pa·'si·βle, -'θi·βle] *adj* unpleasant

desaparecer [de·sa·pa·re·'ser, -'θer] *irr como crecer vi* to disappear; ~ **del mapa** to vanish off the face of the earth; (*en guerra*) to go missing, to be missing in action

desaparecido, -a [de·sa·pa·re·'si·do, -a; -'θi·do, -a] *adj* missing

desaparición [de·sa·pa·ri·'sjon, -'θjon] *f* disappearance

desapego [de·sa·'pe·ɣo] *m* indifference

desapercibido, -a [de·sa·per·si·'βi·do, -a; de·sa·per·θi-] *adj* 1. (*inadvertido*) unnoticed;

pasar ~ to go unnoticed **2.** (*desprevenido*) unprepared; **coger** ~ to catch unawares [*o* off guard]

desaprensivo, -a [de·sa·pren·'si·βo, -a] *adj* unscrupulous

desaprobar <o→ue> [de·sa·pro·'βar] *vt* **1.** (*conducta*) ~ **algo** to disapprove of sth **2.** (*solicitud*) to reject

desaprovechar [de·sa·pro·βe·'tʃar] *vt* to waste

desarmador [des·ar·ma·'dor] *m Méx* (*destornillador*) screwdriver

desarmar [des·ar·'mar] **I.** *vi* POL to disarm **II.** *vt* **1.** (*dejar sin armas*) to disarm; (*argumentos*) to confound **2.** (*desmontar*) to take apart

desarme [des·'ar·me] *m* POL disarmament

desarraigar <g→gu> [de·sa·rrai·'yar] *vt* **1.** (*árbol, persona*) to uproot **2.** (*costumbre, creencia*) to eradicate

desarraigo [de·sa·'rrai·yo] *m* **1.** (*de árbol, persona*) uprooting **2.** (*de costumbre, creencia*) eradication

desarreglo [de·sa·'rre·ylo] *m* **1.** (*desorden: cuarto, persona*) untidiness; (*vida*) confusion **2.** (*desperfecto, molestia*) problem; (*en el coche*) trouble

desarrollar [de·sa·rro·'jar, -'ʎar] **I.** *vt* **1.** (*aumentar*) to develop; ~ **relaciones comerciales** to develop trade relations **2.** (*tratar en detalle*) to expound **II.** *vr:* ~ **se 1.** (*progresar*) to develop **2.** (*tener lugar*) to take place

desarrollo [de·sa·'rro·jo, -ʎo] *m* **1.** *t.* FOTO development; **ayuda al** ~ development aid; **país en vías de** ~ developing country **2.** (*crecimiento*) growth; ~ **profesional** professional development

desarticular [des·ar·ti·ku·'lar] **I.** *vt* **1.** (*mecanismo*) to dismantle **2.** (*articulación*) to dislocate **3.** (*grupo*) to break up **II.** *vr:* ~ **se 1.** (*mecanismo*) to come apart; (*piezas*) to come loose **2.** (*articulación*) to become dislocated **3.** (*grupo*) to break up

desaseado, -a [de·sa·se·'a·do, -a] *adj* (*sucio*) dirty; (*desordenado*) untidy

desasir [de·sa·'sir] *irr como asir* **I.** *vt* ~ **algo** to let go of sth **II.** *vr:* ~ **se 1.** (*desprenderse*) to come off **2.** (*desacostumbrarse*) to let go

desasosegar [de·sa·so·se·'yar] *irr como fregar* **I.** *vt* to worry **II.** *vr:* ~ **se** to become uneasy

desasosiego [de·sa·so·'sje·yo] *m* unease

desastre [de·'sas·tre] *m* disaster; **ser un** ~ *inf* (*alguien*) to be hopeless; (*algo*) to be a flop

desastroso, -a [de·sas·'tro·so, -a] *adj* disastrous

desatado, -a [de·sa·'ta·do, -a] *adj* **1.** (*desligado*) untied **2.** (*desenfrenado*) wild; **estar** ~ to be out of control

desatar [de·sa·'tar] **I.** *vt* **1.** (*soltar*) to untie; (*nudo, paquete, zapatos*) to undo **2.** (*causar*) to unleash **II.** *vr:* ~ **se 1.** (*soltarse*) to untie oneself; (*nudo*) to come undone **2.** (*desligarse*) to free oneself **3.** (*desencadenarse: tormenta*) to

break; (*crisis*) to erupt **4.** (*perder la contención*) ~ **se en improperios** to let loose a stream of abuse

desatascar <c→qu> [de·sa·tas·'kar] *vt* **1.** (*desobstruir*) to unblock **2.** (*sacar del atascadero*) to pull out

desatención [de·sa·ten·'sjon, -'θjon] *f* **1.** (*distracción*) inattention **2.** (*descortesía*) discourtesy

desatender <e→ie> [de·sa·ten·'der] *vt* **1.** (*desoír*) to ignore **2.** (*abandonar*) to neglect

desatento, -a [de·sa·'ten·to, -a] *adj* **1.** (*distraído*) inattentive; (*negligente*) careless **2.** (*descortés*) ~ **con alguien** impolite to sb

desatinar [de·sa·ti·'nar] *vi* (*conducta*) to act foolishly; (*palabras*) to say stupid things

desatino [de·sa·'ti·no] *m* **1.** (*error*) mistake; (*torpeza*) blunder **2.** (*tontería*) rubbish

desatornillador [de·sa·tor·ni·ja·'dor, -ʎa·'dor] *m AmL* screwdriver

desatornillar [de·sa·tor·ni·'jar, -'ʎar] *vt* to unscrew; ~ **un tornillo** to remove a screw

desatrancar <c→qu> [de·sa·tran·'kar] *vt* (*puerta*) to unbolt

desautorizado, -a [des·au·to·ri·'sa·do, -a; -'θa·do, -a] *adj* unauthorized

desautorizar <z→c> [des·au·to·ri·'sar, -'θar] *vt* (*inhabilitar*) to deprive of authority; (*prohibir*) to ban; (*desmentir*) to deny

desavenencia [de·sa·βe·'nen·sja, -θja] *f* **1.** (*desacuerdo*) disagreement **2.** (*discordia*) friction

desavenir [de·sa·βe·'nir] *irr como venir* **I.** *vt* to cause to fall out **II.** *vr:* ~ **se** to fall out

desayunar [de·sa·ju·'nar] **I.** *vi* to have [*o* eat] breakfast; ~ **fuerte** to eat a large breakfast **II.** *vt* ~ **algo** to have sth for breakfast

desayuno [de·sa·'ju·no] *m* breakfast; ~ **buffet** breakfast buffet

desazón [de·sa·'son, -'θon] *f* **1.** (*desasosiego*) unease **2.** (*malestar*) discomfort **3.** (*picor*) itch

desazonar [de·sa·so·'nar, de·sa·θo-] **I.** *vt* (*inquietar*) to worry **II.** *vr:* ~ **se** (*inquietarse*) to worry

desbancar <c→qu> [des·βan·'kar] *vt* to oust

desbandarse [des·βan·'dar·se] *vr* MIL to disband

desbarajuste [des·βa·ra·'xus·te] *m* chaos; **¡esto es un** ~ **total!** this is a total mess!

desbaratar [des·βa·ra·'tar] **I.** *vt* **1.** (*desunir, dispersar*) to break up **2.** (*desmontar*) to take apart **3.** (*arruinar*) to ruin **II.** *vr:* ~ **se 1.** (*separarse*) to break up **2.** (*estropearse*) to break down **3.** (*fracasar*) to fail

desbloquear [des·βlo·ke·'ar] *vt* **1.** (*desatascar*) *t.* POL to unblock **2.** FIN to unfreeze

desbocado, -a [des·βo·'ka·do, -a] *adj* (*caballo*) runaway

desbocar <c→qu> [des·βo·'kar] **I.** *vt* (*enloquecer*) to drive mad [*o* crazy] **II.** *vr:* ~ **se 1.** (*enloquecer*) to go crazy **2.** (*caballo*) to bolt

desbordamiento [des·βor·da·'mjen·to] *m* overflowing; COMPUT overflow; *fig* outbreak

D

desbordante [des·βor·'dan·te] *adj* (*alegría, entusiasmo*) boundless; ~ **de alegría** brimming with happiness
desbordar [des·βor·'dar] **I.** *vr:* ~ **se** 1. (*líquido*) to overflow; (*río*) to overflow 2. (*vicio*) to get out of control **II.** *vi* to overflow; ~ **de alegría** to be brimming with happiness; ~ **de emoción** to be full of emotion **III.** *vt* (*exceder*) to exceed; **esto desborda mi paciencia** this is the final straw
descabellado, -a [des·ka·βe·'ja·do, -a; -'ʎa·do, -a] *adj* preposterous
descabezado, -a [des·ka·βe·'sa·do, -a; -'θa·do, -a] *adj* headless
descabezar <z→c> [des·ka·βe·'sar, -'θar] *vt* ~ **un sueñecito** to take a nap
descafeinado, -a [des·ka·fei·'na·do, -a] *adj* 1. (*café*) decaffeinated 2. *fig* (*falto de fuerzas*) watered-down
descalabro [des·ka·'la·βro] *m* 1. (*herida*) serious injury 2. (*revés*) setback; **sufrir un** ~ (*derrota*) to suffer a defeat
descalcificar <c→qu> [des·kal·si·fi·'kar, -θi·fi·'kar] *vt* decalcify
descalificación [des·ka·li·fi·ka·'sjon, -'θjon] *f* disqualification
descalificar <c→qu> [des·ka·li·fi·'kar] *vt* to disqualify
descalzar <z→c> [des·kal·'sar, -'θar] **I.** *vt* ~ **a alguien** to take sb's shoes off **II.** *vr:* ~ **se** to take one's shoes off
descalzo, -a [des·'kal·so, -a; -θo, -a] *adj* 1. (*sin zapatos*) barefoot 2. *fig* (*indigente*) destitute
descambiar [des·kam·'bjar] *vt inf* to swap, to change back, to exchange
descaminar [des·ka·mi·'nar] **I.** *vt* to misdirect ▸ **ir descaminado** to be on the wrong track **II.** *vr:* ~ **se** 1. (*perderse*) to get lost 2. (*descarriarse*) to go astray
descampado [des·kam·'pa·do] *m* piece of open ground; **en** ~ in the open
descansado, -a [des·kan·'sa·do, -a] *adj* 1. *estar* (*reposado*) rested 2. *ser* (*cómodo*) restful
descansar [des·kan·'sar] **I.** *vi* 1. (*reposar*) to rest; **descanse en paz** (*difunto*) rest in peace 2. (*recuperarse*) to recover 3. (*dormir*) to sleep; **¡que descanses!** sleep well! 4. (*apoyar*) to rest **II.** *vt* 1. (*apoyar*) to rest 2. (*aliviar*) to relieve **III.** *vr:* ~ **se** (*confiarse*) to trust (*en* in)
descansillo [des·kan·'si·jo, -ʎo] *m* landing
descanso [des·'kan·so] *m* 1. (*reposo*) rest; **día de** ~ day of rest, day off 2. (*recuperación*) recovery 3. (*tranquilidad*) peace 4. (*pausa*) *t.* DEP break; (*alto*) pause 5. (*alivio*) relief 6. (*apoyo*) support
descapotable [des·ka·po·'ta·βle] **I.** *adj* **coche** ~ convertible **II.** *m* convertible
descarado, -a [des·ka·'ra·do, -a] *adj* 1. (*desvergonzado*) shameless 2. (*evidente*) blatant
descarga [des·'kar·ɣa] *f* 1. (*de mercancías*) unloading 2. (*disparo*) discharge; (*disparos*) volley; **una** ~ **de golpes** a barrage of strikes

3. ELEC, FÍS, FIN discharge; ~ **eléctrica** (*calambre*) electric shock
descargar <g→gu> [des·kar·'ɣar] **I.** *vi* 1. (*desembocar*) to flow 2. (*tormenta*) to break **II.** *vt* 1. (*carga*) to unload; ~ **el vientre** to have a bowel movement 2. ELEC, FÍS to discharge; (*corriente*) to use up 3. (*disparar*) to fire; ~ **un golpe sobre...** to land a blow on... 4. (*desahogar*) to vent 5. JUR (*absolver*) to acquit (*de* of); (*librar*) to release 6. COMPUT to download; ~ **algo de Internet** to download sth **III.** *vr:* ~ **se** 1. (*vaciarse*) to empty; ELEC, FÍS to discharge; (*pila*) to go flat, to run out 2. (*librarse*) to unburden oneself 3. (*desahogarse*) to let off steam
descarnado, -a [des·kar·'na·do, -a] *adj* 1. (*sin carne*) scrawny; (*huesudo*) bony; (*flaco*) thin 2. (*acre*) brutal
descaro [des·'ka·ro] *m* cheek
descarriar <1. *pres:* descarrío> [des·ka·rri·'ar] **I.** *vt* 1. (*animal*) to separate from the herd 2. (*descaminar*) to misdirect **II.** *vr:* ~ **se** 1. (*perderse*) to get lost 2. (*descaminarse*) to go astray
descarrilar [des·ka·rri·'lar] *vi* to be derailed
descartar [des·kar·'tar] **I.** *vt* (*propuesta*) to reject; (*posibilidad*) to rule out **II.** *vr:* ~ **se** (*naipes*) to discard
descascarar [des·kas·ka·'rar] **I.** *vt* (*pelar*) to peel **II.** *vr:* ~ **se** to chip
descendencia [de·sen·'den·sja, -θen·'den·θja] *f* descendents *pl;* **tener** ~ to have offspring
descendente [de·sen·'den·te, des·θen-] *adj* 1. (*en caída*) descending 2. (*en disminución*) diminishing
descender <e→ie> [de·sen·'der, des·θen-] **I.** *vi* 1. (*ir abajo*) to descend; (*a un valle, una mina*) to go down 2. (*disminuir*) to diminish 3. (*proceder*) to be descended **II.** *vt* 1. (*llevar*) to take down 2. (*una escalera*) to go down
descendiente [de·sen·'djen·te, des·θen-] *mf* descendant
descenso [de·'sen·so, des·'θen·so] *m* 1. (*bajada*) descent; **carrera de** ~ DEP downhill race 2. (*cuesta, pendiente*) slope 3. (*disminución, caída*) decline; ECON downturn
descentralizar <z→c> [de·sen·tra·li·'sar, des·θen·tra·li·'θar] *vt* to decentralize
descifrar [de·si·'frar, des·θi-] *vt* (*mensaje, código*) to decipher; (*problema*) to figure out
descocado, -a [des·ko·'ka·do, -a] *adj* (*descarado*) impudent
descoco [des·'ko·ko] *m* (*descaro*) impudence
descodificador [des·ko·di·fi·ka·'dor] *m* decoder
descodificar <c→qu> [des·ko·di·fi·'kar] *vt* to decode
descojonante [des·ko·xo·'nan·te] *adj inf* hilarious
descojonarse [des·ko·xo·'nar·se] *vr inf* (*reír*) ~ **se de alguien/algo** to piss oneself laughing
descolgar [des·kol·'ɣar] *irr como* colgar **I.** *vt*

1. (*teléfono*) to pick up **2.** (*bajar*) to take down **II.** *vr:* ~ **se 1.** (*bajar*) to come down **2.** (*aparecer*) to turn up **3.** (*dejar caer*) to drop

descolorar [des·ko·lo·'rar] *vt, vr;* **descolorir** [des·ko·lo·'rir] *vt, vr:* ~ **se** *v.* **decolorar**

descomedido, -a [des·ko·me·'di·do, -a] *adj* **1.** (*excesivo*) excessive **2.** (*insolente*) rude

descompensar [des·kom·pen·'sar] **I.** *vt* to unbalance; **estar descompensado** to be unbalanced **II.** *vr:* ~ **se** to unbalance

descomponer [des·kom·po·'ner] *irr como* **poner I.** *vt* **1.** (*desordenar*) to mess up **2.** (*separar*) to take apart **3.** (*corromper*) *t.* QUÍM to decompose **4.** (*enfurecer*) to anger **II.** *vr:* ~ **se 1.** (*desmembrarse*) to come apart **2.** (*corromperse*) to decay **3.** (*enfermar*) to become ill **4.** (*encolerizarse*) to lose one's temper

descomposición [des·kom·po·si·'sjon, -'θjon] *f* **1.** (*separación*) separation; QUÍM decomposition **2.** (*corrupción*) decay **3.** (*diarrea*) ~ (**de vientre**) diarrhea

descompostura [des·kom·pos·'tu·ra] *f* **1.** (*desarreglo*) disorder **2.** (*descomedimiento*) rudeness

descompuesto, -a [des·kom·'pwes·to, -a] **I.** *pp de* **descomponer II.** *adj* **1.** (*desordenado*) untidy **2.** (*podrido*) rotten **3.** (*alterado*) upset; **ponerse ~ de rabia** to lose one's temper **4.** (*enfermo*) ill

descomunal [des·ko·mu·'nal] *adj* enormous

desconcertar <e→ie> [des·kon·ser·'tar, des·kon·θer-] *vt* **1.** (*desbaratar*) to ruin; (*planes*) to upset **2.** (*pasmar*) to confuse; **estar desconcertado** to be disconcerted

desconchado [des·kon·'tʃa·do] *m* (*de loza*) chip; (*en la pared*) *place where paint has come off*

desconcierto [des·kon·'sjer·to, -'θjer·to] *m* **1.** (*desarreglo*) disorder **2.** (*desorientación*) confusion

desconectar [des·ko·nek·'tar] **I.** *vi, vt* to disconnect; (*radio, tele*) to switch off; (*desenchufar*) to unplug **II.** *vi inf* to switch off

desconfiado, -a [des·kon·fi·'a·do, -a] *adj* distrustful

desconfianza [des·kon·fi·'an·sa, -θa] *f* distrust

desconfiar <*1. pres:* desconfío> [des·kon·fi·'ar] *vi* ~ **de alguien/algo** to mistrust sb/sth

descongelar [des·kon·xe·'lar] **I.** *vt* **1.** (*comida*) to thaw out; (*el frigorífico*) to defrost **2.** FIN to unfreeze; ~ **los salarios** to lift a wage freeze **II.** *vr:* ~ **se** (*comida*) to thaw out; (*el frigorífico*) to defrost

descongestionar [des·kon·xes·tjo·'nar] *vt* to unblock; MED to clear

desconocer [des·ko·no·'ser, -'θer] *irr como* **crecer** *vt* **1.** (*ignorar*) ~ **algo** to be unaware of sth **2.** (*no conocer*) to not know; (*no reconocer*) to not recognize **3.** (*no aceptar*) to deny; ~ **la paternidad** to disown one's paternity

desconocido, -a [des·ko·no·'si·do, -a; -'θi·do,

-a] **I.** *adj* unknown; (*correos*) address unknown; **estar** ~ (*cambiado*) to be unrecognizable **II.** *m, f* stranger

desconocimiento [des·ko·no·si·'mjen·to, des·ko·no·θi-] *m* **1.** (*ignorancia*) ignorance; **por ~ de los hechos** without full knowledge of the facts **2.** (*ingratitud*) ingratitude

desconsiderado, -a [des·kon·si·de·'ra·do, -a] *adj* inconsiderate

desconsolado, -a [des·kon·so·'la·do, -a] *adj* disconsolate

desconsolar <o→ue> [des·kon·so·'lar] **I.** *vt* to distress **II.** *vr:* ~ **se** to lose hope

desconsuelo [des·kon·'swe·lo] *m* distress; **daba ~ verlo** it was sad to see him like that

descontado, -a [des·kon·'ta·do, -a] *adj* (*descartado*) discounted ▶ **dar algo por ~** to take sth for granted; **por ~** of course

descontar <o→ue> [des·kon·'tar] *vt* **1.** (*restar*) to take away **2.** (*letras*) to discount **3.** (*descartar*) to disregard; **descontando que fuera...** assuming that it was not...

descontento [des·kon·'ten·to] *m* dissatisfaction

descontento, -a [des·kon·'ten·to, -a] *adj* dissatisfied

descontrol [des·kon·'trol] *m* loss of control

descontrolarse [des·kon·tro·'lar·se] *vr* (*máquina*) to go out of control; (*persona*) to go wild

descorazonar [des·ko·ra·so·'nar, des·ko·ra·θo-] **I.** *vt* to discourage **II.** *vr:* ~ **se** to lose heart

descorchador [des·kor·tʃa·'dor] *m* corkscrew

descorchar [des·kor·'tʃar] *vt* (*botella*) to uncork

descorrer [des·ko·'rrer] **I.** *vt* to draw; (*cortinas, cerrojo*) to draw back; ~ **el cerrojo** to unbolt the door **II.** *vr:* ~ **se** to open

descortés [des·kor·'tes] *adj* impolite

descortesía [des·kor·te·'si·a] *f* discourtesy

descoser [des·ko·'ser] **I.** *vt* (*costura*) to unstitch; **tengo la manga descosida** my sleeve is coming apart at the seam **II.** *vr:* ~ **se** (*costura*) to come apart at the seam; **se me ha descosido un botón** one of my buttons has come off

descosido, -a [des·ko·'si·do] *adj* **como un ~** (*loco*) like mad; **hablar como un ~** to talk one's head off

descoyuntar [des·ko·jun·'tar] *vt* (*dislocar*) to dislocate

descrédito [des·'kre·di·to] *m* discredit; **caer en ~** to fall into disrepute

descreído, -a [des·kre·'i·do, -a] *adj* skeptical

descremar [des·kre·'mar] *vt* (*leche*) to skim

describir [des·kri·'βir] *irr como* **escribir** *vt* **1.** (*explicar*) to describe **2.** (*trazar*) to trace

descripción [des·krip·'sjon, -kriβ·'θjon] *f* description; JUR statement

descuajaringar <g→gu> [des·kwa·xa·rin·'gar] **I.** *vt* to break into pieces **II.** *vr:* ~ **se** *inf* (*cansarse*) to be knackered; ~ **de risa** to laugh one's head off

D

descuartizar <z→c> [des·kwar·ti·'sar, -'θar] *vt* to cut up; (*en cuatro*) to quarter

descubierto [des·ku·'βjer·to] *m* 1.(*lugar*) al ~ in the open; MIN opencast 2.(*bancario*) overdraft; al [*o* en] ~ (*cuenta, cheque*) overdrawn 3.(*en evidencia*) poner algo al ~ to bring sth into the open; quedar al ~ to be revealed

descubierto, -a [des·ku·'βjer·to, -a] I. *pp de* descubrir II. *adj* open; (*sin techo*) open-air; (*cielo*) clear; (*cabeza*) uncovered; (*paisaje*) bare

descubridor(a) [des·ku·βri·'dor, -·'do·ra] *m(f)* discoverer

descubrimiento [des·ku·βri·'mjen·to] *m* 1.(*tierras, invento*) discovery 2.(*revelación*) disclosure; JUR detection

descubrir [des·ku·'βrir] *irr como abrir* I. *vt* 1.(*destapar*) to uncover 2.(*encontrar*) to discover 3.(*averiguar*) to find out 4.(*inventar*) to invent 5.(*revelar*) to reveal 6.(*desenmascarar*) to unmask II. *vr:* ~ se 1.(*salir a la luz*) to come out 2.(*delatarse*) to give oneself away 3.(*desenmascararse*) to reveal oneself

descuento [des·'kwen·to] *m* 1.(*deducción*) discount 2.(*rebaja*) reduction; COM discount; ~ por pago al contado cash discount; ~ por cantidad quantity discount; ~ al por mayor discount on bulk purchase; ~ por no tener siniestros no claims bonus 3.(*de letras de cambio: acción*) discounting; (*cantidad*) discount 4. DEP injury time

descuidado, -a [des·kwi·'da·do, -a] *adj* 1. *ser* (*falto de atención*) inattentive; (*de cuidado*) careless; (*imprudente*) negligent; (*desaseado*) slovenly; (*desaliñado*) untidy 2. *estar* (*abandonado*) neglected; (*desprevenido*) unprepared; aspecto ~ untidiness; coger ~ a alguien to catch sb off his/her guard

descuidar [des·kwi·'dar] I. *vi* ¡descuida! don't worry! II. *vt* 1.(*desatender*) to neglect 2.(*ignorar*) to overlook III. *vr:* ~ se 1.(*abandonarse*) to neglect oneself, to let oneself go 2.(*distraerse*) to be distracted

descuido [des·'kwi·do] *m* 1.(*falta de atención*) inattentiveness; (*de cuidado*) carelessness; (*imprudencia*) negligence 2.(*error*) oversight; por ~ inadvertently

desde ['des·de] I. *prep* 1.(*temporal: pasado*) since; (*a partir de*) from; ~ ...hasta... from... until...; ~ ahora (en adelante) from now on; ¿~ cuándo? since when?; ¿~ cuándo vives aquí? how long have you lived here (for)?; ~ entonces since then; ~ hace un mes for a month; ~ hace poco/mucho for a short/long time; ~ hoy/mañana from today/tomorrow; ~ el principio from the beginning; ~ ya from now on 2.(*local*) from; te llamo ~ el aeropuerto I'm calling from the airport II. *adv* ~ luego (*por supuesto*) of course; hace un tiempo horroroso — ¡~ luego! the weather is dreadful — absolutely! III. *conj* ~ que since

desdecir [des·de·'sir, -'θir] *irr como decir* I. *vi* to be unworthy; ~ de los suyos to let one's

family down II. *vr:* ~ se de algo to withdraw sth, to take sth back; ~ se de una promesa to go back on a promise

desdén [des·'den] *m* disdain

desdentado, -a [des·den·'ta·do, -a] *adj* toothless

desdeñable [des·de·'na·βle] *adj* 1.(*insignificante*) insignificant; nada ~ far from negligible 2.(*despreciable*) despicable

desdeñar [des·de·'nar] *vt* 1.(*despreciar*) to scorn 2.(*rechazar*) to spurn

desdeñoso, -a [des·de·'no·so, -a] *adj* disdainful; (*soberbio*) contemptuous

desdibujar [des·di·βu·'xar] I. *vt* to blur II. *vr:* ~ se to become blurred

desdicha [des·'di·tʃa] *f* 1.(*desgracia*) misfortune; (*suceso*) calamity 2.(*miseria*) misery

desdichado, -a [des·di·'tʃa·do, -a] *adj* unfortunate; es un ~ he is an unfortunate wretch

desdoblar [des·do·'βlar] I. *vt* 1.(*desplegar*) to unfold; (*extender*) to open out, to spread out 2.(*dividir*) to divide 3.(*duplicar*) to double II. *vr:* ~ se 1.(*abrirse*) to open out 2.(*dividirse*) to divide 3.(*duplicarse*) to double

deseable [de·se·'a·βle] *adj* desirable

desear [de·se·'ar] *vt* to want; (*sexualmente*) to desire; ~ suerte a alguien to wish sb luck; hacerse ~ to play hard to get; ¿desea algo más? would you like anything else?; dejar mucho que ~ to leave a lot to be desired

desecar <c→qu> [de·se·'kar] I. *vt* (*pantano*) to dry out; (*alimentos, aire*) to dry II. *vr:* ~ se to dry up

desechable [de·se·'tʃa·βle] *adj* 1.(*de un solo uso*) disposable; guantes ~s disposable gloves; botellas ~s non-returnable bottles 2.(*despreciable*) despicable; nada ~ far from negligible

desechar [de·se·'tʃar] *vt* 1.(*tirar*) to throw away 2.(*descartar*) to rule out; (*desestimar*) to reject

desecho(s) [de·'se·tʃo(s)] *m(pl)* (*restos*) remains *pl*; (*residuos*) residue; (*basura*) waste; ~s tóxicos toxic waste; de ~ waste

desembalar [des·em·ba·'lar] *vt* to unpack

desembarazar <z→c> [des·em·ba·ra·'sar, -'θar] I. *vt* (*librar*) to free II. *vr:* ~ se to free oneself III. *vi Chile* (*dar a luz*) to give birth

desembarazo [des·em·ba·'ra·so, -θo] *m* (*desenvoltura*) ease

desembarcadero [des·em·bar·ka·'de·ro] *m* landing stage; (*puente*) jetty, wharf

desembarcar <c→qu> [des·em·βar·'kar] I. *vi* 1.(*descargar*) to disembark 2.(*una escalera*) to lead to II. *vt* 1.(*descargar*) to unload 2.(*transportar*) to transport

desembarco [des·em·'bar·ko] *m* (*arribada*) landing

desembargar <g→gu> [des·em·bar·'yar] *vt* ~ algo to lift the embargo on sth

desembarque [des·em·'bar·ke] *m* (*arribada*) landing

desembocadura [des·em·bo·ka·'du·ra] *f*

D

1. (*de un río*) mouth 2. (*desagüe*) outlet
desembocar <c→qu> [des·em·bo·'kar] *vi*
1. (*río*) ~ **en** to flow into 2. (*situación*) ~ **en** to result in
desembolsar [des·em·bol·'sar] *vt* 1. (*sacar*) ~ **algo** to take sth out of one's pocket 2. (*pagar*) to pay; (*gastar*) to spend
desembolso [des·em·'bol·so] *m* 1. (*pago*) payment 2. (*gasto*) expense
desembozar <z→c> [des·em·bo·'sar, -'θar] I. *vt* (*descubrir*) to uncover II. *vr:* ~ **se** (*descubrirse*) to uncover oneself
desembragar <g→gu> [des·em·bra·'ʝar] AUTO I. *vi* to release the clutch II. *vt* to release
desembrollar [des·em·bro·'jar, -'ʎar] *vt inf* 1. (*madeja*) to untangle 2. (*asunto*) to sort out
desembuchar [des·em·bu·'tʃar] I. *vi inf* (*confesar*) to come clean; **¡desembucha de una vez!** out with it! II. *vt* ~ **algo** to come clean about sth
desempacar <c→qu> [des·em·pa·'kar] *vt* AmL *Arg, CRi, Hond, Mex, Nic, Urug* (*maleta*) to unpack
desempaquetar [des·em·pa·ke·'tar] *vt* to unwrap
desempate [des·em·'pa·te] *m* breakthrough
desempeñar [des·em·pe·'ɲar] *vt* 1. (*préstamo*) to pay off 2. (*cargo*) to hold; (*trabajo*) tocarry out; ~ **un papel** to play a role
desempeño [des·em·'pe·ɲo] *m* 1. (*de un préstamo*) repayment 2. (*ejercicio*) fulfillment; (*realización*) performance
desempleado, -a [des·em·ple·'a·do, -a] I. *adj* unemployed II. *m, f* unemployed person
desempleo [des·em·'pleo] *m* unemployment; ~ **oculto** hidden unemployment
desempolvar [des·em·pol·'βar] *vt* 1. (*limpiar*) to dust 2. (*lo olvidado*) to revive, to brush up
desencadenar [des·en·ka·de·'nar] I. *vt* 1. (*soltar*) to unleash 2. (*provocar*) to trigger II. *vr:* ~ **se** to break loose
desencajar [des·en·ka·'xar] I. *vt* (*sacar*) to dismantle; MED to dislocate; (*cara*) to distort II. *vr:* ~ **se** (*salirse*) to come apart; MED to dislocate
desencantar [des·en·kan·'tar] I. *vt* 1. (*desilusionar*) to disillusion; (*decepcionar*) to disappoint 2. (*desembrujar*) ~ **algo** to break the spell on sth II. *vr:* ~ **se** to become disillusioned
desencanto [des·en·'kan·to] *m* 1. (*decepción*) disappointment 2. (*desilusión*) disillusion
desenchufar [des·en·tʃu·'far] *vt* to unplug
desencriptar [des·eŋ·krip·'tar] *vt* COMPUT to decrypt
desencuadernar [des·en·kwa·der·'nar] I. *vt* (*libro*) to remove the binding from II. *vr:* ~ **se** *t. fig* to fall apart
desenfadado, -a [des·en·fa·'da·do, -a] *adj* 1. (*desvuelto*) self-assured 2. (*carácter*) easy-going 3. (*ropa*) casual
desenfado [des·en·'fa·do] *m* openness; (*sin inhibiciones*) naturalness
desenfocado, -a [des·en·fo·'ka·do, -a] *adj*

FOTO out of focus
desenfrenado, -a [des·en·fre·'na·do, -a] *adj* frantic
desenfreno [des·en·'fre·no] *m* lack of restraint
desenganchar [des·en·gan·'tʃar] I. *vt* 1. (*gancho*) to unhook 2. (*soltar*) to take off; (*caballos*) to unhitch 3. FERRO to uncouple II. *vr:* ~ **se** *inf* (*de la droga*) to get off drugs
desengañar [des·en·ga·'ɲar] I. *vt* (*desilusionar*) to disillusion; ~ **a alguien** (*abrir los ojos*) to shatter sb's illusions II. *vr:* ~ **se** (*decepcionarse*) to be disappointed; **pronto te** ~ **ás** (*verás claro*) you'll soon see the truth
desengaño [des·en·'ga·ɲo] *m* disillusion; **sufrir un** ~ **amoroso** to have an unhappy love affair
desengrasar [des·en·gra·'sar] *vt* to remove the grease from
desenlace [des·en·'la·se, -θe] *m* outcome; **la película tiene un** ~ **feliz** the film has a happy ending
desenlazar <z→c> [des·en·la·'sar, -'θar] I. *vt* 1. (*desatar*) to untie 2. (*resolver*) to clear up II. *vr:* ~ **se** (*resolverse*) to be resolved; TEAT to end
desenmascarar [des·en·mas·ka·'rar/des·em·mas·ka·'rar] I. *vt* to unmask; *fig* to expose II. *vr:* ~ **se** to remove one's mask; *fig* to reveal oneself
desenredar [des·en·rre·'dar] I. *vt t. fig* to unravel; (*pelo*) to untangle II. *vr:* ~ **se** *inf* (*librarse*) to extricate oneself
desenroscar <c→qu> [des·en·rros·'kar] *vt* 1. (*abrir, sacar de la rosca*) to unscrew 2. (*desenrollar*) to unwind
desentenderse <e→ie> [des·en·ten·'der·se] *vr* 1. (*despreocuparse*) ~ **de algo** to want nothing to do with sth; ~ **de un problema** to wash one's hands of a problem 2. (*fingir ignorancia*) ~ **de algo** to pretend to not know about sth; **hacerse el desentendido** to turn a deaf ear
desenterrar <e→ie> [des·en·te·'rrar] *vt* 1. to dig up; (*cadáver*) to exhume 2. (*encontrar*) to find; ~ **viejos recuerdos** to rake up old memories
desentonar [des·en·to·'nar] *vi* 1. (*cantar*) to sing out of tune; (*tocar*) to play out of tune 2. (*no combinar*) to not go [*o* match]
desentorpecer [des·en·tor·pe·'ser, -'θer] *irr como crecer vt* 1. (*desembarazar*) to clear 2. (*desentumecer*) to loosen up
desentrañar [des·en·tra·'ɲar] *vt* (*descubrir*) to unravel
desentumecer [des·en·tu·me·'ser, -'θer] *irr como crecer vt* to loosen up; DEP to warm up
desenvolver [des·em·bol·'βer] *irr como volver* I. *vt* 1. (*desempaquetar*) to unwrap 2. (*desenrollar*) to unwind; (*desdoblar*) to unfold 3. (*descubrir*) to discover 4. (*desarrollar*) to develop II. *vr:* ~ **se** 1. (*llevarse*) to get on with 2. (*manejarse*) to handle oneself

deseo [de·'seo] *m* **1.**(*anhelo*) wish; ~ **imperioso** burning desire; **tener ~s de venganza** to want to get one's revenge; **tengo grandes ~s de que vengan** I really hope they come; **formular un ~** to make a wish **2.**(*necesidad*) need **3.**(*ansia*) longing **4.**(*sexual*) desire **5.**(*impulso*) whim

deseoso, -a [de·se·'o·so, -a] *adj* **estar ~ de hacer algo** (*ansioso*) to be eager to do sth; **estoy ~ de conocerlo** I'm dying to meet him

desequilibrado, -a [de·se·ki·li·'βra·do, -a] *adj* unbalanced; (*trastornado*) (mentally) disturbed

desequilibrar [de·se·ki·li·'βrar] **I.** *vt* **1.**(*descompensar*) to unbalance **2.**(*trastornar*) to disturb **II.** *vr:* **~se 1.**(*descompensarse*) to unbalance **2.**(*psíquicamente*) to become disturbed

desequilibrio [de·se·ki·'li·βrjo] *m* **1.**(*falta de equilibrio*) lack of balance; (*descompensación, desproporción*) imbalance **2.**(*trastorno*) disturbance; **~ mental** mental instability

desertar [de·ser·'tar] *vi* **1.** MIL to desert; **~ de** to desert from; **~ a** to go over to **2.** *fig* (*abandonar*) to abandon

desértico, -a [de·'ser·ti·ko, -a] *adj* desert

desertor(a) [de·ser·'tor, -·'to·ra] *m(f)* deserter

desesperación [des·es·pe·ra·'sjon, -'θjon] *f* **1.**(*desmoralización*) desperation, despair; **con ~** desperately; **caer en la ~** to become desperate **2.**(*enojo*) exasperation **3.**(*que desespera*) **ser una ~** to be a cause of despair

desesperado, -a [des·es·pe·'ra·do, -a] *adj* **1.**(*desmoralizado*) desperate; (*situación*) hopeless; **correr/gritar como un ~** to run/shout like crazy; **hacer algo a la desesperada** to do sth as a last resort **2.**(*enojado*) exasperated

desesperante [des·es·pe·'ran·te] *adj* **1.**(*sin esperanza*) hopeless; **resulta ~...** there is no point...; **¡eres ~!** you're a disaster! **2.**(*exasperante*) exasperating; **tu comportamiento es ~** your behavior drives me to despair

desesperar [des·es·pe·'rar] **I.** *vt* **1.**(*quitar la esperanza*) **~ a alguien** to cause sb to lose hope **2.**(*exasperar*) to exasperate **II.** *vi* to despair; **no desesperes de que sigan vivos** don't lose hope, they're still alive **III.** *vr:* **~se 1.**(*perder la esperanza*) to give up hope **2.**(*lamentarse*) **~ por algo** to despair of sth **3.**(*despecharse*) to despair

desestimar [des·es·ti·'mar] *vt* **1.**(*despreciar*) **~ algo** to have a low opinion of sth **2.**(*rechazar*) to reject

desfachatez [des·fa·tʃa·'tes, -'teθ] *f* cheek

desfalco [des·'fal·ko] *m* embezzlement

desfallecer [des·fa·je·'ser, -·ʎe·'θer] *irr como crecer* **I.** *vi* **1.**(*debilitarse*) to weaken **2.**(*colapsar*) to collapse; (*desmayarse*) to faint **3.**(*perder el ánimo*) to lose heart; **después de una hora empezó a ~** after an hour he/she began to flag **II.** *vt* **1.**(*debilitar*) to weaken **2.**(*desanimar*) to discourage

desfallecimiento [des·fa·fe·si·'mjen·to, -ʎe·θi·'mjen·to] *m* **1.**(*debilidad*) weakening **2.**(*desmayo*) faint; (*colapso*) collapse; **~ de ánimo** loss of heart; **~ (de las fuerzas)** loss of strength; **poco antes de llegar a la meta le sobrevino el ~** just before reaching the end, he/she collapsed

desfasado, -a [des·fa·'sa·do, -a] *adj* **1.**(*anticuado: persona*) old-fashioned; (*cosa*) antiquated; **estar ~** to be behind the times **2.** TÉC out of phase

desfase [des·'fa·se] *m* (*diferencia*) gap; **~ con la realidad** lack of realism; **¡que ~!** *inf* wild!

desfavorable [des·fa·βo·'ra·βle] *adj* unfavorable

desfavorecer [des·fa·βo·re·'ser, -'θer] *irr como crecer* *vt* **1.**(*perjudicar*) to discriminate against **2.**(*sentar mal*) **este clima me desfavorece** this climate doesn't suit me

desfigurar [des·fi·ɣu·'rar] *vt* **1.**(*afear: las facciones*) to disfigure; (*el cuerpo, el tipo*) to deform **2.**(*deformar*) to deface; (*una imagen, la realidad*) to distort; (*un texto*) to mutilate **3.**(*disfrazar*) to disguise **4.**(*ocultar*) to hide

desfiguro [des·fi·'ɣu·ro] *m* *Méx* (*cosa ridícula*) silly stunt; **hacer un ~** to make a fool of oneself

desfiladero [des·fi·la·'de·ro] *m* GEO gorge

desfilar [des·fi·'lar] *vi* **1.**(*marchar en fila*) *t.* MIL to walk in file; **desfilaron ante la reina** they paraded before the queen **2.**(*salir*) to file out

desfile [des·'fi·le] *m* **1.**(*acción*) marching; (*de tropas*) march-past; (*parada*) parade; POL march; (*en una fiesta*) procession; **~ de modelos** fashion show **2.**(*personas*) procession

desgajar [des·ɣa·'xar] **I.** *vt* **1.**(*arrancar*) to tear off; (*romper*) to break; (*ramas*) to snap off; **~ una página de un libro** to tear a page out of a book **2.**(*separar*) to tear apart **3.**(*despedazar*) to tear to pieces **II.** *vr:* **~se** (*desprenderse*) to come off; (*romperse*) to break off; (*rama*) to snap off

desgana [des·'ɣa·na] *f* **1.**(*inapetencia*) lack of appetite **2.**(*falta de interés*) lack of enthusiasm; **con ~** without enthusiasm

desgarbado, -a [des·ɣar·'βa·do, -a] *adj* (*larguirucho*) gangling

desgarrador(a) [des·ɣa·rra·'dor, -·'do·ra] *adj* heartrending

desgarrar [des·ɣa·'rrar] **I.** *vt* **1.**(*partir*) to tear; (*en muchos pedazos*) to tear to pieces; **~ un paquete** to tear open a parcel **2.**(*causar pena*) **esto me desgarra el corazón** this breaks my heart **II.** *vr:* **~se 1.**(*romperse*) to tear **2.**(*anímicamente*) **se me desgarra el corazón al pensar que no voy a verte más** it breaks my heart to think I'll never see you again

desgarro [des·'ɣa·rro] *m* **1.**(*rotura*) tear **2.** *AmL* (*esputo*) spittle

desgastar [des·ɣas·'tar] **I.** *vt* **1.**(*estropear*) to wear out **2.** (*consumir*) to use up **3.** (*cansar*) to wear out **II.** *vr:* ~ **se 1.** (*consumirse*) to wear out; (*color*) to fade **2.** (*acabarse*) to run out **3.** (*debilitarse*) to wear oneself out

desgaste [des·'ɣas·te] *m* **1.** (*fricción*) wear; ~ **natural** wear and tear **2.** (*consumo*) consumption

desglosar [des·ɣlo·'sar] *vt* **1.** (*una hoja*) to detach **2.** (*una cuestión*) to treat separately; ~ **los gastos** to itemize expenses

desgobernar <e→ie> [des·ɣo·βer·'nar] *vt* **1.** (*un país*) to misgovern; (*de una institución*) to mismanage; ~ **un asunto** to mishandle an affair **2.** (*los huesos*) to dislocate

desgobierno [des·ɣo·'βjer·no] *m* (*de un país*) misgovernment; (*una institución*) mismanagement

desgracia [des·'ɣra·sja, -θja] *f* **1.** (*suerte adversa*) bad luck; **por** ~ unfortunately; **este año estoy de** ~ this year I've had nothing but bad luck; **tiene la** ~ **de ser sordo** he has the misfortune of being deaf; **he tenido la** ~ **de...** I've been unlucky enough to...; **para mayor** ~ to top it off **2.** (*acontecimiento*) misfortune; **llevar una temporada de** ~**s** to have one disaster after another; **en el accidente no hubo** ~**s personales** in the accident nobody was hurt; **es una** ~ **que...** +*subj* it's a terrible shame that...; **eres una verdadera** ~ you're an absolute disgrace **3.** (*pérdida de gracia*) disgrace; **caer en** ~ to fall from grace, to fall into disgrace ►**las** ~**s nunca vienen solas** *prov* when it rains, it pours *prov*

desgraciadamente [des·ɣra·sja·da·'men·te, des·ɣra·θja-] *adv* unfortunately

desgraciado, -a [des·ɣra·'sja·do, -a; des·ɣra·θja-] **I.** *adj* **1.** (*sin suerte*) unlucky; **ser** ~ (*tener mala suerte*) to be unlucky; (*no llegar a nada*) to be a disaster **2.** (*infeliz*) miserable **3.** (*que implica desgracia*) unfortunate; **fue una intervención desgraciada** it was an unfortunate intervention **4.** (*pobre*) poor **II.** *m, f* **1.** (*sin suerte*) unlucky person **2.** (*infeliz*) **es un** ~ he's a poor wretch **3.** (*pobre*) poor person **4.** (*persona sin valor*) **ser un** ~ to be worthless **5.** *pey* (*miserable*) son of a bitch *sl*

desgraciar [des·ɣra·'sjar, -'θjar] **I.** *vt* **1.** (*estropear*) to ruin **2.** (*disgustar*) to displease **II.** *vr:* ~ **se** (*malograrse*) to be ruined

desgranar [des·ɣra·'nar] *vt* **1.** (*maíz, trigo*) to thresh; (*habas*) to shell; ~ (**las cuentas de**) **un rosario** to tell one's beads **2.** (*repetir*) ~ **insultos/palabrotas** to reel off a stream of abuse/ obscenities; ~ **mentiras** to tell a string of lies

desgravable [des·ɣra·'βa·βle] *adj* tax-deductible

desgravación [des·ɣra·'βa·sjon, -θjon] *f* **1.** (*reducción de un impuesto*) tax allowance, tax deduction **2.** (*de un gasto*) tax relief; ~ **sobre bienes de capital** capital allowance; ~ **por cargas familiares** tax allowance [*o* deduction] for dependants

desgravar [des·ɣra·'βar] *vt* **1.** (*suprimir: un*

impuesto, un derecho) to exempt from **2.** (*reducir*) ~ **el tabaco** (*bajar el impuesto*) to reduce the tax on tobacco; (*el arancel*) to reduce the duties on tobacco **3.** (*deducir*) to deduct

desgreñado, -a [des·ɣre·'na·do, -a] *adj* disheveled

desguace [des·'ɣwa·se, -θe] *m* **1.** (*lugar*) junkyard **2.** (*acción*) wrecking **3.** (*materiales*) junk

desguazar <z→c> [des·ɣwa·'sar, -'θar] *vt* (*reducir a chatarra*) to scrap, to wreck; ~ **algo** (*quitar las partes útiles*) to use sth for scrap

deshabitado, -a [des·a·βi·'ta·do, -a] *adj* (*edificio*) empty; **ciudad deshabitada** ghost town; **una región muy deshabitada** a very sparsely populated region

deshabitar [des·a·βi·'tar] *vt* **1.** (*un edificio*) to abandon; ~ **una casa** to vacate a house **2.** (*despoblar*) to empty

deshacer [des·a·'ser, -'θer] *irr como hacer* **I.** *vt* **1.** (*un paquete*) to unwrap; (*una costura*) to unpick; (*un nudo*) to undo; (*la cama*) to mess up; (*un aparato*) to dismantle; (*una maleta*) to unpack; ~ **los puntos** to undo the stitches; ~ **un error** to rectify a mistake **2.** (*romper*) to break; (*en pedazos*) to tear apart; (*cortar*) to cut up; (*una res*) to butcher; (*a golpes*) to knock to pieces **3.** (*arruinar*) to ruin; (*plan*) to spoil **4.** (*disolver*) to dissolve; (*hielo*) to melt; (*contrato, negocio*) to dissolve; ~ **una casa** *fig* to move home **5.** MIL to rout ►**no intentes** ~ **lo hecho** what's done can't be undone; **ser el que hace y deshace** to be the boss **II.** *vr:* ~ **se 1.** (*descomponerse*) to come apart; (*hielo*) melt; (*desaparecer*) to disappear; ~ **se en cumplidos** to be full of praise; ~ **se de impaciencia** to be dying of impatience; ~ **se en lágrimas** to burst into tears; ~ **se en llanto** to cry one's heart out; ~ **se de nervios** to be a nervous wreck; ~ **se por algo** to try one's hardest to do sth; **se deshace por complacernos** he/she does everything possible to please us; ~ **se a trabajar** to work oneself into the ground; ~ **se empollando** *inf* to tire oneself out studying **2.** (*romperse*) to break; (*costura, nudo*) to come undone; (*pastel*) to fall apart; (*silla*) to fall to pieces **3.** (*desprenderse*) to come away; ~ **se de algo** (*venderlo*) to offload sth; ~ **se de alguien** (*librarse de, asesinar*) to get rid of sb; (*despedir*) to say goodbye to sb

deshecho, -a [des·'e·tʃo, -a] **I.** *pp de* **deshacer II.** *adj* **1.** (*deprimido*) devastated; **dejar a alguien** ~ to leave sb shattered **2.** (*cansado*) exhausted; **estar** ~ to be exhausted **3.** (*tormenta*) violent; (*lluvia*) heavy

deshelar <e→ie> [des·e·'lar] **I.** *vt* (*hielo, nieve*) to melt; (*una nevera*) to defrost **II.** *vr:* ~ **se** (*hielo*) to melt; (*nieve*) to thaw; (*nevera*) to defrost

desheredar [des·e·re·'dar] *vt* to disinherit

deshidratar [des·i·dra·'tar] **I.** *vt* to dry; (*cuerpo*) to dehydrate **II.** *vr:* ~ **se** to dry out;

D

(*cuerpo*) to dehydrate
deshielo [des·'je·lo] *m* **1.** (*el deshelar*) thawing; (*de la nevera*) defrosting **2.** (*clima*) *t.* POL thaw
deshilachar [des·i·la·'tʃar] *vt, vr:* ~ **se** to fray
deshilvanado, -a [des·il·βa·'na·do, -a] *adj* (*discurso*) disjointed
deshinchar [des·in·'tʃar] **I.** *vt* **1.** (*sacar el aire*) to deflate **2.** (*una inflamación*) to reduce **II.** *vr:* ~ **se 1.** (*perder aire*) to deflate; **se me ha deshinchado la rueda de la bici** my bicycle tire is flat **2.** (*una inflamación*) to go down **3.** *inf* (*deponer la vanidad*) to get down off one's high horse
deshojado, -a [des·o·'xa·do] *adj* **1.** (*árbol*) leafless **2.** (*libro*) **un libro** ~ a book with pages missing
deshojar [des·o·'xar] **I.** *vt* **1.** BOT to strip the leaves from; ~ **una flor** to pull the petals off a flower **2.** (*un libro*) to tear the pages out of **II.** *vr:* ~ **se 1.** BOT (*un árbol*) to lose its leaves; (*una flor*) to lose its petals **2.** (*un libro*) to lose its pages
deshonesto, -a [des·o·'nes·to, -a] *adj* **1.** (*inmoral*) indecent **2.** (*tramposo*) dishonest
deshonor [des·o·'nor] *m* (*afrenta*) dishonor
deshonra [des·'on·rra] *f* (*afrenta*) disgrace; **tener algo a** ~ (*como insulto*) to take offense at sth; (*como humillante*) to think sth is beneath one
deshonrar [des·on·'rrar] *vt* to disgrace; (*ofender*) to offend; (*humillar*) to humiliate; ~ **a alguien** (*desacreditar*) to bring disgrace on sb
deshonroso, -a [des·on·'rro·so, -a] *adj* **1.** (*que causa deshonra*) disgraceful **2.** (*poco honroso*) dishonest
deshora [des·'o·ra] *f* inconvenient time; **hablar a** ~(**s**) to interrupt; **venir a** ~(**s**) (*en un momento inconveniente*) to come at a bad moment; (*demasiado tarde*) to arrive too late; **dormir a** ~**s** to sleep at odd hours
desidia [de·'si·dja] *f* **1.** (*descuido*) carelessness; **me molesta tu** ~ **en el trabajo** I don't like your lack of attention to your work **2.** (*pereza*) laziness
desierto [de·'sjer·to] *m* **1.** GEO desert **2.** (*lugar despoblado*) wasteland; **predicar en el** ~ *fig* to preach to the winds
desierto, -a [de·'sjer·to, -a] *adj* **1.** (*sin gente*) deserted **2.** (*como un desierto*) desert **3.** (*sin participantes*) **una subasta desierta** an auction without bidders; **el premio fue declarado** ~ the prize was not awarded; **dar por** ~ **un concurso** to declare a competition void
designación [de·siɣ·na·'sjon, -'θjon] *f* **1.** (*nombramiento*) appointment; ~ **de candidatos** selection of candidates **2.** (*nombre*) name; ~ **del contenido** contents
designar [de·siɣ·'nar] *vt* **1.** (*dar un nombre*) to designate; ~ **a alguien con un apodo** to give sb a nickname **2.** (*destinar*) to assign; (*elegir*) to choose; (*fecha*) to set; (*nombrar*) to appoint

(*para* to); ~ **un abogado** to appoint a lawyer; ~ **un candidato** to select a candidate; ~ **un representante** to nominate a representative
designio [de·'siɣ·njo] *m* **1.** (*plan*) plan **2.** (*propósito*) intention **3.** (*deseo*) wish; **su** ~ **es convertirse en multimillonario** his/her ambition is to be a multimillionaire
desigual [de·si·'ɣwal] *adj* **1.** (*distinto*) unequal; **ser muy** ~ to be very different **2.** (*injusto*) unfair **3.** (*irregular*) uneven **4.** (*inconstante*) inconsistent
desigualdad [de·si·ɣwal·'dad] *f* **1.** (*diferencia*) inequality **2.** (*injusticia*) unfairness **3.** (*irregularidad*) unevenness **4.** (*del carácter*) inconsistency; (*del tiempo*) changeability
desilusión [de·si·lu·'sjon] *f* **1.** (*desengaño*) disappointment; **sufrir una** ~ to be disappointed **2.** (*desencanto*) disillusion
desilusionante [de·si·lu·sjo·'nan·te] *adj* (*que desencanta*) disillusioning
desilusionar [de·si·lu·sjo·'nar] **I.** *vt* **1.** (*quitar la ilusión*) to disillusion **2.** (*decepcionar*) to disappoint **II.** *vr:* ~ **se 1.** (*perder la ilusión*) to become disillusioned; (*ver claro*) to see things for what they are **2.** (*decepcionarse*) to be disappointed
desinencia [de·si·'nen·sja, -θja] *f* ending; ~ **nominal** noun ending
desinfectante [des·in·fek·'tan·te] *m* disinfectant
desinfectar [des·in·fek·'tar] *vt* to disinfect
desinflado, -a [des·in·'fla·do, -a] *adj* (*rueda*) flat
desinflar [des·in·'flar] **I.** *vt* (*sacar el aire*) to deflate **II.** *vr:* ~ **se** (*perder aire*) to go down; **se me ha desinflado la rueda de atrás** my back tire is flat
desintegración [des·in·te·ɣra·'sjon, -'θjon] *f* **1.** (*de una cosa*) disintegration; (*debido al clima*) erosion; QUÍM decomposition **2.** (*de un territorio, un grupo*) breakup
desintegrar [des·in·te·'ɣrar] **I.** *vt* **1.** (*disgregarse*) to disintegrate; (*una piedra*) to erode **2.** (*un grupo, un país*) to break up **II.** *vr:* ~ **se 1.** (*disgregarse*) to disintegrate; (*edificio, muro*) to fall down; QUÍM to decompose **2.** (*grupo*) to break up; (*partido*) to fall apart
desinterés [des·in·te·'res] *m* **1.** (*indiferencia*) indifference; **sentir** ~ **por algo** to not be interested in sth **2.** (*altruismo*) altruism; (*generosidad*) generosity
desinteresado, -a [des·in·te·re·'sa·do, -a] *adj* **1.** (*indiferente*) indifferent; (*en un conflicto*) impartial **2.** (*altruista*) altruistic; (*generoso*) generous
desintoxicación [des·in·tok·si·ka·'sjon, -'θjon] *f* detoxification
desintoxicar <c→qu> [des·in·tok·si·'kar] **I.** *vt* to detoxify **II.** *vr:* ~ **se 1.** to undergo detoxification; (*de alcohol*) to dry out **2.** *fig* to get away from it all
desistir [de·sis·'tir] *vi* **1.** (*de un proyecto*) ~ **de algo** to give up sth; **no** ~**é de convencerte**

I'll do my best to persuade you; **no hay manera de hacerles ~ de su propósito** there is no way of getting them to back down **2.** (*renunciar a*) **~ de un derecho** to waive a right; **~ de un cargo** to resign from a position; **~ de una petición** to withdraw a request; **~ de un contrato** to withdraw from a contract
desleal [des·le·'al] *adj* (*infiel*) disloyal; (*traidor*) treacherous; **competencia ~** unfair competition; **publicidad ~** misleading advertising; **ser ~ a su patria** to betray one's country; **ser ~ con su partido** to betray one's party; **has sido ~ a tu familia** you have been disloyal to your family; **ser ~ con** [*o* a] **alguien** (*injusto*) to treat sb unfairly
deslealtad [des·leal·'tad] *f* **1.** (*infidelidad*) disloyalty **2.** (*injusticia*) unfairness
desleír [des·le·'ir] *irr como* reír **I.** *vt* (*disolver*) to dissolve **II.** *vr:* **~se** to dissolve
deslenguado, -a [des·len·'gwa·do, -a] *adj* **1.** (*desvergonzado*) foul-mouthed **2.** (*chismoso*) gossipy; **ser ~** to be a gossip; **¡no seas ~!** don't be such a gossip!
desligar <g→gu> [des·li·'γar] **I.** *vt* (*separar*) to separate; **~ intereses particulares de los de la empresa** to separate private interests from those of the company **II.** *vr:* **~se** (*de un compromiso*) to be released; **no poder ~se de algo** to be unable to get out of sth
deslindar [des·lin·'dar] *vt* **1.** (*un lugar*) to demarcate; **~ una finca** to mark the boundary of a farm; **~ dos provincias** to mark the boundary between two provinces **2.** (*determinar*) to outline; **~ dos temas** to distinguish between two topics
desliz [des·'lis, -'liθ] *m* **1.** (*error*) slip; (*indiscreción*) indiscretion **2.** (*adulterio*) affair
deslizante [des·li·'san·te, -'θan·te] *adj* **1.** (*que desliza, que resbala*) slippery **2.** (*corredizo*) sliding
deslizar <z→c> [des·li·'sar, -'θar] **I.** *vt* **1.** (*pasar*) **~ la mano sobre algo** to run one's hand over sth; **~ un sobre por debajo de una puerta** to slip an envelope under the door **2.** (*incluir con disimulo*) to slip; **~ algo en una conversación** to slip sth into a conversation **II.** *vi* to slip **III.** *vr:* **~se 1.** (*resbalar*) **~ sobre algo** to slide over sth; **~ se por un tobogán** to go down a slide; **las lágrimas se deslizaban por sus mejillas** the tears slid down his/her cheeks; **con la tormenta se han deslizado algunas tejas** the storm has blown a few tiles off **2.** (*escaparse*) to slip away **3.** (*el tiempo*) to slip away **4.** (*cometer un error*) to slip up; (*una indiscreción*) to slip out
deslomar [des·lo·'mar] *vt* **1.** (*dañar*) **~ a alguien** to break sb's back **2.** (*agotar*) to exhaust
deslucido, -a [des·lu·'si·do, -a; -'θi·do, -a] *adj* **1.** (*ropa*) shabby **2.** (*actuación*) lackluster **3.** (*sin gracia*) dull
deslucir [des·lu·'sir, -'θir] *irr como* lucir **I.** *vt* **1.** (*estropear*) to ruin **2.** (*quitar el lustre: metal*) to tarnish; (*una prenda, un tejido,*

colores) to fade **3.** (*desacreditar*) to discredit **II.** *vr:* **~se 1.** (*fracasar*) to fail **2.** (*perder el lustre*) to lose one's shine; (*colores*) to fade; (*metal*) to become dull **3.** (*desacreditarse*) to be discredited
deslumbrador(a) [des·lum·bra·'dor, -·'do·ra] *adj,* **deslumbrante** [des·lum·'bran·te] *adj* (*impresionante*) dazzling; (*despampanante*) stunning
deslumbrar [des·lum·'brar] *vt* to dazzle
deslustrar [des·lus·'trar] *vt* **1.** (*gastar*) to wear out; (*una prenda, un tejido, colores*) to fade **2.** (*estropear*) to ruin **3.** (*desacreditar*) to discredit
desmadrado, -a [des·ma·'dra·do, -a] *adj* (*desenfrenado*) wild
desmadrarse [des·ma·'drar·se] *vr inf* (*desenfrenarse*) to go wild; (*alocarse*) to go crazy; **¡no te desmadres!** don't lose it!
desmadre [des·'ma·dre] *m* **1.** (*comportamiento*) outrageous behavior; **la policía acabó con el ~ entre los hinchas** the police put an end to the mayhem between the fans **2.** (*caos*) chaos; **tus fiestas acaban siendo un ~** your parties are always completely wild
desmalezar <z→c> [des·ma·le·'sar, -'θar] *vt AmL* to weed, to clear brush
desmán [des·'man] *m* **1.** (*salvajada*) outrage; **cometer desmanes contra alguien** to commit outrages against sb **2.** (*exceso*) excess; **debido a sus desmanes con la bebida** due to his/her excessive drinking
desmantelar [des·man·te·'lar] *vt* **1.** (*derribar*) to knock down; (*un edificio*) to demolish **2.** (*desmontar*) to take apart; (*bomba*) to dismantle; (*escenario*) to take down
desmaquillador [des·ma·ki·ja·'dor, des·ma·ki·λa-] *m* make-up remover
desmaquillador(a) [des·ma·ki·ja·'dor, -·'do·ra; des·ma·ki·λa-] *adj* **leche ~a** make-up remover
desmayado, -a [des·ma·'ja·do, -a] *adj* **1.** (*sin conocimiento*) unconscious **2.** (*sin fuerza*) exhausted; (*color*) faded
desmayar [des·ma·'jar] **I.** *vi* (*desanimarse*) to lose heart **II.** *vr:* **~se** (*desvanecerse*) to faint
desmayo [des·'ma·jo] *m* **1.** (*desvanecimiento*) faint; **hablar con ~** to speak in a small voice **2.** (*desánimo*) dismay **3.** (*debilidad*) weakness
desmedido, -a [des·me·'di·do, -a] *adj* excessive; **tener un apetito ~** to have an enormous appetite; **afición desmedida por la bebida** excessive drinking
desmejorar [des·me·xo·'rar] **I.** *vt* (*estropear*) to ruin; (*gastar*) to wear out **II.** *vi* to deteriorate; **con la gripe has desmejorado mucho** the flu has really weakened you **III.** *vr:* **~se 1.** (*estropearse*) to be ruined; (*gastarse*) to wear out, to go downhill *inf* **2.** (*perder la salud*) to deteriorate
desmembrar <e→ie> [des·mem·'brar] **I.** *vt* **1.** (*desunir*) to break up; (*una institución*) to dismantle; (*un cuerpo*) to dismember; **la**

bomba le desmembró la mano the bomb took his/her hand off **2.** (*escindir*) to separate **II.** *vr:* ~ **se 1.** (*desunirse*) to break up **2.** (*escindirse*) to separate (*de* from)

desmentir [des·men·'tir] *irr como sentir* **I.** *vt* **1.** (*negar*) to deny; ~ **a alguien** (*contradecir*) to contradict sb; (*decir que miente*) to accuse sb of lying; **el artículo desmiente la historia** the article disproves the story **2.** (*demostrar que es falso*) to refute; ~ **una sospecha** to refute an accusation; **las pruebas desmienten tus palabras** the evidence contradicts what you have said **3.** (*desdecir*) ~ **algo/a alguien** to be unworthy of sth/sb; **con su comportamiento desmiente a su familia** his/her behavior is a disgrace to the family; **este vino desmiente su marca** this wine doesn't do justice to its label **II.** *vi* to be out of line **III.** *vr* ~ **se** to contradict oneself

desmenuzar <z→c> [des·me·nu·'sar, -'θar] **I.** *vt* **1.** (*deshacer*) to break into small pieces; (*pez*) to flake; (*con un cuchillo*) to chop up; (*con los dedos*) to crumble; (*raspar*) to grate; (*moler*) to grind; (*papel*) to tear up **2.** (*analizar*) to scrutinize **II.** *vr:* ~ **se** to crumble

desmerecer [des·me·re·'ser, -'θer] *irr como crecer* **I.** *vt* (*no merecer*) to not deserve **II.** *vi* **1.** (*decaer*) to decline; (*belleza*) to lose one's looks **2.** (*ser inferior*) ~ **de alguien/algo** to be worse than sb/sth; ~ **en talento de alguien** to be less talented than sb; **tu último libro no desmerece de los anteriores** your latest book maintains the standard of the previous ones; **desmereces de tu familia** your family is too good for you

desmesurado, -a [des·me·su·'ra·do, -a] *adj* **1.** (*enorme*) enormous **2.** (*excesivo*) excessive; (*ambición*) boundless; (*pretensiones*) exaggerated; **beber de una forma desmesurada** to drink to excess **3.** (*desvergonzado*) shameless; (*descortés*) rude; (*ofensivo*) offensive

desmigajar [des·mi·ya·'xar] **I.** *vt* to crumble **II.** *vr:* ~ **se** to crumble

desmilitarizar <z→c> [des·mi·li·ta·ri·'sar, -'θar] *vt* to demilitarize

desmirriado, -a [des·mi·'rrja·do, -a] *adj* (*flaco*) skinny; (*raquítico*) puny

desmontar [des·mon·'tar] **I.** *vt* **1.** (*un mecanismo*) to disassemble **2.** (*una pieza: quitar*) to detach; (*sacar*) to remove **3.** (*una estructura, un edificio*) to take down **4.** (*un bosque*) to cut down **5.** (*una pistola*) to uncock **6.** (*de un caballo, de una moto*) to throw **II.** *vi* (*de un caballo*) to dismount; (*de una moto*) to help get down from **III.** *vr:* ~ **se** (*bajarse*) to dismount

desmonte [des·'mon·te] *m* **1.** (*de un terreno*) leveling **2.** (*de un bosque*) clearance, cut **3.** (*escombros*) heap of soil

desmoralizador(a) [des·mo·ra·li·sa·'dor, -'do·ra; des·mo·ra·li·θa-] *adj* **1.** (*que desanima*) demoralizing **2.** (*que corrompe*) corrupting

desmoralizar <z→c> [de·mo·ra·li·'sar, -'θar] **I.** *vt* **1.** (*desanimar*) to demoralize; **la crítica la ha desmoralizado mucho** the criticism has really gotten to her **2.** (*corromper*) to corrupt **II.** *vr:* ~ **se 1.** (*desanimarse*) to lose heart; (*perder la confianza*) to lose one's confidence; **las tropas se iban desmoralizando** the soldiers were gradually becoming demoralized **2.** (*corromperse*) to be corrupted

desmoronamiento [des·mo·ro·na·'mjen·to] *m* **1.** (*arruinamiento*) ruin; (*de un edificio*) collapse **2.** (*disminución: de un imperio, una ideología*) decline; (*de una persona*) breakdown; (*de un sentimiento*) weakening; **la crisis económica produjo el ~ de mi fortuna** the economic crisis used up all my wealth

desmoronar [des·mo·ro·'nar] **I.** *vt* (*deshacer*) to wear away; (*edificio*) to ruin **II.** *vr:* ~ **se 1.** (*deshacerse*) to fall to pieces; (*un edificio, un muro*) to fall down **2.** (*disminuir*) to decline; (*sentimiento*) to weaken **3.** (*persona*) to fall apart

desnatar [des·na·'tar] *vt* (*la leche*) to skim; **leche sin ~** whole milk

desnaturalizado, -a [des·na·tu·ra·li·'sa·do, -a; -'θa·do, -a] *adj* **1.** (*alimentos*) adulterated **2.** (*hijo*) ungrateful; **madre desnaturalizada** uncaring mother

desnaturalizar <z→c> [des·na·tu·ra·li·'sar, -'θar] **I.** *vt* **1.** (*expatriar*) to denaturalize **2.** (*desvirtuar*) to denature; (*aspecto*) to spoil; (*carácter*) to ruin; ~ **la competencia** to distort the marketplace **II.** *vr:* ~ **se** (*expatriarse*) to abandon one's country

desnivel [des·ni·'βel] *m* **1.** (*diferencia de altura*) drop; (*pendiente*) slope **2.** (*desequilibrio*) imbalance; (*disparidad*) inequality; ~ **cultural** cultural difference [*o* gap] **3.** (*altibajo*) unevenness

desnivelar [des·ni·βe·'lar] **I.** *vt* **1.** (*un terreno*) to make uneven **2.** (*desequilibrar*) to unbalance; (*balanza*) to tip **II.** *vr:* ~ **se 1.** (*torcerse*) to twist; (*calle*) to become uneven **2.** (*perder el equilibrio*) to become unbalanced

desnucar <c→qu> [des·nu·'kar] **I.** *vt* **1.** (*herir*) ~ **a alguien** to break sb's neck **2.** (*matar*) to kill; ~ **una gallina** to wring a chicken's neck; ~ **el conejo de un golpe en el cogote** to kill the rabbit with a blow to its neck **II.** *vr:* ~ **se** to break one's neck

desnudar [des·nu·'dar] **I.** *vt* **1.** (*desvestir*) to undress **2.** (*descubrir*) to strip **II.** *vr:* ~ **se** (*desvestirse*) to undress

desnudez [des·nu·'des, -'deθ] *f* **1.** (*persona*) nudity **2.** *fig* bareness

desnudo [des·'nu·do] *m* ARTE nude

desnudo, -a [des·'nu·do, -a] *adj* **1.** (*desvestido*) naked, nude; ~ **de** (**la**) **cintura para arriba/abajo** naked from the waist up/down **2.** (*con poca ropa*) half-naked **3.** (*despojado*) bare **4.** (*pobre*) penniless; **este mes me he quedado** ~ *inf* this month I'm broke **5.** (*claro*) clear; **al** ~ clearly; **decir a alguien la verdad**

desnuda to tell sb the plain truth **6.**(*desprovisto*) ~ **de algo** devoid of sth

desnutrición [des·nu·tri·'sjon, -'θjon] *f* malnutrition, undernourishment

desnutrido, -a [des·nu·'tri·do, -a] *adj* undernourished

desobedecer [de·so·βe·de·'ser, -'θer] *irr como crecer vi, vt* to disobey

desobediencia [de·so·βe·'djen·sja, -θja] *f* disobedience; MIL insubordination

desobediente [de·so·βe·'djen·te] *adj* disobedient; MIL insubordinate

desocupación [de·so·ku·pa·'sjon, -'θjon] *f* **1.**(*paro*) unemployment **2.**(*ociosidad*) leisure

desocupado, -a [de·so·ku·'pa·do, -a] **I.** *adj* **1.**(*parado*) unemployed **2.**(*vacío*) empty; (*vivienda*) vacant; (*paso, plaza*) clear; (*ocioso*) idle; **estoy ~** I'm not busy **II.** *m, f* unemployed person

desocupar [de·so·ku·'par] **I.** *vt* **1.**(*desembarazar*) to clear; (*evacuar*) to evacuate; ~ **una vivienda** to vacate a property **2.**(*vaciar*) to empty **II.** *vr:* ~ **se 1.**(*de una ocupación*) to get away; **cuando pueda ~me** when I'm free **2.**(*quedarse vacante*) to be vacant **III.** *vi AmL* (*parir*) to give birth

desodorante [de·so·do·'ran·te] **I.** *adj* (*para el cuerpo*) deodorant; **espray ~** (*para el cuerpo*) deodorant spray **II.** *m* (*para el cuerpo*) deodorant; ~ **en barra** stick deodorant; ~ **antitranspirante** antiperspirant

desoír [de·so·'ir] *irr como oír* vt ~ **algo** to not listen to sth

desolación [de·so·la·'sjon, -'θjon] *f* **1.**(*devastación*) desolation **2.**(*desconsuelo*) distress

desolado, -a [de·so·'la·do, -a] *adj* **1.**(*desierto*) desolate **2.**(*desconsolado*) devastated

desolar <o→ue> [de·so·'lar] **I.** *vt* (*destruir, afligir*) to devastate **II.** *vr:* ~ **se** to be devastated

desollar <o→ue> [de·so·'jar, -'ʎar] *vt* (*quitar la piel*) to flay, to skin; ~ **a alguien vivo** *fig* to fleece sb, to skin sb alive

desorbitado, -a [des·or·βi·'ta·do, -a] *adj* **1.**(*ojos*) bulging, bug-eyed *inf* **2.**(*exagerado*) exaggerated; (*desmedido*) exorbitant

desorbitar [des·or·βi·'tar] **I.** *vt* (*exagerar*) to exaggerate; (*dar demasiada importancia*) to blow out of proportion **II.** *vr:* ~ **se** (*asunto*) to get out of control; **se le ~on los ojos** *fig* he/she was flabbergasted

desorden [des·'or·den] *m* **1.**(*desarreglo*) mess; (*confusión*) chaos; ~ **público** public disturbance; **la casa está en ~** the house is in a mess **2.**(*exceso*) excess **3.** *pl* (*alboroto*) disorders *pl*

desordenado, -a [des·or·de·'na·do, -a] *adj* **1.**(*desorganizado*) jumbled; (*persona, cosa*) messy; (*vida*) chaotic **2.**(*excesivo*) excessive

desordenar [des·or·de·'nar] *vt* (*turbar*) to mess up; (*mezclar*) to mix up; (*pelo*) to ruffle

desorganización [des·or·ya·ni·sa·'sjon, -θa·'θjon] *f* lack of organization; **en esta**

empresa llevan una ~ increíble this company is completely disorganized

desorganizar <z→c> [des·or·ya·ni·'sar, -'θar] **I.** *vt* to disrupt; (*planes*) to disturb **II.** *vr:* ~ **se** (*persona, empresa*) to be disorganized

desorientación [de·so·rjen·ta·'sjon, -'θjon] *f* **1.**(*extravío*) disorientation **2.**(*confusión*) confusion **3.**(*falta de orientación*) loss of direction

desorientar [de·so·rjen·'tar] **I.** *vt* **1.**(*extraviar*) to lose one's bearings, to disorient **2.**(*confundir*) to confuse **II.** *vr:* ~ **se 1.**(*extraviarse*) to become disoriented **2.**(*confundirse*) to become confused

desovar [de·so·'βar] *vi* (*pez, anfibio*) to spawn; (*insecto*) to lay eggs

despabilado, -a [des·pa·βi·'la·do, -a] *adj* **1.**(*listo*) smart **2.**(*despierto*) alert

despabilar [des·pa·βi·'lar] **I.** *vt* **1.**(*despertar*) to wake up **2.**(*avivar*) to sharpen up; **es muy perezosa, pero en el colegio ya la ~án** she's very lazy, but at school they'll soon make her sharpen up **3.**(*acabar deprisa*) to finish off; (*fortuna*) to squander; (*comida*) to eat up **4.**(*robar*) to steal **5.**(*matar*) to kill **II.** *vi* **1.**(*darse prisa*) to hurry up **2.**(*avivarse*) **si quieres empezar a trabajar por tu cuenta, tienes que ~** if you want to work for yourself, you'll have to get your act together **III.** *vr:* ~ **se 1.**(*sacudir el sueño*) to waken up **2.**(*darse prisa*) to hurry up **3.**(*avivarse*) to get one's act together; **se ha despabilado desde que va al colegio** he/she has really come to life since starting school **4.** *AmL* (*marcharse*) to leave

despachante [des·pa·'tʃan·te] *mf RíoPl* COM customs officer

despachar [des·pa·'tʃar] **I.** *vt* **1.**(*enviar*) to send, to ship; (*mercancías*) to dispatch **2.**(*concluir*) to finish off; (*buque*) to clear out **3.**(*resolver*) to decide; (*discutir*) to discuss **4.**(*atender*) to serve, to wait on **5.**(*vender*) to sell **6.**(*matar*) to kill **7.** *inf* (*despedir*) to dismiss, to fire **II.** *vi* **1.**(*acabar*) to finish **2.**(*atender*) to do business; **por las tardes no despachan en esta tienda** this shop doesn't open in the evenings **3.**(*conversar*) ~ **con alguien** to consult with sb **III.** *vr:* ~ **se 1.**(*darse prisa*) to hurry up **2.**(*desahogarse*) to let off steam; ~ **se a (su) gusto con alguien** to speak frankly to sb **3.**(*desembarazarse*) ~ **se de alguien** to rid oneself of sb

despacho [des·'pa·tʃo] *m* **1.**(*oficina*) office; (*en casa*) study; **mesa de ~** desk **2.**(*envío*) sending **3.**(*de un asunto*) resolution; (*entrevista*) consultation **4.**(*de clientes*) service; **sólo tenemos ~ por las mañanas** we only see clients in the morning **5.**(*venta*) sale; **no tener buen ~** to sell slowly; **tener buen ~** to sell well **6.**(*despido*) dismissal **7.**(*de un pedido*) dispatch, shipping; (*de la correspondencia, el equipaje*) sending; (*de un buque*) clearance **8.**(*muebles*) office furniture; **comprarse un ~ nuevo** to refurnish one's office **9.**(*taquilla*) ticket office; (*tienda*) shop; ~ **de**

billetes [*o* **boletos** *AmL*] FERRO ticket office; ~ **de localidades** TEAT, CINE box [*o* ticket] office **10.** (*parte*) message; (*telegrama*) telegram; (*entre gobiernos*) dispatch; ~ **judicial** legal dispatch

despacio [des·'pa·sjo, -θjo] I. *adv* **1.** (*lentamente*) slowly **2.** (*calladamente*) quietly II. *interj* take it easy

despampanante [des·pam·pa·'nan·te] *adj* (*mujer*) stunning

despancar <c→qu> [des·pan·'kar] *vt AmS* (*maíz*) to husk

desparejado, -a [des·pa·re·'xa·do, -a] *adj* odd; **este calcetín está** ~ this is an odd sock; **estos calcetines están** ~**s** these socks don't match

desparpajo [des·par·'pa·xo] *m* **1.** (*desenvoltura*) self-confidence; (*en el hablar*) ease; **con** ~ confidently **2.** (*habilidad*) skill; **con** ~ skillfully **3.** (*frescura*) cheek; **con** ~ cheekily

desparramar [des·pa·rra·'mar] I. *vt* **1.** (*dispersar*) to scatter; ~ **su atención** to allow one's attention to wander **2.** (*un líquido*) to spill **3.** (*malgastar*) to waste **4.** (*una noticia*) to spread **5.** *Arg, Méx, PRico* (*diluir*) to dilute II. *vr:* ~**se 1.** (*dispersarse*) to scatter; **el rebaño se desparramó por el campo** the flock spread out across the field; **al pasar el coche los pájaros se** ~**on** when the car went past the birds scattered **2.** (*un líquido*) to spill **3.** (*divertirse*) to enjoy oneself **4.** (*dispersar su atención*) to allow one's attention to wander

desparramo [des·pa·'rra·mo] *m* **1.** *Chile, Cuba* (*desparramamiento*) scattering **2.** *Chile, Urug* (*desbarajuste*) disorder

despatarrado, -a [des·pa·ta·'rra·do, -a] *adj* (*espatarrado*) **estar** ~ to straddle; (*en un sofá*) to sprawl (out)

despavorido, -a [des·pa·βo·'ri·do, -a] *adj* terrified

despechar [des·pe·'tʃar] I. *vt* (*indignar*) to anger II. *vr* ~**se contra alguien** to get angry with sb

despecho [des·'pe·tʃo] *m* (*desesperación*) despair

despectivo, -a [des·pek·'ti·βo] *adj* (*despreciativo*) contemptuous; (*desdeñoso*) disdainful; (*tono*) derogatory; **tratar de manera despectiva** to treat with a lack of respect

despedazar <z→c> [des·pe·da·'sar, -'θar] I. *vt* (*romper*) to smash; (*en mil pedazos*) to tear to pieces; (*con un cuchillo, una tijera*) to cut up; (*con las manos*) to tear up; (*el corazón*) to break; **la bomba le despedazó la mano** the bomb blew his/her hand off II. *vr:* ~**se 1.** (*romperse*) to smash; (*en mil pedazos*) to fall to pieces; (*muro*) to fall down; (*cristal*) to shatter; (*globo*) to burst **2.** (*apenar*) **se me despedazó el alma cuando vi tanta miseria** *fig* seeing such misery broke my heart

despedida [des·pe·'di·da] *f* **1.** (*separación*) goodbye, farewell **2.** (*acto oficial*) send-off; (*fiesta*) leaving party; ~ **de soltero** stag night

[*o* party]; ~ **de soltera** hen night [*o* party]; **cena de** ~ farewell dinner **3.** (*en una carta*) close

despedir [des·pe·'dir] *irr como pedir* I. *vt* **1.** (*decir adiós*) to say goodbye; ~ **a alguien con una fiesta** to give sb a going-away party; **vinieron a** ~**me al aeropuerto** they came to the airport to see me off **2.** (*echar*) to throw out; (*de un empleo*) to dismiss, to fire **3.** (*difundir*) to give off; (*emitir*) to emit; **el volcán despide fuego** the volcano gives off flames **4.** (*lanzar*) to launch; (*flecha*) to fire **5.** (*apartar de sí*) to get rid of II. *vr:* ~**se 1.** (*decir adiós*) to say goodbye **2.** (*dejar un empleo*) to leave; ~**se de un trabajo** to leave a job **3.** (*de obtener, conseguir algo*) **despídete de ese dinero** say goodbye to that money; **despídete este mes de salir por las noches** this month you can forget about going out in the evening

despegado, -a [des·pe·'ɣa·do, -a] *adj* **1.** (*poco cariñoso*) distant **2.** (*áspero*) unfriendly **3.** (*suelto*) unstuck

despegar <g→gu> [des·pe·'ɣar] I. *vt* to unstick; ~ **dos hojas** to separate two pages; **sin** ~ **los labios** without a word II. *vi* to take off; **la economía no despega** the economy is stagnant III. *vr:* ~**se 1.** (*desprenderse*) to come off; (*deshacerse*) to come apart **2.** (*perder el afecto*) ~**se de alguien** to lose one's feelings for sb

despego [des·'pe·ɣo] *m* (*falta de afecto*) lack of feeling; **sentir** ~ **por alguien** to feel nothing for sb

despegue [des·'pe·ɣe] *m* AVIAT, ECON take-off; (*cohete*) blast-off, lift-off

despeinado, -a [des·pei·'na·do, -a] *adj* unkempt

despeinar [des·pei·'nar] I. *vt* to ruffle II. *vr* **me despeiné** I got my hair messed up

despejado, -a [des·pe·'xa·do, -a] *adj* **1.** (*sin nubes, obstáculos*) clear **2.** (*ancho*) wide; (*habitación*) spacious **3.** (*listo*) smart **4.** (*despierto*) alert; (*cabeza*) clear

despejar [des·pe·'xar] I. *vt* **1.** (*un lugar, una mesa*) to clear; (*sala*) to tidy up; ~ **la calle de nieve** to clear the street of snow **2.** (*una situación*) to clarify; (*un misterio*) to clear up **3.** (*una persona*) **el aire fresco despejó mi mente** the fresh air cleared my mind **4.** DEP to clear; ~ **el tiro a córner** to concede a corner II. *vr:* ~**se 1.** (*cielo, misterio*) to clear up **2.** (*despabilarse*) to wake up; (*mentalmente*) to sharpen one's wits **3.** (*adquirir desenvoltura*) to gain self-confidence **4.** (*un enfermo*) to improve; **se ha despejado un poco** he/she is feeling a bit better

despeje [des·'pe·xe] *m* (*en fútbol, hockey*) clearance

despellejar [des·pe·je·'xar, des·pe·ʎe-] I. *vt* **1.** (*desollar*) to flay, to skin **2.** *inf* (*criticar*) to lambaste, to cut to bits, to skin alive **3.** *inf* (*desvalijar*) to fleece II. *vr:* ~**se** to peel

despelotarse [des·pe·lo·'tar·se] *vr inf* **1.** (*desnudarse*) to strip off, to strip down **2.** (*de risa*) to split one's sides

despeluzar <z→c> [des·pe·lu·'sar, -'θar] *vt, vr v.* **despeluznar**

despeluznar [des·pe·lus·'nar, des·pe·luθ-] **I.** *vt* **1.** (*causar miedo*) to terrify **2.** *Cuba* (*desplumar*) to pluck **II.** *vr* to be terrified; **se despeluz(n)ó** (**del miedo que tenía**) it made his/her hair stand on end

despensa [des·'pen·sa] *f* **1.** (*fresquera*) larder, pantry **2.** *Arg* (*almacén*) shop

despeñadero [des·pe·ɲa·'de·ro] *m* **1.** GEO precipice **2.** (*riesgo*) danger; **meterse en un ~** to get into danger

despeñadero, -a [des·pe·ɲa·'de·ro, -a] *adj* sheer

despeñar [des·pe·'ɲar] **I.** *vt* to throw down; **~ a alguien por un precipicio** to throw sb over a cliff **II.** *vr:* **~se** to throw oneself down; **el motorista se despeñó por el talud** the driver went headlong down the slope

desperdiciar [des·per·di·'sjar, -'θjar] *vt* to waste; (*ocasión*) to miss

desperdicio [des·per·'di·sjo, -θjo] *m* **1.** (*residuo*) garbage; **~s biológicos** biological waste **2.** (*malbaratamiento*) waste; **no tener ~** *irón* to be good from start to finish *iron*

desperdigar <g→gu> [des·per·di·'ɣar] *vt, vr:* **~se** to scatter

desperezarse <z→c> [des·pe·re·'sar·se, -'θar·se] *vr* to stretch

desperfecto [des·per·'fek·to] *m* **1.** (*deterioro*) damage **2.** (*defecto*) fault, defect

despertador [des·per·ta·'dor] *m* (*reloj*) alarm clock

despertar <e→ie> [des·per·'tar] **I.** *vt* to wake up **II.** *vr:* **~se** to wake up **III.** *m* awakening

despiadado, -a [des·pja·'da·do, -a] *adj* (*inhumano*) ruthless; (*cruel*) cruel

despichar [des·pi·'ʧar] *vi inf* to peg out, to bite the dust

despido [des·'pi·do] *m* (*descontratación*) dismissal; **~ colectivo** mass layoff

despierto, -a [des·'pjer·to, -a] *adj* **1.** (*insomne*) awake **2.** (*listo*) smart; **mente despierta** sharp mind

despilfarrador(a) [des·pil·fa·rra·'dor, -·'do·ra] **I.** *adj* wasteful; (*con dinero*) spendthrift **II.** *m(f)* wasteful person; (*con dinero*) spendthrift

despilfarrar [des·pil·fa·'rrar] *vt* to waste; (*dinero*) to squander

despilfarro [des·pil·'fa·rro] *m* (*derroche*) waste; (*de dinero*) squandering

despintar [des·pin·'tar] **I.** *vt* **1.** (*colores*) to run **2.** (*la realidad*) to misrepresent **3.** *Chile, PRico* **~ a alguien** (*apartar la mirada*) to look away from sb; (*perder de vista*) to lose sight of sb **II.** *vr:* **~se 1.** (*borrarse*) to fade; **~se con el sol** to fade with the sunlight **2.** *inf* (*de la memoria*) **este asunto no se me despinta** I can't forget what happened

despistado, -a [des·pis·'ta·do, -a] **I.** *adj* absent-minded **II.** *m, f* **eres un ~** you're absent-minded

despistar [des·pis·'tar] **I.** *vt* (*confundir*) to confuse; (*desorientar*) to mislead **II.** *vr:* **~se 1.** (*perderse*) to get lost **2.** (*desconcertarse*) to become confused

despiste [des·'pis·te] *m* **1.** (*distracción*) confusion **2.** (*error*) slip; **un ~ lo tiene cualquiera** anyone can make a mistake

desplante [des·'plan·te] *m* rude remark

desplazado, -a [des·pla·'sa·do, -a; -'θa·do, -a] *adj* (*no integrado*) out of place; (*trasladado*) displaced

desplazamiento [des·pla·sa·'mjen·to, des·pla·θa-] *m* **1.** (*traslado*) displacement **2.** (*remoción*) removal

desplazar <z→c> [des·pla·'sar, -'θar] *vt* **1.** (*mover*) to move **2.** (*suplantar*) to displace

desplegable [des·ple·'ɣa·βle] *adj* folding; **silla ~** folding chair

desplegar [des·ple·'ɣar] *irr como* **fregar** *vt* **1.** (*abrir*) to open out; (*desdoblar*) to unfold; (*bandera*) to unfurl **2.** MIL to deploy **3.** (*desarrollar*) to develop; **~ toda su fantasía** to give free rein to one's imagination

despliegue [des·'plje·ɣe] *m* **1.** (*desdoblamiento*) unfolding **2.** MIL deployment

desplomarse [des·plo·'mar·se] *vr* **1.** (*casa, persona*) to collapse **2.** (*desviarse*) to go off course

desplumar [des·plu·'mar] *vt* **1.** (*plumas*) to pluck **2.** (*robar*) to fleece; **~ a alguien jugando a las cartas** to clean sb out at cards

despoblado [des·po·'βla·do] *m* (*yermo*) deserted place

despoblado, -a [des·po·'βla·do, -a] *adj* depopulated

despoblar <o→ue> [des·po·'βlar] *vt* **1.** (*de habitantes*) to depopulate **2.** (*un bosque*) to clear; **el huracán despobló la zona de árboles** the hurricane blew down all the trees in the area

despojar [des·po·'xar] **I.** *vt* to strip; **la ~on de todo** they took everything she had; **~ de un derecho a alguien** to deprive sb of a right **II.** *vr:* **~se 1.** (*desistir*) **~se de algo** to give sth up **2.** (*quitar*) **~ de algo** to remove sth; (*ropa*) to take off

despojo [des·'po·xo] *m* **1.** (*presa*) spoils *pl;* **~ del mar** flotsam and jetsam **2.** *pl* (*restos*) leftovers *pl;* (*del matadero*) rubble; (*mortales*) mortal remains

desposar [des·po·'sar] **I.** *vt* to marry **II.** *vr:* **~se con** to get married to

desposeer [des·po·se·'er] *irr como* **leer** **I.** *vt* **1.** (*expropiar*) to dispossess **2.** (*no reconocer*) to not recognize; **la desposeyeron de sus derechos** they deprived her of her rights **3.** (*destituir*) to oust; **~ a alguien de su cargo** to remove sb from his/her position **4.** (*desplumar*) **~ a alguien de algo** to fleece sb of sth **II.** *vr:* **~se 1.** (*renunciar*) **~se de algo** to give sth up **2.** (*desapropiarse*) **~se de algo** to relinquish sth

desposorio(s) [des·po·'so·rjo(s)] *m(pl)* **1.** (*esponsales*) engagement **2.** (*matrimonio*) marriage

despostar [des·pos·'tar] *vt AmS* to joint meat

déspota ['des·po·ta] *mf* despot

despotismo [des·po·'tis·mo] *m* despotism

despotricar <c→qu> [des·po·tri·'kar] *vi inf* (*maldecir*) **~ de algo/alguien** to rant and rave about sth/sb

despreciable [des·pre·'sja·βle, -'θja·βle] *adj* contemptible; **nada ~** to not be sneered at

despreciar [des·pre·'sjar, -'θjar] **I.** *vt* **1.** (*menospreciar*) to despise **2.** (*rechazar*) to spurn; (*oferta*) to turn down **II.** *vr:* **~se** to run oneself down

despreciativo, -a [des·pre·sja·'ti·βo, -a; des·pre·θja-] *adj* disdainful

desprecio [des·'pre·sjo, -θjo] *m* contempt

desprender [des·pren·'der] **I.** *vt* **1.** (*soltar*) to release **2.** (*olor, gas*) to give off **3.** (*deducir*) to deduce; **de su aviso desprendemos que...** from his/her warning we can deduce that... **II.** *vr:* **~se 1.** (*soltarse*) to untie oneself **2.** (*deshacerse*) to come undone; (*desembarazarse*) to rid oneself of; **~se de cualquier duda** to get rid of any doubts; (*renunciar*) to part with **3.** (*deducirse*) **de tu comportamiento se desprende que...** your behavior shows that...

desprendido, -a [des·pren·'di·do, -a] *adj* (*generoso*) generous; (*altruista*) disinterested

desprendimiento [des·pren·di·'mjen·to] *m* **1.** (*separación*) separation; **~ de tierras** landslide; **~ de retina** detached retina **2.** (*generosidad*) generosity

despreocupación [des·preo·ku·pa·'sjon, -'θjon] *f* **1.** (*indiferencia*) indifference **2.** (*insensatez*) carelessness

despreocupado, -a [des·preo·ku·'pa·do, -a] *adj* **1.** (*negligente*) careless **2.** (*tranquilo*) unconcerned

despreocuparse [des·preo·ku·'par·se] *vr* **1.** (*tranquilizarse*) to stop worrying **2.** (*desatender*) **~se de algo** to neglect sth

despresar [des·pre·'sar] *vt AmS* to carve

desprestigiar [des·pres·ti·'xjar] **I.** *vt* to discredit **II.** *vr:* **~se 1.** (*rebajarse*) to fall into discredit **2.** (*perder reputación*) to see one's reputation suffer

desprevenido, -a [des·pre·βe·'ni·do, -a] *adj* unprepared; **coger a alguien ~** to catch sb unawares [*o* off guard]

desproporción [des·pro·por·'sjon, -'θjon] *f* disproportion

desproporcionado, -a [des·pro·por·sjo·'na·do, -a; des·pro·por·θjo-] *adj* disproportionate

despropósito [des·pro·'po·si·to] *m* stupid remark; **decir ~s** to make stupid remarks

desproveer [des·pro·βe·'er] *irr como proveer vt* to deprive

desprovisto, -a [des·pro·'βis·to, -a] *adj* **~ de** lacking; **el estadio está ~ de las medidas de**

seguridad necesarias the stadium lacks the necessary safety provisions

después [des·'pwes] **I.** *adv* **1.** (*tiempo*) after; **~ de la cena** after supper; **una hora ~** an hour later **2.** (*espacio*) **~ de la torre** behind the tower **3.** (*concesivo*) **~ de todo** after all **II.** *conj* **~ (de) que** after

despuntar [des·pun·'tar] **I.** *vt* (*gastar la punta*) to blunt; (*quitarla*) to remove the tip of **II.** *vi* **1.** (*amanecer*) to dawn; **al ~ la aurora** at the break of dawn **2.** (*distinguirse*) to stand out; **despunta en inglés** he/she excels at English **III.** *vr:* **~se** (*gastarse*) to become blunt

desquiciado, -a [des·ki·'sja·do, -a; -'θja·do, -a] *adj inf* disturbed

desquiciar [des·ki·'sjar, -'θjar] **I.** *vt* **1.** (*desencajar*) to unhinge **2.** (*alterar*) to disturb **II.** *vr:* **~se** to become unstable

desquitar [des·ki·'tar] *vt, vr:* **~se 1.** (*resarcir*) to win back; **~se de una pérdida** to make good a loss **2.** (*desagraviar*) **~ de algo** to make up for sth **3.** (*vengar*) to get even with

desquite [des·'ki·te] *m* **1.** (*satisfacción*) satisfaction **2.** (*venganza*) revenge; **tomar(se) el ~** to avenge oneself

desrielar [des·rrje·'lar] *vi AmL* to derail

destacable [des·ta·'ka·βle] *adj* outstanding

destacado, -a [des·ta·'ka·do, -a] *adj* outstanding

destacamento [des·ta·ka·'men·to] *m* MIL detachment, detail

destacar <c→qu> [des·ta·'kar] **I.** *vi* to stand out; **~ en el deporte** to excel at sports **II.** *vt* (*realzar*) to emphasize **III.** *vr:* **~se** (*sobresalir*) to stand out

destajo [des·'ta·xo] *m* piecework; **trabajar a ~** to do piecework; *fig* to work hard; **hablar a ~** *inf* to talk nineteen to the dozen; **a ~** *Arg, Chile* (*a ojo*) by guesswork

destapar [des·ta·'par] **I.** *vt* **1.** (*abrir*) to open; **~ la olla** to take the lid off the pot **2.** (*desabrigar*) to uncover **3.** (*secretos*) to reveal **II.** *vr:* **~se 1.** (*perder la tapa*) to lose its lid **2.** (*desabrigarse*) to be uncovered **3.** *inf* (*desnudarse*) to strip off, to strip down **4.** (*descubrirse*) to be revealed **5.** (*desahogarse*) **~se con** [*o* **haciendo**] **algo** to let off steam by doing sth

destaponar [des·ta·po·'nar] *vt Perú* (*abrir*) to open

destartalado, -a [des·tar·ta·'la·do, -a] *adj* ramshackle

destellar [des·te·'jar, -'ʎar] *vi* to sparkle

destello [des·'te·jo, -ʎo] *m* **1.** (*rayo*) ray **2.** (*reflejo*) glint **3.** (*resplandor*) sparkle

destemplado, -a [des·tem·'pla·do, -a] *adj* **1.** (*sonido*) out of tune **2.** (*voz*) harsh **3.** (*tiempo*) unpleasant **4.** (*persona*) bad-tempered

destemplanza [des·tem·'plan·sa, -θa] *f* **1.** (*inmoderación*) excess; **con ~** excessively **2.** (*malestar*) indisposition

desteñido, -a [des·te·'ni·do, -a] *adj* (*descolorido*) faded; (*manchado*) discolored

desteñir [des·te·'nir] *irr como ceñir* **I.** *vi* (*des-*

colorarse) to fade; (*despintar*) to run **II.** *vt* **1.**(*descolorar*) to fade **2.**(*manchar*) to stain **III.** *vr:* ~ **se** (*descolorarse*) to fade; (*despintar*) to run, to bleed

desternillarse [des·ter·ni·'jar·se, -'ʎar·se] *vr* ~ **de risa** to laugh one's head off

desterrar <e→ie> [des·te·'rrar] *vt* **1.**(*exiliar*) to exile; ~ **a alguien del país** to exile sb from the country **2.**(*alejar*) to banish

destetar [des·te·'tar] *vt* to wean

destiempo [des·'tjem·po] *m* **a** ~ at the wrong moment

destierro [des·'tje·rro] *m* **1.**(*pena*) exile **2.**(*lugar*) (place of) exile **3.**(*lugar muy alejado*) remote place

destilación [des·ti·la·'sjon, -'θjon] *f* (*alcohol*) distillation; (*petróleo*) refining

destilar [des·ti·'lar] **I.** *vi* to distill **II.** *vt* **1.**(*alambicar*) to distill **2.**(*filtrar*) to filtrate **3.**(*sentimiento*) to exude; **la crítica destila mala leche** the criticism is full of spite

destilería [des·ti·le·'ri·a] *f* distillery; ~ **de petróleo** oil refinery

destinar [des·ti·'nar] *vt* **1.**(*dedicar*) to dedicate; (*asignar*) to assign **2.**(*enviar*) to send **3.**(*designar*) to appoint; ~ **a alguien para Ministro de Defensa** to appoint sb as Minister of Defense **4.** MIL to post

destinatario, -a [des·ti·na·'ta·rjo, -a] *m, f* (*correo*) addressee; (*mercancía*) consignee

destino [des·'ti·no] *m* **1.**(*hado*) fate; **tuvo un** ~ **muy triste** he/she met an unhappy end **2.**(*empleo*) job; **pedir un importante** ~ **en el gobierno** to apply for an important position in the government **3.**(*destinación*) destination; **estación de** ~ destination station; **el barco sale con** ~ **a México** the boat is bound for Mexico **4.**(*finalidad*) purpose

destitución [des·ti·tu·'sjon, -'θjon] *f* dismissal; ~ **del cargo** removal from office

destituir [des·ti·tu·'ir] *irr como huir* *vt* **1.**(*despedir*) to dismiss; ~ **al jefe de gobierno** to remove the head of the government **2.** elev (*privar*) ~ **a alguien de algo** to deprive sb of sth

destornillador(a) [des·tor·ni·ja·'dor, -ʎa·'dor] *m* (*herramienta*) screwdriver; ~ **de estrella** Philips screwdriver

destornillar [des·tor·ni·'jar, -'ʎar] *vt* to unscrew

destrabar [des·tra·'βar] **I.** *vt* to untie **II.** *vr:* ~**se** to come undone

destreza [des·'tre·sa, -θa] *f* skill; ~ **manual** dexterity; **con** ~ skillfully

destripador(a) [des·tri·pa·'dor, -'do·ra] *m(f)* *fig* murderer; **Jack el** ~ Jack the Ripper

destripar [des·tri·'par] *vt* **1.**(*despanzurrar: persona, animal*) to disembowel; (*pez*) to gut **2.**(*despachurrar*) *t. fig* to crush

destrozar <z→c> [des·tro·'sar, -'θar] *vt* **1.**(*despedazar*) to smash; (*libro*) to rip up; (*ropa*) to tear up; ~ **un vehículo** (*conduciendo*) to smash up a vehicle **2.**(*moralmente*) to shatter; **estar destrozado** to be an

emotional wreck **3.** *inf* (*físicamente*) to shatter; **el viaje me ha destrozado** the trip did me in; **he trabajado todo el día y estoy destrozado** I've been working all day and now I'm beat **4.**(*planes*) to ruin **5.**(*enemigo, cosecha*) to destroy

destrozo [des·'tro·so, -θo] *m* **1.**(*daño*) damage **2.**(*acción*) destruction

destrucción [des·truk·'sjon, -truɣ·'θjon] *f* destruction

destructivo, -a [des·truk·'ti·βo, -a] *adj* destructive

destruir [des·tru·'ir] *irr como huir* *vt* **1.**(*destrozar*) to destroy **2.**(*física o moralmente*) to shatter **3.**(*aniquilar*) to annihilate

desubicado, -a [de·su·βi·'ka·do, -a] *adj AmL* out of place; *fig* disoriented

desunión [de·su·'njon] *f* **1.**(*separación*) separation **2.**(*discordia*) disunity

desunir [de·su·'nir] **I.** *vt* **1.**(*separar*) to separate **2.**(*enemistar*) ~ **a dos personas** to cause discord between two people **II.** *vr:* ~**se 1.**(*separar*) to separate **2.**(*enemistar*) to fall out

desuso [de·'su·so] *m* **caer en** ~ to fall into disuse; (*máquina*) to become obsolete

desvalido, -a [des·βa·'li·do, -a] *adj* needy

desvalijar [des·βa·li·'xar] *vt* to clean out

desvalorización [des·βa·lo·ri·sa·'sjon, -θa·'θjon] *f* depreciation; ~ **monetaria** monetary devaluation

desvalorizar <z→c> [des·βa·lo·ri·'sar, -'θar] *vt* to devalue

desván [des·'βan] *m* loft, attic

desvanecer [des·βa·ne·'ser, -'θer] *irr como crecer* **I.** *vt* **1.**(*color*) to tone down **2.**(*dudas*) to dispel; ~ **las sospechas de alguien** to allay sb's suspicions **II.** *vr:* ~**se 1.**(*desaparecer*) to disappear; (*alcohol*) to evaporate; (*colores, esperanzas*) to fade; (*enojo*) to abate; **el entusiasmo se desvaneció rápidamente** the enthusiasm soon abated **2.**(*desmayarse*) to faint

desvanecimiento [des·βa·ne·si·'mjen·to, -θi·'mjen·to] *m* **1.**(*desaparición*) disappearance **2.**(*mareo*) faint; **tener un** ~ to faint

desvariar <*1. pres:* desvarío> [des·βa·ri·'ar] *vi* (*delirar*) to be delirious; (*decir incoherencias*) to talk nonsense

desvarío [des·βa·'ri·o] *m* **1.**(*locura*) craziness; **los** ~**s de una imaginación enfermiza** the crazed imaginings of a sick mind **2.**(*delirio*) delirium

desvelar [des·βe·'lar] **I.** *vt* **1.**(*sueño*) ~ **a alguien** to keep sb awake **2.**(*revelar*) to reveal **II.** *vr:* ~**se 1.**(*no dormir*) to stay awake **2.**(*esmerarse*) ~**se por algo/alguien** to devote oneself to sth/sb

desvelo [des·'βe·lo] *m* **1.**(*insomnio*) insomnia **2.**(*despabilamiento*) alertness **3.**(*pl*) (*atención*) efforts *pl*

desventaja [des·βen·'ta·xa] *f* disadvantage, drawback

desventura [des·βen·'tu·ra] *f* misfortune

desventurado, -a [des·βen·tu·'ra·do, -a] *adj*

unfortunate; **una familia desventurada** an
ill-fated family
desvergonzado, -a [des·βer·yon·'sa·do, -θa·
do, -a] *adj* **1.** (*sinvergüenza*) shameless
2. (*descarado*) brazen
desvergüenza [des·βer·'ywen·sa, -θa] *f*
shamelessness
desvestir [des·βes·'tir] *irr como pedir vt, vr:*
~ **se** to undress
desviación [des·βja·'sjon, -'θjon] *f* **1.** (*torcedura*) deviation; ~ **de la columna vertebral**
curvature of the spine; ~ **jurídica** miscarriage
of justice **2.** (*del tráfico*) diversion, detour;
(*bocacalle*) turning
desviado, -a [des·βi·'a·do, -a] *adj* (*diferente*)
deviant
desviar <*l. pres:* desvío> [des·βi·'ar] I. *vt* (*del
camino, dinero*) to divert; (*de un propósito*)
to distract; ~ **una cuestión** to avoid a problem
II. *vr:* ~ **se** **1.** (*del camino*) to be diverted; (*del
tema*) to be distracted; (*de una idea, inten-
ción*) to be put off; **la brigada se desvió
hacia la izquierda** the brigade turned
towards the left **2.** (*extraviarse*) to get lost
desvincular [des·βin·ku·'lar] I. *vt* to dissociate
II. *vr:* ~ **se** to dissociate oneself
desvío [des·'βi·o] *m* **1.** (*desviación*) deviation
2. (*carretera*) detour; (*temporal*) diversion, detour
desvirtuar <*l. pres:* desvirtúo> [des·βir·tu·
'ar] *vt* (*argumento, prueba*) to undermine;
(*rumor*) to scotch; ~ **la competencia** to distort the marketplace
desvivirse [des·βi·'βir·se] *vr* **1.** (*chiflarse*) ~
por alguien to be crazy about sb; **se desvive
por ella** he's head over heels in love with her
2. (*afanarse*) ~ **con** [*o* **por**] **alguien** to be utterly devoted to sb; **se desvivió por conse-
guir este documento** he/she went to every
length imaginable to get this document
detallado, -a [de·ta·'ja·do, -a; de·ta·'ʎa-] *adj*
detailed; **una lista detallada** an itemized list
detalle [de·'ta·je, -ʎe] *m* **1.** (*pormenor*) detail;
en [*o* **al**] ~ in detail; **venta al** ~ retail sales;
entrar en ~ **s** to go into details **2.** (*finura*) nice
gesture; **has tenido un** ~ **regalándome las
flores** it was very kind of you to give me the
flowers
detallista [de·ta·'jis·ta, -'ʎis·ta] I. *adj* precise;
pey pedantic II. *mf* **1.** (*minucioso*) perfectionist **2.** COM retailer **3.** (*considerado*) thoughtful
person
detectar [de·tek·'tar] *vt* to detect
detective [de·tek·'ti·βe] *mf* detective
detector [de·tek·'tor] *m* detector; ~ **de humo**
smoke detector
detención [de·ten·'sjon, -'θjon] *f* **1.** (*parada*)
stopping; (*de la correspondencia*) withhold-
ing; ~ **del crecimiento** inhibition of growth
2. JUR arrest; ~ **ilegal** false imprisonment;
~ **preventiva** preventive detention, remand in
custody; ~ **domiciliaria** house arrest **3.** (*dilación*) delay; **sin** ~ without delay **4.** (*prolijidad*)

detail; **describir con** ~ to describe in detail;
ha corregido el examen con ~ he/she took
great care in marking the exam
detener [de·te·'ner] *irr como tener* I. *vt*
1. (*parar*) to stop; (*correspondencia*) to withhold; ~ **los progresos de una enfermedad**
to halt the progression of a disease **2.** JUR to arrest **3.** (*retener*) ~ **(en su poder)** to keep (in
one's power) II. *vr:* ~ **se** **1.** (*pararse*) to stop
2. (*entretenerse*) ~ **se en algo** to spend one's
time doing sth
detenido, -a [de·te·'ni·do, -a] I. *adj* **1.** (*minucioso*) thorough **2.** (*arrestado*) arrested II. *m,
f* person under arrest
detenimiento [de·te·ni·'mjen·to] *m* **1.** (*minuciosidad*) care; **con** ~ thoroughly **2.** (*tardanza*) delay; **con** ~ late **3.** JUR arrest
detergente [de·ter·'xen·te] I. *adj* detergent
II. *m* detergent; ~ **para lavar la ropa** laundry
detergent; ~ **lavavajillas** dish liquid; ~ **en
pastilla** laundry tablet
deteriorar [de·te·rjo·'rar] I. *vt* **1.** (*empeorar*)
to worsen **2.** (*romper*) to break **3.** (*gastar*) to
wear out II. *vr:* ~ **se** **1.** (*empeorarse*) to worsen
2. (*estropearse*) to spoil; **mercancía deterio-
rada** spoiled goods
deterioro [de·te·'rjo·ro] *m* **1.** (*desmejora*) deterioration; ~ **de calidad** decline in quality **2.** (*daño*) damage; **sin** ~ undamaged;
~ **debido al almacenamiento** damaged in
storage **3.** (*desgaste*) wear and tear **4.** (*echarse
a perder*) spoiling; **sujeto a** ~ perishable; **de
fácil** ~ easily spoiled
determinación [de·ter·mi·na·'sjon, -'θjon] *f*
1. (*fijación*) establishment; ~ **de los daños**
ascertainment of damages; ~ **de objetivos** setting of objectives **2.** (*decisión*) decision; **tomar
una** ~ to make a decision; **con** ~ determinedly
3. (*audacia*) determination
determinado, -a [de·ter·mi·'na·do, -a] *adj*
1. (*cierto*) *t.* LING definite **2.** (*atrevido*) determined **3.** (*preciso*) specific
determinante [de·ter·mi·'nan·te] I. *adj* decisive II. *m* decisive factor; MAT determinant
determinar [de·ter·mi·'nar] I. *vt* **1.** (*fijar*) to
establish; (*plazo*) to fix **2.** (*decidir*) to decide;
JUR to settle; ~ **un pleito** to adjudicate a (court)
case **3.** (*motivar*) ~ **a alguien a hacer algo** to
determine sb to do sth II. *vr:* ~ **se por algo** to
decide in favor of sth; ~ **se a hacer algo** to decide to do sth
detestable [de·tes·'ta·βle] *adj* loathsome
detestar [de·tes·'tar] *vt* to detest, to loathe
detonación [de·to·na·'sjon, -'θjon] *f*
1. (*acción*) detonation **2.** (*ruido*) explosion
detonador [de·to·na·'dor] *m* detonator
detonante [de·to·'nan·te] I. *adj* **1.** (*explosivo*)
explosive **2.** AmL (*que molesta*) discordant
II. *m* (*causa*) cause
detonar [de·to·'nar] I. *vi* to detonate, to set off
II. *vt* to detonate
detractor(a) [de·trak·'tor, -·'to·ra] I. *adj* deni-
grating II. *m(f)* detractor

detrás [de·'tras] **I.** *adv* **1.** (*local*) behind; **allí** ~ over there, behind that; **entrar por** ~ to come in through the back; **me asaltaron por** ~ they attacked me from behind **2.** (*en el orden*) **el que está** ~ the next one; **primero estás tú y** ~ **van mis amigos** *fig* you're more important to me than my friends **II.** *prep* **1.** (*local: tras*) ~ **de** behind; ~ **de la carta** on the back of the letter; **quedar** ~ **de los otros** to be behind the others; **ir** ~ **de alguien** to be looking for sb; **hablar mal (por)** ~ **de alguien** to criticize sb behind his/her back **2.** (*en el orden*) **uno** ~ **de otro** one after another

detrimento [de·tri·'men·to] *m* **1.** (*daño*) harm; **causa** ~ **de la salud** it damages your health **2.** (*perjuicio*) detriment; **en** ~ **de alguien** to sb's detriment; **en** ~ **de su salud** at cost to his/her health

deuda ['deu·da] *f* **1.** (*débito*) debt; ~ **activa** productive debt; ~ **contraída** debt; ~ **del Estado** Treasury notes/bonds; ~ **externa** foreign debt; ~ **interna** internal debt; ~ **pública** national debt; ~ **a pagar** debt due; ~ **pendiente** outstanding debt; ~ **vencida** mature debt; **cargado de** ~s burdened with debt; **contraer** ~s to get into debt; **sin** ~s free of debt **2.** (*moral*) debt; **estar en** ~ **con alguien** to be indebted to sb; **lo prometido es** ~ **a** promise is a promise **3.** (*pecado*) **y perdónanos nuestras** ~s... and forgive us our sins...

deudor(a) [deu·'dor, -·'do·ra] **I.** *adj* indebted; **saldo** ~ debit balance **II.** *m(f)* debtor; ~ **solidario** joint debtor

devaluación [de·βa·lwa·'sjon, -'θjon] *f* devaluation

devaluar <*1. pres:* devalúo> [de·βa·lu·'ar] *vt* to devalue

devanar [de·βa·'nar] *vr:* ~**se** *Cuba* (*reírse mucho*) to split one's sides laughing **2.** ~ **se los sesos** to rack one's brains

devaneo [de·βa·'neo] *m* (*amorío*) flirtation

devastación [de·βas·ta·'sjon, -'θjon] *f* devastation

devastar [de·βas·'tar] *vt* to devastate

devenir [de·βe·'nir] *irr como venir vi* **1.** (*acaecer*) to occur **2.** (*convertirse*) ~ **en algo** to become sth

devoción [de·βo·'sjon, -'θjon] *f* **1.** (*religión*) religious belief; **fingir** ~ to feign belief **2.** (*oración*) devotion **3.** (*respeto*) devotion; **rezar con** ~ to pray devoutly **4.** (*obediencia*) obedience; **estar a la** ~ **de alguien** to be at sb's disposal **5.** (*fervor*) fervor; **amar con** ~ to love devotedly; **hacer con** ~ to do with great devotion; **tener** ~ **a un santo** to venerate a saint **6.** (*afición*) attachment

devolución [de·βo·lu·'sjon, -'θjon] *f* return; ~ **a origen** return to sender; FIN refund; ~ **de impuestos** tax refund, tax return; **'no se admiten devoluciones'** 'no refunds'

devolver [de·βol·'βer] *irr como volver* **I.** *vt* **1.** to return; *fig* to restore; ~ **bien por mal** to repay evil with good; ~ **un favor** to return a fa-

vor; **devuélvase al remitente** (*en cartas*) return to sender; **esta máquina no devuelve cambio** this machine does not give change; ~ **la pelota al defensa** to pass the ball back to the defender **2.** (*vomitar*) to throw up **II.** *vr:* ~**se** *AmL* (*volver*) to return; ~**se a casa** to go back home

devorador(a) [de·βo·ra·'dor, -·'do·ra] *adj* **hambre** ~a ravenous hunger

devorar [de·βo·'rar] *vt* to devour; ~ **la comida** to wolf down one's food; **la enfermedad devoró sus fuerzas** the illness consumed his/her strength; **me devora la impaciencia** I am consumed with impatience

devoto, -a [de·'βo·to, -a] **I.** *adj* **1.** (*religioso*) devout **2.** (*adicto*) devoted; ~ **admirador de los Beatles** loyal fan of the Beatles **II.** *m, f* **1.** (*creyente*) devotee **2.** (*admirador*) enthusiast

día ['di·a] *m* day; ~ **de año nuevo** New Year's day; ~ **de cumpleaños** birthday; **el** ~ **D** D-day; ~ **de descanso** rest day; ~ **de los difuntos** All Souls' Day; ~ **festivo** holiday; ~ **hábil** [*o* **laborable**] working day; **el** ~ **del juicio final** judgment day; ~ **lectivo** school day; ~ **libre/de baja** day off; ~ **de Reyes** Epiphany; ~ **del santo** saint's day; **cambio del** ~ today's exchange rate; **al abrir el** ~ at the break of day; **al caer el** ~ at the close of day; **al otro** ~ by the next day; **antes del** ~ before the break of day; **de hoy en ocho** ~s eight days from now; **de un** ~ **a otro** from one day to the next; **cualquier** ~ any day; **durante** ~s **enteros** for days at a time; **una diferencia como del** ~ **a la noche** as different as you can get; **un** ~ **sí y otro no, ~ por medio** *AmL* every other day; **el** ~ **de hoy** nowadays; **el** ~ **de mañana** in the future; **el** ~ **menos pensado** one fine day; **el** ~ **que...** the day that...; **el otro** ~ the other day; **en su** ~ in his/her day; **hoy (en)** ~ nowadays; **un buen** ~ one fine day; **un** ~ **de estos** one of these days; **un** ~ **u otro** some day; **hace buen** ~ it's nice weather; **a** ~s at times; **de** ~ by [*o* during the] day; **del** ~ today's; ~ **a** ~ day by day; ~ **tras** [*o* **por**] ~ day after day; **de** ~ **en** ~ from day to day; **¡buenos** ~s! hello; (*por la mañana*) good morning; **¡hasta otro** ~! until another day! ▶ **mañana** **será otro** ~ tomorrow is another day; **tiene los** ~s **contados** his/her days are numbered; **entrado en** ~s getting on; **un** ~ **y otro** ~ again and again; **todo el santo** ~ the whole day long; **alcanzar a alguien en** ~s to outlive sb; **dar a alguien el** ~ to ruin sb's day; **estar al** ~ to be up to date; **un** ~ **es un** ~ it's just one day; **tener** ~s (*viejo*) to be old; (*de mal humor*) to be bad-tempered

diabetes [dja·'βe·tes] *f inv* diabetes

diabético, -a [dja·'βe·ti·ko, -a] *adj, m, f* diabetic

diablo [di·'a·βlo] *m* devil; **ser un** ~ **de hombre** to be an absolute devil; **tener el** ~ **en el cuerpo** to be a little devil; **abogado del** ~

devil's advocate; **duele como el** ~ it hurts like hell ▶ **de mil** ~**s** hellish; **anda el** ~ **suelto** *inf* there's trouble brewing; **aquí anda el** ~ everything is going wrong; **dar al** ~ *inf* to send to hell; **¡vete al** ~**!** go to hell!; **¿cómo** ~**s...?** how on earth...?; **¡qué** ~**s!** hell!; **¡**~**s!** damn!

diablura [dja·'βlu·ra] *f* prank

diabólico, -a [dja·'βo·li·ko, -a] *adj* **1.**(*maligno*) diabolic(al) **2.**(*complicado*) fiendish

diadema [dja·'de·ma] *f* (*corona*) diadem; (*joya*) tiara; (*del pelo*) hair band

diáfano, -a [di·'a·fa·no, -a] *adj* **1.**(*transparente*) transparent **2.**(*translúcido*) translucent **3.**(*claro*) clear; **un argumento** ~ a clear argument

diafragma [dja·'fraɣ·ma] *m* **1.** FOTO, ANAT diaphragm **2.**(*anticonceptivo*) diaphragm

diagnosis [djaɣ·'no·sis] *f inv* diagnosis

diagnosticar <c→qu> [djaɣ·nos·ti·'kar] *vt* to diagnose

diagnóstico [djaɣ·'nos·ti·ko] *m* (*diagnosis*) diagnosis; ~ **precoz** early diagnosis

diagonal [dja·ɣo·'nal] I. *adj* diagonal; **en** ~ diagonally II. *f* diagonal

diagrama [dja·'ɣra·ma] *m* diagram; ~ **de bloques** block diagram; ~ **esquemático** schematic diagram; ~ **de puntos** scatter diagram; ~ **de flujo** flowchart

dial [di·'al] *m* dial; ~ **de velocidad** AUTO speedometer

dialectal [dja·lek·'tal] *adj* dialect

dialéctica [dja·'lek·ti·ka] *f* dialectics *pl*

dialecto [dja·'lek·to] *m* dialect

diálisis [di·'a·li·sis] *f inv* dialysis

dialogar <g→gu> [dja·lo·'ɣar] *vi* (*hablar*) to talk; ~ **con alguien** to have a conversation with sb; **escrito en forma dialogada** written as a dialog

diálogo [di·'a·lo·ɣo] *m* **1.**(*conversación*) conversation **2.** LIT dialog(ue)

diamante [dja·'man·te] *m* diamond; **bodas de** ~ diamond wedding; ~ **brillante** brilliant; ~ (**en**) **bruto** rough [*o* uncut] diamond

diametralmente [dja·me·tral·'men·te] *adv* diametrically; ~ **opuesto** diametrically opposed

diámetro [di·'a·me·tro] *m* diameter

diana [di·'a·na] *f* **1.** MIL reveille; **a toque de** ~ *fig* highly disciplined **2.**(*objeto*) target **3.**(*del blanco*) bull's-eye; **hacer** ~ to hit the bull's-eye

diapasón [dja·pa·'son] *m* MÚS range; ~ **normal** standard pitch; (*objeto*) tuning fork; (*de voz*) pitch-pipe; (*guitarra*) fingerboard; **bajar/subir el** ~ *inf* to turn the volume down/up

diapositiva [dja·po·si·'ti·βa] *f* slide

diariero, -a [dja·'rje·ro, -a] *m, f AmS* paperboy, newspaper vendor

diario [di·'a·rjo] *m* **1.**(*periódico*) (daily) newspaper; ~ **de avisos** classified advertising newspaper **2.**(*dietario*) journal **3.**(*memorias*) diary

diario, -a [di·'a·rjo, -a] *adj* daily; **a** ~ daily; **de** ~ everyday; **uniforme de** ~ service uniform

diarismo [dja·'ris·mo] *m AmL* (*periodismo*) journalism

diarrea [dja·'rrea] *f* diarrhea

dibujante [di·βu·'xan·te] *mf* (*lineal*) draftsman *m*, draftswoman *f;* ~ **proyectista** architectural draftsman *m*, architectural draftswoman *f;* (*de bocetos*) sketcher; (*de caricaturas, dibujos animados*) cartoonist

dibujar [di·βu·'xar] I. *vt* **1.**(*trazar*) to draw; ~ **copiando** to draw from a copy; ~ **según modelo** to draw from a model; ~ **a pulso** to draw freehand; ~ **a lápiz** to draw in pencil **2.**(*describir*) to describe II. *vr:* ~**se** to be outlined

dibujo [di·'βu·xo] *m* **1.**(*acción*) drawing **2.**(*resultado*) drawing; ~ **acotado** contour drawing; ~**s animados** cartoons **3.**(*muestra*) illustration; **con** ~**s** illustrated **4.**(*estampado*) pattern

dic. *abr de* **diciembre** Dec.

dicción [dik·'sjon, diy·'θjon] *f* **1.**(*declamación*) declamation **2.**(*pronunciación*) diction; (*estilo*) eloquence

diccionario [dik·sjo·'na·rjo, diy·θjo-] *m* dictionary; ~ **de artes y ciencias** dictionary of art and science; ~ **enciclopédico** encyclopedic dictionary; ~ **de inglés-español** English-Spanish dictionary

dicha ['di·tʃa] *f* (*suerte*) luck; ~ **conyugal** marital bliss; **por** ~ fortunately; **nunca es tarde si la** ~ **es buena** *prov* better late than never *prov*

dicharachero, -a [di·tʃa·ra·'tʃe·ro, -a] I. *adj* funny II. *m, f* joker

dicho ['di·tʃo] *m* **1.**(*ocurrencia*) observation **2.**(*refrán*) saying **3.** *pl* (*al casarse*) vows *pl;* **tomarse los** ~**s** to take one's vows

dicho, -a ['di·tʃo, -a] I. *pp de* **decir** II. *adj* **dicha gente** the said people; ~ **y hecho** no sooner said than done

dichoso, -a [di·'tʃo·so, -a] *adj* **1.**(*feliz*) ~ **de algo** happy to sth **2.** *irón* (*maldito*) blessed

diciembre [di·'sjem·bre, -'θjem·bre] *m* December; *v.t.* **marzo**

dictado [dik·'ta·do] *m* **1.**(*escuela*) dictation **2.** *fig* (*inspiración*) dictate; **seguir los** ~**s de la conciencia** to follow one's conscience

dictador(a) [dik·ta·'dor, -'do·ra] *m(f)* dictator

dictadura [dik·ta·'du·ra] *f* dictatorship

dictamen [dik·'ta·men] *m* **1.**(*peritaje*) opinion; ~ **en juicio** legal opinion; **dar** ~ to give advice **2.**(*informe*) report; ~ **facultativo** medical report **3.**(*opinión*) opinion; **tomar** ~ **de alguien** to consult with sb **4.** JUR ~ **judicial** legal judgment

dictaminar [dik·ta·mi·'nar] *vi* to render judgment

dictar [dik·'tar] *vt* **1.**(*un dictado*) to dictate **2.**(*una sentencia*) to pass **3.**(*una ley*) to enact **4.**(*un discurso*) to give **5.** *AmS* (*clases*) to teach

didáctico, -a [di·'dak·ti·ko, -a] *adj* didactic; **material** ~ teaching material

diecinueve [dje·si·'nwe·βe, dje·θi-] *adj inv, m* nineteen; *v.t.* **ocho**

dieciocho [dje·si·'o·tʃo, dje·θi-] *adj inv, m* eighteen; *v.t.* **ocho**

dieciséis [dje·si·'seis, dje·θi-] *adj inv, m* sixteen; *v.t.* **ocho**

dieciseisavo, -a [dje·si·sei·'sa·βo, dje·θi-] *adj, m, f* sixteenth; *v.t.* **octavo**

diecisiete [dje·si·'sje·te, dje·θi-] *adj inv* seventeen; *v.t.* **ocho**

diecisieteavo, -a [dje·si·sje·te·'a·βo, -a; dje· θi-] *adj, m, f* seventeenth; *v.t.* **octavo**

diente ['djen·te] *m* **1.** (*de la boca*) tooth; ~ **canino** canine (tooth); ~ **incisivo** incisor; ~ **de leche** milk tooth; ~ **molar** molar; ~**s postizos** false teeth; ~ **picado** tooth with caries; **armado hasta los** ~**s** armed to the teeth; **daba** ~ **con** ~ his/her teeth were chattering **2.** BOT ~ **de ajo** clove of garlic; ~ **de león** dandelion ▸ **decir algo entre** ~**s** to mumble sth; **poner los** ~**s largos a alguien** to make sb green with envy; **pelar el** ~ *AmL, inf* to smile flirtatiously; **volar** ~ *AmL* (*comer*) to stuff one's face

diesel ['dje·sel] *m* diesel

diestro, -a ['djes·tro, -a] **I.** *adj* <destrísimo *o* diestrísimo> **1.** (*a la derecha*) right; **a** ~ **y siniestro** *fig* left, right and center **2.** (*hábil*) skillful **3.** (*astuto*) cunning **4.** (*que usa la mano derecha*) right-handed **II.** *m, f* matador

dieta [di·'e·ta] *f* **1.** (*para adelgazar*) diet; ~ **absoluta** starvation diet; **estar a** ~ to be on a diet; **poner alguien a** ~ to put sb on a diet **2.** (*alimentación*) ~ **alimenticia** diet; ~ **básica** staple diet **3.** (*asamblea*) diet **4.** *pl* (*retribución*) allowance, expenses *pl*; (*de diputados*) salary

dietético, -a [dje·'te·ti·ko, -a] *adj* dietary; **régimen** ~ diet; **médico** ~ dietician

diez [djes, djeθ] *adj inv, m* ten; *v.t.* **ocho**

diezmar [djes·'mar, djeθ-] *vt* (*aniquilar*) to decimate

difamación [di·fa·ma·'sjon, -'θjon] *f* defamation; (*escrita*) libel; (*oral*) slander

difamar [di·fa·'mar] *vt* to defame; (*por escrito*) to libel; (*hablando*) to slander

difamatorio, -a [di·fa·ma·'to·rjo, -a] *adj* defamatory; (*escrito*) libelous; (*hablando*) slanderous

diferencia [di·fe·'ren·sja, -θja] *f* **1.** (*desigualdad*) difference; ~ **de los tipos de interés** interest differential/margin; **a** ~ **de algo** unlike [*o* in contrast with] sth **2.** (*desacuerdo*) disagreement; **arreglar** (**las**) ~**s** to settle one's differences **3.** MAT difference; ~ **de caja** cash deficit

diferencial¹ [di·fe·ren·'sjal, 'θjal-] **I.** *adj* **1.** (*variable*) variable **2.** MAT differential **II.** *f* MAT differential

diferencial² [di·fe·ren·'sjal, -'θjal] *m* AUTO differential (gear)

diferenciar [di·fe·ren·'sjar, -'θjar] **I.** *vi* to differentiate **II.** *vt* **1.** (*distinguir*) to distinguish

2. MAT to differentiate **III.** *vr:* ~ **se** to differ

diferendo [di·fe·'ren·do] *m AmS* (*disputa*) dispute

diferente [di·fe·'ren·te] **I.** *adj* different; ~**s veces** several times; **España es** ~ Spain is different **II.** *adv* differently; **piensa muy** ~ he/she has a very different way of thinking

diferir [di·fe·'rir] *irr como sentir* **I.** *vi* to differ; ~ **de algo** to be different from sth **II.** *vt* to postpone; ~ **el pago** to delay payment; **transmisión en diferido** pre-recorded broadcast

difícil [di·'fi·sil, -θil] *adj* difficult; ~ **de explicar** difficult to explain; **de** ~ **acceso** hard to get to

difícilmente [di·fi·sil·'men·te, di·fi·θil-] *adv* with difficulty; **un material** ~ **soluble** a substance that is hard to dissolve; (*apenas*) hardly

dificultad [di·fi·kul·'tad] *f* difficulty; **estar en** ~**es** to be in difficulty; **expresarse con** ~ to express oneself with difficulty; **poner** ~**es a alguien** to put sb in a difficult position; **ahí está la** ~ that's where the problem lies

dificultar [di·fi·kul·'tar] *vt* to hinder; ~ **la circulación** to obstruct the traffic

dificultoso, -a [di·fi·kul·'to·so, -a] *adj* difficult; (*laborioso*) arduous

difteria [dif·'te·rja] *f* diphtheria

difuminar [di·fu·mi·'nar] *vt* (*dibujo*) to stump, to blur; (*luz*) to diffuse

difundir [di·fun·'dir] **I.** *vt* to spread; (*gas*) to give off; ~ **por la radio** to broadcast on the radio **II.** *vr:* ~**se** to spread; **la novedad se ha difundido por toda la ciudad** the news has spread throughout the city

difunto, -a [di·'fun·to, -a] **I.** *adj* deceased; **el** ~ **presidente** the late president **II.** *m, f* deceased person; **día de** ~**s** All Souls' Day; **misa de** ~**s** Requiem (mass)

difusión [di·fu·'sjon] *f* **1.** (*expansión, divulgación*) dissemination; TV, RADIO broadcast; ~ **de productos** distribution of products **2.** (*prolijidad*) lengthiness

difuso, -a [di·'fu·so, -a] *adj* **1.** (*extendido*) widespread **2.** (*vago, prolijo*) diffuse

digerir [di·xe·'rir] *irr como sentir vt* **1.** (*la comida*) to digest **2.** (*a una persona*) to stomach; (*noticia, libro*) to absorb

digestión [di·xes·'tjon] *f* (*de alimentos*) digestion; **tener mala** ~ to have stomach problems; **corte de** ~ stomach cramp

digestivo, -a [di·xes·'ti·βo, -a] *adj* digestive; **aparato** ~ ANAT digestive system

digital [di·xi·'tal] *adj* **1.** (*dactilar*) finger; **huellas** ~**es** fingerprints **2.** COMPUT, TÉC digital; **ingreso** ~ digital input; **ordenador** ~ digital computer

digitalizar <z→c> [di·xi·ta·li·'sar, -'θar] *vt* to digitalize

dígito ['di·xi·to] **I.** *adj* digital **II.** *m* MAT, COMPUT digit; ~ **de verificación** verification number; ~ **de control** check bit

dignarse [diɣ·'nar·se] *vr* ~ **hacer algo** to condescend to do sth; **se dignaron invitarnos a su fiesta** *irón* they deigned to invite us to their party

dignidad [diɣ·ni·'dad] *f* **1.** (*respeto*) dignity; **con** ~ with dignity **2.** (*decencia*) decency

digno, -a ['diɣ·no, -a] *adj* **1.** (*merecedor*) deserving; ~ **de compasión** worthy of sympathy; ~ **de confianza** trustworthy; ~ **de fe** worth believing in; ~ **de mención** worth mentioning; ~ **de ver** worth seeing **2.** (*adecuado*) fitting **3.** (*noble*) noble

dije ['di·xe] *m* (*colgante*) charm; **ser un** ~ *inf* (*persona*) to be a treasure [*o* jewel]

dilación [di·la·'sjon, -'θjon] *f* (*aplazamiento*) postponement; (*retraso*) delay; **sin** ~ without delay

dilapidar [di·la·pi·'dar] *vt* to squander; ~ **una fortuna** to squander a fortune

dilatación [di·la·ta·'sjon, -'θjon] *f* **1.** (*ampliación*) expansion; MED dilation; ~ **del mercado** COM expansion of the market **2.** (*desahogo*) calm

dilatar [di·la·'tar] I. *vt* **1.** (*extender*) to expand; MED to dilate **2.** (*aplazar*) to postpone; ~ **la reunión** to postpone the meeting **3.** (*retrasar*) to delay **4.** (*prolongar*) to prolong II. *vr:* ~**se** **1.** (*extenderse*) to expand **2.** *AmL* (*demorar*) to delay

dilema [di·'le·ma] *m* dilemma; **encontrarse en un** ~ to be in a dilemma

diligencia [di·li·'xen·sja, -θja] *f* **1.** (*esmero*) diligence **2.** (*agilidad*) skill **3.** (*trámite*) paperwork; ~**s policiales** police proceedings; **evacuar una** ~ to resolve a matter; **hacer** ~**s** to do business **4.** (*asunto administrativo*) procedure; ~ **judicial/policial** legal/police procedures; ~**s preparatorias** initial proceedings; ~**s de prueba** taking of evidence **5.** (*nota oficial*) communication; ~ **de notificación** official notification **6.** (*carreta*) stagecoach

diligente [di·li·'xen·te] *adj* (*cuidadoso, aplicado*) diligent

dilucidar [di·lu·si·'dar, di·lu·θi-] *vt* to elucidate

diluir [di·lu·'ir] *irr como huir* I. *vt* **1.** (*líquidos, colores*) to dilute; **sin** ~ undiluted **2.** (*sólidos*) to dissolve; **dejar** ~ **en la boca** to allow to dissolve in one's mouth II. *vr:* ~**se** to dissolve

diluviar [di·lu·'βjar] *vimpers* to pour down rain

diluvio [di·'lu·βjo] *m* **1.** (*lluvia*) downpour **2.** *inf* (*abundancia*) shower; ~ **de balas** hail of bullets

dimanar [di·ma·'nar] *vi* to emanate; **tu éxito dimana de tu constancia** your success stems from your perseverance

dimensión [di·men·'sjon] *f* (*extensión, tamaño, medida*) dimension; *fig* magnitude; **de dos dimensiones** in two dimensions; **la** ~ **cultural** the cultural aspect; **una edificio de grandes dimensiones** a large building; **un escándalo de grandes dimensiones** a major scandal; **este asunto está alcanzando dimensiones inesperadas** this affair is turning out to be bigger than people expected

diminutivo [di·mi·nu·'ti·βo] *m* LING diminutive

diminutivo, -a [di·mi·nu·'ti·βo, -a] *adj* di-

minutive; **lente diminutiva** diminishing lens

diminuto, -a [di·mi·'nu·to, -a] *adj* tiny

dimisión [di·mi·'sjon] *f* resignation; **presentar la** ~ to resign

dimitir [di·mi·'tir] *vi, vt* to resign; ~ **de un cargo** to resign (from) a position; **dimitió de presidente del club** he/she resigned as club president

Dinamarca [di·na·'mar·ka] *f* Denmark

dinamarqués, -esa [di·na·mar·'kes, -·'ke·sa] I. *adj* Danish II. *m, f* Dane

dinámica [di·'na·mi·ka] *f* dynamics *pl*

dinámico, -a [di·'na·mi·ko, -a] *adj* dynamic

dinamismo [di·na·'mis·mo] *m* (*energía*) dynamism

dinamita [di·na·'mi·ta] *f* dynamite

dinamitar [di·na·mi·'tar] *vt* to dynamite

dinamizar [di·na·mi·'sar, -'θar] *vt* to vitalize

dinamo [di·'na·mo] *f*, **dínamo** ['di·na·mo] *f* dynamo

dinastía [di·nas·'ti·a] *f* dynasty

dineral [di·ne·'ral] *m* fortune; **costar un** ~ *inf* to cost a fortune

dinero [di·'ne·ro] *m* money; ~ **blanco** silver coins; ~ **en caja** cash in hand; ~ **electrónico** e-cash; ~ **metálico** [*o* **contante y sonante**] hard [*o* ready] cash; ~ **de rescate** ransom money; ~ **de curso legal** legal tender; ~ **negro** undeclared money; ~ **en reserva** cash reserve; ~ **suelto** loose change; **pagar en** ~ to pay in cash; **estar mal de** ~ to be short of money; **ser alguien de** ~ to be rich ▶ ~ **en manos de necio como agua se va** *prov* a fool and his money are soon parted *prov*

dinosaurio [di·no·'sau·rjo] *m* dinosaur

dintel [din·'tel] *m* ARQUIT lintel

diñar [di·'ɲar] *vt inf* to give; ~**la** *inf* to kick the bucket

dio [djo] **3.** *pret de* **dar**

diócesis [di·'o·se·sis, -θe·sis] *f inv* diocese

diodo [di·'o·do] *m* diode

dioptría [djop·'tri·a] *f* diopter

dios(a) [djos, 'djo·sa] *m(f)* god *m*, goddess *f*

Dios [djos] *m* God; ~ **Hombre** Jesus Christ; ~ **mediante** God willing; ~ **te bendiga** God bless you; **¡~ nos libre!** Heaven help us!; **¡~ sabe!** God knows!; ~ **sabe que estuve ahí** I swear I was there; ~ **tenga en su gloria** God rest his/her soul; **¡alabado sea** ~! praise the Lord!; **así** ~ **me asista** JUR so help me God; ~ **lo llamó** he/she went to meet his/her maker; **¡~ mío!** my God!; **¡ay** ~! oh dear!; **¡santo** ~! my God! ▶**a la buena de** ~ at random; **como** ~ **le trajo al mundo** stark naked; **¡~ nos coja confesados!** Lord help us!; **todo** ~ everyone; ~ **aprieta pero no ahoga** *prov* God strikes not with both hands *prov;* ~ **dirá** time will tell; **hacer algo como** ~ **manda** to do sth properly; **si** ~ **quiere** God willing; **¡sabe** ~! God only knows!; **que sea lo que** ~ **quiera** if it is meant to be; **¡válgame** ~! good God!; **¡vaya por** ~! for Heaven's sake!; **venga** ~ **y lo vea** I'll eat my hat; **¡vive** ~! I swear to God!;

vivir como ~ to live like a lord; **¡a** ~**!** goodbye!; **¡por** ~**!** for God's sake!

dióxido [di·'ok·si·do] *m* dioxide

diploma [di·'plo·ma] *m* diploma; ~ **de asistencia** attendance certificate; ~ **de bachiller(ato)** ≈*high school diploma;* ~ **de capitán** captain's commission; ~ **de maestría** teaching certificate; ~ **de reconocimiento** official diploma; ~ **universitario** university diploma

diplomacia [di·plo·'ma·sja, -θja] *f* **1.** (*política, tacto*) diplomacy **2.** (*cuerpo*) diplomatic corps **3.** (*carrera*) diplomatic career

diplomado, -a [di·plo·'ma·do, -a] *adj* qualified; **traductora diplomada** qualified translator

diplomático, -a [di·plo·'ma·ti·ko, -a] **I.** *adj* diplomatic **II.** *m, f* diplomat

diptongo [dip·'ton·go] *m* diphthong

diputación [di·pu·ta·'sjon, -'θjon] *f* **1.** (*delegación*) deputation; ~ **provincial** provincial delegation of government **2.** *Méx* (*edificio*) town hall

diputado, -a [di·pu·'ta·do, -a] *m, f* member of parliament; ~ **independiente** independent (member)

dique ['di·ke] *m* **1.** (*rompeolas*) dike; ~ **de abrigo** breakwater **2.** NÁUT dry dock; ~ **flotante** floating dock **3.** (*freno*) brake; **poner un** ~ **a algo** to restrain sth

dirección [di·rek·'sjon, -reɣ·'θjon] *f* **1.** (*rumbo*) direction; ~ **de la circulación** direction of traffic; ~ **única** one-way; ~ **prohibida** no entry; ~ **de marcha** gear control; ~ **visual** viewing direction; **en** ~ **longitudinal** lengthwise; **en** ~ **opuesta** in the opposition direction; **el viento soplaba en** ~ **oeste** the wind was blowing from the east; **salir con** ~ **a España** to leave for Spain **2.** (*administración, mando*) direction; ~ **central** central control; ~ **general** head office; ~ **comercial** business management; ~ **del Estado** state control; ~ **política** political control; ~ **regional** regional government; **alta** ~ senior management **3.** (*guía*) direction; ~ (**artística**) TEAT artistic direction; ~ **de personal** personnel management; **bajo la** ~ **de** directed by **4.** (*señas*) address; ~ **comercial** business address; ~ **de correo electrónico** e-mail address **5.** AUTO steering; ~ **asistida** power steering

directa [di·'rek·ta] *f* AUTO top gear; (*coche automático*) drive

directiva [di·rek·'ti·βa] *f* **1.** (*dirección*) board (of directors) **2.** (*instrucción*) directive

directivo, -a [di·rek·'ti·βo, -a] **I.** *adj* managing; **junta directiva** managing committee **II.** *m, f* **1.** (*ejecutivo*) director; (*gerente*) manager **2.** (*de la junta directiva*) member of the board of directors

directo [di·'rek·to] *m* **1.** FERRO direct train **2.** DEP straight (punch)

directo, -a [di·'rek·to, -a] *adj* **1.** (*recto*) straight **2.** (*inmediato, franco*) direct; **transmisión en** ~ live broadcast; **un tren** ~ a through train;

seguir el camino más ~ to take the shortest way

director(a) [di·rek·'tor, --'to·ra] **I.** *adj* managing **II.** *m(f)* director; (*jefe*) manager; ~ **accidental** [*o* **en funciones**] acting director; ~ **administrativo** administrative director; ~ **de departamento** department manager; ~ (**de escena**) CINE, TEAT director; ~ (**de escuela**) principal *mf;* ~ **de fábrica** factory manager; ~ **general** managing director; ~ **de la obra** project manager; ~ **de orquesta** conductor; ~ **invitado** guest conductor; ~ **de sucursal** branch manager; ~ **técnico** technical director; ~ **de la tesis** doctoral advisor

directorio [di·rek·'to·rjo] *m* **1.** (*junta*) governing body **2.** (*agenda*) address book **3.** COMPUT directory; ~ **raíz** root [*o* parent] directory **4.** (*guía de teléfonos*) telephone book [*o* directory]

directriz [di·rek·'triθ] *f* **1.** (*orientación*) guideline **2.** MAT directrix

dirigente [di·ri·'xen·te] *mf* leader; **los** ~**s** the leadership; **preparar a los** ~**s** to train the leadership

dirigir <g→j> [di·ri·'xir] **I.** *vt* **1.** (*un coche, un buque*) to steer **2.** (*el tráfico*) to direct **3.** (*un envío, palabras*) to address **4.** (*la vista*) to turn; ~ **todas sus atenciones a algo** *fig* to focus all one's effort on sth **5.** (*una nación*) to lead; (*empresa*) to manage; (*finca*) to run; (*orquesta, debate*) to conduct; ~ **una casa** to run a household **6.** (*por un camino*) to lead **7.** CINE, TEAT, TV to direct **II.** *vr:* ~ **se 1.** (*a un lugar*) ~**se a** to head for/towards **2.** (*a una persona*) ~**se a alguien** to address sb

discapacitado, -a [dis·ka·pa·si·'ta·do, -a; dis·ka·pa·θi·] *adj* disabled, handicapped

discernimiento [di·ser·ni·'mjen·to, dis·θer-] *m* **1.** (*acción de distinguir*) differentiation; (*capacidad de distinguir*) discernment **2.** (*juicio*) discrimination; **obrar sin** ~ to behave indiscriminately

discernir [di·ser·'nir, dis·θer-] *irr como cernir vt* (*diferenciar*) to differentiate; ~ **entre lo bueno y lo malo** to distinguish between good and bad

disciplina [di·si·'pli·na, dis·θi-] *f* discipline

disciplinado, -a [di·si·pli·'na·do, -a; dis·θi-] *adj* disciplined

disciplinar [di·si·pli·'nar, dis·θi-] *vt* (*someter*) to discipline

disciplinario, -a [di·si·pli·'na·rjo, -a; dis·θi-] *adj* disciplinary; **sanción disciplinaria** disciplinary measure

discípulo, -a [di·'si·pu·lo, -a; dis·'θi-] *m, f* **1.** (*alumno*) pupil **2.** (*seguidor*) disciple

disc-jockey <dis yoqueis> [dis 'jo·kei] *mf* DJ, disc jockey

disco ['dis·ko] *m* **1.** (*lámina circular*) disk; (*en el teléfono*) dial; ~ **de freno** brake disk; ~ **de horario** parking permit; ~ **de señales** FERRO signal (disk) **2.** MÚS record; ~ **de larga duración** LP; **siempre pones el mismo** ~ *inf* you always go on about the same thing; **¡cambia el ~ ya!** *inf* give it a break! **3.**(*semáforo*) traffic light **4.** COMPUT disk; **~ de arranque** boot disk; **~ duro** hard disk; **~ flexible** floppy (disk)

discográfico, -a [dis·ko·'γra·fi·ko, -a] *adj* record

díscolo, -a ['dis·ko·lo, -a] *adj* disobedient

disconforme [dis·kon·'for·me] *adj* **1.**(*persona*) in disagreement **2.**(*cosa*) incompatible

disconformidad [dis·kon·for·mi·'dad] *f* **1.**(*con algo, entre personas*) disagreement; **se te nota tu ~ con la decisión** you obviously disagree with the decision **2.**(*de cosas*) incompatibility

discontinuidad [dis·kon·ti·nwi·'dad] *f* **1.**(*inconstancia*) discontinuity **2.**(*interrupción*) interruption

discontinuo, -a [dis·kon·'ti·nwo, -a] *adj* **1.**(*inconstante*) discontinuous **2.**(*interrumpido*) interrupted

discordancia [dis·kor·'dan·sja, -θja] *f* **1.**(*disconformidad*) disagreement; **hubo ~s a la hora de elegir un representante** there was a clash over the choice of representative **2.** MÚS discordance, dissonance

discordante [dis·kor·'dan·te] *adj* **1.**(*opinión*) conflicting **2.** MÚS discordant, dissonant

discordia [dis·'kor·dja] *f* discord

discoteca [dis·ko·'te·ka] *f* **1.**(*local*) disco(theque) **2.**(*discos*) record collection

discreción [dis·kre·'sjon, -'θjon] *f* discretion; **~ absoluta** strict privacy; **a ~** at one's discretion; **bajo ~** confidentially; **con ~** tactfully

discrepancia [dis·kre·'pan·sja, -θja] *f* **1.**(*entre cosas*) discrepancy **2.**(*entre personas*) disagreement

discrepante [dis·kre·'pan·te] *adj* divergent

discrepar [dis·kre·'par] *vi* **1.**(*diferenciarse*) to differ **2.**(*disentir*) to dissent; **discrepo de lo que Ud. piensa sobre eso** I disagree with what you think about that

discreto, -a [dis·'kre·to, -a] *adj* (*reservado*) discreet; (*cantidad*) modest

discriminación [dis·kri·mi·na·'sjon, -'θjon] *f* **1.**(*perjuicio*) discrimination **2.**(*diferenciación*) differentiation; **de difícil ~** difficult to distinguish between

discriminar [dis·kri·mi·'nar] *vt* **1.**(*diferenciar*) to differentiate (between) **2.**(*perjudicar*) to discriminate against

discriminatorio, -a [dis·kri·mi·na·'to·rjo, -a] *adj* discriminatory

disculpa [dis·'kul·pa] *f* **1.**(*perdón*) apology; **admitir una ~** to accept an apology; **pedir ~s** to apologize; **eso no tiene ~** there is no excuse **2.**(*pretexto*) excuse; **¡no valen ~s!** no excuses!

disculpable [dis·kul·'pa·βle] *adj* pardonable

disculpar [dis·kul·'par] I. *vt* **1.**(*perdonar*) to forgive **2.**(*justificar*) to justify; **tu inexperiencia no disculpa ese comportamiento** your inexperience does not excuse such behavior II. *vr:* **~se** to apologize

discurrir [dis·ku·'rrir] I. *vi* **1.**(*pensar*) **~ sobre algo** to ponder sth **2.**(*andar*) to roam; **los niños discurrían por la feria** the children wandered around the fair **3.**(*río*) to flow **4.**(*transcurrir*) to pass II. *vt* to come up with

discurso [dis·'kur·so] *m* **1.**(*arenga*) speech; **~ de clausura** closing speech; **~ de recepción** opening speech; **~ solemne** formal speech; **pronunciar un ~** to make a speech **2.**(*plática*) talk **3.**(*disertación escrita*) dissertation; (*oral*) presentation **4.**(*transcurso*) passing

discusión [dis·ku·'sjon] *f* **1.**(*debate*) discussion; **~ del presupuesto** POL budget debate; **~ pública** public debate **2.**(*riña*) argument; **entablar una ~** to start an argument; **sin ~** without argument [*o* question]

discutible [dis·ku·'ti·βle] *adj* **1.**(*disputable*) debatable **2.**(*dudoso*) doubtful

discutido, -a [dis·ku·'ti·do, -a] *adj* controversial

discutir [dis·ku·'tir] I. *vi, vt* **1.**(*hablar*) to discuss; **~ un asunto** to discuss sth; **~ el recorte del presupuesto** to debate the budget cut; **~ sobre el precio** to argue about the price **2.**(*opinar diferentemente*) **~ de** [*o* sobre] **algo** to argue about [*o* over] sth II. *vt* (*contradecir*) **siempre me discutes lo que digo** you always contradict what I say

disecar <c→qu> [di·se·'kar] *vt* **1.** ANAT to dissect **2.**(*preparar un animal muerto*) to stuff **3.**(*secar una flor*) to press

disección [di·sek·'sjon, -seγ·'θjon] *f* ANAT dissection

diseminar [di·se·mi·'nar] I. *vt* **1.**(*semillas*) to disperse **2.**(*noticias*) to spread II. *vr:* **~se** to spread

disentería [di·sen·te·'ri·a] *f* MED dysentery

disentimiento [di·sen·ti·'mjen·to] *m* disagreement

disentir [di·sen·'tir] *irr como sentir vi* to dissent; **disiento de tu opinión** I disagree with you; **en religión disentimos profundamente** we have deep differences regarding religion

diseñador(a) [di·se·ɲa·'dor, -·'do·ra] *m(f)* **1.**(*dibujante*) artist **2.**(*decorador*) designer

diseñar [di·se·'ɲar] *vt* **1.**(*crear*) to design **2.**(*dibujar*) to draw; (*delinear*) to draft **3.**(*proyectar*) to plan

diseño [di·'se·ɲo] *m* **1.**(*dibujo*) drawing; (*boceto*) sketch; (*esbozo*) outline; **~ de construcción** construction plan; **~ de página** *t.* ′ COMPUT page design **2.**(*forma*) design; **~ ergonómico** ergonomic design **3.**(*en tejidos*) pattern **4.**(*descripción*) description

disertación [di·ser·ta·'sjon, -'θjon] *f* (*escrita*) dissertation; (*oral*) presentation

disertar [di·ser·'tar] *vi* (*por escrito*) to write a dissertation; (*oralmente*) to give a presentation, to expound

disfraz [dis·'fras, -'fraθ] *m* **1.**(*para engañar*) disguise; (*traje*) fancy dress, costume **2.**(*di-*

simulación) pretense; **presentarse sin ~** to be frank

disfrazar <z→c> [dis·fra·'sar, -'θar] I. *vt* **1.** (*enmascarar*) to disguise **2.** (*escándalo*) to cover up; (*voz*) to disguise; (*sentimiento, embarazo*) to hide II. *vr:* ~ **se de** (*enmascararse*) to disguise oneself as

disfrutar [dis·fru·'tar] *vi, vt* **1.** (*gozar*) ~ **de algo** to enjoy sth; ~ **de excelente salud** to enjoy excellent health; ~ **de licencia** to be on leave **2.** (*poseer*) ~ **de algo** to have sth (*de*) **3.** (*utilizar*) to use (sth); (*sacar provecho*) to enjoy (sth)

disfrute [dis·'fru·te] *m* **1.** (*goce*) enjoyment **2.** (*aprovechamiento*) benefit

disgregar <g→gu> [dis·γre·'γar] I. *vt* **1.** (*materia*) to disintegrate **2.** (*gente*) to disperse II. *vr:* ~ **se 1.** (*gente*) to disperse **2.** (*materia*) to disintegrate

disgustar [dis·γus·'tar] I. *vt* **1.** (*desagradar*) to displease; **me disgusta** I don't like it **2.** (*enfadar*) to anger; (*ofender*) to offend II. *vr:* ~ **se 1.** (*enfadarse*) ~ **se por** [*o* **de**] **algo** to get angry about sth **2.** (*ofenderse*) ~ **se por algo** to be offended about sth; **se ha disgustado por tus comentarios** he/she took offense at your comments **3.** (*reñir*) ~ **se con alguien** to quarrel with sb

disgusto [dis·'γus·to] *m* **1.** (*desagrado*) displeasure; (*repugnancia*) repulsion; **estar a ~** to be ill at ease **2.** (*aflicción*) suffering; (*molestia*) annoyance; (*enfado*) anger; **dar un ~ a alguien** (*afligir*) to cause sb suffering; (*causar molestias*) to annoy sb **3.** (*pelea*) quarrel

disidencia [di·si·'den·sja, -θja] *f* POL dissent
disidente [di·si·'den·te] *adj, mf* dissident

disimulación [di·si·mu·la·'sjon, -'θjon] *f* **1.** (*fingimiento*) pretense **2.** (*ocultación*) concealment **3.** (*tolerancia*) tolerance

disimular [di·si·mu·'lar] I. *vi* to pretend II. *vt* **1.** (*ocultar*) to conceal; ~ **el miedo** to hide one's fear; **no ~ algo** to not hide sth **2.** (*tolerar*) to tolerate; ~ **algo a alguien** to tolerate sth from sb

disimulo [di·si·'mu·lo] *m* (*fingimiento*) pretense; (*engaño*) deceit; **con ~** furtively

disipado, -a [di·si·'pa·do, -a] *adj* (*libertino*) dissipated

disipar [di·si·'par] I. *vt* (*nubes, niebla*) to disperse; (*dudas*) to dispel; **el sol disipa las nieblas** the sun disperses the clouds; ~ **el cansancio** to dispel one's tiredness II. *vr:* ~ **se** to disperse; (*dudas*) to vanish; ~ **se en humo** (*desaparecer*) to vanish into thin air; (*fracasar*) to go up in smoke

dislexia [dis·'lek·sja] *f* dyslexia

disléxico, -a [dis·'lek·si·ko, -a] *adj, m, f* dyslexic

dislocación [dis·lo·ka·'sjon, -'θjon] *f* MED dislocation

dislocar <c→qu> [dis·lo·'kar] I. *vt* **1.** MED to **1.** dislocate **2.** (*desplazar*) to displace II. *vr:* ~ **se 1.** (*deshacerse*) to come apart **2.** (*desar-*

ticularse) to be dislocated

disminución [dis·mi·nu·'sjon, -'θjon] *f* decrease; ~ **de los gastos** fall in spending; ~ **de la natalidad** decline in the birth rate; ~ **de la pena** JUR remission of sentence; ~ **de peso** weight loss; ~ **de los precios** fall in prices; ~ **de la presión** TÉC loss of pressure; ~ **de la producción** fall in production; ~ **de riesgo** risk reduction; ~ **de tamaño** reduction in size; ~ **de la tensión** reduction of tension; ~ **del valor** depreciation; ~ **de las ventas** fall in sales; **ir en ~** to diminish

disminuir [dis·mi·nu·'ir] *irr como huir* I. *vi* (*en intensidad*) to diminish; (*número*) to decrease; (*existencias*) to decline; ~ **de tamaño** to shrink II. *vt* to diminish; (*precio, sueldo*) to lower; (*velocidad*) to reduce; ~ **de tamaño** to make smaller; ~ **en duración** to make shorter; ~ **la ganancia** to reduce profits

disociación [di·so·sja·'sjon, -θja·'θjon] *f* separation

disociar [di·so·'sjar, -'θjar] *vt, vr:* ~ **se** to separate

disoluble [di·so·'lu·βle] *adj* **1.** (*contrato*) rescindable **2.** QUÍM soluble

disolución [di·so·lu·'sjon, -'θjon] *f* **1.** (*dilución*) dissolution; (*de la familia*) break-up; (*de las costumbres*) dissoluteness; ~ **de contrato** rescission of a contract **2.** QUÍM solution

disolvente [di·sol·'βen·te] *m* QUÍM solvent; (*para pintura*) thinner

disolver [di·sol·'βer] *irr como volver vt, vr:* ~ **se** (*manifestación*) to dissolve; (*reunión*) to break up

disonancia [di·so·'nan·sja, -θja] *f* **1.** MÚS dissonance **2.** (*discordancia*) discord

dispar [dis·'par] *adj* dissimilar

disparado, -a [dis·pa·'ra·do, -a] *adj* **salir ~** to rush off

disparador [dis·pa·ra·'dor] *m* **1.** (*de un arma*) trigger; **poner en el ~** *inf* to drive to distraction **2.** FOTO shutter release; ~ **automático** automatic shutter release

disparar [dis·pa·'rar] I. *vt* (*un proyectil, el arma*) to fire; ~ **un tiro/flechas a** [*o* **contra**] **alguien** to fire a shot/arrows at sb; ~ **una piedra contra alguien** to throw a stone at sb II. *vi* (*tirar*) to fire; ~ **contra alguien** to fire at sb **2.** *AmL* (*caballo*) to bolt III. *vr:* ~ **se 1.** (*arma*) to go off **2.** (*precios*) to shoot up **3.** (*desbocarse*) to blow one's top

disparatado, -a [dis·pa·ra·'ta·do, -a] *adj* **1.** (*absurdo*) nonsensical **2.** *inf* (*desmesurado*) outrageous

disparatar [dis·pa·ra·'tar] *vi* (*hablar*) to talk nonsense; (*obrar*) to act foolishly

disparate [dis·pa·'ra·te] *m* **1.** (*insensatez: acción*) foolish act; (*comentario*) foolish remark; (*idea*) foolish idea **2.** *inf* (*mucho*) **me gusta un ~** I really love him/her/it; **costar un ~** to cost a fortune

disparidad [dis·pa·ri·'dad] *f* disparity; ~ **de precios** ECON difference in prices

disparo [dis·'pa·ro] *m* **1.**(*el disparar*) firing **2.**(*tiro*) shot; ~ **al aire** shot into the air; ~ **de partida** firing of starting pistol

dispensable [dis·pen·'sa·βle] *adj* (*impedimento*) dispensable; (*error*) forgivable

dispensador [dis·pen·sa·'dor] *m*, **dispensadora** [dis·pen·sa·'do·ra] *f* (*aparato*) dispenser

dispensar [dis·pen·'sar] *vt* **1.**(*otorgar*) to give out; ~ **cuidados a alguien** to care for sb; ~ **favores/atención a alguien** to lavish favors/attention on sb; ~ **ovaciones/elogios a alguien** to shower sb with acclaim/praise **2.**(*librar*) to release; (*de molestias*) to relieve; ~ **a alguien de su cargo** to relieve sb of his/her position; ~ **a alguien del servicio militar** to exempt sb from military service; **me ~on del castigo** they let me off being punished **3.**(*excusar*) to forgive; **dispénseme que le interrumpa** forgive me for interrupting

dispensario [dis·pen·'sa·rjo] *m* dispensary; ~ **sanitario** (health) clinic

dispepsia [dis·'peβ·sja] *f* dyspepsia

dispersar [dis·per·'sar] **I.** *vt* to spread; (*personas, animales*) to disperse; MIL to put to flight; (*una manifestación*) to break up; (*light*) to diffuse; FÍS to scatter; ~ **sus energías** to divide one's energy **II.** *vr:* ~ **se** (*semillas*) to be dispersed; (*personas, animales*) to disperse; MIL to spread out

dispersión [dis·per·'sjon] *f* dispersion; FÍS diffusion; ~ **de la luz** diffusion of light; ~ **de la nubosidad** dispersion of the clouds; **pintura de** ~ emulsion paint; **la** ~ **de las tropas** the dispersal of the troops; **la** ~ **de los manifestantes** the breaking up of the demonstration

disperso, -a [dis·'per·so, -a] *adj* scattered; MIL in disarray

disponer [dis·po·'ner] *irr como poner* **I.** *vi* to have the use; **puede** ~ **de mí cuando Ud. quiera** I am at your disposal; ~ **de tiempo** to have time **II.** *vt* **1.**(*colocar*) to place; ~ **las sillas en círculo** to set out the chairs in a circle **2.**(*preparar*) to prepare; (*la mesa*) to lay; ~ **las camas** to make the beds up **3.**(*determinar*) to stipulate; ~ **en testamento** to dispose of in a will **III.** *vr:* ~ **se 1.**(*colocarse*) to position oneself **2.**(*prepararse*) to get ready

disponibilidad [dis·po·ni·βi·li·'dad] *f* **1.**(*disposición*) availability **2.** *pl* (*dinero*) cash *pl*

disponible [dis·po·'ni·βle] *adj* available

disposición [dis·po·si·'sjon, -'θjon] *f* **1.**(*colocación*) arrangement; ~ **del espacio** organization of space **2.**(*de ánimo, salud*) disposition **3.**(*para algún fin*) preparation; ~ **de servicio** service provision; **estar en** ~ **de hacer algo** to be ready to do sth **4.**(*disponibilidad*) availability; **de libre** ~ freely available; **estoy a su** ~ I am at your disposal; **poner a** ~ to make available **5.**(*talento*) aptitude; **tener** ~ **para la música** to have an aptitude for music **6.**(*resolución*) agreement; ~ **legal** legal provision; **última** ~ last will and testament; **tomar las disposiciones precisas** to take the appropri-

ate measures

dispositivo [dis·po·si·'ti·βo] *m* device; ~ **de alarma** burglar alarm; ~ **antirrobo** anti-theft device; ~ **de cambio de velocidades** AUTO gears *pl*; ~ **de televisión** video security system; ~ **de visualización** COMPUT monitor; ~ **táctico** MIL plan of action

dispuesto, -a [dis·'pwes·to, -a] **I.** *pp de* **disponer II.** *adj* **1.**(*preparado*) ready; ~ **para el uso** ready to use; **estar** ~ **a trabajar/a negociar** to be prepared to work/to negotiate **2.**(*habilidoso*) capable **3.**(*de ánimo, salud*) **estar bien** ~ (*ánimo*) to be in a good frame of mind; (*de salud*) to be well; **estar mal** ~ (*ánimo*) to be in a poor frame of mind; (*de salud*) to be indisposed

disputa [dis·'pu·ta] *f* (*pelea*) fight; (*conversación*) argument; ~ **legal** legal dispute; **sin** ~ without argument [*o* question]; **en** ~ at issue

disputable [dis·pu·'ta·βle] *adj* disputable

disputar [dis·pu·'tar] **I.** *vi* to argue **II.** *vt* (*competir*) to compete for; ~ **una carrera** to contest a race **III.** *vr:* ~ **se** to compete with one another (for); **todos se disputan la foto** they all want the photograph

disquete [dis·'ke·te] *m* COMPUT floppy disk; ~ **de arranque** start-up disk; ~ **de destino** destination drive; ~ **para instalación** setup disk

disquetera [dis·ke·'te·ra] *f* disk drive

disquisición [dis·ki·si·'sjon, -'θjon] *f* treatise

distancia [dis·'tan·sja, -θja] *f t. fig* distance; ~ **entre ruedas** AUTO inter-wheel spacing; ~ **de seguridad** safe distance; ~ **visual** visibility; **a** ~ (*lejos*) far away; (*desde lejos*) from a distance; **¿a qué** ~? how far?; **acortar** ~s to close the gap; **cubrir** ~s to cover a lot of ground; **guardar las** ~s *fig* to keep one's distance; **tener a alguien a** ~ to keep sb at arm's length

distanciado, -a [dis·tan·'sja·do, -a; -'θja·do, -a] *adj t. fig* distant; **están** ~s *fig* they have drifted apart

distanciamiento [dis·tan·sja·'mjen·to, dis·tan·θja-] *m fig* distance

distanciar [dis·tan·'sjar, -'θjar] **I.** *vt* to distance **II.** *vr:* ~ **se 1.**(*de una persona*) to drift apart **2.**(*de un lugar*) to move away

distante [dis·'tan·te] *adj t. fig* distant

distar [dis·'tar] *vi* to be distant; **disto mucho de creerlo** that's very hard for me to believe

distender <e→ie> [dis·ten·'der] *vt* **1.**(*estirar*) to stretch **2.**(*aflojar*) to loosen; *fig* to relax

distensión [dis·ten·'sjon] *f* (*relajación*) easing of tension; POL détente

distinción [dis·tin·'sjon, -'θjon] *f* **1.**(*diferenciación*) distinction; **a** ~ **de algo** in contrast to sth; **no hacer** ~ to make no distinction; **sin** ~ irrespective of **2.**(*claridad*) clarity **3.**(*honor*) distinction **4.**(*elegancia*) refinement; (*educación*) good manners *pl*

distinguido, -a [dis·tin·'gi·do, -a] *adj* **1.**(*ilustre*) distinguished **2.**(*elegante*) refined

3.(*en cartas*) Dear; ~ **amigo:**... Dear Sir,...
distinguir <gu→g> [dis·tin·'gir] I. *vt* 1.(*diferenciar*) to distinguish; **no ~ lo blanco de lo negro** *inf* to not be able to tell left from right 2.(*divisar*) to make out 3.(*condecorar*) to honor; (*tratar mejor*) to favor; ~ **a alguien con su confianza** to bestow one's trust on sb II. *vr:* ~**se** 1.(*poder ser visto*) to be noticeable 2.(*ser diferente*) to be different
distintivo [dis·tin·'ti·βo] *m* emblem
distintivo, -a [dis·tin·'ti·βo, -a] *adj* **característica distintiva** distinguishing characteristic
distinto, -a [dis·'tin·to, -a] *adj* (*diferente*) different; **es ~ a** [*o* **de**] **los demás** he/it is different from the others
distorsión [dis·tor·'sjon] *f* (*falseamiento*) distortion; **distorsiones de competencia** distortion of the market
distorsionar [dis·tor·sjo·'nar] *vt* to distort
distracción [dis·trak·'sjon, -tray·'θjon] *f* 1.(*entretenimiento*) pastime 2.(*falta de atención*) distraction 3. JUR ~ **de fondos** embezzlement
distraer [dis·tra·'er] I. *vt* 1.(*entretener*) to entertain 2.(*dinero*) to embezzle 3.(*desviar*) to divert II. *vr:* ~**se** 1.(*entretenerse*) to amuse oneself 2.(*no atender*) to be distracted
distraído, -a [dis·tra·'i·do, -a] I. *adj* 1.(*desatento*) distracted 2.(*entretenido*) entertaining 3. *Chile, Méx* (*mal vestido*) badly dressed II. *m, f* **hacerse el ~** to pretend to not notice
distribución [dis·tri·βu·'sjon, -'θjon] *f* 1.(*repartición, disposición*) distribution; (*de correo*) delivery; ~ **de agua** water distribution; ~ **de equipajes** baggage reclaim; ~ **del espacio** spatial distribution; ~ **de funciones** division of functions; ~ **de información** distribution of information 2. COM distribution; ~ **exclusiva** exclusive distribution; ~ **mayorista** wholesale distribution 3. FIN sharing out; ~ **de beneficios** profit breakdown 4. CINE, TÉC distribution; **armario de** ~ ELEC connection cabinet
distribuidor [dis·tri·βwi·'dor] *m* 1. TÉC distributor; ~ **automático** automatic dispenser; ~ **automático de billetes** ticket dispenser 2. COM dealer
distribuidor(a) [dis·tri·βwi·'dor, -'do·ra] *m(f)* distributor; ~ **exclusivo** exclusive distributor; ~ **industrial** industrial retailer; ~ **oficial** official dealer
distribuir [dis·tri·βu·'ir] *irr como huir* I. *vt* 1.(*repartir*) to distribute; (*disponer*) to arrange; (*una tarea*) to allocate; (*el correo*) to deliver 2. COM to distribute II. *vr:* ~**se** to divide up
distributivo, -a [dis·tri·βu·'ti·βo, -a] *adj* distributive; **justicia distributiva** retributive justice
distrito [dis·'tri·to] *m* district; ~ **electoral** constituency; ~ **industrial** industrial area; ~ **judicial** jurisdiction; ~ **de policía** police district
disturbio [dis·'tur·βjo] *m* disturbance, riot
disuadir [di·swa·'dir] *vt* to dissuade; ~ **a alguien de algo** to dissuade sb from sth

disuasión [di·swa·'sjon] *f* dissuasion; POL, MIL deterrence
disuasivo, -a [di·swa·'si·βo, -a] *adj* dissuasive; POL, MIL deterrent; **poder** ~ deterrent
disyuntiva [dis·jun·'ti·βa] *f* choice
disyuntivo, -a [dis·jun·'ti·βo, -a] *adj* disjunctive; **conjunción disyuntiva** LING disjunctive (conjunction)
dita ['di·ta] *f AmC, Chile* debt
DIU ['diu] *m* MED *abr de* **dispositivo intrauterino** IUD
diurético, -a [dju·'re·ti·ko, -a] *adj* diuretic
diurno, -a [di·'ur·no, -a] *adj* daily; **trabajo** ~ day work; **luz diurna artificial** artificial daylight
divo, -a ['di·βo, -a] *mf* leading opera singer, diva *f*
divagación [di·βa·ɣa·'sjon, -'θjon] *f* 1.(*desviación*) digression 2. *pl* (*sin concierto*) ramblings *pl*
divagar <g→gu> [di·βa·'ɣar] *vi* 1.(*desviarse*) to digress 2.(*hablar sin concierto*) to ramble
diván [di·'βan] *m* divan
divergencia [di·βer·'xen·sja, -θja] *f* divergence
divergente [di·βer·'xen·te] *adj* divergent; **opiniones ~ s** differing opinions
divergir <g→j> [di·βer·'xir] *vi t.* MAT to diverge; (*opiniones*) to differ; (*personas*) to disagree
diversidad [di·βer·si·'dad] *f* diversity
diversificación [di·βer·si·fi·ka·'sjon, -'θjon] *f* 1.(*variedad*) diversity 2. ECON diversification
diversificar <c→qu> [di·βer·si·fi·'kar] I. *vt* to diversify; ~ **los horizontes** to broaden one's horizons II. *vr:* ~**se** to diversify
diversión [di·βer·'sjon] *f* 1.(*entretenimiento*) entertainment 2.(*pasatiempo*) pastime
diverso, -a [di·'βer·so, -a] *adj* 1.(*distinto*) distinct; (*desemejante*) dissimilar 2. ~**s** (*varios*) various; (*muchos*) many
divertido, -a [di·βer·'ti·do, -a] *adj* 1.(*alegre*) amusing 2.(*que hace reír*) funny 3. *AmL* (*achispado*) tipsy
divertir [di·βer·'tir] *irr como sentir* I. *vt* (*entretener*) to amuse; **sus bromas me divierten** his/her jokes are funny II. *vr:* ~**se** 1.(*alegrarse*) to amuse oneself (*en* with); **¡que te diviertas!** enjoy yourself! 2.(*distraerse*) to be distracted
dividendo [di·βi·'den·do] *m* dividend; **arrojar ~s** to pay dividends
dividir [di·βi·'dir] I. *vt* 1.(*partir*) to divide; ~ **por la mitad** to divide in two 2.(*distribuir*) to distribute 3.(*separar*) to separate; **divide y vencerás** *prov* divide and conquer *prov*; (*sembrando discordia*) to disunite 4.(*agrupar*) to divide up 5. MAT ~ **algo entre** [*o* **por**] **dos** to divide sth by two II. *vr:* ~**se** 1.(*partirse*) to divide 2.(*agruparse*) to divide up into 3.(*enemistarse*) to fall out
divinidad [di·βi·ni·'dad] *f* 1.(*ser divino*) divinity 2.(*deidad*) deity 3. *inf* (*preciosidad*) **esta**

mujer es una ~ that woman is absolutely divine

divinizar <z→c> [di·βi·ni·'sar, -'θar] *vt* (*deificar*) to deify

divino, -a [di·'βi·no, -a] *adj* divine, heavenly

divisa [di·'βi·sa] *f pl* (*moneda*) (foreign) currency

divisar [di·βi·'sar] *vt* (*percibir*) to make out

divisible [di·βi·'si·βle] *adj* divisible

división [di·βi·'sjon] *f* **1.** (*partición*) *t.* MAT division **2.** (*separación*) separation **3.** (*parte*) portion **4.** MIL division

divisor [di·βi·'sor] *m* MAT divisor; **máximo común ~** highest common factor

divisorio, -a [di·βi·'so·rjo, -a] *adj* dividing; **línea divisoria de las aguas** watershed

divorciado, -a [di·βor·'sja·do, -a; -'θja·do, -a] I. *adj* divorced II. *m, f* divorcee

divorciar [di·βor·'sjar, -'θjar] I. *vt* to divorce II. *vr*: **~se** to get divorced; **ella se divorció de él** she divorced him

divorcio [di·'βor·sjo, -θjo] *m* **1.** (*separación*) divorce **2.** (*discrepancia*) disagreement; **~ de opiniones** difference of opinions

divulgación [di·βul·ɣa·'sjon, -'θjon] *f* disclosure; (*publicación*) publication; **libro de ~** popularizing book

divulgar <g→gu> [di·βul·'ɣar] I. *vt* (*propagar*) to spread; (*dar a conocer*) to make known; (*popularizar*) to popularize II. *vr*: **~se** (*propagarse*) to spread; (*conocerse*) to become known

Dn. [don] *abr de* **don** ≈ Mr. (*used before the first name*)

DNI [de·ne·'i/de·e·ne·'i] *m abr de* **Documento Nacional de Identidad** ID

Dña. ['do·ɲa] *abr de doña* ≈ Mrs. (+*first name*)

do <does> [do] *m* (*de la escala diatónica*) C; (*de la solfa*) do; **~ bemol** C flat; **~ de pecho** high C; **~ sostenido** C sharp

dobladillo [do·βla·'di·jo, -ʎo] *m* (*pliegue*) hem; (*del pantalón*) turn-up, cuff

doblaje [do·'βla·xe] *m* CINE dubbing

doblar [do·'βlar] I. *vt* **1.** (*arquear*) to bend **2.** (*plegar*) to fold; **no ~** do not bend **3.** (*duplicar*) to be twice as much as; **mi madre me dobla en edad** my mother is twice my age **4.** (*una película*) to dub **5.** (*rodear*) to go around; **~ la esquina** to turn the corner II. *vi* **1.** (*redoblar*) to double **2.** (*torcer*) to turn (*a* towards) **3.** (*hacer dos papeles*) to play two roles **4.** (*campanas*) to toll III. *vr*: **~se** (*inclinarse*) to bend down

doble¹ ['do·βle] I. *adj inv* (*duplo*) double; **contabilidad por partida ~** double-entry bookkeeping; **tener ~ nacionalidad** to have dual citizenship; **~ personalidad** split personality II. *m f t.* CINE double

doble² ['do·βle] *m* **1.** (*duplo*) double **2.** (*pliegue*) fold **3.** (*toque de campanas*) knell **4.** (*tenis*) (**partido de**) **~s** doubles (match)

doble³ ['do·βle] *f* doubles *pl*

doblegar <g→gu> [do·βle·'ɣar] I. *vt*

1. (*torcer*) to **2.** (*persuadir*) to persuade II. *vr*: **~se 1.** (*torcerse*) to twist **2.** (*someterse*) to give in

doblez¹ [do·'βles, -'βleθ] *m* (*pliegue*) fold

doblez² [do·'βles, -'βleθ] *m o f* (*hipocresía*) duplicity

doce ['do·se, -θe] *adj inv, m* twelve; *v.t.* **ocho**

doceavo, -a [do·se·'a·βo, -a; do·θe-] *adj* twelfth; *v.t.* **octavo**

docena [do·'se·na, -'θe·na] *f* dozen; **una ~ de huevos** a dozen eggs

docencia [do·'sen·sja, -'θen·θja] *f* teaching; **dedicarse a la ~** to be a teacher

doceno, -a [do·'se·no, -a; -'θe·no, -a] *adj* twelfth; *v.t.* **octavo**

docente [do·'sen·te, -'θen·te] I. *adj* teaching II. *mf* teacher; UNIV lecturer, professor

dócil ['do·sil, -θil] *adj* **1.** (*sumiso*) obedient **2.** (*manso*) docile

docilidad [do·si·li·'dad, do·θi-] *f* **1.** (*sumisión*) obedience **2.** (*mansedumbre*) docility

docto, -a ['dok·to, -a] *adj* learned; **~ en leyes** well-versed in the law

doctor(a) [dok·'tor, -'to·ra] *m(f)* doctor

doctorado [dok·to·'ra·do] *m* **1.** (*grado*) doctorate **2.** (*estudios*) **curso de ~** doctoral course

doctoral [dok·to·'ral] *adj* UNIV doctoral; **tesis ~** doctoral thesis

doctorando, -a [dok·to·'ran·do, -a] *m, f* PhD student

doctorar [dok·to·'rar] *vt, vr*: **~se en historia** to do a doctorate [*o* PhD] in history

doctrina [dok·'tri·na] *f* (*teoría*) doctrine

documentación [do·ku·men·ta·'sjon, -'θjon] *f* **1.** (*estudio*) information **2.** (*documentos*) documentation; (*del coche*) vehicle documents *pl*, car papers *pl*

documentado, -a [do·ku·men·'ta·do, -a] *adj* **1.** (*identificado*) documented; (*personas*) with papers **2.** (*informado*) informed

documental [do·ku·men·'tal] *adj, m* documentary

documentar [do·ku·men·'tar] I. *vt* **1.** (*probar*) to document **2.** (*instruir*) to inform II. *vr*: **~se** to inform oneself

documento [do·ku·'men·to] *m* document; **~ descargable** COMPUT downloadable document; **~s de envío** dispatch documents; **Documento Nacional de Identidad** ID, identity card

dodotis® [do·'do·tis] *m inv* diapers, Pampers®

dogma ['doɣ·ma] *m* dogma

dogmático, -a [doɣ·'ma·ti·ko, -a] *adj* dogmatic

dogo ['do·ɣo] *m* bulldog

dólar ['do·lar] *m* dollar

dolencia [do·'len·sja, -θja] *f* ailment; **~ respiratoria** respiratory complaint

doler <o→ue> [do·'ler] I. *vi* to hurt; **me duele la cabeza** I have a headache II. *vr*: **~se 1.** (*quejarse*) **~se de algo** to complain about sth **2.** (*arrepentirse*) to regret (*de*)

dolido, -a [do·'li·do, -a] *adj* hurt

dolo ['do·lo] *m* **1.** (*engaño*) fraud **2.** JUR **con ~** under false pretenses

dolor [do·'lor] *m* pain; **~ de cabeza** headache; **estar con ~es** to have labor pains; **retorcerse de ~** to writhe in pain; **tengo ~ de barriga** I have (a) stomachache

dolorido, -a [do·lo·'ri·do, -a] *adj* **1.** (*dañado*) painful; **tener la rodilla dolorida** to have a sore knee **2.** (*apenado*) sad

doloroso, -a [do·lo·'ro·so, -a] *adj* **1.** (*lastimador*) painful **2.** (*lamentable*) regrettable

doloso, -a [do·'lo·so, -a] *adj* fraudulent

dom. *abr de* **domingo** Sun.

domar [do·'mar] *vt* to tame

domesticado, -a [do·mes·ti·'ka·do, -a] *adj* **animal ~** domestic animal

domesticar <c→qu> [do·mes·ti·'kar] *vt* **1.** (*animales*) to domesticate **2.** (*personas*) to bring under control

doméstico, -a [do·'mes·ti·ko, -a] **I.** *adj* domestic; **vuelo ~** national flight; **animal ~** pet; **gastos ~s** household expenses **II.** *m, f* (domestic) servant

domiciliación [do·mi·si·lja·'sjon, -θi·lja·'θjon] *f* (*orden permanente*) standing order; (*de recibos*) direct debit; (*de una letra de cambio*) bank transfer

domiciliar [do·mi·si·'ljar, -θi·'ljar] **I.** *vt* **1.** (*un recibo*) to pay by direct debit; **~ el alquiler** to pay the rent by standing order; **~ la nómina** to pay the salary direct into sb's account **2.** (*dar domicilio*) to house **II.** *vr:* **~se** to reside

domiciliario, -a [do·mi·si·'lja·rjo, -a; do·mi·θi-] *adj* home; **arresto ~** JUR house arrest

domicilio [do·mi·'si·ljo, -'θi·ljo] *m* (*de alguien*) residence; (*una empresa*) address; **reparto a ~** home delivery; **~ social** registered office

dominación [do·mi·na·'sjon, -'θjon] *f* **1.** (*el dominar*) domination **2.** (*poder*) power

dominante [do·mi·'nan·te] *adj* dominant; **~ en el mercado** dominant in the marketplace

dominar [do·mi·'nar] **I.** *vi* **1.** (*imperar*) to rule **2.** (*sobresalir*) to stand out **3.** (*predominar*) to predominate **II.** *vt* **1.** (*conocer*) to have a good knowledge of; (*idioma*) to have a good command of **2.** (*reprimir*) to control; **~ el odio** to overcome one's hatred **3.** (*sobresalir*) to dominate **4.** (*divisar*) to look out over **III.** *vr:* **~se** to control oneself

domingo [do·'min·go] *m* Sunday; **~ de Resurrección** Easter Sunday; **~ de Ramos** Palm Sunday; *v.t.* **lunes**

dominguero, -a [do·min·'ge·ro, -a] **I.** *adj* Sunday **II.** *m, f pey* Sunday driver

dominical [do·mi·ni·'kal] **I.** *adj* Sunday; **descanso ~** Sunday off; **oración ~** Lord's Prayer **II.** *m* PREN Sunday supplement

dominicano, -a [do·mi·ni·'ka·no, -a] *adj, m, f* GEO, REL Dominican

dominio [do·'mi·njo] *m* **1.** (*dominación*) control; **~ de sí mismo** self-control **2.** (*poder*) authority **3.** (*territorio*) domain **4.** (*campo*) subject **5.** (*posesión*) ownership; **ser de ~ público** *fig* to be common knowledge

dominó <dominós> [do·mi·'no] *m* (*juego*) dominoes *pl*

don [don] *m* gift; **tener ~ de gentes** to have a way with people

don, doña [don, 'do·ɲa] *m, f* ≈ Mr. *m*, ≈ Mrs. *f* (*title of respect used before the first name*)

donación [do·na·'sjon, -'θjon] *f* donation; JUR gift

donador(a) [do·na·'dor, -'do·ra] *m(f)* donor

donaire [do·'nai·re] *m* (*gracia*) grace

donante [do·'nan·te] *mf* donor

donar [do·'nar] *vt* to donate

donativo [do·na·'ti·βo] *m* donation

doncella [don·'se·ja, -'θe·ʎa] *f* (*criada*) maid

donde ['don·de] *adv* where; **a** [*o* **hacia**] **~...** where... to; **de ~...** where... from; **en ~** where; **estuve ~ Luisa** I was at Luisa's

dónde ['don·de] *pron interrog, rel* where; **¿a** [*o* **hacia**] **~?** where to?; **¿de ~?** where from?; **¿en ~?** where?

dondequiera [don·de·'kje·ra] *adv* **1.** (*en cualquier parte*) anywhere **2.** (*donde*) wherever

donut ['do·nu(t)] *m* <donuts> doughnut, donut

doña ['do·ɲa] *f v.* **don**

dopar [do·'par] *vt, vr:* **~se** DEP to take drugs

doping ['do·pin] *m* drug-taking

dorada [do·'ra·da] *f* (*pez*) gilthead

dorado, -a [do·'ra·do] *adj* golden

dorar [do·'rar] **I.** *vt* **1.** (*tostar*) to brown **2.** (*suavizar*) to sweeten; **~ la píldora** to sugar the pill **II.** *vr:* **~se** to go brown

dormilón, -ona [dor·mi·'lon, -·'lo·na] *m, f inf* sleepyhead

dormir [dor·'mir] *irr* **I.** *vi* **1.** (*descansar*) to sleep; **~ a pierna suelta** to be fast [*o* sound] asleep; **~ de un tirón** to sleep right through the night; **quedarse dormido** to fall asleep **2.** (*pernoctar*) to spend the night; **~ en casa de alguien** to sleep at sb's house **3.** (*reposar*) to rest **4.** (*descuidarse*) to let things slide **II.** *vt* (*a un niño*) to get to sleep; (*a un paciente*) to put to sleep; **~ la borrachera/mona** *inf* to sleep off one's hangover; **~ la siesta** to take a nap; **esta monotonía me duerme** this monotony is putting me to sleep **III.** *vr:* **~se 1.** (*adormecerse*) to fall asleep; **se me ha dormido el brazo** my arm fell asleep **2.** (*descuidarse*) to not pay attention

dormitorio [dor·mi·'to·rjo] *m* **1.** (*en una casa*) bedroom; (*muebles*) bedroom furniture [*o* set] **2.** (*en un colegio*) dormitory

dorsal [dor·'sal] **I.** *adj* ANAT dorsal; **espina ~** backbone **II.** *m* DEP number

dorso ['dor·so] *m* (*reverso*) *t.* ANAT back; **~ de la mano** back of the hand; **véase al ~** please turn over

dos [dos] **I.** *adj inv* two; **~ puntos** colon; **de ~**

en ~ two by two; **están a** ~ DEP it's two-all ► cada ~ **por tres** all the time; **en un** ~ **por tres** in a flash II. *m* two; **los/las** ~ both
doscientos, -as [do·'sjen·tos, -as; dos·'θjen-] *adj* two hundred; *v.t.* **ochocientos**
dosificar <c→qu> [do·si·fi·'kar] *vt* to measure out
dosis ['do·sis] *f inv* dose; **una buena** ~ **de paciencia** a lot of patience; (*droga*) fix *sl*
dotación [do·ta·'sjon, -'θjon] *f* 1.(*equipamiento*) equipping 2.(*personal: de un buque*) crew; (*de una fábrica*) workforce; (*de una oficina*) staff 3.(*financiación*) endowment
dotado, -a [do·'ta·do, -a] *adj* (*con talento*) gifted
dotar [do·'tar] *vt* 1.(*constituir dote*) to give as a dowry 2.(*equipar*) ~ **de** [*o* **con**] **algo** to equip with sth 3.(*señalar bienes*) to endow 4.(*con sueldo*) to provide
dote¹ ['do·te] *m o f*(*ajuar*) dowry
dote² ['do·te] *f* (*aptitud*) gift; ~ **de mando** leadership ability
doy [doi] *1. pres de* **dar**
Dpto. [de·par·ta·'men·to] *AmL abr de* **departamento** (*distrito*) administrative district
Dr(a). [dok·'tor, -·'to·ra] *abr de* **doctor**(a) Dr.
dragón [dra·'yon] *m* 1.(*monstruo*) dragon 2.(*reptil*) flying dragon; ~ **marino** (*pez*) weever
drama ['dra·ma] *m* drama; TEAT play
dramático, -a [dra·'ma·ti·ko, -a] *adj* dramatic; **autor** ~ playwright
dramatismo [dra·ma·'tis·mo] *m* drama
dramatizar <z→c> [dra·ma·ti·'sar, -'θar] *vt* dramatize
dramaturgo, -a [dra·ma·'tur·yo, -a] *m, f* playwright
drástico, -a [a ['dras·ti·ko] *adj* drastic
drenaje [dre·'na·xe] *m* drainage
drenar [dre·'nar] *vt* to drain
driblar [dri·'βlar] *vi, vt* DEP to dribble; ~ **a un contrario** to dribble around an opponent
droga ['dro·ya] *f* drug; ~ **sintética** synthetic drug
drogadicto, -a [dro·ya·'dik·to, -a] I. *adj* addicted to drugs II. *m, f* drug addict
drogado, -a [dro·'ya·do, -a] *adj* **estar** ~ to be drugged
drogar <g→gu> [dro·'yar] I. *vt* to drug II. *vr:* ~ **se** to take drugs
drogodependencia [dro·yo·de·pen·'den·sja, -'θja] *f* drug addiction
droguería [dro·ye·'ri·a] *f* drugstore
dromedario [dro·me·'da·rjo] *m* dromedary
dublinés, -esa [du·βli·'nes, -·'ne·sa] I. *adj* of/from Dublin II. *m, f* Dubliner
ducado [du·'ka·do] *m* (*territorio*) duchy
ducha ['du·tʃa] *f* (*para ducharse*) shower
duchar [du·'tʃar] I. *vt* to shower II. *vr:* ~ **se** to take a shower
ducho, -a ['du·tʃo, -a] *adj* skilled
dúctil ['duk·til] *adj* (*dilatable*) stretchable; (*flexible*) pliable

duda ['du·da] *f* (*indecisión, incredulidad*) doubt; **salir de** ~ **s** to dispel one's doubts; **no cabe la menor** ~ there is not the slightest doubt; **poner algo en** ~ to question sth
dudar [du·'dar] I. *vi* 1.(*desconfiar*) ~ **de algo** to doubt sth 2.(*vacilar*) to hesitate II. *vt* to doubt
dudoso, -a [du·'do·so, -a] *adj* 1.(*inseguro*) doubtful 2.(*indeciso*) undecided 3.(*sospechoso*) dubious
duelo ['dwe·lo] *m* 1.(*desafío*) duel; **retar a** ~ to challenge to a duel 2.(*pesar*) grief 3.(*funerales*) mourning 4.(*cortejo*) funeral procession
duende ['dwen·de] *m* 1.(*espíritu*) elf; (*fantasma*) ghost 2. **tener** ~ to have charm
dueño, -a ['dwe·ɲo, -a] *m, f* (*propietario*) owner; (*amo*) boss; ~ **y señor** lord and master; **hacerse** ~ **de algo** (*apropiarse*) to take possession of sth; (*dominar*) to take command of sth; **ser** ~ **de sí mismo** (*empresario*) to be one's own boss; **no ser** ~ **de sí mismo** (*dominarse*) to not be in control of oneself
dulce ['dul·se, -θe] I. *adj* 1.(*referente al sabor*) sweet 2.(*suave*) soft 3.(*agradable*) pleasant 4.(*metal*) soft 5.(*agua*) fresh II. *m* 1.(*postre*) dessert 2.(*almíbar*) syrup 3.(*golosina*) candy
dulcificar <c→qu> [dul·si·fi·'kar, dul·θi-] *vt* (*azucarar*) to sweeten
dulzor [dul·'sor, -'θor] *m*, **dulzura** [dul·'su·ra, -'θu·ra] *f* 1.(*sabor*) sweetness 2.(*suavidad*) softness
duna ['du·na] *f* dune
dundera [dun·'de·ra] *f AmL* (*bobada*) stupidity
dundo, -a ['dun·do, -a] *adj AmL* (*bobo*) silly
dúo ['duo] *m* duet
duodécimo, -a [duo·'de·si·mo, -a; -'de·θi·mo, -a] *adj* twelfth; *v.t.* **octavo**
dúplex ['du·pleks] *m* ARQUIT duplex
duplicado [du·pli·'ka·do] *m* duplicate; **por** ~ in duplicate
duplicar <c→qu> [du·pli·'kar] *vt, vr:* ~ **se** to duplicate
duque(sa) ['du·ke, du·'ke·sa] *m(f)* duke, duchess *m, f*
durabilidad [du·ra·βi·li·'dad] *f* durability
duración [du·ra·'sjon, -'θjon] *f* duration, length; (*de un préstamo*) term; **de larga** ~ long-term
duradero, -a [du·ra·'de·ro, -a] *adj* long-lasting
durante [du·'ran·te] *prep* during; **hablar** ~ **una hora** to talk for an hour
durar [du·'rar] *vi* 1.(*extenderse*) to last 2.(*permanecer*) to stay 3.(*resistir*) to last
durazno [du·'ras·no, -'raθ·no] *m AmL* (*fruta*) peach; (*árbol*) peach tree
dureza [du·'re·sa, -'re·θa] *f* 1.(*rigidez*) hardness; ~ **de vientre** constipation 2.(*callosidad*) hard skin
durmiente [dur·'mjen·te] I. *adj* sleeping II. *mf* sleeper
duro ['du·ro] *adv* hard ► **quedarse** ~ *Arg, inf* to be amazed

duro, -a ['du·ro, -a] *adj* hard; ~ **de corazón** hard-hearted; ~ **de oído** hard of hearing; **a duras penas** barely

DVD [de·u·βe·'de] *abr de* **videodisco digital** DVD

E

e [e], **E** *f* E, e; ~ **de España** E as in Echo

e [e] *conj* (*before 'hi' or 'i'*) **madres** ~ **hijas** mothers and daughters

E ['es·te] *abr de* **Este** E

ea ['e·a] *interj* (*animando*) come on

ebanista [e·βa·'nis·ta] *mf* cabinetmaker, woodworker

ébano ['e·βa·no] *m* ebony

ebrio, -a ['e·βrjo, -a] *adj elev* **1.** (*borracho*) inebriated **2.** (*extasiado*) ~ **de** beside oneself with; (*ciego*) blind with

ebullición [e·βu·ji·'sjon, -ʎi·'θjon] *f* (*de líquidos*) boiling

eccema [ek·'se·ma, eɣ·'θe·ma] *m* MED eczema

echado, -a [e·'tʃa·do] *adj* **1.** (*postrado*) lying down; **estar** ~ to be lying down; ~ **para adelante** *inf* pushy **2.** *Nic, CRi* (*indolente*) idle

echar [e·'tʃar] **I.** *vt* **1.** (*tirar*) to throw; (*carta*) to mail; (*a la basura, al suelo*) to throw out; **la suerte está echada** the die is cast **2.** (*verter*) to pour; ~ **en algo** to pour into sth **3.** (*expulsar*) to throw out; (*despedir*) to fire **4.** *inf* (*crecer: pelo*) to grow; (*hojas, flores*) to sprout **5.** (*emitir*) to give off; ~ **humo** to let out smoke **6.** (*tumbar*) to lie down **7.** (*proyectar*) to show; TEAT to stage **8.** (*calcular*) **te echo 30 años** I bet you're 30 **9.** (*tiempo, esfuerzo*) **eché dos horas en acabar** it took me two hours to finish **10.** *Perú* (*emborracharse*) ~ **le** to get drunk **11.** *Chile* (*echar a correr*) ~ **las** to beat it **II.** *vi* **1.** (*lanzar*) to throw **2.** (*verter*) to pour **3.** (*empezar*) to begin; ~ **a correr** to break into a run **III.** *vr:* ~ **se 1.** (*postrarse*) to lie down **2.** (*lanzarse*) to jump; ~ **se sobre algo/alguien** to fall upon sth/sb; ~ **se a los pies de alguien** to throw oneself down before sb; ~ **se atrás** *fig* to have second thoughts **3.** (*empezar*) to begin; ~ **se a llorar** to burst into tears; ~ **se a la bebida** to take to drink **4.** *inf* (*iniciar una relación*) ~ **se un novio** to get a boyfriend

echarpe [e·'tʃar·pe] *m* stole; *AmL* (*chal*) shawl

echón, -ona [e·'tʃon, -·'tʃo·na] *Ven* **I.** *adj* conceited **II.** *m, f* braggart

eclesiástico [e·kle·'sjas·ti·ko] *m* clergyman

eclesiástico, -a [e·kle·'sjas·ti·ko, -a] *adj* ecclesiastical

eclipsar [e·kliβ·'sar] **I.** *vt* **1.** ASTR to eclipse **2.** (*oscurecer*) to darken **3.** *fig* to outshine **II.** *vr:* ~ **se 1.** (*sufrir un eclipse*) to be eclipsed

2. (*decaer*) to decline

eclipse [e·'kliβ·se] *m* eclipse; ~ **solar** solar eclipse

eco ['e·ko] *m* **1.** *t. fig* echo; **hacer** ~ *fig* to have an impact; **tener** ~ *fig* to arouse interest; ~ **s de sociedad** PREN gossip column **2.** (*repercusión*) consequence

ecografía [e·ko·yra·'fi·a] *f* ultrasound scan

ecología [e·ko·lo·'xi·a] *f* ecology

ecológico, -a [e·ko·'lo·xi·ko, -a] *adj* ecological; **daños** ~ **s** environmental damage; **producción ecológica** AGR organic farming

ecologismo [e·ko·lo·'xis·mo] *m* green movement, environmentalism

ecologista [e·ko·lo·'xis·ta] **I.** *adj* ecological **II.** *mf* ecologist, environmentalist

economía [e·ko·no·'mi·a] *f* **1.** (*situación, sistema*) economy; ~ **de desechos** recycling industry; ~ **forestal** forestry sector; ~ **sumergida** black economy; ~ **de escala** economy of scale; ~ **de oferta** supply-side economy **2.** (*ciencia*) economics; ~ **de la empresa** business economics; ~ **política** political economics **3.** (*ahorro*) saving **4.** (*moderación*) thrift(iness) **5.** (*cosa ahorrada*) savings *pl;* **hacer** ~ **s** to economize

económico, -a [e·ko·'no·mi·ko, -a] *adj* **1.** ECON economic; **año** ~ financial year; **estudiar Ciencias Económicas** to study economics **2.** (*barato*) cheap; (*ahorrador*) economical; (*persona*) thrifty

economista [e·ko·no·'mis·ta] *mf* economist

economizar <z→c> [e·ko·no·mi·'sar, -'θar] *vi, vt* to economize; **no** ~ **esfuerzos** to spare no effort; ~ **esfuerzos** to save one's efforts

ecosistema [e·ko·sis·'te·ma] *m* ecosystem

ecuación [e·kwa·'sjon, -'θjon] *f* equation

ecuador [e·kwa·'dor] *m* equator

Ecuador [e·kwa·'dor] *m* Ecuador

> **i** **Ecuador** is located in the northwestern part of South America. It borders on Colombia to the north, Peru to the east and south, and the Pacific Ocean to the west. The capital is **Quito**. The country's official language is Spanish and the official currency of **Ecuador** is the **sucre**.

ecuánime [e·'kwa·ni·me] *adj* (*justo*) fair; (*imparcial*) impartial

ecuanimidad [e·kwa·ni·mi·'dad] *f* (*imparcialidad*) impartiality

ecuatorial [e·kwa·to·'rjal] *adj* equatorial

ecuatoriano, -a [e·kwa·to·'rja·no, -a] **I.** *adj* of/from Ecuador **II.** *m, f* native/inhabitant of Ecuador

ecuménico, -a [e·ku·'me·ni·ko, -a] *adj* universal

eczema [ek·'se·ma, eɣ·'θe·ma] *m* MED eczema

edad [e·'dad] *f* **1.** (*años*) age; ~ **para jubilarse** retirement age; ~ **del pavo** adolescence; **mayor de** ~ adult; **menor de** ~ minor; **ser**

mayor/menor de ~ to be of/under age; **a la ~ de...** at the age of...; **¿qué ~ tiene?** how old is he/she?; **de mi** ~ of my age; **de cierta** ~ getting up there (in age); **llegar a la mayoría de** ~ to come of age; **de mediana** ~ middle-aged; **la tercera** ~ old [*o* retirement] age **2.** (*época*) age, era; **la Edad Media** the Middle Ages

edema [e·'de·ma] *m* edema

edén [e·'den] *m* Eden; *fig* (*paraíso*) paradise

edición [e·di·'sjon, -'θjon] *f* **1.** (*impresión, conjunto de ejemplares*) edition; ~ **de bolsillo** paperback edition **2.** (*de un acontecimiento*) **la presente ~ del Festival de Cine** this year's Film Festival

edicto [e·'dik·to] *m* **1.** (*aviso*) announcement **2.** JUR edict

edificación [e·di·fi·ka·'sjon, -'θjon] *f* (*construcción*) construction

edificante [e·di·fi·'kan·te] *adj* edifying

edificar <c→qu> [e·di·fi·'kar] *vt* **1.** (*construcción*) to build **2.** (*moral*) to edify

edificio [e·di·'fi·sjo, -θjo] *m* building

edil(a) [e·'dil] *m(f)* councilman *m,* councilwoman *f*

editar [e·di·'tar] *vt* **1.** (*publicar*) to publish **2.** (*preparar*) to edit

editor [e·di·'tor] *m* COMPUT editor

editor(a) [e·di·'tor, -'to·ra] *m(f)* **1.** (*que publica*) publisher **2.** (*que prepara textos*) editor

editorial¹ [e·di·to·'rjal] **I.** *adj* **1.** (*publicar*) publishing **2.** (*preparar*) editing; **casa** ~ publishing house; **éxito** ~ best-seller **II.** *f* publisher

editorial² [e·di·to·'rjal] *m* editorial

editorialista [e·di·to·rja·'lis·ta] *mf* editorialist

Edo. [es·'ta·do] *Méx, Ven abr de* **Estado** State

edredón [e·dre·'don] *m* eiderdown; ~ **nórdico** quilt, comforter

educación [e·du·ka·'sjon, -'θjon] *f* **1.** (*instrucción*) education, teaching; ~ **de adultos** adult education; ~ **ambiental** environmental education; ~ **física** ENS physical education; ~ **a distancia** distance learning; ~ **permanente** permanent education; **Educación General Básica** HIST education for children aged 6 to 14; **educación preescolar** nursery school education; ~ **vial** road education **2.** (*comportamiento*) manners *pl;* **este niño no tiene** ~ this child has no manners **3.** (*crianza*) upbringing

educado, -a [e·du·'ka·do, -a] *adj* **1.** (*culto*) cultured, cultivated **2.** (*cortés*) (**bien**) ~ polite; **mal** ~ rude

educar <c→qu> [e·du·'kar] *vt* **1.** (*dar instrucción*) to educate **2.** (*criar*) to bring up **3.** (*facultades*) to improve; **debes ~ tu oído** you should train your ear

educativo, -a [e·du·ka·'ti·βo, -a] *adj* (*instructivo*) educational

edulcorante [e·dul·ko·'ran·te] *m* sweetener

edutenimiento [e·du·te·ni·'mjen·to] *m* edutainment

EE.UU. [es·'ta·dos u·'ni·dos] *mpl abr de* **Estados Unidos** USA

efe ['e·fe] *f* (*letra*) f; **la letra** ~ the letter f

efectivamente [e·fek·ti·βa·'men·te] *adv* in fact

efectividad [e·fek·ti·βi·'dad] *f* effectiveness

efectivo [e·fek·'ti·βo] *m* (*dinero*) cash; ~ **electrónico** electronic cash; **en** ~ (in) cash

efectivo, -a [e·fek·'ti·βo, -a] *adj* **1.** (*que hace efecto*) effective **2.** (*auténtico*) real; **un éxito** ~ a real success; **hacer** ~ to put into action; (*cheque*) to cash

efecto [e·'fek·to] *m* effect; ~ **invernadero** greenhouse effect; ~ **retardado** delayed reaction; ~**s secundarios** side effects; **hacer** ~ to have an effect; **hacer buen** ~ (*impresión*) to make a good impression; **tener** ~ to take effect; **llevar a** ~ to carry out; **en** ~ indeed; **para los** ~**s** effectively; **con** ~**s retroactivos** retroactively

efectuar <1. pres: efectúo> [e·fek·tu·'ar] **I.** *vt* to carry out; (*viaje*) to go on; ~ **una compra** to make a purchase **II.** *vr:* ~**se** (*tener lugar*) to take place; (*realizarse*) to be carried out

efervescente [e·fer·βe·'sen·te, -'θen·te] *adj* (*líquido*) fizzy; **pastilla** ~ dissoluble tablet

eficacia [e·fi·'ka·sja, -θja] *f* **1.** (*de persona*) efficiency; (*de medida*) effectiveness; ~ **económica** economic efficiency; **con** ~ effectively; **sin** ~ useless **2.** TÉC efficiency

eficaz [e·fi·'kas, -'kaθ] *adj* (*persona*) efficient; (*medida*) effective

eficiencia [e·fi·'sjen·sja, -'θjen·θja] *f* (*persona*) efficiency; (*medida*) effectiveness

eficiente [e·fi·'sjen·te, -'θjen·te] *adj* (*persona*) efficient; (*medida*) effective

efusión [e·fu·'sjon] *f* **1.** (*cordialidad*) effusion; **con gran** ~ very effusively **2.** (*derramamiento*) spillage

efusivo, -a [e·fu·'si·βo, -a] *adj* effusive

EGB [e·xe·'βe] *f* HIST *abr de* **Educación General Básica** education for children aged 6 to 14

Egeo [e·'xe·o] *m* Aegean; **el mar** ~ the Aegean Sea

egipcio, -a [e·'xip·sjo, -a; -'xiβ·θjo, -a] *adj, m, f* Egyptian

Egipto [e·'xip·to] *m* Egypt

ego ['e·yo] *m* PSICO ego

egocéntrico, -a [e·yo·'sen·tri·ko, -a; -'θen·tri·ko, -a] *adj* egocentric, self-centered

egoísmo [e·yo·'is·mo] *m* selfishness, egoism

egoísta [e·yo·'is·ta] **I.** *adj* selfish, egoistical; **ser un** ~ to be very selfish **II.** *mf* selfish person, egoist

egresado, -a [e·yre·'sa·do, -a] *m, f Arg, Chile* (*universidad, escuela*) graduate

egresar [e·yre·'sar] *vi Arg, Chile* (*escuela*) to finish school; (*universidad*) to graduate

eh [e] *interj* **1.** (*advertencia*) OK; **no vuelvas a hacerlo, ¿~?** don't do it again, OK? **2.** (*susto, incomprensión*) **¿~?** eh?

ej. [e·'xem·plo] *abr de* **ejemplo** example

eje ['e·xe] *m* **1.** TÉC, MAT axle **2.** (*centro*) ~ **de la conversación** core of the conversation; **ser el** ~ **de atención** to be the center of attention; **el Eje** HIST the Axis

ejecución [e·xe·ku·'sjon, -'θjon] *f* execution; (*de proyectos*) implementation; ~ **de un pedido** carrying out of an order; ~ **de la sentencia** JUR execution of sentence; **poner en** ~ to carry out

ejecutar [e·xe·ku·'tar] *vt* to execute; (*ley*) to enforce

ejecutivo, -a [e·xe·ku·'ti·βo, -a] **I.** *adj* **1.** (*que decide*) *t.* JUR executive; **comité** ~ executive committee; **poder** ~ executive power **2.** (*urgente*) urgent **II.** *m*, *f* (*en cargo directivo*) executive; (*empleado*) manager; ~ **de marketing** marketing executive, executive committee

ejemplar [e·xem·'plar] **I.** *adj* exemplary; **un alumno** ~ a model student **II.** *m* (*ejemplo*) example; (*de libro*) copy; (*de revista*) issue; ~ **de muestra** sample

ejemplarizar <z→c> [e·xem·pla·ri·'sar, -'θar] *vi AmL* to serve as an example

ejemplificar <c→qu> [e·xem·pli·fi·'kar] *vt* to exemplify

ejemplo [e·'xem·plo] *m* example; **dar buen** ~ to set a good example; **poner por** ~ to give as an example; **por** ~ for example; **sin** ~ unprecedented; **predicar con el** ~ to practice what one preaches; **tomar por** ~ to take as an example

ejercer <c→z> [e·xer·'ser, -'θer] **I.** *vt* (*profesión*) to practice; (*derechos*) to exercise **II.** *vi* (*como abogado, médico*) to practice; (*de profesor*) to work

ejercicio [e·xer·'si·sjo, -'θi·θjo] *m* **1.** (*de una profesión*) practice; **en** ~ practicing **2.** DEP exercise; (*entrenamiento*) training; **tener falta de** ~ to be out of practice **3.** ENS (*para practicar*) exercise; (*prueba*) test **4.** MIL ~ **de las armas** weapons training; ~ **de combate** combat exercise **5.** ECON ~ **contable** tax year; ~ (**económico**) financial year

ejercitar [e·xer·si·'tar, -θi·'tar] **I.** *vt* **1.** (*profesión*) to practice; (*actividad*) to carry out; ~ **la cirugía** to work as a surgeon **2.** (*desarrollar*) to develop **3.** (*adiestrar*) to train **II.** *vr:* ~ **se** to train; ~ **se en natación** to do swimming training

ejército [e·'xer·si·to, -θi·to] *m* MIL (*tropas*) army; (*fuerzas armadas*) armed forces; ~ **del aire** air force

ejote [e·'xo·te] *m AmC, Méx* string bean

el [el], **la** [la], **lo** [lo] <los, las> *art def* **1.** the; **el perro** the dog; **la mesa** the table; **los amigos/las amigas** the friends; **prefiero** ~ **azul al amarillo** I prefer the blue one to the yellow one **2.** *lo* + *adj* **lo bueno/malo** the good/bad thing; **lo antes** [*o* **más pronto**] **posible** as soon as possible; **hazlo lo mejor que puedas** do it the best you can **3.** + *nombres geográficos* **el Canadá** Canada; **la China/India**

China/India **4.** + *días de semana* **llegaré el domingo** I'll arrive on Sunday; **los sábados no trabajo** I don't work on Saturdays **5.** + *nombre propio, inf* **he visto a la Carmen** I saw Carmen **6.** + *que* **lo que digo es...** what I'm saying is...; **lo que pasa es que...** the thing is that... **7.** *como interj* **¡la de gente que vino!** so many people came!

él [el] *pron pers, 3.sing m* **1.** (*sujeto*) he **2.** (*tras preposición*) him; **el libro es de** ~ (*suyo*) the book is his

elaboración [e·la·βo·ra·'sjon, -'θjon] *f* **1.** (*fabricación*) manufacture; (*tratamiento*) treatment **2.** (*de comidas*) preparation; **de** ~ **casera** home-made

elaborar [e·la·βo·'rar] *vt* **1.** (*fabricar*) to manufacture; (*preparar*) to prepare **2.** (*una idea*) to develop

elación [e·la·'sjon, -'θjon] *f AmL* elation, exaltation

elasticidad [e·las·ti·si·'dad, -θi·'dad] *f* elasticity

elástico [e·'las·ti·ko] *m* elastic

elástico, -a [e·'las·ti·ko, -a] *adj* elastic; (*concepto*) ambiguous; (*horario, persona*) flexible; (*tela*) stretch

ele ['e·le] *f* L, l; **la letra** ~ the letter l

elección [e·lek·'sjon, -ley·'θjon] *f* (*selección*) choice; *t.* POL election; **elecciones legislativas** general election; ~ **parcial** by-election; **lo dejo a su** ~ the choice is yours

electo, -a [e·'lek·to, -a] *adj* elect

elector(a) [e·lek·'tor, -·'to·ra] **I.** *adj* electing **II.** *m(f)* voter; **los** ~ **es** the electorate

electorado [e·lek·to·'ra·do] *m* electorate

electoral [e·lek·to·'ral] *adj* electoral; **colegio** ~ electoral college

electricidad [e·lek·tri·si·'dad, -θi·'dad] *f* electricity

electricista [e·lek·tri·'sis·ta, -'θis·ta] **I.** *adj* electrical **II.** *mf* electrician

eléctrico, -a [e·'lek·tri·ko, -a] *adj* (*que usa electricidad*) electric; (*relacionado*) electrical; **máquina eléctrica** electrical appliance

electrificar <c→qu> [e·lek·tri·fi·'kar] *vt* to electrify

electrizar <z→c> [e·lek·tri·'sar, -'θar] *vt t. fig* to electrify

electrocardiograma [e·lek·tro·kar·djo·'yra·ma] *m* electrocardiogram

electrocución [e·lek·tro·ku·'sjon, -'θjon] *f* electrocution

electrocutar [e·lek·tro·ku·'tar] *vt* to electrocute

electrodo [e·lek·'tro·do] *m* electrode; ~ **positivo/negativo** positive/negative electrode

electrodoméstico [e·lek·tro·do·'mes·ti·ko] *m* household [*o* electrical] appliance

electrón [e·lek·'tron] *m* electron

electrónica [e·lek·'tro·ni·ka] *f* electronics

electrónico, -a [e·lek·'tro·ni·ko, -a] *adj* electronic; **microscopio** ~ electron microscope; **correo** ~ e-mail

E

electrotécnico, -a [e·lek·tro·'tey·ni·ko, -a] *adj* related to electrical engineering

elefante, -a [e·le·'fan·te, -a] *m, f* elephant *m;* ~ **marino** elephant seal

elegancia [e·le·'ɣan·sja, -θja] *f* elegance; (*buen gusto*) tastefulness

elegante [e·le·'ɣan·te] *adj* elegant; (*con buen gusto*) tasteful

elegantoso, -a [e·le·ɣan·'to·so, -a] *adj inf* ritzy

elegir [e·le·'xir] *irr* **I.** *vi, vt* (*escoger*) to choose; **a** ~ **entre** to be chosen from **II.** *vt* POL to elect

elementado, -a [e·le·men·'ta·do, -a] *adj Chile, Col* (*alelado*) bewildered

elemental [e·le·men·'tal] *adj* basic; **conocimientos ~es** basic knowledge

elemento [e·le·'men·to] *m* **1.** (*componente, persona*) element; ~ **base** basic element; **tener ~s de juicio** to be able to judge; ~ **decisivo** crucial factor **2.** *pl* (*fuerzas naturales*) elements *pl* **3.** *pl* (*nociones fundamentales*) ~**s de matemáticas** basic mathematics *pl*

elenco [e·'len·ko] *m* **1.** TEAT cast **2.** *AmL* (*personal*) staff **3.** *Chile, Perú* (*equipo*) team

elepé [e·le·'pe] *m* LP, album

elevación [e·le·βa·'sjon, -'θjon] *f* **1.** (*subida*) rise **2.** GEO elevation

elevado, -a [e·le·'βa·do, -a] *adj* (*alto*) elevated; (*nivel, estilo*) refined; MAT raised to the power of

elevador [e·le·βa·'dor] *m* **1.** *AmC* (*ascensor*) elevator **2.** *Arg* (*para cargas*) freight elevator

elevalunas [e·le·βa·'lu·nas] *m inv* AUTO automatic windows

elevar [e·le·'βar] **I.** *vt* **1.** (*subir*) to raise; ~ **al trono** to put on the throne **2.** MAT ~ **a** to raise to the power of **3.** (*enviar*) to present; ~ **una protesta** to lodge a complaint **II.** *vr:* ~**se 1.** (*tener altura*) to rise **2.** (*tener precio*) ~**se a** to amount to; (*cotización*) to stand at

eliminación [e·li·mi·na·'sjon, -'θjon] *f* (*supresión, de errores*) elimination; (*de aranceles*) abolition; (*de basura, residuos*) disposal

eliminar [e·li·mi·'nar] *vt* **1.** (*suprimir, matar*) to eliminate; ~ **la competencia** to eliminate the competition **2.** DEP to knock out; **fueron eliminados en la cuarta prueba** they went out in the fourth round

eliminatoria [e·li·mi·na·'to·rja] *f* **1.** (*competición*) playoff **2.** (*vuelta*) qualifying round; (*atletismo*) heat

elipse [e·'lip·se] *f* ellipse

elipsis [e·'lip·sis] *f inv* ellipsis

elite [e·'li·te] *f*, **élite** [e·'li·te] *f* elite; **de** ~ top-class

elitista [e·li·'tis·ta] *adj* elitist

elixir [e·lik·'sir] *m* elixir

ella ['e·ja, -ʎa] *pron pers, 3. sing f* **1.** (*sujeto*) she **2.** (*tras preposición*) her; **el abrigo es de** ~ (*suyo*) the coat is hers

ellas ['e·jas, -ʎas] *pron pers, 3. pl f* **1.** (*sujeto*) they **2.** (*tras preposición*) them; **el coche es de** ~ (*suyo*) the car is theirs

ello ['e·jo, -ʎo] *pron pers, 3. sing neutro* **1.** (*sujeto*) it **2.** (*tras preposición*) it; **para** ~ for it; **por** ~ that is why; **estar en** ~ to be doing it; **¡a** ~**!** let's do it!

ellos ['e·jos, -ʎos] *pron pers, 3. pl m* **1.** (*sujeto*) they **2.** (*tras preposición*) them; **estos niños son de** ~ (*suyos*) these children are theirs

elocuencia [e·lo·'kwen·sja, -θja] *f* eloquence; **con** ~ eloquently

elocuente [e·lo·'kwen·te] *adj* eloquent; **las pruebas son ~s** *fig* the evidence speaks for itself

elogiar [e·lo·'xjar] *vt* to eulogize *form*, to praise

elogio [e·'lo·xjo] *m* eulogy, praise; **hacer ~s** to eulogize; **recibir ~s** to be praised; **digno de** ~ praiseworthy

elote [e·'lo·te] *m AmC* ear of corn

eludir [e·lu·'dir] *vt* (*evitar*) to elude; (*preguntas*) to evade; ~ **su responsabilidad** to shirk one's responsibility

emanar [e·ma·'nar] *vi* **1.** (*escaparse*) ~ **de** to emanate from *form*; (*líquido*) to ooze from **2.** (*tener su origen*) ~ **de** to stem from

emancipación [e·man·si·pa·'sjon, -θi·pa·'θjon] *f* emancipation

emancipar [e·man·si·'par, e·man·θi·-] **I.** *vt* (*liberar*) to free; (*feminismo*) to emancipate **II.** *vr:* ~**se** to become emancipated

embadurnar [em·ba·dur·'nar] **I.** *vt* (*manchar*) ~ **algo de** [*o* **con**] **algo** to smear sth with sth **II.** *vr* ~**se de** [*o* **con**] **algo** to be smeared with sth

embajada [em·ba·'xa·da] *f* embassy

embajador(a) [em·ba·xa·'dor, --'do·ra] *m(f)* ambassador

embalaje [em·ba·'la·xe] *m* (*envoltorio*) packaging; (*acción*) packing

embalar [em·ba·'lar] **I.** *vt* to pack **II.** *vr:* ~**se** (*correr*) to dash off

embalsamar [em·bal·sa·'mar] *vt* (*cadáveres*) to embalm

embalsar [em·bal·'sar] *vt* to dam

embalse [em·'bal·se] *m* **1.** (*pantano*) reservoir **2.** (*acción*) damming **3.** *Arg* (*presa*) dam

embarazada [em·ba·ra·'sa·da, -'θa·da] **I.** *adj* (*encinta*) pregnant; **estar ~ de seis meses** to be six months pregnant; **quedarse** ~ to get pregnant **II.** *f* pregnant woman

embarazar <z→c> [em·ba·ra·'sar, -'θar] *vt* **1.** (*cohibir*) ~ **a alguien** to make sb feel awkward **2.** (*dejar encinta*) ~ **a alguien** to get sb pregnant

embarazo [em·ba·'ra·so, -θo] *m* **1.** (*gravidez*) pregnancy; **interrupción del** ~ abortion **2.** (*cohibición*) awkwardness; **causar ~ a alguien** to make sb feel awkward

embarazoso, -a [em·ba·ra·'so·so, -a; -'θo·so, -a] *adj* awkward

embarcación [em·bar·ka·'sjon, -'θjon] *f* (*barco*) vessel; ~ **de recreo** pleasure craft

embarcadero [em·bar·ka·'de·ro] *m* pier, wharf

embarcar <c→qu> [em·bar·'kar] **I.** *vi* to go

on board; (*avión*) to board **II.** *vt* **1.** (*en barco*) to stow **2.** (*avión*) to put on board **3.** (*en un asunto*) to involve **III.** *vr:* ~ **se 1.** (*en barco*) to embark **2.** (*avión*) to board **3.** (*en un asunto*) to become involved

embargar <g→gu> [em·bar·'ɣar] *vt* (*retener*) to confiscate

embargo [em·'bar·ɣo] **I.** *m* **1.** COM embargo **2.** (*retención*) confiscation **II.** *conj* **sin** ~ however

embarque [em·'bar·ke] *m* **1.** (*de material*) loading **2.** (*de personas*) boarding; **tarjeta de** ~ boarding card

embarrada [em·ba·'rra·da] *f* Cuba, PRico, And **1.** (*desliz*) blunder **2.** (*tontería*) foolishness, stupid act

embate [em·'ba·te] *m* **1.** (*del mar*) pounding **2.** (*acometida*) onslaught

embaucador(a) [em·bau·ka·'dor, -·'do·ra] **I.** *adj* deceitful **II.** *m(f)* cheat

embaucar <c→qu> [em·bau·'kar] *vt* to cheat

embejucarse [em·be·xu·'kar·se] *vr* Col, *inf* (*disgustarse*) to get upset; (*encolerizarse*) to get angry

embelesar [em·be·le·'sar] **I.** *vi, vt* to captivate **II.** *vr* ~ **se de** [*o* **con**] **algo** to be captivated by sth

embellecer [em·be·je·'ser, -·ʎe·'θer] *irr como* **crecer** *vt* (*hacer más bonito*) to beautify

embestida [em·bes·'ti·da] *f* onslaught

embestir [em·bes·'tir] *irr como* **pedir** **I.** *vi* to charge **II.** *vt* (*atacar*) to attack; (*coche*) to crash into

emblema [em·'ble·ma] *m* emblem; (*de marca*) logo

embobar [em·bo·'βar] **I.** *vt* (*asombrar*) to amaze; (*fascinar*) to fascinate **II.** *vr* ~ **se en** [*o* **con**] **algo** to be amazed by sth; (*de fascinación*) to be fascinated by sth

embocar <c→qu> [em·bo·'kar] *vt* (*enfilar*) ~ **algo** to slip into sth; **embocó la bola** he/she putted the ball

embolador [em·bo·la·'dor] *m* Col, *inf* shoeshine

embolar [em·bo·'lar] **I.** *vt* Col, *inf* (*zapatos*) to shine **II.** *vr:* ~ **se** AmC to get drunk

embolia [em·'bo·lja] *f* embolism; ~ **cerebral** brain clot

embolsar [em·bol·'sar] *vt* to pocket

emborrachar [em·bo·rra·'tʃar] **I.** *vt* **1.** (*a alguien*) to make drunk **2.** CULIN ~ **con algo** to soak in sth **II.** *vr:* ~ **se 1.** (*beber*) to get drunk **2.** (*los colores*) to run

emborronar [em·bo·rro·'nar] *vt* **1.** (*de tachaduras*) to cover with blots and smudges **2.** (*escribir*) to scribble

emboscada [em·bos·'ka·da] *f* ambush

embotellado, -a [em·bo·te·'ja·do, -·ʎa·do] *adj* (*bebida*) bottled; **vino** ~ bottled wine

embotellamiento [em·bo·te·ja·'mjen·to, em·bo·te·ʎa-] *m* **1.** (*de vino*) bottling **2.** (*de tráfico*) jam

embotellar [em·bo·te·'jar, -·'ʎar] **I.** *vt*

1. (*líquido*) to bottle **2.** (*tráfico*) to block **II.** *vr:* ~ **se** (*tráfico*) to get congested

embrague [em·'bra·ɣe] *m* AUTO clutch

embriagar <g→gu> [em·brja·'ɣar] **I.** *vi, vt* **1.** (*emborrachar*) to inebriate **2.** (*enajenar*) to hypnotize; **este perfume embriaga** this perfume is intoxicating **II.** *vr:* ~ **se** (*emborracharse*) to get drunk

embriaguez [em·brja·'ɣes, -·'ɣeθ] *f* **1.** (*borrachera*) inebriation; **en estado de** ~ inebriated **2.** (*enajenación*) delight

embrión [em·bri·'on] *m* BIO embryo; (*idea*) beginnings *pl*

embrionario, -a [em·brjo·'na·rjo, -a] *adj* embryonic

embrollar [em·bro·'jar, -·'ʎar] **I.** *vt* **1.** (*liar*) to mess up; **embrollas todo lo que tocas** you mess everything up; **lo embrollas más de lo necesario** you're overcomplicating things **2.** CSur (*engañar*) to deceive **II.** *vr:* ~ **se** to get tangled up; ~ **se en algo** to get involved in sth

embrollo [em·'bro·jo, -·ʎo] *m* **1.** (*lío*) mess; (*de hilos*) tangle; **meterse en un** ~ to get into a mess **2.** (*embuste*) swindle; **no me vengas con** ~ **s** don't try and fool me

embromado, -a [em·bro·'ma·do, -a] *adj* AmL, *inf* **1.** (*difícil*) hard **2.** (*molesto*) annoyed

embromar [em·bro·'mar] *vt* AmL (*fastidiar*) to annoy

embroncarse [em·bron·'kar·se] <c→qu> *vr* Arg, *inf* to get angry

embrujado, -a [em·bru·'xa·do, -a] *adj* bewitched; **casa embrujada** haunted house

embrujar [em·bru·'xar] *vt* **1.** (*haciendo brujería*) to captivate **2.** (*embelesar*) to hypnotize

embudo [em·'bu·do] *m* (*aparato*) funnel; **en forma de** ~ funnel-shaped; **aplicar la ley del** ~ to apply one-sided rule

embuste [em·'bus·te] *m* **1.** (*mentira*) lie **2.** (*estafa*) swindle

embustero, -a [em·bus·'te·ro, -a] **I.** *adj* lying; **¡qué tío más** ~! what a swindler! **II.** *m, f* **1.** (*mentiroso*) liar **2.** (*estafador*) swindler

embute [em·'bu·te] *m* Méx, *inf* (*soborno*) bribe

embutido [em·bu·'ti·do] *m* sausage

embutir [em·bu·'tir] **I.** *vt* to pack (in), to stuff; ~ **lana en un cojín** to stuff wool into a cushion; **íbamos embutidos en el tranvía** in the tram we were packed in like sardines **II.** *vr* ~ **se de algo** to stuff oneself with sth

eme ['e·me] *f* **1.** (*letra*) M, m; **la letra** ~ the letter m **2.** (*mierda*) **mandar a alguien a la** ~ *inf* to tell sb to "eff" off

emergencia [e·mer·'xen·sja, -·θja] *f* **1.** (*acción*) appearance **2.** (*suceso*) emergency; **estado de** ~ state of emergency; **plan de** ~ emergency plan

emergente [e·mer·'xen·te] *adj* **país** ~ emergent country

emerger <g→j> [e·mer·'xer] *vi* **1.** (*del agua*) to emerge; **mi jefe emergió de la nada** my boss is a self-made man **2.** (*de la superficie*) to surface

emigración [e·mi·ɣra·'sjon, -'θjon] *f* emigration; (*animales*) migration

emigrante [e·mi·'ɣran·te] *mf* emigrant; POL émigré

emigrar [e·mi·'ɣrar] *vi* to emigrate; (*animales*) to migrate

eminencia [e·mi·'nen·sja, -θja] *f* **1.**(*talento*) expert; **ser una ~ en su campo** to be an expert in one's field **2.**(*título*) Eminence

eminente [e·mi·'nen·te] *adj* **1.**(*sobresaliente*) outstanding **2.**(*elevado*) high

emisión [e·mi·'sjon] *f* **1.** TV, RADIO (*difusión*) broadcast; (*en directo*) live broadcast; (*programa*) program **2.**(*de radiación, calor, luz*) emission; **emisiones contaminantes** pollution

emisor(a) [e·mi·'sor] *adj* **1.** TV, RADIO broadcasting **2.** FIN **banco ~** issuing bank

emisora [e·mi·'so·ra] *f* broadcasting station; **~ clandestina** pirate station; **~ de radio** radio station; **~ de televisión** television station

emitir [e·mi·'tir] *vt* **1.** TV, RADIO to broadcast; (*en directo*) to broadcast live **2.**(*luz, calor, olor, radiación*) to emit, to give off; (*humo*) to let off **3.**(*grito*) to let out **4.**(*dictamen*) to give

emoción [e·mo·'sjon, -'θjon] *f* (*sentimiento*) emotion; (*conmoción*) excitement; **lleno de emociones** full of thrills; **palabras llenas de ~** words full of emotion; **llorar de ~** to cry with emotion; **sin ~** without emotion; **sentir una honda ~** to feel a deep emotion; **dar rienda suelta a sus emociones** to give free rein to one's emotions

emocional [e·mo·sjo·'nal, e·mo·θjo-] *adj* emotional

emocionante [e·mo·sjo·'nan·te, e·mo·θjo-] *adj* **1.**(*excitante*) exciting, thrilling **2.**(*conmovedor*) moving

emocionar [e·mo·sjo·'nar, e·mo·θjo-] I. *vt* **1.**(*apasionar*) to excite; **este libro no me emociona** this book doesn't do anything for me **2.**(*conmover*) to move; **los espectadores estaban emocionados** the spectators were moved; **tus palabras me ~on** I found your words very moving II. *vr:* **~ se 1.**(*conmoverse*) to be moved **2.**(*turbarse*) to get flustered; (*alegrarse*) to get excited

emotivo, -a [e·mo·'ti·βo, -a] *adj* **1.**(*persona*) emotional **2.**(*palabras*) moving

empacar <c→qu> [em·pa·'kar] I. *vi AmL* to pack II. *vt* to pack

empachado, -a [em·pa·'tʃa·do, -a] *adj* **estoy ~** (*indigestado*) I have indigestion; (*harto*) I'm so full I feel sick

empachar [em·pa·'tʃar] I. *vt* **1.**(*indigestar*) to give indigestion **2.**(*turbar*) to bother II. *vr:* **~ se 1.**(*indigestarse*) to get indigestion; (*comer demasiado*) to eat too much **2.**(*turbarse*) to get flustered

empacho [em·pa·'tʃo] *m* **1.**(*indigestión*) indigestion; **tengo un ~ de dulces** I've eaten too many sweets; **tengo un ~ de televisión**

I'm sick of watching television **2.**(*turbación*) fluster; **no tengo ~ en...** I don't mind...

empadronamiento [em·pa·dro·na·'mjen·to] *m* registration in local census bureau; **oficina de ~** register office

empadronar [em·pa·dro·'nar] I. *vt* to register (for a census) II. *vr:* **~ se** to register (for a census)

empalagar <g→gu> [em·pa·la·'ɣar] I. *vt* **1.**(*alimento*) to be oversweet **2.**(*persona*) to cloy upon; **esta película empalaga** this movie is too treacly II. *vr* **~ se de** [*o* **con**] **algo** (*hastiarse*) to get sick of sth

empalagoso, -a [em·pa·la·'ɣo·so, -a] *adj* **1.**(*alimento*) oversweet **2.**(*persona*) cloying **3.**(*película*) treacly, corny

empalmar [em·pal·'mar] I. *vi* **1.**(*dos trenes*) to link up **2.**(*dos caminos, ríos*) **~ con algo** to meet sth; **esta carretera empalma con la nacional** this road joins up with the national highway II. *vt* (*teléfono*) to connect; **~ a puerta** DEP to shoot on goal III. *vr:* **~ se** (*sexualmente*) to get a hard-on

empalme [em·'pal·me] *m* **1.**(*del teléfono*) connection **2.**(*punto: de maderos, tubos*) join; (*del teléfono*) connection **3.** *argot* (*erección*) hard-on

empanada [em·pa·'na·da] *f* CULIN pie (*usually containing meat or tuna*)

empanadilla [em·pa·na·'di·ja, -ʎa] *f* small pasty

empanar [em·pa·'nar] *vt* **1.**(*rebozar*) to coat in breadcrumbs **2.**(*rellenar*) to fill

empañetar [em·pa·ɲe·'tar] *vt AmL* (*encalar*) to plaster

empapar [em·pa·'par] I. *vt* **1.**(*mojar*) to soak; **la lluvia ha empapado el suelo** the rain has soaked the floor **2.**(*absorber*) to soak up II. *vr:* **~ se 1.**(*mojarse*) to get soaked **2.**(*un tema*) **~ se de algo** to become versed in sth

empapelar [em·pa·pe·'lar] I. *vi, vt* (*las paredes*) to (wall)paper II. *vt* **1.**(*objeto*) to wrap up **2.** *inf*(*encausar*) to prosecute

empaque [em·'pa·ke] *m* **1.**(*gravedad*) portentousness; **andaba con gran ~** he/she walked with great pomp **2.**(*semblante*) air; (*del rostro*) expression; **su ~ era grave** he/she had a severe expression **3.** *AmL* (*desfachatez*) cheek

empaquetar [em·pa·ke·'tar] *vt* (*objetos*) to pack

emparedado [em·pa·re·'da·do] *m* sandwich

emparejar [em·pa·re·'xar] I. *vi* **1.**(*ponerse al lado*) **~ con alguien** to catch up with sb **2.**(*ponerse al nivel*) to draw level II. *vt* **1.**(*juntar*) to pair up; **ya estoy emparejado** I already have a partner **2.**(*nivelar*) to level **3.**(*ventana*) to leave slightly open III. *vr:* **~ se** (*formar pareja*) to make a pair; (*parejas*) to pair up; **en el siguiente partido quedé emparejado con Juan** in the next game I drew level with Juan

emparentado, -a [em·pa·ren·'ta·do, -a] *adj* **~ con algo** related to sth

emparentar <e→ie> [em·pa·ren·'tar] *vi* ~ **con una familia** to marry into a family

empastador(a) [em·pas·ta·'dor] *m(f) AmL* (book)binder

empastar [em·pas·'tar] *vt* **1.**(*rellenar*) to fill; (*cubrir*) to cover; ~ **un diente** to have a tooth filled **2.**(*libro*) to bind

empaste [em·'pas·te] *m* **1.** MED filling; **tengo dos muelas con** ~ I have fillings in two of my back teeth **2.**(*relleno*) filling; (*cubrir*) covering

empatar [em·pa·'tar] **I.** *vi* **1.** DEP to draw; ~ **a uno** to draw one-all; **estar empatados a puntos en la clasificación** to have the same points in the league table **2.** POL to tie **II.** *vt* **1.** *AmL* (*cuerdas*) to tie together; ~ **mentiras** to tell one lie after another **2.** *CRi, PRico* (*amarrar*) to moor **3.** *Ven, Col* (*importunar*) to annoy

empate [em·'pa·te] *m* **1.** DEP draw; **gol del** ~ the equalizer **2.** POL tie

empatía [em·pa·'ti·a] *f* empathy

empavonar [em·pa·βo·'nar] **I.** *vt AmL* (*pringar*) to grease **II.** *vr:* ~**se** *AmC* to get dressed up

empedernido, -a [em·pe·der·'ni·do, -a] *adj* (*incorregible*) incorrigible; **bebedor** ~ hardened drinker; **fumador** ~ chain smoker; **solterón** ~ confirmed bachelor

empeine [em·'pei·ne] *m* instep

empelotado, -a [em·pe·lo·'ta·do, -a] *adj AmL, inf* (*desnudo*) stark naked; *Méx* (*colado por alguien*) infatuated

empelotarse [em·pe·lo·'tar·se] *vr AmL, inf* (*desnudarse*) to strip

empeñar [em·pe·'ɲar] **I.** *vt* (*objetos*) to pawn; ~ **la palabra** to give one's word **II.** *vr:* ~**se 1.**(*insistir*) to insist; **se empeña en hablar contigo** he/she insists on speaking to you; **no te empeñes** don't go on about it **2.**(*endeudarse*) to get into debt

empeño [em·'pe·ɲo] *m* **1.**(*afán*) determination; **con** ~ determinedly; **tengo** ~ **por** [*o* **en**] **sacar la mejor nota** I'm determined to get the highest mark; **pondré** ~ **en...** I will try my best to... **2.**(*compromiso*) commitment **3.**(*de objetos*) pawning; **casa de** ~**s** pawnbroker's

empeorar [em·peo·'rar] **I.** *vt* to make worse; **con tus palabras lo has acabado de** ~ what you've said has just made it worse **II.** *vi, vr:* ~**se** to worsen

empequeñecer [em·pe·ke·ɲe·'ser, -'θer] *irr como crecer vt* **1.**(*disminuir*) to make smaller **2.**(*quitar importancia*) to trivialize

emperador [em·pe·ra·'dor] *m* **1.** POL emperor **2.** ZOOL swordfish

emperatriz [em·pe·ra·'tris, -'triθ] *f* empress

emperrarse [em·pe·'rrar·se] *vr inf* (*obstinarse*) to be bent [*o* dead set] on

empezar [em·pe·'sar, -'θar] *irr vi, vt* to begin, to start; **empezó de la nada** he/she started with nothing; **¡no empieces!** don't start!; ~ **con buen pie** to get off to a good start; **para** ~ **me leeré el periódico** to begin with, I'll

read the newspaper; **para** ~ **no tengo dinero y, además, no tengo ganas** first of all, I have no money, and what's more, I don't feel like it

empiezo [em·'pje·so, -θo] *m Col, Ecua, Guat* (*comienzo*) beginning

empinado, -a [em·pi·'na·do, -a] *adj* (*pendiente*) steep

empinar [em·pi·'nar] **I.** *vt* **1.**(*poner vertical*) to stand up **2.**(*alzar*) to raise; ~ **una botella** to raise a bottle (*to drink*); ~ **la cabeza** to raise one's head; ~ **el codo** *inf* to take a drink **II.** *vr:* ~**se 1.**(*persona*) to stand on tiptoes; (*animal*) to stand on its hind legs **2.**(*un edificio*) to tower

empipada [em·pi·'pa·da] *f AmL* binge; **darse una** ~ **de chocolate** to go on a chocolate binge

empiparse [em·pi·'par·se] *vr AmL* to go on a binge

empírico, -a [em·'pi·ri·ko, -a] *adj* empirical

emplaste [em·'plas·te] *m* plaster

emplasto [em·'plas·to] *m* poultice

emplazamiento [em·pla·sa·'mjen·to, em·pla·θa-] *m* (*lugar, situación*) location

emplazar <z→c> [em·pla·'sar, -'θar] *vt* **1.**(*citar*) to call; JUR to summon; **le emplazo para darme una respuesta** I want an answer from you by tomorrow **2.**(*situar*) to locate; **este monumento no está bien emplazado aquí** this isn't the best place for this monument

empleabilidad [em·ple·a·βi·li·'dad] *f* (*de trabajadores*) employability *no pl*

empleado, -a [em·ple·'a·do, -a] *m, f* employee; ~ **de oficina** office worker; ~ **de ventanilla** clerk; **los** ~**s de una empresa** company personnel [*o* staff]

empleador(a) [em·plea·'dor, -·'do·ra] *m(f) AmL* employer

emplear [em·ple·'ar] **I.** *vt* **1.**(*usar: medio, técnica, método*) to use; (*tiempo*) to spend; **¡podrías** ~ **mejor el tiempo!** you could use your time better!; **¡ya te está bien empleado!** it serves you right!; **dar algo por bien empleado** to be satisfied with the results of sth **2.**(*dinero*) to invest; **he empleado todo el dinero en la casa** I've put all my money into the house **3.**(*colocar*) to employ; (*ocupar*) to engage; **en estos momentos no estoy empleado** I'm unemployed at the moment **II.** *vr:* ~**se 1.**(*colocarse*) ~**se de** [*o* **como**] **algo** to be employed as sth **2.**(*usarse*) to be used **3.**(*esforzarse*) ~**se a fondo** to put everything into sth

empleo [em·'pleo] *m* **1.**(*trabajo*) job; (*ocupación*) employment; **pleno** ~ full employment; **no tener** ~ to be out of work; **crear** ~ to create employment; **solicitud de** ~ job application **2.**(*uso, técnica, método*) use; (*tiempo*) spending; **modo de** ~ instructions for use

emplomadura [em·plo·ma·'du·ra] *f AmL* (*empaste*) filling

emplomar [em·plo·'mar] *vt* **1.** *AmL* (*empastar*) to fill **2.** *Col, Guat* (*enredar*) to entangle

empobrecer [em·po·βre·'ser, -'θer] *irr como crecer* I. *vt* to impoverish; **la edad empobrece los reflejos** age slows one's reflexes II. *vi, vr:* **~se** to become poorer; **este terreno se ha empobrecido** this soil has become less fertile

empobrecimiento [em·po·βre·si·'mjen·to, -θi·'mjen·to] *m* (*depauperación*) impoverishment

empollar [em·po·'jar, -'ʎar] I. *vi* 1. *inf* (*estudiante*) to work hard 2. *AmL* (*ampollar*) to blister II. *vt* 1. (*ave*) to brood 2. *inf* (*lección*) to work hard at; **estar empollado de algo** to be up on sth

empollón, -ona [em·po·'jon, --'jo·na; -'ʎon, --'ʎo·na] *m, f inf* brain

emponchado, -a [em·pon·'tʃa·do, -a] *adj* 1. *AmL* (*astuto*) sharp, crafty 2. *Arg, Ecua, Perú, Urug* (*con poncho*) wearing a poncho 3. *Arg, Bol, Perú* (*sospechoso*) suspicious

emporio [em·'po·rjo] *m AmC* (*almacén*) store

empotrado, -a [em·po·'tra·do, -a] *adj* fitted, built-in

empotrar [em·po·'trar] *vt* (*en una pared*) to build in

empotrerar *vt AmL* to put out to pasture

emprendedor(a) [em·pren·de·'dor, --'do·ra] *adj* resourceful, enterprising

emprender [em·pren·'der] *vt* 1. (*trabajo*) to begin; (*negocio*) to set up; **~ la marcha** to set out; **~ la vuelta** to go back; **~ el vuelo** to take off; **al anochecer la emprendimos hacia la casa** at nightfall we set off back to the house 2. *inf* (*principiar una acción*) **~la con alguien** to take it out on sb; **~la a insultos con alguien** to begin insulting sb

empresa [em·'pre·sa] *f* ECON enterprise; (*compañía*) company; **~ de mensajería** courier company; **mediana ~** medium-sized company; **pequeña ~** small company; **~ matriz** parent company; **~ privada** private enterprise; **~ pública** state-owned company

empresarial [em·pre·sa·'rjal] *adj* (*de la empresa*) business; (*compañía*) company

empresario, -a [em·pre·'sa·rjo, -a] *m, f* 1. ECON businessman *m*, businesswoman *f* 2. TEAT impresario

empréstito [em·'pres·ti·to] *m* loan; **~ público** government loan

empujar [em·pu·'xar] *vi, vt* 1. (*dar empujón*) to push; (*con violencia*) to shove; (*multitud*) to elbow, to shoulder; **me empujó hacia atrás** he/she pushed me back 2. (*instar*) to urge

empuje [em·'pu·xe] *m* 1. (*acción*) pushing 2. FÍS force; **~ ascensional** upward force 3. (*energía*) energy; (*resolución*) drive; **persona de ~** pushy person; **no tienes el ~ suficiente para llevar la empresa** you don't have enough drive to run the company

empujón [em·pu·'xon] *m* push; (*violento*) shove; **dar un ~ a alguien** to give sb a shove; **entrar en un local a empujones** to push one's way into a place; **si no le damos un ~ al**

trabajo no lo acabaremos if we don't push ahead with the work we won't finish it

empuntar [em·pun·'tar] I. *vi Col, inf* **~las** to beat it *inf* II. *vt Col, Ecua* (*encarrilar*) to direct towards III. *vr:* **~se** *Ven* (*obstinarse*) to dig one's heels in

empuñar [em·pu·'ɲar] *vt* 1. (*tomar*) to take; (*asir*) to grip; **~ las armas** to take up arms 2. *Chile* (*la mano*) to clench

empurrarse [em·pu·'rrar·se] *vr AmC* to get irritated

emulación [e·mu·la·'sjon, -'θjon] *f* (*imitación*) emulation

emular [e·mu·'lar] *vt* (*imitar*) to emulate

emulsión [e·mul·'sjon] *f* emulsion

en [en] *prep* 1. (*lugar: dentro*) in; (*encima de*) on; (*con movimiento*) in, into; **el libro está ~ el cajón** the book is in the drawer; **pon el libro ~ el cajón** put the book in the drawer; **he dejado las llaves ~ la mesa** I left the keys on the table; **coloca el florero ~ la mesa** put the vase on the table; **~ la pared hay un cuadro** there is a painting on the wall; **pon el póster ~ la pared** put the poster on the wall; **estar ~ el campo/~ la ciudad/~ una isla** to be in the countryside/in the city/on an island; **~ Escocia** in Scotland; **vacaciones ~ el mar** holidays at the seaside; **jugar ~ la calle** to play in the street; **estoy ~ casa** I'm at home; **trabajo ~ una empresa japonesa** I work at a Japanese company 2. (*tiempo*) in; **~ el año 2005** in 2005; **~ mayo** in May; **~ otra ocasión** on another occasion; **~ aquellos tiempos** in those times [*o* days]; **~ un mes** in a month; **lo terminaré ~ un momento** I'll finish it in a minute; **~ todo el día** all [*o* the whole] day 3. (*modo, estado*) **~ absoluto** not at all; **~ construcción** under construction; **~ flor** in flower; **~ venta** for sale; **~ vida** while living; **~ voz alta** aloud; **de dos ~ dos** two at a time; **decir algo ~ español** to say something in Spanish; **pagar ~ pesos** to pay in pesos 4. (*medio*) **papá viene ~ tren** dad is coming by train [*o* plane]; **lo reconocí ~ la voz** I recognized him by his voice 5. (*ocupación*) **doctor ~ filosofía** PhD in Philosophy; **trabajo ~ ingeniería** I work in engineering; **estar ~ la policía** to be in the police force; **estar ~ la mili** to be doing military service; **trabajar ~ Correos** to work in the postal service 6. (*con verbo*) **pienso ~ ti** I am thinking of you; **no confío ~ él** I don't trust him; **ingresar ~ un partido** to join a party; **ganar ~ importancia** to gain in importance 7. (*cantidades*) **aumentar la producción ~ un 5%** to increase production by 5%; **me he equivocado sólo ~ 3 dólares** I was off by just 3 dollars

en. *abr de enero* Jan.

enagua(s) [e·'na·ɣwa(s)] *f(pl)* underskirt

enajenación [e·na·xe·na·'sjon, -'θjon] *f* 1. (*de la mente*) derangement; **~ mental** insanity 2. (*embeleso*) delight 3. (*entre personas*) estrangement

enajenar [e·na·xe·'nar] **I.** *vt* **1.** (*enloquecer*) to make crazy **2.** (*turbar*) to disturb; (*fascinar*) to fascinate **II.** *vr:* ~**se 1.** (*enloquecer*) to go crazy **2.** (*de alguien*) to become estranged

enaltecer [e·nal·te·'ser, -'θer] *irr como crecer vt* (*ensalzar*) to praise

enamoradizo, -a [e·na·mo·ra·'di·so, -a; -'di·θo, -a] *adj* romantic

enamorado, -a [e·na·mo·'ra·do, -a] **I.** *adj* ~ (**de alguien/algo**) in love (with sb/sth); **estuvimos un tiempo ~s** we were in love for a time **II.** *m, f* lover *m, f;* **día de los ~s** St Valentine's Day

enamorar [e·na·mo·'rar] **I.** *vt* (*conquistar*) to win the heart of; **mi profesora me ha enamorado** I'm in love with my teacher **II.** *vr* ~ (**de alguien/algo**) to fall in love (with sb/sth)

enano, -a [e·'na·no, -a] **I.** *adj* tiny **II.** *m, f* **1.** (*persona*) dwarf **2.** *inf* (*criatura*) kid; **disfrutar como un** ~ *inf* to have a great time

enarbolar [e·nar·βo·'lar] *vt* (*bandera*) to hoist; (*cartel*) to stick up; (*espada*) to wield

enarcar [e·nar·'kar] <c→qu> *vr Méx* (*caballo*) to rear

enardecer [e·nar·de·'ser, -'θer] *irr como crecer* **I.** *vt* **1.** (*personas*) to fire with enthusiasm; (*pasiones*) to kindle; ~ **los ánimos** to raise spirits **2.** (*enfervorizar*) to inflame **II.** *vr:* ~**se 1.** (*pasiones*) to be kindled **2.** (*entusiasmarse*) ~**se por algo** to become enthusiastic about sth

encabezado [en·ka·βe·'sa·do, -'θa·do] *m Guat, Méx* (*titular*) heading

encabezamiento [en·ka·βe·sa·'mjen·to, -θa·'mjen·to] *m* **1.** (*de un escrito, libro, artículo*) heading **2.** (*de una carta: parte superior*) letterhead; (*tratamiento*) form of address; (*primeras líneas*) opening

encabezar <z→c> [en·ka·βe·'sar, -'θar] *vt* **1.** (*lista, grupo*) to head; (*institución*) to be the head of **2.** (*un escrito*) to be at the top of; (*un artículo*) to be the title of; ~ **un libro con una cita** to open a book with a quotation **3.** (*una carta: la parte superior*) to head; (*el tratamiento*) to title; (*las primeras líneas*) to open

encabritarse [en·ka·βri·'tar·se] *vr* (*persona*) to lose one's temper

encadenar [en·ka·de·'nar] *vt* **1.** (*poner cadenas*) to chain (up) **2.** *fig* (*unir*) to connect, to link up; (*atar*) to tie down

encajar [en·ka·'xar] **I.** *vi* **1.** *t.* TÉC to fit; (*cerradura*) to bolt; **la puerta encaja mal** the door doesn't fit properly **2.** (*datos, hechos*) to fit in; **las dos declaraciones encajan** the two statements fit together; **este chiste no encaja aquí** this joke is out of place here **II.** *vt* **1.** *t.* TÉC to fit; ~ **en algo** to clamp into sth; ~ **dos piezas** to fit two pieces together; ~ **la ventana en el marco** to fit the window into the frame; ~ **el sombrero en la cabeza** to stick a hat on one's head; ~ **la funda en la máquina** to put the covering over the machine **2.** *inf* ~ **un tiro a alguien** to shoot sb; ~ **un golpe a alguien** to hit sb **3.** *inf* (*aceptar*) to take; **no** ~ **la muerte de alguien** not to take sb's death well; **no sabes** ~ **una broma** you don't know how to take a joke **4.** (*gol*) to let in **5.** *inf* (*soltar*) to come out with; ~ **una reprimenda a alguien** to give sb a talking-to **6.** (*endilgar*) to palm off on sb; ~ **una tarea a alguien** to palm a task off on sb **7.** (*insertar*) to fit **III.** *vr:* ~**se 1.** *AmL, inf* (*aprovecharse*) to go too far **2.** (*atascarse*) to jam

encaje [en·'ka·xe] *m* (*tejido*) lace

encajonar [en·ka·xo·'nar] **I.** *vt* **1.** (*en cajones*) to put in a drawer; (*en cajas*) to box (up) **2.** (*a la fuerza*) to cram; **estábamos encajonados en el coche** we were crammed into the car **II.** *vr:* ~**se** (*apretarse*) ~**se en algo** to squeeze into sth

encalambrarse [en·ka·lam·'brar·se] *vr AmL* **1.** (*calambre*) to cramp up **2.** (*de frío*) to become numb

encallar [en·ka·'jar, -'ʎar] *vi* **1.** (*barco*) to run aground **2.** (*asunto*) to founder; (*negociaciones*) to break down

encallecer [en·ka·je·'ser, -ʎe·'θer] *irr como crecer* **I.** *vi, vr:* ~**se** (*piel*) to harden **II.** *vr:* ~**se** (*persona*) to become inured

encaminar [en·ka·mi·'nar] **I.** *vt* (*dirigir*) to direct; ~ **sus pasos hacia el pueblo** to head towards the village; ~ **la mirada/la conversación hacia un punto** to direct one's gaze/the conversation towards a point; ~ **los esfuerzos hacia una meta** to focus one's efforts on a goal; ~ **los negocios hacia algo** to steer one's business towards sth **II.** *vr* ~**se a/hacia algo** to head for/towards sth; ~**se a la meta** to focus on the goal

encamotarse [en·ka·mo·'tar·se] *vr AmL, inf* ~ **de alguien** to fall in love with sb

encandilar [en·kan·di·'lar] **I.** *vt* to dazzle; **tu belleza lo encandiló** your beauty captivated him; **escuchar encandilado** to listen in rapture **II.** *vr:* ~**se 1.** *fig* (*luz, emociones*) to light up **2.** *AmL* (*asustarse*) to be scared **3.** *PRico* (*enfadarse*) to get angry

encanecer [en·ka·ne·'ser, -'θer] *irr como crecer vi, vr:* ~**se** (*pelo*) to go gray; **pelo encanecido** gray hair

encantado, -a [en·kan·'ta·do, -a] *adj* **1.** (*satisfecho*) delighted; **¡~ (de conocerle)!** pleased to meet you!; **estoy ~ con mi nuevo trabajo** I love my new job; **estoy ~ de la vida** I am thrilled **2.** (*embrujado*) haunted

encantador(a) [en·kan·ta·'dor, -·'do·ra] *adj* **1.** (*persona*) charming **2.** (*fiesta, lugar*) lovely

encantamiento [en·kan·ta·'mjen·to] *m* spell

encantar [en·kan·'tar] *vt* **1.** (*hechizar*) to bewitch; (*serpientes*) to charm **2.** (*gustar*) **me encanta viajar** I love to travel; **me encanta que te preocupes por mí** I love the fact that you care about me **3.** (*cautivar*) to captivate; (*fascinar*) to fascinate

encanto [en·'kan·to] *m* **1.** (*hechizo*) spell; **romper el** ~ to break the spell **2.** (*atractivo*) charm; **¡es un ~ de niño!** what an adorable child!

encapricharse [en·ka·pri·'tʃar·se] *vr* **1.**(*con una cosa*) **~se con algo** to be taken by sth **2.**(*con una persona*) to become infatuated, to have a crush on; **te has encaprichado con ella** you're infatuated with her

encapuchado, -a [en·ka·pu·'tʃa·do, -a] *adj* hooded

encarar [en·ka·'rar] **I.** *vt* **1.**(*persona, cosa*) to bring face to face **2.**(*riesgo*) to face up to **3.**(*fusil*) **~ a algo/alguien** to aim at sth/sb **II.** *vr:* **~se 1.**(*dos personas*) to be face to face **2.**(*a una dificultad*) **~se a algo** to face up to sth **3.** *inf* (*a un superior*) **~se a alguien** to stand up to sb

encarcelamiento [en·kar·se·la·'mjen·to, en·kar·θe-] *m* imprisonment

encarcelar [en·kar·se·'lar, en·kar·θe-] *vt* to imprison; **estar encarcelado** to be in prison

encarecer [en·ka·re·'ser, -'θer] *irr como crecer vt* COM to raise the price of

encarecidamente [en·ka·re·si·da·'men·te, en·ka·re·θi-] *adv* strongly; **le ruego ~...** I have to insist...

encarecimiento [en·ka·re·si·'mjen·to, -θi·'mjen·to] *m* **1.** COM price increase; **el ~ de la vida** the increase of the cost of living **2.**(*acentuación*) emphasis **3.**(*insistencia*) **con ~** insistently

encargado, -a [en·kar·'ɣa·do, -a] **I.** *adj* in charge **II.** *m, f* person in charge; **~ de negocios** chargé d'affaires; **~ de campo** groundskeeper; **~ de curso** course director; **~ de obras** site manager; **~ de prensa** press officer

encargar <g→gu> [en·kar·'ɣar] **I.** *vt* **1.**(*encomendar*) to put in charge; **lo ~on del departamento de ventas** they put him in charge of the sales department; **encargó a su hija a una vecina** he asked a neighbor to watch his daughter **2.**(*comprar*) to order **3.**(*mandar*) to ask **4.** JUR to commission **II.** *vr* **~se de algo** to take responsibility for sth; **tengo que ~me aún de un par de cosas** I still have to get a couple of things done

encargo [en·'kar·ɣo] *m* **1.**(*pedido*) order; **~ por anticipado** advance order; **hacer un nuevo ~** to make another order **2.**(*trabajo*) job; **traje de ~** tailor-made suit; **de ~** to order; **por ~ de** at the request of; **hacer ~s** to run errands; **tener ~ de hacer algo** to be commissioned to do sth

encariñado, -a [en·ka·ri·'ɲa·do, -a] *adj* **estar ~ con algo** to be very attached to sth; **estar ~ con alguien** to be fond of sb

encariñarse [en·ka·ri·'ɲar·se] *vr* **~ con algo** to get attached to sth; **~ con alguien** to grow fond of sb; **el niño se ha encariñado con su tía** the child has become attached to his aunt

encarnación [en·kar·na·'sjon, -'θjon] *f* incarnation; **la ~ del horror** the embodiment of horror

encarnado, -a [en·kar·'na·do] *adj* **1.**(*color carne*) skin-tone; (*rosado*) pink; (*rojo*) red **2.**(*persona*) incarnate

encarnar [en·kar·'nar] **I.** *vi* REL to incarnate **II.** *vt* (*representar*) to represent; **~ a** CINE, TEAT to play the role [*o* part] of

encarnizado, -a [en·kar·ni·'sa·do, -a; -'θa·do, -a] *adj* (*lucha*) bloody

encarpetar [en·kar·pe·'tar] *vt AmL* (*dar carpetazo*) to shelve

encarrilar [en·ka·rri·'lar] *vt* (*dirigir*) to guide

encasillar [en·ka·si·'jar, -'ʎar] *vt* **1.**(*meter en casillas*) to pigeonhole **2.**(*clasificar*) to classify **3.** CINE, TEAT to typecast **II.** *vr* **~se en algo** to limit oneself to sth, to be classified as sth

encausar [en·kau·'sar] *vt* JUR to prosecute; (*acusar*) to accuse

encauzar <z→c> [en·kau·'sar, -'θar] *vt* (*corriente*) to channel; (*debate*) to lead; **~ su vida** to sort out one's life

encéfalo [en·'se·fa·lo, en·'θe-] *m* MED brain

encendedor [en·sen·de·'dor, en·θen-] *m* lighter

encender <e→ie> [en·sen·'der, en·θen-] **I.** *vi* (*fuego*) to catch fire; (*motor*) to fire **II.** *vt* **1.**(*cigarrillo*) to light; **~ un conflicto** to stir up a conflict **2.**(*conectar*) to switch on **III.** *vr:* **~se 1.**(*desencadenarse*) to break out **2.**(*inflamarse*) to ignite **3.**(*luz*) go come on; (*ruborizarse*) to blush

encendido [en·sen·'di·do, en·θen-] *m* AUTO, TÉC ignition; **~ automático** automatic ignition

encendido, -a [en·sen·'di·do, -a; en·θen-] *adj* **1.**(*conectado*) **estar ~** to be on **2.**(*ardiente*) burning; (*cigarrillo*) lighted; (*apasionado*) passionate; **estar ~** to be lit

encerado [en·se·'ra·do, en·θe-] *m* blackboard

encerar [en·se·'rar, en·θe-] *vt* to wax; (*lustrar*) to polish

encerrar <e→ie> [en·se·'rrar, en·θe-] **I.** *vt* **1.**(*depositar, recluir*) to lock in [*o* up]; **~ entre paréntesis** to put in brackets **2.**(*contener*) to contain; **la oferta encerraba una trampa** the offer held a trap **II.** *vr:* **~se** to lock oneself in; *fig* to cut oneself off

encerrona [en·se·'rro·na, en·θe-] *f* trap; **preparar una ~ a alguien** to frame [*o* lay a trap for] sb

encestar [en·se·'tar, en·θes-] *vi* DEP to score a basket

enchastrar [en·tʃas·'trar] *vt CSur* to dirty

enchilada [en·tʃi·'la·da] *f AmC* enchilada

enchilado, -a [en·tʃi·'la·do, -a] *adj Méx* **1.**(*bermejo*) ruddy **2.**(*colérico*) angry; (*rabioso*) furious

enchilar [en·tʃi·'lar] **I.** *vt AmC* **1.** CULIN to season with chili **2.**(*molestar*) to annoy **3.**(*decepcionar*) to disappoint **II.** *vr:* **~se** *AmC* (*enfurecerse*) to blow one's top

enchinar [en·tʃi·'nar] **I.** *vt Méx* (*enrizar*) to curl **II.** *vr:* **~se** *Méx* **1.**(*ponerse carne de gallina*) to get gooseflesh **2.**(*acobardarse*) to be frightened

enchinchar [en·tʃin·'tʃar] **I.** *vt* **1.** *Guat, RDom* (*incomodar*) to annoy **2.** *Méx* ~ **a alguien** (*hacer perder el tiempo*) to waste sb's time **II.** *vr:* ~**se 1.** *Arg* (*malhumorarse*) to be in a bad mood; **¿estás enchinchado?** are you in a bad mood? **2.** *Guat, Méx, Perú, PRico* (*llenarse de chinches*) to be infested with bugs

enchironar [en·tʃi·ro·'nar] *vt inf* to throw in jail

enchivarse [en·tʃi·'βar·se] *vr Col, Ecua* to get furious

enchufar [en·'tʃu·far] *vt* **1.** ELEC to plug in **2.** TÉC (*conectar*) to connect **3.** (*acoplar*) to couple **4.** *inf* (*persona*) ~ **a alguien** to get a job for sb (by pulling strings)

enchufe [en·'tʃu·fe] *m* **1.** (*clavija*) plug **2.** (*toma*) socket **3.** *inf* (*contactos*) **tener** ~ *inf* to have connections **4.** COMPUT plug-in

enchutar [en·tʃu·'far] *vt AmC* **1.** (*embutir*) ~ **de algo** to fill with sth **2.** (*introducir*) to introduce

encía [en·'si·a, -'θi·a] *f* ANAT gum

enciclopedia [en·si·klo·'pe·dja, en·θi·] *f* encyclopedia; ~ **en ocho volúmenes** an eight-volume encyclopedia; **ser una** ~ **viviente** to be a walking encyclopedia

enciclopédico, -a [en·si·klo·'pe·di·ko, -a; en·θi·] *adj* encyclopedic; **diccionario** ~ encyclopedic dictionary

encierro [en·'sje·rro, -'θje·rro] *m* **1.** (*reclusión*) confinement; (*prisión*) imprisonment; (*aislamiento*) isolation; (*como protesta*) sit-in **2.** (*lugar*) quiet spot; (*cercado*) enclosure **3.** TAUR *running of bulls in the San Fermín festival in Pamplona*

encima [en·'si·ma, -'θi·ma] **I.** *adv* **1.** (*arriba:* con contacto) on top; (*sin tocar*) above **2.** *fig* **echarse** ~ **de alguien** to attack sb; **se nos echa el tiempo** ~ time is running out; **quitarse algo de** ~ (*librarse*) to get sth off one's back; **quitar a alguien un peso de** ~ to take a weight off sb's mind; **tener algo** ~ to be saddled with sth; **ya tenemos bastante** ~ we have enough on our plate; **llevaba mucho dinero** ~ he/she had a lot of money on him/her **3.** (*además*) besides; **te di el dinero y** ~ **una botella de vino** I gave you the money and a bottle of wine as well **4.** (*superficialmente*) **por** ~ superficial(ly) **II.** *prep* **1.** (*local:* con contacto) ~ **de** on top of; **con queso** ~ with cheese on top; **el libro está** ~ **de la mesa** the book is on the table; **estar** ~ **de alguien** *fig* to be on sb's case [*o* back] **2.** (*local:* sin contacto) (*por*) ~ **de** above; **por** ~ **de todo** above all; **por** ~ **de la media** above average **3.** (*con movimiento*) (*por*) ~ **de** over; **pon esto** ~ **de la cama** put this over the bed; **cuelga la lámpara** ~ **de la mesa** hang the light above the table; **¡por** ~ **de mí!** *fig* over my dead body!; **ése pasa por** ~ **de todo** *fig* he only cares about himself **4.** (*más alto*) **el rascacielos está por** ~ **de la catedral** the skyscraper is higher than the cathedral

encina [en·'si·na, en·'θi·] *f* BOT holm oak

encinta [en·'sin·ta, -'θin·ta] *adj* pregnant;

dejar ~ **a alguien** to get sb pregnant

enclave [en·'kla·βe] *m* enclave

enclenque [en·'klen·ke] *adj* (*enfermizo*) sickly; (*débil*) weak; (*flaco*) puny

encoger <g→j> [en·ko·'xer] **I.** *vi* (*tejido*) to shrink **II.** *vt* **1.** (*reducir*) to shrink **2.** (*desalentar*) to depress; **verlo así me encoge el ánimo** it depresses me to see him like this **III.** *vr:* ~**se 1.** (*contraerse*) to contract; (*persona*) to cringe; ~**se de hombros** *fig, inf* to shrug one's shoulders **2.** (*reducirse*) to shrink **3.** (*acobardarse*) to get scared

encolerizar <z→c> [en·ko·le·ri·'sar, -'θar] **I.** *vt* to incense **II.** *vr:* ~**se** to be incensed

encomendar <e→ie> [en·ko·men·'dar] **I.** *vt* **1.** (*recomendar*) to recommend **2.** (*confiar*) ~ **algo a alguien** to entrust sth to sb **II.** *vr:* ~**se** to commend; ~**se a Dios** to commend one's soul to God

encomendería [en·ko·men·de·'ri·a] *f Perú* COM grocery store

encomiar [en·ko·'mjar] *vt* to praise

encomienda [en·ko·'mjen·da] *f* **1.** (*encargo*) assignment **2.** (*encomio*) praise **3.** *AmL* (*postal*) parcel

encomio [en·'ko·mjo] *m* praise; **digno de** ~ praiseworthy

enconar [en·ko·'nar] **I.** *vt* **1.** (*agravar*) to worsen; (*agudizar*) to intensify; (*espolear*) to spur on **2.** (*exasperar*) to exasperate **3.** (*inflamar*) to inflame **II.** *vr:* ~**se 1.** (*inflamarse*) to become inflamed **2.** (*agravarse*) to worsen; (*agudizarse*) to intensify

encontradizo, -a [en·kon·tra·'di·so, -a; -'di·θo, -a] *adj* **hacerse el** ~ to contrive a meeting

encontrado, -a [en·kon·'tra·do, -a] *adj* (*opuesto*) opposite; **opiniones encontradas** conflicting opinions

encontrar <o→ue> [en·kon·'trar] **I.** *vt* **1.** (*hallar*) to find **2.** (*coincidir con*) to come across **3.** (*considerar*) to find; (*notar*) to be conscious of **II.** *vr:* ~**se 1.** (*estar*) to be **2.** (*sentirse*) to feel **3.** (*citarse*) ~**se con alguien** to meet sb **4.** (*coincidir*) ~**se con alguien** to run [*o* bump] into sb **5.** (*hallar*) to find; ~**se con algo** to come across sth; **me encontré con que el coche se había estropeado** the car broke down on me; ~**se con un problema** to come up against a problem; ~**se con una sorpresa desagradable** to have a nasty surprise; **no sé lo que me** ~**é cuando llegue** I don't know what I'll find when I arrive; ~**se todo hecho** *inf* to be born with a silver spoon in one's mouth

encontronazo [en·kon·tro·'na·so, -θo] *m inf* crash; **darse un** ~ to have a collision; **tener un** ~ **con alguien** to quarrel with sb; (*enfrentamiento*) to clash with sb

encorvado, -a [en·kor·'βa·do, -a] *adj* hunched; **un viejecito** ~ a stooped old man

encorvar [en·kor·'βar] **I.** *vt* (*cosa*) to bend; (*cuerpo*) to stoop **II.** *vr:* ~**se** (*cosa*) to become bent; (*madera*) to warp; (*persona*) to become

E

hunched

encrucijada [en·kru·si·'xa·da, en·kru·θi-] *f* (*cruce*) crossroads *inv*, intersection; **estar en una ~** *fig* to be at a crossroads [*o* turning point]

encuadernación [en·kwa·der·na·'sjon, -'θjon] *f* **1.**(*encuadernado*) binding **2.**(*cubierta*) cover; **~ en pasta** hardback; **~ en rústica** paperback **3.**(*taller*) bookbinder's

encuadernador(a) [en·kwa·der·na·'dor, -·'do·ra] *m(f)* bookbinder

encuadernar [en·kwa·der·'nar] *vt* to bind; **encuadernado en rústica** paperback; **encuadernado en pasta** hardback; **sin ~** unbound

encuadrar [en·kwa·'drar] *vt* **1.** *t.* CINE, FOTO, TV (*enmarcar*) to frame **2.**(*incluir*) to include

encubierto, -a [en·ku·'bjer·to, -a] **I.** *pp de* **encubrir II.** *adj* **tus palabras son una acusación encubierta** what you've said is a veiled accusation

encubrir [en·ku·'brir] *irr como* **abrir** *vt* **1.**(*cubrir*) to cover **2.**(*ocultar*) to hide; (*silenciar*) to hush up; (*escándalo, crimen*) to cover up; (*un delincuente*) to harbor

encuentro [en·'kwen·tro] *m* **1.**(*acción*) encounter; **ir al ~ de alguien** to go to meet sb **2.**(*cita, reunión*) meeting **3.** DEP match, game; **~ amistoso** DEP friendly match [*o* game]

encuerado, -a [en·kwe·'ra·do, -a] *adj Cuba, Méx* **1.**(*desharrapado*) shabby **2.**(*desnudo*) naked

encuerar [en·kwe·'rar] *vt, vr:* **~se** *AmL* to undress, to strip

encuerista [en·kwe·'ris·ta] *mf AmL* stripper

encuesta [en·'kwes·ta] *f* (*sondeo*) opinion poll; **~ estadística** statistical survey; **~ no oficial** straw poll; **hacer una ~** to carry out an opinion poll

encularse [en·ku·'lar·se] *vr Arg, inf* **1.**(*ofenderse*) **~ por algo** to get pissed off about sth **2.**(*enojarse*) to get angry

enculebrado, -a [en·ku·'le·bra·do, -a] *adj Col, inf*(*endeudado*) indebted

encumbrar [en·kum·'brar] **I.** *vt* **1.**(*levantar*) to raise **2.**(*socialmente*) to elevate; **~ a alguien a la fama** to make sb famous **II.** *vr:* **~se** **1.**(*elevarse*) to rise **2.**(*engrandecerse*) to be ennobled

endeble [en·'de·βle] *adj* (*débil*) weak; (*enfermizo*) sickly

endémico, -a [en·'de·mi·ko, -a] *adj* MED endemic

endemoniado, -a [en·de·mo·'nja·do, -a] *adj* **1.**(*poseso*) possessed **2.**(*malo*) bad **3.** *inf*(*difícil, tremendo*) awful; **tienes un genio ~** you have a terrible temper **4.** *inf*(*travieso*) naughty; **¡~s chiquillos!** damn kids! *inf*

endenantes [en·de·'nan·tes] *adv AmL, inf* a bit before

enderezar <z→c> [en·de·re·'sar, -'θar] *vt* **1.**(*poner derecho*) to straighten **2.**(*corregir*) to straighten out

endeudarse [en·deu·'dar·se] *vr* to get into

debt; (*favor*) to be indebted, to owe a favor

endiablado, -a [en·dja·'βla·do, -a] *adj v.* **endemoniado**

endibia [en·'di·βja] *f* endive

endilgar <g→gu> [en·dil·'yar] *vt inf* **1.**(*cargar*) **~ algo a alguien** to offload sth onto sb; **me ~on sus opiniones moralistas** they inflicted their moralistic opinions on me **2.**(*una tarea*) **me ~on el trabajo sucio** I got stuck with the dirty work

endocalidad [en·do·ka·li·'dad] *f* inner worth *no pl*

endosar [en·do·'sar] *vt* FIN to endorse; (*traspasar*) to endorse over to; **~ una letra** to co-sign a document

endrogarse <g→gu> [en·dro·'yar·se] *vr* **1.** *AmL* (*drogarse*) to take drugs **2.** *Méx, Perú* (*endeudarse*) to get into debt

endulzar <z→c> [en·dul·'sar, -'θar] *vt* **1.**(*poner dulce*) to sweeten **2.**(*suavizar*) to soften

endurecer [en·du·re·'ser, -'θer] *irr como* **crecer I.** *vt* **1.**(*poner duro*) to harden; TÉC to chill **2.**(*mente*) to toughen; (*persona*) to inure **3.**(*hacer resistente*) to strengthen **II.** *vr:* **~se** **1.**(*ponerse duro*) to get tough; (*sentimientos*) to become hardened **2.**(*hacerse resistente*) to be strengthened **3.**(*agudizarse*) to become more intense

endurecimiento [en·du·re·si·'mjen·to, -θi·'mjen·to] *m* **1.**(*dureza*) hardness **2.**(*proceso*) hardening; **~ de las arterias** hardening of the arteries **3.**(*resistencia*) harshness

ene ['e·ne] **I.** *adj inv* MAT x; **~ veces** x times **II.** *f* (*letra*) N, n; **la letra ~** the letter n

eneldo [e·'nel·do] *m* dill

enema [e·'ne·ma] *m* (*lavado*) enema; **poner un ~ a alguien** to give sb an enema

enemigo, -a <enemicísimo> [e·ne·'mi·yo, -a] **I.** *adj* enemy; (*hostil*) hostile; **país ~** hostile country **II.** *m, f* enemy; (*contrario*) opponent; **~ acérrimo** sworn enemy; **~s mortales** mortal enemies *pl;* **ser ~ de algo** to be opposed to sth

enemistad [e·ne·mis·'tad] *f* enmity; (*hostilidad*) animosity

enemistar [e·ne·mis·'tar] **I.** *vt* to make enemies of **II.** *vr:* **~se** to become enemies

energético, -a [e·ner·'xe·ti·ko, -a] *adj* energy; **fuentes energéticas** sources of energy; **valor ~** (*de alimentos*) calories *pl*

energía [e·ner·'xi·a] *f t.* FÍS energy; (*fuerza*) force; **~ nuclear** nuclear energy; **~ eólica** wind power; **con ~** *fig* forcefully; **con toda su ~** with all one's force; **sin ~** *fig* feebly; **la glucosa da ~** glucose gives you energy; **emplear todas las ~s en algo** to put all one's energies into sth

enérgico, -a [e·'ner·xi·ko, -a] *adj* **1.**(*fuerte*) energetic **2.**(*decidido*) firm **3.**(*estricto*) tough; **ponerse ~ con alguien** to get tough with sb

energúmeno, -a [e·ner·'yu·me·no, -a] *m, f inf*

lout, boor; **se puso a gritar como un** ~ he started shouting like a maniac

enero [e·'ne·ro] *m* January; **la cuesta de** ~ the post-Christmas slump; *v.t.* **marzo**

enervante [e·ner·'βan·te] *adj* (*irritante*) annoying

enésimo, -a [e·'ne·si·mo, -a] *adj* MAT nth; **por enésima vez** *inf* for the thousandth [*o* umpteenth] time

enfadar [en·fa·'dar] I. *vt* 1. (*irritar*) to anger; **estar enfadado con alguien** to be angry with [*o* mad at] sb 2. *AmL* (*aburrir*) to bore II. *vr:* ~**se** to get angry; ~**se con alguien** to get angry with [*o* mad at] sb

enfado [en·'fa·do] *m* (*enojo*) anger; (*molestia*) annoyance

énfasis ['en·fa·sis] *m inv* emphasis; (*insistencia*) insistence; **poner** ~ **en algo** to emphasize sth

enfático, -a [en·'fa·ti·ko, -a] *adj* emphatic; (*insistente*) insistent

enfatizar <z→c> [en·fa·ti·'sar, -'θar] I. *vt* to emphasize II. *vt* to emphasize

enfermar [en·fer·'mar] I. *vi, vr* to get sick; ~(**se**) **de algo** to come down with sth; (*hartarse*) to get sick of sth II. *vt* to make sick

enfermedad [en·fer·me·'dad] *f* illness; (*específica*) disease; ~ **del hígado** liver disease; **ausencia por** ~ sick leave; **costar una** ~ *fig* to take its toll

enfermera [en·fer·'me·ra] *f* nurse

enfermería [en·fer·me·'ri·a] *f* infirmary

enfermero [en·fer·'me·ro] *m* male nurse; (*camillero*) stretcher-bearer

enfermizo, -a [en·fer·'mi·so, -a; -'mi·θo, -a] *adj* 1. (*de mala salud*) sickly 2. (*morboso*) sick

enfermo, -a [en·'fer·mo, -a] I. *adj* ill, sick; ~ **del corazón** suffering heart disease; ~ **de gravedad** seriously ill; **caer** ~ **de algo** to come down with sth; **ponerse** ~ to get ill; **esta situación me pone** ~ this situation is really getting me down II. *m, f* ill person; (*paciente*) patient

enfilar [en·fi·'lar] I. *vi* to head II. *vt* 1. (*poner en fila*) to put in a row 2. (*enhebrar*) to string 3. (*poner en línea*) to line up 4. (*ruta*) to take; **enfilamos la carretera** we went down the road

enflaquecer [en·fla·ke·'ser, -'θer] *irr como crecer* I. *vi, vr:* ~**se** to become thin II. *vt* to make thin

enfocar <c→qu> [en·fo·'kar] *vt* 1. (*ajustar*) to focus; **mal enfocado** out of focus 2. (*iluminar*) ~ **algo** to shine light upon sth 3. (*una cuestión*) to approach; (*considerar*) to consider; **no enfocas bien el problema** you're not addressing the issue properly

enfoque [en·'fo·ke] *m* 1. (*punto de vista*) opinion, stance 2. (*planteamiento*) approach; (*concepción*) conception

enfrentamiento [en·fren·ta·'mjen·to] *m* confrontation; (*encontronazo*) collision; (*pelea*) fight; ~**s callejeros** street-fighting

enfrentar [en·fren·'tar] I. *vt* 1. (*encarar*) to bring face to face; (*confrontar*) to confront 2. (*hacer frente*) to face up to; ~ **los hechos** to face the facts II. *vr:* ~ **se** 1. (*encararse*) to come face to face 2. (*afrontarse*) ~**se con alguien** to face up to sb 3. (*pelearse*) to fight; **los manifestantes se** ~**on con la policía** the demonstrators clashed with the police 4. (*confrontar*) to confront 5. (*oponerse*) to oppose; **estar enfrentado a alguien** to be up against sb

enfrente [en·'fren·te] I. *adv* 1. (*en el lado opuesto*) opposite; **allí** ~ over there; **la casa de** ~ the house opposite 2. (*en contra*) **tendrás a tu familia** ~ your family will be against you II. *prep* (*local: frente a*) ~ **de** opposite; ~ **del teatro** opposite the theater; **vivo** ~ **del parque** I live opposite the park; **ponerse** ~ **de alguien** *fig* to be opposed to sb

enfriamiento [en·frja·'mjen·to] *m* 1. (*pérdida de temperatura*) cooling; ~ **económico** economic slowdown 2. (*resfriado*) cold; **pillar un** ~ *inf* to catch a cold [*o* chill]

enfriar < *I. pres:* enfrío> [en·fri·'ar] I. *vi* to cool (down) II. *vt* to cool; *fig* to cool down; ~ **el vino** to chill the wine III. *vr:* ~**se** 1. (*perder calor*) to cool (down) 2. (*refrescar, apaciguarse*) to cool off 3. (*acatarrarse*) to catch a cold

enfundar [en·fun·'dar] I. *vt* (*espada, cuchillo*) to sheathe; **pistola** to put back in the holster II. *vr:* ~ **se** (*ropa*) to put on

enfurecer [en·fu·re·'ser, -'θer] *irr como crecer* I. *vt* to enrage II. *vr:* ~**se** 1. (*encolerizarse*) to be furious 2. (*mar*) to become rough

engajado, -a [en·ga·'xa·do, -a] *adj Col, CRi* curly

engalanar [en·ga·la·'nar] I. *vt* (*decorar*) to decorate; (*adornar*) to embellish II. *vr:* ~**se** to do oneself up, to get dressed up

enganchar [en·gan·'tʃar] I. *vt* 1. (*sujetar*) to hook; (*remolque*) to hitch up; (*caballerías*) to harness 2. (*prender*) to catch on; TAUR to impale 3. *inf* (*atrapar*) to catch; (*convencer*) to persuade 4. MIL to recruit 5. FERRO, TÉC to couple II. *vr:* ~ **se** 1. (*sujetarse*) ~**se de algo** to get hooked on sth 2. (*prenderse*) ~**se de** [*o* **con**] **algo** to get caught on sth 3. (*enredarse*) to get caught up; ~**se en una pelea** to get caught up in a fight 4. MIL to sign up for the army 5. *inf* (*drogarse*) ~**se a** to get hooked on; **estar enganchado** to be hooked

enganche [en·'gan·tʃe] *m* 1. (*gancho*) hook 2. (*acto*) hooking 3. MIL recruitment, enlistment

engañabobos [en·ga·ɲa·'βo·βos] *mf inv, inf* (*timador*) con artist

engañar [en·ga·'ɲar] I. *vi* to deceive; **las apariencias engañan** appearances can be deceptive II. *vt* 1. (*desorientar*) to confuse 2. (*mentir*) to deceive; (*estafar*) to cheat; ~ **a alguien** (*ser infiel*) to cheat on sb; (*burlarse*) to laugh at sb; ~ **el hambre** to stave off one's hunger; **dejarse** ~ to fall for it *inf* III. *vr:* ~**se**

1. (*equivocarse*) to be wrong **2.** (*hacerse ilusiones*) to get excited; **¡no te engañes con esta oferta!** don't get all excited about this offer!

engañifa [en·ga·'ɲi·fa] *f inf*, **engañifla** [en·ga·'ɲi·fla] *f Chile* trap

engaño [en·'ga·ɲo] *m* **1.** (*mentira*) deceit **2.** (*truco*) trick **3.** (*ilusión*) illusion

engañoso, -a [en·ga·'ɲo·so, -a] *adj* **1.** (*persona*) deceitful **2.** (*algo: falaz*) false; (*equívoco*) incorrect; **publicidad engañosa** false advertising

engaratusar [en·ga·ra·tu·'sar] *vt AmC, Col* (*engatusar*) to coax

engarce [en·'gar·se, -θe] *m* (*montura*) mounting

engarzar <z→c> [en·gar·'sar, -'θar] **I.** *vt* **1.** (*trabar*) to join together **2.** (*montar*) to set **II.** *vr:* ~ **se** *AmL* to get caught up

engatusar [en·ga·tu·'sar] *vt* to sweet-talk; ~ **a alguien para que haga algo** to coax sb into doing sth

engavetar [en·ga·βe·'tar] *vt Guat* to pigeon-hole; ~ **a alguien** to shelve sb

engendrar [en·xen·'drar] *vt* **1.** (*concebir*) to beget *liter* **2.** (*causar*) to give rise to

engendro [en·'xen·dro] *m* **1.** (*persona fea*) freak **2.** (*idea*) piece of claptrap

englobar [en·glo·'βar] *vt* **1.** (*incluir*) to include, to comprise **2.** (*reunir*) to bring together

engolillarse [en·go·li·'jar·se, -'ʎar·se] *vr* **1.** *Cuba* (*contraer deudas*) to get into debt **2.** *Perú* (*encolerizarse*) to lose one's temper

engomar [en·go·'mar] *vt* **1.** (*con cola*) to put glue on **2.** (*cabello*) to put gel on

engordar [en·gor·'dar] *vi* **1.** (*ponerse gordo*) to get fat **2.** (*aumentar de peso*) to gain weight **3.** (*poner gordo*) to be fattening **4.** *inf* (*enriquecerse*) to get rich

engorroso, -a [en·go·'rro·so, -a] *adj* awkward; (*molesto*) bothersome

engranaje [en·gra·'na·xe] *m* **1.** TÉC gear; (*mecanismo*) cogs *pl* **2.** (*sistema*) gearing

engranar [en·gra·'nar] **I.** *vi* to interlock **II.** *vt* **1.** (*endentar*) to fit **2.** (*enlazar*) to connect

engrandecer [en·gran·de·'ser, -'θer] *irr como* **crecer** *vt* **1.** (*aumentar*) to increase; (*acrecentar*) to enlarge; (*elevar*) to ennoble **2.** (*exagerar*) to exaggerate **3.** (*enaltecer*) to praise

engrasar [en·gra·'sar] *vt* **1.** (*con grasa*) to grease; (*enaceitar*) to oil **2.** AUTO, TÉC (*lubricar*) to lubricate **3.** (*manchar*) to stain

engrase [en·'gra·se] *m* **1.** (*engrasado*) greasing; AUTO, TÉC lubrication **2.** (*grasa*) grease; (*lubricante*) lubrication

engreído, -a [en·gre·'i·do, -a] *adj* **1.** (*envanecido*) conceited **2.** *AmL* (*mimado*) spoiled

engreír [en·gre·'ir] *irr como* **reír** **I.** *vt* **1.** (*envanecer*) to make arrogant **2.** *AmL* (*mimar*) to pamper **II.** *vr:* ~ **se** **1.** (*envanecerse*) to become vain; (*presumir*) to boast **2.** *AmL* (*hacerse mimado*) to get spoiled

engrifarse [en·gri·'far·se] *vr* **1.** *Col* (*volverse*

altivo) to become arrogant **2.** *Méx* (*irritarse*) to get annoyed; (*malhumorarse*) to lose one's temper

engrosar <o→ue> [en·gro·'sar] **I.** *vi*, *vr:* ~ **se** (*aumentar*) to increase **II.** *vt* (*aumentar*) to increase; (*multiplicar*) to multiply

engrudo [en·'gru·do] *m* paste

engualichar [en·gwa·li·'tʃar] *vt Arg* **1.** (*endemoniar*) ~ **a alguien** to put a spell on sb **2.** (*al amante*) ~ **a alguien** to have power over sb

enguandocar [en·gwan·do·'kar] *vt Col* (*adornar*) to adorn; (*recargar*) to overload

enguaraparse [en·gwa·ra·'par·se] *vr AmC* (*fermentar*) to ferment

engubiar [en·gu·'βjar] *vt Urug* to defeat

engullir <3. *pret:* engulló> [en·gu·'jir, -'ʎir] *vt* **1.** (*tragar*) to swallow **2.** (*atropelladamente*) to devour **3.** *pey* (*comer*) to gobble down

enharinar [en·a·ri·'nar] *vt* (*rebozar*) to coat with flour; (*espolvorear*) to sprinkle with flour

enhebrar [en·e·'βrar] *vt* **1.** (*pasar hebra*) to thread **2.** (*ensartar*) to string together

enhiesto, -a [en·'jes·to, -a] *adj* **1.** (*derecho*) straight; (*erguido*) upright **2.** (*alto*) high

enhorabuena [en·o·ra·'βwe·na] *f* congratulations *pl*; **dar la** ~ **a alguien** to congratulate sb; **estar de** ~ to be on top of the world; **¡**~**!** congratulations!

enigma [e·'niɣ·ma] *m* enigma; **descifrar/plantear un** ~ to unravel/to pose an enigma

enigmático, -a [e·niɣ·'ma·ti·ko, -a] *adj* enigmatic; (*misterioso*) mysterious

enjabonar [en·xa·βo·'nar] *vt* **1.** (*al lavar*) to soap **2.** *inf* (*regañar*) to tick off

enjambre [en·'xam·bre] *m* **1.** (*de abejas*) swarm **2.** (*muchedumbre*) throng

enjaular [en·xau·'lar] *vt* (*encerrar*) to lock up; (*en una jaula*) to cage

enjetarse [en·xe·'tar·se] *vr Arg, Méx* **1.** (*enojarse*) to get angry **2.** (*ofenderse*) to take offense

enjuagar <g→gu> [en·xwa·'ɣar] *vt* to rinse

enjuague [en·'xwa·ɣe] *m* **1.** *t.* TÉC rinse **2.** (*manejo*) rinsing **3.** (*líquido*) ~ **bucal** mouthwash

enjugamanos [en·xu·ɣa·'ma·nos] *m inv, AmL* hand-towel

enjugar <g→gu> [en·xu·'ɣar] **I.** *vt* **1.** (*secar*) to dry; (*limpiar*) to wipe (off) **2.** (*una deuda*) to write off **II.** *vr:* ~ **se** **1.** (*secarse*) to dry **2.** (*adelgazar*) to lose weight

enjuiciar [en·xwi·'sjar, -'θjar] *vt* **1.** (*juzgar*) to analyze; (*censurar*) to criticize **2.** (*procesar*) to prosecute; (*sentenciar*) to sentence

enjutarse [en·xu·'tar·se] *vr Guat, Ven* **1.** (*enflaquecerse*) to become thin **2.** (*achicarse*) to get smaller; (*encogerse*) to shrink

enjuto, -a [en·'xu·to, -a] *adj* scrawny; ~ **de carnes** thin

enlace [en·'la·se, -θe] *m* **1.** (*conexión*) connection **2.** *t.* ELEC, FERRO (*empalme*) link; (*unión*) join; ~ **ferroviario** railroad link **3.** (*entrelazado*) joining **4.** (*boda*) wedding

5. (*contacto*) link; ~ **policial** police informer
6. COMPUT link

enlatados [en·la·'ta·dos] *mpl Col* (*comestibles en latas*) canned food

enlatar [en·la·'tar] *vt* to can; **programa enlatado** TV prerecorded program

enlazar <z→c> [en·la·'sar, -'θar] I. *vi* (*transporte*) to link up II. *vt* **1.** (*atar*) to tie; (*unir*) to join; (*entrelazar*) to interlink **2.** *t.* ELEC, TÉC (*empalmar*) to connect III. *vr:* ~ **se** (*casarse*) to marry

enloquecer [en·lo·ke·'ser, -'θer] *irr como crecer* I. *vi, vr:* ~ **se** to go out of one's mind, to go crazy; ~ **de dolor** to be in terrible pain; ~ **de rabia** to be a lunatic; ~ **por alguien** to be crazy about sb II. *vt* to drive crazy

enlozado [en·lo·'sa·do, -'θa·do] *m AmL* enamel finish, glaze

enlozar <z→c> [en·lo·'sar, -'θar] *vt AmL* to enamel, to glaze

enlutar [en·lu·'tar] I. *vt* **1.** (*en el vestir*) to dress in mourning **2.** (*ensombrecer*) to darken; (*entristecer*) to sadden II. *vr:* ~ **se** to wear black

enmarcar <c→qu> [en·mar·'kar, em·mar·'kar] *vt* to frame; (*encajar*) to place

enmascarar [en·mas·ka·'rar, em·mas·ka·'rar] I. *vt* **1.** (*poner máscara*) to mask; (*disfrazar*) to disguise **2.** (*ocultar*) to hide; (*encubrir*) to cover up II. *vr:* ~ **se 1.** (*con una máscara*) to wear a mask; (*disfrazarse*) to disguise oneself **2.** (*encubrirse*) to cover one's tracks

enmendar <e→ie> [en·men·'dar, em·men·'dar] I. *vt* **1.** (*corregir*) to correct; ~ **la plana a alguien** to find fault with sb **2.** (*modificar*) to modify; (*una ley*) to amend II. *vr:* ~ **se** to mend one's ways

enmicar [en·mi·'kar, em·mi·'kar] <c→qu> *vt Méx* (*cubrir con plástico*) to cover in plastic

enmienda [en·'mjen·da, em·'mjen·da] *f* **1.** (*corrección*) correction; **no tener** ~ *fig* to be beyond repair **2.** (*modificación*) modification; (*de una ley*) amendment

enmohecer [en·mo·e·'ser, em·mo·e·'ser; -'θer] *irr como crecer vi, vr:* ~ **se 1.** (*cubrirse de moho*) to go moldy; (*pudrirse*) to rot **2.** (*caer en desuso*) to get rusty

enmudecer [en·mu·de·'ser, em·mu·de·'ser; -'θer] *irr como crecer* I. *vi* **1.** (*perder el habla*) to become speechless; ~ **de miedo** to be speechless with fear **2.** (*callar*) to go silent II. *vt* to silence

ennegrecer [en·ne·ɣre·'ser, -'θer] *irr como crecer* I. *vt* **1.** (*poner negro*) to blacken **2.** (*oscurecer*) to darken; (*ensombrecer*) to sadden II. *vr:* ~ **se 1.** (*ponerse negro*) to blacken **2.** (*oscurecerse*) to darken; (*ensombrecer*) to sadden

ennoblecer [en·no·βle·'ser, -'θer] *irr como crecer vt* **1.** (*conceder el título*) to ennoble **2.** (*enaltecer*) to exalt; **nos ennoblece su presencia** we are honored by your presence

enojar [e·no·'xar] I. *vt* **1.** (*enfadar*) to anger

2. (*molestar*) to annoy II. *vr:* ~ **se 1.** (*enfadarse*) to get angry **2.** (*molestarse*) to get cross

enojo [e·'no·xo] *m* **1.** (*enfado*) anger; **con** ~ angrily **2.** (*molestia*) annoyance

enojón, -ona [e·no·'xon, -·'xo·na] I. *adj Chile, Ecua, Méx* (*enojadizo*) touchy II. *m, f Chile, Ecua, Méx* (*enojadizo*) quick-tempered person

enojoso, -a [e·no·'xo·so, -a] *adj* (*molesto*) annoying

enorgullecer [e·nor·yu·je·'ser, -ʎe·'θer] *irr como crecer* I. *vt* to fill with pride II. *vr:* ~ **se** to be proud

enorme [e·'nor·me] *adj* enormous; (*gigantesco*) huge; (*desmedido, extraordinario*) remarkable, monstrous *pej*

enormidad [e·nor·mi·'dad] *f* **1.** (*tamaño*) enormity; *fig* lot; **trabajó una** ~ he/she worked a lot **2.** (*cantidad*) great number; **una** ~ **de dinero** a lot of money

enrabiar [en·rra·'βjar] I. *vt* to enrage II. *vr:* ~ **se** to get angry

enraizado, -a [en·rrai·'sa·do, -a; -'θa·do, -a] *adj* rooted; **una costumbre muy enraizada** a deep-seated tradition

enraizar [en·rrai·'sar, -'θar] *irr vi* to set [*o* put] down roots

enrastrojarse [en·rras·tro·'xar·se] *vr AmL* to get dirty

enredadera [en·rre·da·'de·ra] *f* climbing plant

enredar [en·rre·'dar] I. *vi* (*niño*) to get into mischief; **¡no andes enredando con las cerillas!** don't play with the matches! II. *vt* **1.** (*liar*) to mix up; (*confundir*) to confuse **2.** (*enemistar*) to make enemies of III. *vr:* ~ **se 1.** (*cuerda, asunto*) to get mixed up **2.** (*planta*) to climb **3.** *inf* (*amancebarse*) to have an affair

enredo [en·'rre·do] *m* **1.** (*de alambres*) tangle **2.** (*mentira*) troublemaking **3.** (*asunto*) muddle **4.** (*intriga*) intrigue **5.** (*engaño*) deceit **6.** (*amorío*) affair **7.** *pl, inf* (*trastos*) stuff

enrejado [en·rre·'xa·do] *m* (*de hierro*) grating; (*de caña*) fence

enrevesado, -a [en·rre·βe·'sa·do, -a] *adj* (*intrincado*) complicated; (*camino, carretera*) winding; (*difícil*) difficult

enriquecer [en·rri·ke·'ser, -'θer] *irr como crecer* I. *vt* **1.** (*hacer rico, engrandecer, metal, tierra*) to enrich **2.** (*adornar*) to embellish II. *vr:* ~ **se** to get rich; ~ **se** (**a costa ajena**) to get rich (at other people's expense)

enriquecimiento [en·rri·ke·si·'mjen·to, -θi·'mjen·to] *m* enrichment; ~ **injusto** JUR embezzlement

enrojecer [en·rro·xe·'ser, -'θer] *irr como crecer* I. *vi* to blush; ~ **de ira** to go red with anger; (*con fiebre*) to flush II. *vt* (*cielo*) to redden III. *vr:* ~ **se** (*persona*) to blush; (*cielo*) to redden

enrolar [en·rro·'lar] *vt* **1.** NÁUT to enroll **2.** MIL to enlist

enrollar [en·rro·'jar, -'ʎar] I. *vt* (*cartel*) to roll up; (*cuerda*) to coil II. *vr:* ~ **se** *inf* **1.** (*exten-*

derse demasiado) to go on and on **2.**(*ligar*) **~se con alguien** to take up with sb **3.**(*saber estar*) to get on well

enroscar <c→qu> [en·rros·'kar] **I.** *vt* **1.**(*tornillo*) to screw in **2.**(*tapa*) to twist on **II.** *vr:* **~se** to curl up; **la serpiente se enroscó en la rama** the snake coiled itself around the branch

enrostrar [en·rros·'trar] *vt AmL* to throw in one's face

enrular [en·rru·'lar] *vt CSur* to curl

ensaimada [en·sai·'ma·da] *f light, spiral-shaped pastry from Mallorca*

ensalada [en·sa·'la·da] *f* salad; **~ de frutas** fruit salad

ensaladera [en·sa·la·'de·ra] *f* salad bowl

ensalzar <z→c> [en·sal·'sar, -'θar] **I.** *vt* (*dignificar*) to dignify; (*alabar*) to praise **II.** *vr:* **~se** to boast

ensamblar [en·sam·'blar] *vt* to assemble

ensanchar [en·san·'tʃar] **I.** *vt* to widen **II.** *vr:* **~se** to widen

ensanche [en·'san·tʃe] *m* (*ampliación*) enlargement; (*de anchura*) widening

ensangrentar <e→ie> [en·san·gren·'tar] *vt* to cover in blood

ensartar [en·sar·'tar] *vt* **1.**(*perlas*) to string **2.**(*pinchar*) to skewer **3.**(*hablar*) to reel off

ensayar [en·sa·'jar] **I.** *vt* **1.** TEAT to rehearse **2.**(*probar*) to test; (*examinar*) to examine **II.** *vr* **~se en algo** to rehearse sth

ensayo [en·'sa·jo] *m* **1.** TEAT rehearsal; **~ general** dress rehearsal **2.** LIT essay **3.**(*prueba*) test; (*experimento*) experiment; **tubo de ~** test tube

enseguida [en·se·'ɣi·da] *adv* at once, right away

ensenada [en·se·'na·da] *f* **1.**(*mar*) inlet **2.** *Arg* (*corral*) meadow

enseña [en·'se·ɲa] *f* insignia; (*estandarte*) standard

enseñanza [en·se·'ɲan·sa, -θa] *f* **1.**(*sistema*) education; **~ primaria** primary education; **~ privada** private education; **~ pública** public education; **~ secundaria** secondary education; **~ superior** higher education **2.**(*docencia*) teaching; **~ a distancia** distance learning; **~ universitaria** university education; **método de ~** teaching method; **dedicarse a la ~** to be a teacher **3.**(*lección*) lesson

enseñar [en·se·'ɲar] *vt* **1.**(*instruir, dar clases*) to teach; (*explicar*) to explain; **ella me enseñó a tocar la flauta** she taught me how to play the flute; **hay que ~ con el ejemplo** you have to lead by example; **¡la vida te ~á!** life is the best teacher!; **¡ya te ~é yo a obedecer!** I'll teach you a bit of obedience! **2.**(*mostrar*) to show; **~ el camino a alguien** to show sb the way **3.**(*dejar ver*) to show; (*presentar*) to present; (*exhibir*) to exhibit

enseres [en·'se·res] *mpl* belongings *pl*; (*útiles*) tools *pl*; (*mobiliario*) goods *pl*

ensillar [en·si·'jar, -'ʎar] *vt* to saddle

ensimismarse [en·si·mis·'mar·se] *vr*

1.(*absorberse*) to become absorbed; **~ en recuerdos/una lectura** to become engrossed in one's memories/reading **2.** *Col, Chile* (*engreírse*) to become vain

ensombrecer [en·som·bre·'ser, -'θer] *irr como crecer* **I.** *vt* (*oscurecer*) to darken; (*ofuscar*) to cast a shadow over **II.** *vr:* **~se 1.**(*entristecerse*) to become sad **2.**(*oscurecerse*) to darken

ensopar [en·so·'par] **I.** *vt AmS* (*empapar*) to soak **II.** *vr:* **~se** *AmS* to get soaked

ensordecedor(a) [en·sor·de·se'dor, -·'dor·; en·sor·de·θe-] *adj* deafening

ensordecer [en·sor·de·'ser, -'θer] *irr como crecer* **I.** *vi* (*quedarse sordo*) to go deaf **II.** *vt* (*ruido*) to deafen

ensortijado, -a [en·sor·ti·'xa·do, -a] *adj* curly

ensortijar [en·sor·ti·'xar] *vt* (*pelo*) to curl

ensuciar [en·su·'sjar, -'θjar] **I.** *vt* to dirty **II.** *vr:* **~se 1.**(*mancharse*) to get dirty; **~se de algo** to be stained with sth **2.**(*reputación*) to tarnish **3.** *inf* (*excremento*) to soil oneself

ensueño [en·'swe·ɲo] *m* dream; **de ~** fantastic

entablar [en·ta·'βlar] *vt* **1.**(*conversación*) to strike up; (*negociaciones*) to begin; (*amistad*) to establish; (*juicio*) to file; **~ relaciones comerciales** to establish trade links **2.**(*suelo*) to put floorboards on **3.**(*ajedrez*) to set up

entablillar [en·ta·βli·'jar, -'ʎar] *vt* to splint

entallado, -a [en·ta·'ja·do, -a; en·ta·'ʎa-] *adj* taken in at the waist

entallar [en·ta·'jar, -'ʎar] **I.** *vt* (*vestido*) to take in at the waist **II.** *vi, vr:* **~se** to fit; **la chaqueta entalla bien** the jacket fits well

entarimado [en·ta·ri·'ma·do] *m* floorboards *pl*

ente ['en·te] *m* **1.** FILOS being **2.**(*autoridad*) body; **el Ente Público** the public sector

entecarse [en·te·'kar·se] <c→qu> *vr Chile* (*emperrarse*) to be stubborn

entendederas [en·ten·de·'de·ras] *fpl inf* brains *pl*; **es muy corto de ~** he's pretty dumb

entender <e→ie> [en·ten·'der] **I.** *vi* **1.**(*comprender*) to understand; **si entiendo bien Ud. quiere decir que...** am I right in saying that what you mean is that... **2.**(*saber*) **~ mucho de algo** to know a lot about sth; **no ~ nada de algo** to know nothing about sth **II.** *vt* **1.**(*comprender*) to understand; **dar a ~ que...** to imply that...; **dar a ~ a alguien que...** to lead sb to believe that...; **lo entendieron mal** they misunderstood it; **¿qué entiende Ud. por 'acuerdo'?** what do you understand by 'agreement'?; **ellos ya se harán ~** they'll soon make themselves understood; **no ~ ni jota/papa** *inf* not to understand a thing; **no entiende una broma** he/she can't take a joke **2.**(*creer*) to think; **yo entiendo que sería mejor si** +*subj* I think it would be better if; **yo no lo entiendo así** that's not the way I see it; **tengo entendido que...** (*según creo*) I believe that...; (*según he oído*) I've heard that... **III.** *vr:* **~se 1.**(*llevarse bien*) to get on **2.**(*ponerse de acuerdo*) to agree; **para el precio entiéndete con mi socio** as regards the price, reach an agreement with my partner **3.** *inf* (*liarse*) to have an affair **4.** *inf* (*desenvolverse*) to manage; **¡que se las entienda!** let him/her get on with it! **5.** (*expresiones*) **¡yo me entiendo!** I know what I'm doing!; **pero ¿cómo se entiende?** *inf* but what does it mean?; **eso se entiende por sí mismo** this is self-explanatory **IV.** *m* opinion; **a mi ~** the way I see it

entendido, -a [en·ten·'di·do, -a] **I.** *adj* **1.** (*listo*) clever, smart **2.** (*experto*) **~ en algo** expert on sth; **no se dio por ~** he pretended he hadn't heard **3.** (*claro*) **queda ~ que...** it is clear that...; **queda ~ que te acompaño a casa** of course I'll take you home; **bien ~ que...** on the understanding that... **II.** *m, f* expert; (*vinos*) connoisseur; **es un gran ~ en informática** he's a real expert on computers; **hacerse el ~** to act smart

entendimiento [en·ten·di·'mjen·to] *m* **1.** (*razón*) reason; (*facilidad de comprensión*) understanding; **obrar con ~** to go about things reasonably; **un hombre de mucho ~** a very reasonable man **2.** (*acuerdo*) agreement

enterado, -a [en·te·'ra·do, -a] *adj* **~ de algo** (*iniciado*) aware of sth; (*conocedor*) knowledgeable about sth; **yo ya estaba ~ del incidente** I already knew about the incident; **no se dio por ~** he pretended he didn't understand

enteramente [en·te·ra·'men·te] *adv* wholly

enterar [en·te·'rar] **I.** *vt* **1.** (*informar*) **~ de algo** to tell about sth **2.** *Méx, CRi, Hond* COM to pay **II.** *vr* **~ de algo** (*descubrir*) to find out about sth; (*saber*) to hear about sth; **no me enteré de nada hasta que me lo dijeron** I wasn't aware of anything until they told me; **pasa las hojas sin ~se de lo que lee** he/she turns the pages without taking anything in; **¡para que se entere!** *inf* that'll teach him/her/you!; **para que te enteres...** for your information...

entereza [en·te·'re·sa, -'re·θa] *f* **1.** (*determinación*) strength of mind **2.** (*aplomo*) aplomb **3.** (*integridad*) integrity; **a la muerte de su madre demostraron mucha ~** they showed great fortitude when their mother died

enternecer [e·ter·ne·'ser, - 'θer] *irr como crecer* **I.** *vt* **1.** (*ablandar*) to soften **2.** (*conmover*) to move; (*hacer ceder*) to make relent **II.** *vr:* **~se** (*conmoverse*) to be touched; (*ceder*) to relent

entero, -a [en·'te·ro] *adj* (*completo*) *t.* MAT whole, entire; **por ~** completely; **se pasa días ~s sin decir ni una palabra** he/she goes for days at a time without speaking; **el espejo salió ~ de aquí** when the mirror left here it was in one piece; **la comisión entera se declaró a favor** the whole committee declared themselves in favor; **el juego de café no está ~** some of the coffee service is missing

enterrador(a) [en·te·rra·'dor] *m(f)* (*sepul-*

turero) gravedigger

enterrar <e→ie> [en·te·'rrar] **I.** *vt* **1.** (*a un muerto*) to bury; **¡ésa nos ~á a todos!** *inf* she will outlive the lot of us! **2.** (*un objeto*) to bury; (*no muy profundo*) to cover up **3.** (*ilusiones, esperanzas*) to abandon **II.** *vr:* **~se** (*recluirse*) to hide oneself away

enterratorio [en·te·rra·'to·rjo] *m AmS* (*cementerio*) Indian burial ground

entibiar [en·ti·'βjar] **I.** *vt* (*líquido*) to cool; *fig* to soften **II.** *vr:* **~se** (*líquido*) to become lukewarm; *fig* to soften

entidad [en·ti·'dad] *f* (*asociación*) organization; **~ aseguradora** insurance firm; **~ crediticia** credit company; **~ jurídica** legal entity; **~ bancaria** bank

entierro [en·'tje·rro] *m* **1.** (*inhumación*) burial; **¡no pongas esa cara de ~!** don't look so glum! **2.** (*funeral*) funeral

entonación [en·to·na·'sjon, -'θjon] *f* LING, MÚS intonation

entonar [en·to·'nar] **I.** *vi* **1.** (*canción*) to sing in tune **2.** (*armonizar*) to go well **II.** *vt* (*canción*) to sing

entonces [en·'ton·ses, -θes] *adv* **1.** (*temporal*) then; **desde ~** from then on; **hasta ~** until then; **en** [*o por*] **aquel ~** at that time **2.** (*modal*) then; **¿y ~ qué pasó?** and what happened next?; **¿pues ~ por qué te extraña si no vienen?** then why are you surprised that they don't come?; **¡~!** well, then!

entornar [en·tor·'nar] *vt* (*puerta*) to leave slightly open

entorno [en·'tor·no] *m* surroundings *pl;* (*medio ambiente*) environment; (*mundillo*) world, sphere

entorpecer [en·tor·pe·'ser, -'θer] *irr como crecer* *vt* **1.** (*movimiento*) to make slow [*o* clumsy]; (*frío*) to numb **2.** (*dificultar*) to hamper; (*retrasar*) to slow down **3.** (*sentidos*) to dull

entrabar [en·tra·'βar] *vt AmS* to interfere

entrada [en·'tra·da] *f* **1.** (*puerta*) entrance; (*para coche*) door; **~ a la autopista** (*entry*) ramp; **~ trasera** back door **2.** (*acción*) entrance; **hacer una ~** to make an entrance; **se prohíbe la ~** no entry [*o* admittance] **3.** (*comienzo*) entry; (*en un cargo*) start; **~ en funciones** starting date; **~ en vigor** coming into force; **de ~** right from the start; **así de ~ tu idea no me pareció mal** at first your idea didn't strike me as bad **4.** (*cine, teatro*) ticket; **~ gratuita** free entry [*o* admission] **5.** (*público*) audience; **en el estreno hubo una gran ~** the premiere was packed **6.** CULIN first course, entrée **7.** *pl* (*pelo*) **tiene ~s** his/her hair is receding **8.** MÚS entry; **dar la ~** to enter **9.** (*en diccionario*) entry **10.** (*depósito*) deposit; **ya hemos dado la ~ para el coche** we've already made the down-payment on the car **11.** COM income; **~ de pedidos** orders *pl* **12.** FIN **~s y salidas** income and costs **13.** COMPUT input

entrado, -a [enˈtraˌðo, -a] *adj* **un señor ~ en años** an elderly gentleman; **llegamos entrada la noche** we arrived when it was already dark; **hasta muy ~ el siglo XVII** until well into the seventeenth century

entrador(a) [enˌtraˈðor, -ˈðoˌra] *adj* **1.** *AmS* (*animoso*) spirited; (*atrevido*) daring **2.** *Arg* (*simpático*) friendly **3.** *AmL* (*enamoradizo*) romantic **4.** *Chile* (*entremetido*) interfering **5.** *Guat, Nic* (*compañero*) companionable

entrampar [enˌtramˈpar] **I.** *vt* **1.** (*animal*) to trap **2.** (*engañar*) to deceive **3.** *inf* (*embrollar*) to mess up **II.** *vr:* **~ se** to get into debt

entrante¹ [enˈtranˌte] *adj* (*próximo*) next; **a primeros del mes ~** at the start of next month

entrante² [enˈtranˌte] *m* CULIN first course, starter

entraña [enˈtraˌɲa] *f* **1.** *pl* (*órganos*) entrails *pl;* **echar las ~ s** *inf* to throw up; **¡hijo de mis ~ s!** *inf* my darling child! **2.** (*lo esencial*) core **3.** *pl* (*carácter*) nature; **de buenas ~ s** good-natured **4.** *pl* (*interior*) core; **las ~ s de la tierra** the bowels of the earth

entrañable [enˌtraˈɲaˌβle] *adj* (*amistad*) intimate; (*película, persona*) endearing; (*recuerdo*) fond

entrañar [enˌtraˈɲar] *vt* to involve; **~ graves peligros** to entail serious dangers

entrar [enˈtrar] **I.** *vi* **1.** (*pasar*) to enter; **~ por la ventana** to come in through the window; **~ por la fuerza** to break in; **el tren entra en la estación** the train enters the station; **me entró por un oído y me salió por otro** it went in one ear and out the other; **~ con buen pie** to start off on the right foot; **¡entre!** come in! **2.** (*caber*) to fit; **no me entra el anillo** I can't get the ring on; **el corcho no entra en la botella** the cork won't fit into the bottle; **por fin he hecho ~ el tapón** I finally got the lid on **3.** (*penetrar*) to go in; **el clavo entró en la pared** the nail went into the wall; **¡no me entra en la cabeza cómo pudiste hacer eso!** I can't understand how you could do this! **4.** (*empezar*) to begin; **~ en relaciones** to start a relationship; **el verano entra el 21 de junio** summer begins on the 21st of June; **después entré a trabajar en una casa más rica** afterwards I started working in a wealthier household; **cuando entró de alcalde** when he was elected mayor; **no ~ en detalles** not to go into details; **~ en calor** to warm up; **~ en vigor** to come into force; **me entró la tentación** I was tempted; **me entró un mareo** I became dizzy; **me entró el hambre** I became hungry **5.** (*como miembro*) **~ en algo** to become a member of sth; **~ en la Academia de Ciencias** to be admitted to the Royal Academy of Science **6.** (*formar parte*) **en un kilo entran tres panochas** you can get three corncobs with the kilo; **eso no entraba en mis cálculos** I hadn't planned on this **7.** MÚS to come in **8.** DEP to tackle **9.** COMPUT to access **10.** (*dar*) **esperemos que no te entre la gripe** we hope you don't get the flu; **le ha entrado la costumbre de...** he/she's gotten into the habit of... **11.** *inf* (*entender*) **las matemáticas no me entran** I can't get the hang of mathematics **12.** *inf* (*soportar*) **su hermano no me entra** I can't stand his/her brother **13.** *inf* (*relacionarse, tratar*) **no sabe ~ a las chicas** he doesn't know how to pick up girls; **a él no sabes como ~ le** you don't know how to deal with him **14.** (*opinar*) **yo en eso no entro** [*o* **ni entro ni salgo**] *inf* I have nothing to do with this **II.** *vt* to put; **~ el coche en el garaje** to put the car into the garage

entre [ˈenˌtre] *prep* **1.** (*dos cosas*) between; (*más de dos cosas*) among; **salir de ~ las ramas** to emerge from the branches; **pasar por ~ las mesas** to go between the tables; **~ semana** during the week; **ven ~ las cinco y las seis** come between five and six; **~ tanto** meanwhile; **lo cuento ~ mis amigos** I consider him as one of my friends; **un ejemplo ~ muchos** one of many examples; **el peor ~ todos** the worst of the lot; **llegaron veinte ~ hombres y mujeres** twenty men and women arrived; **se la llevaron ~ cuatro hombres** she was carried off by four men; **lo hablaremos ~ nosotros** we'll talk it over with each other; **~ el taxi y la entrada me quedé sin dinero** what with the taxi and the ticket I had no money left; **¡guárdalo ~ los libros!** keep it with your books; **me senté ~ los dos** I sat down between the two of them **2.** MAT **ocho ~ dos son cuatro** eight divided by two is four

entreabierto, -a [enˌtreaˈβjerˌto, -a] *adj* ajar

entreabrir [enˌtreaˈβrir] *irr como* abrir *vt* to open slightly

entreacto [enˌtreˈakˌto] *m* (*intermedio*) interval

entrecano, -a [enˌtreˈkaˌno, -a] *adj* graying

entrecejo [enˌtreˈsexo, -ˈθeˌxo] *m* (*ceño*) brow; **fruncir el ~** to frown

entrecomillar [enˌtrekomiˈʎar, -ˈʎar] *vt* to put in quotes [*o* quotation marks]

entrecortado, -a [enˌtrekorˈtaˌðo, -a] *adj* (*respiración*) uneven, labored; (*voz*) halting; **con la voz entrecortada por los sollozos** with a voice broken with sobs

entrecruzar <z→c> [enˌtrekruˈsar, -ˈθar] *vt, vr:* **~ se** to interweave; (*miradas*) to cross; (*cintas*) to interlace

entredicho [enˌtreˈðiˌtʃo] *m* (*duda*) **poner algo en ~** to put sth in question; **poner en ~ la veracidad** to question the truth

entrega [enˈtreˌɣa] *f* **1.** (*dedicación*) dedication **2.** (*fascículo*) installment; **novela por ~ s** serialized novel **3.** (*de documentos*) delivery; (*ceremonia*) giving; **~ de premios** giving of prizes; **~ de títulos** UNIV graduation ceremony; **hacer ~ de algo** to hand sth over **4.** COM delivery; **~ a domicilio** home delivery; **talón de ~** delivery sheet; **pagadero a la ~** payable on delivery; **~ contra reembolso** collect on deliv-

ery **5.** MIL surrender; (*de prisioneros*) release
entregar <g→gu> [en·tre·'ɣar] I. *vt* **1.** (*dar*)
to give, to hand over [*o* in]; ~ **la** *inf* to kick the
bucket **2.** (*carta*) to deliver **3.** MIL to surrender;
(*prisioneros*) to hand over II. *vr:* ~ **se 1.** (*desvivirse*) to take to; ~ **se a la bebida** to take to
drink **2.** (*delincuente*) to give oneself up **3.** MIL
to surrender **4.** (*sexo*) to yield
entrelazar <z→c> [en·tre·la·'sar, -'θar] *vt, vr:*
~ **se** to join, to (inter)weave
entremedias [en·tre·'me·djas] *adv* **1.** (*local*)
between; (*más de dos cosas*) among; ~ **de...**
somewhere between... **2.** (*temporal*) meanwhile
entremeses [en·tre·'me·ses] *mpl* hors
d'oeuvres *pl*, appetizers *pl*
entremeterse [en·tre·me·'ser·se, -'θer·se] *vr*
to interfere, to butt in *inf*
entremetido, -a [en·tre·me·'ti·do, -a] I. *adj*
interfering II. *m, f* busybody
entremezclar [en·tre·mes·'klar, en·tre·meθ-]
vt to intermingle
entrenador(a) [en·tre·na·'dor] *m(f)* DEP coach
entrenamiento [en·tre·na·'mjen·to] *m* **1.** DEP
training session **2.** (*práctica*) training
entrenar [en·tre·'nar] *vt, vr:* ~ **se** to train
entrepierna [en·tre·'pjer·na] *f* **1.** (*muslo, pantalón*) crotch **2.** *Chile* (*de baño*) swimsuit
entresacar <c→qu> [en·tre·sa·'kar] *vt*
(*escoger*) to pick out; (*elegir*) to choose
entresuelo [en·tre·'swe·lo] *m* mezzanine, first
floor
entretanto [en·tre·'tan·to] *adv* meanwhile
entretecho [en·tre·'te·tʃo] *m CSur* (*desván*) attic
entretejer [en·tre·te·'xer] *vt* (*entrelazar*) to
interweave
entretela [en·tre·'te·la] *f* inner lining
entretener [en·tre·te·'ner] *irr como* tener I. *vt*
1. (*divertir*) to entertain **2.** (*apartar la atención*) to distract **3.** (*asunto*) to delay; ~ **a alguien con excusas** to keep giving sb excuses
4. (*detener*) to hold up II. *vr:* ~ **se 1.** (*pasar el
rato*) to amuse oneself **2.** (*tardar*) to delay; **¡no
te entretengas!** don't dilly dally! **3.** (*apartar la
atención*) to be distracted
entretenido, -a [en·tre·te·'ni·do, -a] *adj* entertaining
entretenimiento [en·tre·te·ni·'mjen·to] *m*
(*diversión*) entertainment; (*pasatiempo*) activity; **en el bosque hay mucho ~ para los
niños** children can have a great time in the forest
entretiempo [en·tre·'tjem·po] *m* between season; (*primavera*) spring; (*otoño*) autumn
entrever [en·tre·'βer] *irr como* ver *vt*
1. (*objeto*) to glimpse **2.** (*sospechar*) to surmise; (*intenciones*) to guess
entreverar [en·tre·βe·'rar] *vr:* ~ **se** *Arg, Perú* to
jumble together
entrevero [en·tre·'βe·ro] *m CSur* **1.** (*confusión*) jumble **2.** (*riña*) brawl **3.** (*escaramuza*)
skirmish

entrevista [en·tre·'βis·ta] *f* **1.** (*interviú*) interview; **hacer una ~ a alguien** to interview sb;
~ **de trabajo** job interview **2.** (*reunión*) meeting
entrevistar [en·tre·βis·'tar] I. *vt* to interview
II. *vr:* ~ **se** (*entrevista*) to be interviewed; (*reunión*) to have a meeting
entristecer [en·tris·te·'ser, -'θer] *irr como*
crecer I. *vt* to sadden II. *vr:* ~ **se** to be saddened
entrometerse [en·tro·me·'ter·se] *vr* to interfere
entrometido, -a [en·tro·me·'ti·do, -a] *adj, m, f*
v. entremetido
entroncar <c→qu> [en·tron·'kar] *vi* **1.** (*tener
parentesco*) ~ **con alguien** to be related to sb
2. *AmL* (*tren*) to connect
entronque [en·'tron·ke] *m AmL* (*tren*) connection
entrucharse [en·tru·'tʃar·se] *vr Méx*
1. (*entremeterse*) ~ **en algo** to interfere with
sth **2.** (*enamorarse*) ~ **de alguien** to fall in
love with sb
entuerto [en·'twer·to] *m* (*agravios*) wrongdoing, offense
entumecerse [en·tu·me·'ser·se, -'θer·se] *irr
como* crecer *vr* (*frío*) to go numb; (*músculo*)
to stiffen; (*hinchazón*) to swell
entumecido, -a [en·tu·me·'si·do, -a; -'θi·do,
-a] *adj* (*frío*) numb; (*pierna, rígido*) stiff; (*hinchado*) swollen
enturbiar [en·tur·'βjar] *vt* to darken
entusiasmar [en·tu·sjas·'mar] I. *vt* to enthuse
II. *vr:* ~ **se** to get enthusiastic
entusiasmo [en·tu·'sjas·mo] *m* enthusiasm
entusiasta [en·tu·'sjas·ta] I. *adj* enthusiastic
II. *mf* enthusiast
entusiástico, -a [en·tu·'sjas·ti·ko, -a] *adj* enthusiastic
enumeración [e·nu·me·ra·'sjon, -'θjon] *f* enumeration
enumerar [e·nu·me·'rar] *vt* to enumerate;
(*escrito*) to set down
enunciado [e·nun·'sja·do, -'θja·do] *m* (*de
problema*) setting out
enunciar [e·nun·'sjar, -'θjar] *vt* (*explicar*) to
set out; (*expresar*) to state
enunciativo, -a [e·nun·sja·'ti·βo, -a; e·nun·
θja-] *adj* **oración enunciativa** declarative
sentence
envanecer [em·ba·ne·'ser, -'θer] *irr como*
crecer I. *vt* to make vain II. *vr:* ~ **se 1.** (*enorgullecerse*) to become proud **2.** (*engreírse*) to
become vain
envasar [em·ba·'sar] *vt* to package; (*en latas*)
to can; (*en botellas*) to bottle
envase [em·'ba·se] *m* **1.** (*paquete*) package; (*recipiente*) container; (*botella*) bottle
2. (*casco*) bottle; ~ **sin retorno** non-returnable bottle **3.** (*acción*) packing; ~ **al vacío** vacuum packing
envejecer [em·be·xe·'ser, -'θer] *irr como*
crecer *vt, vr:* ~ **se** to age

envenenar [em·be·ne·'nar] *vt* to poison

envergadura [em·ber·ɣa·'du·ra] *f* (*importancia*) magnitude; (*alcance*) scope; **de gran ~** far-reaching

envés [em·'bes] *m* back

enviado, -a [em·bi·'a·do, -a] *m, f* envoy; **~ especial** PREN, TV, RADIO special correspondent

enviar <*1. pres:* envío> [em·bi·'ar] *vt* to send; **~ por correo** to mail

envidia [em·'bi·dja] *f* envy; **tener ~ a alguien** to envy sb; **tener ~ de algo** to be jealous of sth; **daba ~ verlo de lo guapo que iba** it made me envious to see how handsome he looked; **lo corroe la ~** he is eaten up by jealousy

envidiable [em·bi·'dja·βle] *adj* enviable

envidiar [em·bi·'djar] *vt* to envy; **¡mucho tienes tú que ~le a ella!** *irón* you have no reason to be jealous of her!

envidioso, -a [em·bi·'djo·so, -a] *adj* envious

envío [em·'bi·o] *m* sending; (*expedición*) issue; **~ a domicilio** home delivery; **~ contra reembolso** cash on delivery; **~ urgente** urgent delivery; **~ con valor declarado** declared value delivery; **gastos de ~** shipping and handling

enviudar [em·bju·'dar] *vi* to be widowed; (*una mujer*) to become a widow; (*un hombre*) to become a widower

envoltorio [em·bol·'to·rjo] *m* 1. (*embalaje*) wrapping 2. (*caramelo*) wrapper

envoltura [em·bol·'tu·ra] *f* (*capa exterior*) covering; (*embalaje*) wrapping

envolver [em·bol·'βer] *irr como* volver I. *vt* 1. (*en papel*) to wrap; **~ con** [*o* en] **algo** to wrap up in sth 2. (*empaquetar, ropa*) to pack; **~ con** [*o* en] **algo** to pack in sth; (*para regalo*) to gift-wrap 3. (*implicar*) to involve 4. (*rodear*) to envelop II. *vr* **~se** to get involved

envuelto, -a [em·'bwel·to] *pp de* envolver

enyesar [en·je·'sar] *vt* to plaster

enzarzar [en·sar·'sar, -θar·'θar] *vr:* **~se en** to get involved [*o* entangled] in

enzima [en·'si·ma, -'θi·ma] *m o f* enzyme

eñe ['e·ɲe] *f* Ñ, ñ; **la letra ~** *15th letter of the Spanish alphabet*

eólico, -a [e·'o·li·ko, -a] *adj* wind; **central eólica** wind power plant

epa ['e·pa] *interj AmL* (*saludo*) hi!; (*llamar la atención*) hey!; (*accidente*) (wh)oops!

épica ['e·pi·ka] *f* epic

epicentro [e·pi·'sen·tro, -'θen·tro] *m* epicenter

épico, -a ['e·pi·ko, -a] *adj* epic; **poema ~** epic poem

epidemia [e·pi·'de·mja] *f* epidemic

epidermis [e·pi·'der·mis] *f inv* epidermis

epígrafe [e·'pi·ɣra·fe] *m* 1. (*título*) title 2. (*inscripción*) epigraph

epilepsia [e·pi·'leβ·sja] *f* epilepsy

epiléptico, -a [e·pi·'lep·ti·ko, -a] *adj, m, f* epileptic

epílogo [e·'pi·lo·ɣo] *m* (*de libro*) epilogue, epilog

episcopal [e·pis·ko·'pal] *adj* episcopal; **sede ~** bishop's palace

episodio [e·pi·'so·djo] *m* 1. *t.* MÚS, LIT, TV episode 2. (*etapa*) stage 3. (*suceso*) incident

epitafio [e·pi·'ta·fjo] *m* epitaph

época ['e·po·ka] *f* 1. HIST epoch, age; **coches de ~** classic cars *pl;* **muebles de ~** antique furniture; **trajes de ~** period costumes *pl;* **un invento que hizo ~** a revolutionary invention 2. (*tiempo*) time; **~ de las lluvias** rainy season; **es la ~ más calurosa del año** it is the hottest time of the year; **en aquella ~** at that time

epopeya [e·po·'pe·ja] *f* LIT epic

equidad [e·ki·'dad] *f* 1. (*justicia*) fairness 2. (*de precios*) equity

equilátero, -a [e·ki·'la·te·ro, -a] *adj* MAT equilateral

equilibrado, -a [e·ki·li·'βra·do, -a] *adj* balanced; (*sensato*) sensible

equilibrar [e·ki·li·'βrar] *vt, vr:* **~se** to balance

equilibrio [e·ki·'li·βrjo] *m* 1. (*en general*) balance; **mantener el ~** to keep one's balance; **perder el ~** to lose one's balance; **llego a fin de mes con muchos ~s** *fig* I can barely make do on my monthly budget 2. (*contrapeso*) counterweight 3. (*armonía, mesura*) balance

equilibrista [e·ki·li·'βris·ta] *mf* tightrope artist

equino, -a [e·'ki·no] *adj* equine

equipaje [e·ki·'pa·xe] *m* (*maletas*) baggage, luggage; **entrega de ~s** baggage check-in; **exceso de ~** excess baggage; **registro de ~** baggage inspection; **hacer el ~** to pack; **~ de mano** hand baggage [*o* luggage]

equipal [e·ki·'pal] *m Méx* 1. (*silla de mimbre*) rustic wicker chair 2. (*silla de cuero*) leather chair

equipamiento [e·ki·pa·'mjen·to] *m* **~ de serie** AUTO standard equipment

equipar [e·ki·'par] *vt* to equip; (*de ropa*) to fit out

equiparable [e·ki·pa·'ra·βle] *adj* comparable

equiparar [e·ki·pa·'rar] *vt* 1. (*igualar*) to put on the same level 2. (*comparar*) to compare, to liken

equipo [e·'ki·po] *m* 1. (*grupo*) team; (*turno*) shift; **~ gestor** management team; **~ de investigadores** research team; **~ de trabajo** teamwork 2. DEP team; **carrera por ~s** team race; **el ~ de casa/de fuera** the home/visiting team 3. (*utensilios*) equipment; **~ de alta fidelidad** hi-fi system; **~ productivo** productive equipment; **bienes de ~** capital goods *pl*

equis ['e·kis] I. *adj inv* X; **~ dólares** X number of dollars; **el señor ~** Mr. so-and-so II. *f inv* 1. (*letra*) X, x; **la letra ~** the letter x 2. *Col* (*serpiente*) snake

equitación [e·ki·ta·'sjon, -'θjon] *f* horseback riding; **escuela de ~** (horseback) riding school

equitativamente [e·ki·ta·ti·βa·'men·te] *adv* equitably

equitativo, -a [e·ki·ta·'ti·βo, -a] *adj* equitable; **hicieron un reparto ~ de las ganancias** they split the profits equally

equivalencia [e·ki·βa·'len·sja, -θja] *f* equivalence

equivalente [e·ki·βa·'len·te] **I.** *adj* equivalent; **una cantidad ~ a diez dólares** an amount equivalent to ten dollars **II.** *m* equivalent; **el ~ a diez días de trabajo** the equivalent of ten days' work

equivaler [e·ki·βa·'ler] *irr como valer vi* to be equivalent; **la negativa equivaldría a la ruptura de las negociaciones** saying no would mean the breakdown of negotiations; **lo que equivale a decir que...** which is the same as saying that...

equivocación [e·ki·βo·ka·'sjon, -'θjon] *f* mistake; (*error*) error; (*malentendido*) misunderstanding; (*confusión*) mix-up; **por ~** by mistake

equivocado, -a [e·ki·βo·'ka·do, -a] *adj* mistaken; **número ~** wrong number

equivocar <c→qu> [e·ki·βo·'kar] **I.** *vt* **1.** (*confundir*) to get wrong; **equivoqué los sobres de las cartas** I mixed up the envelopes for the letters **2.** (*desconcertar*) to throw **II.** *vr:* **~se** to be wrong; **~se en** [*o de*] **algo** to be wrong about sth; **~se de camino** to take the wrong way; **~se al escribir/al hablar** to make a mistake (when) writing/when speaking; **~se al leer** to misread; **~se de número** (**de teléfono**) to dial the wrong number; **~se de tranvía** to take the wrong tram; **~se de puerta** to take the wrong door

equívoco [e·'ki·βo·ko] *m* (*doble sentido*) ambiguity; (*malentendido*) misunderstanding

equívoco, -a [e·'ki·βo·ko, -a] *adj* **1.** (*con dos sentidos*) ambiguous **2.** (*dudoso*) doubtful

era[1] ['e·ra] *f* **1.** (*período*) era; **~ postcomunista** the post-communist era **2.** (*para trigo*) threshing floor

era[2] ['e·ra] *3. imp de* **ser**

erario [e·'ra·rjo] *m* revenue; **el ~ público** the public treasury

ere ['e·re] *f* R, r; **la letra ~** the letter r

erección [e·rek·'sjon, -rey·'θjon] *f* **1.** (*del pene*) erection **2.** (*de monumentos*) building

erecto, -a [e·'rek·to, -a] *adj* (*tieso*) erect; (*cuerpo*) upright

eremita [e·re·'mi·ta] *mf* hermit

eres ['e·res] *2. pres de* **ser**

erguido, -a [er·'yi·do, -a] *adj* (*derecho*) upright

erguir [er·'yir] *irr* **I.** *vt* to raise; **~ el cuello** to straighten one's neck; **con la cabeza erguida** with one's head held high **II.** *vr:* **~se** (*ponerse de pie*) to stand up straight; (*en una silla*) to sit up (straight); **el perro se irguió sobre las patas traseras** the dog rose up on its hind legs

erigir <g→j> [e·ri·'xir] **I.** *vt* **1.** (*construir*) to build; **~ un andamio** to put up scaffolding **2.** (*fundar*) to establish **3.** (*nombrar*) to appoint; **la erigieron presidenta** she was

named president **II.** *vr:* **~se 1.** (*declararse*) **~se en algo** to declare oneself to be sth **2.** (*hacer de*) **~se en algo** to act as sth

erizado, -a [e·ri·'sa·do, -a; e·ri·'θa-] *adj* **1.** BOT prickly **2.** (*pelo*) on end

erizar <z→c> [e·ri·'sar, -'θar] **I.** *vt* **1.** (*el pelo*) to make stand on end; **el frío me erizó el vello** the cold gave me goose pimples; **el miedo me erizó los cabellos** I was so frightened my hair stood on end **2.** (*un asunto*) to complicate; **estar erizado de dificultades** to be full of problems; **la vida está erizada de espinas** life is full of difficulties; **el camino está erizado de obstáculos** the way is littered with obstacles **II.** *vr:* **~se** (*pelo*) to stand on end; **mis cabellos se ~on del susto** I was so shocked my hair stood on end; **se me erizó el vello de tanto frío** it was so cold I had goose pimples

erizo [e·'ri·so, -θo] *m* **1.** (*mamífero*) hedgehog **2.** (*pez*) globefish **3.** (*de mar*) sea urchin

ermita [er·'mi·ta] *f* hermitage

ermitaño [er·mi·'ta·ɲo] *m* hermit crab

ermitaño, -a [er·mi·'ta·ɲo, -a] *m, f* hermit

erogación [e·ro·ya·'sjon, -'θjon] *f* **1.** *Arg, Méx, Par* (*pago*) costs *pl* **2.** *Ven, Col* (*donativo*) contribution

erogar <g→gu> [e·ro·'yar] *vt Arg, Col* (*pagar*) to pay; (*bienes*) to distribute

erógeno, -a [e·'ro·xe·no, -a] *adj* erogenous

erosión [e·ro·'sjon] *f* **1.** (*desgaste*) wear and tear; (*desaparición*) disappearance; **~ monetaria** gradual devaluation **2.** GEO erosion **3.** (*de la piel*) graze **4.** (*de alguien*) decline; **sufrir ~** to go into decline; (*perder influencia*) to lose influence; (*perder prestigio*) to lose prestige

erosionar [e·ro·sjo·'nar] **I.** *vt* **1.** (*desgastar*) to wear away **2.** GEO to erode **3.** (*la piel*) to abrade **4.** (*a alguien*) to harm; **el artículo erosionó al partido** the article damaged the party **II.** *vr:* **~se** to decline; (*perder prestigio*) to lose prestige; (*perder influencia*) to lose influence

erótico, -a [e·'ro·ti·ko, -a] *adj* erotic

erotismo [e·ro·'tis·mo] *m* eroticism

erradicar <c→qu> [e·rra·di·'kar] *vt* to eradicate; (*una planta*) to uproot; (*una institución*) to abolish; (*una enfermedad*) to stamp out

errar [e·'rrar] *irr* **I.** *vi* **1.** (*equivocarse*) to err; **~ en algo** to make a mistake in sth; **~ en la respuesta** to give the wrong answer; **~ en el camino** to take the wrong road; *fig* to make the wrong choice **2.** (*andar vagando*) to wander; (*vagabundear*) to live on the streets; **~ por algo** to roam around sth; **ir errando por las calles** to wander the streets **II.** *vt* (*no acertar*) to miss; **~ la vocación** to choose the wrong career **III.** *vr* **~se en algo** to make a mistake in sth

errata [e·'rra·ta] *f* errata

erre ['e·rre] *f* RR, rr; **la letra ~** the letter "rr"; **~ que ~** *inf* stubbornly; **él está, ~ que ~, empeñado en subir** he absolutely insists on climbing up

E

erróneo, -a [e·'rro·neo, -a] *adj* erroneous; **decisión errónea** wrong decision

error [e·'rror] *m* 1.(*falta*) fault; ~ **de cálculo** miscalculation; ~ **de operación** COMPUT operative error; ~ **ortográfico** spelling mistake; ~ **freudiano** Freudian slip; **cometer un** ~ to make a mistake; **has cometido un** ~ **muy grave** you have made a very serious mistake 2.(*equivocación*) mistake; (*descuido*) oversight; **estar en el** ~ to be wrong; **por** ~ by mistake 3.FÍS, MAT (*diferencia*) error 4.(*conducta reprochable*) misconduct 5.JUR ~ **judicial** miscarriage of justice 6.TIPO ~ **de imprenta** misprint

eructar [e·ruk·'tar] *vi* to belch, to burp

eructo [e·'ruk·to] *m* belch, burp

erudición [e·ru·di·'sjon, -'θjon] *f* erudition; (*sabiduría*) wisdom

erudito, -a [e·ru·'di·to, -a] **I.** *adj* 1.(*persona*) erudite; ~ **a la violeta** *pey* pseudo-intellectual; (*sabio*) wise 2.(*obra*) scholarly; **conocimientos** ~**s** extensive knowledge **II.** *m, f* scholar; (*sabio*) man of learning *m*, woman of learning *f*; (*experto*) expert; **es un** ~ **en filosofía** he is a philosophy scholar

erupción [e·rup·'sjon, -ruβ·'θjon] *f* 1.GEO eruption; ~ **volcánica** volcanic eruption 2.MED rash

es [es] 3. *pres de* **ser**

esa(s) ['e·sa(s)] *adj, pron dem v.* **ese, -a**

ésa(s) ['e·sa(s)] *pron dem v.* **ése**

esbeltez [es·βel·'tes, -'teθ] *f* 1.(*delgadez*) slenderness 2.(*altura*) height 3.(*elegancia*) elegance

esbelto, -a [es·'βel·to, -a] *adj* 1.(*delgado*) slender 2.(*alto*) tall 3.(*grácil*) graceful 4.(*elegante*) elegant; **un hombre** ~ a well-proportioned man

esbozar <z→c> [es·βo·'sar, -'θar] *vt* 1.(*dibujo*) to sketch 2.(*un tema*) to outline; ~ **un discurso** to summarize a speech 3.(*una sonrisa*) **esbozó una sonrisa** a smile formed upon his/her lips

esbozo [es·'βo·so, -θo] *m* 1.(*dibujo*) sketch 2.(*de un proyecto*) outline

escabechar [es·ka·βe·'tʃar] *vt* CULIN to marinate

escabeche [es·ka·'βe·tʃe] *m* 1.(*adobo*) marinade; **atún en** ~ pickled tuna; **poner en** ~ to marinade 2.(*alimento: pescado*) pickled fish; ~ **de pollo** marinated chicken

escabroso, -a [es·ka·'βro·so, -a] *adj* 1.(*áspero*) rough; (*terreno*) uneven 2.(*asunto*) thorny

escabullirse <3. *pret:* se escabulló> [es·ka·βu·'ʝir·se, -'ʎir·se] *vr* 1.(*desaparecer*) to slip away; ~ (**por**) **entre la multitud** to slip away [*o* sneak off] through the crowd 2.(*escurrirse*) to slip through

escacharrar [es·ka·tʃa·'rrar] *inf* **I.** *vt* 1.(*objeto*) to break 2.(*plan, proyecto*) to spoil; **la lluvia nos escacharró la fiesta** the rain spoiled the party; **escacharró nuestros planes** it wrecked our plans **II.** *vr:* ~**se**

1.(*objeto*) to break 2.(*plan, proyecto*) to be spoiled; **nuestros planes se** ~**on por culpa de la lluvia** our plans were spoiled by the rain

escafandra [es·ka·'fan·dra] *f* diving [*o* wet] suit; ~ **autónoma** scuba diving outfit; ~ **espacial** space suit

escala [es·'ka·la] *f* 1. *t.* MÚS (*serie, proporción, de mapa*) scale; ~ **de colores** range of colors, color scale; ~ **de cuotas** payment scale; ~ **de descuentos** range of discounts; ~ **de grados** degree scale; ~ **impositiva** tax bracketing; ~ **de reproducción** scale of reproduction; ~ **de Richter** Richter scale; ~ **de salarios** salary scale; ~ **de valores** set of values; **a** ~ to scale; **hacer** ~**s** to do scales; **un mapa a** ~ **1:100.000** a map with a scale of 1:100,000; ~ **milimétrica** millimeter scale 2.(*medida*) level; **a** ~ **mundial** on a world scale; ~ **nacional** on a national scale; **en gran** ~ on a large scale; **comprar en gran** ~ to buy in bulk; **fabricación en gran** ~ large-scale production; **ser de mayor** ~ to be on a large scale 3.(*parada, puerto*) stop; AVIAT stopover; ~ **forzada** forced landing; **el avión tuvo que hacer** ~ **en París** the plane had to land in Paris; **hacer** ~ **en un puerto** to make a stop at a port 4.(*escalera*) ladder; ~ **de cuerda** rope ladder

escalada [es·ka·'la·da] *f* 1.(*subida*) climb, ascent; ~ **libre** free climbing; ~ **en roca** rock climbing 2.(*a una posición, cargo*) promotion 3.(*aumento*) increase; (*de un conflicto, la violencia*) escalation

escalafón [es·ka·la·'fon] *m* (*de cargos*) ranking; (*de sueldos*) salary scale; **subir en el** ~ to move up in the ranking

escalar [es·ka·'lar] **I.** *vi* 1.(*en las montañas, socialmente*) to climb 2.(*profesionalmente*) to rise **II.** *vt* 1.(*subir*) to go up; (*una montaña*) to climb; **has escalado las cimas del poder** you have reached the height of power 2.(*ladrón*) to break into; ~ **on la habitación por la ventana** they got into the room through the window 3.(*una posición*) to rise to

escaldado, -a [es·kal·'da·do, -a] *adj* 1.(*quemado*) scalded 2.(*escarmentado*) cautious; **salir** ~ to learn one's lesson

escaldadura [es·kal·da·'du·ra] *f Arg* (*lastimadura*) chafing

escaldar [es·kal·'dar] **I.** *vt* (*metal*) to make red hot **II.** *vr:* ~**se** (*persona*) to be scalded

escalera [es·ka·'le·ra] *f* 1.(*escalones*) staircase, stairs; AVIAT stairway; ~ **abajo** downstairs; ~ **arriba** upstairs; ~ **de caracol** spiral staircase; ~ **mecánica** [*o* **automática**] escalator; ~ **de servicio** service stairs 2.(*escala*) ladder; ~ **de bomberos** firemen's ladder; ~ **de cuerda** rope ladder; ~ **doble** stepladder; ~ **de incendios** fire escape; ~ **de mano** ladder; ~ **de tijera** stepladder; **subir la** ~ to go up the ladder 3.(*naipes*) run; ~ **de color real** royal flush

escalinata [es·ka·li·'na·ta] *f* main staircase;

(*fuera*) outside steps *pl*

escalofriante [es·ka·lo·ˈfrjan·te] *adj* (*pavoroso*) chilling; **película** ~ scary movie

escalofrío [es·ka·lo·ˈfri·o] *m* **1.** (*sensación*) chill; **al abrir la ventana sentí** ~**s** I felt a chill when I opened the window; **el libro me produjo** ~**s** the book sent shivers down my spine; **cierra la puerta, tengo** ~**s** close the door, I feel chilly **2.** MED shiver

escalón [es·ka·ˈlon] *m* **1.** (*de una escala*) rung; ~ **lateral** side step **2.** (*nivel*) step; **subir un** ~ (*profesionalmente*) to move up the ladder; **este libro es un** ~ **hacia el éxito** this book is a stepping stone on the way to success; **descender un** ~ **en la opinión pública** to go down in the eyes of the public

escalonado, -a [es·ka·lo·ˈna·do, -a] *adj* **1.** (*terreno*) terraced **2.** (*precio*) graded; **tarifa escalonada** graded fare **3.** (*horario, vacaciones*) staggered

escalonar [es·ka·lo·ˈnar] *vt* **1.** (*terreno*) to terrace **2.** (*precio*) to grade

escalope [es·ka·ˈlo·pe] *m* escalope; ~ **a la vienesa** Wiener schnitzel

escalpelo [es·kal·ˈpe·lo] *m* scalpel

escama [es·ˈka·ma] *f* (*placa*) *t.* ZOOL, BOT scale; ~**s de jabón** soap flakes

escamado, -a [es·ka·ˈma·do, -a] *adj* **1.** (*piel, superficie*) scaly **2.** *inf* (*receloso*) cautious

escamar [es·ka·ˈmar] **I.** *vt* **1.** (*el pescado*) to scale **2.** *inf* (*inquietar*) to make suspicious **II.** *vr:* ~**se** *inf* to smell a rat; **me escamé al oír la noticia** I was worried when I heard the news; **me escamé de tu respuesta** I was suspicious of your response

escamocha [es·ka·ˈmo·tʃa] *f Méx* (*sobras*) leftovers *pl*

escampar [es·kam·ˈpar] *v impers* **espera hasta que escampe** wait until it clears

escandalizar <z→c> [es·kan·da·li·ˈsar, -ˈθar] **I.** *vi* to cause an upset **II.** *vt* **1.** (*indignar*) to shock **2.** (*horrorizar*) to horrify **3.** (*impactar*) to shock **4.** (*alborotar*) **ayer por la noche escandalizaste la casa con tus gritos** last night you woke up the whole house with your shouting **III.** *vr:* ~**se 1.** (*indignarse*) ~**se de** [*o por*] **algo** to be shocked by sth **2.** (*estar horrorizado*) ~**se de** [*o por*] **algo** to be horrified at sth

escándalo [es·ˈkan·da·lo] *m* **1.** (*ruido*) uproar; **armar un** [*o* **dar el**] ~ to make a scene; **se armó un** ~ there was a terrible uproar **2.** (*hecho inmoral*) scandal; ~ **público** public scandal; **causar** ~ to cause a scandal; **la piedra del** ~ the root of the scandal; **estos precios son un** ~ these prices are outrageous; **tu comportamiento es un** ~ your behavior is a disgrace; **de** ~ scandalous **3.** (*pasmo*) **¡qué** ~! can you believe it?

escandaloso, -a [es·kan·da·ˈlo·so, -a] *adj* **1.** (*ruidoso*) noisy; (*alborotado*) uproarious **2.** (*inmoral, irritante*) scandalous; **precios** ~**s** outrageous prices **3.** (*revoltoso*) unruly; **esta**

clase es escandalosa this class is rowdy [*o* out of control]

Escandinavia [es·kan·di·ˈna·βja] *f* Scandinavia

escandinavo, -a [es·kan·di·ˈna·βo, -a] *adj, m, f* Scandinavian

escanear [es·ka·ne·ˈar] *vt* to scan

escáner [es·ˈka·ner] *m* scanner

escaño [es·ˈka·ɲo] *m* **1.** (*banco*) bench **2.** POL (*acta de diputado*) seat

escapada [es·ka·ˈpa·da] *f* (*huida*) escape; (*viaje*) short trip

escapar [es·ka·ˈpar] **I.** *vi* **1.** (*de la cárcel, de un peligro*) to escape; (*de un encierro*) to evade; **logré** ~ I managed to escape; **es imposible** ~ **a esta ley** it is impossible to dodge this law **2.** (*deprisa, ocultamente*) to get away; ~ **de casa** to run away from home **II.** *vr:* ~**se 1.** (*de la cárcel, de un peligro*) to escape; (*de un encierro*) to evade **2.** (*deprisa, ocultamente*) to get away; ~**se de casa** to run away from home; **algunas cosas se escapan al poder de la voluntad** some things are beyond one's power **3.** (*agua, gas*) to leak **4.** (*decir*) to come out; **se me ha escapado que te vas a casar** I let it slip that you were getting married **5.** (*soltarse*) to get away; **se escapó un tiro** a shot was let loose; **se me ha escapado su nombre** I've forgotten your name; **se me ha escapado el autobús** I missed the bus; **se me ha escapado la mano** my hand slipped; **se me ha escapado la risa** I couldn't help laughing; **se me escapó un suspiro** I let out a sigh **6.** (*pasar inadvertido*) to go unnoticed; **no se te escapa ni una** you don't miss a thing

escaparate [es·ka·pa·ˈra·te] *m* **1.** (*de una tienda*) shop window; **estar en el** ~ *fig* to be in the limelight **2.** (*estantería*) bookcase **3.** *AmL* (*armario*) dresser **4.** *inf* (*pecho*) cleavage

escapatoria [es·ka·pa·ˈto·rja] *f* **1.** (*lugar*) escape; **no hay** ~ *fig* there's no way out **2.** (*excusa*) excuse **3.** (*solución*) way out; **no tener** ~ to have no way out; (*cláusula*) loophole

escape [es·ˈka·pe] *m* **1.** (*de un gas, líquido*) leak **2.** (*solución*) way out; **no tenía** ~ (*de una amenaza*) there was no way out **3.** (*rápidamente*) **a** ~ like a shot; **dame a** ~ **las tijeras** quickly, pass me the scissors

escarabajo [es·ka·ra·ˈβa·xo] *m* beetle

escaramujo [es·ka·ra·ˈmu·xo] *m* **1.** BOT dog rose **2.** ZOOL goose barnacle

escaramuza [es·ka·ra·ˈmu·sa, -θa] *f* (*lucha*) skirmish

escarapelar [es·ka·ra·pe·ˈlar] **I.** *vt* **1.** *Col, CRi, Méx* (*descascarar*) to peel **2.** *Col* (*manosear*) to handle; (*ajar*) to wear out **II.** *vr:* ~**se** *Méx, Perú* (*atemorizarse*) to be scared **2.** (*temblar*) to shudder

escarbar [es·kar·ˈβar] **I.** *vi* **1.** (*en la tierra*) ~ **en algo** to dig sth **2.** (*escudriñar*) ~ **en algo** to investigate sth; (*entremeterse*) to pry into sth

II. *vt* **1.** (*la tierra*) to dig up; ~ **la arena** to dig up sand **2.** (*la lumbre*) to poke **3.** (*tocar*) ~ **algo** to pick at sth **4.** (*limpiar*) to clean; ~ **los dientes** to pick one's teeth **5.** (*investigar*) to investigate; (*entremeterse*) to pry into **III.** *vr:* ~ **se** to pick; ~ **se las orejas** to scratch [*o* pick] one's ears

escarceo [es·kar·'seo, -'θeo] *m* **1.** *pl* (*divagaciones*) distractions *pl;* ~ **s políticos** political comings and goings; **sin ~ s** without hesitation; ~ **amoroso** fling **2.** *pl* (*vueltas*) prancing; **el caballo dio ~ s** the horse pranced around

escarcha [es·'kar·ʧa] *f* frost

escarchar [es·kar·'ʧar] *vt* (*frutas*) to crystallize

escarlata [es·kar·'la·ta] *adj* scarlet

escarlatina [es·kar·la·'ti·na] *f* MED scarlet fever

escarmentar <e→ie> [es·kar·men·'tar] **I.** *vi* **1.** (*desengañarse*) to realize the truth; ~ **en cabeza ajena** to learn from sb else's mistakes **2.** (*enmendarse*) to learn one's lesson **II.** *vt* **1.** (*castigar*) to punish **2.** (*reprender*) to reprimand **3.** (*desengañar*) to teach a lesson; **quedar** [*o* estar] **escarmentado de algo** to learn one's lesson from sth

escarmiento [es·kar·'mjen·to] *m* (*lección*) lesson; **me sirvió de ~** it taught me a lesson

escarnecer [es·kar·ne·'ser, -'θer] *irr como* **crecer** *vt* (*burlarse*) to mock; (*ridiculizar*) to deride

escarnio [es·'kar·njo] *m* scorn; **con ~** scornfully

escarola [es·ka·'ro·la] *f* curly endive

escarpado, -a [es·kar·'pa·do, -a] *adj* (*terreno*) rugged; (*montaña*) steep and craggy

escasamente [es·ka·sa·'men·te] *adv* scarcely; **hace ~ dos horas que se han ido** they left barely two hours ago

escasear [es·ka·se·'ar] **I.** *vi* (*faltar*) to be scarce; **escasea la leche** milk is scarce **II.** *vt* (*dar con escasez*) to skimp on

escasez [es·ka·'ses, -'seθ] *f* **1.** (*insuficiencia*) shortage; **comprar con ~** to spend sparingly **2.** (*falta*) shortage; ~ **de lluvias** lack of rain; ~ **de viviendas** housing shortage; **una región con ~ de agua** a region with scarce rainfall **3.** (*pobreza*) neediness; **vivir con ~** to live in need

escaso, -a [es·'ka·so, -a] *adj* (*insuficiente*) insufficient, scant(y); (*tiempo*) little; ~ **de palabras** of few words; **viento ~** light wind; **andar ~ de dinero** to be short of money; **estar ~ de tiempo** to be short of time; **tener escasas posibilidades de ganar** to have little chance of winning; **en dos horas escasas** in only two hours

escatimar [es·ka·ti·'mar] *vt* to skimp on; ~ **el aplauso a alguien/algo** to be sparing in the applause for sb/sth; **me escatimó parte del dinero** he/she kept part of my money

escayola [es·ka·'jo·la] *f* **1.** (*yeso*) plaster **2.** MED cast

escayolar [es·ka·jo·'lar] *vt* MED to put a cast on; **llevar el brazo escayolado** to have an arm in a cast

escena [e·'se·na, es·'θe-] *f* **1.** (*parte del teatro*) stage; **aparecer en ~** to appear on stage; **poner en ~** to stage; **puesta en ~** staging; **salir a la ~** to go on stage; **salir de la ~** to go off stage **2.** (*lugar, parte de una obra*) scene; ~ **final** final scene; **cambio de ~** change of scene; ~ **del crimen** scene of the crime; **desaparecer de ~** (*marcharse*) to leave the scene; (*morirse*) to pass away; **poner en ~** to put on stage; **salir a ~** (*aparecer*) to make an appearance **3.** (*arte*) theater; **dedicarse a la ~** to devote oneself to the stage **4.** LIT scene **5.** (*suceso, reproche*) scene; ~ **de celos** display of jealousy; **hacer una ~ ridícula** to make a ridiculous scene

escenario [e·se·'na·rjo, es·'θe-] *m* **1.** (*parte del teatro*) stage **2.** (*lugar, situación*) scene; ~ **del crimen** scene of the crime; **un cambio de ~** a change of scene

escénico, -a [e·'se·ni·ko, -a; es·'θe-] *adj* scenic; **efectos ~ s** stage effects *pl;* **escuela de arte ~** drama school; **palco ~** stage

escenografía [e·se·no·ɣra·'fi·a, es·θe-] *f* **1.** (*decoración*) set design **2.** (*decorados*) set

escepticismo [e·sep·ti·'sis·mo, es·θep·ti·'θis-] *m* (*desconfianza*) skepticism

escéptico, -a [e·'sep·ti·ko, -a; es·'θep-] **I.** *adj* (*desconfiado*) skeptical; **ser ~ respecto a algo** to be skeptical about sth **II.** *m, f* skeptic; **es un ~ de la homeopatía** he doesn't take homeopathy seriously

escindir [e·sin·'dir, es·θin-] **I.** *vt* **1.** (*dividir*) to divide; (*partido*) *t.* FÍS to split **2.** (*separar*) to separate **3.** (*cortar*) to split **II.** *vr:* ~ **se 1.** (*dividirse*) ~ **se en algo** to divide into sth; (*partido*) to split into sth **2.** (*separarse*) to separate

escisión [e·si·'sjon, es·θi-] *f* **1.** (*división*) division; (*de un partido*) split; *t.* FÍS splitting **2.** (*separación*) separation; MED excision

esclarecer [es·kla·re·'ser, -'θer] *irr como* **crecer** *vt* **1.** (*explicar*) to clear up; (*un crimen, misterio*) to shed light upon; ~ **un asunto** to clear up a matter **2.** (*iluminar*) to illuminate

esclarecimiento [es·kla·re·si·'mjen·to, -θi·'mjen·to] *m* **1.** (*explicación*) explanation **2.** (*iluminación*) illumination

esclavitud [es·kla·βi·'tud] *f* **1.** (*sistema*) slavery, servitude; **someter a la ~** to submit to slavery **2.** (*dependencia*) dependence

esclavizar <z→c> [es·kla·βi·'sar, -'θar] **I.** *vt* **1.** (*cautivar*) to enslave **2.** (*dominar*) to control; ~ **a alguien** (*hacer depender*) to make sb dependent; **la empresa te ha esclavizado** you're a slave to the company **II.** *vr:* ~ **se** to become a slave

esclavo, -a [es·'kla·βo, -a] **I.** *adj* **1.** (*cautivo*) slave **2.** (*dominado*) dependent; (*obediente*) obedient; **eres esclava de tu familia** you do everything your family wants; **ser ~ del alcohol** to be a slave to alcohol **II.** *m, f* slave; (*estar enamorado*) to be at sb's command; **ser un ~ de algo** *fig* to be dependent on sth

esclerosis [es·kle·'ro·sis] *f inv* sclerosis; **~ múltiple** multiple sclerosis

esclusa [es·'klu·sa] *f* **1.** (*recinto*) lock; TÉC sluice **2.** (*puerta*) lock gate

escoba [es·'ko·βa] *f* **1.** (*para barrer*) broom; (*de bruja*) broomstick **2.** *pey* (*mujer*) frump

escobazo [es·ko·'βa·so, -θo] *m* **1.** (*golpe*) **dar un ~ a alguien** to hit sb with a broom **2.** *Arg, Chile* (*barredura*) **dar un ~ al suelo** to give the floor a quick sweep

escobilla [es·ko·'βi·ja, -ʎa] *f* **1.** (*cepillo*) *t.* ELEC brush; (*de baño*) toilet brush **2.** (*escoba*) broom **3.** (*del limpiaparabrisas*) windshield wiper blade **4.** (*plumero*) feather duster

escobillar [es·ko·βi·'jar, -'ʎar] I. *vi AmL* (*zapatear*) to tap or shuffle the feet II. *vt* to brush

escocedura [es·ko·se·'du·ra, es·ko·θe·] *f* **1.** (*picor*) smarting, stinging **2.** (*irritación*) inflammation; (*ampolla*) blister

escocer [es·ko·'ser, -'θer] *irr como cocer* I. *vi* **1.** (*picar*) to sting **2.** (*ofender*) to be offended; (*irritar*) to be annoyed; **no me escuece que no me hayan invitado** I'm not annoyed at not being invited II. *vr:* **~se 1.** (*inflamarse*) to redden **2.** (*dolerse*) to be sore; (*enfadarse*) to get angry

escocés [es·ko·'ses, -'θes] *m* **1.** (*lengua*) (Scottish) Gaelic **2.** (*bebida*) Scotch

escocés, -esa [es·ko·'ses, --'se·sa; -'θes, --'θe·sa] I. *adj* Scottish II. *m, f* Scot, Scotsman *m*, Scotswoman *f*

Escocia [es·'ko·sja, -θja] *f* Scotland

escoger <g→j> [es·ko·'xer] I. *vi* to choose; **no has sabido ~** you've made the wrong choice II. *vt* **1.** (*elegir, seleccionar*) to choose **2.** (*decidirse*) to decide

escogido, -a [es·ko·'xi·do, -a] *adj* **1.** *ser* (*selecto*) finest; (*persona*) upper class; **mercancías escogidas** top quality goods **2.** *estar* (*elegido*) taken; **estos plátanos están ya muy ~s** all the good bananas have gone

escolar [es·ko·'lar] I. *adj* academic; **curso ~** academic year; **edad ~** school age II. *mf* schoolboy *m*, schoolgirl *f*

escolaridad [es·ko·la·ri·'dad] *f* (*en una escuela*) schooling, education; **libro de ~** reports *pl*; **la ~ es obligatoria** education is compulsory; **perder la ~** not to be eligible to take an exam

escolarización [es·ko·la·ri·sa·'sjon, -θa·'θjon] *f* education; **~ obligatoria** compulsory education; **esta región tiene una tasa de ~ muy baja** this area has a very low enrollment

escolarizar <z→c> [es·ko·la·ri·'sar, -'θar] *vt* to educate; **~ una región** to educate a region

escolero, -a [es·ko·'le·ro, -a] *m, f Perú* (*escolar*) schoolboy *m*, schoolgirl *f*

escollar [es·ko·'jar, -'ʎar] *vi Arg, Chile* (*proyecto*) to fail

escollo [es·'ko·jo, -ʎo] *m* (*riesgo*) pitfall; **sortear un ~** to overcome an obstacle

escolta [es·'kol·ta] *f* **1.** MIL (*acompañante*) escort; **dar ~ a alguien** to escort sb **2.** (*acompa-*

ñamiento) escort **3.** (*guardaespaldas*) bodyguard; (*guardia*) guard

escoltar [es·kol·'tar] *vt* to escort

escombro(s) [es·'kom·bro(s)] *m(pl)* rubble; **hacer ~** *Arg* to exaggerate

esconder [es·kon·'der] I. *vt* (*ocultar*) to hide; (*tapar*) cover up; **el fondo del mar esconde muchas riquezas** the ocean bed has many secret treasures II. *vr:* **~se** (*persona, cosas*) to hide

escondidas [es·kon·'di·das] *adv* **a ~** secretly; **a ~ del profesor** behind the teacher's back

escondido(s) [es·kon·'di·do(s)] *m(pl) AmL* hide and seek

escondite [es·kon·'di·te] *m* **1.** (*juego*) hide and seek **2.** (*lugar*) hiding place

escondrijo [es·kon·'dri·xo] *m* hideout

escopeta [es·ko·'pe·ta] *f* (*arma*) shotgun; **~ de aire comprimido** air gun; **~ de cañones recortados** sawed-off shotgun

escopetear [es·ko·pe·te·'ar] *vt* **1.** *Méx* (*con indirectas*) to be snide about **2.** *Ven* (*contestar mal*) to give an unpleasant reply to

escorbuto [es·kor·'βu·to] *m* scurvy

escorchar [es·kor·'tʃar] *vt Arg* (*molestar*) to annoy; (*enfadar*) to anger; **¡no me escorches la paciencia!** don't try my patience!

escoria [es·'ko·rja] *f* **1.** (*hez*) dregs *pl* **2.** (*despreciable*) scum

Escorpio [es·'kor·pjo] *m* Scorpio

escorpión [es·kor·'pjon] *m* (*alacrán*) scorpion

escotado [es·ko·'ta·do] *m* neckline

escotado, -a [es·ko·'ta·do, -a] *adj* with a low neckline; **lleva un vestido muy ~** she's wearing a dress with a plunging neckline

escotar [es·ko·'tar] I. *vt* **1.** (*cortar un escote*) to cut **2.** (*ajustar*) to cut to fit II. *vi* **~ entre todos** to club together (to buy sth)

escote [es·'ko·te] *m* **1.** (*en el cuello*) neckline; **~ en pico** V-neck **2.** (*busto*) bust

escotilla [es·ko·'ti·ja, -ʎa] *f* hatchway

escozor [es·ko·'sor, -'θor] *m* **1.** (*picor*) burning **2.** (*resentimiento*) resentment

escrachar [es·kra·'tʃar] *vt* **1.** *AmL* (*tachar*) to strike out, to eliminate **2.** *PRico* (*estropear*) to ruin **3.** *Arg, inf* (*arruinar*) to wreck

escracho [es·'kra·tʃo] *m RíoPl* **1.** (*cara fea*) mug *inf* **2.** (*esperpento*) fright

escribanía [es·kri·βa·'ni·a] *f AmL* (*notaría*) notary

escribano [es·kri·'βa·no] *m* **1.** (*notario*) notary **2.** (*secretario judicial*) court clerk

escribir [es·kri·'βir] *irr* I. *vi, vt* write; **~ algo a mano** to write sth by hand; **~ algo a máquina** to typewrite sth; **escrito a mano** handwritten; **escrito a máquina** typewritten; **¿cómo se escribe tu nombre?** how do you spell your name? II. *vr:* **~se** to write (to each other); **se escriben mucho** they write to each other a lot; **estaba escrito que acabarían casándose** it was in their stars to get married

escrito [es·'kri·to] *m* **1.** (*carta*) letter; (*nota*) note **2.** (*literario, científico*) text; JUR brief, writ

3. *pl* (*obras*) writings *pl*

escrito, -a [es·'kri·to, -a] **I.** *pp de* **escribir II.** *adj* written; **por** ~ in writing; **con la emoción escrita en su cara** with excitement written all over his/her face

escritor(a) [es·kri·'tor, -·'to·ra] *m(f)* writer

escritorio [es·kri·'to·rjo] *m* **1.** (*mesa*) desk **2.** COMPUT desktop

escritura [es·kri·'tu·ra] *f* **1.** (*acto*) writing **2.** (*signos*) script; ~ **fonética** phonetic script **3.** (*documento*) deed; ~ **de propiedad** title deeds; ~ **de hipoteca** mortgage deeds; ~ **de seguro** insurance certificate; ~ **social** company registration; **mediante** ~ in writing; **las Sagradas Escrituras** REL the Holy Scriptures

escriturar [es·kri·tu·'rar] *vt* to execute by deed

escroto [es·'kro·to] *m* scrotum

escrúpulo [es·'kru·pu·lo] *m* **1.** (*duda*) scruple; ~**s de conciencia** pangs of conscience; **ser una persona sin** ~**s** to be completely unscrupulous; **no tener** ~**s en hacer algo** to have no qualms about doing sth **2.** (*asco*) disgust; **me da** ~ **beber de latas** I think it's disgusting to drink out of cans

escrupulosidad [es·kru·pu·lo·si·'dad] *f* scrupulousness

escrupuloso, -a [es·kru·pu·'lo·so, -a] *adj* **1.** (*meticuloso*) scrupulous **2.** (*quisquilloso*) fussy

escrutar [es·kru·'tar] *vt* **1.** (*mirar*) to scrutinize **2.** (*recontar*) to count

escrutinio [es·kru·'ti·njo] *m* **1.** (*examen*) scrutiny **2.** (*recuento*) count **3.** (*votación*) vote

escuadra [es·'kwa·dra] *f* **1.** (*para dibujar*) set square; ~ **de delineante** draftsman's square; **a** ~ at right angles **2.** (*de apoyo, fijación*) bracket **3.** DEP corner (of the net)

escuadrilla [es·kwa·'dri·ja, -Aa] *f* AVIAT squadron

escuadrón [es·kwa·'dron] *m* MIL squadron

escuálido, -a [es·'kwa·li·do] *adj* (*flaco*) scrawny; (*macilento*) emaciated

escucha¹ [es·'ku·ʧa] *m* MIL scout

escucha² [es·'ku·ʧa] *f* (*de conversaciones*) listening; ~ **telefónica** telephone tapping; **servicio de** ~ monitoring service; **estar a la** ~ to be listening; ~ **electrónica** electronic surveillance

escuchar [es·ku·'ʧar] **I.** *vi* **1.** (*atender*) to listen **2.** (*en secreto*) to eavesdrop **3.** (*obedecer*) to pay attention **II.** *vt* **1.** (*oír*) to listen to; (*seguir*) to follow; (*en secreto*) to eavesdrop; ~ **un concierto** to listen to a concert; ~ **una conversación telefónica** to tap into a telephone conversation; ~ (**la**) **radio** to listen to the radio **2.** (*prestar atención*) to pay attention; **¡escúchame bien!** pay attention to what I'm saying! **III.** *vr:* ~**se** to like the sound of one's own voice

escudar [es·ku·'dar] **I.** *vt* (*proteger*) to shield **II.** *vr* (*excusarse*) ~**se en algo** to use sth as an excuse

escudo [es·'ku·do] *m* **1.** (*arma*) shield

2. (*amparo*) defense; (*persona*) protector **3.** (*emblema*) ~ (**de armas**) coat of arms **4.** (*moneda*) escudo (*monetary unit of Chile and Portugal*)

escudriñar [es·ku·dri·'ɲar] **I.** *vt* **1.** (*examinar*) to scrutinize; (*una habitación*) to search **2.** (*mirar*) to scour **II.** *vi* ~ **en la intimidad de alguien** to invade sb's privacy

escuela [es·'kwe·la] *f* **1.** (*institución, edificio*) school; (*de enseñanza primaria*) primary school, elementary school; **Escuela de Bellas Artes** School of Fine Arts; ~ **de conducir** driving school; ~ **de idiomas** language school; ~ **normal** teacher training college; ~ **de párvulos** nursery school; ~ **superior técnica** polytechnic; ~ **taller** workshop **2.** (*método de enseñanza*) method **3.** (*conocimientos*) teaching; **ha tenido buena** ~ he/she has been well taught; **la vida es la mejor** ~ life is the best teacher **4.** (*estilo, seguidores*) school; **la** ~ **holandesa/de Durero** the Dutch school/the Dürer school; **su ejemplo ha hecho** ~ his/her work has set an example

escueto, -a [es·'kwe·to, -a] *adj* **1.** (*sin adornos*) bare **2.** (*lenguaje*) concise; *pey* curt; **explicar algo de forma escueta** to explain sth briefly

escuincle [es·'kwin·kle, -a] *m Méx, inf* (*chiquillo*) baby, kid

esculcar <c→qu> [es·kul·'kar] *vt AmC, Col, Méx* (*registrar*) to go through

esculpir [es·kul·'pir] *vt* (*modelar*) to sculpt; ~ **a cincel** to sculpt using a chisel; ~ **en madera** to carve in wood; ~ **una figura en mármol** to sculpt a figure in marble

escultor(a) [es·kul·'tor, -·'to·ra] *m(f)* sculptor *m*, sculptress *f;* ~ **de madera** wood carver

escultura [es·kul·'tu·ra] *f* sculpture; ~ **de madera** wood carving

escultural [es·kul·tu·'ral] *adj* **1.** (*escultórico*) sculptural **2.** (*bello*) statuesque; **esta chica tiene medidas** ~**es** this girl has beautiful curves

escupidera [es·ku·pi·'de·ra] *f* **1.** (*para escupir*) spittoon **2.** *AmL* (*orinal*) chamber pot

escupir [es·ku·'pir] **I.** *vi* **1.** (*por la boca*) to spit **2.** *inf* (*contar*) to spit it out **II.** *vt* **1.** (*por la boca*) to spit out; ~ **sangre** to spit blood **2.** (*pagar*) to cough up **3.** (*arrojar*) to give out; ~ **fuego** to belch smoke; **el volcán escupe lava** the volcano spits lava **4.** (*tratar mal*) to abuse; ~ **a alguien** to insult sb **5.** *inf* (*decir*) to spit out; **escupe lo que sabes** spill the beans

escurreplatos [es·ku·rre·'pla·tos] *m inv* plate rack

escurridizo, -a [es·ku·rri·'di·so, -a; -'di·θo, -a] *adj* slippery; (*idea*) elusive; **lazo** ~ slipknot

escurrido, -a [es·ku·'rri·do] *adj* **1.** (*flaco*) thin **2.** *Méx, PRico* (*avergonzado*) embarrassed

escurridor [es·ku·rri·'dor] *m* (*colador*) drainer, colander

escurrir [es·ku·'rrir] **I.** *vi* (*gotear, ropa*) to drip;

(*verdura*) to drain **II.** *vt* **1.** (*ropa*) to wring out; (*platos, verdura*) to drain **2.** (*deslizar*) to slip; ~ **la mano por encima de algo** to run one's hand over sth; **escurrió el dinero en mi bolsillo** he/she slipped the money into my pocket **3.** (*una vasija*) to empty; ~ **la** (**botella de**) **cerveza** to empty the bottle of beer **III.** *vr:* ~ **se 1.** (*resbalar*) to slip **2.** (*escaparse*) to slip out; **el pez se me escurrió de** (**entre**) **las manos** the fish slipped out of my hands; ~ **se por un agujero** to slip through a hole; ~ **el bulto** *inf* to dodge the issue **3.** (*desaparecer*) to slip away; ~ **se** (**por**) **entre la gente** to slip away in the crowd **4.** (*gotear*) to drip; (*lágrima*) to trickle

esdrújulo, -a [es·'dru·xu·lo] *adj* LING proparoxytonic

ese ['e·se] *f* S, s; **la letra** ~ the letter s; **ir haciendo** ~**s** *inf* to stagger from side to side

ese, -a ['e·se, -a] **I.** *adj* <esos, -as> that; ¿~ **coche es tuyo?** is that car yours?; **esas sillas están en el medio** those chairs are in the way; **el chico** ~ **no me cae bien** I don't like that boy **II.** *pron dem v.* **ése, ésa, eso**

ése, ésa, eso <ésos, -as> *pron dem* that, that one; **me lo ha dicho ésa** that girl told me; ¿**por qué no vamos a otro bar?** — ~ **no me gusta** why don't we go to another bar? — I don't like that one; **llegaré a eso de las doce** I'll arrive at about twelve o'clock; **estaba trabajando, en eso** (**que**) **tocaron al timbre** I was working when I heard the bell; ¡**a** ~! get him!; ¡**no me vengas con ésas!** come off it!; **me ofrecieron mucho dinero pero, ¡ni por ésas!** they offered to pay me a lot, but not on your life!; **eso mismo te acabo de decir** that's what I've just said; **aun con eso prefiero quedarme en casa** even so, I'd rather stay at home; **lejos de eso** just the opposite; **no es eso** it's not that; **por eso** (**mismo**) that's why; ¿**y eso?** what do you mean?; ¿**y eso qué?** so what?; ¡**eso sí que no!** definitely not!; *v.t.* **ese, -a**

esencia [e·'sen·sja, -θja] *f* **1.** (*naturaleza*) essence; **se dice que el irlandés es por** ~ **hablador** it is said that the Irish are talkative by nature **2.** (*fondo*) base; **ser de** ~ to be very pure; **en** ~ in essence **3.** QUÍM essence; ~ **de café** coffee essence; ~ **de rosas** essence of roses

esencial [e·sen·'sjal, -'θjal] *adj* **1.** (*sustancial*) fundamental; **elemento** ~ essential element; **lo** ~ the main thing **2.** (*indispensable*) essential; **alimento/aceite** ~ essential food/oil

esencialmente [e·sen·sjal·'men·te, e·sen·θjal-] *adv* essentially

esfera [es·'fe·ra] *f* **1.** MAT sphere **2.** (*del reloj*) face, dial **3.** (*ámbito*) *t.* ASTR field; ~ **de actividad** area of activity; ~ **de influencia** sphere of influence **4.** (*clase*) class; **las altas** ~**s de la sociedad** the upper classes

esférico [es·'fe·ri·ko] *m* DEP ball

esférico, -a [es·'fe·ri·ko, -a] *adj* spherical

esferográfico [es·fe·ro·'yra·fi·ko, -a] *m AmS*

(*bolígrafo*) ball-point pen

esfinge [es·'fin·xe] *f* (*animal fabuloso*) sphinx; **ser una** ~ *fig* to be inscrutable

esforzar [es·for·'sar, -'θar] *irr como* **forzar I.** *vt* **1.** (*forzar*) to force; (*vista, voz*) to strain **2.** (*dar ánimo*) to encourage **II.** *vr:* ~ **se** (*moralmente*) to strive; (*físicamente*) to make an effort

esfuerzo [es·'fwer·so, -θo] *m* **1.** (*acción de esforzarse*) effort; **sin** ~ effortlessly; **hacer un** ~ to make an effort; **me ha costado muchos** ~**s conseguirlo** it took me a lot of effort to manage it **2.** (*económico*) strain; **hacer un** ~ to tighten one's belt **3.** (*valor*) courage **4.** TÉC stress

esfumar [es·fu·'mar] **I.** *vt* (*contornos*) to blur; (*colores*) to tone down **II.** *vr:* ~ **se 1.** (*desaparecer*) to fade away; (*contornos*) to blur **2.** *inf* (*marcharse*) to beat it

esgrima [es·'yri·ma] *f* fencing; **practicar la** ~ to do fencing

esgrimir [es·yri·'mir] *vt* **1.** (*blandir*) to wield **2.** (*argumento*) to use

esgrimista [es·yri·'mis·ta] *mf AmL* fencer

esguince [es·'yin·se, -θe] *m* **1.** MED sprain; **hacerse un** ~ **en el tobillo** to sprain one's ankle **2.** (*movimiento*) sidestep

eslabón [es·la·'βon] *m* **1.** (*de una cadena*) link **2.** (*entre acontecimientos*) step; **el** ~ **perdido** the missing link

eslavo, -a [es·'la·βo, -a] *adj, m, f* Slav

eslogan [es·'lo·yan] *m* slogan

eslovaco, -a [es·lo·'βa·ko, -a] **I.** *adj* Slovakian **II.** *m, f* Slovak

Eslovaquia [es·lo·'βa·kja] *f* Slovakia

Eslovenia [es·lo·'βe·nja] *f* Slovenia

esloveno, -a [es·lo·'βe·no, -a] *adj, m, f* Slovenian

esmaltar [es·mal·'tar] *vt* **1.** (*metal, cerámica*) to enamel **2.** (*adornar de colores*) to paint

esmalte [es·'mal·te] *m* **1.** (*barniz*) varnish; (*sobre metal, porcelana*) enamel; ~ **de laca** lacquer enamel; **sin** ~ flat, mat(te) **2.** (*de uñas*) nail polish **3.** (*color*) smalt **4.** (*de los dientes*) enamel

esmerado, -a [es·me·'ra·do, -a] *adj* **1.** (*persona*) painstaking **2.** (*obra*) professional

esmeralda [es·me·'ral·da] **I.** *adj* emerald **II.** *f* emerald; ~ **oriental** corundum

esmerarse [es·me·'rar·se] *vr* (*esforzarse*) ~ **en algo** to make an effort with sth

esmero [es·'me·ro] *m* care; **con** ~ with great care

esmirriado, -a [es·mi·'rrja·do, -a] *adj* (*flaco*) scrawny; (*raquítico*) puny

esmoquin [es·'mo·kin] *m* tuxedo

esnifar [es·ni·'far] *vt inf* (*cocaína*) to snort; (*pegamento, pintura*) to sniff

esnob [es·'noβ] **I.** *adj* snobbish **II.** *mf* snob

esnobismo [es·no·'βis·mo] *m* snobbery

eso ['e·so] *pron dem v.* **ése**

esófago [e·'so·fa·yo] *m* esophagus

esos ['e·sos] *adj v.* **ese**

ésos ['e·sos] *pron dem v.* **ése**

esotérico, -a [e·so·'te·ri·ko, -a] *adj* esoteric

esoterismo [e·so·te·'ris·mo] *m* esoteric nature

espabilada [es·pa·βi·'la·da] *f Col* (*parpadeo*) blink; en una ~ in a second

espabilado, -a [es·pa·βi·'la·do, -a] *adj* 1.(*listo*) smart 2.(*despierto*) awake

espabilar [es·pa·βi·'lar] I. *vi* 1.(*darse prisa*) to hurry up 2.(*avivarse*) to liven up; si quieres montar una empresa, tienes que ~ if you want to be self-employed, you'll have to shape up II. *vt* 1.(*despertar*) to wake up 2.(*avivar*) to get one's act together *inf*, to shape up; en la mili ya lo ~án he's having to straighten up in the army; es muy perezosa, pero en el colegio ya la ~án she's very lazy, but when she gets to school she'll have to change her act 3.(*acabar deprisa*) to hurry; (*fortuna*) to squander; (*comida*) to wolf down 4.(*robar*) to swipe 5.(*matar*) to bump off III. *vr:* ~se 1.(*sacudir el sueño*) to wake oneself up; (*la pereza*) to get busy; tómate un café para ~te have a coffee to wake yourself up 2.(*darse prisa*) to hurry up 3.(*avivarse*) se han espabilado desde que van al colegio they've livened up since they started school 4.*AmL* (*marcharse*) to head off

espaciador [es·pa·sja·'dor, es·pa·θja-] *m* space bar

espacial [es·pa·'sjal, -'θjal] *adj* space; estación ~ space station

espaciar [es·pa·'sjar, -'θjar] I. *vt* (*sillas*) to separate; (*alumnos*) to distribute; (*letras*) to space out; ~ las visitas to spread out [*o* to stagger] the visits; ~ los árboles to space out the trees II. *vr:* ~se (*en un discurso*) to go on at length, to expatiate

espacio [es·'pa·sjo, -θjo] *m* 1.(*área*) *t.* ASTR space; (*superficie*) area; (*trayecto*) distance; ~ sideral outer space; ~ verde green belt; ~ virtual cyberspace; ~ vital living space; ~ web web site; a doble ~ double-spaced 2.(*que ocupa un cuerpo*) room, space 3.(*de tiempo*) period; en el ~ de dos meses in a period of two months; por ~ de tres horas for a three-hour period 4.(*programa*) program; ~ informativo news bulletin; ~ publicitario advertising spot

espacioso, -a [es·pa·'sjo·so, -a, es·pa·'θjo-] *adj* (*lugar*) spacious, roomy

espada¹ [es·'pa·da] *m* 1.TAUR bullfighter 2.ZOOL swordfish

espada² [es·'pa·da] *f* 1.(*arma*) sword; ~ negra foil; desnudar la ~ to unsheathe one's sword; tu respuesta es una ~ de dos filos [*o* de doble filo] your answer is a double-edged sword; de capa y ~ cloak-and-dagger 2.(*naipes*) spade; pintan ~s spades are trumps

espadachín [es·pa·da·'tʃin] *m* (*esgrimidor*) swordsman

espagueti(s) [es·pa·'ye·ti(s)] *m(pl)* spaghetti

espalda [es·'pal·da] *f* 1.ANAT back; ancho de ~s broad-shouldered; ser cargado de ~s to be hunched; andar de ~s to walk backwards; con las manos en la ~ with one's hands clasped behind one's back; estar a ~s de alguien to be behind sb; estar de ~s a la pared to have one's back to the wall; atacar por la ~ to attack from the rear; coger a alguien por la ~ *fig* to take sb by surprise; doblar la ~ *fig* to put one's back into a task; volver la ~ a alguien *fig* to turn one's back on sb; hablar a ~s de alguien to talk behind sb's back; me caí de ~s al oír eso *inf* I was astonished to hear that; tener las ~s muy anchas *fig* to put up with a lot; tener las ~s bien guardadas *inf* to have friends in high places; la responsabilidad recae sobre mis ~s the responsibility is on my shoulders; vivir de ~s a la realidad to live in the clouds 2.DEP backstroke; 100 metros ~ 100-meters backstroke; ¿sabes nadar ~? can you do the backstroke? 3.(*de un edificio*) back 4.(*de un animal*) back; (*para el consumo*) shoulder

espaldero [es·pal·'de·ro] *m Ven* 1.(*guardaespaldas*) bodyguard 2.(*asistente de un militar*) henchman

espaldilla [es·pal·'di·ja, -ʎa] *f* (*de una res*) shoulder

espanglis [es·'pan·lis] *m* Spanglish

espantadizo, -a [es·pan·ta·'di·so, -a; -'di·θo, -a] *adj* 1.(*persona*) jittery 2.(*caballo*) skittish

espantamoscas [es·pan·ta·'mos·kas] *m inv* fly-swatter

espantapájaros [es·pan·ta·'pa·xa·ros] *m inv* scarecrow

espantar [es·pan·'tar] I. *vt* 1.(*dar susto*) to shock; (*dar miedo*) to frighten 2.(*ahuyentar a un animal*) to shoo away; (*asustándolo*) to frighten off 3.(*asombrar*) to awe II. *vr:* ~se 1.(*personas*) ~se de [*o* por] algo to be scared of sth 2.(*animales*) to be shooed away; (*asustándolos*) to be frightened off

espanto [es·'pan·to] *m* 1.(*miedo*) fright; ¡qué ~! how awful!; hace un calor de ~ it's terribly hot; los precios son de ~ prices are outrageous; estar curado de ~s *inf* to have been around a few years 2.(*terror*) horror 3.*AmL* (*fantasma*) ghost

espantosidad [es·pan·to·si·'dad] *f AmC, Col, PRico* (*horror*) horror

espantoso, -a [es·pan·'to·so, -a] *adj* 1.(*horroroso*) horrible 2.(*feo*) hideous 3.(*asombroso*) awesome

España [es·'pa·ɲa] *f* Spain

i España (formally named Reino de España) is a constitutional monarchy with a two-chamber system. Juan Carlos I became the King of Spain on November 22, 1975. The successor to the throne is Crown Prince Felipe de Asturias. The country's official language is Spanish. Since 1978, el gallego (Galician), **el catalán** (Catalan) and **el euskera/el vasco** (Basque), have also been recognized as national languages.

español [es·pa·'ɲol] *m* Spanish; **clases de ~** Spanish classes; **aprender ~** to learn Spanish; **traducir al ~** to translate into Spanish
español(a) [es·pa·'ɲol, -'ɲo·la] **I.** *adj* Spanish; **a la ~a** Spanish-style **II.** *m(f)* Spaniard
esparadrapo [es·pa·ra·'dra·po] *m* adhesive [*o* medical] tape
esparcimiento [es·par·si·'mjen·to, -θi·'mjen·to] *m* **1.** (*acción*) spreading **2.** (*diversión*) fun
esparcir <c→z> [es·par·'sir, -'θir] **I.** *vt* **1.** (*cosas*) to spread out; (*líquido*) to spill; **el viento ha esparcido los papeles de la mesa** the wind has blown the papers off the table **2.** (*mancha*) to spread over **3.** (*noticia*) to spread **4.** (*distraer*) **~ el ánimo** to amuse oneself **II.** *vr:* **~se 1.** (*cosas*) to spread out **2.** (*noticias*) to spread **3.** (*distraerse*) to relax; **¿qué haces para ~te?** what do you do for fun?
espárrago [es·'pa·rra·yo] *m* asparagus; **~ triguero** wild asparagus; **¡vete a freír ~s!** *inf* get lost!; **estar hecho un ~** *fig* to be as thin as a rake
espartillo [es·par·'ti·jo, -ʎo] *m AmL*, **esparto** [es·'par·to] *m* esparto
espasmo [es·'pas·mo] *m* spasm
espasmódico, -a [es·pas·'mo·di·ko, -a] *adj* spasmodic
espátula [es·'pa·tu·la] *f* spatula
especia [es·'pe·sja, -θja] *f* spice
especial [es·pe·'sjal, -'θjal] *adj* **1.** (*no habitual*) special; (*adecuado*) perfect; **edición/comisión/escuela ~** special edition/committee/school; **en ~** in particular; **no pensaba en nada en ~** I wasn't thinking of anything in particular; **él es para mí alguien muy ~** he means a lot to me **2.** (*raro*) peculiar
especialidad [es·pe·sja·li·'dad, es·pe·θja-] *f* **1.** (*de un restaurante, una empresa*) specialty **2.** (*rama*) field; DEP specialty
especialista [es·pe·sja·'lis·ta, es·pe·θja-] *mf* **1.** (*experto*) specialist **2.** (*médico*) specialist **3.** CINE stuntman *m*, stuntwoman *f*
especialización [es·pe·sja·li·sa·'sjon, -θja·li·θa·'θjon] *f* specialization; **mi ~ es la física cuántica** my field is quantum physics
especializar <z→c> [es·pe·sja·li·'sar, es·pe·θja·li·'θar] *vi, vr:* **~se** to specialize; **personal especializado** skilled staff
especialmente [es·pe·sjal·'men·te, es·pe·θjal-] *adv* **lo he hecho ~ para ti** I made it especially for you
especie [es·'pe·sje, -'pe·θje] *f* **1.** *t.* BOT, ZOOL (*clase*) species *invr*; **~ amenazada de extinción** endangered species; **la ~ animal** animals *pl*; **gente de todas las ~s** all kinds of people; **un hombre de mala ~** an unpleasant man **2.** COM **pagar en ~s** to pay in kind **3.** (*rumor*) rumor

especificación [es·pe·si·fi·ka·'sjon, -θi·fi·ka·'θjon] *f* **1.** (*precisión*) specification; **especificaciones técnicas** technical specifications **2.** (*explicación*) explanation
especificar <c→qu> [es·pe·si·fi·'kar, es·pe·θi-] *vt* **1.** (*explicar*) to explain; **el ministro especificó los problemas actuales de la economía** the minister spelled out the present economic problems; **no ~ los pormenores de las negociaciones** not to give details of the negotiations **2.** (*citar*) to specify; (*enumerar*) to enumerate
específico, -a [es·pe·'si·fi·ko, -'θi·fi·ko] *adj* specific; **el significado ~ de una palabra** the specific meaning of a word
espécimen [es·'pe·si·men, -θi·men] *m* <especímenes> **1.** (*ejemplar*) specimen; **~ de lujo** prime example **2.** (*muestra*) sample
espectacular [es·pek·ta·ku·'lar] *adj* spectacular
espectáculo [es·pek·'ta·ku·lo] *m* **1.** TEAT show; (*de variedades*) variety show; **~ de circo** circus; **~ deportivo** sporting event **2.** (*visión*) sight **3.** *inf* (*escándalo*) **dar el ~** to make a scene
espectador(a) [es·pek·ta·'dor, -'do·ra] *m(f)* spectator
espectro [es·'pek·tro] *m* (*fantasma*) phantom, specter
especulación [es·pe·ku·la·'sjon, -'θjon] *f* speculation
especulador(a) [es·pe·ku·la·'dor, -'do·ra] *m(f)* speculator
especular [es·pe·ku·'lar] *vi t.* FIN (*conjeturar*) to speculate; **~ en la Bolsa** to speculate on the stock market **2.** (*meditar*) to speculate
especulativo, -a [es·pe·ku·la·'ti·βo, -a] *adj* **1.** (*que especula*) speculative **2.** (*teórico*) theoretical
espejado [es·pe·'xa·do] *m AmL* mirror-like
espejismo [es·pe·'xis·mo] *m* **1.** (*óptico*) mirage **2.** (*de la imaginación*) illusion
espejo [es·'pe·xo] *m* mirror; **~ retrovisor** car mirror, rear-view mirror; **mirarse al ~** to look at oneself in the mirror; **el cine es el ~ de la vida** the cinema reflects real life
espeluznante [es·pe·lus·'nan·te, es·pe·luθ-] *adj* horrific
espera [es·'pe·ra] *f* **1.** (*acción, duración*) wait; **tuvimos dos horas de ~** we had a two-hour wait; **estoy a la ~ de recibir la beca** I'm waiting to hear about the grant; **esta ~ me saca de quicio** this waiting around is really getting to me **2.** (*estado*) waiting; **lista de ~** waiting list; **en ~ de su respuesta** (*final de carta*) looking forward to hearing from you **3.** (*paciencia*) patience **4.** (*plazo*) period; **no tener ~** to be urgent; **sin ~** immediate
esperanza [es·pe·'ran·sa, -θa] *f* hope; **~ de vida** life expectancy; **no tener ~s** to have no hope; **abrigar ~s** to foster hopes; **estar en estado de buena ~** to be pregnant [*o* expecting]; **poner las ~s en algo** to put one's hopes

into sth; **tener ~s de conseguir un puesto de trabajo** to have hopes of getting a job; **veo el futuro con ~** I'm hopeful about the future; **con ~ no se come** *prov* who lives by hope will die by hunger

esperanzador(a) [es·pe·ran·sa·'dor, -·'do·ra; -θa·dor, -·'do·ra] *adj* hopeful

esperanzar <z→c> [es·pe·ran·'sar, -'θar] **I.** *vt* to give hope to **II.** *vr ~***se en algo** to become hopeful about sth

esperar [es·pe·'rar] **I.** *vi* **1.** (*aguardar*) to wait; **~ al aparato** (*teléfono*) to stay on the line; **hacerse ~** to keep people waiting; **es de ~ que** +*subj* it is to be expected that; **¡que se espere!** let him wait!; **¿a qué esperas?** what are you waiting for?; **no lo encuentro** hold on, I can't find it; **ganaron la copa tan esperada** they won the long-awaited cup; **uno sólo tiene que ~ a que las cosas lleguen** all things come to those who wait **2.** (*confiar*) to hope; **~ en alguien** to place one's hope in sb **II.** *vt* **1.** (*aguardar*) to wait for; **hace una hora que lo espero** I've been waiting for him for an hour; **hacer ~ a alguien** to keep sb waiting; **la respuesta no se hizo ~** the answer was not long in coming; **me van a ~ al aeropuerto** they're meeting me at the airport; **nos esperan malos tiempos** there are bad times in store for us; **espero su decisión con impaciencia** (*final de carta*) I'm looking forward to hearing from you; **te espera una prueba dura** a hard test awaits you **2.** (*un bebé, recibir, pensar*) to expect; **ya me lo esperaba** I expected it **3.** (*confiar*) to hope; **espero que nos veamos pronto** I hope to see you soon; **esperando recibir noticias tuyas...** looking forward to hearing from you...; **espero que sí** I hope so

esperma [es·'per·ma] *m* sperm

esperpento [es·per·'pen·to] *m* **1.** (*persona*) fright **2.** (*desatino*) piece of nonsense **3.** (*estilo literario*) literary style coined by Valle Inclán

espesar [es·pe·'sar] **I.** *vt* (*líquido*) to thicken **II.** *vr:* **~se** (*bosque*) to become denser

espeso, -a [es·'pe·so, -a] *adj* **1.** (*cabello, niebla, bosque, líquido*) thick **2.** (*persona*) untidy **3.** *Arg, Perú, Ven* (*molesto*) bothersome

espesor [es·pe·'sor] *m* **1.** (*grosor*) thickness; (*nieve*) depth **2.** (*densidad*) density

espesura [es·pe·'su·ra] *f* **1.** (*del cabello, bosque*) thickness; (*de un líquido*) density **2.** (*bosque*) thicket

espetar [es·pe·'tar] *vt* **1.** (*ave, objeto*) to skewer **2.** *inf* (*de repente*) to come out with; **~ cuatro verdades a alguien** *fig* to give sb a piece of one's mind

espía [es·'pi·a] *mf* spy; (*de la policía*) informer; (*infiltrado*) infiltrator; **~ doble** double agent

espiantar [es·pjan·'tar] **I.** *vi, vr:* **~se** *CSur, inf* (*alejarse*) to head off; (*huir*) to escape **II.** *vt CSur* (*hurtar*) to steal

espiar < *1. pres:* espío> [es·pi·'ar] **I.** *vi* (*hacer espionaje*) to spy **II.** *vt* to spy on; (*para la poli-*

cía) to inform on

espichar [es·pi·'tʃar] *vt Col, inf* (*aplastar*) to squash

espiga [es·'pi·ɣa] *f* **1.** BOT ear; **dibujo de ~** herringbone **2.** (*madera*) dowel

espina [es·'pi·na] *f* **1.** (*de pescado*) bone **2.** BOT thorn **3.** ANAT **~** (**dorsal**) spine **4.** (*inconveniente*) problem; **esto me da mala ~** *inf* I don't like the look of this **5.** (*pesar*) frustration; **sacarse una ~** *inf* (*desquitarse*) to get even; (*desahogarse*) to let it all out; **tener una ~ clavada** to have sth hanging over one

espinaca [es·pi·'na·ka] *f* spinach

espinal [es·pi·'nal] *adj* spinal; **médula ~** spinal chord

espinazo [es·pi·'na·so, -θo] *m* ANAT spinal column; **doblar el ~** *fig* to work hard

espinilla [es·pi·'ni·ja, -ʎa] *f* **1.** ANAT shin; **dar a alguien una patada en la ~** to kick sb in the shin **2.** (*grano*) blackhead

espino [es·'pi·no] *m* TÉC **alambre de ~** barbed wire

espinoso, -a [es·pi·'no·so, -a] *adj*, **espinudo, -a** [es·pi·'nu·do, -a] *adj AmC, CSur* **1.** (*planta*) thorny; (*pescado*) bony **2.** (*problema*) tricky

espionaje [es·pjo·'na·xe] *m* espionage; **~ industrial** industrial espionage; **servicio de ~ británico** British secret service

espiración [es·pi·ra·'sjon, -'θjon] *f* MED exhalation

espiral [es·pi·'ral] **I.** *adj* spiral; **escalera ~** spiral staircase **II.** *f* spiral

espirar [es·pi·'rar] **I.** *vi* (*aire*) to exhale **II.** *vt* (*olor*) to give off

espiritismo [es·pi·ri·'tis·mo] *m* spiritualism; **sesión de ~** séance

espiritista [es·pi·ri·'tis·ta] *adj* spiritualist

espíritu [es·'pi·ri·tu] *m* spirit; (*alma*) soul; (*inteligencia*) mind; (*idea principal*) essence, nature; **~ de compañerismo** brotherly spirit; **~ de contradicción** contrariness; **~ emprendedor** hardworking nature; **~ deportivo** sportsmanship; **~ de la época** spirit of the age; **~ de observación** (*don*) gift of observation; **el Espíritu Santo** REL the Holy Spirit; **~ de solidaridad** spirit of solidarity; **pobre de ~** mean-spirited; **exhalar el ~** to breathe one's last; **levantar el ~ a alguien** to lift sb's spirits; **tener un ~ de rebelión** to have a spirit of rebellion; **hacer algo con ~ alegre** to go about sth cheerfully; **evocar los ~s** to call upon the spirits

espiritual [es·pi·ri·tu·'al] *adj* spiritual; **vida ~** spiritual life; **mantenemos una relación puramente ~** we have a purely Platonic relationship

espita [es·'pi·ta] *f* **1.** (*de una cuba*) faucet; (*del gas*) gas spigot; () **2.** (*palmo*) span **3.** *inf* (*borracho*) drunk

esplendidez [es·plen·di·'des, -'deθ] *f* **1.** (*generosidad*) generosity **2.** (*magnificencia*) splendor

espléndido, -a [es·'plen·di·do, -a] adj 1.(generoso) generous 2.(aspecto) splendid; (día) beautiful; (comida) lovely; (ocasión, idea, resultado) excellent
esplendor [es·plen·'dor] m splendor
esplendoroso, -a [es·plen·do·'ro·so, -a] adj splendid
espliego [es·'plje·ɣo] m lavender
espolear [es·po·le·'ar] vt 1.(al caballo) to spur 2.(a alguien) to spur on
espolvorear [es·pol·βo·re·'ar] vt to sprinkle
esponja [es·'pon·xa] f 1.(para lavar) t. ZOOL sponge; ~ de baño bath sponge; beber como una ~ inf to drink like a fish 2.(persona) sponge, leech
esponjoso, -a [es·pon·'xo·so, -a] adj (masa) fluffy; (pan) light
espontaneidad [es·pon·ta·nei·'dad] f spontaneity
espontáneo, -a [es·pon·'ta·neo, -a] I. adj spontaneous; (saludo) natural; curación espontánea spontaneous healing II. m, f TAUR bullfight spectator who enters the ring to participate
espora [es·'po·ra] f spore
esporádico, -a [es·po·'ra·di·ko, -a] adj sporadic
esportivo, -a [es·por·'ti·βo, -a] adj AmL 1.(deportivo) sporting 2.(afectando descuido) casual
esposar [es·po·'sar] vt to handcuff
esposas [es·'po·sas] fpl (manillas) handcuffs pl; colocar las ~ a alguien to handcuff sb
esposo, -a [es·'po·so, -a] m, f spouse; (marido) husband; (mujer) wife; salude a su ~ de mi parte give my regards to your husband; los ~s the bride and groom
espray [es·'prai] m 1.(líquido) spray 2.(envase) aerosol
esprint [es·'prin(t)] m sprint
esprintar [es·prin·'tar] vt to sprint
esprínter [es·'prin·ter] mf sprinter
espuela [es·'pwe·la] f 1.(de caballo) spur 2.inf(la última copa) one for the road; tomar la ~ to have one for the road
espuma [es·'pu·ma] f (burbujas) foam; (de las olas) spray; (de jabón) lather; (de cerveza) head; ~ de afeitar shaving foam; crecer como la ~ inf(persona) to shoot up; (cosa) to grow very quickly
espumarajo [es·pu·ma·'ra·xo] m 1.pey (espuma) froth 2.(de la boca) foam
espumilla [es·pu·'mi·ja, -ʎa] f AmL CULIN (merengue) meringue
espumoso, -a [es·pu·'mo·so, -a] adj (masa) foamy; (líquido) sparkling; vino ~ sparkling wine
esputo [es·'pu·to] m spit(tle); MED sputum
esqueje [es·'ke·xe] m cutting
esquela [es·'ke·la] f 1.(nota) notice of death 2.(necrológica) ~ (mortuoria) obituary notice
esquelético, -a [es·ke·'le·ti·ko, -a] adj 1.ANAT

skeletal 2.(persona) scrawny
esqueleto [es·ke·'le·to] m 1.ANAT skeleton; después de la operación quedé hecho un ~ after the operation I was so thin I looked like a skeleton 2.(de un avión, barco) shell; (de un edificio) framework
esquema [es·'ke·ma] m 1.(gráfico) sketch; en ~ in rough 2.(de una clase) summary; tengo que hacer el ~ del discurso I have to make an outline for the speech 3.(idea) idea; romper los ~s to shake up sb's ideas
esquemático, -a [es·ke·'ma·ti·ko, -a] adj schematic
esquematizar [es·ke·ma·ti·'sar, -'θar] vt to outline
esquí [es·'ki] m 1.(patín) ski; ~ de fondo cross-country ski 2.(deporte) skiing; ~ acuático water-skiing; ~ parabólico carve skiing, carving
esquiador(a) [es·kja·'dor, -·'do·ra] m(f) skier; ~ de fondo cross-country skier
esquiar < 1. pres: esquío> [es·ki·'ar] vi to ski
esquilar [es·ki·'lar] vt 1.(ovejas) to shear; (perros) to clip 2.(timar) to rip off
esquimal [es·ki·'mal] I. adj Eskimo; perro ~ husky II. mf Eskimo
esquina [es·'ki·na] f corner; casa que hace ~ house on the corner; hacer un saque de ~ DEP to take a corner; a la vuelta de la ~ around the corner; doblar la ~ to turn the corner
esquinar [es·ki·'nar] I. vi to be on the corner II. vt 1.(objetos) to turn around 2.(maderos) to square III. vr: ~se to have a quarrel
esquinazo [es·ki·'na·so, -θo] m inf corner; dar ~ a alguien (dejar plantado) to stand sb up; (rehuir) to avoid sb
esquirla [es·'kir·la] f splinter, chip
esquirol [es·ki·'rol] mf scab, blackleg
esquivar [es·ki·'βar] I. vt 1.(golpe) to dodge 2.(problema) to shirk 3.(encuentro) ~ algo to get out of sth 4.(a alguien) to avoid II. vr: ~se to back out
esquivo, -a [es·'ki·βo, -a] adj 1.(huidizo) evasive 2.(arisco) aloof
esquizofrenia [es·ki·so·'fre·nja, es·ki·θo-] f schizophrenia
esquizofrénico, -a [es·ki·so·'fre·ni·ko, -a; es·ki·θo-] adj, m, f schizophrenic
esta ['es·ta] adj v. este, -a
ésta ['es·ta] pron dem v. éste
estabilidad [es·ta·βi·li·'dad] f stability; (de una amistad) firmness; (del carácter) steadiness, stability; ~ de los precios price stability
estabilización [es·ta·βi·li·sa·'sjon, -θa·'θjon] f stability
estabilizar <z→c> [es·ta·βi·li·'sar, -'θar] I. vt to stabilize; (amistad) to establish II. vr: ~se to stabilize
estable [es·'ta·βle] adj stable; (trabajo) steady; (carácter) steadfast, stable
establecer [es·ta·βle·'ser, -'θer] irr como crecer I. vt 1.(fundar) to establish; (grupo de

trabajo) to set up; (*sucursal, tienda*) to open; (*principio, récord*) to set; (*orden, escuela*) to found **2.**(*colocar*) to place; (*campamento*) to set up; (*colonos*) to settle; (*conexión*) to establish **II.** *vr* ~**se de algo** (*instalarse*) to set oneself up as sth

establecimiento [es·ta·βle·si·'mjen·to, -θi· 'mjen·to] *m* **1.**(*fundación, relaciones*) establishment; (*de un grupo de trabajo*) setting-up; (*de una sucursal*) opening; (*de un principio, récord*) setting; (*del orden, de una escuela*) founding **2.**(*de colonia*) settlement

establo [es·'ta·βlo] *m* **1.**(*cuadra*) stable, barn **2.** *Cuba* (*cochera*) depot; (*para alquilar*) garage

estaca [es·'ta·ka] *f* (*palo*) post; (*para tienda*) peg; (*garrote*) stick

estacada [es·ta·'ka·da] *f* fence; **dejar a alguien en la** ~ to leave sb in the lurch; **quedarse en la** ~ to be left in the lurch

estación [es·ta·'sjon, -'θjon] *f* **1.**(*año, temporada*) season; ~ **de las lluvias** rainy season **2.** *t.* RADIO, TV, FERRO station; (*parada*) stop; ~ **de autobuses** bus station; ~ **central** central station; ~ **de destino** destination; ~ **de metro** subway station **3.**(*centro*) *t.* REL station, center; ~ **meteorológica** weather station; ~ **orbital** orbiting space station; ~ **de servicio** service [*o* gas] station

estacionamiento [es·ta·sjo·na·'mjen·to, es·ta·θjo-] *m* **1.** AUTO (*acción*) parking; (*espacio*) parking place [*o* space]; (*lugar*) car park **2.**(*colocación*) placing **3.** MIL (*posición*) positioning **4.**(*estabilización*) stabilization

estacionar [es·ta·sjo·'nar, es·ta·θjo-] **I.** *vt* **1.** AUTO to park **2.**(*colocar*) to place **3.** MIL to position **II.** *vr:* ~**se 1.** AUTO to park **2.**(*alguien*) to stabilize **3.**(*parar*) to stabilize; **la producción se ha estacionado** production has stabilized

estada [es·'ta·da] *f AmL*, **estadía** [es·ta·'di·a] *f* **1.**(*estancia*) stay **2.**(*de un modelo*) session **3.** COM (*tiempo*) demurrage; (*tarifa*) cost of such a delay

estadía [es·ta·'di·a] *f AmL* (*estancia*) stay

estadio [es·'ta·djo] *m* **1.** DEP stadium **2.** MED stage

estadística [es·ta·'dis·ti·ka] *f* statistics *pl*

estadístico, -a [es·ta·'dis·ti·ko, -a] **I.** *adj* statistical **II.** *m, f* statistician

estado [es·'ta·do] *m* **1.**(*condición*) condition; (*situación*) state; ~ **de alarma** state of alert; ~ **civil** marital status; ~ **de las cosas** (*general*) state of affairs; ~ **de gracia** state of grace; ~ **de la economía** state of the economy; ~ **de derecho** constitutional state; ~ **de emergencia** state of emergency; ~ **financiero** financial situation; ~ **gaseoso** gaseous state; ~ **de guerra** state of war; **el cuarto** ~ (*periodismo*) the press; ~ **de necesidad** JUR state of necessity; **en buen** ~ **de conservación** in a good state of upkeep; **en** ~ **de embriaguez** in a state of inebriation; **en** ~ **de merecer** mar-

riageable **2.** POL state; ~ **comunitario** community state; ~ **miembro** member state; **presupuestos del** ~ state budget; ~ **totalitario** police state

Estados Unidos [es·'ta·dos u·'ni·dos] *mpl* United States *pl* + *sing vb* of America

estadounidense [es·ta·do·u·ni·'den·se] **I.** *adj* of/from the United States, American **II.** *mf* native/inhabitant of the United States, American

estafa [es·'ta·fa] *f* swindle

estafador(a) [es·ta·fa·'dor, -·'do·ra] *m(f)* swindler

estafar [es·ta·'far] *vt* to swindle; **la cajera me ha estafado el cambio** the checkout assistant has shortchanged me

estafeta [es·ta·'fe·ta] *f* (*correos*) post office branch

estagnación [es·tay·na·'sjon, -'θjon] *f AmC* stagnation

estaje [es·'ta·xe] *m AmL* piecework

estajear [es·ta·xe·'ar] *vi AmL* to do as piecework

estajero, -a [es·ta·'xe·ro, -a] *m, f AmL* pieceworker, freelancer

estalactita [es·ta·lak·'ti·ta] *f* stalactite

estalagmita [es·ta·lay·'mi·ta] *f* stalagmite

estallar [es·ta·'jar, -·'ʎar] *vi* **1.**(*globo, neumático*) to burst; (*bomba*) to explode, to go off; (*cristales*) to shatter; (*látigo*) to crack; **estalló una ovación** applause broke out; **me estalla la cabeza** I have a splitting headache **2.**(*revolución, incendio*) to break out; (*tormenta*) to break; **al** ~ **la guerra** when the war broke out **3.**(*risa*) to burst out; ~ **en llanto** burst into tears; **estaba enfadado y al final estalló** he was angry and he finally snapped

estallido [es·ta·'ji·do, -'ʎi·do] *m* **1.**(*ruido*) explosion; (*de un globo*) bursting **2.**(*de una revolución*) outbreak; ~ **de cólera** outbreak of cholera

Estambul [es·tam·'bul] *m* Istanbul

estampa [es·'tam·pa] *f* **1.**(*dibujo*) illustration; ~ **de la Virgen** image of the Virgin Mary **2.**(*huella*) imprint **3.**(*impresión*) impression; (*aspecto*) appearance; **un caballo de magnífica** ~ a splendid-looking horse; **¡maldita sea tu** ~! damn you!; **ser la viva** ~ **de la pobreza** to be the incarnation of poverty; **ser la viva** ~ **de su padre** *inf* to be the spitting image of one's father

estampado [es·tam·'pa·do] *m* **1.**(*tejido*) print; **no me gusta este** ~ I don't like this design **2.**(*metal*) engraving

estampado, -a [es·tam·'pa·do, -a] *adj* printed

estampar [es·tam·'par] **I.** *vt* **1.**(*en papel, tela*) to print; (*con relieve*) to stamp; ~ **un dibujo en una camiseta** to print a design on a T-shirt **2.** TÉC (*una chapa*) to press; (*un motivo en una chapa*) to stamp; **se me quedó estampado en la cabeza** *fig* it imprinted itself on my memory **3.**(*huella*) to imprint; ~ **una firma** to sign one's name **4.** *inf* (*arrojar*) to hurl **5.** *inf* (*dar*) to give; ~ **una bofetada a alguien** to give sb a slap; ~**le un beso a alguien en la cara** to plant a kiss on sb's face **II**. *vr* ~**se con algo** *inf* to crash into sth

estampido [es·tam·'pi·do] *m* bang; ~ **del trueno** peal of thunder; **dar un** ~ to bang

estampilla [es·tam·'pi·ja, -ʎa] *f* **1**. (*sello*) rubber stamp **2**. *AmL* (*de correos*) stamp

estancamiento [es·tan·ka·'mjen·to] *m* **1**. (*del agua*) stagnation **2**. (*de una mercancía*) monopolization **3**. (*de los negocios*) breakdown; (*de un proceso*) deadlock **4**. ECON recession

estancar <c→qu> [es·tan·'kar] **I**. *vt* **1**. (*un río*) to stagnate; **aguas estancadas** stagnant water **2**. (*mercancía*) to monopolize **3**. (*proceso*) to hold up **II**. *vr:* ~**se 1**. (*río*) to be held back **2**. (*negocio*) to falter; **quedarse estancado** to get stuck; **me he estancado en los estudios** I'm bogged down in my studies

estancia [es·'tan·sja, -θja] *f* **1**. (*permanencia*) stay **2**. (*habitación*) room **3**. *AmL* (*hacienda*) estate **4**. *Cuba, Ven* (*quinta*) country house **5**. (*poesía*) stanza

estanciera [es·tan·'sje·ra, -'θje·ra] *f Arg* (*furgoneta*) station wagon

estanciero, -a [es·tan·'sje·ro, -a; -'θje·ro, -a] *m, f CSur, Col, Ven* **1**. (*de ganado*) cattle farmer **2**. (*de latifundios*) landowner

estanco [es·'tan·ko] *m* **1**. (*establecimiento*) state store **2**. (*monopolio*) monopoly

estanco, -a [es·'tan·ko, -a] *adj* **1**. NÁUT watertight **2**. (*separado*) independent

estándar [es·'tan·dar] **I**. *adj* standard; **tipo** ~ standard version **II**. *m* standard

estandarizar <z→c> [es·tan·da·ri·'sar, -'θar] *vt* to standardize

estandarte [es·tan·'dar·te] *m* banner

estanque [es·'tan·ke] *m* **1**. (*en un parque*) pool, pond **2**. (*para el riego*) tank

estanquillo [es·tan·'ki·jo, -ʎo] *m* **1**. *Ecua* (*taberna*) tavern **2**. *Méx* (*tienda*) small shop or stall

estante [es·'tan·te] *m* **1**. (*tabla*) shelf; (*para libros*) bookshelf **2**. (*estantería para libros*) bookcase

estantería [es·tan·te·'ri·a] *f* shelves *pl;* (*para libros*) bookcase

estañar [es·ta·'ɲar] *vt Ven* (*herir*) to wound

estaño [es·'ta·ɲo] *m* tin; ~ **para soldar** solder

estar [es·'tar] *irr* **I**. *vi* **1**. (*hallarse*) to be; (*un objeto: derecho*) to stand; (*tumbado*) to lie; (*colgando*) to hang; **Valencia está en la costa** Valencia is on the coast; **¿está Pepe?** is Pepe there?; **como estamos aquí tú y yo** as you and I are here; **ya lo hago yo, para eso estoy** I'll do it, that's why I'm here; **¿está la comida?** is lunch ready? **2**. (*sentirse*) to be; **¿cómo estás?** how are you?; **ya estoy mejor** I'm better **3**. (+ *adjetivo, participio*) to be; ~ **asomado al balcón** to be looking out over the balcony; ~ **cansado** to be tired; ~ **sentado** to be sitting; ~ **ubicado** *AmL* to be located; ~ **viejo** to be old; **el asado está delicioso** the roast is delicious; **está visto que...** it is obvious that...

4. (+ *bien, mal*) ~ **mal de azúcar** to be running out of sugar; ~ **mal de la cabeza** to be out of one's mind; ~ **mal de dinero** to be short of money; **eso te está bien empleado** *inf* it serves you right; **esa blusa te está bien** that blouse suits you **5**. (+ *a*) ~ **al caer** (*persona*) to be about to arrive; (*suceso*) to be about to happen; **están al caer las diez** it's almost ten o'clock; ~ **al día** to be up to date; **estamos a uno de enero** it's the first of January; **¿a qué estamos?** what day is it?; **las peras están a 10 pesos el kilo** pears cost 10 pesos a kilo; **las acciones están a 12 dólares** the shares are at 12 dollars; **Caracas está a 40 grados** it is 40 degrees in Caracas; **el termómetro está a diez grados** the thermometer shows ten degrees; **están uno a uno** they're tied; ~ **a examen** to be under examination; **estoy a lo que decida la asamblea** I will follow whatever the assembly decides; **estoy a oscuras en este tema** I'm in the dark about this matter **6**. (+ *con*) to be; **estoy con mi novio** I'm with my boyfriend; **en la casa estoy con dos más** I share the house with two others; **estoy contigo en este punto** I agree with you on that point **7**. (+ *de*) to be; ~ **de broma** to be joking; ~ **de charla** to be chatting; ~ **de mal humor** to be in a bad mood; ~ **de parto** to be in labor; ~ **de pie** to be standing; ~ **de suerte** to be lucky; ~ **de secretario** to be working as a secretary; ~ **de viaje** to be traveling; **en esta reunión estoy de más** I'm not needed in this meeting; **esto que has dicho estaba de más** there's no call for what you've just said **8**. (+ *en*) **el problema está en el dinero** the problem is the money; **yo estoy en que él no dice la verdad** I believe he's not telling the truth; **no estaba en sí cuando lo hizo** he wasn't in control of himself when he did it; **siempre estás en todo** you don't miss a thing **9**. (+ *para*) ~ **para morir** to feel like dying; **hoy no estoy para bromas** today I'm in no mood for jokes; **el tren está para salir** the train is about to leave **10**. (+ *por*) **estoy por llamarle** I think we should call him; **eso está por ver** we don't know that yet; **la historia de esta ciudad está por escribir** the history of this city has not been written yet; **este partido está por la democracia** this party believes in democracy **11**. (+ *gerundio*) to be; **¿qué estás haciendo?** what are you doing?; **estoy haciendo la comida** I'm making lunch; **siempre estás viendo la tele** you're always watching television; **estoy escribiendo una carta** I'm writing a letter; **¡lo estaba viendo venir!** I saw it coming!; **este pastel está diciendo cómeme** this cake is crying out to be eaten **12**. (+ *que*) **estoy que no me tengo** I can hardly stand up, I'm so tired; **está que trina** he/she's furious **13**. (+ *sobre*) **estate sobre este asunto** look after this matter; **ser una persona que siempre está sobre sí** (*serena*) to always be in control of oneself

14. (*entendido*) **a las 10 en casa, ¿estamos?** 10 o'clock at home, OK? **II.** *vr:* ~ **se 1.** (*hallarse*) to be **2.** (*permanecer*) to stay; ~ **se de charla** to be chatting; **te puedes ~ con nosotros** you can stay with us; **me estuve con ellos toda la tarde** I spent the whole afternoon with them; **¡estate quieto!** keep still; **¡estate callado!** shut up!

estatal [es·ta·'tal] *adj* state

estática [es·'ta·ti·ka] *f* statics

estático, -a [es·'ta·ti·ko, -a] *adj* static; (*pasmado*) rooted to the spot

estatua [es·'ta·twa] *f* statue

estatuilla [es·ta·'twi·ja, -ʎa] *f* statuette; CINE Oscar

estatura [es·ta·'tu·ra] *f* stature; (*altura*) height; **¿qué ~ tienes?** how tall are you?; **es un hombre de ~ pequeña** he's a short man; **su ~ política** his/her political stature

estatus [es·'ta·tus] *m inv* status

estatutario, -a [es·ta·tu·'ta·rjo, -a] *adj* statutory

estatuto [es·ta·'tu·to] *m* **1.** (*de una sociedad*) rule **2.** JUR, POL statute; (*de autonomía*) statute of autonomy; **~ de los trabajadores** employment legislation

este ['es·te] *m* **1.** (*punto*) east; HIST **Alemania del Este** East Germany **2.** (*viento*) easterly

este, -a ['es·te, -a] **I.** *adj* <estos, -as> this; **~ perro es mío** this dog is mine; **esta casa es nuestra** this house is ours; **estos guantes son míos** these gloves are mine **II.** *pron dem v.* **éste, ésta, esto**

éste, ésta, esto <éstos, -as> *pron dem* him, her, this; (a) **éstos no los he visto nunca** I've never seen them; **~ se cree muy importante** this guy thinks he's very important; **antes yo también tenía una camisa como ésta** I used to have a shirt like this before, too; (**estando**) **en esto** [*o* **en éstas**], **llamaron a la puerta** and then, someone called at the door; **¡ésta sí que es buena!** *irón* that's a good one!, that's brilliant!; **te lo juro, por ésta(s)** I swear to God!; *v.t.* **este, -a**

estela [es·'te·la] *f* **1.** NÁUT wake **2.** (*de avión*) slipstream, vapor trail **3.** (*rastro*) trail; **dejar una ~ de recuerdos** to leave a lot of memories in one's wake

estelar [es·te·'lar] *adj* **1.** ASTR stellar; **sistema ~** stellar system **2.** (*extraordinario*) **invitado ~** star guest; **programa ~** TV star program

estelaridad [es·te·la·ri·'dad] *f* Chile (*popularidad*) stardom; **tener una gran ~** to be a star

estenografía [es·te·no·ɣra·'fi·a] *f* shorthand

estenografiar [es·te·no·ɣra·fi·'ar] <*1. pres:* estenografío> *vt* to take down in shorthand

estentóreo, -a [es·ten·'to·reo, -a] *adj* (*voz, risa*) booming

estepa [es·'te·pa] *f* GEO steppe

estera [es·'te·ra] *f* matting

estéreo [es·'te·reo] **I.** *adj inf* stereo **II.** *m* stereo

estereofónico, -a [es·te·reo·'fo·ni·ko, -a] *adj* stereophonic

estereotipado, -a [es·te·reo·ti·'pa·do, -a] *adj* stereotyped; **frase estereotipada** hackneyed expression

estereotipo [es·te·reo·'ti·po] *m* stereotype

estéril [es·'te·ril] *adj* **1.** (*persona*) sterile; (*mujer*) infertile **2.** (*tierra*) barren **3.** (*trabajo*) mundane; (*esfuerzo*) useless; (*discusión*) pointless

esterilidad [es·te·ri·li·'dad] *f* **1.** (*de una persona*) sterility **2.** (*tierra*) barrenness

esterilizar [es·te·ri·li·'sar, -'θar] <z→c> *vt* to sterilize

esterilla [es·te·'ri·ja, -ʎa] *f* **1.** (*estera*) mat; **~ eléctrica** electric blanket; **~ del camping** camping mat **2.** *Ecua* (*rejilla*) **silla de ~** wicker chair

esterlina [es·ter·'li·na] *adj* **libra ~** pound sterling

esternón [es·ter·'non] *m* MED sternum, breastbone

estero [es·'te·ro] *m* **1.** *AmL* (*pantano*) bog **2.** *Cuba* (*ría*) estuary **3.** *Chile, Ecua* (*arroyo*) stream **4.** *Ven* (*aguazal*) pool; **estar en el ~** to be up the creek without a paddle

esteroide [es·te·'roi·de] *m* steroid

esteta [es·'te·ta] *mf* esthete

estética [es·'te·ti·ka] *f* esthetics

estético, -a [es·'te·ti·ko, -a] *adj* esthetic; **cirugía estética** plastic [*o* cosmetic] surgery; **no ~** unesthetic

estetoscopio [es·te·tos·'ko·pjo] *m* stethoscope

estiércol [es·'tjer·kol] *m* manure; **sacar el ~** *fig* to do the dirty work

estigma [es·'tiɣ·ma] *m* stigma; (*en el cuerpo*) mark; REL stigmata *pl*

estigmatizar [es·tiɣ·ma·'ti·sar, -θar] <z→c> *vt t.* REL to stigmatize

estilar [es·ti·'lar] **I.** *vt* to usually do **II.** *vr:* ~ **se** to be in fashion

estilista [es·ti·'lis·ta] *mf* **1.** LIT stylist **2.** (*diseño*) designer, stylist

estilístico, -a [es·ti·'lis·ti·ko, -a] *adj* stylistic

estilizar [es·ti·li·'sar, -'θar] <z→c> *vt* to stylize; (*adelgazar*) to make slim

estilo [es·'ti·lo] *m* **1.** *t.* ARTE, LIT (*modo*) style; **~ de la época** COMPUT font style; **al ~ de** in the style of; **~ de vida** lifestyle; **por el ~** like that; **¿estás mal?, pues yo estoy por el ~** are you not feeling well? neither am I; **algo por el ~** something similar **2.** DEP style; **~ libre** freestyle; **~ (de) pecho** breaststroke **3.** LING **~ directo/indirecto** direct/indirect speech

estilográfica [es·ti·lo·'ɣra·fi·ka] *f* fountain pen

estima [es·'ti·ma] *f* esteem; **tener a alguien en mucha ~** to hold sb in high esteem

estimación [es·ti·ma·'sjon, -'θjon] *f* **1.** (*aprecio*) esteem; **~ propia** self-esteem **2.** (*evaluación*) estimate; **~ de ventas** sales forecast

estimado, -a [es·ti·'ma·do, -a] *adj* **1.** (*apreciado*) respected **2.** (*en cartas*) **~ Señor** Dear Sir

estimar [es·ti·'mar] I. *vt* **1.** (*apreciar*) to appreciate, to value; ~ **mucho a alguien** to appreciate sb a lot; ~ **poco a alguien** not to think much of sb; ~ **en demasía** to overrate **2.** (*tasar*) to estimate **3.** (*valorar*) ~ **en algo** to value at sth **4.** (*juzgar*) to judge; **lo estimó oportuno** he/she considered it appropriate; ~ **que...** to consider that... **5.** JUR (*una demanda*) to admit II. *vr:* ~**se 1.** (*apreciarse*) to value each other **2.** (*calcularse*) ~**se en algo** to be valued at sth

estimulante [es·ti·mu·'lan·te] *m* stimulant

estimular [es·ti·mu·'lar] *vt* **1.** (*excitar*) to stimulate; (*en la sexualidad*) to excite, to turn on *inf* **2.** (*animar*) to encourage; ECON to stimulate

estímulo [es·'ti·mu·lo] *m* **1.** (*incentivo*) incentive; ECON boost; ~ **de la exportación** an export incentive **2.** MED stimulus

estío [es·'ti·o] *m elev* summer

estipendio [es·ti·'pen·djo] *m* stipend

esti(p)tiquez [es·ti(p)·ti·'kes, -'keθ] *f AmL* (*estreñimiento*) constipation

estipulación [es·ti·pu·la·'sjon, -'θjon] *f* **1.** (*convenio*) agreement **2.** JUR stipulation

estipular [es·ti·pu·'lar] *vt* **1.** (*acordar*) to stipulate **2.** (*fijar*) to fix

estirado, -a [es·ti·'ra·do, -a] *adj* (*adusto*) severe; (*engreído*) haughty, snooty *inf*

estirar [es·ti·'rar] I. *vi* to stretch; **no estires más que se rompe la cuerda** if you stretch it any more the rope will break II. *vt* **1.** (*alargar*) to stretch out; (*suma*) to spin out; (*un discurso*) to draw out; ~ **el bolsillo** to spin out one's resources **2.** (*alisar*) to smoothen; ~ **la masa** to roll out the dough; **aún tengo que ~ la cama** I still have to make the bed **3.** (*extender*) to stretch **4.** (*tensar*) to tighten; ~ **la piel** to have a face-lift **5.** (*piernas, brazos*) to stretch out; **voy a salir a ~ un poco las piernas** I'm going to stretch my legs a little; ~ **demasiado un músculo** to overstretch a muscle; ~ **el cuello** to crane (one's neck); ~ **la pata** *inf* to kick the bucket *inf* **6.** (*alambre*) to draw III. *vr:* ~**se** to stretch; (*crecer*) to shoot up

estirón [es·ti·'ron] *m* **1.** (*tirón*) pull **2.** (*crecimiento*) **dar un ~** *inf* to shoot up

estirpe [es·'tir·pe] *f* stock; JUR stirps *pl*

estival [es·ti·'βal] *adj* summer

esto ['es·to] *pron dem v.* **éste**

estocada [es·to·'ka·da] *f* **1.** *t.* TAUR lunge **2.** (*herida*) stab wound

Estocolmo [es·to·'kol·mo] *m* Stockholm

estofado [es·to·'fa·do] *m* (meat) stew

estofar [es·to·'far] *vt* **1.** (*guisar*) to stew **2.** (*enguatar*) to quilt

estoico, -a [es·'toi·ko, -a] *adj* stoical

estola [es·'to·la] *f* stole

estomacal [es·to·ma·'kal] *adj* stomach; **trastorno ~** stomach upset

estómago [es·'to·ma·ɣo] *m* stomach; **dolor de ~** stomach-ache; **tener buen ~** *fig* to be

tough; **tener a alguien sentado en el ~** *fig* not to like sb; **se me revolvió el ~** it turned my stomach

Estonia [es·'to·nja] *f* Estonia

estonio, -a [es·'to·njo, -a] *adj, m, f* Estonian

estorbar [es·tor·'βar] I. *vi* **1.** (*obstaculizar*) to get in the way **2.** (*molestar*) to be annoying II. *vt* **1.** (*impedir*) to stop **2.** (*obstaculizar*) to hinder **3.** (*molestar*) to bother

estorbo [es·'tor·βo] *m* **1.** (*molestia*) nuisance; **sal de casa, que sólo eres un ~** leave the house, you're only getting in the way **2.** (*obstáculo*) obstacle

estornino [es·tor·'ni·no] *m* starling

estornudar [es·tor·nu·'dar] *vi* to sneeze

estornudo [es·tor·'nu·do] *m* sneeze

estos ['es·tos] *adj v.* **este, -a**

estrabismo [es·tra·'βis·mo] *m* squint

estrado [es·'tra·do] *m* dais; ~ **del testigo** JUR witness box; **citar a alguien para ~s** to subpoena [*o* call as a witness]

estrafalario, -a [es·tra·fa·'la·rjo, -a] *adj inf* **1.** (*ropa*) shabby **2.** (*extravagante*) outlandish; (*ridículo*) preposterous

estragar <g→gu> [es·tra·'ɣar] *vt* **1.** (*dañar*) to damage **2.** (*embotar*) to numb; (*gusto*) to pervert

estrago [es·'tra·ɣo] *m* damage; **hacer grandes ~s en la población civil** to wreak havoc upon the civil population

estragón [es·tra·'ɣon] *m* tarragon

estrambótico, -a [es·tram·'bo·ti·ko, -a] *adj* eccentric

estramonio [es·tra·'mo·njo] *m* thorn apple

estrangulación [es·tran·gu·la·'sjon, -'θjon] *f t.* MED strangulation; ~ **de intestinos** strangulation of the intestines

estrangulador [es·tran·gu·la·'dor] *m* AUTO ~ **de aire** choke; TEC throttle

estrangulador(a) [es·tran·gu·la·'dor, -·'do·ra] *m(f)* (*asesino*) strangler

estrangulamiento [es·tran·gu·la·'mjen·to] *m* **1.** (*de persona*) strangulation **2.** (*estorbo*) blockage **3.** (*estrechamiento*) bottleneck

estrangular [es·tran·gu·'lar] I. *vt* **1.** (*asesinar*) to strangle **2.** MED to strangulate **3.** TÉC to throttle II. *vr:* ~**se** to be strangled

estraperlista [es·tra·per·'lis·ta] *mf* black marketeer

estraperlo [es·tra·'per·lo] *m* **1.** (*tráfico*) black market; **adquirir algo de ~** to buy sth on the black market **2.** (*mercancía*) black market goods *pl*

Estrasburgo [es·tras·'βur·ɣo] *m* Strasbourg

estratagema [es·tra·ta·'xe·ma] *m* **1.** (*artimaña*) ploy **2.** MIL strategy

estratega [es·tra·'te·ɣa] *mf* strategist

estrategia [es·tra·'te·xja] *f* strategy

estratégico, -a [es·tra·'te·xi·ko, -a] *adj* strategic

estrato [es·'tra·to] *m t.* GEO stratum; ~ **social** social stratum

estrechamente [es·tre·tʃa·'men·te] *adv*

1.(*pobremente*) in austerity; **vivimos ~ we barely make ends meet 2.**(*íntimamente*) closely **3.**(*rigurosamente*) strictly

estrechar [es·tre·'t∫ar] I. *vt* **1.**(*angostar*) to narrow; (*ropa*) to take in **2.**(*abrazar*) to hug; (*la mano*) to shake **3.**(*amistad*) to deepen **4.**(*obligar*) to oblige II. *vr:* **~ se 1.**(*camino*) to become narrower **2.** *inf* (*en un asiento*) to squeeze in **3.**(*dos personas*) to become close; **~ se las manos** to shake hands **4.**(*amistad*) to deepen **5.**(*económicamente*) to live on a minimum

estrechez [es·tre·'t∫es, -'t∫eθ] *f* **1.**(*espacial*) narrowness; **~ de espíritu** mean-spiritedness **2.**(*rigidez*) strictness **3.**(*de amistad*) deepening **4.**(*escasez*) shortage; (*apuro*) jam; **~ de dinero** lack of money **5.** *pl* (*económicamente*) neediness

estrecho [es·'tre·t∫o] *m* GEO strait

estrecho, -a [es·'tre·t∫o, -a] *adj* **1.**(*angosto*) narrow; **él es muy ~ de caderas** he has very narrow hips; **hacérselas pasar estrechas a alguien** *inf* to give sb a hard time **2.**(*amistad*) close **3.**(*ropa, lugar*) tight **4.**(*rígido*) strict **5.** *inf* (*sexualmente*) prudish

estregar [es·tre·'ɣar] *irr como fregar* I. *vt* **1.**(*frotar*) to rub; (*cepillar, para limpiar*) to scrub **2.**(*sacar brillo*) to shine II. *vr:* **la ~ se** to rub

estrella [es·'tre·ja, -ʎa] *f* **1.**ASTR, CINE star; **~ fija** fixed star; **~ fugaz** shooting star; **~ de Venus** the planet Venus; **una nueva ~ del teatro** a new star of the stage; **querer contar las ~s** *fig* to aim for the moon; **poner a alguien por las ~s** to praise sb to the skies; **ver las ~s** (**de dolor**) *fig* to see stars **2.**(*destino*) fate; **tener buena/mala ~** to be lucky/unlucky **3.** TIPO asterisk **4.** ZOOL **~ de mar** starfish

estrellado, -a [es·tre·'ja·do, -a; es·tre·'ʎa-] *adj* **1.**(*esteliforme*) star-shaped **2.**(*noche, cielo*) starry; **cielo ~** starry sky **3.**(*avión*) crashed

estrellar [es·tre·'jar, -'ʎar] I. *adj* star II. *vt* (*romper*) to smash; (*arrojar*) to hurl; **~ huevos en una sartén** to break eggs in a frying pan III. *vr:* **~ se 1.**(*chocar*) **~ se contra** [*o* en] **algo** to crash into sth; **~ se con alguien** *fig* to bump into sb **2.**(*avión*) to crash; (*barco*) to break up; (*globo*) to burst; **~ se contra** [*o* en] **algo** to collide with sth **3.**(*fracasar*) to fail

estremecedor(a) [es·tre·me·se·'dor, -'do·ra, es·tre·me·θe-] *adj* **1.**(*emoción*) moving **2.**(*horrible*) harrowing

estremecer [es·tre·me·'ser, -'θer] *irr como crecer* I. *vt* **1.**(*conmover*) to move **2.**(*hacer tiritar*) to make tremble II. *vr:* **~ se 1.**(*por un suceso, de un susto*) to be shocked; **se estremecieron sus creencias** his/her/their beliefs were rocked **2.**(*temblar*) to shiver

estremecimiento [es·tre·me·si·'mjen·to, -θi·'mjen·to] *m* **1.**(*emoción*) shock **2.**(*de cañonazo, terremoto*) rumble **3.**(*de frío, miedo*) shivering **4.**(*de susto*) shock

estrenar [es·tre·'nar] I. *vt* **1.**(*usar*) to use for the first time; (*ropa*) to wear for the first time; (*edificio*) to inaugurate; **~ un piso** to move into a new flat; **sin ~** brand new **2.** CINE, TEAT première **3.**(*trabajo*) to start; **~ un cargo** to have one's first day in a job II. *vr:* **~ se 1.**(*carrera artística*) to make one's debut **2.**CINE, TEAT to be premièred **3.**(*trabajo*) to open, to start work

estreno [es·'tre·no] *m* **1.**(*uso*) first use; (*edificio*) opening; **~ de piso** housewarming; **ser de ~** to be brand new **2.**(*de un actor, un músico*) debut; (*de una obra*) première

estreñido, -a [es·tre·'ɲi·do, -a] *adj* constipated

estreñimiento [es·tre·ɲi·'mjen·to] *m* constipation

estreñir [es·tre·'ɲir] *irr como ceñir vt* (*comida*) to constipate; **las judías me estriñen** green beans give me constipation

estrépito [es·'tre·pi·to] *m* **1.**(*ruido*) din; **reírse con ~** to laugh loudly **2.**(*ostentación*) fanfare; **con gran ~** ostentatiously

estrepitoso, -a [es·tre·pi·'to·so, -a] *adj* (*risa, aplausos*) loud; (*fracaso*) spectacular

estrés [es·'tres] *m* stress; **producir ~** to be stressful

estresante [es·tre·'san·te] *adj* stressful

estresar [es·tre·'sar] *vt* to stress

estría [es·'tri·a] *f pl* (*rayas*) grooves *pl*; **~ s del embarazo** stretch marks *pl* from pregnancy

estribar [es·tri·'βar] *vi* to lie; **nuestro éxito estriba en nuestra larga experiencia** our success is due to our lengthy experience

estribillo [es·tri·'βi·jo, -ʎo] *m* **1.** MÚS chorus **2.** LIT refrain **3.**(*frase*) catchphrase; **siempre (con) el mismo ~** *fig* always the same old story

estribo [es·'tri·βo] *m* **1.**(*de jinete*) stirrup; **estar sobre los ~s** *fig* to be careful; **perder los ~s** *fig* to fly off the handle **2.**(*del coche*) running board; (*de moto*) footrest **3.**(*entibo*) buttress **4.**(*respaldo*) grip

estribor [es·tri·'βor] *m* NÁUT starboard

estricto, -a [es·'trik·to, -a] *adj* **1.**(*severo*) strict **2.**(*exacto*) exact

estridente [es·tri·'den·te] *adj* shrill; (*vestir*) loud

estripazón [es·tri·pa·'son, -'θon] *m AmC* **1.**(*apertura*) opening **2.**(*destrozo*) mutilation

estrofa [es·'tro·fa] *f* (*de poema*) stanza; (*de canción*) verse

estrógeno [es·'tro·xe·no] *m* estrogen

estroncio [es·'tron·sjo, -θjo] *m* strontium

estropajo [es·tro·'pa·xo] *m* (*de fregar*) scourer; **poner a alguien como un ~** to lay into sb; **servir de ~** *fig* to work like a slave

estropear [es·tro·pe·'ar] I. *vt* **1.**(*deteriorar: planes, comida*) to spoil; (*televisor*) to break; (*cosecha*) to ruin; **con lo que dijiste, lo has estropeado todo** by saying that, you have ruined everything **2.**(*aspecto*) to spoil; **desde la muerte de su mujer está muy estropeado** since his wife died he looks terrible II. *vr:* **~ se 1.**(*deteriorarse*) to spoil **2.**(*averiarse*) to break down; (*comida*) to go off; (*planes*) to be

spoiled
estructura [es·truk·'tu·ra] *f* structure; (*edificio*) framework
estructural [es·truk·tu·'ral] *adj* structural; **problemas ~es** structural [*o* organizational] problems *pl*
estructurar [es·truk·tu·'rar] **I.** *vt* to structure; (*clasificar*) to classify **II.** *vr:* ~**se** to be structured
estruendo [es·'trwen·do] *m* **1.** (*ruido*) din **2.** (*alboroto*) uproar **3.** (*ostentación*) ostentation
estruendoso, -a [es·trwen·'do·so, -a] *adj* deafening; (*aplauso*) thunderous
estrujar [es·tru·'xar] **I.** *vt* **1.** (*apretar, naranja*) to squeeze **2.** (*machacar*) to crush; (*papel*) to crumple up **3.** (*al saludar*) to hug **II.** *vr:* ~**se** **1.** (*entre mucha gente*) to push **2.** (*apretujarse*) to squeeze together; ~**se los sesos** *inf* to rack one's brains
estuche [es·'tu·ʧe] *m* case; (*cajita*) little box; ~ **de gafas** glasses case; ~ **de joyas** jewel box; ~ **de violín** violin case
estudiante [es·tu·'djan·te] *mf* **1.** (*de universidad*) student; ~ **de ciencias** science student **2.** (*de escuela*) pupil
estudiantil [es·tu·djan·'til] *adj* student; **movimiento** ~ student movement
estudiar [es·tu·'djar] **I.** *vi, vt* **1.** (*aprender, observar*) to study; ~ **para médico** to study to be a doctor; **dejar de** ~ to drop out **2.** (*analizar*) to analyze, to study **II.** *vt* **1.** (*reflexionar*) to think about; **lo** ~ **é** I'll think about it **2.** (*obra de teatro*) to learn
estudio [es·'tu·djo] *m* **1.** (*trabajo intelectual*) studying **2.** (*ensayo, obra*) study; (*informe*) report; (*investigación*) research; ~ **de impacto ambiental** environmental impact study; **estar en** ~ to be under study **3.** MÚS etude **4.** ARTE, TV studio; ~ **cinematográfico** cinema studio; ~ **radiofónico** radio studio; ~ **de registro de sonido** sound studio **5.** MED (*prueba*) test **6.** (*taller*) studio **7.** *pl* (*carrera*) studies *pl;* **cursar** ~**s** to study; **tener** ~**s** to have an education
estudioso, -a [es·tu·'djo·so, -a] **I.** *adj* studious **II.** *m, f* scholar
estufa [es·'tu·fa] *f* heater; ~ **eléctrica** electric fire [*o* heater]
estupefacción [es·tu·pe·fak·'sjon, -faɣ·'θjon] *f* **1.** (*asombro*) amazement; (*sorpresa*) surprise **2.** (*espanto*) fright **3.** MED stupefaction
estupefaciente [es·tu·pe·fa·'sjen·te, -'θjen·te] *m* MED narcotic; (*droga*) drug
estupefacto, -a [es·tu·pe·'fak·to, -a] *adj* **1.** (*atónito*) amazed **2.** (*espantado*) shocked
estupendo, -a [es·tu·'pen·do, -a] *adj* fantastic; ¡~! great!
estupidez [es·tu·pi·'des, -'deθ] *f* stupidity
estúpido, -a [es·'tu·pi·do, -a] **I.** *adj* stupid **II.** *m, f* idiot
estupor [es·tu·'por] *m* **1.** (*asombro*) amazement **2.** (*espanto*) shock

estupro [es·'tu·pro] *m* JUR rape
esturión [es·tu·'rjon] *m* sturgeon
esvástica [es·'βas·ti·ka] *f* swastika
etapa [e·'ta·pa] *f* (*fase*) stage; (*época*) phase; **por** ~ **s** in stages; **quemar** ~ **s** *fig* to come along quickly; **quemar** ~ **s con el coche** *fig* to speed along
etarra [e·'ta·rra] **I.** *adj* **un comando** ~ an ETA cell **II.** *mf* ETA member
etc. [et·'se·te·ra, et·'θe-] *abr de* **etcétera** etc.
etcétera [et·'se·te·ra, et·'θe-] etcetera
éter ['e·ter] *m* ether
etéreo, -a [e·'te·reo, -a] *adj* ethereal
eternidad [e·ter·ni·'dad] *f* eternity; **tardar una** ~ to take a lifetime
eternizar <z→c> [e·ter·ni·'sar, -'θar] **I.** *vt* to make last forever; *pey* (*alargar*) to spin out **II.** *vr:* ~**se** to take ages; ~**se en algo** to take ages doing sth
eterno, -a [e·'ter·no, -a] *adj* eternal; (*discurso*) long-winded
ética ['e·ti·ka] *f* **1.** *t.* FILOS (*moral*) ethics; ~ **profesional** professional code of conduct **2.** (*decencia*) decency; **no tener** ~ to have no sense of decency
ético, -a ['e·ti·ko, -a] *adj* ethical
etílico, -a [e·'ti·li·ko, -a] *adj* **1.** QUÍM ethyl **2.** (*alcohólico*) alcoholic; **borrachera etílica** drunkenness; **en estado** ~ drunk
etimología [e·ti·mo·lo·'xi·a] *f* etymology
etimológico, -a [e·ti·mo·'lo·xi·ko, -a] *adj* etymological
etíope [e·'ti·o·pe] *adj, mf* Ethiopian
Etiopía [e·tjo·'pi·a] *f* Ethiopia
etiqueta [e·ti·'ke·ta] *f* **1.** (*rótulo*) label; ~ **del precio** price tag **2.** (*convenciones*) etiquette; ~ **de la red** netiquette; ~ **de palacio** court etiquette; **de** ~ (*solemne*) formal; (*ceremonioso*) ceremonial; **función de** ~ formal function; **traje de** ~ formal [*o* evening] dress; **ir de** ~ *inf* to be dressed up
etiquetar [e·ti·ke·'tar] *vt* to label; (*encasillar*) to stereotype
etnia ['ed·nja] *f* (*pueblo*) ethnic group
étnico, -a ['et·ni·ko, -a] *adj* ethnic
etnología [et·no·lo·'xi·a] *f* ethnology
eucalipto [eu·ka·'lip·to] *m* eucalyptus
eucaristía [eu·ka·ris·'ti·a] *f* Eucharist
eufemismo [eu·fe·'mis·mo] *m* euphemism
euforia [eu·'fo·rja] *f* euphoria
eufórico, -a [eu·'fo·ri·ko, -a] *adj* euphoric
Eurasia [eu·'ra·sja] *f* Eurasia
euro ['eu·ro] *m* euro
Europa [eu·'ro·pa] *f* Europe
europarlamentario, -a [eu·ro·par·la·men·'ta·rjo, -a] *m, f* member of the European Parliament, MEP
europeidad [eu·ro·pei·'dad] *f* Europeanness
europeísmo [eu·ro·pe·'is·mo] *m* Europeanism
europeísta [eu·ro·pe·'is·ta] *adj, mf* pro-European
europeizar [eu·ro·pei·'sar, -'θar] *irr como*

enraizar vt to Europeanize

europeo, -a [eu·ro·'peo, -a] **I.** *adj* European; **Consejo Europeo** Council of Europe **II.** *m, f* European

eurotúnel [eu·ro·'tu·nel] *m* Channel tunnel

euscaldún, -una [eus·kal·'dun, -·'du·na] *adj* Basque-speaking

Euskadi [eus·'ka·di] *m* Basque Provinces

euskera [eus·'ke·ra] *m*, **eusquera** [eus·'ke·ra] *m* Basque language

eutanasia [eu·ta·'na·sja] *f* euthanasia, mercy killing

evacuación [e·βa·kwa·'sjon, -'θjon] *f* **1.**(*personas, edificios*) evacuation **2.** MED excretion

evacuar [e·βa·'kwar] *vt* **1.**(*ciudad, población*) to evacuate **2.**(*diligencias, trámites*) to carry out; (*deber*) to fulfill; (*consulta*) to perform; (*negocio, trato*) to conclude **3.** MED ~ (**el vientre**) to have a bowel movement

evadir [e·βa·'dir] **I.** *vt* (*evitar: problema, persona*) to avoid; (*peligro, riesgo*) to avert; ~ **la mirada de alguien** to avoid sb's gaze **II.** *vr:* ~**se** to get away

evaluación [e·βa·lwa·'sjon, -'θjon] *f* **1.**(*valoración*) valuation **2.** ENS assessment; (*examen*) exam(ination)

evaluar < *I. pres:* evalúo> [e·βa·lu·'ar] *vt* **1.**(*valorar*) to value **2.**(*apreciar*) ~ **en algo** to price at sth **3.**(*analizar*) *t.* ENS to assess

evangélico, -a [e·βan·'xe·li·ko, -a] **I.** *adj* evangelical **II.** *m, f* evangelist

evangelio [e·βan·'xe·ljo] *m* Gospel; **el Evangelio según San Mateo** the Gospel according to St Matthew; **decir el** ~ *fig* to speak the truth

evaporación [e·βa·po·ra·'sjon, -'θjon] *f* evaporation

evaporar [e·βa·po·'rar] **I.** *vt* (*convertir en vapor*) to evaporate **II.** *vr:* ~**se 1.**(*convertirse en vapor*) to evaporate **2.**(*desaparecer*) to vanish; (*persona*) to disappear into thin air

evasión [e·βa·'sjon] *f* evasion; ~ **de impuestos** ECON tax evasion; (*fuga*) escape; **lectura de** ~ escapist literature; ~ **de la realidad** escape from reality

evasiva [e·βa·'si·βa] *f* **1.**(*rodeo*) evasions *pl;* **dar** ~**s** to hedge **2.**(*pretexto*) excuse **3.**(*escapatoria*) way out

evasivo, -a [e·βa·'si·βo, -a] *adj* evasive; (*ambiguo*) ambiguous, non-committal

evento [e·'βen·to] *m* **1.**(*incidente*) incident, event; **a todo** ~ in any event; ~ **social** social event **2.** DEP meeting

eventual [e·βen·'twal] *adj* **1.**(*posible*) possible; (*accidental*) fortuitous; (*provisional*) temporary; **trabajo** ~ casual job **2.**(*adicional*) extra; **ingresos** ~**es** extra income

eventualidad [e·βen·twa·li·'dad] *f* **1.**(*cualidad*) contingency **2.**(*inseguridad*) insecurity **3.**(*hecho*) eventuality

eventualmente [e·βen·twal·'men·te] *adv* fortuitously; (*tal vez*) possibly

evidencia [e·βi·'den·sja, -θja] *f* (*certidumbre*)

evidence; **poner algo en** ~ (*probar*) to prove sth; (*hacer claro*) to make sth clear; **poner a alguien en** ~ to make sb look bad

evidenciar [e·βi·den·'sjar, -'θjar] *vt* (*demostrar*) to show; (*patentizar*) to indicate

evidente [e·βi·'den·te] *adj* evident; (*pruebas*) manifest

evidentemente [e·βi·den·te·'men·te] *adv* evidently; **¡~!** of course!

evitar [e·βi·'tar] **I.** *vt* **1.**(*prevenir*) to prevent; (*molestias, disgustos*) to avoid; **no pude** ~ **que declarasen** I couldn't keep [*o* prevent] them from testifying; **pude** ~ **mayores estragos** I was able to prevent further damage **2.**(*rehuir*) to avoid; **antes de los exámenes evito salir por la noche** I try not to go out at night before the exams **II.** *vr:* ~**se 1.**(*cosas*) to avoid **2.**(*personas*) to avoid each other

evocación [e·βo·ka·'sjon, -'θjon] *f* **1.**(*de espíritus*) invocation **2.**(*recuerdo*) evocation

evocar <c→qu> [e·βo·'kar] *vt* **1.**(*espíritus*) to invoke **2.**(*recordar*) to evoke; (*revivir*) to relive; **estuvimos toda la tarde evocando nuestra niñez** we spent the whole afternoon remembering our childhood

evolución [e·βo·lu·'sjon, -'θjon] *f* **1.** *t.* MED (*desarrollo*) progress **2.**(*cambio*) transformation; **experimentar una** ~ to undergo a transformation **3.** BIO evolution **4.** MIL maneuver **5.** *pl* (*vueltas*) turns *pl*

evolucionar [e·βo·lu·sjo·'nar, -θjo·'nar] *vi* **1.**(*desarrollarse*) to progress **2.**(*cambiar*) to transform **3.** MED to evolve **4.**(*dar vueltas*) to turn **5.** MIL to maneuver

ex [eks] **I.** *adj* ~ **novia** ex-girlfriend **II.** *mf inf* ex

exacerbar [ek·sa·ser·'βar, ek·sa·θer·] **I.** *vt* **1.**(*dolor*) to intensify; (*crisis*) to deepen, to exacerbate **2.**(*irritar*) to aggravate **II.** *vr:* ~**se 1.**(*dolor*) to intensify; (*crisis*) to deepen **2.**(*irritarse*) to become irritated

exactitud [ek·sak·ti·'tud] *f* **1.**(*precisión*) accuracy **2.**(*veracidad*) exactitude **3.**(*puntualidad*) punctuality

exacto, -a [ek·'sak·to, -a] *adj* **1.**(*con precisión*) accurate; (*al copiar algo*) faithful **2.**(*correcto*) correct; **eso no es del todo** ~ that's not exactly true **3.**(*puntual*) punctual

exageración [ek·sa·xe·ra·'sjon, -'θjon] *f* exaggeration

exagerado, -a [ek·sa·xe·'ra·do, -a] **I.** *adj* exaggerated; (*publicidad*) distorted; (*precio*) steep; (*en los gestos*) theatrical **II.** *m, f* **¡eres un** ~**!** don't exaggerate!

exagerar [ek·sa·xe·'rar] *vi, vt* **1.**(*sobrepasarse*) to exaggerate; ~ **los precios** to charge excessive prices; ~ **los gestos** to behave theatrically; **pienso que ese paso sería** ~ I think such a step would be going too far **2.**(*al relatar*) to exaggerate; **¡anda, anda, no exageres tanto!** *inf* come on, stop exaggerating!

exaltación [ek·sal·ta·'sjon, -'θjon] *f* **1.**(*gloria*) exaltation **2.**(*entusiasmo*) enthusiasm; (*pasión*) fervor; (*excitación*) excitement

exaltado, -a [ek·sal·'ta·do, -a] **I.** *adj* **1.**(*sobreexcitado*) over-excited; (*apasionado*) passionate; (*entusiasmado*) enthusiastic **2.**(*violento*) extreme **3.**(*radical*) radical **II.** *m, f* **1.**(*nervioso*) excitable person **2.** POL extremist **3.**(*loco*) lunatic

exaltar [ek·sal·'tar] **I.** *vt* **1.**(*elevar*) to exalt **2.**(*realzar*) ~ **a alguien** to praise sb **II.** *vr* ~**se con algo** (*apasionarse*) to become excited about sth; (*obsesionarse*) to become obsessed with sth

examen [ek·'sa·men] *m* **1.**(*prueba, reflexión*) examination; ~ **de conciencia** soul-searching; ~ **de conducir** driving test; ~ **de ingreso** entrance exam; ~ **de selectividad** *university entrance exam;* **presentarse a un** ~ to sit for an exam; **tribunal de exámenes** examination board; **aprobar/suspender un** ~ to pass/fail an exam **2.**(*médico*) examination; **someterse a un** ~ to have a check-up **3.** TÉC test; AUTO check **4.**(*estudio*) examination; (*indagación*) research

examinador(a) [ek·sa·mi·na·'dor, -'do·ra] *m(f)* examiner

examinar [ek·sa·mi·'nar] **I.** *vt* **1.** *t.* MED (*poner un examen, reflexionar*) to examine **2.** TÉC, AUTO to inspect **3.**(*estudiar*) to study, to examine; (*observar*) to observe **4.** ADMIN, JUR to examine; **para ~lo** for examination; **al ~lo** upon examination **II.** *vr:* ~**se** (*en una prueba*) to take an exam; **mañana me examino de francés** tomorrow I have a French exam; **volver a** ~**se** to retake an exam

exánime [ek·'sa·ni·me] *adj* **1.**(*inánime*) lifeless **2.**(*debilitado*) weak

exasperación [ek·sas·pe·ra·'sjon, -'θjon] *f* (*ira*) exasperation

exasperante [ek·sas·pe·'ran·te] *adj* exasperating

exasperar [ek·sas·pe·'rar] **I.** *vt* to exasperate **II.** *vr:* ~**se** to get exasperated

excarcelar [es·kar·se·'lar, es·kar·θe·-] *vt* to release from prison

excavación [es·ka·βa·'sjon, -'θjon] *f* excavation; (*arqueológica*) dig

excavadora [es·ka·βa·'do·ra] *f* excavator

excavar [es·ka·'βar] *vt* to excavate; (*en arqueología*) to dig

excedencia [es·e·'den·sja, es·θe·'den·θja] *f* (*laboral*) leave

excedente [e·se·'den·te, es·θe·-] **I.** *adj* **1.**(*sobrante*) surplus **2.**(*funcionario*) redundant; (*temporalmente*) on (extended) leave **II.** *m* surplus; ~ **en la balanza comercial** trade surplus

exceder [e·se·'der, es·θe·-] **I.** *vi* to be greater; ~ **de algo** to exceed sth **II.** *vt* (*aventajar: persona*) to outdo; (*cosa*) to be better than **III.** *vr:* ~**se 1.**(*sobrepasar*) ~**se en algo** to excel at sth; ~**se a sí mismo** to outdo oneself **2.**(*pasarse*) to go too far; **has vuelto a ~te** you've overstepped the mark again; **te excedes en el uso de tacos** you swear too much

excelencia [e·se·'len·sja, es·θe·'len·θja] *f* **1.**(*exquisitez*) excellence; **por** ~ par excellence **2.**(*cargo*) Excellency

excelente [e·se·'len·te, es·θe·-] *adj* excellent

excelentísimo, -a [e·se·len·'ti·si·mo, -a; es·θe-] *adj* honorable; **el** ~ **Ayuntamiento de Cádiz** the Cadiz city council; **el Excelentísimo Señor Presidente** His Excellency, the President

excelso, -a [e·'sel·so, -a; es·'θel-] *adj* (*excelente*) excellent

excentricidad [e·sen·tri·si·'dad, es·θen·tri·θi-] *f* eccentricity; **estoy harta de tus ~es** I've had it up to here with your weirdness

excéntrico, -a [e·'sen·tri·ko, -a; es·'θen-] *adj, m, f* eccentric

excepción [e·sep·'sjon, es·θeβ·'θjon] *f* exception; ~ **de la regla** exception to the rule; **con** ~ **de algunos casos** with a few exceptions; **sin** ~ (**ninguna**) without exception; **de** ~ unique; **un vino de** ~ an exceptionally good wine; **a** [*o* con] ~ **de** with the exception of; **todo el mundo a** [*o* con] ~ **de mí** everybody except me

excepcional [e·sep·sjo·'nal, es·θeβ·θjo-] *adj* (*extraordinario*) exceptional; (*raro*) unusual

excepto [e·'sep·to, es·'θep-] *adv* except; **todo el mundo** ~ **yo** everybody except me; ~ **algunos casos** with the exception of some cases

exceptuar <*1. pres:* exceptúo> [e·sep·tu·'ar, es·θep-] *vt* to except; ~ **de un deber** to release sb from a duty

excesivo, -a [e·se·'si·βo, -a; es·θe·-] *adj* excessive; **exposición excesiva** FOTO over-exposure

exceso [e·'se·so, -'θe·so] *m* **1.**(*abuso, demasía*) excess; ~ **de alcohol** excessive drinking; ~ **de capacidad** overcapacity; ~ **de demanda** excess demand; ~ **de deudas** too many debts; ~ **de equipaje** excess baggage; ~ **de peso** excess weight; ~ **de velocidad** speeding; **en** ~ in excess; **comer con** [*o* **en**] ~ to overeat; **solía beber hasta el** ~ he/she used to drink to excess **2.** FIN surplus **3.** *pl* (*libertinaje*) indulgence; **en su juventud cometió muchos ~s** in his youth he indulged in a lot of excess **4.** *pl* (*desorden*) chaos

excitable [e·si·'ta·βle, es·θi-] *adj* excitable; (*irritable*) temperamental; **muy** ~ very highly-strung

excitación [e·si·ta·'sjon, es·θi·ta·'θjon] *f* **1.**(*exaltación*) excitement; (*sexual*) arousal **2.**(*irritación*) nervousness **3.**(*incitación*) stimulation

excitar [e·si·'tar, es·θi-] **I.** *vt* **1.**(*incitar*) to incite; (*apetito*) to stimulate **2.**(*poner nervioso*) to put on edge **3.**(*sexualmente*) to arouse **II.** *vr:* ~**se 1.**(*enojarse*) to become agitated, to get all worked up *inf* **2.**(*sexualmente*) to become aroused

exclamación [es·kla·ma·'sjon, -'θjon] *f* **1.**(*frase*) exclamation; **signo de** ~ exclamation mark **2.**(*grito*) cry; **lanzar una** ~ **de sorpresa** to cry out in surprise

exclamar [es·kla·'mar] *vi, vt* **1.** (*declamar*) to exclaim **2.** (*gritar*) to cry

excluir [es·klu·'ir] *irr como huir vt* **1.** (*expulsar, eliminar*) to exclude; (*descartar*) to rule out **2.** (*rechazar*) to reject

exclusión [es·klu·'sjon] *f* **1.** (*eliminación*) exclusion; **con ~ de** excluding; **con ~ de la prensa** press-free **2.** (*expulsión*) expulsion **3.** (*rechazo*) rejection

exclusiva [es·klu·'si·βa] *f* **1.** (*privilegio*) sole rights *pl* **2.** (*monopolio*) monopoly **3.** PREN exclusive; (*primicia*) scoop

exclusivamente [es·klu·si·βa·'men·te] *adv* exclusively

exclusive [es·klu·'si·βe] *adv* exclusively; **cerrado hasta el 27 de agosto ~** closed up to and including the 26th of August

exclusivo, -a [es·klu·'si·βo, -a] *adj* exclusive; **contrato/modelo ~** exclusive contract/model

Excma. [e·se·len·'ti·si·ma, es·θe-] *adj abr de* **excelentísima** honorable

Excmo. [e·se·len·'ti·si·mo, es·θe-] *adj abr de* **excelentísimo** honorable

excomulgar <g→gu> [es·ko·mul·'ɣar] *vt* REL to excommunicate

excomunión [es·ko·mu·'njon] *f* REL excommunication

excoriación [es·ko·rja·'sjon, -'θjon] *f* graze

excremento [es·kre·'men·to] *m* excretion

exculpar [es·kul·'par] **I.** *vt* JUR to acquit **II.** *vr:* **~ se** to be acquitted

excursión [es·kur·'sjon] *f* **1.** (*paseo*) excursion, trip; **~ a pie** hike; **ir de ~** to go on an excursion [*o* outing] **2.** (*de estudios*) field trip

excursionista [es·kur·sjo·'nis·ta] *mf* day-tripper, excursionist; (*a pie*) hiker; (*turista*) sightseer

excusa [es·'ku·sa] *f* **1.** (*pretexto*) excuse **2.** (*disculpa*) apology; **presentar sus ~s** to apologize **3.** (*justificación*) justification

excusable [es·ku·'sa·βle] *adj* justifiable

excusar [es·ku·'sar] **I.** *vt* **1.** (*justificar*) to justify **2.** (*disculpar*) to excuse **3.** (*eximir*) to let off **4.** (*evitar*) to avoid **5.** (+ *inf*) **excusas venir** you don't have to come **II.** *vr* **~se de algo** to apologize for sth

exención [ek·sen·'sjon, -'θjon] *f* exemption; **~ de derechos de aduana** exemption from import/export duty; **~ de impuestos** tax exemption; **~ del servicio militar** exemption from military service

exento, -a [ek·'sen·to, -a] *adj* exempt, free; **~ de aranceles** duty-free; **~ de averías** free of breakdowns; **~ de impuestos** tax free; **~ de mantenimiento** free of maintenance; **rentas exentas del impuesto** tax-free income; **estar ~ de la jurisdicción local** to be beyond local jurisdiction

exfoliar [es·fo·'ljar] **I.** *vt* to exfoliate; **la falta de humedad exfolia la piel** lack of moisture dries out the skin **II.** *vr:* **~se** (*pintura*) to peel; (*corteza*) to flake

exhalación [ek·sa·la·'sjon, -'θjon] *f* (*aire*) exhalation

exhalar [ek·sa·'lar] **I.** *vt* **1.** (*aire*) to exhale, to breathe out **2.** (*emanar*) to give off **3.** (*suspiros, quejas*) to let out **II.** *vr* **~se** to hurry

exhaustivo, -a [ek·saus·'ti·βo, -a] *adj* exhaustive; **de forma exhaustiva** thoroughly

exhausto, -a [ek·'saus·to, -a] *adj* exhausted

exhibición [ek·si·βi·'sjon, -'θjon] *f* **1.** (*ostentación*) display **2.** (*exposición*) exhibition **3.** (*presentación*) show; **~ cinematográfica** film festival; **~ deportiva** sports festival

exhibicionismo [ek·si·βi·sjo·'nis·mo, -θjo·'nis·mo] *m* **1.** (*sexual*) indecent exposure, flashing *inf* **2.** (*deseo de exhibirse*) showing-off

exhibicionista [ek·si·βi·sjo·'nis·ta, -θjo·'nis·ta] *mf* **1.** (*sexual*) flasher **2.** (*presuntuoso*) show-off

exhibir [ek·si·'βir] **I.** *vt* **1.** (*mostrar*) to exhibit **2.** (*ostentar*) to show off **3.** JUR to show **II.** *vr:* **~se** to put on a show; **~se en público** to expose oneself

exhortación [ek·sor·ta·'sjon, -'θjon] *f* **1.** (*ruego*) exhortation **2.** (*amonestación*) warning

exhortar [ek·sor·'tar] *vt* **1.** (*rogar*) to exhort **2.** (*amonestar*) to warn

exhumar [ek·su·'mar] *vt* **1.** (*cadáver*) to exhume **2.** (*recordar*) to relive

exigencia [ek·si·'xen·sja, -θja] *f* **1.** (*demanda*) demand; **tener ~s** *inf* to be very demanding **2.** (*requisito*) requirement

exigente [ek·si·'xen·te] *adj* demanding

exigible [ek·si·'xi·βle] *adj* (*obligación*) enforceable; JUR payable on demand

exigir <g→j> [ek·si·'xir] *vt* **1.** (*solicitar*) to ask for, to demand; **el docente exige demasiado** the teacher is asking for too much **2.** (*reclamar, pedir*) to demand; **la carta exige contestación** the letter needs to be answered

exil(i)ado, -a [ek·si·'la·do/ek·si·'lja·do, -a] **I.** *adj* exiled **II.** *m, f* exile

exil(i)ar [ek·si·'lar/ek·si·'ljar] **I.** *vt* to exile **II.** *vr:* **~se** to go into exile; **muchos chilenos se ~on en España** many Chilean sought exile in Spain

exilio [ek·'si·ljo] *m* exile

eximir [ek·si·'mir] **I.** *vt* to exempt; **~ de obligaciones** to free from obligations; **~ de responsabilidades** to release from responsibilities **II.** *vr:* **~se** to be exempted

existencia [ek·sis·'ten·sja, -θja] *f* **1.** (*vida*) existence **2.** *pl* COM stock; **en ~** in stock; **liquidación de ~s** liquidation of stock; **renovar las ~s** to renew stocks; **en tanto haya ~s** as soon as stocks are in

existencial [ek·sis·ten·'sjal, -'θjal] *adj* existential

existente [ek·sis·'ten·te] *adj* **1.** (*que existe*) existing **2.** COM in stock

existir [ek·sis·'tir] *vi* to exist, to be; **existen numerosas actividades** there are many activities; **cree que existen ovnis** he/she believes

that UFOs exist
éxito ['ek·si·to] *m* success; ~ **de taquilla** box office hit; ~ **de ventas** sales success; **con** ~ successfully; **sin** ~ without success; **tener** ~ to be successful
exitoso, -a [ek·si·'to·so, -a] *adj* successful
éxodo ['ek·so·do] *m* exodus; ~ **rural** rural depopulation; ~ **urbano** urban depopulation; (*de técnicos, científicos, etc.*) brain drain
exonerar [ek·so·ne·'rar] *vt* **1.** (*eximir*) to exempt **2.** (*culpa*) to exonerate **3.** (*relevar*) to relieve; ~ **a alguien de su cargo** to remove sb from his/her position
exorbitante [ek·sor·βi·'tan·te] *adj* **1.** (*excesivo*) excessive; (*precio*) exorbitant **2.** (*exagerado*) exaggerated
exótico, -a [ek·'so·ti·ko, -a] *adj* exotic
exotismo [ek·so·'tis·mo] *m* exoticism
expandir [es·pan·'dir] **I.** *vt* **1.** (*dilatar*) to expand **2.** (*divulgar*) to spread **II.** *vr:* ~**se** **1.** (*dilatarse*) to expand **2.** (*extenderse, divulgarse*) to spread
expansión [es·pan·'sjon] *f* **1.** (*dilatación*) expansion; POL enlargement **2.** (*extensión*) extension **3.** (*crecimiento*) growth **4.** (*difusión*) spread **5.** (*diversión*) recreation
expansionarse [es·pan·sjo·'nar·se] *vr* **1.** (*dilatarse*) to expand **2.** *inf* (*sincerarse*) to talk openly **3.** *inf* (*divertirse*) to relax
expansivo, -a [es·pan·'si·βo, -a] *adj* (*dilatable*) expansive
expatriar < *1. pres:* expatrío> [es·pa·tri·'ar] **I.** *vt* **1.** (*exiliar*) to exile **2.** (*quitar la ciudadanía*) to deprive of citizenship **II.** *vr:* ~**se** **1.** (*exiliarse*) to go into exile **2.** (*renunciar a la ciudadanía*) to renounce one's citizenship
expectación [es·pek·ta·'sjon, -'θjon] *f* **1.** (*expectativa*) expectation; **con** ~ expectantly **2.** (*emoción*) excitement
expectante [es·pek·'tan·te] *adj* (*atento*) expectant
expectativa [es·pek·ta·'ti·βa] *f* **1.** (*expectación*) expectation; **estar a la** ~ **de algo** to be on the lookout for sth **2.** (*perspectiva*) prospect; ~ **de vida** life expectancy
expectorar [es·pek·to·'rar] *vt* to expectorate
expedición [es·pe·di·'sjon, -'θjon] *f* **1.** (*viaje*) expedition; ~ **científica** scientific expedition; ~ **militar** military expedition **2.** (*grupo*) expedition **3.** (*remesa*) shipment; (*acción*) shipping; (**empresa de**) ~ shipping agent; **oficina de** ~ issuing [*o* shipping] office **4.** (*documento*) issue
expediente [es·pe·'djen·te] *m* **1.** (*asunto judicial*) proceedings *pl;* **instruir un** ~ to open proceedings **2.** (*legajo*) file; (*sumario*) record; ~ **académico** academic [*o* student] record **3.** (*administrativo*) file **4.** (*trámite*) requirement; **cubrir el** ~ *inf* to keep up appearances
expedir [es·pe·'dir] *irr como pedir vt* **1.** (*carta*) to send; (*pedido*) to ship; ~ **por avión** to send by air mail; ~ **por correo** to send by mail **2.** (*documento*) to issue

expeditar [es·pe·di·'tar] *vt* **1.** *AmL* (*acelerar*) to speed up **2.** *AmC, Méx* (*despachar*) to send
expeler [es·pe·'ler] *vt* (*sangre, excreto*) to expel; (*aire, humo*) to give out
expendedor [es·pen·de·'dor] *m* ~ **automático** vending machine; ~ **de bebidas/cigarrillos** soft drink/cigarette vending machine
expendedor(a) [es·pen·de·'dor, -'do·ra] **I.** *adj* **máquina** ~**a de billetes/tabaco** ticket/cigarette vending machine **II.** *m(f)* vendor
expendio [es·'pen·djo] *m And, Méx, Ven* (*estanco*) shop
expensas [es·'pen·sas] *fpl* costs *pl;* **a** ~ **de** at the expense of; **vivir a** ~ **de alguien** to live off sb
experiencia [es·pe·'rjen·sja, -θja] *f* **1.** (*práctica, vivencia*) experience; ~ **docente** teaching experience; **falta de** ~ **laboral** lack of work experience; **saber algo por** ~ **propia** to know sth from experience **2.** (*experimento*) experiment
experimentado, -a [es·pe·ri·men·'ta·do, -a] *adj* **1.** (*con experiencia*) experienced **2.** (*comprobado*) tested; **no** ~ **en animales** (*en etiquetas*) not tested on animals
experimental [es·pe·ri·men·'tal] *adj* experimental
experimentar [es·pe·ri·men·'tar] **I.** *vi* to experiment **II.** *vt* **1.** (*sentir*) to experience **2.** (*hacer experimentos*) to experiment with; (*probar*) to test **3.** (*sufrir*) to register; ~ **un alza** to register a rise; ~ **un aumento** to register an increase; ~ **una caída** to register a fall; ~ **una pérdida** to register a loss
experimento [es·pe·ri·'men·to] *m* experiment
experto, -a [es·'per·to, -a] **I.** *adj* expert **II.** *m, f* **1.** (*conocedor*) expert **2.** (*perito*) specialist
expiación [es·pja·'sjon, -'θjon] *f* **1.** (*purgación*) expiation **2.** (*castigo*) serving
expiar < *1. pres:* expío> [es·pi·'ar] *vt* **1.** (*purgar*) to expiate **2.** (*pena*) to serve
expirar [es·pi·'rar] *vi* **1.** (*morir*) to expire; (*cultura*) to die out **2.** (*plazo*) to expire; **antes de** ~ **el mes** before the end of the month
explanada [es·pla·'na·da] *f* (*espacio*) flat area
explanar [es·pla·'nar] *vt* **1.** (*allanar*) to level, to grade **2.** (*explicar*) to explain
explayar [es·pla·'jar] **I.** *vt* to extend; ~ **la mirada** to look around **II.** *vr:* ~**se** **1.** (*extenderse*) to spread **2.** (*expresarse*) to speak at length; ~**se con alguien** (*confiarse*) to talk openly to sb **3.** (*divertirse*) to enjoy oneself
explicable [es·pli·'ka·βle] *adj* **1.** (*que se puede explicar*) explicable, explainable **2.** (*comprensible*) understandable
explicación [es·pli·ka·'sjon, -'θjon] *f* **1.** (*aclaración*) explanation; **pedir explicaciones** to ask for explanations **2.** (*motivo*) reason; **sin dar explicaciones** without giving reasons **3.** (*interpretación*) interpretation **4.** *pl* (*excusas*) reason; **dar explicaciones** to justify
explicar <c→qu> [es·pli·'kar] **I.** *vt* **1.** (*manifestar*) to tell **2.** (*aclarar, exponer*) to explain

3. (*interpretar*) to interpret **4.** (*justificar*) to justify **II.** *vr:* ~**se 1.** (*comprender*) to understand; **no me lo explico** I don't understand it **2.** (*disculparse*) to apologize **3.** (*articularse*) to express oneself; **¿me explico?** do I make myself clear?; **ella se explica muy bien** she expresses herself very clearly

explicativo, -a [es·pli·ka·'ti·βo, -a] *adj* explanatory

explícito, -a [es·'pli·si·to, -a; -θi·to, -a] *adj* explicit

exploración [es·plo·ra·'sjon, -'θjon] *f* **1.** MIL reconnaissance (mission) **2.** MED examination **3.** (*investigación*) exploration

explorador(a) [es·plo·ra·'dor] **I.** *adj* **1.** MIL reconnaissance **2.** (*investigador*) explorative **II.** *m(f)* **1.** MIL scout **2.** (*scout*) Boy Scout *m*, Girl Scout *f* **3.** (*investigador*) explorer

explorar [es·plo·'rar] *vt* **1.** MIL to reconnoiter **2.** MED to analyze **3.** (*investigar*) to explore

explosión [es·plo·'sjon] *f* **1.** (*estallido*) explosion, boom; ~ **demográfica** population boom; **motor de** ~ internal combustion engine; **hacer** ~ to explode **2.** (*detonación*) detonation; (*voladura*) blasting; ~ **fallida** dud **3.** (*arrebato*) outburst; ~ **de carcajadas** guffaw

explosionar [es·plo·sjo·'nar] *vi, vt* to explode

explosivo [es·plo·'si·βo] *m* explosive

explosivo, -a [es·plo·'si·βo, -a] *adj* explosive; **artefacto** ~ explosive device

explotación [es·plo·ta·'sjon, -'θjon] *f* **1.** (*aprovechamiento*) exploitation; AGR plantation; MIN working; ~ **abusiva** exploitation; ~ **a cielo abierto** opencast mining; ~ **de la energía** harnessing of energy; ~ **minera** mine **2.** (*empresa*) management **3.** (*abuso*) exploitation

explotar [es·plo·'tar] **I.** *vi* **1.** (*estallar*) to explode; ~ **en carcajadas** to burst out laughing **2.** (*tener un arrebato*) to blow up *inf* **II.** *vt* **1.** (*recursos, terreno*) to exploit; AGR to cultivate; MIN to exploit; ~ **pozos petrolíferos** to exploit oil wells **2.** (*empresa*) to manage **3.** (*abusar*) to exploit

expoliar [es·po·'ljar] *vt* to ransack

expolio [es·'po·ljo] *m* **1.** (*acción*) ransacking **2.** (*botín*) loot **3.** *inf* (*alboroto*) din

exponente [es·po·'nen·te] *m* **1.** (*ejemplo*) example; (*índice*) index **2.** MAT exponent

exponer [es·po·'ner] *irr como* **poner I.** *vt* **1.** (*mostrar*) to show, to display **2.** (*hablar*) to set out **3.** (*exhibir*) to exhibit **4.** (*proponer*) to put forward **5.** (*explicar*) to explain **6.** (*arriesgar*) to endanger **7.** (*abandonar*) to abandon **8.** FOTO to expose **II.** *vr:* ~**se 1.** (*descubrirse*) to expose oneself **2.** (*arriesgarse*) to endanger oneself

exportación [es·por·ta·'sjon, -'θjon] *f* export

exportador(a) [es·por·ta·'dor, -'do·ra] **I.** *adj* exporting **II.** *m(f)* exporter

exportar [es·por·'tar] *vt* to export

exposición [es·po·si·'sjon, -'θjon] *f* **1.** (*expli-*

cación) explanation **2.** (*informe*) report **3.** (*exhibición*) exhibition; ~ **universal** world('s) fair **4.** FOTO exposure

expósito, -a [es·'po·si·to, -a] **I.** *adj* abandoned **II.** *m, f* abandoned child, foundling *liter*

expositor(a) [es·po·si·'tor, -·'to·ra] *m(f)* **1.** (*que exhibe*) exhibitor **2.** (*que aclara*) exponent **3.** (*mueble*) display case

exprés [es·'pres] **I.** *adj inv* express; **café** ~ espresso; **olla** ~ pressure cooker **II.** *m* (*tren*) express

expresamente [es·pre·sa·'men·te] *adv* **1.** (*literalmente*) clearly **2.** (*deliberadamente*) expressly

expresar [es·pre·'sar] **I.** *vt* to express **II.** *vr:* ~**se** to express oneself

expresión [es·pre·'sjon] *f* **1.** expression; **reducir a la mínima** ~ to reduce to the bare minimum **2.** *pl* (*saludos*) greetings *pl*

expresionismo [es·pre·sjo·'nis·mo] *m* ARTE expressionism

expresionista [es·pre·sjo·'nis·ta] *adj, mf* expressionist

expresivo, -a [es·pre·'si·βo, -a] *adj* **1.** (*vivo*) expressive **2.** (*revelador*) revealing **3.** (*significativo*) meaningful **4.** (*afectuoso*) affectionate

expreso [es·'pre·so] **I.** *m* **1.** (*tren*) express **2.** (*correo*) special delivery **II.** *adv* express

expreso, -a [es·'pre·so, -a] *adj* **1.** (*explícito*) express **2.** (*claro*) clear **3.** (*rápido*) express; **tren** ~ express train; **enviar una carta por** (*correo*) ~ to send a letter by special delivery

exprimidor [es·pri·mi·'dor] *m* squeezer

exprimir [es·pri·'mir] *vt* **1.** (*frutas*) to squeeze **2.** (*ropa*) to wring **3.** (*persona*) to exploit, to bleed (dry) *inf*

expropiación [es·pro·pja·'sjon, -'θjon] *f* expropriation; ~ **forzosa** compulsory purchase

expropiar [es·pro·'pjar] *vt* to expropriate

expuesto, -a [es·'pwes·to, -a] **I.** *pp de* **exponer II.** *adj* **1.** (*peligroso*) risky **2.** (*sin protección*) exposed **3.** (*sensible*) vulnerable; ~ **a perturbaciones** vulnerable to disturbances; (~ *a la vista*) on display

expulsar [es·pul·'sar] *vt* **1.** (*a alguien*) to expel, to kick out *inf*; (*del país*) to deport; (*excluir*) to bar; ~ **a alguien de la escuela** to expel sb from school; ~ **a alguien del campo de juego** DEP to send sb off the pitch [*o* field]; ~ **de la sala** to eject from the room **2.** (*emitir*) to give off, to expel

expulsión [es·pul·'sjon] *f* **1.** (*de alguien*) expulsion; (*del país*) deportation; DEP expulsion; ~ **de la escuela** expulsion from school **2.** (*emisión*) expulsion

expurgar <g→gu> [es·pur·'γar] *vt* **1.** (*purificar*) to clean out **2.** (*censurar*) to expurgate

exquisitez [es·ki·si·'tes, -'teθ] *f* exquisiteness; (*manjar*) delicacy

exquisito, -a [es·ki·'si·to, -a] *adj* exquisite; (*comida*) delicious

éxtasis ['es·ta·sis] *m inv* ecstasy

extemporáneo, -a [es·tem·po·'ra·neo, -a] *adj*

1. (*a destiempo*) unseasonable; **son unas temperaturas extemporáneas para esta altura del año** these are unusual temperatures for this time of year 2. (*inoportuno*) inopportune; (*inadecuado*) inappropriate

extender <e→ie> [es·ten·'der] I. *vt* 1. (*papeles, mantequilla, pintura*) to spread 2. (*desplegar*) to unfold; ~ **la mano** to reach out one's hand 3. (*ensanchar*) to widen; (*agrandar*) to enlarge; ~ **la vista** to look around 4. (*propagar*) to spread 5. (*escribir*) to write out; (*documento*) to draw up II. *vr:* ~ **se** 1. (*terreno*) to extend; (*en la cama*) to stretch out 2. (*prolongarse*) to last 3. (*difundirse, expresarse*) ~ **se por algo** to extend over sth; ~ **se en discusiones interminables** to get bogged down in endless discussions

extendido, -a [es·ten·'di·do, -a] *adj* 1. (*amplio*) widespread; **un parentesco muy** ~ a far-reaching set of family relations 2. (*prolongado*) long 3. (*conocido*) well-known; **estar muy** ~ to be very well-known 4. (*detallado*) extensive 5. (*mano, brazos*) outstretched

extensible [es·ten·'si·βle] *adj* 1. (*ampliable*) extensible; **cable** ~ extension cord 2. (*desplegable*) folding; **mesa** ~ folding table 3. (*elástico*) elastic 4. (*plazo*) extendible

extensión [es·ten·'sjon] *f* 1. (*dimensión*) extent; (*longitud*) length; **en toda la** ~ **de la palabra** in all senses of the word; **por** ~ by extension 2. (*difusión*) spreading 3. (*duración*) length 4. (*ampliación*) *t.* POL expansion; ~ **hacia el este** expansion to the east 5. TEL, ELEC extension; ~ **eléctrica** extension cord

extenso, -a [es·'ten·so, -a] *adj* (*amplio*) extensive

extenuar <1. pres: extenúo> [es·te·nu·'ar] *vt* 1. (*agotar*) to exhaust 2. (*debilitar*) to weaken

exterior [es·te·'rjor] I. *adj* 1. (*de fuera*) external, exterior; **aspecto** ~ external appearance; **espacio** ~ outer space 2. (*extranjero*) foreign; **Ministerio de Asuntos Exteriores** State Department; **relaciones** ~ **es** foreign relations *pl* II. *m* 1. (*parte de afuera, apariencia*) exterior 2. *pl* CINE location shots *pl*

exteriorizar <z→c> [es·te·rjo·ri·'sar, -'θar] *vt* (*manifestar*) to show; (*revelar*) to reveal

exteriormente [es·te·rjor·'men·te] *adv* externally, outwardly

exterminar [es·ter·mi·'nar] *vt* 1. (*aniquilar*) to exterminate 2. (*devastar*) to destroy

exterminio [es·ter·'mi·njo] *m* 1. (*aniquilación*) extermination 2. (*devastación*) destruction

externo, -a [es·'ter·no, -a] *adj* external; **consultorios** ~ **s** outpatients' department; **de uso** ~ MED external use only

extinción [es·tin·'sjon, -'θjon] *f* 1. (*apagado*) extinguishing; ~ **de incendios** fire extinguishing 2. ECOL extinction; **en vías de** ~ threatened by extinction 3. (*de obligación, derecho*) end; (*de contrato*) termination

extinguir <gu→g> [es·tin·'gir] I. *vt* 1. (*apagar*) to extinguish 2. (*finalizar*) to terminate II. *vr:* ~ **se** 1. (*apagarse*) to be extinguished 2. (*finalizar*) to be terminated; ECOL to become extinct

extinto, -a [es·'tin·to, -a] I. *adj* 1. (*especie, volcán*) extinct 2. (*fuego*) extinguished 3. AmS, Méx (*muerto*) deceased II. *m, f* AmS, Méx deceased

extintor [es·tin·'tor] *m* ~ **de incendios** fire extinguisher

extirpación [es·tir·pa·'sjon, -'θjon] *f* 1. MED extraction; (*de un miembro*) amputation 2. (*erradicación*) eradication 3. (*desarraigo*) extirpation

extirpar [es·tir·'par] *vt* 1. MED to extract; (*miembro*) to amputate 2. (*erradicar*) to eradicate 3. (*arrancar*) to extirpate

extorsión [es·tor·'sjon] *f* 1. (*chantaje*) extortion 2. (*molestia*) nuisance; **ser una** ~ to be a pain *inf*

extorsionar [es·tor·sjo·'nar] *vt* 1. (*chantajear*) to extort 2. (*molestar*) to bother

extra[1] ['es·tra] I. *adj* 1. (*adicional*) extra; **horas** ~ **s** overtime; **paga** ~ bonus 2. (*excelente*) extra special; **de calidad** ~ top quality II. *prep* ~ **de** in addition to III. *m* 1. (*complemento*) extra; (*en periódico, revista*) special supplement 2. (*paga*) bonus

extra[2] ['es·tra] *mf* 1. CINE, TV extra 2. (*ayudante*) helper

extracción [es·trak·'sjon, -'θjon] *f* 1. (*sacar*) removal; (*de un diente*) extraction; ~ **de sangre** drawing of blood 2. (*lotería*) draw 3. *t.* MIN (*origen*) extraction

extraconyugal [es·tra·kon·ju·'ɣal] *adj* extramarital

extractar [es·trak·'tar] *vt* to extract; (*resumir*) to summarize

extracto [es·'trak·to, -a] *m* 1. (*resumen*) summary 2. (*pasaje*) extract; ~ **impreso** COMPUT printed extract 3. QUÍM extract

extractor [es·trak·'tor] *m* ~ **de humo** exhaust fan

extradición [es·tra·di·'sjon, -'θjon] *f* extradition

extraditar [es·tra·di·'tar] *vt* to extradite

extraer [es·tra·'er] *irr como traer* *v* 1. (*sacar*) to remove; (*dientes*) to extract; ~ **de un libro** to extract from a book 2. QUÍM, MIN to extract 3. MAT to extract

extraescolar [es·tra·es·ko·'lar] *adj* extracurricular

extrajudicial [es·tra·xu·di·'sjal, -'θjal] *adj* extrajudicial

extralimitarse [es·tra·li·mi·'tar·se] *vr* to go too far; ~ **en sus funciones** to overstep one's bounds; ~ **en sus esfuerzos** to make a superhuman effort

extranjería [es·tran·xe·'ri·a] *f* status of aliens; **ley de** ~ immigration law

extranjero [es·tran·'xe·ro] *m* abroad

extranjero, -a [es·tran·'xe·ro, -a] I. *adj* foreign;

lengua extranjera foreign language **II.** *m, f* foreigner

extrañamente [es·tra·ɲa·'men·te] *adv* strangely

extrañar [es·tra·'ɲar] **I.** *vt* **1.** (*desterrar*) to deport **2.** (*sorprender*) to surprise **3.** (*echar de menos*) to miss **II.** *vr* ~**se de algo** to find sth strange

extrañeza [es·tra·'ɲe·sa, -θa] *f* **1.** (*rareza*) strangeness; **causar** ~ to cause surprise **2.** (*perplejidad*) surprise

extraño, -a [es·'tra·ɲo, -a] **I.** *adj* **1.** (*raro, forastero*) strange, odd; (*extranjero*) foreign **2.** (*peculiar*) peculiar; (*extraordinario*) remarkable **II.** *m, f* (*forastero*) outsider, stranger; (*extranjero*) foreigner

extraoficial [es·tra·o·fi·'sjal, -'θjal] *adj* unofficial; **una declaración** ~ an off-the-record statement

extraordinario [es·tra·or·di·'na·rjo] *m* PREN special supplement

extraordinario, -a [es·tra·or·di·'na·rjo, -a] *adj* **1.** (*fuera de lo normal*) extraordinary; (*muy bueno*) fantastic **2.** (*por añadidura*) special **3.** (*raro*) strange **4.** (*sorprendente*) surprising

extrarradio [es·tra·'rra·djo] *m* outskirts *pl*

extrasensorial [es·tra·sen·so·'rjal] *adj* extrasensory

extraterrestre [es·tra·te·'rres·tre] **I.** *adj* extraterrestrial **II.** *mf* extraterrestrial, alien

extravagancia [es·tra·βa·'ɣan·sja, -θja] *f* **1.** (*rareza*) strangeness **2.** (*excentricidad*) eccentricity

extravagante [es·tra·βa·'ɣan·te] **I.** *adj* **1.** (*raro*) odd **2.** (*excéntrico*) eccentric **II.** *mf* eccentric

extraviado, -a [es·tra·βi·'a·do, -a] *adj* **1.** (*cosa*) lost **2.** (*animal*) stray

extraviar <1. *pres:* extravío> [es·tra·βi·'ar] **I.** *vt* **1.** (*despistar*) to confuse **2.** (*perder*) to lose; (*dejar*) to leave **II.** *vr:* ~ **se 1.** (*errar el camino*) to get lost **2.** (*perderse*) to get lost; (*carta*) to get lost in the mail **3.** (*descarriarse*) to stray; *fig* to go astray

extremado, -a [es·tre·'ma·do, -a] *adj* **1.** (*excesivo*) excessive **2.** (*exagerado*) extreme

extremar [es·tre·'mar] **I.** *vt* to carry to extremes; ~ **la prudencia** to be extremely cautious; **la policía extremó las medidas de seguridad** the police tightened security measures **II.** *vr* ~ **se en algo** to put a lot of work into sth

extremaunción [es·tre·ma·un·'sjon, -'θjon] *f* REL extreme unction

extremidad [es·tre·mi·'dad] *f* **1.** (*cabo*) end; (*punta*) tip **2.** *pl* ANAT limb

extremismo [es·tre·'mis·mo] *m* extremism; (*religioso*) fundamentalism; ~ **derechista** right-wing extremism

extremista [es·tre·'mis·ta] *adj, mf* extremist

extremo [es·'tre·mo] *m* **1.** (*cabo*) end; **a tal** ~ to such an extreme; **con** [*o* **en**] ~ a lot; **en**

último ~ in the last resort; **pasar de un** ~ **a otro** to go from one extreme to another; **los** ~**s se tocan** opposite ends of the spectrum meet up **2.** (*asunto*) matter; **en este** ~ on this point **3.** (*punto límite*) extreme; **esto llega hasta el** ~ **de...** this goes so far as... **4.** *pl* (*aspavientos*) **hacer** ~**s** to go wild

extremo, -a [es·'tre·mo, -a] **I.** *adj* **1.** (*intenso*) extreme **2.** (*distante*) furthest; **los barrios más** ~**s** the outermost areas **3.** (*límite*) extreme **II.** *m, f* DEP winger, outside forward; ~ **derecho** right winger, right outside forward

extrínseco, -a [es·'trin·se·ko, -a] *adj* (*externo*) extrinsic(al); **circunstancias extrínsecas** extrinsic circumstances

extrovertido, -a [es·tro·βer·'ti·do, -a] *adj* PSICO outgoing

exuberancia [ek·su·βe·'ran·sja, -θja] *f* exuberance

exuberante [ek·su·βe·'ran·te] *adj* exuberant; (*vegetación*) lush

exultar [ek·sul·'tar] *vi* to exult

eyaculación [e·ja·ku·la·'sjon, -'θjon] *f* ejaculation

eyacular [e·ja·ku·'lar] *vi* to ejaculate

F

F, f ['e·fe] *f* F, f; ~ **de Francia** F as in Foxtrot

fa [fa] *m inv* MÚS F; ~ **sostenido** F sharp

fabada [fa·'βa·da] *f* bean stew (*typical dish of Asturias prepared with pork products*)

fábrica ['fa·βri·ka] *f* **1.** (*lugar de producción*) factory; ~ **de cerveza** brewery; **en** [*o* **ex**] ~ direct from the factory **2.** (*de ladrillo, piedra*) masonry; **obra de** ~ stonework **3.** (*invención*) fabrication; ~ **de mentiras** pack of lies **4.** (*edificio*) building

fabricación [fa·βri·ka·'sjon, -'θjon] *f* manufacturing; ~ **en masa** mass production

fabricante [fa·βri·'kan·te] *mf* **1.** (*que fabrica*) manufacturer **2.** (*dueño*) factory owner

fabricar <c→qu> [fa·βri·'kar] *vt* **1.** (*producir*) to manufacture; ~ **cerveza** to brew beer **2.** (*construir*) to build **3.** (*inventar*) to fabricate

fábula ['fa·βu·la] *f* **1.** LIT fable **2.** *inf* (*invención*) tale **3.** (*relato mitológico*) myth **4.** ¡**de** ~! terrific!, smashing!

fabulador(a) [fa·βu·la·'dor, -'do·ra] *m(f)* **1.** (*fabulista*) writer of fables **2.** (*que inventa cosas fabulosas*) storyteller

fabuloso, -a [fa·βu·'lo·so, -a] *adj* **1.** (*inventado*) fabulous; **personaje** ~ fictitious character **2.** (*extraordinario*) fabulous

facción [fak·'sjon, -'θjon] *f* **1.** (*banda*) guerrilla band **2.** (*de un partido*) faction **3.** *pl* (*rasgos*) (facial) features *pl*

faceta [fa·'se·ta, fa·'θe-] *f* facet; (*aspecto*) aspect, side

faceto, -a [fa·'se·to, -a; fa·'θe-] *adj Méx* **1.**(*chistoso*) facetious **2.**(*presuntuoso*) cocksure

facha¹ ['fa·tʃa] **I.** *adj pey, inf* fascist **II.** *mf pey, inf* fascist

facha² ['fa·tʃa] *f inf* appearance, look; **tener una ~ sospechosa** to look suspicious; **estar hecho una ~** to look a sight

fachada [fa·'tʃa·da] *f* **1.**(*de un edificio*) façade **2.**(*apariencia*) façade, front; **su buen humor es pura ~** his/her good mood is pure pretense

fachendoso, -a [fa·tʃen·'do·so, -a] **I.** *adj inf* swanky *inf* **II.** *m, f inf* swank *inf*

fachero [fa·'tʃe·ro] *m Arg, inf* good-looking man

fachinal [fa·tʃi·'nal] *m Arg* marshland

facial [fa·'sjal, -'θjal] *adj* facial

fácil ['fa·sil, -θil] *adj* **1.**(*sin dificultades*) easy, simple; **es más ~ de decir que de hacer** *prov* easier said than done *prov* **2.**(*cómodo*) undemanding **3.**(*probable*) probable; **es ~ que** +*subj* it is likely that; **es ~ que nieve** it may well snow **4.**(*carácter*) easy-going **5.**(*mujer*) loose *pej*

facilidad [fa·si·li·'dad, fa·θi-] *f* **1.**(*sin dificultad*) ease **2.**(*dotes*) facility; **tener ~ para algo** to have an ability for sth; **tener ~ para los idiomas** to have a flair for languages **3.** *pl* (*de pago*) payment arrangements *pl*; **ofrecer** [*o* **dar**] **~es a alguien para algo** to facilitate sth for sb

facilitar [fa·si·li·'tar] *vt* **1.**(*favorecer*) to facilitate; (*posibilitar*) to make possible **2.**(*suministrar*) to furnish, to supply

fácilmente [fa·sil·'men·te, fa·θil-] *adv* **1.**(*sin dificultad*) easily **2.**(*con probabilidad*) probably

facineroso, -a [fa·si·ne·'ro·so, -a; fa·θi-] *m, f* **1.**(*delincuente*) criminal **2.**(*malvado*) wicked person

facón [fa·'kon] *m RíoPl: gaucho's knife*

facsímil(e) [fak·'si·mil, --mi·le] *m* (*reproducción*) facsimile

factibilidad [fak·ti·βi·li·'dad] *f* feasibility

factible [fak·'ti·βle] *adj* feasible, viable

fáctico, -a ['fak·ti·ko, -a] *adj* factual; **los poderes ~s** the institutions holding effective control

factor [fak·'tor] *m t.* MAT (*causa*) factor; **~ de riesgo** risk factor

factoría [fak·to·'ri·a] *f* factory

factura [fak·'tu·ra] *f* **1.**(*cuenta*) bill; (*recibo*) receipt; **pasar ~** to render an account; **su holgazanería le pasa ahora ~** *inf* he/she is now having to pay the price for his/her idleness **2.**(*hechura*) **esta chaqueta es de buena ~** this jacket is well made

facturación [fak·tu·ra·θjon, -θjon] *f* **1.**(*elaboración de una factura*) invoicing **2.** FERRO registration **3.** COM turnover **4.**(*equipaje*) check-in

facturar [fak·tu·'rar] *vt* **1.**(*cobrar*) to bill; **~ los**

gastos de transporte to bill for transport costs **2.** COM (*ganar*) to earn; **nuestra compañía factura tres millones de pesos al mes** our company is bringing in three million pesos a month **3.** FERRO to register **4.** AVIAT **~** (**el equipaje**) to check in

facultad [fa·kul·'tad] *f* **1.**(*atribuciones*) authority; **tener ~ para hacer algo** to have the authority to do sth; **conceder ~es a alguien (para hacer algo)** to authorize sb (to do sth) **2.**(*aptitud*) faculty; **recobró sus ~es** he/she recovered his/her faculties **3.** UNIV faculty **4.** *pl* (*dotes*) faculties *pl*

facultar [fa·kul·'tar] *vt* to authorize; **este título me faculta para ejercer la abogacía** this qualification entitles me to practice law

facultativo, -a [fa·kul·ta·'ti·βo, -a] **I.** *adj* **1.**(*potestativo*) optional **2.** UNIV faculty **3.**(*del médico*) medical **II.** *m, f* doctor

fado ['fa·do] *m* MÚS fado (*melancholic Portuguese folksong*)

faena [fa·'e·na] *f* **1.**(*tarea*) task; **~s domésticas** chores *pl* **2.** *inf* (*mala pasada*) dirty trick; **hacer una ~ a alguien** to play a dirty trick on sb **3.** TAUR *bullfighter's performance, especially with the cape*

faenar [fae·'nar] **I.** *vi* **1.**(*pescar*) to fish **2.**(*laborar*) to work **II.** *vt* (*matar reses*) to slaughter animals

faenero, -a [fae·'ne·ro, -a] *m, f Chile* field worker

fagot¹ [fa·'ɣot] *mf* MÚS bassoonist

fagot² [fa·'ɣot] *m* MÚS bassoon

fagotista [fa·ɣo·'tis·ta] *mf* MÚS bassoonist

failear [fai·le·'ar] *vt AmC, RíoPl* COM (*documentos*) to file; (*en una carpeta*) to put in a folder

faíno, -a [fa·'i·no, -a] *adj Cuba* simple

fair play [fer plei] *m* DEP fair play

faisán [fai·'san] *m* pheasant

faja ['fa·xa] *f* **1.**(*para ceñir*) corset, girdle; (*para abrigar*) sash **2.**(*distintivo honorífico*) sash **3.**(*franja*) strip **4.**(*de libros*) promotional band

fajada [fa·'xa·da] *f* **1.** *Ant* (*ataque*) attack, assault **2.** *Arg, inf* (*paliza*) beating; **le han dado una buena ~** they gave him a hell of a beating **3.** *Ven* (*chasco*) disappointment

fajar [fa·'xar] **I.** *vt* **1.**(*envolver*) to wrap; (*periódicos*) to put a wrapper on **2.** *AmL* (*golpear*) to strike **II.** *vr:* **~se 1.**(*ponerse una faja*) to put on a girdle [*o* sash] **2.** *AmL* (*pelearse*) to fight **III.** *vi* **~ con alguien** to fight with sb

fajilla [fa·'xi·ja, -ʎa] *f AmL* wrapper

fajín [fa·'xin] *m* **1.** *diminutivo de* **faja 2.**(*de generales, funcionarios*) sash

fajita [fa·'xi·ta] *f* CULIN *appetizer of grilled meat wrapped in a corn tortilla*

fajo ['fa·xo] *m* **1.**(*papeles*) bundle; **~ de billetes** *inf* wad of dough *inf* **2.** *pl* (*de bebé*) baby's swaddling clothes

falacia [fa·'la·sja, -θja] *f* deceit

falange [fa·'lan·xe] *f* **1.** MIL, HIST, ANAT phalanx

2. POL **la Falange (Española)** the Falange
falangista [fa·lan·'xis·ta] *adj, mf* Falangist
falaz [fa·'las, -'laθ] *adj* false; **apariencia** ~ deceptive appearance
falca ['fal·ka] *f* wedge
falda ['fal·da] *f* **1.** (*vestido*) skirt; ~ **pantalón** culottes; ~ **plisada** pleated skirt; ~ **tubo/recta** straight skirt **2.** (*regazo*) lap **3.** (*de una mesa camilla*) table cover **4.** (*de una montaña*) lower slope **5.** CULIN brisket **6.** (*de sombrero*) brim **7.** *inf* (*mujer*) **es asunto de** ~s it is to do with women; **le tiran mucho las** ~s he is a real ladies' man
faldellín [fal·de·'jin, -'ʎin] *m Ant, Ven* christening robe
faldeo [fal·'deo] *m Arg, Chile* (*ladera*) mountainside
faldero [fal·'de·ro] *m* **1.** (*hombre*) womanizer **2.** (*animal*) **perro** ~ lapdog
faldón [fal·'don] *m* **1.** (*de una camisa*) (shirt-)tail **2.** (*de una funda*) flap
falencia [fa·'len·sja, -θja] *f Col* bankruptcy, insolvency
falible [fa·'li·βle] *adj* (*erróneo*) fallible; (*engañoso*) deceitful
fálico, -a ['fa·li·ko, -a] *adj* phallic
falla ['fa·ja, -ʎa] *f* **1.** (*defecto*) defect; (*en un sistema*) fault; ~ **en tiempo de ejecución** COMPUT runtime failure **2.** GEO fault **3.** *Col* ENS day absent (*from school*)
fallar [fa·'jar, -'ʎar] **I.** *vi* **1.** JUR to render judgment, to find **2.** (*malograrse: proyecto*) to fail; (*plan, intento*) to miscarry **3.** (*no funcionar*) to go wrong; **le** ~**on los nervios** his/her nerves let him/her down; **algo le falla** there is sth wrong with him/her; **no falla nunca** (*cosa*) it never fails; (*persona*) you can always count on her/him **4.** (*romperse*) to break **5.** (*no cumplir con su palabra*) ~ **a alguien** to let sb down; (*en una cita*) to stand sb up **II.** *vt* **1.** JUR to render judgment on; ~ **la absolución** to acquit; ~ **un pleito** to rule on a case **2.** (*premio*) to award **3.** DEP to miss **4.** (*en el juego de naipes*) to trump
fallecer [fa·je·'ser, -ʎe·'θer] *irr como crecer vi* to pass away, to die
fallecido, -a [fa·je·'si·do, -a; -ʎe·'θi·do, -a] **I.** *adj* deceased, late **II.** *m, f* deceased
fallecimiento [fa·je·si·'mjen·to, -ʎe·θi·'mjen·to] *m* death
fallero, -a [fa·'je·ro, -a; fa·'ʎe-] *m, f person who participates in las Fallas*
fallido, -a [fa·'ji·do, -a; fa·'ʎi-] **I.** *adj* **1.** (*proyecto*) unsuccessful; (*intento*) abortive **2.** COM (*deuda*) bad **3.** (*en quiebra*) bankrupt **II.** *m, f* irrecoverable loan
fallo ['fa·jo, -ʎo] *m* **1.** JUR sentence **2.** (*error*) error; (*omisión*) omission; ~ **humano** human error; **este asunto solo tiene un pequeño** ~ this matter only has one small shortcoming [*o* hitch] **3.** (*certamen*) decision **4.** TÉC breakdown **5.** (*en el juego de naipes*) void **6.** (*fracaso*) failure **7.** MED ~ **cardíaco/renal** heart/

kidney failure
falluto, -a [fa·'ju·to, -a; fa·'ʎu-] *adj RíoPl, inf* (*en el comportamiento*) unreliable; (*en el modo de ser*) two-faced, hypocritical
falo ['fa·lo] *m elev* phallus
falocracia [fa·lo·'kra·sja, -θja] *f* male chauvinism
falopa [fa·'lo·pa] *f Arg, Urug, inf* (*droga*) drugs *pl*
falopero, -a [fa·'lo·pe·ro, -a] *m, f Arg, Urug, inf* (*adicto*) addict
falsario, -a [fal·'sa·rjo, -a] **I.** *adj* counterfeit **II.** *m, f* (*mentiroso*) liar
falseable [fal·se·'a·βle] *adj* falsifiable, forgeable
falseador(a) [fal·sea·'dor, -'do·ra] *m(f)* forger
falseamiento [fal·sea·'mjen·to] *m* forgery
falsear [fal·se·'ar] **I.** *vi* **1.** (*flaquear*) to weaken **2.** MÚS to be out of tune **II.** *vt* **1.** (*adulterar al referir*) to misrepresent; (*verdad*) to distort **2.** (*falsificar materialmente*) to counterfeit
falsedad [fal·se·'dad] *f* (*en el carácter*) falseness; (*hipocresía*) hypocrisy
falsete [fal·'se·te] *m* MÚS falsetto; **cantar en** ~ to sing falsetto
falsificación [fal·si·fi·ka·'sjon, -'θjon] *f* (*acto, objeto*) forgery; ~ **de billetes** counterfeiting of banknotes
falsificador(a) [fal·si·fi·ka·'dor, -'do·ra] *m(f)* (*de documentos*) forger; (*de moneda*) counterfeiter
falsificar <c→qu> [fal·si·fi·'kar] *vt* to forge, to falsify; ~ **la verdad** to distort the truth
falso ['fal·so] *adv* **en** ~ (*falsamente*) falsely; **jurar en** ~ to commit perjury; **coger a alguien en** ~ to catch sb out [*o* in a lie]; **dar un golpe en** ~ (*movimiento*) to miss the mark; **dar un paso en** ~ (*tropezar*) to stumble; (*equivocarse*) to make a mistake; **sonar** ~ to ring false
falso, -a ['fal·so, -a] **I.** *adj* **1.** (*no cierto, no auténtico*) false; **¡**~**!** not true! **2.** (*no natural*) artificial; (*pseudo*) pseudo; **llave falsa** fake key; **puerta falsa** false door **3.** (*caballería*) vicious **II.** *m, f* (*mentiroso*) liar; (*hipócrita*) hypocrite
falta ['fal·ta] *f* **1.** (*carencia*) lack; (*ausencia*) absence; ~ **de dinero** shortage of money; ~ **de educación** lack of education; ~ **de liquidez** liquidity problem; **echar en** ~ **algo/a alguien** to miss sth/sb; **me hace** ~ **dinero** I need money; **¡ni** ~ **que hace!** there is absolutely no need! **2.** (*equivocación*) error; ~ **ortográfica** spelling error; **sin** ~**s** with no mistakes; **sin** ~ without fail **3.** DEP foul **4.** JUR default; (*omisión censurable*) misdemeanor
faltar [fal·'tar] *vi* **1.** (*no estar*) to be missing; (*persona*) to be absent; ~ **a clase** to miss class; ~ **a una cita** not to turn up to an appointment; **me faltan mis llaves** my keys are missing **2.** (*necesitarse*) ~ (**por**) **hacer** to be still to be done; **nos falta dinero para...** we do not have enough money to...; **me falta tiempo para hacerlo** I need time to do it; **no falta quien...**

there is always sb who...; **falta (por) saber si...** we need to know if...; **¡no ~ía** [*o* **faltaba**] **más!** that is the limit!; (*respuesta a agradecimiento*) you are welcome!; (*asentir amablemente*) of course!; **por si algo faltaba...** as if it were not enough already...; **¡lo que faltaba!** that is the last straw! **3.** (*temporal: quedar*) to be left; **faltan cuatro días para tu cumpleaños** your birthday is in four days; **falta poco para las doce** it is nearly twelve o'clock; **faltan diez para las nueve** *AmL* it is ten to nine; **poco le faltó para llorar** he/she was on the verge of tears **4.** (*no cumplir*) ~ **a una promesa** to break a promise; **nunca falta a su palabra** he/she never goes back on his/her word **5.** (*ofender*) to be rude; **~ a alguien** to be disrespectful [*o* rude] to sb **6.** (*cometer una falta*) ~ **en algo** to make a mistake

falto, -a ['fal·to, -a] *adj* (*escaso*) ~ **de algo** short of sth; (*desprovisto*) lacking in sth; **~ de recursos** lacking in resources; **estar ~ de cariño** to be in need of love [*o* lacking affection]

faltón, -ona [fal·'ton, -'to·na] *adj inf* **1.** (*que falta a su palabra*) unreliable, fly-by-night *inf* **2.** (*negligente*) negligent, remiss **3.** *AmL* (*vago*) idle, do-nothing **4.** (*grosero*) rude

faltriquera [fal·tri·'ke·ra] *f* pocket; (*a la cintura*) *a pouch tied around the waist and under the apron or skirt*

fama ['fa·ma] *f* **1.** (*gloria*) glory; (*celebridad*) fame; **tener ~** to be famous; **dar ~ a algo/alguien** to make sth/sb famous; **unos tienen la ~ y otros cardan la lana** *prov* some do all the work while others get all the glory *prov* **2.** (*reputación*) reputation; **tener ~ de fanfarrón** to have a reputation of being boastful; **ser de mala ~** to have a bad reputation **3.** (*rumor*) rumor; **corre la ~ de que...** there is a rumor going around that...

famélico, -a [fa·'me·li·ko, -a] *adj* starving

familia [fa·'mi·lja] *f* **1.** (*pareja e hijos*) family; (*que comparten una casa*) household; **~ numerosa** large family, (*with three or more children*); **cabeza de ~** head of the household **2.** (*parentela*) relatives *pl;* **~ política** in-laws *pl;* **libro de ~** *book recording the details of a family, including births, deaths, marriages, etc.;* **de buena ~** from a good family; **eso viene de ~** that runs in the family; **en ~** with the family; **ser de la ~** to be one of the family; **acordarse de la ~ de alguien** *inf* to insult sb **3.** (*hijos*) family

familiar [fa·mi·'ljar] **I.** *adj* **1.** (*íntimo*) intimate; **asunto ~** personal matter; **economía ~** domestic economy **2.** (*conocido*) familiar **II.** *mf* (*pariente*) relative

familiaridad [fa·mi·lja·ri·'dad] *f* (*confianza*) intimacy; (*trato familiar*) familiarity

familiarizar <z→c> [fa·mi·lja·ri·'sar, -'θar] **I.** *vt* (*acostumbrar*) to familiarize **II.** *vr:* **~se** to familiarize oneself, to get to know

famoso, -a [fa·'mo·so, -a] *adj* **1.** (*conocido*) ~ **por algo** famous for sth **2.** *inf* (*sonado*) talked-of

fan [fan] *mf* <fans> (*admirador*) fan; (*de fútbol*) supporter

fanático, -a [fa·'na·ti·ko, -a] **I.** *adj* fanatical **II.** *m, f* **1.** *inf* (*hincha*) fan; **es una fanática del rock** she is crazy about rock **2.** *pey* (*extremista*) fanatic

fanatismo [fa·na·'tis·mo] *m* fanaticism

fané [fa·'ne] *adj AmL, inf* (*arrugado*) crumpled, rumpled; (*marchito*) withered

fanfarrón, -ona [fan·fa·'rron, -'rro·na] *inf* **I.** *adj* (*chulo*) swanky **II.** *m, f* (*bravucón*) braggart, swank

fanfarronada [fan·fa·rro·'na·da] *f inf* brag, baloney

fanfarronear [fan·fa·rro·ne·'ar] *vi inf* to brag

fangal [fan·'gal] *m* quagmire

fango ['fan·go] *m* **1.** (*lodo*) mud; **baños de ~** MED mud bath **2.** (*deshonra*) dishonor

fangoso, -a [fan·'go·so, -a] *adj* muddy

fantasear [fan·ta·se·'ar] **I.** *vi* **1.** (*soñar*) to fantasize **2.** (*presumir*) to boast, to pose **3.** (*soñar despierto*) to daydream **II.** *vt* to invent

fantaseo [fan·ta·'seo] *m* fantasizing

fantasía [fan·ta·'si·a] *f* **1.** (*imaginación*) imagination; (*cosa imaginada*) fantasy; **joyas de ~** costume jewelry; **¡déjate de ~s!** come down to earth! *inf* **2.** LIT fantastic tale **3.** MÚS fantasia

fantasioso, -a [fan·ta·'sjo·so, -a] **I.** *adj* **1.** (*inventado*) fanciful; **idea fantasiosa** fanciful idea **2.** (*fachendoso*) swanky *inf* **II.** *m, f* poseur *form*, show-off

fantasma [fan·'tas·ma] **I.** *m* **1.** (*aparición*) ghost; **andar como un ~** to be lifeless; **aparecer como un ~** to appear from [*o* out of] nowhere **2.** (*visión*) phantom **3.** *inf* (*fanfarrón*) boaster, poseur *form* **II.** *adj* ghost; **empresa ~** dummy company

fantasmada [fan·tas·'ma·da] *f inf* pose

fantasmagórico, -a [fan·tas·ma·'yo·ri·ko, -a] *adj* phantasmagorical; TEAT with optical illusion

fantasmal [fan·tas·'mal] *adj* phantom, illusory

fantasmón, -ona [fan·tas·'mon, -'mo·na] **I.** *adj inf* presumptuous **II.** *m, f* poseur *form*, show-off

fantástico, -a [fan·'tas·ti·ko, -a] *adj* **1.** (*irreal*) fantastic, imaginary **2.** *inf* (*fabuloso*) fantastic, fabulous

fantochada [fan·to·'tʃa·da] *f* **1.** (*fantasmada*) pose **2.** (*tontería*) silly act [*o* remark]

fantoche [fan·'to·tʃe] *m* **1.** (*títere*) puppet **2.** (*mamarracho*) sight **3.** (*fantasmón*) poseur; *form* phony *inf*

fañoso, -a [fa·'ɲo·so, -a] *adj Ven* twanging

FAO ['fao] *f abr de* **Organización de las Naciones Unidas para la Agricultura y la Alimentación** FAO

faquir [fa·'kir] *m* fakir

faralá [fa·ra·'la] *f* <faralaes> **1.** (*volante*) flounce **2.** *inf* (*oropel*) frills *pl*, frippery

faramallear [fa·ra·ma·je·'ar; -ʎe·'ar] *vi Chile, Méx* to brag

farándula [fa·'ran·du·la] *f* **1.**(*farsa*) farce **2.** TEAT the stage, theater world **3.** *inf*(*palabrería*) nonsense

faraón [fa·ra·'on] *m* Pharaoh

faraónico, -a [fa·ra·'o·ni·ko, -a] *adj* pharaonic

fardada [far·'da·da] *f inf* showing off

fardar [far·'dar] *vi inf* (*presumir*) to boast; (*impresionar*) to make an impression

fardo ['far·do] *m* (*bulto*) package; (*de ropa*) bundle

fardón, -ona [far·'don, -·'do·na] *adj inf* **1.**(*chulo*) swanky *inf,* boastful **2.**(*vistoso*) showy; (*coche*) swish, flashy *inf*

farero, -a [fa·'re·ro, -a] *m, f* lighthouse keeper

farfullar [far·fu·'jar, -·'ʎar] **I.** *vi inf* (*balbucear*) to stutter **II.** *vt inf* (*chapucear*) to botch

farfullero, -a [far·fu·'je·ro, -a; -·'ʎe·ro, -a] *m, f inf* **1.**(*tartamudo*) stutterer **2.**(*chapucero*) botcher

faringe [fa·'rin·xe] *f* ANAT pharynx, throat

faringitis [fa·rin·'xi·tis] *f inv* MED pharyngitis

fariña [fa·'ri·ɲa] *f AmS* coarse cassava flour

farisaico, -a [fa·ri·'sai·ko, -a] *adj* **1.**(*fariseo*) Pharisaic(al) **2.**(*falso*) hypocritical

fariseo, -a [fa·ri·'seo, -a] *m, f* **1.**(*de la secta judía*) Pharisee **2.**(*hipócrita*) hypocrite

farmacéutico, -a [far·ma·'seu·ti·ko, -a; far·ma·'θeu-] **I.** *adj* pharmaceutical; **industria farmacéutica** pharmaceutical industry; **productos ~s** pharmaceutical products **II.** *m, f* druggist

farmacia [far·'ma·sja, -θja] *f* **1.**(*tienda*) drugstore; **~ de guardia** ≈ 24-hour drugstore **2.**(*ciencia*) pharmacy

fármaco ['far·ma·ko] *m* medicine, drug

farmacodependencia [far·ma·ko·de·pen·'den·sja, -θja] *f* drug dependence

farmacólogo, -a [far·ma·'ko·lo·ɣo, -a] *m, f* pharmacologist

faro ['fa·ro] *m* **1.** AUTO headlight; **~ antiniebla** fog light [*o* lamp] **2.** NÁUT lighthouse

farol [fa·'rol] *m* **1.**(*lámpara*) lamp; (*de papel*) Chinese lantern; **~ (de calle)** streetlight **2.** DEP bluff **3.** *inf* (*fanfarronada*) idle boast, swank *inf*; (*patraña*) tall story; **tirarse un ~** to show off **4.** *pl AmL* (*ojos*) eyes; **¡adelante con los ~es!** *inf* go for it!

farola [fa·'ro·la] *f* street light [*o* lamp]; (*poste*) lamppost

farolazo [fa·ro·'la·so, -θo] *m AmC, Méx* swig of liquor

farolear [fa·ro·le·'ar] *vi inf* to brag, to swank *inf*

farolero, -a [fa·ro·'le·ro, -a] **I.** *adj inf* bragging **II.** *m, f* **1.**(*oficio*) lamplighter **2.**(*fanfarrón*) show-off

farolillo [fa·ro·'li·jo, -ʎo] *m* Chinese lantern; **~ rojo** *inf* team [*o* competitor] in last place

farra ['fa·rra] *f* **estar** [*o* **ir**] **de ~** *inf* to party

fárrago ['fa·rra·ɣo] *m* jumble

farragoso, -a [fa·rra·'ɣo·so, -a] *adj* jumbled-up

farrear [fa·rre·'ar] **I.** *vi CSur, inf* to paint the town red **II.** *vr:* **~se** *RíoPl* (*dinero*) to squander, to blow *inf*

farrista [fa·'rris·ta] **I.** *adj CSur* fun-loving; **mi hija es muy ~** my daughter is always out living it up **II.** *mf CSur* (*que le gusta ir a fiestas*) party-loving

farruco, -a [fa·'rru·ko, -a] **I.** *adj* defiant **II.** *m, f RíoPl:* Galician or Asturian immigrant

farruto, -a [fa·'rru·to, -a] *adj Bol, Chile* puny

farsa ['far·sa] *f* **1.** TEAT (*farándula*) theater; (*sainete*) farce **2.**(*engaño*) sham

farsante [far·'san·te] **I.** *adj inf* sham **II.** *mf inf* charlatan

FAS [fas] *fpl* MIL *abr de* **Fuerzas Armadas** the (armed) forces

fascículo [fa·'si·ku·lo, fas·'θi-] *m* (*de libro*) installment

fascinación [fa·si·na·'sjon, fas·θi·na·'θjon] *f* fascination; **sentir ~ por algo** to be fascinated by [*o* drawn to] sth

fascinador(a) [fa·si·na·'dor, -·'do·ra, fas·θi-] *adj,* **fascinante** [fas·θi·'nan·te] *adj* fascinating; (*persona*) captivating; (*libro*) enthralling

fascinar [fa·si·'nar, fas·θi-] **I.** *vi, vt* (*encantar*) to fascinate; (*libro*) enthrall **II.** *vr:* **~se** to be fascinated

fascismo [fa·'sis·mo, fas·'θis-] *m* fascism

fascista [fa·'sis·ta, fas·'θis-] **I.** *adj* fascist(ic) **II.** *mf* fascist

fascistoide [fa·sis·'toi·de, fas·'θis-] *adj* fascist-like

fase ['fa·se] *f* **1.**(*período, estado*) phase **2.** ELEC, FÍS, QUÍM phase; **de tres ~s** three-phase; (*nave espacial*) stage

fast food [fas fud] *m o f* fast food

fastidiado, -a [fas·ti·'dja·do, -a] *adj inf* **1.**(*enfermo*) unwell **2.**(*molesto*) annoyed **3.**(*estropeado*) broken; **andar ~ de...** to have a bad...; **ando ~ de dinero/tiempo estos días** I don't have enough money/time these days; **anda ~ de la rodilla** he has a bad knee

fastidiar [fas·ti·'djar] **I.** *vt* **1.**(*molestar*) to annoy; **¡no te fastidia!** *inf* you must be kidding! **2.** *inf* (*estropear*) ruin **3.**(*causar hastío*) to sicken **4.**(*aburrir*) to bore **II.** *vr:* **~se** *inf* **1.**(*enojarse*) to get cross; **¡fastídiate!** stuff it! *inf;* **¡hay que ~se!** it's unbelievable! **2.**(*aguantarse*) to put up with it **3.** *AmL* (*perjudicarse*) to harm

fastidio [fas·'ti·djo] *m* **1.**(*disgusto*) bother; **¡vaya ~!** what a nuisance; (*mala suerte*) misfortune **2.**(*aburrimiento*) bore **3.**(*hastío*) repugnance

fastidioso, -a [fas·ti·'djo·so, -a] *adj* **1.**(*molesto*) annoying **2.**(*aburrido*) boring **3.**(*pesado*) dull; **persona fastidiosa** a bore

fasto ['fas·to] *m* **1.**(*pompa*) pomp **2.** *pl* (*anales*) annals *pl*

fastuosidad [fas·two·si·'dad] *f* lavishness

fastuoso, -a [fas·tu·'o·so, -a] *adj* (*casa, boda*) sumptuous; (*persona*) showy, flashy

fatal [fa·'tal] **I.** *adj* **1.**(*inevitable*) unavoidable; **el momento ~** the inevitable [*o* fateful moment] **2.**(*desagradable*) disagreeable **3.**(*funesto*) fatal; (*mortal*) mortal; **mujer ~**

femme fatale **4.**JUR not extendable **5.** *inf* (*muy mal*) awful **II.** *adv inf* awfully; **el examen me fue** ~ my exam was a disaster
fatalidad [fa·ta·li·'dad] *f* **1.** (*desgracia*) misfortune **2.** (*destino*) fate
fatalismo [fa·ta·'lis·mo] *m* fatalism
fatalista [fa·ta·'lis·ta] **I.** *adj* fatalistic **II.** *mf* **1.** (*que sigue el fatalismo*) fatalist **2.** *inf* (*pesimista*) pessimist
fatídico, -a [fa·'ti·di·ko, -a] *adj* **1.** (*que predice el futuro*) prophetic **2.** *inf* (*algo*) fateful **3.** (*terrible*) horrible
fatiga [fa·'ti·ɣa] *f* **1.** (*cansancio*) weariness, fatigue; ~ **visual** eye strain **2.** (*sofocos*) shortness of breath **3.** *pl* (*sacrificios*) hardship
fatigado, -a [fa·ti·'ɣa·do, -a] *adj* **1.** (*agotado*) worn-out **2.** (*sofocado*) short of breath
fatigador(a) [fa·ti·ɣa·'dor, -·'do·ra] *adj* (*que cansa*) tiring; (*que molesta*) annoying
fatigar <g →gu> [fa·ti·'ɣar] **I.** *vt* **1.** (*cansar*) to tire, to fatigue **2.** (*molestar*) to annoy; (*importunar*) to pester **II.** *vr:* ~**se 1.** (*agotarse*) to wear oneself out; (*ojos*) to strain **2.** (*esforzarse*) to exert oneself **3.** (*sofocarse*) to get short of breath
fatigoso, -a [fa·ti·'ɣo·so, -a] *adj* **1.** (*trabajo*) tiring **2.** (*persona*) tiresome; (*jadeante*) panting
fatuidad [fa·twi·'dad] *f* (*vanidad*) conceit; (*inmodestia*) immodesty
fatuo, -a ['fa·two, -a] *adj* **1.** (*presumido*) conceited; (*jactancioso*) boastful **2.** (*necio*) fatuous
fauces ['fau·ses, -θes] *fpl* **1.** ZOOL fauces *pl* **2.** *AmL* (*dientes*) teeth
fauna ['fau·na] *f* fauna
fauno ['fau·no] *m* faun
favela [fa·'βe·la] *f* *AmL* **1.** (*casucha*) shanty **2.** *pl* (*barrio*) shanty town
favor [fa·'βor] *m* **1.** (*servicio*) favor; (*ayuda*) good turn; **por** ~ please; **hacer un** ~ **a alguien** to do sb a favor; **¡hágame el** ~ **de dejarme en paz!** would you please leave me alone!; **te lo pido por** ~ I am begging you; **hagan el** ~ **de venir puntualmente** please be punctual **2.** (*gracia*) favor; **a** [*o* **en**] ~ **de alguien** in sb's favor; **tener a alguien a su** ~ to have sb on your side; **a** ~ **del viento/de la corriente** with the wind/the current **3.** (*beneficio*) **voto a** ~ vote for; **estar a** ~ **de algo** to be in favor of sth; **votar a** ~ **de alguien** to vote for sb
favorable [fa·βo·'ra·βle] *adj* **1.** (*propicio*) favorable **2.** (*optimista*) promising **3.** (*benévolo*) kind
favorecedor(a) [fa·βo·re·se·'dor, -·'do·ra, fa·βo·re·θe-] *adj* becoming; **es un vestido muy** ~ **para ti** the dress is very becoming on you
favorecer [fa·βo·re·'ser, -'θer] *irr como crecer* **I.** *vt* **1.** (*beneficiar*) to benefit **2.** (*ayudar*) to help **3.** (*dar preferencia*) to favor **4.** (*prendas de vestir*) to become **II.** *vr:* ~**se** to benefit
favorecido, -a [fa·βo·re·'si·do, -a; -'θi·do, -a] *adj* **1.** (*propiciado*) favored **2.** (*fotografía*) **has**

salido ~ **en la foto** you came out well in the picture
favoritismo [fa·βo·ri·'tis·mo] *m* (*nepotismo*) nepotism; (*parcialidad*) favoritism
favorito, -a [fa·βo·'ri·to, -a] **I.** *adj* favorite; **plato** ~ favorite dish **II.** *m, f* **1.** (*del rey*) favorite; ~ **del público** the public's darling; **la favorita del rey** the king's mistress **2.** DEP (the) favorite
fax [faks] *m inv* fax; **mandar un** ~ **a una empresa/a Suecia** to send a fax to a company/to Sweden
faxear [fak·se·'ar] *vt* to fax
fayuca [fa·'ju·ka] *f Méx, inf* black market; **tabaco de** ~ contraband tobacco
fayuquero, -a [fa·ju·'ke·ro, -a] *m, f Méx, inf* smuggler
faz [fas, faθ] *f* (*anverso*) obverse
FCC [e·fe·se·'se, -θe·'θe] *abr de* **fluorclorocarbonados** CFC
fe [fe] *f* **1.** (*religión*) faith; ~ **en Dios** faith in God; **doy profesión de** ~ I profess my faith **2.** (*confianza*) faith; **digno de** ~ worthy of trust; **dar** ~ **a algo/alguien** to vouch for sth/sb; **dar** ~ **de algo** to certify sth; **tener** ~ **en alguien** to believe in sb; **de buena/mala** ~ in good/bad faith **3.** (*lealtad*) fidelity **4.** (*certificado*) certificate; ~ **de bautismo/de matrimonio** certificate of baptism/marriage; ~ **de erratas** errata
fealdad [feal·'dad] *f* **1.** (*monstruosidad*) ugliness **2.** (*indignidad*) indignity
feb. *abr de* **febrero** Feb.
febrero [fe·'βre·ro] *m* February; *v.t.* **marzo**
febril [fe·'βril] *adj* (*fiebre*) feverish; **acceso** ~ sudden temperature; (*actividad*) hectic
fecal [fe·'kal] *adj* fecal; **sustancias** ~**es** fecal matter
fecha ['fe·tʃa] *f* **1.** (*data*) date; (*señalada*) day; ~ **de caducidad** expiration date; (*de comida*) sell-by date; ~ **de cierre** closing date; ~ **clave** decisive day; ~ **de las elecciones** Election day; ~ **de entrega** date of delivery; ~ **límite** [*o* **tope**] deadline; **sin** ~ undated; **en la** ~ **fijada** on the agreed day; **hasta la** ~ until now, so far; **adelantar/atrasar la** ~ **de algo** to bring forward/put back the date of sth; **¿cuál es la** ~ **de hoy?** what is the date today? **2.** ECON date; **a 30 días** ~ at 30 days' sight **3.** *pl* (*época*) days *pl*; **en estas** ~**s** around this time
fechable [fe·'tʃa·βle] *adj* datable
fechado, -a [fe·'tʃa·do, -a] *adj* (*en cartas*) ~ **el...** dated...
fechador [fe·tʃa·'dor] *m* date-stamp
fechar [fe·'tʃar] *vt* to date
fechoría [fe·tʃo·'ri·a] *f* **1.** (*delito*) misdemeanor **2.** (*travesura*) prank
fécula ['fe·ku·la] *f* starch
fecundación [fe·kun·da·'sjon, -'θjon] *f* fertilization
fecundar [fe·kun·'dar] *vt t.* BIO to fertilize
fecundidad [fe·kun·di·'dad] *f* **1.** (*fertilidad*) fertility **2.** (*abundancia*) abundance **3.** (*pro-*

ductividad) productiveness

fecundizar <z→c> [fe·kun·di·'sar, -'θar] *vt* to fertilize

fecundo, -a [fe·'kun·do, -a] *adj* **1.**(*prolífico*) prolific **2.**(*tierra*) fertile; (*campo*) productive **3.**(*creador*) fertile

fedatario [fe·da·'ta·rjo] *m* (public) notary

federación [fe·de·ra·'sjon, -'θjon] *f* federation

federado, -a [fe·de·'ra·do, -a] *adj* federate; **estado** ~ federate state

federal [fe·de·'ral] **I.** *adj* federal; (*partidario del federalismo*) federalist; **estado** ~ federal state; **república** ~ federal republic **II.** *mf* federalist

federalismo [fe·de·ra·'lis·mo] *m* federalism

federalista [fe·de·ra·'lis·ta] *adj, mf* federalist

federalizar <z→c> [fe·de·ra·li·'sar, -'θar] **I.** *vt* to federalize **II.** *vr:* ~**se** to form a federation

federar [fe·de·'rar] **I.** *vt* (*aliarse*) to unite; (*federalizar*) to federate **II.** *vr:* ~**se** (*unirse*) to become a member; (*federalizarse*) to form a federation

federativo, -a [fe·de·ra·'ti·βo, -a] *adj* federative

fehaciente [fea·'sjen·te, -'θjen·te] *adj* indisputable; JUR irrefutable; **copia** ~ certified copy

felación [fe·la·'sjon, -'θjon] *f* fellatio

felicidad [fe·li·si·'dad, fe·li·θi-] *f* **1.**(*alegría*) happiness **2.**(*dicha*) good fortune; **¡~es!** (*boda, nacimiento, etc.*) congratulations!; (*Navidad*) Merry Christmas; (*cumpleaños*) happy birthday; **te deseamos muchas ~es** we wish you all the best

felicitación [fe·li·si·ta·'sjon, -θi·ta·'θjon] *f* **1.**(*enhorabuena*) congratulation **2.**(*tarjeta*) greetings card

felicitar [fe·li·si·'tar, fe·li·θi-] **I.** *vt* ~ **a alguien por algo** to congratulate sb on sth **II.** *vr* ~**se por algo** to be glad about sth; ~**se de que** +*subj* to be glad that

feligrés, -esa [fe·li·'ɣres, -·'ɣre·sa] *m, f* parishioner, church member

felino, -a [fe·'li·no, -a] *adj* feline

feliz [fe·'lis, -'liθ] *adj* **1.**(*dichoso*) happy; **¡~ Navidad!** merry Christmas!; **¡~ viaje!** have a good trip! **2.**(*exitoso*) fortunate, successful

felonía [fe·lo·'ni·a] *f* **1.**(*deslealtad*) disloyalty **2.**(*infamia*) infamy *form* **3.** AmL JUR felony

felpa ['fel·pa] *f* **1.**(*peluche*) plush **2.** *inf* (*paliza*) beating, licking **3.** *inf* (*reprimenda*) telling-off

felpeada [fel·pe·'a·da] *f Arg, Urug, CSur, inf* dressing-down

felpudo [fel·'pu·do] *m* doormat

felpudo, -a [fel·'pu·do, -a] *adj* (*tela*) plushy; (*moqueta*) shaggy

femenino [fe·me·'ni·no] *m* LING feminine

femenino, -a [fe·me·'ni·no, -a] *adj* **1.**(*de sexo femenino*) female; **equipo** ~ women's team **2.**(*afeminado*) effeminate **3.** LING feminine

feminidad [fe·mi·ni·'dad] *f* femininity

feminismo [fe·mi·'nis·mo] *m* (*doctrina*) feminism; (*movimiento*) feminist movement

feminista [fe·mi·'nis·ta] *adj, mf* feminist

fémur ['fe·mur] *m* ANAT femur, thigh-bone *inf*

fenecer [fe·ne·'ser, -'θer] *irr como crecer vi* (*morirse*) to die

fenicio, -a [fe·'ni·sjo, -θjo] *adj, m, f* Phoenician

fénix ['fe·niks] *m* phoenix

fenomenal [fe·no·me·'nal] **I.** *adj* **1.**(*extraordinario*) incredible; (*estupendo*) terrific **2.** *inf* (*tremendo*) tremendous **3.**(*fenoménico*) phenomenal **II.** *adv inf* terrifically

fenómeno [fe·'no·me·no] **I.** *adj inv, inf* marvelous; **¡~!** terrific! **II.** *m* **1.** *t.* FILOS, MED (*suceso*) phenomenon; (*maravilla*) marvel **2.**(*genio*) genius **3.**(*monstruo*) freak **III.** *adv* marvelously

feo ['feo] **I.** *m inf* **I.**(*grosería*) insult; **hacer un** ~ **a alguien** to snub [*o* slight] sb **II.** *adv inf* bad, badly

feo, -a ['feo, -a] **I.** *adj* **1.**(*espantoso*) ugly; **dejar** ~ **a alguien** *fig* to show sb up [*o* in a bad light]; **la cosa se está poniendo fea** things aren't looking too good **2.**(*reprobable*) bad; **está muy** ~ **lo que hiciste** what you did was really nasty [*o* rotten] **II.** *m, f* ugly man m, ugly woman *f*

féretro ['fe·re·tro] *m* coffin

feria ['fe·rja] *f* **1.**(*exposición*) fair, show; ~ **de muestras** trade fair **2.**(*fiesta*) festival **3.**(*verbena*) fair; **puesto de** ~ stand

feriado, -a [fe·'rja·do, -a] *adj AmL* holiday; **día** ~ bank [*o* legal] holiday

ferial [fe·'rjal] **I.** *adj* (*de exposición*) fair, show; **recinto** ~ trade fair pavilion **II.** *m* fair; (*lugar*) fairground

feriante [fe·'rjan·te] *mf* **1.**(*que exhibe*) exhibitor; (*en la verbena*) stall holder **2.**(*que compra*) fairgoer

feriar [fe·'rjar] **I.** *vi* to take time off **II.** *vt* **1.**(*comprar*) to buy **2.**(*vender*) to sell **3.**(*permutar*) to exchange, to barter

fermentación [fer·men·ta·'sjon, -'θjon] *f* fermentation

fermentar [fer·men·'tar] **I.** *vi* **1.**(*vino*) to ferment **2.**(*agitarse*) to get in a state, to work oneself up **II.** *vt* to ferment

fermento [fer·'men·to] *m* **1.**(*sustancia*) fermenting agent **2.**(*origen*) cause

ferocidad [fe·ro·si·'dad, fe·ro·θi-] *f* **1.**(*salvajismo*) ferocity **2.**(*crueldad*) savagery

feroz [fe·'ros, -'roθ] *adj* **1.**(*salvaje*) fierce **2.**(*cruel, violento*) savage **3.** *inf* (*muy grande*) huge

férreo, -a ['fe·rreo, -a] *adj* **1.**(*de hierro, tenaz*) iron **2.**(*del ferrocarril*) railroad

ferretería [fe·rre·te·'ri·a] *f* **1.**(*tienda*) hardware store **2.**(*ferrería*) ironworks *pl*

ferretero, -a [fe·rre·'te·ro, -a] *m, f* hardware dealer

férrico, -a ['fe·rri·ko, -a] *adj* ferrous

ferrocarril [fe·rro·ka·'rril] *m* **1.**(*vía*) railroad **2.**(*tren*) railroad; ~ **de cremallera** rack railway; ~ **de vía ancha** wide-gauge railroad; **por** ~ by rail

ferrocarrilero, -a [fe·rro·ka·rri·'le·ro, -a] *adj*

AmL, inf (ferroviario) railroad; **el transporte ~** rail transport

ferroviario, -a [fe·rro·'βja·rjo, -a] I. *adj* railroad II. *m, f* railroad worker

ferry ['fe·rri] *m* ferry

fértil ['fer·til] *adj* 1. *(tierra)* fertile; **estar en edad ~** to be of reproductive age 2. *(rico)* rich

fertilidad [fer·ti·li·'dad] *f* fertility; *(t. de tierra)* productiveness

fertilización [fer·ti·li·sa·'sjon, -θa·'θjon] *f (de tierra)* fertilization; **~ in vitro** in vitro fertilization

fertilizante [fer·ti·li·'san·te, -'θan·te] *m* fertilizer

fertilizar <z→c> [fer·ti·li·'sar, -'θar] *vt* to fertilize

ferviente [fer·'βjen·te] *adj* fervent

fervor [fer·'βor] *m* 1. *t.* REL fervor 2. *(calor)* intense heat 3. *(entusiasmo)* enthusiasm; **con ~** ardently

fervoroso, -a [fer·βo·'ro·so, -a] *adj* fervent

festejar [fes·te·'xar] I. *vt* 1. *(celebrar)* to celebrate 2. *(galantear)* to court, to woo 3. *AmL (azotar)* to beat II. *vr:* **~se** to enjoy oneself

festejo [fes·'te·xo] *m* 1. *(conmemoración)* celebration 2. *(galanteo)* courtship 3. *pl (actos públicos)* festival, public festivities *pl*

festín [fes·'tin] *m* 1. *(celebración)* celebration 2. *(banquete)* feast

festinar [fes·ti·'nar] *vt AmC* 1. *(agasajar)* to wine and dine 2. *(arruinar)* to ruin 3. *(apremiar)* to hasten

festival [fes·ti·'βal] *m* festival; **~ de cine** film festival

festividad [fes·ti·βi·'dad] *f* 1. *(conmemoración)* festivity 2. *(día)* feast

festivo, -a [fes·'ti·βo, -a] *adj* 1. *(de fiesta)* festive, celebratory; **día ~** bank holiday 2. *(humorístico)* humorous, entertaining; *(persona)* witty

festón [fes·'ton] *m* 1. *(guirnalda)* garland 2. *(remate cosido)* scallop

feta ['fe·ta] *f Arg* slice

fetal [fe·'tal] *adj* fetal

fetiche [fe·'ti·tʃe] *m* fetish

fetichismo [fe·ti·'tʃis·mo] *m* fetishism

fetichista [fe·ti·'tʃis·ta] I. *adj* fetishistic II. *mf* fetishist

fetidez [fe·ti·'des, -'deθ] *f* stench

fétido, -a ['fe·ti·do, -a] *adj* foul smelling; **bomba fétida** stink bomb

feto ['fe·to] *m* 1. MED fetus 2. *inf (feo)* ugly sod *inf*

feúcho, -a [fe·'u·tʃo, -a] *adj inf* unattractive, plain

feudal [feu·'dal] *adj* feudal, manorial; **señor ~** feudal lord

feudalismo [feu·da·'lis·mo] *m* 1. *(sistema)* feudalism 2. *(época)* feudal era

feudo ['feu·do] *m* fief; **este pueblo es un ~ de los socialistas** this town is a socialist stronghold

fiabilidad [fja·βi·li·'dad] *f* 1. *(de una persona)* trustworthiness 2. *(de una empresa, de datos)* reliability

fiable [fi·'a·βle] *adj* 1. *(persona)* trustworthy 2. *(empresa)* reliable

fiaca [fi·'a·ka] *f Arg, inf (pereza)* laziness

fiado, -a [fi·'a·do, -a] *adj* trusting; **comprar al ~** to buy on credit

fiador [fja·'dor] *m (de puerta)* catch; *(de pistola)* safety catch

fiador(a) [fja·'dor, -'do·ra] *m(f)* backer, bondsman; **salir ~ por alguien** to stand surety [*o* bail] for sb

fiambre [fi·'am·bre] I. *adj* 1. CULIN cold 2. *inf (noticia)* stale; *(discurso)* old hat II. *m* 1. CULIN cold meat 2. *inf (cadáver)* stiff; **ese está ~** that one is stone-dead

fiambrera [fjam·'bre·ra] *f (cesta)* picnic basket; *(para el almuerzo)* lunch pail [*o* box]; *(caja)* Tupperware® container

fianza [fi·'an·sa, -θa] *f* 1. *(depósito)* deposit 2. *(garantía)* security 3. *(fiador)* surety, bail; **en libertad bajo ~** free [*o* out] on bail

fiar <1. pres: fío> [fi·'ar] I. *vi* 1. *(al vender)* to give credit 2. *(confiar)* to trust; **es de ~** he/she is trustworthy II. *vt* 1. *(garantizar)* to stand surety [*o* bail] for 2. *(dar crédito)* to sell on credit 3. *(confiar)* to entrust III. *vr* **~se de algo/alguien** to trust sth/sb; **no te fíes de lo que dice** don't trust what he/she says

fiasco ['fjas·ko] *m* fiasco

fibra ['fi·βra] *f* 1. *t.* BIO, MED *(filamento)* fiber; **~ muscular** muscle fiber; **~ de vidrio** fiberglass 2. *(vigor)* energy; **no tiene ~ suficiente para llevar la empresa** he/she doesn't have the drive to run the business

fibroso, -a [fi·'βro·so, -a] *adj t.* MED fibrous

ficción [fik·'sjon, -'θjon] *f* 1. *(simulación)* simulation 2. *(invención)* invention; **~ novelesca** fiction

ficha ['fi·tʃa] *f* 1. *(de ruleta)* chip; *(de dominó)* domino; *(de ajedrez)* piece, man 2. *(para una máquina)* token; *(de teléfono)* telephone token; *(de guardarropa)* checkroom token 3. *(tarjeta informativa)* (index) card; *(en el trabajo)* card; **~ perforada** COMPUT punched card; **~ policial** police record; **~ técnica** technical specifications 4. DEP signing 5. *(bribón)* rascal

fichaje [fi·'tʃa·xe] *m* DEP signing (up)

fichar [fi·'tʃar] I. *vi* 1. DEP to sign 2. *(en el trabajo)* to clock in II. *vt* 1. *(registrar)* to enter; **~ a alguien** *(la policía)* to open a file on sb; **estar fichado** to have a police record 2. *inf (desconfiar)* to mistrust 3. DEP to sign up 4. *(anotar informaciones)* to record

fichero [fi·'tʃe·ro] *m* 1. *(archivador)* filing-cabinet; *(caja)* box file 2. COMPUT file

ficticio, -a [fik·'ti·sjo, -a; -θjo, -a] *adj* fictitious

fidedigno, -a [fi·de·'diɣ·no, -a] *adj* reliable

fideicomiso [fi·dei·ko·'mi·so] *m* trust

fidelidad [fi·de·li·'dad] *f* 1. *(lealtad)* fidelity, faithfulness 2. *(precisión)* precision; **alta ~** high fidelity

fideo [fi·'deo] *m* CULIN fine noodle

fiduciario, -a [fi·du·si·'da·rjo, -a; fi·du·θi-]

I. *adj* fiduciary II. *m, f* trustee

fiebre ['fje·βre] *f* fever; ~ **del heno** hay fever; ~ **del juego** compulsive gambling; ~ **del oro** gold rush; ~ **palúdica** malaria; **tener poca** ~ to have a slight temperature

fiel [fjel] I. *adj* 1. (*persona*) faithful; **ser** ~ **a una promesa** to keep a promise; **siempre me han sido ~es** they have always been loyal to me 2. (*retrato*) faithful 3. (*memoria*) accurate II. *m* 1. (*seguidor*) faithful 2. (*de una balanza*) needle, pointer; **él podría inclinar el ~ de la balanza** he could tip the scales 3. *pl* REL the faithful

fieltro ['fjel·tro] *m* felt

fiera ['fje·ra] *f* 1. ZOOL wild animal 2. (*persona*) animal; (*persona astuta*) wizard, whiz

fiereza [fje·'re·sa, -'re·θa] *f* 1. (*de un animal*) ferocity, ferociousness 2. (*de una persona*) cruelty

fiero, -a ['fje·ro, -a] *adj* 1. (*feroz*) fierce 2. (*cruel*) cruel 3. (*feo*) ugly 4. (*fuerte*) terrible

fierro ['fje·rro] *m AmL* 1. (*hierro*) iron 2. (*del ganado*) branding iron

fiesta ['fjes·ta] *f* 1. (*día*) holiday; **¡Felices Fiestas!** Merry Christmas and a Happy New Year!; **hoy hago** ~ I have taken the day off today 2. (*celebración*) celebration; ~ (**mayor**) festival; **aguar la** ~ *inf* to be a wet blanket 3. *inf* (*humor*) **estar de** ~ to be in a very cheerful mood 4. *inf* (*asunto*) **tengamos la** ~ **en paz** let's agree to differ

fifí [fi·'fi] *m AmL* (*señorito*) playboy, man-about-town

fifiriche [fi·fi·'ri·tʃe] *adj AmL* (*enclenque*) weak

fig. [fi·ɣu·ra·'ti·βo] *abr de* **figurativo** fig

figura [fi·'ɣu·ra] *f* 1. *t.* ARTE, MAT (*de un cuerpo*) figure; ~ **decorativa** (*persona*) formal figure; **un vestido que realza la** ~ (*que adelgaza*) a dress that enhances the figure 2. (*cara, mueca*) face; (*aspecto*) countenance 3. (*imagen*) image; **se distinguía la** ~ **de un barco** you could make out the shape of a boat 4. TEAT character 5. (*personaje*) figure; **las grandes ~s del deporte** great sports figures 6. (*ilustración*) illustration 7. (*de la baraja*) court card 8. MÚS note

figuración [fi·ɣu·ra·'sjon, -'θjon] *f* 1. ARTE representational art 2. (*imaginación*) imagination 3. CINE extras *pl*

figurado, -a [fi·ɣu·'ra·do, -a] *adj* 1. (*lenguaje*) metaphorical 2. (*uso*) figurative; **en sentido** ~ in a figurative sense

figurante [fi·ɣu·'ran·te] *mf* CINE, TEAT extra

figurar [fi·ɣu·'rar] I. *vi* 1. (*encontrarse*) to figure; **no figura en la lista** it is not on the list; **figura en el puesto número tres** he appears in third place 2. (*destacar*) to stand out 3. (*aparentar*) to pose; **le gusta un montón** ~ he loves putting on airs II. *vt* 1. (*representar*) to represent 2. TEAT to appear 3. (*simular*) to pretend III. *vr:* ~**se** to imagine; **¡figúrate!** just think!; **no vayas a ~te que...** don't go thinking that...

figurativo, -a [fi·ɣu·ra·'ti·βo, -a] *adj* figurative; **no** ~ non-figurative

figurín [fi·ɣu·'rin] *m* 1. (*dibujo*) fashion design; (*modelo*) model 2. (*persona*) flashy person 3. (*revista*) fashion magazine

figurita [fi·ɣu·'ri·ta] *f Arg* picture card

figuroso, -a [fi·ɣu·'ro·so, -a] *adj Chile, Méx* (*extravagante en el vestir*) loud-dressing

fija ['fi·xa] *f* 1. *CSur* (*en una apuesta*) sure bet 2. *Arg* (*arpón*) harpoon

fijación [fi·xa·'sjon, -'θjon] *f* 1. (*sujeción*) fixation; (*con chinchetas*) sticking up; (*con cuerdas*) tying up; (*con cola*) gluing on; (*con clavos*) nailing; (*con cadenas*) chaining; (*con tornillos*) screwing on 2. (*de precio, regla*) fixing 3. (*de la mirada*) fixedness 4. (*de esquíes*) ski binding 5. (*obsesión*) **tener una ~ por alguien** to have a fixation on sb

fijado [fi·'xa·do] *m* FOTO fixing

fijador [fi·xa·'dor] *m* 1. (*para el pelo*) hair gel 2. (*de pintura*) fixative 3. FOTO fixer

fijar [fi·'xar] I. *vt* 1. (*sujetar*) to fix; (*con cuerdas*) to tie up; (*con cola*) to glue on; (*con clavos*) to nail; (*con cadenas*) to chain; (*con tornillos*) to screw on; ~ **con chinchetas** to stick up with drawing pins; ~ **una placa en la pared** to fix a plaque on the wall; **prohibido ~ carteles** bill posters prohibited 2. (*la mirada*) to fix; ~ **la atención en algo** to concentrate on sth 3. (*residencia, precio*) to establish 4. *t.* QUÍM to fix II. *vr:* ~**se** 1. (*en un lugar*) to establish oneself 2. (*atender*) to pay attention; **no se ha fijado en mi nuevo peinado** he/she has not noticed my new hairdo; **ese se fija en todo** nothing escapes him; **fíjate bien en lo que te digo** listen carefully to what I have to say 3. (*mirar*) to notice; **no se fijó en mí** he/she did not notice me

fijeza [fi·'xe·sa, -θa] *f* (*persistencia*) persistence; **mirar con ~ a alguien** to stare fixedly at sb

fijo, -a ['fi·xo, -a] I. *adj* 1. (*estable*) stable; **cliente** ~ regular client; **precio** ~ fixed price 2. (*idea*) fixed 3. (*mirada*) steady 4. (*trabajador*) permanent II. *adv* with certainty; **saber algo de** ~ to know sth for sure

fila ['fi·la] *f* 1. (*hilera*) row; ~ **de coches** line of cars; **en** ~ **india** in single file; **aparcar en doble** ~ to double-park; **en** ~ **india; salir de la** ~ to step out of line 2. MIL rank; **¡en ~s!** fall in!; **¡rompan ~s!** fall out!; **llamar a ~s** to draft 3. *inf* (*tirria*) dislike 4. MAT row 5. *pl* (*de un partido*) ranks *pl*

filamento [fi·la·'men·to] *m* 1. (*de un tejido*) thread 2. ELEC filament

filantropía [fi·lan·tro·'pi·a] *f* philanthropy

filántropo [fi·'lan·tro·po, -a] *mf* philanthropist

filarmónico, -a [fi·lar·'mo·ni·ko, -a] *adj* Philharmonic; **orquesta filarmónica** Philharmonic Orchestra

filatelia [fi·la·'te·lja] *f* philately, stamp collecting

filatelista [fi·la·te·'lis·ta] *mf* philatelist, stamp

collector

filete [fi·'le·te] *m* **1.** CULIN (*solomillo*) steak; (*lonja*) filet **2.** (*ribete*) edging

filetear [fi·le·te·'ar] *vt* **1.** (*un vestido*) to hem **2.** CULIN to filet **3.** (*tornillo*) to thread

filiación [fi·lja·'sjon, -'θjon] *f* **1.** (*origen*) filiation; (*de ideas*) relation **2.** (*datos personales*) particulars *pl* **3.** (*en un partido*) affiliation

filial [fi·'ljal] **I.** *adj* filial; **equipo ~** DEP sister club **II.** *f* **1.** COM subsidiary **2.** REL dependency

filigrana [fi·li·'γra·na] *f* **1.** (*de orfebrería*) filigree **2.** (*en un papel*) watermark

Filipinas [fi·li·'pi·nas] *fpl* **las ~** the Philippines

filipino, -a [fi·li·'pi·no, -a] *adj, m, f* Philippine

film [film] *m* CINE, FOTO film, movie; **~ transparente** plastic wrap®

filmación [fil·ma·'sjon, -'θjon] *f* **1.** (*de reportaje*) footage **2.** (*rodaje*) filming, shooting

filmadora [fil·ma·'do·ra] *f* camera

filmar [fil·'mar] *vt* to film, to shoot

filme ['fil·me] *m* film, movie

filmina [fil·'mi·na] *f* slide

filmografía [fil·mo·γra·'fi·a] *f* films, movies

filmoteca [fil·mo·'te·ka] *f* film archive

filo ['fi·lo] *m* **1.** (*de cuchillo*) blade; **un arma de dos ~s** *fig* a double-edged sword **2.** (*entre dos partes*) dividing line **3.** *AmC* (*hambre*) hunger

filología [fi·lo·lo·'xi·a] *f* philology; **~ germánica** Germanic language and literature; **~ hispánica** Hispanic language and literature

filólogo, -a [fi·'lo·lo·γo, -a] *m, f* philologist

filón [fi·'lon] *m* **1.** MIN seam **2.** (*negocio*) gold mine

filoso, -a [fi·'lo·so, -a] *adj AmL* (*afilado*) sharp

filosofar [fi·lo·so·'far] *vi* to philosophize

filosofía [fi·lo·so·'fi·a] *f* **1.** (*disciplina*) philosophy **2.** (*serenidad*) calm; **tomar las cosas con ~** to be philosophical about things

filosófico, -a [fi·lo·'so·fi·ko, -a] *adj* philosophical

filósofo, -a [fi·'lo·so·fo, -a] *m, f* philosopher

filoxera [fi·lok·'se·ra] *f* (*insecto*) phylloxera

filtración [fil·tra·'sjon, -'θjon] *f* **1.** (*de un líquido*) leak, seepage; (*de la luz*) filtration **2.** (*de información*) leak

filtrar [fil·'trar] **I.** *vi* **1.** (*líquido*) to leak (out), to seep; (*luz*) to filter **2.** (*tubería*) to leak **II.** *vt* **1.** (*por un filtro*) to filter; (*llamadas*) to screen **2.** (*datos*) to leak **3.** (*noticia*) to percolate **III.** *vr:* **~se 1.** (*líquido*) to seep; (*luz*) to filter **2.** (*noticia*) to percolate **3.** (*dinero*) to dwindle

filtro ['fil·tro] *m* **1.** (*tamiz*) filter; **cigarrillo con ~** filter tip cigarette; **~ solar** sunscreen **2.** (*poción*) philter

filudo, -a [fi·'lu·do, -a] *adj AmL* sharp

fin [fin] *m* **1.** (*término*) end; **~ de semana** weekend; **a ~(es) de mes** at the end of the month; **algo toca a su ~** sth is coming to an end; **poner ~ a algo** to put an end to sth; **sin ~** never-ending; **al ~ y al cabo, a ~ de cuentas** after all **2.** (*propósito*) aim; **~es deshonestos** immoral purposes; **a ~ de que** +*subj*

so that

finado, -a [fi·'na·do, -a] *m, f* deceased

final¹ [fi·'nal] **I.** *adj* (*producto, resultado*) end; (*fase, examen*) final; (*solución*) ultimate; **el juicio ~** REL the Final [*o* Last] Judgment; **palabras ~es** last words **II.** *m* end; (*de un libro*) ending; MÚS finale; **película con ~ feliz** film with a happy ending; **al ~ no nos lo dijo** in the end he did not tell us

final² [fi·'nal] *f* DEP (*partido*) final; (*ronda*) finals *pl*

finalidad [fi·na·li·'dad] *f* purpose; FILOS finality

finalista [fi·na·'lis·ta] *mf t.* FILOS finalist

finalización [fi·na·li·sa·'sjon, -θa·'θjon] *f* finalization; **~ de contrato** completion of a contract

finalizar <z→c> [fi·na·li·'sar, -'θar] **I.** *vi* to finish; (*plazo*) to end **II.** *vt* to end; (*discurso*) to conclude

finalmente [fi·nal·'men·te] *adv* finally, at last

financiación [fi·nan·sja·'sjon, -θja·'θjon] *f* financing, funding; **~ de los partidos** political party financial backing

financiador(a) [fi·nan·sja·'dor, -·'do·ra, fi·nan·θja-] *m(f)* financial backer

financiar [fi·nan·'sjar, -'θjar] *vt* to finance

financiera [fi·nan·'sje·ra, -'θje·ra] *f* finance company

financiero, -a [fi·nan·'sje·ro, -a; -'θje·ro, -a] **I.** *adj* financial **II.** *m, f* financier

financista [fi·nan·'sis·ta, -'θis·ta] *mf AmL* **1.** (*experto en finanzas*) financial expert **2.** (*el que financia*) financier

finanzas [fi·'nan·sas, -θas] *fpl* finances *pl*

finar [fi·'nar] *vi* to die

finca ['fin·ka] *f* (*urbana*) (town) property; (*rústica*) (country) estate

finés, -esa [fi·'nes] **I.** *adj* Finnish **II.** *m, f* Finn

fineza [fi·'ne·sa, -θa] *f* **1.** (*delgadez*) fineness **2.** (*suavidad*) softness **3.** (*de calidad*) excellence **4.** (*cumplido*) compliment **5.** (*regalo*) gift **6.** (*primor*) exquisiteness

fingido, -a [fin·'xi·do, -a] *adj* fake, make-believe; (*persona*) false

fingidor(a) [fin·xi·'dor, -·'do·ra] *m(f)* (*de una enfermedad*) *person who pretends to be ill;* (*de sentimientos*) *person who feigns a feeling*

fingimiento [fin·xi·'mjen·to] *m* **1.** (*de una enfermedad*) pretense; (*de un sentimiento*) feigning **2.** (*engaño*) trick; (*hipocresía*) hypocrisy

fingir <g→j> [fin·'xir] **I.** *vi* to pretend **II.** *vt* to pretend; (*sentimiento*) to feign

finiquitar [fi·ni·ki·'tar] *vt* **1.** (*cuenta*) to settle **2.** *inf* (*asunto*) to wind up

finiquito [fi·ni·'ki·to] *m* settlement; (*documento*) final discharge

finisecular [fi·ni·se·ku·'lar] *adj* turn-of-the-century

finito, -a [fi·'ni·to, -a] *adj* finite; **número ~** MAT finite number

finlandés, -esa [fin·lan·'des] **I.** *adj* Finnish **II.** *m, f* Finn

Finlandia [fin·'lan·dja] *f* Finland
fino ['fi·no] *m* dry sherry
fino, -a ['fi·no, -a] *adj* **1.**(*delgado*) fine; **lluvia fina** fine rain **2.**(*liso*) smooth, even **3.**(*de calidad*) excellent; **oro** ~ refined gold; **tener un paladar** ~ to have a discriminating palate **4.**(*sentido*) acute **5.**(*cortés*) polite; **modales** ~s refined manners **6.**(*astuto*) shrewd **7.**(*metal*) precious
finolis [fi·'no·lis] **I.** *adj inv, inf* la-di-da, hoity-toity **II.** *mf inv, inf* affected person
finura [fi·'nu·ra] *f* **1.**(*delgadez*) fineness **2.**(*suavidad*) smoothness **3.**(*calidad*) excellence **4.**(*cortesía*) refinement **5.**(*astucia*) shrewdness
fiordo ['fjor·do] *m* fjord, fiord
fique ['fi·ke] *m Col* BOT sisal
firma ['fir·ma] *f* **1.**(*en documentos*) signature **2.**(*de un acuerdo*) signing **3.**(*empresa*) firm
firmamento [fir·ma·'men·to] *m* firmament
firmante [fir·'man·te] *mf* signatory, signer; **el/la abajo** ~ the undersigned
firmar [fir·'mar] *vi, vt* to sign; ~ **autógrafos** to sign autographs; ~ **un cheque** (*para pagar*) to sign a check; (*para cobrar*) to endorse a check; ~ **un tratado /acuerdo** to sign a treaty/an agreement
firme ['fir·me] **I.** *adj* (*fijo*) firm; (*estable*) steady; (*seguro*) secure; (*carácter*) resolute; (*postura corporal*) straight; (*amistad*) strong; **con mano** ~ with a firm hand; **esta mesa no está** ~ this table is unsteady; **es** ~ **en sus propósitos** he/she is resolute in his/her intentions **II.** *m* **1.**(*de la carretera*) road surface **2.**(*de guijo*) roadbed **III.** *adv* **de** ~ (*fuertemente*) strongly; (*sin parar*) steadily; **el calor aprieta de** ~ the heat is intense
firmeza [fir·'me·sa, -θa] *f* **1.**(*solidez*) solidity; (*de un mueble*) sturdiness **2.**(*de una creencia*) firmness; ~ **de carácter** resolution **3.**(*perseverancia*) perseverance
firulete [fi·ru·'le·te] *m* **1.** *CSur* (*adorno*) cheap adornment **2.** *RíoPl* (*paso de tango*) tango step
fiscal [fis·'kal] **I.** *adj* **1.**(*del fisco*) fiscal **2.**(*de los impuestos*) tax **II.** *mf* **1.** JUR public prosecutor; **Fiscal General del Estado** Attorney General **2.**(*interventor*) auditor, inspector
fiscalía [fis·ka·'li·a] *f* office of the public prosecutor
fiscalidad [fis·ka·li·'dad] *f* taxation
fiscalización [fis·ka·li·sa·'sjon, -θa·'θjon] *f* audit; (*de impuestos*) tax inspection
fiscalizador(a) [fis·ka·li·sa·'dor, --'do·ra; fis·ka·li·θa-] *m(f)* auditor; (*de impuestos*) tax inspector
fiscalizar <z→c> [fis·ka·li·'sar, -'θar] *vt* to audit; (*lo fiscal*) to inspect
fisco ['fis·ko] *m* public treasury
fisgar <g→gu> [fis·'yar] **I.** *vi* (*indagar*) ~ **en algo** to snoop around sth; **le encanta** ~ **en mis asuntos** he/she loves prying into my affairs **II.** *vt* **1.**(*pescar*) to harpoon **2.**(*con el olfato*) to sniff out

fisgón, -ona [fis·'yon, --'yo·na] *m, f pey* **1.**(*que indaga*) nosy Parker **2.**(*que se burla*) mocker
fisgonear [fis·yo·ne·'ar] *vi pey* ~ **en algo** to pry into sth
física ['fi·si·ka] *f* physics *pl*
físicamente [fi·si·ka·'men·te] *adv* physically
físico ['fi·si·ko] *m* physique; **tener un buen** ~ (*cuerpo*) to have a good physique; (*aspecto general*) to be good-looking
físico, -a ['fi·si·ko, -a] **I.** *adj t.* FÍS physical; **educación física** ENS physical education **II.** *m, f* physicist
fisiología [fi·sjo·lo·'xi·a] *f* physiology
fisiólogo, -a [fi·'sjo·lo·yo, -a] *m, f* physiologist
fisión [fi·'sjon] *f* FÍS, BIO fission
fisionomía [fi·sjo·no·'mi·a] *f v.* **fisonomía**
fisioterapeuta [fi·sjo·te·ra·'peu·ta] *mf* physiotherapist
fisioterapia [fi·sjo·te·'ra·pja] *f* physiotherapy
fisonomía [fi·so·no·'mi·a] *f* **1.**(*general*) physiognomy **2.**(*del rostro*) face **3.**(*aspecto*) appearance **4.**(*rasgos*) features *pl*
fisonomista [fi·so·no·'mis·ta] *mf* **¿eres un buen** ~? do you have a good memory for faces?
fístula ['fis·tu·la] *f* **1.** MED fistula **2.**(*tubo*) tube
fisura [fi·'su·ra] *f* **1.**(*grieta*) fissure, crack **2.** MED (*en un hueso*) hairline fracture **3.** MED (*en el ano*) fissure
flac(c)idez [flak·si·'des, flay·θi·'deθ] *f* **1.**(*de las carnes*) flabbiness **2.**(*de la piel*) flaccidity
flác(c)ido, -a ['flak·si·do, -a; 'flay·θi·do, -a] *adj* **1.**(*carnes*) flabby **2.**(*piel*) flaccid **3.**(*vestiduras*) loose
flaco ['fla·ko] *m* weak spot
flaco, -a ['fla·ko, -a] *adj* **1.**(*delgado*) thin; **los años de las vacas flacas** the lean years **2.**(*escaso*) poor; **rendimientos** ~s poor performance **3.**(*débil*) weak; **punto** ~ weak spot
flacucho, -a [fla·'ku·tʃo, -a] *adj pey, inf* skinny
flagelar [fla·xe·'lar] **I.** *vt* **1.**(*azotar*) to flog; REL to flagellate **2.**(*verbalmente*) to censure **II.** *vr:* ~ **se** to flagellate oneself
flagelo [fla·'xe·lo] *m* whip; (*azote*) scourge
flagrante [fla·'yran·te] **I.** *adj* (*evidente*) flagrant **II.** *adv* **en** ~ red-handed
flamante [fla·'man·te] *adj inf* **1.**(*vistoso*) flamboyant **2.**(*nuevo*) brand-new
flamear [fla·me·'ar] **I.** *vi* **1.**(*llamear*) to flame **2.**(*bandera*) to flap **II.** *vt* **1.** CULIN to flambé **2.** MED to disinfect (*using a flame*)
flamenco [fla·'men·ko] *m* **1.** ZOOL flamingo **2.**(*cante, baile*) flamenco **3.**(*lengua*) Flemish

> **i** The **flamenco**, a traditional form of song and dance from **Andalucía**, is known the world over. The origins of the **flamenco** can be found in the rich traditions of three national groups: the Andalusians, the Moors, and the Gypsies. The song and dance movements (solos or duets) are always accompanied by a

rhythmic clapping of the hands and clicking of the fingers, as well as various cries, such as "Ole!"

flamenco, -a [fla·'men·ko, -a] I. *adj* 1.(*andaluz*) flamenco; **cante** ~ flamenco 2.(*de Flandes*) Flemish 3.(*chulo*) cocky II. *m, f* Fleming

flan [flan] *m* crème caramel; **estar hecho un ~** to be shaking like a leaf

flanco ['flan·ko] *m* flank, side

Flandes ['flan·des] *m* Flanders

flanquear [flan·ke·'ar] *vt* 1.(*estar al lado*) to flank 2. MIL to outflank

flaquear [fla·ke·'ar] *vi* 1.(*fuerzas*) to flag; (*salud*) to decline 2.(*en un examen*) to be poor 3.(*demanda*) to slacken 4.(*edificio*) to be on the point of giving way 5.(*ánimo*) to lose heart

flaqueza [fla·'ke·sa, -θa] *f* 1.(*de flaco*) thinness 2.(*debilidad*) weakness

flash [flaʃ] *m inv* 1. FOTO flash 2.(*noticia*) newsflash

flato ['fla·to] *m* 1. MED flatulence 2. *AmC* (*melancolía*) melancholy

flatoso, -a [fla·'to·so, -a] *adj AmL* (*miedoso*) apprehensive

flatulencia [fla·tu·'len·sja, -θja] *f* MED flatulence

flauta¹ ['flau·ta] *f* ~ (**dulce**) recorder; ~ (**travesera**) flute

flauta² ['flau·ta] *mf*, **flautista** [flau·'tis·ta] *mf* flutist

flebitis [fle·'βi·tis] *f inv* MED phlebitis

flecha ['fle·tʃa] *f* 1.(*arma*) arrow; **ser rápido como una ~** *fig* to be as quick as lightning 2.(*de torre*) spire 3.(*de viga*) rise

flechar [fle·'tʃar] I. *vi* to shoot (with an arrow) II. *vt* 1.(*un arco*) to draw 2. *inf*(*enamorar*) to sweep sb off his/her feet

flechazo [fle·'tʃa·so, -θo] *m* 1.(*de flecha*) arrow shot 2. *inf*(*de amor*) **lo nuestro fue un ~** ours was love at first sight

fleco ['fle·ko] *m* 1.(*adorno*) fringe 2.(*del pelo*) fringe 3. *pl* (*de vestido*) frayed edges *pl* 4. *pl fig* (*asunto*) fine print

flema ['fle·ma] *f* 1.(*calma*) imperturbability 2.(*mucosidad*) phlegm

flemático, -a [fle·'ma·ti·ko, -a] I. *adj* phlegmatic II. *m, f* phlegmatic person

flemón [fle·'mon] *m* 1. MED conjunctivitis 2.(*dental*) gumboil

flequillo [fle·'ki·jo, -ʎo] *m* fringe; ()

fleta ['fle·ta] *f AmC* 1.(*friega*) rubbing 2.(*zurra*) thrashing; (*castigo*) spanking

fletador(a) [fle·ta·'dor, -'do·ra] *m(f)* 1.(*de avión*) charterer 2. COM freighter 3.(*pasajeros*) carrier

fletamento [fle·ta·'men·to] *m* 1.(*de avión*) charter 2.(*contrato*) freight 3.(*pasajeros*) carrier

fletar [fle·'tar] I. *vt* 1.(*avión*) to charter 2. COM

to freight 3. *AmL* (*vehículo*) to hire, to rent 4. *CSur* (*despedir*) to fire II. *vr*: ~ **se** *AmC* (*fastidiarse*) to get annoyed

flete ['fle·te] *m* 1.(*carga*) cargo, freight 2. COM (*tasa*) freight 3. *AmL* (*tarifa*) hire charge

flexibilidad [flek·si·βi·li·'dad] *f* 1.(*de palo*) flexibility; (*de músculo*) suppleness 2.(*de una persona*) flexibility; ~ **de precios** price flexibility

flexibilizar <z→c> [flek·si·βi·li·'sar, -'θar] *vt* to make (more) flexible

flexible [flek·'si·βle] *adj* 1.(*palo*) flexible; (*músculo*) supple 2.(*persona*) flexible; **horario** ~ flextime

flexión [flek·'sjon] *f* (*del cuerpo*) flexion, bending; (*plancha*) press-up; ~ **de brazos en la espaldera** pull-up

flexionar [flek·sjo·'nar] *vt* to flex, to bend

flexo ['flek·so] *m* flexible table lamp

flipado, -a [fli·'pa·do, -a] *adj inf* freaked *inf;* (*drogado*) stoned, high

flipante [fli·'pan·te] *adj inf* amazing, far-out *inf,* awesome *inf;* (*drogas*) mind-bending

flipar [fli·'par] I. *vt inf* **este actor me flipa** I love this actor II. *vi, vr:* ~ **se** *inf* (*drogas*) to be spaced-out [*o* on a high], to get high [*o* stoned]

flirt [flirt] *m* <flirts> flirt

flirtear [flir·te·'ar] *vi* to flirt

flirteo [flir·'teo] *m* flirtation

flojear [flo·xe·'ar] *vi* 1.(*disminuir*) to diminish; (*calor*) to ease up 2.(*en una materia*) ~ **en algo** to be poor at sth

flojera [flo·'xe·ra] *f inf* 1.(*debilidad*) weakness; **cogió ~ de piernas** his legs went weak 2.(*pereza*) slackness

flojo, -a ['flo·xo, -a] *adj* 1.(*cuerda*) slack; (*nudo*) loose 2.(*vino, café, argumento*) weak; (*viento*) light; (*luz*) feeble; ~ **de carácter** spineless; **estoy ~ en inglés** I am weak in English 3.(*cosecha*) poor 4.(*obrero*) slack 5. *AmL* (*cobarde*) cowardly

flor [flor] *f* 1. BOT (*planta*) flowering plant; (*parte de la planta*) flower, bloom; **estar en ~** to be in flower [*o* bloom]; **camisa de ~ es** flowery shirt 2.(*lo más selecto*) flower; **la ~ y nata de la sociedad** the cream of society; **la ~ de la canela** *fig* the best; **la ~ de la vida** the prime of life 3.(*piropo*) compliment 4.(*de los metales*) iridescence 5.(*de las pieles*) grain 6.(*virginidad*) virginity 7.(*del vino*) lees *pl* 8.(*nivel*) **pasó volando a ~ de tierra** the plane skimmed over the ground; **tengo los nervios a ~ de piel** my nerves are frayed

flora ['flo·ra] *f* flora

floración [flo·ra·'sjon, -'θjon] *f* 1.(*acción*) flowering 2.(*tiempo*) flowering season

florear [flo·re·'ar] I. *vi* 1.(*la espada*) to flourish 2. MÚS to play a trill 3. *AmL* (*florecer*) to flower II. *vt* 1.(*adornar*) to adorn with flowers 2.(*harina*) to sift 3.(*naipes*) to stack 4.(*piropear*) to compliment

florecer [flo·re·'ser, -'θer] *irr como crecer* I. *vi* 1.(*planta*) to flower, to bloom 2.(*industria*) to

flourish **II.** *vr:* ~ **se** to grow mold
floreciente [flo·re·'sjen·te, -'θjen·te] *adj*
1. (*planta*) flowering **2.** (*industria*) flourishing
florecimiento [flo·re·si·'mjen·to, -θi·'mjen·to]
m **1.** (*de una planta*) flowering **2.** (*de una industria*) flourishing
floreo [flo·'reo] *m* **1.** (*conversación*) empty talk **2.** MÚS ornament
florería [flo·re·'ri·a] *f CSur, Bol, Perú* (*floristería*) florist's, flower shop
florero [flo·'re·ro] *m* **1.** (*jarrón*) vase; **estar de** ~ *fig* to be just for decoration **2.** (*maceta*) flowerpot
florete [flo·'re·te] *m* DEP foil
floricultor(a) [flo·ri·kul·'tor, --'to·ra] *m(f)* floriculturist
floricultura [flo·ri·kul·'tu·ra] *f* flower growing
florido, -a [flo·'ri·do, -a] *adj* **1.** (*con flores*) flowery; (*floreciente*) flowering; **árbol** ~ tree in flower [*o* bloom] **2.** (*selecto*) select **3.** (*lenguaje*) florid
florín [flo·'rin] *m* florin
floripondio [flo·ri·'pon·djo] *m pey* **1.** (*flor*) large flower **2.** (*adorno*) gaudy decoration
florista [flo·'ris·ta] *mf* florist
floristería [flo·ris·te·'ri·a] *f* florist's, flower shop
flota ['flo·ta] *f* fleet
flotación [flo·ta·'sjon, -'θjon] *f* **1.** floating, flotation, floatation; **línea de** ~ NÁUT waterline **2.** FIN flotation, floatation
flotador [flo·ta·'dor] *m* **1.** TÉC (*de pesca*) float **2.** (*en barcos*) float; (*para niños*) rubber ring **3.** (*cisterna*) ballcock **4.** *RíoPl, inf* (*michelines*) roll of fat
flotar [flo·'tar] *vi* **1.** (*en agua: activamente*) to stay afloat; (*pasivamente*) to be suspended; (*en aire*) to float **2.** (*bandera*) to wave
flote ['flo·te] *m* **estar a** ~ to be afloat; **mantenerse a** ~ *t. fig* to manage to keep one's head above water; **sacar a** ~ **una empresa** to get a business going
fluctuación [fluk·twa·'sjon, -'θjon] *f* **1.** (*oscilación*) fluctuation **2.** (*irresolución*) uncertainty
fluctuante [fluk·tu·'an·te] *adj* fluctuating
fluctuar <*1. pres:* fluctúo> [fluk·tu·'ar] *vi* to fluctuate; **estoy fluctuando entre comprarme un coche o no** I can't decide whether to buy a car or not
fluidez [flwi·'des, -'deθ] *f* **1.** (*de líquido*) fluidity **2.** (*de expresión*) **hablar con** ~ **un idioma extranjero** to speak a foreign language fluently
fluido ['flwi·do] *m* **1.** (*líquido*) fluid **2.** ELEC current **3.** (*expresión*) fluent
fluido, -a ['flwi·do, -a] *adj* **1.** (*alimento*) liquid; **es** ~ **de palabra** he speaks with ease **2.** (*tráfico*) free-flowing
fluir [flu·'ir] *irr como huir vi* **1.** (*correr*) to run; (*brotar*) to flow **2.** (*palabras*) to flow
flujo ['flu·xo] *m* **1.** (*de un líquido*) flow; ~ **de datos** *t.* COMPUT data flow; ~ **de palabras** stream of words **2.** (*de la marea*) rising tide

3. MED discharge; ~ **de vientre** diarrhea; ~ **menstrual** menstrual flow
fluminense [flu·mi·'nen·se] **I.** *adj* of/from Rio de Janeiro **II.** *mf* native/inhabitant of Rio de Janeiro
flúor ['fluor] *m* fluorine
fluorescente [flwo·re·'sen·te, -s'θen·te] **I.** *adj* fluorescent; **tubo** ~ fluorescent tube **II.** *m* fluorescent light
flus [flus] *m* **1.** *Ant, Col, Ven* (*terno*) suit of clothes **2.** *ElSal* (*racha de buena suerte*) lucky streak
fluvial [flu·'βjal] *adj* fluvial; **puerto** ~ river port
FM [e·'fe·me/e·fe·'e·me] *f abr de* **Frecuencia Modulada** FM
FMI [e·fe·m·e'i] *m abr de* **Fondo Monetario Internacional** IMF
fobia ['fo·βja] *f* **1.** MED phobia **2.** (*aversión*) aversion
foca ['fo·ka] *f* **1.** ZOOL seal **2.** (*piel*) sealskin **3.** *pey* (*gordo*) whale
focal [fo·'kal] *adj* focal; **distancia** ~ focal length
focalizar <z→c> [fo·ka·li·'sar, -'θar] *vt* to focus on
foche ['fo·tʃe] **I.** *adj Chile* (*maloliente*) smelly **II.** *mf Chile* (*persona corrompida*) corrupt person, rotten apple *inf*
foco ['fo·ko] *m* **1.** FÍS, MAT focus **2.** (*centro*) focal point; ~ **de infección** source of infection **3.** (*lámpara*) light; (*estadio*) floodlight; (*teatro*) spotlight **4.** *AmL* (*bombilla*) light bulb
fofo, -a ['fo·fo, -a] *adj* flabby; **estoy** ~ I am flabby
fogaje [fo·'ya·xe] *m Arg, Col, PRico, Ven* (*bochorno*) stifling heat
fogata [fo·'ya·ta] *f* (*en el campo*) bonfire; (*de alegría*) blaze; (*como baliza*) flare
fogón [fo·'yon] *m* **1.** (*de la cocina*) stove **2.** (*de máquinas de vapor*) furnace; FERRO firebox **3.** (*de un cañón*) vent **4.** *AmL* (*fogata*) fire
fogonazo [fo·yo·'na·so, -θo] *m* **1.** (*de arma*) flash **2.** (*de pólvora*) flare
fogosidad [fo·yo·si·'dad] *f* **1.** (*de pasión*) passion **2.** (*de persona*) ardor **3.** (*de debate*) animation
fogoso, -a [fo·'yo·so, -a] *adj* **1.** (*pasión*) passionate **2.** (*persona*) ardent **3.** (*debate*) animated **4.** (*caballo*) spirited
fogueado, -a [fo·ye·'a·do, -a] *adj AmL* expert
foguear [fo·ye·'ar] **I.** *vt* **1.** (*un arma*) to fire a blank (cartridge) **2.** MIL to get used to gunfire **3.** (*a penalidades*) to harden **II.** *vr:* ~ **se** to become hardened
fogueo [fo·'yeo] *m* **bala de** ~ blank (cartridge)
foguerear [fo·ye·re·'ar] **I.** *vt Chile, Cuba* (*quemar*) to burn off **II.** *vi* (*hacer una hoguera*) to make a fire
foja ['fo·xa] *f AmL* sheet; ~ **de servicios** record
folclor(e) [fol·'klor, --'klo·re] *m* folklore
folclórico, -a [fol·'klo·ri·ko, -a] **I.** *adj* folk **II.** *m, f* flamenco singer
fólder ['fol·der] *f AmL* (*carpeta*) folder

foliación [fo·lja'sjon, -'θjon] *f* foliation

folio ['fo·ljo] *m* **1.** (*hoja de papel*) sheet (of paper) **2.** (*de un libro*) leaf

folk [folk] *m* MÚS folk music

follador [fo·ja·'dor, fo·ʎa·] *m* (*que afuella*) bellows operator

follaje [fo·'ja·xe, fo·'ʎa-] *m* **1.** (*de árbol, bosque*) foliage **2.** (*adorno*) decoration of branches and leaves **3.** (*en un texto, al hablar*) waffle, wordiness

follar¹ [fo·'jar, -'ʎar] **I.** *vi vulg* to fuck **II.** *vt* **1.** *vulg* (*coitar*) to fuck **2.** *vulg* (*fastidiar*) to bug *inf* **3.** (*deshacer*) to destroy

follar² <o→ue> [fo·'jar, -'ʎar] *vt* **1.** (*soplar*) to blow with bellows **2.** *inf* (*suspender*) to screw up

folletín [fo·je·'tin, fo·ʎe-] *m* newspaper serial; **novela de ~** pulp novel

folleto [fo·'je·to, fo·'ʎe-] *m* pamphlet; **~ publicitario** advertising leaflet, flier

follón [fo·'jon, -'ʎon] *m inf* **1.** (*alboroto*) fight; **armar un ~** to cause a commotion **2.** (*asunto enojoso*) trouble

follón, -ona [fo·'jon, --'jo·na; -'ʎon, --'ʎo·na] *adj* **1.** (*chulo*) swaggering **2.** (*holgazán*) lazy

follonero, -a [fo·jo·'ne·ro, -a; fo·ʎo-] *m, f* troublemaker

fome ['fo·me] *adj Arg, Chile* (*aburrido*) boring; **más ~ que jugar solo a la escondida** duller than playing hide-and-seek by yourself

fomentar [fo·men·'tar] *vt* **1.** (*empleo*) to promote; (*economía*) to boost **2.** (*discordias*) to foment

fomento [fo·'men·to] *m* **1.** (*del empleo*) promotion; (*de la economía*) boosting; **Banco Internacional de Reconstrucción y Fomento** International Bank for Reconstruction and Development **2.** (*de discordias*) fueling

fonda ['fon·da] *f* inn

fondeadero [fon·dea·'de·ro] *m* anchorage

fondeado, -a [fon·de·'a·do, -a] *adj AmL* well-off, well-heeled

fondear [fon·de·'ar] **I.** *vi* NÁUT to anchor **II.** *vt* **1.** (*anclar*) to anchor **2.** (*sondear*) to sound **3.** (*registrar*) to search; (*una cuestión*) to examine thoroughly; **~ un asunto** to examine a matter thoroughly

fondeo [fon·'deo] *m* **1.** NÁUT anchoring; (*sondeo*) sounding **2.** (*registro*) search

fondillos [fon·'di·jos, -ʎos] *mpl* (*pantalones*) seat; (*trasero*) behind

fondo ['fon·do] *m* **1.** (*de un cajón*) back; (*del río*) bed; (*de un valle*) bottom; **los bajos ~s** the underworld [o low life]; **en el ~ de su corazón** in his/her heart of hearts; **en este asunto hay mar de ~** there are underlying issues in this matter; **tocar ~** ECON to hit bottom **2.** (*de un edificio*) depth; **al ~ del pasillo** at the end of the corridor; **mi habitación está al ~ de la casa** my bedroom is at the back of the house **3.** (*lo esencial*) essence; **artículo de ~** editorial; **en el ~** at bottom; **ir al ~ de un**

asunto to go to the heart of the matter; **tratar un tema a ~** to seriously discuss a subject; **hay un ~ de verdad en lo que dices** there is sth of truth in what you say **4.** (*índole*) nature, disposition; **persona de buen ~** a good person at heart; **tiene un buen ~** he/she has a happy disposition **5.** (*de un cuadro*) background; (*de una tela*) background color; **ruido/música de ~** background noise/music **6.** (*conjunto de cosas, biblioteca*) collection **7.** DEP long-distance; **corredor de ~** long-distance runner; **esquiador de ~** cross-country skier **8.** FIN, POL fund; **~ común** kitty; **Fondo Monetario Internacional** International Monetary Fund; **a ~ perdido** non-recoverable **9.** *pl* (*medios*) funds *pl*; **~s públicos** public funds; **cheque sin ~s** bad check **10.** NÁUT sea bed; **tocar ~** to touch bottom; **irse a ~** to sink

fondón, -ona [fon·'don, --'do·na] *adj pey, inf* big-bottomed

fonema [fo·'ne·ma] *m* LING phoneme

fonética [fo·'ne·ti·ka] *f* phonetics *pl*

fono ['fo·no] *m Chile* (*auricular del teléfono*) receiver

fonología [fo·no·lo·'xi·a] *f* LING phonology

fonoteca [fo·no·'te·ka] *f* sound archive, sound [o music] library

fontanería [fon·ta·ne·'ri·a] *f* **1.** (*acción, conducto*) plumbing **2.** (*establecimiento*) plumber's

fontanero, -a [fon·ta·'ne·ro, -a] **I.** *adj* (*natural*) spring; (*artificial*) fountain **II.** *m, f* plumber

footing ['fu·tin] *m* jogging; **hacer ~** to jog

forajido, -a [fo·ra·'xi·do, -a] **I.** *adj* outlawed **II.** *m, f* outlaw, bandit

foral [fo·'ral] *adj* **1.** (*de los privilegios*) *referring to the privileges obtained by the granting of charters in the Middle Ages to certain towns* **2.** (*de la jurisdicción*) jurisdictional **3.** (*de las leyes*) statutory

foráneo, -a [fo·'ra·neo, -a] *adj* **1.** (*de otro lugar*) outside **2.** (*extraño*) alien

forastero, -a [fo·ras·'te·ro, -a] **I.** *adj* **1.** (*de otro lugar*) outside; (*extranjero*) foreign **2.** (*extraño*) alien **II.** *m, f* stranger; (*extranjero*) foreigner

forcejear [for·se·xe·'ar, for·θe-] *vi* **1.** (*esforzarse*) to struggle **2.** (*resistir*) to resist

forcejeo [for·se·'xeo, for·θe-] *m* **1.** (*esfuerzo*) struggle **2.** (*resistencia*) resistance

forense [fo·'ren·se] **I.** *adj* forensic; **médico ~** forensic surgeon **II.** *mf* pathologist

forestal [fo·res·'tal] *adj* forest, woodland; **camino ~** forest track; **repoblación ~** reforestation; **guarda ~** forest ranger

forestar [fo·res·'tar] *vt* to reforest

forfait [for·'fait] *m* **1.** COM fixed price **2.** (*esquiar*) ski pass

forja ['for·xa] *f* **1.** (*fragua*) forge **2.** (*ferrería*) ironworks *pl* **3.** (*creación*) forging **4.** (*argamasa*) mortar

forjar [for·'xar] **I.** *vt* **1.** (*metal*) to forge **2.** (*muro*) to build; (*revocar*) to render

3.(*inventar*) to invent **4.**(*crear*) to forge; (*imperio*) to build **II.** *vr:* ~ **se 1.**(*imaginarse*) to imagine; ~ **ilusiones** to build castles in the air **2.**(*crear*) to make

forma ['for·ma] *f* **1.**(*figura*) form, shape; **las ~s de una mujer** a woman's curves; **en ~ de gota** in the shape of a drop; **dar ~ a algo** (*formar*) to shape sth; (*precisar*) to spell out **2.**(*manera*) way; ~ **de comportamiento** demeanor; ~ **de pago** method of payment; **defecto de ~** JUR defect of form; **de ~ libre** freely; **en (buena) y escrita** written; **en (buena) y debida ~** duly; **de ~ que** so that; **de todas ~s,...** anyway,...; **lo haré de una ~ u otra** I will do it one way or another; **no hay ~ de abrir la puerta** this door is impossible to open **3.**(*comportamiento*) manners *pl* **4.**(*molde*) mold **5.**(*condición*) **estar en ~** to be fit [*o* in good shape] **6.** DEP form

formación [for·ma·'sjon, -'θjon] *f* **1.**(*creación*) creation; (*de una sociedad*) organization; ~ **del balance** preparation of the balance sheet; ~ **de humo** forming of smoke **2.** *t.* MIL (*de personas*) formation; ~ **política** political group; ~ **de tropas** military force; **desfilar en ~ cerrada** to march past in close formation **3.**(*educación*) education; ~ **de adultos** adult education; ~ **escolar** school education; ~ **profesional** vocational training **4.** GEO formation **5.**(*forma*) form

formal [for·'mal] *adj* **1.**(*relativo a la forma*) formal; **requisito ~** formal requirement **2.**(*serio*) serious; (*educado*) educated; (*cumplidor*) reliable **3.**(*oficial*) official; **una invitación ~** a formal invitation; **tiene novio ~** she has a steady boyfriend

formalidad [for·ma·li·'dad] *f* **1.**(*seriedad*) seriousness; (*exactitud*) correctness **2.** *pl* ADMIN, JUR formalities *pl* **3.**(*norma de comportamiento*) formality

formalismo [for·ma·'lis·mo] *m* formalism

formalizar <z→c> [for·ma·li·'sar, -'θar] **I.** *vt* **1.**(*dar forma*) to formalize **2.**(*solemnizar*) to solemnize; ~ **un noviazgo** (*comprometerse*) to become engaged; (*casarse*) to marry **3.** JUR to formalize; ~ **un contrato** to formalize a contract; ~ **una solicitud** to formalize a motion **II.** *vr:* ~ **se 1.**(*formarse*) to be formalized **2.**(*volverse formal*) to grow up

formar [for·'mar] **I.** *vi* **1.** MIL to fall in **2.**(*figurar*) to figure **II.** *vt* **1.**(*dar forma*) to form, to shape **2.**(*constituir*) to form; MIL to form up; ~ **parte de** to form part of **3.**(*educar*) to train; (*enseñar*) to teach **III.** *vr:* ~ **se 1.**(*crearse*) to form; MIL to fall in **2.**(*ser educado*) to be educated; **se ha formado a sí mismo** he is self-taught **3.**(*desarrollarse*) to develop **4.**(*hacerse*) to form; ~ **se una idea de algo** to form an impression of sth

formatear [for·ma·te·'ar] *vt* COMPUT to format

formateo [for·ma·'teo] *m* COMPUT formatting

formativo, -a [for·ma·'ti·βo, -a] *adj* (*educativo*) educational; (*instructivo*) instructive

formato [for·'ma·to] *m* format; (*tamaño*) size; ~ **de datos** COMPUT data format; ~ **de texto** COMPUT text format; ~ **vertical** vertical format

formica® [for·'mi·ka] *f* Formica®

formidable [for·mi·'da·βle] *adj* **1.** *inf* (*estupendo*) fantastic **2.**(*enorme*) enormous **3.**(*temible*) awesome

fórmula ['for·mu·la] *f* **1.** *t.* MAT, QUÍM formula; ~ **de despedida** (*carta*) closing formula, close; **coche de ~ 1** DEP Formula One car **2.** *AmL* MED prescription

formulación [for·mu·la·'sjon, -'θjon] *f* **1.**(*de una idea*) formulation; ~ **de balances** drawing up of the balance; ~ **de la propuesta** drawing up of a proposal **2.** FÍS formula

formular [for·mu·'lar] **I.** *adj* formulaic **II.** *vt* **1.**(*expresar con una fórmula*) to express with a formula **2.**(*manifestar*) to formulate; ~ **demanda** to file a claim [*o* suit]; ~ **denuncia** to lodge a complaint **3.**(*recetar*) to prescribe

formulario [for·mu·'la·rjo] *m* **1.**(*impreso*) form; ~ **para giro postal** postal order form **2.**(*colección de fórmulas*) formulary; (*de recetas*) recipe book

formulario, -a [for·mu·'la·rjo, -a] *adj* **1.**(*cortés*) formal **2.**(*formular*) formulaic

formulismo [for·mu·'lis·mo] *m* formalism; (*burocrático*) red tape

fornicar <c→qu> [for·ni·'kar] *vi* **1.**(*realizar el acto sexual*) to fornicate **2.**(*cometer adulterio*) to commit adultery

fornido, -a [for·'ni·do, -a] *adj* well-built, husky

foro ['fo·ro] *m* **1.**(*plaza*) forum; ~ **romano** Roman forum **2.** JUR (*lugar*) court of law **3.** JUR (*curia*) the Bar **4.** TEAT upstage area; **irse por el ~** *inf* to slip away unnoticed

forofo, -a [fo·'ro·fo, -a] *m, f* fan, buff

forraje [fo·'rra·xe] *m* **1.**(*pasto*) hay; (*verde*) grass; *AmL* (*seco*) feed **2.** *inf* (*fárrago*) hodge-podge

forrar [fo·'rrar] **I.** *vt* (*el exterior, una pared*) to face; (*el interior, una prenda*) to line; (*una butaca*) to upholster; (*un libro*) to cover; ~ **con algodón** to cover with cotton **II.** *vr:* ~ **se** *inf* (*enriquecerse*) to make a packet

forro ['fo·rro] *m* **1.**(*exterior, de una pared*) facing; (*interior, de una prenda*) lining; (*de una butaca*) upholstery; (*de un libro*) cover **2.** AUTO ~ **de freno** brake lining **3.** *inf* (*en absoluto*) **ni por el ~** at all **4.** *AmL, vulg* (*preservativo*) condom, rubber

fortachón, -ona [for·ta·'tʃon, -'tʃo·na] *adj inf* beefy

fortalecedor(a) [for·ta·le·se·'dor, -'do·ra, for·ta·le·θe-] *adj* **1.**(*vigorizador*) invigorating **2.**(*que da ánimo*) encouraging **3.**(*reforzante*) fortifying, revitalizing

fortalecer [for·ta·le·'ser, -'θer] *irr como crecer* **I.** *vt* **1.**(*vigorizar*) to invigorate **2.**(*animar*) to encourage **3.**(*reforzar*) to fortify **II.** *vr:* ~ **se 1.**(*vigorizarse*) to fortify oneself **2.**(*volverse más fuerte*) to become stronger

fortalecimiento [for·ta·le·si·'mjen·to, -θi· 'mjen·to] *m* **1.**(*de una cosa*) fortifying **2.**(*del cuerpo*) toughening **3.**(*del ánimo*) encouragement

fortaleza [for·ta·'le·sa, -θa] *f* **1.**(*fuerza*) strength; **de poca** ~ not very tough **2.**(*virtud*) fortitude **3.**(*robustez*) robustness **4.**MIL fortress, stronghold

fortificación [for·ti·fi·ka·'sjon, -'θjon] *f* **1.**(*fortalecimiento*) strengthening **2.**MIL (*acción*) fortifying **3.**MIL (*obra*) fortification

fortificar <c→qu> [for·ti·fi·'kar] I. *vt* **1.**(*fortalecer*) to strengthen **2.**MIL to fortify II. *vr:* ~**se** **1.**(*fortalecerse*) to fortify oneself **2.**MIL to build fortifications

fortísimo, -a [for·'ti·si·mo, -a] *adj superl de* **fuerte**

fortuito, -a [for·'twi·to, -a/for·tu·'i·to, -a] *adj* fortuitous, chance

fortuna [for·'tu·na] *f* **1.**(*suerte*) fortune; **por** ~ (*afortunadamente*) fortunately; (*por casualidad*) luckily; **probar** ~ to try one's luck **2.**(*destino*) fate **3.**(*capital*) fortune; **su voz era su** ~ his/her voice was his/her asset

fórum ['fo·run] *m* forum

forúnculo [fo·'run·ku·lo] *m* MED boil, furuncle

forzado [for·'sa·do, -'θa·do] *m* **1.**(*presidiario*) convict **2.**(*galeote*) galley slave

forzado, -a [for·'sa·do, -a; -'θa·do, -a] *adj* **1.**(*artificial*) forced; **trabajos** ~**s** hard labor **2.**(*ocupado*) occupied

forzar [for·'sar, -'θar] *irr* I. *vt* **1.**(*obligar*) to force **2.**(*un acontecimiento*) to bring about **3.**(*violar*) to rape **4.**(*esforzar*) to force; (*voz*) to strain **5.**(*obligar a entrar*) to push in; (*a abrirse*) to force open II. *vr:* ~**se** **1.**(*obligarse*) to force oneself **2.**(*esforzarse*) to push oneself

forzosamente [for·so·sa·'men·te, for·θo-] *adv* (*inevitablemente*) unavoidably; (*obligatoriamente*) necessarily

forzoso, -a [for·'so·so, -a; for·'θo-] *adj* forced, necessary; **aterrizaje** ~ forced landing; **venta forzosa** forced sale

forzudo, -a [for·'su·do, -a; for·'θu-] *adj* strong

fosa ['fo·sa] *f* **1.**(*hoyo*) pit; (*alargado*) MIL, GEO trench; ~ **séptica** septic tank **2.**(*sepultura*) grave; ~ **común** common grave **3.**ANAT fossa; ~ **nasal** nostril

fosfato [fos·'fa·to] *m* phosphate

fosforecer [fos·fo·res·'ser, -'θer] *irr como* **crecer** *vi* to phosphoresce

fosforescencia [fos·fo·re·'sen·sja, -res·'θen·θja] *f* phosphorescence

fosforescente [fos·fo·re·'sen·te, -res·'θen·te] *adj* phosphorescent; **pintura** ~ luminous paint

fósforo ['fos·fo·ro] *m* **1.**QUÍM phosphorus **2.**(*cerilla*) match

fósil ['fo·sil] I. *adj* **1.**GEO fossil **2.***inf* (*anticuado*) antiquated II. *m* fossil

fosilizarse <z→c> [fo·si·li·'sar·se, -'θar·se] *vr* **1.**GEO to fossilize **2.***inf* (*persona*) to turn into an old fossil

foso ['fo·so] *m* **1.**(*hoyo*) hole; (*alargado*) ditch;

MIL trench; (*fortaleza*) moat **2.**MÚS, TEAT orchestra pit **3.**DEP pit **4.**(*en un garaje*) inspection pit

foto ['fo·to] *f* photo; ~ (**tamaño**) **carnet** passport photo

fotocopia [fo·to·'ko·pja] *f* photocopy

fotocopiadora [fo·to·ko·pja·'do·ra] *f* photocopier

fotocopiar [fo·to·ko·'pjar] *vt* to photocopy

fotogénico, -a [fo·to·'xe·ni·ko, -a] *adj* photogenic

fotografía [fo·to·ɣra·'fi·a] *f* **1.**(*imagen*) photograph; ~ **aérea** aerial photograph; ~ **en color** color photograph; ~ (**tamaño**) **carnet** passport photograph; **álbum de** ~**s** photo(graph) album **2.**(*arte*) photography

fotografiar <*1. pres:* fotografío> [fo·to·ɣra·fi·'ar] I. *vi* to photograph II. *vt* **1.**(*hacer fotos*) to photograph **2.**(*describir*) to describe in detail III. *vr:* ~**se** to have one's picture taken

fotográfico, -a [fo·to·'ɣra·fi·ko, -a] *adj* photographic; **máquina fotográfica** camera; **papel** ~ photographic paper

fotógrafo, -a [fo·'to·ɣra·fo, -a] *m, f* photographer

fotograma [fo·to·'ɣra·ma] *m* **1.**CINE still **2.**FOTO photogram

fotomatón [fo·to·ma·'ton] *m* **1.**(*mecanismo*) photo automaton **2.**(*cabina*) photo booth **3.**(*foto*) passport-size photo

fotomodelo [fo·to·mo·'de·lo] *mf* photographic model

fotomontaje [fo·to·mon·'ta·xe] *m* photomontage

fotonovela [fo·to·no·'βe·la] *f* photo(-)essay

fotoquímica [fo·to·'ki·mi·ka] *f* photochemistry

fotorreportaje [fo·to·rre·por·'ta·xe] *m* report with photographs, illustrated feature

fotosíntesis [fo·to·'sin·te·sis] *f inv* photosynthesis

fotovoltaico, -a [fo·to·βol·'tai·ko, -a] *adj* photovoltaic

FP [e·fe·'pe] *f abr de* **Formación Profesional** vocational training, technical education

frac [frak] *m* <fracs *o* fraques> tails *pl*

fracasar [fra·ka·'sar] *vi* **1.**(*no tener éxito*) to fail; **la película fracasó** the film was a flop; ~ **un examen** to fail an exam **2.**NÁUT to break up

fracaso [fra·'ka·so] *m* **1.**(*acción*) failure **2.**(*fiasco*) fiasco **3.**(*desastre*) disaster

fracción [frak·'sjon, -'θjon] *f* **1.**(*división*) division; (*ruptura*) rupture; (*de una cantidad*) splitting up **2.**(*parte*) fraction; (*de un objeto*) fragment; (*de una organización*) splinter group; ~ **parlamentaria** parliamentary faction **3.**MAT, QUÍM fraction

fraccionamiento [frak·sjo·na·'mjen·to, frak·θjo-] *m* (*división*) division; (*ruptura*) rupturing; (*de una cantidad*) splitting up; (*de una organización*) splintering

fraccionar [frak·sjo·'nar, frak·θjo-] I. *vt* (*dividir*) to divide; (*romper*) to break up; (*una cantidad*) to split up; ~ **el pago** to pay in installments; (una organización) to break away II. vr: ~se to fractionalize; (grupo) to split up

fraccionario, -a [frak·sjo·'na·rjo, -a; frak·θjo-] adj 1. MAT fractional; **número** ~ fraction 2. POL factional 3. (incompleto) incomplete

fractura [frak·'tu·ra] f 1. (rotura) break; MED fracture; ~ **simple/complicada** closed/compound fracture 2. GEO (falla) fault

fracturar [frak·tu·'rar] I. vt to break; (una caja fuerte) to force II. vr: ~se to fracture

fragancia [fra·'ɣan·sja, -θja] f fragrance; (perfume) perfume; (vino) bouquet

fragata [fra·'ɣa·ta] f 1. NÁUT frigate 2. ZOOL frigate bird

frágil ['fra·xil] adj 1. (objeto) fragile 2. (constitución, salud) delicate; (anciano) frail 3. (carácter) weak; **tener una memoria** ~ to have a bad memory

fragilidad [fra·xi·li·'dad] f 1. (de un objeto) fragility 2. (de la constitución, salud) delicacy; (de un anciano) frailty 3. (del carácter) weakness

fragmentación [fraɣ·men·ta·'sjon, -'θjon] f fragmentation; (en muchos pedazos) breaking up; (de un cristal) shattering

fragmentar [fraɣ·men·'tar] I. vt (dividir) to fragment, to divide; (en muchos pedazos) to break up; (romper) to break; (una roca) to split II. vr: ~se (cristal) to shatter; (roca) to split

fragmentario, -a [fraɣ·men·'ta·rjo, -a] adj 1. (compuesto) compound 2. (incompleto) fragmentary

fragmento [fraɣ·'men·to] m 1. (parte) fragment; (de un cristal) splinter; (de una roca) chip; (de un tejido) remnant; (de un papel) scrap 2. LIT, MÚS (parte) fragment, excerpt

fragor [fra·'ɣor] m din

fragoso, -a [fra·'ɣo·so, -a] adj 1. (áspero) rough 2. (ruidoso) noisy

fragua ['fra·ɣwa] f forge

fraguar <gu→gü> [fra·'ɣwar] I. vi 1. (cemento) to set 2. (idea) to devise II. vt (metal) to forge; ¿qué estás fraguando? fig what are you scheming?

fraile ['frai·le] m 1. REL friar 2. (en un vestido) accidental turn-up 3. PREN white space

frambuesa [fram·'bwe·sa] f raspberry

francés, -esa [fran·'ses, --'se·sa; -'θes, --'θe·sa] I. adj French; **tortilla francesa** plain omelet II. m, f Frenchman m, Frenchwoman f

Francfort ['frank·fort] m Frankfurt

Francia ['fran·sja, -θja] f France

franciscano, -a [fran·sis·'ka·no, -a; fran·θis-] I. adj 1. REL Franciscan 2. AmL (pardo) dun II. m, f Franciscan

franco ['fran·ko] m 1. (moneda francesa, belga, suiza) franc 2. HIST (lengua) Frankish

franco, -a ['fran·ko, -a] I. adj 1. (sincero) frank 2. (generoso) generous 3. (libre) free; **puerto** ~ free port; ~ **a bordo** free on board; ~ **de derechos** duty-free; ~ **en fábrica** ex-factory 4. (claro) patent 5. HIST Frankish 6. (francés)

French II. m, f Frank

francófilo, -a [fran·'ko·fi·lo, -a] adj Francophile

francotirador [fran·ko·ti·ra·'dor] m 1. (guerrillero) guerrilla; (tirador emboscado) sniper 2. (persona aislada) loner

franela [fra·'ne·la] f 1. (tejido) flannel 2. AmL (camiseta) T-shirt

franelear [fra·ne·le·'ar] vi Arg, Urug, inf (manosear) to pet

franja ['fran·xa] f 1. (guarnición) border 2. (tira) strip; **en la misma** ~ **horaria** in the same time zone

franquear [fran·ke·'ar] I. vt 1. (carta) to pay postage on; **a** ~ **en destino** postage paid at destination 2. (desobstruir) to clear 3. (río) to cross; ~ **el paso** to open the way; (obstáculo) to get around sth 4. (conceder) to grant 5. (dar libertad) to free II. vr: ~se to have a heart-to-heart talk

franqueo [fran·'keo] m 1. (sellos) postage; **sin** ~ without stamps 2. (acción: de una carta) franking 3. (de una salida) opening

franqueza [fran·'ke·sa, -θa] f 1. (sinceridad) frankness; **admitir algo con** ~ to openly admit sth 2. (generosidad) generosity 3. (familiaridad) intimacy 4. (exención) exemption

franquicia [fran·'ki·sja, -θja] f 1. (de franqueo) exemption; ~ **postal** free postage 2. ECON franchise

franquismo [fran·'kis·mo] m 1. (régimen) Franco's regime 2. (movimiento) Francoism

franquista [fran·'kis·ta] I. adj Francoist II. mf Francoist

frasco ['fras·ko] m 1. (botella) flask; (de perfume) perfume bottle; ~ **pulverizador** sprayer 2. AmL: measurement of liquids, 2.37 liters

frase ['fra·se] f 1. (oración) sentence 2. (locución) expression; (refrán) saying; (expresión famosa) well-known phrase; ~ **hecha** idiom; ~ **proverbial** proverb 3. (sin valor) cliché 4. (estilo) style 5. MÚS phrase

fraseología [fra·seo·lo·'xi·a] f (verbosidad) verbiage

fraternal [fra·ter·'nal] adj fraternal, brotherly

fraternidad [fra·ter·ni·'dad] f fraternity

fraternizar <z→c> [fra·ter·ni·'sar, -'θar] vi 1. (unirse) to mingle with; POL to sympathize with 2. (alternar) to fraternize

fratricidio [fra·tri·'si·djo, -'θi·djo] m fratricide

fraude ['frau·de] m fraud; ~ **fiscal** tax fraud [o evasion]; **cometer** ~ to commit a fraudulent act

fraudulento, -a [frau·du·'len·to, -a] adj fraudulent; **publicidad fraudulenta** misleading advertising

fray [frai] m REL Brother

frazada [fra·'sa·da, -'θa·da] f AmL blanket; (de lana) wool blanket

frecuencia [fre·'kwen·sja, -θja] f t. FÍS frequency; **con** ~ frequently

frecuentar [fre·kwen·'tar] vt 1. (lugar) to frequent 2. (a alguien) to be in touch with

3. (*acción*) to do sth frequently
frecuente [fre·'kwen·te] *adj* **1.** (*repetido*) frequent **2.** (*usual*) common
fregadero [fre·ɣa·'de·ro] *m* (kitchen) sink
fregado [fre·'ɣa·do] *m* **1.** (*limpieza*) cleaning; (*de los platos*) (doing) the dishes **2.** *inf* (*enredo*) mess **3.** *pey* (*pelea*) brawl
fregado, -a [fre·'ɣa·do, -a] *adj* **1.** *AmL* (*descarado*) cheeky; (*fastidioso*) tiresome **2.** *AmL* (*astuto*) sly **3.** *AmC* (*severo*) strict
fregar [fre·'ɣar] *irr vt* **1.** (*frotar*) to rub **2.** (*limpiar: el suelo*) to scrub; (*con fregona*) to mop; (*los platos*) to wash [*o* to do] the dishes **3.** *AmL, inf* (*molestar*) to annoy
fregona [fre·'ɣo·na] *f* **1.** (*utensilio*) mop **2.** *pey* (*sirvienta*) drudge **3.** *pey* (*mujer ordinaria*) common woman
freidora [frei·'do·ra] *f* fryer
freír [fre·'ir] *irr* **I.** *vt* **1.** (*guisar*) to fry; (*en mucho aceite*) to deep-fry **2.** *inf* (*molestar*) to annoy **3.** *inf* (*matar*) to bump off *inf;* ~ **a balazos** to shoot dead **II.** *vr:* ~ **se 1.** (*alimento*) to fry **2.** *inf* (*persona*) to find it hot; **aquí te fríes** it's boiling here
fréjol ['fre·xol] *m Perú* BOT, CULIN (*frijol*) bean
frenada [fre·'na·da] *f Arg, Chile* (*frenazo*) sudden braking
frenar [fre·'nar] **I.** *vt* **1.** (*hacer parar*) to stop **2.** (*un impulso, persona*) to restrain; (*un desarrollo*) to check, to curb **II.** *vi* to brake; ~ **en seco** to slam on the brakes **III.** *vr* ~ **se en algo** to restrain oneself from (doing) sth
frenazo [fre·'na·so, -θo] *m* AUTO sudden braking; **pegar un** ~ to step on the brakes **2.** (*del desarrollo*) curb; **sufrir un** ~ *fig* to suffer a setback
frenesí [fre·ne·'si] *m* **1.** (*exaltación*) frenzy **2.** (*locura*) wildness; (*delirio furioso*) passion
frenético, -a [fre·'ne·ti·ko, -a] *adj* **1.** (*exaltado*) frenzied; **aplauso** ~ frenzied applause **2.** (*loco*) wild **3.** (*furioso*) furious
freno ['fre·no] *m* **1.** TÉC brake; ~ **de mano** hand [*o* emergency] brake **2.** (*para un caballo*) bit **3.** (*contención*) curb; **tirar del** ~ **a alguien** to hold sb back; **no tener** ~ not to hold back **frente¹** ['fren·te] *f* **1.** (*parte de la cara*) forehead; **fruncir la** ~ to frown **2.** (*cara*) face; ~ **a** ~ face to face; **bajó la** ~ he/she bowed his/her head
frente² ['fren·te] **I.** *m* **1.** (*delantera*) front; (*de un edificio*) façade, face; **al** ~ (*dirección*) ahead; (*lugar*) in front; **de** ~ head-on; ¡de ~! MIL forward march!; **estar al** ~ **de algo** to be in charge of sth; **hacer** ~ **a alguien** to stand up to sb; **hacer** ~ **a algo** to face up to sth; **no tener dos dedos de** ~ *inf* to be as thick as two short planks; **ponerse al** ~ to take charge **2.** POL, METEO, MIL front; **un** ~ **frío** a cold front **3.** (*de un escrito*) top margin **II.** *prep* **1.** ~ **a** (*enfrente de*) opposite; (*delante de*) in front of; (*contra*) as opposed to; (*ante*) in the face of **2.** **en** ~ **de** opposite
fresa ['fre·sa] **I.** *adj* strawberry-colored **II.** *f* BOT

strawberry
fresadora [fre·sa·'do·ra] *f* milling machine, miller
fresar [fre·'sar] *vt* to mill
fresco ['fres·ko] *m* **1.** (*frescor*) freshness, cool air; (*frío moderado*) coolness; (*viento*) cool; **salir a tomar el** ~ to go out to get some fresh air **2.** ARTE fresco **3.** *AmL* (*refresco*) soft drink
fresco, -a ['fres·ko, -a] **I.** *adj* **1.** (*frío*) cool; (*prenda*) lightweight, cool; (*cutis*) fresh, rosy **2.** (*reciente*) fresh; **noticia fresca** up-to-date news; **queso** ~ cottage cheese **3.** (*descansado*) fresh **4.** *inf* (*desvergonzado*) fresh, cheeky **5.** (*impasible*) cool **6.** (*equivocado*) **estar** ~ *inf* to be wrong **II.** *m, f inf* cheeky person
frescor [fres·'kor] *m* **1.** (*frío moderado*) coolness; (*frescura*) freshness **2.** ARTE skin-tone
frescura [fres·'ku·ra] *f* **1.** (*frescor*) freshness, cool air; (*frío moderado*) coolness **2.** (*desvergüenza*) cheek **3.** (*desembarazo*) naturalness; **con** ~ freely
fresno ['fres·no] *m* ash
fresquería [fres·ke·'ri·a] *f AmL: establishment where drinks are made and sold*
frialdad [frjal·'dad] *f* **1.** (*frío*) coldness **2.** (*despego*) coolness; **me trató con** ~ he/she was cool towards me **3.** (*impasibilidad*) coolness **4.** (*falta de sentimientos*) indifference; (*frigidez*) frigidity **5.** (*estilo*) impersonality; (*del ambiente*) lack of warmth
fricandó [fri·kan·'do] *m* CULIN fricandeau
fricción [frik·'sjon, -'θjon] *f* **1.** (*resistencia*) friction **2.** (*del cuerpo*) rub; (*con linimento*) massage **3.** (*desavenencia*) friction; (*disputa*) fight
friccionar [frik·sjo·'nar, frik·θjo-] *vt* (*en seco*) to rub; (*con linimento*) to massage
friega ['frje·ɣa] *f* **1.** (*fricción*) rub **2.** *AmL* (*molestia*) bother **3.** *inf* (*zurra*) beating
friegaplatos [frje·ɣa·'pla·tos] *m inv* dishwasher
frigidez [fri·xi·'des, -'deθ] *f* frigidity
frígido, -a ['fri·xi·do, -a] *adj* frigid
frigorífico [fri·ɣo·'ri·fi·ko] *m* **1.** (*nevera*) fridge, refrigerator **2.** (*local*) cold store
frigorífico, -a [fri·ɣo·'ri·fi·ko, -a] *adj* refrigerated; **camión** ~ refrigerated truck
frijol [fri·'xol] *m*, **fríjol** ['fri·xol] *m AmL* bean

> **i** In Central America, **frijoles** are the primary source of protein, especially for the poor, who cannot afford meat. **Frijoles** are stewed pinto beans that are served with **tortillas** and accompany every warm meal.

friki ['fri·ki] **I.** *adj* freaky **II.** *m inf* freak
frío ['fri·o] *m* cold; **hace** ~ it is cold; **hace un** ~ **que pela** it is bitterly cold; **coger** ~ to catch cold; **tener** ~ to be cold
frío, -a ['fri·o, -a] *adj* **1.** (*no caliente*) cold **2.** (*relación*) cool **3.** (*falto de sentimientos*) in-

different; (*frígido*) frigid **4.**(*impasible*) impassive **5.**(*inexpresivo*) inexpressive; (*ambiente*) impersonal

friolento, -a [frjo·'len·to, -a] *adj AmL* (*friolero*) sensitive to the cold

friolera [frjo·'le·ra] *f* **1.** *irón* (*insignificante*) trifle; **ganaron la ~ de 50 millones en la loto** they won a mere fifty million in the lottery **2.** *inf* (*montón*) pile

friolero, -a [frjo·'le·ro, -a] *adj* sensitive to the cold

frisa ['fri·sa] *f* **1.** *Arg, Chile* (*pelo*) nap **2.** *PRico, RDom* (*manta*) blanket

friso ['fri·so] *m* (*de la pared*) wainscot

fritanga [fri·'tan·ga] *f pey* (*comida frita*) (greasy) fried food; **hueles a ~** you reek of fried food

frito ['fri·to] *m* fry

frito, -a ['fri·to, -a] **I.** *pp de* **freír II.** *adj* **1.**(*comida*) fried **2.** *inf* (*dormido*) **quedarse ~** to fall fast asleep **3.** *inf* (*muerto*) dead; **quedarse ~** to kick the bucket; **dejar a alguien ~** to snuff sb **4.** *inf* (*harto*) **estar ~ con algo** to be fed up with sth

frivolidad [fri·βo·li·'dad] *f* **1.**(*ligereza*) frivolity **2.**(*coquetería*) flirtatiousness **3.**(*trivialidad*) triviality **4.**(*sensualidad*) sensuality

frívolo, -a ['fri·βo·lo, -a] *adj* **1.**(*ligero*) light **2.**(*coqueto*) flirtatious **3.**(*superficial*) frivolous, superficial **4.**(*sensual*) sensual

frondosidad [fron·do·si·'dad] *f* **1.**(*de una planta*) leafiness; (*de un bosque*) lushness **2.**(*follaje*) foliage

frondoso, -a [fron·'do·so, -a] *adj* (*planta, árbol*) leafy; (*bosque*) lush

frontal [fron·'tal] **I.** *adj* **1.** ANAT frontal **2.**(*relativo al frente*) front **3.**(*de frente*) head-on **II.** *m* **1.** ANAT frontal bone **2.** REL frontal

frontera [fron·'te·ra] *f* **1.**(*límite*) border; **atravesar la ~** to cross the frontier **2.**(*frontispicio*) frontispiece; (*de un edificio*) façade

fronterizo, -a [fron·te·'ri·so, -a; -'ri·θo, -a] *adj* (*en la frontera*) frontier; (*país*) border(ing); **paso ~** border post

frontón [fron·'ton] *m* **1.**(*juego*) pelota, jai alai **2.**(*pared*) front wall **3.**(*pista*) court **4.** ARQUIT frontispiece, pediment

frotación [fro·ta·'sjon, -'θjon] *f*, **frotadura** [fro·ta·'du·ra] *f* **1.**(*acción*) rubbing; (*con cepillo*) brushing **2.**(*efecto*) friction

frotamiento [fro·ta·'mjen·to] *m* (*acción de frotar*) rubbing; (*con cepillo*) brushing

frotar [fro·'tar] **I.** *vt* to rub; (*con cepillo*) to brush; (*con un estropajo*) to scrub **II.** *vr:* **~ se** to rub oneself; **~ se con una toalla** to rub oneself with a towel

fructífero, -a [fruk·'ti·fe·ro, -a] *adj* fruitful

fructificación [fruk·ti·fi·ka·'sjon, -'θjon] *f* **1.**(*de una planta*) fruitfulness **2.**(*de un esfuerzo*) fruition

fructificar <c→qu> [fruk·ti·fi·'kar] *vi* **1.**(*planta*) to bear fruit **2.**(*esfuerzo*) to come to fruition

frugal [fru·'γal] *adj* frugal

frugalidad [fru·γa·li·'dad] *f* frugality

fruición [frwi·'sjon, -'θjon] *f* delight

frunce ['frun·se, -θe] *m* gather, shirr

fruncimiento [frun·si·'mjen·to, -θi·'mjen·to] *m* (*de los labios*) pursing; (*de la frente*) wrinkling; (*del entrecejo*) frowning

fruncir <c→z> [frun·'sir, -'θir] **I.** *vt* **1.**(*tela*) to gather, to shirr; (*arrugar*) to pucker **2.**(*labios*) to purse; (*frente*) to wrinkle; **~ el entrecejo** to frown **II.** *vr:* **~ se** to affect modesty

fruslería [frus·le·'ri·a] *f* **1.**(*baratija*) trifle **2.** *inf* (*bagatela*) nothing **3.** *inf* (*tontería*) silly thing

frustración [frus·tra·'sjon, -'θjon] *f* **1.**(*de planes*) thwarting; (*fracaso*) failure; (*de una esperanza*) frustration **2.**(*desilusión*) disappointment

frustrado, -a [frus·'tra·do, -a] *adj* (*persona*) frustrated; (*intento*) failed

frustrar [frus·'trar] **I.** *vt* **1.**(*estropear*) to thwart; **~ las esperanzas de alguien** to frustrate sb's hopes **2.**(*decepcionar*) to discourage **II.** *vr:* **~ se 1.**(*plan*) to fail **2.**(*esperanzas*) to be disappointed

fruta ['fru·ta] *f* fruit; **~ de Aragón** passion fruit; **~ del tiempo** seasonal fruit; **~s tropicales** tropical fruits

frutal [fru·'tal] **I.** *adj* fruit **II.** *m* fruit tree

frutería [fru·te·'ri·a] *f* greengrocer's

frutero [fru·'te·ro] *m* **1.**(*recipiente*) fruit bowl **2.** ARTE still life

frutero, -a [fru·'te·ro, -a] **I.** *adj* fruit; **es muy ~** he eats a lot of fruit **II.** *m, f* fruit seller

fruticultura [fru·ti·kul·'tu·ra] *f* fruit growing

frutilla [fru·'ti·ja, -ʎa] *f AmL* (*fresón*) strawberry

fruto ['fru·to] *m* **1.** BOT fruit **2.**(*hijo*) offspring **3.**(*rendimiento*) fruit; (*resultado*) result **4.**(*ganancia*) profit; *t.* JUR (*provecho*) benefit

fucsia¹ ['fuk·sja] **I.** *adj* (*color*) fuchsia-colored **II.** *m* fuchsia

fucsia² ['fuk·sja] *f* BOT fuchsia

fue [fwe] **1.** *3. pret de* **ir 2.** *3. pret de* **ser**

fuego ['fwe·γo] *m* **1.** fire; **¿me das ~?** can you give me a light?; **~s artificiales** fireworks *pl;* **a ~ lento** CULIN over a low heat; *fig* little by little; **prender** [*o* **pegar**] **~ a algo** to set sth on fire [*o* on fire]; **echar ~ por los ojos** to look daggers at sb **2.** MIL firing; **estar entre dos ~s** to be caught in the crossfire [*o* middle]; **arma de ~** firearm **3.**(*ardor*) ardor; **en el ~ de la discusión** in the heat of the discussion

fuel [fwel] *m* refined oil

fuelle ['fwe·je, -ʎe] *m* **1.**(*instrumento, de una cámara*) bellows *pl* **2.**(*de un vestido*) fold **3.**(*de un carruaje*) folding top **4.** *inf* (*pulmones*) lungs *pl;* (*aguante*) stamina **5.** *inf* (*soplón*) telltale, tattletale

fuente ['fwen·te] *f* **1.**(*manantial*) spring **2.**(*construcción*) fountain **3.**(*plato llano*) platter; (*plato hondo*) (serving) dish **4.**(*origen*) source; **~s bien informadas** reliable sources

fuera ['fwe·ra] I. *adv* 1. (*lugar*) outside; **por ~** on the outside; **de ~** from the outside; **el nuevo maestro es de ~** the new teacher is not from here; **estar ~ de lugar** to be irrelevant [*o* out of place] 2. (*dirección*) out; **¡~!** out!; **¡~ con esto!** no way!; **¡~ de mi vista!** out of my sight!; **echar a alguien ~** to throw sb out; **hacia ~** outwards; **salir ~** to go out 3. (*tiempo*) out; **~ de plazo** past the deadline 4. *inf* (*de viaje*) away; **me voy ~ una semana** I am going away for a week II. *prep* 1. *t. fig* (*local*) out of; **estar ~ de casa** to be away from home; **~ de juego** DEP offside; **~ de serie** exceptional 2. (*excepto*) **~ de** outside of III. *conj* **~ de que** +*subj* apart from the fact that IV. *m* boo

fueraborda [fwe·ra·'βor·da] *m* 1. (*motor*) outboard motor 2. (*embarcación*) outboard motor boat

fuereño, -a [fwe·'re·ɲo, -a] I. *adj AmL*, *inf* (*forastero*) outside, foreign II. *m*, *f AmL*, *inf* (*forastero*) outsider

fuero ['fwe·ro] *m* 1. (*privilegio*) privilege 2. (*jurisdicción*) jurisdiction; **en mi ~ interno** inwardly 3. (*código*) code

fuerte ['fwer·te] I. *adj* <fortísimo> 1. (*resistente*) strong; (*robusto*) tough; **caja ~** safe; **hacerse ~** to entrench oneself; **ser ~ de carácter** to be strong-willed 2. (*musculoso*) strong; (*gordo*) fat 3. (*intenso*) intense; (*sonido*) loud; (*comida, golpe*) heavy; (*abrazo, beso*) big; **un vino ~** a full-bodied wine 4. (*valiente*) brave 5. (*sólido*) solid; (*duro*) hard; (*tela*) thick 6. (*genio*) **tener un carácter** [*o* **genio**] **muy ~** to be quick-tempered 7. (*poderoso*) powerful 8. (*versado*) **estar ~ en matemáticas** to be good at mathematics 9. (*considerable*) considerable 10. (*violento*) disturbing; (*expresión*) nasty; **palabra ~** rude word 11. (*terreno*) rough 12. LING (*vocal*) *the Spanish vowels a, e, o;* (*forma*) *when the word stress falls on the word stem* 13. MIL fortified II. *m* 1. (*de una persona*) strong point 2. MIL fort 3. MÚS forte III. *adv* 1. (*con fuerza*) strongly; (*con intensidad*) intensely 2. (*en voz alta*) aloud 3. (*en abundancia*) copiously; **desayunar ~** to have a large breakfast

fuerza ['fwer·sa, -θa] *f* 1. *t. Fís* (*capacidad física*) strength; *t. Fís* (*potencia*) force; **~ de ánimo** strength of mind; **~ de voluntad** willpower; **sin ~s** weak, drained; **se le va la ~ por la boca** he/she is all talk [*o* hot air] 2. (*capacidad de soportar*) toughness; (*eficacia*) effectiveness 3. (*poder*) power; **~ de disuasión** powers of dissuasion; **~ mayor** act of God, force majeure 4. (*violencia*) force; **a** [*o* **por**] **la ~** any which way; **por ~** (*por necesidad*) out of necessity; (*con violencia*) by force; **recurrir a la ~** to resort to violence 5. (*intensidad*) intensity 6. (*expresividad*) expressiveness 7. *pl* POL political groups *pl*; MIL forces *pl*; **~s del orden público** forces of law and order

8. ELEC power 9. (*usando*) **a ~ de** by means of; **lo ha conseguido todo a ~ de trabajo** he/she has achieved everything through hard work

fuete ['fwe·te] *m AmL* (*látigo*) whip

fuga ['fu·ɣa] *f* 1. (*huida*) flight; (*de la cárcel*) escape; **darse a la ~** to escape, to run away; **~ de capital** flight of capital; **~ de cerebros** brain drain 2. (*en tubos*) leak; (*de líquido*) leakage; (*de gas*) escape; **la cañería tiene una ~** the pipe has a leak 3. MÚS fugue 4. (*auge*) peak

fugacidad [fu·ɣa·si·'dad, -θi·'dad] *f* brevity; (*caducidad*) transitoriness

fugarse <g→gu> [fu·'ɣar·se] *vr* to flee; (*de casa*) to run away; (*para casarse*) to elope; **~ de la cárcel** to escape from prison

fugaz [fu·'ɣas, -'ɣaθ] *adj* fleeting; (*caduco*) short-lived; **estrella ~** shooting star

fugitivo, -a [fu·xi·'ti·βo, -a] I. *adj* fugitive; (*belleza*) transitory II. *m*, *f* fugitive; (*de la cárcel*) escapee

fulana [fu·'la·na] *f pey* whore

fulano, -a [fu·'la·no, -a] *m*, *f* 1. (*evitando el nombre*) so-and-so 2. (*persona indeterminada*) guy, John Doe; **no me importa lo que digan ~ y mengano** I do not care what Tom, Dick or Harry say 3. (*amante*) lover

fular [fu·'lar] *m* 1. (*tela*) fine silk 2. (*pañuelo*) foulard, silky scarf

fulero, -a [fu·'le·ro, -a] *adj inf* 1. (*embustero*) lying 2. (*chapucero*) **eres muy ~** you are a bungler

fulgor [ful·'ɣor] *m* (*resplandor*) radiance; (*centelleo*) sparkle; (*de una superficie*) gleam

fulgurante [ful·ɣu·'ran·te] *adj* 1. (*rápido*) rapid; **su carrera fue ~** he/she rose rapidly in his/her career 2. (*dolor*) intense

fulgurar [ful·ɣu·'rar] *vi* (*resplandecer*) to shine; (*centellear*) to sparkle; (*espejear*) to gleam

fullería [fu·je·'ri·a, fu·ʎe-] *f* 1. (*trampa*) trick; (*en el juego*) cheating; **hacer ~s** to cheat 2. (*treta*) ruse

fullero, -a [fu·'je·ro, -a; fu·'ʎe-] I. *adj* 1. (*tramposo*) tricky 2. *inf* (*astuto*) crafty II. *m*, *f* 1. (*tramposo*) trickster; (*en el juego*) cheat, cardsharper 2. *inf* (*astuto*) crafty individual

fulminación [ful·mi·na·'sjon, -'θjon] *f* (*aniquilación*) destruction

fulminante [ful·mi·'nan·te] I. *adj* 1. *t.* MED (*inesperado*) sudden 2. (*explosivo*) explosive 3. (*mirada*) withering II. *m* gunpowder

fulminar [ful·mi·'nar] I. *vi* to explode II. *vt* 1. (*dañar*) to strike down; (*aniquilar*) to destroy; (*matar*) to electrocute; **un rayo/el cáncer lo fulminó** he was struck down by lightning/cancer 2. (*arrojar*) to hurl 3. (*imponer*) to impose; **~ una censura** to impose censorship 4. (*amenazar*) to threaten angrily

fumadero [fu·ma·'de·ro] *m* smoking room; **~ de opio** opium den

fumador(a) [fu·ma·'dor, -·'do·ra] I. *adj* **zona de no ~es** no-smoking area II. *m(f)* smoker; **no ~** non-smoker

fumar [fu·'mar] I. *vi, vt* to smoke II. *vr:* **~se** 1. (*fumar*) to smoke 2. *inf* (*gastar*) to squander 3. *inf* (*faltar*) to cut; **~se la clase** to play hooky from school

fumigar <g→gu> [fu·mi·'ɣar] *vt* to fumigate

funambulesco, -a [fu·nam·bu·'les·ko, -a] *adj* 1. (*extravagante*) extravagant 2. (*relativo al funámbulo*) acrobatic; (*como un funámbulo*) like a tightrope walker

funámbulo, -a [fu·'nam·bu·lo, -a] *m, f* tightrope walker

función [fun·'sjon, -'θjon] *f* 1. *t.* BIO, MAT (*papel*) function; **el precio está en ~ de la calidad** the price depends on the quality 2. (*cargo*) office; (*tarea*) duty; **entrará en ~ mañana** he/she will start work tomorrow; (*cargo*) he/she will take office tomorrow; **el ministro en funciones** the acting minister 3. (*acto formal*) function; CINE showing; TEAT performance; **~ doble** double feature; **~ de noche** late show

funcional [fun·sjo·'nal, fun·θjo·] *adj* functional

funcionalidad [fun·sjo·na·li·'dad, fun·θjo·] *f* functionality

funcionamiento [fun·sjo·na·'mjen·to, fun·θjo·] *m* 1. (*marcha*) running; **~ administrativo** running of the administration; **~ del mercado** market organization; **poner en ~** to bring into operation 2. (*rendimiento*) performance; (*manera de funcionar*) operation; **en estado de ~** in working order; (*máquina*) working

funcionar [fun·sjo·'nar, fun·θjo·] *vi* to function; (*estar trabajando*) to be working; **la televisión no funciona** the television does not work; **'no funciona'** 'out of order'

funcionario, -a [fun·sjo·'na·rjo, -a; fun·θjo·] *m, f* (*de una organización*) employee; (*del Estado*) civil servant

funda ['fun·da] *f* (*cubierta*) cover; (*para gafas*) glasses case; (*de libro*) (dust) jacket; (*de almohada*) pillowcase; (*de butaca*) loose cover; (*de revólver*) holster; **~ nórdica** duvet

fundación [fun·da·'sjon, -'θjon] *f* 1. (*creación*) foundation, founding 2. (*institución*) foundation 3. (*justificación*) foundation, fundament 4. (*de una estructura*) foundations *pl*

fundado, -a [fun·'da·do, -a] *adj* well-founded

fundador(a) [fun·da·'dor, -·'do·ra] I. *adj* founder, founding II. *m(f)* founder

fundamental [fun·da·men·'tal] *adj* 1. fundamental; (*esencial*) essential; (*básico*) basic; **argumento ~** key argument; **conocimientos ~es** rudimentary knowledge 2. MAT cardinal

fundamentalismo [fun·da·men·ta·'lis·mo] *m* fundamentalism

fundamentalista [fun·da·men·ta·'lis·ta] *adj, mf* fundamentalist

fundamentar [fun·da·men·'tar] *vt* 1. ARQUIT to

lay the foundations of 2. (*basar*) to base 3. (*establecer*) to establish

fundamento [fun·da·'men·to] *m* 1. ARQUIT foundations *pl* 2. (*base*) basis 3. (*motivo*) grounds; **sin ~** groundless 4. (*formalidad*) sensibleness; (*seriedad*) seriousness; **hablar sin ~** not to talk seriously 5. *pl* (*conocimientos*) fundamentals *pl*

fundar [fun·'dar] I. *vt* 1. (*crear*) to found 2. TÉC to found 3. (*basar*) to base; (*justificar*) to found II. *vr:* **~se** 1. (*basarse*) to base oneself; (*tener su justificación*) to be founded 2. (*asentarse*) to be established

fundición [fun·di·'sjon, -'θjon] *f* 1. (*de un metal*) smelting 2. (*en una forma*) casting 3. (*de ideas*) fusion 4. (*taller*) foundry 5. (*hierro*) cast iron 6. TIPO font

fundidor [fun·di·'dor] *m* founder

fundillo [fun·'di·jo, -ʎo] *m* 1. AmL (*fondillos*) seat (of one's pants) 2. *Méx* (*trasero*) bottom

fundir [fun·'dir] I. *vt* 1. (*deshacer*) to melt 2. (*dar forma*) to found, to cast 3. (*bombilla*) to fuse; (*plomo*) to blow 4. (*unir*) to unite; (*empresas*) to merge 5. *inf* (*gastar*) to squander II. *vr:* **~se** 1. (*deshacerse*) to melt 2. (*bombilla*) to fuse; (*plomo*) to blow 3. (*unirse*) to unite; (*empresas*) to merge 4. *inf* (*arruinarse*) to become ruined; (*negocio*) to go bankrupt

fundo ['fun·do] *m* Chile, Perú (*finca*) country property

fúnebre ['fu·ne·βre] *adj* 1. (*triste*) mournful 2. (*sombrío*) gloomy 3. (*de los difuntos*) funerary; **coche ~** hearse; **pompas ~s** (*ceremonia*) funeral; (*empresa*) undertaker's

funeral [fu·ne·'ral] I. *adj* funerary, funereal II. *m* 1. (*entierro*) burial 2. *pl* (*misa*) funeral, obsequies *pl*

funeraria [fu·ne·'ra·rja] *f* funeral parlor

funerario, -a [fu·ne·'ra·rjo, -a] *adj* funeral

funesto, -a [fu·'nes·to, -a] *adj* 1. (*aciago*) ill-fated 2. (*desgraciado*) terrible 3. *inf* (*sin talento*) inept

fungicida [fun·xi·'si·da, -'θi·da] I. *adj* fungicidal II. *m* fungicide

fungir <g→j> [fun·'xir] *vi* 1. AmL (*un cargo*) to hold the post 2. AmC (*presumir*) to put on airs

funicular [fu·ni·ku·'lar] I. *adj* funicular; (*de cable aéreo*) cable; **tren ~** cable [*o* funicular] railway II. *m* funicular; **~ aéreo** cable car

furcia ['fur·sja, -θja] *f pey* whore, tart *inf*

furgón [fur·'ɣon] *m* 1. (*carro*) wagon; (*camioneta*) van 2. FERRO (*para el equipaje*) baggage car; (*para mercancías*) freight car; **~ de cola** caboose

furgoneta [fur·ɣo·'ne·ta] *f* van

furia ['fu·rja] *f* 1. (*ira, ímpetu*) fury 2. (*persona*) **estaba hecha una ~** she was furious 3. *inf* (*energía*) energy 4. (*auge*) zenith

furibundo, -a [fu·ri·'βun·do, -a] *adj* 1. (*furioso*) furious 2. *inf* (*entusiasta*) enthusiastic; (*extremado*) extreme

furioso, -a [fu·'rjo·so, -a] *adj* 1. (*furibundo*) furious **2.** (*loco*) beside oneself **3.** (*violento*) violent; (*tempestad*) raging **4.** (*tremendo*) tremendous; (*sentimiento*) intense

furor [fu·'ror] *m* **1.** (*ira*) fury **2.** (*ímpetu*) impulse **3.** (*energía*) drive **4.** (*auge*) craze; **hacer** ~ to be the (latest) thing **5.** (*afición*) passion **6.** (*locura*) frenzy **7.** MED ~ **uterino** nymphomania

furtivo, -a [fur·'ti·βo, -a] *adj* furtive; **cazador** ~ poacher

furúnculo [fu·'run·ku·lo] *m* MED boil

fuselaje [fu·se·'la·xe] *m* AVIAT fuselage

fusible [fu·'si·βle] **I.** *adj* fusible **II.** *m* fuse

fusil [fu·'sil] *m* rifle

fusilamiento [fu·si·la·'mjen·to] *m* **1.** (*ejecución*) execution (by firing squad) **2.** *inf* (*de textos*) cribbing

fusilar [fu·si·'lar] *vt* **1.** (*ejecutar*) to execute, to shoot **2.** *inf* (*copiar*) to crib

fusilería [fu·si·le·'ri·a] *f* **1.** (*fusiles*) rifles **2.** (*soldados*) fusiliers **3.** (*fuego*) gunfire

fusilero [fu·si·'le·ro] *m* fusilier, rifleman

fusión [fu·'sjon] *f* **1.** (*fundición*) fusion **2.** (*unión*) union; ECON merger

fusionar [fu·sjo·'nar] **I.** *vi* to fuse **II.** *vt* **1.** (*deshacer*) to fuse **2.** (*unir*) to fuse; (*empresas*) to merge **III.** *vr:* ~**se** to fuse; (*empresas*) to merge

fusta ['fus·ta] *f* **1.** (*látigo*) riding whip **2.** (*leña*) brushwood **3.** (*tejido*) woolen cloth

fustán [fus·'tan] *m* AmL (*combinación*) lady's slip

fuste ['fus·te] *m* **1.** (*madera*) wood **2.** (*vara*) pole; (*de una lanza*) shaft **3.** (*importancia*) importance; (*sustancia*) solidity; (*de una persona*) consequence

fustigar <g→gu> [fus·ti·'ɣar] *vt* **1.** (*azotar*) to whip **2.** (*reprender*) to reprimand

fútbol ['fud·βol] *m* soccer; ~ **americano** football

futbolín [fud·βo·'lin] *m* table football

futbolista [fud·βo·'lis·ta] *mf* DEP soccer player

futbolístico, -a [fud·βo·'lis·ti·ko, -a] *adj* soccer

fútbol-sala ['fud·βol-'sa·la] *m* DEP indoor soccer

fútil ['fu·til] *adj* trivial

futileza [fu·ti·'le·sa, -θa] *f* Chile (*pequeñez*) trifle

futilidad [fu·ti·li·'dad] *f* triviality

futre ['fu·tre] *m* AmL, *pey* stuck-up person

futurible [fu·tu·'ri·βle] **I.** *adj* possible; (*acontecimiento*) likely; (*persona*) potential **II.** *mf* potential candidate

futuro [fu·'tu·ro] *m t.* LING (*tiempo*) future

futuro, -a [fu·'tu·ro, -a] **I.** *adj* future **II.** *m, f inf* intended

futurólogo, -a [fu·tu·'ro·lo·ɣo, -a] *m, f* futurologist

G

G, g [xe] *f* G, g; ~ **de Granada** G as in Golf

gabacho, -a [ga·'βa·ʧo, -a] *m, f pey* (*francés*) frog *sl*

gabán [ga·'βan] *m* overcoat

gabardina [ga·βar·'di·na] *f* **1.** (*tela*) gabardine **2.** (*prenda*) raincoat

gabinete [ga·βi·'ne·te] *m* **1.** (*estudio*) study; (*salita*) private sitting room; ~ **de prensa** press office **2.** POL cabinet **3.** (*tocador*) dressing room **4.** (*museo*) museum **5.** (*de médico*) office

Gabón [ga·'βon] *m* Gabon

gabonés, -esa [ga·βo·'nes, --'ne·sa] *adj, m, f* Gabonese

gacela [ga·'se·la, ga·'θe-] *f* gazelle

gaceta [ga·'se·ta, ga·'θe-] *f* **1.** (*publicación*) gazette **2.** *inf* (*persona*) gossip, grapevine

gacha ['ga·ʧa] *f* **1.** *pl* (*comida*) ≈ porridge **2.** *inf* (*barro*) mud

gachí <gachís> [ga·'ʧi] *f inf* bird, chick

gacho, -a ['ga·ʧo, -a] *adj* drooping; **orejas gachas** floppy ears; **sombrero** ~ slouch hat

gachó [ga·'ʧo] *m inf* guy, bloke

gachumbo [ga·'ʧum·bo] *m* Col, Ecua hollowed-out fruit shell

gaditano, -a [ga·di·'ta·no, -a] **I.** *adj* of/from Cadiz **II.** *m, f* native/inhabitant of Cadiz

gaélico, -a [ɣa·'e·li·ko, -a] *adj* Gaelic

gafa ['ga·fa] *f* **1.** *pl* (*anteojos*) glasses *pl*; ~**s de bucear** diving mask; **llevar** ~**s** to wear glasses; **ponerse las** ~**s** to put one's glasses on **2.** (*varilla*) earpiece

gafar [ga·'far] *vt* **1.** *inf* (*mala suerte*) to jinx **2.** (*con las uñas*) to claw **3.** (*con grapas*) to staple

gafe ['ga·fe] *m* **1.** (*cenizo*) jinx **2.** (*aguafiestas*) party-pooper, wet-blanket

gag [gaɣ] *m* <gags> gag

gago, -a ['ga·ɣo, -a] **I.** *adj AmL* stuttering **II.** *m, f* stutterer

gaita ['gai·ta] *f* **1.** MÚS (*gallega*) bagpipes *pl*; (*zamorana*) hurdy-gurdy **2.** *inf* (*cuello*) neck **3.** *inf* (*lata*) **vaya** ~ **tener que hacer eso** having to do that is a real pain

gaitero, -a [gai·'te·ro, -a] *m, f* (*de gaita gallega*) bagpiper; (*de gaita zamorana*) hurdy-gurdy player

gajo ['ga·xo] *m* **1.** (*de naranja*) segment **2.** (*racimo*) bunch **3.** (*rama*) branch

gala ['ga·la] *f* **1.** (*fiesta*) gala **2.** (*garbo*) elegance **3.** (*selecto*) best **4.** *pl* (*vestido*) finery, (fine) clothes *pl* ► **hacer** ~ **de algo** to take pride in sth

galáctico, -a [ga·'lak·ti·ko, -a] *adj* galactic

galaico, -a [ga·'lai·ko, -a] *adj* Galician

galán [ga·'lan] *m* **1.** (*hombre*) handsome man **2.** (*novio*) beau

galante [ga·'lan·te] *adj* **1.** (*hombre*) gallant **2.** (*mujer*) flirtatious

galantear [ga·lan·te·'ar] *vt* to woo
galantería [ga·lan·te·'ri·a] *f* **1.** (*hacia una mujer*) gallantry **2.** (*amabilidad*) politeness **3.** (*cumplido*) compliment
galápago [ga·'la·pa·γo] *m* seaturtle
galardón [ga·lar·'don] *m* prize
galardonar [ga·lar·do·'nar] *vt* to award a prize to; ~ **a alguien con un título** to confer a title on sb
galaxia [ga·'lak·sja] *f* (*universo*) galaxy
galbana [gal·'βa·na] *f inf* laziness
galeón [ga·le·'on] *m* NÁUT galleon
galeote [ga·le·'o·te] *m* galley slave
galera [ga·'le·ra] *f* **1.** ZOOL mantis shrimp **2.** TIPO galley **3.** *AmL* (*cobertizo*) shed **4.** *AmL* (*sombrero: de copa*) top hat; (*de hongo*) bowler hat
galería [ga·le·'ri·a] *f* **1.** (*corredor, de arte*) gallery **2.** *pl* (*grandes almacenes*) department store; (*centro comercial*) shopping center, mall **3.** *pl* (*bulevar*) arcade **4.** MIN, TEAT gallery; **hablar para la** ~ to play to the gallery
galerón [ga·le·'ron] *m* **1.** *AmS* (*romance*) ballad **2.** *Col, Ven* MÚS folkdance and song **3.** *CRi, ElSal* (*cobertizo*) shed
galés, -esa [ga·'les, -·'le·sa] **I.** *adj* Welsh **II.** *m, f* Welshman *m*, Welshwoman *f*
Gales ['ga·les] *m* (**el País de**) ~ Wales
galgo, -a ['gal·γo, -a] *m, f* greyhound; ~ **inglés** whippet
galguerías [gal·γe·'ri·as] *fpl Col* (*golosinas*) candies *pl*
Galia ['ga·lja] *f* Gaul
Galicia [ga·'li·sja, -θja] *f* Galicia
galicismo [ga·li·'sis·mo, -'θis·mo] *m* French loan word(s), Gallicism
galimatías [ga·li·ma·'ti·as] *m inv* (*lenguaje*) gibberish
gallardear [ga·jar·de·'ar, ga·ʎar-] *vi* (*presumir*) to show off, to strut
gallardía [ga·jar·'di·a, ga·ʎar-] *f* **1.** (*garbo*) style, elegance **2.** (*valentía*) bravery
gallardo, -a [ga·'jar·do, -a; ga·'ʎar-] *adj* **1.** (*de aspecto*) elegant **2.** (*garboso*) dashing **3.** (*valiente*) brave **4.** (*generoso*) noble
gallear [ga·je·'ar, -ʎe·'ar] **I.** *vi* **1.** (*fanfarronear*) to brag **2.** (*alzar la voz*) to shout **3.** (*creerse importante*) to strut around **II.** *vt* (*el gallo a la gallina*) to tread
gallego, -a [ga·'je·γo, -a; ga·'ʎe-] *m, f* **1.** *AmS, pey* (*español*) Spaniard **2.** Galician
galleta [ga·'je·ta, -'ʎe·ta] *f* **1.** (*dulce*) biscuit, cookie; (*salada*) cracker **2.** *inf* (*bofetada*) slap, smack
gallina [ga·'ji·na, -'ʎi·na] *f* **1.** (*hembra del gallo*) hen; ~ **clueca** brooding hen **2.** *inf* (*cobarde*) chicken **3.** (*juego*) **jugar a la ~ ciega** to play blind man's buff ► **acostarse con las ~s** to go to bed very early
gallinazo [ga·ji·'na·so, -ʎi·'na·θo] *m* turkey buzzard
gallinero [ga·ji·'ne·ro, ga·ʎi-] *m* (*corral*) chicken coop, henhouse

gallito [ga·'ji·to, -'ʎi·to] *m inf* **ser un** ~ to be a tough guy; **ponerse** ~ to act tough
gallo ['ga·jo, -ʎo] *m* **1.** (*ave*) cock, rooster; ~ **de pelea** fighting cock; ~ **silvestre** wood grouse **2.** (*engreído*) show-off **3.** MÚS false note; **soltar un** ~ to let out a squeak **4.** *AmL* (*hombre fuerte*) tough guy ► **en menos que canta un** ~ in an instant [*o* a flash]
galo, -a ['ga·lo, -a] **I.** *adj* (*francés*) French **II.** *m, f* (*francés*) Frenchman *m*, Frenchwoman *f*
galón [ga·'lon] *m* **1.** (*cinta*) braid **2.** (*medida inglesa*) gallon
galopar [ga·lo·'par] *vi* to gallop
galope [ga·'lo·pe] *m* gallop
galpón [gal·'pon] *m AmL* shed
galuchar [ga·lu·'tʃar] *vi Col, Cuba, PRico, Ven* to gallop
galvanizar <z→c> [gal·βa·ni·'sar, -'θar] *vt* TÉC to electroplate
gama ['ga·ma] *f* **1.** MÚS gamut; (*escala*) scale **2.** (*escala*) range; **una ~ amplia/reducida de productos** a wide/narrow range of products
gamada [ga·'ma·da] *adj* **cruz** ~ swastika
gamba ['gam·ba] *f* prawn, shrimp
gamberrada [gam·be·'rra·da] *f* act of hooliganism; **hacer ~s** to horse around *inf*
gamberro, -a [gam·'be·rro, -a] *m, f* hooligan
gambeta [gam·'be·ta] *f AmL* **1.** (*distensión*) swerve **2.** (*evasiva*) dodge **3.** (*fútbol*) dummy; **hacer ~s** to dribble
gamín, -ina [ga·'min, -'mi·na] *m, f Col* (*pilluelo*) urchin
gamma ['ga·ma/'gam·ma] *f* gamma
gamo ['ga·mo] *m* fallow deer
gamonal [ga·mo·'nal] *m AmL*: *local political boss*
gamonalismo [ga·mo·na·'lis·mo] *m AmL* caciquism
gamuza [ga·'mu·sa, -θa] *f* **1.** (*piel*) chamois (leather) **2.** (*paño*) duster
gana ['ga·na] *f* desire; **tener ~s de hacer algo** to feel like doing sth; **tengo ~s de irme de vacaciones** I feel like going on holiday; **son ~s de fastidiar** *inf* they're just trying to be difficult; **de buena/mala** ~ willingly/unwillingly; **me quedé con las ~s de verlo** I wish I'd been able to see him; **no me da la (real)** ~ *inf* I can't be bothered; **venir en** ~ to feel like
ganadería [ga·na·de·'ri·a] *f* **1.** (*ganado*) livestock **2.** (*crianza*) livestock farming
ganadero, -a [ga·na·'de·ro, -a] **I.** *adj* livestock **II.** *m, f* **1.** (*criador: de vacas*) cattle farmer **2.** (*tratante: de vacas*) cattle merchant
ganado [ga·'na·do, -a] *m* **1.** (*reses*) livestock *pl;* ~ **bovino** [*o* **vacuno**] cattle *pl;* ~ **cabrío** goats *pl;* ~ **ovino** sheep *inv;* ~ **porcino** pigs *pl* **2.** *AmL* (~ **vacuno**) cattle *pl* **3.** *inf* (*de personas*) crowd
ganador(a) [ga·na·'dor, -·'do·ra] **I.** *adj* winning **II.** *m(f)* winner
ganancia [ga·'nan·sja, -θja] *f* **1.** (*beneficio*) profit **2.** (*sueldo*) earnings *pl*

ganancial [ga·nan·'sjal, -'θjal] *adj* pertaining to earnings or profit; **bienes ~es** property acquired during marriage

gananioso, -a [ga·nan·'sjo·so, -a; -'θjo·so, -a] *adj* **1.**(*que da ganancia*) profitable **2.**(*beneficiado*) **salir ~ de algo** to make a profit from sth

ganar [ga·'nar] **I.** *vi* **1.**(*vencer*) to win **2.**(*mejorar*) **~ en algo** to improve at sth; **~ en condición social** to better oneself socially; **con esto sólo puedes salir ganando** you can't lose with this; **no gana para sustos** with him/her it is one thing after another **II.** *vt* **1.**(*trabajando*) to earn; **con ese negocio consiguió ~ mucho dinero** he/she made a lot of money out of that business **2.**(*jugando*) win; (*a alguien*) to beat; **le he ganado 30 pesos I** won 30 pesos from him/her **3.**(*adquirir*) to gain; (*libertad*) to win; **~ conocimientos de algo** to acquire knowledge of sth; **~ experiencia** to gain experience; **~ peso** to put on weight; **¿qué esperas ~ con esto?** what do you hope to gain by that? **4.**(*llegar a*) to reach; **~ la orilla** to reach the shore **5.**(*aventajar*) **~ a alguien en algo** to be better than sb at sth **III.** *vr:* **~se 1.**(*dinero*) to earn; **¡te la vas a ~!** *inf* you're for it **2.**(*a alguien*) to win over

ganchillo [gan·'tʃi·jo, -ʎo] *m* **1.**(*gancho*) hook **2.**(*labor*) crochet; **hacer ~** to crochet

gancho ['gan·tʃo] *m* **1.**(*instrumento*) hook **2.** DEP (*boxeo*) hook; (*baloncesto*) hook shot **3.**(*algo que atrae*) bait **4.** AmL (*horquilla*) hairpin **5.**(*atractivo*) **tener ~** to be attractive **6.**(*persona*) decoy

ganchudo, -a [gan·'tʃu·do, -a] *adj* hooked

gandido, -a [gan·'di·do, -a] *adj Col, pey* (*glotón*) gluttonous

gandinga [gan·'din·ga] *f Cuba, PRico* CULIN liver stew

gandul(a) [gan·'dul, -'du·la] **I.** *adj* lazy **II.** *m(f)* loafer

gandulear [gan·du·le·'ar] *vi* to loaf around

gandulería [gan·du·le·'ri·a] *f* loafing

ganga ['gan·ga] *f* (*oferta*) bargain; **a precio de ~** at a bargain price

ganglio ['gan·gljo] *m* ANAT ganglion; **~ linfático** lymph gland

gangosear [gan·go·se·'ar] *vi* to speak through one's nose

gangoso, -a [gan·'go·so, -a] **I.** *adj* nasal **II.** *adv* **hablar ~** to speak through one's nose

gangrena [gan·'gre·na] *f* MED gangrene

gangrenarse [gan·gre·'nar·se] *vr* to become gangrenous

gángster ['gans·ter] *mf* gangster

ganguear [gan·ge·'ar] *vi* to speak through one's nose

gangueo [gan·'geo] *m* twang

gansada [gan·'sa·da] *f* silly thing; **hacer ~s** to clown around; **decir ~s** to talk nonsense

gansear [gan·se·'ar] *vi inf* **1.**(*hacer gansadas*) to clown [*o* to goof] around **2.**(*decir gansadas*) to talk nonsense

ganso, -a ['gan·so, -a] *m, f* **1.**(*ave: hembra*) goose; (*macho*) gander **2.** *inf* (*estúpido*) dummy; **hacer el ~** to clown around

ganzúa¹ [gan·'su·a, -'θu·a] *f* (*llave*) picklock

ganzúa² [gan·'su·a, -'θu·a] *m* (*ladrón*) burglar

gañán [ga·'ɲan] *m* **1.**(*mozo*) farmhand **2.**(*tosco*) brute

gañir <3. pret: gañó> [ga·'ɲir] *vi* (*animal, persona*) to howl; (*perro*) to yelp; (*ave*) to squawk

gañote [ga·'ɲo·te] *m* throat

garabatear [ga·ra·βa·te·'ar] **I.** *vt* (*al escribir*) to scribble; (*dibujando*) to doodle **II.** *vi* (*al escribir*) to scribble

garabato [ga·ra·'βa·to] *m* **1.**(*al escribir*) scribble **2.**(*al dibujar*) doodle

garaje [ga·'ra·xe] *m* garage

garandumba [ga·ran·'dum·ba] *f AmS* flat river boat

garante [ga·'ran·te] **I.** *adj* responsible **II.** *mf* guarantor

garantía [ga·ran·'ti·a] *f* **1.**(*seguridad*) guarantee; **sin ~** (*en la lotería*) no liability assumed **2.** FIN (*aval*) guarantee, collateral; (*caución*) surety **3.** COM guarantee; **~s constitucionales** POL constitutional rights

garantizador(a) [ga·ran·ti·sa·'dor, -'do·ra; ga·ran·ti·θa-] *m(f)* guarantor

garantizar <z→c> [ga·ran·ti·'sar, -'θar] *vt* **1.**(*asegurar*) to guarantee; **no está garantizado que él sea el orador** it's not certain that he'll be the speaker **2.** JUR to act as guarantor for

garañón [ga·ra·'ɲon] *m AmL* (*caballo semental*) stud

garapiña [ga·ra·'pi·ɲa] *f* **1.**(*galón*) braid **2.** CULIN sugar icing [*o* coating]

> **i** In Latin America, **garapiña** (or **garrapiña**) is a refreshing drink prepared from pineapple rinds, water, and milk.

garapiñar [ga·ra·pi·'ɲar] *vt* to coat with sugar

garbanzo [gar·'βan·so, -θo] *m* chickpea

garbeo [gar·'βeo] *m* stroll

garbo ['gar·βo] *m* **1.**(*elegancia*) elegance; (*de movimiento*) grace(fulness) **2.**(*brío*) dash **3.**(*generosidad*) generosity **4.**(*de un escrito*) style

garboso, -a [gar·'βo·so, -a] *adj* **1.**(*elegante*) elegant **2.**(*brioso*) dashing **3.**(*generoso*) generous

gardenia [gar·'de·nja] *f* gardenia

garete [ga·'re·te] *inf* **ir(se) al ~** (*proyecto*) to go down the tubes; NÁUT to go adrift

garfa ['gar·fa] *f* claw

garfio ['gar·fjo] *m* hook

gargajear [gar·ya·xe·'ar] *vi* to hawk

gargajo [gar·'ya·xo] *m* phlegm

garganta [gar·'yan·ta] *f* **1.**(*gaznate*) throat; (*cuello*) neck; (*empeine*) instep; **tener buena ~** to have a good voice; **se me hizo un nudo**

en la ~ de lo nervioso que estaba I was so nervous I had a lump in my throat **2.**(*de un objeto*) neck

gargantilla [gar·ɣan·'ti·ja, -ʎa] *f* **1.**(*collar*) (short) necklace; (*de perlas*) string of pearls **2.**(*cinta*) choker

gárgaras ['gar·ɣa·ras] *fpl* gargles *pl*; **hacer ~** to gargle; **¡vete a hacer ~!** *inf* get lost!

gargarear [gar·ɣa·re·'ar] *vi Chile, Guat, Perú* (*barbotear*) to gargle

gárgola ['gar·ɣo·la] *f* ARQUIT gargoyle

garita [ga·'ri·ta] *f* **1.**(*de centinelas*) sentry box **2.**(*de portero*) lodge **3.** FERRO signal box **4.**(*de fortificación*) lookout post, watch tower

garito [ga·'ri·to] *m* **1.**(*local*) nightclub; (*de juego*) gambling den; (*antro*) dive, joint **2.**(*ganancia*) winnings *pl*

garlar [gar·'lar] *vi inf* to chatter

garlito [gar·'li·to] *m* trap; **caer en el ~** *fig* to fall into the trap

garlopa [gar·'lo·pa] *f* jack plane

garnacha [gar·'na·tʃa] *f* (*uva, vino*) Grenache

garra ['ga·rra] *f* **1.**(*de animal*) claw; **caer en las ~ s de alguien** to fall into sb's clutches; **la policía le echó la ~** the police got hold of him **2.** *pey* (*mano*) paw **3.** NÁUT hook **4.** *pl, AmL* (*harapos*) rags, tatters *pl* **5.** *inf* (*brío*) **tener ~** to be compelling [*o* appealing]

garrafa [ga·'rra·fa] *f* (*pequeña*) carafe; (*más grande*) demijohn; **vino de ~** cheap wine

garrafal [ga·rra·'fal] *adj* (*muy grande*) enormous; (*muy malo*) terrible

garrapata [ga·rra·'pa·ta] *f* tick

garrapatear [ga·rra·pa·te·'ar] *vi, vt* to scribble, to scrawl

garrapiña [ga·rra·'pi·ɲa] *f v.* **garapiña**

garrapiñar [ga·rra·pi·'ɲar] *vt v.* **garapiñar**

garrocha [ga·'rro·tʃa] *f* TAUR goad

garronear [ga·rro·ne·'ar] *vi Arg* to goad

garrotazo [ga·rro·'ta·so, -θo] *m* blow with a stick [*o* club]

garrote [ga·'rro·te] *m* **1.**(*palo*) stick **2.**(*ligadura*) tourniquet **3.**(*de ejecución*) garotte

garrotillo [ga·rro·'ti·jo, -ʎo] *m* MED croup

garrucha [ga·'rru·tʃa] *f* pulley

garrulería [ga·rru·le·'ri·a] *f* chatter

garúa [ga·'ru·a] *f AmL* (*llovizna*) drizzle

garuar [ga·'rwar] *vimpers AmL* (*lloviznar*) to drizzle

garza ['gar·sa, -θa] *f* heron

garzón, -ona [gar·'son, -'so·na; -'θon, -'θo·na] *m, f AmL* (*camarero*) waiter *m*, waitress *f*

gas [gas] *m* **1.**(*fluido*) gas; **~ natural** natural gas; **bombona de ~** gas cylinder; **cartucho de ~** gas cartridge; **cocina de ~** gas stove; **agua con ~** carbonated water; **agua sin ~** noncarbonated [*o* still] water **2.** *inf* AUTO **dar ~** to accelerate; **ir a todo ~** to go at full speed; **quedarse sin ~** *fig* to run out of steam **3.** *pl* (*en el estómago*) **~es** wind

gasa ['ga·sa] *f* **1.**(*tela*) gauze; **~ hidrófila** surgical gauze **2.** MED lint **3.**(*pañal*) diaper liner **4.**(*de luto*) crape

gasear [ga·se·'ar] *vt* **1.**(*agua*) to carbonate **2.** QUÍM to gasify **3.**(*matar*) to gas

gaseiforme [ga·sei·'for·me] *adj* gaseous

gaseosa [ga·se·'o·sa] *f* lemonade, soda

gaseoso, -a [ga·se·'o·so, -a] *adj* **1.**(*bebida*) fizzy **2.**(*gaseiforme*) gaseous

gasfitería [gas·fi·te·'ri·a] *f AmL* plumbing

gasificación [ga·si·fi·ka·'sjon, -'θjon] *f* **1.**(*de bebida*) carbonation **2.** QUÍM gasification

gasificar <c→qu> [ga·si·fi·'kar] *vt* **1.**(*bebida*) to carbonate **2.** QUÍM (*transformar en gas*) to gasify

gasoducto [ga·so·'duk·to] *m* gas pipeline

gasoil [gas·'oil] *m* diesel

gasóleo [ga·'so·leo] *m* diesel

gasolina [ga·so·'li·na] *f* gas(oline); **~ sin plomo** unleaded gasoline; **~ súper** premium gasoline; **echar ~** to get gas

gasolinera [ga·so·li·'ne·ra] *f* **1.**(*establecimiento*) gas station **2.**(*lancha*) motorboat

gastado, -a [gas·'ta·do, -a] *adj* **1.**(*vestido, zapato*) worn out; (*cuello*) frayed; (*talón*) worn down; (*suelo*) worn; (*neumático*) bare; (*pilas*) used up **2.**(*expresión*) hackneyed **3.**(*persona*) worn out

gastador [gas·ta·'dor] *m* **1.** MIL (*zapador*) sapper **2.**(*condenado*) convict

gastador(a) [gas·ta·'dor, -·'do·ra] **I.** *adj* extravagant, lavish **II.** *m(f)* spendthrift

gastar [gas·'tar] **I.** *vt* **1.**(*dinero*) to spend **2.**(*vestido, zapato, neumático*) to wear out; (*talón, suelo*) to wear down **3.**(*tiempo*) to spend **4.**(*electricidad*) to use **5.**(*consumir, usar*) use; **¿qué talla/número gastas?** what size are you? **6.**(*tener*) **~ mal/buen humor** to be bad/good-humored **7.**(*poseer*) to have **II.** *vr:* **~ se 1.**(*dinero*) to spend **2.**(*vestido*) to wear out **3.**(*consumirse*) to run out

gasto ['gas·to] *m* **1.** *pl* (*de dinero*) spending; (*en un negocio*) costs *pl*; ECON, COM (*desembolso*) expenditure; (*costos adicionales*) expenses *pl*; **~s adicionales** extra charges; **~s pagados** all expenses paid; **~s corrientes** running costs; **~s de inscripción** registration fees *pl*; **~s de personal** staff costs *pl*; **~s generales** overhead (expenses); **el ~ público** public expenditure; **~s de representación** expenses *pl* **2.**(*de fuerza*) expenditure; **no merece el ~ de tanto tiempo** it's not worth spending so much time on it **3.**(*consumo*) consumption **4.**(*de una fuente*) flow

gástrico, -a ['gas·tri·ko, -a] *adj* gastric

gastritis [gas·'tri·tis] *f inv* MED gastritis

gastroenteritis [gas·tro·en·te·'ri·tis] *f inv* MED gastroenteritis

gastronomía [gas·tro·no·'mi·a] *f* (*arte culinaria*) gastronomy

gastronómico, -a [gas·tro·'no·mi·ko, -a] *adj* gastronomic

gastrónomo, -a [gas·'tro·no·mo, -a] *m, f* **1.**(*que trabaja en gastronomía*) gastronome **2.**(*gourmet*) gourmet

gatas ['ga·tas] **andar a ~** to crawl

gatear [ga·te·'ar] **I.** *vi* **1.**(*trepar*) to climb, to clamber **2.**(*ir a gatas*) to crawl **3.***AmL* (*enamorar*) to seduce **II.** *vt* **1.**(*arañar*) to scratch **2.** *inf*(*robar*) to swipe

gatera [ga·'te·ra] *f AmL* (*verdulera*) vegetable seller

gatillo [ga·'ti·jo, -ʎo] *m* **1.**(*percusor*) trigger; **apretar el ~** to pull the trigger **2.**(*de dentista*) forceps *pl* **3.**(*de cuadrúpedo*) nape (of the neck) **4.**(*ratero*) petty thief

gato ['ga·to] *m* **1.**(*minino*) cat; (*macho*) tomcat **2.**(*astuto*) fox **3.**(*madrileño*) man from Madrid **4.** TÉC (*de coche*) jack; (*de carpintero*) vice **5.**(*para dinero*) moneybag ▶ **dar ~ por liebre a alguien** *inf* to rip sb off; **aquí hay ~ encerrado** *inf* there's something fishy going on here

GATT [gat] *m abr de* **Acuerdo General sobre Aranceles y Comercio** GATT

gatuno, -a [ga·'tu·no, -a] *adj* feline, catlike

gauchaje [gau·'tʃa·xe] *m CSur* gauchos *pl*

gauchear [gau·tʃe·'ar] *vi* **1.**Arg, *Urug* (*vivir como un gaucho*) to live as a gaucho **2.***Arg* (*errar*) to rove

gaucho ['gau·tʃo] *m AmL* **1.**(*campesino*) gaucho **2.**(*jinete*) skilled horseman

> **i** **Gauchos** were the cowboys of the South American **Pampa**.

gaucho, -a ['gau·tʃo, -a] *adj* **1.**(*de gaucho*) gaucho **2.***AmL* (*grosero*) coarse **3.***AmL* (*astuto*) cunning

gaveta [ga·'βe·ta] *f* drawer

gavia ['ga·βja] *f* (*zanja*) ditch

gavilán [ga·'βi·lan] *m* **1.**(*ave*) sparrow hawk **2.**(*de pluma*) nib **3.**(*de espada*) quillon **4.**(*del cardo*) thistle flower

gavilla [ga·'βi·ja, -ʎa] *f* **1.**(*fajo*) bundle, sheaf **2.**(*cuadrilla*) band

gaviota [ga·'βjo·ta] *f* (sea)gull

gay [gai] *m* gay

gazapera [ga·sa·'pe·ra, ga·θa-] *f* (*madriguera*) warren

gazapo [ga·'sa·po, -'θa·po] *m* **1.**(*conejo*) young rabbit **2.**(*en un periódico*) misprint **3.** *inf*(*al hablar*) slip

gazmoño, -a [gas·'mo·ɲo, -a; gaθ-] *adj* **1.**(*mojigato*) prudish **2.**(*hipócrita*) hypocritical

gaznápiro, -a [gas·'na·pi·ro, -a; gaθ-] *m, f* simpleton

gaznatada [gas·na·'ta·da, gaθ-] *f AmL* blow to the throat

gaznate [gas·'na·te, gaθ-] *m* gullet

gazpacho [gas·'pa·tʃo, gaθ-] *m* CULIN gazpacho (*cold soup made of tomatoes, cucumbers, peppers, olive oil and a little bread*)

GB [dʒi·ɣa·'bait] *m* **1.** *abr de* **gigabyte** GB **2.** *abr de* **Gran Bretaña** GB

Gbit [dʒi·ɣa·'bit] *m abr de* **gigabit** Gbit

Gbyte [dʒi·ɣa·'bait] *m abr de* **gigabyte** GB

géiser ['xei·ser] *m* geyser

geisha ['gei·sa] *f* geisha

gel [xel] *m* gel

gelatina [xe·la·'ti·na] *f* **1.**(*sustancia*) gelatin **2.** CULIN jelly

gelatinoso, -a [xe·la·ti·'no·so, -a] *adj* **1.**(*como la gelatina*) gelatinous **2.**(*de gelatina*) jelly

gélido, -a ['xe·li·do, -a] *adj* icy

gema ['xe·ma] *f* (*piedra preciosa*) gem, jewel

gemelo, -a [xe·'me·lo, -a] **I.** *adj* twin; **hermanos ~s** twin brothers **II.** *m, f* (*mellizo*) twin

gemelos [xe·'me·los] *mpl* **1.**(*anteojos*) binoculars *pl*; **~ de teatro** opera glasses **2.**(*de la camisa*) cufflinks *pl* **3.** ASTR **Gemelos** Gemini **4.** ANAT calves *pl*

gemido [xe·'mi·do] *m* **1.**(*de dolor*) groan; (*de pena, de placer*) moan; (*al llorar*) wail **2.**(*de animal*) whimper

geminación [xe·mi·na·'sjon, -'θjon] *f* (*duplicación*) duplication

Géminis ['xe·mi·nis] *m* Gemini

gemir [xe·'mir] *irr como pedir* *vi* **1.**(*de dolor*) to groan; (*de pena, de placer*) to moan **2.**(*animal*) to whine

gen [xen] *m* BIO gene

gendarme [xen·'dar·me] *mf* police officer

genealogía [xe·nea·lo·'xi·a] *f* genealogy

genealógico, -a [xe·nea·'lo·xi·ko, -a] *adj* genealogical; **árbol ~** family tree

generación [xe·ne·ra·'sjon, -'θjon] *f* **1.**(*producción*) generation; **instrucción de ~** COMPUT generative instruction **2.**(*descendientes*) generation

generacional [xe·ne·ra·sjo·'nal, -θjo·'nal] *adj* generational

generador [xe·ne·ra·'dor] *m* ELEC generator

generador(a) [xe·ne·ra·dor, -·'do·ra] *adj* **1.**(*productivo*) productive; **medidas ~as de empleo** employment creation measures **2.** ELEC generating

general [xe·ne·'ral] **I.** *adj* **1.**(*universal*) general; **cuartel ~** headquarters; **cultura ~** general knowledge; **junta ~** (**extraordinaria**) (extraordinary) general meeting; **regla ~** general rule; **de uso ~** (*para todo uso*) multi-purpose, all-purpose; (*para todo el mundo*) for general use; **por lo ~**, **en ~** in general, generally; **por regla ~** as a (general) rule; **en ~ me siento satisfecho** overall, I'm satisfied **2.**(*vago*) general; **tengo una idea ~ del tema** I have a general idea about the subject **II.** *m* general

generalidad [xe·ne·ra·li·'dad] *f* **1.**(*calidad general, validez general*) generality; **en la ~ de los casos** in most cases **2.**(*vaguedad*) **respondió con una ~** he/she gave a vague reply; **hablar de ~es** to talk about nothing in particular **3.** *pl* (*conocimientos generales*) basic knowledge

generalización [xe·ne·ra·li·sa·'sjon, -θa·'θjon] *f* **1.**(*universalización*) generalization **2.**(*difusión*) spread

generalizador(a) [xe·ne·ra·li·sa·'dor, -·'do·ra;

xe·ne·ra·li·θa-] *adj* generalizing
generalizar <z→c> [xe·ne·ra·li·'sar, -'θar] *vt*
1. (*hacer general*) to generalize **2.** (*difundir*) to
spread
generalmente [xe·ne·ral·'men·te] *adv* **1.** (*en*
general) generally **2.** (*ampliamente*) widely
3. (*habitualmente*) generally
generar [xe·ne·'rar] *vt* **1.** (*producir*) to generate; ~ **beneficios** to generate profits **2.** (*provocar*) to create; ~ **un clima de confianza** to
create a climate of trust
generativo, -a [xe·ne·ra·'ti·βo, -a] *adj* generative
generatriz [xe·ne·ra·'tris, -'triθ] *f* **1.** FÍS generator **2.** MAT generatrix
genérico, -a [xe·'ne·ri·ko, -a] *adj* **1.** (*de la*
especie) generic; **medicamentos** ~**s** generic
drugs **2.** LING **nombre** ~ common noun
género ['xe·ne·ro] *m* **1.** BIO genus; ~ **humano**
mankind, human race **2.** (*clase*) type, sort;
¿**qué** ~ **de hombre es?** what sort of man is
he?; **sin ningún** ~ **de dudas** without a shadow of a doubt; **tomar todo** ~ **de precauciones** to take every possible precaution
3. LING gender **4.** LIT, ARTE genre; **el** ~ **novelís-
tico** fiction; **el** ~ **lírico** lyric poetry **5.** COM (*artículo*) article; (*mercancía*) merchandise, goods
pl; (*tela*) cloth; ~**s de punto** knitwear **6.** MÚS
el ~ **lírico** opera **7.** (*manera*) manner
generosidad [xe·ne·ro·si·'dad] *f* **1.** (*dadivosi-
dad*) generosity **2.** (*magnanimidad*) magnanimity
generoso, -a [xe·ne·'ro·so, -a] *adj* **1.** (*dadivoso*) generous; **ser** ~ **con** [*o* **para con**] **alguien** to be generous to sb **2.** (*magnánimo*)
magnanimous **3.** (*abundante*) generous
génesis ['xe·ne·sis] *f inv* genesis
Génesis ['xe·ne·sis] *m* Genesis
genética [xe·'ne·ti·ka] *f* BIO genetics
genético, -a [xe·'ne·ti·ko, -a] *adj* genetic
genial [xe·'njal] *adj* **1.** (*idea*) brilliant **2.** (*gracioso*) funny **3.** (*estupendo*) great
genialidad [xe·nja·li·'dad] *f* **1.** (*cualidad*)
genius **2.** (*acción*) stroke of genius
genio ['xe·njo] *m* **1.** (*carácter*) character;
tener mal ~ to be bad-tempered; **tener
mucho** ~ to be very temperamental **2.** (*persona*) genius; **el** ~ **de Cervantes** Cervantes
the genius **3.** (*empuje*) drive **4.** (*de una época*)
spirit **5.** (*ser fabuloso*) genie **6.** ARTE genius
genital [xe·ni·'tal] *adj* genital
genitales [xe·ni·'ta·les] *mpl* genitals *pl*
genitivo [xe·ni·'ti·βo] *m* LING genitive
genocidio [xe·no·'si·djo, -'θi·djo] *m* genocide
genoteca [xe·no·'te·ka] *f* BIOL gene bank
Génova ['xe·no·βa] *f* Genoa
gente ['xen·te] *f* **1.** (*personas*) people *pl*; ~ **de
armas** men at arms; **la** ~ **joven/mayor**
young/old people; ~ **menuda** (*niños*) children; **a este partido le preocupa la** ~ this
party cares about people; **tienes que tratar
más con la** ~ you should spend more time
with other people; ¿**qué dirá la** ~? what will

people say?; **tener don de** ~**s** to have a way
with people **2.** (*personal*) staff **3.** *inf* (*parentela*) family; ¿**qué tal tu** ~? how are your
folks? **4.** *AmL* (*honrado*) honest people
gentil [xen·'til] I. *adj* **1.** (*pagano*) pagan
2. (*apuesto*) dashing; (*elegante*) elegant
3. (*amable*) considerate II. *mf* pagan, heathen
gentileza [xen·ti·'le·sa, -θa] *f* **1.** (*garbo*) elegance **2.** (*cortesía*) kindness; ¿**tendría Ud. la**
~ **de ayudarme?** would you be so kind as to
help me?
gentilicio, -a [xen·ti·'li·sjo, -a; -li·θjo, -a] *adj*
nombre ~ *noun describing people from a particular place*
gentío [xen·'ti·o] *m* crowd
gentuza [xen·'tu·sa, -θa] *f pey* rabble; ¡**qué** ~!
what a rabble!
genuflexión [xe·nu·flek·'sjon] *f* genuflection
genuino, -a [xe·'nwi·no, -a] *adj* (*persona*)
genuine; (*manuscrito*) authentic; (*amor*) true;
es un caso ~ **de histeria** it is a genuine case
of hysteria
geodesia [xeo·'de·sja] *f* geodesy
geografía [xeo·yra·'fi·a] *f* geography
geográfico, -a [xeo·'yra·fi·ko, -a] *adj* geographical
geógrafo, -a [xe·'o·yra·fo, -a] *m, f* geographer
geología [xeo·lo·'xi·a] *f* geology
geológico, -a [xeo·'lo·xi·ko, -a] *adj* geological
geólogo, -a [xe·'o·lo·yo, -a] *m, f* geologist
geometría [xeo·me·'tri·a] *f* geometry
geométrico, -a [xeo·'me·tri·ko, -a] *adj* geo-
metric(al)
geopolítico, -a [xeo·po·'li·ti·ko, -a] *adj* geopo-
litical
Georgia [xe·'or·xja] *f* Georgia
georgiano, -a [xeor·'xja·no, -a] *adj, m, f* Geor-
gian
geranio [xe·'ra·njo] *m* geranium
gerencia [xe·'ren·sja, -θja] *f* (*de una empresa*,
un teatro) management; (*de un banco*) directors *pl*
gerente [xe·'ren·te] *mf* (*de una gran empresa*)
director, general manager; (*de una pequeña
empresa*) manager; (*de un departamento*)
head
geriatra [xe·'rja·tra] *mf* geriatrician
geriatría [xe·rja·'tri·a] *f* geriatrics *pl*
geriátrico, -a [xe·'rja·tri·ko, -a] *adj* geriatric;
clínica geriátrica geriatric hospital
gerifalte [xe·ri·'fal·te] *m* **1.** (*persona*) bigwig
2. (*halcón*) gyrfalcon, gerfalcon
germánico, -a [xer·'ma·ni·ko, -a] I. *adj* **1.** (*de
Germania*) Germanic **2.** (*de Alemania*) German II. *m, f* German
germanio [xer·'ma·njo] *m* germanium
germanismo [xer·ma·'nis·mo] *m* word or
phrase of German origin
germanista [xer·ma·'nis·ta] *mf* Germanist,
German scholar
germanización [xer·ma·ni·sa·'sjon, -θa·'θjon]
f Germanization
germanizar <z→c> [xer·ma·ni·'sar, -'θar] *vt*

to Germanize, to make German

germano, -a [xer·'ma·no, -a] *adj, m, f v.* **germánico**

germanófilo, -a [xer·ma·'no·fi·lo, -a] *adj* Germanophile

germanófobo, -a [xer·ma·'no·fo·βo, -a] *adj* Germanophobe

germanooccidental [xer·ma·nok·si·den·'tal/ xer·ma·no·ok·si·den·'tal, -θi·den·'tal] HIST *adj, mf* West German

germanooriental [xer·ma·no·rjen·'tal/xer·ma·no·o·rjen·'tal] HIST *adj, mf* East German

germen ['xer·men] *m* **1.** BIO germ; **~ de trigo** wheat germ **2.** (*origen*) origin

germicida [xer·mi·'si·da, -'θi·da] *m* germicide

germinación [xer·mi·na·'sjon, -'θjon] *f* germination

germinar [xer·mi·'nar] *vi* **1.** BOT to germinate **2.** (*sospechas*) to arouse; **~ en** to give rise to

gerontología [xe·ron·to·lo·'xi·a] *f* gerontology

gerundio [xe·'run·djo] *m* LING gerund

gesta ['xes·ta] *f* heroic deed, exploit; LIT epic poem or narrative

gestación [xes·ta·'sjon, -'θjon] *f* **1.** (*de una persona, un animal*) gestation **2.** (*de un plan, proyecto*) preparation; (*de un complot*) hatching; **el proyecto está en ~** the project is at the planning stage

gestar [xes·'tar] **I.** *vt* to gestate **II.** *vr:* **~ se** (*proceso*) to develop; (*plan, proyecto*) to be prepared; (*complot*) to be hatched

gesticulación [xes·ti·ku·la·'sjon, -'θjon] *f* **1.** (*con las manos*) gesticulation **2.** (*con la cara*) face-pulling; (*de dolor*) grimace

gesticular [xes·ti·ku·'lar] *vi* **1.** (*con las manos*) to gesticulate **2.** (*con la cara*) to pull faces; (*de dolor*) to grimace

gestión [xes·'tjon] *f* **1.** (*diligencia*) measure; **hacer gestiones** to take measures [*o* steps] **2.** (*de una empresa*) management; **~ del conocimiento** knowledge management; **~ de crisis** crisis management; **la ~ del gobierno** the government's management of the country; **la ~ al frente de la escuela** the school management **3.** COMPUT **~ de ficheros** file management

gestionar [xes·tjo·'nar] *vt* **1.** (*asunto*) to conduct **2.** (*negocio*) to manage

gesto ['xes·to] *m* **1.** (*con el cuerpo*) movement; (*con la mano*) gesture; (*con el rostro*) expression; **torcer el ~** to scowl **2.** (*semblante*) face **3.** (*acto*) gesture; **un ~ de apoyo** a gesture of support

gestor(a) [xes·'tor, -·'to·ra] **I.** *adj* managing **II.** *m(f)* person who handles official matters on the behalf of his/her client; **~ del conocimiento** knowledge manager

gestual [xes·'twal] *adj* gestural; **lenguaje ~** body language

gestualidad [xes·twa·li·'dad] *f* (*del rostro*) expressiveness; (*del cuerpo*) body language

ghanés, -esa [ga·'nes, -·'ne·sa] *adj, m, f* Ghanian

giba ['xi·βa] *f* **1.** (*chepa*) hump, hunch **2.** (*bulto*) lump **3.** (*molestia*) nuisance

gibar [xi·'βar] *vt* **1.** (*corcorvar*) to bend **2.** *inf* (*jorobar*) to bother, to hassle

gibón [xi·'βon] *m* gibbon

Giga ['dʒi·ɣa] *m* Giga

gigabyte [dʒi·ɣa·'bait] *m* gigabyte; **~s por segundo** gigabytes per second

gigante [xi·'ɣan·te] **I.** *adj* giant, gigantic **II.** *m* **1.** (*ser*) giant **2.** (*en fiesta popular*) papier-mâché giant

gigantesco, -a [xi·ɣan·'tes·ko, -a] *adj* gigantic

gigantismo [xi·ɣan·'tis·mo] *m* MED giantism, gigantism

gigoló [dʒi·ɣo·'lo] *m* gigolo

gilipollas [xi·li·'po·jas, -ʎas] *mf inv, vulg* dimwit

gilipollez [xi·li·po·'jes, -'ʎeθ] *f inf* nonsense; **decir gilipolleces** to talk nonsense

gimnasia [xim·'na·sja] *f* **1.** DEP gymnastics *pl;* **~ rítmica** rhythm gymnastics **2.** ENS gym **3.** (*ejercicio*) **hacer ~** to do exercises

gimnasio [xim·'na·sjo] *m* gymnasium; **~ (de musculación)** gym

gimnasta [xim·'nas·ta] *mf* gymnast

gimnástico, -a [xim·'nas·ti·ko, -a] *adj* gymnastic

gimotear [xi·mo·te·'ar] *vi* **1.** *pey* (*gemir*) to groan **2.** (*lloriquear*) to whimper, to whine

gimoteo [xi·mo·'teo] *m* **1.** (*gemidos*) groan **2.** (*lloriqueo*) whimper, whining

ginebra [xi·'ne·βra] *f* gin

Ginebra [xi·'ne·βra] *f* Geneva

ginebrino, -a [xi·ne·'βri·no, -a] **I.** *adj* of/from Geneva **II.** *m, f* native/inhabitant of Geneva

ginecología [xi·ne·ko·lo·'xi·a] *f* gynecology

ginecológico, -a [xi·ne·ko·'lo·xi·ko, -a] *adj* gynecological

ginecólogo, -a [xi·ne·'ko·lo·ɣo, -a] *m, f* gynecologist

ginesta [xi·'nes·ta] *f* broom

gingivitis [xin·xi·'βi·tis] *f inv* MED gingivitis

gira ['xi·ra] *f* **1.** (*de un día*) (day)trip, excursion; (*más larga*) tour **2.** (*de un artista*) tour; **estar de ~** to be on tour

girado, -a [xi·'ra·do, -a] *m, f* FIN drawee

giralda [xi·'ral·da] *f* weathervane; (*en forma de gallo*) weathercock

girar [xi·'rar] **I.** *vi* **1.** (*dar vueltas*) to revolve; (*con rapidez*) to spin **2.** (*conversación*) **~ en torno a algo** to revolve around sth **3.** (*beneficios*) **este negocio gira mucho** this business has a big turnover **4.** (*torcer*) to turn **II.** *vt* **1.** (*dar la vuelta*) to turn; **~ la vista** to look around **2.** COM (*dinero*) to send; **~ a cargo de alguien** (*letra*) to draw on sb

girasol [xi·ra·'sol] *m* sunflower

giratorio, -a [xi·ra·'to·rjo, -a] *adj* revolving

giro ['xi·ro] *m* **1.** (*vuelta, cariz*) turn; **un ~ de volante** a turn of the steering wheel; **tomar un ~ favorable/negativo** to take a turn for the better/worse; **me preocupa el ~ que toma este asunto** I don't like the way this issue is developing **2.** COM (*letra*) draft; ~ **postal** money order

gitanada [xi·ta·'na·da] *f* **1.** (*engaño*) contemptible trick **2.** (*zalamería*) wheedling

gitanería [xi·ta·ne·'ri·a] *f* **1.** *inf* (*halago*) cajolement **2.** (*grupo*) band of gypsies **3.** (*vida*) gypsy way of life **4.** (*acción*) gypsy saying

gitano, -a [xi·'ta·no, -a] **I.** *adj* **1.** (*de los gitanos*) gypsy **2.** *inf* (*zalamero*) wheedling **II.** *m, f* **1.** (*calé*) gypsy **2.** *inf* (*estafador*) swindler **3.** CULIN **brazo de** ~ jelly roll

glaciación [gla·sja·'sjon, -θja·'θjon] *f* glaciation

glacial [gla·'sjal, -'θjal] *adj* **1.** (*helado*) icy cold; **zona** ~ polar region **2.** (*persona*) cold

glaciar [gla·'sjar, -'θjar] *m* GEO glacier

gladiolo [gla·'djo·lo] *m*, **gladíolo** [gla·'dio·lo] *m* gladiolus

glande ['glan·de] *m* ANAT glans penis

glándula ['glan·du·la] *f* ANAT gland

glandular [glan·du·'lar] *adj* glandular

glasear [gla·se·'ar] *vt* (*alimentos, papel*) to glaze; (*tarta*) to ice

glaucoma [glau·'ko·ma] *m* MED glaucoma

glicerina [gli·se·'ri·na, gli·θe-] *f* glycerin

global [glo·'βal] *adj* **1.** (*total*) overall; **valoración** ~ total value **2.** (*cantidad*) total **3.** (*informe*) comprehensive **4.** (*mundial*) global

globalidad [glo·βa·li·'dad] *f* totality

globalifóbico, -a [glo·βa·li·'fo·βi·ko] **I.** *adj* antiglobalization; **movimiento** ~ antiglobalization movement **II.** *m, f* antiglobalization activist, globalization critic

globalización [glo·βa·li·sa·'sjon, -θa·'θjon] *f* **1.** (*de un problema*) overall treatment **2.** (*generalización*) generalization **3.** (*mundialización*) globalization

globalizante [glo·βa·li·'san·te, -'θan·te] *adj* generalizing

globalizar <z→c> [glo·βa·li·'sar, -'θar] *vt* **1.** (*problema*) to give an overall view of **2.** (*generalizar*) to generalize **3.** (*mundializar*) to globalize

globo ['glo·βo] *m* **1.** (*esfera*) sphere; ~ **de una lámpara** (round) lampshade; ~ **ocular** eyeball **2.** (*tierra, mapa*) globe **3.** (*para niños*) balloon; ~ (**aerostático**) hot-air balloon **4.** *inf* (*enfado*) anger **5.** *inf* (*preservativo*) condom, rubber **6.** DEP (*tenis*) lob **7.** (*cómics, tebeos*) speech balloon [*o* bubble]

globular [glo·βu·'lar] *adj* **1.** (*de globo*) spherical **2.** (*de glóbulo*) globular

glóbulo ['glo·βu·lo] *m* ANAT corpuscle; ~ **blanco/rojo** white/red corpuscle

gloria[1] ['glo·rja] *f* **1.** (*fama*) glory; **Goya es una** ~ **nacional** Goya is a national treasure **2.** (*paraíso*) heaven; **conseguir la** ~ to go to heaven; **estar en la** ~ *inf* to be in seventh heaven **3.** (*esplendor*) glory

gloria[2] ['glo·rja] *m* REL Gloria, doxology

gloriarse <1. *pres:* me glorío> [glo·ri·'ar·se] *vr* (*presumir*) ~**se de algo** to boast about sth

glorieta [glo·'rje·ta] *f* **1.** (*cenador*) arbor **2.** (*plazoleta*) (small) square **3.** (*rotonda*) traffic circle

glorificación [glo·ri·fi·ka·'sjon, -'θjon] *f* glorification

glorificar <c→qu> [glo·ri·fi·'kar] **I.** *vt* to glorify **II.** *vr* ~ **se de algo** to boast about sth

glorioso, -a [glo·'rjo·so, -a] *adj* **1.** *t.* REL glorious **2.** (*jactancioso*) boastful

glosa ['glo·sa] *f* **1.** ~ **a algo** (*aclaración*) explanation on sth; (*anotación*) note on sth; (*comentario*) comment on sth **2.** LIT gloss **3.** MÚS variation

glosar [glo·'sar] *vt* **1.** (*anotar*) to annotate **2.** (*comentar*) to comment on; LIT to gloss **3.** (*tergiversar*) to deliberately misinterpret

glosario [glo·'sa·rjo] *m* glossary

glotis ['glo·tis] *f inv* ANAT glottis

glotón [glo·'ton] *m* glutton

glotón, -ona [glo·'ton, -·'to·na] **I.** *adj* gluttonous, greedy **II.** *m, f* glutton

glotonear [glo·to·ne·'ar] *vi* to be gluttonous

glotonería [glo·to·ne·'ri·a] *f* gluttony

glucemia [glu·'se·mja, -'θe·mja] *f* MED glycemia

glucosa [glu·'ko·sa] *f* glucose

gluten ['glu·ten] *m* **1.** (*cola*) glue **2.** BOT gluten

glúteo ['glu·teo] *m* ANAT gluteus; ~**s** (*nalgas*) buttocks *pl*

glutinoso, -a [glu·ti·'no·so, -a] *adj* glutinous

gnomo ['no·mo] *m* gnome

gnosticismo [nos·ti·'sis·mo, -'θis·mo] *m* REL Gnosticism

gobernabilidad [go·βer·na·βi·li·'dad] *f* governability

gobernable [go·βer·'na·βle] *adj* **1.** (*país*) governable **2.** (*nave*) steerable

gobernación [go·βer·na·'sjon, -'θjon] *f* government

gobernador(a) [go·βer·na·'dor, -·'do·ra] **I.** *adj* governing **II.** *m(f)* governor

gobernanta [go·βer·'nan·ta] *f* AmL **1.** (*niñera*) nanny **2.** (*institutriz*) governess **3.** (*ama de llaves*) housekeeper

gobernante [go·βer·'nan·te] *mf* ruler

gobernar <e→ie> [go·βer·'nar] *vt* **1.** POL (*mandar*) to govern **2.** (*dirigir*) to manage; (*nave*) to steer; ~ **una casa** to run a household **3.** (*máquina*) to handle, to run **4.** (*a una persona*) to rule

gobierno [go·'βjer·no] *m* **1.** POL government; ~ **autonómico** regional government; ~ **central** central government; **en círculos afines al** ~ in the corridors of power **2.** (*ministros*) cabinet; ~ **en la sombra** shadow cabinet **3.** (*del gobernador*) governorship; (*residencia*) governor's residence **4.** (*dirección*) management **5.** (*de una nave*) steering **6.** (*de una máquina*) handling

goce ['go·se, -θe] *m* pleasure, enjoyment

godo, -a ['go·do, -a] **I.** *adj* Gothic **II.** *m, f* **1.** HIST Goth **2.** AmC, *pey* (*español*) Spaniard

gofre ['go·fre] *m* waffle

gol [gol] *m* DEP goal; ~ **del empate** equalizer; **meter un** ~ to score (a goal)

gola ['go·la] *f* **1.** (*gorguera*) ruff **2.** (*garganta*) throat

golazo [go·'la·so, -θo] *m* DEP great goal

goleador(a) [go·lea·'dor, -·'do·ra] *m(f)* DEP goal scorer

golear [go·le·'ar] *vt* DEP to score a lot of goals against, to hammer

golf [golf] *m* DEP golf

golfa ['gol·fa] *f* **1.** *inf* (*puta*) slut, hussy **2.** *v.* **golfo, -a**

golfear [gol·fe·'ar] *vi* to loaf around

golfista [gol·'fis·ta] *mf* DEP golfer

golfo ['gol·fo] *m* GEO gulf

golfo, -a ['gol·fo, -a] **I.** *adj* (*niño*) naughty **II.** *m, f* **1.** (*pilluelo*) urchin **2.** (*vagabundo*) tramp **3.** (*sinvergüenza*) scoundrel

gollete [go·'ʎe·te, 'ʎe·te] *m* **1.** ANAT (*garganta*) throat **2.** (*de vasija*) neck

golondrina [go·lon·'dri·na] *f* **1.** (*pájaro*) swallow **2.** *reg* (*barca*) motorboat

golosina [go·lo·'si·na] *f* **1.** (*manjar*) delicacy **2.** (*dulce*) candy **3.** (*deseo*) desire **4.** (*cosa apetitosa*) tidbit

golosinear [go·lo·si·ne·'ar] *vi* to have treats

goloso, -a [go·'lo·so, -a] **I.** *adj* **1.** (*de dulces*) sweet-toothed **2.** (*apetitoso*) appetizing; **es una oferta muy golosa** it's a very tempting offer **II.** *m, f* **ser un** ~ to have a sweet tooth

golpe ['gol·pe] *m* **1.** (*impacto*) blow; (*choque*) bump; ~ **de Estado** coup (d'état); ~ **de pincel** brushstroke; **un** ~ **de tos** a fit of coughing; **andar a** ~**s** to be always fighting; **abrirse de** ~ (*puerta, ventana*) to fly open; **cerrar la puerta de** ~ to slam the door shut; **dar un** ~ to strike; **me ha dado un** ~ **en la cabeza** I banged my head; **parar un** ~ to stop a blow; **me lo tragué de un** ~ I downed it in one go [*o* all at once] **2.** (*ruido*) bang **3.** (*ocurrencia*) witty remark **4.** (*atraco*) hold-up **5.** (*gran cantidad*) crowd; ~ **de gente** slew of people **6.** (*sorpresa*) shock **7.** (*de vestido*) flap **8.** (*en el boxeo*) punch; ~ **bajo** blow below the belt; ~ **franco** free kick ▶ **a** ~ **de vista** at a glance

golpear [gol·pe·'ar] **I.** *vi* **1.** (*dar un golpe*) to hit **2.** (*latir*) to throb, to beat **3.** TÉC (*motor*) to knock **II.** *vt* to hit; (*puerta*) to knock on **III.** *vr* ~**se la cabeza** to bang one's head

golpetear [gol·pe·te·'ar] **I.** *vi* **1.** (*dar golpes*) to hammer **2.** (*traquetear*) to rattle **II.** *vt* to hammer

golpista [gol·'pis·ta] *mf* participant in a coup (d'état)

goma ['go·ma] *f* **1.** (*sustancia*) rubber; ~ **de borrar** eraser; ~ **elástica** (*sustancia*) rubber; (*objeto*) elastic band; ~ **de pegar** glue **2.** *inf* (*preservativo*) condom, rubber **3.** AmL (*resaca*) hangover

goma-dos ['go·ma-dos] *f* plastic explosive

gomaespuma [go·ma·es·'pu·ma] *f* foam rubber

gomería [go·me·'ri·a] *f* Arg COM tire shop

gomero [go·'me·ro] *m* AmL (*árbol*) rubber tree

gomina® [go·'mi·na] *f* hair [*o* styling] gel

gominola [go·mi·'no·la] *f* gumdrop

gomosidad [go·mo·si·'dad] *f* **1.** (*elasticidad*) elasticity **2.** (*adherencia*) stickiness

gomoso [go·'mo·so] *m* sticky

gónada ['go·na·da] *f* ANAT gonad

góndola ['gon·do·la] *f* **1.** (*de Venecia*) gondola **2.** AmL bus

gondolero [gon·do·'le·ro] *m* gondolier

gong [gon] *m* <gongs>, **gongo** ['gon·go] *m* gong

gonorrea [go·no·'rrea] *f* MED gonorrhea

gordo ['gor·do] *m* **1.** (*grasa*) fat **2.** (*lotería*) **el** ~ the first prize (in the lottery), the jackpot; **sacar el** ~ *fig* to bring home the bacon

gordo, -a ['gor·do, -a] **I.** *adj* **1.** (*persona*) fat; (*comida*) fatty; (*tejido*) thick **2.** (*suceso*) important; (*salario*) big; **una mentira gorda** a big lie; **ha pasado algo muy** ~ sth serious has happened **II.** *m, f* fat man, fat woman *m, f*

gordura [gor·'du·ra] *f* (*obesidad*) fatness; (*corpulencia*) corpulence; (*grasa*) fat

gorgojo [gor·'yo·xo] *m* **1.** (*insecto*) weevil **2.** *inf* (*persona*) midget

gorgotear [gor·yo·te·'ar] *vi* **1.** (*hacer ruido*) to gurgle; (*arroyo*) to babble **2.** (*burbujear*) to bubble

gorgoteo [gor·yo·'teo] *m* **1.** (*ruido*) gurgle; (*de un arroyo*) babbling **2.** (*borboteo*) bubbling

gorila [go·'ri·la] *m* **1.** (*animal*) gorilla **2.** *inf* (*portero*) bouncer **3.** *inf* (*guardaespaldas*) bodyguard **4.** *inf* (*matón*) thug

gorjear [gor·xe·'ar] **I.** *vi* **1.** (*personas*) to twitter **2.** (*pájaros*) to chirp **II.** *vr*: ~ **se 1.** (*niño*) to gurgle **2.** AmL (*burlarse*) to make fun of

gorjeo [gor·'xeo] *m* **1.** (*de personas*) twittering; (*de bebés*) gurgling **2.** (*de pájaros*) chirping

gorra ['go·rra] *f* **1.** (*prenda*) cap; ~ **de visera** baseball cap **2.** (*para niños*) bonnet ▶ **de** ~ *inf* (*gratis*) free

gorrear [go·rre·'ar] *vi, vt inf* to scrounge; **¿te puedo** ~ **un cigarrillo?** can I get a cigarette from you?

gorrero [go·'rre·ro] *m inf* scrounger

gorrinada [go·rri·'na·da] *f* (*acción injusta*) dirty trick

gorrino, -a [go·'rri·no, -a] *m, f* **1.** (*cochinillo*) suckling pig; (*cerdo*) pig; (*cerda*) sow **2.** *pey* (*persona*) pig

gorrión [go·rri·'on] *m* **1.** (*pardal*) sparrow **2.** AmC (*colibrí*) hummingbird

gorro ['go·rro] *m* hat; (*de uniforme*) cap; ~ **para bebés** baby's bonnet; ~ **de natación** bathing cap; ~ **de papel** paper hat

gorrón [go·'rron] *m* **1.** (*piedra*) pebble, cobblestone **2.** TÉC pivot

gorrón, -ona [go·'rron, -·'rro·na] *m, f* **1.** *inf* (*aprovechado*) scrounger **2.** AmC (*egoísta*) selfish person

gorronear [go·rro·ne·'ar] *vi v.* **gorrear**

G

gorronería [go·rro·ne·'ri·a] *f inf* scrounging

gota ['go·ta] *f* **1.** (*de líquido*) drop; **café con unas ~s de ron** coffee with a dash of rum; **el agua salía ~ a ~ del grifo** the water dripped out of the tap; **apurar el vaso hasta la última ~** to drain the glass to the last drop; **parecerse como dos ~s de agua** to be like two peas in a pod **2.** (*pizca*) drop; **no queda ni ~ de agua** there's not a drop of water left **3.** METEO **~ fría** cold front **4.** MED (*enfermedad*) gout **5.** (*gotero*) **el ~ la ~ que colma el vaso** the last straw

gotear [go·te·'ar] **I.** *vi* **1.** (*líquido*) to drip; (*escurrir*) trickle **2.** (*salirse*) to leak **II.** *v impers* **está goteando** it's drizzling

goteo [go·'teo] *m* **1.** (*gotear*) drip(ping) **2.** MED (intravenous) drip

gotera [go·'te·ra] *f* **1.** (*filtración, grieta*) leak **2.** (*mancha*) stain **3.** (*achaque*) complaint **4.** *pl, AmL* (*afueras*) outskirts *pl*

gotero [go·'te·ro] *m* **1.** MED drip **2.** AmL (*cuentagotas*) dropper

gótico, -a ['go·ti·ko, -a] *adj* Gothic

gotoso, -a [go·'to·so, -a] **I.** *adj* MED gouty **II.** *m, f* MED gout-sufferer

gozada [go·'sa·da, -'θa·da] *f inf* delight

gozar <z→c> [go·'sar, -'θar] **I.** *vi* **1.** (*divertirse*) to enjoy oneself **2.** (*disfrutar*) **~ de algo** to enjoy sth; **~ de una increíble fortuna** to be incredibly wealthy **II.** *vt* **1.** (*disfrutar*) to enjoy **2.** (*poseer carnalmente*) to possess **III.** *vr:* **~se** to enjoy oneself; **~se en** to take pleasure in

gozne ['gos·ne, 'goθ-] *m* hinge

gozo ['go·so, -θo] *m* **1.** (*delicia*) delight; (*placer*) pleasure **2.** (*alegría*) joy **3.** (*del fuego*) flame

gr. ['gra·mo] *abr de* **gramo** g.

grabación [gra·βa·'sjon, -'θjon] *f* **1.** (*de disco*) recording **2.** TV (*de una serie*) shooting **3.** COMPUT copying

grabado [gra·'βa·do] *m* **1.** ARTE (*acción*) engraving **2.** ARTE (*copia*) print; **~ al agua fuerte** etching; **~ en madera** woodcut **3.** (*ilustración*) illustration

grabador(a) [gra·βa·'dor] *m(f)* engraver

grabadora [gra·βa·'do·ra] *f* TÉC tape recorder

grabar [gra·'βar] **I.** *vt* **1.** ARTE to engrave; (*en madera*) to cut **2.** (*disco*) to record **3.** COMPUT to copy **4.** (*fijar*) to engrave **II.** *vr:* **~se** to become engraved

gracia ['gra·sja, -θja] *f* **1.** *pl* (*agradecimiento*) ¡~s! thanks!; ¡muchas ~s! thanks a lot!; ¡~s a Dios! thank God!; **te debo las ~s** I owe you my thanks; **no me ha dado ni las ~s** he/she didn't even say "thank you"; **~s a tus esfuerzos lo conseguí** thanks to your efforts, I managed it **2.** REL grace **3.** (*perdón*) mercy **4.** (*favor*) favor **5.** (*agrado*) **me cae en ~** I like him/her **6.** (*garbo*) elegance; **está escrito con ~** it's elegantly written **7.** (*chiste*) joke; **no tiene (ni) pizca de ~** it's not in the least bit funny; **no me hace nada de ~** I don't find it funny in the least; **si lo haces se va la ~** if you

do it, it loses its charm; **este cómico tiene poca ~** this comedian isn't very funny; **la ~ es que...** the funny thing is that...; **no estoy hoy para ~s** I'm not in a mood for jokes today **8.** *irón* (*ocurrencia*) **hoy ha hecho otra de sus ~s** he/she has been up to his/her tricks again

grácil ['gra·sil, -θil] *adj* graceful

gracioso, -a [gra·'sjo·so, -a; gra·'θjo·-] **I.** *adj* **1.** (*atractivo*) attractive **2.** (*chistoso*) funny; **para mí no fue nada ~** I didn't find it at all funny **3.** (*gratis*) free **II.** *m, f* TEAT comic character; **no te hagas el ~ conmigo** don't try to play the clown with me

grada ['gra·da] *f* **1.** (*de un estadio*) tier; **las ~s** the terraces **2.** (*peldaño*) step **3.** *pl* (*escalinata*) steps *pl* **4.** *pl, AmL* (*atrio*) courtyard

gradación [gra·da·'sjon, -'θjon] *f* **1.** (*escalonamiento*) gradation **2.** MÚS gradation **3.** (*retórica*) climax

gradería [gra·de·'ri·a] *f*, **graderío** [gra·de·'ri·o] *m* **1.** (*de un estadio*) terraces *pl* **2.** *fig* crowd

grado ['gra·do] *m* **1.** (*nivel*) degree; **~ de confianza** degree of trust; **quemaduras de primer ~** MED first-degree burns; **en ~ sumo** greatly, highly **2.** (*parentesco*) degree **3.** ENS year; **~ elemental** basic level **4.** UNIV degree; **~ de doctor** doctorate **5.** MAT degree; **~ centígrado** degree centigrade **6.** LING **~ comparativo** degree of comparison **7.** MIL (*rango*) rank **8.** (*de alcohol*) degree

graduable [gra·du·'a·βle] *adj* adjustable

graduación [gra·dwa·'sjon, -'θjon] *f* **1.** (*regulación*) adjustment **2.** (*en grados*) graduation; (*en niveles, de personas*) grading; (*de precios*) regulation **3.** (*de un vino*) strength; **~ alcohólica** alcohol content **4.** MIL rank **5.** UNIV graduation

graduado, -a [gra·du·'a·do, -a] **I.** *adj* graduate(d) **II.** *m, f* **1.** UNIV graduate; **~ en ingeniería** engineering graduate **2.** ENS **~ escolar** school diploma

gradual [gra·du·'al] *adj* gradual

gradualmente [gra·dwal·'men·te] *adv* **1.** (*en grados*) by degrees **2.** (*progresivamente*) gradually

graduar <1. pres: gradúo> [gra·du·'ar] **I.** *vt* **1.** (*regular*) to regulate **2.** TÉC to graduate; **~ la vista a alguien** to test sb's eyesight **3.** (*en niveles*) to classify; (*precios*) to regulate **4.** UNIV to confer a degree on **5.** MIL to confer a rank on **II.** *vr:* **~se** to graduate; **se graduó en económicas** he/she graduated in economics

grafía [gra·'fi·a] *f* (*escritura*) writing; (*ortografía*) spelling

gráfica ['gra·fi·ka] *f* graph

gráfico ['gra·fi·ko] *m* graph; **~ de tarta** pie chart; **tarjeta de ~s** COMPUT graphics card

gráfico, -a ['gra·fi·ko, -a] *adj* **1.** (*de la escritura*) written **2.** (*del dibujo*) illustrated; **diccionario ~** visual dictionary **3.** (*claro*) graphic **4.** *fig* expressive

grafismo [gra·'fis·mo] *m* **1.** (*grafía*) handwriting **2.** (*aspecto estético*) vivid writing style **3.** COMPUT computer graphics

grafista [gra·'fis·ta] *mf* graphic artist [*o* designer]

grafito [gra·'fi·to] *m* MIN graphite

grafología [gra·fo·lo·'xi·a] *f* graphology

grafólogo, -a [gra·'fo·lo·yo, -a] *m, f* graphologist

gragea [gra·'xea] *f* MED (sugar-coated) pill

grajo ['gra·xo] *m* **1.** (*ave*) rook **2.** (*charlatán*) chatterbox **3.** *AmL* (*sobaquina*) body odor

gral. [xe·ne·'ral] *adj abr de* **general** gen.

gramática [gra·'ma·ti·ka] *f* LING grammar; **~ generativa** transformational grammar

gramatical [gra·ma·ti·'kal] *adj* grammatical; **regla ~** grammatical rule

gramático, -a [gra·'ma·ti·ko, -a] *m, f* grammarian

gramilla [gra·'mi·ja, -ʎa] *f AmL* (*hierba*) lawn, grass

gramo ['gra·mo] *m* gram

gramófono [gra·'mo·fo·no] *m* phonograph

gramola [gra·'mo·la] *f* **1.** (*gramófono*) phonograph **2.** (*en un bar*) jukebox

gran [gran] *adj v.* **grande**

granada [gra·'na·da] *f* **1.** (*fruto*) pomegranate **2.** (*proyectil: de mano*) grenade; (*de artillería*) shell

granadilla [gra·na·'di·ja, -ʎa] *f AmC* (*planta*) passionflower

granado [gra·'na·do] *m* pomegranate tree

granado, -a [gra·'na·do, -a] *adj* **1.** (*ilustre*) distinguished **2.** (*maduro*) mature **3.** (*alto*) tall

granar [gra·'nar] *vi* to seed

granate [gra·'na·te] **I.** *adj* burgundy **II.** *m* MIN garnet

Gran Bretaña [gram bre·'ta·ɲa] *f* Great Britain

grancanario, -a [gran·ka·'na·rjo, -a] **I.** *adj* of/from Grand Canary **II.** *m, f* native/inhabitant of Grand Canary

grande ['gran·de] **I.** *adj* <más grande *o* mayor, grandísimo> (*precediendo un sustantivo singular: gran*) **1.** (*de tamaño*) big; (*número, cantidad*) large; **gran ciudad** big city; **una habitación ~** a large room; **una gran suma de dinero** a large sum of money; **una gran mentira** a big lie; **gran velocidad** high speed; **vino gran cantidad de gente** a lot of people came; **tengo un gran interés por...** I'm very interested in...; **no me preocupa gran cosa** I'm not very worried about it **2.** *inf* (*de edad*) grown-up **3.** (*moralmente*) great; **un gran hombre** a great man; **una gran idea** a great idea ► **pasarlo en ~** to have a great time **II.** *m* (*prócer*) great; **los ~s de la industria** the major industrial players

grandeza [gran·'de·sa, -θa] *f* **1.** (*tamaño*) size; **delirio de ~** delusions of grandeur **2.** (*excelencia de cosas, de personas*) greatness **3.** (*de un Grande*) status of grandee

grandilocuencia [gran·di·lo·'kwen·sja, -θja] *f* grandiloquence

grandilocuente [gran·di·lo·'kwen·te] *adj* grandiloquent

grandiosidad [gran·djo·si·'dad] *f* impressiveness, grandeur

grandioso, -a [gran·'djo·so, -a] *adj* impressive; (*rimbombante*) grandiose

grandullón, -ona [gran·du·'jon, --'jo·na; -'ʎon, --'ʎo·na] *adj* oversized

granel [gra·'nel] **carga a ~** bulk order; **a ~** (*sin envase*) loose; (*líquido*) by volume; (*en abundancia*) in abundance

granero [gra·'ne·ro] *m* granary; (*de granja*) barn

granítico, -a [gra·'ni·ti·ko, -a] *adj* **1.** (*de granito*) granite **2.** (*parecido al granito*) granitic

granito [gra'nito] *m* MIN granite

granizada [gra·ni·'sa·da, -'θa·da] *f* **1.** (*pedrisco*) hailstorm **2.** (*de balas*) hail

granizado [gra·ni·'sa·do, -'θa·do] *m* iced drink; **~ de café** ≈ iced coffee

granizar <z→c> [gra·ni·'sar, -'θar] *vimpers* to hail

granizo [gra·'ni·so, -θo] *m* hail

granja ['gran·xa] *f* **1.** (*finca*) farm **2.** (*establecimiento*) dairy store

granjear [gran·xe·'ar] **I.** *vt* **1.** (*ganado*) to farm **2.** (*adquirir*) to earn **II.** *vr:* **~se** to earn

granjero, -a [gran·'xe·ro, -a] *m, f* farmer

grano ['gra·no] *m* **1.** (*de cereales, sal, arena*) grain; (*de café*) bean; (*de mostaza*) seed; **~s** grain; (*de uva*) grape **2.** (*de piel*) spot, pimple **3.** TÉC grain; **de ~ duro** coarse-grained; **de ~ fino** fine-grained ► **de un ~** (*de arena*) **hace una montaña** he/she always makes a mountain out of a molehill; **apartar el ~ de la paja** to separate the wheat from the chaff; **ir al ~** to get to the point

granuja¹ [gra·'nu·xa] *m* **1.** (*pilluelo*) rascal **2.** (*bribón*) scoundrel; **el muy ~ me ha engañado** that scoundrel has cheated me

granuja² [gra·'nu·xa] *f* **1.** (*uva*) grapes *pl* **2.** (*de las frutas*) seeds *pl*

granujada [gra·nu·'xa·da] *f* **1.** (*travesura*) prank **2.** (*bribonada*) dirty trick

granujería [gra·nu·xe·'ri·a] *f* **1.** (*travesura*) prank **2.** (*bribonada*) dirty trick **3.** (*de pillos*) bunch of ragamuffins **4.** (*de bribones*) bunch of scoundrels

granulado [gra·nu·'la·do] *m* granules *pl*

granular [gra·nu·'lar] **I.** *adj* grainy **II.** *vt* to granulate

granuloso, -a [gra·nu·'lo·so, -a] *adj* grainy

grapa ['gra·pa] *f* **1.** (*para papeles, madera*) staple **2.** (*licor*) grappa

grapadora [gra·pa·'do·ra] *f* stapler

grapar [gra·'par] *vt* to staple

grasa¹ ['gra·sa] *f* **1.** ANAT fat; **~ de cerdo** pork fat; **cocinar sin ~** to cook without fat [*o* grease]; **tener mucha ~ en los muslos** to have fat thighs **2.** TÉC (*lubricante*) oil, grease **3.** (*mugre*) grime

G

grasa² ['gra·sa] *Arg* **I.** *adj inf, pey* common **II.** *m inf, pey* **ser un** ~ to be common

grasiento, -a [gra·'sjen·to, -a] *adj* fatty; (*de aceite*) greasy

graso, -a ['gra·so, -a] *adj* **1.**(*grasiento*) fatty; **piel grasa** oily skin; **pelo** ~ greasy hair **2.**(*gordo*) fat

gratén [gra·'ten] *m* CULIN **al** ~ au gratin

gratificación [gra·ti·fi·ka·'sjon, -'θjon] *f* **1.**(*recompensa*) reward; (*sobre objetos perdidos*) compensation **2.**(*del sueldo*) bonus; ~ **de Navidad** Christmas bonus **3.**(*propina*) tip **4.**(*satisfacción*) gratification

gratificante [gra·ti·fi·'kan·te] *adj* gratifying

gratificar <c→qu> [gra·ti·fi·'kar] *vt* **1.**(*recompensar*) ~ **a alguien por algo** to reward sb for sth **2.**(*en el trabajo*) ~ **a alguien** to give sb a bonus **3.**(*complacer*) to gratify

gratinador [gra·ti·na·'dor] *m* grill

gratinar [gra·ti·'nar] *vt* CULIN to cook au gratin, to brown on top

gratis ['gra·tis] *adv* free

gratitud [gra·ti·'tud] *f* gratitude

grato, -a ['gra·to, -a] *adj* **1.**(*agradable*) pleasant; ~ **al paladar** tasty; **tu novio me ha dado una grata impresión** *elev* your boyfriend seems very nice; **tu visita me es muy grata** I'm very glad you could come **2.**(*en una carta*) **me es** ~ **comunicarle que...** I am pleased to inform you that...

gratuidad [gra·twi·'dad] *f* **1.**(*de gratis*) **reclamar la** ~ **de la enseñanza/la sanidad** to demand free education/health services **2.**(*arbitrariedad*) arbitrariness **3.**(*algo infundado*) unjustified remark

gratuito, -a [gra·'twi·to, -a] *adj* **1.**(*gratis*) free **2.**(*arbitrario*) arbitrary **3.**(*infundado*) groundless; **es una acusación gratuita** the accusation is groundless; **este rumor es** ~ this rumor is without foundation

grava ['gra·βa] *f* gravel

gravable [gra·'βa·βle] *adj* taxable

gravamen [gra·'βa·men] *m* **1.**(*carga*) burden **2.**(*de los ingresos*) tax

gravar [gra·'βar] *vt* **1.**(*cargar*) to burden **2.** FIN to tax; ~ **algo con un impuesto** to impose a tax on sth

grave ['gra·βe] *adj* **1.**(*objeto*) heavy **2.**(*enfermedad*) serious; **está** ~ he/she is very sick **3.**(*persona, situación*) serious; **este es un momento** ~ **para la industria** this is a difficult time for the industry **4.**(*estilo*) solemn **5.**(*sonido*) deep

gravedad [gra·βe·'dad] *f* **1.** FÍS gravity; **centro de** ~ center of gravity **2.** MED seriousness; **estar herido de** ~ to be seriously injured **3.** MÚS (*de los sonidos*) depth **4.**(*de un estilo*) solemnity **5.**(*de una situación, de un asunto*) seriousness

gravilla [gra·'βi·ja, -ʎa] *f* gravel

gravitación [gra·βi·ta·'sjon, -'θjon] *f* FÍS gravitation

gravitar [gra·βi·'tar] *vi* **1.** FÍS to gravitate **2.**(*un cuerpo*) ~ **sobre algo** to rest on sth **3.**(*recaer*) ~ **sobre** to loom over

gravitatorio, -a [gra·βi·ta·'to·rjo, -a] *adj* gravitational

graznar [gras·'nar, graθ-] *vi* (*cuervo*) to caw; (*ganso*) to honk; (*pato*) to quack

graznido [gras·'ni·do, graθ-] *m* (*de cuervo*) caw; (*de ganso*) honk; (*de pato*) quack

greca ['gre·ka] *f* **1.**(*adorno*) frieze **2.** *AmL* (*cafetera eléctrica*) coffee machine

Grecia ['gre·sja, -θja] *f* Greece

grecolatino, -a [gre·ko·la·'ti·no, -a] *adj* Greco-Latin

grecorromano, -a [gre·ko·rro·'ma·no, -a] *adj* Greco-Roman

gregoriano, -a [gre·yo·'rja·no, -a] *adj* Gregorian

gremial [gre·'mjal] **I.** *adj* **1.**(*de una asociación*) relating to an association **2.**(*de un sindicato*) relating to a trade union **3.** HIST guild **II.** *mf* **1.**(*de una asociación*) association member **2.**(*de un sindicato*) union member

gremio ['gre·mjo] *m* **1.**(*asociación*) association **2.**(*sindicato*) trade union **3.** HIST guild

greña ['gre·ɲa] *f* mop [*o* mat] of hair, rats' tails *pl*

greñudo, -a [gre·'ɲu·do, -a] *adj* (*pelo*) tangled, matted

gres [gres] *m* **1.**(*arcilla*) potter's clay **2.**(*producto*) earthenware

gresca ['gres·ka] *f* **1.**(*bulla*) uproar, racket **2.**(*riña*) quarrel

grial [gri·'al] *m* grail

griego, -a ['grje·yo] *adj, m, f* Greek

grieta ['grje·ta] *f* **1.**(*en la pared, una taza*) crack; (*en la piel*) chap **2.**(*desacuerdo*) rift

grifa ['gri·fa] *f* hash, dope, pot

grifo ['gri·fo] *m* **1.** TÉC tap, faucet; **agua del** ~ tap water; **he dejado el** ~ **abierto** I left the faucet running **2.** *Perú, Ecua, Bol* (*gasolinera*) gas station

grifo, -a ['gri·fo, -a] *adj inf* stoned, high (on dope)

grillarse [gri·'jar·se, -'ʎar·se] *vr* **1.** *inf* (*persona*) to go nuts **2.**(*tubérculo*) to sprout

grillete [gri·'je·te, -'ʎe·te] *m t.* NÁUT shackle

grillo ['gri·jo, -ʎo] *m* **1.**(*insecto*) cricket **2.**(*de tubérculo*) shoot **3.** *pl* (*grilletes*) shackles *pl*

grima ['gri·ma] *f* **me da** ~ (*asco*) it's disgusting; (*dentera*) it sets my teeth on edge

grimillón [gri·mi·'jon, -'ʎon] *m Chile* multitude

gringada [grin·'ga·da] *f AmL, inf* **1.**(*truco sucio*) dirty trick **2.**(*grupo de gringos*) group of gringos

gringo ['grin·go] *m inf* gibberish; **hablar en** ~ to speak gibberish

gringo, -a ['grin·go, -a] *m, f AmL, inf* **1.**(*persona*) gringo (*North American or North European*) **2.**(*de EE.UU.*) Yank(ee)

gripa ['gri·pa] *f AmL* flu, influenza

gripal [gri·'pal] *adj* MED flu, influenza

griparse [gri·'par·se] *vr* TÉC to seize up

gripe ['gri·pe] *f* MED flu, influenza; ~ **aviar** bird flu, avian influenza

griposo, -a [gri·'po·so, -a] I. *adj* MED **estar** ~ to have the flu II. *m, f* flu patient

gris [gris] I. *adj* **1.** (*color*) gray; ~ **marengo** charcoal gray; **de ojos** ~**es** gray-eyed **2.** (*persona*) boring II. *m* **1.** (*color*) gray **2.** (*viento*) cold wind **3.** HIST (*policía*) *member of Spanish National Police*

grisáceo, -a [gri·'sa·seo, -θeo] *adj* grayish

grisma ['gris·ma] *f* Chile, Guat, Hond (*pizca*) pinch

grisú [gri·'su] *m* <grisúes *o* grisús> MIN firedamp

gritadera [gri·ta·'de·ra] *f* Col, Ven (*griterío*) loud shouting

gritar [gri·'tar] I. *vt* **1.** (*dar gritos*) to shout at **2.** (*reprender*) to tell off **3.** (*en un concierto*) to boo II. *vi* to shout, to yell

griterío [gri·te·'ri·o] *m* uproar

grito ['gri·to] *m* shout; ~ **de protesta** cry of protest; **pegar un** ~ to shout, to yell; **me lo dijo a** ~**s** he/she told me in a very loud voice; **a** ~ **limpio** [*o* **pelado**] at the top of one's voice; **la región está pidiendo a** ~**s ayuda internacional** the region is crying out for international support ▶ **ser el último** ~ to be the (latest) rage

groenlandés, -esa [groen·lan·'des, -·'de·sa] I. *adj* Greenland II. *m, f* Greenlander

Groenlandia [groen·'lan·dja] *f* Greenland

grogui ['gro·ɣi] *adj* groggy, half-asleep

grosella [gro·'se·ja, -ʎa] *f* currant

grosería [gro·se·'ri·a] *f* **1.** (*descortesía*) rudeness **2.** (*ordinariez*) vulgarity **3.** (*tosquedad*) crudeness **4.** (*estupidez*) stupidity **5.** (*observación*) rude comment; (*palabrota*) swearword

grosero, -a [gro·'se·ro, -a] *adj* **1.** (*descortés*) rude **2.** (*ordinario*) vulgar **3.** (*tosco*) crude

grosor [gro·'sor] *m* thickness

grotesco, -a [gro·'tes·ko, -a] *adj* grotesque

grúa ['gru·a] *f* **1.** (*máquina*) crane **2.** (*vehículo*) tow truck, wrecker

grueso, -a ['grwe·so] *m* **1.** (*espesor*) thickness **2.** (*parte principal*) main part **3.** MED (*intestino*) large intestine **4.** COM **vender en** ~ to sell in bulk **5.** TIPO stem

grueso, -a ['grwe·so, -a] *adj* **1.** (*persona*) stout **2.** (*objeto, tela*) thick **3.** (*mar*) **mar gruesa** heavy seas **4.** (*broma*) crude

grulla ['gru·ja, -ʎa] *f* crane

grumete [gru·'me·te] *m* NÁUT cabin boy

grumo ['gru·mo] *m* **1.** (*coágulo*) lump; ~ **de sangre** blood clot **2.** (*de lechuga*) heart **3.** (*de planta*) shoot

grumoso, -a [gru·'mo·so, -a] *adj* lumpy

gruñido [gru·'ɲi·do] *m* **1.** (*de cerdo, persona*) grunt **2.** (*del perro*) growl **3.** *fig* (*queja*) grumble **4.** (*de puerta*) creak

gruñir <3. pret: gruñó> [gru·'ɲir] *vi* **1.** (*cerdo, persona*) to grunt **2.** (*perro*) to growl **3.** *fig* (*quejarse*) to grumble **4.** (*puerta*) to creak

gruñón, -ona [gru·'ɲon, -·'ɲo·na] I. *adj inf*

grumbling, whining II. *m, f inf* grumbler; **es un viejo** ~ he's a grumpy old man

grupa ['gru·pa] *f* hindquarters *pl;* **volver** ~**s** MIL to turn around

grupo ['gru·po] *m* **1.** (*conjunto*) group; ~ (**industrial**) COM corporation; ~ **parlamentario** POL parliamentary group; ~ **de presión** POL pressure group; ~ **principal** COMPUT main group; **trabajo en** ~ group work **2.** TÉC unit

gruta ['gru·ta] *f* (*artificial*) grotto; (*natural*) cave

guaca ['gwa·ka] *f* AmL **1.** (*tumba*) tomb **2.** (*tesoro*) buried treasure **3.** (*hucha*) money box; **hacer** ~ to make money

guacal [gwa·'kal] *m* AmC, Col, Ven (*calabaza, jícara*) gourd

guacamayo [gwa·ka·'ma·jo] *m* macaw

guacamol(e) [gwa·ka·'mol, -·'mo·le] *m* AmL CULIN guacamole

guacamote [gwa·ka·'mo·te] *m* Méx manioc

guachada [gwa·'tʃa·da] *f* AmL, inf (*canallada*) dirty trick

guachimán [gwa·tʃi·'man] *m* AmL (*vigilante*) watchman

guacho, -a ['gwa·tʃo, -a] *m, f* AmS (*huérfano*) orphan; (*expósito*) abandoned child

guadal [gwa·'dal] *m* Arg sandy bog

guadalajareño, -a [gwa·da·la·xa·'re·ɲo, -a] I. *adj* of/from Guadalajara II. *m, f* native/inhabitant of Guadalajara

guadaña [gwa·'da·ɲa] *f* **1.** (*herramienta*) scythe **2.** (*muerte*) **la Guadaña** the Grim Reaper

guagua ['gwa·ɣwa] *f* **1.** AmC (*autobús*) bus **2.** CSur (*bebé*) baby **3.** (*trivialidad*) trifle

guajiro, -a [gwa·'xi·ro, -a] I. *adj* peasant II. *m, f* Cuba white peasant

gualdo, -a [gwa·'do, -a] *adj* yellow; **la bandera roja y gualda** the Spanish flag

guamazo [gwa·'ma·so, -θo] *m* Méx punch

guamúchil [gwa·'mu·tʃil] *m* Méx (*planta*) camachile

guanábano [gwa·'na·βa·no] *m* AmL (*árbol*) soursop tree; (*fruta*) custard apple

guanaco [gwa·'na·ko] *m* (*mamífero*) guanaco

guanaco, -a [gwa·'na·ko, -a] I. *adj* AmL (*tonto*) simple; (*lento*) slow II. *m, f* **1.** AmL (*tonto*) simpleton **2.** AmC, pey native of El Salvador

guanajo, -a [gwa·'na·xo, -a] *m, f* Cuba, PRico (*pavo, bobo*) turkey

guandoca [guan·'do·ka] *f* Col (*cárcel*) prison

guango, -a ['guan·go, -a] *adj* Méx baggy

guano ['gwa·no] *m* **1.** (*excrementos*) guano **2.** CSur (*estiércol*) dung

---

i At the beginning of the 20th century, Chile was still meeting more than two thirds of the international market's needs for manure with saltpeter and **guano**, the dried excrement of seabirds and bats. Huge piles of guano could be found in the northern part of the country and on offshore islands. A dispute over guano deposits in the region was even one of the causes of the War of the Pacific, which led to Bolivia losing its only access to the sea in 1884.

guantada [gwan·'ta·da] *f* slap; **dar una ~ a alguien** to slap sb

guantazo [gwan·'ta·so, -θo] *m v.* **guantada**

guante ['gwan·te] *m* glove; **~ cibernético** COMPUT data glove ► **ir** [*o* **sentar**] **como un ~** to fit like a glove

guantear [gwan·te·'ar] *vt AmL* (*abofetear*) to slap (around)

guantera [gwan·'te·ra] *f* AUTO glove box [*o* compartment]

guaperas [gwa·'pe·ras] **I.** *adj inf* good-looking **II.** *m inv, inf* heart-throb; **va de ~** he thinks he's a real heart-throb

guaperío [gwa·pe·'ri·o] *m* **el ~** the jet set

guapo ['gwa·po] *m* **1.** (*galán*) handsome man **2.** *AmL, pey* (*pendenciero*) bully

guapo, -a ['gwa·po, -a] *adj* **1.** (*atractivo: en general*) good-looking; (*mujer*) pretty; (*hombre*) handsome **2.** (*en el vestir*) **estar** [*o* **ir**] **~** to look smart **3.** *AmL* (*valiente*) brave

guaquero, -a [gwa·'ke·ro, -a] *m, f AmL* grave robber; (*ilegal*) plunderer (*person who digs for ancient Indian archaeological valuables*)

guaraca [gwa·'ra·ka] *f AmL* (*honda*) catapult; (*látigo*) whip

guaraná [gwa·ra·'na] *f* BOT guarana

guarangada [gwa·ran·'ga·da] *f AmL* (*grosería*) rude comment

guaraní [gwa·ra·'ni] *adj, m* (*pueblo, lengua*) Guarani; (*moneda*) guarani

guarapo [gwa·'ra·po] *m AmL* (*jugo*) sugar-cane juice; (*bebida*) sugar-cane liquor

guarapón [gua·ra·'pon] *m AmS* broad-brimmed hat

guarda¹ ['gwar·da] *mf* guard; **~ forestal** forest ranger; (*cuidador*) custodian, keeper; **~ jurado** security guard

guarda² ['gwar·da] *f* **1.** (*acto*) guarding, safekeeping **2.** (*protección*) protection **3.** (*de un libro*) flyleaf **4.** (*de la ley*) observance **5.** *pl* (*de llave*) guard; (*de cerradura*) ward **6.** *pl* (*de abanico*) outer ribs *pl*

guardabarros [gwar·da·'βa·rros] *m inv* fender

guardabosque(s) [gwar·da·'βos·ke(s)] *mf* (*inv*) **1.** (*de caza*) gamekeeper **2.** (*guarda forestal*) forest ranger

guardacostas [gwar·da·'kos·tas] *m inv* coastguard

guardaespaldas [gwar·da·es·'pal·das] *mf inv* bodyguard

guardameta [gwar·da·'me·ta] *mf* DEP goalkeeper, goalie

guardapolvo [gwar·da·'pol·βo] *m* (*mono*) overalls *pl*

guardar [gwar·'dar] **I.** *vt* **1.** (*vigilar*) to guard

2. (*proteger*) to protect **3.** (*ley*) to observe **4.** (*conservar*) to keep; **~ un sitio** to keep a place; **~ un trozo de pastel a alguien** to save a piece of cake for sb; **guárdame esto, que ahora vengo** keep this for me, I'll be back soon [*o* right back] **5.** (*poner*) **¿dónde has guardado las servilletas?** where did you put the napkins?; **~ el dinero en el banco** to keep money in the bank; **~ algo en el bolsillo** to put sth in one's pocket **6.** (*quedarse con*) to keep **7.** (*ahorrar*) to save; **~ las fuerzas** to save one's strength **8.** COMPUT to save **II.** *vr:* **~se 1.** (*evitar*) **~se de hacer algo** to be careful not to do sth **2.** (*protegerse*) **~se de algo/alguien** to be on one's guard against sth/sb

guardarropa¹ [gwar·da·'rro·pa] *m* **1.** (*cuarto*) checkroom **2.** (*armario*) wardrobe

guardarropa² [gwar·da·'rro·pa] *mf* **1.** (*de vestuario*) checkroom attendant **2.** TEAT (*guardarropía*) wardrobe

guardarropía [gwar·da·rro·'pi·a] *m* **1.** TEAT (*accesorios*) props *pl* **2.** TEAT (*cuarto*) wardrobe

guardería [gwar·de·'ri·a] *f* (*centro educativo*) nursery; (*en hipermercado*) crèche

guardia¹ ['gwar·dja] *f* **1.** (*vigilancia*) duty; **¿cuál es la farmacia de ~?** which pharmacy is open tonight?; **estar de ~** to be on duty; MIL to be on guard duty **2.** (*protección*) **estar en ~** to be on one's guard **3.** DEP guard; **bajar la ~** to lower one's guard; **en ~** (*esgrima*) en garde **4.** (*instituciones*) **la Guardia Civil** the Civil Guard; **~ municipal** [*o* **urbana**] local police

guardia² ['gwar·dja] *mf* **~ civil** civil guard; **~ municipal** [*o* **urbano**] local policeman; **~ de tráfico** traffic policeman *m*, traffic policewoman *f*

guardián, -ana [gwar·'djan, -'dja·na] *m, f* **1.** (*protector*) guardian; **perro ~** watchdog **2.** (*en el zoo*) (zoo)keeper

guardilla [gwar·'di·ja, -ʎa] *f* **1.** (*habitación*) attic room **2.** (*ventana*) attic window **3.** (*buhardilla*) attic, garret

guarecer [gwa·re·'ser, -'θer] *irr como crecer* **I.** *vt* **1.** (*proteger*) to protect **2.** (*albergar*) to shelter; **lo guarecí en mi casa** I took him in **3.** (*curar*) to cure **II.** *vr:* **~se** (*cobijarse*) to take refuge; **~se de la lluvia** to take shelter from the rain

guarida [gwa·'ri·da] *f* **1.** (*de animales*) den, lair **2.** (*refugio*) hideout

guarnecer [gwar·ne·'ser, -'θer] *irr como crecer vt* **1.** (*adornar*) **~ algo con** [*o* **de**] **algo** to decorate sth with sth; CULIN to garnish sth with sth; (*vestido*) to trim sth with sth **2.** MIL (*ciudad*) to garrison **3.** (*equipar*) **~ con** [*o* **de**] **algo** to equip with sth; (*proveer*) to provide with sth

guarnición [gwar·ni·'sjon, -'θjon] *f* **1.** CULIN accompaniment to a main dish; (*adorno*) garnish; **chuletas de cordero con ~** (**de patatas y ensalada**) lamb chops served with salad and potatoes **2.** (*adorno*) adornment; (*en vestido*) trimming; (*en joya*) setting **3.** MIL garrison **4.** *pl* (*arreos*) harness

guarro, -a ['gwa·rro, -a] **I.** *adj* **1.** (*cosa*) disgusting; **chiste ~** dirty joke **2.** (*persona*) dirty; (*moralmente*) smutty **II.** *m, f* pig

guasa ['gwa·sa] *f* **1.** (*burla*) joke; **estar de ~** to be joking; **tiene ~ que... +** *subj* it's ironic that... **2.** (*sosería*) dullness

guasanga [gwa·'san·ga] *f* AmL (*bullanga*) hubbub

guasca ['gwas·ka] *f* AmL (*látigo*) whip

guasearse [gwa·se·'ar·se] *vr* to joke; **~ de alguien/algo** to make fun of sb/sth

guasería [gwa·se·'ri·a] *f* Arg, Chile (*grosería*) rudeness, obscenity

guaso, -a ['gwa·so, -a] *adj CSur* **1.** (*rústico*) peasant **2.** (*tosco*) coarse

guasón, -ona [gwa·'son, -·'so·na] *m, f* joker

guata ['gwa·ta] *f* **1.** (*algodón*) cotton padding **2.** AmL (*barriga*) belly

guate ['gwa·te] *m* AmC, Méx cornstalks for fodder

Guatemala [gwa·te·'ma·la] *f* Guatemala

---

i **Guatemala** (formally named **República de Guatemala**) is located in Central America. The capital is also called **Guatemala**. The country's official language is Spanish and the official currency of **Guatemala** is the **quetzal**.

---

guatemalteco, -a [gwa·te·mal·'te·ko, -a] *adj, m, f* Guatemalan

guateque [gwa·'te·ke] *m inf* party

guatero [gwa·'te·ro] *m Chile* hot-water bottle

guay [gwai] *adj inf* great, cool

guayaba [gwa·'ja·βa] *f* **1.** (*fruto*) guava **2.** (*jalea*) guava jelly **3.** AmL (*mentira*) lie

guayabo [gwa·'ja·βo] *m* guava tree

guayacán [gwa·ja·'kan] *m AmL* BOT lignum-vitae tree

Guayana [gwa·'ja·na] *f* Guyana

guayanés, -esa [gwa·ja·'nes, -·'ne·sa] *adj, m, f* Guyanese

guayar [gwa·'jar] **I.** *vt Ant* to grate **II.** *vr:* **~ se** *PRico* to get drunk

gubernamental [gu·βer·na·men·'tal] *adj* **1.** (*relativo a*) governmental **2.** (*partidario*) loyalist

gubernativo, -a [gu·βer·na·'ti·βo, -a] *adj* governmental; **policía gubernativa** national police

gubia ['gu·βja] *f* TÉC gouge

guepardo [ge·'par·do] *m* cheetah

güero, -a ['gwe·ro, -a] **I.** *adj AmL* (*rubio: pelo, persona*) blond(e); (*tez*) fair **II.** *m, f AmL* (*rubio*) blond *m*, blonde *f*

guerra ['ge·rra] *f* war; **la ~ civil española** the Spanish Civil War; **la ~ de las galaxias** star wars; **~ mediática** media war; **~ de precios/ tarifas** price/tariff war; **~ santa** holy war; **la**

Primera/Segunda Guerra Mundial the First/Second World War; **~ química/psicológica/biológica** chemical/psychological/ biological warfare; **ir a la ~** to go to war; **estar en pie de ~** to be on a war footing; **tener la ~ declarada a alguien** *inf* to have it in for sb; **dar mucha ~** *inf* to be a real handful; **en ~** at war

guerrear [ge·rre·'ar] *vi* **1.** (*hacer guerra*) to wage war **2.** (*resistir*) to resist

guerrera [ge·'rre·ra] *f* trench coat

guerrero, -a [ge·'rre·ro, -a] **I.** *adj* **1.** (*de guerra*) warlike **2.** (*travieso*) naughty **3.** (*revoltoso*) rebellious **II.** *m, f* warrior

guerrilla [ge·'rri·ja, -ʎa] *f* **1.** (*guerra*) guerrilla warfare **2.** (*partida*) guerrilla band

guerrillear [ge·rri·ʎe·'ar, -ʎe·'ar] *vi* to wage guerrilla warfare

guerrillero, -a [ge·rri·'je·ro, -a, 'ʎe·ro, -a] *m, f* guerrilla (fighter)

gueto ['ge·to] *m* ghetto

guía[1] ['gi·a] *mf* (*de un grupo*) guide; **~ turística** tourist guide

guía[2] ['gi·a] *m* **1.** MIL scout **2.** (*manillar*) handlebar

guía[3] ['gi·a] *f* **1.** (*pauta*) guidance, guideline **2.** (*persona*) guide **3.** (*manual*) handbook; **~ comercial** trade directory; **~ de ferrocarriles** train schedule; **~ telefónica** telephone directory [*o* book]; **~ turística** travel guide(book) **4.** (*de planta*) main stem **5.** TÉC guide **6.** (*del bigote*) end **7.** PRico (*volante*) steering wheel **8.** *pl* (*riendas*) reins *pl*

guiar < *1. pres:* guío> [gi·'ar] **I.** *vt* **1.** (*a alguien*) to guide **2.** (*conversación*) to direct **3.** (*planta*) to train **II.** *vr:* **~ se por algo** to be guided by sth; **me guío por mi instinto** I follow my instincts

guija ['gi·xa] *f* pebble

guijarro [gi·'xa·rro] *m* **1.** (*canto*) pebble **2.** *pl* (*en playa*) pebbles *pl*

guijo ['gi·xo] *m* gravel

guillarse [gi·'jar·se, -'ʎar·se] *vr inf* **1.** (*chiflarse*) to go nuts **2.** (*irse*) **guillárselas** to beat it

guillotina [gi·jo·'ti·na, gi·ʎo·] *f* **1.** (*de ejecución, para papel*) guillotine **2.** TÉC **ventana de ~** sash window

guillotinar [gi·jo·ti·'nar, gi·ʎo·] *vt* to guillotine

guinda ['gin·da] *f* **1.** (*fruta*) morello cherry **2.** *inf* (*remate*) **poner la ~ a algo** to top sth off

guindilla [gin·'di·ja, -ʎa] *f* CULIN chili pepper

guineo [gi·'neo] *m AmL* (*banana*) banana

guiñapo [gi·'na·po] *m* **1.** (*trapo*) rag **2.** (*andrajoso*) ragged person; **estar hecho un ~** to be a wreck **3.** (*degradado*) down-and-out **4.** (*debilucho*) weakling

guiñar [gi·'nar] **I.** *vt* **~ el ojo a alguien** to wink at sb **II.** *vi* (*con el ojo*) to wink

guiño [gi·'no] *m* wink; **hacer un ~ a alguien** to wink at sb

guiñol [gi·'nol] *m* **1.** (*teatro*) puppet show **2.** (*títere*) puppet

guión [gi·'on] *m* **1.** CINE, TV script **2.** (*de una* *conferencia*) outline **3.** LING (*de compuesto, al fin de renglón*) hyphen; (*en diálogo*) dash **4.** (*persona*) scriptwriter **5.** (*real*) standard **6.** (*de procesión*) banner

guionista [gjo·'nis·ta] *mf* CINE screenwriter; TV scriptwriter

guipar [gi·'par] *vt inf* **1.** (*ver*) to see, to spot **2.** (*entender*) to catch on to, to see through

guiri ['gi·ri] *mf pey* **1.** (*extranjero*) foreigner **2.** (*guardia*) civil guard

guirigay [gi·ri·'yai] *m* <guirigayes *o* guri­gáis> *inf* **1.** (*lenguaje*) gibberish **2.** (*griterío*) uproar **3.** (*barullo*) hubbub

guirlache [gir·'la·tʃe] *m* (hard) nougat

guirnalda [gir·'nal·da] *f* garland

guisa ['gi·sa] *f* **a ~ de** like; **de tal ~** in such a way; **no puedes hacerlo de esta ~** you can't do it like that

guisado [gi·'sa·do] *m* stew

guisante [gi·'san·te] *m* pea

guisar [gi·'sar] **I.** *vt* **1.** (*cocinar*) to cook; (*con salsa*) to stew, to braise **2.** (*tramar*) to prepare **II.** *vr:* **~se** to cook; **se está guisando** it's cooking

guiso ['gi·so] *m* **1.** (*plato*) dish **2.** (*en salsa*) stew

güisqui ['gwis·ki] *m* whisky, whiskey

guita ['gi·ta] *f* **1.** (*cuerda*) twine **2.** *inf* (*dinero*) dough, curd

guitarra [gi·'ta·rra] *f* (*instrumento*) guitar

guitarrista [gi·ta·'rris·ta] *mf* guitarist

gula ['gu·la] *f* gluttony

guripa [gu·'ri·pa] *mf inf* (*guardia*) cop

gurrumino, -a [gu·rru·'mi·no, -a] *adj* **1.** (*tacaño*) stingy **2.** (*pequeño*) puny

gurú [gu·'ru] *m* guru

gusanillo [gu·sa·'ni·jo, -ʎo] *m* worm ▶ **matar el ~** *inf* (*comiendo*) to kill one's hunger; (*bebiendo*) to quench one's thirst

gusano [gu·'sa·no] *m* **1.** (*lombriz*) worm; **~ informático** COMPUT computer worm; **~ de tierra** earthworm; **~ de luz** glow-worm **2.** (*oruga*) caterpillar **3.** (*larva de mosca*) maggot **4.** *fig* (*persona despreciable*) worm

gustar [gus·'tar] **I.** *vi* **1.** (*agradar*) **me gusta nadar/el helado** I like swimming/ice cream; **me gustan estos zapatos** I like these shoes; **¡así me gusta!** well done!; **como Ud. guste** as you wish; **cuando guste** whenever you like [*o* want] **2.** (*apasionarse*) **~ de** +*infin* to enjoy **3.** (*atraer*) **me gusta tu hermano** I fancy your brother **4.** (*querer*) **me gustas** I like you **5.** (*condicional*) **me ~ía saber...** I would like to know... **II.** *vt* (*probar*) to taste

gustativo, -a [gus·ta·'ti·βo, -a] *adj* taste

gustazo [gus·'ta·so, -θo] *m* **1.** (*placer*) great pleasure; **tuve el ~ de darle la mano** I had the great pleasure of shaking his/her hand; **darse el ~ de algo** to treat oneself to sth **2.** (*ante una desgracia*) satisfaction

gustillo [gus·'ti·jo, -ʎo] *m* **1.** (*sabor*) aftertaste, tang **2.** (*sensación*) kick; **da ~ ver que le regañan a ella también** I get a kick out of

seeing her criticized for a change

gusto ['gus·to] *m* **1.** (*sentido*) taste; **una broma de mal ~** a joke in bad taste; **no hago nada a su ~** nothing I do pleases him/her; **lo ha hecho a mi ~** he/she did it to my satisfaction **2.** (*sabor*) taste, flavor; **~ a algo** taste of sth; **huevos al ~** eggs cooked to order **3.** (*placer*) pleasure; **con ~** with pleasure; **~s caros** expensive tastes *pl;* **coger ~ a algo** to take [*o* develop] a liking to sth; **encontrar ~ en algo** to find enjoyment in sth; **estar a ~** to feel comfortable; **tanto ~ en conocerla — el ~ es mío** pleased to meet you — the pleasure is all mine; **cantan que da ~** they sing wonderfully

gustoso, -a [gus·'to·so, -a] *adj* **1.** (*sabroso*) tasty, savory **2.** (*con gusto*) **te acompañaré ~** I'd be glad to accompany you **3.** (*agradable*) pleasant

gutural [gu·tu·'ral] *adj* guttural, throaty

gymkhana [dʒin·'ka·na] *f* gymkhana

H

H, h ['a·tʃe] *f* H, h; **~ de Huelva** H as in Hotel

ha [xa] *interj* ah, ha; **¡~, ~!** Ha, ha!

haba ['a·βa] *f* broad bean

Habana [a·'βa·na] *f* **La ~** Havana

habanero, -a [a·βa·'ne·ro, -a] *adj, m, f* Havanan

habano [a·'βa·no] *m* (*cigarro*) Havana cigar

haber [a·'βer] *irr* **I.** *aux* **1.** (*en tiempos compuestos*) to have; **ha ido al cine** he/she has gone to the cinema; **he comprado el periódico** I bought the newspaper **2.** (*de obligación*) **~ de hacer algo** to have to do sth; **has de hacerlo** (*sin falta*) you must do it **3.** (*futuro*) **han de llegar pronto** they should be here soon **4.** (*imperativo*) **no tengo sitio — ¡~ venido antes!** there's no room — you should have come earlier! **II.** *vimpers* **1.** (*ocurrir*) **ha habido un terremoto en Japón** there has been an earthquake in Japan; **¿qué hay?** what's the news?; **¿qué hay, Pepe?** how's it going, Pepe? **2.** (*efectuarse*) to take place; **hoy no hay cine** the cinema is closed today; **ayer hubo reunión** there was a meeting yesterday; **después habrá baile** there'll be a dance afterwards **3.** (*existir*) **aquí no hay agua** there is no water here; **eso es todo... ¡y ya no hay más!** that's all... and nothing more!; **¿hay algo entre tú y ella?** is there something going on between you two?; **hay poca gente que...** there are few people who...; **hay quien cree que...** some people think that...; **¡muchas gracias! — no hay de qué** thanks a lot! — not at all; **no hay quien me gane al pingpong** nobody can beat me at table tennis

4.(*hallarse, estar*) **hay un cuadro en la pared** there is a painting on the wall; **había un papel en el suelo** there was a piece of paper on the floor; **no hay leche/platos en la mesa** there is no milk/there are no plates on the table **5.**(*tiempo*) **había una vez...** once upon a time... **6.**(*obligatoriedad*) **¡hay que ver cómo están los precios!** my God! look at those prices!; **hay que trabajar más** we have to work harder; **no hay que olvidar que...** we must not forget that... **III.***vt* **compra cuantos sellos pueda** ~ buy as many stamps as you can **IV.** *vr* **habérselas con alguien** to be up against sb **V.** *m* **1.**(*capital*) assets *pl;* **tener algo en su** ~ *fig* to have sth to one's credit **2.**(*en cuenta corriente*) balance, account; **pasaré la cantidad a tu** ~ I'll pay the amount into your account **3.** *pl* (*emolumentos*) assets *pl*

habichuela [a·βi·ˈʧwe·la] *f* (kidney) bean; (*judía blanca*) haricot bean

hábil [ˈa·βil] *adj* **1.**(*diestro*) skilled; **ser ~ para algo** to be skilled at sth **2.**(*en el oficio*) **ser ~ en algo** to be good at sth **3.**(*astuto*) shrewd; **una respuesta** ~ a clever response **4.**JUR working; **días ~es** working days

habilidad [a·βi·li·ˈdad] *f* **1.**(*destreza*) skill; **no tengo gran ~ con las manos** I'm not very skillful with my hands **2.**(*facultad*) ability **3.**(*astucia*) shrewdness **4.**(*gracia*) grace; **se mueve con** ~ she moves gracefully

habilidoso, -a [a·βi·li·ˈdo·so, -a] *adj* **1.**(*diestro*) skillful, able **2.**(*astuto*) shrewd **3.**(*gracioso*) graceful

habilitación [a·βi·li·ta·ˈsjon, -ˈθjon] *f* **1.**JUR (*de personas*) ~ **para algo** entitlement to sth **2.**(*de empleo*) paymaster's duties **3.**(*oficina*) paymaster's office **4.**(*de un espacio*) fitting out

habilitar [a·βi·li·ˈtar] *vt* **1.**(*a personas*) train, to teach; JUR to entitle, to empower; (*documentos*) to authorize **2.**COM (*dar capital*) to fund, to finance **3.**(*proveer*) ~ **de algo** to provide with sth **4.**(*espacio*) to fit out

habiloso, -a [a·βi·ˈlo·so, -a] *adj AmL* **1.**(*hábil*) skilled, skillful **2.**(*astuto*) shrewd

habitabilidad [a·βi·ta·βi·li·ˈdad] *f* (in)habitability

habitable [a·βi·ta·ˈβle] *adj* (in)habitable

habitación [a·βi·ta·ˈsjon, -ˈθjon] *f* **1.**(*cuarto*) room; (*dormitorio*) bedroom; ~ **individual** single room **2.**(*vivienda*) dwelling **3.**(*acción*) living

habitáculo [a·βi·ˈta·ku·lo] *m* **1.**(*vivienda*) dwelling **2.**ECOL (*espacio*) habitat **3.**AUTO interior

habitante [a·βi·ˈtan·te] *mf* inhabitant; **¿cuántos habitantes tiene Chile?** what is the population of Chile?

habitar [a·βi·ˈtar] **I.** *vi* to live **II.** *vt* to live in

hábitat [ˈa·βi·tat] *m* <hábitats> habitat

hábito [ˈa·βi·to] *m* **1.**(*costumbre*) habit; **he dejado el ~ de fumar** I gave up smoking

2.REL (*sotana*) habit; (*orden*) insignia

habitual [a·βi·tu·ˈal] *adj* regular; **cliente** ~ regular client; **bebedor** ~ habitual drinker; **lo dijo con su ironía** ~ he said it with his customary irony

habituar <*1. pres:* habitúo> [a·βi·tu·ˈar] *vt, vr* ~(**se**) **a algo** to get used to sth

habla [ˈa·βla] *f* **1.**(*facultad*) speech, diction; **quedarse sin** ~ to be left speechless **2.**(*acto*) speech; **un país de** ~ **inglesa** an English-speaking country; **¡Juan al ~!** TEL Juan speaking! **3.**(*manera, dialecto*) way of speaking

hablado, -a [a·ˈβla·do, -a] *adj* spoken; **bien** ~ well-spoken; **el francés** ~ spoken French; **ser mal** ~ to be foul-mouthed

hablador(a) [a·βla·ˈdor, -ˈdo·ra] **I.** *adj* talkative **II.** *m(f)* **1.**(*cotorra*) chatterbox **2.**(*chismoso*) gossip

habladuría [a·βla·du·ˈri·a] *f* rumor; ~**s** gossip

hablante [a·ˈβlan·te] *mf* speaker

hablantina [a·βlan·ˈti·na] *f Col, Ven* talkative

hablar [a·ˈβlar] **I.** *vi* **1.**(*decir*) to speak, to talk; ~ **a gritos** to shout; ~ **alto/bajo** to speak loudly/softly; ~ **entre dientes** to mutter; **déjeme terminar de** ~ let me finish; ~ **claro** to speak frankly; **el autor no habla de este tema** the author does not address this topic; **la policía le ha hecho** ~ the police made him talk; **los números hablan por sí solos** the figures speak for themselves; **¡no ~ás en serio!** you must be joking!; **por no ~ de...** not to mention...; **¡y no se hable más!** and that's an end to it; **¡ni ~!** no way! **2.**(*conversar*) ~ **con alguien** to talk to sb; ~ **con franqueza** to talk sincerely; ~ **por teléfono** to talk on the telephone; **no he podido ~ con él** I haven't managed to speak to him; ~ **por los codos** *inf* to talk nineteen to the dozen **II.** *vt* **1.**(*idioma*) to speak **2.**(*decir*) to say; ~ **a alguien** (*de algo/alguien*) to talk to sb (about sth/sb); **no me habló en toda la noche** he/she didn't say a word to me all night **3.**(*asunto*) **lo hablaré con tu padre** I'll talk about it with your father **III.** *vr:* ~ **se** to talk to each other; **no se hablan** they are not on speaking terms; **nos hablamos de tú** we are on familiar terms

hablilla [a·ˈβli·ja, -ʎa] *f* rumor

hacendado, -a [a·sen·ˈda·do, -a; a·θen-] **I.** *adj* landowning **II.** *m, f* **1.**(*de una hacienda*) landowner **2.**AmS (*de ganado*) livestock farmer, rancher

hacendoso, -a [a·sen·ˈdo·so, -a; a·θen-] *adj* hard-working

hacer [a·ˈser, -ˈθer] *irr* **I.** *vt* **1.**(*producir*) to make; (*coche t.*) to manufacture; **la casa está hecha de madera** the house is made of wood; **Dios hizo al hombre** God created man **2.**(*realizar*) to do; (*libro*) to write; **¿qué hacemos hoy?** what shall we do today?; ~ **una llamada** to make a phone call; **demuestra lo que sabes** ~ show us what you can do; **hazlo por mí** do it for me; **a medio** ~ half-finished;

hicimos la trayectoria en tres horas we did the trip in three hours; **lo hecho, hecho está** there's no use crying over spilled milk; **puedes ~ lo que quieras** you can do whatever you want; **¿qué haces por aquí?** what are you doing around here?; **¡me la has hecho!** you've let me in for it; **la ha hecho buena** he's/she's really messed things up **3.** (*pregunta*) to ask; (*observación*) to make; (*discurso*) to make, to give **4.** (*ocasionar: ruido*) to make; (*daño*) to cause; **~ destrozos** to wreak havoc; **~ sombra** to cast a shadow; **no puedes ~me esto** you can't do this to me **5.** (*construir*) to build **6.** (*procurar*) to make; **¿puedes ~me sitio?** can you fit me in? **7.** (*transformar*) **~ pedazos algo** to smash sth up; **estás hecho un hombre** you're a man now **8.** (*conseguir: dinero, amigos*) to make **9.** (*llegar*) **~ puerto** to clear harbor; **~ noche en...** to spend the night in... **10.** (*más sustantivo*) **~ el amor** to make love; **~ caso a alguien** to pay heed to sb; **~ cumplidos** to pay compliments; **~ deporte** to do sport; **~ frente a algo/alguien** to face up to sth/sb; **~ la maleta** to pack; **~ uso de algo** to make use of sth **11.** (*más verbo*) **~ creer algo a alguien** to make [*o* have] sb believe sth; **~ venir a alguien** to make sb come; **hazle pasar** let him in; **no me hagas contarlo** don't make me say it **12.** (*limpiar*) **hacer las escaleras** *inf* to do the steps **III.** TEAT **~ una obra** to do [*o* put on] a play; **~ el papel de Antígona** to play the role of Antigone **14.** ENS (*carrera*) to study, to do; **¿haces francés o inglés?** are you doing French or English? **15.** CULIN (*comida, pastel*) to make; (*patatas*) to do; **quiero la carne bien hecha** I want the meat well done **II.** *vi* **1.** (*convenir*) **eso no hace al caso** that's not relevant **2.** (*oficio*) **~ de algo** to work as sth **3.** (*con preposición*) **por lo que hace a Juan...** regarding Juan...; **hizo como que no me vio** he/she pretended he/she didn't seen me **III.** *vr:* **~ se 1.** (*volverse*) to become; **~se del Madrid** to become a Madrid fan **2.** (*crecer*) to grow **3.** (*simular*) to pretend; **se hace a todo** he's/she's always pretending; **~se la víctima** to act like a victim **4.** (*habituarse*) **~se a algo** to get used to sth **5.** (*dejarse hacer*) **~se una foto** to have one's picture taken **6.** (*conseguir*) **~se respetar** to instill respect; **~se con el poder** to seize power **7.** (*resultar*) to be; **se me hace muy difícil creer eso** it's very difficult for me to believe that **IV.** *vimpers* **1.** (*tiempo*) **hace frío/calor** it is cold/hot; **hoy hace un buen día** it's a nice day today **2.** (*temporal*) **hace tres días** three days ago; **no hace mucho** not long ago; **desde hace un día** since yesterday
hacha ['a·tʃa] *f* **1.** (*herramienta*) axe, hatchet **2.** (*antorcha*) torch **3.** (*vela*) large candle
hachazo [a·'tʃa·so, -θo] *m* stroke of the axe
hache ['a·tʃe] *f* H, h; **la ~** the letter h
hachís [xa·'tʃis] *m* hashish
hacia ['a·sja, -θja] *prep* **1.** (*dirección*) towards,

to; **el pueblo está más ~ el sur** the village lies further to the south; **el pueblo está yendo ~ Cuzco** the village is on the way to Cuzco; **fuimos ~ allí** we went that way; **vino ~ mí** he/she came towards me **2.** (*cerca de*) near **3.** (*respecto a*) regarding
hacienda [a·'sjen·da, a·'θjen-] *f* **1.** (*finca*) country estate **2.** (*bienes*) **~ pública** public finance
Hacienda [a·'sjen·da, a·'θjen-] *f* (*ministerio*) Treasury; (*administración*) Internal Revenue Service; **el Ministro de Economía y ~** the Minister of Finance; **¿pagas mucho a ~?** do you pay a lot of tax?
hacinamiento [a·si·na·'mjen·to, a·θi-] *m* **1.** (*de haces*) piling **2.** (*de objetos*) stacking; (*de personas*) (over)crowding
hacinar [a·si·'nar, a·θi-] **I.** *vt* to pile **II.** *vr:* **~se** (*personas*) to (over)crowd; (*objetos*) to stack
hacker ['xa·ker] *mf* (*pirata informático*) hacker
hada ['a·da] *f* fairy; **cuento de ~s** fairy tale; **~ madrina** fairy godmother
hado ['a·do] *m* fate
Haití [ai·'ti] *m* Haiti
haitiano, -a [ai·'tja·no, -a] *adj, m, f* Haitian
hala ['a·la] *interj* **1.** (*sorpresa*) well, well **2.** (*prisa*) come on
halagador(a) [a·la·ɣa·'dor, -·'do·ra] *adj* flattering
halagar <g→gu> [a·la·'ɣar] *vt* to flatter
halago [a·'la·ɣo] *m* **1.** (*acción*) flattery **2.** (*palabras*) flattering words *pl*, compliment
halagüeño, -a [a·la·'ɣwe·ɲo, -a] *adj* **1.** (*halagador*) flattering **2.** (*prometedor*) encouraging
halcón [al·'kon] *m* **1.** ZOOL falcon **2.** POL hawk
hálito ['a·li·to] *m* **1.** (*aliento*) breath **2.** (*vapor*) steam
hall [xol] *m* hall
hallar [a·'jar, -'ʎar] **I.** *vt* **1.** (*encontrar*) to find; (*sin buscar*) to come across **2.** (*inventar*) to invent **3.** (*averiguar*) to check **4.** (*darse cuenta*) to realize **5.** (*tierra*) to discover **II.** *vr:* **~se 1.** (*sitio*) to be **2.** (*estado*) to feel; **se halló con la resistencia de su partido** he/she met opposition from his/her party
hallazgo [a·'jas·ɣo, a·'ʎaθ-] *m* **1.** discovery **2.** *pl* findings *pl*
halo ['a·lo] *m* halo
halógeno [a·'lo·xe·no] *m* halogen
halterofilia [al·te·ro·'fi·lja] *f* DEP weightlifting
halterófilo, -a [al·te·'ro·fi·lo, -a] *m, f* DEP weightlifter
hamaca [a·'ma·ka] *f* **1.** (*cama*) hammock **2.** (*tumbona*) deckchair **3.** *AmL* (*mecedora*) rocking chair
hamacar <c→qu> [a·ma·'kar] *vt, vr:* **~(se)** *AmS, Guat* to rock
hambre ['am·bre] *f* **1.** (*apetito*) hunger; **huelga de ~** hunger strike; **matar el ~** to kill one's hunger; **me ha entrado (el) ~** I'm getting hungry; **morirse de ~** to die of hunger; **tener ~** to be hungry **2.** (*de la población*) starvation **3.** (*deseo*) **~ de algo** longing for sth;

~ de poder hunger for power

hambrear [am·bre·'ar] *vi AmL* **1.** (*hacer pasar hambre*) to starve **2.** (*mendigar*) to be hungry

hambriento, -a [am·'brjen·to, -a] *adj* **1.** (*con hambre*) hungry **2.** (*muerto de hambre*) starving **3.** (*deseoso*) **estar ~ de poder** to be hungry for power

hambruna [am·'bru·na] *f AmL* famine

hamburguesa [am·bur·'ɟe·sa] *f* CULIN hamburger; **~ con queso** cheeseburger

hamburguesería [am·bur·ɟe·se·'ri·a] *f* hamburger bar

hampa ['am·pa] *f* **1.** (*gente*) underworld **2.** (*modo de vida*) criminal class

handicap ['xan·di·kap] *m* handicap

hangar [an·'gar] *m* AVIAT hangar

haragán, -ana [a·ra·'ɣan, --'ɣa·na] *m, f* loafer

haraganear [a·ra·ɣa·ne·'ar] *vi* to loaf around

haraganería [a·ra·ɣa·ne·'ri·a] *f* loafing around

harakiri [a·ra·'ki·ri] *m* hara-kiri

harapiento, -a [a·ra·'pjen·to, -a] *adj* ragged, in tatters

harapo [a·'ra·po] *m* rag

hardware ['xard·wer] *m* hardware

harem [a·'ren] *m*, **harén** [a·'ren] *m* harem

harina [a·'ri·na] *f* **1.** CULIN flour; **~ integral** whole-wheat flour; **~ de trigo** wheat flour **2.** (*polvo*) powder

harinear [a·ri·ne·'ar] *vimpers Ven* to drizzle

harinoso, -a [a·ri·'no·so, -a] *adj* **1.** (*parecido a la harina*) floury **2.** (*con harina*) with flour

harmonía [ar·mo·'ni·a] *f* harmony

hartar [ar·'tar] *irr* I. *vt* **1.** (*saciar*) **~ a alguien** to give sb their fill **2.** (*fastidiar*) **me harta con sus chistes** I'm getting sick of his/her jokes II. *vr*: **~ se 1.** (*saciarse*) to eat one's fill; (*en exceso*) to eat too much **2.** (*cansarse*) to get fed up; **~ se de reír** to laugh oneself silly; **me he hartado del tiempo que hace en Nueva York** I'm sick of [*o* fed up with] this New York weather

harto, -a ['ar·to, -a] I. *adj* **1.** (*repleto*) full; (*en exceso*) too full **2.** (*sobrado*) **tengo hartas razones** I have plenty of reasons **3.** (*cansado*) **estar ~ de alguien/algo** to be sick of [*o* fed up with] sb/sth II. *adv* (*sobrado*) (more than) enough; (*muy*) a lot of

hartura [ar·'tu·ra] *f* (over)abundance

hasta ['as·ta] I. *prep* **1.** (*de lugar*) to; **te llevo ~ la estación** I'll give you a lift to the station; **volamos ~ Madrid** we're flying to Madrid; **~ cierto punto** to a certain degree, up to a point **2.** (*de tiempo*) until, up to until; **~ ahora** up to now; **~ el próximo año** up until next year **3.** (*en despedidas*) **¡~ luego!** see you later!; **¡~ la vista!** see you again!; **¡~ la próxima!** until next time! II. *adv* even III. *conj* **~ cuando come lee el periódico** he/she even reads the newspaper while he's/she's eating; **no consiguió un trabajo fijo ~ que cumplió 40 años** he/she didn't get a steady job until he/she was forty

hastiar <*1. pres:* hastío> [as·ti·'ar] I. *vt*

1. (*aburrir*) to bore **2.** (*hartar, repugnar*) to sicken II. *vr* **~ se de alguien/algo** to get fed up with sb/sth

hastío [as·'ti·o] *m* **1.** (*tedio*) boredom; **¡qué ~!** what a bore! **2.** (*repugnancia*) disgust

hatajo [a·'ta·xo] *m* **1.** (*de ganado*) small herd **2.** (*de personas*) bunch, cluster

Hawai [xa·'wai] *m* Hawaii

hawaiano, -a [xa·wa·'ja·no, -a] *adj, m, f* Hawaiian

haya ['a·ja] *f* **1.** (*árbol*) beech **2.** (*madera*) beechwood

Haya ['a·ja] *f* **La ~** the Hague

hayal [a·'jal] *m* beech grove

haz [as, aθ] *m* (*hato*) bunch; (*de papeles*) sheaf

hazaña [a·'sa·ɲa, a·'θa-] *f* feat, exploit

hazmerreír [as·me·rre·'ir, aθ·me-] *m inv* laughing stock; **es el ~ de la gente** he's/she's the butt of everyone's jokes

HB [a·'ʧe·'βe] *m abr de* **Herri Batasuna** *Basque nationalist political coalition*

he [e] *1. pres de* **haber**

hebilla [e·'βi·ja, -ʎa] *f* buckle

hebra ['e·βra] *f* **1.** (*hilo*) thread **2.** (*fibra*) fiber; **tabaco de ~** loose tobacco

hebreo [e·'βreo] *m* **1.** (*lengua*) Hebrew **2.** *inf* (*mercader*) merchant **3.** *inf* (*usurero*) usurer

hebreo, -a [e·'βreo, -a] *adj, m, f* Hebrew

hecatombe [e·ka·'tom·be] *f* hecatomb

hechicería [e·ʧi·se·'ri·a, -θe·'ri·a] *f* **1.** (*arte*) witchcraft **2.** (*hechizo*) spell

hechicero, -a [e·ʧi·'se·ro, -a; -'θe·ro, -a] *m, f* **1.** (*brujo*) sorcerer **2.** (*de tribu*) witch doctor

hechizar <z→c> [e·ʧi·'sar, -'θar] *vt* **1.** (*encantar*) to cast a spell on **2.** (*fascinar*) captivate, to enchant

hechizo [e·'ʧi·so, -θo] *m* spell; **romper el ~** to break the spell

hecho ['e·ʧo] *m* **1.** (*circunstancia*) fact **2.** (*acto*) action, deed; **~ delictivo** criminal act; **los Hechos de los Apóstoles** the Acts of the Apostles **3.** (*suceso*) event; JUR deed; **exposición de los ~s** statement of events; **lugar de los ~s** scene of the crime; **los ~s que causaron el incendio** the events that gave rise to the fire ► **de ~** in fact

hecho, -a ['e·ʧo, -a] *adj* **1.** (*maduro*) mature; **vino ~** mature wine **2.** (*cocido*) cooked; **me gusta la carne hecha** I like meat well done; **el pollo está demasiado ~** the chicken is overcooked **3.** (*acabado*) finished; **frase hecha** idiom; **traje ~** ready-made suit **4.** (*adulto*) **un hombre ~ y derecho** a real man

hechura [e·'ʧu·ra] *f* **1.** (*factura*) making; **de buena ~** well-made **2.** (*de un vestido*) tailoring **3.** (*obra*) work; (*de Dios*) creation **4.** (*del cuerpo*) shape

hectárea [ek·'ta·rea] *f* hectare

hectogramo [ek·to·'ɣra·mo] *m* hectogram

hectolitro [ek·to·'li·tro] *m* hectoliter

hectómetro [ek·'to·me·tro] *m* hectometer

H

heder <e→ie> [e·'der] *vi* ~ **a algo** to stink of sth

hediondo, -a [e·'djon·do] *adj* **1.** (*fétido*) fetid **2.** (*repugnante*) repulsive **3.** (*obsceno*) obscene

hedonismo [e·do·'nis·mo] *m* hedonism

hedonista [e·do·'nis·ta] **I.** *adj* hedonistic **II.** *mf* hedonist

hedor [e·'dor] *m* stench; ~ **a huevos podridos** stench of rotten eggs

hegemonía [e·xe·mo·'ni·a] *f* hegemony

hegemónico, -a [e·xe·'mo·ni·ko, -a] *adj* hegemonic

helada [e·'la·da] *f* frost; **las primeras ~s del año** the first frosts of the year; **anoche cayó una ~** there was a frost last night

heladera [e·la·'de·ra] *f* (*nevera*) refrigerator, fridge; **este sitio es una ~** it's absolutely freezing here

heladería [e·la·de·'ri·a] *f* ice cream parlor

helado [e·'la·do] *m* **1.** (*postre*) ice cream **2.** (*sorbete*) sorbet

helado, -a [e·'la·do, -a] *adj* **1.** (*frío*) freezing; (*congelado*) frozen; **estoy ~** I'm freezing; **el lago está ~** the lake is frozen; **las cañerías están heladas** the pipes are frozen **2.** (*pasmado*) **me quedé ~** I was left speechless; (*de miedo*) I was petrified **3.** (*altivo*) aloof

helador(a) [e·la·'dor, -·'do·ra] *adj* (*viento*) freezing

heladora [e·la·'do·ra] *f* ice cream maker [*o* machine]

helaje [e·'la·xe] *m Col* intense cold, frost

helar <e→ie> [e·'lar] **I.** *vt* **1.** (*congelar*) to freeze **2.** (*pasmar*) to astonish **II.** *vimpers* to freeze **III.** *vr:* ~**se 1.** (*congelarse*) to freeze; **el lago se ha helado** the lake has frozen over **2.** (*morir*) to freeze to death **3.** (*pasar frío*) to be frozen [*o* ice cold]; ~**se de frío** to get chilled to the bone

helecho [e·'le·tʃo] *m* fern, bracken

helénico, -a [e·'le·ni·ko, -a] *adj* **1.** (*antiguo*) Hellenic **2.** (*actual*) Greek

helenista [e·le·'nis·ta] *mf* Hellenist

hélice ['e·li·se, -θe] *f* TÉC propeller

helicoidal [e·li·koi·'dal] *adj* helicoid

helicóptero [e·li·'kop·te·ro] *m* helicopter

helio ['e·ljo] *m* helium

heliocéntrico, -a [e·ljo·'sen·tri·ko, -a; e·ljo·'θen-] *adj* heliocentric

helipuerto [e·li·'pwer·to] *m* heliport

helvético, -a [el·'βe·ti·ko, -a] *adj, m, f* Swiss

hematoma [e·ma·'to·ma] *m* bruise; MED hematoma

hembra ['em·bra] *f* **1.** *t.* ZOOL, ELEC female **2.** TÉC female; (*tornillo*) nut

hembraje [em·'bra·xe] *m AmS* **1.** (*de ganado*) herd of female animals **2.** *pey* (*de mujeres*) gaggle

hemeroteca [e·me·ro·'te·ka] *f* archive of periodicals

hemiciclo [e·mi·'si·klo, e·mi·'θi-] *m* **1.** (*semicírculo*) semicircle **2.** (*sala*) semicircular hall;

(*parlamento*) floor **3.** POL (*en España, Congreso de Diputados*) Parliament chamber

hemiplejia [e·mi·'ple·xja] *f*, **hemiplejía** [e·mi·ple·'xi·a] *f* MED hemiplegia, semi-paralysis

hemipléjico, -a [e·mi·'ple·xi·ko, -a] **I.** *adj* hemiplegic, semi-paralyzed **II.** *m, f* hemiplegic, person with partial paralysis

hemisférico, -a [e·mis·'fe·ri·ko, -a] *adj* hemispherical

hemisferio [e·mis·'fe·rjo] *m* hemisphere

hemofilia [e·mo·'fi·lja] *f* MED hemophilia

hemoglobina [e·mo·ɣlo·'βi·na] *f* BIO hemoglobin

hemorragia [e·mo·'rra·xja] *f* MED hemorrhage

hemorroides [e·mo·'rroi·des] *fpl* hemorrhoids *pl*

henchir [en·'tʃir] *irr como pedir* **I.** *vt* to fill; ~ **los pulmones de aire** to fill one's lungs with air **II.** *vr:* ~**se** (*hartarse de comida*) to stuff oneself

hender <e→ie> [en·'der] **I.** *vt* **1.** (*algo de madera*) to split; (*algo de plástico*) to cut **2.** (*abrirse paso*) to make one's way through **3.** (*mar*) to plough; **el barco hendía las aguas** the ship ploughed the waves **II.** *vr:* ~**se** to split

hendidura [en·di·'du·ra] *f* **1.** (*raja*) split; (*en la pared, en un jarrón*) crack **2.** (*de una guía*) groove

hendija [en·'di·xa] *f AmL* (*rendija*) crack

hendir [en·'dir] *irr como cernir vt v.* **hender**

henequén [en·e·'ken] *m AmL* henequen (*plant and fabric derived from it*)

heno ['e·no] *m* hay; **fiebre del ~** hay fever

hepático, -a [e·'pa·ti·ko, -a] *adj* hepatic; **cirrosis hepática** cirrhosis of the liver

hepatitis [e·pa·'ti·tis] *f inv* MED hepatitis

heptágono [ep·'ta·ɣo·no] **I.** *adj* heptagonal **II.** *m* heptagon

heptatlón ['ep·tat·lon] *m* DEP heptathlon

heráldica [e·'ral·di·ka] *f* heraldry

heráldico, -a [e·'ral·di·ko] *adj* heraldic

herbáceo, -a [e·r·'βa·seo, -a; -θeo, -a] *adj* **1.** (*de hierba*) herbaceous **2.** (*de hierbas medicinales*) homeopathic

herbaje [er·'βa·xe] *m* **1.** (*lugar*) pasture **2.** (*comida*) grass

herbario [er·'βa·rjo] **I.** *adj* herbal **II.** *m* herbalist

herbicida [er·βi·'si·da, -'θi·da] *m* herbicide

herbívoro [er·'βi·βo·ro] *m* herbivore

herbolario [er·βo·'la·rjo] *m* health food shop

herbolario, -a [er·βo·'la·rjo, -a] *m, f* herbalist

herboristería [er·βo·ris·te·'ri·a] *f v.* **herbolario**

hercio ['er·sjo, -θjo] *m* FÍS hertz

hercúleo, -a [er·'ku·leo, -a] *adj* Herculean; **una empresa hercúlea** a Herculean task

heredable [e·re·'da·βle] *adj* able to be inherited

heredar [e·re·'dar] *vt* to inherit; **propiedad heredada** inherited property; **problemas heredados del franquismo** problems handed down from Franco's time

heredero, -a [e·re·'de·ro, -a] *m, f* heir; **el ~ del trono** the heir to the throne; **el príncipe ~** the crown prince

hereditario, -a [e·re·di·'ta·rjo, -a] *adj* hereditary; **enfermedad hereditaria** hereditary disease

hereje [e·'re·xe] *mf* REL heretic

herejía [e·re·'xi·a] *f* **1.** (*calumnia*) insult **3.** (*fechoría*) evil deed **4.** (*rebeldía*) rebellion

herencia [e·'ren·sja, -θja] *f* **1.** JUR inheritance **2.** (*legado*) legacy; **una ~ de la antigüedad** a legacy of the past

herético, -a [e·'re·ti·ko, -a] *adj* heretical

herida [e·'ri·da] *f* **1.** (*lesión*) wound; **tocar a alguien en la ~** *fig* to find somebody's weak [*o* sore] spot **2.** (*ofensa*) affront

herido, -a [e·'ri·do, -a] **I.** *adj* **1.** (*lesionado*) injured; MIL wounded; **~ de gravedad** seriously injured; MIL mortally wounded **2.** (*ofendido*) hurt, offended **II.** *m, f* injured person; MIL wounded soldier; **los ~s** the wounded; **en el atentado no hubo ~s** nobody was wounded in the attack

herir [e·'rir] *irr como sentir* **I.** *vt* **1.** (*lesionar*) to injure; MIL to wound **2.** (*golpear*) to hit **3.** (*flecha*) to sink into **4.** MÚS (*instrumento de cuerda*) to pluck; (*instrumento de tecla*) to strike **5.** (*sol*) to beat down **6.** (*ofender*) to hurt, to offend **7.** (*acertar*) to hit **II.** *vr:* **~se** to be injured

hermafrodita [er·ma·fro·'di·ta] *adj, m* hermaphrodite

hermanamiento [er·ma·na·'mjen·to] *m* **1.** (*de ciudades*) twinning **2.** (*acción*) joining

hermanar [er·ma·'nar] **I.** *vt* (*unir*) to join; (*ciudades*) to twin; **Santiago está hermanada con...** Santiago is twinned with... **II.** *vr:* **~se** to be twinned

hermanastro, -a [er·ma·'nas·tro, -a] *m, f* stepbrother *m*, stepsister *f*

hermandad [er·man·'dad] *f* (*de hombres*) brotherhood; (*de mujeres*) sisterhood; REL religious association

hermano, -a [er·'ma·no, -a] *m, f* (*pariente*) brother *m*, sister *f*; **~ de padre** paternal half-brother; **~ político** brother-in-law; **~ de leche** foster brother; **~s siameses** Siamese twins; **mi ~ mayor/pequeño** my elder/younger brother; **tengo tres ~s** (*sólo chicos*) I have three brothers; (*chicos y chicas*) I have three brothers and sisters; **medio ~** half-brother; **lenguas hermanas** sister tongues

hermético, -a [er·'me·ti·ko, -a] *adj* hermetic(al); (*al aire*) airtight; (*al agua*) watertight

hermetismo [er·me·'tis·mo] *m* secrecy; **el ~ entre las personas de su confianza es absurdo** it's absurd for people he/she trusts to behave so secretively

hermetizar <z→c> [er·me·ti·'sar, -'θar] *vt* to seal (hermetically)

hermosear [er·mo·se·'ar] *vt* **1.** (*a una persona*) to beautify **2.** (*a una cosa*) to embellish, to adorn

hermoso, -a [er·'mo·so, -a] *adj* **1.** (*paisaje, mujer*) beautiful; (*hombre*) handsome **2.** (*día*) lovely **3.** (*niño*) pretty; (*sanote*) robust **4.** (*persona*) good **5.** (*gesto*) nice

hermosura [er·mo·'su·ra] *f* beauty

hernia ['er·nja] *f* MED hernia

herniarse [er·'njar·se] *vr* to rupture oneself; *irón* to work very hard; **¡no te herniarás, no!** *irón* don't burst a blood vessel!

héroe ['e·roe] *m* hero; (*protagonista*) main character

heroicidad [e·roi·si·'dad, e·roi·θi·-] *f* **1.** (*hazaña*) feat (of heroism) **2.** (*cualidad*) heroic qualities

heroico, -a [e·'roi·ko, -a] *adj* heroic

heroína [e·ro·'i·na] *f* **1.** (*de héroe*) heroine; (*protagonista*) main character **2.** (*droga*) heroin

heroinómano, -a [e·roi·'no·ma·no, -a] *m, f* heroin addict

heroísmo [e·ro·'is·mo] *m* heroism

herpes ['er·pes] *m o f inv* MED herpes

herrador [e·rra·'dor] *m* (black)smith

herradura [e·rra·'du·ra] *f* **1.** (*de caballo*) horseshoe; **camino de ~** bridle path **2.** ZOOL horseshoe bat

herraje(s) [e·'rra·xe(s)] *m(pl)* ironwork

herramienta [e·rra·'mjen·ta] *f* tool; **~ agrícola** agricultural machinery; **caja de (las) ~s** tool box

herrar <e→ie> [e·'rrar] *vt* **1.** (*caballo*) to shoe **2.** (*a un animal*) to brand

herrería [e·rre·'ri·a] *f* blacksmith's, smithy

herrero [e·'rre·ro] *m* blacksmith

herrumbre [e·'rrum·bre] *f* rust

herrumbroso, -a [e·rrum·'bro·so, -a] *adj* rusty

hervidero [er·βi·'de·ro] *m* **1.** (*manantial*) hot spring; **un ~ de intrigas** a hotbed of intrigue **2.** (*multitud*) throng

hervido [er·'βi·do] *m* **1.** (*de los alimentos, líquidos*) boiling; (*a fuego lento*) simmering **2.** (*burbujeo*) bubbling **3.** AmS (*cocido*) stew

hervidor [er·βi·'dor] *m* **1.** (*de cocina, para el agua*) kettle; (*de cocina, para la leche*) milk pan **2.** TÉC boiler

hervir [er·'βir] *irr como sentir* **I.** *vi* **1.** (*alimentos*) to boil; (*a fuego lento*) to simmer **2.** (*burbujear*) to bubble **3.** (*el mar*) to be choppy **4.** (*persona*) to get angry; **~ en cólera** to lose one's temper; **le hierve la sangre** his/her blood is boiling **5.** (*abundar*) **esta calle hierve en rumores** the street is bubbling with rumors **II.** *vt* **1.** (*bullir*) to boil **2.** (*desinfectar*) to sterilize

hervor [er·'βor] *m* **1.** (*acción*) boil; **dar un ~ a algo** to bring sth to the boil; **levantar el ~** to come to the boil; **le falta un ~** *fig* he's has a loose screw **2.** (*burbujeo*) bubbling **3.** (*de la juventud*) fervor

heterodoxo, -a [e·te·ro·'dok·so, -a] *adj* heterodox

heterogeneidad [e·te·ro·xe·nei·'dad] *f* heterogeneity

heterogéneo, -a [e·te·ro·'xe·neo, -a] *adj* heterogeneous

heterosexual [e·te·ro·sek·su·'al] *adj, mf* heterosexual

heterosexualidad [e·te·ro·sek·swa·li·'dad] *f* heterosexuality

hexagonal [ek·sa·ɣo·'nal] *adj* hexagonal

hexágono [ek·'sa·ɣo·no] *m* hexagon

hez [es, eθ] *f* 1.(*poso*) sediment 2. *pl* (*escoria*) dregs *pl* 3. *pl* (*excrementos*) feces *pl*

hibernación [i·βer·na·'sjon, -'θjon] *f* 1.ZOOL hibernation 2. MED deep sleep

hibernal [i·βer·'nal] *adj* 1.(*temporada*) winter 2. ZOOL hibernating

hibernar [i·βer·'nar] *vi* to hibernate

hibisco [i'βis·ko] *m* hibiscus

hibridación [i·βri·da·'sjon, -'θjon] *f* hybridization

híbrido ['i·βri·do] *m* BIO hybrid

híbrido, -a ['i·βri·do, -a] *adj* hybrid; **computador** ~ hybrid computer

hidalgo [i·'dal·ɣo] *m* HIST nobleman

hidalgo, -a [i·'dal·ɣo, -a] *adj* 1.(*de los nobles, noble*) noble 2.(*generoso*) gentlemanly

hidratante [i·dra·'tan·te] *adj* moisturizing; **crema** ~ moisturizer

hidratar [i·dra·'tar] *vt* (*piel*) to moisturize

hidrato [i·'dra·to] *m* hydrate

hidráulica [i·'drau·li·ka] *f* hydraulics *pl*

hidráulico, -a [i·'drau·li·ko, -a] *adj* hydraulic

hídrico, -a ['i·dri·ko, -a] *adj* 1.(*relativo al agua*) water 2.(*que contiene agua*) hydric

hidroavión [i·dro·a·βi·'on] *m* seaplane

hidrocarburo [i·dro·kar·'βu·ro] *m* hydrocarbon

hidrodinámico, -a [i·dro·di·'na·mi·ko, -a] *adj* hydrodynamic

hidroeléctrico, -a [i·dro·e·'lek·tri·ko, -a] *adj* hydroelectric; **central hidroeléctrica** hydroelectric power station

hidrofobia [i·dro·'fo·βja] *f* 1.MED (*fobia al agua*) hydrophobia 2.(*rabia*) rabies

hidrófobo, -a [i·'dro·fo·βo, -a] *adj* 1.QUÍM hydrophobic 2.(*rabioso*) rabid

hidrófugo, -a [i·'dro·fu·ɣo, -a] *adj* water-resistant

hidrogenar [i·dro·xe·'nar] *vt* to hydrogenize

hidrógeno [i·'dro·xe·no] *m* hydrogen

hidrografía [i·dro·ɣra·'fi·a] *f* hydrography

hidrográfico, -a [i·dro·'ɣra·fi·ko, -a] *adj* hydrographic

hidrológico, -a [i·dro·'lo·xi·ko, -a] *adj* hydrological

hidroplano [i·dro·'pla·no] *m* 1.AVIAT seaplane 2.NÁUT hydroplane

hidrosfera [i·dros·'fe·ra] *f* GEO hydrosphere

hidrosoluble [i·dro·so·'lu·βle] *adj* water-soluble

hidrostático, -a [i·dros·'ta·ti·ko, -a] *adj* hydrostatic

hidroterapia [i·dro·te·'ra·pja] *f* MED hydrotherapy

hidróxido [i·'drok·si·do] *m* hydroxide

hiedra ['je·dra] *f* ivy

hiel [jel] *f* 1.(*bilis*) bile 2.(*amargura*) bitterness; **echar la** ~ to sweat blood 3. *pl* (*adversidades*) troubles *pl*

hielera [je·'le·ra] *f* 1. Chile, Méx (*nevera portátil*) ice chest 2. Arg (*cubitera*) ice cube tray

hielo ['je·lo] *m* 1.(*del agua*) ice; ~ **en la carretera** black ice; ~ **picado** crushed ice; **el barco ha quedado aprisionado en el** ~ the ship is trapped in the ice; **capa** [*o* **manta**] **de** ~ icecap 2. *pl* (*helada*) frost, cold spell 3.(*frialdad*) coldness; **romper el** ~ to break the ice

hiena ['je·na] *f* hyena

hierático, -a [je·'ra·ti·ko, -a] *adj* hieratic

hierba ['jer·βa] *f* 1.(*planta*) grass; *t.* MED herb; ~ **medicinal** medicinal herb; **infusión de** ~s herbal tea; **mala** ~ weed; **tenis sobre** ~ lawn tennis 2. *inf* (*droga*) grass ▶ **como la mala** ~ like wildfire

hierbabuena [jer·βa·'βwe·na] *f* mint

hierbajo [jer·'βa·xo] *m* weed

hierra ['je·rra] *f* AmL branding

hierro ['je·rro] *m* 1.(*metal*) *t.* DEP iron; **edad del** ~ Iron Age; **salud de** ~ iron constitution; **voluntad de** ~ iron will 2.(*del ganado*) branding iron 3.(*para marcar*) brand 4.(*de lanza*) tip of spear 5.(*arma*) weapon 6.(*herramienta, golf*) iron 7. *pl* (*grilletes*) shackles *pl* 8. *pl* (*cadenas*) chains *pl*

hígado ['i·ɣa·do] *m* 1.ANAT liver 2. *pl* (*valor*) guts *pl*

higiene [i·'xje·ne] *f* hygiene; ~ **personal** personal cleanliness [*o* hygiene]

higiénico, -a [i·'xje·ni·ko, -a] *adj* hygienic; **compresa higiénica** sanitary napkin; **papel** ~ toilet paper

higienización [i·xje·ni·sa·'sjon, -θa·'θjon] *f* cleaning

higienizar <z→c> [i·xje·ni·'sar, -'θar] *vt* to clean

higo ['i·ɣo] *m* 1.(*fruto*) fig; ~ **chumbo** prickly pear 2. *inf* (*cosa sin valor*) **esto me importa un** ~ I don't give a hoot; **esto no vale un** ~ this is pure nonsense 3.(*algo arrugado*) **estar hecho un** ~ (*persona*) to be withered (up); (*ropa*) to be crumpled

higuera [i·'ɣe·ra] *f* fig tree

hijastro, -a [i·'xas·tro, -a] *m, f* stepson *m*, stepdaughter *f*

hijo, -a ['i·xo, -a] *m, f* 1.(*parentesco*) son *m*, daughter *f*; ~ **adoptivo** adopted son; **un** ~ **de papá** Daddy's boy; ~ **político** son-in-law; ~ **predilecto** (**de una ciudad**) favorite son; ~ **de puta** *vulg* bastard; ~ **único** only child; **pareja sin** ~**s** childless couple; **como cualquier** ~ **de vecino** just like everybody else; **es** ~ **de Madrid** he's from Madrid 2. *pl* (*descendencia*) children *pl*, offspring

híjole ['i·xo·le] *interj Méx, inf* (*caramba*) Jesus

hijuelar [i·xwe·'lar] *vt* Chile to parcel

hilacha [i·'la·tʃa] *f*, **hilacho** [i·'la·tʃo] *m*

raveled thread
hilada [i·'la·da] *f* (*hilera*) line
hilado [i·'la·do] *m* **1.** (*acción*) spinning **2.** (*hilo*) thread; (*en la industria*) yarn; **fábrica de ~s** yarn factory
hilador(a) [i·la·'dor, --'do·ra] *m(f)* spinning machine
hiladora [i·la·'do·ra] *f* spinner
hilandería [i·lan·de·'ri·a] *f* **1.** (*actividad, arte*) spinning **2.** (*fábrica*) textile mill
hilandero, -a [i·lan·'de·ro, -a] *m, f* spinner's
hilar [i·'lar] *vt* **1.** (*hilo, araña*) to spin **2.** (*inferir*) to work out **3.** (*cavilar*) to ponder; **~ fino** *fig* to split hairs
hilarante [i·la·'ran·te] *adj* hilarious; **gas ~** laughing gas
hilaridad [i·la·ri·'dad] *f* hilarity; **esta comedia provoca la ~ del público** this comedy has the audience in stitches
hilatura [i·la·'tu·ra] *f* **1.** (*fábrica*) textile mill **2.** (*fabricación*) spinning
hilaza [i·'la·sa, -θa] *f* **1.** (*hilo*) thread **2.** (*en la industria*) yarn
hilera [i·'le·ra] *f* **1.** (*fila, de cosas iguales*) row, line; MIL file; **colocarse en la ~** to get into line **2.** TÉC drawplate **3.** ARQUIT ridgepole
hilo ['i·lo] *m* **1.** (*para coser*) thread; (*para bordar*) yarn; (*para bordar*) floss; **~ bramante** twine; **~ dental** dental floss; **~ de perlas** string of pearls; **cortar el ~ de la vida a alguien** *fig* to cut short sb's life; **mover los ~s** *fig* to pull the strings; **pender de un ~** *fig* to hang by a thread **2.** (*tela*) linen **3.** TÉC wire; **~ conductor** thread; **telegrafía sin ~s** wireless telegraphy **4.** (*de un discurso*) gist; **no sigo el ~ de la película** I'm not following this film; **perder el ~** (*de la conversación*) to lose the thread (of the conversation) **5.** (*de un líquido*) trickle **6.** MÚS **~ musical** piped music
hilván [il·'βan] *m* **1.** (*costura*) basting **2.** (*hilo*) basting thread
hilvanado [il·βa·'na·do] *m* basting
hilvanar [il·βa·'nar] *vt* **1.** (*vestido*) to baste **2.** (*frases*) to weave together; **un discurso mal hilvanado** an incoherent speech
himen ['i·men] *m* ANAT hymen
himno ['im·no] *m* hymn; **~ nacional** national anthem
hincapié [in·ka·'pje] *m* hold; **hacer ~ en algo** to emphasize sth
hincar <c→qu> [in·'kar] **I.** *vt* **1.** (*clavar*) to stick; **~ el diente en algo** *fig, inf* to get one's teeth into sth **2.** (*pie*) to get a strong foothold, to stand firmly **II.** *vr* **~se de rodillas** to kneel down
hincha[1] ['in·tʃa] *mf* (*seguidor*) fan
hincha[2] ['in·tʃa] *f inf* (*tirria*) grudge
hinchable [in·'tʃa·βle] *adj* inflatable; **colchón ~** inflatable mattress; **muñeca ~** blow-up doll
hinchado, -a [in·'tʃa·do, -a] *adj* **1.** (*pie, madera*) swollen **2.** (*estilo*) wordy, verbose **3.** (*persona*) pompous

hinchamiento [in·tʃa·'mjen·to] *m* swelling
hinchar [in·'tʃar] **I.** *vt* **1.** (*globo*) to blow up; (*neumático*) to inflate; (*estómago*) to swell; **~ la bici** to inflate the bike tires **2.** (*exagerar*) to exaggerate; **¡no lo hinches!** come off it! **3.** (*río*) to swell **4.** AmL (*molestar*) to bother **II.** *vr:* **~ se 1.** (*pierna*) to swell; **se me ha hinchado mucho el pie** my foot's really swollen **2.** (*engreírse*) to become conceited **3.** *inf* (*de comer*) **~se** (**de algo**) to stuff oneself (with sth) **4.** (*hacer mucho*) **~se a mirar/a escuchar algo** to look at/to listen to sth non-stop; **~se a insultar a alguien** to go overboard insulting sb
hinchazón [in·tʃa·'son, -'θon] *f* **1.** (*del pie, madera*) swelling; (*del río*) flooding **2.** (*soberbia*) conceit **3.** (*de un estilo*) pomposity
hindi ['in·di] *m* Hindi
hindú [in·'du] *mf* **1.** (*indio*) Indian **2.** (*del hinduismo*) Hindu
hinduismo [in·du·'is·mo] *m* REL Hinduism
hinojo [i·'no·xo] *m* **1.** (*planta*) fennel **2.** HIST (*rodilla*) knee; **de ~s** on one's knees; **ponerse de ~s** to get down on one's knees
hipar [i·'par] *vi* **1.** (*tener hipo*) to have the hiccups **2.** (*perros*) to pant **3.** (*fatigarse*) to get tired **4.** (*sollozar*) to whine **5.** (*desear*) **~ por algo/alguien** to long for sth/sb
hiperactividad [i·per·ak·ti·βi·'dad] *f* hyperactivity
hiperactivo, -a [i·per·ak·'ti·βo, -a] *adj* hyperactive
hipérbola [i·'per·βo·la] *f* MAT hyperbola
hipérbole [i·'per·βo·le] *f* LIT hyperbole
hiperbólico, -a [i·per·'βo·li·ko, -a] *adj* MAT hyperbolic
hipercrítico, -a [i·per·'kri·ti·ko, -a] *adj* hypercritical, overcritical
hiperenlace [i·per·en·'la·se, -θe] *m* hyperlink
hipermercado [i·per·mer·'ka·do] *m* superstore
hipermétrope [i·per·'me·tro·pe] *adj* MED far-sighted
hipermetropía [i·per·me·tro·'pi·a] *f* MED far-sightedness
hiperrealismo [i·per·rrea·'lis·mo] *m* hyperrealism
hipersensibilidad [i·per·sen·si·βi·li·'dad] *f* hypersensitivity
hipersensible [i·per·sen·'si·βle] *adj* hypersensitive, oversensitive
hipertensión [i·per·ten·'sjon] *f* MED high blood pressure
hipertenso, -a [i·per·'ten·so, -a] **I.** *adj* suffering from high blood pressure **II.** *m, f* person with high blood pressure; **mi padre es ~** my father has high blood pressure
hipertexto [i·per·'tes·to] *m* hypertext
hipertrofia [i·per·'tro·fja] *f* MED hypertrophy
hipertrofiarse [i·per·tro·'fjar·se] *vr* MED to hypertrophy
hípica ['i·pi·ka] *f* (*general*) horsemanship; (*montar*) riding; (*carreras*) horse racing

H

hípico, -a ['i·pi·ko, -a] *adj* equestrian, horse

hipido [i·'pi·do] *m* whimper, sob

hipnosis [ip·'no·sis] *f inv* hypnosis

hipnótico [iβ·'no·ti·ko] *m* MED sedative

hipnótico, -a [iβ·'no·ti·ko, -a] *adj* hypnotic

hipnotismo [iβ·no·'tis·mo] *m* hypnotism

hipnotización [iβ·no·ti·sa·'sjon, -θa·'θjon] *f* hypnotizing

hipnotizador(a) [iβ·no·ti·sa·'dor, -·'do·ra; iβ·no·ti·θa-] *m(f)* hypnotizer

hipnotizar <z→c> [iβ·no·ti·'sar, -'θar] *vt* to hypnotize

hipo ['ipo] *m* 1. (*fisiológico*) hiccup; **tener ~** to have the hiccups 2. (*deseo*) **~ de algo** longing for sth; **...que quita el ~** *fig* ... that takes your breath away 3. (*tirria*) grudge

hipocondría [i·po·kon·'dri·a] *f* MED hypochondria

hipocondríaco, -a [i·po·kon·'dri·a·ko, -a] *adj, m, f* hypochondriac

hipocrático, -a [i·po·'kra·ti·ko, -a] *adj* Hippocratic; **el juramento ~** the Hippocratic oath

hipocresía [i·po·kre·'si·a] *f* hypocrisy

hipócrita [i·'po·kri·ta] I. *adj* hypocritical II. *mf* hypocrite

hipodérmico, -a [i·po·'der·mi·ko, -a] *adj* MED hypodermic

hipódromo [i·'po·dro·mo] *m* DEP racetrack

hipófisis [i·'po·fi·sis] *f inv* ANAT pituitary gland

hipopótamo [i·po·'po·ta·mo] *m* hippopotamus

hipoteca [i·po·'te·ka] *f* mortgage

hipotecable [i·po·te·'ka·βle] *adj* mortgageable

hipotecar <c→qu> [i·po·te·'kar] *vt* to mortgage; **si haces eso ~ás tu libertad** if you do that you're signing away your freedom

hipotecario, -a [i·po·te·'ka·rjo, -a] *adj* mortgage; **crédito ~** mortgage loan

hipotensión [i·po·ten·'sjon] *f* MED low blood pressure

hipotenso, -a [i·po·'ten·so, -a] I. *adj* suffering from low blood pressure II. *m, f* **ser ~** to have low blood pressure

hipotenusa [i·po·te·'nu·sa] *f* MAT hypotenuse

hipotermia [i·po·'ter·mja] *f* MED hypothermia; **muerte por ~** death from hypothermia

hipótesis [i·'po·te·sis] *f inv* hypothesis

hipotético, -a [i·po·'te·ti·ko, -a] *adj* hypothetical; **es totalmente ~ que...** we cannot be at all sure that...

hippie ['xi·pi], **hippy** ['xi·pi] I. *adj* hippy; **moda ~** hippy style II. *mf* hippy

hiriente [i·'rjen·te] *adj* hurtful

hirsuto, -a [ir·'su·to, -a] *adj* 1. (*pelo*) hairy, shaggy 2. (*planta*) bristly 3. (*carácter*) surly, brusque

hirviente [ir·'βjen·te] *adj* boiling

hisopo [i·'so·po] *m* 1. (*planta*) hyssop 2. (*de iglesia*) aspergillum

hispánico, -a [is·'pa·ni·ko, -a] *adj* 1. (*de España*) Spanish 2. (*de Hispania*) Hispanic; **Filología Hispánica** Spanish Language and Literature

hispanidad [is·pa·ni·'dad] *f* 1. (*calidad*) Spanishness 2. (*conjunto*) Spanish-speaking world

hispanismo [is·pa·'nis·mo] *m* UNIV Hispanicism

hispanista [is·pa·'nis·ta] *mf* Hispanist, Hispanicist

hispanizar <z→c> [is·pa·ni·'sar, -'θar] *vt, vr:* **~se** to adopt Spanish ways

hispano, -a [is·'pa·no, -a] I. *adj* 1. (*español*) Spanish 2. (*en EE.UU.*) Hispanic II. *m, f* 1. (*español*) Spaniard 2. (*en EE.UU.*) Hispanic

Hispanoamérica [is·pa·no·a·'me·ri·ka] *f* Spanish America

> **ⓘ Hispanoamérica** is a generic term that includes all the countries in Central and South America where Spanish is (officially) spoken. There are nineteen nations in all: **Argentina, Bolivia, Chile, Colombia, Costa Rica, Cuba, Ecuador, El Salvador, Guatemala, Honduras, México, Nicaragua, Panamá, Paraguay, Perú, Puerto Rico, República Dominicana, Uruguay** and **Venezuela**. In contrast, the collective term **Latinoamérica** (or **América Latina**) applies to all the countries in Central and South America that were colonized by the Spaniards, Portuguese, and French.

---

hispanoamericano, -a [is·pa·no·a·me·ri·'ka·no, -a] *adj, m, f* Spanish American

hispanohablante [is·pa·no·a·'βlan·te] I. *adj* Spanish-speaking; **los países ~s** Spanish-speaking countries II. *mf* Spanish speaker

histeria [is·'te·rja] *f* hysteria

histérico, -a [is·'te·ri·ko, -a] I. *adj* hysterical II. *m, f* hysterical person

histerismo [is·te·'ris·mo] *m* hysteria

historia [is·'to·rja] *f* 1. (*antigüedad*) history; **~ natural** natural history; **~ universal** universal [*o* world] history; **pasar a la ~** (*ser importante*) to go down in history; (*no ser actual*) to be out of date 2. *t. inf* story; **cuenta la ~ completa** tell the whole story; **ésa es la misma ~ de siempre** it's the same old story; **eso sólo son ~s** that doesn't prove anything; **ya sabes la ~** you know what I'm talking about; **¡déjate de ~s!** stop fooling around; **¡no me vengas con ~s!** come off it

historiador(a) [is·to·rja·'dor, -·'do·ra] *m(f)* historian

historial [is·to·'rjal] I. *adj* historical II. *m* 1. (*antecedentes*) file, record; **~ delictivo** police record 2. (*currículo*) curriculum vitae; **~ profesional** professional background; **este hecho no empañará el ~ de esta institución** this will not tarnish the reputation of this institution; **él tiene un ~ intachable** he has an impeccable record

historiar [is·to·'rjar] *vt* 1. (*contar*) to tell the

story of **2.** ARTE to paint **3.** *AmL* (*enmarañar*) to complicate

historicismo [is·to·ri·'sis·mo, -'θis·mo] *m* historicism

histórico, -a [is·'to·ri·ko, -a] *adj* (*que tiene que ver con la historia*) historical; (*acontecimiento*) historic; **un miembro ~ del partido** a longstanding party member

historieta [is·to·'rje·ta] *f* **1.** (*anécdota*) anecdote **2.** (*con viñetas*) comic strip

historiografía [is·to·rjo·ɣra·'fi·a] *f* historiography

historiógrafo, -a [is·to·'rjo·ɣra·fo, -a] *m, f* historiographer

histrión [is·'trjon] *m* **1.** (*actor*) actor **2.** (*payaso*) clown

histriónico, -a [is·'trjo·ni·ko, -a] *adj* histrionic

hito ['i·to] *m* (*mojón*) milestone

hobby ['xo·βi] *m* <hobbies> hobby

hocicar <c→qu> [o·si·'kar, o·θi-] I. *vt* (*hozar*) **~ algo** to root around in sth II. *vi* **1.** (*caerse*) to fall flat on one's face **2.** *inf* (*dificultad*) to run into trouble **3.** (*dar de bruces*) to run [*o* bump] into III. *vi, vt* (*tocar(se)*) to nuzzle

hocico [o·'si·ko, o·'θi-] *m* **1.** (*morro*) muzzle; (*de cerdo*) snout **2.** *inf* (*cara*) mug; **caer de ~ s** to fall on one's face; **estar de ~ s** to be in a bad mood; **meter el ~ en todo** *fig* to stick one's nose in everything

hocicudo, -a [o·si·'ku·do, -a; o·'θi-] *adj AmL* **1.** (*persona*) thick-lipped **2.** (*animal*) long-snouted

hockey ['xo·kei] *m* hockey; **~ sobre hielo/hierba** ice/field hockey

hogar [o·'ɣar] *m* **1.** (*casa*) home; **~ del pensionista** old people's home; **~ de adopción** foster home; **artículos para el ~** household items; **persona sin ~** homeless person **2.** (*familia*) family; **la vida del ~** family life; **crear un ~** to start a family **3.** (*de cocina, de tren*) boiler; (*de chimenea*) hearth; (*de fundición*) furnace

hogareño, -a [o·ɣa·'re·ɲo, -a] *adj* **1.** (*ambiente*) family **2.** (*persona*) domestic

hogaza [o·'ɣa·sa, -θa] *f large loaf of bread*

hoguera [o·'ɣe·ra] *f* **1.** (*en un campamento*) bonfire; (*de alegría*) blaze **2.** HIST (*ejecución*) stake; **morir en la ~** to be burnt at the stake

hoja ['o·xa] *f* **1.** (*de una planta*) leaf; (*pétalo*) petal; **~ s del bosque** forest leaves; **árbol sin ~ s** leafless tree; **los árboles vuelven a echar ~ s** the leaves on the trees are sprouting again **2.** (*de papel*) sheet; **~ de lata** tinplate; **~ volante** leaflet, flyer; **~ de una mesa** (*extensible*) table flap; **pasar la ~** to turn the page; **~ de movilización** MIL call-up paper; **no hay** [*o* tiene] **vuelta de ~** *fig* there's no doubt about it **3.** (*formulario*) form; **~ de estudios** educational record; **~ de pedido** order form; **~ de servicios** service record **4.** (*de arma*) blade; **~ de afeitar** razor blade **5.** (*de ventana*) pane

hojalata [o·xa·'la·ta] *f* tinplate

hojalatería [o·xa·la·te·'ri·a] *f* (*local*) tinsmith's (shop); (*mercancía*) tinware

hojaldre [o·'xal·dre] *m* puff pastry; **pastel de ~** puff

hojarasca [o·xa·'ras·ka] *f* **1.** (*hojas*) fallen [*o* dead] leaves **2.** (*estilo*) waffle

hojear [o·xe·'ar] *vt* to browse through

hojoso, -a [o·'xo·so, -a] *adj* leafy

hojuela [o·'xwe·la] *f* **1.** (*hoja*) small leaf **2.** CULIN pancake; (*aceitunas*) crushed olives **3.** *AmC* (*hojaldre*) puff pastry

hola ['o·la] *interj* hello

holán [o·'lan] *m AmC* (*lienzo*) canvas

holanda [o·'lan·da] *f* cheese; (*tela*) fine linen

Holanda [o·'lan·da] *f* the Netherlands

holandés, -esa [o·lan·des, -·'de·sa] I. *adj* Dutch; **la escuela holandesa** ARTE the Dutch school II. *m, f* Dutchman *m,* Dutchwoman *f*

holding ['xol·din] *m* <holdings> COM holding company; **el ~ de empresas fiduciarias** the holding of fiduciary companies

holgado, -a [ol·'ɣa·do, -a] *adj* **1.** (*vestido*) loose **2.** (*espacioso*) spacious; **en este coche se va ~** there's lots of space in this car; **ir ~ de tiempo** to have plenty of time

holganza [ol·'ɣan·sa, -θa] *f* **1.** (*ociosidad*) leisure; (*agradable*) rest **2.** (*diversión*) enjoyment; (*regocijo*) merriment

holgar [ol·'ɣar] *irr como colgar* I. *vi* **1.** (*sobrar*) to be unnecessary; **huelgan las palabras** what can you say?; **huelga decir que...** needless to say that... **2.** (*descansar*) to relax II. *vr:* **~ se 1.** (*alegrarse*) **~ se de** [*o* con] algo to be pleased with sth **2.** (*divertirse*) **~ se de algo** to have a good time with sth

holgazán, -ana [ol·ɣa·'san, -·'sa·na; -'θan, -·'θa·na] *m, f* loafer

holgazanear [ol·ɣa·sa·ne·'ar, ol·ɣa·θa-] *vi* to loaf around

holgazanería [ol·ɣa·sa·ne·'ri·a, ol·ɣa·θa-] *f* laziness

holgorio [ol·'ɣo·rjo] *m v.* **jolgorio**

holgura [ol·'ɣu·ra] *f* **1.** (*de vestido*) looseness **2.** (*bienestar*) **vivir con ~** to live comfortably

hollín [o·'ʎin] *m* soot

holocausto [o·lo·'kaus·to] *m* **1.** (*genocidio*) holocaust **2.** REL sacrifice

holografía [o·lo·ɣra·'fi·a] *f* holography

holograma [o·lo·'ɣra·ma] *m* hologram

hombracho [om·'bra·tʃo] *m,* **hombrachón** [om·bra·'tʃon] *m* strong man; *pey* brute

hombre ['om·bre] I. *m* **1.** (*varón*) man; **el ~ de la calle** *fig* the man in the street; **~ de las cavernas** caveman; **~ de confianza** right-hand man; **~ de estado** statesman; **~ del montón** nobody special; **~ de negocios** businessman; **~ de paja** front man; **el ~ medio** the average man; **el ~ del saco** the boogeyman; **ser ~ de dos caras** to be two-faced; **el ~ del tiempo** the weatherman; **el defensa fue al ~** DEP the defender went for the man; **¡está hecho un ~!** he's become a man!; **hacer un ~ de alguien** to make a man out of sb; **se comportó**

como un ~ he behaved like a man; **¡~ al agua!** man overboard! **2.** (*especie humana*) **el ~** mankind **II.** *interj* (*sorpresa*) well, well; (*duda*) well...; **¡~!, ¿qué tal?** hey! how's it going?; **¡cállate, ~!** c'mon, give it a rest; **¡pero, ~!** but, come on!; **¡sí, ~!** yes, of course!

hombre-anuncio ['om·bre-a·'nun·sjo, -θjo] *m* <hombres-anuncio> sandwich man

hombre-lobo ['om·bre-'lo·βo] *m* <hombres-lobo> werewolf

hombrera [om·'bre·ra] *f* **1.** (*almohadilla*) shoulder pad **2.** (*de uniforme*) epaulet(te) **3.** (*de armadura*) shoulder plate

hombre-rana ['om·bre-'rra·na] *m* <hombres-rana> frogman

hombría [om·'bri·a] *f* **1.** (*conducta*) uprightness **2.** (*comportamiento*) manliness; **un acto de ~** a worthy action

hombro ['om·bro] *m* ANAT, TIPO shoulder; **ancho de ~s** broad-shouldered; **cargado de ~s** round-shouldered; **encogerse de ~s** to shrug one's shoulders; **llevar algo a ~s** carry sth on one's shoulders ▸ **arrimar el ~** to lend a hand; **mirar a alguien por encima del ~** to snub sb

hombruno, -a [om·'bru·no, -a] *adj* mannish; **mujer hombruna** mannish woman

homenaje [o·me·'na·xe] *m* **1.** (*el honrar*) tribute; **hacer una fiesta en ~ de alguien** to celebrate in honor of sb; **rendir ~ a alguien** to pay homage to sb **2.** HIST obedience, allegiance

homenajear [o·me·na·xe·'ar] *vt* to pay tribute to

homeópata [o·me·'o·pa·ta] *mf* homeopath

homeopatía [o·meo·pa·'ti·a] *f* homeopathic medicine

homeopático, -a [o·meo·'pa·ti·ko, -a] *adj* homeopathic

homicida [o·mi·'si·da, -'θi·da] **I.** *adj* homicidal; **el arma ~** the murder weapon **II.** *mf* (*planeado*) murderer *m*, murderess *f*; (*no planeado*) person guilty of manslaughter

homicidio [o·mi·'si·djo, -'θi·djo] *m* homicide; (*planeado*) murder; (*no planeado*) manslaughter; **~ frustrado** attempted murder; **brigada de ~s** murder squad

homínido [o·'mi·ni·do] *m* BIO hominid

homo ['o·mo] *adj inf* gay

homogeneidad [o·mo·xe·nei·'dad] *f* homogeneity

homogeneización [o·mo·xe·nei·sa·'sjon, -θa·'θjon] *f* homogenization

homogeneizar <z→c> [o·mo·xe·nei·'sar, -'θar] *vt* **1.** *t.* QUÍM to homogenize **2.** (*uniformar*) to standardize

homogéneo, -a [o·mo·'xe·neo, -a] *adj* homogeneous, uniform

homógrafo [o·'mo·ɣra·fo] *m* homograph

homógrafo, -a [o·'mo·ɣra·fo, -a] *adj* homographic

homologable [o·mo·lo·'ɣa·βle] *adj* equivalent; **el récord no es ~** the record cannot be accepted

homologación [o·mo·lo·ɣa·'sjon, -'θjon] *f* **1.** (*de una escuela*) validation, accreditation **2.** DEP (*de un récord*) official recognition **3.** TÉC (*de un casco*) authorization **4.** JUR (*de un arreglo*) confirmation; (*de un convenio*) ratification

homologar <g→gu> [o·mo·lo·'ɣar] **I.** *vt* **1.** (*escuela*) to validate **2.** DEP (*récord*) to recognize officially **3.** TÉC to authorize **4.** JUR (*arreglo*) to confirm; (*convenio*) to ratify **II.** *vr:* **~se** to be officially recognized

homólogo, -a [o·'mo·lo·ɣo, -a] **I.** *adj* equivalent **II.** *m, f* counterpart

homónimo [o·'mo·ni·mo] *m* namesake

homónimo, -a [o·'mo·ni·mo, -a] **I.** *adj* homonymous **II.** *m, f* homonym

homosexual [o·mo·sek·'swal] *adj, mf* homosexual

homosexualidad [o·mo·sek·swa·li·'dad] *f* homosexuality

honda ['on·da] *f* sling

hondo ['on·do] *m* depth

hondo, -a ['on·do, -a] *adj* deep; **en lo ~ del valle** in the depths of the valley; **respirar ~** to breathe deeply; **cante ~** *purist Flamenco musical style*

hondonada [on·do·'na·da] *f* GEO depression, hollow

hondura [on·'du·ra] *f* depth; **meterse en ~s** *fig* to get into deep water

Honduras [on·'du·ras] *f* Honduras

i **Honduras** is located in Central America and borders on **Nicaragua**, **El Salvador**, and **Guatemala**, as well as the Caribbean Sea and the Pacific Ocean. The capital is **Tegucigalpa**. The country's official language is Spanish and the official currency of **Honduras** is the **lempira**.

hondureño, -a [on·du·'re·ɲo, -a] *adj, m, f* Honduran

honestidad [o·nes·ti·'dad] *f* honesty

honesto, -a [o·'nes·to, -a] *adj* honest

hongo ['on·go] *m* **1.** BOT fungus; (*comestible*) mushroom **2.** (*sombrero*) derby (hat)

honor [o·'nor] *m* honor; **cuestión de ~** matter of honor; **¡palabra de ~!** word of honor!; **¡por mi ~!** on my honor!; **hacer ~ a su fama** to honor his/her name; **es para mí un gran ~** it is a great honor for me; **hacer los ~es** to do the honors

honorabilidad [o·no·ra·βi·li·'dad] *f* honor

honorable [o·no·'ra·βle] *adj* honorable

honorario, -a [o·no·'ra·rjo] *adj* honorary; **cónsul ~** honorary consul

honorífico, -a [o·no·'ri·fi·ko, -a] *adj* honorary

honra ['on·rra] *f* **1.** (*honor, reputación*) honor; **¡a mucha ~!** I'm proud of it! **2.** REL **~s fúnebres** funeral proceedings

honradez [on·rra·'des, -'deθ] *f* (*honestidad*) honesty; (*integridad*) integrity; **falta de ~** lack of integrity

honrado, -a [on·'rra·do, -a] *adj* (*íntegro, moral*) honorable; (*decente*) upright; **llevar una vida honrada** to lead an honorable life

honrar [on·'rrar] **I.** *vt* to honor; **nos honra con su presencia** he/she honors us with his/her presence **II.** *vr* ~**se con** [*o* **de**] **algo** to be an honor for sb

honroso, -a [on·'rro·so, -a] *adj* honorable

hora ['o·ra] *f* **1.** (*de un día*) hour; ~**s de consulta** surgery hours; ~**s extraordinarias** overtime; ~ **feliz** happy hour; ~(**s**) **punta** rush hour; **un cuarto de** ~ a quarter of an hour; **media** ~ half an hour; **una** ~ **y media** an hour and a half; **a última** ~ at the last minute; **a primera/última** ~ **de la tarde** in the early/ late afternoon; **noticias de última** ~ last-minute news; **el pueblo está a dos** ~**s de camino** the village is a two-hour walk from here; **estuve esperando** ~**s y** ~**s** I was waiting for hours and hours; **a la** ~ on time **2.** (*del reloj*) time; **¿qué** ~ **es?** what time is it?, what's the time?; **¿a qué** ~ **vendrás?** what time are you coming?; **adelantar la** ~ to put [*o* set] the clock forward; **poner el reloj en** ~ to set one's watch; **retrasar la** ~ to put [*o* set] the clock back; **me ha dado** [*o* **tengo**] ~ **para el martes** I have an appointment for Tuesday **3.** (*tiempo*) time; **a la** ~ **de la verdad...** when it comes down to it...; **comer entre** ~**s** to eat between meals; **estar en** ~**s bajas** to be feeling down; **no lo dejes para última** ~ don't leave it till the last minute; **tener** (**muchas**) ~**s de vuelo** *fig* to be (very) experienced; **ven a cualquier** ~ come at any time; **ya va siendo** ~ **que tomes tus propias decisiones** it is about time that you made your own decisions **4.** *pl* (*mitología*) **las** ~**s** the seasons

horario ['o·ra·rjo] *m* **1.** (*escolar, de medio de transporte*) timetable, schedule; (*de consulta*) surgery hours; ~ **de atención al público** opening hours; ~ **flexible** flextime; ~ **de oficina** office hours; **¿qué** ~ **hacen?** what hours do they work?; **tenemos** ~ **de tarde** we work evenings **2.** (*manecilla del reloj*) hour hand

horario, -a ['o·ra·rjo, -a] *adj* hourly

horca ['or·ka] *f* **1.** (*para colgar*) gallows *pl* **2.** (*bieldo*) winnowing fork **3.** (*horquilla*) pitchfork

horcajadas [or·ka·'xa·das] **a** ~ astride

horchata [or·'tʃa·ta] *f* **1.** orgeat (*refreshing drink made of tiger nut juice, water and sugar*) **2.** *Méx:* rice drink with sugar and cinnammon

horda ['or·da] *f* **1.** (*de salvajes*) horde **2.** (*banda*) violent group

horizontal [o·ri·son·'tal, o·ri·θon-] **I.** *adj* horizontal **II.** *f* horizontal position

horizontalidad [o·ri·son·ta·li·'dad, o·ri·θon-] *f* horizontality

horizonte [o·ri·'son·te, -'θon·te] *m* horizon

horma ['or·ma] *f* **1.** TÉC (*molde*) mold **2.** (*muelle*) ~ **de zapatos** shoetree

hormiga [or·'mi·ɣa] *f* ant; ~ **blanca** white ant; **ser una** ~ *fig* to be always working

hormigón [or·mi·'ɣon] *m* concrete; ~ **armado** reinforced concrete

hormigonera [or·mi·ɣo·'ne·ra] *f* concrete mixer

hormiguear [or·mi·ɣe·'ar] *vi* **1.** (*picar*) to tingle, to itch **2.** (*gente, insectos*) to swarm; ~ **de algo** to seethe [*o* teem] with sth

hormigueo [or·mi·'ɣeo] *m* **1.** (*picor*) pins and needles; **tengo un** ~ **en la espalda** my back is itching **2.** (*multitud*) swarming

hormiguero [or·mi·'ɣe·ro] *m* **1.** (*de hormigas*) anthill **2.** (*de gente*) swarm; **la plaza era un** ~ **de gente** the square was seething with people

hormiguero, -a [or·mi·'ɣe·ro, -a] *adj* related to ants; **oso** ~ anteater

hormona [or·'mo·na] *f* hormone

hormonal [or·mo·'nal] *adj* hormone, hormonal

hornacina [or·na·'si·na, -'θi·na] *f* ARQUIT (vaulted) niche

hornada [or·'na·da] *f* **1.** (*de horno*) batch **2.** (*conjunto*) **una** ~ **de médicos** a group of doctors

hornalla [or·'na·ja, -ʎa] *f* *AmL* **1.** (*parrilla*) barbecue **2.** (*del fogón*) hot plate **3.** (*horno*) oven

hornear [or·ne·'ar] *vt* to bake

hornero, -a [or·'ne·ro, -a] *m, f* baker

hornillo [or·'ni·to·pjo, -ʎo] *m* (*cocina*) stove; (*de una cocina*) ring; ~ **de gas** gas ring; ~ **portátil** portable cooker

horno ['or·no] *m* **1.** (*cocina*) oven; ~ **microondas** microwave oven; **recién salido del** ~ straight from [*o* out of] the oven; **asar al** ~ to oven roast **2.** TÉC furnace; ~ **crematorio** cremation furnace; **alto** ~ blast furnace; (*para cerámica*) kiln

horóscopo [o·'ros·ko·po] *m* horoscope

horqueta [or·'ke·ta] *f* **1.** (*horca*) winnowing fork **2.** (*horquilla*) pitchfork **3.** (*de un árbol*) fork

horquilla [or·'ki·ja, -ʎa] *f* **1.** (*del pelo*) bobby pin; (*de moño*) hairpin **2.** (*de bicicleta, árbol*) fork **3.** TÉC yoke

horrendo, -a [o·'rren·do, -a] *adj v.* **horroroso**

hórreo ['o·rreo] *m* raised granary

horrible [o·'rri·βle] *adj* **1.** (*horroroso*) horrible; **un crimen** ~ a ghastly crime; **una historia** ~ a horrible story **2.** (*muy feo*) grotesque

horripilante [o·rri·pi·'lan·te] *adj* horrifying

horripilar [o·rri·pi·'lar] **I.** *vt* **1.** (*erizar*) ~ **a alguien** to make sb's hair stand on end; **estas historias me horripilan** I'm horrified by these stories **2.** (*horrorizar*) to horrify **II.** *vr:* ~**se** to be horrified

horror [o·'rror] *m* **1.** (*miedo, aversión*) horror; **tener** ~ **a algo** to have a horror of sth; **siento** ~ **a la oscuridad** I'm terrified of the dark; **me da** ~ **verte con esta corbata** you look terrible with that tie on; **el diseño moderno me parece un** ~ I don't like modern design at all; **¡qué** ~**!** *inf* how horrible! **2.** *pl* (*actos*) **los**

H

~**es de la guerra** the atrocities of war **3.** *inf* (*mucho*) **ganar un ~ de dinero** to earn a lot of money; **hoy hace un ~ de frío** it's hellishly cold today; **me cuesta ~es** it's very hard for me; **me gusta ~es el regalo** I absolutely love the gift

horrorizar <z→c> [o·rro·ri·'sar, -'θar] **I.** *vt* to horrify; **me horrorizó ver el accidente** I was horrified by the accident **II.** *vr* **~ se de algo** to be horrified [*o* terrified] by sth

horroroso, -a [o·rro·'ro·so, -a] *adj* horrifying; **una escena horrorosa** a terrible scene; **su última novela es horrorosa** his/her last novel is awful

hortaliza [or·ta·'li·sa, -θa] *f* vegetable

hortelano, -a [or·te·'la·no, -a] *m, f* truck gardener; **~ aficionado** amateur gardener

hortensia [or·'ten·sja] *f* hydrangea

hortera¹ [or·'te·ra] *inf* **I.** *adj* vulgar, tasteless, tacky **II.** *m* vulgar person

hortera² [or·'te·ra] *f* wooden bowl

horterada [or·te·'ra·da] *f inf* tasteless thing; **esta película es una ~** this film is so tacky

hortícola [or·'ti·ko·la] *adj* horticultural; **productos ~s** horticultural produce

horticultor(a) [or·ti·kul·'tor, -·'to·ra] *m(f)* gardener

horticultura [or·ti·kul·'tu·ra] *f* horticulture

hortofrutícola [or·to·fru·'ti·ko·la] *adj* fruit and vegetable gardening

hortofruticultura [or·to·fru·ti·kul·'tu·ra] *f* fruit and vegetable growing

hosco, -a ['os·ko, -a] *adj* **1.** (*persona*) gruff **2.** (*ambiente*) unpleasant, hostile

hospedaje [os·pe·'da·xe] *m* **1.** (*acción, situación*) residence; **dar ~ a alguien** to put sb up **2.** (*coste*) rent

hospedar [os·pe·'dar] **I.** *vt* to accommodate **II.** *vr:* **~se** to stay

hospedería [os·pe·de·'ri·a] *f* **1.** (*fonda*) inn **2.** (*en convento*) hospice

hospicio [os·'pi·sjo, -θjo] *m* **1.** (*para niños*) children's home **2.** (*para pobres, en un monasterio*) hospice

hospital [os·pi·'tal] *m* hospital; **~ militar** military hospital

hospitalario, -a [os·pi·ta·'la·rjo, -a] *adj* **1.** (*acogedor*) welcoming, hospitable **2.** (*de hospital*) hospital

hospitalidad [os·pi·ta·li·'dad] *f* hospitality

hospitalización [os·pi·ta·li·sa·'sjon, -θa·'θjon] *f* **1.** (*envío*) hospitalization **2.** (*estancia*) stay in hospital

hospitalizar <z→c> [os·pi·ta·li·'sar, -'θar] *vt* to hospitalize; **ayer ~on a mi madre** yesterday my mother went into hospital; **estoy hospitalizado desde el domingo** I've been in hospital since Sunday

hosquedad [os·ke·'dad] *f* **1.** (*de una persona*) gruffness **2.** (*de un lugar*) dismalness

hostal [os·'tal] *m* cheap hotel

hostelería [os·te·le·'ri·a] *f* **1.** ECON hotel business **2.** ENS hotel management; **escuela**

superior de ~ school of hotel management

hostelero, -a [os·te·'le·ro, -a] **I.** *adj* hotel **II.** *m, f* hotelier

hostería [os·te·'ri·a] *f* inn

hostia ['os·tja] *f* **1.** REL host; (*sin consagrar*) wafer **2.** *inf* smack; (*golpe*) bash; **darse una ~** (*chocar*) to smash

hostiar [os·'tjar] *vt vulg* (*bofetada, golpe*) to belt

hostigador(a) [os·ti·ɣa·'dor, -·'do·ra] *adj* annoying

hostigamiento [os·ti·ɣa·'mjen·to] *m* **1.** (*fustigación*) whipping **2.** (*molestia*) annoyance **3.** (*apremio*) harassment

hostigante [os·ti·'ɣan·te] *adj Col* (*sabor*) sickly; (*persona*) annoying

hostigar <g→gu> [os·ti·'ɣar] *vt* **1.** (*fustigar*) to whip **2.** (*molestar*) to bother; (*con observaciones*) to harass **3.** (*incitar*) to incite **4.** MIL to make small attacks

hostigoso, -a [os·ti·'ɣo·so, -a] *adj Chile, Guat, Perú* cloying

hostil [os·'til] *adj* hostile; **le hicieron un recibimiento ~** he was given a hostile reception

hostilidad [os·ti·li·'dad] *f* hostility

hostión [os·'tjon] *m vulg* heavy clout

hotel [o·'tel] *m* **1.** (*establecimiento*) hotel; **~ residencia** boarding house, guesthouse **2.** (*casa*) country house, villa; (*mansión*) mansion

hotelero, -a [o·te·'le·ro, -a] *adj* hotel; **industria hotelera** hotel business **II.** *m, f* hotelier, hotelkeeper

hovercraft [o·βer·'kraf] *m* <hovercrafts> hovercraft

hoy [oi] *adv* today; **~ (en) día** nowadays; **llegará de ~ a mañana** it will arrive any time now; **de ~ en adelante** from now on; **los niños de ~ (en día)** children nowadays; **llegará de ~ a mañana** it will arrive today or tomorrow

hoyo ['o·jo] *m* **1.** (*concavidad*) hollow **2.** (*agujero*) hole **3.** (*sepultura*) grave

hoyuelo [o·'jwe·lo] *m* dimple

hoz [os, oθ] *f* AGR sickle

huacal [wa·'kal] *m And, Méx: wooden box*

huachafoso, -a [wa·ʧa·'fo·so, -a] *adj Perú* affected, pretentious

huaico ['wai·ko] *m Perú* landslide

huarache [wa·'ra·ʧe] *m Méx* **1.** (*sandalia*) sandal **2.** CULIN *corn dough filled with fried beans*

huarmi ['war·mi] *f AmS* **1.** (*mujer muy trabajadora*) hardworking woman **2.** (*ama de casa*) housewife

huasca ['was·ka] *f AmL* (*látigo*) whip

huaso, -a ['wa·so, -a] **I.** *adj AmS* (*campesino*) peasant **II.** *m, f AmS* (*campesino*) peasant

hubo ['u·βo] *3. pret de* **haber**

hucha ['u·ʧa] *f* **1.** (*alcancía*) moneybox, piggy bank **2.** (*ahorros*) savings

hueco ['we·ko] *m* **1.** (*agujero*) hole; **~ del ascensor** elevator shaft; **~ de la mano** hollow of the hand; **~ de la ventana** window space **2.** (*lugar*) space; **hazme un ~** move over **3.** (*tiempo*) time; **hazme un ~ para mañana** make time for me tomorrow

hueco, -a ['we·ko, -a] *adj* **1.** (*ahuecado*) hole; (*vacío*) empty **2.** (*sonido*) resonant **3.** (*tierra*) soft **4.** (*palabras*) empty **5.** (*persona*) vain; **ponerse ~** to become vain; **tener la cabeza hueca** *pey* to be thick **6.** (*estilo*) trite

huelga ['wel·ɣa] *f* strike; **~ de advertencia** warning strike; **~ de brazos caídos** sit-down strike; **~ general** general strike; **~ de hambre** hunger strike; **~ salvaje** wildcat strike; **convocar una ~** to call a strike; **declararse en** [*o* **hacer**] **~** to go on strike

huelguista [wel·'ɣis·ta] *mf* striker

huella ['we·ja, -ʎa] *f* **1.** (*señal*) mark; **~ de un animal** animal track; **~ dactilar** fingerprint **2.** (*vestigio*) trace; (*pasos*) footsteps; **seguir las ~s de alguien** to follow sb's footsteps

huérfano, -a ['wer·fa·no, -a] **I.** *adj* orphan; **ser ~ de padre** to have no father; **quedarse ~** to become an orphan; **la ciudad se queda huérfana en invierno** the city empties in winter **II.** *m, f* orphan

huerta ['wer·ta] *f* (*frutales*) orchard; (*hortalizas*) truck garden

huertero, -a [wer·'te·ro, -a] *m, f Arg, Nic, Perú* truck gardener

huerto ['wer·to] *m* (*hortalizas*) vegetable patch; (*frutales*) orchard; **~ familiar** allotment

huesera [we·'se·ra] *f Chile* ossuary

hueso ['we·so] *m* **1.** ANAT bone; **carne sin ~** boneless meat; **estar en los ~s** to be a rack of bones **2.** (*de fruto*) pit **3.** (*faena*) task; **un ~ duro de roer** a hard nut to crack; **este profesor es un ~** this teacher's really strict **4.** *AmL* (*trabajo*) hard work

huésped ['wes·ped] *m t.* BIO host

huésped(a) ['wes·ped, ··pe·da] *m(f)* guest

hueste ['wes·te] *f* **1.** HIST (*ejército*) host **2.** (*de un partido*) supporters

huesudo, -a [we·'su·do, -a] *adj* **1.** (*persona*) big-boned **2.** (*carne*) bony

hueva ['we·βa] *f* roe

huevada [we·'βa·da] *f AmL, inf* (*estupidez*) stupid thing

huevear [we·βe·'ar] *vi AmS, inf* (*hacer tonterías*) to fool around

huevera [we·'βe·ra] *f* egg cup; (*cartón*) egg crate

huevería [we·βe·'ri·a] *f shop that sells eggs*

huevero, -a [we·'βe·ro, -a] *m, f* (*que vende*) egg seller

huevo ['we·βo] *m* **1.** BIO egg; **~ duro** hard-boiled egg; **~s fritos** fried eggs; **~ pasado por agua** soft-boiled egg; **~s revueltos** scrambled eggs; **clara de ~** egg white; **ir pisando ~s** to go very slowly and/or carefully; **poner un ~** to lay an egg; *vulg* to take a crap **2.** *AmL* (*valor*) guts *pl* **3.** *vulg* (*testículo*) ball; **¡estoy hasta los ~s!** I've had it up to here!; **me importa un ~** I don't give a crap; **¡tiene ~s la cosa!** that's

quite something!; **poner algo a alguien a ~** to make sth very easy for sb; **me costó un ~** (*de dinero*) it cost loads; (*de dificultades*) it was damn difficult; **¡y un ~!** like hell!

huevonear [we·βo·ne·'ar] *vi Méx, vulg* to piss around

huida [u·'i·da] *f* flight; **~ del lugar del accidente** flight from the scene of the accident; **no hay ~ posible** there's no way out

huidizo, -a [ui·'di·so, -a; -θo, -a] *adj* **1.** (*persona*) elusive **2.** (*momento*) fleeting

huido, -a [u·'i·do, -a] *m, f* escaped prisoner

huir [u·'ir] *irr* **I.** *vi* (*escapar*) to flee; **~ de casa** to run away from home; **el tiempo huye** time flies; **pudieron ~ de sus perseguidores** they managed to give their pursuers the slip **II.** *vi, vt* (*evitar*) **~ (de)** algo to keep away from sth; **~ (de) alguien** to avoid sb

huiro ['wi·ro] *m AmS* (*alga*) seaweed

hule ['u·le] *m* **1.** (*para la mesa*) tablecloth **2.** (*tela*) oilcloth **3.** *AmL* (*caucho*) rubber

hulero, -a [u·'le·ro, -a] *m, f AmL* rubber gatherer, rubber tapper

hulla ['u·ja, -ʎa] *f* fossil coal; **~ blanca** hydroelectric power

humanamente [u·ma·na·'men·te] *adv* humanly; **hacer todo lo ~ posible** to do everything humanly possible

humanidad [u·ma·ni·'dad] *f* **1.** (*género humano*) **la ~** mankind; **un crimen contra la ~** a crime against humanity **2.** (*naturaleza, caridad humana*) humanity **3.** *inf* (*corpulencia*) fatness **4.** *pl* (*letras*) arts

humanismo [u·ma·'nis·mo] *m* humanism

humanista [u·ma·'nis·ta] *mf* humanist

humanístico, -a [u·ma·'nis·ti·ko, -a] *adj* humanistic

humanitario, -a [u·ma·ni·'ta·rjo, -a] *adj* humanitarian; **organización humanitaria** humanitarian organization

humanitarismo [u·ma·ni·ta·'ris·mo] *m* humanitarianism

humanización [u·ma·ni·sa·'sjon, -θa·'θjon] *f* **1.** (*dignificación*) humanization **2.** ARTE humanizing

humanizador(a) [u·ma·ni·sa·'dor, -·'do·ra; u·ma·ni·θa-] *adj* humanizing

humanizar <z→c> [u·ma·ni·'sar, -'θar] **I.** *vt* (*dignificar, arte*) to humanize **II.** *vr:* **~se** to become human

humano, -a [u·'ma·no, -a] *adj* **1.** (*del hombre*) human **2.** (*manera de ser*) humane

humanoide [u·ma·'noi·de] *m* humanoid

humareda [u·ma·'re·da] *f* cloud of smoke

humazo [u·'ma·so, -θo] *m* thick smoke

humear [u·me·'ar] **I.** *vi* **1.** (*humo*) to smoke **2.** (*vapor*) to steam **3.** (*enemistad*) to linger on, to smolder **4.** (*engreírse*) to act vain **II.** *vr:* **~se** to put on airs

humectante [u·mek·'tan·te] *adj* moisturizing

humedad [u·me·'dad] *f* humidity; (*agradable*) moisture; (*desagradable*) dampness

humedal [u·me·'dal] *m* wetland

humedecer [u·me·de·'ser, -'θer] *irr como crecer vt* to moisten

húmedo, -a ['u·me·do, -a] *adj* (*mojado*) wet; (*agradable*) moist; (*desagradable*) damp; (*con vapor*) humid; (*aire*) muggy

húmero ['u·me·ro] *m* ANAT humerus

humidificar <c→qu> [u·mi·di·fi·'kar] *vt* to humidify

humildad [u·mil·'dad] *f* 1.(*modestia*) humility, humbleness 2.(*religiosa*) meekness 3.(*social*) lowliness

humilde [u·'mil·de] *adj* 1.(*modesto*) humble; un ~ trabajador a humble worker 2.(*en sentido religioso*) meek 3.(*condición social*) poor; ser de orígenes ~s to be of humble origin

humillación [u·mi·ʎa·'sjon, -ʎa·'θjon] *f* 1.(*degradación*) humiliation 2.(*vergüenza*) shame

humillante [u·mi·'jan·te, -'ʎan·te] *adj* humiliating

humillar [u·mi·'jar, -'ʎar] I. *vt* 1.(*degradar*) to humiliate 2.(*avergonzar*) to shame II. *vr:* ~ se to lower oneself

humo ['u·mo] *m* 1.(*de combustión*) smoke; señal de ~ smoke signal; en ese bar siempre hay ~ it's always smoky in that bar; la chimenea echa ~ the chimney pours out smoke; tragar el ~ al fumar to inhale cigarette smoke 2.(*vapor*) steam 3.(*al cocinar*) smoke, steam 4. *pl* (*vanidad*) conceit; bajar los ~s a alguien to take sb down a peg; subirse los ~s a la cabeza to put on airs

humor [u·'mor] *m* 1.(*cualidad, humorismo*) humor; ~ negro black humor; ¡pero no tienes sentido del ~ o qué! don't you have a sense of humor? 2.(*ánimo*) mood; estar de buen/mal ~ to be in a good/bad mood; no estoy de ~ para bailar I'm not in the mood for dancing

humorado, -a [u·mo·'ra·do, -a] *adj* bien/mal ~ (*por un momento*) in a good/bad mood; (*carácter*) even-tempered/bad-tempered

humorista [u·mo·'ris·ta] *mf* comic, humorist; (*dibujante*) cartoonist

humorístico, -a [u·mo·'ris·ti·ko, -a] *adj* comic

humus ['u·mus] *m* humus

hundido, -a [un·'di·do, -a] *adj* 1.(*ojos*) deep-set; (*techo*) collapsed 2.(*persona*) downcast, demoralized

hundimiento [un·di·'mjen·to] *m* 1.(*de un barco*) sinking 2.(*de un edificio*) *t.* ECON collapse 3. GEO (*depresión*) hollow

hundir [un·'dir] I. *vt* 1.(*barco*) to sink 2.(*sumergir*) ~ la mano en el agua to put one's hand in the water; ~ los pies en el barro to sink one's feet into the mud 3.(*suelo*) to cave in 4.(*arruinar*) to ruin; (*proyecto*) to cause to fail; (*empresa*) to bankrupt; (*esperanzas*) to destroy; la crisis económica ha hundido a muchos empresarios the economic crisis has ruined many businessmen II. *vr:* ~ se 1.(*barco*) to sink 2.(*edificio*) to collapse;

(*suelo*) to cave in; el rublo se hunde the ruble is plummeting 3.(*fracasar*) to fail, to lose it; me he hundido en el tercer set I lost it in the third set

húngaro, -a ['un·ga·ro, -a] *adj, m, f* Hungarian

Hungría [un·'gri·a] *f* Hungary

huno, -a ['u·no, -a] I. *adj* HIST Hun II. *m, f* HIST Hun

huracán [u·ra·'kan] *m* hurricane; las tropas pasaron como un ~ por la ciudad the troops stampeded through the city; (*persona*) whirlwind of energy

huracanado, -a [u·ra·ka·'na·do, -a] *adj* tempestuous; vientos ~s hurricane winds

huraño, -a [u·'ra·no, -a] *adj* 1.(*insociable*) unsociable 2.(*hosco*) surly

hurgar <g→gu> [ur·'yar] I. *vi, vt* 1.(*remover*) ~ en algo to poke around in sth; ~ el fuego to poke the fire 2.(*fisgonear*) ~ en algo to look [*o* rummage] through sth II. *vr:* ~ se la nariz to pick one's nose

hurgón [ur·'yon] *m* (*de fuego*) poker

hurguetear [ur·ye·te·'ar] *vt AmL* ~ algo rummage around in sth

hurón, -ona [u·'ron, -'ro·na] *m, f* 1.(*animal*) ferret 2. *inf* (*husmeador*) nosy parker 3. *inf* (*huraño*) unsociable

huronera [u·ro·'ne·ra] *f* 1.(*madriguera*) ferret hole 2.(*escondrijo*) hiding place; (*de ladrones*) den; (*escondite*) hideout

hurra ['u·rra] *interj* hooray

hurtadillas [ur·ta·'di·jas, -ʎas] a ~ secretly; lo hizo a ~ de su novia he did it behind his girlfriend's back

hurtar [ur·'tar] I. *vt* 1.(*robar*) to steal; (*en tiendas*) to shoplift 2.(*con el peso*) to give sb short measure 3.(*mar*) to eat away 4.(*cuerpo*) to avoid 5.(*ocultar*) to hide II. *vr:* ~ se a algo to keep away from sth

hurto ['ur·to] *m* 1.(*acción*) stealing; (*en tiendas*) shoplifting 2.(*cosa*) stolen property

husmear [us·me·'ar] I. *vt* (*perro*) to sniff II. *vi* (*perro*) to sniff around; (*fisgonear*) to nose around

husmeo [us·'meo] *m* 1.(*de un perro*) sniffing 2.(*fisgoneo*) nosing around, snooping

huso ['u·so] *m* 1.(*textil*) spindle 2. GEO ~ horario time zone

huy [ui] *interj* (*de asombro*) wow

I

I, i [i] *f* I, i; ~ de Italia I as in India; ~ griega y

ibérico, -a [i·'βe·ri·ko, -a] *adj* Iberian; Península Ibérica Iberian Peninsula

Iberoamérica [i·βe·ro·a·'me·ri·ka] *f* Latin America

iberoamericano, -a [i·βe·ro·a·me·ri·ka·no,

-a] *adj*, *m*, *f* Latin American

iceberg [i·se·'βery, i·θe-] *m* <icebergs> iceberg; **la punta del** ~ the tip of the iceberg

icono [i·'ko·no] *m*, **ícono** ['i·ko·no] *m* REL, COMPUT icon

iconoclasta [i·ko·no·'klas·ta] *adj* iconoclastic

iconografía [i·ko·no·yra·'fi·a] *f* iconography

ictericia [ik·te·'ri·sja, -·'ri·θja] *f* MED jaundice

I+D [i mas de] *abr de* **Investigación y Desarrollo** R & D

ida ['i·da] *f* departure; **billete de** ~ single (ticket); **billete de** ~ **y vuelta** return (ticket)

idea [i·'dea] *f* **1.** *t.* FILOS idea; **ni** ~ no idea; **tener la** ~ **de hacer algo** to have the idea of doing sth **2.** (*propósito*) intention; **tener** ~ **de hacer algo** to have the intention of doing sth

ideal [i·de·'al] *adj*, *m* ideal

idealismo [i·dea·'lis·mo] *m* idealism

idealista [i·dea·'lis·ta] *adj* idealistic

idealizar <z→c> [i·dea·li·'sar, -'θar] *vt* to idealize

idear [i·de·'ar] *vt* **1.** (*concebir*) to conceive **2.** (*inventar*) to think up **3.** (*un plan*) to devise

ídem ['i·den] *pron* ditto

idéntico, -a [i·'den·ti·ko, -a] *adj* identical; **es** ~ **a su madre** he is just like his mother

identidad [i·den·ti·'dad] *f* identity; **carné de** ~ identity card

identificable [i·den·ti·fi·'ka·βle] *adj* identifiable

identificación [i·den·ti·fi·ka·'sjon, -'θjon] *f* identification; COMPUT password; ~ **de llamadas** TEL caller ID

identificar <c→qu> [i·den·ti·fi·'kar] **I.** *vt* to identify **II.** *vr:* ~**se** to identify; ~**se con alguien/algo** to identify oneself with sb/sth

ideología [i·deo·lo·'xi·a] *f* ideology

idílico, -a [i·'di·li·ko, -a] *adj* idyllic

idilio [i·'di·ljo] *m* idyll; (*relación amorosa*) love affair

idioma [i·'djo·ma] *m* language; **hablar el mismo** ~ *fig* to be on the same wavelength

idiomático, -a [i·djo·'ma·ti·ko, -a] *adj* idiomatic

idiosincrasia [i·djo·sin·'kra·sja] *f* idiosyncrasy

idiota [i·'djo·ta] **I.** *adj* idiotic, stupid **II.** *mf* idiot

idiotez [i·djo·'tes, -'teθ] *f* idiocy

ido, -a ['i·do, -a] *adj inf* crazy; *AmC* (*borracho*) drunk

idólatra [i·'do·la·tra] *mf* idolater *m*, idolatress *f*

idolatrar [i·do·la·'trar] *vt* to worship; (*adorar*) to adore; (*amar*) to idolize

ídolo ['i·do·lo] *m* idol

idóneo, -a [i·'do·neo, -a] *adj* apt

iglesia [i·'yle·sja] *f* church; **casarse por la** ~ to have a church wedding

iglú [i·'ylu] *m* igloo

ignición [iy·ni·'sjon, -'θjon] *f* (*inicio de combustión*) ignition

ignífugo, -a [iy·'ni·fu·yo, -a] *adj* fireproof

ignorancia [iy·no·'ran·sja, -θja] *f* ignorance; (*incultura*) lack of culture [*o* education]

ignorante [iy·no·'ran·te] *adj* **1.** (*desconoce-*

dor) ~ **de algo** ignorant about [*o* of] sth **2.** (*inculto*) uncultured, uneducated

ignorar [iy·no·'rar] *vt* **1.** (*desconocer*) ~ **algo** to be ignorant of sth **2.** (*no hacer caso*) to ignore

igual [i·'ywal] **I.** *adj* **1.** (*idéntico*) identical; (*semejante*) same; MAT equal; **nunca he visto cosa** ~ I've never seen anything like it **2.** (*lo mismo*) **habla** ~ **que su padre** he/she speaks just like his/her father; **¡es** ~**!** it doesn't matter ▶ **al** ~ **que...** as well as... **II.** *mf* equal; **no tiene** ~ he/she has no equal **III.** *adv inf* (*quizá*) ~ **no viene** he/she might not come

igualado, -a [i·ywa·'la·do, -a] *adj* **1.** (*parecido*) similar **2.** (*empatado*) level

igualar [i·ywa·'lar] **I.** *vt* **1.** (*hacer igual*) to equalize; (*equiparar*) to match **2.** (*allanar*) to flatten (out); (*nivelar*) to level **3.** (*ajustar*) to even out **II.** *vi* (*equivaler*) to be equal **III.** *vr:* ~**se 1.** (*parecerse*) ~**se a** [*o* con] **alguien** to be similar to sb **2.** (*ponerse al igual*) to make equal, to equate

igualdad [i·ywal·'dad] *f* equality; (*semejanza*); ~ **de derechos** equal rights; **estar en** ~ **de condiciones** to be on an equal footing

igualitario, -a [i·ywa·li·'ta·rjo, -a] *adj* egalitarian

igualitarismo [i·ywa·li·ta·'ris·mo] *m* egalitarianism

igualmente [i·ywal·'men·te] **I.** *interj* and the same to you **II.** *adv* equally

iguana [i·'ywa·na] *f* iguana

ilegal [i·le·'yal] *adj* illegal, unlawful

ilegalidad [i·le·ya·li·'dad] *f* illegality

ilegible [i·le·'xi·βle] *adj* (*letra*) illegible; (*contenido*) unreadable

ilegitimar [i·le·xi·ti·'mar] *vt* (*asunto*) to invalidate; (*hijo*) to disinherit

ilegitimidad [i·le·xi·ti·mi·'dad] *f* (*asunto*) illegality; (*hijo*) illegitimacy

ilegítimo, -a [i·le·'xi·ti·mo, -a] *adj* (*asunto*) illegal; (*hijo*) illegitimate

ileso, -a [i·'le·so, -a] *adj* unharmed, unhurt; **salir** [*o* resultar] ~ to be unscathed

iletrado, -a [i·le·'tra·do, -a] *adj* uncultured; (*analfabeto*) uneducated

ilícito, -a [i·'li·si·to, -a; -θi·to, -a] *adj* illegal, illicit

ilimitado, -a [i·li·mi·'ta·do, -a] *adj* unlimited

ilocalizable [i·lo·ka·li·'sa·βle, -'θa·βle] *adj* **el médico está** ~ the doctor cannot be found

ilógico, -a [i·'lo·xi·ko, -a] *adj* illogical

iluminación [i·lu·mi·na·'sjon, -'θjon] *f* illumination; (*alumbrado*) lighting; (*como adorno*) illuminations *pl*

iluminado, -a [i·lu·mi·'na·do] *adj* illuminated; (*un monumento*) lit up

iluminar [i·lu·mi·'nar] *vt* to illuminate; *fig* to enlighten; (*un monumento*) to light up

ilusión [i·lu·'sjon] *f* **1.** (*alegría*) excitement; **ese viaje me hace mucha** ~ I'm excited about the journey **2.** (*esperanza*) hope; **hacerse ilusiones** to get one's hopes up

3. (*sueño*) illusion; (*espejismo*) (optical) illusion

ilusionante [i·lu·sjo·'nan·te] *adj* exciting

ilusionar [i·lu·sjo·'nar] **I.** *vt* **1.** (*entusiasmar*) to excite; **estar ilusionado con algo** to be excited about sth **2.** (*hacer ilusiones*) to raise false hopes **II.** *vr:* ~ **se 1.** (*alegrarse*) to be excited **2.** (*esperanzarse*) **el proyecto le ilusiona mucho** the project got his hopes up

ilusionismo [i·lu·sjo·'nis·mo] *m* illusionism, conjuring

ilusionista [i·lu·sjo·'nis·ta] *mf* illusionist

iluso, -a [i·'lu·so, -a] *adj* gullible

ilusorio, -a [i·lu·'so·rjo, -a] *adj* illusory

ilustración [i·lus·tra·'sjon, -'θjon] *f* **1.** (*imagen, instrucción*) illustration; ~ **gráfica** graphic illustration; (*explicación*) explanation **2.** HIST **la Ilustración** the Enlightenment

ilustrado, -a [i·lus·'tra·do, -a] **I.** *adj* **1.** (*con imágenes*) illustrated **2.** (*instruido*) enlightened **II.** *m, f* learned [*o* erudite] person

ilustrador(a) [i·lus·tra·'dor, --'do·ra] *m(f)* illustrator

ilustrar [i·lus·'trar] **I.** *vt* **1.** (*con imágenes*) to illustrate **2.** (*instruir*) to enlighten **II.** *vr:* ~ **se** to enlighten oneself

ilustrativo, -a [i·lus·tra·'ti·βo, -a] *adj* illustrative

ilustre [i·'lus·tre] *adj* (*famoso*) illustrious

imagen [i·'ma·xen] *f* **1.** (*representación mental*) image; **ser la viva ~ de alguien** to be the spitting [*o* living] image of sb **2.** TV picture **3.** (*escultura sagrada*) idol, graven image; (*pintura*) icon

imaginable [i·ma·xi·'na·βle] *adj* imaginable

imaginación [i·ma·xi·na·'sjon, -'θjon] *f* imagination; **ni por ~** on no account

imaginar [i·ma·xi·'nar] **I.** *vt* to imagine; ~ **fantasmas** to imagine things **II.** *vr:* ~ **se 1.** (*representarse*) to imagine oneself; **me lo imagino** I can imagine [*o* picture] it **2.** (*figurarse*) to imagine, to suppose

imaginario, -a [i·ma·xi·'na·rjo, -a] *adj* imaginary

imaginativo, -a [i·ma·xi·na·'ti·βo, -a] *adj* imaginative

imán [i·'man] *m* **1.** *t. fig* (*hierro*) magnet **2.** REL imam

iman(t)ar [i·ma·'nar/i·man·'tar] *vt* to magnetize

imbatible [im·ba·'ti·βle] *adj* unbeatable

imbebible [im·be·'βi·βle] *adj* undrinkable

imbécil [im·'be·sil, -θil] *adj, mf t.* MED imbecile

imbecilidad [im·be·si·li·'dad, im·be·θi·li-] *f t.* MED imbecility, subnormality

imberbe [im·'ber·βe] *adj* clean-shaven; *pey* (*inmaduro*) beardless

imborrable [im·bo·'rra·βle] *adj* indelible; (*acontecimiento*) unforgettable

imbricación [im·bri·ka·'sjon, -'θjon] *f* ARQUIT imbrication, overlapping

imbricar <c→qu> [im·bri·'kar] **I.** *vt* to imbricate **II.** *vr:* ~ **se** (*superponerse*) to overlap

imbuido, -a [im·bu·i·do, -a] *adj* imbued; ~ **de algo** imbued with sth

imbuir [im·bu·ir] *irr como huir* **I.** *vt* to imbue **II.** *vr* ~ **se de algo** to imbibe sth

imitable [i·mi·'ta·βle] *adj* imitable

imitación [i·mi·ta·'sjon, -'θjon] *f* imitation; **perlas de ~** imitation pearls

imitador(a) [i·mi·ta·'dor, --'do·ra] *m(f)* imitator; (*parodista*) impersonator

imitar [i·mi·'tar] *vt* to imitate, to copy; (*parodiar*) to impersonate; ~ **una firma** to forge a signature

impaciencia [im·pa·'sjen·sja, -'θjen·θja] *f* impatience

impacientar [im·pa·sjen·'tar, -θjen·'tar] **I.** *vt* to make impatient **II.** *vr:* ~ **se** to become impatient

impaciente [im·pa·'sjen·te, -'θjen·te] *adj* impatient; **estamos ~s por empezar** we are eager to start

impactar [im·pak·'tar] *vt* **1.** (*un acontecimiento*) to make an impact **2.** (*un proyectil*) to strike

impacto [im·'pak·to] *m* **1.** (*choque*) impact; (*golpe emocional*) shock; (*huella*) damage; *fig* repercussions *pl;* ~ **(medio)ambiental** environmental impact **2.** *AmL* (*en el boxeo*) punch

impagable [im·pa·'ya·βle] *adj* unpayable

impago [im·'pa·yo] *m* nonpayment

impalpable [im·pal·'pa·βle] *adj* impalpable

impar [im·'par] *adj* (*número*) odd

imparable [im·pa·'ra·βle] *adj* unstoppable

imparcial [im·par·'sjal, -'θjal] *adj* impartial; (*sin prejuicios*) unbiased

imparcialidad [im·par·sja·li·'dad, -θja·li·'dad] *f* impartiality, fairness

impartir [im·par·'tir] *vt* to give; (*conferir*) to impart *form*

impasible [im·pa·'si·βle] *adj* impassive

impavidez [im·pa·βi·'des, -'deθ] *f* sangfroid, intrepidness

impávido, -a [im·'pa·βi·do, -a] *adj* self-possessed, intrepid

impecable [im·pe·'ka·βle] *adj* **1.** *ser* (*correcto*) impeccable **2.** *estar* (*nuevo*) **el motor está ~** the engine is in perfect condition

impedido, -a [im·pe·'di·do, -a] *adj* disabled; **estar ~ para algo** to be incapacitated for sth

impedimento [im·pe·di·'men·to] *m* **1.** (*que imposibilita algo*) restraint **2.** (*obstáculo*) impediment, hindrance **3.** MED handicap

impedir [im·pe·'dir] *irr como pedir* *vt* **1.** (*imposibilitar*) to prevent, to keep from **2.** (*obstaculizar*) to impede, to hinder

impeler [im·pe·'ler] *vt* (*impulsar*) to impel, to drive; **fue impelido a robar por sus amigos** he was pushed into stealing by his friends

impenetrable [im·pe·ne·'tra·βle] *adj* impenetrable

impensable [im·pen·'sa·βle] *adj* unthinkable

impensado, -a [im·pen·'sa·do, -a] *adj* (*imprevisto*) unforeseen; (*inesperado*) unexpected

impepinable [im·pe·pi·'na·βle] *adj inf* unquestionable

imperar [im·pe·'rar] *vi* to reign; *fig* to prevail

imperativo [im·pe·ra·'ti·βo] *m* **1.** LING imperative **2.** *pl* (*necesidad*) imperative

imperativo, -a [im·pe·ra·'ti·βo, -a] *adj* imperative

imperceptible [im·per·sep·'ti·βle, im·per·θep-] *adj* **1.** (*inapreciable*) imperceptible **2.** (*minúsculo*) minute

imperdible [im·per·'di·βle] **I.** *adj* that can't be missed **II.** *m* safety pin

imperdonable [im·per·do·'na·βle] *adj* unpardonable, inexcusable

imperecedero, -a [im·pe·re·se·'de·ro, -a, im·pe·re·θe-] *adj* imperishable; *fig* everlasting

imperfección [im·per·fek·'sjon, -'θjon] *f* imperfection, flaw

imperfecto [im·per·'fek·to] *m* LING imperfect

imperfecto, -a [im·per·'fek·to, -a] *adj* imperfect, flawed

imperial [im·pe·'rjal] *adj* imperial

imperialismo [im·pe·rja·'lis·mo] *m* POL imperialism

imperio [im·'pe·rjo] *m* **1.** (*territorio*) empire; *t. fig* realm **2.** (*mandato*) reign

imperioso, -a [im·pe·'rjo·so, -a] *adj* **1.** (*autoritario*) imperious **2.** (*urgente*) imperative

impermeabilidad [im·per·mea·βi·li·'dad] *f* impermeability

impermeable [im·per·me·a·βle] **I.** *adj* impermeable **II.** *m* raincoat

impersonal [im·per·so·'nal] *adj t.* LING impersonal

impertérrito, -a [im·per·'te·rri·to, -a] *adj* (*impávido*) imperturbable; (*sin miedo*) fearless

impertinencia [im·per·ti·'nen·sja, -'nen·θja] *f* **1.** (*insolencia*) impertinence, impudence **2.** (*inoportunidad*) inappropriateness

impertinente [im·per·ti·'nen·te] *adj* **1.** (*insolente*) impertinent, impudent **2.** (*inoportuno*) inopportune

imperturbable [im·per·tur·'βa·βle] *adj* imperturbable

ímpetu ['im·pe·tu] *m* **1.** (*vehemencia*) vehemence **2.** (*brío*) impetus, energy

impetuosidad [im·pe·two·si·'dad] *f* rashness

impetuoso, -a [im·pe·tu·o·so, -a] *adj* rash

impiedad [im·pje·'dad] *f* impiety

impío, -a [im·'pi·o, -a] *adj* impious; (*inclemente*) pitiless

implacable [im·pla·'ka·βle] *adj* implacable; (*riguroso*) relentless

implantar [im·plan·'tar] **I.** *vt* **1.** *t.* MED to implant **2.** (*asentar*) to establish **3.** (*instituir*) to found, to institute **4.** (*introducir*) to introduce **II.** *vr:* ~ **se** to become established

implementar [im·ple·men·'tar] *vt* AmL (*método*) to introduce; (*plan*) to implement

implemento [im·ple·'men·to] *m* AmL (*utensilio*) tool; (*accesorio*) implement; ~**s agrícolas** farming equipment

implicación [im·pli·ka·'sjon, -'θjon] *f* inclusion; (*en un delito*) implication

implicar <c→qu> [im·pli·'kar] **I.** *vt* **1.** (*incluir*) to involve **2.** (*significar*) to imply; **eso implica que...** this means that... **II.** *vr:* ~ **se** to be [*o* become] involved

implícito, -a [im·'pli·si·to, -a; -θi·to, -a] *adj* implicit

implorar [im·plo·'rar] *vt* (*a alguien*) to implore; (*algo*) to beg; ~ (**el**) **perdón** to beg forgiveness

impoluto, -a [im·po·'lu·to, -a] *adj* immaculate

imponderable [im·pon·de·'ra·βle] *adj* imponderable

imponente [im·po·'nen·te] *adj* (*impresionante*) imposing; (*que infunde respeto*) awesome; (*grandioso*) grand

imponer [im·po·'ner] *irr como* poner **I.** *vt* to impose; (*respeto*) to command; ~ **a** [*o* **sobre**] **alguien** (*carga, impuestos*) to impose on [*o* upon] sb **II.** *vi* to impress **III.** *vr:* ~ **se 1.** (*hacerse ineludible*) to become unavoidable **2.** (*hacerse obedecer*) **se impuso a los demás** he/she made his/her authority felt **3.** (*prevalecer*) ~ **se a algo** to prevail over sth

imponible [im·po·'ni·βle] *adj* FIN taxable; **no** ~ tax exempt

impopular [im·po·pu·'lar] *adj* unpopular

importación [im·por·ta·'sjon, -'θjon] *f* **1.** (*acción*) importation **2.** (*producto*) import

importador(a) [im·por·ta·'dor, -·'do·ra] *m(f)* importer

importancia [im·por·'tan·sja, -θja] *f* **1.** (*interés*) importance; **sin** ~ unimportant; **restar** [*o* **quitar**] ~ **a algo** to play sth down **2.** (*extensión*) scope, magnitude **3.** (*trascendencia*) significance

importante [im·por·'tan·te] *adj* **1.** (*de gran interés*) important; **lo** ~ **es** +*infin* the important thing is +*infin* **2.** (*dimensión*) considerable **3.** (*cantidad*) significant

importar [im·por·'tar] **I.** *vt* (*mercancía*) to import **II.** *vi* to matter, to mind; **no importa la hora que sea** it doesn't matter what time it is; **¿a ti qué te importa?** what does it have to do with you?; **¿te importa esperar?** do you mind waiting?; **me importa un pepino** *inf* I couldn't care less

importe [im·'por·te] *m* (*cuantía*) value; (*total*) amount

importunar [im·por·tu·'nar] *vt* to pester, to importune *form*

imposibilidad [im·po·si·βi·li·'dad] *f* impossibility

imposibilitado, -a [im·po·si·βi·li·'ta·do, -a] *adj* disabled; **el despegue se vio** ~ **por la niebla** the take-off was impeded by the fog

imposibilitar [im·po·si·βi·li·'tar] *vt* (*impedir*) to impede, to make impossible

imposible [im·po·'si·βle] *adj* **1.** (*irrealizable*) impossible **2.** *inf* (*insoportable*) impossible, unbearable **3.** AmL (*repugnante*) horrid

imposición [im·po·si·'sjon, -'θjon] *f* imposition; (*de impuestos*) taxation

impositiva [im·po·si·'ti·βa] *f* AmL tax office

impositivo, -a [im·po·si·'ti·βo, -a] *adj* **1.** FIN tax **2.** *CSur* (*imperativo*) imperative

impostergable [im·pos·ter·'γa·βle] *adj* that cannot be postponed

impostor(a) [im·pos·'tor, --to·ra] *m(f)* impostor, imposter

impotencia [im·po·'ten·sja, -θja] *f* **1.** (*falta de poder*) *t.* MED impotence **2.** (*incapacidad*) incapacity; (*indefensión*) helplessness

impotente [im·po·'ten·te] *adj* **1.** (*sin poder*) impotent, powerless **2.** (*incapaz*) incapable **3.** (*desvalido*) helpless **4.** MED impotent

impracticable [im·prak·ti·'ka·βle] *adj* **1.** (*irrealizable*) unfeasible **2.** (*intransitable*) impassable

imprecar [im·pre·'kar] <c→qu> *vt* to curse, to imprecate *form*

imprecisión [im·pre·si·'sjon, -θi·'sjon] *f* **1.** (*falta de precisión*) inexactness **2.** (*falta de determinación*) vagueness

impreciso, -a [im·pre·'si·so, -a; -'θi·so, -a] *adj* **1.** (*no preciso*) imprecise **2.** (*indefinido*) vague

impredecible [im·pre·de·'si·βle, -'θi·βle] *adj* unpredictable; (*suceso*) unforeseeable

impregnar [im·preγ·'nar] **I.** *vt* **1.** (*empapar*) to impregnate, to saturate **2.** (*penetrar*) to penetrate **II.** *vr:* ~ **se** to become impregnated

impremeditado, -a [im·pre·me·di·'ta·do, -a] *adj* (*impensado*) unpremeditated; (*irreflexivo*) unintentional; (*involuntario*) inadvertent

imprenta [im·'pren·ta] *f* printing; (*taller*) printer's; (*impresión*) print; ~ **genética** genetic imprint

imprescindible [im·pre·sin·'di·βle, im·pres·θin-] *adj* (*ineludible*) essential; (*insustituible*) indispensable

impresentable [im·pre·sen·'ta·βle] *adj* unpresentable

impresión [im·pre·'sjon] *f* **1.** (*huella*) imprint **2.** TIPO printing, impression; COMPUT print-out **3.** (*sensación*) impression; **cambiar impresiones** to compare notes

impresionable [im·pre·sjo·'na·βle] *adj* impressionable

impresionante [im·pre·sjo·'nan·te] *adj* (*emocionante*) impressive, striking; (*magnífico*) magnificent

impresionar [im·pre·sjo·'nar] **I.** *vt* to impress **II.** *vr:* ~ **se** to be impressed

impresionismo [im·pre·sjo·'nis·mo] *m* ARTE impressionism

impreso [im·'pre·so] *m* **1.** (*formulario*) form **2.** (*envío*) printed matter; ~ **publicitario** flyer

impreso, -a [im·'pre·so, -a] *pp de* **imprimir**

impresora [im·pre·'so·ra] *f* COMPUT printer; ~ **de inyección de tinta** ink-jet printer; ~ **láser** laser printer

imprevisible [im·pre·βi·'si·βle] *adj* unforeseeable; (*persona*) unpredictable

imprevisión [im·pre·βi·'sjon] *f* **1.** (*despreocupación*) thoughtlessness; (*descuido*) carelessness **2.** (*ligereza*) imprudence

imprevisto [im·pre·'βis·to] *m* **1.** (*algo inespe-*

rado) contingency, sth unexpected **2.** *pl* (*gastos*) unexpected expenses

imprevisto, -a [im·pre·'βis·to, -a] *adj* (*no previsto*) unforeseen; (*inesperado*) unexpected

imprimir [im·pri·'mir] *irr vt* **1.** TIPO, COMPUT to print **2.** (*editar*) to publish **3.** *t. fig* (*un sello*) to stamp

improbabilidad [im·pro·βa·βi·li·'dad] *f* improbability, unlikelihood

improbable [im·pro·'βa·βle] *adj* improbable, unlikely

improcedente [im·pro·se·'den·te, im·proθe-] *adj* **1.** (*inoportuno*) inopportune; (*extemporáneo*) ill-timed **2.** (*inadecuado*) inappropriate **3.** (*antirreglamentario*) irregular; JUR inadmissible

improductividad [im·pro·duk·ti·βi·'dad] *f* **1.** (*falta de productividad*) unproductiveness **2.** (*falta de rentabilidad*) unprofitability

improductivo, -a [im·pro·duk·'ti·βo, -a] *adj* **1.** (*no productivo*) unproductive **2.** (*antieconómico*) unprofitable

impronunciable [im·pro·nun·'sja·βle, -'θja·βle] *adj* unpronounceable

improperio [im·pro·'pe·rjo] *m* (*ofensa*) offense; (*insulto*) insult

impropio, -a [im·'pro·pjo, -a] *adj* improper, unfitting; (*inadecuado*) inappropriate; **ese comportamiento es ~ en él** that behavior is unusual for him

improrrogable [im·pro·rro·'γa·βle] *adj* **1.** (*no prolongable*) non-extendable, non-extendible **2.** (*no aplazable*) that cannot be postponed

improvisación [im·pro·βi·sa·'sjon, -'θjon] *f* improvisation

improvisar [im·pro·βi·'sar] *vt* to improvise; TEAT to ad-lib

improviso, -a [im·pro·'βi·so, -a] *adj* unexpected; **de** ~ unexpectedly; **coger a alguien de** ~ to surprise sb

imprudencia [im·pru·'den·sja, -θja] *f* **1.** (*irreflexión*) imprudence, carelessness **2.** JUR negligence; ~ **temeraria** criminal negligence; (*conduciendo*) reckless driving

imprudente [im·pru·'den·te] *adj* **1.** (*irreflexivo*) imprudent; (*insensato*) unwise **2.** (*incauto*) incautious **3.** (*indiscreto*) indiscreet **4.** JUR negligent

impúdico, -a [im·'pu·di·ko, -a] *adj* indecent, immodest; (*obsceno*) lewd

impuesto [im·'pwes·to] *m* FIN tax; ~ **sobre la renta** income tax; ~ **sobre la propiedad** property tax; **Impuesto sobre el Valor Añadido** Value Added Tax; **libre de** ~**s** tax-free, duty-free; **sujeto a** ~**s** taxable, dutiable

impugnar [im·puγ·'nar] *vt* **1.** *t.* JUR to contest **2.** (*combatir*) to dispute; (*una teoría*) to challenge

impulsar [im·pul·'sar] *vt* **1.** (*empujar*) to impel **2.** (*estimular*) to motivate; (*promover*) to instigate

impulsión [im·pul·'sjon] *f* TÉC drive

impulsivo, -a [im·pul·'si·βo, -a] *adj* impulsive

impulso [im·'pul·so] *m* (*estímulo*) impulse, stimulus; ~ **sexual** sex drive
impulsor(a) [im·pul·'sor] **I.** *adj* **fuerza ~a** driving force **II.** *m(f)* catalyst
impune [im·'pu·ne] *adj* unpunished
impunidad [im·pu·ni·'dad] *f* impunity
impureza [im·pu·'re·sa, -'re·θa] *f t.* REL impurity
impuro, -a [im·'pu·ro, -a] *adj t.* REL impure
imputable [im·pu·'ta·βle] *adj* imputable, attributable
imputación [im·pu·ta·'sjon, -'θjon] *f* imputation
imputar [im·pu·'tar] *vt* to impute
inabarcable [in·a·βar·'ka·βle] *adj* impossible to encompass; (*inmenso*) vast
inacabable [in·a·ka·'βa·βle] *adj* never-ending, interminable
inaccesible [in·ak·se·'si·βle, in·ak·θe-] *adj* inaccessible, unapproachable; (*inalcanzable*) beyond one's reach
inaceptable [in·a·sep·'ta·βle, in·a·θep-] *adj* unacceptable
inactividad [in·ak·ti·βi·'dad] *f* inactivity; (*desocupación*) unemployment
inactivo, -a [in·ak·'ti·βo, -a] *adj* inactive; (*desocupado*) jobless; (*volcán*) dormant
inadaptable [in·a·dap·'ta·βle] *adj* unadaptable
inadecuado, -a [in·a·de·'kwa·do, -a] *adj* inadequate
inadmisible [in·ad·mi·'si·βle] *adj* inadmissible
inadvertido, -a [in·ad·βer·'ti·do, -a] *adj* **1.** (*descuidado*) inadvertent; **me cogió ~** it caught me unprepared **2.** (*desapercibido*) unnoticed
inagotable [in·a·γo·'ta·βle] *adj* inexhaustible; (*persona*) tireless
inaguantable [in·a·γwan·'ta·βle] *adj* unbearable, intolerable
inalámbrico, -a [in·a·'lam·bri·ko, -a] *adj* TEL cordless, wireless
inalcanzable [in·al·kan·'sa·βle, -'θa·βle] *adj* unattainable, beyond one's reach
inalienable [in·a·lje·'na·βle] *adj* inalienable
inalterable [in·al·te·'ra·βle] *adj* unalterable; (*imperturbable*) impassive
inalterado, -a [in·al·te·'ra·do, -a] *adj* unchanged
inamovible [in·a·mo·'βi·βle] *adj* fixed, immovable
inanición [i·na·ni·'sjon, -'θjon] *f* starvation
inanimado, -a [in·a·ni·'ma·do, -a] *adj*, **inánime** [i·'na·ni·me] *adj* inanimate
inapelable [in·a·pe·'la·βle] *adj* **1.** JUR unappealable, not open to appeal **2.** (*inevitable*) inevitable
inapetencia [in·a·pe·'ten·sja, -θja] *f* loss [*o* lack] of appetite
inaplazable [in·a·pla·'sa·βle, -'θa·βle] *adj* unpostponable, undeferrable
inaplicable [in·a·pli·'ka·βle] *adj* inapplicable
inapreciable [in·a·pre·'sja·βle, -'θja·βle] *adj* **1.** (*imperceptible*) inappreciable **2.** (*de gran valor*) priceless
inaprensible [in·a·pren·'si·βle] *adj* (*inasible*) elusive
inasequible [in·a·se·'ki·βle] *adj* out of reach; **eso es ~ para mi bolsillo** that is beyond my means
inaudible [in·au·'di·βle] *adj* inaudible
inaudito, -a [in·au·'di·to, -a] *adj* **1.** (*sin precedente*) unprecedented **2.** (*vituperable*) outrageous
inauguración [in·au·yu·ra·'sjon, -'θjon] *f* **1.** (*puente, exposición*) opening; (*estatua*) unveiling **2.** (*comienzo*) inauguration
inaugurar [in·au·yu·'rar] *vt* **1.** (*puente*) to open; (*estatua*) to unveil **2.** (*comenzar*) to inaugurate
inca ['in·ka] *adj, m* Inca

> **i** The **Incas** were originally a small indigenous tribe that lived in **Perú**. In the 15th century, however, they expanded their empire, which ultimately covered present-day Colombia, Ecuador, Peru, and Bolivia, and extended south into the northern part of Argentina and Chile.

incaico, -a [in·'kai·ko, -a] *m, f* Inca
incalculable [in·kal·ku·'la·βle] *adj* incalculable
incalificable [in·ka·li·fi·'ka·βle] *adj* (*reprobable*) reproachable
incanato [in·ka·'na·to] *m Chile, Perú* HIST Incan period
incandescente [in·kan·de·'sen·te, -des·'θen·te] *adj* FÍS (*metal*) incandescent; (*temperamento*) fiery
incansable [in·kan·'sa·βle] *adj* tireless
incapacidad [in·ka·pa·si·'dad, in·ka·paθi-] *f* **1.** (*ineptitud*) incompetence **2.** (*psíquica*) incapacity; (*física*) disability **3.** (*falta de habilidad*) inability, incapability
incapacitado, -a [in·ka·pa·si·'ta·do, -a; -θi·'ta·do, -a] **I.** *adj* (*incapaz*) incapacitated; (*incompetente*) incompetent **II.** *m, f* (*minusválido*) disabled person
incapacitar [in·ka·pa·si·'tar, -θi·'tar] *vt* (*para negocios*) to incapacitate
incapaz [in·ka·'pas, -'paθ] *adj* **1.** (*inepto*) incapable **2.** JUR (*sin capacidad legal*) incapacitated, incompetent **3.** (*sin talento*) inept
incautación [in·kau·ta·'sjon, -'θjon] *f* seizure, confiscation
incautarse [in·kau·'tar·se] *vr* **~se de algo** (*confiscar*) to confiscate sth; (*adueñarse*) to appropriate sth
incauto, -a [in·'kau·to, -a] *adj* (*sin cautela*) incautious; (*confiado*) credulous
incendiar [in·sen·'djar, in·θen-] **I.** *vt* **~ algo** (*sin intención*) to unintentionally set sth on fire; (*intencionalmente*) to set fire to sth, to commit arson **II.** *vr:* **~se** to catch fire

incendiario, -a [in·sen·'dja·rjo, -a; in·θen-] *adj, m, f* incendiary

incendio [in·'sen·djo, in·'θen-] *m* fire; ~ **intencionado** arson

incentivar [in·sen·ti·'βar, in·θen-] *vt* to motivate, to offer incentives to

incentivo [in·sen·'ti·βo, in·θen-] *m* incentive

incertidumbre [in·ser·ti·'dum·bre, in·θer-] *f* incertitude

incesante [in·se·'san·te, in·θe-] *adj* incessant

incesto [in·'ses·to, in·'θes-] *m* incest

incestuoso, -a [in·ses·tu·o·so, -a; in·'θes-] *adj* incestuous

incidencia [in·si·'den·sja, in·θi-] *f* 1. *t.* MAT incidence 2. (*consecuencia*) repercussion

incidente [in·si·'den·te, in·θi-] *m* incident

incidir [in·si·'dir, in·θi-] *vi* ~ **en algo** (*consecuencias*) to impinge on [*o* affect] sth; (*tema*) to touch on sth

incienso [in·'sjen·so, -'θjen·so] *m* incense

incierto, -a [in·'sjer·to, -a; in·'θjer-] *adj* (*dudoso*) doubtful, uncertain; (*falso*) untrue

incineración [in·si·ne·ra·'sjon, in·θi·ne·ra·'θjon] *f* incineration; (*de personas*) cremation

incinerador [in·si·ne·ra·'dor, in·θi-] *m* incinerator; (*para cadáveres*) crematorium

incineradora [in·si·ne·ra·'do·ra, in·θi-] *f* (*para basuras*) incinerator

incinerar [in·si·ne·'rar, in·θi-] *vt* to incinerate; (*cadáveres*) to cremate

incipiente [in·si·'pjen·te, in·θi-] *adj* incipient

incisión [in·si·'sjon, in·θi-] *f t.* MED incision

inciso [in·'si·so, in·'θi-] *m* (*al relatar*) aside

incitación [in·si·ta·'sjon, in·θi·ta·'θjon] *f* (*instigación*) incitement

incitar [in·si·'tar, in·θi-] *vt* (*instigar*) to incite

incívico, -a [in·'si·βi·ko, -a; in·'θi-] *adj* antisocial

incivilizado, -a [in·si·βi·li·'sa·do, -a; in·θi·βi·li·'θa] *adj* 1. (*inculto*) uncivilized 2. (*rudo*) uncivil

inclemencia [in·kle·'men·sja, -θja] *f* inclemency

inclinación [in·kli·na·'sjon, -'θjon] *f* 1. (*declive*) slope 2. (*reverencia*) bow 3. (*afecto*) ~ **por alguien/algo** inclination for [*o* to] sb/sth 4. (*tendencias*) propensity, tendency

inclinado, -a [in·kli·'na·do, -a] *adj* inclined; ~ **a algo** inclined to [*o* towards] sth

inclinar [in·kli·'nar] I. *vt* to incline II. *vr:* ~ **se** 1. (*reverencia*) to bow; (*árboles*) to bend 2. (*propender*) to incline 3. (*preferir*) ~ **se por algo** to have a penchant for sth

incluir [in·klu·ir] *irr como huir vt* to include, to enclose, to contain; **todo incluido** all-inclusive

inclusión [in·klu·'sjon] *f* inclusion; **con** ~ **de...** with the inclusion of...

inclusive [in·klu·'si·βe] *adv* inclusively

incluso [in·'klu·so] I. *adv* inclusively II. *prep* including; **han aprobado todos,** ~ **tú** you have all passed, even you

incluso, -a [in·'klu·so, -a] *adj* included

incoar [in·ko·'ar] *vt* JUR (*proceso*) to institute proceedings

incógnita [in·'koɣ·ni·ta] *f* enigma; (*secreto*) secret; **despejar la** ~ (*enigma*) to solve the enigma; (*secreto*) to disclose the secret

incógnito, -a [in·'koɣ·ni·to] *adj* incognito

incoherencia [in·ko·e·'ren·sja, -θja] *f* incoherence

incoherente [in·ko·e·'ren·te] *adj* incoherent

incoloro, -a [in·ko·'lo·ro, -a] *adj* colorless

incólume [in·'ko·lu·me] *adj* intact, unscathed

incombustible [in·kom·bus·'ti·βle] *adj* incombustible

incomible [in·ko·'mi·βle] *adj* inedible, uneatable

incomodar [in·ko·mo·'dar] I. *vt* to inconvenience, to incommode *form* II. *vr:* ~ **se** 1. (*molestarse*) **no te incomodes, que abro yo** don't trouble yourself, I'll open the door 2. *CSur* (*enfadarse*) to become angry

incomodidad [in·ko·mo·di·'dad] *f*, **incomodo** [in·ko·'mo·do] *m* uncomfortableness, discomfort

incómodo, -a [in·'ko·mo·do, -a] *adj* 1. (*inconfortable*) uncomfortable 2. (*molesto*) tiresome

incomparable [in·kom·pa·'ra·βle] *adj* incomparable

incompatibilidad [in·kom·pa·ti·βi·li·'dad] *f* incompatibility

incompatible [in·kom·pa·'ti·βle] *adj* incompatible

incompetencia [in·kom·pe·'ten·sja, -θja] *f* incompetence

incompetente [in·kom·pe·'ten·te] *adj* incompetent

incompleto, -a [in·kom·'ple·to, -a] *adj* incomplete

incomprensible [in·kom·pren·'si·βle] *adj* incomprehensible

incomprensión [in·kom·pren·'sjon] *f* (*no querer comprender*) unwillingness to understand; (*no poder comprender*) incomprehension

incomunicación [in·ko·mu·ni·ka·'sjon, -'θjon] *f* 1. (*aislamiento*) isolation; (*en prisión*) solitary confinement 2. (*falta de comunicación*) lack of communication

incomunicado, -a [in·ko·mu·ni·'ka·do, -a] *adj* incommunicado; **el preso estuvo 6 días** ~ the prisoner spent 6 days in solitary confinement

incomunicar <c→qu> [in·ko·mu·ni·'kar] *vt* 1. (*aislar*) to isolate 2. (*bloquear*) to cut off

inconcebible [in·kon·se·'βi·βle, -θe·'βi·βle] *adj* 1. (*inimaginable*) inconceivable 2. (*inadmisible*) unacceptable

inconciliable [in·kon·si·'lja·βle, -θi·'lja·βle] *adj* irreconcilable

inconcluso, -a [in·kon·'klu·so, -a] *adj* unfinished

inconcreción [in·kon·kre·'sjon, -'θjon] *f* imprecision

inconcreto, -a [in·kon·'kre·to, -a] *adj* imprecise

incondicional [in·kon·di·sjo·'nal, -θjo·'nal] *adj* unconditional

inconexo, -a [in·ko·'nek·so, -a] *adj* unconnected

inconformista [in·kon·for·'mis·ta] *mf* nonconformist

inconfundible [in·kon·fun·'di·βle] *adj* unmistakable

incongruencia [in·kon·'grwen·sja, -θja] *f* incongruity

incongruente [in·kon·'grwen·te] *adj* incongruous

inconmensurable [in·kon·men·su·'ra·βle, in·kom·men-] *adj* incommensurate

inconmovible [in·kon·mo·'βi·βle, in·kom·mo-] *adj* (*personas*) steadfast

inconsciencia [in·kon·'sjen·sja, -kons·'θjen·θja] *f* 1.(*desmayo*) unconsciousness 2.(*insensatez*) senselessness; (*irresponsabilidad*) thoughtlessness

inconsciente [in·kon·'sjen·te, -kons·'θjen·te] *adj* 1. *estar* (*desmayado*) unconscious 2. *ser* (*insensato*) senseless; (*irresponsable*) thoughtless 3. *ser* (*gesto*) involuntary

inconsistencia [in·kon·sis·'ten·sja, -θja] *f* flimsiness

inconsistente [in·kon·sis·'ten·te] *adj* 1.(*irregular*) uneven 2.(*poco sólido*) flimsy; (*argumento*) weak

inconsolable [in·kon·so·'la·βle] *adj* inconsolable, broken-hearted

inconstante [in·kons·'tan·te] *adj* inconstant; (*caprichoso*) changeable

inconstitucionalidad [in·kons·ti·tu·sjo·na·li·'dad, -θjo·na·li·'dad] *f* unconstitutionality

incontable [in·kon·'ta·βle] *adj* 1.(*innumerable*) countless 2.(*inenarrable*) unmentionable; LING uncountable

incontenible [in·kon·te·'ni·βle] *adj* (*irrefrenable*) uncontainable, unrestrainable; (*risa, júbilo, impulso*) irrepressible

incontestable [in·kon·tes·'ta·βle] *adj* incontestable; (*pregunta*) unanswerable

incontinencia [in·kon·ti·'nen·sja, -θja] *f t.* MED incontinence

incontrolado, -a [in·kon·tro·'la·do, -a] *adj* uncontrolled; (*violento*) violent

incontrovertible [in·kon·tro·βer·'ti·βle] *adj* incontrovertible

inconveniencia [in·kom·be·'njen·sja, -θja] *f* 1.(*descortesía*) discourtesy 2.(*disparate*) absurd remark 3.(*no adecuado*) inappropriateness

inconveniente [in·kom·be·'njen·te] I. *adj* 1.(*descortés*) discourteous; (*disparate*) absurd 2.(*no adecuado*) inappropriate 3.(*no aconsejable*) unadvisable II. *m* disadvantage; (*obstáculo*) inconvenience

incordiar [in·kor·'djar] *vt* to bother; ¡**deja de** ~! stop being so irritating!

incordio [in·'kor·djo] *m inf* bother, pest

incorporación [in·kor·po·ra·'sjon, -'θjon] *f*

1.(*al enderezarse*) straightening up; (*al sentarse*) sitting up 2.(*integración*) incorporation; ~ **a filas** MIL induction

incorporar [in·kor·po·'rar] I. *vt* 1.(*a un grupo*) ~ **a** [*o* **en**] **algo** to incorporate in [*o* into] sth 2.(*a una persona*) to include II. *vr:* ~**se** 1.(*enderezarse*) to sit up 2.(*en el trabajo*) ~**se al trabajo** to start a new job 3.(*agregarse*) ~**se a** [*o* **en**] **algo** to join sth 4. MIL (*a filas*) to enlist

incorrecto, -a [in·ko·'rrek·to, -a] *adj* 1.(*erróneo*) erroneous 2.(*descortés*) impolite

incorregible [in·ko·rre·'xi·βle] *adj* incorrigible

incorruptible [in·ko·rrup·'ti·βle] *adj* incorruptible

incredulidad [in·kre·du·li·'dad] *f* incredulity

incrédulo, -a [in·'kre·du·lo, -a] I. *adj* incredulous II. *m, f* incredulous person; (*escéptico*) skeptic

increíble [in·kre·'i·βle] *adj* incredible

incrementar [in·kre·men·'tar] *vt, vr:* ~**se** to increase

incremento [in·kre·'men·to] *m* (*aumento*) increment; (*crecimiento*) increase

increpar [in·kre·'par] *vt* to rebuke

incriminar [in·kri·mi·'nar] *vt* JUR to incriminate

incrustación [in·krus·ta·'sjon, -'θjon] *f* (*proceso*) embedding; ARTE inlaying; MED incrustation

incrustar [in·krus·'tar] I. *vt* (*con madera*) to inlay II. *vr:* ~ **se** to embed itself; MED to encrust

incubación [in·ku·βa·'sjon, -'θjon] *f* incubation (period)

incubadora [in·ku·βa·'do·ra] *f* incubator

incubar [in·ku·'βar] *vt, vr:* ~**se** to incubate

incuestionable [in·kwes·tjo·'na·βle] *adj* unquestionable

inculcar <c→qu> [in·kul·'kar] I. *vt* (*enseñar*) to instill; (*infundir*) to inculcate II. *vr:* ~**se en algo** to be obstinate about sth

inculpación [in·kul·pa·'sjon, -'θjon] *f* accusation

inculpar [in·kul·'par] *vt* ~ **a alguien de algo** to accuse sb of sth; JUR to charge sb with sth

inculto, -a [in·'kul·to, -a] *adj* uneducated

incultura [in·kul·'tu·ra] *f* lack of education [*o* culture]

incumbencia [in·kum·'ben·sja, -θja] *f* responsibility, incumbency *form*; **no es de tu** ~ it's none of your business

incumbir [in·kum·'bir] *vi* to concern; ~ **a alguien** ADMIN to be incumbent on [*o* upon] sb

incumplimiento [in·kum·pli·'mjen·to] *m* non-compliance; ~ **de contrato** breach of contract

incumplir [in·kum·'plir] *vt* to breach

incurable [in·ku·'ra·βle] I. *adj* incurable II. *mf* incurable person

incurrir [in·ku·'rrir] *vi* ~ **en una falta** to commit an error; ~ **en viejas costumbres** to go back to old habits

incursión [in·kur·'sjon] *f* incursion, strike

indagación [in·da·ɣa·'sjon, -'θjon] *f* inquiry

indagar <g→gu> [in·da·'γar] *vt* ~ **algo** to look into sth
indebido, -a [in·de·'βi·do, -a] *adj* wrongful; (*ilícito*) illicit; **respuesta indebida** inappropriate reply
indecencia [in·de·'sen·sja, -'θen·θja] *f* indecency
indecente [in·de·'sen·te, -'θen·te] *adj* indecent; (*sin vergüenza*) shameless
indecisión [in·de·si·'sjon, in·de·θi-] *f* (*vacilación*) indecision
indeciso, -a [in·de·'si·so, -a; 'θi·so, -a] *adj* **1.** (*irresoluto*) irresolute **2.** (*que vacila*) indecisive
indecoroso, -a [in·de·ko·'ro·so, -a] *adj* indecorous
indefendible [in·de·fen·'di·βle] *adj* indefensible
indefensión [in·de·fen·'sjon] *f* defenselessness
indefenso, -a [in·de·'fen·so, -a] *adj* defenseless
indefinible [in·de·fi·'ni·βle] *adj* indefinable, undefinable
indefinidamente [in·de·fi·ni·da·'men·te] *adv* indefinitely
indefinido, -a [in·de·fi·'ni·do, -a] *adj t.* LING indefinite
indeformable [in·de·for·'ma·βle] *adj* that keeps its shape
indemne [in·'dem·ne] *adj* (*persona*) unharmed; (*cosa*) undamaged
indemnización [in·dem·ni·sa·'sjon, -θa·'θjon] *f* indemnity, indemnification; ~ **de despido** unemployment compensation, severance pay
indemnizar <z→c> [in·dem·ni·'sar, -'θar] *vt* **1.** (*daños y perjuicios*) to indemnify; ~ **de** [o **por**] **algo** to indemnify for sth **2.** (*gastos*) to reimburse
independencia [in·de·pen·'den·sja, -θja] *f* independence; **con** ~ **de algo** independently of sth
independiente [in·de·pen·'djen·te] *adj* independent; **un piso** ~ a self-contained apartment
independización [in·de·pen·di·sa·'sjon, θa·'θjon] *f* liberation; (*adolescente*) emancipation
independizar <z→c> [in·de·pen·di·'sar, -'θar] **I.** *vt* to make independent **II.** *vr:* ~ **se** to become independent
indescifrable [in·de·si·'fra·βle, in·des·θi·'fra·βle] *adj* indecipherable
indescriptible [in·des·krip·'ti·βle] *adj* indescribable
indeseable [in·de·se·'a·βle] *adj* undesirable
indestructible [in·des·truk·'ti·βle] *adj* indestructible
indeterminación [in·de·ter·mi·na·'sjon, -'θjon] *f* indeterminacy; (*indecisión*) indecision
indeterminado, -a [in·de·ter·mi·'na·do, -a] *adj* indeterminate; (*indeciso*) indecisive

indexación [in·dek·sa·'sjon, -'θjon] *f* indexation; COMPUT indexing
indexar [in·dek·'sar] *vt* COMPUT to index
India ['in·dja] *f* **la** ~ India; **las** ~**s** the Indies
indiada [in·'dja·da] *f AmL: a group of Indians*
indicación [in·di·ka·'sjon, -'θjon] *f* **1.** (*señal*) indication; (*por escrito*) observation; (*consejo*) advice; ~ **de las fuentes** source reference; **por** ~ **de...** on the advice of... **2.** *pl* (*instrucciones*) instructions *pl*
indicado, -a [in·di·'ka·do, -a] *adj* **1.** (*aconsejable*) advisable; (*adecuado*) indicated; **eso es lo más** ~ that is the most suitable **2.** MED (*tratamiento*) recommended
indicador [in·di·ka·'dor] *m* indicator; TÉC gauge, gage; ECON index; ~ **de carretera** road sign; ~ **de gasolina** fuel gauge
indicar <c→qu> [in·di·'kar] *vt* **1.** TÉC (*aparato*) to register **2.** (*señalar, sugerir*) to indicate; (*mostrar*) to show **3.** MED to prescribe
indicativo, -a [in·di·ka·'ti·βo] *adj t.* LING indicative
índice ['in·di·se, -θe] *m* **1.** (*biblioteca, catálogo*) index, catalog; (*libro*) table of contents **2.** (*dedo*) index finger, forefinger **3.** (*estadísticas*) rate; ~ **de audiencia** audience ratings; ~ **de paro** unemployment rate; **Índice de Precios al Consumidor** Consumer Price Index
indicio [in·'di·sjo, -θjo] *m* sign; JUR indication; (*vestigio*) trace
indiferencia [in·di·fe·'ren·sja, -θja] *f* indifference
indiferente [in·di·fe·'ren·te] *adj* indifferent; **me es** ~ it doesn't make any difference to me
indígena [in·'di·xe·na] **I.** *adj* indigenous, native; (*en Latinoamérica*) Indian **II.** *mf* native; (*en Latinoamérica*) Indian
indigencia [in·di·'xen·sja, -θja] *f* poverty
indigente [in·di·'xen·te] *mf* destitute person
indigestar [in·di·xes·'tar] **I.** *vt* to cause indigestion to **II.** *vr:* ~**se 1.** (*empacharse*) ~**se de** [o **por**] **algo** to get indigestion from sth **2.** *inf* (*hacerse antipático*) to be detestable **3.** *AmL* (*inquietarse*) to worry
indigestión [in·di·xes·'tjon] *f* MED indigestion; **contraer una** ~ to get indigestion
indigesto, -a [in·di·'xes·to, -a] *adj ser* indigestible, hard to digest
indignación [in·diγ·na·'sjon, -'θjon] *f* indignation
indignado, -a [in·diγ·'na·do, -a] *adj* ~ **por algo** indignant about [o at] sth
indignante [in·diγ·'nan·te] *adj* infuriating, outrageous
indignar [in·diγ·'nar] **I.** *vt* to infuriate, to outrage **II.** *vr* ~**se por algo** to become indignant [o infuriated] about sth
indigno, -a [in·'diγ·no, -a] *adj* **1.** (*desmerecedor*) unworthy **2.** (*vil*) contemptible
índigo ['in·di·γo] *m* indigo
indio, -a ['in·djo, -a] **I.** *adj* **1.** (*de la India*) Indian **2.** (*de América*) American Indian **II.** *m, f* **1.** (*de la India*) Indian **2.** (*de América*) Ameri-

can Indian ▶**hacer el** ~ (*tonterías*) to fool around [*o* about]; (*el ridículo*) to act the fool

ℹ️ When Columbus discovered America, he believed he landed in India. Therefore, he named the native inhabitants **indios**. The word "**indio**" should be used carefully, since it also means "tonto," (stupid) and is a discriminatory term for describing the rural population.

indirecta [in·di·'rek·ta] *f inf* hint, insinuation; **lanzar** [*o* **soltar**] **una** ~ to drop a hint
indirecto, -a [in·di·'rek·to, -a] *adj* indirect; **complemento** ~ LING indirect object
indisciplinado, -a [in·di·si·pli·'na·do, -a; in·dis·θi-] *adj* undisciplined
indiscreción [in·dis·kre·'sjon, -'θjon] *f* indiscretion
indiscreto, -a [in·dis·'kre·to, -a] *adj* imprudent; (*que no guarda secretos*) indiscreet
indiscriminado, -a [in·dis·kri·mi·'na·do, -a] *adj* indiscriminate
indiscutible [in·dis·ku·'ti·βle] *adj* indisputable
indisociable [in·di·so·'sja·βle, -'θja·βle] *adj* inseparable; QUÍM indissoluble
indispensable [in·dis·pen·'sa·βle] *adj* indispensable; **lo** (**más**) ~ the most essential; **el requisito** ~ **es...** the key requisite is...
indisponer [in·dis·po·'ner] *irr como poner* I. *vt* 1. (*enemistar*) ~ **a uno contra otro** to set one person against another 2. (*de salud*) to indispose II. *vr:* ~ **se** 1. (*enemistarse*) to quarrel 2. (*ponerse mal*) to become indisposed
indisposición [in·dis·po·si·'sjon, -'θjon] *f* indisposition
indispuesto, -a [in·dis·'pwes·to, -a] *adj* indisposed; (*reacio*) unwilling
indistintamente [in·dis·tin·ta·'men·te] *adv* indiscriminately; **se aplica a todos los niños** ~ it applies to all the children without distinction
indistinto, -a [in·dis·'tin·to, -a] *adj* indistinguishable
individual [in·di·βi·'dwal] *adj* 1. (*personal*) personal; (*peculiar*) individual 2. (*simple*) single 3. *CSur* (*idéntico*) identical
individualista [in·di·βi·dwa·'lis·ta] *mf* individualist
individualizar <z→c> [in·di·βi·dwa·li·'sar, -'θar] *vt* to individualize
individuo [in·di·'βi·dwo] *m* individual; *pey* (*sujeto*) individual, character
indivisible [in·di·βi·'si·βle] *adj* indivisible
indócil [in·'do·sil, -'do·θil] *adj* (*desobediente*) unruly
indoctrinar [in·dok·tri·'nar] *vt AmL* to indoctrinate; *fig* to brainwash
indocumentado, -a [in·do·ku·men·'ta·do, -a] *adj* **estar** ~ to be without papers [*o* means of identification]
índole ['in·do·le] *f* nature, kind
indolencia [in·do·'len·sja, -θja] *f* (*desgana*)

indolence
indolente [in·do·'len·te] *adj* (*con desgana*) indolent
indomable [in·do·'ma·βle] *adj* (*que no se somete*) indomitable; (*indomesticable*) untameable
indómito, -a [in·'do·mi·to, -a] *adj* (*indomable*) indomitable; (*rebelde*) rebellious
Indonesia [in·do·'ne·sja] *f* Indonesia
indonesio, -a [in·do·'ne·sjo, -a] *adj, m, f* Indonesian
inducir [in·du·'sir, -'θir] *irr como traducir vt* 1. ELEC (*corriente*) to induce 2. (*instigar*) to induce; ~ **a error** to lead astray, to mislead 3. FILOS (*razonar*) to induce; **de todo esto induzco que...** from all this I induce that...
indudable [in·du·'da·βle] *adj* undeniable; **es** ~ **que...** it is certain that...
indulgencia [in·dul·'xen·sja, -θja] *f t.* REL indulgence; **proceder sin** ~ **contra...** to proceed without leniency against...
indultar [in·dul·'tar] *vt* JUR (*perdonar*) to pardon; ~ **a alguien de la pena de muerte** to grant sb a reprieve from the death penalty
indulto [in·'dul·to] *m* (*perdón total*) pardon; (*perdón parcial*) remission
indumentaria [in·du·men·'ta·rja] *f* clothing, clothes *pl*; (*vestir*) dress
industria [in·'dus·trja] *f* industry; ~ **del automóvil** automobile industry
industrial [in·dus·'trjal] I. *adj* industrial; **nave** ~ industrial warehouse; **planta** ~ industrial plant; **polígono** ~ industrial estate, industrial park II. *mf* industrialist; (*fabricante*) manufacturer
industrialización [in·dus·trja·li·sa·'sjon, -θa·'θjon] *f* industrialization
industrializar <z→c> [in·dus·trja·li·'sar, -'θar] *vt, vr:* ~ **se** to industrialize
inédito, -a [i·'ne·di·to, -a] *adj* (*no publicado*) unpublished
inefable [i·ne·'fa·βle] *adj* ineffable, inexpressible
ineficacia [in·e·fi·'ka·sja, -θja] *f* 1. (*sin resultado*) ineffectiveness 2. COM (*sin rentabilidad*) lack of profitability 3. (*de una persona*) inefficiency
ineficaz [in·e·fi·'kas -'kaθ] *adj* 1. (*cosa*) ineffective 2. (*persona*) ineffectual
ineficiente [in·e·fi·'sjen·te, -'θjente] *adj* inefficient
INEM [i·'nem] *m abr de* **Instituto Nacional de Empleo** *national employment agency*
inenarrable [i·ne·na·'rra·βle] *adj* indescribable
inepcia [i·'nep·sja, -neβ·θja] *f AmL* ineptitude; (*necedad*) imbecility
ineptitud [i·nep·ti·'tud] *f* ~ **para algo** (*incapacidad*) ineptitude in sth; (*incompetencia*) incompetence in sth
inepto, -a [i·'nep·to, -a] *adj* ~ **para algo** (*incapaz*) inept at sth; (*incompetente*) incompetent at sth

inequívoco, -a [in·e·'ki·βo·ko, -a] *adj* unequivocal; (*inconfundible*) unmistakable

inercia [i·'ner·sja, -θja] *f t.* Fís inertia; **por ~** mechanically

inerme [i·'ner·me] *adj* (*desarmado*) unarmed; (*indefenso*) defenseless

inerte [i·'ner·te] *adj* (*sin vida*) inanimate; (*inmóvil*) inert

inesperado, -a [in·es·pe·'ra·do, -a] *adj* unexpected

inestable [in·es·'ta·βle] *adj* **1.** (*frágil*) *t.* TÉC fragile **2.** (*variable*) unstable

inestimable [in·es·ti·'ma·βle] *adj* inestimable

inevitable [in·e·βi·'ta·βle] *adj* inevitable, unavoidable

inexacto, -a [in·ek·'sak·to, -a] *adj* inexact; (*erróneo*) inaccurate

inexcusable [in·es·ku·'sa·βle] *adj* (*sin disculpa*) inexcusable

inexistencia [in·ek·sis·'ten·sja, -θja] *f* non-existence

inexistente [in·ek·sis·'ten·te] *adj* non-existent

inexorable [in·ek·so·'ra·βle] *adj* elev inexorable

inexperiencia [in·es·pe·'rjen·sja, -θja] *f* inexperience

inexperto, -a [in·es·'per·to, -a] *adj* inexpert; (*sin experiencia*) inexperienced

inexplicable [in·es·pli·'ka·βle] *adj* inexplicable

inexpresivo, -a [in·es·pre·'si·βo, -a] *adj* inexpressive

inextricable [in·es·tri·'ka·βle] *adj* inextricable; (*complicado*) intricate

infalible [in·fa·'li·βle] *adj* infallible

infame [in·'fa·me] *adj* **1.** (*vil*) wicked **2.** (*muy malo*) vile

infamia [in·'fa·mja] *f* infamy; (*deshonra*) dishonor

infancia [in·'fan·sja, -θja] *f* **1.** (*niñez, niños*) childhood **2.** (*etapa inicial*) infancy

infante, -a [in·'fan·te, -a] *m, f* **1.** elev (*niño, niña*) infant; **jardín de ~s** AmL kindergarten **2.** (*príncipe, princesa*) infante *m*, infanta *f*

infantería [in·fan·te·'ri·a] *f* MIL infantry

infanticida [in·fan·ti·'si·da, -'θi·da] **I.** *adj* infanticidal **II.** *mf person who commits infanticide*

infantil [in·fan·'til] *adj* **1.** (*referente a la infancia*) infant; **trabajo ~** child labor **2.** pey (*ingenuo*) infantile

infarto [in·'far·to] *m* heart attack

infatigable [in·fa·ti·'ɣa·βle] *adj* tireless

infección [in·fek·'sjon, -'θjon] *f* contagion; (*afección*) infection

infeccioso, -a [in·fek·'sjo·so, -a; -'θjo·so, -a] *adj* infectious; **enfermedad infecciosa** contagious illness

infectar [in·fek·'tar] **I.** *vt* (*contagiar*) to transmit; inf (*contaminar*) to infect; (*corromper*) to corrupt **II.** *vr:* **~se 1.** (*contagiarse*) **~se de SIDA** to catch AIDS **2.** (*inflamarse*) to become infected

infecto, -a [in·'fek·to, -a] *adj* **1.** (*contagiado*) **~ de algo** infected with sth **2.** (*nauseabundo*) nauseating **3.** (*corrupto*) corrupt, tainted

infelicidad [in·fe·li·si·'dad, -θi·'dad] *f* unhappiness

infeliz [in·fe·'lis, -'liθ] *adj* **1.** (*no feliz*) unhappy **2.** inf (*ingenuo*) ingenuous

inferior [in·fe·'rjor] **I.** *adj* **1.** (*debajo*) lower; **labio ~** lower lip **2.** (*de menos calidad*) inferior **3.** (*menos*) **~ a algo** lesser than sth **4.** (*subordinado*) subordinate **II.** *mf* inferior

inferioridad [in·fe·rjo·ri·'dad] *f* inferiority; **estar en ~ de condiciones** to be at a disadvantage

inferir [in·fe·'rir] *irr como sentir vt* **1.** (*deducir*) to infer; **~ de** [o por] **algo** to infer from sth **2.** (*causar*) to cause

infernal [in·fer·'nal] *adj* infernal; **ruido ~** infernal din

infértil [in·'fer·til] *adj* infertile

infestar [in·fes·'tar] *vt* **~ de algo** (*inundar*) to overrun with sth; (*infectar*) to infect with sth; (*corromper*) to corrupt with sth

infidelidad [in·fi·de·li·'dad] *f* infidelity, unfaithfulness

infiel [in·'fjel] **I.** *adj* <infidelísimo> **1.** (*desleal*) unfaithful **2.** (*pagano*) heathen **II.** *mf* pagan

infiernillo [in·fjer·'ni·jo, -ʎo] *m* camping [o portable] stove

infierno [in·'fjer·no] *m* **1.** *t.* REL hell; **me mandó al ~** he/she told me to go to hell **2.** (*en la mitología*) underworld

infiltrar [in·fil·'trar] **I.** *vt* to infiltrate, to penetrate **II.** *vr:* **~se en algo** (*penetrar*) to penetrate sth; (*introducirse*) to infiltrate sth

ínfimo, -a ['in·fi·mo, -a] *adj* **1.** (*muy bajo*) very low **2.** (*mínimo*) minimal **3.** (*vil*) vile

infinidad [in·fi·ni·'dad] *f* **1.** (*cualidad de infinito*) infinity **2.** (*gran número*) enormous quantity

infinitivo [in·fi·ni·'ti·βo] *m* infinitive

infinito [in·fi·'ni·to] *m t.* MAT infinity

infinito, -a [in·fi·'ni·to, -a] *adj* **1.** (*ilimitado*) limitless; (*cosas no materiales*) boundless **2.** (*incontable*) infinite

inflable [in·'fla·βle] *adj* inflatable

inflación [in·fla·'sjon, -'θjon] *f t.* ECON inflation

inflacionista [in·fla·sjo·'nis·ta, -θjo·'nis·ta] *adj* ECON inflationist

inflamable [in·fla·'ma·βle] *adj* (in)flammable

inflamación [in·fla·ma·'sjon, -'θjon] *f* **1.** *t.* MED inflammation **2.** TÉC ignition; **punto de ~** ignition point

inflamar [in·fla·'mar] **I.** *vt* **1.** (*encender*) to ignite **2.** (*excitar*) *t.* MED to inflame **II.** *vr:* **~se** *t.* MED to become inflamed

inflamatorio, -a [in·fla·ma·'to·rjo, -a] *adj* inflammatory

inflar [in·'flar] **I.** *vt* **1.** (*llenar de aire*) to inflate **2.** (*exagerar*) to exaggerate **II.** *vr* **1.** (*hincharse*) **~se de algo** to swell with sth **2.** inf (*de comida*) to stuff oneself

inflexible [in·flek·'si·βle] *adj* **1.** (*rígido*) inflex ible **2.** (*firme*) firm

inflexión [in·flek·'sjon] *f* **1.** (*de la voz*) *t.* MAT, LING inflection, inflexion **2.** (*torcimiento*) bend

infligir <g→j> [in·fli·'xir] *vt* (*dolor*) to inflict; ~ **un castigo** to inflict a punishment; ~ **daño** to cause injury

influencia [in·'flwen·sja, -θja] *f* influence; **tener** ~ to be influential

influenciar [in·flwen·'sjar, -θjar] *vt* to influence; **dejarse** ~ to be influenced

influir [in·flu·'ir] *irr como huir* **I.** *vi* ~ **en** [*o sobre*] **algo** (*contribuir*) to have a hand in sth; (*actuar*) to have an influence on sth **II.** *vt* to influence

influjo [in·'flu·xo] *m* influence

influyente [in·flu·'jen·te] *adj* influential

infoguerra [in·fo·'γer·ra] *f* COMPUT, POL information war

infonomía [in·fo·no·'mi·a] *f* information management *no pl*

infonomista [in·fo·no·'mis·ta] *mf* information manager

información [in·for·ma·'sjon, -'θjon] *f* information; TEL directory assistance

informal [in·for·'mal] *adj* **1.** (*desenfadado*) informal, casual; **lenguaje** ~ informal language **2.** (*no cumplidor*) unreliable

informante [in·for·'man·te] *mf* informant

informar [in·for·'mar] **I.** *vt* to inform **II.** *vi* JUR to plead **III.** *vr* ~ **se de algo** to find out about sth

informática [in·for·'ma·ti·ka] *f* computer [*o* computing] science

informático, -a [in·for·'ma·ti·ko, -a] **I.** *adj* **fallo** ~ computer error **II.** *m, f* computer expert

informativo [in·for·ma·'ti·βo] *m* news broadcast; **el** ~ **de las nueve** the nine o'clock news

informativo, -a [in·for·ma·'ti·βo, -a] *adj* informative; **boletín** ~ (*por escrito, radial*) (news) bulletin

informatización [in·for·ma·ti·sa·'sjon, -θa·'θjon] *f* computerization

informatizar <z→c> [in·for·ma·ti·'sar, -'θar] *vt* to computerize

informe [in·'for·me] *m* report

infortunado, -a [in·for·tu·'na·do, -a] *adj* unfortunate

infortunio [in·for·'tu·njo] *m* misfortune, adversity

infotainment [in·fo·'tain·ment] *m* infotainment

infracción [in·frak·'sjon, -'θjon] *f* infraction; (*administrativa*) breach; ~ **de tráfico** traffic violation

infractor(a) [in·frak·'tor, -'to·ra] *m(f)* offender

infraestructura [in·fra·es·truk·'tu·ra] *f* infrastructure

infrahumano, -a [in·fra·u·'ma·no, -a] *adj* subhuman

infranqueable [in·fran·ke·'a·βle] *adj* impassable, insurmountable *fig*

infrarrojo, -a [in·fra·'rro·xo, -a] *adj* infrared

infrautilizar <z→c> [in·fra·u·ti·li·'sar, -'θar] *vt* to underuse

infravalorar [in·fra·βa·lo·'rar] *vt* to undervalue, to underestimate

infrecuente [in·fre·'kwen·te] *adj* infrequent

infringir <g→j> [in·frin·'xir] *vt* to infringe; ~ **la ley** to break the law

infructuoso, -a [in·fruk·tu·'o·so, -a] *adj* fruitless

ínfula ['in·fu·la] *f pl* **darse** ~**s** to put on airs (and graces)

infundado, -a [in·fun·'da·do, -a] *adj* unfounded

infundir [in·fun·'dir] *vt* (*deseo*) to infuse; (*respeto*) to command; (*sospechas*) to instill

infusión [in·fu·'sjon] *f* infusion; (*de hierbas*) herb(al) tea

ingeniar [in·xe·'njar] **I.** *vt* to devise **II.** *vr:* ~ **se** to contrive, to manage

ingeniería [in·xe·nje·'ria] *f* engineering; **escuela de** ~ school of engineering

ingeniero [in·xe·'nje·ro, -a] *m, f* engineer

ingenio [in·'xe·njo] *m* (*inventiva*) ingenuity; (*maña*) aptitude

ingenioso, -a [in·xe·'njo·so, -a] *adj* **1.** (*hábil*) skillful **2.** (*listo*) ingenious

ingenuidad [in·xe·nwi·'dad] *f* **1.** (*inocencia*) candor **2.** (*torpeza*) naivety

ingenuo, -a [in·'xe·nwo, -a] *adj* ingenuous, candid

ingerir [in·xe·'rir] *irr como sentir vt* to ingest; (*medicamentos*) to take

ingestión [in·xes·'tjon] *f* ingestion, consumption; (*medicamentos*) taking, intake

Inglaterra [in·gla·'te·rra] *f* England

ingle ['in·gle] *f* ANAT groin

inglés, -esa [in·'gles, -'gle·sa] **I.** *adj* English **II.** *m, f* Englishman *m*, Englishwoman *f*

ingratitud [in·gra·ti·'tud] *f* ingratitude

ingrato, -a [in·'gra·to, -a] *adj* ungrateful; ~ (**para**) **con alguien** ungrateful to sb; (*tarea*) thankless

ingravidez [in·gra·βi·'des, -'deθ] *f* weightlessness, lack of gravity

ingrávido, -a [in·'gra·βi·do, -a] *adj* lacking in gravity, weightless

ingrediente [in·gre·'djen·te] *m* ingredient

ingresar [in·gre·'sar] **I.** *vi* **1.** (*inscribirse*) ~ **en algo** to become a member of sth **2.** (*hospitalizarse*) to be admitted to hospital **II.** *vt* **1.** FIN (*cheque*) to pay in, to deposit **2.** (*hospitalizar*) to hospitalize **3.** (*percibir*) to earn

ingreso [in·'gre·so] *m* **1.** (*inscripción*) entry; (*alta*) incorporation; **examen de** ~ entrance exam **2.** (*en una cuenta*) deposit **3.** *pl* (*retribuciones*) income

íngrimo, -a ['in·gri·mo, -a] *adj AmL* solitary

inhábil [in·'a·βil] *adj* JUR **día** ~ non-working day

inhabilitar [in·a·βi·li·'tar] *vt* JUR **1.** (*incapacitar*) ~ **para algo** to incapacitate for sth **2.** (*prohibir*) ~ **a** (**hacer**) **algo** to disqualify from (doing) sth

inhabitable [in·a·βi·'ta·βle] *adj* uninhabitable
inhabitado, -a [in·a·βi·'ta·do, -a] *adj* uninhabited
inhabitual [in·a·βi·tu·'al] *adj* unusual
inhalador [in·a·la·'dor] *m* MED inhaler
inhalar [in·a·'lar] *vt t.* MED to inhale, to breathe in
inherente [in·e·'ren·te] *adj* inherent; ~ **a algo** inherent in sth
inhibición [in·i·βi·'sjon, -'θjon] *f* (*represión*) repression; (*abstención*) abstention; MED, JUR inhibition
inhibir [in·i·'βir] **I.** *vt* to repress; BIO, JUR to inhibit **II.** *vr* ~**se de algo** to abstain from sth; ~**se de hacer algo** to refrain from doing sth
inhospitalario, -a [in·os·pi·ta·'la·rjo, -a] *adj* inhospitable, unfriendly
inhóspito, -a [in·'os·pi·to, -a] *adj* inhospitable
inhumación [in·u·ma·'sjon, -'θjon] *f* inhumation, burial
inhumano, -a [in·u·'ma·no, -a] *adj* (*no humano*) inhuman; (*sin compasión*) inhumane
inhumar [in·u·'mar] *vt elev* to inhume, to bury
iniciación [i·ni·sja·'sjon, -θja·'θjon] *f* **1.** (*comienzo*) beginning, commencement **2.** (*introducción*) ~ **a** [*o* **en**] **algo** initiation to sth
iniciado, -a [i·ni·'sja·do, -a; -'θja·do, -a] **I.** *adj* initiated **II.** *m, f* initiate
inicial [i·ni·'sjal, -'θjal] *adj* initial; **fase** ~ initial phase
iniciar [i·ni·'sjar, -'θjar] **I.** *vt* **1.** (*comenzar*) to begin **2.** (*introducir*) to initiate; COMPUT to log in [*o* on] **II.** *vr:* ~**se 1.** (*comenzar*) to begin **2.** (*introducirse en*) ~ **en algo** to learn sth on one's own
iniciativa [i·ni·sja·'ti·βa, i·ni·θja-] *f* initiative; ~ **privada** ECON private enterprise
inicio [i·'ni·sjo, -θjo] *m* beginning
inigualable [in·i·ɣwa·'la·βle] *adj* incomparable, unrivaled
inimaginable [in·i·ma·xi·'na·βle] *adj* unimaginable
ininteligible [in·in·te·li·'xen·te] *adj* unintelligible; (*escritura*) illegible
ininterrumpido, -a [in·in·te·rrum·'pi·do, -a] *adj* uninterrupted
iniquidad [i·ni·ki·'dad] *f* iniquity; (*infamia*) wickedness
injerencia [in·xe·'ren·sja, -θja] *f* interference
injerir [in·xe·'rir] *irr como sentir* **I.** *vt* **1.** (*introducir*) to introduce; ~ **en algo** to introduce into sth **2.** (*injertar*) to graft **II.** *vr:* ~**se** to interfere
injertar [in·xer·'tar] *vt* (*plantas*) *t.* MED to graft
injerto [in·'xer·to] *m* (*brote*) *t.* MED graft
injuria [in·'xu·rja] *f* (*con palabras*) insult, affront; (*con acciones*) harm; JUR slander
injuriar [in·xu·'rjar] *vt* (*con palabras*) to insult; (*con acciones*) to injure
injusticia [in·xus·'ti·sja, -θja] *f* injustice, unfairness

injustificado, -a [in·xus·ti·fi·'ka·do, -a] *adj* unjustified
injusto, -a [in·'xus·to, -a] *adj* **1.** (*no justo*) unjust, unfair **2.** (*injustificado*) *t.* JUR inequitable
inmaculado, -a [in·ma·ku·'la·do, -a, im·ma-] *adj* immaculate
inmadurez [in·ma·du·'res, -reθ; im·ma-] *f* immaturity
inmaduro, -a [in·ma·'du·ro, -a; im·ma-] *adj* immature
inmediaciones [in·me·dja·'sjo·nes, -'θjo·nes; im·me-] *fpl* surroundings *pl*, vicinity
inmediatamente [in·me·dja·ta·'men·te, im·me-] *adv* **1.** (*sin demora*) immediately **2.** (*directamente*) directly
inmediato, -a [in·me·'dja·to, -a, im·me-] *adj* **1.** (*sin demora*) immediate; **de** ~ immediately, right away **2.** (*directo*) direct **3.** (*próximo*) adjacent
inmejorable [in·me·xo·'ra·βle, im·me-] *adj* unbeatable, excellent
inmemorable [in·me·mo·'ra·βle, im·me-] *adj*, **inmemorial** [in·me·mo·'rjal, im·me-] *adj* immemorial; **desde tiempos** ~**es** since [*o* from] time immemorial
inmensidad [in·men·si·'dad, im·men-] *f* **1.** (*extensión*) immensity **2.** (*cantidad*) vastness
inmenso, -a [in·'men·so, -a/im·'men·so, -a] *adj* immense
inmerecido, -a [in·me·re·'si·do, -a, -'θi·do, -a; im·me- ime-] *adj* undeserved
inmersión [in·mer·'sjon, im·mer-] *f* (*sumersión*) *t.* ASTR immersion
inmerso, -a [in·'mer·so, -a/im'mer·so, -a] *adj* immersed; *fig* involved
inmigración [in·mi·ɣra·'sjon, -'θjon; im·mi-] *f* immigration
inmigrante [in·mi·'ɣran·te, im·mi-] *mf* immigrant
inmigrar [in·mi·'ɣrar, im·mi-] *vi* to immigrate
inminente [in·mi·'nen·te; im·mi·'nen·te] *adj* imminent
inmiscuir [in·mis·ku·'ir, im·mi-] *irr como huir* **I.** *vt* to put in **II.** *vr:* ~ **se** to interfere, to meddle
inmobiliaria [in·mo·βi·'lja·rja, im·mo-] *f* real estate agency
inmobiliario, -a [in·mo·βi·'lja·rjo, -a; im·mo-] *adj* property
inmolación [in·mo·la·'sjon, 'θjon; im·mo-] *f* immolation, sacrifice
inmoral [in·mo·'ral, im·mo-] *adj* immoral; (*en cuestiones sexuales*) indecent
inmortal [in·mor·'tal, im·mor-] *adj* immortal
inmortalidad [in·mor·ta·li·'dad, im·mor-] *f* immortality
inmortalizar <z→c> [in·mor·ta·li·'sar, -'θar; im·mor-] **I.** *vt* to immortalize **II.** *vr:* ~**se** to be immortalized
inmóvil [in·'mo·βil, im·'mo-] *adj* immobile
inmovilizar <z→c> [in·mo·βi·li·'sar, -'θar; im·mo-] *vt* **1.** (*paralizar*) to paralyze; ~ **a alguien** to put sb out of action **2.** MED to immobi-

lize

inmueble [in·'mwe·βle, im·'mwe-] *adj*, *m* property

inmundicia [in·mun·'di·sja, -θja; im·mun-] *f* (*suciedad*) filth; (*basura*) garbage

inmundo, -a [in·'mun·do, -a; im·'mun·do, -a] *adj* filthy; (*asqueroso*) disgusting

inmune [in·'mu·ne/im·'mu·ne] *adj* immune; ~ **de algo** (*exento*) exempt from sth

inmunidad [in·mu·ni·'dad, im·mu·ni-] *f* immunity

inmunizar <z→c> [in·mu·ni·'θar, im·mu·ni-] I. *vt* to immunize II. *vr:* ~**se** to safeguard oneself

inmunodeficiencia [in·mu·no·de·fi·'sjen·sja, -'θjen·θja; im·mu·no-] *f* MED immunodeficiency; **síndrome de** ~ **adquirida** Acquired Immune Deficiency Syndrome

inmunoestimulante [in·mu·no·es·ti·mu·'lan·te] I. *adj* immunostimulant; **terapia** ~ immunostimulant therapy II. *m* immunostimulant

inmunología [in·mu·no·lo·'xi·a, im·mu·no-] *f* MED immunology

inmutable [in·mu·'ta·βle, im·mu-] *adj* immutable

inmutar [in·mu·'tar, im·mu·'tar] I. *vt* 1. (*afectar*) to affect 2. (*variar*) to alter II. *vr:* ~**se** to be affected; **sin** ~ **se** without turning a hair [*o* batting an eye], impassively

innato, -a [in·'na·to, -a] *adj* innate, inborn; **tiene un talento** ~ he/she has a natural talent

innecesario, -a [in·ne·se·'sa·rjo, -a; in·ne·θe-] *adj* unnecessary

innegable [in·ne·'ɣa·βle] *adj* undeniable

innoble [in·'no·βle] *adj* ignoble

innovación [in·no·βa·'sjon, -'θjon] *f* innovation

innovador(a) [in·no·βa·'dor, -'do·ra] I. *adj* innovative, novel II. *m(f)* innovator

innovar [in·no·'βar] *vt* to innovate

innumerable [in·nu·me·'ra·βle] *adj* innumerable; **un gentío** ~ countless people

inocencia [i·no·'sen·sja, -'θen·θja] *f* (*falta de culpabilidad, falta de malicia*) innocence

inocentada [i·no·sen·'ta·da, i·no·θen-] *f* (*engaño*) blunder; (*broma*); **gastar una** ~ **a alguien** to play a practical joke on sb

inocente [i·no·'sen·te, -'θen·te] *adj* innocent

inocuo, -a [i·'no·kwo, -a] *adj* innocuous, harmless

inodoro [i·no·'do·ro] *m* toilet

inodoro, -a [i·no·'do·ro, -a] *adj* odorless

inofensivo, -a [in·o·fen·'si·βo, -a] *adj* inoffensive

inoficioso, -a [in·o·fi·'sjo·so, -a; -θjo·so, -a] *adj AmL* useless, idle

inolvidable [in·ol·βi·'da·βle] *adj* unforgettable

inoperante [in·o·pe·'ran·te] *adj* ineffective

inopinado, -a [in·o·pi·'na·do, -a] *adj* unexpected

inoportuno, -a [in·o·por·'tu·no, -a] *adj* (*fuera de lugar*) inappropriate; (*fuera de tiempo*) inopportune, untimely

inorgánico, -a [in·or·'ɣa·ni·ko, -a] *adj* 1. (*no viviente*) inorganic 2. (*no organizado*) disorganized

inoxidable [in·ok·si·'da·βle] *adj* rustproof; (*acero*) stainless

input ['im·put] *m* <inputs> COMPUT input

inquebrantable [in·ke·βran·'ta·βle] *adj* (*decisión*) unwavering; (*cosa*) unbreakable

inquietante [in·kje·'tan·te] *adj* (*preocupante*) worrying; (*perturbador*) disturbing

inquietar [in·kje·'tar] I. *vt* to worry II. *vr* ~**se con** [*o* **por**] **algo** to worry about sth

inquieto, -a [in·'kje·to, -a] *adj* 1. *estar* (*intranquilo*) anxious 2. *ser* (*desasosegado*) restless

inquietud [in·kje·'tud] *f* 1. (*intranquilidad*) anxiety 2. (*desasosiego*) restlessness 3. *pl* (*anhelos*) aspirations *pl*

inquilino, -a [in·ki·'li·no] *m*, *f* tenant, lessee

inquirir [in·ki·'rir] *irr como* **adquirir** *vt* to inquire

inquisición [in·ki·si·'sjon, -'θjon] *f* investigation

Inquisición [in·ki·si·'sjon, -'θjon] *f* Inquisition

inri ['in·rri] *m* REL INRI; **para más** ~ *fig* to make matters worse

insaciable [in·sa·'sja·βle, -'θja·βle] *adj* insatiable; (*sed*) unquenchable

insalubre [in·sa·'lu·βre] *adj* unhealthy, insalubrious *form*

insalvable [in·sal·'βa·βle] *adj* unsalvageable; (*obstáculo*) insuperable

insanable [in·sa·'na·βle] *adj* incurable

insano, -a [in·'sa·no, -a] *adj* 1. (*insalubre*) unhealthy 2. (*loco*) insane

insatisfacción [in·sa·tis·fak·'sjon, -'θjon] *f* dissatisfaction

insatisfactorio, -a [in·sa·tis·fak·'to·rjo, -a] *adj* unsatisfactory

insatisfecho, -a [in·sa·tis·'fe·tʃo, -a] *adj* dissatisfied

inscribir [ins·kri·'βir] *irr como* **escribir** I. *vt* 1. (*registrar*) to register; ~ **en el Registro Civil** to report a birth to the Office of Vital Statistics 2. (*grabar*) to inscribe; ~ **en algo** to inscribe on sth 3. (*alistar*) to enroll; ~ **en algo** to enroll in sth II. *vr:* ~**se** 1. (*registrarse*) to register; **se inscribió en la oficina de empleo** he registered with the employment agency 2. *t. UNIV* (*alistarse*) to enroll; ~**se en algo** to enroll in sth

inscripción [ins·krip·'sjon, -kriβ·'θjon] *f* 1. (*registro*) registration 2. (*alistamiento*) *t. UNIV* enrollment; ~ **en la universidad** university enrollment; ~ **en un curso** matriculation in a course 3. (*escrito grabado*) inscription

inscrito, -a [ins·'kri·to, -a] *pp de* **inscribir**

insecticida [in·sek·ti·'si·da, -'θi·da] *m* insecticide

insecto [in·'sek·to] *m* insect

inseguridad [in·se·yu·ri·'dad] *f* insecurity

inseguro, -a [in·se·'ɣu·ro, -a] *adj* insecure

inseminación [in·se·mi·na·'sjon, -'θjon] *f* insemination

inseminar [in·semi'nar] *vt* to inseminate
insensatez [in·sen·sa·'tes, -'teθ] *f* **1.** (*falta de sensatez*) foolishness **2.** (*disparate*) stupidity
insensato, -a [in·sen·'sa·to, -a] *adj* foolish
insensibilidad [in·sen·si·βi·li'dad] *f* **1.** (*física o afectiva*) insensitivity **2.** (*resistencia*) immunity
insensibilizar <z→c> [in·sen·si·βi·li·'sar, -'θar] I. *vt* to render insensitive; MED to desensitize II. *vr:* ~ **se 1.** (*no sentir*) to become insensitive **2.** (*resistir*) to become immune
insensible [in·sen·'si·βle] *adj* **1.** (*física o afectivamente*) insensitive **2.** (*resistente*) immune
inseparable [in·se·pa·'ra·βle] *adj* inseparable
inserción [in·ser·'sjon, -'θjon] *f* (*inclusión*) inclusion; ~ **laboral** assisted employment services *pl;* ~ **social** social insertion
insertar [in·ser·'tar] I. *vt* **1.** (*llave, moneda, texto*) to insert **2.** (*anuncio*) to place II. *vr:* ~ **se en algo** to invade sth
inservible [in·ser·'βi·βle] *adj* useless
insidia [in·'si·dja] *f* **1.** (*trampa*) trap **2.** (*engaño*) deception, trick
insignia [in·'siɣ·nja] *f* **1.** (*de asociación*) badge; (*honorífica*) decoration; (*militar*) insignia **2.** (*bandera*) flag, ensign
insignificante [in·siɣ·ni·fi·'kan·te] *adj* insignificant
insinuación [in·si·nwa·'sjon, -'θjon] *f* **1.** (*alusión*) allusion **2.** (*engatusamiento*) insinuation
insinuar <1. *pres:* insinúo> [in·si·nu·'ar] I. *vt* to insinuate; ¿**qué estás insinuando?** what are you insinuating?; ¿**quién te ha insinuado eso?** who has put that into your head? II. *vr:* ~ **se 1.** (*engatusar*) ~ **se a alguien** to get in with sb; *inf* (*amorosamente*) to flirt with sb **2.** (*cosa*) to be discernible
insípido, -a [in·'si·pi·do, -a] *adj* **1.** (*comida*) insipid **2.** (*persona: aburrida*) dull; (*sin espíritu*) listless
insistencia [in·sis·'ten·sja, -θja] *f* **1.** (*perseverancia*) persistence **2.** (*énfasis*) insistence; **pedir algo con** ~ to press for sth
insistente [in·sis·'ten·te] *adj* **1.** (*perseverante*) persistent; (*machacón*) insistent **2.** (*con énfasis*) pressing
insistir [in·sis·'tir] *vi* to persist; ~ **en algo** (*perseverar*) to persist in sth; (*exigir*) to insist on sth
insobornable [in·so·βor·'na·βle] *adj* incorruptible
insolación [in·so·la·'sjon, -'θjon] *f* MED sunstroke
insolencia [in·so·'len·sja, -θja] *f* impertinence, disrespect; (*arrogancia*) arrogance
insolente [in·so·'len·te] *adj* impertinent; (*arrogante*) insolent
insolidario, -a [in·so·li·'da·rjo, -a] *adj* unsupportive; (*egoísta*) selfish
insólito, -a [in·'so·li·to, -a] *adj* **1.** (*inhabitual*) unusual, uncommon **2.** (*extraordinario*) unwonted *form*
insoluble [in·so·'lu·βle] *adj* insoluble

insolvencia [in·sol·'βen·sja, -θja] *f* bankruptcy; ECON insolvency
insolvente [in·sol·'βen·te] *adj* bankrupt; ECON insolvent
insomnio [in·'som·njo] *m* MED insomnia, sleeplessness
insondable [in·son·'da·βle] *adj* bottomless, unfathomable *fig*
insonorización [in·so·no·ri·sa·'sjon, -'θjon] *f* soundproofing
insonorizar <z→c> [in·so·no·ri·'sar, -'θar] *vt* to soundproof
insoportable [in·so·por·'ta·βle] *adj* unbearable
insoslayable [in·sos·la·'ja·βle] *adj* unavoidable, inevitable
insospechable [in·sos·pe·'tʃa·βle] *adj* **1.** (*imprevisible*) unforeseeable **2.** (*sorprendente*) surprising
insospechado, -a [in·sos·pe·'tʃa·do, -a] *adj* **1.** (*no esperado*) unexpected **2.** (*no sospechado*) unsuspected, unforeseen
insostenible [in·sos·te·'ni·βle] *adj* unsustainable
inspección [ins·pek·'sjon, -'θjon] *f* TÉC inspection; (*de equipaje*) check; (*de trabajo*) supervision; **Inspección de Trabajo** labor inspector; **Inspección Técnica de Vehículos** motor vehicle inspection
inspeccionar [ins·pek·sjo·'nar, -θjo·'nar] *vt* TÉC to inspect; (*equipaje*) to check; (*trabajo*) to supervise
inspector(a) [ins·pek·'tor, -'to·ra] *m(f)* inspector; ENS school inspector
inspiración [ins·pi·ra·'sjon, -'θjon] *f* **1.** (*de aire*) inhalation **2.** (*ideas*) inspiration
inspirar [ins·pi·'rar] I. *vt* **1.** (*aire*) to inhale **2.** (*ideas, confianza*) to inspire II. *vr:* ~ **se en algo/alguien** to be inspired by sth/sb
instalación [ins·ta·la·'sjon, -'θjon] *f* **1.** (*acción*) installation; (*de baño*) plumbing **2.** (*lo instalado*) TÉC fitting; (*objeto fijo*) fixture **3.** *pl* (*edificio*) facility; **instalaciones deportivas** sports facilities *pl*
instalador(a) [ins·ta·la·'dor, -'do·ra] *m(f)* installer, fitter
instalar [ins·ta·'lar] I. *vt* **1.** (*calefacción, teléfono*) to install; (*baño*) to plumb, to fit **2.** (*alojar*) to accommodate II. *vr:* ~ **se** to settle; (*negocio*) to set up; **me instalé en un sillón** I installed myself in an armchair
instancia [ins·'tan·sja, -θja] *f* **1.** (*acción de instar*) urging **2.** (*solicitud*) application; (*petición formal*) petition **3.** JUR instance; **en última** ~ *fig* as a last resort
instantánea [ins·tan·'ta·nea] *f* FOTO snapshot
instantáneo, -a [ins·tan·'ta·neo, -a] *adj* instantaneous; (*efecto, café*) instant
instante [ins·'tan·te] *m* instant; **al cabo de un** ~ the next instant; **en un** ~ in an instant; **a cada** ~ constantly; ¡**un** ~! one moment!
instar [ins·'tar] *vi, vt* to urge; ~ **a algo** to press for sth

instaurar [ins·tau·'rar] *vt* (*imperio*) to found; (*democracia*) to establish; (*plan*) to implement

instigar <g→gu> [ins·ti·'ɣar] *vt* to instigate; (*a algo malo*) to incite; (*a las masas*) to rouse

instintivo, -a [ins·tin·'ti·βo, -a] *adj* instinctive

instinto [ins·'tin·to] *m* instinct; ~ **de supervivencia** survival instinct

institución [ins·ti·tu·'sjon, -'θjon] *f* **1.** (*social*) institution; ~ **penitenciaria** prison **2.** (*fundación*) foundation

institucional [ins·ti·tu·sjo·'nal, -θjo·'nal] *adj* institutional

institucionalizar <z→c> [ins·ti·tu·sjo·na·li·'sar, -θjo·na·li·'θar] *vt* to institutionalize

instituir [ins·ti·tu·'ir] *irr como huir vt* **1.** (*fundar*) to found **2.** (*establecer: comisión*) to set up; (*derecho*) to institute; (*beca*) to create; (*norma*) to introduce

instituto [ins·ti·'tu·to] *m* **1.** ENS (*de bachillerato*) secondary school, high school **2.** (*científico*) institute **3.** (*establecimiento*) ~ **de belleza** beauty salon

institutriz [ins·ti·tu·'tris, -'triθ] *f* governess

instrucción [ins·truk·'sjon, -'θjon] *f* **1.** (*enseñanza*) teaching; (*en una máquina*) instruction **2.** *pl* (*órdenes*) instructions *pl*, directions *pl*; (*directrices*) guidelines *pl*

instructivo, -a [ins·truk·'ti·βo, -a] *adj* instructive, educational

instructor(a) [ins·truk·'tor, -·'to·ra] **I.** *m(f)* instructor **II.** *adj* instructional

instruido, -a [ins·tru·'i·do, -a] *adj* educated

instruir [ins·tru·'ir] *irr como huir vt* **1.** (*enseñar*) to teach; (*en una máquina*) to instruct; (*en tarea específica*) to train **2.** (*informar*) to inform **3.** JUR (*proceso*) to prepare

instrumental [ins·tru·men·'tal] *adj t.* MÚS instrumental

instrumentista [ins·tru·men·'tis·ta] *mf* (*músico*) instrumentalist

instrumento [ins·tru·'men·to] *m* instrument

insubsanable [in·suβ·sa·'na·βle] *adj* (*daño*) irreparable; (*dificultad*) insurmountable

insuficiencia [in·su·fi·'sjen·sja, -'θjen·θja] *f* insufficiency; MED failure

insuficiente [in·su·fi·'sjen·te, -'θjen·te] **I.** *adj* insufficient **II.** *m* ENS fail; **sacar un** ~ to get an F

insufrible [in·su·'fri·βle] *adj* insufferable

insular [in·su·'lar] *adj* insular

insulina [in·su·'li·na] *f* insulin

insulso, -a [in·'sul·so, -a] *adj* (*comida*) insipid, tasteless; (*persona, película*) dull

insultante [in·sul·'tan·te] *adj* insulting

insultar [in·sul·'tar] *vt* to insult; (*con injurias*) to abuse

insulto [in·'sul·to] *m* insult; (*injuria*) abuse

insumisión [in·su·mi·'sjon] *f* **1.** (*de un pueblo*) rebelliousness **2.** MIL *refusal to do military service or its alternative*

insumiso [in·su·'mi·so] *m one who refuses to do military service or its alternative*

insuperable [in·su·pe·'ra·βle] *adj* insuperable,

insurmountable; (*resultado*) unbeatable

insurgente [in·sur·'xen·te] *adj* insurgent

insurrección [in·su·rrek·'sjon, -'θjon] *f* insurrection; ~ **militar** mutiny

insustancial [in·sus·tan·'sjal, -'θjal] *adj* **1.** (*sin sustancia*) insubstantial **2.** (*sin interés*) uninteresting **3.** (*no importante*) unimportant, insignificant

insustituible [in·sus·ti·tu·'i·βle] *adj* irreplaceable

intachable [in·ta·'ʧa·βle] *adj* irreproachable; (*comportamiento*) faultless

intacto, -a [in·'tak·to, -a] *adj* (*no tocado*) untouched; (*no dañado*) intact

intangible [in·tan·'xi·βle] *adj* (*inviolable*) inviolable; (*intocable, inmaterial*) intangible

integración [in·te·ɣra·'sjon, -'θjon] *f* integration

integral [in·te·'ɣral] *adj* **1.** (*completo*) integral, full **2.** (*pan*) wholegrain **3.** (*elemento*) integral, intrinsic **4.** MAT integral; **cálculo** ~ integral calculus

integrar [in·te·'ɣrar] **I.** *vt* **1.** (*constituir*) to constitute, to comprise **2.** (*en conjunto*) *t.* MAT to integrate **II.** *vr:* ~ **se** to integrate

integridad [in·te·ɣri·'dad] *f* **1.** (*totalidad*) entirety **2.** (*honradez*) integrity **3.** (*física*) physical well-being

integrismo [in·te·'ɣris·mo] *m* (*ideológico*) fundamentalism

íntegro, -a ['in·te·ɣro, -a] *adj* (*completo*) whole; (*persona*) honest, upright

intelecto [in·te·'lek·to, -a] *m* intellect

intelectual [in·te·lek·tu·'al] **I.** *adj* intellectual **II.** *mf* intellectual

inteligencia [in·te·li·'xen·sja, -θja] *f t.* POL intelligence; **servicio de** ~ intelligence agency [*o bureau*]

inteligente [in·te·li·'xen·te] *adj* intelligent

inteligible [in·te·li·'xi·βle] *adj* comprehensible; (*sonido*) *t.* FILOS intelligible

intemperie [in·tem·'pe·rje] *f* **1.** (*el aire libre*) **a la** ~ out in the open; **dormir a la** ~ to sleep outdoors **2.** (*del clima*) harsh climate; (*mal tiempo*) inclement weather

intempestivo, -a [in·tem·pes·'ti·βo, -a] *adj* (*observación*) inopportune; (*visita*) ill-timed

intención [in·ten·'sjon, -'θjon] *f* intention; (*propósito firme*) resolution; **sin** ~ unintentionally; **con** ~ deliberately; **tener segundas intenciones** to have an ulterior motive; **tener buenas intenciones** to mean well

intencionado, -a [in·ten·sjo·'na·do, -a; -θjo·'na·do, -a] *adj* intentional; JUR premeditated; **bien** ~ (*acción*) well-meant; (*persona*) well-meaning; **mal** ~ unkind; (*persona*) malicious

intendencia [in·ten·'den·sja, -θja] *f* **1.** MIL service corps, quartermaster corps **2.** (*dirección*) management **3.** CSur (*distrito*) district

intendente [in·ten·'den·te] *m* **1.** MIL quartermaster-general **2.** (*de empresa*) manager **3.** CSur (*de un distrito*) mayor

intensidad [in·ten·si·'dad] *f t*. FÍS intensity; (*de tormenta*) severity; (*de viento*) force; (*de palabras*) vehemence

intensificar <c→qu> [in·ten·si·fi·'kar] **I.** *vt* to intensify **II.** *vr:* ~ **se** (*tensión*) to heighten; (*tráfico, calor*) to increase; (*conflicto*) to intensify

intensivo, -a [in·ten·'si·βo, -a] *adj* intensive

intenso, -a [in·'ten·so, -a] *adj* (*fuerza, olor*) strong; (*palabras*) vehement; (*tormenta*) severe; (*frío, calor*) intense

intentar [in·ten·'tar] *vt* **1.** (*probar*) to attempt, to try **2.** (*proponerse*) to intend, to mean

intento [in·'ten·to] *m* attempt, try; (*propósito*) aim

intentona [in·ten·'to·na] *f inf* reckless attempt

interacción [in·ter·ak·'sjon, -'θjon] *f* interaction

interactivo, -a [in·ter·ak·'ti·βo, -a] *adj* interactive

intercalación [in·ter·ka·la·'sjon, -'θjon] *f* insertion; ~ **de líneas** insert

intercalar [in·ter·ka·'lar] *vt* (*en un periódico*) to insert

intercambiar [in·ter·kam·'bjar] *vt* to interchange; (*opiniones*) to exchange; (*cosas*) to swap; ~ **correspondencia con alguien** to correspond with sb

intercambio [in·ter·'kam·bjo] *m* exchange

interceder [in·ter·se·'der, -θe·'der] *vi* to intercede; ~ **en favor de alguien** to intercede on behalf of sb

interceptar [in·ter·sep·'tar, -θep·'tar] *vt* (*comunicaciones*) to cut off; (*el paso de algo*) to intercept; (*tráfico*) to hold up, to stop

intercesión [in·ter·se·'sjon, -θe·'sjon] *f* (*en favor de alguien*) intercession

intercomunicador [in·ter·ko·mu·ni·ka·'dor] *m* intercom

intercomunicar <c→qu> [in·ter·ko·mu·ni·'kar] *vt* to intercommunicate

intercontinental [in·ter·kon·ti·nen·'tal] *adj* intercontinental

intercultural [in·ter·kul·tu·'ral] *adj* intercultural

interdisciplinar [in·ter·di·si·pli·'nar, -dis·θi·pli·'nar] *adj*, **interdisciplinario, -a** [in·ter·di·si·pli·'na·rjo, -a; in·ter·dis·θi-] *adj* interdisciplinary

interés [in·te·'res] *m* **1.** (*importancia*) concern **2.** (*deseo, atención*) interest; **tengo mucho ~ en que...** it is of interest to me that...; **tengo ~ por saber...** I'm interested in knowing... **3.** (*provecho*) interest; **el ~ público** the public's interest; **esto redunda en ~ tuyo** this redounds to your credit **4.** FIN interest; (*rendimiento*) yield; **un 10% de ~** 10% interest

interesadamente [in·te·re·sa·da·'men·te] *adv* **actuar ~** (*por propio interés*) to act selfishly; (*por interés material*) to act in one's own interest

interesado, -a [in·te·re·'sa·do, -a] **I.** *adj* **1.** (*con interés*) interested **2.** (*egoísta*) selfish,

self-seeking **II.** *m, f* **1.** the interested party, the person concerned **2.** (*egoísta*) selfish person

interesante [in·te·re·'san·te] *adj* interesting

interesar [in·te·re·'sar] **I.** *vi* to be of interest; **este tema no me interesa** this subject is of no interest to me **II.** *vr:* ~ **se 1.** (*mostrar interés*) ~ **se por algo** to become interested in sth **2.** (*preguntar por*) ~ **se por algo** to ask about sth; ~ **se por la salud de alguien** to ask after sb's health

interferencia [in·ter·fe·'ren·sja, -θja] *f t*. FÍS, LING interference

interferir [in·ter·fe·'rir] *irr como sentir vi t*. FÍS to interfere; ~ **en algo** to interfere with [*o* in] sth; **eso no interfiere en mi decisión** that does not influence my decision

interfono [in·ter·'fo·no] *m* intercom

intergubernamental [in·ter·yu·βer·na·men·'tal] *adj* intergovernmental

interino, -a [in·te·'ri·no, -a] **I.** *adj* **1.** (*funcionario*) temporary **2.** POL interim **II.** *m, f* **1.** (*suplente*) stand-in **2.** (*funcionario*) temporary [*o* acting] incumbent; (*maestro*) substitute teacher

interior [in·te·'rjor] **I.** *adj* interior; (*sin costa*) inland; **decoración ~** interior decoration; **mercado ~** COM (*de la UE*) internal market; (*de Inglaterra*) home [*o* domestic] market; **ropa ~** underwear; **la vida ~ de una persona** a person's inner life **II.** *m* interior; **el ~ de un país** the interior of a country; **Ministerio del Interior** POL Department of the Interior; **en el ~ de...** inside...

interiores [in·te·'rjo·res] *mpl Col* (*calzoncillos*) men's underpants *pl*

interiorista [in·te·rjo·'ris·ta] *mf* interior designer

interiorizar <z→c> [in·te·rjo·ri·'sar, -'θar] *vt* to internalize

interiormente [in·te·rjor·'men·te] *adv* **1.** (*en su interior*) inside **2.** (*internamente*) internally

interjección [in·ter·xek·'sjon, -'θjon] *f* LING interjection, exclamation

interlocutor(a) [in·ter·lo·ku·'tor, -·'to·ra] *m(f)* speaker, interlocutor *form;* ~ **es sociales** ECON management and workers' representatives

intermediario, -a [in·ter·me·'dja·rjo, -a] *m, f* **1.** (*mediador*) mediator, intermediary; (*enlace*) go-between **2.** (*comerciante*) middleman

intermedio [in·ter·'me·djo] *m* interval

intermedio, -a [in·ter·'me·djo, -a] *adj* **1.** (*capa*) intermediate **2.** (*período de tiempo*) intervening **3.** (*calidad*) **mandos ~s** middle management

interminable [in·ter·mi·'na·βle] *adj* interminable, endless

intermitencia [in·ter·mi·'ten·sja, -θja] *f* **1.** (*calidad*) intermittency **2.** MED intermittence

intermitente [in·ter·mi·'ten·te] *m* intermittence; AUTO turn signal

internacional [in·ter·na·sjo·'nal, -θjo·'nal] *adj* international; **partido ~** DEP international game

internacionalización [in·ter·na·sjo·na·li·sa· 'sjon, -θjo·na·li·θa·'θjon] *f* internationalization

internado [in·ter·'na·do] *m* boarding school

internado, -a [in·ter·'na·do, -a] **I.** *adj* boarding **II.** *m, f* **1.** (*alumno*) boarder **2.** (*demente*) inmate

internamiento [in·ter·na·'mjen·to] *m* (*en hospital*) admission, confinement; ~ **en algo** admission to sth; MIL internment in sth

internar [in·ter·'nar] **I.** *vt* ~ **en** (*hospital*) to admit to; (*asilo*) to commit to **II.** *vr:* ~ **se** (*en tema*) ~ **se en algo** to delve into sth

internauta [in·ter·'nau·ta] *mf* COMPUT Internet user

internet [in·ter·'net] *f* COMPUT Internet; ~ **localizada** localized Internet

interno, -a [in·'ter·no, -a] *adj* internal; **régimen** ~ (*de una empresa*) internal management; (*de un partido*) internal affairs

interponer [in·ter·po·'ner] *irr como poner* **I.** *vt* **1.** (*entre varias cosas*) to interpose; (*entre dos cosas: silla*) to place; (*papel*) to insert; (*alguien*) to come **2.** (*en un asunto*) to intervene **3.** JUR to bring, to lodge **II.** *vr:* ~ **se** to intervene

interposición [in·ter·po·si·'sjon, -'θjon] *f* **1.** (*entre varias cosas*) interposition; (*de una silla*) placing between; (*de un papel*) insertion; (*de alguien*) coming between **2.** (*en un asunto*) intervention **3.** JUR bringing, lodging

interpretación [in·ter·pre·ta·'sjon, -'θjon] *f* **1.** (*de texto*) interpretation; (*traducción oral*) interpreting **2.** TEAT performance; MÚS rendering; **escuela de** ~ TEAT stage [*o* acting] school

interpretar [in·ter·pre·'tar] *vt* **1.** (*texto, traducir oralmente*) to interpret **2.** TEAT to perform; MÚS to render

interpretativo, -a [in·ter·pre·ta·'ti·βo, -a] *adj* interpretative, interpretive; **fuerza interpretativa** interpretative ability

intérprete[1] [in·'ter·pre·te] *mf* (*actor*) performer; (*traductor*) interpreter, translator

intérprete[2] [in·'ter·pre·te] *m* COMPUT interpreter

interprofesional [in·ter·pro·fe·sjo·'nal] *adj* **Salario Mínimo Interprofesional** minimum wage

interpuesto, -a [in·ter·'pwes·to, -a] *pp de* **interponer**

interrelacionado, -a [in·te·rre·la·sjo·'na·do, -a; -θjo·'na·do, -a] *adj* interrelated

interrogación [in·te·rro·ɣa·'sjon, -'θjon] *f* (*signo*) question mark

interrogante[1] [in·te·rro·'ɣan·te] *m* question

interrogante[2] [in·te·rro·'ɣan·te] *m o f* questioner

interrogar <g→gu> [in·te·rro·'ɣar] *vt* to question; (*policía*) to interrogate

interrogatorio [in·te·rro·ɣa·'to·rjo] *m* interrogation, (cross-)examination

interrumpir [in·te·rrum·'pir] *vt* **1.** (*cortar*) to interrupt; (*bruscamente al hablar*) to break;

(*tráfico*) to hold up **2.** (*estudios*) to terminate; ~ **las vacaciones** (*por unos días*) to temporarily interrupt one's holidays; (*definitivamente*) to cut short one's holidays

interrupción [in·te·rrup·'sjon, -rruβ·'θjon] *f* **1.** (*corte*) break; (*del tráfico*) stoppage, holdup; **sin** ~ uninterruptedly **2.** (*de los estudios*) termination

interruptor [in·te·rrup·'tor] *m* ELEC switch

intersección [in·ter·sek·'sjon, -'θjon] *f* intersection

interurbano, -a [in·ter·ur·'βa·no, -a] *adj* intercity; **conferencia (interurbana)** TEL long-distance call

intervalo [in·ter·'βa·lo] *m t.* MÚS interval; **a** ~ **s** at intervals

intervención [in·ter·βen·'sjon, -'θjon] *f* **1.** (*participación*) participation **2.** (*en conflicto*) intervention; (*en temas familiares*) involvement **3.** (*mediación*) mediation **4.** POL intervention **5.** MED operation **6.** (*del teléfono*) tapping; (*del correo*) interception

intervencionismo [in·ter·βen·sjo·'nis·mo, -θjo·'nis·mo] *m* POL interventionism

intervenir [in·ter·βe·'nir] *irr como venir* **I.** *vi* **1.** (*tomar parte*) to participate **2.** (*en conflicto*) to intervene **3.** (*mediar*) to mediate **4.** (*suceder*) to occur **II.** *vt* **1.** MED to operate on **2.** (*incautar*) to seize **3.** (*teléfono*) to tap; (*correo*) to intercept **4.** COM to audit

interviú [in·ter·'βju] *m o f* interview

intestinal [in·tes·ti·'nal] *adj* intestinal

intestino [in·tes·'ti·no] *m* **1.** ANAT intestine; **el** ~ **grueso** the large intestine; **el** ~ **delgado** the small intestine **2.** *pl* (*tripas*) intestines *pl,* bowels *pl*

intimar [in·ti·'mar] **I.** *vi* to become intimate [*o* friendly] **II.** *vt* to require

intimidación [in·ti·mi·da·'sjon, -'θjon] *f* intimidation

intimidad [in·ti·mi·'dad] *f* **1.** (*personal*) heart of hearts **2.** *pl* (*sexuales*) private parts *pl;* (*asuntos*) personal matters *pl;* (*privacidad*) privacy **3.** (*vida privada*) private life

intimidar [in·ti·mi·'dar] **I.** *vt* to intimidate **II.** *vr:* ~ **se** to be intimidated

intimidatorio, -a [in·ti·mi·da·'to·rjo, -a] *adj* intimidating

íntimo, -a ['in·ti·mo, -a] *adj* **1.** (*interior, interno*) inner, innermost **2.** (*amigo*) intimate, close **3.** (*velada*) intimate **4.** (*conversación*) private

intocable [in·to·'ka·βle] **I.** *adj* untouchable **II.** *mf* untouchable

intolerable [in·to·le·'ra·βle] *adj* intolerable

intolerancia [in·to·le·'ran·sja, -θja] *f* intolerance; ~ **medicamentosa** medication intolerance

intolerante [in·to·le·'ran·te] *adj* intolerant

intoxicación [in·tok·si·ka·'sjon, -'θjon] *f* (*alimentos*) food poisoning; (*alcohol*) intoxication

intoxicar <c→qu> [in·tok·si·'kar] *vt, vr:* ~(**se**) to poison

intraducible [in·tra·du·'si·βle, -'θi·βle] *adj* untranslatable

intranquilizar <z→c> [in·tran·ki·li·'sar, -'θar] *vt, vr:* ~(**se**) to worry

intranquilo, -a [in·tran·'ki·lo, -a] *adj* **1.**(*nervioso*) edgy **2.**(*preocupado*) worried, uneasy **3.**(*excitado*) agitated, restless

intransferible [in·trans·fe·'ri·βle] *adj* untransferable

intransigencia [in·tran·si·'xen·sja, -θja] *f* intransigence; (*intolerancia*) intolerance

intransigente [in·tran·si·'xen·te] *adj* intransigent; (*intolerante*) intolerant

intransitable [in·tran·si·'ta·βle] *adj* impassable

intransitivo, -a [in·tran·si·'ti·βo, -a] *adj* LING intransitive

intrascendencia [in·tra·sen·'den·sja, -tras·θen·'den·θja] *f* triviality

intrascendente [in·tra·sen·'den·te, -tras·θen·'den·te] *adj* trivial

intrascendente [in·tra·sen·'den·te, -tras·θen·'den·te] *adj* trivial

intratable [in·tra·'ta·βle] *adj* (*persona*) impossible; (*material*) unusable; (*asunto*) intractable; (*enfermedad*) untreatable

intrépido, -a [in·'tre·pi·do, -a] *adj* intrepid

intriga [in·'tri·ɣa] *f* **1.**(*maquinación*) intrigue **2.**(*de una película*) suspense

intrigante [in·tri·'ɣan·te] *adj* **1.**(*persona*) scheming **2.**(*película*) gripping

intrigar <g→gu> [in·tri·'ɣar] **I.** *vi* to scheme **II.** *vt* to intrigue

intrincado, -a [in·trin·'ka·do, -a] *adj* (*bosque*) thick; (*camino*) twisting; (*nudo*) intricate; (*situación*) complicated

intrínseco, -a [in·'trin·se·ko, -a] *adj* **1.**(*interior*) intrinsic; **valor** ~ intrinsic value **2.**(*propio*) inherent **3.**(*esencial*) intrinsic

introducción [in·tro·duk·'sjon, -'θjon] *f* introduction; (*de clavo*) hammering in; COMPUT (*de datos*) input; (*de mercancías*) launching; (*de libro*) preface

introducir [in·tro·du·'sir, -'θir] *irr como traducir* **I.** *vt* (*llave*) to insert, to put in; (*clavo*) to hammer in; (*medidas*) to introduce; COMPUT (*datos*) to enter, to input; (*moda*) to introduce **II.** *vr:* ~**se** (*meterse*) to get in(to); (*en un ambiente*); ~ **se en algo** to enter into sth

introductor(a) [introduk'tor(a)] *m(f)* ~ **de datos** COMPUT data entry keyer

introductorio, -a [in·tro·duk·'to·rjo, -a] *adj* introductory; **capítulo** ~ introduction

intromisión [in·tro·mi·'sjon] *f* interference

introspección [in·tros·pek·'sjon, -'θjon] *f* introspection

introvertido, -a [in·tro·βer·'ti·do, -a] *adj* introverted

intrusión [in·tru·'sjon] *f* trespass; (*en la vida privada*) intrusion

intruso, -a [in·'tru·so, -a] *m, f* intruder; (*en reunión*) interloper; (*en fiesta*) gatecrasher

intuición [in·twi·'sjon, -'θjon] *f* intuition;

saber algo por ~ to know sth intuitively

intuir [in·tu·'ir] *irr como huir* *vt* **1.**(*reconocer*) to intuit *form* **2.**(*presentir*) to sense; **intuyo que...** I have a hunch that...

intuitivo, -a [in·twi·'ti·βo, -a] *adj* intuitive

inundación [i·nun·da·'sjon, -'θjon] *f* flood(ing)

inundar [i·nun·'dar] *vt* to flood

inusitado, -a [i·nu·si·'ta·do, -a] *adj* **1.**(*no habitual*) unusual, uncommon **2.**(*extraordinario*) unwonted

inusual [i·nu·su·'al] *adj* **1.**(*nohabitual*) unusual **2.**(*extraordinario*) unwonted

inútil [in·'u·til] **I.** *adj* **1.**(*que no sirve*) useless **2.**(*esfuerzo*) vain **3.**(*sin sentido*) futile **II.** *mf* (*torpe*) incompetent person

inutilizar <z→c> [in·u·ti·li·'sar, -'θar] *vt* **1.**(*objeto*) to render useless; (*instalaciones*) to render unusable **2.**(*al enemigo*) to defeat

invadir [im·ba·'dir] *vt* (*país*) to invade; (*entrar en gran número*) to overrun; (*privacidad*) to intrude on; **los hinchas invadieron el campo** the fans invaded the pitch [*o* field]

invalidar [im·ba·li·'dar] *vt* to invalidate

invalidez [im·ba·li·'des, -'deθ] *f* invalidity; MED disability; **pensión de** ~ disability allowance

inválido, -a [im·'ba·li·do, -a] **I.** *adj* invalid; MED disabled **II.** *m, f* disabled person, invalid

invariable [im·ba·'rja·βle] *adj t.* MAT invariable

invasión [im·ba·'sjon] *f t.* MIL, MED invasion; (*de plaga*) plague; (*en privacidad*) intrusion

invasor(a) [im·ba·'sor, -·so·ra] *m(f)* invader

invectiva [im·bek·'ti·βa] *f* invective

invencible [im·ben·'si·βle, -'θi·βle] *adj* invincible; (*insuperable*) unbeatable; (*obstáculo*) insurmountable

invención [im·ben·'sjon, -'θjon] *f* invention

inventar [im·ben·'tar] *vt* to invent

inventariar <*1. pres:* inventarío> [im·ben·ta·'rjar] *vt* to make an inventory of

inventario [im·ben·'ta·rjo] *m* inventory

inventiva [im·ben·'ti·βa] *f* inventiveness

invento [im·'ben·to] *m* invention

inventor(a) [im·ben·'tor, -·to·ra] *m(f)* inventor

invernada [im·ber·'na·da] *f* **1.** CSur (*invernadero*) winter pasture **2.** Méx (*cosecha*) winter crop **3.** Ven (*aguacero*) heavy rainstorm

invernadero [im·ber·na·'de·ro] *m* greenhouse, hothouse; **el efecto** ~ the greenhouse effect

invernal [im·ber·'nal] *adj* winter; (*tiempo*) wintry; **sueño** ~ ZOOL winter sleep, hibernation

invernar <e→ie> [im·ber·'nar] *vi* ZOOL to winter; (*los que duermen*) to hibernate

inverosímil [im·be·ro·'si·mil] *adj* implausible; (*que no parece verdad*) improbable, hard to believe

inversión [im·ber·'sjon] *f* **1.** COM, FIN investment **2.**(*efecto de invertir*) inversion

inversionista [im·ber·sjo·'nis·ta] *mf* investor

inverso, -a [im·'ber·so] *adj* inverse, opposite; **a la inversa** inversely; **y a la inversa** vice versa; **en orden** ~ in reverse order

inversor(a) [im·ber·'sor, --so·ra] *m(f)* investor

invertebrado, -a [im·ber·te·'βra·do, -a] *adj* ZOOL invertebrate

invertido, -a [im·ber·'ti·do, -a] *adj* (*al revés*) inverted; (*volcado*) upside-down

invertir [im·ber·'tir] *irr como sentir vt* **1.** (*orden*) to invert **2.** (*volcar*) to turn upside down **3.** (*dinero*) to invest

investidura [im·bes·ti·'du·ra] *f* (*en un cargo*) investiture; REL ordination

investigación [im·bes·ti·ɣa·'sjon, -'θjon] *f* **1.** (*indagación*) investigation; (*averiguación*) inquiry; ~ **de campo** field research; ~ **de mercado** market research **2.** (*ciencia*) research **3.** (*estudio*) study

investigador(a) [im·bes·ti·ɣa·'dor, --do·ra] **I.** *adj* investigative; **comisión** ~ **a** investigatory commission **II.** *m(f)* investigator, researcher; ~ **privado** private detective

investigar <g→gu> [im·bes·ti·'ɣar] *vt* **1.** (*indagar*) to investigate; (*averiguar*) to inquire **2.** (*en la ciencia*) to research

investir [im·bes·'tir] *irr como pedir vt* (*en un cargo*) to confer

inviabilidad [im·bja·βi·li·'dad] *f* non-viability

inviable [im·bi·'a·βle] *adj* non-viable, unfeasible

invicto, -a [im·'bik·to, -a] *adj* unbeaten

invidencia [im·bi·'den·sja, -θja] *f* blindness

invidente [im·bi·'den·te] *adj* blind

invierno [im·'bjer·no] *m* winter; *AmL* (*lluvias*) rainy season; *AmC* (*aguacero*) shower

inviolable [im·bjo·'la·βle] *adj* POL (*derechos*) inviolable

invisibilidad [im·bi·si·βi·li·'dad] *f* invisibility

invisible [im·bi·'si·βle] *adj* invisible

invitación [im·bi·ta·'sjon, -'θjon] *f* invitation; (*tarjeta*) invitation card

invitado, -a [im·bi·'ta·do, -a] *m, f* guest; ~ **de honor** guest of honor

invitar [im·bi·'tar] **I.** *vt* **1.** (*convidar*) to invite **2.** (*instar*) to press; (*rogar*) to beg **II.** *vi* to invite; **esta vez invito yo** this time it's on me

invocar <c→qu> [im·bo·'kar] *vt* to invoke; (*suplicar*) to implore, to appeal; (*alegar*) to allege

involución [im·bo·lu·'sjon, -'θjon] *f* **1.** POL reaction **2.** BIO involution, regression

involucionista [im·bo·lu·sjo·'nis·ta, -θjo·'nis·ta] *adj, mf* POL reactionary

involucrar [im·bo·lu·'krar] **I.** *vt* to involve **II.** *vr:* ~**se** to interfere; (*intervenir*) to become [o get] involved

involuntario, -a [im·bo·lun·'ta·rjo, -a] *adj* involuntary; (*sin querer*) unintentional

invulnerable [im·bul·ne·'ra·βle] *adj* invulnerable; **es** ~ **a las críticas** he/she is insensitive to the criticism

inyección [in·jek·'sjon, -'θjon] *f* **1.** MED injection **2.** TÉC fuel injection; **motor de** ~ fuel-injected engine

inyectar [in·jek·'tar] *vt* to inject

ión [i·'on] *m* ion

ir [ir] *irr* **I.** *vi* **1.** (*general*) to go; **¡voy!** I'm coming!; **¡vamos!** let's go!, come on!; ~ **a pie** to go on foot; ~ **en bicicleta** to go by bicycle; ~ **a caballo** to go on horseback; **tengo que** ~ **a París** I have to go to Paris; ~ **detrás de una chica** to chase after a girl **2.** (*ir a buscar*) **iré por el pan** I'll go and get the bread **3.** (*progresar*) to go; **¿cómo va la tesina?** how is the dissertation going?; **¿cómo te va?** how are things?; **en lo que va de año** so far this year **4.** (*diferencia*) **de dos a cinco van tres** two from five leaves three **5.** (*referirse*) **eso no va por ti** I'm not referring to you; **¿tú sabes de lo que va?** do you know what it is about? **6.** (*interj: sorpresa*) **¡vaya coche!** what a car!; **¡qué va!** of course not! **7.** (*con verbo*) **iban charlando** they were chatting; **voy a hacerlo** I'm going to do it **8.** (*edad*) ~ **para viejo** to be getting on **II.** *vr:* ~**se 1.** (*marcharse*) to leave **2.** (*dirección*) to go; ~**se para el sur** to go southwards; ~**se por las ramas** to beat about the bush

ira ['i·ra] *f* anger

iracundo, -a [i·ra·'kun·do, -a] *adj* irate

Irán [i·'ran] *m* Iran

iraní [i·ra·'ni] *adj, mf* Iranian

Iraq [i·'rak] *m* Iraq

iraquí [i·ra·'ki] *adj, mf* Iraqi

irascible [i·ra·'si·βle, --ras'θi·βle] *adj* irascible

irgo ['ir·ɣo] *1. pres de* **erguir**

irguió [ir·'ɣjo] *3. pret de* **erguir**

iridio [i·'ri·djo] *m* iridium

iridiscente [i·ri·di·'sen·te, --dis·'θen·te] *adj* iridescent

iris ['i·ris] *m inv* ANAT iris; **arco** ~ rainbow

Irlanda [ir·'lan·da] *f* Ireland

irlandés, -esa [ir·lan·'des, --'de·sa] **I.** *adj* Irish **II.** *m, f* Irishman *m*, Irishwoman *f*

ironía [i·ro·'ni·a] *f* irony; ~ **del destino** quirks of fate

irónico, -a [i·'ro·ni·ko, -a] *adj* ironic

ironizar <z→c> [i·ro·ni·'sar, -'θar] *vt* to be ironic

IRPF [i·e·rre·pe·'e·fe/i·e·rre·'pe·fe] *m abr de* **Impuesto sobre la Renta de las Personas Físicas** personal income tax

irracional [i·rra·sjo·'nal, -θjo·'nal] *adj* irrational; (*contra la lógica*) illogical; **número** ~ MAT irrational number; **ser** ~ to be unreasonable

irradiar [i·rra·'djar] **I.** *vt* **1.** (*emitir*) to radiate **2.** (*difundir*) to diffuse **3.** (*tratamiento*) to irradiate **II.** *vi* to radiate **III.** *vr:* ~**se** to be diffused, to be disseminated *form*

irrazonable [i·rra·so·'na·βle, -θo·'na·βle] *adj* irrational

irreal [i·rre·'al] *adj* unreal

irrealizable [i·rrea·li·'θa·βle, -'θa·βle] *adj* unrealizable, unfeasible

irrebatible [i·rre·βa·'ti·βle] *adj*, **irrechazable** [i·rre·tʃa·'sa·βle, -'θa·βle] *adj* irrefutable

irreconciliable [i·rre·kon·si·'lja·βle, -θi·'lja·βle] *adj* irreconcilable

irreconocible [i·rre·ko·no·'si·βle, -'θi·βle] *adj* unrecognizable

irrecuperable [i·rre·ku·pe·'ra·βle] *adj* irretrievable

irreflexión [i·rre·flek·'sjon] *f* recklessness, thoughtlessness

irreflexivo, -a [i·rre·flek·'si·βo, -a] *adj* reckless; (*persona*) rash

irrefrenable [i·rre·fre·'na·βle] *adj* (*desarrollo*) uncontrollable; (*persona*) irrepressible

irrefutable [i·rre·fu·'ta·βle] *adj* irrefutable

irregular [i·rre·yu·'lar] *adj* irregular

irregularidad [i·rre·yu·la·ri·'dad] *f* irregularity

irrelevante [i·rre·le·'βan·te] *adj* irrelevant

irremediable [i·rre·me·'dja·βle] *adj* irremediable; (*daño físico*) irreversible

irrenunciable [i·rre·nun·'sja·βle, -'θja·βle] *adj* (*imprescindible*) indispensable

irreparable [i·rre·pa·'ra·βle] *adj* irreparable; (*incompensable*) that cannot be compensated

irrepetible [i·rre·pe·'ti·βle] *adj* unique

irreprimible [i·rre·pri·'mi·βle] *adj* irrepressible

irreprochable [i·rre·pro·'ʧa·βle] *adj* irreproachable

irreproducible [i·rre·pro·du·'si·βle, -'θi·βle] *adj* (*que ya no se puede fabricar*) irreplaceable

irresistible [i·rre·sis·'ti·βle] *adj* (*atractivo*) irresistible

irresoluble [i·rre·so·'lu·βle] *adj* unsolvable

irresoluto, -a [i·rre·so·'lu·to, -a] *adj* (*vacilante*) irresolute

irrespetuoso, -a [i·rres·pe·tu·'o·so, -a] *adj* disrespectful

irrespirable [i·rres·pi·'ra·βle] *adj* (*por tóxico*) unbreathable; (*aire*) stale, suffocating

irresponsabilidad [i·rres·pon·sa·βi·li·'dad] *f* 1. (*falta de responsabilidad*) absence of responsibility 2. (*desconsideración*) irresponsibility

irresponsable [i·rres·pon·'sa·βle] *adj* irresponsible; ~ **de algo** not responsible for sth

irreverencia [i·rre·βe·'ren·sja, -θja] *f* irreverence

irreverente [i·rre·βe·'ren·te] *adj* irreverent

irreversible [i·rre·βer·'si·βle] *adj* irreversible

irrevocable [i·rre·βo·'ka·βle] *adj* irrevocable

irrigar <g→gu> [i·rri·'yar] *vt* (*regar*) to irrigate; (*la sangre*) to oxygenate

irrisorio, -a [i·rri·'so·rjo, -a] *adj* derisory; **a precios ~s** at ridiculous [*o* ridiculously low] prices

irritabilidad [i·rri·ta·βi·li·'dad] *f* irritability

irritable [i·rri·'ta·βle] *adj* irritable

irritación [i·rri·ta·'sjon, -'θjon] *f* 1. MED (*órgano*) inflammation; (*de piel*) irritation 2. (*enfado*) irritation

irritante [i·rri·'tan·te] *adj* irritating

irritar [i·rri·'tar] I. *vt* 1. (*enojar, molestar*) to irritate 2. MED (*órgano*) to inflame II. *vr:* ~**se** 1. (*enojarse*) to become irritated 2. MED (*órgano*) to become inflamed

irrompible [i·rrom·'pi·βle] *adj* unbreakable

irrumpir [i·rrum·'pir] *vi* ~ **en algo** to burst into sth

irrupción [i·rrup·'sjon, -rruβ·'θjon] *f* irruption; MIL invasion

isla ['is·la] *f* island

Islam [is·'lan] *m* REL Islam

islámico, -a [is·'la·mi·ko, -a] *adj* Islamic

islamización [is·la·mi·sa·'sjon, -θa·'θjon] *f* Islamization

islandés, -esa [is·lan·'des, -·'de·sa] I. *adj* Icelandic II. *m, f* Icelander

Islandia [is·'lan·dja] *f* Iceland

isleño, -a [is·'le·ɲo, -a] *m, f* islander

islote [is·'lo·te] *m* islet

isotónico, -a [i·so·'to·ni·ko, -a] *adj* isotonic

Israel [i·rra·'el/is·rra·'el] *m* Israel

israelí [i·rrae·'li/is·rrae·'li] *adj, mf* Israeli

israelita [i·rrae·'li·ta/is·rrae·'li·ta] *adj, mf* Israelite

istmo ['is·mo] *m* GEO isthmus

itacate [i·ta·'ka·te] *m Méx* travel(ling) provisions

Italia [i·'ta·lja] *f* Italy

italiano, -a [i·ta·'lja·no, -a] *adj, m, f* Italian

itálico, -a [i·'ta·li·ko, -a] *adj* HIST Italic

itinerancia [i·ti·ne·'ran·sja, -θja] *f* TEL roaming *no pl*

itinerante [i·ti·ne·'ran·te] *adj* itinerant, traveling

itinerario [i·ti·ne·'ra·rjo] *m* itinerary; FERRO (*horario*) schedule; AVIAT (*vuelo*) route

ITV [i·te·'u·βe] *f abr de* **Inspección Técnica de Vehículos** MOT test

IVA ['i·βa] *m abr de* **Impuesto sobre el Valor Añadido** VAT

izada [i·'sa·da, -θa·da] *f AmL* raising

izar <z→c> [i·'sar, -'θar] *vt* to hoist

izcuinche [is·'kwin·ʧe, iθ-] *m Méx* (*perro callejero*) mangy stray dog; (*niño callejero*) street urchin

izqda. *adj,* **izqdo.** [is·'kjer·da, iθ-] *adj abr de* **izquierda, izquierdo** left

izquierda [iθ·'kjer·da, iθ-] *f* 1. (*mano*) left hand 2. POL left 3. (*lado*) left side; **a la ~** to the left

izquierdista [is·kjer·'dis·ta, iθ-] *mf* POL left-winger, leftist

izquierdo, -a [is·'kjer·do, -a; iθ-] *adj* left; *fig* crooked; (*zurdo*) left-handed; **levantarse con el pie ~** to get up on the wrong side of the bed

J

J, j ['xo·ta] *f* J, j; ~ **de Juan** J as in Juliet

ja [xa] *interj* ha

jabalí [xa·βa·'li] *m* <jabalíes> wild boar

jabalina [xa·βa·'li·na] *f* DEP javelin

jabato, -a [xa·'βa·to, -a] *adj* brave

jabón [xa·'βon] *m* 1. (*para lavar*) soap; **pastilla**

de ~ bar of soap **2.** *PRico, Arg* (*susto*) fright ▶**dar** ~ **a alguien** to soft-soap sb; **dar un** ~ **a alguien** to give sb a hard time

jabonar [xa·βo·'nar] *vt* to soap

jaboncillo [xa·βon·'si·jo, -'θi·ʎo] *m* (*de tocador*) (bar of) toilet soap

jabonera [xa·βo·'ne·ra] *f* (*para depositar jabón*) soap dish

jabonoso, -a [xa·βo·'no·so, -a] *adj* soapy

jabugo [xa·'βu·ɣo] *m* type of Spanish ham (*from Jabugo*)

jaca ['xa·ka] *f AmL* (*gallo*) (fighting) cock

jacal [xa·'kal] *m Méx, Ven* hut

jacalear [xa·ka·le·'ar] *vi Méx* to spread rumors

jacarandá [xa·ka·ran·da] *m AmL* ʙᴏᴛ jacaranda

jacarandoso, -a [xa·ka·ran·'do·so, -a] *adj* merry

jacinto [xa·'sin·to, -'θin·to] *m* hyacinth

jaco ['xa·ko] *m pey* (*caballo*) nag

jactancia [xak·'tan·sja, -θja] *f* boasting, boastfulness

jactancioso, -a [xak·tan·'sjo·so, -a; -θjo·so, -a] *adj* boastful

jactarse [xak·'tar·se] *vr* **jactarse de algo** to boast of [*o* about] sth

jaculatoria [xa·ku·la·'to·rja] *f* short prayer

jacuz(z)i® [ja·'kud·si] *m* Jacuzzi®

jade ['xa·de] *m* jade

jadear [xa·de·'ar] *vi* to pant

jaguar [xa·'ɣwar] *m* jaguar

jagüel [xa·'ɣwel] *m*, **jagüey** [xa·'ɣwei] *m AmL* (*balsa*) pool; (*cisterna*) cistern

jaiba ['xai·βa] **I.** *adj* **1.** *Ant, Méx* (*astuto*) cunning **2.** *Cuba* (*perezoso*) lazy **II.** *f AmL* (*cangrejo*) crab

jáibol ['xai·βol] *m Méx* whisky and soda, highball

jalada [xa·'la·da] *f Méx, Ven, inf* (*exageración*) exaggeration

jalado, -a [xa·'la·do, -a] *adj* **1.** *Méx, Ven* (*exagerado*) exaggerated **2.** *AmL* (*demacrado*) emaciated **3.** *AmL* (*obsequioso*) obliging **4.** *AmL* (*borracho*) drunk

jalar [xa·'lar] **I.** *vt* **1.** *AmL* (*una cuerda*) to pull **2.** *AmL* (*una persona*) to attract **3.** *inf* (*comer*) to guzzle, to wolf down **II.** *vi Bol, PRico, Urug, Ven* (*largarse*) to clear off **III.** *vr:* ~**se** *AmL* to get drunk

jalea [xa·'lea] *f* jelly

jalear [xa·le·'ar] *vt* (*animar*) to encourage

jaleo [xa·'leo] *m* **1.** (*barullo*) commotion; **armar** ~ to make a scene **2.** (*desorden*) confusion; **me he armado un** ~ **con los nombres** *inf* I got the names all mixed up

jalonar [xa·lo·'nar] *vt* (*un terreno*) to stake out

jamar [xa·'mar] **I.** *vt inf* (*comer*) to wolf (down) **II.** *vr:* ~**se** *inf* (*atracarse*) to stuff oneself

jamás [xa·'mas] *adv* never; ~ **de los jamases** never in your life; **¿habías leído** ~ **algo parecido?** had you ever read anything like it?; **nunca digas nunca** ~ never (ever) say never; **nunca** ~ never again

jamelgo [xa·'mel·ɣo] *m inf* (*caballo*) nag

jamón [xa·'mon] *m* ham; ~ **dulce** [*o* **de York**] boiled ham; ~ **serrano** cured ham ▶**¡y un** ~**!** *inf* get away!

Japón [xa·'pon] *m* Japan

japonés, -esa [xa·po·'nes, -·'ne·sa] *adj, m, f* Japanese

jaque ['xa·ke] *m* check; ~ **mate** checkmate; **dar** ~ to check ▶**tener a alguien en** ~ *fig* to keep sb in check

jaquear [xa·ke·'ar] *vt* to check

jaqueca [xa·'ke·ka] *f* (severe) headache, migraine; **este tipo me da** ~ *inf* this guy's getting to me

jara ['xa·ra] *f Guat, Méx* (*flecha*) arrow

jarabe [xa·'ra·βe] *m* syrup; (*para la tos*) cough mixture [*o* syrup] ▶**dar** ~ **de palo a alguien** *inf* to give sb a thrashing; ~ **de pico** *inf* empty talk

jarana [xa·'ra·na] *f* **1.** *inf* (*juerga*) spree; **ir de** ~ *inf* to go on a spree **2.** *Méx* ᴍᴜ́ꜱ small guitar **3.** *AmL* (*burla*) joke **4.** *AmC* (*deuda*) debt **5.** *Col* (*embuste*) trick

jaranear [xa·ra·ne·'ar] **I.** *vi inf* (*ir de copas*) to go out on the town; (*divertirse*) to live it up **II.** *vt Col* (*importunar*) to pester

jaranero, -a [xa·ra·'ne·ro, -a] *m, f* **ser un** ~ to be a reveler

jardín [xar·'din] *m* garden; ~ **de infancia** (*hasta los tres años*) nursery school; (*a partir de tres años*) kindergarten; **los jardines de una ciudad** the municipal parks; **trabajar en el** ~ to garden

jardinear [xar·di·ne·'ar] *vt AmL* to garden

jardinera [xar·di·'ne·ra] *f* **1.** (*profesión*) (woman) gardener **2.** (*maceta*) window box ▶**a la** ~ jardinière (*with diced, cooked vegetables*)

jardinería [xar·di·ne·'ri·a] *f* gardening

jardinero, -a [xar·di·'ne·ro, -a] *m, f* gardener

jareta [xa·'re·ta] *f CRi, Par* (*bragueta*) fly, zipper

jarocho, -a [xa·'ro·tʃo, -a] *adj AmL* (*arrogante*) rude

jarra ['xa·rra] *f* jar; (*de agua*) jug, pitcher ▶**ponerse de** [*o* **en**] ~**s** to stand with arms akimbo

jarro ['xa·rro] *m* jug, pitcher; **echar un** ~ **de agua fría** *fig* to pour cold water on

jarrón [xa·'rron] *m* vase

jartón, -ona [xar·'ton, -·'to·na] *m, f AmC, Méx* (*comilón*) greedy-guts *inf*

jaspeado, -a [xas·pe·'a·do] *adj* speckled; (*tela, lana*) variegated

jauja ['xau·xa] *f* earthly paradise; **para ti la vida es Jauja** you're living in clover

jaula ['xau·la] *f* (*para animales*) cage

jauría [xau·'ri·a] *f* pack of hounds

jazmín [xas·'min, xaθ-] *m* jasmine

jazz [dʒas] *m* jazz; **tocar** ~ to jazz

J.C. [xe·su·'kris·to] *abr de* **Jesucristo** J.C.

jebe ['xe·βe] *m AmL* (*caucho*) rubber

jeep [dʒip] *m* <jeeps> jeep

jefatura [xe·fa·'tu·ra] *f* **1.** (*cargo*) leadership **2.** (*sede*) ~ **del gobierno** seat of government; ~ **de policía** police headquarters

jefazo, -a [xe·'fa·so, -a; -θo, -θa] *m, f inf* big boss

jefe, -a ['xe·fe, -a] *m, f* head, boss; (*de una banda*) leader; ~ **de filas** DEP team captain; ~ **de gobierno** head of the government; ~ **de(l) Estado** head of state; ~ **de partido** party leader; **redactor** ~ editor-in-chief

jengibre [xen·'xi·βre] *m* ginger

jeque ['xe·ke] *m* sheik(h)

jerarca [xe·'rar·ka] *mf* high official

jerarquía [xe·rar·'ki·a] *f* hierarchy

jerárquico, -a [xe·'rar·ki·ko, -a] *adj* hierarchical

jerez [xe·'res, -'reθ] *m* sherry

jerga ['xer·ɣa] *f* jargon

jergón [xer·'ɣon] *m* (*colchón*) rough mattress, pallet

jeringa [xe·'rin·ga] *f* (*instrumento*) syringe

jeringar <g→gu> [xe·rin·'gar] *vt* (*con la jeringa*) to syringe

jeringuilla [xe·rin·'gi·ja, -ʎa] *f* syringe

jeroglífico [xe·ro·'ɣli·fi·ko] *m* hieroglyph(ic); (*pasatiempo*) rebus, puzzle

jeroglífico, -a [xe·ro·'ɣli·fi·ko, -a] *adj* hieroglyphic

jersey [xer·'sei] *m* pullover; ~ **de cuello alto** turtleneck sweater

Jesucristo [xe·su·'kris·to] *m* Jesus Christ

jesuita [xe·su·'i·ta] *adj, m* Jesuit

Jesús [xe·'sus] *m* Jesus ▸ **en un** (**decir**) ~ **in** a flash; **¡~!** (*al estornudar*) bless you!; (*interjección*) good heavens!

jeta ['xe·ta] *f inf* (*cara*) mug, dial; **ése tiene una ~ increíble** *fig* what incredible cheek that guy has

ji [xi] *interj* ha

jíbaro, -a ['xi·βa·ro, -a] *adj* **1.** *AmL* (*campesino*) country, peasant; (*costumbres, vida*) rural **2.** *AmL* (*planta, animal*) wild **3.** *Ant, Méx* (*huraño*) shy

jibia ['xi·βja] *f* cuttlefish

jícama ['xi·ka·ma] *f Méx* BOT edible tuber

jícaro ['xi·ka·ro] *m AmC* (*árbol*) calabash tree

jicotera [xi·ko·'te·ra] *f AmC, Méx* wasps' nest

jijona [xi·'xo·na] *m* soft nougat (*made in Jijona*)

jilguero [xil·'ɣe·ro] *m* goldfinch

jincho, -a ['xin·tʃo, -a] *adj Col, inf* (*borracho*) drunk

jineta [xi·'ne·ta] *f* genet

jinete [xi·'ne·te] *m* (*persona*) horseman; (*profesional*) rider

jinetear [xi·ne·te·'ar] *vt AmL* to break in (horses)

jinetera [xi·ne·'te·ra] *f Cuba, inf* prostitute

jiote ['xjo·te] *m Méx* MED impetigo

jipa ['xi·pa] *f Col* Panama hat

jirafa [xi·'ra·fa] *f* giraffe

jirón [xi·'ron] *m* shred; **hacer algo jirones** to tear sth to shreds

jitazo [xi·'ta·so, -θo] *m Méx, inf* hit

jitomate [xi·to·'ma·te] *m Méx* (*tomate*) tomato

JJ.OO. ['xwe·ɣos o·'lim·pi·kos] *abr de* **Juegos Olímpicos** Olympic Games

jo [xo] *interj* **1.** (*so*) whoa **2.** (*sorpresa*) **¡~!** well, well!

jobillo [xo·'βi·jo, -ʎo] *m PRico, inf* **irse de ~s** to play truant

jockey ['xo·kei] *m* jockey

jocoso, -a [xo·'ko·so, -a] *adj* humorous, jocular

jocundo, -a [xo·'kun·do, -a] *adj* jovial

joda ['xo·da] *f Arg, vulg* joke; **lo dije en ~** I was only joking

joder [xo·'der] **I.** *vt vulg* **1.** (*copular*) to fuck, to screw **2.** (*fastidiar*) to be an asshole to; **¡no me jodas!** stop being an asshole! **3.** (*echar a perder*) to fuck up **4.** (*robar*) to swipe *inf* **II.** *vi vulg* to fuck **III.** *vr:* ~ **se** *vulg* **1.** (*fastidiarse*) to get pissed off; **¡jódete!** fuck off! **2.** (*echar a perder*) **nuestra amistad se ha jodido** our friendship's gone down the drain; **la tele se ha jodido** the TV is all screwed up **IV.** *interj vulg* shit

jodido, -a [xo·'di·do, -a] **I.** *pp de* **joder II.** *adj vulg* **1.** (*cansado*) beat *inf;* **estoy ~** I'm beat **2.** (*difícil*) **es ~ tener que trabajar tanto** it's damned hard having to work so much

jodón, -ona [xo·'don, -'do·na] *adj Méx, inf* pain in the ass

joint-venture ['dʒoim 'ben·tʃa] *f* ECON joint venture

jojoba [xo·'xo·βa] *f AmL* BOT jojoba

jolgorio [xol·'ɣo·rjo] *m* merriment

jolín [xo·'lin] *interj,* **jolines** [xo·'li·nes] *interj* sugar

jopé [xo·'pe] *interj* sugar

Jordania [xor·'da·nja] *f* Jordan

jordano, -a [xor·'da·no, -a] *adj, m, f* Jordanian

jornada [xor·'na·da] *f* **1.** (*de trabajo*) working day; (*tiempo trabajado*) hours of work; ~ **continua** *continuous schedule without lunch break, finishing early;* ~ **partida** split shift; **trabajo media ~** I work half a day [*o* part-time] **2.** (*viaje*) day's journey; (*andando*) day's march [*o* walk]; **este pueblo está a dos ~s de viaje** this village is two days' away **3.** *pl* (*congreso, simposio*) conference

jornal [xor·'nal] *m* (*paga*) day's wage [*o* pay]; **trabajar a ~** to be paid by the day

jornalero, -a [xor·na·'le·ro, -a] *m, f* day laborer

joroba [xo·'ro·βa] *f* **1.** (*de persona*) hunched back; (*de camello*) hump **2.** *inf* (*molestia*) nuisance

jorobado, -a [xo·ro·'βa·do, -a] *adj* hunchbacked

jorobar [xo·ro·'βar] **I.** *vt inf* to annoy **II.** *vr:* ~ **se** *inf* **1.** (*enojarse*) to get annoyed **2.** (*aguantar*) to put up with it; **si no le gusta, ¡que se jorobe!** if he doesn't like it, he can lump it!

jorongo [xo·'ron·go] *m Méx* poncho

joropo [xo·'ro·po] *m Col: popular dance of the Colombian lowlanders*

jota ['xo·ta] *f* (*letra*) j ▸ **no entender** [*o* **saber**] **ni ~** *inf* not to have a clue; **no ver ni ~** *inf* not to see a thing

joto ['xo·to] *m* 1. *Col* (*paquete*) bundle 2. *Méx, pey* (*homosexual*) queer
joven ['xo·βen] I. *adj* young; **de muy ~** in early youth II. *mf* young man *m*, young woman *f*; **los jóvenes** young people
jovial [xo·'βjal] *adj* cheerful, jovial
joya ['xo·ja] *f* (*alhaja*) jewel; (*piedra*) gem; **las ~s** jewelry; **esta mujer de la limpieza es una ~** this cleaning lady is a gem
joyería [xo·je·'ri·a] *f* (*tienda*) jeweler's (shop)
joyero [xo·'je·ro] *m* jewel case
joyero, -a [xo·'je·ro, -a] *m, f* jeweler
juanete [xwa·'ne·te] *m* (*del pie*) bunion
jubilación [xu·βi·la·'sjon, -'θjon] *f* 1. (*acción*) retirement 2. (*pensión*) pension
jubilado, -a [xu·βi·'la·do, -a] *m, f* pensioner, retiree
jubilar [xu·βi·'lar] I. *vt* to pension off II. *vr:* ~**se** 1. (*retirarse*) to retire 2. *AmC* (*hacer novillos*) to play truant
júbilo ['xu·βi·lo] *m* joy, jubilation
jubiloso, -a [xu·βi·'lo·so, -a] *adj* jubilant; **estar ~** to be joyful
judaico, -a [xu·'dai·ko, -a] *adj* Jewish, Judaic
judía [xu·'di·a] *f* 1. (*mujer*) Jewess 2. bean; **~ verde** green bean
judicial [xu·di·'sjal, -'θjal] *adj* judicial
judío, -a [xu·'di·o, -a] I. *adj* Jewish II. *m, f* Jew
judo ['dʒu·do] *m* DEP judo
juego ['xwe·ɣo] *m* 1. (*diversión*) game; **~ de mesa** board game; **~ de los roles** role-playing; **hacer ~s malabares** to juggle 2. DEP play; **~ en blanco** nil draw; **~ limpio** fair play; **~ sucio** foul play; **fuera de ~** (*persona*) offside; (*balón*) out of play 3. (*conjunto*) set; **~ de café** coffee set; **~ de mesa** dinner service; **hacer ~** to match ▶ **desgraciado en el ~, afortunado en amores** *prov* lucky at cards, unlucky in love *prov*; **tomarse algo a ~** to take sth as a joke; **vérsele a alguien el ~** to know what sb is up to
juerga ['xwer·ɣa] *f* spree; **ayer estuve de ~** *inf* I was (out) partying [*o* on a spree] yesterday; **correrse unas cuantas ~s** *inf* to go out at night quite a bit
juev. *abr de* **jueves** Thurs.
jueves ['xwe·βes] *m inv* Thursday; **Jueves Santo** Maundy Thursday ▶ **no es nada del otro lunes** ~ it's nothing to write home about; *v.t.* **lunes**
juez [xwes, xweθ] *mf t.* JUR judge; **~ de instrucción** JUR examining magistrate; **~ de paz** justice of the peace; **ser ~ y parte** to be biased; **~ de línea** [*o* de banda] DEP linesman
jugada [xu·'ɣa·da] *f* 1. DEP play; **~ de ajedrez** chess move; **~ antirreglamentaria** foul play; **Ronaldo hizo una ~ genial** Ronaldo made a great move 2. (*jugarreta*) bad turn; **hacer** [*o* **gastar**] **una ~ a alguien** to play a dirty trick on sb
jugador(a) [xu·ɣa·'do, -'do·ra] I. *adj* **ser muy ~** to gamble a lot II. *m(f) t.* DEP player
jugar [xu·'ɣar] *irr* I. *vi* 1. (*a un juego, deporte*)

to play; **~ limpio/sucio** to play fair/unfairly; **¿quién juega?** (*juego de mesa*) whose move is it?; (*partido en la TV, radio*) who's playing?; **¿puedo ~?** can I join in? 2. (*bromear*) to play about; **hacer algo por ~** to do sth for fun 3. (*en un negocio*) to speculate; **~ a la bolsa** to speculate on the stock exchange 4. (*hacer juego*) to match II. *vt* 1. (*un juego, una partida*) to play 2. (*apostar*) to gamble; **~ fuerte** to play for high stakes III. *vr:* **~ se** 1. (*la lotería*) to be drawn 2. (*apostar*) **~se algo** to gamble [*o* to bet] on sth 3. (*arriesgar*) **~se el todo por el todo** to stake one's all ▶ **jugársela a alguien** to take sb for a ride
jugarreta [xu·ɣa·'rre·ta] *f inf* dirty trick; **hacer una ~ a alguien** to pull a fast one on sb
jugo ['xu·ɣo] *m* 1. (*de fruta, carne*) juice 2. (*esencia*) essence; **declaraciones con mucho ~** *fig* important declarations ▶ **sacar el ~ a alguien** to squeeze sb dry
jugoso, -a [xu·'ɣo·so, -a] *adj* juicy
juguete [xu·'ɣe·te] *m* toy
juguetear [xu·ɣe·te·'ar] *vi* 1. (*con las llaves, una pelota*) to play 2. (*los niños*) to romp
juguetería [xu·ɣe·te·'ri·a] *f* toyshop
juguetón, -ona [xu·ɣe·'ton, -'to·na] *adj* playful
juicio ['xwi·sjo, -θjo] *m* 1. (*facultad para juzgar*) reason 2. (*razón*) sense; **falta de ~** lack of common sense; **recobrar el ~** to come to one's senses; **tú no estás en tu sano ~** you're not in your right mind 3. (*opinión*) opinion; **a mi ~** to my mind; **emitir un ~ sobre algo** to pass judgment on sth 4. JUR trial; **~ criminal** criminal proceedings; **llevar a alguien a ~** to take sb to court; **el (día del) Juicio final** REL the Last Judgment
juicioso, -a [xwi·'sjo·so, -a; -θjo·so, -a] *adj* (*sensato*) sensible; (*acertado*) fitting
juil [xwil] *m Méx* ZOOL Mexican lake trout; **si el ~ no abriera la boca, no lo pescarían** *prov* silence is golden *prov*
jul. *abr de* **julio** Jul.
julepe [xu·'le·pe] *m AmL* 1. (*miedo*) scare 2. (*ajetreo*) drudgery; **dar un ~ a alguien** *inf* to make sb sweat
julia ['xu·lja] *f Méx, inf* (*coche celular*) police van [*o* wagon]
julio ['xu·ljo] *m* 1. (*mes*) July; *v.t.* **marzo** 2. FÍS joule
juma ['xu·ma] *f AmL, inf* drunkenness
jumado, -a [xu·'ma·do, -a] *adj AmL, inf* drunk
jumarse [xu·'mar·se] *vr Col, Cuba* to get drunk
jumento [xu·'men·to] *m* donkey
jumo ['xu·mo] *m PRico* drunkenness
jumo, -a ['xu·mo, -a] *adj AmL* (*borracho*) drunk
jun. *abr de* **junio** Jun.
juncal [xun·'kal] *adj* (*gallardo*) slim
junco ['xun·ko] *m* BOT reed
jungla ['xun·gla] *f* jungle
junio ['xu·njo] *m* June; *v.t.* **marzo**
júnior ['dʒu·njor] *m* <juniors> junior

J

junta ['xun·ta] *f* **1.** (*comité*) committee; (*consejo*) council; ~ **directiva** COM board of directors; ~ **militar** MIL military junta; ~ **municipal** POL district council **2.** (*reunión*) meeting; ~ **general** general meeting; **celebrar** ~ to hold a board meeting; ~ **de accionistas** shareholders' meeting

juntar [xun·'tar] **I.** *vt* **1.** (*aproximar*) ~ **la mesa a la pared** to move the table over to the wall; ~ **las sillas** to put the chairs together **2.** (*unir*) to join **3.** (*reunir: personas*) to assemble; (*objetos*) to put together; (*dinero*) to collect **II.** *vr:* ~**se 1.** (*reunirse*) to meet **2.** (*unirse*) to come together **3.** (*aproximarse*) to come closer **4.** (*vivir juntos*) to move in (together)

junto ['xun·to] **I.** *adv* **hacerlo todo** ~ to do it all at the same time **II.** *prep* **1.** (*local*) ~ **a** near to; **¿quién es el que está ~ a ella?** who's the man at her side?; **estábamos ~ a la entrada** we were at the entrance; **pasaron ~ a nosotros** they walked past us **2.** (*con movimiento*) ~ **a** beside; **pon la silla ~ a la mesa** put the chair next to the table **3.** (*con, en compañía de*) ~ **con** together with

junto, -a ['xun·to, -a] *adj* joined; **nos sentamos todos ~s** we all sat together

juntura [xun·'tu·ra] *f* TÉC (*de dos ladrillos*) joint; (*de dos tubos*) junction; (*sellado*) seal

jupiarse [xu·'pjar·se] *vr AmC* to get drunk

jura ['xu·ra] *f* oath; (*acto*) swearing in

juraco [xu·'ra·ko] *m AmL, inf* hole

jurado [xu·'ra·do] *m* **1.** JUR (*miembro*) juror; (*tribunal*) jury **2.** (*de un examen*) qualified examiner **3.** (*de un concurso*) panel member

jurado, -a [xu·'ra·do, -a] *adj* qualified; **intérprete** ~ sworn interpreter

juramentar [xu·ra·men·'tar] **I.** *vt* to swear in **II.** *vr:* ~**se** to be sworn in

juramento [xu·ra·'men·to] *m* **1.** *t.* JUR (*jura*) oath; **falso** ~ perjury; **estar bajo** ~ to be on oath; **tomar** ~ **a alguien** to swear sb in **2.** (*blasfemia*) swearword

jurar [xu·'rar] *vi, vt* to swear; ~ **por alguien** to swear by sb; ~ **en falso** to commit perjury; ~ **por todos los santos** to swear blind; **jurársela(s) a alguien** *inf* to swear vengeance on sb

jurel [xu·'rel] *m* horse mackerel

jurero, -a [xu·'re·ro, -a] *m, f Chile, Ecua* (*testigo falso contratado*) false witness

jurídico, -a [xu·'ri·di·ko, -a] *adj* legal, lawful

jurisdicción [xu·ris·dik·'sjon, -'θjon] *f* **1.** JUR (*potestad*) jurisdiction; ~ **militar** military law **2.** (*territorio*) administrative district

jurisdiccional [xu·ris·dik·sjo·'nal, -θjo·'nal] *adj* jurisdictional, judicial; **aguas** ~**es** territorial waters

jurisprudencia [xu·ris·pru·'den·sja, -θja] *f* **1.** (*legislación*) jurisprudence **2.** (*ciencia*) science of law

jurista [xu·'ris·ta] *mf* jurist

jurungar <g→gu> [xu·run·'gar] *Ven* **I.** *vt* to bore **II.** *vr:* ~**se** to get bored

justamente [xus·ta·'men·te] *adv* justly; (*precisamente*) precisely

justicia [xus·'ti·sja, -θja] *f* justice; (*derecho*) law; **administrar** ~ to administer justice; **hacer** ~ **a alguien** to do sb justice

justiciero, -a [xus·ti·'θje·ro, -a; -'θje·ro, -a] *adj* (*justo*) just; (*severo*) strict

justificable [xus·ti·fi·'ka·βle] *adj* justifiable

justificación [xus·ti·fi·ka·'sjon, -'θjon] *f* justification; **no hay ~ para lo que has hecho** there's no excuse for what you've done

justificante [xus·ti·fi·'kan·te] *m* supporting evidence; (*de ausencia*) note of absence

justificar <c→qu> [xus·ti·fi·'kar] **I.** *vt* **1.** (*disculpar*) to justify; **mi desconfianza es justificada** my distrust is vindicated **2.** (*probar*) to prove; (*con documentos*) to substantiate **II.** *vr:* ~**se** to justify oneself

justo ['xus·to] *adv* **1.** (*exactamente*) right; **llegué ~ a tiempo** I arrived just in time **2.** (*escasamente*) scarcely; **tengo ~ para vivir** I have just enough to live on

justo, -a ['xus·to, -a] *adj* **1.** (*persona, decisión*) just **2.** (*exacto*) exact; (*acertado*) correct; **el peso** ~ the correct weight; **tener el dinero** ~ to have exact change **3.** (*escaso*) **ha venido muy justo de dinero** money's been very tight **4.** (*ajustado*) close-fitting; **este abrigo me viene** ~ this coat is rather tight for me

juvenil [xu·βe·'nil] **I.** *adj* youthful, young **II.** *mf* DEP **juego con los** ~**es** I'm in the junior team

juventud [xu·βen·'tud] *f* **1.** (*edad*) youth **2.** (*estado*) early life **3.** (*jóvenes*) young people

juzgado [xus·'γa·do, xuθ-] *m* court; ~ **de guardia** police court

juzgar <g→gu> [xus·'γar, xuθ-] **I.** *vt* **1.** (*juez: decidir*) to judge; (*condenar*) to sentence **2.** (*opinar sobre*) to judge; (*considerar*) to consider, to deem; ~ **mal a alguien** to misjudge sb; **le ~on de maleducado** they considered him ill-mannered; **no te juzgo capaz de hacerlo** I don't think you're capable of doing it **II.** *vi* **1.** (*juez*) to judge **2.** (*opinar*) ~ **sobre apariencias** to judge by appearances

K

K, k [ka] *f* K, k; ~ **de Kenia** K as in Kilo

kaki ['ka·ki] *adj* khaki

karaoke [ka·ra·'o·ke] *m* karaoke

karate [ka·'ra·te] *m*, **kárate** ['ka·ra·te] *m* DEP karate

kart [kart] *m* <karts> go-cart

karting ['kar·tin] *m* <kartings> DEP go-carting

kayak [ka·'jak] *m* <kayaks> DEP kayak

Kazajstán [ka·saks·'tan, ka·θaks-] *m* Kazakhstan

KB [ki·lo·'βait] *m* COMPUT *abr de* **kilobyte** KB

keniata [ke·'nja·ta] *adj, mf* Kenyan
kerosén [ke·ro·'sen] *m AmS* kerosene
keroseno [ke·ro·'se·no] *m* kerosene, paraffin
ketchup ['ked·ʧup] *m* <ketchups> ketchup
kg [ki·lo·'ɣra·mo] *abr de* **kilogramo** kg
kikirikí [ki·ki·ri·'ki] *m* cock-a-doodle-doo
kilo ['ki·lo] *m* kilo
kilocaloría [ki·lo·ka·lo·'ri·a] *f* kilocalorie
kilogramo [ki·lo·'ɣra·mo] *m* kilogram
kilohercio [ki·lo·'er·sjo, -θjo] *m* kilohertz
kilolitro [ki·lo·'li·tro] *m* kiloliter
kilometraje [ki·lo·me·'tra·xe] *m* AUTO mileage
kilométrico, -a [ki·lo·'me·tri·ko] *adj* kilometric
kilómetro [ki·'lo·me·tro] *m* kilometer
kilovatio [ki·lo·'βa·tjo] *m* kilowatt
kinder ['kin·der] *m inv, AmL,* **kindergarten** [kin·der·'ɣar·ten] *m inv* kindergarten, nursery school
kit [kit] *m* <kits> kit
kleenex® ['kli·neks] *m inv,* **klínex** ['kli·neks] *m inv* Kleenex®, tissue
km [ki·'lo·me·tro] *abr de* **kilómetro** km.
km/h [ki·'lo·me·tro por 'o·ra] *abr de* **kilómetro por hora** km/h
k.o. ['ka·o] *adj abr de* **knock-out** knock-out; **dejar ~ a alguien** to knock sb out
kw [ki·lo·'βa·tjo] *abr de* **kilovatio** kV

L

L, l ['e·le] *f* L,l; **~ de Lisboa** L as in Lima
l ['li·tro] *abr de* **litro(s)** l
la [la] **I.** *art def v.* **el, la, lo II.** *pron pers, f sing* **1.** *objeto directo: f sing* her; (*cosa*) it; **¡tráeme~!** bring her/it to me!; **mi bicicleta y ~ tuya** my bicycle and yours **2.** (*con relativo*) **~ que...** the one that...; **~ cual** which **III.** *m* MÚS A; **en ~ bemol menor** in A flat minor
laberíntico, -a [la·βe·'rin·ti·ko, -a] *adj* labyrinthine; *fig* rambling
laberinto [la·βe·'rin·to] *m* **1.** (*lugar*) labyrinth, maze **2.** (*maraña*) tangle
labia ['la·βja] *f inf* glibness; **tener mucha ~** to be a smooth talker
labial [la·'βjal] *adj* labial
lábil ['la·βil] *adj* **1.** *t.* QUÍM (*carácter*) labile **2.** (*frágil*) frail
labio ['la·βjo] *m* **1.** (*boca*) lip; **~ leporino** harelip; **morderse los ~s** *fig* to keep back what one thinks; **estar sin despegar los ~s** to not say a word **2.** (*borde*) rim **3.** *pl* (*vulva*) labia *pl*
labioso, -a [la·'βjo·so, -a] *adj Ecua* honey-tongued
labor [la·'βor] *f* work; (*de coser*) needlework; (*labranza*) plowing; **no estoy por la ~** I don't feel like it; **ocupación: sus ~es** occupation: housewife; **hacer ~es** to do needlework

laborable [la·βo·'ra·βle] *adj* **día ~** working day
laboral [la·βo·'ral] *adj* labor
laborar [la·βo·'rar] *vi* **~ por** [*o* **en favor de**] **algo** to strive for sth
laboratorio [la·βo·ra·'to·rjo] *m* laboratory, lab
laboreo [la·βo·'reo] *m* farm work; MIN working
laborioso, -a [la·βo·'rjo·so, -a] *adj* hard-working, industrious; (*difícil*) arduous
laborista [la·βo·'ris·ta] **I.** *adj* **partido ~** Labor Party, **II.** *mf* member of the Labor Party
labrado [la·'βra·do] *m* (*acción*) working; AGR tillage
labrado, -a [la·'βra·do, -a] *adj* AGR tilled; **campo ~** ploughed field
labrador(a) [la·βra·'dor, --do·ra] *m(f)* farmhand
labrantío [la·βran·'ti·o] *m* land for cultivation
labranza [la·'βran·sa, -θa] *f* (*cultivo*) tillage
labrar [la·'βrar] *vt* **1.** (*un material*) to work; (*un dibujo*) to draw; (*cristal*) to etch; **sin ~** plain; **~ la felicidad de alguien** to make sb happy; **~ la perdición de alguien** to bring sb to ruin **2.** (*cultivar, en jardín*) to work; (*arar*) to plow
labriego, -a [la·'βrje·ɣo, -a] *m, f* farm worker
laburante [la·βu·'ran·te] *mf Arg, Urug, inf* worker
laburar [la·βu·'rar] *vi Arg, Urug, inf* to work
laburo [la·'βu·ro] *m Arg, Urug, inf* work
laca ['la·ka] *f* **1.** (*pintura*) lacquer, shellac **2.** (*para el pelo*) hairspray
lacayo [la·'ka·jo] *m* footman; *pey* (*adulador*) lackey
lachear [la·ʧe·'ar] *vt Chile* to chat up
lacho ['la·ʧo] *m Chile, Perú* (*enamorado*) lover; (*pisaverde*) dandy
lacio, -a ['la·sjo, -a; 'la·θjo-] *adj* (*cabello*) straight, lank
lacón [la·'kon] *m* ham
lacónico, -a [la·'ko·ni·ko, -a] *adj* brief; (*persona*) laconic
lacra ['la·kra] *f* **1.** (*de una enfermedad*) mark **2.** (*vicio*) blight
lacrar [la·'krar] *vt* (*cerrar*) to seal
lacre ['la·kre] *m* sealing wax
lacrimógeno, -a [la·kri·'mo·xe·no, -a] *adj* tear; **gas ~** tear gas; **película lacrimógena** *pey* tearjerker
lacrimoso, -a [la·kri·'mo·so, -a] *adj* (*lloroso*) tearful; (*lastimoso*) sorrowful; (*quejumbroso*) whining
lactancia [lak·'tan·sja, -θja] *f* nursing, breastfeeding; (*período*) pre-weaning period
lactante [lak·'tan·te] *mf* nursing infant, nursling
lacteado, -a [lak·te·'a·do, -a] *adj* milk; **papilla lacteada** milk-based baby formula
lácteo, -a ['lak·teo, -a] *adj* milk, dairy; *fig* milky; **vía láctea** ASTR Milky Way
láctico, -a ['lak·ti·ko, -a] *adj* lactic
lactosa [lak·'to·sa] *f* lactose
lacustre [la·'kus·tre] *adj* lacustrine, of lakes; **construcciones ~s** lake dwellings

K
L

ladeado, -a [la·de·'a·do, -a] *adj* tilted; **el cuadro está ~** the picture is lopsided
ladear [la·de·'ar] **I.** *vt* **1.**(*inclinar*) to slant **2.**(*desviar*) to skirt; **~ un problema** to get around a problem **II.** *vr:* **~se 1.**(*inclinarse*) to lean **2.** *Chile* (*enamorarse*) **~se de alguien** to fall in love with sb
ladera [la·'de·ra] *f* slope, hillside
ladilla [la·'di·ja, -ʎa] *f* crab louse
ladino, -a [la·'di·no] *adj* cunning
lado ['la·do] *m* **1.** *t.* MAT side; **a ambos ~s** on both sides; **por el ~ materno** on the mother's side; **ir de un ~ a otro** to go back and forth; **por todos ~s** everywhere; **al ~** nearby; **la casa de al ~** the house next-door; **al ~ de** (*junto a*) beside, next to; **al ~ mío, a mi ~** next to me, by my side; **por un ~..., y por el otro ~...** on the one hand..., and on the other hand... **2.**(*lugar*) **por el ~ del río** by the river; **ir a algún otro ~** to go somewhere else; **~ a ~** side by side **3.**(*punto de vista*) side; **el ~ bueno de la vida** the good side of life; **su ~ débil** his/her weak spot **4.**(*camino*) direction; **tomar por otro ~** to go another way **5.**(*partido*) **me puse de tu ~** I sided with you ▸ **dejar de ~ a alguien** to ignore sb; **mirar de ~ a alguien** to look out of the corner of one's eye at sb
ladrar [la·'drar] *vi* to bark ▸ **perro que ladra no muerde** *prov* his bark is worse than his bite
ladrido [la·'dri·do] *m* bark
ladrillo [la·'dri·jo, -ʎo] *m* brick; **ser un ~** *inf* (*película, libro*) to be deadly dull
ladrón [la·'dron] *m* (*enchufe*) multiple socket
ladrón, -ona [la·'dron, -'dro·na] *m, f* thief, robber; **~ cuatrero** treacherous thief ▸ **piensa el ~ que todos son de su condición** *prov* we all judge others by our own standards; **la ocasión hace al ~** *prov* opportunity makes the thief *prov*
ladronzuelo, -a [la·dron·'swe·lo, -a; -'θwe·lo, -a] *m, f* (*ratero*) petty thief
lagar [la·'ɣar] *m* **1.**(*aceite*) oil press; (*vino*) winepress **2.**(*edificio*) press house
lagartear [la·ɣar·te·'ar] **I.** *vt* **1.** *Chile* to pinion **2.** *Col* (*hacer chanchullos*) to finagle **II.** *vi* *Guat, Méx* (*cazar lagartos*) to catch lizards
lagartija [la·ɣar·'ti·xa] *f* small lizard
lagarto [la·'ɣar·to] **I.** *m* **1.**(*reptil*) lizard **2.** *AmL* (*caimán*) alligator **II.** *interj* knock on wood!
lagarto, -a [la·'ɣar·to, -a] *m, f* (*persona*) crafty fellow
lagartón, -ona [la·ɣar·'ton, -'to·na] *m, f* sharp fellow; *pey* sly devil *m*, sly bitch *f*
lago ['la·ɣo] *m* lake

> **i** **Lago de Titicaca** (Lake Titicaca), located at an altitude of nearly 4,000 meters (12,500 ft.), surrounded by the snowcapped peaks of the Andes, and covering over 8,000 square km. (3,200 square miles), is a lake that is steeped in legend. Incan culture supposedly originated at **Lake Titicaca**. The two-ton gold chain of the Inca **Huáscar** is said to lie on the lake's bottom, placed there in an effort to save it from the attacking **conquistadores**.

lágrima ['la·ɣri·ma] *f* tear ▸ **llorar ~s de sangre por algo** to shed bitter tears for sth; **llorar a ~ viva** to weep bitterly; **deshacerse en ~s** to burst into tears
lagrimal [la·ɣri·'mal] **I.** *adj* lachrymal **II.** *m* corner of the eye
lagrimear [la·ɣri·me·'ar] *vi* **1.**(*llorar*) to cry easily **2.**(*ojos*) to water
lagrimoso, -a [la·ɣri·'mo·so, -a] *adj* (*ojos*) watery
laguna [la·'ɣu·na] *f* **1.**(*agua salada*) lagoon; (*dulce*) small lake **2.**(*omisión*) gap; **~ en la memoria** memory lapse
laicalización [lai·ka·li·sa·'sjon, -θa·'θjon] *f* *Chile* secularization
laicalizar <z→c> [lai·ka·li·'sar, -'θar] *vt* *Chile* to secularize
laico, -a ['lai·ko, -a] **I.** *adj* lay **II.** *m, f* layman *m*, laywoman *f*
laísmo [la·'is·mo] *m*

> **i** The term **laísmo** refers to the incorrect use of **la(s)** as the indirect object instead of **le(s)**, as in the sentence "**La regalé una novela de Borges**," which should read "**Le regalé una novela de Borges.**" Though such use is common in some regions, most Spanish speakers do not consider it to be correct.

laja ['la·xa] *f* flat stone; **~ de pizarra** slate slab
lama ['la·ma] *f* **1.**(*cieno*) silt **2.**(*de metal*) slat
lambiche [lam·'bi·tʃe] *adj* *Méx, vulg* (*adulador*) ass-kissing
lameculos [la·me·'ku·los] *mf inv, vulg* kiss-ass
lamedura [la·me·'du·ra] *f* licking
lamentable [la·men·'ta·βle] *adj* regrettable
lamentación [la·men·ta·'sjon, -'θjon] *f* lamentation
lamentar [la·men·'tar] **I.** *vt* to regret; **lo lamento** I'm sorry **II.** *vr* **~se de algo** to complain about sth
lamento [la·'men·to] *m* lament
lameplatos [la·me·'pla·tos] *mf inv* **1.** *inf* (*goloso*) glutton **2.**(*pobre*) scrounger
lamer [la·'mer] **I.** *vt* to lick; **las olas lamen las arenas** the waves lap against the shore ▸ **mejor lamiendo que mordiendo** it's easier to catch a bear with honey than with vinegar **II.** *vr:* **~se** to lick oneself; **~se de gusto** to lick one's lips

lamido [la·'mi·do] *m* licking

lamido, -a [la·'mi·do, -a] *adj* (*flaco*) scrawny; (*relamido*) affected; (*gastado*) worn out

lámina ['la·mi·na] *f* 1. (*hojalata*) tin plate; (*hoja de metal*) sheet; (*segmento*) lamina; ~ **para proyector** projector plate 2. (*ilustración*) print; **con ~s** illustrated

laminar [la·mi·'nar] I. *adj* 1. (*en forma de lámina*) laminar 2. (*formado de láminas*) laminated II. *vt* 1. (*cortar*) to split 2. (*guarnecer*) to laminate

lampa ['lam·pa] *f* And (*pala*) shovel; (*azada*) pick

lámpara ['lam·pa·ra] *f* lamp, light; ~ **fluorescente** fluorescent lamp; ~ **de pie** standard lamp

lamparazo [lam·pa·'ra·so, -θo] *m* Col drink

lamparilla [lam·pa·'ri·ja, -ʎa] *f* (*luz*) small lamp

lamparón [lam·pa·'ron] *m* 1. (*mancha*) grease stain 2. MED scrofula

lampiño, -a [lam·'pi·ɲo, -a] *adj* (*sin barba*) beardless; (*sin pelo*) hairless

lana ['la·na] *f* 1. (*material, tela*) wool; ~ **esquilada** fleece 2. *Méx, inf* (*dinero*) dough; **tienen mucha ~** they're loaded ▶ **unos cardan la ~ y otros cobran la fama** some do all the work and others get all the credit; **cardar la ~ a alguien** to tell sb off

lanar [la·'nar] *adj* wool-bearing; **ganado ~** sheep

lance ['lan·se, 'lan·θe] *m* throw; ~ **de honor** duel; **comprar de ~** *inf* to buy secondhand; **de ~** *inf* at a bargain price; ~ **de amor** love affair; ~ **de fortuna** stroke of luck

lancha ['lan·tʃa] *f* motorboat; ~ **a remolque** barge; ~ **de salvamento** lifeboat

lanchar [lan·'tʃar] *vi* Ecua 1. (*nublarse*) to become overcast 2. (*helar*) to freeze

lancinante [lan·si·'nan·te, lan·θi-] *adj* (*dolor*) stabbing

landa ['lan·da] *f* moorland

lanero, -a [la·'ne·ro, -a] *adj* wool

langosta [lan·'gos·ta] *f* 1. (*insecto*) locust 2. (*crustáceo*) lobster

langostino [lan·gos·'ti·no] *m* prawn

langucia [lan·'gu·sja, -θja] *f AmL* hunger

languidecer [lan·gi·de·'ser, -'θer] *irr como crecer vi* to languish; ~ **de amor** to pine; **la conversación languideció** the conversation flagged

languidez [lan·gi·'des, -'deθ] *f* 1. (*debilidad*) weakness 2. (*espíritu*) listlessness

lánguido, -a ['lan·gi·do, -a] *adj* 1. (*débil*) weak 2. (*espíritu*) languid

lanilla [la·'ni·ja, -ʎa] *f* nap

lanolina [la·no·'li·na] *f* lanolin

lanoso, -a [la·'no·so, -a] *adj*, lanudo, -a [la·'nu·do, -a] *adj* woolly; (*oveja*) wool-bearing

lanza ['lan·sa, -θa] *f* lance ▶ **quebrar ~s** to cross swords, to argue; **romper una ~ en favor de alguien** to stick up for sb

lanzabengalas [lan·sa·βen·'ga·las, lan·θa-] *m inv* flare gun

lanzacohetes [lan·sa·ko·'e·tes, lan·θa-] *m inv* rocket launcher

lanzada [lan·'sa·da, -'θa·da] *f* (*golpe*) spear thrust; (*herida*) lance wound

lanzadera [lan·sa·'de·ra, lan·θa-] *f* shuttle; (*plataforma*) platform, launch(ing) pad

lanzado, -a [lan·'sa·do, -a; lan·'θa-] *adj* 1. (*decidido*) determined; (*emprendedor*) enterprising 2. (*impetuoso*) impetuous; (*fogoso*) forward

lanzador(a) [lan·sa·'dor, lan·'θa-] *m(f)* thrower; (*béisbol*) bowler, pitcher

lanzallamas [lan·sa·'ja·mas, lan·'θa·ʎa-] *m inv* flamethrower

lanzamiento [lan·sa·'mjen·to, lan·θa-] *m* throw; ~ **de bombas** dropping of bombs; ~ **comercial** commercial promotion, product launch; ~ **espacial** space launch; ~ **de peso** DEP shot put

lanzamisiles [lan·sa·mi·'si·les, lan·θa-] *m inv* missile-launcher

lanzar <z→c> [lan·'sar, -'θar] I. *vt* 1. (*arrojar*) ~ **a algo/alguien** to throw at [o to] sth/sb; ~ **peso** to put the shot 2. (*al mercado*) to launch II. *vr* ~**se a/sobre algo/alguien** to throw oneself at/against sth/sb; ~**se a correr** to break into a run; ~**se al agua** to dive into the water; ~**se en paracaídas** to parachute; ~**se en picado** to nosedive; ~**se a algo** to undertake sth

lapa ['la·pa] *f* ZOOL limpet; **pegarse como una ~** *inf* (*persona*) to stick like a leech

La Paz *f* La Paz

lapicera [la·pi·'θe·ra, -'se·ra] *f Arg, Urug* ballpoint pen

lapicero [la·pi·'θe·ro, -'θe·ro] *m* pencil; (*recipiente*) penholder

lápida ['la·pi·da] *f* stone tablet; ~ **conmemorativa** memorial tablet; ~ **mortuoria** gravestone

lapidar [la·pi·'dar] *vt* to stone

lapidario, -a [la·pi·'da·rjo] *adj* categorical, scathing; **frase lapidaria** *memorable phrase*

lápiz ['la·pis, 'la·piθ] *m* pencil; ~ **de labios** lipstick; ~ **de ojos** eye pencil; ~ **de color** crayon

lapón, -ona [la·'pon] I. *adj* Lapp II. *m, f* Lapp, Laplander

Laponia [la·'po·nja] *f* Lapland

lapso ['laβ·so] *m* 1. (*período*) ~ (**de tiempo**) lapse 2. *v.* lapsus

lapsus ['laβ·sus] *m inv* blunder; ~ **linguae** slip of the tongue

laquear [la·ke·'ar] *vt* to lacquer

lar [lar] *m* (*fuego*) hearth; (*hogar*) home

largar <g→gu> [lar·'ɣar] I. *vt* 1. (*soltar*) to release 2. *inf* (*golpe*) to land; (*bofetada*) to let fly 3. *inf* (*discurso*) to give 4. *inf* (*deshacerse de*) ~ **algo a alguien** to unload sth on sb II. *vr*: ~**se** 1. (*irse*) to leave; (*de casa*) to leave home 2. *AmL* (*comenzar*) to begin; ~**se a hacer algo** to start to do sth III. *vi inf* to yak

largo ['lar·ɣo] I. *adv* plenty; **tenemos comida**

para ~ we have plenty of food; ~ **y tendido** at length ▶ **a lo** ~ **de la playa** along the beach; **a lo** ~ **del día** throughout the day; **¡**~ **(de aquí)!** clear off! **II.** *m* length; **nadar tres** ~**s** to swim three lengths of the pool; **diez metros de** ~ ten meters long

largo, -a ['lar·ɣo, -a] *adj* long; **a** ~ **plazo, a la larga** in the long term [*o* run]; **a lo** ~ **de los años** throughout the years; **dar largas a algo** to put off doing sth; **el pantalón te está** ~ your pants are too long for you; **ir de** ~ to be in a long dress; **(de gala)** to be in formal dress; **pasar de** ~ to pass by; *fig* to ignore; **tener cincuenta años** ~**s** to be well past 50; **tener las manos largas (***pegar***)** to be free with one's hands; **(***robar***)** to be light-fingered; **por** ~ for a long time

largometraje [lar·ɣo·me·'tra·xe] *m* full-length [*o* feature] film

larguero [lar·'ɣe·ro] *m* DEP crossbar

larguirucho, -a [lar·ɣi·'ru·tʃo, -a] *adj inf* lanky

largura [lar·'ɣu·ra] *f* length

laringe [la·'rin·xe] *f* larynx

laringitis [la·rin·'xi·tis] *f inv* laryngitis

larva ['lar·βa] *f* larva

larvado, -a [lar·'βa·do, -a] *adj* latent

las [las] **I.** *art def v.* **el, la, lo II.** *pron pers f pl* **1.** (*objeto directo*) them; **¡míra~!** look at them! **2.** (*con relativo*) ~ **que...** the ones that...; ~ **cuales** those which **3.** (*laísmo*) improper use of '*la*' and '*las*' as indirect objects instead of '*le*' and '*les*'

lascar <c→qu> [las·'kar] *vt Méx* (*lastimar*) to bruise

lascivia [la·'si·βja, las·'θi·βja] *f* lasciviousness

lascivo, -a [la·'si·βo, las·'θi·βo, -a] *adj* lascivious

láser ['la·ser] *m* laser

lasitud [la·si·'tud] *f* lassitude

lástima ['las·ti·ma] *f* pity; **dar** [*o* causar] ~ to inspire pity; **su último libro da** ~ his/her latest book is pathetic; **de** [*o* por] ~ out of pity; **estar hecho una** ~ to be a sorry sight; **¡qué** ~**!** what a pity!

lastimar [las·ti·'mar] **I.** *vt* **1.** (*herir*) to hurt **2.** (*agraviar*) to offend **II.** *vr:* ~**se 1.** (*herirse*) to hurt oneself **2.** (*quejarse*) ~**se de algo** to complain about sth

lastimero, -a [las·ti·'me·ro, -a] *adj,* **lastimoso, -a** [las·ti·'mo·so, -a] *adj* pitiful

lastra ['las·tra] *f* flagstone

lastre ['las·tre] *m* (*estorbo*) dead weight; **ser un** ~ to be a burden

lata ['la·ta] *f* **1.** (*metal*) tin **2.** (*envase*) can **3.** *inf* (*pesadez*) bore; **dar la** ~ to be a nuisance; **¡vaya** ~**!** (*fastidio*) what a pain!

latazo [la·'ta·so, -θo] *m inf* **ser un** ~ (*pesado*) to be a drag; (*fastidioso*) bother; (*aburrido*) bore; **dar el** ~ to be a nuisance

latear [la·te·'ar] *vi AmL* to bore; **se pasa el día lateando** he/she spends all day blabbing away

latente [la·'ten·te] *adj* latent

lateral [la·te·'ral] *adj* lateral; (*secundario*) sec-

ondary

latería [la·te·'ri·a] *f* **1.** (*conjunto de latas*) cans *pl* of preserves; **la** ~ **de su despensa** the canned goods in her pantry **2.** *AmL* (*hojalatería*) tinsmith's shop

latido [la·'ti·do] *m* (*corazón*) heartbeat; (*herida, arteria*) throbbing

latifundio [la·ti·'fun·djo] *m large landed estate*

latifundista [la·ti·fun·'dis·ta] *mf owner of a large estate*

latigazo [la·ti·'ɣa·so, '-ɣa·θo] *m* **1.** (*golpe*) whiplash; (*chasquido*) crack of a whip **2.** (*destino*) stroke of fate

látigo ['la·ti·ɣo] *m* whip

latiguear [la·ti·ɣe·'ar] **I.** *vi* to crack a whip **II.** *vt AmL* to flog

latiguillo [la·ti·'ɣi·jo, -ʎo] *m* **1.** (*efectismo*) hamming **2.** (*muletilla*) catchphrase; (*expresión*) platitude

latín [la·'tin] *m* Latin; **saber (mucho)** ~ *inf* to know what's what, to know a thing or two

latino, -a [la·'ti·no, -a] **I.** *adj* Latin; **América Latina** Latin America **II.** *m, f* Latin; *AmL* (*latinoamericano*) Latin American

Latinoamérica [la·ti·no·a·'me·ri·ka] *f* Latin America

latinoamericano, -a [la·ti·no·a·me·ri·'ka·no, -a] *adj, m, f* Latin American

latir [la·'tir] *vi* (*corazón*) to beat; (*arteria, herida*) to throb

latitud [la·ti·'tud] *f* latitude; (*extensión*) breadth

lato, -a ['la·to, -a] *adj* **en sentido** ~ in the broad sense

latón [la·'ton] *m* brass

latoso, -a [la·'to·so, -a] *adj* bothersome

latrocinio [la·tro·'si·njo, -'θi·njo] *m* larceny

laúd [la·'ud] *m MÚS* lute

laudatorio, -a [lau·da·'to·rjo, -a] *adj* laudatory; **discurso** ~ eulogistic speech

laudo ['lau·do] *m* decision

laureado, -a [lau·re·'a·do, -a] *adj* (*coronado*) crowned with laurel; (*premiado*) laureate, prize-winning

laurear [lau·re·'ar] *vt* (*coronar*) to crown with laurel; (*premiar*) to award

laurel [lau·'rel] *m* (*árbol*) laurel; (*condimento*) bay leaf; **dormirse en los** ~**es** to rest on one's laurels

lava ['la·βa] *f* (*volcán*) lava

lavable [la·'βa·βle] *adj* washable; (*color*) colorfast

lavabo [la·'βa·βo] *m* **1.** (*pila*) sink **2.** (*cuarto*) lavatory

lavacoches [la·βa·'ko·tʃes] *m inv* (*instalación*) car wash

lavacristales [la·βa·kris·'ta·les] *mf inv* window cleaner

lavadero [la·βa·'de·ro] *m* (*de ropa*) laundry; (*en el río*) washing place

lavado [la·'βa·do] *m* wash; ~ **en seco** dry-cleaning; MED lavage, washing; ~ **de cerebro** *fig* brainwashing; ~ **de cara** *fig* facelift

lavadora [la·βa·'do·ra] *f* washing machine
lavanda [la·'βan·da] *f* lavender
lavandería [la·βan·de·'ri·a] *f* laundromat
lavaplatos [la·βa·'pla·tos] *m inv* **1.** (*electrodoméstico*) dishwasher **2.** *Col, inf* (*fregadero*) (kitchen) sink
lavar [la·'βar] **I.** *vt* to wash; **~ la cabeza** to wash one's hair; **~ los platos** to do the dishes **II.** *vr:* **~se** to wash; **~se los dientes** to brush one's teeth
lavarropas [la·βa·'rro·pas] *f inv, Arg* washing machine
lavativa [la·βa·'ti·βa] *f* (*enema*) enema
lavatorio [la·βa·'to·rjo] *m AmL* washroom
lavavajillas [la·βa·βa·'xi·jas, -ʎas] *m inv* **1.** (*electrodoméstico*) dishwasher **2.** (*detergente*) dish detergent
lavotear [la·βo·te·'ar] **I.** *vt* to wash sloppily **II.** *vr:* **~se** *inf* to take a sponge bath
laxante [lak·'san·te] *m* laxative
laxar [lak·'sar] *vt* (*vientre*) to loosen up
laxitud [lak·si·'tud] *f* laxity
laxo, -a ['lak·so, -a] *adj* slack; (*moral*) lax
lazada [la·'sa·da, -'θa·da] *f* (*de zapato*) bow
lazareto [la·sa·'re·to, la·θa-] *m* (*de contagiosos*) quarantine station
lazo ['la·so, 'la·θo] *m* **1.** (*nudo*) bow **2.** (*para caballos*) lasso; (*para conejos*) snare **3.** (*cinta*) ribbon **4.** (*vínculo*) tie; **~s afectivos** emotional bonds
lda., ldo. *abr de* **licenciada, -o** graduate
le [le] *pron pers* **1.** *objeto indirecto:* m sing him; *f sing* her; *forma cortés* you; **¡da~ un beso!** give him/her a kiss!; **~ puedo llamar el lunes** I can call you on Monday **2.** *reg, objeto directo:* m sing him **3.** *forma cortés* you
leal [le·'al] *adj* loyal
lealtad [le·al·'tad] *f* loyalty
lebrel [le·'βrel] *m* greyhound
lección [lek·'sjon, -'θjon] *f* lesson; **tomar lecciones de matemáticas** to take mathematics classes; **¿te tomo la ~?** *inf* should I test you?; **dar una ~ a alguien** to teach sb a lesson; **¡que te sirva de ~!** let that be a lesson to you!
lechada [le·'tʃa·da] *f* (*argamasa*) grout
lechal [le·'tʃal] **I.** *adj* (*cachorro*) suckling; **cordero ~** suckling lamb **II.** *m* (*cordero*) baby lamb
leche ['le·tʃe] *f* **1.** (*líquido*) milk; **~ en polvo** powdered milk; **~ entera** whole milk; **~ desnatada** skimmed milk; **~ semidesnatada** low fat milk **2.** *vulg* (*esperma*) spunk **3.** *inf* (*golpe*) blow; **¡te doy una ~!** I'm going to belt you one! **4.** *inf* (*hostia*) **¡~s!** damn it!; **ser la ~** to be too much; **estar de mala ~** to be in a foul mood; **tener mala ~** to be vindictive; **a toda ~** at full speed
lechera [le·'tʃe·ra] *adj, f v.* **lechero**
lechería [le·tʃe·'ri·a] *f* dairy
lechero, -a [le·'tʃe·ro, -a] *m, f* milkman *m*, milkwoman *f*
lechigada [le·tʃi·'ɣa·da] *f* litter
lecho ['le·tʃo] *m* bed; (*río*) riverbed

lechón, -ona [le·'tʃon, -·'tʃo·na] *m, f* suckling pig
lechosa [le·'tʃo·sa] *f AmL* BOT papaya
lechoso, -a [le·'tʃo·so] *adj* milky
lechuga [le·'tʃu·ɣa] *f* lettuce ▶ **como una ~** as fresh as a daisy; **ser más fresco que una ~** *inf* to have a lot of nerve
lechuza [le·'tʃu·sa, -θa] *f* barn owl
lectivo, -a [lek·'ti·βo, -a] *adj* **ciclo ~** ENS school cycle; UNIV academic cycle; **día ~** school day
lector [lek·'tor] *m* COMPUT reader; **~ de CD** CD player
lector(a) [lek·'tor, -·to·ra] *m(f)* **1.** (*que lee*) reader; (*en voz alta*) lector **2.** (*profesor*) conversation assistant
lectorado [lek·to·'ra·do] *m* assistantship
lectura [lek·'tu·ra] *f* **1.** *t.* COMPUT reading; **dar ~ a algo** to read sth aloud; **ser de mucha ~** to be well-read **2.** (*obra*) reading material
leer [le·'er] *irr vt* to read; **~ en voz alta** to read aloud; **~ en la cara de alguien** to see from sb's expression
legación [le·ɣa·'sjon, -'θjon] *f* legation
legado [le·'ɣa·do] *m* legacy
legajo [le·'ɣa·xo] *m* dossier
legal [le·'ɣal] *adj* **1.** (*determinado por la ley*) legal; (*conforme a la ley*) lawful **2.** (*fiel*) trustworthy
legalidad [le·ɣa·li·'dad] *f* legality; **al filo de la ~** semi-legal; **fuera de la ~** unlawful
legalista [le·ɣa·'lis·ta] *adj* legalistic
legalización [le·ɣa·li·θa·'θjon] *f* **1.** (*autorización*) legalization **2.** (*atestamiento*) authentication
legalizar <z→c> [le·ɣa·li·'sar, -'θar] *vt* **1.** (*autorizar*) to legalize **2.** (*atestar*) to authenticate
légamo ['le·ɣa·mo] *m* mud
legaña [le·'ɣa·ɲa] *f* sleep, rheum; **tienes ~s** you have sleep in your eyes
legar <g→gu> [le·'ɣar] *vt* (*legado*) to bequeath
legendario, -a [le·xen·'da·rjo] *adj* legendary; (*famoso*) renowned
legible [le·'xi·βle] *adj* legible
legión [le·'xjon] *f* legion; **hay comida para una ~** there's enough food to feed an army
legionario, -a [le·xjo·'na·rjo, -a] **I.** *adj* legionary **II.** *m, f* legionnaire
legionella [le·xjo·'ne·la] *f* MED Legionnaire's disease
legislación [le·xis·la·'sjon, -'θjon] *f* legislation
legislador(a) [le·xis·la·'dor, -·'do·ra] **I.** *adj* legislative **II.** *m(f)* **1.** (*que legisla*) legislator **2.** *AmL* (*parlamentario*) member of parliament
legislar [le·xis·'lar] *vi* to legislate
legislativo, -a [le·xis·la·'ti·βo, -a] *adj* legislative; **poder ~** legislative power
legislatura [le·xis·la·'tu·ra] *f* **1.** (*período*) term of office **2.** *AmL* (*parlamento*) legislative body
legitimación [le·xi·ti·ma·'sjon, -'θjon] *f* **1.** (*legalización*) authentication **2.** (*habilita-*

ción) recognition **3.** (*hijo*) legitimization

legitimar [le·xi·ti·'mar] *vt* **1.** (*dar legitimidad*) to authenticate **2.** (*habilitar*) to recognize **3.** (*hijo*) to make legitimate

legítimo, -a [le·'xi·ti·mo, -a] *adj* **1.** (*legal*) legitimate; **defensa legítima** self-defense **2.** (*verdadero*) genuine **3.** (*hijo*) legitimate

lego, -a ['le·γo, -a] *adj* **ser un ~ en el tema** to know nothing about the subject

legua ['le·γwa] *f* league; **a la ~** miles away

leguleyo, -a [le·γu·'le·jo, -a] *m, f pey* pettifogging lawyer, shyster

legumbre [le·'γum·bre] *f* **1.** (*planta*) legume **2.** (*seca*) pulse; (*hortaliza*) vegetable; **frutas y ~s** fruit and vegetables

leíble [le·'i·βle] *adj* readable

leído, -a [le·'i·do, -a] *adj* **1.** (*persona*) well-read **2.** (*revista*) widely-read

leísmo [le·'is·mo]

i The term **leísmo** refers to the incorrect or perhaps non-standard use of **le(s)** as the direct object instead of **lo(s)** or **la(s)**, as in the sentence "**Les visité ayer, a mis hermanas,**" which should read "**Las visité ayer, a mis hermanas.**" Although such use is common in some regions, most Spanish speakers do not accept it as being correct.

lejanía [le·xa·'ni·a] *f* distance

lejano, -a [le·'xa·no, -a] *adj* faraway; (*parentesco*) distant; **en un futuro no muy ~** in the not-so-distant future

lejía [le·'xi·a] *f* (*para lavar*) bleach

lejos ['le·xos] I. *adv* far; **~ de algo** far from sth; **a lo ~** in the distance; **de ~** from afar; **ir demasiado ~** *t. fig* to go too far; **es de ~ la mejor soprano** she is by far the best soprano; **llegar ~** *fig* to go far; **sin ir más ~** *fig* to take an obvious example II. *prep* **~ de** far from; **está muy ~ de mí hacer algo** *fig* I have no intention of intervening in sth

lelo, -a ['le·lo, -a] *adj inf* **1.** *ser* (*tonto*) silly, goofy **2.** *estar* (*pasmado*) stunned; (*mareado*) dizzy

lema ['le·ma] *m* (*tema*) theme; (*mote*) motto

lencería [len·se·'ri·a, len·θe·] *f* (*de ropa interior*) lingerie shop; (*ropa interior*) underwear; **~ de un almacén** linen room

lengón, -ona [len·'gon, -·'go·na] *adj Col* outspoken

lengua ['len·gwa] *f* **1.** ANAT tongue; **lo tengo en la punta de la ~** I have it on the tip of my tongue; **morderse la ~** *t. fig* to bite one's tongue; **sacar la ~ a alguien** to stick ones tongue out at sb; **se me trabó la ~** I got tongue-tied; **tener la ~ demasiado larga** *fig* to talk too much **2.** LING tongue; **~ materna** mother tongue; **~ oficial** official language **3.** (*forma*) tongue; **~ de agua** tongue of water ▶ **tener la ~ de trapo** *inf* to stutter and stam-

mer; **estar con la ~ fuera** to be out of breath; **tener una ~ viperina** to be a backbiter; **atar la ~ a alguien** to silence sb; **dar a la ~** to gab; **aquí alguien se ha ido de la ~** sb here has spilled the beans; **tirar a alguien de la ~** to pump sb for information; **volar ~** *AmC* (*hablar*) to gossip

lenguado [len·'gwa·do] *m* sole

lenguaje [len·'gwa·xe] *m* language

lenguaraz [len·gwa·'ras, -'raθ] *adj* talkative

lenguaz [len·'gwas, -'gwaθ] *adj* garrulous

lengüeta [len·'gwe·ta] *f* (*zapato*) tongue; (*balanza*) pointer; MÚS reed

lengüetear [len·gwe·te·'ar] *vi AmL, inf* to stick one's tongue out

lengüilargo, -a [len·gwi·'lar·γo, -a] *adj inf* impudent

lengüón, -ona [len·'gwon, -·'gwo·na] *adj AmL* (*calumniador*) backbiting; (*chismoso*) gossipy

lenificar <c→qu> [le·ni·fi·'kar] *vt* to soothe

lenitivo, -a [le·ni·'ti·βo] *adj* alleviating

lente ['len·te] *f* **1.** (*gafas*) eyeglasses *pl*; **llevar ~s** to wear glasses **2.** *t.* FOTO (*cristal*) lens; **~ de aumento** magnifying glass

lenteja [len·'te·xa] *f* lentil; **ganarse las ~s** *fig* to earn one's daily bread

lentejuela [len·te·'xwe·la] *f* sequin, spangle

lenticular [len·ti·ku·'lar] *adj* lenticular

lentilla [len·'ti·ja, -ʎa] *f* contact lens

lentitud [len·ti·'tud] *f* slowness; *fig* slow-wittedness; **con ~** slowly

lento, -a ['len·to] *adj* slow; *fig* slow-witted; **a paso ~** slowly; **cocinar a fuego ~** to cook over low heat [*o* a low flame]; **quemar a fuego ~** *fig* to burn slowly

leña ['le·ɲa] *f* **1.** (*madera*) firewood; **echar ~ al fuego** to add more firewood; *fig* to add fuel to the flames **2.** (*castigo*) beating; **¡~ con él!** let him have it!; **dar ~** to give a beating; **repartir ~** to dish out blows; **recibir ~** to get beaten up ▶ **hacer ~ del árbol caído** to kick somebody when he is down; **llevar ~ al monte** to carry coals to Newcastle

leñador(a) [le·ɲa·'dor, -·'do·ra] *m(f)* woodcutter, lumberjack

leñazo [le·'ɲa·so, -θo] *m inf* bash; **darse un ~ en la cabeza** to bash one's head

leñoso, -a [le·'ɲo·so, -a] *adj* woody

Leo ['le·o] *m* Leo

león [le·'on] *m* lion; *AmL* (*puma*) puma, panther; **~ (marino)** sea lion ▶ **no es tan fiero el ~ como lo pintan** *inf* it's not as bad as it looks

leonera [leo·'ne·ra] *f* **1.** (*jaula*) lion's cage **2.** (*habitación*) messy room

leonino, -a [leo·'ni·no, -a] *adj* **1.** (*animal*) leonine **2.** (*contrato*) unfair

leopardo [leo·'par·do] *m* leopard

leotardo(s) [leo·'tar·do(s)] *m(pl)* leotards *pl*, tights *pl*

lépero, -a ['le·pe·ro, -a] I. *adj* **1.** *AmC* (*grosero*) coarse; (*vil*) rotten **2.** *Cuba* (*perspicaz*) shrewd **3.** *Ecua. inf* (*arruinado*) broke

II. *m, f AmC* pauper

leporino, -a [le·po·'ri·no, -a] *adj* **labio** ~ harelip

lepra ['le·pra] *f* MED leprosy

leproso, -a [le·'pro·so, -a] **I.** *adj* leprous **II.** *m, f* leper

lerdear [ler·de·'ar] *vi AmC, Arg* to be sluggish; (*demorarse*) to take a long time

lerdo, -a ['ler·do, -a] *adj* slow, sluggish

les [les] *pron pers* **1.** *m pl, reg* (*objeto directo*) them; (*forma cortés*) you **2.** *mf pl* (*objeto indirecto*) them; (*forma cortés*) you

lesbiana [les·'βja·na] *f* lesbian

lésbico, -a ['les·βi·ko, -a] *adj* lesbian

lesear [le·se·'ar] *vi Chile* to fool around

lesera [le·'se·ra] *f AmL* stupidity

lesión [le·'sjon] *f* injury; ~ **cardiaca** heart damage

lesionar [le·sjo·'nar] **I.** *vt* (*herir*) to injure; (*dañar*) to damage **II.** *vr:* ~ **se** to get hurt

lesivo, -a [le·'si·βo, -a] *adj* harmful

leso, -a ['le·so, -a] *adj* injured

letal [le·'tal] *adj elev* lethal

letanía [le·ta·'ni·a] *f* litany; **¡ya está éste con su ~!** there he goes again with his usual story

letárgico, -a [le·'tar·xi·ko, -a] *adj* lethargic

letargo [le·'tar·ɣo] *m* lethargy

letón, -ona [le·'ton] **I.** *adj* Latvian, Lettish **II.** *m, f* Latvian, Lett

Letonia [le·'to·nja] *f* Latvia

letra ['le·tra] *f* **1.** (*signo*) letter; **con ~ mayúscula/minúscula** in capitals/small letters; **al pie de la ~** to the letter; **~ por ~** word for word; **poner cuatro ~s a alguien** to drop sb a line; **tener las ~s gordas** *fig* to be perfectly clear **2.** (*escritura*) handwriting; **de su puño y ~** in his own handwriting **3.** *pl* (*saber*) learning, letters; UNIV arts *pl;* **hombre de ~s** man of letters **4.** MÚS lyrics *pl* **5.** COM ~ (**de cambio**) bill of exchange; ~ **al portador** draft payable to the bearer; ~ **a la vista** sight draft; **girar una ~ a cargo de alguien** to draw a bill on sb

letrado, -a [le·'tra·do, -a] *m, f* lawyer

letrero [le·'tre·ro] *m* notice, sign

leucemia [leu·'se·mja, -'θe·mja] *f* MED leukemia

leucocito [leu·ko·'si·to, -'θi·to] *m* leukocyte

leva ['le·βa] *f* MIL levy

levadizo, -a [le·βa·'di·so, -a; -'di·θo, -a] *adj* **puente** ~ drawbridge

levadura [le·βa·'du·ra] *f* leavening yeast; ~ **en polvo** baking powder

levantamiento [le·βan·ta·'mjen·to] *m* **1.** (*amotinamiento*) uprising **2.** (*alzar*) lifting; ~ **del cadáver** removal of the corpse

levantar [le·βan·'tar] **I.** *vt* **1.** (*alzar*) to lift, to raise; (*del suelo*) to pick up; (*polvo, telón*) to raise; (*un campamento*) to strike; (*las anclas*) to weigh; ~ **el vuelo** to take off; **después del fracaso ya no levantó cabeza** he/she never recovered from the fiasco **2.** (*despertar, provocar*) to awaken; **no queremos ~ sospe-** chas we don't want to arouse suspicion; ~ **polémica** to give rise to controversy **3.** (*construir*) to build; (*monumento*) to erect; (*muro*) to put up **4.** (*suprimir*) to remove; (*embargo, castigo*) to lift **5.** (*mapa*) to draw up; ~ **acta de algo** to draw up a report on sth **6.** (*voz, mirada*) to raise; ~ **la voz a alguien** to raise one's voice to sb **II.** *vr:* ~ **se 1.** (*de la cama*) to get up; ~ **se con el pie izquierdo** *fig* to get out of bed on the wrong side **2.** (*sobresalir*) to stand out **3.** (*sublevarse*) to rebel; **se ~on pocas voces críticas** very few protested **4.** (*viento, telón*) to rise **5.** (*sesión*) to adjourn; **se levanta la sesión** the meeting is closed, court is adjourned

levante [le·'βan·te] *m* east; (*viento*) east wind

levantisco, -a [le·βan·'tis·ko, -a] *adj* rebellious

levar [le·'βar] *vt* ~ (**las**) **anclas** to weigh anchor

leve ['le·βe] *adj* (*enfermedad*) mild; (*peso, sanción*) light; (*error*) slight; (*pecado*) venial

levitar [le·βi·'tar] *vi* to levitate

lexicalizar <z→c> [lek·si·ka·li·'sar, -'θar] *vt* to lexicalize

léxico ['lek·siko] *m* vocabulary

ley [lei] *f* **1.** JUR, REL, FÍS law; **Ley Fundamental** Fundamental Law; **Ley General Tributaria** Tax Law; ~ **orgánica** constitutional law; **la ~ de la oferta y demanda** the law of supply and demand; ~ **de prescripción** statute of limitations; **la ~ seca** the Prohibition; **la ~ de la selva, la ~ del más fuerte** the law of the jungle; **fuerza de ~** force of law; **proyecto de ~** bill; **hacer algo con todas las de la ~** to do sth properly; **hecha la ~, hecha la trampa** every law has its loophole; **respetar las ~es del juego** to follow the rules of the game; **regirse por la ~ del embudo** to have one law for oneself, and one for everyone else; **según la ~ vigente** in accordance with the law currently in force; **se le aplicó la ~ de la fuga al reo** the prisoner was shot while trying to escape; **ser de ~** *inf* to be reliable **2.** (*oro*) legal standard of fineness; (*monedas*) genuine; **oro de ~** standard gold; **ser de buena ~** *fig* to be genuine

leyenda [le·'jen·da] *f* LIT, REL legend

lezna ['les·na, 'leθ·na] *f* awl

liana [li·'a·na] *f* liana

liar <1. pres: lío> [li·'ar] **I.** *vt* **1.** (*fardo*) to tie up; (*paquete*) to wrap up **2.** (*cigarrillo*) to roll **3.** *inf* (*engañar*) to take in; (*enredar*) to mix up; **¡ahora sí que la hemos liado!** we've really done it now! **II.** *vr:* ~ **se 1.** *inf* (*juntarse*) to become lovers **2.** (*embarullarse*) to get complicated; ~ **se la manta a la cabeza** *inf* to take the plunge **3.** (*ponerse a*) ~ **se a golpes con alguien** to start fighting with sb

libanés, -esa [li·βa·'nes, -esa] *adj, m, f* Lebanese

Líbano ['li·βa·no] *m* **El** ~ Lebanon

libar [li·'βar] *vi* (*abeja*) to suck

libelo [li·'βe·lo] *m* libel

libélula [li·'βe·lu·la] *f* dragonfly

liberación [li·βe·ra·'sjon, -'θjon] *f* liberation, release

liberal [li·βe·'ral] *adj t.* POL liberal

liberalización [li·βe·ra·li·sa·'sjon, -θa·'θjon] *f* liberalization

liberalizar <z→c> [li·βe·ra·li·'sar, -'θar] *vt* to liberalize

liberar [li·βe·'rar] *vt* to liberate, to set free; (*eximir*) to exempt

liberiano, -a [li·βe·'rja·no, -a] *adj, m, f* Liberian

líbero ['li·βe·ro] *m* DEP sweeper

libérrimo, -a [li·'βe·rri·mo, -a] *adj superl de* libre

libertad [li·βer·'tad] *f* 1. (*libre arbitrio*) liberty; ~ **de culto** freedom of worship; ~ **de expresión** freedom of speech; ~ **de prensa** freedom of the press; **en** ~ **bajo fianza** on bail; **en** ~ **condicional** on parole; **poner en** ~ to set free; **tomarse demasiadas** ~**es** to take too many liberties 2. (*naturalidad*) familiarity

libertar [li·βer·'tar] *vt* to liberate

libertario, -a [li·βer·'ta·rjo, -a] *adj, m, f* libertarian

libertinaje [li·βer·ti·'na·xe] *m* libertinage

libertino, -a [li·βer·'ti·no, -a] *adj* dissolute

Libia ['li·βja] *f* Libya

libidinoso, -a [li·βi·di·'no·so, -a] *adj* lustful

libido [li·'βi·do] *f* libido

libio, -a ['li·βjo, -a] *adj, m, f* Libyan

libra ['li·βra] *f* pound; ~ **esterlina** pound sterling; **una** ~ **de judías** a pound of beans

Libra ['li·βra] *f* Libra

librado, -a [li·'βra·do, -a] *adj* **salir bien** ~ **de algo** to come out of sth unscathed, to be successful in sth; **salir mal** ~ to come out the worse for wear, to fail

libramiento [li·βra·'mjen·to] *m*, **libranza** [li·'βran·sa, -θa] *f* order of payment; (*de un cheque*) payment

librar [li·'βrar] I. *vt* 1. (*dejar libre*) ~ **de algo/ alguien** to free from sth/sb; (*salvar*) to save from sth/sb; **¡líbreme Dios!** God [*o* Heaven] forbid!; **y líbranos del mal** and deliver us from evil 2. COM to draw; ~ **una letra a cargo de alguien** to draw a draft on sb II. *vi inf* (*tener libre*) **hoy libro** I have today off III. *vr:* ~ **se de algo/alguien** (*deshacerse*) to get rid of sth/sb; (*salvarse*) to escape from sth/sb

libre <libérrimo> ['li·βre] *adj* free; **zona de** ~ **cambio** free trade area; ~ **de franqueo** no postage necessary; **dar vía** ~ to give the green light; **eres bien** ~ **de hacerlo** you are quite free to do so

librea [li·'βrea] *f* (*traje*) livery

librecambio [li·βre·'kam·bjo] *m* free trade

librería [li·βre·'ri·a] *f* bookshop; ~ **de ocasión** secondhand bookshop

librero, -a [li·'βre·ro] *m, f* bookseller

libreta [li·'βre·ta] *f* 1. (*cuaderno*) notebook; (*para notas*) notepad 2. (*de ahorros*) bank book

libro ['li·βro] *m* book; ~ **de bolsillo** paperback; ~ **blanco** white paper; ~ **científico** science book; ~ **de cocina** cookbook; ~ **de consulta** reference book; ~**s de contabilidad** accounting books; ~ **de escolaridad** school record; ~ **ilustrado** picture book; **los Libros Sagrados** the Holy Scriptures; ~ **de texto** textbook ▶**hablar como un** ~ <u>abierto</u> to express oneself clearly; **hablar como un** ~ <u>cerrado</u> not to express oneself clearly; <u>colgar</u> **los** ~**s** to abandon one's studies

licencia [li·'sen·sja, -'θen·θja] *f* 1. (*permiso*) license; (*para un libro*) authorization; ~ **de conducir** *Méx, Cuba* driver's license; ~ **de obras** building permit 2. (*soldado*) **estar tres días de** ~ to be on leave for three days

licenciado, -a [li·sen·'sja·do, -a; li·θen·'θja-] *m, f* 1. (*estudiante*) graduate; ~ **en economía** Economics graduate 2. (*soldado*) discharged soldier

licenciar [li·sen·'sjar, -'θjar] I. *vt* (*despedir*) to dismiss; (*soldado*) to discharge II. *vr:* ~ **se** to graduate; **se licenció en psicología** he got a degree in psychology

licenciatura [li·sen·sja·'tu·ra, li·θen·θja-] *f* (*título*) degree; (*carrera*) university studies *pl*

licencioso, -a [li·sen·'sjo·so, -a , -θen·'θjo·so, -a] *adj* (*persona*) licentious

liceo [li·'θeo] *m* *AmL* (*colegio*) secondary school

licitación [li·si·ta·'sjon, li·θi·ta·'θjon] *f* 1. (*concurso*) tender; **sacaron el proyecto a** ~ the project was put out to tender 2. (*subasta*) bidding

licitador(a) [li·si·ta·'dor, -·'do·ra; li·θi·-] *m(f)* bidder

licitar [li·si·'tar, li·θi-] *vt* to bid

lícito, -a ['li·si·to, -a; -θi·to, -a] *adj* allowed; (*justo*) fair

licor [li·'kor] *m* liquor; (*de frutas*) liqueur

licuadora [li·kwa·'do·ra] *f* (*batidora*) blender; (*para fruta*) liquidizer

licuar <*1. pres:* licúo> [li·'kwar] *vt* 1. FÍS to liquate 2. (*fruta*) to liquefy

líder ['li·der] *mf* leader; **la empresa** ~ the leading company

liderar [li·de·'rar] *vt* to lead; (*dirigir*) to head; **el equipo que lidera la clasificación** the team at the top of the table

liderato [li·de·'ra·to] *m*, **liderazgo** [li·de·'ras·yo, -'raθ·yo] *m* leadership; **capacidad de** ~ leadership capability

lidia ['li·dja] *f* fight; TAUR bullfight

lidiar [li·'djar] *vi, vt* to fight; ~ **con los niños** *fig* to contend with the kids

liebre [lje·'βre] *f* hare; ~ **marina** sea hare ▶<u>levantar</u> **la** ~ to let the cat out of the bag; **donde menos se piensa** <u>salta</u> **la** ~ things always happen when you least expect them to

lienzo ['ljen·so, -θo] *m* (*tela*) cloth; (*para cuadros*) canvas; (*óleo*) painting

liga ['li·ya] *f* 1. (*alianza*) *t.* DEP league 2. (*prenda*) suspender, garter

ligamento [li·ɣa·'men·to] *m* ANAT ligament
ligar <g→gu> [li·'ɣar] **I.** *vi inf* (*tontear*) to flirt; ~ **con alguien** (*conocer*) to get off with sb, to pick sb up **II.** *vt* **1.** (*atar*) to tie **2.** (*metal*) to alloy **3.** (*unir*) to join **III.** *vr:* ~**se 1.** (*unirse*) to join **2.** *inf* (*tontear*) to flirt
ligerear [li·xe·re·'ar] *vi Chile* to walk quickly
ligereza [li·xe·'re·sa , -θa] *f* **1.** (*rapidez*) swiftness **2.** (*levedad*) lightness
ligero, -a [li·'xe·ro, -a] *adj* **1.** (*leve, ingrávido*) light; (*ruido*) soft; **ir muy ~ de ropa** to be lightly clad **2.** (*ágil*) nimble ▶ **hacer algo a la ligera** to do sth without thinking; **tomarse algo a la ligera** to not take sth seriously
ligón [li·'ɣon, -ona] *m* womanizer; **ser un ~** to be a Don Juan
ligona [li·'ɣo·na] *f inf* flirt
ligue ['li·ɣe] *m inf* **1.** (*acción*) pick-up; **tener un ~ con alguien** to have an affair with sb **2.** (*persona*) chat-up, pick-up
liguero [li·'ɣe·ro] *m* garter belt
liguero, -a [li·'ɣe·ro, -a] *adj* DEP league; **competición liguera** league competition
lija ['li·xa] *f* sandpaper; ~ **esmeril** emery board
lijadora [li·xa·'do·ra] *f* sander
lijar [li·'xar] *vt* to sand
lijoso, -a [li·'xo·so, -a] *adj Cuba* stuck-up
lila[1] ['li·la] **I.** *adj* lilac **II.** *f* BOT lilac
lila[2] ['li·la] *m* (*color*) lilac
lile ['li·le] *adj Chile* weak
liliputiense [li·li·pu·'tjen·se] *adj, mf* Lilliputian
lima ['li·ma] *f* **1.** (*instrumento*) file; **rebajar con la ~** to file down **2.** BOT (*fruta*) lime; (*árbol*) lime tree ▶ **comer como una ~** *inf* to eat like a horse
limadura [li·ma·'du·ra] *f* **1.** (*pulido*) polishing **2.** *pl* (*partículas*) filings
limar [li·'mar] *vt* to file; *fig* to perfect
limaza [li·'ma·sa, -θa] *f* slug
limbo ['lim·bo] *m* REL limbo; **estar en el ~** (*distraído*) to be distracted; (*atontado*) to be bewildered; (*no enterarse*) to be oblivious
limeño, -a [li·'me·ɲo, -a] **I.** *adj* of/from Lima **II.** *m, f* native/inhabitant of Lima
limitación [li·mi·ta·'sjon, -'θjon] *f* limitation; (*de una norma*) restriction; **sin limitaciones** unlimited; **el plan tiene sus limitaciones** the plan has its shortcomings
limitado, -a [li·mi·'ta·do, -a] *adj* **1.** (*poco*) scant; (*medios*) limited; **un número ~** a limited number **2.** (*tonto*) slow-witted
limitar [li·mi·'tar] **I.** *vi ~* **con algo** to border on sth **II.** *vt* to limit; (*libertad*) to restrict **III.** *vr:* ~**se** to confine oneself
límite ['li·mi·te] *m* limit; **situación ~** extreme situation; **sin ~s** limitless; **fecha ~ de entrega** delivery deadline
limítrofe [li·'mi·tro·fe] *adj* bordering; **países ~s** neighboring countries
limón [li·'mon] *adj, m* lemon
limonada [li·mo·'na·da] *f* lemonade
limonar [li·mo·'nar] *m Guat* lemon tree
limonero [li·mo·'ne·ro] *m* lemon tree

limosna [li·'mos·na] *f* alms *pl;* **pedir ~** to beg
limosnear [li·mos·ne·'ar] *vi* to beg
limosnero, -a [li·mos·'ne·ro, -a] *m, f AmL* (*pedigüeño*) beggar
limoso, -a [li·'mo·so, -a] *adj* muddy
limpiabotas [lim·pja·'βo·tas] *mf inv* bootblack
limpiachimeneas [lim·pja·tʃi·me·'neas] *mf inv* chimney sweep
limpiacristales[1] [lim·pja·kris·'ta·les] *mf inv* (*persona*) window cleaner
limpiacristales[2] [lim·pja·kris·'ta·les] *m inv* (*producto*) window cleaning fluid
limpiador [lim·pja·'dor] *m* cleaner
limpiador(a) [lim·pja·'dor, ··do·ra] *adj* cleaning; **leche ~a** cleansing milk
limpiamuebles [lim·pja·'mwe·βles] *m inv* furniture polish
limpiaparabrisas [lim·pja·pa·ra·'βri·sas] *m inv* windshield wiper
limpiar [lim·'pjar] **I.** *vt* to clean; (*dientes*) to brush; (*chimenea*) to sweep; ~ **el polvo** to dust; ~ **en seco** to dry-clean; ~ **de culpas** to exonerate **II.** *vi* to clean **III.** *vr:* ~**se** to clean; (*nariz*) to wipe; (*dientes*) to brush
limpieza [lim·'pje·sa, -θa] *f* **1.** (*lavar*) washing; (*casa, zapatos*) cleaning; ~ **de cutis** facial; ~ **a fondo** thorough cleaning; **señora de la ~** cleaning lady **2.** (*estado*) cleanness, cleanliness **3.** (*eliminación*) cleansing; POL purge
limpio ['lim·pjo] *adv* (*sin trampas*) fairly; **jugar ~** to play fair ▶ **escribir en ~** to make a clean copy; **¿qué has sacado en ~ de todo este asunto?** what do you make of all this?; **en ~** (*dinero*) net
limpio, -a ['lim·pjo, -a] *adj* clean; (*aire*) pure ▶ **lo dejaron ~** *inf* (*sin dinero*) they cleaned him out; **no sacar nada en ~ de algo** to make neither head nor tail of sth
limpión [lim·'pjon] *m AmL* (*trapo*) dishcloth
limusina [li·mu·'si·na] *f* AUTO limousine
linaje [li·'na·xe] *m* lineage; **de rancio ~** of ancient descent
linaza [li·'na·sa, -θa] *f* flax seed; **aceite de ~** linseed oil
lince ['lin·se, -θe] *m* lynx; **tener ojos de ~** to be sharp-eyed
linchamiento [lin·tʃa·'mjen·to] *m* lynching
linchar [lin·'tʃar] *vt* to lynch
lindar [lin·'dar] *vi ~* **con algo** to border on sth
linde ['lin·de] *m o f*, **lindero** [lin·'de·ro] *m* boundary
lindo, -a ['lin·do, -a] *adj* pretty; (*niño*) lovely, cute; **divertirse a lo ~** to have a great time
línea ['li·nea] *f* **1.** *t.* MAT, MIL, ECON (*raya*) line; ~ **de meta** DEP (*fútbol*) goal line; (*atletismo*) finishing line; ~ **recta** straight line; **fracasar en toda la ~** to fail completely **2.** (*renglón*) line; ~ **en blanco** blank line; **leer entre ~s** to read between the lines **3.** (*de transporte*) line; (*trayecto*) route; ~ **aérea** airline; ~ **férrea** railroad line; **coche de ~** long-distance bus **4.** TEL telephone line; ~ **para el fax** fax line; ~ **roja** hotline; **no hay ~** the line is dead [*o* down]

L

5. (*pariente*) line; **por ~ materna** on his mother's side **6.** (*tipo*) figure; **guardar la ~** to watch one's figure **7.** (*fábrica*) **~ de montaje** assembly line

lineal [li·ne·'al] *adj t.* MAT, ARTE linear

linfa ['lin·fa] *f* BIO lymph

linfático, -a [lin·'fa·ti·ko, -a] *adj* lymphatic; **ganglio ~** lymph node

lingotazo [lin·go·'ta·so, -'ta·θo] *m inf* swig; **pegarse un ~** to take a swig

lingote [lin·'go·te] *m* ingot; (*de acero*) pig

lingüista [lin·'gwis·ta] *mf* linguist

lingüística [lin·'gwis·ti·ka] *f* linguistics

lingüístico, -a [lin·'gwis·ti·ko, -a] *adj* linguistic

linimento [li·ni·'men·to] *m* liniment

lino ['li·no] *m* **1.** BOT flax **2.** (*tela*) linen

linóleo [li·'no·leo] *m* linoleum

linterna [lin·'ter·na] *f* torch, flashlight; **~ mágica** magic lantern

lío ['li·o] *m* **1.** (*embrollo*) mess; **¡déjame de ~s!** don't come to me with your problems!; **hacerse un ~ con algo** to get into a jam with sth **2.** *inf* (*relación*) affair; **sé que tienes un ~ por ahí** I know you're having an affair

liofilizar <z→c> [ljo·fi·li·'sar, -'θar] *vt* to freeze-dry, to lyophilize

lioso, -a [li·'o·so, -a] *adj* (*difícil*) complicated; **persona liosa** troublemaker

lipidia [li·'pi·dja] *f* **1.** *AmC* (*pobreza*) poverty; (*miseria*) misery **2.** *Cuba, Méx* (*impertinencia*) impertinence

lipidiar [li·pi·'djar] *vt Cuba, Méx, PRico* to annoy

lipotimia [li·po·'ti·mja] *f* blackout

liquelique [li·ke·'li·ke] *m Col, Ven* white linen jacket

liquen ['li·ken] *m* lichen

liquidación [li·ki·da·'sjon, -'θjon] *f* **1.** (*de una mercancía*) sale; **~ por fin de temporada** (*invierno*) end of season sale; (*verano*) summer sale; **~ total** clearance sale **2.** (*de una empresa*) liquidation **3.** (*de una factura*) payment; (*cuenta*) settlement

liquidar [li·ki·'dar] *vt* **1.** *inf* (*acabar*) to liquidate; (*matar*) to kill; **lo ~on** *inf* they bumped him off **2.** (*mercancía*) to sell; **~ las existencias** to sell off all merchandise **3.** (*cerrar*) to close **4.** (*factura*) to settle

liquidez [li·ki·'des, 'deθ] *f* **1.** (*agua*) fluidity **2.** COM liquidity

líquido ['li·ki·do] *m* **1.** (*agua*) liquid; **~ de frenos** brake fluid **2.** (*saldo*) cash; **~ imponible** taxable income

líquido, -a ['li·ki·do, -a] *adj* **1.** (*material*) liquid **2.** (*dinero*) cash; **renta líquida** disposable income

lira ['li·ra] *f* **1.** (*moneda*) lira **2.** (*instrumento*) lyre

lírica ['li·ri·ka] *f* poetry

lírico, -a ['li·ri·ko, -a] **I.** *adj* **1.** LIT lyric(al) **2.** MÚS lyrical **II.** *m, f* utopian; *AmL* lyric poet

lirio ['li·rjo] *m* lily; **~ de los valles** lily of the valley

lirón [li·'ron] *m* dormouse; **dormir como un ~** to sleep like a log

Lisboa [lis·'βoa] *f* Lisbon

lisboeta [lis·βo·'e·ta] **I.** *adj* of/from Lisbon **II.** *mf* native/inhabitant of Lisbon

lisiado, -a [li·'sja·do, -a] *adj* crippled

lisiar [li·'sjar] *vr:* **~se** to become disabled

liso, -a ['li·so, -a] *adj* **1.** (*superficie*) smooth; (*pelo*) straight; **los 100 metros ~s** the 100 meter flat race **2.** (*tela*) plain

lisonja [li·'son·xa] *f* flattery

lisonjear [li·son·xe·'ar] *vt* to flatter

lisonjero, -a [li·son·'xe·ro, -a] **I.** *adj* flattering **II.** *m, f* flatterer

lista ['lis·ta] *f* **1.** (*enumeración*) list; **~ de la compra** shopping list; **~ del censo electoral** electoral roll; **estar en la ~ de espera** to be on the waiting list; **pasar ~** (*leer*) to take roll call; (*controlar siempre*) to check on **2.** (*tira, de madera*) strip; (*estampado*) stripe; **a ~s** striped

listado [lis·'ta·do] *m* list

listado, -a [lis·'ta·do, -a] *adj* striped

listar [lis·'tar] *vt* to list

listillo, -a [lis·'ti·jo, -a; -ʎo, -a] *m, f* smart aleck

listín [lis·'tin] *m* (*de teléfonos*) directory

listo, -a ['lis·to, -a] *adj* **1.** *ser* (*inteligente*) clever; (*sagaz*) shrewd; (*hábil*) skilful; **pasarse de ~** to be too clever by half **2.** *estar* (*preparado*) ready; **~ para enviar** *t.* COMPUT ready to send; **~ para despegar** ready for takeoff; **estás ~ si crees que...** *inf* you have another think coming if you think that...

listón [lis·'ton] *m* lath; **poner el ~ muy alto** *fig* to set very high standards

lisura [li·'su·ra] *f AmL* (*frescura*) impudent remark

litera [li·'te·ra] *f* (*cama*) bunk; FERRO couchette; NÁUT berth

literal [li·te·'ral] *adj* literal

literario, -a [li·te·'ra·rjo, -a] *adj* literary; **lenguaje ~** literary language

literato, -a [li·te·'ra·to, -a] *m, f* man *m* of letters, woman *f* of letters

literatura [li·te·ra·'tu·ra] *f* literature; **~ barata** pulp fiction; **¡eso es sólo hacer ~!** that's only words, but no action!

litigar <g→gu> [li·ti·'yar] *vt t.* JUR to dispute

litigio [li·'ti·xjo] *m* **1.** (*disputa*) dispute; **en ~** in dispute **2.** (*juicio*) lawsuit

litografía [li·to·yra·'fi·a] *f* (*proceso*) lithography; (*grabado*) lithograph

litoral [li·to·'ral] **I.** *adj* coastal **II.** *m* (*costa*) coast; (*playa*) shore

litri ['li·tri] *adj inf* pretentious, hoity-toity

litro ['li·tro] *m* liter; **un ~ de leche** a liter of milk

litrona [li·'tro·na] *f inf* liter bottle of beer

Lituania [li·'twa·nja] *f* Lithuania

lituano, -a [li·'twa·no] *adj, m, f* Lithuanian

liturgia [li·'tur·xja] *f* liturgy

liviano, -a [li·'βja·no, -a] *adj* light; (*error*)

trivial

lívido, -a ['li·βi·do, -a] *adj* **1.** (*amoratado*) livid; **~ de frío** livid with cold **2.** (*pálido*) ashen

llaga ['ja·γa, ʎa-] *f* (*herida*) wound

llagar <g→gu> [ja·'γar, ʎa-] **I.** *vt* to wound **II.** *vr:* **~se** to get hurt; **~se** (**los pies**) to get sores (on your feet)

llama ['ja·ma, ʎa-] *f* **1.** (*fuego*) flame; *fig* burning passion **2.** zool llama

llamada [ja·'ma·da , ʎa-] *f* **1.** (*voz*) call; **~ al orden** call to order; **~ del programa** comput program call **2.** (*de teléfono*) phone call; **~ urbana** local call; **~ a cobro revertido** reverse charge call **3.** (*a la puerta golpeando*) knock; (*con el timbre*) ring

llamado, -a [ja·'ma·do, ʎa-] *adj* (*conocido como*) called; (*supuesto*) so-called

llamado [ja·'ma·do, -a; ʎa-] *m AmS v.* **llamamiento**

llamador [ja·ma·'dor, ʎa-] *m* doorknocker

llamamiento [ja·ma·'mjen·to, ʎa-] *m* **1.** (*exhortación*) appeal; (*soldado*) call-up; **hacer un ~ a todos** to issue an appeal to all **2.** mil **~ a filas** call to arms **3.** jur (*citación*) summons, subpoena

llamar [ja·'mar, ʎa-] **I.** *vt* **1.** (*voz, teléfono*) to call; **~ a filas** mil to draft; **te llaman al teléfono** you're wanted on the phone; **~ a capítulo a alguien** to tell sb off **2.** (*denominar*) to call; **lo llamé idiota** I called him an idiot **3.** (*despertar*) to wake up; **~ la atención** (*reprender*) to reprimand; (*ser llamativo*) to attract attention; **~ la atención sobre algo** to draw attention to sth **II.** *vi* (*a la puerta golpeando*) to knock; (*con el timbre*) to ring; **¿quién llama?** who is it? **III.** *vr:* **~se** to be called; **¿cómo te llamas?** what's your name?

llamarada [ja·ma·'ra·da, ʎa-] *f* blaze

llamarón [ja·ma·'ron, ʎa-] *m Chile, Col, Ecua* sudden blaze

llamativo, -a [ja·ma·'ti·βo, -a; ʎa-] *adj* (*traje*) flashy; (*color*) loud

llamear [ja·me·'ar, ʎa-] *vi* to blaze

llana ['ja·na, 'ʎa-] *f* trowel

llanca ['jan·ka, 'ʎa-] *f Chile: bluish-green copper ore*

llanito, -a [ja·'ni·to, -a; ʎa-] *m, f inf* Gibraltarian

llano ['ja·no, 'ʎa-] *m* plain

llano, -a ['ja·no, -a; 'ʎa-] *adj* **1.** (*liso*) flat; (*terreno*) level **2.** ling paroxytone **3.** (*sencillo*) **el pueblo ~** the common people

llanta ['janta, 'ʎan-] *f* **1.** *AmL* (*rueda*) tire **2.** (*cerco*) (metal) rim; **~ de aleación** alloy wheel

llantería [jan·te·'ri·a, ʎan-] *f AmL* wailing

llanto ['jan·to, 'ʎan-] *m* crying

llanura [ja·'nu·ra, ʎa-] *f* plain

llapa ['ja·pa, 'ʎa-] *f AmS* extra

llave ['ja·βe, 'ʎa-] *f* **1.** *t. fig* (*instrumento*) key; **~ de contacto** auto ignition key; **ama de ~s** housekeeper; **~ en mano** (*coche*) on the road; **~s en mano** (*casa*) available for immediate

occupancy; **echar la ~** to lock; **estar bajo ~** to be under lock and key; **la ~ no entra** the key doesn't fit; **la ~ para descubrir el secreto** the key to the secret; **meter/sacar la ~** to put in/pull out the key **2.** (*grifo*) faucet **3.** (*tuerca*) wrench; **~ inglesa** monkey wrench **4.** (*interruptor*) switch

llavero [ja·'βe·ro, ʎa-] *m* key ring

llegada [je·'γa·da, ʎe-] *f* arrival; (*meta*) finishing line

llegar <g→gu> [je·'γar, ʎe-] **I.** *vi* **1.** (*al destino, el correo*) to arrive; (*avión*) to land; (*barco*) to dock; **~ a la meta** dep to reach the finishing line; **estar al ~** to be about to arrive; **~ a Madrid/al hotel** to arrive in Madrid/at the hotel; **~ tarde** to be late; **¡todo llegará!** all in good time!; **¡hasta ahí podíamos ~!** that's the limit! **2.** (*recibir*) **no me ha llegado el dinero** I haven't received the money **3.** (*durar*) to live; **~ a viejo** to live to old age; **~ a los ochenta** to reach the age of eighty; **el enfermo no ~á a la primavera** the patient won't make it to spring; **este gobierno no ~á a 2 años** this government won't last two years **4.** (*ascender*) to amount to; **no llega a 20 dólares** it's less than 20 dollars **5.** (*lograr*) **ese ~á lejos** that fellow will go far; **~ a ser muy rico** to become very rich; **llegamos a recoger 8.000 firmas** we managed to get 8,000 signatures; **~ a ministro** to succeeding in becoming a minister; **nunca ~é a entenderte** I'll never understand you **6.** (*ser suficiente*) to be enough **7.** (*tocar*) **~ a** [*o* **hasta**] **algo** to reach sth; **no me llegas ni a la suela de los zapatos** you can't hold a candle to me **II.** *vr:* **~se** (*ir*) to go; **~se por casa de alguien** to stop by sb's house

llenador(a) [je·na·'dor, -·'do·ra, ʎe-] *adj Csur* filling; **esta tarta es muy llenadora** this pie is very filling

llenar [je·'nar, ʎe-] **I.** *vt* **1.** (*atestar*) to fill; **~ de algo** to fill with sth; **~ el suelo de papeles** to scatter papers all over the floor; **~se los bolsillos de caramelos** to fill one's pockets with candy **2.** (*cumplimentar*) to fill in [*o* out] **3.** (*colmar*) **~ de algo** to overwhelm with sth; **nos llenó de regalos** we were showered with gifts **4.** (*satisfacer*) to satisfy **5.** (*agradecer*) to be grateful for **II.** *vi* (*comida*) to be filling; **la pasta llena mucho** pasta is very filling **III.** *vr:* **~se de algo** *inf* **1.** (*comida*) to stuff oneself with sth **2.** (*irritarse*) to be fed up with sth

lleno ['je·no, 'ʎe-] *m* (*teatro, auditorio*) full house

lleno, -a ['je·no, -a; 'ʎe-] *adj* full; **luna llena** full moon; **~ de** full of, filled with; **el autobús iba ~** the bus was full; **estoy ~** *inf* I'm full; **el escritorio estaba ~ de papeles** the desk was covered with papers

llevadero, -a [je·βa·'de·ro, -a; ʎe-] *adj* bearable

llevar [je·'βar, ʎe-] **I.** *vt* **1.** (*a un destino, acompañar*) to take; (*transportar*) to transport; (*en* *brazos*) to carry; (*viento*) to blow; (*comida*) to take out; ~ **a alguien en el coche** to give sb a lift; ~ **algo a alguien** to take sth to sb; **dos pizzas para ~, por favor** two pizzas to go, please **2.** (*exigir, cobrar*) to charge; (*costar*) to cost; **este trabajo lleva mucho tiempo** this work takes a lot of time **3.** (*tener*) ~ **consigo** to be carrying, to have **4.** (*conducir*) to lead; ~ **de la mano** to lead by the hand; ~ **consigo** [*o* **aparejado**] to include; **esto no lleva a ninguna parte** this isn't getting us anywhere **5.** (*ropa*) to wear **6.** (*coche*) to drive **7.** (*finca*) to run **8.** (*estar*) to have been; **llevo cuatro días aquí** I've been here for four days **9.** (*gestionar*) to manage; ~ **las cuentas** to manage the accounts; **el abogado que lleva el caso** the lawyer handling the case **10.** (*inducir*) ~ **a algo** to lead to sth, to induce sth; **me llevó a pensar que...** it led me to think that... **11.** (*exceder*) to exceed; **te llevo dos años** I'm two years older than you **12.** (*tener como ingrediente*) **esta receta lleva 12 huevos** this recipe calls for 12 eggs; **¿lleva picante?** does it have hot pepper? ▶ **dejarse** ~ **por algo** to be carried away with sth; **dejarse** ~ **por alguien** to let sb influence you; ~ **las de perder** to look like losing; **¿qué tal lo llevas?** how are you holding up? **II.** *vr:* ~ **se 1.** (*coger*) to take; ~ **se algo por delante** to crush sth; ~ **se dos años** to be two years older **2.** (*ganar*) to win; ~ **se la mayor/peor parte** to get the best/worst of it **3.** (*estar de moda*) to be in fashion; **ya no se llevan estos zapatos** those shoes are no longer in fashion **4.** (*soportarse*) to get along; ~ **se bien** my boss and I get along well; ~ **se a matar** to hate each other ▶ **...y me llevo cuatro** MAT ... and carry four

lliclla ['jik·ja, 'ʎik·ʎa] *f Bol, Ecua, Perú* blanket (*carried on the back by Indian women*)

llicta ['jik·ta, 'ʎik-] *f Bol* potato meal cake (*type of hard cake eaten while chewing coca to give flavor to the coca ball*)

llorar [jo·'rar, ʎo-] **I.** *vi* to cry, to weep; **me lloran los ojos** my eyes are watering; ~ **de alegría** to cry for joy; **de** ~ enough to make one cry; **lloramos de risa** we laughed until we cried ▶ **quien no llora no mama** *inf* the squeaky wheel gets the oil *prov* **II.** *vt* **1.** (*lágrimas*) ~ **por algo/alguien** to cry over sth/sb; *fig* to mourn sth/sb; ~ **la muerte de alguien** to mourn sb's death **2.** (*quejarse*) to whine; (*lamentar*) to bemoan

llorica [jo·'ri·ka, ʎo-] *mf inf* crybaby, whiner

lloriquear [jo·ri·ke·'ar, ʎo-] *vi* to whimper, to snivel

lloriqueo [jo·ri·'keo, ʎo-] *m* whimpering

lloro(s) ['jo·ro(s), ʎo-] *m(pl)* crying; **con estos** ~ **s no conseguirás nada** this crying won't get you anywhere

llorón, -ona [jo·'ron, -o·na; ʎo-] **I.** *adj* always crying; **sauce** ~ weeping willow **II.** *m, f* crybaby, whiner

lloroso, -a [jo·'ro·so, -a; ʎo-] *adj* tearful

llovedizo, -a [jo·βe·'di·so, -a; ʎo·βe·'di·θo, -a] *adj* (*techo*) leaky; **agua llovediza** rainwater

llover <o→ue> [jo·'βer, ʎo-] *vi, vt, vimpers* to rain; **está lloviendo** it's raining; **llueve a mares** [*o* **a cántaros**] it's pouring; **siempre llueve sobre mojado** it never rains but it pours; **como llovido del cielo** heaven sent; **llueven las malas noticias** it's one piece of bad news after another; **me escucha como quien oye** ~ *inf* it's water off a duck's back to him/her, in one ear and out the other; **ya ha llovido mucho desde entonces** *fig* a lot has happened since then

llovida [jo·'βi·da, ʎo-] *f AmL* rain; **¡qué ~!** what a downpour!

llovizna [jo·'βis·na, ʎo·'βiθ·na] *f* drizzle

lloviznar [jo·βis·'nar, ʎo·βiθ·'nar] *vimpers* **está lloviznando** it's drizzling

lluqui ['ju·ki, 'ʎu-] *adj Ecua* (*zurdo*) left-handed

lluvia ['ju·βja, 'ʎu-] *f* **1.** (*chubasco*) rain; ~ **de estrellas** meteor shower; **época de las ~s** rainy season; ~ **ácida** acid rain; ~ **radiactiva** fallout; **hubo una ~ de protestas** there was a shower of protests **2.** *AmL* (*ducha*) shower

lluvioso, -a [ju·'βjo·so, -a; ʎu-] *adj* rainy; **tiempo** ~ rainy weather

lo [lo] **I.** *art def v.* **el, la, lo II.** *pron pers m y neutro sing* **1.** (*objeto: masculino*) him; (*neutro*) it; **¡lláma~!** call him!; **¡haz~!** do it! **2.** (*con relativo*) ~ **que...** what; ~ **cual** which; ~ **que quiero decir es que...** what I mean is that...

loa ['loa] *f* praise

loable [lo·'a·βle] *adj* commendable

loar [lo·'ar] *vt* to praise

lobezno [lo·'βes·no, -'βeθ·no] *m* wolf cub

lobisón [lo·βi·'son] *m Arg, Par, Urug* werewolf

lobo, -a ['lo·βo] *m, f* wolf; ~ **cerval** lynx; ~ **de mar** old salt; ~ **marino** seal; **meterse en la boca del** ~ to go into the lion's den; **ser un** ~ **con piel de oveja** to be a wolf in sheep's clothing; **tener un hambre de ~s** to be as hungry as a wolf

lóbrego, -a ['lo·βre·ɣo, -a] *adj* gloomy

lóbulo ['lo·βu·lo] *m ANAT* lobe; ~ **de la oreja** earlobe

local [lo·'kal] **I.** *adj* local; **periódico** ~ local newspaper **II.** *m* locale; COM premises *pl*; ~ **público** public building

localidad [lo·ka·li·'dad] *f* **1.** (*municipio*) town **2.** (*entrada*) ticket; (*asiento*) seat

localismo [lo·ka·'lis·mo] *m pey* (*chovinismo*) provincialism, parochialism

localista [lo·ka·'lis·ta] *adj pey* parochial, of local interest; **escritor** ~ parochial writer

localización [lo·ka·li·sa·'sjon, -θa·'θjon] *f* **1.** (*búsqueda*) finding; AVIAT tracking; ~ **de software** COMPUT software localization **2.** (*posición*) location

localizar <z→c> [lo·ka·li·'sar, -'θar] *vt* **1.** (*encontrar*) to find; ~ **por teléfono** to get in touch by phone **2.** (*limitar*) to localize; (*fuego, epidemia*) to confine

locería [lo·se·'ri·a, lo0e-] *f AmL* crockery

loche ['lo·tʃe] *m Col* ZOOL loach

loción [lo·'sjon, -'0jon] *f* lotion; ~ **capilar** hair lotion; ~ **bronceadora** suntan lotion; ~ **hidratante** moisturizing cream

loco, -a ['lo·ko, -a] **I.** *adj* mad, crazy; **a lo ~, a tontas y a locas** any old way; **estar ~ de atar** to be raving [*o* stark staring] mad; **estar ~ por la música** to be crazy about music; **estar ~ de contento** to be elated; **estar medio ~** to be not all there; **tener una suerte loca** to be incredibly lucky **II.** *m, f* madman *m*, madwoman *f*; **casa de ~s** *t. fig* madhouse; **cada ~ con su tema** to each his own; **hacerse el ~** to act dumb; **hacer el ~** to act the fool

locomoción [lo·ko·mo·'sjon, -'0jon] *f* locomotion

locomotor(a) [lo·ko·mo·'tor, --to·ra] *adj* locomotive

locomotora [lo·ko·mo·'to·ra] *f* locomotive

locro ['lo·kro] *m AmS: meat and vegetable stew*

locuacidad [lo·kwa·si·'dad, lo·kwa·0i-] *f* talkativeness

locuaz [lo·'kwas, -'kwa0] *adj* loquacious; (*charlatán*) talkative

locución [lo·ku·'sjon, -'0jon] *f* (*expresión*) phrase

locura [lo·'ku·ra] *f* **1.** (*enajenación mental*) madness; **querer con ~** to be madly in love with; **una casa de ~** a dream house **2.** (*disparate*) crazy thing; **andar haciendo ~s** to be doing foolish things

locutor(a) [lo·ku·'tor, --to·ra] *m(f)* speaker

locutorio [lo·ku·'to·rjo] *m* TEL telephone booth

lodazal [lo·da·'sal, -'0al] *m* quagmire

lodo ['lo·do] *m* mud

lógica ['lo·xi·ka] *f* logic

lógico, -a ['lo·xi·ko, -a] *adj* logical; (*normal*) natural

logística [lo·'xis·ti·ka] *f* logistics *pl*

logístico, -a [lo·'xis·ti·ko, -a] *adj* logistic

logopeda [lo·yo·'pe·da] *mf* speech therapist

logopedia [lo·yo·'pe·dja] *f* speech therapy

logotipo [lo·yo·'ti·po] *m* logotype; (*de una empresa, un producto*) logo

lograr [lo·'yra·do, -a] *adj* successful, well done

lograr [lo·'yrar] **I.** *vt* to achieve; **logré convencerla** I managed to convince her **II.** *vr:* ~**se** to be successful

logro ['lo·yro] *m* achievement

loma ['lo·ma] *f* hill

lomada [lo·'ma·da] *f AmS* hill

lombriz [lom·'bris, -'bri0] *f* worm; ~ **intestinal** tapeworm; ~ **de tierra** earthworm

lomo ['lo·mo] *m* back; (*de libro*) spine; (*solomillo*) loin; **agachar el ~** *inf* to work very hard; **sobar el ~ a alguien** *inf* to butter sb up

lona ['lo·na] *f* canvas

loncha ['lon·tʃa] *f* slice; (*beicon*) rasher

lonchería [lon·tʃe·'ri·a] *f AmC, Méx* lunch counter

londinense [lon·di·'nen·se] **I.** *adj* London **II.** *mf* Londoner

Londres ['lon·dres] *m* London

longaniza [lon·ga·'ni·sa, -'ni·0a] *f spicy pork sausage;* **hay más días que ~s** there's all the time in the world

longevidad [lon·xe·βi·'dad] *f* longevity

longevo, -a [lon·'xe·βo, -a] *adj* (*que dura*) long-lived; (*viejo*) very old

longitud [lon·xi·'tud] *f* length; **salto de ~** DEP long jump; **cuatro metros de ~** four meters long; **cincuenta grados ~ este/oeste** fifty degrees longitude east/west; **estar en la misma ~ de onda** *fig* to be on the same wavelength

longitudinal [lon·xi·tu·di·'nal] *adj* **corte ~** longitudinal section

longui(s) ['lon·gi(s)] *mf inv* **hacerse el ~** *inf* to play dumb

lonja ['lon·xa] *f* COM public exchange

lonjear [lon·xe·'ar] *vt* **1.** *Arg* (*cortar*) to slice **2.** *Arg, inf* (*azotar*) to give (sb) a good beating

loquera [lo·'ke·ra] *f AmL* madness

lora ['lo·ra] *f Col* (*loro*) parrot

Lorena [lo·'re·na] *f* Lorraine

loro ['lo·ro] *m* **1.** ZOOL parrot; **repetir como un ~** to repeat parrot fashion; **hablar como un ~** to talk non-stop **2.** *pey, inf* (*mujer*) old hag

los [los] **I.** *art def v.* **el, la, lo II.** *pron pers m y neutro pl* **1.** (*objeto directo*) them; **¡lláma~!** call them! **2.** (*con relativo*) ~ **que...** the ones that...; ~ **cuales** which

losa ['lo·sa] *f* **1.** (*piedra*) slab; (*lápida*) gravestone **2.** (*baldosa*) tile

lote ['lo·te] *m* **1.** (*parte*) share; COM lot **2.** (*toqueteo*) **darse** [*o* **pegarse**] **el ~** to get off with

lotería [lo·te·'ri·a] *f* lottery; ~ **primitiva** weekly lottery; **administración de ~** office selling lottery tickets; **me tocó la ~** I won the lottery; **un décimo de la ~** a tenth share of a lottery number; **¡con ese hijo te tocó la ~!** you really struck gold with that son of yours!; **jugar a la ~** to play the lottery

loto¹ ['lo·to] *m* (*planta*) lotus; (*flor*) lotus flower

loto² ['lo·to] *f inf* lottery

loza ['lo·sa, 'lo·0a] *f* earthenware; (*vajilla*) crockery; ~ **fina** china

lozano, -a [lo·'sa·no, -a; lo·'0a-] *adj* (*persona: robusta*) vigorous; (*saludable*) healthy

lubina [lu·'βi·na] *f* sea bass

lubricante [lu·βri·'kan·te] *m* lubricant

lubricar <c→qu> [lu·βri·'kar] *vt* to lubricate

lubrificante [lu·βri·fi·'kan·te] *m* lubricant

lubrificar <c→qu> [lu·βri·fi·'kar] *vt* to lubricate

Lucayas [lu·'ka·jas] *fpl* **islas ~** the Bahamas

lucero [lu·'se·ro, -'0e·ro] *m* (*estrella*) bright star

lucha ['lu·tʃa] *f* fight; DEP wrestling; ~ **cuerpo a cuerpo** hand-to-hand fighting [*o* combat]; ~ **contra la droga** the fight against drugs

L

luchador(a) [lu·ˈtʃa·ˈdor, -·ˈdo·ra] *m(f)* fighter; DEP wrestler

luchar [lu·ˈtʃar] *vi* ~ **por algo** to fight for sth, to struggle for sth

luche [ˈlu·tʃe] *m Chile* 1.(*juego*) hopscotch 2.BOT, CULIN sea lettuce

lucidez [lu·si·ˈdes, lu·θi·ˈdeθ] *f* 1.(*estado*) lucidity; **antes de morir tuvo todavía un momento de** ~ before dying he/she had one last moment of lucidness 2.(*clarividencia*) clarity; (*sagacidad*) clear-headedness

lucido, -a [lu·ˈsi·do, -a; lu·ˈθi-] *adj* (*brillante*) outstanding

lúcido, -a [ˈlu·si·do, -a; ˈlu·θi-] *adj* 1.(*clarividente*) clear-sighted; (*sagaz*) astute 2.(*sobrio*) clear-headed

luciérnaga [lu·ˈsjer·na·ɣa, lu·ˈθjer-] *f* firefly

lucio [ˈlu·sjo, -θjo] *m* pike

lucir [lu·ˈsir, -ˈθir] *irr* **I.** *vi* 1.(*brillar*) to shine 2.(*compensar*) to compensate; (*verse*) to look good; **el vestido no le luce** the dress doesn't look good on her; **es un trabajo pesado y que no luce** it's hard work, though it doesn't look it; **este jersey hecho a mano no luce** this handmade sweater doesn't look much; **no te luce el dinero que tienes** no one would ever know you are wealthy **II.** *vt* (*exhibir*) to display; **lucía un bronceado impecable** he/she was showing off his/her perfect tan **III.** *vr:* ~**se** 1.(*exhibirse*) to display 2.(*destacarse*) to stand out; **¡ahora sí que nos hemos lucido!** *irón* now we've really made a mess of it!

lucrativo, -a [lu·kra·ˈti·βo, -a] *adj* lucrative; **no** ~ not profitable; **sin fines** ~**s** non-profit making

lucro [ˈlu·kro] *m* profit; **con ánimo de** ~ for profit; **organización sin ánimo de** ~ non-profit organization

lúdico, -a [ˈlu·di·ko, -a] *adj* ludic; **el aspecto** ~ **de la vida** the fun side of life

luego [ˈlwe·ɣo] **I.** *adv* 1.(*después*) later; **¡hasta** ~! see you later! 2.(*entonces*) then 3.(*por supuesto*) **desde** ~ of course **II.** *conj* 1.(*así que*) and so 2.(*después de*) ~ **que** as soon as

lugar [lu·ˈɣar] *m* place; **en primer/segundo** ~ first/second; **tener** ~ to take place; **en algún** ~ **de la casa** somewhere in the house; **la observación está fuera de** ~ that comment is out of place; **en** ~ **de** instead of; **yo en** ~ **de usted...** if I were you...; **no des** ~ **a que te reprendan** don't give them any cause for reproach; **dar** ~ **a un escándalo** to give rise to a scandal

lugareño, -a [lu·ɣa·ˈre·ɲo, -a] *adj, m, f* local

lugarteniente [lu·ɣar·te·ˈnjen·te] *m* deputy

lúgubre [ˈlu·ɣu·βre] *adj* gloomy

lujo [ˈlu·xo] *m* luxury; **permitirse el** ~ **de...** to treat oneself to the luxury of...; **un** ~ **asiático** the ultimate in luxury; **con gran** ~ **de detalles** with a wealth of detail; **darse el** ~ **de** to give oneself the pleasure of

lujoso, -a [lu·ˈxo·so, -a] *adj* luxurious

lujuria [lu·ˈxu·rja] *f* lechery, lust

lujurioso, -a [lu·xu·ˈrjo·so, -a] *adj* lecherous

lulo [ˈlu·lo] *m Chile* small cylindrical bundle

lumbago [lum·ˈba·ɣo] *m* MED lumbago

lumbar [lum·ˈbar] *adj* lumbar

lumbre [ˈlum·bre] *f* (*llamas*) fire; (*brasa*) glow

lumbrera [lum·ˈbre·ra] *f* 1.(*claraboya*) skylight 2.(*talento*) leading light

luminosidad [lu·mi·no·si·ˈdad] *f* luminosity; (*astro, día*) brightness

luminoso, -a [lu·mi·ˈno·so, -a] *adj* (*brillante*) bright, luminous; (*día*) light; **anuncio** ~ illuminated [*o* neon] sign

lun. *abr de* **lunes** Mon.

luna [ˈlu·na] *f* 1.ASTR moon; (*luz*) moonlight; ~ **creciente/menguante** waxing/waning moon; ~ **llena/nueva** full/new moon; ~ **de miel** honeymoon; **media** ~ half moon; **a la luz de la** ~ in the moonlight; **estar en la** ~ to be daydreaming 2.(*cristal*) plate glass; (*espejo*) mirror; ~**s del coche** car windows ▶ **quedarse a la** ~ **de** **Valencia** to be disappointed

lunar [lu·ˈnar] **I.** *adj* lunar **II.** *m* (*en la piel*) mole; (*en una tela*) polka-dot

lunarejo, -a [lu·na·ˈre·xo, -a] *adj AmL* (*persona*) with moles on the face; (*animal*) spotted

lunático, -a [lu·ˈna·ti·ko, -a] *adj* lunatic

lunes [ˈlu·nes] *m inv* Monday; ~ **de carnaval** the last Monday before Lent; ~ **de Pascua** Easter Monday; **el** ~ on Monday; **el** ~ **pasado** last Monday; **el** ~ **que viene** next Monday; **el** ~ **por la noche/al mediodía/por la mañana/por la tarde** Monday night/at midday/morning/afternoon; (*todos*) **los** ~ every Monday, on Mondays; **en la noche del** ~ **al martes** in the small hours of Monday; **el** ~ **entero** all day Monday; **cada dos** ~ (**del mes**) every other Monday; **hoy es** ~, once de marzo today is Monday, March 11th

luneta [lu·ˈne·ta] *f* (*adorno*) crescent-shaped ornament

lunfardismo [lun·far·ˈdis·mo] *m Arg* slang word

lupa [ˈlu·pa] *f* magnifying glass; **mirar con** ~ *fig* to examine meticulously

lupanar [lu·pa·ˈnar] *m* brothel

lúpulo [ˈlu·pu·lo] *m* hop plant; (*cerveza*) hops

lustrabotas [lus·tra·ˈβo·tas] *mf inv, AmL* shoeshine

lustrador [lus·tra·ˈdor] *m Arg, Nic* shoeshine boy

lustrar [lus·ˈtrar] *vt* to polish; (*zapatos*) to shine

lustre [ˈlus·tre] *m* 1.(*brillo*) luster; **sacar** ~ **a los zapatos/a los muebles** to polish one's shoes/the furniture; **tener** ~ *fig* to be famous or noble 2.*AmL* (*betún*) shoe polish

lustrín [lus·ˈtrin] *m Chile* shoeshine stall

lustrina [lus·ˈtri·na] *f Chile* (*betún*) shoe polish

lustro [ˈlus·tro] *m* lustrum; **en el último** ~ *elev* in the last five years

lustroso, -a [lus·ˈtro·so, -a] *adj* shiny; **estar** ~

fig to be radiant

luto ['lu·to] *m* mourning; (*vestido*) mourning clothes; **ir de ~** to wear mourning; **estar de ~ por alguien** to be in mourning for sb

luxación [luk·sa·'sjon, -'θjon] *f* MED dislocation

Luxemburgo [luk·sem·'bur·γo] *m* Luxembourg

luxemburgués, -esa [luk·sem·bur·'γes, --'γe·sa] *adj* Luxembourgish, Luxembourgian

luz [lus, luθ] *f* 1. (*resplandor*) light; **~ corta** dipped headlights; **~ larga** full beam; **~ natural** natural light; **~ trasera** tail light; **traje de luces** bullfighter's suit; **a la ~ del día** in daylight; **a media ~** in subdued light; **dar a ~** to give birth; **¡~ de mis ojos!** the apple of my eye!; **sacar a la ~** *fig* to bring to light; **salir a la ~** *fig* to come to light; **a la ~ de los nuevos datos...** in the light of the new data... 2. (*energía*) electricity; **¡da la ~!** turn on the light!; **se fue la ~** the power went off; **apagar/encender la ~** to turn off/on the light 3. *pl* (*inteligencia*) intelligence; **el Siglo de las Luces** the Age of Enlightenment; **ser de pocas luces** to be dim-witted; **tener pocas luces** to be stupid; **a todas luces** evidently

lycra® ['li·kra] *f* Lycra®

M

M, m ['eme] *f* M, m; **~ de María** M as in Mike

Mª [ma·'ri·a] *abr de* **María** *abbreviation for the name Mary*

macabí [ma·ka·'βi] *m Cuba* cunning person, shark *fig*

macabro, -a [ma·'ka·βro, -a] *adj* macabre

macaco, -a [ma·'ka·ko, -a] **I.** *adj Cuba, Chile* (*feo*) ugly **II.** *m, f* 1. ZOOL macaque 2. *AmL, pey* Chink

macagua [ma·'ka·γwa] *f* 1. *AmS* (*ave*) laughing falcon 2. *Ven* (*serpiente*) large poisonous snake 3. *Cuba* BOT macaw-tree

macana [ma·'ka·na] *f* 1. (*tontería*) nonsense 2. *AmL* (*porra*) baton

macaneador(a) [ma·ka·nea·'dor, --'do·ra] *m(f) Arg, inf* fibber

macanear [ma·ka·ne·'ar] *vi CSur* (*hacer tonterías*) to act foolishly; (*decir tonterías*) to talk nonsense

macanudo, -a [ma·ka·'nu·do, -a] *adj AmL, inf* fantastic, super

macarra [ma·'ka·rra] *m inf* 1. (*chorizo*) roughneck 2. (*chulo*) pimp

macarrón [ma·ka·'rron] *m* (*pasta*) macaroni

macedonia [ma·se·'do·nja, ma·θe-] *f* **~** (**de frutas**) fruit salad

macerar [ma·se·'rar, ma·θe-] *vt* 1. (*con golpes*) to macerate 2. CULIN to marinate 3. (*mortificar*) to mortify

maceta [ma·'se·ta, -'θe·ta] *f* 1. (*tiesto*) flowerpot 2. *Chile* (*ramo*) bunch of flowers

macetero [ma·se·'te·ro, ma·θe-] *m* flowerpot stand; *AmL* flowerpot

machacar <c→qu> [ma·tʃa·'kar] **I.** *vt* 1. (*triturar*) to pound 2. (*insistir*) to insist on, to harp on 3. *inf* (*estudiar*) to cram 4. *inf* (*destruir*) to crush **II.** *vr:* **~se** *inf* to wear oneself out; **machacársela** *vulg* to jerk [*o* to beat] off

machacón, -ona [ma·tʃa·'kon, --'ko·na] *adj pey* insistent

machamartillo [ma·tʃa·mar·'ti·jo, -ʎo] **a ~** very firmly; **creer algo a ~** to firmly believe sth; **repetir algo a ~** to repeat sth ad nauseam

machete [ma·'tʃe·te] *m* 1. machete 2. *Arg, Urug, Col, inf* (*chuleta*) crib (sheet)

machetear [ma·tʃe·te·'ar] **I.** *vi, vt Arg, Col, inf* (*copiar*) to copy **II.** *vr:* **~se** *Méx* (*trabajar*) to work; *inf* (*empollar*) to cram

machetero, -a [ma·tʃe·'te·ro, -a] *m, f* 1. *Arg, inf* (*copión*) copycat 2. *Méx* (*empollón*) plodder

machismo [ma·'tʃis·mo] *m* male chauvinism; (*virilidad*) manliness, masculinity

machista [ma·'tʃis·ta] *adj* (male) chauvinistic

macho ['ma·tʃo] *m* 1. ZOOL (*masculino*) male; **~ cabrío** male goat, billy goat *inf* 2. *inf* (*machote*) tough guy

machona [ma·'tʃo·na] *f AmL, inf* butch

machote [ma·'tʃo·te] *m* 1. *inf* (*hombre*) (tough) guy 2. *AmL* (*borrador*) (rough) draft; (*modelo*) model

machucar <c→qu> [ma·tʃu·'kar] *vt* (*aplastar*) to crush

macizo [ma·'si·so, -'θi·θo] *m* GEO massif

macizo, -a [ma·'si·so, -a; -'θi·θo, -a] *adj* 1. (*puerta*) solid; **de plata maciza** of solid silver 2. (*persona*) robust; **estar ~** to be robust

macramé [ma·kra·'me] *m* macramé

macroinstrucción [ma·kro·ins·truk·'sjon, -'θjon] *f* COMPUT macro

mácula ['ma·ku·la] *f* spot; *fig* stain; **sin ~** *fig* pure

macuto [ma·'ku·to] *m* 1. (*mochila*) backpack; MIL knapsack 2. *Ven* (*de los mendigos*) begging basket

madama [ma·'da·ma] *f RíoPl* (*de burdel*) madam

madeja [ma·'de·xa] *f* skein, hank; **enredar la ~** *fig* to complicate matters

madera [ma·'de·ra] *f* 1. (*de los árboles*) wood; **~ prensada** particle board, chipboard; (*cortada*) timber, lumber; **de ~** wooden; **¡toca ~!** knock on wood!; **ser de la misma ~** to be just the same; **tener ~ de** to have the makings of; **tener** [*o* ser de] **buena/mala ~** (not) to have what it takes 2. *inf* (*policía*) **la ~** the law

maderaje [ma·de·'ra·xe] *m*, **maderamen** [ma·de·'ra·men] *m* timbers *pl*; **~ de techo** roof timbers

maderería [ma·de·re·'ri·a] *f* lumber yard

madero [ma·'de·ro] *m* (*viga*) beam; (*tablón*) board

madona [ma·'do·na] *f* Madonna
madrastra [ma·'dras·tra] *f* stepmother; *pey* (*mala madre*) bad mother
madraza [ma·'dra·sa, -θa] *f inf* mother hen *fig;* **es una verdadera ~** she is a really devoted mother
madre ['ma·dre] *f* mother; **~ superiora** REL Mother Superior; **~ de alquiler** surrogate mother; **~ de leche** wet nurse; **~ política** mother-in-law; **futura ~** mother-to-be; **¡~ (mía)!** goodness me!; **¡~ de Dios!** Holy Mary!; **como su ~ lo/la parió** *inf* in his/her birthday suit; **¡la ~ que te parió!** *vulg* you bastard!; **¡viva la ~ que te parió!** *inf* well done!; **¡tu ~!** *inf* up yours! *vulg;* **de puta ~** *vulg* fucking great! *vulg;* **sacar a alguien de ~** *inf* to drive sb mad [*o* nuts]; **los alquileres se están saliendo de ~** *inf* rents are becoming ridiculously high
madrear [ma·dre·'ar] *vt* **1.** *Méx* (*romper a golpes*) to bash up **2.** *Méx, vulg* (*pegar fuerte*) to beat up
madrejón [ma·dre·'xon] *m Arg* watercourse
madreperla [ma·dre·'per·la] *f* mother of pearl
madreselva [ma·dre·'sel·βa] *f* honeysuckle
Madrid [ma·'drid] *m* Madrid
madriguera [ma·dri·'ɣe·ra] *f* **1.** (*guarida*) den; (*de conejo*) burrow; (*de ratón*) hole; (*de zorro*) earth; (*de tejón*) set **2.** (*escondrijo*) lair
madrileño, -a [ma·dri·'le·ɲo, -a] *adj* of/from Madrid; **las noches madrileñas** the Madrid nights
madrina [ma·'dri·na] *f* (*de bautismo*) godmother; (*de un artista, una asociación*) patroness; **~ (de boda)** maid of honor
madrugada [ma·dru·'ɣa·da] *f* dawn; **en la** [*o* **de**] **~** in the early morning; **salimos de viaje de ~** we set off in the early hours; **a las cinco de la ~** at five in the morning; **pegarse una ~** to get up very early
madrugador(a) [ma·dru·ɣa·'dor, -'do·ra] *adj* **ser muy ~** to be an early riser [*o* early bird]
madrugar <g→gu> [ma·dru·'ɣar] *vi* to get up early ▶ **a quien madruga, Dios le ayuda** *prov* the early bird catches the worm *prov;* **no por mucho ~ amanece más temprano** *prov* ≈ everything will happen at its appointed time
madrugón [ma·dru·'ɣon] *m* **darse un ~** to get up very early
maduración [ma·du·ra·'sjon, -'θjon] *f* (*de fruta*) ripening
madurar [ma·du·'rar] **I.** *vt* **1.** (*hacer maduro: fruta*) to ripen; (*persona*) to mature **2.** (*reflexionar sobre*) to think over **II.** *vi, vr:* **~se** (*volverse maduro: fruta*) to ripen; (*persona*) to mature
madurez [ma·du·'res, -'reθ] *f* (*de fruta*) ripeness; (*de persona*) maturity; (*de un plan*) readiness; **estar en la ~** to be middle-aged
maduro, -a [ma·'du·ro, -a] *adj* (*fruta*) ripe; (*persona: prudente*) mature; (*plan*) ready; **una manzana demasiado madura** an over-ripe apple; **estar a las duras y a las maduras**

to take the bad with the good
maestría [maes·'tri·a] *f* **1.** (*habilidad*) mastery; **con ~** skillfully **2.** (*título*) Master's degree
maestro, -a [ma·'es·tro, -a] **I.** *adj* **obra maestra** masterpiece **II.** *m, f* **1.** (*profesor*) teacher; **la vida es la mejor maestra** life is the best school **2.** (*persona de gran conocimiento*) master **3.** (*capataz*) overseer; **~ de cocina** master chef; **~ de obras** foreman
mafia ['ma·fja] *f* **la Mafia** the Mafia
mafioso, -a [ma·'fjo·so, -a] *m, f* Mafioso
maganzón, -ona [ma·ɣan·'son, -'so·na; -'θo·na] *m, f Col, CRi* lazybones *inv inf*
magdalena [maɣ·da·'le·na] *f* (*pastel*) sweet muffin ▶ **estar como una Magdalena** to be inconsolable; **llorar como una Magdalena** to cry like a child
magia ['ma·xja] *f* magic; **como por arte de ~** as if by magic
mágico, -a ['ma·xi·ko, -a] *adj* **1.** (*misterioso*) magic; **varita mágica** magic wand **2.** (*maravilloso*) marvelous
magín [ma·'xin] *m inf* creativity
magisterio [ma·xis·'te·rjo] *m* **dedicarse al ~** to be a teacher; **estudiar ~** to study to become a teacher
magistrado, -a [ma·xis·'tra·do, -a] *m, f* JUR (*juez*) magistrate; (*miembro del Tribunal Supremo*) Supreme Court judge
magistral [ma·xis·'tral] *adj* (*con maestría*) masterly
magma ['maɣ·ma] *m* magma
magnánimo, -a [maɣ·'na·ni·mo, -a] *adj* magnanimous
magnate [maɣ·'na·te] *m* tycoon; **~ de las finanzas** finance magnate; **~ de la prensa** press baron
magnesio [maɣ·'ne·sjo] *m* magnesium
magnético, -a [maɣ·'ne·ti·ko, -a] *adj* magnetic
magnetismo [maɣ·ne·'tis·mo] *m* magnetism
magnetizar <z→c> [maɣ·ne·ti·'sar, -'θar] *vt* to magnetize; (*hipnotizar*) to hypnotize; (*retener la atención*) to captivate
magnetofónico, -a [maɣ·ne·to·'fo·ni·ko, -a] *adj* **cinta magnetofónica** (recording) tape
magnetófono [maɣ·ne·'to·fo·no] *m* tape recorder
magnífico, -a [maɣ·'ni·fi·ko, -a] *adj* (*excelente*) magnificent
magnitud [maɣ·ni·'tud] *f* magnitude
magno, -a ['maɣ·no, -a] *adj* great; **Alejandro Magno** Alexander the Great; **aula magna** main hall
magnolia [maɣ·'no·lja] *f* magnolia
magnolio [maɣ·'no·lio] *m* magnolia
mago, -a ['ma·ɣo, -a] *m, f* magician; **los Reyes Magos** the Magi, the Three Wise Men
magra ['ma·ɣra] *f* slice of ham
magrear [ma·ɣre·'ar] *vt vulg* to feel up
magro ['ma·ɣro] *m* (*como el lomo*) tenderloin; *inf* (*carne magra*) lean meat
magro, -a ['ma·ɣro, -a] *adj* lean
magua ['ma·ɣwa] *f Cuba, PRico, Ven* (*contra-*

riedad) setback

maguey [ma·'ɣei] *m AmL* вот maguey

magulladura [ma·ɣu·ja·'du·ra, ma·ɣu·ʎa-] *f* bruising

magullar [ma·ɣu·'jar, -ʎar] *vt* to bruise

mahometano, -a [ma·o·me·'ta·no, -a] *adj, m, f* Muslim, Mohammedan

mahonesa [ma·o'ne·sa] *f* mayonnaise

maicena® [mai·'se·na, -'θe·na] *f* cornstarch

maíz [ma·'is, -'iθ] *m* corn

maizal [mai·'sal, -'θal] *m* cornfield

majada [ma·'xa·da] *f* **1.**(*aprisco*) fold **2.**(*estiércol*) dung

majaderear [ma·xa·de·re·'ar] *vt AmL* to annoy

majadería [ma·xa·de·'ri·a] *f* (*tontería*) idiocy

majadero, -a [ma·xa·'de·ro] *adj* (*porfiado*) pestering; (*imprudente*) foolish; (*loco*) crazy

majagua [ma·'xa·ɣwa] *f Cuba* **1.**(*árbol*) type of linden tree **2.**(*chaqueta*) suit jacket

majamama [ma·xa·'ma·ma] *f Chile* jumble

majar [ma·'xar] *vt* (*en un mortero*) to crush; (*en la era*) to thresh

majara [ma·'xa·ra], **majareta** [ma·xa·'re·ta] *adj inf* crazy, nuts

majarete [ma·xa·'re·te] *m* **1.** *Cuba* (*galanteador*) Don Juan **2.** *PRico* (*confusión*) commotion **3.** *Ant, Ven* (*postre*) blancmange (*made with corn, milk and sugar*)

maje ['ma·xe] *adj Méx, inf* gullible

majestad [ma·xes·'tad] *f* Majesty; **Su Majestad** Your Majesty

majestuosidad [ma·xes·two·si·'dad] *f* majesty

majestuoso, -a [ma·xes·tu·'o·so, -a] *adj* majestic

majo, -a ['ma·xo, -a] *adj* **1.**(*bonito*) lovely; (*guapo*) attractive **2.**(*agradable*) pleasant **3.**(*ataviado*) stylish; **ponte maja para la fiesta** dress up for the party

mal [mal] **I.** *adj v.* **malo II.** *m* **1.**(*daño*) harm; (*injusticia*) wrong; (*sufrimiento*) suffering; **hacer ~ a alguien** to do sb harm **2.**(*lo malo*) bad thing; **el ~ menor** the lesser evil; **decir ~ de alguien** to talk badly of sb; **menos ~** thank goodness **3.**(*inconveniente*) problem; **el ~ está en que...** the problem is that... **4.**(*enfermedad*) illness; **~ de montaña** mountain sickness; **~ de vientre** stomach complaint **5.**(*desgracia*) misfortune ▶ **el ~ de ojo** the evil eye; **bien vengas, ~, si vienes solo** *prov* it never rains but it pours; **no hay ~ que por bien no venga** *prov* every cloud has a silver lining; **el que escucha su ~ oye** *prov* those who listen at doors never hear good of themselves **III.** *adv* **1.**(*de mala manera, insuficientemente*) badly; **dejar ~ a alguien** to show sb in a bad light; **estar ~ de dinero** to be badly off; **esto acabará ~** this will end badly; **ir de ~ en peor** to go from bad to worse; **sentar ~** to upset; **ella me cae ~** I don't like her **2.**(*equivocadamente*) wrongly **3.**(*difícilmente*) **~ podrás ganar con esta moto** you'll be hard-pressed to win with this motorbike **4.**(*+ a mal*) **to-**

marse algo a ~ to take sth badly; **estoy a ~ con mi vecino** I'm on bad terms with my neighbor **5.**(*mal que bien*) **~ que bien, el negocio sigue funcionando** better or worse, the business is still working; **~ que bien, tendré que ir al dentista este mes** whether I like it or not, I will have to go to the dentist this month; **aprobar los exámenes más ~ que bien** to scrape through the exams

malabarismo [ma·la·βa·'ris·mo] *m* juggling; **hacer ~s para mantener su puesto de trabajo** *fig* to do a balancing act to keep one's job

malabarista [ma·la·βa·'ris·ta] *mf* juggler

malaconsejar [mal·a·kon·se·'xar] *vt* to badly advise

malacostumbrado, -a [mal·a·kos·tum·'bra·do, -a] *adj* **estar ~** (*mimado*) to be spoiled; (*vicioso*) to have bad habits

malacostumbrar [mal·a·kos·tum·'brar] **I.** *vt* **1.**(*mimar*) to spoil **2.**(*educar mal*) to bring up badly **II.** *vr:* **~ se** to get into a bad habit

malagradecido, -a [mal·a·ɣra·de·'si·do, -a; -·'θi·do, -a] *adj* ungrateful

malandante [mal·an·'dan·te] *adj* **persona ~** unfortunate person

malandrín, -ina [ma·lan·'drin, -·'dri·na] *adj* roguish

malanga [ma·'lan·ga] **I.** *adj Cuba* cowardly **II.** *f* **1.**(*sombrero de paja*) straw hat **2.** *RDom* (*pelo*) **pelar a alguien la ~** to cut sb's hair **3.** *AmC, Méx* (*planta*) taro

malapata [ma·la·'pa·ta] *mf* clumsy oaf; **tener ~** (*poca destreza*) to be maladroit; (*malas intenciones*) to have wicked intentions; (*mala suerte*) to be unlucky; **la cosa tiene ~** *fig* it is ill-starred [*o* fated]

malaria [ma·'la·rja] *f* malaria

Malasia [ma·'la·sja] *f* Malaysia

malaventura [ma·la·βen·'tu·ra] *f* **1.**(*desgracia*) unhappiness; (*golpe*) blow **2.**(*mala suerte*) misfortune

malayo, -a [ma·'la·jo] *adj, m, f* Malay, Malayan

malbaratar [mal·βa·ra·'tar] *vt* (*malgastar*) to squander

malcarado, -a [mal·ka·'ra·do, -a] *adj* (*enfadado*) cross; (*furioso*) furious; (*malhumorado*) grumpy

malcomer [mal·ko·'mer] *vi* to eat badly; (*sin ganas*) to eat without appetite; **el dinero sólo da para ~** the money isn't sufficient to eat properly

malcriadez [mal·kria·'des, -'deθ] *f AmC, AmS* ill-breeding; (*descortesía*) rudeness

malcriado, -a [mal·kri·'a·do, -a] *adj* (*mal educado*) spoiled; (*descortés*) rude

malcriar <*1. pres:* malcrío> [mal·kri·'ar] *vt* to bring up badly; (*mimar*) to spoil

maldad [mal·'dad] *f* evil, wickedness

maldecir [mal·de·'sir, -'θir] *irr* **I.** *vt* to curse, to damn; **¡te maldigo!** I curse you! **II.** *vi* **1.**(*jurar*) to swear **2.**(*hablar mal*) to speak ill; (*difamar*) to speak evil **3.**(*quejarse*) **~ de**

algo/alguien to complain about sth/sb
maldición [mal·di·'sjon, -'θjon] *f* **1.** (*imprecación*) curse; **me ha caído una ~** a curse has been put on me **2.** (*juramento*) swear word; **soltar una ~ contra alguien** to swear at sb
maldito, -a [mal·'di·to] I. *pp de* **maldecir** II. *adj* **1.** (*endemoniado*) damned; **¡maldita sea!** *inf* damn (it)!; **¡~ seas!** *vulg* damn you!; **~ el caso que me hacen** *inf* they are completely ignoring me; **no vale la maldita pena** *inf* there's absolutely no point; **¡maldita la gracia (que me hace)!** I don't find it funny at all! **2.** (*maligno*) wicked; **¡vete, ~!** get out of here!; **soltar la maldita** to talk a mile a minute
maldoso, -a [mal·'do·so, -a] *adj Méx* wicked
maleable [ma·le·'a·βle] *adj* **1.** (*forjable*) malleable; (*flexible*) pliable **2.** (*dócil*) pliant
maleante [ma·le·'an·te] *adj* (*delincuente*) delinquent; (*persona maligna*) miscreant
malear [ma·le·'ar] I. *vt* **1.** (*pervertir*) to pervert **2.** (*dañar: a alguien*) to harm; (*algo*) to spoil II. *vr:* **~se** to go to the dogs
malecón [ma·le·'kon] *m* dyke; (*rompeolas*) breakwater
maleducado, -a [mal·e·du·'ka·do, -a] *adj* ill-mannered; (*niño*) ill-bred; (*mimado*) spoiled; (*descortés*) rude
maleducar [mal·e·du·'kar] *vt* to spoil
maleficio [ma·le·'fi·sjo, -θjo] *m* (*hechizo*) curse; (*daño*) harm
maléfico, -a [ma·'le·fi·ko, -a] *adj* **poder ~** evil power
malentendido [mal·en·ten·'di·do] *m* misunderstanding
malestar [ma·les·'tar] *m* malaise; (*espiritual*) uneasiness
maleta [ma·'le·ta] *f* suitcase; **hacer la ~** to pack one's suitcase
maletera [ma·le·'te·ra] *f Col, Méx*, **maletero** [ma·le·'te·ro] *m AUTO* trunk
maletero, -a [ma·le·'te·ro, -a] *m, f Chile* (*ladrón*) thief
maletín [ma·le·'tin] *m* (*de aseo*) toilet bag; ~ (*de viaje*) overnight bag
malevaje [ma·le·'βa·xe] *m Arg* ruffians *pl*
malévolo, -a [ma·'le·βo·lo, -a] *adj* malevolent
maleza [ma·'le·sa, -θa] *f* weeds *pl*; (*matorral*) thicket
malgastador(a) [mal·γas·ta·'dor, -·'do·ra] *m(f)* spendthrift
malgastar [mal·γas·'tar] *vt* to waste; **~ todo el dinero en tabaco** to squander all the money on cigarettes; **~ dinero en el bingo** to waste money on bingo; **~ el tiempo charlando** to waste time chatting; **~ una oportunidad** to waste an opportunity
malhechor(a) [mal·e·'tʃor(a)] *m(f)* delinquent, wrongdoer
malherir [mal·e·'rir] *irr como sentir vt* to seriously injure
malhumorado, -a [mal·u·mo·'ra·do, -a] *adj* bad-tempered; **estar ~** to be in a bad mood
malicia [ma·'li·sja, -θja] *f* **1.** (*intención malé-*

vola) malice **2.** (*maldad*) wickedness **3.** (*picardía*) mischievousness; **tener mucha ~** to be full of mischief; **no tener ~** to be very trusting
maliciar [ma·li·'sjar, -'θjar] *vt, vr:* **~se** (*sospechar*) to suspect; **~ de todo** to be suspicious of everything
malicioso, -a [ma·li·'sjo·so, -a; -θjo·so, -a] *adj* malicious; (*maligno*) malign; (*que sospecha malicia*) suspicious
maligno, -a [ma·'liγ·no] *adj* (*pernicioso*) malign; (*persona*) spiteful; (*sonrisa*) malicious; MED malignant
malinchista [ma·lin·'tʃis·ta] *mf Méx* person who prefers foreign things
malintencionado, -a [mal·in·ten·sjo·'na·do, -a, -θjo·'na·do, -a] *adj* unkind
malinterpretar [mal·in·ter·pre·'tar] *vt* to misinterpret
malla ['ma·ja, -ʎa] *f* **1.** (*de un tejido*) mesh, weave; **de ~(s) ancha(s)/estrecha(s)/fina(s)** open/close/fine weave; **caer en las ~s de alguien** *fig* to fall prey to sb **2.** *pl* (*pantalones*) leggings *pl* **3.** *AmL* (*de baño*) swimsuit
mallo ['ma·jo, -ʎo] *m Chile* (*guiso de patatas*) potato stew
Mallorca [ma·jor·ka, ma·ʎor·] *f* Majorca
mallorquín, -ina [ma·jor·kin, ma·ʎor-] *adj* of/from Majorca
malnutrido, -a [mal·nu·'tri·do, -a] *adj* malnourished
malo, -a ['ma·lo, -a] I. *adj* <peor, pésimo> (*precediendo un sustantivo masc. sing.: mal*) **1.** (*en general*) bad; **mala gestión** mismanagement; **malas palabras** bad words; **eres ~ de entender** you are difficult to understand; **fumar es ~ para la salud** smoking is bad for your health; **de mala gana** unwillingly; **me gusta la casa, lo ~ es que es demasiado cara** I like the house, the problem is that it is too expensive; **tener mala mano para algo** to have no talent for sth; **siempre anda con malas mujeres** he is always with flighty women; **es ~ para madrugar** he is bad at getting up early; **tener mala suerte** to be unlucky; **hace un tiempo malísimo** the weather is really bad; **el trabajo en las minas es muy ~** the work in the mines is very hard; **me vino de malas** it happened at a very inconvenient time for me; **la chapa de este coche es mala** the bodywork of this car is poor; **hacer un trabajo de mala manera** to do a job badly **2.** *ser* (*falso*) false **3.** *ser* (*malévolo*) nasty; **tener mal genio** to have a bad temper; **una mala persona** a nasty person; **venir de malas** to have a hostile attitude **4.** *estar* (*enfermo*) ill; **caer ~** to become ill **5.** *ser* (*travieso*) naughty **6.** *estar* (*estropeado*) spoiled; (*leche*) sour; (*ropa*) worn-out ▶ **más vale ~ conocido que bueno por conocer** *prov* better the devil you know II. *adv* **si no pagas voluntariamente tendré que intentarlo por las malas** if you don't pay voluntarily I will have to take steps to force you to; **hoy te llevo al dentista aunque sea por**

las malas today I am taking you to the dentist even if I have to drag you there; **podemos llegar a un acuerdo por las buenas o por las malas** we can reach an agreement by fair means or foul; **estoy a malas con mi jefe** I am at daggers drawn with my boss; **andar a malas** to be on bad terms; **han vuelto a fallar un penalti, hoy están de ~s** they have failed to score a penalty again, today they are out of luck **III.** *m, f (persona)* bad man *m,* bad woman *f;* CINE baddie; **los ~s de la peli** the bad guys

malograr [ma·lo·'ɣrar] **I.** *vt* **1.** *(desaprovechar)* to waste; *(frustrar)* to frustrate; **has malogrado la ocasión** you have wasted the occasion **2.** *(estropear)* to ruin **II.** *vr:* **~ se 1.** *(fallar)* to fail; **se han malogrado mis esperanzas** my hopes have come to nothing **2.** *(estropearse)* to be ruined

maloliente [mal·o·'ljen·te] *adj* foul-smelling; **me molestan tus cigarros ~s** your smelly cigarettes annoy me

malparar [mal·pa·'rar] *vt (persona)* to come off badly; **salió malparado de la pelea** he came off worse in the fight

malparir [mal·pa·'rir] *vi* to have a miscarriage

malpensado, -a [mal·pen·'sa·do, -a] *adj* evil-minded; **no seas tan ~** don't be so cynical

malsano, -a [mal·'sa·no, -a] *adj* unhealthy; *(moralmente)* unwholesome

malsonante [mal·so·'nan·te] *adj (sonido)* jarring; *(palabra)* nasty; **ruidos ~s** jarring noises

malta ['mal·ta] *f* **1.** *t.* AGR malt **2.** *Arg (cerveza)* beer

maltés, -esa [mal·'tes] *adj, m, f* Maltese

maltón, -ona [mal·'ton -'to·na] *m, f AmS* overgrown youth

maltraído, -a [mal·tra·'i·do, -a] *adj Bol, Chile, Perú* disheveled

maltratar [mal·tra·'tar] *vt* to maltreat; **~ (de palabra)** to abuse (verbally)

maltrato [mal·'tra·to] *m* maltreatment, abuse; *(insulto)* (verbal) abuse

maltrecho, -a [mal·'tre·tʃo, -a] *adj (golpeado)* battered

malura [ma·'lu·ra] *f Chile* pain or discomfort

malva ['mal·βa] **I.** *adj* mauve **II.** *f* mallow; **estar criando ~s** *inf* to be pushing up daisies; **ser (como) una ~** *inf* to be meek and mild

malvado, -a [mal·'βa·do, -a] *adj* wicked; **una persona malvada** a wicked person

malvavisco [mal·'βis·ko] *m* marsh mallow

malvender [mal·βen·'der] *vt* to sell at a loss

malversar [mal·βer·'sar] *vt* to misappropriate, to embezzle

malversión [mal·βer·'sjon] *f* embezzlement, misappropriation

Malvinas [mal·'βi·nas] *fpl* Falkland Islands *pl*

malvís [mal·'βis] *m inv* song thrush

malvón [mal·'βon] *m Arg, Méx, Par, Urug* BOT geranium

mama ['ma·ma] *f* **1.** *(pecho)* breast; *(ubre)* udder **2.** *inf (mamá)* mom(my)

mamá [ma·'ma] *f inf* mom(my)

mamada [ma·'ma·da] *f* **1.** *(acción)* breastfeeding **2.** *(cantidad mamada)* breastfeed **3.** *AmL (ganga)* bargain; **¡vaya ~!** what a bargain! **4.** *vulg (felación)* blow job; **dar una ~ a alguien** to give sb a blow job, to go down on sb

mamadera [ma·ma·'de·ra] *f AmL* baby bottle

mamar [ma·'mar] **I.** *vi, vt* **1.** *(en el pecho)* to breastfeed **2.** *(adquirir)* **has mamado la pereza (con la leche)** you acquired your laziness at your mother's breast **3.** *inf (comer)* to wolf (down) **4.** *vulg* **mamársela a alguien** to give sb a blow job **II.** *vr:* **~se** *vulg (emborracharse)* to get sloshed

mamarracho [ma·ma·'rra·tʃo] *m inf* ridiculous person

mameluco [ma·me·'lu·ko] *m* **1.** *(bobo)* idiot **2.** *AmL (de bebé)* romper suit

mamífero [ma·'mi·fe·ro] *m* mammal

mamila [ma·'mi·la] *f Méx* baby bottle

mamografía [ma·mo·ɣra·'fi·a] *f* MED mammogram, mammography

mamón, -ona [ma·'mon] *m, f* **1.** *vulg* jerk; *(hombre)* prick; *(mujer)* bitch **2.** *AmL, inf (borracho)* drunk

mamonear [ma·mo·ne·'ar] *vt Guat, Hond* **1.** *(golpear)* to beat **2.** *(retardar)* to postpone **3.** *(pasar el tiempo con futilezas)* to waste time

mamotreto [ma·mo·'tre·to] *m pey* **1.** *(libro)* hefty tome **2.** *(armatoste)* cumbersome object; **esta butaca es un ~** this armchair is a cumbersome piece of furniture

mampara [mam·'pa·ra] *f* screen (door), (room) divider

mamporro [mam·'po·rro] *m inf* clout; **darse un ~ contra algo** to bash oneself against sth

mampostería [mam·pos·te·'ri·a] *f* rubblework; **~ de ladrillos en bruto** brickwork

mamúa [ma·'mu·a] *f Arg, Urug, vulg (borrachera)* **agarrarse una ~** to get smashed

mamut <mamuts> [ma·'mut] *m* mammoth

manada [ma·'na·da] *f (rebaño de vacas, ciervos)* herd; *(de ovejas, aves)* flock; *(de peces)* shoal; *(de lobos)* pack; **~ de gallinas** brood of hens; **~ de gente** crowd of people; **una ~ de curiosos** a crowd of onlookers; **pasamos la frontera en ~** we crossed over the border en masse

Managua [ma·'na·ɣwa] *m* Managua

manantial [ma·nan·'tjal] *m* spring; **~ caliente** hot spring; **~ medicinal** health spa

manar [ma·'nar] **I.** *vt* to flow with; **la fuente mana agua fría** the fountain flows with cold water; **la herida no paraba de ~ sangre** the wound wouldn't stop flowing with blood **II.** *vi* **1.** *(surgir)* to well; **el agua manaba sucia de la fuente** dirty water welled from the fountain **2.** *(fluir fácilmente)* to flow; **las palabras manaban de su boca** the words flowed from his/her mouth

manazas [ma·'nasas, -θas] *mf inv, inf* clumsy person, klutz; **ser un ~** to be clumsy

mancha ['man·t∫a] *f* **1.**(*en la ropa, piel*) dirty mark; (*de tinta*) stain; (*salpicadura*) spot; (*de maquillaje*) smudge **2.**(*toque de color*) fleck; **este perro es blanco con ~s negras** this dog is white with black patches; **la corbata tiene ~s azules y blancas** the tie has splashes of blue and white

Mancha ['man·t∫a] *f* **el canal de la ~** the (English) Channel

manchado, -a [man·'t∫a·do, -a] *adj* (*ropa, mantel*) stained; (*cara, fruta*) dirty

manchar [man·'t∫ar] **I.** *vt* to dirty **II.** *vr:* **~se** (*ensuciarse*) to get dirty

mancilla [man·'si·ja, -'θi·ʎa] *f* stain; **sin ~** pure

mancillar [man·si·'jar, -θi·'ʎar] *vt* to sully

manco, -a ['man·ko] *adj* (*de un brazo*) one-armed; (*de una mano*) one-handed; **es ~ de la mano derecha** (*le falta*) he/she is missing his/her right hand; (*la tiene inutilizada*) his/her right hand is useless; **no ser (cojo ni) ~** (*ser hábil*) to be dexterous; (*ser largo de manos*) to be light-fingered

mancomunidad [man·ko·mu·ni·'dad] *f* (*comunidad*) community

mancornas [man·'kor·nas] *fpl Col, Chile* cuff links *pl*

mancuernillas [man·kwer·'ni·jas, -ʎas] *fpl Méx* cuff links *pl*

manda ['man·da] *f* legacy, bequest

mandado [man·'da·do] *m* **hacer un ~** to run an errand

mandamás [man·da·'mas] *mf pey, inf* big shot

mandamiento [man·da·'mjen·to] *m* **1.**(*orden*) order; **~ de detención** arrest warrant; **~ judicial** court order **2.**(*precepto*) precept **3.** REL commandment

mandar [man·'dar] *vt* **1.**(*ordenar*) to order; **~ a alguien que** +*subj* to order sb to; **lo que Ud. mande** whatever you say **2.**(*prescribir*) to prescribe **3.**(*dirigir*) to lead; (*gobernar*) to govern **4.**(*encargar*) **~ buscar/hacer/venir** to ask to get/do/come **5.**(*enviar*) to send; **~ al cuerno** *inf* to send to hell **6.** TÉC to control; **mandado a distancia** remote controlled

mandarina [man·da·'ri·na] *f* mandarin, tangerine

mandatario, -a [man·da·'ta·rjo, -a] *m, f* agent; **primer ~** POL head of state; JUR attorney

mandato [man·'da·to] *m* **1.**(*orden*) order; **~ judicial** injunction; **~ de pago** warrant for payment; **por ~ de las leyes** by law **2.** POL mandate; **~ internacional** international mandate; **~ parlamentario** parliamentary mandate

mandíbula [man·'di·βu·la] *f* **1.** ANAT jaw; **reír(se) a ~ batiente** to laugh one's head off **2.** TÉC clamp; **~ prensora** vice; **~ de sujeción** clamp

mandil [man·'dil] *m AmL* (*de caballería*) cloth (*used to rub down a horse*)

mandilón [man·di·'lon] *m pey, inf* wimp

mandinga [man·'din·ga] *m* **1.** *AmL, inf* (*diablo*) devil **2.** *Arg, inf* (*muchacho*) scamp

mando ['man·do] *m* **1.**(*poder*) control; MIL command; (*del presidente*) term of office; **don de ~** leadership qualities; **estar al ~ de** to be in command of; **estar bajo el ~ de alguien** to be under sb's command **2.**(*quien lo tiene*) **~s intermedios de una empresa** middle management of a business; **alto ~** MIL high command **3.** TÉC control; **~ a distancia** remote control; **~ manual** manual control; **botón de ~** control button

mandolina [man·do·'li·na] *f* MÚS mandolin

mandón, -ona [man·'don, -·'do·na] *adj* bossy

manecilla [ma·ne·'si·ja, -'θi·ʎa] *f* (*del reloj*) hand; TÉC pointer

manejable [ma·ne·'xa·βle] *adj* user-friendly; (*persona*) tractable

manejar [ma·ne·'xar] **I.** *vt* **1.**(*usar*) to use; (*máquina*) to operate; *fig* to handle; **~ un cuchillo** to use a knife; **manejas bien las cifras** you are good with numbers; **'¡manéjese con cuidado!'** 'handle with care!' **2.**(*dirigir*) to handle; **~ intereses** to manage interests **3.**(*a alguien*) to manage; **maneja al marido a su antojo** she can twist her husband around her little finger **4.** *AmL* (*un coche*) to drive **II.** *vr:* **~se** to manage; **saber ~se en la vida** to know how to get on in life; **manejárselas** *inf* to get by

manejo [ma·'ne·xo] *m* **1.**(*uso*) use; (*de una máquina*) operation; *fig* handling; **~ de animales** handling of animals; **~ a distancia** remote control **2.** COMPUT management; **~ de errores** error management; **~ de la memoria** memory management; **~ de información** information management **3.** *AmL* (*de un coche*) driving

manera [ma·'ne·ra] *f* **1.**(*forma, modo*) manner, way; **~ de decir** way of saying; **~ de pensar** way of thinking; **~ de proceder** way of acting; **es su ~ de ser** that's the way he/she is; **a la ~ de sus abuelos** in the way their grandparents did; **a la ~ de la casa** in the habitual way; **a ~ de** a sort of; **a mi ~** my way; **de la ~ que sea** somehow or other; **de cualquier ~, de todas ~s** anyway; **de esta ~** that way; **de ~ que** (*finalidad*) so that; **¿de ~ que sacaste mala nota?** so you got a bad mark, did you?; **de ninguna ~** no way; **se echó a gritar de tal ~ que...** *inf* he/she started to shout in such a way that...; **de una ~ o de otra** one way or another; **en cierta ~** in a way; **en gran ~** largely; **no hay ~ de...** there is no way that...; **¡qué ~ de llover!** just look at the rain!; **sobre ~** a lot; **primero se lo dije de buena ~** first I said it to him nicely; **contestar de mala ~** to answer rudely; **hacer las cosas de mala ~** to do things badly **2.** *pl* (*modales*) manners *pl;* **¡estas no son ~s!** this is no way to behave!

maneto, -a [ma·'ne·to, -a] *adj* **1.** *Hond* (*manos*) one-handed **2.** *Guat, Ven* (*piernas*) knock-kneed

manga ['man·ga] *f* **1.**(*del vestido*) sleeve; **de**

~s cortas/largas short-/long-sleeved; estar en ~s de camisa to be in shirt-sleeves; andar ~ por hombro *inf* to be a mess; poner algo ~ por hombro *inf* to turn sth inside out; sacarse algo de la ~ *fig* to come up with sth; hacer un corte de ~s a alguien ≈ to give sb the finger; tener (la) [*o* ser de] ~ ancha *fig* to be lenient; tienen algo en la manga they are keeping sth up their sleeve 2. AVIAT ~ de aire windsock 3. METEO ~ de viento tornado; ~ de agua waterspout 4. *Arg, pey* (*grupo de personas*) mob ▶ hacer ~s y capirotes to completely ignore; tirar la ~ to ask for a loan

manganeta [man·ga·'ne·ta] *f Hond* trick

mangante [man·'gan·te] *mf inf* (*ladrón*) thief

manganzón, -ona [man·gan·'son, -·'so·na; -·'θon, -·'θo·na] *m, f AmL* loafer

mangar <g→gu> [man·'gar] *vt inf* to swipe, to nick; (*en tiendas*) to shoplift

mangle ['man·gle] *m AmL* BOT mangrove tree

mango ['man·go] *m* 1. (*puño*) knob; (*alargado*) handle; tener la sartén por el ~ *fig* to hold the reins 2. (*árbol*) mango tree; (*fruta*) mango

mangoneador(a) [man·go·nea·'dor, -·'do·ra] *adj* 1. (*entrometido*) meddlesome 2. (*vago*) idle

mangonear [man·go·ne·'ar] *inf* I. *vi* 1. (*entrometerse*) to meddle 2. (*vaguear*) to loaf II. *vt* to wangle; está mangoneando todo he/she has a finger in every pie

mangoneo [man·go·'neo] *m inf* 1. (*entremetimiento*) meddling 2. (*vagancia*) idleness

manguear [man·ge·'ar] *vt Arg, inf* (*dinero*) to scrounge

manguera [man·'ge·ra] *f* (*tubo*) hose

maní [ma·'ni] *m* peanut

manía [ma·'ni·a] *f* 1. (*locura*) mania 2. (*extravagancia*) eccentricity, quirk 3. (*obsesión*) obsession; tener ~ por la moda to be obsessed with fashion 4. *inf* (*aversión*) aversion; tener ~ a alguien not to be able to stand sb; coger ~ a alguien to take a dislike to sb

maniaco, -a [ma·'nja·ko, -a], maníaco, -a [ma·'ni·a·ko, -a] *m, f* maniac; ~ sexual sex maniac

maniatar [ma·nja·'tar] *vt* ~ a alguien to tie sb's hands up; lo ~on a la silla they tied his hands to the chair

maniático, -a [ma·'nja·ti·ko, -a] *m, f* 1. (*extravagante*) fusspot 2. (*loco*) maniac; un ~ del fútbol a football fanatic; ser un ~ del cine to be crazy about films; un ~ de la limpieza a cleaning maniac

manicomio [ma·ni·'ko·mjo] *m* psychiatric hospital; *fig* (*casa de locos*) madhouse

manicura [ma·ni·'ku·ra] *f* manicure

manicuro, -a [ma·ni·'ku·ro, -a] *m, f* manicurist

manido, -a [ma·'ni·do, -a] *adj* 1. (*alimentos*) off; (*fruta*) overripe 2. (*objetos*) worn; (*libro*) tatty; (*ropa*) shabby

manifestación [ma·ni·fes·ta·'sjon, -'θjon] *f*

1. (*expresión*) expression; como ~ de cariño as an expression of love 2. (*reunión*) demonstration

manifestante [ma·ni·fes·'tan·te] *mf* demonstrator

manifestar <e→ie> [ma·ni·fes·'tar] I. *vt* 1. (*declarar*) to declare 2. (*mostrar*) to show II. *vr:* ~se 1. (*declararse*) to declare oneself; ~se a favor/en contra de algo to declare oneself for/against sth 2. (*revelarse*) to show oneself 3. (*política*) to demonstrate

manifiesto [ma·ni·'fjes·to] *m* manifesto

manifiesto, -a [ma·ni·'fjes·to, -a] *adj* (*evidente*) manifest; poner de ~ (*revelar*) to show [*o* make clear]; (*expresar*) to declare

manigua [ma·'ni·ɣwa] *f Cuba* jungle

manija [ma·'ni·xa] *f* handle

manilargo, -a [ma·ni·'lar·ɣo, -a] *m, f* petty thief

manilla [ma·'ni·ja, -ʎa] *f* (*del reloj*) hand

manillar [ma·ni·'jar, -ʎar] *m* handlebars *pl*

maniobra [ma·ni·'o·βra] *f* 1. (*operación manual*) handling 2. (*ardid*) ploy; ~s fraudulentas fraudulent tactics 3. MIL maneuver; estar de ~s to be on maneuvers 4. (*vehículo*) maneuver; FERRO switch

maniobrable [ma·njo·'βra·βle] *adj* maneuverable; un vehículo fácilmente ~ a highly maneuverable car

maniobrar [ma·njo·'βrar] I. *vi* 1. MIL to carry out maneuvers 2. (*intrigar*) to scheme II. *vt* 1. (*manejar*) to handle 2. (*manipular*) to manipulate

manipulación [ma·ni·pu·la·'sjon, -'θjon] *f* 1. (*empleo*) use, handling 2. (*alteración*) manipulation

manipular [ma·ni·pu·'lar] *vt* 1. (*máquina*) to operate 2. (*alterar*) to manipulate 3. (*interferir*) ~ algo to interfere with sth 4. (*manosear*) ~ algo to fiddle with sth

maniquí <maniquíes> [ma·ni·'ki] *m* (*para ropa*) mannequin

manir [ma·'nir] *irr como abolir vt* (*carne*) to hang

manirroto, -a [ma·ni·'rro·to, -a] *adj* spendthrift

manitas [ma·'ni·tas] hacer ~ *inf* to neck hands; ser un ~ *inf* to be dexterous, to be good with one's hands

manito [ma·'ni·to] *m Méx* pal

manivela [ma·ni·'βe·la] *f* handle

manjar [man·'xar] *m* food; (*exquisitez*) delicacy

mano ['ma·no] *f* 1. ANAT hand; a ~ alzada (*votación*) by a show of hands; a ~ armada armed; a ~s llenas in abundance; alzar la ~ contra alguien to raise one's hand to sb; apretón de ~s handshake; bajo ~ underhand; coger a alguien con las ~s en la masa to catch sb red-handed; cogidos de las ~s hand in hand; comer de la ~ de alguien *fig* to eat out of sb's hand; me lo prometió con la ~ en el corazón he/she promised me with his/her

M

hand on his/her heart; **dar de ~** (*al trabajo*) to leave work; **echar una ~ a alguien** to give sb a hand; **dejar algo en ~s de alguien** to leave sth in sb's hands; **echar ~ de alguien** to make use of sb; **ser de ~ abierta/cerrada** *fig* to be generous/tight-fisted; **estar al alcance de la ~** to be within (arm's) reach; **estar ~ sobre ~** *fig* to be idle; **hecho a ~** hand-made; **su vida se le había ido de las ~s** his/her life has gotten out of hand; **se le ha ido la ~** (*desmesura*) he/she has overdone it; (*violencia*) he/she has lost control; **lavarse las ~s (en algo)** to wash one's hands of sth; **llevar a alguien de la ~** to lead sb by the hand; *fig* to guide sb; **~ a ~** *fig* hand in hand; **¡~s a la obra!** to work!; **meter ~** to take action; **meter ~ a alguien** *inf* to touch sb up; **pedir la ~ de alguien** to ask for sb's hand in marriage; **poner las ~s en el fuego por alguien** to stick one's neck out for someone; **si a ~ viene...** if it drops into my lap...; **echar ~ de algo** to draw on sth; **traer algo entre ~s** to be up to sth; **tomarle la ~ a algo** *inf* to take sth up; **untar la ~ a alguien** to grease sb's palm; **¡venga esa ~!** let's shake on it! **2.** zool (*de un mono*) hand; (*de un perro*) paw; **~ de ave** bird's claw; **~ de cerdo** pig's trotter **3.** (*lado*) **~ derecha/izquierda** right-/left-hand side; **a [o de] la ~ derecha** on the right(-hand side) **4.** (*capa*) coat; **una ~ de pintura** a coat of paint **5.** (*trabajador*) hand; **~ de obra** labor **6.** (*habilidad*) skill; **tener buena ~ para coser** to be good at sewing; **tener ~ izquierda** to be tactful; **tener ~ con** to have a way with; **~ de santo** sure remedy **7.** (*de naipes*) hand; **ser ~** to lead ▶ **muchas ~s en un plato hacen mucho garabato** *prov* too many cooks spoil the broth

manojo [ma·'no·xo] *m* bunch; **~ de llaves** bunch of keys; **ser un ~ de nervios** to be a bundle of nerves

manopla [ma·'no·pla] *f* mitten; (*para lavarse*) washcloth

manoseado, -a [ma·no·se·'a·do, -a] *adj* (*sobado*) worn; (*trillado*) hackneyed

manosear [ma·no·se·'ar] *vt* to handle; *pey* to paw

manotazo [ma·no·'ta·so, -θo] *m* smack; **dar ~s** to smack

manoteador(a) [ma·no·tea·'dor, -'dora] *m(f)* *Arg, Méx* (*ratero*) thief

manotear [ma·no·te·'ar] *vi* to gesticulate

mansalva [man·'sal·βa] *adv* **a ~** (*sobre seguro*) without risk; (*traidoramente*) point-blank; (*en gran cantidad*) in abundance

mansarda [man·'sar·da] *f* *AmC, AmS* attic

mansedumbre [man·se·'dum·bre] *f* **1.** (*suavidad*) gentleness **2.** (*sumisión*) meekness

mansión [man·'sjon] *f* (*casa suntuosa*) mansion

manso, -a ['man·so] *adj* docile; (*animales*) tame; (*aguas*) quiet

manta¹ ['man·ta] *f* blanket; **a ~** in abundance; **liarse la ~ a la cabeza** (*actuar con decisión*)

to take it on oneself to do sth; (*de modo irreflexivo*) to recklessly decide to do sth; **tirar de la ~** to let the cat out of the bag

manta² ['man·ta] *mf* (*persona torpe*) oaf

manteca [man·'te·ka] *f* **1.** (*grasa*) fat; **~ de cerdo** lard **2.** *RíoPl* (*mantequilla*) butter; **como ~** as soft as butter

mantecado [man·te·'ka·do] *m* **1.** (*bollo*) pastry cake (*type of shortbread*) **2.** (*helado*) ice cream (*made from a custard base*)

mantecoso, -a [man·te·'ko·so, -a] *adj* **1.** (*de manteca*) greasy; (*sabor*) buttery **2.** (*consistencia*) soft; (*carne*) fatty

mantel [man·'tel] *m* tablecloth; **comer a ~es** to dine formally; **estar a mesa y ~** to have free board; **poner/levantar los ~es** *fig* to lay/clear the table

mantelería [man·te·le·'ri·a] *f* table linen

mantener [man·te·'ner] *irr como* tener **I.** *vt* **1.** (*conservar, relaciones*) to maintain; (*orden*) to keep; **~ a punto** to keep in working order; **mantiene la línea** he/she keeps his/her figure; **~ la calma** to keep calm **2.** (*perseverar*) **~ algo** to keep sth up **3.** (*sustentar*) to maintain; **~ correspondencia con alguien** to keep up a correspondence with sb **4.** (*sostener*) to support **5.** (*proseguir*) to continue; **una conversación con alguien** to hold a conversation with sb **II.** *vr:* **~se 1.** (*sostenerse*) to support oneself **2.** (*continuar*) to continue **3.** (*perseverar*) to keep; **se mantiene en sus trece** *inf* he/she is sticking to his/her guns **4.** (*sustentarse*) to support oneself

mantenido, -a [man·te·'ni·do, -a] *adj* kept

mantenimiento [man·te·ni·'mjen·to] *m* **1.** (*alimentos*) sustenance **2.** téc maintenance; **~ de datos** comput database update; **sin ~** maintenance-free **3.** (*de una propiedad*) upkeep

mantequilla [man·te·'ki·ja, -ʎa] *f* butter

mantequillera [man·te·ki·'je·ra, -'ʎe·ra] *f* *AmL:* butter dish

mantilla [man·'ti·ja, -ʎa] *f* **1.** (*de mujer*) mantilla **2.** (*de niño*) swaddling clothes *pl*; **el negocio está en ~s** *inf* the business is in its infancy; **estar en ~s sobre algo** *inf* to be in the dark about sth

manto ['man·to] *m* **1.** (*prenda*) cloak; (*talar*) gown **2.** (*capa*) layer; **el ~ ácido de la piel** the acid layer of the skin; **~ terrestre** earth's crust; **~ vegetal** humus

mantón [man·'ton] *m* shawl

mantudo, -a [man·'tu·do, -a] *m, f* *AmC* masked [*o* disguised] person

manual [ma·nu·'al] **I.** *adj* manual, hand; **trabajos ~es** handicrafts *pl* **II.** *m* manual, handbook; **~ de referencia** reference book; **~ de instrucciones** instruction manual

manufactura [ma·nu·fak·'tu·ra] *f* manufacture

manufacturar [ma·nu·fak·tu·'rar] *vt* to manufacture

manuscrito [ma·nus·'kri·to] *m* manuscript

manuscrito, -a [ma·nus·'kri·to, -a] *adj* handwritten
manutención [ma·nu·ten·'sjon, -'θjon] *f* 1. (*alimentos*) keep 2. TÉC maintenance
manzana [man·'sa·na, -'θa·na] *f* 1. (*fruta*) apple; **la ~ de la discordia** the bone of contention; **sano como una ~** as fit as a fiddle 2. (*conjunto de casas*) block; **dar la vuelta a la ~** to go around the block 3. *AmL* ANAT (*nuez*) Adam's apple
manzanilla [man·sa·'ni·ja, man·θa·'ni·ʎa] *f* 1. (*planta*) chamomile; (*flor*) chamomile flower; (*infusión*) chamomile tea 2. (*vino*) manzanilla
manzano [man·'sa·no, -'θa·no] *m* apple tree
maña ['ma·ɲa] *f* 1. (*habilidad*) skill, dexterity; **tener ~ para algo** to have a knack for sth 2. (*astucia*) craftiness 3. *pl* (*caprichos*) whims *pl*; **tiene ~s** he/she has his/her little whims ▶ **más vale ~ que fuerza** *prov* better brains than brawn
mañana¹ [ma'·ɲa·na] I. *f* (*temprano*) early morning; (*hasta el mediodía*) morning; **a las 5 de la ~** at 5 a.m.; **de la noche a la ~** overnight; **de ~** in the early morning; **por la ~** in the morning; **todas las ~s** every morning; **~ por la ~** tomorrow morning II. *adv* 1. (*día*) tomorrow; **¡hasta ~!** see you tomorrow!; **~ será otro día** tomorrow is another day 2. (*futuro*) tomorrow ▶ **no dejes para ~ lo que puedas hacer hoy** *prov* do not leave for tomorrow what you can do today
mañana² [ma'·ɲa·na] *m* tomorrow; **pasado ~** the day after tomorrow; **el día de ~** in the future
mañanero, -a [ma·ɲa·'ne·ro, -a] *adj* 1. (*madrugador*) early-rising 2. (*de la mañana*) morning
mañanita [ma·ɲa·'ni·ta] *f Méx* (*canción*) serenade
mañero, -a [ma·'ɲe·ro, -a] *adj Arg, inf* fussy
mañosear [ma·ɲo·se·'ar] *vi* 1. *Chile, Perú* to act craftily 2. *CSur, Méx* to be finicky
mañoso, -a [ma·'ɲo·so, -a] *adj* (*hábil*) dexterous, handy
mapa ['ma·pa] *m* map; **~ astronómico** map of the stars; **~ del tiempo** weather map; **borrar del ~** (*matar*) to wipe off the map [*o* the face of the earth]; **desaparecer del ~** to vanish into thin air; **no estar en el ~** *fig* to be out of this world
mapache [ma·'pa·tʃe] *m*, **mapachín** [ma·pa·'tʃin] *m AmL* raccoon
maqueta [ma·'ke·ta] *f* 1. ARQUIT (scale) model 2. (*formato*) format; (*de libro*) dummy
maquetación [ma·ke·ta·'sjon, -'θjon] *f* layout
maquetar [ma·ke·'tar] *vt* to lay out
maquiavélico, -a [ma·kja·'βe·li·ko, -a] *adj* Machiavellian
maquillador(a) [ma·ki·ja·'dor, -·'do·ra; ma·ki·ʎa-] *m(f) t.* TEAT make-up artist
maquillaje [ma·ki·'ja·xe, -ʎa·xe] *m* 1. (*acción*) application of make-up 2. (*producto*) make-up

maquillar [ma·ki·'jar, -ʎar] I. *vt* 1. (*poner base de fondo*) to apply foundation to; (*con pinturas*) to apply make-up to 2. (*disimular*) to disguise II. *vr*: **~ se** (*con base de fondo*) to put on foundation; (*con pinturas*) to put on make-up
máquina ['ma·ki·na] *f* 1. (*artefacto*) machine; **~ de afeitar** electric shaver [*o* razor]; **~ de coser/lavar** sewing/washing machine; **~ fotográfica** camera; **~ de escribir automática** electric typewriter; **a toda ~** (at) full speed; **escrito a ~** typed; **hecho a ~** machine-made 2. (*aparato de monedas*) vending machine; **~ de tabaco** cigarette dispenser; **~ tragaperras** *inf* slot-machine
maquinación [ma·ki·na·'sjon, -'θjon] *f* plot
maquinar [ma·ki·'nar] *vt* (*urdir*) to scheme
maquinaria [ma·ki·'na·rja] *f* (*máquinas*) machinery
maquinilla [ma·ki·'ni·ja, -ʎa] *f* (safety) razor
maquinista [ma·ki·'nis·ta] *mf* (*conductor*) machinist; **~ de trenes** engineer
maquinizar <z→c> [ma·ki·ni·'sar, -'θar] *vt* to mechanize
mar [mar] *m o f* 1. GEO sea; **Mar Antártico** Antarctic Ocean; **Mar de las Antillas** Caribbean Sea; **Mar Báltico** Baltic Sea; **Mar de Irlanda** Irish Sea; **Mar Mediterráneo** Mediterranean Sea; **Mar del Norte** North Sea; **en alta ~** offshore; **~ adentro** high seas; **~ de fondo** swell; **~ gruesa/picada/rizada** heavy/rough/choppy sea; *fig* unrest; **por ~** by sea; **hacerse a la ~** to put out to sea; **al otro lado del ~** overseas; **arar en el ~** *fig* to labor in vain; **arrojarse a la ~** *fig* to venture forth 2. *inf* **la ~ de...** loads of...; **llueve a ~es** it is pouring with rain; **lloró a ~es** he/she cried his/her eyes out; **sudar a ~es** to pour with sweat; **ser la ~ de aburrido** to be excruciatingly boring; **ser la ~ de bonita** to be incredibly pretty ▶ **quien no se aventura no pasa la ~** *prov* nothing ventured, nothing gained; **echar pelillos al ~** to let bygones be bygones
mar. *abr de* **marzo** Mar.
maraca [ma·'ra·ka] *f* maraca
maraña [ma·'ra·ɲa] *f* (*lío*) mess; **~ de cabello** tangle of hair; **~ de hilo** tangle of threads
marasmo [ma·'ras·mo] *m* (*debilitamiento*) weakening
maratón [ma·ra·'ton] *m o f* marathon
maravilla [ma·ra·'βi·ja, -ʎa] *f* 1. (*portento*) marvel; **a las mil ~s/de ~** marvelously; **hablar ~s de alguien** to speak extremely well of sb; **hacer ~s** *fig* to work wonders 2. (*admiración*) wonder
maravillar [ma·ra·βi·'jar, -ʎar] I. *vt* to amaze II. *vr* **~ se de algo** to marvel at sth
maravilloso, -a [ma·ra·βi·'jo·so, -a; -ʎo·so, -a] *adj* marvelous
marca ['mar·ka] *f* 1. (*distintivo*) mark; **~ de agua** watermark; **~ de ganado** brand 2. (*de productos*) brand; **~ registrada** registered trademark; **ropa de ~** designer label 3. (*huella*) impression 4. DEP record

M

marcación *f* ~ **por voz** TEL voice dialing

marcado, -a [mar·'ka·do] *adj* (*señalado*) marked; (*evidente*) clear

marcador [mar·ka·'dor] *m* **1.** (*tablero*) scoreboard; **abrir el** ~ to open the scoring; **cerraron el** ~ **con tres tantos** they finished the game with three goals **2.** *Arg* (*rotulador*) marker pen

marcaje [mar·'ka·xe] *m* DEP marking, cover(age)

marcapaso(s) [mar·ka·'pa·so(s)] *m* (*inv*) pacemaker

marcar <c→qu> [mar·'kar] **I.** *vt* **1.** (*señalar*) to mark; (*ganado*) to brand; (*mercancías*) to label; ~ **una época** to denote an era; ~ **el compás** to beat time **2.** (*resaltar*) to emphasize **3.** (*teléfono*) to dial **4.** (*cabello*) to style **5.** DEP ~ **un gol** to score a goal; ~ **un punto** to score a point **6.** DEP (*a un jugador*) to mark, to cover **II.** *vr:* ~ **se** to show

marcha ['mar·tʃa] *f* **1.** (*movimiento*) progress; **poner en** ~ to start **2.** (*caminata*) hike **3.** (*curso*) course; ~ **de los negocios** business trend; **la** ~ **de los acontecimientos** the course of events; **sobre la** ~ along the way **4.** (*velocidad*) gear; ~ **atrás** reverse; **a toda** ~ at full speed **5.** *t.* MIL, MÚS march; ~ **silenciosa** silent march **6.** (*salida*) departure; **¡en** ~**!** let's go! **7.** *inf* (*acción*) action; **¡aquí hay mucha** ~**!** this is where the action is!; **ir de** ~ to go out on the town; **tener** ~ to be full of go

marchante [mar·'tʃan·te] *mf* dealer; ~ **de obras de arte** art dealer

marchantía [mar·tʃan·'ti·a] *f AmC, PRico, Ven* clientele

marchar [mar·'tʃar] **I.** *vi* **1.** (*ir*) to go; **¡marchando!** let's go! **2.** (*funcionar*) to work; ~ **sobre ruedas** *fig* to go like clockwork **II.** *vr:* ~ **se 1.** (*irse*) to leave **2.** (*huir*) to flee; ~ **se del país** to flee the country

marchitar [mar·tʃi·'tar] **I.** *vi* (*plantas*) to wither; (*personas*) to be on the wane **II.** *vr:* ~ **se** to wither

marchito, -a [mar·'tʃi·to, -a] *adj* withered

marchoso, -a [mar·'tʃo·so, -a] *adj inf* fun-loving

marcial [mar·'sjal, -'θjal] *adj* martial; **artes** ~ **es** martial arts; **ley** ~ martial law

marciano, -a [mar·'sja·no, -a; 'θja·no, -a] *adj, m, f* Martian

marco ['mar·ko] *m* **1.** (*recuadro*) frame; (*armazón*) framework; **el** ~ **legal** the legal framework **2.** (*ambiente*) background **3.** (*moneda*) mark

marea [ma·'rea] *f* (*mar*) tide; ~ **alta** high tide; ~ **baja** low tide; ~ **creciente** rising tide; ~ **menguante** ebb tide; ~ **negra** oil slick [*o* spill]; ~ **viva** spring tide; **una** ~ **humana** a flood of people

mareado, -a [ma·re·'a·do, -a] *adj* **1.** (*indispuesto*) sick; (*en el mar*) seasick; (*en el coche*) carsick; (*al viajar*) travel-sick; **estoy** ~ **I** feel sick **2.** (*aturdido*) dizzy; *fig* confused

3. (*bebido*) tipsy

marear [ma·re·'ar] **I.** *vt* **1.** *inf* (*molestar*) to pester **2.** MED to nauseate **3.** (*aturdir*) to make dizzy; *fig* to confuse **II.** *vr:* ~ **se 1.** (*enfermarse*) to feel sick; (*en el mar*) to get seasick; (*al viajar*) to get travel-sick **2.** (*quedar aturdido*) to become dizzy; *fig* to become confused **3.** (*emborracharse*) to get tipsy

marejada [ma·re·'xa·da] *f* swell

maremagno [ma·re·'may·no] *m*, **maremágnum** [ma·re·'may·nun] *m inv* (*multitud*) multitude

maremoto [ma·re·'mo·to] *m* tidal wave; (*seísmo*) seaquake

mareo [ma·'reo] *m* **1.** (*malestar*) nausea; (*en el mar*) seasickness; (*al viajar*) travel-sickness, motion sickness **2.** (*vértigo*) dizziness; **¡qué** ~ **de hombre!** *inf* what a nuisance that man is!

marfil [mar·'fil] *m* ivory

margarina [mar·ya·'ri·na] *f* margarine

margarita [mar·ya·'ri·ta] *f* **1.** BOT daisy; **deshojar la** ~ to play 'she loves me, she loves me not' **2.** (*bebida*) margarita **3.** ZOOL periwinkle **4.** (*perla*) pearl; **echar** ~ **s a puercos** to cast pearls before swine **5.** TIPO daisywheel

margen ['mar·xen] *m o f* **1.** (*borde*) margin; **el** ~ **del río** the riverside [*o* riverbank]; **al** ~ apart; **dejar al** ~ to leave out; **mantenerse al** ~ **de algo** *fig* to keep out of sth **2.** (*página*) margin **3.** (*libertad*) leeway; **dar** ~ to give leeway **4.** (*ganancia*) profit margin; ~ **de costos** margin of costs; ~ **de seguridad** safety margin

marginado, -a [mar·xi·'na·do, -a] **I.** *adj* **1.** (*excluido*) excluded, marginalized **2.** (*aislado*) isolated **II.** *m, f* outcast

marginal [mar·xi·'nal] *adj* **1.** (*al margen*) apart **2.** (*secundario*) secondary

marginar [mar·xi·'nar] *vt* (*ignorar algo*) to disregard; (*a alguien*) to marginalize

maría [ma·'ri·a] *f* **1.** *inf* (*ama de casa*) housewife **2.** *inf* (*marihuana*) grass, pot

mariachi [ma·'rja·tʃi] *m Méx* mariachi musician

> [i] The **mariachi**, a musical phenomenon that is truly typical of Mexico, are groups of musicians who play guitars, **vihuelas** (a 5-string guitar), trumpets, basses, and violins. They wear silver-studded outfits and stroll through the streets or go around playing from table to table in restaurants. Their songs deal with such topics as love, death, and rebellion.

marica [ma·'ri·ka] *m vulg* **1.** (*homosexual*) fag(got) **2.** (*cobarde*) sissy **3.** (*insulto grosero*) asshole

Maricastaña [ma·ri·kas·'ta·na] *f* **tiempos de** ~ *inf* years ago; **este chiste es de los tiempos de** ~ that joke is as old as the hills

maricón [ma·ri·'kon] *m vulg v.* **marica**

mariconada [ma·ri·ko·'na·da] *f vulg* **1.** (*acción malintencionada*) dirty trick; **hacer una ~ a alguien** to play a dirty trick on sb **2.** (*tontería*) dumb thing to do

marido [ma·'ri·do] *m* husband

mariguana [ma·ri·'ɣwa·na], **marihuana** [ma·ri·'wa·na] *f* marijuana, marihuana

marimacho [ma·ri·'ma·tʃo] *m inf* butch (woman)

marimandón, -ona [ma·ri·man·'don, -·'do·na] *m, f inf* battle-ax (woman)

marimba [ma·'rim·ba] *f* **1.** MÚS (*de maderas*) marimba; (*tambor*) African drum **2.** *Arg* (*paliza*) beating

marimorena [ma·ri·mo·'re·na] *f inf* rumpus; **armar la ~** to kick up a fuss; **se armó la ~** all Hell broke loose

marina [ma·'ri·na] *f* navy; **la ~ mercante** the merchant marine

marinero [ma·ri·'ne·ro] *m* sailor; **~ de agua dulce** *irón* landlubber

marinero, -a [ma·ri·'ne·ro, -a] *adj* **1.** (*relativo al mar*) marine; **buque ~** seagoing boat; **pueblo ~** coastal town; **pescado a la marinera** *fish in a sauce with tomatoes, mussels and wine* **2.** (*relativo a la marina*) marine; **nudo ~** sailor's knot

marino [ma·'ri·no] *m* sailor, seaman

marino, -a [ma·'ri·no, -a] *adj* marine

marioneta [ma·rjo·'ne·ta] *f* **1.** (*títere*) puppet, marionette **2.** *pl* (*teatro*) puppet show

mariposa [ma·ri·'po·sa] *f* ZOOL butterfly; **~ nocturna** moth ▸ **¡a otra <u>cosa</u> ~!** let's change the subject!

mariposear [ma·ri·po·se·'ar] *vi* **1.** (*ser inconstante*) to be fickle **2.** (*rondar*) **~ a alguien** to dance attendance on sb

mariquita[1] [ma·ri·'ki·ta] *f* (*insecto*) ladybug

mariquita[2] [ma·ri·'ki·ta] *m inf* fag(got)

marisabidilla [ma·ri·sa·βi·'di·ja, -ʎa] *f inf* know-all

mariscal [ma·ris·'kal] *m* marshal

marisco [ma·'ris·ko] *m* seafood

marisma [ma·'ris·ma] *f* marsh

marisquería [ma·ris·ke·'ri·a] *f* (*tienda*) seafood shop; (*restaurante*) seafood restaurant

marital [ma·ri·'tal] *adj* marital; **vida ~** married life

maritatas [ma·ri·'ta·tas] *fpl Guat, Hond* junk

marítimo, -a [ma·'ri·ti·mo, -a] *adj* maritime, marine; **ciudad marítima** seaside town; **seguro ~** marine insurance

marjal [mar·'xal] *m* fen

marmita [mar·'mi·ta] *f* pot

mármol ['mar·mol] *m* marble; **frío como el ~** as cold as stone; **de ~** of marble

marmóreo, -a [mar·'mo·reo, -a] *adj* marble(-like)

marmota [mar·'mo·ta] *f* marmot; **~ de América** groundhog

maroma [ma·'ro·ma] *f* **1.** *AmL* (*pirueta*) somersault **2.** *AmL* (*cambio de partido político*) change of political allegiance; (*de opinión*) change of opinion

maromo [ma·'ro·mo] *m inf* guy

marqués, -esa [mar·'kes, -·'ke·sa] *m, f* marquis *m*, marquise *f*

marquesina [mar·ke·'si·na] *f* (glass) canopy, marquee

marquetería [mar·ke·te·'ri·a] *f* marquetry; (*ebanistería*) cabinet-making

marrajo [ma·'rra·xo] *m* shark

marrana [ma·'rra·na] *f* (*cerda*) sow; *pey, inf* (*mujer sucia*) slut; (*vil*) despicable woman

marranada [ma·rra·'na·da] *f inf* filthiness

marrano [ma·'rra·no] *m* (*cerdo*) pig; *pey, inf* (*hombre sucio*) dirty man; (*grosero*) rude man; (*vil*) despicable man

marrano, -a [ma·'rra·no, -a] *adj* filthy

marras ['ma·rras] *adv* **tema de ~** the same old subject; **la persona de ~** the person in question; **lo de ~** the same old thing

marrón [ma·'rron] **I.** *adj* brown **II.** *m* **1.** (*color*) brown **2.** *AmC* (*martillo*) hammer

marroquí [ma·rro·'ki] *adj, mf* Moroccan

Marruecos [ma·'rrwe·kos] *m* Morocco

marrullero, -a [ma·rru·'je·ro, a-; -ʎe·ro, -a] *adj* flattering; (*con labia*) glib

Marsella [mar·'se·ja, -ʎa] *f* Marseilles

marsellés, -esa [mar·se·'jes, -'ʎes] *adj, m, f* Marseillaise

marsopa [mar·'so·pa] *f* porpoise

marsupial [mar·su·'pjal] **I.** *adj* **animal ~** marsupial **II.** *m* marsupial

mart. *abr de* **martes** Tues.

marta ['mar·ta] *f* ZOOL marten; **~ cebellina** sable

Marte ['mar·te] *m* Mars

martes ['mar·tes] *m inv* Tuesday; **~ y trece** ≈ Friday the thirteenth; *v.t.* **lunes**

martill(e)ar [mar·ti·'jar, -ʎar; mar·ti·je·'ar, -ʎe·'ar] *vt* to hammer

martilleo [mar·ti·'jeo, -ʎeo] *m* hammering

martillero [mar·ti·'je·ro, -ʎe·ro] *m Arg, Chile* auctioneer

martillo [mar·'ti·jo, -ʎo] *m* hammer; **pez ~** hammerhead; **creer algo a macha ~** to firmly believe sth; **repetir algo a macha ~** to repeat sth ad nauseam

martín [mar·'tin] *m* **~ pescador** kingfisher; **~ del río** heron

martingala [mar·tin·'ga·la] *f inf* sly trick, dodge

mártir ['mar·tir] *mf* martyr

martirio [mar·'ti·rjo] *m* REL martyrdom; *fig* torture

martirizar <z→c> [mar·ti·ri·'sar, -'θar] *vt* to torture

maruja [ma·'ru·xa] *f pey, inf* housewife (*used to refer to women whose sole interests are their homes, family, personal appearance and gossip*)

marxismo [mar·'sis·mo] *m* Marxism

marxista [mar·'sis·ta] *adj, mf* Marxist

marzo ['mar·so, -θo] *m* March; **en ~** in March; **a principios/a mediados/a fin(al)es de ~** at

M

the beginning/in the middle/at the end of March; **el 21 de** ~ the 21st of March; **el mes de ~ tiene 31 días** the month of March has 31 days; **el pasado ~ fue muy frío** last March was very cold

mas [mas] **I.** *m* manor **II.** *conj* LIT but, yet

más [mas] **I.** *adv* **1.** (*cantidad*) more; ~ **dinero/zapatos** more money/shoes **2.** (*comparativo*) more; ~ **inteligente/complicado** more intelligent/complicated; ~ **grande/pequeño** bigger/smaller; ~ **temprano/tarde** earlier/later; **correr** ~ to run more; **esto me gusta** ~ I like this better; ~ **acá** closer; ~ **adelante** (*local*) further forward [*o* on]; (*temporal*) later; **es ~ guapo que tú** he is more handsome than you; **cada día** [*o* **vez**] ~ more and more; **cuanto ~ mejor** the more the merrier; ~ **allá de esto** beyond this; ~ **de la cuenta** too much **3.** (*superlativo*) **el/la ~** the most; **la ~ bella** the most beautiful; **el ~ listo de la clase** the cleverest in the class; **lo que ~ me gusta** what I most like [*o* like most]; **lo que ~ quieras** what you most want; **lo ~ probable es que llueva** it is likely to rain; **lo ~ pronto posible** as early as possible; ~ **que nunca** more than ever; **a lo ~** at (the) most; **a ~ no poder** to the utmost; **a ~ tardar** at the latest; **todo lo ~** at most **4.** (*con numerales, cantidad*) ~ **de treinta** more than thirty; **son ~ de las diez** it is after ten **5.** (*preferencia*) ~ **quiero la muerte que la esclavitud** I prefer death to slavery **6.** (*tan*) **¡está ~ guapa!** she looks so beautiful; **¡qué tarde ~ apacible!** what a peaceful afternoon! **7.** (*con pronombre interrogativo, indefinido*) **¿algo ~?** anything else?; **no, nada ~** no, nothing else **8.** (*en frases negativas*) **no puedo ~** I have had it; **nunca ~** never again **9.** MAT plus; **tengo tres libros, ~ los que he prestado** I have three books, plus those I have lent **10.** (*a más*) **a ~ y mejor** really; **llueve a ~ y mejor** it is raining with a vengeance **11.** (*de más*) **de ~** spare, more than enough; **hay comida de ~** there is food to spare; **estar de ~** not to be needed; **de lo ~** very **12.** (*más bien*) ~ **bien** rather; **no es muy delgado; es ~ bien gordo** he is not very thin; rather he is fat **13.** (*más o menos*) ~ **o menos** (*aproximadamente*) more or less; **le va ~ o menos** he/she is doing so-so; **ni ~ ni menos** exactly **14.** (*por más que*) **por ~ que lo intento, no consigo dormirme** however hard I try, I cannot sleep ▸ **tener sus ~ y sus menos** to have one's good and one's bad points; **sin ~ acá ni ~ allá** without more ado; **el ~ allá** the beyond; **el que ~ y el que menos** every single one; **quien ~ y quien menos** everyone; **es ~ aún** what is more; **el no va ~** the last word; **el no va ~** (*de la moda*) the latest fashion; **como el que ~** as well as the next man; **sin ~ ni ~** without more ado; **¿qué ~ da?** what difference does it make? **II.** *m* MAT plus sign

masa ['ma·sa] *f* **1.** (*pasta*) mixture; (*para hor-*

near) dough; **coger a alguien con las manos en la** ~ to catch sb red-handed **2.** (*volumen, muchedumbre*) mass; ~ **monetaria** money supply; **medios de comunicación de ~s** mass media; **en ~** en masse

masacrar [ma·sa·'krar] *vt* to massacre

masacre [ma·'sa·kre] *f* massacre

masaje [ma·'sa·xe] *m* massage; **dar ~s** to massage; **darse ~s** to be massaged

masajista [ma·sa·'xis·ta] *mf* masseur *m*, masseuse *f*

masato [ma·'sa·to] *m* AmS **1.** (*mazamorra*) coconut candy **2.** (*bebida*) fermented corn or rice drink

mascada [mas·'ka·da] *f* **1.** AmL (*tabaco*) quid of chewing tobacco **2.** Col, Cuba, Chile (*bocado*) bite **3.** Méx (*pañuelo*) silk kerchief

mascar <c→qu> [mas·'kar] *vt* (*masticar*) to chew

máscara ['mas·ka·ra] *f* mask; **traje de ~** fancy dress; **quitar la ~ a alguien** *fig* to unmask sb; **quitarse la ~** *fig* to reveal oneself

mascarada [mas·ka·'ra·da] *f* **1.** (*baile*) masquerade **2.** (*farsa*) farce

mascarilla [mas·ka·'ri·ja, -ʎa] *f* **1.** (*máscara*) mask **2.** (*protección*) face mask **3.** (*cosmética*) ~ **exfoliante** face scrub; ~ **facial** face pack

mascota [mas·'ko·ta] *f* mascot; (*animal de compañía*) pet

masculinidad [mas·ku·li·ni·'dad] *f* masculinity

masculino [mas·ku·'li·no] *m* LING masculine

masculino, -a [mas·ku·'li·no, -a] *adj* **1.** (*de hombre*) masculine; **moda masculina** men's fashion **2.** LING **género ~** masculine form

mascullar [mas·ku·'jar, -ʎar] *vt* to mumble

masificación [ma·si·fi·ka·'sjon, -'θjon] *f* overcrowding

masilla [ma·'si·ja, -ʎa] *f* putty

masita [ma·'si·ta] *f* AmS CULIN small cake

masivo, -a [ma·'si·βo, -a] *adj* (*grande*) massive; (*fuerte*) strong; (*de masas*) mass

masón, -ona [ma·'son, -·'so·na] *m, f* Mason, Freemason

masoquista [ma·so·'kis·ta] *adj* masochistic

mastectomía [mas·tek·to·'mi·a] *f* mastectomy

máster <másters> ['mas·ter] *m* master's degree

masticar <c→qu> [mas·ti·'kar] *vt* to chew; (*meditar*) to ponder

mástil ['mas·til] *m* mast, spar; (*poste*) post, pole

mastín [mas·'tin] *m* mastiff

masturbación [mas·tur·βa·'sjon, -'θjon] *f* masturbation

masturbarse [mas·tur·'βar·se] *vr* to masturbate

mata ['ma·ta] *f* clump; (*arbusto*) bush

matadero [ma·ta·'de·ro] *m* slaughterhouse; **ir al ~** *fig* to put one's life in danger; **llevar al ~** *fig* to send sb to his/her death

matador(a) [ma·ta·'dor, -·'do·ra] *m(f)* TAUR

matador
matamoscas [ma·ta·'mos·kas] *m inv* (*insecticida*) fly-spray; (*objeto*) fly swatter
matanza [ma·'tan·sa, -θa] *f* 1.(*el matar*) killing; (*en batallas*) slaughter; **hacer una** ~ to massacre 2.(*carneada*) slaughter; **hacer la** ~ to slaughter an animal
matar [ma·'tar] I. *vt* 1.(*quitar la vida*) to kill; ~ **a golpes** to beat to death; ~ **a palos** to club to death; ~ **a puñaladas** to knife [*o* stab] to death; ~ **a tiros** to shoot dead; ~ **a disgustos** to be the death of 2.(*carnear*) to slaughter 3.(*saciar*) to assuage; (*hambre*) to satisfy; (*sed*) to quench 4.(*el tiempo*) to kill; (*el aburrimiento*) to alleviate II. *vr:* ~ **se** 1.(*suicidarse*) to kill oneself 2.(*aniquilarse*) **te estás matando trabajando así** you are wearing yourself out working like that 3.(*trabajar sin descanso*) ~ **se a trabajar** to work oneself to death; ~ **se por algo** to go out of one's way to do sth 4.(*por accidente*) to get killed
matarife [ma·ta·'ri·fe] *mf* butcher
matarratas [ma·ta·'rra·tas] *m inv* 1.(*raticida*) rat poison 2. *pey, inf* (*aguardiente*) firewater; (*alcohol de mala calidad*) rotgut, hooch
matasanos [ma·ta·'sa·nos] *mf inv, irón, inf* quack
matasellos [ma·ta·'se·jos, -ʎos] *m inv* postmark
matasuegras [ma·ta·'swe·ɣras] *m inv, inf* party blower
matazón [ma·ta·'son, -'θon] *m AmL* (*matanza*) massacre
match [matʃ] *m* match
mate ['ma·te] I. *adj* dull II. *m* 1.(*ajedrez*) mate; **jaque** ~ checkmate 2.(*acabado*) matte 3. *pl inf* (*matemáticas*) math 4.*AmS* (*bebida*) maté

> **i** In South America **mate** has four meanings. It can refer to the maté plant; the leaves of the maté plant, from which tea is made; the tea itself; or a container in which the tea is kept.

matemáticas [ma·te·'ma·ti·kas] *fpl* mathematics
matemático, -a [ma·te·'ma·ti·ko, -a] I. *adj* mathematical II. *m, f* mathematician
materia [ma·'te·rja] *f* 1. *t.* FÍS matter; ~ **gris** ANAT grey matter; ~ **prima** raw material 2.(*tema*) subject, matter; **en** ~ **de** in the matter of 3. *t.* ENS (*disciplina*) subject
material [ma·te·'rjal] I. *adj* (*real*) tangible; **daño** ~ physical damage; **el autor** ~ **del hecho** the actual perpetrator of the deed II. *m* material; ~ **es de construcción** building materials; ~ **de oficina** office equipment
materialismo [ma·te·rja·'lis·mo] *m* materialism
materialista [ma·te·rja·'lis·ta] *adj* materialistic
materializar <z→c> [ma·te·rja·li·'sar, -'θar]

I. *vt* to bring into being; (*realizar*) to carry out; (*hacer aparecer*) to produce II. *vr:* ~ **se** to materialize
materialmente [ma·te·rjal·'men·te] *adv* materially; **ser** ~ **posible** to be physically possible
maternal [ma·ter·'nal] *adj* maternal, motherly
maternidad [ma·ter·ni·'dad] *f* maternity; (*hospital*) maternity hospital; (*sala*) maternity ward
materno, -a [ma·'ter·no, -a] *adj* maternal; **abuelo** ~ maternal grandfather; **lengua materna** mother tongue
matero, -a [ma·'te·ro, -a] *m, f AmS* mate-drinker
matinal [ma·ti·'nal] *adj* morning; **sesión** ~ (*congreso*) morning session; CINE, TEAT matinee
matiné [ma·ti·'ne] *f* matinee
matiz [ma·'tis, -'tiθ] *m* 1.(*gradación*) shade; (*toque*) touch 2.(*sentido*) nuance
matizar <z→c> [ma·ti·'sar, -'θar] *vt* 1.(*combinar colores o tonos*) to blend; ~ **de rojo** to tinge with red 2.(*graduar*) to tint 3.(*de un sentido*) to tinge
matón, -ona [ma·'ton, --'to·na] *m, f* thug (*asesino*) murderer
matorral [ma·to·'rral] *m* thicket
matraca [ma·'tra·ka] *f* rattle, noisemaker; **dar la** ~ *inf* to pester; **ser** ~ *inf* to be a bore
matraz [ma·'tras, -'traθ] *m* flask
matrero, -a [ma·'tre·ro, -a] *adj AmS* fugitive
matrícula [ma·'tri·ku·la] *f* 1.(*documento*) registration document 2.(*inscripción*) enrollment; UNIV matriculation 3.AUTO (*placa*) license plate; **número de la** ~ license number 4.(*conjunto de alumnos*) student enrollment
matricular [ma·tri·ku·'lar] I. *vt* to register; UNIV to enroll II. *vr* ~ **se en la universidad** to enroll in the university
matrimonial [ma·tri·mo·'njal] *adj* matrimonial, marriage; **agencia** ~ dating agency; **vida** ~ married life
matrimonio [ma·tri·'mo·njo] *m* 1.(*institución*) marriage; ~ **canónico** church wedding; ~ **civil** civil wedding; **contraer** ~ to marry 2.(*marido y mujer*) married couple; **cama de** ~ double bed
matriz [ma·'tris, -'triθ] I. *f* 1.(*útero*) womb 2.(*molde*) cast 3.TIPO, MAT matrix II. *adj* **la casa** ~ **está en Sevilla** the parent company is in Seville; **lengua** ~ primal language
matrona [ma·'tro·na] *f* (*comadrona*) midwife
maturrango, -a [ma·tu·'rran·go, -a] *adj* 1.*AmS* (*mal jinete*) **ser** ~ to be a poor rider 2.*Chile* (*tosco*) clumsy
matutino, -a [ma·tu·'ti·no, -a] *adj* morning; **periódico** ~ morning paper; **sesión matutina** morning session
maula[1] ['mau·la] *mf inf* 1.(*tramposo*) cheat 2.(*inútil*) good-for-nothing
maula[2] ['mau·la] *f* 1.(*baratija*) a piece of junk 2.(*engaño*) trick
maullar [mau·'jar, -ʎar] *irr como aullar vi* to meow

M

maullido [mau·'ji·do, -Ái̯do] *m* meow
mauritano, -a [mau·ri·'ta·no, -a] *adj, m, f* Mauritanian
mausoleo [mau·so·'leo] *m* mausoleum
maxilar [mak·si·'lar] **I.** *adj* maxillary **II.** *m* jaw
máxima ['mak·si·ma] *f* maxim
máxime ['mak·si·me] *adv* particularly
máximo, -a ['mak·si·mo, -a] **I.** *adj* maximum; **rendimiento** ~ maximum output; **triunfo** ~ greatest triumph; **pon la radio al** ~ turn the radio as high as it goes **II.** *m, f* maximum; **como** ~ at most; (*temporal*) at the latest
maya[1] ['ma·ja] *f* BOT daisy
maya[2] ['ma·ja] *adj, m* Maya, Mayan; **los** ~**s** the Maya [*o* Mayas]

---

i The **Mayas** were native peoples of North and Central America and lived in what is today Mexico, Guatemala, and Honduras. The great number of Mayan ruins, such as the impressive pyramids constructed from blocks of stone, the numerous inscriptions and drawings that they left behind, and their extremely accurate calendar all bear witness to the fact that Mayan civilization was highly advanced in many fields.

---

mayestático, -a [ma·jes·'ta·ti·ko, -a] *adj* majestic; **plural** ~ the royal we
mayo ['ma·jo] *m* May; *v.t.* **marzo**
mayonesa [ma·jo·'ne·sa] *f* mayonnaise
mayor [ma·'jor] *adj* **1.** (*tamaño*) bigger; **la** ~ **parte** the majority, most; **el** ~ **barco** the largest boat; **mal** ~ greater evil; ~ **que** bigger than; **comercio al por** ~ wholesale trade **2.** (*edad*) older; ~ **que** older than; **mi hermano** ~ my older [*o* big] brother; **el** ~ **de mis hermanos** the eldest of my brothers and sisters; **ser** ~ to be grown-up; **ser** ~ **de edad** to be an adult, to be of legal age; **persona** ~ elderly person; **los** ~**es** the adults, the grown-ups; **ya es** ~ **para esos juguetes** he/she is too old for [*o* has outgrown] those toys **3.** MÚS major; **tono** ~ major key; **tercera** ~ major third; **escala en do** ~ scale of C major
mayoral [ma·jo·'ral] *m* (*capataz*) foreman
mayorcito, -a [ma·jor·'si·to, -a; -θi·to, -a] *adj inf* ¡**si ya eres** ~! what a big boy/girl you are now!
mayordomo, -a [ma·jor·'do·mo] *m, f* administrator; (*de una mansión*) butler
mayoría [ma·jo·'ri·a] *f* majority; ~ **de edad** (age of) majority; **llegar a la** ~ **de edad** to come of age; ~ **relativa** relative majority
mayorista [ma·jo·'ris·ta] **I.** *adj* wholesale; **comercio** ~ wholesale business **II.** *mf* wholesaler
mayoritariamente [ma·jo·ri·ta·rja·'men·te] *adv* mainly, preponderantly *form*
mayoritario, -a [ma·jo·ri·'ta·rjo, -a] *adj* majority; **tener el apoyo** ~ to have majority support

mayormente [ma·jor·'men·te] *adv* especially, particularly
mayúscula [ma·'jus·ku·la] *f* capital (letter); **escribirse con** ~ to be written with a capital (letter)
mayúsculo, -a [ma·'jus·ku·lo, -a] *adj* big; **letra mayúscula** capital letter
maza ['ma·sa, -θa] *f* (*porra*) club; (*para machacar*) pestle; (*percusor*) hammer
mazacote [ma·sa·'ko·te, ma·θa-] *m* **1.** (*hormigón*) concrete; **esta esponja está hecha un** ~ this sponge is rock hard **2.** *inf* (*comida*) stodgy food
mazacotudo, -a [ma·sa·ko·'tu·do, -a; ma·θa-] *adj AmL* dense
mazapán [ma·sa·'pan, ma·θa-] *m* marzipan
mazmorra [mas·'mo·rra, maθ-] *f* dungeon
mazo ['ma·so, 'ma·θo] *m* **1.** (*martillo*) mallet **2.** (*del mortero*) pestle; (*grande*) sledgehammer
mazorca [ma·'sor·ka, -'θor·ka] *f* (*del maíz*) cob; ~ **de maíz** corncob, ear of corn
me [me] **I.** *pron pers* **1.** (*objeto directo*) me; ¡**míra**~! look at me! **2.** (*objeto indirecto*) me; **da**~ **el libro** give me the book **II.** *pron reflexivo* ~ **lavo** I wash myself; ~ **voy** I am going; ~ **he comprado un piso** I have bought myself an apartment; ~ **lavo el pelo** I wash my hair
meada [me·'a·da] *f* **1.** *inf* (*pis*) pee; **echar una** ~ to take a piss **2.** (*mancha de orina*) piss; **aquí hay una** ~ **de gato** a cat took a piss here
meadero [mea·'de·ro] *m vulg* urinal
meandro [me·'an·dro] *m* (*curva*) meander
mear [me·'ar] *vi, vr:* ~**se** *inf* to piss; ~**se de risa** to die laughing
mecánica [me·'ka·ni·ka] *f* mechanics
mecánico, -a [me·'ka·ni·ko, -a] **I.** *adj* mechanical **II.** *m, f* mechanic
mecanismo [me·ka·'nis·mo] *m* mechanism; (*dispositivo*) device
mecanizar <z→c> [me·ka·ni·'sar, -'θar] *vt* to mechanize
mecanografía [me·ka·no·γra·'fi·a] *f* typewriting
mecanógrafo, -a [me·ka·'no·γra·fo, -a] *m, f* typist
mecate [me·'ka·te] *m AmC, Col, Méx, Ven* rope
mecedora [me·se·'do·ra, me·θe-] *f* rocking chair
mecenas [me·'se·nas, -'θe·nas] *mf inv* patron
mecer <c→z> [me·'ser, -'θer] **I.** *vt* (*balancear*) to rock; (*columpiar*) to swing **II.** *vr:* ~**se** (*balancearse*) to rock; (*columpiarse*) to swing
mecha ['me·tʃa] *f* **1.** (*pabilo*) wick; (*de explosivos*) fuse **2.** (*gasa*) swab **3.** (*mechón*) tuft **4.** *pl* (*mechones teñidos*) highlights *pl*, streaks *pl*; **hacerse** ~**s** to have highlights [*o* streaks] put in **5.** *inf* (*prisa*) **a toda** ~ very fast **6.** *inf* (*fastidio*) **aguantar** ~ to grin and bear it
mechero [me·'tʃe·ro] *m* (*encendedor*) lighter
mechificar <c→qu> [me·tʃi·fi·'kar] *vi AmS* to trick

mechón [me·'tʃon] *m* tuft

mechudo, -a [me·'tʃu·do, -a] *adj AmL* (*desgreñado*) unkempt

meco, -a ['me·ko, -a] *adj* 1. *Méx* (*grosero*) rude 2. *Méx* (*bermejo con negro*) blackish red; **toro** ~ blackish red bull

medalla [me·'da·ja, -ʎa] *f* medal; ~ **militar** military decoration

medallista [me·da·'jis·ta, -ʎis·ta] *mf* medal winner, medalist

medallón [me·'da·jon, -ʎon] *m* medallion

médano ['me·da·no] *m* dune; (*bajío*) sandbank

media ['me·dja] *f* 1. (*promedio*) average 2. (*calceta*) stocking; *AmL* (*calcetín*) sock

mediacaña [me·dja·'ka·ɲa] *f* bead

mediación [me·dja·'sjon, -'θjon] *f* mediation

mediado, -a [me·'dja·do, -a] *adj* (*medio lleno*) half full; (*trabajo*) half-completed; **para ~s de semana** by the middle of the week [*o* by midweek]

mediador(a) [me·dja·'dor, -'do·ra] *m(f)* mediator

mediano, -a [me·'dja·no, -a] *adj* 1. (*calidad*) average 2. (*tamaño*) medium; **talla mediana** medium

medianoche [me·dja·'no·tʃe] *f* 1. (*hora*) midnight; **a ~** at midnight 2. (*panecillo*) small soft roll

mediante [me·'djan·te] I. *adj* **Dios** ~ God willing II. *prep* by means of; (*a través de*) through

mediar [me·'djar] *vi* 1. (*intermediar*) to mediate 2. (*interceder*) ~ **por alguien** to intercede on behalf of sb

mediato, -a [me·'dja·to, -a] *adj* next but one

medicación [me·di·ka·'sjon, -'θjon] *f* medication

medicamento [me·di·ka·'men·to] *m* medicine

medicar <c→qu> [me·di·'kar] I. *vt* to medicate II. *vr:* ~ **se** to take medicine

medicina [me·di·'si·na, -'θi·na] *f* medicine; **la ~ naturista** natural remedies

medicinal [me·di·si·'nal, -θi·'nal] *adj* medicinal; **balón** ~ medicine ball; **hierba** ~ medicinal plant

medición [me·di·'sjon, -'θjon] *f* measurement

médico, -a ['me·di·ko, -a] I. *adj* medical; **cuerpo** ~ medical corps II. *m, f* doctor; **Colegio de Médicos** Medical Association; ~ **de cabecera** general practitioner; ~ **forense** forensic surgeon; ~ **naturista** homeopath

medida [me·'di·da] *f* 1. (*medición*) measurement 2. (*dimensión*) measurement; **a la ~** (*ropa*) made-to-measure; **tomar la(s) ~(s)** to take the measurement(s); **hasta cierta ~** up to a point; **en la ~ de lo posible** as far as possible; **a ~ que** as 3. (*moderación*) moderation; **con ~** with care; **sin ~** without moderation 4. (*acción*) measure; **tomar ~s** to take measures

medidor [me·di·'dor] *m* 1. (*instrumento*) gauge 2. *AmL* (*contador*) meter

medidor(a) [me·di·'dor(a)] *adj* measuring; **reloj** ~ stopwatch

medieval [me·dje·'βal] *adj* medieval

medio ['me·djo] *m* 1. (*mitad*) middle; **en ~ de** in the middle of; **meterse por** ~ to intervene; **quitar de en** ~ to get rid of; **quitarse de en** ~ to get out of the way 2. (*instrumento*) means; ~ **de transporte** means of transport; **por** ~ **de** by means of 3. PREN, RADIO, TV medium; **los ~s de comunicación** the media 4. (*entorno*) surroundings *pl;* ~ **ambiente** environment 5. *Cuba* (*moneda*) five cent coin 6. *pl* (*fuentes*) sources *pl;* (*capital*) means *pl;* **estar corto de ~s** to be hard-up

medio, -a ['me·djo, -a] I. *adj* 1. (*mitad*) half; **a las cuatro y media** at half past four; **litro y** ~ one and a half liters; **mi media naranja** *fig* my better half 2. (*promedio*) **ciudadano** ~ average person II. *adv* half; ~ **vestido** half dressed; **a** ~ **asar** half done; ~ **dormido** half asleep; **tomar a medias** to share; **ir a medias** to go halves

medioambiental [me·djo·am·bjen·'tal] *adj* environmental

mediocre [me·'djo·kre] *adj* mediocre

mediocridad [me·djo·kri·'dad] *f* mediocrity

mediodía [me·djo·'di·a] *m* midday; **al** ~ at noon

medir [me·'dir] *irr como pedir* I. *vt* 1. (*calcular*) to measure; **¿cuánto mides?** how tall are you? 2. (*sopesar*) to weigh; ~ **los riesgos** to weigh up the risks 3. (*moderar*) to moderate II. *vi* to measure III. *vr:* ~ **se** to be moderate; ~ **se con alguien** to measure oneself against sb

meditación [me·di·ta·'sjon, -'θjon] *f* meditation

meditar [me·di·'tar] *vi, vt* to meditate

mediterráneo, -a [me·di·te·'rra·neo, -a] *adj* Mediterranean; **isla mediterránea** Mediterranean island

Mediterráneo [me·di·te·'rra·neo] *m* Mediterranean

medrar [me·'drar] *vi* (*crecer*) to grow; (*avanzar*) to thrive

medroso, -a [me·'dro·so, -a] *adj* 1. *estar* frightened 2. *ser* apprehensive

médula ['me·du·la] *f* 1. ANAT marrow; ~ **espinal** spinal cord 2. (*meollo*) core; **hasta la** ~ to the core; **estar hasta la** ~ *inf* to be fed up

medusa [me·'du·sa] *f* jellyfish

megáfono [me·'ya·fo·no] *m* megaphone

megalomanía [me·ya·lo·ma·'ni·a] *f* megalomania

megalómano, -a [me·ya·'lo·ma·no, -a] *adj* megalomaniac

megavatio [me·ya·'βa·tjo] *m* megawatt

mejicano, -a [me·xi·'ka·no, -a] *adj, m, f* Mexican

Méjico ['me·xi·ko] *m* Mexico

mejilla [me·'xi·ja, -ʎa] *f* cheek; **poner la otra** ~ to turn the other cheek

mejillón [me·xi·'jon, -ʎon] *m* mussel

mejor [me·'xor] I. *adj* 1. (*compar*) better;

~ **que** better than; **es ~ que no vayas** +*subj* it is better that you don't go; **cambiar a ~ to** change for the better; **pasar a ~ vida** to pass away **2.**(*superl*) **el/la/lo ~** the best; **el ~ alumno** the best student; **la ~ nota** the best mark; **~ postor** highest bidder **II.** *adv* better; **a lo ~** maybe; **~ que ~** better still [*o* yet]; **en el ~ de los casos** at best; **~ quiero un coche viejo que una moto** I prefer to have an old car than a motorbike

mejora [me·'xo·ra] *f* improvement; **~ salarial** (pay) raise

mejorable [me·xo·'ra·βle] *adj* improvable

mejorana [me·xo·'ra·na] *f* marjoram

mejorar [me·xo·'rar] **I.** *vt* **1.**(*perfeccionar*) to improve **2.**(*superar*) to surpass; (*subasta*) to outbid **II.** *vi, vr:* **~se 1.**(*enfermo*) to get better; **¡que se mejore!** I hope you get better soon! **2.**(*tiempo*) to improve

mejoría [me·xo·'ri·a] *f* improvement

mejunje [me·'xun·xe] *m* mixture; *pey* concoction

melancolía [me·lan·ko·'li·a] *f* melancholy

melancólico, -a [me·lan·'ko·li·ko, -a] *adj* melancholic

melanina [me·la·'ni·na] *f* melanin

melanoma [me·la·'no·ma] *m* MED melanoma

melena [me·'le·na] *f* **1.**(*crin*) mane **2.**(*pelo*) long hair (*shoulder-length or longer; worn loose*); **soltarse la ~** *t. fig* to let one's hair down

melenudo, -a [me·le·'nu·do, -a] *adj* long-haired

melifluo, -a [me·'li·flwo, -a] *adj* mellifluous

melindre [me·'lin·dre] *m* **hacer ~s** to affect

melindroso, -a [me·lin·'dro·so, -a] *adj* (*afectado*) affected

melisa [me·'li·sa] *f* lemon balm

mella ['me·ja, -ʎa] *f* **hacer ~** to make an impression

mellar [me·'jar, -ʎar] *vt* (*disminuir*) to shrink

mellizo, -a [me·'ji·so, -a; -ʎi·θo, -a] *m, f* twin

melocotón [me·lo·ko·'ton] *m* peach; **anoche cogí un melocotón** *inf* (*borrachera*) I got plastered last night

melocotonero [me·lo·ko·to·'ne·ro] *m* peach tree

melodía [me·lo·'di·a] *f* melody

melódico, -a [me·'lo·di·ko, -a] *adj* melodic

melodrama [me·lo·'dra·ma] *m* melodrama

melodramático, -a [me·lo·dra·'ma·ti·ko, -a] *adj* melodramatic

melómano, -a [me·'lo·ma·no, -a] *m, f* music lover

melón [me·'lon] *m* melon; *inf* (*cabeza*) noggin

melón, -ona [me·'lon, -ona] *m, f inf* loony

melopea [me·lo·'pea] *f inf* drunkenness

meloso, -a [me·'lo·so, -a] *adj* sweet

membrana [mem·'bra·na] *f* membrane; **~ mucosa** mucous membrane

membresía [mem·bre·'sia] *f* membership

membrete [mem·'bre·te] *m* letterhead

membrillo [mem·'bri·jo, -ʎo] *m* (*árbol*) quince

tree; (*fruto*) quince; **carne** [*o* **dulce**] **de ~** quince jelly

memela [me·'me·la] *f Méx* CULIN thin corn tortilla

memo, -a ['me·mo, -a] *adj* idiotic

memorable [me·mo·'ra·βle] *adj* memorable

memorándum [me·mo·'ran·dun] *m* <memorandos> memorandum

memoria [me·'mo·rja] *f* **1.**(*facultad, recuerdo*) memory; **a la** [*o* **en**] **~ de** in memory of; **de ~** by heart; **flaco de ~** forgetful; **hacer ~** to try and remember; **traer a la ~** to bring to mind; **venir a la ~** to come to mind **2.**(*informe*) report **3.** COMPUT memory **4.** *pl* (*autobiografía*) autobiography

memorizar <z→c> [me·mo·ri·'sar, -'θar] *vt* to memorize

menaje [me·'na·xe] *m* household furnishings *pl;* **~ de cocina** kitchen utensils

mención [men·'sjon, -'θjon] *f* mention; **digno de ~** worth mentioning; **hacer ~ de** to mention

mencionar [men·sjo·'nar, -θjo·'nar] *vt* to mention

menda ['men·da] **I.** *pron pers, inf* yours truly; **aquí el** [*o* **este**] **~ no dijo nada** yours truly didn't say anything **II.** *pron indef, inf* **un ~ a** guy

mendicidad [men·di·si·'dad, -θi·'dad] *f* begging; **vivir de la ~** to live by begging

mendigar <g→gu> [men·di·'ɣar] *vi, vt* **~ algo** to beg for sth

mendigo, -a [men·'di·ɣo, -a] *m, f* beggar

mendrugo [men·'dru·ɣo] *m* (*trozo de pan*) crust

menear [me·ne·'ar] **I.** *vt* to move; (*cabeza*) to shake; **~ la cola** to wag one's tail **II.** *vr:* **~se** to move; *inf* (*apresurarse*) to get a move on

meneo [me·'neo] *m* **1.**(*brusco*) jolt **2.** *inf* (*vapuleo*) beating; **dar un ~ a alguien** to give sb a beating

menester [me·nes·'ter] *m* **1.**(*necesidad*) need; **ser ~** to be necessary; **haber ~ de algo** to need sth **2.** *pl* (*tareas*) jobs *pl*

menesteroso, -a [me·nes·te·'ro·so, -a] *adj* needy

menestra [me·'nes·tra] *f* vegetable stew

mengano, -a [men·'ga·no, -a] *m, f* **fulano y ~** so-and-so

mengua ['men·gwa] *f* **1.**(*disminución*) decrease; **sin ~ de** without a diminishing of; JUR without detriment to **2.**(*carencia*) lack; **sin ~** sufficient

menguante [men·'gwan·te] *f* **1.**(*marea*) ebb; (*estiaje*) low water level **2.**(*mengua*) decrease

menguar <gu→gü> [men·'gwar] **I.** *vi* to diminish **II.** *vt* to decrease; (*punto*) to reduce

meninge [me·'nin·xe] *f* ANAT meninx, meninges *pl;* **me estrujé las ~s** *inf* I racked my brains

meningitis [me·nin·'xi·tis] *f inv* MED meningitis

menisco [me·'nis·ko] *m* ANAT meniscus

menopausia [me·no·'pau·sja] *f* MED menopause, change of life

menor [me·'nor] **I.** adj **1.** (tamaño) smaller; ~ que smaller than; (número) smaller; **al por** ~ COM retail; **no dar la ~ importancia a algo** not to give sth the least importance; **Asia Menor** Asia Minor **2.** (edad) younger; ~ **que** younger than; ~ **de edad** underage; **el ~ de mis hermanos** the youngest of my brothers **3.** MÚS minor; **tono** ~ minor key; **tercera ~** minor third **II.** mf (persona) minor; **no apto para ~es** not suitable for children

Menorca [me·'nor·ka] f Minorca

menorista [me·no·'ris·ta] **I.** adj Chile, Méx retail **II.** mf Chile, Méx (minorista) retailer

menos ['me·nos] **I.** adv **1.** (contrario de más) less; **a ~ que** unless; **el/la ~** the least; **el coche (el)** ~ **caro** the least expensive car; **eso es lo de ~** that is the least important thing; **lo ~** the least; **al** [o **por lo**] ~ at least; **aún ~** even less; **cuanto ~...** (tanto) **más** the less... the more; **de ~** short; **echar de ~** to miss; **en ~ de nada** in no time; **ir a ~** to decrease; ~ **de 20 personas** fewer than 20 people; ~ **de una hora** less than an hour; ~ **mal** thank goodness; **¡ni mucho ~!** not at all!; **son las ocho ~ diez** it's ten minutes to eight; **cada vez ~ tiempo/casos** less and less time/fewer and fewer cases **2.** MAT minus **3.** (excepto) **todo ~ eso** anything but that **II.** m MAT minus

menoscabo [me·nos·'ka·βo] m **1.** (disminución) decrease **2.** (daño) impairment; fig damage; **sufrir ~** to suffer damage

menospreciable [me·nos·pre·'sja·βle, -'θja·βle] adj despicable

menospreciar [me·nos·pre·'sjar, -'θjar] vt to underrate; (subestimar) to underestimate

menosprecio [me·nos·'pre·sjo, -θjo] m underrating; (subestimación) underestimate

mensaje [men·'sa·xe] m message; ~ **de error** COMPUT error message; ~ (**de**) **radio** radio communication; ~ **de socorro** SOS message

mensajería [men·sa·xe·'ri·a] f messenger [o courier] service

mensajero, -a [men·sa·'xe·ro, -a] **I.** adj messenger; **paloma mensajera** messenger [o carrier] pigeon **II.** m, f messenger

menso, -a ['men·so, -a] adj Méx (necio) stupid

menstruación [mens·trwa·'sjon, -'θjon] f menstruation

menstruar <1. pres: **menstrúo**> [mens·tru·'ar] vi to menstruate

mensual [men·su·'al] adj monthly; **revista ~** monthly (magazine)

mensualidad [men·swa·li·'dad] f **1.** (sueldo) monthly salary **2.** (paga) monthly payment; (compra aplazada) monthly installment; ~ **del alquiler** month's rent

menta ['men·ta] f mint; (infusión) mint tea; (extracto) menthol; **caramelo de ~** mint

mental [men·'tal] adj mental; **cálculo ~** mental arithmetic

mentalidad [men·ta·li·'dad] f mentality

mentalizar <z→c> [men·ta·li·'sar, -'θar] **I.** vt

(preparar) to prepare (mentally); (concienciar) to make aware; ~ **a alguien de algo** to make sb aware of sth **II.** vr: ~ **se** (prepararse) to prepare oneself (mentally); (concienciarse) to make oneself aware

mentar <e→ie> [men·'tar] vt to mention

mente ['men·te] f **1.** (pensamiento) mind; **tener en** (**la**) ~ to have in mind; **quitarse algo de la** ~ to get sth out of one's head; **tengo la ~ en blanco** my mind is a complete blank; **traer a la** ~ to bring to mind **2.** (intelecto) intellect

mentecato, -a [men·te·'ka·to, -a] **I.** adj silly **II.** m, f fool

mentir [men·'tir] irr como sentir vi to lie; **miente más que habla** he/she is a compulsive liar; **¡miento!** I tell a lie!, I am wrong!

mentira [men·'ti·ra] f lie; ~ **piadosa** white lie; **¡parece ~!** I can hardly believe it!

mentiroso, -a [men·ti·'ro·so, -a] **I.** adj (persona) lying **II.** m, f liar

mentís [men·'tis] m inv denial; **dar un ~ a algo** to deny sth

mentol [men·'tol] m menthol

mentón [men·'ton] m chin

mentor [men·'tor] m mentor

menú [me·'nu] m <menús> t. COMPUT menu; ~ **de navegación** navigation menu

menudear [me·nu·de·'ar] vt ~ **sus visitas** to make frequent visits

menudencia [me·nu·'den·sja, -θja] f (pequeñez) trifle; (meticulosidad) meticulousness

menudillos [me·nu·'di·jos, -ʎos] mpl giblets pl

menudo, -a [me·'nu·do, -a] adj minuscule; (pequeño y delgado) slight; (fútil) futile; **¡menuda película!** what a film!; **¡~ lío has armado!** what a fuss you have created! ▶ **a ~** often

meñique [me·'ɲi·ke] m little finger, pinky

meollo [me·'o·jo, -ʎo] m **1.** (sesos) brains pl **2.** (médula) marrow **3.** (fundamento) essence, crux

mequetrefe [me·ke·'tre·fe] m inf good-for-nothing

meramente [me·ra·'men·te] adv merely

mercachifle [mer·ka·'tʃi·fle] m pey **1.** (comerciante) hawker **2.** (avaro) moneygrubber

mercader [mer·ka·'der] m merchant; ~ **de grueso** wholesaler

mercadería [mer·ka·de·'ri·a] f merchandise

mercadillo [mer·ka·'di·jo, -ʎo] m street market, flea market

mercado [mer·'ka·do] m market; ~ **de capitales** investment market; ~ **de divisas** foreign exchange market; ~ **exterior/interior** overseas/domestic market; **el ~ de Madrid** the Madrid market; ~ **alcista/bajista** bull/bear market; ~ **de trabajo** labor market; ~ **único europeo** European Single Market; ~ **de valores** securities market; **hay ~ los sábados** there is a market on Saturdays

mercancía [mer·kan·'si·a, -'θi·a] f goods pl;

M

tren de ~s goods [*o* freight] train
mercante [mer·'kan·te] **I.** *adj* mercantile
II. *mf* merchantman
mercantil [mer·kan·'til] *adj* mercantile
merced [mer·'sed, -'θed] *f* mercy; **~ a** thanks
to; **estar a ~ de alguien** to be at sb's mercy
mercenario, -a [mer·se·'na·rjo, -a; mer·θe·]
adj, m, f mercenary
mercería [mer·se·'ri·a, mer·θe·] *f* notions *pl;*
(*tienda*) notions store

---

i In 1991, **Mercosur** (**Mercado Común
del Sur**, or Common Market of the South)
was created by Argentina, Brazil, Paraguay,
and Uruguay. This free-trade zone (or customs union) was designed to strengthen the
economies of the member countries and lead
to a united policy of democracy. The bloc has
since granted associate member status to
Chile (in 1996), Bolivia (in 1997), and Peru
(in 2001), and Venezuela has just recently
become a full member (in 2005).

---

mercurio [mer·'ku·rjo] *m* mercury
Mercurio [mer·'ku·rjo] *m* Mercury
merecedor(a) [me·re·se·'dor, -'do·ra; me·re·
θe·] *adj* deserving; **hacerse ~ de algo** to earn
sth
merecer [me·re·'ser, -'θer] *irr como crecer* **I.** *vt*
to deserve; (*valer*) to be worthy of; **merece
respeto de nuestra parte** he/she deserves
our respect; **este libro merece mención** this
book deserves a mention; **no merece la pena**
it is not worth it **II.** *vr:* **~se** to deserve
merecido [me·re·'si·do, -'θi·do] *m* deserts *pl;*
se llevó su ~ he/she got his/her just deserts
merendar <e→ie> [me·ren·'dar] **I.** *vt* to have
for tea, to have for an afternoon snack **II.** *vi* to
have tea, to have an afternoon snack; (*en el
campo*) to picnic **III.** *vr:* **~se** *inf* to wangle;
~se a alguien to get the better of sb
merendero [me·ren·'de·ro] *m* picnic area
merengue [me·'ren·ge] *m* **1.** (*dulce*) meringue **2.** *CSur, inf* (*lío*) mess
meridiano [me·ri·'dja·no] *m* meridian
meridiana, -a [me·ri·'dja·no, -a] *adj* midday
meridional [me·ri·djo·'nal] *adj* south; **Andalucía está en la España ~** Andalusia is in
southern Spain
merienda [me·'rjen·da] *f* **1.** (*comida por la
tarde*) tea, afternoon snack **2.** (*picnic*) picnic;
ir de ~ to go for a picnic; **~ de negros** *fig* free-
for-all
mérito ['me·ri·to] *m* merit; (*valor*) worth;
hacer ~s to prove oneself worthy; **de ~** (*obra*)
excellent; (*persona*) worthy
merlo ['mer·lo] *m AmL* ZOOL wrasse
merluza [mer·'lu·sa, -θa] *f* **1.** ZOOL hake **2.** *inf*
(*borrachera*) **coger una buena ~** to get
sloshed
merluzo, -a [mer·'lu·so, -a; -θo, -a] *adj inf* silly

merma ['mer·ma] *f* decrease; **~ de peso** loss of
weight
mermar [mer·'mar] *vt* to lessen; (*sueldo*) to
cut; **~ peso** to reduce weight
mermelada [mer·me·'la·da] *f* jam; **~ de naranja** marmalade
mero ['me·ro] **I.** *adv* **1.** *AmC, Méx* (*pronto*)
soon **2.** *Méx* (*muy*) very **3.** *Méx* (*precisamente*) precisely **II.** *m* **1.** ZOOL grouper **2.** *Méx*
(*jefe*) boss
mero, -a ['me·ro, -a] *adj* **1.** (*sencillo*) simple
2. (*sin nada más*) mere; **la mera verdad** the
plain truth **3.** *Méx* (*preciso*) precise **4.** *Méx*
(*propio*) own
merodear [me·ro·de·'ar] *vi* to prowl; **~ por un
sitio** to hang about a place
merolico, -a [me·ro·'li·ko, -a] *m, f Méx*
1. (*vendedor charlatán*) quack **2.** (*persona
charlatana*) chatterer
mes [mes] *m* month; **a principios/a me-
diados/a fin(al)es de ~** at the beginning/in
the middle/at the end of the month; **5.000
pesos al ~** 5,000 pesos a month; **todos los
~es** every month; **el ~ corriente** this month;
el ~ que viene next month; **el ~ pasado** last
month; **hace un ~** a month ago; **con un ~ de
anticipo** a month's salary in advance; **~ (de
trabajo)** (*sueldo*) monthly salary; **tengo el ~**
inf I have my period
mesa ['me·sa] *f* **1.** (*mueble*) table; **~ de despacho** office desk; **~ de tertulia** coffee table;
vino de ~ table wine; **bendecir la ~** to say
grace; **poner la ~** to lay [*o* set] the table; **quitar la ~** to clear the table; **en la ~** (*comiendo*)
at the table; **¡a la ~!** food's ready!; **servir una
~** to serve a table; **tener a alguien a ~ y a
mantel** to give sb free board; **vivir** [*o* estar] **a
~ puesta** to live a life of leisure **2.** POL **~ electoral** *officials in charge of a polling station*
3. (*pensión*) board; **~ y cama** board and lodging
mesero, -a [me·'se·ro, -a] *m, f Méx*
(*camarero*) waiter *m,* waitress *f*
meseta [me·'se·ta] *f* GEO plateau
Mesías [me·'si·as] *m* Messiah
mesilla [me·'si·ja, -ʎa] *f* small table; **~ de
noche** nightstand
mesón [me·'son] *m* inn, tavern
mesonero, -a [me·so·'ne·ro, -a] *m, f* inn-
keeper
mestizo, -a [mes·'ti·so, -a; -θo, -a] **I.** *adj*
1. (*entre blancos e indios*) mestizo **2.** (*entre
dos razas*) mixed-race **II.** *m, f* **1.** (*entre blancos e indios*) mestizo **2.** (*entre dos razas*) person of mixed race
mesura [me·'su·ra] *f* **1.** (*moderación*) moderation **2.** (*cortesía*) courtesy, civility **3.** (*calma*)
calm
meta¹ ['me·ta] *f t. fig* winning post; (*portería*)
goal; **la ~ de su vida** his/her aim in life;
fijarse una ~ to set oneself a goal
meta² ['me·ta] *mf* (*portero*) goaltender
metabolismo [me·ta·βo·'lis·mo] *m* metabo-

lism

metadona [me·ta·'do·na] *f* methadone

metafísica [me·ta·'fi·si·ka] *f* FILOS metaphysics

metafísico, -a [me·ta·'fi·si·ko, -a] *adj* metaphysical

metáfora [me·'ta·fo·ra] *f* metaphor

metafórico, -a [me·ta·'fo·ri·ko, -a] *adj* metaphorical

metal [me·'tal] *m* metal; ~ **noble** precious metal; ~ **pesado** heavy metal; **el vil ~** (*dinero*) filthy lucre

metálico [me·'ta·li·ko] *m* **en ~** in cash; **premio en ~** cash prize

metálico, -a [me·'ta·li·ko, -a] *adj* metallic; **tela metálica** (metal) screening

metalurgia [me·ta·'lur·xja] *f* metallurgy

metalúrgico, -a [me·ta·'lur·xi·ko, -a] *adj* metallurgical; **industria metalúrgica** metallurgical industry

metamorfosear [me·ta·mor·fo·se·'ar] **I.** *vt* to transform **II.** *vr:* ~**se** to metamorphose

metamorfosis [me·ta·mor·'fo·sis] *f inv* metamorphosis; (*en una persona*) transformation

metano [me·'ta·no] *m* methane

metástasis [me·'tas·ta·sis] *f inv* MED metastasis

metedura [me·te·'du·ra] *f* **¡vaya ~ de pata!** *inf* what a blooper

metelón, -ona [me·te·'lon, -·'lo·na] *adj Méx* meddling

meteórico, -a [me·te·'o·ri·ko, -a] *adj* (*rápido*) meteoric

meteorito [me·teo·'ri·to] *m* meteorite

meteorología [me·teo·ro·lo·'xi·a] *f* meteorology

meteorológico, -a [me·teo·ro·'lo·xi·ko, -a] *adj* meteorological; **informe ~** weather forecast; **estación meteorológica** weather station

meteorólogo, -a [me·teo·'ro·lo·yo, -a] *m, f* meteorologist

meter [me·'ter] **I.** *vt* **1.** (*introducir*) to insert; (*poner*) to put; ~ **en una caja** to put in a box; **¡mete el enchufe!** put the plug in!; ~ **un clavo en la pared** to hammer a nail into the wall; ~ **a alguien en la cárcel** to put sb in jail; ~ **un gol** DEP to score a goal; ~ **dinero en el banco** to put money in the bank **2.** *inf* (*encasquetar*) to palm off; (*vender*) to sell; (*enjaretar*) to foist; **nos metió una película aburridísima** he/she foisted a really boring film on us; **le metieron tres meses de cárcel** they gave him/her three months in jail **3.** *inf* (*pegar*) ~ **un puñetazo a alguien** to punch sb **4.** (*provocar*) ~ **miedo/un susto a alguien** to frighten/startle sb; ~ **prisa a alguien** to hurry sb (up) **5.** (*hacer participar*) to involve; ~ **a toda la familia en el asunto** to involve the whole family in the matter **6.** (*emplear*) to employ; ~ **a alguien a fregar platos** to put sb to work washing dishes; ~ **a una chica de peluquera** to put a girl to work as a hairdresser ▶ **a todo ~** *inf* as fast as possible **II.** *vr:* ~**se 1.** (*introducirse*) to put; ~**se el dedo en la nariz** to stick one's finger in one's nose; **se le**

ha metido en la cabeza que... he/she has gotten it into his/her head that... **2.** (*entrar en un lugar*) to enter; **lo vi ~se en un cine** I saw him go into a cinema; ~**se entre la gente** to mingle with the people; **se metió en el armario** he/she got into the wardrobe; **¿dónde se habrá metido?** where has he/she gotten to? **3.** (*entrar indebidamente*) to enter unlawfully **4.** (*inmiscuirse*) to meddle; **¡no te metas donde no te llaman!** mind your own business! **5.** (*provocar*) ~**se con alguien** to provoke sb **6.** (*comenzar un oficio*) ~**se a monja** to become a nun; ~**se a actor** to become an actor

metiche [me·'ti·tʃe] *adj Méx* (*entrometido*) meddlesome

meticuloso, -a [me·ti·ku·'lo·so, -a] *adj* meticulous

metida [me·'ti·da] *f inf* **dar una ~ a algo** to give sth a boost; **¡vaya ~ de pata!** *AmL, inf* what a blooper!

metido, -a [me·'ti·do, -a] *adj* **estar ~ en un negocio** to be involved in a business; **está muy ~ con esa chica** *inf* he hooked on that girl; ~ **en carnes** chubby; ~ **en años** elderly; **la llave está metida** the key is in

metl [metl] *m Méx* agave

metódico, -a [me·'to·di·ko, -a] *adj* methodical

metodismo [me·to·'dis·mo] *m* Methodism

metodista [me·to·'dis·ta] *adj, mf* Methodist

método ['me·to·do] *m* method; **proceder con ~** to proceed methodically; **un ~ de guitarra** (*libro*) a guitar manual

metodología [me·to·do·lo·'xi·a] *f* methodology

metomentodo [me·to·men·'to·do] *mf inv, inf* nosy parker; **ser un ~** to be a real busybody

metraje [me·'tra·xe] *m* length; **película de largo ~** feature-length film; **película de corto ~** short (film)

metralla [me·'tra·ja, -ʎa] *f* **1.** (*munición*) shell; **fuego de ~** shellfire **2.** (*trozos*) shrapnel

metralleta [me·tra·'je·ta, -ʎeta] *f* submachine gun, Tommy gun

métrica ['me·tri·ka] *f* LIT metrics

métrico, -a ['me·tri·ko, -a] *adj* metric

metro ['me·tro] *m* **1.** (*unidad*) meter; ~ **cuadrado** square meter; ~ **cúbico** cubic meter **2.** (*para medir*) ruler; ~ **de cinta** tape measure; ~ **plegable** folding ruler **3.** FERRO subway

metrópoli [me·'tro·po·li] *f* (*urbe*) metropolis; (*capital*) capital

metropolitano [me·tro·po·li·'ta·no] *m* subway

metropolitano, -a [me·tro·po·li·'ta·no, -a] *adj* (*de la capital*) metropolitan; (*de la urbe*) city

mexicano, -a [me·xi·'ka·no, -a] *adj, m, f v.* **mejicano**

México ['me·xi·ko] *m* Mexico

> **i** | **México**, or **Méjico**, (formally named **Estados Unidos Mexicanos**) is located in North America and borders on the United States in the north. The capital, **Ciudad de**

M

México (Mexico City), has almost twenty million inhabitants. The country's official language is Spanish and the official currency is the **peso**. The original inhabitants of Mexico, the **aztecas** (Aztecs), referred to themselves as **Mexica**.

mezcal [mes·'kal, meθ-] *m Méx* BOT mescal
mezcla ['mes·kla, 'meθ-] *f* mixture; ~ **de carburantes** blend of fuel; ~ **explosiva** *t. fig* explosive mixture; **sin** ~ (*tela*) pure
mezclar [mes·'klar, meθ-] **I.** *vt* **1.** (*unir*) to blend; CULIN (*añadir*) to mix **2.** (*revolver*) to muddle; (*confundir*) to mix up **3.** (*involucrar*) to involve **II.** *vr:* ~**se 1.** (*inmiscuirse*) to meddle; ~**se entre los espectadores** to mingle with the spectators; ~**se con gente de mucho dinero** to mix with wealthy people **2.** (*revolverse*) to mix
mezcolanza [mes·ko·'lan·sa, meθ·ko·'lan·θa] *f pey* hodgepodge
mezquindad [mes·kin·'dad, meθ-] *f* **1.** (*tacañería*) stinginess **2.** (*acto vil*) meanness
mezquino, -a [mes·'ki·no, -a; meθ-] **I.** *adj* **1.** (*tacaño*) stingy **2.** (*innoble*) ignoble; (*miserable*) small-minded **II.** *m, f* miser
mezquita [mes·'ki·ta; meθ-] *f* mosque
mg. *abr de* **miligramo** mg
mi [mi] **I.** *adj* (*antepuesto*) my; ~ **amigo/casa** my friend/house; ~**s amigos** my friends **II.** *m inv* MÚS E; ~ **mayor** E major; ~ **menor** E minor
mí [mi] *pron pers* me; **a** ~ (*objeto directo*) me; (*objeto indirecto*) to me; **para** ~ for me; **¿y a** ~ **qué?** so what?; **para** ~ (**que**)... I think (that)...; **por** ~ as far as I'm concerned; **por** ~ **mismo** by myself; **¡a** ~ **con esas!** don't give me that!; **¡a** ~ **!** (*¡socorro!*) on help!
miaja ['mja·xa] *f* crumb
miau [mjau] meow
mica ['mi·ka] *f AmC, inf* drunkenness
micción [mik·'sjon, -'θjon] *f* urination
miche ['mi·tʃe] *m* **1.** *CRi* (*pendencia*) brawl **2.** *Chile* (*juego*) game of marbles
michelín [mi·tʃe·'lin] *m inf* (*pliegue de grasa*) spare tire
mico ['mi·ko] *m* **1.** ZOOL long-tailed monkey **2.** *inf* (*persona fea*) hideous person ► **dar** ~ **a alguien** *inf* (*dejar plantado*) to stand sb up; **dar el** ~ **a alguien** *inf* (*engañar*) to take sb in; **quedarse hecho un** ~ *inf* (*avergonzado*) to be ashamed; **volverse** ~ **para hacer algo** *inf* to go mad [*o* crazy] trying to do sth
micro ['mi·kro] *m* (*micrófono*) mike
microbio [mi·'kro·βjo] *m* microbe
microbús [mi·kro·'βus] *m* minibus
microchip [mi·kro·'tʃip] *m* microchip
microficha [mi·kro·'fi·tʃa] *f* microfiche
microfilm [mi·kro·'film] *m* <microfilm(e)s> microfilm
microfilmar [mi·kro·fil·'mar] *vt* to microfilm

micrófono [mi·'kro·fo·no] *m* microphone
microonda [mi·kro·'on·da/mi·'kron·da] *f t.* FÍS (*cocina*) microwave; **horno** (**de**) ~**s** microwave (oven)
microorganismo [mi·kro·or·ɣa·'nis·mo] *m* micro-organism
microscópico, -a [mi·kros·'ko·pi·ko, -a] *adj* microscopic
microscopio [mi·kros·'ko·pjo] *m* microscope; ~ **de 60 aumentos** microscope with x60 magnification; ~ **electrónico** electron microscope
microtenis [mi·kro·'te·nis] *m inv, AmL* table tennis
miedo ['mje·do] *m* fear; **por** ~ **a** [*o* **de**] for fear of; **por** ~ **de que** +*subj* for fear that; **meter** ~ **a alguien** to frighten sb; **dar** ~ to be frightening; **morirse de** ~ to be petrified; **de** ~ *inf* (*maravilloso*) terrific; **el concierto estuvo de** ~ the concert was terrific; **hace un frío de** ~ *inf* (*terrible*) it is dreadfully cold ► **al que mal vive, el** ~ **le sigue** *prov* ≈ those who act badly always live in fear
miedoso, -a [mje·'do·so, -a] *adj ser* fearful
miel [mjel] *f* honey; ~ **blanca** bees' honey; **luna de** ~ honeymoon; **quedarse con la** ~ **en los labios** to be left wanting more; **hacerse de** ~ to go all sugary ► **no hay** ~ **sin hiel** *prov* there is no rose without a thorn; ~ **sobre hojuelas** even better; **hazte de** ~ **y te comerán las moscas** *prov* ≈ if you are too good people will take advantage of you
miembro ['mjem·bro] *m* **1.** *pl* (*extremidades*) limbs *pl* **2.** (*pene*) ~ (**viril**) male member **3.** *t.* LING, MAT (*socio*) member; **no** ~ non-member; ~ **de pleno derecho** full member; **hacerse** ~ **de** to join
mientras ['mjen·tras] **I.** *adv* meanwhile; ~ (**tanto**) in the meantime **II.** *conj* ~ (**que**) while; ~ (**que**) +*subj* as long as; ~ **se ríe no se llora** you cannot laugh and cry at the same time; ~ **más le dan más pide el niño** the more the child gets, the more he/she wants
miérc. *abr de* **miércoles** Wed.
miércoles ['mjer·koles] *m inv* Wednesday; ~ **de ceniza** Ash Wednesday; ~ **santo** Easter Wednesday; *v.t.* **lunes**
mierda ['mjer·da] *f vulg* shit; (*porquería*) muck; **¡** ~ **!** shit!; **¡una** ~ **!** like hell!; **¡a la** ~ **!** to hell with it!; **¡(vete) a la** ~ **!** get lost!; **¡eso te importa una** ~ **!** you don't give a damn about that!; **mandar a alguien a la** ~ to tell sb to go to hell; **¿qué** ~ **ocurre?** what the hell is going on?; **irse a la** ~ to go to the dogs; **no comerse ni** (**una**) ~ to get absolutely nowhere; **el maestro nuevo es una** ~ the new teacher is lousy; **¡2.000 pesos, una** ~ **!** 2,000 pesos, that's peanuts!; **es una** ~ **de coche** the car is a piece of junk; **no valer una** ~ to be a load of crap; **cubrirse de** ~ to discredit oneself
mies [mjes] *f* **1.** (*cereal maduro*) (ripe) corn **2.** (*temporada*) harvest (time) **3.** *pl* (*campos*) cornfields *pl*
miga ['mi·ɣa] *f* bread (*not the crust*); (*trocito*)

crumb; **hacer buenas/malas ~s con al-guien** to get on well/badly with sb; **hacer ~s a alguien** to leave sb in a sorry state; **estar hecho ~** (*cansado*) to be shattered; **hacer ~s** to destroy; **esto tiene su ~** (*esencia*) there is something to this

migaja [mi·'ɣa·xa] *f* 1.(*trocito*) crumb; **una ~ de algo** a scrap of sth 2. *pl* (*sobras*) leftovers *pl*

migración [mi·ɣra·'sjon, -'θjon] *f* ZOOL migration

migraña [mi·'ɣra·ɲa] *f* migraine

mijo ['mi·xo] *m* millet

mil [mil] I. *adj inv* thousand; **dos ~ millones** two billion; **ya se lo he dicho ~ veces** I have already told him/her hundreds of times II. *m* thousand; **~es** thousands; **a ~es** by the thousand; **~es y ~es** thousands and thousands; **varios ~es de dólares** several thousand dollars; **a las ~** (**y quinientas**) very late; **pasar las ~ y una** to be a huge amount

milagro [mi·'la·ɣro] *m* miracle; **hacer ~s** to work wonders; **contar la vida y ~s de al-guien** to tell all the gory details about sb's life; **esta vez se escapó de ~** this time he/she had a lucky escape; **si sales de ésta, solo saldrás de ~** if you get out of this, it will be a miracle

milagroso, -a [mi·la·'ɣro·so, -a] *adj* miraculous; (*maravilloso*) marvelous

Milán [mi·'lan] *m* Milan

milanesa [mi·la·'ne·sa] *f* breaded escalope

milenario, -a [mi·le·'na·rjo, -a] *adj* millennial

milenio [mi·'le·njo] *m* millennium

milenrama [mi·len·'rra·ma] *f* yarrow

mili ['mi·li] *f inf* military service; **ir a** [*o* **hacer**] **la ~** to do military service; **tener mucha ~** *inf* to be an old hand

milibar [mi·li·'βar] *m* FÍS millibar

milicia [mi·'li·sja, -θja] *f* military; **~ nacional** (*ciudadanos*) militia

miligramo [mi·li·'ɣra·mo] *m* milligram

mililitro [mi·li·'li·tro] *m* milliliter

milímetro [mi·'li·me·tro] *m* millimeter

militante [mi·li·'tan·te] *adj* militant

militar [mi·li·'tar] I. *vi* 1.(*cumplir el servicio*) to serve 2.(*en un partido*) to be an active member of; **~ en favor de/contra algo** to campaign for/against sth II. *adj* military; **los altos mandos ~es** the military high command III. *m* soldier

milla ['mi·ja, -ʎa] *f* mile; **~ marina** nautical mile

millar [mi·'jar, -ʎar] *m* thousand; **protestaron a ~es** they protested by the thousands

millo ['mi·jo, -ʎo] *m AmC, Méx* type of millet

millón [mi·'jon, -'ʎon] *m* million; **mil millones** a billion; **cuatro millones de habitantes** four million inhabitants

millonada [mi·jo·'na·da, mi·ʎo-] *f inf* fortune

millonario, -a [mi·jo·'na·rjo, -a; mi·ʎo-] *m, f* millionaire

milonga [mi·'lon·ga] *f* 1.MÚS popular dance 2. *And, CSur* (*fiesta*) party 3. *And, CSur, inf*

(*trola, mentira*) tall story

milpa ['mil·pa] *f AmL* 1.(*campo*) cornfield 2.(*planta*) corn

milpiés [mil·'pjes] *m inv* millipede

mimar [mi·'mar] *vt* to indulge; (*excesivamente*) to spoil

mimbre ['mim·bre] *m* wicker; **muebles de ~** wicker furniture

mimbrera [mim·'bre·ra] *f* osier; (*sauce*) willow

mimeografiar <*1. pres:* mimeografío> [mi·meo·ɣra·fi·'ar] *vt AmL* to mimeograph

mimeógrafo [mi·me·'o·ɣra·fo] *m AmL* mimeograph

mímica ['mi·mi·ka] *f* 1.(*facial*) mime 2.(*señas*) sign language 3.(*ademanes*) gesticulation

mímico, -a ['mi·mi·ko, -a] *adj* imitative; TEAT mimetic

mimo ['mi·mo] *m* 1.(*actor*) mimic; **hacer ~ de alguien** to mimic sb 2.(*caricia*) caress; (*condescendencia*) spoiling; **necesitar mucho ~** to need a lot of affection; **le dan demasiado ~** they spoil him/her; **realizo mi trabajo con ~** I carry out my work with love

mimosa [mi·'mo·sa] *f* mimosa

mimoso, -a [mi·'mo·so, -a] *adj* 1.(*mimado*) spoiled 2. *ser* (*cariñoso*) affectionate 3. *estar* (*apegado*) clinging

mina ['mi·na] *f* 1.MIN mine; **~ de carbón** coal mine; **este negocio es una ~** this business is a gold mine 2.(*explosivo*) mine; **~ de mar** underwater mine; **~ de tierra** landmine 3.(*de lápiz*) lead

minar [mi·'nar] I. *vt* 1.(*excavar, colocar minas*) to mine 2.(*debilitar*) to undermine II. *vr:* **~se** *inf* (*hartarse*) to become fed up

minarete [mi·na·'re·te] *m* minaret

mineral [mi·ne·'ral] I. *adj* mineral; **agua ~** mineral water II. *m* GEO mineral

mineralogía [mi·ne·ra·lo·'xi·a] *f* mineralogy

minería [mi·ne·'ri·a] *f* mining

minero, -a [mi·'ne·ro, -a] *m, f* miner

minga ['min·ga] I. *interj RíoPl, inf* no way!, like hell! II. *f And* communal work

mingaco [min·'ga·ko] *m Chile: communal work done by neighbors*

miniatura [mi·nja·'tu·ra] *f* miniature

minibús [mi·ni·'βus] *m* minibus

minifalda [mi·ni·'fal·da] *f* miniskirt

minifundio [mi·ni·'fun·djo] *m* smallholding

minifundista [mi·ni·'fun·dis·ta] *mf* smallholder

minigolf [mi·ni·'ɣolf] *m* miniature golf

minimizar <z→c> [mi·ni·mi·'sar, -'θar] *vt* to minimize

mínimo ['mi·ni·mo] *m* minimum; **un ~ de respeto** a minimum of respect; **como ~** (*cantidad*) as a minimum; **como ~ podrías llamar por teléfono** you could at least phone; **reducir al ~** to reduce to the bare minimum

mínimo, -a ['mi·ni·mo, -a] *adj superl de* **pequeño** minimum; **cifra mínima** minimum

M

figure; **la mínima obligación posible** the slightest obligation possible; **sin el más ~ ruido** without the least noise; **no ayudar en lo más ~** to be no help at all

minino, -a [mi·'ni·no, -a] *m, f inf* pussy [*o* kitty] (cat)

miniserie [mi·ni·'se·rje] *f* miniseries

ministerio [mi·nis·'te·rjo] *m* **1.** (*cartera, edificio*) ministry **2.** (*cargo*) ministerial office

ministro, -a [mi·'nis·tro, -a] *m, f* minister; **primera ministra** prime minister; **~ sin cartera** minister without portfolio; **Ministro de Economía y Hacienda** Treasury Secretary; **Ministro de Educación y Ciencia** Education Secretary; **Ministro del Interior** Secretary of the Interior

minivacaciones [mi·ni·βa·ka·'sjo·nes, -'θjo·nes] *fpl* short break

minoría [mi·no·'ri·a] *f* minority; **~ de edad** minority

minoridad [mi·no·ri·'dad] *f* minority

minorista [mi·no·'ris·ta] **I.** *adj* retail **II.** *mf* retailer

minoritario, -a [mi·no·ri·'ta·rjo, -a] *adj* minority

minucia [mi·'nu·sja, -θja] *f* trifle

minuciosidad [mi·nu·sjo·si·'dad, mi·nu·θjo-] *f* meticulousness

minucioso, -a [mi·nu·'sjo·so, -a; -θjo·so, -a] *adj* meticulous

minúscula [mi·'nus·ku·la] *f* LING lower case; **en ~s** in lower case [*o* small] letters; **escribirse con ~** to be written in lower case

minúsculo, -a [mi·'nus·ku·lo, -a] *adj* minuscule, minute; **letra minúscula** lower-case [*o* small] letter

minusvalía [mi·nus·βa·'li·a] *f* **1.** (*física*) handicap, disability **2.** COM capital loss

minusválido, -a [mi·nus·'βa·li·do, -a] **I.** *adj* handicapped **II.** *m, f* handicapped person

minusvalorar [mi·nus·βa·lo·'rar] *vt* to undervalue

minuta [mi·'nu·ta] *f* (*cuenta*) lawyer's bill

minutero [mi·nu·'te·ro] *m* minute hand

minuto [mi·'nu·to] *m* minute; **sin perder un ~** at once; **vuelvo en un ~** I will be right back [*o* back in a minute]

mío, -a ['mi·o, -a] *pron pos* **1.** (*de mi propiedad*) mine; **la botella es mía** the bottle is mine; **¡ya es ~!** I have it! **2.** (*tras artículo*) **el ~/la mía** mine; **los ~s** (*cosas*) mine; (*parientes*) my family; **ésta es la mía** *inf* this is just what I want; **he vuelto a hacer una de las mías** I have been up to it again; **eso es lo ~** that is my strong point **3.** (*tras sustantivo*) of mine; **una amiga mía** a friend of mine; **¡amor ~!** my darling!; (**no**) **es culpa mía** it is (not) my fault

miocardio [mjo·'kar·djo] *m* ANAT myocardium

mioma [mi·'o·ma] *m* MED myoma

miope [mi·'o·pe] **I.** *adj* myopic, short-sighted **II.** *mf* short-sighted person

miopía [mjo·'pi·a] *f* myopia, short-sightedness

mira ['mi·ra] *f* **1.** MIL watchtower; **estar en la ~ de alguien** to be in sb's sights **2.** (*mirada*) gaze; **con amplias ~s** broad-minded; **de ~s estrechas** narrow-minded; **con ~s a** with a view to **3.** (*pl*) (*intención*) intention; **con ~s desinteresadas** disinterestedly

mirada [mi·'ra·da] *f* look; **~ perdida** faraway look; **devorar con la ~** to gaze hungrily at; **echar una ~ a algo** to glance at sth; **levantar la ~** to look up; **apartar la ~** to look away; **volver la ~ atrás** to look back

mirado, -a [mi·'ra·do, -a] *adj* **estar bien/mal ~** (*persona*) to be well/badly thought of; **está mal ~ ir sin regalo** it is not the done thing to go without a present; **bien ~,...** all things considering [*o* considered],...

mirador [mi·ra·'dor] *m* (*atalaya*) viewpoint

miramiento [mi·ra·'mjen·to] *m* **1.** (*consideración*) consideration; **tener ~ con alguien** to have[*o* show] consideration for sb; **sin ~** inconsiderately; **andar con ~s** to tread carefully; **sin ~s de** without considering **2.** (*cuidado*) discretion; **sin ~** indiscreetly

mirar [mi·'rar] **I.** *vt* **1.** (*observar*) to observe; (*ver*) to look at; **~ fijamente a alguien** to stare at sb; **~ algo por encima** to give sth a quick look (over) **2.** (*buscar*) to look for **3.** (*prestar atención*) to watch; **¡mira el bolso!** keep an eye on the bag!; **¡pero mira lo que estás haciendo!** but look what you are doing! **4.** (*meditar*) to think about; **mirándolo bien/bien mirado** taking everything into consideration **5.** (*tener en cuenta*) to take into account; **~ el dinero** to be careful of the money **6.** (*estimar*) **~ bien/mal** to have a good/poor opinion of; **~ con buena/mala cara** to approve/disapprove of **II.** *vi* **1.** (*dirigir la vista*) to look; **~ por la ventana** to look out of the window; **~ por un agujero** to look through a hole; **~ atrás** to look back; **~ alrededor** to look around **2.** (*buscar*) to look for; **siempre miramos por nuestros hijos** we always look out for our children **3.** (*dar*) **la casa mira al este** the house faces east; **la ventana mira al mar** the window overlooks the sea **4.** (*de aviso, exclamativo*) **¡mira! ya llega** look! here he/she/it comes; **mira, mira, déjate de tonterías** that is enough, stop being silly; **¡pues, mira por donde...!** surprise, surprise...!; **mire, ya se lo he explicado tres veces** look, I have already explained it to you three times **5.** (*tener en cuenta*) **mira que si se cae este jarrón** just imagine if the vase fell **6.** (*mira que*) **mira que es tonta, ¿eh?** she really is silly, isn't she? ► **ser de mírame y no me toques** to be very delicate **III.** *vr:* **~se** (*verse*) to look at oneself; **~se a los ojos** to look into another's eyes; **~se en el espejo** to look at oneself in the mirror

mirilla [mi·'ri·ja, -ʎa] *f* (*en la puerta*) peephole; FOTO viewer

miriñaque [mi·ri·'ɲa·ke] *m* CSur FERRO cowcatcher

mirlo ['mir·lo] *m* blackbird; **achantar el ~** *inf* to hold one's tongue

mirón, -ona [mi·'ron, -ona] *m*, *f* **1.** (*espectador curioso*) onlooker; *pey* (*de intimidades*) snoop; (*voyeur*) peeping Tom **2.** COMPUT lurker

mirra ['mi·rra] *f* myrrh

misa ['mi·sa] *f* mass; **~ de difuntos** requiem mass; **~ del gallo** midnight mass; **ir a ~** to go to mass; **cantar ~** to sing mass; **decir ~** to say mass ▸**no saber de la ~ la media** [*o* la **mitad**] *inf* not to know the half [*o* the first thing] of it; **no se puede estar en ~ y repicando** you can't be in two places at once; **eso va a ~** *inf* and that's a fact

miscelánea [mi·se·'la·nea, mis·θe-] *f* miscellany

miserable [mi·se·'ra·βle] *adj* **1.** (*pobre*) poor **2.** (*lamentable*) pitiful **3.** (*tacaño*) stingy **4.** (*poco, mísero*) miserable; **un sueldo ~** a miserable wage

miseria [mi·'se·rja] *f* **1.** (*pobreza*) poverty; **caer en la ~** to become impoverished; **vivir en la ~** to live in poverty **2.** (*poco dinero*) pittance

misericordia [mi·se·ri·'kor·dja] *f* **1.** (*compasión*) compassion **2.** (*perdón*) forgiveness

misericordioso, -a [mi·se·ri·kor·'djo·so, -a] *adj* **1.** (*que siente*) compassionate **2.** (*que perdona*) forgiving

mísero, -a ['mi·se·ro, -a] *adj v.* **miserable**

misil [mi·'sil] *m* missile; **~ antiaéreo** anti-aircraft missile

misión [mi·'sjon] *f* mission

misionero, -a [mi·sjo·'ne·ro, -a] *m*, *f* missionary

mismo ['mis·mo] *adv* **1.** (*incluso*) even; **me duele sentado ~** it hurts me even when I am sitting down **2.** (*manera*) **así ~** in that way **3.** (*justamente*) **ahí ~** just there; **aquí ~** right here; **ayer ~** only yesterday; **nos podemos ver el miércoles ~** we could meet on Wednesday, say

mismo, -a ['mis·mo, -a] *adj* **1.** (*idéntico*) **el/lo ~/la misma** the same; **al ~ tiempo** at the same time; **da lo ~** it does not matter; **por lo ~** for that reason; **lo ~ José como** [*o* que] **María** both José and María; **lo ~ no vienen** they might not come; **quedamos** [*o* seguimos] **en las mismas** we are where we were **2.** (*semejante*) **el ~/la misma/lo ~** the same; **llevar la misma falda** to wear an identical skirt **3.** (*reflexivo*) myself; **te perjudicas a ti ~** you harm yourself; **yo misma lo vi** I myself saw him/it; **lo hizo por sí misma** she did it (all) by herself; **lo podemos hacer nosotros ~s** we can do it ourselves **4.** (*precisamente*) **este ~ perro fue el que me mordió** that very dog was the one that bit me; **¡eso ~!** exactly! **5.** (*hasta*) actual; **el ~ embajador asistió a la fiesta** the ambassador himself attended the party

misterio [mis·'te·rjo] *m* mystery; **obrar con ~** to act mysteriously

misterioso, -a [mis·te·'rjo·so, -a] *adj* mysterious

mística ['mis·ti·ka] *f* mysticism

místico, -a ['mis·ti·ko] *adj* mystical

mistificar <c→qu> [mis·ti·fi·'kar] *vt* **1.** (*burlarse*) to hoax **2.** (*falsear*) to misrepresent

mistol [mis·'tol] *m* Arg, Par BOT jujube tree

mitad [mi·'tad] *f* **1.** (*parte igual*) half; **~ hombre ~ bestia** half man, half beast; **a ~ de precio** at half price; **mezcla harina y agua, ~ y ~** mix flour and water, half and half [*o* in equal amounts]; **reducir a la ~** to halve **2.** (*medio*) middle; **en ~ del bosque** in the middle of the forest; **cortar por la ~** to cut in half

mítico, -a ['mi·ti·ko, -a] *adj* mythical, mythological

mitigar <g→gu> [mi·ti·'γar] **I.** *vt* **1.** (*dolores*) to alleviate; (*sed*) to quench; (*hambre*) to take the edge off; (*temperamento*) to pacify; **~ la inquietud de alguien** to put sb's mind at rest **2.** (*colores, luz*) to subdue; (*calor*) to mitigate **II.** *vr:* **~se 1.** (*dolores*) to lessen **2.** (*color, luz*) to become subdued

mitin ['mi·tin] *m* political meeting, rally

mito ['mi·to] *m* myth

mitología [mi·to·lo·'xi·a] *f* mythology

mitológico, -a [mi·to·'lo·xi·ko, -a] *adj* mythological

mitote [mi·'to·te] *m* Méx **1.** (*jaleo*) uproar; (*caos*) riot **2.** (*danza*) ritual Aztec dance

mixto, -a ['mis·to, -a] *adj* mixed

mixtura [mis·'tu·ra] *f* mixture

ml. [mi·li·'li·tro] *abr de* **mililitro** ml

mm. *abr de* **milímetro** mm

mobiliario [mo·βi·'lja·rjo] *m* furniture

moca ['mo·ka] *m* **1.** (*café*) mocha **2.** Ecua (*ciénaga*) quagmire

mocasín [mo·ka·'sin] *m* moccasin

mocedad [mo·se·'dad, mo·θe-] *f* youth

mocetón, -ona [mo·se·'ton, -·'to·na; mo·θe-] *m*, *f* (*chico*) strapping lad; (*chica*) big girl

mochales [mo·'tʃa·les] *adj inv*, *inf* **estar ~** to be crazy

mochila [mo·'tʃi·la] *f* backpack

mochilero, -a [mo·tʃi·'le·ro, -a] *m*, *f* backpacker; **ir de mochilera** to go backpacking

mocho, -a ['mo·tʃo] *adj* AmL (*mutilado*) mutilated

mochuelo [mo·'tʃwe·lo] *m* small owl; **cargar a alguien con el ~** *inf* to stick sb with the dirty work; **cada ~ a su olivo** *fig* to each his own

moción [mo·'sjon, -·'θjon] *f t.* POL motion; **presentar una ~ de censura** to put forward a censure motion

moco ['mo·ko] *m* **1.** (*materia*) mucus; (*de la nariz*) snot; **limpiarse los ~s** to wipe one's nose **2.** (*del pavo*) wattle; **no es ~ de pavo** *fig* it's nothing to sneeze [*o* sniff] at **3.** (*de una mecha*) snuff; **a ~ de candil** by candlelight ▸**llorar a ~ tendido** *inf* to cry one's eyes out

mocoso, -a [mo·'ko·so, -a] *m*, *f pey* brat

moda ['mo·da] *f* fashion; **vestido/peinado de**

~ fashionable dress/hairstyle; **estar de** ~ to be fashionable; **ponerse/pasar de** ~ to come into/go out of fashion; **ir a la (última)** ~ to follow the (latest) fashion

modal [mo'·dal] **I.** *adj* modal **II.** *mpl* manners *pl;* ~ **es de la mesa** table manners; **¡qué** ~ **es son estos!** what manners are these!

modalidad [mo·da·li·'dad] *f* form; ~ **es de un contrato** types of contract

modelar [mo·de·'lar] *vt* to model; *fig* to fashion

modelo [mo·'de·lo] *mf* **1.** (*de modas*) model **2.** ARTE, FOTO model; ~ **vivo** live model

modelo [mo·'de·lo] *m* **1.** (*ejemplo*) model; **un político** ~ a model politician; **hacer algo según el** ~ to do sth according to the model **2.** (*esquema*) design

módem ['mo·dem] *m* COMPUT modem

moderación [mo·de·ra·'sjon, -'θjon] *f* moderation; **comer con** ~ to eat in moderation

moderado, -a [mo·de·'ra·do, -a] *adj* (*propuesta, persona, velocidad*) moderate; (*precio, petición*) reasonable; (*castigo*) light

moderador(a) [mo·de·ra·'dor] *m(f)* TV, RADIO moderator

moderar [mo·de·'rar] **I.** *vt* **1.** (*disminuir*) to moderate **2.** TV, RADIO to present; (*debate*) to chair **II.** *vr:* ~ **se** to calm down

modernismo [mo·der·'nis·mo] *m* modernism

modernización [mo·der·ni·sa·'sjon, -θa·'θjon] *f* modernization

modernizar <z→c> [mo·der·ni·'sar, -'θar] **I.** *vt* to modernize **II.** *vr:* ~ **se** to modernize oneself, to come up to date

moderno, -a [mo·'der·no, -a] *adj* modern; **edad moderna** present day; **historia moderna** modern history

modestia [mo·'des·tja] *f* modesty; ~ **aparte** modesty apart [*o* aside]; **vestir con** ~ to dress discreetly

modesto, -a [mo·'des·to, -a] *adj* modest

módico, -a ['mo·di·ko, -a] *adj* modest

modificación [mo·di·fi·ka·'sjon, -'θjon] *f* (*de plan*) modification; (*de tema*) alteration; LING qualification

modificar <c→qu> [mo·di·fi·'kar] **I.** *vt* (*plan*) to modify; (*texto*) to revise; (*tema*) to alter; LING to qualify **II.** *vr:* ~ **se** to adapt

modismo [mo·'dis·mo] *m* idiom

modista [mo·'dis·ta] *mf* dressmaker

modisto [mo·'dis·to] *m* fashion designer

modo ['mo·do] *m* **1.** (*manera*) way; ~ **de andar/hablar/pensar** way of walking/talking/thinking; **hazlo a tu** ~ do it your way; **de este** ~ in this way; **de ningún** ~ no way; **hacer algo de cualquier** ~ to do sth any old how; **encontrar un** ~ **de resolver el problema** to find a way to solve the problem; **de cualquier** ~ **no hubieran ido** anyway they would not have gone; **de** ~ **que lo has conseguido** so you have managed it; **utilizar el paraguas a** ~ **de espada** to use the umbrella as a sword; **en cierto** ~ in a way; **de un** ~ **u**

otro one way or another; **de todos** ~ **s no hubo heridos** at any rate no one was injured; **de todos** ~ **s, lo volvería a intentar** anyway, I would try again; **de todos** ~ **s es mejor que te vayas** in spite of everything it would be better for you to go **2.** LING mood **3.** COMPUT mode; ~ **de operación** operational mode **4.** *pl* (*comportamiento*) manners *pl;* **tener buenos/malos** ~ **s** to have good/bad manners; **decir algo con buenos/malos** ~ **s** to say sth politely/rudely

modorra [mo·'do·rra] *f* drowsiness

modorro, -a [mo·'do·rro, -a] *adj* (*somnoliento*) drowsy

modoso, -a [mo·'do·so, -a] *adj* **ser** [*o* **estar**] ~ to be well-mannered

modular [mo·du·'lar] *vi, vt* to modulate

módulo ['mo·du·lo] *m* **1.** *t.* ARQUIT, ELEC (*de un mueble*) unit **2.** (*de una prisión*) wing **3.** ENS, COMPUT module **4.** AVIAT ~ **de mando** command module

mofa ['mo·fa] *f* mockery; **hacer** ~ **de algo** to scoff at sth

mofar [mo·'far] *vi, vr* ~ **se de algo/alguien** to scoff at sth/sb

mofeta [mo·'fe·ta] *f* ZOOL skunk

moflete [mo·'fle·te] *m* chubby cheek

mofletudo, -a [mo·fle·'tu·do, -a] *adj* chubby-cheeked

mogolla [mo·'yo·ja, -ʎa] *m Col* CULIN dark wholegrain bread

mogollón [mo·yo·'jon, -'ʎon] *m inf* **1.** (*cantidad*) load(s); **había** ~ **de público en el pabellón** there were masses of spectators in the pavilion **2.** (*lío*) mess

mohín [mo·'in] *m* face; **hacer un** ~ **gracioso** to pull a funny face

mohíno, -a [mo·'i·no, -a] *adj* **1.** (*enfadado*) sulky; (*de mal humor*) grumpy **2.** (*triste*) glum

moho ['mo(o)] *m* mold; **no (dejar) criar** ~ (*alimentos*) to be eaten immediately; (*un objeto*) to be in constant use

mohoso, -a [mo·'o·so, -a] *adj* moldy

mojama [mo·'xa·ma] *f* salted dried tuna

mojar [mo·'xar] **I.** *vt* to wet; (*ligeramente*) to moisten; (*para planchar*) to dampen; (*el pan*) to dunk **II.** *vi inf* (*en un asunto*) to get involved **III.** *vr:* ~ **se 1.** (*con un líquido*) to get wet **2.** *inf* (*comprometerse*) to get involved

mojarra [mo·'xa·rra] *f Arg* short broad knife

mojigato, -a [mo·xi·'ya·to, -a] *adj* (*gazmoño*) prudish; (*hipócrita*) hypocritical

mojón [mo·'xon] *m* boundary stone; ~ **kilométrico** milestone

mol [mol] *m* mole

molar [mo·'lar] **I.** *adj* **1.** (*de muela*) **diente** ~ molar **2.** (*de moler*) grinding **II.** *m* molar **III.** *vi inf* **1.** (*gustar*) **este libro mola** this book is really cool; **me molan las rubias** I am into [*o* I go for] blonds **2.** (*llevarse*) to be in; **ahora mola llevar pelo corto** nowadays short hair is in

Moldavia [mol·'da·βja] *f* Moldavia

moldavo, -a [mol·'da·βo] *adj, m, f* Moldavian
molde ['mol·de] *m* TÉC, CULIN mold; TIPO form;
pan de ~ sliced bread; **letras de** ~ block letters; **romper ~s** to break the mold
moldear [mol·de·'ar] *vt* to mold; **diversas
circunstancias han moldeado su vida** various circumstances have shaped his/her life
moldura [mol·'du·ra] *f* 1.(*listón*) trim
2. ARQUIT molding
mole¹ ['mo·le] *f* (*masa*) mass
mole² ['mo·le] *m Méx* CULIN 1.(*salsa*) sauce;
~ **verde** green sauce 2.(*guiso*) stew

> **i** **Mole** is the name given to a Mexican chili
> sauce. Cayenne pepper from the chili plant
> gives this sauce its characteristic spicy taste.

molécula [mo·'le·ku·la] *f* molecule
molecular [mo·le·ku·'lar] *adj* molecular;
biología ~ molecular biology
moler <o→ue> [mo·'ler] *vt* 1.(*café, trigo*) to
grind; (*aceitunas*) to press 2.(*fatigar*) to exhaust; **estoy molido de la excursión** the trip
has exhausted me
molestar [mo·les·'tar] I. *vt* (*estorbar*) to inconvenience; (*fastidiar*) to bother; (*dolores*) to
hurt; (*enfadar*) to annoy; **esta camisa me
molesta** this shirt annoys me II. *vr:* ~**se**
1.(*tomarse la molestia*) to bother; **ni siquiera
te has molestado en comprobarlo** you
didn't even bother check it; **no te molestes
por mí** don't mind me; **no tendrías que
haberte molestado** you shouldn't have bothered 2.(*ofenderse*) to take offense; **se ha
molestado por tu comentario** he/she has
taken offense at what you said
molestia [mo·'les·tja] *f* 1.(*fastidio*) bother;
(*por dolores*) discomfort; **ser una** ~ to be a
nuisance; **no es ninguna** ~ it doesn't bother
me 2.(*inconveniente*) trouble; **no es ninguna** ~ (**para mí**) it is no trouble (for me);
tomarse la ~ to take the trouble; **perdonen
las ~s** we apologize for the inconvenience
caused
molesto, -a [mo·'les·to, -a] *adj* 1.*ser* (*desagradable*) unpleasant; (*fastidioso*) troublesome 2.*estar* (*enfadado*) ~ **por algo** annoyed
about sth; (*ofendido*) hurt by sth 3.*estar*
(*incómodo*) uncomfortable
molicie [mo·'li·sje, -θje] *f* **vivir en la** ~ to live
a life of luxury
molido, -a [mo·'li·do, -a] *adj inf* (*cansado*)
estoy ~ I am worn out
molinero, -a [mo·li·'ne·ro, -a] *m, f* miller
molinete [mo·li·'ne·te] *m* (*juguete*) pinwheel
molinillo [mo·li·'ni·jo, -ʎo] *m* ~ **de café** coffee
grinder
molino [mo·'li·no] *m* mill; ~ **de papel** paper
mill
mollejas [mo·'je·xas, -'ʎe·xas] *fpl* sweet-
breads *pl*
mollera [mo·'je·ra, -'ʎe·ra] *f* (*fontanela*) fonta-

nel; (*seso*) brain; **tener la** ~ **cerrada** *fig* to be
old enough to reason; **eso no me entra en la**
~ I just don't get it; **ser duro de** ~ to be stubborn
mollete [mo·'je·te, -'ʎe·te] *m* 1.(*pan*) muffin
2. *Bol* CULIN *bread made quickly and poorly*
molo ['mo·lo] *m Chile* (*rompeolas*) breakwater; (*dique*) seawall
molón, -ona [mo·'lon, -'lo·na] *adj inf* cool;
Guat, Ecua, Méx tiresome
molusco [mo·'lus·ko] *m* mollusk
momentáneo, -a [mo·men·'ta·neo, -a] *adj*
1.(*instantáneo*) momentary 2.(*provisional*)
provisional; **hacer un arreglo** ~ to find a provisional solution 3.(*temporal*) temporary
momento [mo·'men·to] *m* 1.(*instante*) instant, moment; **¡espera un** ~! wait a moment!; **de un** ~ **a otro** at any time now; **al** ~
immediately; **en cualquier** [*o* **en todo**] ~ at
any time; **en el** ~ **adecuado** at the appropriate
time; **en este** ~ **estaba pensando en ti** I was
just thinking about you; **de** ~, **no te puedo
decir nada** for the moment, I can't tell you
anything; **de** ~ **leeré el periódico y luego...**
for the time being I'll read the newspaper and
then...; **de** [*o* **por el**] ~ **no sé nada de él** for
the moment I haven't heard from him; **en un**
~ **de flaqueza** in a moment of weakness; **la
tensión aumentaba por ~s** the tension was
growing ever stronger [*o* stronger and
stronger]; **aparecer en el último** ~ to arrive at
the last moment; **en todo** ~ **mantuvo la
calma** at all times he/she remained calm; **no
tengo un** ~ **libre** I do not have one free moment; **hace un** ~ **que ha salido** he/she left a
moment ago; **a cada** ~ all the time 2.(*período*) period; **atravieso un mal** ~ I am going
through a bad patch 3.(*actualidad*) present;
la música del ~ present-day music
momia ['mo·mja] *f* mummy
momificar <c→qu> [mo·mi·fi·'kar] *vt* to
mummify
momio, -a ['mo·mjo, -a] *adj* lean
mona ['mo·na] *f* 1. ZOOL female monkey; (*especie*) Barbary ape 2. *inf* (*borrachera*) drunken
state; **coger una** ~ to get drunk; **estar como
una** ~ to be drunk; **dormir la** ~ to sleep off a
hangover ▶ **aunque la** ~ **se vista de seda,**
se queda *prov* you can't make a silk purse
from a sow's ear; **vete a freír ~s** *inf* go jump in
the lake; **estar hecho una** ~ to feel mortified
Mónaco ['mo·na·ko] *m* Monaco
monada [mo·'na·da] *f* **es una** ~ **de chica** that
girl is a beauty; **¡qué** ~ **de vestido!** what a gorgeous dress!; **este bebé es una** ~ this baby is
a cute little thing
monaguillo, -a [mo·na·'γi·jo, -a; -ʎo, -a] *m, f*
altar boy
monarca [mo·'nar·ka] *mf* monarch
monarquía [mo·nar·'ki·a] *f* monarchy
monárquico, -a [mo·'nar·ki·ko, -a] *adj* 1.(*de
la monarquía*) monarchic 2.(*partidario*) monarchist

M

monasterio [mo·nas·'te·rjo] *m* monastery
monda ['mon·da] *f* **1.** (*acción*) peeling **2.** (*peladura*) peel ► **ser la** ~ *inf* to be terrific
mondadientes [mon·da·'djen·tes] *m inv* toothpick
mondadura [mon·da·'du·ra] *f* **1.** (*acción*) peeling **2.** *pl* (*peladuras*) peelings *pl*
mondar [mon·'dar] I. *vt* **1.** (*plátano, patata, palo*) to peel; (*guisantes*) to shell; (*rama*) to pare **2.** (*árbol*) to prune II. *vr:* ~ **se** to peel; ~ **se los dientes** to clean one's teeth with a toothpick; ~ **se** (**de risa**) *inf* to die laughing
mondo, -a ['mon·do, -a] *adj* (*cabeza*) shaven; **quedarse** ~ (**y lirondo**) *inf* (*de dinero*) to be broke ► ~ **y lirondo** *inf* plain, pure and simple
mondongo [mon·'don·go] *m* entrails *pl*, innards *pl*
moneda [mo·'ne·da] *f* **1.** (*pieza*) coin; ~ **de cinco peniques** five pence coin; ~ **de 5/10/ 25 centavos** nickel/dime/quarter; ~ **suelta** change; **teléfono de** ~**s** pay phone; **pagar a alguien con la misma** ~ *fig* to pay sb back tit for tat; **la otra cara de la** ~ the other side of the coin; **esto es** ~ **corriente** *fig* that is the norm **2.** (*de un país*) currency; ~ **base** base currency; ~ **de curso legal** legal tender; ~ **extranjera** foreign currency; ~ **fuerte/ débil** strong/weak currency; ~ **nacional** local currency; ~ **única europea** European single currency
monedero [mo·ne·'de·ro] *m* purse; ~ **falso** (*persona*) counterfeiter
monegasco, -a [mo·ne·'yas·ko, -a] *adj* of/ from Monaco
monería [mo·ne·'ri·a] *f* (*gracia*) antics *pl*
monetario, -a [mo·ne·'ta·rjo] *adj* monetary; **institución monetaria** monetary institution; **tormentas monetarias** monetary turmoil
mongólico, -a [mon·'go·li·ko, -a] *adj* MED of Down syndrome; **ser un** ~ to have Down syndrome
mongolismo [mon·go·'lis·mo] *m* MED Down's syndrome
monigote [mo·ni·'yo·te] *m* **hacer** ~**s** (*figuras humanas*) to draw stick figures; (*borrones*) to doodle
monitor [mo·ni·'tor] *m* TÉC, TV, COMPUT monitor; (*pantalla*) screen
monitor(a) [mo·ni·'tor(a)] *m(f)* (*de un deporte*) coach, trainer; (*de un campamento*) camp leader; ~ **de natación** swimming instructor
monitorio, -a [mo·ni·'to·rjo] *adj* admonitory; **carta monitoria** admonitory letter
monja ['mon·xa] *f* nun, sister
monje ['mon·xe] *m* monk, brother
mono ['mo·no] *m* **1.** ZOOL monkey; **¿tengo** ~**s en la cara?** *inf* what are you staring at?; **en esta casa soy el último** ~ in this house I am a nobody **2.** (*traje*) overalls *pl*; (*de mecánico*) coveralls *pl*; (*de calle*) jumpsuit **3.** *inf* (*de drogas*) withdrawal symptoms *pl*; **tener el** ~ to be suffering from withdrawal symptoms

mono, -a ['mo·no, -a] *adj* **1.** (*niño*) cute; (*chico/a*) good-locking; (*vestido*) lovely **2.** *Col, inf* (*rubio*) blonde
monóculo [mo·'no·ku·lo] *m* monocle
monocultivo [mo·no·kul·'ti·βo] *m* monoculture
monogamia [mo·no·'ya·mja] *f* monogamy
monógamo, -a [mo·'no·ya·mo, -a] *adj* monogamous
monografía [mo·no·yra·'fi·a] *f* monograph
monograma [mo·no·'yra·ma] *m* monogram
monolingüe [mo·no·'lin·gwe] *adj* monolingual
monólogo [mo·'no·lo·yo] *m* monologue; TEAT soliloquy
monopatín [mo·no·pa·'tin] *m* skateboard
monopolio [mo·no·'po·ljo] *m* monopoly
monopolizar <z→c> [mo·no·po·li·'sar, -'θar] *vt* COM to monopolize, to corner (a market); ~ **la atención de alguien** to monopolize sb's attention
monosílabo [mo·no·'si·la·βo] *m* monosyllable; **responder con** ~**s** to answer in monosyllables
monosílabo, -a [mo·no·'si·la·βo, -a] *adj* monosyllabic
monotonía [mo·no·to·'ni·a] *f* monotony
monótono, -a [mo·'no·to·no, -a] *adj* monotonous
monóxido [mo·'nok·si·do, -a] *m* monoxide
monseñor [mon·se·'ɲor] *m* monsignor
monstruo ['mons·trwo] I. *m* monster; (*persona fea*) hideous person; (*persona perversa*) fiend; (*artista*) superstar II. *adj inv* **una actuación** ~ a magnificent performance
monstruosidad [mons·trwo·si·'dad] *f* monstrosity; **eso que dices es una** ~ what you are saying is a monstrosity
monstruoso, -a [mons·tru·'o·so, -a] *adj* (*desfigurado*) disfigured; (*terrible*) monstrous; (*enorme*) huge
monta ['mon·ta] *f* **de poca** ~ unimportant
montacargas [mon·ta·'kar·yas] *m inv* (freight) elevator
montador(a) [mon·ta·'dor] *m(f)* **1.** TÉC (*de máquinas*) fitter, assembler **2.** CINE editor
montaje [mon·'ta·xe] *m* **1.** TÉC assembly; CINE editing; FOTO montage; TEAT decor **2.** (*engaño*) set-up
montante [mon·'tan·te] *m* **1.** (*importe*) total **2.** (*de puerta*) jamb; (*de ventana*) mullion
montaña [mon·'ta·ɲa] *f* (*monte*) mountain; (*zona*) mountains *pl*; ~ **rusa** big dipper; **la fe mueve** ~**s** faith will move mountains ► **hacer una** ~ **de un grano de arena** to make a mountain out of a molehill; **grande como una** ~ as big as a house
montañero, -a [mon·ta·'ɲe·ro, -a] *m, f* mountaineer
montañés, -esa [mon·ta·'ɲes, --'ɲe·sa] *adj* highlander
montañismo [mon·ta·'ɲis·mo] *m* mountaineering

montañoso, -a [mon·ta·'ɲo·so, -a] *adj* mountainous

montar [mon·'tar] **I.** *vi* **1.** (*subir a una bici, un caballo*) to get on; (*en un coche*) to get in; ~ **en** (*una bici, un caballo*) to get onto; (*en un coche*) to get into **2.** (*ir a caballo*) to ride; ~ **en bici** to ride a bicycle **II.** *vt* **1.** (*subir en un caballo*) to mount; **no montes al niño en el alféizar** don't sit the lad on the windowsill **2.** (*ir a caballo*) to ride **3.** (*acaballar, cubrir*) to cover **4.** (*máquina*) to assemble; (*tienda*) to open **5.** (*clara de huevo*) to beat; (*nata*) to whip **6.** (*casa*) to furnish **7.** (*negocio*) to set up **8.** *inf* (*lío*) ~**la** to kick up a fuss; ~ **un número** to make a scene **III.** *vr:* ~**se 1.** (*subir*) to climb; **no te montes ahí** no don't climb up there **2.** *inf* (*arreglárselas*) **¿cómo te lo montas con el trabajo?** how do you manage with the work?

monte ['mon·te] *m* **1.** (*montaña*) mountain; **el ~ de los Olivos** the Mount of Olives **2.** (*bosque*) ~ **alto** woodland; ~ **bajo** scrub; **batir el ~** (*cazar*) to go hunting; (*buscar*) to beat the undergrowth; **echarse al ~** to take to the hills **3.** *pl* (*cordillera*) mountain range **4.** (*establecimiento*) ~ **de piedad** state-owned pawnshop ► **no todo el ~ es** <u>orégano</u> *prov* all that glitters is not gold

montera [mon·'te·ra] *f* **ponerse el mundo por ~** *fig* not to be affected by the opinion of others

montería [mon·te·'ri·a] *f* hunting

montés, -esa [mon·'tes, -·'te·sa] *adj* wild; **cabra montesa** mountain goat; **gato ~** wildcat

montículo [mon·'ti·ku·lo] *m* mound

monto ['mon·to] *m* total

montón [mon·'ton] *m* heap; **un ~ de ropa** a heap of clothes; **había un ~ de gente** there were a lot of people; **tengo problemas a montones** *inf* I have loads of problems; **tomar montones de pastillas** *inf* to take loads of pills; **ser del ~** to be ordinary; **tener una cara del ~** to have a run-of-the-mill face

montura [mon·'tu·ra] *f* (*arnés*) harness; (*silla*) saddle; (*de gafas*) frame

monumental [mo·nu·men·'tal] *adj* **1.** (*grande, de importancia*) monumental; (*error*) tremendous **2.** (*de monumento*) **el Madrid ~** the sights of Madrid

monumento [mo·nu·'men·to] *m* memorial; (*grande*) monument; ~ **funerario** gravestone; ~ **de la literatura** literary work of art; **los ~s de una ciudad** the sights of a city; **esta casa es un ~ nacional** this house is a listed building; **esta chica es un ~** this girl is beautiful

monzón [mon·'son, -·'θon] *m* monsoon

moña ['mo·ɲa] *f* **estar ~** *inf* to be drunk

moño ['mo·ɲo] *m* **1.** (*pelo*) bun **2.** (*lazo*) bow **3.** (*plumas*) crest **4.** *Col* (*capricho*) whim **5.** *Chile* (*pelo*) hair; (*copete*) forelock **6.** *inf* (*expresiones*) **quitar ~s a alguien** to bring sb down a peg (or two); **ponerse ~s** to put on airs (and graces); **estar hasta el ~ de algo** to be fed up to the back teeth with sth

moquear [mo·ke·'ar] *vi* to have a runny nose

moqueta [mo·'ke·ta] *f* carpet

mora ['mo·ra] *f* (*del moral*) mulberry; (*de la zarzamora*) blackberry

morada [mo·'ra·da] *f* **1.** (*casa*) abode **2.** (*residencia*) residence **3.** (*estancia*) stay; **la eterna ~** heaven

morado, -a [mo·'ra·do, -a] *adj* purple; **poner un ojo ~ a alguien** to give sb a black eye; **pasarlas moradas** to have a bad time; **ponerse ~** (*comiendo*) *inf* to gorge [*o* stuff] oneself

moral [mo·'ral] **I.** *adj* **1.** (*ético*) moral; **código ~** code of ethics **2.** (*espiritual*) spiritual **II.** *f* morals *pl*; ~ **relajada** relaxed morals; **levantar la ~ a alguien** to boost sb's morale; **hay que tener ~ para hacer eso** you have to be sure of yourself to do that

moraleja [mo·ra·'le·xa] *f* moral

moralista [mo·ra·'lis·ta] *mf* moralist

moralizar <z→c> [mo·ra·li·'sar, -·'θar] **I.** *vi* to moralize **II.** *vt* to improve the morals of

moratón [mo·ra·'ton] *m* bruise

moratoria [mo·ra·'to·rja] *f t.* FIN moratorium; ~ **nuclear** moratorium on nuclear weapons testing

mórbido, -a ['mor·βi·do, -a] *adj* **1.** (*enfermo*) ill **2.** (*suave*) soft

morbo ['mor·βo] *m* **1.** (*enfermedad*) illness **2.** (*interés malsano*) morbid fascination; **esto tiene mucho ~** this has created a lot of unhealthy interest

morbosidad [mor·βo·si·'dad] *f* morbidity

morboso, -a [mor·'βo·so, -a] *adj* **1.** (*clima*) unhealthy **2.** (*placer, imaginación*) morbid

morcilla [mor·'si·ja, -·'θi·ʎa] *f* **1.** CULIN blood sausage **2.** *Cuba* (*mentira*) lie **3.** *inf* (*fastidiar*) **¡que te den ~!** go fly a kite!

morcillo [mor·'si·jo, -·'θi·ʎo] *m* shin

mordaz [mor·'das, -·'daθ] *adj* (*comentario*) caustic; (*crítica*) scathing

mordaza [mor·'da·sa, -·'da·θa] *f* gag; **quieren ponerme una ~** *fig* they want to shut me up

mordedor(a) [mor·de·dor, -·'do·ra] *adj* **perro ladrador, poco ~** *prov* his bark is worse than his bite

mordedura [mor·de·'du·ra] *f* bite

morder <o→ue> [mor·'der] **I.** *vt* **1.** (*con los dientes*) to bite; **está que muerde** *inf* he/she is furious **2.** *AmL* (*estafar*) to cheat **II.** *vr:* ~**se** to bite; **¡no te muerdas las uñas!** don't bite your nails; **tuve que ~me la lengua** I had to bite my tongue; **no ~se la lengua** to say what one thinks

mordida [mor·'di·da] *f* **1.** *Méx, inf* (*acción*) bite; (*dinero*) bribe **2.** *Arg v.* **mordisco**

mordisco [mor·'dis·ko] *m* bite, nibble

mordisquear [mor·dis·ke·'ar] *vt* ~ **algo** to nibble at sth

morena [mo·'re·na] *f* **1.** ZOOL moray eel **2.** GEO moraine

moreno, -a [mo·'re·no, -a] **I.** *adj* brown; (*de piel*) dark-skinned; (*de cabello*) dark-haired;

(*de ojos*) brown-eyed **II.** *m*, *f* **1.** (*negro*) black person **2.** *Cuba* (*mulato*) mulatto

morera [mo·'re·ra] *f* mulberry tree

morete [mo·'re·te] *m AmC*, **moretón** [mo·re·'ton] *m inf* bruise

morfema [mor·'fe·ma] *m* LING morpheme

morfina [mor·'fi·na] *f* morphine

morfinómano, -a [mor·fi·'no·ma·no, -a] *m*, *f* morphine addict

morgue ['mor·ɣe] *f AmL* morgue

moribundo, -a [mo·ri·'βun·do, -a] *adj* dying

morir [mo·'rir] *irr* **I.** *vi* **1.** (*perecer*) to die; (*en catástrofe, guerra, accidente*) to be killed; **~ de hambre/sed** to die of starvation/thirst; **~ ahogado** (*en agua*) to drown; (*en humo*) to asphyxiate, to suffocate; **~ de viejo** to die of old age; **murió al pie del cañón** he died with his boots on **2.** (*tarde*) to draw to a close; (*luz*) to fade away; (*tradición*) to die out; (*camino*) to peter out; (*río*) to finish; (*sonido*) to die away **II.** *vr:* **~se 1.** (*perecer*) to die; (*planta*) to wither; **¡así te mueras!** *inf* good riddance to you! **2.** (*con 'de'*) **~se de hambre/de sed** to die of starvation/thirst; **~se de frío** to freeze to death; **~se de risa** to die laughing; **~se de pena** to pine away **3.** (*con 'por'*) **me muero (de ganas) por saber lo que te dijo** I am dying to know what she/he said to you; **me muero por ella** I am crazy about her

mormón, -ona [mor·'mon, -·'mo·na] *adj*, *m*, *f* Mormon

moro, -a ['mo·ro, -a] **I.** *adj* (*musulmán*) Muslim **II.** *m*, *f* Muslim; **ser un ~** *inf* to be chauvinistic; **¡hay ~s en la costa!** *fig* watch out!; **¡no hay ~s en la costa!** *fig* the coast is clear!

morochos [mo·'ro·tʃos] *mpl Ven* twins *pl*

moroso, -a [mo·'ro·so, -a] *m*, *f* debtor in arrears, defaulter

morral [mo·'rral] *m* **1.** (*de las caballerías*) nosebag **2.** (*zurrón*) knapsack

morrear [mo·rre·'ar] *vt, vr:* **~se** *vulg* to French-kiss

morriña [mo·'rri·na] *f inf* homesickness

morro ['mo·rro] *m* **1.** ZOOL (*hocico*) snout **2.** (*de persona*) **~s** (*labios*) lips; (*boca*) mouth; **beber a ~** to drink straight from the bottle; **me caí de ~s** I fell flat on my face; **estar de ~(s)** *fig* to be angry; **torcer el ~** *fig* to pout; **tiene un ~ que se lo pisa** *inf* he/she has a real nerve; **lo hizo así, por el ~** *inf* he/she did it like that, quite brazenly; **se quedó el dinero por (todo) el ~** *inf* he/she brazenly kept all the money

morrocotudo, -a [mo·rro·ko·'tu·do, -a] *adj inf* (*formidable*) terrific; (*susto, disgusto*) dreadful

morrón [mo·'rron] *adj* **pimiento ~** sweet red pepper

morsa ['mor·sa] *f* walrus

morse ['mor·se] *m* Morse code; **señal ~** Morse code signal

mortadela [mor·ta·'de·la] *f* mortadella, ≈ bologna

mortaja [mor·'ta·xa] *f* **1.** (*sábana*) shroud;

(*vestidura*) burial garments *pl* **2.** *AmL* (*de cigarrillo*) cigarette paper

mortal [mor·'tal] **I.** *adj* **1.** (*sujeto a la muerte*) mortal; **los restos ~es** the mortal remains **2.** (*que la causa*) mortal, lethal; **pecado ~** mortal sin; **peligro ~** mortal danger; **tener un odio ~ a alguien** to have a deadly hatred of sb **II.** *mf* mortal; **los ~es** mankind

mortalidad [mor·ta·li·'dad] *f* (*cualidad*) mortality; (*número*) mortality rate

mortandad [mor·tan·'dad] *f* loss of life; **la ~ de la guerra en Ruanda** the bloodbath during the war in Rwanda

mortecino, -a [mor·te·'si·no, -a; -'θi·no, -a] *adj* (*luz*) dim; (*color*) muted; (*fuego*) dull

mortero [mor·'te·ro] *m t.* MIL (*cuenco*) mortar

mortífero, -a [mor·'ti·fe·ro, -a] *adj* deadly

mortificar <c→qu> [mor·ti·fi·'kar] **I.** *vt* **1.** (*atormentar*) to torment **2.** *t.* REL (*humillar*) to mortify **II.** *vr:* **~se 1.** (*atormentarse*) to be tormented **2.** REL to mortify oneself **3.** *Méx* (*avergonzarse*) to be ashamed

mortuorio, -a [mor·tu·'o·rjo, -a] *adj* death

moruno, -a [mo·'ru·no, -a] *adj* Moorish; **pincho ~** spicy meat kebab

mosaico [mo·'sai·ko] *m* mosaic

mosca ['mos·ka] *f* **1.** ZOOL fly; **por si las ~s** *inf* just in case; **tener la ~ detrás de la oreja** *inf* to be nagged by sth; **estar ~** *inf* (*receloso*) to be suspicious; (*enfadado*) to be cross; **papar ~s** *inf* to be spellbound; **¿qué ~ te ha picado?** what's bugging you?; **andar cazando ~s** to spend time on futile things; **~ cojonera** *vulg* pest; **~ muerta** hypocrite **2.** *inf* (*dinero*) dough; **aflojar la ~** to shell out

moscada [mos·'ka·da] *adj* **nuez ~** nutmeg

moscarda [mos·'kar·da] *f* blowfly, bluebottle

moscardón [mos·kar·'don] *m* **1.** ZOOL (*moscarda*) blowfly, bluebottle; (*tábano*) horsefly **2.** (*persona*) pest

moscatel [mos·ka·'tel] *m* Muscatel

moscón [mos·'kon] *m v.* **moscardón**

moscón, -ona [mos·'kon, -·'ko·na] *m*, *f* blowfly

moscovita [mos·ko·'βi·ta] *adj*, *mf* Muscovite

Moscú [mos·'ku] *m* Moscow

mosqueado, -a [mos·ke·'a·do, -a] *adj inf* cross; **estar ~ con alguien** to be cross with sb

mosquearse [mos·ke·'ar·se] *vr inf* (*ofenderse*) to take offense; (*enfadarse*) to get angry

mosqueo [mos·'keo] *m* anger

mosquetero [mos·ke·'te·ro] *m* **1.** (*soldado*) musketeer **2.** *Arg, Bol* (*en una fiesta*) party-crasher

mosquita [mos·'ki·ta] *f* **~ muerta** hypocrite

mosquitero [mos·ki·'te·ro] *m* mosquito net(ting)

mosquito [mos·'ki·to] *m* mosquito; (*pequeño*) gnat

mostaza [mos·'ta·sa, -'ta·θa] *f* mustard; (*de*) **color ~** mustard(-yellow)

mosto ['mos·to] *m* must

mostrador [mos·tra·'dor] *m* (*tienda*) counter;

(*bar*) bar; (*ventanilla*) window

mostrar <o→ue> [mos·'trar] I. *vt* (*enseñar*) to show; (*presentar*) to display; **¡no muestres tu miedo!** do not reveal your fear! II. *vr:* ~ **se** to appear; ~ **se amigo** to be friendly

mota ['mo·ta] *f* (*partícula*) speck; ~ (**de polvo**) speck of dust

mote ['mote] *m* **1.** (*apodo*) nickname; ~ **cariñoso** pet name **2.** *AmL* (*maíz*) boiled corn

moteado, -a [mo·te·'a·do, -a] *adj* (*ojos*) flecked; (*tela*) dotted; (*huevos*) speckled

motear [mo·te·'ar] *vt* to fleck, to speckle

motejar [mo·te·'xar] *vt* (*tildar*) to brand

motel [mo·'tel] *m* motel

motero, -a [mo·'te·ro, -a] *m, f* biker

motete [mo·'te·te] *m AmS* bundle

motín [mo·'tin] *m* uprising; (*militar*) mutiny; **un ~ en la cárcel** a prison riot

motivación [mo·ti·βa·'sjon, -'θjon] *f* motivation

motivar [mo·ti·'βar] *vt* **1.** (*incitar*) to motivate **2.** (*explicar*) to explain **3.** (*provocar*) to cause

motivo [mo·'ti·βo] *m* **1.** (*causa*) reason behind; (*crimen*) motive; **con ~ de...** on the occasion of...; **por este ~** for this reason **2.** (*tela*) motif

moto ['mo·to] *f inf* motorbike; ~ **acuática** Jet Ski®; ~ **para la nieve** snowmobile; **ir en ~** to ride a motorbike; **iba como una ~** *inf* he/she was going like a bat out of hell; **estar como una ~** to be very attractive; **ponerse como una ~** (*sexual*) to get horny; (*enfadado*) to get furious

motocicleta [mo·to·si·'kle·ta, -θi·'kle·ta] *f* motorcycle; **ir en ~** to go by motorcycle

motociclismo [mo·to·si·'klis·mo, -θi·'klis·mo] *m* motorcycling

motociclista [mo·to·si·'klis·ta, -θi·'klis·ta] *mf* motorcyclist

motoneta [mo·to·'ne·ta] *f AmL* motor scooter

motor [mo·'tor] *m t. fig* motor; ~ **de búsqueda** COMPUT search engine; ~ **de reacción** jet engine; **vehículo de ~** motor vehicle **motor(a)** [mo·'tor, -·'to·ra] *adj* motor; **nervio ~** motor nerve

motora [mo·'to·ra] *f* motorboat

motorismo [mo·to·'ris·mo] *m* motorcycling

motorista [mo·to·'ris·ta] *mf* **1.** DEP motorcyclist **2.** (*chófer*) motorist, driver **3.** (*policía*) motorized policeman

motorizar <z→c> [mo·to·ri·'sar, -'θar] *vt* to motorize; **estar motorizado** *inf* to have wheels [*o* a car]

motosierra [mo·to·'sje·rra] *f* chain saw

motriz [mo·'tris, -'triθ] *adj* driving; **fuerza ~** driving force

movedizo, -a [mo·βe·'di·so, -a; -'di·θo, -a] *adj* **1.** (*móvil*) moving; **arenas movedizas** quicksand; *fig* dangerous ground **2.** (*inconstante*) changeable

mover <o→ue> [mo·'βer] I. *vt* **1.** (*desplazar*) to move; ~ **archivo** COMPUT move file; ~ **la cola** to wag one's tail; ~ **la cabeza** (*asentir*) to nod (one's head); (*negar*) to shake one's head

2. (*incitar*) to rouse; ~ **a alguien a lágrimas** to move sb to tears II. *vr:* ~ **se** to move; **¡venga, muévete!** come on! get a move on!

movida [mo·'βi·da] *f* **1.** *inf* fuss; **¡qué ~!** (*lío*) what a business! **2.** (*ambiente*) scene

movido, -a [mo·'βi·do, -a] *adj* **1.** (*foto*) blurred **2.** (*activo*) active; (*vivo*) lively; **he tenido un día muy ~** I have had a very busy day **3.** MÚS rhythmic

móvil ['mo·βil] *m* **1.** (*para colgar*) mobile **2.** (*crimen*) motive **3.** TEL mobile phone, cell phone

movilidad [mo·βi·li·'dad] *f* mobility

movilización [mo·βi·li·sa·'sjon, -θa·'θjon] *f* **1.** (*recursos, tropas*) mobilization **2.** (*huelga*) industrial action **3.** (*dinero*) release

movilizar <z→c> [mo·βi·li·'sar, -'θar] *vt* to mobilize; (*dinero*) to release

movimiento [mo·βi·'mjen·to] *m* **1.** *t.* FÍS movement; ~ **vibratorio** vibratory movement; **hacer ~s** ARQUIT to subside; **poner en ~** to put [*o* set] in motion; **había mucho ~ en las tiendas** the shops were busy **2.** COM movement; ~ **s bursátiles** stock-market movements

mozambiqueño, -a [mo·θam·bi·'ke·ɲo, -a; mo·θam-] *adj, m, f* Mozambican

mozo ['mo·so, -θo] *m* servant; ~ (**de café**) waiter; ~ (**de estación**) porter; ~ **de hotel** bellboy

mozo, -a ['mo·θo, -a; -θo, -a] *m, f* (*chico*) lad; (*chica*) girl; (*joven*) youth, young person; **¡pero si estás hecho un ~!** (*a un chico*) what a strapping lad you are!; (*a un adulto*) you are nothing but a lad!

mu [mu] I. *interj* (*vaca*) moo II. *m* **no decir ni ~** *inf* not to say a word

mucamo, -a [mu·'ka·mo, -a] *m, f AmL* (*criado*) servant; (*criada*) maid

muchachada [mu·tʃa·'tʃa·da] *f AmL* group of youths

muchacho, -a [mu·'tʃa·tʃo, -a] *m, f* (*chico*) boy; (*chica*) girl

muchedumbre [mu·tʃe·'dum·bre] *f* (*de personas*) crowd; (*de cosas*) collection; **salió volando una ~ de pájaros** a flock of birds flew off

mucho, -a ['mu·tʃo, -a] I. *adj* a lot of; ~ **vino** a lot of wine, much wine; ~ **s libros** a lot of books, many books; **esto es ~ para ella** this is too much for her; **hace ya ~ tiempo que...** it has been a long time since...; **muchas veces** lots of times II. *adv* (*intensidad*) very; **trabajar/esforzarse** ~ to work/to try hard; (*cantidad*) a lot; (*mucho tiempo*) for a long time; (*muchas veces*) many times; (*a menudo*) often; **lo sentimos** ~ we are very sorry; **no hace ~ estuvo aquí** he/she was here not long ago; **es con** ~ **el más simpático** he is by far the most pleasant; **por** ~ **que se esfuercen, no lo conseguirán** however hard they try, they will not manage it; **ni** ~ **menos** far from it; **como** ~ at (the) most

mucosa [mu·'ko·sa] *f* mucus

M

mucosidad [mu·ko·si·'dad] *f* mucosity
mucoso, -a [mu·'ko·so, -a] *adj* mucous; **membrana mucosa** mucous membrane
muda ['mu·da] *f* 1.(*ropa interior*) change of underwear; (*cama*) change of sheets 2.(*serpiente*) slough, shedding of skin 3.(*pájaro, pelo*) molt 4.(*voz*) **está de** ~ his voice is breaking
mudable [mu·'da·βle] *adj* changeable
mudanza [mu·'dan·sa, -θa] *f* move; **camión de** ~**s** moving van; **estar de** ~ to be in the middle of a move
mudar [mu·'dar] I. *vi, vt* to change; ~ (**de**) **pluma** to molt; ~ (**de**) **piel** to slough, to shed II. *vr:* ~**se** 1.(*casa*) to move; **nos mudamos (de aquí)** we are moving (away); ~**se a Ecuador** to move to Ecuador 2.(*ropa*) ~**se** (**de ropa**) to change clothes
mudo, -a ['mu·do, -a] *adj* mute; **cine** ~ silent movies; **quedarse** ~ **de asombro** to be speechless with amazement
mueble ['mwe·βle] I. *m* 1.(*pieza*) piece of furniture; ~ **bar** drinks cabinet; **cama** ~ foldaway bed; ~ **zapatero** shoe cupboard; ~ **de cocina** kitchen unit 2. *pl* furniture; **con/sin** ~**s** furnished/unfurnished; ~**s de cocina** kitchen units [*o* cabinets]; ~**s de época** period furniture II. *adj* JUR **bienes** ~**s** movable goods, personal property
mueca ['mwe·ka] *f* face; **hacer** ~**s** to pull faces; (*de dolor, disgusto*) grimace
muela ['mwe·la] *f* (*diente*) molar; ~**s del juicio** wisdom teeth; ~ **picada** molar with tooth decay; **dolor de** ~**s** toothache
muelle ['mwe·je, -ʎe] *m* 1.(*resorte*) spring 2.(*puerto*) wharf; ~ **flotante** floating quay
muérdago ['mwer·da·ɣo] *m* mistletoe
muerte ['mwer·te] *f* death; ~ **forestal** forest destruction; ~ **súbita** MED crib death; **pena de** ~ death penalty; **condenar a** ~ to condemn [*o* sentence] to death; **morir de** ~ **natural** to die of natural causes; **está luchando contra la** ~ he/she is fighting for his/her life; **estar enfermo de** ~ to be at death's door; **está en su lecho de** ~ he/she is on his/her deathbed; **hasta que la** ~ **os separe** (*matrimonio*) till death do you part ▶ **cada** ~ **de un obispo** once in a blue moon; **de mala** ~ lousy, crummy; **a** ~ to death; **a ese tipo lo odio a** ~ I detest that man; **llevarse un susto de** ~ to be scared to death
muerto, -a ['mwer·to, -a] I. *pp de* **morir** II. *adj* dead; **horas muertas** period of inactivity; **naturaleza muerta** still life; **estar** ~ (**de cansancio**) to be exhausted; **estar** ~ **de hambre/sed** to be ravenous/dying of thirst; **caerse** ~ to drop dead; **no tener dónde caerse** ~ *inf* to be penniless; **punto** ~ AUTO neutral III. *m, f* dead person; (*difunto*) deceased; (*cadáver*) corpse; **están tocando a** ~**s** the bells are tolling for a death; **ahora me cargan el** ~ **a mí** *inf* now they are laying the blame on me; **hacerse el** ~ (*callado*) to keep

as quiet as a mouse; (*quieto, t. fig*) to play dead; (*nadando*) to float; **ser un** ~ **de hambre** to be a nobody

▌**i** The **Día de los Muertos** (Day of the Dead) is a big feast in Mexico. Entire families visit cemeteries to eat and drink with the dead at their gravesites. The food eaten during the celebration includes cookies and candy in the shape of skulls and skeletons. Whatever is left over (the **"ofrenda,"** or offering), is supposed to nourish and strengthen the dead. This tradition is part of the culture of death that traces its roots back thousands of years and is still very much alive in Mexico today.

muesca ['mwes·ka] *f* nick; (*ranura*) groove
muesli ['mwes·li] *m* muesli
muestra ['mwes·tra] *f* 1.(*mercancía*) sample; ~ **gratuita** free sample; **feria de** ~**s** trade fair 2.(*prueba*) proof; ~ **de amistad** token of friendship 3.(*demostración*) demonstration; **dar** ~(**s**) **de valor** to give a demonstration of courage 4.(*de labores*) example; ~ **de bordado/punto** example of embroidery/knitting 5. MED ~ **de sangre/orina** blood/urine sample [*o* specimen] ▶ **por la** ~ **se conoce el paño** *prov* a friend in need is a friend indeed
muestrario [mwes·'tra·rjo] *m* collection of samples
muestreo [mwes·'treo] *m* sampling
mugido [mu·'xi·do] *m* (*vaca*) moo
mugir <g→j> [mu·'xir] *vi* (*vaca*) to moo
mugre ['mu·ɣre] *f* grime
mugriento, -a [mu·'ɣrjen·to, -a] *adj* grubby
mujer [mu·'xer] *f* woman (*esposa*) wife; ~ **de edad** elderly lady; ~ **fácil** loose woman; ~ **fatal** femme fatale; ~ **de la limpieza** cleaning lady; ~ **de la calle** prostitute; **una** ~ **de rompe y rasga** a woman who knows what she wants (and how to get it); **ser una** ~ **de su casa** to be a good housewife; **tomar** ~ to take a wife; **está hecha toda una** ~ she really is grown-up; **esto es cosa de** ~**es** this is women's stuff
mujerero, -a [mu·xe·'re·ro, -a] *adj* AmC, AmS (*mujeriego*) woman-chasing, skirt-chasing
mujeriego [mu·xe·'rje·ɣo] *m* womanizer
mulato, -a [mu·'la·to, -a] *m, f* mulatto
mulero, -a [mu·'le·ro, -a] *m, f* RíoPl, inf 1.(*mentiroso*) liar 2.(*tramposo*) cheat
muleta [mu·'le·ta] *f* 1.(*apoyo*) crutch; **andar con** ~**s** to walk with crutches 2. TAUR *red cloth attached to a stick used by a matador*
muletilla [mu·le·'ti·ja, -ʎa] *f* (*coletilla*) tag; (*palabra*) pet word; (*frase*) catch phrase
mullido, -a [mu·'ji·do, -ʎi·do] *adj* soft
mullo ['mu·jo, -ʎo] *m* Ecua (*abalorio*) colored bead
mulo, -a ['mu·lo, -a] *m, f* (*caballo y asna*)

hinny; (*asno y yegua*) mule

multa ['mul·ta] *f* fine; **poner una ~ a alguien** to fine sb

multar [mul·'tar] *vt* to fine; **me han multado con 3.000 pesos** I've been fined 3,000 pesos

multicines [mul·ti·'si·nes, -'θi·nes] *mpl* multiplex

multicolor [mul·ti·ko·'lor] *adj* multicolored; TIPO polychromatic

multicopista [mul·ti·ko·'pis·ta] *f* duplicator

multiforme [mul·ti·'for·me] *adj* multifarious

multilateralismo [mul·ti·la·te·ra·'lis·mo] *m* POL multilateralism *no pl*

multilingüe [mul·ti·'lin·gwe] *adj* multilingual

multimedia [mul·ti·'me·dja] *adj inv* multimedia; **programa ~ de computadora** multimedia computer program

multimillonario, -a [mul·ti·mi·jo·'na·rjo, -a, mul·ti·mi·ʎo-] *m, f* multimillionaire

multinacional [mul·ti·na·sjo·'nal, -θjo·'nal] *adj, f* multinational

múltiple ['mul·ti·ple] *adj* multiple; (*variado*) multifarious; **~s veces** numerous times

multiplicación [mul·ti·pli·ka·'sjon, -'θjon] *f t.* MAT multiplication

multiplicar <c→qu> [mul·ti·pli·'kar] I. *vi, vt* 1. MAT **~ por algo** to multiply by sth; **tabla de ~** multiplication table 2. (*reproducir, aumentar*) to multiply II. *vr:* **~se** 1. (*reproducirse*) to multiply; **¡creced y multiplicaos!** REL go forth and multiply! 2. (*desvivirse*) to be everywhere at the same time

múltiplo, -a ['mul·ti·plo, -a] *adj, m, f* multiple

multitud [mul·ti·'tud] *f* 1. (*cantidad*) multitude; **una ~ de flores** a great number of flowers 2. (*gente*) multitude, crowd; (*vulgo*) masses *pl*

multitudinario, -a [mul·ti·tu·di·'na·rjo, -a] *adj* multitudinous

multiuso [mul·ti·'u·so] *adj inv* multi-purpose

mundanal [mun·da·'nal] *adj*, **mundano, -a** [mun·'da·no, -a] *adj* 1. (*del mundo*) of the world; (*terrenal*) worldly 2. (*extravagante*) society

mundial [mun·'djal] *adj* world; **campeonato ~ de fútbol** World Cup; **guerra ~** world war; **a nivel ~** worldwide

mundillo [mun·'di·jo, -ʎo] *m inf* (*ambiente*) world; **el ~ de la música** the world of music; **ella se maneja bien en ese ~** she gets on well in that circle

mundo ['mun·do] *m* 1. (*tierra*) earth; (*planeta*) planet; (*globo*) world; **~ profesional** professional world; **el ~ antiguo** the ancient world; **el otro ~** the next world; **dar la vuelta al ~** to go around the world; **echar al ~** to give birth to; **venir al ~** to be born; **irse de este ~** to die; **nadó como Dios lo trajo al ~** he went swimming in the nude; **ver ~** to travel a lot; **andar por esos ~s de Dios** *inf* (*estar de viaje*) to be traveling all over the place; (*estar perdido*) to be lost; **recorrer medio ~** to visit many countries; **con la mayor tranquilidad**

del ~ with the utmost calm; **rápidamente se le cae el ~ encima** he/she quickly gets discouraged; **vive en otro ~** *fig* he/she lives in a world of his/her own; **este ~ es un pañuelo** it is a small world; **desde que el ~ es ~** since the world began; **ponerse el ~ por montera, reírse del ~** not to care what others think/say; **hacer un ~ de algo** to make a mountain out of a molehill; **así va [*o anda*] el ~** that is the way things are; **no es nada del otro ~** it is nothing out of this world; **por nada del ~** not for the world 2. (*humanidad*) **todo el ~** everyone, everybody; **a la vista de todo el ~** for the whole world to see; **lo sabe medio ~** nearly everyone knows that 3. (*experiencia*) worldliness; **Lola tiene mucho ~** Lola is worldly-wise

mundología [mun·do·lo·'xi·a] *f inf* worldly wisdom

munición [mu·ni·'sjon, -'θjon] *f* ammunition

municipal [mu·ni·si·'pal, -θi·pal] *adj* municipal; **parque ~** municipal park; **término ~** municipality

municipio [mu·ni·'si·pjo, -θi·pjo] *m* 1. (*población*) municipality, borough 2. (*ayuntamiento*) town hall 3. (*concejo*) town council

munificencia [mu·ni·fi·'sen·sja, -θen·θja] *f* munificence

munir [mu·'nir] I. *vt CSur* **~ de algo** to provide with sth; **ir munido de los documentos necesarios** to have the necessary documents II. *vr CSur* **~se de algo** to provide oneself with sth; **~se de suficientes provisiones** to equip oneself with sufficient provisions

muñeca [mu·'ɲe·ka] *f* 1. (*brazo*) wrist 2. (*juguete*) doll; **~ hinchable** inflatable doll 3. *fig* (*niña*) doll, cutie

muñeco [mu·'ɲe·ko] *m* 1. (*juguete*) doll; **~ articulado** jointed doll; **~ de nieve** snowman 2. *pey* (*monigote*) puppet

muñequera [mu·ɲe·'ke·ra] *f* wristband

muñón [mu·'ɲon] *m* stump

mural [mu·'ral] *m* mural

ℹ After the Mexican Revolution, the minister of education, José Vasconcelos, allowed **murales** (murals) depicting scenes from Mexican society to be painted on the walls of public buildings in Mexico City. The most famous muralist painter is **Diego Rivera**. The **murales** that have been found in Mexico date back as far as the pre-Hispanic age and include those discovered at the temples in Bonampak and Teotihuacán.

---

muralla [mu·'ra·ja, -ʎa] *f* wall

murciélago [mur·'sje·la·ɣo, -mur·'θje] *m* bat

murga ['mur·ɣa] *f inf* (*banda*) street band; **dar la ~ a alguien** to bother sb

murmullo [mur·'mu·jo, -ʎo] *m* 1. (*voz*) whisper; (*cuchicheo*) murmur 2. (*hojas*) rustling; (*agua*) murmur

murmuración [mur·mu·ra·'sjon, -'θjon] *f* (*calumnia*) slander; (*cotilleo*) gossip

murmurar [mur·mu·'rar] **I.** *vi, vt* (*entre dientes*) to mutter; (*susurrar*) to murmur; ~ **al oído de alguien** to whisper in sb's ear **II.** *vi* **1.** (*gruñir*) to grumble **2.** (*criticar*) to criticize; (*chismorrear*) to gossip **3.** (*agua*) to murmur; (*hojas*) to rustle

muro ['mu·ro] *m* wall; ~ **de contención** retaining wall; **Muro de las Lamentaciones** the Wailing Wall; ~ **medianero** party [*o* dividing] wall

mus [mus] *m card game*

musa ['mu·sa] *f* muse; **le sopló la** ~ he/she was inspired; (*en un juego*) he/she was on a lucky streak

musaraña [mu·sa·'ra·ɲa] *f* **1.** ZOOL shrew **2.** *fig* (*bicho*) small animal; **pensar en las ~s** *fig* to have one's head in the clouds

muscular [mus·ku·'lar] *adj* muscular

musculatura [mus·ku·la·'tu·ra] *f* musculature

músculo ['mus·ku·lo] *m* muscle; ~ **deltoides** deltoid muscle; **ser ~ puro** to be all muscle

musculoso, -a [mus·ku·'lo·so, -a] *adj* muscular

muselina [mu·se·'li·na] *f* muslin

museo [mu·'seo] *m* museum; ~ **etnográfico** museum of ethnography

musgo ['mus·ɣo] *m* moss

música ['mu·si·ka] *f* music; ~ **folclórica** traditional music; ~ **ratonera** *inf* cabaret [*o* pub] music; ~ **sacra** sacred music; ~ **de cámara** chamber music; ~ **ambiental** Muzak®, canned [*o* piped] music; ~ **ligera** easy listening; **banda de** ~ band; **caja de** ~ music box; **tus palabras nos sonaron a** ~ **celestial** you were spouting nonsense; **tener talento para la** ~ to be musical

musical [mu·si·'kal] **I.** *adj* musical; **composición** ~ musical composition **II.** *m* musical

músico, -a ['mu·si·ko, -a] *m, f* musician; (*compositor*) composer

musitar [mu·si·'tar] *vi* **1.** (*balbucear*) to mumble; (*susurrar*) to whisper; ~ **al oído de alguien** to whisper in sb's ear **2.** (*hojas*) to rustle

muslo ['mus·lo] *m* (*persona*) thigh; (*animal*) leg

mustela [mus·'te·la] *f* weasel

mustio, -a ['mus·tjo, -a] *adj* **1.** (*flores*) wilting **2.** (*triste*) low

musulmán, -ana [mu·sul·'man, -·'ma·na] *adj, m, f* Muslim

mutable [mu·'ta·βle] *adj* mutable

mutación [mu·ta·'sjon, -'θjon] *f* mutation

mutilado, -a [mu·ti·'la·do, -a] *m, f* cripple; ~ **de guerra** disabled war veteran

mutilar [mu·ti·'lar] *vt* **1.** (*cuerpo*) to mutilate **2.** (*recortar*) to cut

mutis ['mu·tis] *m inv* TEAT exit; ~ **por el foro** quick exit; **hacer** ~ to exit

mutismo [mu·'tis·mo] *m* silence; **no hay manera de sacarlo de su** ~ there is no way of making him break his silence

mutual [mu·tu·'al] **I.** *adj* mutual **II.** *f CSur* mutual benefit society

mutualidad [mu·twa·li·'dad] *f* **1.** (*cooperativa*) mutual benefit society; ~ **de accidentes de trabajo** mutual insurance company **2.** (*reciprocidad*) mutuality

mutuo, -a ['mu·two, -a] *adj* mutual

muy [mwi] *adv* very; **es ~ improbable que...** +*subj* it is very unlikely that...; ~ **a pesar mío** much to my dismay; ~ **de tarde en tarde** once in a blue moon; ~ **de mañana** in the very early morning; **le saluda ~ atentamente,** (*en cartas*) sincerely yours,; **¡dejarnos plantados: eso es ~ de María!** she didn't show up — how typical of María!; **es Ud. ~ libre de hacer lo que quiera** you are completely free to do as you please

N

N, n ['e·ne] *f* N, n; ~ **de Navarra** N as in November

nabo ['na·βo] *m* **1.** BOT turnip **2.** *vulg* (*pene*) cock

nácar ['na·kar] *m* mother-of-pearl, nacre; **de** ~ nacreous, pearly

nacarado, -a [na·ka·'ra·do, -a] *adj*, **nacarino, -a** [na·ka·'ri·no, -a] *adj* nacreous, pearly

nacatamal [na·ka·ta·'mal] *m AmC, Méx* CULIN pork tamale

nacer [na·'ser, -θer] *irr como crecer vi* **1.** (*venir al mundo*) to be born; **nací el 29 de febrero** I was born on the 29th of February; **haber nacido para la música** to be a natural for music; **volver a** ~ to have a very narrow escape **2.** ASTR to be created; (*día*) to rise; **nace una estrella** a star is born; **al ~ el día** at the break of day **3.** (*originarse*) to stem; (*arroyo*) to begin; (*surgir*) to arise; **nació una duda en su mente** *elev* a doubt was sown in his/her mind ▸**nadie nace** <u>enseñado</u> *prov* we all have to learn; **no con quien naces, sino con quien paces** *prov* it's your environment that counts, not your birth

nacido, -a [na·'si·do, -a; -θi·do, -a] **I.** *adj* **bien** ~ (*origen*) born into a good family; (*comportamiento*) noble **II.** *m, f* **recién** ~ newborn; **los ~s el 2 de abril** those born on the 2nd of April; **un mal** ~ a born villain

naciente¹ [na·'sjen·te, 'θjen·te] *m* (*oriente*) orient; (*este*) east

naciente² [na·'sjen·te, 'θjen·te] *f Arg, Par* spring

nacimiento [na·si·'mjen·to, na·θi-] *m* **1.** (*venida al mundo*) birth; **de** ~ by birth; **ciego de** ~ born blind; **lugar de** ~ birthplace; **partida de** ~ birth certificate; (*belén*) Nativity scene **2.** (*linaje*) family; **ser de humilde** ~ to

be of humble birth **3.**(*comienzo*) beginning;
~ **del pelo** root (of hair)
nación [na·'sjon, -'θjon] *f* nation; (**la Orga-nización de**) **las Naciones Unidas** the Unit-ed Nations (Organization)
nacional [na·sjo·'nal, -θjo·'nal] *adj* national;
carretera ~ (*en los Estados Unidos*) highway;
moneda ~ national currency; **renta** ~ nation-al income; **vuelos** ~**es** domestic flights
nacionalidad [na·sjo·na·li·'dad, na·θjo-] *f*
(*ciudadanía*) nationality, citizenship; **ser de** ~ **española** to have Spanish nationality, to be a Spanish national
nacionalismo [na·sjo·na·'lis·mo, na·θjo-] *m*
nationalism
nacionalista [na·sjo·na·'lis·ta, na·θjo-] *adj, mf*
nationalist
nacionalización [na·sjo·na·li·sa·'sjon, na·θjo·na·li·θa·'θjon] *f* (*persona*) naturalization, na-tionalization
nacionalizar <z→c> [na·sjo·na·li·'sar, na·θjo·na·li·'θar] **I.** *vt* (*persona*) to naturalize, to nationalize **II.** *vr* ~ **se español** to obtain Span-ish nationality
naco ['na·ko] *m* **1.***AmC* (*cobarde*) coward;
AmC (*marica*) queer **2.** *Arg* (*miedo*) fear
nada ['na·da] **I.** *pron indef* nothing; **¡gracias!**
— **¡de** ~**!** thank you! — you're welcome!;
¡pues ~**!** well all right then; **por** ~ **se queja** he/she complains about the slightest thing;
como si ~ as if nothing had happened;
~ **menos que el director** the director him-self; **no servir para** ~ to be useless **II.** *adv* not at all; ~ **más** (*solamente*) only; (*no más*) no more; **¡** ~ **más!** enough!; ~ **de** ~ absolutely nothing; **no ser** ~ **difícil** not to be difficult at all; **¡** ~ **de eso!** none of that!; **¡y** ~ **de llegar tarde!** no arriving late!; **¡casi** ~**!** hardly any-thing!; **antes de** ~ (*sobre todo*) above all;
(*primero*) first of all; **para** ~ not in the slightest **III.** *f* nothing, nothingness; **salir de la** ~ to ap-pear out of nowhere
nadador(a) [na·da·'dor, -·'do·ra] *m(f)* swimmer
nadar [na·'dar] *vi* to swim; ~ **en deudas** to be swimming in debt
nadería [na·de·'ri·a] *f* nothing important
nadie ['na·dje] *pron indef* nobody, anybody, no one; **no vi a** ~ I didn't see anybody, I saw no-body; **no vino** ~ nobody came; **tú no eres** ~ **para decir...** who are you to say...?; **un don** ~ a nobody; **tierra de** ~ no man's land
nadita [na·'di·ta] **I.** *f Ecua, Méx* **en** ~ **estuvo que lo mataran** they almost killed him **II.** *adv Méx* in no time
nado ['na·do] *adv* **a** ~ afloat, swimming; **cru-zar algo a** ~ to swim across sth
nafta ['naf·ta] *f CSur* (*gasolina*) gasoline
nagual [na·'ywal] *f Méx, Hond* witch doctor
nagualear [na·ywa·le·'ar] *vi Méx* **1.**(*mentir*)
to lie **2.**(*robar*) to swipe
naif [na·'if] *adj* naive
nailon ['nai·lon] *m* nylon
naipe ['nai·pe] *m* **1.**(*carta*) card **2.** *pl* (*baraja*)

pack of cards
najarse [na·'xar·se] *vr inf* to beat it, to scram
nalga ['nal·ya] *f* buttock; ~**s** bottom
namibio, -a [na·'mi·βjo, -a] *adj, m, f* Namibian
nana ['na·na] *f* **1.**(*canción*) lullaby **2.**(*niñera*)
nanny
nanay [na·nai] *interj inf* no way!
nanotecnología [na·no·tek·no·lo·'xi·a] *f*
nanotechnology
nanotecnólogo, -a [na·no·tek·'no·lo·yo, -a]
m, f nanotechnologist
napia(s) ['na·pja(s)] *f(pl) inf* conk
napolitano, -a [na·po·li·'ta·no, -a] *adj, m, f*
Neapolitan
naranja [na·'ran·xa] **I.** *f* orange; **media** ~
ARQUIT dome ▶ **¡** ~ **s** (**de la China**)**!** no way!; **tu media** ~ your better half **II.** *adj* (**de color**) ~
orange
naranjada [na·ran·'xa·da] *f* orangeade
naranjado, -a [na·ran·'xa·do, -a] *adj* orangey
naranjal [na·ran·'xal] *m* orange grove
naranjo [na·'ran·xo] *m* orange tree
narcisismo [nar·si·'sis·mo, nar·θi-] *m* narcis-sism, egoism
narcisista [nar·si·'sis·ta, nar·θi-] *adj* narcissis-tic
narciso [nar·'si·so, 'θi·so] *m* **1.**BOT daffodil,
narcissus *inv* **2.**(*persona*) narcissist
narco ['nar·ko] *m inf* drug dealer [*o* trafficker]
narcoterrorismo [nar·ko·te·rro·'ris·mo] *m*
drugs terrorism
narcótico [nar·'ko·ti·ko] *m* narcotic
narcótico, -a [nar·'ko·ti·ko, -a] *adj* narcotic
narcotizar <z→c> [nar·ko·ti·'sar, -'θar] *vt* to narcotize
narcotraficante [nar·ko·tra·fi·'kan·te] *mf*
drug dealer [*o* trafficker]
narcotráfico [nar·ko·'tra·fi·ko] *m* drug dealing
[*o* trafficking]
narigada [na·ri·'ya·da] *f Ecua* pinch of snuff
narigón, -ona [na·ri·'yon, -·'yo·na] *adj* big-nosed
narigudo, -a [na·ri·'yu·do, -a] *adj* big-nosed
nariz [na·'riθ] *f* **1.**ANAT nose; ~ **chata** flat nose;
~ **ganchuda** hooked nose; ~ **respingona** turned-up nose; ~ **aguileña** aquiline nose; **dar a alguien con la puerta en las narices** to slam the door in sb's face; **darse de narices con alguien** *inf* to bump straight into sb; **so-narse/limpiarse la** ~ to blow/wipe one's nose; **romper las narices a alguien** to smash sb's face in; **no ver más allá de sus narices** *inf* to not be able to see further than the end of one's nose; **quedarse con un palmo de narices** *inf* to be let down; **me da en la** ~ **que...** I have a funny feeling that... **2.** *inf*
(*eufemismo por 'cojones'*) **estar hasta las narices** to have had it up to here; **lo hizo por narices** he/she did it because he/she felt like it; **¡(qué) narices!** no way; **tener narices** to be too much; **¡tócate las narices!** would you believe it?
narizudo, -a [na·ri·'θu·do, -a] *adj Méx* large-

nosed

narración [na·rra·'sjon, -'θjon] *f* narration

narrador(a) [na·rra·'dor, --'do·ra] *m(f)* narrator; (*que cuenta la historia*) storyteller

narrar [na·'rrar] *vt* to narrate; (*informar*) to tell

narrativa [na·rra·'ti·βa] *f* literature

nasal [na·'sal] *adj* nasal

nata ['na·ta] *f* 1.(*producto*) cream; ~ **montada** whipped cream; **la crema y ~ de la sociedad** the crème de la crème of society 2.(*sobre un líquido*) film

natación [na·ta·'sjon, -'θjon] *f* DEP swimming

natal [na·'tal] *adj* native, home; **ciudad ~** home town; **país ~** native country [*o* land]

natalicio, -a [na·ta·'li·sjo, -θjo] *adj* birthday

natalidad [na·ta·li·'dad] *f* birth; **índice de ~** birth rate

natillas [na·'ti·jas, -ʎas] *fpl* custard

Natividad [na·ti·βi·'dad] *f* nativity

nativo, -a [na·'ti·βo, -a] I. *adj* native, home; **lengua nativa** native [*o* mother] tongue; **profesor ~** native teacher II. *m, f AmL* native

nato, -a ['na·to, -a] *adj* born; **un triunfador ~** a born winner

natural [na·tu·'ral] *adj* 1.(*no artificial, sencillo*) natural; **de tamaño ~** life-sized; **esto es lo más ~ del mundo** (*normal*) it is the most natural thing in the world; (*lógico*) it makes perfect sense 2.(*nacido*) **ser ~ del Reino Unido** to be a British natural; **hijo ~** illegitimate child

naturaleza [na·tu·ra·'le·sa, -θa] *f* 1.(*campo*) nature; **~ muerta** still life; **en plena ~ in** the heart of the countryside 2.(*manera*) nature 3.(*índole*) type; **de ~ pública** of the public domain

naturalidad [na·tu·ra·li·'dad] *f* naturalness; **lo dijo con mucha ~** he/she said it very naturally

naturalizar <z→c> [na·tu·ra·li·'sar, -'θar] I. *vt* to naturalize; **~ costumbres** to take on customs II. *vr* **~ se a algo** (*habituarse*) to get used to sth

naufragar <g→gu> [nau·fra·'γar] *vi* 1.(*hundirse*) to sink 2.(*no hundir del todo*) to be wrecked; (*personas*) to be shipwrecked 3.(*fracasar*) to fall through

naufragio [nau·'fra·xjo] *m* (*accidente*) shipwreck

náufrago, -a ['nau·fra·γo, -a] I. *adj* shipwrecked II. *m, f* shipwrecked sailor, castaway

nauseabundo, -a [nau·sea·'βun·do, -a] *adj* nauseating

náuseas ['nau·seas] *fpl* sick feeling; **tengo ~** I feel sick; **dar ~ a alguien** to make sb feel sick

náutica ['nau·ti·ka] *f* navigation

náutico, -a ['nau·ti·ko, -a] *adj* nautical; **club ~** yacht club

nava ['na·βa] *f* plain

navaja [na·'βa·xa] *f* (pocket) knife; **~ de afeitar** razor; **~ automática** switchblade

navajada [na·βa·'xa·da] *f*, **navajazo** [na·βa·'xa·θo] *m* 1.(*golpe*) stabbing 2.(*herida*) stab [*o* knife] wound, gash

naval [na·'βal] *adj* naval

nave ['na·βe] *f* 1.NÁUT, AVIAT ship, vessel; **~** (**espacial**) spaceship, spacecraft 2.(*en una iglesia*) nave; **~ central** main nave 3.(*almacén*) warehouse ▸ **quemar las ~s** to burn one's bridges

navegable [na·βe·'γa·βle] *adj* navigable; **rutas ~s** navigable routes

navegación [na·βe·γa·'sjon, -'θjon] *f* navigation

navegador [na·βe·γa·'dor] *m* COMPUT browser

navegante [na·βe·'γan·te] *mf* navigator; **~ de internet** Net surfer

navegar <g→gu> [na·βe·'γar] *vi, vt* to navigate; **~ veinte nudos por hora** to sail at 20 knots an hour; **~ contra la corriente** to go against the flow; **~ por la web** to surf the net

Navidad [na·βi·'dad] *f* Christmas; **¡feliz ~!** merry Christmas!

navideño, -a [na·βi·'de·no, -a] *adj* Christmas; (*ambiente*) festive

naviero, -a [na·'βje·ro, -a] *m, f* ship owner

navío [na·'βi·o] *m* ship

nazismo [na·'θis·mo] *m* Nazism

NE [nor·'des·te] *abr de* **Nordeste** NE

neblina [ne·'βli·na] *f* mist; *fig* haze

nebuloso, -a [ne·βu·'lo·so, -a] *adj* 1.(*brumoso*) misty 2.(*nuboso*) cloudy 3.(*vago*) hazy 4.(*oscuro*) obscure

necedad [ne·θe·'dad] *f* stupidity; **no decir más que ~es** to talk a lot of nonsense

necesariamente [ne·θe·sa·rja·'men·te] *adv* necessarily

necesario, -a [ne·θe·'sa·rjo, -a] *adj* necessary; **es ~ que haya más acuerdo** there is a need for more agreement

neceser [ne·θe·'ser] *m* (*de aseo*) toilet bag; (*de afeitar*) shaving kit; (*de maquillaje*) cosmetic bag

necesidad [ne·θe·si·'dad] *f* 1.(*ser preciso*) need, necessity; **de primera ~** essential 2.(*requerimiento*) need; **tener ~ de algo** to be in need of sth 3.*pl* (*evacuación corporal*) **hacer sus ~es** to relieve oneself

necesitado, -a [ne·θe·si·'ta·do, -a] I. *adj* (*pobre*) needy; **estar ~ de amor** to be in need of love II. *m, f* poor person; **los ~s** the poor

necesitar [ne·θe·si·'tar] I. *vt* 1.(*precisar*) to need; **se necesita piso** apartment wanted 2.(*tener que*) to need to; **necesitas comer algo** you have to eat something II. *vi* (*precisar*) **~ de algo** to need sth

necio, -a [ne·'sjo, -a; neθ-] *adj* idiotic

nécora ['ne·ko·ra] *f* fiddler crab

necrología [ne·kro·lo·'xi·a] *f* 1.(*biografía*) obituary 2.(*nota*) list of deaths

necrológico, -a [ne·kro·'lo·xi·ko, -a] *adj* necrological

néctar ['nek·tar] *m* nectar

nectarina [nek·ta·'ri·na] *f* nectarine

neerlandés, -esa [ne·(e)r·lan·'des, --'de·sa] I. *adj* Dutch II. *m, f* Dutchman *m*, Dutchwoman *f*

nefasto, -a [ne·'fas·to, -a] *adj* awful; (*día*) horrible
nefritis [ne·'fri·tis] *f inv* MED nephritis
negación [ne·ɣa·'sjon, -'θjon] *f* 1.(*desmentir*) denial 2.(*denegar*) refusal 3. LING negative; **es la ~ del arte** it is anything but art
negado, -a [ne·'ɣa·do, -a] I. *adj* ~ **para algo** useless at sth II. *m, f* **ser un ~ para las matemáticas** to be no good at math
negar [ne·'ɣar] *irr como fregar* I. *vt* 1.(*desmentir*) to deny 2.(*rehusar*) to refuse; (*rechazar*) to reject; ~ **con la cabeza** to shake one's head II. *vr:* ~ **se** to refuse
negativa [ne·ɣa·'ti·βa] *f* (*negación*) denial; (*rehusamiento*) refusal; (*rechazo*) rejection
negativo [ne·ɣa·'ti·βo] *m* FOTO negative
negativo, -a [ne·ɣa·'ti·βo, -a] *adj* negative; **tu respuesta fue negativa** your answer was negative
negligencia [ne·ɣli·'xen·sja, -θja] *f* (*descuido*) carelessness; JUR negligence
negligente [ne·ɣli·'xen·te] *adj* 1.(*descuidado*) careless; **ser ~ en** [*o* **para**] **su trabajo** to be a careless worker 2. JUR negligent
negociable [ne·ɣo·'θja·βle] *adj* negotiable; **el precio es ~** the price is open to negotiation
negociación [ne·ɣo·sja·'sjon, -θja·'θjon] *f* negotiation; ~ **colectiva** collective bargaining; **entrar en negociaciones con alguien** to enter into negotiations with sb
negociado [ne·ɣo·'θja·do] *m* 1.(*dependencia*) section; **jefe de ~** head of department 2. AmS (*negocio*) suspicious deal
negociador(a) [ne·ɣo·θja·'dor, -'do·ra] *m(f)* 1.(*comerciante*) merchant 2.(*mediador*) negotiator
negociante [ne·ɣo·'θjan·te] *mf* (*comerciante*) dealer
negociar [ne·ɣo·'sjar, -'θjar] I. *vi* (*comerciar*) to deal II. *vi, vt* (*dialogar, concertar*) to negotiate
negocio [ne·'ɣo·sjo, -θjo] *m* 1.(*comercio*) business; ~ **al detalle** retail business; **hombre/mujer de ~s** businessman/businesswoman 2.(*asunto*) matter; **eso no es ~ mío** it's none of my business ▶ **hacer un ~ redondo** *inf* to do a good bit of business
negrada [ne·'ɣra·da] *f Cuba* HIST slaves (*body of slaves belonging to a plantation*)
negrero, -a [ne·'ɣre·ro, -a] *m, f* 1.(*que trata con esclavos*) slave dealer; (*tirano*) slave driver 2. CSur (*aprovechado*) parasite
negrilla [ne·'ɣri·ja, -ʎa] *f*, **negrita** [ne·'ɣri·ta] *f* TIPO bold face
negro, -a ['ne·ɣro] I. *adj* black; ~ **del sol** suntanned; ~ **como la boca del lobo** pitch-black; ~ **como el carbón** as black as coal ▶ **estar/ponerse ~** *inf* to be/get furious; **pasarlas negras** *inf* to have a terrible time; **verse para hacer algo** *inf* to have a hard time doing sth; **verlo todo ~** to be very pessimistic II. *m, f* 1.(*persona*) black; **trabajar como un ~** *inf* to work like a slave 2.(*escritor*) ghost writer

3. *Arg, inf* (*cariño*) darling
negrura [ne·'ɣru·ra] *f* blackness
negruzco, -a [ne·'ɣruθ·ko, -a] *adj* blackish
neme ['ne·me] *m Col* asphalt
nene, -a ['ne·ne, -a] *m, f inf* (*niño*) baby; (*expresión de cariño*) dear
nenúfar [ne·'nu·far] *m* water lily
neocapitalismo [neo·ka·pi·ta·'lis·mo] *m* ECON neocapitalism
neoclasicismo [neo·kla·si·'θis·mo] *m* neoclassicism
neoclásico, -a [neo·'kla·si·ko, -a] *adj* neoclassical
neolítico [neo·'li·ti·ko] *m* Neolithic (Period)
neologismo [neo·lo·'xis·mo] *m* neologism
neón [ne·'on] *m* neon
neoyorquino, -a [neo·jor·'ki·no, -a] *m, f* New Yorker
neozelandés, -esa [neo·θe·lan·'des, --'de·sa] *m, f* New Zealander
nepalés, -esa [ne·pa·'les, --'le·sa] *m, f* Nepalese person
nepotismo [ne·po·'tis·mo] *m* nepotism
nervio ['ner·βjo] *m* 1.(*conductor*) nerve; **ataque de ~s** nervous breakdown; **crispar los ~s a alguien, poner a alguien los ~s de punta** *inf* (*enfadar*) to drive sb mad [*o* crazy]; (*poner nervioso*) to get on sb's nerves; **ponerse de los ~s** to get nervous [*o* flustered]; **estar atacado de los ~s** to be a nervous wreck; **tener ~s de acero** to have nerves of steel 2.(*tendón*) sinew 3.(*ímpetu*) impetus; **esta empresa tiene ~** this company is dynamic
nerviosismo [ner·βjo·'sis·mo] *m* nervousness
nervioso, -a [ner·'βjo·so, -a] *adj* 1. ANAT nervous; **el sistema ~** the nervous system 2.(*intranquilo*) excitable
neto, -a ['ne·to] *adj* 1.(*claro*) clear 2.(*no bruto*) net
neumático [neu·'ma·ti·ko] I. *adj* pneumatic; **martillo ~** pneumatic drill II. *m* tire
neumonía [neu·mo·'ni·a] *f* MED pneumonia
neurología [neu·ro·lo·'xi·a] *f* MED neurology
neurólogo, -a [neu·'ro·lo·ɣo, -a] *m, f* MED neurologist
neurona [neu·'ro·na] *f* ANAT neuron
neurosis [neu·'ro·sis] *f inv* neurosis
neurótico, -a [neu·'ro·ti·ko, -a] *adj, m, f* neurotic
neutral [neu·'tral] *adj, mf* neutral
neutralidad [neu·tra·li·'dad] *f* neutrality
neutralización [neu·tra·li·sa·'sjon, -θa·θjon] *f* neutralization
neutralizar <z→c> [neu·tra·li·'sar, -'θar] I. *vt* to neutralize II. *vr:* ~ **se** to be neutralized
neutro, -a ['neu·tro, -a] *adj* 1. *t.* QUÍM neutral 2. ZOOL sexless 3. LING neuter; **género ~** neuter gender
neutrón [neu·'tron] *m* FÍS neutron
nevada [ne·'βa·da] *f* snowfall; (*tormenta*) snowstorm
nevado, -a [ne·'βa·do] *adj* 1.(*cubierto*)

snow-covered; (*montaña*) snow-capped **2.** (*blanco*) snow-white
nevar <e→ie> [ne·'βar] *v impers* to snow
nevazón [ne·βa·'θon] *f Arg, Chile, Ecua* METEO blizzard, snowstorm
nevera [ne·'βe·ra] *f* (*frigorífico*) fridge; **este cuarto es una ~** this room is freezing
nevisca [ne·'βis·ka] *f* light snowfall
neviscar <c→qu> [ne·βis·'kar] *v impers* to snow lightly
nexo ['nek·so] *m* nexus; LING connective
ni [ni] *conj* ~ ... ~ ... neither... nor...; **no fumo ~ bebo** I don't smoke or drink, I neither smoke nor drink; ~ (**siquiera**) not even; **¡~ lo pienses!** don't even let it cross your mind!; **sin más ~ más** without any further ado; **~ bien...** *Arg* as soon as...
nica ['ni·ka] *adj Nic*, *inf* Nicaraguan
Nicaragua [ni·ka·'ra·ɣwa] *f* Nicaragua

i **Nicaragua**, located in Central America, borders on Honduras to the north, Costa Rica to the south, the Caribbean Sea to the east, and the Pacific Ocean to the west. The capital of Nicaragua is **Managua**. The country's official language is Spanish and the official currency is the **córdoba**.

nicaragüense [ni·ka·ra·'ɣwen·se] *adj, mf* Nicaraguan
nicho ['ni·tʃo] *m* niche
nicotina [ni·ko·'ti·na] *f* nicotine
nidada [ni·'da·da] *f* **1.** (*huevos*) clutch (of eggs) **2.** (*polluelos*) brood
nidal [ni·'dal] *m* **1.** (*lugar*) nest; (*huevo*) sitting **2.** (*escondite*) hiding place
nido ['ni·do] *m* **1.** (*lecho*) den; ~ **de ladrones** den of thieves; ~ **de discordias** hotbed of dissent; **caerse del ~** *fig* to come down to earth with a bump **2.** (*nidal*) nest
niebla ['nje·βla] *f* fog; **hay ~** it is foggy
nieto, -a ['nje·to, -a] *m, f* grandchild, grandson *m*, grand-daughter *f*; **los nietos** the grandchildren
nieve ['nje·βe] *f* **1.** (*precipitación*) snow; ~ **carbónica** dry ice; **a punto de ~** CULIN stiff; **copo de ~** snowflake **2.** *inf* (*cocaína*) coke, snow **3.** *AmC* (*helado*) ice cream
NIF [nif] *m abr de* **Número de Identificación Fiscal** Fiscal Identity Number
nigeriano, -a [ni·xe·'rja·no, -a] *adj, m, f* Nigerian
nigua ['ni·ɣwa] *f AmC* ZOOL jigger flea
Nilo ['ni·lo] *m* Nile
nimbo ['nim·bo] *m* METEO nimbus
nimiedad [ni·mje·'dad] *f* (*insignificancia*) trifle
nimio, -a ['ni·mjo, -a] *adj* insignificant
ninfa ['nin·fa] *f* **1.** (*mitología*) *t.* ZOOL nymph **2.** (*joven*) girl
ninfómana [nin·'fo·ma·na] *f* nymphomaniac
ningún [nin·'gun] *adj indef v.* **ninguno**

ninguno, -a [nin·'gu·no, -a] **I.** *adj indef* (*precediendo un sustantivo masculino singular: ningún*) any; **por ningún lado** anywhere; **de ninguna manera** no way; **ninguna vez** never; **en ningún sitio** nowhere; **no hay ningún peligro** there is no danger **II.** *pron indef* anything, nothing; (*personas*) anybody, nobody; **no quiso venir ~** nobody wanted to come
niña ['ni·na] *f* **1.** (*chica, persona no adulta*) girl **2.** ANAT pupil; **eres como las ~s de mis ojos** *fig* you are the apple of my eye
niñera [ni·'ne·ra] *f* nanny; (*canguro*) babysitter
niñería [ni·ne·'ri·a] *f* **1.** (*de niños*) childish act **2.** *inf* (*pequeñez*) triviality
niñez [ni·'neθ] *f* childhood; *fig* infancy
niño ['ni·no] *m* boy; ~ **bien** *inf* rich kid; ~ **de la bola** the baby Jesus; ~ **mimado** (*favorito*) spoiled child; ~ **de pecho** babe-in-arms; ~ **probeta** test tube baby; **¡no seas ~!** don't act like a child!
nipón, -ona [ni·'pon, -'po·na] **I.** *adj* Japanese **II.** *m, f* native/inhabitant of Japan
níquel ['ni·kel] *m* nickel
niqui ['ni·ki] *m* (*camiseta*) T-shirt
nitidez [ni·ti·'deθ] *f* brightness; FOTO clarity
nítido, -a ['ni·ti·do, -a] *adj* bright; FOTO clear
nitrato [ni·'tra·to] *m* nitrate; ~ **de plata** silver nitrate
nítrico, -a ['ni·tri·ko, -a] *adj* nitric; **ácido ~** nitric acid
nitrógeno [ni·'tro·xe·no] *m* nitrogen
nitroglicerina [ni·tro·ɣli·θe·'ri·na] *f* nitroglycerine
nitroso, -a [ni·'tro·so, -a] *adj* nitrous
nivel [ni·'βel] *m* **1.** (*estándar*) standard; ~ **de vida** standard of living; **estar al ~** to come up to scratch; **estar al ~ de lo exigido** to rise to the occasion **2.** (*horizontalidad, grado, cota*) level; ~ **estilístico** stylistic level; **paso a ~** grade crossing; **sobre el ~ del mar** above sea level
nivelación [ni·βe·la·'sjon, -'θjon] *f* leveling; ~ **del presupuesto** balancing the budget
nivelar [ni·βe·'lar] **I.** *vt* to level **II.** *vr*: ~**se** to level out; ~**se con alguien** to catch up with sb
níveo, -a ['ni·βeo, -a] *adj elev* snowy, snow-white
nixtamal [nis·ta·'mal] *m Méx* corn (*specially processed for tortilla-making*)
NO [no·ro·'es·te] *abr de* **Noroeste** NW
no [no] *adv* **1.** (*respuesta*) no; **¡que ~!** I tell you it isn't! **2.** + *adjetivo* non-; ~ **protegido** non-protected **3.** + *verbo* not; ~ **... nada** not... anything; ~ **... nadie** not... anyone; ~ **... nunca** not... ever, never; ~ **ya** not only; **ya ~** not any more, no longer; **hoy ~ tengo clase** I don't have class today; ~ **tiene más que un abrigo** he/she only has one coat; ~ **quiero hablar más de esto** I don't want to talk about this any more **4.** (*retórica*) **¿~?** isn't he/she/it?, don't we/they? ► ~ **bien** + *subj* as soon as; **el ~ va** _más_ the best, the state-of-the-art; **tener**

un ~ **sé qué** to have something special; **a ~ ser que** +*subj* unless; **¡a que ~!** do you want to bet?; **¿cómo ~?** of course; **o, sí** ~ otherwise

nº ['nu·me·ro] *abr de* **número** No.

nobiliario, -a [no·βi·'lja·rjo] *adj* noble

noble ['no·βle] **I.** *adj* <nobilísimo> **1.** *t.* QUÍM (*aristócrata*) noble **2.** (*bueno*) upright **3.** (*honesto*) honest **II.** *mf* nobleman *m*, noblewoman *f*

nobleza [no·'βle·sa, -θa] *f* **1.** (*linaje, hidalguía*) nobility **2.** (*bondad*) uprightness **3.** (*honestidad*) honesty

noche ['no·tʃe] *f* **1.** (*contrario de día*) night; ~**vieja** New Year's Eve; **buenas** ~**s** (*saludo*) good evening; (*despedida*) good night; **turno de** ~ night shift; **media** ~ midnight; **a media** ~ at midnight; **por la** ~ at night; **toda la** ~ all night long; **ayer** (**por la**) ~ last night; **hacerse de** ~ to get dark; **hacer** ~ **en** to spend the night in **2.** (*tarde*) evening **3.** (*oscuridad*) darkness; **es de** ~ it's dark ▶ **ser como la** ~ **y el día** to be like night and day; **de la** ~ **a la mañana** overnight; **pasar la** ~ **en blanco** to stay up all night

Nochebuena [no·tʃe·'bwe·na] *f* Christmas Eve; **en** ~ on Christmas Eve

nochecita [no·tʃe·'θi·ta] *f AmL* dusk, nightfall

nochero [no·'tʃe·ro] *m* **1.** *CSur* (*vigilante*) night watchman **2.** *Col* (*mesilla*) bedside table

Nochevieja [no·tʃe·'βje·xa] *f* New Year's Eve

noción [no·'sjon, -'θjon] *f* **1.** (*idea*) idea; **perder la** ~ **del tiempo** to lose track of the time **2.** *pl* (*fundamentos*) base; **tengo nociones de francés** I know a little French

nocivo, -a [no·'θi·βo, -a] *adj* harmful; ~ **para la salud** damaging to health

noctámbulo, -a [nok·'tam·bu·lo, -a] **I.** *adj* **ser** ~ to be a night-bird; (*salir*) to go out at night **II.** *m, f* (*trasnochador*) night worker; (*que sale*) night owl

nocturno [nok·'tur·no] *m* MÚS nocturne

nocturno, -a [nok·'tur·no, -a] *adj* **1.** (*de noche*) night; **la vida nocturna** nightlife **2.** BOT, ZOOL nocturnal

nodo ['no·do] *m* node

nodriza [no·'dri·sa, -θa] *f* **1.** (*ama*) wet-nurse **2.** (*transporte*) **avión** ~ mother airplane; **buque** ~ supply ship

Noé *m* REL Noah; **el arca de** ~ Noah's ark

nogal [no·'ɣal] *m*, **noguera** [no·'ɣe·ra] *f* walnut tree

nómada ['no·ma·da] **I.** *adj* nomadic; **pueblo** ~ nomadic people **II.** *mf* nomad

nomás [no·'mas] *adv AmL* **1.** (*solamente*) only; ~ **que** +*subj* unless; **¡pase** ~! come straight in! **2.** (*nada más*) and that was all **3.** (*apenas*) hardly

nombrado, -a [nom·'bra·do, -a] *adj* famous

nombramiento [nom·bra·'mjen·to] *m* (*designación*) appointment; (*militar*) commission

nombrar [nom·'brar] *vt* **1.** (*citar*) to quote; (*mencionar*) to mention **2.** (*llamar*) to call **3.** (*designar*) to appoint; (*militar*) to commis-

sion

nombre ['nom·bre] *m* **1.** (*designación*) name; ~ **y apellido** name and surname, full name; ~ **de familia** surname, last name; ~ **de pila**, **primer** ~ first name; ~ **de soltera** maiden name; **de** ~ by name; ~ **artístico** stage name; **sin** ~ nameless; **en** ~ **de** on behalf of; **a su propio** ~ in his/her own name; **conocer a alguien de** ~ to know sb by name; **dar su** ~ to give one's name; **poner un** ~ **a alguien** to give sb a name; **llamar a las cosas por su** ~ *fig* to call a spade a spade; **tu conducta no tiene** ~ your behavior is a disgrace; **reservar a** ~ **de X** to book in X's name **2.** (*reputación*) reputation; **de** ~ famous **3.** LING noun; ~ **común** common noun; ~ **propio** proper noun

nomenclátor [no·men·'kla·tor] *m* catalogue of names

nomenclatura [no·men·kla·'tu·ra] *f* nomenclature

nomeolvides [no·meol·'βi·des] *f inv* forget-me-not

nómina ['no·mi·na] *f* **1.** (*lista*) list; (*de sueldos*) payroll **2.** (*haberes*) salary

nominación [no·mi·na·'sjon, -'θjon] *f* appointment, nomination

nominal [no·mi·'nal] *adj* **1.** (*relativo al nombre*) nominal; **citación** ~ personal summons; **valor** ~ nominal value **2.** LING noun

nominar [no·mi·'nar] *vt* to nominate

nominativo [no·mi·na·'ti·βo] *m* LING nominative

nominativo, -a [no·mi·na·'ti·βo, -a] *adj* nominative

non [non] **I.** *adj* odd **II.** *m* odd number; **de** ~ odd; **estar** [*o* **quedar**] **de** ~ *inf* to be the odd one out; **decir** (**que**) ~**es** *fig* to say no

noquear [no·ke·'ar] *vt* to knock out

nordeste [nor·'des·te] *m* (*dirección*) North East; (*viento*) northeasterly

nórdico, -a ['nor·di·ko, -a] *adj* northern, northerly

noreste [nor·'es·te] *m v.* **nordeste**

noria ['no·rja] *f* **1.** (*para agua*) water wheel **2.** *inf* (*trabajo*) treadmill *fig*; **este trabajo es una** ~ this job is a pain in the neck **3.** (*columpio*) Ferris wheel

norirlandés, -esa [no·rir·lan·'des, -·'de·sa] *adj* Northern Irish

norma ['nor·ma] *f* rule; (*general*) norm, standard; ~**s de circulación** road safety manual; ~ **técnica** technical norm; **observar la** ~ to follow the rules; **como** ~ (*general*) as a rule

normal [nor·'mal] *adj* normal; **gasolina** ~ regular gas

normalizar <z→c> [nor·ma·li·'sar, -'θar] *vt* **1.** (*volver normal*) to normalize **2.** (*reglar*) to regulate

normalmente [nor·mal·'men·te] *adv* normally; (*habitualmente*) usually

normando, -a [nor·'man·do, -a] *adj, m, f* Norman

N

normativa [nor·ma·'ti·βa] *f* rules *pl;* **~ comunitaria** POL Community regulations *pl;* **según la ~ vigente** according to current rules

normativo, -a [nor·ma·'ti·βo, -a] *adj* normative

noroeste [no·ro·'es·te] *m* (*dirección*) North West; (*viento*) northwesterly

norte ['nor·te] *m* **1.** (*punto cardinal*) north; **el ~ de España** Northern Spain; **al ~ de** north of **2.** (*viento*) northerly **3.** (*guía*) aim; **ha perdido el ~** *fig* he/she has lost his/her way; **sin ~** aimless

norteamericano, -a [nor·te·a·me·ri·'ka·no, -a] *adj, m, f* North American; (*de los EE.UU.*) American

nortear [nor·te·'ar] *vr:* **~ se** *Méx* to get lost

norteño, -a [nor·'te·ɲo, -a] *adj* Northern

nortino, -a [nor·'ti·no, -a] *adj, m, f Chile, Perú* (*norteño*) northern

Noruega [no·'rwe·ɣa] *f* Norway

noruego, -a [no·'rwe·ɣo] *adj, m, f* Norwegian

nos [nos] **I.** *pron pers* us; **tu primo nos pegó** your cousin hit us; **nos escribieron una carta** they wrote a letter to us **II.** *pron reflexivo* ourselves, each other

nosocomio [no·so·'ko·mjo] *m AmL* hospital

nosotros, -as [no·'so·tros, -as] *pron pers, 1. pl* **1.** (*sujeto*) we **2.** (*tras preposición*) us

nostalgia [nos·'tal·xja] *f* (*de lugar*) homesickness; (*del pasado*) nostalgia; **~ de alguien** longing for sb

nostálgico, -a [nos·'tal·xi·ko, -a] *adj* (*de un lugar*) homesick; (*del pasado*) nostalgic; **~ de alguien** longing (for) sb; **sentimiento ~** sentimental longing

nota ['no·ta] *f* **1.** (*anotación*) note; **~ al pie de la página** footnote **2.** (*apunte*) note; **tomar ~** to take notes; **tomar (buena) ~ de algo** to take (good) note of sth **3.** (*aviso*) letter; **~ circular** circular **4.** (*calificación*) mark, grade; **sacar malas ~s** to get bad marks [*o* grades] **5.** (*factura*) receipt; **~ de caja** receipt **6.** (*cuenta*) bill **7.** (*detalle*) touch; **una ~ individual** a personal touch **8.** MÚS note ▶ **dar la ~** to stand out (in a negative way); **dejar mala ~** to leave a bad impression; **forzar la ~** to go too far

notable [no·'ta·βle] **I.** *adj* remarkable; (*suma*) considerable **II.** *m* ENS *in the Spanish education system the qualification equivalent to 7 or 8 on a scale of ten*

notación [no·ta·'sjon, -'θjon] *f* **1.** (*sistema*) notation; **~ musical** musical notation; **~ fonética** phonetic script **2.** MAT, QUÍM annotation

notar [no·'tar] *vt* to notice; (*calor*) to feel; **hacer ~** to point out; **hacerse ~** to stand out

notaría [no·ta·'ria] *f* notary's office

notariado, -a [no·ta·'rja·do, -a] *adj* profession of notary

notarial [no·ta·'rjal] *adj* JUR legal; (*hecho por el notario*) notarial

notario, -a [no·'ta·rjo, -a] *m, f* notary

noticia [no·'ti·sja, -θja] *f* (piece of) news; **las ~s** the news; **~ falsa** a false news item; **~ de prensa** press report; **ser ~** to be in the news; **~s de última hora** latest news; **tener ~ de algo** to have heard about sth; **andar atrasado de ~s** not to be up to date (with the news)

noticiario [no·ti·'sja·rjo, -'θja·rjo] *m* RADIO, TV news program; **~ deportivo** sports news

notificación [no·ti·fi·ka·'sjon, -'θjon] *f* notification; **~ de accidentes** accident report; **~ por escrito** written notification

notificar <c→qu> [no·ti·fi·'kar] *vt* to notify; **hacer ~** to let it be known

notorio, -a [no·'to·rjo, -a] *adj* **1.** (*conocido*) well-known **2.** (*evidente*) obvious

nov. *abr de* **noviembre** Nov.

novatada [no·βa·'ta·da] *f* **1.** (*broma*) hazing; **gastar la ~ a alguien** to play a trick on sb; **pagar la ~** to learn the hard way **2.** *inf* (*complicación*) beginner's mistake

novato, -a [no·'βa·to, -a] *m, f* (*en un lugar*) new guy *m,* new girl *f;* (*en una actividad*) beginner

novecientos, -as [no·βe·'θjen·tos, -as] *adj* nine hundred; *v.t.* **ochocientos**

novedad [no·βe·'dad] *f* **1.** (*acontecimiento*) new development; **¿hay alguna ~?** anything new?; **las últimas ~es** the latest; **el enfermo sigue sin ~es** the patient's condition is unchanged **2.** (*cosa*) novelty; (*libro*) new publication

novedoso, -a [no·βe·'do·so, -a] *adj AmL* novel

novel [no·'βel] **I.** *adj* new; (*sin experiencia*) inexperienced **II.** *mf* beginner

novela [no·'βe·la] *f* novel; **~ corta** novella; **~ por entregas** serialized novel; **~ policíaca** detective story; **~ rosa** romance; **¡déjate de ~s!** stop dreaming!

novelesco, -a [no·βe·'les·ko, -a] *adj* novel; *fig* amazing

novelista [no·βe·'lis·ta] *mf* novelist

novelística [no·βe·'lis·ti·ka] *f* fiction

noveno, -a [no·'βe·no, -a] *adj, m, f* ninth; *v.t.* **octavo**

noventa [no·'βen·ta] *adj inv, m* ninety; *v.t.* **ochenta**

novia *f v.* **novio**

noviar [no·'βjar] *vi CSur* to go steady; **~ con alguien** to be going out with sb

noviazgo [no·'βjaθ·ɣo] *m* **1.** (*para casarse*) engagement **2.** *inf* (*relación*) relationship

novicio, -a [no·'βi·sjo, a; -θjo, -a] *m, f* **1.** REL novice **2.** (*principiante*) beginner

noviembre [no·'βjem·bre] *m* November; *v.t.* **marzo**

novillada [no·βi·'ja·da, -'ʎa·da] *f* TAUR bullfight with young bulls and less experienced bullfighters

novillero, -a [no·βi·'je·ro, -'ʎe·ro, -a] *m, f* **1.** (*torero*) apprentice bullfighter **2.** (*escuela*) truant

novillo, -a [no·'βi·jo, -a; -ʎo, -a] *m, f* young

bull ▸ **hacer** ~**s** to play truant
novio, -a ['no·βjo, -a] *m, f* **1.** (*para casarse*) bridegroom *m*, bride *f*; **los** ~**s** (*en la boda*) the bride and groom; (*después de la boda*) the newly-weds; **viaje de** ~**s** honeymoon **2.** (*en relación amorosa*) boyfriend *m*, girlfriend *f*; **echarse novia** to get a girlfriend ▸ **compuesta y sin** ~ all dressed up and nowhere to go
novísimo, -a [no·'βi·si·mo] *adj* brand new; (*noticia*) latest
nubarrón [nu·βa·'rron] *m* storm cloud
nube ['nu·βe] *f* cloud; ~ **de mosquitos** cloud of mosquitoes; ~ **de verano** *t. fig* passing cloud; (*pequeñez*) trifle; **descargar una** ~ to rain ▸ **bajar de las** ~**s** to come back down to earth; **estar por las** ~**s** (*precios*) to be sky-high; **poner a alguien por las** ~**s** to praise sb to the skies; **ponerse por las** ~**s** *inf* (*persona*) to go up the wall; **vivir en las** ~**s** to have one's head in the clouds
núbil ['nu·βil] *adj* nubile
nublado [nu·'βla·do] **I.** *adj* cloudy **II.** *m* METEO cloud cover
nublar [nu·'βlar] **I.** *vt* **1.** (*nubes*) to cloud **2.** (*mente*) to get confused; (*ojos*) to mist over **II.** *vr:* ~**se 1.** (*nubes*) to cloud over **2.** (*mente*) to get confused; (*ojos*) to mist over; **se me nubló la vista** my eyes clouded over
nubosidad [nu·βo·si·'dad] *f* cloudiness
nuboso, -a [nu·'βo·so, -a] *adj* cloudy
nuca ['nu·ka] *f* ANAT nape, back of the neck
nuclear [nu·kle·'ar] *adj* nuclear; **energía** ~ nuclear energy [*o* power]
núcleo ['nu·kleo] *m* **1.** QUÍM nucleus **2.** (*centro*) hub; ~ **de una idea** core of an idea; ~ **urbano** town
nudillo [nu·'di·jo, -ʎo] *m* ANAT knuckle
nudo ['nu·do] *m* **1.** *t.* NÁUT (*atadura*) knot; ~ **corredizo** slipknot; **deshacer el** ~ to untie the knot **2.** (*madera*) knot; ~ **de rama** fork in a branch; **sin** ~**s** smooth **3.** (*punto de reunión*) center; ~ **de comunicaciones** communications center; ~ **ferroviario** junction **4.** (*cosa que une*) **el** ~ **de la amistad** the ties of friendship **5.** (*dificultad*) **el** ~ **del problema es...** the crux of the problem is...
nudoso, -a [nu·'do·so, -a] *adj* knotty; (*madera*) gnarled
nuera ['nwe·ra] *f* daughter-in-law
nuestro, -a ['nwes·tro, -a] **I.** *adj pos antepuesto* our; ~ **hijo/nuestra hija** our son/daughter; ~**s nietos** our grandchildren; **por nuestra parte** on our side **II.** *pron pos* **1.** (*propiedad*) **la casa es nuestra** the house is ours; **¡ya es** ~**!** *fig* we got it/him! **2.** *tras artículo* **el** ~/**la nuestra/lo** ~ ours; **los** ~**s** our people; (*parientes*) our family **3.** *tras substantivo* of ours, our; **una amiga nuestra** a friend of ours; **es culpa nuestra** it is our fault
nueva ['nwe·βa] *f* piece of news; **esto me coge de** ~**s** this is news to me; **la buena** ~ good tidings *pl*

nuevamente [nwe·βa·'men·te] *adv* **1.** (*otra vez*) again **2.** (*últimamente*) recently
Nueva York [nwe·βa·'jork] *f* New York
Nueva Zelanda [nwe·βa·se·'lan·da] *f* New Zealand
nueve ['nwe·βe] *adj inv, m* nine; *v.t.* **ocho**
nuevo, -a ['nwe·βo, -a] *adj* new; **de** ~ again; **sentirse como** ~ to feel like a new man; **¿qué hay de** ~**?** what's new?; **hasta** ~ **aviso** until further notice
nuez [nweθ] *f* **1.** BOT walnut; ~ **de anacardo** cashew nut; ~ **de coco** coconut; ~ **moscada** nutmeg; **cascar nueces** to crack nuts **2.** ANAT Adam's apple; **apretar la** ~ **a alguien** *inf* to wring sb's neck
nulidad [nu·li·'dad] *f* **1.** (*no válido*) nullity; **declarar la** ~ **de algo** to declare sth invalid **2.** *inf* (*persona*) nonentity; **ser una** ~ to be useless
nulo, -a ['nu·lo, -a] *adj* **1.** (*inválido*) null; **voto** ~ invalid vote **2.** (*incapaz*) useless; **soy** ~ **para el deporte** I'm no good at sports
numeración [nu·me·ra·'sjon, -'θjon] *f* (*sistema*) numbering system; ~ **arábiga** Arabic numerals; ~ **correlativa** correlated sequence; ~ **decimal** decimal system
numeral [nu·me·'ral] **I.** *adj* numeral **II.** *m* LING number
numerar [nu·me·'rar] *vt* to number; ~ **correlativamente** to make a correlated sequence; (*paginar*) to paginate; **sin** ~ unnumbered
numerario, -a [nu·me·'ra·rjo, -a] *adj* **1.** (*de números*) full **2.** (*fijo*) permanent; (*profesor*) tenured
numérico, -a [nu·'me·ri·ko, -a] *adj* numerical
número ['nu·me·ro] *m* **1.** MAT number; ~ **cardinal** cardinal number; ~ **primo** prime number; ~ **quebrado** fraction; **en** ~**s redondos** in round numbers; **aprender de** ~**s** *inf* to learn one's sums; **hacer** ~**s** to do one's sums **2.** (*cantidad*) number; ~ **de habitantes** number of inhabitants; **sin** ~ innumerable **3.** *t.* LING (*cifra, edición*) number; ~ **de matrícula** enrollment number; ~ **de identificación personal** PIN (personal identification number); ~ **de zapatos** shoe size; ~ **suelto** odd number **4.** (*ejemplar*) copy; ~ **atrasado** back issue **5.** (*actuación*) ~ **de baile** dance number; **montar un** ~ to make a scene
numeroso, -a [nu·me·'ro·so, -a] *adj* numerous; **familia numerosa** large family
nunca ['nun·ka] *adv* never; ~ **jamás** never ever; **más que** ~ more than ever
nupcial [nup·'sjal, -'β·θjal] *adj* nuptial; **corona** ~ bridal wreath
nupcias ['nup·sjas, -β·θjas] *fpl* nuptials *pl*; **segundas** ~ remarriage; **posteriores** ~ later wedding
nurse ['nur·se] *f AmL* **1.** (*niñera*) nanny; (*extranjera*) au-pair **2.** (*enfermera*) nurse
nutria ['nu·trja] *f* otter
nutrición [nu·tri·'sjon, -'θjon] *f* nutrition
nutrido, -a [nu·'tri·do, -a] *adj* **1.** (*alimentado*)

N

fed; **bien** ~ well-fed; **mal** ~ undernourished **2.** (*numeroso*) ample; (*biblioteca*) well-stocked
nutrir [nu·'trir] **I.** *vt* **1.** (*alimentar*) to feed; (*piel*) to nourish **2.** (*fortalecer*) to strengthen **II.** *vr* ~**se de** [*o* con] **algo** to feed off sth
nutritivo, -a [nu·tri·'ti·βo, -a] *adj* nutritious; **valor** ~ nutritional value

Ñ

Ñ, ñ ['e·ɲe] *f* Ñ, ñ

> **i** The **eñe** is the trademark of the Spanish **alfabeto**. Up until a few years ago, the "ch" (**la che**), which followed in the alphabet directly after the "c," and the "ll" (**la elle**), which came directly after the "l," were also part of the alphabet, as they are both independent sounds in their own right. The two sounds were dropped as separate letters of the alphabet in order to internationalize the Spanish alphabet.

ña [ɲa] *f AmC, AmS, inf* (*señora*) lady, Missis
ñácara ['ɲa·ka·ra] *f Chile* sore, ulcer
ñandutí [ɲan·du·'ti] *m CSur* Paraguayan lace
ñangotarse [ɲan·go·'tar·se] *vr* **1.** *PRico, RDom* (*ponerse en cuclillas*) to squat **2.** *PRico* (*someterse*) to yield **3.** *PRico* (*perder el ánimo*) to lose heart
ñaña ['ɲa·ɲa] *f Chile, Perú* elder sister
ñapango, -a [ɲa·'pan·go, -a] *adj Col* mestizo, half-breed
ñata ['ɲa·ta] *f AmL, inf* beak
ñato, -a ['ɲa·to, -a] **I.** *adj* **1.** *CSur* (*chato*) snub-nosed **2.** *Col* (*gangoso*) nasal **II.** *m, f AmL* guy
ñeque ['ɲe·ke] **I.** *adj AmC* strong **II.** *m* **1.** *Chile, Ecua, Perú* (*fuerza*) strength; (*energía*) vim **2.** *Perú* (*valor, coraje*) courage
ñire ['ɲi·re] *m Chile* BOT Antarctic beech
ño [ɲo] *m AmC, AmS, inf* (*señor*) abbreviated form of 'señor' used only before the first name
ñoco, -a ['ɲo·ko, -a] *adj AmS* (*sin dedo*) missing a finger; (*sin mano*) missing a hand
ñoñería [ɲo·ɲe·'ri·a] *f* **1.** (*simpleza*) inanity **2.** (*dengues*) silliness
ñoño, -a ['ɲo·ɲo, -a] **I.** *adj inf* **1.** (*soso*) insipid; (*aburrido*) boring **2.** (*tonto*) inane **3.** (*remilgado*) prudish **II.** *m, f inf* **1.** (*tonto*) idiot **2.** (*aburrido*) bore
ñoqui ['ɲo·ki] *m* gnocchi
ñorbo ['ɲor·βo] *m Ecua, Perú* BOT passion-flower
ñu [ɲu] *m* gnu

ñudo ['ɲu·do] *m* knot; **al** ~ *AmL, inf* in vain
ñuto, -a ['ɲu·to, -a] *adj AmS, Arg, Perú* (*ablandado*) tenderized

O

O, o [o] *f* O, o; ~ **de Oviedo** O as in Oscar
▶ **no saber hacer la 'o' con un <u>canuto</u>** not to know a thing
o, ó [o] *conj* or; ~**...,** ~**...** either..., or...; ~ **sea** in other words; ~ **bien** or else
O [o·'es·te] *abr de* **oeste** W
oasis [o·'a·sis] *m inv* oasis
obcecación [oβ·θe·ka·'θjon] *f* stubborn insistence
obcecar <c→qu> [oβ·θe·'kar] **I.** *vt* to blind **II.** *vr:* ~**se** to be blinded, to stubbornly insist
obedecer [o·βe·de·'ser, -θer] *irr como crecer* **I.** *vt* (*orden, a alguien*) to obey; (*instrucciones*) to follow; **hacerse** ~ to make people obey **II.** *vi* (*provenir*) to be due; (*responder*) to respond
obediencia [o·βe·'djen·sja, -θja] *f* obedience
obediente [o·βe·'djen·te] *adj* obedient
obelisco [o·βe·'lis·ko] *m* obelisk
obertura [o·βer·'tu·ra] *f t.* MÚS overture
obesidad [o·βe·si·'dad] *f* obesity
obeso, -a [o·'βe·so, -a] *adj* obese
obispado [o·βis·'pa·do] *m* REL **1.** (*cargo*) bishopric **2.** (*diócesis*) diocese
obispo [o·'βis·po] *m* REL bishop ▶ **<u>trabajar</u> para el** ~ to work for nothing
óbito ['o·βi·to] *m* death, demise *form*
obituario [o·βi·'twa·rjo] *m* **1.** *AmL* (*defunción*) demise **2.** *AmL* (*del periódico*) obituary
objeción [oβ·xe·'sjon, -'θjon] *f* objection; ~ **de conciencia** conscientious objection; **poner** ~ **a algo** to object to sth
objetar [oβ·xe·'tar] *vt* to object; **tengo algo que** ~ I have an objection
objetividad [oβ·xe·ti·βi·'dad] *f* objectivity
objetivo [oβ·xe·'ti·βo] *m* **1.** (*finalidad*) goal; **tener como** ~ to have as one's goal **2.** FOTO lens **3.** (*blanco*) target
objetivo, -a [oβ·xe·'ti·βo, -a] *adj* objective
objeto [oβ·'xe·to] *m* **1.** (*cosa*) object; ~ **de enseñanza** teaching aid; ~ **de lujo** luxury item; ~ **de valor** valuables *pl;* **la mujer** ~ woman as an object; ~**s perdidos** lost property **2.** (*motivo*) purpose; **el** ~ **de la presente es...** the purpose of this letter is...; **con (el)** [*o* **al**] ~ **de...** in order to...; **tener por** ~ to have as one's aim **3.** LING object
objetor(a) [oβ·xe·'tor, -·'to·ra] *m(f)* dissenter; ~ **de conciencia** conscientious objector
oblea [o·'βlea] *f* (*hostia*) wafer
oblicuo, -a [o·'βli·kwo, -a] *adj* oblique, slanted
obligación [o·βli·ɣa·'sjon, -'θjon] *f* **1.** (*deber*)

obligation; ~ **alimenticia** duty to provide maintenance; **contraer una** ~ to undertake an obligation; **cumplir con una** ~ to fulfill an obligation; **dedicarse a sus obligaciones** to devote oneself to one's duties; **faltar a sus obligaciones** to neglect one's duties; **tener la** ~ **de hacer algo** to be obliged to do sth **2.** (*deuda*) liability; (*documento*) bond

obligado, -a [o·βli·'ɣa·do, -a] *adj* **1.** *estar* obliged **2.** *ser* (*imprescindible*) obligatory; **tema** ~ compulsory topic

obligar <g→gu> [o·βli·'ɣar] **I.** *vt* **1.** (*forzar*) to force; (*comprometer*) to oblige **2.** *Chile, Arg* (*invitar*) to invite to drink **II.** *vr:* ~ **se** to commit oneself

obligatoriedad [o·βli·ɣa·to·rje·'dad] *f* obligation; **de** ~ **general** universally compulsory; ~ **del voto** requirement to vote

obligatorio, -a [o·βli·ɣa·'to·rjo, -a] *adj* obligatory; **asignatura obligatoria** compulsory subject; **compromiso** ~ binding commitment; **es** ~ **llevar puesto el casco** helmets must be worn

oblongo, -a [o·'βlon·go, -a] *adj* oblong

obnubilación [oβ·nu·βi·la·'sjon, -'θjon] *f* (*trastorno*) confusion; (*ofuscación*) fascination

obnubilar [oβ·nu·βi·'lar] *vt* (*trastornar*) to confuse; (*ofuscar*) to fascinate

oboe [o·'βoe] *m* MÚS oboe; (*músico*) oboist

obra ['o·βra] *f* **1.** (*creación, labor*) work; ~ **de arte** work of art; ~ **benéfica** charitable act; ~**s completas** collected [*o* complete] works; ~ **de consulta** reference work; ~ **maestra** masterpiece; ~ **de teatro** play; **por** ~ **(y gracia) de** thanks to; **¡manos a la** ~**!** let's get to work! **2.** (*construcción*) building work; (*lugar en construcción*) construction site; (*edificio*) building; ~ **de caminos, canales y puertos** civil engineering; ~**s públicas** public works; **mano de** ~ labor; **estar en** ~**s** to be under construction ▶ ~**s son amores** y **no buenas razones** *prov* actions speak louder than words; ~ **empezada, medio** acabada *prov* the hardest part is getting started *prov*

obradera [o·βra·'de·ra] *f Col, Guat, Pan* (*diarrea*) diarrhea

obraje [o·'βra·xe] *m* **1.** *CSur* sawmill **2.** *Méx* butcher's shop

obrajero, -a [o·βra·'xe·ro, -a] *m, f* **1.** *AmL* (*propietario*) sawmill owner **2.** *Arg, Par* (*peón*) sawmill worker **3.** *AmL* (*artesano*) craftsman **4.** *Méx* (*carnicero*) pork butcher

obrar [o·'βrar] **I.** *vi* **1.** (*actuar*) to act; ~ **a tontas** y **a locas** *inf* to act rashly **2.** *vulg* (*defecar*) to move one's bowels **II.** *vi, vt* **1.** (*hacer efecto*) to have an effect on; ~ **buen efecto** to be effective; ~ **sobre alguien/algo** to act on sb/sth **2.** (*construir*) to build **3.** (*hacer*) to do; (*trabajar*) to work; **sin** ~ unworked

obrero, -a [o·'βre·ro, -a] **I.** *adj* (*relativo al trabajo*) working; (*relativo al obrero*) working-class **II.** *m, f* worker; ~ **agrícola** farm laborer; ~ **asalariado** day laborer; ~ **eventual**

temporary worker; ~ **especializado** |*o* **cualificado**| skilled worker; ~ **fijo** permanent employee; **ser alguien** ~ **de su propia ruina** to be the author of one's own downfall

obscenidad [oβs·θe·ni·'dad] *f* obscenity

obsceno, -a [oβs·'θe·no, -a] *adj* obscene

obscuro, -a [oβs·'ku·ro, -a] *adj v.* **oscuro**

obsequiar [oβ·se·'kjar] *vt* **1.** (*con atenciones*) to honor; (*con bebidas*) to toast; (*con regalos*) to bestow **2.** (*agasajar*) to lavish attention on; (*festejar*) to celebrate; ~ **con su presencia** to honor with one's presence **3.** *AmL* (*regalar*) to give

obsequio [oβ·'se·kjo] *m* **1.** (*regalo*) gift **2.** (*agasajo*) attention; **¡hágame Ud. este** ~**!** please do this favor for me!; **en** ~ **de alguien** in honor of sb

obsequioso, -a [oβ·se·'kjo·so, -a] *adj* attentive

observación [oβ·ser·βa·'sjon, -'θjon] *f* **1.** (*contemplación, vigilancia*) observation **2.** (*comentario*) remark; ~ **marginal** note

observador(a) [oβ·ser·βa·'dor, -·'do·ra] **I.** *adj* observant **II.** *m(f)* observer

observancia [oβ·ser·'βan·sja, -θja] *f* observance

observar [oβ·ser·'βar] *vt* **1.** (*contemplar, cumplir*) to observe **2.** (*orden*) to follow; (*normas, plazos*) to adhere to **3.** (*notar*) to notice; **hacer** ~ **algo a alguien** to bring sth to sb's attention

observatorio [oβ·ser·βa·'to·rjo] *m* observatory; ~ **astronómico** observatory; ~ **meteorológico** weather station

obsesión [oβ·se·'sjon] *f* obsession

obsesionado, -a [oβ·se·sjo·'na·do, -a] *adj* obsessed; **está** ~ **con ella** he is obsessed with [*o* by] her

obsesionar [oβ·se·sjo·'nar] **I.** *vt* to obsess; **el fútbol lo obsesiona** he is obsessed with [*o* by] soccer **II.** *vr:* ~ **se** to be obsessed; ~ **se con algo/alguien** to be obsessed by [*o* with] sth/sb

obsesivo, -a [oβ·se·'si·βo, -a] *adj* obsessive

obseso, -a [oβ·'se·so, -a] **I.** *adj* obsessed **II.** *m, f* obsessive person; ~ **del sexo** sex maniac

obsoleto, -a [oβ·so·'le·to, -a] *adj* obsolete

obstaculizar <z→c> [oβs·ta·ku·li·'sar, -'θar] *vt* to hinder; ~ **la carretera** to obstruct [*o* block] the road; ~ **el progreso** to hinder progress

obstáculo [oβs·'ta·ku·lo] *m* obstacle; DEP hurdle; ~**s comerciales** trade barriers; **salvar un** ~ to overcome an obstacle; **poner** ~**s a alguien** to hinder sb

obstante [oβs·'tan·te] *adv* **no** ~ nevertheless

obstetricia [oβs·te·'tri·sja, -θja] *f* MED obstetrics *pl*

obstinación [oβs·ti·na·'sjon, -'θjon] *f* obstinacy

obstinado, -a [oβs·ti·'na·do, -a] *adj* obstinate

obstinarse [oβs·ti·'nar·se] *vr* to persist; ~ **en su silencio** to remain silent; ~ **contra algo/**

alguien to hold firm against sth/sb

obstrucción [oβs·truk·'sjon, -'θjon] *f* obstruction; MED blockage

obstruir [oβs·tru·'ir] *irr como huir* **I.** *vt* **1.** (*el paso, acción*) to obstruct **2.** (*una tubería*) to block **II.** *vr:* ~ **se** to get blocked

obtención [oβ·ten·'sjon, -'θjon] *f* obtaining; QUÍM extraction; ~ **de datos** data collection

obtener [oβ·te·'ner] *irr como tener vt* to obtain; QUÍM to extract; (*resultado, ventaja*) to gain; ~ **un pedido** to receive an order; **difícil de** ~ not easily obtainable

obtenible [oβ·te·'ni·βle] *adj* obtainable

obturación [oβ·tu·ra·'sjon, -'θjon] *f* **1.** (*cierre*) closure; (*bloqueo*) blockage **2.** (*de dientes*) filling

obturar [oβ·tu·'rar] *vt* to close; (*bloquear*) to block; (*los dientes*) to fill

obtuso, -a [oβ·'tu·so, -a] *adj* (*cosa*) blunt; (*persona*) obtuse

obviar [oβ·'βjar] **I.** *vi* to stand in the way **II.** *vt* (*evitar*) to avoid; (*eliminar*) to remove; ~ **un problema** to get around a problem

obvio, -a ['oβ·βjo, -a] *adj* obvious; **es** ~ it's obvious

oca ['o·ka] *f* **1.** ZOOL goose; **¡es la** ~! *inf* it's the best! **2.** (*juego*) snakes *pl* and ladders

ocasión [o·ka·'sjon] *f* occasion; **coche de** ~ second hand car; **libros de** ~ bargain [*o* cutprice] books; **aprovechar la** ~ to make the most of the opportunity; **desperdiciar la** ~ to waste the opportunity; **en esta** ~ on this occasion; **en ocasiones** sometimes; **con** ~ **de** on the occasion of ▶ **la** ~ **hace al ladrón** *prov* opportunity makes the thief *prov*

ocasional [o·ka·sjo·'nal] *adj* **1.** (*no habitual*) occasional; **trabajo** ~ temporary work **2.** (*causante*) causative; **enfermedad** ~ underlying illness

ocasionar [o·ka·sjo·'nar] *vt* ~ **algo** to cause sth, to bring sth about

ocaso [o·'ka·so] *m* ASTR setting; (*del sol*) sunset; (*oeste*) west

occidental [ok·θi·den·'tal] *adj* western; **potencias** ~ **es** Western powers

occidente [ok·θi·'den·te] *m* GEO west; **el** ~ the West

occipucio [ok·θi·'pu·sjo, -θjo] *m* MED occiput

OCDE [o·θe·de·'e] *f abr de* **Organización para la Cooperación y el Desarrollo Económicos** OECD

Oceanía [o·θea·'ni·a] *f* Oceania

océano [o·'θea·no] *m* **1.** (*mar*) ocean; **Océano Austral** Southern Ocean; **Océano Boreal** Arctic Ocean **2.** *fig* (*cantidad*) sea; **un** ~ **de gente** a sea of people

oceanografía [o·θea·no·ɣra·'fi·a] *f* oceanography

ocelote [o·θe·'lo·te] *m* ocelot

ochava [o·'tʃa·βa] *f AmL* (*chaflán*) corner house; (*de un edificio*) cant

ochenta [o·'tʃen·ta] **I.** *adj inv* **1.** eighty; **los años** ~ the eighties; **un hombre de alrede-**

dor de ~ **años** a man of about eighty years of age; **una mujer en sus** ~ a woman in her eighties **2.** (*octogésimo*) eightieth **II.** *m* eighty

ocho ['o·tʃo] **I.** *adj inv* eight; **jornada de** ~ **horas** eight-hour day; ~ **veces mayor/ menor que...** eight times bigger/smaller than...; **a las** ~ at eight (o'clock); **son las** ~ **y media de la mañana/tarde** it is half past eight in the morning/evening; **las** ~ **y cuarto/ menos cuarto** a quarter past/to eight; **a las** ~ **en punto** at eight o'clock precisely [*o* on the dot]; **el** ~ **de agosto** the eighth of August; **dentro de** ~ **días** in a week's time; **de aquí a** ~ **días** a week from now ▶ **ser más chulo que un** ~ *inf* to be a real showoff; **dar igual** ~ **que** ~ not to care less **II.** *m* eight

ochocientos, -as [o·tʃo·'θjen·tos, -as] *adj* eight hundred

ocio ['o·sjo, -θjo] *m* leisure; **horas de** ~ spare time

ociosear [o·sjo·se·'ar, o·θjo-] *vi AmS* to be at leisure, to loaf (around) *inf*

ociosidad [o·sjo·si·'dad, o·θjo-] *f* idleness ▶ **la** ~ **es la madre de todos los vicios** *prov* the devil makes work for idle hands *prov*, idleness is the root of all evil *prov*

ocioso, -a [o·'sjo·so, -a; -'θjo·so, -a] *adj* **1.** *estar* (*inactivo*) idle **2.** *ser* (*inútil*) useless; **palabras ociosas** idle talk

oclusión [o·klu·'sjon] *f* LING, METEO occlusion

ocote [o·'ko·te] *m Méx* BOT ocote pine

ocre ['o·kre] *adj* ocher

oct. *abr de* **octubre** Oct.

octágono [ok·'ta·ɣo·no] *m* octagon

octava [ok·'ta·βa] *f* LIT, MÚS octave

octavilla [ok·ta·'βi·ja, -ʎa] *f* (*volante*) leaflet

octavo, -a [ok·'ta·βo] **I.** *adj* eighth; **en** ~ **lugar** in eighth place; (*enumeración*) eighth; **la octava parte** an eighth **II.** *m, f* eighth

octogésimo, -a [ok·to·'xe·si·mo, -a] *adj* eightieth; *v.t.* **octavo**

octubre [ok·'tu·βre] *m* October; *v.t.* **marzo**

óctuplo, -a ['ok·tu·plo, -a] *adj* eightfold

ocular [o·ku·'lar] *adj* ocular; **examen** ~ eye test; **testigo** ~ eyewitness

oculista [o·ku·'lis·ta] *mf* MED ophthalmologist

ocultar [o·kul·'tar] **I.** *vt* (*cosa*) to hide; (*información, delito*) to conceal; ~ **la cara entre** [*o* con] **las manos** to cover one's face with one's hands **II.** *vr:* ~ **se** to hide

ocultismo [o·kul·'tis·mo] *m* **el** ~ the occult

oculto, -a [o·'kul·to, -a] *adj* (*escondido*) hidden; (*secreto*) secret; **de** ~ incognito; **en** ~ in secret; **traerse algo** ~ to keep sth hidden

ocupación [o·ku·pa·'sjon, -'θjon] *f* **1.** (*trabajo*) occupation; ~ **lucrativa** well-paid job; ~ **temporal** temporary job; **sin** ~ unemployed **2.** (*apoderamiento*) *t.* MIL occupation; ~ **hotelera** hotel occupancy; **zona de** ~ occupied zone

ocupado, -a [o·ku·'pa·do, -a] *adj* **1.** (*sitio*) occupied **2.** (*persona*) busy **3.** (*línea de teléfono*) busy

ocupante [o·ku·'pan·te] I. *adj* MIL occupying II. *mf* 1.(*de vehículo*) occupant; (*de tren, avión*) passenger 2.(*de un edificio*) resident
ocupar [o·ku·'par] I. *vt* 1.(*lugar, teléfono*) t. MIL to occupy 2.(*un cargo*) to hold; (*vacante*) to fill 3.(*tiempo, espacio, asiento*) to take up 4.(*a una persona*) to keep busy II. *vr* ~**se de** [o con] **algo** to busy oneself with sth; ~**se de alguien** (*cuidar*) to look after sb; **ella se ocupó de todo** she took care of everything
ocurrencia [o·ku·'rren·sja, -θja] *f* (*idea*) idea; **dijo que podía comerse 20 panecillos, ¡qué ~!** he/she said that he/she could eat 20 rolls, what nonsense!; **se bañó en el mar en pleno invierno, ¡qué ~!** he/she swam in the sea in the middle of winter, what a thing to do!; **tener la ~ de...** to have the bright idea of...
ocurrente [o·ku·'rren·te] *adj* witty
ocurrir [o·ku·'rrir] I. *vi* to happen; **¿qué ocurre?** what's wrong?; **¿qué te ocurre?** what's the matter?; **lo que ocurre es que...** the thing is that... II. *vr:* ~**se** to occur; **no se me ocurre nada** I can't think of anything; **¿cómo se te ocurrió esa tontería?** what on earth made you think of a stupid thing like that?; **nunca se me hubiese ocurrido pensar que...** I never would have imagined that...
odiar [o·'djar] *vt* to hate; ~ **a alguien a muerte** to have an undying hatred for sb, to hate sb's guts *inf*
odio ['o·djo] *m* hate, hatred
odioso, -a [o·'djo·so, -a] *adj* 1.(*hostil*) nasty 2.(*repugnante*) horrible 3.*AmL* (*fastidioso*) annoying
odisea [o·di·'sea] *f* odyssey
odontología [o·don·to·lo·'xi·a] *f* MED dentistry
odontólogo, -a [o·don·'to·lo·ɣo, -a] *m, f* MED dentist
odre ['o·dre] *m* wineskin
OEA [o·e·'a] *f abr de* **Organización de los Estados Americanos** OAS
oeste [o·'es·te] *m* 1.(*punto*) west; **el lejano ~** the wild [o far] west; **película del ~** western; **hacia el ~** westward(s); **al ~ de...** west of... 2.(*viento*) westerly
ofender [o·fen·'der] I. *vt* 1.(*humillar*) to offend; **hacerse el ofendido** to take offense 2.(*herir*) to insult II. *vr:* ~**se** to take offense; **¡no te ofendas conmigo!** don't get angry with me!
ofensa [o·'fen·sa] *f* offense
ofensiva [o·fen·'si·βa] *f* offensive; **tomar la ~** to go on the offensive
ofensivo, -a [o·fen·'si·βo, -a] *adj* 1.(*hiriente*) offensive 2.(*dañino*) damaging; ~ **para el medio ambiente** environmentally damaging 3.(*que ataca*) attacking
oferta [o·'fer·ta] *f* 1.(*propuesta*) offer; ~ **de empleo** job offer; **estar de ~** to be on special offer; **hacer mayor ~** to outbid 2.COM tender, bid 3.ECON supply; ~ **y demanda** supply and demand; ~ **excesiva** oversupply
ofertar [o·fer·'tar] *vt* to offer; **invitar a alguien**

a ~ to invite sb to bid
oficial [o·fi·'θjal] *adj* official; **boletín ~** official gazette
oficial(a) [o·fi·'θjal, -·'θja·la] *m(f)* 1.(*oficio manual*) (skilled) worker; (*administrativo*) clerk; ~ **de albañil** builder's mate; ~ **de obra** building worker 2.MIL officer; ~ **de complemento** reserve officer; ~ **marinero** ship's officer 3.(*funcionario*) civil servant; ~ **del juzgado** court clerk; ~ **de la justicia** sheriff; ~ **del registro civil** registry clerk
oficialismo [o·fi·sja·'lis·mo, o·fiθ-] *m* 1.*Arg* (*burocracia*) bureaucracy 2.*AmL* (*del gobierno*) the government and its party members
oficialista [o·fi·sja·'lis·ta, o·fiθ-] *adj* 1.*AmL* (*burocrático*) bureaucratic 2.*AmL* (*del gobierno*) governmental
oficializar <z→c> [o·fi·sja·li·'sar, -θja·li·'θar] *vt* to make official
oficiar [o·fi·'sjar, -'θjar] I. *vt* REL to celebrate II. *vi inf* (*obrar*) to act; ~ **de intérprete** to act as interpreter
oficina [o·fi·'θi·na] *f* office; ~ **de asistencia social** social security office; ~ **de correos** post office; ~ **de cuenta** accounting office; ~ **de empleo** employment agency; ~ **de maquinaria** machine room; ~ **de objetos perdidos** lost property (office)
oficinista [o·fi·si·'nis·ta, o·fiθ-] *mf* office worker
oficio [o·'fi·sjo, -θjo] *m* 1.(*trabajo manual*) trade; ~ **especializado** skilled trade; **ejercer un ~** to have a trade; **sin ~ ni beneficio** out of work; **tomar algo por ~** *fig* to do sth out of habit; **ser del ~** *inf* to be on the game 2.(*profesión*) profession; **de ~** by trade; **gajes del ~** occupational hazards 3.(*función*) function; **defensor de ~** JUR public defender; **de ~** ex officio 4.(*escrito*) official document 5.REL service; ~ **de difuntos** funeral service; **Santo Oficio** Holy Office
oficioso, -a [o·fi·'sjo, -a; -θjo·so, -a] *adj* 1.(*extraoficial*) unofficial; **mentira oficiosa** white lie 2.(*servicial*) obliging
ofidios [o·'fi·djos] *mpl* snakes *pl*
ofimática [o·fi·'ma·ti·ka] *f* COMPUT office automation
ofrecer [o·fre·'ser, -θer] *irr como crecer* I. *vt* to offer; ~ **un banquete** to give a meal; ~ **grandes dificultades** to present a lot of difficulties; ~ **un sacrificio** to offer up a sacrifice II. *vr:* ~**se** (*brindarse*) to offer oneself; **¿se le ofrece algo?** do you need anything?; **¿qué se le ofrece?** may I help you?
ofrecimiento [o·fre·θi·'mjen·to] *m* offer; REL offering
ofrenda [o·'fren·da] *f* offering; (*sacrificio*) sacrifice
oftalmología [of·tal·mo·lo·'xi·a] *f* MED ophthalmology
oftalmólogo, -a [of·tal·'mo·lo·ɣo, -a] *m, f* MED ophthalmologist

O

ofuscar <c→qu> [o·fus·'kar] **I.** *vt* **1.** (*cegar*) to blind **2.** (*la mente*) to confuse; ~ (**la mente**) **a alguien** to confuse sb **II.** *vr* ~**se en algo** to insist on sth; ~**se con una idea** to be obsessed by an idea

ogro ['o·ɣro] *m t. fig* ogre

ohmio ['o·mjo] *m* Fís ohm

oída [o·'i·da] *f* **conocer a alguien de** ~**s** to have heard about sb; **saber algo de** ~**s** to have heard about sth

oído [o·'i·do] *m* **1.** (*sentido*) hearing; **aprender de** ~ to learn by ear; **aplicar el** ~ to listen carefully; **aguzar el** ~ to prick up one's ears; **tener buen** ~ to have a good ear; **duro de** ~ hard of hearing **2.** ANAT ear; ~ **interno/medio/externo** inner/middle/outer ear; **zumbido de** ~**s** buzzing in the ears; **cerrar los** ~**s a algo** to turn a deaf ear to sth; **dar** ~**s a alguien** (*escuchar*) to listen to sb; (*creer*) to believe sb; **hacer** ~**s de mercader** to pretend not to hear; **ladrar a alguien al** ~ to yell into sb's ear; **llegar a** ~**s de alguien** to come to sb's notice [*o* attention]; **pegarse al** ~ to be catchy; **ser todo** ~**s** to be all ears ▶¡~ **al parche!** look out!; **regalar los** ~**s** to flatter

oír [o·'ir] *irr vt* (*sentir*) to hear; (*escuchar*) to listen; **¡oye!** hey!; **¿oyes?** do you understand?; **¡oiga!** excuse me!; **¡Dios te oiga!** may your prayers be answered!; **como lo oyes** believe it or not; ~ **decir que...** to hear that...; **ya me oirá** he/she hasn't heard the last of me; **no se oye el vuelo de una mosca** you could hear a pin drop ▶~, **ver y callar** *prov* hear no evil, see no evil, speak no evil; ~ **como quien oye llover** not to be listening

ojal [o·'xal] *m* **1.** (*para botones*) buttonhole **2.** (*ojete*) eyelet

ojalá [o·xa·'la] *interj* I hope so, I wish; **¡~ tuvieras razón!** if only you were right!

ojeada [o·xe·'a·da] *f* glance; **echar una** ~ **a algo** to glance at sth; **¿puedes echar una** ~ **a mi maleta?** (*vigilar*) could you keep an eye on my suitcase?

ojear [o·xe·'ar] *vt* **1.** (*mirar con atención*) to stare at **2.** (*pasar la vista*) to glance at **3.** (*la caza*) to beat

ojeras [o·'xe·ras] *fpl* bags *pl* (under the eyes); **tener** ~ to have dark circles under one's eyes

ojete [o·'xe·te] *m* **1.** (*ojal*) eyelet **2.** *vulg* (*ano*) asshole **3.** *Arg, Méx* (*vagina*) vagina

ojímetro [o·'xi·me·tro] *m inf* **a** ~ at a rough guess

ojo ['o·xo] **I.** *m* **1.** ANAT eye; ~ **de buey** NÁUT porthole; ~ **de gallo** *fig* corn; ~ **morado** black eye; ~**s rasgados** almond [*o* slanting] eyes; ~**s saltones** [*o* **de rana**] bulging eyes; **a** ~ by eye; **mirar con buenos/malos** ~**s** to approve/disapprove of; **pasar los** ~**s por algo** to run one's eyes over sth; **¡qué** ~ **tienes!** you don't miss a thing!; **tener** ~ **clínico** to be a good diagnostician; *fig* to be very observant **2.** (*agujero*) hole; ~ **de aguja** eye of a needle; ~ **de cerradura** keyhole; ~ **del huracán** eye of the storm;

meterse por el ~ **de una aguja** to be very sharp ▶ **donde pone el** ~, **pone la bala** he/she is a good shot; **no parecerse ni en el blanco de los** ~**s** to be like night and day; **poner los** ~**s en blanco** to roll one's eyes; **costar un** ~ **de la cara** to cost an arm and a leg; **no tener** ~**s en la cara** to be blind; ~**s que no ven, corazón que no siente** *prov* out of sight, out of mind *prov*; **a** ~ **de buen cubero** roughly; **mirar con unos** ~**s redondos como platos** to look wide-eyed; **a** ~**s cerrados** without thinking; **con los** ~**s cerrados** with complete confidence; **andar con cien** ~**s** to be on one's guard; **cuatro** ~**s** *pey* four-eyes; **cuatro** ~**s ven más que dos** *prov* two heads are better than one *prov*; **poner delante de los** ~**s de alguien** to make clear to sb; **ser el** ~ **derecho de alguien** to be the apple of sb's eye; **¡dichosos los** ~**s que te ven!** *irón* it's great to see you after so long!; **estar entrampado hasta los** ~**s** to be up to one's neck in debt; **a** ~**s vistas** visibly; **en un abrir y cerrar de** ~**s** in a flash; **andar con** ~ to be careful; **cerrar los** ~**s a algo** to shut one's eyes to sth; **clavar los** ~**s en algo** to lay eyes on sth; **comerse con los** ~**s** to devour with one's eyes; **echar el** ~ **a algo/alguien** to have one's eye on sth/sb; **echar un** ~ **a algo/alguien** to take a look at sth/sb; (*vigilar*) to keep an eye on sth/sb; **meter algo a alguien por los** ~**s** to shove sth down sb's throat; **no pegar** ~ to not sleep a wink; **no saber dónde poner los** ~**s** not to know which way to turn; **sacarle los** ~**s a alguien** to kill sb; **ser todo** ~**s** to give one's full attention; **tener** ~ (*cuidado*) to be careful; **tener a alguien entre** ~**s** (*estar enfadado*) to be angry with sb; (*tener manía*) to have it in for sb; **¡mis** ~**s!** my darling!; ~ **por** ~ (**y diente por diente**) *prov* an eye for an eye (a tooth for a tooth) **II.** *interj* (be) careful, look out; **¡~ con ese tipo!** watch out for that guy! ▶**¡~ al dinero que es el amor verdadero!** you can't live on thin air!

ojota [o·'xo·ta] *f AmL* (*sandalia*) sandal

okey [o·'ke·i] **I.** *adj* okay **II.** *m AmL* okay; **dar el** ~ to give the go ahead **III.** *adv* okay

okupa [o·'ku·pa] *mf inf* squatter

ola ['o·la] *f* wave; ~ **de calor** heat wave; ~ **de frío** cold spell

olé [o·'le] *interj* ≈ bravo

oleada [o·le·'a·da] *f t. fig* wave; ~ **de gente** throng of people

oleaginoso, -a [o·lea·xi·'no·so, -a] *adj* oily

oleaje [o·le·'a·xe] *m* swell, surf

óleo ['o·leo] *m* **1.** ARTE oil paint; **cuadro al** ~ oil painting; **pintar al** ~ to paint in oil **2.** REL **administrar los** ~**s** to anoint sb with holy oil

oleoso, -a [o·le·'o·so, -a] *adj* oily

oler [o·'ler] *irr* **I.** *vi* to smell; ~ **a algo** to smell of sth; ~ **bien** to smell good **II.** *vt* to smell; ~ **una flor** to smell a flower; ~ **el peligro** to smell danger

olfa ['ol·fa] *mf RíoPl* **1.** *inf* (*chupamedias*) bootlicker **2.** *inf* (*persona servil*) toady

olfatear [ol·fa·te·'ar] **I.** *vt* to sniff; (*husmear*) to smell out **II.** *vi* to sniff; (*curiosear*) to pry

olfato [ol·'fa·to] *m* sense of smell; **tener (buen)** ~ *fig* to have a good nose [*o* instinct]

oligarquía [o·li·γar·'ki·a] *f* oligarchy

oligofrenia [o·li·γo·'fre·nja] *f* mental deficiency

olimpiada [o·lim·'pja·da] *f*, **olimpíada** [o·lim·'pi·a·da] *f* Olympics + *pl vb*

olímpico, -a [o·'lim·pi·ko, -a] *adj* Olympic

olisquear [o·lis·ke·'ar] *vi, vt v.* olfatear

oliva [o·'li·βa] **I.** *adj* (**verde**) ~ olive (green) **II.** *f* **1.** BOT (*árbol*) olive tree; (*fruta*) olive **2.** (*color*) olive (green)

oliváceo, -a [o·li·'βa·θeo, -a] *adj* olive-green

olivo [o·'li·βo] *m* olive tree; **el Monte de los Olivos** REL the Mount of Olives

olla ['o·ja, -ʎa] *f* **1.** (*para cocinar*) pot; ~ **exprés** pressure cooker; ~ **de grillos** *inf* madhouse **2.** CULIN stew

olmo ['ol·mo] *m* elm

olor [o·'lor] *m* smell; **buen** ~ good smell; (*fragancia*) scent; ~ **corporal** body odor; **tener** ~ **a** to smell of

olores [o·'lo·res] *mpl Chile* (*especias*) spices *pl*

oloroso, -a [o·lo·'ro·so] *adj* fragrant

olote [o·'lo·te] *m Méx* corncob

OLP [o·e·le·'pe] *f abr de* **Organización para la Liberación de Palestina** PLO

olvidadizo, -a [ol·βi·da·'di·so, -a; -'di·θo, -a] *adj* forgetful

olvidar [ol·βi·'dar] *vt, vr:* ~**se** to forget; **no** ~ **que...** (*considerar*) to remember that...; **se me ha olvidado tu nombre** I forgot your name

olvido [ol·'βi·do] *m* **1.** (*falta de memoria*) forgetfulness **2.** (*omisión*) oversight, forgetting; **caer en** (**el**) ~ to sink into oblivion; **enterrar en el** ~ to forget forever

ombligo [om·'bli·γo] *m* navel, belly button *inf*; **se me encoge el** ~ *fig* I'm getting cold feet; **el** ~ **del mundo** the center of the world; **contemplarse el** ~ to self-gratify

ombú [om·'bu] *m Arg* BOT umbra tree, ombu

ominoso, -a [o·mi·'no·so, -a] *adj* despicable

omisión [o·mi·'sjon] *f* **1.** (*supresión*) omission **2.** (*negligencia*) negligence

omiso, -a [o·'mi·so, -a] *adj* (*negligente*) negligent; **hacer caso** ~ **de algo** to take no notice of sth

omitir [o·mi·'tir] *vt* **1.** (*no hacer*) to fail to do; **no** ~ **esfuerzos** to spare no effort **2.** (*pasar por alto*) to omit

ómnibus ['om·ni·βus] *m* AUTO bus

omnipotente [om·ni·po·'ten·te] *adj* almighty, omnipotent

omnipresente [om·ni·pre·'sen·te] *adj* ubiquitous

omoplato [o·mo·'pla·to] *m*, **omóplato** [o·'mo·pla·to] *m* ANAT scapula, shoulder blade

OMS [oms] *f abr de* **Organización Mundial de la Salud** WHO

once ['on·θe] **I.** *adj inv* eleven ▸ **estar a las** ~ **y cuarto** to have a screw loose; **estar a las** ~ (*ropa*) to be askew **II.** *m* eleven; *v.t.* **ocho**

ONCE ['on·θe] *f abr de* **Organización Nacional de Ciegos Españoles** *Spanish national organization for the blind*

onceno, -a [on·'θe·no, -a] *adj* eleventh; *v.t.* **octavo** ▸ **el** ~, **no estorbar** *inf* don't get in the way

onda ['on·da] *f t.* FÍS, RADIO wave; ~ **explosiva** [*o* **expansiva**] shockwave; ~**s del pelo** waves *pl* of hair ▸ **¡qué buena** ~**!** *inf* that's really cool!; **estar en la misma** ~ to be on the same wavelength; **estar en la** ~ **de algo** *inf* (*comprender*) to be on top of sth; (*seguir*) to keep up with sth

ondear [on·de·'ar] *vi* (*formar*) to undulate; (*moverse*) to ripple; (*bandera*) to flutter

ondulado, -a [on·du·'la·do, -a] *adj* wavy; **cartón** ~ corrugated cardboard

ondular [on·du·'lar] **I.** *vi* (*formar ondas*) to ripple; (*moverse*) to undulate; (*bandera*) to flutter; (*culebra*) to slither **II.** *vt* to wave

oneroso, -a [o·ne·'ro·so, -a] *adj* **1.** (*molesto*) onerous; (*gravoso*) burdensome **2.** (*costoso*) costly

ONG [o·e·ne·'xe] *f abr de* **Organización No Gubernamental** NGO

onomástica [o·no·'mas·ti·ka] *f* **1.** (*materia*) onomastics *pl* **2.** (*día*) name-day, saint's day

ONU ['o·nu] *f abr de* **Organización de las Naciones Unidas** UNO

onza ['on·sa, -θa] *f* ounce

opa ['o·pa] *mf CSur* **1.** (*retrasado mental*) mental retard **2.** (*simple*) fool

opacar <c→qu> [o·pa·'kar] *vt* **1.** AmL (*hacer opaco*) to darken **2.** Méx (*superar*) to outshine; **su belleza opaca a las de las demás** her beauty eclipses that of all others

opaco, -a [o·'pa·ko, -a] *adj* **1.** (*no transparente*) opaque; **proyector de cuerpos** ~**s** overhead projector **2.** (*sin brillo*) dull; (*oscuro*) gloomy **3.** (*persona, voz*) gloomy

opción [op·'sjon, -β·'θjon] *f* **1.** (*elección*) choice; (*posibilidad*) option; ~ **del menú** COMPUT menu option **2.** (*derecho*) right; ~ **al cambio** right to exchange **3.** ECON, JUR option; ~ **de compra** option to purchase

opcional [op·sjo·'nal, oβ·θjo-] *adj* optional

OPEP [o·'pep] *f abr de* **Organización de Países Exportadores de Petróleo** OPEC

ópera ['o·pe·ra] *f* opera; **teatro de la** ~ opera house; ~ **prima** CINE, LIT author's first work

operación [o·pe·ra·'sjon, -'θjon] *f* **1.** MAT, MED operation; ~ **quirúrgica** surgical operation **2.** (*actividad*) activity; (*negocio*) transaction; ~ **por acciones** share trading; ~ **de saneamiento** clean-up operation

operador(a) [o·pe·ra·'dor] *m(f)* **1.** CINE projectionist; ~ **de cámara** cameraman **2.** COMPUT, TEL operator

operar [o·pe·'rar] **I.** *vi* **1.** (*actuar*) *t.* MIL to operate **2.** COM to do business; ~ **con bancos** to do business with banks **3.**(*tener efecto*) to take effect **II.** *vt* **1.** MED to operate on **2.**(*producir un efecto*) to bring about; ~ **milagros** to work miracles **III.** *vr:* ~ **se** to have an operation

operario, -a [o·pe·'ra·rjo, -a] *m, f* worker; ~ **sin cualificar** unskilled worker

operativo, -a [o·pe·ra·'ti·βo] *adj* **1.**(*efectivo*) operative **2.** COMPUT **sistema** ~ operating system

opinar [o·pi·'nar] *vi, vt* to think; ~ **bien/mal de algo/alguien** to have a good/bad opinion of sth/sb; ¿**tú qué opinas de** [*o* sobre] **esto?** what do you think about this?; ¿**puedo** ~? can I say what I think?

opinión [o·pi·'njon] *f* opinion; (*postura*) stance; (*punto de vista*) viewpoint; **en mi** ~ in my opinion; **cambiar de** ~ to change one's opinion [*o* mind]; **dar su** ~ (**sobre algo**) to express an opinion (about sth); **ser de otra/la misma** ~ to be of a different/the same opinion; **tener buena/mala** ~ **de algo/alguien** to have a good/bad opinion of sth/sb

opio ['o·pjo] *m* opium

oponente [o·po·'nen·te] *mf* opponent

oponer [o·po·'ner] *irr como poner* **I.** *vt* **1.**(*enfrentar*) to oppose; (*confrontar*) to confront **2.**(*objetar*) to object; ~ **reparos** to raise objections; ~ **resistencia** to offer resistance **II.** *vr:* ~**se 1.**(*rechazar*) to object; ~**se a algo** to oppose sth **2.**(*enfrentarse*) to oppose each other **3.**(*obstaculizar*) to hinder **4.**(*ser contrario*) to be opposed **5.**(*estar enfrente*) to be opposite

oporto [o·'por·to] *m* CULIN port (wine)

oportunidad [o·por·tu·ni·'dad] *f* **1.**(*posibilidad*) chance; (*ocasión*) opportunity; **una segunda** ~ a second chance; **aprovechar la** ~ to make the most of the opportunity; (**no**) **tener** ~ **de...** (not) to have the opportunity of... **2.**(*cualidad*) opportuneness; (*temporal*) timeliness; (*adecuación*) appropriateness **3.** *pl* (*ofertas*) bargains *pl*

oportuno, -a [o·por·'tu·no, -a] *adj* **1.**(*adecuado, apropiado*) appropriate; **en el momento** ~ at the right moment **2.**(*propicio*) opportune **3.**(*al caso*) relevant **4.**(*permisible*) permissible

oposición [o·po·si·'sjon, -'θjon] *f* **1.**(*resistencia*) *t.* POL opposition; **encontrar** ~ to meet opposition; **presentar** ~ to oppose **2.**(*objeción*) objection **3.**(*contraposición*) comparison **4.** (*pl*) UNIV (competitive) examination (*for a public-sector job*)*; **por** ~ by examination

opositar [o·po·si·'tar] *vi* ~ **a algo** to sit an examination for sth

opositor(a) [o·po·si·'tor, -'to·ra] **I.** *adj* opposing; **partido** ~ opposing party **II.** *m(f)* **1.**(*oponente*) *t.* POL opponent **2.**(*candidato*) candidate (*in examination for a public-sector job*)

opresión [o·pre·'sjon] *f* **1.**(*angustia*) anxiety **2.**(*represión*) oppression **3.**(*presión*) pressure; (*compresión*) compression

opresor(a) [o·pre·'sor, -'so·ra] **I.** *adj* oppres-

sive **II.** *m(f)* oppressor

oprimir [o·pri·'mir] *vt* **1.**(*presionar*) to press; (*comprimir*) to compress **2.**(*agobiar*) to weigh down **3.**(*reprimir*) to oppress; (*constreñir*) to restrict

oprobio [o·'pro·βjo] *m* disgrace

oprobioso, -a [o·pro·'βjo·so, -a] *adj* disgraceful

optar [op·'tar] *vi* **1.**(*escoger*) ~ **por algo/alguien** to opt for sth/sb **2.**(*aspirar*) to aspire **3.**(*solicitar*) ~ **a un cargo** to apply for a position **4.**(*tener acceso*) to have access

optativo, -a [op·ta·'ti·βo, -a] *adj* optional; (*asignatura*) **optativa** optional subject

óptica ['op·ti·ka] *f* **1.** FÍS optics *pl* **2.**(*establecimiento*) optician's **3.**(*punto de vista*) viewpoint; **bajo esta** ~ according to this point of view

óptico, -a ['op·ti·ko, -a] **I.** *adj* **1.** ANAT optic; **nervio** ~ optic nerve **2.** FÍS optical **II.** *m, f* optician

optimismo [op·ti·'mis·mo] *m* optimism

optimista [op·ti·'mis·ta] **I.** *adj* optimistic **II.** *mf* optimist

optimizar [op·ti·mi·'sar, -'θar] *vt* to optimize

óptimo ['op·ti·mo] *m* optimum

óptimo, -a ['op·ti·mo, -a] **I.** *superl de* **bueno** **II.** *adj* (very) best; (*excelente*) excellent

opuesto, -a [o·'pwes·to] **I.** *pp de* **oponer** **II.** *adj* **1.**(*enfrente*) opposite; **al lado** ~ on the other side; **en dirección opuesta** in the opposite direction **2.**(*diverso*) different; (*contrario, enfrentado*) opposing; **polo** ~ *t. fig* opposite pole; **el sexo** ~ the opposite sex **3.**(*enemigo*) enemy

opulencia [o·pu·'len·sja, -θja] *f* opulence

opulento, -a [o·pu·'len·to, -a] *adj* opulent

oración [o·ra·'sjon, -'θjon] *f* **1.** REL prayer; **decir una** ~ to say a prayer **2.**(*frase*) sentence; LING clause; (*discurso*) speech; ~ **coordinada** coordinate clause; ~ **subordinada** subordinate clause; ~ **simple/compuesta** simple/compound sentence

oráculo [o·'ra·ku·lo] *m* oracle

orador(a) [o·ra·'dor, -'do·ra] *m(f)* orator

oral [o·'ral] *adj* oral; **por vía** ~ MED orally

órale ['o·ra·le] *interj Méx* (*animar*) come on; (*oiga*) hey; (*acuerdo*) OK, right

orangután [o·ran·gu·'tan] *m* orangutan

orar [o·'rar] *vi elev* ~ **por algo** to pray for sth; (*rogar*) to plead for sth

oratoria [o·ra·'to·rja] *f* oratory

oratorio [o·ra·'to·rjo] *m* REL chapel

órbita ['or·βi·ta] *f* **1.** ASTR, FÍS orbit; ~ **terrestre** terrestrial orbit; **poner en** ~ to put into orbit; **estar en** ~ *fig* to be up to date; **estar fuera de** ~ *fig* to be out of touch **2.**(*ámbito*) sphere **3.** ANAT eye socket; **se me salían los ojos de las** ~**s** *fig* I couldn't believe my eyes

orca ['or·ka] *f* killer whale

órdago ['or·da·ɣo] *m* **de** ~ *inf* terrific

orden¹ <órdenes> ['or·den] *m* **1.**(*organización*) *t.* REL, ARQUIT order; **en** ~ in order; **llamar**

al ~ to call to order; **poner en** ~ to put in order; **ser persona de** ~ to be orderly; *fig* to be upright **2.** (*sucesión*) order; **en** [*o* por] **su** (**debido**) ~ in the right order; **por** ~ by order; **por** ~ **de antigüedad** in order of seniority **3.** (*categoría*) rank; **de primer**/**segundo** ~ first-rate/second-rate; **del** ~ **de** in the order of **orden²** <órdenes> ['or·den] *f* **1.** (*mandato*) order; ~ **ministerial** ministerial decree; ~ **de registro** search warrant; **órdenes son órdenes** orders are orders; **¡a la** ~**!** yes, sir!; **contrario a las órdenes** against orders; **dar una** ~ to give an order; **cumplir una** ~ to obey an order; **estar a las órdenes de alguien** to be at sb's command; **hasta nueva** ~ until further notice; **estar a la** ~ **del día** *fig* to be the order of the day **2.** COM, REL order; ~ **de entrega** delivery order; ~ **de pago** payment order; ~ **permanente** standing order; **por** ~ by order; **por** ~ **de** to the order of; **entrar en una** ~ (**religiosa**) to join a religious order; ~ **de caballería** HIST order of knighthood **3.** *pl* REL (*sacramento*) orders *pl;* **las órdenes mayores**/**menores** the major/minor orders
ordenación [or·de·na·'sjon, -'θjon] *f* **1.** (*disposición*) arrangement **2.** (*ordenanza*) order; (*regulación*) regulation; ~ **jurídica** legal system; ~ **territorial** regional development **3.** REL ordination
ordenado, -a [or·de·'na·do, -a] *adj* **1.** *estar* (*en orden*) tidy, neat **2.** *ser* (*persona*) organized
ordenador [or·de·na·'dor] *m* computer; ~ **de a bordo** car computer; ~ **personal** personal computer; ~ **portátil** laptop computer; **asistido por** ~ computer-aided
ordenanza¹ [or·de·'nan·sa, -θa] *f* **1.** (*ordenación*) organization; (*medida*) order **2.** *pl* ADMIN, MIL regulations *pl*
ordenanza² [or·de·'nan·sa, -θa] *m* **1.** MIL orderly **2.** (*botones*) office assistant
ordenar [or·de·'nar] *vt* **1.** (*arreglar*) to organize; (*habitación, armario*) to tidy; (*colocar*) to arrange; (*clasificar*) to order **2.** (*mandar*) to order **3.** REL to ordain
ordeña [or·'de·ɲa] *f AmC, CSur, Méx* milking
ordeñar [or·de·'ɲar] *vt* to milk
ordeñe [or·'de·ɲe] *m Arg, Cuba* milking
ordinal [or·di·'nal] *adj, m* ordinal
ordinariez [or·di·na·'rjeθ] *f* (*vulgaridad*) vulgarity
ordinario, -a [or·di·'na·rjo, -a] *adj* **1.** (*habitual*) usual; **de** ~ usually **2.** (*grosero*) rude **3.** *t.* JUR (*regular*) ordinary
orégano [o·'re·ɣa·no] *m* oregano
oreja [o·'re·xa] *f* **1.** ANAT ear; **aguzar las** ~**s** to prick up one's ears; **calentar las** ~**s a alguien** to box sb's ears; *fig* to give sb an earful **2.** (*lateral*) flap; (*lengüeta*) tongue; (*del zapato*) eyelet tab; **sillón de** ~**s** wing chair ▶ **ver las** ~**s al** lobo to have a close shave; **con las** ~**s** gachas with one's tail between one's legs; **agachar las** ~**s** to lose heart; **enseñar la** ~ to

show one's true colors
orejera [o·re·'xe·ra] *f* **1.** (*en una gorra*) earflap **2.** *pl* (*en una cinta*) earmuffs *pl*
orejero, -a [o·re·'xe·ro, -a] *m, f Chile, pey* telltale
orejón [o·re·'xon] *m* CULIN dried apricot
orfanato [or·fa·'na·to] *m* orphanage
orfanatorio [or·fa·na·'to·rjo] *m Méx* orphanage
orfandad [or·fan·'dad] *f* **1.** (*estado*) orphanhood **2.** (*pensión*) orphan's allowance
orfebre [or·'fe·βre] *mf* (*orífice*) goldsmith; (*platero*) silversmith
orfelinato [or·fe·li·'na·to] *m* orphanage
orfeón [or·fe·'on] *m* MÚS choral society
orgánico, -a [or·'ɣa·ni·ko, -a] *adj* organic; **Ley Orgánica del Estado** basic law
organigrama [or·ɣa·ni·'ɣra·ma] *m* organization chart; ~ **del programa** COMPUT flowchart
organillo [or·ɣa·'ni·jo, -ʎo] *m* barrel organ
organismo [or·ɣa·'nis·mo] *m* **1.** ANAT, BIO organism **2.** (*institución*) body; ~ **oficial** official body
organización [or·ɣa·ni·sa·'sjon, -θa·'θjon] *f* organization; **Organización del Tratado del Atlántico Norte** North Atlantic Treaty Organization; **Organización No Gubernamental** Non-Governmental Organization
organizado, -a [or·ɣa·ni·'sa·do, -a; --'θa·do, -a] *adj* organized
organizador(a) [or·ɣa·ni·sa·'dor, -θa·'dor] **I.** *adj* organizing; **comité** ~ organizing committee **II.** *m(f)* (*de un evento*) organizer; ~ **de despacho** office organizer
organizar <z→c> [or·ɣa·ni·'sar, -'θar] **I.** *vt* to organize; (*una fiesta*) to hold **II.** *vr:* ~**se** **1.** (*asociarse*) to organize oneself **2.** (*surgir*) to break out; **¡menuda se organizó!** all hell broke loose! **3.** (*ordenar*) to arrange; ~**se el tiempo** to organize one's time
organizativo, -a [or·ɣa·ni·sa·'ti·βo, -a; or·ɣa·ni·θa-] *adj* organizing
órgano ['or·ɣa·no] *m* **1.** (*organismo*) *t.* ANAT organ; ~ **judicial** judicial body; ~**s sexuales** sexual organs **2.** MÚS organ; ~ **electrónico** electric organ
orgasmo [or·'ɣas·mo] *m* orgasm
orgía [or·'xi·a] *f* orgy; (*desenfreno*) wildness, disinhibition
orgullo [or·'ɣu·jo, -ʎo] *m* **1.** (*satisfacción*) pride; ~ **por** [*o* de] **algo** pride in sth; **sentir** ~ **por alguien**/**algo** to be proud of sb/sth; **tener el** ~ **de...** to be proud to...; ~ **propio** self-respect **2.** (*soberbia*) arrogance
orgulloso, -a [or·ɣu·'jo·so, a; -ʎo·so, -a] *adj* **1.** *estar* (*satisfecho*) proud; **sentirse** ~ **de algo**/**alguien** to feel proud of sth/sb **2.** *ser* proud; (*soberbio*) arrogant
orientación [o·rjen·ta·'sjon, -'θjon] *f* **1.** (*situación*) situation **2.** (*posición*) position **3.** (*ajuste*) adjustment **4.** (*asesoramiento*) advice; (*dirección*) management; ~ **profesional** career [*o* vocational] guidance **5.** (*tendencia*)

inclination; ~ **política** political orientation; ~ **sexual** sexual orientation
oriental [o·rjen·'tal] I. *adj* 1. (*del Este*) eastern; **Alemania Oriental** East Germany; **alfombra** ~ Persian rug 2. (*del Extremo Oriente*) oriental II. *mf* Oriental
orientar [o·rjen·'tar] I. *vt* 1. (*dirigir*) to direct; **orientado a la práctica** with a practical focus 2. (*ajustar*) to adjust 3. (*asesorar*) to advise 4. (*dirigir*) to manage II. *vr:* ~ **se** 1. (*dirigirse*) to orient oneself; *fig* to find one's bearings; ~ **se bien** to have a good sense of direction; **se orientó muy bien en el trabajo** he/she settled in well in the job 2. (*tender*) to tend
oriente [o·'rjen·te] *m* 1. GEO east; **el Oriente Próximo, el Cercano Oriente** the Near East; **el Extremo Oriente, el Lejano Oriente** the Far East 2. (*viento*) easterly
orificio [o·ri·'fi·sjo, -θjo] *m* orifice; (*abertura*) opening; ~ **de salida** outlet
origen [o·'ri·xen] *m* 1. (*principio*) origin; **texto/idioma de** ~ source text/language 2. (*causa*) cause; **dar** ~ **a algo** to give rise to sth; **tener su** ~ **en algo** to have its origins in sth 3. (*ascendencia*) descent 4. (*procedencia*) origin; **de** ~ **español** of Spanish origin
original [o·ri·xi·'nal] I. *adj* 1. (*auténtico, creativo*) original; **versión** ~ original version 2. (*originario*) originating 3. (*singular*) peculiar II. *m* original; **fiel al** ~ faithful to the original
originalidad [o·ri·xi·na·li·'dad] *f* 1. (*autenticidad, creatividad*) originality 2. (*singularidad*) peculiarity
originar [o·ri·xi·'nar] I. *vt* 1. (*causar*) to cause 2. (*provocar*) to provoke II. *vr:* ~ **se** 1. (*tener el origen*) to originate 2. (*surgir*) to arise 3. (*proceder*) ~ **se en algo** to spring from sth
originario, -a [o·ri·xi·'na·rjo, -a] *adj* 1. (*oriundo*) native; **es** ~ **de Chile** he comes from Chile 2. (*de origen*) **país** ~ country of origin
orilla [o·'ri·ja, -ʎa] *f* 1. (*borde*) edge 2. (*ribera*) bank; **a** ~ **s del Orinoco** on the banks of the Orinoco; ~ **de** *inf* on the edge of 3. *pl, AmL* (*arrabales*) outskirts *pl*
orillero, -a [o·ri·'je·ro, -a; -ʎe·ro, -a] I. *adj AmL, pey* 1. (*arrabalero*) low class 2. (*grosero*) coarse II. *m, f AmL, pey* 1. (*arrabalero*) common person 2. (*grosero*) ill-bred person
orín [o·'rin] *m* rust; **cubierto de** ~ rusty
orina [o·'ri·na] *f* <orines> urine
orinal [o·ri·'nal] *m* chamber pot; (*de niño*) potty
orinar [o·ri·'nar] I. *vi, vt* to urinate; **ir a** ~ to go to the lavatory II. *vr:* ~ **se** to wet oneself; ~ **se en la cama** to wet the bed; **estoy orinándome** I need to urinate
oriundo, -a [o·'rjun·do, -a] *adj* ~ **de** native to; **es** ~ **de Méjico** he comes from Mexico
orla ['or·la] *f* 1. (*de tela*) edge; ~ **de luto** black border 2. (*foto*) graduating-class photo [*o* picture]

ornamentación [or·na·men·ta·'sjon, -'θjon] *f* adornment
ornamentar [or·na·men·'tar] *vt* to adorn
ornamento [or·na·'men·to] *m* ornament
ornitorrinco [or·ni·to·'rrin·ko] *m* duck-billed platypus
oro ['o·ro] *m* gold; ~ **de ley** fine gold; **bañado en** ~ gold-plated; **de** ~ gold; **color** ~ golden; **hacerse de** ~ to make one's fortune; **nadar en** ~ to be swimming in money ▶ **prometer a alguien el** ~ **y el moro** to promise sb the earth; **mi palabra es** ~ my word is my honor; **guardar como** ~ **en paño** to treasure; **no es** ~ **todo lo que reluce** *prov* all that glitters is not gold *prov*
orondo, -a [o·'ron·do, -a] *adj* (*gordo*) fat
oropel [o·ro·'pel] *m* (*latón*) imitation gold leaf
orquesta [or·'kes·ta] *f* MÚS orchestra
orquestar [or·kes·'tar] *vt t. fig* to orchestrate
orquídea [or·'ki·dea] *f* orchid
ortiga [or·'ti·ya] *f* nettle
ortodoncia [or·to·'don·sja, -θja] *f* MED orthodontics *pl*
ortodoxo, -a [or·to·'dok·so, -a] I. *adj* orthodox; **ser católico** ~ to be a devout Catholic II. *m, f* orthodox
ortogonal [or·to·yo·'nal] *adj* right-angled
ortografía [or·to·yra·'fi·a] *f* spelling; **falta de** ~ spelling mistake
ortográfico, -a [or·to·'yra·fi·ko, -a] *adj* spelling; **reglas ortográficas** spelling rules; **reforma ortográfica** spelling reform
ortopeda [or·to·'pe·da] *mf* MED orthopedist
ortopedia [or·to·'pe·dja] *f* MED orthopedics
ortopédico, -a [or·to·'pe·di·ko, -a] MED I. *adj* orthopedic; **pierna ortopédica** artificial leg II. *m, f* orthopedist
oruga [o·'ru·ya] *f* 1. ZOOL caterpillar 2. TÉC caterpillar track
orujo [o·'ru·xo] *m* 1. (*residuo*) marc 2. (*aguardiente*) strong Spanish liqueur made from residue of grape skins after pressing
orzuelo [or·'swe·lo, -θwe·lo] *m* MED sty(e)
os [os] I. *pron pers* (*objeto directo e indirecto*) you II. *pron reflexivo* yourselves; **¿~ marcháis?** are you leaving?
osa ['o·sa] *f* ASTR **la Osa Mayor/Menor** the Great/Little Bear ▶ **¡anda la ~!** *inf* good heavens!
osadía [o·sa·'di·a] *f* daring
osado, -a [o·'sa·do, -a] *adj* daring
osamenta [o·sa·'men·ta] *f* skeleton; (*restos mortales*) bones *pl*
osar [o·'sar] *vi* to dare; **¿cómo osas decir esto?** how dare you say that!
oscilación [o·si·la·'sjon, os·θi·la·'θjon] *f* 1. (*vaivén*) oscillation 2. (*variación*) fluctuation 3. (*indecisión*) indecision
oscilar [o·si·'lar, os·θi·'lar] *vi* 1. (*en vaivén*) to oscillate 2. (*péndulo*) to swing 3. (*variar*) to fluctuate
oscilatorio, -a [o·si·la·'·to·rjo, os·θi·la·'to·rjo, -a] *adj* oscillatory

oscurecer [os·ku·re·'ser, -θer] *irr como crecer* **I.** *vimpers* to get dark **II.** *vt t. fig* (*privar de luz*) to darken **III.** *vr:* ~**se** *t. fig* (*volverse oscuro*) to darken **IV.** *m* dusk; **al** ~ at dusk

oscurecimiento [os·ku·re·θi·'mjen·to] *m t. fig* darkening

oscuridad [os·ku·ri·'dad] *f* **1.** (*falta de luz*) darkness; **en la** ~ in the dark **2.** (*falta de claridad*) obscurity; **en la** ~ in obscurity

oscuro, -a [os·'ku·ro, -a] *adj* dark; *fig* obscure; **azul** ~ dark blue; **a oscuras** in the dark; **de** ~ **origen** of obscure origin

óseo, -a ['o·seo, -a] *adj* bony; **restos** ~**s** skeletal remains

osificar [o·si·fi·'kar] <c→qu> *vt, vr:* ~**se** to ossify

osmosis [os·'mo·sis] *f*, **ósmosis** ['os·mo·sis] *f inv* osmosis

oso ['o·so] *m* bear; ~ **blanco** polar bear; ~ **de peluche** teddy bear; **fuerte como un** ~ as strong as an ox

ostensible [os·ten·'si·βle] *adj* obvious; **hacer** ~ to make evident

ostentación [os·ten·ta·'sjon, -'θjon] *f* display; (*jactancia*) ostentation; **hacer** ~ **de algo** to show sth; (*jactarse*) to flaunt sth

ostentar [os·ten·'tar] *vt* **1.** (*mostrar*) to show; (*jactarse*) to flaunt **2.** (*poseer*) to have; (*puesto, poder*) to hold

ostentoso, -a [os·ten·'to·so, -a] *adj* **1.** (*jactancioso*) ostentatious **2.** (*llamativo*) showy; (*provocativo*) provocative

ostra ['os·tra] *f* oyster ▶ **aburrirse como una** ~ *inf* to be bored to death; **¡~s!** *inf* Jesus!

ostracismo [os·tra·'sis·mo, -·'θis·mo] *m* ostracism; **condenar al** ~ *fig* to ostracize

OTAN [o·'tan] *f abr de* **Organización del Tratado del Atlántico Norte** NATO

otario, -a [o·'ta·rjo, -a] *adj CSur* foolish

otate [o·'ta·te] *m Méx* BOT reed, rush

otear [o·te·'ar] **I.** *vt* to scan; (*escudriñar*) to scrutinize **II.** *vi* to look

otitis [o·'ti·tis] *f inv* MED inflammation of the ear; ~ **media** inflammation of the middle ear

otomano, -a [o·to·'ma·no, -a] *adj, m, f* Ottoman

otomía [o·to·'mi·a] *f Arg, Col* atrocity

otoñal [o·to·'ɲal] *adj* autumnal; **un amor** ~ *fig* late love

otoño [o·'to·ɲo] *m* autumn, fall; **a fin(al)es de** ~ at the end of autumn [*o* fall]; **el** ~ **(de la vida)** the autumn (of one's life)

otorgamiento [o·tor·ɣa·'mjen·to] *m* **1.** (*concesión*) concession; JUR execution; (*de documento*) drawing up; (*de contrato*) award; (*de licencia*) grant; ~ **de poder** bestowal of power **2.** (*consentimiento*) consent

otorgar <g→gu> [o·tor·'ɣar] *vt* **1.** (*conferir*) to confer; ~ **poderes** to confer powers **2.** (*conceder*) to concede; (*ayudas*) to offer; ~ **un plazo** to set a time limit **3.** (*expedir*) to issue; ~ **licencia** to grant a license **4.** (*acceder*) ~ **algo** to agree to sth; ~ **su consentimiento** to give one's consent

otorrinolaringólogo, -a [o·to·rri·no·la·rin·'go·lo·ɣo, -a] *m, f* MED ear, nose and throat specialist

otro, -a ['o·tro, -a] **I.** *adj* another, other; **al** ~ **día** the next day; **el** ~ **día** the other day; **en otra ocasión** another time; **la otra semana** the other week; **en** ~ **sitio** in another place, somewhere else; **otra cosa** another thing; ~ **tanto** as much again; **otra vez** again; **¡otra vez será!** maybe another time!; **eso ya es otra cosa** that is much better; **¡hasta otra (vez)!** until the next time! **II.** *pron indef* **1.** (*distinto: cosa*) another (one); (*persona*) someone else; ~**s** others; **el** ~/**la otra**/**lo** ~ the other (one); **ninguna otra persona, ningún** ~ nobody else; **de un sitio a** ~ from one place to another; **no** ~ **que...** none other than...; **ésa es otra** (*cosa distinta*) that is different; *irón* (*aún peor*) that is even worse **2.** (*uno más*) another; **otras tres personas** three more people; **¡otra, otra!** more!

otrora [o·'tro·ra] *adv* formerly

otrosí [o·tro·'si] *adv* furthermore

ovación [o·βa·'sjon, -'θjon] *f* ovation; **dar/recibir una** ~ to give/receive an ovation

ovacionar [o·βa·sjo·'nar, -θjo·'nar] *vt* to give an ovation

oval [o·'βal] *adj*, **ovalado, -a** [o·βa·'la·do, -a] *adj* oval

ovario [o·'βa·rjo] *m* ANAT ovary

oveja [o·'βe·xa] *f* sheep *inv*; (*hembra*) ewe; **la** ~ **negra de la familia** the black sheep of the family ▶ **cada** ~ **con su pareja** *prov* birds of a feather flock together *prov*

ovejero, -a [o·βe·'xe·ro, -a] **I.** *adj* sheep; **perro** ~ sheep dog **II.** *m, f* **1.** (*ganadero*) sheep breeder; (*pastor*) shepherd **2.** *AmL* (*perro*) sheep dog

overol [o·βe·'rol] *m AmL* overall

ovillo [o·'βi·jo, -ʎo] *m* ball; *fig* tangle; **hacerse un** ~ (*enredarse*) to get tangled up; (*encogerse*) to curl up into a ball; (*al hablar*) to get all tangled up

ovino, -a [o·'βi·no, -a] **I.** *adj* sheep; **ganado** ~ sheep *pl* **II.** *m, f* sheep *inv*

ovni ['oβ·ni] *m* UFO

ovulación [o·βu·la·'sjon, -'θjon] *f* ovulation

ovular [o·βu·'lar] *vi* to ovulate

óvulo ['o·βu·lo] *m* ANAT ovule

oxidación [ok·si·da·'sjon, -'θjon] *f* **1.** QUÍM oxidation **2.** (*metal*) rusting

oxidar [ok·si·'dar] **I.** *vt* **1.** QUÍM to oxidize **2.** (*metal*) to rust; **un hierro oxidado** a piece of rusty iron **II.** *vr:* ~**se 1.** (*metal*) to rust; (*mente*) to go rusty **2.** QUÍM to oxidize

óxido ['ok·si·do] *m* **1.** QUÍM oxide **2.** (*orín*) rust

oxigenar [ok·si·xe·'nar] **I.** *vt* **1.** (*cabello*) to bleach; (*rubio*) **oxigenado** platinum [*o* peroxide] blond(e) **2.** QUÍM to oxygenate; **agua oxigenada** (hydrogen) peroxide **II.** *vr:* ~**se** *inf* to get some fresh air

oxígeno [ok·'si·xe·no] *m* QUÍM oxygen

O

oyente [o·'jen·te] *mf* listener; (**libre**) ~ UNIV auditor

ozono [o·'θo·no] *m* QUÍM ozone; **el agujero en la capa de** ~ the hole in the ozone layer

P

P, p [pe] *f* P, p; ~ **de París** P as in Papa

pabellón [pa·βe·'jon, -'ʎon] *m* **1.** (*tienda*) bell tent **2.** (*bandera*) flag **3.** ARQUIT pavilion

pacer [pa·'ser, -θer] *irr como crecer vi, vt* to graze

pacha ['pa·ʧa] *f* **1.** *Nic, Méx* (*botella aplanada*) flask **2.** *Nic* (*biberón*) baby's bottle

pachacho, -a [pa·'ʧa·ʧo, -a] *adj Chile* short-legged

pachaco, -a [pa·'ʧa·ko, -a] *adj* **1.** *AmC* (*aplastado*) flattened **2.** *CRi* (*inútil, enclenque*) feeble

pachamama [pa·ʧa·'ma·na] *f And* (*Madre Tierra*) Mother Earth

pachamanca [pa·ʧa·'man·ka] *f And* **1.** (*plato*) barbecued meat **2.** (*horno*) barbecue pit

pachanga [pa·'ʧan·ga] *f* **1.** *Cuba* (*danza*) Cuban dance **2.** *Col, inf* (*fiesta*) party

pacho, -a ['pa·ʧo, -a] *adj Nic* (*flaco*) skinny

pachón, -ona [pa·'ʧon, -'ʧo·na] *adj AmL* (*peludo*) hairy

pachorra [pa·'ʧo·rra] *f inf* slowness; **tener** ~ to be lackadaisical [*o* laid-back]

pachorriento, -a [pa·ʧo·'rrjen·to, -a] *adj AmS, inf* phlegmatic, lackadaisical

pachucho, -a [pa·'ʧu·ʧo, -a] *adj* **1.** *inf* (*persona*) off-color **2.** (*fruta*) overripe

paciencia [pa·'sjen·sja, -'θjen·θja] *f* patience; **se me ha acabado la** ~ I've run out of patience

paciente [pa·'sjen·te, 'θjen·te] **I.** *adj* patient; **ser** ~ **con alguien** to be patient with sb **II.** *mf* patient

pacificación [pa·si·fi·ka·sjon, -θi·fi·ka·'θjon] *f* pacification

pacificar <c→qu> [pa·si·fi·kar, -θi·fi·'kar] *vt* to pacify

pacífico, -a [pa·'si·fi·ko, -a, -θi·fi·ko, -a] *adj* peaceful; **carácter** ~ (*nación*) peacefulness

Pacífico [pa·'si·fi·ko, -θi·fi·ko] *m* Pacific (Ocean)

pacifismo [pa·si·fis·mo, -θi·'fis·mo] *m* pacifism

pacifista [pa·si·fis·ta, -θi'fista] *adj, mf* pacifist

paco, -a ['pa·ko] *adj AmL* reddish

pacota [pa·'ko·ta] *f Méx* (*pacotilla*) rabble

pacotilla [pa·ko·'ti·ja, -ʎa] *f* **1.** (*calidad inferior*) trashiness; **tienda de** ~**s** junk shop; **de** ~ (*mercancía*) shoddy; (*restaurante*) second-rate; **ser de** ~ to be shoddy **2.** *AmL* (*chusma*) rabble

pacotillero, -a [pa·ko·ti·'je·ro, -a; -ʎe·ro, -a] **I.** *adj* second-rate; **tienda pacotillera** shop selling shoddy goods **II.** *m, f* **1.** (*vendedor*) street vendor **2.** *AmL* (*negociante que viaja*) street hawker

pactar [pak·'tar] **I.** *vi* to come to an agreement **II.** *vt* to agree on

pacto ['pak·to] *m* agreement; (*contrato*) contract; ~ **antiterrorista** antiterrorism pact

padecer [pa·de·'ser, -θer] *irr como crecer* **I.** *vi* to suffer **II.** *vt* **1.** (*sufrir*) to suffer; ~ **algo** to suffer from sth **2.** (*soportar*) to endure

padecimiento [pa·de·θi·'mjen·to] *m* **1.** (*sufrimiento*) suffering **2.** (*enfermedad*) ailment

padrastro [pa·'dras·tro] *m* **1.** (*marido de madre*) stepfather **2.** (*mal padre*) cruel father

padrazo [pa·'dra·so, -θo] *m* **es un** ~ *inf* he's a great dad

padre ['pa·dre] *m* **1.** *t.* REL father; ~ **espiritual** confessor; **¡tu** ~! *inf* up yours! **2.** *pl* (*padre y madre*) parents *pl* ► **tal** ~, **tal hijo** *prov* like father, like son

padrenuestro [pa·dre·'nwes·tro] *m* Lord's Prayer

padrillo [pa·'dri·jo, -ʎo] *m CSur* stallion

padrino [pa·'dri·no] *m* (*de bautizo*) godfather; (*de boda*) best man; **tener buenos** ~**s** *fig* to know the right people

padrón [pa·'dron] *m* **1.** ADMIN (*registro*) (census) register **2.** *AmL* (*caballo*) stallion

padrote [pa·'dro·te] *m AmC, Méx* **1.** (*equino*) stallion; (*bovino*) breeding bull **2.** *inf* (*alcahuete*) pimp

paella [pa·'e·ja, -ʎa] *f* paella (*Spanish dish of rice, meat and fish, flavored and colored with saffron*)

paellera [pae·'je·ra, -'ʎera] *f* paella dish

pág. ['pa·xi·na] *abr de* **página** p.

paga [pa·ɣa] *f* **1.** (*sueldo*) pay **2.** (*acto*) payment

pagadero, -a [pa·ɣa·'de·ro, -a] *adj* **1.** (*a pagar*) due **2.** (*pagable*) payable

pagado, -a [pa·'ɣa·do, -a] *adj* paid; ~ **de sí mismo** full of oneself

paganismo [pa·ɣa·'nis·mo] *m* paganism

pagano, -a [pa·'ɣa·no, -a] *adj* pagan

pagar <g→gu> [pa·'ɣar] **I.** *vt* **1.** (*gastos*) to pay; (*una deuda*) to repay; ~ **un anticipo** to make an advance payment **2.** (*expiar*) to atone for; ~ **una condena** to serve a sentence; **¡me las** ~**ás!** you'll pay for this! **3.** (*recompensar*) to repay; (*una visita*) to return; **¡Dios se lo pague!** God will reward you! **II.** *vr* **1.** (*aficionarse*) ~ **se de algo** to take a liking to sth **2.** (*presumir*) to boast; ~ **se de algo** to boast about sth

pagaré [pa·ɣa·'re] *m* promissory note, IOU

página ['pa·xi·na] *f* page; **pasar la** ~ (**adelante**) to turn the page; ~**s blancas** telephone directory; ~**s amarillas** TEL yellow pages; ~ **web** COMPUT web site

paginación [pa·xi·na·'sjon, -'θjon] *f* pagination

paginar [pa·xi·'nar] *vt* to paginate
pago ['pa·ɣo] *m* **1.** (*reintegro*) payment; ~ **adicional** supplement; ~ **extraordinario** one-off payment, bonus; ~ **inicial** down payment; ~ **a plazos** payment in installments; **día de** ~ pay day; **anticipar el** ~ to pay in advance; **sujeto a** ~ subject to payment **2.** (*salario*) pay; ~ **anticipado** advance payment; ~ **por hora** hourly pay; ~ **por incapacidad** sick pay **3.** *fig* (*recompensa*) reward; ¿**éste es el** ~ **que me das?** is this how you repay me? **4.** *Arg, Perú* (*de nacimiento*) home region
pai [pai] *m AmL* CULIN pie
paila ['pai·la] *f AmL* (*sartén*) frying pan
país [pa·'is] *m* country; ~ **comunitario** member state (*of the European Union*); ~ **industrializado** industrialized country; ~ **limítrofe** neighboring country; ~ **en vías de desarrollo** developing country; ~ **en vías de industrialización** industrializing country
paisa ['pai·sa] *m AmL v.* **paisano**
paisaje [pai·'sa·xe] *m* landscape
paisajista [pai·sa·'xis·ta] *mf* landscape artist
paisanada [pai·sa·'na·da] *f CSur* peasants *pl*
paisano, -a [pai·'sa·no, -a] *m, f* **1.** (*no militar*) civilian; **ir de** ~ to be in plain clothes **2.** (*compatriota*) compatriot **3.** (*campesino*) peasant
Países Bajos [pa·'i·ses 'βa·xos] *mpl* Netherlands
paja ['pa·xa] *f* straw; **cama de** ~ straw bed; **no dormirse en las** ~**s** *inf* to be alert; **hacerse una** ~ *vulg* to jerk off
pajar [pa·'xar] *m* haystack; (*lugar*) hayloft; **buscar una aguja en un** ~ *fig* to search for a needle in a haystack
pajarero, -a [pa·xa·'re·ro, -a] *adj* **1.** (*de pájaros*) bird; **redes pajareras** bird nets **2.** *AmL* (*caballos*) skittish
pajarita [pa·xa·'ri·ta] *f* bow tie
pájaro ['pa·xa·ro] *m* bird; ~ **bobo** penguin; ~ **carpintero** woodpecker; ~ **mosca** hummingbird; **tener la cabeza llena de** ~**s** to be scatterbrained; **voló el** ~ *inf* the chance has gone ▸ **más vale** ~ **en** mano **que ciento volando** *prov* a bird in the hand is worth two in the bush
pajarón, -ona [pa·xa·'ron, -'ro·na] *adj Arg, Chile, pey, inf* scatterbrained
pajarraco [pa·xa·'rra·ko] *m inf* (*pillo*) rogue
paje ['pa·xe] *m* (*criado*) page
pajero [pa·'xe·ro] *m CSur, vulg* jerk-off
pajita [pa·'xi·ta] *f* (drinking) straw
pajizo, -a [pa·'xi·so, -a; -θo, -a] *adj* straw; (*color, cabello*) straw-colored
pajolero, -a [pa·xo·'le·ro, -a] *adj inf* damned
pajonal [pa·xo·'nal] *m CSur* scrubland
pajuela [pa·'xwe·la] *f* **1.** *Bol* (*cerilla*) match **2.** *Bol, Col* (*mondadientes*) toothpick
pajuerano, -a [pa·xwe·'ra·no, -a] *m, f Arg, Bol, Urug, pey* (*paleto*) country bumpkin, hick
Pakistán [pa·kis·'tan] *m* Pakistan
pakistaní [pa·kis·ta·'ni] *adj, mf* Pakistani
pala ['pa·la] *f* **1.** (*para cavar*) spade; (*cuadrada*)

shovel; ~ **mecánica** mechanical shovel; *AmL* bulldozer **2.** (*del timón*) rudder **3.** (*raqueta*) racket; (*bate*) bat
palabra [pa·'la·βra] *f* word; ~ **clave** *t.* COMPUT keyword, password; ~**s cruzadas** crossword; ~**s insultantes** rude words; ~ **de matrimonio** promise of marriage; ~**s mayores** strong words; ~ **técnica** technical term; **juego de** ~**s** pun, play on words; **libertad de** ~ freedom of speech; **bajo** ~ on one's word of honor; **buenas** ~**s** empty words; **de pocas** ~**s** quiet; **ahorrar** ~**s** not to waste one's words; **aprender las** ~**s** to learn one's lines; **coger a alguien la** ~ to take sb at his/her word; **cumplir la** ~ to be as good as one's word; **dirigir la** ~ **a alguien** to speak to sb; **faltar a la** ~ to go back on one's word; **llevar la** ~ to speak; **medir las** ~**s** to choose one's words carefully; **no entender** ~ not to understand a single word; **quitar a alguien la** ~ **de la boca** to take the words right out of sb's mouth ▸ **dejar a alguien con la** ~ **en la** boca to interrupt sb; **a** ~**s necias** oídos **sordos** *prov* sticks and stones will break my bones, but names will never hurt me *prov;* **poner dos** ~**s a alguien** to write sb a short note; **hablar a medias** ~**s** to drop hints; **decir la** última ~ to have the last word; **de** ~ (*oral*) by word of mouth; (*que cumple sus promesas*) honorable
palabrería [pa·la·βre·'ri·a] *f* (empty) words, hot air
palabrota [pa·la·'βro·ta] *f* swearword
palaciego, -a [pa·la·'sje·ɣo, -a; -'θje·ɣo, -a] **I.** *adj* palace **II.** *m, f* courtier
palacio [pa·'la·sjo, -θjo] *m* palace; **Palacio de las Cortes** Spanish parliament building; **Palacio de Justicia** law courts; ~ **municipal** town hall
paladar [pa·la·'dar] *m* palate; **tener buen** ~ (*vino*) to be smooth on the palate; (*persona*) to have a discerning palate
paladear [pa·la·de·'ar] *vt* to savor; ~ **un dulce** to allow a sweet to dissolve in one's mouth
palanca [pa·'lan·ka] *f* **1.** (*pértiga*) lever; (*palanqueta*) crowbar; ~ **de mando** AVIAT, COMPUT joystick; ~ **de cambio** gearshift **2.** *AmL* (*influencia*) influence; **tener mucha** ~ to have a lot of influence
palangana [pa·lan·'ga·na] *f* washbasin
palanganear [pa·lan·ga·ne·'ar] *vi AmL, inf* to brag
palanquear [pa·lan·ke·'ar] *vt AmL* **1.** (*apalancar*) to lever **2.** (*influenciar*) to influence
palapa [pa·'la·pa] *f Méx* sunshade
palatal [pa·la·'tal] *adj* palatal
palatino, -a [pa·la·'ti·no, -a] *adj* **1.** ANAT palatal; **hueso** ~ hard palate **2.** (*del palacio*) palace; **vida palatina** palace life
palco ['pal·ko] *m* TEAT box
palenque [pa·'len·ke] *m* (*estacada*) fence
palenquear [pa·len·ke·'ar] *vt Arg, Urug* to tether
paleontología [pa·leon·to·lo·'xi·a] *f* paleon-

tology
Palestina [pa·les·'ti·na] *m* Palestine
palestino, -a [pa·les·'ti·no, -a] *adj, m, f* Palestinian
paleta [pa·'le·ta] *f* **1.** (*pala*) (small) shovel; (*del albañil*) trowel **2.** (*del pintor*) palette **3.** (*de turbinas*) blade **4.** (*omóplato*) shoulder blade **5.** *Col, inf* (*helado*) popsicle
paletilla [pa·le·'ti·ja, -ʎa] *f* (*omóplato*) shoulder blade
paleto [pa·'le·to] *m* fallow deer
paleto, -a [pa·'le·to, -a] *m, f* yokel, hick
paliacate [pa·lja·'ka·te] *m Méx* large brightly colored scarf
paliar <*1. pres:* palío, palio> [pa·'ljar] *vt* (*enfermedad*) to alleviate
paliativo [pa·lja·'ti·βo] *m* palliative
paliativo, -a [pa·lja·'ti·βo, -a] *adj* MED palliative; **remedio** ~ palliative remedy
palidecer [pa·li·de·'ser, -θer] *irr como crecer vi* **1.** (*persona*) to turn pale **2.** (*cosa*) to fade
palidez [pa·li·'des, -'deθ] *f* paleness
pálido, -a ['pa·li·do, -a] *adj* pale; (*estilo*) flat
palillo [pa·'li·jo, -ʎo] *m* (small) stick; (*para los dientes*) toothpick; (*para el tambor*) drumstick; **tocar todos los ~s** *inf* to pull out all the stops
palique [pa·'li·ke] *m inf* chat; **estar de ~ con alguien** to chat to sb
palisandro [pa·li·'san·dro] *m* rosewood
paliza [pa·'li·sa, -θa] *f* beating; *inf* (*esfuerzo*) slog; **dar una buena ~** (*pegar*) to beat up; (*derrotar*) to thrash; **¡no me des la ~!** *fig* give me a break!; **pegarse una ~ con algo** *inf* to exhaust oneself with sth
palma ['pal·ma] *f* **1.** (*palmera*) palm (tree); (*hoja de palmera*) palm leaf; **llevarse la ~** to be the best **2.** ANAT palm; **conocer algo como la ~ de su mano** *inf* to know sth like the back of one's hand; **llevar a alguien en ~s** to handle sb with kid gloves **3.** *pl* (*ruido*) clapping; (*aplauso*) applause; **tocar las ~s** to clap; (*aplaudir*) to applaud
palmada [pal·'ma·da] *f* (*golpe*) pat
palmar [pal·'mar] **I.** *m* palm grove **II.** *vi inf* ~ **la** to kick the bucket
palmera [pal·'me·ra] *f* palm (tree)
palmeral [pal·me·'ral] *m* palm grove
palmo ['pal·mo] *m* (hand)span; **con un ~ de la lengua fuera** *inf* with one's tongue hanging out ▶ **dejar a alguien con un ~ de narices** to disappoint sb badly; **~ a ~** inch by inch
palmotear [pal·mo·te·'ar] *vi* to clap
palmoteo [pal·mo·'te·o] *m* clapping
palo ['pa·lo] *m* **1.** (*bastón*) stick; (*vara*) pole; (*garrote*) club; (*estaca*) post; **~ de la escoba** broomstick; **~ de hockey** hockey stick; **~ de la portería** goalpost **2.** (*paliza*) beating; **andar a ~s** to be at each another's throats; **dar ~s de ciego** to thrash around wildly; *fig* to grope in the dark; **dar un ~ a alguien** *fig* to tear a strip off sb; (*cobrar mucho*) to rip sb off; **echar a alguien a ~s** to throw sb out; **liarse a ~s con**

alguien to come to blows with sb; **moler a alguien a ~s** to beat sb black and blue ▶ ~ **de agua** *AmL* downpour; **no dar un ~ al agua** not to do a stick of work; **de tal ~, tal astilla** *prov* like father, like son; **cada ~ que aguante su vela** *prov* everyone must face up to their responsibilities; **ser un ~** to be a setback
paloma [pa·'lo·ma] *f* (*ave*) pigeon; (*blanca, como símbolo*) dove; ~ **mensajera** carrier pigeon
palomar [pa·lo·'mar] *m* dovecote, pigeon loft
palomilla [pa·lo·'mi·ja, -ʎa] *f* ZOOL moth
palomitas [pa·lo·'mi·tas] *fpl* CULIN popcorn
palote [pa·'lo·te] *m* drumstick
palpable [pal·'pa·βle] *adj* palpable; (*evidente*) clear
palpar [pal·'par] *vt* **1.** (*tocar*) to touch; *inf* (*magrear*) to feel up **2.** (*percibir*) to feel; **se palpaba el entusiasmo** you could feel the enthusiasm
palpitación [pal·pi·ta·'sjon, -'θjon] *f* **1.** (*del pulso*) throb; (*del corazón*) beating; (*por estar excitado*) palpitation **2.** (*estremecimiento*) shudder
palpitante [pal·pi·'tan·te] *adj* **1.** (*corazón*) throbbing **2.** *fig* (*emocionante*) exciting; (*interés*) burning; **un problema de ~ actualidad** a problem of the utmost relevance
palpitar [pal·pi·'tar] *vi* (*contraerse*) to shudder; (*corazón, pulso*) to throb
palta ['pal·ta] *f AmS* BOT avocado (pear)
palto ['pal·to] *m CSur* BOT avocado pear tree
paludismo [pa·lu·'dis·mo] *m* MED malaria
palurdo, -a [pa·'lur·do, -a] *m, f* yokel, hick
pamela [pa·'me·la] *f* broad-brimmed ladies' hat
pamema [pa·'me·ma] *f* trifle; *inf* fuss
pampa ['pam·pa] *f* GEO pampas + *sing/pl vb*

ⓘ The **pampas** is the vast, flat, grassy plain of Argentina. The moist, sandy soil of the region is very fertile and ideally suited to the cultivation of grains.

pámpano ['pam·pa·no] *m* vine shoot; **echar ~s** to put out shoots
pampear [pam·pe·'ar] *vi CSur* to travel over the pampas
pampero, -a [pam·'pe·ro] *adj* of/from the Pampas
pampino, -a [pam·'pi·no, -a] *adj Chile* of/from the Chilean pampas
pamplina [pam·'pli·na] *f inf* (*pamema*) silly thing
pan [pan] *m* bread; ~ **de azúcar** sugar loaf; ~ **integral** wholegrain bread; ~ **con mantequilla** bread and butter; ~ **de molde** sliced bread; ~ **de munición** (army) ration bread; ~ **rallado** breadcrumbs *pl;* **estar a ~ y agua** to be on (a strict diet of) bread and water; **ganarse el ~** to earn one's living; **un ~ de jabón** (*pieza*) a bar of soap ▶ **comer ~ con corteza**

(*ser independiente*) to fend for oneself; (*recuperar la salud*) to be on the mend; **¡el ~ de cada día!** the same old thing!; **no sólo de ~ vive el hombre** man cannot live by bread alone; **a falta de ~, buenas son tortas** *prov* half a loaf is better than none, beggars can't be choosers; (**llamar**) **al ~, ~ y al vino, vino** *inf* to call a spade a spade; **ser más bueno que el ~** to be very good-natured; **ser ~ comido** *inf* to be dead easy; **con su ~ se lo coma** *inf* that's his/her lookout [*o* problem]; **comer el ~ de alguien** to live off sb
pana ['pa·na] *f* corduroy
panacea [pa·na·'sea, -'θea] *f* panacea, cure-all
panadería [pa·na·de·'ri·a] *f* bakery
panadero, -a [pa·na·'de·ro, -a] *m, f* baker
panal [pa·'nal] *m* honeycomb
Panamá [pa·na·'ma] *m* Panama

> [i] **Panamá** is divided into two parts by the Panama Canal and links Central America to South America. The capital, also called **Panamá**, is the largest city in the country. The country's official language is Spanish, although English is widely spoken. The official currency of Panama is the **balboa**.

panameño, -a [pa·na·'me·ɲo, -a] *adj, m, f* Panamanian

> [i] The **Panamericana** (Pan-American Highway) is the name of the roadway that stretches throughout the entire American continent and connects Alaska in the North with Tierra del Fuego in the South. The idea for the road arose in the first half of the 20th century. Many sections of the **Panamericana** and roads that connect to it remain unpaved to this day.

pancarta [pan·'kar·ta] *f* placard
pancho ['pan·tʃo] *m Arg* (*perrito caliente*) hotdog
pancho, -a ['pan·tʃo, -a] *adj* calm
pancista [pan·'sis·ta, -'θis·ta] *mf* opportunist
pancita [pan·'si·ta, -'θi·ta] *f Méx* CULIN tripe
páncreas ['pan·kreas] *m inv* pancreas
panda[1] ['pan·da] *m* ZOOL panda
panda[2] ['pan·da] *f v.* **pandilla**
pandereta [pan·de·'re·ta] *f*, **pandero** [pan·'de·ro] *m* MÚS tambourine
pandilla [pan·'di·ja, -ʎa] *f* band; (*de amigos*) group; **~ de ladrones** gang of thieves
pandorga [pan·'dor·ɣa] *f Col* (*diablura*) prank
panecillo [pa·ne·'si·jo, -'θi·ʎo] *m* roll
panel [pa·'nel] *m* panel; **~ de control** control panel
panela [pa·'ne·la] *f* **1.** (*bizcocho*) corn cake **2.** *Col, CRi, Hond* (*azúcar*) brown sugar loaf
panera [pa·'ne·ra] *f* (*cesto*) breadbox

pánfilo, -a ['pan·fi·lo, -a] *adj* **1.** (*fácil de engañar*) gullible **2.** (*lento*) slow
panfleto [pan·'fle·to] *m* pamphlet; *fig* propaganda
pánico ['pa·ni·ko] *m* panic; **entrar en ~** to panic; **tener ~ a algo** to be terrified of sth
pánico, -a ['pa·ni·ko, -a] *adj* panic
panificar <c→qu> [pa·ni·fi·'kar] *vt* **~ algo** to make bread from sth
panocha [pa·'no·tʃa] *f*, **panoja** [pa·'no·xa] *f* **1.** (*de maíz*) corncob **2.** (*espiga*) ear of corn; (*racimo*) cornstalk
panoli [pa·'no·li] *adj inf* idiotic
panorama [pa·no·'ra·ma] *m* panorama; *fig* outlook
panqué [pan·'ke] *m Cuba, Méx*, **panqueque** [pan·'ke·ke] *m AmS* CULIN pancake
pantaleta(s) [pan·ta·'le·ta(s)] *f(pl) Méx, Ven* (*bragas*) panties *pl*
pantalla [pan·'ta·ja, -ʎa] *f* **1.** (*de la lámpara*) shade **2.** (*protección*) screen; **servir de ~** (*testaferro*) to be a figurehead **3.** COMPUT, TV, CINE screen; **~ cromática** color screen; **~ panorámica** wide screen; **pequeña ~** *inf* TV
pantalón [pan·ta·'lon] *m* trousers *pl*, pants *pl*, pair of pants; **~ tejano** [*o* **vaquero**] jeans *pl*; **llevar los pantalones** *fig* to wear the trousers [*o* pants]
pantano [pan·'ta·no] *m* (*ciénaga*) marsh; (*laguna*) swamp
pantanoso, -a [pan·ta·'no·so, -a] *adj* marshy
panteón [pan·te·'on] *m* **1.** HIST pantheon **2.** (*sepultura*) tomb; **~ de familia** family vault **3.** *AmL* (*cementerio*) cemetery
panteonero, -a [pan·teo·'ne·ro, -a] *m, f AmL* gravedigger
pantera [pan·'te·ra] *f* panther
pantimedia(s) [pan·ti·'me·dja(s)] *f(pl) Méx* pantyhose
pantis ['pan·tis] *mpl inf* pantyhose
pantomima [pan·to·'mi·ma] *f* pantomime
pantorrilla [pan·to·'rri·ja, -ʎa] *f* calf
pantufla [pan·'tu·fla] *f* slipper
panucho [pa·'nu·tʃo] *m Méx* meat and bean stuffed tortilla
panul [pa·'nul] *m CSur* BOT (*apio*) celery
panza ['pan·sa, -θa] *f* **1.** (*barriga*) belly; (*de un recipiente*) bulge **2.** ZOOL stomach; (*rumiantes*) rumen
pañal [pa·'ɲal] *m* diaper; **estar aún en ~es** *fig* to be still in its infancy
pañetar [pa·'ɲe·tar] *vt Col* (*una pared*) to plaster
paño ['pa·ɲo] *m* (*tejido, trapo*) cloth; **~ de cocina** (*para fregar*) dishcloth; (*para secar*) dish towel ▶ **ser el ~ de lágrimas de alguien** to be sb's shoulder to cry on; **andarse con ~s calientes** to do things by halves; **aplicar ~s calientes** to apply half measures; **~s menores** underwear; **¡conozco el ~!** *inf* I know what's what!; **hay ~ que cortar** there's plenty to be getting on with
pañoleta [pa·ɲo·'le·ta] *f* fichu

pañuelo [pa·'nwe·lo] *m* **1.** (*moquero*) handkerchief; **el mundo es un ~** it's a small world **2.** (*pañoleta*) fichu; (*de cabeza*) headscarf, scarf

papa¹ ['pa·pa] *m* pope

papa² ['pa·pa] *f* **1.** *reg, AmL* (*patata*) potato; **no entender ni ~** not to understand a thing **2.** *pl* (*comida*) purée

papá [pa·'pa] *m inf* dad; **Papá Noel** Santa Claus; **los ~s** mom and dad

papachar [pa·pa·'tʃar] *vt Méx* (*mimar*) to spoil

papada [pa·'pa·da] *f* (*de la persona*) double chin, jowl; (*del animal*) dewlap

papagayo [pa·pa·'ya·jo] *m* **1.** (*loro*) parrot **2.** (*hablador*) chatterbox

papal [pa·'pal] **I.** *adj* papal **II.** *m AmL* potato field

papalote [pa·pa·'lo·te] *m Ant, Méx* paper kite

papamóvil [pa·pa·'mo·βil] *m inf* popemobile

papanatas [pa·pa·'na·tas] *m inv, inf* halfwit

paparrucha [pa·pa·'rru·tʃa] *f inf,* **paparruchada** [pa·pa·rru·'tʃa·da] *f inf* **1.** (*noticia falsa*) piece of nonsense; (*patraña*) lie **2.** (*obra sin valor*) piece of trash; **ese libro es una ~** this book is trash

papaya [pa·'pa·ja] *f* pawpaw, papaya

papel [pa·'pel] *m* **1.** (*para escribir, material*) paper; (*hoja*) piece of paper; (*escritura*) piece of writing; **~ de calcar** tracing paper; **~ de envolver** wrapping paper; **~ de regalo** giftwrap; **~ de estraza** brown paper; **~ de aluminio** aluminum [*o* tin] foil; **~ de seda** tissue paper; **~ higiénico** toilet paper; **~ de hilo** parchment paper; **~ de lija** sandpaper; **~ maché** papier-mâché; **~ moneda** banknotes *pl,* bills *pl;* **~ pintado** wallpaper; **~ de plata** silver paper; **~ reciclado** recycled paper; **~ secante** blotting paper; **~ mojado** *fig* worthless scrap of paper; **ponerse más blanco que el ~** to go as white as a sheet **2.** (*rol*) role; **~ protagonista** leading role; **~ secundario** supporting role; **hacer su ~** to play one's part; **hacer un ~ ridículo** to make a fool of oneself; **hacer buen/mal ~** to make a good/bad impression; **repartir los ~es** to assign the parts **3.** *pl* (*documentos*) documentation; (*de identidad*) identity papers *pl*

papeleo [pa·pe·'leo] *m* paperwork; **~ burocrático** red tape

papelera [pa·pe·'le·ra] *f* **1.** (*cesto*) wastepaper basket; (*en la calle*) litter bin **2.** (*fábrica*) paper mill

papelería [pa·pe·le·'ri·a] *f* stationer's

papelerío [pa·pe·le·'ri·a] *m AmL* mass of papers

papeleta [pa·pe·'le·ta] *f* (*cédula*) slip of paper; (*en el examen*) result slip; **~ de propaganda** flier

papelón [pa·pe·'lon] *m inf* blunder; **¡qué ~!** how embarrassing!

papera [pa·'pe·ra] *f MED* **1.** *pl* (*enfermedad*) mumps *pl* **2.** (*bocio*) goiter

papilla [pa·'pi·ja, -ʎa] *f* baby food; **dar ~ a al-**

guien *fig* to con sb; **echar la (primera) ~** *inf* to be as sick as a dog; **hacer ~ a alguien** *fig* to beat hell out of sb; **estar hecho ~** *fig* to be smashed to a pulp

papiro [pa·'pi·ro] *m* papyrus

papo ['pa·po] *m* **1.** *inf* (*bocio*) goiter **2.** (*papada*) double chin, jowl

paquebote [pa·ke·'βo·te] *m* packet boat

paquete [pa·'ke·te] *m* **1.** *t. fig* (*atado*) packet; **~ postal** parcel **2.** *inf* (*castigo*) **meter un ~ a alguien** (*reprender*) to tell sb off; (*castigar*) to punish sb heavily **3.** *vulg* (*genitales*) basket; **marcar ~** to show one's basket

paquete, -a [pa·'ke·te, -a] *adj Arg* smart

paquetear [pa·ke·te·'ar] *vi Arg, Urug, inf:* to show off one's outfit

paquete-bomba [pa·'ke·te-·'βom·ba] *m* <paquetes-bomba> mail [*o* letter] bomb

paquetería [pa·ke·te·'ri·a] *f Arg* (*vanidad*) vanity

paquistaní [pa·kis·ta·'ni] *adj, mf v.* **pakistaní**

par [par] **I.** *adj* **1.** (*número*) even; **~es o nones** odds or evens **2.** (*igual*) equal; **a la ~** at the same time; **sin ~** without equal ▶ **de ~ en ~** wide open **II.** *m* **1.** (*dos cosas*) pair; **un ~ de zapatos/pantalones** a pair of shoes/pants **2.** (*algunos*) **un ~ de minutos** a couple of minutes

para ['pa·ra] **I.** *prep* **1.** (*destino*) for; **asilo ~ ancianos** old people's home; **un regalo ~ el niño** a present for the child **2.** (*finalidad*) for; **gafas ~ bucear** diving goggles; **servir ~ algo** to be useful for sth; **¿~ qué es esto?** what is this for? **3.** (*dirección*) to; **voy ~ Madrid** I'm going to Madrid; **mira ~ acá** look over here **4.** (*duración*) for; **~ siempre** forever; **vendrá ~ Navidad/finales de marzo** he/she will come for Christmas/towards the end of March; **estará listo ~ el viernes** it will be ready for [*o* by] Friday; **diez minutos ~ las once** *AmL* ten to eleven **5.** (*contraposición*) for; **es muy activo ~ la edad que tiene** he is very active for his age **6.** (*trato*) ~ (**con**) with; **es muy amable ~ con nosotros** he/she is very kind to us **7.** (+ *estar*) **estar ~...** (*disposición*) to be ready to...; (*a punto de*) about to...; **no estoy ~ bromas** I'm in no mood for jokes; **está ~ llegar** he/she is about to arrive **8.** (*a juicio de*) **~ mí, esto no es lo mismo** in my opinion, this is not the same; **~ mí que va a llover** I think it's going to rain **II.** *conj* **1.** + *infin* to; **he venido ~ darte las gracias** I came to thank you **2.** **~ que** + *subj* so that; **te mando al colegio ~ que aprendas algo** I send you to school so that you learn sth

parábola [pa·'ra·βo·la] *f* **1.** (*alegoría*) parable **2.** *MAT* curve, parabola

parabólica [pa·ra·'βo·li·ka] *f* satellite dish

parabrisas [pa·ra·'βri·sas] *m inv AUTO* windshield

paraca [pa·'ra·ka] *f AmL* strong breeze from the Pacific

paracaídas [pa·ra·ka·'i·das] *m inv* parachute

paracaidismo [pa·ra·kai·'dis·mo] *m* parachuting

paracaidista [pa·ra·kai·'dis·ta] *mf* DEP parachutist; MIL paratrooper

parachoques [pa·ra·'tʃo·kes] *m inv* AUTO bumper

parada [pa·'ra·da] *f* **1.** (*de un autobús*) stop; ~ **de taxis** taxi rank **2.** (*acción de parar*) stopping; ~ **de una fábrica** factory stoppage; **hacer una** ~ **para descansar** to make a rest stop **3.** DEP, MIL parade; **paso de** ~ marching step

paradero [pa·ra·'de·ro] *m* (*de una persona*) whereabouts; (*de una cosa*) destination; **está en** ~ **desconocido** his/her whereabouts are unknown

paradisíaco, -a [pa·ra·di·'si·a·ko, -a] *adj* heavenly; **un placer** ~ a heavenly delight

parado, -a [pa·'ra·do, -a] **I.** *adj* **1.** (*que no se mueve*) stationary; **estar** ~ to be motionless; (*fábrica*) to be at a standstill; **quedarse** ~ to remain motionless; *fig* to be surprised **2.** (*sin empleo*) unemployed **3.** (*remiso*) slow **4.** (*tímido*) shy **5.** *AmL* standing (up) ▶ **salir bien/mal** ~ **de algo** to come out of sth well/badly; **ser el peor** ~ **en algo** to be the one who comes off worst in sth **II.** *m, f* unemployed person; **los** ~**s** the unemployed

paradoja [pa·ra·'do·xa] *f* paradox; **esto es una** ~ this is absurd

parador [pa·ra·'dor] *m* inn; (*en España*) state-run luxury hotel

paraestatal [pa·ra·es·ta·'tal] *adj* semi-official

parafina [pa·ra·'fi·na] *f* paraffin

parafrasear [pa·ra·fra·se·'ar] *vt* to paraphrase

paráfrasis [pa·'ra·fra·sis] *f inv* paraphrase

paragolpes [pa·ra·'ɣol·pes] *m inv, AmL* bumper

parágrafo [pa·'ra·ɣra·fo] *m* paragraph; ..., ~ **aparte** ..., new paragraph; *fig* ..., to change the subject

paraguas [pa·'ra·ɣwas] *m inv* umbrella

Paraguay [pa·ra·'ɣwai] *m* Paraguay

> **i** Paraguay, a landlocked country located in South America, borders on Bolivia, Brazil, and Argentina. The capital is **Asunción**. The country's official languages are Spanish and **guaraní**. The official currency of the country is also called the **guaraní**.

paraguayo, -a [pa·ra·'ɣwa·jo, -a] *adj, m, f* Paraguayan

paragüero [pa·ra·'ɣwe·ro] *m* umbrella stand

paraíso [pa·ra·'i·so] *m* **1.** (*en el cielo*) heaven; ~ **terrenal** earthly paradise **2.** *Méx* (*gallinero*) henhouse

paraje [pa·'ra·xe] *m* (*lugar*) place; (*punto*) spot

paralela [pa·ra·'le·la] *f* **1.** MAT parallel **2.** *pl* DEP parallel bars *pl*

paralelo [pa·ra·'le·lo] *m* **conexión en** ~ ELEC parallel connection; **establecer un** ~ **entre dos cosas** to compare two things

paralelo, -a [pa·ra·'le·lo, -a] *adj* parallel; **líneas paralelas** parallel lines; **seguir caminos** ~**s** to develop along similar lines

paralelogramo [pa·ra·le·lo·'ɣra·mo] *m* parallelogram

parálisis [pa·'ra·li·sis] *f inv* paralysis

paralítico, -a [pa·ra·'li·ti·ko, -a] *adj* (*persona*) paralyzed

paralización [pa·ra·li·sa·'sjon, -θa·'θjon] *f* **1.** (*del cuerpo*) paralysis **2.** (*de un proceso*) halting; ~ **de una obra** halting of construction

paralizar <z→c> [pa·ra·li·'sar, -'θar] **I.** *vt* **1.** (*persona*) to paralyze; **el miedo/el frío la paralizó** she was paralyzed by fear/by the cold **2.** (*cosa*) to stop; ~ **un transporte** to paralyze a means of transport **II.** *vr* **1.** (*persona*) to be paralyzed **2.** (*cosa*) to stop

parámetro [pa·'ra·me·tro] *m* parameter

paramilitar [pa·ra·mi·li·'tar] *adj* paramilitary; **fuerzas** ~**es** paramilitary forces

páramo ['pa·ra·mo] *m* **1.** (*terreno desierto*) wilderness; (*infértil*) wasteland **2.** (*lugar desamparado*) exposed place

parangón [pa·ran·'gon] *m* **sin** ~ incomparable

paraninfo [pa·ra·'nin·fo] *m* UNIV auditorium, assembly hall

paranoia [pa·ra·'noja] *f* paranoia

paranoico, -a [pa·ra·'noi·ko, -a] *adj* paranoid

parapente [pa·ra·'pen·te] *m* paragliding

parapetarse [pa·ra·pe·'tar·se] *vr* to protect oneself; ~ **tras una excusa** to hide behind an excuse

parapeto [pa·ra·'pe·to] *m* **1.** MIL parapet; (*barricada*) barricade **2.** (*baranda*) railing

paraplejía [pa·ra·ple·'xi·a] *f* paraplegia

parapléjico, -a [pa·ra·'ple·xi·ko, -a] *adj, m, f* paraplegic

parapsicología [pa·raβ·si·ko·lo·'xi·a] *f* parapsychology

parar ['pa·rar] **I.** *vi* **1.** (*detenerse, cesar*) to stop; **la máquina funciona sin** ~ the machine works non-stop; **mis hijos no me dejan** ~ my kids never give me a break; **mis remordimientos de conciencia no me dejan** ~ my guilty conscience doesn't give me any peace; **ha parado de llover** it has stopped raining; **no para** (**de trabajar**) he/she never stops (working) **2.** (*acabar*) to finish; **ir a** ~ **a...** to end up in...; **¿dónde iremos a** ~**?** what's the world coming to?; **¿en qué irá a** ~ **esto?** where will it all end?; **salir bien/mal parado de algo** to come out of sth well/badly; **¿dónde quieres ir a** ~**?** what are you getting at? **3.** (*alojarse, estar*) to live; **nunca para en casa** he/she is never at home; **siempre para en el mismo hotel** he/she always stays at the same hotel **II.** *vt* **1.** (*detener*) to stop; (*un golpe*) to block; (*un gol*) to save; (*el motor*) to turn off **2.** (*en el juego*) to bet **III.** *vr* **1.** (*detenerse*) to stop; ~**se a pensar** to stop and think; ~**se a descansar** to stop to rest **2.** *AmL* (*levantarse*) to get up

pararrayos [pa·ra·'rra·jos] *m inv* lightning

conductor

parásito, -a [pa·'ra·si·to, -a] **I.** *adj t. fig* parasitic **II.** *m, f t. fig* parasite

parasol [pa·ra·'sol] *m* sunshade; (*en el coche*) sun visor

parcela [par·'se·la, -'θe·la] *f* plot; ~ **edificable** building plot

parcelar [par·se·'lar, par·θe-] *vt* to parcel out

parche ['par·tʃe] *m* **1.** (*pegote*) patch; (*para una herida*) Band-aid®; ~ **para el ojo** eye patch; **poner un** ~ to patch up **2.** (*retoque*) makeshift remedy; (*de pintura*) dab; **poner ~s** to patch up; *fig* to paper over the cracks

parchear [par·tʃe·'ar] *vt* **1.** (*poner parches*) to patch (up) **2.** *inf* (*manosear*) to feel (sb) up *sl*

parchís [par·'tʃis] *m* Parcheesi®

parcial [par·'sjal, -'θjal] **I.** *adj* **1.** (*incompleto*) partial; **la venta ~ del terreno** the partial sale of the land **2.** (*arbitrario*) biased **II.** *mf* supporter

parcialidad [par·sja·li·'dad, par·θja-] *f* bias, favoritism

parco, -a ['par·ko, -a] *adj* **1.** (*moderado*) moderate; (*sobrio*) frugal **2.** (*escaso*) meager; ~ **en palabras** of few words; **ser ~ en conceder favores** to be sparing with one's favors

pardiez [par·'djes, -'djeθ] *interj* HIST good gracious

pardillo [par·'di·jo, -ʎo] *m* linnet

pardillo, -a [par·'di·jo, -a; -ʎo, -a] **I.** *adj inf* **1.** (*palurdo*) uncouth **2.** (*ingenuo*) simple **II.** *m, f* **1.** (*palurdo*) yokel **2.** (*ingenuo*) simpleton

pardo, -a ['par·do] **I.** *adj* grayish-brown; **oso ~** brown bear; **de ojos ~s** brown-eyed **II.** *m, f AmL* mulatto

parear [pa·re·'ar] *vt* **1.** (*formar parejas*) to pair; (*atar*) to tie together; (*ropa*) to match up **2.** BIO to mate **3.** (*igualar*) to match

parecer [pa·re·'ser, -θer] **I.** *irr como crecer vi* to seem; (*aparentar*) to appear; **a lo que parece** as far as one can tell; **parece mayor de lo que es** he/she seems older than he/she is; **parece mentira que** +*subj* it seems incredible that; **aunque parezca mentira** though it may seem incredible; **me parece que no tienes ganas** I don't think you want to; **parece que va a llover** it looks like rain; **¿qué te parece?** what do you think?; **si te parece bien,...** if you agree,...; **parecen hermanos** they look like brothers ▶ **quien no parece, perece** *prov* if you don't look after your own interests, nobody else will **II.** *irr como crecer vr* to look alike; **te pareces mucho a tu madre** you look very much like your mother; **¡esto se te parece!** this looks like you! **III.** *m* **1.** (*opinión*) opinion; (*juicio*) judgment; **a mi ~** in my opinion; **esto es cuestión de ~es** this is a matter of opinion **2.** (*aspecto, apariencia*) appearance; **ser de buen ~** to be good-looking; **al ~** apparently

parecido, -a [pa·re·'si·do, -'θi·do] *m* similarity, likeness

parecido, -a [pa·re·'si·do, -a; -θi·do, -a] *adj* **1.** (*semejante*) similar **2.** (*de aspecto*) **ser bien/mal ~** (*persona*) to be good/bad-looking; (*cosa*) to be appropriate/inappropriate

pared [pa·'red] *f* wall; (*de una montaña*) face; (*separación*) partition; ~ **abdominal** stomach wall; ~ **maestra** (load-)bearing wall ▶ **vivimos ~ por medio** we live next door; **estar blanco como la ~** to be as white as a sheet [*o* ghost]; **entre cuatro ~es** cooped up; **dejar a alguien pegado a la ~** to put sb on the spot; **quedarse pegado a la ~** to be put on the spot; **hablar a la ~** to talk to a brick wall; **¡cuidado, que estas ~es oyen!** careful, walls have ears!; **subirse por las ~es** to go up the wall; (*enfadarse*) to blow one's top; (*estar nervioso*) to be [*o* go] stir crazy

paredón [pa·re·'don] *m* thick wall; **llevar a alguien al ~** to take sb before a firing squad

pareja [pa·'re·xa] *f* **1.** (*par*) couple; ~ **de hecho** common law couple; **~s mixtas** DEP mixed doubles; **hacen buena ~** they make a good partnership [*o* couple]; **¿dónde está la ~ de este guante?** where is the other glove?; **no correr ~s** to be dissimilar **2.** (*compañero*) partner **3.** (*en los dados*) pair

parejo, -a [pa·'re·xo, -a] *adj* **1.** (*igual*) equal; (*semejante*) similar; **los caballos iban ~s** the horses were neck and neck **2.** (*llano*) smooth

parentela [pa·ren·'te·la] *f* relations *pl*

parentesco [pa·ren·'tes·ko] *m* relationship, kinship; ~ **por consanguinidad** blood relationship

paréntesis [pa·'ren·te·sis] *m inv* **1.** (*signo*) bracket; **poner algo entre ~** to put sth in brackets; **entre ~** *fig* by the way; **abrir/cerrar el ~** to open/close brackets; *fig* to introduce/finish a digression **2.** (*interrupción*) interruption; **hicimos un ~ para almorzar** we had a break for lunch

paridad [pa·ri·'dad] *f* **1.** FIN, ECON parity; ~ **(de cambio)** exchange parity **2.** (*igualdad*) equality; (*semejanza*) similarity; ~ **de fuerzas** parity of strength; **competir a ~ de medios** to compete on an equal basis

pariente, -a [pa·'rjen·te, -a] **I.** *adj* related **II.** *m, f* **1.** (*familiar*) relative; **los ~s** the relations, the relatives; **~lejano/cercano** distant/close relative **2.** *inf* (*marido, mujer*) other half; **mi parienta** my missus

paripé [pa·ri·'pe] *m* show; **hacer el ~** to put on a show; (*presumir*) to show off; (*fingir*) to pretend

parir [pa·'rir] **I.** *vt* to give birth to **II.** *vi* to give birth ▶ **poner a alguien a ~** *inf* to run sb down

París [pa·'ris] *m* Paris

parisiense [pa·ri·'sjen·se] *adj, mf* Parisian

paritario, -a [pa·ri·'ta·rjo, -a] *adj* equal; **comité ~** joint committee

paritorio [pa·ri·'to·rjo] *m* **1.** (*sala*) delivery room **2.** *AmC* (*parto*) birth

parking ['par·kin] *m* <parkings> parking lot

parlamentario, -a [par·la·men·'ta·rjo, -a] **I.** *adj* parliamentary; **debate ~** parliamentary debate **II.** *m, f* member of parliament

parlamento [par·la·'men·to] *m* parliament; **Parlamento Europeo** European Parliament

parlanchín, -ina [par·lan·'tʃin, -·'tʃi·na] **I.** *adj inf* talkative **II.** *m, f inf* (*persona*) chatterbox; (*indiscreta*) gossip

parlotear [par·lo·te·'ar] *vi* to chatter

parloteo [par·lo·'teo] *m* chat

paro ['pa·ro] *m* **1.** (*parar: una fábrica*) shutdown; (*de trabajar*) stopping **2.** (*huelga*) ~ **laboral** strike; (*por parte de los empresarios*) lockout **3.** (*desempleo*) unemployment; **estar en ~** to be unemployed; **cobrar el ~** to be on the dole

parodia [pa·'ro·dja] *f* parody

parodiar [pa·ro·'djar] *vt* to parody

parpadear [par·pa·de·'ar] *vi* **1.** (*ojos*) to blink; **sin ~** *fig* without a second thought **2.** (*luz, llama*) to flicker

parpadeo [par·pa·'deo] *m* **1.** (*de los ojos*) blinking **2.** (*de luz, llama*) flicker

párpado ['par·pa·do] *m* eyelid

parque ['par·ke] *m* **1.** (*jardín*) park; **~ de atracciones** amusement park; **~ natural** National Park; **~ zoológico** zoo **2.** (*depósito*) depot; **~ de bomberos** fire department; **~ militar** military depot **3.** (*conjunto*) collection; **~ industrial** industrial park; **~ de maquinaria** pool of machinery; **~ de vehículos** fleet of vehicles, car pool **4.** (*para niños*) playpen

parqué [par·'ke] *m* parquet

parqueadero [par·kea·'de·ro] *m AmL* parking lot

parquear [par·ke·'ar] *vt AmL* to park

parquedad [par·ke·'dad] *f* frugality; **hablar con ~** to be sparing with one's words

parquímetro [par·'ki·me·tro] *m* parking meter

parra ['pa·rra] *f* (grape)vine; **subirse a la ~** (*enfadarse*) to hit the roof; (*darse importancia*) to put on airs

párrafo ['pa·rra·fo] *m v.* **parágrafo**

parral [pa·'rral] *m* **1.** (*parras*) vine; (*techo*) vine arbor **2.** (*viña*) vineyard

parranda [pa·'rran·da] *f* spree; **ir de ~** to go out on the town

parrilla [pa·'rri·ja, -·ʎa] *f* **1.** (*para la brasa*) grill; (*de un horno*) oven rack **2.** (*establecimiento*) grill(room) **3.** DEP ~ (**de salida**) (starting) grid **4.** *AmL* AUTO roof-rack

parrillada [pa·rri·'ja·da, -·ʎa·da] *f* grill; **~ de pescado** grilled fish; **~ de carne** mixed grill

párroco ['pa·rro·ko] **I.** *adj* parish **II.** *m* parish priest

parroquia [pa·'rro·kja] *f* **1.** (*territorio, fieles*) parish **2.** (*iglesia*) parish church

parroquial [pa·rro·'kjal] *adj* parish; **iglesia ~** parish church

parsimonia [par·si·'monja] *f* **1.** (*calma*) calm; (*lentitud*) deliberation; **con ~** calmly **2.** (*en los gastos*) economy **3.** (*prudencia*) care; (*moderación*) moderation

parsimonioso, -a [par·si·mo·'njo·so, -a] *adj* **1.** (*tranquilo*) calm; (*flemático*) phlegmatic **2.** (*ahorrador*) economical **3.** (*prudente*) careful; (*moderado*) moderate

parte¹ ['par·te] *f* **1.** (*porción, elemento*) part; (*de repuesto*) spare (part); **~ alícuota** proportion; **~ del mundo** part of the world; **una cuarta ~** a quarter; **de varias ~s** of several parts; **en ~** in part; **en gran ~** largely; **en mayor ~** for the most part; **~ por ~** bit by bit; **tomar ~ en algo** to be involved in sth **2.** (*repartición*) division; **~ hereditaria** share of the inheritance; **tener ~ en algo** to have a share in sth; **llevarse la peor/mejor ~** to come off (the) worst/best **3.** (*lugar*) part; **¿a qué ~ vas?** where are you going?; **a ninguna ~** nowhere; **en ninguna ~** nowhere; **en cualquier ~** anywhere; **por todas (las) ~s** everywhere; **en otra ~** somewhere else; **¿de qué ~ de Colombia eres?** which part of Colombia is your family from?; **no llevar a ninguna ~** *fig* to lead nowhere **4.** *t.* JUR (*bando*) party; (*en una discusión*) participant; **~ contratante** contracting party **5.** (*lado*) side; **dale recuerdos de mi ~** give him/her my regards; **estar de ~ de alguien** to be on sb's side; **ponerse de ~ de alguien** to take sb's side; **saber de buena ~** to know from a reliable source; **me tienes de tu ~** I'm on your side; **de ~ a ~** (*de un lado a otro*) from side to side; (*de arriba a abajo*) from top to bottom; **por otra ~** on the other hand; (*además*) what's more **6.** (*sección*) section; (*tomo*) volume; (*capítulo*) chapter **7.** TEAT, MÚS (*papel*) part **8.** *pl* (*genitales*) (private) parts *pl* ► **tomar** [*o* **echar**] **algo a mala ~** to take sth as an insult

parte² ['par·te] *m* **1.** (*comunicado*) message; **dar ~** to report **2.** RADIO, TV report; **~ meteorológico** weather report

partero, -a [par·'te·ro, -a] *m, f* midwife *f*, male midwife *m*

partición [par·ti·'sjon, -'θjon] *f* partition; MAT division

participación [par·ti·si·pa·'sjon, -θi·pa·'θjon] *f* **1.** (*intervención*) participation; **~ en los beneficios** profit-sharing **2.** (*parte*) share **3.** (*anuncio*) notice; (*aviso*) warning

participante [par·ti·si·'pan·te, par·ti·θi-] *mf* participant

participar [par·ti·si·'par, par·ti·θi-] **I.** *vi* **1.** (*tomar parte*) to participate; **~ en un juego** to take part in a game; **participo en tu alegría** I share your happiness **2.** (*tener parte*) to have a part; **~ en una herencia** to share in an inheritance **3.** (*tener en común*) **~ de algo** to share sth **II.** *vt* (*comunicar*) to inform

partícipe [par·'ti·si·pe, -θi·pe] **I.** *adj* involved **II.** *mf* participant; **~ de algo** person involved in sth; **hacer a alguien ~ de algo** (*compartir*) to share sth with sb; (*informar*) to inform sb of sth

participio [par·ti·'si·pjo, -'θi·pjo] *m* LING participle; **~ activo** [*o* **de presente**] present partici-

ple; ~ **pasivo** [*o* de **pretérito**] past participle
partícula [par·'ti·ku·la] *f* **1.** *t.* FÍS, QUÍM particle;
~**s de polvo** dust particles **2.** LING particle;
~ **prepositiva** prefix
particular¹ [par·ti·ku·'lar] **I.** *adj* **1.** (*propio*) peculiar; (*individual*) individual; (*típico*) typical;
(*personal*) personal; **el sabor ~ del azafrán**
the special flavor of saffron **2.** (*raro*) peculiar
3. (*extraordinario*) unusual; **caso ~** unusual
case; **en ~** in particular **4.** (*privado*) private;
envíamelo a mi domicilio ~ send it to my
home address **5.** (*determinado*) particular; **un
problema ~** a particular problem **II.** *mf* private individual; (*civil*) civilian
particular² [par·ti·ku·'lar] *m* matter
particularidad [par·ti·ku·la·ri·'dad] *f* **1.** (*especialidad*) specialty; (*singularidad*) distinctive
feature; (*peculiaridad*) peculiarity **2.** (*rareza*)
peculiarity **3.** (*detalle*) detail; (*circunstancia*)
circumstance; **las ~es del crimen** the circumstances of the crime
particularmente [par·ti·ku·lar·'men·te] *adv*
particularly
partida [par·'ti·da] *f* **1.** (*salida*) departure
2. (*envío*) consignment **3.** FIN item; ~ **doble**
double entry **4.** (*anotación*) entry; (*certificado*) certificate; ~ **de defunción** death certificate **5.** (*juego*) game; **jugar una ~ de ajedrez** to play a game of chess
partidario, -a [par·ti·'da·rjo, -a] **I.** *adj* **1.** (*parcial*) biased **2.** (*seguidor*) **ser ~ de algo** to be
in favor of sth **II.** *m, f* **1.** (*seguidor*) follower;
(*afiliado*) member; (*de una idea*) supporter
2. (*guerrillero*) partisan
partido [par·'ti·do] *m* **1.** POL party; ~ **de dere-
cha(s)/de izquierda(s)** right-wing/left-wing
party; ~ **obrero** worker's party; ~ **pequeño**
minority party; ~ **popular** people's party; **sistema de ~ único** one-party system **2.** (*grupo*)
group; **formar ~** to band together; **esta idea
tiene mucho ~** this idea has a lot of supporters **3.** DEP (*juego*) match; ~ **amistoso**
friendly **4.** (*para casarse*) match; **encontrar
un buen ~** to make quite a catch **5.** ADMIN district; ~ **judicial** administrative area **6.** (*determinación*) determination; **tomar ~ a favor de
algo/alguien** (*inclinarse*) to lean towards
sth/sb; (*opinar*) to express an opinion on sth/
sb **7.** (*provecho*) advantage; **sacar ~ de algo**
to put sth to use; **saqué ~ del asunto** I
profited from the affair **8.** *AmL* (*del pelo*) parting
partir [par·'tir] **I.** *vt* **1.** *t.* MAT (*dividir*) to divide;
~ **por la mitad** to divide into two halves
2. (*romper*) to break; (*madera*) to chop; (*una
nuez*) to crack; ~ **el pan** REL to break bread;
~ **la cabeza a alguien** to crack sb's head open
3. (*repartir*) to share out **4.** (*compartir*) to
share **5.** (*una baraja*) to cut **II.** *vi* **1.** (*tomar
como base*) to start; **a ~ de ahora** from now
on; **a ~ de mañana** from tomorrow; **a ~ de
las seis** from six o'clock onwards; **a ~ de
entonces** since then **2.** (*salir de viaje*) to

leave; (*ponerse en marcha*) to start; **partimos
de Cádiz a las cinco** we left Cadiz at five
o'clock **III.** *vr* to split; (*cristal*) to crack; ~**se**
(**de risa**) *inf* to split one's sides laughing
partisano, -a [par·ti·'sa·no, -a] *m, f* partisan
partitivo, -a [par·ti·'ti·βo] *adj* LING partitive
partitura [par·ti·'tu·ra] *f* MÚS score; (*hojas*)
sheet music
parto ['par·to] *m* birth; ~ **prematuro** premature birth; **dolores de ~** labor pains *pl;* **estar
de ~** to be in labor
parturienta [par·tu·'rjen·ta] *f* **1.** (*que está de
parto*) woman in labor **2.** (*que acaba de parir*)
woman who has just given birth
parvo, -a ['par·βo, -a] *adj* (*pequeño*) small;
(*escaso*) scarce
parvulario [par·βu·'la·rjo] *m* kindergarten;
(*educación preescolar*) nursery school, preschool
párvulo, -a ['par·βu·lo, -a] *m, f* infant;
escuela de ~s nursery school, preschool
pasa ['pa·sa] *f* raisin; ~ **de Corinto** currant;
estar hecho una ~ *inf* to be as shriveled as a
prune
pasable [pa·'sa·βle] *adj* passable
pasabocas [pa·sa·'βo·kas] *m inv, Col* (*tapas*)
appetizer
pasada [pa·'sa·da] *f* **1.** (*paso*) passing; **hacer
varias ~s** to make several passes; **de ~** when
passing; *fig* in passing **2.** (*mano*) going-over;
(*pintura*) coat; **dar una ~ a algo** to give sth another going-over **3.** *inf* (*comportamiento*) excess; **¡vaya (mala) ~!** what a thing to do!;
hacer una mala ~ a alguien to play a dirty
trick on sb **4.** *inf* (*exageración*) **¡es una ~!** it's
way over the top! **5.** (*en un juego*) pass
pasadizo [pa·sa·'di·so, -θo] *m* (*pasillo*) corridor; (*entre dos calles*) alley; ~ **secreto** secret
passageway
pasado [pa·'sa·do] *m* past; LING past (tense);
en el ~ in the past; **son cosas del ~** it's all in
the past
pasado, -a [pa·'sa·do, -a] *adj* **1.** (*de atrás*)
past; **el año ~** last year; ~ **mañana** the day after tomorrow; ~**s dos meses** after two
months; ~ **de moda** out of fashion; (*vestido*)
unfashionable **2.** (*estropeado: alimentos*) bad;
(*fruta*) overripe; (*leche*) off, sour; (*mantequilla*) rancid; (*ropa*) worn-out; (*flores*)
wilted; **el yogur está ~ de fecha** the yogurt is
past its sell-by date **3.** (*muy cocido*) overcooked; **¿quieres el filete muy ~?** do you
want the steak very well done?; **un huevo ~
por agua** a soft-boiled egg
pasador [pa·sa·'dor] *m* **1.** (*alfiler*) pin; (*imperdible*) safety pin; (*broche*) clip; (*de corbata*)
tiepin **2.** (*para el cabello*) hairclip, barrette
3. (*cerrojo*) bolt **4.** (*colador*) colander
pasadores [pa·sa·'do·res] *mpl* **1.** (*alfiler*) cufflinks *pl* **2.** *Perú* (*cordones*) shoelaces *pl*
pasaje [pa·'sa·xe] *m* **1.** (*acción de pasar*) passing; (*de una calle*) crossing **2.** (*derecho*) toll
3. (*en barco*) voyage **4.** (*billete de avión*)

(plane) ticket; (*de barco*) (boat) ticket; (*precio*) fare **5.** (*pasajeros*) passengers *pl* **6.** (*pasillo*) passage; ~ **subterráneo** underground passage **7.** (*estrecho*) strait

pasajero, -a [pa·sa·'xe·ro, -a] **I.** *adj* **1.** (*transitorio, breve*) passing; (*fugaz*) fleeting **2.** (*calle, plaza*) busy **II.** *m, f* (*viajero*) passenger; **tren de ~ s** passenger train

pasamano(s) [pa·sa·'ma·no(s)] *m(pl)* handrail

pasamontañas [pa·sa·mon·'ta·ɲas] *m inv* ski mask

pasapalos [pa·sa·'pa·los] *m inv, Méx, Ven* appetizer

pasaporte [pa·sa·'por·te] *m* passport; **dar** (**el**) ~ **a alguien** *inf* (*despedirlo*) to give sb their marching orders; (*matarlo*) to bump sb off

pasapuré(s) [pa·sa·pu·'re(s)] *m* (*inv*) vegetable mill; (*patatas*) potato masher

pasar [pa·'sar] **I.** *vi* **1.** (*por delante*) to pass; ~ **desapercibido** to go unnoticed; ~ **de largo** to go past; **pásate por mi casa** drop by my house; **dejar** ~ (*por delante*) to allow to go past; ~ **por encima de** (*un obstáculo*) to overcome; (*una persona*) to overlook; ~ **por alto** *fig* to leave out; **no dejes** ~ **la oportunidad** don't miss the opportunity **2.** (*por un hueco*) to go through; **el sofá no pasa por la puerta** the sofa won't go through the door; **el Ebro pasa por Zaragoza** the Ebro flows through Zaragoza; ~ **por una crisis** to go through a crisis **3.** (*trasladarse*) to move; **pasemos al comedor** let's go to the dining room **4.** (*acaecer*) to happen; **¿qué pasa?** what's up?; **¿qué te pasa?** what's wrong?; **pase lo que pase** whatever happens; **dejar** ~ **algo** to allow sth to happen; **lo que pasa es que...** the thing is that... **5.** (*acabar*) to pass; **cuando pasen las vacaciones...** when the holidays are over... **6.** (*el tiempo*) to pass; **lo pasado, pasado** what's done is done **7.** (*ser transferido*) to be transferred **8.** (*poder existir*) to get by; **vamos pasando** we manage **9.** (*aparentar*) to pass for; **pasa por nuevo** it looks new; **hacerse** ~ **por médico** to pass oneself off as a doctor **10.** (*cambiar*) to go; **paso a explicar porqué** and now I will (go on to) explain why; ~ **a mayores** to go from bad to worse **11.** (*ser admisible*) to pass; **arreglándolo aún puede** ~ if we fix it, it should still be okay **12.** (*no jugar*) to pass **13.** *inf* (*no necesitar*) **yo paso de salir** I don't want to go out; **pasa de todo** he/she couldn't care less about anything **II.** *vt* **1.** (*atravesar*) to cross; ~ **el puente** to cross the bridge; ~ **el semáforo en rojo** to go through a red light **2.** (*por un hueco*) to go through; ~ **la tarjeta por la ranura** to swipe the card through the slot; ~ **algo por debajo de la puerta** to slide sth under the door **3.** (*trasladar*) to transfer; ~ **a limpio** to make a fair copy **4.** (*dar*) to pass; ~ **la pelota** to pass the ball **5.** (*una temporada*) to spend; ~ **el invierno en el Caribe** to spend the winter in the Caribbean; ~ **lo bien/mal** to have a good/ bad time; ~ **lo en grande** to have a whale of a time; **¡que lo paséis bien!** enjoy yourselves! **6.** (*sufrir*) to experience; ~ **hambre** to go hungry; ~ **frío** to feel the cold; **pasé un mal rato** I went through a difficult time **7.** (*transmitir*) to send; (*una película*) to show; (*una noticia*) to broadcast; (*dinero*) to give; ~ **un recado** to pass on a message; **me has pasado el resfriado** you've given me your cold; **le paso a la Sra. Ortega** I'll put you through to Mrs. Ortega **8.** (*sobrepasar*) to exceed; **he pasado los treinta** I am over thirty; **te paso en altura** I am taller than you **9.** (*hacer deslizar*) ~ **la mano por la mesa** to run one's hand over the table; ~ **la aspiradora** to vacuum **10.** (*tolerar*) to allow to pass **11.** (*aprobar*) to pass **12.** (*omitir*) to overlook **13.** (*colar*) to strain **14.** (*las hojas de un libro*) to turn **III.** *vr* **1.** (*acabarse*) to pass; **ya se le** ~**á el enfado** his anger will soon subside; ~ **se de fecha** to miss a deadline **2.** (*exagerar*) to go too far; ~ **se de la raya** to go over the line; ~ **se de listo** to be too clever by half **3.** (*por un sitio*) to visit; **me pasé un rato por casa de mi tía** I popped by my aunt's house for a while; **se me pasó por la cabeza que...** it occurred to me that...; ~ **se la mano por el pelo** to run one's hand through one's hair **4.** *t.* MIL (*cambiar*) to go over; **se ha pasado de trabajadora a perezosa** she has gone from being hard-working to being lazy **5.** (*olvidarse*) to be forgotten; **se me pasó tu cumpleaños** I forgot your birthday **6.** (*estropearse: alimentos, leche*) to spoil, to go off; (*fruta*) to overripen; (*mantequilla*) to go rancid; (*flores*) to wilt; **se ha pasado el arroz** the rice is overcooked **7.** (*escaparse*) to be missed; **se me pasó la oportunidad** I missed my chance

pasarela [pa·sa·'re·la] *f* **1.** (*para desfiles*) catwalk **2.** (*de un barco*) gangway **3.** COMPUT gateway **4.** (*puente provisional*) temporary bridge; (*para peatones*) walkway

pasatiempo [pa·sa·'tjem·po] *m* **1.** (*diversión*) pastime; **los pasatiempos del periódico** the games and puzzles section of the newspaper **2.** (*hobby*) hobby

pascana [pas·'ka·na] *f* **1.** *AmS* (*etapa de un viaje*) stage **2.** *Arg, Bol, Perú* (*posada*) wayside inn

Pascua ['pas·kwa] *f* **1.** (*de resurrección*) Easter; **de ~ s a Ramos** once in a blue moon; **hacer la ~ a alguien** *inf* to do the dirty on sb **2.** *pl* (*navidad*) Christmas time; **dar las ~ s a alguien** to wish sb a merry Christmas **3.** *pl* (*pentecostés*) Whitsun ▶ **tener cara de ~** (**s**) *inf* to be glowing with happiness; **¡y santas ~ s!** and that's that!; **estar como una(s) ~** (**s**) to be over the moon

pase ['pa·se] *m* **1.** (*desfile*) parade; (*de moda*) fashion show **2.** DEP pass **3.** (*en los naipes*) pass **4.** *t.* MIL pass; (*licencia*) license; (*para entrar gratis*) free pass; ~ (**de transporte**) travel pass

5. *AmL* (*pasaporte*) passport

paseandero, -a [pa·sean·'de·ro, -a] *adj CSur* fond of walking

paseante [pa·se·'an·te] *mf* walker; ~ (**en corte**) *inf* loafer

pasear [pa·se·'ar] **I.** *vt* (*en coche*) to take for a ride; (*a pie*) to take for a walk; ~ **al perro** to walk the dog **II.** *vi, vr* (*a pie*) to go for a walk; (*en coche*) to go for a drive; (*a caballo*) to ride

paseo [pa·'seo] *m* **1.** (*a pie*) walk; (*en coche, a caballo*) ride; (*en barco*) trip; **dar un** ~ to go for a walk; **¡vete a** ~! get lost! **2.** (*para pasear*) avenue; ~ **marítimo** promenade, esplanade

pasillo [pa·'si·jo, -ʎo] *m* (*corredor*) passage; (*entre habitaciones*) corridor, hallway

pasión [pa·'sjon] *f* passion; **con** ~ passionately; **sin** ~ without enthusiasm; **sentir** ~ **por el fútbol** to be passionate about soccer

pasional [pa·sjo·'nal] *adj* passionate; **crimen** ~ crime of passion

pasiva [pa·'si·βa] *f* LING passive

pasividad [pa·si·βi·'dad] *f* passivity, passiveness

pasivo [pa·'si·βo] *m* liabilities *pl;* (*en el balance*) debit side

pasivo, -a [pa·'si·βo, -a] *adj t.* LING passive; **verbo** ~ passive verb; **voz pasiva** passive

pasmado, -a [pas·'ma·do, -a] *adj* (*asombrado*) amazed

pasmar [pas·'mar] **I.** *vt* (*asombrar*) to astonish; **me has dejado pasmado** you have left me completely stunned **II.** *vr* to be astonished; ~ **se ante algo** to be fascinated by sth

paso ['pa·so] *m* **1.** (*acción de pasar*) passing; (*en coche*) overtaking; **al** ~ on the way; **ceder el** ~ (*a una persona*) to make way; (*en el tráfico*) to yield; **estar de** ~ to be passing through; **al** ~ **que come ve la tele** when eating, he/she watches TV; **de** ~ (*indirectamente*) by the way; **nadie salió al** ~ **de sus mentiras** nobody put a stop to his/her lies **2.** (*movimiento*) step; (*progreso*) progress; **ir al** ~ to keep in step; **marcar el** ~ to mark the rhythm [*o* time]; **a cada** ~ at every step; **a** ~ **llano** smoothly; ~ **a** ~ step by step; **contar los** ~**s a alguien** to watch sb's every move; **dar un** ~ **adelante/atrás** to take a step forwards/backwards; **dar un** ~ **en falso** to trip; *fig* to make a false move; **vive a dos** ~**s de mi casa** he/she lives very near to my house; **dar todos los** ~**s necesarios** *fig* to take all the necessary steps **3.** (*velocidad*) pace; **a** ~**s agigantados** with giant steps; *fig* by leaps and bounds; **a buen** ~ quickly; **a** ~ **de tortuga** at snail's pace; **a este** ~ **no llegarás** at this speed you'll never get there; **a este** ~ **no conseguirás nada** *fig* at this rate you won't achieve anything **4.** (*pisada*) footprint; (*de un animal*) track; **seguir los** ~**s de alguien** to follow sb; *fig* to follow in sb's footsteps **5.** (*pasillo*) passage; (*en el mar*) strait; (*entre montañas*) pass; ~ **subterráneo** underground passage; **abrirse** ~ to open up a path for oneself; *fig* to make one's

way; **¡prohibido el** ~! (*pasar*) no thoroughfare!; (*entrar*) no entry!; **salir del** ~ (**con algo**) to get out of a jam (with sth) **6.** (*para atravesar algo*) crossing; ~ **de cebra** zebra crossing; ~ **a nivel** level crossing; **¡**~**!** make way!; ~ **de ecuador** halfway point **7.** (*de un contador*) unit; **marcar los** ~**s** to count the units **8.** (*de un escrito*) passage

pasota [pa·'so·ta] *mf inf* drop-out; **es un** ~ **total** he doesn't give a damn about anything

paspadura [pas·pa·'du·ra] *f AmS* chapped skin

pasta ['pas·ta] *f* **1.** (*masa*) paste; (*para un pastel*) pastry; (*para paredes*) filler; (*para madera*) putty; ~ **de dientes** toothpaste **2.** (*comida italiana*) pasta **3.** (*pastelería*) pastries *pl* **4.** (*encuadernación*) cover; **de** ~ **dura/blanda** hardback/softback **5.** *inf* (*dinero*) dough **6.** (*madera*) pulp; **tener** ~ **para algo** to be cut out for sth; **tener buena** ~ to be good-natured

pastar [pas·'tar] *vi, vt* to graze

pastel [pas·'tel] *m* **1.** (*tarta*) cake; (*bollo*) pastry; (*de carne*) pie; **descubrir el** ~ to catch on **2.** (*lápiz*) pastel crayon **3.** (*pintura*) pastel

pastelería [pas·te·le·'ri·a] *f* pastry shop

pastelero, -a [pas·te·'le·ro, -a] *m, f* **1.** (*repostero*) pastry chef **2.** (*contemporizador*) staller; **ser un** ~ to go with the flow, to be spineless

pastelón [pas·te·'lon] *m AmL* (*loseta para pavimentar*) large paving stone

pastilla [pas·'ti·ja, -ʎa] *f* **1.** (*medicinal*) tablet; ~ **contra el dolor** painkiller; ~ **para la garganta** throat lozenge; ~ **para la tos** cough drop **2.** (*dulce*) candy **3.** (*trozo*) piece; ~ **de caldo** stock cube; ~ **de chocolate** bar of chocolate; ~ **de jabón** bar of soap; **ir a toda** ~ *inf* to go at full speed

pastizal [pas·ti·'sal, -θal] *m* pasture

pasto ['pas·to] *m* **1.** (*pastizal*) pasture **2.** (*hierba*) grass; ~ **seco** fodder; **ser** ~ **de las llamas** to go up in flames; **ser** ~ **de la murmuración** to be the subject of gossip; **a todo** ~ at full pelt **3.** (*vino*) **de** ~ ordinary; **vino de** ~ table wine

pastor [pas·'tor] *m* **1.** REL minister **2.** ZOOL **perro** ~ sheepdog

pastor(a) [pas·'tor, -·'to·ra] *m(f)* (*de ganado*) herdsman *m;* (*de ovejas*) shepherd

pastorear [pas·to·re·'ar] *vt* **1.** (*el ganado*) to graze **2.** *AmC* (*mimar*) to spoil **3.** *AmL* (*atisbar*) to spy on

pastoso, -a [pas·'to·so, -a] *adj* **1.** (*voz*) mellow; **lengua pastosa** furred tongue **2.** *AmL* (*región*) grassy

pata ['pa·ta] *f* (*de un perro*) paw; (*de una silla*) leg; ~**s de gallo** (*en el rostro*) crow's feet; ~ **de palo** wooden leg; **mala** ~ *inf* bad luck; **estirar la** ~ *inf* to kick the bucket; **ir a** ~ *inf* to go on foot; ~**s arriba** upside down; **a la** ~ **coja** hopping; **a (la)** ~ **llana** simply; **a cuatro** ~**s** on all fours; **meter la** ~ *inf* to put one's foot in it; **poner a alguien de** ~**s en la calle** *inf* to

throw sb out
patada [pa·'ta·da] *f* (*contra algo*) kick; (*en el suelo*) stamp; **dar una ~ contra la pared** to kick the wall; **dar ~s en el suelo** to stamp one's feet; **romper una puerta a ~s** to kick a door down; **echar a alguien a ~s** to kick sb out; **tratar a alguien a ~s** to treat sb like dirt; **a ~s** *fig* by the bucket load
Patagonia [pa·ta·'go·ni·a] *f* Patagonia; **ir a la ~** to go to Patagonia

ⓘ **Patagonia** is located in the southernmost part of Chile and Argentina, south of the Pampas. Unlike the Pampas, this vast, sparsely settled, barren plateau is unsuited for growing grains and is used mainly for raising sheep.

patalear [pa·ta·le·'ar] *vi* to kick; (*en el suelo*) to stamp one's feet; **está que patalea** he/she is furious
patata [pa·'ta·ta] *f* potato; **~s fritas** French fries *pl;* **una bolsa de ~s fritas** a bag of potato chips; **tortilla de ~** Spanish omelet; **puré de ~(s)** mashed potatoes ▸ **no entender ni ~** *inf* (*palabra*) not to understand a single word; (*ser tonto*) to be completely stupid; **¡~!** (*al hacer una foto*) cheese!
patatús [pa·ta·'tus] *m inv, inf* (*desmayo*) faint; **le dio un ~** he/she fainted
patear [pa·te·'ar] **I.** *vt* **1.** (*dar golpes*) to kick; **~ el estómago a alguien** to kick sb in the stomach **2.** (*pisotear*) to trample **3.** (*tratar rudamente*) to trample on **II.** *vi* **1.** (*en el suelo*) to stamp; (*estar enfadado*) to be furious **2.** (*andar mucho*) to tramp around; **estar pateando todo el día** to spend the whole day walking; **tuve que ~ para tener este éxito** I had to work really hard for this success
patentar [pa·ten·'tar] *vt* to patent
patente [pa·'ten·te] **I.** *adj* **1.** (*visible*) clear **2.** (*evidente*) patent; **hacer ~** to establish; (*comprobar*) to prove; (*revelar*) to reveal **II.** *f* **1.** (*documento*) license; (*permiso*) permit; **~ de comercio** business license; **~ de sanidad** bill of health **2.** (*título*) title; **~ de piloto** pilot's license **3.** JUR patent; **~ industrial** industrial patent; **solicitar la ~** to apply for a patent
patera [pa·'te·ra] *f* small boat
paternal [pa·ter·'nal] *adj* paternal; **amor ~** paternal [*o* fatherly] love
paternidad [pa·ter·ni·'dad] *f* **1.** (*relación*) fatherhood; JUR paternity **2.** (*calidad*) fatherliness
paterno, -a [pa·'ter·no, -a] *adj* paternal; **mi abuelo ~** my paternal grandfather
patero, -a [pa·'te·ro, -a] **I.** *adj Chile* bootlicking **II.** *m, f Chile* bootlicker
patético, -a [pa·'te·ti·ko, -a] *adj pey* pathetic
patibulario, -a [pa·ti·βu·'la·rjo, -a] *adj* gallows; **horca patibularia** gallows *pl;* **novela patibularia** (*terrible*) horrifying novel
patíbulo [pa·'ti·βu·lo] *m* scaffold; (*horca*) gal-

lows *pl*
patidifuso, -a [pa·ti·di·'fu·so, -a] *adj* stunned; **me quedé ~** I was aghast
patilla [pa·'ti·ja, -ʎa] *f* **1.** (*de gafas*) sidepiece; (*de madero*) peg **2.** *pl* (*pelo*) sideburns *pl*
patín [pa·'tin] *m* **1.** (*de hielo*) ice skate; (*de ruedas*) roller skate; **patines en línea** roller-blades **2.** (*patinete*) scooter **3.** TÉC shoe
patinaje [pa·ti·'na·xe] *m* **1.** (*sobre hielo*) (ice) skating; (*sobre ruedas*) (roller) skating; **~ artístico** (*sobre hielo*) figure skating; **~ de velocidad** speed skating **2.** (*deslizamiento*) slip; (*de un vehículo*) skid
patinar [pa·ti·'nar] *vi* **1.** (*sobre patines de hielo*) to (ice) skate; (*sobre patines de ruedas*) to (roller) skate **2.** (*deslizarse*) to slip; (*un vehículo*) to skid **3.** (*equivocarse*) to slip up
patinazo [pa·ti·'na·so, -θo] *m* **1.** (*deslizamiento*) slip; (*de un vehículo*) skid **2.** *inf* (*equivocación*) blunder
patinete [pa·ti·'ne·te] *m* scooter
patio ['pa·tjo] *m* (*interior*) courtyard; (*entre dos casas*) back yard; **~ de recreo** playground
patiperrear [pa·ti·pe·rre·'ar] *vi Chile* to traipse around
pato, -a ['pa·to] *m, f* **1.** ZOOL duck; (*macho*) drake **2.** *inf* (*torpe*) clumsy person ▸ **estar hecho un ~** (*de agua*) *inf* to be extremely dull; **pagar el ~** *inf* to carry the can
patochada [pa·to·'tʃa·da] *f* piece of nonsense; **decir ~s** to talk rubbish
patógeno, -a [pa·'to·xe·no, -a] *adj* MED pathogen; **germen ~** harmful germ
patojo, -a [pa·'to·xo, -a] *m, f Col, Guat* kid *inf*
patología [pa·to·lo·'xi·a] *f* MED pathology
patológico, -a [pa·to·'lo·xi·ko, -a] *adj t. fig* pathological
patoso, -a [pa·'to·so, -a] *adj* **1.** (*soso*) boring **2.** (*torpe*) clumsy
patraña [pa·'tra·ɲa] *f* lie, pack of lies
patria ['pa·trja] *f* native land; **~ adoptiva** adoptive homeland; **~ celestial** heaven; **madre ~** mother country; *AmL* Spain
patriada [pa·'trja·da] *f CSur* rising
patriarca [pa·'trjar·ka] *m t.* REL patriarch
patrimonial [pa·tri·mo·'njal] *adj* hereditary; **bien ~** inheritance
patrimonio [pa·tri·'mo·njo] *m* **1.** (*herencia*) inheritance; **~ cultural** cultural heritage **2.** (*riqueza*) wealth
patriota [pa·'trjo·ta] **I.** *adj* patriotic **II.** *mf* patriot
patriótico, -a [pa·'trjo·ti·ko, -a] *adj* patriotic
patriotismo [pa·trjo·'tis·mo] *m* patriotism
patrocinador(a) [pa·tro·si·na·'dor, -·'do·ra; patroθi-] *m(f) t.* DEP sponsor
patrocinar [pa·tro·si·'nar, pa·tro·θi·] *vt t.* DEP to sponsor
patrocinio [pa·tro·'si·njo, -'θi·njo] *m* **1.** (*protección*) patronage **2.** DEP sponsorship
patrón [pa·'tron] *m* **1.** (*modelo*) model; (*de costura*) pattern **2.** FIN **~ monetario** monetary standard

P

patrón, -ona [pa·'tron, -·'tro·na] *m, f* **1.** (*que protege*) patron *m*, patroness *f* **2.** (*jefe*) boss **3.** (*de una casa*) head; (*de una pensión*) landlord *m*, landlady *f*

patronal [pa·tro·'nal] **I.** *adj* (*empresario*) employers'; **cierre ~** lockout **II.** *f* **1.** (*asociación*) employers' organization **2.** (*fiesta*) **fiesta ~** patron saint's day

patronato [pa·tro·'na·to] *m* **1.** (*protección*) patronage **2.** ECON employers' organization **3.** (*fundación*) foundation

patrono, -a [pa·'tro·no, -a] *m, f* **1.** (*jefe*) boss **2.** (*de un feudo*) landowner **3.** (*miembro del patronato*) board member **4.** REL patron saint

patrulla [pa·'tru·ja, -ʎa] *f t.* MIL patrol; **estar de ~** to be on patrol

patrullar [pa·tru·'jar, -'ʎar] *vi, vt* to patrol

patucos [pa·'tu·kos] *mpl* (*para bebés*) bootees *pl*

patuleco, -a [pa·tu·'le·ko, -a] *adj AmC, AmS* (*de pies*) lame; (*de piernas*) bow-legged

paturro, -a [pa·'tu·rro, -a] *adj Col* short and stocky

paulatino, -a [pau·la·'ti·no, -a] *adj* gradual

paupérrimo, -a [pau·'pe·rri·mo, -a] *adj superl de* **pobre**

pausa ['pau·sa] *f* pause

pausado, -a [pau·'sa·do, -a] *adj* deliberate

pauta ['pau·ta] *f* **1.** (*modelo*) guide **2.** (*normas*) standard; **marcar la ~** to set the example [*o* standard] **3.** (*regla*) rule

pautado, -a [pau·'ta·do, -a] *adj* lined

pava ['pa·βa] *f* **1.** ZOOL *v.* **pavo, -a 2.** *AmL* (*olla*) pot; (*tetera*) tea kettle **3.** *AmL* (*sombrero*) straw hat **4.** *And, AmC* (*flecos*) fringe ▶ **pelar la ~** *inf* (*los enamorados*) to court

pavada [pa·'βa·da] *f* **1.** *CSur* (*disparate*) piece of foolishness **2.** *CSur* (*poquísimo*) pittance **3.** *AmC* (*mala suerte*) piece of bad luck

pavear [pa·βe·'ar] **I.** *vi* **1.** *CSur* (*hacer el tonto*) to goof off **2.** *CSur* (*pelar la pava*) to court **II.** *vt* **1.** *And, CSur* (*bromear*) to play a joke on **2.** *And* (*asesinar*) to bump off

pavimentar [pa·βi·men·'tar] *vt* (*con losas*) to pave; (*con asfalto*) to surface

pavimento [pa·βi·'men·to] *m* **1.** (*recubrimiento: en una casa*) flooring; (*en la carretera*) surfacing **2.** (*material: en una casa*) floor; (*en una carretera*) surface

pavo ['pa·βo] *m inf* **1.** (*un duro*) five pesetas; **¡dame diez ~s!** give me fifty pesetas! **2.** (*dólar*) buck; **soltar el ~** to pay up

pavo, -a ['pa·βo, -a] *m, f* turkey; (*persona*) idiot; **~ real** peacock; **estar en la edad del ~** *inf* to be at an awkward stage (*of one's adolescence*); **comer ~** *inf* to be a wallflower; **no es moco de ~** *inf* it's not to be scoffed at [*o* sneezed]; **ir de ~** *AmL* to mooch a ride

pavonearse [pa·βo·ne·'ar·se] *vr* to strut (about); **~se de algo** to show off about sth

pavor [pa·'βor] *m* terror

pavoroso, -a [pa·βo·'ro·so, -a] *adj* terrifying

payada [pa·'ja·da] *f CSur* MÚS improvised song between two competing musicians, accompanied by guitars

payador [pa·ja·'dor] *m CSur:* improvisational guitar-playing singer, competing with another

payasada [pa·ja·'sa·da] *f* clowning; *pey* idiotic behavior; **hacer ~s** to clown around

payasear [pa·ja·se·'ar] *vi* to clown around

payaso, -a [pa·'ja·so, -a] *m, f* clown; **¡deja de hacer el ~!** stop fooling around!

payo, -a ['pa·jo, -a] *m, f* non-gypsy (*gypsy term to refer to people who are not gypsies*)

paz [pas, paθ] *f* peace; **hacer las paces** to make up; **estar en ~ con alguien** to be even with sb; **¡a la ~ de Dios!** God be with you!; **¡déjame en ~!** leave me alone!; **¡...y en ~!** ... and that's that!; **que en ~ descanse** may he/she rest in peace

pazguato, -a [pas·'ɣwa·to, -a; paθ-] *m, f* simpleton

PCE *m abr de* **Partido Comunista Español** *Spanish Communist Party*

P.D. [pos·'da·ta] *abr de* **posdata** P.S.

pe [pe] *f* p; **de ~ a pa** *inf* from A to Z

peaje [pe·'a·xe] *m* toll

peatón, -ona [pea·'ton, -·'to·na] *m, f* pedestrian

peca ['pe·ka] *f* freckle

pecado [pe·'ka·do] *m* sin; **~ capital** deadly sin; **~ original** original sin; **pagar sus ~s** to pay for one's sins; **sería un ~ rechazarlos** it would be a crying shame to reject them; **¡estos niños de mis ~s!** *irón, inf* these children of mine!; **¡ay, José de mis ~s!** *irón, inf* oh, my beloved José!

pecador(a) [pe·ka·'dor, -·'do·ra] **I.** *adj* sinning **II.** *m(f)* sinner

pecar <c→qu> [pe·'kar] *vi* to sin; **~ por exceso** to go too far; **peca por exceso de confianza** he/she is too confident by half; **éste no peca de hablador** he's not exactly talkative

pecarí [pe·ka·'ri] *m AmL* ZOOL peccary

pecera [pe·'se·ra, -θe·ra] *f* fish tank; (*en forma de globo*) fishbowl

pechada [pe·'tʃa·da] *f* **1.** *AmS* (*empujón*) shove **2.** *Arg, inf* (*sablazo*) touch for a loan

pechador(a) [pe·tʃa·'dor, -·'do·ra] *m(f) Arg, inf* sponger, moocher

pechar [pe·'tʃar] *vt Arg, inf* to sponge, to mooch; **~ a alguien** to sponge off sb

pechazo [pe·'tʃa·θo] *m AmS, inf* sponging, mooching

pecho ['pe·tʃo] *m* breast, chest; **dar el ~ al bebé** to breastfeed the baby; **a ~ descubierto** (*sin armas*) unarmed; *fig* openly; **dar el ~ a alguien** *fig* to face up to sb; **gritar a todo ~** to shout at the top of one's voice; **partirse el ~ por alguien** to slog one's guts out for sb; **abrir su ~ a alguien** to open one's heart to sb; **tomarse algo muy a ~** to take sth to heart; **¡~ al agua!** courage!

pechuga [pe·'tʃu·ɣa] *f* (*de ave*) breast; **~ de pollo** chicken breast

pechugón, -ona [pe·tʃu·ˈɣon] *adj* **1.** *AmL* (*descarado*) shameless **2.** *AmL* (*franco*) outspoken

pecoso, -a [pe·ˈko·so, -a] *adj* freckly

pectoral [pek·to·ˈral] **I.** *adj* **1.** ANAT pectoral **2.** (*contra la tos*) cough **II.** *m* MED pectoral

pecueca [pe·ˈkwe·ka] *f Col, Ecua, Ven* **1.** (*pezuña*) hoof **2.** (*olor*) smell of feet

peculiar [pe·ku·ˈljar] *adj* **1.** (*especial*) distinctive **2.** (*raro*) peculiar

peculiaridad [pe·ku·lja·ri·ˈdad] *f* **1.** (*singularidad*) peculiarity **2.** (*distintivo*) distinguishing feature

pedagogía [pe·da·ɣo·ˈxi·a] *f* pedagogy

pedagógico, -a [pe·da·ˈɣo·xi·ko, -a] *adj* pedagogical

pedagogo, -a [pe·da·ˈɣo·ɣo, -a] *m, f* educator, teacher

pedal [pe·ˈdal] *m* pedal; **pisar el ~** AUTO to accelerate

pedalear [pe·da·le·ˈar] *vi* to pedal

pedante [pe·ˈdan·te] *adj* pretentious, pedantic

pedantería [pe·dan·te·ˈri·a] *f* pedantry

pedazo [pe·ˈda·θo] *m* (big) piece; **~ de papel** piece of paper; **caerse a ~s** to fall apart, to fall to pieces; **hacerse ~s** to fall to pieces; **hacer ~s** to break; (*madera*) to smash up; (*papel*) to tear up; **ser un ~ de pan** to be very good-natured; **¡~ de bruto!** *inf* you brute!

pederasta [pe·de·ˈras·ta] *m* pederast

pedestal [pe·des·ˈtal] *m* pedestal; (*apoyo*) base; **poner a alguien en un ~** to put sb on a pedestal

pedestre [pe·ˈdes·tre] *adj* pedestrian; **carrera ~** foot race

pediatra [pe·ˈdja·tra] *mf* pediatrician

pediatría [pe·dja·ˈtri·a] *f* pediatrics

pedicura [pe·di·ˈku·ra] *f* pedicure; **hacerse la ~** to get a pedicure

pedida [pe·ˈdi·da] *f* **~ de mano** asking for sb's hand in marriage

pedido [pe·ˈdi·do] *m* COM order; (*de un servicio*) reservation; **enviar sobre ~** to supply on request; **a ~** to order; **a ~ de** at the request of

pedido, -a [pe·ˈdi·do, -a] *adj* (*solicitado*) requested; (*encargado*) ordered

pedigrí [pe·di·ˈɣri] *m* pedigree

pedigüeño, -a [pe·di·ˈɣwe·ɲo, -a] *adj* persistent

pedilón, -ona [pe·di·ˈlon, -·ˈlo·na] *adj AmL* persistent

pedinche [pe·ˈdin·tʃe] *mf Méx* scrounger

pedir [pe·ˈdir] *irr vt* **1.** (*rogar*) to ask for; **~ algo a alguien** to ask sb for sth; **~ prestado** to borrow; **a ~ de boca** just right; **~ la mano de alguien** to ask for sb's hand in marriage; **~ limosna** to beg **2.** (*exigir*) to demand; (*necesitar*) to need; (*solicitar*) to request; **~ a gritos algo** *fig* to be crying out for sth **3.** (*encargar*) to order

pedo [ˈpe·do] *m inf* **1.** (*ventosidad*) fart; **tirarse un ~** to fart **2.** (*borrachera*) drunkenness; **estar en ~** to be blind drunk

pedorrear [pe·do·rre·ˈar] *vi inf* to fart repeatedly

pedorro, -a [pe·ˈdo·rro, -a] *m, f* (*que tira pedos*) farter; (*tonto*) stupid fart; (*pelmazo*) bore, drag

pedrada [pe·ˈdra·da] *f* throw of a stone; **matar a alguien a ~s** to stone sb to death ▶ **sentar algo como una ~** to take sth very badly; **venir como ~ en ojo de boticario** to be just what the doctor ordered

pedrea [pe·ˈdrea] *f* **1.** METEO hailstorm **2.** (*lotería*) small prizes *pl* (*in lottery*)

pedregal [pe·dre·ˈɣal] *m* stony [*o* rocky] ground

pedregoso, -a [pe·dre·ˈɣo·so, -a] *adj* stony

pedregullo [pe·dre·ˈɣu·jo, -ʎo] *m CSur* gravel

pedrera [pe·ˈdre·ra] *f* stone quarry

pedrería [pe·dre·ˈri·a] *f* precious stones *pl*

pedrisco [pe·ˈdris·ko] *m* METEO hail

pedrusco [pe·ˈdrus·ko] *m AmL v.* **pedregal**

pedúnculo [pe·ˈdun·ku·lo] *m* stalk

pega [ˈpe·ɣa] *f* **1.** *inf* (*dificultades*) difficulty; **poner ~s a** to find fault with; **de ~** fake **2.** *CSur, Méx, inf* (*trabajo*) job

pegada [pe·ˈɣa·da] *f CSur* **1.** (*mentira*) lie **2.** (*suerte*) piece of luck

pegadizo, -a [pe·ɣa·ˈdi·so, -a; -di·θo, -a] *adj* (*pegajoso*) sticky; (*enfermedad*) contagious; **melodía pegadiza** catchy tune

pegajoso, -a [pe·ɣa·ˈxo·so, -a] *adj* **1.** (*adhesivo*) sticky, adhesive **2.** (*persona*) tiresome; (*niño*) clinging

pegamento [pe·ɣa·ˈmen·to] *m* glue; **~ en barra** stick glue; **~ de contacto** bonding cement

pegar <g→gu> [pe·ˈɣar] **I.** *vt* **1.** (*aglutinar*) to stick; **~ un sello** to attach a stamp; **no ~ ojo** not to sleep a wink **2.** (*con hilo, grapa*) to attach **3.** (*muebles*) **la mesilla a la cama** to put the side table right next to the bed **4.** (*contagiar*) to give **5.** (*fuego*) **~ fuego a algo** to set fire to sth **6.** (*golpear*) to hit; **~ una paliza a alguien** to beat sb up **7.** (*un grito*) to let out; (*un tiro*) to fire; **~ una bofetada** to slap; **~ un salto** to jump; **~ un susto a alguien** to frighten sb **8.** COMPUT to paste **9.** *AmL, inf* (*tener suerte*) to be lucky; **~la** to get what one wants **10.** *Méx* (*atar*) to tie **II.** *vi* **1.** (*hacer juego*) to go together; **esto no pega ni con cola** this really doesn't go **2.** (*rozar*) **~ en algo** to brush against sth; (*tocar*) to touch sth **3.** (*golpear*) to beat; **¡cómo pega el sol!** *inf* the sun is burning hot! **4.** *inf* (*currar*) to work hard; **no ~ golpe** not to do a thing **III.** *vr* **1.** (*impactar*) **~se con algo** to bump into sth; **~se con alguien** to fight with sb **2.** (*quemarse*) to stick to the pot **3.** (*entrometerse*) **~se a algo** to interfere in sth **4.** (*aficionarse*) **~se a algo** to acquire a liking for sth **5.** (*acompañar siempre*) **~se a alguien** to stick to sb (like glue); (*perseguir*) to follow sb **6.** (*contagiarse*) **se me pegó el sarampión** I caught [*o* got] the measles **7.** *inf* (*engañar*) **pegársela a alguien** *inf* to trick sb **8.** *inf* (*darse*) ~ **se la gran vida** to live it up; ~ **se un tiro** to shoot oneself

pegatina [pe·ɣa·'ti·na] *f* sticker

pegote [pe·'ɣo·te] *m* **esa corbata es un** ~ that tie just doesn't go; **tirarse** ~ **s** to show off

peinado [pei·'na·do] *m* hairstyle, hairdo; **hacerse un** ~ to have one's hair done

peinado, -a [pei·'na·do, -a] *adj* combed

peinador [pei·na·'dor] *m* (*tocador*) dressing table

peinar [pei·'nar] **I.** *vt* to comb; (*acicalar*) to style **II.** *vr* to comb one's hair; (*arreglar el pelo*) to style [*o* to do] one's hair

peine ['pei·ne] *m* comb; **¡te vas a enterar de lo que vale un** ~! *fig* you'll soon find out what's what!; **¡ya apareció el** ~! *fig* so that's it!

peineta [pei·'ne·ta] *f* Spanish ornamental comb

peinilla [pei·'ni·ja, -ʎa] *f* **1.** *Col, Ecua* (*peine*) dressing comb **2.** *Col, Ecua, Pan, Ven* (*especie de machete*) large machete

p.ej. [por e·'xem·plo] *abr de* **por ejemplo** e.g.

pejiguera [pe·xi·'ɣe·ra] *f inf* nuisance

pela ['pe·la] *f inf* (*dinero*) **no me quedan más** ~ **s** I have no money left; ~ **larga** lots of dough

pelada [pe·'la·da] *f* **1.** (*rapada*) haircut **2.** *CSur* (*calva*) bald head **3.** *AmL* (*error*) blunder

peladez [pe·la·'des, -'deθ] *f* **1.** *And* (*pobreza*) poverty **2.** *Méx* (*palabrota*) obscenity

pelado [pe·'la·do] *m inf* poor wretch

pelado, -a [pe·'la·do, -a] *adj* **1.** (*rapado*) shorn **2.** (*escueto*) bare **3.** *AmL, inf* (*sin dinero*) broke

peladuras [pe·la·'du·ras] *fpl* (*cáscaras*) peelings *pl*

pelagatos [pe·la·'ɣa·tos] *m inv, inf* poor wretch

pelaje [pe·'la·xe] *m* coat, fur

pelambre [pe·'lam·bre] *m o f* **1.** (*pelo*) thick hair; (*de animales*) fur **2.** *AmL* (*habladurías*) rumors *pl*

pelambrera [pe·lam·'bre·ra] *f* mop

pelandusca [pe·lan·'dus·ka] *f inf* floozy *sl*

pelapatatas [pe·la·pa·'ta·tas] *m inv* potato peeler

pelar [pe·'lar] **I.** *vt* **1.** (*pelo*) to cut; (*rapar*) to shear; (*plumas*) to pluck; (*frutas*) to peel; (*animales*) to skin; **ser duro de** ~ to be a hard nut to crack **2.** *AmL, inf* (*dar una paliza*) to beat up **3.** *And, inf* (*morir*) ~ **la** to kick the bucket **II.** *vr* **1.** (*el pelo*) to have one's hair cut; **ir a** ~ **se** to go for a haircut **2.** (*la piel*) to peel **3.** *inf* (*intensificador*) **corre que se las pela he/**she is a really fast runner; **pelárselas por algo** to be crazy about sth

pelaverduras [pe·la·βer·'du·ras] *m inv* vegetable peeler

peldaño [pel·'da·ɲo] *m* step

pelea [pe·'lea] *f* fight; (*verbal*) quarrel, argument; **buscar** ~ to be looking for trouble

pelear [pe·le·'ar] **I.** *vi* to fight; (*discutir*) to argue; ~ **por algo** (*trabajar*) to struggle for sth

II. *vr* **1.** (*con violencia*) ~ **se por algo** to fight over sth; (*verbal*) to argue about sth **2.** (*enemistarse*) to fall out

pelele [pe·'le·le] *m* **1.** (*muñeco*) rag doll **2.** (*de bebés*) rompers *pl* **3.** *inf* (*persona*) puppet

peleón [pe·le·'on] *m inf* troublemaker

peleón, -ona [pe·le·'on, -·'o·na] *adj* quarrelsome; **vino** ~ cheap wine

peletería [pe·le·te·'ri·a] *f* **1.** (*costura*) furrier's; (*venta*) fur shop **2.** *AmC* (*zapatería*) shoe store

peliagudo, -a [pe·lja·'ɣu·do, -a] *adj* tricky

pelícano [pe·'li·ka·no] *m*, **pelicano** [pe·li·'ka·no, -a] *m* pelican

película [pe·'li·ku·la] *f* film, movie; ~ **en blanco y negro** black and white movie; ~ **hablada** talkie; ~ **muda** silent film [*o* movie]; ~ **de suspense** thriller; ~ **de terror** horror film [*o* movie]; ~ **del oeste** western; **de** ~ *inf* sensational; **como de** ~ like sth out of the movies; **poner en** ~ to film; **echar una** ~ to show a film; **¡allí** ~ **s!** it's nothing to do with me!; **no saber de qué va la** ~ not to have a clue

peligrar [pe·li·'ɣrar] *vi* to be in danger; **hacer** ~ to endanger

peligro [pe·'li·ɣro] *m* danger; ~ **de incendio** fire risk; **puesta en** ~ endangering; **correr** ~ to run a risk; **correr** ~ **de hacer algo** to run the risk of doing sth; **estar en** ~ **de muerte** to be in mortal danger; **fuera de** ~ out of danger; **poner en** ~ to endanger; **poniendo en** ~ **su propia vida** risking his/her own life

peligroso, -a [pe·li·'ɣro·so, -a] *adj* dangerous

pelillo [pe·'li·jo, -ʎo] *m inf* trifle; **echar** ~ **s a la mar** to make up; **¡** ~ **s a la mar!** let bygones be bygones!

pelirrojo, -a [pe·li·'rro·xo, -a] *adj* red-haired

pella ['pe·ja, -ʎa] *f* lump; ~ **de algodón** ball of cotton wool

pelleja [pe·'je·xa, -ʎe·xa] *f inf* **ser una** ~ to be all skin and bones

pellejerías [pe·je·xe·'ri·as, pe·ʎe-] *fpl Chile* hard times *pl*

pellejo [pe·'je·xo, -'ʎe·xo] *m* **1.** (*de animal*) hide **2.** (*de persona*) skin; **no tener más que el** ~ to be all skin and bones; **no caber en su** ~ *fig* to be bursting with pride; **quitar el** ~ **a alguien** *fig* to criticize sb; **si yo estuviera en tu** ~... *inf* if I were in your shoes...; **salvar(se)** el ~ *inf* to save one's skin; **arriesgar el** ~ to risk one's neck; **pagar con el** ~ to pay with one's life; **perder el** ~ to lose one's life **3.** (*odre*) wineskin **4.** (*fruta*) peel; (*salchicha*) skin

pellizcar <c→qu> [pe·jis·'kar, -ʎiθ·'kar] **I.** *vt* **1.** (*repizcar*) to pinch **2.** *inf* (*pizcar algo*) to take a pinch of; (*comida*) to nibble **II.** *vr* to pinch oneself

pellizco [pe·'jis·ko, -ʎiθ·ko] *m* **1.** (*pizco*) pinch; **dar un** ~ **a alguien** to pinch sb **2.** (*poquito: de sal*) pinch; (*de bocadillo*) nibble

pelma ['pel·ma] *m inf*, **pelmazo, -a** [pel·'ma·

so, -θo, -a] *m inf* bore, drag

pelo ['pe·lo] *m* **1.** (*cabello*) hair; (*de animal*) fur; (*de ave*) plumage; (*de barba*) whisker; **tener el ~ rubio** to have fair hair; **tirar el ~** (*perro*) to molt; **cortarse el ~** to get one's hair cut; **soltarse el ~** to take one's hair down; *fig* to let one's hair down **2.** (*vello*) down; (*pelusa*) fluff; (*de alfombra*) pile **3.** (+ *al*) **al ~** perfectly; **todo irá al ~** everything will be fine; **el traje ha quedado al ~** the suit looks great; **venir al ~** to be just right, to happen [*o* come] at just the right time; **sin venir al ~** inconveniently **4.** *inf* (*poco*) **por un ~ te caes** you very nearly fell; **escaparse por un ~** to escape by the skin of one's teeth; **no se mueve ni un ~ de aire** the air is completely still ▶ **cortar un ~ en el aire** (*cuchillo*) to be as sharp as a razor; (*listo*) to be very clever; **no tener ~s en la lengua** *inf* not to mince words; **un hombre de ~ en pecho** a real man; **ponerle a uno los ~s de punta** to make one's hair stand on end; **no tocar un ~ (de la ropa) a alguien** *inf* not to lay a finger on sb; **contar algo con ~s y señales** *inf* to describe sth in great detail; **colgado de un ~** hanging from a thread; **no tener (un) ~ de tonto** *inf* to be nobody's fool; **agarrarse a un ~** to clutch at straws; **estar hasta los ~s** *inf* to be fed up; **tomar el ~ a alguien** *inf* to pull sb's leg; **no se te ve el ~, ¿por dónde andas?** *inf* I/we haven't seen you for ages, where have you been hiding?; **a ~** (*la cabeza descubierta*) bare-headed; (*sin prepararse*) unprepared

pelón, -ona [pe·'lon] *m, f inf* poor wretch

pelota¹ [pe·'lo·ta] *f* **1.** (*balón*) ball; **echar la ~ a alguien** *fig* to leave sb holding the baby; **devolver la ~ a alguien** (*argumentar*) to turn the tables on sb; (*vengarse*) to give sb a taste of their own medicine; **la ~ sigue en el tejado** *fig* things are still up in the air **2.** (*juego*) pelota **3.** *pl, vulg* (*testículos*) balls *pl;* **tocar las ~s a alguien** to irritate sb; **tocarse las ~s** to do absolutely nothing; **¡fíjate, que tiene ~s!** I'll tell you one thing, he's got balls!; **¡y esto es así, por ~s!** that's how it is, and no arguing!; **de ~s** cool **4.** *vulg* (*desnudo*) **en ~s** stark naked; **dejar a alguien en ~s** (*juego*) to clean sb out; (*ropa*) to strip sb naked; **pillar a alguien en ~s** *fig* to catch sb with their pants down ▶ **hacer la ~ a alguien** to suck up to sb

pelota² [pe·'lo·ta] *m inf* crawler

pelotazo [pe·lo·'ta·so, -θo] *m* **1.** (*con el pie*) shot; (*tirando*) throw; (*con la raqueta*) stroke **2.** *inf* (*bebida*) slug; **meterse un ~** to have a drink

pelotear [pe·lo·te·'ar] *vi* (*tenis*) to toss back and forth; (*fútbol*) to kick around

pelotera [pe·lo·'te·ra] *f inf* fight

pelotón [pe·lo·'ton] *m* (*de gente*) crowd; (*en carreras*) pack; **~ de ejecución** firing squad

pelotudo, -a [pe·lo·'tu·do, -a] *m, f CSur, vulg* jerk

peluca [pe·'lu·ka] *f* wig; **usar ~** to wear a wig

peluche [pe·'lu·tʃe] *m* **1.** (*tejido*) plush **2.** (*juguete*) soft toy; **oso ~** teddy bear

pelucón [pe·lu·'kon] *m And, inf* bigwig

pelucón, -ona [pe·lu·'kon, -·'ko·na] *adj And, inf* long-haired

peludo, -a [pe·'lu·do] *adj* **1.** hairy; (*con una barba*) bearded **2.** *AmC, inf* (*difícil*) tricky

peluquería [pe·lu·ke·'ri·a] *f* hairdresser's; **~ de señoras/señores** ladies'/gents' [*o* men's] hairdressers; **ir a la ~** to go to the hairdresser's

peluquero, -a [pe·lu·'ke·ro, -a] *m, f* hairdresser

peluquín [pe·lu·'kin] *m* toupee; **¡ni hablar del ~!** it's out of the question!

pelusa [pe·'lu·sa] *f* (*vello*) down; (*tejido*) fluff; (*de polvo*) fluff; **sentir ~** *inf* (*celos*) to be jealous; (*envidia*) to be envious

pelvis ['pel·βis] *f inv* pelvis

pena ['pe·na] *f* **1.** (*tristeza*) sorrow; **ahogar las ~s** to drown one's sorrows **2.** (*lástima*) **ser una ~** to be a pity; **¡qué ~!** what a shame!; **ella me da ~** I feel really sorry for her; **me da ~ verlo así** it upsets me to see him like that **3.** (*sanción*) punishment; **~ de cadena perpetua** life sentence; **~ capital** capital punishment; **~ pecuniaria** fine **4.** (*dificultad*) trouble; **pasar las ~s del purgatorio** to go through hell; **a duras ~s** with great difficulty; (*apenas*) scarcely; **sin ~ ni gloria** undistinguished; **valer la ~** to be worth the effort [*o* the trouble]; **¡allá ~s!** it's not my problem! **5.** *AmL* (*vergüenza*) shame; **tener ~** to be ashamed ▶ **so ~ ~ que** + *subj* under pain of

penable [pe·'na·βle] *adj* punishable

penacho [pe·'na·tʃo] *m* crest

penado, -a [pe·'na·do, -a] **I.** *adj AmL* (*tímido*) shy **II.** *m, f* convict

penal [pe·'nal] **I.** *adj JUR* penal; **antecedentes ~es** criminal record **II.** *m* **1.** (*prisión*) prison **2.** *AmL* (*falta*) foul (*inside the penalty area*)

penalidad [pe·na·li·'dad] *f* **1.** (*molestia*) hardship **2.** (*sanción*) punishment

penalización [pe·na·li·sa·'sjon, -θa·'θjon] *f* penalization

penalizar <z→c> [pe·na·li·'sar, -'θar] *vt* to penalize

penalti [pe·'nal·ti] *m* **1.** (*falta*) foul (*inside the penalty area*)*;* **área de ~s** penalty area **2.** (*sanción*) penalty; (*en baloncesto*) free throw; **casarse de ~** *inf* to have a shotgun wedding

penar [pe·'nar] **I.** *vt* to punish **II.** *vi* **1.** (*padecer*) to suffer; **~ de amores** to be unhappy in love **2.** (*ansiar*) **~ por algo** to long for sth

penca ['pen·ka] *f* **1.** *AmL* (*borrachera*) **agarrarse una ~** to get drunk **2.** *And* (*atractivo*) **una ~ de mujer** an attractive woman; **una ~ de casa** a gorgeous house

penco ['pen·ko] *m And, inf* (*atractivo*) **un ~ de hombre** an attractive man

pendejada [pen·de·'xa·da] *f AmL, inf* **1.** (*disparate*) stupidity **2.** (*acto cobarde*) cowardly act

P

pendejear [pen·de·xe·'ar] *vi Col, Méx, inf* to mess [*o* to fool] around

pendejo, -a [pen·'de·xo] *m, f Arg, inf* fool

pendencia [pen·'den·sja, -θja] *f* fight; **armar ~** to start a fight

pendenciero, -a [pen·den·'sje·ro, -a; -'θje·ro, -a] I. *adj* quarrelsome II. *m, f* troublemaker

pender [pen·'der] *vi* to hang

pendiente¹ [pen·'djen·te] I. *adj* 1.(*colgado*) hanging 2.(*problema, asunto*) unresolved; (*trabajo, pedido*) outstanding; **una cuenta ~ de pago** an outstanding account; **quedar ~ una asignatura** to have one subject left to pass (*as a resit or carried over to next year*) 3. *inf* (*ocuparse*) **estate ~ del arroz** keep an eye on the rice; **¡tú estate ~ de lo tuyo!** mind your own business!; **estar ~ de los labios de alguien** (*estar atento*) to be hanging on sb's every word 4.(*depender*) **estamos ~s de lo que digan nuestros padres** it all depends on what our parents say II. *m* (*de oreja*) earring; (*de nariz*) nose ring

pendiente² [pen·'djen·te] *f* (*cuesta, del tejado*) slope; **de mucha ~** steep

pendón [pen·'don] *m* banner

péndulo ['pen·du·lo] *m* pendulum

pene ['pe·ne] *m* penis

penetración [pe·ne·tra·'sjon, -'θjon] *f* penetration

penetrante [pe·ne·'tran·te] *adj* 1.(*profundo*) deep; (*dolor*) fierce 2.(*frío*) biting; (*hedor*) strong; (*olor*) pervasive 3.(*sonido*) penetrating; (*grito*) piercing

penetrar [pe·ne·'trar] I. *vi* to penetrate II. *vt* 1.(*atravesar*) to penetrate 2.(*entender*) to understand; **~ un misterio** to unravel a mystery; **~ una intención** to fathom an intention; **~ los pensamientos de alguien** to penetrate sb's thoughts

penicilina [pe·ni·si·'li·na, pe·ni·θi-] *f* MED penicillin

península [pe·'nin·su·la] *f* GEO peninsula; **la Península Ibérica** the Iberian Peninsula

i The **Península Ibérica** (Iberian Peninsula) includes Spain and Portugal. Spanish speakers make use of this term (and the corresponding adjective **peninsular**) in order to differentiate the Spanish mainland from the two Spanish island groups (**Baleares y Canarias**) and the country's African territories (**Ceuta y Melilla**).

peninsular [pe·nin·su·'lar] *adj* peninsular; **las temperaturas ~es** temperatures in the Iberian peninsula

penique [pe·'ni·ke] *m* penny

penitencia [pe·ni·'ten·sja, -θja] *f* 1.(*pena*) punishment; **imponer una ~ a alguien** to impose a punishment on sb 2. REL penance; **hacer ~** to do penance 3.(*arrepentimiento*) penitence

penitenciaría [pe·ni·ten·sja·'ri·a, -θja·'ri·a] *f* prison, penitentiary

penitenciario, -a [pe·ni·ten·'sja·rjo, -'θja·rjo] *adj* 1.(*relativo a la penitenciaría*) penitentiary 2.(*relativo a la penitencia*) penitential

penitente [pe·ni·'ten·te] *adj, mf* penitent

penoso, -a [pe·'no·so, -a] *adj* 1.(*arduo*) laborious 2.(*dificultoso*) difficult 3.(*con pena*) upset 4. *AmL* (*vergonzoso*) shameful

pensado, -a [pen·'sa·do, -a] *adj* 1.(*reflexionado*) considered; **esto está poco ~** this hasn't been properly thought out; **lo tengo bien ~** I have thought it through thoroughly; **tener ~ hacer algo** to have it in mind to do sth; **el día menos ~ volverá** just when it's least expected he/she will return 2.(*persona*) **ser un mal ~** to always be ready to think the worst

pensador(a) [pen·sa·'dor, -·'do·ra] *m(f)* thinker

pensamiento [pen·sa·'mjen·to] *m* 1.(*acción, idea, objeto*) thought 2.(*intención*) intention 3.(*mente*) mind; **¿cuándo te vino esa idea al ~?** when did that idea occur to you? 4. BOT pansy

pensar <e→ie> [pen·'sar] I. *vi, vt* 1.(*formar un juicio, reflexionar*) **~ (en) algo** to think (about) sth; **¡ni ~lo!** don't even think about it!; **¡no quiero ni ~lo!** I don't even want to think about it!; **dar mucho que ~** to give people a lot to think about; **esto hay que ~lo bien** this needs to be thought out carefully; **lo hicimos sin ~lo** we did it without thinking; **sin ~lo me dio una bofetada** he/she suddenly slapped me; **pensándolo bien** on reflection 2.(*considerar*) to consider II. *vi* (*opinar, suponer*) to think; **pienso que deberíamos irnos** I think we should go; **~ muy mal de alguien** to think very badly of sb III. *vt* 1.(*intención*) to think of; **pensábamos venir este fin de semana** we were thinking of coming this weekend 2.(*inventar, tramar*) to think up

pensativo, -a [pen·sa·'ti·βo, -a] *adj* thoughtful, pensive

pensión [pen·'sjon] *f* 1.(*paga*) pension; **~ de viudez** widow's pension; **~ alimenticia** maintenance; **aún no cobra la ~** (*no recibe la paga*) he/she doesn't get a pension yet; (*no tiene la edad*) he/she isn't a pensioner yet 2.(*para huéspedes*) guesthouse 3.(*precio por alojamiento*) (charge for) board and lodging; **~ completa** full board

pensionado [pen·sjo·'na·do] *m* ENS boarding school

pensionado, -a [pen·sjo·'na·do, -a] *m, f* pensioner

pensionar [pen·sjo·'nar] *vt* to give a pension to

pensionista [pen·sjo·'nis·ta] *mf* 1.(*jubilado*) pensioner 2.(*huésped*) guest (*at boarding house*) 3.(*alumno*) boarder

pentagonal [pen·ta·γo·'nal] *adj* pentagonal

pentágono [pen·'ta·γo·no] *m* pentagon

pentagrama [pen·ta·'γra·ma] *m* MÚS stave, staff

pentatlón [pen·tat·'lon] *m* pentathlon

Pentecostés [pen·te·kos·'tes] *m* REL **1.** (*cristiano*) Whitsun; **Pascua de ~** Whit Sunday **2.** (*judío*) Pentecost

penúltimo, -a [pe·'nul·ti·mo, -a] *adj* penultimate, next-to-last

penumbra [pe·'num·bra] *f* semi-darkness; ASTR penumbra

penuria [pe·'nu·rja] *f* **1.** (*escasez*) scarcity; **pasar muchas ~s** to suffer great hardship **2.** (*pobreza*) poverty

peña ['pe·ɲa] *f* **1.** (*roca*) crag **2.** (*grupo*) group; (*de aficionados*) club; (*tertulia*) circle; *inf* (*de jóvenes*) gang

peñasco [pe·'ɲas·ko] *m* boulder

peñascoso, -a [pe·ɲas·'ko·so, -a] *adj* rocky

peñón [pe·'ɲon] *m* **1.** (*peñasco*) crag; **el Peñón** the Rock (of Gibraltar) **2.** (*monte*) mountain

peón [pe·'on] *m* **1.** (*obrero*) unskilled laborer; (*jornalero*) farmhand; *Méx* (*aprendiz*) apprentice **2.** (*en juegos*) piece; (*en ajedrez*) pawn

peonza [pe·'on·sa, -θa] *f* (*juguete*) top

peor [pe·'or] *adv, adj comp de* **mal(o)** worse; **en matemáticas soy ~ que tú** I am worse at math than you are; **el ~ de la clase** the worst in the class; **y verás, será ~ aún** you'll see, it will get even worse; **el ~ día, verás como te hablará** just when you least expect it, he/she will speak to you; **en el ~ de los casos** at worst; **si pasa lo ~** if worst comes to worst; **pero lo ~ de todo fue...** but the worst thing of all was...; **vas de mal en ~** you're going from bad to worse; **~ es nada** it's better than nothing

pepa ['pe·pa] *f* **1.** *AmL* (*pepita*) seed **2.** *And* (*mentira*) fib

Pepa ['pe·pa] *f inf* **¡viva la ~!** (*indiferencia*) who cares!; (*regocijo*) hurray!

Pepe ['pe·pe] *m* **ponerse como un ~** *inf* to have a great time; **ver menos que ~ Leches** *inf* to be as blind as a bat

pepena [pe·'pe·na] *f* **1.** *Col* (*abanico*) fan **2.** *Méx* (*lo recogido*) collection; (*vísceras*) viscera

pepinillo [pe·pi·'ni·ʎo, -ʎo] *m* gherkin

pepino [pe·'pi·no] *m* cucumber; **eso me importa un ~** *inf* I don't give a hoot about that

pepita [pe·'pi·ta] *f* seed

pepsina [peβ·'si·na] *f* pepsin

pequeñajo, -a [pe·ke·'ɲa·xo, -a] *m, f inf* kid

pequeñez [pe·ke·'ɲes, -'ɲeθ] *f* **1.** (*tamaño*) smallness **2.** (*minucia*) trifle

pequeño, -a [pe·'ke·ɲo, -a] **I.** *adj* small, little; **ya desde ~ solía venir a este sitio** I've been coming here since I was little; **esta camisa me queda pequeña** this shirt is too small for me **II.** *m, f* little one

pequeñoburgués, -esa [pe·ke·ɲo·βur·'ɣes, -·'ɣe·sa] *adj, m, f* petit bourgeois

pequinés [pe·ki·'nes] *m* ZOOL Pekinese

pequinés, -esa [pe·ki·'nes, -·'ne·sa] *adj, m, f* Pekinese

pera ['pe·ra] **I.** *adj* posh; **niño ~** little rich kid **II.** *f* BOT pear ▶ **pedir ~s al olmo** *inf* to ask for the impossible; **poner a alguien las ~s a cuarto** *inf* to read sb the Riot Act; **eso es la ~** *inf* that's the limit; **tocarse la ~** *vulg* to sit on one's backside

peral [pe·'ral] *m* pear tree

perca ['per·ka] *f* perch

percance [per·'kan·se, -θe] *m* (*contratiempo*) setback; (*por culpa propia*) blunder; (*de plan, proyecto*) hitch

per cápita [per 'ka·pi·ta] *adv* per capita; **consumo ~** per capita consumption

percatarse [per·ka·'tar·se] *vr* **~se de algo** (*darse cuenta*) to notice sth; (*comprender*) to realize sth

percebe [per·'θe·βe, -'θe·βe] *m* goose barnacle

percepción [per·sep·'sjon, -θeβ·'θjon] *f* **1.** (*acción*) perception **2.** (*idea*) notion; (*impresión*) impression **3.** FIN receipt

perceptible [per·sep·'ti·βle, per·θep-] *adj* perceptible

perceptivo, -a [per·sep·'ti·βo, -a; per·θep-] *adj* perceptive

perceptor(a) [per·sep·'tor, -·'to·ra; perθep-] *m(f)* recipient

percha ['per·tʃa] *f* **1.** (*en el armario*) hanger **2.** (*perchero*) coat stand; (*en la tienda*) clothes rail; **vestido de ~** ready-made dress **3.** *AmC* (*chaqueta*) jacket **4.** *inf* (*tipo*) build; **tener buena ~** to have a good figure

perchero [per·'tʃe·ro] *m* **~ (de pared)** coat rack; **~ (de pie)** coat stand

percibir [per·si·'βir, per·θi-] *vt* **1.** (*notar*) to perceive **2.** (*darse cuenta*) to notice **3.** (*comprender*) to realize **4.** (*cobrar*) to receive

percusión [per·ku·'sjon] *f* MÚS percussion; **instrumento de ~** percussion instrument

percusionista [per·ku·sjo·'nis·ta] *mf* (*de bongos, congas*) percussionist; (*de batería*) drummer

perdedor(a) [per·de·dor, -·'do·ra] *m(f)* loser

perder <e→ie> [per·'der] **I.** *vt* **1.** (*en general, peso, costumbre*) to lose; **~ la cuenta** to lose count; **he perdido mis gafas** I lost my glasses; **~ terreno** *fig* to lose ground **2.** (*malgastar*) to waste **3.** (*oportunidad, tren*) to miss **4.** (*ocasionar daños*) to destroy; **esa equivocación nos perdió** that mistake was our undoing; **el juego lo ~á** gambling will be his undoing **II.** *vi* **1.** (*en general*) to lose; **Portugal perdió por 1 a 2 frente a Italia** Portugal lost 2-1 against Italy; **vas a salir perdiendo** you're going to come off worst; **llevar todas las de ~** to be fighting a losing battle; **lo echó todo a ~** he/she spoiled everything; **la comida se echó a ~** the food was completely ruined **2.** (*decaer*) to decline; **~ en salud** to decline in health **3.** (*desteñir*) to fade **III.** *vr* **1.** (*extraviarse*) to get lost; **¡qué se le habrá perdido por allí?**

P

fig what is he/she doing there? **2.** (*bailando, leyendo*) to lose oneself; **~ se en palabrerías complicadas** (*hablando*) to get bogged down in complicated wordplay **3.** (*desaparecer*) to disappear **4.** (*arruinarse*) **~ se por algo/alguien** to be ruined by sth/sb **5.** (*desperdiciarse*) to be wasted; **se pierde mucha agua por falta de conciencia ecológica** a lot of water is wasted through lack of environmental awareness **6.** (*ocasión*) to miss out; **si no te vienes, tú te lo pierdes** if you don't come, you'll be the one who misses out **7.** (*extinguirse*) to die out; **poco a poco la minifalda se va perdiendo** miniskirts are slowly going out of fashion **8.** (*anhelar*) **~ se por algo/alguien** to be crazy about sth/sb

perdición [per·di·'sjon, -'θjon] *f* **1.** (*acción*) loss; (*daño*) ruin **2.** (*moral*) perdition

pérdida ['per·di·da] *f* loss; **~ de cabellos** hair loss; **~ de conciencia** loss of consciousness; **~ por fricción** wear; **esto es una ~ de tiempo** this is a waste of time; **es fácil de encontrar, no tiene ~** it's easy to find, you can't miss it; **el edificio sufrió grandes ~s** the building was badly damaged; **~ s humanas** victims; **no hubo que lamentar ~s humanas** fortunately there were no lives lost

perdidamente [per·di·da·'men·te] *adv* **estar ~ enamorado** to be madly in love

perdido, -a [per·'di·do, -a] **I.** *adj* **1.** (*que no se encuentra*) lost; **dar a alguien por ~** to give sb up for lost; **dar algo por ~** to give sth up for lost; *fig* to give up on sth; **estar ~** to be lost **2.** (*vicioso, sin salida*) lost; **estar loco ~** *inf* to be completely insane **3.** (*sucio*) **poner algo ~** *inf* to make sth completely dirty; **ponerse ~ de pintura** *inf* to get covered in paint **II.** *m, f inf* (*vago*) loafer; (*pobre*) poor wretch; **hacerse el ~** *inf* to make oneself scarce

perdiz [per·'dis, -'diθ] *f* partridge; **...y fueron felices y comieron perdices** ...and they lived happily ever after

perdón [per·'don] *m* **1.** (*absolución, indulto*) pardon **2.** (*disculpa*) **¡~!** sorry!; **¿~?** pardon?; **¡con ~!** if you'll excuse me!; **no cabe ~** it's inexcusable; **pedir ~ a alguien** to ask for sb's forgiveness; (*disculparse*) to apologize to sb

perdonable [per·do·'na·βle] *adj* forgivable

perdonar [per·do·'nar] *vt* **1.** (*ofensa, deuda*) to forgive; (*pecado, pena*) to pardon; **no te perdono** I don't forgive you; **perdona que te interrumpa** forgive me for interrupting; **perdona, ¿puedo pasar?** excuse me, can I come through? **2.** (*obligación*) to let off; **te perdono los 20 dólares** I'll forget about the 20 dollars you owe me; **les he perdonado la tarde a mis empleados** I have given my employees the afternoon off **3.** (*dejar pasar*) **no ~ ningún esfuerzo** to spare no effort; **no ~ ningún medio** to use all possible means; **la guerra no perdona a nadie** war spares no-one

perdurable [per·du·'ra·βle] *adj* long-lasting; (*eterno*) everlasting

perdurar [per·du·'rar] *vi* **1.** (*todavía*) to persist **2.** (*indefinidamente*) to last for ever; **su recuerdo ~á para siempre entre nosotros** his/her memory will always be with us

perecedero, -a [pe·re·se·'de·ro, -a; pe·re·θe-] *adj* **1.** (*pasajero*) transitory **2.** (*alimento*) perishable

perecer [pe·re·'ser, -θer] *irr como crecer vi* **1.** (*morir*) to perish; **~ de sed** to die of thirst **2.** (*daño, sufrimiento*) to suffer

peregrinación [pe·re·ɣri·na·'sjon, -'θjon] *f* REL pilgrimage; **ir en ~** to make a pilgrimage

peregrinar [pe·re·ɣri·'nar] *vi* **1.** REL to make a pilgrimage **2.** (*viajar: a pie*) to wander; (*con vehículo*) to drive around; **para matricularme tuve que ~ por cientos de oficinas** to register I had to trek through hundreds of offices

peregrino, -a [pe·re·'ɣri·no, -a] *m, f* pilgrim

perejil [pe·re·'xil] *m* BOT parsley

perenne [pe·'ren·ne] *adj* everlasting; BOT perennial

perentorio, -a [pe·ren·'to·rjo, -a] *adj* **plazo ~** fixed time limit

pereza [pe·'re·sa, -θa] *f* (*gandulería*) laziness; (*de movimientos*) slowness; **me dio ~ ir** I didn't feel like going

perezosa [pe·re·'so·sa, -'θo·sa] *f Arg, Perú, Urug* deck chair

perezoso, -a [pe·re·'so·so, -'θo·so] *adj* (*gandul*) lazy; (*movimiento*) unhurried; **y ni corto ni ~** *inf* without giving it a thought

perfección [per·fek·'sjon, -'θjon] *f* perfection; **estilo de gran ~** highly polished style; **hacer algo a la ~** to do sth to perfection

perfeccionamiento [per·fek·sjo·na·'mjen·to, -θjo·na·'mjen·to] *m* perfection; (*técnica, sistema*) improvement; (*profesional*) further training

perfeccionar [per·fek·sjo·'nar, -θjo·'nar] *vt* to perfect; (*de técnica, sistema*) to improve

perfeccionista [per·fek·sjo·'nis·ta, -θjo·'nis·ta] *adj, mf* perfectionist

perfectamente [per·fek·ta·'men·te] *adv* perfectly; **sabes ~ que...** you know perfectly well that...; **te entiendo ~** I understand you perfectly; **¡~!** exactly!

perfecto [per·'fek·to] *m* LING perfect tense

perfecto, -a [per·'fek·to, -a] *adj* **1.** perfect; **nadie es ~** nobody is perfect; **habla un inglés ~** he/she speaks perfect English; **un ~ caballero** a perfect gentleman; **eres un ~ idiota** you are a complete idiot **2.** LING **pretérito ~** past perfect

perfidia [per·'fi·dja] *f* disloyalty; (*traición*) betrayal

pérfido, -a ['per·fi·do, -a] *adj* disloyal; (*traidor*) treacherous

perfil [per·'fil] *m* **1.** *t.* TÉC (*de cara*) profile; **de ~** in profile; **~ genético** genetic profile **2.** (*contorno*) outline **3.** (*de personalidad*) characteristics *pl;* **el ~ del candidato** the description of the candidate

perfilar [per·fi·'lar] I. *vt* 1.(*retocar*) to touch up 2.(*sacar perfil*) to outline; TÉC to streamline II. *vr* 1.(*distinguirse*) to stand out 2.(*tomar forma*) to take shape

perforación [per·fo·ra·'sjon, -'θjon] *f* 1.(*con máquina*) drilling; (*de oreja*) piercing; (*de papel*) punching; (*con muchos agujeros*) perforation 2.(*agujeros, línea*) perforation

perforar [per·fo·'rar] *vt* (*con máquina*) to drill; (*oreja*) to pierce; (*papel*) to punch; (*para decorar, arrancar*) to perforate

perfumador [per·fu·ma·'dor] *m* (*utensilio*) perfume spray

perfumar [per·fu·'mar] I. *vt* to perfume; **las flores perfuman la habitación** the smell of flowers fills the room II. *vi* to be fragrant

perfume [per·'fu·me] *m* 1.(*sustancia*) perfume 2.(*olor*) fragrance

perfumería [per·fu·me·'ri·a] *f* perfume shop

pergamino [per·ɣa·'mi·no] *m* parchment; **libro en ~** parchment-bound book; **familia de ~s** ancient family

pericia [pe·'ri·sja, -θja] *f* 1.(*habilidad*) expertise 2.(*práctica*) skill

pericial [pe·ri·'sjal, -'θjal] *adj* expert; **informe ~** expert report

perico [pe·'ri·ko] *m* ZOOL parakeet

periferia [pe·ri·'fe·rja] *f* periphery; (*de ciudad*) outskirts *pl*

perifollo [pe·ri·'fo·jo, -ʎo] *m* BOT chervil

perífrasis [pe·'ri·fra·sis] *f inv* circumlocution, wordiness

perifrástico, -a [pe·ri·'fras·ti·ko, -a] *adj* circumlocutory, long-winded

perilla [pe·'ri·ja, -ʎa] *f* goatee ▶ **venir de ~s** to be just what was needed

perímetro [pe·'ri·me·tro] *m* MAT perimeter

perineo [pe·ri·'neo] *m* perineum

perinola [pe·ri·'no·la] *f* (small) spinning top

periodicidad [pe·rjo·di·si·'dad, -θi·'dad] *f* frequency

periódico [pe·'rjo·di·ko] *m* newspaper

periódico, -a [pe·'rjo·di·ko, -a] *adj* periodic; **sistema ~** QUÍM periodic table

periodicucho [pe·rjo·di·'ku·tʃo] *m pey* scandal sheet, rag

periodismo [pe·rjo·'dis·mo] *m* journalism

periodista [pe·rjo·'dis·ta] *mf* journalist

periodístico, -a [pe·rjo·'dis·ti·ko, -a] *adj* 1.(*de los periodistas*) journalistic 2.(*de los periódicos*) newspaper; **reportaje ~** newspaper report

periodo [pe·'rjo·do] *m*, **período** [pe·'ri·o·do] *m t.* MAT, FÍS, GEO period; **~ álgido** critical period; **~ glacial** ice age; **~ productivo** productive period; **~ de prueba** trial period

peripecia [pe·ri·'pe·sja, -θja] *f* vicissitude; **pasar por muchas ~s** to go through many ups and downs

periquete [pe·ri·'ke·te] *m* **esto lo hago yo en un ~** I can do that in no time; **estoy lista en un ~** I'll be ready in a jiffy

periquito [pe·ri·'ki·to] *m* parakeet

periscopio [pe·ris·'ko·pjo] *m* periscope

perito, -a [pe·'ri·to, -a] I. *adj* expert II. *m, f* 1.(*experto*) expert 2. UNIV graduate; **~ agrónomo** agronomist; **~ mercantil** accountant; **Escuela de Peritos** professional training college

peritoneo [pe·ri·to·'neo] *m* peritoneum

perjudicar <c→qu> [per·xu·di·'kar] I. *vt* 1.(*causar daño*) to damage; (*naturaleza, intereses*) to harm; (*proceso, desarrollo*) to hinder; **fumar perjudica la salud** smoking is bad for your health 2.(*causar desventaja*) to disadvantage II. *vr* to harm oneself

perjudicial [per·xu·di·'sjal, -'θjal] *adj* 1.(*que causa daño*) harmful; **~ para la salud** harmful to health 2.(*desventajoso*) disadvantageous

perjuicio [per·'xwi·sjo, -θjo] *m* 1.(*daño: de imagen, naturaleza*) harm; (*de objeto*) damage; (*de libertad*) infringement; **causar ~s** to cause harm; **sin ~ de que** +*subj* despite the fact that 2.(*detrimento*) detriment; **ir en ~ de alguien** to be to sb's detriment

perjurar [per·xu·'rar] *vi* 1.(*en falso*) to commit perjury 2.(*faltar al juramento*) to break one's oath

perjurio [per·'xu·rjo] *m* 1.(*en falso*) perjury 2.(*faltar al juramento*) breaking one's word

perla ['per·la] *f* pearl; **~ cultivada** cultured pearl; **eso viene de ~s** that is just what was needed

permanecer [per·ma·ne·'ser, -θer] *irr como* **crecer** *vi* to remain; **~ quieto** to keep still; **~ invariable** to remain unchanged; **~ dormido** to carry on sleeping; **~ sentado** to remain seated

permanencia [per·ma·'nen·sja, -θja] *f* 1.(*estancia*) stay; (*duración*) duration; **lograr la ~ en primera** DEP to hold on to first place 2.(*persistencia*) persistence 3.(*continuación*) continuation

permanente [per·ma·'nen·te] I. *adj* permanent; **estado ~** permanent state II. *f* perm

permeabilidad [per·mea·βi·li·'dad] *f* permeability

permeable [per·me·'a·βle] *adj* permeable; **~ al agua** permeable to water

permisible [per·mi·'si·βle] *adj* permissible

permisión [per·mi·'sjon] *f* permission

permisionario, -a [per·mi·sjo·'na·rjo, -a] *m, f* *AmL* official agent

permisividad [per·mi·si·βi·'dad] *f* permissiveness

permisivo, -a [per·mi·'si·βo, -a] *adj* permissive

permiso [per·'mi·so] *m* 1.(*aprobación, autorización*) permission; **me dio ~ para hacerlo** he/she gave me permission to do it; **pedir ~ a alguien** to ask sb for permission 2.(*licencia*) permit; **~ de conducir** driver's license; **~ de residencia/de trabajo** residence/work permit 3.(*vacaciones*) leave; **pedir ~** to request leave; **estar de ~** MIL to be on leave

permitir [per·mi·'tir] I. *vt* 1.(*consentir*) to permit; ¿**me permite pasar/entrar/salir?** may I get past/enter/leave?; **no está permitido fumar** smoking is not allowed; **si me permite la expresión** if you will excuse the phrase **2.** (*autorizar*) to authorize **3.** (*hacer posible, tolerar*) to allow; **esta máquina permite trabajar el doble** this machine allows you to do twice as much work; **no permito que me levantes la voz** I won't allow you to raise your voice to me **II.** *vr* to allow oneself

permuta [per·'mu·ta] *f* exchange

permutar [per·mu·'tar] *vt* to exchange

pernera [per·'ne·ra] *f* (pant) leg

pernicioso, -a [per·ni·'sjo·so, -a; -'θjo·so, -a] *adj* damaging; ~ **para algo/alguien** damaging to sth/sb

pernil [per·'nil] *m* (*del cerdo*) leg of ham

pernio ['per·njo] *m* hinge

perno ['per·no] *m* bolt

pernoctar [per·nok·'tar] *vi* to spend the night

pero ['pe·ro] **I.** *conj* but; (*sin embargo*) however; **¡~ si todavía es una niña!** but she is still only a child!; **¡~ si ya la conoces!** but you already know her!; **¿~ qué es lo que quieres?** what do you want? **II.** *m* (*objeción*) objection; **el proyecto tiene sus ~s** there are lots of problems with the project; **sin un ~** no buts; **poner ~s a algo** to object to sth; **¡no hay ~ que valga!** there are no buts about it!; **poner ~s a todo** to object to everything

perogrullada [pe·ro·ɣru·'ja·da, -'ʎa·da] *f* obvious truth

perol [pe·'rol] *m* (metal) cooking pot

peroné [pe·ro·'ne] *m* fibula

peronista [pe·ro·'nis·ta] *adj, mf* Peronist

peroración [pe·ro·ra·'sjon, -'θjon] *f* speech

perorar [pe·ro·'rar] *vi* to make a speech; *pey* to hold forth

peróxido [pe·'rok·si·do] *m* peroxide

perpendicular [per·pen·di·ku·'lar] *adj, f* perpendicular

perpetrar [per·pe·'trar] *vt* to perpetrate

perpetuar < *1. pres:* perpetúo> [per·pe·tu·'ar] **I.** *vt* **1.** (*recuerdo, memoria, nombre*) to preserve **2.** (*situación, error, mentira*) to perpetuate **II.** *vr* to be perpetuated

perpetuidad [per·pe·twi·'dad] *f* **1.** (*continuidad*) continuity **2.** (*eternidad*) perpetuity; **a ~** in perpetuity; **condenar a ~** to condemn to life imprisonment

perpetuo, -a [per·'pe·two, -a] *adj* **1.** (*incesante*) perpetual; **nieves perpetuas** permanent snow **2.** (*vitalicio*) life; **cadena perpetua** life sentence

perplejo, -a [per·'ple·xo, -a] *adj* perplexed

perra ['pe·rra] *f* **1.** zool bitch; *v.t.* **perro** I. **2.** *inf* (*rabieta*) tantrum; **coger una ~** to throw a tantrum **3.** *inf* (*modorra*) sleepiness; (*pereza*) laziness **4.** (*mujer malvada*) bitch **5.** *inf* (*dinero*) penny; **no tener una ~** to be broke **6.** *inf* (*borrachera*) drunkenness; **cogerse una ~** *argot* to get plastered

perramus [pe·'rra·mus] *m inv, Arg, Bol, Urug* raincoat

perrera [pe·'rre·ra] *f* (*de perros callejeros*) dog pound

perrería [pe·rre·'ri·a] *f* (*vileza*) dirty trick

perrilla [pe·'rri·ja, -ʎa] *f Méx* (*orzuelo*) snare

perrito [pe·'rri·to] *m* ~ **caliente** hot dog

perro, -a [pe·'rro] **I.** *m, f* (*macho*) dog; (*hembra*) bitch; ~ **callejero** stray dog; ~ **faldero** lapdog; ~ **lazarillo** guide-dog; **echar los ~s a alguien** *inf* to tear sb to shreds; **morir como un ~** *inf* to die a lonely death ▸ **se llevan como el ~ y el gato** *inf* they fight like cat and dog; **ser como el ~ del hortelano** to be a dog in the manger; **¡venga ya, a otro ~ con ese hueso!** *inf* pull the other one!; **humor de ~s** *inf* filthy mood; **a ~ flaco todo son pulgas** *prov* misfortunes never come singly; **tiempo de ~s** *inf* filthy weather; ~ **ladrador, poco mordedor** *prov* his bark is worse than his bite; **muerto el ~ se acabó la rabia** *prov* dead dogs don't bite; **ser ~ viejo** *inf* to be an old hand **II.** *adj* lousy; **llevar una vida perra** to lead a wretched life

persa ['per·sa] *adj* Persian; **alfombra ~** Persian rug

persecución [per·se·ku·'sjon, -'θjon] *f* pursuit; (*acoso*) persecution; ~ **en coche** car chase

perseguir [per·se·'ɣir] *irr como seguir vt* to chase; (*contrato, chica*) to pursue; **la policía persigue al fugitivo** the police are pursuing the fugitive; **me persigue la mala suerte** I am dogged by bad luck; **me persiguen los remordimientos** I am tormented by remorse; **el jefe me persigue todo el día** the boss is always on my back; **¿qué persigues con esto?** what do you hope to achieve by this?

perseverancia [per·se·βe·'ransja, -θja] *f* **1.** (*insistencia*) ~ **en algo** insistence on sth **2.** (*en trabajo, actividad*) ~ **en algo** perseverance in sth **3.** (*firmeza*) resolve

perseverante [per·se·βe·'ran·te] *adj* **1.** (*insistente*) insistent **2.** (*constante*) persevering **3.** (*firme*) determined

perseverar [per·se·βe·'rar] *vi* **1.** (*insistir*) to insist **2.** (*mantener*) ~ **en algo** to persevere in sth

Persia ['per·sja] *f* Persia

persiana [per·'sja·na] *f* blind

pérsico, -a ['per·si·ko] *adj* Persian

persignarse [per·siɣ·'nar·se] *vr* to cross oneself

persistencia [per·sis·'ten·sja, -θja] *f* persistence

persistente [per·sis·'ten·te] *adj* persistent

persistir [per·sis·'tir] *vi* to persist

persona [per·'so·na] *f* person; ~ **de contacto** contact; ~ **(non) grata** persona (non) grata; **en ~** in person; ~ **jurídica** legal entity; ~ **mayor** adult, grown-up; ~ **física** individual; **ser buena/mala ~** to be good/bad; **había muchas ~s** there were a lot of people; **no había ninguna ~ allí** there was nobody there;

se apareció en la ~ de... he/she appeared in the form of...; **ese es una ~ de cuidado** you need to be careful with him

personaje [per·so·'na·xe] *m* personality; TEAT, LIT character; ~ **de culto** cult figure; **es todo un ~** he/she is a real character

personal [per·so·'nal] **I.** *adj* personal; **datos ~es** personal details; **pronombre ~** personal pronoun **II.** *m* **1.** (*plantilla*) personnel; (*en empresa*) staff; ~ **de a bordo** AVIAT aircrew; ~ **docente** teaching staff; ~ **de tierra** AVIAT ground crew **2.** *inf* (*gente*) people *pl*

personalidad [per·so·na·li·'dad] *f* personality

personalizable [per·so·na·li·'saβ·le, -'θaβ·le] *adj t.* INFOR personalizable; **productos ~s** COMPUT personalizable products

personalizar <z→c> [per·so·na·li·'sar, -'θar] *vt* **1.** (*hacer personal*) to personalize **2.** (*aludir*) to get personal

personarse [per·so·'nar·se] *vr* to appear; ~ **en juicio** to appear before the court; **persónese ante el director** report to the director

personero, -a [per·so·'ne·ro, -a] *m, f AmL* government representative

personificar <c→qu> [per·so·ni·fi·'kar] *vt* to personify; **personifica la maldad** he/she is evil personified

perspectiva [pers·pek·'ti·βa] *f* **1.** (*general*) perspective **2.** (*vista*) view **3.** *pl* (*posibilidad*) prospects *pl*

perspicacia [pers·pi·'ka·sja, -θja] *f* insight

perspicaz [pers·pi·'kas, -'kaθ] *adj* **1.** (*vista*) keen **2.** (*persona*) perceptive

persuadir [per·swa·'dir] **I.** *vt* **1.** (*inducir*) to encourage; **lo ~é para que no lo haga** I will persuade him not to do it **2.** (*convencer*) to persuade **II.** *vr* to be persuaded

persuasión [per·swa·'sjon] *f* **1.** (*acto*) persuasion; **emplear todo su poder de ~** to use all one's powers of persuasion **2.** (*convencimiento*) belief

persuasivo, -a [per·swa·'si·βo, -a] *adj* persuasive

pertenecer [per·te·ne·'ser, -θer] *irr como crecer vi* **1.** (*ser de*) to belong; **esta casa me pertenece** this house belongs to me; **esta cita pertenece a Hamlet** this is a quotation from Hamlet **2.** (*tener obligación*) **te pertenece a ti hacerlo** it is your duty to do it

perteneciente [per·te·ne·'sjen·te, 'θjen·te] *adj* ~ **a** belonging to; **los países ~s a la ONU** the countries that are members of the UN; **todo lo ~ al caso** everything that is relevant to the case; **un cuadro ~ a la colección de Thyssen** a picture that belongs to the Thyssen collection

pertenencia [per·te·'nen·sja, -θja] *f* **1.** (*acción*) belonging **2.** *pl* (*bienes*) belongings *pl* **3.** *pl* (*accesorios*) accessories *pl*

pértiga ['per·ti·ya] *f t.* DEP pole; **salto de ~** pole vault; **saltar con ~** to pole vault; ~ **del trole** current-collecting pole, trolley pole

pertinacia [per·ti·'na·sja, -θja] *f* (*de lluvia,*

persona) persistence

pertinaz [per·ti·'nas, -'naθ] *adj* (*lluvia, tos, persona*) persistent

pertinente [per·ti·'nen·te] *adj* **1.** (*oportuno*) appropriate **2.** (*datos, pregunta, comentario*) relevant, pertinent **3.** (*relativo*) **en lo ~ a...** with regard to...

pertrechar [per·tre·'tʃar] **I.** *vt* to supply **II.** *vr* ~ **se de algo** (*de alimentos*) to supply oneself with sth; (*de equipamiento*) to equip oneself with sth

pertrechos [per·'tre·tʃos] *mpl* MIL supplies *pl*

perturbación [per·tur·βa·'sjon, -'θjon] *f* disturbance

perturbado, -a [per·tur·'βa·do, -a] *m, f* ~ (**mental**) mentally disturbed person

perturbador(a) [per·tur·βa·'dor, -'do·ra] *m(f)* troublemaker

perturbar [per·tur·'βar] *vt* to disturb; (*confundir*) to confuse

Perú [pe·'ru] *m* Peru

i **Perú** is located in the western part of South America and is the continent's third largest country, after Brazil and Argentina. The capital, which is also the largest city in Peru, is **Lima**. Both Spanish and **quechua** are the country's official languages and the official currency is the **sol**. The original inhabitants of Peru were the **Incas**.

peruano, -a [pe·'rwa·no, -a] *adj, m, f* Peruvian

perversidad [per·βer·si·'dad] *f* (*sexual*) perversity

perversión [per·βer·'sjon] *f* **1.** (*acción*) perversion; ~ **de menores** corruption of minors **2.** (*cualidad*) perversity

perverso, -a [per·'βer·so, -a] *adj* (*sexual*) perverse

pervertido, -a [per·βer·'ti·do, -a] *adj* perverted

pervertir [per·βer·'tir] *irr como sentir* **I.** *vt* to corrupt **II.** *vr* to become corrupt; (*depravarse*) to become perverted

pesa ['pe·sa] *f t.* DEP weight; ~ **del reloj** clock weight; **hacer ~s** to do weight training; **levantamiento de ~s** weightlifting

pesadez [pe·sa·'des, -'deθ] *f* **1.** (*de objeto*) heaviness **2.** (*de movimiento*) slowness, sluggishness **3.** (*de sueño*) drowsiness **4.** (*de tarea*) boring nature **5.** (*de persona*) tiresome nature **6.** (*de viaje*) tediousness **7.** (*de lectura*) density; (*aburrido*) dullness **8.** (*de dibujo*) over-elaboration **9.** (*de estómago*) (acid) indigestion

pesadilla [pe·sa·'di·ja, -ʎa] *f* nightmare

pesado, -a [pe·'sa·do, -a] *adj* **1.** (*que pesa*) heavy; **tengo la cabeza pesada** my head feels rather stuffy; **tengo el estómago ~** my stomach is uncomfortably full **2.** (*lento*) slow **3.** (*molesto*) tiresome **4.** (*duro*) hard; **un tra-**

P

bajo ~ hard work **5.** (*aburrido*) boring **6.** (*sueño*) deep; (*tiempo*) oppressive; (*viaje*) tedious; (*lectura*) heavy going

pesadumbre [pe·sa·'dum·bre] *f* affliction

pésame ['pe·sa·me] *m* condolences *pl;* **dar el** ~ to offer one's condolences; **reciba mi más sincero** ~ please accept my heartfelt condolences

pesantez [pe·san·'tes, -'teθ] *f* gravity

pesar [pe·'sar] **I.** *vi* to weigh; **esta caja pesa mucho** this box is very heavy; **pon encima lo que no pese** put the lightest things on top; ~ **sobre alguien** to weigh heavily on sb; (*problemas*) to weigh sb down **II.** *vt* to weigh; (*cantidad concreta*) to weigh out; **¿me puede** ~ **la fruta?** could you weigh this fruit for me?; **me pesa haberte mentido** I regret having lied to you; **mal que te pese...** much as you may dislike it...; **pese a quien pese** come what may; **pese a que...** although... **III.** *m* **1.** (*pena*) sorrow; **muy a** ~ **mío** to my great sadness **2.** (*remordimiento*) regret ▶ **a** ~ **de** in spite of

pesaroso, -a [pe·sa·'ro·so, -a] *adj* **1.** (*afligido*) sad; **está** ~ **por haberlo dicho** he really regrets having said it **2.** (*disgustado*) upset

pesca ['pes·ka] *f* fishing; (*captura*) capture; **ir de** ~ to go fishing; ~ **de altura** deep-sea fishing; ~ **de arrastre** trawling; ~ **de bajura** inshore fishing; **y toda la** ~ *fig, inf* and all the rest of the crew

pescadería [pes·ka·de·'ri·a] *f* (*tienda*) fish market

pescadilla [pes·ka·'di·ja, -ʎa] *f* whiting; **ser la** ~ **que se muerde la cola** *inf* to be a vicious circle

pescado [pes·'ka·do] *m* fish

pescador(a) [pes·ka·'dor, -·'do·ra] *m(f)* (*de caña*) angler; (*de mar*) fisherman

pescar <c→qu> [pes·'kar] *vt* **1.** (*con caña, en barco*) to fish for; **ir a** ~ **sardinas** to fish for sardines **2.** (*sorprender*) to catch out; (*resfriado*) to catch **3.** *inf* (*novio*) to land **4.** *inf* (*entender*) to understand

pescuezo [pes·'kwe·so, -θo] *m* (scruff of the) neck; **retorcer el** ~ **a alguien** *inf* to wring sb's neck; **sacar el** ~ *inf* to be snooty; **salvar el** ~ *fig* to save one's skin

pese ['pe·se] *adv* ~ **a** in spite of, despite

pesebre [pe·'se·βre] *m* manger; (*de Navidad*) Nativity scene

pesero [pe·'se·ro] *m Méx* minibus

peseta [pe·'se·ta] *f* peseta; **cambiar la** ~ *inf* to throw up

pesetero, -a [pe·se·'te·ro, -a] *m, f* money-grubbing; **eres un** ~ all you think about is money

pesimismo [pe·si·'mis·mo] *m* pessimism

pesimista [pe·si·'mis·ta] **I.** *adj* pessimistic **II.** *mf* pessimist

pésimo, -a ['pe·si·mo, -a] *adj* dreadful

peso ['pe·so] *m* **1.** (*de objeto*) weight; **coger/perder** ~ to gain/lose weight; **¿qué** ~ **tiene?** how much does it weigh?; **vender a** ~ to sell by weight; **eso cae por su propio** ~ that goes without saying **2.** (*pesadez*) heaviness; **tener** ~ **en las piernas** to have heavy legs **3.** (*importancia*) weight; **es un gran** ~ **dentro de la empresa** he/she has a lot of influence within the business; **tener una razón de** ~ to have a good reason **4.** (*carga*) burden; **llevar el** ~ **de algo** to bear the burden of sth; **me saco un** ~ **de encima** that's taken a load off my mind **5.** DEP (*bola*) shot **6.** DEP (*boxeo*) ~ **gallo** bantamweight **7.** (*moneda*) peso ▶ **comprar a** ~ **de oro** to pay way over the odds; **pagar a** ~ **de oro** to pay the earth

pespuntar [pes·pun·'tar] *vt* to backstitch

pespunte [pes·'pun·te] *m* **1.** (*acción, costura*) backstitching **2.** (*puntada*) backstitch

pespuntear [pes·pun·te·'ar] *vt* to backstitch

pesquero [pes·'ke·ro] *m* fishing boat

pesquero, -a [pes·'ke·ro, -a] *adj* fishing

pesquisa¹ [pes·'ki·sa] *f* inquiry; **hacer** ~**s** to make inquiries

pesquisa² [pes·'ki·sa] *m Arg, Ecua, Par* detective

pestaña [pes·'ta·ɲa] *f* eyelash; **quemarse las** ~**s** *fig* to burn the midnight oil

pestañear [pes·ta·'ɲar/pes·ta·ɲe·'ar] *vi* to blink; **sin** ~ without batting an eyelid

pestañeo [pes·ta·'ɲeo] *m* blinking

peste ['pes·te] *f* **1.** *t.* MED (*plaga*) plague; ~ **bubónica** bubonic plague **2.** (*olor*) stench; **aquí hay una** ~ **increíble** it really stinks here **3.** (*crítica*) **echar** ~**s de alguien** to heap abuse on sb

pesticida [pes·ti·'si·da, -'θi·da] *m* pesticide

pestífero, -a [pes·'ti·fe·ro, -a] *adj* (*fétido*) foul-smelling

pestilencia [pes·ti·'len·sja, -θja] *f* stench; MED pestilence

pestilente [pes·ti·'len·te] *adj v.* **pestífero**

pestillo [pes·'ti·jo, -ʎo] *m* bolt; **echar el** ~ to shoot the bolt; ~ **de golpe** spring bolt

petaca [pe·'ta·ka] *f* **1.** (*para cigarros*) cigarette case; (*para tabaco*) tobacco pouch **2.** *AmL* (*caja*) box; (*baúl*) chest; (*cesto*) basket **3.** *AmC* (*joroba*) hump

petacón, -ona [pe·ta·'kon, -·'ko·na] *adj AmL* tubby

pétalo ['pe·ta·lo] *m* petal

petanca [pe·'tan·ka] *f* DEP lawn bowling

petardo [pe·'tar·do] *m* **1.** (*de fiesta*) firecracker; **tirar** ~**s** to set off firecrackers **2.** (*estafa*) swindle; **pegar un** ~ **a alguien** to take sb for a ride **3.** *inf* (*persona o cosa mala*) **ser un** ~ to be a pain

petate [pe·'ta·te] *m* (*de soldado, marinero*) kit bag; **liar el** ~ *fig* to pack up and go

petatearse [pe·ta·te·'ar·se] *vr Méx* (*morirse*) to croak *sl*

petenera [pe·te·'ne·ra] *f* MÚS *Andalusian song;* **salirse por** ~**s** to go off on a tangent

petición [pe·ti·'sjon, -'θjon] *f* (*ruego, solicitud*) request; (*escrito*) petition; **a** ~ **de...** at the request of...; ¿**has hecho ya la ~ de mano?** have you asked her to marry you yet?

peticionar [pe·ti·sjo·'nar, -θjo·'nar] *vt AmL* to petition

petirrojo [pe·ti·'rro·xo] *m* robin (redbreast)

petiso, -a [pe·'ti·so] **I.** *adj Arg, Urug (pequeño)* small; *(muy pequeño)* tiny; *(enano)* short **II.** *m, f* short person

petisú [pe·ti·'su] *m* éclair

petitorio, -a [pe·ti·'to·rjo, -a] *adj* petitionary

peto ['pe·to] *m (de bebé, delantal)* bib

pétreo, -a ['pe·treo, -a] *adj* stony; *(duro)* rock-hard

petrificación [pe·tri·fi·ka·'sjon, -'θjon] *f* petrifaction

petrificar <c→qu> [pe·tri·fi·'kar] **I.** *vt t. fig* to petrify **II.** *vr:* ~ **se** to turn to stone

petrodólar [pe·tro·'do·lar] *m* ECON petrodollar

petróleo [pe·'tro·leo] *m* **1.** *(carburante)* petroleum, (crude) oil **2.** *(de lámpara)* paraffin

petrolero [pe·tro·'le·ro] *m (barco)* oil tanker

petrolero, -a [pe·tro·'le·ro, -a] *adj* **1.** *(del carburante)* oil **2.** *(de la lámpara)* paraffin

petrolífero, -a [pe·tro·'li·fe·ro, -a] *adj* oil-bearing; **campo** ~ oilfield; **industria petrolífera** oil industry

petroquímica [pe·tro·'ki·mi·ka] *f* petrochemistry

petulancia [pe·tu·'lan·sja, -θja] *f* **1.** *(arrogancia)* arrogance **2.** *(insolencia)* insolence

petulante [pe·tu·'lan·te] *adj* **1.** *(arrogante)* arrogant **2.** *(insolente)* insolent

petunia [pe·'tu·nja] *f* petunia

peyorativo, -a [pe·jo·ra·'ti·βo, -a] *adj* pejorative; **un comentario** ~ a derogatory remark

peyote [pe·'jo·te] *m AmL* BOT peyote cactus

pez[1] [pes, peθ] *m* ZOOL fish; ~ **rojo** [*o* **dorado**] goldfish; **estar como (el)** ~ **en el agua** to be in one's element; **estar** ~ **en español** *inf* to have no idea of Spanish; **ese es un buen** ~ he's a wily bird; **un** ~ **gordo** a big shot

pez[2] [pes, peθ] *f* **1.** *(betún)* pitch **2.** *(excremento)* meconium

pezón [pe·'son, -'θon] *m* **1.** *(de mujer)* nipple **2.** *(de animal)* teat **3.** BOT stalk

pezuña [pe·'su·ɲa, pe·'θu-] *f* **1.** *(de vaca, oveja)* hoof **2.** *pl, inf (de persona)* feet *pl*

PHN [plan i·dro·'lo·xi·ko na·sjo·'nal, na·θjo·ᵞnal] *abr de* **Plan Hidrológico Nacional** *national water plan*

pi [pi] *f* MAT pi

piadoso, -a [pja·'do·so, -a] *adj* **1.** *(misericordioso)* merciful; *(bondadoso)* compassionate **2.** *(devoto)* pious

pialar [pja·'lar] *vt AmL* to lasso

pianista [pja·'nis·ta] *mf* pianist

piano [pi·'a·no] *m* piano; ~ **de cola** grand piano

piar <*1. pres:* pío> [pi·'ar] *vi (pájaro)* to chirp; ~ **por algo** *(clamar)* to cry out for sth

piara [pi·'a·ra] *f* herd (of pigs)

PIB [pe·i·'βe] *m abr de* **Producto Interior Bruto** GDP

pibe, -a ['pi·βe, -a] *m, f Arg (chico)* boy; *(chica)* girl

pibil [pi·'βil] *m Méx* CULIN chili sauce

pica ['pi·ka] *f* **1.** *(lanza)* pike **2.** *pl (de cartas)* spades *pl*

picacho [pi·'ka·tʃo] *m* peak

picada [pi·'ka·da] *f* **1.** *(de avispa)* sting; *(de serpiente)* bite **2.** *(de pez)* bite **3.** *CSur (tapas)* snack

picadero [pi·ka·'de·ro] *m (para adiestrar)* ring; *(escuela)* riding school

picadillo [pi·ka·'di·jo, -ʎo] *m (carne picada)* ground meat; *(para embutido)* filling; **hacer** ~ **a alguien** *inf* to make mincemeat of sb

picado [pi·'ka·do] *m* dive; **caer en** ~ *(acciones)* to slump; *(fama)* to plummet

picado, -a [pi·'ka·do, -a] *adj* **1.** *(con picaduras: abrigo)* moth-eaten; *(fruta)* rotten; *(muela)* decayed; *(cara)* pockmarked **2.** *(con agujeros)* perforated **3.** *(mar)* choppy **4.** *inf (enfadado)* annoyed

picador [pi·ka·'dor] *m* **1.** *(adiestrador)* horse-breaker **2.** TAUR picador *(mounted bullfighter who goads the bull with a lance)* **3.** MIN miner

picadura [pi·ka·'du·ra] *f* **1.** *(de insecto)* sting; *(de serpiente)* bite **2.** *(en ropa, metal)* hole **3.** *(caries)* cavity

picaflor [pi·ka·'flor] *m* **1.** ZOOL hummingbird **2.** *AmL (tenorio)* Don Juan

picante [pi·'kan·te] **I.** *adj* spicy, hot; *fig* risqué **II.** *m* **1.** CULIN spicy food **2.** *(de comida)* spiciness; *(de expresión)* sauciness

picantería [pi·kan·te·'ri·a] *f And* small restaurant

picapica [pi·ka·'pi·ka] *f (polvos)* ~ *(de picores)* itching powder; *(de estornudos)* sneezing powder

picapleitos [pi·ka·'plei·tos] *m inv, pey* pettifogger, shyster

picaporte [pi·ka·'por·te] *m* **1.** *(aldaba)* doorknocker **2.** *(tirador)* door handle **3.** *(pestillo)* latch

picar <c→qu> [pi·'kar] **I.** *vi* **1.** *(sol)* to sting **2.** *(pimienta)* to be hot **3.** *(pez)* to take the bait **4.** *(de la comida)* to snack **5.** *(tener picazón)* to itch; **me pica la espalda** my back is itchy **6.** *(golpear)* ~ **a la puerta** to knock on the door **7.** *(aspirar)* ~ **muy alto** to aim too high **II.** *vt* **1.** *(con punzón)* to prick, to pierce **2.** *(sacar)* ~ **una aceituna de la lata** to fish an olive from the tin **3.** *(insecto)* to sting; *(serpiente)* to bite **4.** *(ave)* to peck **5.** *(desmenuzar)* to chop up; *(carne)* to mince **6.** *(ofender)* to irritate; **estar picado con alguien** to be annoyed with sb; **¿qué mosca te ha picado?** what's eating you? **7.** *(incitar)* to goad **III.** *vr* **1.** *(metal)* to rust; *(muela)* to decay; *(ropa)* to get moth-eaten; *(vino)* to turn sour **2.** *(mar)* to become choppy **3.** *(ofenderse)* to become irritated; *(mosquearse)* to become angry; ~ **se por nada** to get irritated about the slightest thing; **siempre se pica cuando juega** he/she

P

always becomes angry when playing **4.** *AmL* (*embriagarse*) to get tipsy

picardear [pi·kar·de·'ar] **I.** *vi* to get into mischief **II.** *vr* to fall into bad ways

picardía [pi·kar·'di·a] *f* **1.** (*malicia*) roguishness; **lo dije con ~** I said it out of a sense of mischief **2.** (*travesura*) naughty trick **3.** (*broma*) joke

picaresco, -a [pi·ka·'res·ko, -a] *adj* **1.** (*astuto*) cunning **2.** (*comentario*) mischievous

pícaro, -a ['pi·ka·ro, -a] **I.** *adj* **1.** (*granuja*) roguish **2.** (*astuto*) cunning **3.** (*comentario*) naughty **II.** *m, f* rogue ▶ **~ de siete suelas** *inf* out-and-out rogue

picarón [pi·ka·'ron] *m AmL* fritter

picatoste [pi·ka·'tos·te] *m* crouton

picazón [pi·ka·'son, -'θon] *f* itch

picha ['pi·tʃa] *f vulg* dick, prick

pichanga [pi·'tʃan·ga] *f* **1.** *Arg* (*vino*) wine (*not fully fermented*) **2.** *Bol* (*fácil*) **ser ~** to be a cinch *inf*

pichi ['pi·tʃi] *m CSur, inf* (*pipí*) pee *sl*

pichicata [pi·tʃi·'ka·ta] *f Arg, inf* drugs *pl*

pichicatearse [pi·tʃi·ka·te·'ar·se] *vr Arg, inf* to take drugs

pichicatero, -a [pi·tʃi·ka·'te·ro, -a] *m, f Arg, inf* drug addict

pichicato, -a [pi·tʃi·'ka·to, -a] *adj AmC* stingy

pichichi [pi·'tʃi·tʃi] *m* DEP top goal-scorer

pichín [pi·'tʃin] *m CSur, inf* pee

pichincha [pi·'tʃin·tʃa] *f* **1.** *Arg* (*ganga*) bargain **2.** *Chile* (*cantidad pequeña*) tiny bit; **con sólo una ~ de leche** with just a drop of milk

pichirre [pi·'tʃi·rre] *adj Ven* (*tacaño*) stingy

pichón [pi·'tʃon] *m* young pigeon

pichón, -ona [pi·'tʃon, -·'tʃo·na] *m, f* (*querido*) darling

pichoso, -a [pi·'tʃo·so, -a] *adj* **1.** *Col* (*de ojos llorosos*) watery-eyed **2.** *Ven* (*sucio*) dirty

pichula [pi·'tʃu·la] *f Arg, Chile, Perú, vulg* dick

pichulear [pi·tʃu·le·'ar] *vt* **1.** *Chile* (*engañar*) to cheat **2.** *CSur* (*negociar*) to buy and sell (*on a small scale*)

picnic ['piɣ·nik] *m* picnic

pico ['pi·ko] *m* **1.** (*del pájaro*) beak **2.** *inf* (*boca*) mouth; **¡cierra el ~!** shut up!; **~ de oro** the gift of gab; **tener un buen ~** to be a smooth talker; **¡él de ~ todo lo que quieras!** he's always promising the earth!; **alguien se fue del ~** sb let the cat out of the bag; **¡ese se perderá por el ~!** his big mouth will be the end of him! **3.** (*herramienta*) pickax **4.** (*montaña*) peak; **cortado a ~** sheer **5.** (*de jarra*) lip **6.** (*cantidad*) **llegar a las cuatro y ~** to arrive just after four o'clock; **tiene cuarenta y ~ de años** he/she is forty-something; **salir por un ~** to cost a lot

picor [pi·'kor] *m* (*en la piel*) itching; (*en la boca*) stinging, burning

picota [pi·'ko·ta] *f* pillory; **poner en la ~ a alguien** *fig* to pillory sb

picotada [pi·ko·'ta·da] *f*, **picotazo** [pi·ko·'ta·so, -θo] *m* **pegar una ~** (*ave*) to peck; **arran-**

car a ~s to peck off

picotear [pi·ko·te·'ar] **I.** *vi* **1.** (*comer*) to nibble **2.** (*hablar*) to chatter **II.** *vt* to peck

pictórico, -a [pik·'to·ri·ko, -a] *adj* pictorial; **técnica pictórica** painting technique

picudo, -a [pi·'ku·do, -a] *adj* pointed; (*anguloso*) angled

pie [pje] *m* **1.** (*extremidad, medida*) foot; **~s planos** flat feet; **~ de atleta** MED athlete's foot; **~ equino** clubfoot; **¿qué ~ calza Ud.?** what shoe size do you take?; **al ~ del árbol** at the foot of the tree; **al ~ de la carta** at the bottom of the letter; **a(l) ~ de (la) obra** on the spot; **a ~** on foot; **a ~ firme** steadfastly; **quedarse de ~** to remain standing; **estar de ~** to be standing; **ponerse de ~** to stand up; **caer de ~s** to land on one's feet; **ya sabemos de qué ~ cojea** *fig* now we know his/her weak spot; **tener los ~s en el suelo** *fig* to be realistic; **echar ~ a tierra** (*salir de coche*) to get out; (*salir de tren, autobús*) to get off; **se marchó por su propio ~** he/she left on his own; **no hacer ~** (*en una piscina*) to be out of one's depth; **perder ~** (*en una piscina*) to get out of one's depth; **estoy cansada: no me tengo en ~** I am so tired I can barely stand; **con buen ~** *fig* on the right footing; **estar en ~ de guerra** to be on a war footing; **en ~ de igualdad** on an equal footing; **trabajo hecho con los ~s** *inf* slipshod work; **ya tiene un ~ en el hoyo** *inf* he/she already has one foot in the grave; **este nació de ~** *inf* this one was born lucky **2.** TIPO **~ de imprenta** imprint; **~ de página** foot of the page **3.** (*planta*) stem; (*tronco*) trunk; **~ de vid** vine stock **4.** (*métrica*) foot **5.** TEAT cue **6.** (*trípode*) leg ▶ **~ de banco** *inf* stupid idea; **hoy no doy ~ con bola** I can't seem to do anything right today; **no tener ni ~s ni cabeza** to make no sense; **estar al ~ del cañón** to be ready for action; **~ de fuerza** *AmL* armed forces; **buscar tres ~s al gato** (*daño*) to ask for trouble; (*complicaciones*) to complicate matters; **seguir algo al ~ de la letra** to follow sth to the letter; **andarse con ~s de plomo** to tread very carefully; **poner ~s en polvorosa** to cut and run; **creer a ~(s) juntillas** to believe unquestioningly; **parar los ~s a alguien** *inf* to put sb in his/her place; **~s, ¿para qué os quiero?** time to leave!; **salir por ~s** *inf* to beat it; **de a ~** ordinary

piedad [pje·'dad] *f* **1.** REL piety; (*compasión*) pity; **¡ten ~ de nosotros!** have pity on us! **2.** ECON **monte de ~** pawnshop

piedra ['pje·dra] *f* stone; **~ pómez** pumice stone; **~ preciosa** precious stone; **cartón ~** papier-mâché; **Edad de Piedra** Stone Age; **poner la primera ~** to lay the foundation stone; **lo saben hasta las ~s** the whole world knows; **lavado a la ~** stonewashed; **~ angular** *fig* cornerstone; **~ filosofal** *fig* philosopher's stone; **~ de toque** *fig* touchstone; **no dejar ~ por mover** *fig* to leave no stone unturned; **no dejar ~ sobre ~** to raze to the ground; **que-**

darse de ~ to be stunned; **tirar la ~ y esconder la mano** to play the innocent; **tirarse ~s a su propio tejado** to foul one's own nest; **pasar a alguien por la ~** *inf* to lay sb

piel [pjel] *f* (*de persona, fruta*) skin; (*de animal*) skin, hide; (*con pelo*) fur; (*cuero*) leather; **dejarse la ~ en algo** *inf* to work oneself into the ground for sth; **un abrigo de ~es** a fur coat ►~ **de gallina** goose-pimples *pl*

pienso ['pjen·so] *m* fodder; ~ **completo** compound feed

pierna ['pjer·na] *f* leg; ~ **ortopédica** artificial leg; **estirar las ~s** to stretch one's legs; **con las ~s cruzadas** with one's legs crossed; **dormir a ~ suelta** to be fast asleep; **en ~s** bare-legged

pieza ['pje·sa, -θa] *f* 1.(*pedazo*) *t.* MÚS, TEAT piece; ~ **de artillería** artillery piece; ~ **de recambio** spare part; ~ **suelta** individual part; **un traje de dos ~s** a two-piece suit; ~ **por ~** piece by piece; **vender a ~s** to sell by the piece; **¡menuda ~ está hecho ese!** *inf* what a little rascal he is! 2. *AmL* (*habitación*) room ► **quedarse de una ~** to be absolutely dumbfounded

pifia ['pi·fja] *f* 1.(*error*) blunder 2. *And* (*escarnio*) mockery

pigmentación [piɣ·men·ta·'sjon, -'θjon] *f* pigmentation

pigmento [piɣ·'men·to] *m* pigment

pignorar [piɣ·no·'rar] *vt* to pawn

pija ['pi·xa] *f AmL, vulg* dick

pijada [pi·'xa·da] *f* piece of nonsense; **¡eso son ~s!** what a load of nonsense!

pijama [pi·'xa·ma] *m* pajamas *pl*

pije ['pi·xe] *m Chile, Perú, inf* la-di-da

pijo ['pi·xo] *m vulg* dick; **¡y un ~!** like hell!

pijo, -a ['pi·xo, -a] *pey, inf* I. *adj* posh; **niño ~** upper -class twit II. *m, f* posh youth

pijotero, -a [pi·xo·'te·ro, -a] *adj AmL* (*tacaño*) stingy

pila ['pi·la] *f* 1.(*recipiente*) basin; (*lavadero*) sink; (*bautismal*) font; **nombre de ~** first name, Christian name 2. FÍS battery; ~ **reversible** reversible battery; **ponerse las ~s** *inf* to get one's act together 3.(*montón*) pile; **una ~ de libros** a pile of books

pila-botón ['pi·la-βo·'ton] *f* <pilas-botón> watch battery

pilar [pi·'lar] *m* 1.(*columna*) pillar 2.(*apoyo*) prop 3.(*en camino*) milestone

pilcha ['pil·tʃa] *f CSur, inf* fine clothes *pl*

pilche ['pil·tʃe] *m And* wooden bowl

píldora ['pil·do·ra] *f* pill; **la ~** (**anticonceptiva**) the pill; **dorar la ~ a alguien** *inf* to sweeten the pill; **me tragué la ~** *fig* I fell for it

pileta [pi·'le·ta] *f* 1. *Arg* (*de cocina*) kitchen sink 2. *Arg* (*piscina*) swimming pool; **tirarse a la ~** to go headlong into sth 3. *RíoPl* (*abrevadero*) water trough

pilila [pi·'li·la] *f infantil* (*pene de niño*) weenie

pililo, -a [pi·'li·lo, -a] *m, f CSur, pey* tramp

pillaje [pi·'ja·xe, -'ʎa·xe] *m* pillage

pillapilla [pi·ja·'pi·ja, pi·ʎa·'pi·'ʎa] *m inf* **jugar al ~** to play tag

pillar [pi·'jar, -'ʎar] *vt* 1.(*atropellar*) to knock down, to run over 2.(*encontrar*) to find; (*en flagrante*) to catch; **me pillas de buen humor** you've caught me in a good mood; **eso no me pilla de sorpresa** that doesn't surprise me; **tu casa nos pilla de camino** your house is on our way; **aquí te pillo, aquí te mato** *fig* to strike while the iron is hot 3.(*entender*) to grasp 4.(*robar*) to steal 5. *Arg* (*orinar*) to piss

pillastre [pi·'jas·tre, -'ʎas·tre] *m inf* rascal

pillín, -ina [pi·'jin, --'ji·na; --'ʎin, --'ʎi·na] *adj inf* crafty

pillo, -a ['pi·jo, -a; -'ʎo, -a] I. *adj inf* crafty II. *m, f inf* rascal

pilmama [pil·'ma·na] *f Méx* nanny

pilme ['pil·me] *m Chile* ZOOL blister beetle

pilón [pi·'lon] *m* 1.(*lavadero*) basin; (*abrevadero*) drinking trough 2. ARQUIT pillar

piloncillo [pi·lon·'si·jo, -'θi·ʎo] *m Méx* brown sugar

piloso, -a [pi·'lo·so, -a] *adj* hairy

pilotar [pi·lo·'tar] *vt* (*barco*) to steer; (*coche*) to drive; (*avión*) to fly

pilote [pi·'lo·te] *m* ARQUIT pile

pilotear [pi·lo·te·'ar] *vt AmL* 1.(*ayudar*) to guide 2.(*negocio*) to run 3. *Chile* (*explotar*) to exploit

piloto¹ [pi·'lo·to] I. *mf* 1. NÁUT navigator; (*oficial*) first mate; (*práctico*) (coast) pilot 2. AVIAT pilot; **poner el ~ automático** to set the automatic pilot 3. AUTO driver; ~ **de carreras** racing driver II. *adj* (*de prueba*) test; (*de modelo*) show, model; **piso ~** model apartment; **experiencia ~** test

piloto² [pi·'lo·to] *m Arg* (*impermeable*) raincoat

piltrafa [pil·'tra·fa] *f* (*persona*) wreck

pilucho, -a [pi·'lu·tʃo, -a] *adj Chile* naked

pimentero [pi·men·'te·ro] *m* 1. BOT pepper plant 2.(*vasija*) pepper pot

pimentón [pi·men·'ton] *m* paprika

pimienta [pi·'mjen·ta] *f* pepper; ~ **en grano** peppercorns *pl*

pimiento [pi·'mjen·to] *m* pepper; ~ **encarnado** red pepper; **me importa un ~** I couldn't care less

pimpante [pim·'pan·te] *adj inf* (*despreocupado*) unconcerned; **tan ~** as if nothing had happened

pimpón [pim·'pon] *m* DEP ping-pong

pinacate [pi·na·'ka·te] *m Méx* ZOOL black stinkbug

pinacoteca [pi·na·ko·'te·ka] *f* art gallery

pináculo [pi·'na·ku·lo] *m* pinnacle

pinar [pi·'nar] *m* pine grove

pincel [pin·'sel, -'θel] *m* (paint)brush; **estar hecho un ~** to be stylishly dressed

pincelada [pin·se·'la·da, pin·θe-] *f* brushstroke; **dar las últimas ~s** *fig* to apply the finishing touches

pinchar [pin·'tʃar] **I.** *vi* (*rueda*) to get a flat (tire) ► **ni ~ ni cortar** *inf* to not count for anything **II.** *vt* **1.** (*alfiler*) to prick **2.** (*estimular*) to prod; (*mortificar*) to wound **3.** (*inyección*) to give an injection; **tengo que ir al médico para que me pinche** I have to go the doctor's for an injection **4.** (*teléfono*) to tap **III.** *vr* **1.** (*alfiler*) to prick oneself **2.** (*rueda*) **se nos ha pinchado una rueda** one of our wheels has a puncture **3.** (*insulina*) to give oneself an injection **4.** *inf* (*drogarse*) to shoot up

pinchazo [pin·'tʃa·so, -'tʃa·θo] *m* **1.** (*espina*) prick; **me dieron unos ~s en el estómago** I had some shooting pains in the stomach **2.** (*neumático*) flat (tire); **tuvimos un ~ tras la curva** we got a flat after the bend

pinche ['pin·tʃe] *mf* cook's helper

pinchito [pin·'tʃi·to] *m* (*tapa*) snack; (*en un palillo*) hors d'oeuvre on a stick

pincho ['pin·tʃo] *m* **1.** (*erizo*) sting; (*rosa*) thorn **2.** *v.* **pinchito**

pinedo [pi·'ne·do] *m AmC* pine grove

pinga ['pin·ga] *f Col, Méx, Perú, vulg* prick *vulg;* **¡de ~!** unreal!

pingajo [pin·'ga·xo] *m inf* rag

pingo ['pin·go] *m* **1.** *inf* (*harapo*) rag **2.** *CSur* (*caballo*) horse ► **ir de ~** to go out on the town; **poner a alguien hecho un ~** to run sb down

pingonear [pin·go·ne·'ar] *vi inf* to loaf around

ping-pong [pin·'pon] *m* ping-pong

pingüe ['pin·gwe] *adj* (*negocio*) lucrative; **~s beneficios** fat profits

pingüino [pin·'gwi·no] *m* penguin

pino ['pi·no] *m* **1.** (*árbol, madera*) pine; **~ piñonero** stone pine **2.** DEP handstand ► **en el quinto ~** in the back of beyond

pinol(e) [pi·'nol, ·'no·le] *m AmC* pinole (*toasted, ground corn meal mixed into chocolate drink*)

pinta ['pin·ta] *f* **1.** *t.* ZOOL (*mancha*) spot; (*gota*) drop; **a ~s** spotted **2.** *inf* (*aspecto*) appearance; **tener ~ de caro** to look expensive; **tener buena ~** (*dish*) to look tasty; (*persona*) to be attractive; **sacar por la ~** to recognize

pintada [pin·'ta·da] *f* (*pared*) (piece of) graffiti

pintado, -a [pin·'ta·do] *adj* (*animal*) spotted; **papel ~** wallpaper; **eso viene como ~** that is just what was needed; **el traje te sienta que ni ~** *inf* the suit really suits you; **no lo puedo ver ni ~** *inf* I can't stand even the sight of him

pintalabios [pin·ta·'la·βjos] *m inv* lipstick

pintar [pin·'tar] **I.** *vi* **1.** ARTE to paint **2.** (*bolígrafo*) to write **II.** *vt* **1.** (*pared*) to paint; (*con dibujos*) to decorate; **~ de azul** to paint blue; **¡recién pintado!** wet paint! **2.** (*cuadro*) to paint; **¿qué pinta eso aquí?** *fig* what's that doing here?; **no ~ nada** *fig* (*persona*) to have no influence; (*asunto*) to be completely irrelevant **3.** (*describir*) to describe **III.** *vr* to do one's make-up

pinto, -a ['pin·to, -a] *adj* spotted

pintor(a) [pin·'tor, ·'to·ra] *m(f)* painter

pintoresco, -a [pin·to·'res·ko, -a] *adj* picturesque, colorful

pintura [pin·'tu·ra] *f* **1.** (*arte, cuadro*) painting; **~ a la aguada** watercolor; **~ al óleo** oil painting; **~ rupestre** cave painting; **voy a clases de ~** I go to painting classes; **no lo puedo ver ni en ~** *inf* I can't stand him **2.** (*color*) paint; **caja de ~s** paint box; **dar una capa de ~ a algo** to give sth a coat of paint

pinturero, -a [pin·tu·'re·ro, -a] *adj* fashion-conscious

pinza(s) ['pin·sa(s), -θa(s)] *f(pl)* **1.** (*tenacilla*) tongs *pl*; TÉC pincers *pl* **2.** (*para la ropa*) clothespin **3.** (*para depilar*) tweezers *pl* **4.** (*costura*) pleat **5.** (*de cangrejo*) claw

pinzón [pin·'son, ·'θon] *m* finch

piña ['pi·ɲa] *f* **1.** (*pino*) pine cone **2.** (*fruta*) pineapple

piñón [pi·'ɲon] *m* **1.** (*pino*) pine nut; **estar a partir un ~ con alguien** *inf* to be thick as thieves **2.** TÉC pinion

pío [pi·o] *m* cheep; **no decir ni ~** not to say a word; **¡~, ~, ~!** tweet, tweet!

pío, -a [pi·o, -a] *adj* pious; **monte ~** benefit fund; **obra pía** charitable deed

piocha ['pjo·tʃa] *adj Méx, inf* (*magnífico*) great

piojo ['pjo·xo] *m* louse; **estar como ~s en costura** *inf* to be packed in like sardines

piojoso, -a [pjo·'xo·so, -a] *adj* louse-infested; (*sucio*) seedy

piola ['pjo·la] **I.** *adj Arg, inf* (*astuto*) clever **II.** *f AmS* (*cuerda*) cord

piolet [pjo·'let] *m* ice axe

piolín [pjo·'lin] *m AmS* twine

pionero, -a [pjo·'ne·ro, -a] *m, f* pioneer

pipa ['pi·pa] *f* **1.** (*fumador*) pipe; **preparar la ~** to fill one's pipe; **fumar en ~** to smoke a pipe **2.** (*tonel*) barrel **3.** (*de fruta*) pip, seed **4.** CRi, inf (*cabeza*) head **5.** inf (*muy bien*) **lo pasamos ~** we had a great time

pipe ['pi·pe] *m AmC* buddy

pipeta [pi·'pe·ta] *f* pipette

pipí [pi·'pi] *m inf* pee *sl*

pipil [pi·'pil] *adj AmC* Mexican

pipiolo, -a [pi·'pjo·lo, -a] *m, f Méx* kid

pipón, -ona [pi·'pon, ·'po·na] **I.** *adj Ant, Arg, Ecua, inf* pot-bellied **II.** *m, f PRico, inf* (*niño*) boy; (*niña*) girl

pique ['pi·ke] *m* **1.** (*rivalidad*) rivalry; **menudo ~ se traen entre ellos** they really hate each other **2.** *Arg, Par, Nic* (*camino*) trail **3.** (*hundirse*) **irse a ~** (*barco*) to sink; (*plan*) to fail

piqueta [pi·'ke·ta] *f* pickax

piquete [pi·'ke·te] *m* (*strike*) picket

pira ['pi·ra] *f* pyre; **~ funeraria** funeral pyre

pirado, -a [pi·'ra·do, -a] **I.** *adj inf* crazy **II.** *m, f inf* nutcase

piragua [pi·'ra·ɣwa] *f* canoe

piragüismo [pi·ra·'ɣwis·mo] *m* canoeing

piramidal [pi·ra·mi·'dal] *adj* pyramidal

pirámide [pi·'ra·mi·de] *f* pyramid

piraña [pi·'ra·ɲa] *f* piranha

pirarse [pi·'rar·se] *vr inf* to clear off; **~ de la**

clase to skip class
pirata [pi·'ra·ta] I. *mf* pirate; ~ **aéreo** hijacker
II. *adj* pirate; **emisora** ~ pirate radio station
pirca ['pir·ka] *f AmC* stone wall
pirco ['pir·ko] *m Chile* CULIN succotash
pirenaico, -a [pi·re·'nai·ko, -a] *adj* Pyrenean;
   pico ~ the highest mountain in the Pyrenees
Pirineos [pi·ri·'neos] *mpl* Pyrenees
piripi [pi·'ri·pi] *adj inf* tipsy
pirómano, -a [pi·'ro·ma·no, -a] *m, f* pyromaniac
piropear [pi·ro·pe·'ar] *vt inf* to make flirtatious
   comments to
piropo [pi·'ro·po] *m inf* flirtatious comment;
   echar ~ **s** to make flirtatious comments
pirotecnia [pi·ro·'teɣ·nja] *f* pyrotechnics
pirrarse [pi·'rrar·se] *vr inf* ~ **se por alguien** to
   be crazy about sb
pirueta [pi·'rwe·ta] *f* pirouette
piruja [pi·'ru·xa] *f Méx, inf* hooker
piruleta [pi·ru·'le·ta] *f*, **pirulí** [pi·ru·'li] *m*
   <pirulís> lollipop
pis [pis] *m inf* piss
pisada [pi·'sa·da] *f* 1. (*acción*) footstep
   2. (*huella*) footprint; **seguir las ~ s de alguien**
   fig to follow in sb's footsteps
pisapapeles [pi·sa·pa·'pe·les] *m inv* paperweight
pisar [pi·'sar] *vt* 1. (*poner el pie*) to tread; ¡**no**
   pises las flores! don't tread on the flowers!;
   me han pisado en el bus sb trod on my foot
   on the bus; **ir pisando huevos** *fig* to tread
   carefully; ~ **los talones a alguien** *fig* to follow
   on sb's heels; ~ **fuerte** *fig* to make a big impact
   2. (*entrar*) to enter 3. (*humillar*) to walk all
   over 4. *inf* (*planes*) to pre-empt; **con su**
   proyecto me pisan el terreno their plan has
   beaten me to it; **me han pisado el tema** they
   have stolen my topic
piscicultura [pi·si·kul·'tu·ra, pis·θi-] *f* fish
   farming
piscina [pi·'si·na, pis·'θi·na] *f* swimming pool;
   ~ **cubierta** indoor swimming pool
Piscis ['pi·sis, 'pis·θis] *m inv* Pisces
pisco ['pis·ko] *m* 1. (*aguardiente*) *strong Peru-*
   vian liquor; ~ **sour** *cocktail made with pisco,*
   lemon and sugar 2. *Col, Ven* (*pavo*) turkey
   3. *Col, pey* (*hombre*) guy
piscolabis [pis·ko·'la·βis] *m inv, inf* snack
piso ['pi·so] *m* 1. (*pavimento*) floor; (*calle*) surface 2. (*planta*) floor, story; **de dos ~ s** with
   two floors 3. (*vivienda*) apartment
pisotear [pi·so·te·'ar] *vt* to trample; *fig* to walk
   all over
pisotón [pi·so·'ton] *m* stamp; **dar un ~ a al-**
   guien to tread on sb's foot
pispear [pis·pe·'ar] *vt Arg* to swipe
pista ['pis·ta] *f* 1. (*huella*) trail; (*indicio*) clue;
   estar sobre la buena ~ to be on the right
   lines; **seguir la ~ a alguien** to follow sb's trail
   2. (*de circo*) ring; (*para atletismo, coches*)
   track; (*de tenis*) court; (*de baile*) floor; ~ **de**
   aterrizaje runway; ~ **de esquí** ski slope; ~ **de**

hielo ice rink 3. (*camino*) trail 4. COMPUT track
pistache [pis·'ta·tʃe] *m* 1. CULIN (*helado*) pistachio ice cream; (*dulce*) pistachio sweet 2. *Méx*
   (*pistacho*) pistachio
pistacho [pis·'ta·tʃo] *m* pistachio
pistero [pis·'te·ro] *m* (*taza*) cup with spout
pistilo [pis·'ti·lo] *m* pistil
pisto ['pis·to] *m* 1. (*caldo*) chicken broth
   2. (*fritada*) vegetable stew (*made with tomato,*
   onion, pepper and zucchini) 3. *AmC* (*dinero*)
   dough ▶ **darse** ~ to show off
pistola [pis·'to·la] *f* 1. (*arma*) pistol 2. (*del pin-*
   tor) spray gun
pistolera [pis·to·'le·ra] *f* (*funda*) holster
pistolero [pis·to·'le·ro, -a] *m* gunman
pistoletazo [pis·to·le·'ta·so, -'ta·θo] *m* pistol
   shot; ~ **de salida** *fig: starting signal*
pistón [pis·'ton] *m* 1. (*émbolo*) piston 2. (*de*
   arma) percussion cap 3. MÚS key
pistonudo, -a [pis·to·'nu·do, -a] *adj inf* great
pita ['pi·ta] *f* BOT agave, century plant
pitada [pi·'ta·da] *f Arg, inf* puff; ¿**me das una**
   ~ ? will you let me have a puff?
pitanza [pi·'tan·sa, -θa] *f* (*ración*) daily ration;
   inf (*alimentos*) grub
pitar [pi·'tar] I. *vi, vt* 1. (*claxon*) to blow; **me**
   pitan los oídos my ears are buzzing 2. *AmS*
   (*fumar*) to smoke 3. *Chile* (*engañar*) to cheat
   II. *vi* 1. *inf* (*deprisa*) **salir pitando** to rush off
   2. *inf* (*ser suficiente*) ¡**con la mitad vas que**
   pitas! half of it should be more than enough!
pitido [pi·'ti·do] *m* whistle
pitillera [pi·ti·'ʎe·ra, -'ʎe·ra] *f* cigarette case
pitillo [pi·'ti·jo, -ʎo] *m* cigarette
pitiminí [pi·ti·mi·'ni] *m* (*persona*) finicky person
pitiyanqui [pi·ti·'jan·ki] *m PRico* Yankee-lover
pito [pi·'to] *m* 1. (*silbato*) whistle; (*claxon*)
   horn; **tocar** ~ **s** to click one's fingers; **entre ~ s**
   y flautas *inf* what with one thing and another;
   por ~ **s o por flautas** *inf* for one reason or another; **tomar a alguien por el** ~ **del sereno**
   inf to take no notice of sb; **no me importa un**
   ~ *inf* I don't give a damn about it/him/her;
   no valer un ~ *inf* to be completely worthless
   2. (*cigarro*) cigarette 3. *inf* (*pene*) dick
pito, -a ['pi·to, -a] *adj inf* smart; **iba todo** ~ he
   looked really smart
pitón [pi·'ton] *m* 1. ZOOL python 2. (*cuerno*)
   budding horn
pitonisa [pi·to·'ni·sa] *f* fortune teller
pitopausia [pi·to·'pau·sja] *f inf* men's midlife
   crisis
pitorrearse [pi·to·rre·'ar·se] *vr inf* to make fun
pitorreo [pi·to·'rreo] *m inf* joking; ¡**esto es un**
   ~ ! this is a joke!
pitorro [pi·'to·rro] *m* spout
pituco, -a [pi·'tu·ko, -a] *adj CSur* 1. (*cursi*) affected, snooty 2. (*nuevo rico*) nouveau riche
pitufo [pi·'tu·fo] *m inf* shrimp
pituita [pi·'twi·ta] *f* mucus
pituitario, -a [pi·twi·'ta·rjo, -a] *adj* pituitary;
   glándula pituitaria pituitary gland

P

pivote [pi·'βo·te] *m* TÉC pivot
píxel ['pik·sel] *m* COMPUT pixel
piyama [pi·'ja·ma] *m AmL* pajamas *pl*
pizarra [pi·'sa·rra, -'θa·rra] *f* **1.** (*roca*) slate **2.** (*encerado*) blackboard
pizarrín [pi·sa·'rrin, pi·θa-] *m* slate pencil
pizarrón [pi·sa·'rron, pi·θa-] *m AmL* blackboard
pizca ['pis·ka, 'piθ-] *f* **1.** *inf* (*poco*) pinch, little bit; **una ~ de sal** a pinch of salt; **no tienes ni ~ de vergüenza** you have no shame whatsoever **2.** *Méx* (*cosecha*) harvest
pizcar <c→qu> [pis·'kar, piθ-] *vt Méx* to pick
pizco ['pis·ko, 'piθ-] *m inf* (*pellizco*) pinch
pizpireta [pis·pi·'re·ta, piθ-] *adj* (*mujer*) vivacious
pizza ['pi·tsa] *f* pizza
placa ['pla·ka] *f* **1.** (*lámina, plancha*) sheet; FOTO plate; COMPUT board; **~ base** COMPUT motherboard; **~ giratoria** FERRO turntable **2.** (*cartel*) plaque; **~ conmemorativa** commemorative plaque **3.** AUTO license plate **4.** MED **~ dental** (dental) plaque
placar [pla·'kar] *m*, **placard** [pla·'kar] *m Arg, Urug* built-in cupboard, built-in closet
placebo [pla·'se·βo, -'θe·βo] *m* MED placebo
pláceme ['pla·se·me, -θe·me] *m* congratulations *pl;* **dar el ~ a alguien** to congratulate sb
placenta [pla·'sen·ta, -'θen·ta] *f* placenta
placentero, -a [pla·sen·'te·ro, -a; pla·θen-] *adj* pleasant
placer [pla·'ser, -'θer] I. *m* pleasure; **con sumo ~** with great pleasure; **casa de ~** brothel II. *irr como crecer vi* to please; **¡haré lo que me plazca!** I will do as I please!
placero, -a [pla·'se·ro, -a; -'θe·ro, -a] *m, f AmL* street trader
plácet ['pla·set, -θet] *m form* approval; **dar el ~ a un embajador** to accept an ambassador's credentials
placidez [pla·si·'des, pla·θi·'deθ] *f* calmness
plácido, -a ['pla·si·do, -a; -θi·do, -a] *adj* calm
plaga ['pla·ya] *f* **1.** AGR plague **2.** (*calamidades*) disaster; (*lacra*) blight **3.** (*abundancia*) glut; **este año hemos tenido una ~ de cerezas** this year we've had a glut of cherries
plagado, -a [pla·'ya·do -a] *adj* infested; **el texto estaba ~ de faltas** the text was full of mistakes; **la casa está plagada de cucarachas** the house is infested with cockroaches
plagar <g→gu> [pla·'yar] I. *vt* to infest; **~ de algo** to fill with sth; **~on la ciudad de carteles** they covered the city with posters II. *vr:* **~se** to become infested; **el pueblo se plagó de ratas** the village became infested with rats
plagiar [pla·'xjar] *vt* **1.** (*copiar*) to plagiarize **2.** *AmL* (*secuestrar*) to kidnap
plagio ['pla·xjo] *m* **1.** (*copia*) plagiarism **2.** *AmL* (*secuestro*) kidnapping
plan [plan] *m* **1.** (*proyecto*) plan; **~ de emergencia** emergency plan; **¿tienes ~ para esta noche?** do you have any plans for tonight **2.** *inf* (*ligue*) date **3.** *inf* (*actitud*) **esto no es ~**

it's just not on; **en ~ de... as...; está en un ~ que no lo soporto** I can't stand him/her when he/she behaves like this
plana ['pla·na] *f* **1.** (*folio*) page; **a toda ~** full-page; **un artículo en primera ~** a front-page article **2.** (*en una organización*) **la ~ mayor del partido** the party leadership
plancha ['plan·tʃa] *f* **1.** (*lámina*) sheet; TIPO plate **2.** (*para ropa*) iron **3.** *inf* (*desacierto*) blunder; **hacer** [*o* **tirarse**] **una ~** to put one's foot in it **4.** CULIN grill; **a la ~** grilled
planchado [plan·'tʃa·do] *m* ironing
planchado, -a [plan·'tʃa·do, -a] *adj* **1.** *AmC* (*acicalado*) neat **2.** (*anonadado*) flattened; **lo dejé ~** *inf* I left him speechless
planchar [plan·'tʃar] *vt* to iron
plancton ['plank·ton] *m* BIO plankton
planeador [pla·nea·'dor] *m* AVIAT glider
planear [pla·ne·'ar] I. *vi* (*ave*) to hover; AVIAT to glide II. *vt* to plan
planeta [pla·'ne·ta] *m* planet
planetario [pla·ne·'ta·rjo] *m* planetarium
planetario, -a [pla·ne·'ta·rjo, -a] *adj* planetary
planicie [pla·'ni·sje, -θje] *f* plain
planificación [pla·ni·fi·ka·'sjon, -'θjon] *f* planning; **~ regional** local planning
planificar <c→qu> [pla·ni·fi·'kar] *vt* to plan
planilla [pla·'ni·ja, -Áa] *f* **1.** (*impreso*) form; **~ de cálculo** COMPUT spreadsheet **2.** *AmL* (*nómina*) payroll
planisferio [pla·nis·'fe·rjo] *m* planisphere
plano ['pla·no] *m* **1.** MAT plane; **~ inclinado** inclined plane **2.** (*mapa*) map; **levantar un ~** to draw a map **3.** CINE **primer ~** close-up; **en primer ~** (*delante*) in the foreground **4.** (*totalmente*) **de ~** directly; (*negar*) flatly; **aceptar algo de ~** to accept sth without hesitation
plano, -a ['pla·no, -a] *adj* flat; **superficie plana** flat surface
planta ['plan·ta] *f* **1.** BOT plant; **~ anual** annual; **~ de interior** houseplant; **~ medicinal** medicinal plant; **~ trepadora** climbing plant **2.** (*pie*) sole **3.** (*fábrica*) plant; **~ de abastecimientos de agua** waterworks; **~ atómica/hidráulica** atomic/hydraulic power station; **~ incineradora** incineration plant; **~ de reciclaje de basuras** recycling plant; **~ siderúrgica** steel plant **4.** (*piso*) floor, story; **~ alta** top floor; **~ baja** ground floor, first floor *Am* **5.** (*aspecto*) **tener buena ~** to be good-looking
plantación [plan·ta·'sjon, -'θjon] *f* plantation
plantado, -a [plan·'ta·do, -a] *adj inf* **bien ~** good-looking
plantar [plan·'tar] I. *vt* **1.** (*bulbo*) to plant; **han plantado el monte** they have planted trees on the hillside **2.** (*clavar*) to stick in; **~ una tienda de campaña** to pitch a tent **3.** *inf* (*golpe*) to land; **~ un tortazo a alguien** to slap sb **4.** *inf* (*cita*) to stand up; **desapareció y me dejó plantado** he/she disappeared and left me standing; **dejó plantada a su novia** he stood his girlfriend up; **lo ~on en la calle** they

chucked him out **5.**(*abandonar*) to abandon **II.** *vr:* ~ **se 1.**(*resistirse*) ~ **se ante algo** to stand firm in the face of sth **2.**(*asno*) to refuse to move **3.**(*aparecer*) to get to; **se ~ on en mi casa en un periquete** they arrived at my house in no time **4.**(*en los naipes*) to stick; **aquí me planto** I'm sticking

planteamiento [plan·tea·'mjen·to] *m* **1.**(*enfoque*) approach **2.** MAT solution

plantear [plan·te·'ar] **I.** *vt* **1.**(*asunto, problema*) to approach; **este problema está mal planteado** this problem has been incorrectly formulated **2.**(*causar*) to cause; (*discusión*) to provoke **3.**(*proponer*) to put forward, to pose **II.** *vr* **1.**(*reflexionar*) to think about **2.**(*cuestión*) to ask oneself; **ahora me planteo si...** now I ask myself whether...

plantel [plan·'tel] *m Arg* (*plantilla*) staff

planteo [plan·'teo] *m Arg* demand

plantilla [plan·'ti·ja, -ʎa] *f* **1.**(*empleados*) staff; ~ **de profesores** teaching staff **2.**(*de zapato*) insole **3.**(*zapatero*) sole **4.**(*patrón*) pattern **5.**(*equipo*) squad

plantón [plan·'ton] *m inf* long wait; **dar un ~ a alguien** to stand sb up; **y ahora estoy de ~** I've been left waiting around

plañir <3. *pret:* plañó> [pla·'ɲir] *vi* to wail

plaqué [pla·'ke] *m* (*de oro*) gold-plating; (*de plata*) silver-plating

plaqueta [pla·'ke·ta] *f* MED platelet

plasma ['plas·ma] *m* plasma

plasmar [plas·'mar] *vt* **1.**(*moldear*) to mold **2.**(*representar*) to represent

plasta¹ ['plas·ta] *mf pey* bore, drag

plasta² ['plas·ta] *f* **1.**(*mal hecha*) botch **2.**(*blanda*) soft mass

plástica ['plas·ti·ka] *f* plastic arts *pl*; (*escultura*) sculpture

plasticidad [plas·ti·si·'dad, plas·ti·θi-] *f* plasticity; *fig* expressiveness

plástico ['plas·ti·ko] *m* plastic; (*para envolver*) plastic wrap

plástico, -a ['plas·ti·ko, -a] *adj* **1.**(*materia*) plastic **2.**(*expresivo*) expressive; **las artes plásticas** the plastic arts

plastificar <c→qu> [plas·ti·fi·'kar] *vt* to laminate

plastilina® [plas·ti·'li·na] *f* modeling clay

plata ['pla·ta] *f* **1.**(*metal*) silver; ~ **labrada** silverwork; ~ **de ley** sterling silver; **bodas de ~** silver wedding anniversary **2.**(*moneda*) silver coins *pl* **3.** *AmL* (*dinero*) money; **¡adiós mi ~!** *CSur, inf* what a disaster! ▸ **hablar en ~** to talk bluntly

plataforma [pla·ta·'for·ma] *f t.* POL platform; ~ **giratoria** turntable; ~ **petrolífera** oil rig; ~ **de lanzamiento** launch pad; ~ **continental** GEO continental shelf

platal [pla·'tal] *m AmL* fortune

plátano ['pla·ta·no] *m* (*árbol*) banana tree; (*fruta*) banana; ~ **guineo** plantain

platea [pla·'tea] *f* TEAT orchestra (section)

plateado, -a [pla·te·'a·do] *adj* silver-plated;

(*color*) silver

platear [pla·te·'ar] *vt* to silver-plate

platense [pla·'ten·se] *adj* **1.**(*de La Plata*) of/from La Plata **2.**(*de Río de La Plata*) native/inhabitant of the River Plate region

platería [pla·te·'ri·a] *f* (*tienda*) jeweler's; (*vajilla*) silverware

platero, -a [pla·'te·ro] *m, f* silversmith

plática ['pla·ti·ka] *f* chat; **estar de ~** to be chatting

platicar <c→qu> [pla·ti·'kar] *vi inf* to chat

platija [pla·'ti·xa] *f* flounder

platillo [pla·'ti·jo, -ʎo] *m* **1.**(*de taza*) saucer **2.**(*de balanza*) pan **3.** MÚS cymbal

platino [pla·'ti·no] *m* QUÍM platinum

plato ['pla·to] *m* **1.**(*vajilla*) plate; (*para taza*) saucer; **tiro al** ~ DEP clay pigeon shooting; **pagar los ~s rotos** *fig* to pay the consequences; **comer en un mismo ~** *fig* to be bosom pals **2.**(*comida*) dish; ~ **combinado** *dish usually consisting of meat or fish and vegetables*; ~ **fuerte** main dish; *fig* main part; **hoy hay ~ único** today there is only one dish **3.**(*de balanza*) pan

plató [pla·'to] *m* CINE (film) set

platón [pla·'ton] *m AmL* serving dish

platónico, -a [pla·'to·ni·ko, -a] *adj* platonic

platudo, -a [pla·'tu·do, -a] *adj AmL* well-heeled

plausible [plau·'si·βle] *adj* (*admisible*) acceptable

playa ['pla·ja] *f* **1.**(*mar*) beach; ~ **naturista** nudist beach **2.** *AmL* (*espacio*) open space; ~ **de estacionamiento** parking lot

play-back ['plei·βak] *m* <play-backs> play-back; **cantar en ~** to mime a song

play-boy [plei·'βoi] *m* <play-boys> playboy

playera [pla·'je·ra] *f Guat, Méx* T-shirt

playeras [pla·'je·ras] *fpl* gym shoes *pl*

playo, -a ['pla·jo, -a] *adj CSur* shallow; **plato ~** dinner plate

plaza ['pla·sa, -θa] *f* **1.**(*espacio*) square; (*de mercado*) marketplace; (*de toros*) bullring; ~ **de abastos** (central) food market; **fuimos a la ~ a comprar** we went to the market to do the shopping **2.**(*asiento*) seat; (*de garage*) space **3.**(*empleo*) position **4.**(*en instituciones, viajes*) place

plazo ['pla·so, -θo] *m* **1.**(*vencimiento*) period; ~ **de entrega** delivery date; ~ **de preaviso** notice period; **a corto/largo ~** in the short/long term; **fuera del ~** after the closing date; **en el ~ de un mes** within a month; **depósito a ~ fijo** fixed-term deposit; **el ~ vence el día...** the deadline is on... **2.**(*cantidad*) installment; **a ~s** in installments

plazoleta [pla·so·'le·ta, pla·θo-] *f diminutivo de* **plaza**

pleamar [plea·'mar] *f* high tide

plebe ['ple·βe] *f pey* (*chusma*) rabble

plebeyo, -a [ple·'βe·jo, -a] **I.** *adj* **1.** *t.* HIST plebeian **2.**(*sin linaje*) common **3.**(*inculto*) uneducated; (*grosero*) uncouth **II.** *m, f* **1.** *t.* HIST

P

plebeian 2. (*sin linaje*) commoner **3.** (*grosero*) lout

plebiscito [ple·βi·'si·to, -'θi·to] *m* plebiscite

plegable [ple·'ya·βle] *adj* (*papel*) foldable; (*mueble*) folding; **silla** ~ folding chair

plegar [ple·'yar] *irr como fregar* **I.** *vt* (*doblar*) to fold; (*muebles*) to fold away **II.** *vr:* ~**se** to yield

plegaria [ple·'ya·rja] *f* prayer

pleitear [plei·te·'ar] *vi* JUR to bring a lawsuit, to sue

pleito ['plei·to] *m* **1.** JUR lawsuit **2.** (*disputa*) dispute

plenario, -a [ple·'na·rjo] *adj* plenary; **sesión plenaria** plenary session

plenipotenciario, -a [ple·ni·po·ten·'sja·rjo, -a; -'θja·rjo, -a] *adj, m, f* plenipotentiary

plenitud [ple·ni·'tud] *f* **1.** (*totalidad*) fullness; **sensación de** ~ sensation of fullness **2.** (*apogeo*) height; ~ **vital** full vigor

pleno ['ple·no] *m* plenary session; **aprobar algo en** ~ to approve sth in a full session

pleno, -a ['ple·no, -a] *adj* full; ~ **empleo** full employment; **en** ~ **uso de sus facultades mentales** in full command of his/her faculties; **a plena luz del día** in broad daylight; **en** ~ **verano** at the height of summer

pletórico, -a [ple·'to·ri·ko, -a] *adj* full; ~ **de salud** bursting with health

pleura ['pleu·ra] *f* pleura

pleuresía [pleu·re·'si·a] *f* MED pleurisy

plexiglás® [plek·si·'ylas] *m* Plexiglas®

plica ['pli·ka] *f* sealed envelope

pliego ['plje·yo] *m* **1.** (*hoja*) sheet **2.** (*documento*) document; ~ **de cargos** list of charges; ~ **de condiciones** specifications *pl*

pliegue ['plje·ye] *m t.* GEO fold

plinto ['plin·to] *m* ARQUIT plinth

plisar [pli·'sar] *vt* to pleat

plomada [plo·'ma·da] *f* plumb line; **echar la** ~ to drop the plumb line

plomazo [plo·'ma·so, -θo] *m inf* (*pesado*) drag

plomería [plo·me·'ri·a] *f Arg* plumber's

plomero [plo·'me·ro] *m Arg* plumber

plomizo, -a [plo·'mi·so, -a; -θo, -a] *adj* leaden

plomo ['plo·mo] *m* **1.** (*metal*) lead; **gasolina sin** ~ unleaded gas; **caer a** ~ to fall heavily **2.** *inf* (*pesado*) **ser un** ~ to be a real drag **3.** *pl* ELEC fuse

pluma ['plu·ma] *f* **1.** (*ave*) feather; **cambiar la** ~ to molt **2.** (*escribir*) pen; ~ **estilográfica** fountain pen ▶ **vestirse de** ~**s ajenas** to dress in borrowed finery; **quedarse cacareando y sin** ~**s** to remain defiant in defeat

plumada [plu·'ma·da] *f* stroke of the pen

plumaje [plu·'ma·xe] *m* (*ave*) plumage

plumario, -a [plu·'ma·rjo, -a] *m, f AmC, Méx, pey* (*periodista*) hack

plumazo [plu·'ma·so, -θo] *m* stroke of the pen; **suprimieron de un** ~ **las subvenciones** they abolished the subsidies at a stroke

plúmbeo, -a ['plum·beo, -a] *adj* heavy; *fig* tedious

plumear [plu·me·'ar] *vt AmC* to write

plumero [plu·'me·ro] *m* **1.** (*para limpiar*) feather duster **2.** (*estuche*) pencil case; (*caja*) pencil box **3.** (*adorno*) plume ▶ **vérsele el** ~ **a alguien** to be obvious what sb is up to

plumier [plu·'mjer] *m* (*estuche*) pencil case; (*caja*) pencil box

plumilla [plu·'mi·ja, -ʎa] *f* nib

plumón [plu·'mon] *m* **1.** (*ave*) down **2.** (*cama*) feather bed

plural [plu·'ral] **I.** *adj* plural; **número** ~ plural **II.** *m* plural; ~ **mayestático** royal 'we'

pluralidad [plu·ra·li·'dad] *f* plurality; **a** ~ **de votos** by majority vote

pluralizar <z→c> [plu·ra·li·'sar, -'θar] *vt* (*generalizar*) to generalize; **cuenta lo tuyo y no pluralices** tell your side and don't speak for the rest of us

pluriempleo [plu·ri·em·'pleo] *m situation where various positions are filled by the same person*

plurifamiliar [plu·ri·fa·mi·'ljar] *adj* for several families

pluripartidismo [plu·ri·par·ti·'dis·mo] *m* multi-party system

plus [plus] *m* **1.** (*gratificación*) bonus; **de** ~ extra; ~ **de peligrosidad** high-risk allowance; ~ **de festivos** overtime for holidays **2.** (*ventaja*) advantage

pluscuamperfecto [plus·kwam·per·'fek·to] *m* LING pluperfect

plusmarquista [plus·mar·'kis·ta] *mf* record holder; **el** ~ **mundial de maratón** the world record holder for marathon

plusvalía [plus·βa·'li·a] *f* ECON appreciation

plutonio [plu·'to·njo] *m* plutonium

pluvial [plu·'βjal] *adj* rain

pluviosidad [plu·βjo·si·'dad] *f* rainfall

p.m. [pe·'e·me] *abr de* **post meridiem** pm

P.M. [pe·'e·me] *f abr de* **policía militar** MP

PN ['pe·so 'ne·to] *m abr de* **peso neto** net weight

PNB [pe·ne·'be, pe·en·e-] *m abr de* **producto nacional bruto** GNP

PNN [pe·'ne·ne] *m abr de* **producto nacional neto** NNP

PNV [pe·ne·'u·βe] *m abr de* **Partido Nacionalista Vasco** *Basque Nationalist Party*

p.o. [por 'or·den] *abr de* **por orden** by order

población [po·βla·'sjon, -'θjon] *f* **1.** *t.* BIO (*habitantes*) population; ~ **activa** ECON working population **2.** (*localidad: ciudad*) city; (*ciudad pequeña*) town; (*pueblo*) village

poblado [po·'βla·do] *m* (*pueblo*) village; (*colonia*) settlement

poblado, -a [po·'βla·do, -a] *adj* **1.** (*habitado*) inhabited **2.** (*cejas*) bushy

poblador(a [po·βla·'dor, -'do·ra] *m(f)* (*habitante*) inhabitant; (*colono*) settler

poblar <o→ue> [po·'βlar] **I.** *vi, vt* **1.** (*colonizar*) to colonize **2.** (*de plantas*) to plant; (*de peces*) to stock; ~ **el monte de pinos** to plant the hillside with pines **3.** (*habitar*) to inhabit;

distintas especies pueblan el fondo del mar various species inhabit the sea bed **II.** *vr:* ~**se** to fill; **la costa se pobló rápidamente** the coast quickly filled with people

pobre ['po·βre] **I.** *adj* **1.**(*no rico*) poor; ~ **de algo** poor in sth **2.**(*desgraciado*) unfortunate **3.**(*humilde*) humble **4.**(*exclamaciones*) **¡~ de ti si dices mentiras!** you'll be sorry if you lie! **II.** *mf* poor person; **los pobres** the poor *pl*

pobremente [po·βre·'men·te] *adv* poorly

pobreza [po·'βre·sa, -θa] *f* **1.**(*necesidad*) poverty **2.**(*pusilanimidad*) cowardliness

pochismo [po·'tʃis·mo] *m Méx* **1.**(*anglo-americanismo*) *Anglicism introduced into Spanish* **2.** *inf* (*característica de los pochos*) *characteristic of Americanized Mexicans*

pocho, -a ['po·tʃo, -a] **I.** *m*, *f Méx, pey* Americanized Mexican **II.** *adj* **1.**(*fruta*) overripe **2.**(*persona*) off-color

pochoclo [po·'tʃo·klo] *m Arg* popcorn

pocilga [po·'sil·ɣa, po·'θil-] *f t. fig* pigsty

pócima ['po·si·ma, -θi·ma] *f*, **poción** [po·'sjon, -'θjon] *f* potion; *pey*(*brebaje*) brew; **la ~ mágica** the magic potion

poco ['po·ko] **I.** *m* **1.**(*cantidad*) **un ~ de azúcar** a little sugar; **espera un ~** wait a little **2.** *pl* few; ~**s de los presentes lo sabían** few of those present knew it; **los ~s que vinieron...** the few who came...; **es un envidioso como hay ~s** there are few people who are as jealous as him **II.** *adv* little; **escribir ~** to write little; **es ~ simpático** he is not very friendly; ~ **a ~** bit by bit, little by little; ~ **a ~ dejamos de creerle** we gradually stopped believing him; **a ~ de llegar...** shortly after arriving...; ~ **después** shortly afterwards; **dentro de ~** soon; **desde hace ~** since recently; **hace ~** recently, not long ago; **a/con/por ~ que se esfuerce lo conseguirá** with a little bit of effort he/she will get it; **por ~ me estrello** I very nearly crashed; **tener en ~ a alguien** to have a low opinion of sb; **y por si fuera ~...** and as if that wasn't enough...

poco, -a <poquísimo> ['po·ko, -a] *adj* little; ~**s** few; **queda poca comida** there's not much food left; **hay pocas colecciones mejores que ésta** there are few collections better than this one; **tiene pocas probabilidades de aprobar** he/she has little chance of passing

podadera [po·da·'de·ra] *f* pruning shears *pl*

podar [po·'dar] *vt* to prune

podenco [po·'den·ko] *m breed of Spanish hunting dog*

poder [po·'der] **I.** *irr vi* to be able to; **puedo** I can; **puedes** you can; **no ~ más de hambre** to be starving; **yo a ti te puedo** *inf* I'm stronger than you; **no ~ con el alma** to be completely exhausted; **no puedes cogerlo sin permiso** you can't take it without permission; **no podemos abandonarlo** we can't abandon him; **¡bien pod(r)ías habérmelo dicho!** you could have told me!; **bien puede**

haber aquí un millón de abejas there could easily be a million bees here; **no puedo verlo todo el día sin hacer nada** I can't stand seeing him do nothing all day long; **no puedo con mi madre** I can't cope with my mother; **la sala se llenó a más no ~** the room filled to bursting point; **de ~ ser, no dudes que lo hará** if it is at all possible, have no doubt that he/she will do it; **no pude menos que preguntar** I couldn't help but asking; **lo menos que puedes hacer es llamar** the least you can do is call; **no puede ser** it is impossible; **a ~ ser** if possible **II.** *irr vimpers* **puede ser** maybe; **¡puede!** maybe!; **¿se puede?** may I (come in)? **III.** *m* **1.** *t.* POL (*autoridad*) power; ~ **absoluto** absolute power; ~ **ejecutivo** executive power; ~ **judicial** judicial power; ~ **legislativo** legislative power; **los ~es fácticos** the powers that be; **los ~es públicos** the public authorities; **la división de ~es** the separation of powers; **el partido en el ~** the party in power; **subir al ~** to achieve power; **los documentos están en ~ del juez** the documents are in the hands of the judge; **haré todo lo que está en mi ~** I will do everything in my power **2.**(*autorización*) authority; ~ **notarial** power of attorney; **por ~es** by proxy; ~ **de decisión** decision-making power **3.**(*fuerza*) strength; ~ **adquisitivo** ECON buying [*o* purchasing] power

poderío [po·de·'ri·o] *m* **1.**(*autoridad*) power **2.**(*riqueza*) wealth **3.**(*fuerza*) strength

poderoso, -a [po·de·'ro·so, -a] *adj* **1.**(*influyente*) powerful **2.**(*rico*) wealthy **3.**(*eficaz*) effective

podio ['po·djo] *m* podium

podólogo, -a [po·'do·lo·ɣo, -a] *m*, *f* podiatrist, chiropodist

podredumbre [po·dre·'dum·bre] *f* (*putrefacción*) decay

podrido, -a [po·'dri·do, -a] *adj* **1.**(*descompuesto*) *t. fig* rotten; **estar ~ de dinero** *inf*, **estar ~ en plata** *Arg*, *inf* to be filthy rich **2.** *Arg*, *inf*(*aburrido*) fed up

podrir [po·'drir] *irr vt, vr v.* **pudrir**

poema [po·'e·ma] *m* poem; ~ **épico** epic poem; ~ **en prosa** prose poem; **¡fue todo un ~!** it was really funny!; **estar hecho un ~** to be a real sight

poesía [poe·'si·a] *f* **1.**(*género*) poetry **2.**(*poema*) poem; **libro de ~(s)** poetry book

poeta, -isa [po·'e·ta, poe·'ti·sa] *m*, *f* poet *m(f)*, poetess *f*

poética [po·'e·ti·ka] *f* poetics

poético, -a [po·'e·ti·ko, -a] *adj t. fig* poetic; **arte poética** poetics

poetisa [poe·'ti·sa] *f v.* **poeta**

póker ['po·ker] *m* poker; **poner cara de ~** to look poker-faced

polaco, -a [po·'la·ko, -a] *adj* Polish

polaina [po·'lai·na] *f* gaiter

polar [po·'lar] *adj* polar; **Círculo Polar Ártico/Antártico** Arctic/Antarctic Circle; **la**

P

estrella ~ Polaris, Pole Star
polaridad [po·la·ri·'dad] *f* polarity
polarización [po·la·ri·sa·'sjon, -θa·θjon] *f* polarization
polarizar <z→c> [po·la·ri·'sar, -'θar] *vt t.* Fís to polarize; (*atención*) to focus
polca ['pol·ka] *f* MÚS polka
polea [po·'lea] *f* pulley; **sistema de ~s** pulley system
polémica [po·'le·mi·ka] *f* controversy, polemic
polémico, -a [po·'le·mi·ko, -a] *adj* polemical
polemizar <z→c> [po·le·mi·'sar, -'θar] *vi* to argue; **~ con alguien** to have an argument with sb
polen ['po·len] *m* pollen; **alergia al ~** hay fever
polera [po·'le·ra] *f* **1.** *Chile* (*camiseta*) t-shirt **2.** *Arg* (*de cuello alto*) turtleneck
poli ['po·li] *f inf abr de* **policía** cops *pl*
poliamida [po·lja·'mi·da] *f* polyamide
policía¹ [po·li·'si·a, -'θi·a] *f* police; **agente de ~** police officer; **coche de ~** police car; **comisaría de ~** police station; **jefatura de ~** police headquarters
policía² [po·li·'si·a, -'θi·a] *mf* policeman *m*, policewoman *f*; **perro ~** police dog
policiaco, -a [po·li·'sja·ko, -a; -'θja·ko, -a] *adj*, **policíaco, -a** [po·li·'si·a·ko, -a] *adj* police; **estado ~** police state; **película/novela policíaca** detective film/novel
policial [po·li·'sjal, -'θjal] *adj v.* **policíaco**
policlínica [po·li·'kli·ni·ka] *f*, **policlínico** [po·li·'kli·ni·ko] *m* hospital
polideportivo [po·li·de·por·'ti·βo] *m* sports center
poliéster [po·'ljes·ter] *m* polyester
polietileno [po·lje·ti·'le·no] *m* polyethylene
polifacético, -a [po·li·fa·'se·ti·ko, -a; po·li·fa·'θe·] *adj* multi-faceted; (*persona*) many-sided
poligamia [po·li·'ya·mja] *f* polygamy
polígamo, -a [po·'li·ya·mo, -a] *adj* polygamous
políglota [po·'li·ylo·ta] *adj* polyglot
poligonal [po·li·yo·'nal] *adj* polygonal
polígono [po·'li·yo·no] *m* **1.** MAT polygon **2.** (*terreno*) site; **~ industrial** industrial estate [*o* park]
polilla [po·'li·ja, -ʎa] *f* moth; **no tener ~ en la lengua** *inf* not to mince one's words
polimorfo, -a [po·li·'mor·fo, -a] *adj* polymorphous
polinesio, -a [po·li·'ne·sjo, -a] *adj, m, f* Polynesian
polinización [po·li·ni·sa·'sjon, -θa·θjon] *f* pollination
polio ['po·ljo] *f inv* MED polio, poliomyelitis
pólipo ['po·li·po] *m* MED polyp
polisemia [po·li·'se·mja] *f* LING polysemy
polisílabo, -a [po·li·'si·la·βo] *adj* LING polysyllabic
politécnica [po·li·'tek·ni·ka] *f* polytechnic, technical school
politécnico, -a [po·li·'tek·ni·ko, -a] *adj* poly-

technic
política [po·'li·ti·ka] *f* politics; **Política Agraria Común** Common Agricultural Policy; **~ interior/exterior** domestic/foreign policy; **~ monetaria** monetary policy; **~ pesquera** fishing policy
político, -a [po·'li·ti·ko, -a] **I.** *adj* **1.** POL political; **ciencias políticas** political science; **economía política** political economy **2.** (*parentesco*) in-law; **hermano ~** brother-in-law; **hermana política** sister-in-law **II.** *m, f* politician
politizar <z→c> [po·li·ti·'sar, -'θar] *vt, vr* to become politicized
politólogo, -a [po·li·'to·lo·yo, -a] *m, f* political scientist
póliza ['po·li·sa, -θa] *f* policy; **~ de seguros** insurance policy
polizón [po·li·'son, -'θon] *mf* stowaway
polizonte [po·li·'son·te, -'θon·te] *m pey* cop
polla ['po·ja, -ʎa] *f* **1.** *inf* (*chica*) chick **2.** *vulg* (*pene*) dick; **¡y una ~!** like hell! **3.** *AmL* (*carrera*) horse race
pollera [po·'je·ra, -'ʎe·ra] *f Arg* (*falda*) skirt
pollería [po·je·'ri·a, po·ʎe-] *f* poultry shop
pollerudo [po·je·'ru·do, po·ʎe-] **I.** *adj CSur* (*blando*) weak; **niño ~** sissy; **hombre ~** wimp **II.** *m CSur, pey* (*clérigo*) priest
pollina [po·'ji·na, -'ʎi·na] *f PRico, Ven* (*del pelo*) bangs *pl*
pollino, -a [po·'ji·no, -a; -'ʎi·no, -a] *m, f* **1.** (*borrico*) (young) donkey **2.** *fig* (*tonto*) fool
pollito, -a [po·'ji·to, -a; -'ʎi·to, -a] *m, f* (*ave*) chick; *fig* (*niño*) kid
pollo ['po·jo, -ʎo] *m* **1.** CULIN chicken; **~ asado** roast chicken; **voló el ~** *fig* the chance has gone **2.** *inf* (*mozo*) boy; **¿quién es ese ~?** who's that guy?
polluelo [po·'jwe·lo , -'ʎwe·lo] *m* chick
polo ['po·lo] *m* **1.** GEO, Fís, ASTR pole; **~ norte/ártico/boreal** North Pole; **~ sur/antártico/austral** South Pole; **~ industrial** development region **2.** DEP polo **3.** (*camiseta*) polo neck **4.** (*helado*) popsicle
pololear [po·lo·le·'ar] *vi AmS* to flirt
pololo, -a [po·'lo·lo] *m, f And* (*novio*) boyfriend *m*; (*novia*) girlfriend *f*
polonesa [po·lo·'ne·sa] *f* MÚS polonaise
Polonia [po·'lo·nja] *f* Poland
poltrón, -ona [pol·'tron, -'tro·na] *adj* lazy
poltrona [pol·'tro·na] *f* easy chair, recliner
polución [po·lu·'sjon, -'θjon] *f* pollution; **~ ambiental** environmental pollution
polvareda [pol·βa·'re·da] *f* dust cloud; **levantar una ~** *fig* to cause an uproar
polvera [pol·'βe·ra] *f* powder compact
polvo ['pol·βo] *m* **1.** (*suciedad*) dust; **quitar el ~** to dust; **hacer ~** (*algo*) to smash; (*a alguien*) to annihilate; **estoy hecho ~** *inf* I'm exhausted; **hacer morder el ~ a alguien** to humiliate sb; **sacudir a alguien el ~** *fig* to give sb a beating **2.** (*sustancia*) powder; **levadura en ~** powdered yeast **3.** *vulg* (*coito*) screw; **echar**

un ~ to screw **4.** *pl* (*cosmética*) powder
pólvora ['pol·βo·ra] *f* gunpowder; **no haber inventado la ~** *inf* to be a bit dim
polvoriento, -a [pol·βo·'rjen·to, -a] *adj* dusty
polvorín [pol·βo·'rin] *m* powder magazine; **estamos sentados sobre un ~** *fig* we're sitting on a powder keg
polvorón [pol·βo·'ron] *m crumbly shortbread, eaten at Christmas*
polvoso, -a [pol·'βo·so, -a] *adj AmL* dusty
pomada [po·'ma·da] *f* ointment; **~ contra mosquitos** mosquito repellent
pomelo [po·'me·lo] *m* grapefruit
pómez ['po·mes, -meθ] *f* pumice
pompa ['pom·pa] *f* (*esplendor*) pomp; (*ostentación*) display; **~s fúnebres** (*ceremonia*) funeral ceremony; (*funeraria*) funeral parlor
pompis ['pom·pis] *m inv, inf* bottom, tush(y) *sl*
pompo, -a ['pom·po, -a] *adj Col, Ecua* (*sin filo*) blunt
pomposidad [pom·po·si·'dad] *f* pomposity
pomposo, -a [pom·'po·so, -a] *adj* magnificent; (*estilo*) pompous
pómulo ['po·mu·lo] *m* cheekbone
ponchada [pon·'tʃa·da] *f CSur, inf* stack; **una ~ de** a load of
ponche ['pon·tʃe] *m* punch
poncho ['pon·tʃo] *m* poncho
poncho, -a ['pon·tʃo, -a] *adj AmL* lazy
ponderación [pon·de·ra·'sjon, -'θjon] *f* **1.** (*elogio*) eulogy **2.** (*el sopesar*) deliberation; **con ~** carefully
ponderar [pon·de·'rar] *vt* **1.** (*sopesar*) to weigh up **2.** (*encomiar*) to praise
ponencia [po·'nen·sja, -θja] *f* (*conferencia*) paper; (*informe*) report
ponente [po·'nen·te] *mf* (*en conferencia*) speaker; (*informador*) reporter; **~ alternativo** UE opposition spokesperson, shadow rapporteur
poner [po·'ner] *irr* **I.** *vt* **1.** (*colocar*) to put; (*horizontalmente*) to lie; (*inyección*) to give; (*sellos, etiqueta*) to stick on; (*tirita*) to put on; (*huevos*) to lay; **pon la ropa en el tendedero** hang the clothes on the line; **¿dónde habré puesto...?** where can I have put...?; **lo pongo en tus manos** *fig* I leave it in your hands **2.** (*disponer*) to place; (*la mesa*) to lay, to set; **~ algo a disposición de alguien** to make sth available to sb **3.** (*encender*) to switch on; **pon el despertador para las cuatro** set the alarm for four o'clock; **~ en marcha** to start **4.** (*convertir*) to make; **~ de mal humor a alguien** to put sb in a bad mood; **~ colorado a alguien** to make sb blush; **el sol te pondrá moreno** the sun will give you a tan **5.** (*suponer*) to assume; **pon que no viene** let's assume he/she doesn't come; **pongamos el/por caso que no llegue a tiempo** let's consider what happens if he/she doesn't arrive on time **6.** (*exponer*) **~ la ropa a secar al sol** to put the clothes out to dry in the sun; **~ la leche al fuego** to put the milk on the stove; **~ en peligro** to endanger **7.** (*contribuir*) to put in;

(*juego*) to bet; **pusimos todo de nuestra parte** we did all that we could **8.** (*una expresión*) to take on; **~ mala cara** to look angry **9.** (*tratar*) to treat; **~ de idiota** *pey* to treat sb like a fool **10.** (*denominar*) to give; **le pusieron por** [*o de*] **nombre Manolo** they called him Manolo; **¿qué nombre le van a ~?** what are they going to call him/her? **11.** (*espectáculo*) to put on; **~ en escena** to stage; **¿qué ponen hoy en el cine?** what's on at the cinema today? **12.** (*imponer*) to impose; **nos han puesto muchos deberes** they have given us a lot of homework; **~ una multa** to impose a fine; **~ condiciones** to impose conditions **13.** (*instalar*) to install **14.** (*a trabajar*) **tendré que ~te a trabajar** I will have to put you to work; **puse a mi hijo de aprendiz de panadero** I found my son a position as an apprentice baker **15.** (*añadir*) to add **16.** (*escribir*) to write; (*un telegrama*) to send; **~ entre comillas** to put in inverted commas; **~ la firma** to sign; **~ un anuncio** to place an advertisement; **~ por escrito** to put in writing; **te pongo cuatro letras para decirte que...** this is just a short note to tell you that... **17.** (*estar escrito*) to say **18.** (*vestido, zapato*) to put on; **le pusieron el collar** they put its collar on **19.** (*teléfono*) to put through; **me puse al habla con mi amigo** I got through to my friend **II.** *vr:* **~ se 1.** (*vestido, zapato*) to put on; **ponte guapo** make yourself look nice; **~ se de invierno** to dress warmly; **~ se de luto** to wear mourning clothes; **~ se de largo** to dress up **2.** ASTR to set; **el sol se pone por el oeste** the sun sets in the west **3.** (*comenzar*) to begin; **se puso a llover** it started to rain **4.** (*con adjetivo o adverbio*) to become; **ponte cómodo** make yourself comfortable
póney ['po·ni] *m* pony
pongo ['pon·go] *1. pres de* **poner**
poni ['po·ni] *m* pony
poniente [po·'njen·te] *m* **1.** (*oeste*) west **2.** (*viento*) west wind
ponzoña [pon·'so·ɲa, -'θo·ɲa] *f* poison
ponzoñoso, -a [pon·so·'ɲo·so, -a; pon·θo-] *adj* poisonous; *fig* harmful
pop [pop] **I.** *adj inv* pop **II.** *m inv* pop (music)
popa ['po·pa] *f* (*barco*) stern; **viento en ~** following wind; **a ~** astern
popero, -a [po·'pe·ro] *m, f inf* pop music fan
popó [po·'po] *m infantil* poop
popocho, -a [po·'po·tʃo, -a] *adj Col* **1.** (*repleto*) stuffed **2.** (*rico*) loaded *inf* **3.** (*gordo*) pudgy *inf*
popoff [po·'pof] *adj inv, Méx, inf* posh
popote [po·'po·te] *m Méx* (*paja*) straw
populacho [po·pu·'la·tʃo] *m* masses *pl*
popular [po·pu·'lar] *adj* **1.** (*del pueblo*) folk; **aire ~** folk song **2.** (*conocido*) well-known; (*admirado*) popular
popularidad [po·pu·la·ri·'dad] *f* popularity
popularizar <z→c> [po·pu·la·ri·'sar, -'θar] **I.** *vt* to popularize; (*extender*) to spread **II.** *vr:*

P

~se to become popular
populoso, -a [po·pu·'lo·so, -a] *adj* populous
popurrí [po·pu·'rri] *m* potpourri
póquer ['po·ker] *m* poker
poquito [po·'ki·to] *adv* a little; **bébelo ~ a poco** drink it a little bit at a time
por [por] *prep* **1.** (*lugar: a través de*) through; (*vía*) via; (*en*) in; **~ aquí** near here; **limpia la botella ~ dentro/fuera** clean the inside/outside of the bottle; **pasé ~ Madrid** I passed through Madrid; **adelantar ~ la izquierda** to overtake on the left; **volar ~ encima de los Alpes** to fly over the Alps; **ese pueblo está ~ Castilla** that town is in Castile; **la cogió ~ la cintura** he grasped her waist **2.** (*tiempo*) in; **~ la(s) mañana(s)** in the morning; **mañana ~ la mañana** tomorrow morning; **~ la tarde** in the evening; **ayer ~ la noche** last night; **~ noviembre** in November; **~ fin** finally **3.** (*a cambio de*) for; (*en lugar de*) instead of; (*sustituyendo a alguien*) in place of; **cambié el libro ~ el álbum** I exchanged the book for the album **4.** (*agente*) by; **una novela ~ Dickens** a novel by Dickens **5.** MAT (*multiplicación*) by **6.** (*reparto*) per; **toca a cuatro ~ cabeza** it comes out at four each; **el ocho ~ ciento** eight per cent **7.** (*finalidad*) for **8.** (*causa*) because of; (*en cuanto a*) regarding; **lo hago ~ ti** I'm doing it for you; **~ desesperación** out of desperation; **~ consiguiente** consequently; **~ eso, ~ (lo) tanto** therefore, because of that; **~ lo que a eso se refiere** as far as that is concerned; **~ mí que se vayan** as far as I'm concerned, they can go **9.** (*preferencia*) in favor; **estoy ~ comprarlo** I think I should buy it; **estar loco ~ alguien** to be crazy about sb **10.** (*dirección*) **voy (a) ~ tabaco** I'm going to get some cigarettes **11.** (*pendiente*) **este pantalón está ~ lavar** these pants need to be washed **12.** (*aunque*) however; **~ muy cansado que esté lo haré** however tired I am, I'll get it done **13.** (*medio*) by means of; (*alguien*) through; **poner ~ escrito** to put in writing; **al ~ mayor** wholesale **14.** (*interrogativo*) **¿~ (qué)?** why? **15.** **~ si acaso** just in case **16.** (*casi*) **~ poco** almost; **por ~ me ahogo** I nearly drowned
porcelana [por·se·'la·na, por·θe-] *f* porcelain
porcentaje [por·sen·'ta·xe, por·θen-] *m* percentage; **~ de derechos del autor** author's royalties
porcentual [por·sen·tu·'al, por·θen-] *adj* percentage
porche ['por·tʃe] *m* **1.** (*pórtico*) porch **2.** (*cobertizo*) arcade
porcino, -a [por·'si·no, -'θi·no] *adj* pig; **ganado ~** swine *pl*
porción [por·'sjon, -'θjon] *f* portion; CULIN serving
pordiosear [por·djo·se·'ar] *vi* to beg
pordiosero, -a [por·djo·'se·ro, -a] *m, f* beggar
porfía [por·'fi·a] *f* persistence; **a ~** in competition

porfiador(a) [por·fja·'dor, -·'do·ra] **I.** *adj* obstinate **II.** *m(f)* obstinate person
porfiar <*1. pres:* porfío> [por·fi·'ar] *vi* **1.** (*insistir*) **~ en algo** to insist on sth **2.** (*disputar*) to quarrel
pormenor [por·me·'nor] *m* detail
pormenorizado, -a [por·me·no·ri·'sa·do, -a; -θa·do, -a] *adj* detailed
pormenorizar <z→c> [por·me·no·ri·'sar, -'θar] *vt* to describe in detail
porno ['por·no] *adj inv, m inf* porn
pornografía [por·no·ɣra·'fi·a] *f* pornography
pornográfico, -a [por·no·'ɣra·fi·ko, -a] *adj* pornographic
poro ['po·ro] *m* pore
porongo [po·'ron·go] *m* **1.** *CSur* (*calabaza para el mate*) calabash **2.** *Perú* (*lechera*) milk can
pororó [po·ro·'ro] *m CSur* popcorn
poroso, -a [po·'ro·so, -a] *adj* porous
poroto [po·'ro·to] *m Chile* bean
porque ['por·ke] *conj* **1.** (*causal*) because; **lo hizo ~ sí** he/she did it because he/she wanted to **2.** +*subj* (*final*) so that; **recemos ~ llueva** let us pray that it rains
porqué [por·'ke] *m* reason
porquería [por·ke·'ri·a] *f inf* **1.** (*suciedad*) filth **2.** (*acto*) disgusting act **3.** (*comida*) pigswill **4.** (*cacharro*) piece of junk **5.** (*pequeñez*) trifle
porqueriza [por·ke·'ri·sa, -θa] *f* pigsty
porra ['po·rra] *f* (*bastón*) truncheon; **¡vete a la ~!** go to hell!; **¡~(s)!** damn!
porrazo [po·'rra·so, -θo] *m* blow; **de golpe y ~** all of a sudden; **de un ~** in one go
porreta [po·'rre·ta] *f* **en ~(s)** *inf* stark naked
porrista [po·'rris·ta] *mf Méx* fan
porro ['po·rro] *m inf* (*canuto*) joint
porrón [po·'rron] *m bottle with a long neck*
porrudo, -a [po·'rru·do, -a] *adj Arg* big-headed
porsiaca [por·si·'a·ka] *adv inf* just in case
portaaviones [por·ta·βi·'o·nes; por·ta·a·βi-] *m inv* aircraft carrier
portada [por·'ta·da] *f* TIPO title page; PREN cover
portador(a) [por·ta·'dor] *m(f)* **1.** (*de gérmenes*) carrier **2.** COM bearer
portaequipaje(s) [por·ta·e·ki·'pa·xe(s)] *m (inv)* **1.** (*maletero*) trunk **2.** (*baca, en tren*) luggage rack; (*en bicicleta*) carrier
portafolios [por·ta·'fo·ljos] *m inv* briefcase
portal [por·'tal] *m* (*zaguán*) hall; COMPUT portal; **~ de Belén** REL Nativity scene
portalámpara(s) [por·ta·'lam·pa·ra(s)] *m (inv)* (*de bombilla*) socket
portaligas [por·ta·'li·ɣas] *m inv, AmL* garter belt
portamaletas [por·ta·ma·'le·tas] *m inv* AUTO trunk
portaminas [por·ta·'mi·nas] *m inv* mechanical pencil
portamonedas [por·ta·mo·'ne·das] *m inv* purse
portante [por·'tan·te] *m* **tomar el ~** *inf* to clear off; **dar el ~ a alguien** *inf* to fire sb

portar [por·'tar] I. *vt* (*perro*) to fetch II. *vr:* ~ **se** to behave; ~ **se bien con alguien** to treat sb well; **el niño se porta bien/mal** the child is well-/badly behaved; ~ **se como un hombre** to act like a man; **nuestro equipo se ha portado** our team performed well

portátil [por·'ta·til] *adj* portable; **máquina de escribir** ~ portable typewriter; **ordenador** ~ laptop

portavoz [por·ta·'βos, -'βoθ] *mf* spokesperson, spokesman *m*, spokeswoman *f*

portazo [por·'ta·so, -θo] *m* slam (*of the door*); **dar un** ~ to slam the door; **despedirse con un** ~ to slam one's door on the way out; **dar a alguien un** ~ **en las narices** *inf* to slam the door in sb's face

porte ['por·te] *m* 1. (*transporte*) transport; ~ **aéreo** air freight; **gastos de** ~ shipping costs; **a** ~ **debido** carriage forward 2. (*gastos de transporte*) shipping costs *pl* 3. (*correo*) postage; ~ **por expreso** express postage; ~ **de un paquete** parcel post; ~ **suplementario** additional postage 4. (*de buque*) capacity; **buque de gran** ~ large vessel 5. (*aspecto*) appearance; **es un hombre de** ~ **distinguido** he has a distinguished air; **mostrar un** ~ **severo** to look strict

portear [por·te·'ar] I. *vi* to slam the door II. *vt* to transport, to ship

portento [por·'ten·to] *m* marvel; **niño** ~ child prodigy; **ser un** ~ **de energía** to be full of energy

portentoso, -a [por·ten·'to·so, -a] *adj* marvelous

porteño, -a [por·'te·ɲo, -a] I. *adj* of/from Buenos Aires II. *m, f* native/inhabitant of Buenos Aires

portería [por·te·'ri·a] *f* 1. (*en edificio*) porter's lodge 2. DEP goal

portero, -a [por·'te·ro, -a] *m, f* 1. (*conserje*) caretaker; (*en un edificio de viviendas*) porter; ~ **automático** intercom 2. *Arg* (*administrador*) building manager 3. DEP goalkeeper

portezuelo [por·te·'swe·lo, -'θwe·lo] *m Arg, Chile* (*paso de montaña*) pass

pórtico ['por·ti·ko] *m* (*porche*) porch; (*galería*) arcade

portillo [por·'ti·jo, -ʎo] *m* (*abertura*) gap; (*entre montañas*) narrow pass

portorriqueño, -a [por·to·rri·'ke·ɲo, -a] *adj, m, f* Puerto Rican

portuario, -a [por·'twa·rjo, -a] *adj* port

portugués, -esa [por·tu·'ʝes, -·'ʝe·sa] *adj, m, f* Portuguese

porvenir [por·βe·'nir] *m* future; **lleno de** ~ full of promise; **tener el** ~ **asegurado** to have a secure future; **un joven de** ~ a young man with great prospects

pos [pos] I. *adv* **ir en** ~ **de algo/alguien** to pursue sth/sb; **van en** ~ **del éxito** they are striving for success II. *conj Méx, inf v.* **pues**

posada [po·'sa·da] *f* 1. (*parador, fonda*) inn; (*pensión*) guest house 2. (*hospedaje*) lodging; **dar** ~ **a alguien** to give sb lodging; **hacer** ~ to stop for the night; **pedir** ~ to ask for shelter

posaderas [po·sa·'de·ras] *fpl inf* bottom, backside

posadero, -a [po·sa·'de·ro, -a] *m, f* landlord *m*, landlady *f*

posar [po·'sar] I. *vi* (*modelo*) to pose II. *vt* (*poner suavemente*) to place; (*mirada*) to rest III. *vr:* ~ **se** to settle; **el sol se posaba en el mar** the sun set over the sea; **el gorrión se posó en la rama** the sparrow alighted on the branch

posdata [pos·'da·ta] *f* postscript

pose ['po·se] *f* (*postura*) pose

poseedor(a) [po·se·'dor/po·se·e·'dor, --'do·ra] *m(f)* owner

poseer [po·'ser/po·se·'er] *irr como leer vt* to possess, to have; ~ **una importante posición social** to occupy an important position in society; ~ **a alguien a la fuerza** to rape sb

poseído, -a [po·se·'i·do, -a] I. *adj* possessed; ~ **de odio** full of hatred; **una chica poseída de su belleza** a girl obsessed by her own beauty II. *m, f* madman *m*, madwoman *f*; **gritar como un** ~ to shout like one possessed

posesión [po·se·'sjon] *f* possession; **estar en** ~ **de algo** to be in possession of sth

posesionar [po·se·sjo·'nar] *vr:* ~ **se** to take possession; ~ **se de un nuevo cargo** to take up a new position

posesivo, -a [po·se·'si·βo, -a] *adj t.* LING possessive

poseso, -a [po·'se·so, -a] I. *adj* possessed II. *m, f* madman *m*, madwoman *f*

posguerra [pos·'ʝe·rra] *f* postwar period

posibilidad [po·si·βi·li·'dad] *f* 1. (*lo posible*) possibility; **tener grandes** ~ **es de éxito** to have a good chance of success 2. (*aptitud, facultad*) capability; **tienes** ~ **es de llegar a ser un buen actor** you have the ability to become a good actor; **esto está por encima de mis** ~ **es** this is beyond my capabilities 3. *pl* (*medios económicos*) means *pl*; **estás viviendo por encima de tus** ~ **es** you are living beyond your means

posibilitar [po·si·βi·li·'tar] *vt* to make possible

posible [po·'si·βle] *adj* possible; **hacer** ~ to make possible; **hacer lo** ~ **para que** +*subj* to do everything possible so that; **hacer todo lo** ~ to do everything one can; **es muy** ~ **que lleguen tarde** they may very well arrive late; **es** ~ **que** +*subj* it is possible that; **es muy** ~ **que** +*subj* it is very likely that; **¡no es** ~ **!** I can't believe it!; **¿será** ~ **?** surely not?; **si es** ~ **if** possible; **en lo** ~ as far as possible; **lo antes** ~ as soon as possible; **no lo veo** ~ I don't think it's possible

posiblemente [po·si·βle·'men·te] *adv* possibly

posición [po·si·'sjon, -'θjon] *f t.* MIL position; ~ **clave** vital position; ~ **del cuerpo** posture; **la** ~ **económica** the economic situation; ~ **de empleado** position of employment; **la** ~ **geográfica** the geographic location; **en buena** ~

in a good position; **de** ~ of high social standing; **mi** ~ **ante este asunto...** my opinion on this affair...; **tomar** ~ to adopt a stance

positivo [po·si·'ti·βo] *m* FOTO print

positivo, -a [po·si·'ti·βo, -a] *adj* **1.** *t.* MAT, FÍS positive **2.** (*práctico*) practical; **un hombre** ~ a practical man

poso ['po·so] *m* sediment; (*de café*) grounds *pl;* (*de vino*) lees *pl;* **hasta los ~s** *fig* to the very last drop

posponer [pos·po·'ner] *irr como poner vt* **1.** (*postergar*) to relegate **2.** (*aplazar*) to postpone

postal [pos·'tal] **I.** *adj* mail; **envío** ~ parcel post **II.** *f* postcard

poste ['pos·te] *m t.* TEL post; ELEC pylon; ~ **indicador** signpost; ~ **kilométrico** ≈ milestone
▶ **más serio que un** ~ *inf* dead serious

postema [pos·'te·ma] *f Méx* pus

póster ['pos·ter] *m* poster

postergar <g→gu> [pos·ter·'ɣar] *vt* **1.** (*aplazar*) to postpone; ~ **la fecha** to put back the date **2.** (*posponer injustamente*) to delay; ~ **el ascenso de alguien** to pass sb over for promotion

posteridad [pos·te·ri·'dad] *f* **1.** (*descendencia*) descendants *pl;* (*generaciones venideras*) future generations *pl* **2.** (*futuro*) posterity; **pasar a la** ~ to be remembered by posterity

posterior [pos·te·'rjor] *adj* **1.** (*de tiempo*) later; ~ **a** after **2.** (*de lugar*) back; ~ **a alguien** behind sb; **la parte** ~ **de la cabeza** the back of the head

posterioridad [pos·te·rjo·ri·'dad] *f* posteriority; **con** ~ **de fecha** at a later date; **con** ~ subsequently

posteriormente [pos·te·rjor·'men·te] *adv* subsequently, later

postigo [pos·'ti·ɣo] *m* **1.** (*puerta falsa*) blind door **2.** (*contraventana*) shutter

postín [pos·'tin] *m* **de** ~ luxurious; **darse mucho** ~ to show off

postinear [pos·ti·ne·'ar] *vi* to show off

postinero, -a [pos·ti·'ne·ro, -a] *adj inf* vain

postizo [pos·'ti·so, -θo] *m* hairpiece

postizo, -a [pos·'ti·so, -a; -θo, -a] *adj* artificial; **cuello** ~ detachable collar; **dentadura postiza** false teeth; **nombre** ~ false name; **ojo** ~ artificial eye; **pelo** ~ wig

postor(a) [pos·'tor, -'to·ra] *m(f)* bidder; **mejor** ~ highest bidder

postración [pos·tra·'sjon, -'θjon] *f* prostration; ~ **nerviosa** nervous breakdown

postrado, -a [pos·'tra·do, -a] *adj* prostrate; ~ **de dolor** (*dolor físico*) in great pain; (*pena*) beside oneself with grief; ~ **en cama** laid up in bed; **quedar** ~ **por una enfermedad** to be struck down by an illness

postrar [pos·'trar] **I.** *vt* to prostrate **II.** *vr:* ~ **se** to prostrate oneself

postre ['pos·tre] *m* dessert; **a** (**la**) ~ *fig* in the end, when all is said and done; **llegar a los ~s** *fig* to arrive too late

postrero, -a [pos·'tre·ro, -a] *adj* last

postrimerías [pos·tri·me·'ri·as] *fpl* (*de persona*) final years *pl;* (*tiempo*) final stages *pl;* **estar en sus** ~ to be at the end of one's life; **en las** ~ **del siglo pasado** at the end of the last century

postulado [pos·tu·'la·do] *m* proposition

postular [pos·tu·'lar] *vt* **1.** (*pedir*) to request; (*donativos*) to collect **2.** (*solicitar*) ~ **algo** to petition for sth

póstumo, -a ['pos·tu·mo, -a] **I.** *adj* posthumous; **fama póstuma** posthumous fame **II.** *m,* **f** posthumous son *m,* posthumous daughter *f*

postura [pos·'tu·ra] *f* **1.** (*colocación*) position; (*del cuerpo*) posture **2.** (*actitud*) attitude **3.** (*subasta*) bid; ~ **mayor** highest bad; **hacer** ~ to bid **4.** (*apuesta*) amount bet **5.** (*conjunto de huevos*) clutch

post-venta [pos·'βen·ta] **I.** *adj* after-sales; **servicio** ~ after-sales service **II.** *f* warranty period

potable [po·'ta·βle] *adj* drinkable; **agua** ~ drinking water; **Juan es una persona** ~ *inf* (*aceptable*) Juan is a nice guy

potaje [po·'ta·xe] *m* **1.** CULIN (*sopa*) soup; (*guiso*) stew (*containing pulses and vegetables*) **2.** *inf* (*mezcla*) mixture

potar [po·'tar] *vi, vt inf* to puke

potasio [po·'ta·sjo] *m* potassium

pote ['po·te] *m* pot; (*para plantas*) flowerpot
▶ **darse** ~ to show off

potencia [po·'ten·sja, -θja] *f* **1.** (*fuerza*) strength; (*capacidad*) capacity; ~ **de carga** capacity; ~ **explosiva** explosive power; ~ **generativa** generative power; ~ **imaginativa** imaginative power; ~ **intelectual** intellectual power; ~ **mágica** magic power; ~ **del motor** engine capacity; ~ **motriz** motive power; ~ **visual** visual acuity **2.** (*poder*) power; **gran** ~ great power **3.** COMPUT ~ **de entrada/de salida** input/output capacity **4.** FILOS possibility; **en** ~ potential **5.** MAT power; **elevar a la cuarta** ~ to raise to the power of four

potencial [po·ten·'sjal, -'θjal] **I.** *adj* **1.** (*que tiene potencia*) powerful **2.** (*posible*) potential **3.** LING **el modo** ~ the conditional tense **II.** *m* **1.** (*poder, capacidad*) power; ~ **financiero** financial muscle **2.** FÍS potential energy; ELEC potential difference **3.** LING conditional

potente [po·'ten·te] *adj* **1.** (*poderoso*) powerful **2.** (*eficiente*) efficient **3.** (*sexualidad*) potent

potestad [po·tes·'tad] *f* authority; ~ **electoral** electoral authority; ~ **legislativa** legislative jurisdiction; ~ **reglamentaria** regulatory authority; **patria** ~ paternal authority

potingue [po·'tin·ge] *m pey* **1.** *inf* (*cosmético*) lotion; **darse ~s** to put on one's war paint **2.** (*bebida*) concoction

poto ['po·to] *m* **1.** *Perú* (*vaso*) clay bowl **2.** *And, inf* (*trasero*) butt

---

ⓘ "Vale un **Potosí**" (as rich as a Potosí) is a saying that describes unimaginable wealth.

The city of Potosí in Bolivia was built by the conquistadores to exploit the largest silver mine of that time, the **Cerro Rico**. Thousands of indigenous people lost their lives in the mine.

---

potranca [po·'tran·ka] *f* filly
potranco [po·'tran·ko, -a] *m* colt
potrear [po·tre·'ar] *vt* **1.** *AmL* (*domar*) to break **2.** *Guat, Perú* (*pegar*) to beat
potro ['po·tro] *m* **1.** ZOOL colt **2.** DEP vaulting horse **3.** (*de tortura*) rack; **tener a alguien en el ~** *fig* to have sb on the rack
poza ['po·sa, -θa] *f* (*charca*) puddle
pozal [po·'sal, -θal] *m* (*cubo*) well-bucket
pozo ['po·so, -θo] *m* **1.** (*manantial*) well **2.** (*hoyo profundo*) shaft; **~ airón** ventilation shaft; **~ de extracción** extraction shaft; **~ de lobos** trap; **~ negro** cesspool; **~ petrolífero** oil well; **~ de retrete** latrine; **~ séptico** septic tank; **caer en un ~** *fig* to fall into oblivion; **ser un ~ sin fondo** *fig* to be a bottomless pit; **ser un ~ de ciencia** *fig* to be a fount of knowledge **3.** *CSur* (*bache*) pothole
pozole [po·'so·le, -θo·le] *m* *Méx* CULIN ≈ hominy; (*guiso*) posole (*stew of hominy, meat and chili*)
PP [pe·'pe] *m* *abr de* **Partido Popular** Popular Party (*Spanish conservative party*)
p.p. [por po·'der] *abr de* **por poder** pp
práctica ['prak·ti·ka] *f* **1.** (*experiencia*) experience; **una ~ de muchos años** many years' experience; **adquirir ~** to gain experience; **perder la ~** to get out of practice; **tener ~ en algo** to have experience of sth **2.** (*ejercitación*) practice; **~ profesional** professional practice **3.** (*cursillo*) practical course; **~ preprofesional** vocational training **4.** (*realización*) practice; **en la ~** in practice; **llevar a la ~** to carry out; **poner en ~** to put into practice **5.** (*costumbre*) practice; **~ judicial** normal legal practice; **la ~ de los negocios** business norms **6.** (*modo*) manner; (*método*) method; **la ~ comercial** business methods ▸ **la ~ hace al maestro** *prov* practice makes perfect
practicable [prak·ti·'ka·βle] *adj* **1.** (*realizable*) feasible **2.** (*camino, calle*) passable **3.** (*puerta, ventana*) that opens
practicar <c→qu> [prak·ti·'kar] *vi, vt* to practice; **~ deporte** to play sport, to do sports; **estudió medicina, pero no practica** he/she studied medicine, but he/she doesn't work as a doctor; **~ el español** to practice Spanish; **~ una operación** to perform an operation
práctico ['prak·ti·ko] *m* NÁUT pilot; **~ de puerto** coast pilot
práctico, -a ['prak·ti·ko, -a] *adj* practical
pradera [pra·'de·ra] *f* grassland, prairie
pradería [pra·de·'ri·a] *f* meadowlands *pl*
prado ['pra·do] *m* grassy field; (*para ganado*) meadow; (*para pasear*) park

Praga ['pra·γa] *f* Prague
pragmático, -a [praγ·'ma·ti·ko, -a] *adj* pragmatic
prángana ['pran·ga·na] *f* *Méx, PRico* extreme poverty
preámbulo [pre·'am·bu·lo] *m* introduction, preamble; **sin ~s** *fig* without further ado; **no andarse con ~s** not to beat around the bush; **¡déjese de ~s!** get to the point!
preaviso [pre·a·'βi·so] *m* forewarning
prebenda [pre·'βen·da] *f* REL prebend
precalentar <e→ie> [pre·ka·len·'tar] *vt* to preheat
precario, -a [pre·'ka·rjo, -a] *adj* precarious
precaución [pre·kau·'sjon, -'θjon] *f* precaution; **tomar precauciones** to take precautions
precaver [pre·ka·'βer] **I.** *vt* (*prevenir*) to prevent; (*evitar*) to avoid **II.** *vr* **~se de algo/alguien** to take precautions against sth/sb; **hay que ~se de todas las eventualidades** you have to be prepared for all eventualities
precavido, -a [pre·ka·'βi·do, -a] *adj* cautious
precedencia [pre·se·'den·sja, pre·θe·'den·θja] *f* precedence; **dar ~ a alguien** to give precedence to sb
precedente [pre·se·'den·te, pre·θe-] **I.** *adj* preceding **II.** *m* precedent; **sentar un ~** to establish a precedent; **sin ~s** unprecedented
preceder [pre·se·'der, pre·θe-] *vt* **1.** (*anteceder*) to precede; **un banquete precedido de varios discursos** a banquet preceded by several speeches **2.** (*tener primacía*) **~ a algo/alguien** to have priority over sth/sb; **~ en categoría** to have a higher position
preceptista [pre·sep·'tis·ta, pre·θep-] *adj* preceptive
preceptiva [pre·sep·'ti·βa, pre·θep-] *f* precepts *pl*
preceptivo, -a [pre·sep·'ti·βo, -a; pre·θep-] *adj* compulsory
precepto [pre·'sep·to, -'θep·to] *m* (*mandamiento*) order; (*norma*) precept; **~ básico** basic principle; **~ de conducta** rule of behavior; **~ jurídico** law; **~ de ley** legal doctrine
preceptor(a) [pre·sep·'tor, --to·ra; pre·θep-] *m(f)* tutor
preceptuar <1. *pres:* preceptúo> [pre·sep·tu·'ar, pre·θep-] *vt* to establish
preces ['pre·ses, -θes] *fpl* prayers *pl*; (*súplicas*) pleas *pl*
preciado, -a [pre·'sja·do, -a; -'θja·do, -a] *adj* prized; **~ de sí mismo** boastful
preciarse [pre·'sjar·se, -'θjar·se] *vr* **~ de algo** to boast about sth
precintar [pre·'sin·tar, -'θin·tar] *vt* to seal
precinto [pre·'sin·to, 'θin·to] *m* seal; **~ de aduana** customs seal
precio ['pre·sjo, -θjo] *m* price; **~ abordable** reasonable price; **~ alzado** fixed price; **~ al consumidor** retail price; **~ al contado** cash price; **~ de conversión** conversion rate; **~ de coste** cost price; **~ al detalle** retail price; **~ de fábrica** price ex-works, factory price; **~ irriso-**

rio bargain price; ~ **al por mayor** wholesale price; ~ **preferente** preferential price; ~ **de presentación** introductory price; ~ **recomendado** recommended price; ~ **de rescate** ransom; ~ **de tarifa** list price; ~ **de temporada** seasonal price; ~ **unitario** single price; ~ **de venta al público** retail price; **a buen** ~ for a good price; **a** ~ **controlado** at a controlled price; **a mitad de** ~ at half price; **a poco** ~ cheaply; **a** ~ **de oro** for a very high price; **poner el** ~ to set the price; **¿qué** ~ **tiene el libro?** how much does this book cost?; **de todos los** ~**s** at all prices; **no tener** ~ *fig* to be priceless; **al** ~ **de la salud** at the cost of one's health; **querer conseguir algo a cualquier** ~ to want sth at any price; **poner** ~ **a la cabeza de alguien** to put a price on sb's head

preciosidad [pre·sjo·si·'dad, pre·θjo-] *f* value; **este cuadro es una** ~ this picture is very valuable; *fig* this picture is delightful; **esta chica es una** ~ this girl is lovely

precioso, -a [pre·'sjo·so, -a; pre·'θjo-] *adj* **1.** (*valioso*) valuable **2.** (*hermoso*) lovely

precipicio [pre·si·'pi·sjo, -θi·'pi·θjo] *m* precipice; **estar al borde del** ~ *fig* to be on the brink of disaster

precipitación [pre·si·pi·ta·'sjon, -θi·pi·ta·'θjon] *f* **1.** (*prisa*) haste; **con** ~ hastily **2.** METEO rainfall

precipitadamente [pre·si·pi·ta·da·'men·te, pre·θi-] *adv* hastily

precipitado, -a [pre·si·pi·'ta·do, pre·θi-] *adj* hasty; **ser** ~ **en el hablar** to talk too soon

precipitar [pre·si·pi·'tar, pre·θi-] I. *vt* **1.** (*arrojar*) to throw down; **lo** ~**on por la ventana** they threw him out of the window **2.** (*apresurar*) to hasten; (*acelerar*) to hurry II. *vr:* ~**se** **1.** (*arrojarse*) to throw oneself down; ~**se sobre algo/alguien** to hurl oneself at sth/sb **2.** (*acontecimientos*) to happen very quickly; (*personas*) to act hastily; **¡no se precipite!** don't be hasty!

precisamente [pre·si·sa·'men·te, pre·θi-] *adv* exactly; **¿tiene que ser** ~ **hoy?** does it have to be today, of all days?; ~ **por eso** for that very reason

precisar [pre·si·'sar, pre·θi-] I. *vi* to be necessary II. *vt* **1.** (*determinar*) to specify; **no lo puedo** ~ I can't put my finger on it **2.** (*necesitar*) to need; **preciso tu ayuda** I need your help

precisión [pre·si·'sjon, pre·θi-] *f* **1.** (*exactitud*) precision; ~ **de funcionamiento** reliability; ~ **de tiro** accuracy; **instrumento de** ~ precision instrument; **hablar con** ~ to speak clearly **2.** (*determinación*) clarification; **hacer precisiones** to clarify matters **3.** (*necesidad*) need; **tener** ~ **de hacer algo** to need to do sth

preciso, -a [pre·'θi·so, -a, pre·'θi-] *adj* **1.** (*necesario*) necessary; **es** ~ **que** +*subj* it is necessary to; **es** ~ **que nos veamos** we need to see each other; **si es** ~**...** if necessary... **2.** (*exacto*) precise; **a la hora precisa** punctu-

ally

preclaro, -a [pre·'kla·ro, -a] *adj* illustrious

precocidad [pre·ko·si·'dad, pre·ko·θi-] *f* (*del niño*) precociousness

precocinado, -a [pre·ko·si·'na·do, -a, pre·ko·θi-] *adj* pre-cooked; **plato** ~ ready-cooked dish, convenience food

preconcebido, -a [pre·kon·se·'βi·do, -a; pre·kon·θe-] *adj* preconceived; **tener ideas preconcebidas** to have preconceived ideas

preconizable [pre·ko·ni·'sa·βle, -θa·βle] *adj* foreseeable

preconizar <z→c> [pre·ko·ni·'sar, -'θar] *vt* to recommend

precordillera [pre·kor·di·'je·ra, -'ʎe·ra] *f* *Arg* Andean foothills *pl*

precoz [pre·'kos, -'koθ] *adj* precocious; (*diagnóstico, cosecha*) early; **eyaculación** ~ premature ejaculation

precursor(a) [pre·kur·'sor, --'so·ra] I. *adj* preceding II. *m(f)* precursor

predecesor(a) [pre·de·se·'sor --'so·ra; -θe·'sor, --'so·ra --so·ra] *m(f)* **1.** (*en el cargo*) predecessor **2.** (*antepasados*) ancestor

predecir [pre·de·'sir, -'θir] *irr como decir vt* to predict; (*tiempo*) to forecast

predestinado, -a [pre·des·ti·'na·do, -a] *adj* predestined; **estar** ~ **al crimen** to be destined for a life of crime

predestinar [pre·des·ti·'nar] *vt* to predestine

predeterminar [pre·de·ter·mi·'nar] *vt* to predetermine

prédica ['pre·di·ka] *f* (*sermón*) sermon

predicación [pre·di·ka·'sjon, -'θjon] *f* **1.** (*sermonear*) preaching **2.** (*sermón*) sermon

predicado [pre·di·'ka·do] *m* LING predicate

predicador(a) [pre·di·ka·'dor, --do·ra] *m(f)* preacher

predicar <c→qu> [pre·di·'kar] *vt* to preach; ~ **en desierto** to preach in the wilderness; ~ **con el ejemplo** to practice what one preaches ▶**no se puede** ~ **y andar en la procesión** *prov* you can't be in two places at once; **una cosa es** ~ **y otra dar trigo** *prov* actions speak louder than words

predicativo, -a [pre·di·ka·'ti·βo, -a] *adj* LING predicative

predicción [pre·dik·'sjon, -'θjon] *f* prediction; ~ **económica** economic forecast

predilección [pre·di·lek·'sjon, -'θjon] *f* predilection

predilecto, -a [pre·di·'lek·to, -a] *adj* favorite; **hijo** ~ favorite son; **plato** ~ favorite dish

predio ['pre·djo] *m* **1.** JUR estate; ~ **familiar** family estate; ~ **grande** large estate **2.** (*finca*) piece of land; ~ **familiar** family holding

predisponer [pre·dis·po·'ner] *irr como poner* I. *vt* **1.** (*fijar por anticipado*) to agree beforehand; **venía predispuesto a pelearse** he arrived in a mood for a quarrel **2.** (*influir*) to predispose; ~ **a alguien a favor/en contra de alguien** to bias sb in favor of/against sb **3.** (*inclinar*) to make receptive; MED to predispose **II.** *vr* **1.**(*prepararse*) ~**se a algo** to prepare oneself for sth **2.**(*tomar partido*) to have a bias; ~**se a favor/en contra de alguien** to be biased in favor of/against sb

predisposición [pre·dis·po·si·'sjon, -'θjon] *f t.* MED predisposition; (*tendencia*) tendency; ~ **al crimen** criminal predisposition; **tener** ~ **a engordar** to have a tendency to put on weight

predispuesto, -a [pre·dis·'pwes·to, -a] **I.** *pp de* **predisponer II.** *adj* **1.** *ser* (*sensible*) predisposed; **ser** ~ **a coger los virus** to have a tendency to catch viruses **2.** *estar* (*prevenido*) prejudiced; **estar** (**mal**) ~ **contra alguien** to be prejudiced against sb

predominar [pre·do·mi·'nar] *vi, vt* **1.**(*prevalecer*) to predominate; **aquí predomina la corrupción** corruption is very common here; ~ **en número** to be most numerous **2.**(*sobresalir*) to stand out; ~ **en algo/sobre alguien** to stand out at sth/over sb

predominio [pre·do·'mi·njo] *m* **1.**(*poder*) predominance **2.**(*preponderancia*) preponderance **3.**(*superioridad*) ~ **sobre alguien** superiority over sb

preeminencia [pre·mi·'nen·sja/pre·e·mi·'nen·sja, -θja -θja] *f* pre-eminence

preeminente [pre·mi·'nen·te/pre·e·mi·'nen·te] *adj* pre-eminent

preescolar [pres·ko·'lar/pre·es·ko·'lar] *adj* preschool; **edad** ~ pre-school age

preestreno [pres·'tre·no/pre·es·tre·no] *m* preview

preexistir [prek·sis·'tir/pre·ek·sis·tir] *vi* to pre-exist

prefabricado, -a [pre·fa·βri·'ka·do, -a] *adj* prefabricated; **casa prefabricada** prefabricated house

prefacio [pre·'fa·sjo, -θjo] *m* (*libro*) preface

preferencia [pre·fe·'ren·sja, -θja] *f* **1.**(*elección, trato*) preference; **mostrar** ~ **por alguien** to show a preference for sb **2.**(*predilección*) predilection; **sentir** ~ **por alguien** to be biased in favor of sb **3.**(*prioridad*) priority; ~ **de paso** right of way; **precio de** ~ preferential price; **tener** ~ **ante alguien** to have priority over sb; **dar** ~ to give preference; **de** ~ preferably

preferentemente [pre·fe·ren·te·'men·te] *adv* preferably

preferible [pre·fe·'ri·βle] *adj* preferable; **sería** ~ **que lo hicieras** it would be best if you did it

preferiblemente [pre·fe·ri·βle·'men·te] *adv* preferably

preferido, -a [pre·fe·'ri·do, -a] *adj* favorite

preferir [pre·fe·'rir] *irr como sentir vt* to prefer; **prefiero ir a pie** I prefer to walk; **prefiero que no venga** I would rather he/she didn't come

prefijar [pre·fi·'xar] *vt* to decide (in advance), to prearrange

prefijo [pre·'fi·xo] *m* **1.** LING prefix **2.** TEL area code

pregón [pre·'yon] *m* proclamation; **con** ~ *fig* with much ado; **sin** ~ *fig* without a lot of fuss

pregonar [pre·yo·'nar] *vt* **1.**(*en público*) to proclaim; ~ **mercancías** to publicize goods **2.**(*lo que estaba oculto*) to make public; ~ **a los cuatro vientos** *inf* to proclaim for all to hear; ~ **a tambor batiente** to proclaim loudly **3.**(*alabar*) to praise publicly

pregonero, -a [pre·yo·'ne·ro, -a] *m, f* (*público*) town crier

pregunta [pre·'yun·ta] *f* **1.**(*demanda*) question; ~ **capciosa** trick question; **estrechar a** ~**s a alguien** to bombard sb with questions; **a tal** ~ **tal respuesta** ask a silly question, get a silly answer; **estar a la cuarta** ~ *inf* to be broke **2.**(*de datos*) inquiry

preguntar [pre·yun·'tar] **I.** *vt* to ask; ~ **a alguien la lección** to test sb; ~ **a un sospechoso** to question a suspect; ~ **por alguien** to ask after sb ▶ **quien pregunta no yerra** *prov* he who asks questions won't go far wrong **II.** *vr* ~**se si/cuándo/qué...** to wonder if/when/what...

preguntón, -ona [pre·yun·'ton, -·to·na] *adj* inquisitive, nosy *pej*

prehistórico, -a [pre·is·'to·ri·ko, -a] *adj* prehistoric

prejubilación [pre·xu·βi·la·'sjon, -'θjon] *f* early retirement

prejuicio [pre·'xwi·sjo, -θjo] *m* prejudice

prejuzgar <g→gu> [pre·xus·'yar, pre·xuθ-] *vt* to prejudge

preliminar [pre·li·mi·'nar] *adj* preliminary

preludio [pre·'lu·djo] *m t.* MÚS prelude

premamá [pre·ma·'ma] *adj inv* **vestido** ~ maternity dress

prematuro, -a [pre·ma·'tu·ro, -a] *adj* premature; (*persona*) precocious; **detección prematura del cáncer** early detection of cancer; **nacimiento** ~ premature birth

premeditación [pre·me·di·ta·'sjon, -'θjon] *f* premeditation; **con** ~ premeditated

premeditadamente [pre·me·di·ta·da·'men·te] *adv* with premeditation

premeditado, -a [pre·me·di·'ta·do, -a] *adj* premeditated

premeditar [pre·me·di·'tar] *vt* **1.**(*pensar*) to think about **2.**(*planear*) to plan; JUR to premeditate

premiación [pre·mja·'sjon, -'θjon] *f And* awarding (of prizes)

premiado, -a [pre·'mja·do, -a] **I.** *adj* prizewinning **II.** *m, f* prizewinner; (*literatura, ciencias*) laureate

premiar [pre·'mjar] *vt* to reward; (*dar un premio*) to give [o award] a prize to

premier [pre·'mjer] *mf* premier

premio ['pre·mjo] *m* **1.**(*galardón*) prize; ~ **Nobel** (**de literatura**) Nobel Prize (for/in literature); **conceder un** ~ to award a prize **2.**(*recompensa*) reward; ~ **por hallazgo** finder's reward **3.**(*remuneración*) bonus; ~ **al ahorro** savings bonus; ~ **de antigüedad**

P

long-service bonus **4.**(*lotería*) prize; **el ~ gordo** the jackpot
premisa [pre·'mi·sa] *f* **1.**(*condición*) premise **2.**(*indicio*) indication
premonición [pre·mo·ni·'sjon, -'θjon] *f* premonition
premunir [pre·mu·'nir] **I.** *vt AmL* **~ de algo** to provide with sth **II.** *vr AmL* **~se de algo** to provide oneself with sth
prenatal [pre·na·'tal] *adj* prenatal
prenda ['pren·da] *f* **1.**(*fianza*) guarantee; **en ~** as security; **en ~s** as evidence; **hacer ~** to hold as security; **soltar ~** to commit oneself; **no soltar ~** *inf* not to say a word; **a mí no me duelen ~s** I don't mind admitting it **2.**(*pieza de ropa*) garment; **~s interiores** underwear; **~ protectora** protective clothing **3.**(*cariño*) darling; **la ~ de mi corazón** my darling **4.**(*cualidades*) talent; **~s del espíritu** spiritual qualities; **un hombre de ~s** a talented man
prendar [pren·'dar] **I.** *vt* **1.**(*tomar como prenda*) to take as security **2.**(*ganar el afecto*) to captivate **II.** *vr* **~se de alguien** *elev* to fall in love with sb
prendedor [pren·de·'dor] *m* (*broche*) brooch, pin; (*de corbata*) tiepin
prender [pren·'der] **I.** *vi* (*planta, ideas*) to take root; (*medicamentos*) to take effect; **sus ideas prendieron** his/her ideas took root **II.** *vt* **1.**(*sujetar*) to hold down; (*con alfileres*) to pin; (*con cola*) to stick; (*en un gancho*) to hang; (*el pelo*) to tie back; **~ un alfiler de corbata** to put a tiepin on **2.**(*detener*) to catch **3.**(*fuego*) **el coche prendió fuego** the car caught fire **4.** *AmL* (*encender*) to light; (*luz*) to turn on; **~ un cigarrillo** to light a cigarette **III.** *vr PRico* (*emborracharse*) to get drunk
prendimiento [pren·di·'mjen·to] *m* **1.** *Col, Ven* (*irritación*) irritation **2.** *CSur* (*estreñimiento*) constipation
prensa ['pren·sa] *f* **1.**(*máquina*) press; **~ de uvas** wine press **2.**(*imprenta*) printer's, press; **dar a la ~** to send to the printer's; **estar en ~** to be at the printer's **3.** PREN press; **~ amarilla** tabloids *pl;* **~ especializada** specialist publications; **rueda de ~** press conference; **libertad de ~** freedom of the press; **secretario de ~** press secretary; **Prensa y Relaciones Públicas** Public Relations; **tener buena/mala ~** *fig* to get a good/bad press
prensar [pren·'sar] *vt* to press
prensil [pren·'sil] *adj* prehensile
preñada [pre·'ɲa·da] *adj* (*mujer*) pregnant
preñado, -a [pre·'ɲa·do] *adj* **1.**(*animal*) pregnant **2.**(*lleno*) full; **una nube preñada de agua** a cloud full of water; **una palabra preñada** a word loaded with meaning; **~ de dificultades** full of difficulties; **~ de emoción** full of emotion
preñar [pre·'ɲar] *vt* **1.**(*mujer*) to make pregnant **2.**(*animal*) to impregnate **3.**(*llenar*) to fill
preñez [pre·'ɲes, -'ɲeθ] *f* (*de la mujer, del animal*) pregnancy

preocupación [preo·ku·pa·'sjon, -'θjon] *f* **1.**(*desvelo*) worry; **~ por algo/alguien** worry about sth/sb; **¡déjate de preocupaciones!** stop worrying!; **sin preocupaciones** unworried **2.**(*pesadumbre*) worry; **causar preocupaciones a alguien** to be a cause of concern for sb **3.**(*obsesión*) concern; **tu única ~ es el dinero** the only thing you care about is money
preocupado, -a [preo·ku·'pa·do, -a] *adj* worried; **~ por algo/alguien** worried about sth/sb; **mi padre anda bastante ~** my father is quite worried
preocupante [preo·ku·'pan·te] *adj* worrying
preocupar [preo·ku·'par] **I.** *vt* to worry; **~ a alguien** to make sb worry **II.** *vr* **1.**(*inquietarse*) **~se por algo/alguien** to worry about sth/sb; **¡no se preocupe!** don't worry!; **¡no te preocupes tanto!** don't worry so much! **2.**(*encargarse*) to take care; **no se preocupa de arreglar el asunto** he/she doesn't do anything to solve the problem
prepa ['pre·pa] *f Méx* (*preparatoria*) secondary school
preparación [pre·pa·ra·'sjon, -'θjon] *f* **1.**(*de asunto, comida*) preparation; **~ de datos** COMPUT data processing **2.**(*formación*) training; **~ académica** education; **~ especializada** specialist training; **~ profesional** professional training; **sin ~** untrained
preparado [pre·pa·'ra·do] *m* preparation; **~ listo** ready-made medicine
preparado, -a [pre·pa·'ra·do, -a] *adj* (*listo*) ready; **~ (para funcionar)** ready for use; **tener ~** to have ready
preparar [pre·pa·'rar] **I.** *vt* **1.**(*disponer*) to prepare; **~ un buque para zarpar** to get a boat ready for a journey; **~ el camino** to prepare the way; **~ una casa para vivir en ella** to make a house ready for living in; **~ un discurso** to write a speech; **~ las maletas** to pack one's bags; **ya puedes ~ la maleta** *inf* it's time you were leaving; **~ la tierra** to prepare the ground **2.** QUÍM, ANAT to prepare **3.** COMPUT (*datos*) to process; (*programa*) to compile **II.** *vr* to get ready; **prepárate para salir** get ready to leave; **se prepara una tormenta** there's a storm brewing; **~se para cualquier eventualidad** to prepare oneself for any eventuality
preparativo [pre·pa·ra·'ti·βo] *m* preparation
preparativo, -a [pre·pa·ra·'ti·βo, -a] *adj* preparatory
preparatoria [pre·pa·ra·'to·rja] *f Méx* prep school
preparatorio, -a [pre·pa·ra·'to·rjo, -a] *adj* preparatory; **curso ~** introductory course; **trabajos ~s** preliminary work
prepo ['pre·po] *Arg* **de ~** by force
preponderancia [pre·pon·de·'ran·sja, -θja] *f* preponderance
preponderante [pre·pon·de·'ran·te] *adj* preponderant
preponderar [pre·pon·de·'rar] *vi* to prevail
preposición [pre·po·si·'sjon, -'θjon] *f* preposi-

tion
prepotente [pre·po·'ten·te] *adj* arrogant
prerrogativa [pre·rro·ya·'ti·βa] *f* prerogative
presa ['pre·sa] *f* 1.(*acción*) capture; **las llamas hicieron ~ en la casa** the house went up in flames; **ser ~ del terror** to be seized by terror 2.(*objeto, de caza*) prey; **animal de ~** prey; **ave de ~** bird of prey; **hacer una ~** to make a kill 3.(*dique*) dam 4.(*colmillo*) fang 5.(*uña*) talon 6.(*acequia*) channel 7. DEP hold; **~ de brazo** (*judo*) arm hold
presagiar [pre·sa·'xjar] *vt* to betoken *form;* **estas nubes presagian tormenta** these clouds mean there will be a storm
presagio [pre·'sa·xjo] *m* 1.(*señal*) warning sign 2.(*presentimiento*) premonition
presbicia [pres·'βi·sja, -θja] *f* MED long-sightedness
presbiterio [pres·βi·'te·rjo] *m* presbytery
presbítero [pres·'βi·te·ro] *m* priest
prescindible [pre·sin·'di·βle, pres·θin-] *adj* dispensable
prescindir [pre·sin·'dir, pres·θin-] *vi* 1.(*renunciar a*) **~ de algo/alguien** to do without sth/sb; **no podemos ~ de él** we can't do without him 2.(*pasar por alto*) **~ de algo/alguien** to overlook sth/sb; **han prescindido de mi opinión** they have ignored my opinion 3.(*no contar*) **~ de algo/alguien** to disregard sth/sb
prescribir [pres·kri·'βir] *irr como escribir* I. *vi* (*plazo*) to expire II. *vt* (*indicar*) t. MED to prescribe; **prescrito por la ley** prescribed by law
prescripción [pres·krip·'sjon, -kriβ·'θjon] *f* 1.(*indicación*) indication 2. MED prescription 3.(*plazo*) expiry
presencia [pre·'sen·sja, -θja] *f* 1.(*asistencia*) presence; **~ en Internet** Internet presence; **sin la ~ del ministro** without the minister being present; **hacer acto de ~** to put in an appearance 2.(*aspecto*) appearance; **buena ~** good looks
presencial [pre·sen·'sjal, -'θjal] *adj* **testigo ~** eyewitness
presenciar [pre·sen·'sjar, -'θjar] *vt* 1.(*ver*) to witness 2.(*asistir*) to attend; **10.000 personas ~on el concierto** 10,000 people attended the concert
presentable [pre·sen·'ta·βle] *adj* presentable; **ponerse ~** to make oneself presentable
presentación [pre·sen·ta·'sjon, -'θjon] *f* 1.(*de una novela, una película*) launch(ing) 2.(*de un número artístico*) presentation; TEAT show 3.(*de instancia, dimisión*) submission; **el plazo de ~ de solicitudes finaliza hoy** the period for presenting requests ends today 4.(*de argumentos, documento, propuesta*) presentation 5.(*de personas*) introduction 6.(*aspecto*) appearance 7. AmL (*súplica*) petition
presentador(a) [pre·sen·ta·'dor, -·'do·ra] *m(f)* (*de programa*) presenter; (*de telediario*) newsreader

presentar [pre·sen·'tar] I. *vt* 1.(*mostrar*) to show 2.(*ofrecer*) to offer; **el viaje presenta dificultades** the journey poses difficulties; **la ciudad presenta un aspecto de gala** the city is in festive mood 3. TV, RADIO to present; TEAT to put on; (*presentador*) to introduce 4.(*instancia, dimisión*) to submit 5.(*argumentos*) to put forward; (*pruebas, propuestas*) to submit 6.(*pasaporte, documento*) to show 7.(*persona*) to introduce; **te presento a mi marido** may I introduce you to my husband? 8.(*candidato*) to propose II. *vr:* **~se** 1.(*comparecer*) to present oneself; (*aparecer*) to turn up 2.(*para elecciones*) **~se a** to run for
presente [pre·'sen·te] I. *adj* 1.(*que está*) present; **¡~!** present!; **estar ~** to be present 2.(*actual*) current 3.(*este*) **la ~ edición** this edition 4.(*a considerar*) **hay que tener ~ s las circunstancias** one must consider the circumstances; **ten ~ lo que te he dicho** bear in mind what I have told you 5.(*en una carta*) **por la ~ deseo comunicarle que...** I write in order to tell you that... II. *m* 1.(*actualidad*) present; **hasta el ~** until now; **por el ~** for the moment 2. LING present (tense) 3.(*regalo*) present, gift
presentimiento [pre·sen·ti·'mjen·to] *m* premonition; **tengo el ~ de que...** I have a feeling that...
presentir [pre·sen·'tir] *irr como sentir* *vt* to have a premonition of; **presiento que mañana lloverá** I have a feeling it's going to rain tomorrow
preservación [pre·ser·βa·'sjon, -'θjon] *f* preservation
preservar [pre·ser·'βar] I. *vt* to protect II. *vr* to protect oneself
preservativo [pre·ser·βa·'ti·βo] *m* condom
presidencia [pre·si·'den·sja, -θja] *f* 1.(*mandato*) presidency; **asumir la ~** to take over the presidency; **esta orden viene de la ~** this order comes from the president 2.(*edificio*) presidential palace 3.(*de organización, asamblea: conjunto*) board; (*individuo*) chairperson, president; **asumir la ~** to take the chair
presidencial [pre·si·den·'sjal, -·'θjal] *adj* POL presidential
presidente [pre·si·'den·te, -a] *mf* 1. POL president; **~ del gobierno** prime minister 2.(*de asociación*) chairperson
presidiario, -a [pre·si·'dja·rjo, -a] *m, f* convict
presidio [pre·'si·djo] *m* prison; **condenar a 20 años de ~** to sentence to 20 years in prison
presidir [pre·si·'dir] *vt* 1.(*ocupar presidencia*) to be president of 2.(*mandar*) to rule 3.(*dominar*) to dominate
presilla [pre·'si·ja, -ʎa] *f* fastener
presión [pre·'sjon] *f* pressure; **~ arterial** blood pressure; **~ competitiva** competition; **~ fiscal** tax burden; **~ social** social pressure; **grupo de ~** pressure group; **zona de altas presiones** METEO high pressure area; **cerrado a ~** pressurized; **¿a qué ~ llevas las ruedas?** what is

your tire pressure?; **estar bajo** ~ to be under pressure; **hacer** ~ **sobre alguien** to put pressure on sb; **no acepto presiones de nadie** I don't let anyone pressure me

presionar [pre·sjo·'nar] *vt* **1.** (*apretar*) to press **2.** (*coaccionar*) to put pressure on

preso, -a ['pre·so, -a] *m, f* prisoner, (prison) inmate

prestación [pres·ta·'sjon, -'θjon] *f* **1.** (*de ayuda, servicio*) provision; ~ **por desempleo** unemployment benefit; **prestaciones en especie** payment in kind; ~ **de servicios** provision of services; **Prestación Social Sustitutoria** social service (*as an alternative to military service*) **2.** *pl* (*de coche*) features *pl;* **un coche con todas las últimas prestaciones** a car with all the latest features

prestado, -a [pres·'ta·do, -a] *adj* borrowed; **voy de ~, el traje me lo han dejado** I'm wearing borrowed finery, sb lent me the suit; **vivir de ~ en casa de alguien** to live off sb else

prestamista [pres·ta·'mis·ta] *mf* moneylender

préstamo ['pres·ta·mo] *m* **1.** (*acción*) lending **2.** *t.* FIN (*lo prestado: para exposición*) loan; ~ **hipotecario** mortgage; ~ **a interés fijo** fixed-interest loan; **la duración de un** ~ the period of a loan

prestancia [pres·'tan·sja, -θja] *f* (*distinción*) distinction

prestar [pres·'tar] **I.** *vt* **1.** (*dejar*) to lend; **¿me prestas la bici, por favor?** can I borrow your bike?; **el banco me ha prestado el dinero** I have borrowed money from the bank **2.** (*dedicar*) ~ **ayuda** to help; ~ **servicios** to provide services; ~ **colaboración** to cooperate; ~ **apoyo** to support **3.** (*declaración*) to make; (*juramento*) to swear **4.** (*atención*) to pay; ~ **silencio** to remain silent; ~ **paciencia** to be patient; ~ **oídos** to lend an ear **II.** *vr:* ~**se 1.** (*ofrecerse*) to offer oneself; **se prestó a ayudarme** he/she offered to help me **2.** (*avenirse*) to accept **3.** (*dar motivo*) to give rise to; **tus palabras se prestan a confusión** your words lend themselves to misinterpretation

prestatario, -a [pres·ta·'ta·rjo, -a] *m, f* borrower

presteza [pres·'te·sa, -θa] *f* speed

prestidigitación [pres·ti·di·xi·ta·'sjon, -'θjon] *f* conjuring; **un número de** ~ a conjuring trick

prestidigitador(a) [pres·ti·di·xi·ta·'dor, -·'do·ra] *m(f)* conjurer

prestigio [pres·'ti·xjo] *m* prestige; **una cuestión de** ~ a matter of honor; **una persona de** ~ a noteworthy person

prestigioso, -a [pres·ti·'xjo·so, -a] *adj* prestigious

presumido, -a [pre·su·'mi·do, -a] *adj* **1.** (*arrogante*) arrogant **2.** (*vanidoso*) vain

presumir [pre·su·'mir] **I.** *vi* ~ **de algo** to boast about sth; ~ **más que una mona** *inf* to be as vain as a peacock **II.** *vt* to presume

presunción [pre·sun·'sjon, -'θjon] *f* **1.** (*sospe-*

cha) assumption **2.** (*petulancia*) arrogance **3.** (*vanidad*) vanity

presunto, -a [pre·'sun·to, -a] *adj* **1.** (*supuesto*) presumed; **el** ~ **asesino** the alleged murderer **2.** (*equivocadamente*) so-called

presuntuoso, -a [pre·sun·tu·'o·so] *adj* conceited

presuponer [pre·su·po·'ner] *irr como poner vt* **1.** (*suponer*) to presuppose **2.** (*calcular*) to suppose

presupuestar [pre·su·pwes·'tar] *vt* **1.** POL, ECON to budget (for) **2.** (*gastos*) to calculate; ~ **los gastos en tres millones** to calculate the costs to be three million

presupuestario, -a [pre·su·pwes·'ta·rjo, -a] *adj* budget(ary)

presupuesto [pre·su·'pwes·to] *m* **1.** POL, ECON budget; ~ **anual** annual budget; **Presupuesto General del Estado** National Budget; **la confección del** ~ the drawing up of the budget **2.** (*cálculo*) estimate **3.** (*suposición*) assumption

presuroso, -a [pre·su·'ro·so, -a] *adj* hurried; **iba** ~ **por la calle** he hurried down the street

pretender [pre·ten·'der] *vt* **1.** (*aspirar a*) to aspire to; ~ **subir de categoría** to be seeking promotion **2.** (*pedir*) to expect; **¿qué pretendes que haga?** what do you want me to do? **3.** (*tener intención*) to mean; **no pretendía molestar** I didn't mean to disturb you **4.** (*intentar*) to try to **5.** (*afirmar*) to affirm

pretendiente [pre·ten·'djen·te] *m* (*de trabajo*) applicant; (*de mujer*) suitor; (*a la corona*) pretender

pretensión [pre·ten·'sjon] *f* **1.** (*derecho*) claim; ~ **económica** financial demand **2.** (*ambición*) ambition; (*aspiración*) aim; **es una persona con muchas pretensiones** he/she is very ambitious; **es una persona con pocas pretensiones** he/she is easily pleased; **tener muchas pretensiones laborales** to be ambitious at work; **tiene la** ~ **de que vaya con él** he wants me to go with him **3.** *pl* (*vanidad*) **tiene pretensiones de actor** he fancies himself as an actor

pretérito [pre·'te·ri·to] *m* LING past

pretérito, -a [pre·'te·ri·to, -a] *adj* past

pretextar [pre·tes·'tar] *vt* to use as an excuse; **pretextó que estaba enfermo** he pretended that he was ill; **siempre pretexta algo** he/she always has some excuse

pretexto [pre·'tes·to] *m* pretext; **a** ~ **de...** on the pretext of...

pretil [pre·'til] *m* AmL (*atrio*) forecourt

pretina [pre·'ti·na] *f* (*cinta*) band; (*de calzoncillos*) waistband; (*de prenda*) elastic

prevalecer [pre·βa·le·'ser, -'θer] *irr como crecer vi* **1.** (*imponerse*) to prevail; **la verdad prevaleció sobre la mentira** truth prevailed over lies **2.** (*predominar*) to predominate; **esta regla prevalece sobre las demás** this rule takes precedence over the others

prevaleciente [pre·βa·le·'sjen·te, ·'θjen·te] *adj* (*costumbre*) prevailing

prevaricación [pre·βa·ri·ka·'sjon, ·'θjon] *f* **1.** JUR perversion of the course of justice **2.** (*del deber*) dereliction of duty

prevaricar <c→qu> [pre·βa·ri·'kar] *vi* **1.** JUR to pervert the course of justice **2.** (*faltar al deber*) to fail to do one's duty

prevención [pre·βen·'sjon, ·'θjon] *f* **1.** (*precaución*) precaution **2.** *t.* MED (*acción*) prevention; **~ del cáncer** cancer prevention; **~ de accidentes** accident prevention; **~ de siniestros** crash prevention

prevenido, -a [pre·βe·'ni·do, -a] *adj* **1.** *estar* (*alerta*) **estar ~** to be prepared **2.** *ser* (*previsor*) prudent ▸ **hombre ~ vale por dos** *prov* forewarned is forearmed *prov*

prevenir [pre·βe·'nir] *irr como venir* I. *vt* **1.** (*protegerse de*) to prevent **2.** (*advertir*) to warn **3.** (*predisponer*) to prejudice; **~ a alguien a favor de alguien/en contra de alguien** to bias sb in sb's favor/against sb **4.** (*proveer*) **~ de algo** to provide with sth ▸ **más vale ~ que curar** *prov* prevention is better than cure, a stitch in time saves nine *prov* II. *vr:* **~se 1.** (*tomar precauciones*) to take precautions **2.** (*contra alguien*) to protect oneself **3.** (*proveerse*) **~se de algo** to provide oneself with sth

preventivo, -a [pre·βen·'ti·βo, -a] *adj* preventive, preventative; **medida preventiva** preventive measure; **prisión preventiva** remand

prever [pre·'βer] *irr como ver vt* to foresee

previo ['pre·βjo] *m* TV, CINE playback

previo, -a ['pre·βjo, -a] *adj* previous; **(sin) ~ aviso** (without) prior warning; **previa presentación del D.N.I.** on presentation of identity documents; **~ pago de la matrícula** on payment of the matriculation fee; **tuve una entrevista previa con él** I had a preliminary interview with him

previsible [pre·βi·'si·βle] *adj* **1.** (*probable*) predictable **2.** (*que se puede prever*) foreseeable; **era ~** it was to be expected

previsión [pre·βi·'sjon] *f* **1.** (*de prever*) prediction; **esto supera todas las previsiones** this surpasses all the predictions **2.** (*precaución*) precaution; **hay que tener ~ de futuro** one must plan for the future; **en ~ de...** as a precaution against... **3.** (*cálculo*) forecast; **las previsiones económicas** the economic forecasts

previsor(a) [pre·βi·'sor, ·'so·ra] *adj* **1.** (*con visión*) far-sighted **2.** (*precavido*) prudent

previsto, -a [pre·'βis·to, -a] *adj* predicted; **el éxito estaba ~** the success had been expected; **todo lo necesario está ~** everything necessary has been prepared

PRI [pe·rre·'i/pe·e·rre·i] *m abr de* **Partido Revolucionario Institucional** *Mexican ruling party from 1929 onwards*

prieto, -a ['prje·to, -a] *adj* **1.** (*apretado*) tight **2.** (*negro*) black

prima ['pri·ma] *f* **1.** (*pariente*) (girl) cousin; **~ hermana/segunda** first/second cousin **2.** FIN bonus; (*seguro*) insurance premium

primacía [pri·ma·'sia, ·'θia] *f* **1.** *t.* MIL, POL supremacy **2.** (*prioridad*) priority

primada [pri·'ma·da] *f inf* piece of foolishness; **me han hecho una ~** they've ripped me off

primar [pri·'mar] I. *vi* to be of great importance; **en esta escuela prima el orden** in this school the most important thing is good behavior; **aquí priman los enchufes sobre la capacidad personal** here contacts are more important than ability II. *vt* to reward

primario, -a [pri·'ma·rjo, -a] *adj* primary; **corriente primaria** ELEC primary current; **enseñanza primaria** primary education; **necesidades primarias** basic necessities

primate [pri·'ma·te] *m* primate

primavera [pri·ma·'βe·ra] *f* spring; **estar en la ~ de la vida** *fig* to be in the prime of life

primaveral [pri·ma·βe·'ral] *adj* spring(like)

primer [pri·'mer] *adj v.* **primero, -a**

primera [pri·'me·ra] *f* **1.** AUTO first (gear); **ir en ~** to be in first (gear) **2.** FERRO, AVIAT first class; **viajar en ~** to travel first class

primeriza [pri·me·'ri·sa, -θa] *f* first-time mother

primerizo, -a [pri·me·'ri·so, -a; -θo, -a] *m, f* (*novato*) novice

primero [pri·'me·ro] *adv* **1.** (*en primer lugar*) first; **~..., segundo...** first..., second...; **~ dice una cosa, luego otra** first he/she says one thing, then another **2.** (*antes*) rather

primero, -a [pri·'me·ro, -a] I. *adj* (*ante sustantivo masc. sing.: primer*) first; **primera calidad** top quality; **primera edición** first edition; **el Primer Ministro** the Prime Minister; **primera representación** première (performance); **estado ~** initial state; **a primera hora (de la mañana)** first thing (in the morning); **a ~s de mes** at the beginning of the month; **de primera** first-rate; **de primera calidad** top quality; **ser/estar de primera** to be really good; **desde un primer momento** from the outset; **en primer lugar** in the first place; **ocupar una de las primeras posiciones** to occupy one of the top positions; **lo ~ es lo ~** first things first; **para mí tú eres lo ~** for me you are more important than anything else; **lo ~ es ahora la familia** the most important thing now is the family II. *m, f* first; **el ~ de la carrera** the winner of the race; **el ~ de la clase** the top of the class; **estar entre los ~s** to be among the leaders; **eres el ~ en llegar** you are the first to arrive

primicia [pri·'mi·sja, -θja] *f* PREN, TV, RADIO scoop

primitivo, -a [pri·mi·'ti·βo, -a] *adj* primitive; **los habitantes ~s** the original inhabitants; **lotería primitiva** *Spanish state lottery;* **palabra primitiva** LING non-derived word

primo ['pri·mo] *m* **1.** (*pariente*) (boy) cousin; **~ hermano/segundo** first/second cousin

2. *inf* (*ingenuo*) mug; **hacer el** ~ to get taken for a ride; **¡no seas** ~! don't be such a fool!

primo, -a ['pri·mo, -a] *adj* **materia prima** raw material; **número** ~ MAT prime number

primogénito, -a [pri·mo·'xe·ni·to, -a] *adj, m, f* first-born

primor [pri·'mor] *m* **1.** (*habilidad*) skill **2.** (*esmero*) care; **hacer algo con** ~ to take great care in doing sth

primordial [pri·mor·'djal] *adj* **1.** (*más importante*) supreme; **este asunto es de interés** ~ this affair is of fundamental concern **2.** (*fundamental*) essential, fundamental

primoroso, -a [pri·mo·'ro·so, -a] *adj* **1.** (*hábil*) skillful **2.** (*con esmero*) careful; **es un bordado** ~ ~ it is a delicate piece of embroidery **3.** (*excelente*) excellent; **labios** ~ **s** beautiful lips

prímula ['pri·mu·la] *f* primrose

princesa [prin·'se·sa, -'θe·sa] *f v.* **príncipe, princesa**

principado [prin·si·'pa·do, prin·θi·] *m* principality; **el Principado** Asturias; **el Principado de Andorra** the Principality of Andorra

principal [prin·si·'pal, prin·θi·] *adj* **1.** (*más importante*) principal; **el problema** ~ the main problem; **lo** ~ **es que...** the main priority is ... **2.** (*esencial*) essential

principalmente [prin·si·pal·'men·te, prin·θi·] *adv* mainly, principally; **él ha sido** ~ **el que ha hecho el trabajo** he is the one who did most of the work

príncipe ['prin·si·pe, -θi·pe] *adj* **edición** ~ first edition

príncipe, princesa ['prin·si·pe, -θi·pe; prin·'se·sa, -'θe·sa] *m, f* prince *m*, princess *f*; ~ **heredero** crown prince; **el Príncipe de Asturias** the Prince of Asturias (*title held by the heir to the Spanish throne*); ~ **azul** Prince Charming

principesco, -a [prin·si·'pes·ko, -a; prin·θi·] *adj* princely

principiante [prin·si·'pjan·te, prin·θi·] *mf* beginner, novice

principio [prin·'si·pjo, -'θi·pjo] *m* **1.** (*comienzo*) beginning; **al** ~ at the beginning; **ya desde el** ~ right from the beginning; **desde un** ~ from the first; **a** ~ **s de diciembre** at the beginning of December; **dar** ~ **a algo** to start sth **2.** (*causa*) cause; (*origen*) origin; **el** ~ **de la discusión** the cause of the argument **3.** (*de ética*) principle; **sin** ~ **s** unprincipled; **hombre de** ~ **s** a man of principle(s); **por** ~ on principle **4.** *t.* FÍS (*fundamento*) principle; **en** ~ in principle

pringado, -a [prin·'ga·do, -a] *m, f inf* chump

pringar <g→gu> [prin·'gar] **I.** *vt* **1.** (*manchar*) ~ **de/con algo** to smear with sth **2.** (*mojar*) to dip **II.** *vi AmL* (*lloviznar*) to drizzle **III.** *vr:* ~**se 1.** (*mancharse*) ~**se de/con algo** to cover oneself with sth **2.** (*en negocio*) to make a bit on the side; **se ha pringado en 200 marcos** *pey* he/she has raked off 200 marks

pringoso, -a [prin·'go·so, -a] *adj* greasy

pringue ['prin·ge] *m* **1.** (*grasa*) grease **2.** (*suciedad*) grime **3.** *inf* (*jugada*) **¡vaya** ~! *inf* what a drag!

prioridad [prjo·ri·'dad] *f* **1.** (*anterioridad*) priority; **de máxima** ~ top priority; **dar** ~ **a un asunto** to give an affair priority **2.** AUTO right of way

prioritario, -a [prjo·ri·'ta·rjo, -a] *adj* priority; **este plan es** ~ this plan has priority

prisa ['pri·sa] *f* hurry; **a toda** ~ at full speed; **de** ~ quickly; **de** ~ **y corriendo** (*con demasiada prisa*) in a rush; (*rápidamente*) quickly; **no corre** ~ there's no hurry; **¡date** ~! hurry up!; **meter** ~ **a alguien** to hurry sb; **tengo** ~ I'm in a hurry; **no tengas** ~ take your time

prisión [pri·'sjon] *f* **1.** (*reclusión*) imprisonment; ~ **celular** confinement in cells; ~ **preventiva** remand **2.** (*edificio*) prison; ~ **de alta seguridad** high-security prison; **estar en** ~ to be in prison

prisionero, -a [pri·sjo·'ne·ro, -a] *m, f* prisoner; **hacer** ~ **a alguien** to take sb prisoner

prisma ['pris·ma] *m* (*figura*) prism

prismáticos [pris·'ma·ti·kos] *mpl* binoculars *pl*

privación [pri·βa·'sjon, -'θjon] *f* **1.** (*desposesión*) deprivation; ~ **de libertad** JUR loss of liberty **2.** (*carencia*) privation

privado [pri·'βa·do] *m* (*de rey*) royal favorite; (*de ministro*) protégé

privado, -a [pri·'βa·do, -a] *adj* **1.** (*reunión, fiesta*) private; (*sesión*) closed **2.** (*personal, confidencial*) private; **vida privada** private life; **en** ~ in private **3.** (*falto*) ~ **de...** without...; ~ **de flexibilidad** (*cosa*) inelastic; (*persona*) inflexible; ~ **de inteligencia** slow-witted; ~ **de la libertad** deprived of one's freedom; ~ **de medios** without means

privanza [pri·'βan·sa, -θa] *f* (*de príncipe*) favor; (*de ministro*) protection

privar [pri·'βar] **I.** *vt* **1.** (*desposeer*) to deprive; ~ **a alguien del permiso de conducir** to revoke sb's driver's license; ~ **a alguien de un derecho** to deprive sb of a right; ~ **a alguien de un cargo** to remove sb from a position **2.** (*prohibir*) to forbid; **no me prives de visitarte** don't stop me from visiting you **3.** (*gustar*) to delight; **está privado por esa chica** he's crazy about that girl **II.** *vr* to deny oneself; **no se privan de nada** they don't want for anything

privativo, -a [pri·βa·'ti·βo, -a] *adj* (*propio*) exclusive; ~ **de alguien** exclusive to sb

privatización [pri·βa·ti·sa·'sjon, -θa·'θjon] *f* privatization

privatizar <z→c> [pri·βa·ti·'sar, -'θar] *vt* to privatize

privilegiado, -a [pri·βi·le·'xja·do, -a] **I.** *adj* privileged; (*memoria*) exceptional **II.** *m, f* privileged person

privilegiar [pri·βi·le·'xjar] *vt* to grant a privilege to

privilegio [pri·βi·'le·xjo] *m* privilege; ~ **fiscal** tax concession

pro [pro] **I.** *m o f* **1.** (*provecho*) advantage; **valorar los ~s y los contras** to weigh the pros and cons; **en ~ de** in favor of **2.** (*de bien*) **un hombre de ~** an honest man **II.** *prep* for

proa ['proa] *f* NÁUT bow; AVIAT nose; **poner la ~ en un asunto** to tackle an affair; **poner la ~ a alguien** to take a stand against sb

probabilidad [pro·βa·βi·li·'dad] *f* **1.** (*verosimilitud*) probability; **con toda ~** in all likelihood **2.** (*posibilidad*) prospect; **hay ~es de ganar** there is a good chance of winning

probable [pro·'βa·βle] *adj* **1.** (*verosímil*) probable; **un resultado ~** a likely result; **lo más ~ es que...** chances are that...; **el ~ campeón** the likely winner **2.** (*que se puede probar*) provable

probablemente [pro·βa·βle·'men·te] *adv* probably

probado, -a [pro·'βa·do, -a] *adj* proven

probador [pro·βa·'dor] *m* fitting room

probar <o→ue> [pro·'βar] **I.** *vt* **1.** (*demostrar*) to prove; **todavía no está probado que sea culpable** it still hasn't been proved that he is guilty **2.** (*experimentar*) to try; (*aparato*) to test **3.** (*a alguien*) to test **4.** (*vestido*) to try on **5.** CULIN to taste; **no he probado nunca una paella** I have never tried paella **II.** *vi* (*intentar*) to try

probatorio, -a [pro·βa·'to·rjo, -a] *adj* evidential

probeta [pro·'βe·ta] *f* (*tubo*) test tube; ~ **graduada** graduated flask

problema [pro·'βle·ma] *m* problem; ~**s de adaptación** teething problems; ~ **de liquidez** cash flow problem; **el planteamiento del ~** the way in which the problem is presented

problemática [pro·βle·'ma·ti·ka] *f* problems *pl*, questions *pl*

problemático, -a [pro·βle·'ma·ti·ko, -a] *adj* problematic

procacidad [pro·ka·si·'dad, -θi·'dad] *f* **1.** (*insolencia*) shamelessness **2.** (*grosería*) obscenity

procaz [pro·'kas, -'kaθ] *adj* **1.** (*insolente*) shameless **2.** (*grosero*) obscene

procedencia [pro·se·'den·sja, pro·θe·'den·θja] *f* **1.** (*origen*) origin; **anunciar la ~ del tren** to announce where the train has come from **2.** JUR legitimacy

procedente [pro·se·'den·te, pro·θe·] *adj* **1.** (*oportuno*) appropriate **2.** (*que viene de*) ~ **de** from; **el tren ~ de Nueva York con destino a Chicago** the train from New York to Chicago **3.** JUR fitting

proceder [pro·se·'der, pro·θe·] **I.** *m* **1.** (*comportamiento*) behavior **2.** (*actuación*) (course of) action **II.** *vi* **1.** (*familia*) to descend; (*de un lugar*) to come; (*pasión*) to spring **2.** (*actuar*) to act **3.** (*ser oportuno*) to be appropriate; **no ~** to be inappropriate; **ahora procede guardar silencio** now we/you should remain

silent; **táchese lo que no proceda** delete as applicable **4.** (*pasar a*) to proceed

procedimiento [pro·se·di·'mjen·to, pro·θe·] *m* **1.** (*actuación*) procedure; **seguir un ~** to follow a procedure **2.** (*método*) method **3.** JUR proceedings *pl*

prócer ['pro·ser, -θer] **I.** *adj* illustrious **II.** *m* national hero

procesado, -a [pro·se·'sa·do, -a; pro·θe·] *m*, *f* JUR defendant; **el ~** the accused

procesador [pro·se·sa·'dor, pro·θe·] *m* computer; ~ **de textos** word processor

procesal [pro·se·'sal, pro·θe·] *adj* (*costos, actuación*) legal; (*regla, derecho*) procedural

procesamiento [pro·se·sa·'mjen·to, pro·θe·] *m* **1.** JUR prosecution **2.** COMPUT processing; ~ **en línea** on-line processing

procesar [pro·se·'sar, pro·θe·] *vt* **1.** JUR to prosecute; **le procesan por violación** he is being prosecuted for rape **2.** TÉC to process

procesión [pro·se·'sjon, pro·θe·] *f* **1.** *t.* REL (*marcha*) procession **2.** (*hilera*) line; (*de personas*) procession **3.** *inf* (*preocupación*) **permaneció tranquilo aunque la ~ iba por dentro** he remained outwardly calm, but he was actually rather worried

proceso [pro·'se·so, pro·'θe·] *m* **1.** (*método*) process; ~ **de una enfermedad** development of an illness **2.** (*procedimiento*) procedure **3.** JUR (*causa*) trial

proclama [pro·'kla·ma] *f* **1.** (*matrimonial*) banns *pl* **2.** (*política*) proclamation

proclamación [pro·kla·ma·'sjon, -'θjon] *f* proclamation

proclamar [pro·kla·'mar] **I.** *vt* **1.** (*hacer público*) to announce; ~ **la República** to proclaim a Republic **2.** (*aclamar*) to acclaim **3.** (*sentimiento*) to declare **4.** (*ganador*) to declare; **fue proclamado Premio Nobel** he was awarded the Nobel Prize **II.** *vr* ~**se presidente** to proclaim oneself president; ~**se ganador** to declare oneself the winner

proclive [pro·'kli·βe] *adj* prone

procrear [pro·kre·'ar] *vt* to procreate

proctólogo, -a [prok·'to·lo·γo, -a] *m*, *f* MED proctologist *m*, *f*

procura [pro·'ku·ra] *f Méx* **en ~ de** in an attempt to

procurador(a) [pro·ku·ra·'dor, -·'do·ra] *m(f)* attorney; (*en negocios*) agent

procurar [pro·ku·'rar] **I.** *vt* **1.** (*intentar*) to try; **procura hacerlo lo mejor que puedas** do it to the best of your abilities; **procura que no te oigan** make sure they don't hear you **2.** (*proporcionar*) to obtain **II.** *vr* to secure (for oneself)

prodigar <g→gu> [pro·di·'γar] **I.** *vt* **1.** (*malgastar*) to waste **2.** (*dar*) to lavish **II.** *vr* **se prodigó en toda clase de atenciones con nosotros** he attended to our every need; **se prodigó en elogios hacia él** he/she showered him with praise; **se prodiga tanto en las explicaciones que nadie la entiende**

her explanations are so detailed that nobody understands her

prodigio [pro·'di·xjo] *m* prodigy; **niño ~** child prodigy

prodigioso, -a [pro·di·'xjo·so, -a] *adj* **1.** (*sobrenatural*) miraculous **2.** (*extraordinario*) marvelous

pródigo, -a ['pro·di·γo, -a] *adj* **1.** (*malgastador*) wasteful; **el hijo ~** the prodigal son **2.** (*generoso*) generous; **la pródiga naturaleza** bountiful nature

producción [pro·duk·'sjon, -'θjon] *f* **1.** *t.* TÉC, CINE production; **~ en cadena** assembly line production; **~ por encargo** manufacture to order; **~ en masa** mass production; **~ a medida** made-to-measure fabrication **2.** (*productos*) output

producir [pro·du·'sir, -'θir] *irr como* traducir **I.** *vt* **1.** *t.* TÉC, CINE to produce; (*energía*) to generate **2.** (*beneficios*) to generate; (*intereses*) to yield **3.** (*alegría, impresión*) to create; (*aburrimiento, miedo*) to produce; (*daño, tristeza*) to cause **II.** *vr:* **~se 1.** (*fabricarse*) to be produced **2.** (*tener lugar*) to take place; **se produjo una crisis** a crisis occurred; **se ha producido una mejora** there has been an improvement **3.** (*ocurrir*) to occur; **cuando se produzca el caso...** as the case arises...

productividad [pro·duk·ti·β i·'dad] *f* productivity

productivo, -a [pro·duk·'ti·β o, -a] *adj* productive

producto [pro·'duk·to] *m* **1.** *t.* QUÍM, MAT product; **~s básicos** commodities; **~s agrícolas** agricultural produce; **~ alimenticio** food item; **~s alimenticios** foodstuffs *pl;* **~ de belleza** beauty product; **~ estancado** product sold by state monopoly; **~s a granel** goods sold by bulk; **~ de línea blanca** no-name product; **~ de marca** brand-name product; **~s químicos** chemicals *pl;* **~ (semi)manufacturado** manufactured good; **~ terminado** finished product; **~ derivado** [*o* secundario] by-product **2.** (*de un negocio*) profit; (*de una venta*) proceeds *pl;* **Producto Interior Bruto** Gross Domestic Product; **Producto Nacional Bruto** Gross National Product

productor(a) [pro·duk·'tor, -·'to·ra] **I.** *adj* producing **II.** *m(f)* producer

proemio [pro·'e·mjo] *m* preface

proeza [pro·'e·sa, -θa] *f* exploit

profanar [pro·fa·'nar] *vt* (*templo*) to desecrate; (*memoria, nombre*) to profane

profano, -a [pro·'fa·no, -a] *adj* **1.** (*secular*) secular **2.** (*irreverente*) irreverent **3.** (*ignorante*) ignorant; **soy ~ en esta materia** I am not an expert in this subject

profecía [pro·fe·'si·a, -'θi·a] *f* prophecy

proferir [pro·fe·'rir] *irr como sentir vt* (*grito*) to utter; (*insulto*) to hurl; (*queja*) to express

profesar [pro·fe·'sar] **I.** *vt* (*religión, doctrina*) to profess **II.** *vi, vr:* **~se** to take one's vows

profesión [pro·fe·'sjon] *f* **1.** (*empleo*) profes-

sion; **la ~ más antigua del mundo** the world's oldest profession; **las profesiones liberales** the professions; **de ~** by profession **2.** (*de religión, doctrina*) profession; **~ de fe** profession of one's faith ▶ **hacer ~ de algo** to boast about sth

profesional [pro·fe·sjo·'nal] **I.** *adj* professional; **deportista ~** professional sportsman, sportswoman *m, f;* **ética ~** professional ethics; **secreto ~** trade secret **II.** *mf* professional

profesionista [pro·fe·sjo·'nis·ta] *mf Méx* professional

profesor(a) [pro·fe·'sor, -·'so·ra] *m(f)* (*no universitario*) teacher; (*universitario*) professor; (*catedrático*) senior teacher; **~ agregado** assistant professor; **~ numerario** [*o* titular] full professor

profesorado [pro·fe·so·'ra·do] *m* **1.** (*cargo no universitario*) teaching position; (*cargo universitario*) professorship **2.** (*conjunto*) faculty

profeta, -isa [pro·'fe·ta, pro·fe·'ti·sa] *m, f* prophet *m(f)*, prophetess *f;* **nadie es ~ en su tierra** no one is a prophet in his own land

profetizar <z→c> [pro·fe·ti·'sar, -'θar] *vt* to prophesy; *fig* (*adivinar*) to conjecture

profiláctico [pro·fi·'lak·ti·ko] *m* condom

profiláctico, -a [pro·fi·'lak·ti·ko, -a] *adj* preventive, preventative

profilaxis [pro·fi·'lak·sis] *f inv* prophylaxis

prófugo ['pro·fu·γo] *m* MIL deserter

prófugo, -a ['pro·fu·γo, -a] *m, f* JUR fugitive

profundamente [pro·fun·da·'men·te] *adv* profoundly; **~ ofendido** deeply offended; **~ sentido** heartfelt; **una persona ~ moral** a profoundly moral person

profundidad [pro·fun·di·'dad] *f* depth; **analizar en ~** to analyze in depth; **tener mucha/ poca ~** to be very deep/not very deep; **una cueva de cinco metros de ~** a cave five meters deep

profundizar <z→c> [pro·fun·di·'sar, -'θar] **I.** *vt* (*hoyo, zanja*) to make deeper; *fig* to study in depth **II.** *vi* **~ en algo** to study [*o* to go into] sth in depth

profundo, -a [pro·'fun·do] *adj* (*hoyo, lago, voz*) deep; (*capa, estrato*) deep-lying; (*observación*) incisive; (*pena*) heartfelt; (*dificultad*) extreme; (*pensamiento, misterio*) profound; (*conocimiento*) thorough; **psicología profunda** deep psychology; **en lo más ~ de mi corazón** from the very bottom of my heart

profusión [pro·fu·'sjon] *f* profusion; **~ de ideas** profusion of ideas; **~ de trabajo** surplus of work; **con ~ de detalles** with a wealth of details; **hay gran ~ de noticias** there is a lot of news

profuso, -a [pro·'fu·so, -a] *adj* profuse

progenie [pro·'xe·nje] *f* (*descendencia*) offspring, progeny

progenitor(a) [pro·xe·ni·'tor, -·'to·ra] *m(f)* **1.** (*antepasado*) for(e)bear **2.** (*mayor*) father *m*, mother *f;* **los ~es** the parents

programa [pro·'γra·ma] *m* program; **~ de las**

clases (**de la Universidad**) (university) class schedule; ~ **de estudios** study plan; ~ **de trabajo** work schedule; ~ **antivirus** COMPUT antivirus program; ~ **aplicativo** COMPUT application; ~ **contaminado** COMPUT infected program; ~ **de demostración** COMPUT trial software; ~ **de gráficas** COMPUT graphics program; ~ **de tratamiento de textos** COMPUT word-processing program; ~**s utilitarios** COMPUT utilities *pl*

programación [pro·γra·ma·'sjon, -'θjon] *f* 1. (*acción*) programming 2. TV, RADIO program

programador(a) [pro·γra·ma·'dor, -·'do·ra] *m(f)* programmer

programar [pro·γra·'mar] *vt* to plan; **la conferencia está programada para el domingo** the talk is scheduled for Sunday; **¿qué tienes programado para esta tarde?** what do you have planned for this evening?

progre ['pro·γre] I. *adj inf* trendy; POL left-wing; **sus ideas son ~s** he/she is a lefty II. *mf* trendy liberal; POL lefty

progresar [pro·γre·'sar] *vi* to make progress; (*enfermedad, ciencia*) to develop; ~ **profesionalmente** to progress [*o* get ahead] in one's career

progresión [pro·γre·'sjon] *f* 1. (*avance*) progress 2. MAT, MÚS progression

progresista [pro·γre·'sis·ta] *adj* progressive

progresivamente [pro·γre·si·βa·'men·te] *adv* progressively; **recuperarse ~** to recover gradually

progresivo, -a [pro·γre·'si·βo, -a] *adj t.* FIN (*que progresa*) progressive; (*que aumenta*) increasing; **aspecto ~** LING continuous tense

progreso [pro·'γre·so] *m* progress

prohibición [pro·i·βi·'sjon, -'θjon] *f* prohibition

prohibido, -a [pro·i·'βi·do, -a] *adj* ~ **fumar** no smoking; **fruto ~** forbidden fruit; **prohibida la entrada** no entry

prohibir [pro·i·'βir] *irr vt* to prohibit, to ban; **en los hospitales prohíben fumar** in hospitals smoking is not allowed

prohibitivo, -a [pro·i·βi·'ti·βo, -a] *adj* prohibitive; **a precio ~** prohibitively expensive

prohijar [pro·i·'xar] *irr como airar vt t. fig* to adopt

prójimo ['pro·xi·mo] *m* 1. (*semejante*) fellow man; **amor al ~** love of one's neighbor 2. *pey* (*sujeto*) specimen; **¡menudo ~ tenemos de vecino!** what a neighbor we have!

prole ['pro·le] *f* offspring *pl;* **padre con numerosa ~** father of many children

prolegómeno [pro·le·'γo·me·no] *m* (*a un escrito*) preface; (*al hablar*) introduction; **déjate de ~s y ve al grano** *inf* stop beating around the bush and get to the point

proletariado [pro·le·ta·'rja·do] *m* proletariat

proletario, -a [pro·le·'ta·rjo, -a] I. *adj* proletarian; **barrio ~** working-class area II. *m, f* proletarian

proliferación [pro·li·fe·ra·'sjon, -'θjon] *f* 1. (*en cantidad*) proliferation; ~ **tecnológica** technology proliferation; **tratado de no ~ de armas nucleares** nuclear non-proliferation treaty 2. *t.* MED (*incontrolada*) spread

proliferar [pro·li·fe·'rar] *vi* 1. (*en cantidad*) to proliferate 2. (*epidemia, rumor*) to spread

prolífico, -a [pro·'li·fi·ko, -a] *adj* prolific

prolijo, -a [pro·'li·xo, -a] *adj* (*esmerado*) detailed

prólogo ['pro·lo·γo] *m* (*de libro*) foreword; TEAT, DEP prelude

prolongación [pro·lon·ga·'sjon, -'θjon] *f* extension; (*de decisión*) postponement

prolongado, -a [pro·lon·'ga·do, -a] *adj* prolonged; **un sobre ~** a long envelope

prolongar <g→gu> [pro·lon·'gar] I. *vt* to extend; (*decisión*) to postpone; (*un estado*) to prolong II. *vr:* ~ **se** to continue; (*un estado*) to be prolonged; (*reunión*) to overrun; **la fiesta se prolongó hasta bien entrada la noche** the party carried on well into the night; **las negociaciones se están prolongando demasiado** the negotiations are dragging on for too long

promediar [pro·me·'djar] I. *vt* 1. (*repartir*) to divide in two 2. (*sacar promedio*) to average out II. *vi* 1. (*mediar*) to mediate 2. (*temporal*) **antes de ~ el año** before the year was halfway through; **promediaba el mes cuando...** the month was halfway through when...

promedio [pro·'me·djo] *m* average; **veo la tele un ~ de dos horas al día** I watch an average of two hours' TV a day

promesa [pro·'me·sa] *f* promise; REL vow; ~ **de matrimonio** promise of marriage; **el jefe me ha dado su ~ de que...** the boss has promised me that...

prometedor(a) [pro·me·te·'dor, -·'do·ra] *adj* promising

prometer [pro·me·'ter] I. *vt* to promise; REL to vow; **te prometo que lo haré** I promise you I'll do it; **te prometo por mis muertos que...** I promise on my mother's grave that...; ~ **el oro y el moro** to promise the earth ▶ **lo prometido es deuda** *prov* a promise is a promise II. *vi* **este negocio promete** this business is promising III. *vr* (*novios*) to get engaged

prometido, -a [pro·me·'ti·do] *m, f* fiancé *m,* fiancée *f*

prominencia [pro·mi·'nen·sja, -θja] *f* (*abultamiento*) bulge

prominente [pro·mi·'nen·te] *adj* prominent

promiscuidad [pro·mis·kwi·'dad] *f* (*sexual*) promiscuity

promiscuo, -a [pro·'mis·kwo, -a] *adj* (*sexualmente*) promiscuous

promoción [pro·mo·'sjon, -'θjon] *f* 1. (*de empresa, categoría, producto*) promotion 2. (*de licenciados*) year, graduating class; **ser de la misma ~** to have graduated in the same year

promocionar [pro·mo·sjo·'nar, -θjo·'nar] *vt* (*a empresa, de categoría, a producto*) to pro-

P

mote; **está promocionando su nueva película** she is promoting her new film

promontorio [pro·mon·'to·rjo] *m* (*terreno*) promontory

promotor(a) [pro·mo·'tor] *m(f)* **1.** (*de altercado*) instigator **2.** (*patrocinador*) sponsor; (*deportivo, artístico, de espectáculo*) promoter

promover <o→ue> [pro·mo·'βer] *vt* **1.** (*querella, escándalo*) to cause; (*proceso*) to advance **2.** (*en el cargo*) to promote **3.** (*aplausos*) to bring forth; (*altercado*) to instigate

promulgación [pro·mul·ɣa·'sjon, -'θjon] *f* enactment; (*divulgación*) announcement

promulgar <g→gu> [pro·mul·'ɣar] *vt* to enact; (*divulgar*) to announce

pronombre [pro·'nom·bre] *m* LING pronoun

pronominal [pro·no·mi·'nal] *adj* LING pronominal; **verbo** ~ reflexive verb

pronosticar <c→qu> [pro·nos·ti·'kar] *vt* to forecast

pronóstico [pro·'nos·ti·ko] *m t.* ECON forecast; MED prognosis; DEP prediction; **lesiones de ~ reservado** injuries of unknown seriousness

prontitud [pron·ti·'tud] *f* (*de ejecución*) promptness

pronto ['pron·to] **I.** *adv* **1.** (*rápido*) quickly **2.** (*enseguida*) at once **3.** (*temprano*) early ▶**al** ~ at first; **de** ~ suddenly; **¡hasta** ~! see you!; **por de** [*o* **por lo**] ~ for the time being **II.** *conj* **tan** ~ **como** as soon as; **tan** ~ **como llegaron/lleguen** as soon as they arrived/arrive

pronto, -a ['pron·to, -a] *adj* **1.** (*rápido*) quick; (*despierto*) sharp; **inteligencia pronta** lively intelligence **2.** (*dispuesto*) ready; **estar** ~ CSur to be ready

prontuario [pron·'twa·rjo] *m* (*resumen*) summary

pronunciación [pro·nun·sja·'sjon, -θja·'θjon] *f* LING pronunciation

pronunciado, -a [pro·nun·'sja·do, -a; -'θja·do, -a] *adj* pronounced; (*pendiente, cuesta*) steep; **arrugas pronunciadas** deep lines; **acento** ~ strong [*o* marked] accent; **una curva pronunciada** a sharp bend; **rasgos** ~**s** strong features

pronunciamiento [pro·nun·sja·'mjen·to, -θja·'mjen·to] *m* JUR pronouncement; ~ **judicial** court judgment; ~ **de sentencia** sentencing

pronunciar [pro·nun·'sjar, -'θjar] **I.** *vt* **1.** (*articular*) to pronounce; ~ **un brindis por alguien** to propose a toast in sb's honor; ~ **un discurso** to make a speech; ~ **unas palabras** to say a few words; ~ **sentencia** to pass sentence **2.** (*resaltar*) to emphasize **II.** *vr:* ~ **se** **1.** (*opinar*) ~ **se sobre algo** to state one's opinion on sth **2.** (*acentuarse*) to become more pronounced

propagación [pro·pa·ɣa·'sjon, -'θjon] *f* (*multiplicación, reproducción*) propagation

propaganda [pro·pa·'ɣan·da] *f* **1.** (*publici-*

dad) publicity; **hacer** ~ to advertise, to publicize **2.** MIL, POL propaganda

propagar <g→gu> [pro·pa·'ɣar] **I.** *vt* (*multiplicar*) to propagate; ~ **un rumor** to spread a rumor **II.** *vr:* ~ **se** (*multiplicarse*) to propagate

propalar [pro·pa·'lar] *vt, vr:* ~ **se** to spread

propano [pro·'pa·no] *m* propane

propasar [pro·pa·'sar] **I.** *vt* to overstep **II.** *vr:* ~ **se** (*extralimitarse*) to go too far; ~ **se con alguien** to take liberties with sb

propender [pro·pen·'der] *vi* ~ **a algo** to tend towards sth; MED to be prone to sth

propensión [pro·pen·'sjon] *f* ~ **a algo** tendency towards sth; MED predisposition to sth; **tener gran** ~ **a resfriarse** to catch colds very easily

propenso, -a [pro·'pen·so, -a] *adj* (*a enfermedades*) susceptible; (*dispuesto*) inclined; **ser** ~ **a algo** to be prone to sth

propiamente [pro·pja·'men·te] *adv* ~ **dicho** strictly speaking

propiciar [pro·pi·'sjar, -'θjar] **I.** *vt* (*favorecer*) to favor; (*posibilitar*) to make possible; **el viento propició la extensión de las llamas** the wind helped the flames to spread **II.** *vr:* ~ **se** (*conseguir*) to gain; **con sus palabras se propició el respeto de todos** with his/her words he/she won everyone's respect

propicio, -a [pro·'pi·sjo, -a; -'θjo, -a] *adj* **1.** (*favorable*) favorable; **en el momento** ~ at the right moment **2.** (*dispuesto*) inclined; **mostrarse (poco)** ~ **para...** (not) to be prepared to...

propiedad [pro·pje·'dad] *f* **1.** (*pertenencia, cualidad*) *t.* FÍS property; ~ **exclusiva** exclusive ownership; ~ **horizontal** joint ownership; ~ **industrial** patent rights; ~ **intelectual** intellectual property; ~ **inmobiliaria** real estate; ~ **mobiliaria** movable property; ~ **rústica** farm property; **un piso de mi** ~ an apartment that I own; **tener algo en** ~ to own sth; **ser** ~ **de alguien** to be sb's property **2.** (*corrección*) correctness; (*exactitud*) precision; **expresarse con** ~ to speak correctly

propietario, -a [pro·pje·'ta·rjo, -a] *m, f* owner; (*terrateniente*) landowner; (*casero*) landlord

propina [pro·'pi·na] *f* tip; **dejar** ~ to leave a tip; **de** ~ *fig* for good measure

propinar [pro·pi·'nar] *vt* (*golpes*) to give

propio, -a ['pro·pjo, -a] *adj* **1.** (*de uno mismo*) own; **con la propia mano** with one's own hand; **en defensa propia** in self-defense; **es tu propia culpa** it's your own fault; **lo he visto con mis** ~**s ojos** I have seen it with my own eyes; **tengo piso** ~ I own my apartment **2.** (*mismo*) same; **lo** ~ the same; **el** ~ **jefe** the boss himself; **al** ~ **tiempo** at the same time; **nombre** ~ LING proper noun **3.** (*característico*) characteristic; **los productos** ~**s del país** the products of the country; **eso (no) es** ~ **de ti** that is (not) like you **4.** (*apropiado*) proper

proponer [pro·po·'ner] *irr como poner* **I.** *vt*

1. (*sugerir, presentar*) to propose; ~ **un brindis por alguien** to propose a toast in sb's honor **2.** (*plantear*) to put forward; ~ **un acertijo** to ask a riddle; ~ **una cuestión** to set out a matter **II.** *vr* to propose; (*tener intención*) to intend; **¿qué te propones?** what are you trying to do?

proporción [pro·por·'sjon, -'θjon] *f* **1.** (*relación, porcentaje*) proportion; **no guardar ~ con algo** to be out of proportion with sth; **en una ~ de 8 a 1** in a ratio of 8 to 1 **2.** *pl* (*dimensión*) proportions *pl;* **un accidente de enormes proporciones** a major accident

proporcional [pro·por·sjo·'nal, -θjo·'nal] *adj* proportional; **reparto ~** proportional distribution; **sistema ~** POL proportional representation

proporcionar [pro·por·sjo·'nar, -θjo·'nar] *vt* **1.** (*facilitar*) to provide; ~ **víveres a alguien** to provide sb with supplies **2.** (*ocasionar*) to cause; ~ **disgustos a alguien** to upset sb **3.** (*dar proporción*) to proportion

proposición [pro·po·si·'sjon, -'θjon] *f* **1.** (*propuesta*) proposal; ~ **de ley** bill; ~ **de matrimonio** marriage proposal **2.** LING (*oración*) sentence; (*parte*) clause

propósito [pro·'po·si·to] **I.** *m* **1.** (*intención*) intention; **buenos ~s** good intentions; **tener el ~ de...** to intend to... **2.** (*objetivo*) objective ▶ **fuera de ~** irrelevant; **a ~** (*adrede*) on purpose; (*por cierto*) by the way **II.** *prep* **a ~ de** with regard to

propuesta [pro·'pwes·ta] *f* proposal; (*oferta*) offer; **a ~ de alguien** on sb's suggestion; **formular una ~** to draw up a proposal

propugnar [pro·puɣ·'nar] *vt* (*promover*) to advocate

propulsar [pro·pul·'sar] *vt* **1.** TÉC to propel **2.** (*fomentar*) to promote

propulsión [pro·pul·'sjon] *f* TÉC propulsion; ~ **a hélice** propeller power; ~ **por reacción** jet propulsion; ~ **total** AUTO four-wheel drive

prorrata [pro·'rra·ta] *f* portion; (*cuota*) quota

prórroga ['pro·rro·ɣa] *f* **1.** ECON extension; ~ **de pago** extension of payment deadline **2.** (*aplazamiento*) deferral **3.** DEP extra time, overtime

prorrogación [pro·rro·ɣa·'sjon, -'θjon] *f* extension

prorrogar <g→gu> [pro·rro·'ɣar] *vt* **1.** ECON to extend **2.** *t.* JUR (*aplazar*) to defer

prorrumpir [pro·rrum·'pir] *vi* ~ **en algo** to break out into sth

prosa ['pro·sa] *f* prose; **texto en ~** piece of prose

prosaico, -a [pro·'sai·ko, -a] *adj* prosaic

prosapia [pro·'sa·pja] *f* ancestry; **de mucha ~** from an illustrious family

proscribir [pros·kri·'βir] *irr como escribir vt* to ban

proscrito, -a [pros·'kri·to, -a] *pp de* **proscribir**

prosecución [pro·se·ku·'sjon, -'θjon] *f* **1.** (*continuación*) continuation **2.** *t.* JUR prosecution; ~ **criminal** pursuit of a criminal

proseguir [pro·se·'ɣir] *irr como seguir* **I.** *vi* to continue; ~ **con/en algo** to persist with sth **II.** *vt* **1.** (*continuar*) *t.* JUR to continue; ~ **diligencias** to continue proceedings **2.** (*un fin*) to pursue

prosista [pro·'sis·ta] *mf* prose writer

prospección [pros·pek·'sjon, -'θjon] *f t.* MIN prospecting; ~ **petrolífera** oil prospecting; ~ **de mercado** ECON market research

prospecto [pros·'pek·to] *m* prospectus; (*de un medicamento*) directions *pl* for use

prosperar [pros·pe·'rar] *vi* (*florecer*) to thrive; (*tener éxito*) to prosper

prosperidad [pros·pe·ri·'dad] *f* (*bienestar*) prosperity; ~ **económica** economic prosperity

próspero, -a ['pros·pe·ro, -a] *adj* (*floreciente*) thriving; (*con éxito*) prosperous; **¡Próspero Año Nuevo!** Happy New Year!

próstata ['pros·ta·ta] *f* prostate

prosternarse [pros·ter·'nar·se] *vr* to prostrate oneself

prostíbulo [pros·'ti·βu·lo] *m* brothel

prostitución [pros·ti·tu·'sjon, -'θjon] *f* prostitution; **ejercer la ~** to be a prostitute

prostituir [pros·ti·tu·'ir] *irr como huir* **I.** *vt* to prostitute **II.** *vr:* ~ **se** *t. fig* to prostitute oneself

prostituto, -a [pros·ti·'tu·to, -a] *m, f* male prostitute *m*, prostitute *f*

prosudo, -a [pro·'su·do, -a] *adj Chile, Ecua, Perú* affectedly formal

protagonista [pro·ta·ɣo·'nis·ta] **I.** *adj* **la actriz ~** the leading actress; **el papel ~** the leading role **II.** *mf* key participant; CINE, TEAT leading actor *m*, leading actress *f;* LIT main character

protagonizar <z→c> [pro·ta·ɣo·ni·'sar, -'θar] *vt* to play; ~ **una película** to star in a film

protección [pro·tek·'sjon, -'θjon] *f* protection; ~ **acústica** sound-proofing; ~ **antiaérea** anti-aircraft defenses; ~ **contra incendios** fire protection; ~ **sanitaria** health cover; **crema de alta ~** high-protection sun cream; **poner a alguien bajo ~** to place sb under protection; **tomar a alguien bajo su ~** to take sb into one's protection

protector [pro·tek·'tor] *m* protector; ~ **labial** lip salve; ~ **solar** sunscreen

protector(a) [pro·tek·'tor, -·'to·ra] **I.** *adj* protective; **casco ~** protective helmet; **sociedad ~a de animales** society for the prevention of cruelty to animals **II.** *m(f)* protector; (*mecenas*) patron

protectorado [pro·tek·to·'ra·do] *m* protectorate

proteger <g→j> [pro·te·'xer] **I.** *vt* to protect **II.** *vr:* ~ **se** to protect oneself; ~ **se los ojos** to protect one's eyes

protegido, -a [pro·te·'xi·do, -a] **I.** *adj* protected; ~ **contra escritura** COMPUT write-protected; ~ **por patente** protected by patent **II.** *m, f* protégé *m*, protégée *f*

proteína [pro·te·'i·na] *f* protein

prótesis ['pro·te·sis] *f inv* prosthesis; ~ **auditiva** hearing aid

protesta [pro·'tes·ta] *f* protest; JUR objection

protestante [pro·tes·'tan·te] *adj, mf* REL Protestant

protestar [pro·tes·'tar] I. *vi* to protest II. *vt* JUR to raise an objection

protestón, -ona [pro·tes·'ton, -·'to·na] *adj inf* grumbling

protocolo [pro·to·'ko·lo] *m* protocol; **de** ~ formal

protón [pro·'ton] *m* proton

prototipo [pro·to·'ti·po] *m* prototype

protuberancia [pro·tu·βe·'ran·sja, -θja] *f* protuberance

protuberante [pro·tu·βe·'ran·te] *adj* protuberant

provecho [pro·'βe·ʧo] *m* use; (*ventaja*) advantage; (*beneficio*) benefit; **para su propio** ~ for one's own use; **de** ~ useful; **nada de** ~ nothing of use; **en** ~ **de alguien** to sb's advantage; **sacar** ~ **de algo/alguien** to do benefit from sth/sb, to profit from sth/sb; **¡buen** ~! enjoy your meal!, bon appétit!

provechoso, -a [pro·βe·'ʧo·so, -a] *adj* beneficial; (*útil*) useful

proveedor(a) [pro·βe·'dor/pro·βe·'e·dor] *m(f)* **1.** (*suministrador*) supplier **2.** COMPUT provider

proveer [pro·'βer/pro·βe·'er] *irr* I. *vi* to provide; ~ **a algo** to provide for sth; ~ **a las necesidades de alguien** to attend to sb's needs; **¡Dios** ~**á!** the Lord will provide! II. *vt:* ~**se 1.** (*abastecer*) to supply; ~ **de algo** to furnish with sth; (*dotar*) to provide with sth **2.** (*un puesto*) to fill III. *vr* to supply oneself; ~**se de algo** to provide oneself with sth

proveniente [pro·βe·'njen·te] *adj* **el tren** ~ **de Madrid** the train from Madrid

provenir [pro·βe·'nir] *irr como venir vi* ~ **de** to come from, to stem from

proverbial [pro·βer·'βjal] *adj* proverbial

proverbio [pro·'βer·βjo] *m* proverb

providencia [pro·βi·'den·sja, -θja] *f* **1.** (*medida*) precaution **2.** JUR ruling; ~ **ejecutoria** writ of execution **3.** REL Providence

provincia [pro·'βin·sja, -θja] *f* province; *AmS* (*estado*) state; **ciudad de** ~**s** provincial town

provincial [pro·βin·'sjal, -'θjal] *adj* provincial; **capital** ~ provincial capital; **delegación** ~ provincial authority

provincialismo [pro·βin·sja·'lis·mo, -θja·lis·mo] *m* provincialism; *pey* parochialism

provinciano, -a [pro·βin·'sja·no, -a; -'θja·no, -a] *adj, m, f t. pey* provincial

provisión [pro·βi·'sjon] *f* (*reserva*) supply; **provisiones** provisions *pl*

provisional [pro·βi·sjo·'nal] *adj* provisional; **gobierno** ~ provisional government; **medida** ~ temporary measure

provisto, -a [pro·'βis·to, -a] I. *pp de* **proveer** II. *adj* provided; ~ **al efecto** provided for the purpose

provocación [pro·βo·ka·'sjon, -'θjon] *f* provocation

provocador [pro·βo·ka·'dor] *m* stirrer

provocador(a) [pro·βo·ka·'dor, -·'do·ra] I. *adj* provocative II. *m(f)* POL agitator

provocar <c→qu> [pro·βo·'kar] I. *vt* **1.** (*incitar*) to provoke; **¡no me provoques!** don't provoke me! **2.** (*causar*) *t.* MED to cause, to induce; ~ **risa a alguien** to make sb laugh; ~ **lástima a alguien** to make sb feel sorry for one; ~ **un cambio** to bring about a change; ~ **una guerra** to start a war; ~ **una escena** to create a scene; ~ **un incendio** to start a fire II. *vi AmL* (*apetecer*) (**no**) **me provoca** I (don't) feel like it

provocativo, -a [pro·βo·ka·'ti·βo, -a] *adj* provocative

proxeneta [prok·se·'ne·ta] *mf* (*de prostitutas*) pimp *m;* (*alcahuete*) procurer *m,* procuress *f*

próximamente [prok·si·ma·'men·te] *adv* soon

proximidad [prok·si·mi·'dad] *f* proximity; **en las** ~**es** in the vicinity

próximo, -a ['prok·si·mo, -a] *adj* **1.** (*cercano*) near, neighboring; (*temporal*) close; **en fecha próxima** shortly, soon; **estar** ~ **a...** to be close to... **2.** (*siguiente*) next; **el** ~ **año** next year; **el** ~ **viernes** next Friday; **el** ~ **3 de octubre** on the 3rd of October this year; **la próxima vez** the next time; **¡hasta la próxima!** see you soon!

proyección [pro·jek·'sjon, -'θjon] *f* **1.** FÍS, ARQUIT, CINE, PSICO projection; (*sesión*) screening; ~ **de sombras** casting of shadows **2.** (*influencia*) influence; **una empresa de** ~ **internacional** a business with a global presence

proyectable [pro·jek·'ta·βle] *adj* **asiento** ~ AVIAT ejector seat

proyectar [pro·jek·'tar] I. *vt* **1.** FÍS, FOTO, CINE to project **2.** (*lanzar*) to throw **3.** (*luz*) to shine; (*sombra*) to cast **4.** (*planear*) to plan **5.** *t.* TÉC (*diseñar*) to design II. *vr:* ~**se 1.** (*luz*) to be shone; (*sombra*) to be cast **2.** PSICO ~**se en algo** to project onto sth

proyectil [pro·jek·'til] *m* projectile; ~ **anticarro** anti-tank missile

proyecto [pro·'jek·to] *m* plan; ~ **de fin de carrera** UNIV final year project; (*en Letras*) final year dissertation; ~ **de ley** bill; **en** ~ planned; **tener** ~**s** to have plans; **tener algo en** ~ to be planning sth

proyector [pro·jek·'tor] *m* FOTO, CINE projector; ~ **de cine** film projector; **de diapositivas** slide projector; ~ **de cuerpos opacos** overhead projector; ~ **de luz** floodlight

prudencia [pru·'den·sja, -θja] *f* prudence

prudencial [pru·den·'sjal, -'θjal] *adj* (*razonable*) reasonable; **una cantidad** ~ an adequate amount

prudenciarse [pru·den·'sjar·se, -'θjar·se] *vr AmL* **1.** (*ser prudente*) to be cautious **2.** (*moderarse*) to be moderate

prudente [pru·'den·te] *adj* prudent

prueba ['prwe·βa] *f* **1.** *t.* TÉC (*test*) test; (*experimento*) experiment; ~ **de alcohole-mia** Breathalyzer® test; ~ **de aptitud** aptitude test; ~ **al azar** random trial; ~ **de azúcar en la sangre** blood sugar test; ~**s nucleares** nuclear tests; ~ **de paternidad** paternity test; **período de** ~ trial period; **poner a** ~ to try out; **someter a** ~ to test; **sufrir una dura** ~ to be put through a stern test; **a** ~ **de agua** waterproof; **a** ~ **de balas** bullet-proof; **a** ~ **de robo** theft-proof; **a título de** ~ as a test; **a toda** ~ fully tested; *fig* cast-iron; ~ **de fuego** *fig* acid test **2.** (*comprobación*) proof; (*de ropa*) trying on; ~ **de degustación** tasting **3.** (*examen*) exam; ~ **de acceso** entry exam **4.** DEP (*competición*) event; ~ **clasificatoria/eliminatoria** qualifier/eliminator **5.** TIPO proof; ~ **de imprenta** proof **6.** (*testimonio*) piece of evidence; ~ **circunstancial** circumstantial evidence; ~ **documental** documentary evidence; **dar** ~**s de afecto** to show one's affection; **en** ~ **de nuestro reconocimiento** as a token of our gratitude; **presentar la** ~ to present the evidence; **ser** ~ **de algo** to be proof of sth; **tener** ~**s de que...** to have evidence that...

prurito [pru·'ri·to] *m* **1.** MED (*picor*) itch **2.** (*afán*) urge

Prusia ['pru·sja] *f* Prussia

prusiano, -a [pru·'sja·no, -a] *adj, m, f* Prussian

P.S. [pos es·'krip·tun] *abr de* **post scriptum** PS

(p)seudónimo [seu·'do·ni·mo] *m* pseudonym

(p)sicoanálisis [si·ko·a·'na·li·sis] *m* psychoanalysis

(p)sicoanalista [si·ko·a·na·'lis·ta] *mf* psychoanalyst

(p)sicodélico, -a [si·ko·'de·li·ko, -a] *adj* psychedelic

(p)sicofármaco [si·ko·'far·ma·ko, -a] *m* psychotropic drug

(p)sicología [si·ko·lo·'xi·a] *f* psychology; ~ **infantil** child psychology; ~ **evolutiva** developmental psychology

(p)sicológico, -a [si·ko·lo·'xi·ko, -a] *adj* psychological; **terror** ~ psychological terror

(p)sicólogo, -a [si·'ko·lo·γo, -a] *m, f* psychologist; **es muy/poco** ~ *inf* he is very/not very perceptive

(p)sicópata [si·'ko·pa·ta] *mf* psychopath; ~ **sexual** sexual psychopath

(p)sicosis [si·'ko·sis] *f inv* psychosis; ~ **colectiva** collective psychosis

(p)sicosomático, -a [si·ko·so·'ma·ti·ko, -a] *adj* psychosomatic

(p)sicoterapeuta [si·ko·te·ra·'peu·ta] *mf* psychotherapist

(p)sicoterapia [si·ko·te·'ra·pja] *f* psychotherapy

(p)sique ['si·ke] *f* psyche

(p)siquiatra [si·'kja·tra] *mf* psychiatrist

(p)siquiatría [si·kja·'tri·a] *f* psychiatry

(p)siquiátrico [si·'kja·tri·ko] *m* (*hospital*) mental [*o* psychiatric] hospital

(p)siquiátrico, -a [si·'kja·tri·ko, -a] *adj* psychiatric

(p)síquico, -a ['si·ki·ko, -a] *adj* psychic, mental; **problemas** ~**s** mental problems

PSOE [pe·'soe] *m abr de* **Partido Socialista Obrero Español** *Spanish Socialist Party*

pta. [pe·'se·ta] *f* <pt(a)s.> *abr de* **peseta** peseta

púa ['pu·a] *f* (*de planta*) thorn; (*de animal*) spine, quill; (*del peine*) tooth; (*de tenedor*) prong; MÚS plectrum

pub <pubs> [paβ] *m* bar, cocktail lounge

púber ['pu·βer] *adj* adolescent

pubertad [pu·βer·'tad] *f* puberty

púbico, -a ['pu·βi·ko, -a] *adj* pubic; **zona púbica** pubic area

pubis ['pu·βis] *m inv* pubis

publicable [pu·βli·'ka·βle] *adj* publishable

publicación [pu·βli·ka·'sjon, -'θjon] *f* publication; ~ **electrónica** e-publication; ~ **reciente** recent publication

publicar <c→qu> [pu·βli·'kar] I. *vt* to publish II. *vr:* ~**se** to be published

publicidad [pu·βli·si·'dad, -θi·'dad] *f* **1.** (*carácter público*) publicity; **dar** ~ to publicize; **este programa le ha dado mucha** ~ this program has given him/her a lot of publicity **2.** (*propaganda*) advertising; ~ **disimulada** subliminal advertising; ~ **sobreimpresa** press advertising; ~ **en TV** TV advertisements *pl*; **hacer** ~ **de algo** to advertise sth

publicista [pu·βli·'sis·ta, -'θis·ta] *mf* publicist

publicitario, -a [pu·βli·si·'ta·rjo, -a; pu·βli·θi-] *adj* advertising

público ['pu·βli·ko] *m* public; **en** ~ in public; **aparecer en** ~ to appear in public; **el gran** ~ the general public; **para todos los** ~**s** for all audiences; CINE G-rated; **abierto/cerrado al** ~ open/closed to the public; **hoy hay poco** ~ there aren't many people today

público, -a ['pu·βli·ko, -a] *adj* public; **deuda pública** national debt; **relaciones públicas** public relations; **el sector** ~ the public sector; **transporte** ~ public transport; **de utilidad pública** of general use; **escándalo** ~ public scandal; **hacer** ~ to make public; **hacerse** ~ to become known; **ser del dominio** ~ to be public domain

pucha ['pu·tʃa] *interj CSur* ¡**la** ~! damn!

pucherazo [pu·tʃe·'ra·so, -θo] *m* ~ **electoral** electoral fraud

puchero [pu·'tʃe·ro] *m* (*olla*) pot; CULIN stew; **ganarse el** ~ to earn a crust; **hacer** ~**s** *inf* (*gestos*) to pout

pucho ['pu·tʃo] *m AmL* (*colilla*) cigarette butt

pudibundo, -a [pu·di'βun·do, -a] *adj pey* prudish

púdico, -a ['pu·di·ko, -a] *adj v.* **pudoroso**

pudiente [pu·'djen·te] *adj* (*rico*) well-off

pudin ['pu·din] *m* pudding

pudor [pu·'dor] *m* (*recato*) shyness; (*vergüenza*) shame

pudoroso, -a [pu·do·'ro·so, -a] *adj* (*recatado*) shy; (*vergonzoso*) bashful

P

pudridero [pu·dri·'de·ro, -a] *m* (*estercolero*) compost heap

pudrir [pu·'drir] *irr* **I.** *vt t. fig* to rot **II.** *vr:* ~**se** *t. fig* to rot; *Arg, inf* (*aburrirse*) to get bored; ~**se en la cárcel** *inf* to rot in prison; **¡ahí te pudras!** *vulg* go to hell!

pueblerino, -a [pwe·βle·'ri·no, -a] *m, f* villager; *pey* yokel

pueblo ['pwe·βlo] *m* **1.** (*nación*) people; **el ~ bajo** the common people; **un hombre del ~** a man of the people **2.** (*aldea*) village; (*población*) (small) town; ~ **costero** seaside town; ~ **de mala muerte** *inf* dead-end town; ~ **joven** *AmL* shanty town; **de ~** from a small town; *pey* small-town

puente ['pwen·te] *m. t.* NÁUT, ELEC (*construcción, de las gafas*) bridge; ~ **levadizo** drawbridge; ~ **colgante** suspension bridge; ~ **aéreo** (*servicio*) shuttle; MIL airlift; ~ **dental** bridge; ~ **de mando** (compass) bridge; ~ **de maniobras** working deck; ~ **de paseo** promenade deck, bridge (circuit); **hacer un ~ a un coche** to hot-wire a car **2.** (*fiesta*) long weekend (*a public holiday plus an additional day off*); **hacer/tener ~** to take/have a long weekend

puenting ['pwen·tin] *m* bungee jumping

puerco, -a ['pwer·ko, -a] *m, f* **1.** (*cerdo*) pig; (*macho*) hog; (*hembra*) sow; ~ **espín** porcupine **2.** *inf* (*persona sucia u obscena*) pig **3.** *inf* (*canalla*) swine

puericultor(a) [pwe·ri·kul·'tor, -·'to·ra] *m(f)* MED pediatrician

puericultura [pwe·ri·kul·'tu·ra] *f* (*general*) childcare, pediatrics

pueril [pwe·'ril] *adj* infant; **edad ~** childhood

puerro ['pwe·rro] *m* leek

puerta ['pwer·ta] *f* door; ~ **de la calle** front door; ~ **corredera** sliding door; ~ **cortafuego** fire door; ~ **de servicio** service door; ~ **de socorro** emergency exit; ~ **giratoria** revolving door; **día de ~s abiertas** open day; **quinta ~** AUTO rear door; **entrar por la ~ grande** to make a grand entrance; **escuchar detrás de la ~** to eavesdrop; **a la ~ de casa** at the front door; **a ~ abierta** *t.* JUR in public; **a ~ cerrada** *t.* JUR in private; **a las ~s de la muerte** at death's door; **enseñar la ~ a alguien** to show sb the door; **estar a las ~s** *fig* to be on the brink; **dar a alguien con la ~ en las narices** to slam the door in sb's face; **de ~s adentro** *fig* in private; **ir de ~ en ~** to go from door to door; **cerrar las ~s a alguien** *fig* to block sb's path; **poner a alguien en la ~ (de la calle)** to throw sb out; **eso es querer poner ~s al campo** *fig* that is like trying to turn back the waves; **por la ~ grande** *t. fig* in triumph; **tiene todas las ~s abiertas** *fig* he has a wealth of opportunities; **disparo a ~** DEP shot at goal

puerto ['pwer·to] *m* **1.** NÁUT harbor; (*ciudad*) port; ~ **deportivo** marina; ~ **franco** free port; ~ **interior** river port; ~ **marítimo** seaport; ~ **de matrícula** home port; **tomar ~** to come into port **2.** (*de montaña*) pass **3.** COMPUT port; ~ **para módem** modem port; ~ **de transmisión en paralelo/en serie** parallel/serial port

Puerto Rico [pwer·to'rri·ko] *m* Puerto Rico

> **i** **Puerto Rico**, a self-governing territory of the United States since 1952, consists of a main island and several small islands situated in the Greater Antilles. The capital of Puerto Rico is San Juan. The country's official languages are both Spanish and English.

puertorriqueño, -a [pwer·to·rri·'ke·no, -a] *adj, m, f* Puerto Rican

pues [pwes] **I.** *adv* **1.** (*entonces*) then; (*así que*) so; **he vuelto a suspender — ~ estudia más** I've failed again — well, you should study more; ~ **entonces, nada** well that's it, then **2.** (*ilativo*) so; ~ **bien** okay; **la consecuencia es, ~,...** so the result is...; **dejémoslo, ~** let's leave it, then **3.** (*causal*) **estudio inglés — ¡ah, ~ yo también!** I study English — ah, me too!; **¿quién es? — ~ no sé** who is it? — I don't know **4.** (*expletivo*) well; **¿estuvisteis por fin en Toledo? — ~ no/sí** did you end up going to Toledo? — no, I didn't/yes, I did; **¡~ esto no es nada!** this is nothing compared with what's to come! **5.** (*exclamativo*) **¡~ vaya lata!** what a pain!; **¡~ no faltaría más!** (*naturalmente*) but of course!; (*el colmo*) that's all we (etc.) need! **6.** (*interrogativo*) **¿~ qué quieres?** what do you want, then?; **¿y ~?** and?; **¿~ qué ha pasado?** so what happened? **7.** (*atenuación*) well; **¿nos vemos mañana? — ~ no sé todavía** shall we meet tomorrow? — well, I'm not sure yet **8.** (*insistencia*) ~ **así es** well that's how it is; ~ **claro** but of course; **¡vamos ~!** come on then!; **¡~ entonces!** for that very reason! **II.** *conj* **no voy de viaje, ~ no tengo dinero** I'm not going on holiday because I don't have any money

puesta ['pwes·ta] *f* putting; (*de aves*) laying; ~ **a cero** resetting; ~ **al día** updating; ~ **en escena** TEAT staging; ~ **en funcionamiento** activation; ~ **en hora** setting (*of time*); ~ **en libertad** release; ~ **en marcha** start button; AUTO starter; ~ **en práctica** putting into effect; ~ **a punto** final check; AUTO service; ~ **de sol** sunset

puestero, -a [pwes·'te·ro, -a] *m, f* stallholder

puesto ['pwes·to] *m* **1.** (*lugar*) place; (*posición*) position; ~ **de información** information point; ~ **de observación** ASTR observation station; MED observation post; **ceder/mantener el ~** DEP to lose/keep one's place **2.** (*empleo*) job; (*cargo, posición*) position **3.** (*tenderete*) stall; (*feria de muestras*) stand; (*chiringuito*) open-air bar; ~ **de periódicos** newspaper stand **4.** MIL post **5.** (*guardia*) post; ~ **de policía** police station; ~ **de socorro** first-aid station

puesto, -a ['pwes·to, -a] I. *pp de* **poner** II. *adj*
1. COM (*ex*) from; ~ **en fábrica** ex works **2.** *inf*
(*arreglado*) **ir muy bien** ~ to be very smartly
dressed; **tenerlos muy bien** ~**s** *vulg* to be a
real man **3.** *inf* (*entendido*) **estar** ~ **en un**
tema to be well-informed about a subject; ~ **al**
día up to date III. *conj* ~ **que** given that
pufo ['pu·fo] *m inf* dirty trick; **meter un** ~ **a al-**
guien to pull a fast one on sb
pugna ['puɣ·na] *f* struggle
pugnar [puɣ·'nar] *vi t. fig* to fight; ~ **por algo/**
alguien to struggle for sth/sb; (*intentar*) to
strive for sth
puja ['pu·xa] *f* (*en una subasta*) bid; ~ **mínima**
minimum bid
pujante [pu·'xan·te] *adj* strong; *fig* vigorous
pujanza [pu·'xan·sa, -θa] *f* strength; (*brío*)
vigor
pujar [pu·'xar] *vi* (*en una subasta*) to bid
pulcritud [pul·kri·'tud] *f* (*aseo*) tidiness
pulcro, -a <pulquérrimo> ['pul·kro, -a] *adj*
(*aseado*) tidy
pulga ['pul·ɣa] *f* flea; COMPUT bug; **tener** ~**s** to
be restless; **tener malas** ~**s** *inf* to be bad-tempered; **buscar las** ~**s a alguien** *inf* to tease sb
pulgada [pul·'ɣa·da] *f* (*medida*) inch
pulgar [pul·'ɣar] I. *adj* **dedo** ~ thumb II. *m*
thumb
Pulgarcito [pul·ɣar·'si·to, -'θi·to] *m* LIT Tom
Thumb
pulgón [pul·'ɣon] *m* aphid
pulguiento, -a [pul·'ɣjen·to, -a] *adj* AmL
flea-ridden
pulido [pu·'li·do] *m* polishing
pulido, -a [pu·'li·do, -a] *adj* polished
pulidor [pu·li·'dor] *m* TÉC polisher
pulidor(a) [pu·li·'dor, -'do·ra] *adj* TÉC
polishing
pulir [pu·'lir] *vt* to polish; (*perfeccionar*) to polish up
pulla ['pu·ja, -ʎa] *f* gibe
pullman ['pul·man] *m AmL* (*coche cama*)
sleeping car
pullover [pu·'lo·βer] *m AmL* pullover
pulmón [pul·'mon] *m* lung; ~ **de acero** iron
lung; ~ **acuático** aqualung; **gritar a pleno** ~
to shout at the top of one's voice [o lungs];
enfermo de ~ lung patient; **padecer de los**
pulmones to have bad lungs
pulmonar [pul·mo·'nar] *adj* MED pulmonary
pulmonía [pul·mo·'ni·a] *f* MED pneumonia
pulóver [pu·'lo·βer] *m AmL* pullover
pulpa ['pul·pa] *f* (*de la fruta*) flesh; ~ **de ma-**
dera wood pulp
pulpería [pul·pe·'ria] *f AmL* local shop, general
store

> ℹ️ In Latin America, a **pulpería** is a general
> store selling alcoholic beverages and all sorts
> of other items. **Pulperías** are very similar to
> the small **tiendas de pueblo** that are still
> frequently found in small villages in Spain.

pulpero, -a [pul·'pe·ro, -a] *m, f AmL* grocer
púlpito ['pul·pi·to] *m* pulpit
pulpo ['pul·po] *m* octopus
pulque ['pul·ke] *m Méx* CULIN *drink made from*
fermented agave cactus juice
pulquería [pul·ke·'ri·a] *f AmC, Méx* (*pulpería*)
general store
pulquero, -a [pul·'ke·ro, -a] *m, f AmS, Méx*
storekeeper
pulquérrimo, -a [pul·'ke·rri·mo, -a] *adj superl*
de **pulcro**
pulsación [pul·sa·'sjon, -'θjon] *f* **1.** ANAT
(*latido*) beat, throbbing **2.** (*de una tecla*) striking; (*mecanografía*) keystroke; ~ **doble** COM-
PUT strikeover
pulsar [pul·'sar] *vt* to press; (*teclado*) to strike;
~ **el timbre** to ring the bell; ~ **la opinión**
pública to gage public opinion
pulsera [pul·'se·ra] *f* bracelet; **reloj de** ~
wristwatch
pulso ['pul·so] *m* wrist; *fig* steadiness of hand;
a ~ (*sin apoyarse*) freehand; (*por su propio*
esfuerzo) on one's own; **con** ~ carefully;
tener buen ~ to have a steady hand; **tomar el**
~ **a alguien** to take sb's pulse; **echar un** ~ **a**
alguien to arm wrestle sb
pulular [pu·lu·'lar] *vi* **los turistas pululaban**
por la plaza the square was swarming with
tourists
pulverizador [pul·βe·ri·sa·'dor, -θa·'dor] *m*
sprayer; (*atomizador*) atomizing spray
pulverizar <z→c> [pul·βe·ri·'sar, -'θar] I. *vt*
1. (*reducir a polvo*) to pulverize **2.** (*atomizar*)
to atomize II. *vr:* ~**se** to be pulverized
pum [pun] *interj* bang; **ni** ~ *inf* not a thing
puma ['pu·ma] *m* puma
pumita [pu·'mi·ta] *f* MIN pumice stone
puna [pu·na] *f AmS* **1.** (*altiplano*) Andean plateau **2.** (*malestar*) altitude sickness
punción [pun·'sjon, -'θjon] *f* MED puncture
pundonor [pun·do·'nor] *m* sense of honor
pundonoroso, -a [pun·do·no·'ro·so, -a] *adj*
honorable
punga ['pun·ga] *f Arg, inf*, **punguista** ['pun·
gis·ta] *m Arg, inf* pickpocket
punible [pu·'ni·βle] *adj* punishable
punición [pu·ni·'sjon, -'θjon] *f* punishment
punitivo, -a [pu·ni·'ti·βo, -a] *adj* punitive
punki ['pun·ki] *adj, mf* punk
punta ['pun·ta] *f* **1.** (*extremo*) end; (*de lengua,*
iceberg) tip; (*de tierra*) headland; **hora(s)** ~
rush hour; **de** ~ **a** ~ from end to end; **lo tenía**
en la ~ **de la lengua** it was on the tip of my
tongue **2.** (*pico*) point; **a** ~ **de navaja** at knifepoint; **a** ~ **de pistola** at gunpoint; **acabar en**
~ to come to a point; **sacar** ~ (*afilar*) to sharp-
en ▶ **de** ~ **en blanco** all dressed up; **estar de**
~ **con alguien** to be annoyed with sb;
ponerse de ~ **con alguien** to fall out with sb
puntada [pun·'ta·da] *f* (*costura*) stitch; (*pin-*
chazo) prick; *fig* hint
puntaje [pun·'ta·xe] *m AmL v.* **puntuación**
puntal [pun·'tal] *m AmL* (*refrigerio*) snack

puntapié [pun·ta·'pje] *m* kick; **pegar un ~ a alguien** to kick sb; **tratar a alguien a ~s** *fig* to walk all over sb

puntear [pun·te·'ar] *vt* **1.** (*motear*) to dot **2.** (*dar puntadas*) to stitch **3.** MÚS to pluck

puntería [pun·te·'ri·a] *f* (*destreza*) marksmanship; **tener buena/mala ~** to be a good/bad shot

puntero [pun·'te·ro] *m* (*vara*) pointer

puntero, -a [pun·'te·ro, -a] *adj* leading; **tecnología puntera** cutting-edge technology; **el equipo ~** DEP the top team

puntiagudo, -a [pun·tja·'ɣu·do, -a] *adj* (sharp-)pointed

puntilla [pun·'ti·ja, -ʎa] *f* **1.** (*encaje*) lace (edging) **2.** (*del pie*) **de ~s** on tiptoe; **andar de ~s** to walk on tiptoe; **ponerse de ~s** to stand on tiptoe

punto ['pun·to] *m* **1.** (*general*) point; **~ álgido** crucial moment; **~ de arranque** starting point; **~ cardinal** point of the compass; **~ cero** starting point; **~ clave** key point; **no hay ~ de comparación** there's no comparison; **~ de destino** destination; **~ de ebullición** boiling point; **~ de encuentro** meeting place; **~ esencial** main point; **~ fuerte** strong point; **~ de intersección** intersection; **~ máximo** high point; **~ muerto** AUTO neutral; **~ de referencia** reference point; **~ a tratar** item (on the agenda); **~ de venta** point of sale; **~ de vista** point of view; **dar el ~ a algo** to get sth just right; **ganar por ~s** to win on points; **al ~** (*en seguida*) at once; **hasta tal ~ que...** to such a degree that...; **de todo ~** absolutely; **la una en ~** exactly one o'clock; **en ~ a** with reference to; **hasta cierto ~** up to a point; **¿hasta qué ~?** how far?; **¡vamos por ~s!** let's take it step by step!; **a ~ de** on the point of; **está a ~ de llover** it's about to rain; **a ~ fijo** exactly; **¡~ en boca!** *inf* mum's the word!; **¡y ~!** *inf* and that's that!; **en su ~** *fig* just right **2.** TIPO full stop; **~ y aparte** full stop, new paragraph; **~ y coma** semicolon; **~ final** full stop (*end of paragraph*); **poner ~ final a algo** *fig* to bring sth to an end; **~ y seguido** full stop (*no new paragraph*); **~s suspensivos** suspension points, dot, dot, dot *inf*; **dos ~s** colon; **poner los ~s sobre las íes** *fig* to dot one's i's and cross one's t's; **con ~s y comas** very precise **3.** (*calceta, labor*) knitting; **~ de media** plain stitch; **chaqueta de ~** knitted jacket; **hacer ~** to knit **4.** (*puntada*) stitch; **~ de sutura** MED stitch **5.** CULIN **a/en su ~** done; **batir a ~ de nieve** to beat until stiff **6.** (*preparado*) **a ~** ready; **poner a ~** TÉC to fine-tune; (*ajustar*) to adjust; **tener a ~** to have ready **7.** COMPUT dot; **~ .com** dot.com

puntocom [pun·to·'kom] *f* COMPUT (**compañía**) [*o* **empresa**] ~ dotcom company

puntuación [pun·twa·'sjon, -'θjon] *f* **1.** LING punctuation; **signo de ~** punctuation mark **2.** (*calificación*) mark, grade; DEP score; **sistema de ~** scoring system

puntual [pun·tu·'al] *adj* **1.** (*concreto*) specific **2.** (*exacto*) precise **3.** (*sin retraso*) punctual

puntualidad [pun·twa·li·'dad] *f* punctuality

puntualizar <z→c> [pun·twa·li·'sar, -'θar] *vt* to specify; (*aclarar*) to clarify

puntuar <*1. pres:* puntúo> [pun·tu·'ar] *vt* **1.** (*un escrito*) to punctuate **2.** (*conseguir puntos*) to score **3.** (*calificar*) to mark, to grade; DEP to score

punzada [pun·'sa·da, -θa·da] *f* (*dolor*) sharp pain; (*en los costados*) stitch

punzante [pun·'san·te, -θan·te] *adj* **1.** (*puntiagudo*) sharp **2.** (*mordaz*) scathing

punzar <z→c> [pun·'sar, -'θar] **I.** *vt* (*agujerear*) to puncture **II.** *vi* (*doler*) to stab

punzó [pun·'so, -'θo] *adj* CSur, Col **rojo ~** bright red

punzón [pun·'son, -'θon] *m* punch; **~ para cuero** awl

puñado [pu·'ɲa·do] *m* handful; **a ~s** (*mucho*) by the handful; **un ~** *inf* (*mucho*) a lot

puñal [pu·'ɲal] *m* dagger; **poner a alguien el ~ al pecho** *fig* to hold a gun to sb's head

puñalada [pu·ɲa·'la·da] *f* stab; (*herida*) stab wound; *fig* blow; **coser a ~s** to stab repeatedly; **dar una ~ trapera a alguien** *fig* to stab sb in the back

puñeta [pu·'ɲe·ta] *f vulg* **1.** (*molestia*) **¡(qué) ~(s)!** hell!; **hacer la ~ a alguien** to screw things up for sb **2.** (*bobada*) stupid thing; **¡déjate de ~s!** stop messing about!; **¿qué ~s estás diciendo?** what the hell are you on about?; **en la quinta ~** in never-never land **3.** *AmL* (*masturbación*) jerk-off **4.** *vulg* (*expresión de enfado*) **mandar a alguien a hacer ~s** to tell sb to go to hell; **¡vete a hacer ~s!** go to hell!

puñetazo [pu·ɲe·'ta·so, -θo] *m* punch

puñetero, -a [pu·ɲe·'te·ro, -a] *adj inf* damn(ed); **el muy ~ no me ayudó** the bastard didn't help me

puño ['pu·ɲo] *m* **1.** (*mano*) fist; **~ cerrado** clenched fist; **con el ~ en alto** with one's fist raised; **apretar los ~s** *fig* to struggle hard; **comerse los ~s** *fig* to be starving; **como un ~** (*huevo, mentira*) enormous; (*casa, habitación*) tiny; **verdades como ~s** fundamental truths; **de su ~ y letra** in his/her own hand; **meter a alguien en un ~** *fig* to intimidate sb; **tener a alguien en un ~** *fig* to have sb under one's thumb **2.** (*mango*) handle; (*pomo*) hilt **3.** (*de la ropa*) cuff; **~ vuelto** turned-up cuff

pupa ['pu·pa] *f* **1.** (*ampolla*) blister; (*heridilla*) small wound **2.** *inf* (*dolor*) pain; **¡~!** ouch! **3.** ZOOL pupa

pupila [pu·'pi·la] *f* pupil; **tener ~** *inf* to be sharp

pupilaje [pu·pi·'la·xe] *m* (*tutela*) pupilage

pupilar [pu·pi·'lar] *adj* pupillary

pupilo, -a [pu·'pi·lo, -a] *m, f* ward

pupitre [pu·'pi·tre] *m* **1.** (*escritorio*) desk **2.** TÉC console; **~ de control** control panel

pupo ['pu·po] *m Arg, Bol, Chile* navel

purasangre [pu·ra·'san·gre] *adj, m* thoroughbred

puré [pu·'re] *m* purée; **~ de patatas** mashed potatoes; **hacer ~** to purée; *fig* to beat to a pulp; **estar hecho ~** *fig* to be exhausted

pureza [pu·'re·sa, -θa] *f* purity

purga ['pur·ya] *f (eliminación)* purge

purgación [pur·ya·'sjon, -'θjon] *f* **1.** MED purging **2.** TÉC draining

purgante [pur·'yan·te] *adj, m* purgative

purgar <g→gu> [pur·'yar] **I.** *vt t. fig* to clean; MED to purge; *(evacuar)* to empty; *(aguas)* to drain **II.** *vr:* **~se** *t. fig* to clean oneself; MED to take a purge

purgativo, -a [pur·ya·'ti·βo, -a] *adj* purgative

purgatorio [pur·ya·'to·rjo] *m* purgatory

purificador [pu·ri·fi·ka·'dor] *m* purifier; **~ de humos** smoke filter

purificador(a) [pu·ri·fi·ka·'dor, -'do·ra] *adj* **planta ~a** water treatment plant

purificar <c→qu> [pu·ri·fi·'kar] **I.** *vt t. fig* to purify **II.** *vr:* **~se** to be purified; *fig* to purify oneself

Purísima [pu·'ri·si·ma] *f* **la ~** the Virgin (Mary)

purista [pu·'ris·ta] *adj, mf* purist

puritano, -a [pu·ri·'ta·no, -a] **I.** *adj* puritanical **II.** *m, f* puritan

puro ['pu·ro] *m* cigar

puro, -a ['pu·ro, -a] *adj* pure; *(auténtico)* authentic; **por pura cortesía** as a matter of courtesy; **pura lana** pure wool; **la pura verdad** the honest truth; **pura casualidad** sheer chance; **de ~ miedo** from sheer terror; **se cae de ~ bueno/tonto** he is unbelievably kind/stupid

púrpura ['pur·pu·ra] *adj, f* purple

purpúreo, -a [pur·'pu·reo, -a] *adj* purple

purrete, -a [pu·'rre·te, -a] *m, f RíoPl, inf* kid *inf*

purulento, -a [pu·ru·'len·to, -a] *adj* purulent

pus [pus] *m* MED pus

pusilánime [pu·si·'la·ni·me] *adj* cowardly

pústula ['pus·tu·la] *f* MED pustule

puta ['pu·ta] *f vulg* whore; **casa de ~s** brothel; **ir de ~s** to go whoring; **hijo de ~** son of a bitch; **pasarlas ~s** to go through hell

putada [pu·'ta·da] *f vulg* ¡qué **~!** what a bloody nuisance!; **hacer una ~ a alguien** to play a dirty trick on sb

putañear [pu·ta·ɲe·'ar] *vi inf* to go whoring

putativo, -a [pu·ta·'ti·βo, -a] *adj* putative

puteada [pu·te·'a·da] *f AmS, vulg* swearword; **dar ~s** to swear

putear [pu·te·'ar] **I.** *vi vulg (ir de putas)* to go whoring **II.** *vt vulg (fastidiar)* to annoy; **me putea tanta gilipollez** all this stupidity really pisses me off; **estoy puteado** I'm really pissed off; **¡te han puteado bien!** they've really messed you about!

puticlub [pu·ti·'kluβ] *m inf* singles bar

puto, -a ['pu·to] *adj vulg* damned; **¡de puta madre!** brilliant!; **¡qué puta suerte!** what damn awful luck!; **el ~ coche no arranca** the damn car won't start; **ni puta idea** not a damn

clue; **las estoy pasando putas** I'm having a really shitty time

putrefacción [pu·tre·fak·'sjon, -'θjon] *f* decay

putrefacto, -a [pu·tre·'fak·to, -a] *adj* rotten

pútrido, -a ['pu·tri·do, -a] *adj* putrid

puya ['pu·ja] *f* **echar una ~ a alguien** to make a gibe at sb

puzzle ['pus·le, 'puθ-] *m* jigsaw (puzzle)

PVP ['pre·sjo de 'βen·ta al 'pu·βli·ko, 'pre·θjo] *m abr de* **Precio de Venta al Público** RRP

Q

Q, q [ku] *f* Q, q; **~ de Quebec** Q as in Quebec

qm [kin·'tal 'me·tri·ko] *abr de* **quintal métrico** 100 kg

que [ke] **I.** *pron rel* **1.** *(con antecedente: personas, cosas)* that, which *(often omitted when referring to object)*; **la pelota ~ está pinchada** the ball that is punctured; **la pelota ~ compraste** the ball you bought; **la historia de ~ te hablé** the story I told you about; **reacciones a las ~ estamos acostumbrados** reactions which we are accustomed to; **el proyecto en el ~ trabajo** the project that I am working on; **la empresa para la ~ trabajo** the company that I work for **2.** *(con antecedente: personas)* who, whom *(often omitted when referring to the object)*; **la mujer que trabaja conmigo** the woman who works with me; **el rey al ~ sirvo** the king (whom) I serve **3.** *(sin antecedente)* **el/la/lo ~...** the one (that/who/which)...; **los ~ hayan terminado** those who have finished; **el ~ quiera, ~ se marche** whoever wants to, can leave; **es de los ~...** he/she/it is the type that...; **el ~ más y el ~ menos** every single one; **es todo lo ~ sé** that's all I know; **lo ~ haces** what you do; **no sabes lo difícil ~ es** you don't know how difficult it is **4.** *(con preposición)* **de lo ~ habláis** what you are talking about **II.** *conj* **1.** *(completivo)* that; **me pidió ~ le ayudara** he/she asked me to help him/her **2.** *(estilo indirecto)* that; **ha dicho ~...** he/she said that... **3.** *(comparativo)* **más alto ~** taller than; **lo mismo ~** the same as **4.** *(porque)* because; **le ayudaré, seguro, ~ se lo he prometido** I'll help him/her, of course, because I promised **5.** *(para que)* **dio órdenes a los trabajadores ~ trabajaran más rápido** he/she ordered the workers to work faster **6.** *(sin que)* **no voy de vacaciones, ~ no me roben** I can't go on vacation without getting robbed **7.** *(de manera que)* **corre ~ vuela** he/she runs like the wind **8.** *(o, ya)* **~ paguen, ~ no paguen, eso ya se verá** we'll see whether they pay or not **9.** *(y)* **lo hizo él, ~ no yo** he did it, not me **10.** *(frecuentativo)* **y él dale ~ dale con la guitarra**

and he kept on playing and playing the guitar **11.** (*explicativo*) **hoy no vendré, es ~ estoy cansado** I'm not coming in today because I'm tired; **no es ~ no pueda, es ~ no quiero** it's not that I can't, it's that I don't want to; **¿es ~ no puedes venir?** can't you come then? **12.** (*enfático*) **¡~ sí/no!** I said "yes"/"no"!; **sí ~ lo hice** I did do it! **13.** (*de duda*) **¿~ no está en casa?** are you saying he/she isn't at home? **14.** (*exclamativo*) **¡~ me canso!** I'm getting tired!; **¡~ sea yo el que tenga que hacerlo!** I would be the one who has to do it! **15.** (*con verbo*) **hay ~ trabajar más** you/we/they have to work harder; **tener ~ hacer algo** to have to do something; **dar ~ hablar** to give people something to talk about ▸ **a la ~ llegue** as soon as he/she arrives; **a menos ~ +***subj* unless; **antes ~** before; **con tal (de) ~ +***subj* as long as; **por mucho ~ tú digas...** no matter what you say...; **yo ~ tú...** if I were you...

qué [ke] *adj, pron interrog* **1.** (*general*) what; (*cuál*) which; (*qué clase de*) what kind of; **¿por ~?** why?; **¿en ~ piensas?** what are you thinking about?; **¿para ~?** what for?; **¿de ~ hablas?** what are you talking about?; **¿a ~ esperas?** what are you waiting for?; **¿~ día llega?** what day is he/she arriving?; **¿~ cerveza tomas?** what kind of beer do you drink?; **¿a ~ vienes?** what are you here for?; **¿~ edad tienes?** how old are you?; **según ~ gente no la soporto** some people I just can't stand **2.** (*exclamativo*) **¡~ alegría!** how nice!; **¡~ gracia!** how funny!; **¡~ suerte!** what luck! **3.** (*cuán*) **¡~ magnífica vista!** what a magnificent view!; **¡mira ~ contento está!** look how happy he is! **4.** (*cuánto*) **¡~ de gente!** what a lot of people! ▸ **¿~ tal?** how are you [*o* things]?; **¿~ tal si salimos a cenar?** how about going out to dinner?; **¿y ~?** so what?; **¿y a mí ~?** and what about me?; **¿~?** well?; **~, ¿vienes o no?** well, are you coming, or not?

quebrada [ke·'βra·da] *f* **1.** (*paso*) ravine **2.** (*hendidura*) gap **3.** *AmL* (*arroyo*) stream

quebradizo, -a [ke·βra·'di·so, -a; -'di·θo, -a] *adj* **1.** (*objeto*) brittle **2.** (*de salud*) sickly; (*persona mayor*) frail **3.** (*voz*) faltering

quebrado [ke·'βra·do] *m* MAT fraction

quebrado, -a [ke·'βra·do, -a] *adj* **1.** (*empresa*) bankrupt **2.** (*herniado*) ruptured **3.** (*terreno*) rough

quebrantar [ke·βran·'tar] I. *vt* **1.** (*romper*) to break; (*cascar*) to crack; (*machacar*) to crush **2.** (*ley, secreto*) to break; (*obligación*) to violate **3.** (*autoridad*) to breach; (*salud*) to debilitate II. *vr:* **~se** (*estado de salud*) to be ruined; (*fuerza*) to be weakened

quebranto [ke·'βran·to] *m* **1.** (*de romper*) breaking; (*de cascar*) cracking; (*de machacar*) crushing **2.** (*económico*) heavy loss **3.** (*moral*) breakdown; (*físico*) weakening **4.** (*pena*) suffering

quebrar <e→ie> [ke·'βrar] I. *vt* **1.** (*romper*) to break **2.** (*interrumpir*) to interrupt **3.** (*el*

cuerpo) to bend **4.** (*rostro*) to distort **5.** (*ley*) to break **6.** (*suavizar*) to moderate II. *vi* **1.** (*con alguien*) to break up **2.** (*ceder*) to break down **3.** COM to go bankrupt **4.** (*intento*) to fail **5.** *Méx* (*darse por vencido*) to give in III. *vr:* **~se 1.** MED to rupture oneself **2.** (*la voz*) to go hoarse **3.** (*cuerpo*) to bend; **~se de dolor** to double over with pain

quebrazón [ke·βra·'son, -'θon] *m AmL* **1.** (*resultado*) breakage **2.** (*acción*) shattering

quechua ['ke·tʃwa] I. *adj* Quechua II. *mf* Quechuan

> **ⓘ Quechua** is both the name of the original inhabitants of **Perú** as well as the name of their language. **Quechua** is the second official language of **Perú**.

quedada [ke·'da·da] *f* **1.** *inf* (*burla*) joke **2.** *Méx, pey* (*solterona*) old maid

quedado, -a [ke·'da·do, -a] *adj Arg, Chile* slow

quedar [ke·'dar] I. *vi* **1.** (*permanecer*) to remain; **los problemas quedan atrás** the problems are a thing of the past; **¿cuánta gente queda?** how many people are left?; **~ a deber algo** to owe sth **2.** (*sobrar*) to be left; **no nos queda otro remedio que...** there's nothing left for us to do but...; **no queda ningún ejemplar de este libro** there are no copies of this book left **3.** (*resultar*) **todo quedó en una simple discusión** it ended up in a mere argument; **~ acordado** to be arranged; **~ cojo** to go lame; **~ eliminado** to be eliminated; **~ en ridículo** to make a fool of oneself **4.** (*acordar*) **~ en algo** to agree to sth; **¡en qué habéis quedado?** what have you decided?; **quedamos a las 10** we agreed to meet at 10; **primero dices una cosa y luego otra, ¿en qué quedamos?** first you say one thing and then another, make up your mind! **5.** (*estar situado*) to lie; **queda por/hacia el norte** it lies to the north; **quedar lejos de aquí** to be a long way from here **6.** (*faltar*) **quedan aún 100 km para llegar a casa** there are still 100 km left before we get home; **aún queda mucho por hacer** there's still a lot to do; **por mí que no quede** I'll do all that I can **7.** (*terminar*) to end; **... y ahí quedó el concierto** the concert ended there **8.** (*en una subasta*) **el cuadro queda por un millón de dólares** the painting goes for one million dollars **9.** (+ *por*) **~ por cobarde** to come across as a coward; **algo queda por ver** sth remains to be seen **10.** (+ *bien/mal*) **~ bien/mal** to turn out well/badly **11.** (+ *como*) **~ como un señor** to behave like a real gentleman; **~ como un idiota** to look like a fool II. *vr:* **~se 1.** (*permanecer*) to stay; **~se atrás** to stay behind; **~se colgado** (*ordenador*) to block; **durante la tormenta nos quedamos a oscuras** during the storm the lights went out; **cuando me lo dijo me quedé mudo** when he told me I was speechless **2.** (*resultar*) ~**se ciego** to go blind; ~**se viuda/viudo** to become a widow/widower; **al freír la carne se ha quedado en nada** when the meat was fried it shrunk to almost nothing **3.** (*conservar, adquirir*) **me quedo con el coche pequeño** I'll take the small car; **quédate con el libro** keep the book; ~**se sin nada** to be left with nothing; **entre el mar y la montaña me quedo con el mar** if I have to choose between the sea and the mountains, I'll take the sea **4.** (*burlarse*) ~**se con alguien** to make fun of sb

quehacer [ke·a·'ser, -'θer] *m* chores *pl;* **los** ~**es de la casa** housework; **dar** ~ **a alguien** to assign work to sb

queja ['ke·xa] *f* complaint; **no tengo** ~ **de él** I have nothing against him

quejarse [ke·'xar·se] *vr* **1.** (*formular queja*) ~ **de algo** to complain about sth; **se queja del frío** he complains about the cold; **¿qué tal te va el negocio? — bien, gracias, no puedo quejarme** how's business? — fine, thanks, I can't complain **2.** (*gemir*) ~ **de algo** to moan about sth

quejica [ke·'xi·ka] **I.** *adj* (*por dolor*) moaning; (*por manera de ser*) complaining; **¡no seas** ~**, hombre!** stop whining! **II.** *mf* complainer; (*criticón*) picky

quejido [ke·'xi·do] *m* moan; (*constante*) lament; ~ **de dolor** cry of pain; **dar** ~**s** to groan

quejoso, -a [ke·'xo·so, -a] *adj* complaining; **estar** ~ **de alguien** to be annoyed at sb

quejumbroso, -a [ke·xum·'bro·so, -a] *adj* (*voz*) whining; (*por dolor*) moaning

quelite [ke·'li·te] *m Méx* greens *pl*

queltehue [kel·'te·we] *m Chile* ZOOL teruteru

quema ['ke·ma] *f* **1.** (*acción*) burning; (*completa*) incineration **2.** (*incendio, fuego*) fire; **huir de la** ~ *fig* to flee from danger

quemada [ke·'ma·da] *f* **1.** *Arg, Méx* (*acción que pone en ridículo*) embarrassment **2.** *Méx* (*quemadura*) burn

quemado, -a [ke·'ma·do] *adj* burnt; **este político está** ~ *inf* this politician is finished; **estar** ~ **con alguien** *inf* to have had it with sb

quemadura [ke·ma·'du·ra] *f* burn; ~ **de primer grado** first-degree burn

quemar [ke·'mar] **I.** *vi* to burn; **cuidado, esta sopa quema** be careful, the soup is boiling hot **II.** *vt* **1.** (*comida, sol*) to burn; (*casa: completamente*) to burn down; ~ **un bosque** to set fire to a forest; **este chili quema la garganta/la lengua** this chili burns my throat/tongue **2.** (*planta: calor*) to scorch; (*frío*) to frostbite **3.** (*fortuna*) to squander **4.** (*fastidiar*) to mess up **5.** *AmC* (*denunciar*) ~ **a alguien** to inform against sb **III.** *vr:* ~**se 1.** (*arder*) to burn; **el bosque se quema** the forest is on fire; **me he quemado los cabellos** I've singed my hair **2.** (*herir*) to be hurt **3.** (*comida*) to burn; (*ligeramente*) to singe **4.** (*tener calor*) **me estoy quemando** I'm burning up **5.** (*por una pasión*) ~**se de amor** to burn with love

6. (*acertar*) **¡que te quemas!** you're getting warmer!

quemarropa [ke·ma·'rro·pa] **disparar a** ~ to shoot at close range; **hacerle preguntas a alguien a** ~ to fire questions (at sb)

quemazón [ke·ma·'son, -'θon] *f* **1.** (*quema*) burning **2.** (*calor*) intense heat **3.** (*ardor*) **siento una** ~ **en el estómago** I have a burning sensation in my stomach

quemo ['ke·mo] *m Arg* **¡que** ~**!** how embarrassing!

quemón [ke·'mon] *m Méx* dope smoker

quena ['ke·na] *f* MÚS *reed flute used in Andean music*

quepis ['ke·pis] *m* (*inv*) (*gorro militar*) kepi

quepo ['ke·po] *1. pres de* **caber**

queque ['ke·ke] *m Chile, Perú, AmC* (*bollo*) cake

querella [ke·'re·ja, -ʎa] *f* **1.** JUR lawsuit; ~ **criminal** criminal action; **poner una** ~ **contra alguien** to sue sb **2.** (*discordia*) dispute

querellarse [ke·re·'jar·se, -'ʎar·se] *vr* **1.** (*quejarse*) to complain; ~ **por algo** to complain about sth **2.** JUR to bring an action

querencia [ke·'ren·sja, -θja] *f* (*aprecio*) attachment; (*cariño*) affection; (*afición*) liking; **tomar** ~ **a algo/alguien** to take a liking to sth/sb

querendón, -ona [ke·ren·'don,·-'do·na] *adj AmL* loving, affectionate

querer [ke·'rer] *irr* **I.** *vt* **1.** (*desear*) to desire; (*más suave*) to want; **como tú quieras** as you like; **has ganado, ¿qué más quieres?** you win, what more do you want?; **hacer algo queriendo/sin** ~ to do something on purpose/unintentionally; **quisiera tener 20 años menos** I wish I were 20 years younger; **eso es lo que quería decir** that's what I meant to say; **quiero que sepáis que...** I want you to know that ...; **donde quiera que esté** wherever he/she/it may be; **¡por lo que más quieras, deja ese tema!** for God's sake, change the subject! **2.** (*amar*) to like; (*más fuerte*) to love; **te quiero con locura** I love you madly **3.** (*pedir*) to require **4.** (*requerir*) **estas plantas quieren mucha agua** these plants need a lot of water ▶~ **es poder** *prov* where there's a will, there's a way; **como quiera que sea** anyhow **II.** *v impers* **parece que quiere llover** it looks like rain **III.** *m* love

querido, -a [ke·'ri·do, -a] **I.** *adj* dear **II.** *m, f* (*amante*) lover; (*como vocativo*) darling

queroseno [ke·ro·'se·no] *m* kerosene

quesadilla [ke·sa·'di·ja, -ʎa] *f* CULIN **1.** (*pastel*) cheesecake **2.** (*pastelillo*) pastry **3.** *AmL* (*tortilla*) quesadilla (*folded tortilla filled with a spicy mixture and topped with cheese*)

quesera [ke·'se·ra] *f* (*plato*) cheese dish

queso ['ke·so] *m* **1.** CULIN cheese; ~ **de bola** Edam cheese; ~ **rallado** grated cheese **2.** *inf* (*pie*) foot; **te huelen los** ~**s** your feet smell

quicio ['ki·sjo, -θjo] *m* (*de puerta, ventana*)

Q

hinge post ▶ **sacar las cosas de** ~ to make a mountain out of a molehill; **estar fuera de** ~ to be in disorder; **sacar a alguien de** ~ to drive sb up the wall *sl*

quico ['ki·ko] *m inf* toasted corn snack

quid [kid] *m* crux; **ese es el ~ de la cuestión** that is the crux of the matter; **dar en el ~** to hit the nail on the head

quiebra ['kje·βra] *f* 1. com bankruptcy; **dar en ~** to go bankrupt 2. (*hendidura*) fissure; (*rotura*) break 3. (*pérdida*) loss, breakdown; **la ~ de los valores** the breakdown of values; **este asunto no tiene ~** this can't go wrong

quiebro ['kje·βro] *m* (*movimiento*) dodge; **hacer un ~ al defensa** (*fútbol*) to dribble around the defender

quien [kjen] *pron rel* 1. (*con antecedente*) who, that, whom (*often omitted when referring to object*); **el chico de ~ te hablé** that boy I told you about; **las chicas con ~es...** the girls with whom ... 2. (*sin antecedente*) that; **hay ~ dice que...** some people say that...; **no hay ~ lo aguante** nobody can stand him; **~ opine eso...** whoever thinks so...; **~ más, ~ menos, todos tenemos problemas** everybody has problems

quién [kjen] *pron interrog* who; **¿~ es?** (*llama*) who is it?; **¿~ es son tus padres?** who are your parents?; **¿a ~ has visto?** who did you see?; **¿a ~ se lo has dado?** who did you give it to?; **¿~ eres tú para decirme esto?** who are you to tell me this?; **¿por ~ me tomas?** what do you take me for?; **¡~ tuviera 20 años!** If only I were 20!

quienquiera <quienesquiera> [kjen·'kje·ra] *pron indef* whoever; **~ que sea que pase** whoever it is, come in

quieto, -a [kje·to, -a] *adj* 1. (*tranquilo*) calm; **no puede estar nunca ~** (*niño*) he/she can never keep still 2. (*parado*) motionless; **quedarse ~** to stand still

quietud [kje·'tud] *f* 1. (*calma*) calm 2. (*inmovilidad*) stillness

quijada [ki·'xa·da] *f* jaw(bone)

quilate [ki·'la·te] *m* karat; **de muchos ~s** *t. fig* of great value

quilco ['kil·ko] *m Chile* (large) basket

quilla [ki·ja, -ʎa] *f* NÁUT keel

quillango [ki·'jan·go, -'ʎan·go] *m CSur* (*manta de pieles*) fur blanket

quillay [ki·'jai, -'ʎai] *m Arg, Chile* BOT soapbark tree

quilo ['ki·lo] *m* 1. (*peso*) kilo(gram); **sudar el ~** *inf* to sweat blood 2. *inf* (*dinero*) million

quilombo [ki·'lom·bo] *m* 1. *Chile* (*burdel*) whorehouse 2. *Ven* (*choza*) hut 3. *Arg* (*lío*) mess

quiltro ['kil·tro] *m Chile, pey* (*perro*) mutt

quimba ['kim·ba] *f* 1. *AmL* (*garbo*) grace 2. *AmL* (*sandalia*) sandal 3. *pl Col* (*conflicto*) difficulties *pl*

quimbo ['kim·bo] *m Cuba* knife, machete

quimera [ki·'me·ra] *f* (*ilusión*) chimera *form*

química ['ki·mi·ka] *f* chemistry

químico, -a ['ki·mi·ko, -a] I. *adj* chemical; **productos ~s** chemicals *pl* II. *m, f* chemist

quimioterapia [ki·mjo·te·'ra·pja] *f* chemotherapy

quimono [ki·'mo·no] *m* kimono

quincalla [kin·'ka·ja, -ʎa] *f* 1. (*objetos*) scrap metal 2. (*adornos*) trinkets *pl*

quince ['kin·se, -θe] I. *adj inv* fifteen; **dentro de ~ días** in two weeks II. *m* fifteen; *v.t.* **ocho**

quincena [kin·'se·na, kin·'θe-] *f* (*días*) two weeks

quincenal [kin·se·'nal, kin·θe-] *adj* every two weeks; **revista ~** semimonthly journal

quincuagésimo, -a [kin·kwa·'xe·si·mo, -a] *adj* fiftieth; *v.t.* **octavo**

quingos ['kin·gos] *m inv, AmL* zigzag

quiniela [ki·'nje·la] *f* 1. (*juego*) sports pools *pl;* **jugar a las ~s** to do the pools 2. (*boleto*) pools coupon 3. *CSur* (*lotería*) lottery

quinientos, -as [ki·'njen·tos, -as] *adj* five hundred; *v.t.* **ochocientos**

quinina [ki·'ni·na] *f* quinine

quino ['ki·no] *m AmL* BOT cinchona tree

quinqué [kin·'ke] *m* oil lamp

quinqui ['kin·ki] *mf inf* delinquent

quinta ['kin·ta] *f* 1. (*casa*) country house 2. MIL draft; **entrar en ~s** to be drafted

quintal [kin·'tal] *m* quintal; **~ métrico** 100 kg

quintar [kin·'tar] *vt* MIL to draft

quinteto [kin·'te·to] *m* MÚS quintet

quintillizo, -a [kin·ti·'ji·so, -a; -'ʎi·θo, -a] *m, f* quintuplet

quinto ['kin·to] *m* conscript, draftee

quinto, -a ['kin·to, -a] *adj, m, f* fifth; *v.t.* **octavo**

quintuplicar <c→qu> [kin·tu·pli·'kar] *vt* to quintuple

quiosco ['kjos·ko] *m* 1. (*de jardín*) gazebo 2. (*de periódicos*) news-stand

quipo(s) ['ki·po(s)] *m(pl)*, **quipu(s)** ['ki·pu(s)] *m(pl) AmL* HIST quipu (*ancient Peruvian system of colored threads and knots for recording facts and events*)

quirófano [ki·'ro·fa·no] *m* operating room; **pasar por el ~** to be operated on

quirquincho [kir·'kin·tʃo] *m CSur* 1. ZOOL (*armadillo*) small armadillo 2. (*guitarra*) charango

quirúrgico, -a [ki·'rur·xi·ko, -a] *adj* surgical

quiso ['ki·so] 3. *pret de* **querer**

quisque ['kis·ke] *pron indef, inf*, **quisqui** ['kis·ki] *pron indef, vulg* **cada ~** each and every one; **todo ~** anyone and everyone; **se lo dijo a todo ~** he told every Tom, Dick and Harry

quisquilloso, -a [kis·ki·'jo·so, -a; -'ʎo·so, -a] *adj* 1. (*susceptible*) touchy 2. (*meticuloso*) fussy

quiste ['kis·te] *m* MED cyst

quitaesmalte [ki·ta·es·'mal·te] *m* nail varnish remover

quitagusto [ki·ta·'yus·to] *m Ecua, Perú* (*intruso*) killjoy

quitamanchas [ki·ta·'man·tʃas] *m inv* stain

remover

quitanieves [ki·ta·'nje·βes] *f inv* snowplow

quitar [ki·'tar] **I.** *vt* **1.** (*piel, funda*) to remove; (*sombrero, tapa, ropa*) to take off; (*botón*) to pull off; **~ la mesa** to clear the table; **una capucha de quita y pon** a detachable hood **2.** (*desposeer*) to take; (*robar*) to steal; **me lo has quitado de la boca** *fig* you took the words right out of my mouth; **el café me quita el sueño** coffee keeps me awake; **ese asunto me quita el sueño** that matter is keeping me awake at night **3.** (*mancha*) to get out; (*obstáculo*) to remove; (*dolor*) to relieve; (*vida*) to take **4.** (*de plan, horario, texto*) to leave out **5.** (*regla*) to do away with **6.** (*apartar*) to get out of the way; (*mueble*) to remove; **¡quita!** (*no me molestes*) don't bother me!; (*deja eso*) leave that alone!; (*déjate de tonterías*) stop it! **7.** MAT to subtract; **quitando dos** taking away two ▸ **ni ~ ni poner en algo** not to have any say in sth **II.** *vr:* **~se** (*sombrero, gafas, ropa*) to take off; (*barba*) to shave off; **~se la vida** to commit suicide; **~se de la bebida** to give up drinking; **~se de encima algo/a alguien** to get rid of sth/sb; **quítate de mi vista** get out of my sight; **~se años** (*de encima*) to look years younger

Quito ['ki·to] *m* Quito

quizá(s) [ki·'sa(s), -'θa(s)] *adv* perhaps, maybe; **~ y sin ~** without a doubt

R

R, r ['e·rre] *f* R, r; **~ de Ramón** R as in Romeo

rabadilla [rra·βa·'di·ja, -ʎa] *f* ANAT coccyx

rabanito [rra·βa·'ni·to] *m* radish

rábano ['rra·βa·no] *m* radish; **~ picante** [*o* blanco] horseradish ▸ **tomar el ~ por las hojas** *inf* (*interpretación*) to get the wrong end of the stick; (*ejecución*) to get it back to front; **me importa un ~** *inf* I couldn't care less; **¡y un ~!** no way!; **déjame tu coche — ¡y un ~!** *inf* can I borrow your car? — no way!

rabí <rabíes> [rra·'βi] *m* REL rabbi

rabia ['rra·βja] *f* **1.** MED (*hidrofobia*) rabies *pl* **2.** (*furia*) rage; **¡qué ~!** how infuriating! **3.** (*enfado, manía*) **tener ~ a alguien** (*enfado*) to be furious with sb; (*manía*) not to be able to stand sb; **tomar ~ a alguien** (*enfado*) to become furious with sb; (*manía*) to take a dislike to sb; **me da ~ sólo pensarlo** just thinking about it makes me mad; **con ~** angrily

rabiar [rra·'βjar] *vi* **1.** (*padecer rabia: animal*) to be rabid, to have rabies; (*persona*) to have rabies **2.** (*enfadarse*) to be furious; **hacer ~ a alguien** to infuriate sb **3.** (*sufrir*) to be in great pain; **~ de...** to be dying of... ▸ **está que rabia**

inf (*picante*) it's incredibly hot; **a ~** (*mucho*) incredibly

rabieta [rra·'βje·ta] *f* tantrum; **coger una ~** to throw a tantrum [*o* fit]

rabimocho, -a [rra·βi·'mo·tʃo, -a] *adj AmL* (*rabón*) short

rabino [rra·'βi·no] *m* rabbi

rabioso, -a [rra·'βjo·so, -a] *adj* **1.** (*hidrofóbico*) rabid **2.** (*furioso*) furious; (*desconsiderado*) inconsiderate **3.** *inf* (*picante*) really hot **4.** *fig* (*vehemente*) fervent; **un tema de rabiosa actualidad** a highly topical issue

rabo ['rra·βo] *m* **1.** (*cola*) tail; **salir con el ~ entre las piernas** *inf* to go away with one's tail between one's legs; **aún queda el ~ por desollar** *inf* the worst is yet to come **2.** (*extremo*) end **3.** (*tallo*) stem **4.** *vulg* (*pene*) cock

rabona [rra·'βo·na] *f CSur, inf* (*faltar a la escuela*) truant; **hacer(se) la ~** to play hook(e)y

rácano, -a ['rra·ka·no, -a] *adj* **1.** *inf* (*tacaño*) mean **2.** *inf* (*gandul*) lazy

racha ['rra·tʃa] *f* **1.** (*de aire*) gust of wind **2.** (*fase*) series; **tener buena/mala ~** to have a good/bad run; **a** [*o* por] **~s** in fits and starts; **arrancar un coche a ~s, dar una ~ a un coche** to jump-start a car

racial [rra·'sjal, -'θjal] *adj* (*étnico*) racial; **disturbios ~es** race riots

racimo [rra·'si·mo, rra·'θi-] *m* bunch; **~ de uvas** bunch of grapes

raciocinio [rra·sjo·'si·njo, -θjo·'θi·njo] *m* **1.** (*facultad, razón*) reason **2.** (*proceso mental*) reasoning

ración [rra·'sjon, -'θjon] *f* **1.** (*tapa*) portion (*portion of food served as a large snack in a bar or restaurant*); **una ~ de patatas fritas** a side of French fries; **una ~ de queso** a plate of cheese **2.** (*en casa*), helping, serving; (*en restaurante*) plate, portion **3.** MIL ration ▸ **poner a alguien a media ~** to put sb on half rations

racional [rra·sjo·'nal, rra·θjo-] *adj* rational; (*razonable*) reasonable

racionalización [rra·sjo·na·li·sa·'sjon, -θjo·na·li·θa·'θjon] *f* ECON, PSICO rationalization

racionalizar <z→c> [rra·sjo·na·li·'sar, -θjo·na·li·'θar] *vt* to rationalize

racionamiento [rra·sjo·na·'mjen·to, rra·θjo-] *m* rationing

racionar [rra·sjo·'nar, rra·θjo-] *vt* **1.** (*repartir*) to ration out **2.** (*limitar*) to ration

racismo [rra·'sis·mo, -'θis·mo] *m* racism

racista [rra·'sis·ta, -'θis·ta] *adj, mf* racist

radar [rra·'dar] *m* ELEC radar; **por ~** by radar

radiación [rra·dja·'sjon, -'θjon] *f* FÍS radiation; **~ solar** solar radiation

radiactividad [rra·djak·ti·βi·'dad] *f* FÍS radioactivity

radiactivo, -a [rra·djak·'ti·βo, -a] *adj* radioactive

radiador [rra·dja·'dor] *m* (*de casa, coche*) radiator

radial [rra·'djal] *adj* **1.** (*forma*) radial; **músculo** ~ ANAT radial muscle **2.** *AmL* RADIO radio

radiante [rra·'djan·te] *adj* (*brillante*) radiant; ~ **de alegría/felicidad** radiant with joy/happiness; **estás ~ con ese vestido** you look wonderful in that dress

radiar [rra·'djar] **I.** *vi* (*irradiar*) to radiate **II.** *vt* **1.** (*irradiar*) to radiate **2.** RADIO to broadcast; **un debate radiado** a radio debate **3.** MED to treat with X-rays **4.** *AmL* (*eliminar*) to delete

radical [rra·di·'kal] **I.** *adj* **1.** BOT, MAT (*t. extremado*) radical **2.** (*fundamental*) drastic **II.** *m* **1.** LING root **2.** MAT, QUÍM, PSICO radical **3.** MAT (*signo*) radical (sign) **III.** *mf* POL radical; ~ **de derecha** extreme right-winger

radicalizar <z→c> [rra·di·ka·li·'sar, -'θar] **I.** *vt* to radicalize **II.** *vr:* ~ **se** (*extremar*) to become radical

radicar <c→qu> [rra·di·'kar] **I.** *vi* **1.** *fig* (*arraigar*) to take root; **el problema radica en su comportamiento** the problem lies in his/her behavior **2.** (*estar asentado*) to reside **3.** (*basarse*) ~ **en algo** to be based on sth **4.** (*consistir*) ~ **en algo** to consist of sth **II.** *vr:* ~ **se** (*establecerse*) to settle

radicheta [rra·di·'tʃe·ta] *f Arg, Urug* (*achicoria*) chicory

radio¹ ['rra·djo] *f* RADIO, TEL **1.** (*radiodifusión*) radio; **hablar por la ~** to talk by radio; **retransmitir por ~** to send by radio **2.** (*receptor*) radio; (*radiotelefonía*) radiophone; ~ **del coche** car radio; **dirigido por ~** radio-controlled **3.** (*emisora*) radio station; ~ **pirata** pirate radio ▶~ **macuto** *inf* the grapevine

radio² ['rra·djo] *m* **1.** MAT, ANAT radius; **en un ~ de varios kilómetros** within a radius of several kilometers **2.** (*en la rueda*) spoke **3.** QUÍM radium **4.** (*ámbito*) range; (*esfera*) field; ~ **de acción** operational range; *fig* sphere of influence; ~ **de alcance** reach; ~ **visual** field of vision

radioactivo, -a [rra·djo·ak·'ti·βo, -a] *adj* radioactive

radioaficionado, -a [rra·djo·a·fi·sjo·'na·do, -a; -θjo·'na·do, -a] *m, f* radio ham

radiocomunicación [rra·djo·ko·mu·ni·ka·'sjon, -'θjon] *f* radio communication

radiodespertador [rra·djo·des·per·ta·'dor] *m* radio alarm (clock)

radiodifusión [rra·djo·di·fu·'sjon] *f* broadcasting

radiodifusora [rra·djo·di·fu·'so·ra] *f AmL* radio transmitter

radioescucha [rra·djo·es·'ku·tʃa] *mf v.* **radioyente**

radiografía [rra·djo·ɣra·'fi·a] *f* **1.** (*técnica*) radiography **2.** (*placa*) radiograph, X-ray photograph

radiografiar <*1. pres:* radiografío> [rra·djo·ɣra·fi·'ar] *vt* **1.** RADIO, TEL to radiograph **2.** MED to X-ray

radiólogo, -a [rra·'djo·lo·ɣo, -a] *m, f* MED radiologist

radiopatrulla [rra·djo·pa·'tru·ja, -ʎa] *f* patrol car

radiotaxi [rra·djo·'tak·si] *m* radio taxi

radioterapia [rra·djo·te·'ra·pja] *f* MED radiotherapy

radioyente [rra·djo·'jen·te] *mf* RADIO listener; ~ **clandestino** illegal listener

R.A.E. ['rra·e] *f abr de* **Real Academia Española** Spanish Royal Academy (*organization which is responsible for setting linguistic standards for Spanish*)

ⓘ Since it was founded in 1713, the **Real Academia Española** (**RAE**) has made the standardization and purification of the Spanish language one of its objectives.

raedura [rrae·'du·ra] *f* **1.** (*rascado*) scrape **2.** (*brizna*) scraping

raer [rra·'er] *irr vt* **1.** (*raspar*) to scrape **2.** MED to graze **3.** (*desgastar*) to wear out

ráfaga ['rra·fa·ɣa] *f* **1.** (*de aire*) gust **2.** (*de luz, inspiración*) flash **3.** (*de disparos*) burst

ragú <ragús> [rra·'ɣu] *m* ragout

raído, -a [rra·'i·do, -a] *adj* (*deslucido*) spoilt; (*gastado*) worn-out

raíl [rra·'il] *m* FERRO rail

raíz [rra·'is, -'iθ] *f* **1.** ANAT, BOT *t. fig* root; **echar raíces** (*persona*) to put down roots; (*costumbre*) to take root; **como si hubiera echado raíces** *fig* well-established; **tener sus raíces en un lugar** *fig* to have one's roots in a place **2.** (*causa*) cause; (*origen*) origin; **a ~ de** because of; **tener su ~ en algo** to be due to sth **3.** MAT, LING root; ~ **cuadrada/cúbica** square/cube root; **extraer la ~** to calculate the root ▶ **de** ~ completely; **arrancar de** ~ to destroy

raja ['rra·xa] *f* **1.** (*grieta*) crack; (*hendedura*) split **2.** (*abertura*) opening; (*separación*) gap **3.** *vulg* (*vulva*) pussy **4.** (*rodaja*) slice

rajada [rra·'xa·da] *f inf* **1.** *Arg* (*fuga*) flight **2.** *Méx* (*cobardía*) chickening out **3.** *Col* (*examen*) fail

rajadiablo(s) [rra·xa·'dja·βlos] *m* (*inv*), *Chile* young rogue

rajante [rra·'xan·te] *adj Arg* (*definitivo*) definitive

rajar [rra·'xar] **I.** *vi* **1.** *inf* (*charlar*) to chatter **2.** *AmL, pey* (*hablar mal*) ~ **de alguien** to slag sb off **II.** *vt* **1.** (*cortar*) to cut; (*abrir*) to cut open; (*hender*) to split; (*quitar*) to cut off; (*partir*) to cut up; (*en rajas*) to slice **2.** *inf* (*apuñalar*) to knife **III.** *vr:* ~ **se 1.** (*abrirse*) to split open; (*agrietarse*) to crack **2.** *inf* (*echarse atrás*) to back out **3.** *inf* (*disculparse*) to apologize

rajatabla [rra·xa·'ta·βla] **a ~** (*estrictamente*) strictly; (*exactamente*) to the letter; (*a toda costa*) at all costs

raje ['rra·xe] *m Arg* **1.** *inf* (*huída*) flight; **al ~** in a rush **2.** *inf* (*el despedir*) sacking, firing; **dar**

el ~ a alguien to get rid of sb
rajo ['rra·xo] *m AmC* (*desgarrón*) tear; (*rotura*) rip
rajón, -ona [rra·'xon, -·'xo·na] *adj* **1.** *AmC, Méx* (*fanfarrón*) bragging **2.** *AmC* (*ostentoso*) lavish **3.** *Cuba, Méx* (*cobarde*) chicken *inf* **4.** *Méx* (*poco fiable*) unreliable
ralea [rra·'lea] *f pey* sort; **son todos de la misma ~** they're all as bad as each other
ralentí [rra·len·'ti] *m* **1.** AUTO timing; **al ~** ticking over **2.** CINE slow motion; **al ~** in slow motion
rallador [rra·ja·'dor, rra·ʎa-] *m* grater
ralladura [rra·ja·'du·ra, rra·ʎa-] *f* gratings *pl;* **~ de queso** grated cheese
rallar [rra·'jar, -'ʎar] *vt* (*fino*) to grate; (*menos fino*) to shred
rally(e) <rallys> ['rra·li] *m* rally
ralo, -a ['rra·lo, -a] *adj* **1.** (*escaso*) scarce; (*árboles*) sparse; (*cabello*) thin; (*tejido*) threadbare **2.** *CSur* (*insustancial*) flimsy
rama ['rra·ma] *f* **1.** BOT, MAT (*t. de árbol*) branch; **~ florida** flowering branch; **~s secas** brushwood **2.** (*ámbito*) branch; ECON (*t. sector*) sector **3.** (*derivación*) branch **4.** (*parentesco*) branch; **por la ~ materna/paterna** on the mother's/father's side ▶ **andarse por las ~s** (*rodeos*) to beat about the bush; **irse por las ~s** (*desviarse*) to go off on a tangent
ramada [rra·'ma·da] *f Chile* (*puesto de feria*) festival stand
ramaje [rra·'ma·xe] *m* **1.** (*ramas*) branches **2.** (*follaje*) foliage
ramal [rra·'mal] *m* **1.** (*cabo*) strand **2.** (*ramificación*) branch; FERRO branch line
rambla ['rram·bla] *f* (*paseo*) boulevard
ramera [rra·'me·ra] *f pey* whore
ramificación [rra·mi·fi·ka·'sjon, -'θjon] *f* ramification; **ramificaciones** consequences *pl*
ramificarse [rra·mi·fi·'kar·se] <c→qu> *vr* to branch out
ramillete [rra·mi·'je·te, -'ʎe·te] *m* bouquet
ramo ['rra·mo] *m* **1.** (*de flores*) bunch **2.** (*de árbol*) (small) branch **3.** (*ámbito*) area; ECON (*t. sector*) sector; **~ de la construcción** construction sector **4.** REL **Domingo de Ramos** Palm Sunday
rampa ['rram·pa] *f* (*inclinación*) ramp; (*en carretera*) ramp; **en ~** sloping
rampla ['rram·pla] *f Chile* (*carrito de mano*) hand truck
rana ['rra·na] *f* frog; **~ de San Antonio** jumping frog; **hombre ~** frogman; **el príncipe ~** the frog prince ▶ **cuando las ~s críen pelo** when pigs fly
ranchera [rran·'tʃe·ra] *f AmL* **1.** (*canción*) typical popular Mexican song **2.** (*furgoneta*) station wagon
ranchería [rran·tʃe·'ri·a] *f* **1.** *Col* (*chabolas*) shantytown **2.** (*barraca*) bunkhouse
ranchero, -a [rran·'tʃe·ro, -a] *m, f* **1.** (*granjero*) rancher **2.** (*colono*) settler
rancho ['rran·tʃo] *m* **1.** (*comida*) food; MIL

mess; *pey* (*de mala calidad*) swill **2.** (*granja*) ranch ▶ **hacer ~ aparte** to go one's own way
ranciarse [rran·'sjar·se, -'θjar·se] *vr* to go rancid
rancio, -a ['rran·sjo, -a; -·θjo, -a] *adj* **1.** (*grasas*) rancid **2.** (*antiguo*) ancient; *pey* (*anticuado*) old-fashioned
rancotán [rran·ko·'tan] *adv AmL* (*al contado*) in cash
rango ['rran·go] *m* **1.** (*categoría, puesto*) rank; **de primer/segundo ~** first/second-level; **según el ~** according to rank; **de (alto) ~** high-ranking; **de ~ abolengo** of ancient lineage **2.** (*ordenación*) order
rangoso, -a [rran·'go·so, -a] *adj AmC* **1.** (*generoso*) generous **2.** (*ostentoso*) ostentatious
ranura [rra·'nu·ra] *f* groove; (*junta*) joint; (*fisura*) slot
rapacidad [rra·pa·si·'dad, rra·pa·θi-] *f* rapacity
rapar [rra·'par] *vt* **1.** **~se el pelo** (*afeitar*) to shave one's head; (*cortar*) to have one's hair cut very short **2.** *inf* (*mangar*) to snatch
rapaz [rra·'pas, -'paθ] **I.** *adj* **1.** (*ávido*) greedy **2.** (*explotador*) rapacious **II.** *f* bird of prey
rapaz(a) [rra·'pas, -·'pa·sa; -'pa·θ, -·'pa·tha] *m(f)* kid; (*muchacho*) boy; (*niña*) girl
rape ['rra·pe] *m* **1.** ZOOL (*pescado*) monkfish **2.** *inf* (*afeitado*) quick shave; **al ~** (*pelo*) closely cropped
rapear [rra·pe·'ar] *vi* MÚS to rap
rapidez [rra·pi·'des, -'deθ] *f* speed; **~ de reflejos** quick reflexes; **con (gran) ~** (very) quickly
rápido ['rra·pi·do] *m* **1.** (*tren*) express **2.** *pl* (*de un río*) rapids *pl*
rápido, -a ['rra·pi·do, -a] *adj* **1.** (*veloz*) fast **2.** (*breve*) quick **3.** (*corriente*) running
rapiña [rra·'pi·ɲa] *f* robbery; (*saqueo*) pillage
raposo, -a [rra·'po·so, -a] *m, f* **1.** (*zorro*) fox **2.** (*astuto*) sly fox
raptar [rrap·'tar] *vt* to kidnap
rapto ['rrap·to] *m* **1.** (*secuestro*) kidnapping; **~ de un niño** child abduction **2.** (*arrebato*) fit; **en un ~ de celos/generosidad** in a fit of jealousy/generosity
raptor(a) [rrap·'tor, -·'to·ra] *m(f)* kidnapper
raque ['rra·ke] *adj Ven* scrawny
raqueta [rra·'ke·ta] *f* **1.** DEP (*pala*) bat **2.** DEP (*tenista*) racket **3.** (*para nieve*) snowshoe
raquítico, -a [rra·'ki·ti·ko, -a] *adj* **1.** MED suffering from rickets **2.** *inf* (*enclenque*) sickly **3.** (*débil*) weak
raquitismo [rra·ki·'tis·mo] *m* MED rickets *pl*
raramente [rra·ra·'men·te] *adv* **1.** (*casi nunca*) rarely, seldom **2.** (*extrañamente*) strangely
rareza [rra·'re·sa, -θa] *f* **1.** (*cualidad*) rarity **2.** (*curiosidad*) strangeness **3.** (*peculiaridad*) peculiarity; (*manía*) eccentricity; **tener sus ~s** (*ser caprichoso*) to be a bit odd
rarífico, -a [rra·'ri·fi·ko, -a] *adj Chile* implausible
raro, -a ['rra·ro, -a] *adj* **1.** (*extraño, inesperado*) strange; **¡(qué) cosa más rara!** how

strange! **2.** (*inusual*) unusual; (*poco común*) rare; **rara vez** rarely; **no es ~ que...** +*subj* it's not surprising that... **3.** FÍS, QUÍM rarefied; **gases ~ s** rarefied gases

ras [rras] *m* level; **a**(I) **~ de** on a level with; **a ~ de agua** at water level; **a ~ de tierra** at ground level; **volar a ~ de suelo** to hedgehop; **al ~** level

rasante [rra·'san·te] **I.** *adj* close **II.** *f* slope; **cambio de ~** brow of a hill

rasar [rra·'sar] **I.** *vt* **1.** (*igualar*) to level **2.** (*rozar*) to skim **II.** *vr:* **~ se** (*cielo*) to clear

rasca ['rras·ka] *f* **1.** *inf* (*frío*) cold; **¡vaya ~ que hace!** it's freezing! **2.** *AmL* (*mona*) drunkenness; **pegarse una ~** to get plastered

rascacielos [rras·ka·'sje·los, -'θje·los] *m inv* skyscraper

rascar <c→qu> [rras·'kar] **I.** *vt* **1.** (*con las uñas*) to scratch **2.** (*raspar*) to scrape **3.** *irón, inf* (*instrumento*) **~ la guitarra** to bash away at the guitar; **~ el violín** to scrape away on the violin **II.** *vr:* **~ se 1.** (*con las uñas*) to scratch **2.** *AmS* (*achisparse*) to get tipsy

rascón, -ona [rras·'kon, -·'ko·na] *adj Méx* (*pendenciero*) troublemaker

rascuache [rras·'kwa·ʧe] *adj Méx, inf* **1.** (*miserable, pobre*) wretched **2.** (*de baja calidad*) cheap

rasgadura [rras·ɣa·'du·ra] *f* tear, rip

rasgar <g→gu> [rras·'ɣar] **I.** *vt* **1.** (*romper por un lado*) to tear; (*en dos*) to tear in two; (*en pedazos*) to tear to pieces; **ojos rasgados** almond [*o* slanting] eyes **2.** (*cortar*) to cut **II.** *vr:* **~ se 1.** (*desgarrarse*) to tear **2.** *AmL, vulg* (*diñarla*) to kick the bucket

rasgo ['rras·ɣo] *m* **1.** (*del rostro*) feature; (*del carácter*) trait **2.** (*acción*) deed; **un ~ de generosidad** a fit of generosity **3.** (*trazo*) stroke; **a grandes ~ s** in outline, in general

rasguear [rras·ɣe·'ar] **I.** *vi* (*en la escritura*) to write with a flourish **II.** *vt* MÚS to strum

rasguñar [rras·ɣu·'ɲar] **I.** *vt* **1.** (*arañar*) to scratch; (*herir*) to wound; (*cortar*) to cut **2.** ARTE to sketch **II.** *vr:* **~ se** (*arañarse*) to scratch oneself; (*herirse*) to wound oneself; **~ se con algo** (*excoriarse*) to graze oneself against sth

rasguño [rras·'ɣu·ɲo] *m* (*arañazo*) scratch; (*rasponazo*) scrape; (*excoriación*) chafing; **sin un ~** *fig* unscathed

raso ['rra·so] *m* satin

raso, -a ['rra·so, -a] *adj* **1.** (*liso*) smooth; (*llano*) flat **2.** (*cielo*) clear; **al ~** in the open air **3.** (*al borde*) level; **una cucharada rasa** a level spoonful

raspa ['rras·pa] *f* **1.** (*del pescado*) backbone **2.** (*del cereal*) beard; (*de uva*) stalk **3.** *AmL* (*ratero*) pickpocket; (*ramera*) prostitute **4.** *fig, inf* (*delgado*) beanstalk

raspada [rras·'pa·da] *f Méx, PRico* (*reprimenda*) scolding

raspado [rras·'pa·do] *m* **1.** TÉC scraping; (*limado*) filing **2.** MED dilatation and curettage,

D and C

raspador [rras·pa·'dor] *m* **1.** (*instrumento*) scraper; (*lima*) file; MED curette **2.** (*de fósforos*) friction strip

raspadura [rras·pa·'du·ra] *f* (*raspado*) scratching; (*con espátula*) scraping

raspaje [rras·'pa·xe] *m Arg* MED curettage

raspar [rras·'par] **I.** *vi* (*ser rasposo*) to be rough; (*en sorteos*) to scratch **II.** *vt* **1.** (*rascar*) to scratch **2.** MED to scrape **3.** *AmL, inf* (*mangar*) to swipe **4.** *AmS, inf* (*abroncar*) to yell at **III.** *vr:* **~ se** to scratch oneself

raspón [rras·'pon] *m* **1.** (*arañazo*) scratch; (*excoriación*) chafing; (*rasguño*) scrape; (*de bala*) graze **2.** *Col* (*sombrero*) (large) straw hat

rasposo, -a [rras·'po·so, -a] *adj* rough

rasquetear [rras·ke·te·'ar] *vt* **1.** *AmL* (*almohazar*) to groom **2.** *Arg* (*raer*) to scrape **3.** *AmS* (*caballo*) to curry

rasquiña [rras·'ki·ɲa] *f AmL* (*comezón*) itch

rastra ['rras·tra] *f* (*rastrillo*) rake ►**a ~ s** unwillingly; **ir a ~ s** *inf* to drag along behind; **llevar a alguien a ~ s** to drag sb along

rastrear [rras·tre·'ar] **I.** *vt* **1.** (*seguir*) to track **2.** (*investigar*) **~ algo** to make inquiries about sth **3.** (*llevar arrastrando*) to drag **4.** (*minas*) to sweep **II.** *vi* **1.** (*investigar*) to make inquiries **2.** (*rastrillar*) to rake

rastrero, -a [rras·'tre·ro, -a] *adj* **1.** (*por el suelo*) creeping; **planta rastrera** creeper **2.** *pey* (*servil*) cringing **3.** *pey* (*despreciable*) despicable; (*canallesco*) base

rastrillo [rras·'tri·jo, -ʎo] *m* (*herramienta*) rake

rastro ['rras·tro] *m* **1.** (*indicio, pista*) trace; **ni ~** not a trace; **sin dejar** (**ni**) **~** without trace; **seguir el ~ a** [*o* **de**] **alguien** to follow sb's trail **2.** (*mercadillo*) flea market **3.** (*herramienta*) rake

rastrojo [rras·'tro·xo] *m* (*de paja*) stubble

rasurar [rra·su·'rar] **I.** *vt* to shave **II.** *vr:* **~ se** to shave

rata¹ ['rra·ta] *f* ZOOL rat; **~ de alcantarilla** sewer rat; **escabullirse como una ~** to run and hide ►**~ de biblioteca** bookworm; **más pobre que las ~ s** as poor as a church mouse; **hacerse la ~** *AmL* to play truant

rata² ['rra·ta] *mf* **1.** *inf* (*rácano*) miser **2.** (*descuidero*) pickpocket

ratear [rra·te·'ar] **I.** *vi* (*gatear*) to crawl **II.** *vt* **1.** *inf* (*mangar*) to nick **2.** *inf* (*racanear*) **~ algo** to be stingy with sth **3.** (*prorratear*) to share out

ratería [rra·te·'ri·a] *f* **1.** (*hurto*) theft **2.** (*racanería*) stinginess

ratero, -a [rra·'te·ro, -a] *m, f* petty thief

raticida [rra·ti·'si·da, -'θi·da] *m* rat poison

ratificación [rra·ti·fi·ka·'sjon, -'θjon] *f* **1.** JUR, POL ratification **2.** (*confirmación*) confirmation

ratificar <c→qu> [rra·ti·fi·'kar] **I.** *vt* **1.** JUR, POL to ratify **2.** (*confirmar*) to confirm **II.** *vr:* **~ se** JUR, POL to be ratified

rato ['rra·to] *m* while; (*momento*) moment; **a ~ s** from time to time; **a cada ~** all the time; **al**

(**poco**) ~ shortly after; **de ~ en ~** from time to time; **todo el ~** the whole time; **un buen ~** for quite a time; **pasar un buen/mal ~** to have a good/bad time; **hacer pasar un mal ~ a alguien** to give sb a rough [*o* hard] time; **pasar el ~** to pass the time ▸ **¡hasta otro ~!** see you later!; **ser un ~ tonto** *inf* to be a bit stupid; **aún hay para ~** there's still plenty left to do; **tener para ~** to have lots to do; **un ~ (largo)** *inf* a lot

ratón [rra·'ton] *m* mouse; **~ de campo** field mouse; **~ (electrónico)** COMPUT mouse ▸ **~ de biblioteca** bookworm

ratonera [rra·to·'ne·ra] *f* **1.** (*trampa*) mouse-trap; *fig* trap; **caer en la ~** *fig* to fall into the trap **2.** (*agujero*) mousehole

raudal [rrau·'dal] *m* torrent; **~ de palabras** flood of words ▸ **a ~es** in floods; **por la ventana entra la luz a ~es** the light came flooding through the window

raya ['rra·ja] *f* **1.** (*línea*) line; (*guión*) dash; **a ~s** (*papel*) lined; (*jersey*) striped; **tres en ~** (*juego*) tic(k)-tac(k)-toe **2.** (*franja*) edge; (*cortafuegos*) firebreak **3.** (*del pelo*) part; **~ al lado/en medio** side/center part; **hacer la ~** to part one's hair **4.** ZOOL ray, skate **5.** (*doblez*) fold **6.** (*cocaína*) line ▸ **pasar(se) de la ~** to go too far

rayado [rra·'ja·do, -a] *m* **1.** (*líneas*) lines **2.** (*plumeado*) hatching **3.** (*rayajo*) scrawl

rayar [rra·'jar] **I.** *vi* **1.** (*lindar*) **~ con algo** to border on sth **2.** (*asemejarse*) **~ en algo** to come close to sth **3.** (*amanecer*) to break; **está rayando el alba** dawn is breaking; **al ~ el día** at the break of day **II.** *vt* **1.** (*marcar con rayas*) to line; (*plumear*) to hatch **2.** (*tachar*) to cross out **3.** (*arañar*) to scratch **III.** *vr*: **~se** to get scratched

rayo ['rra·jo] *m* **1.** (*de luz*) ray; **~ de luna** shaft of moonlight **2.** (*radiación*) **~s infrarrojos** infrared rays; **~s X** X-rays; **~ láser** laser beam; **emitir ~s** to give out radiation **3.** (*relámpago*) (bolt of)lightning; **ha caído un ~ en la torre** the tower was hit by lightning **4.** (*radio*) spoke ▸ **¡~s (y centellas)!** good heavens!; **echar ~s y centellas** to be furious; **¡mal ~ te parta!** *inf* go to hell!; **que me parta un ~ si no es verdad** *inf* I swear it on my mother's grave

raza ['rra·sa, -θa] *f* **1.** (*casta*) race; (*estirpe*) strain; **de ~** (*perro*) pedigree; (*caballo*) thoroughbred; **de ~ blanca/negra** white/black **2.** (*temperamento*) character; **de (pura) ~** true

razón [rra·'son, -'θon] **I.** *f* **1.** (*discernimiento*) reason; (*entendimiento*) understanding; **puesto en ~** reasonable; (**no**) **atender a razones** (not) to listen to reason; **privar de la ~ a alguien** to drive sb out of his/her mind **2.** (*argumento*) argument; (*razonamiento*) reasoning; **venirse a razones con alguien** to reach an agreement with sb **3.** (*motivo*) reason; (*justificación*) justification; **~ de Estado** reasons *pl* of State; **~ de ser** raison d'être;

~ de más para +*infin*, **~ de más para que** +*subj* more than enough reason to +*infin;* **la ~ por la que...** the reason why...; **fuera de ~** unreasonable; **por ~ de algo** due to sth; **por razones de seguridad** for security reasons; **por una u otra ~** for one reason or another; **tener razones para... ~** +*infin* to have cause to... **4.** (*acierto*) right; **la ~ de la fuerza** the doctrine that might is right; **¡con (mucha) ~!** quite rightly!; **sin ~** without justification; **dar la ~ a alguien** to agree with sb; **llevar la ~** to be right; **tener (mucha) ~** to be (absolutely) right; **me asiste la ~** most people would agree with me **5.** (*información*) information; (*recado*) message; **~ aquí** inquire here; **dar ~ de alguien** to give information about sb; **mandar ~ a alguien de algo** to send sb a message about sth; **pedir ~ de alguien** to ask sb for information **6.** MAT (*proporción*) ratio; **a ~ de tres por persona** at a rate of three per person; **a ~ de 2 pesos el kilo** at 2 pesos per kilo **7.** JUR **~ social** trade name ▸ **entrar en ~** to come to one's senses; **hacer perder la ~ a alguien** to make sb lose control; **meter a alguien en ~** to make sb see sense; **perder la ~** to take leave of one's senses **II.** *prep* **en ~ de** (*en cuanto a*) as far as; (*a causa de*) because of

razonable [rra·so·'na·βle, rra·θo-] *adj* **1.** (*sensato*) reasonable **2.** (*justo*) fair; (*adecuado*) sufficient

razonamiento [rra·θo·na·'mjen·to, rra·θo-] *m* **1.** (*pensamientos, argumentación*) reasoning; (*reflexión*) reflection; **tus ~s no son convincentes** your argument is not convincing **2.** (*conversación*) discussion

razonar [rra·θo·'nar, rra·θo-] **I.** *vi* **1.** (*pensar, deducir, argumentar*) to reason **2.** (*reflexionar*) to reflect **II.** *vt* **1.** (*exponer*) to show **2.** (*fundamentar*) to establish

RDSI [e·rre·de·se·'i/e·rre·de·e·se·'i] *f abr de* **Red Digital de Servicios Integrados** ISDN

re [rre] *m* MÚS (*de la escala diatónica*) D; (*de la solfa*) re; **~ bemol** D flat; **~ sostenido** D sharp

reabrir [rre·a·'βrir] *irr como* **abrir** *vt t.* JUR to reopen

reacción [rre·ak·'sjon, -aɣ·'θjon] *f* reaction; **~ en cadena** chain reaction; **~ excesiva** overreaction

reaccionar [rre·ak·sjo·'nar, -aɣ·θjo·'nar] *vi* **1.** (*ante un estímulo*) **~ a** [*o* **ante**] **algo** to react to sth **2.** (*responder*) **~ a algo** to respond to sth **3.** (*repercutir*) **~ en** [*o* **sobre**] **algo** to have repercussions on sth

reaccionario, -a [rre·ak·sjo·'na·rjo, -a; -aɣ·θjo·'na·rjo, -a] *adj, m, f* reactionary

reacio, -a [rre·'a·sjo, -a; -θjo, -a] *adj* reluctant; **el pintor era ~ a mostrarse en público** the painter was reluctant to show his work

reactivar [rre·ak·ti·'βar] *vt* to reactivate; ECON to revive, to boost

reactivo [rre·ak·'ti·βo] *m* QUÍM reagent; (*indicador*) indicator; *fig* stimulant

R

reactor [rre·ak·'tor] *m* **1.** (*motor*) jet engine **2.** (*avión*) jet **3.** FÍS reactor

readaptación [rre·a·dap·ta·'sjon, -'θjon] *f* **1.** (*adaptación*) readaptation, readjustment **2.** (*reintegración*) ~ **a algo** reintegration into sth; ~ **profesional** professional retraining

readaptar [rre·a·dap·'tar] I. *vt* **1.** (*volver a adaptar*) to readapt **2.** (*reintegrar*) ~ **a algo** to reintegrate into sth **3.** (*profesión*) to retrain II. *vr:* ~**se 1.** (*adaptarse*) to readapt **2.** (*reintegrarse*) ~**se a algo** to reintegrate into sth

readmisión [rre·ad·mi·'sjon] *f* readmission; (*de despedidos*) re-employment

readmitir [rre·ad·mi·'tir] *vt* to readmit; (*despedidos*) to re-employ

reafirmar [rre·a·fir·'mar] I. *vt* **1.** (*apoyar*) to re-affirm **2.** (*poner firme*) to make firm; (*la piel*) to tone up II. *vr:* ~**se 1.** (*confirmarse*) to reaffirm **2.** (*insistir*) ~**se en algo** to insist on sth

reagrupar [rre·a·ɣru·'par] I. *vt* to regroup; (*redistribuir*) to redistribute II. *vr:* ~**se** to re-group

reajustar [rre·a·xus·'tar] *vt* **1.** (*adaptar*) to re-adjust **2.** (*reestructurar*) to restructure **3.** (*reorganizar*) to reorganize **4.** TÉC, ECON to adjust

reajuste [rre·a·'xus·te] *m* **1.** (*adaptación*) readjustment **2.** (*reestructuración*) restructuring **3.** (*reorganización*) reorganization; , ~ **de gobierno** cabinet reshuffle **4.** TÉC, ECON adjustment; ~ **salarial** wage settlement

real [rre·'al] I. *adj* **1.** (*verdadero*) real; **basado en hechos** ~**es** based on a true story; **no me da la** ~ **gana** *inf* I don't feel like it **2.** (*del rey*) royal; **Alteza** ~ Royal Highness; **palacio** ~ royal palace **3.** (*espléndido*) splendid II. *m* (*de la feria*) fairground; (*moneda*) real

realce [rre·'al·se, -θe] *m* **1.** (*relieve*) relief **2.** (*esplendor*) splendor; (*acento*) accent; **dar** ~ to highlight

realengo, -a [rrea·'len·go, -a] *adj* **1.** HIST Crown **2.** AmL (*sin amo*) ownerless; (*vagabundo*) stray

realeza [rrea·'le·sa, -θa] *f* (*dignidad*) royalty

realidad [rrea·li·'dad] *f* reality; (*verdad*) truth; ~ **virtual** virtual reality; **ajeno a la** ~ far removed from reality; **hacer** ~ to make come true; **hacerse** ~ to happen; **en** ~ in fact

realismo [rrea·'lis·mo] *m* **1.** ARTE, LIT, CINE realism **2.** POL royalism

realista [rrea·'lis·ta] I. *adj* **1.** ARTE, LIT, CINE realistic **2.** POL royalist II. *mf* **1.** ARTE, LIT, FILOS, CINE realist **2.** POL royalist

realizable [rrea·li·'sa·βle, -'θa·βle] *adj* **1.** (*practicable*) practical; (*factible*) feasible **2.** ECON saleable; **bienes** ~**s** saleable goods

realización [rrea·li·sa·'sjon, -θa·'θjon] *f* **1.** (*ejecución*) execution **2.** (*materialización*) realization; (*cumplimiento*) fulfillment **3.** (*organización*) organization **4.** ECON realization; ~ **de un pedido** fulfillment of an order; ~ **de plusvalías** realization of capital gains

realizador(a) [rrea·li·sa·'dor, -'do·ra; rrea·li·θa-] *m(f)* CINE, TV producer

realizar <z→c> [rrea·li·'sar, -'θar] I. *vt* **1.** (*efectuar*) to carry out; (*hacer*) to make **2.** (*hacer realidad*) to make real; (*sueños*) to fulfill **3.** ECON to realize; (*ganancia, aportaciones*) to take **4.** CINE, TV to produce **5.** AmL (*notar*) to notice II. *vr:* ~**se 1.** (*desarrollarse*) to be carried out **2.** (*materializarse*) to happen; (*hacerse realidad*) to come true

realmente [rre·al·'men·te] *adv* (*en efecto, verdaderamente*) really; (*de hecho*) in fact

realquilar [rre·al·ki·'lar] *vt* to sublet; **vivir en una vivienda realquilada** to live in a sublet property

realzar <z→c> [rre·al·'sar, -'θar] *vt* **1.** (*labrar*) to emboss **2.** (*acentuar*) to bring out **3.** (*subrayar*) to highlight

reamargo, -a [rre·a·'mar·ɣo, -a] *adj AmL* very bitter

reamigo, -a [rre·a·'mi·ɣo, -a] *m, f AmL* very close friend; **son** ~**s del director** they are very close friends of the director

reanimación [rre·a·ni·ma·'sjon, -'θjon] *f* **1.** revival **2.** MED resuscitation; (*posoperatorio*) reanimation; **unidad de** ~ intensive care unit

reanimar [rre·a·ni·'mar] I. *vt* **1.** (*reavivar*) to revive **2.** (*reactivar*) to reactivate **3.** (*animar*) to liven up **4.** MED to resuscitate II. *vr:* ~**se 1.** (*recuperar el conocimiento*) to regain consciousness **2.** (*animarse*) to liven up

reanudar [rre·a·nu·'dar] *vt* to resume

reaparición [rre·a·pa·ri·'sjon, -'θjon] *f* reappearance; TEAT, CINE comeback

reapertura [rre·a·per·'tu·ra] *f* reopening

reata [rre·'a·ta] *f* **1.** (*correa*) rope (*used to keep animals in file*); (*animales*) pack train; **una** ~ **de mulos** a pack of mules **2.** AmL (*de flores*) border ▶ **de** ~ (*sucesivamente*) one after the other; (*en hilera*) in single file

reavivar [rre·a·βi·'βar] *vt, vr:* ~**se** to revive

rebaja [rre·'βa·xa] *f* **1.** (*oferta*) sale; ~**s de verano** summer sales; **estar de** ~**s** to have a sale on **2.** (*descuento*) discount

rebajar [rre·βa·'xar] I. *vt* **1.** (*abaratar*) to reduce **2.** (*humillar*) to put down **3.** *t.* FOTO (*mitigar*) to soften; (*debilitar*) to weaken; (*disminuir*) to lessen **4.** (*una bebida*) to dilute II. *vr:* ~**se 1.** (*humillarse*) to be humiliated **2.** (*condescender*) to lower oneself **3.** (*dispensarse*) to be let off

rebanada [rre·βa·'na·da] *f* slice

rebanar [rre·βa·'nar] *vt* **1.** (*hacer rebanadas*) to slice **2.** (*partir*) to cut up

rebañar [rre·βa·'ɲar] *vt* (*apurar*) to finish off; ~ **el plato** to wipe the plate clean

rebaño [rre·'βa·ɲo] *m t. fig* herd

rebasar [rre·βa·'sar] *vt* (*sobrepasar*) to exceed; MIL to overrun; ~ **el límite** *fig* to overstep the mark; **esto rebasa los límites de mi paciencia** this is trying my patience

rebatir [rre·βa·'tir] *vt* **1.** (*discutir*) to contest; (*refutar*) to refute; (*rechazar*) to reject **2.** (*repeler*) to repel **3.** (*abatir*) to knock down

rebelarse [rre·βe·'lar·se] *vr* to rebel; (*opo-*

nerse) to be opposed

rebelde [rre·'βel·de] I. *adj* 1. (*indócil*) unruly; (*levantisco*) restless 2. (*insurrecto*) rebellious 3. (*persistente*) persistent 4. (*difícil*) troublesome 5. JUR defaulting II. *mf* 1. rebel 2. JUR defaulter

rebeldía [rre·βel·'di·a] *f* 1. (*cualidad*) rebelliousness 2. (*oposición*) opposition 3. *t.* MIL (*insubordinación*) insubordination 4. JUR default; **declarar a alguien en** ~ to declare sb to be in default; **juzgar en** ~ to judge by default

rebelión [rre·βe·'ljon] *f* rebellion

rebenque [rre·'βen·ke] *m CSur* riding crop

reblandecer [rre·βlan·de·'ser, -'θer] *irr como crecer vt, vr:* ~ **se** to soften

rebobinar [rre·βo·βi·'nar] *vt* (*retroceder*) to rewind

rebosar [rre·βo·'sar] *vi* 1. (*desbordar*) to overflow 2. (*tener mucho*) ~ **de** to be brimming with; **le rebosa el dinero** he/she is rolling in money; **le rebosa la soberbia** he/she is very arrogant; **la gota que hizo** ~ **el vaso** the final straw, the straw which broke the camel's back 3. (*estar lleno*) to be full to the brim; (**lleno**) **a** ~ full to the brim 4. (*abundar*) to abound

rebotar [rre·βo·'tar] I. *vi* 1. (*botar*) to bounce; (*bala*) to ricochet 2. (*chocar*) ~ **en** [*o* **contra**] **algo** to bump into sth 3. COMPUT to be returned as undeliverable; **me rebota el mensaje que he enviado** the message I sent has been returned as undeliverable II. *vt* 1. (*botar*) to bounce 2. *inf* (*enfadar*) to anger III. *vr:* ~ **se** 1. (*vino*) to turn 2. *inf*(*enfadarse*) to get angry

rebote [rre·'βo·te] *m* (*bote*) bounce; DEP rebound; (*golpe*) blow; (*de bala*) ricochet; **de** ~ on the rebound

rebozar <z→c> [rre·βo·'sar, -'θar] *vt* CULIN (*con pan rallado*) to coat with breadcrumbs

rebullir <3. *pret:* rebulló> [rre·βu·'jir, -'ʎir] *vi, vr:* ~ **se** to stir; **sin** ~ **se** very quietly

rebumbio [rre·'βum·bjo] *m Méx* (*alboroto*) commotion

rebuscado, -a [rre·βus·'ka·do, -a] *adj* pedantic; (*palabras*) obscure; (*estilo*) contrived

rebuscar <c→qu> [rre·βus·'kar] I. *vi* to search thoroughly II. *vt* (*buscar*) to search for III. *vr* **rebuscárselas** *CSur* (*defenderse*) to get by

rebuznar [rre·βus·'nar, rre·βuθ-] *vi* (*burro*) to bray

rebuzno [rre·'βus·no, -βuθ·no] *m* bray

recabar [rre·ka·'βar] *vt* 1. (*obtener*) to manage to obtain 2. (*pedir*) to ask for

recadero, -a [rre·ka·'de·ro, -a] *m, f* messenger

recado [rre·'ka·do] *m* 1. (*mensaje*) message; **dar un** ~ **a alguien** to give a message to sb 2. (*encargo*) errand; **hacer** ~s to do errands

recaer [rre·ka·'er] *irr como caer vi* 1. (*enfermedad*) to relapse 2. (*delito*) to commit a repeat offense; ~ **en el mismo error una y otra vez** to repeat the same mistake again and again 3. (*culpa*) to fall

recaída [rre·ka·'i·da] *f* relapse

recalar [rre·ka·'lar] I. *vi* 1. NÁUT to put in 2. (*persona*) to appear II. *vt* to soak III. *vr:* ~ **se** to get soaked

recalcar <c→qu> [rre·kal·'kar] *vt* (*palabras*) to stress

recalcitrante [rre·kal·si·'tran·te, rre·kal·θi-] *adj* recalcitrant

recalentado [rre·ka·len·'ta·do] *m Méx, inf* leftovers *pl*

recalentar <e→ie> [rre·ka·len·'tar] I. *vt* 1. (*comida*) to reheat 2. (*aparato*) to overheat II. *vr:* ~ **se** (*motor*) to overheat

recámara [rre·'ka·ma·ra] *f* 1. (*para ropa*) dressing room 2. (*arma*) chamber

recamarera [rre·ka·ma·'re·ra] *f Méx* chambermaid

recambiar [rre·kam·bi·'ar] *vt* (*sustituir*) to substitute

recambio [rre·'kam·bjo] *m* (*repuesto*) spare (part); (*envase*) refill

recapacitar [rre·ka·pa·si·'tar, -θi·'tar] I. *vt* to consider II. *vi* to think things over

recapitulación [rre·ka·pi·tu·la·'sjon, -'θjon] *f* summary, summing up

recapitular [rre·ka·pi·tu·'lar] *vt* to summarize

recargado, -a [rre·kar·'ɣa·do, -a] *adj* (*exagerado*) overelaborate; (*lenguaje*) overblown

recargar <g→gu> [rre·kar·'ɣar] *vt* 1. (*pila*) to recharge 2. (*decorar*) to overdecorate; **el vestido recargado de lazos y botones no se vendió** nobody bought the dress which was dripping with laces and buttons 3. (*impuesto*) to increase 4. (*carga*) to overload; ~ **de trabajo** to overload with work

recargo [rre·'kar·ɣo] *m* (*tasas*) increase; (*sobreprecio*) surcharge; **llamada sin** ~ tollfree call

recatado, -a [rre·ka·'ta·do, -a] *adj* 1. (*modesto*) modest 2. (*cauto*) cautious

recato [rre·'ka·to] *m* (*cautela*) caution; (*pudor*) modesty

recauchutar [rre·kau·tʃu·'tar] *vt* AUTO (*llanta*) to retread

recaudación [rre·kau·da·'sjon, -'θjon] *f* 1. (*cobro*) collection; (*cantidad*) takings *pl*; ~ **diaria** daily takings 2. (*de impuestos*) collection; (*cantidad*) receipts *pl*

recaudar [rre·kau·'dar] *vt* (*impuestos, dinero*) to collect

recaudería [rre·kau·de·'ri·a] *f Méx* (*especiería*) grocery store

recelo [rre·'se·lo, rre·'θe-] *m* mistrust; **mirar algo con** ~ to be suspicious of sth

receloso, -a [rre·se·'lo·so, -a; rre·'θe-] *adj* distrustful; **estar** ~ **de alguien** to be suspicious of sb; **ponerse** ~ to become suspicious

recensión [rre·sen·'sjon, rre·'θe-] *f* PREN review

recepción [rre·sep·'sjon, -θeβ·'θjon] *f* reception

recepcionista [rre·sep·sjo·'nis·ta, -θeβ·θjo·'nis·ta] *mf* receptionist

receptividad [rre·sep·ti·βi·'dad, rre·θep-] *f*

R

receptiveness

receptivo, -a [rre·sep·'ti·βo, -a; rre·θep-] *adj* (*sensible*) receptive

receptor [rre·sep·'tor, rre·θep-] *m* (*radio, teléfono*) receiver; ~ **de televisión** TV set

receptor(a) [rre·sep·'tor, --'to·ra, rre·θep-] *m(f)* recipient

recesión [rre·se·'sjon, rre·θe-] *f* ECON recession

receso [rre·'se·so, -'θe·so] *m AmL* (*vacaciones*) recess

receta [rre·'se·ta, rre·'θe-] *f* **1.** CULIN recipe; ¿**cuál es tu ~ para ser feliz?** *fig* what's your formula for happiness? **2.** MED prescription; **con ~ médica** on prescription

recetar [rre·θe·'tar, rre·θe-] *vt* MED to prescribe

recetario [rre·θe·'ta·rjo, rre·θe-] *m* **1.** CULIN cookbook **2.** MED (*libro*) pharmacopoeia; (*talonario*) prescription pad

rechazar <z→c> [rre·tʃa·'sar, -'θar] *vt* **1.** (*no aceptar*) to reject **2.** (*denegar, no tolerar*) to refuse; ~ **de plano las acusaciones** to flatly deny the accusations **3.** (*ataque*) to repel, to push back

rechazo [rre·'tʃa·so, -θo] *m* rejection; (*denegación*) refusal

rechinamiento [rre·tʃi·na·'mjen·to] *m* squeaking; ~ **de dientes** grinding of teeth

rechinar [rre·tʃi·'nar] **I.** *vi* to squeak; (*puerta*) to creak **II.** *vt* ~ **los dientes** to grind one's teeth

rechistar [rre·tʃis·'tar] *vi* to grumble; **sin ~** without complaining

rechupete [rre·tʃu·'pe·te] **de ~** delicious

recibidor [rre·si·βi·'dor, rre·θi-] *m* **1.** (*hotel, oficinas*) lobby **2.** (*casa*) entry (hall)

recibimiento [rre·si·βi·'mjen·to, rre·θi-] *m* **1.** (*acogida*) welcome; **dispensar un ~ multitudinario** they gave him/her a tumultuous welcome **2.** (*recibidor*) lobby

recibir [rre·si·'βir, rre·θi-] **I.** *vt* **1.** (*tomar*) to receive **2.** (*personas*) to welcome **3.** (*aceptar*) to accept **II.** *vi* (*médico*) to see patients; (*ministro*) to see people **III.** *vr:* ~**se de algo** *AmL* to graduate as sth; (*médico, abogado*) to qualify as sth

recibo [rre·'si·βo, rre·θi-] *m* **1.** (*en tienda*) receipt; (*de la luz, del agua*) bill; ~ **de entrega** delivery note **2.** (*de una carta*) receipt; **acusar ~** to acknowledge receipt **3.** (*recibidor*) lobby

reciclaje [rre·si·'kla·xe, rre·θi-] *m* **1.** (*de materiales*) recycling **2.** ENS ~ **profesional** *fig* professional retraining

reciclar [rre·si·'klar, rre·θi-] *vt* **1.** TÉC to recycle **2.** (*formación*) to retrain

recién [rre·'sjen, -'θjen] *adv* **1.** (*acabado de*) recently; ~ **pintado** freshly painted; **los ~ casados** the newly weds; **el ~ nacido** the newborn baby **2.** *AmL* (*en cuanto*) as soon as

reciente [rre·'sjen·te, rre·'θjen-] *adj* **1.** (*nuevo*) new **2.** (*que acaba de suceder*) recent; **un libro de ~ publicación** a book which has recently been published

recientemente [rre·sjen·te·'men·te, rre·θjen-] *adv* recently

recinto [rre·'sin·to, rre·'θin-] *m* enclosure; ~ **fortificado** fortified enclosure; ~ **universitario** university campus; ~ **ferial** fairgrounds *pl*

recio, -a ['rre·sjo, -a; -θjo, -a] **I.** *adj* **1.** (*fuerte*) strong **2.** (*rígido*) stiff; **en lo más ~ del invierno** in the depths of winter **II.** *adv* (*hablar*) loudly

recipiente [rre·si·'pjen·te, rre·θi-] *m* container; (*de vidrio, barro*) vessel

reciprocidad [rre·si·pro·si·'dad, rre·θi·pro·θi-] *f* reciprocity

recíproco, -a [rre·'si·pro·ko, -a; rre·'θi-] *adj* reciprocal; **...y a la recíproca** ...and vice versa

recital [rre·θi·'tal, rre·θi-] *m* MÚS concert

recitar [rre·si·'tar, rre·θi-] *vt* to recite; ~ **maquinalmente el menú** to recite the menu from memory

reclamación [rre·kla·ma·'sjon, -'θjon] *f* **1.** (*recurso*) protest; (*queja*) complaint **2.** (*exigencia*) claim

reclamar [rre·kla·'mar] **I.** *vi* **1.** (*protestar*) to protest **2.** (*quejarse*) ~ **por algo** to complain about sth **II.** *vt* (*pedir*) to claim; (*una deuda*) to demand; ~ **daños** to sue for damages; **nos reclaman el dinero que nos prestaron** they want us to repay the money which they lent us; **el terrorista es reclamado por la justicia sueca a Italia** the Swedish courts have asked Italy to hand over the terrorist

reclame [rre·'kla·me] *m Arg, Urug* ad(vertisement)

reclamo [rre·'kla·mo] *m* **1.** (*grito*) decoy call; **acudir al ~** to answer the call **2.** COM ad(vertisement)

reclinar [rre·kli·'nar] **I.** *vt* to lean; (*hacia atrás*) to lean back; **reclinó su cabeza contra** [*o* **sobre**] **mis hombros** he/she rested his/her head on my shoulders **II.** *vr:* ~**se** (*inclinarse*) to lean; (*apoyarse*) to rest

recluir [rre·klu·'ir] *irr como huir* **I.** *vt* (*cárcel*) to imprison **II.** *vr:* ~**se** to shut oneself away

reclusión [rre·klu·'sjon] *f* **1.** JUR imprisonment **2.** (*aislamiento*) seclusion

recluso, -a [rre·'klu·so, -a] **I.** *adj* (*preso*) imprisoned; **la población reclusa vive en condiciones inhumanas** the prisoners live in inhuman conditions **II.** *m, f* prisoner

recluta [rre·'klu·ta] *mf* (*voluntario*) recruit; (*obligado*) conscript, draftee

reclutamiento [rre·klu·ta·'mjen·to] *m* recruiting

reclutar [rre·klu·'tar] *vt* MIL to recruit; (*obligar*) to conscript, to draft

recobrar [rre·ko·'βrar] **I.** *vt* to recover; ~ **las fuerzas** to regain one's strength; ~ **las pérdidas** to make good one's losses; ~ **el sentido** to regain consciousness; ~ **las ganas de vivir** to recover one's enthusiasm for life **II.** *vr:* ~**se** to recover

recodo [rre·'ko·do] *m* (*río*) bend

recoger <g→j> [rre·ko·'xer] **I.** *vt* **1.** (*buscar*) to collect; **te voy a ~ a la estación** I'll meet you at the station; **recogen las cartas a las ocho** they pick up the mail at eight **2.** (*coger*) to collect; (*guardar*) to keep; **~ del suelo** to pick up from the floor; **¡es hora de ~!** let's call it a day! **3.** (*juntar*) to gather together **4.** (*cosecha*) to gather; **~ el fruto de su trabajo** to reap the fruits of one's labor **5.** (*acoger*) to take in **6.** (*arremangar: vestido*) to lift up; (*pantalón*) to roll up **7.** (*cabello*) to gather up **8.** (*cortinas*) to roll up **II.** *vr:* **~se 1.** (*a casa*) to go home; (*a la cama*) to go to bed **2.** REL to withdraw

recogida [rre·ko·'xi·da] *f* collection; **~ de basuras** garbage collection; **~ de beneficios** FIN profit taking; **~ de equipajes** AVIAT baggage claim

recogido, -a [rre·ko·'xi·do] *adj* (*retirado*) secluded

recolección [rre·ko·lek·'sjon, -leɣ·'θjon] *f* AGR harvest; (*periodo*) harvest time

recolectar [rre·ko·lek·'tar] *vt* **1.** (*cosas*) to gather **2.** (*frutos*) to harvest

recolocación [rre·ko·lo·ka·'sjon, -'θjon] *f* (*en empleo*) outplacement; **~ diferida** temporary layoff

recomendable [rre·ko·men·'da·βle] *adj* recommendable

recomendación [rre·ko·men·da·'sjon, -'θjon] *f* recommendation; **con la ayuda de tu ~** with the help of your recommendation; **por ~ de mi médico** on my doctor's advice

recomendado, -a [rre·ko·men·'da·do, -a] **I.** *adj* (*precio*) recommended; **precio de venta al público ~** recommended retail price **II.** *m, f person who has obtained a job by means of contacts*

recomendar <e→ie> [rre·ko·men·'dar] *vt* to advise; **nos recomendó no salir de casa** he/ she advised us not to leave the house

recompensa [rre·kom·'pen·sa] *f* reward; **ofrecer una ~ de 100 dólares por algo** to offer a reward of 100 dollars for sth; **en ~** as a reward

recompensar [rre·kom·pen·'sar] *vt* **1.** (*a alguien, un servicio*) **~ por** [*o* de] **algo** to reward for sth **2.** (*de un daño*) to compensate; **fue recompensado por sus gastos** his/her expenses were paid

reconciliación [rre·kon·si·lja·'sjon, -θi·lja·'θjon] *f* reconciliation; **darse la mano en señal de ~** to shake hands as a sign of reconciliation

reconciliar [rre·kon·si·'ljar, rre·kon·θi·-] **I.** *vt* to reconcile **II.** *vr:* **~se** to be reconciled

recóndito, -a [rre·'kon·di·to, -a] *adj* hidden; **la casa está en lo más ~ del bosque** the house is hidden away in the depths of the forest; **en lo más ~ de mi corazón** in my heart of hearts

reconfortar [rre·kon·for·'tar] *vt* to comfort

reconocer [rre·ko·no·'ser, -'θer] *irr como crecer* **I.** *vt* **1.** (*identificar*) to recognize; **~ a alguien por la voz** to recognize sb by his/her

voice **2.** (*admitir*) to accept; (*un error*) to acknowledge; **~ como hijo** to recognize as one's son **3.** (*examinar*) to check; MED to examine **II.** *vr:* **~se 1.** (*declararse*) to admit; **~se culpable** to admit one's guilt **2.** (*identificarse*) **no se reconoció a sí misma** she no longer knew who she was; **no me reconocí en la novela** I didn't recognize myself in the novel

reconocimiento [rre·ko·no·si·'mjen·to, -θi·'mjen·to] *m* **1.** POL, JUR recognition; **el no ~ de Bosnia-Herzegovina** the non-recognition of Bosnia-Herzegovina; **~ de firma** authorization of signature **2.** (*exploración*) inspection; **~ médico** medical examination; **vuelo de ~** reconnaissance flight **3.** (*gratitud*) gratefulness; **en ~ de mi labor** in recognition of my work **4.** COMPUT **~ de errores** error recognition

reconquista [rre·kon·'kis·ta] *f* reconquest

reconquistar [rre·kon·kis·'tar] *vt* to reconquer; *fig* to win back

reconstituir [rre·kons·ti·tu·'ir/rre·kons·ti·'twir] *irr como huir vt* (*restablecer*) to re-establish

reconstituyente [rre·kons·ti·tu·'jen·te] *m* MED tonic, restorative

reconstrucción [rre·kons·truk·'sjon, -truɣ·'θjon] *f* **1.** (*país*) rebuilding **2.** JUR reconstruction

reconstruir [rre·kons·tru·'ir/rre·kons·'trwir] *irr como huir vt* **1.** (*reedificar*) to rebuild **2.** (*componer*) to reconstruct; (*completar*) to complete

recontra [rre·'kon·tra] *AmL, inf* **¡idiota! — ¡que te ~!** idiot! — the same to you!

recontrabueno, -a [rre·kon·tra·'βwe·no, -a] *adj AmL, inf* really good

recontracaro, -a [rre·kon·tra·'ka·ro, -a] *adj AmL, inf* really expensive

Recopa [rre·'ko·pa] *f* DEP Cup-Winners' Cup

recopilación [rre·ko·pi·la·'sjon, -'θjon] *f* compilation

recopilar [rre·ko·pi·'lar] *vt* to compile

récord <*récords*> ['rre·kord] *m* record

recordar <o→ue> [rre·kor·'dar] **I.** *vi, vt* **1.** (*acordarse*) to remember **2.** (*traer a la memoria, semejar*) to remind; **recuérdale a mamá que me traiga el libro** remind mom to bring me the book; **este paisaje me recuerda (a) la Toscana** this landscape reminds me of Tuscany; **si mal no recuerdo** if I remember correctly **II.** *vi, vr:* **~se** *Arg, Méx* (*despertarse*) to wake up **III.** *vr:* **~se** (*acordarse*) to remember

recordatorio [rre·kor·da·'to·rjo] *m* **1.** (*comunión*) communion card; (*fallecimiento*) in memoriam card **2.** (*advertencia*) reminder

recorrer [rre·ko·'rrer] *vt* **1.** (*atravesar*) to cross; (*viajar por*) to travel around; **~ la América del Sur en bicicleta** to travel around South America by bicycle **2.** (*trayecto*) to travel; **recorrimos tres kilómetros a pie** we walked three kilometers **3.** (*registrar*) to check; (*terreno*) to search

recortado, -a [rre·kor·'ta·do, -a] *adj* (*hoja*) un-

recortar [rre·kor·'tar] I. *vt* 1.(*figuras*) to cut out; (*barba, uñas*) to trim; (*quitar*) to cut off 2.(*disminuir*) to cut (down) II. *vr:* ~ **se** to stand out; **el perfil de las montañas se recorta sobre el horizonte** the outline of the mountains stands out against the horizon

recorte [rre·'kor·te] *m* 1.(*periódico*) cutting 2.(*rebajamiento*) cut(back); ~ **de personal** downsizing

recostar <o→ue> [rre·kos·'tar] I. *vt* 1.(*apoyar*) to rest 2.(*inclinar*) ~ **contra/en algo** to lean against/on sth; ~ **la espalda contra una columna** to lean one's back against a column II. *vr:* ~ **se** 1.(*inclinarse*) ~ **se contra/en algo** to lean against/on sth 2.(*apoyarse*) to rest

recova [rre·'ko·βa] *f* 1. *CSur* (*arcadas*) arcade 2. *And, Urug* (*mercado*) market

recoveco [rre·ko·'βe·ko] *m* 1.(*escondrijo*) nook 2. **sin** ~ **s** frankly; **persona con** ~ complicated person 3.(*vuelta*) bend

recreación [rre·krea·'sjon, -'θjon] *f* 1.(*reproducción*) reproduction 2.(*diversión*) recreation

recrear [rre·kre·'ar] I. *vt* 1.(*reproducir*) to reproduce 2.(*divertir*) to entertain II. *vr:* ~ **se** to entertain oneself; **se recrea contemplando cuadros** he/she enjoys looking at pictures

recreativo, -a [rre·krea·'ti·βo, -a] *adj* recreational; (**salón de juegos**) ~ **s** amusement arcade

recreo [rre·'kreo] *m* 1. recreation; **de** ~ recreational; **casa de** ~ holiday home; **puerto de** ~ marina 2.(*en el colegio*) break, recess

recriminación [rre·kri·mi·na·'sjon, -'θjon] *f* (*reproche*) reproach

recriminar [rre·kri·mi·'nar] *vt* (*reprochar*) to reproach

recrudecer [rre·kru·de·'ser, -'θer] *irr como crecer vi, vr:* ~ **se** to worsen; (*conflicto*) to intensify

recta ['rek·ta] *f* straight; **entrar en la** ~ **final** *t.* DEP to enter the final straight

rectamente [rek·ta·'men·te] *adv* (*honradamente*) justly

rectangular [rek·tan·gu·'lar] *adj* rectangular

rectángulo [rek·'tan·gu·lo] *m* rectangle

rectángulo, -a [rek·'tan·gu·lo, -a] *adj* rectangular

rectificación [rek·ti·fi·ka·'sjon, -'θjon] *f* (*corrección*) correction

rectificar <c→qu> [rek·ti·fi·'kar] *vt* 1.(*corregir*) to correct 2.(*carretera*) to straighten

rectilíneo, -a [rek·ti·'li·neo, -a] *adj* 1.(*forma*) rectilinear 2.(*persona*) rigid

rectitud [rek·ti·'tud] *f* (*honradez*) uprightness

recto¹ ['rek·to] *adv* straight; **siga todo** ~ go straight ahead

recto² ['rek·to, -a] *m* ANAT rectum

recto, -a ['rek·to, -a] *adj* 1. *t.* MAT (*forma*) straight; **ángulo** ~ right angle; **línea recta** straight line 2.(*honrado*) upright

rector(a) [rek·'tor, -·'to·ra] I. *adj* principal; (*responsable*) governing II. *m(f)* ENS, REL rector; (*universidad*) president

rectorado [rek·to·'ra·do] *m* rectorship; (*lugar*) rectorate; (*cargo*) UNIV presidency

recuadro [rre·'kwa·dro] *m* (*casilla*) box

recubrimiento [rre·ku·βri·'mjen·to] *m* covering

recubrir [rre·ku·'βrir] *irr como abrir vt* to cover

recuento [rre·'kwen·to] *m* count; **hacer el** ~ **de votos** to count the votes

recuerdo [rre·'kwer·do] *m* 1.(*evocación*) memory; **en** [*o* **como**] ~ **de nuestro encuentro** in memory of our meeting; **tener un buen** ~ **de algo** to have good memories of sth 2.(*de un viaje*) souvenir 3. *pl* (*saludos*) regards *pl;* **dales muchos** ~ **s de mi parte** send them my regards

recular [rre·ku·'lar] *vi* 1.(*retroceder*) to go back; (*automóvil*) to back up 2. *inf* (*ceder*) to give way

recuperación [rre·ku·pe·ra·'sjon, -'θjon] *f* 1.(*recobrar*) recovery; MIL recapture; ~ **de datos** COMPUT data retrieval 2. ECON recovery; ~ **de las cotizaciones** share price recovery; **la** ~ **de los precios** rally of prices 3.(*enfermo*) recovery 4.(*asignatura*) pass (*in a re-take exam*); **examen de** ~ makeup (exam) 5.(*rescate*) rescue

recuperar [rre·ku·pe·'rar] I. *vt* 1.(*recobrar*) to recover; MIL to recapture 2.(*tiempo*) to make up 3.(*rescatar*) to rescue 4.(*asignatura*) to pass (*a makeup examination*); **mi hijo no recuperó la física en el examen de septiembre** my son failed his physics makeup II. *vr:* ~ **se** to recover

recurrir [rre·ku·'rrir] *vi* 1. JUR to appeal 2.(*acudir*) ~ **a** (*una persona*) to turn to; (*una institución*) to resort to; ~ **a la justicia** to turn to the law; ~ **a todos los medios** to resort to every measure available; **no tener a quien** ~ to have nobody to turn to

recursivo, -a [rre·kur·'si·βo, -a] *adj Col* (*ocurrente*) resourceful

recurso [rre·'kur·so] *m* 1. JUR appeal; ~ **de apelación** appeal; ~ **contencioso administrativo** action against the administration; **interponer un** ~ **contra la sentencia** to lodge an appeal against the sentence 2.(*remedio*) solution; **no me queda otro** ~ **que...** I have no alternative but...; **como último** ~ as a last resort 3. *pl* (*bienes*) means *pl;* **familias sin** ~ **s** families without means 4. *pl* (*reservas*) resources *pl;* ~ **s naturales** natural resources; **el país cuenta con abundantes** ~ **s minerales** the country has rich mineral resources

recusar [rre·ku·'sar] *vt* to reject; JUR to challenge

red [rred] *f* 1.(*malla*) net; ~ **de arrastre** trawl net; **echar las** ~ **es** to cast the nets 2.(*sistema*) network; ~ **comercial** business [*o* sales] network; ~ **vial** road network; **han desarticu-**

lado una ~ de carteristas they have broken up a gang of pickpockets **3.** ELEC power lines *pl;* **avería en la ~** power failure ▸ **caer en la ~** to fall into the trap

redacción [rre·dak·'sjon, -daɣ·'θjon] *f* **1.** ENS writing; **hacer una ~ sobre el mar** to write a composition on the sea **2.** PREN editing

redactar [rre·dak·'tar] *vt* to write; (*documento*) to edit; (*testamento*) to draw up

redactor(a) [rre·dak·'tor, -·'to·ra] *m(f)* writer; PREN editor

redada [rre·'da·da] *f* (*de la policía*) roundup, raid

rededor [rre·de·'dor] *m* al [*o* en] ~ around; **al ~ de la casa** around the house

redención [rre·den·'sjon, -'θjon] *f* **1.** REL redemption **2.** (*cautivo*) freeing

redentor(a) [rre·den·'tor, -·'to·ra] *m(f)* redeemer

redimir [rre·di·'mir] *vt* **1.** REL to redeem **2.** (*esclavo*) to purchase the freedom of

redistribución [rre·dis·tri·βu·'sjon, -'θjon] *f* redistribution

rédito ['rre·di·to] *m* yield, revenue

redituar <*3. pres:* reditúa> [rre·di·tu·'ar] *vt* to yield

redoblar [rre·do·'βlar] **I.** *vt* **1.** (*aumentar*) to intensify **2.** (*clavo*) to clinch, to bend back **II.** *vi* (*tambor*) to play a roll on the drums

redoble [rre·'do·βle] *m* drum roll

redomón [rre·do·'mon] *adj AmS* half-trained

redonda [rre·'don·da] *f* **1.** (*dehesa*) pasture; **en tres kilómetros a la ~** for three kilometers in all directions **2.** MÚS whole note

redondear [rre·don·de·'ar] *vt* to round off; **~ por defecto/por exceso** to round up/down

redondel [rre·don·'del] *m* circle

redondela [rre·don·'de·la] *f* **1.** *Arg, Chile* (*objeto circular*) round object **2.** *Chile, inf* (*círculo*) circle

redondez [rre·don·'des, -'deθ] *f* roundness

redondo, -a [rre·'don·do] *adj t.* MAT (*circular*) round; (*redondeado*) rounded ▸ **un negocio ~** a great deal; **caer(se) ~** (*derrumbarse*) to fall flat; (*quedarse mudo*) to be struck dumb; **negarse en ~** to flatly deny

reducción [rre·duk·'sjon, -duɣ·'θjon] *f* **1.** *t.* QUÍM, ECON (*disminución*) reduction; (*rebaja*) discount; (*de personal*) cut; **~ de la jornada laboral** reduction of the working day **2.** JUR remission **3.** FÍS, MAT reduction; **~ de quebrados** reduction of fractions

reducido, -a [rre·du·'si·do, -a; -'θi·do, -a] *adj* (*pequeño*) small; (*estrecho*) narrow; **tarifas reducidas** reduced rates

reducidor(a) [rre·du·θi·'dor, -·'do·ra; rre·du·θi-] *m(f) AmS* (*perista*) fence

reducir [rre·du·'sir, -'θir] *irr como traducir* **I.** *vt* **1.** *t.* QUÍM (*disminuir*) to reduce; (*personal, gastos*) to cut; (*precios*) to lower **2.** (*foto, dibujo*) to reduce; **~ de escala** to scale down **3.** (*someter*) to subdue; **la policía redujo al**

agresor the police overpowered the assailant **4.** (*convertir*) to reduce; **el fuego redujo la casa a cenizas** the fire reduced the house to ashes; **~/quedar reducido a escombros** to reduce/be reduced to rubble **5.** (*limitar*) to reduce **6.** (*resumir*) to summarize; (*acortar*) to abbreviate **7.** MAT to reduce; **~ al común denominador** *t. fig* to reduce to the lowest common denominator **II.** *vi* AUTO to downshift **III.** *vr:* **~se** to come down

redundancia [rre·dun·'dan·sja, -θja] *f* redundancy

redundante [rre·dun·'dan·te] *adj* redundant

redundar [rre·dun·'dar] *vi* **eso redunda en beneficio nuestro** this works in our interest; **eso ~á en perjuicio vuestro** this will work against you

reeditar [rre·di·'tar/rre·e·di·'tar] *vt* to republish; (*imprimir*) to reprint

reelección [rre·lek·'sjon/rre·e·lek·'sjon, -leɣ·'θjon] *f* re-election

reelegir [rre·le·'xir/rre·e·le·'xir] *irr como elegir vt* to re-elect

reembolsar [rrem·bol·'sar/rre·em·bol·'sar] *vt* to repay, to reimburse

reembolso [rrem·'bol·so/rre·em·'bol·so] *m* (*devolución*) repayment; **enviar algo contra ~** to send sth cash on delivery

reemplazante [rrem·pla·'san·te, -'θan·te; rre·em-] *mf Méx* replacement

reemplazar <z→c> [rrem·pla·'sar/rre·em·pla·'sar, -'θar] *vt* to replace; (*representar*) to substitute

reemplazo [rrem·'pla·so/rre·em·'pla·so, -θo] *m* (*sustitución*) replacement; DEP substitution

reencarnación [rren·kar·na·'sjon/rre·en·kar·na·'sjon, -'θjon] *f* reincarnation

reencauchar [rren·kau·'tʃar, rre·en-] *vt Col, Perú* AUTO to retread

reencontrar <o→ue> [rren·kon·'trar, rre·en-] **I.** *vt* to find again **II.** *vr:* **~se** to meet again

reencuentro [rren·'kwen·tro/rre·en·'kwen·tro] *m* (*encuentro*) reunion

reenviar <*1. pres:* reenvío> [rrem·bi·'ar/rre·em·bi·'ar] *vt* (*al remitente*) to return; (*a un nuevo destinatario*) to forward

reestreno [rres·'tre·no/rre·es·'tre·no] *m* TEAT revival; TV rerun; CINE reshowing

reestructurar [rres·truk·tu·'rar/rre·es·truk·tu·'rar] *vt* to restructure

refacción [rre·fak·'sjon, -faɣ·'θjon] *f* snack

refaccionar [rre·fak·sjo·'nar, -faɣ·θjo·'nar] *vt AmL* (*edificios*) to refurbish

refectorio [rre·fek·'to·rjo] *m* refectory

referencia [rre·fe·'ren·sja, -θja] *f* **1.** reference; **punto de ~** point of reference; **con ~ a** with reference to; **hacer una pequeña ~ a alguien** to make a slight reference to sb; **hacer una ~ a algo** to refer to sth **2.** *pl* (*informes*) report **3.** (*nota*) reference; **nuestra/su ~** (*en un escrito*) our/your ref.

referéndum <referéndums> [rre·fe·'ren·dun] *m* POL (*popular*) referendum

R

referente [rre·fe·'ren·te] *adj* regarding; (**en lo**) ~ **a su queja** with regard to your complaint

referí [rre·fe·'ri] *m AmL* DEP referee

referir [rre·fe·'rir] *irr como sentir* I. *vt* 1. (*relatar*) to recount 2. (*remitir*) to refer II. *vr:* ~**se** to refer; **en** [*o* **por**] **lo que se refiere a nuestras relaciones** with regard to our relationship

refinado, -a [rre·fi·'na·do] *adj* refined

refinar [rre·fi·'nar] I. *vt* to refine II. *vr:* ~**se** to become refined

refinería [rre·fi·ne·'ri·a] *f* refinery

reflector [rre·flek·'tor] *m* (*foco*) spotlight; DEP floodlight; MIL searchlight

reflector(a) [rre·flek·'tor, -·'to·ra] *adj* reflective

reflejar [rre·fle·'xar] I. *vi, vt* to reflect; **tus palabras reflejan miedo** your words show fear II. *vr:* ~**se** to be reflected

reflejo [rre·'fle·xo] *m* 1. (*luz, imagen*) reflection; **las esmeraldas despiden unos preciosos** ~**s verdes** emeralds give off lovely green sparkles; **su comportamiento es un fiel** ~ **de su estado de ánimo** his/her behavior is an accurate reflection of how he/she is feeling 2. MED, PSICO reflex; **para ello hay que ser rápido de** ~**s** you need fast reflexes for that

reflejo, -a [rre·'fle·xo, -a] *adj* reflective; **movimiento** ~ reflex

reflexión [rre·flek·'sjon,] *f* 1. (*consideraciones*) reflection; **con** ~ on reflection; **sin** ~ without thinking 2. (*rayos*) reflection

reflexionar [rre·flek·sjo·'nar] *vi, vt* to reflect; **reflexiona bien antes de dar ese paso** think carefully before doing that

reflexivo, -a [rre·flek·'si·βo, -a] *adj* 1. (*sensato*) thoughtful 2. LING reflexive

reflujo [rre·'flu·xo] *m* 1. (*marea*) ebb 2. MED reflux; ~ **gástrico** gastric reflux

reforma [rre·'for·ma] *f* 1. (*mejora, modificación*) reform; ~ **educativa** educational reform; ~ **monetaria** monetary reform 2. ARQUIT (*reestructuración*) rebuilding; (*renovación*) renovation; **hacer una** ~ **en el cuarto de baño** to have one's bathroom refurbished 3. REL **la Reforma Protestante** the Reformation

reformar [rre·for·'mar] I. *vt* 1. REL (*t. mejorar, modificar*) to reform; ~ **su conducta** to change one's ways 2. (*a alguien*) to reform 3. ARQUIT (*reestructurar*) to rebuild; (*renovar*) to renovate, to reform 4. (*rehacer*) to redo II. *vr:* ~**se** to mend one's ways; ~**se en el vestir** to dress better

reformatorio [rre·for·ma·'to·rjo] *m* reformatory; ~ **para delincuentes juveniles** reform school (for juvenile delinquents)

reformatorio, -a [rre·for·ma·'to·rjo, -a] *adj* reforming

reformista [rre·for·'mis·ta] I. *adj* reformist; **tendencias** ~**s** reformist tendencies; **ser** ~ to be a reformist II. *mf* reformist

reforzar [rre·for·'sar, -'θar] *irr como forzar* I. *vt* (*fortalecer*) to reinforce; (*con vigas*) to strengthen II. *vr:* ~**se** to be reinforced

refractar [rre·frak·'tar] I. *vt* to refract II. *vr:* ~**se** to be refracted

refrán [rre·'fran] *m* saying, proverb; **como dice el** ~ as the saying goes

refregar [rre·fre·'ɣar] *irr como fregar* I. *vt* 1. (*frotar*) to rub; ~ **con un cepillo** to scrub with a brush; ~ **la cacerola con un estropajo** to scrub the saucepan with a scouring pad 2. *inf* (*reprochar*) ~ **algo a alguien** (**por las narices**) to rub sb's nose in sth II. *vr:* ~**se** to rub; ~**se los ojos** to rub one's eyes

refrendar [rre·fren·'dar] *vt* 1. (*un pasaporte*) to stamp 2. (*aceptar*) to accept

refrescante [rre·fres·'kan·te] *adj* refreshing

refrescar [rre·fres·'kar] I. *vt* 1. (*algo, a alguien*) to refresh; **el baño me ha refrescado** the bath has revived me 2. (*cosas olvidadas*) to brush up; ~ **la memoria** to refresh one's memory II. *vi* 1. (*aire, viento*) to cool down 2. (*dar fresco*) to refresh; **esta bebida refresca mucho** this drink is very refreshing 3. (*beber*) to have a refreshing drink III. *vr:* ~**se** 1. (*aire, viento, cosa*) to cool down; **el día se ha refrescado** the weather has become cooler 2. (*persona*) to cool down; (*beber*) to have a refreshing drink; **voy a ducharme para** ~**me** I'm going to have a shower to cool down; ~**se con una cerveza** to have a nice cool drink of beer 3. (*tomar el fresco*) to get some fresh air IV. *vimpers* **por la tarde refresca** in the evening it gets cooler

refresco [rre·'fres·ko] *m* (*bebida*) soft drink; (*gaseosa, naranjada*) fizzy drink

refriega [rre·'frje·ɣa] *f inf* (*pelea*) scuffle; (*violenta*) brawl

refrigeración [rre·fri·xe·ra·'sjon, -'θjon] *f* refrigeration; (*de una habitación*) air conditioning; ~ **por aire/agua** air/water-cooling

refrigerador [rre·fri·xe·ra·'dor] *m* 1. (*nevera*) refrigerator; (*cámara*) cool room; (*líquido*) coolant, refrigerant 2. (*de un automóvil*) cooling system

refrigerador(a) [rre·fri·xe·ra·'dor, -·'do·ra] *adj* cooling; **aparato** ~ (*para comestibles*) refrigerator; (*para habitaciones*) air-cooling unit

refrigeradora [rre·fri·xe·ra·'do·ra] *f Perú* (*nevera*) refrigerator

refrigerar [rre·fri·xe·'rar] I. *vt* (*enfriar*) to refrigerate; (*una habitación*) to air-condition II. *vr:* ~**se** (*enfriarse*) to cool down

refrigerio [rre·fri·'xe·rjo] *m* snack

refuerzo [rre·'fwer·so, -θo] *m* 1. (*viga*) strengthening; (*parche*) patch 2. (*ayuda*) support 3. *pl* MIL reinforcements *pl*

refugiado, -a [rre·fu·'xja·do, -a] *m, f* refugee; **el Alto Comisionado de las Naciones Unidas para los Refugiados** (**ACNUR**) United Nations High Commission for Refugees (UNHCR)

refugiarse [rre·fu·'xjar·se] *vr* (*en un lugar*) to take refuge; ~ **de algo** to flee from sth; ~ **en una mentira** to hide behind a lie; **se refugió en la bebida** he/she turned to drink

refugio [rre·'fu·xjo] *m* **1.** (*protección, consuelo, lugar*) ~ **de algo** refuge from sth **2.** *t.* MIL (*construcción*) shelter; ~ (**montañero**) mountain shelter; ~ **nuclear** [*o* **atómico**] fallout shelter **3.** (*persona*) protector **4.** (*tráfico*) traffic island

refundir [rre·fun·'dir] I. *vt* **1.** (*metal: fundir*) to recast **2.** (*revisar*) to revise **3.** (*reunir*) to join **4.** (*perder*) to lose II. *vr:* ~**se 1.** (*reunirse*) to be joined **2.** *AmC* (*perderse*) to be lost

refunfuñar [rre·fun·fu·'ɲar] *vi* to grumble

refutación [rre·fu·ta·'sjon, -'θjon] *f* refutation

refutar [rre·fu·'tar] *vt* to refute

regadera [rre·ɣa·'de·ra] *f* **1.** (*recipiente*) watering can **2.** (*reguera*) irrigation channel **3.** *Amc, Col, Méx, Ven* (*ducha*) shower

regaderazo [rre·ɣa·de·'ra·so, -θo] *m Méx* shower

regadío [rre·ɣa·'di·o, -a] *m* irrigation; **estos campos son de** ~ these fields are irrigated

regadío, -a [rre·ɣa·'di·o, -a] *adj* (*de riego*) irrigation

regalado, -a [rre·ɣa·'la·do, -a] *adj* **1.** (*cómodo*) easy; **llevar una vida regalada** to lead a life of luxury **2.** (*barato*) very cheap; **vender algo a precio** ~ to sell sth for a knockdown price

regalar [rre·ɣa·'lar] I. *vt* **1.** (*obsequiar*) to give; **en esta tienda regalan la fruta** *fig* in this shop the fruit is dirt-cheap; ~ **los oídos a alguien** to flatter sb **2.** (*mimar*) to pamper **3.** (*deleitar*) to delight II. *vr:* ~**se 1.** (*llevar buena vida*) to live very well **2.** (*deleitarse*) ~ **con algo** to delight in sth

regalía [rre·ɣa·'li·a] *f* **1.** (*privilegio*) privilege; (*del Estado, la Corona*) prerogative **2.** (*pago*) bonus

regaliz [rre·ɣa·'lis, -'liθ] *m* **1.** (*golosina*) licorice **2.** BOT licorice plant

regalo [rre·'ɣa·lo] *m* **1.** (*obsequio*) present, gift; **a este precio el coche es un** ~ at this price the car is a steal; **una cesta de fruta de** ~ **en cada habitación** a complimentary basket of fruit in each room **2.** (*gusto*) pleasure; **un** ~ **para la vista** a sight for sore eyes

regañadientes [rre·ɣa·ɲa·'djen·tes] **a** ~ reluctantly, grudgingly

regañar [rre·ɣa·'ɲar] I. *vt inf* to scold II. *vi* **1.** (*reñir*) to argue; (*dejar de tener trato*) to fall out; **ha regañado con su novio** (*reñir*) she has had a fight with her boyfriend; (*separarse*) she has split up with her boyfriend **2.** (*refunfuñar*) to grumble

regañina [rre·ɣa·'ɲi·na] *f* **1.** (*represión*) reprimand; **echar una** ~ **a alguien** to tell sb off **2.** (*riña*) quarrel; **tener una** ~ **por algo** to quarrel about sth

regar [rre·'ɣar] *irr como fregar vt* **1.** (*con agua: una planta, el jardín*) to water; (*las calles*) to hose down; AGR to irrigate **2.** (*con un líquido*) to wet; (*mojar*) to soak; (*con algo menudo*) to sprinkle; ~ **el suelo con arena** to sprinkle sand on the ground; ~ **algo con lágrimas** to

bathe sth with tears **3.** (*atravesar*) to cross

regata [rre·'ɣa·ta] *f* DEP regatta

regatear [rre·ɣa·te·'ar] I. *vi* **1.** (*mercadear*) to haggle **2.** (*hacer regates*) to dodge; (*con el balón*) to dribble II. *vt* to haggle over

regateo [rre·ɣa·'teo] *m* **1.** (*negociar*) haggling **2.** DEP dribbling

regazo [rre·'ɣa·so, -θo] *m* lap; *fig* warmth

regencia [rre·'xen·sja, -θja] *f* **1.** (*gobierno*) regency **2.** (*dirección*) direction; (*de un negocio*) management

regeneración [rre·xe·ne·ra·'sjon, -'θjon] *f* regeneration

regenerar [rre·xe·ne·'rar] I. *vt* **1.** *t.* ELEC (*algo*) to regenerate **2.** (*a alguien*) to reform II. *vr:* ~**se** (*renovarse*) to regenerate; (*cabello*) to grow back

regentar [rre·xen·'tar] *vt* **1.** (*dirigir*) to manage **2.** POL to govern

regente [rre·'xen·te] *mf* **1.** (*que gobierna*) regent **2.** (*que dirige*) director; (*un negocio*) manager

régimen ['rre·xi·men] *m* <regímenes> **1.** (*sistema*) system; (*reglamentos*) regulations *pl*; ~ **abierto** (*en una prisión*) open regime; ~ **legal de la seguridad social para jubilación e invalidez** social security system for retirement and disability; ~ **penitenciario** prison system **2.** POL government **3.** (*dieta*) diet; ~ **de adelgazamiento** diet (to lose weight); **estar a** ~ to be on a diet; **poner a alguien a** ~ to put sb on a diet **4.** (*manera de vivir*) lifestyle; **llevar un** ~ **de austeridad** to have an austere lifestyle

regimiento [rre·xi·'mjen·to] *m* MIL regiment

región [rre·'xjon] *f* **1.** (*territorio*) region **2.** (*espacio*) area; (*del cuerpo*) region; ~ **abdominal** abdominal region

regional [rre·xjo·'nal] *adj* regional

regir [rre·'xir] *irr como elegir* I. *vt* **1.** (*gobernar*) to govern; (*dirigir*) to direct **2.** (*guiar*) to lead; (*ley*) to govern **3.** LING to take II. *vi* **1.** (*tener validez*) to apply **2.** *inf* (*estar cuerdo*) to be sane; **¡tú no riges!** you're out of your mind! III. *vr:* ~**se** to be guided

registrador(a) [rre·xis·tra·'dor, -'do·ra] I. *adj* registering; **caja** ~**a** cash register II. *m(f)* **1.** (*funcionario*) registrar; ~ **de la propiedad** property [*o* land] registrar **2.** TÉC recorder; ~ **de sonidos** sound recorder

registrar [rre·xis·'trar] I. *vt* **1.** (*examinar*) to search **2.** (*inscribir*) to record; (*una empresa, un patente*) to register **3.** (*señalar*) to note; (*grabar*) to record II. *vr:* ~**se 1.** (*inscribirse*) to register **2.** (*observarse*) to be reported

registro [rre·'xis·tro] *m* **1.** (*inspección*) search; ~ **de la casa** house search **2.** (*con un instrumento*) measurement; (*grabación*) recording **3.** (*inscripción*) recording; (*inclusión*) inclusion; (*de una empresa, una patente*) registration **4.** (*nota*) note; (*protocolo*) record; ~ **de entrada/de salida** note of arrival/departure; ~ **de inventario** inventory **5.** (*libro*) register;

R

~ electoral electoral register; **~ de la propiedad** land register **6.**(*oficina, archivo*) registry; **~ civil** registry office; **~ de la propiedad** land registry **7.**(*abertura*) inspection hatch **8.**(*de un mecanismo*) regulator **9.**(*de un libro*) entry **10.**MÚS register; (*órgano*) stop; **tiene un ~ muy amplio** he/she has a very wide range

regla ['rre·ɣla] *f* **1.**(*instrumento*) ruler; **~ de cálculo** slide rule **2.**(*norma*) rule; **~s de exportación** COM export regulations; **por ~ general** as a general rule; **ser la ~** to be the rule; **la ~ es que** +*subj* the rule is that **3.**MAT **~ de tres** rule of three; **las cuatro ~s** addition, subtraction, multiplication and division **4.**(*menstruación*) period; **está con la ~** she has her period ▶ **la excepción confirma la ~** *prov* the exception confirms the rule; **estar en ~** to be in order; **poner en ~** to put in order; **salir de la ~** to go too far

reglamentación [rre·ɣla·men·ta·'sjon, -'θjon] *f* **1.**(*acción*) regulation; *pey* regimentation **2.**(*reglas*) rules *pl*

reglamentar [rre·ɣla·men·'tar] *vt* to regulate; *pey* to regiment

reglamento [rre·ɣla·'men·to] *m* rules *pl*; (*de una organización*) regulations *pl*; **~** (**de funcionarios**) civil service regulations; (**interno**) rules *pl*; **~ de tráfico** traffic regulations

reglar [rre·'ɣlar] **I.** *vt* **1.**(*reglamentar*) to regulate **2.**(*con líneas*) to line **II.** *vr:* **~se** (*sujetarse*) to be regulated

regocijar [rre·ɣo·si·'xar, rre·ɣo·θi-] **I.** *vr:* **~se 1.**(*alegrarse*) **~se con algo** to delight in sth **2.**(*divertirse*) to amuse oneself **II.** *vt* to delight

regocijo [rre·ɣo·'si·xo, -'θi·xo] *m* **1.**(*alegría*) delight; **esperar algo con ~** to be really looking forward to sth **2.**(*júbilo*) rejoicing

regodeón, -ona [rre·ɣo·de·'on] *adj Chile, Col, inf* hard to please, fussy

regresar [rre·ɣre·'sar] **I.** *vi* (*volver*) to return, to go back **II.** *vt Méx* (*devolver*) to give back **III.** *vr:* **~se** *AmL* (*volver*) to return

regresión [rre·ɣre·'sjon] *f* (*retroceso*) regression

regresivo, -a [rre·ɣre·'si·βo, -a] *adj* regressive

regreso [rre·'ɣre·so] *m* (*vuelta*) return; (**viaje de**) **~** return journey; **estar de ~** to have returned

reguero [rre·'ɣe·ro] *m* (*chorro*) irrigation channel ▶ **expandirse como un ~ de pólvora** to spread like wildfire

regulación [rre·ɣu·la·'sjon, -'θjon] *f* **1.**(*reglamentación*) regulation; **~ administrativa** administrative regulations **2.** *t.* TÉC (*organización, ajuste*) adjustment; (*de un río*) channeling; **de ~ automática** self-regulating; **~ de la demanda** ECON management of demand

regulador [rre·ɣu·la·'dor] *m* regulator; (*mecanismo*) control knob

regular [rre·ɣu·'lar] **I.** *vt* **1.** *t.* TÉC (*organizar, ajustar*) to adjust **2.**(*reglamentar*) to regulate **3.**(*poner en orden*) to put in order **II.** *adj* **1.**(*conforme a una regla*) regular; **verbos ~es** regular verbs **2.**(*ordenado*) ordered **3.**(*estable*) stable **4.**(*uniforme*) regular **5.**(*mediano*) average; (*mediocre*) mediocre; (*nota*) satisfactory; **de tamaño ~** normal size ▶ **tu comportamiento no me parece ni medio ~** *inf* your behavior strikes me as most irregular **III.** *adv* so-so

regularidad [rre·ɣu·la·ri·'dad] *f* **1.**(*conformidad, uniformidad*) compliance; **con ~** regularly **2.**(*mediocridad*) mediocrity

regularizar <z→c> [rre·ɣu·la·ri·'sar, -'θar] **I.** *vt* (*poner en orden*) to regularize; (*normalizar*) to standardize **II.** *vr:* **~se** (*regularse*) to be regulated; (*normalizarse*) to become standardized

regularmente [rre·ɣu·lar·'men·te] *adv* (*normalmente*) usually

rehabilitación [rre·a·βi·li·ta·'sjon, -'θjon] *f* **1.** *t.* JUR, MED (*de alguien*) rehabilitation; (*restitución*) restitution **2.**(*de una cosa*) repair; (*de un edificio*) refurbishment

rehabilitar [rre·a·βi·li·'tar] **I.** *vt* **1.** *t.* JUR, MED (*a alguien*) to rehabilitate; (*restituir*) to return **2.**(*una cosa*) to repair; (*un edificio*) to refurbish; **~ la memoria** [*o* **la buena fama**] **de alguien** to restore sb's reputation **II.** *vr:* **~se** to be rehabilitated

rehacer [rre·a·'ser, -'θer] *irr como hacer* **I.** *vt* **1.**(*volver a hacer*) to redo; **~ una carta** to rewrite a letter **2.**(*reconstruir*) to rebuild; (*reparar*) to repair; (*un edificio*) to refurbish; **~ su vida con alguien** to rebuild one's life with sb **II.** *vr:* **~se** (*recuperar las fuerzas*) to recover one's strength; (*la salud*) to regain one's health; (*la tranquilidad*) to regain one's peace of mind; **~se de una desgracia** to recover from a misfortune

rehecho, -a [rre·'e·tʃo, -a] **I.** *pp de* **rehacer II.** *adj* (*robusto*) thickset

rehén [rre·'en] *m* (*persona*) hostage

rehogar <g→gu> [rre·o·'ɣar] *vt* to sauté

rehuir [rre·u·'ir] *irr como huir* *vt* **1.**(*eludir*) to avoid; **~ a alguien** to avoid sb; **~ una obligación** to shirk an obligation; **rehuye decir la verdad** he/she avoids telling the truth **2.**(*rechazar*) to reject

rehusar [rre·u·'sar] *vt* to refuse; (*una reclamación*) to reject; **¡rehusado!** rejected!; **rehúsa verme** he/she refuses to see me; **~ una invitación** to decline an invitation

reimpresión [rre·im·pre·'sjon] *f* reprint; **~ pirata** pirate copy

reimprimir [rre·im·pri·'mir] *irr como imprimir* *vt* to reprint

reina ['rrei·na] *f t.* ZOOL (*soberana, la mejor*) queen; **~ madre** queen mother; **abeja ~** queen bee

reinado [rrei·'na·do] *m t. fig* (*tiempo*) reign

reinar [rrei·'nar] *vi* **1.** *t. fig* (*gobernar*) to reign **2.**(*dominar*) to prevail

reincidencia [rre·in·si·'den·sja, -θi·'den·θja] *f* relapse; JUR repeat offense

reincidente [rre·in·si·'den·te, rre·in·θi-] I. *adj*
repeat II. *mf* (*delincuente*) repeat offender
reincidir [rre·in·si·'dir, rre·in·θi-] *vi* (*error*) ~
en algo to relapse into sth; ~ **en un delito** to
repeat an offence
reincorporar [rre·in·kor·po·'rar] I. *vt* ~ **a algo**
to reincorporate into sth; ~ **a alguien a un**
puesto to restore sb to a position II. *vr:* ~ **se** (*a*
un sitio) to return; (*a una organización*) to rejoin
reino ['rrei·no] *m* realm; (*de un monarca*)
kingdom; **Reino Unido** United Kingdom
reintegración [rre·in·te·γra·'sjon, -'θjon] *f*
1.(*reincorporación*) reintegration; (*en un*
cargo) reinstatement **2.**(*de gastos*) reimbursement; ~ **de los daños** reimbursement for
damages
reintegrar [rre·in·te·'γrar] I. *vt* **1.**(*reincor-*
porar) to reintegrate; (*en un cargo*) to reinstate; ~ **a alguien a su puesto de trabajo** to
reinstate sb in his/her job **2.**(*devolver*) to return; (*dinero*) to repay; (*desembolsos*) to reimburse II. *vr:* ~ **se** (*reincorporarse*) to return;
(*a una organización*) to rejoin
reintegro [rre·in·'te·γro] *m* **1.**(*reintegración*)
reintegration; (*en un cargo*) reinstatement
2.(*premio*) **me tocó un** ~ I won back my
stake **3.**(*pago*) reimbursement; (*de la cuenta*)
withdrawal; (*devolución*) repayment
reír [rre·'ir] *irr* I. *vi* **1.**(*desternillarse*) to laugh;
echarse a ~ to burst out laughing; **no me**
hagas ~ *fig* don't make me laugh **2.**(*sonreír*)
to smile ▶ **el que ríe último ríe mejor** *prov*
he who laughs last laughs longest [*o* best] *prov*
II. *vr:* ~ **se 1.**(*desternillarse*) ~ **se de algo** to
laugh at sth; ~ **se a carcajadas** to laugh loudly;
me río de tu dinero *fig* I don't give a damn
about your money; ~ **se para sus adentros** to
chuckle; ~ **se tontamente** to giggle **2.**(*son-*
reír) to smile **3.**(*burlarse*) ~ **se de algo** to
laugh at sth **4.** *inf* (*romperse*) to come apart
III. *vt* ~ **algo** to laugh at sth
reiteradamente [rrei·te·ra·da·'men·te] *adv* repeatedly
reiterar [rrei·te·'rar] I. *vt* to repeat; **te reitero**
las gracias I thank you once again; **reiteró su**
intención de ayudarme he/she repeated
his/her intention of helping me II. *vr:* ~ **se** to
repeat; **se reiteró en su decisión de dejar**
de fumar he/she reaffirmed his/her decision
to stop smoking
reivindicación [rrei·βin·di·ka·'sjon, -'θjon] *f*
~ **de algo** claim to sth
reivindicar <c→qu> [rrei·βin·di·'kar] *vt*
1.(*pedir*) to claim; (*exigir*) to demand **2.**(*re-*
cobrar) to recover **3.**(*una acción*) to claim;
~ **un atentado** to claim responsibility for an attack
reja ['rre·xa] *f* **1.**(*barras*) grill; **estar entre** ~ s
fig, *inf* to be behind bars **2.**(*del arado*) plow-
share
rejego [rre·'xe·γo] *adj* *AmC*, *Méx* **1.**(*indom-*
able) wild; (*alzado*) untamed **2.**(*intratable*)

unmanageable; (*enojadizo*) cranky
rejilla [rre·'xi·ja, -ʎa] *f* **1.**(*enrejado*) grating
2.(*parrilla*) grill **3.**(*brasero*) brazier **4.**(*tejido*)
wickerwork **5.**(*para equipaje*) luggage rack
rejo ['rre·xo] *m* **1.**(*punta*) spike **2.** *AmL*
(*látigo*) whip
rejuvenecer [rre·xu·βe·ne·'ser, -'θer] *irr como*
crecer I. *vt* (*hacer más joven*) to rejuvenate;
este peinado te rejuvenece this haircut
makes you look much younger II. *vr:* ~ **se** to be
rejuvenated
relación [rre·la·'sjon, -'θjon] *f* **1.**(*entre cosas,*
hechos) relationship, relation; ~ **entre la**
causa y el efecto relationship between cause
and effect; **hacer** ~ **a algo** to refer to sth; **con**
~ **a su petición** with regard to your/his/her
request **2.**(*entre dos magnitudes*) relationship; ~ **calidad-precio** value for money; **los**
gastos no guardan ~ **con el presupuesto**
the expenses bear no relation to the budget
3.(*entre personas*) relationship; **relaciones**
públicas public relations; **tener relaciones**
con alguien to be in contact with sb; **tener**
muchas relaciones (*amigos*) to have lots of
friends; (*influyentes*) to have lots of contacts
4. *pl* (*noviazgo, amorío*) relationship; **han**
roto sus relaciones they have broken up;
mantienen relaciones they are going out
with each other; **mantener relaciones se-**
xuales con alguien to have a sexual relationship with sb
relacionar [rre·la·sjo·'nar, rre·la·θjo-] I. *vt*
(*poner en relación*) to relate II. *vr:* ~ **se**
1.(*estar relacionado*) to be related **2.**(*iniciar*
relaciones) to strike up a relationship; (*man-*
tener relaciones) to mix; ~ **se mucho** (*tener*
amigos) to have lots of friends; (*influyentes*) to
have lots of contacts
relajación [rre·la·xa·'sjon, -'θjon] *f* **1.**(*disten-*
sión, distracción) relaxation **2.**(*malas cos-*
tumbres) slackness **3.**(*debilitación*) weakening **4.**(*atenuación*) easing; ~ **de la pena**
reduction of the sentence
relajadura [rre·la·xa·'du·ra] *f* *Méx* (*hernia*)
rupture
relajar [rre·la·'xar] I. *vt* **1.**(*distender, distraer*)
to relax **2.**(*suavizar*) to ease; (*la pena*) to reduce II. *vr:* ~ **se 1.**(*distenderse, descansar*) to
relax **2.**(*debilitarse*) to weaken **3.**(*suavizarse*)
to ease
relamer [rre·la·'mer] I. *vt* to lick II. *vr:* ~ **se**
1.(*los labios*) to lick one's lips **2.**(*gozar*) ~ **se**
con algo to relish sth; ~ **se con un manjar** to
eat a delicacy with great relish **3.**(*gloriarse*)
~ **se de algo** to gloat over sth **4.**(*arreglarse*) to
clean oneself up **5.**(*animal*) to lick its chops
relámpago [rre·'lam·pa·γo] *m* flash of lightning; **ser** (**veloz como**) **un** ~ to be as fast as
lightning
relampaguear [rre·lam·pa·γe·'ar] I. *vi* to sparkle II. *vimpers* **relampagueaba** there was
lightning
relance [rre·'lan·se, -θe] *m* **1.** *Chile* (*piropo*)

R

flirtatious compliment **2.** *Col* **de ~** (*al contado*) in cash

relatar [rre·la·'tar] *vt* (*información*) to report; (*una historia*) to tell

relatividad [rre·la·ti·βi·'dad] *f* FÍS relativity

relativizar <z→c> [rre·la·ti·βi·'sar, -'θar] *vt* to play down

relativo [rre·la·'ti·βo] *m* LING (*pronombre*) relative pronoun; **oración de ~** relative clause

relativo, -a [rre·la·'ti·βo, -a] *adj* **1.** (*referente*) relative; **un artículo ~ a...** an article about... **2.** (*dependiente*) relative; **pronombre ~** relative pronoun; **ser ~ a algo** to be relative to sth **3.** (*poco*) limited

relato [rre·'la·to] *m* report; LIT story; **~ corto** short story

relegar <g→gu> [rre·le·'γar] *vt* (*apartar*) to relegate; **ser relegado al olvido** to be consigned to oblivion; **~ algo a un plano secundario** to push sth into the background

relente [rre·'len·te] *f* night dew; **dormir al ~** to sleep out in the open

relevancia [rre·le·'βan·sja, -θja] *f* importance, relevance

relevante [rre·le·'βan·te] *adj* **1.** (*importante*) important **2.** (*sobresaliente*) outstanding

relevar [rre·le·'βar] **I.** *vt* **1.** (*liberar*) to exempt; **~ a alguien de un juramento** to release sb from an oath; **~ a alguien de sus deudas** to release sb from his/her debts; **~ a alguien de sus culpas** to exonerate sb from blame for his/her actions **2.** JUR (*destituir*) to remove; **~ a alguien de un cargo** to relieve sb of his/her post **3.** (*reemplazar*) to place; MIL to relieve; DEP to substitute **4.** (*acentuar*) to highlight **II.** *vr:* **~se** to take turns

relevo [rre·'le·βo] *m* **1.** (*reemplazo*) change; **tomar el ~ de alguien** to take over from sb **2.** (*pl*) DEP (*competición*) relay; **carrera de ~s** relay race **3.** MIL change of the guard

relicario [rre·li·'ka·rjo] *m* **1.** (*para reliquias*) reliquary **2.** *AmL* (*medallón*) locket

relieve [rre·'lje·βe] *m* **1.** ARTE, GEO relief; **en bajo ~** in bas-relief **2.** (*renombre*) prominence ► **poner de ~** to emphasize

religión [rre·li·'xjon] *f* **1.** (*creencia, doctrina*) religion; **~ reformada** Protestantism; **sin ~** godless **2.** (*virtud*) virtue **3.** (*orden*) **entrar en ~** to take vows

religiosidad [rre·li·xjo·si·'dad] *f* **1.** (*observancia*) religiosity, religiousness **2.** (*piedad*) piety **3.** (*puntualidad*) punctuality; (*exactitud*) thoroughness

religioso, -a [rre·li·'xjo·so, -a] **I.** *adj* **1.** (*relativo a la religión*) religious **2.** (*pío*) pious **3.** (*puntual*) punctual; (*exacto*) thorough **II.** *m, f* member of a religious order, monk *m*, nun *f*

reliquia [rre·'li·kja] *f* **1.** *t.* REL relic; **una ~ de familia** a family heirloom **2.** (*antigüedad*) collector's item **3.** MED after-effect

rellano [rre·'ja·no, -'λano] *m* (*de escalera*) landing

rellena [rre·'je·na, -'λe·na] *f Col, Méx* (*morcilla*) blood sausage

rellenar [rre·je·'nar, rre·λe-] *vt* **1.** (*llenar*) **~ de** [*o* con] **algo** to fill with sth; CULIN to stuff with sth; **~ los agujeros de yeso** to fill in the holes with plaster **2.** (*por completo*) to fill up; (*demasiado*) to overfill **3.** (*volver a llenar*) to refill **4.** (*completar*) to fill out **5.** *inf* (*dar de comer*) to stuff (sb) (with food)

relleno [rre·'je·no, rre·'λe-] *m* **1.** (*material*) filling; CULIN stuffing **2.** (*superfluidad*) padding; **palabra de ~** filler

relleno, -a [rre·'je·no, -a; rre·'λe-] *adj* **1.** (*lleno*) full; (*demasiado*) stuffed full; CULIN stuffed **2.** *inf* (*gordo*) chubby

reloj [rre·'lox] *m* clock; (*de pulsera*) watch; **~ despertador** alarm clock; **~ para fichar** time clock; **~ de arena** hourglass; **~ de caja** [*o* **de péndulo**] grandfather clock; **carrera contra ~** race against the clock; **trabajar contra ~** to work against the clock; **ser (como) un ~** (*mecanismo*) to go like clockwork

relojear [rre·lo·xe·'ar] *vt Arg* **1.** (*tomar el tiempo*) to time **2.** *inf* (*controlar, espiar*) to keep tabs on; **~ a alguien de arriba abajo** to look sb up and down

relojería [rre·lo·xe·'ri·a] *f* clockmaker's; (*de relojes de pulsera*) watchmaker's

relojero, -a [rre·lo·'xe·ro, -a] *m, f* clockmaker; (*de relojes de pulsera*) watchmaker

reluciente [rre·lu·'sjen·te, -'θjen·te] *adj* shining; **~ de limpio** shiny clean

relucir [rre·lu·'sir, -'θir] *irr como lucir vi* **1.** (*despedir, reflejar luz*) to shine **2.** (*sobresalir*) to stand out ► **sacar algo a ~** to bring sth up; **salir a ~** to come up

relumbrar [rre·lum·'brar] *vi* **1.** (*emitir, reflejar luz*) to shine **2.** (*sobresalir*) to stand out

remachado, -a [rre·ma·'tʃa·do] *adj* **1.** (*nariz*) flat **2.** *Col* (*callado*) quiet

remachar [rre·ma·'tʃar] **I.** *vt* **1.** (*golpear*) to hammer **2.** (*doblar*) to bend; (*aplastar*) to flatten **3.** (*sujetar*) to rivet **4.** (*subrayar*) to stress; **~ algo a alguien** to stress sth to sb **II.** *vr:* **~se** *Col* to remain silent

remanente [rre·ma·'nen·te] **I.** *adj* remaining **II.** *m* remainder; COM surplus; (*contabilidad*) carry-over

remangar <g→gu> [rre·man·'gar] **I.** *vt* to roll up **II.** *vr:* **~se** *t. fig* to roll up one's sleeves

remanso [rre·'man·so] *m* (*represa*) pool; (*agua muerta*) stagnant water ► **~ de paz** haven of peace

remar [rre·'mar] *vi* (*bogar*) to row

rematar [rre·ma·'tar] **I.** *vt* **1.** (*concluir*) to finish (off); (*terminar de hacer*) to put the finishing touches to; **nunca rematas lo que has empezado** you never finish what you start **2.** (*matar: animal*) to put out of its misery; (*persona*) to finish off **3.** (*una costura*) to finish off **4.** (*gastar*) to use up **5.** DEP to shoot **6.** (*en subasta*) to knock down **7.** (*vender*) to sell off (cheap) **II.** *vi* **1.** DEP to shoot **2.** (*terminar*) to end; **la torre remata en punta** the tower ends in a point

remate [rre·'ma·te] *m* **1.**(*conclusión*) conclusion; (*de un producto*) finishing touch; **dar ~ a un edificio** to put the finishing touches to a building **2.**(*final, extremo*) end; **poner ~ a un mueble** to ornament a piece of furniture **3.**(*matanza*) killing off, coup de grâce **4.**(*adjudicación*) sale by auction **5.**(*oferta*) highest bid **6.** DEP shot **7.**(*consumo*) consumption; **dar ~** to use up **8.**(*venta*) sale (*at a low price*) ▶ **estar loco de ~** to be as mad as a hatter; **para ~** to top it all off; **por ~** finally

remecer [rre·me·'ser, -'θer] *irr como crecer vt, vr: ~ se AmL* (*sacudir*) to shake

remedar [rre·me·'dar] *vt* (*imitar*) to imitate; (*parodiar*) to mimic

remediar [rre·me·'djar] *vt* **1.**(*evitar*) to prevent; **no me cae bien, no puedo ~lo** I don't like him/her, I can't help it **2.**(*acabar con*) to finish off; (*reparar*) to repair; (*compensar*) to make up for; **llorando no remedias nada** crying won't solve anything **3.**(*corregir*) to correct **4.**(*ayudar*) to help

remedio [rre·'me·djo] *m* **1.**(*arreglo*) remedy; (*compensación*) compensation; (*corrección*) correction; **no tener ~** to be a hopeless case; **mi hermano no tiene ~** my brother is beyond help; **tu problema/la crisis no tiene ~** there is no solution to your problem/to the crisis; **no hay ~** there's nothing we can do; **no tenemos** [*o* **no hay**] **más ~ que...** the only solution is..., there is no choice but to...; **poner ~ a un mal** to right a wrong; **sin ~** (*inútil*) hopeless; (*sin falta*) inevitable; **un idealista sin ~** an incurable idealist **2.**(*ayuda*) help; **buscar ~ en sus amigos** to turn to one's friends for help; **buscar ~ en la bebida** to turn to drink **3.** MED (*medio*) remedy; **~ naturalista** natural remedy; **~ casero** household [*o* home] remedy ▶ **es peor el ~ que la enfermedad** *prov* the remedy is worse than the disease; **¿qué ~?** what choice is there?

rememorar [rre·me·mo·'rar] *vt* to remember

remendar <e→ie> [rre·men·'dar] *vt* (*reparar*) to mend; (*con parches*) to patch; (*zurcir*) to darn

remera [rre·'me·ra] *f* **1.** ZOOL flight feather **2.** *Arg* (*camiseta*) T-shirt

remero, -a [rre·'me·ro, -a] *m, f* rower, oarsman

remesa [rre·'me·sa] *f* consignment, shipment; FIN remittance

remezón [rre·me·'son, -'θon] *m AmL* (*sacudida*) shake

remiendo [rre·'mjen·do] *m* **1.**(*reparación*) mending; (*con parches*) patching; (*zurcidura*) darning **2.**(*corrección*) correction **3.**(*extra*) addition **4.**(*parche*) patch

remilgo [rre·'mil·γo] *m* primness; (*quisquilloso*) fussiness; **sin ~s** without making a fuss; **hacer ~s** to make a fuss

reminiscencia [rre·mi·ni·'sen·sja, -'θen·θja] *f* **1.**(*en una obra*) influence; **la ópera tiene ~s**

wagnerianas the opera shows Wagnerian influences **2.**(*lo que sobrevive*) remainder **3.**(*recuerdo*) reminiscence

remisible [rre·mi·'si·βle] *adj* (*deuda, pena, pecado*) forgivable

remisión [rre·mi·'sjon] *f* **1.**(*envío*) consignment **2.**(*referencia*) reference **3.**(*atenuación*) slackening **4.**(*de una obligación*) excusal; (*de pecados, deuda*) forgiveness; (*de una pena*) release; **sin ~** without fail

remite [rre·'mi·te] *m* sender's name and address

remitente [rre·mi·'ten·te] *mf* sender

remitir [rre·mi·'tir] **I.** *vt* **1.**(*enviar*) to send; FIN to remit; **~ algo a alguien** to send sth to sb **2.**(*referirse*) to refer **3.**(*de una obligación*) to forgive; **~ a alguien de una pena** to release sb from a punishment; **~ a alguien de una deuda** to cancel sb's debt; **~ a alguien de sus pecados** to forgive sb his/her sins **4.**(*aplazar*) to postpone; (*un juicio*) to adjourn **5.**(*confiar*) to entrust **6.**(*ceder*) to hand over **II.** *vi* (*calmarse*) to let up **III.** *vr:* **~ se 1.**(*referirse*) to refer **2.**(*confiarse*) to trust; **~ se al juez** to abide by the ruling of the judge

remo ['rre·mo] *m* **1.**(*pala: con soporte*) oar; (*sin soporte*) paddle; **a(l) ~** by rowboat; *fig* with difficulty **2.** DEP rowing ▶ **a ~ y vela** *inf* speedily; **andar al ~** *inf* to work like a slave; **tomar el ~** *inf* to take the helm

remodelación [rre·mo·de·la·'sjon, -'θjon] *f* redesign, remodeling; **~ del gabinete** cabinet reshuffle

remodelar [rre·mo·de·'lar] *vt* to redesign, remodel; (*gobierno*) to reshuffle

remojar [rre·mo·'xar] **I.** *vt* (*mojar, sumergir*) to soak; (*empapar*) to drench; (*ablandar*) to soften; (*galleta*) to dip **II.** *vr:* **~ se** (*mojarse*) to get wet; (*bañarse*) to have a dip

remojo [rre·'mo·xo] *m* (*empapamiento, sumersión*) soaking; (*baño*) dip; **poner en ~** to leave to soak

remolacha [rre·mo·'la·ʧa] *f* beet; (*roja*) beetroot; (*de azúcar*) (sugar) beet

remolcador [rre·mol·ka·'dor] *m* **1.**(*camión*) tow truck **2.**(*barco*) tug

remolcador(a) [rre·mol·ka·'dor, -'do·ra] *adj* **grúa ~a** tow truck

remolcar <c→qu> [rre·mol·'kar] *vt* **1.**(*un barco*) to tug; (*un vehículo averiado*) to tow **2.**(*convencer*) to rope in

remolienda [rre·mo·'ljen·da] *f Arg, Urug, inf* (*juerga*) binge

remolino [rre·mo·'li·no] *m* **1.**(*movimiento*) whirl; (*de agua*) whirlpool; **~ de viento** whirlwind **2.**(*pelo*) cowlick **3.**(*gente*) throng **4.**(*confusión*) commotion **5.** *inf* (*persona*) whirlwind

remolonear [rre·mo·lo·ne·'ar] *vi, vr:* **~ se 1.**(*vaguear*) to be lazy **2.**(*evitar*) to shirk

remolque [rre·'mol·ke] *m* **1.**(*arrastre*) tow **2.**(*vehículo*) trailer **3.**(*cuerda*) towrope; **llevar a ~** to tow ▶ **hacer algo a ~** to do sth re-

R

luctantly

remontar [rre·mon·'tar] I. *vt* **1.**(*superar*) to overcome **2.**(*subir*) to go up; ~ **un río** (*navegar*) to go up a river; (*nadar*) to swim up a river **3.**(*elevar*) to fly; ~ **el vuelo** to soar **4.**(*la caza*) to beat II. *vr:* ~**se** **1.**(*volar*) to climb; (*ave*) to soar **2.**(*gastos*) to amount **3.**(*pertenecer, retroceder*) to go back to; **la construcción de la iglesia se remonta al siglo pasado** the construction of the church dates from the past century

remorder <o→ue> [rre·mor·'der] I. *vt* **1.**(*atormentar*) to torment **2.**(*morder*) to bite again II. *vr:* ~**se** to suffer remorse

remordimiento [rre·mor·di·'mjen·to] *m* remorse; **tener ~s (de conciencia) por algo** to feel remorseful about sth; **el ~ no lo deja dormir** he can't sleep for remorse

remoto, -a [rre·'mo·to, -a] *adj* **1.**(*lejano*) remote; **en tiempos ~s** long ago **2.**(*improbable*) remote; **no existe ni la más remota posibilidad** there is not the slightest possibility; **no tener ni la más remota idea** to not have the slightest idea

remover <o→ue> [rre·mo·'βer] I. *vt* **1.**(*mover*) to remove **2.**(*agitar*) to shake; (*dar vueltas*) to stir; (*la ensalada*) to toss **3.**(*activar*) to stir up II. *vi* to investigate III. *vr:* ~**se** **1.**(*moverse*) to roll about **2.**(*aguas*) to move about

remunerable [rre·mu·ne·'ra·βle] *adj* remunerable

remuneración [rre·mu·ne·ra·'sjon, -'θjon] *f* **1.**(*pago*) remuneration **2.**(*recompensa*) compensation

remunerar [rre·mu·ne·'rar] *vt* **1.**(*pagar*) to remunerate; ~ **a alguien por un servicio** to pay sb for a service **2.**(*recompensar*) to compensate

renacer [rre·na·'ser, -'θer] *irr como crecer vi* **1.**(*volver a nacer*) to be reborn **2.**(*regenerarse*) to revive; **sentirse ~** to feel completely revived

renacimiento [rre·na·si·'mjen·to, -θi·'mjen·to] *m* **1.**ARTE, LIT renaissance **2.** *t.* FILOS, REL (*regeneración*) revival

renacuajo, -a [rre·na·'kwa·xo, -a] *m, f pey* shrimp

renal [rre·'nal] *adj* renal

rencor [rren·'kor] *m* ill feeling; **guardar ~ a alguien** to bear a grudge against sb

rencoroso, -a [rren·ko·'ro·so, -a] *adj* **1.**(*vengativo*) spiteful **2.**(*resentido*) resentful

rendición [rren·di·'sjon, -'θjon] *f* **1.**(*capitulación, sumisión*) surrender **2.**(*entrega*) yield; **~ de cuentas** balance **3.**(*utilidad*) usefulness **4.**(*fatiga*) exhaustion **5.**(*conquista*) conquest

rendidamente [rren·di·da·'men·te] *adv* devotedly; **estar ~ enamorado de** to be besotted with

rendido, -a [rren·'di·do, -a] *adj* **1.**(*cansado*) exhausted **2.**(*sumiso*) submissive; **cayó ~ ante su belleza** he was enchanted by her beauty

rendija [rren·'di·xa] *f* crack

rendimiento [rren·di·'mjen·to] *m* **1.**(*productividad*) yield; ECON (*máximo*) capacity; **a pleno ~** at full capacity **2.**(*beneficio*) profit; **de gran ~** very profitable **3.**(*cansancio*) exhaustion **4.** *pl* (*ingresos*) income **5.**(*humildad*) humility **6.**(*obsequiosidad*) servility

rendir [rren·'dir] *irr como pedir* I. *vt* **1.**(*rentar*) to yield; ~ **utilidad** to be useful; ~ **fruto** to bear fruit; **la inversión ha rendido mucho** the investment has been very profitable **2.**(*trabajar*) to produce; **estas máquinas rinden mucho** these machines are very productive **3.**(*tributar*) to attribute; ~ **las gracias a alguien** to thank sb; ~ **importancia a algo** to attribute importance to sth **4.**(*entregar*) to hand over; (*pruebas*) to bring; (*una confesión*) to make; ~ **cuentas** to settle the accounts; *fig* to account for one's actions; ~ **obsequios a alguien** to praise sb; ~ **las armas** to surrender one's arms **5.**(*vencer*) to defeat **6.**(*cansar*) to exhaust; **me rindió el sueño** I was overcome by tiredness **7.**(*sustituir*) to replace II. *vr:* ~ **se** **1.**(*entregarse*) to surrender; ~ **se al enemigo** to surrender to the enemy; ~ **se a la evidencia de algo** to bow to the evidence of sth; ~ **se a las razones de alguien** to yield to sb's arguments **2.**(*cansarse*) ~ **se de cansancio** to give in to one's exhaustion

renegado, -a [rre·ne·'ya·do] I. *adj* **1.**(*religión*) apostate **2.** *inf* (*carácter*) bad-tempered II. *m, f* **1.**(*religión*) apostate **2.** *inf* (*carácter*) grouch

renegar [rre·ne·'yar] *irr como fregar* I. *vi* **1.**(*protestar*) ~ **de algo** to protest against sth **2.**(*renunciar*) to renounce; ~ **de la fe** to renounce one's faith; ~ **del partido** to renounce the party II. *vt* **1.**(*negar*) to deny **2.**(*detestar*) to detest

RENFE ['rren·fe] *f abr de* **Red Nacional de Ferrocarriles Españoles** *Spanish state railway company*

renglón [rren·'glon] *m* **1.**(*línea*) line; **poner cuatro renglones a alguien** to drop sb a line; **a ~ seguido** on the next line; *fig* straight away **2.**(*partida*) share

rengo, -a ['rren·go, -a] *adj CSur* (*cojo*) lame

renguear [rren·ge·'ar] *vi CSur* (*cojear*) to limp

renguera [rren·'ge·ra] *f CSur* limp

reno ['rre·no] *m* reindeer

renombrado, -a [rre·nom·'bra·do, -a] *adj* (*célebre*) renowned

renombre [rre·'nom·bre] *m* renown; **una empresa de gran ~** a very well-known company; **una persona de ~** a famous person; **adquirir ~** to become renowned; **gozar de ~** to be renowned

renovación [rre·no·βa·'sjon, -'θjon] *f* renewal; (*de un edificio*) renovation

renovar <o→ue> [rre·no·'βar] *vt* to renew; (*una casa*) to renovate; (*un país*) to modernize; ~ **un pedido** to repeat a request; ~ **la pin-**

tura to touch up the paintwork; **~ la memoria** to refresh one's memory; **~ un aviso** to repeat a warning

renta ['rren·ta] *f* **1.**(*beneficio*) profit; (*ingresos*) income; **~ per cápita** per capita income; **~s públicas** national revenue **2.**(*pensión*) pension; **~ por incapacidad laboral** disability benefit; **~ vitalicia** life annuity; **~ de viudez** widow's pension **3.**(*alquiler*) rent; **en ~** for rent; **tomar a ~ un negocio** to lease out a business

rentabilidad [rren·ta·βi·li·'dad] *f* profitability; **~ competitiva** cost-effectiveness; **dar una ~ de...** to yield profits of...

rentable [rren·'ta·βle] *adj* profitable

rentar [rren·'tar] **I.** *vt* **1.**(*beneficio*) to yield **2.** *AmL* (*alquilar*) to rent **II.** *vi* to be profitable; **~ bien** to yield a good profit

rentero, -a [rren·'te·ro, -a] *m, f* **1.**(*arrendatario*) tenant farmer **2.** *Arg* (*contribuyente*) taxpayer

renuencia [rre·'nwen·sja, -θja] *f* reluctance

renuente [rre·'nwen·te] *adj* reluctant

renuncia [rre·'nun·sja, -θja] *f* **1.**(*abandono*) **~ a** [*o* **de**] **algo** resignation from sth; **~ del cargo** resignation from the post; **~ al contrato** withdrawal from the contract; **presentar su ~** to resign **2.**(*escrito*) waiver

renunciar [rre·nun·'sjar, -'θjar] *vi* **1.**(*desistir*) **~ a** [*o* **de**] **algo** to renounce sth; **~ al trono** to abdicate the throne; **~ a un cargo** to resign from a post; **~ a una herencia** to renounce an inheritance **2.**(*rechazar*) **~ a algo** to reject sth

reñido, -a [rre·'ɲi·do, -a] *adj* **1.**(*enojado*) angry; **estoy ~ con él** I have fallen out with him **2.**(*en oposición*) **estar ~** *fig* to be incompatible **3.**(*encarnizado*) bitter

reñir [rre·'ɲir] *irr como ceñir* **I.** *vi* to quarrel; **¿has reñido con tu novio?** did you fight with your boyfriend? ▶ **dos no riñen si uno no quiere** it takes two to tango **II.** *vt* to scold

reo, -a ['rreo, -a] **I.** *adj* accused **II.** *m, f* (*culpado*) defendant; (*autor*) culprit; **~ de asesinato** murderer; **~ habitual** persistent offender; **~ preventivo** remand prisoner

reojo [rre·'o·xo] *m* **mirar de ~** (*con hostilidad*) to look askance at; (*con disimulo*) to look out of the corner of one's eye at

reorganización [rre·or·ya·ni·sa·'sjon, -θa·'θjon] *f* reorganization; **~ del gobierno** government reshuffle

reorganizar <z→c> [rre·or·ya·ni·'sar, -'θar] *vt* to reorganize; (*gobierno*) to reshuffle

reorientación [rre·o·rjen·ta·'sjon, -'θjon] *f* reorientation; **~ política** political realignment

reparable [rre·pa·'ra·βle] *adj* (*arreglable*) repairable

reparación [rre·pa·ra·'sjon, -'θjon] *f* **1.**(*arreglo*) repair **2.**(*indemnización, enmienda*) compensation; **~ de perjuicios** damages *pl*

reparar [rre·pa·'rar] **I.** *vt* **1.**(*arreglar*) to repair; **~ el daño** to repair the damage **2.**(*indemni-*

zar, enmendar) to compensate **3.**(*recuperar*) **~ fuerzas** to recover one's strength; **con la siesta reparo fuerzas** a nap refreshes me **II.** *vi* **~ en** (*advertir*) to notice; (*considerar*) to consider; **sin ~ en gastos** regardless of the cost; **no ~ en sacrificios/gastos** to spare no effort/expense **III.** *vr:* **~se** to restrain oneself

reparo [rre·'pa·ro] *m* **1.**(*arreglo*) repair **2.**(*inconveniente*) problem; **sin ~ alguno** without any difficulty; **tener ~s para** to be reluctant [*o* hesitant] to **3.**(*objeción*) objection; **sin ~** without reservation; **no andar con ~s** to have no reservations; **poner ~s a algo** to raise objections to sth

repartición [rre·par·ti·'sjon, -'θjon] *f* **1.** *v.* **repartimiento 2.** *AmL* (*oficina*) office

repartimiento [rre·par·ti·'mjen·to] *m* (*distribución*) distribution; (*división*) division

repartir [rre·par·'tir] **I.** *vt* to distribute; (*correos*) to deliver **II.** *vr:* **~se** (*dividir*) to divide up; **~se el mercado** to divide up the market

reparto [rre·'par·to] *m* **1.**(*distribución*) distribution; (*división*) division; **~ de contribuciones** allotment of taxes; **~ domiciliario** home delivery; **~ de equipajes** baggage reclaim; **~ postal** mail delivery; **camión de ~** (*furgoneta*) delivery van; (*grande*) delivery truck **2.**(*relación*) division; **~ de poderes** ECON division of power

repasador [rre·pa·sa·'dor] *m Arg, Urug* (*paño de cocina*) dish cloth

repasar [rre·pa·'sar] *vt* **1.**(*la ropa*) to mend **2.**(*un texto, la lección*) to revise; **segunda edición repasada y corregida** second edition, revised and amended **3.**(*la cuenta*) to check **4.**(*una carta*) to reread

repaso [rre·'pa·so] *m* **1.**(*revisión*) review **2.**(*inspección*) check

repatriar [rre·pa·'trjar] *vt* to repatriate

repe ['rre·pe] *m Ecua* CULIN *mashed cooked bananas with milk and cheese*

repecho [rre·'pe·tʃo] *m* (steep) slope; **a ~** uphill

repeinar [rre·pei·'nar] **I.** *vt* to comb carefully **II.** *vr:* **~se** to comb one's hair carefully

repelente [rre·pe·'len·te] **I.** *adj* **1.**(*rechazador*) repellent; **~ al agua** water-repellent **2.**(*repugnante*) repulsive **3.**(*redicho*) affected **II.** *mf* (*sabelotodo*) know-it-all

repeler [rre·pe·'ler] *vt* **1.**(*rechazar*) to repel; **los imanes se repelen mutuamente** magnets repel one another **2.**(*repugnar*) to disgust

repensar <e→ie> [rre·pen·'sar] *vt* to reconsider

repente [rre·'pen·te] *m inf*(*movimiento*) start; (*ataque*) fit ▶ **de ~** suddenly, all of a sudden; **de ~ se echó a llorar** suddenly he/she started to cry

repentino, -a [rre·pen·'ti·no, -a] *adj* sudden

repercusión [rre·per·ku·'sjon] *f* **1.**(*efecto*) repercussion; **tener gran ~** (*éxito*) to meet with great success **2.**(*del choque*) reverberation

repercutir [rre·per·ku·'tir] *vi* **1.**(*efecto*) **~ en algo** to have an effect on sth; **~ en la salud** to

R

affect one's health **2.**(*del choque*) to rebound **3.**(*eco*) to reverberate

repertorio [rre·per·'to·rjo] *m* **1.**(*lista*) list; ~ **legislativo** legislative program **2.** *t.* TEAT repertoire, repertory

repetición [rre·pe·ti·'sjon, -'θjon] *f* repetition; ~ **de orden** repeat order; **fusil de** ~ repeating rifle; **en caso de** ~ in case of repetition

repetido, -a [rre·pe·'ti·do, -a] *adj* repeated; **repetidas veces** again and again; **tengo muchos sellos ~ s** I have doubles of lots of my stamps

repetir [rre·pe·'tir] *irr como pedir* **I.** *vi* **1.**(*sabor*) to repeat; **los ajos repiten mucho** garlic comes back on you **2.**(*plato*) ~ **de un plato de comida** to have second helpings of a dish **II.** *vt* (*reiterar, recitar*) to repeat; ~ **curso** to stay down; ~ **un pedido de mercancía** to reorder goods **III.** *vr:* ~ **se** to repeat oneself

repicar <c→qu> [rre·pi·'kar] **I.** *vi* (*campanas*) to ring, to peal; (*castañuelas*) to click **II.** *vt* **1.**(*campanas*) to ring; (*instrumento*) to play **2.**(*despedazar*) to mince **III.** *vr:* ~ **se** to boast

repique [rre·'pi·ke] *m* **1.**(*de las campanas*) peal **2.** *inf* (*riña*) squabble

repiquetear [rre·pi·ke·te·'ar] *vi, vt* to ring; (*castañuelas*) to click

repisa [rre·'pi·sa] *f* shelf; ~ **de chimenea** mantelpiece; ~ **de ventana** window ledge

replantear [rre·plan·te·'ar] *vt* (*asunto*) to raise again; (*plan*) to revise; (*reconsiderar*) to rethink

replegar [rre·ple·'γar] *irr como fregar* **I.** *vt* **1.**(*doblar*) to fold **2.**(*para atrás*) to fold back **II.** *vr:* ~ **se** MIL to fall back

repleto, -a [rre·'ple·to, -a] *adj* ~ **de algo** full of sth; (*demasiado*) crammed with sth; **tener una cartera repleta de billetes** to have a wallet full of bills; **el tren está** ~ the train is packed; **estoy** ~ I'm full up; **está repleta de energía** she is full of energy

réplica ['rre·pli·ka] *f* **1.**(*respuesta*) reply; (*objeción*) rebuttal **2.** ARTE replica

replicar <c→qu> [rre·pli·'kar] **I.** *vt* to answer **II.** *vi* **1.**(*replicar*) to reply **2.**(*contradecir*) to contradict; **obedecer sin** ~ to obey without argument

repliegue [rre·'plje·γe] *m* **1.**(*dobladura*) fold **2.** MIL withdrawal

repoblación [rre·po·βla·'sjon, -'θjon] *f* (*de personas*) repopulation; (*de plantas*) replanting; ~ **forestal** reforestation

repoblar <o→ue> [rre·po·'βlar] *vt* (*personas*) to repopulate; (*plantas*) to replant; (*árboles*) to reforest

repollo [rre·'po·jo, -ʎo] *m* cabbage

reponer [rre·po·'ner] *irr como poner* **I.** *vt* **1.**(*volver a poner*) to put back; (*teléfono*) to hang up; (*máquina*) to put back into service; (*en su cargo*) to reinstate **2.**(*replicar*) to reply **3.** CINE to rerelease; TEAT to revive; TV to rerun **II.** *vr:* ~ **se** to recover

reportaje [rre·por·'ta·xe] *m* report; PREN article; ~ **gráfico** illustrated report; (*documental*) documentary

reportar [rre·por·'tar] **I.** *vt* **1.**(*proporcionar*) to bring **2.** *AmL* (*informar*) to report **II.** *vr:* ~ **se** to restrain oneself

reportear [rre·por·te·'ar] *vt AmL* (*entrevistar*) to interview

reportero, -a [rre·por·'te·ro, -a] *m, f* reporter; ~ **gráfico** press photographer

reposado, -a [rre·po·'sa·do, -a] *adj* peaceful; (*agua*) calm

reposar [rre·po·'sar] **I.** *vi* to rest; **aquí reposan los restos mortales de...** here lie the mortal remains of... **II.** *vt* to settle; ~ **la comida** to let one's food settle **III.** *vr:* ~ **se** (*líquidos*) to settle; (*vino*) to lie

reposera [rre·po·'se·ra] *f AmL* (*tumbona*) deckchair

reposición [rre·po·si·'sjon, -'θjon] *f* **1.**(*de un objeto*) replacement; ~ **de existencias** replenishment of stocks; ~ **de maquinaria** replacement of machinery **2.**(*del mercado, de una persona*) recovery **3.**(*de una situación*) stabilization **4.** TEAT revival; TV rerun; CINE rerelease

reposo [rre·'po·so] *m* (*tranquilidad*) peace; (*descanso*) rest; ~ **en cama** rest in bed, bed rest; **una máquina en** ~ a machine at rest

repostada [rre·pos·'ta·da] *f AmC* (*contestación*) rude reply

repostar [rre·pos·'tar] *vt* **1.**(*provisiones*) to stock up with **2.**(*vehículo*) to refuel; (*combustible*) to fill up with

repostería [rre·pos·te·'ri·a] *f* **1.**(*pastelería*) pastry shop **2.**(*oficio*) pastry-making **3.**(*productos*) pastries *pl*

reprender [rre·pren·'der] *vt* to reprimand; ~ **algo a alguien** to scold [*o* to reprimand] sb for sth

represa [rre·'pre·sa] *f* **1.**(*estancamiento*) pool **2.**(*construcción*) dam

represalia [rre·pre·'sa·lja] *f* reprisal; **en** ~ **por...** in retaliation for...

representación [rre·pre·sen·ta·'sjon, -'θjon] *f* **1.**(*substitución, delegación*) representation; ~ **colectiva** collective representation; ~ **exclusiva** exclusive representation; ~ **mayoritaria** majority representation; ~ **proporcional** POL proportional representation; **por** [*o* **en**] ~ **de** representing **2.** TEAT performance **3.**(*reproducción*) reproduction; (*ilustración*) illustration; ~ **digital** digital display

representante [rre·pre·sen·'tan·te] *mf* **1.**(*delegado, suplente*) representative; ~ **especial** special representative **2.** TEAT, CINE agent, manager; (*actor*) actor, actress *m, f* **3.** COM dealer, salesman *m*, saleswoman *f*

representar [rre·pre·sen·'tar] **I.** *vt* **1.**(*substituir*) to represent **2.**(*actuar*) to act; (*una obra*) to perform; ~ **el papel de amante** to play the role of lover **3.**(*significar*) to mean **4.**(*encarnar, personificar*) to embody; (*reproducir*) to reproduce; (*ilustrar*) to illustrate; ~ **visual-**

mente COMPUT to display visually **5.** (*aparentar*) to seem; **representa ser más joven** he/she seems younger **II.** *vr:* ~**se** to imagine

representativo, -a [rre·pre·sen·ta·'ti·βo, -a] *adj* representative; **gobierno** ~ representative government

represión [rre·pre·'sjon] *f* (*contención*) suppression; (*limitación*) repression; ~ **de crímenes** anti-crime measures

reprimenda [rre·pri·'men·da] *f* reprimand

reprimir [rre·pri·'mir] **I.** *vt* to suppress **II.** *vr:* ~**se** (*contenerse*) to control oneself; ~**se de hablar** to refrain from speaking

reprobable [rre·pro·'βa·βle] *adj* reprehensible

reprobación [rre·pro·βa·'sjon, -'θjon] *f* **1.** (*condenación*) condemnation **2.** (*rechazamiento*) rejection

reprobar <o→ue> [rre·pro·'βar] *vt* to condemn

reprochable [rre·pro·'tʃa·βle] *adj* reprehensible

reprochar [rre·pro·'tʃar] *vt* to reproach

reproche [rre·'pro·tʃe] *m* reproach; **en son de** ~ in a reproachful tone; **hacer ~s a alguien por algo** to reproach sb for sth

reproducción [rre·pro·duk·'sjon, -duɣ·'θjon] *f* **1.** (*procreación*) reproduction; ~ **bovina** cattle breeding **2.** (*repetición*) repetition; (*copia*) reproduction; ~ (**de un libro**) copy (of a book); ~ **de un discurso** repeat of a speech; (*documentos*) duplication **3.** (*representación*) reproduction; ~ **magnetofónica** tape recording; ~ **radiofónica** radio reproduction

reproducir [rre·pro·du·'sir, -'θir] *irr como traducir* **I.** *vt* **1.** (*procrear*) to reproduce **2.** (*repetir*) to repeat; (*copiar*) to reproduce; (*un libro*) to print; (*documento*) to duplicate **3.** (*representar*) to represent; (*imitar*) to imitate; (*contar*) to recount **II.** *vr:* ~**se** to reproduce

reproductor [rre·pro·duk·'tor] *m* (*aparato*) playback machine; ~ **de discos compactos** compact disc player; ~ **de video** video recorder

reproductor(a) [rre·pro·duk·'tor, -·'to·ra] **I.** *adj* reproductive **II.** *m(f)* (*animal*) breeder

reptar [rrep·'tar] *vi* to crawl

reptil [rrep·'til] *m* reptile

república [rre·'pu·βli·ka] *f* republic; ~ **miembro** member republic; ~ **bananera** *pey* banana republic

republicano, -a [rre·pu·βli·'ka·no, -a] *adj, m, f* republican

repudiar [rre·pu·'djar] *vt* **1.** (*rechazar*) to reject **2.** (*parientes*) to disown

repudio [rre·'pu·djo] *m* **1.** (*rechazo*) rejection **2.** (*de parientes*) repudiation

repuesto [rre·'pwes·to] *m* **1.** (*pieza*) spare part; **rueda de** ~ spare tire **2.** (*de alimentos*) supply

repuesto, -a [rre·'pwes·to, -a] *pp de* **reponer**

repugnancia [rre·puɣ·'nan·sja, -θja] *f* **1.** (*repulsión*) ~ **a algo** repugnance for sth

2. (*asco*) ~ **a algo** disgust for sth; **tener ~ al pescado** to loathe fish **3.** (*resistencia*) reluctance; **hacer algo con** ~ to do sth reluctantly

repugnante [rre·puɣ·'nan·te] *adj* disgusting

repugnar [rre·puɣ·'nar] **I.** *vi* **1.** (*producir aversión*) to repel; (*asquear*) to disgust; **me repugna la carne grasosa** fatty meat makes me sick **2.** (*disgustar*) to disgust **II.** *vt* (*rehusar*) to refuse

repulsión [rre·pul·'sjon] *f* (*aversión*) aversion; (*asco*) disgust

repulsivo, -a [rre·pul·'si·βo, -a] *adj* repulsive

repunte [rre·'pun·te] *m RíoPl* (*alza*) rise; **el ~ del dólar causó sensación hoy en la bolsa** the dollar's upturn caused a sensation in the stock market today

reputación [rre·pu·ta·'sjon, -'θjon] *f* reputation; **mujer de mala** ~ woman of ill repute; **tener muy buena/mala** ~ to have a very good/bad reputation; **un local con mala** ~ a place with a bad reputation

reputar [rre·pu·'tar] *vt* **1.** (*considerar*) ~ **a alguien de** [*o por*] **algo** to consider sb to be sth **2.** (*apreciar*) to respect

requemar [rre·ke·'mar] **I.** *vt* **1.** (*asar bien*) to roast; (*demasiado*) to burn **2.** (*plantas*) to scorch **3.** (*doler*) ~ **la garganta/la lengua** to burn one's throat/tongue **II.** *vr:* ~**se 1.** (*quemarse*) to scorch **2.** (*enfadarse*) to become angry **3.** (*plantas*) to scorch

requenete [rre·ke·'ne·te] *adj Ven* (*rechoncho*) tubby

requerimiento [rre·ke·ri·'mjen·to] *m* **1.** (*requisitoria*) ~ **de algo** demand for sth; (*escrito*) writ for sth; ~ **de información** request for information; **a ~ de...** on the request of...; **hacer el ~ para la publicación de las proclamas** to publish the (matrimonial) banns **2.** (*exigencia*) demand

requerir [rre·ke·'rir] *irr como sentir vt* **1.** (*necesitar*) to require; **esto requiere toda la atención** this calls for our fullest attention **2.** (*amorosamente*) to woo; ~ **de amores** to woo **3.** (*intimar*) to urge; ~ **a alguien que...** +*subj* to urge sb to...

requesón [rre·ke·'son] *m* cottage [*o* curd] cheese

requetebueno, -a [rre·ke·te·'βwe·no, -a] *adj AmL, inf* really good

requetecaro, -a [rre·ke·te·'ka·ro, -a] *adj AmL, inf* really expensive

réquiem ['rre·kjen] *m* MÚS requiem

requisar [rre·ki·'sar] *vt* to confiscate

requisito [rre·ki·'si·to] *m* (*requerimiento*) requirement; (*condición*) condition; **ser** ~ **indispensable** to be absolutely essential; ~ **previo** prerequisite; **exigir ciertos ~s** to demand certain requirements; **cumplir con los ~s** to fulfill the requirements

res [rres] *f* **1.** (*animal*) beast; **~es de matadero** animals for slaughter; **carne de** ~ beef **2.** *AmL* (*vaca*) head of cattle

resabio [rre·'sa·βjo] *m* **1.** (*sabor*) unpleasant

aftertaste **2.** (*costumbre*) bad habit

resaca [rre·'sa·ka] *f* **1.** (*olas*) undertow, undercurrent **2.** *inf* (*malestar*) hangover

resaltar [rre·sal·'tar] **I.** *vi* (*sobresalir, distinguirse*) to stand out **II.** *vt* **hacer ~** to highlight

resalte [rre·'sal·te] *m*, **resalto** [rre·'sal·to] *m* (*saliente*) projection, ledge

resarcir <c→z> [rre·sar·'sir, -'θir] **I.** *vt* **1.** (*compensar*) **~ de algo** to compensate for sth **2.** (*reparar*) to repay **II.** *vr* **~ se de algo** to make up for sth

resbalada [rres·βa·'la·da] *f AmL, inf* slip

resbaladilla [rres·βa·la·'di·ja, -ʎa] *f Méx* slide

resbaladizo, -a [rres·βa·la·'di·so, -a; -θo, -a] *adj* slippery

resbalar [rres·βa·'lar] *vi* to slide; (*sin querer*) to slip; (*coche*) to skid; **¡cuidado con no ~!** be careful not to slip!

resbalín [rres·βa·'lin] *m Chile* slide

rescatar [rres·ka·'tar] *vt* **1.** (*a un prisionero*) to rescue; (*con dinero*) to pay the ransom for **2.** (*a un náufrago*) to pick up **3.** (*un cadáver*) to recover **4.** (*algo perdido*) to recover **5.** (*una deuda*) to pay off **6.** (*tiempo*) to win back; **quisiera ~ mi juventud** I wish I could relive my youth **7.** ECON (*bonos*) to redeem **8.** *AmL* (*mercancías*) to peddle

rescate [rres·'ka·te] *m* **1.** (*de un prisionero*) rescue; (*con dinero*) ransoming **2.** (*de una prenda*) revival **3.** (*recuperación*) recovery; **con facultad de ~** redeemable

rescindir [rre·sin·'dir, rres·θin·] *vt* (*la ley*) to repeal; (*un contrato*) to annul

rescisión [rresi'sjon, rresθi-] *f* (*la ley*) repeal; (*un contrato*) annulment; **~ de una deuda** debt cancellation

resecar <c→qu> [rre·se·'kar] *vt* (*secar mucho*) to dry out; (*plantas*) to parch

resentido, -a [rre·sen·'ti·do, -a] *adj* **1.** *estar* (*ofendido*) resentful **2.** *estar* (*débil*) worn out **3.** *ser* (*rencoroso*) bitter

resentimiento [rre·sen·ti·'mjen·to] *m* resentment

resentirse [rre·sen·'tir·se] *irr como sentir vr* **1.** (*ofenderse*) **~ por** [*o* de] **algo** to feel resentful about sth **2.** (*sentir dolor*) **~ de** [*o* con] **algo** to suffer from sth; **~ del costado** to have a sore side; **todavía se resiente de las heridas del accidente** he/she is still suffering from the injuries he/she received in the accident **3.** (*debilitarse*) to be weakened; **los edificios se resintieron cuando abrieron el túnel** the buildings were weakened when they dug the tunnel

reseña [rre·'se·ɲa] *f* **1.** (*de un libro*) review **2.** (*de una persona*) description **3.** (*narración*) report

reseñar [rre·se·'ɲar] *vt* **1.** (*un libro*) to review **2.** (*una persona*) to describe **3.** (*resumir*) to summarize

resero, -a [rre·'se·ro, -a] *m, f CSur* (*arreador*) cowhand

reserva [rre·'ser·βa] *f* **1.** (*previsión*) reserva-

tion; **~ de equipajes** *AmL* left luggage; **tener algo en ~** to hold sth in reserve **2.** FIN reserve; (*fondos*) reserves *pl* **3.** (*de plazas*) reservation; **hacer una ~** to reserve, to book **4.** (*biológica*) reserve **5.** MIL reserves *pl*; **pasar a la ~** to join the reserves **6.** (*discreción*) secrecy; **guardar la ~** to be discrete **7.** (*vino*) vintage **8.** (*lugar protegido*) reserve; (*para personas*) reservation; (*para animales*) wildlife reserve

reservado [rre·ser·'βa·do] *m* **1.** FERRO reserved compartment **2.** (*habitación*) reserved room

reservado, -a [rre·ser·'βa·do, -a] *adj* **1.** (*derecho*) reserved; **quedan ~s todos los derechos** all rights reserved **2.** (*callado*) reserved **3.** (*confidencial*) confidential; **fondos ~s** reptilian funds **4.** (*cauteloso*) cautious

reservar [rre·ser·'βar] **I.** *vt* **1.** (*retener plaza*) to reserve; **~ un asiento** (*ocupar*) to save a seat; (*para un viaje*) to reserve a seat **2.** (*guardar*) to put by **3.** (*ocultar*) to conceal **II.** *vr:* **~ se** (*conservarse*) to save oneself

resfriado [rres·fri·'a·do] *m* MED cold

resfriar <3. *pres:* resfría> [rres·fri·'ar] **I.** *vi* to cool **II.** *vt* to cool off **III.** *vr:* **~ se 1.** (*enfriarse*) to get cold **2.** MED to catch a cold

resfrío [rres·'fri·o] *m AmL* cold

resguardar [rres·ɣwar·'dar] **I.** *vt* **1.** (*proteger*) **~ de algo** to protect from sth **2.** (*poner en seguridad*) to safeguard; **~ los derechos** to reserve the rights **II.** *vr* **~ se de algo** to protect oneself from sth; **~ se con un muro** to shelter behind a wall

resguardo [rres·'ɣwar·do] *m* **1.** (*protección*) protection **2.** (*recibo*) receipt; **~ de entrega/ de transferencia** proof of delivery/transfer

residencia [rre·si·'den·sja, -θja] *f* **1.** (*domicilio, estancia*) residence; **~ habitual** usual place of residence; **cambiar de ~** to change one's address **2.** (*casa lujosa*) residence; **~ real** royal residence; **~ señorial** palatial residence **3.** (*internado*) residence; (*colegio*) boarding school; **~ de ancianos** old people's home; **~ universitaria** dormitory

residente [rre·si·'den·te] **I.** *adj* resident; **no ~** non-resident; **~ en el lugar** resident locally **II.** *mf* resident

residir [rre·si·'dir] *vi* **1.** (*habitar*) to reside **2.** (*radicar*) **~ en** to lie in

residual [rre·si·du·'al] *adj* residual; **aguas ~es** sewage

residuo [rre·'si·dwo] *m* **1.** (*resto*) residue; QUÍM residuum **2.** *pl* (*basura*) waste; (*géneros defectuosos*) leftovers *pl*; **~ s de las fábricas** industrial waste; **~ s radiactivos** radioactive waste

resignación [rre·siɣ·na·'sjon, -'θjon] *f* resignation

resignar [rre·siɣ·'nar] **I.** *vt* to resign from **II.** *vr:* **~ se** to resign oneself; **~ se con** [*o* a] **algo** to resign oneself to sth

resina [rre·'si·na] *f* resin

resistencia [rre·sis·'ten·sja, -θja] *f* **1.** resistance; **~ a la autoridad** opposition to the

authorities; **oponer** ~ to offer resistance; **formar parte de la** ~ to be part of the resistance; **la** ~ **francesa** the French Resistance **2.**(*aguante*) ~ **física** stamina; ~ **al choque** shock resistance; ~ **al frío** resistance to the cold; ~ **al pago** non-payment; ~ **a la publicidad** publicity fatigue **3.** DEP **carrera de** ~ endurance race **4.** ELEC resistor, resistance
resistente [rre·sis·'ten·te] **I.** *adj* resistant; ~ **al calor** heat-resistant; ~ **a la intemperie** weatherproof; ~ **a la lavadora** machine-washable; ~ **a la luz** light-resistant **II.** *mf* resistance fighter
resistir [rre·sis·'tir] **I.** *vi, vt* **1.**(*oponer resistencia*) to resist; ~ **a una tentación** to resist a temptation; ~ **al enemigo** to resist the enemy; **resistió la enfermedad** he/she overcame the illness; **¡no resisto más!** I can't take any more! **2.**(*aguantar*) **no resisto la comida pesada** I can't cope with heavy food; **no puedo** ~ **a esta persona** I can't stand this person **II.** *vr:* ~**se** to resist
resolana [rre·so·'la·na] *f* AmL **1.**(*sol reflejado*) reflection **2.**(*lugar a pleno sol*) sunny, windless spot **3.**(*resplandor*) sun glare
resolución [rre·so·lu·'sjon, -'θjon] *f* **1.**(*firmeza*) resolve **2.**(*decisión*) decision; POL resolution; ~ **administrativa** administrative decision; ~ **judicial** adjudication; **tomar una** ~ to take [*o* reach] a decision **3.**(*solución*) solution
resolver [rre·sol·'βer] *irr como volver* **I.** *vt* **1.**(*acordar*) to agree **2.**(*solucionar*) to solve; (*dudas*) to resolve **3.**(*decidir*) to decide **II.** *vr:* ~**se 1.**(*solucionarse*) to be solved **2.**(*decidirse*) to decide
resonancia [rre·so·'nan·sja, -θja] *f* resonance; **caja de** ~ MÚS sound box; **de** ~ **universal** of great importance; **tener** ~ (*suceso*) to have an impact
resonante [rre·so·'nan·te] *adj* (*importante*) important; **con éxito** ~ with tremendous success
resonar <o→ue> [rre·so·'nar] *vi* to resound; **los gritos de angustia resuenan todavía en mis oídos** I can still hear the cries of anguish
resorte [rre·'sor·te] *m* **1.**(*muelle*) spring **2.** *fig* (*medio*) means *pl* **3.** *Méx* elastic
resortera [rre·sor·'te·ra] *f Méx* slingshot
respaldar [rres·pal·'dar] **I.** *vt* **1.**(*apoyar*) to support **2.**(*proteger*) to protect **II.** *vr:* ~**se** (*apoyarse*) to lean; (*hacia atrás*) to lean back; ~**se en el sillón** to sit back in one's chair **III.** *m* support
respaldo [rres·'pal·do] *m* **1.**(*respaldar*) support **2.**(*reverso*) back; **en el** ~ on the back **3.**(*apoyo*) support; (*protección*) protection
respectar [rres·pek·'tar] *vi* (*verbo defectivo*) to regard; **por** [*o* en] **lo que respecta a él...** with regard to him...
respectivamente [rres·pek·ti·βa·'men·te] *adv* respectively
respectivo, -a [rres·pek·'ti·βo, -a] *adj* respective

respecto [rres·'pek·to] *m* (**con**) ~ **a** with regard to; **al** ~, **con** ~ **a eso** in that regard; **a este** ~ in this regard
respetable [rres·pe·'ta·βle] *adj* **1.**(*digno de respeto*) respectable **2.**(*notable*) considerable
respetar [rres·pe·'tar] *vt* **1.**(*honrar*) to respect; **hacerse** ~ to command respect **2.**(*considerar*) to consider **3.**(*cumplir*) to observe
respeto [rres·'pe·to] *m* (*veneración*) respect; ~ **a las leyes** respect for the law; ~ **de un plazo** compliance with a time limit; **falta de** ~ lack of respect; **tener mucho** ~ **a las tormentas** to be well aware of the dangers of storms; **¡mis** ~**s a su señora!** give your wife my regards! ▸**faltar al** ~ **a alguien** to be disrespectful to(wards) sb; **ofrecer los** ~**s a alguien** to pay one's respects to sb; **de** ~ respectable
respetuoso, -a [rres·pe·tu·'o·so, -a] *adj* respectful; **ser** ~ **con las leyes** to respect the law
respiración [rres·pi·ra·'sjon, -'θjon] *f* (*inhalación*) breathing; (*aliento*) breath; ~ **artificial** artificial respiration; ~ **boca a boca** mouth to mouth resuscitation; **dificultad de** ~ breathing difficulties; **faltar a uno la** ~ to be breathless, to be short of breath
respirar [rres·pi·'rar] *vi* to breathe; ~ **aliviado** to breathe easily; ~ **trabajosamente** to gasp for breath; **no me atrevo a** ~ **delante de él** I don't dare to open my mouth when he's around ▸**¡déjame que respire!** give me a break!; **sin** ~ without stopping
respiratorio, -a [rres·pi·ra·'to·rjo, -a] *adj* respiratory; **vías respiratorias** air passages
resplandecer [rres·plan·de·'ser, -'θer] *irr como crecer vi* (*lucir, reflejar*) to shine; ~ **de alegría** to glow with happiness; ~ **por su inteligencia** to stand out for one's intelligence
resplandor [rres·plan·'dor] *m* brightness
responder [rres·pon·'der] *vi* **1.**(*contestar*) to reply; **el perro responde al nombre de...** the dog answers to the name of... **2.**(*contradecir*) to contradict **3.**(*corresponder*) to correspond; (*cumplir con*) to obey **4.**(*ser responsable*) ~ **por algo** to answer for sth
responsabilidad [rres·pon·sa·βi·li·'dad] *f* **1.**(*por un niño*) ~ **de** [*o* por] **alguien** responsibility for sb; ~ **propia** personal responsibility; **exigir** ~ to demand that sb accept responsibility **2.**(*por un daño*) liability; ~ **civil** civil liability; ~ **del daño** liability for damages; **incurrir en** ~ to become liable; **no acepto la** ~ it has nothing to do with me
responsabilizar <z→c> [rres·pon·sa·βi·li·'sar, -'θar] **I.** *vt* ~ **de algo** to make responsible for sth **II.** *vr:* ~**se** (*asumir la responsabilidad*) ~**se de algo** to accept the responsibility for sth
responsable [rres·pon·'sa·βle] **I.** *adj* ~ **de algo** responsible for sth; **ser civilmente** ~ to be liable **II.** *mf* (*encargado*) person in charge; (*culpable*) culprit
respuesta [rres·'pwes·ta] *f* answer; ~ **negativa** negative reply; **en** ~ **a su carta**

del... in reply to your letter of...; **por toda ~ se encogió de hombros** his/her only answer was a shrug of the shoulders

resquicio [rres·'ki·sjo, -θjo] *m* **1.**(*abertura*) crack **2.**(*ocasión*) opening; **~ de esperanza** glimmer of hope

resta ['rres·ta] *f* MAT subtraction

restablecer [rres·ta·βle·'ser, -'θer] *irr como crecer* I. *vt* to re-establish; (*democracia, paz*) to restore II. *vr:* **~se** to recover

restablecimiento [rres·ta·βle·si·'mjen·to, -θi·'mjen·to] *m* (*recuperación*) re-establishment; (*de democracia, paz*) restoration

restante [rres·'tan·te] I. *adj* remaining; **cantidad ~** remainder II. *m* remainder

restar [rres·'tar] I. *vi* to remain; **aún restan algunos días para finalizar el año** there are still a few days left until the end of the year II. *vt* to take away; **~ energías a alguien** to drain sb's strength; **~se años** to seem much younger; **~ importancia a algo** to play sth down; MAT to subtract

restauración [rres·tau·ra·'sjon, -'θjon] *f* **1.** *t.* ARTE restoration; **~ de la monarquía** restoration of the monarchy **2.** COM the restaurant business

restaurante [rres·tau·'ran·te] *m* restaurant

restaurar [rres·tau·'rar] *vt t.* ARTE to restore

restitución [rres·ti·tu·'sjon, -'θjon] *f* **1.**(*devolución*) *t.* FIN return **2.**(*reposición*) replacement

resto ['rres·to] *m* (*lo que sobra*) rest; MAT remainder; **~s de un buque** wreckage; **los ~s mortales** the mortal remains; **los ~s de la torre** the tower ruins; **lo recordaré el ~ de mis días** I will remember him for the rest of my life

restregar [rres·tre·'yar] *irr como fregar* I. *vt* to rub II. *vr:* **~se** to rub; **~se los ojos** to rub one's eyes

restricción [rres·trik·'sjon, -triy·'θjon] *f* (*limitación*) restriction; (*recorte*) cutback; **~ de la natalidad** reduction of the birth rate; **~ mental** evasiveness; **sin restricciones** freely

restringir <g→j> [rres·trin·'xir] *vt* to restrict

resucitar [rre·su·θi·'tar, rre·su·θi-] I. *vi* to resuscitate II. *vt* (*de la muerte*) to resuscitate

resuelto, -a [rre·'swel·to, -a] I. *pp de* **resolver** II. *adj* determined

resultado [rre·sul·'ta·do] *m* result, outcome; **~ del reconocimiento** (**médico**) results of the medical examination; **dar buen ~** (*funcionar*) to work; (*no desgastarse*) to last; **dar mal ~** (*no funcionar*) to fail; (*desgastarse*) to wear out fast; **tener por ~** to lead to

resultar [rre·sul·'tar] *vi* **1.**(*deducirse*) **~ de algo** to result from sth **2.**(*surtir*) to be; **~ muerto en un accidente** to be killed in an accident; **~ en beneficio de alguien** to be to sb's benefit **3.**(*tener éxito*) to succeed, to work well

resumen [rre·'su·men] *m* (*sumario*) summary; **en ~** in short

resumidero [rre·su·mi·'de·ro] *m* *AmL* **1.**(*alcantarilla*) drain **2.**(*pozo ciego*) cesspool

resumir [rre·su·'mir] I. *vt* to summarize II. *vr* **~se en algo** to amount to sth

resurgir <g→j> [rre·sur·'xir] *vi* **1.**(*reaparecer*) to reappear **2.**(*renacer*) to be resurrected **3.**(*revivir*) to revive

resurrección [rre·su·rrek·'sjon, -rey·'θjon] *f* REL resurrection; **Pascua de Resurrección** Easter; **Domingo de Resurrección** Easter Sunday

retablo [rre·'ta·βlo] *m* ARTE altarpiece, retable

retacón, -ona [rre·ta·'kon, --'ko·na] *adj CSur* stubby

retaguardia [rre·ta·'ywar·dja] *f* MIL rearguard
▸ **estar a la ~ de algo** to lag behind sth; **ir a la ~** to bring up the rear; **quedarse en la ~** to stay in the background; **a** [*o* **en**] **~** (*tarde*) late

retar [rre·'tar] *vt* to challenge

retardar [rre·tar·'dar] I. *vt* to delay II. *vr:* **~se** to be late; **me he retardado** I was delayed

retardo [rre·'tar·do] *m* delay; **sufrir un ~** to be delayed; **tener ~ con algo** to be late doing sth

retazo [rre·'ta·so, -θo] *m* **1.**(*retal*) remnant **2.**(*fragmento*) fragment

rete ['rre·te] *adj Méx* (*muy*) very; **su hija es ~ alta** their daughter is very tall

retemblar <e→ie> [rre·tem·'blar] *vi* to shake; **hacer ~** to shake

retén [rre·'ten] *m* MIL reserves *pl*; (*refuerzos*) reinforcements *pl*

retención [rre·ten·'sjon, -'θjon] *f* **1.**(*custodia*) retention; (*deducción*) deduction; **~ fiscal** tax retention; **certificado de retenciones** certificate of tax retention **2.**(*memorizar*) retention **3.**(*moderación*) moderation

retener [rre·te·'ner] *irr como* **tener** I. *vt* **1.**(*conservar*) to retain; (*el pasaporte*) to withhold; (*la respiración*) to hold **2.**(*recordar*) to retain; (*detener*) to detain II. *vr:* **~se** to restrain oneself

reticencia [rre·ti·'sen·sja, -'θen·θja] *f* **1.**(*indirecta*) insinuation; **andar con ~s** to drop hints **2.**(*renuencia*) reluctance **3.**(*reserva*) **~ ante** reticence towards

reticente [rre·ti·'sen·te, -'θen·te] *adj* **1.**(*discurso*) insinuating **2.**(*reacio*) reluctant

retina [rre·'ti·na] *f* ANAT retina; **desprendimiento de ~** detached retina

retintín [rre·tin·'tin] *m* **1.**(*tonillo*) sarcastic tone **2.**(*son*) ringing

retirada [rre·ti·'ra·da] *f* **1.**(*abandono*) abandonment; MIL retreat **2.**(*eliminación*) withdrawal

retirado, -a [rre·ti·'ra·do, -a] I. *adj* **1.**(*lejos*) remote **2.**(*jubilado*) retired II. *m, f* retired person

retirar [rre·ti·'rar] I. *vt* **1.**(*apartar*) to remove; (*tropas, dinero*) to withdraw **2.**(*echar*) to remove; **~ on de la sala a los manifestantes** they removed the demonstrators from the hall **3.**(*recoger, quitar*) to take away **4.**(*negar*) to deny **5.**(*jubilar*) to retire II. *vr:* **~se 1.**(*aban-*

donar; **~se de algo** to withdraw from sth **2.** *t.* MIL (*retroceder*) to retreat **3.** (*jubilarse*) to retire

retiro [rre·'ti·ro] *m* **1.** (*pensión*) pension **2.** (*refugio*) retreat **3.** (*retraimiento*) withdrawal

reto ['rre·to] *m* challenge

retobado, -a [rre·to·'βa·do, -a] *adj* **1.** *AmC, Méx, Ecua* (*respondón*) insolent **2.** *AmC, Cuba, Ecua* (*indómito*) wild **3.** *Arg, Méx, Urug* (*enconado*) ticked off *inf*

retobar [rre·to·'βar] **I.** *vt CSur* (*forrar*) to cover with leather **II.** *vi Méx* (*rezongar*) to talk back

retocar <c→qu> [rre·to·'kar] *vt* **1.** (*corregir*) FOTO to retouch, to touch up **2.** (*perfeccionar*) to perfect

retoñar [rre·to·'ɲar] *vi* to sprout

retoque [rre·'to·ke] *m* (*corrección*) alteration; FOTO retouch

retorcer [rre·tor·'ser, -'θer] *irr como cocer* **I.** *vt* **1.** (*torcer*) to twist **2.** (*enroscar*) to twine **II.** *vr:* ~se **1.** (*enroscarse*) to twist **2.** (*de dolor*) to writhe

retorcido, -a [rre·tor·'si·do, -a; rre·tor·'θi-] *adj* **1.** (*complicado*) **pensar de manera retorcida** to think in a very confused way; **¡qué ~!** how complicated! **2.** (*maligno*) twisted; **una mente retorcida** a warped mind

retórica [rre·'to·ri·ka] *f* rhetoric

retornable [rre·tor·'na·βle] *adj* **botella (no) ~** (non-)returnable bottle

retornar [rre·tor·'nar] **I.** *vi* to return **II.** *vt* to give back

retorno [rre·'tor·no] *m* return

retracción [rre·trak·'sjon, -tray·'θjon] *f* **1.** JUR retraction **2.** (*retroceso, retiro*) withdrawal **3.** (*impedimento*) obstacle **4.** MED retraction

retractar [rre·trak·'tar] **I.** *vt* (*desdecirse*) to take back; JUR to retract **II.** *vr* ~se de algo to withdraw from sth

retraer [rre·tra·'er] *irr como traer* **I.** *vt* **1.** (*encoger*) to withdraw **2.** (*traer*) to bring back **3.** (*impedir*) to hinder **4.** JUR to retract **II.** *vr:* ~se **1.** (*aislarse*) ~se a [*o* en] algo to withdraw into sth **2.** (*retirarse*) ~se de algo to withdraw from sth **3.** (*retroceder*) to retreat

retraído, -a [rre·tra·'i·do, -a] *adj* (*reservado*) reserved; (*poco sociable*) withdrawn

retraimiento [rre·trai·'mjen·to] *m* reserve

retransmisión [rre·trans·mi·'sjon] *f* broadcast; ~ **deportiva** sports program; ~ **por televisión** television broadcast; ~ **en directo/diferido** live/pre-recorded broadcast

retransmitir [rre·trans·mi·'tir] *vt* to broadcast

retrasado, -a [rre·tra·'sa·do, -a] *adj* **1.** (*atrasado*) backward; ~ **en tecnología** technologically backward **2.** (*anticuado*) old-fashioned **3.** (*no actual*) out of date **4.** (*subdesarrollado*) underdeveloped; ~ **mental** mentally retarded

retrasar [rre·tra·'sar] **I.** *vt* **1.** (*demorar*) to delay **2.** (*el reloj*) to put [*o* set] back **II.** *vi* **1.** (*el reloj*) to be slow **2.** (*no estar al día*) to be out of touch **III.** *vr:* ~se to be late

retraso [rre·'tra·so] *m* **1.** (*demora*) delay **2.** (*del desarrollo*) underdevelopment **3.** (*de la deuda*) arrears *pl;* **tener ~ en los pagos** to be in arrears

retratar [rre·tra·'tar] *vt* **1.** (*describir*) to depict, to portray **2.** (*fotografiar*) to photograph **3.** (*pintar*) to paint a portrait of

retrato [rre·'tra·to] *m* (*representación*) *t.* FOTO portrait ▶ **ser el vivo ~ de alguien** to be the spitting image of sb

retrete [rre·'tre·te] *m* lavatory, toilet

retribución [rre·tri·βu·'sjon, -'θjon] *f* reward; (*sueldo*) remuneration; **retribuciones dinerarias** money payment

retribuir [rre·tri·βu·'ir] *irr como huir vt* **1.** (*remunerar*) to remunerate **2.** *AmL* (*compensar*) to compensate

retroactivo, -a [rre·tro·ak·'ti·βo, -a] *adj* retroactive

retroalimentación [rre·tro·a·li·men·ta·'sjon, -'θjon] *f* feedback

retroceder [rre·tro·se·'der, -θe·'der] *vi* **1.** (*regresar*) to go back **2.** (*desistir*) to give up; (*echarse atrás*) to back down

retroceso [rre·tro·'se·so, -'θe·so] *m* **1.** (*regresión*) reversal; ~ **en las negociaciones** setback in the negotiations **2.** MED relapse

retrógrado, -a [rre·'tro·yra·do, -a] *adj, m, f* reactionary

retroproyector [rre·tro·pro·jek·'tor] *m* overhead projector

retrospectivo, -a [rre·tros·pek·'ti·βo, -a] *adj* retrospective

retrovisor [rre·tro·βi·'sor] *m* AUTO rearview mirror; ~ **exterior** side mirror; **mirar por el espejo** ~ to look in the rearview mirror

retumbar [rre·tum·'bar] *vi* to boom; (*resonar*) to resound

reuma ['rreu·ma] *m o f*, **reúma** [rre·'u·ma] *m o f* MED rheumatism

reumático, -a [rreu·'ma·ti·ko, -a] *adj* rheumatic

reumatismo [rreu·ma·'tis·mo] *m* MED rheumatism

reunificación [rre·u·ni·fi·ka·'sjon, -'θjon] *f* reunification

reunificar <c→qu> [rre·u·ni·fi·'kar] *vt* to reunify

reunión [rreu·'njon] *f* **1.** (*encuentro, asamblea*) meeting; ~ **de los trabajadores** employees' meeting; ~ **de antiguos alumnos** class reunion; ~ **en la cumbre** summit meeting **2.** (*conferencia*) meeting; **estar en** ~ to be in a meeting; **celebrar una** ~ to hold a meeting **3.** (*el juntar*) collection **4.** (*grupo, invitados*) gathering

reunir [rreu·'nir] *irr* **I.** *vt* **1.** (*congregar*) to assemble **2.** (*unir*) to gather **3.** (*juntar*) to reunite **4.** (*poseer*) to have; ~ **las cualidades necesarias** to have the necessary qualities **II.** *vr:* ~se **1.** (*congregarse*) to meet; (*informal*) to get together **2.** (*unir*) to gather **3.** (*juntarse*) to reunite

R

reválida [rre·'βa·li·da] *f* **1.**(*confirmación*) confirmation **2.**(*examen*) final examination

revalidar [rre·βa·li·'dar] **I.** *vt* to confirm **II.** *vr:* ~ **se** to be recognized

revaloración [rre·βa·lo·ra·'sjon, -'θjon] *f* re-evaluation; FIN revaluation

revalorización [rre·βa·lo·ri·sa·'sjon, -θa·'θjon] *f* FIN appreciation

revalorizar <z→c> [rre·βa·lo·ri·'sar, -'θar] *vt* **1.** to re-evaluate **2.** FIN to appreciate; (*subir el valor*) to increase the value of

revancha [rre·'βan·tʃa] *f* **1.**revenge; **tomarse la ~ por algo** to get one's own back for sth; **tomarse la ~** to take one's revenge **2.** DEP return match

revelación [rre·βe·la·'sjon, -'θjon] *f t.* REL revelation

revelado [rre·βe·'la·do] *m* FOTO developing

revelar [rre·βe·'lar] *vt* **1.**(*dar a conocer*) to reveal, to disclose **2.** FOTO to develop

revellín [rre·βe·'jin, -'ʎin] *m Cuba* (*dificultad*) difficulty ▶ **echar** ~ to provoke anger

revenir [rre·βe·'nir] *irr como venir vi, vr:* ~ **se** **1.**(*encoger*) to shrink **2.**(*agriarse*) to sour **3.**(*secarse*) to dry out

reventa [rre·'βen·ta] *f* resale; (*entradas*) scalping

reventadero [rre·βen·ta·'de·ro] *m* **1.** *Col, Méx* (*hervidero*) bubbling spring **2.** *Chile* (*rompiente*) shoal

reventado, -a [rre·βen·'ta·do, -a] *adj* **1.** *inf* (*hecho polvo*) wiped out **2.** *Arg* (*sinuoso*) devious

reventar <e→ie> [rre·βen·'tar] **I.** *vi* **1.**(*romperse*) to break; (*globo, neumático*) to burst; **lleno hasta ~** full to bursting **2.** *inf* (*morir*) to croak; **¡que reviente!** I hope he/she drops dead! **II.** *vt* **1.**(*romper*) to break; (*globo, neumático*) to burst **2.** *inf* (*molestar*) to annoy **III.** *vr:* ~ **se** (*romperse*) to break; (*globo, neumático*) to burst

reverbero [rre·βer·'βe·ro] *m* **1.**(*de la luz*) reflection **2.** (*farol*) reflecting light; AUTO reflector **3.** *AmL* (*hornillo*) spirit stove

reverdecer [rre·βer·de·'ser, -'θer] *irr como crecer vi* **1.**(*verdear*) to become green **2.**(*vigorizar*) to revive

reverencia [rre·βe·'ren·sja, -θja] *f* **1.**(*veneración*) reverence; **Su Reverencia** Your Reverence **2.**(*inclinación*) bow

reverenciar [rre·βe·ren·'sjar, -'θjar] *vt* to revere

reverendo, -a [rre·βe·'ren·do, -a] **I.** *adj* revered; REL Reverend **II.** *m, f* Reverend

reversa [rre·'βer·sa] *f Chile, Col, Méx* AUTO reverse

reversible [rre·βer·'si·βle] *adj* reversible

reversión [rre·βer·'sjon] *f* reversion

reverso [rre·'βer·so] *m* other side ▶ **el ~ de la medalla** the other side of the coin

revertir [rre·βer·'tir] *irr como sentir vi* to revert; **revirtió en su beneficio** it worked to his/her advantage

revés [rre·'βes] *m* **1.**(*reverso*) other side; **al** [*o* **del**] ~ back to front; (*con lo de arriba abajo*) upside down; **te has puesto el jersey del ~** you have put your jumper on back to front; (*dentro para fuera*) inside out **2.**(*golpe*) blow with the back of the hand **3.** DEP backhand **4.**(*infortunio*) setback; ~ **de fortuna** stroke of bad luck

revestir [rre·βes·'tir] *irr como pedir* **I.** *vt* (*recubrir*) ~ **con** [*o* **de**] **algo** to cover with sth; ~ **de cinc** to coat with zinc **II.** *vr:* ~ **se** (*aparentar*) ~ **se con** [*o* **de**] **algo** to arm oneself with sth

revirado, -a [rre·βi·'ra·do, -a] *adj Arg, Urug* (*loco*) nutty

revire [rre·'βi·re] *m Arg, Urug, inf* crazy idea; **le dio uno de sus ~s** he/she had one of his/her crazy ideas

revisada [rre·βi·'sa·da] *f AmL* (*revisión*) check, review

revisar [rre·βi·'sar] *vt* to check; TÉC to inspect; (*textos, edición*) to revise

revisión [rre·βi·'sjon] *f* check; TÉC inspection; JUR, TIPO revision

revisor(a) [rre·βi·'sor, -'so·ra] *m(f)* **1.**(*controlador*) inspector; ~ **de cuentas** auditor **2.** FERRO ticket inspector

revista [rre·'βis·ta] *f* **1.** PREN magazine; **las ~s del corazón** the gossip magazines; ~ **electrónica** e-zine; ~ **especializada** special interest magazine; ~ **ilustrada** illustrated magazine **2.**(*espectáculo*) revue, variety show

revivificar <c→qu> [rre·βi·βi·fi·'kar] *vt* to revive

revivir [rre·βi·'βir] **I.** *vi* to revive **II.** *vt* to revive; (*evocar*) to relive

revocar <c→qu> [rre·βo·'kar] **I.** *vt* **1.**(*anular*) to annul **2.**(*apartar*) to dismiss **3.**(*enlucir*) to plaster **II.** *vi* (*humo*) to blow back

revolcar [rre·βol·'kar] *irr como volcar* **I.** *vt* **1.**(*derribar*) to knock over **2.** *inf* (*vencer*) to defeat **3.** *inf* (*suspender*) to fail **II.** *vr:* ~ **se** (*restregarse*) ~ **se por algo** to roll around in sth

revolear [rre·βo·le·'ar] *vt Méx, CSur* to whirl around

revoloteo [rre·βo·lo·'teo] *m* fluttering

revoltijo [rre·βol·'ti·xo] *m* **1.**(*embrollo*) jumble **2.**(*tripas*) tripe

revoltoso, -a [rre·βol·'to·so, -a] **I.** *adj* **1.**(*travieso*) mischievous **2.**(*rebelde*) rebellious **II.** *m, f* troublemaker

revoltura [rre·βol·'tu·ra] *f Méx* mixture

revolución [rre·βo·lu·'sjon, -'θjon] *f* **1.** *t.* POL, ASTR (*cambio, rotación*) revolution; **número de revoluciones** number of revolutions **2.**(*inquietud*) disturbance

revolucionar [rre·βo·lu·sjo·'nar, rre·βo·lu·θjo-] *vt* **1.**(*amotinar*) to stir up **2.**(*transformar*) to revolutionize **3.**(*excitar*) to arouse interest in **4.** TÉC to increase the number of revolutions of

revolucionario, -a [rre·βo·lu·sjo·'na·rjo, -a; rre·βo·lu·θjo-] *adj, m, f* revolutionary

revoluta [rre·βo·'lu·ta] *f AmC v.* **revolución**

revolvedora [rre·βol·βe·'do·ra] *f Arg, Méx (de cemento)* cement mixer

revolver [rre·βol·'βer] *irr como volver* **I.** *vt* **1.** (*mezclar*) to mix **2.** (*desordenar*) to mess up **3.** (*investigar*) to investigate **II.** *vr:* ~ **se 1.** (*moverse*) to toss and turn; **se me revuelve el estómago** it makes my stomach turn **2.** (*enfrentarse*) to turn **3.** (*el tiempo*) to break

revólver [rre·'βol·βer] *m* revolver

revoque [rre·'βo·ke] *m* **1.** (*acción*) plastering **2.** (*material*) plaster

revuelo [rre·'βwe·lo] *m* (*turbación*) disturbance; **causar** ~ to disturb

revuelta [rre·'βwel·ta] *f* **1.** (*tumulto*) disturbance **2.** (*rebelión*) revolt **3.** (*encorvadura*) bend; **carretera con muchas ~ s** windy road

revuelto, -a [rre·'βwel·to, -a] **I.** *pp de* **revolver II.** *adj* **1.** (*agitado*) shaken **2.** (*desordenado*) chaotic **3.** (*tiempo*) unsettled **4.** (*irritado*) annoyed **5.** (*intrincado*) tangled **6.** (*huevos*) scrambled

revulsar [rre·βul·'sar] *vi, vt Méx* (*vomitar*) to throw up

rey [rrei] *m* king; **los Reyes** The King and Queen; **los Reyes Católicos, los Reyes Magos** the Magi, the Three Wise Men; **el día de Reyes** Epiphany, Twelfth Night ▶ **a ~ muerto ~ puesto** off with the old, on with the new

rezagado, -a [re·sa·'ya·do, -a; re·θa-] *m, f* straggler

rezar <z→c> [rre·'sar, -'θar] **I.** *vt* ~ **por alguien** to pray for sb; ~ **una oración** to say a prayer **II.** *vi* **1.** (*decir*) to pray **2.** (*corresponder*) ~ **con algo** to apply to sth

rezo ['rre·so, -θo] *m* **1.** (*el rezar*) praying **2.** (*oración*) prayer

rezongar <g→gu> [rre·son·'gar, rre·θon-] *vi* to grumble

RFA [e·rre·fe·'a/e·rre·e·fe·'a] *f v.* **República Federal de Alemania** FRG

ría ['rri·a] *f* **1.** GEO ≈ estuary **2.** DEP water break

riachuelo [rrja·'t͡ʃwe·lo] *m* stream

riada [rri·'a·da] *f* flood

ribazo [rri·'βa·so, -θo] *m* steep bank

ribera [rri·'βe·ra] *f* **1.** (*orilla*) bank **2.** (*tierra*) riverside **3.** (*vega*) fertile plain

ricamente [rri·ka·'men·te] *adv* **1.** (*con abundancia*) richly **2.** (*con placer*) splendidly

ricino [ri·'si·no, ri·'θi-] *m* castor oil plant

rico, -a ['rri·ko, -a] **I.** *adj* **1.** (*acaudalado*) rich; **es muy ~** he/she is very rich **2.** (*sabroso*) delicious; **la comida está muy rica** the food is delicious **3.** (*abundante*) rich **4.** (*fructífero*) fertile **5.** (*simpático*) lovely, cute **II.** *m, f* (*rico*) rich person; **los ricos** the rich; **nuevo ~** nouveau riche

ricota [rri·'ko·ta] *f Arg* CULIN ricotta cheese

ridiculizar <z→c> [rri·di·ku·li·'sar, -'θar] *vt* to ridicule

ridículo, -a [rri·'di·ku·lo, -a] *adj* (*risorio*) ridiculous; **poner(se) en** ~ to make a fool of (oneself)

riego ['rrje·yo] *m* irrigation; ~ **sanguíneo** blood flow

riel [rrjel] *m* **1.** FERRO rail **2.** (*para cortinas*) bar; **los ~ es de la cortina** the curtain rod

rienda ['rrjen·da] *f* **1.** (*correa*) rein; **tener las ~ s del poder** *fig* to hold the reins of power **2.** *pl* (*gobierno*) reins *pl* ▶ **a ~ suelta** *fig* wildly; **dar ~ suelta a** to give free rein to; **llevar las ~ s** to be in control; **tirar de la ~** to pressure

riesgo ['rrjes·yo] *m* risk; ~ **monetario** monetary risk; **a ~ de que...** +*subj* at the risk of...; **a ~ y ventura de...** at the risk of...; **por cuenta y ~ propios** at one's own risk and expense; **asumir un ~** to assume a risk; **estar asegurado a todo ~** AUTO to have full coverage insurance; **exponer a un ~** to expose to a risk; **exponerse a un ~** to run a risk; ~ **profesional** occupational hazard

riesgoso, -a [rrjes·'yo·so, -a] *adj AmL* **1.** (*arriesgado*) risky **2.** (*peligroso*) dangerous

rifa ['rri·fa] *f* (*sorteo*) raffle

rifar [rri·'far] *vt* to raffle

rifle ['rri·fle] *m* rifle

rigidez [rri·xi·'des, -'deθ] *f* **1.** (*inflexibilidad*) rigidity **2.** (*severidad*) strictness

rígido, -a ['rri·xi·do, -a] *adj* **1.** (*inflexible*) rigid **2.** (*severo*) strict

rigor [rri·'yor] *m* **1.** (*severidad*) strictness **2.** (*exactitud*) rigorousness **3.** METEO ~ **del invierno** depths of winter ▶ **de** ~ de rigueur

riguroso, -a [rri·yu·'ro·so, -a] *adj* **1.** (*severo*) strict **2.** (*exacto*) rigorous

rima ['rri·ma] *f* LIT rhyme; **tener** ~ to rhyme

rimar [rri·'mar] **I.** *vi* **1.** (*versificar*) to write poetry **2.** (*tener rima*) to rhyme **II.** *vt* to rhyme

rímel® ['rri·mel] *m* mascara

rin [rrin] *m* **1.** *Ven* (*llanta*) rim **2.** *Perú* (*ficha telefónica*) telephone token

rincón [rrin·'kon] *m* **1.** (*esquina*) corner **2.** (*escondrijo, lugar tranquilo*) nook; **por todos los rincones** *fig* in every nook and cranny

rinitis [rri·'ni·tis] *f* MED rhinitis; ~ **alérgica** hay fever

rinoceronte [rri·no·se·'ron·te, rri·no·θe·] *m* rhinoceros

riña ['rri·ɲa] *f* quarrel; ~ **de gallos** cockfight

riñón [rri·'ɲon] *m* **1.** ANAT kidney; **tener piedras en el** ~ to have kidney stones **2.** *pl* (*parte de la espalda*) lower back **3.** *fig* (*centro*) heart ▶ **tener el ~ bien cubierto** to be well off; **costar un** ~ to cost an arm and a leg

riñonera [rri·ɲo·'ne·ra] *f* **1.** (*faja*) cummerbund **2.** (*cinturón con bolsa*) fanny pack *inf*

río ['rri·o] *m* river; ~ **abajo** downstream; ~ **arriba** upstream ▶ **tener un ~ de oro** to have a goldmine; **pescar en ~ revuelto** to fish in troubled waters; **cuando el ~ suena, agua lleva** *prov* where there's smoke, there's fire

rioplatense [rrio·pla·'ten·se] **I.** *adj* of/from the River Plate region **II.** *mf* native/inhabitant

of the River Plate region
riqueza [rri·'ke·sa, -θa] *f* riches *pl*
risa [rri·'sa] *f* laughter; **digno de** ~ laughable; **estar muerto de** ~ to be laughing one's head off; **llorar de** ~ to laugh until one cries; **tener un ataque de** ~ to have a fit of the giggles; **tomar algo a** ~ to treat sth as a joke; **¡qué** ~! what a joke!; **no estoy para** ~**s** I'm in no mood for jokes
risco ['rris·ko] *m* crag
ríspido, -a ['rris·pi·do, -a] *adj AmL* (*rudo*) coarse
ristra ['rris·tra] *f* **1.**(*trenza*) string; **una** ~ **de ajos/cebollas** a string of garlic/onions **2.** *inf* (*sarta*) string; **una** ~ **de mentiras** a string of lies
risueño, -a [rri·'swe·ɲo, -a] *adj* **1.**(*alegre*) smiling **2.**(*próspero*) favorable
rítmico, -a ['rrid·mi·ko, -a] *adj* rhythmic
ritmo ['rrid·mo] *m* rhythm
rito ['rri·to] *m* (*costumbre*) ritual; REL rite
ritual [rri·tu·'al] *adj, m* ritual
rival [rri·'βal] *adj, mf* rival
rivalidad [rri·βa·li·'dad] *f* rivalry
rizado, -a [rri·'sa·do, rri·'θa-] *adj* (*cabello*) curly
rizo ['rri·so, -θo] *m* **1.**(*mechón*) curl; **rizar el** ~ (*imponerse*) to win through; (*complicar*) to overcomplicate things **2.**(*tela*) velvet; **tela de** ~ (*felpa*) terrycloth
rizo, -a ['rri·θo, -a] *adj* curly
RNE ['rra·djo na·sjo'nal de es·'pa·ɲa, na·θjo-] *f* *abr de* **Radio Nacional de España** Spanish national radio network
robar [rro·'βar] *vt* **1.**(*hurtar: algo*) to steal; (*a alguien*) to rob; (*a alguien con violencia*) to mug; **me** ~**on en París** I was robbed in Paris; **me robó la novia** *inf* he stole my girlfriend **2.**(*estafar*) to cheat **3.**(*en juegos*) to draw
roble ['rro·βle] *m* oak; **estar como un** ~ to be as fit as a fiddle
robo ['rro·βo] *m* **1.**(*hurto*) robbery; ~ **con homicidio** theft and murder; ~ **a mano armada** armed robbery; ~ **con allanamiento** breaking and entering **2.**(*estafa*) swindle; **ser un** ~ *fig* (*muy caro*) to be a rip-off; **¿20 pesos? ¡qué** ~! twenty pesos? what a rip-off!
robot <robots> [rro·'βot] *m* robot; ~ **de cocina** food processor
robustecer [rro·βus·te·'ser, -'θer] *irr como crecer* I. *vt* to strengthen II. *vr:* ~ **se** to become strong
robusto, -a [rro·'βus·to, -a] *adj* robust
roca ['rro·ka] *f* (*materia, peña*) rock; **ese hombre es una** ~ that man is as solid as a rock
roce ['rro·θe, -θe] *m* **1.**(*fricción*) brush **2.**(*huella*) scrape **3.**(*contacto*) contact; **tener mucho** ~ **con alguien** to have a lot of contact with sb **4.**(*pelea*) scrape
rochar [rro·'tʃar] *vt* **1.** AGR to clear ground **2.** *Chile* (*sorprender*) to catch red-handed
rochela [rro·'tʃe·la] *f Col, PRico, Ven* hullaba-

loo
rociar <3. *pres:* rocía> [rro·si·'ar, rro·θi-] I. *vimpers* **ha rociado** dew has fallen II. *vt* (*regar*) to wash down
rocío [rro·'si·o, -'θi·o] *m* **1.**(*relente*) dew; **cae** ~ dew is forming **2.**(*lluvia*) drizzle
rock [rrok] I. *adj* rock; **grupo de música** ~ rock group II. *m* MÚS rock
rocoso, -a [rro·'ko·so, -a] *adj* rocky; **Montañas Rocosas** Rocky Mountains, Rockies
rocote [rro·'ko·te] *m*, **rocoto** [rro·'ko·to] *m Bol, Ecua, Perú* (*pimiento*) (large) green pepper
rodada [rro·'da·da] *f* wheel track
rodado, -a [rro·'da·do, -a] *adj* **1.**(*fluido*) smooth; **venir** ~ (*sin dificultades*) to go smoothly; (*de perlas*) to come in very handy **2.** AUTO **tráfico** ~ vehicular traffic
rodaja [rro·'da·xa] *f* **1.**(*rueda*) small wheel **2.**(*trozo*) slice
rodaje [rro·'da·xe] *m* **1.** CINE shooting **2.**(*rodar*) rolling; **cuando tengamos más** ~ when we are ready **3.**(*ruedas*) wheels *pl*
rodar <o→ue> [rro·'dar] I. *vi* **1.**(*dar vueltas, moverse sobre ruedas*) to roll; ~ **por el suelo** to roll across the floor **2.**(*girar sobre el eje*) to turn **3.**(*deslizarse*) to slide ▶ **echarlo todo a** ~ to spoil everything II. *vt* **1.**(*hacer dar vueltas*) to roll **2.**(*película*) to shoot **3.**(*coche*) to run in
rodear [rro·de·'ar] I. *vi* (*circunvalar*) to go around II. *vt* **1.**(*cercar*) ~ **de algo** to surround with sth **2.**(*hacer dar vueltas*) to turn **3.**(*un tema*) to avoid III. *vr* ~ **se de algo/alguien** to surround oneself with sth/sb
rodeo [rro·'deo] *m* **1.**(*desvío*) detour; **dar un** ~ to take a detour; **conseguir algo con** ~**s** to achieve sth in a roundabout way **2.**(*evasiva*) evasion **3.** DEP rodeo ▶ **andar(se) con** ~**s** to beat about the bush; **dejarse de** ~**s** stop beating about the bush; **sin** ~**s** without beating about the bush
rodilla [rro·'di·ja, -ʎa] *f* **1.** ANAT knee; **de** ~**s** on one's knees; **ponerse de** ~**s** to kneel **2.**(*paño*) cloth
rodillo [rro·'di·jo, -ʎo] *m* **1.** TÉC roller **2.**(*de cocina*) rolling pin
roedor [rroe·'dor] *m* rodent
roer [rro·'er] *irr vt* **1.**(*ratonar*) ~ **algo** to gnaw at sth; **los ratones royeron mi libro** the mice gnawed my book; ~ **se las uñas** to bite one's nails **2.**(*concomer*) **las preocupaciones me roen el alma** I'm worrying my life away
rogar <o→ue> [rro·'ɣar] *vt* to request; (*con humildad*) to beg; JUR to plead; **rogamos nos contesten inmediatamente nuestra carta** we would be grateful if you could give us an immediate reply; **¡te ruego que me escuches!** I beg you to listen to me!; **le gusta hacerse de** ~ he/she likes playing hard to get
rojizo, -a [rro·'xi·so, -a; -θo, -a] *adj* reddish
rojo, -a ['rro·xo] *adj* red; (*persona*) red-headed; ~ **chillón/subido** bright/deep red; ~ **bur-**

deos maroon ▸ **al** ~ (**vivo**) red-hot; **poner** ~ **a alguien** to make sb blush; **ponerse** ~ to go red

rol [rrol] *m* **1.** (*papel*) role; **desempeñar un** ~ to play a role **2.** (*lista*) list; ~ **de pago** payroll

rollito ['rro·ji·to, -λi-] *m* ~ **de primavera** CULIN spring roll, egg roll

rollo ['rro·jo, -λo] *m* **1.** *t.* FOTO (*de papel, alambre*) roll; **hacer un** ~ **de algo** to roll sth up **2.** *inf* (*cosa aburrida*) bore; **¡qué** ~ **de película!** what a boring film!; **soltar siempre el mismo** ~ to always come out with the same old stuff **3.** *inf* (*tipo de vida*) lifestyle; (*asunto*) affair; **montarse el** ~ to organize one's life; **ir a su** ~ to do as one likes; **tener un** ~ **con alguien** *argot* to have a fling with sb *inf*; **tener mucho** ~ to be full of crap *sl*; **traerse un mal** ~ to be in a mess; **acaba con el** ~, **muchacho** get on with it, son; **corta el** ~ (*palabrería, mentiras*) cut the crap *inf* **4.** (*del cuerpo*) roll (of fat)

Roma ['rro·ma] *f* Rome

romance [rro·'man·se, -θe] **I.** *adj* LING Romance **II.** *m t.* LIT (*aventura*) romance; ~ **de ciego** popular ballad; **tiene un** ~ **con la vecina** he's having an affair with his neighbor

románico, -a [rro·'ma·ni·ko, -a] *adj* Romanesque

romanista [rro·ma·'nis·ta] *mf* Romanist

romano, -a [rro·'ma·no] **I.** *adj* **1.** (*de Roma*) Roman **2.** REL Roman Catholic **3.** (*latín*) Latin **II.** *m, f* (*de Roma*) Roman

romanticismo [rro·man·ti·'sis·mo, -'θis·mo] *m* romanticism; (*movimiento*) Romanticism

romántico, -a [rro·'man·ti·ko, -a] *adj, m, f* romantic

rombo ['rrom·bo] *m* rhombus; **en forma de** ~ diamond-shaped

romería [rro·me·'ri·a] *f* **1.** (*peregrinaje*) pilgrimage **2.** (*fiesta*) festival **3.** (*muchedumbre*) throng

romerito [rro·me·'ri·to] *m Méx* vegetables *pl*

romero [rro·'me·ro] *m* rosemary

romero, -a [rro·'me·ro, -a] *adj, m, f* pilgrim

romo, -a ['rro·mo, -a] *adj* **1.** (*sin punta*) blunt **2.** (*de nariz pequeña*) snub-nosed **3.** (*tosco*) coarse

rompecabezas [rrom·pe·ka·'βe·sas, -θas] *m inv* (*juego*) brainteaser; (*acertijo*) riddle

romper [rrom·'per] **I.** *vi* **1.** (*las olas*) to break **2.** (*empezar bruscamente*) to burst; ~ **a llorar** to burst into tears **3.** (*el día*) to break; **al** ~ **el día** at the break of day **4.** (*separarse*) to break up **II.** *vt* **1.** (*destrozar, quebrar*) to break; (*un cristal*) to shatter; (*un plato*) to smash; (*papel, tela*) to tear; (*los zapatos*) to wear out; (*un terreno*) to plough; ~ **algo a martillazos** to smash sth with a hammer; ~ **algo a golpes** to bash sth to pieces; ~ **una ventana a pedradas** to break a window by throwing stones at it **2.** (*negociaciones, relaciones*) to break off; (*contrato, promesa*) to break; ~ **el silencio/el encanto** to break the silence/the spell; ~ **el**

hilo del discurso to interrupt the speech **3.** (*iniciar*) ~ **el fuego** to open fire ▸ **de rompe y rasga** determined; **una persona de rompe y rasga** a very determined person **III.** *vr:* ~**se 1.** (*hacerse pedazos*) to break **2.** (*fracturarse*) to break; ~**se la pierna** to break one's leg; ~**se la cabeza** *fig* to rack one's brains

rompope [rrom·'po·pe] *m AmC, Ecua, Méx* CULIN eggnog

ron [rron] *m* rum

roncar <c→qu> [rron·'kar] *vi* (*persona*) to snore

roncear [rron·se·'ar, rron·θe-] *vt Arg, Chile, Méx* to move by levering

roncha ['rron·tʃa] *f* (*hinchazón*) swilling; (*cardenal*) bruise; (*picadura*) sting

ronco, -a ['rron·ko, -a] *adj* (*afónico*) voiceless; (*áspero*) hoarse

roncón, -ona [rron·'kon, -'ko·na] *m, f Col, Ven* bragging

ronda ['rron·da] *f* **1.** (*de vigilancia*) round; **hacer una** ~ **de inspección por la fábrica** to do an inspection tour of the factory **2.** (*de copas*) round; **pagar una** ~ to buy a round **3.** POL round (*of voting*) **4.** (*jóvenes*) group of serenaders; (*serenata*) serenade; **andar de** ~ (*tocar música*) to go serenading **5.** (*avenida*) beltway

rondalla [rron·'da·ja, -λa] *f* **1.** (*música*) street music **2.** (*conjunto musical*) street musicians

rondar [rron·'dar] **I.** *vi* **1.** (*vigilar*) to be on patrol **2.** (*andar paseando de noche*) to prowl about **II.** *vt* **1.** (*a las mujeres*) to court **2.** (*rodear*) to surround; **las mariposas nocturnas rondan la luz** moths are drawn to the light; **anda rodando los setenta años** he/she is about seventy years old

rondín [rron·'din] *m* **1.** *Bol, Ecua, Perú* (*armónica*) harmonica **2.** *Bol, Chile* (*vigilante*) watchman

ronquido [rron·'ki·do] *m* (*de una persona*) snore

ronronear [rron·rro·ne·'ar] *vi* (*gato*) to purr

roña ['rro·ɲa] *f* **1.** (*mugre*) filth **2.** (*mezquindad*) meanness; (*tacañería*) stinginess **3.** (*orín*) rust **4.** (*sarna de carneros*) scab

roñoso, -a [rro·'ɲo·so, -a] *adj* **1.** (*tacaño*) mean, tight **2.** (*sucio*) filthy **3.** (*sarnoso*) scabby **4.** (*oxidado*) rusty

ropa ['rro·pa] *f* **1.** (*géneros de tela*) ~ **blanca** white wash *pl;* ~ **de color** colored wash *pl;* ~ **delicada** delicates *pl;* ~ **interior** underwear; **cambiar la** ~ **de cama** to change the sheets **2.** (*vestidos, traje*) clothes *pl;* ~**s hechas** ready-made clothes; **cambiar(se) la** ~ to change one's clothes; **estar en** ~**s menores** to be in one's underwear; **poner(se) la** ~ to get dressed; **ponerse** ~ **de abrigo** to put on warm clothing; **ligero de** ~ lightly dressed ▸ **a quema** ~ point-blank; **disparar a quema** ~ to shoot at close range; **¡cuidado que hay** ~ **tendida!** be careful what you say!

R

ropero [rro·'pe·ro] *m* (*armario*) wardrobe

rosa ['rro·sa] **I.** *adj* pink **II.** *f* BOT rose; ~ **de azafrán** saffron crocus; **color de** ~ pink; **esencia de** ~**s** rose essence ▸ **no hay** ~ **sin espinas** *prov* every rose has its thorn *prov*

rosado, -a [rro·'sa·do, -a] *adj* (*color*) pink; **vino** ~ rosé (wine)

rosal [rro·'sal] *m* rosebush

rosario [rro·'sa·rjo] *m* REL rosary; **rezar el** ~ to say the rosary ▸ **acabar como el** ~ **de la aurora** to end in confusion; **tener el** ~ **al cuello y el diablo en el cuerpo** to be a complete hypocrite

rosca ['rros·ka] *f* **1.** TÉC thread; **el tornillo se pasó de** ~ the screw broke the thread **2.** (*forma de espiral*) coil; **hecho una** ~ rolled up into a ball; **hacerse** ~ (*gato, serpiente*) to roll up into a ball **3.** (*forma de anillo*) ring; (*bollo*) (ring-shaped) bread roll; (*torta*) sponge ring; ~ **de Reyes** *Méx* Christmas cake eaten on Epiphany ▸ **no comerse una** ~ not to get off with anyone; **hacer la** ~ **a alguien** to suck up to sb; **pasarse de** ~ to go too far

roscón [rros·'kon] *m* sponge ring; ~ **de Reyes** Christmas cake eaten on Epiphany

rosedal [rro·se·'dal] *m Arg, Urug* BOT rose garden

rosquete [rros·'ke·te] *adj, m Perú, vulg* queer

rosquilla [rros·'ki·ja, -ʎa] *f* doughnut ▸ **venderse como** ~**s** to sell like hot cakes

rosticería [rros·ti·se·'ri·a, rros·ti·θe-] *f Chile, Méx: shop that sells roast chicken, beef and other dishes*

rostro ['rros·tro] *m* (*cara*) face

rotación [rro·ta·'sjon, -'θjon] *f* rotation; ~ **de cultivos** AGR crop rotation; ~ **del capital** capital movement

rotativo [rro·ta·'ti·βo] *m* newspaper

rotativo, -a [rro·ta·'ti·βo, -a] *adj* rotary; **impresión rotativa** TIPO rotary printing

rotería [rro·te·'ri·a] *f Chile* **1.** (*acción*) inconsiderate act **2.** (*plebe*) the masses

rotisería [rro·ti·se·'ri·a] *f Arg: shop that sells roast chicken, beef and other dishes*

roto ['rro·to] *m* (*desgarrón*) tear; (*agujero*) hole

roto, -a ['rro·to, -a] **I.** *pp* **de romper II.** *adj* **1.** (*despedazado*) broken; **un vestido** ~ a torn dress; **un florero/un cristal** ~ a broken vase/ glass **2.** (*andrajoso*) wretched **3.** (*destrozado*) destroyed

rotonda [rro·'ton·da] *f* AUTO traffic circle

rotoso, -a [rro·'to·so, -a] **I.** *adj AmL* tattered **II.** *m, f* wretch

rótula ['rro·tu·la] *f* **1.** ANAT knee joint **2.** TÉC ball-and-socket joint

rotulador [rro·tu·la·'dor] *m* felt-tip pen

rótulo ['rro·tu·lo] *m* sign; (*encabezamiento*) heading; (*etiqueta*) ticket; (*letrero*) sign; (*anuncio público*) notice; CINE subtitle; ~ **de población** town sign

rotundo, -a [rro·'tun·do, -a] *adj* **1.** (*terminante*) emphatic; **un éxito** ~ a resounding

success; **una negativa rotunda** a flat refusal **2.** (*lleno y sonoro*) sonorous; **palabras rotundas** resounding words

rotura [rro·'tu·ra] *f* (*acción*) breaking; (*parte quebrada*) break; ~ **de hueso** fracture; ~ **de ligamento** torn ligament

rouge [rruʃ] *m Arg, Chile* (*colorete*) blusher, rouge

roza ['rro·sa, -θa] *f*, **rozado** [rro·'sa·do, -'θa·do] *m Arg* AGR cleared ground

rozar <z→c> [rro·'sar, -'θar] **I.** *vi* to rub; **rozar (por) los cincuenta** *fig* to be pushing fifty **II.** *vt* **1.** *t. fig* (*tocar ligeramente*) to brush; ~ **la ridiculez** *fig* to border on the ridiculous **2.** (*frotar*) to rub **3.** AGR to clear; (*animales*) to graze **III.** *vr:* ~**se 1.** (*restregarse*) to rub **2.** (*relacionarse*) to rub shoulders

rte. [rre·mi·'ten·te] *abr de* **remitente** sender

RTVE [e·rre·te·u·βe·'e] *f abr de* **Radio Televisión Española** Spanish state broadcasting corporation

ruana ['rrwa·na] *f AmS* (*poncho*) poncho

rubéola [rru·'βeo·la] *f* MED German measles

rubí [rru·'βi] *m* MIN ruby

rubio, -a ['rru·βjo, -a] **I.** *adj* fair; **tabaco** ~ Virginia tobacco **II.** *m, f* blond; (*mujer*) blonde

rublo ['rru·βlo] *m* (*moneda*) ruble

rubor [rru·'βor] *m* **1.** (*color*) bright red; (*de vergüenza*) blush **2.** (*vergüenza*) shame; (*bochorno*) embarrassment; **lo confieso con el** ~ **de mi cara** my blushing face leaves me no choice but to confess

ruborizado, -a [rru·βo·ri·'sa·do, -a; -'θa·do, -a] *adj* blushing

ruborizar <z→c> [rru·βo·ri·'sar, -'θar] **I.** *vt* to cause to blush **II.** *vr:* ~**se** to blush

rúbrica ['rru·βri·ka] *f* **1.** (*firma*) signature; (*después del nombre*) flourish **2.** (*epígrafe*) heading

rubro ['rru·βro] *m AmL* **1.** (*título*) heading, title **2.** COM (*asiento, partida*) area

ruca ['rru·ka] *f Arg, Chile* (*choza*) shack

ruco, -a ['rru·ko, -a] *adj AmC* old

rudeza [rru·'de·sa, -θa] *f* **1.** (*brusquedad*) rudeness **2.** (*tosquedad*) coarseness **3.** (*torpeza*) stupidity

rudimentario, -a [rru·di·men·'ta·rjo, -a] *adj* rudimentary

rudo, -a ['rru·do, -a] *adj* **1.** (*material*) rough; (*sin trabajar*) raw **2.** (*persona tosca*) coarse; (*brusca*) rude; (*torpe*) clumsy; (*poco inteligente*) stupid

rueda ['rrwe·da] *f* **1.** (*que gira*) wheel; (*de mueble*) castor; ~ **de aspas** wheel (*of windmill*); ~ **de paletas** paddle wheel; ~ **de repuesto** spare tire; **vapor de** ~**s** paddle steamer; **hacer la** ~ DEP to do a cartwheel **2.** (*de personas*) ring; ~ **de prensa** press conference; ~ **de identificación** (*sospechosos*) police line-up **3.** (*orden sucesivo*) ring ▸ **todo marcha sobre** ~**s** everything is going smoothly

ruedo ['rrwe·do] *m* **1.** (*contorno*) ring

2.(*borde*) edge; (*del vestido*) hem **3.** TAUR bull-ring **4.**(*estera*) (round) mat **5.** AmL (*dobla-dillo*) hem; (*de pantalón*) cuff ► **echarse al ~** to enter the fray

ruego ['rrwe·yo] *m* request ► **~s y preguntas** POL any other business; **no valen ~s ni súpli-cas** there is no point pleading

rufián [rru·'fjan] *m* **1.**(*chulo*) pimp **2.**(*gra-nuja*) scoundrel

rugby ['rruɣ·βi] *m* DEP rugby

rugido [rru·'xi·do] *m* **1.**(*del león*) roar **2.**(*del viento*) howl

rugir <g→j> [rru·'xir] **I.** *vi* **1.**(*león*) to roar; (*viento*) to howl **2.**(*persona*) **este hombre está que ruge** this man is beside himself with rage **II.** *v impers* to become known; **rugía que...** it became known that...

rugoso, -a [rru·'yo·so, -a] *adj* **1.**(*arrugado*) wrinkled **2.**(*áspero*) rough **3.**(*ondulado*) wavy

ruido ['rrwi·do] *m* **1.**(*sonido*) *t.* ELEC noise; **~s parásitos** interference, static **2.**(*estrépito*) noise; **nivel de ~** noise level; **~ de fondo** background noise ► **mucho ~ y pocas nueces** much ado about nothing; **hacer ~** to cause a stir; **querer ~** to be looking for trouble

ruidoso, -a [rrwi·'do·so, -a] *adj* noisy; *fig* sensational; **una carcajada ruidosa** a loud guffaw

ruin [rrwin] *adj* **1.**(*malvado*) wicked; (*vil*) despicable **2.**(*tacaño*) mean

ruina ['rrwi·na] *f* **1.**(*destrucción*) destruction; **este hombre está hecho una ~** *fig* this man is a wreck **2.** ARQUIT ruin; **las ~s de un castillo** the ruins of a castle **3.** *pl* (*escombros*) ruins *pl*; **convertir una ciudad en ~s** to raze a city to the ground; **declarar una casa en ~s** to condemn a house **4.**(*perdición*) downfall; **causar la ~ de alguien** to cause sb's downfall; **estar en la ~** to be bankrupt; **salvar a alguien de la ~** to save sb from disaster

ruinoso, -a [rrwi·'no·so, -a] *adj* **1.**(*edificios*) dilapidated **2.**(*perjudicial*) disastrous; ECON ruinous

ruiseñor [rrwi·se·'ɲor] *m* nightingale

rulenco, -a [rru·'len·ko, -a] *adj Chile* weak; (*raquítico*) stunted

rulero [rru·'le·ro] *m AmS* hair curler, roller

ruleta [rru·'le·ta] *f* (*juego*) roulette

ruletear [rru·le·te·'ar] *vi AmC, Méx* (*conducir un taxi*) to drive a taxi

ruletero, -a [rru·le·'te·ro, -a] *m, f AmC, Méx* (*conductor*) taxi driver

rulo ['rru·lo] *m* **1.**(*del cabello*) curl **2.**(*rizador*) *t.* TÉC roller

rulota ['rru·lo·ta] *f* (*caravana*) trailer

ruma ['rru·ma] *f AmS* (*montón*) **una ~ de...** a pile of...; **~s de...** lots of...

Rumania [rru·'ma·nja] *f*, **Rumanía** [rru·ma·'ni·a] *f* Romania

rumano, -a [rru·'ma·no] *adj, m, f* Romanian

rumba ['rrum·ba] *f* MÚS rumba

rumbo ['rrum·bo] *m* (*dirección*) direction; *t. fig* AVIAT, NÁUT course; **tomar ~ a un puerto** to

head for a port; **con ~ a** bound [*o* headed] for; **dar otro ~ a la conversación** to change the topic of the conversation; **no tengo ~ fijo** I'm not going anywhere in particular; **la negocia-ción está tomando un ~ favorable** the negotiation is taking a turn for the better; **tomar otro ~** POL to change course

rumiante [rru·'mjan·te] *m* ruminant

rumor [rru·'mor] *m* **1.**(*chisme*) rumor; **a título de ~** as a rumor; **poner un ~ en circu-lación** to start a rumor; **corren ~es de que...** it is rumored that... **2.**(*ruido*) murmur; (*del viento*) whistle; (*del bosque*) rustle; **~ de voces** buzz of conversation

rumorearse [rru·mo·re·'ar·se] *vr* **se rumorea que...** it is rumored that...

rumoroso, -a [rru·mo·'ro·so, -a] *adj* murmuring; (*viento*) whistling; (*bosque*) rustling

runcho ['rrun·tʃo] *m Col* ZOOL opossum

rundún [rrun·'dun] *m Arg* **1.**(*pájaro mosca*) tiny hummingbird **2.** *Arg, Chile, Méx, Perú* (*juguete*) bullroarer

rupestre [rru·'pes·tre] *adj* rock; **pintura ~** cave painting

rupia ['rru·pja] *f* (*moneda*) rupee

ruptura [rrup·'tu·ra] *f* breaking; (*de rela-ciones*) breaking-off

rural [rru·'ral] **I.** *adj* rural; **vida ~** country life **II.** *m* **1.** AmL, *t. pey* (*rústico*) yokel **2.** *pl, Méx* (*policía*) rural police

Rusia ['rru·sja] *f* Russia

ruso, -a ['rru·so, -a] **I.** *adj* Russian; **ensaladilla rusa** Russian salad (*potato salad with carrots, eggs and tuna*) **II.** *m, f* Russian

rústico, -a ['rrus·ti·ko, -a] **I.** *adj* **1.**(*campestre*) rural; **finca rústica** farmhouse **2.**(*tosco*) rough **II.** *m, f* peasant; *pey* yokel

ruta ['rru·ta] *f* **1.**(*camino*) route; **~ federal** AmL federal highway; **~ de itinerario** itinerary; **~ de vuelo** flight path **2.**(*conducta*) **tienes que cambiar de ~** you'll have to change your ways

rutina [rru·'ti·na] *f* **1.**(*costumbre*) routine; **~ cotidiana** daily routine **2.** COMPUT routine

rutinario, -a [rru·ti·'na·rjo, -a] *adj* routine; **un hombre ~** (*de costumbres*) a man of habit; (*aburrido*) an unimaginative man

S

S, s ['e·se] *f* S, s; **~ de Soria** S as in Sierra

S. [san] *abr de* **San** St

S.A. [e·se·'a] *f* **1.** *abr de* **Sociedad Anónima** ≈ Inc., *stock corporation* **2.** *abr de* **Su Alteza** Your Highness

sáb. *abr de* **sábado** Sat.

sábado ['sa·βa·do] *m* **1.**(*día*) Saturday; *v.t.* **lunes 2.**(*judaísmo*) Sabbath

sabana [sa·'βa·na] *f* savanna(h)

sábana ['sa·βa·na] *f* sheet; ~ **ajustable** fitted sheet; **se me han pegado las ~s** *inf* I've overslept

sabandija [sa·βan·'di·xa] *f* **1.** (*insecto*) bug **2.** *pey* (*persona*) wretch; **¡qué ~s!** little wretches!

sabanear [sa·βa·ne·'ar] *vi AmL* to ride the plains

sabático, -a [sa·'βa·ti·ko, -a] *adj* **1.** (*judaísmo*) sabbatical **2.** (*universidad*) **un año ~** a sabbatical year

sabelotodo [sa·βe·lo·'to·do] *mf inv, inf* know-it-all

saber [sa·'βer] *irr* **I.** *vt* **1.** (*estar informado*) to know; **¿se puede ~ si... ?** could you tell me if ...?; **¿se puede ~ dónde/cómo/quién...?** can sb tell me where/how/who ...?; **sin ~lo yo** without my knowing; **se sabe que...** it is known that...; **vete tú/vaya usted a ~** it's anyone's guess; **¡véte tu a ~ si es cierto!** your guess is as good as mine!; (**al menos**) **que yo sepa** as far as I know; **para que lo sepas** for your information; **¡pues no sé qué te diga!** I wouldn't be so sure!; **tener (un) no sé qué de raro** to have sth strange about one; **¡no sé ni por dónde ando!** *inf* I don't know whether I'm coming or going!; **¡y qué sé yo!** how should I know! **2.** (*tener habilidad*) **sabe** (**hablar**) **ruso** he/she can speak Russian; **no ~(se) la poesía** not to know the poem by heart **3.** (*conocer*) to know; **¿sabes mi nombre?** do you know my name?; **~ de algo** to know about sth; **~ mucho de literatura** to know a lot about literature **4.** (*noticia*) to find out; **lo supe por mi hermano** I heard about it from my brother; **la prensa hizo ~ anoche la noticia** the papers gave out the news last night; **¡va a ~ quién soy yo!** he/she will find out who he/she is dealing with! ▶ **a ~** namely **II.** *vi* **1.** (*tener sabor*) **~ a algo** to taste of sth; **sabe mal** it tastes bad; (**me**) **supo a quemado** it tasted burnt; **~ a gloria** to taste [*o* be] divine **2.** (*agradar*) **la conferencia me supo a poco** the conference was really good but it should have been longer; **me supo mal aquella respuesta** that reply upset me **3.** (*tener noticia*) to have news; **no sé nada de mi hermano** I have no news of my brother **4.** (*tener la habilidad*) **~ de algo** to know how to do sth; **él no sabe resolver ni los ejercicios más fáciles** he can't do even the simplest exercises **III.** *vr* **sabérselas todas** *inf* she knows all the tricks **IV.** *m* knowledge ▶ **el ~ no ocupa lugar** *prov* you can't know too much

sabichoso, -a [sa·βi·'tʃo·so, -a] *adj Cuba, PRico* pedantic; (*sabiondo*) know-it-all

sabido, -a [sa·'βi·do, -a] *adj* **1.** (*conocido*) known; **es cosa sabida** it's well known; **dar por ~** to take for granted **2.** (*leído*) learned

sabiduría [sa·βi·du·'ri·a] *f* **1.** (*conocimientos*) knowledge **2.** (*sensatez*) wisdom

sabiendas [sa·'βjen·das] **a ~** knowingly; **lo hizo a ~ de que me molestaba** he/she did it knowing full well that it annoyed me

sabihondo, -a [sa·'βjon·do, -a] *m, f* know-it-all; (*niño*) smart-aleck, smarty pants

sabio, -a ['sa·βjo, -a] **I.** *adj* wise **II.** *m, f* scholar ▶ **errar es de ~s** *prov* to err is human

sabiondo, -a [sa·'βjon·do, -a] *m, f v.* **sabihondo**

sable ['sa·βle] *m* saber

sabor [sa·'βor] *m* taste; **tiene (un) ~ a naranja** it tastes of orange; **de ~ romántico** with a romantic flavor; **dejar un mal ~ de boca** to leave a nasty taste in one's mouth

saborear [sa·βo·re·'ar] *vt* to savor; (*triunfo*) to relish

sabotaje [sa·βo·'ta·xe] *m* sabotage

sabotear [sa·βo·te·'ar] *vt* to sabotage

sabroso, -a [sa·'βro·so, -a] *adj* (*sazonado*) tasty

sabueso [sa·'βwe·so, -a] *m* **1.** ZOOL bloodhound **2.** *fig* sleuth

saca ['sa·ka] *f* **1.** (*saco*) sack; **~ de correos** mailbag **2.** (*extracción*) withdrawal **3.** (*exportación*) export **4.** (*copia*) authorized copy

sacabuche [sa·ka·'βu·tʃe] *m* **1.** MÚS sackbut **2.** NÁUT hand pump **3.** *Méx* (*navaja*) pointed knife

sacacorchos [sa·ka·'kor·tʃos] *m inv* corkscrew

sacamanchas [sa·ka·'man·tʃas] *m inv* stain remover

sacapuntas [sa·ka·'pun·tas] *m inv* pencil sharpener

sacar <c→qu> [sa·'kar] **I.** *vt* **1.** (*de un sitio*) to take out, to remove; (*agua, espada*) to draw; (*diente*) to pull (out); **~ a bailar** to invite to dance; **~ a alguien de la cama/de la cárcel** to get sb out of bed/of jail; **~ a pasear** to take out for a walk; **sácalo del garage** take it out of the garage; **¿de dónde lo has sacado?** where did you get it from?; **recién sacado del horno** freshly baked; **¡te voy a ~ los ojos!** *fig* I'll teach you (to do that)! **2.** (*de una situación*) to get; **~ adelante** (*persona*) to look after; (*negocio*) to run; (*niño*) to bring up; **~ a alguien del atolladero** to get sb out of a jam; **~ a alguien de la pobreza** to rescue sb from poverty **3.** (*solucionar*) to solve **4.** (*reconocer*) to recognize **5.** (*entrada*) to get **6.** (*obtener*) to obtain; (*premio, votos*) to get; **~ las consecuencias** to come to conclusions; **~ en claro** (**de**) to gather (from); **no ~ ni para vivir** not to make enough to live on; **~ a alguien 10 dólares** to squeeze 10 dollars out of sb **7.** MIN to extract **8.** (*parte del cuerpo*) to stick out **9.** *inf* (*foto*) to take; (*dibujo*) to do; **¡sácame una foto!** take a photo of me! **10.** (*mancha*) to remove **11.** (*producto*) to bring out; **~ a la venta** to put on sale [*o* the market]; (*libro*) to publish **12.** (*mostrar*) to show; (*desenterrar*) to unearth; **~ en hombros** to carry out shoulder-high; **~ algo a relucir** to bring out the dirty linen **13.** (*ventaja*) **el ganador me sacó**

dos minutos the winner was two minutes quicker than me II. *vi* (*tenis*) to serve; (*fútbol: portero*) to take a goal kick; (*fútbol: saque de banda*) to take a throw-in III. *vr* se sacó una pestaña del ojo he/she took an eyelash out of his/her eye

sacarina [sa·ka·'ri·na] *f* saccharin

sacerdote [sa·ser·'do·te, sa·θer-] *m* priest

sacho ['sa·tʃo] *m* 1. (*para sachar*) weeder 2. *Chile* (*ancla*) anchor

saciar [sa·'sjar, -'θjar] I. *vt* (*hambre, curiosidad*) to satisfy; (*instintos sexuales*) to satiate; (*sed*) to quench II. *vr:* ~ se *t. fig* to satiate oneself

saciedad [sa·sje·'dad, sa·θje-] *f* satiation; repetir hasta la ~ to repeat over and over

saco ['sa·ko] *m* 1. (*bolsa*) bag; (*costal*) sack; ~ de trigo sack of wheat; ~ de dormir sleeping bag 2. *AmL* (*prenda*) jacket 3. (*saqueo*) sacking; entrar a ~ to loot 4. *DEP* (*boxeo*) punching bag ▸ en el mismo ~ in the same boat; caer en ~ roto to fall on deaf ears; no echar algo en ~ roto to take note of sth

sacón, -ona [sa·'kon, -·'ko·na] *m, f Méx, inf* (*miedica*) chicken

sacramento [sa·kra·'men·to] *m* sacrament; el ~ de la Eucaristía the Blessed Sacrament; administrar a alguien los últimos ~s to give sb the last rites

sacrificar <c→qu> [sa·kri·fi·'kar] I. *vt* 1. (*ofrecer*) to sacrifice; *t. fig* to give up 2. (*animal*) to slaughter II. *vr* ~ se por algo/alguien to sacrifice oneself for sth/sb

sacrificio [sa·kri·'fi·sjo, -·'fi·θjo] *m* sacrifice; el Santo Sacrificio Holy Communion

sacrilegio [sa·kri·'le·xjo] *m* sacrilege

sacristán [sa·kris·'tan] *m* sacristan

sacristía [sa·kris·'ti·a] *f* vestry, sacristy

sacro, -a ['sa·kro, -a] *adj* 1. (*sagrado*) sacred 2. *ANAT* hueso ~ sacrum

sacudida [sa·ku·'di·da] *f* shake; ~ eléctrica electric shock; ~ sísmica earthquake; el coche pegaba ~s the car was jolting; dale una ~ a la alfombra shake the carpet [*o* rug]

sacudir [sa·ku·'dir] I. *vt* 1. (*agitar*) to shake; (*moscas*) to brush off; ~ el rabo to swish its tail; ~ a alguien por los hombros to shake sb by the shoulders 2. (*pegar*) to belt II. *vr:* ~ se to shake oneself

sádico, -a ['sa·di·ko, -a] I. *adj* sadistic II. *m, f* sadist

sadomasoquismo [sa·do·ma·so·'kis·mo] *m* sadomasochism

saeta [sa·'e·ta] *f* 1. (*flecha*) arrow 2. (*reloj*) hand; (*brújula*) magnetic needle 3. *MÚS pious song in flamenco style typically sung in the religious processions in Spain during Easter week*

safari [sa·'fa·ri] *m* safari

sagaz [sa·'ɣas, -'ɣaθ] *adj* astute

sagitario [sa·xi·'ta·rjo] *m* Sagittarius

sagrado, -a <sacratísimo> [sa·'ɣra·do] *adj* sacred

sagú [sa·'ɣu] *m AmC* 1. (*planta*) arrowroot 2. (*harina*) sago

Sahara [sa·'xa·ra] *m* el ~ the Sahara

sal [sal] *f* 1. (*condimento*) salt; ~ común table salt; poner demasiada ~ a algo to put too much salt in sth; ~ marina sea [*o* bay] salt; ~ gorda [*o* gruesa *Méx*] coarse [*o* rock] salt 2. *pl* (*perfume*) smelling salts *pl;* ~ es de baño bath salts 3. (*gracia*) wit; (*encanto*) charm; la ~ de la vida the spice of life 4. *AmL* (*mala suerte*) bad luck

sala ['sa·la] *f* 1. (*habitación*) room; (*grande*) hall; ~ de espera waiting room; ~ de estar living room 2. *JUR* courtroom; Sala de lo Civil/Penal Civil/Criminal Court

salado, -a [sa·'la·do, -a] *adj* 1. (*comida*) salty 2. (*gracioso*) witty; (*encantador*) charming 3. *AmL* (*infortunado*) unfortunate

salamanca [sa·la·'man·ka] *f* 1. *Arg* ZOOL *flat-headed salamander* 2. *CSur* (*cueva natural*) natural cave

salamandra [sa·la·'man·dra] *f* salamander; ~ acuática newt

salame [sa·'la·me] *adj Arg, inf* (*tonto*) fool

salar [sa·'lar] *vt* 1. (*condimentar*) to add salt to; ~ algo demasiado to put too much salt in sth 2. (*para conservar*) to salt 3. *AmL* (*echar a perder*) to spoil

salarial [sa·la·'rjal] *adj* wage

salario [sa·'la·rjo] *m* wages *pl;* ~ en especie payment in kind

salchicha [sal·'tʃi·tʃa] *f* sausage; perro ~ *inf* hotdog

salchichón [sal·tʃi·'tʃon] *m salami-type cured sausage*

saldar [sal·'dar] *vt* (*cuenta*) to pay; (*deuda*) to pay off; todavía no hemos saldado nuestras diferencias we still haven't settled our differences

saldo ['sal·do] *m* 1. (*diferencia*) balance; (*pago*) payment; ~ acreedor credit balance; ~ de la cuenta account balance 2. *pl* (*rebajas*) sales *pl*

salero [sa·'le·ro] *m* 1. (*objeto*) salt shaker 2. (*gracia*) wit

saleroso, -a [sa·le·'ro·so, -a] *adj inf* (*ingenioso*) witty; (*encantador*) charming

salida [sa·'li·da] *f* 1. (*puerta*) way out; ~ para coches car exit; a la ~ del teatro coming out of the theater; callejón sin ~ dead end; ~ de emergencia emergency exit 2. (*de un tren, avión*) departure; (*de un barco*) sailing 3. *ASTR* rising; ~ del sol sunrise 4. *DEP* start; dar la ~ to start the race 5. *COM* sale; (*partida*) consignment; este producto no tiene ~ there is no market for this product; ~ de capital capital outflow 6. *inf* (*ocurrencia*) witty remark; ¡menuda ~! what a crazy idea! 7. (*solución*) way out; en este asunto no hay ~ there is no way out of this

salidor(a) [sa·li·'dor, -·'do·ra] *adj AmL* party-loving; es muy ~ he likes to go out a lot

salina [sa·'li·na] *f* 1. (*instalación*) salt works

2.(*mina*) salt mine
salino, -a [sa·'li·no, -a] *adj* saline
salir [sa·'lir] *irr* **I.** *vi* **1.**(*ir al exterior*) to go out;
(*ir fuera*) to go away; ~ **a dar una vuelta** to go
out for a stroll [*o* walk]; ~ **con alguien** *inf* to
go out with sb; ~ **adelante** to make progress;
~ **mal con alguien** to fall out with sb **2.**(*de
viaje*) to leave; (*avión*) to depart; ~ **del cascarón** [*o* **del huevo**] to come out of the egg;
para ~ de dudas le pregunté directamente
to clear up any doubts I asked him/her directly; ~ **ileso** [*o* **bien librado**] to come out unscathed; ~ **ganando/perdiendo** to come out
the better/the worse **3.**(*flores, fuente*) to
come out; (*sol*) to rise; ~ **a la luz** to come to
light; ~ **en la tele** to be on TV **4.**(*convertirse*)
to turn into; **salió un buen artista** he became
a good artist **5.**(*parecerse*) ~ **a alguien** to look
like sb; **este niño ha salido a su padre** the
boy takes after his father **6.**COMPUT ~ **de un
programa** to exit a program **7.**DEP to start
8.(*costar*) to cost; **nos sale a 4 pesos el
metro** it costs us 4 pesos per meter ▶ **salga lo
que salga** whatever happens **II.** *vr:* ~ **se** (*de un
recipiente*) to spill; (*líquido*) to overflow;
(*leche*) to boil over; (*vasija*) to leak; **el río se
salió (de madre)** the river burst its banks
▶ ~ **se con la suya** to get one's own way
saliva [sa·'li·βa] *f* saliva; **gastar ~ en balde** *fig*
to waste one's breath
salivadera [sa·li·βa·'de·ra] *f Arg, Urug* (*escupidera*) spittoon
salmo ['sal·mo] *m* psalm; **cantar a alguien el
~ ** *fig* to tell sb a few home truths
salmón [sal·'mon] **I.** *adj* salmon-pink **II.** *m*
salmon
salmuera [sal·'mwe·ra] *f* brine
salón [sa·'lon] *m* **1.**(*de casa*) living-room
2.(*local*) hall; ~ **de actos** assembly hall; ~ **de
baile** dancehall
salpicadera [sal·pi·ka·'de·ra] *f Méx* AUTO mudguard, fender
salpicar <c→qu> [sal·pi·'kar] *vt* **1.**(*rociar*) to
sprinkle; (*con pintura*) to splash; ~ **la mesa de
flores** to decorate the table with flowers
2.(*manchar*) to spatter
salpicón [sal·pi·'kon] *m* **1.** CULIN ≈ salmagundi
(*chopped seafood or meat with oil, vinegar
and seasoning*) **2.** *Col, Ecua* (*bebida*) cold
drink of fruit juice **3.**(*mancha*) spatter

> **i** In **Colombia** and **Ecuador** the **salpicón**
> is a cold fruit drink. In Spain, however, **salpi-
> cón** is a cold meat, fish or seafood dish.

salpimentar <e→ie> [sal·pi·men·'tar] *vt* to
season, to add salt and pepper; ~ **algo con
algo** *fig* to liven sth up with sth
salsa ['sal·sa] *f* **1.** CULIN sauce; (*caldo*) gravy;
~ **mayonesa** mayonnaise; ~ **verde** parsley
sauce; ~ **de tomate** (*de aderezo*) ketchup;
(*para cocinar*) tomato sauce **2.**(*gracia*) hu-

mor; **este libro tiene mucha ~** this book is
very amusing; **esa es la ~ de la vida** she is the
spice of life **3.** MÚS salsa ▶ **estar en su propia
~** to be in one's element
salsamentaría [sal·sa·men·ta·'ri·a] *f Col* COM
delicatessen
saltador(a) [sal·ta·'dor, ·'do·ra] **I.** *adj* jumping **II.** *m(f)* (*atleta*) jumper; ~ **de altura**
high-jumper; ~ **de longitud** long-jumper; ~ **de
pértiga** pole-vaulter
saltamontes [sal·ta·'mon·tes] *m inv* grasshopper
saltaperico [sal·ta·pe·'ri·ko] *m Cuba* BOT min-
nieroot
saltar [sal·'tar] **I.** *vi* **1.**(*botar*) to jump; (*chispas*) to fly up; ~ **por los aires** to blow up; *fig*
to get furious; ~ **de alegría** to jump for joy; ~ **a
la cuerda** to skip; ~ **en pedazos** to break into
pieces; **los jugadores ~ on al terreno de
juego** the players ran out onto the field
2.(*lanzarse*) to jump; ~ **al agua** to jump into
the water; ~ **con paracaídas** to make a parachute jump **3.**(*explotar*) to explode; (*costura*)
to burst; (*los plomos*) to blow **4.**(*trabajo*) to
be promoted rapidly; (*ser destituido*) to be
kicked out **5.**(*desprenderse*) to come off ▶ **estar a la que salta** to look out for an opportunity **II.** *vt* **1.**(*movimiento*) to jump (over)
2.(*animal*) to cover **III.** *vr:* ~ **se 1.**(*ley, norma*)
to break **2.**(*línea, párrafo*) to miss out, to skip
3.(*desprenderse*) to come off; **se me saltó un
botón** one of my buttons came off; **se me ~ on
las lágrimas** my eyes filled with tears
saltear [sal·te·'ar] *vt* **1.**(*asaltar*) to hold up
2. CULIN to sauté **3.**(*interrumpir*) to do in fits
and starts
salto ['sal·to] *m* **1.**(*bote*) jump; **de** [*o* **en**] **un ~**
with one jump; **apartarse de un ~** to jump
away; **dar un ~** to jump; *fig* to jump with
fright; **dar ~s de alegría** to jump for joy; **dar
un ~ atrás** to jump backwards; **me pegó un ~
el corazón** my heart pounded **2.** DEP jump;
~ **de altura** high jump; ~ **de longitud** long
jump; ~ **mortal** somersault; ~ **del potro** vault;
a ~s in leaps and bounds **3.**(*trabajo*) rapid promotion **4.**(*bata*) ~ **de cama** negligee **5.** COM-
PUT ~ **de página** page break **6.**(*omisión*) gap,
omission ▶ ~ **de agua** waterfall
salubridad [sa·lu·βri·'dad] *f* healthiness; *AmL*
(*higiene*) hygiene
salud [sa·'lud] *f* (*estado físico*) health; **¡~!** (*al
estornudar*) bless you!; (*al brindar*) good
health!; **beber a la ~ de...** to drink to the
health of...; **rebosante de ~** bursting with
health; **¡~, dinero y amor!** *inf* cheers!; **gastar
~** to be in good health; **lo juro por la ~ de
mis hijos** I swear on the Bible
saludable [sa·lu·'da·βle] *adj* **1.**(*sano*) healthy
2.(*provechoso*) beneficial
saludar [sa·lu·'dar] *vt* **1.**(*al encontrar*) to
greet; (*con la mano*) to wave; MIL to salute; **le
saluda atentamente su...** *form* yours faithfully...; **he ido a ~ a mis padres** I went to visit

my parents; **estos ya ni se saludan** they don't even speak to each other now **2.** (*recibir*) to welcome **3.** (*mandar saludos*) to send regards to

saludo [sa·'lu·do] *m* **1.** (*palabras*) greeting; **con un cordial ~** *form* yours sincerely; **¡dele ~s de mi parte!** give him/her my regards; **tu madre te manda ~s** your mother sends her love **2.** (*recibimiento*) welcome

salvación [sal·βa·'sjon, -'θjon] *f* rescue; REL salvation; **Ejército de Salvación** Salvation Army

salvado [sal·'βa·do] *m* bran

Salvador [sal·βa·'dor] *m* **El ~** El Salvador

---

i The Republic of **El Salvador** is located in the northeastern part of Central America. The capital is **San Salvador**. The official language of the country is Spanish and the official currency of **El Salvador** is the **colón**. It is the smallest and most densely populated country in Central America.

---

salvadoreño, -a [sal·βa·do·'re·ɲo, -a] *adj, m, f* Salvadoran

salvaguardar [sal·βa·ɣwar·'dar] *vt* to safeguard; (*derechos, intereses*) to protect

salvaguardia [sal·βa·'ɣwar·dja] *f* **1.** (*protección*) safeguard; (*de intereses*) safekeeping **2.** (*salvoconducto*) safe-conduct

salvaje [sal·'βa·xe] **I.** *adj* (*planta, animal*) wild; (*persona*) uncivilized; (*acto*) savage; **huelga ~** wildcat strike **II.** *mf* savage; (*persona ruda*) barbarian

salvajismo [sal·βa·'xis·mo] *m* **1.** (*animal*) wild nature **2.** (*gamberrismo*) vandalism **3.** (*crueldad*) savagery

salvamento [sal·βa·'men·to] *m* salvation; (*accidente, naufragio*) rescue

salvar [sal·'βar] **I.** *vt. t.* REL (*del peligro*) to save; **~ del peligro** to save from danger **2.** (*foso*) to jump across; (*distancia*) to cover; (*obstáculo, problema*) to overcome; **~ las apariencias** to keep up appearances **II.** *vr:* **~se** to save oneself; (*en sentido religioso*) to be saved; **¡sálvese quien pueda!** every man for himself!

salvavidas [sal·βa·'βi·das] *m inv* (*cinturón*) lifebelt; **bote ~** lifeboat; **chaleco ~** lifejacket

salvavidas [sal·βa·'βi·das] *mf* lifeguard

salvedad [sal·βe·'dad] *f* **1.** (*excepción*) exception **2.** (*condición*) reservation; **con la ~ de que...** with the proviso that...

salvilla [sal·'βi·ja, -ʎa] *f Chile* cruet

salvo ['sal·βo] *prep* except; **~ que** +*subj* unless; **~ error u omisión** *form* errors and omissions excepted; **~ aviso en contrario** *form* unless otherwise informed

salvo, -a [sal·βo, -a] *adj* safe; **poner a ~** to put in a safe place; **sano y ~** safe and sound

samba ['sam·ba] *f* samba

sambumbia [sam·'bum·bja] *f* **1.** *Col* (*cosa*

desmoronada*) **volver algo ~ to smash sth to pieces **2.** *Cuba* CULIN *drink of cane syrup, water and peppers* **3.** *Méx* CULIN pineapple cordial

san [san] *adj* Saint

sanar [sa·'nar] **I.** *vi* **~ de algo** to recover from sth **II.** *vt* to cure

sanatorio [sa·na·'to·rjo] *m* sanatorium

sanción [san·'sjon, -'θjon] *f* **1.** (*multa*) penalty; ECON sanction **2.** (*ley*) passing **3.** (*autorización*) endorsement

sancionar [san·sjo·'nar, san·θjo-] *vt* **1.** (*castigar*) to punish; ECON (*aplicar sanciones*) to impose sanctions on **2.** (*aprobar*) to authorize; JUR to ratify

sancochar [san·ko·'tʃar] *vt AmL* (*rehogar*) to parboil

sancocho [san·'ko·tʃo] *m* **1.** *AmC, PRico, Ven* (*lío*) fuss **2.** *And, Ven* parboiled meat

sandalia [san·'da·lja] *f* sandal

sándalo ['san·da·lo] *m* **1.** (*árbol*) sandalwood tree **2.** (*madera*) sandalwood

sandez [san·'des, -'deθ] *f* stupid action; **no decir más que sandeces** to say nothing but foolish things

sandía [san·'di·a] *f* watermelon

sandinista [san·di·'nis·ta] *adj, mf Nic* Sandinista

sandunga [san·'dun·ga] *f* **inf 1.** (*gracia*) charm **2.** *Col, Chile, PRico* celebration

sándwich ['san·gwitʃ] *m* CULIN toasted sandwich; **día ~** *Arg, inf: day off between a holiday and another day off*

saneamiento [sa·nea·'mjen·to] *m* **1.** (*de un edificio*) repair; (*de un terreno*) drainage **2.** (*de economía*) reform

sanear [sa·ne·'ar] *vt* **1.** (*edificio*) to clean up; (*tierra*) to drain **2.** (*economía*) to reform; **~ un vicio** to break a bad habit

sanfermines [san·fer·'mi·nes] *mpl* running of the bulls (*Pamplona, Spain*)

sangrar [san·'grar] **I.** *vi* to bleed; **estar sangrando por la nariz** to have a nosebleed; **estar sangrando** *fig* to be very fresh **II.** *vt* **1.** MED to bleed **2.** (*dinero*) to bleed dry **3.** (*agua, resina*) to drain off **4.** TIPO to indent

sangre ['san·gre] *f* **1.** (*líquido*) blood; **a ~ fría** in cold blood; **de ~ azul** blue-blooded; **animales de ~ caliente/fría** warm/cold-blooded animals; (*caballo de*) **pura ~** thoroughbred (horse); **chupar la ~ (de las venas) a alguien** *inf* to bleed sb dry; **dar** [*o* **donar*] **~** to give [*o* donate] blood; **dar la ~ de sus venas** *fig* to give everything one has; **hacer ~** (*en una pelea, lucha*) to draw blood; **aportar ~ nueva a algo** to inject new blood [*o* life] into sth; **llevar algo en la ~** to have sth in the blood; (*de familia*) to run in the family; **le hierve la ~** *fig* his/her blood boils **2.** (*linaje*) lineage ▶ **no llegar la ~ al río** not to have disastrous results; **hacerse mala ~** to get bitter; **sudar ~** to go through hardships; **tener mala ~** to be bad-tempered

sangría [san·'gri·a] *f* **1.** MED bleeding; **una ~**

de votos a continuous loss of votes **2.**(*brazo*) inner angle of the elbow **3.**(*aguas*) irrigation channel **4.** TIPO indentation **5.**(*bebida*) sangria (*cold drink made of red wine, water, sugar, lemon and orange*)

sangriento, -a [san·'grjen·to, -a] *adj* bloody; (*injusticia*) cruel; **hecho ~** bloody event

sangriligero, -a [san·gri·li·'xe·ro, -a] *adj AmC* friendly, nice

sangripesado, -a [san·gri·pe·'sa·do, -a] *adj AmC* unpleasant, disagreeable

sangrón, -ona [san·'gron, -·'gro·na] *adj Méx, inf* boring; **su novio es un ~, no lo soporto** her boyfriend is a bore, I can't stand him

sanguaraña [san·gwa·'ra·ɲa] *f* **1.** *Ecua, Perú* (*circunloquio*) evasion; **déjate de ~s** stop beating around the bush **2.** *Perú: popular Peruvian dance*

sanguijuela [san·gi·'xwe·la] *f* **1.** ZOOL leech **2.** *pey* (*persona*) bloodsucker

sanguíneo, -a [san·'gi·neo, -a] *adj* **1.** MED blood; **rojo ~** blood-red; **grupo ~** blood type [*o* group] **2.**(*temperamento*) sanguine

sanidad [sa·ni·'dad] *f* health; **~ (pública)** public health

sanitario [sa·ni·'ta·rjo] *m* (*wáter*) toilet

sanitario, -a [sa·ni·'ta·rjo, -a] **I.** *adj* health; (*aparatos, medidas*) sanitary **II.** *m, f* health worker

sano, -a ['sa·no, -a] *adj* **1.**(*robusto, saludable*) healthy; **~ de juicio** of sound mind; **cortar por lo ~** to take extreme measures; **salir ~ y salvo** to emerge safe and sound **2.**(*no roto*) intact

santería [san·te·'ri·a] *f Arg, Urug: shop selling religious items*

Santiago [san·'tja·ɣo] *m* **~ (de Chile)** Santiago

santiaguino, -a [san·tja·'ɣi·no, -a] **I.** *adj* of/from Santiago (in Chile) **II.** *m, f* native/inhabitant of Santiago (in Chile)

santiamén [san·tja·'men] *m* **en un ~** in a jiffy

santidad [san·ti·'dad] *f* holiness; **Su Santidad** His Holiness, the Pope

santificar <c→qu> [san·ti·fi·'kar] *vt* **1.**(*consagrar*) to consecrate **2.**(*canonizar*) to sanctify

santiguar <gu→gü> [san·ti·'ɣwar] **I.** *vt* **1.**(*signarse*) to make the sign of the cross over **2.** *inf* (*maltratar*) to hit **II.** *vr:* **~se** to cross oneself

santo, -a ['san·to, -a] **I.** *adj* sacred, holy; (*piadoso*) saintly; (*inviolable*) consecrated; **la Santa Sede** the Holy See; **el Santo Oficio** HIST the Inquisition; **campo ~** cemetery; **Jueves Santo** Maundy Thursday; **Semana Santa** Holy Week, Easter; **Viernes Santo** Good Friday; **¿qué haces en Semana Santa?** what are you doing over Easter?; **se pasó todo el ~ día haciendo...** he/she spent the whole blessed day doing... **II.** *m, f* **1.**(*personaje*) saint; **día de Todos los Santos** All Saint's Day **2.**(*fiesta*) saint's day, name day; **el día de mi ~** my saint's day **3.**(*imagen*) (religious) illustration;

ver los ~s de un libro to look at the pictures in a book ► **hoy tengo el ~ de cara/espalda** I'm in/out of luck today; **no ser ~ de la devoción de alguien** to not be particularly fond of sb; **ser mano de ~** to be good at everything; **desnudar a un ~ para vestir a otro** to rob Peter to pay Paul; **dormirse como un ~** (*bendito*) to sleep like a baby; **llegar y besar el ~** (*sin esfuerzo*) to pull it off at the first attempt; (*fácil*) like taking candy from a baby; **quedarse para vestir ~s** (*mujer*) to be left on the shelf, to remain an old maid

santuario [san·tu·'a·rjo] *m* **1.**(*templo*) shrine; (*capilla*) chapel **2.**(*refugio*) sanctuary, refuge **3.** *Col* (*tesoro*) buried treasure

saña ['sa·ɲa] *f* **1.**(*ira*) anger **2.**(*rencor*) viciousness; **lo hizo con toda la mala ~** he/she did it with great cruelty

sapaneco, -a [sa·pa·'ne·ko, -a] *adj Hond* chubby

sapiencia [sa·'pjen·sja, -θja] *f* **1.**(*conocimientos*) wisdom **2.**(*sensatez*) good sense

sapo ['sa·po] *m* **1.** ZOOL toad **2.**(*persona*) nasty bit of work **3.** *inf* (*bicho*) small animal

saque ['sa·ke] *m* DEP (*fútbol*) goal kick, throw-in; (*fútbol americano*) kick-off; (*tenis*) serve; **~ de esquina** corner kick

saquear [sa·ke·'ar] *vt* to loot

saqueo [sa·'keo] *m* looting

sarampión [sa·ram·'pjon] *m* MED measles

sarape [sa·'ra·pe] *m Méx* blanket

sarazo, -a [sa·'ra·so, -a; -θo, -a] *adj Col, Cuba, Méx, Ven* (*fruto, maíz*) ripening

sarcasmo [sar·'kas·mo] *m* sarcasm

sarcástico, -a [sar·'kas·ti·ko, -a] *adj* sarcastic

sarcófago [sar·'ko·fa·ɣo] *m* sarcophagus; (*tumba*) tomb

sardina [sar·'di·na] *f* sardine; **~s en aceite** sardines in oil; (*estar*) **como ~s en lata** to be packed like sardines

sardo, -a ['sar·do] *adj, m, f* Sardinian

sargento [sar·'xen·to] *m* sergeant

sarna ['sar·na] *f* MED scabies; (*de los animales*) mange ► **~ con gusto no pica(, pero mortifica** *prov* if you like sth you'll do it whatever the cost

sarpullido [sar·pu·'ji·do, -'ʎi·do] *m* MED (*irritación*) rash

sarro ['sa·rro] *m* MED (*de los dientes*) tartar

SARS ['sars] *m* MED (*síndrome respiratorio agudo severo*) SARS

sarta ['sar·ta] *f* **1.**(*hilo*) string **2.**(*serie*) row; **una ~ de mentiras** a string [*o* pack] of lies

sartén [sar·'ten] *f* frying pan ► **tener la ~ por el mango** to have the whip [*o* upper] hand

sastre, -a ['sas·tre, -a] *m, f* tailor; **traje ~** tailor-made suit; **de eso, será lo que tase un ~** *inf* that's more than doubtful

sastrería [sas·tre·'ri·a] *f* tailor's shop; (*oficio*) tailoring

satánico, -a [sa·'ta·ni·ko, -a] *adj* satanic

satélite [sa·'te·li·te] *m* ASTR, TÉC satellite; (*país*) **~ satellite** (state)

satén [sa·'ten] *m* satin

satinado, -a [sa·ti·'na·do, -a] *adj* shiny, glossy; **papel** ~ shiny paper

sátira ['sa·ti·ra] *f* LIT satire

satírico, -a [sa·'ti·ri·ko, -a] I. *adj* satirical II. *m*, *f* satirist

satirizar <z→c> [sa·ti·ri·'sar, -'θar] *vt* to satirize

sátiro ['sa·ti·ro] *m* satyr; (*hombre lascivo*) lecher

satisfacción [sa·tis·fak·'sjon, -faɣ·'θjon] *f* 1. (*estado*) satisfaction; (*alegría*) happiness; **a mi entera** ~ to my complete satisfaction 2. REL fulfillment

satisfacer [sa·tis·fa·'ser, -'θer] *irr como* hacer I. *vt* 1. (*pagar*) to honor; ~ **la penitencia por sus pecados** to do penitence for one's sins 2. (*deseo, curiosidad, hambre*) to satisfy; (*sed*) to quench; (*demanda*) to settle; ~ **todos los caprichos de sus hijos** to gratify all one's children's whims 3. (*requisitos*) to meet 4. (*agravio*) ~ **algo** to make amends for sth II. *vr:* ~**se** 1. (*contentarse*) to satisfy oneself 2. (*agravio*) to obtain redress

satisfactorio, -a [sa·tis·fak·'to·rjo, -a] *adj* (*solución*) satisfactory; **no ser** ~ to be unsatisfactory; **resulta** ~ **comprobar que...** it is pleasing to confirm that...

satisfecho, -a [sa·tis·'fe·tʃo, -a] I. *pp de* **satisfacer** II. *adj* (*contento*) contented; (*exigencias, deseo sexual*) satisfied; ~ **de sí mismo** self-satisfied; **estar** ~ (*harto*) to have had enough

saturación [sa·tu·ra·'sjon, -'θjon] *f* saturation

saturar [sa·tu·'rar] *vt* to saturate

sauce ['sau·se, 'sau·θe] *m* willow; ~ **llorón** weeping willow

saúco [sa·'u·ko] *m* elder tree

saudí <saudíes> [sau·'di], **saudita** [sau·'di·ta] I. *adj* Saudi; **Arabia Saudí** Saudi Arabia II. *mf* Saudi

sauna ['sau·na] *f* sauna

savia ['sa·βja] *f* 1. (*de árbol*) sap 2. (*energía*) vitality

saxofón [sak·so·'fon] *m*, **saxófono** [sak·'so·fo·no] *m* saxophone

sazón [sa·'son, -'θon] *f* 1. (*condimento*) flavor 2. (*madurez*) ripeness; **estar en** ~ to be ripe ▶**fuera** de ~ out of season; **a la** ~ at that time

sazonar [sa·so·'nar, sa·θo-] *vt* 1. (*comida*) to season 2. (*madurar*) to ripen

se [se] *pron pers* 1. *forma reflexiva:* *m sing* himself; *f sing* herself; *de cosa* itself; *pl* themselves; *de Ud.* yourself; *de Uds.* yourselves 2. *objeto indirecto:* *m sing* to him; *f sing* to her; *a una cosa* to it; *pl* to them; *a Ud., Uds.* to you; **mi hermana** ~ **lo prestó a su amiga** my sister lent it to her friend 3. (*oración impers*) you; ~ **aprende mucho en esta clase** you learn a lot in this class 4. (*oración pasiva*) ~ **confirmó la sentencia** the sentence was confirmed

sé [se] *1. pres de* **saber**

SE *abr de* **sudeste** SE

sebo ['se·βo] *m* grease; (*vela*) tallow; **hacer** ~ *Arg, inf* to idle

seboso, -a [se·'βo·so, -a] *adj* greasy

seca ['se·ka] *f* 1. (*sequía*) drought; *AmL* (*temporada*) dry season 2. (*banco de arena*) dry sandbank

secador [se·ka·'dor] *m* (*para la ropa*) clothes horse; (*para las manos*) hand-dryer; (*para el pelo*) hairdryer; ~ (**de mano**) hand-dryer

secadora [se·ka·'do·ra] *f* tumble dryer, spin dryer

secante[1] [se·'kan·te] I. *adj* drying; **línea** ~ secant; **papel** ~ blotting paper II. *m* 1. (*pintura*) paint dryer 2. (*papel*) blotting paper

secante[2] [se·'kan·te] *f* MAT secant

secar <c→qu> [se'kar] I. *vt* 1. (*deshumedecer*) to dry 2. (*enjugar*) to wipe 3. (*cicatrizar*) to heal II. *vr:* ~**se** 1. (*deshumedecer*) to dry up 2. (*enjugar*) to wipe up 3. (*desecarse*) to dry up; (*fuente*) to run dry 4. (*curarse*) to heal up 5. (*insensibilizarse*) to become hardened 6. (*estar sediento*) to be very thirsty; ~**se de sed** to have a raging thirst

sección [sek·'sjon, seɣ·'θjon] *f* 1. (*cortadura, perfil*) cross-section 2. (*parte*) section 3. (*departamento*) branch

secesión [se·se·'sjon, se·θe-] *f* (*separación*) split; (*fracción de Estado*) secession

seco, -a ['se·ko, -a] *adj* 1. (*sin agua*) dry; **golpe** ~ dull blow; **estar** ~ to be very thirsty; **limpiar en** ~ to dry clean 2. (*desecado*) dried up; **frutos** ~**s** dried fruit and nuts 3. (*río*) dried up 4. (*marchito*) withered 5. (*flaco*) skinny 6. (*cicatriz*) healed 7. (*tajante*) curt 8. (*vino*) dry 9. (*pasmado*) **dejar** ~ **a alguien** to dumbfound sb; (*matar*) to kill sb; **quedarse** ~ to be dumbfounded ▶**a secas** on its own; **en** ~ suddenly; **frenar en** ~ to pull up sharply

secreción [se·kre·'sjon, -'θjon] *f* 1. (*sustancia*) secretion 2. (*el segregar*) segregation

secretaría [se·kre·ta·'ri·a] *f* 1. (*oficina*) secretary's office 2. (*cargo*) secretary position 3. (*gobierno, organismo*) secretariat

secretariado [se·kre·ta·'rja·do] *m* 1. (*oficina*) secretary's office 2. (*cargo*) secretary position 3. (*carrera*) secretary profession 4. (*organismo*) secretariat

secretario, -a [se·kre·'ta·rjo] *m*, *f* (*de oficina, gobierno*) secretary

secretear [se·kre·te·'ar] *vi inf* to exchange secrets

secreto [se·'kre·to] *m* 1. (*misterio*) secret; ~ **profesional** trade secret; ~ **a voces** open secret; **en** ~ in secret; **mantener en** ~ to keep secret; **guardar un** ~ to keep a secret; ~ **de confesión** REL seal of confession 2. (*reserva*) secrecy 3. (*lugar*) secret drawer

secreto, -a [se·'kre·to, -a] *adj* 1. (*oculto*) secret 2. (*callado*) secretive

secta ['sek·ta] *f* (*grupo*) sect

sectario, -a ['sek·ta·rjo, -a] I. *adj* 1. (*de secta*) sectarian 2. (*fanático*) fanatical II. *m*, *f* 1. (*de*

S

una secta) member of a sect **2.** (*fanático*) fanatic

sector [sek·'tor] *m* **1.** *t.* MAT sector; ~ **económico** economic sector; ~ **hotelero** hotel [*o* hospitality] industry; ~ **de la informática** computing sector; ~ **multimedia** multimedia sector; ~ **servicios** service sector **2.** (*grupo*) group

secuela [se·'kwe·la] *f* consequence; ~ (**de una enfermedad**) after-effect (of an illness); **dejar** ~**s** to have after-effects

secuencia [se·'kwen·sja, -θja] *f* **1.** (*serie*) *t.* CINE sequence; ~ **de caracteres** *t.* COMPUT series of characters **2.** (*orden de las palabras*) word order

secuestrador(a) [se·kwes·tra·'dor, -·'do·ra] *m(f)* kidnapper

secuestrar [se·kwes·'trar] *vt* **1.** (*raptar*) to kidnap **2.** (*embargar*) to confiscate

secuestro [se·'kwes·tro] *m* **1.** (*rapto*) kidnapping **2.** (*bienes*) confiscation **3.** (*embargo*) seizure

secular [se·ku·'lar] *adj* secular; *fig* age-old

secundar [se·kun·'dar] *vt* to second

secundario, -a [se·kun·'da·rjo] *adj* (*segundo*) secondary; (*cargo*) minor; **papel** ~ CINE, TEAT supporting role; **esto es** ~ that's of minor importance

sed [sed] *f* **1.** (*falta de agua*) thirst **2.** (*de plantas*) dryness; **tener** ~ to be thirsty **3.** (*afán*) ~ **de algo** longing for sth; ~ **de poder** thirst for power

seda ['se·da] *f* **1.** ZOOL bristle **2.** (*tela, hilo*) silk; **de** ~ **natural** of pure silk; **como una** ~ (*tacto*) as smooth as silk; (*persona*) sweet-tempered; (*sin tropiezos*) smoothly

sedante [se·'dan·te] **I.** *adj* (**de efecto**) ~ soothing **II.** *m* sedative

sedar [se·'dar] *vt* to sedate

sede ['se·de] *f* (*residencia*) seat; (*empresa*) headquarters *pl;* **la Santa Sede** the Holy See

sedentario, -a [se·den·'ta·rjo, -a] *adj* sedentary

sediento, -a [se·'djen·to, -a] *adj* thirsty; ~ **de algo** thirsty for sth; ~ **de poder** eager for power

sedimentación [se·di·men·ta·'sjon, -'θjon] *f* sedimentation

sedimento [se·di·'men·to] *m* sediment, deposit

sedoso, -a [se·'do·so, -a] *adj* silky, silken

seducción [se·duk·'sjon, -duɣ·'θjon] *f* **1.** (*persuasión*) seduction **2.** (*tentación*) fascination

seducir [se·du·'sir, -'θir] *irr como traducir vt* **1.** (*persuadir*) to seduce **2.** (*fascinar*) to charm

seductor(a) [se·duk·'tor, -·'to·ra] **I.** *adj* seductive; **artes** ~**as** wiles; (*idea*) captivating; (*tentador*) tempting **II.** *m(f)* (*que seduce*) seducer; (*que encanta*) charmer

segar [se·'ɣar] *irr como fregar vt* (*cortar*) to reap; (*hierba*) to mow; ~ **algo en flor** *fig* to mow sth down

segmentar [seɣ·men·'tar] *vt* to divide into segments

segmento [seɣ·'men·to] *m* (*parte*) segment; (*motor*) piston rings *pl*

segregar <g→gu> [se·ɣre·'ɣar] *vt* to segregate

seguido, -a [se·'ɣi·do, -a] *adj* **1.** (*continuo*) consecutive; **un año** ~ a whole year **2.** (*en línea recta*) straight; **todo** ~ straight on

seguidor(a) [se·ɣi·'dor] *m(f)* follower, supporter; DEP fan

seguimiento [se·ɣi·'mjen·to] *m* (*persecución*) chase; (*sucesión*) continuation; (*estudio*) follow-up; ~ **médico** medical follow-up

seguir [se·'ɣir] *irr* **I.** *vt* **1.** (*suceder, ser adepto*) to follow **2.** (*perseguir*) to chase **3.** (*acompañar, cursar*) to follow; ~ **un curso de informática** to take a computing course **4.** (*continuar*) ~ **adelante** to carry on; **¡que sigas bien!** I hope you keep well! **II.** *vi* **sigue por esta calle** follow this street **III.** *vr:* ~**se** to ensue

según [se·'ɣun] **I.** *prep* according to; ~ **eso** according to that; ~ **la ley** in accordance with the law; ~ **tus propias palabras/tu sonrisa** judging by your own words/your smile **II.** *adv* **1.** (*como*) as; ~ **lo convenido** as we agreed **2.** (*mientras*) while; **podemos hablar** ~ **vamos andando** we can talk as we walk **3.** (*eventualidad*) ~ (**y como**) it depends; ~ **el trabajo iré o no** I'll go if work permits

segunda [se·'ɣun·da] *f* AUTO second gear; FERRO second class ►**con** ~**s** with veiled meaning

segundo [se·'ɣun·do] *m* (*tiempo*) second

segundo, -a [se·'ɣun·do, -a] **I.** *adj* second; **primo** ~ second cousin; **segunda intención** implied second meaning; **vivir en el** ~ to live on the second floor **II.** *m, f* second (one); *v.t.* **octavo**

seguramente [se·ɣu·ra·'men·te] *adv* **1.** (*de modo seguro*) certainly **2.** (*probablemente*) probably

seguridad [se·ɣu·ri·'dad] *f* **1.** (*protección*) security; **Seguridad Social** ADMIN Social Security; **agente de** ~ security guard **2.** (*certeza*) certainty; **para mayor** ~ to be sure of it **3.** (*firmeza*) confidence; **habla con mucha** ~ he/she speaks with great self-confidence **4.** (*confiabilidad*) trustworthiness

seguro [se·'ɣu·ro] **I.** *m* **1.** (*contrato*) insurance; ~ **médico** medical [*o* health] insurance; ~ **de protección jurídica** legal insurance; ~ **a riesgo parcial** AUTO third-party insurance; ~ **a todo riesgo** AUTO comprehensive insurance **2.** (*mecanismo*) safety device **II.** *adv* for sure; **a buen** [*o* **de**] ~ surely; **sobre** ~ on safe ground; **en** ~ in a safe place; **tener** ~ **algo** to have sth firmly fastened

seguro, -a [se·'ɣu·ro, -a] *adj* **1.** (*exento de peligro*) safe **2.** (*firme*) secure **3.** (*sólido*) solid **4.** (*convencido*) certain; ~ **de sí mismo** confident; **¿estás** ~**?** are you sure?

seis [seis] *adj inv, m* six; *v.t.* **ocho**

seisavo, -a [sei·'sa·βo] *adj* sixth; *v.t.* **octavo**

seiscientos, -as [sei·'sjen·tos, -as; -'θjen·tos, -as] *adj* six hundred; *v.t.* **ochocientos**

seísmo [se·'is·mo] *m* (*temblor*) tremor; (*terremoto*) earthquake

selección [se·lek·'sjon, -ley·'θjon] *f* selection; ~ **nacional** national team; ~ **natural** natural selection

seleccionar [se·lek·sjo·'nar, -ley·θjo·'nar] *vt* to select

selectividad [se·lek·ti·βi·'dad] *f* UNIV *university entrance exam*

i The **selectividad** is a state school exam, which all students wishing to attend a Spanish university must successfully take after having completed the **bachillerato**.

selectivo, -a [se·lek·'ti·βo] *adj* selective; **método** ~ selective criterion

selecto, -a [se·'lek·to, -a] *adj* select; (*ambiente*) exclusive

sellar [se·'jar, -'ʎar] *vt* **1.** (*timbrar*) to stamp **2.** (*dejar huella*) to leave a mark **3.** (*concluir*) to end **4.** (*precintar*) to seal; (*cerrar*) to close; ~ **los labios** to seal one's lips

sello ['se·jo, -ʎo] *m* **1.** (*instrumento, marca*) stamp; ~ **de garantía** mark [*o* seal] of guarantee; ~ **oficial** official stamp **2.** (*correo*) (postage) stamp **3.** (*precinto*) seal; **cerrar con un** ~ to seal **4.** (*distintivo*) stamp, hallmark; **esta película lleva el** ~ **de su director** this film carries the stamp of its director **5.** (*anillo*) signet ring **6.** MED capsule

selva ['sel·βa] *f* (*bosque*) forest; (*tropical*) jungle; ~ **virgen** virgin forest

selvático, -a [sel·'βa·ti·ko, -a] *adj* **1.** (*de la selva*) woodland; (*de jungla*) jungle **2.** (*salvaje*) wild

semáforo [se·'ma·fo·ro] *m* (*de circulación*) traffic lights *pl*

semana [se·'ma·na] *f* week; **Semana Santa** Easter, Holy Week; **fin de** ~ weekend; **durante** ~**s** (**enteras**) for weeks (on end)

semanal [se·ma·'nal] *adj* weekly; **revista** ~ weekly magazine

semanario [se·ma·'na·rjo] *m* weekly (magazine)

semanario, -a [se·ma·'na·rjo, -a] *adj* weekly

semántica [se·'man·ti·ka] *f* LING semantics

semblante [sem·'blan·te] *m* **1.** (*cara*) face **2.** (*expresión*) appearance; **tener un** ~ **alegre** to look cheerful

semblanza [sem·'blan·sa, -θa] *f* **1.** (*parecido*) similarity **2.** (*bosquejo biográfico*) biographical sketch

sembrar <e→ie> [sem·'brar] *vt* **1.** (*plantar*) to sow **2.** (*esparcir*) to scatter; ~ **una calle de flores** to strew a street with flowers; ~ **para el futuro** to sow for the future; ~ **el terror** to spread terror ▶ **quien mal siembra, mal coge** *prov* as you sow, so shall you reap

semejante [se·me·'xan·te] I. *adj* **1.** (*similar*)

similar **2.** (*tal*) such; ~ **persona** such a person II. *m* fellow man

semejanza [se·me·'xan·sa, -θa] *f* **1.** (*similitud*) similarity; (*físico*) resemblance **2.** MED mimesis

semejar [se·me·'xar] I. *vi* to resemble II. *vr:* ~**se** to look alike; ~**se a alguien** to look like sb

semen ['se·men] *m* **1.** (*espermatozoide*) semen **2.** (*semilla*) seed

semental [se·men·'tal] I. *adj* **1.** AGR sowing **2.** ZOOL breeding; **caballo** ~ stud II. *m* stud

sementar <e→ie> [se·men·'tar] *vt* to sow

semestral [se·mes·'tral] *adj* half-yearly

semestre [se·'mes·tre] *m* six-month period; UNIV semester

semiautomático, -a [se·mi·au·to·'ma·ti·ko, -a] *adj* semi-automatic

semicírculo [se·mi·'sir·ku·lo, -'θir·ku·lo] *m* semicircle

semidiós, -osa [se·mi·'djos, -·'djo·sa] *m, f* demigod

semidormido, -a [se·mi·dor·'mi·do, -a] *adj* half-asleep

semifinal [se·mi·fi·'nal] *f* semi-final; **pasar a la** ~ to get through to the semi-final

semilla [se·'mi·ja, -ʎa] *f* seed

semillero [se·mi·'je·ro, -'ʎe·ro] *m* **1.** (*sementera*) seedbed **2.** (*origen*) breeding ground

seminario [se·mi·'na·rjo] *m* **1.** ENS, REL seminary **2.** (*sementera*) seedbed

semioscuridad [se·mi·os·ku·ri·'dad] *f* half-darkness

semiótica [se·'mjo·ti·ka] *f* LING semiotics

semiprecioso, -a [se·mi·pre·'sjo·so, -a; -'θjo·so, -a] *adj* **piedra semipreciosa** semi-precious stone

semiseco, -a [se·mi·'se·ko, -a] *adj* medium-dry

sémola ['se·mo·la] *f* semolina

senado [se·'na·do] *m* senate

senador(a) [se·na·'dor, -·'do·ra] *m(f)* senator

sencillamente [sen·si·ja·'men·te, sen·θi·ʎa-] *adv* simply

sencillez [sen·si·'jes, sen·θi·'ʎeθ] *f* **1.** (*simplicidad*) simplicity **2.** (*naturalidad*) naturalness **3.** (*sinceridad*) sincerity

sencillo, -a [sen·'si·jo, -a; -'θi·ʎo, -a] *adj* **1.** (*simple*) simple; (*fácil*) easy **2.** (*natural*) natural; **gente sencilla** unaffected people **3.** (*sincero*) straightforward

senda ['sen·da] *f*, **sendero** [sen·'de·ro] *m* **1.** (*camino*) path; ~ **del jardín** garden path **2.** (*método*) way

sendos, -as ['sen·dos, -as] *adj* each of two; **llegamos en** ~ **coches** we both arrived by car

senectud [se·nek·'tud] *f* old age

senil [se·'nil] *adj* senile

senilidad [se·ni·li·'dad] *f* (*decrepitud*) senility

seno ['se·no] *m* **1.** (*concavidad*) hollow; **un fregadero de dos** ~**s** a two-basin sink, a double sink **2.** ANAT, MAT sinus; ~ **frontal** frontal sinus **3.** (*matriz*) womb **4.** (*pecho*) breast

S

sensación [sen·sa·'sjon, -'θjon] *f* **1.**(*sentimiento*) feeling **2.**(*novedad*) sensation **3.**(*reacción*) **causar** ~ to cause a sensation

sensacional [sen·sa·sjo·'nal, sen·sa·θjo-] *adj* sensational

sensacionalismo [sen·sa·sjo·na·'lis·mo, sen·sa·θjo-] *m* sensationalism

sensacionalista [sen·sa·sjo·na·'lis·ta, sen·sa·θjo-] *adj* sensationalist; **prensa** ~ gutter [*o* tabloid] press

sensatez [sen·sa·'tes, -'teθ] *f* good sense

sensato, -a [sen·'sa·to, -a] *adj* sensible

sensibilidad [sen·si·βi·li·'dad] *f* sensitivity

sensibilizar <z→c> [sen·si·βi·li·'sar, -'θar] *vt* to sensitize

sensible [sen·'si·βle] *adj* (*sensitivo*) sensitive; (*impresionable*) impressionable; ~ **a los cambios de tiempo** sensitive to changes in the weather; ~ **a la luz** sensitive to light

sensiblemente [sen·si·βle·'men·te] *adv* **1.**(*perceptible*) perceptibly **2.**(*evidente*) markedly

sensitivo, -a [sen·si·'ti·βo, -a] *adj* **1.**(*sensorial*) sensory; **tacto** ~ sense of touch **2.**(*sensible*) sensitive **3.**(*sensual*) sensual

sensor [sen·'sor] *m* sensor

sensorial [sen·so·'rjal] *adj* sensory; **órgano** ~ sense organ

sensual [sen·su·'al] *adj* sensual

sensualidad [sen·swa·li·'dad] *f* sensuality

sentado, -a [sen·'ta·do, -a] **I.** *pp de* **sentar** **II.** *adj* (*sensato*) sensible ▸ **dar algo por** ~ to take sth for granted

sentador(a) [sen·ta·'dor, -'do·ra] *adj Arg, Chile* (*prenda de vestir*) becoming, well-fitting

sentar <e→ie> [sen·'tar] **I.** *vi* (*ropa*) to suit; ~ **bien/mal a alguien** (*comida*) to agree/disagree with sb; ~ **como un tiro** to be as welcome as a hole in the head; **esa chaqueta me siente bien/mal** that jacket suits/doesn't suit me **II.** *vt* to sit; **estar sentado** to be sitting down; **estar bien sentado** *fig* to be well established **III.** *vr:* ~**se 1.**(*asentarse*) to sit down; **¡siéntese!** have a seat! **2.**(*establecerse*) to settle down

sentencia [sen·'ten·sja, -θja] *f* **1.**(*proverbio*) maxim **2.**JUR sentence; **dictar** ~ to pronounce sentence; ~ **de divorcio** decree of divorce

sentenciar [sen·ten·'sja, -θja] *vt* **1.**(*decidir*) ~ **algo** to give one's opinion on [*o* about] sth **2.**(*condenar*) to sentence

sentido [sen·'ti·do] *m* **1.**(*facultad, significado*) sense; ~ **común** common sense; ~ **del deber** sense of duty; ~ **del humor** sense of humor; **doble** ~ (*significado*) double meaning; (*dirección*) two-way; **costar un** ~ to cost the earth; **estar con los cinco** ~**s en el asunto** to be totally absorbed in the subject; **estar sin** ~ to be unconscious; **perder el** ~ to lose consciousness; **sexto** ~ intuition, sixth sense **2.**(*dirección*) direction; **en el** ~ **de la flecha** in the direction of the arrow; **en el** ~ **de las agujas del reloj** clockwise; ~ **único** one-way **3.**(*significado*) meaning

sentido, -a [sen·'ti·do, -a] *adj* **1.**(*conmovido*) deeply felt **2.**(*sensible*) sensitive; **ser muy** ~ to be easily hurt

sentimental [sen·ti·men·'tal] *adj* sentimental

sentimentalismo [sen·ti·men·ta·'lis·mo] *m* sentimentality

sentimiento [sen·ti·'mjen·to] *m* **1.**(*emoción*) feeling; **sin** ~**s** unfeeling **2.**(*pena*) sorrow; **le acompaño en el** ~ please accept my condolences

sentir [sen·'tir] *irr* **I.** *vt* **1.**(*percibir*) to feel; ~ **frío** to feel cold; **sin** ~ without noticing **2.**(*lamentar*) to be sorry for; **lo siento mucho** I am very sorry; **siento que** +*subj* I'm sorry that **II.** *vr:* ~**se 1.**(*estar*) to feel; ~**se bien/mal** to feel good/bad **2.**(*padecer*) ~**se de algo** to suffer from sth **III.** *m* **1.**(*opinión*) opinion; ~ **popular** public opinion; **en mi** ~ in my view **2.**(*sentimiento*) feeling

seña ['se·ɲa] *f* **1.**(*gesto*) sign; **hacer** ~**s** to make signs, to signal; **hablar por** ~**s** to use [*o* talk in] sign language **2.**(*particularidad*) distinguishing mark; **las** ~**s son mortales** the signs are unmistakable

señal [se·'ɲal] *f* **1.**(*particularidad*) distinguishing mark **2.**(*signo*) sign; ~ **de tráfico** road sign; **en** ~ **de** as a sign [*o* token] of; **dar** ~**es de vida** *fig* to show oneself **3.**(*teléfono*) tone; ~ **de comunicar** busy signal **4.**(*huella*) mark; **ni** ~ no trace **5.**(*adelanto*) deposit; **paga y** ~ first payment; **dejar una** ~ to leave a deposit

señalado, -a [se·ɲa·'la·do, -a] *adj* **1.**(*famoso*) distinguished **2.**(*importante*) special

señalar [se·ɲa·'lar] **I.** *vt* **1.**(*anunciar*) to announce **2.**(*marcar*) to mark **3.**(*estigmatizar*) to mark (for life) **4.**(*mostrar*) to show **5.**(*indicar*) to point out **6.**(*fijar*) to fix **II.** *vr* ~**se por algo** to distinguish oneself by sth

señalización [se·ɲa·li·sa·'sjon, -θa·'θjon] *f* signposting

señalizar <z→c> [se·ɲa·li·'sar, -'θar] *vt* to signpost

señor(a) [se·'ɲor, -·'ɲo·ra] **I.** *adj inf* **1.**(*noble*) lordly **2.**(*enorme*) huge **II.** *m(f)* **1.**(*dueño*) owner **2.**(*hombre*) (gentle)man; (*mujer*) wife; (*dama*) lady; ~**a de compañía** companion; **¡**~**as y** ~**es!** ladies and gentlemen! **3.**(*título*) Mister *m*; **el** ~**/la** ~**a García** Mr./Mrs. García; **los** ~**es García** the Garcías; **muy** ~ **mío** Dear Sir; **¡no,** ~**!** absolutely not!; **¡sí,** ~**!** it certainly is! **4.**REL **el Señor** Our Lord; **nuestra Señora** Our Lady; **descansar en el Señor** to rest in peace

señoría [se·ɲo·'ri·a] *f* rule; **Su Señoría** Your Lordship

señori(a)l [se·ɲo·'ril/se·ɲo·'rjal] *adj* lordly; **casa** ~ stately home

señorío [se·ɲo·'ri·o] *m* **1.**(*dominio*) rule **2.**(*territorio*) domain **3.**(*dignidad*) stateliness **4.**(*personas*) gentry

señorita [se·ɲo·'ri·ta] *f* **1.**(*tratamiento*) Miss **2.**(*chica*) young lady

señorito [se‧ɲo‧'ri‧to] *m* young man

señuelo [se‧'nwe‧lo] *m* decoy; *fig* lure

separación [se‧pa‧ra‧'sjon, -'θjon] *f* **1.** (*desunión*) separation **2.** (*espacio*) distance

separado [se‧pa‧'ra‧do] *adv* **por** ~ separately; **contar por** ~ to count one by one

separar [se‧pa‧'rar] **I.** *vt* **1.** (*desunir*) to separate; ~ **algo de algo** to separate sth from sth **2.** (*apartar*) to remove **3.** (*destituir*) to dismiss **II.** *vr:* ~**se** (*personas*) to separate

separo [se‧'pa‧ro] *m Méx* (*celda*) cell

sepelio [se‧'pe‧ljo] *m elev* religious funeral, Christian burial

sepia ['se‧pja] *f* cuttlefish; **de color** ~ sepia

sept. *abr de* **septiembre** September

septentrión [sep‧ten‧'trjon] *m elev* (*norte*) north; (**viento**) ~ north wind

septentrional [sep‧ten‧trjo‧'nal] *adj elev* northern

septiembre [sep‧'tjem‧bre] *m* September; *v.t.* **marzo**

séptimo, -a ['sep‧ti‧mo, -a] *adj, m, f* seventh; *v.t.* **octavo**

sepulcral [se‧pul‧'kral] *adj* sepulchral; **silencio** ~ deathly silence

sepulcro [se‧'pul‧kro] *m* **1.** (*tumba*) tomb; **es un** ~ *fig* he/she can keep a secret **2.** (*relicario*) reliquary

sepultar [se‧pul‧'tar] **I.** *vt* **1.** *t. fig* (*inhumar*) to bury **2.** (*cubrir*) to conceal **II.** *vr:* ~**se** (*sumergir*) to hide away

sepultura [se‧pul‧'tu‧ra] *f* **1.** (*sepelio*) burial **2.** (*tumba*) grave; **dar** ~ **a alguien** to bury sb; **estar cavando su propia** ~ to be digging one's own grave

sequía [se‧'ki‧a] *f* drought

séquito ['se‧ki‧to] *m* retinue

ser [ser] *irr* **I.** *aux* **1.** (*construcción de la pasiva*) **las casas fueron vendidas** the houses were sold; **el triunfo fue celebrado** the triumph was celebrated **2.** (*en frases pasivas*) **era de esperar** it was to be expected; **es de esperar que** +*subj* it is to be hoped that **II.** *vi* **1.** (*absoluto, copulativo, existir, constituir*) to be; **cuatro y cuatro son ocho** four and four make eight; **éramos cuatro** there were four of us; **¿quién es?** (*puerta*) who is it?; (*teléfono*) who's calling?; **soy Pepe** (*a la puerta*) it's me, Pepe; (*al teléfono*) this is Pepe; **es de noche** it's night time; **son las cuatro** it's four o'clock; **el que fue director del teatro** the former theater director **2.** (*tener lugar*) **el examen es mañana** the exam is tomorrow; **el concierto es en el pabellón** the concert is in the pavilion; **eso fue en 2000** that was in 2000 **3.** (*costar*) **¿a cuánto es el pollo?** how much is the chicken?; **¿cuánto es todo?** how much is everything? **4.** (*estar*) **el cine es en la otra calle** the cinema is in the next street **5.** (*convertirse en*) **¿qué quieres ~ de mayor?** what do you want to be when you grow up?; **¿qué es de él?** what's he doing now?; **¿qué ha sido de ella?** whatever happened to her?; **llegó a** ~ **ministro** he became a minister **6.** (*depender*) **todo es que se decida pronto** everything depends on a quick decision **7.** (*con 'de': posesión*) **¿de quién es esto?** whose is this?; **el paquete es de él** the parcel belongs to him; **el anillo es de plata** the ring is made of silver; **el coche es de color azul** the car is blue; ~ **de Escocia** to be from Scotland; ~ **de 2 euros** to cost 2 euros; **es de 30 años** he/she is thirty years old; **lo que ha hecho es muy de ella** that's typical of her; **esta manera de hablar no es de un catedrático** that's no way for a lecturer to talk; **es de lo más guay** it's really great; **eres de lo que no hay** there's nobody like you; **es de un cobarde que no veas** he's a terrible coward **8.** (*con 'para'*) **este estilo no es para ti** that's not your style; **¿para quién es el vino?** who is the wine for?; **la película no es para niños** it's not a film for children; **no es para ponerse así** there's no need to get so angry; **es como para no hablarte más** it's enough to never speak to you again **9.** (*con 'que'*) **esto es que no lo has visto bien** you can't have seen it properly; **es que ahora no puedo** the thing is I can't at the moment; **si es que merece la pena** if it's worthwhile; **¡y es que tenía unas ganas de acabarlo!** I was longing to finish it! **10.** (*oraciones enfáticas, interrogativas*) **¡esto es!** (*así se hace*) that's the way!; (*correcto*) that's right!; **¿pero qué es esto?** what's this then?; **¿cómo es eso?** how is that possible?; **¡como debe** ~**!** that's as it should be!; **¡no puede** ~**!** that can't be!; **¿no puede** ~**?** isn't that possible?; **¡eso es cantar!** that's what I call singing! **11.** (*en futuro*) **¿~á capaz?** will he/she be up to it?; **¡~á capaz!** trust him/her!; **~á lo que sea** we can't change things now **12.** (*en infinitivo*) **manera de** ~ manner; **razón de** ~ raison d'être; **a no** ~ **que** +*subj* unless; **todo puede** ~ everything is possible; **quizá ganemos el campeonato — todo puede** ~ we may yet win the championship — all is not over; **por lo que pueda** ~ just in case **13.** (*en indicativo, condicional*) **es más** what is more; **siendo así** that being so; **y eso es todo** and that's that; ~ **más/menos que alguien** to be better/worse than sb; **es igual** (*no importa*) it doesn't matter; **yo soy de los que piensan que...** I'm one of those who think that...; **de no haber sido por ti** if it hadn't been for you; **con el carisma que tiene sería un buen líder** (*de un partido*) with his charisma he'd be a fine leader **14.** (*en subjuntivo*) **si yo fuera tú** if I were you; **si no fuera por eso...** if it weren't for that...; **si por mí fuera** if it were up to me; **me tratas como si fuera un niño** you treat me like a child; **sea lo que sea** whatever it is; **lo que sea** ~**á** whatever will be will be; **hazlo sea como sea** do it whatever; **sea quien sea** whoever it is; **dos pesos, o sea, 50 céntimos** two pesos, I mean, 50 cents; **el color que quieras, pero que no**

sea rojo any color you like other than red; **cómprame un chupa-chups o lo que sea** buy me a lollipop or something; **por listo que sea...** however clever he is...; **cualquiera que sea el día** whatever day it is **III.** *m* **1.**(*criatura*) being; ~ **vivo** living creature; ~ **humano** human being **2.**(*esencia*) essence **3.** FILOS life

serenar [se·re·'nar] **I.** *vt* (*calmar*) to calm **II.** *vi, vr:* ~ **se** (*calmarse*) to calm down; (*tiempo*) to clear up

serenata [se·re·'na·ta] *f* MÚS serenade

serenidad [se·re·ni·'dad] *f* **1.**(*sosiego*) calmness **2.**(*príncipe*) **Su Serenidad** His Serene Highness

sereno [se·'re·no] *m* **1.**(*humedad*) night dew; **al** ~ out in the open **2.**(*vigilante*) night watchman

sereno, -a [se·'re·no, -a] *adj* **1.**(*sosegado*) calm **2.**(*sin nubes*) clear

serial [se·'rjal] *m* RADIO, TV serial

serie ['se·rje] *f* **1.**(*sucesión*) series *inv;* **asesino en** ~ serial killer; ~ **televisiva** TV series *inv;* **fuera de** ~ out of order; *fig* outstanding, special **2.** *t.* MAT (*gran cantidad*) set; **fabricar en** ~ to mass produce **3.** DEP competition

seriedad [se·rje·'dad] *f* seriousness; **falta de** ~ irresponsibility

serio, -a ['se·rjo, -a] *adj* **1.**(*grave*) serious **2.**(*severo*) solemn **3.**(*formal*) reliable **4.**(*responsable*) trustworthy **5.**(*sin burla*) serious; **esto va en** ~ this is in earnest; **¿en** ~**?** are you serious?

sermón [ser·'mon] *m* sermon; **echar un** ~ **a alguien** to give sb a ticking off, to preach to sb

sermonear [ser·mo·ne·'ar] **I.** *vi* to sermonize **II.** *vt inf* to lecture

seropositivo, -a [se·ro·po·si·'ti·βo, -a] *adj* HIV-positive

serpear [ser·pe·'ar] *vi* to creep

serpentear [ser·pen·te·'ar] *vi* to creep; *fig* to wind

serpentina [ser·pen·'ti·na] *f* (*de papel*) streamer

serpiente [ser·'pjen·te] *f* snake; ~ **de cascabel** rattlesnake; ~ **de vidrio** slow worm; ~ **de verano** *fig* made-up story

serranía [se·rra·'ni·a] *f* mountainous area

serrano, -a [se·'rra·no, -a] *adj* highland; **jamón** ~ cured ham

serrar <e→ie> [se·'rrar] *vt* to saw

serrín [se·'rrin] *m* sawdust

serruchar [se·rru·'tʃar] *vt Arg, Chile, PRico* to saw

serrucho [se·'rru·tʃo] *m* (*sierra*) handsaw

servible [ser·'βi·βle] *adj* serviceable

servicial [ser·βi·'sjal, -'θjal] *adj* obliging

servicio [ser·'βi·sjo, -θjo] *m* **1.**(*acción de servir*) service; ~ **civil sustitutorio** community service; ~ **a domicilio** home delivery; ~ **de información telefónica** telephone answering service; ~ **en línea** online service; ~ **militar** military service; ~ **posventa** after-sales service; **estar de** ~ to be on duty; **hacer un** ~ **a al-**

guien to do sb a service; **hacer un flaco** ~ **a alguien** to do sb more harm than good **2.**(*servidumbre*) (domestic) service; **entrada de** ~ service entrance **3.**(*culto*) service **4.**(*cubierto*) set; ~ **de té** tea set **5.**(*retrete*) lavatory **6.** DEP serve

servidor [ser·βi·'dor] *m* COMPUT server

servidor(a) [ser·βi·'dor, -·'do·ra] *m(f)* (*criado*) servant; **un** ~ yours truly; **¿quién es el último?** — ~ who is the last in the line? — I am

servidumbre [ser·βi·'dum·bre] *f* **1.**(*personal*) servants *pl* **2.**(*esclavitud*) servitude **3.**(*trabajo de siervo*) slave labor **4.**(*sujeción*) compulsion **5.** JUR obligation

servil [ser·'βil] **I.** *adj* servile **II.** *m* crawler

servilismo [ser·βi·'lis·mo] *m* servility

servilleta [ser·βi·'je·ta, -'ʎe·ta] *f* napkin; **doblar la** ~ *fig, inf* to kick the bucket

servir [ser·'βir] *irr como pedir* **I.** *vi* **1.**(*ser útil*) to be of use; **no sirve de nada** it's no use; **no sirve para nada** it's useless [*o* no use at all] **2.**(*ser soldado, criado*) to serve **3.**(*ayudar*) to assist; **¿en qué puedo** ~ **le?** can I help you?; **¡para** ~ **le!** at your service! **4.**(*atender a alguien*) to serve **5.** DEP to serve **6.**(*suministrar*) to supply **7.**(*poner en el plato*) to serve; (*en el vaso*) to pour out **II.** *vr:* ~ **se 1.**(*utilizar*) to make use **2.**(*dignarse*) **sírvase cerrar la ventana** please close the window

sésamo ['se·sa·mo] *m* **1.** BOT sesame **2.** TV **barrio** ~ Sesame Street ▶ **¡ábrete,** ~**!** open sesame!

sesear [se·se·'ar] *vi* to pronounce the Spanish 'c' before 'e' and 'i' and of 'z' in all positions as 's'

sesenta [se·'sen·ta] *adj inv, m* sixty; *v.t.* **ochenta**

seseo [se·'seo] *m* pronunciation of the Spanish 'z' in all occurrences and of 'c' before 'e' and 'i' as 's'

sesera [se·'se·ra] *f inf* **1.**(*cerebro*) brainpan **2.**(*cabeza*) brains *pl;* (*inteligencia*) intelligence

sesgar <g→gu> [ses·'ɣar] *vt* **1.**(*cortar*) to cut down **2.**(*torcer*) to slant **3.** TÉC to bevel **4.**(*estudio*) to bias

sesgo ['ses·ɣo] *m* **1.**(*oblicuidad*) slant; **al** ~ aslant **2.**(*orientación*) direction

sesión [se·'sjon] *f* **1.**(*reunión*) session; ~ **a puerta cerrada** private session; **abrir/levantar la** ~ to open/close [*o* adjourn] the meeting **2.**(*representación*) show(ing); ~ **de tarde** matinee

seso ['se·so] *m* **1.** ANAT brain **2.**(*inteligencia*) brains *pl;* **beber(se) los** ~**s** *fig* to drive (oneself) mad; **calentarse los** ~**s** *inf* to rack one's brains **3.** *pl* CULIN brains *pl* ▶ **tener sorbido el** ~ **a alguien** *inf* to have complete control over sb

set [set] *m* <sets> **1.** DEP set **2.**(*conjunto*) service

seta ['se·ta] *f* mushroom; (*no comestible*)

toadstool; **crecer como ~s** to mushroom
setecientos, -as [se·te·'sjen·tos, -as; se·te·
'θjen-] *adj* seven hundred; *v.t.* **ochocientos**
setenta [se·'ten·ta] *adj inv, m* seventy; *v.t.*
ochenta
setiembre [se·'tjem·bre] *m v.* **septiembre**
seto ['se·to] *m* fence; **~ vivo** hedge
seudónimo [seu·'do·ni·mo] *m* pseudonym;
(*escritor*) pen name
severidad [se·βe·ri·'dad] *f* severity; (*brusquedad*) roughness; (*rigurosidad*) strictness
severo, -a [se·'βe·ro, -a] *adj* harsh; (*brusco*)
rough; (*riguroso*) strict; (*austero*) austere;
(*grave*) serious
sexismo [sek·'sis·mo] *m* sexism, gender bias
sexista [sek·'sis·ta] I. *adj* sexist II. *mf* sexist;
(*machista*) male chauvinist
sexo ['sek·so] *m* 1. (*individuos, actividad*) sex;
~ seguro safe sex 2. (*órganos*) genitals *pl*
sexteto [ses·'te·to] *m* MÚS sextet
sexto, -a ['ses·to, -a] *adj, m, f* sixth; *v.t.* **octavo**
sexual [sek·su·'al] *adj* sexual; **órganos ~es**
sex organs
sexualidad [sek·swa·li·'dad] *f* sexuality
shock [ʃok/tʃok] *m* shock
short *m* shorts *pl*
si [si] I. *conj* 1. (*condicional*) if; **~ acaso** maybe; **~ no** if not, otherwise; **por ~ ...** in case...;
por ~ acaso just in case 2. (*en preguntas indirectas*) whether, if; **¿y si ...?** what if ...? 3. (*en
oraciones concesivas*) **~ bien** although
4. (*comparación*) **como ~... +*subj* as if...; **el
padre está más nervioso que ~ fuera él
mismo a dar a luz** the father is as nervous as
if he were going to give birth himself 5. (*en
frases desiderativas*) **¡~ hiciera un poco más
de calor!** if only it were a little warmer!
6. (*protesta, sorpresa*) but; **¡pero ~ ella se
está riendo!** but she's laughing! 7. (*énfasis*)
fíjate ~ es tonto que... he's so stupid that...
II. *m* MÚS B; **en Si bemol mayor** in B flat major
sí [si] I. *adv* yes; **¡~, señor!** yes sir!; **¡~ que
está buena la tarta!** the cake tastes really
good!; **¡(claro) que ~!** of course!; **creo que ~**
I think so; **¡eso ~ que no!** certainly not!; **por
~ o por no** in any case; **porque ~** (*es así*) because that's the way it is; (*lo digo yo*) because I
say so; **volver en ~** to regain consciousness
II. *pron pers: m sing* himself; *f sing* herself;
cosa, objeto itself; **a ~ mismo** to himself; **de ~**
in itself; **dar de ~** to be extensive; (*tela*) to
give; **el tema da mucho de ~** it's a wide subject; **en** [*o* **de por**] **~** separately; **estar fuera
de ~** to be beside oneself; **hablar entre ~** to
talk among themselves; **por ~** in itself; **mirar
por ~** to be selfish III. *m* consent; **dar el ~** to
agree; (*casamiento*) to accept the proposal;
tener el ~ de la madre to have the mother's
consent; **no hay entre ellos ni un ~ ni un no**
they get on extremely well
siamés, -esa [sja·'mes, -·'me·sa] *adj* Siamese;
gato ~ Siamese cat; **hermanos siameses** Sia-

mese twins
Sicilia [si·'si·lja, si·'θi-] *f* Sicily
siciliano, -a [si·si·'lja·no, -a; si·θi-] *adj, m, f* Sicilian
sicología [si·ko·lo·'xi·a] *f v.* (**p**)**sicología**
sida ['si·da], **SIDA** ['si·da] *m abr de* **síndrome
de inmunodeficiencia adquirida** AIDS
siderurgia [si·de·'rur·xja] *f* iron and steel industry
sidoso, -a [si·'do·so, -a] I. *adj* AIDS; **enfermo
~** AIDS sufferer II. *m, f* AIDS sufferer
sidra ['si·dra] *f* cider
siega ['sje·ɣa] *f* 1. (*el segar*) reaping
2. (*tiempo*) harvest time 3. (*mieses*) cornfields *pl*
siembra ['sjem·bra] *f* 1. (*el sembrar*) sowing
2. (*tiempo*) sowing time 3. (*terreno*) sown
field
siempre ['sjem·pre] *adv* always; **de ~** always;
a la hora de ~ at the usual time; **una amistad
de ~** a lifelong friendship; **~ pasa lo mismo**
the same thing always happens; **¡hasta ~!** see
you!; **por ~** for ever; **por ~ jamás** for ever and
ever; **~ que** +*subj* provided that, as long as
sien [sjen] *f* ANAT temple
sierra ['sje·rra] *f* 1. (*herramienta*) saw; **~ continua** chainsaw; **~ mecánica** power saw
2. (*lugar*) sawmill 3. GEO mountain range; **~ de
peñascos cortados** ridge
siervo, -a ['sjer·βo, -a] *m, f* 1. (*esclavo*) slave;
~ de la gleba serf 2. (*servidor*) servant
siesta ['sjes·ta] *f* 1. (*descanso*) siesta; **echar** [*o*
dormir] **la ~** to have a nap 2. (*hora de calor*)
hottest part of the day
siete ['sje·te] I. *adj inv* seven II. *m* 1. (*número*)
seven; *v.t.* **ocho** 2. *inf* (*rasgón*) rent 3. (*carpintería*) G-clamp 4. *AmS, Méx, vulg* (*ano*) ass
sietemesino, -a [sje·te·me·'si·no, -a] I. *adj*
niño ~ baby born 2 months premature II. *m, f*
(*prematuro*) baby born 2 months premature
sífilis ['si·fi·lis] *f* syphilis
sifón [si·'fon] *m* 1. TÉC (*tubo, tubería*) trap
2. (*botella*) siphon 3. (*soda*) club soda
siga ['si·ɣa] *f* Chile chase
sigilar [si·xi·'lar] *vt* (*ocultar*) to conceal
sigilo [si·'xi·lo] *m* 1. (*discreción*) discretion; **~ profesional** client confidentiality
2. (*secreto*) stealth; **~ sacramental** secrecy of
the confessional, seal of confession
sigla ['si·ɣla] *f* 1. (*letra inicial*) initial 2. (*rótulo
de siglas*) acronym; **~ de fabricante** manufacturer's mark
siglo ['si·ɣlo] *m* century; **Siglo de las Luces**
Age of Enlightenment; **el ~ XXI** the 21st century; **el Siglo de Oro** the Golden Age; **por los
~s de los ~s** for ever and ever; **hace un ~
que no te veo** I haven't seen you for ages;
retirarse del ~ to withdraw from the world
signar [siɣ·'nar] I. *vt* 1. (*marcar*) to put one's
mark on 2. (*firmar*) to sign 3. REL to make the
sign of the cross over II. *vr:* **~se** to cross oneself
signatario, -a [siɣ·na·'ta·rjo] I. *adj* signatory;

poder ~ JUR power of attorney **II.** *m, f* signatory

signatura [siɣ·na·'tu·ra] *f* **1.** (*firma*) *t.* TIPO signature **2.** (*en biblioteca*) catalog number

significación [siɣ·ni·fi·ka·'sjon, -'θjon] *f* **1.** (*importancia*) significance **2.** (*sentido*) meaning

significado [siɣ·ni·fi·'ka·do] *m* meaning

significar <c→qu> [siɣ·ni·fi·'kar] **I.** *vi, vt* to mean; **¿qué significa eso?** what's the meaning of this? **II.** *vr* ~**se por algo** to become known for sth

signo ['siɣ·no] *m* **1.** *t.* LING, MAT (*señal*) sign; ~ **de enfermedad** sign of illness; ~ **de más/menos** plus/minus sign; ~ **de la multiplicación** multiplication sign; ~ **de puntuación** punctuation mark **2.** (*escrito*) mark **3.** (*destino*) fate

siguiente [si·'ɣjen·te] **I.** *adj* following; **de la** ~ **manera** in the following way **II.** *mf* next; **¡el** ~**!** next please!

sílaba ['si·la·βa] *f* syllable; ~ **aguda** stressed syllable; **de dos** ~ **s** two-syllable

silbar [sil·'βar] *vi, vt* **1.** (*persona*) to whistle; (*serpiente*) to hiss; (*sirena*) to blow; (*una flecha, bala*) to whiz(z) **2.** (*abuchear*) to boo

silbato [sil·'βa·to] *m* whistle

silbido [sil·'βi·do] *m* whistle; (*serpiente*) hiss; (*sirena*) blast; (*viento*) whistling; ~ **de los oídos** ringing in the ears

silenciador [si·len·sja·'dor, si·len·θja-] *m* silencer

silenciar [si·len·'sjar, -'θjar] *vt* **1.** (*suceso*) to hush up **2.** (*persona*) to silence

silencio [si·'len·sjo, -θjo] *m* **1.** silence; **en** ~ in silence; **guardar** ~ to remain silent; **guardar** ~ **sobre algo** to keep silent about sth; **imponer** ~ to impose silence; **pasar algo en** ~ to pass over sth in silence; **romper el** ~ to break the silence; **¡~!** quiet! **2.** MÚS rest

silencioso, -a [si·len·'sjo·so, -a; -'θjo·so, -a] **I.** *adj* **1.** (*poco hablador*) quiet **2.** (*callado*) silent **3.** (*sin ruido*) soundless; (*motor*) noiseless **II.** *m, f* silencer

silicona [si·li·'ko·na] *f* silicone

silla ['si·ja, -ʎa] *f* **1.** *t.* REL (*asiento*) chair; ~ **de manos** litter; ~ **de lona** deckchair; ~ **giratoria** swivel chair; ~ **plegable** folding chair; ~ **de ruedas** wheelchair **2.** (*montura*) saddle

sillón [si·'jon, -'ʎon] *m* (*butaca*) armchair

silueta [si·'lwe·ta] *f* silhouette; **cuidar la** ~ to look after one's figure; **la** ~ **de Nueva York** the New York skyline

silvestre [sil·'βes·tre] *adj* wild

sima ['si·ma] *f* GEO abyss

simbólico, -a [sim·'bo·li·ko, -a] *adj* symbolic

simbolismo [sim·bo·'lis·mo] *m* symbolism

simbolizar <z→c> [sim·bo·li·'sar, -'θar] *vt* to symbolize

símbolo ['sim·bo·lo] *m* symbol; ~ **de prestigio** status symbol

simetría [si·me·'tri·a] *f* symmetry

simétrico, -a [si·'me·tri·ko, -a] *adj* symmetri-

cal

símil ['si·mil] **I.** *adj* similar **II.** *m* simile

similar [si·mi·'lar] *adj* similar

similitud [si·mi·li·'tud] *f* similarity; (*física*) resemblance

simio ['si·mjo] *m* ape

simpatía [sim·pa·'ti·a] *f* **1.** (*agrado*) liking; **sentir** ~ **por algo** to be attracted to sth; **tener** ~ **por alguien** to have a liking for sb **2.** (*carácter*) friendliness

simpático, -a [sim·'pa·ti·ko] *adj* friendly; **hacerse el** ~ to ingratiate oneself

simpatizar <z→c> [sim·pa·ti·'sar, -'θar] *vi* **1.** (*congeniar*) to get along (with sb) **2.** (*identificarse con*) to sympathize

simple <simplísimo> ['sim·ple] **I.** *adj* **1.** (*sencillo*) simple **2.** (*fácil*) easy, straightforward **3.** (*mero*) pure; **a** ~ **vista** with the naked eye **4.** (*mentecato*) simple **II.** *m* **1.** (*persona*) simpleton **2.** (*tenis*) singles *inv*

simpleza [sim·'ple·sa, -θa] *f* **1.** (*tontería*) silliness **2.** (*insignificancia*) trifle

simplicidad [sim·pli·si·'dad, sim·pli·θi-] *f* **1.** (*sencillez*) simplicity **2.** (*ingenuidad*) plainness

simplificar <c→qu> [sim·pli·fi·'kar] *vt* **1.** (*facilitar*) to simplify **2.** MAT to break down

simposio [sim·'po·sjo] *m* symposium

simulación [si·mu·la·'sjon, -'θjon] *f* simulation; (*fingir*) feigning

simulacro [si·mu·'la·kro] *m* **1.** (*apariencia*) simulacrum; ~ **de incendio** fire drill **2.** (*acción simulada*) sham

simulador [si·mu·la·'dor] *m* TÉC simulator; ~ **de vuelo** flight simulator

simulador(a) [si·mu·la·'dor, -·'do·ra] *m(f)* faker

simular [si·mu·'lar] *vt* to simulate

simultaneidad [si·mul·ta·nei·'dad] *f* simultaneity

simultáneo, -a [si·mul·'ta·neo, -a] *adj* simultaneous; **interpretación simultánea** simultaneous interpreting

sin [sin] *prep* without; ~ **dormir** without sleep; ~ **querer** unintentionally; ~ **más** nothing more; ~ **más ni más** without thinking about it, without further ado; **estar** ~ **algo** to be out of sth

sinagoga [si·na·'ɣo·ɣa] *f* REL synagogue

sincerarse [sin·se·'rar·se, sin·θe-] *vr* (*exculparse*) ~ **ante alguien** to justify oneself to sb; (*abrirse*) to be completely honest with sb

sinceridad [sin·se·ri·'dad, sin·θe-] *f* sincerity; **con toda** ~ in all sincerity

sincero, -a [sin·'se·ro, -a; sin·'θe-] *adj* sincere; **seré** ~ **contigo** I'll be honest with you

sincrónico, -a [sin·'kro·ni·ko, -a] *adj* synchronous

sincronizar <z→c> [sin·kro·ni·'sar, -'θar] *vt* to synchronize

sindical [sin·di·'kal] *adj* union

sindicalismo [sin·di·ka·'lis·mo] *m* **1.** (*movimiento*) trade unionism **2.** (*doctrina*) syndicalism

sindicalista [sin·di·ka·'lis·ta] I. *adj* (*sindical*) union II. *mf* (*miembro*) trade unionist

sindicar <c→qu> [sin·di·'kar] I. *vt* 1.(*obreros*) to unionize 2.(*delatar*) to betray 3.(*poner bajo sospecha*) to place under suspicion II. *vr:* ~ **se** to join a union

sindicato [sin·di·'ka·to] *m* labor union

síndrome ['sin·dro·me] *m* syndrome; ~ **de abstinencia** withdrawal symptoms; ~ **de burnout** [*o* **del trabajador quemado**] burnout syndrome; ~ **de Estocolmo** Stockholm syndrome

sinfonía [sin·fo·'ni·a] *f* symphony

sinfónico, -a [sin·'fo·ni·ko, -a] *adj* symphonic; **orquesta sinfónica** symphony orchestra

singular [sin·gu·'lar] I. *adj* 1.(*único*) singular; **ejemplar** ~ unique example 2.(*excepcional*) outstanding; **en** ~ in the singular; *fig* in particular 3.(*extraño*) peculiar II. *m* LING singular; **¡habla en** ~! *fig* speak for yourself!

singularidad [sin·gu·la·ri·'dad] *f* 1.(*unicidad*) singularity 2.(*excepcionalidad*) exceptional nature 3.(*distinción*) peculiarity

singularmente [sin·gu·lar·'men·te] *adv* especially

siniestro [si·'njes·tro] *m* (*accidente*) accident; (*catástrofe*) natural disaster; (*incendio*) fire

siniestro, -a [si·'njes·tro, -a] *adj elev* 1.(*maligno*) evil; **un personaje** ~ a sinister character 2.(*funesto*) disastrous 3.(*izquierdo*) left; **a diestra y siniestra** right and left

sinnúmero [sin·'nu·me·ro] *m* huge number

sino ['si·no] I. *m* fate II. *conj* 1.(*al contrario*) but 2.(*solamente*) **no espero** ~ **que me creas** I only hope that you believe me 3.(*excepto*) except

sinónimo [si·'no·ni·mo] *m* synonym

sinónimo, -a [si·'no·ni·mo, -a] *adj* synonymous

sinopsis [si·'noβ·sis] *f inv* 1.(*resumen*) synopsis 2.(*esquema*) diagram

sinóptico, -a [si·'nop·ti·ko, -a] *adj* 1.(*resumido*) synoptic 2.(*esquemático*) diagrammatic

sinrazón [sin·rra·'son, -'θon] *f* injustice; (*absurdo*) unreasonableness

sinsentido [sin·sen·'ti·do] *m* absurdity

sinsonte [sin·'son·te] *m AmL* ZOOL mockingbird

sintáctico, -a [sin·'tak·ti·ko, -a] *adj* syntactic

sintaxis [sin·'tak·sis] *f inv* syntax

síntesis ['sin·te·sis] *f inv* synthesis; **en** ~ in a word

sintético, -a [sin·'te·ti·ko, -a] *adj* synthetic

sintetizador [sin·te·ti·sa·'dor, sin·te·ti·θa-] *m* MÚS synthesizer

sintetizar <z→c> [sin·te·ti·'sar, -'θar] *vt* 1.QUÍM to synthesize 2.(*resumir*) to summarize

síntoma ['sin·to·ma] *m* symptom

sintomático, -a [sin·to·'ma·ti·ko, -a] *adj* symptomatic

sintonía [sin·to·'ni·a] *f* 1.(*adecuación*) tuning 2.(*señal sonora, melodía*) signature tune 3.(*entendimiento*) **estar en** ~ (**con alguien**) to be on the same wavelength (as sb)

sintonizar <z→c> [sin·to·ni·'sar, -'θar] I. *vt* to tune in to; ~ **una emisora** to pick up a radio station II. *vi* to tune in

sinuosidad [si·nwo·si·'dad] *f* 1.(*curvación*) sinuosity 2.(*concavidad*) curve

sinuoso, -a [si·nu·'o·so, -a] *adj* 1.(*curvado*) winding 2.(*retorcido*) devious

sinvergüenza [sim·ber·'ɣwen·sa, -θa] *pey* I. *adj* shameless II. *mf* lowlife

síquico, -a ['si·ki·ko, -a] *adj v.* (p)**síquico**

siquiera [si·'kje·ra] I. *adv* at least; **ni** ~ not even II. *conj* + *subj* even if

sirena [si·'re·na] *f* 1.(*bocina*) siren 2.(*mujer pez*) mermaid

sirope [si·'ro·pe] *m AmC, Col* (*jarabe*) syrup

sirviente [sir·'βjen·te] *mf* (*criado*) servant

sisa ['si·sa] *f* 1.(*corte*) armhole 2.(*dinero*) petty theft

sisar [si·'sar] *vt* 1.(*cortar una sisa*) to take in 2.(*hurtar*) to pilfer

sisirisco [si·si·'ris·ko] *m Méx* 1.(*ano*) anus 2.(*miedo*) fright

sísmico, -a ['sis·mi·ko, -a] *adj* seismic; **movimiento** ~ earth tremor

sismo ['sis·mo] *m* (*temblor*) tremor; (*terremoto*) earthquake

sistema [sis·'te·ma] *m* system; ~ **antibloqueo de frenos** AUTO antilock brake system; ~ **inmunitario** immune system; ~ **montañoso** mountain range; ~ **operativo** COMPUT operating system; ~ **periódico** QUÍM periodic table; ~ **planetario** ASTR solar system

sistemático, -a [sis·te·'ma·ti·ko, -a] *adj* systematic

sistematizar <z→c> [sis·te·ma·ti·'sar, -'θar] *vt* to systematize

sitio ['si·tjo] *m* 1.(*lugar*) place; (*espacio*) room; ~ **de veraneo** holiday resort; **en cualquier** ~ anywhere; **en ningún** ~ nowhere; **en todos los** ~**s** everywhere; **guardar el** ~ **a alguien** to keep sb's place; **hacer** ~ to make room; **ocupar mucho** ~ to take up a lot of room; **poner a alguien en su** ~ *fig* to put sb in his/her place 2.MIL siege 3.*Méx* ~ (**de taxis**) taxi stand

sito, -a ['si·to, -a] *adj* ~ **en** situated in

situación [si·twa·'sjon, -'θjon] *f* 1.(*ubicación*) location 2.(*estado*) situation; **estar en** ~ **desahogada** to be comfortably off

situado, -a [si·tu·'a·do, -a] *adj* situated; **estar** ~ to be financially secure; **estar bien** ~ (*trabajo*) to have a good job

situar < *1. pres:* situó> [si·tu·'ar] I. *vt* (*colocar*) to place; (*emplazar*) to locate II. *vr:* ~ **se** 1.(*ponerse en un lugar*) to situate oneself 2.(*abrirse paso*) to make one's way

siútico, -a [si·'u·ti·ko, -a] *adj Chile, inf* 1.(*de mal gusto*) vulgar 2.(*de nuevo rico*) affected

S.M. [e·se·'e·me] *mf abr de* **Su Majestad** H.M.

SME [e·se·me·'e] *m abr de* **Sistema Monetario Europeo** EMS
smog [es·'moy] *m* smog
s/n *abr de* **sin número** no street number
snorkeling [es·'nor·ke·lin] *m* snorkeling *no pl;* **practicar ~** to snorkel
so [so] **I.** *interj* whoa! **II.** *prep* under; **~ pena de...** on pain of...; **~ pretexto de que...** under the pretext of... **III.** *m inf* **¡~ imbécil!** you idiot!
SO [su·do·'es·te] *abr de* **sudoeste** SW
soba ['so·βa] *f inf* **1.** (*a persona*) pawing, feeling up **2.** (*de un objeto*) handling, fingering **3.** (*zurra*) beating
sobaco [so·'βa·ko] *m* armpit
sobado, -a [so·'βa·do, -a] *adj* **1.** (*objetos*) worn **2.** (*papel*) dog-eared **3.** (*tema*) well worn
sobajar [so·βa·'xar] *vt* **1.** (*manosear con fuerza*) to paw **2.** *Méx* (*humillar*) to humiliate
sobandero [so·βan·'de·ro] *m Col* bonesetter
sobar [so·'βar] **I.** *vt* **1.** *inf* (*a persona*) to paw, to feel up **2.** (*un objeto*) to handle, to finger **3.** (*ablandar*) to knead **4.** (*pegar*) to wallop **5.** (*molestar*) to pester **II.** *vi inf* (*dormir*) to sleep
soberanamente [so·βe·ra·na·'men·te] *adv* (*extremadamente*) supremely; **divertirse ~** to have a whale of a time
soberanía [so·βe·ra·'ni·a] *f* sovereignty
soberano, -a [so·βe·'ra·no, -a] **I.** *adj* **1.** POL sovereign **2.** (*excelente*) supreme **II.** *m, f* (*monarca*) sovereign
soberbia [so·'βer·βja] *f* **1.** (*orgullo*) pride **2.** (*suntuosidad*) magnificence **3.** (*ira*) anger
soberbio, -a [so·'βer·βjo, -a] *adj* **1.** (*orgulloso*) proud **2.** (*suntuoso*) magnificent
sobornar [so·βor·'nar] *vt* to bribe
soborno [so·'βor·no] *m* **1.** (*acción*) bribery **2.** (*dinero, objeto*) bribe
sobra ['so·βra] *f* **1.** (*exceso*) surplus; **de ~** (*en abundancia*) more than enough; (*inútilmente*) in the way; **saber algo de ~** to know sth only too well **2.** *pl* (*desperdicios*) leftovers *pl;* (*restos*) remnants *pl*
sobrador(a) [so·βra·'dor, -'do·ra] *m(f) Arg, Urug* conceited person
sobrante [so·'βran·te] **I.** *adj* **1.** (*que sobra*) spare; COM, FIN surplus **2.** (*de más*) excess **II.** *m* (*que sobra*) remainder; (*superávit*) surplus; (*saldo*) balance in hand
sobrar [so·'βrar] *vi* **1.** (*quedar*) to remain; **nos sobra bastante tiempo** we have plenty of time **2.** (*abundar*) to be more than enough; **me sobran cinco kilos** I've got five kilos left over; (*perder peso*) I've got to lose five kilos; **aquí sobran las palabras** nothing more needs to be said **3.** (*estar de más*) to be superfluous; **creo que sobras aquí** I think you're in the way [o not needed] here
sobre ['so·βre] **I.** *m* **1.** (*para una carta*) envelope; **~ monedero** special delivery envelope; **un ~ de levadura** a packet of yeast **2.** *inf* (*cama*) bed; **irse al ~** to go off to bed

II. *prep* **1.** (*por encima de*) on; **deja el periódico ~ la mesa** leave the newspaper on the table; **marchar ~ la ciudad** to march on the town; **estar ~ alguien** to keep constant watch on sb **2.** (*cantidad aproximada*) **pesar ~ los cien kilos** to weigh about a hundred kilos **3.** (*aproximación temporal*) **llegar ~ las tres** to arrive at about three o'clock **4.** (*tema, asunto*) about; **~ ello** about it **5.** (*reiteración*) on top of; **le caía lágrima ~ lágrima** he/she shed tear after tear **6.** (*además de*) as well as **7.** (*superioridad*) **el boxeador triunfó ~ su adversario** the boxer triumphed over his opponent; **destacar ~ alguien por su estatura** to tower over sb **8.** (*porcentajes*) out of; **tres ~ cien** three out of a hundred **9.** FIN **un préstamo ~ una casa** a loan on a house
sobreabundancia [so·βre·a·βun·'dan·sja, -θja] *f* superabundance, overabundance
sobrealimentación [so·βre·a·li·men·ta·'sjon, -'θjon] *f* overfeeding
sobrecarga [so·βre·'kar·ya] *f* excess; (*persona*) added burden; ELEC overload; COM surcharge
sobrecargar [so·βre·'kar·yar] **I.** *vt* (*por peso*) to overload; (*por esfuerzo*) to overburden **II.** *vr:* **~se** to overload oneself; **~se de trabajo** to take on too much work
sobrecoger [so·βre·'ko·xer] **I.** *vt* **1.** (*sorprender*) to take by surprise **2.** (*espantar*) to frighten **II.** *vr:* **~se 1.** (*asustarse*) to be startled **2.** (*sorprenderse*) **~se de algo** to be surprised by sth
sobredosis [so·βre·'do·sis] *f inv* overdose
sobreentender [so·βre·en·ten·'der] <e→ie> **I.** *vt* **1.** (*adivinar*) to infer; **de todo ello sobreentendemos que...** we understand from all this that... **2.** (*presuponer*) to presuppose **II.** *vr:* **~se** (*ser evidente*) to be obvious; **aquí queda sobreentendido que...** (*implicado*) it is implied here that...
sobreestimar [so·βre·es·ti·'mar] *vt* to overestimate
sobrehumano, -a [so·βre·u·'ma·no, -a] *adj* superhuman
sobrellevar [so·βre·je·'βar, -ʎe·'βar] *vt* **1.** (*aguantar*) to bear; **~ mal** to take badly; **~ bien** to take well **2.** (*peso*) **~ algo a alguien** to help sb with sth
sobremanera [so·βre·ma·'ne·ra] *adv* exceedingly
sobremesa [so·βre·'me·sa] *f* **1.** (*mantel*) table cover **2.** (*postre*) dessert **3.** (*tras la comida*) **de ~** after-dinner; COMPUT desktop; **conversación de ~** table talk; **programa de ~** TV afternoon program; **estar de ~** to be gathered after a meal
sobrenatural [so·βre·na·tu·'ral] *adj* **1.** (*fenómenos*) supernatural; **ciencias ~es** occult sciences; **la vida ~** life after death **2.** (*extraordinario*) incredible
sobrenombre [so·βre·'nom·bre] *m* **1.** (*calificativo*) epithet **2.** (*apodo*) nickname

sobrentender <e→ie> [so·βren·ten·'der/so· βre·en·ten·'der] *vt, vr v.* **sobreentender**

sobrepasar [so·βre·pa·'sar] *vt* **1.** (*en cantidad*) to surpass; (*límite*) to exceed; ~ **su ámbito de responsabilidades** to go beyond one's powers **2.** (*aventajar*) to pass; (*un récord, el mejor*) to beat

sobreponer [so·βre·po·'ner] *irr como poner* **I.** *vt* **1.** (*encima de algo*) to superimpose, to put on top; (*cubierta, funda*) cover **2.** (*en consideración, rango*) ~ **a algo/alguien** to place above sth/sb; (*anteponer*) to prefer to sth/sb; ~ **a alguien a todos los demás** to put sb before everyone else **II.** *vr:* ~**se 1.** (*calmarse*) to pull oneself together **2.** (*al enemigo, a una enfermedad*) to overcome; (*al miedo, a un susto*) to recover from

sobreprecio [so·βre·'pre·sjo, -·θjo] *m* surcharge

sobresaliente [so·βre·sa·'ljen·te] **I.** *adj* **1.** (*excelente*) outstanding **2.** ENS (*en títulos superiores*) first class; (*nota: nine or better on a scale of one to ten*) excellent **II.** *m* ENS (*nota*) distinction

sobresalir [so·βre·sa·'lir] *irr como salir vi* **1.** *t.* ARQUIT (*por tamaño, estatura*) ~ **de algo** to stand out from sth **2.** (*distinguirse*) to stand out **3.** (*ser excelente*) ~ **en algo** to be outstanding at sth

sobresaltar [so·βre·sal·'tar] **I.** *vi* to start **II.** *vt* to startle **III.** *vr* ~**se con** [*o de*] **algo** to be startled at sth

sobresalto [so·βre·'sal·to] *m* **1.** (*susto*) scare **2.** (*turbación*) sudden shock; **con** ~ shocked; **de** ~ suddenly

sobreseimiento [so·βre·sei·'mjen·to] *m* JUR stay of proceedings; (*aplazamiento*) discontinuance

sobrestimar [so·βres·ti·'mar] *vt* to overestimate

sobresueldo [so·βre·'swel·do] *m* extra pay [*o* wage]

sobretasa [so·βre·'ta·sa] *f* (*suplemento*) surcharge; ~ **por retraso** surcharge for delayed payment

sobretodo [so·βre·'to·do] *m* (*abrigo*) overcoat; (*mono*) overall

sobrevenir [so·βre·βe·'nir] *irr como venir vi* (*epidemia*) to ensue; (*desgracia, guerra*) to happen unexpectedly; (*tormenta*) to break; **le sobrevino una sensación de gran tristeza** a feeling of deep sadness took [*o* came over] him/her

sobrevida [soβ·re·'βida] *f* MED survival time

sobreviviente [so·βre·βi·'βjen·te] *mf* survivor

sobrevivir [so·βre·βi·'βir] *vi* (*acontecimientos*) to survive; (*a alguien*) to outlive; **pero ella sigue sobreviviendo en mi recuerdo** but she lives on in my memory

sobrevolar <o→ue> [so·βre·βo·'lar] *vt* to fly over

sobriedad [so·βrje·'dad] *f* **1.** (*sin beber*) soberness **2.** (*moderación*) moderation **3.** (*pru-*

dencia) restraint **4.** (*estilo*) plainness

sobrino, -a [so·'βri·no, -a] *m, f* nephew *m*, niece *f*

sobrinonieto, -a [so·βri·no·'nje·to, -a] *m, f* great-nephew *m*, great-niece *f*

sobrio, -a ['so·βrjo, -a] *adj* **1.** (*no borracho*) sober **2.** (*moderado*) moderate **3.** (*prudente*) restrained; ~ **de palabras** of few words **4.** (*estilo*) plain

soca ['so·ka] *f AmL* AGR ratoon

socar <c→qu> [so·'kar] **I.** *vt AmC* to compress **II.** *vr:* ~**se** *AmC* to get drunk

socavar [so·ka·'βar] *vt* to dig under; *fig* to undermine

sociable [so·'sja·βle, so·'θja-] *adj* **1.** (*tratable*) sociable; (*que no discute*) easy-going **2.** (*afable*) friendly

social [so·'sjal, -'θjal] *adj* **1.** (*relativo a la sociedad*) society; (*a la convivencia*) social **2.** (*por parte del estado*) **asistencia** ~ social work; **asistente** ~ social worker; **Estado Social** Welfare State **3.** JUR, ECON company, corporate; **razón** ~ company name

socialdemócrata [so·sjal·de·'mo·kra·ta, so· θjal-] **I.** *adj* social-democratic **II.** *mf* social democrat

socialismo [so·sja·'lis·mo, so·θja-] *m* socialism

socialista [so·sja·'lis·ta, so·θja-] *adj, mf* socialist

socializar <z→c> [so·sja·li·'sar, -θja·li·'θar] *vt* to socialize

sociedad [so·sje·'dad, so·θje-] *f* **1.** (*población, humanidad*) society; ~ **del bienestar** welfare society [*o* state] **2.** (*trato*) company; **la** ~ **con la que tratas** the company you keep **3.** (*empresa*) company; ~ **anónima** corporation **4.** (*asociación*) association; ~ **protectora** (**de animales**) society for the prevention of cruelty to animals **5.** JUR ~ **conyugal** property held jointly by spouses **6.** (*mundo elegante*) society; **la buena** [*o* **alta**] ~ high society

socio, -a ['so·sjo, -a; -θjo, -a] *m, f* **1.** (*de una asociación*) member **2.** (*en sociedad comercial*) partner; ~ **comercial** business partner

socioeconómico, -a [so·sjo·e·ko·'no·mi·ko, -a; so·θjo-] *adj* socioeconomic

sociología [so·sjo·lo·'xi·a, so·θjo-] *f* sociology

sociólogo, -a [so·'sjo·lo·γo, -a; so·'θjo-] *m, f* sociologist

sociopolítico, -a [so·sjo·po·'li·ti·ko, -a; so· θjo-] *adj* sociopolitical

socolar [so·ko·'lar] *vt Col, Ecua, Hond, Nic* to clear land

socollón [so·ko·'jon, -'ʎon] *m AmC, Cuba* jolt

socorrer [so·ko·'rrer] *vt* to help, to come to the aid of

socorrido, -a [so·ko·'rri·do, -a] *adj* **1.** (*útil*) useful **2.** (*que ayuda*) helpful **3.** (*comprobado*) tried and tested **4.** (*común*) ordinary

socorrista [so·ko·'rris·ta] *mf* (*de playas*) lifeguard; (*en piscinas*) pool attendant

socorro [so·'ko·rro] *m* **1.** (*ayuda*) help; (*salva-*

S

mento) rescue; **pedir** ~ to ask for help; **puesto de** ~ first-aid post; **señal de** ~ distress signal, SOS **2.** (*dinero*) money towards sth

socoyote [so·ko·'jo·te] *m Méx* (*benjamín*) youngest child

soda ['so·da] *f* (*bebida*) soda water

sodio ['so·djo] *m* sodium

sofá <sofás> [so·'fa] *m* sofa

sofá-cama <sofás-cama> [so·'fa-'ka·ma] *m* sofa-bed

sofisticado, -a [so·fis·ti·'ka·do, -a] *adj* **1.** (*afectado*) affected **2.** TÉC sophisticated

sofocado, -a [so·fo·'ka·do, -a] *adj* **estar** ~ to be stifled

sofocante [so·fo·'kan·te] *adj* **1.** (*asfixiante*) stifling; (*ambiente, aire*) suffocating; **hace un calor** ~ the heat is stifling **2.** (*avergonzante*) shameless

sofocar <c→qu> [so·fo·'kar] I. *vt* **1.** (*asfixiar*) to suffocate **2.** (*impedir que progrese*) to stifle; (*fuego*) to put out; (*revolución*) to crush; (*epidemia*) to stop **3.** (*avergonzar*) to embarrass **4.** (*enojar*) to upset II. *vr:* ~**se 1.** (*sonrojar*) to blush **2.** (*excitarse*) to get worked up; (*enojarse*) to get angry **3.** (*ahogarse*) to suffocate

sofoco [so·'fo·ko] *m* **1.** (*ahogo*) suffocation; (*después de un esfuerzo*) panting **2.** (*excitación*) shock **3.** (*calor*) heat flush

soga ['so·ɣa] *f* rope; (*para ahorcar*) noose; **dar** ~ to pay out rope; **dar** ~ **a alguien** (*mofarse*) to make fun of sb; (*llevar la corriente*) to humor sb; **Pedro está con la** ~ **al cuello** *fig* Pedro has his back to the wall

sois [sois] *2. pres pl de* **ser**

soja ['so·xa] *f* soy; ~ **transgénica** GM soybean; **semilla de** ~ soybean

sol [sol] *m* **1.** (*astro*) sun; (*luz*) sunlight; **al** ~ **puesto** de dusk; **de** ~ **a** ~ from dawn to dusk; **día de** ~ sunny day; **ponerse al** ~ (*tumbarse*) to lie in the sun; (*sentarse*) to sit in the sun; **tomar el** ~ to sunbathe; **hoy hace** ~ it's sunny today **2.** (*bebida*) ~ **y sombra** brandy and anisette **3.** (*moneda*) sol **4.** *inf* (*alabanza*) **es un** ~ he/she is an angel **5.** MÚS G; ~ **mayor** G major ▶ **no dejar a alguien ni a** ~ **ni a sombra** not to leave sb alone; **arrimarse al** ~ **que más calienta** to know which side one's bread is buttered on

solamente [so·la·'men·te] *adv* **1.** (*únicamente*) only **2.** (*expresamente*) expressly

solapa [so·'la·pa] *f* **1.** (*chaqueta*) lapel **2.** (*libro*) flap

solapar [so·la·'par] I. *vi* to overlap II. *vt* **1.** (*cubrir*) to cover up **2.** (*chaqueta, vestido*) to put lapels on **3.** (*disimular*) to conceal

solar [so·'lar] I. *adj* solar; **plexo** ~ solar plexus II. *m* **1.** (*terreno*) plot; ~ **para edificaciones** building site **2.** (*casa*) family seat **3.** (*linaje*) line; **venir del** ~ **de...** to come from the... family **4.** *AmC* (*patio*) yard III. <o→ue> *vt* **1.** (*pavimentar*) to tile **2.** (*calzado*) to sole

soldado, -a [sol·'da·do, -a] *m, f* **1.** MIL soldier;

~ **de infantería** infantryman, foot soldier; ~ **de caballería** cavalryman; ~ **raso** private **2.** (*defensor*) defender

soldador [sol·da·'dor] *m* TÉC soldering iron [o gun]

soldador [sol·da·'dor, -'do·ra] *mf* welder

soldadura [sol·da·'du·ra] *f* TÉC **1.** (*trabajo*) welding **2.** (*punto de unión*) soldered [o welded] joint **3.** (*material*) solder

soldar <o→ue> [sol·'dar] I. *vt* (*con metal fundido*) to weld; (*unir*) to join II. *vr:* ~**se** (*herida*) to heal; (*huesos*) to knit together

soleado, -a [so·le·'a·do, -a] *adj* sunny

soledad [so·le·'dad] *f* (*estado*) solitude; (*sentimiento*) loneliness

solemne [so·'lem·ne] *adj* **1.** (*ceremonioso*) solemn; **discurso** ~ formal speech **2.** (*mentira*) monstrous; (*error*) monumental

solemnidad [so·lem·ni·'dad] *f* **1.** (*cualidad*) solemnity **2.** REL (*festividad*) religious ceremony **3.** *pl* (*formalidades*) formalities *pl*

solemnizar <z→c> [so·lem·ni·'sar, -'θar] *vt* to celebrate

soler <o→ue> [so·'ler] *vi* ~ **hacer** to be in the habit of doing; **se suelen celebrar los santos** saints' days are usually celebrated; **suele ocurrir que...** it often occurs that...; **solemos coger el tren** we usually catch the train; **solíamos coger el tren, pero ya no** we used to catch the train, but not any more

solera [so·'le·ra] *f* **1.** (*puntal*) support **2.** (*del molino*) lower millstone **3.** (*del vino*) mature wine mixed with younger wine to give it flavor

solfa ['sol·fa] *f* **1.** MÚS (*signos*) musical notation; (*arte de solfear*) sol-fa; (*melodía*) music; **estar** (**escrito**) **en** ~ to be in musical notation **2.** *inf* (*zurra*) hiding ▶ **poner algo en** ~ (*ridiculizar*) to hold sth up to mockery; (*con arte y orden*) to put sth in order

solfear [sol·fe·'ar] *vt* **1.** MÚS to practice sol-fa **2.** (*pegar*) to tan **3.** *inf* (*reprender*) to tell off

solfeo [sol·'feo] *m* **1.** MÚS (*acción*) solfeggio, singing of scales; (*fragmento*) sol-fa **2.** *inf* (*zurra*) hiding

solicitante [so·li·si·'tan·te, so·li·θi·-] *mf* **1.** (*de una petición*) petitioner; ~ **de asilo** asylum seeker **2.** (*para un trabajo*) applicant

solicitar [so·li·si·'tar, so·li·θi·-] *vt* **1.** (*pedir*) to ask for; (*gestionar*) to solicit; (*un trabajo*) to apply for; ~ **un médico** to call for a doctor **2.** (*compañía, atención*) to seek; ~ **la mano de una mujer** to ask for a woman's hand in marriage; **te solicitan en todas partes** you're in great demand

solícito, -a [so·'li·si·to, -a; so·li·θi·-] *adj* (*diligente*) diligent; (*cuidadoso*) solicitous

solicitud [so·li·si·'tud, so·li·θi·-] *f* **1.** (*diligencia*) diligence; (*cuidado*) solicitude **2.** (*petición*) request; (*formal*) petition; ~ **de empleo** job application

solidaridad [so·li·da·ri·'dad] *f* solidarity; **por** ~ **con** out of solidarity with

solidario, -a [so·li·'da·rjo, -a] *adj* shared;

hacerse ~ de alguien to sympathize with sb
solidarizarse <z→c> [so·li·da·ri·'sar·se, 'θar·se] *vr* to feel solidarity with; **me solidarizo con tu opinión** I share your view
solidez [so·li·'des, -'deθ] *f* solidity; (*estabilidad*) firmness
solidificar <c→qu> [so·li·di·fi·'kar] I. *vt* to solidify; *fig* to harden II. *vr:* ~ **se** to solidify
sólido ['so·li·do] *m* 1. FÍS solid 2. (*geometría*) solid shape
sólido, -a ['so·li·do, -a] *adj t.* FÍS solid; (*colores*) fast; (*ingreso*) steady; (*precios*) stable; (*voz*) strong
solista [so·'lis·ta] *mf* MÚS soloist
solitaria [so·li·'ta·rja] *f* ZOOL tapeworm
solitario [so·li·'ta·rjo] *m* 1. (*diamante*) solitaire 2. (*cartas*) solitaire
solitario, -a [so·li·'ta·rjo, -a] I. *adj* 1. (*sin compañía*) alone; (*abandonado*) lonely; **en** ~ single-handed 2. (*lugar*) isolated II. *m, f* loner
sollozar <z→c> [so·jo·'sar, so·ʎo·'θar] *vi* to sob
sollozo [so·'jo·so, -'ʎo·θo] *m* sob
solo ['so·lo] *m* 1. *t.* MÚS (*baile*) solo 2. (*cartas*) solitaire
solo, -a ['so·lo, -a] *adj* 1. (*sin compañía*) alone; (*sin familia*) orphaned; (*solitario*) lonely; **a solas** alone; **por sí** ~ on one's own; **lo hace como ella sola** she does it as only she can 2. (*único*) only; **ni una sola vez** not once 3. (*sin añadir nada*) on its own; (*café*) black; (*alcohol*) straight, neat; **comer el pan** ~ to eat plain bread ▶ **estar más ~ que la una** to be completely on one's own; **más vale ~ que mal acompañado** better to be alone than in bad company
sólo ['so·lo] *adv* 1. (*únicamente*) only; ~ **que...** except that...; **tan** ~ just; **aunque ~ sean 10 minutos de deporte al día** even if it's only 10 minutes sport a day 2. (*expresamente*) expressly
solsticio [sols·'ti·sjo, -θjo] *m* solstice
soltar [sol·'tar] *irr* I. *vt* 1. (*dejar de sujetar*) to let go of; (*liberar*) to free; (*dejar caer*) to drop; **no ~ prenda** not to say a word about sth, to give nothing away; **¡suéltame!** let me go!, let go of me! 2. (*nudo*) to untie 3. (*expresión, grito*) to let out; (*tacos*) to come out with; ~ **una carcajada** to burst out laughing 4. (*golpe*) ~ **un golpe** to strike; ~ **una bofetada a alguien** to cuff [*o* slap] sb 5. (*puesto*) to give up 6. (*lágrimas*) to shed 7. AUTO (*embrague*) to let out; (*frenos*) to release; (*cinturón*) to undo 8. (*gases*) ~ **un pedo** *inf* to let out a fart 9. *inf* (*dinero*) to cough up; ~ **la mosca** to fork out II. *vr:* ~ **se** 1. (*liberarse*) to escape; (*de unas ataduras*) to free oneself; ~ **se de la mano** to let go of sb's hand 2. (*un nudo*) to come undone; (*un tiro*) to go off 3. (*al hablar*) to let oneself go; (*una palabra, expresión*) to let out; **se me soltó la lengua** I found my tongue 4. (*desenvoltura*) to become expert; ~ **se a hacer algo** to become expert at

sth 5. (*para independizarse*) to achieve independence
soltero, -a [sol·'te·ro, -a] I. *adj* single II. *m, f* bachelor *m*, single woman *f*; **apellido de soltera** maiden name; **de solteras solíamos salir mucho** we used to go out a lot before we got married
solterón, -ona [sol·te·'ron, -'ro·na] *m, f* confirmed bachelor *m*, old maid *f*, spinster *f*
soltura [sol·'tu·ra] *f* 1. (*de una cuerda, del pelo*) looseness 2. (*de forma relajada*) ease; (*al hablar*) fluency
soluble [so·'lu·βle] *adj* 1. (*líquido*) soluble; ~ **en agua** water-soluble; **café** ~ instant coffee 2. (*problema*) solvable
solución [so·lu·'sjon, -'θjon] *f* 1. (*líquido*) solution; ~ **anticongelante** antifreeze 2. (*de un problema*) solution; **este problema no tiene** ~ there's no solution to this problem; **no hay más** ~ there's nothing more to be done
solucionar [so·lu·sjo·'nar, so·lu·θjo-] *vt* to solve
solvencia [sol·'βen·sja, -θja] *f* 1. FIN solvency 2. (*responsabilidad*) trustworthiness; ~ **moral** character; **de toda** ~ **moral** of excellent character
solventar [sol·βen·'tar] *vt* 1. (*problema*) to resolve; (*asunto*) to settle; (*desavenencia*) to end 2. (*deuda, cuenta*) to pay
solvente [sol·'βen·te] I. *adj* 1. FIN solvent 2. (*sin deudas*) free of debts 3. (*reputación*) respectable II. *m* solvent
somatada [so·ma·'ta·da] *f* AmC blow
sombra ['som·bra] *f* 1. (*proyección*) shadow; ~s **chinescas** shadow play; ~ **de ojos** (*producto cosmético*) eye shadow; **se ha convertido en mi** ~ he/she follows me everywhere; **no es** ~ **de lo que era** he/she is a shadow of his/her former self 2. (*contrario de sol*) shade; **hacer** ~ to give shade; **hacer** ~ **a alguien** *fig* to put sb in the shade; **dar (una) buena** ~ to give good shade; **sentarse a la** ~ **de un árbol** to sit in the shade of a tree; **quita de ahí que me haces** ~ move over, you're blocking my light; **no ver más que** ~s **a su alrededor** to be pessimistic about everything; **no fiarse ni de su (propia)** ~ to be extremely suspicious 3. *pl* (*oscuridad*) darkness 4. (*clandestinidad*) **trabajar en la** ~ to work illegally 5. ARTE shading 6. (*cantidad mínima*) trace; **esto no tiene la más mínima** ~ **de verdad** there's not the slightest truth in this; **una** ~ **de tristeza** a trace of sadness; ~ **de duda** shadow of doubt 7. (*de un difunto*) ghost 8. (*defecto*) stain 9. *inf* (*cárcel*) **a la** ~ in the slammer; **poner a la** ~ to lock up ▶ **tener buena** ~ (*tener chiste*) to be witty; (*ser simpático*) to have charm; (*tener suerte*) to be lucky; **tener mala** ~ (*ser antipático*) to be a nasty bit of work; (*tener mala suerte*) to be unlucky; **¡vete por la** ~! watch how you go!; **ni por** ~ not in the least
sombrear [som·bre·'ar] *vt* 1. (*dar sombra*) to shade; (*a alguien*) to cast a shadow over; ~ **los**

ojos to put eye shadow on **2.** ARTE to shade
sombrero [som·'bre·ro] *m* (*prenda*) hat; ~ **de
copa** top hat; ~ **hongo** derby; **quitarse el ~
ante algo** to take one's hat off to sth
sombrilla [som·'bri·ja, -ʎa] *f* parasol
sombrío, -a [som·'bri·o, -a] *adj* **1.** (*en la sombra*) shady; (*oscuro*) dark **2.** (*triste*) sad; (*pesimista*) gloomy
somero, -a [so·'me·ro, -a] *adj* **1.** (*superficial*)
superficial; (*vago*) imprecise **2.** (*aguas*) shallow
someter [so·me·'ter] **I.** *vt* **1.** (*dominar*) to force
to submit; (*subyugar*) to conquer; ~ **la volun-
tad** to subjugate one's will **2.** (*proyecto, ideas,
a un tratamiento*) to submit **3.** (*encomendar*)
el asunto es sometido a los tribunales the
matter is referred to the courts **4.** (*subordinar*)
to subordinate; **todo está sometido a tu
decisión** everything is subject to your decision
II. *vr:* ~ **se 1.** (*en una lucha*) to give in **2.** (*a una
acción, un tratamiento*) ~ **se a algo** to under-
go sth **3.** (*a una decisión, opinión*) to bow;
~ **se a las órdenes/la voluntad de alguien**
to bow to sb's orders/will
somnífero [som·'ni·fe·ro] *m* sleeping pill
somnífero, -a [som·'ni·fe·ro, -a] *adj* sleep-in-
ducing
somnolencia [som·no·'len·sja, -θja] *f* (*sueño*)
drowsiness
somos ['so·mos] *1. pres pl de* **ser**
son [son] **I.** *m* **1.** (*sonido*) sound **2.** (*rumor,
voz*) rumor; **corre el ~ de que...** rumor has it
that... **3.** (*en actitud*) **venir en ~ de paz** to
come in peace; **en ~ de broma** as a joke
▶ **bailar al ~ que tocan** to toe the line; **hacer
algo a su ~** to do sth one's own way; **¿a ~ de
qué?, ¿a qué ~?** why?; **sin ~** for no reason at
all **II.** *3. pres pl de* **ser**
sonajero [so·na·'xe·ro] *m* (baby's) rattle
sonambulismo [so·nam·bu·'lis·mo] *m* sleep-
walking
sonámbulo, -a [so·'nam·bu·lo, -a] **I.** *adj* sleep-
walking **II.** *m, f* sleepwalker
sonante [so·'nan·te] *adj* **dinero contante y ~**
(hard) cash
sonar <o→ue> [so·'nar] **I.** *vi* **1.** (*timbre, teléfono, campana*) to ring; (*instrumento*) to be
heard; **me suenan las tripas** my stomach is
rumbling **2.** *t.* LING, MÚS (*parecerse*) to sound;
~ **a algo** to sound like sth; ~ **a hueco** to sound
hollow; **esto me suena** this sounds familiar;
(**tal y**) **como suena** as I'm telling you; **lo que
sea** ~**á** what will be, will be **II.** *vt* **1.** (*instrumento*) to play **2.** (*la nariz*) to blow; ~ **la nariz
a un niño** to blow a child's nose **III.** *vr:* ~ **se** to
blow one's nose
sonata [so·'na·ta] *f* sonata
sonda ['son·da] *f* **1.** (*acción*) sounding **2.** MED
probe, catheter
sondar [son·'dar] *vt* **1.** MED to probe **2.** MIN ~
algo to bore into sth **3.** (*explorar*) to explore,
to investigate
sondear [son·de·'ar] *vt* **1.** (*una persona*) to
sound out **2.** *v.* **sondar**

sondeo [son·'deo] *m* **1.** MED probing **2.** MIN
boring **3.** NÁUT sounding **4.** (*averiguación*) investigation; ~ **de mercado** ECON market survey; ~ **de la opinión pública** public opinion
survey
soneto [so·'ne·to] *m* LIT sonnet
songa-songa ['son·ga-'son·ga] *AmC, Chile,
Ecua* **a la** ~ underhand
songo, -a ['son·go] *adj Col, Méx* **1.** (*tonto*)
stupid **2.** (*taimado*) sly
sonido [so·'ni·do] *m* **1.** (*ruido*) sound **2.** *t.* MÚS
(*manera de sonar*) tone **3.** FÍS resonance
4. RADIO sound; ~ **estereofónico** stereo sound
sonoridad [so·no·ri·'dad] *f t.* MÚS (*características*) sonority; (*agradable*) sonorousness
sonoro, -a [so·'no·ro, -a] *adj* **1.** (*que puede
sonar*) resonant; (*acústico*) acoustic; (*bóveda*)
echoing **2.** (*fuerte*) loud; (*agradable*) sonorous;
una voz sonora/poco sonora a rich/thin
voice **3.** LING voiced **4.** FÍS resonant **5.** CINE
banda sonora soundtrack; **película sonora**
talkie
sonreír [son·rre·'ir] *irr como* **reír I.** *vi, vr:* ~ **se**
(*reír levemente*) to smile; ~ **a alguien** to smile
at sb; ~ **maliciosamente** to smile maliciously;
~ **de felicidad** to beam with happiness **II.** *vi*
(*la vida, la suerte*) to smile; **le sonríe la fortuna** fortune smiles on him/her
sonrisa [son·'rri·sa] *f* (*leve*) smile; (*maliciosa*)
smirk; ~ **de oreja a oreja** (broad) grin
sonrojar [son·rro·'xar] **I.** *vt* to make blush
II. *vr:* ~ **se** to blush
sonrojo [son·'rro·xo] *m* **1.** (*acción*) blushing
2. (*rubor*) blush **3.** (*causa*) naughty remark
sonsear [son·se·'ar] *vi CSur* (*tontear*) to behave stupidly
sonsera [son·'se·ra] *f Arg* foolishness
sonso, -a ['son·so, -a] *m, f CSur* (*tonto*) stupid
soñado, -a [so·'ɲa·do, -a] *adj* (*con que se
sueña*) dreamt-of; **el hombre** ~ Mr. Right
soñador(a) [so·ɲa·'dor, --'do·ra] **I.** *adj* dreamy
II. *m(f)* dreamer
soñar <o→ue> [so·'ɲar] *vi, vt* to dream;
~ **con algo** to dream of sth; ~ **despierto** to
daydream; **¡ni ~ lo!** no way!; **siempre he
soñado con ser médico** I've always dreamt
of being a doctor; **¡sueña** [*o que sueñes*] **con
los angelitos!** sweet dreams!
soñoliento, -a [so·ɲo·'ljen·to, -a] *adj* drowsy
sopa ['so·pa] *f* **1.** (*caldo*) soup **2.** *pl* (*pan*) ~ **s
de leche** bread and milk ▶ **ése os da** ~ **s con
honda a todos vosotros** he's streets ahead of
all of you; **poner a alguien como la** ~ **de
Pascua** to give sb a ticking off; **comer la** [*o
andar a la*] ~ **boba** to live off other people;
estar ~ to be tight; **ver hasta en la** ~ to see
everywhere; **como** [*o* **hecho**] **una** ~ (*mojado*)
soaked to the skin
sopera [so·'pe·ra] *f* soup tureen
sopero, -a [so·'pe·ro, -a] **I.** *adj* soup; **ser muy**
~ to be very fond of soup **II.** *m, f* soup plate
soplar [so·'plar] **I.** *vi* to blow ▶ ~ **y beber, no
puede ser** *prov* you can't have your cake and

eat it too; **¡sopla!** It beats me! **II.** *vt* **1.** (*con la boca*) to blow on; (*apartar*) to blow away; (*velas*) to blow out; (*hinchar*) to blow up; (*fuego*) to blow on; **soplado a boca** (*vidrio*) hand-blown **2.** (*en un examen*) to whisper; TEAT to prompt **3.** *inf* (*delatar*) to inform [*o* squeal] on; (*entre alumnos*) to tell on **4.** *inf* (*hurtar*) to swipe; (*cobrar*) to sting for **5.** (*golpe*) to deal **6.** (*inspirar*) to inspire **III.** *vr:* **~se** *inf* **1.** (*comer*) to wolf down; (*beber*) to knock back **2.** (*engreírse*) to get conceited

soplete [so·'ple·te] *m* blow torch; **~ soldador** welding torch

soplo ['so·plo] *m* **1.** (*acción*) puff; **apagar las velas de un ~** to blow out the candles with one puff **2.** (*viento leve*) breeze; **~ de viento** breath of wind **3.** (*tiempo*) **como un ~** like a flash **4.** (*denuncia*) tip-off **5.** (*sonido*) murmur; (*corazón*) heart murmur

soplón, -ona [so·'plon, -·'plo·na] *m, f* **1.** (*de la policía*) informer **2.** TEAT prompter **3.** (*entre alumnos*) tattletale

sopor [so·'por] *m* lethargy

soportable [so·por·'ta·βle] *adj* bearable

soportar [so·por·'tar] *vt* **1.** (*sostener*) to support **2.** (*aguantar*) to stand

soporte [so·'por·te] *m* **1.** *t. fig* (*apoyo*) support **2.** (*pilar*) support pillar; (*de madera*) beam; **~ para bicicletas** bike rack **3.** COMPUT **~ físico** hardware; **~ lógico** software

soprano[1] [so·'pra·no] *m* MÚS (*voz*) soprano

soprano[2] [so·'pra·no] *f* MÚS soprano

soquete [so·'ke·te] *m AmL* (*calcetín*) (short) sock, anklet

sor [sor] *f* REL sister

sorber [sor·'βer] *vt* **1.** (*con los labios*) to sip; (*por una pajita*) to suck; (*por la nariz*) to sniff; MED to inhale; **~ tabaco** to take snuff **2.** (*empaparse de*) to soak up **3.** (*escuchar*) to drink in

sorbo ['sor·βo] *m* (*cantidad, trago*) sip; **beber a ~s** to sip; **tomar de un ~** to drink in one go; **échame otro ~** give me another drop

sordera [sor·'de·ra] *f* **1.** (*privación*) deafness **2.** (*disminución*) loss of hearing

sordidez [sor·di·'des, -'deθ] *f* sordidness

sordo, -a ['sor·do, -a] **I.** *adj* **1.** (*que no oye*) deaf; **~ de un oído** deaf in one ear; **hacer oídos ~s** to turn a deaf ear; **~ como una tapia** as deaf as a post, stone deaf; **quedarse ~** to go deaf **2.** (*que oye mal*) hard of hearing **3.** (*algo que no hace ruido*) noiseless; **a sordas, a lo ~** on the quiet **4.** (*de timbre oscuro*) dull; **un golpe ~** a dull thud **5.** (*que no presta atención*) inattentive **6.** (*sentimiento, pasión*) repressed **7.** LING voiceless **II.** *m, f* deaf person; **los ~s** the deaf, deaf people; **hacerse el ~** to pretend not to hear; **no hay peor ~ que el que no quiere oír** *prov* there are none so deaf as those who will not hear

sordomudo, -a [sor·do·'mu·do, -a] **I.** *adj* deaf and dumb **II.** *m, f* deaf mute

sorna ['sor·na] *f* **1.** (*al obrar*) slyness; **con ~** slyly **2.** (*al hablar*) sarcasm; **con ~** sarcastically

sorprendente [sor·pren·'den·te] *adj* **1.** (*inesperado*) unexpected; (*desarrollo, evolución*) surprising; (*asombroso*) amazing; **es ~ que** +*subj* it's surprising that **2.** (*que salta a la vista*) striking; **poseer una estatura ~** to be surprisingly tall **3.** (*extraordinario*) incredible; **no es ~ que** +*subj* it's hardly surprising that

sorprender [sor·pren·'der] **I.** *vt* **1.** (*coger desprevenido*) to take by surprise; (*asombrar*) to startle, to amaze; (*extrañar*) to surprise; **no me ~ía que viniera** I wouldn't be surprised if he/she came; **durante un momento me quedé sorprendida** I was surprised for a moment **2.** (*descubrir algo*) to come across **3.** (*pillar*) to catch (in the act) **4.** MIL (*atacar*) to surprise **II.** *vr:* **~se 1.** (*asombrarse*) **~se de algo** to be amazed at sth **2.** (*extrañarse*) to be surprised

sorpresa [sor·'pre·sa] *f* **1.** (*acción*) surprise; **coger a alguien de** [*o* por] **~** to take sb by surprise **2.** (*efecto*) suddenness; (*asombro*) amazement; (*extrañeza*) surprise

sorpresivo, -a [sor·pre·'si·βo, -a] *adj* **1.** (*inesperado*) surprising; (*asombroso*) amazing **2.** (*repentino*) sudden

sortear [sor·te·'ar] *vt* **1.** (*decidir*) to draw lots for; (*destino*) to toss up for; (*rifar*) to raffle **2.** (*esquivar*) to avoid

sorteo [sor·'te·o] *m* **1.** (*decisión*) drawing of lots; (*rifa*) raffle; (*lotería*) draw **2.** (*esquivación*) avoidance

sortija [sor·'ti·xa] *f* **1.** (*joya*) ring; (*con sello*) signet ring **2.** (*rizo*) curl

sosegado, -a [so·se·'ɣa·do, -a] *adj* **1.** (*apacible*) peaceful **2.** (*tranquilo*) calm

sosegar [so·se·'ɣar] *irr como fregar* **I.** *vt* (*calmar*) to calm **II.** *vi, vr:* **~se** (*descansar*) to rest **III.** *vr:* **~se** (*calmarse*) to calm down

sosegate [so·se·'ɣa·te] *m Arg, Urug* **dar** [*o* **pegar**] **un ~ a alguien** to tell sb off

sosiego [so·'sje·ɣo] *m* calm; **hacer algo con ~** to do sth calmly

soslayar [sos·la·'jar] *vt* **1.** (*objeto*) to put sideways **2.** (*evitar*) to avoid

soso, -a ['so·so, -a] *adj* **1.** (*sin sal*) unsalted; (*sin sabor*) tasteless, insipid **2.** (*persona*) dull

sospecha [sos·'pe·tʃa] *f* **1.** (*suposición*) supposition **2.** (*desconfianza*) mistrust **3.** (*de un crimen*) suspicion; (*contra alguien concreto*) accusation; **bajo ~ de asesinato** suspected of murder

sospechar [sos·pe·'tʃar] **I.** *vt* **1.** (*creer posible*) to suppose; **¡ya lo sospechaba!** I thought as much! **2.** (*recelar*) to suspect **II.** *vi* to be suspicious

sospechoso, -a [sos·pe·'tʃo·so, -a] **I.** *adj* suspicious; **me resulta ~ que** +*subj* I find it suspicious that **II.** *m, f* suspect

sostén [sos·'ten] *m* **1.** *t. fig* (*apoyo*) support; **pilar de ~** support pillar **2.** (*prenda*) bra **3.** (*de familia*) support; (*alimentos*) sustenance

sostener [sos·te·'ner] *irr como tener* **I.** *vt*

1. (*sujetar*) to support 2. (*aguantar*) to bear; (*por debajo*) to hold up 3. (*afirmar*) to maintain; (*idea, teoría*) to stick to 4. (*persona*) to support 5. (*lucha, velocidad, posición*) to keep up; ~ **una larga conversación** to have a long conversation II. *vr:* ~ **se** 1. (*sujetarse*) to hold oneself up 2. (*aguantarse*) to keep going 3. (*en pie*) to stand up 4. (*económicamente*) **apenas me puedo** ~ I can hardly support myself 5. (*en opinión*) ~**se en algo** to insist on sth

sostenido [sos·te·'ni·do] *m* MÚS sharp; **poner un** ~ to raise by a semitone

sostenido, -a [sos·te·'ni·do, -a] *adj* 1. (*esfuerzo*) sustained 2. MÚS sharp; **fa** ~ F sharp

sota ['so·ta] *f* (*naipe*) jack

sotana [so·'ta·na] *f* cassock, soutane

sótano ['so·ta·no] *m* 1. (*piso*) basement 2. (*habitación*) cellar

sotreta [so·'tre·ta] *adj Arg, Bol, Urug* 1. (*caballo*) old and useless 2. (*holgazán*) idle; (*no fiable*) untrustworthy

soturno, -a [so·'tur·no, -a] *adj Ven* (*taciturno*) taciturn

soy [soi] *1. pres de* **ser**

spaguetti [es·pa·'ye·ti] *mpl* spaghetti

spray [es·'prai] *m* <sprays> spray

squash [es·'kwaʃ] *m* DEP squash

Sr. [se·'ɲor] *abr de* **señor** Mr.

Sra. [se·'ɲo·ra] *abr de* **señora** Mrs.

Srta. [se·ɲo·'ri·ta] *f abr de* **señorita** Miss

Sta. ['san·ta] *f abr de* **santa** St.

status [es·'ta·tus] *m inv* status

Sto. ['san·to] *abr de* **santo** St.

su [su] *adj* (*de él*) his; (*de ella*) her; (*de cosa, animal*) its; (*de ellos*) their; (*de Ud., Uds.*) your; (*de uno*) one's; ~ **familia** his/her/their family

suampo ['swam·po] *m AmC* (*ciénaga*) swamp

suave [su·'a·βe] *adj* 1. (*superficie, piel*) smooth; (*jersey, cabello, droga*) soft; (*viento, noche, sopa, salsa*) gentle; (*sopa, salsa*) mild 2. (*aterrizaje*) smooth; (*curva, subida*) gentle; (*temperatura, tabaco*) mild 3. (*carácter*) docile; (*maneras*) refined; (*palabras*) kind

suavidad [swa·βi·'dad] *f* 1. (*de superficie, piel*) smoothness; (*de jersey, cabello*) softness; (*de viento, noche, temperatura*) gentleness; (*de sopa*) mildness 2. (*de aterrizaje*) smoothness; (*de caricia, subida*) gentleness 3. (*de carácter*) docility; (*de palabras*) kindness

suavizante [swa·βi·'san·te, -'θan·te] I. *adj* **crema** ~ conditioner II. *m* 1. (*para la ropa*) fabric softener 2. (*para el cabello*) conditioner

suavizar [swa·βi·'sar, -'θar] <z→c> *vt* 1. (*hacer suave*) to smooth; (*pelo, piel*) to soften; (*superficie*) to smooth out; (*navaja*) to strop 2. (*expresión*) to soften; (*situación*) to relax, to ease 3. (*persona*) to mollify 4. (*recorrido, trabajo*) to make easy; (*velocidad*) to moderate

suba ['su·βa] *f Arg* (*alza*) rise

subalimentación [suβ·a·li·men·ta·'sjon,

-'θjon] *f* undernourishment

subalterno, -a [suβ·al·'ter·no] I. *adj* secondary II. *m, f* (*empleado*) subordinate

subarrendar <e→ie> [suβ·a·rren·'dar] *vt* (*ceder: piso*) to sublet; (*finca*) to sublease

subarriendo [suβ·a·'rrjen·do] *m* (*cesión: de piso*) subletting; (*de finca*) sublease

subasta [su·'βas·ta] *f* 1. (*venta*) auction; ~ **forzada** forced auction; **sacar a** ~ **pública** to put up for auction 2. (*de contrato público*) tender

subastador(a) [su·βas·ta·'dor, --'do·ra] *m(f)* auctioneer

subastar [su·βas·'tar] *vt* 1. (*vender*) to auction 2. (*contrato público*) to put out to tender

subcampeón, -ona [suβ·kam·pe·'on, --'o·na] *m, f* runner-up; ~ **mundial** world number two

subconsciencia [suβ·kon·'sjen·sja, -'θjen·θja] *f* subconscious

subconsciente [suβ·kon·'sjen·te, -'θjen·te] *adj* subconscious

subcultura [suβ·kul·'tu·ra] *f* subculture

subdesarrollado, -a [suβ·de·sa·rro·'ja·do, -a; -'ʎa·do, -a] *adj* underdeveloped

subdirector(a) [suβ·di·rek·'tor, --'to·ra] *m(f)* assistant director [*o* manager]

súbdito, -a ['suβ·di·to, -a] *m, f* 1. (*sometido*) vassal 2. POL (*de un rey*) subject; (*ciudadano*) citizen

subdividir [suβ·di·βi·'dir] *vt* to subdivide

subempleo [suβ·em·'pleo] *m* underemployment

subestimar [suβ·es·ti·'mar] I. *vt* to underestimate; (*propiedad*) to undervalue II. *vr:* ~ **se** to underestimate oneself

subida [su·'βi·da] *f* 1. (*de una calle, un río*) rise 2. (*cuesta*) slope; **la calle hace** ~ the street is on a slope 3. (*de precios, temperaturas, costes*) increase 4. (*acción de subir*) ascent; (*en coche, teleférico*) climb 5. POL ~ **al poder** rise to power; ~ **al trono** ascent to the throne

subir [su·'βir] I. *vi* 1. (*ascender: calle, cuesta*) to go up; (*sol, pastel, globo, río*) to rise; ~ **a la cima** to climb to the peak; ~ **a primera** DEP to go up to the first division; **la marea ha subido** the tide has come in 2. (*andando*) to go up; **sube a por tus cosas** go up and get your things 3. (*aumentar*) ~ **en algo** to increase by sth; **la gasolina ha subido** gas has gone up 4. (*montar: al coche*) to get in; (*al caballo, tren, a la bici*) to get on; ~ **a un árbol** to climb a tree II. *vt* 1. (*precio*) to raise; **hacer** ~ **los precios** to put up the prices 2. (*música*) to turn up; (*voz*) to raise 3. (*en coche*) to go up; (*montaña*) to climb 4. (*poner más alto: brazos*) to lift up; (*cortina, persiana*) to raise; (*cuello de abrigo*) to turn up; (*cabeza, pesas*) to lift; ~ **a un niño en brazos** to lift up a child 5. (*llevar*) to take up; ~ **al tercer piso** to go up to the third floor 6. (*pared*) to build III. *vr:* ~**se** (*al coche*) to get in; (*al tren, a la bici*) to get on; ~**se a un árbol/a una silla** to climb a tree/onto a chair; **se me ha subido el vino a**

la cabeza the wine has gone to my head

súbito ['su·βi·to] *adv* suddenly; **de ~** (*repentinamente*) suddenly; (*inesperadamente*) unexpectedly

súbito, -a ['su·βi·to, -a] *adj* **1.** (*repentino*) sudden; **muerte súbita** MED sudden death; (*de bebés*) crib death **2.** (*inesperado*) unexpected **3.** (*carácter, genio*) irritable

subjefe, -a [suβ·'xe·fe, -a] *m, f* assistant manager

subjetividad [suβ·xe·ti·βi·'dad] *f* subjectivity

subjetivo, -a [suβ·xe·'ti·βo, -a] *adj* subjective

subjuntivo [suβ·xun·'ti·βo] *m* subjunctive

sublevación [su·βle·βa·'sjon, -'θjon] *f* uprising

sublevar [su·βle·'βar] **I.** *vt* **1.** (*amotinar*) to rouse to revolt **2.** (*irritar*) to upset **II.** *vr:* **~ se** to revolt

sublimación [su·βli·ma·'sjon, -'θjon] *f* **1.** (*de alguien*) praise **2.** PSICO, QUÍM sublimation

sublimar [su·βli·'mar] *vt* **1.** (*a alguien*) to praise **2.** PSICO, QUÍM to sublimate

sublime [su·'βli·me] *adj* sublime

subliminal [su·βli·mi·'nal] *adj* subliminal

submarinismo [suβ·ma·ri·'nis·mo/sum·ma·ri·'nis·mo] *m* scuba-diving, skin-diving; **hacer ~** to go scuba-diving [*o* skin-diving]

submarino [suβ·ma·'ri·no/sum·ma·'ri·no] *m* submarine

submarino, -a [suβ·ma·'ri·no, -a/sum·ma·'ri·no, -a] *adj* submarine; (*vida*) underwater

subnormal [suβ·nor·'mal] **I.** *adj* subnormal **II.** *mf* (*persona*) subnormal person; **¡eres un ~!** *pey* you moron!

subordinación [su·βor·di·na·'sjon, -'θjon] *f* subordination; (*obediencia*) obedience

subordinado, -a [su·βor·di·'na·do, -a] **I.** *adj* **1.** (*en el trabajo*) subordinate **2.** LING **oración subordinada** subordinate clause **II.** *m, f* (*en el trabajo*) subordinate

subordinar [su·βor·di·'nar] *vt* to subordinate

subrayado [suβ·rra·'ja·do] *m* underlining

subrayar [suβ·rra·'jar] *vt* **1.** (*con raya*) to underline **2.** (*recalcar*) to emphasize

subrogante [suβ·rro·'yan·te] *adj* Chile (*interino*) substitute

subsanar [suβ·sa·'nar] *vt* **1.** (*falta*) to make up for **2.** (*error*) to rectify; (*defecto*) to repair; (*mal*) to remedy **3.** (*dificultad*) to overcome

subscripción [suβs·krip·'sjon, -kriβ·'θjon] *f v.* **suscripción**

subsecretario, -a [suβ·se·kre·'ta·rjo, -a] *m, f* **1.** POL undersecretary **2.** (*en oficina*) assistant

subsidiar [suβ·si·'djar] *vt* to subsidize

subsidiario, -a [suβ·si·'dja·rjo, -a] *adj* **1.** (*de subsidio*) subsidiary; **órgano ~** (*institución*) subsidiary company **2.** (*secundario*) complementary

subsidio [suβ·'si·djo] *m* subsidy; **~ de paro** [*o* **de desempleo**] unemployment compensation

subsiguiente [suβ·si·'yjen·te] *adj* subsequent

subsistencia [suβ·sis·'ten·sja,   -θja] *f* **1.** (*hecho*) subsistence **2.** *pl* (*alimentos*) suste-

nance

subsistente [suβ·sis·'ten·te] *adj* (*existente*) surviving

subsistir [suβ·sis·'tir] *vi* **1.** (*vivir*) to subsist **2.** (*perdurar*) to endure; (*creencia*) to exist; (*empresa*) to survive

substancia [suβs·'tan·sja, -θja] *f v.* **sustancia**

substantivo [suβs·tan·'ti·βo] *adj, m v.* **sustantivo**

substitución [suβs·ti·tu·'sjon, -'θjon] *f v.* **sustitución**

substraer [suβs·tra·'er] *irr como traer vt v.* **sustraer**

subsuelo [suβ·'swe·lo] *m* subsoil

subte ['suβ·te] *m Arg, inf* (*metro*) subway

subterráneo, -a [suβ·te·'rra·neo, -a] *adj* underground, subterranean

subtítulo [suβ·'ti·tu·lo] *m t.* CINE subtitle

subtropical [suβ·tro·pi·'kal] *adj* subtropical

suburbano, -a [suβ·ur·'βa·no] *adj* suburban; **línea suburbana** suburban line

suburbio [su·'βur·βjo] *m* **1.** (*alrededores*) (poor) suburb; **vivir en los ~s de París** to live on the edge of Paris **2.** (*barrio*) slum area

subvención [suβ·βen·'sjon, -'θjon] *f* grant; POL subsidy

subvencionar [suβ·βen·sjo·'nar, -θjo·'nar] *vt* to aid; POL to subsidize; ADMIN to finance with a grant

subversión [suβ·βer·'sjon] *f* subversion

subversivo, -a [suβ·βer·'si·βo, -a] *adj* subversive

subyacente [suβ·ja·'sen·te, -'θen·te] *adj elev* **1.** (*capa*) underlying **2.** (*problema*) hidden

subyugar <g→gu> [suβ·ju·'yar] *vt* **1.** (*oprimir*) to subjugate **2.** (*sugestionar*) to dominate

succionar [suk·sjo·'nar, suɣ·θjo·] *vt* to suck; (*tierra, esponja*) to soak up

sucedáneo [su·se·'da·neo, su·θe-] *m* substitute; (*imitación*) imitation

sucedáneo, -a [su·se·'da·neo, -a; su·θe-] *adj* substitute

suceder [su·se·'der, su·θe-] **I.** *vi* **1.** (*seguir*) to succeed **2.** (*ocurrir*) to happen; **¿qué sucede?** what's happening?; **por lo que pueda ~** just in case; **suceda lo que suceda** whatever happens; **lo más que puede ~ es que** +*subj* the worst thing that can happen is **3.** (*en cargo*) to follow on **II.** *vt* (*heredar*) to inherit; (*seguir*) to succeed; **~ al rey** to succeed the king

sucesión [su·se·'sjon, su·θe-] *f* **1.** (*acción*) succession **2.** (*serie*) series *inv* **3.** (*cargo, trono*) succession **4.** (*herencia*) inheritance **5.** (*descendencia*) issue

sucesivo, -a [su·se·'si·βo, -a; su·θe-] *adj* following; **en lo ~** henceforth; **hicimos el examen en dos días ~s** we did the exam on two consecutive days

suceso [su·'se·so, -'θe·so] *m* **1.** (*hecho*) event; (*repentino*) incident **2.** (*transcurso*) outcome **3.** (*crimen*) crime; **página** [*o* **sección**] **de ~s** PREN accident and crime reports

S

sucesor(a) [su·se·'sor, -·'so·ra; su·θe-] *m(f)*
1. (*a un cargo*) successor **2.** (*heredero*) heir
suche ['su·tʃe] **I.** *adj Ven* (*agrio*) bitter **II.** *m
Chile* **1.** (*subalterno*) assistant **2.** (*rufián*) pimp
suciedad [su·sje·'dad, su·θje-] *f* **1.** (*cualidad*)
dirtiness **2.** (*porquería*) dirt **3.** (*jugada*) dirty
act
sucio ['su·sjo, -θjo] *adv* **jugar ~** to play dirty
sucio, -a ['su·sjo, -a; -θjo, -a] *adj* dirty;
(*jugada*) foul; **tengo los apuntes en ~** I've
got the notes in rough; **hacer el trabajo ~** to
do the dirty work
Sucre ['su·kre] *m* Sucre
sucucho [su·'ku·tʃo] *m AmL* (*vivienda miserable*) shanty
suculento, -a [su·ku·'len·to, -a] *adj*
1. (*sabroso*) tasty **2.** (*nutritivo*) nutritious
3. (*jugoso*) juicy, succulent
sucumbir [su·kum·'bir] *vi* **1.** (*rendirse*) to succumb; JUR to lose; **~ ante alguien** DEP to succumb to sb **2.** (*morir*) to die
sucursal [su·kur·'sal] *f* **1.** (*de empresa*) subsidiary; (*de banco, negocio*) branch **2.** (*negociado*) department
sucusumucu [su·ku·su·'mu·ku] *adv Col,
Cuba, PRico* **a lo ~** (*fingiéndose tonto*) playing
dumb *inf*
Sudáfrica [su·'da·fri·ka] *f* South Africa
sudafricano, -a [su·da·fri·'ka·no, -a] *adj, m, f*
South African
Sudamérica [su·da·'me·ri·ka] *f* South America
sudamericano, -a [su·da·me·ri·'ka·no, -a]
adj, m, f South American
sudar [su·'dar] **I.** *vi, vt* to sweat; **me sudan los
pies** my feet are sweating; **estoy sudando a
chorros** I'm dripping with sweat **II.** *vi inf* (*trabajar*) to sweat it out **III.** *vt* **1.** (*camisa*) to
make sweaty **2.** (*conseguir*) **gano mucho
pero lo sudo** I earn good money but I have to
work for it
sudeste [su·'des·te] *m* south-east
sudoeste [su·do·'es·te] *m* south-west
sudor [su·'dor] *m* (*de la piel*) sweat; **con el ~
de mi frente** with the sweat of my brow
sudoroso, -a [su·do·'ro·so, -a] *adj* sweaty
Suecia ['swe·sja, -θja] *f* Sweden
sueco, -a ['swe·ko] **I.** *adj* Swedish **II.** *m, f*
Swede ▶ **hacerse el ~** to pretend not to hear
[*o see*]
suegro, -a ['swe·yro, -a] *m, f* father-in-law *m*,
mother-in-law *f;* **los ~s** the in-laws
suela ['swe·la] *f* sole; **echar las medias ~s** to
patch up; **tú no me llegas a la ~ del zapato**
fig you can't hold a candle to me; **de siete ~s**
out-and-out; **es un tonto de siete ~s** *inf* he's
a total idiot; **como la ~ de un zapato** tough as
shoe leather
suelazo [swe·'la·so, -θo] *m Chile, Col, Ecua,
Ven* hard fall
sueldo ['swel·do] *m* pay; (*mensual*) salary;
(*semanal*) wage; **~ base** basic salary; **~ fijo**
regular wage; **un aumento de ~** a pay raise;

¿qué ~ ganas? how much do you earn?
suelo ['swe·lo] *m* **1.** (*de la tierra*) ground;
~ natal native soil; **poner una maleta en el
~** to put a suitcase on the ground; **besar el ~**
to kiss the ground; **está muy hondo, no toco
(el) ~** it's very deep, I can't reach the bottom
2. (*de casa*) floor; **~ de tarima** wood flooring,
floorboards *pl* **3.** (*terreno*) land; **~ edificable**
building land **4.** (*de vasija*) bottom **5.** (*poso*)
dregs *pl* ▶ **no te dejes arrastrar por el ~**
don't let them run you down; **estar por los ~s**
(*deprimido*) to feel very down; (*de precio*) to
be dirt cheap; **irse al ~** to fail
suelto ['swel·to] *m* **1.** (*dinero*) loose change
2. (*artículo*) short item
suelto, -a ['swel·to, -a] *adj* **1.** (*desengan-
chado: tornillo, lana*) loose **2.** (*desatado: cordón, pelo, perro*) loose; (*broche*) unfastened;
(*arroz*) fluffy; **dinero ~** ready money; **no
dejar ni un cabo ~** to leave no loose ends; **un
prisionero anda ~** a prisoner is on the loose;
voy ~ de vientre *fig* I have diarrhea **3.** (*separado*) separate; **pieza suelta** individual piece
4. (*vestido*) loose-fitting **5.** (*incontrolado*)
tener la lengua suelta to have a ready tongue
6. (*estilo*) free; (*lenguaje*) fluent; **dibujar con
mano suelta** to draw free-hand **7.** (*no envasado*) loose **8.** *inf* (*no agarrotado*) free; **eso lo
hago yo fácil y ~** I'll do that in a jiffy
sueño ['swe·ɲo] *m* **1.** (*acto de dormir*) sleep;
me cogió el ~ sleep overcame me; **descabezar** [*o* **echarse**] **un ~** to have a nap; **entre ~s**
half asleep; **tener el ~ ligero/pesado** to be a
light/heavy sleeper **2.** (*ganas de dormir*)
sleepiness; **tener ~** to be sleepy; **entrar ~ a
uno** to get sleepy [*o* drowsy]; **caerse de ~** to
be falling asleep; **me quita el ~** it keeps me
awake **3.** (*fantasía*) dream; **ni en** [*o* por] **~s**
not even in your wildest dreams; **un coche
que es un ~** a dream car; **los ~s, ~s son**
dreams are dreams; **~ húmedo** wet dream
suero ['swe·ro] *m* **1.** (*de leche*) whey **2.** MED
serum
suerte ['swer·te] *f* **1.** (*fortuna*) luck; **¡**(**buena**)
~! good luck!; **estar de ~** to be in luck; **no
estar de ~** to be out of luck; **tener buena/
mala ~** to be lucky/unlucky; **traer/dar
buena/mala ~** to bring/give good/bad luck;
por ~ fortunately; **probar ~** to try one's luck;
ser cuestión de ~ to be a matter of luck;
¡deséame ~! wish me luck!; **la ~ está
echada** the die is cast **2.** (*destino*) fate; **echar
algo a ~(s)** to draw lots for sth; **¿quién sabe
la ~ que te espera?** who knows what
fate awaits you? **3.** (*casualidad*) chance
4. (*manera*) way; **de ~ que...** in such a way
that...; **de esta ~** in this way **5.** (*tipo*) kind;
tratar con toda ~ de gente to deal with all
sorts of people **6.** (*condición*) state; **de tal ~
que** so that
suertero, -a [swer·'te·ro, -a] **I.** *adj Ecua, Hond,
Perú* lucky **II.** *m, f Perú* lottery ticket seller
suéter ['swe·ter] *m* sweater

suficiencia [su·fi·'sen·sja, -'θjen·θja] *f* **1.** (*lo bastante*) sufficiency **2.** (*presunción*) self-importance, smugness; **decir con aires de ~** to say with a superior air

suficiente [su·fi·'sjen·te, -'θjen·te] **I.** *adj* **1.** (*bastante*) enough; **ser ~** to be sufficient; **~ que conozco eso yo** I know that well enough **2.** (*presumido*) self-important, smug **II.** *m* ENS (*nota*) pass

sufijo [su·'fi·xo] *m* suffix

sufragar <g→gu> [su·fra·'ɣar] **I.** *vt* **1.** (*ayudar*) to aid **2.** (*costear: gastos*) to meet; (*tasa*) to pay; (*beca*) to finance **II.** *vi* AmL (*votar*) **~ por alguien** to vote for sb

sufragio [su·'fra·xjo] *m* **1.** (*voto*) vote **2.** (*derecho*) suffrage; **~ universal** universal suffrage **3.** (*sistema*) election **4.** REL suffrage

sufrido, -a [su·'fri·ðo, -a] *adj* **1.** (*persona*) patient, uncomplaining; **eres demasiado ~** you're too long-suffering **2.** (*color*) fast; **una tela sufrida** a hard-wearing material **3.** (*marido*) complaisant

sufrimiento [su·fri·'mjen·to] *m* **1.** (*acción*) suffering **2.** (*moral*) tolerance; (*físico*) toughness

sufrir [su·'frir] *vt* **1.** (*aguantar*) to bear; (*peso*) to support; (*a alguien*) to put up with **2.** (*padecer*) to suffer; **~ de celos** to suffer from jealousy; **~ de la espalda** to have back trouble; **~ quejas** to receive complaints; **~ las consecuencias** to suffer the consequences **3.** (*experimentar: cambio*) to undergo; (*examen*) to take; (*desengaño, accidente*) to have; (*pena*) to be stricken with; **~ una operación** to have an operation

sugerencia [su·xe·'ren·sja, -θja] *f* **1.** (*propuesta*) suggestion **2.** (*recomendación*) recommendation **3.** (*inspiración*) inspiration

sugerir [su·xe·'rir] *irr como sentir vt* **1.** (*proponer*) to suggest **2.** (*insinuar*) to hint **3.** (*evocar*) to prompt **4.** (*inspirar*) to inspire

sugestión [su·xes·'tjon] *f* **1.** (*de sugestionar*) hypnotic power **2.** (*propuesta*) suggestion **3.** (*inspiración*) inspiration

sugestionar [su·xes·tjo·'nar] **I.** *vt* (*influenciar*) to influence; (*dominar*) to dominate **II.** *vr:* **~se** to indulge in autosuggestion

suiche ['swi·tʃe] *m Méx* (*botón*) switch; (*de un coche*) ignition key

suicida [swi·'si·ða, swi·'θi-] **I.** *adj* suicidal **II.** *mf* **1.** (*muerto*) person who has committed suicide **2.** (*loco*) suicidal person

suicidarse [swi·si·'ðar·se, swi·'θi-] *vr* to commit suicide

suicidio [swi·'θi·djo, swi·'θi-] *m* suicide; **intento de ~** suicide attempt

suite [swit] *f* suite; **~ nupcial** bridal suite

Suiza ['swi·sa, -θa] *f* Switzerland

suizo, -a ['swi·θo, -a; -θo, -a] **I.** *adj* Swiss; **chocolate ~** Swiss chocolate **II.** *m, f* Swiss

sujetador [su·xe·ta·'ðor] *m* **1.** (*sostén*) bra **2.** (*del bikini*) fastener

sujetar [su·xe·'tar] **I.** *vt* **1.** (*agarrar*) **~ por algo** to seize by sth **2.** (*dominar*) to dominate **3.** (*someter*) to subject **4.** (*asegurar*) to support; (*pelo*) to hold in place; (*con clavos*) to nail down; (*con tornillos*) to screw down **II.** *vr:* **~se 1.** (*agarrarse*) to subject oneself **2.** (*a reglamento*) **~se a algo** to abide by sth

sujeto [su·'xe·to] *m* **1.** (*tema*) subject **2.** *pey* (*individuo*) individual

sujeto, -a [su·'xe·to, -a] *adj* (*expuesto a*) subject; **~ a comprobación** subject to checking; **~ a la inflación** affected by inflation; **estar ~ a fluctuaciones** to be subject to fluctuation

sulfato [sul·'fa·to] *m* sulfate

sulfuro [sul·'fu·ro] *m* sulfide

sultán, -ana [sul·'tan, -·'ta·na] *m, f* sultan *m*, sultana *f*

suma ['su·ma] *f* **1.** MAT (*acción*) adding (up); (*resultado*) total; **~ y sigue** (*cuenta*) carried forward; *fig* it's still going on **2.** (*cantidad*) sum **3.** (*esencia*) summary

sumamente [su·ma·'men·te] *adv* extremely

sumar [su·'mar] **I.** *vt* **1.** MAT to add (up) **2.** (*una obra*) to gather; (*hechos*) to summarize **II.** *vr:* **~se** (*a una manifestación, a una idea*) to join; (*a una discusión*) to participate in

sumario [su·'ma·rjo] *m* JUR criminal proceedings *pl*

sumario, -a [su·'ma·rjo, -a] *adj* **1.** (*explicación*) concise **2.** JUR **juicio ~** summary trial

sumergible [su·mer·'xi·βle] **I.** *adj* **1.** (*reloj*) waterproof **2.** (*submarino*) submersible **II.** *m* submarine

sumergir <g→j> [su·mer·'xir] **I.** *vt* to submerge **II.** *vr:* **~se** to submerge

sumidero [su·mi·'de·ro] *m* (*rejilla*) drain; (*de la calle*) sewer

suministrar [su·mi·nis·'trar] *vt* **1.** *t.* COM (*datos, información*) to supply **2.** (*abastecer*) to stock **3.** (*facilitar*) to supply

suministro [su·mi·'nis·tro] *m* **1.** *t.* COM (*de datos, información*) supply **2.** (*abastecimiento*) stock **3.** *pl* MIL supplies *pl*

sumir [su·'mir] **I.** *vt* (*hundir*) to sink; **~ en la miseria a alguien** to plunge sb into poverty **II.** *vr:* **~se** to sink; **~se en el trabajo** to become absorbed in one's work

sumisión [su·mi·'sjon] *f* **1.** (*acción*) submission **2.** (*carácter*) submissiveness **3.** (*obediencia*) obedience

sumo, -a ['su·mo] *adj* **1.** (*más alto*) high(est); **~ sacerdote** high priest; **a lo ~** at most; **en grado ~** highly **2.** (*mayor*) great

sunco, -a ['sun·ko, -a] **I.** *adj Chile* (*de un brazo*) one-armed; (*de una mano*) one-handed **II.** *m, f Chile* (*de un brazo*) one-armed person; (*de una mano*) one-handed person

sungo, -a ['sun·go, -a] *adj Col* (*de raza negra*) Black

suntuosidad [sun·two·si·'dad] *f* **1.** (*lujo*) sumptuousness **2.** (*opulencia*) lavishness **3.** (*aparatosidad*) magnificence

suntuoso, -a [sun·tu·'o·so, -a] *adj* **1.** (*lujoso*) sumptuous **2.** (*opulento*) lavish **3.** (*aparatoso*)

S

magnificent

supeditar [su·pe·di·'tar] I. *vt* 1. (*subordinar*) to subordinate 2. (*someter*) to subdue 3. (*condicionar*) to condition II. *vr:* ~ **se** to submit

súper¹ ['su·per] I. *adj inf* super II. *m* supermarket

súper² ['su·per] *f* Premium (gas)

superable [su·pe·'ra·βle] *adj* 1. (*récord*) beatable 2. (*situación*) surmountable

superabundancia [su·per·a·βun·'dan·sja, -θja] *f* (*en cantidad*) superabundance; (*en diversidad*) great variety

superabundante [su·per·a·βun·'dan·te] *adj* superabundant; (*negativo*) excessive

superación [su·pe·ra·'sjon, -'θjon] *f* 1. (*de récord*) improvement 2. (*de situación*) surmounting

superar [su·pe·'rar] I. *vt* 1. (*sobrepasar: a alguien*) to surpass; (*límite*) to exceed; (*récord*) to beat; ~ **todo lo que se había visto hasta ahora** to go beyond anything seen before 2. (*prueba*) to pass 3. (*situación*) to overcome II. *vr:* ~ **se** to excel oneself

superávit [su·pe·'ra·βit] *m* <superávit(s)> surplus

superdotado, -a [su·per·do·'ta·do, -a] *adj* extremely gifted

superficial [su·per·fi·'sjal, -'θjal] *adj* superficial; (*detalle*) minor; **herida** ~ flesh wound

superficie [su·per·'fi·sje, -θje] *f* 1. (*parte externa*) surface; ~ **cultivable** arable area; **salir a la** ~ (*submarino*) to surface; (*minero*) to come to the surface; *fig* to come to light 2. MAT surface; (*área*) surface area 3. (*apariencia*) external appearance

superfluo, -a [su·'per·flwo, -a] *adj* superfluous; (*gastos*) unnecessary

superior [su·pe·'rjor] *adj* 1. (*más alto*) higher; **el curso** ~ **de un río** the upper course of a river; **el piso** ~ **al mío** the apartment above mine 2. (*en calidad*) better; (*en inteligencia, rango*) superior 3. (*excelente*) excellent; **mujer** ~ superwoman

superior(a) [su·pe·'rjor, -·'rjo·ra] *m(f)* superior

superioridad [su·pe·rjo·ri·'dad] *f* superiority; ~ **sobre alguien** superiority over sb; **hablar con un tono de** ~ to speak in a superior tone of voice

superlativo [su·per·la·'ti·βo] *m* LING superlative

superlativo, -a [su·per·la·'ti·βo, -a] *adj t.* LING superlative

supermercado [su·per·mer·'ka·do] *m* supermarket

superpoblación [su·per·po·βla·'sjon, -'θjon] *f* overpopulation

superponer [su·per·po·'ner] *irr como poner vt* 1. (*dos cosas*) to superimpose; ~ **algo a algo** to superimpose sth on sth 2. (*dar prioridad*) to give more importance to

superpotencia [su·per·po·'ten·sja, -θja] *f* superpower

superproducción [su·per·pro·duk·'sjon,

-duɣ·'θjon] *f* 1. COM overproduction 2. CINE big-budget movie

supersónico, -a [su·per·'so·ni·ko, -a] *adj* supersonic

superstición [su·pers·ti·'sjon, -'θjon] *f* superstition

supersticioso, -a [su·pers·ti·'sjo·so, -a; -'θjo·so, -a] *adj* superstitious

supervisar [su·per·βi·'sar] *vt* to supervise; (*en un examen*) to invigilate

supervisión [su·per·βi·'sjon] *f* 1. (*vigilancia*) supervision 2. (*en examen*) invigilation

supervisor(a) [su·per·βi·'sor, -·'so·ra] *m(f)* supervisor; (*funcionario*) inspector

supervivencia [su·per·βi·'βen·sja, -θja] *f* survival

superviviente [su·per·βi·'βjen·te] I. *adj* surviving II. *mf* survivor

suplantar [su·plan·'tar] *vt* 1. (*en el trabajo*) to supplant 2. (*escrito*) to forge

suplementario, -a [su·ple·men·'ta·rjo, -a] *adj* supplementary; **tomo** ~ additional volume

suplementero [su·ple·men·'te·ro] *m Chile* newspaper vendor

suplemento [su·ple·'men·to] *m* 1. (*complemento*) supplement 2. (*tomo*) supplementary volume 3. (*de periódico*) ~ **en color** color supplement 4. (*precio*) extra charge; (*del tren*) excess fare; (*plus*) bonus; ~ **por turnos** shift bonus

suplencia [su·'plen·sja, -θja] *f* substitution

suplente [su·'plen·te] I. *adj* substitute; **maestro** ~ substitute teacher II. *mf t.* DEP substitute

súplica ['su·pli·ka] *f* plea; (*escrito*) request; JUR petition

suplicar <c→qu> [su·pli·'kar] *vt* 1. (*rogar*) to implore; ~ **algo de rodillas** to beg on one's knees for sth 2. JUR ~ **algo** to appeal against sth

suplicio [su·'pli·sjo, -θjo] *m* 1. (*tortura*) torture 2. (*tormento*) torment; **el viaje fue un** ~ we had a terrible journey

suplir [su·'plir] *vt* 1. (*completar*) to make up for 2. (*sustituir*) to substitute; ~ **el bolígrafo por un lápiz** to change the pen for a pencil 3. (*en el trabajo*) to replace

supo ['su·po] 3. *pret de* **saber**

suponer [su·po·'ner] *irr como poner vt* 1. (*dar por sentado*) to suppose; **vamos a** ~ **que...** let's suppose that...; **se supone que...** it is assumed that...; **suponiendo que...** supposing that...; **supongamos que...** let us assume that...; **dar algo por supuesto** to take sth for granted 2. (*figurar*) to imagine; **supongo que vendrá Gema, no? — supongo que sí** I imagine Gema will come, won't she? — I suppose so; **no supongo que** +*subj* I don't imagine; **puedes** ~ **que...** you can imagine that... 3. (*atribuir*) **le supongo unos 40 años** I imagine him/her to be about 40; **no le suponía tan fuerte** I didn't realize he/she was so strong 4. (*significar*) to mean; ~ **un duro golpe para alguien** to be a real blow for sb; **esto me supone 60 pesos al mes** this amounts to 60 pesos a month for me; **no ~ molestia alguna** to be no trouble

suposición [su·po·si·'sjon, -'θjon] *f* supposition; (*presunción*) assumption

supositorio [su·po·si·'to·rjo] *m* MED suppository

supremacía [su·pre·ma·'si·a, -'θi·a] *f* **1.** (*superioridad*) supremacy **2.** (*prioridad*) priority

supremo, -a [su·'pre·mo] *adj* (*altísimo*) highest; *fig* supreme; **el instante ~** the culminating moment; **el Tribunal Supremo** the Supreme Court

suprimir [su·pri·'mir] *vt* **1.** (*poner fin*) to suppress; (*fronteras*) to eliminate; (*controles, obstáculos, amenaza*) to remove; (*regla*) to abolish **2.** (*omitir*) to omit **3.** (*silenciar*) to silence

supuesto [su·'pwes·to] *m* **1.** (*suposición*) assumption, supposition **2.** (*hipótesis*) hypothesis

supuesto, -a [su·'pwes·to, -a] *adj* (*ladrón, asesino*) alleged; (*testigo, nombre*) assumed; (*causa*) supposed; **por ~** of course; **dar algo por ~** to take sth for granted; (*pretendido*) so-called; **~ que** since, as

supurar [su·pu·'rar] *vi* MED to suppurate

sur [sur] *m* **1.** (*punto*) south; **la América del Sur** South America **2.** (*viento*) south wind

surafricano, -a [sur·a·fri·'ka·no, -a] *adj, m, f* South African

surazo [su·'ra·so, -θo] *m Arg, Bol* (*viento*) strong southerly wind

surcar <c→qu> [sur·'kar] *vt* **1.** (*tierra*) to plow **2.** *elev* (*mar*) **~ el mar** to sail the seas

surco ['sur·ko] *m* **1.** (*en tierra*) furrow **2.** (*arruga*) wrinkle **3.** (*en disco*) groove

sureste [sur·'es·te] *m* south-east

surf [surf] *m* DEP surfing; **hacer ~** to windsurf

surgir <g→j> [sur·'xir] *vi* **1.** (*agua*) to gush **2.** (*aparecer: dificultad, posibilidad*) to arise; (*pregunta*) to come up; (*persona*) to appear unexpectedly **3.** (*edificio*) to rise up

suroeste [sur·o·'es·te] *m* south-west

surrealismo [su·rrea·'lis·mo] *m* ARTE surrealism

surrealista [su·rrea·'lis·ta] *adj, mf* surrealist

surtido [sur·'ti·do] *m* selection, assortment

surtido, -a [sur·'ti·do, -a] *adj* **1.** (*mezclado*) mixed; **galletas surtidas** assorted biscuits **2.** (*variado*) varied **3.** (*bien provisto*) well-stocked

surtidor [sur·ti·'dor] *m* **1.** (*lugar*) gas station **2.** (*aparato*) gas pump

surtir [sur·'tir] **I.** *vt* **1.** (*proveer*) **~ de algo** to supply with sth **2.** (*tener*) **~ efecto** (*palabras*) to have the desired effect; (*medicamento*) to work **II.** *vi* to spout **III.** *vr* **~se de algo** to provide oneself with sth

suruco [su·'ru·ko] *m CSur, vulg* crap

surumbo, -a [su·'rum·bo, -a] *adj Guat, Hond* stunned

surupa [su·'ru·pa] *f Ven* (*cucaracha*) cockroach

susceptibilidad [su·sep·ti·βi·li·'dad, sus·θep-] *f* (*sensibilidad*) *t.* MED susceptibility

susceptible [su·sep·'ti·βle, sus·θep-] *adj* **1.** (*cosa*) **~ de mejora** capable of improvement; **materiales ~s de ser reutilizados** material which can be reused **2.** (*persona: sensible*) sensitive; (*irritable*) touchy

suscitar [su·si·'tar, sus·θi-] *vt* (*sospecha, discordia*) to cause; (*discusión*) to start; (*escándalo, comentarios*) to provoke; (*odio, conflicto*) to stir up; (*problema*) to raise; (*antipatías, curiosidad*) to arouse

suscribir [sus·kri·'βir] *irr como escribir* **I.** *vt* **1.** (*escrito*) to sign **2.** (*opinión*) to endorse **3.** (*acciones*) to take out an option on **II.** *vr* **~se a una revista** to subscribe to a magazine

suscripción [sus·krip·'sjon, -kriβ-'θjon] *f* **1.** (*firma*) signature **2.** (*de acciones*) taking up **3.** (*a una revista*) subscription

suscri(p)tor(a) [sus·krip·'tor, -'to·ra] *m(f)* **1.** (*firmante*) signatory **2.** (*de acciones*) subscriber **3.** (*de una revista*) subscriber

suspender [sus·pen·'der] *vt* **1.** (*tener en el aire*) **~ de algo** to hang from sth **2.** (*trabajador, deportista*) to suspend **3.** (*en un examen*) to fail; **he suspendido matemáticas** I've flunked math **4.** (*interrumpir: sesión*) to adjourn; (*tratamiento*) to break off; (*embargo*) to lift; (*servicio*) to discontinue; **~ las disputas** to end the dispute; **se ha suspendido la función de esta noche** tonight's show has been called off

suspensión [sus·pen·'sjon] *f* **1.** (*acción de colgar*) suspension **2.** (*interrupción: de sesión*) adjournment; (*de tratamiento*) interruption; (*de disputas*) end; (*de producción*) break; (*de embargo*) lifting; **~ de armas** truce; **~ de la pena** annulment of the penalty; **~ de pagos** temporary receivership, suspension of payment

suspenso [sus·'pen·so] *m* **1.** ENS fail; **sacar un ~** to fail, to flunk **2.** *AmL* suspense

suspenso, -a [sus·'pen·so, -a] *adj* (*perplejo*) perplexed

suspicacia [sus·pi·'ka·sja, -θja] *f* suspicion

suspicaz [sus·pi·'kas, -'kaθ] *adj* suspicious

suspirar [sus·pi·'rar] *vi* **1.** (*dar suspiros*) to sigh **2.** (*anhelar*) **~ por algo** to long for sth

suspiro [sus·'pi·ro] *m* (*de persona*) sigh; (*del viento*) breath

sustancia [sus·'tan·sja, -θja] *f* **1.** (*materia, esencia*) substance; **~ activa** active ingredient; **~ gris** ANAT gray matter; **en ~** in essence; **este ensayo no tiene ~** this essay is lacking in substance **2.** (*de alimentos*) stock **3.** (*juicio*) **un fundamento sin ~** an unconvincing reason; **decir cosas sin ~** to say superficial things; **un comentario sin ~** a shallow commentary

sustancial [sus·tan·'sjal, -'θjal] *adj* **1.** (*esencial*) vital; (*fundamental*) essential **2.** (*comida*) substantial **3.** (*libro*) meaty

sustancioso, -a [sus·tan·'sjo·so, -a; -'θjo·so,

-a] *adj* **1.**(*comida*) substantial **2.**(*libro*) meaty
sustantivo [sus·tan·'ti·βo] *m* noun
sustantivo, -a [sus·tan·'ti·βo, -a] *adj* **1.**(*esencial*) vital; (*fundamental*) essential **2.**LING nominal
sustentar [sus·ten·'tar] **I.** *vt* **1.**(*una cosa*) to hold up; (*columna*) to support **2.**(*esperanza*) to sustain **3.**(*familia*) to feed **II.** *vr:* ~ **se 1.**(*alimentarse*) to sustain oneself **2.**(*aguantarse*) ~ **se en algo** to rely on sth
sustento [sus·'ten·to] *m* **1.**(*mantenimiento*) maintenance **2.**(*apoyo*) support
sustitución [sus·ti·tu·'sjon, -'θjon] *f* replacement; (*temporal*) substitution
sustituir [sus·ti·tu·'ir] *irr como huir* *vt* **t.** DEP to substitute; ~ **a alguien** (*temporalmente*) to stand in for sb; (*definitivamente*) to replace sb
sustitutivo, -a [sus·ti·tu·'ti·βo, -a] *adj* substitute
sustituto, -a [sus·ti·'tu·to, -a] *m, f* substitute, replacement
susto ['sus·to] *m* scare; **poner cara de** ~ to look scared; **darle un** ~ **a alguien** to give sb a fright; **pegarse** [*o* **llevarse**] **un** ~ to get scared; **pegarle un** ~ **a alguien** to scare sb; **no ganar para** ~ **s** to have one problem after another
sustraer [sus·tra·'er] *irr como traer* **I.** *vt* **1.**(*restar*) to subtract **2.**(*robar*) to steal **3.**(*privar*) to remove **4.**(*separar*) to abduct **II.** *vr* ~ **se de algo** to get away from sth; ~ **se de los periodistas** to avoid the journalists
susurrar [su·su·'rrar] **I.** *vi* **1.**(*hablar bajo*) to whisper; (*no claro*) to mutter; ~ **algo a alguien** to whisper sth to sb **2.**(*viento*) to murmur **II.** *vr:* ~ **se** to be rumored **III.** *vimpers* **se susurra que...** it is rumored that...
susurro [su·'su·rro] *m* **1.**(*al hablar: bajo*) whisper; (*no claro*) mutter **2.**(*del viento*) murmur
sutil [su·'til] *adj* **1.**(*velo, hilo*) delicate; (*rebanada*) thin **2.**(*sabor*) subtle; (*aroma*) delicate **3.**(*diferencia, ironía*) fine; (*jugada, sistema*) refined
sutileza [su·ti·'le·sa, -θa] *f*, **sutilidad** [su·ti·li·'dad] *f* **1.**(*de velo, hilo*) delicacy **2.**(*de sabor*) subtlety; (*de aroma*) delicacy **3.**(*de diferencia, ironía*) fineness; (*de jugada, sistema*) refinement **4.**(*de persona*) sharpness
suturar [su·tu·'rar] *vt* to stitch
suyo, -a ['su·jo, -a] *adj, pron* (*de él*) his; (*de ella*) hers; (*de cosa, animal*) its; (*de ellos*) theirs; (*de Ud., Uds.*) yours; (*de uno*) one's; **este encendedor es** ~ this lighter is his/hers; **siempre habla de los** ~ **s** he/she is always talking about his/her family; ~ **afectísimo** yours truly; **darle a alguien lo** ~ to give sb what belongs to him/her; *fig* to give sb what he/she deserves; **ya ha hecho otra de las suyas** *inf* he/she has been up to his/her tricks again; **leer Hamlet tiene lo** ~ (*es difícil*) reading Hamlet is not easy; (*es interesante*) reading Hamlet is rewarding; **el problema es ya de** ~ **difícil de resolver** (by its nature) the

problem is hard to solve; **hacer suyas las quejas de los alumnos** to echo the pupils' complaints; **Albert es muy** ~ Albert keeps to himself; **eso es muy** ~ that's typical of him/her; **ir a lo** ~ to go one's own way

T

T, t [te] *f* T, t; ~ **de Tarragona** T as in Tango
tabacal [ta·βa·'kal] *m* AmL tobacco plantation
tabaco [ta·'βa·ko] *m* **1.**(*planta, producto*) tobacco; **de color** ~ tobacco; ~ **rubio** Virginia tobacco; ~ **de mascar** chewing tobacco **2.**(*cigarrillo*) cigarettes *pl;* (*cigarro, puro*) cigar; **¿tienes** ~**?** do you have any cigarettes?
tabanco [ta·'βan·ko] *m* AmC (*desván*) attic
tábano ['ta·βa·no] *m* **1.**ZOOL horsefly **2.**(*persona*) nuisance
taberna [ta·'βer·na] *f* tavern, bar
tabernero, -a [ta·βer·'ne·ro, -a] *m, f* (*dueño*) landlord; (*camarero*) barkeeper
tabique [ta·'βi·ke] *m* partition; ~ **nasal** nasal septum
tabla ['ta·βla] *f* **1.**(*plancha*) board; ~ **de cocina** cutting board; ~ **de planchar** ironing board; **ser la única** ~ **de salvación** *fig* to be the last resort; ~ **de surf** surfboard; ~ **de windsurf** sailboard **2.**(*de libro*) table of contents **3.**(*lista*) list; (*cuadro*) table; **las Tablas de la Ley** the Tables of the Law; **decir la** ~ to recite the multiplication table **4.**(*de vestido*) pleat **5.**(*pintura*) panel **6.**AGR (*para plantas*) garden patch; (*más grande*) plot **7.***pl* DEP draw, tie **8.***pl* TEAT stage **9.***pl* (*experiencia*) **un político con muchas** ~**s** an experienced politician ▶ **a raja** ~ to the letter; **hacer** ~ **rasa de algo** to wipe the slate clean
tablada [ta·'βla·da] *f* **1.** CSur (*lugar*) stockyard **2.** Par (*matadero*) slaughterhouse
tablao [ta·'βlao] *m* (*escenario*) stage
tablero [ta·'βle·ro] *m* **1.**(*de madera*) board; ~ **de anuncios** bulletin board **2.**(*pizarra*) blackboard **3.** DEP ~ **de ajedrez** chess board; ~ **de damas** checkers board **4.**(*de mesa*) table top **5.**AUTO dashboard **6.**AVIAT ~ **de mandos** instrument panel **7.**(*ábaco*) abacus
tableta [ta·'βle·ta] *f* **1.**(*de chocolate*) bar **2.**MED tablet
tabloide [ta·'βloi·de] *m* AmL tabloid
tablón [ta·'βlon] *m* **1.**(*de andamio*) plank; (*de anuncios*) bulletin board **2.** *inf* (*borrachera*) **coger** [*o* **agarrar**] **un** ~ to get smashed **3.** AmL (*para plantas*) patch; (*más grande*) plot
tabú [ta·'βu] *m* <tabúes> taboo
tabulador [ta·βu·la·'dor] *m* (*tecla*) tab
tacañería [ta·ka·ɲe·'ri·a] *f* stinginess, miserliness
tacaño, -a [ta·'ka·ɲo, -a] **I.** *adj* stingy **II.** *m, f*

miser, tightwad *inf*

tachar [ta·'tʃar] *vt* **1.** (*rayar*) to cross out **2.** (*atribuir*) ~ **de algo** to brand as sth **3.** (*acusar*) to accuse; **le ~on de incompetente** they accused him of being incompetent

tachero [ta·'tʃe·ro] *m Arg, inf* (*taxista*) taxi driver

tacho ['ta·tʃo] *m* **1.** *AmL* (*vasija*) metal basin **2.** *AmL* (*hojalata*) tin **3.** *AmL* (*cubo*) trash can **4.** *Arg, inf* (*taxi*) taxi ▶ **irse al ~** *Arg, inf* to collapse

tachón [ta·'tʃon] *m* **1.** (*borrón*) crossing out **2.** (*tachuela*) large stud

tácito, -a ['ta·si·to, -a; 'ta·θi-] *adj* tacit

taciturno, -a [ta·si·'tur·no, -a; 'ta·θi-] *adj* **1.** (*callado*) taciturn **2.** (*melancólico*) melancholy, glum

taco ['ta·ko] *m* **1.** (*pedazo*) piece; ~**s de salida** DEP starting block **2.** (*de arma*) wad **3.** (*de billar*) cue **4.** (*de bota*) stud; ~ **de rosca** screw-in stud **5.** (*de papel*) pad; (*calendario*) tear-off desk, calendar; (*fajo*) wad **6.** (*de jamón*) cube; (*bocado*) bite to eat **7.** TÉC plug; (*para tornillo*) anchor bolt **8.** *inf* (*palabrota*) swearword, four-letter word; **decir** [*o* **soltar**] ~**s** to swear **9.** *inf* (*lío*) mess; **estar hecho un** ~ to be all mixed up **10.** *AmL* (*tacón*) heel **11.** *pl inf* (*años*) years; **¡ya tengo mis 40 ~s!** I'm already past 40!

tacón [ta·'kon] *m* heel; ~ **de aguja** spike heel; **zapatos de ~ alto** high-heel(ed) shoes

taconear [ta·ko·ne·'ar] *vi* **1.** (*suelo*) to tap one's heel **2.** (*arrogantemente*) to strut

táctica ['tak·ti·ka] *f* tactic(s); **ir con ~** to move strategically

táctico, -a ['tak·ti·ko, -a] **I.** *adj* tactical **II.** *m, f* tactician

táctil ['tak·til] *adj* tactile

tacto ['tak·to] *m* **1.** (*sentido*) sense of touch; **al** ~ to the touch; **ser áspero al** ~ to feel rough **2.** (*contacto*) touch **3.** (*habilidad*) tact; **no tener** ~ to be tactless

tacuache [ta·'kwa·tʃe] *m Cuba, Méx* ZOOL (*Solenodon*) almique

tacuaco, -a [ta·'kwa·ko, -a] *adj Chile* (*rechoncho*) chubby

taita ['tai·ta] *m* **1.** *CSur* expert **2.** *Arg* (*matón*) bully, tough **3.** *Ven* (*jefe de familia*) head of the family

tajada [ta·'xa·da] *f* **1.** (*porción*) slice; **llevarse la mejor ~** to take the lion's share; **sacar ~ de algo** to get something out of sth **2.** *inf* (*ronquera*) **tener una ~** to be hoarse **3.** *inf* (*borrachera*) **anoche pilló una buena ~** last night he/she got smashed **4.** (*corte*) cut

tajante [ta·'xan·te] *adj* **1.** (*respuesta*) categorical; (*actitud*) dogmatic; (*medidas*) unequivocal **2.** (*absoluto*) in no uncertain terms **3.** (*cortante*) sharp

tajar [ta·'xar] *vt* **1.** (*cortar*) to cut; (*en lonchas*) to slice; (*trocear*) to chop **2.** *AmL* (*afilar*) to sharpen

tajo ['ta·xo] *m* **1.** (*corte*) cut; **darse un ~ en el**

dedo to cut one's finger **2.** GEO gorge **3.** (*filo*) cutting edge **4.** *inf* (*trabajo*) work; **ir al ~** to go to work **5.** (*de carnicero*) butcher's block; (*para decapitar*) executioner's block

tal [tal] **I.** *adj* **1.** (*igual*) such; ~ **día hace un año** a day like this a year ago; **en ~ caso** in that case; **no digas ~ cosa** don't say any such thing; **no he dicho nunca ~ cosa** I never said anything of the kind **2.** (*tanto*) so; **la distancia es ~ que...** it's so far away that..., it's such a long way that... **3.** (*cierto*) certain; **un ~ Pérez... llamó...** somebody called Perez called... **II.** *pron* **1.** (*alguien*) ~ **habrá que piense así** there's bound to be sb who thinks so; **el ~** that fellow; ~ **o cual** someone or other; **¡ése es otro que ~!** he's another one! **2.** (*cosa*) **no haré ~** I won't do anything of the sort; **¡no hay ~!** there's no such thing!; **hablar de ~ y cual** to talk about one thing and another; **... y ~ y cual** (*enumeración*) and so on and so forth **III.** *adv* **1.** (*así*) so **2.** (*de la misma manera*) just; **es ~ cual lo buscaba** it's just what I was looking for; **son ~ para cual** they're two of a kind, they're made for each other; **estar ~ cual** to be just as it was; **lo dejé ~ cual** I left it just as I found it; ~ **y como** just as; ~ **y como suena** just as I'm telling you **3.** (*cómo*) **¿qué ~ (te va)?** how are things?; **¿qué ~ el viaje?** how was the trip?; **¿qué ~ te lo has pasado?** did you have a good time?; **¿qué ~ si tomamos una copa?** why don't we have sth to drink?; **¿qué ~ es tu nuevo jefe?** what's your new boss like?; ~ **y como están las cosas** the way things are now **IV.** *conj* **con** ~ **de** +*infin*, **con** ~ **de que** +*subj* (*mientras*) as long as; (*condición*) provided; ~ **vez** (*quizás*) perhaps, maybe

tala ['ta·la] *f* **1.** (*de árboles*) felling **2.** (*destrucción*) destruction

taladrar [ta·la·'drar] *vt* **1.** (*con taladro*) to drill **2.** (*oídos*) to pierce; **un ruido que taladra los oídos** an ear-splitting noise

taladro [ta·'la·dro] *m* drill; (*agujero*) (drill) hole

talamoco, -a [ta·la·'mo·ko, -a] *adj Ecua* albino

talante [ta·'lan·te] *m* **1.** (*modo*) disposition **2.** (*humor*) mood; **de buen ~** in a good mood; **de mal ~** in a bad mood **3.** (*gana*) **de buen ~** willingly

talar [ta·'lar] **I.** *adj* **túnica ~** full-length tunic **II.** *vt* **1.** (*árboles*) to fell **2.** (*destruir*) to lay waste

talco ['tal·ko] *m* **1.** (*mineral*) talc **2.** (*polvos*) talcum powder

talento [ta·'len·to] *m* (*capacidad*) talent; **de gran ~** very talented; **tener ~ para los idiomas** to have a gift for languages

talentoso, -a [ta·len·'to·so, -a] *adj* talented

talero [ta·'le·ro] *m Arg, Chile, Urug* whip

Talgo ['tal·ɣo] *m abr de* **Tren Articulado Ligero Goicoechea Oriol** *high speed light articulated intercity train in Spain*

talismán [ta·lis·'man] *m* talisman, lucky charm

T

talla ['ta·ja, -ʎa] *f* **1.**(*de diamante*) cutting **2.**(*en madera*) carving; (*en piedra*) sculpting **3.**(*estatura*) height; **ser de poca ~** to be short; **no dar la ~** MIL not to be qualified; *fig* not to be good enough **4.**(*medidor*) measuring stick **5.**(*de vestido*) size; **un abrigo de la ~ 42** a size 42 coat **6.**(*moral, intelectual*) stature

tallar [ta·'jar, -'ʎar] *vt* **1.**(*diamante*) to cut **2.**(*madera*) to carve; (*en piedra*) to sculpt

tallarín [ta·ja·'rin, ta·ʎa-] *m* noodle

talle ['ta·je, -ʎe] *m* **1.**(*cintura, del vestido*) waist **2.**(*figura*) figure

taller [ta·'jer, -'ʎer] *m* **1.**TÉC workshop; **~ artesanal** craft workshop; **~es gráficos** printing works **2.**(*seminario*) seminar **3.**(*estudio*) studio **4.**(*auto*) garage

tallo ['ta·jo, -ʎo] *m* **1.**BOT stem, stalk **2.**(*renuevo*) shoot, sprout

talón [ta·'lon] *m* **1.**(*del pie, zapato, calcetín*) heel; **pisar a alguien los talones** *inf* (*perseguir*) to be hot on sb's heels; (*emular*) to follow in sb's footsteps; **~ de Aquiles** Achilles' heel; *fig* weak point **2.**(*cheque*) check; **hazme un ~ de 10.000 pesos** make me out a check for 10,000 pesos; **~ sin fondos** bad [*o* bounced] check **3.**(*resguardo*) voucher; (*recibo*) receipt

tamal [ta·'mal] *m* *AmC, Méx* tamale (*dish made of cornmeal, meat or chicken, and chili wrapped in corn husks or banana leaves*)

tamalada [ta·ma·'la·da] *f* *Méx* CULIN tamale party

tamango [ta·'man·go] *m* *CSur* (*calzado*) coarse leather shoe

tamaño [ta·'ma·ɲo] *m* **1.**(*medida*) size; **de ~ natural** life size; **¿de qué ~ es?** what size is it?, how big is it?; **de gran ~** large **2.**(*formato*) size; **en ~ grande** large size; **en ~ bolsillo** pocket size

tamaño, -a [ta·'ma·ɲo, -a] *adj* **1.**(*grande*) such a big, so big a **2.**(*pequeño*) such a small, so small a **3.**(*semejante*) such a; **tamaña tontería** such a stupid thing; **sólo a ti se te ocurre ~ disparate** only you would think of such an absurd idea

tambache [tam·'ba·tʃe] *m* *Méx, inf* bundle; **un ~ de ropa/de hojas de papel** a pile of clothes/of papers; **hacer ~ a alguien** to play a dirty trick on sb

tambalear [tam·ba·le·'ar] *vi, vr:* **~se** to stagger; *fig* to totter

tambarria [tam·'ba·rrja] *f* *Perú* (*fiesta*) party

tambembe [tam·'bem·be] *m* *Chile* (*trasero*) bottom, butt *inf*

tambero, -a [tam·'be·ro, -a] **I.** *adj* *Arg* dairy; **vaca tambera** milking cow **II.** *m, f* *Arg* (*ganado manso*) tame livestock; (*vaca lechera*) milk cow

también [tam·'bjen] *adv* also, as well, too; **yo lo ví ~** I also saw him, I saw him too [*o* as well]

tambocha [tam·'bo·tʃa] *f* *Col, Ven* (*hormiga*) poisonous red-headed ant

tambor [tam·'bor] *m* **1.**(*cilindro, instrumento*) drum; **tocar el ~** to play the drum;

proclamar algo a ~ batiente to proclaim sth triumphantly **2.**(*músico*) drummer **3.**ANAT eardrum

tamiz [ta·'mis, -'miθ] *m* sieve, sifter; **pasar por el ~** to sift

tamizar <z→c> [ta·mi·'sar, -'θar] *vt* to sift, to sieve; *fig* to screen

tampoco [tam·'po·ko] *adv* not either, nor, neither; **ni puedo ni ~ quiero** I neither can nor do I want to; **~ me gusta éste** I don't like this one either; **si tú no lo haces yo ~** if you don't do it, neither will I

tampón [tam·'pon] *m* **1.**(*de tinta*) ink pad **2.**(*para la mujer*) tampon

tamuga [ta·'mu·ɣa] *f* **1.***AmC* (*fardo*) bundle; (*mochila*) knapsack **2.***AmL* (*marihuana*) joint *inf*

tan [tan] *adv* so; **~... como...** as... as...; **~ es así que no he podido hacerlo** so much so that I haven't been able to do it; **de ~ simpático me resulta insoportable** he/she is so nice I find him/her unbearable; **~ siquiera una vez** just once

tanate [ta·'na·te] *m* **1.***AmC, Méx* (*cesto*) pannier **2.***AmC* (*fardo*) bundle **3.***pl, Méx, vulg* (*testículos*) balls *pl* **4.***pl, AmC* (*cachivaches*) gear, stuff

tanda ['tan·da] *f* **1.**(*turno*) shift, turn; **estar en la ~ de día** to be on the day shift; **¿me puedes guardar la ~?** will you keep my place for me? **2.**(*serie*) series *inv*; **por ~s** in batches; **en ~s de ocho** (*en filas*) in rows of eight; (*en grupos*) in groups of eight; **~ de palos** thrashing **3.**(*de trabajo, capa*) layer **4.**(*trabajo*) job, task

tándem ['tan·den] *m* tandem

tanga ['tan·ga] *m* thong

tangente [tan·'xen·te] *f* tangent; **salirse** [*o* **irse**] **por la ~** *fig* to go off on a tangent

tangible [tan·'xi·βle] *adj* tangible; *fig* concrete

tango ['tan·go] *m* MÚS tango

---

i The **tango**, said to be "a sad thought that you can dance," was born in the streets of La Boca, a district in Buenos Aires. The tango was the child of the immigrants' feelings of desolation, despair, and disappointment due to unfulfilled dreams. It was not until the 1920's that **tango** songs and dances were no longer considered obscene and became chic even in Europe. Carlos Gardel, who died in 1935, is still considered the world's greatest tango singer.

---

tano, -a ['ta·no, -a] *adj, m, f Arg, Urug, inf* (*italiano*) Italian

tanque ['tan·ke] *m* **1.**MIL tank **2.**(*cisterna*) tanker **3.**(*vehículo*) road-tanker **4.***inf* (*de cerveza*) large glass **5.***vulg* (*gordo*) fatso **6.***AmL* (*estanque*) pool

tanquear [tan·ke·'ar] *vi Col* (*echar gasolina*) to

get gas

tantear [tan·te·'ar] *vt* **1.** (*calcular: cantidad*) to calculate; (*tamaño, volumen*) to gauge, to weigh up; (*a ojo*) to size up; (*precio*) to estimate **2.** (*probar*) to try out; (*persona: sondear*) to sound out; ~ **el terreno** *fig* to get the lay of the land **3.** (*dibujo*) to sketch **4.** DEP (*puntos*) to keep the score of; (*goles*) to score **5.** (*ir a tientas*) to grope; **tuvimos que bajar la escalera tanteando** we had to feel our way down the stairs

tanteo [tan·'teo] *m* **1.** (*cálculo: cantidad*) calculation; (*de tamaño, volumen*) weighing up; (*a ojo*) sizing up, gauging; (*de precio*) estimate; **al** [*o* **por**] ~ by trial and error **2.** (*sondeo*) sounding out **3.** DEP (*de puntos*) score; (*de goles*) scoring; ~ **final** final score

tanto ['tan·to] **I.** *m* **1.** (*cantidad*) certain amount; COM rate; ~ **alzado** lump sum basis; ~ **por ciento** percentage; **me pagan a ~ la hora** I'm paid so much the hour; **costar otro** ~ to cost as much again; **un** ~ a bit; **estar un** ~ **harto de algo** to be rather fed up with sth; **estoy un** ~ **sorprendido** I'm somewhat surprised **2.** (*punto*) point; (*gol*) goal; **un** ~ **a favor de algo** a point in sb's favor; **apuntarse un** ~ **a favor** to score a point ▸ **estar al** ~ **de algo** to be up to date on sth **II.** *adv* **1.** (*de tal modo*) so much, to such an extent; **no es para** ~ there's no need to make such a fuss; **pensé que vendrías**; ~ **es así que no salí de casa** I thought you'd come; in fact, I was so sure, I stayed home **2.** (*en tal cantidad*) **no me das ni** ~ **así de pena** I don't feel the least bit sorry for you **3.** (*de duración*) so long; **tu respuesta tardó** ~ **que...** your answer took so long that... **4.** (*comparativo*) ~ **mejor/peor** so much the better/worse; ~ **como** as much as; **eso era** ~ **como no decir nada** that was the same as not saying anything; ~ **cuanto necesito para vivir** all I need to live on; ~ **si llueve como si no...** whether it rains or not... ▸ **¡ni** ~ **ni tan calvo!** neither one extreme nor the other!; ~ **...como...** both ... and...; ~ **él como su hermano juegan al baloncesto** both he and his brother play basketball; **en** ~ (**que** +*subj*) (*mientras*) as long as, provided; **entre** ~ meanwhile, in the meantime; **por** (**lo**) ~ therefore, so; **por lo** ~ **mejor callar** so best keep quiet

tanto, -a ['tan·to, -a] **I.** *adj* **1.** (*comparativo*) as much, as many; **no tengo** ~ **dinero como tú** I don't have as much money as you; **tenemos** ~**s días de vacación como ellos** we have as many vacation days as they do **2.** (*tal cantidad, ponderativo*) so much; **tantas posibilidades** so many possibilities; **¡hace** ~ **tiempo!** such a long time ago!; **¡hace** ~ **tiempo que no te veo!** I haven't seen you for so long!; ~ **gusto en conocerle** a pleasure to meet you; **¿a qué se debe tanta risa?** what's so funny? **3.** *pl* (*número indefinido*) **en mil novecientos ochenta y** ~**s** in nineteen eighty-something; **uno de** ~**s** one of many; **a** ~**s de enero** on

such and such a day of January; **tener 40 y** ~**s años** to be 40-odd years old; **a las tantas de la madrugada** *inf* in the wee hours of the morning; **quedarse despierto hasta las tantas** to stay up until all hours ▸ ~ **tienes**, ~ **vales** *prov* a man's worth is the worth of his land **II.** *pron dem* ~**s** as many; **coge** ~**s como quieras** take as many as you like; **no llego a** ~ I won't go that far; **no me imaginaba que iba a llegar a** ~ I never thought it would come to that; **jamás podré llegar a** ~ I'll never be able to go so far

tañer <3. *pret*: tañó> [ta·'ɲer] **I.** *vt* **1.** (*instrumento*) to play **2.** (*campanas*) to ring **II.** *vi* to toll

tapa ['ta·pa] *f* **1.** (*cubierta*) lid; ~ **de rosca** screw-top; **libro de** ~**s duras** hardback; **levantar** [*o* **saltar**] **a alguien la** ~ **de los sesos** *inf* to blow sb's brains out **2.** (*de zapato*) heelpiece **3.** CULIN appetizer; **una** ~ **de aceitunas** a side of olives **4.** (*carne*) **tapa de ternera** round of beef

tapada [ta·'pa·da] *f And, inf* save, stop

tapado [ta·'pa·do] *m Arg* (*abrigo*) coat

tapado, -a [ta·'pa·do, -a] *adj AmL* (*animal*) all one color

tapaporos [ta·pa·'po·ros] *m inv* (*pintura*) sealer, primer

tapar [ta·'par] **I.** *vt* **1.** (*cuerpo*) to cover; (*cazuela*) to put a lid on; (*en cama*) to cover up **2.** (*puerta*) to wall up; (*desagüe*) to obstruct; (*agujero*) to fill in; (*botella*) to put the cap on **3.** (*vista*) **¿te tapo?** am I blocking your view?; **la pared nos tapa el viento** the wall protects us from the wind **4.** (*ocultar*) to hide **II.** *vr*: ~**se 1.** (*con ropa*) to wrap up; (*en cama*) to cover up; (*completamente*) to hide; (*con velo*) to shroud **2.** (*oídos, nariz*) to get blocked; ~**se la cara/los ojos** to cover one's face/eyes

taparrabo(s) [ta·pa·'rra·βo(s)] *m* (*inv*) **1.** (*de Tarzán*) loincloth **2.** (*bañador*) swimming trunks *pl*

tapayagua [ta·pa·'ja·ɣwa] *f Hond* drizzle

tape ['ta·pe] *m* **1.** *Arg, Urug* (*aindiado*) Indian-looking person **2.** *Cuba, PRico* (*tapa*) lid **3.** *RíoPl* (*cinta de video*) tape

tapeo [ta·'peo] *m ir de* ~ to go barhopping (*for beer or wine and tapas*)

tapia ['ta·pja] *f* wall; (*de jardín*) garden wall; **estar más sordo que una** ~ to be as deaf as a doorknob

tapicería [ta·pi·se·'ri·a, ta·pi·θe·-] *f* **1.** (*tapices*) tapestries *pl*, wall-hangings *pl* **2.** (*tienda: de tapices*) tapestry shop; (*de muebles*) upholstery; (*taller*) upholsterer's **3.** (*arte*) tapestry-making **4.** (*tela*) upholstery material; **muebles de** ~ upholstered furniture

tapisca [ta·'pis·ka] *f AmC* AGR corn harvest

tapiz [ta·'pis, -'piθ] *m* tapestry, wall-hanging; (*en el suelo*) rug

tapizar <z→c> [ta·pi·'sar, -'θar] *vt* (*muebles*) to upholster; (*acolchar*) to quilt

tapón [ta·'pon] *m* **1.** (*obturador*) stopper; (*cilindro, de fregadero*) drain plug; (*de corcho*) cork; (*de cuba*) bung; AUTO oil drain plug **2.** *inf* (*persona*) short stubby person **3.** MED tampon; (*para el oído*) earplug **4.** (*cerumen*) wax in the ear **5.** (*de tráfico*) traffic jam

taponar [ta·po·'nar] *vt* **1.** (*cerrar*) to plug; (*con corcho*) to cork; (*de plástico*) to seal; (*cuba*) to bung; (*desagüe*) to clog **2.** (*herida*) to plug

tapujo [ta·'pu·xo] *m* **1.** (*embozo*) muffler **2.** *inf* (*disimulo*) false pretext; **andar con ~s** (*obrar*) to behave deceitfully; **no andarse con ~s** (*hablar*) to speak plainly

taquear [ta·ke·'ar] **I.** *vi AmL* **1.** *inf* (*jugar*) to shoot pool **2.** (*arma*) to ram **3.** (*llenar*) to stuff **II.** *vr:* **~se** *AmL* to tap one's heels

taquería [ta·ke·'ri·a] *f* **1.** *Cuba* (*descaro*) cheek **2.** *Méx* (*tacos*) taco stand

taquicardia [ta·ki·'kar·dja] *f* MED tachycardia

taquigrafía [ta·ki·ɣra·'fi·a] *f* shorthand, stenography

taquilla [ta·'ki·ja, -ʎa] *f* **1.** TEAT, CINE box office; DEP gate money; FERRO ticket window; (*de apuestas*) tote window; **éxito de ~** box-office hit **2.** (*recaudación*) receipts *pl*, takings *pl*

tara ['ta·ra] *f* **1.** (*defecto*) defect **2.** COM (*peso*) tare

tarado, -a [ta·'ra·do, -a] **I.** *adj* **1.** (*objeto*) defective, imperfect **2.** (*alocado*) crazy; (*imbécil*) stupid **II.** *m, f* (*loco*) nitwit

tarantín <tarantines> [ta·ran·'tin] *m* **1.** *Ven* (*tenducha*) stall **2.** *pl, AmC, Cuba, PRico* (*cachivaches*) odds *pl* and ends

tarántula [ta·'ran·tu·la] *f* tarantula

tararear [ta·ra·re·'ar] *vt* to la-la-la, to croon; (*con labios cerrados*) to hum

tarascón [ta·ras·'kon] *m AmS* (*mordedura*) bite; (*herida*) bite wound

tardanza [tar·'dan·sa, -θa] *f* delay; **perdona la ~ en escribirte** forgive me for taking so long to write

tardar [tar·'dar] *vi* to take time; **~ en llegar** to take a long time to arrive; FERRO to be late arriving; **~ en responder** to take a long time to answer; **~ on tres semanas en contestar** it took them three weeks to answer; **~ on mucho en arreglarlo** it took them a long time to fix it; **no tardo nada** I won't be long; **no ~é en volver** I'll be right back; **¡no tardes!** don't be gone long!; **a más ~** at the latest; **sin ~** without taking long

tarde ['tar·de] **I.** *f* **1.** (*primeras horas*) afternoon; **por la ~** in the afternoon; **¡buenas ~s!** good afternoon! **2.** (*últimas horas*) evening; **¡buenas ~s!** good evening!; (**todos**) **los viernes por la ~** Friday evenings **II.** *adv* late; **~ o temprano** sooner or later; **de ~ en ~** now and then, occasionally; **se me hace ~** it's getting late ▸ **más vale ~ que nunca** *prov* better late than never *prov*

tardío, -a [tar·'di·o, -a] *adj* **1.** (*atrasado*) late; **es un consejo ~** a belated piece of advice **2.** (*lento*) slow

tarea [ta·'rea] *f* **1.** (*faena*) task **2.** (*trabajo*) job; **~s de la casa** housework **3.** *pl* ENS homework; **¿has hecho tus ~s?** have you done your homework?

tareco [ta·'re·ko] *m Cuba, Ecua, Ven* **1.** (*herramienta*) tool of trade **2.** (*trasto*) old thing

tarifa [ta·'ri·fa] *f* rate; (*transporte*) fare; **¿cuál es su ~?** how much does he/she charge?

tarima [ta·'ri·ma] *f* platform

tarja ['tar·xa] *f* **1.** HIST (*escudo*) shield **2.** *AmL* (*tarjeta de visita*) business card ▸ **beber sobre ~** to drink on a tab

tarjar [tar·'xar] *vt Chile* to cross out

tarjeta [tar·'xe·ta] *f* **1.** card; **~ de crédito** credit card; **~ de embarque** AVIAT boarding pass; **~ postal** postcard; **~ de visita** calling card **2.** COMPUT **~ de gráficos** graphics card; **~ de memoria** memory chip

tarro ['ta·rro] *m* **1.** (*envase*) pot; (*de cristal*) jar; (*de metal*) tin, can **2.** *inf* (*cabeza*) head; **comer el ~ a alguien** to brainwash sb; **¿estás mal del ~?** are you off your head?

tarta ['tar·ta] *f* cake; (*pastel*) pie

tartamudear [tar·ta·mu·de·'ar] *vi* to stammer, to stutter

tartamudo, -a [tar·ta·'mu·do, -a] **I.** *adj* stammering, stuttering **II.** *m, f* stutterer

tartera [tar·'te·ra] *f* **1.** (*para tartas*) cake pan **2.** (*fiambrera*) lunchbox

tasa ['ta·sa] *f* **1.** (*valoración*) valuation **2.** (*precio, derechos*) fee; (*de impuesto*) tax **3.** (*de joya*) appraisal **4.** (*porcentaje*) rate; **~ de desempleo** unemployment rate; **~ de interés** interest rate; **~ impositiva** tax rate; **~ de natalidad** birth rate

tasación [ta·sa·'sjon, -'θjon] *f* **1.** (*de producto*) fixing of a price; (*de impuesto*) tax regulation **2.** (*de joya*) appraisement

tasajear [ta·sa·xe·'ar] *vt AmL* **1.** (*tajear*) to cut **2.** (*carne*) to jerk

tasar [ta·'sar] *vt* **1.** (*precio*) to fix the price of; (*impuesto*) to tax **2.** (*valorar*) to value; (*trabajo*) to regulate; **~ en exceso** to overrate **3.** (*tabaco, comida*) to ration; (*libertad*) to limit

tasca ['tas·ka] *f* (*taberna*) bar

tata ['ta·ta] *m AmL* (*papá*) daddy

tatarabuelo, -a [ta·ta·ra·'βwe·lo, -a] *m, f* great-great-grandfather

tataranieto, -a [ta·ta·ra·'nje·to, -a] *m, f* great-great-grandson

tatuaje [ta·tu·'a·xe] *m* tattoo

tatuar < *I. pres:* tatúo> [ta·tu·'ar] *vt* to tattoo

tauca ['tau·ka] *f* **1.** *Bol, Chile, Ecua* (*montón*) heap; **una ~ de papeles** a pile of papers **2.** *Chile* (*talega grande*) sack

taurino, -a [tau·'ri·no, -a] *adj* **1.** (*del toro*) bull-like **2.** (*de la corrida*) bullfighting

Tauro ['tau·ro] *m* Taurus

tauromaquia [tau·ro·'ma·kja] *f* art of bullfighting

taxi ['tak·si] *m* taxi, taxicab

taxista [tak·'sis·ta] *mf* taxi driver, cabdriver

taza ['ta·sa, -θa] *f* **1.** (*de café*) cup; **una ~ de café** (*con café*) a cup of coffee; (*para el café*) coffee cup **2.** (*grande*) mug **3.** (*del wáter*) toilet bowl **4.** (*de fuente*) basin

te [te] **I.** *f* **la letra ~** the letter t **II.** *pron pers* (*objeto directo, indirecto*) you; **¡míra~!** look at yourself! **III.** *pron reflexivo* **~ vistes** you get dressed; **~ levantas** you get up; **no ~ hagas daño** don't hurt yourself; **¿~ has lavado los dientes?** have you brushed your teeth?

té [te] *m* tea

teatral [tea·'tral] *adj* theatre; (*efecto, experiencia, autor*) stage; *fig* theatrical

teatro [te·'a·tro] *m* **1.** (*t. fig*) TEAT theater; **obra de ~** play; **el ~ de Calderón** Calderon's plays; **hacer ~** to work in the theater; *fig* to playact; (*exagerar*) to exaggerate **2.** (*escenario*) stage

techar [te·'tʃar] *vt* to roof

techo ['te·tʃo] *m* **1.** (*de habitación*) ceiling **2.** (*de casa*) roof; **vivir bajo el mismo ~** to live under the same roof **3.** (*tope*) maximum; (*de evolución*) peak

tecla ['te·kla] *f* **1.** (*de piano, ordenador*) key; **~ de mayúsculas** shift key; **~ de retroceso** backspace key; **~ de intro** enter key; **tocar una ~** (*piano, ordenador*) to press a key; **dar en la ~** *inf* to hit the nail on the head; **hay que tocar muchas ~s para averiguar eso** a lot of strings will have to be pulled to find that out; **tocar demasiadas ~s** *fig* to do too many things at once **2.** (*materia*) weak point; **tocar la ~ sensible** to touch a nerve

teclado [te·'kla·do] *m* keyboard; **tocar los ~s en un grupo** to play the keyboards in a group

teclear [te·kle·'ar] *vi* **1.** (*piano*) to play; (*ordenador*) to type **2.** (*dedos*) to drum

técnica ['tek·ni·ka] *f* **1.** (*método*) technique **2.** (*tecnología*) technology

tecnicismo [tek·ni·'sis·mo, -θis·mo] *m* **1.** (*término*) technical term **2.** (*detalle*) technicality

técnico, -a ['tek·ni·ko, -a] **I.** *adj* **1.** (*de la técnica*) technical **2.** (*de especialidad*) technical; **término ~** technical term **II.** *m, f* **1.** TÉC technician; (*de lavadoras*) repairman, engineer **2.** (*especialista*) expert, specialist; **~ de inserción laboral** employment services assistant; **~ de métodos y tiempos** business process consultant **3.** DEP trainer, coach

tecnología [tek·no·lo·'xi·a] *f* **1.** TÉC, ECON technology; **~ punta** leading-edge technology **2.** (*técnica*) technique

tecnológico, -a [tek·no·'lo·xi·ko, -a] *adj* **1.** TÉC technological; (*desarrollo*) technological; **parque ~** technology park **2.** (*técnico*) technical

tecolote [te·ko·'lo·te] *m* AmC, Méx ZOOL (*búho*) owl

tedioso, -a [te·'djo·so, -a] *adj* tedious, wearisome

teja ['te·xa] *f* **1.** (*del tejado*) roof tile; **de color ~** brownish-orange **2.** (*sombrero*) shovel hat ▸ **pagar a toca ~** to pay cash on the nail; **de ~s** (*para*) **abajo** in this world; **de ~s** (*para*) **arriba** in heaven

tejado [te·'xa·do] *m* roof; **empezar la casa por el ~** *fig* to put the cart before the horse; **la pelota sigue en el ~** *fig* it is still in the air ▸ **quien tiene el ~ de vidrio, no tire piedras al de su vecino** *prov* people who live in glass houses shouldn't throw stones *prov*

tejano, -a [te·'xa·no] **I.** *adj* **1.** (*de Tejas*) Texan **2.** (*ropa*) denim; **pantalón ~** jeans **II.** *m, f* Texan

tejaván [te·xa·'βan] *m* AmL **1.** (*cobertizo*) shed **2.** (*corredor*) corridor **3.** (*alero*) eaves *pl* **4.** (*casa*) rustic house with tiled roof

tejedor(a) [te·xe·'dor, --'do·ra] *m(f)* **1.** weaver **2.** ZOOL water strider

tejemaneje [te·xe·ma·'ne·xe] *m inf* **1.** (*actividad*) to-do; **traerse un ~ increíble con los papeles** to make such a fuss with the papers **2.** (*intriga*) scheming; **se deben de traer algún ~** they must be up to sth

tejer [te·'xer] *vt* **1.** (*tela*) to weave; (*tricotar*) to knit; **~ y destejer** *fig* to blow hot and cold **2.** (*cestos, trenzas*) to plait **3.** ZOOL (*araña*) to spin **4.** (*intrigas, plan*) to plot

tejido [te·'xi·do] *m* **1.** *t.* ANAT (*textura*) tissue **2.** (*tela*) fabric; **los ~s** textiles *pl*

tela ['te·la] *f* **1.** (*tejido*) material, fabric; **~ de araña** spider web; **~ metálica** wire screen; **~ de punto** knit; **~ de saco** sackcloth, burlap; **lo cubrieron con una ~ blanca** they covered it with a white cloth **2.** (*en leche*) film; **llegar a las ~s del corazón** *fig* to pull heartstrings **3.** *inf* (*asunto*) matter; **hay ~ para rato** (*para discutir*) there's plenty to talk about; (*para trabajar*) there's a lot to be done; **este asunto trae ~** it's a complicated matter; **este problema tiene ~** this isn't an easy problem **4.** (*lienzo*) canvas; **una ~ de Barceló** a painting by Barceló **5.** *inf* (*dinero*) dough ▸ **poner algo en ~ de juicio** (*dudar*) to question sth; (*tener reparos*) to raise objections about sth

telar [te·'lar] *m* (*máquina*) loom

telaraña [te·la·'ra·ɲa] *f* cobweb, spiderweb; **mirar las ~s** *fig* to have one's head in the clouds; **tener ~s en los ojos** *fig* to be blind to what is going on

tele ['te·le] *f inf abr de* **televisión** TV; **ver la ~** to watch TV

teleadicto, -a [te·le·a·'dik·to, -a] *adj inf* couch potato

telecabina [te·le·ka·'βi·na] *f* cable car

telecomedia [te·le·ko·'me·dja] *f* **1.** (*serie*) sitcom, TV comedy show **2.** (*película*) TV film

telecompra [te·le·'kom·pra] *f* teleshopping

telecomunicación [te·le·ko·mu·ni·ka·'sjon, -'θjon] *f* **1.** (*sistema*) telecommunication; **ingeniero de Telecomunicaciones** telecommunications engineer **2.** *pl* (*empresa*) telecommunications *pl*

teleconferencia [te·le·kon·fe·'ren·sja, -θja] *f* COM teleconference, video-phone conference

telediario [te·le·di·'a·rjo] *m* TV news; **el ~ de las 3** the 3 o'clock news

teléf. [te·'le·fo·no] *abr de* **teléfono** tel.

teleférico [te·le·'fe·ri·ko] *m* cable car
telefonazo [te·le·fo·'na·so, -θo] *m inf* ring; **dar un ~ a alguien** to give sb a ring
telefonía [te·le·fo·'ni·a] *f* telephony
telefónico, -a [te·le·'fo·ni·ko, -a] *adj* **1.** (*de teléfono*) telephone; **cabina telefónica** phone booth; **guía telefónica** telephone directory, phone book; **llamada telefónica** phone call **2.** (*de telefonía*) telephonic
teléfono [te·'le·fo·no] *m* **1.** (*sistema, aparato*) telephone; **~ móvil** cell phone; **~ público** public phone; **~ rojo** *fig* hotline; **~ de tarjeta** card phone; **por ~** over the phone; **hablar por ~** to talk on the phone; **llamar por ~** to telephone **2.** (*número*) phone number **3.** *pl* (*compañía*) telephone company
telegrafiar <3. *pret:* telegrafió> [te·le·ɣra·fi·'ar] *vi, vt* to telegraph
telégrafo [te·'le·ɣra·fo] *m* **1.** (*aparato*) telegraph **2.** *pl* (*administración*) post office
telegrama [te·le·'ɣra·ma] *m* telegram
telenovela [te·le·no·'βe·la] *f* TV soap opera
telenque [te·'len·ke] **I.** *adj* **1.** *Chile* (*temblón*) shaking; (*enfermizo*) sickly **2.** *ElSal* (*torcido*) crooked **II.** *m Guat* (*cachivache*) junk
teleobjetivo [te·le·oβ·xe·'ti·βo] *m* FOTO telephoto lens
telepatía [te·le·pa·'ti·a] *f* telepathy
telepático, -a [te·le·'pa·ti·ko, -a] *adj* telepathic
telescópico, -a [te·les·'ko·pi·ko, -a] *adj* telescopic
telescopio [te·les·'ko·pjo] *m* telescope
telespectador(a [te·les·pek·ta·'dor, -·'do·ra] *m(f)* TV viewer
televidente [te·le·βi·'den·te] *mf v.* **telespectador**
televisar [te·le·βi·'sar] *vt* to televise, to broadcast; (*en directo*) to televise live
televisión [te·le·βi·'sjon] *f* **1.** (*sistema, organización*) television; **~ digital** digital television; **~ de pago** pay-television **2.** *inf* (*televisor*) television, TV set; **~ en color** color TV
televisor [te·le·βi·'sor] *m* television set
télex ['te·leks] *m* telex
telón [te·'lon] *m* curtain; **el ~ de acero** the iron curtain; **~ de fondo** backdrop
tema ['te·ma] *m t.* MÚS, LIT theme; **cada loco con su ~** to each his own; **ése es el ~ de mi sermón** *fig* that's just what I'm always saying; **alejarse del ~** to stray from the issue; **~s de actualidad** current issues
temario [te·'ma·rjo] *m* **1.** (*lista de temas*) program **2.** (*para un examen*) list of topics **3.** (*de una conferencia*) agenda
temática [te·'ma·ti·ka] *f* subjects *pl*
temblar <e→ie> [tem·'blar] *vi* to tremble; **~ de miedo** to tremble with fear; **~ por alguien** to fear for sb; **dejar temblando** (*comer*) to polish off; **~ de frío** to shiver (with cold); **~ de pensarlo** to shudder just to think of it; **~ como un flan** to shake like a leaf; **me tiembla el ojo** my eye is twitching
tembleque [tem·'ble·ke] *m inf* **1.** (*temblor*)

shaking; **me dio un ~** I got the shakes **2.** (*persona*) weakling
temblor [tem·'blor] *m* (*tembleque*) tremor; (*escalofrío*) shiver; **~ de frío** shivers; **~** (**de tierra**) earthquake
tembloroso, -a [tem·blo·'ro·so] *adj* shaky
temer [te·'mer] **I.** *vt* **1.** (*sentir temor*) to fear **2.** (*sospechar*) to be afraid **II.** *vi* to be afraid; **~ por alguien** to fear for sb **III.** *vr:* **~se** to be afraid; **me temo que si/no** I'm afraid so/not
temeroso, -a [te·me·'ro·so, -a] *adj* **1.** (*medroso*) fearful; **~ de Dios** God-fearing; **~ de que...** +*subj* fearful that... **2.** (*temible*) dreadful
temible [te·'mi·βle] *adj* fearsome
temor [te·'mor] *m* **1.** (*miedo*) fear; **por ~ a lo que diga la gente** for fear of what people will say **2.** (*sospecha*) suspicion
témpano ['tem·pa·no] *m* **1.** (*pedazo*) chunk; (*de hielo*) ice floe; **quedarse como un ~** to be chilled to the bone; **tener las manos como un ~** to have ice-cold hands; **él es como un ~** *fig* he is as cold as stone **2.** (*tambor*) kettledrum; (*piel*) drumhead
temperamental [tem·pe·ra·men·'tal] *adj* **1.** (*del temperamento*) temperamental; **característica ~** characteristic of one's nature **2.** (*persona*) spirited
temperamento [tem·pe·ra·'men·to] *m* (*carácter, vivacidad*) temperament; **tener mucho ~** to have a strong character
temperante [tem·pe·'ran·te] **I.** *adj AmS* (*abstemio*) abstemious **II.** *mf AmS* teetotaler
temperatura [tem·pe·ra·'tu·ra] *f* temperature; (*de una persona*) temperature; (*fiebre*) fever; **el niño tiene mucha ~** the boy's running a very high temperature
tempestad [tem·pes·'tad] *f* (*tormenta*) storm; (*marejada*) gale; (*agitación*) turmoil; **~ de injurias** storm of insults; **~ de silbidos** outburst of whistling; **levantar ~es** to produce turmoil; **levantar una ~ de protestas** to raise a storm of protest; **una ~ en un vaso de agua** a storm in a teacup
tempestuoso, -a [tem·pes·tu·'o·so, -a] *adj* tempestuous; (*ambiente*) stormy
templado, -a [tem·'pla·do, -a] *adj* **1.** (*tibio*) lukewarm **2.** (*temperado*) tempered **3.** (*moderado*) moderate; **ser ~ en la bebida** to drink with moderation **4.** (*sereno*) composed **5.** (*valiente*) courageous **6.** *inf* (*bebido*) tipsy; **estar ~** to be drunk **7.** MÚS tuned
templar [tem·'plar] **I.** *vt* **1.** (*moderar*) to moderate; (*suavizar*) to soften; (*calmar*) to calm down **2.** (*calentar*) to warm up **3.** (*entibiar*) to cool down **4.** MÚS (*afinar*) to tune; **~ a alguien la gaita** *fig* to calm sb down **5.** (*apretar*) to tighten **6.** (*mezclar*) to blend **7.** (*acero*) to temper **II.** *vr:* **~se 1.** (*moderarse*) to control oneself **2.** (*calentarse*) to get warm; (*enfriarse*) to cool off **3.** *AmL* (*enamorarse*) to fall in love **4.** *Col, Perú* (*emborracharse*) to get drunk
temple ['tem·ple] *m* **1.** (*valentía*) courage

2. (*carácter*) disposition; (*humor*) mood; **estar de buen/mal ~** to be in a good/bad mood **3.** (*temperatura*) temperature; (*tiempo*) weather **4.** (*del acero: proceso*) tempering; (*dureza*) hardness **5.** MÚS tuning **6.** ARTE tempera

templo ['tem·plo] *m* temple; (*iglesia*) church; **una verdad como un ~** *inf* the naked truth

temporada [tem·po·'ra·da] *f* (*tiempo*) season; (*época*) period; **~ alta** high season; **~ baja** low season; **~ de caza/pesca** hunting/fishing season; **fruta de ~** seasonal fruit; **están pasando por una ~ difícil** they're going through a difficult period

temporal [tem·po·'ral] **I.** *adj* **1.** (*relativo al tiempo*) stormy **2.** (*no permanente*) temporary, provisional; (*no eterno*) temporal; **contrato ~** temporary contract **3.** (*secular*) worldly **4.** ANAT **hueso ~** temporal **II.** *m* **1.** (*tormenta*) storm; (*marejada*) stormy seas *pl*; **capear el ~** *fig* to weather the storm **2.** ANAT temporal bone

temporario, -a [tem·po·'ra·rjo, -a] *adj AmL* temporary

temprano [tem·'pra·no] *adv* **1.** (*a primera hora*) early; **~ por la mañana** early in the morning **2.** (*antes*) early; **llegar (demasiado) ~** to arrive (too) early

temprano, -a [tem·'pra·no, -a] *adj* early; **a edad temprana** at an early age

tenacidad [te·na·si·'dad, te·na·θi-] *f* **1.** (*persona*) tenacity; (*porfía*) perseverance **2.** (*material*) resilience **3.** (*dolor*) persistence; (*mancha*) stubbornness

tenaz [te·'nas, -'naθ] *adj* **1.** (*perseverante*) persevering; (*cabezota*) stubborn; **ser ~ en sus decisiones** to be firm in his/her decisions **2.** (*resistente*) resistant **3.** (*persistente*) persistent; (*niebla*) clinging

tenaza(s) [te·'na·sa(s), -θa(s)] *f(pl)* pliers *pl*

tencha ['ten·tʃa] *f Guat* (*cárcel*) jail

tendajón [ten·da·'xon] *m Méx* small shop

tendear [ten·de·'ar] *vi Méx* to window-shop

tendencia [ten·'den·sja, -θja] *f* **1.** (*inclinación*) tendency; **tener ~ a** to have a tendency to **2.** (*dirección*) trend; **~ alcista** upward [*o* bullish] trend; **~ al alza/a la baja** upward/downward trend, bullish/bearish; **las últimas ~s de la moda** the latest fashion trends **3.** (*aspiración*) **~ a algo** drift toward sth; **~s autonomistas** trend toward self-government

tender <e→ie> [ten·'der] **I.** *vt* **1.** (*desdoblar, esparcir*) **~ sobre algo** to spread over sth; **~ la cama** *AmL* to make the bed; **~ la mesa** *AmL* to lay the table **2.** (*tumbar*) to lay; (*de golpe*) to throw down **3.** (*colocar: ropa*) to hang out; (*cuerda*) to stretch; (*puente*) to build; (*línea, vía*) to lay **4.** (*aproximar*) to hold out; **~ la mano a alguien** *fig* to give sb a hand **II.** *vi* **1.** (*inclinarse, aspirar*) to tend; **tu cabello tiende a rojizo** your hair is slightly reddish; **tiendo a ser optimista** I tend to be optimistic **2.** MAT to tend toward **III.** *vr:* **~se 1.** (*tum-*

barse) to stretch out **2.** (*abandonarse*) to let oneself go

tendido [ten·'di·do] *m* **1.** (*de un cable*) laying **2.** (*cables*) cables *pl*, wiring **3.** (*ropa*) wash **4.** TAUR *front rows of seats* **5.** *AmL* (*de la cama*) bed linen

tendón [ten·'don] *m* ANAT tendon

tenebroso, -a [te·ne·'βro·so, -a] *adj t. fig* (*oscuro*) dark; (*tétrico*) gloomy

tenedor [te·ne·'dor] *m* (*para comer*) fork

tenedor(a) [te·ne·'dor, -'do·ra] *m(f)* **1.** (*propietario*) holder; **~ de tierras** landowner **2.** FIN **~ de libros** bookkeeper

tenencia [te·'nen·sja, -θja] *f* JUR possession; **~ ilícita de armas** illegal possession of arms

tener [te·'ner] *irr* **I.** *vt* **1.** (*poseer, disfrutar, sentir, padecer*) to have; **~ los ojos azules** to have blue eyes; **~ 29 años** to be 29 years old; **~ hambre/sed/calor/sueño** to be hungry/thirsty/hot/sleepy; **~ poco de tonto** to be no fool; **¿(con que) ésas tenemos?** so that's the way it is?; **~la tomada con alguien** *inf* to have it in for sb; **no ~las todas consigo** not to be sure of something; **no ~ nada que perder** to have nothing to lose; **no ~ precio** to be priceless; **~ cariño a alguien** to be fond of sb; **~ la culpa de algo** to be to blame for sth; **¿tienes frío?** are you cold?; **le tengo lástima** I feel sorry for him/her; **~ sueño** to be sleepy **2.** (*considerar*) **~ por algo** to consider sth; **~ a alguien en menos/mucho** to think all the less/more of sb; **ten por seguro que...** rest assured that...; **tengo para mí que...** I think tha... **3.** (*guardar*) to keep **4.** (*contener*) to have; **el frasco ya no tiene miel** there's no honey left in the jar **5.** (*coger*) to take; **ten esto** take this **6.** (*sujetar*) to hold; **~ a alguien por el brazo** to hold sb by the arm **7.** (*recibir*) to have; **~ un niño** to have a baby **8.** (*hacer sentir*) **me tienes preocupada** I'm worried about you; **me tienes loca** you're driving me mad! **9.** (*cumplir*) **~ su palabra** to keep one's word **II.** *vr:* **~se 1.** (*considerarse*) **~se por algo** to consider oneself sth; **~ se en mucho** to think highly of oneself **2.** (*sostenerse*) to stand; **~se de pie** to stand; **~se firme** to stand upright; *fig* to stand firm; **estoy que no me tengo** I'm exhausted **3.** (*dominarse*) to control oneself **4.** (*atenerse*) to adhere **III.** *aux* **1.** (*con participio concordante*) **~ pensado hacer algo** to plan to do sth; **ya tengo comprado todo** I've bought everything already; **~se algo callado** to keep quiet about sth; **ya me lo tenía pensado** I had already thought of that **2.** (*obligación, necesidad*) **~ que** to have to; **~ mucho que hacer** to have a lot to do; **¿qué tiene que ver esto conmigo?** what does this have to do with me?

tenida [te·'ni·da] *f Chile* meeting; (*traje*) suit; (*uniforme*) uniform

teniente [te·'njen·te] *m* MIL lieutenant; **~ coronel** lieutenant-colonel

tenis ['te·nis] *m* tennis; **~ de mesa** table tennis

T

tenor [te·'nor] *m* **1.** *t.* MÚS (*contenido*) tenor; **a este** ~ at this rate; **a** ~ **de** according to **2.** (*constitución*) constitution

tensar [ten·'sar] *vt* (*músculo*) to tense; (*cuerda*) to tighten

tensión [ten·'sjon] *f* **1.** FÍS tension **2.** (*estado: cosa*) stress; (*cuerda, piel*) tautness; (*nervios, músculos*) tension; (*impaciencia*) anxiety; **película de** ~ thriller; **estar en** ~ (*nervioso*) to be nervous; (*impaciente*) to be anxious **3.** MED ~ **arterial** blood pressure **4.** ELEC voltage **5.** *pl* (*conflicto*) strained relations *pl*

tenso, -a ['ten·so, -a] *adj* (*cosa, situación*) tense; (*cuerda, piel*) taut; (*músculos, nervios*) tense; (*impaciente*) anxious

tentación [ten·ta·'sjon, -'θjon] *f* temptation; **me dan tentaciones de...** I'm tempted to...; **caer en la** ~ to succumb [*o* give in] to the temptation

tentáculo [ten·'ta·ku·lo] *m* tentacle

tentar <e→ie> [ten·'tar] *vt* **1.** (*palpar*) to feel; (*reconocer*) to probe **2.** (*atraer*) to tempt; (*seducir*) to entice; **no me tientes** don't tempt me

tentativa [ten·ta·'ti·βa] *f* attempt; ~ **de robo** attempted robbery

tenue ['te·nwe] *adj* **1.** (*delgado*) fine; (*delicado*) delicate **2.** (*sutil*) subtle; (*débil*) weak; **luz** ~ faint light **3.** (*sencillo*) simple

teñir [te·'nir] *irr como ceñir vt, vr:* ~**se** to dye; ~**(se) de rojo** to dye red; ~ **de tristeza** to tinge with sadness

teología [teo·lo·'xi·a] *f* theology

teólogo, -a [te·'o·lo·γo, -a] **I.** *adj* theological **II.** *m, f* theologian; (*estudiante*) divinity student

teorema [teo·'re·ma] *m* theorem

teoría [teo·'ri·a] *f* theory; ~ **del caos** the chaos theory; **en** ~ in theory

teórica [te·'o·ri·ka] *f* theoretics *pl*

teórico, -a [te·'o·ri·ko, -a] **I.** *adj* theoretical **II.** *m, f* theorist, theoretician

tepache [te·'pa·tʃe] *m Méx* CULIN tepache (*drink made of fermented agave cactus juice, water, pineapple and cloves*)

tequesquite [te·kes·'ki·te] *m Méx* rock salt

tequiche [te·'ki·tʃe] *m Ven* CULIN *dish made with toasted corn, coconut milk and butter*

tequila [te·'ki·la] *m* tequila

tequio ['te·kjo] *m AmC, Méx* **1.** (*molestia*) bother **2.** (*daño*) harm

tequioso, -a [te·'kjo·so, -a] *adj AmC* **1.** (*travieso*) mischievous; (*niño*) trying **2.** (*molesto*) bothersome

TER [ter] *m abr de* **Tren Español Rápido** express train (*Spanish intercity high-speed train*)

terapeuta [te·ra·'peu·ta] *mf* therapist

terapéutica [te·ra·'peu·ti·ka] *f* therapeutics *pl*

terapia [te·'ra·pja] *f* therapy; ~ **en** [*o* de] **grupo** group therapy

tercena [ter·'se·na, -'θe·na] *f Ecua* butcher's shop

tercer [ter·'ser, -'θer] *adj v.* **tercero**

tercermundista [ter·ser·mun·'dis·ta, ter·θer-] *adj* third-world, underdeveloped

Tercer Mundo [ter·'ser 'mun·do, -'θer] *m* Third World

tercero [ter·'se·ro, ter·'θe-] **I.** *m* **1.** *t.* JUR third party **2.** (*alcahuete*) procurer **II.** *adv* third

tercero, -a [ter·'se·ro, -a; ter·'θe-] **I.** *adj* (*delante de un sustantivo masculino: tercer*) third; **terceras personas** third parties; **en tercer lugar** thirdly; **ser** ~ to be the odd man out; **viven en el** ~ they live on the third floor; **tercera edad** senior citizens, retirement years ▶**a la tercera va la vencida** *prov* third time lucky *prov* **II.** *m, f* third; *v.t.* **octavo**

terciar [ter·'sjar, -'θjar] **I.** *vt* **1.** (*dividir*) to divide into three parts **2.** (*atravesar*) to place diagonally across **3.** (*la carga*) to balance **4.** *AmL* (*aguar*) to water down **II.** *vi* **1.** (*intervenir*) to intervene **2.** (*mediar*) to have a word **3.** (*participar*) to take part; ~ **en un juego** to join in a game **III.** *vr, vimpers:* ~**se 1.** (*ocurrir*) to arise; **si se tercia** should the occasion arise; **prepararse por lo que se pueda** ~ to get ready for what may happen **2.** (*ponerse*) to make up the number

tercio ['ter·sjo, -θjo] *m* (*parte*) third; *v.t.* **octavo** ▶**hacer buen/mal** ~ **a alguien** to do sb a good/bad turn

terciopelo [ter·sjo·'pe·lo, ter·θjo-] *m* velvet; **lazo de** ~ velvet bow

terco, -a ['ter·ko, -a] **I.** *adj* **1.** (*persona*) stubborn, obstinate **2.** (*niño*) unruly **3.** (*animal*) balky **4.** (*cosa*) tough **II.** *m, f* stubborn person

tereque [te·'re·ke] *m Col, RDom, PRico, Ven* (*cachivache*) utensil

tergiversar [ter·xi·βer·'sar] *vt* (*hechos*) to misrepresent; (*la verdad*) to distort

termas ['ter·mas] *fpl* (*baños*) hot baths *pl*

térmico, -a ['ter·mi·ko, -a] *adj* thermal; **central térmica** thermal power plant

terminación [ter·mi·na·'sjon, -'θjon] *f* **1.** (*acción*) termination; (*de un proyecto*) completion; (*producción*) finish; (*de un plazo*) end **2.** (*final*) end; (*borde*) end, edge

terminal¹ [ter·mi·'nal] **I.** *adj* terminal; **parte** ~ final part; **un enfermo** ~ a terminally ill patient **II.** *m* COMPUT terminal

terminal² [ter·mi·'nal] *f* **1.** (*estación*) terminal, terminus; FERRO station **2.** (*de aeropuerto*) terminal; ~ **aérea** air terminal

terminar [ter·mi·'nar] **I.** *vt* **1.** (*finalizar*) to finish; (*proyecto*) to complete; **¿cuándo terminas?** when will you be done? **2.** (*producir*) to finish; **¿cuándo van a ~ el puerto?** when are they going to finish the port?; **estar bien terminado** to be well finished **3.** (*consumir*) to finish up; (*beber*) to drink up; (*comer*) to eat up **II.** *vi* **1.** (*tener fin*) to finish, to end; (*plazo, contrato*) to end; ~ **bien/mal** to have a happy/unhappy ending; ~ **en punta** to end in a point; ~ **de construir** to finish building; ~ **de hacer/coser/comer** to finish doing/sewing/eating; **cuando termines de comer...** when you finish eating...; **¿cuándo termina la película?** what time does the film end?; **la escuela termina a las dos** school is out at 2 pm **2.** (*acercarse al final*) to be ending; **ya termina la película** the film is almost over **3.** (*poner fin*) to put an end to **4.** (*destruir*) to do away; **el tabaco va a ~ contigo** tobacco is going to be the end of you! **5.** (*separarse*) to break up **6.** (*llegar a*) **~ por hacer algo** to end up doing sth; **terminaron peleándose** they wound up fighting **7.** (*haber hecho*) **~ de hacer algo** to have just done sth **III.** *vr:* **~se 1.** (*aproximarse al final*) to be almost over **2.** (*no haber más*) (for) there to be no more; **me está terminando la paciencia** I'm running out of patience; **se terminaron las galletas** there aren't any more biscuits (left)

término [ter·'mi·no] *m* **1.** (*fin*) end; **dar ~ a algo** to finish sth off; **llevar a ~** to carry out; **poner ~ a algo** to put an end to sth; **sin ~** endless; **me bajé en el ~** I got off at the terminus; **he llegado al ~ de mi paciencia** I've reached the end of my patience **2.** (*plazo*) period; **en el ~ de quince días** within 15 days **3.** (*linde*) boundary **4.** ADMIN district; **~ municipal** township **5.** (*vocablo*) word; (*especial*) term; **en buenos ~s** on good terms; **en otros ~s** in other words; **contestar en malos ~s** to answer rudely **6.** (*parte*) term **7.** *pl* (*de un contrato*) terms *pl*, conditions *pl* ▶ **estar en buenos/malos ~s** to be on good/bad terms; **separarse en buenos/malos ~s** to separate on good/bad terms; **en ~s generales** generally speaking; **~ medio** compromise; **en medios ~s** with vague half-answers; **en primer ~** first of all; **en último ~** as a last resort; **por ~ medio** on the average

terminología [ter·mi·no·lo·'xi·a] *f* terminology
terminótica [ter·mi·'no·ti·ka] *f* LING terminotics
termita [ter·'mi·ta] *f* termite
termo ['ter·mo] *m* thermos
termómetro [ter·'mo·me·tro] *m* thermometer; **~ clínico** clinical thermometer
termostato [ter·mos·'ta·to] *m*, **termóstato** [ter·'mos·ta·to] *m* thermostat, thermal switch
ternejo, -a [ter·'ne·xo, -a] *adj* Ecua, Perú (*persona*) lively
ternera [ter·'ne·ra] *f* (*carne*) beef, veal
ternero, -a [ter·'ne·ro, -a] *m, f* calf
ternura [ter·'nu·ra] *f* **1.** (*cariño*) tenderness **2.** (*dulzura*) sweetness **3.** (*delicadeza, sensibilidad*) gentleness **4.** Chile, Ecua, Guat (*inmadurez*) greenness
terquedad [ter·ke·'dad] *f* **1.** (*testarudez*) stubbornness, obstinacy **2.** (*porfía*) willfulness **3.** (*de un niño*) unruliness
terracota [te·rra·'ko·ta] *f* terracotta
terraplén [te·rra·'plen] *m* **1.** (*montón*) mound; (*protección*) rampart **2.** (*desnivel*) slope; **~ de un ferrocarril** railway embankment
terráqueo, -a [te·'rra·keo, -a] **I.** *adj* terraqueous; **globo ~** globe **II.** *m, f* earthling

terrateniente [te·rra·te·'njen·te] *mf* landowner, landholder
terraza [te·'rra·sa, -θa] *f* **1.** (*jardín*) terrace; (*balcón*) balcony; (*azotea*) flat roof **2.** (*de una cafetería*) terrace (*area outside a bar or café where tables are placed to serve customers in good weather*)
terregal [te·rre·'γal] *m* Méx loose topsoil
terremoto [te·rre·'mo·to] *m* earthquake
terrenal [te·rre·'nal] *adj* worldly; **paraíso ~** earthly paradise
terreno [te·'rre·no] *m* **1.** (*suelo*) land; GEO terrain; **~ arcilloso** clayey ground **2.** (*espacio*) lot; (*parcela*) plot of land; (*campo*) field; DEP playing field; **~ de fútbol** soccer field; **~ edificable** buildable land; **vehículo todo ~** all-terrain vehicle **3.** (*esfera*) sphere; **~ desconocido** unfamiliar territory; **estar en su propio ~** to be on one's own ground ▶ **ceder ~** to give up ground; **explorar el ~** to see how the land lies; **ganar/perder ~** to gain/lose ground; **minar el ~ a alguien** to undermine sb's plans; **preparar el ~ para algo** to pave the way for sth; **ser ~ abonado para...** to be ideal for...
terrestre [te·'rres·tre] **I.** *adj* **1.** (*de la Tierra*) terrestrial; **globo ~** globe **2.** (*en la tierra*) earthly; **animal ~** land animal; **transporte ~** ground transport **3.** (*terrenal*) earthly **II.** *mf* terrestrial
terrible [te·'rri·βle] *adj* terrible; **hace un frío ~** it's terribly cold; **tener un hambre ~** to be terribly hungry
terrícola [te·'rri·ko·la] *mf* earthling, earth dweller
territorial [te·rri·to·'rjal] *adj* territorial; **división ~** territorial division
territorio [te·rri·'to·rjo] *m* **1.** (*región*) territory; POL region/district; JUR district; **~ jurisdiccional** jurisdictional territory; **en todo el ~ nacional** over the whole country, nationwide **2.** ZOOL territory
terror [te·'rror] *m* **1.** (*miedo*) terror; **película de ~** horror film; **las arañas me dan ~** I'm terrified of spiders; **me domina el ~** I'm terrified **2.** (*que provoca miedo*) terror **3.** POL terror; **reino de ~** reign of terror
terrorismo [te·rro·'ris·mo] *m* terrorism
terrorista [te·rro·'ris·ta] **I.** *adj* terrorist; **organización ~** terrorist organization **II.** *mf* terrorist
terso, -a ['ter·so, -a] *adj* **1.** (*liso*) smooth; (*tirante*) taut **2.** (*limpio*) clean; (*transparente*) clear; (*brillante*) shiny
tertulia [ter·'tu·lja] *f* **1.** (*reunión*) gathering; **estar de ~** to talk; **hacer ~** to meet informally to talk; **~ literaria** literary circle **2.** (*para jugar*) games room
tesis ['te·sis] *f inv* **1.** (*proposición*) theory **2.** (*trabajo*) thesis; **~ doctoral** doctorate [*o* doctoral] thesis
tesón [te·'son] *m* tenacity; **trabajar con ~** to work diligently

tesonero, -a [te·so·'ne·ro, -a] *adj AmL* **1.** (*perseverante*) persevering **2.** (*tenaz*) tenacious

tesorería [te·so·re·'ri·a] *f* **1.** (*cargo*) treasury **2.** *t.* FIN (*despacho*) treasurer's office

tesoro [te·'so·ro] *m* **1.** (*de gran valor*) treasure; **ser un ~ de una persona** to be a real treasure; **valer un ~** to be worth a fortune **2.** (*fortuna*) fortune; **~ (público)** (public) treasury **3.** (*cariño*) dear

testamentario, -a [tes·ta·men·'ta·rjo, -a] **I.** *adj* testamentary **II.** *m, f* executor *m,* executrix *f*

testamento [tes·ta·'men·to] *m* will, testament; **~ abierto** nuncupative will; **hacer ~** to make one's will

testar [tes·'tar] *vi* to make a will

testarudez [tes·ta·ru·'des, -'deθ] *f* **1.** (*cualidad*) pigheadedness **2.** (*acción*) an act of stubbornness

testículo [tes·'ti·ku·lo] *m* ANAT testicle

testificar <c→qu> [tes·ti·fi·'kar] **I.** *vt* **1.** (*declarar*) to testify; (*testigo*) to witness **2.** (*afirmar: testigo*) to attest; (*documento*) to bear witness **3.** (*demostrar*) to give evidence **II.** *vi* to testify

testigo[1] [tes·'ti·ɣo] *mf t.* JUR witness; **~ de cargo/de descargo** witness for the prosecution/defense; **~ de matrimonio** witness at sb's wedding; **~ ocular** eyewitness; **fui ~ del accidente** I witnessed the accident; **examinar ~s** to examine witnesses; **poner a alguien por ~** to cite sb as witness

testigo[2] [tes·'ti·ɣo] *m* **1.** (*prueba*) proof; **ser ~ de algo** to bear witness to sth **2.** DEP baton

testimonial [tes·ti·mo·'njal] *adj* **1.** (*que afirma*) attesting; **declaración ~** testimony **2.** (*que prueba*) evidentiary

testimoniar [tes·ti·mo·'njar] **I.** *vt* **1.** (*declarar*) to testify **2.** (*afirmar*) to attest **3.** (*dar muestra*) to show **4.** (*probar*) to evidence **II.** *vi* to bear witness

testimonio [tes·ti·'mo·njo] *m* **1.** (*declaración*) testimony; **dar ~** to bear witness; **no levantarás falso ~** thou shalt not bear false witness **2.** (*afirmación*) statement **3.** (*muestra, prueba*) evidence

testosterona [tes·tos·te·'ro·na] *m* **1.** (*hormona*) testosterone **2.** *inf* (*violencia brutal*) **es una película con mucha ~** it's a film with a lot of violence

teta ['te·ta] *f* **1.** *inf* (*pecho*) breast; **niño de ~** *inf* babe-in-arms; **dar la ~** to breast-feed; **quitar la ~** to wean **2.** (*ubre*) udder **3.** (*pezón: mujer*) nipple; (*animal*) teat

tétano(s) ['te·ta·no(s)] *m* (*inv*) MED tetanus

tetera [te·'te·ra] *f* **1.** (*para té*) teapot; (*para hervir*) kettle **2.** *AmL* (*tetilla*) nipple **3.** *AmL v.* **tetero**

tetero [te·'te·ro] *m AmL* baby's bottle

tétrico, -a ['te·tri·ko, -a] *adj* dismal

textil [tes·'til] **I.** *adj* textile; **planta ~** textile mill **II.** *m* textile

texto ['tes·to] *m* text; (*pasaje*) extract; (**libro de**) **~** textbook

textual [tes·tu·'al] *adj* **1.** (*relativo al texto*) textual; (*escrito*) written **2.** (*conforme al texto*) textual; (*literal*) word-for-word; (*exacto*) exact; **con las palabras ~es** with those exact words

textura [tes·'tu·ra] *f* **1.** (*tejido*) weave **2.** (*estructura*) structure; GEO, QUÍM texture

tez [tes, teθ] *f* complexion; **de ~ morena** dark

ti [ti] *pron pers* **a ~** (*objeto directo, indirecto*) you; **de ~** from you; **de ~ para mí** from you for me; **para ~** for you; **por ~** for you

tía ['ti·a] *f* **1.** (*pariente*) aunt; **~ abuela** great-aunt; **¡(cuéntaselo a) tu ~!** *inf* tell that to the marines!; **no hay tu ~** *inf* nothing doing! **2.** *inf* (*mujer*) woman; **ser una ~ buena** to be a good-looking woman; **vaya ~ más tonta** what a stupid woman!; **pero ~, ¿qué te pasa?** hey, girl, what's the matter with you?

tianguis ['tjan·gis] *m inv, Méx* (*rastro indígena*) street market

tibia ['ti·βja] *f* ANAT tibia, shinbone *inf*

tibiarse [ti·'βjar·se] *vr AmC, Ven* (*irritarse*) to get cross

tibiera [ti·'βje·ra] *f Ven* **1.** (*molestia*) irritation **2.** (*fastidio*) nuisance

tibieza [ti·'βje·sa, -θa] *f* tepidness; (*apatía*) halfheartedness; (*frialdad en el trato*) coolness

tibio, -a ['ti·βjo, -a] *adj* **1.** (*temperatura*) lukewarm **2.** (*carácter, sentimiento*) unenthusiastic **3.** *AmL, inf* (*enfadado*) angry ▸ **poner ~ a alguien** to lay in to sb

tibor [ti·'βor] *m* **1.** (*vasija*) vase **2.** *AmL* (*orinal*) chamber pot

tiburón [ti·βu·'ron] *m* **1.** ZOOL shark **2.** FIN raider

tico, -a ['ti·ko, -a] *adj, m, f AmL, inf* (*costarricense*) Costa Rican

tiempo ['tjem·po] *m* **1.** (*momento, duración, periodo*) time; **~ libre/de ocio** spare/leisure time; **al poco ~** shortly after; **~ de pago** payday; **los buenos ~s** the good old days; **a ~** in time; **a ~ parcial** part-time; **a su ~** in due course; **todo a su ~** all in good time; **al (mismo) ~, a un ~** at the same time; **al que...** while...; **antes de ~** early; **llegar antes de ~** to arrive ahead of time; **andando el ~** in the course of time; **con ~** in good time; **llegué a la estación con ~** I reached the station early; **hazlo con ~** don't leave it for the last minute; **de ~ en ~** from time to time; **desde hace mucho ~** for a long time; **durante cierto ~** for some time; **en estos ~s** nowadays; **en ~s de paz** in peacetime; **en ~s de Franco** in the Franco era; **en mis ~s** in my time [*o* day]; **en otros ~s** in the past; **el ~ pasa volando** time flies; **amanecerán ~s mejores** better days are coming; **dar ~ al ~** to give it time; **hace ~ que...** it's a long time since...; **hace ~ que no voy al cine** I haven't been to the cinema for a long time; **¡cuánto ~ sin verte!** long time no see!; **les faltó ~ para decirlo a todos** it didn't take them long to tell everyone; **hay** ~ there's time; **matar el/hacer** ~ to kill time; **mucho/ demasiado** ~ long/too long; **perder el** ~ to waste time; **sin perder** ~ losing no time; **si me da** ~... if I have enough time; **ya es** ~ **que** +*subj* it's about time; **tomarse** ~ to take one's time **2.**(*época*) time; (*estación*) season **3.** METEO weather; **cerveza del** ~ beer at room temperature; ~ **de perros** filthy weather; **si el** ~ **no lo impide** weather permitting; **hoy hace mal** ~ the weather is bad today **4.** LING tense; ~ **presente** present tense **5.**(*edad*) age; **¿cuánto** ~ **tiene el niño?** how old is the child? **6.** DEP (**medio**) ~ half-time; ~ **muerto** time out **7.** MÚS time, beat; (*parte*) movement; TÉC stroke; **motor de dos** ~s two-stroke engine ▸ **a(l) mal** ~ **buena cara** *prov* you have to look on the bright side of things *prov;* **el** ~ **es oro** *prov* time is money *prov;* **el** ~ **no perdona** *prov* time and tide wait for no man *prov*

tienda ['tjen·da] *f* **1.**(*establecimiento*) shop, store; ~ **de comestibles** grocery store; **ir de** ~s to go shopping **2.**(*alojamiento*) ~ (**de campaña**) tent; **montar/desmontar una** ~ to put up [*o* pitch]/take down a tent

tiento ['tjen·to] *m* **1.**(*acción*) touch; **a** ~ gropingly **2.**(*tacto*) tact; (*cautela*) caution; **con** ~ carefully; (*cuidado*) care

tierno, -a ['tjer·no, -a] **I.** *adj* **1.**(*blando*) soft; (*pan, dulces*) fresh **2.**(*suave, delicado, sensible*) tender; **a tierna edad** at a tender age; **desde mi más tierna edad...** since I was very young...; **en mi más tierna niñez** in early childhood; **¡qué** ~**!** how tender! **3.**(*cariñoso*) affectionate **4.** *Chile, Ecua, Guat* (*inmaduro*) green **II.** *m, f Guat, Nic* newborn or very young child

tierra ['tje·rra] *f* **1.**(*materia, superficie, planeta*) earth; ~ **vegetal** humus; **toma de** ~ ELEC ground; **bajo** ~ MIN underground; **estar bajo** ~ to be buried; ~ **de nadie** no-man's-land; ~s **altas/bajas** highlands/lowlands; **dar en** ~ to fall; **caer por** ~ *fig* to crumble; **echar** ~ **a algo** *fig* to cover sth up; **echar por** ~ to knock down; *fig* to ruin; **me falta** ~ *fig* I'm not sure; **¡trágame,** ~**!** *inf* I wish the ground would open up and swallow me!; **parece que se lo ha tragado la** ~ *inf* it is as if he had vanished off the face of the earth **2.**(*firme*) mainland; ~ **adentro** inland; **poner** ~ **por medio** to make oneself scarce; **tomar** ~ AVIAT to land, to touch down; NÁUT to land; **como no lleguemos pronto a la estación, nos vamos a quedar en** ~ if we don't get to the station soon, the train will leave without us **3.**(*región*) land; **Tierra Santa** Holy Land; ~ (**natal**) native land **4.**(*hacienda*) property; ~ **de labor** agricultural land; ~ **de pastos** grazing land; **poseer** ~s to own land; **aquí, como en toda la** ~ **de garbanzos...** *inf* here, like everywhere in the world

tierral [tje·'rral] *m AmL* (*polvareda*) cloud of dust

tieso, -a ['tje·so, -a] *adj* **1.**(*rígido*) stiff; **dejar** ~ **a alguien** *inf* (*matar*) to bump sb off; (*sorprender*) to dumbfound; **quedarse** ~ (*de frío*) to be frozen stiff; (*miedo*) to be scared stiff; (*morirse*) to croak; (*dormirse*) to fall asleep **2.**(*erguido*) erect; (*orejas*) pricked up **3.**(*terco*) unbending; **tenérselas tiesas** to hold firm **4.**(*serio*) stiff **5.**(*engreído*) conceited; **no te pongas** ~ don't act so stuck up **6.**(*tirante*) taut

tiesto ['tjes·to] *m* **1.**(*maceta*) flowerpot **2.** *Chile* (*vasija*) pot, bowl

tifón [ti·'fon] *m* **1.**(*huracán*) typhoon **2.**(*tromba*) waterspout

tifus ['ti·fus] *m inv* MED typhus

tigre, -a ['ti·γre, ti·'γre·sa] *m, f AmL* ZOOL jaguar

tigre(sa) ['ti·γre, -a] *m(f)* **1.** ZOOL tiger *m*, tigress *f;* **oler a** ~ *inf* to stink **2.**(*persona*) tiger

tijera [ti·'xe·ra] *f* **1.**(*pl*) (*utensilio, con esta forma*) scissors *pl;* (*más grandes*) shears *pl;* **silla de** ~ folding chair; **echar** ~ **a algo** *inf* to start cutting sth **2.**(*persona*) gossip **3.** DEP scissor-kick

tildar [til·'dar] *vt* **1.**(*con acento*) to put an accent on **2.**(*la ñ*) to put a tilde over **3.**(*a alguien*) ~ **de algo** to brand as sth **4.**(*tachar*) to cross out

tilde ['til·de] *f* **1.**(*acento*) accent **2.**(*de la ñ*) tilde **3.**(*tacha*) flaw **4.**(*cosa mínima*) jot

tiliches [ti·'li·tʃes] *mpl AmC, Méx* (*trastos*) junk

tilingo, -a [ti·'lin·go, -a] *adj* **1.** *CSur, Méx* (*atolondrado*) silly **2.** *Arg* (*demente*) soft in the head

timar [ti·'mar] **I.** *vt* to con **II.** *vr:* ~ **se** (*hacerse guiños*) to make eyes at each other; (*tontear*) to flirt

timba ['tim·ba] *f inf* **1.**(*partida*) game **2.**(*lugar*) gambling den **3.** *AmL* (*barriga*) belly

timbrar [tim·'brar] *vt* (*pegar*) to put a stamp on; (*estampar*) to postmark

timbre ['tim·bre] *m* **1.**(*aparato*) bell; (*de la puerta*) doorbell; **han tocado el** ~ somebody rang the bell **2.** *t.* MÚS (*sonido*) timbre **3.**(*sello que se pega*) stamp; (*que se estampa*) seal **4.**(*acción*) action to one's credit; ~ **de gloria** mark of honor; **ser un** ~ **de gloria para alguien** to be a credit to sb

timidez [ti·mi·'des, -'deθ] *f* shyness

tímido, -a ['ti·mi·do, -a] *adj* shy, timid

timón [ti·'mon] *m* rudder; **llevar el** ~ **de una empresa** *inf* to be at the helm of a business

tímpano ['tim·pa·no] *m* **1.** ANAT (*membrana*) eardrum **2.**(*instrumento*) kettledrum

tina ['ti·na] *f* vat; *AmL* (*bañera*) bathtub

tincanque [tin·'kan·ke] *m Chile, inf* flip

tincar <c→qu> [tin·'kar] *vt* **1.** *Chile* (*presentir*) to have a hunch **2.** *Arg, Chile* (*pelota*) to drive

tincazo [tin·'ka·so, -θo] *m Arg, Ecua, inf* flick

tinga ['tin·ga] *f Méx* (*alboroto*) uproar

tingo ['tin·go] *Méx* **del** ~ **al tango** from pillar to post

T

tiniebla [ti·'nje·βla] *f* darkness

tino ['ti·no] *m* 1.(*puntería*) aim 2.(*destreza*) skill 3.(*moderación*) moderation; **a buen ~** by guesswork; **sin ~** recklessly; **estar a ~** to be guessing; **sacar de ~ a alguien** to exasperate sb 4.(*tina*) vat

tinoso, -a [ti·'no·so, -a] *adj Col, Ven* 1.(*hábil*) skillful 2.(*sensato*) sensible

tinta ['tin·ta] *f* 1.(*para escribir*) ink; **~ china** Indian ink; **~ de imprenta** printer's ink; **a dos ~s** in two colors; **cargar las ~s** to exaggerate; **sobre este asunto han corrido ríos de ~** much has been written about this matter 2.(*color*) hue; **medias ~s** half-tones; *fig* half measures

tinte ['tin·te] *m* 1.(*teñidura*) dye 2.(*colorante*) coloring 3.(*tintorería*) dry cleaner's 4.(*matiz*) tinge; (*apariencia*) touch; **un cierto ~ de escepticismo** a certain tint of skepticism; **tus palabras tenían un cierto ~ de ironía** his words were tinged with irony

tinterillo [tin·te·'ri·jo, -ʎo] *m pey* 1.(*chupatintas*) pencil pusher 2.*AmL* (*picapleitos*) shyster lawyer

tintero [tin·'te·ro] *m* inkwell; **dejar(se) algo en el ~** *fig* to leave sth unsaid

tinto, -a ['tin·to, -a] *adj* (*rojo oscuro*) dark red; (*uvas*) red; **vino ~** red wine

tintorería [tin·to·re·'ri·a] *f* dry cleaner's

tintura [tin·'tu·ra] *f* 1.(*tinte*) tint 2.(*colorante*) dye 3.(*maquillaje*) rouge 4.MED tincture

tío ['ti·o, -a] *m* 1.(*pariente*) uncle; **~ abuelo** great-uncle; **mis ~s** my aunt and uncle; **tener un ~ en América** to have a rich friend or relative 2.*inf* (*hombre*) guy; **¡oye ~!** hey, man!; **ser un ~ bueno** to be a good-looking guy

tipear [ti·pe·'ar] *vi AmC, AmS* to type

típico, -a ['ti·pi·ko, -a] *adj* typical; **plato ~** local or traditional dish

tipificar [ti·pi·fi·'kar] *vt* 1.(*normalizar*) to standardize 2.(*caracterizar*) to typify

tipo ['ti·po] *m* 1.(*modelo*) model 2.(*muestra*) sample; (*espécimen*) type; **un impreso/una carta ~** a standard form/letter 3.(*cuerpo*) build; **aguantar el ~** to hold out; **mover el ~** *inf* to get moving; **tener buen ~** to have a good figure; **él tiene buen ~** he's well-built 4.(*clase*) type, kind 5.FIN rate; **~ de cambio** exchange rate 6.TIPO type

tipo, -a ['ti·po, -a] *m, f* 1.*inf* guy *m,* woman *f* 2.*pey* character; **~ raro** weirdo; **no soporto esa tipa** I can't stand that bitch

tipografía [ti·po·ɣra·'fi·a] *f* (*impresión*) printing; (*taller*) printing press

tipógrafo, -a [ti·'po·ɣra·fo] *m, f* printer

tiquear [ti·ke·'ar] *vt* 1.*AmC, PRico, Col* (*chequear*) to check 2.*Chile* (*perforar*) to punch

tira ['ti·ra] *f* (*banda*) strip, band; **~ cómica** comic strip; **hacer ~s algo** to tear sth to shreds

tirabuzón [ti·ra·βu·'son, -'θon] *m* 1.(*rizo*) ringlet, curl 2.(*sacacorchos*) corkscrew

tirada [ti·'ra·da] *f* 1.(*edición*) print run; **el**

periódico local tiene una ~ de 10.000 ejemplares the local paper has a circulation of 10,000 copies; **de una ~** *fig* without stopping 2.(*distancia*) stretch

tiradero [ti·ra·'de·ro] *m Méx* (*vertedero*) garbage dump

tirado, -a [ti·'ra·do, -a] I. *adj* 1.estar *inf* (*barato*) dirt cheap; **dejar ~ a alguien** (*decepcionar*) to let sb down; (*en situación difícil*) to leave in the lurch 2.ser *pey* (*descuidado*) slovenly 3.estar *inf* (*fácil*) very easy; **ese ejercicio está ~** that exercise is dead easy II. *m, f inf* bum

tirador [ti·ra·'dor] *m* 1.(*agarradero*) handle, knob 2.(*cordón*) pull chain 3.(*tirachinas*) slingshot

tirador(a) [ti·ra·'dor, -'do·ra] *m(f)* (*disparador*) shot, marksman

tiranía [ti·ra·'ni·a] *f* tyranny; **someterse a la ~ de la moda** to be a slave to fashion

tiranizar <z→c> [ti·ra·ni·'sar, -'θar] *vt* to tyrannize

tirano, -a [ti·'ra·no, -a] I. *adj* tyrannical II. *m, f* tyrant, despot

tirante [ti·'ran·te] I. *adj* 1.(*tieso*) taut; **el pantalón me está ~** the pants are tight on me 2.(*conflictivo*) tense; **estar ~ con alguien** to have strained relations with sb II. *m* 1.(*travesaño*) strut; **se me caen los ~s de este vestido** the straps on this dress keep slipping; **~s** (*elásticos*) suspenders *pl* 2.(*de caballería*) trace

tirantez [ti·ran·'tes, -'teθ] *f* (*tensión*) tension, strain

tirar [ti·'rar] I. *vi* 1.(*arrastrar*) **~ de algo** to pull on sth; **tira y afloja** give and take; **a todo ~** at the most; **~ de la lengua a alguien** to draw sb out 2.(*atraer*) to attract; **no me tiran los libros** I'm not very interested in books 3.(*sacar*) **~ de algo** to pull out sth 4.(*chimenea*) to draw 5.(*colores*) **~ a rojo** to tend toward red 6.(*vestidos*) **esta camisa me tira de los hombros** this shirt is tight in the shoulders 7.(*querer lograr*) **~ para director** to be aiming at being director 8.(*parecerse*) to take after; **él tira a su padre** he takes after his father 9.(*torcer*) to turn; **aquí cada uno tira por su lado** here everyone takes his/her own turning 10.(*disparar*) to shoot; **~ al blanco** to target shoot ▶ **¿qué tal? — vamos tirando** *inf* how are you? — we're managing II. *vt* 1.(*lanzar*) to throw; **~ piedras a alguien** to throw stones at sb 2.(*malgastar*) to waste 3.(*desechar*) to throw away 4.(*disparar*) to shoot; (*bombas*) to drop; (*cohetes*) to launch 5.(*derribar*) to knock down; (*árbol*) to fell; (*edificio*) to pull down 6.(*trazar*) to draw 7.(*imprimir*) to print 8.(*extender*) to stretch 9.FOTO to take 10.(*derramar*) to spill III. *vr*: **~se** 1.(*lanzarse*) to throw oneself 2.(*echarse*) to lie down 3.*inf* (*pasar*) to spend; **~se una hora esperando** to spend an hour waiting 4.(*acometer*) to throw oneself 5.*vulg* (*copu-*

lar) ~ **se a alguien** to lay sb

tiritar [ti·ri·'tar] *vi* to shiver; **se me ha quedado la cuenta del banco tiritando** there isn't much left in my bank account

tiro ['ti·ro] *m* **1.** (*lanzamiento, disparo*) shot; ~ **a portería** shot at goal; ~ **al aire** warning shot; **barraca de** ~ **al blanco** shooting range; ~ **con arco** archery; **a** ~ in range; *fig* accessible; **a** ~ **limpio** guns blazing; **dar un** ~ to fire a shot; **¡que le den un** ~**!** *inf* somebody shoot him!; **pegarse un** ~ to shoot oneself; **me salió el** ~ **por la culata** *inf* it backfired on me **2.** (*munición*) round **3.** (*daño*) injury **4.** (*alcance*) range **5.** (*arrastre*) pull **6.** (*caballerías*) team **7.** (*arreos*) trace; **poner el** ~ **a los caballos** to harness the horses **8.** (*corriente de aire*) draft **9.** *inf* (*heroína*) heroin ▸ **a** ~ **hecho** deliberately; **de** ~**s largos** all dressed up, dressed to kill; **sentar a alguien como un** ~ (*comida*) to disagree with sb; (*noticia*) to upset sb; **ni a** ~**s** not on a long shot

tiroides [ti·'roi·des] **I.** *adj inv* ANAT **glándula** ~ thyroid gland **II.** *m inv* MED thyroid

tirotear [ti·ro·te·'ar] **I.** *vt* to shoot at **II.** *vr:* ~ **se 1.** (*disparar*) to shoot at each other **2.** (*disputar*) to quarrel

tiroteo [ti·ro·'teo] *m* shooting

tísico, -a ['ti·si·ko, -a] **I.** *adj* MED tubercular **II.** *m, f* consumptive person

titanio [ti·'ta·njo] *m* QUÍM titanium

titeo [ti·'teo] *m Arg, Bol, Urug* **1.** (*burla*) mocking **2.** (*tomadura de pelo*) teasing; **tomar a alguien para el** ~ to make fun of sb

títere ['ti·te·re] *m* **1.** *t. fig* (*muñeco*) puppet; **no dejar** ~ **con cabeza** to spare no one **2.** (*tipejo*) weakling **3.** *pl* (*espectáculo*) puppet show

titipuchal [ti·ti·pu·'tʃal] *m Méx, inf* (*tropel*) throng

titubear [ti·tu·βe·'ar] *vi* **1.** (*vacilar*) to waver; *fig* to hesitate **2.** (*balbucear*) to stutter

titubeo [ti·tu·'βeo] *m* **1.** (*vacilación*) tottering; *fig* hesitation; **deja a un lado tus** ~**s** put your doubts aside **2.** (*balbuceo*) stammering

titulación [ti·tu·la·'sjon, -'θjon] *f* (*denominación*) title; (*académica*) qualifications *pl*

titulado, -a [ti·tu·'la·do, -a] **I.** *adj* titled **II.** *m, f* degree holder; ~ (**universitario**) university graduate

titular¹ [ti·tu·'lar] **I.** *adj* **profesor** ~ full professor **II.** *mf* holder; ~ **de acciones** shareholder

titular² [ti·tu·'lar] **I.** *m* headline; **aparecer en los** ~**es** to appear in the newspaper headlines; **ocupar los** ~**es** to be in all the newspapers **II.** *vt* (*poner título*) to title **III.** *vr:* ~ **se** to be entitled; **el libro se titula...** the book is titled...

título ['ti·tu·lo] *m* **1.** (*rótulo, dignidad*) title; ~ **de crédito** credits **2.** (*diploma*) diploma; ~ **universitario** university degree **3.** (*motivo*) reason; **¿a** ~ **de qué hace Ud. eso?** why are you doing that?; **a justo** ~ rightly **4.** (*en calidad de*) **a** ~ **de** by way of; **a** ~ **de devolución** as a refund; **a** ~ **gratuito** for free; **a** ~ **de**

prueba as a trial **5.** (*valor comercial*) bond **6.** ~ **de propiedad** (property) deeds *pl*

tiza ['ti·sa, -θa] *f* chalk

tizate [ti·'sa·te, -'θa·te] *m Guat, Hond, Nic* chalk

tiznado, -a [tis·'na·do, -a; tiθ-] *adj AmC* drunk

tizne ['tis·ne, 'tiθ-] *m o f* (*hollín*) soot

tlachique [tla·'tʃi·ke] *m Méx* CULIN *agave cactus juice before fermentation to pulque*

tlacote [tla·'ko·te] *m Méx* MED **1.** (*absceso*) boil **2.** (*tumor*) tumor

tlapalería [tla·pa·le·'ri·a] *f Méx* (*ferretería*) hardware store

TLCAN *abr de* **Tratado de Libre Comercio de América del Norte** NAFTA

toalla [to·'a·ja, -ʎa] *f* towel; ~ **de lavabo/ baño** hand/bath towel; **arrojar la** ~ *fig* to throw in the towel

tobillera [to·βi·'je·ra, -'ʎe·ra] *f* ankle support

tobillo [to·'βi·jo, -ʎo] *m* ankle

tobo ['to·βo] *m Ven* (*cubo*) bucket

tobogán [to·βo·'ɣan] *m* **1.** (*deslizadero*) slide **2.** (*pista*) chute

tocadiscos [to·ka·'dis·kos] *m inv* record player

tocado [to·'ka·do] *m* (*peinado*) hairdo

tocado, -a [to·'ka·do, -a] *adj* **1.** (*perturbado*) slightly touched; **estar** ~ (**de la cabeza**) to be not all there **2.** (*lesionado*) injured **3.** (*medio podrido*) going bad **4.** (*cubierto en la cabeza*) **ir** ~ **de un sombrero** to be wearing a hat

tocador [to·ka·'dor] *m* **1.** (*mueble*) dressing table **2.** (*habitación*) ladies' dressing room; (*servicios*) ladies' room

tocar <c→qu> [to·'kar] **I.** *vt* **1.** (*contacto*) to touch, to feel; **tócame la frente** (**y dime si está caliente**) feel my forehead (and tell me if it's hot); ~ **de cerca algo** *fig* to hit home; ~ **fondo** to hit bottom; **¡no lo toques!** don't touch it! **2.** MÚS to play; (*campana*) to ring; (*tambor*) to beat; ~ **la bocina** to blow the horn; ~ **alarma** to sound the alarm; ~ **a muerto** to toll (a death knell); **el reloj tocó las tres** the clock struck three; ~ **el timbre** to ring the doorbell **3.** (*modificar*) to change **4.** (*chocar*) to run into **5.** (*afectar*) to affect; ~ **en el corazón** to touch one's heart **II.** *vi* **1.** (*corresponder*) **te toca a ti decidir** it's up to you to decide; **te toca jugar** it's your turn; **hoy me toca salir** today I have to go out **2.** (*obligación*) **me toca barrer el patio todas las mañanas** I have to sweep the courtyard every morning **3.** (*llegar el momento oportuno*) to be time; **toca ir a la compra** it's time to do the shopping **4.** (*caer en suerte*) to fall; **le tocó a él hacerlo** it fell to him to do it; **le tocó el premio gordo** he/she won the grand prize **5.** (*estar muy cerca*) to verge on **6.** (*ser parientes*) to be related **III.** *vr:* ~ **se 1.** (*estar en contacto*) to touch **2.** (*peinarse*) to do one's hair **3.** (*cubrirse la cabeza*) ~ **se con un sombrero** to wear a hat; ~ **se con un pañuelo** to cover one's head with a scarf ▸ **los**

T

extremos se tocan *prov* extremes meet *prov;* **tocárselas** *inf* to beat it

tocayo, -a [to·'ka·jo, -a] *m, f* namesake

tocineta [to·si·'ne·ta, to·θi-] *f Col v.* **tocino**

tocino [to·'si·no, to·'θi-] *m (lardo)* pork fat; *(carne)* bacon; **confundir la velocidad con el ~** *inf* to mix up two completely different things

todavía [to·da·'βi·a] *adv* **1.** *(aún)* still; **~ no** not yet; **es ~ más caro que...** it is even more expensive than... **2.** *(sin embargo)* **pero ~** however

todo ['to·do] **I.** *pron indef* all; **~ lo que...**, **~ cuanto...** al...; **(o) ~ o nada** all or nothing; **es ~ uno** it's all one and the same; **ante** *[o* **sobre|** **~** above all; **~ lo contrario** quite the contrary; **después de ~** *inf* after all; **con ~** nevertheless; **en ~ y por ~** absolutely; **y ~** and all; **estar en ~** *inf* to be on the ball, not to miss a thing; **me invitaron a comer y ~** they even invited me to eat (and all); **para ~** all-purpose; **me es ~ uno** it's all the same to me **II.** *adv inf* all, completely **III.** *m (la totalidad)* the whole; **del ~** completely; **no del ~** not entirely; **jugarse el ~ por el ~** to risk all; **ser el ~** to be the chief

todo, -a ['to·do, -a] *art indef* **1.** *(entero)* all; **toda la familia** the whole family; **toda Argentina** all of Argentina; **en toda Europa** all over Europe; **a toda prisa**, **a ~ correr** as fast as possible **2.** *(cada)* every; **a toda costa** at all cost; **~ Dios** *[o* **quisqui|** *inf* absolutely everyone; **toda precaución es poca** you can't be careful enough **3.** *pl* all; **día de Todos los Santos** All Saints' Day; **a ~s los niños les gusta el chocolate** all children like chocolate; **~s los niños de la clase tomaron chocolate** all of the children in the class had chocolate; **~s y cada uno** each and every one; **a todas horas** at all hours; **en todas partes** everywhere; **de ~s modos** anyway **4.** *(intensificación)* **su cara es toda nariz** his face is all nose; **ser ~ nervios** to be a bundle of nerves

todopoderoso, -a [to·do·po·de·'ro·so] *adj* almighty

todoterreno [to·do·te·'rre·no] **I.** *adj inv* all-purpose, versatile **II.** *m* AUTO all-terrain vehicle; **ser un ~** *fig* to be a Jack-of-all-trades

toldillo [tol·'di·jo, -ʎo] *m Col* mosquito net

toldo ['tol·do] *m (marquesina)* marquee; *(en un balcón)* canopy; *(en una tienda)* awning

tolerancia [to·le·'ran·sja, -θja] *f* **1.** *(indulgencia)* tolerance **2.** *(resistencia)* tolerance

tolerar [to·le·'rar] *vt* **1.** *(soportar)* to bear, to tolerate; *(alimentos, medicinas)* to be able to take **2.** *(permitir)* **~ algo** to be lenient with sth, to allow sth; **una película tolerada para menores** a film suitable for children **3.** *(aceptar)* tolerate

tolete [to·'le·te] *m* **1.** *AmL (garrote)* bludgeon **2.** *Col, Cuba (trozo)* piece

tolvanera [tol·βa·'ne·ra] *f AmC, Méx (polvareda)* cloud of dust

toma [to·ma] *f* **1.** *(adquisición)* taking; **~ de conciencia** awareness; **~ de declaración** taking of evidence; **~ de datos** COMPUT data acquisition; **~ de decisiones** decision making; **~ de poder** takeover; **~ de posesión** taking office **2.** *(conquista)* capture; **~ por asalto** to take by storm **3.** *(dosis)* dose **4.** TÉC inlet; **~ de tierra** ground **5.** *(grabación)* take **6.** *(ingesta)* intake **7.** FOTO shot

tomacorriente [to·ma·ko·'rrjen·te] *m* **1.** *AmL (colector)* collector **2.** *Arg, Perú (enchufe)* socket, plug

tomar [to·'mar] **I.** *vi* to turn; **~ por la derecha** to take a right **II.** *vt* **1.** *(coger, quitar, llevar)* to take; *(préstamo)* to borrow; *(aliento)* to catch; *(fuerzas)* to gather; **~ las armas** to take up arms; **~ una decisión** to make a decision; **~ medidas** to take measures **2.** *(beber)* to have, to drink; **~ café** to have coffee; **no tomes ese agua** don't drink that water **3.** *(comer)* to have, to eat **4.** *(interpretar)* to take; **~ a la ligera** to take lightly; **~ algo a mal** to take offense at sth; **~ muy a pecho** to take to heart; **~ a risa** to take as a joke; **~ en serio** to take seriously; **~ a alguien por ladrón** to take sb for a thief; **¿por quién me tomas?** what do you take me for? **5.** *(adquirir)* to take; **~ conciencia de algo** to become aware of sth **6.** *(sentir)* to take; **~ cariño/odio a alguien** to take a like/dislike to sb; **~ confianza a alguien** to treat sb as a friend **7.** *(conquistar)* to take, to capture **8.** *(copiar)* to copy **9.** *(contratar)* to hire; **~ un abogado** to hire a lawyer **10.** *(alquilar)* to rent **11.** *(adoptar)* adopt; **~ una actitud de...** to adopt an attitude of ... **12.** *(hacerse cargo)* to take over; **~ sobre sí** to take upon oneself **13.** *(filmar)* to shoot **14.** *(sobrevenir)* to come over **15.** *(transporte)* to take **16.** *(medir)* to take; **le ~ron la tensión** they measured [*o* took] his/her blood pressure **17.** *AmL (beber alcohol)* to drink; **no debes ~ ni fumar** you shouldn't drink or smoke; **~la** *(emborracharse)* to get drunk **18.** ZOOL *(copular)* to cover; **¡vete a ~ por culo!** *vulg* fuck off! ▶ **~la con algo/alguien** to take it out on sth/sb; **¡toma!** well! **III.** *vr:* **~se 1.** *(coger)* to take; **~se libertades** to take liberties; **~se unas vacaciones** to take a vacation **2.** *(beber)* to drink, to have; **me he tomado un vaso de leche** I had a glass of milk **3.** *(comer)* to eat, to have **4.** *(ponerse la voz ronca)* **se me ha tomado la voz** I'm hoarse **5.** *AmL (emborracharse)* **tomársela** to get drunk

tomate [to·'ma·te] *m* **1.** BOT tomato **2.** *inf (agujero)* hole ▶ **ponerse rojo como un ~** to turn as red as a beetroot

tómbola ['tom·bo·la] *f* charity raffle

tomillo [to·'mi·jo, -ʎo] *m* thyme

tomo [to·mo] *m (volumen)* volume; **de cuatro ~s** in four volumes ▶ **de ~ y lomo** out-and-out

tomografía [to·mo·ɣra·'fi·a] *f* MED CAT scan; **tomografía axial computerizada (TAC)** computerized axial tomograph (CAT)

tonada [to·'na·da] *f* 1.(*canción*) song 2.(*melodía*) tune, melody 3.*AmL* (*tonillo*) accent
tonalidad [to·na·li·'dad] *f* 1.LING intonation 2.MÚS tonality, tone; ~ **menor** minor key 3.ARTE shade
tonel [to·'nel] *m* 1.(*barril*) barrel 2. *inf* (*persona gorda*) fatso
tonelada [to·ne·'la·da] *f* (*peso*) ton
tónica ['to·ni·ka] *f* 1.(*bebida*) tonic water 2.(*tono general*) general trend
tónico ['to·ni·ko] *m* 1.MED tonic 2.(*para el cabello*) hair tonic
tonificar <c→qu> [to·ni·fi·'kar] *vt* to tone up
tonina [to·'ni·na] *f Arg, Urug* ZOOL dolphin
tono ['to·no] *m* 1.(*altura*) tone, pitch; ~ **agudo/grave** high/low pitch 2.(*señal*) tone; ~ **de marcar** TEL dial tone 3.(*intensidad*) **bajar el** ~ to lower one's voice 4.(*deje, estilo*) tone; **en** ~ **de reproche** reproachfully; **bajar el** ~ to tone down; **dar el** ~ to set the tone; **darse** ~ to put on airs; **fuera de** ~ out of place; **estar a** ~ **con algo** to be in tune with sth; **subirse de** ~ to become heated 5.(*atmósfera*) tone 6.(*maneras*) **el buen** ~ refinement; **de buen** ~ tasteful; **de mal** ~ vulgar 7.MED tone 8.MÚS (*modo*) key; ~ **mayor/menor** major/minor key; ~**s y semitonos** whole tones and halftones
tontear [ton·te·'ar] *vi* 1.(*bobear*) to fool around 2.*inf* to flirt
tontería [ton·te·'ri·a] *f* 1.(*memez*) stupidity, foolishness 2.(*nadería*) trifle
tonto, -a ['ton·to] I. *adj* silly; **ser más** ~ **que Picio** *inf* to be as dumb as they come; **hacer algo a tontas y a locas** to do sth without thinking; **ponerse** ~ *inf* to get silly; **ser** ~ **del culo** *inf* to be a complete idiot; **ser** ~ **perdido** to be dead from the neck up II. *m, f* fool; **hacer el** ~ to clown around; **le gusta más que a un** ~ **un lápiz** he/she is crazy about it; **hacerse el** ~ to play dumb; **el** ~ **del pueblo** the village idiot
topacio [to·'pa·sjo, -θjo] *m* MIN topaz
topadora [to·pa·'do·ra] *f Arg, Méx, Urug* (*buldózer*) bulldozer
topar [to·'par] I. *vi* 1.(*chocar*) ~ **con algo** to run into sth; ~ **contra algo** to bump against [*o* into] sth 2.(*hallar*) ~ **con alguien** to bump into sb II. *vt* 1.(*chocar*) ~ **algo** to butt 2.(*hallar: algo*) to come across; (*a alguien*) to bump into III. *vr:* ~**se** 1.(*chocar*) ~**se con algo** to run into sth; ~**se contra algo** to bump against [*o* into] sth 2.(*hallar*) ~**se con alguien** to bump into sb
tope ['to·pe] I. *adj* top, maximum; **fecha** ~ latest date, at the latest II. *m* 1.(*extremo*) end; **estar hasta el** ~ (*lleno*) to be jam-packed; (*harto*) to be fed up; **estoy a** ~ **de trabajo** I'm swamped with work 2.(*parachoques*) buffer, AUTO bumper 3.(*para impedir un movimiento*) check; (*puerta*) doorstop 4.(*obstáculo*) obstacle
tópico ['to·pi·ko] *m* 1.(*lugar común*) com-

monplace 2.(*estereotipo*) cliché 3.MED **uso** ~ external application
tópico, -a ['to·pi·ko, -a] *adj* 1.(*trivial*) trite 2.(*local*) local 3.MED for external application; **de uso** ~ for external use only
topinambur [to·pi·nam·'bur] *m Arg, Bol* BOT Jerusalem artichoke
topo ['to·po] *m* (*roedor, espía*) mole; **ver menos que un** ~ *inf* to be as blind as a bat; **ser un** ~ *inf* to be a klutz
topocho, -a [to·'po·tʃo, -a] *adj Ven* plump
topografía [to·po·ɣra·'fi·a] *f* topography, surveying
topón [to·'pon] *m* 1. *Chile, Col, Hond* (*topetazo*) butt 2. *Col* (*puñetazo*) punch
topónimo [to·'po·ni·mo] *m* place name
toposo, -a [to·'po·so, -a] *adj Ven* 1.(*entrometido*) meddlesome 2.(*pedante*) pretentious
toque ['to·ke] *m* 1.(*roce*) touch 2.(*golpe*) tap; **dar un** ~ **en la puerta** to tap on the door 3.(*sonido*) ~ **de campanas** ringing of bells; ~ **de queda** curfew; ~ **de tambor** drumbeat; ~ **de atención** warning note; **dáme un** ~ **más tarde** give me a ring later 4.(*advertencia*) warning 5.(*matiz*) touch; **el** ~ **femenino** a woman's touch 6.(*modificación*) touch up; **dar los últimos** ~**s a algo** to put the finishing touches on sth 7.(*pincelada*) dab 8.(*ensayo*) test; **piedra de** ~ touchstone 9.(*lo principal*) crux 10.(*aplicación medicinal*) painting of throat
toquetear [to·ke·te·'ar] *vt inf* to fiddle with, to finger
tórax ['to·raks] *m inv* thorax
torbellino [tor·βe·'ji·no, -'ʎi·no] *m* whirlwind; **ser un** ~ *inf* to be a bundle of energy
torcedura [tor·se·'du·ra, tor·θe-] *f* MED sprain
torcer [tor·'ser, -'θer] *irr como cocer* I. *vi* to turn; ~ **a la izquierda** to turn left II. *vt* 1.(*encorvar*) to bend 2.(*dar vueltas, desviar*) to wind; ~ **el cuello a alguien** to wring sb's neck; ~ **las manos** to wring one's hands; ~ **la vista** to squint 3.(*referente al gesto*) ~ **el gesto** to scowl III. *vr:* ~**se** 1.(*encorvarse*) to bend; **la madera se ha torcido con la humedad** the dampness has warped the wood 2.(*dislocarse*) to sprain; **me he torcido el pie** I've twisted my ankle 3.(*corromperse*) to go astray; (*fracasar*) to go wrong 4.(*agriarse*) to go sour
torcida [tor·'si·da, tor·'θi-] *f* wick
torcido, -a [tor·'si·do, tor·'θi-] *adj* 1.(*ladeado*) lopsided 2.(*encorvado*) crooked 3.(*artero*) devious
torear [to·re·'ar] I. *vi* (*lidiar*) to fight; (*toros*) to bullfight II. *vt* 1.(*lidiar*) to fight; (*toros*) to bullfight 2.(*evitar*) to dodge 3.(*engañar*) to string along 4.(*tomar el pelo*) to tease
toreo [to·'reo] *m* 1.(*tauromaquia*) bullfighting 2.(*lidia*) fighting 3.(*burla*) covert mockery
torero, -a [to·'re·ro, -a] I. *adj* bullfighting; **valor** ~ outstanding figure in bullfighting II. *m, f* bullfighter, matador; **saltarse algo a la**

torera *inf* to blatantly ignore sth; **tener más suerte que un ~** *inf* to have the luck of the devil

tormenta [tor·'men·ta] *f* **1.** *t. fig* (*temporal*) storm **2.** (*agitación*) turmoil; **una ~ de celos** a fit of jealousy; **~ de ideas** brainstorm; **una ~ en un vaso de agua** a storm in a teacup

tormento [tor·'men·to] *m* **1.** (*castigo*) torment; **potro de ~** torture rack; **dar ~ a alguien** to torture sb **2.** (*congoja*) anguish

torna ['tor·na] *f* **1.** (*devolución*) restitution **2.** (*regreso*) return ▶ **se han cambiado las ~s** the shoe's on the other foot; **volver las ~s a alguien** to turn the tables on sb; **volverse las ~s** to turn the tables

tornado [tor·'na·do] *m* METEO tornado

tornar [tor·'nar] **I.** *vi* to return; **~ en sí** to regain consciousness; **~ a hacer algo** to do sth again **II.** *vt* **1.** (*devolver*) to return **2.** (*cambiar*) to make; **~ triste** to make sad **III.** *vr:* **~se** to turn; **~se azul** to turn blue

torneo [tor·'neo] *m* tournament

tornero, -a [tor·'ne·ro, -a] *m, f* (*de metal*) machinist; (*de madera*) lathe operator

tornillo [tor·'ni·jo, -ʎo] *m* **1.** (*clavo con rosca*) screw; **apretar un ~** to tighten a screw; **apretar los ~s a alguien** *fig* to put pressure on sb; **te falta un ~** *inf* you have a screw loose; **beso de ~** French kiss **2.** *inf* (*deserción*) desertion

torniquete [tor·ni·'ke·te] *m* **1.** (*puerta*) turnstile **2.** MED tourniquet

torno ['tor·no] *m* **1.** (*máquina, para madera*) lathe; (*de alfarero*) potter's wheel; (*de banco*) vise **2.** (*cabrestante*) winch **3.** (*giro*) turn **4.** (*freno*) brake **5.** (*de un río*) bend in a river ▶ **en ~ a** about; **en ~ a ese tema** with regard to this subject

toro ['to·ro] *m* **1.** (*animal*) bull; **~ bravo** [*o de lidia*] *bull raised to fight in the bullring*; **coger el ~ por los cuernos** *fig* to take the bull by the horns; **fuerte como un ~** strong as an ox; **¡otro ~!** *fig* change the subject! **2.** *pl* (*toreo*) bullfighting; **ir a los ~s** to go to bullfights; **ver los ~s desde la barrera** *fig* to watch sth from the sidelines **3.** (*hombre*) strong man

torpe ['tor·pe] *adj* **1.** (*inhábil*) clumsy **2.** (*pesado*) sluggish **3.** (*obsceno*) lewd

torpedo [tor·'pe·do] *m* torpedo

torpeza [tor·'pe·sa, -θa] *f* **1.** (*pesadez*) heaviness **2.** (*inhabilidad*) clumsiness **3.** (*obscenidad*) baseness **4.** (*tontería*) stupidity

torre ['to·rre] *f* tower; **~ de alta tensión** electricity pylon; **~ de extracción** [*o de perforación*] derrick; **~ de mando** control tower; **~ del homenaje** donjon; **~ de marfil** *fig* ivory tower; (*campanario*) bell tower; (*ajedrez*) rook, castle

torreja [to·'rre·xa] *f AmL* CULIN ≈ French toast

torrencial [to·rren·'sjal, -'θjal] *adj* **lluvia ~** torrential rains

torrente [to·'rren·te] *m* **1.** (*corriente*) torrent **2.** (*multitud*) flood

torrentoso, -a [to·rren·'to·so, -a] *adj AmL* (*llu-*

via) torrential; (*caudal*) fast-flowing

torsión [tor·'sjon] *f* (*desviación*) torsion; **~ hacia la izquierda** twisting to the left

torso ['tor·so] *m* torso; ARTE bust

torta ['tor·ta] *f* **1.** (*tarta*) cake; *AmL* (*pastel*) pie **2.** *inf* (*bofetada*) slap; (*golpe*) punch; **darse una ~** to bang oneself **3.** *inf* (*borrachera*) drunkenness ▶ **ser ~s y pan pintado** *inf* to be child's play; **no saber ni ~** *inf* not to know a thing

tortilla [tor·'ti·ja, -ʎa] *f* (*de huevos*) ≈ omelet; *AmL* (*de harina*) tortilla ▶ **dar la vuelta a la ~** to change things completely; **se ha vuelto la ~** the tables have turned

i In Spain, a **tortilla** is a type of omelette. A **tortilla de patatas**, for example, is an omelette with potatoes and onions. **Tortillas** are also made with such ingredients as spinach, tuna, and asparagus. In Latin America, particularly in Mexico, a **tortilla** is a flat pancake made out of corn and is one of the staple foods of the region.

tórtola ['tor·to·la] *f* turtledove

tórtolo ['tor·to·lo] *m* **1.** (*ave*) lovebird **2.** (*hombre*) loverboy **3.** *pl* (*enamorados*) lovebirds *pl*

tortuga [tor·'tu·ɣa] *f* turtle; **a paso de ~** to walk at a snail's pace

tortuoso, -a [tor·tu·'o·so, -a] *adj* **1.** (*sinuoso*) winding **2.** (*astuto*) tortuous

tortura [tor·'tu·ra] *f* (*suplicio*) torture; **sufrir ~s** to be tortured

torturar [tor·tu·'rar] *vt* to torture

tos [tos] *f* cough; **~ ferina** whooping cough

tosco, -a ['tos·ko, -a] *adj* rough, coarse

tosedera [to·se·'de·ra] *f AmL* nagging cough

toser [to·'ser] *vi* to cough; **no hay quien te tosa** *inf* nobody can compete with you

tostada [tos·'ta·da] *f* **1.** (*para desayuno*) toast **2.** *Méx:* fried tortilla

tostador [tos·ta·'dor] *m* toaster

tostar <o→ue> [tos·'tar] **I.** *vt* **1.** (*torrar*) to roast; (*pan*) to toast **2.** (*curtir*) to brown **II.** *vr:* **~se** to tan

total [to·'tal] **I.** *adj* total; **importe ~** total amount; **en ~** in all; **un cambio ~** a complete change; **¡ha sido ~!** *inf* it was great! **II.** *m* MAT sum **III.** *adv* so, in the end

totalidad [to·ta·li·'dad] *f* totality, whole; **en su ~** in its entirety

totalitario, -a [to·ta·li·'ta·rjo, -a] *adj* **1.** (*completo*) total **2.** (*dictatorial*) totalitarian

totora [to·'to·ra] *f AmS* BOT (*junco*) reed

toxicidad [tok·si·si·'dad, tok·si·θi-] *f* toxicity

tóxico [tok·si·ko] *m* toxic substance

tóxico, -a ['tok·si·ko, -a] *adj* toxic

toxicomanía [tok·si·ko·ma·'ni·a] *f* drug addiction

toxicómano, -a [tok·si·'ko·ma·no, -a] **I.** *adj*

addicted to drugs **II.** *m, f* drug addict, substance abuser

toxina [tok·'si·na] *f* toxin

traba ['tra·βa] *f* **1.** (*trabamiento*) tie
2. (*cuerda*) hobble **3.** (*obstáculo*) hindrance;
poner ~s a... to put obstacles in the way of...
4. *AmL, inf* (*marihuana*) grass; (*efecto*) high

trabajado, -a [tra·βa·'xa·do, -a] *adj* **1.** (*cansado*) worn-out **2.** (*con esmero*) well-crafted

trabajador(a) [tra·βa·xa·'dor, --'do·ra] **I.** *adj*
hard-working **II.** *m(f)* worker

trabajar [tra·βa·'xar] **I.** *vi* to work; **~ de vendedora** to work as a saleswoman; **en edad de
~** of working age; **~ como un condenado** to
work like a slave; **~ en balde** to work in vain;
~ por horas to be paid by the hour; **~ por
cuenta propia** to be self-employed; **~ a
tiempo completo/parcial** to work full-time/
part-time **II.** *vt* **1.** (*tratar*) to work; (*caballo*) to
train **2.** (*perfeccionar*) to work on; **tienes que
~ el acento** you have to work on your accent
3. (*inquietar*) to disturb **4.** (*amasar*) to knead
5. (*máquina*) to run, to operate **III.** *vr:* **~se** to
work

trabajo [tra·'βa·xo] *m* (*acción*) work; (*puesto*)
job; **~ en cadena** assembly-line work; **~ a
destajo** piecework; **~ estacional** seasonal
work; **~s manuales** handicrafts *pl;* **~s forzados** hard labor; **con/sin** ~ employed/unem-
ployed; **~ en equipo** teamwork; **~ perdido**
wasted effort; **puesto de** ~ post/job; **~ de chinos** intricate laborious work; **~ fijo** steady job;
~ cualificado skilled work; **~ de campo** field
work; **~ negro** illegal work; **~ eventual** temporary [*o* casual] work; **~ intelectual** brainwork; **hacer un buen** ~ to do a good job;
almuerzo de ~ working lunch; **tener** ~ **atrasado** to have a backlog; **¡buen** ~! well done!;
quedarse sin ~ to be let go; **mucha gente se
quedó sin** ~ **cuando instalaron la nueva
maquinaria** many people were made redundant when the new machinery was installed;
costar ~ to be difficult; **tomarse el** ~ **de
hacer algo** to take the trouble to do sth; **aho-
rrarse el** ~ **de hacer algo** to spare oneself the
trouble of doing sth

trabalenguas [tra·βa·'len·gwas] *m inv* tongue
twister

trabar [tra·'βar] **I.** *vt* **1.** (*juntar*) to join
2. (*coger*) to seize **3.** (*atar*) to tie **4.** (*impedir*)
to impede **5.** (*espesar*) to thicken **6.** (*comenzar*) to start; (*contactos*) to strike up
7. (*embargar bienes*) to put a lien on **II.** *vi* to
take hold **III.** *vr:* **~se** to get stuck; **~se la lengua** to get tongue-tied

trabilla [tra·'βi·ja, -ʎa] *f* belt loop; (*en la pernera*) foot strap

trácala ['tra·ka·la] *f* **1.** *Ecua* (*multitud*) mob
2. *Méx, PRico* (*fullería*) fraud **3.** *Méx* (*persona
tramposa*) trickster

tracalada [tra·ka·'la·da] *f* **1.** *AmC, AmS*
(*multitud*) crowd, lot **2.** *Méx* (*fullería*) trickery

tracalero, -a [tra·ka·'le·ro, -a] *m, f Méx, PRico*

cheat

tracción [trak·'sjon, -'θjon] *f* **1.** (*tirar*) pulling
2. (*accionar*) drive, traction; **~ a cuatro ruedas** four-wheel drive; **~ delantera/trasera**
front/rear-wheel drive

tractor [trak·'tor] *m* tractor

tradición [tra·di·'sjon, -'θjon] *f* tradition

tradicional [tra·di·sjo·'nal, tra·di·θjo-] *adj* traditional

traducción [tra·duk·'sjon, -duɣ-'θjon] *f* translation; **~ al/del inglés** translation into/from
English; **~ automática** machine [*o* automatic]
translation; **~ directa/inversa** translation
from/into a foreign language; **~ libre** free
translation; **~ simultánea** simultaneous translation

traducir [tra·du·'sir, -'θir] *irr vt* to translate

traductología [tra·'duk·to·lo·'xi·a] *f* translation studies [*o* science]

traductor(a) [tra·duk·'tor, --'to·ra] **I.** *adj* translating **II.** *m(f)* translator; **~ de bolsillo** pock-
et-size electronic translating device; **~ jurado**
sworn translator

traer [tra·'er] *irr* **I.** *vt* **1.** (*llevar: a alguien*) to
bring along; (*consigo*) to bring; (*vestido*) to
wear; **tengo una carta para ti — trae** I have
a letter for you · give it to me; **¿has traído la
carta?** did you bring the letter?; **lo traigo en
la cartera** I've got it in my briefcase; **~ a alguien arrastra(n)do** to drag sb; **¿qué te trae
por aquí?** what brings you here?; **el jefe me
trae de aquí para allí todo el día** my boss
has me running all day; **me trae floja** *vulg* I
don't give a damn; **me trae sin cuidado** I
couldn't care less **2.** (*ir a por*) to fetch
3. (*atraer*) to attract **4.** (*ocasionar*) to cause
5. (*implicar*) involve **6.** (*más adjetivo*) **~ convencido a alguien** to have sb convinced;
~ preocupado a alguien to have sb worried;
~ de cabeza a alguien *inf* to be driving sb
mad; **esta mujer me trae perdido** this woman will be my ruin **7.** (*más sustantivo*) **~
retraso** to be late; **~ prisa** to be in a hurry;
~ hambre to be hungry; **traes cara de
circunstancias** *inf* you look very serious
8. (*razones, ejemplos*) to adduce **9.** (*más 'a'*)
~ a colación to bring up; **~ a cuento** to mention; **~ a alguien a razones** to get sb to listen
to reason; **~ a la memoria** to bring to mind
II. *vr:* **~se 1.** (*llevar a cabo*) **~se algo entre
manos** to be up to something **2.** (*vestirse*) **~se
bien** to dress well **3.** (*ser difícil, intenso*) **este
examen se las trae** the exam is really tough;
hace un frío que se las trae it's really cold

traficante [tra·fi·'kan·te] *mf* dealer, trader; (*de
drogas*) drug dealer; (*de personas, coches*)
smuggler

traficar <c→qu> [tra·fi·'kar] *vi* to deal; (*con
drogas*) to traffic; (*con personas*) to smuggle

tráfico ['tra·fi·ko] *m* **1.** (*de vehículos*) traffic;
~ por carretera road traffic **2.** COM trade; (*de
drogas*) traffic; (*de personas, coches*) smuggling; **~ de contrabando** smuggling; **~ de**

T

blancas white-slave traffic; **~ de influencias** graft

tragaluz [tra·ya·'lus, -'luθ] *m* (*grande*) skylight; (*pequeño*) transom

traganíqueles [tra·ya·'ni·ke·les] *f inv*, *Nic, inf* (*tragaperras*) slot machine

tragar <g→gu> [tra·'yar] **I.** *vt, vr:* **~se** (*comida, bebida, crítica*) to swallow; (*historia, mentira*) to fall for; **tuve que ~me el enfado** I had to hold back my anger; **ése se lo traga todo** *fig* he believes everything you tell him; **¡trágame tierra!** I wish the ground would open up and swallow me! **II.** *vt* **1.** (*soportar*) **no ~ a alguien** to not be able to stand sb **2.** (*consumir*) to down; (*absorber*) to soak up **3.** (*aguantar*) **tuvimos que ~ toda la conferencia** we had to sit through the whole conference; **~ saliva** to eat crow

tragedia [tra·'xe·dja] *f* tragedy

trágico, -a ['tra·xi·ko, -a] **I.** *adj* tragic; **no te pongas ~** don't get all melodramatic **II.** *m, f* TEAT, LIT tragedian *m*, tragedienne *f*

trago ['tra·yo] *m* **1.** (*de bebida*) swig; **a ~s cortos** in sips; **a ~s largos** in long drinks; **de un ~** in one gulp **2.** (*bebida*) drink; **tomar un ~ de más** *inf* to have one drink too many **3.** (*vicio*) bottle, drink **4.** (*experiencia*) experience; **pasar un mal ~** to have a bad time of it

traición [trai·'sjon, -'θjon] *f* **1.** (*acto desleal*) treachery, betrayal **2.** JUR treason; **matar a ~ to** kill treacherously

traicionar [trai·sjo·'nar, trai·θjo-] *vt* to betray; (*adulterio*) to be unfaithful; **la memoria me traiciona** my memory fails me; **le traicionó su acento** his/her accent gave him/her away

traicionero, -a [trai·sjo·'ne·ro, -a; trai·θjo-] **I.** *adj* (*persona*) perfidious; (*acción*) traitorous; (*memoria*) unreliable; (*animal*) dangerous **II.** *m, f* traitor

traidor(a) [trai·'dor, -·'do·ra] **I.** *adj* traitorous; (*falso*) deceitful **II.** *m(f)* traitor

traje ['tra·xe] *m* **1.** (*vestidura*) dress; **~ de baño** bathing suit; **~ de luces** bullfighter's costume **2.** (*de hombre*) suit; **~ de etiqueta** formal dress; **~ hecho a la medida** custom-made suit; **~ de confección** ready-to-wear suit **3.** (*de mujer*) outfit; **~ de noche** evening dress; **~ (de) chaqueta** suit **4.** (*popular*) regional costume **5.** (*de época*) period costume

trajeado, -a [tra·xe·'a·do, -a] *adj* **ir bien/mal ~** to be well/badly dressed

trajín [tra·'xin] *m* **1.** (*de mercancías*) haulage **2.** (*ajetreo*) rush; **el ~ de la ciudad** the hustle and bustle of the city; **había un gran ~** there was a lot of commotion

trajinera [tra·xi·'ne·ra] *f Méx* (*canoa*) ≈ canoe (*small boat typical for canals that carries up to 15 people and is moved with the help of a long stick*)

trama ['tra·ma] *f* **1.** (*de hilos*) weft **2.** LIT plot **3.** (*intriga*) scheme

tramar [tra·'mar] *vt* **1.** (*traición*) to plot; (*intriga, plan*) to scheme; **¿qué estarán tra-**

mando? what are they up to?; **aquí se está tramando algo** something's cooking here **2.** (*tejidos*) to weave

tramitar [tra·mi·'tar] *vt* **1.** (*asunto*) to attend to; (*negocio*) to transact; **está tramitando el divorcio** he/she has started divorce proceedings **2.** (*expediente*) to process

trámite ['tra·mi·te] *m* **1.** (*diligencias*) **~ burocrático** administrative proceedings; **pasar por todos los ~s** to go through the whole procedure **2.** (*formalidad*) formality; **estar en ~s de hacer algo** to be in the process of doing sth; **esto es puro ~** this is just a formality; **¿has hecho los ~s para el pasaporte?** have you taken the necessary steps to obtain your passport?

tramo ['tra·mo] *m* **1.** (*de camino*) stretch; FERRO section **2.** (*de escalera*) flight

trampa ['tram·pa] *f* **1.** (*para personas, animales*) trap; **~ mortal** death trap; **caer en la ~** (*animal*) to be caught in the snare; (*persona*) to fall into the trap; **poner una ~ a un animal/a alguien** to set a trap for an animal/for sb **2.** (*trampilla*) trapdoor **3.** (*del mostrador*) hinged section of a counter **4.** (*engaño*) trick; (*en los juegos*) cheating; **hacer ~** (*engañar*) to cheat; (*en el deporte*) fixing **5.** *inf* (*deuda*) bad debt ►**sin ~ ni cartón** with no catches; **hecha la ley hecha la ~** *prov* laws are made to be broken *prov*

trampear [tram·pe·'ar] *vi* **1.** *inf* (*estafar*) to swindle **2.** (*de penuria*) to get by **3.** (*ir tirando*) to manage

trampolín [tram·po·'lin] *m* (*de piscina*) diving board; (*de gimnasia*) trampoline; (*de esquí*) ski jump

tramposo, -a [tram·'po·so, -a] **I.** *adj* cheating **II.** *m, f* **1.** (*estafador*) swindler **2.** (*en los juegos*) cheat

tranca ['tran·ka] *f* **1.** (*palo*) cudgel; (*de la puerta*) crossbar **2.** *inf* (*borrachera*) binge; **coger una ~** *inf* to get plastered

trance ['tran·se, -θe] *m* **1.** (*momento*) **pasar un ~ difícil** to go through a difficult time **2.** (*hipnótico*) trance **3.** (*situación*) **estar en ~ de hacer algo** to be on the point of doing sth; **estar en ~ de muerte** to be at death's door ►**hacer algo a todo ~** to do sth at any cost

tranque [tran·ke] *m Chile* (*embalse*) reservoir

tranquilidad [tran·ki·li·'dad] *f* **1.** (*calma, serenidad*) tranquility; (*del mar*) calm; **para mayor ~** to be on the safe side; **~ de conciencia** ease of mind; **trabajar con ~** to work calmly; **debo decirte para tu ~ que...** I must tell you, to put your mind at rest, that... **2.** (*autocontrol*) calmness **3.** (*despreocupación*) lack of concern

tranquilizante [tran·ki·li·'san·te, -'θan·te] *m* tranquilizer

tranquilizar <z→c> [tran·ki·li·'sar, -'θar] **I.** *vt* to calm down; (*con palabras*) to reassure **II.** *vr:* **~se** to calm down

tranquilla [tran·'ki·ja, -·ʎa] *f* **1.** (*pasador*) bolt

2. (*para desorientar*) red herring

tranquillo [tran·'ki·jo, -ʎo] *m* **coger el ~ a algo** to get the knack of sth

tranquilo, -a [tran·'ki·lo, -a] *adj* **1.** (*no agitado, mar*) calm; **¡déjame ~!** leave me alone!; **mientras no te digan nada, tú ~** as long as they don't mention anything to you, don't worry **2.** (*persona: serena*) serene; (*con autocontrol*) calm; (*despreocupada*) unconcerned; **tú ~, que no pasará nada** don't worry, everything will be all right

transa ['tran·sa] *f* **1.** *AmL* (*espíritu de compromiso*) commitment **2.** *Méx* (*engaño*) deceit **3.** *RíoPl* (*transacción*) transaction; (*tráfico de droga*) drug dealing

transacción [tran·sak·'sjon, -'θjon] *f* **1.** JUR settlement **2.** POL agreement **3.** COM deal **4.** FIN transaction

transandino, -a [trans·an·'di·no, -a] *adj* trans-Andean

transar [tran·'sar] *vi AmL* (*transigir*) to compromise; **no pienso ~ en eso** I'm not giving in on that

transatlántico [trans·at·'lan·ti·ko] *m* ocean liner

transbordador [trans·βor·da·'dor] *m* **1.** NÁUT ferry **2.** AVIAT shuttle

transbordar [trans·βor·'dar] **I.** *vt* **1.** (*por río*) to ferry across **2.** (*mercancías*) to transfer **II.** *vi* to change, to transfer

transbordo [trans·'βor·do] *m* **1.** (*cambio*) change; **hay que hacer ~ en el aeropuerto** you have to change planes at the airport **2.** (*mercancías*) transfer

transcender <e→ie> [tran·sen·'der, trans·θen-] *vi v.* **trascender**

transcribir [trans·kri·'βir] *irr como escribir vt* **1.** (*copiar*) to transcribe **2.** *t.* MÚS (*transliterar*) to transpose

transcripción [trans·krip·'sjon, -kriβ·'θjon] *f* (*acción*) transcription; (*resultado*) transcript

transcurrir [trans·ku·'rrir] *vi* **1.** (*el tiempo*) to elapse, to pass **2.** (*acontecer*) to take place

transeúnte [tran·se·'un·te] *mf* (*peatón*) passer-by, pedestrian

transferencia [trans·fe·'ren·sja, -θja] *f* **1.** (*traslado*) transfer **2.** FIN transfer; **a través de una ~ bancaria** by bank draft **3.** (*de propiedad*) transfer **4.** PSICO transference

transferir [trans·fe·'rir] *irr como sentir vt* **1.** (*trasladar*) to transfer **2.** (*posponer*) to postpone **3.** FIN to make over **4.** (*propiedad, derecho*) to transfer

transformación [trans·for·ma·'sjon, -'θjon] *f* transformation; (*de costumbres*) change

transformar [trans·for·'mar] *vt* to transform; (*costumbres*) to change; **desde el accidente está transformado** he/she has changed completely since the accident

tránsfuga ['trans·fu·ɣa] *mf* **1.** (*fugitivo*) fugitive **2.** POL turncoat

transfusión [trans·fu·'sjon] *f t.* MED transfusion

transgredir [trans·ɣre·'dir] *irr como abolir vt*

(*ley*) to violate, to break; (*orden*) to disobey

transgresión [trans·ɣre·'sjon] *f* (*ley*) transgression, violation; (*orden*) disobedience

transición [tran·si·'sjon, -'θjon] *f* transition

transigencia [tran·si·'xen·sja, -θja] *f* **1.** (*condescendencia*) obligingness **2.** (*tolerancia*) tolerance **3.** POL compromise

transigente [tran·si·'xen·te] *adj* **1.** (*condescendiente*) broad-minded **2.** (*tolerante*) tolerant **3.** POL compromising

transigir <g→j> [tran·si·'xir] *vi* **1.** (*ceder*) to yield **2.** (*tolerar*) ~ **con algo** to tolerate sth **3.** JUR, POL to compromise; ~ **sobre algo** to reach a settlement on sth

transistor [tran·sis·'tor] *m* ELEC transistor

transitable [tran·si·'ta·βle] *adj* (*en coche*) open to traffic; (*a pie*) passable

transitar [tran·si·'tar] *vi* ~ **por algo** (*en coche*) to go along sth; (*por un túnel*) to go through sth; (*a pie*) to walk along sth; **una calle muy transitada** a very busy street; **nadie transitaba por la calle** there was no one on the streets

transitivo, -a [tran·si·'ti·βo, -a] *adj* LING transitive

tránsito ['tran·si·to] *m* **1.** (*circulación*) traffic; **de mucho ~** very busy; **el ~ por esta calle es algo complicado** transit along this road is rather complicated **2.** (*de personas*) transit; COM transit

transitorio, -a [tran·si·'to·rjo, -a] *adj* **1.** (*temporal*) temporary; (*ley, periodo, disposición*) transitional **2.** (*pasajero*) fleeting, transitory

translúcido, -a [trans·'lu·si·do, -a; -θi·do, -a] *adj* translucent

transmisible [trans·mi·'si·βle] *adj* transmissible

transmisión [trans·mi·'sjon] *f* **1.** (*de noticia*) broadcast; ~ **en directo/diferida** live/pre-recorded transmission [*o* broadcast] **2.** TV, AUTO, COMPUT transmission **3.** (*enfermedad*) transmission **4.** TÉC drive; (*mecanismo*) transmission; (*propulsión*) drive **5.** JUR transfer **6.** (*por herencia*) descent

transmisor [trans·mi·'sor] *m* TÉC transmitter

transmisor(a) [trans·mi·'sor, -·'so·ra] *adj* **estación ~a** transmitter, radio/TV station

transmitir [trans·mi·'tir] *vt* **1.** (*noticia*) to broadcast **2.** TV, RADIO, TÉC to transmit **3.** (*enfermedad*) to give **4.** (*por herencia*) to pass on **5.** FÍS to transmit

transparencia [trans·pa·'ren·sja, -θja] *f* **1.** (*calidad*) transparency **2.** (*de intención*) openness **3.** FOTO slide **4.** (*para un proyector*) overhead transparency

transparentar [trans·pa·ren·'tar] **I.** *vt* to reveal **II.** *vi, vr:* ~ **se** (*ser transparente*) to be transparent **III.** *vr:* ~ **se** (*dejarse ver, adivinar*) to show through

transparente [trans·pa·'ren·te] **I.** *adj* **1.** (*material*) transparent **2.** (*intenciones*) clear **II.** *m* curtain, blind

transpirar [trans·pi·'rar] *vi* (*persona*) to perspire

transponer [trans·po·'ner] *irr como poner* **I.** *vt* (*persona, cosa*) to move; (*trasplantar*) to transplant **II.** *vr:* ~ **se 1.** (*persona*) to move **2.** (*sol*) to go out of sight **3.** (*dormirse*) to doze off

transportar [trans·por·'tar] **I.** *vt* **1.** (*trasladar*) to transport; (*en brazos*) to carry; (*en un vehículo*) to take; ~ **por barco** to ship **2.** MÚS to transpose **II.** *vr:* ~ **se** to be transported

transporte [trans·'por·te] *m* **1.** COM transport; *t.* TÉC (*de personas*) carriage; ~ **aéreo/marítimo** air/sea transport; ~ **por carretera** road transport; **compañía de** ~s transport company **2.** (*vehículo*) ~s **públicos** public transportation; **¿qué** ~ **utilizas para ir a la ciudad?** how do you get into town? **3.** *pl* (*conjunto*) carriage **4.** (*exaltación*) rapture **5.** MÚS transposition

transportista [trans·por·'tis·ta] *mf* (*empresa, agente*) carrier, transporter

transpuesto, -a [trans·'pwes·to, -a] **I.** *pp de* **transponer II.** *adj* **quedarse** ~ to doze off

transversal [trans·βer·'sal] *adj* (*atravesado, perpendicular*) transverse, crosswise; **calle** ~ cross street

transverso, -a [trans·'βer·so, -a] *adj v.* **transversal**

tranvía [tram·'bi·a] *m* streetcar

trapacero, -a [tra·pa·'se·ro, -a; -'θe·ro, -a] *m, f* cheating

trapear [tra·pe·'ar] *vt AmL* (*limpiar*) to mop

trapecio [tra·'pe·sjo, -θjo] *m* **1.** (*de circo*) trapeze **2.** MAT trapezoid **3.** ANAT (*hueso*) trapezium; (*músculo*) trapezius

trapecista [tra·pe·'sis·ta, -'θis·ta] *mf* trapeze artist

trapiche [tra·'pi·tʃe] *m AmL* (*exprimidor de caña*) sugar mill

trapichear [tra·pi·tʃe·'ar] *vi* **1.** *inf* (*enredos*) to be mixed up in shady business; (*intrigar*) to scheme; (*artimaña*) to contrive; ~ **en los negocios** to have crooked dealings **2.** (*comerciar*) to buy and sell small scale

trapo ['tra·po] *m* **1.** (*tela*) rag **2.** (*para limpiar*) cleaning cloth; ~ **de cocina** dish towel; **pasar el** ~ **por algo** to wipe sth off **3.** *pl, inf* (*vestidos*) clothes *pl* **4.** NÁUT sails *pl;* **a todo** ~ under full sail; *inf* (*a toda velocidad*) at top speed; **el coche iba a todo** ~ *inf* the car was going at full speed; **poner la música a todo** ~ *inf* to put music on full blast **5.** TEAT curtain ▸ **tener lengua de** ~ to mumble; **tener manos de** ~ to be a butterfingers; **estar hecho un** ~ to be worn out; **sacar los** ~s **sucios a relucir** to wash one's dirty linen in public; **entrar al** ~ to fall into the trap; **poner a alguien como un** ~ to rag (on) sb; **soltar el** ~ (*reír*) to burst out laughing; (*llorar*) to burst into tears; **tratar a alguien como un** ~ to treat sb like dirt

tráquea ['tra·kea] *f* ANAT trachea, windpipe *inf*

traquetear [tra·ke·te·'ar] **I.** *vi* (*chapa, vajilla*) to clatter; (*motor, ametralladora*) to rattle; (*si-*

llas, carro) to jolt **II.** *vt* to shake

tras [tras] **I.** *prep* **1.** (*temporal*) after; **día** ~ **día** day after day **2.** (*espacial: detrás de*) behind; (*orden*) after; **voy** ~ **tuyo** (*en la cola*) I'm behind you, I'm after you; (*en el coche*) behind; **ir** ~ **alguien** (*perseguir*) to go after sb **3.** (*con movimiento*) after; **ponerse uno** ~ **otro** to put one after the other **4.** (*además de*) besides; ~ **de ser de pésima calidad es caro** it's not just terrible quality but it's expensive too **II.** *m inf* bottom **III.** *interj* **¡**~ ~**!** knock knock!

trasbocar <c→qu> [tras·βo·'kar] *vt AmC, AmS* to throw up

trasbordar [tras·βor·'dar] *vi, vt v.* **transbordar**

trascendencia [tra·sen·'den·sja, -θen·'den·θja] *f* (*importancia*) consequence; **no tener** ~ to be of little importance; **un incidente sin más** ~ an insignificant incident

trascendental [tra·sen·den·'tal, tras·θen·-] *adj* **1.** (*importante*) important **2.** FILOS transcendental

trascender <e→ie> [tra·sen·'der, tras·θen·-] *vi* **1.** (*hecho, noticia*) to become known **2.** (*efecto, consecuencias*) ~ **a algo** to have a wide effect on sth **3.** (*ir más allá*) ~ **de algo** to go beyond sth **4.** (*olor*) to smell **5.** (*extenderse*) to spread; **el discurso transciende a fascismo** the speech reeks of fascism

trasera [tra·'se·ra] *f* back

trasero [tra·'se·ro] *m* **1.** (*animal*) hindquarters *pl* **2.** *inf* (*persona*) bottom, backside

trasero, -a [tra·'se·ro, -a] *adj* back; **asiento** ~ back seat; **luz trasera** rear light; **parte trasera** rear; **propulsión trasera** rear-wheel drive; **rueda trasera** rear wheel

trasfondo [tras·'fon·do] *m* background

traslación [tras·la·'sjon, -'θjon] *f* (*de cosas*) transfer; (*de cuerpo*) moving; (*de tropa*) transfer

trasladar [tras·la·'dar] **I.** *vt* **1.** (*cosas*) to move; (*cuerpo*) to go; (*tropa, tienda*) to relocate; (*prisionero: a otra prisión*) to transfer; (*a otra comisaría*) to move **2.** (*funcionario*) to transfer **3.** (*fecha*) to postpone **4.** (*idea, obra*) ~ **al papel** to put on paper; ~ **a la pantalla** to make into a film **5.** (*orden, medida*) to notify **6.** (*escrito*) to copy **II.** *vr:* ~ **se 1.** (*mudarse*) to move **2.** (*ir a*) to go to; ~ **se en coche** to drive

traslado [tras·'la·do] *m* **1.** (*de cosas, cuerpo*) movement; (*tropa*) relocation; (*prisionero: de prisión*) transfer; (*de comisaría*) move **2.** (*de funcionario*) transfer **3.** (*de fecha*) postponement **4.** (*mudanza*) removal **5.** (*copia*) copy **6.** (*de orden, medida*) notification

traslucir [tras·lu·'sir, -'θir] *irr como lucir* **I.** *vt* (*cara*) to reveal; **dejar** ~ **algo** (*alguien*) to hint at sth **II.** *vr:* ~ **se 1.** (*ser translúcido*) to be translucent **2.** (*verse, notarse*) to show through **3.** (*hecho, intención*) to become evident

trasluz [tras·'lus, -'luθ] *m* diffused or reflected light; **mirar algo al** ~ to hold sth up to the light

trasmutar [tras·mu·'tar] *vt* to transmute

trasnochado, -a [tras·no·'tʃa·do,-a] *adj* **1.** (*comida*) stale **2.** (*idea, plan*) outdated **3.** (*persona*) drawn

trasnochar [tras·no·'tʃar] **I.** *vi* **1.** (*no dormir*) to spend a sleepless night; (*ir de juerga*) to have a night out; (*trabajando*) to sleep on sth **2.** (*acostarse tarde*) to stay up late **3.** (*pernoctar*) to spend the night **II.** *vt* to sleep on

traspapelar [tras·pa·pe·'lar] **I.** *vt* to misplace, to mislay **II.** *vr:* ~ **se** to get mislaid

traspasar [tras·pa·'sar] *vt* **1.** (*atravesar: arma, rayos*) to go through; (*penetrar, perforar*) to pierce; (*líquido*) to soak through; (*calle, río*) to cross **2.** (*pasar a*) to transfer; FIN to make over; **se traspasa tienda** shop for sale **3.** (*sentidos*) ~ **el corazón** to break sb's heart **4.** (*límite*) to go beyond; (*ley*) to break

traspaso [tras·'pa·so] *m* **1.** (*de piso, negocio, dinero*) transfer **2.** (*de límite*) exceeding; (*ley*) infringement **3.** (*de arma, rayos*) passage; (*de líquido*) soaking through; (*de calle, río*) crossing

traspatio [tras·'pa·tjo] *m AmL* backyard

traspié(s) [tras·'pje(s)] *m* (*inv*) stumble; *fig* slip-up; **dar un** ~ (*tropezar*) to stumble; (*resbalar*) to slip; (*meter la pata*) to slip up; (*en sociedad*) to make a faux pas

trasplantar [tras·plan·'tar] **I.** *vt* **1.** (*planta*) to transplant **2.** (*personas*) to transfer **3.** MED to transplant **II.** *vr:* ~ **se** to migrate

trasplante [tras·'plan·te] *m* **1.** (*de plantas*) transplanting **2.** (*de persona*) transfer **3.** MED transplant

trastada [tras·'ta·da] *f* **1.** *inf* (*travesura*) prank; **hacer una** ~ **a alguien** to play a prank on sb **2.** (*mala pasada*) dirty trick

traste ['tras·te] *m* **1.** (*de guitarra*) fret **2.** *AmL* (*trasto*) piece of junk ▶ **dar al** ~ **con algo** to spoil sth; **irse al** ~ to fall through

trastero, -a [tras·'te·ro, -a] *adj* **cuarto** ~ lumber room

trastienda [tras·'tjen·da] *f* **1.** (*de tienda*) back room **2.** *inf* (*astucia*) **tener mucha** ~ to be very crafty; (*reserva*) to be a dark horse

trasto ['tras·to] *m* **1.** (*mueble*) piece of furniture; (*utensilio*) utensil; **tirarse los** ~**s a la cabeza** to have a knock down drag out fight **2.** *pl* (*herramientas*) gear **3.** *pl* (*para tirar*) junk **4.** *inf* (*persona*) **mi hijo es un** ~ my son is a holy terror; **tratar como un** ~ to treat like a dog

trastornado, -a [tras·tor·'na·do, -a] *adj* (*confundido*) confused; (*sicológicamente*) disturbed; (*loco*) mad, crazy

trastornar [tras·tor·'nar] **I.** *vt* **1.** (*cosa*) to disarrange; (*de arriba abajo*) to turn upside down **2.** (*orden, plan, ideas*) disrupt; (*orden público*) to disturb **3.** (*psicológicamente*) to traumatize; (*por amor*) to lose one's head over sb; **la muerte de su marido la trastornó** she was traumatized by her husband's death **4.** (*encantar*) **me trastornan los coches** I'm

crazy about cars **II.** *vr:* ~ **se 1.** (*enloquecer*) to go mad **2.** (*estropearse*) to fall through **3.** (*turbarse*) to get upset

trasvasijar [tras·βa·si·'xar] *vt Chile* (*trasvasar*) to pour from one container to another, to decant

tratable [tra·'ta·βle] *adj* sociable

tratado [tra·'ta·do] *m* **1.** *t.* POL treaty; ~ **de no agresión** non-aggression treaty; ~ **comercial** trade agreement **2.** (*científico*) ~ **de algo** treatise on sth

tratamiento [tra·ta·'mjen·to] *m* **1.** *t.* MED, QUÍM (*de asunto*) treatment **2.** *t.* COMPUT (*elaboración*) processing; ~ **de texto** word processing; ~ **de agua potable** drinking-water processing **3.** (*de cortesía*) form of address; **el** ~ **de usted** the polite 'you' form; **¿qué** ~ **se le da a un cardenal?** what is the correct way to address a cardinal?

tratante [tra·'tan·te] *mf* dealer

tratar [tra·'tar] **I.** *vt* **1.** (*manejar, portarse*) to deal with; **no es una persona fácil de** ~ he/she is not an easy person to deal with **2.** MED, QUÍM to treat **3.** *t.* COMPUT (*elaborar, agua, minerales*) to process **4.** (*dar tratamiento*) to address; ~ **de tú/usted** to address sb informally/formally using tú/usted **5.** (*tema, asunto*) to discuss **II.** *vi* **1.** (*libro, película*) ~ **de** [*o* **sobre**] **algo** to be about sth, to deal with sth **2.** (*intentar*) to try; **trata de concentrarte** try to concentrate **3.** (*con alguien*) to have contact with **4.** COM to deal **III.** *vr:* ~ **se 1.** (*tener trato*) to have to do; **no me trato con él** I don't have anything to do with him **2.** (*ser cuestión de*) to be a question; **¿de qué se trata?** what's it about?; **tratándose de ti...** in your case...

tratativas [tra·ta·'ti·βas] *fpl Arg, Par* (*negociación*) negotiations *pl;* **siguen en** ~ they are still discussing terms

trato ['tra·to] *m* **1.** (*manejo, comportamiento*) treatment; **malos** ~**s** ill-treatment, abuse; **recibir un buen** ~ to be well-treated **2.** (*contacto*) contact; ~ **carnal** sexual relations; **tener** ~ **de gentes** to have a way with people; **romper el** ~ **con alguien** to break off relations with sb; **no querer** ~**s con alguien** to want nothing to do with sb; **es una señora de un** ~ **exquisito** she is a lady of exquisite manners **3.** (*pacto*) agreement; (*negocio*) deal; **cerrar un** ~ **con alguien** to close a deal with sb; **entrar en** ~**s con alguien** to open negotiations with sb; **¡**~ **hecho!** it's a deal!

trauma ['trau·ma] *m* trauma

traumático, -a [trau·'ma·ti·ko, -a] *adj* traumatic

traumatismo [trau·ma·'tis·mo] *m* injury; ~ **cervical** whiplash injury; MED traumatism

través [tra·'βes] **I.** *m* **1.** (*inclinación*) slant **2.** (*contratiempo*) setback ▶ **dar al** ~ **con algo** to hit sth broadsides; (*arruinar*) to ruin sth; **mirar a alguien de** ~ to look at sb out of the corner of one's eye; **de** ~ crossways, crosswise **II.** *prep* **a** ~ **de** (*de un lugar*) across; (*de la radio*) on; (*de una persona*) from, through

travesaño [tra·βe·'sa·ɲo] *m* **1.** ARQUIT crosspiece **2.** DEP crossbar **3.** (*de una escalera*) rung

travesía [tra·βe·'si·a] *f* **1.** (*por aire*) flight; (*por mar*) crossing **2.** (*distancia*) distance **3.** (*calle*) cross street

travesti [tra·'βes·ti] *mf*, **travestí** [tra·βes·'ti] *mf*, **travestido, -a** [tra·βes·'ti·do, -a] *m*, *f* transvestite

travesura [tra·βe·'su·ra] *f* prank

travieso, -a [tra·'βje·so, -a] *adj* **1.** (*de través*) across; **correr a campo traviesa** to run cross-country **2.** (*niño*) mischievous, naughty; **Daniel el Travieso** Dennis the Menace **3.** (*adulto*) dissolute

trayecto [tra·'jek·to] *m* (*trecho*) distance; (*ruta*) route; (*recorrido*) itinerary; **final de** ~ end of the line

trayectoria [tra·jek·'to·rja] *f* **1.** (*de cuerpo*) path; ~ **de la Luna** the moon's trajectory **2.** (*profesional*) career

traza ['tra·sa, -θa] *f* **1.** *t.* ARQUIT (*plan*) plan **2.** (*habilidad*) ability; **tener** ~ **para escribir** to be good at writing; **tener** ~ **para hablar** to have a knack for speaking **3.** (*aspecto*) appearance; **por las** ~**s** from the look of things; **lleva todas las** ~**s de acabar mal** it clearly looks as though it isn't going to turn out well **4.** (*rastro*) trace

trazado [tra·'sa·do, tra·'θa-] *m* **1.** *t.* ARQUIT (*de plan*) design **2.** (*recorrido*) route; FERRO line **3.** (*dirección*) direction **4.** (*disposición*) layout

trazar <z→c> [tra·'sar, -'θar] *vt* **1.** (*líneas*) to trace; (*esquemáticamente*) to outline; (*dibujos*) to sketch **2.** *t.* ARQUIT (*plan*) to draw up **3.** (*describir*) to describe

trazo ['tra·so, -θo] *m* **1.** (*de bolígrafo, lápiz*) mark; **dibujar al** ~ to outline **2.** (*de escritura*) stroke **3.** (*dibujo*) sketch **4.** (*de la cara*) **de** ~**s suaves** with soft features

trébol ['tre·βol] *m* **1.** (*planta*) clover; (*hoja*) clover leaf; (*emblema nacional de Irlanda*) shamrock **2.** (*cartas*) clubs

trece ['tre·se, -θe] **I.** *adj inv* thirteen; **seguir en sus** ~ to stand firm; **en el siglo** ~ in the thirteenth century; **martes y** ~ ≈ Friday the thirteenth **II.** *m* thirteen; *v.t.* **ocho**

trecho ['tre·tʃo] *m* **1.** (*distancia*) distance, way **2.** (*tramo*) stretch **3.** (*tiempo*) period, spell **4.** (*trozo*) piece; **de** ~ **a** [*o* **en**] ~ every so often; **a** ~**s** at intervals; **hacer algo a** ~**s** to do sth in fits and starts

tregua ['tre·ɣwa] *f* **1.** MIL truce **2.** (*descanso*) respite; **dar** ~**s** (*dolor*) to let up now and then; **la muela le daba** ~**s** his/her toothache would come and go; **sin** ~ relentlessly

treinta ['trein·ta] *adj inv*, *m* thirty; *v.t.* **ochenta**

treintavo, -a [trein·'ta·βo, -a] *adj* thirtieth; *v.t.* **ochentavo**

tremendo, -a [tre·'men·do, -a] *adj* **1.** (*temible*) frightful **2.** (*enorme*) tremendous

3. (*niño*) full of mischief **4.** (*respetable*) imposing ▶ **conseguir** algo por la tremenda to want to get sth by whatever means; **tomar las cosas a la tremenda** to make such a fuss over things

tremolar [tre·mo·'lar] *vi* to wave, to flutter

tren [tren] *m* **1.** FERRO train; ~ **interurbano** intercity train; ~ **de juguete** toy train; ~ **rápido** express train; ~ **de cercanías** suburban train; ~ **de alta velocidad** high-speed train; ~ **directo** through train; **coger el** ~ to catch [*o* take] the train; **ir en** ~ to go by train; **todas quieren subirse al** ~ *fig* everyone wants to get in on it, everyone wants to climb on the bandwagon; **perder el último** ~ *fig* to miss the boat **2.** TÉC ~ **de lavado** carwash **3.** (*lujo*) ~ **de vida** lifestyle; **llevar un gran** ~ **de vida** to live in style **4.** (*ritmo*) **imponer un fuerte** ~ **en la carrera** to set a fast pace in the race **5.** *inf* (*muy bien*) **estar como un** ~ (*persona*) to be very good-looking **6.** *inf* (*en abundancia*) **hay sangría como para parar un** ~ there's plenty of sangria

trenza ['tren·sa, -θa] *f* **1.** (*de pelo*) braid **2.** (*de cintas*) braid

trenzar <z→c> [tren·'sar, -'θar] *vt* **1.** (*pelo*) to braid **2.** (*fibras*) to plait

trepa¹ ['tre·pa] *f* (*astucia*) cunning

trepa² ['tre·pa] *m pey*, *inf* climber; **esta oficina esta llena de** ~**s luchando por llegar a la cima** this office is full of ambitious go-getters scrambling to reach the top

trepador(a) [tre·pa·'dor] **I.** *adj* **planta** ~**a** climbing plant **II.** *m(f)* (*arribista*) social climber, go-getter

trepar [tre·'par] **I.** *vi*, *vt* **1.** (*al árbol*) to climb **2.** (*planta*) to creep **II.** *vt* to climb

trepe ['tre·pe] *m* CRi (*regaño*) scolding; **echar un** ~ **a alguien por algo** to tell sb off for sth

trepidar [tre·pi·'dar] *vi* **1.** (*temblar*) to vibrate **2.** *AmL* (*vacilar*) to hesitate

treque ['tre·ke] *adj Ven* **1.** (*ingenioso*) witty **2.** (*chistoso*) funny

tres [tres] **I.** *adj inv* three; **esta traducción no me sale ni a la de** ~ I just can't do this translation no matter how I try; **como** ~ **y dos son cinco** as sure as you are born; **de** ~ **al cuarto** two-bit; ~ **en raya** (*juego*) tic(k)-tac(k)-toe **II.** *m inv* three; *v.t.* **ocho**

trescientos, -as [tres·'sjen·tos, -as; -'θjen·tos, -as] *adj* three hundred; *v.t.* **ochocientos**

triangular [trian·gu·'lar] *adj* triangular

triángulo [tri·'an·ɣu·lo] *m* **1.** (*figura*) triangle **2.** MÚS triangle **3.** (*sentimental*) ~ **amoroso** eternal triangle

triates ['trja·tes] *mpl Méx* (*trillizos*) triplets *pl*

tribu ['tri·βu] *f* tribe

tribulación [tri·βu·la·'sjon, -'θjon] *f* **1.** tribulation; (*pena*) grief **2.** (*sufrimiento*) suffering **3.** (*adversidad*) hardship

tribuna [tri·'βu·na] *f* **1.** (*en parlamento*) rostrum **2.** (*en desfile, estadio*) stand **3.** JUR ~ **de jurados** jury box **4.** ~ **de la prensa** press box

tribunal [tri·βu·'nal] *m* **1.**JUR court; **Tribunal de Cuentas** General Accounting Office; **Tribunal de Justicia Europeo** European Court of Justice; **llevar a los ~es** to take to court **2.** (*comisión*) ~ **examinador** board of examiners

tributar [tri·βu·'tar] *vt* **1.** (*impuestos*) to pay **2.** (*honor*) to render; (*respeto*) to show; ~ **un homenaje a alguien** to pay tribute to sb

tributario, -a [tri·βu·'ta·rjo, -a] *adj* tributary; (*imponible*) tax; **agencia tributaria** Inland Revenue

tributo [tri·'βu·to] *m* **1.** (*impuesto*) tax **2.** (*homenaje*) tribute; **pagar** ~ to pay tribute

triciclo [tri·'si·klo, tri·'θi-] *m* tricycle

tricolor [tri·ko·'lor] *adj* tricolor

tricota [tri·'ko·ta] *f AmL* (*chaqueta*) sweater

tridimensional [tri·di·men·sjo·'nal] *adj* three-dimensional

trifulca [tri·'ful·ka] *f inf* rumpus

trigal [tri·'ɣal] *m* wheat field

trigo ['tri·ɣo] *m* **1.** (*planta*) wheat **2.** (*grano*) wheat; **no ser** ~ **limpio** *fig* not to be totally above board

trigueño, -a [tri·'ɣe·ɲo, -a] **I.** *adj* light brown; (*pelo*) dark blond; (*piel*) olive-skinned **II.** *m, f AmL* colored person

trilingüe [tri·'lin·gwe] *adj* trilingual

trilla ['tri·ja, -ʎa] *f* **1.** (*acción*) threshing **2.** (*época*) threshing season **3.** *AmL, inf* (*paliza*) thrashing **4.** (*trillo*) thresher

trillar [tri·'jar, -'ʎar] *vt* **1.** (*grano*) to thresh **2.** (*usar*) to overuse **3.** *AmL, inf* (*golpear*) to beat

trillizo [tri·'ji·so, -a; -'ʎi·θo, -a] *m* triplet

trillo ['tri·jo, -ʎo] *m* **1.** AGR (*máquina*) thresher **2.** *AmC* (*senda*) narrow path

trimestral [tri·mes·'tral] *adj* **1.** (*duración*) three-month **2.** (*cada tres meses*) three-monthly, quarterly

trimestre [tri·'mes·tre] *m* **1.** (*período*) quarter **2.** (*educación*) term **3.** (*paga*) quarterly payment

trinar [tri·'nar] *vi* **1.** (*persona*) to sing; (*pájaro*) to warble **2.** *inf* (*rabiar*) to fume; **está que trina** he/she is completely crazy **3.** MÚS to trill

trinca ['trin·ka] *f* **1.** (*tres*) threesome **2.** *And, CSur* (*pandilla*) gang **3.** *AmL, inf* (*embriaguez*) drunkenness **4.** *CSur* (*canicas*) game of marbles

trincar <c→qu> [trin·'kar] **I.** *vt* **1.** (*con cuerdas*) to tie up **2.** (*detener*) to nab **3.** (*romper*) to break up; (*papel*) to tear up **4.** *inf* (*robar*) to steal **5.** *inf* (*matar*) to bump off **6.** *AmL* (*apretar*) to be too tight **II.** *vr:* ~ **se 1.** *inf* (*emborracharse*) to get plastered **2.** *vulg* (*copular*) to screw

trinchera [trin·'tʃe·ra] *f* **1.** MIL trench; **guerra de ~s** trench warfare **2.** (*gabardina*) trench coat

trineo [tri·'neo] *m* sled

trinidad [tri·ni·'dad] *f* trinity; **la Santísima Trinidad** the Holy Trinity

trinitaria [tri·ni·'ta·rja] *f* **1.** BOT (*pensamiento*) pansy **2.** *Col, PRico, Ven* BOT bougainvillea

trino ['tri·no] *m* **1.** MÚS trill **2.** (*pájaro*) warble

trío ['tri·o] *m* trio

tripa ['tri·pa] *f* **1.** (*intestino*) intestine, gut; **quitar las ~s a un pez** to gut a fish **2.** *pl* (*vísceras*) entrails *pl*, innards *pl*; (*comestibles*) tripe; **me suenan las ~s** my stomach's rumbling; **echar las ~s** *inf* (*vomitar*) to throw up; **hacer de ~s corazón** *inf* to pluck up courage, to grin and bear it; **¿qué ~ se te ha roto?** *inf* what's up with you?; **se me revuelven las ~s** it turns my stomach; **¡te voy a sacar las ~s!** *inf* I'm going to tear you to pieces!; **tener malas ~s** *inf* to be cruel **3.** (*vientre*) tummy; **echar ~** *inf* to get a paunch; **llenar(se) la ~** *inf* to eat one's fill; **estar con ~** (*embarazada*) to be in the family way; **dejar con ~** *inf* to get sb pregnant **4.** *pl* (*interior*) insides *pl*; (*de fruta*) core

triple ['tri·ple] **I.** *adj* triple; (*de tres capas*) three-ply **II.** *m* (*cantidad*) triple; **ser el ~ de grande** to be three times as large

triplicar <c→qu> [tri·pli·'kar] **I.** *vt* to triple, to treble **II.** *vr:* ~ **se** to triple, to treble

trípode ['tri·po·de] *m* FOTO tripod

tripón, -ona [tri·'pon, -'po·na] **I.** *adj inf* pot-bellied **II.** *m, f* **1.** *Méx, inf* little boy or girl; **los tripones** the kids **2.** *inf* (*persona gorda*) fatty

tríptico ['trip·ti·ko, -a] *m* (*documento*) three-page leaflet

tripulación [tri·pu·la·'sjon, -'θjon] *f* (*avión, barco*) crew

tripulante [tri·pu·'lan·te] *m* crew member

tripular [tri·pu·'lar] *vt* **1.** (*proveer de tripulación*) to man **2.** (*conducir: coche*) to drive; (*avión, barco*) to pilot

tripulina [tri·pu·'li·na] *f Chile* hubbub

trisca ['tris·ka] *f* **1.** (*crujido*) crunch **2.** (*jaleo*) racket **3.** *AmC* (*mofa*) surreptitious sneer

triscar <c→qu> [tris·'kar] **I.** *vi* **1.** (*patalear*) to stamp **2.** (*jugar*) to romp **II.** *vt* **1.** (*mezclar*) to mingle **2.** (*confundir*) to mix up **3.** *AmC* (*mofar*) to make fun of

triste ['tris·te] *adj* sad; (*mustio, pálido*) gloomy; (*descolorido*) dreary; (*paisaje*) dismal; (*flor*) withered; **un ~ sueldo** a sorry salary; **aún no he comido ni un ~ bocadillo** I haven't even had a measly sandwich yet; **aún no he ganado ni un ~ peso** I've yet to earn a single peso; **es ~ que no podamos ir** it's too bad we can't go; **el caballero de la ~ figura** (**Don Quijote**) the knight of the sad countenance

tristeza [tris·'te·sa, -θa] *f* sadness, sorrow

tristura [tris·'tu·ra] *f AmL* sadness

trituradora [tri·tu·ra·'do·ra] *f* TÉC crusher; (*de la cocina*) grinder; ~ **de carne** meat grinder; ~ **de forraje** forage chopper; ~ **de papel** paper shredder; ~ **de basura** waste-disposal unit; ~ **de hielo** ice crusher

triturar [tri·tu·'rar] *vt* **1.** (*desmenuzar*) to chop; (*moler*) to grind; (*al masticar*) to chew **2.** (*mal-*

T

tratar) to beat to a pulp; (*destruir*) to pulverize **3.** (*criticar*) to tear to pieces

triunfador(a [trjun·fa·'dor, -·'do·ra] *m(f)* winner

triunfar [trjun·'far] *vi* **1.** (*salir triunfador*) to triumph **2.** (*ganar*) ~ **en algo** to win at sth; (*tener éxito*) to succeed; ~ **en la vida** to succeed in life **3.** (*exultar*) ~ **de algo** to exult over sth **4.** (*naipes*) to trump; (*jugar un triunfo*) to play a trump; **triunfan corazones** hearts are trumps

triunfo ['trjun·fo] *m* **1.** (*victoria*) triumph, victory; (*éxito*) success; **arco de ~** victory arch; **costar un ~** to be no easy task **2.** (*naipe*) trump

trivialidad [tri·βja·li·'dad] *f* **1.** (*cualidad*) triviality, pettiness **2.** (*dicho*) trite remark

trivializar <z→c> [tri·βja·li·'sar, -'θar] *vt* **1.** (*restar importancia*) to trivialize **2.** (*simplificar*) to play down

triza ['tri·sa, -θa] *f* shred; **estar hecho ~s** to feel washed out; **hacer ~s** to tear into shreds; (*papel*) to shred; (*película*) to tear to pieces; **hacerse ~s** to smash to bits; (*jarrón*) to shatter; **hacer ~s a alguien** to tear sb apart

trocar [tro·'kar] *irr como volcar* **I.** *vt* **1.** (*cambiar*) ~ **por algo** to exchange for sth, to barter for sth; (*palabras*) to interchange **2.** (*dinero*) to change **3.** (*confundir*) to confuse **4.** (*vomitar*) to vomit **5.** *CSur* (*vender*) to sell **II.** *vr:* ~ **se** (*cambiar*) to change; (*transformarse*) to turn

trocha ['tro·tʃa] *f* **1.** (*senda*) trail; (*atajo*) shortcut **2.** *AmL* FERRO gauge

trofeo [tro·'feo] *m* **1.** (*señal*) trophy; ~ **de guerra** war trophy **2.** (*victoria*) victory, triumph; (*éxito*) success

troglodita [tro·ɣlo·'di·ta] **I.** *adj* **1.** (*cavernícola*) cave-dwelling **2.** *inf* (*burdo*) brutish **II.** *m* **1.** (*cavernícola*) troglodyte, cave-dweller **2.** *inf* (*burdo*) lout

tromba ['trom·ba] *f* METEO ~ (**de agua**) water spout; (*aguacero*) downpour; ~ (**terrestre**) whirlwind; **en ~** en masse

trombón [trom·'bon] *m* MÚS **1.** (*instrumento*) trombone **2.** (*músico*) trombonist

trombosis [trom·'bo·sis] *f inv* MED thrombosis

trompa[1] ['trom·pa] *f* **1.** ZOOL (*elefante*) trunk; (*insectos*) proboscis; ~ **de Falopio** Fallopian tube **2.** *inf* (*nariz*) conk **3.** *AmL, inf* (*labios*) lips *pl;* **¡cierra la ~!** shut your trap! **4.** MÚS (*instrumento*) horn **5.** (*peonza*) top **6.** *inf* (*borrachera*) drunkenness; **coger una ~** to get smashed; **estar ~** to be drunk **7.** METEO *v.* **tromba**

trompa[2] ['trom·pa] *mf* **1.** (*músico*) horn player **2.** *CSur, inf* (*patrón*) boss

trompada [trom·'pa·da] *f*, **trompazo** [trom·'pa·so, -θo] *m* (*porrazo*) bash; (*choque*) crash; (*puñetazo*) punch

trompear [trom·pe·'ar] **I.** *vt AmL, inf* to punch **II.** *vr:* ~ **se** *inf* **1.** (*emborracharse*) to get plastered **2.** *AmL* (*pelearse*) to fight

trompeta [trom·'pe·ta] *f* (*instrumento*) trumpet

trompicón [trom·pi·'kon] *m* **1.** (*tropezón*) stumble; **a trompicones** in fits and starts **2.** *AmC* (*puñetazo*) punch

trompis ['trom·pis] *m inv, Arg, Urug* (*trompada*) punch; **agarrarse a ~** to start punching each other

trompiza [trom·'pi·sa, -θa] *f AmS* fight

trompo ['trom·po] *m* spinning top

trompudo, -a [trom·'pu·do, -a] *adj AmL* thick-lipped

tronado, -a [tro·'na·do, -a] *adj* **1.** (*desgastado*) worn **2.** *inf* (*loco*) **estar ~** to be cracked; (*arruinado*) to be broke; *AmL* (*drogado*) to be high on drugs

tronar <o→ue> [tro·'nar] **I.** *vimpers* METEO to thunder **II.** *vi* **1.** (*ruido*) to thunder; (*gritar*) to roar **2.** (*oponerse*) to denounce violently, to thunder

troncha ['tron·tʃa] *f Arg, Chile, Perú* (*lonja*) slice

tronchar [tron·'tʃar] **I.** *vt* **1.** (*tronco*) to cut down; (*rama*) to snap **2.** (*vida*) to cut short; (*esperanzas*) to shatter **II.** *vr:* ~ **se** to split; ~ **se de risa** *inf* to split one's sides laughing

troncho ['tron·tʃo] *m* **1.** BOT stem; (*de hortaliza*) stalk **2.** *CSur* (*trozo*) chunk

tronco ['tron·ko] *m* **1.** (*árbol*) trunk; (*flor*) stem; (*hortaliza*) stalk; (*de un árbol talado*) stump; (*leño*) log; **dormir como un ~** *inf* to sleep like a log **2.** (*cuerpo*) torso, trunk **3.** (*de familia*) stock **4.** *inf* (*amigo*) buddy; **tranqui ~** cool it, pal **5.** (*conducto*) main line

tronera [tro·'ne·ra] *f* **1.** (*ventana*) dormer; (*en el tejado*) small skylight **2.** MIL crenel **3.** (*billar*) pocket **4.** *Méx* (*chimenea*) chimney

trono ['tro·no] *m* **1.** (*asiento*) throne; **ser leal al ~** to be loyal to the crown; **subir al ~** to come to the throne; **sucesor al ~** heir to the throne **2.** *inf* (*inodoro*) john

tropa ['tro·pa] *f* **1.** (*multitud*) crowd; *pey* (*grupo*) horde; **se presentaron Pepe y Clara y toda la ~** Pepe and Clara and the whole crew showed up; **en ~** in disorganized groups **2.** MIL troop

tropear [tro·pe·'ar] *vi Arg* (*conducir el ganado*) to herd

tropel [tro·'pel] *m* **1.** (*mucha gente*) throng; **en ~** in a mad rush; **salieron en ~ del estadio** they came pouring out of the stadium **2.** (*prisa*) rush **3.** (*desorden*) jumble

tropero [tro·'pe·ro] *m Arg* (*vaquero*) cowboy

tropezar [tro·pe·'sar, -'θar] *irr como empezar* **I.** *vi* **1.** (*con los pies*) to trip **2.** (*topar*) to come across **3.** (*cometer un error*) to make a mistake; (*moralmente*) to go astray **4.** (*reñir*) to quarrel **II.** *vr:* ~ **se** (*encontrarse*) to run into

tropezón [tro·pe·'son, -'θon] *m* **1.** (*acción*) stumble; **dar un ~** to trip; **a tropezones** by fits and starts; *fig* falling and rising; **hablaba a tropezones** he/she spoke falteringly **2.** (*error*) mistake; (*desliz*) lapse **3.** (*persona*) run-in **4.** (*en sopas, legumbres*) small chunks of meat, vegetables or seafood

tropical [tro·pi·'kal] *adj* tropical; **clima ~** tropical climate; **fantasías ~es** exotic fantasies

trópico ['tro·pi·ko] *m* tropic; **~ de Cáncer** Tropic of Cancer; **pasar los ~s** *AmC, fig* to have a hard time

tropiezo [tro·'pje·so, -θo] *m* **1.** (*en el camino*) stumbling block; **dar un ~** to trip **2.** (*error*) blunder; (*moralmente*) moral lapse **3.** (*revés*) setback **4.** (*desgracia*) misfortune; (*en el amor*) thwarting **5.** (*discusión*) quarrel

tropilla [tro·'pi·ja, -ʎa] *f CSur* drove

trotamundos [tro·ta·'mun·dos] *mf inv* globetrotter

trotar [tro·'tar] *vi* **1.** (*caballos*) to trot; (*jinete*) to trot **2.** (*con prisas*) to hustle

trovador [tro·βa·'dor] *m* troubadour

trozo ['tro·so, -θo] *m* **1.** (*pedazo*) piece, bit; **a ~s** in pieces; **la pared se está cayendo a ~s** the wall is falling apart bit by bit **2.** LIT, MÚS excerpt, passage

trucar [tru·'kar] *vt* **1.** (*amañar*) to fix, to rig; FOTO to alter **2.** *inf* AUTO to soup up

trucha ['tru·tʃa] *f* **1.** (*pez*) trout; **~ asalmonada** salmon trout **2.** *AmC* COM (*caseta*) stand

trucho, -a ['tru·tʃo, -a] *adj Arg, Col* (*astuto*) crafty

truco ['tru·ko] *m* trick; **esto tiene ~** there's a trick [*o* a catch] to this; **ése tiene muchos ~s** he's full of tricks ▶ **coger el ~ a algo** to get the hang of sth; **coger el ~ a alguien** to catch on to sb

trueno ['trwe·no] *m* **1.** (*ruido*) clap of thunder **2.** *inf* (*alborotador*) wild youth; **ir de ~** to go on a spree

trueque ['trwe·ke] *m* exchange; COM (*sin dinero*) barter; **a ~ de** in exchange for

trufa ['tru·fa] *f* **1.** *t.* BOT truffle **2.** (*mentira*) lie; (*embuste*) hoax; (*fanfarronada*) bluster **3.** (*bombón*) (chocolate) truffle

truhán [tru·'an] *m* (*estafador*) rogue; (*charlatán*) mountebank

truncar <c→qu> [trun·'kar] *vt* **1.** (*cortar*) to truncate; (*la cabeza*) to cut off **2.** (*texto*) to abridge; (*significado*) to destroy; (*cita*) to mutilate **3.** (*desarrollo*) to stunt; (*esperanzas, ilusiones*) to shatter

trusa ['tru·sa] *f Méx, Perú* (*faja*) girdle

tu [tu] *art pos* your; **~ padre/blusa/libro** your father/blouse/book; **~s hermanos/hermanas** your brothers/sisters

tú [tu] *pron pers* you; **yo que ~** if I were you; **tratar de ~** to address in the familiar manner using 'tú'; **de ~ a ~** on equal footing

tuba ['tu·βa] *f* tuba

tubérculo [tu·'βer·ku·lo] *m* **1.** BOT tuber **2.** *t.* MED (*bulto*) tubercle

tuberculosis [tu·βer·ku·'lo·sis] *f inv* tuberculosis

tubería [tu·βe·'ri·a] *f* **1.** (*tubo*) pipe **2.** (*conjunto*) pipes *pl*

tubo ['tu·βo] *m* **1.** (*para fluidos, gases*) tube; **~ de chimenea** flue; **~ digestivo** alimentary

canal; **~ de ensayo** test tube; **~ de escape** exhaust pipe, tailpipe; **~ de respiración** breathing tube; **tienes que pasar por el ~** *inf* you have to knuckle under; **fue como por un ~** *inf* it was a cinch; **alucinar por un ~** *inf* to really flip; **tenemos trabajo por un ~** *inf* we have loads of work to do **2.** RADIO, TV tube **3.** (*recipiente*) tube; **~ de pasta de dientes** tube of toothpaste **4.** *AmL* TEL (*auricular*) receiver **5.** *inf* (*metro*) subway

tucán [tu·'kan] *m* toucan

tuerca ['twer·ka] *f* nut; **~ mariposa** wing nut

tuerto, -a ['twer·to] I. *adj* **1.** (*de sólo un ojo*) one-eyed **2.** (*torcido*) crooked, twisted II. *m, f* injustice

tuétano ['twe·ta·no] *m* **1.** (*médula*) marrow **2.** (*corazón, esencia*) core, heart; **hasta los ~s** through and through; **enamorado hasta los ~s** head over heels in love; **llegar al ~ de un asunto** to get to the crux of a matter; **calado hasta los ~s** soaked to the skin

tufo ['tu·fo] *m* **1.** (*olor malo*) foul smell; (*de cuerpo*) body odor; (*halitosis*) bad breath; (*a alcohol*) reek; (*a cerrado*) stuffy **2.** (*vapor*) fume **3.** (*rizo*) curl **4.** *pl* (*vanidad*) airs *pl*; **tener ~** *inf* to be conceited

tul [tul] *m* tulle

tulipa [tu·'li·pa] *f* tulip-shaped lampshade

tulipán [tu·li·'pan] *m* tulip

tullido, -a [tu·'ji·do, -a; tu·'ʎi-] I. *adj* (*persona*) disabled; *pey* crippled; (*brazo*) maimed II. *m, f* cripple

tullir <3. *pret:* tulló> [tu·'jir, -'ʎir] *vt* **1.** (*maltratar*) to maltreat **2.** (*herir*) to injure; (*lisiar*) to cripple; **te voy a ~ a palos** I'm going to beat you to a pulp **3.** (*paralizar*) to paralyze **4.** (*agotar*) to wear out, to exhaust

tumba ['tum·ba] *f* **1.** (*sepulcro*) grave, tomb; **ser (como) una ~** (*callado*) to keep quiet; **soy una ~** my lips are sealed; **llevar a alguien a la ~** to carry sb off; **hablar a ~ abierta** to speak openly; **lanzarse a ~ abierta en algo** to go headlong into sth; **tu abuelo se revolvería en su ~** your grandfather would turn in his grave; **cavar su propia ~** to drive a nail into one's own coffin **2.** (*voltereta*) somersault **3.** *AmL* (*tala*) felling of trees; (*claro*) tree clearing

tumbar [tum·'bar] I. *vt* **1.** (*tirar*) to knock down; (*pegando*) to flatten; **el campeón le tumbó en el tercer asalto** the champ knocked him out in the third round; *inf* (*matar*) to bump off; **estar tumbado** to be lying down **2.** *inf* ENS (*suspender*) to fail, to flunk **3.** *inf* (*perturbar, impresionar*) to bowl over **4.** *AmL* (*árboles*) to fell; (*tierra*) to clear **5.** *vulg* (*copular*) to screw II. *vr:* **~se 1.** (*acostarse*) to lie down; **~se en la cama** to lie down on the bed **2.** (*desistir*) to give up **3.** *inf* (*en el trabajo*) to ease up

tumbo ['tum·bo] *m* **1.** (*caída*) fall, tumble **2.** (*vaivén*) roll; **dar un ~** to jolt; **ir por la vida dando ~s** to go through life moving from one hardship to another **3.** (*voltereta*) somersault

T

tumor [tu·'mor] *m* MED tumor
tumulto [tu·'mul·to] *m* tumult; **un ~ de gente** a crowd of people
tuna ['tu·na] *f* **1.** MÚS *in Spain, a type of fraternity in which students get together to sing and play music* **2.** (*vida picaresca*) **correr la ~** to live it up
tunda ['tun·da] *f* **1.** (*paliza*) beating **2.** (*esfuerzo*) exhausting effort; **darse una ~** to wear oneself out **3.** (*de paños*) clipping
túnel ['tu·nel] *m* tunnel; **~ aerodinámico** wind tunnel; **~ de lavado** car wash; **salir del ~** *fig* to see the light at the end of the tunnel
túnica ['tu·ni·ka] *f* **1.** (*vestidura*) tunic, robe **2.** (*membrana*) tunica
tuno, -a ['tu·no] **I.** *adj* **1.** (*astuto*) cunning **2.** (*pícaro*) roguish **II.** *m, f* **1.** (*truhán*) rogue **2.** (*astuto*) crook **3.** (*niño*) scamp **4.** (*de la tuna*) member of a student 'tuna'
tuntún [tun·'tun] *m inf* **al** (**buen**) **~** any old way; **juzgar al buen ~** to jump to conclusions
tupé [tu·'pe] *m* **1.** (*cabello*) pompadour **2.** (*frescura*) cheek
tupí [tu·'pi] *mf AmL* (*aborigen del Brasil*) Tupi
tupido, -a [tu·'pi·do, -a] **I.** *adj* **1.** (*denso*) thick; **correr un ~ velo** to draw a veil over sth; *fig* to keep sth quiet **2.** *AmL* (*obstruido*) blocked **3.** *Méx* (*frecuente*) frequent **4.** (*con tesón*) persistently **II.** *adv* (*a menudo*) often
tupir [tu·'pir] **I.** *vt* **1.** (*apretar*) to pack tightly; (*tapar agujeros*) to fill in **2.** (*obstruir*) to obstruct **II.** *vr:* **~se 1.** (*comer mucho*) to gorge oneself; (*beber mucho*) to guzzle down **2.** *AmL* (*obstruirse*) to get blocked up
turba ['tur·βa] *f* **1.** (*materia*) peat **2.** (*personas*) crowd; *pey* mob
turbación [tur·βa·'sjon, -'θjon] *f* **1.** (*disturbio*) disturbance **2.** (*alarma*) concern **3.** (*vergüenza*) embarrassment **4.** (*confusión*) confusion
turbante [tur·'βan·te] *m* turban
turbar [tur·'βar] **I.** *vt* **1.** (*perturbar*) to disturb **2.** (*alarmar*) to worry **3.** (*avergonzar*) to embarrass **4.** (*desconcertar*) to unsettle **5.** (*agua*) to stir up **II.** *vr:* **~se 1.** (*ser disturbado*) to be disturbed **2.** (*alarmarse*) to get worried **3.** (*avergonzarse*) to get embarrassed **4.** (*desconcertarse*) to become confused **5.** (*agua*) to get stirred up
turbina [tur·'βi·na] *f* turbine
turbio, -a ['tur·βjo, -a] *adj* (*líquido*) cloudy; (*asunto*) turbid, shady; (*sin transparencia, carácter*) opaque; (*negocio*) shady; (*vista*) blurry, unclear
turbulencia [tur·βu·'len·sja, -θja] *f* **1.** (*agua, aire*) turbulence **2.** (*alboroto*) commotion; (*confusión*) turmoil **3.** (*sin transparencia*) murkiness
turbulento, -a [tur·βu·'len·to, -a] *adj* **1.** (*agua, aire*) turbulent **2.** (*alborotado*) stormy; (*confuso*) confused **3.** (*rebelde*) disorderly **4.** (*turbio*) cloudy
turgente [tur·'xen·te] *adj* **1.** (*hinchado*) swol-

len **2.** (*abultado*) protuberant; (*pechos*) firm
turismo [tu·'ris·mo] *m* **1.** (*viajar*) tourism; **~ activo** adventure tourism; **~ de salud** health tourism; **~ verde** ecotourism; **industria del ~** tourist trade; **oficina de ~** visitors' bureau; **hacer ~** to travel as a tourist **2.** AUTO private car
turista [tu·'ris·ta] *mf* tourist
turístico, -a [tu·'ris·ti·ko, -a] *adj* tourist; **viaje ~** sightseeing trip
turnar [tur·'nar] *vi, vr:* **~se** to take turns
turno ['tur·no] *m* **1.** (*en la fábrica*) shift; **cambio de ~** shift change; **estar de ~** to be on duty; **trabajar por ~s** to work shifts; **~ de día/noche** day/night shift **2.** (*orden*) turn; **a** [*o* **por**] **~s** by turns; **es tu ~** it's your turn; **pedir ~** to ask who is last in line; **aguardar su ~** to wait one's turn; **~ de preguntas** question and answer session; **hacer algo por ~s** to take turns doing sth; **de ~** current; **apareció con la novia de ~** he showed up with his latest girlfriend
turquesa¹ [tur·'ke·sa] **I.** *adj* turquoise **II.** *m* (*color*) turquoise blue
turquesa² [tur·'ke·sa] *f* MIN (*piedra*) turquoise
turrón [tu·'rron] *m* **1.** (*dulce*) ≈ nougat **2.** (*puesto*) cushy job; **comer del ~** *fig* to fill a government post

> **i** **Turrón** is an absolute must in Spain at Christmastime. The nougat-like candy comes in both hard and soft varieties and is commonly flavored with peanuts, honey-coated almonds, or roasted hazelnuts. The two most famous kinds come from **Jijona** and **Alicante**.

turulato, -a [tu·ru·'la·to, -a] *adj inf* dazed, stunned; **dejar a alguien ~** to leave sb flabbergasted
tusar [tu·'sar] **I.** *vi Guat* (*murmurar*) to murmur **II.** *vt AmL* (*cortar mal el pelo*) to scalp *fig*
tuso, -a ['tu·so, -a] *adj* **1.** *Col, PRico* (*pelón*) cropped, shorn **2.** *Col, Ven* (*picado de viruelas*) pockmarked **3.** *PRico* (*rabón*) tailless, bobtailed
tutear [tu·te·'ar] **I.** *vt* to address in the familiar manner using 'tú' **II.** *vr:* **~se** to be on familiar terms
tutela [tu·'te·la] *f* **1.** (*cargo*) guardianship; **poner bajo ~** to place in ward **2.** (*amparo*) protection; **estar bajo la ~ de alguien** to be under the protection of sb
tutelaje [tu·te·'la·xe] *m CSur, Guat, Méx* (*tutela*) guardianship, protection
tutelar [tu·te·'lar] **I.** *adj* **1.** JUR tutelary; **juez ~** tutelary judge **2.** (*protector*) protective, guardian **II.** *vt* **1.** (*ejercer la tutela*) to have the charge of **2.** (*proteger*) to protect, to guard **3.** (*velar*) to supervise
tuteo [tu·'teo] *m* familiar use of 'tú'
tutilimundi [tu·ti·li·'mun·di] *m AmL, inf* every-

body

tutor(a) [tu·'tor, -·'to·ra] *m(f)* **1.** JUR guardian; **firma/consentimiento del padre o ~** signature/consent of parent or guardian **2.** (*protector*) protector **3.** (*profesor*) teacher **4.** ENS, UNIV tutor

tutoría [tu·to·'ri·a] *f* **1.** JUR guardianship, tutelage **2.** UNIV tutorship; (*clase*) tutorial

tuyo, -a ['tu·jo, -a] *pron pos* **1.** (*propiedad*) **el perro es ~** the dog is yours; **la botella/la casa es tuya** the bottle/the house is yours; **¡ya es ~!** all yours! **2.** (*tras artículo*) **el ~/la tuya/lo ~** yours; **mi coche está roto, vamos en el ~** my car isn't working, let's take yours; **no cojas mi lápiz, tienes el ~** don't take my pencil, you have your own; **los ~s** yours; (*parientes*) your family; **ésta es la tuya** *fig* this is your chance; **una de las tuyas** (*travesura*) one of your tricks **3.** (*tras sustantivo*) of yours; **una amiga tuya** a friend of yours; **una hermana tuya** one of your sisters; **es culpa tuya** it's your fault **4.** (*tras impersonal 'lo'*) **lo ~** what is yours; **tú a lo ~** you mind your own business; **esto no es lo ~** this isn't your strong point

TVE [te·u·βe·'e] *f abr de* **Televisión Española** *the Spanish state-owned television broadcasting company*

U

U, u [u] *f* <úes> U, u; **~ de Uruguay** U as in Uniform

u [u] *conj placed before words beginning with 'o' or 'ho'* or; **diez u once** ten or eleven

U *abr de* **Universidad** U., Univ.

ubicación [u·βi·ka·'sjon, -'θjon] *f* **1.** (*lugar*) location; (*de una empresa*) site **2.** (*situación*) situation **3.** (*empleo*) position **4.** AmL (*colocación*) placing

ubicar <c→qu> [u·βi·'kar] **I.** *vi* to be (situated) **II.** *vt* AmL (*situar*) to situate; (*guardar*) to place **III.** *vr:* **~ se** to be (situated)

ubre [u·'βre] *f* udder

UC [u·'se, -'θe] *f abr de* **Unión de Consumidores** *Consumers Association*

UCI ['u·si, -θi] *abr de* **Unidad de Cuidados Intesivos** ICU

Ud(s). [us·'ted, -·'te·des] *abr de* usted(es) you

UE [u·'e] *f abr de* **Unión Europea** EU

UEFA [u·'e·fa] *f abr de* **Unión de Asociaciones Europeas de Fútbol** UEFA

UEME [u·e·'e·me·e] *abr de* **Unión Económica y Monetaria Europea** EEMU

UEO [u·e·'o] *f abr de* **Unión Europea Occidental** WEU

ufano, -a [u·'fa·no, -a] *adj* **1.** (*orgulloso*) proud **2.** (*engreído*) conceited; (*arrogante*) arrogant

3. (*satisfecho*) complacent; **va muy ~ con su nueva moto** he is very smug about his new motorbike **4.** (*planta*) lush, luxuriant

ufología [u·fo·lo·'xi·a] *f* ufology

úlcera ['ul·se·ra, 'ul·θe-] *f* MED ulcer; (*pupa*) sore

ulcerar [ul·se·'rar, ul·θe-] *vt, vr:* **~ se** to ulcerate, to fester

ulterior [ul·te·'rjor] *adj* (*posterior*) later, subsequent; (*más*) further

ulteriormente [ul·te·rjor·'men·te] *adv* later, subsequently

últimamente ['ul·ti·ma·'men·te] *adv* **1.** (*recientemente, hace poco*) recently, lately **2.** (*por último*) lastly, finally

ultimar [ul·ti·'mar] *vt* **1.** (*proyecto, obra*) to finish, to complete; (*acuerdo*) to conclude **2.** AmL (*matar*) to murder

ultimátum [ul·ti·'ma·tun] *m* <inv *o* ultimatos> ultimatum; **dar el ~ a alguien** to give sb an ultimatum

último, -a ['ul·ti·mo, -a] *adj* **1.** (*en orden*) last; **el ~ de cada mes** the last day of each month; **a ~ s de mes** at the end of the month; **soy el ~ de la clase** I'm the worst student in the class; **fue el ~ en firmar** he was the last to sign; **siempre llega el ~** he/she is always the last to arrive; **por última vez** for the last time; **hacia la última parte la película mejora** the film gets better towards the end; **la última moda** the latest fashion; **por ~** lastly, finally; **¿quién es el ~?** (*en una cola*) who's the last in line?; **unos estudian ciencias, otros letras; los ~ s...** some study science, others Arts; the latter... **2.** (*espacio*) **la última fila** the last row; **en el ~ piso** on the top floor; **ocupar la última posición de la tabla** to be at the bottom of the chart; **el ~ rincón del mundo** *inf* the boondocks *pl* ► **estar en las últimas** (*muriéndose*) to be at death's door; (*arruinado*) to be on one's last legs; **ser lo ~** (*lo mejor*) to be great; (*lo peor*) to be the end

ultra ['ul·tra] **I.** *adj* extreme **II.** *mf* extreme right-winger, neo-fascist **III.** *adv* extremely

ultracongelado, -a [ul·tra·kon·xe·'la·do, -a] *adj* deep-frozen

ultraconservador(a) [ul·tra·kon·ser·βa·'dor, -·'do·ra] *adj* ultraconservative

ultrafino, -a [ul·tra·'fi·no, -a] *adj* exceedingly fine

ultrajar [ul·tra·'xar] *vt* **1.** (*insultar*) to insult; (*monumento*) to spoil; **~ de palabra** to revile **2.** (*humillar*) to humiliate **3.** (*ajar*) to crumple

ultraje [ul·'tra·xe] *m* abuse; **un ~ a la bandera** a disgrace to the flag

ultramar [ul·tra·'mar] *m* foreign parts *pl*; **pasé mi infancia en ~** I spent my childhood in foreign parts [*o* overseas]; **han venido de ~** they have come from overseas

ultramarino, -a [ul·tra·ma·'ri·no, -a] *adj* overseas

ultramarinos [ul·tra·ma·'ri·nos] *mpl* **1.** (*tienda*) grocery store **2.** (*víveres*) gro-

U

ceries *pl*

ultramoderno, -a [ul·tra·mo·'der·no, -a] *adj* extremely modern

ultranza [ul·'tran·sa, -θa] **1.** (*a muerte*) **el padre defendió el honor de su familia a ~** the father defended his family's honor with his life; **luchar a ~** to fight to the death **2.** (*resueltamente*) **ser de izquierda a ~** to be an out-and-out left-winger; **ser un ecologista a ~** to be a radical ecologist

ultrarrápido, -a [ul·tra·'rra·pi·do, -a] *adj* extra fast; **tren ~** a high-speed train

ultrasónico, -a [ul·tra·'so·ni·ko, -a] *adj* ultrasonic

ultrasonido [ul·tra·so·'ni·do] *m* ultrasound

ultravioleta [ul·tra·βjo·'le·ta] *adj inv* ultraviolet; **rayos ~** ultraviolet rays

ulular [u·lu·'lar] *vi* **1.** (*animal, viento*) to howl; (*búho*) to hoot **2.** (*persona*) to shriek

umbilical [um·bi·li·'kal] *adj* umbilical

umbral [um·'bral] *m* **1.** (*de puerta*) threshold; **atravesar los ~es de una casa** to set foot in a house **2.** (*principio*) beginning, outset **3.** ECON **~ de rentabilidad** break even point

umbrío, -a [um·'bri·o, -a] *adj* shady

UME ['u·me] *f abr de* **Unión Monetaria Europea** EMU

un [un], **una** ['u·na] <unos, -as> **I.** *art indef* **1.** (*no determinado*) a; (*before a vowel or initial silent h*) an; **un perro** a dog; **una chica** a girl; **un elefante** an elephant; **¡tiene una jeta!** he/she's got a nerve! **2.** *pl* (*algunos*) some, a few **3.** *pl* (*aproximadamente*) approximately, about; **unos 30 pesos** about 30 pesos **II.** *adj v.* **uno, -a**

unánime [u·'na·ni·me] *adj* (*opinión, decisión*) unanimous

unanimidad [u·na·ni·mi·'dad] *f* (*de opinión, decisión*) unanimity; **aprobar algo por ~** to approve sth unanimously

unción [un·'sjon, -'θjon] *f* anointing

uncir <c→z> [un·'sir, -'θir] *vt* to yoke

UNED [u·'ned] *f abr de* **Universidad Nacional de Educación a Distancia** ≈ OU

ungir <g→j> [un·'xir] *vt t.* REL to anoint

ungüento [un·'gwen·to] *m* **1.** MED ointment **2.** (*remedio*) salve

únicamente [u·ni·ka·'men·te] *adv* only, solely

unicameral [u·ni·ka·me·'ral] *adj* single-chamber

unicelular [u·ni·se·lu·'lar, u·ni·θe-] *adj* unicellular

único, -a ['u·ni·ko, -a] *adj* **1.** (*solo*) only; **hijo ~** only child; **heredero ~** sole heir; **calle de dirección única** one-way street; **hoy hay plato ~** today there is only one main course **2.** (*extraordinario*) unique

unicornio [u·ni·'kor·njo] *m* unicorn

unidad [u·ni·'dad] *f* **1.** *t.* MIL, MAT unit; **~ familiar** family unit; **Unidad de Cuidados Intensivos** intensive care unit; **~ de medida** unit of measure; **~ monetaria** currency unit **2.** LIT unity **3.** TÉC (*aparato*) unit; **~ de control**

control unit; **~ externa de disco duro** COMPUT external hard disc unit [*o* drive]; **~ de visualización** visual display unit; **~ periférica** peripheral (device); TV, RADIO mobile unit

unidimensional [u·ni·di·men·sjo·'nal] *adj* one-dimensional

unido, -a [u·'ni·do, -a] *adj* united; **estamos muy ~s** we are very close; **mantenerse ~s** to stay together

unifamiliar [u·ni·fa·mi·'ljar] *adj* single-family; **una casa ~** a detached house

unificación [u·ni·fi·ka·'sjon, -'θjon] *f* **1.** (*unión*) unification; **la ~ política** political unification **2.** (*uniformización*) standardization

unificar <c→qu> [u·ni·fi·'kar] *vt* **1.** (*pueblos, esfuerzos*) to unite; **~ posiciones** to unify positions **2.** (*uniformar*) to standardize

uniformar [u·ni·for·'mar] *vt* **1.** (*hacer unitario, impreso*) to standardize **2.** (*vestir*) **~ a alguien** to put sb into uniform; **ir uniformado** to be dressed in uniform

uniforme [u·ni·'for·me] **I.** *adj* (*igual, de la misma forma*) uniform, same; (*movimiento*) steady **II.** *m* uniform; **vestir de ~** to wear a uniform

uniformidad [u·ni·for·mi·'dad] *f* **1.** (*constancia*) regularity; (*movimiento*) steadiness **2.** (*similaridad*) uniformity

uniformizar <z→c> [u·ni·for·mi·'sar, -'θar] *vt* to standardize; (*mezclar*) to blend

unilateral [u·ni·la·te·'ral] *adj* (*visión*) one-sided; POL unilateral

unilateralismo [u·ni·la·te·ra·'lis·mo] *m* POL unilateralism *no pl*

unión [u·'njon] *f* **1.** *t.* TÉC (*de dos elementos*) joint; **no hay muchos puntos de ~ entre nosotros** we haven't much in common **2.** *t.* ECON, POL (*territorial*) union; **Unión Europea** European Union; **~ monetaria** monetary union; **en ~ con** (together) with **3.** (*matrimonio*) marriage **4.** COM merger **5.** (*armonía*) unity, closeness ▸ **la ~ hace la <u>fuerza</u>** *prov* united we stand

unipersonal [u·ni·per·so·'nal] *adj* **1.** (*de una persona*) one-person; (*de un hombre*) one-man; (*de una mujer*) one-woman **2.** (*individual*) single, individual **3.** LING *applying to a verb used only in the infinitive form or the 3rd person singular*

unir [u·'nir] **I.** *vt* **1.** *t.* TÉC (*dos elementos*) to join **2.** (*territorios, familia*) to unite; **nos une una gran amistad** there is a great bond of affection between us **3.** (*ingredientes*) to mix **4.** (*esfuerzos*) to combine **II.** *vr:* **~se** (*territorios, dos personas*) to join together, to unite; ECON to merge; **~se en matrimonio** to marry

unisex [u·ni·'seks] *adj* unisex; **moda ~** unisex fashion; **peluquería ~** unisex hairdresser's

unísono [u·'ni·so·no] *m* MÚS unison; **protestaron al ~** they unanimously protested; **trabajar al ~** to work in harmony; **actuar al ~** to act in complete agreement

unísono, -a [u·'ni·so·no, -a] *adj* in unison

unitario, -a [u·ni·'ta·rjo, -a] *adj* unitary

universal [u·ni·βer·'sal] *adj* **1.**(*del universo*) universal; **receptor ~** RADIO universal receiver **2.**(*del mundo*) worldwide; **de renombre ~** internationally known; **historia ~** world history; **de fama ~** world famous **3.**(*general, amplio*) widespread; **regla ~** general rule **4.** TÉC (*máquina*) multi-purpose machine; **detergente ~** all-purpose detergent

universalidad [u·ni·βer·sa·li·'dad] *f* (*de regla*) universality

universalizar <z→c> [u·ni·βer·sa·li·'sar, -'θar] *vt* to make universal

universidad [u·ni·βer·si·'dad] *f* university; **ir a la ~** to be at university; **¿a qué ~ vas?** which university do you go to?

universitario, -a [u·ni·βer·si·'ta·rjo, -a] **I.** *adj* university; **estudiante ~** university student; **profesor ~** university teacher; **tener estudios ~s** to have studied at university **II.** *m, f* **1.**(*estudiante*) university student **2.**(*no licenciado*) undergraduate; (*licenciado*) graduate

universo [u·ni·'βer·so] *m* (*cosmos*) universe

unívoco, -a [u·'ni·βo·ko, -a] *adj* unanimous

uno ['u·no] *m* one

uno, -a ['u·no, -a] **I.** *adj* **1.**(*número*) one; **a la una** (*hora*) at one o'clock; **¡(a la) una, (a las) dos y (a las) tres!** ready, set, go!; **fila ~** front row **2.**(*único*) **sólo hay una calle** there's only one street ►**andar a una** to agree **II.** *pron indef* **1.**(*alguno*) one, somebody; **cada ~** each (one), every one; **~s cuantos** some, a few; **~..., el otro...** one..., the other...; **~ de tantos** one of many; **aquí hay ~ que pregunta por ti** there's sb here asking for you; **una de dos, o... o...** the choice is simple, either... or....; **una que otra vez** once in a while; **de ~ en ~** one by one, one at a time; **cantar a una** to sing all together; **luchar todos a una** to fight as one; **no acierto una** I can't do anything right; **lo ~ por lo otro** what goes around comes around **2.** *pl* (*algunos*) some **3.**(*indeterminado*) one, you

untar [un·'tar] **I.** *vt* **1.**(*con mantequilla*) to spread **2.**(*mojar*) to dip **3.**(*con grasa*) to grease; (*con aceite*) to oil; (*el cuerpo*) to smear **4.**(*sobornar*) to bribe **II.** *vr* **1.**(*mancharse*) to smear; **~ se de algo** to become smeared with sth **2.**(*crema*) **~ se con/de algo** to rub sth in **3.**(*dinero*) to line one's pocket

unto ['un·to] *m* **1.**(*grasa*) grease **2.** MED ointment **3.** *Chile* (*betún*) shoe polish

untura [un·'tu·ra] *f* **1.** MED ointment **2.**(*grasa*) grease

uña ['u·ɲa] *f* **1.**(*de persona*) nail; **~ encarnada** ingrown nail; (*de gato*) claw; **~s de los pies** toenails *pl*; **afilarse las ~s** *fig* to sharpen one's claws; **limarse las ~s** to file one's nails; **fue a la peluquería a hacerse las ~s** she went to the hairdresser's to have her nails done; **comerse las ~s** to bite one's nails; *fig* to become furious; **estar de ~s con alguien** *inf* to be at loggerheads with sb; **enseñar las ~s**

(*mostrarse agresivo*) to show one's teeth; **para triunfar se dejó las ~s en el trabajo** *fig* to triumph at work he/she wore his/her fingers to the bone **2.**(*pezuña*) hoof **3.**(*del alacrán*) sting ►**ser ~ y carne** to be inseparable; **defenderse con ~s y dientes** to fight tooth and nail to defend oneself; **ser largo de ~s** to be light-fingered

upa ['u·pa] **I.** *interj infantil* upsy-daisy, upsa-daisy; **llevar a ~ un niño** to carry a child **II.** *adj Ecua, Perú* (*tonto*) idiot

uranio [u·'ra·njo] *m* uranium

urbanícola [ur·βa·'ni·ko·la] *mf* city dweller

urbanidad [ur·βa·ni·'dad] *f* urbanity, courtesy

urbanismo [ur·βa·'nis·mo] *m* (*planificación*) town planning

urbanístico, -a [ur·βa·'nis·ti·ko, -a] *adj* town-planning; **desarrollo ~** urban development; **plan ~** development plan

urbanización [ur·βa·ni·sa·'sjon, -θa·'θjon] *f* **1.**(*acción*) urbanization **2.**(*de casas*) housing estate [*o* development]

urbanizar <z→c> [ur·βa·ni·'sar, -'θar] **I.** *vt* to urbanize **II.** *vt, vr:* **~ se** (*de personas*) to become civilized

urbano [ur·'βa·no] *m* traffic policeman

urbano, -a [ur·'βa·no, -a] *adj* **1.**(*de la ciudad*) urban; **conferencia urbana** TEL local call; **un hombre ~** a city man; **planificación urbana** town [*o* city] planning **2.**(*cortés*) urbane, courteous

urbe ['ur·βe] *f* large city, metropolis

urgencia [ur·'xen·sja, -θja] *f* **1.**(*cualidad*) urgency **2.**(*caso*) emergency; **llamada de ~** urgent call; **en caso de ~** in case of emergency; **tratar algo con la debida ~** to handle sth with due speed **3.** *pl* (*en el hospital*) emergency room; **servicio de ~s** (*en ambulatorio*) emergency service

urgente [ur·'xen·te] *adj* urgent, pressing; (*carta, telegrama, pedido*) express; **un pedido ~** a rush order; **¿es ~?** is it urgent?

urgir <g→j> [ur·'xir] *vi* to be urgent, to be pressing

urinario [u·ri·'na·rjo] *m* urinal, public lavatory

urinario, -a [u·ri·'na·rjo, -a] *adj* urinary; **aparato ~** MED urinary tract

urna ['ur·na] *f* **1.**(*caja de cristal*) glass case **2.**(*para cenizas*) urn **3.** POL ballot box; **acudir a las ~s** to go and vote, to go to the polls

urogallo [u·ro·'ɣa·jo, -ʎo] *m* capercaillie

urología [u·ro·lo·'xi·a] *f* urology

urraca [u·'rra·ka] *f* **1.** ZOOL magpie **2.**(*cotorra*) chatterbox; **hablar más que una ~** to talk one's head off

URSS [urs] *f abr de* **Unión de Repúblicas Socialistas Soviéticas** USSR

urticaria [ur·ti·'ka·rja] *f* MED hives *pl*, skin rash

Uruguay [u·ru·'ɣwai] *m* Uruguay

i **Uruguay** (formally named **República Oriental del Uruguay**) is located in the southeastern part of South America. The

U

capital is **Montevideo**, which is also the country's most important city. The official language is Spanish and the official currency is the **peso uruguayo**.

uruguayo, -a [u·ru·'γwa·jo, -a] *adj, m, f* Uruguayan

usado, -a [u·'sa·do, -a] *adj* **1.**(*no nuevo*) secondhand; (*sello*) used **2.**(*gastado*) worn; (*expresión*) common, everyday

usanza [u·'san·sa, -θa] *f* usage, custom

usar [u·'sar] I. *vt* **1.**(*utilizar*) ~ **algo** to use sth, to make use of sth; (*palabra*) to speak; (*libro*) to consult, to look up; (*ropa, gafas*) to wear; ~ **la razón** to reason; **tuve que ~ (de) mis influencias** I had to use all my influence; **de ~ y tirar** disposable; **sin ~** brand new **2.**(*cargo*) to hold; (*oficio*) to discharge II. *vr* **1.**(*utilizar*) to use; **esta palabra ya no se usa** this word is no longer in use **2.**(*ropa*) top be in fashion; **los escotes ya no se usan** low necklines are out of fashion

usina [u·'si·na] *f AmL* (*de gas*) gasworks; (*de electricidad*) power plant

uso ['u·so] *m* **1.**(*utilización*) use; (*gramática*) usage; ~ **ilegal** MED illegal use; **de ~ externo** MED for external application; **hacer ~ de algo** to make use of sth; **hacer ~ de la palabra** (*en parlamento, senado*) to take the floor, to speak; **una expresión de ~ corriente** an everyday expression; **tener muchos ~s** to have many uses; **en buen ~** *inf* in good condition; **desde que tengo ~ de razón...** since I have been old enough to reason...; **estar en pleno ~ de sus facultades** to be sound of mind **2.**(*moda*) fashion **3.**(*costumbre*) custom, usage; **métodos al ~** methods; **al ~ francés** French style; **el dedal todavía está en ~** the thimble is still used; **encalar las fachadas está fuera de ~** whitewashing the outside of houses is no longer done

usted [us·'ted] *pron* **1.** *sing* you; ~ **es** you; **tratar de ~ a alguien** to address sb courteously; **gracias — a ~** thank you — you're welcome **2.** *pl, AmL* (*vosotros*) you

usual [u·su·'al] *adj* **1.**(*de siempre*) usual **2.**(*común*) common **3.**(*tradicional*) customary

usuario, -a [u·su·'a·rjo, -a] *m, f t.* COMPUT user

usura [u·'su·ra] *f* usury; **pagar con ~ un favor** to pay back a favor on unequal terms

usurario, -a [usu·'ra·rjo, -a] *adj* usurious

usurero, -a [u·su·'re·ro, -a] *m, f* usurer

usurpador(a) [u·sur·pa·'dor, -·'do·ra] I. *adj* usurping II. *m(f)* usurper

usurpar [u·sur·'par] *vt* to usurp; (*derecho*) to encroach on sth

utensilio [u·ten·'si·ljo] *m* utensil; (*herramienta*) tool; ~**s de pintor** painter's materials

uterino, -a [u·te·'ri·no, -a] *adj* ANAT, MED uterine; **furor ~** nymphomania; **hermano ~** *a* brother born of the same mother

útero ['u·te·ro] *m* uterus, womb; **el cuello del ~** the cervix

útil ['u·til] I. *adj* **1.**(*objeto*) useful, handy **2.**(*persona*) useful; **ser declarado ~** MIL to be fit for military service **3.**(*ayuda*) helpful; **¿en qué puedo serle ~?** can I be of any help to you? **4.**(*inversión*) profitable II. *mpl* tools *pl*, implements *pl*

utilidad [u·ti·li·'dad] *f* **1.** *t.* COMPUT (*de objeto*) utility; **ser de ~** to be useful **2.**(*de persona*) usefulness **3.**(*de inversión*) profit

utilitario [u·ti·li·'ta·rjo] *m* **1.**(*calidad de útil*) utility **2.**(*coche*) small car

utilitario, -a [u·ti·li·'ta·rjo, -a] *adj* (*edificio*) utilitarian; (*coche, tela*) utility; (*persona, punto de vista*) practical; **pensamiento ~** utilitarian thinking

utilizable [u·ti·li·'sa·βle, -'θa·βle] *adj* usable; (*terreno*) available; (*restos*) reusable

utilización [u·ti·li·sa·'sjon, -θa·'θjon] *f* utilization; (*de un derecho*) application; (*de una persona*) employment

utilizar <z→c> [u·ti·li·'sar, -'θar] I. *vt* to use; (*derecho, hospitalidad*) to avail oneself of sth; (*tiempo, a alguien*) to make use of sth II. *vr:* ~**se** to be used

utopía [u·to·'pi·a] *f* utopia

utópico, -a [u·'to·pi·ko, -a] *adj* utopian

uva ['u·βa] *f* grape; ~ **pasa** raisin ▶ **de ~s a peras** *inf* once in a blue moon; **estar de mala ~** *inf* to be in a bad mood; **tener mala ~** *inf* to be bad-tempered

uve ['u·βe] *f* v; ~ **doble** w

UVI ['u·βi] *f abr de* **Unidad de Vigilancia Intensiva** ICU

V

V, v ['u·βe] *f* V, v; ~ **de Valencia** V as in Victor

vaca ['ba·ka] *f* **1.** ZOOL cow; ~ **marina** manatee; ~ **de San Antón** ladybug; **síndrome de las ~s locas** mad cow disease; ~**s gordas/flacas** *fig* prosperous/lean period; **ponerse como una ~** to get as fat as a cow [*o* pig] **2.**(*carne*) beef **3.**(*cuero*) cowhide

vacaciones [ba·ka·'sjo·nes, -'θjo·nes] *fpl* vacation; **estar de ~** to be on vacation; **irse de ~ al Caribe** to take a vacation in the Caribbean; ~ **a la sombra** *inf* time served in jail

vacante [ba·'kan·te] I. *adj* vacant II. *f* vacancy; (*puesto*) unfilled post; **cubrir (las) ~s** to fill (the) vacancies

vaciado [ba·si·'a·do, ba·θi·-] *m* **1.**(*molde*) cast **2.**(*ahuecamiento*) hollowing out **3.**(*de datos*) extraction of information **4.** COMPUT dumping

vaciar <1. *pres:* vacío> [ba·si·'ar, ba·θi·-] *vt* **1.**(*dejar vacío*) to empty; (*con bomba de agua*) to pump out **2.**(*verter*) to pour

3. (*hueco*) to hollow out **4.** (*escultura*) to cast **5.** (*afilar*) to sharpen **6.** (*información*) to extract **7.** *Col, inf* (*vituperar*) to give a dressing-down

vacilación [ba·si·la·'sjon, -θi·la·'θjon] *f* hesitation; **sin vacilaciones** unhesitatingly

vacilada [ba·si·'la·da, ba·θi·] *f Méx, inf* (*borrachera*) binge, spree; (*chiste*) joke; (*chiste verde*) dirty joke; (*timo*) rip-off; **me dieron una ~** they really ripped me off

vacilante [ba·si·'lan·te, ba·θi·] *adj* **1.** (*persona*) hesitant **2.** (*estructura*) unsteady **3.** (*voz*) faltering

vacilar [ba·si·'lar, ba·θi·] *vi* **1.** (*balancearse: objeto*) to sway; (*borracho*) to stagger; (*llama*) to flicker **2.** (*dudar*) to hesitate **3.** *inf* (*tomar el pelo*) **~ a alguien** to have sb on, to pull sb's leg; **¡no me vaciles!** don't give me that!

vacío [ba·'si·o, -'θi·o] *m* **1.** (*espacio, ausencia*) emptiness; Fís vacuum; (*hueco*) gap; (*abismo*) void; **~ legal** gap in the law, legal void; **~ de poder** political vacuum; **envasado al ~** vacuum-packed; **hacer el ~** Fís to make a vacuum; **hacer el ~ a alguien** to give sb the cold shoulder; **la propuesta cayó en el ~** the proposal fell flat **2.** ANAT side

vacío, -a [ba·'si·o, -a; -'θi·o, -a] *adj* **1.** (*sin contenido, sin gente*) empty; (*hueco*) hollow; **con las manos vacías** empty-handed; **volver de ~** *fig* to come back empty-handed **2.** (*insustancial*) insubstantial; (*superficial*) superficial

vacuna [ba·'ku·na] *f* **1.** (*sustancia*) vaccine; **~ anticolérica** cholera vaccine **2.** (*vacunación*) vaccination; **poner una ~** to vaccinate; **~ antirrábica** rabies vaccination; **eso te servirá de ~** *fig* that should teach you a lesson **3.** (*de las vacas*) cowpox

vacunación [ba·ku·na·'sjon, -'θjon] *f* vaccination; **cartilla de ~** vaccination certificate

vacunar [ba·ku·'nar] **I.** *vt* to vaccinate **II.** *vr:* **~se** to get vaccinated; **se ha vacunado contra la gripe** he/she got vaccinated against flu

vacuno [ba·'ku·no] *m* cattle

vacuno, -a [ba·'ku·no, -a] *adj* cow, bovine; (**carne de**) **~** beef; **ganado ~** cattle

vadear [ba·de·'ar] *vt* **1.** (*río*) to ford **2.** (*dificultad*) to overcome **3.** (*a pie*) to wade across

vado ['ba·do] *m* **1.** (*río*) ford **2.** AUTO **~ permanente** no parking (garage entrance), keep clear ▶ **tentar el ~** to examine possible solutions

vagabundear [ba·ɣa·βun·de·'ar] *vi* **1.** (*vagar*) to wander **2.** (*gandulear*) to lay about **3.** *pey* to be a tramp [*o* bum]

vagabundo, -a [ba·ɣa·'βun·do, -a] **I.** *adj* wandering; (*perro*) stray; *fig, pey* vagrant **II.** *m, f* wanderer; *fig* tramp, bum

vagancia [ba·'ɣan·sja, -θja] *f* laziness; JUR vagrancy

vagar [ba·'ɣar] **I.** <g→gu> *vi* **1.** (*vagabundear*) to wander **2.** (*descansar*) to be idle **II.** *m* leisure, free time

vagina [ba·'xi·na] *f* ANAT vagina

vago, -a ['ba·ɣo] **I.** *adj* **1.** (*perezoso*) lazy **2.** (*impreciso*) vague **3.** (*vagante*) vagrant **II.** *m, f* **1.** (*vagabundo*) tramp **2.** (*holgazán*) lazybones; **hacer el ~** to laze [*o* loaf] about

vagón [ba·'ɣon] *m* (*de pasajeros*) car; (*de mercancías*) freight car; **~ de cola** caboose; **~ restaurante** dining car

vaguear [ba·ɣe·'ar] *vi* **1.** (*holgazanear*) to laze about **2.** (*vagar*) to wander

vaguedad [ba·ɣe·'dad] *f* **1.** (*imprecisión*) vagueness **2.** (*palabras*) vague remark

vahído [ba·'i·do] *m* dizzy spell; **me dio un ~** I felt dizzy

vaho ['ba·o] *m* **1.** (*vapor*) vapor **2.** (*aliento*) breath **3.** *pl* inhalation

vaina¹ ['bai·na] *f* **1.** (*de la espada*) sheath **2.** BOT pod

vaina² ['bai·na] *m pey* (*persona despreciable*) dork

vainica [bai·'ni·ka] *f CRi* (*judía verde*) string bean

vainilla [bai·'ni·ja, -ʎa] *f* vanilla; **~ azucarada** vanilla sugar

vaivén [bai·'βen] *m* (*balanceo*) swaying; (*sacudida*) lurch; **los vaivenes de la vida** life's ups and downs

vajilla [ba·'xi·ja, -ʎa] *f* crockery, dishes *pl*

vale ['ba·le] *m* voucher; FIN promissory note; (*pagaré*) I.O.U. *inf*

valedero, -a [ba·le·'de·ro, -a] *adj* (*válido*) valid; (*vigente*) in force; **ser ~ por seis meses** to be valid for six months

valedor(a) [ba·le·'dor, -'do·ra] *m(f)* (*que protege*) protector; (*que favorece*) patron

valedura [ba·le·'du·ra] *f Méx* (*favor*) favor; (*protección*) protection; (*ayuda*) help

valenciana [ba·len·'sja·na, -'θja·na] *f* **1.** *CSur* (*encaje*) fine cotton lace **2.** *Méx* (*del pantalón*) pant cuff

valentía [ba·len·'ti·a] *f* **1.** (*valor*) bravery **2.** (*hazaña*) brave deed

valer [ba·'ler] *irr* **I.** *vt* **1.** (*costar*) to cost **2.** (*equivaler*) to equal **3.** (*producir*) to earn **4.** (*proteger*) to protect ▶ **valga la expresión** so to speak; **vale tanto oro como pesa** it/he/she is worth its/his/her weight in gold; **hacer ~ sus derechos** to assert one's rights; **vale más que te olvides de él** you'd best forget him; **¡vale ya!** that's enough!; **¡vale!** OK! **II.** *vi* **1.** (*ropa*) to be of use **2.** (*tener validez*) to be valid; **no vale** it's no good **3.** (*funcionar*) to be of use; **esta vez no te valdrán tus excusas** your excuses won't help you this time; **no sé para qué vale este trasto** I don't know what this piece of junk is for; **esta vez no hay peros que valgan** this time, no ifs, ands or buts! **4.** (*tener mérito*) to be worthy; **no ~ nada** to be worthless; **~ poco** to be worth little **5.** (*estar permitido*) to be allowed; **¡eso no vale!** that's not allowed!, that's not fair! **III.** *vr:* **~se 1.** (*servirse*) to make use; **~se de los servicios de alguien** to avail oneself of sb's services; **~se de sus contactos** to take advantage of one's contacts **2.**(*desenvolverse*) to manage; **ya no puede ~ se** he/she can't fend for him/herself any longer

valeriana [ba·le·'rja·na] *f* valerian

valeroso, -a [ba·le·'ro·so, -a] *adj* brave

valía [ba·'li·a] *f* worth

validar [ba·li·'dar] *vt* to validate

validez [ba·li·'des, -'deθ] *f* validity; **dar ~ a algo** to validate sth; **tener ~** to be valid; (*ley*) to be in force; **no tener ~** to be invalid; (*ley*) to be inapplicable

válido, -a ['ba·li·do, -a] *adj* valid; **no ser ~** to be invalid

valiente [ba·'ljen·te] *adj* brave; **¡~ amigo tienes!** *irón* a fine friend you've got!

valija [ba·'li·xa] *f* case; (*del cartero*) mailbag; **~ diplomática** diplomatic bag

valioso, -a [ba·'ljo·so, -a] *adj* valuable

valla ['ba·ja, -ʎa] *f* **1.**(*tapia*) wall; (*barrera*) barrier; (*alambrada*) fence; (*defensa*) barricade **2.**(*publicitaria*) billboard **3.** DEP hurdle

vallado [ba·'ja·do, -'ʎa·do] *m* fence

vallar [ba·'jar, -'ʎar] *vt* to fence in; **~ con un muro** to put a wall around

valle ['ba·je, -ʎe] *m* valley; **~ de lágrimas** vale of tears; **lirio del ~** BOT lily-of-the-valley

vallunco, -a [ba·'jun·ko, -a; ba·'ʎun-] *adj AmC* **1.**(*rústico*) rustic **2.**(*campesino*) peasant

valona [ba·'lo·na] *f Méx* **hacer a alguien la ~** *inf* to put in a good word for sb

valor [ba·'lor] *m* **1.**(*valentía*) bravery; **~ cívico** civil duty; **armarse de ~** to pluck up courage **2.**(*desvergüenza*) cheek **3.**(*valía*) *t.* COM, MÚS value; (*cuantía*) amount; **~ nutritivo/alimenticio** nutritional/food value; **~ adquisitivo** purchasing power; **~ nominal** face value; **~ probatorio** JUR value as evidence **4.**(*significado*) meaning; **~ actual** current meaning **5.** *pl* FIN securities *pl;* **~es bursátiles** stock exchange securities; **~es inmuebles** real estate **6.** *pl* (*ética*) **~es morales** moral principles; **escala de ~es** scale of values

valoración [ba·lo·ra·'sjon, -'θjon] *f* valuation; (*del precio*) value; (*análisis*) assessment

valorar [ba·lo·'rar] *vt* **~ en algo** to value at sth; **valoro muchísimo tu generosidad** I greatly appreciate your generosity

valorizar <z→c> [ba·lo·ri·'sar, -'θar] *vt v.* **valorar**

vals [bals] *m* MÚS waltz

valse ['bal·se] *m AmL v.* **vals**

valva ['bal·βa] *f* valve

válvula ['bal·βu·la] *f* ANAT, TÉC valve; **~ de seguridad** safety valve

vampiresa [bam·pi·'re·sa] *f* vamp, femme fatale

vampiro [bam·'pi·ro] *m* vampire; *fig* bloodsucker

vanagloriarse [ba·na·ɣlo·'rjar·se] *vr* to boast

vanamente [ba·na·'men·te] *adv* vainly

vandalismo [ban·da·'lis·mo] *m* vandalism

vándalo, -a ['ban·da·lo, -a] **I.** *adj* HIST Vandal **II.** *m, f* HIST Vandal; *fig* vandal, hooligan

vanguardia [ban·'gwar·dja] *f* **1.** MIL van **2.**(*movimiento*) forefront; LIT avant-garde; **de ~** ultra-modern

vanguardista [ban·gwar·'dis·ta] **I.** *adj* ultra-modern **II.** *mf* ultra-modern individual; *fig* pioneer

vanidad [ba·ni·'dad] *f* vanity

vanidoso, -a [ba·ni·'do·so, -a] *adj* vain

vano ['ba·no] *m* ARQUIT space

vano, -a ['ba·no, -a] *adj* **1.**(*ineficaz*) vain, useless; **en ~** in vain **2.**(*infundado*) groundless; **es una vana ilusión** it's a mere illusion

vánova ['ba·no·βa] *f Arg* bedspread

vapor [ba·'por] *m* (*vaho*) vapor; (*de agua*) steam; (**barco de**) **~** steamer; **cocer al ~** to steam

vaporizador [ba·po·ri·sa·'dor, ba·po·ri·θa-] *m* vaporizer; (*perfume*) atomizer

vaporizar <z→c> [ba·po·ri·'sar, -'θar] **I.** *vt* **1.**(*evaporar*) to vaporize **2.**(*perfume*) to spray **II.** *vr:* **~ se** to vaporize

vaporizo [ba·po·'ri·so, -θo] *m Méx, PRico* **1.**(*vaho*) vapor; (*para inhalar*) inhalation **2.**(*calor*) sultry heat

vaporoso, -a [ba·po·'ro·so, -a] *adj* **1.**(*tela*) light, diaphanous *liter* **2.**(*humeante*) steamy

vapulear [ba·pu·le·'ar] *vt* **1.**(*zurrar*) to beat; (*zarandear*) to shake **2.**(*criticar*) to slam

vapuleo [ba·pu·'leo] *m* **1.**(*paliza*) beating **2.**(*crítica*) tongue-lashing

vaquería [ba·ke·'ri·a] *f AmS* (*explotación*) cattle-rearing; (*lechería*) dairy

vaquero, -a [ba·'ke·ro, -a] **I.** *adj* cattle **II.** *m, f* cowherd; (*americano*) cowboy *m*, cowgirl *f*

vaquero(s) [ba·'ke·ro(s)] *m(pl)* jeans *pl*

vaquetón, -ona [ba·ke·'ton, -·'to·na] *adj Méx* **1.** *inf* (*lento*) sluggish **2.**(*vago*) shiftless **3.**(*descarado*) shameless

vaquilla [ba·'ki·ja, -ʎa] *f*, **vaquillona** [ba·ki·'jo·na, -'ʎo·na] *f Arg, Chile, Nic, Perú* heifer

vara ['ba·ra] *f* **1.**(*rama*) branch; (*palo*) stick; **~ mágica** magic wand **2.**(*medida*) ≈ yard (*approximately*) **3.** ADMIN wand (of office); **tener alta ~** to have authority [*o* influence]; **doblar la ~ de la justicia** to pervert the course of justice **4.** TÉC (*bastón de mando*) rod **5.**(*del trombón*) slide **6.** TAUR pike

varado, -a [ba·'ra·do, -a] *adj* (*anclado*) stranded

varar [ba·'rar] **I.** *vi* **1.**(*encallar*) to run aground; *fig* to get bogged down **2.** *AmL* (*coche*) to break down **II.** *vt* to beach

varear [ba·re·'ar] *vt* **1.**(*fruta*) to knock down **2.**(*lana*) to sell by the yard

varejón [ba·re·'xon] *m* **1.** *AmS, Nic* (*verdasca*) switch **2.** *Col* BOT type of yucca

variable [ba·ri·'a·βle] **I.** *adj* variable; (*carácter*) changeable **II.** *f* MAT variable

variación [ba·rja·'sjon, -'θjon] *f* **1.** MAT, MÚS variation **2.**(*cambio*) change; (*oscilación*) oscillation

variado, -a [ba·ri·'a·do, -a] *adj* (*no siempre igual*) varied; (*distinto*) mixed, assorted;

(*colores*) variegated
variante [ba·ri·'an·te] *f* **1.** (*variedad*) variety;
(*versión*) version **2.** (*diferencia*) variation
3. (*carretera*) bypass **4.** LING variant
variar <*1. pres:* varío> [ba·ri·'ar] I. *vi*
1. (*modificarse*) to vary **2.** (*cambiar*) to
change; ~ **de comida** to vary one's diet; ~ **de**
peinado to change one's hairstyle; **y para** ~...
and for a change... II. *vt* **1.** (*cambiar*) to
change **2.** (*dar variedad*) to vary
varicela [ba·ri·'se·la, -'θe·la] *f* MED chickenpox
variedad [ba·rje·'dad] *f* **1.** (*clase*) variety
2. (*pluralidad*) variation; **una gran ~ de ofer-**
tas a wide range of offers **3.** *pl* (*espectáculo*)
variety show; **teatro de ~es** music hall ▶ **en**
la ~ está el gusto *prov* variety is the spice of
life
vario, -a ['ba·rjo, -a] *adj pl* **1.** (*diferente*) several; **asuntos ~s** other business **2.** (*algunos*)
some; **varias veces** several times
variopinto, -a [ba·rjo·'pin·to, -a] *adj*
1. (*diverso*) diverse **2.** (*color*) colorful
variz [ba·'ris, -'riθ] *f* MED varicose vein
varón [ba·'ron] *m* **1.** (*hombre*) male; (*niño*)
boy; **santo ~** *fig* extremely kind and patient
man **2.** NÁUT rudder chain
varonil [ba·ro·'nil] *adj* (*hombre*) manly, virile;
voz ~ deep voice; (*mujer*) mannish
vasallo, -a [ba·'sa·jo, -a; -ʎo, -a] *m, f* HIST vassal
vasija [ba·'si·xa] *f* (*recipiente*) container
vaso ['ba·so] *m* **1.** (*recipiente*) glass; **un ~ de**
agua a glass of water; ~ **de papel** paper cup
2. ANAT vessel
vástago ['bas·ta·ɣo] *m* **1.** BOT shoot **2.** *fig*
(*hijo*) scion *liter;* ~ **s** offspring **3.** TÉC rod
vasto, -a ['bas·to, -a] *adj* vast; (*saber*) wide
váter ['ba·ter] *m* toilet
vaticano, -a [ba·ti·'ka·no, -a] *adj* Vatican
Vaticano [ba·ti·'ka·no] *m* Vatican; **la Ciudad**
del ~ the Vatican City
vaticinar [ba·ti·si·'nar, ba·ti·θi-] *vt* to predict,
to prophesy
vaticinio [ba·ti·'si·njo, -'θi·njo] *m* prediction,
prophecy
vatio ['ba·tjo] *m* watt; **una bombilla de 100**
~ **s** a 100-watt bulb
Vd. [us·'ted] *pron pers abr de* **usted** you
vda. ['bju·da] *abr de* **viuda** widow
Vds. [us·'te·des] *pron pers abr de* **ustedes** you
V.E. ['bwes·tra e·se·'len·sja, es·θe·'len·θja] *abr*
de **Vuestra Excelencia** Your Excellency
vecindad [be·sin·'dad, be·θin-] *f* neighborhood; **chisme de ~** neighborhood gossip
vecindario [be·sin·'da·rjo, be·θin-] *m*
1. (*vecindad*) neighborhood; (*ciudadanos*)
neighbors *pl;* (*comunidad*) local community
2. (*padrón*) residence
vecino, -a [be·'si·no, -a; be·'θi-] I. *adj* **1.** (*cer-*
cano) ~ **de algo** near sth; **pueblo ~** next village **2.** (*parecido*) ~ **a algo** similar to sth II. *m,*
f **1.** (*que vive cerca*) neighbor **2.** (*habitante*)
inhabitant; **José García, ~ de Villavieja** José

García, a Villavieja resident ▶ **cada hijo de ~**
inf anyone
vector [bek·'tor] *m* vector
veda ['beda] *f* **1.** (*prohibición*) prohibition;
levantar la ~ de animales de caza to open
the hunting season **2.** (*temporada*) close season
vedado [be·'da·do] *m* reserve; ~ **de caza**
game preserve; **cazar/pescar en ~** to poach
vedar [be·'dar] *vt* to prohibit, to ban
vedette [be·'det/be·'de·te] *f* (music hall) star
vega ['be·ya] *f* **1.** (*de un río*) fertile plain
2. *Cuba* (*tabacal*) tobacco plantation **3.** *Chile*
(*terreno pantanoso*) marshland
vegetación [be·xe·ta·'sjon, -'θjon] *f* **1.** BOT
vegetation **2.** *pl* ANAT adenoids *pl*
vegetal [be·xe·'tal] I. *adj* plant; **aceite ~** vegetable oil; **carbón ~** charcoal II. *m* vegetable
vegetar [be·xe·'tar] *vi* **1.** BOT to grow
2. (*enfermo*) to be like a vegetable **3.** *pey* (*per-*
sona) to vegetate
vegetariano, -a [be·xe·ta·'rja·no, -a] *adj, m, f*
vegetarian
vehemencia [be·'men·sja/be·e·'men·sja,
-θja] *f* **1.** (*ímpetu*) impetuosity **2.** (*entu-*
siasmo) eagerness **3.** (*fervor*) vehemence
vehemente [be·'men·te/be·e·'men·te] *adj*
1. (*impetuoso*) impetuous **2.** (*ardiente*) passionate **3.** (*persona*) forceful
vehículo [be·'i·ku·lo] *m* **1.** (*transporte*) vehicle; ~ **de motor** motor vehicle **2.** (*medio*) vehicle; MED carrier
veinte ['bein·te] *adj inv* twenty; *v.t.* **ochenta**
veintena [bein·'te·na] *f* (*unidades*) about
twenty; **una ~ de personas** about twenty
people
vejación [be·xa·'sjon, -'θjon] *f,* **vejamen**
[be·'xa·men] *m* **1.** (*molestia*) annoyance
2. (*humillación*) humiliation
vejar [be·'xar] *vt* **1.** (*molestar*) to annoy
2. (*humillar*) to humiliate
vejatorio, -a [be·xa·'to·rjo, -a] *adj*
1. (*molesto*) annoying **2.** (*humillante*) humiliating
vejestorio, -a [be·xes·'to·rjo, -a] *m, f pey* old
crock [*o* geezer]
vejez [be·'xes, -'xeθ] *f* **1.** (*ancianidad*) old age;
pasar su ~ en el Caribe to retire in the Caribbean **2.** (*envejecimiento*) aging ▶ **a la ~,**
viruelas *prov* there's no fool like an old fool
prov
vejiga [be·'xi·ɣa] *f* **1.** ANAT bladder **2.** (*ampolla*)
blister
vela ['be·la] *f* **1.** NÁUT sail; ~ **cuadra** square sail;
~ **mayor** mainsail; **alzar ~s** to raise the sails;
fig to prepare to depart; **a toda ~** at full sail; *fig*
energetically; **ser un aficionado a la ~** to be a
sailing enthusiast; **recoger ~s** *fig* to back
down **2.** (*luz*) candle; **se está acabando la ~**
the candle is coming to an end; **derecho**
como una ~ *fig* straight as a ramrod ▶ **poner**
una ~ a San Miguel y otra al diablo to have
a foot in both camps; **¿a ti quién te ha dado ~**

en este **entierro?** who gave you any say in this matter?; **pasar la noche en** ~ to have a sleepless night; **estar a dos** ~**s** to be broke

velada [be·'la·da] *f* evening gathering; LIT, MÚS, TEAT soirée

velador [be·la·'dor] *m* **1.**(*mesita*) pedestal table **2.**(*candelero*) candlestick

veladora [be·la·'do·ra] *f AmL* (*vela*) candlestick

velar [be·'lar] **I.** *vi* **1.**(*no dormir*) to stay awake; (*trabajar*) to work late **2.**(*cuidar*) ~ **por algo** to watch over sth; ~ **bien por sus intereses** to look after one's interests **II.** *vt* **1.**(*vigilar*) to keep watch over; ~ **al enfermo** to sit up with an ill person; ~ **a un muerto** to hold a wake **2.**(*ocultar*) to hide; (*tapar*) to veil **III.** *vr:* ~**se** (*ocultarse*) to hide; (*foto*) to blur

velatorio [be·la·'to·rjo] *m* wake, vigil

velero [be·'le·ro] *m* NÁUT sailing ship

veleta¹ [be·'le·ta] *f* (*para el viento*) weather vane

veleta² [be·'le·ta] *mf* (*persona*) changeable person; **ser un** ~ to blow hot and cold

veliz [be·'lis, -'liθ] *m Méx* (*de cuero*) valise; (*de metal*) case

vello ['be·jo, -ʎo] *m* **1.**(*corporal*) (body) hair; ~ **de las axilas** hair under the armpits **2.** BOT, ZOOL down, fuzz

velloso, -a [be·'jo·so, -a; -'ʎo·so, -a] *adj* BOT, ZOOL downy; (*corporal*) hairy

velludo, -a [be·'ju·do, -a; -'ʎu·do, -a] *adj* hairy

velo ['be·lo] *m* **1.**(*tela, prenda*) veil; **correr un** (*tupido*) ~ **sobre** *fig* to draw a veil over; **descorrer el** ~ **sobre** to reveal; **tomar el** ~ to take the veil **2.** ANAT ~ **del paladar** soft palate

velocidad [be·lo·θi·'dad] *f* **1.** *t.* FÍS, COMPUT speed; ~ **de crucero** cruising speed; ~ **de obturación** FOTO shutter speed; ~ **de transmisión de datos** COMPUT data transfer rate; **exceso de** ~ speeding; **a gran** ~ at high speed; **a toda** ~ at full speed **2.**(*marcha*) gear; **cambio de** ~**es** changing speeds

velocímetro [be·lo·'si·me·tro, be·lo·'θi-] *m* speedometer

velódromo [be·'lo·dro·mo] *m* cycle track

veloz [be·'los, -'loθ] *adj* swift; **raudo y** ~ in a flash

vena ['be·na] *f* **1.** ANAT vein; ~ **yugular** jugular vein **2.** BOT vein **3.**(*filón*) lode; ~ **de agua** underground stream **4.**(*inspiración*) talent **5.** *inf* (*disposición*) mood; **dar la** ~ **a alguien** to take it into one's head

venado [be·'na·do] *m* **1.**(*ciervo*) deer **2.**(*carne*) venison **3.**(*caza mayor*) big game

venal [be·'nal] *adj* **1.** ANAT venous **2.**(*vendible*) salable **3.**(*sobornable*) corrupt

vencedor(a) [ben·se·'dor, -·'do·ra, ben·θe·] **I.** *adj* winning; **equipo** ~ winning team **II.** *m(f)* winner

vencejo [ben·'se·xo, -'θe·xo] *m* swift

vencer <c→z> [ben·'ser, -'θer] **I.** *vi* **1.**(*ganar*) to win **2.**(*plazo*) to expire **II.** *vt* **1.**(*ganar*) to win; (*enemigos*) to defeat; **¡no te dejes** ~**!**

don't let them beat you! **2.**(*obstáculo, sueño*) to overcome; **me venció el sueño** sleep overcame me **3.**(*bajo peso*) to break ▸**a la tercera va la vencida** *prov* third time lucky **III.** *vr:* ~**se** to collapse

vencimiento [ben·si·'mjen·to, -θi·'mjen·to] *m* COM expiry

venda ['ben·da] *f* MED bandage; **tener una** ~ **en los ojos** to have a bandage over one's eyes; *fig* to be blinkered; **caerse a uno la** ~ **de los ojos** to see the truth

vendaje [ben·'da·xe] *m* bandaging

vendar [ben·'dar] *vt* to bandage

vendaval [ben·da·'βal] *m* (*viento*) strong wind; (*huracán*) hurricane

vendedor(a) [ben·de·'dor, -·'do·ra] *m(f)* seller; (*comerciante*) salesman *m*, saleswoman *f*; ~ **ambulante** hawker; ~ **a domicilio** door-to-door salesman

vender [ben·'der] **I.** *vt* to sell **II.** *vr:* ~**se 1.** COM to sell, to be for sale; **se vende** for sale; ~**se al por menor/mayor** to sell (at) retail/wholesale; **se ha vendido todo** everything has been sold; ~**se muy caro** *fig* to play hard to get **2.**(*persona*) to give oneself away; **estar vendido** *inf* to be in a real fix

vendible [ben·'di·βle] *adj* salable

vendimia [ben·'di·mja] *f* grape harvest

vendimiar [ben·di·'mjar] *vi* to harvest grapes

Venecia [be·'ne·sja, -θja] *f* Venice

veneciano, -a [be·ne·'sja·no, -a; -'θja·no, -a] *adj, m, f* Venetian

veneno [be·'ne·no] *m* poison

venenoso, -a [be·ne·'no·so, -a] *adj* poisonous; **serpiente venenosa** poisonous snake

venerable [be·ne·'ra·βle] *adj* venerable

veneración [be·ne·ra·'sjon, -'θjon] *f* (*adoración*) worship; (*respeto*) veneration

venerar [be·ne·'rar] *vt* **1.**(*adorar*) to worship **2.**(*respetar*) to venerate

venéreo, -a [be·'ne·reo, -a] *adj* MED venereal

venezolano, -a [be·ne·so·'la·no, -a; be·ne·θo-] *adj, m, f* Venezuelan

Venezuela [be·ne·'swe·la, -'θwe·la] *f* Venezuela

---

i **Venezuela** (formally named **República de Venezuela**) borders on the Caribbean Sea and the Atlantic Ocean to the north, Guyana to the east, Brazil to the south, and Colombia to the west. The capital is **Caracas**. The country's official language is Spanish and the official currency is the **bolívar**.

---

vengador(a) [ben·ga·'dor, -·'do·ra] **I.** *adj* (*que se venga*) avenging; (*propenso a*) vindictive **II.** *m(f)* avenger

venganza [ben·'gan·sa, -θa] *f* vengeance; **deseo de** ~ thirst for vengeance

vengar <g→gu> [ben·'gar] **I.** *vt* to avenge; ~ **la muerte de alguien** to avenge sb's death **II.** *vr:* ~**se** to take revenge

vengativo, -a [ben·ga·'ti·βo, -a] *adj* **1.**(*vengador*) avenging **2.**(*rencoroso*) vindictive, vengeful

venia ['be·nja] *f elev* permission

venial [be·'njal] *adj* (*pecado*) venial

venida [be·'ni·da] *f* **1.**(*llegada*) arrival; (*vuelta*) return **2.**(*de un río*) floodwater

venidero, -a [a·be·ni·'de·ro, -a] *adj* future; **en años venideros** in years to come

venir [be·'nir] *irr* **I.** *vi* **1.**(*trasladarse*) to come; (*llegar*) to arrive; **vengo (a) por la leche** I've come to fetch the milk **2.**(*ocurrir*) to happen; **vino la guerra** the war came **3.**(*proceder*) to come; **el dinero me viene de mi padre** I inherited the money from my father; **~ de una familia muy rica** to come from a very rich family **4.**(*idea, ganas*) to come; **me vinieron ganas de reír** I felt like laughing; **no sé por qué me vino eso a la memoria** I don't know why that came to my mind **5.**(*tiempo*) to come; (*seguir*) to follow; **el mes que viene** next month; **ya viene la primavera** spring is on its way **6.**(*figurar*) to appear; **no viene en la guía** it's not in the guide **7.**(*prenda*) to suit **8.**(*aproximadamente*) **vienen a ser unas 300 pesos para cada uno** it works out at about 300 pesos each **9.** *elev* (*servir para*) **aquel suceso vino a turbar nuestra tranquilidad** that event served to destroy our peace **10.**(*terminar por*) **vino a dar con sus huesos en la cárcel** *inf* he/she ended up in jail; **viene a querer decir que...** it amounts to saying that... **11.**(*persistir*) to keep on; **ya te lo vengo advirtiendo hace mucho tiempo** I've been warning you for a long time ► **el dinero me viene muy bien** the money comes in very handy; **¿te viene bien mañana después de comer?** would tomorrow after lunch suit you?; **el que venga detrás, que arree** every man for himself; **me viene mal darte la clase por la tarde** teaching you in the afternoon doesn't suit me; **es una familia venida a menos** that family has come down in the world; **a mí eso ni me va ni me viene** to me that's neither here nor there; **¿a qué viene ahora hacerme esos reproches?** why reproach me like that now? **II.** *vr:* **~se 1.**(*volver*) to come back **2.**(*hundirse*) **~se abajo** to collapse; *fig* to fail

venta ['ben·ta] *f* **1.** COM sale; **~ callejera** street sale; **~ a domicilio** door-to-door selling; **~ al contado** cash sale; **~ al por menor/mayor** retail/wholesale; **~ por catálogo** mail order; **~ a plazos** hire purchase; **precio de ~ al público** retail price; **volumen de ~s** sales volume; **en ~** for sale; **estar a la** [*o* **en**] **~** to be for sale; **poner a la** [*o* **en**] **~** to put sth up for sale **2.**(*posada*) inn

ventaja [ben·'ta·xa] *f t.* DEP advantage; **~ competitiva** competitive advantage; **sacar ~ de la debilidad del contrincante** to take advantage of the opponent's weakness; **tener ~ sobre alguien** to have an advantage over sb;

dar 300 metros de ~ to give (sb) a 300-meter head start

ventajoso, -a [ben·ta·'xo·so, -a] *adj* advantageous; (*negocio*) profitable

ventana [ben·'ta·na] *f* **1.**(*abertura*) window; **~ corrediza** sliding window; **~ de doble cristal** double-glazed window; **~ de guillotina** sash window **2.** ANAT **~ de la nariz** nostril ► **echar la casa por la ~** to go to great expense

ventanal [ben·ta·'nal] *m* large window

ventanilla [ben·ta·'ni·ja, -ʎa] *f* **1.**(*ventana*) small window; (*de coche*) side window; **sobre con ~** window envelope **2.**(*taquilla*) ticket office **3.**(*mostrador*) counter

ventilación [ben·ti·la·'sjon, -'θjon] *f* ventilation

ventilador [ben·ti·la·'dor] *m* **1.**(*aparato*) fan **2.**(*conducto*) ventilator (shaft)

ventilar [ben·ti·'lar] **I.** *vt* **1.**(*airear*) to ventilate **2.**(*resolver*) to clear up **II.** *vr:* **~se** (*persona*) to get some air

ventisca [ben·'tis·ka] *f* blizzard

ventolera [ben·to·'le·ra] *f* **1.**(*viento*) gust of wind; **le ha dado la ~ de...** *fig* he/she has taken it into his/her head to... **2.**(*juguete*) windmill

ventosa [ben·'to·sa] *f* **1.**(*objeto*) suction cup, sucker **2.** ZOOL sucker **3.**(*abertura*) vent

ventosear [ben·to·se·'ar] *vi* to break wind

ventosidad [ben·to·si·'dad] *f* fart

ventoso, -a [ben·'to·so] *adj* windy; (*persona*) flatulent

ventrículo [ben·'tri·ku·lo] *m* ANAT ventricle

ventrílocuo, -a [ben·'tri·lo·kwo, -a] *m, f* ventriloquist

ventura [ben·'tu·ra] *f* (good) fortune; **mala ~** ill luck; **a la** (**buena**) **~** with no fixed plan; **echar la buena ~ a alguien** to tell sb's fortune; **por ~** fortunately; **probar ~** to try one's luck

venturoso, -a [ben·tu·'ro·so, -a] *adj* fortunate

veo-veo ['beo-βeo] *m* **jugar al ~** to play I-spy

ver [ber] *irr* **I.** *vi, vt* **1.**(*con los ojos*) to see; **no se ve ni torta** you can't see a thing; **véase la página dos** see page two; **¡que se vean los forzudos!** let's see what you're made of!; **lo nunca visto** something unheard of; **¡habráse visto!** did you ever!; **como vimos ayer en la conferencia** as we saw in the lecture yesterday; **no veas lo contenta que se puso** you should have seen how happy she was; **si no lo veo, no lo creo** if I hadn't seen it with my own eyes, I wouldn't have believed it; **a ~** let's see **2.**(*con la inteligencia*) to see, to understand; **a mi modo de ~** as I see it; **¿no ves que...?** don't you see that ...?; **quiero hacerte ~ esto** I want you to understand this; **veo bien que te cases** I approve of your getting married; **ya lo veo** I can see that; **bueno, ya ~emos** well, we'll see **3.**(*observar*) to watch; (*documentos, información*) to examine **4.**(*visitar*) to see; (*encontrarse*) to meet; **es de**

~ *inf* you can see that **5.** (*comprobar*) to check **6.** (*algo desagradable*) to see; **te veo venir** *fig* I know what you're up to; **veo que hoy me tocará a mí** I can see that it'll be my turn to-day; **~ás como al final te engaña** he/she will trick you in the end, you'll see **7.** JUR (*causa*) to hear **8.** (*relación*) **tener que ~ con alguien/algo** to have to do with sb/sth **9.** (*duda*) **eso está por ~** that remains to be seen; **estoy por ~ si me dan el crédito** I'll have to see if they give me credit; **habrá que ~ si eso es verdad** it remains to be seen whether that's true **10.** (*intentar*) **~é de hablarle** I'll try to speak to him/her ▶ **tengo** un hambre/un sueño **que no veo** I'm really tired/hungry; **no haberlas visto nunca más gordas** to never have been in such a spot; **si te he visto, no me** acuerdo out of sight, out of mind *prov;* **no veas la que se** armó **allí** there was a huge fight; **¡hay que ~!** it just goes to show!; **hay que ~ lo tranquilo que es Pedro** Pedro is such a quiet fellow; **¡vamos a ~!** let's see!; **¡a ~, escuchadme todos!** come on, listen to me everybody!; **a ~**, **venga** come on, hurry up; **a ~ cómo lo hacemos** let's see how we can do this; **¡para que veas!** so there!; **luego ya ~emos** we'll see about that later; **~emos,...** let me see,...; **veamos,...** let me see,...; **¡~ás!** just you wait! **II.** *vr:* **~ se 1.** (*encontrarse*) to meet **2.** (*estado*) to be; **~se apurado** to be in a jam; **se ve enfermo** he thinks he's ill; **~se negro** to be in a fix; **~se pobre** to feel poor **3.** (*imaginarse*) to imagine; **me lo estoy viendo de médico** I can just see him as a doctor **4.** (*parecer*) **se ve que no tienen tiempo** it seems they have no time **5.** *AmL* (*tener aspecto*) to look **III.** *m* **1.** (*aspecto*) appear-ance; **tener buen ~** to be good-looking **2.** (*opinión*) opinion; **a mi ~** in my view

vera ['be·ra] *f* **1.** (*orilla*) bank; **~ de un río** riv-er bank **2.** (*lado*) edge; **a la ~ de** beside
veracidad [be·ra·si·'dad, be·ra·θi·] *f* truthful-ness; (*de una declaración*) veracity
veraneante [be·ra·ne·'an·te] *mf* vacationer
veranear [be·ra·ne·'ar] *vi* ▶ **en Punta del Este** to spend the summer in Punta del Este
veraneo [be·ra·'neo] *m* summer vacation; **lugar de ~** vacation spot; **estar de ~** to be on summer vacation
veraniego, -a [be·ra·'nje·ɣo, -a] *adj* summer
veranillo [be·ra·'ni·jo, -ʎo] *m* **~ de San Miguel** [*o* **de San Juan** *AmL*] Indian summer
verano [be·'ra·no] *m* summer
veras ['be·ras] *fpl* **de ~** (*de verdad*) really; (*en serio*) in earnest; **esto va de ~** this is serious
veraz [be·'ras, -'raθ] *adj* **1.** (*hechos*) true **2.** (*persona*) truthful
verbal [ber·'βal] *adj* **1.** (*del verbo*) verbal; **frase ~** verb phrase **2.** (*oral*) oral
verbalizar <z→c> [ber·βa·li·'sar, -'θar] *vt* (*expresar*) to verbalize
verbena [ber·'βe·na] *f* **1.** (*fiesta*) street party **2.** BOT verbena

verbo ['ber·βo] *m* **1.** (*expresa acción*) verb; **~ auxiliar** auxiliary verb **2.** (*palabra*) curse
verborrea [ber·βo·'rrea] *f*, **verbosidad** [ber·βo·si·'dad] *f* **1.** (*locuacidad*) verbosity; *pey* verbal diarrhea **2.** (*palabras*) verbiage
verdad [ber·'dad] *f* truth; **una ~ a medias** a half truth; **a la ~** in truth; **bien es ~ que...** it is certainly true that...; **bueno, a decir ~,...** well, to tell you the truth,...; **¡de ~!** really!; **¡es ~!** it's true!; **faltar a la ~** to be untruthful; **hay una parte de ~ en esto** there's some truth in this; **la ~ lisa y llana** the plain and simple truth; **pues la ~, no lo sé** I don't know, to tell you the truth; **si bien es ~ que...** although it's true that...; **un héroe de ~** a real hero; **¿~?** isn't it?, aren't you?; **¿~ que no fuiste tú?** it wasn't you, was it?; **la ~ es que hace frío** it certainly is cold ▶ **~ de** Perogrullo truism; **~es como** puños self-evident truths; **decir** cuatro **~es a alguien** to give sb a piece of one's mind; **la ~, toda la ~, y nada más que la ~** the truth, the whole truth, and nothing but the truth
verdaderamente [ber·da·de·ra·'men·te] *adv* truly
verdadero, -a [ber·da·'de·ro, -a] *adj* **1.** (*cierto*) true **2.** (*real*) real **3.** (*persona*) truthful
verde ['ber·de] **I.** *adj* **1.** (*color*) *t.* POL green; **~ oliva** olive-green **2.** (*fruta*) unripe, green; (*leña*) green **3.** (*chistes, canciones*) dirty **4.** (*personas*) randy; **viejo ~** *inf* dirty old man ▶ **estar ~ de** envidia to be green with envy; **poner ~ a alguien** to badmouth sb **II.** *m* **1.** (*color*) green **2.** (*hierba*) green grass; (*pienso*) green fodder **3.** (*del árbol*) foliage **4.** *CSur* (*pasto*) pasture **5.** *CSur* (*mate*) maté **6.** *CSur* (*ensalada*) salad **7.** *AmC, Méx* (*campo*) countryside
verdear [ber·de·'ar] *vi* **1.** (*mostrarse verde*) to look green **2.** (*tirar a verde*) to be greenish **3.** (*ponerse verde*) to turn green **4.** *CSur* (*beber*) to drink maté
verdecer [ber·de·'ser, -'θer] *irr como crecer vi* to turn green
verdín [ber·'din] *m* **1.** (*del cobre*) verdigris **2.** (*verde*) fresh green **3.** (*musgo*) moss
verdor [ber·'dor] *m* **1.** (*verde*) greenness, ver-dure *form* **2.** BOT lushness **3.** (*juventud*) youth
verdoso, -a [ber·'do·so, -a] *adj* greenish
verdugo [ber·'du·ɣo] *m* **1.** (*de ejecuciones*) executioner **2.** (*tirano*) slave driver; (*ator-mentador*) tormentor **3.** (*tormento*) torment **4.** (*látigo*) lash **5.** (*hematoma*) weal **6.** BOT shoot **7.** (*gorro*) balaclava
verdulero, -a [ber·du·'le·ro, -a] *m, f* greengro-cer
verdura [ber·'du·ra] *f* **1.** (*hortalizas*) veg-etable, greens *pl* **2.** (*verdor*) greenness **3.** (*obscenidad*) smuttiness
verdusco, -a [ber·'dus·ko, -a] *adj* dark green
vereda [be·'re·da] *f* **1.** (*sendero*) path **2.** *AmL* (*acera*) sidewalk ▶ **entrar en ~** to start to lead

an orderly life; **hacer** <u>entrar</u> **en** ~ **a alguien** to make sb toe the line; **ir por la** ~ to do the right thing

veredicto [be·re·'dik·to] *m* JUR verdict; ~ **de culpabilidad/inculpabilidad** guilty/not guilty verdict

verga ['ber·ɣa] *f* **1.** (*vara*) rod **2.** *vulg* (*pene*) cock

vergajo [ber·'ɣa·xo] *m* **1.** (*verga del toro*) pizzle **2.** *vulg* (*pene*) cock **3.** (*látigo*) whip **4.** *And, vulg* (*canalla*) bastard, son of a bitch

vergel [ber·'xel] *m elev* orchard

vergonzoso, -a [ber·ɣon·'so·so, -a; 'θo·so, -a] *adj* **1.** (*persona*) bashful; (*tímido*) shy **2.** (*acción*) disgraceful

vergüenza [ber·'ɣwen·sa, -θa] *f* **1.** (*rubor*) shame; **se me cae la cara de** ~ I feel so ashamed; **me da** ~... I'm ashamed to...; **¿no te da** ~? aren't you ashamed?; **pasar** ~ to feel embarrassed; **¡qué** ~! shame on you!; **tener poca** ~ to have no shame, to be shameless; **pasar** ~ **ajena** to be embarrassed for sb else **2.** (*pundonor*) shyness; **perder la** ~ to lose one's shyness **3.** (*persona, acción*) timidity; (*escándalo*) disgrace; **sacar a alguien a la** ~ (**pública**) to disgrace sb publicly **4.** (*cortedad*) modesty; (*sexual*) (sexual) shame; **le da** ~ **al hablar** he/she is embarrassed to speak **5.** *pl* ANAT private parts *pl*

verídico, -a [be·'ri·di·ko, -a] *adj* **1.** (*verdadero*) true **2.** (*muy probable*) credible **3.** (*sincero*) truthful

verificación [be·ri·fi·ka·'sjon, -'θjon] *f* **1.** (*inspección*) inspection **2.** (*prueba*) testing **3.** (*realización*) realization **4.** (*de una profecía*) fulfillment

verificar <c→qu> [be·ri·fi·'kar] **I.** *vt* **1.** (*comprobar*) to check **2.** (*controlar*) to verify **3.** (*realizar*) to carry out; (*ceremonia*) to perform **II.** *vr:* ~ **se 1.** (*acto solemne*) to be held **2.** (*una profecía*) to come true; (*deseos*) to be fulfilled; (*temores*) to be realized

verja ['ber·xa] *f* (*rejas*) grating; (*cerca*) grille; (*puerta*) iron gate

vermú [ber·'mu] *m*, **vermut** [ber·'mu] *m* <vermús> **1.** (*licor*) vermouth **2.** *And, CSur* TEAT early performance

vernáculo, -a [ber·'na·ku·lo, -a] *adj* vernacular; **lengua vernácula** vernacular

verosímil [be·ro·'si·mil] *adj* **1.** (*probable*) likely **2.** (*creíble*) credible

verosimilitud [be·ro·si·mi·li·'tud] *f* likelihood

verraco [be·'rra·ko] *m* **1.** (*para procrear*) boar **2.** *AmC, CSur* (*jabalí*) wild boar

verraquera [be·rra·'ke·ra] *f inf* **1.** (*llanto*) crying spell **2.** *AmC, Col* (*borrachera*) drunken bout

verruga [be·'rru·ɣa] *f* wart; *fig* defect

verrugoso, -a [be·rru·'ɣo·so, -a] *adj* warty

versado, -a [ber·'sa·do, -a] *adj* ~ **en algo** expert in sth

versar [ber·'sar] *vi* **1.** (*tratar*) ~ **sobre algo** to deal with sth; **la conferencia** ~**á sobre las**

vacunas the lecture is about vaccines **2.** (*dar vueltas*) to go around **3.** *AmC* (*escribir*) to versify **4.** *AmC* (*charlar*) to chat **5.** *Méx* (*bromear*) to crack jokes

versátil [ber·'sa·til] *adj* **1.** (*persona*) versatile **2.** (*que se dobla*) flexible

versatilidad [ber·sa·ti·li·'dad] *f* **1.** (*inconstancia*) changeableness **2.** (*flexibilidad*) versatility

versículo [ber·'si·ku·lo] *m* REL verse

versificar <c→qu> [ber·si·fi·'kar] **I.** *vt* to put into verse **II.** *vi* to write verses

versión [ber·'sjon] *f* **1.** (*interpretación*) version; (*descripción*) account; ~ **resumida** abridged version **2.** (*traducción*) translation **3.** CINE ~ **original** in the original language

verso ['ber·so] *m* **1.** (*palabras*) line; **en** ~ in verse **2.** (*género*) verse **3.** (*poema*) poem

vértebra ['ber·te·βra] *f* ANAT vertebra

vertebrado [ber·te·'βra·do] *m* vertebrate

vertebral [ber·te·'βral] *adj* vertebral; **columna** ~ spinal column

vertedero [ber·te·'de·ro] *m* (*escombrero*) garbage dump

verter <e→ie> [ber·'ter] **I.** *vt* **1.** (*vaciar*) to empty; (*líquido*) to pour; (*sin querer*) to spill; (*basura*) to dump; ~ **el café en las tazas** to pour the coffee into the cups **2.** (*traducir*) to translate **3.** (*ideas, conceptos*) to transfer **II.** *vi* to flow

vertical [ber·ti·'kal] *adj, f* vertical

vértice ['ber·ti·se, -θe] *m* vertex

vertiente [ber·'tjen·te] *f* **1.** (*declive*) slope; (*lado*) side **2.** (*punto de vista*) perspective **3.** *And, CSur, Méx* (*fuente*) fountain

vertiginoso, -a [ber·ti·xi·'no·so, -a] *adj* **1.** (*que marea*) giddy **2.** (*velocidad*) excessive

vértigo ['ber·ti·ɣo] *m* **1.** (*mareo*) dizziness; (*por las alturas*) vertigo; **causar** ~(**s**) to cause dizziness; **de** ~ *inf* (*jaleo*) tremendous; (*increíble*) extraordinary; (*fantástico*) wonderful; (*velocidad*) giddy **2.** (*desmayo*) fainting fit **3.** (*frenesí*) frenzy; (*locura*) fit of madness

vesícula [be·'si·ku·la] *f* ANAT vesicle; (*en la epidermis*) blister; ~ **biliar** gall bladder

vespa® ['bes·pa] *f* motor scooter

vespasiana [bes·pa·'sja·na] *f Arg, Chile* public toilet

vespertino, -a [bes·per·'ti·no] *adj* evening, crepuscular *liter*

vestíbulo [bes·'ti·βu·lo] *m* (*de un piso*) hall; (*de un hotel*) lobby; TEAT foyer; (*atrio*) atrium

vestido [bes·'ti·do] *m* **1.** (*prenda*) item of clothing; (*de mujer*) dress **2.** (*ropa*) clothing; ~ **de etiqueta** [*o* **noche**] evening [*o* formal] dress

vestidor [bes·ti·'dor] *m* dressing room

vestidura [bes·ti·'du·ra] *f* **1.** *elev* (*ropa*) apparel **2.** *pl* REL vestments *pl* ▶ **rasgarse las** ~**s** to make a great show of being shocked

vestigio [bes·'ti·xjo] *m* **1.** (*huella*) vestige **2.** (*señal*) trace

vestimenta [bes·ti·'men·ta] *f* clothing

vestir [bes·'tir] *irr como pedir* **I.** *vt* **1.** (*cuerpo,* *persona*) to dress; ~ **de algo** to dress in sth; (*estatua*) to cover in sth; (*pared*) to hang with sth; (*adornar*) to adorn with sth; **estar vestido de pirata** (*disfrazado*) to be dressed as a pirate; ~ **a alguien con un abrigo** to dress sb in a coat **2.** (*llevar*) to wear; (*ponerse*) to put on **3.** (*confeccionar*) to make; **¿qué sastre le viste?** which tailor makes your clothes? **4.** (*expresión*) ~ **el rostro de seriedad** to put on a serious expression ▶ **vísteme despacio que tengo prisa** *prov* make haste slowly **II.** *vi* to dress; ~ **de blanco** to dress in white; ~ **de uniforme** to wear a uniform; ~ **siempre muy bien** to always be very well-dressed; **de ~** (*elegante*) formal; (*para una ocasión*) for special occasions; ~ **mucho** to be dressy ▶ **el mismo que viste y calza** the self-same **III.** *vr:* ~ **se 1.** (*la ropa*) to get dressed; (*cubrirse*) to cover oneself; ~ **se a la moda** to dress according to fashion; ~ **se de azul** to dress in blue; **los árboles se visten de verde** the trees are coming out in leaf; **los campos se visten de blanco** the fields are turning white with snow; ~ **se en Milán** (*comprar*) to buy one's clothes in Milan **2.** (*estado de ánimo*) ~ **se de cierta actitud** to adopt a certain attitude; ~ **se de severidad** to adopt a severe tone

vestón [bes·'ton] *m Chile* (*chaqueta*) jacket

vestuario [bes·'twa·rjo] *m* **1.** (*conjunto*) clothes *pl*; (*de una misma persona*) wardrobe **2.** (*lugar*) TEAT dressing room; DEP changing room

veta ['be·ta] *f* **1.** MIN seam **2.** (*en madera*) grain; (*en mármol*) vein

vetar [be·'tar] *vt* to veto

vetarro, -a [be·'ta·rro, -a] *adj Méx, inf* old; **ya están muy ~ s** they're getting up there

vetazo [be·'ta·so, -θo] *m Ecua* whiplash

vetear [be·te·'ar] *vt* **1.** (*como la madera*) to grain **2.** (*como el mármol*) to streak

veterano [be·te·'ra·no] *m* MIL veteran

veterano, -a [be·te·'ra·no, -a] **I.** *adj* **1.** MIL veteran **2.** (*experimentado*) experienced **II.** *m, f* **1.** MIL veteran **2.** (*experto*) old hand

veterinaria [be·te·ri·'na·rja] *f* veterinary science

veterinario, -a [be·te·ri·'na·rjo, -a] *m, f* veterinarian, vet *inf*

veto ['be·to] *m* veto; (**inter**)**poner** (**su**) ~ **a algo** to veto sth

vetusto, -a [be·'tus·to, -a] *adj elev* **1.** (*persona*) venerable **2.** (*cosa*) very old; *pey* ancient

vez [bes, beθ] *f* **1.** (*acto repetido*) time; **a la ~** at the same time; **a veces** sometimes; **alguna que otra ~** occasionally; **cada ~ me gusta menos** I like him/it less and less; **cada ~ que...** each time that...; **de una ~** (*en un solo acto*) in one go; (*sin interrupción*) without a break; (*definitivamente*) once and for all; **de ~ en cuando** from time to time; **dilo otra ~** say it again; **acabemos de una ~** let's get it over with; **por primera ~** for the first time; **aquella ~** on that occasion; **esta ~** this time;

alguna ~ sometimes; **muchas veces** many times; **¿cuántas veces ...?** how many times ...?, how often ...?; **repetidas veces** over and over again; **otra ~ será** it'll have to wait for another occasion; **pocas veces, rara ~** seldom; **tal ~** perhaps; **una y otra ~** time and time again; **de una ~ por todas** once and for all; **una ~ que haya terminado,...** once it is over,...; **érase una ~...** once upon a time... **2.** (*con número*) time; **una ~** once; **dos veces** twice; **una y mil veces** a thousand times; **3 veces 9** MAT 3 times 9; **dos veces más que** twice as much as; **por enésima ~** for the umpteenth time **3.** (*turno*) **cuando llegue mi ~...** when it's my turn...; **él a su ~ no respondió** he didn't reply in his turn; **en ~ de** instead of; **hacer las veces de alguien** to take sb's place; **ceder la ~ en una cola** to give up one's place in line ▶ **una ~ al año no hace daño** *prov* once won't do any harm

vía ['bi·a] *f* **1.** (*camino*) road; (*calle*) street; ~ **aérea** (*correos*) airmail; **Vía Láctea** Milky Way; ~ **pública** public thoroughfare; **por ~ aérea** by air; (*correos*) by air mail; **¡~ libre!** make way!; **la tradición está en ~ s de recuperación** the tradition is being recovered **2.** (*ruta*) via; **a Montevideo ~ Buenos Aires** to Montevideo via Buenos Aires **3.** (*carril*) line; FERRO track; ~ **férrea** railroad; **por ~ férrea** by rail; ~ **muerta** siding; **de ~ estrecha** narrow gauge; *fig* narrow-minded; **de ~ única** single track **4.** ANAT passage; ~ **s digestivas** digestive tract; ~ **s respiratorias** breathing passage; ~ **s urinarias** urinary tract; **por ~ oral** by mouth **5.** (*procedimiento*) proceedings *pl*; **por ~ judicial** by legal means **6.** COMPUT track

viable [bi·'a·βle] *adj* viable

vía crucis [bi·a 'kru·sis, -θis] *m inv* Stations *pl* of the Cross; *fig* terrible ordeal

viada [bi·'a·da] *f And* speed

viaducto [bja·'duk·to] *m* viaduct

viajante [bja·'xan·te] *mf* COM traveling salesman

viajar [bja·'xar] *vi* to travel; ~ **por Italia** to travel around Italy; ~ **en avión** to travel by plane

viaje [bi·'a·xe] *m* **1.** (*general*) travel; **estar de ~** to be away (on a trip); **irse de ~** to go on a trip; ~ **de negocios** business trip; ~ **de novios** honeymoon; ~ **organizado** package tour; ~ **de ida** outgoing trip; ~ **de ida y vuelta** round trip; **cheque de ~** traveler's check; **¡buen ~!** bon voyage!, have a good trip! **2.** (*carga*) load; (*recorrido*) trip; **un ~ de leña** a load of firewood; **hacer la mudanza en cinco ~ s** to move house in five trips; **de un ~** *AmC, fig* in one go **3.** *inf* (*drogas*) trip

viajero, -a [bja·'xe·ro, -a] **I.** *adj* traveling; ZOOL migratory; **ave viajera** migratory bird **II.** *m, f* traveler; (*pasajero*) passenger; ~ **diario** commuter

vial [bi·'al] **I.** *adj* (*caminos*) road; FERRO rail; **circulación** ~ road traffic; **fluidez** ~ traffic flow;

reglamento ~ rules of the road **II.** *m* avenue

viaraza [bja·'ra·sa, -θa] *f AmL* (*rapto de ira*) fit of rage; **me dio la** ~ I just felt like it

viático [bi·'a·ti·ko] *m* **1.** REL viaticum **2.** (*subvención*) travel allowance

víbora ['bi·βo·ra] *f* **1.** ZOOL viper **2.** *pey* (*persona*) snake; **lengua de** ~ *fig* venomous tongue; **nido de** ~ **s** *fig* nest of vipers

viborear [bi·βo·re·'ar] *vi* **1.** *AmL, inf* (*murmurar*) to backbite **2.** *CSur* (*serpentear*) to snake, to twist and turn

vibración [bi·βra·'sjon, -'θjon] *f* **1.** (*vaivén*) vibration **2.** (*sentimiento*) vibe *inf*, vibration; **ese tío me da buenas/malas vibraciones** that guy gives me good/bad vibes

vibrador [bi·βra·'dor] *m* vibrator

vibrante [bi·'βran·te] *adj* **1.** (*sonoro*) resonant **2.** (*entusiasta*) vibrant; (*emoción*) quivering

vibrar [bi·'βrar] **I.** *vi* **1.** (*oscilar*) to vibrate **2.** (*voz*) to quiver **II.** *vt* (*agitar*) to shake

vicario [bi·'ka·rjo] *m* vicar

vicedirector(a) [bi·se·di·rek·'tor, -·'to·ra; bi·θe-] *m(f)* **1.** COM deputy manager **2.** ENS vice principal

vicepresidente, -a [bi·se·pre·si·'den·te, -a; bi·θe-] *m, f* POL vice president; (*en juntas*) vice chairperson

vicerrector(a) [bi·se·rrek·'tor, -·'to·ra, bi·θe-] *m(f)* UNIV vice president

viceversa [bi·se·'βer·sa, bi·θe-] *adv* vice versa

vichar [bi·'tʃar] *vt Arg, Urug* **1.** (*espiar*) to spy on **2.** (*ver*) to peep at **3.** (*buscar con la mirada*) to look around for

viciado, -a [bi·'sja·do, -a; bi·'θja-] *adj* (*aire*) stuffy

viciar [bi·'sjar, -'θjar] **I.** *vt* **1.** (*falsear*) to falsify; (*deformar*) to distort **2.** (*anular*) to invalidate **II.** *vr:* ~**se 1.** (*costumbres*) to deteriorate; (*persona*) to get a bad habit **2.** (*ser adicto*) ~**se con algo** to become addicted to sth; ~**se con la televisión** to get hooked on television **3.** (*deformarse*) to warp; (*romperse*) to break

vicio ['bi·sjo, -θjo] *m* **1.** (*mala costumbre*) bad habit; **el** ~ **de siempre** the same old bad habit; **hacer algo por** ~ to do sth for the hell of it; **tener el** ~ **de comerse las uñas** to have the bad habit of biting one's nails **2.** (*adicción*) vice; **no poder quitarse el** ~ **de fumar** to be unable to kick the smoking habit **3.** (*objeto*) defect **4.** JUR (*error*) flaw **5.** (*capricho*) whim; **quejarse de** ~ to complain out of sheer habit **6.** BOT **tener mucho** ~ to grow abundantly

vicioso, -a [bi·'sjo·so, -a; bi·'θjo-] **I.** *adj* **1.** (*carácter*) dissolute **2.** (*que produce vicio*) habit-forming **3.** (*defecto*) defective **4.** (*consentido*) spoilt **5.** BOT luxuriant **II.** *m, f* **en lo que respecta a la bebida es un** ~ he drinks too much

vicisitud [bi·si·si·'tud, bi·θi-] *f* **1.** (*acontecimiento*) important event; (*desgracia*) mishap **2.** (*cambio*) change **3.** *pl* (*alternancia*) ups *pl* and downs

víctima ['bik·ti·ma] *f* victim; (*afectado*) person

affected; **ser** ~ **de un fraude** to be the victim of fraud; **no hubo que lamentar** ~**s** fortunately there were no casualties; ~ **propiciatoria** scapegoat

victimar [bik·ti·'mar] *vt AmL* **1.** (*herir*) to injure **2.** (*matar*) to kill

victimario, -a [bik·ti·'ma·rjo, -a] *m, f* **1.** (*el que daña*) victimizer **2.** *AmL* (*el que mata*) killer, murderer

victoria [bik·'to·rja] *f* victory; ~ **por puntos** victory on points; **cantar** ~ to count one's chickens

victorioso, -a [bik·to·'rjo·so, -a] *adj* victorious

vid [bid] *f* (*parra*) (grape)vine

vida ['bi·da] *f* **1.** (*existencia, actividad*) life; ~ **afectiva** emotional life; ~ **íntima** private life; ~ **perra** dog's life; **amargar la** ~ **a alguien** to make sb's life miserable; **(grape)¿cómo te va la** ~**?** how's life treating you?; **complicarse la** ~ to make life difficult for oneself; **costo de la** ~ cost of living; **dar** ~ **a** TEAT, CINE to portray; (*animar*) to enliven; **dejarse la** ~ **en algo** to dedicate one's life to sth; **esperanza de** ~ life expectancy; **estar aún con** ~ to still be alive; **este material es de corta** ~ this material doesn't last; **hacer** ~ **marital** to live together; **llevar una** ~ **miserable** to lead a wretched existence; **me va la** ~ **en este asunto** this is a matter of life or death for me; **partir de esta** ~ to depart this life; **pasar a mejor** ~ to pass away; **pasarse la** ~ **haciendo algo** to spend one's life doing sth; **perder la** ~ to lose one's life; **¿qué es de tu** ~**?** what have you been up to lately?; **quitar la** ~ **a alguien** to take sb's life; **quitarse la** ~ to take one's own life; **salir con** ~ to survive; **tener siete** ~**s** to have the nine lives of a cat; **tren de** ~ lifestyle **2.** (*sustento*) livelihood; **buscarse la** ~ to get by on one's own **3.** (*biografía*) life; **de toda la** ~ all my life; **la** ~ **y milagros de alguien** sb's life story; **la otra** ~ afterlife **4.** (*placer*) pleasure; **este sol es** ~ this sun is a delight **5.** (*alegría*) joy **6.** (*cariño*) **¡mi** ~**!** my darling! **7.** (*prostituta*) **mujer de la** ~ prostitute; **hacer la** ~ *inf* to be on the game ▸ **estar entre la** ~ **y la** <u>muerte</u> to be fighting for one's life; (*a punto de morir*) to be at death's door; **darse la** ~ <u>padre</u> to live the life of Riley; **hacer por la** ~ *inf* to eat; **de por** ~ for life; **¡en** ~**!** not on your life!

vidente [bi·'den·te] *mf* (*que ve*) sighted person; (*que adivina*) clairvoyant

vídeo ['bi·deo] *m* **1.** (*aparato*) video (cassette) recorder, VCR; **cámara de** ~ video camera; **editar en** ~ to edit on video; **grabar en** ~ to record on video **2.** (*película*) video

videocámara [bi·deo·'ka·ma·ra] *f* video camera

videocasete [bi·deo·ka·'se·te] *m* videocassette

videoclip [bi·deo·'klip] *m* music video

videoconferencia [bi·deo·kon·fe·'ren·sja, -θja] *f* COMPUT video conference

V

videojuego [bi·deo·'xwe·yo] *m* video game
videotex(t) [bi·deo·'tes·(t)] *m* teletext
vidorria [bi·'do·rrja] *f* **1.** *Chile, RíoPl* (*vida fácil*) easy life **2.** *Col, PRico, Ven* (*vida dura*) dog's life
vidriado [bi·'drja·do] *m* **1.** (*barniz*) glaze **2.** (*loza*) (piece of) glazed pottery
vidriar [bi·'drjar] **I.** *vt* (*loza*) to glaze **II.** *vr:* ~ **se** (*hacerse transparente*) to become clear
vidriera [bi·'drje·ra] *f* **1.** (*ventana*) stained-glass window; **puerta** ~ glazed door **2.** *AmL* (*escaparate*) shop window
vidriero, -a [bi·'drje·ro, -a] *m, f* glazier
vidrio ['bi·drjo] *m* **1.** (*material*) glass; ~ **de color** colored glass; ¡~! (*frágil*) fragile — handle with care **2.** (*placa*) sheet of glass; (*de una ventana*) window pane **3.** (*objeto*) piece of glassware; (*productos*) glassware ▶ **pagar los** ~ **s** <u>rotos</u> *inf* to take the rap
vidrioso, -a [bi·'drjo·so, -a] *adj* **1.** (*como vidrio*) glassy; (*mirada*) glazed **2.** (*transparente*) like glass; **ojos** ~ **s** glassy eyes **3.** (*frágil*) fragile **4.** (*superficie*) slippery **5.** (*persona*) easily discouraged **6.** (*asunto*) delicate
vidurria [bi·'du·rrja] *f Arg, inf* (*vidorra*) life of leisure
viejales [bje·'xa·les] *m inv, inf* old boy
viejera [bje·'xe·ra] *f PRico* **1.** (*vejez*) old age **2.** (*cosa inservible*) old piece of junk
viejo, -a ['bje·xo, -a] **I.** *adj* old; (*usado*) used; (*gastado*) worn-out; **hacerse** ~ to grow [*o* get] old; **Noche Vieja** New year's Eve ▶ **tan** ~ **como** <u>Canalillo</u> *inf* as old as Moses **II.** *m, f* old man *m,* old woman *f;* **mi** ~ my old man; **mi vieja** my old lady; **mis** ~ **s** *AmL* (*padres*) my folks, my parents
Viena ['bje·na] *f* Vienna
vienés, -esa [bje·'nes, -·'ne·sa] *adj, m, f* Viennese
viento ['bjen·to] *m* **1.** (*corriente*) wind; ~ **s alisios** trade winds; ~ **ascendente** rising wind; ~ **de cola** tail wind; ~ **de frente** head wind; ~ **huracanado** hurricane; **instrumento de** ~ wind instrument; **hace** ~ it's windy; **como el** ~ like the wind; **corre un poquito de** ~ there's a slight breeze; **un pequeño soplo de** ~ a gentle breeze; **estar lleno de** ~ (*vacío*) to be full of (hot) air; (*vanidoso*) to be vain **2.** NÁUT (*rumbo*) course; (*dirección*) direction; **a los cuatro** ~ **s** in all directions; **pregonar algo a los cuatro** ~ **s** to shout sth from the rooftops **3.** *inf* (*irse*) **tomar** ~ to be off; ¡**vete a tomar** ~! *inf* get lost! **4.** (*olor*) scent; (*olfato*) sense of smell; **me da el** ~ **que...** I have a feeling that... **5.** *AmC* MED flatulence ▶ **contra** ~ **y** <u>marea</u> against all odds, come hell or high water; **el negocio va** ~ **en** <u>popa</u> business is going well; **quien siembra** ~ **s, recoge** <u>tempestades</u> *prov* sow the wind and reap the whirlwind *prov;* **echar a alguien con** ~ <u>fresco</u> to tell sb to get lost; **corren** <u>malos</u> ~ **s para...** it's a bad time for...; <u>beber</u> **los** ~ **s por algo** to crazy about sth

vientre ['bjen·tre] *m* **1.** (*abdomen*) abdomen; **hacer de** ~ to have a bowel movement **2.** (*barriga*) belly; **danza del** ~ belly-dancing **3.** (*matriz*) womb
viern. *abr de* **viernes** Fri.
viernes ['bjer·nes] *m inv* Friday; **Viernes Santo** Good Friday; *v.t.* **lunes** ▶ **la** <u>semana</u> **que no tenga** ~ when pigs fly
viga ['bi·ɣa] *f* (*de madera*) beam; (*de metal*) girder
vigencia [bi·'xen·sja, -θja] *f* validity; **estar en** ~ to be valid; **entrar en** ~ to come into effect; **perder** ~ to become invalid
vigente [bi·'xen·te] *adj* valid
vigía¹ [bi·'xi·a] *f* watchtower
vigía² [bi·'xi·a] *mf* lookout
vigilancia [bi·xi·'lan·sja, -θja] *f* **1.** (*cuidado*) vigilance **2.** (*observación*) surveillance; (*servicio*) security service; **tener a alguien bajo** ~ to have sb under surveillance
vigilante [bi·xi·'lan·te] **I.** *adj* (*despierto*) awake; (*en alerta*) alert **II.** *mf* **1.** (*guardián*) guard; (*de cárcel*) warden; (*en museo*) attendant; ~ **nocturno** night watchman; ~ **de seguridad** security guard **2.** *CSur* (*policía*) policeman *m,* policewoman *f*
vigilar [bi·xi·'lar] **I.** *vt* to guard; (*niños*) to watch **II.** *vi* ~ **por algo** to keep watch over sth
vigilia [bi·'xi·lja] *f* **1.** (*no dormir*) wakefulness **2.** (*falta de sueño*) insomnia **3.** (*víspera*) vigil **4.** (*sin comer*) abstinence; (*comida*) meal without meat; **día de** ~ day of abstinence; **comer de** ~ to eat without meat **5.** (*en el trabajo*) late-night work
vigor [bi·'ɣor] *m* **1.** (*fuerza*) vigor; (*energía*) energy; **con** ~ vigorously; **sin** ~ without vigor **2.** (*vitalidad*) vitality; (*empuje*) drive **3.** (*vigencia*) validity; **entrar en** ~ to come into effect; **poner en** ~ to bring into effect
vigorizar <z→c> [bi·ɣo·ri·'sar, -'θar] *vt* **1.** (*fortalecer*) to strengthen **2.** (*revitalizar*) to invigorate **3.** (*animar*) to encourage
vigoroso, -a [bi·ɣo·'ro·so, -a] *adj* **1.** (*fuerte*) vigorous; (*resistente*) tough **2.** (*animado*) lively; (*vital*) energetic **3.** (*protesta*) strong
VIH [u·βe·i·'a·tʃe] *m abr de* **virus de inmunodeficiencia humana** HIV
vil [bil] *adj* (*malo*) vile; (*bajo*) base; (*infame*) despicable
vileza [bi·'le·sa, -θa] *f* **1.** (*cualidad*) vileness **2.** (*acción*) vile act
villa ['bi·ja, -ʎa] *f* **1.** HIST (*población*) town **2.** (*casa*) villa
villancico [bi·jan·'si·ko, bi·ʎan·'θi·ko] *m* (Christmas) carol
villanía [bi·ja·'ni·a, bi·ʎa-] *f* **1.** (*bajeza*) vile act **2.** (*expresión*) obscenity
villano, -a [bi·'ja·no, -a; -'ʎa·no, -a] **I.** *adj* **1.** (*bajo*) villainous **2.** (*rústico*) HIST peasant; (*expresión*) obscene **II.** *m, f* **1.** *pey* (*grosero*) rogue **2.** HIST villein; (*campesino*) peasant
vilo ['bi·lo] *adv* **en** ~ suspended; *fig* in suspense; **tener en** ~ to keep in suspense; **estar**

en ~ to be up in the air
vinagre [bi·'na·ɣre] *m* **1.** (*condimento*) vinegar **2.** (*persona*) disagreeable person
vinagrera [bi·na·'ɣre·ra] *f* **1.** (*recipiente*) vinegar bottle **2.** *pl* (*para la mesa*) cruet set **3.** *AmL* (*ardor*) indigestion
vinagreta [bi·na·'ɣre·ta] *f* vinaigrette
vincha ['bin·tʃa] *f AmS* (*cinta*) hair band
vinchuca [bin·'tʃu·ka] *f Arg, Chile, Par* zooɬ barbeiro, assassin bug
vinculación [bin·ku·la·'sjon, -'θjon] *f* link
vincular [bin·ku·'lar] *vt* **1.** (*ligar*) to link; (*unir*) to join; **~ a** [*o* con] **algo** to link to sth **2.** (*obligar*) to bind
vínculo ['bin·ku·lo] *m* **1.** (*unión*) tie; **el ~ conyugal** the bond of matrimony; **~s familiares** family ties; **~s naturales** blood relations; **los ~s con el extranjero** links with foreign countries **2.** comput link; **~ caduco** invalid [*o* broken] link **3.** (*obligación*) bond
vindicación [bin·di·ka·'sjon, -'θjon] *f* **1.** (*venganza*) vengeance **2.** (*justificación*) vindication **3.** (*reivindicación*) claim
vinería [bi·ne·'ri·a] *f And, CSur* (*vinatería*) wine store
vinícola [bi·'ni·ko·la] **I.** *adj* wine; (*cultivo*) wine-growing **II.** *mf* wine-grower
vinicultor(a) [bi·ni·kul·'tor, --'to·ra] *m(f)* wine producer
vinicultura [bi·ni·kul·'tu·ra] *f* wine production
vino ['bi·no] *m* **1.** wine; **~ rosado** rosé wine; **~ tinto** red wine; **~ caliente** hot punch; **~ de mesa** table wine; **~ de Jerez** sherry; **~ generoso** full-bodied wine; **~ de la casa** house wine; **~ de Oporto** port; **~ espumoso** [*o* de aguja] sparkling wine; **~ peleón** cheap wine **2.** (*recepción*) reception; **~ de honor** reception ►**echar agua al ~** to tone things down; **tener buen ~** to hold one's drink well; **tiene mal ~** he/she can't hold his/her drink
viña ['bi·ɲa] *f* **1.** (*monte*) vineyard **2.** (*planta*) vine ►**de todo hay en la ~ del Señor** *prov* it takes all sorts to make a world; **ser una ~** to be useful; **tener una ~ con algo** to have a goldmine in sth
viñador(a) [bi·ɲa·'dor, --'do·ra] *m(f)* vineyard worker
viñatero, -a [bi·ɲa·'te·ro, -a] *m, f Arg, Perú* winegrower
viñedo [bi·'ɲe·do] *m* **1.** (*monte*) vineyard **2.** (*planta*) vine
viola ['bjo·la] *f* **1.** mús viola **2.** bot violet
violáceo, -a [bjo·'la·θeo, -a; -seo, -a] *adj* purplish
violación [bjo·la·'sjon, -'θjon] *f* **1.** (*infracción*) violation; (*de una ley*) breaking; **~ de contrato** breach of contract **2.** (*de una mujer*) rape **3.** (*invasión*) invasion
violar [bjo·'lar] *vt* **1.** (*mujer*) to rape **2.** (*ley, principio, sepultura*) to violate; (*contrato*) to break
violencia [bjo·'len·sja, -θja] *f* **1.** (*condición*) violence; (*fuerza*) force; **~ de género** gender

violence; **~ vial** road rage; **no ~** non-violence; **con ~** by force; **sin ~** peacefully **2.** (*acción*) violent action
violentar [bjo·len·'tar] **I.** *vt* **1.** (*obligar*) to force; (*sexualmente*) to assault **2.** (*una casa*) to break into; (*un banco*) to rob **3.** (*principio*) to break **4.** (*al interpretar*) to distort **II.** *vr:* **~se** (*obligarse*) to force oneself
violento, -a [bjo·'len·to, -a] *adj* **1.** (*impetuoso*) impetuous; (*esfuerzo*) violent; (*discusión*) heated; (*temperamento*) fiery **2.** (*brutal*) aggressive; (*con violencia*) violent; **acto ~** act of violence **3.** (*persona*) violent **4.** (*postura*) unnatural **5.** (*acto*) embarrassing; (*cohibido*) embarrassed; (*duro*) difficult; **me es muy ~ tener que aceptarlo** I'm embarrassed to have to accept it; **me resulta ~ decirle que no** I find it very hard to say no to him/her **6.** (*tergiversado*) distorted **7.** *AmL* (*de repente*) suddenly
violeta [bjo·'le·ta] *adj, f* violet
violín [bjo·'lin] *m* mús violin, fiddle *inf*
violinista [bjo·li·'nis·ta] *mf* violinist
violonc(h)elo [bjo·lon·'se·lo, -'θe·lo/bjo·lon·'tʃe·lo] *m* mús cello
vip [bip], **VIP** [bip] *m abr de* **Very Important Person** VIP; **sala ~** VIP lounge
Viracocha [bi·ra·'ko·tʃa] *m And* **1.** (*dios inca*) Incan god of creation **2.** (*apelativo de conquistadores*) conquistador (*name applied to the Spanish conquistadors by the Incans*)
viraje [bi·'ra·xe] *m* **1.** (*giro*) turn; (*curva*) bend; **~ en horquilla** hairpin bend; **hacer** [*o* dar] **un ~** to swerve **2.** (*cambio*) switch; (*de opinión*) shift; (*de dirección*) change **3.** náut tack
virar [bi·'rar] **I.** *vi* **1.** (*girar*) to turn; (*curva*) to bend; **~ en redondo** *t. fig* to retrace one's steps; **el coche viró a la izquierda** the car swerved to the left **2.** (*cambiar*) to switch, to change; (*de opinión*) to shift **3.** náut to tack **II.** *vt* (*girar*) to turn
virgen ['bir·xen] **I.** *adj* virgin; *fig* pure; (*cinta*) blank; (*tierras*) virgin **II.** *f* rel **la Virgen** the Virgin; **la Santísima Virgen María** the Blessed Virgin Mary; **¡Santísima Virgen!** *inf* my goodness! ► **ser de la Virgen del puño** *inf* to be tight-fisted; **aparecérsele a uno la Virgen** *inf* to hit the jackpot; **ser un viva la Virgen** *inf* to be happy-go-lucky
virginal [bir·xi·'nal] *adj* (*inmaculado*) virginal; (*puro*) pure
virginidad [bir·xi·ni·'dad] *f* virginity
Virgo ['bir·ɣo] *m* Virgo
viril [bi·'ril] *adj* **1.** (*masculino*) virile; **edad ~** adulthood **2.** (*enérgico*) vigorous
virilidad [bi·ri·li·'dad] *f* **1.** (*masculinidad*) virility **2.** (*energía*) vigor **3.** (*potencia*) strength **4.** (*edad*) adulthood
viringo, -a [bi·'rin·go, -a] *adj Col* (*sin ropa*) naked; (*sin piel*) skinned; (*sin pelo*) hairless
virrey, -reina [bi·'rrei] *m, f* viceroy *m,* vicereine *f*

V

virtual [bir·tu·'al] *adj* virtual

virtud [bir·'tud] *f* 1.(*en las personas*) virtue; **en ~ de** by virtue of 2.(*poder*) power; **tener la ~ de aliviar** to bring relief

virtuoso, -a [bir·tu·'o·so, -a] *adj* 1.(*con gran habilidad*) virtuoso 2.(*lleno de virtudes*) virtuous

viruela [bi·'rwe·la] *f* MED 1.(*enfermedad*) smallpox; **~ loca** scarlet fever 2.(*pústula*) pustule; **picado de ~s** pockmarked; **señales de (la) ~** marks of smallpox

virulento, -a [bi·ru·'len·to, -a] *adj* 1.MED virulent 2.(*maligno*) infected

virus ['bi·rus] *m inv* MED, COMPUT virus

viruta [bi·'ru·ta] *f* shaving; **un ~s irón** (*carpintero*) a carpenter; **echando ~s** *inf* very fast

vis [bis] *f* ~ **cómica** comic effect

visa ['bi·sa] *m o f AmL*, **visado** [bi·'sa·do] *m* visa; **~ de entrada/de salida** entry/exit visa

vísceras ['bi·se·ras, 'bis·θe-] *fpl* entrails *pl*, viscera *pl*

viscosa [bis·'ko·sa] *f* QUÍM viscose

viscosidad [bis·ko·si·'dad] *f* 1.(*consistencia*) thickness 2.(*mucosidad*) viscosity

viscoso, -a [bis·'ko·so, -a] *adj* 1.(*espeso*) thick 2.(*glutinoso*) viscous; (*blando*) soft

visera [bi·'se·ra] *f* 1.HIST, MIL visor 2.(*de una gorra*) peak

visibilidad [bi·si·βi·li·'dad] *f* (*cualidad*) visibility

visible [bi·'si·βle] *adj* 1.(*perceptible*) visible 2.(*obvio*) clear 3.(*persona*) striking 4.*inf* (*presentable*) presentable

visillo [bi·'si·jo, -ʎo] *m* net curtain

visión [bi·'sjon] *f* 1.(*vista*) sight, vision; **perder la ~ de un ojo** to lose the sight in one eye 2.(*aparición*) vision; **ver visiones** *fig* to be seeing things; **me quedé (como) viendo visiones** *fig* I was stunned 3.(*punto de vista*) view; **~ de conjunto** overview; **~ del mundo** view of the world 4.*pey, inf* (*mamarracho*) sight; **ir hecho una ~** to look a sight

visionario, -a [bi·sjo·'na·rjo, -a] I. *adj* 1.(*con imaginación*) visionary 2.(*adivinatorio*) prophetic 3.(*soñador*) idealistic, dreamy *pej* II. *m, f* 1.(*con imaginación*) vision 2.(*adivinador*) prophet 3.(*soñador*) idealist; *pey* dreamer

visita [bi·'si·ta] *f* 1.(*visitante*) visitor 2.(*acción*) visit; **~ del médico** doctor's call; **~ de médico** *fig* flying visit; **~ guiada** guided tour; **~ oficial** POL official visit; **estar de ~ en casa de alguien** to be staying with sb; **ir de ~** to go visiting; **rendir ~ a alguien** to pay sb a visit; **tener (a alguien de) ~** to have visitors

visitante [bi·si·'tan·te] I. *adj* visiting; **comisión ~** visiting commission II. *mf* visitor

visitar [bi·si·'tar] *vt* 1.(*ir a ver*) to visit 2.MED to call (on)

vislumbrar [bis·lum·'brar] *vt* (*ver*) to make out, to distinguish

vislumbre [bis·'lum·bre] *f* 1.(*resplandor*) glimmer 2.(*idea*) sign

visón [bi·'son] *m* mink

visor [bi·'sor] *m* 1.MIL sights *pl*; **~ de luz infrarroja** infrared sights 2.FOTO (*cámara*) viewfinder; (*para diapositivas*) slide viewer

víspera ['bis·pe·ra] *f* (*noche anterior*) night before, eve; (*día anterior*) day before; **en ~s de** just before; **estar en ~s de hacer algo** to be on the point of doing sth

vista ['bis·ta] *f* 1.(*visión*) sight, vision; **tener la ~ cansada** to have eye strain; (*mirada*) look; **~ de lince** eyes like a hawk; **aguzar la ~** to keep one's eyes peeled; **al alcance de la ~** within view; **fuera del alcance de la ~** out of sight; **a la ~** (*al parecer*) from what can be seen; (*visible*) visible; (*previsible*) in full view; **a la ~ de todos** in full view of everyone; **a la ~ está** anyone can see that; **alzar/bajar la ~** to look up/down; **apartar la ~** to look away; **no apartar la ~ de alguien** not to take one's eyes off sb; **no perder de ~ a alguien/algo** not to lose sight of sb/sth; **a primera ~** at first sight; **a simple ~** just by looking; *fig* superficially; **comerse a alguien con la ~** to devour sb with one's eyes; **con la ~ puesta en algo** with one's sights set on sth; **con ~s a...** with a view to...; **corto de ~** short-sighted; **dejar vagar la ~** to let one's eyes wander; **dirigir la ~ a algo** to look towards sth; **a Paco no hay quien le eche la ~ encima** Paco's nowhere to be seen; **de ~** by sight; **en ~ de que...** in view of...; **está a la ~ quién va a ganar** it's obvious who's going to win; **¡fuera de mi ~!** get out of my sight!; **¡hasta la ~!** see you!; **hasta donde alcanza la ~** as far as the eye can see; **se me nubló la ~** my eyes clouded over; **no perder de ~** not to lose sight of; **pagadero a la ~** COM due on demand; **perder de ~** to lose sight of; **quedar a la ~** to remain in sight; **saltar a la ~** to be patently obvious; **tener buena ~** to have good eyesight; **volver la ~ (atrás)** to look back 2.(*panorama*) view; **~ panorámica** panoramic view; (*mirador*) viewpoint; **con ~s al mar** with sea views, overlooking the sea 3.(*imagen, perspectiva*) image; FOTO picture; **~ aérea** aerial view; ARQUIT perspective; **~ general** overall view 4.(*aspecto*) appearance; **tener buena ~** to look good 5.JUR hearing; **~ oral** hearing ▶ **~ de pájaro** bird's-eye view; **ver algo a ~ de pájaro** to have a bird's-eye view of sth; **hacer la ~ gorda** to turn a blind eye; **tener ~** to be shrewd

vistazo [bis·'ta·so, -θo] *m* look; **de un ~** at a glance; **echar [o dar] un ~ a algo** to have a (quick) look at sth

visto, -a ['bis·to, -a] I. *pp de* **ver** II. *adj* 1.(*poco original*) common; **está muy ~** that's been seen before, that's old hat 2.(*obvio*) **está ~ que no puede ser de otra forma** it's clear that things can't be otherwise 3.JUR **~ para sentencia** conclusion of the trial ▶ **nunca ~** unknown; (*inaudito*) unheard of; **el pastel desapareció ~ y no** ~ the cake disappeared in a flash; **por lo ~** apparently III. *conj* ~ **que...**

since...

visto bueno ['bis·to 'βwe·no] *m* ADMIN, JUR approval; **dar el ~ a algo** to give sth the go-ahead

vistoso, -a [bis·'to·so, -a] *adj* (*atractivo*) colorful; (*llamativo*) striking; (*hermoso*) attractive

visual [bi·su·'al] **I.** *adj* visual; **campo ~** field of vision **II.** *f* line of sight

visualización [bi·swa·li·sa·'sjon, -θa·'θjon] *f* visualization; (*display*) *t.* COMPUT visual display

visualizador [bi·swa·li·sa·'dor, -θa·'dor] *m* COMPUT display (screen)

visualizar <z→c> [bi·swa·li·'sar, -'θar] *vt* **1.** (*representar*) to visualize **2.** AmL (*divisar*) to make out **3.** COMPUT to display

vital [bi·'tal] *adj* **1.** *t.* MED vital; **constantes ~es** vital signs, basic functions; **fuerza ~** life force **2.** (*necesario*) essential **3.** (*vivaz*) lively

vitalicio, -a [bi·ta·'li·sjo, -a; -θjo, -a] *adj* ADMIN, FIN life; **renta vitalicia** life pension; **seguro ~** life insurance

vitalidad [bi·ta·li·'dad] *f* **1.** (*alegría de vivir*) vitality **2.** (*importancia*) vital importance

vitalizar <z→c> [bi·ta·li·'sar, -'θar] *vt* **1.** (*vivificar*) to revitalize **2.** (*fortalecer*) to strengthen

vitamina [bi·ta·'mi·na] *f* vitamin; **pobre/rico en ~s** low/rich in vitamins

vitícola [bi·'ti·ko·la] *adj* vine growing

viticultor(a) [bi·ti·kul·'tor, -'to·ra] *m(f)* vine grower

viticultura [bi·ti·kul·'tu·ra] *f* viticulture

vítor ['bi·tor] *m* cheer, hurrah; **prorrumpir en ~es** to cheer

vitorear [bi·to·re·'ar] *vt* to cheer

vitrina [bi·'tri·na] *f* glass cabinet; AmL (*escaparate*) shop window

vituperable [bi·tu·pe·'ra·βle] *adj* **1.** (*inmoral*) reproachable **2.** (*censurable*) reprehensible **3.** (*despreciable*) despicable

vituperar [bi·tu·pe·'rar] *vt* **1.** (*reprobar*) to condemn **2.** (*censurar*) to censure **3.** (*injuriar*) **~ a alguien** to vituperate against sb

vituperio [bi·tu·'pe·rjo] *m* **1.** (*censura*) criticism **2.** (*injuria*) vituperation *liter*

viudedad [bju·de·'dad] *f* **1.** (*viudez*) widowhood **2.** (*pensión: de viuda*) widow's pension; (*de viudo*) widower's pension

viudez [bju·'des, -'deθ] *f* widowhood

viudo, -a ['bju·do, -a] **I.** *adj* widowed; **quedarse ~** to be widowed **II.** *m, f* widower *m*, widow *f*

viva ['bi·βa] **I.** *interj* hurray!; **¡~ el rey!** long live the King!; **¡~n los novios!** three cheers for the bride and groom! **II.** *m* cheer; **dar ~s a alguien** to cheer sb; **recibir con ~s** to welcome with cheers

vivacidad [bi·βa·si·'dad, bi·βa·θi·] *f* **1.** (*viveza*) vivacity **2.** (*energía*) vigor **3.** (*agilidad*) liveliness **4.** (*agudeza*) sharpness

vivales [bi·'βa·les] *m inv, inf* rogue

vivar [bi·'βar] **I.** *m* **1.** (*conejera*) warren **2.** (*criadero*) nursery, breeding place; (*de peces*) hatchery **II.** *vt* AmL (*vitorear*) to cheer

vivaracho, -a [bi·βa·'ra·tʃo, -a] *adj* **1.** (*vivo*) vivacious **2.** (*despierto*) bright

vivaz [bi·'βas, -'βaθ] *adj* **1.** BOT perennial **2.** (*vivaracho*) vivacious **3.** (*enérgico*) lively **4.** (*despierto*) bright

vivencia [bi·'βen·sja, -θja] *f* experience

víveres ['bi·βe·res] *mpl* provisions *pl*; MIL supplies *pl*

vivero [bi·'βe·ro] *m* **1.** (*de plantas*) nursery **2.** (*de peces*) hatchery; (*en un restaurante*) holding tank

viveza [bi·'βe·sa, -θa] *f* **1.** (*celeridad*) swiftness; (*agilidad*) liveliness **2.** (*energía*) vigor **3.** (*agudeza*) sharpness **4.** (*de colores*) brightness

vívido, -a ['bi·βi·do, -a] *adj* vivid

vivienda [bi·'βjen·da] *f* **1.** (*residencia*) residence; (*casa*) house; (*apartamento*) apartment; **sin ~** homeless; **el problema de la ~** the housing problem **2.** AmL (*modo de vida*) way of life

viviente [bi·'βjen·te] *adj* living; **seres ~s** living beings; **ni alma ~** *fig* not a living soul; **todo bicho ~** every living creature

vivificar <c→qu> [bi·βi·fi·'kar] *vt* **1.** (*vitalizar*) to revitalize **2.** (*animar*) to invigorate

vivir [bi·'βir] **I.** *vi* **1.** (*estar vivo*) to be alive; **~ al día** to live from day to day; **~ a lo grande** to live it up; **~ como un rey** to live like a lord; **~ de rentas** to live off the rent; **¡~ para ver!** (*asombro*) who would believe it!, live and learn; **no dejar ~ a alguien** not to leave sb alone; **no ~ de preocupación** to be worried to death; **¿quién vive?** MIL who goes there? **2.** (*habitar*) to live **3.** (*durar*) to last; (*perdurar*) to live on **II.** *vt* to live; **~ su (propia) vida** to live one's own life **III.** *m* life; (*modo de vida*) way of life; **gente de mal ~** (*vicio*) dissolute characters; (*delincuencia*) shady characters

vivo ['bi·βo] *m* **1.** (*borde*) edge, trim **2.** (*tira*) strip

vivo, -a ['bi·βo, -a] *adj* **1.** (*viviente*) alive; **cal viva** quicklime; **ser ~** living being; **a fuego ~** CULIN on a high heat; **a lo ~** vividly; **al rojo ~** red-hot; **en ~** MÚS live; **estar ~** to be alive; **tener el ~ deseo de que** +*subj* to really hope that; **herir en lo más ~** to cut to the quick; **ser la viva imagen de alguien** to be the spitting image of sb; **~ o muerto** dead or alive **2.** (*vivaz*) lively **3.** (*enérgico*) vigorous; **de genio ~** quick-tempered **4.** (*color*) bright **5.** (*actual*) current; (*presente*) present; (*duradero*) lasting **6.** (*vívido*) vivid **7.** (*avispado*) sharp; *pey* crafty

V.O. [ber·'sjon o·ri·xi·'nal] *abr de* **versión original** original version

vocablo [bo·'ka·βlo] *m* word, term

vocabulario [bo·ka·βu·'la·rjo] *m* **1.** (*léxico*) vocabulary; **~ especializado** technical vocabulary; **~ tener un buen ~** to have a wide vocabulary **2.** (*lista*) vocabulary (list)

vocación [bo·ka·'sjon, -'θjon] *f* vocation; **~ artística** artistic vocation; **por ~** from a sense of vocation; **sentir** ~ to feel an inclination; **tener** ~ to have a calling

vocal¹ [bo·'kal] I. *adj* MÚS vocal II. *f* LING vowel

vocal² [bo·'kal] *mf* 1. (*de consejo, tribunal*) member 2. (*portavoz*) spokesperson, spokesman *m*, spokeswoman *f*

voceador(a) [bo·se·a·'dor, -·'do·ra, bo·θe-] I. *adj* shouting II. *m(f)* 1. (*pregonero*) town crier 2. *AmL* (*de periódicos*) news hawker

vocear [bo·se·'ar, bo·θe-] I. *vi* to shout II. *vt* 1. (*manifestar*) to express 2. (*llamar*) to call 3. (*pregonar*) to cry 4. (*divulgar*) to spread 5. (*aclamar*) to acclaim 6. (*presumir*) ~ **algo** to boast of sth

vocerío [bo·se·'ri·o, bo·θe-] *m* (*griterío*) clamor

vocero, -a [bo·'se·ro, -a; bo·'θe-] *m, f AmL* (*portavoz*) spokesperson, spokesman *m*, spokeswoman *f*

vociferar [bo·si·fe·'rar, bo·θi-] I. *vi* to yell II. *vt* 1. (*gritar*) to shout 2. *pey* (*proclamar*) to shout from the rooftops

vodka ['bod·ka] *m o f* vodka

vol. *abr de* **volumen** vol.

volado, -a [bo·'la·do] *adj* 1. ARQUIT projecting 2. *inf* (*loco*) crazy 3. TIPO superior 4. *AmL* (*ausente*) absent-minded; (*enamorado*) lovesick 5. *CSur* ~ **de genio** *inf* quick-tempered 6. (*inquieto*) uneasy

volador(a) [bo·la·'dor, -·'do·ra] *adj* flying

volandas [bo·'lan·das] *fpl* **en** ~ (*en el aire*) up in the air; (*deprisa*) in a rush; **llevar en** ~ to carry shoulder-high

volante [bo·'lan·te] I. *adj* (*móvil*) flying; **rueda** ~ band wheel; **platillo** ~ flying saucer II. *m* 1. AUTO steering wheel; **ir al** ~ to be at the wheel; **ponerse al** ~ to take the wheel 2. TÉC flywheel; (*manual*) handwheel 3. (*del reloj*) balance wheel 4. (*adorno*) flounce 5. (*escrito*) leaflet 6. MED referral note 7. DEP shuttlecock 8. *AmL* (*conductor*) racing driver; DEP winger

volantón [bo·lan·'ton, -·'to·na] *m* 1. (*sedal*) fishing line 2. *AmL* (*cometa*) kite 3. *AmL* (*voltereta*) somersault; (*acrobacia*) acrobatics *pl*

volar <o→ue> [bo·'lar] I. *vi* 1. (*en el aire*) to fly; **echar a** ~ to fly off; **el tiempo vuela** time flies; **las malas noticias vuelan** bad news travels fast, no news is good news 2. (*desaparecer*) to disappear; **el dinero ha volado** the money has vanished 3. (*apresurarse*) to dash; **¡voy volando!** I'm on my way!; ~ **a hacer algo** to rush off to do sth 4. *inf* (*con drogas*) to be high II. *vt* 1. (*hacer explotar*) to blow up 2. (*enfadar*) to drive mad 3. (*hacer volar*) to fly; (*ave*) to frighten off; **hacer** ~ **una cometa** to fly a kite 4. TIPO to write in superscript III. *vr:* ~ **se** 1. (*huir*) to run away 2. (*desaparecer*) to vanish 3. *AmL* (*enfadarse*) to get mad 4. (*hacer novillos*) to play hooky

volátil [bo·'la·til] I. *adj* 1. (*volador*) flying 2. QUÍM volatile 3. (*inconstante*) unpredictable II. *m* poultry

volatilizar <z→c> [bo·la·ti·li·'sar, -'θar] *vt, vr:*

~**se** QUÍM to volatilize

volcán [bol·'kan] *m* 1. GEO volcano; **un** ~ **activo/inactivo** an active/dormant volcano; **ser un** ~ **de pasión** *fig* to be afire with passion 2. *AmL, fig* (*montón*) loads *pl*

volcánico, -a [bol·'ka·ni·ko, -a] *adj* 1. GEO volcanic 2. (*ardiente*) fiery

volcar [bol·'kar] *irr* I. *vi* (*tumbarse*) to overturn; (*barco*) to capsize II. *vt* 1. (*hacer caer*) to knock over; (*verter*) to spill 2. (*dar la vuelta*) to turn over III. *vr:* ~**se** 1. (*darse la vuelta*) to overturn; (*caer*) to get knocked over; (*dar una voltereta*) to turn a somersault 2. (*esforzarse*) to make an effort; ~**se en** [*o* **con**] **alguien** to be extremely kind to sb; ~**se en algo** to throw oneself into sth

volea [bo·'lea] *f v.* **voleo**

volear [bo·le·'ar] I. *vi, vt* (*dep*) to volley II. *vt* (*semillas*) scatter

voleibol [bo·lei·'βol] *m* DEP volleyball

voleiplaya [bo·lei·'pla·ja] *m* DEP beach volleyball

voleo [bo·'leo] *m* DEP volley; **a** ~ on the volley; *fig* at random

voltaje [bol·'ta·xe] *m* voltage

voltario, -a [bol·'ta·rjo, -a] *adj Chile* 1. (*gastador*) spendthrift; (*dadivoso*) generous 2. (*obstinado*) self-willed

volteado [bol·te·'a·do] *m Méx, inf* (*homosexual*) fag

voltear [bol·te·'ar] I. *vi* 1. (*dar vueltas: persona*) to roll over; (*cosa*) to spin; (*campana*) to peal 2. (*volcar*) to overturn 3. *AmL* (*torcer*) to turn; (*girarse*) to turn around; ~ **a hacer algo** to do sth again 4. *AmL* (*pasear*) to go for a walk II. *vt* 1. (*invertir*) to turn over; (*volver del revés*) to turn the right way up 2. (*hacer girar*) to spin; ~ **las campanas** to ring the bells 3. *AmL* (*volcar*) to knock over; (*volver*) to turn; ~ **la espalda a alguien** to turn one's back on sb 4. *AmL* (*lanzar al aire*) to throw into the air; (*el lazo*) to swing III. *vr:* ~**se** 1. (*dar vueltas*) to turn over 2. (*cambiar de ideas*) to change one's ideas 3. *AmL* (*volcar*) to overturn; (*darse la vuelta*) to turn around

voltereta [bol·te·'re·ta] *f* 1. (*cabriola*) handspring; (*en el aire*) somersault; **dar una** ~ to do a handspring; (*en el aire*) to turn a somersault 2. (*vuelco*) (sudden) change

voltio ['bol·tjo] *m* volt

volubilidad [bo·lu·βi·li·'dad] *f* 1. QUÍM instability 2. (*inconstancia*) fickleness; (*imprevisibilidad*) changeableness

voluble [bo·'lu·βle] *adj* 1. QUÍM unstable 2. (*inconstante*) fickle; (*imprevisible*) changeable 3. BOT climbing

volumen [bo·'lu·men] *m* 1. (*tamaño*) size; *t.* FÍS, MAT volume 2. (*cantidad*) amount; (*del pelo*) body; ~ **de ventas** turnover; **de gran** ~ large, bulky 3. (*de sonido*) volume; **a todo** ~ (at) full volume; **poner la música a todo** ~ to put the music on full blast 4. (*tomo*) volume; **en dos/varios volúmenes** in two/several volumes

voluminoso, -a [bo·lu·mi·'no·so, -a] *adj* sizeable; (*poco manejable*) bulky; (*grueso*) thick; (*corpulento*) heavy

voluntad [bo·lun·'tad] *f* **1.**(*intención*) will; (*fuerza de voluntad*) will-power; ~ **de vivir** will to live; **buena** ~ goodwill; **mala** ~ evil intent; **a** ~ at one's discretion; **con buena** ~ with good intentions; **con mucha/poca** ~ willingly/unwillingly; **contra su** ~ against one's will; **de última** ~ as a last wish; **hacer su santa** ~ to do exactly as one pleases; **poner** ~ **en algo** to put one's heart into sth; **por causas ajenas a nuestra** ~ for reasons beyond our control; **por propia** ~ of one's own free will; **quitar a alguien la** ~ **de algo** to stop sb feeling like doing sth; **tener mucha/poca** ~ to have a lot of/not very much will-power; **última** ~ JUR last will **2.**(*cariño*) affection; **ganarse la** ~ **de alguien** to win sb's affection

voluntariedad [bo·lun·ta·rje·'dad] *f* **1.**(*carácter voluntario*) voluntary nature; JUR intent **2.**(*arbitrariedad*) arbitrary nature **3.**(*fuerza de voluntad*) willingness; (*perseverancia*) persistence

voluntario, -a [bo·lun·'ta·rjo, -a] **I.** *adj* **1.**(*libre*) voluntary **2.**(*arbitrario*) arbitrary **II.** *m, f* volunteer; **ofrecerse** ~ **para algo** to volunteer for sth

voluntarioso, -a [bo·lun·ta·'rjo·so, -a] *adj* willing; (*perseverante*) persistent; (*caprichoso*) self-willed

voluptuosidad [bo·lup·two·si·'dad] *f* voluptuousness

voluptuoso, -a [bo·lup·tu·'o·so, -a] *adj* voluptuous

volver [bol·'βer] *irr* **I.** *vi* **1.**(*dar la vuelta*) to go back; ~ **atrás** to turn back **2.**(*regresar*) to return; ~ **a casa** to go home; **al** ~ **a casa me acosté** when I got home I went to bed; **al** ~ **compra el pan** buy the bread on the way back; **al** ~ **me llamó** he/she called me when he/she got back; **he vuelto por la autopista** I came back on the motorway; ~ **en sí** to come to; ~ **sobre sí** to turn around; **volviendo al tema** to come back to the subject **3.**(*repetir*) ~ **a hacer algo** to do sth again; **he vuelto a cometer el mismo error** I've made the same mistake again; **he vuelto a casarme** I've remarried **II.** *vt* **1.**(*dar la vuelta*) to turn over; ~ **la espalda a alguien** *t. fig* to turn one's back on sb; ~ **la vista a algo** to look back at sth **2.**(*poner del revés*) to turn inside out; (*manga*) to roll up **3.**(*transformar*) to make; ~ **furioso** to make mad; ~ **a su estado original** to revert to its original state; ~ **loco a alguien** to drive sb crazy **4.**(*devolver*) to return; ~ **algo a su sitio** to put sth back in its place; ~ **a la vida** to revive **III.** *vr:* ~**se 1.**(*darse la vuelta*) ~**se a** [*o* hacia] algo to turn around towards sth **2.**(*dirigirse*) ~**se a** [*o* hacia] algo to turn towards sth; ~**se contra alguien** to turn against sb; ~**se** (**para**) **atrás** to retrace

one's steps; *fig* to back out; **no tengo dónde** ~ **me** I've got no place to go **3.**(*regresar*) to return **4.**(*convertirse*) to become; (*ponerse*) to grow; ~**se viejo** to grow old; ~**se rico** to get rich

vomitar [bo·mi·'tar] **I.** *vi* to vomit; **es para** ~ *vulg* it's enough to make you sick; **este salchichón me da ganas de** ~ this sausage is making me sick **II.** *vt* **1.**(*comida*) to bring up; *fig* to spew out; (*insultos*) to hurl; (*sangre*) to cough up **2.** *fig* (*desembuchar*) to spit out

vomitivo, -a [bo·mi·'ti·βo] *adj* **1.** MED emetic **2.** *inf* (*asqueroso*) revolting; **ese es** ~ that's disgusting

vómito ['bo·mi·to] *m* (*acción*) vomiting; (*lo vomitado*) vomit; ~ **de sangre** coughing up of blood; **provocar** ~**s a alguien** to make sb throw up *inf*

voracidad [bo·ra·si·'dad, bo·ra·θi-] *f* voraciousness; (*avaricia*) greed

vorágine [bo·'ra·xi·ne] *f* **1.**(*remolino*) whirlpool **2.**(*confusión*) whirl, vortex

voraz [bo·'ras, -'raθ] *adj t. fig* voracious; (*hambriento*) ravenous; **apetito** ~ voracious appetite; (*avaro*) greedy

vos [bos] *pron pers* **1.** *AmL* (*tú*) you; **esto es para** ~ this is for you; **voy con** ~ I'll go with you **2.** HIST (*usted*) thou

vosear [bo·se·'ar]

vosotros, -as [bo·'so·tros, -as] *pron pers, pl* you; ~ **sois muy listos** you are very clever; **esto es para** ~ this is for you

votación [bo·ta·'sjon, -'θjon] *f* vote; ~ **a mano alzada** vote by show of hands; **someter algo a** ~ to put sth to the vote

votar [bo·'tar] **I.** *vi* (*elegir*) to vote; ~ **a** [*o* por] alguien/algo to vote for sb/sth **II.** *vt* (*decidir*) ~ **a alguien** to vote for sb; ~ **un presupuesto** to approve a budget

voto ['bo·to] *m* **1.** POL (*opinión*) vote; (*acción*) voting; ~ **afirmativo** [*o* **a favor**] vote in favor; ~ **de castigo** protest vote; ~ **en blanco** unmarked ballot (paper) (*as a protest*); ~ **de censura** vote of no confidence; ~ **por correo** mail vote; ~ **negativo** [*o* **en contra**] vote against;

V

derecho a ~ right to vote; **dar su ~ a algo** to vote for sth; **emitir su ~** to cast one's vote; **tener** (**derecho a**) ~ to have the (right to) vote **2.** REL (*promesa*) vow; **hacer ~s por** +*infin*, **hacer ~s por que** +*subj t. fig* to vow to

voy [boi] *I. pres de* **ir**

voz [bos, boθ] *f* **1.** (*sonido, facultad, voto*) voice; ~ **afeminada** effeminate voice; ~ **aguardentosa** gravelly voice; ~ **cantante** melody line; ~ **de mando** voice of command; **a dos/cuatro voces** MÚS for two/four voices; **aclarar la ~** to clear one's throat; **ahuecar la ~** to deepen one's voice; **levantar/bajar la ~** to raise/lower one's voice; **levantar la ~ a alguien** to raise one's voice to sb; **a media ~** in a whisper; **de viva ~** in person; **hablar en ~ alta/baja** to speak loudly/softly; **leer en ~ alta** to read aloud; **hacer oír su ~** to make one's voice heard; **no tener ni ~ ni voto** to have no right to vote; *fig* to have no say in the matter; **se me quebró la ~** I lost my voice; *fig* words failed me; **tener ~ en algo** to have a say in sth **2.** (*grito*) shouting; **voces** shouts; **a voces** in a loud voice; **a ~ en grito** at the top of one's voice; **dar una ~ a alguien** to give a shout to sb; **dar voces** to shout; **dar la ~ de alarma** to raise the alarm; **pegar** (**cuatro**) **voces** to shout; **pedir algo a voces** to cry out for sth **3.** (*sonido*) tone **4.** (*rumor*) rumor; **corre la ~ de que...** rumor has it that... **5.** (*vocablo*) word; ~ **técnica** technical term **6.** LING ~ **activa/pasiva** active/passive voice ▶**llevar la ~ cantante** to call the tune

vozarrón [bo·sa·'rron, bo·θa-] *m* booming voice

vudú [bu·'du] *m* voodoo

vuelco ['bwel·ko] *m* **1.** (*tumbo*) turning over; (*voltereta*) somersault **2.** (*cambio*) drastic change; **dar un ~** to overturn; *fig* to change completely ▶**me dio un ~ el corazón** my heart missed a beat

vuelo ['bwe·lo] *m* **1.** (*en el aire*) flight; ~ **acrobático** acrobatic flight; ~ **en globo** balloon flight; ~ **sin motor** gliding; ~ **nacional/internacional** domestic/international flight; ~ **rasante** low-level flight; ~ **regular** scheduled flight; **levantar** [*o* **alzar**] **el ~** (*pájaro*) to fly off; (*avión*) to take off; **al ~** in flight; *fig* quickly; **tomar ~** to take flight; *fig* to leave **2.** (*de la ropa*) looseness; **falda de ~** full skirt ▶ **oír el ~ de una mosca** to hear a pin drop; **de altos ~s** high-powered; **cogerlas al ~** to be very quick on the uptake; **cortar los ~s a alguien** to clip sb's wings

vuelta ['bwel·ta] *f* **1.** (*giro*) turn; **el camión dio una ~ de campana** the truck flipped over; **andar a ~s con algo** *inf* to be working on sth; **a la ~ de** (*lugar*) near; (*tiempo*) after; **a la ~ de la esquina** around the corner; **dar la ~** (*rodear*) to go around; (*volver*) to turn back; (*poner cabeza abajo*) to put face down; (*llave*) to turn; **darse la ~** to turn over; **dar media ~** to turn around; **dar una ~** to have a walk

around; **dar ~s a algo** to turn sth over; **dar mil ~s a alguien** to run circles around sb; **no dar más ~s al tema** to stop worrying about sth; **la cabeza me da ~s** my head is spinning **2.** (*regreso*) return; (*viaje*) trip; ~ **atrás** return (trip); *fig* look back; CINE, LIT flashback; **a la ~ pasaremos por vuestra casa** we'll pass by your house on the way back; **a la ~ empezaré a trabajar** I'll start work when I get back; **de ~ a casa** back home; **estar de ~** to be back; **la ~ al cole**(**gio**) back to school **3.** (*curva*) bend; **dar ~s y revueltas** to turn this way and that **4.** (*dinero*) change; **dar la ~** to give change **5.** (*cambio*) change; **la vida da muchas ~s** life has many ups and downs; **¡las ~s que da la vida!** how things change! **6.** DEP lap; ~ **ciclista** cycle race; **partida de ~** return match **7.** POL round **8.** (*devolución*) refund **9.** (*reverso*) back **10.** (*de la ropa*) facing ▶ **a ~ de correo** by return of post; **esto no tiene ~ de hoja** (*está claro*) there's no doubt about it; (*no hay otra solución*) it's the only way; **poner a alguien de ~ y media** to tell sb off; **estar de ~ de todo** to have seen it all before; **buscar las ~s a alguien** to try to catch sb out; **dar muchas ~s a algo** to think over sth again and again

vuelto ['bwel·to, -a] *m AmL* (*cambio*) change; **dar el ~** to give change

vuelto, -a ['bwel·to, -a] *pp de* **volver**

vuestro, -a ['bwes·tro, -a] **I.** *adj* your; ~ **coche** your car; **vuestra hija** your daughter; ~**s libros** your books **II.** *pron pos* **1.** (*de vuestra propiedad*) yours; **¿es ~?** is this yours? **2.** (*tras artículo*) **el** ~ yours; **los ~s** yours; (*parientes*) your family; **mi radio no funciona, ¿me dejáis la vuestra?** my radio doesn't work, can I borrow yours? **3.** (*tras sustantivo*) (of) yours; **un amigo ~** a friend of yours; (**no**) **es culpa vuestra** it's not your fault ▶ **ésta es la vuestra** *inf* this is your chance

vulcanizadora [bul·ka·ni·sa·'do·ra, bul·ka·ni·θa-] *f Méx* vulcanizer

vulgar [bul·'γar] *adj* **1.** (*común*) common **2.** (*ordinario*) vulgar **3.** (*ramplón*) coarse

vulgaridad [bul·γa·ri·'dad] *f* **1.** (*normalidad*) ordinariness **2.** *pey* (*grosería*) vulgarity **3.** (*ramplonería*) coarseness

vulgarizar <z →c> [bul·γa·ri·'sar, -'θar] **I.** *vt* **1.** (*simplificar*) to vulgarize **2.** (*popularizar*) to popularize **II.** *vr:* ~**se 1.** *pey* (*persona*) to become vulgar **2.** (*trivializarse*) to become trivial **3.** (*popularizarse*) to become popular

vulnerabilidad [bul·ne·ra·βi·li·'dad] *f* vulnerability; (*de la salud*) delicate nature; (*de máquinas*) poor quality

vulnerable [bul·ne·'ra·βle] *adj* vulnerable

vulneración [bul·ne·ra·'sjon, -'θjon] *f* violation

vulnerar [bul·ne·'rar] *vt* (*persona*) to hurt; (*derecho*) to violate

vulva ['bul·βa] *f* ANAT vulva

W

W, w ['u·βe 'do·βle] _f_ W, w; ~ **de Washington** W as in Whisky
walkie-talkie ['wal·ki 'tal·ki] _m_ walkie-talkie
wampa ['wam·pa] _f Méx_ (_ciénaga_) swamp
wáter ['ba·ter] _m_ (_recipiente_) toilet; (_servicio_) washroom
waterpolo [ba·ter·'po·lo] _m_ DEP water polo
watt [bat] _m_ ELEC watt
W.C. ['u·βe se, -θe] _m abr de_ **water-closet** toilet
web [ueb] _m o f_ COMPUT web
wélter ['bel·ter] I. _adj AmL_ DEP **peso** ~ welterweight II. _m AmL_ DEP welterweight
whisky ['wis·ki] _m_ whisky
windsurf ['win(d)·surf] _m_ 1. DEP windsurfing 2. (_tabla_) windsurfer
wing [win] _m AmL_ 1. (_extremo delantero_) winger 2. (_extrema delantera_) wing
WWW _abr de_ **World Wide Web** WWW

X

X, x ['e·kis] _f_ 1. (_letra_) X, x; ~ **de xilófono** X as in X-ray; **rayos** ~ X-rays _pl;_ **en** (**forma de**) ~ X-shaped 2. MAT x; ~ **veces** x times 3. _fig_ (_indeterminado_) x; **le presté x pesos** I lent him/her x pesos 4. (_numeración romana_) ten
xenofobia [se·no·'fo·βja] _f_ xenophobia
xenófobo, -a [se·'no·fo·βo, -a] _adj_ xenophobic
xilófono [si·'lo·fo·no] _m_ MÚS xylophone
xilografía [si·lo·γra·'fi·a] _f_ xylography
xirgo, -a ['sir·γo, -a] _adj Méx_ 1. (_desaseado_) untidy 2. (_hirsuto_) hairy
xocoyote [so·ko·'jo·te] _m Méx_ (_benjamín_) youngest child

Y

Y, y [i 'γrje·γa] _f_ Y, y; ~ **de yema** Y as in Yankee **y** [i] _conj_ and; **días** ~ **días** days and days; ¿~ **qué?** so what?; **me voy de vacaciones — ¿~ tu trabajo?** I'm going on holiday — what about your job?; ¿~ **tu marido**(, **qué tal?**) and how is your husband?; ¿~ **mi monedero? — en el coche** where's my purse? — it's in the car; ¿~ **este paquete? — de mis padres** whose is this packet? — it's my parents'; ~ **eso que...** despite that,...; ¡~ **tanto!** you bet!, you can say that again!

ya [ja] I. _adv_ 1. (_en el pasado_) already; ~ **es hora de que cambies** it's time you changed; ~ **en 1800** as early as 1800 2. (_pronto_) soon, right away; !~ **voy!** coming!; ~ **verás** you'll see 3. (_ahora_) now; ~ **falta poco para Navidades** Christmas is near now 4. (_negación_) ~ **no fumo** I don't smoke any more; ~ **no... sino...** not only..., but... 5. (_afirmación_) yes; ~, ~ all right, OK; _irón_ oh, sure!; ¡**ah** ~! I get it now!; ¡**anda** ~! come off it!; ¡**pues** ~! right now! II. _conj_ 1. (_porque_) ~ **que** since, as 2. (_aprovechando que_) ~ **que estás aquí...** now that you're here ...; ~ **que lo mencionas...** now that you mention it... 3. (_o_) ~ **por...,** ~ **por...** either by... or... III. _interj_ that's it!
yacaré [ja·ka·'re] _m Arg, Bol, Par, Urug_ ZOOL caiman
yacer [ja·'ser, -'θer] _irr vi elev_ 1. (_estar echado_) to lie; **aquí yace el conde** here lies the count 2. (_acostarse_) to lie down 3. (_estar_) to be
yacimiento [ja·si·'mjen·to, -θi·'mjen·to] _m_ GEO, MIN deposit; (_capa_) layer
yagua ['ja·γwa] _f_ 1. _AmL_ BOT royal palm 2. (_fibras_) palm leaf
yagual [ja·'γwal] _m AmC_ padded ring (_for carrying heavy loads on the head_)
yaguré [ja·γu·'re] _m AmL_ ZOOL skunk
yanqui ['jan·ki] I. _adj_ Yankee II. _mf_ Yank
yapa ['ja·pa] _f AmL_ 1. (_a un precio_) bonus 2. (_objeto_) extra; **de** ~ as an addition
yapar [ja·'par] _vt AmL_ 1. (_el precio_) ~ **algo** to give sth as a bonus 2. (_un objeto_) ~ **algo** to add sth as an extra
yarda ['jar·da] _f_ (_medida_) yard
yate ['ja·te] _m_ yacht
ye [je] _f_ letter Y
yedra ['je·dra] _f_ ivy
yegua ['je·γwa] _f_ 1. ZOOL mare 2. _AmC_ (_colilla_) cigar stub
yeísmo [je·'is·mo]

> ⓘ The term **yeísmo** signifies the pronunciation of the 'll' as a 'y,' as in '**gayo**' (instead of '**gallo**').

yelmo ['jel·mo] _m_ helmet
yema ['je·ma] _f_ 1. (_de un huevo_) yolk 2. (_de un dedo_) fingertip 3. CULIN egg yolk 4. BOT young shoot 5. (_parte mejor_) best part; ~**s de espárrago** asparagus tips
yendo [jen·do] _gerundio de_ **ir**
yerba ['jer·βa] _f_ 1. (_planta_) grass; ~ **mate** _AmS_ maté herb 2. (_césped_) lawn; (_pasto_) pasture; (_seco_) dry grass
yerbal [jer·'βal] _m RíoPl_ maté plantation
yerbatal [jer·βa·'tal] _m Arg_ (_yerbal_) maté plantation
yerbatero, -a [jer·βa·'te·ro, -a] I. _adj AmL_ maté II. _m, f AmS_ 1. (_curandero_) folk healer 2. (_vendedor: de hierbas_) herbalist; (_de forraje_) person who sells fodder; (_de mate_)

W
X
Y

grower of maté

yerbear [jer·βe·'ar] *vi AmL* to drink maté

yerbera [jer·'βe·ra] *f RíoPl* maté (tea) gourd

yerbero, -a [jer·'βe·ro, -a] *m, f Méx* (*curandero*) herb doctor

yergo ['jer·ɣo] *1. pres de* **erguir**

yermo ['jer·mo] *m* **1.** (*terreno*) waste land **2.** AGR uncultivated land

yermo, -a ['jer·mo, -a] *adj* **1.** (*inhabitado*) uninhabited **2.** AGR uncultivated; **dejar ~** to leave uncultivated

yerno ['jer·no] *m* son-in-law

yerra ['je·rra] *f RíoPl* branding

yérsey ['jer·sei] *m*, **yersí** [jer·'si] *m AmC, AmS* jersey

yeso ['je·so] *m* **1.** (*material*) plaster; **dar de ~ una pared** to plaster a wall **2.** GEO gypsum

yeta ['je·ta] *f Arg, Urug* bad luck

yé-yé [je·'je] *adj inf* cool; **hoy vas muy ~** you look very hip today

yin ['jin] *yines m* jeans *pl*

yira ['ji·ra] *f Arg, Urug, pey, inf* slut

yo [jo] I. *pron pers* I; **~ que tú...** if I were you...; **esto queda entre tú y ~** this is between you and me; **¿quién lo hizo? — ~ no** who did it? — not me; **soy ~, Susan** it's me, Susan; **~ mismo** myself II. *m t.* PSICO ego

yocalla [jo·'ka·ja, -ʎa] *m Bol* **1.** (*niño callejero*) street urchin **2.** (*niño mestizo*) half-breed

yod [jod] *f* LING yod

yodo ['jo·do] *m* iodine

yoga ['jo·ɣa] *m* yoga

yogui ['jo·ɣi] *mf* yogi

yogur ['jo·ɣur] *m* **1.** CULIN yogurt; **~ natural** plain yogurt; **~ desnatado** low-fat yogurt **2.** *inf* (*genio*) **estar de mal ~** to be like a bear with a sore head; **tener muy mal ~** to be very hot-tempered

yolo ['jo·lo] *m Méx, inf* (*corazón*) darling; **¡~ mío!** my darling!

yonqui ['jon·ki] *mf inf* (*drogata*) junkie

yoyó [jo·'jo] *m* yoyo

yuca ['ju·ka] *f* yucca

yudo ['ju·do] *m* judo

yugo ['ju·ɣo] *m* **1.** *t.* AGR (*dominio*) yoke; **someterse al ~** to bow to the yoke **2.** (*de la campana*) bell cage

yugular¹ [ju·ɣu·'lar] *f* ANAT jugular vein

yugular² [ju·ɣu·'lar] I. *vt* **1.** (*decapitar*) to decapitate **2.** (*detener*) to break off II. *adj* jugular

yunga ['jun·ɡa] *mf Bol, Chile, Ecua, Perú* valley native (*native or resident of the warm valleys on either side of the Andes*)

yungas ['jun·ɡas] *fpl Bol, Chile, Ecua, Perú* warm valleys *pl*

yunque ['jun·ke] *m t.* ANAT anvil

yunta ['jun·ta] *f* **1.** (*par*) yoke (of oxen), couple **2.** *pl, PRico, Urug, Ven* cufflinks *pl*

yuppy ['ju·pi] *mf* yuppy

yute ['ju·te] *m* jute

yuxtaponer [jus·ta·po·'ner] *irr como poner* I. *vt* (*a otra cosa*) to join; (*dos cosas*) to juxtapose II. *vr:* **~se** to join together

yuxtaposición [jus·ta·po·si·'sjon, -'θjon] *f* juxtaposition

yuxtapuesto, -a [jus·ta·'pwes·to, -a] *adj* juxtaposed

yuyal [ju·'jal] *m CSur* weed-covered ground

yuyero, -a [ju·'je·ro, -a] *m, f Arg, CSur* herbalist

yuyo ['ju·jo] *m* **1.** *CSur* (*yerbajo*) weed **2.** *pl, Col, Ecua* (*condimento*) seasoning **3.** *pl, Perú* (*verdura*) herbs *pl* **4.** *AmC* (*ampolla*) blister

Z

Z, z ['se·ta, 'θe-/'se·da, 'θe-] *f* Z, z; **~ de Zaragoza** Z as in Zulu

zabuir [sa·'bwir, θa-] *vi PRico* (*zambullir*) to plunge

zacatal [sa·ka·'tal, θa-] *m AmC, Méx* pasture

zacate [sa·'ka·te, θa-] *m AmL* (*paja*) hay

zafacoca [sa·fa·'ko·ka, θa-] *f* **1.** *AmC, AmS, Méx* (*pelea*) fight **2.** *Chile* (*alboroto*) commotion

zafacón [sa·fa·'kon, θa-] *m PRico, RDom* (*cubo de la basura*) trash can

zafado, -a [sa·'fa·do, -a; θa-] *adj Arg* (*descarado*) sassy

zafadura [sa·fa·'du·ra, θa-] *f AmL* MED (*luxación*) dislocation

zafar [sa·'far, θa-] I. *vt* NÁUT to free II. *vr:* **~se** **1.** (*de una persona*) to get away; **el ladrón se zafó del policía** the thief gave the policeman the slip **2.** (*de un compromiso*) **~se de** to get out of **3.** TÉC (*correa*) to come off **4.** *AmL* (*dislocarse*) to dislocate

zafarrancho [sa·fa·'rran·tʃo, θa-] *m* **1.** NÁUT clearing of the decks **2.** *inf* (*limpieza*) clearing up **3.** *inf* (*riña*) quarrel **4.** *inf* (*destrozo*) mess

zafio, -a ['sa·fjo, -a; 'θa-] *adj* **1.** (*grosero*) rude **2.** (*tosco*) rough, uncouth

zafiro [sa·'fi·ro, θa-] *m* MIN sapphire

zafo ['θa·fo, 'θa-] *adv AmL* (*salvo*) except

zaga ['sa·ɣa, 'θa-] *f* **1.** (*parte posterior*) rear; **ir a la ~ de alguien** to be behind sb; **el vicepresidente no le va a la ~ al presidente** the vice president is every bit as good as the president **2.** DEP defense

zagal(a) [sa·'ɣal, --'ɣa·la; θa-] *m(f)* (*muchacho*) boy; (*muchacha*) girl

zaguán [sa·'ɣwan, θa-] *m* **1.** (*vestíbulo*) hall **2.** (*exterior*) entrance

zahorí <zahoríes> [sa·o·'ri, θa-] *m* **1.** (*vidente*) seer **2.** (*perspicaz*) very perceptive person **3.** (*buscar agua*) water diviner

zaino, -a ['saj·no, -a; 'θaj-] *adj* **1.** (*persona*) treacherous; **mirar a lo ~** to look shifty **2.** (*res*) black; (*caballo*) chestnut

zalamería [sa·la·me·'ri·a, θa-] *f* flattery

zalamero, -a [sa·la·'me·ro, -a; θa-] I. *adj* flattering **II.** *m, f* flatterer

zamarra [sa·'ma·rra, θa-] *f* **1.** (*de pastor*) shepherd's waistcoat **2.** (*chaqueta*) sheepskin jacket **3.** (*piel*) sheepskin

zamarro [sa·'ma·rro, θa-] *m* **1.** (*chaqueta*) sheepskin jacket **2.** (*piel*) sheepskin **3.** (*rústico*) yokel **4.** (*bribón*) sly individual **5.** *pl, AmL* (*pantalones*) breeches *pl*

zambo, -a [sam·bo, -a; θam-] *adj* (*piernas*) knock-kneed, bow-legged

zambomba [sam·'bom·ba, θam-] *f* MÚS *drumlike instrument played by rubbing a stick through the center of the drumskin*

zambra ['sam·bra, 'θam-] *f* **1.** (*bulla*) racket; (*riña*) quarrel **2.** HIST (*fiesta gitana*) gypsy festivity

zambullir <*3. pret:* zambulló> [sam·bu·'jir, θam·bu·'ʎir] **I.** *vt* to submerge **II.** *vr:* ~**se** **1.** (*en el agua*) to dive **2.** (*en un asunto*) ~**se en algo** to plunge into sth **3.** (*ocultarse*) to hide; (*cubrirse*) to cover oneself

zambullón [sam·bu·'jon, θam·bu·'ʎon] *m AmS* (*zambullida*) dip, dive

zampar [sam·'par, θam-] **I.** *vt* **1.** (*comer*) to scarf down **2.** (*ocultar*) to whip out of sight **3.** (*tirar*) to dash (to the ground) **II.** *vr:* ~**se** **1.** (*comer*) to scoff **2.** (*en un lugar*) to crash **3.** *pey* (*invitarse*) to gatecrash

zampón, -ona [sam·'pon, -·'po·na; θam-] **I.** *adj inf* greedy **II.** *m, f inf* glutton

zamuro [sa·'mu·ro, θa-] *m Ven* (*buitre*) turkey vulture

zanahoria[1] [sa·na·'o·rja, θa-] *f* BOT carrot

zanahoria[2] [sa·na·'o·rja, θa-] *m RíoPl* (*imbécil*) idiot

zanca ['san·ka, 'θan-] *f* **1.** (*del ave*) shank **2.** *inf* (*del hombre*) long leg

zancada [san·'ka·da, θan-] *f* stride; **dar** ~**s** to stride; **se recorrió la ciudad en dos** ~**s** he/she walked around the town in no time

zancadilla [san·ka·'di·ja, θan·ka·'di·ʎa] *f* **poner la** ~ **a alguien** to trip sb up; *fig* to ruin sb's chances

zanco ['san·ko, 'θan-] *m* stilt

zancón, -ona [san·'kon, -·'ko·na; θan-] *adj* **1.** (*zancudo*) long-legged **2.** *Col, Guat, Méx* (*demasiado corto*) too short; **el vestido le queda** ~ the dress is too short on her

zancudo [san·'ku·do, θan-] *m AmL* **1.** (*insecto*) mosquito **2.** (*ave*) wader

zancudo, -a [san·'ku·do, -a; θan-] *adj* long-legged

zanganear [san·ga·ne·'ar, θan-] *vi inf* to idle

zángano ['san·ga·no, 'θan-] *m* **1.** (*vago*) idler **2.** *t.* ZOOL drone **3.** (*torpe*) bore

zanja ['san·xa, 'θan-] *f* **1.** (*excavación*) ditch **2.** *AmL* (*arroyada*) watercourse

zanjar [san·'xar, θan-] *vt* **1.** (*abrir zanjas*) to dig ditches **2.** (*asunto*) to settle; (*disputa*) to end

zanjón [san·'xon, θan-] *m* **1.** (*zanja*) gully, ditch **2.** *AmL* (*despeñadero*) gorge

zapa ['sa·pa, 'θa-] *f* **1.** (*pala*) hoe **2.** MIL sap;

labor de ~ *fig* scheming

zapallo [sa·'pa·jo, θa·'pa·ʎo] *m* **1.** *AmL* (*calabaza*) pumpkin **2.** *Arg, Chile* (*chiripa*) fluke

zapata [sa·'pa·ta, θa-] *f* TÉC shoe; (*arandela*) washer; ~ **de freno** brake shoe

zapatear [sa·pa·te·'ar, θa-] **I.** *vt* (*golpear*) to kick **II.** *vi* **1.** (*bailando*) to tap dance **2.** (*velas*) to flap violently

zapatería [sa·pa·te·'ri·a, θa-] *f* **1.** (*tienda*) shoe store **2.** (*fábrica*) shoe factory **3.** (*taller*) shoemaker's **4.** (*oficio*) shoemaking

zapatero [sa·pa·'te·ro, θa-] *m* (*mueble*) shoe rack

zapatero, -a [sa·pa·'te·ro, -a; θa-] **I.** *adj* (*patatas*) hard **II.** *m, f* shoemaker ▶ ~ **a tus zapatos** *prov* cobbler, stick to your last *prov;* (*no meterse*) mind your own business

zapatilla [sa·pa·'ti·ja, θa·pa·'ti·ʎa] *f* **1.** (*para casa*) slipper **2.** (*de deporte*) sneaker; ~**s de clavos** spikes; ~**s de tenis** tennis shoes

zapato [sa·'pa·to, θa-] *m* shoe; ~ **de salón** pump; ~**s de tacón** high-heeled shoes; **un par de** ~**s** a pair of shoes ▶ **tú no me llegas a la suela del** ~ you can't hold a candle to me; **saber dónde aprieta el** ~ to know which side one's bread is buttered on; **meter a alguien en un** ~ to intimidate sb

zape ['sa·pe, θa-] *interj* **1.** (*animal*) shoo! **2.** (*peligro*) look out!

zapear [sa·pe·'ar, θa-] *vt* **1.** (*espantar*) to scare away **2.** *inf* TV to channel surf

zapotazo [sa·po·'ta·so, θa·po·'ta·θo] *m Méx, inf* thump

zapote [sa·'po·te, θa-] *m AmC, Méx* BOT sapodilla

zapping ['sa·pin, 'θa-] *m* channel surfing

zar, zarina [sar, θar] *m, f* tsar *m*, tsarina *f*

zaramullo [sa·ra·'mu·jo, θa·ra·'mu·ʎo] *m Perú, Ven* silly thing

zarandajas [sa·ran·'da·xas, θa-] *fpl* trifles *pl*

zarandear [sarande'ar, θa-] **I.** *vt* **1.** (*sacudir*) to shake hard **2.** (*ajetrear*) to keep busy **3.** (*cribar*) to sieve **4.** *AmL* (*ridiculizar*) to mock **II.** *vr:* ~**se** **1.** (*ajetrearse*) to busy oneself **2.** (*burlarse*) to make fun

zarco, -a ['sar·ko, -a; 'θar-] *adj* light blue

zarina [sa·'ri·na, θa-] *f v.* **zar**

zarpa ['sar·pa, 'θar-] *f* **1.** (*del león*) paw; *inf* (*del hombre*) huge hand, mitt; **echar la** ~ (*animal*) to claw; *inf* (*persona*) to grab **2.** (*barco*) weighing anchor

zarpar [sar·'par, θar-] *vi* NÁUT to set sail

zarrapastroso, -a [sa·rra·pas·'tro·so, -a; θar-] *adj inf* dirty

zarza ['sar·sa, 'θar·θa] *f* bramble, blackberry bush

zarzal [sar·'sal, θar·'θal] *m* bramble patch

zarzo ['sar·so, 'θar·θo] *m Col* loft ▶ **ser caído del** ~ *inf* to be a sucker

zarzuela [sar·'swe·la, θar·'θwe·la] *f* **1.** MÚS zarzuela (*Spanish musical comedy or operetta*) **2.** CULIN *dish made of fish and shellfish*

zas [sas, θas] *interj* **1.** (*de rapidez*) whoosh!

Z

2. (*de golpe*) bang!

zascandilear [sas·kan·di·le·'ar, θas-] *vi* **1.** (*tontear*) to do foolish things **2.** (*entrometerse*) to meddle

zeta ['se·ta, 'θe-] *f* zed

zigzag [siɣ·'saɣ, θiɣ·'θaɣ] *m* <zigzagues *o* zigzags> zigzag

zigzaguear [siɣ·sa·ɣe·'ar, θiɣ·θa-] *vi* to zigzag

zinc [sin, θin] *m* <cines *o* zines> zinc; **óxido de** ~ zinc oxide

zíper ['si·per, 'θi-] *m Méx* (*cremallera*) zip fastener

zócalo ['so·ka·lo, 'θo-] *m* **1.** ARQUIT pedestal **2.** (*de pared*) skirting board **3.** *Méx* (*plaza*) (town) square

> **i** There are **zócalos** in every Mexican city. In the evenings, young and old alike meet in these public plazas that often resemble parks and are square shaped in accordance with the grid-like layout of the cities. Those who show up sit in groups, jog around, chat, flirt, and practice the art of seeing and being seen.

zodíaco [so·'dia·ko, θo-] *m* zodiac; **signos del** ~ signs of the Zodiac

zombi ['som·bi, 'θom-] *m* **1.** (*muerto*) zombie **2.** (*atontado*) **estar** ~ to be like a zombie

zona ['so·na, 'θo-] *f* **1.** *t.* POL, GEO, METEO (*general*) zone; (*terreno*) belt; (*área*) region; ~ **de ensanche** area to be built up; ~ **euro** euro area; ~ **franca** (duty-)free zone; ~ **de influencia** area of influence; ~ **peatonal** pedestrian precinct; ~ **urbana** urban area; ~ **verde** green belt **2.** DEP (*baloncesto: área*) area; (*defensa*) zone defender; (*falta*) zone fault

zoncera [son·'se·ra, θon·'θe-] *f AmL*, **zoncería** [son·se·'ri·a, θon·θe-] *f* (*tontería*) foolishness

zonzo, -a ['son·so, -a; 'θon·θo, -a] *adj* **1.** (*aburrido*) dull **2.** *AmL* (*tonto*) stupid

zoo ['so·o, 'θo·o] *m* zoo

zoología [so·lo·'xi·a/so·o·lo·'xi·a; θo-] *f* zoology

zoológico, -a [so·'lo·xi·ko/so·o·'lo·xi·ko, -a; θo-] *adj* zoological; **parque** ~ zoo

zoólogo, -a [so·'o·lo·ɣo, -a; θo-] *m, f* zoologist

zopenco, -a [so·'pen·ko, -a; θo-] **I.** *adj* oafish **II.** *m, f* dolt

zopilote [so·pi·'lo·te, θo-] *m Méx* ZOOL turkey vulture

zoquete [so·'ke·te, θo-] *m* **1.** (*madera*) block **2.** (*tonto*) blockhead **3.** *Arg* (*calcetín*) sock

zorra ['so·rra, 'θo-] *f* **1.** ZOOL vixen **2.** *inf* (*prostituta*) whore; (*insulto*) bitch **3.** *inf* (*borrachera*) drunkenness

zorrera [so·'rre·ra, θo-] *f* **1.** (*de zorros*) earth **2.** (*habitación*) smoky room **3.** (*modorra*) drowsiness

zorrillo [so·'rri·jo, θo·'rri·ʎo] *m AmL* (*mofeta*) skunk

zorro ['so·rro, 'θo-] *m* **1.** ZOOL fox **2.** (*piel*) fox skin **3.** *inf* (*astuto*) crafty fellow ▶ **hacerse el** ~ to act stupid; **estar** **hecho** **unos** ~**s** to be dead beat; **poner a alguien hecho unos** ~**s** to tire sb to death

zorzal [sor·'sal, θor·'θal] *m* **1.** ZOOL thrush **2.** (*listo*) shrewd person **3.** *AmL* (*papanatas*) simpleton

zote ['so·te, 'θo-] **I.** *adj* foolish **II.** *mf* fool

zozobra [so·'so·βra, θo·'θo-] *f* anxiety

zozobrar [so·so·'brar, θo·'θo-] **I.** *vi* **1.** (*barco*) to capsize **2.** (*plan*) to fail **3.** (*persona*) to hesitate **II.** *vt* **1.** (*barco*) to sink **2.** (*plan*) to spoil

zueco ['swe·ko, 'θwe-] *m* clog

zumba ['sum·ba, 'θum-] *f* **1.** (*cencerro*) mule bell **2.** (*juguete*) rattle **3.** (*burla*) teasing **4.** *AmL* (*paliza*) beating

zumbado, -a [sum·'ba·do, -a; θum-] *adj* **estar** ~ *inf* to be nuts

zumbar [sum·'bar, θum-] **I.** *vi* **1.** (*abejorro, máquina*) to buzz; **salir zumbando** to rush [*o* zoom] off **2.** (*oídos*) to hum **II.** *vt* **1.** (*golpe*) to deal **2.** *AmL* (*arrojar*) to throw; (*expulsar*) to chuck out **3.** (*guasear*) to mock **III.** *vr:* ~**se** to make fun

zumbido [sum··'bi··do, θum-] *m* **1.** (*ruido*) hum; ~ **de los oídos** ringing in the ears **2.** *inf* (*golpe*) clout

zumo ['su··mo, 'θu-] *m* **1.** (*de frutas*) juice **2.** *fig* (*utilidad*) profit; **sacar** ~ **de algo** to get benefit from sth

zupay [su·'pai, θu-] *m AmL* (*demonio*) devil

zurcir <c→z> [sur·'sir, θur·'θir] *vt* to mend; **¡que te zurzan!** *inf* to hell with you!

zurdo, -a ['sur·do, -a; 'θur-] **I.** *adj* left-handed **II.** *m, f* left-handed person

zurra ['su··rra, 'θur-] *f* **1.** (*de la piel*) tanning **2.** (*paliza*) hiding; **dar una** ~ **a alguien** to give sb a hiding

zurrar [su·'rrar, θur-] *vt* **1.** (*pieles*) to tan **2.** *inf* (*apalizar*) to beat **3.** *inf* (*criticar*) to knock

zurriago [su·'rrja·ɣo, θur-] *m* (*látigo*) whip

zurrumbanco, -a [su·rrum·'ba·ko, -a; θur-] *adj CRi, Méx* half-drunk, light-headed

zurullo [su·'ru·jo, θur·'ru·ʎo] *m inf* **1.** (*grumo*) lump **2.** (*excremento*) turd *vulg*

zutano, -a [su·'ta·no, -a; θur-] *m, f* fulano y ~ Tom, Dick and Harry; **fulano y ~ se han casado** what's-his-name and you-know-who have gotten married (*when you can't remember sb's name*)

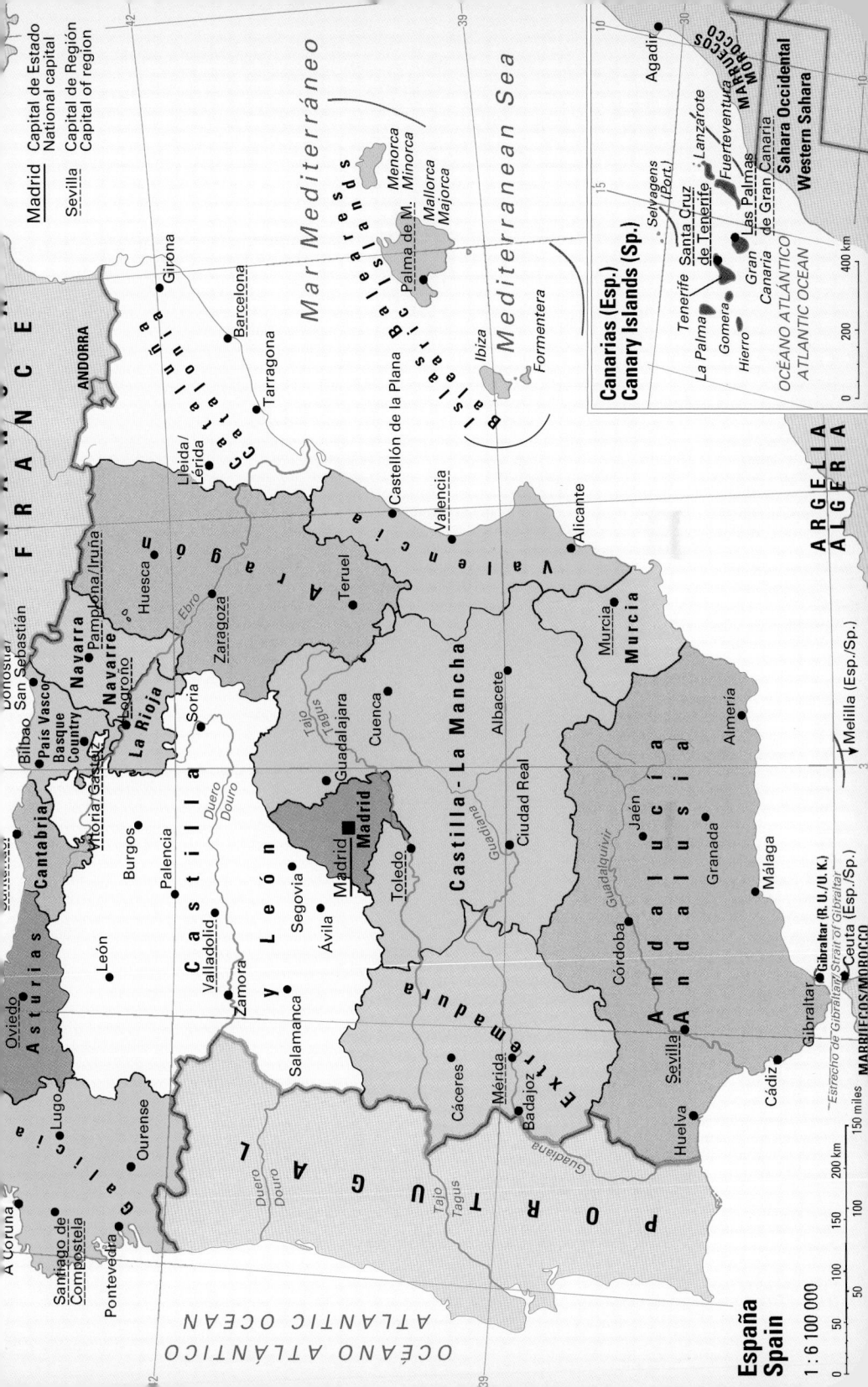

España
Spain
1 : 6 100 000

Capital de Estado
National capital
Capital de Región
Capital of region

Madrid

Sevilla

OCÉANO ATLÁNTICO
ATLANTIC OCEAN

Mar Mediterráneo

Mediterranean Sea

F R A N C E

ANDORRA

A R G E L I A
A L G E R I A

MARRUECOS/MOROCCO

P O R T U G A L

Galicia

Asturias

Cantabria

País Vasco
Basque Country

Navarra
Navarre

La Rioja

Castilla y León

Castilla-La Mancha

Extremadura

Andalucía

Murcia

Comunidad Valenciana

Aragón

Cataluña

Islas Baleares

Canarias (Esp.)
Canary Islands (Sp.)

OCÉANO ATLÁNTICO
ATLANTIC OCEAN

MARRUECOS
MOROCCO

Sahara Occidental
Western Sahara

A Coruña
Santiago de Compostela
Pontevedra
Ourense
Lugo
Oviedo
Gijón
Santander
Bilbao
Donostia/San Sebastián
Vitoria-Gasteiz
Pamplona/Iruña
Logroño
Huesca
Soria
Burgos
Palencia
León
Zamora
Valladolid
Salamanca
Segovia
Ávila
Madrid
Guadalajara
Zaragoza
Teruel
Cuenca
Toledo
Ciudad Real
Albacete
Cáceres
Mérida
Badajoz
Córdoba
Jaén
Granada
Sevilla
Huelva
Cádiz
Málaga
Almería
Murcia
Alicante
Valencia
Castellón de la Plana
Tarragona
Barcelona
Girona
Lleida/Lérida
Gibraltar (R.U./U.K.)
Ceuta (Esp./Sp.)
Melilla (Esp./Sp.)

Duero
Douro
Ebro
Tajo
Tagus
Guadiana
Guadalquivir

Estrecho de Gibraltar
Strait of Gibraltar

Ibiza
Formentera
Mallorca
Majorca
Menorca
Minorca
Palma de M.
Palma de Mallorca
Majorca

Agadir
Selvagens (Port.)
La Palma
Tenerife
Gomera
Hierro
Santa Cruz de Tenerife
Gran Canaria
Las Palmas de Gran Canaria
Fuerteventura
Lanzarote

El mundo hispanohablante
The Spanish-speaking world

: 91 500 000

1000	2000	3000 km
1000		2000 miles

Países donde el español es
lengua oficial y materna

Countries where Spanish is official language
and mother tongue

Países donde el español es lengua oficial

Countries where Spanish is official language

Labels on map:

ESPAÑA
SPAIN

Islas Canarias (Esp.)
Canary Islands (Sp.)

Trópico de Cáncer
Tropic of Cancer

Círculo Polar Ártico
Arctic Circle

MÉXICO
MEXICO

CUBA

P. R.

D.

GUATEMALA
EL SALVADOR

HONDURAS
NICARAGUA

COSTA RICA   P.

VENEZUELA

COLOMBIA

Ecuador
Equator

G.

ECUADOR

G.-E.

OCÉANO
PACÍFICO

PACIFIC
OCEAN

OCÉANO
ATLÁNTICO

ATLANTIC
OCEAN

PERÚ
PERU

BOLIVIA

PARAGUAY

Trópico de Capricornio
Tropic of Capricorn

Isla de Pascua (Chile)
Easter Island (Chile)

CHILE

ARGENTINA

URUGUAY

B.

OCÉANO
PACÍFICO

PACIFIC
OCEAN

FILIPINAS
PHILIPPINES

Ecuador
Equator

OCÉANO
ÍNDICO

INDIAN
OCEAN

Países donde el español es practicado por una minoría
Countries where Spanish is spoken by a minority

B.   Islas Baleares (Esp.)
       Balearic Islands (Sp.)
D.   REPÚBLICA DOMINICANA
       DOMINICAN REPUBLIC
G.   Islas de los Galápagos (Esp.)
       Galapagos Islands (Sp.)
G.-E. GUINEA ECUATORIAL
       EQUATORIAL GUINEA
P.   PANAMÁ
       PANAMA
P. R. Puerto Rico (EE. UU./U. S.)

Hispanoamérica
Spanish America

ESTADOS UNIDOS/UNITED STATES

M É X I C O

Golfo de México
Gulf of Mexico

La Habana
Havana

CUBA

JAMAICA

Mar Caribe
Caribbean Sea

Trópico de Cáncer
Tropic of Cancer

OCÉANO
ATLÁNTICO

Santo Domingo
H. D.
San Juan
P. R.

Cd. de México
Mexico City

Cd. de Guatemala
Guatemala City
San Salvador

G.
HONDURAS
Tegucigalpa
E.
NICARAGUA
Managua

Caracas

VENEZUELA

Orinoco

GUYANA

SURI-
NAME
G. F.

San José

COSTA RICA
P.
Panamá
Panama City

Santa Fe de Bogotá
Bogotá

COLOMBIA

Quito

ECUADOR

Amazonas

Ecuador
Equator

P
E
R
Ú

B R A S I L
B R A Z I L

Lima

La Paz

BOLIVIA

OCÉANO PACÍFICO
PACIFIC OCEAN

PARAGUAY

P
a
r
a
g
u
a
y

P
a
r
a
n
á

Asunción

Trópico de Capricornio
Tropic of Capricorn

A
R
G
E
N
T
I
N
A

C
H
I
L
E

P
a
r
a
n
á

Santiago

Buenos
Aires

URUGUAY
Montevideo

Río de la Plata

ATLANTIC
OCEAN

Est. de Drake
Drake Passage

Círculo Polar Antártico   Antarctic Circle

1 : 58 100 000

0   500   1000   1500   2000 km

0   500   1000 miles

D.   REPÚBLICA DOMINICANA
     DOMINICAN REPUBLIC
E.   EL SALVADOR
G.   GUATEMALA
G. F. Guayana Francesa
     French Guiana

H.   HAITÍ
     HAITI
P.   PANAMÁ
     PANAMA
P. R. Puerto Rico
     (EE. UU./U. S.)

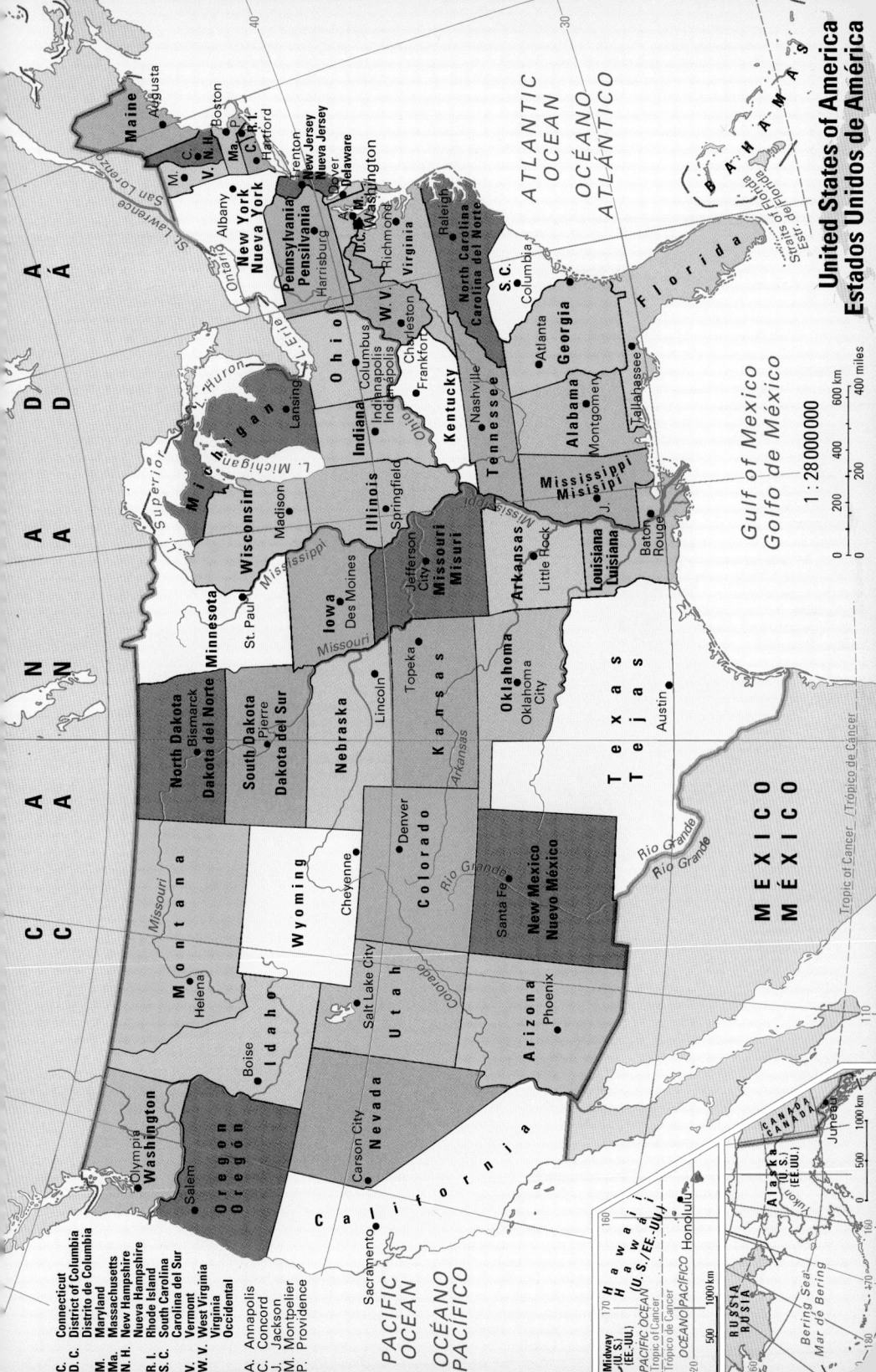

United States of America
Estados Unidos de América

1 : 28 000 000

C.   Connecticut
D. C.   District of Columbia / Distrito de Columbia
M.   Maryland
Ma.   Massachusetts
N. H.   New Hampshire / Nueva Hampshire
R. I.   Rhode Island
S. C.   South Carolina / Carolina del Sur
V.   Vermont
W. V.   West Virginia / Occidental

A.   Annapolis
J.   Jackson
M.   Montpelier
P.   Providence

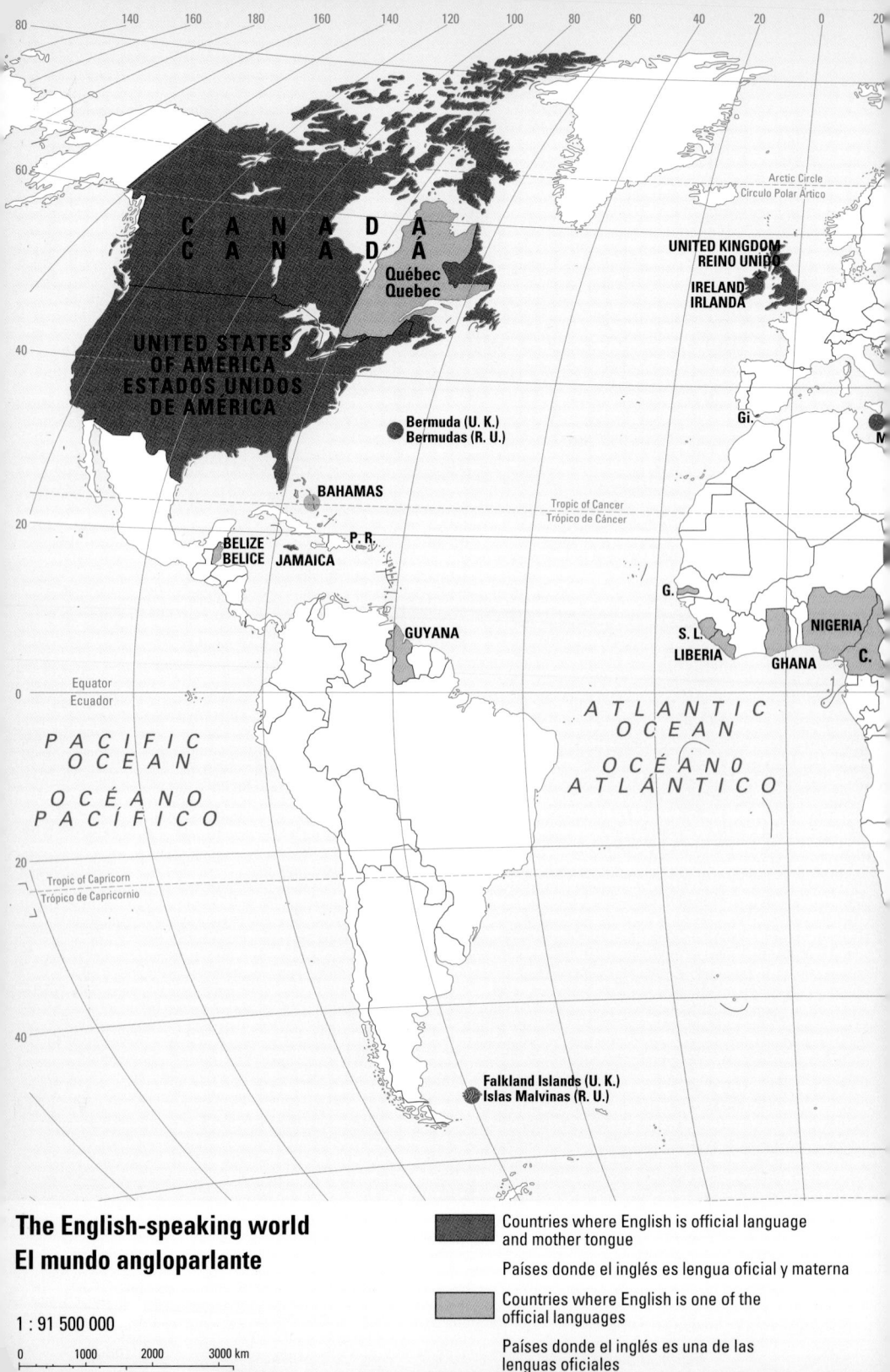

The English-speaking world
El mundo angloparlante

1 : 91 500 000

| 0 | 1000 | 2000 | 3000 km |

| 1000 | | 2000 miles |

Countries where English is official language
and mother tongue

Países donde el inglés es lengua oficial y materna

Countries where English is one of the
official languages

Países donde el inglés es una de las
lenguas oficiales

CANADA
CANADÁ

Québec
Quebec

UNITED STATES
OF AMERICA
ESTADOS UNIDOS
DE AMÉRICA

UNITED KINGDOM
REINO UNIDO

IRELAND
IRLANDA

Arctic Circle
Círculo Polar Ártico

Gi.

M

Bermuda (U. K.)
Bermudas (R. U.)

BAHAMAS

Tropic of Cancer
Trópico de Cáncer

BELIZE
BELICE

P. R.

JAMAICA

G.

S. L.

LIBERIA

NIGERIA

GHANA

C.

GUYANA

Equator
Ecuador

ATLANTIC
OCEAN

OCÉANO
ATLÁNTICO

PACIFIC
OCEAN

OCÉANO
PACÍFICO

Tropic of Capricorn
Trópico de Capricornio

Falkland Islands (U. K.)
Islas Malvinas (R. U.)

PAKISTAN
PAKISTÁN

INDIA

SRI
LANKA

HONGKONG

PACIFIC
OCEAN

OCÉANO
PACÍFICO

N.

Gu.

PALAU

S.

KENYA
KENIA

TANZANIA

SEYCHELLES

INDIAN
OCEAN

OCÉANO
ÍNDICO

MALAWI

MAURITIUS
MAURICIO

SW.

AUSTRALIA

Equator
Ecuador

P.

VANUATU

S. I.

NEW ZEALAND
NUEVA ZELANDA

60   80   100   120   140   160   180   160   140   120   100   80   60

60

40

20

0

40

ANDA

MBIA

Z.

1

2

3
4

5

6
7

8
9

BOTSWANA
BOTSUANA
CAMEROON
CAMERÚN
THE GAMBIA
GAMBIA
Gibraltar (U. K./R. U.)
Guam (U.S./EE.UU.)
LESOTHO
LESOTO

N. Northern Mariana Is. (U. S.)
    Is. Marianas del Norte
    (EE. UU.)
P. PAPUA NEW GUINEA
    PAPÚA NUEVA GUINEA
P. R. Puerto Rico (U. S./EE. UU.)
S. SINGAPORE
    SINGAPUR
SW. SWAZILAND
    SWAZILANDIA

S. A. SOUTH AFRICA
       SUDÁFRICA
S. I. SOLOMON ISLANDS
       ISLAS SALOMÓN
S. L. SIERRA LEONE
       SIERRA LEONA
Z.   ZIMBABWE

Countries in the Pacific Ocean:
Países en el Océano Pacífico:

① Midway (U. S./EE. UU.)
② MARSHALL ISLANDS
   ISLAS MARSHALL
③ NAURU
④ KIRIBATI
⑤ TUVALU

⑥ Western Samoa
   Samoa Occidental
⑦ American Samoa
   Samoa Americana
⑧ FIJI
⑨ TONGA

Canada
Canadá

1 : 30 000 000

0   500   1000   1500 km

RUSSIA
RUSIA

ICELAND
ISLANDIA

Bering Sea
Mar de Bering

Beaufort Sea
Mar de Beaufort

A l a s k a
(USA)
(EE.UU.)

Yukon River
R. Yukón

Gulf of Alaska
Golfo de Alaska

PACIFIC OCEAN
OCÉANO PACÍFICO

Whitehorse

Yukon
Territory
Territorio
del Yukón

Mackenzie River
R. Mackenzie

Northwest Territories
Territorios del Noroeste

Yellowknife

Great Bear Lake
Gran Lago del Oso

Gt. Slave L.
Gran Lago
del Esclavo

British
Columbia
Columbia
Británica

Victoria

Peace River
R. de la Paz

Athabasca

Columbia

Alberta

Edmonton

Lake Athabasca
Lago Athabasca

Saskatchewan

Regina

Manitoba

Nelson

Lake Winnipeg
Lago Winnipeg

Winnipeg

Nunavut

Iqaluit

Baffin Island
Tierra de Baffin

Baffin Bay
Bahía de Baffin

Arctic Circle
Círculo Polar Ártico

Greenland
(Denm.)
Groenlandia
(Dinam.)

Labrador Sea
Mar del Labrador

ATLANTIC OCEAN
OCÉANO
ATLÁNTICO

Hudson Bay
Bahía /
Mar de Hudson

C A N A D A
C A N A D Á

Newfoundland and Labrador
Terranova y Labrador

St. John's
Saint John's

St. Pierre and
Miquelon (Fr.)
Saint Pierre y
Miquelon (Fr.)

Charlottetown

Fredericton

Halifax

P.E.I.

N. B.

N. S.

N. B.   New Brunswick
        Nuevo Brunswick
N. S.   Nova Scotia
        Nueva Escocia
P. E. I. Prince Edward Island

Quebec

Québec
Quebec

St. Lawrence River
R. San Lorenzo

Ottawa

Ontario

Toronto

Lake Ontario
Lago Ontario

Lake Erie
Lago Erie

Lake Huron
Lago Huron

Lake Michigan
Lago Michigan

Lake Superior
Lago Superior

Missouri

Mississippi

U N I T E D   S T A T E S

A

A, a [eɪ] *n* **1.** (*letter*) A, a *f;* ~ **as in Alpha** A de Antonio; **to get from** ~ **to B** ir de un lugar a otro; **from** ~ **to Z** de cabo a rabo **2.** MUS (*note*) la *m* **3.** SCHOOL ≈ sobresaliente *m*

a [ə, *stressed:* eɪ] *indef art before consonant,* **an** [ən, *stressed:* æn] *before vowel* **1.** (*in general*) un, una; ~ **car** un coche; ~ **house** una casa; **in** ~ **day or two** en unos días **2.** (*not translated*) **do you have** ~ **car?** ¿tienes coche?; **she is** ~ **teacher** es maestra; **a hundred days** cien días **3.** (*to express prices, rates*) **$2** ~ **dozen** 2 dólares la docena; **$6** ~ **week** 6 dólares por semana **4.** (*before person's name*) ~ **Mr. Robinson** un tal Sr. Robinson

a. *abbr of* **answer** R

AA [ˌeɪ·ˈeɪ] *abbr of* **Alcoholics Anonymous** AA

AAA [ˈeɪ·eɪ·ˈeɪ] **1.** AUTO *abbr of* **American Automobile Association** ≈ RACE *m* **2.** *abbr of* **Amateur Athletic Association** *federación de atletismo aficionado*

aback [ə·ˈbæk] *adv* **to take sb** ~ coger a alguien de improviso; **to be taken** ~ (**by sth**) quedarse desconcertado (por algo)

abacus [ˈæb·ə·kəs] *n* ábaco *m*

abandon [ə·ˈbæn·dən] **I.** *vt* **1.** (*vehicle, place, person*) abandonar, dejar; **to** ~ **ship** evacuar el barco **2.** (*give up: plan*) renunciar a; (*game*) suspender **3.** (*lose self-control*) **to** ~ **oneself to sth** entregarse a algo **II.** *n* abandono *m;* **with** (**wild**) ~ con desenfreno

abandoned [ə·ˈbæn·dənd] *adj* **1.** (*place, vehicle*) abandonado, -a **2.** (*person*) desamparado, -a

abashed [ə·ˈbæʃt] *adj* avergonzado, -a; **to be** ~ **at sth** avergonzarse de algo

abate [ə·ˈbeɪt] *vi* **1.** (*noise, anger*) disminuir **2.** (*wind*) amainar

abatement *n* disminución *f*

abattoir [ˈæb·ə·twar] *n* matadero *m*

abbess [ˈæb·əs] *n* REL abadesa *f*

abbey [ˈæb·i] *n* abadía *f*

abbot [ˈæb·ət] *n* REL abad *m*

abbreviate [ə·ˈbri·vi·eɪt] *vt* abreviar

abbreviation [ə·ˌbri·vɪ·ˈeɪ·ʃən] *n* abreviatura *f*

ABC[1] [ˌeɪ·bi·ˈsi] *n pl* **1.** (*alphabet*) abecedario *m* **2.** *pl* (*rudiments*) abecé *m,* nociones *fpl* básicas

ABC[2] [ˌeɪ·bi·ˈsi] *n* TV *abbr of* **American Broadcasting Company** *compañía estadounidense de radiotelevisión*

abdicate [ˈæb·dɪ·keɪt] **I.** *vi* abdicar **II.** *vt* (*right*) renunciar a; (*throne*) abdicar (de)

abdication [ˌæb·dɪ·ˈkeɪ·ʃən] *n* **1.** (*of right*) renuncia *f* **2.** (*of throne*) abdicación *f*

abdomen [ˈæb·də·mən] *n* ANAT abdomen *m*

abdominal [æb·ˈdam·ə·nəl] *adj* abdominal

abduct [æb·ˈdʌkt] *vt* secuestrar, plagiar *AmL*

abduction [æb·ˈdʌk·ʃən] *n* secuestro *m,* plagio *m AmL*

aberration [ˌæb·ə·ˈreɪ·ʃən] *n* aberración *f*

abet [ə·ˈbet] <-tt-> *vt* instigar, incitar; **to aid and** ~ **sb** ser cómplice de alguien

abeyance [ə·ˈbeɪ·əns] *n* **to fall into** ~ (*custom*) caer en desuso

abhor [æb·ˈhɔr] <-rr-> *vt* aborrecer

abhorrence [æb·ˈhɔr·əns] *n* aborrecimiento *m*

abhorrent *adj* aborrecible

abide [ə·ˈbaɪd] <-d *o* abode, -d *o* abode> *vt* soportar; **I can't** ~ **her** no la soporto
 ◆**abide by** *vt* **1.** (*rule, decision*) atenerse a **2.** (*promise*) cumplir

abiding *adj* duradero, -a

ability [ə·ˈbɪl·ə·t̬i] <-ies> *n* **1.** (*capability*) capacidad *f;* **to the best of one's** ~ lo mejor que uno pueda **2.** (*talent*) aptitud *f* **3.** *pl* (*skills*) dotes *fupl*

abject [ˈæb·dʒekt] *adj* **1.** (*wretched*) abyecto, -a **2.** (*absolute: poverty, failure*) absoluto, -a

ablaze [ə·ˈbleɪz] *adj* en llamas; *fig* resplandeciente

able [ˈeɪ·bəl] *adj* (*capable: politician, student*) capaz; **to be** ~ **to do sth** (*have ability, manage*) poder hacer algo; (*have knowledge*) saber hacer algo

able-bodied *adj* sano, -a y fuerte; ~ **seaman** marinero *m* de primera

ABM [ˌeɪ·bi·ˈem] *n abbr of* **antiballistic missile** misil *m* antibalístico

abnormal [æb·ˈnɔr·məl] *adj* **1.** (*feature*) anómalo, -a **2.** (*person*) anormal

abnormality [ˌæb·nɔr·ˈmæl·ə·t̬i] <-ies> *n* **1.** (*abnormal feature*) anomalía *f* **2.** (*unusualness*) anormalidad *f*

aboard [ə·ˈbɔrd] **I.** *adv* a bordo; **all** ~! ¡pasajeros a bordo! **II.** *prep* a bordo de; **to go** ~ **a boat** subir a una barca; **to go** ~ **a plane** embarcar en un avión, subir a un avión

abode [ə·ˈboud] **I.** *vi pt, pp of* **abide II.** *n form* domicilio *m*

abolish [ə·ˈbal·ɪʃ] *vt* abolir

abolition [ˌæb·ə·ˈlɪʃ·ən] *n* abolición *f*

abominable [ə·ˈbam·ə·nə·bəl] *adj* abominable

abominate [ə·ˈbam·ə·neɪt] *vt* abominar (de)

abomination [ə·ˌbam·ə·ˈneɪ·ʃən] *n* **1.** (*abominable thing*) abominación *f* **2.** (*disgust*) aversión *f*

aboriginal [ˌæb·ə·ˈrɪdʒ·ə·nəl] **I.** *adj* aborigen **II.** *n* aborigen *mf* (de Australia)

Aborigine [ˌæb·ə·ˈrɪdʒ·ə·ni] *n* aborigen *mf* (de Australia)

abort [ə·ˈbɔrt] **I.** *vt* **1.** MED abortar **2.** *a.* COMPUT abandonar **II.** *vi* **1.** MED abortar **2.** (*fail*) fracasar

abortion [ə·ˈbɔr·ʃən] *n* MED aborto *m* (provocado); **to have an** ~ abortar, tener un aborto

abortive [ə·ˈbɔr·t̬ɪv] *adj* malogrado, -a

abound [ə·ˈbaʊnd] *vi* abundar (en)

about [ə·ˈbaʊt] **I.** *prep* **1.** (*on subject of*) sobre, acerca de; **a book** ~ **football** un libro sobre fútbol; **what is the film** ~? ¿de qué trata la película? **2.**(*characteristic of*) **that's what I like ~ him** eso es lo que me gusta de él **3.**(*surrounding*) alrededor de; **the garden ~ the house** el jardín alrededor de la casa **4.**(*in and through*) por; **to go ~ a place** andar por un lugar ▶ **how ~ that!** ¡vaya!; **how ~ a drink?** ¿qué tal si tomamos algo?; **what ~ it?** (*suggestion*) ¿quieres/queréis?; (*so what?*) ¿y qué? **II.** *adv* **1.**(*approximately*) aproximadamente; **~ my size** más o menos de mi tamaño; **~ 5 lbs.** cerca de 5 libras; **~ here** más o menos aquí; **~ 5 years ago** hace unos cinco años; **~ twenty** unos veinte; **to have had just ~ enough of sth** estar harto de algo; **that's ~ it for today** eso es todo por hoy **2.**(*almost*) casi; **to be (just) ~ ready** estar casi listo **3.**(*on the point of*) **to be ~ to do sth** estar a punto de hacer algo **4.**(*around*) **all ~** por todas partes; **to be somewhere ~** estar por aquí; **is Paul ~?** ¿está Paul por ahí? **5.**(*willing to*) **not to be ~ to do sth** no estar dispuesto a hacer algo

about-face *n* **1.**MIL media vuelta *f* **2.**(*on opinion*) cambio *m* drástico de opinión; (*in position*) cambio *m* drástico de postura

above [ə·'bʌv] **I.** *prep* **1.**(*on the top of*) encima de **2.**(*over*) sobre; **~ suspicion** por encima de toda sospecha **3.**(*greater than, superior to*) por encima de; **~ 3** más de 3; **those ~ the age of 70** los mayores de 70 años; **he is not ~ lying** es muy capaz de mentir; **~ all** sobre todo; **to shout ~ the noise** tener que gritar porque hay ruido; **it's ~ me** no lo entiendo **4.**GEO (*upstream*) más arriba de; (*north of*) al norte de **II.** *adv* encima, arriba; **the floor ~** la planta de arriba; **up ~ sth** por encima de algo; **from ~** de las alturas; **see ~** (*in text*) véase más arriba **III.** *adj* susodicho, -a **IV.** *n* **the ~** lo antedicho

aboveboard *adj* legítimo, -a

abovementioned *adj* anteriormente mencionado, -a

abrasion [ə·'breɪ·ʒən] *n* MED abrasión *f*

abrasive [ə·'breɪ·sɪv] **I.** *adj* **1.**(*rough*) abrasivo, -a **2.**(*in manner*) agresivo, -a **II.** *n* abrasivo *m*

abreast [ə·'brest] *adv* **1.**(*side by side*) **two/three ~** en fila de a dos/tres **2.**(*up to date*) **to be/keep ~ of sth** estar/mantenerse al corriente de algo

abridge [ə·'brɪdʒ] *vt* abreviar; **an ~d version** una versión abreviada

abridgement *n*, **abridgment** [ə·'brɪdʒ·mənt] *n* **1.**(*version*) compendio *m* **2.**(*action*) abreviación *f*

abroad [ə·'brɔd] *adv* **1.**(*in foreign country*) en el extranjero; **from ~** del extranjero; **to be ~** estar en el extranjero; **to go ~** ir al extranjero; **at home and ~** dentro y fuera del país **2.** *form* (*outside*) fuera; **the news quickly spread ~** la noticia se divulgó rápidamente

abrupt [ə·'brʌpt] *adj* **1.**(*sudden*) repentino, -a; (*change*) brusco, -a; (*end*) inesperado, -a **2.**(*brusque*) brusco, -a **3.**(*steep*) abrupto, -a

ABS [ˌeɪ·bi·'es] *n abbr of* **antilock braking system** ABS *m*

abscess ['æb·ses] *n* absceso *m*

abscond [əb·'skand] *vi* fugarse; **to ~ with sb/sth** fugarse con alguien/algo

absence ['æb·səns] *n* **1.**(*not being present: of person, thing*) ausencia *f*; **in the ~ of** en ausencia de; **on leave of ~** MIL de permiso **2.**(*lack of: of money, information*) carencia *f*; **in the ~ of** a falta de

absent[1] ['æb·sənt] *adj* **1.**(*not present*) ausente; **~ without leave** MIL ausente sin permiso **2.**(*lacking*) que falta; **to be ~ in sth** no estar presente en algo **3.**(*distracted*) ausente, distraído, -a

absent[2] [əb·'sent] *vt form* **to ~ oneself (from sth)** ausentarse (de algo)

absentee [ˌæb·sən·'ti] *n* ausente *mf*

absentee ballot *n* voto *m* por correo

absenteeism *n* absentismo *m*

absentee owner *n* propietario, , -a *m*, *f* absentista (*que apenas reside en su propiedad*)

absentee voting *n* voto *m* por correo

absent-minded *adj* despistado, -a, volado, -a *AmL*

absolute ['æb·sə·lut] **I.** *adj* **1.**(*total, not relative*) *a.* POL absoluto, -a; (*denial*) rotundo, -a; (*trust, power, confidence*) pleno, -a; (*disaster*) absoluto, -a, completo, -a **2.** CHEM puro, -a **II.** *n* **the ~** PHILOS lo absoluto

absolutely *adv* **1.**(*comprehensively*) absolutamente; **~!** *inf* ¡claro que sí!; **~ not!** ¡de ninguna manera! **2.**(*very*) totalmente

absolution [ˌæb·sə·'lu·ʃən] *n* REL absolución *f*

absolutism ['æb·sə·lu·ˌtɪz·əm] *n* POL absolutismo *m*

absolve [əb·'zalv] *vt* absolver

absorb [əb·'sɔrb] *vt* **1.**(*liquid*) absorber; (*shock*) amortiguar **2.**(*understand*) asimilar **3.**(*engross*) ocupar; **to get ~ed in sth** estar completamente absorbido por algo; **to be ~ed in one's thoughts** estar abstraído [*o* absorto] en sus pensamientos

absorbent [əb·'sɔr·bənt] *adj* absorbente

absorbing *adj* (*book, story*) absorbente, apasionante

absorption [əb·'sɔrp·ʃən] *n* **1.**(*of liquid*) absorción *f* **2.**(*in book, story*) concentración *f* **3.**(*in work*) dedicación *f* absoluta

abstain [əb·'steɪn] *vi a.* POL abstenerse; **to ~ from (doing) sth** abstenerse de (hacer) algo

abstemious [əb·'sti·mi·əs] *adj* mesurado, -a, comedido, -a

abstention [əb·'sten·ʃən] *n a.* POL abstención *f*

abstinence ['æb·stə·nəns] *n* abstinencia *f*

abstract[1] ['æb·strækt] **I.** *adj* abstracto, -a; **~ art/painting** arte abstracto/pintura abstracta **II.** *n* **1.**(*not concrete*) abstracto *m*; **in the ~** en abstracto **2.**(*summary*) extracto *m*

abstract[2] [əb·'strækt] *vt* **1.** *a.* CHEM extraer **2.**(*summarize*) resumir **3.**(*steal*) robar

abstracted [æb·'stræk·tɪd] *adj* distraído, -a

abstraction [əb·'stræk·ʃən] *n* **1.**(*abstract con-*

cept) abstracción *f* **2.**(*absent-mindedness*) distracción *f*

abstruse [əb·'strus] *adj* abstruso, -a

absurd [əb·'sɜrd] *adj* absurdo, -a

absurdity [əb·'sɜr·də·ṭi] <-ies> *n* **1.**(*absurd state*) absurdo *m;* (*of idea, situation*) ridiculez *f* **2.**(*absurd thing*) disparate *m*, candinga *f Chile*

abundance [ə·'bʌn·dəns] *n* abundancia *f*

abundant [ə·'bʌn·dənt] *adj* abundante

abuse¹ [ə·'bjus] *n* **1.**(*insults*) insultos *mpl,* insultadas *fpl AmL;* **to hurl ~ at sb** lanzar improperios a alguien **2.**(*mistreatment*) maltrato *m* **3.**(*misuse*) abuso *m;* **sexual ~** abuso sexual **4.**(*infringement*) infracción *f; ~ of human rights* violación de los derechos humanos

abuse² [ə·'bjuz] *vt* **1.**(*insult*) insultar **2.**(*mistreat*) maltratar **3.**(*sexually*) abusar de **4.**(*misuse*) abusar de **5.**(*infringe*) infringir

abusive [ə·'bju·sɪv] *adj* **1.**(*language*) insultante, ofensivo, -a **2.**(*person*) agresivo, -a

abut [ə·'bʌt] <-tt-> I. *vt* lindar con II. *vi* **to ~ on** lindar con

abysmal [ə·'bɪz·məl] *adj* pésimo, -a

abyss [ə·'bɪs] *n a. fig* abismo *m*

AC [ˌeɪ·'si] *n abbr of* **alternating current** CA *f*

a/c [ˌeɪ·'si] **1.** *abbr of* **account** c/, cta. **2.** *abbr of* **air conditioning** aire *m* acondicionado, climatización *f*

academic [ˌæk·ə·'dem·ɪk] I. *adj* **1.** UNIV académico, -a; SCHOOL escolar **2.**(*intellectual*) erudito, -a **3.**(*theoretical*) teórico, -a; (*argument*) especulativo **4.**(*irrelevant*) irrelevante II. *n* académico, -a *m, f*

academy [ə·'kæd·ə·mi] <-ies> *n* **1.**(*for special training*) academia *f* **2.**(*prep school*) instituto *m* (*de enseñanza secundaria*) **3.** CINE **the Academy Awards** los Óscars

accede [æk·'sid] *vi* **1.**(*agree*) **to ~ to sth** acceder a algo **2.**(*to a position*) acceder a; **to ~ to the throne** subir al trono

accelerate [ək·'sel·ə·reɪt] I. *vi* (*car*) acelerar; (*growth*) acelerarse II. *vt* acelerar

acceleration [ək·ˌsel·ə·'reɪ·ʃən] *n* aceleración *f*

accelerator [ək·'sel·ə·reɪ·ṭər] *n* **1.** AUTO (*gas pedal*) acelerador *m*, chancleta *f Ven, Col* **2.** PHYS acelerador *m* de partículas

accent [ˈæk·sent] I. *n* **1.** LING, MUS acento *m* **2.** LIT énfasis *m inv* II. *vt* **1.** LIT, MUS acentuar **2.**(*emphasize*) enfatizar

accentuate [æk·'sen·tʃʊ·eɪt] *vt* acentuar

accept [ək·'sept] I. *vt* **1.**(*take when offered*) aceptar **2.**(*approve*) aprobar **3.**(*believe*) creer en **4.**(*acknowledge*) reconocer **5.**(*include socially*) acoger, dar acogida a II. *vi* aceptar

acceptable *adj* (*behavior, suggestion*) aceptable; (*explanation*) admisible

acceptance [ək·'sep·təns] *n* **1.**(*of gift, help*) aceptación *f* **2.**(*approval*) aprobación *f* **3.**(*social*) aceptación *f*

accepted *adj* aceptado, -a; **the ~ procedure** el procedimiento habitual

access [ˈæk·ses] I. *n* entrada *f*, aproches *mpl AmL; a.* COMPUT acceso *m; ~ road* vía *f* de acceso; **to gain ~ to sth** acceder a algo; **to have ~ to sth** tener acceso a algo; **with easy ~** de fácil acceso II. *vt* COMPUT entrar en, acceder a

accessibility [æk·ˌses·ə·'bɪl·ə·ṭi] *n* **1.** accesibilidad *f* **2.** *fig* carácter *m* accesible

accessible [ək·'ses·ə·bəl] *adj* **1.**(*place, work of art*) accesible; (*for the handicapped*) de fácil acceso **2.**(*person*) tratable, accesible

accession [æk·'seʃ·ən] *n* ascenso *m*

accessory [ək·'ses·ə·ri] <-ies> *n* **1.**(*for outfit*) complemento *m*, accesorio *m* **2.**(*for machine, toy*) accesorio *m* **3.** LAW cómplice *mf*

access road *n* (carretera *f* de) acceso *m*, aproches *mpl AmL*

accident [ˈæk·sɪ·dənt] *n* accidente *m; ~ insurance* seguro *m* contra accidentes; **by ~** (*unintended*) sin querer; (*by chance*) por casualidad; **more by ~ than design** más por casualidad que por otra cosa; **~s will happen** son cosas que pasan

accidental [ˌæk·sɪ·'den·təl] *adj* **1.**(*unintentional*) casual, accidental; LAW (*death*) accidental **2.**(*discovery*) fortuito, -a

accident-prone *n* propenso, -a a tener accidentes

acclaim [ə·'kleɪm] I. *vt* aclamar; **critically ~ed** elogiado por la crítica II. *n* aclamación *f*

acclamation [ˌæk·lə·'meɪ·ʃən] *n* aclamación *f*

acclimate [ə·'k·laɪ·mɪt] I. *vi* aclimatarse II. *vt* aclimatar

acclimation [ˌæk·lə·'meɪ·ʃən] *n* aclimatación *f*

accolade [ˈæk·ə·leɪd] *n* elogio *m*

accommodate [ə·'kam·ə·deɪt] *vt* **1.**(*give place to stay*) alojar, hospedar; (*have room for*) albergar, alojar **2.** *form* (*adapt*) adaptar, acomodar; **to ~ oneself to sth** adaptarse a algo **3.**(*satisfy*) complacer

accommodating [ə·'kam·ə·deɪ·ṭɪŋ] *adj* complaciente

accommodation [ə·ˌkam·ə·'deɪ·ʃən] *n* **1.** *pl* (*lodgings*) alojamiento *m* **2.**(*on vehicle, plane*) asientos *mpl* **3.** *form* (*compromise*) acuerdo *m*

accompaniment [ə·'kʌm·pə·nɪ·mənt] *n a.* MUS acompañamiento *m*

accompanist [ə·'kʌm·pə·nɪst] *n* MUS acompañante *mf*

accompany [ə·'kʌm·pə·ni] <-ie-> *vt* (*go with*) acompañar; **to ~ sb on the violin** acompañar a alguien al violín

accomplice [ə·'kam·plɪs] *n* cómplice *mf*

accomplish [ə·'kam·plɪʃ] *vt* **1.**(*achieve*) lograr **2.**(*finish*) concluir; **to ~ a task** realizar una tarea

accomplished [ə·'kam·plɪʃt] *adj* consumado, -a

accomplishment *n* **1.**(*achievement*) logro *m* **2.**(*completion*) conclusión *f; ~ of a task* realización *f* de una tarea **3.**(*skill*) talento *m*

accord [ə·'kɔrd] I. *n* **1.**(*treaty*) convenio *m*

2. (*agreement, harmony*) acuerdo *m;* **on** [*o* **of**] **one's own** ~ de propio acuerdo, voluntariamente; **to be in** ~ **with** estar de acuerdo con **II.** *vt form* conceder **III.** *vi* **to** ~ **with sth** concordar con algo

accordance [ə·'kɔr·dəns] *n* **in** ~ **with** de conformidad con, conforme a

accordingly *adv* **1.** (*appropriately*) en consecuencia **2.** (*therefore*) por consiguiente

according to [ə·'kɔr·dɪŋ·tə] *prep* **1.** (*as told by*) según; ~ **her/what I read** según ella/lo que leí; **to go** ~ **plan** salir según lo previsto **2.** (*as basis*) con arreglo a; ~ **the law** con arreglo a la ley; ~ **the recipe** según la receta

accordion [ə·'kɔr·di·ən] *n* MUS acordeón *m,* filarmónica *f Méx*

accost [ə·'kɔst] *vt* abordar

account [ə·'kaʊnt] **I.** *n* **1.** (*with bank*) cuenta *f* **2.** (*bill*) factura *f;* **to settle an** ~ liquidar una cuenta *f.* *pl* (*financial records*) cuentas *fpl;* **to keep** ~**s** llevar las cuentas; **to keep an** ~ **of sth** llevar la cuenta de algo **4.** (*customer*) cliente *mf* **5.** (*description*) relato *m;* **an** ~ **of sth** un relato [*o* una relación] de algo; **to give an** ~ **of sth** informar sobre algo; **by all** ~**s** a decir de todos; **by her own** ~ según ella misma **6.** (*consideration*) **to take sth into** ~ tomar [*o* tener] algo en cuenta; **to take no** ~ **of sth** no tomar [*o* tener] en cuenta algo, no hacer caso de algo; **on** ~ **of sth** por causa de algo; **on no** ~ de ninguna manera **7.** *form* (*importance*) **of little/no** ~ de poca/ninguna importancia **8.** (*responsibility*) responsabilidad *f;* **on one's own** ~ por cuenta propia; **on sb's** ~ a cuenta de alguien ▶ **to be called to** ~ (**for sth**) tener que rendir cuentas (de algo); **to settle** ~**s with sb** ajustar cuentas con alguien; **to turn sth to** ~ sacar provecho de algo **II.** *vt form* considerar ◆ **account for** *vt* **1.** (*explain*) explicar **2.** (*constitute*) representar

accountability [ə·ˌkaʊn·tə·'bɪl·ɪ·t̬i] *n* responsabilidad *f*

accountable [ə·'kaʊn·tə·bəl] *adj* responsable

accountancy [ə·'kaʊn·tən·si] *n* contabilidad *f*

accountant [ə·'kaʊn·tənt] *n* contable *mf,* contador(a) *m(f) And*

account book *n* libro *m* de contabilidad [*o* de cuentas]

accredit [ə·'kred·ɪt] *vt* **1.** (*recognize: school*) certificar **2.** POL acreditar **3.** (*attribute to*) atribuir

accrue [ə·'kru] *vi* (*increase*) aumentar; (*interest*) acumularse

accumulate [ə·'kjum·jə·leɪt] **I.** *vt* acumular **II.** *vi* acumularse

accumulation [ə·ˌkjum·jə·'leɪ·ʃən] *n* **1.** (*process*) acumulación *f* **2.** (*quantity*) cúmulo *m,* montón *m*

accuracy ['æk·jər·ə·si] *n* precisión *f,* exactitud *f*

accurate ['æk·jər·ɪt] *adj* **1.** (*on target*) certero, -a **2.** (*correct*) preciso, -a, exacto, -a **3.** (*careful*) cuidadoso, -a

accusation [ˌæk·ju·'zeɪ·ʃən] *n* acusación *f*

accusative [ə·'kju·zə·t̬ɪv] LING **I.** *n* acusativo *m* **II.** *adj* acusativo, -a

accusatory [ə·'kju·zə·tɔr·i] *adj form* acusador(a)

accuse [ə·'kjuz] *vt* acusar; **she is** ~**d of...** se la acusa de...

accused [ə·'kjuzd] *n* **the** ~ el acusado, la acusada

accustom [ə·'kʌs·təm] *vt* acostumbrar

accustomed [ə·'kʌs·təmd] *adj* **1.** (*in habit of*) acostumbrado, -a; **to be** ~ **to doing sth** estar acostumbrado a hacer algo; **to grow** ~ **to doing sth** acostumbrarse a hacer algo **2.** (*usual*) usual

AC/DC [ˌeɪ·si·'di·si] *n* **1.** ELEC *abbr of* **alternating current/direct current** corriente *f* alterna/corriente *f* continua **2.** *sl* bisexual *mf,* bi *mf*

ace [eɪs] **I.** *n* **1.** (*playing card*) as *m* **2.** *inf* (*expert*) as *m,* experto, -a *m, f* ▶ **to have an** ~ **up one's sleeve** esconder un as debajo de la manga; **to come within an** ~ **of doing sth** estar a punto de hacer algo **II.** *adj inf* (*expert*) experto, -a **III.** *vt sl* (*perform well in: exam, interview*) bordar

acetate ['æs·ɪ·teɪt] *n* acetato *m*

acetic [ə·'si·t̬ɪk] *adj* acético, -a

acetone ['æs·ɪ·ˌtoʊn] *n* acetona *f*

acetylene [ə·'set·əl·in] *n* acetileno *m*

ache [eɪk] **I.** *n* dolor *m;* ~**s and pains** dolores y achaques **II.** *vi* doler; **I am aching to see her again** me muero de ganas de volver a verla

achieve [ə·'tʃiv] *vt* (*goal, objective*) lograr; (*task*) llevar a cabo; (*victory*) conseguir; (*success*) alcanzar

achievement *n* **1.** (*feat*) hazaña *f;* (*success*) éxito *m,* logro *m* **2.** (*achieving*) realización *f*

acid ['æs·ɪd] **I.** *n* **1.** CHEM ácido *m* **2.** *sl* (*LSD*) ácido *m* **II.** *adj* **1.** CHEM ácido, -a **2.** (*sarcastic*) mordaz

acid house *n* MUS música *f* acid

acidic [ə·'sɪd·ɪk] *adj* ácido, -a

acidify [ə·'sɪd·ɪ·faɪ] <-ie-> **I.** *vt* acidificar **II.** *vi* acidificarse

acidity [ə·'sɪd·ə·t̬i] *n* **1.** CHEM acidez *f* **2.** *fig* mordacidad *f*

acid rain *n* lluvia *f* ácida

acid rock *n* MUS acid rock *m*

acid test *n* prueba *f* de fuego

acid-washed *adj* (*jeans, denim*) deslavado, -a, destintado, -a *Méx*

acknowledge [ək·'nal·ɪdʒ] *vt* **1.** (*admit*) admitir; (*guilt*) confesar **2.** (*recognize*) reconocer; (*letter*) acusar recibo de; (*favor*) agradecer **3.** (*reply to: smile*) devolver; **she refused to** ~ **him** no le devolvió el saludo

acknowledg(e)ment *n* **1.** (*admission*) admisión *f;* (*of guilt*) confesión *f* **2.** (*recognition*) reconocimiento *m* **3.** (*reply*) acuse *m* de recibo **4.** *pl* (*in book*) agradecimientos *mpl*

ACLU [ˌeɪ·si·el·'ju] *n abbr of* **American Civil Liberties Union** *asociación estadounidense* *para la defensa de los derechos civiles*

acne ['æk·ni] *n* acné *m*

acorn ['eɪ·kɔrn] *n* BOT bellota *f*

acorn squash *n* calabaza con forma de bellota de color verde oscuro que se da en invierno

acoustic(al) [ə·'ku·stɪk(əl)] I. *adj* acústico, -a II. *npl* acústica *f*

acoustic guitar *n* guitarra *f* acústica

acoustic nerve *n* ANAT nervio *m* auditivo

acquaint [ə·'kweɪnt] *vt* 1. (*know*) **to be/ become ~ed with sb/sth** conocer a alguien 2. (*familiarize*) familiarizar; **to ~ oneself with sth** familiarizarse con algo; **to be ~ed with sth** estar al corriente de algo

acquaintance [ə·'kweɪn·təns] *n* 1. (*person*) conocido, -a *m, f* 2. (*relationship*) relación *f;* **to make sb's ~** conocer a alguien 3. (*knowledge*) conocimiento *m*

acquiesce [ˌæk·wɪ·'es] *vi form* **to ~ in sth** estar conforme con algo

acquiescence [ˌæk·wɪ·'es·əns] *n form* conformidad *f,* aquiescencia *f*

acquiescent [ˌæk·wɪ·'es·ənt] *adj form* conforme, aquiescente

acquire [ə·'kwaɪr] *vt* adquirir; **to ~ a taste for sth** tomarle el gusto a algo

acquired immunity deficiency syndrome *n* síndrome *m* de inmunodeficiencia adquirida

acquisition [ˌæk·wɪ·'zɪʃ·ən] *n* adquisición *f*

acquisitive [ə·'kwɪz·ɪ·tɪv] *adj* codicioso, -a

acquit [ə·'kwɪt] <-tt-> *vt* 1. LAW absolver; **to ~ sb of a charge** absolver a alguien de una acusación 2. **to ~ oneself well/badly** salir bien/mal parado

acquittal [ə·'kwɪt̮·əl] *n* LAW absolución *f*

acre ['eɪ·kər] *n* acre *m* (*4840 sq. yards; 4047 sq. meters);* **~s of space** *inf* un montón de espacio

acreage ['eɪ·krədʒ] *n* superficie (en acres) *f*

acrid ['æk·rɪd] *adj* 1. (*smell, taste*) acre 2. *fig* áspero, -a

acrimonious [ˌæk·rɪ·'moʊ·ni·əs] *adj* (*remark*) mordaz; (*debate*) reñido, -a

acrimony ['æk·rɪ·moʊ·ni] *n form* acrimonia *f*

acrobat ['æk·rə·bæt] *n* acróbata *mf*

acrobatic [ˌæk·rə·'bæt̮·ɪk] *adj* acrobático, -a

acronym ['æk·rə·nɪm] *n* sigla *f*

acrophobia [ˌæk·rə·'foʊ·bi·ə] *n* PSYCH acrofobia *f*

across [ə·'krɔs] I. *prep* 1. (*on other side of*) al otro lado de; **just ~ the street** justo al otro lado de la calle; **~ from sb/sth** enfrente de alguien/algo 2. (*from one side to other*) a través de; **to walk ~ the bridge** cruzar el puente andando; **the bridge ~ the river** el puente que cruza el río; **to go ~ the ocean to Europe** ir a Europa cruzando el océano II. *adv* 1. (*in distance*) de un lado a otro; **to run/swim ~** cruzar corriendo/a nado; **to be 10 feet ~** tener 10 pies de ancho 2. **to come ~ sth** (*find: an old photo*) encontrar(se) algo 3. (*conveying meaning*) **to get a point ~** hacer entender una idea

across-the-board *adj* (*pay hike, ruling*) general, global

acrylic [ə·'krɪl·ɪk] *n* acrílico *m*

acrylic paint *n* pintura *f* acrílica

act [ækt] I. *n* 1. (*action*) acto *m;* **~ of charity** obra *f* de caridad; **an ~ of God** LAW un caso de fuerza mayor; **the Acts of the Apostles** REL los Hechos de los Apóstoles 2. **to catch sb in the ~** coger a alguien con las manos en la masa 2. (*performance*) número *m;* **a hard ~ to follow** un número difícil de repetir 3. (*pretence*) fingimiento *m* 4. THEAT acto *m* 5. LAW ley *f* ▶ **to get one's ~ together** *inf* arreglárselas; **to get in on the ~** lograr tomar parte en el asunto II. *vi* 1. (*take action*) actuar; **to ~ for sb** representar a alguien 2. (*behave*) portarse 3. (*take effect*) dar resultado 4. THEAT actuar 5. (*pretend*) fingir III. *vt* THEAT representar; **to ~ the part of sb** hacer el papel de alguien; **to ~ the fool** hacer el tonto

◆ **act on** *vt* obrar de acuerdo con

◆ **act out** *vt* (*scene*) representar

◆ **act up** *vi inf* 1. (*person*) hacer de las suyas 2. (*machine*) fallar, no funcionar 3. (*knee, elbow, back*) (*hurt*) doler

acting ['æk·tɪŋ] I. *adj* en funciones II. *n* THEAT arte *m* dramático

action ['æk·ʃən] *n* 1. (*activeness*) acción *f;* **to be out of ~** (*person*) estar inactivo; (*machine*) no funcionar; **to put sth out of ~** inutilizar algo; **to spring into ~** ponerse en marcha; **to take ~** tomar medidas; **to take no ~** no hacer nada 2. MIL acción *f;* **to see ~** servir; **to go into ~** entrar en combate; **killed in ~** muerto en combate 3. (*mechanism*) mecanismo *m* 4. (*motion*) movimiento *m* 5. LAW (*case*) demanda *f;* **civil ~** demanda civil; **to bring an ~ against sb** interponer una demanda contra alguien 6. *inf* (*exciting events*) bullicio *m;* (*fun*) jarana *f* ▶ **~s speak louder than words** *prov* hechos [*o* obras] son amores y no buenas razones *prov*

action-packed *adj* lleno, -a de acción

activate ['æk·tə·veɪt] *vt a.* CHEM activar

active ['æk·tɪv] *adj* 1. (*lively, not passive*) activo, -a; **to be ~ in sth** participar en algo; **to take an ~ part in sth** participar activamente en algo 2. (*energetic*) enérgico, -a

actively *adv* 1. (*in a lively manner*) activamente 2. (*energetically*) enérgicamente 3. (*consciously*) de forma activa

activist ['æk·tə·vɪst] *n* POL activista *mf*

activity [æk·'tɪv·ɪ·ti] <-ies> *n* 1. (*state*) actividad *f* 2. *pl* (*pursuits*) actividades *fpl*

actor ['æk·tər] *n* actor *m*

actress ['æk·trɪs] *n* actriz *f*

actual ['æk·tʃʊ·əl] *adj* 1. (*real*) verdadero, -a; **in ~ fact** en realidad 2. (*precise*) exacto, -a; **what were her ~ words?** ¿cuáles fueron sus palabras exactas?

actually ['æk·tʃʊ·ə·li] *adv* 1. (*in fact*) en realidad 2. (*by the way*) **~ I saw her yesterday** pues la vi ayer

actuate ['æk·tʃʊ·eɪt] *vt* **1.**(*set going: mechanism*) accionar **2.** *form* (*motivate*) estimular
acumen [ə·'kju·mən] *n* perspicacia *f;* **business ~** perspicacia para los negocios
acupuncture ['æk·jʊ·pʌŋk·tʃər] *n* acupuntura *f*
acute [ə·'kjut] **I.** *adj* **1.**(*serious: pain, disease*) agudo, -a **2.**(*extreme: anxiety*) extremo, -a; (*embarrassment*) hondo, -a; (*difficulties*) grande; (*shortage*) fuerte **3.**(*sensitive: hearing, sight*) agudo, -a **4.** MATH (*angle*) agudo, -a **II.** *n* LING acento *m* agudo
acutely *adv* extremadamente; **to be ~ aware of sth** ser plenamente consciente de algo
ad [æd] *n inf abbr of* **advertisement** anuncio *m*
A.D. [,eɪ·'di] *abbr of* **anno Domini** d. (de) C.
adage ['æd·ɪdʒ] *n* dicho *m*
adagio [ə·'da·dʒoʊ] MUS **I.** *adv* adagio **II.** *n* adagio *m*
Adam ['æd·əm] *n* Adán *m*
adamant ['æd·ə·mənt] *adj* firme, categórico, -a
Adam's apple *n* ANAT nuez *f*
adapt [ə·'dæpt] **I.** *vt* adaptar; **to ~ oneself** adaptarse **II.** *vi* adaptarse
adaptable *adj* adaptable
adaptation [,æd·æp·'teɪ·ʃən] *n* **1.** THEAT, MUS, CINE, LIT adaptación *f,* versión *f* **2.**(*act of adapting*) adaptación *f*
adapter *n*, **adaptor** [ə·'dæp·tər] *n* ELEC adaptador *m;* (*for several plugs*) ladrón *m*
ADD [,eɪ·di·'di] *n abbr of* **Attention Deficit Disorder** trastorno *m* por déficit de atención
add [æd] *vt* **1.**(*put with*) añadir, agregar *AmL* **2.**(*say*) añadir, agregar **3.** MATH sumar
◆**add up I.** *vi* sumar; **to ~ to...** ascender a...; **it doesn't ~ to much** *fig* no significa mucho **II.** *vt* sumar
addendum [ə·'den·dəm] <-da> *n* adenda *f*
adder ['æd·ər] *n* ZOOL víbora *f*
addict ['æd·ɪkt] *n* **1.** MED adicto, -a *m, f;* **drug ~** drogadicto *m* **2.** *fig* partidario, -a *m, f;* **to be a movie ~** ser un apasionado del cine
addicted [ə·'dɪk·tɪd] *adj* adicto, -a; **~ to drugs** drogadicto, -a; **to be ~ to sth** ser adicto a algo; *fig* ser muy aficionado a algo
addiction [ə·'dɪk·ʃən] *n* adicción *f;* **drug ~** drogadicción *f*
addictive [ə·'dɪk·tɪv] *adj* adictivo, -a
addition [ə·'dɪʃ·ən] *n* **1.** MATH suma *f* **2.**(*act of adding*) adición *f;* **in ~** además; **in ~ to...** además de... **3.**(*added thing*) añadido *m,* añadidura *f;* **an ~ to the family** uno más en la familia
additional [ə·'dɪʃ·ən·əl] *adj* adicional
additionally [ə·'dɪʃ·ən·əl·i] *adv* por añadidura; **and ~** y además
additive ['æd·ɪ·tɪv] *n* aditivo *m*
address¹ ['æd·res] *n* a. COMPUT dirección *f*
address² [ə·'dres] **I.** *vt* **1.**(*write address on*) dirigir; **to ~ sth wrong** mandar algo a una dirección equivocada **2.**(*speak to*) dirigirse a **3.**(*use title*) **to ~ sb (as sth)** dar a alguien el

tratamiento (de algo) **4.**(*deal with: issue*) abordar **II.** *n* **1.**(*speech*) discurso *m* **2.**(*title*) **form of ~** tratamiento *m*
addressee [,æd·re·'si] *n* destinatario, -a *m, f*
adenoids ['æd·ə·nɔɪdz] *npl* ANAT vegetaciones *f* (adenoideas) *pl*
adept [ə·'dept] *adj* experto, -a; **to be ~ at sth** ser hábil para algo
adequacy ['æd·ɪ·kwə·si] *n* **1.**(*being enough*) suficiencia *f* **2.**(*being good enough*) idoneidad *f*
adequate ['æd·ɪ·kwət] *adj* **1.**(*sufficient*) suficiente **2.**(*good enough*) adecuado, -a
ADHD [,eɪ·di·aɪtʃ·'di] *abbr of* **attention deficit hyperactivity disorder** trastorno *m* por déficit de atención con hiperactividad
adhere [æd·'hɪr] *vi* **1.** *form* (*stick to*) adherirse **2.**(*follow*) **to ~ to sth** (*rule*) observar; (*belief, plan*) aferrarse a
adherence [æd·'hɪr·əns] *n* (*to rule*) observancia *f;* (*to belief*) adhesión *f*
adherent [æd·'hɪr·ənt] *n form* partidario, -a *m, f*
adhesive [æd·'hi·sɪv] **I.** *adj* adhesivo, -a **II.** *n* adhesivo *m*
ad hoc [æd·'hak] **I.** *adj* ad hoc **II.** *adv* ad hoc
ad infinitum [æd·ɪn·fə·'naɪ·təm] *adv* ad infinítum
adipose tissue [,æd·ə·pous·'tɪʃ·ju] *n* tejido *m* adiposo
adjacent [ə·'dʒeɪ·sənt] *adj* contiguo, -a; MATH adyacente
adjectival [,ædʒ·ɪk·'taɪ·vəl] *adj* adjetivo, -a, adjetival
adjective ['ædʒ·ɪk·tɪv] *n* LING adjetivo *m*
adjoin [ə·'dʒɔɪn] **I.** *vt* lindar con **II.** *vi* colindar
adjoining *adj* (*room*) contiguo, -a; (*field*) colindante
adjourn [ə·'dʒɜrn] **I.** *vt* aplazar, posponer **II.** *vi* **1.**(*pause: meeting*) aplazarse **2.** *form* (*go to*) **to ~ to another room** trasladarse a otra habitación
adjudicate [ə·'dʒu·dɪ·keɪt] **I.** *vt* juzgar **II.** *vi* arbitrar
adjust [ə·'dʒʌst] **I.** *vt* **1.** *a.* TECH ajustar, regular **2.**(*rearrange*) arreglar **3.**(*change*) modificar **4.**(*adapt*) adaptar **II.** *vi* adaptarse; **to ~ to sth** adaptarse a algo
adjustable *adj* ajustable
adjustable-rate mortgage *n* hipoteca *f* de interés variable
adjustable wrench *n* llave *f* inglesa
adjustment *n* **1.**(*mechanical*) ajuste *m* **2.**(*mental*) adaptación *f*
adjutant ['ædʒ·ə·tənt] *n* ayudante *mf*
ad lib [,æd·'lɪb] *adv* improvisando
ad-lib [,æd·'lɪb] <-bb-> *vi, vt* improvisar
adman ['æd·mæn] <-men> *n* ECON publicista *m*
admin [əd·'mɪn] *abbr of* **administration** admón.
administer [æd·'mɪn·ɪ·stər] *vt* **1.** *a.* POL (*manage: funds, estate*) administrar; **to ~ sth** estar

al cargo de algo **2.**(*dispense: punishment*) aplicar; (*medicine*) administrar; **to ~ aid to sb** asistir a alguien; **to ~ first aid to sb** prestar primeros auxilios a alguien; **to ~ an oath** tomar juramento

administration [æd·,mɪn·ɪ·'streɪ·ʃən] *n* **1.**(*organization*) administración *f*; (*management*) gerencia *f*; **the ~** la dirección **2.** POL (*time in power*) mandato *m* **3.** POL (*government*) gobierno *m*, administración *f* **4.**(*dispensing: of medicine*) administración *f*; **the ~ of an oath** la toma de un juramento

administrative [æd·'mɪn·ɪ·streɪ·tɪv] *adj* administrativo, -a

administrator [æd·'mɪn·ɪ·streɪ·tər] *n* **1.**(*of organization, institution*) administrador(a) *m(f)* **2.** LAW albacea *mf*

admirable ['æd·mər·ə·bəl] *adj* admirable

admiral ['æd·mər·əl] *n* MIL almirante *m*

admiration [,æd·mə·'reɪ·ʃən] *n* admiración *f*; **in ~** lleno de admiración

admire [əd·'maɪr] *vt* admirar; **to ~ sb for sth** admirar a alguien por algo; **to ~ sb from afar** embobarse con alguien desde lejos

admirer [əd·'maɪr·ər] *n* admirador(a) *m(f)*

admissible [æd·'mɪs·ə·bəl] *adj* admisible

admission [æd·'mɪʃ·ən] *n* **1.**(*entry: to place, building*) entrada *f*; (*to college, organization*) ingreso *m*, admisión *f* **2.**(*entrance fee*) entrada *f* **3.**(*acknowledgement*) confesión *f*; **by** [*o* **on**] **his own ~,...** por confesión propia... **4.** *pl* UNIV departamento *m* de admisión

admit [æd·'mɪt] <-tt-> I. *vt* **1.**(*acknowledge: error*) reconocer; (*crime*) confesar; **to ~ that...** reconocer que... **2.**(*allow entrance to*) dejar entrar **3.**(*permit*) admitir II. *vi* **to ~ to sth** confesarse culpable de algo

admittance [æd·'mɪt·əns] *n* entrada *f*; **to refuse sb ~** negar la entrada a alguien; **no ~** se prohíbe la entrada

admittedly [æd·'mɪt̬·ɪd·li] *adv* **~,...** es cierto que...

admonish [æd·'man·ɪʃ] *vt* amonestar

admonishment *n*, **admonition** [,æd·mə·'nɪʃ·ən] *n* amonestación *f*

ado [ə·'du] *n* **1.**(*commotion*) embrollo *m* **2.**(*delay*) demora *f*; **without further ~** sin más preámbulos ▸ **much ~ about nothing** mucho ruido y pocas nueces

adobe [ə·'dou·bi] *n* (*brick*) adobe *m*; (*building*) construcción *f* de adobe

adolescence [,æd·əl·'es·əns] *n* adolescencia *f*

adolescent [,æd·əl·'es·ənt] I. *adj* **1.**(*relating to adolescence*) adolescente **2.**(*immature*) inmaduro, -a II. *n* adolescente *mf*

adopt [ə·'dapt] *vt* **1.**(*child, strategy*) adoptar **2.**(*candidate*) nombrar

adoption [ə·'dap·ʃən] *n* **1.**(*of child, strategy*) adopción *f* **2.**(*of candidate*) nombramiento *m*

adorable [ə·'dɔr·ə·bəl] *adj* encantador(a); **just ~** irresistible

adoration [,æd·ə·'reɪ·ʃən] *n* adoración *f*; **the ~ of the Virgin Mary** REL la adoración a la virgen María

adore [ə·'dɔr] *vt* **1.**(*love strongly: person*) adorar; (*like very much*); **I just ~ the theater** me encanta el teatro **2.** REL venerar

adoring [ə·'dɔr·ɪŋ] *adj* cariñoso, -a

adorn [ə·'dɔrn] *vt form* adornar

adornment *n form* adorno *m*

adrenaline [ə·'dren·ə·lɪn] *n* adrenalina *f*

Adriatic [,eɪ·dri·'æt·ɪk] *n* **the ~ (Sea)** el (mar) Adriático

adrift [ə·'drɪft] *adv* a la deriva; **to cut sth ~** cortar las amarras de algo; **to go ~** *fig* fallar

adroit [ə·'drɔɪt] *adj* mañoso, -a; (*mentally*) hábil; **to be ~ at sth** ser diestro en algo; **to be ~ at doing sth** ser habilidoso haciendo algo

adulation [,ædʒ·ə·'leɪ·ʃən] *n* adulación *f*

adult [ə·'dʌlt] I. *n* (*person*) adulto, -a *m, f*; (*animal*) animal *m* adulto II. *adj* **1.**(*fully grown*) adulto, -a **2.**(*mature*) maduro, -a; **let's try to be ~ about this problem** seamos razonables con este problema **3.**(*sexually explicit*) para adultos

adult education *n* educación *f* para adultos

adulterate [ə·'dʌl·tə·reɪt] *vt* adulterar

adulterer [ə·'dʌl·tər·ər] *n* adúltero *m*

adulteress [ə·'dʌl·trɪs] <-es> *n* adúltera *f*

adulterous [ə·'dʌl·tər·əs] *adj* adúltero, -a

adultery [ə·'dʌl·tə·ri] <-ies> *n* adulterio *m*; **to commit ~** cometer adulterio

adulthood [ə·'dʌlt·hʊd] *n* edad *f* adulta

advance [əd·'væns] I. *vi* avanzar; **to ~ on sb/ sth** avanzar hacia alguien/algo II. *vt* **1.**(*cause to move forward*) avanzar; (*interest, cause*) promover, fomentar **2.**(*pay in advance*) anticipar III. *n* **1.**(*forward movement*) avance *m*, progreso *m*; **in ~** de antemano, por adelantado **2.** FIN anticipo *m* **3.** *pl* (*sexual flirtation*) insinuaciones *fpl*; **unwelcome ~s** molestias *fpl*; **to reject sb's ~s** rechazar las insinuaciones de alguien IV. *adj* avanzado, -a; **without ~ warning** sin previo aviso

advanced [əd·'vænst] *adj* (*country, course, student*) avanzado, -a; (*level*) superior; (*stage*) avanzado, -a

advancement [əd·'væns·mənt] *n* **1.**(*improvement*) avance *m* **2.**(*promotion*) fomento *m*; **an opportunity for ~** una oportunidad para mejorar

advance notice *n* aviso *m* (previo)

advance payment *n* anticipo *m*

advantage [əd·'væn·tɪdʒ] *n a.* SPORTS ventaja *f*; **~ Jackson** ventaja para Jackson; **to have an ~ over sb** tener ventaja sobre alguien; **to take ~ of sb/sth** aprovecharse de alguien/algo

advantageous [,æd·væn·'teɪ·dʒəs] *adj* ventajoso, -a

advent ['æd·vənt] *n* **1.**(*coming*) llegada *f* **2.** REL **Advent** Adviento *m*

adventure [æd·'ven·tʃər] *n* aventura *f*; **to look for ~** buscar el riesgo

adventurer *n* **1.**(*seeker of excitement*) aventurero, -a *m, f* **2.**(*opportunist*) aprovechado, -a *m, f*

adventurous [əd·'ven·tʃər·əs] *adj* (*person*) aventurero, -a; (*decision*) arriesgado, -a
adverb ['æd·vɜrb] *n* LING adverbio *m*
adverbial [æd·'vɜr·bi·əl] *adj* adverbial
adversary ['æd·vər·ser·i] <-ies> *n* adversario, -a *m,f*
adverse [æd·'vɜrs] *adj* (*decision, criticism, effect*) adverso, -a; (*conditions*) adverso, -a, desfavorable; (*reaction*) hostil
adversity [æd·'vɜr·sə·t̬i] <-ies> *n* adversidad *f*; **in the face of** ~ frente a la adversidad
advertent [æd·'vɜr·tənt] *adj* atento, -a
advertise ['æd·vər·taɪz] I. *vt* anunciar II. *vi* hacer publicidad
advertisement [ˌæd·vər·'taɪz·mənt] *n* COM anuncio *m*, aviso *m AmL;* **to be a good/bad** ~ **for sth** *fig* decir/no decir mucho en favor de algo; **job** ~ oferta *f* de empleo
advertiser ['æd·vər·taɪ·zər] *n* anunciante *mf*
advertising ['æd·vər·ˌtaɪ·zɪŋ] *n* publicidad *f*
advertising agency <-ies> *n* agencia *f* de publicidad
advertising campaign *n* campaña *f* publicitaria
advice [æd·'vaɪs] *n* 1. (*suggestion, opinion*) consejo *m;* **a piece of** ~ un consejo; **to ask for** ~ pedir consejo; **to ask sb for** ~ **on sth** pedir consejo a alguien sobre algo; **to give some good** ~ dar buenos consejos; **on sb's** ~ siguiendo el consejo de alguien 2. COM aviso *m*
advisable [æd·'vaɪ·zə·bəl] *adj* aconsejable; **it is (not)** ~ (no) es recomendable [*o* aconsejable]
advise [æd·'vaɪz] I. *vt* aconsejar; (*specialist*) asesorar; **to** ~ **sb against sth** desaconsejar algo a alguien; **to** ~ **sb on sth** aconsejar a alguien sobre algo; **to** ~ **sb of sth** informar a alguien sobre algo II. *vi* dar un consejo; **to** ~ **against sth** desaconsejar algo; **to** ~ **on sth** asesorar en algo
adviser *n*, **advisor** [əd·'vaɪ·zər] *n* asesor(a) *m(f)*
advisory [æd·'vaɪ·zə·ri] *adj* 1. consultivo, -a; **in an** ~ **capacity** en calidad de asesor; ~ **committee** comité consultivo 2. (*warning*) **hurricane** ~ alerta por huracán
advocacy ['æd·və·kəsi] *n* (*of cause, idea*) defensa *f*
advocate¹ ['æd·və·keɪt] *vt* recomendar; **to** ~ **doing sth** recomendar hacer algo
advocate² ['æd·və·kət] *n* 1. (*supporter*) defensor(a) *m(f)* 2. (*lawyer*) abogado, -a *m, f* defensor(a)
AEC [eɪ·ise·'si] *n abbr of* **Atomic Energy Commission** CEA *f*
Aegean [i·'dʒi·ən] *n* **the** ~ **(Sea)** el (mar) Egeo
aegis ['i·dʒɪs] *n form* **under the** ~ **of...** bajo los auspicios de...
aerate ['er·eɪt] *vt* 1. (*lawn*) airear 2. (*milk*) espumar 3. (*blood*) oxigenar 4. (*air out: shoes*) airear; (*room*) ventilar
aerial ['er·i·əl] I. *adj* aéreo,-a; ~ **photography** fotografía *f* aérea II. *n* antena *f*
aerobatic [ˌer·ə·'bæt̬·ɪk] *adj* de acrobacia

aérea
aerobatics *npl* acrobacia *f* aérea
aerobics [ə·'roʊ·bɪks] *n* + *sing/pl vb* aeróbic *m*, aerobic *m;* **to do** ~ hacer aeróbic
aerodynamic [ˌer·oʊ·daɪ·'næm·ɪk] *adj* aerodinámico, -a
aerodynamics *n* + *sing vb* aerodinámica *f*
aeronautic ['er·ə·nɔ·t̬ik] *adj* aeronáutico, -a
aeronautics *n* + *sing vb* aeronáutica *f*
aerosol ['er·ə·sɔl] *n* aerosol *m*
aerospace industry ['er·oʊ·speɪs·'ɪn·də·stri] *n* industria *f* aeroespacial
aesthetic [es·'θet̬·ɪk] *adj* estético, -a
aesthetics *n* + *sing vb* estética *f*
afar [ə·'far] *adv* lejos; **from** ~ desde lejos
affable ['æf·ə·bəl] *adj* afable
affair [ə·'fer] *n* 1. (*matter*) asunto *m;* ~ **s of state** asuntos de estado; **financial** ~ **s** asuntos financieros; **to meddle in sb's** ~ **s** meterse en los asuntos de alguien; **it's his own** ~ eso es asunto suyo 2. (*controversial situation*) episodio *m* controvertido; (*scandal*) escándalo *m* 3. (*sexual relationship*) aventura *f* (amorosa); **to have an** ~ **(with sb)** tener una aventura (con alguien) 4. (*event, occasion*) acontecimiento *m*
affect [ə·'fekt] *vt* 1. (*have affect on*) afectar; **to be** ~ **ed by sth** (*be moved*) conmoverse por algo 2. (*influence: decision*) afectar a, influir en 3. (*simulate*) fingir
affectation [ˌæf·ek·'teɪ·ʃən] *n* afectación *f*, amaneramiento *m*
affected [ə·'fek·tɪd] *adj* (*behavior, accent*) afectado, -a, amanerado, -a; (*emotion*) fingido, -a; (*smile*) falso, -a; (*style*) forzado, -a
affection [ə·'fek·ʃən] *n* afecto *m*, cariño *m;* **to have a deep** ~ **for sb** tener mucho cariño a alguien
affectionate [ə·'fek·ʃə·nɪt] *adj* afectuoso, -a, cariñoso, -a
affidavit [ˌæf·ɪ·'deɪ·vɪt] *n* declaración *f* jurada
affiliate¹ [ə·'fɪl·i·eɪt] *vt* afiliar; **to be** ~ **d with sb/sth** estar afiliado a alguien/algo
affiliate² [ə·'fɪl·i·ɪt] *n a.* ECON filial *f*
affiliation [ə·ˌfɪl·i·'eɪ·ʃən] *n* afiliación *f*
affinity [ə·'fɪn·ə·t̬i] <-ies> *n* afinidad *f*
affirm [ə·'fɜrm] *vt* afirmar
affirmation [ˌæf·ər·'meɪ·ʃən] *n* afirmación *f*
affirmative [ə·'fɜr·mə·t̬ɪv] I. *adj* afirmativo, -a II. *n* **to answer** [*o* reply] **in the** ~ contestar afirmativamente, dar una respuesta afirmativa; ~ **action** discriminación *f* positiva
affix¹ [ə·'fɪks] *vt* (*attach*) poner; (*stick on*) pegar; (*clip on*) clavar
affix² ['æf·ɪks] *n* <-es> LING afijo *m*
afflict [ə·'flɪkt] *vt* afligir; **to be** ~ **ed with sth** padecer de algo
affliction [ə·'flɪk·ʃən] *n* aflicción *f*
affluence ['æf·lʊ·əns] *n* riqueza *f*
affluent ['æf·lʊ·ənt] *adj* rico, -a; **an** ~ **lifestyle** una vida acomodada; ~ **society** sociedad opulenta
afford [ə·'fɔrd] *vt* 1. (*have money, time for*)

permitirse; **to be able to** ~ **sth** poder permitirse algo; **he can hardly** ~ **it** a duras penas se lo puede permitir **2.** (*provide*) proporcionar, dar; **to** ~ **protection** ofrecer protección

affordable [ə·'fɔr·də·bəl] *adj* (*price, purchase*) asequible

afforest [ə·'fɔr·əst] *vt* forestar

afforestation [ə·ˌfɔr·ə·'steɪ·ʃən] *n* forestación *f*

affront [ə·'frʌnt] **I.** *n* afrenta *f*; **an** ~ **to sb's dignity** una afrenta [*o* ofensa] a la dignidad de alguien **II.** *vt* afrentar; **to be** ~**ed at** [*o* **by**] **sth** ofenderse por algo

Afghan ['æf·gæn] **I.** *n* 1. (*person*) afgano, -a *m, f* **2.** LING afgano *m* **3.** (*dog*) galgo *m* afgano **4.** (*shawl*) mantón *m* de punto; (*blanket*) cubrecama *m* de punto **II.** *adj* afgano, -a

Afghanistan [æf·'gæn·ɪ·stæn] *n* Afganistán *m*

afield [ə·'fild] *adv* **far/further** ~ muy/más lejos

afloat [ə·'floʊt] *adj* a flote; **to keep** [*o* **stay**] ~ *a. fig* mantenerse a flote

afoot [ə·'fʊt] *adj* **there's sth** ~ se está tramando algo

aforementioned [ə·ˌfɔr·'men·ʃənd], **aforesaid** [ə·'fɔr·sed] *form* **I.** *adj* (*in text*) anteriormente mencionado, -a; (*in conversation*) dicho, -a **II.** *n inv* **the** ~ el mencionado/la mencionada; (*person mentioned in conversation*) el susodicho/la susodicha

afraid [ə·'freɪd] *adj* 1. (*scared*) **to be** ~ tener miedo; **to be** ~ **of doing** [*o* **to do**] **sth** tener miedo de hacer algo; **to be** ~ **of sb/sth** tener miedo a algo/alguien **2.** (*sorry*) **I'm** ~ **so** lo siento, pero así es; **I'm** ~ **not** lo siento, pero no; **I'm** ~ **I haven't got the time** me temo que no tengo tiempo

afresh [ə·'freʃ] *adv* de nuevo; **to start** ~ empezar de nuevo

Africa ['æf·rɪ·kə] *n* África *f*

African ['æf·rɪ·kən] **I.** *n* africano, -a *m, f* **II.** *adj* africano, -a

African American I. *adj* afroamericano, -a **II.** *n* afroamericano, -a *m, f*

Afrikaans [ˌæf·rɪ·'kans] *n* LING afrikáans *m inv*

Afro-American *adj, n s.* **African American**

Afro-Caribbean [ˌæf·roʊ·ˌkær·ə·'bi·ən] **I.** *adj* afrocaribeño, -a **II.** *n* afrocaribeño, -a *m, f*

aft [æft] *n* NAUT popa *f*

after ['æf·tər] **I.** *prep* 1. (*at later time*) después de; ~ **two days** al cabo de dos días; (*shortly*) ~ **breakfast** (poco) después de desayunar **2.** (*behind*) detrás de; **to run** ~ **sb** correr detrás de alguien **3.** (*following*) después de; **D comes** ~ **C** la D viene después [*o* detrás] de la C; **to have argument** ~ **argument** tener pelea tras pelea **4.** (*about*) por; **to ask** ~ **sb** preguntar por alguien **5.** (*despite*) ~ **all** después de todo **6.** (*in the style of*) **a drawing** ~ **Picasso** un dibujo al estilo de Picasso **7.** (*in honor of*) **to name sth/sb** ~ **sb** llamar a algo/a alguien como alguien **II.** *adv* después; **soon** ~ poco después; **the day** ~ el día después **III.** *conj* después de que +*subj*; **he spoke** ~

she went out habló después de que ella se fuera; **I'll call him** (**right**) ~ **I've taken a shower** le llamaré tan pronto (como) me haya duchado

afterbirth *n* MED placenta *f*

aftercare ['æf·tər·ker] *n* MED asistencia *f* postoperatoria

after-dinner *adj* de sobremesa

aftereffects ['æf·tər·ɪ·ˌfekts] *npl* (*of drugs, treatment*) efectos *mpl* secundarios; (*of accident*) secuelas *fpl*

afterglow *n* 1. (*after sunset*) arrebol *m* **2.** PHYS luminiscencia *f*

after-hours *adj* fuera de horas

afterlife ['æf·tər·laɪf] *n* vida *f* más allá de la muerte; **the** ~ el más allá

after-market *n* venta *f* de repuestos y accesorios, venta *f* de refacción *Méx*

aftermath ['æf·tər·mæθ] *n* secuelas *fpl*

afternoon [ˌæf·tər·'nun] **I.** *n* tarde *f*; **this** ~ esta tarde; **in the** ~ por la tarde; **all** ~ toda la tarde; **tomorrow/yesterday** ~ mañana/ayer por la tarde; **4 o'clock in the** ~ las 4 de la tarde; **good** ~**!** ¡buenas tardes! **II.** *adj* de la tarde; ~ **nap** siesta *f*

after-sales service *n* servicio *m* postventa

after-shave ['æf·tər·ʃeɪv] *n* loción *f* para después del afeitado

aftershock *n* GEO réplica *f*

aftertaste ['æf·tər·teɪst] *n a. fig* regusto *m*

after-tax *adj* después de impuestos

afterthought ['æf·tər·θɔt] *n* idea *f* tardía

afterward *adv*, **afterwards** ['æf·tər·wərdz] *adv* (*later*) más tarde; (*after something*) después; **shortly** ~ poco después

again [ə·'gen] *adv* 1. (*as a repetition*) otra vez; (*one more time*) de nuevo; **never** ~ nunca más; **once** ~ otra vez; **then** ~ por otra parte; **yet** ~ una vez más; ~ **and** ~ una y otra vez **2.** (*anew*) de nuevo

against [ə·'genst] **I.** *prep* 1. (*in opposition to*) (en) contra (de); **to be** ~ **sth/sb** estar en contra de algo/alguien; ~ **my will** en contra de mi voluntad **2.** (*as protection from*) contra; **to protect oneself** ~ **rain** protegerse de la lluvia **3.** (*in contact with*) contra; **to lean** ~ **a tree** apoyarse en un árbol; **to run** ~ **a wall** estrellarse contra una pared **4.** (*in front of*) ~ **the light** a contraluz **5.** (*in competition with*) contra; ~ **time/the clock** contra el tiempo/el reloj **6.** (*in comparison with*) **the dollar rose/fell** ~ **the euro** el dólar subió/bajó respecto al euro **II.** *adv a.* POL en contra; **there were 10 votes** ~ hubo 10 votos en contra

agate ['æg·ət] *n* ágata *f*

age [eɪdʒ] **I.** *n* 1. (*of person, object*) edad *f*; **old** ~ vejez *f*; ~ **of consent** edad núbil; **what is your** ~**?** ¿qué edad tienes?; **when I was her** ~ cuando tenía su edad; **to be seven years of** ~ tener siete años; **to be under** ~ ser menor de edad; **to come of** ~ alcanzar la madurez; **to improve with** ~ mejorar con los años [*o* la edad] **2.** (*era*) época *f*; **in this day and** ~ en estos tiempos **3.** (*long time*) siglos *mpl;* **I haven't seen you in ~s!** ¡hace siglos que no te veo! **II.** *vi* **1.** (*become older*) envejecer **2.** CULIN (*mature*) madurar **III.** *vt* **1.** (*make older*) envejecer **2.** CULIN (*mature*) madurar

age bracket *n s.* **age group**

aged¹ [ɛɪdʒd] *adj* **1.** CULIN curado, -a; (*wine*) añejo, -a **2.** (*with age of*) de ... años de edad; **this game is for children ~ 8 to 12** este juego es para niños de entre 8 y 12 años de edad

aged² ['eɪ·dʒɪd] **I.** *adj* (*old*) viejo, -a **II.** *n* **the ~** los ancianos

age group *n* grupo *m* de edad

ageless ['eɪdʒ·lɪs] *adj* eterno, -a

age limit *n* límite *m* de edad

agency ['eɪ·dʒən·si] <-ies> *n* **1.** COM agencia *f;* **travel ~** agencia de viajes **2.** ADMIN agencia *f,* organismo *m;* **government ~** agencia [*o* organismo] gubernamental **3.** *form* **through the ~ of** por acción de

agenda [ə·'dʒen·də] *n* (*for meeting*) orden *m* del día; **to be at the top of the ~** *fig* ser un asunto prioritario

agent ['eɪ·dʒənt] *n* agente *mf;* **secret ~** agente secreto

Agent Orange *n* agente *m* naranja

Age of Aquarius *n* era *f* de acuario

age-old *adj* antiguo, -a, secular

agglomerate [ə·'glam·ə·reɪt] *n,* **agglomeration** [ə·ˌglam·ə·'reɪ·ʃən] *n* aglomeración *f*

aggravate ['æg·rə·veɪt] *vt* **1.** (*make worse*) agravar **2.** *inf* (*annoy*) fastidiar

aggravating *adj* (*annoying*) molesto, -a

aggravation [ˌæg·rə·'veɪ·ʃən] *n inf* fastidio *m*

aggregate¹ ['æg·rɪ·gɪt] **I.** *n* **1.** FIN, ECON conglomerado *m;* (*sum total*) suma *f* total; (*total value*) valor *f* total **2.** MATH suma *f* **II.** *adj* FIN, ECON total

aggregate² ['æg·rɪ·geɪt] *vt* FIN, ECON sumar

aggression [ə·'greʃ·ən] *n* **1.** (*feelings*) agresividad *f* **2.** (*violence*) agresión *f;* **an act of ~** una agresión

aggressive [ə·'gres·ɪv] *adj* agresivo, -a

aggressor [ə·'gres·ər] *n* agresor(a) *m(f)*

aggrieved [ə·'grivd] *adj* ofendido, -a

aghast [ə·'gæst] *adj* horrorizado, -a; **to be ~ at sth** estar horrorizado por algo

agile ['ædʒ·əl] *adj* ágil

agility [ə·'dʒɪl·ə·t̬i] *n* agilidad *f*

aging I. *adj* envejecido, -a **II.** *n* envejecimiento *m;* **the process of ~** el proceso de envejecimiento

agitate ['ædʒ·ɪ·teɪt] **I.** *vt* **1.** (*make nervous*) inquietar; **to become ~d** inquietarse, ponerse inquieto **2.** TECH (*shake*) agitar **II.** *vi* **to ~ for/against sth** hacer campaña en favor de/en contra de algo

agitation [ˌædʒ·ɪ·'teɪ·ʃən] *n a.* POL agitación *f*

agitator ['ædʒ·ɪ·teɪ·t̬ər] *n* agitador(a) *m(f),* violentista *mf* Chile

agnostic [æg·'nas·tɪk] **I.** *n* agnóstico, -a *m, f* **II.** *adj* agnóstico, -a

ago [ə·'goʊ] *adv* **a minute/a year ~** hace un minuto/un año; **a long time ~, long ~** hace mucho tiempo; **how long ~ was that?** ¿cuánto tiempo hace de eso?

agog [ə·'gag] *adj* **to watch/listen ~** mirar/ escuchar con avidez

agonize ['æg·ə·naɪz] *vi* atormentarse; **to ~ about whether to do sth** atormentarse respecto a hacer algo o no; **an ~d cry** un grito de angustia

agonizing ['æg·ə·naɪ·zɪŋ] *adj* **1.** (*pain*) atroz; **to die an ~ death** tener una muerte espantosa **2.** (*delay, decision*) angustiante

agony ['æg·ə·ni] <-ies> *n* agonía *f;* **to be in ~** sufrir fuertes dolores; **to prolong the ~** (of sth) prolongar la agonía (de algo)

agony column *n* PUBL sección *f* de desaparecidos

agoraphobia [ˌæg·ər·ə·'foʊ·bi·ə] *n* PSYCH agorafobia *f*

agrarian [ə·'grer·i·ən] *adj* agrario, -a

agree [ə·'gri] **I.** *vi* **1.** (*hold same opinion*) estar de acuerdo; **to ~ on sth** (*be in agreement*) estar de acuerdo en algo; (*reach agreement*) acordar algo; **to ~ to do sth** (*reach agreement*) acordar hacer algo; (*consent*) acceder a hacer algo; **to ~ to a suggestion** aceptar una sugerencia; **we don't ~ on many things** no estamos de acuerdo en muchas cosas; **they can't ~** no pueden ponerse de acuerdo; **to ~ to disagree** estar en desacuerdo amistoso **2.** (*be good for*) **to ~ with sb** sentar bien a alguien **3.** (*match up*) casar, concordar **4.** LING concordar **II.** *vt* (*concur*) acordar; **it is ~d that...** se ha acordado que...; **at the ~d time** a la hora fijada

agreeable *adj* **1.** (*pleasant*) agradable; **he's quite an ~ guy** es un tipo muy agradable **2.** (*consenting*) **to be ~ (to sth)** estar conforme (con algo) **3.** (*acceptable*) **is that ~ to you?** ¿está/estás de acuerdo?

agreement *n* **1.** (*contract, arrangement*) acuerdo *m;* **to break an ~** romper un acuerdo **2.** (*shared opinion*) acuerdo *m;* **to be in ~ with sb/sth** estar de acuerdo con alguien/ algo; **to reach an ~** llegar a un acuerdo **3.** LING concordancia *f*

agribusiness ['æg·rɪ·ˌbɪz·nɪs] *n* industria *f* agropecuaria

agricultural [ˌæg·rɪ·'kʌl·tʃər·əl] *adj* agrícola; **~ science** agronomía *f*

agriculture ['æg·rɪ·kʌl·tʃər] *n* agricultura *f*

agritourism [ˌæg·rɪ·'tʊr·ɪzəm] *n* agroturismo

aground [ə·'graʊnd] *adv* NAUT **to run ~** encallar; *fig* fracasar

ah [a] *interj* ah

aha [a·'ha] *interj* ajá

ahead [ə·'hed] *adv* **1.** (*in front*) delante; **the road ~ was blocked** había atasco en la carretera delante de nosotros **2.** (*advanced position, forwards*) adelante; **to go ~** adelantarse; **to move ~ quickly** avanzar rápidamente; **to press ~ with the plan** tirar adelante con el plan **3.** (*in the future*) **to look** ~ anticiparse; **to plan** ~ hacer planes con antelación

ahead of *prep* **1.** (*in front of*) delante de; **to walk** ~ **sb** caminar delante de alguien; (**way**) ~ **sb/sth** (muy) por delante de alguien/algo **2.** (*before*) antes de; **to decide/arrive** ~ **time** decidir/llegar antes de tiempo **3.** (*more advanced than*) **to be a minute** ~ **sb** llevar un minuto de ventaja sobre alguien; **to be** ~ **one's time** anticiparse a su época **4.** (*informed about*) **to keep** ~ **sth** mantenerse al tanto de algo

ahem [ə·ˈhəm] *interj* ejem

ahoy [ə·ˈhɔɪ] *interj* **land/ship** ~! ¡tierra/barco a la vista!; ~ **there!** ¡ah del barco!

AI [ˌeɪ·ˈaɪ] *n* **1.** COMPUT *abbr of* **artificial intelligence** IA **2.** MED, BIO *abbr of* **artificial insemination** inseminación *f* artificial

aid [eɪd] **I.** *n* **1.** (*assistance, support*) ayuda *f*; **to come/go to the** ~ **of sb** ir en ayuda de alguien; **with the** ~ **of sb/sth** con (la) ayuda de alguien/algo **2.** POL, ECON ayuda *f*; **emergency** ~ ayuda de emergencia; **financial** ~ asistencia *f* financiera **3.** (*device*) ayuda *f*; **hearing** ~ audífono *m*; **visual** ~**s** recursos *mpl* visuales **II.** *vt* ayudar; **to** ~ **and abet sb** LAW ser cómplice de alguien

aid convoy *n* convoy *m* humanitario

aide [eɪd] *n* asistente *mf*

AIDS [eɪdz] *n abbr of* **Acquired Immune Deficiency Syndrome** sida *m*

ail [eɪl] *form* **I.** *vi* estar enfermo, -a **II.** *vt* afligir; **what** ~**s you?** *a. iron* ¿qué te pasa?

ailing [ˈeɪl·ɪŋ] *adj* **1.** (*person*) enfermo, -a **2.** (*company, economy*) debilitado, -a

ailment [ˈeɪl·mənt] *n* dolencia *f*

aim [eɪm] **I.** *vi* **1.** (*point: weapon*) apuntar; **to** ~ **at sb/sth** apuntar a alguien/algo **2.** (*plan to achieve*) **to** ~ **at** [*o* **for**] **sth** tener algo como objetivo; **to** ~ **to do sth** poner como objetivo hacer algo **II.** *vt* **1.** (*point a weapon*) apuntar; **to** ~ **sth at sb/sth** apuntar algo hacia alguien/algo **2.** (*direct at*) **to** ~ **sth at sb** dirigir algo hacia alguien **3.** (*intend to*) **to be** ~**ed at doing sth** ir encaminado a hacer algo **III.** *n* **1.** (*ability to shoot*) puntería *f*; **to take** ~ apuntar **2.** (*goal*) objetivo *m*, meta *f*; **his** ~ **was to make fun of us** su objetivo era burlarse de nosotros; **sb's** ~ **in life** la meta de alguien en la vida; **with the** ~ **of doing sth** con el objetivo de hacer algo

aimless [ˈeɪm·lɪs] *adj* sin objetivo(s)

ain't [eɪnt] *inf* **1.** (*to be*) *s.* **am not, are not, is not 2.** (*to have*) *s.* **have not, has not**

air [er] **I.** *n* **1.** (*earth's atmosphere*) aire *m* **2.** (*space overhead, sky*) aire *m*; **to fire into the** ~ disparar al aire; **to be up in the** ~ *fig* estar en el aire **3.** AVIAT **by** ~ por avión; **to travel by** ~ viajar en avión **4.** TV, RADIO, CINE **to be on the** ~ estar en antena [*o* en el aire]; **to be taken off the** ~ ser retirado de antena **5.** (*aura, quality*) aire *m*; **to have an** ~ **of confidence/danger** envolverle un aire de con-

fianza/peligro **6.** MUS aire *m*, tonada *f* ▶ **out of thin** ~ de la nada; **to disappear into thin** ~ desaparecer como por arte de magia **II.** *adj* aéreo, -a **III.** *vt* **1.** TV, RADIO emitir; **the program will be** ~**ed on Saturday** el programa se emitirá el sábado **2.** (*expose to air*) airear **3.** (*publicize*) **to** ~ **one's grievances** ventilar sus quejas **IV.** *vi* **1.** TV, RADIO emitirse **2.** (*be exposed to air*) ventilarse

air bag *n* airbag *m*

air ball *n* (*in basketball*) pelota que no toca ni el aro

air base *n* base *f* aérea

airborne [ˈer·bɔrn] *adj* **1.** (*transported by aircraft*) aerotransportado, -a **2.** (*in the air*) **to be** ~ volar

air brake *n* freno *m* neumático

airbrush I. *n* aerógrafo *m* **II.** *vt* pintar con aerógrafo

air bubble *n* burbuja *f* de aire

air bus *n* AVIAT aerobús *m*

air-conditioned *adj* climatizado, -a

air conditioner *n* acondicionador *m* de aire

air conditioning *n* aire *m* acondicionado, climatización *f*

air-cooled *adj* enfriado, -a por aire

air corridor *n* corredor *m* aéreo

aircraft [ˈer·kræft] *n* (*airplane*) avión *m*; (*in general*) aeronave *f*

aircraft carrier *n* portaaviones *m inv*

aircraft industry *n* industria *f* aeronáutica

aircrew *n* + *sing/pl vb* tripulación *f* de vuelo

air cushion *n* cojín *m* de aire

airdrome [ˈer·droʊm] *n* aeródromo *m*

air-dry *vt* secar al aire

airfare *n* precio *m* del billete de avión [*o Méx, Col* del tiquete]

airfield *n* aeródromo *m*

air filter *n* filtro *m* de aire

air force *n* fuerza *f* aérea

airframe *n* armazón *m*

airfreight *n* carga *f* aérea

air gun *n* pistola *f* de aire comprimido

airhead *n inf* cabeza *mf* hueca

air hole *n* respiradero *m*

air lane *n* vía *f* aérea

airless [ˈer·lɪs] *n* (*room*) mal ventilado, -a; (*day*) sin viento

airlift I. *n* puente *m* aéreo **II.** *vt* aerotransportar

airline *n* línea *f* aérea, aerolínea *f AmL*

airliner *n* avión *m* de pasajeros

airmail I. *n* correo *m* aéreo **II.** *vt* enviar por correo aéreo

airman <-men> *n* **1.** (*pilot*) aviador *m*; (*crew member*) tripulante *mf* **2.** MIL soldado *m* de las fuerzas aéreas

air mass *n* METEO masa *f* de aire

air mattress *n* colchón *m* inflable

air piracy *n* piratería *f* aérea

airplane *n* avión *m*

air pocket *n* bolsa *f* de aire

air pollutant *n* agente *m* contaminante (del aire)

air pollution *n* contaminación *f* atmosférica
airport *n* aeropuerto *m*
airport terminal *n* terminal *f* aérea
air pump *n* bomba *f* de aire
air quality *n* calidad *f* del aire
air raid *n* ataque *m* aéreo
air rifle *n* rifle *m* de aire comprimido
airship *n* zepelín *m*, dirigible *m*
air show *n* exhibición *f* aérea
airsick *adj* mareado, -a; **to get** ~ marearse (en avión)
airspace *n* espacio *m* aéreo
airstrip *n* pista *f* de aterrizaje
air taxi *n* aerotaxi *m*
airtight *adj* hermético, -a
airtime *n* TV tiempo *m* en antena
air traffic *n* tráfico *m* aéreo
air-traffic controller *n* controlador(a) *m(f)* aéreo, -a
airway ['er·weɪ] *n* **1.** ANAT vía *f* respiratoria **2.** (*route of aircraft*) ruta *f* aérea
airworthy ['er·ˌwɜr·ði] *adj* en condiciones para el vuelo
airy ['er·i] *adj* **1.** ARCHIT espacioso, -a **2.** (*light*) ligero, -a; **with an** ~ **step** con un paso grácil **3.** (*lacking substance*) etéreo, -a
aisle [aɪl] *n* pasillo *m*; (*in church*) nave *f* lateral
▶ **to have sb** <u>rolling</u> **in the** ~**s** tener a alguien riéndose a carcajadas; **to** <u>take</u> **sb down the** ~ llevar al altar a alguien
ajar [ə·'dʒɑr] *adj* entreabierto, -a
AK *n abbr of* **Alaska** Alaska
AKA, aka *abbr of* **also known as** alias
akimbo [ə·'kɪm·boʊ] *adj* (**with**) **arms** ~ (con) los brazos en jarras
akin [ə·'kɪn] *adj* ~ **to** parecido a
AL *n*, **Ala.** [ˌæl·ə·'bæm·ə] *n abbr of* **Alabama** Alabama *f*
Alabama [ˌæl·ə·'bæm·ə] *n* Alabama *f*
à la carte [a·lə·'kart] *adj, adv* a la carta
alacrity [ə·'læk·rə·t̬i] *n* prontitud *f*

> ℹ️ El **Alamo**, construido en el siglo XVIII como capilla franciscana, fue escenario de la batalla del 6 de marzo de 1836 por la independencia de Tejas con respecto a México, en la que cerca de 180 soldados tejanos, entre ellos W. B. Travis, Jim Bowie y Davy Crockett, murieron en combate contra varios miles de militares mexicanos comandados por el general Santa Anna. Seis semanas después, otras tropas tejanas, bajo el grito "Remember the Alamo" (Recuerden el Álamo), obtuvieron finalmente la independencia al derrotar a los mexicanos en San Jacinto.

à la mode [a·lə·'moʊd] *adj* CULIN con helado
alarm [ə·'larm] **I.** *n* **1.** (*worry*) alarma *f*; **to cause sb** ~ alarmar a alguien **2.** (*warning*)

alarma *f*; **fire** ~ alarma contra incendios; **burglar** ~ dispositivo *m* antirrobo; **a false** ~ una falsa alarma; **to give** [*o* **sound**] **the** ~ dar la (voz de) alarma; *a. fig* alertar **3.** (*clock*) reloj *m* despertador **II.** *vt* alarmar; **to be** ~**ed** estar alarmado
alarm clock *n* reloj *m* despertador
alarming *adj* alarmante
alarmist [ə·'lar·mɪst] **I.** *adj* alarmista **II.** *n* alarmista *mf*
Alas. [ə·'læs·kə] *n abbr of* **Alaska** Alaska
Alaska [ə·'læs·kə] *n* Alaska
albacore ['æl·bə·ˌkɔr] *n* ZOOL atún *m* blanco, albacora *f*
Albania [æl·'beɪ·ni·ə] *n* Albania *f*
Albanian **I.** *n* **1.** (*person*) albanés, -esa *m, f* **2.** LING albanés *m* **II.** *adj* albanés, -esa
albatross ['æl·bə·trɔs] *n* albatros *m*
albeit [ɔl·'bi·ɪt] *conj* aunque
albino [æl·'baɪ·noʊ] **I.** *adj* albino, -a, ruaco, -a *Ven* **II.** *n* albino, -a *m, f*
album ['æl·bəm] *n a.* MUS álbum *m*; **the family** ~ el álbum de familia

> ℹ️ **Alcatraz** es una antigua cárcel situada en la Isla de Alcatraz, en la bahía de San Francisco (California). La isla, con cinco hectáreas de extensión, se alza sobre una base de acantilados, por lo cual también recibe el nombre de **'The Rock'**. En esta cárcel se recluían presos particularmente peligrosos.

alcohol ['æl·kə·hɔl] *n* alcohol *m*
alcohol-free *adj* sin alcohol
alcoholic [ˌæl·kə·'hɔ·lɪk] **I.** *n* alcohólico, -a *m, f* **II.** *adj* alcohólico, -a
alcoholism *n* alcoholismo *m*
alcove ['æl·koʊv] *n* nicho *m* (*para estantería o cama*)
alder ['ɔl·dər] *n* BOT aliso *m*
alderman ['ɔl·dər·mən] <-men> *n* POL regidor(a) *m(f)*
ale [eɪl] *n* cerveza *f*
alert [ə·'lɜrt] **I.** *adj* despierto, -a; **to keep** ~ mantenerse alerta **II.** *n* **1.** (*alarm*) alarma *f* **2.** (*period of watchfulness*) alerta *f*; **state of** ~ estado *m* de alerta; **to be on the** ~ estar alerta **III.** *vt* (*notify*) alertar
alfalfa [æl·'fæl·fə] *n* alfalfa *f*
alfresco [æl·'fres·koʊ] *adv* al aire libre
alga ['æl·gə] *n* <*pl* algae> alga *f*
algebra ['æl·dʒə·brə] *n* MATH álgebra *f*
algebraic [ˌæl·dʒə·'breɪ·ɪk] *adj* algebraico, -a
Algeria [æl·'dʒɪr·i·ə] *n* Argelia *f*
Algerian **I.** *n* argelino, -a *m, f* **II.** *adj* argelino, -a
Algiers [æl·'dʒɪrz] *n* Argel *m*
alias ['eɪ·li·əs] **I.** *n* alias *m inv* **II.** *adv* alias
alibi ['æl·ə·baɪ] *n* coartada *f*
alien ['eɪ·li·ən] **I.** *adj* **1.** (*foreign*) extranjero, -a **2.** (*strange*) extraño, -a; ~ **to sb** ajeno a alguien; **an** ~ **idea** una idea poco normal **II.** *n* **1.** *form* (*foreigner*) extranjero, -a *m, f*; **illegal**

~ (extranjero) ilegal **2.**(*extraterrestrial*) extraterrestre *mf*
alienate ['eɪ·li·ə·neɪt] *vt* **1.**(*person*) distanciar;
to ~ sb from sb/sth hacer que alguien se dis-
tancie de alguien/algo **2.** LAW (*property*) enajenar
alienation [ˌeɪ·li·ə·'neɪ·ʃən] *n* **1.**(*of people*)
distanciamiento *m* **2.** LAW (*of property*) enajenación *f*
alight¹ [ə·'laɪt] *adj* **1.**(*on fire*) quemando; **to
be ~** estar ardiendo; **to set sth ~** prender
fuego a algo **2.** *fig* (*with enthusiasm, joy*)
resplandeciente; **to set sb's imagination ~**
despertar la imaginación a alguien
alight² [ə·'laɪt] *vi form* **1.**(*on branch*) posarse
2. (*from vehicle*) apearse, bajarse
♦ **alight on** *vi* **to ~ sth** dar con [*o* encontrar]
algo
align [ə·'laɪn] *vt* **1.**(*two things*) poner en línea
(recta); (*wheels*) alinear **2.** *fig* **to ~ oneself
with sb/sth** alinearse con alguien/algo
alignment *n* alineación *f;* **to be out of ~** no
estar alineado
alike [ə·'laɪk] **I.** *adj* **1.**parecido, -a; **to look ~**
parecerse **2. Clara and Carl ~...** (*both*) tanto
Clara como Carl... **II.** *adv* (*similarly*) de un
modo parecido; **to think ~** pensar de forma
parecida
alimony ['æl·ɪ·moʊ·ni] *n* pensión *f* alimenticia
alive [ə·'laɪv] *adj* **1.**(*not dead*) vivo, -a; **to be ~**
estar vivo; **to be buried ~** ser enterrado vivo;
to keep sb ~ mantener a alguien con vida; **to
keep sb's hopes ~** mantener vivas las esperanzas de alguien **2.**(*active*) activo, -a; **to
make sth come ~** dar vida a algo **3.**(*aware*)
to be ~ to sth ser consciente de algo
alkali ['æl·kə·laɪ] **I.**<-s *o* -es> *n* álcali *m* **II.** *adj*
alcalino, -a
alkaline ['æl·kə·laɪn] *adj* alcalino, -a
all [ɔl] **I.** *adj* todo, -a; ~ **the butter** toda la
mantequilla; ~ **the wine** todo el vino; ~ **my
sisters** todas mis hermanas; **with ~ possible
speed** con la máxima velocidad posible
II. *pron* **1.**(*everybody*) todos, -as; ~ **aboard!**
¡todos a bordo!; ~ **but him** todos menos él;
he's got four daughters, ~ with blue eyes
tiene cuatro hijas, todas con ojos azules; **once
and for ~** de una vez por todas **2.**(*everything*)
todo; ~ **but...** todo menos...; **most of ~** sobre
todo; **the best of ~ would be...** lo mejor de
todo sería...; **for ~ I know** que yo sepa **3.**(*the
whole quantity*) todo, -a; **they took/drank it
~** se lo tomaron/bebieron todo; ~ **of France**
toda Francia **4.**(*the only thing*) todo, -a; ~ **I
want is...** lo único que quiero es...; **I am ~ the
family she has** soy toda la familia que ella
tiene **5.** SPORTS **two ~** dos a dos; **to tie two ~**
empatar a dos **III.** *adv* totalmente; ~ **around**
completo, no del todo; **not as stupid as ~ that** no del todo
estúpido; **it's ~ the same** me da igual
Allah ['æl·ə] *n* Alá *m*
all-around [ɔl·ə·'raʊnd] *adj* completo, -a;
~ **talent** talento *m* para todo

allay [ə·'leɪ] *vt* (*fear*) calmar; (*doubt*) despejar
all clear *n* cese *m* de alarma; **to give/get the ~**
dar/oír el cese de alarma; **to give sth the ~** *fig*
dar la luz verde a algo
all-day *adj* que dura todo el día
allegation [ˌæl·ɪ·'geɪ·ʃən] *n* acusación *f;* **to
make an ~ against sb** acusar a alguien
allege [ə·'ledʒ] *vt* afirmar; **she is ~d to have
stolen the money** se dice que ha robado el
dinero; **it is ~d that...** se dice que...
alleged [ə·'ledʒd] *adj* supuesto, -a
allegedly [ə·'ledʒ·ɪd·li] *adv* (*según*) se dice
allegiance [ə·'li·dʒəns] *n* lealtad *f;* **to pledge
~ to sb/sth** jurar lealtad a alguien/algo
allegorical [ˌæl·ɪ·'gɔr·ɪk·əl] *adj* alegórico, -a
allegory ['æl·ɪ·gɔr·i] <-ies> *n* alegoría *f*
allergen ['æl·ər·dʒən] *n* alergeno *m,*
alérgeno *m*
allergenic [æl·ər·'dʒen·ɪk] *adj* alergénico, -a
allergic [ə·'lɜr·dʒɪk] *adj* alérgico, -a; ~ **reaction** reacción *f* alérgica
allergist ['æl·ər·dʒɪst] *n* alergólogo, -a *m, f*
allergy ['æl·ər·dʒi] <-ies> *n* alergia *f*
alleviate [ə·'li·vi·eɪt] *vt* aliviar
alley ['æl·i] *n* **1.**(*between buildings*) callejón
m; **blind ~** callejón sin salida **2.**(*in garden*)
paseo *m* ▶ **to be** (**right**) **up one's ~** ser lo suyo
inf
alley cat *n* gato *m* callejero
alleyway *n* callejón *m*
alliance [ə·'laɪ·əns] *n* alianza *f;* **to form an ~**
formar una alianza
allied ['æl·aɪd] *adj* **1.** *a.* MIL aliado, -a; **the
Allied forces** las fuerzas aliadas **2.**(*combined*) ~ **with** [*o* to] **sth** unido a algo
alligator ['æl·ɪ·geɪ· t̬ər] *n* caimán *m*
alligator pear *n* aguacate *m,* palta *f Arg, Bol,
Chile, Ecua, Perú, Urug*
all-inclusive [ɔl·ɪn·'klu·sɪv] *adj* todo incluido;
~ **rate** precio *m* con todo incluido
alliteration *n* LIT aliteración *f*
all-night *adj* (*taking all night*) que dura toda la
noche; (*open all night*) abierto, -a toda la
noche
all-nighter *n inf* **to pull an ~** tirarse toda la
noche (haciendo algo), pasar la noche derecho
(haciendo algo)
allocate ['æl·ə·keɪt] *vt* **1.**(*assign*) asignar
2.(*distribute*) repartir; **to ~ blame for sth to
sb** echar las culpas a alguien de algo
allocation [æl·ə·'keɪ·ʃən] *n* **1.**(*assignment*)
asignación *f* **2.**(*act of distributing*) distribución *f*
allot [ə·'lat] <-tt-> *vt* asignar
allotment *n* **1.**(*assignment*) asignación *f*
2.(*distribution*) distribución *f* **3.**(*allotted
thing*) asignación *f*
all-out [ɔl·'aʊt] *adj* total; **to make an ~ effort**
hacer un esfuerzo supremo; ~ **attack** ataque
m total
allow [ə·'laʊ] *vt* **1.**(*permit*) permitir; **to ~
access** permitir el acceso; **to ~ sb to do sth**
dejar a alguien hacer algo; ~ **me** permíta(n)me;

please ~ me through *form* déje(n)me pasar, por favor; **smoking is not ~ed** se prohíbe fumar **2.**(*allocate*) asignar; **please ~ up to 7 days for delivery** entrega en un plazo máximo de 7 días **3.**(*admit*) **to ~ that...** reconocer que...
◆ **allow for** *vt* tener en cuenta
allowable *adj* **1.**(*error*) permisible **2.**(*expenses*) deducible
allowance [ə·'laʊ·əns] *n* **1.**(*permitted amount*) cantidad *f* permitida; **baggage ~** equipaje *m* no sujeto a tasas **2.**(*pocket money*) paga *f* **3.**(*preparation*) **to make ~(s) for sth** tener algo en cuenta **4.**(*excuse*) **to make ~s for sb** ser indulgente con alguien; **to make ~s for sth** tolerar algo
alloy ['æl·ɔɪ] I. *n* aleación *f*; **~ wheels** llantas *fpl* de aleación II. *vt form* empañar
all-purpose [ɔl·'pɜr·pəs] *adj* universal, multiuso
all right I. *adj* **1.**(*okay*) bien; **that's ~** (*after thanks*) de nada; (*after excuse*) no pasa nada; **what do you think of the book? — it was ~, nothing special** ¿qué te parece el libro? — ah, pasable, nada del otro mundo; **to be ~ with sb** comportarse bien con alguien **2.**(*healthy*) bien; **to be ~** estar bien (de salud); (*safe*) estar sano y salvo; **to get home ~** llegar a casa sin ningún percance II. *interj* (*expressing agreement*) de acuerdo III. *adv* **1.**(*well*) bien **2.**(*certainly*) con (toda) seguridad **3.**(*in answer*) vale
All Saints' Day *n* día *m* de Todos los Santos
All Souls' Day *n* día *m* de (los) Difuntos
allspice ['ɔl·spaɪs] *n* CULIN pimienta *f* de Jamaica
all-star I. *adj* (*cast*) estelar II. *n* SPORTS miembro *mf* de un equipo all-star
all-terrain vehicle *n* vehículo *m* todoterreno
all-time high *n* máximo *m* histórico
all-time low *n* mínimo *m* histórico
allude [ə·'lud] *vi* **to ~ to sth** aludir a algo
allure [ə·'lʊr] I. *n* (*attractiveness*) atractivo *m*; (*charm*) encanto *m*; **sexual ~** atractivo sexual II. *vt* atraer
alluring [ə·'lʊr·ɪŋ] *adj* (*attractive*) atractivo, -a; (*enticing*) tentador(a)
allusion [ə·'lu·ʒən] *n* alusión *f*
all-weather *adj* para todo tiempo
ally ['æl·aɪ] I.<-ies> *n* **1.**(*country*) aliado, -a *m, f* **2.**(*supporter*) partidario, -a *m, f* II.<-ie-> *vt* **to ~ oneself with sb** POL aliarse con alguien
alma mater ['æl·mə·ma·t̪ər] *n* alma máter *f*
almanac ['ɔl·mə·næk] *n* almanaque *m*
almighty [ɔl·'maɪ·t̪i] I. *adj inf* todopoderoso, -a II. *n* **the Almighty** el Todopoderoso
almond ['a·mənd] *n* **1.**(*nut*) almendra *f* **2.**(*tree*) almendro *m*
almost ['ɔl·moʊst] *adv* casi; **~ half** casi la mitad; **we're ~ there** casi hemos llegado
alms [amz] *npl* limosna *f*
aloe vera [,al·oʊ·'ver·ə] *n* áloe *m* vera
aloha [ə·'loʊ·ə] *interj reg: Hawaiian* (*greeting,*

farewell) aloha
alone [ə·'loʊn] I. *adj* **1.**(*without others*) solo, -a; **to do sth ~** hacer algo solo; **to go it ~** *inf* hacerlo por su cuenta; **to leave sb ~** dejar a alguien en paz; **to leave sth ~** dejar algo como está **2.**(*unique*) **to be ~ in doing sth** ser el único/los únicos en hacer algo; **Jane ~ can do that** Jane es la única que puede hacerlo ► **let ~...** mucho menos... II. *adv* solamente, sólo
along [ə·'lɑŋ] I. *prep*; **all ~** a lo largo de; **all ~ the river** a lo largo del río; **~ the road** por la carretera; **I lost it ~ the way** lo perdí por el camino; **it's ~ here** está por aquí II. *adv* **all ~** todo el tiempo; **to bring/take sb ~** traer/llevar a alguien; **to go ~** seguir adelante; **he will be ~ in an hour** llegará en una hora; **come ~!** ¡ven con nosotros!
alongside [ə·'lɑŋ·saɪd] I. *prep* **1.**(*next to*) junto a; **to draw up ~ sb/sth** pararse al lado de alguien/algo; **~ each other** uno junto al otro; **to fight ~ sb** luchar al lado de alguien **2.** NAUT al costado de II. *adv* al lado; NAUT de costado
aloof [ə·'luf] *adj* distante; **to remain ~ from sth** mantenerse alejado de algo
aloud [ə·'laʊd] *adv* en voz alta; **to think ~** pensar en voz alta
alpha ['æl·fə] *n* alfa *f*
alphabet ['æl·fə·bet] *n* alfabeto *m*
alphabetical [,æl·fə·'bet̪·ɪ·kəl] *adj* alfabético, -a; **in ~ order** en orden alfabético
alphabetize *vt* alfabetizar
alphanumeric [,æl·fə·nu·'mer·ɪk] *adj* alfanumérico, -a
alpha particle *n* partícula *f* alfa
alpha ray *n* rayo *m* alfa
alpine ['æl·paɪn] *adj* alpino, -a
Alps [ælps] *npl* the ~ los Alpes
already [ɔl·'red·i] *adv* ya
alright [ɔl·'raɪt] *adv s.* **all right**
Alsace ['æl·sæs] *n* Alsacia *f*
Alsatian [æl·'seɪ·ʃən] I. *n* (*person*) alsaciano, -a *m, f* II. *adj* alsaciano, -a
also ['ɔl·soʊ] *adv* también
altar ['ɔl·t̪ər] *n* altar *m*
altar boy *n* monaguillo *m*
altar girl *n* monaguilla *f*
alter ['ɔl·t̪ər] I. *vt* **1.**(*change: text, plan*) cambiar; (*option*) cambiar de; (*paint*) retocar **2.** FASHION (*dress, suit*) hacer ajustes a **3.**(*castrate: dog, cat*) castrar II. *vi* cambiarse
alterable ['ɔl·t̪ər·ə·bəl] *adj* modificable
alteration [,ɔl·t̪ər·'eɪ·ʃən] *n* **1.**(*change*) modificación *f*; (*in house*) reforma *f* **2.**(*act of changing*) modificación *f*
altercation [,ɔl·t̪ər·'keɪ·ʃən] *n* altercado *m*
alter ego ['al·t̪ər·i·goʊ] *n* **1.**(*second identity*) álter ego *m* **2.**(*close friend*) amigo íntimo, álter ego *m elev*
alternate¹ ['ɔl·t̪ər·neɪt] *vi, vt* alternar
alternate² ['ɔl·t̪ər·nɪt] *adj* **1.**(*by turns*) alterno, -a; **on ~ days** en días alternos **2.**(*alternative*) alternativo, -a

alternating ['ɔl·tər·neɪ·t̬ɪŋ] *adj* alterno, -a
alternating current *n* ELEC corriente *f* alterna
alternative [ɔl·'tɜr·nə·t̬ɪv] I. *n* alternativa *f;* to have no ~ but to do sth no tener otra alternativa que hacer algo II. *adj* alternativo, -a
alternative-fuel *adj* (*car*) que utiliza combustibles alternativos
alternatively *adv* 1. (*on the other hand*) si no 2. (*as a substitute*) en lugar de esto
alternator ['ɔl·tər·neɪ·t̬ər] *n* alternador *m*
alt-fuel *adj inf abbr of* **alternative-fuel** (*car*) que utiliza combustibles alternativos
although [ɔl·'ðoʊ] *conj* aunque; **he is stingy ~ he is rich** es tacaño a pesar de que es rico; **~ it's snowing...** aunque está nevando...
altimeter [æl·'tɪm·ɪ·t̬ər] *n* AVIAT altímetro *m*
altitude ['æl·tə·tud] *n* altitud *f*
alto ['æl·toʊ] *n* 1. (*woman*) contralto *f* 2. (*man*) contralto *m*
altogether [ɔl·tə·'geð·ər] I. *adv* 1. (*completely*) totalmente; **not ~** no del todo 2. (*in total*) en total II. *n* **in the ~** en cueros *inf*
alto saxophone *n* saxofón *m* alto
altruism ['æl·tru·ɪz·əm] *n* altruismo *m*
altruist ['æl·tru·ɪst] *n* altruista *mf*
altruistic [æl·tru·'ɪs·tɪk] *adj* altruista
aluminum [ə·'lu·mə·nəm] *n* aluminio *m*
aluminum foil *n* papel *m* de plata
aluminum oxide *n* alúmina *f*
always ['ɔl·weɪz] *adv* 1. (*at all times*) siempre 2. (*alternatively*) siempre, en todo caso
Alzheimer's disease ['alts·haɪ·mərz] *n* enfermedad *f* de Alzheimer
am [əm, *stressed:* æm] *vi* 1. *pers sing of* **be**
A.M. [eɪ·'em], **a.m.** *abbr of* **ante meridiem** a.m.
amalgam [ə·'mæl·gəm] *n* amalgama *f*
amalgamate [ə·'mæl·gə·meɪt] I. *vt* 1. (*metals*) amalgamar II. *vi* 1. (*metals*) amalgamarse 2. COM fusionarse
amalgamation [ə·mæl·gə·'meɪ·ʃən] *n* 1. (*process*) amalgamación *f* 2. COM fusión *f*
amass [ə·'mæs] *vt* (*money*) amasar; (*information*) acumular
amateur ['æm·ə·tʃər] I. *n* 1. (*not professional*) aficionado, -a *m, f* 2. *offensive* (*lacking skill*) chapucero, -a *m, f* II. *adj* aficionado, -a; **~ sport** deporte *m* de aficionados
amateurish [æm·ə·'tʃɜr·ɪʃ] *adj* chapucero, -a
amaze [ə·'meɪz] *vt* 1. (*astound*) asombrar; **to be ~d that...** quedar asombrado porque...; **to be ~d by sth** estar asombrado por algo 2. (*surprise*) sorprender; **to be ~d by sth** estar sorprendido por algo
amazement *n* asombro *m;* **to stare at sth in ~** quedarse boquiabierto mirando algo; **to my ~** para mi gran asombro
amazing *adj* asombroso, -a, sorpresivo, -a *AmL;* **truly ~** realmente increíble
Amazon ['æm·ə·zan] *n* 1. (*river*) **the ~** el Amazonas 2. (*female warrior*) amazona *f*
ambassador [æm·'bæs·ə·dər] *n* embajador(a) *m(f)*

amber ['æm·bər] I. *n* ámbar *m* II. *adj* ambarino, -a
ambidextrous [æm·bɪ·'dek·strəs] *adj* ambidextro, -a
ambient ['æm·bi·ənt] *adj* ambiental
ambiguity [æm·bə·'gju·ə·t̬i] <-ies> *n* ambigüedad *f*
ambiguous [æm·'bɪg·ju·əs] *adj* ambiguo, -a
ambition [æm·'bɪʃ·ən] *n* ambición *f;* **she has no ~** no es nada ambiciosa
ambitious [æm·'bɪʃ·əs] *adj* ambicioso, -a; **to be ~ for sth** tener ambición de algo; **to be ~ to do sth** tener la ambición de hacer algo
ambivalent [æm·'bɪv·ə·lənt] *adj* ambivalente; **to feel ~ about** [*o* towards] **sth/sb** tener sentimientos encontrados hacia algo/alguien
amble ['æm·bəl] I. *vi* andar [*o* pasear] tranquilamente II. *n* 1. (*stroll*) paseo *m* 2. (*of horse*) ambladura *f*
ambulance ['æm·bju·ləns] *n* ambulancia *f*
ambush ['æm·buʃ] I. *vt* **to ~ sb** tender una emboscada a alguien II. *n* <-es> emboscada *f;* **to lie in ~ for sb** aguardar emboscado a alguien
ameba <-bas *o* -bae> *n s.* **amoeba**
amebiasis [æm·ə·'baɪ·ə·sɪs] *n* amebiasis *f inv,* disentería *f* amebiana
amebic *adj s.* **amoebic**
ameliorate [ə·'mil·jə·reɪt] *vt form* mejorar
amelioration [ə·mil·jə·'reɪ·ʃən] *n form* mejora *f*
amen [eɪ·'men] *interj* amén; **~ to that!** ¡así es!
amenable [ə·'mi·nə·bəl] *adj* receptivo, -a; **to be ~ to sth** mostrarse receptivo a (aceptar) algo; **to be ~ to reason** estar dispuesto a entrar en razón
amend [ə·'mend] *vt* 1. (*text, constitution*) enmendar; (*plan*) modificar 2. BOT (*soil*) mejorar
amendment *n* 1. (*to text, constitution*) enmienda *f;* (*to plan*) modificación *f* 2. (*to soil*) mejora *f* (de la tierra)
amends *npl* **to make ~ for sth** reparar algo
amenities [ə·'men·ə·t̬iz] *npl* comodidades *fpl*
America [ə·'mer·ɪ·kə] *n* América *f* (del Norte), Estados *m* Unidos *pl;* **the ~s** las Américas
American [ə·'mer·ɪ·kən] I. *n* 1. (*person from USA*) estadounidense *mf;* americano, -a *m, f* 2. (*person from American continent*) americano, -a *m, f* 3. LING inglés *m* americano II. *adj* americano, -a
American Indian *n s.* **Native American**
Americanism *n* americanismo *m*
Americanize *vt* americanizar
amethyst ['æm·ɪ·θɪst] I. *n* 1. (*stone*) amatista *f* 2. (*color*) amatista *m* II. *adj* amatista
amiability [eɪ·mi·ə·'bɪl·ə·t̬i] *n* amabilidad *f*
amiable ['eɪ·mi·ə·bəl] *adj* amable
amicable ['æm·ɪ·kə·bəl] *adj* amistoso, -a; **to reach an ~ settlement** llegar a un arreglo amistoso
amid(st) [ə·'mɪd(st)] *prep* en medio de, entre
amino acid [ə·'mi·noʊ·'æs·ɪd] *n* ami-

noácido *m*
amiss [ə·'mɪs] I. *adj* there's something ~
algo va mal II. *adv* to take sth ~ tomar algo a
mal; a little courtesy would not go ~ no
vendría mal un poco de cortesía
ammeter ['æm·mi·ţər] *n* ELEC amperímetro *m*
ammonia [ə·'moʊn·jə] *n* 1. (*gas*) amoniaco *m*,
amoníaco *m* 2. (*liquid*) amoniaco *m* (líquido),
amoníaco *m* (líquido)
ammunition [ˌæm·jə·'nɪʃ·ən] *n* 1. (*for guns*)
munición *f* 2. *fig* argumentos *mpl*
ammunition depot *n* depósito *m* de municiones
amnesia [æm·'ni·ʒə] *n* amnesia *f*
amnesty ['æm·nɪ·sti] <-ies> *n* amnistía *f*
amoeba [ə·'mi·bə] <-bas *o* -bae> *n* ameba *f*
amoebiasis *n s.* amebiasis
amoebic [ə·'mi·bɪk] *adj* amébico, -a
amok [ə·'mʌk] *adv s.* amuck
among(st) [ə·'mʌɲ(st)] *prep* entre; ~ friends
entre amigos; (just) one ~ many (sólo) uno
entre tantos; ~ Canadians entre los canadienses; to divide sth up ~ us dividir algo
entre nosotros; ~ the flowers/the pupils
entre las flores/los alumnos; ~ other things
entre otras cosas
amoral [ˌeɪ·'mɔr·əl] *adj* amoral
amorous ['æm·ər·əs] *adj* amoroso, -a
amorphous [ə·'mɔr·fəs] *adj* amorfo, -a
amortization [æm·ˌər·ţɪ·'zeɪ·ʃən] *n* amortización *f*
amortize [ə·'mɔr·taɪz] *vt* amortizar
amount [ə·'maʊnt] I. *n* 1. (*quantity*) cantidad
f; a certain ~ of difficulty alguna [*o* cierta]
dificultad 2. (*very much*) any ~ of grandes
cantidades de; any ~ of people mucha gente
3. (*of money*) suma *f*, importe *m*; a check in
the ~ of... un cheque por valor de...; ~ carried forward traslado a cuenta nueva II. *vi*
1. (*add up to*) to ~ to sth ascender a algo; that
~s to a refusal eso viene a ser una negativa
2. (*be successful*) to ~ to sth llegar a algo; he
will never ~ to much nunca llegará a nada
amp 1. *abbr of* ampere amp 2. MUS *inf abbr of*
amplifier amplificador *m*, ampli *m*
ampere ['æm·pɪr] *n* amperio *m*
ampersand [ˌæm·pər·'sænd] *n* COMPUT arroba *f*
ampersat [ˌæm·pər·'sæt] *n* COMPUT arroba *f*
amphetamine [æm·'fet·ə·min] *n* anfetamina *f*
amphibian [æm·'fɪb·i·ən] I. *adj* anfibio, -a II. *n*
1. ZOOL anfibio *m* 2. AUTO vehículo *m* anfibio
amphibious [æm·'fɪb·i·əs] *adj* anfibio, -a
amphitheater ['æm·fə‚θi·ə·ţər] *n* anfiteatro *m*
ample ['æm·pəl] *adj* 1. (*plentiful*) abundante
2. (*large*) amplio, -a 3. (*enough*) suficiente
amplification [ˌæm·plə·fɪ·'keɪ·ʃən] *n* 1. MUS
amplificación *f* 2. (*increased detail*) ampliación *f*
amplifier ['æm·plə·faɪ·ər] *n* amplificador *m*
amplify ['æm·plə·faɪ] <-ie-> I. *vt* 1. MUS
amplificar 2. (*enlarge upon: statement*)
ampliar; (*idea*) desarrollar; (*remark*) aclarar
II. *vi* to ~ upon sth extenderse sobre algo

amplitude ['æm·plɪ·tud] *n* amplitud *f*
ampoule *n*, ampule ['æm·pul] *n* MED
ampolla *f*
amputate ['æm·pju·teɪt] *vt* amputar
amputation [ˌæm·pju·'teɪ·ʃən] *n* amputación *f*
amputee [ˌæm·pju·'ti] *n* mutilado, -a *m, f*
amuck [ə·'mʌk] *adv* de forma descontrolada; to
run ~ descontrolarse
amulet ['æm·jʊ·lɪt] *n* amuleto *m*, cábula *f Arg,
Méx, Par*
amuse [ə·'mjuz] *vt* 1. (*entertain*) entretener;
to ~ oneself distraerse; to keep sb ~d entretener a alguien 2. (*cause laughter*) divertir,
hacer gracia; I'm not ~d no me hace gracia
amusement [ə·'mjuz·mənt] *n* 1. (*entertainment*) entretenimiento *m*, entretención *f AmL;
for one's own ~ para entretenerse 2. (*mirth*)
diversión *f*; (much) to my ~ con (gran)
regocijo por mi parte; he looked on in ~ miró
divertido 3. (*laughter*) risa *f*; to conceal one's
~ aguantarse la risa
amusement park *n* parque *m* de atracciones
amusing *adj* divertido, -a, gracioso, -a
an [ən, *stressed:* æn] *indef art before vowel s.* a
anabolic steroid [æn·ə·'bɔl·ɪk·'ster·ɔɪd] *n*
esteroide *m* anabolizante
anachronism [ə·'næk·rə·nɪz·əm] *n* anacro-
nismo *m*
anachronistic [ə·ˌnæk·rə·'nɪs·tɪk] *adj* ana-
crónico, -a
anaconda [ˌæn·ə·'kan·də] *n* anaconda *f*
anagram ['æn·ə·græm] *n* anagrama *m*
anal ['eɪ·nəl] *adj* anal
analgesic [æn·əl·'dʒi·zɪk] I. *adj* analgésico, -a
II. *n* analgésico *m*
analog ['æn·ə·lag] *n* equivalente *m*
analog computer *n* ordenador *m* analógico,
computadora *f* analógica *AmL*
analogous [ə·'næl·ə·gəs] *adj* análogo, -a; to
be ~ to sth ser análogo a algo
analogy [ə·'næl·ə·dʒi] <-ies> *n* analogía *f*; to
draw an ~ between establecer una analogía
entre; by ~ with sth por analogía con algo
analysis [ə·'næl·ə·sɪs] <-ses> *n* 1. (*examination*) análisis *m inv* 2. (*psychoanalysis*) psicoanálisis *m inv*; to be in ~ seguir un tratamiento de psicoanálisis ▶ in the final [*o* last] ~
a fin de cuentas
analyst ['æn·ə·lɪst] *n* 1. (*analyzer*) analista *mf*;
food ~ analista de alimentos; financial ~ analista de inversiones 2. PSYCH psicoanalista *mf*
analytic [ˌæn·ə·'lɪţ·ɪk], analytical [ˌæn·ə·'lɪţ·
ɪ·kəl] *adj* analítico, -a
analyze ['æn·ə·laɪz] *vt* analizar; PSYCH psicoanalizar
anarchic [æn·'ar·kɪk] *adj*, anarchical [æn·'ar·
kɪ·kəl] *adj* anárquico, -a
anarchism ['æn·ər·kɪ·zəm] *n* anarquismo *m*
anarchist ['æn·ər·kɪst] I. *adj* anarquista II. *n*
anarquista *mf*
anarchistic [ˌæn·ər·'kɪs·tɪk] *adj* anarquista
anarchy ['æn·ər·ki] *n* anarquía *f*
anathema [ə·'næθ·ə·mə] *n* 1. REL anatema *m*

2. *fig* **the very idea was ~ to her** la sola idea le resultaba odiosa

anatomical [ˌæn·ə·'tam·ɪ·kəl] *adj* anatómico, -a

anatomy [ə·'næṱ·ə·mi] <-ies> *n* **1.** BIO anatomía *f* **2.** *iron* (*body*) anatomía *f*, cuerpo *m* **3.** (*analysis*) análisis *m inv*

ancestor ['æn·ses·tər] *n* **1.** (*of person*) antepasado, -a *m, f* **2.** (*of idea, organization*) precursor(a) *m(f)*

ancestral [æn·'ses·trəl] *adj* ancestral; **the ~ home** la casa solariega

ancestry ['æn·ses·tri] <-ies> *n* ascendencia *f*; **she is of Polish ~** es de ascendencia polaca

anchor ['æŋ·kər] **I.** *n* **1.** NAUT ancla *f*, sacho *m* *Chile;* **to be at ~** estar anclado; **to drop/ weigh ~** echar/levar anclas **2.** *fig* sostén *m* **3.** (*news ~*) presentador(a) *m(f)* de un boletín informativo **II.** *vt* **1.** NAUT anclar **2.** (*rope, tent*) sujetar **3.** RADIO, TV **to ~ a radio/TV program** presentar un programa de radio/de televisión **III.** *vi* NAUT echar anclas

anchorage ['æŋ·kər·ɪdʒ] *n* **1.** (*place*) fondeadero *m* **2.** (*fee*) anclaje *m*

anchorman ['æŋ·kər·mæn] <-men> *n* **1.** RADIO, TV presentador *m* **2.** *fig* hombre *m* clave

anchorwoman ['æŋ·kər·ˌwʊm·ən] <-men> *n* **1.** RADIO, TV presentadora *f* **2.** *fig* mujer *f* clave

anchovy ['æn·tʃoʊ·vi] <-ies> *n* (*fresh*) boquerón *m;* (*canned, smoked*) anchoa *f*

ancient ['eɪn·ʃənt] **I.** *adj* **1.** *a.* HIST antiguo, -a; **~ since ~ times** desde tiempos remotos; **~ history** historia antigua; **to be ~ history** *fig* haber pasado a la historia **2.** *inf* (*very old*) prehistórico, -a, del año de la pera; **I feel pretty ~** me siento viejísimo **II.** *n* **the ~s** los antiguos

ancillary ['æn·sə·ler·i] *adj* **1.** (*staff*) auxiliar **2.** (*road*) secundario, -a; **to be ~ to sth** estar subordinado a algo

and [ən, ənd, *stressed:* ænd] *conj* **1.** (*also*) y; (*before 'i' or 'hi'*) e; **black ~ white** blanco y negro; **food ~ drink** comida y bebida; **parents ~ children** padres e hijos **2.** MATH y; **2 ~ 3 is 5** 2 más 3 son 5; **four hundred ~ twelve** cuatrocientos doce **3.** (*then*) **he left ~ everybody was relieved** todo el mundo se alivió cuando él se fue **4.** (*increase*) **more ~ more** cada vez más; **better ~ better** cada vez mejor **5.** (*repetition*) **I tried ~ tried** lo intenté una y otra vez [*o* repetidas veces] **6.** (*continuation*) **he cried ~ cried** lloraba sin parar ▸ **~ so on** [*o* **forth**] etcétera

Andalusia [ˌæn·də·'lu·ʒə] *n* Andalucía *f*

Andalusian I. *adj* andaluz(a) **II.** *n* **1.** (*person*) andaluz(a) *m(f)* **2.** LING andaluz *m*

Andean ['æn·di·ən] *adj* andino, -a

Andes ['æn·diz] *npl* Andes *mpl*

Andorra [æn·'dɔr·ə] *n* Andorra *f*

Andorran I. *adj* andorrano, -a **II.** *n* andorrano, -a *m, f*

androgynous [æn·'dradʒ·ə·nəs] *adj* andrógino, -a

android ['æn·drɔɪd] *n* androide *m*

anecdotal [ˌæn·ɪk·'doʊṱ·əl] *adj* anecdótico, -a

anecdote ['æn·ɪk·doʊt] *n* anécdota *f*

anemia [ə·'ni·mi·ə] *n* anemia *f*

anemic [ə·'ni·mɪk] *adj* anémico, -a

anemone [ə·'nem·ə·ni] *n* anémona *f*

anesthesia [ˌæn·ɪs·'θi·ʒə] *n* anestesia *f*

anesthetic [ˌæn·ɪs·'θeṱ·ɪk] **I.** *adj* anestésico, -a **II.** *n* anestésico *m;* **to be under ~** estar bajo los efectos de la anestesia; **to give sb an ~** anestesiar a alguien

anesthetist [ə·'nes·θɪ·tɪst] *n* anestesista *mf*

anesthetize [ə·'nes·θɪ·taɪz] *vt* anestesiar

anew [ə·'nu] *adv* de nuevo; **to begin ~** volver a empezar (de nuevo)

angel ['eɪn·dʒl] *n* ángel *m;* **~ of death** ángel exterminador; **to be no ~** no ser ningún ángel

angelic [æn·'dʒel·ɪk] *adj* angelical

anger ['æŋ·gər] **I.** *n* enfado *m*, enojo *m AmL;* (*stronger*) ira *f*, cólera *f;* **to speak in ~** hablar indignado **II.** *vt* enfadar, enojar *AmL*

angina [æn·'dʒaɪ·nə] *n* angina *f;* **~ pectoris** angina de pecho

angle¹ ['æŋ·gəl] **I.** *n* **1.** *a.* MATH ángulo *m;* **at an ~ of 90 degrees, at a 90 degree ~** en ángulo recto, en ángulo de 90 grados; **to be at an ~ (to sth)** formar un ángulo (con algo); **the picture was hanging at an ~** el cuadro estaba torcido; **he wore his hat at an ~** llevaba el sombrero ladeado **2.** (*perspective*) perspectiva *f;* **to see sth from a different ~** ver algo desde otro ángulo; **what is the best news ~ for this story?** ¿cuál es el mejor enfoque informativo para esta historia? **3.** (*opinion*) punto *m* de vista; **what's your ~ on this issue?** ¿qué opina(s) sobre esta cuestión? **4.** *inf* (*scheme, ploy*) **she knows all the ~s** se las sabe todas **II.** *vt* **1.** (*turn at an angle: shot*) ladear **2.** (*information*) dirigir; **this article is ~d towards teenagers** este artículo se dirige a los adolescentes

angle² ['æŋ·gəl] *vi* **1.** (*to fish*) pescar (con caña); **to go ~** ir a pescar **2.** *fig* **to ~ for sth** *inf* tratar de pescar algo

angler ['æŋ·glər] *n* pescador(a) *m(f)* de caña

Anglican ['æŋ·glɪ·kən] **I.** *adj* anglicano, -a **II.** *n* anglicano, -a *m, f*

Anglican Church *n* Iglesia *f* anglicana

Anglicist ['æŋ·glɪ·sɪst] *n* anglicista *mf*

Anglicize ['æŋ·glɪ·saɪz] *vt* anglicanizar

Anglo-American [ˌæŋ·gloʊ·ə·'mer·ɪ·kən] **I.** *n* angloamericano, -a *m, f* **II.** *adj* angloamericano, -a

Anglophile ['æŋ·glə·faɪl] *n* anglófilo, -a *m, f*

Anglophobe [ˌæŋ·glə·'foʊb] *n* anglófobo, -a *m, f*

Anglophone *n Can* Anglohablante *mf* en el Canadá

Anglo-Saxon [ˌæŋ·gloʊ·'sæk·sən] **I.** *adj* anglosajón, -ona **II.** *n* **1.** (*person*) anglosajón, -ona *m, f* **2.** LING anglosajón *m*

Angola [æŋ·'goʊ·lə] *n* Angola *f*

Angolan I. *adj* angoleño, -a **II.** *n* angoleño, -a

m, f

angora [æŋ·ˈgɔ·rə] n 1.(fabric) angora f 2.(cat) gato m de angora

angry [ˈæŋ·gri] adj 1.(person) enfadado, -a, enojado, -a AmL; (crowd) enfurecido, -a; (sky) tormentoso, -a; (sea) embravecido, -a; **to make sb ~** enfadar [o enojar AmL] a alguien; **to get ~ with sb** enfadarse con alguien, enojarse con alguien AmL; **to get ~ about sth** enfadarse por algo, enojarse por algo AmL; **to exchange ~ words** intercambiar palabras llenas de ira 2. MED inflamado, -a

angst [æŋkst] n angustia f

anguish [ˈæŋ·gwɪʃ] n angustia f; **to be in ~ (over sth)** estar angustiado (por algo); **to cause sb ~** angustiar a alguien

angular [ˈæŋ·gjʊ·lər] adj (shape) angular; (face) anguloso, -a

animal [ˈæn·ɪ·məl] I. n 1. ZOOL animal m; **~ fat** grasa f animal 2. fig (person) animal m, bestia mf II. adj (instincts) animal; (desires) carnal

animal cracker n CULIN galletita con forma de animal, galletita f de animalitos Méx

animal husbandry n cría f de animales

animal kingdom n reino m animal

animal rights npl derechos mpl de los animales

animate¹ [ˈæn·ɪ·meɪt] vt animar

animate² [ˈæn·ɪ·mɪt] adj animado, -a

animated adj animado, -a; **to become ~** animarse

animation [ˌæn·ɪ·ˈmeɪ·ʃən] n animación f; **computer ~** animación por ordenador [o por computadora AmL]

animator [ˈæn·ɪ·meɪ·tər] n animador(a) m(f)

anime [əˈnim] n anime m, dibujos animados japoneses

animosity [ˌæn·ɪ·ˈmas·ə·t̬i] n animosidad f

anise [ˈæn·ɪs] n (planta f de) anís m

aniseed n, **anise seed** [ˈæn·ɪ·sid] n (semilla f de) anís m

ankle [ˈæŋ·kəl] n tobillo m

anklebone [ˈæŋ·kəl·boʊn] n hueso m del tobillo

ankle-deep adj **to be ~ in sth** estar metido hasta los tobillos en algo

anklet [ˈæŋ·klɪt] n 1.(chain) pulsera f tobillera 2.(short sock) calcetín m corto

annals [ˈæn·əlz] npl anales mpl

annex [ˈæn·eks] I. n <-es> 1.(of building) edificio m anexo 2.(of document) anexo m, apéndice m II. vt 1.(territory) anexionar 2.(document) adjuntar (como anexo); (clause) añadir

annexation [ˌæn·ɪk·ˈseɪ·ʃən] n anexión f

annihilate [əˈnaɪ·ə·leɪt] vt a. fig aniquilar

annihilation [əˌnaɪ·ə·ˈleɪ·ʃən] n a. fig aniquilación f

anniversary [ˌæn·ə·ˈvɜr·sə·ri] <-ies> n aniversario m

annotate [ˈæn·ə·teɪt] vt anotar; **~d edition** edición f comentada

annotation [ˌæn·ə·ˈteɪ·ʃən] n 1.(act of writ-

ing) anotación f 2.(note) anotación f, nota f

announce [əˈnaʊns] vt anunciar; (result) comunicar

announcement n anuncio m; **official ~** comunicado m oficial; **to make an ~ about sth** anunciar algo

announcer [əˈnaʊn·sər] n locutor(a) m(f)

annoy [əˈnɔɪ] vt molestar, fastidiar, embromar AmL, enchilar AmC; **to get ~ed with sb** enfadarse [o enojarse AmL] con alguien

annoyance [əˈnɔɪ·əns] n 1.(irritation) fastidio m, enojo m AmL; **much to my ~, she won** me fastidia que haya ganado 2.(irritating thing) molestia f, fastidio m

annoying adj (noise, fact) molesto, -a, chocante AmL; (person) pesado, -a; (habit) fastidioso, -a; **it's ~ to think that...** me da rabia pensar que...; **how ~!** ¡qué fastidio!

annual [ˈæn·ju·əl] I. adj anual II. n 1.(book) anuario m 2. BOT planta f anual

annually [ˈæn·ju·ə·li] adv anualmente

annuity [əˈnu·ə·t̬i] <-ies> n renta f anual

annul [əˈnʌl] <-ll-> vt anular

annulment [əˈnʌl·mənt] n anulación f

Annunciation [əˌnʌn·si·ˈeɪ·ʃən] n **the ~** la Anunciación

anode [ˈæn·oʊd] n ánodo m

anodyne [ˈæn·ə·daɪn] I. adj anodino, -a II. n MED analgésico m

anoint [əˈnɔɪnt] vt untar; (oil) ungir

anointing n unción f

anomalous [əˈnam·ə·ləs] adj anómalo, -a

anomaly [əˈnam·ə·li] <-ies> n anomalía f

anonymity [ˌæn·ə·ˈnɪm·ɪ·t̬i] n anonimato m

anonymous [əˈnan·ə·məs] adj anónimo, -a; **~ letter** carta f anónima; **to remain ~** permanecer en el anonimato

anorexia [ˌæn·ə·ˈrek·si·ə] n anorexia f

anorexia nervosa n anorexia f nerviosa

anorexic [ˌæn·ə·ˈrek·sɪk] adj anoréxico, -a

another [əˈnʌð·ər] I. pron 1.(one more) otro, -a; **it's always one thing or ~** siempre pasa algo inf 2.(mutual) **one ~** uno a otro; **they love one ~** se quieren II. adj otro, -a; **~ pastry?** ¿otro pastel?; **~ $30** otros 30 dólares; **could he be ~ Mozart?** ¿podría ser otro Mozart?

answer [ˈæn·sər] I. n 1.(reply) respuesta f, contestación f; **in ~ to your question** como respuesta a tu pregunta; **I called but there was no ~** llamé pero no contestaron; **the short ~ is 'no'** en una palabra: no 2.(solution) solución f 3. LAW contestación f 4.(equivalent) **to be the French ~ to the Beatles** ser el equivalente francés de los Beatles II. vt 1.(respond to) contestar a; **to ~ the telephone** contestar al teléfono; **to ~ the door** abrir la puerta 2.(fit, suit: description) responder a; (need) satisfacer; (prayers) escuchar III. vi contestar, responder

◆**answer back** vi contestar, replicar; **don't ~!** ¡no repliques!

◆**answer for** vt (action, situation) responder

de; (*person*) responder por; **to ~ oneself** responder por sí mismo; **to have a lot to ~** tener mucha culpa

◆**answer to** *vt* **1.** (*obey*) obedecer a **2.** (*fit: description*) corresponder a **3.** (*be named*) **to ~ the name of Billy** responder al nombre de Billy

answerable ['æn·sər·ə·bəl] *adj* **1.** (*responsible*) **to be ~ for sth** ser responsable de algo **2.** (*accountable*) **to be ~ to sb** tener que rendir cuentas a alguien; **to be ~ to nobody** no tener que rendir cuentas a nadie

answering machine *n* contestador *m* automático

answering service *n* servicio *m* de mensajes

ant [ænt] *n* hormiga *f* ▶**to have ~s in one's pants** *inf* tener hormigas en el culo, ser un manojo de nervios

antagonism [æn·'tæg·ə·nɪz·əm] *n* **1.** (*towards sb*) animadversión *f*; (*between people*) rivalidad *f* **2.** (*of ideas, systems*) antagonismo *m*

antagonistic [æn·ˌtæg·ə·'nɪs·tɪk] *adj* **1.** (*person, attitude*) antagónico, -a **2.** ANAT antagonista

antagonize [æn·'tæg·ə·naɪz] *vt* enfadar, enojar *AmL*

Antarctic [ænt·'ark·tɪk] I. *adj* antártico, -a II. *n* **the ~** el Antártico

Antarctica [ænt·'ark·tɪ·kə] *n* la Antártida

Antarctic Circle *n* círculo *m* polar antártico

Antarctic Ocean *n* Océano *m* Antártico

ante ['æn·ti] *n* apuesta *f*; **to raise the ~** subir la apuesta

anteater ['ænt·ˌi·tər] *n* oso *m* hormiguero

antecedent [ˌæn·tɪ·'si·dənt] I. *n* **1.** (*forerunner*) antecedente *m*, precedente *m* **2.** *pl* (*past history*) antecedentes *mpl* II. *adj* antecedente, precedente

antechamber ['æn·tɪ·ˌtʃeɪm·bər] *n* antecámara *f*

antediluvian [ˌæn·tɪ·də·'lu·vi·ən] *adj a. fig* antediluviano, -a

antelope ['æn·tɪ·loʊp] <-(s)> *n* antílope *m*

antenna [æn·'ten·ə] <-nae *o* -s> *n* antena *f*

anterior [æn·'tɪr·i·ər] *adj* anterior

anteroom ['æn·tɪ·rum] *n* antesala *f*

anthem ['æn·θəm] *n* himno *m*

anthill ['ænt·hɪl] *n* hormiguero *m*

anthology [æn·'θɑl·ə·dʒi] <-ies> *n* antología *f*

anthracite ['æn·θrə·saɪt] *n* antracita *f*

anthropoid ['æn·θrə·pɔɪd] I. *n* antropoide *mf* II. *adj* antropoide

anthropological [ˌæn·θrə·pə·'lɑdʒ·ɪ·kəl] *adj* antropológico, -a

anthropologist [ˌæn·θrə·'pɑl·ə·dʒɪst] *n* antropólogo, -a *m, f*

anthropology [ˌæn·θrə·'pɑl·ə·dʒi] *n* antropología *f*

anti ['æn·ti] I. *adj* en contra; **to be ~** estar en contra II. *prep* en contra de

antiabortion [ˌæn·ti·ə·'bɔr·ʃən] *adj* antiabortista, contrario, -a al aborto

antiaging cream *n* crema *f* antiarrugas

antiaircraft [ˌæn·tɪ·'er·kræft] *adj* antiaéreo, -a

anti-American *adj* antiamericano, -a

antibiotic [ˌæn·tɪ·baɪ·'ɑt̬·ɪk] I. *n* antibiótico *m* II. *adj* antibiótico, -a

antibody ['æn·tɪ·bɑd·i] <-ies> *n* anticuerpo *m*

anticipate [æn·'tɪs·ə·peɪt] *vt* **1.** (*expect, foresee*) prever; **to ~ doing/being sth** tener previsto hacer/ser algo **2.** (*look forward to*) esperar (con ilusión) **3.** (*act in advance of*) anticiparse a; **to ~ one's inheritance** gastarse de antemano la herencia

anticipation [æn·ˌtɪs·ə·'peɪ·ʃən] *n* **1.** (*foresight*) previsión *f*; **in ~ of** en previsión de **2.** (*funds*) anticipo *m* **3.** (*excitement*) ilusión *f*; **to wait in ~** esperar con gran ilusión

anticipatory [æn·'tɪs·ə·pə·tɔr·i] *adj* previsor(a)

anticlerical [ˌæn·tɪ·'kler·ɪ·kəl] *adj* anticlerical

anticlimactic [ˌæn·tɪ·klɪ·'mæk·tɪk] *adj* decepcionante

anticlimax [ˌæn·tɪ·'klaɪ·mæks] <-es> *n* anticlímax *m inv*; (*disappointment*) decepción *f*

anticoagulant [ˌæn·tɪ·koʊ·'æg·jə·lənt] I. *n* anticoagulante *m* II. *adj* anticoagulante

antics ['æn·tɪks] *npl* **1.** (*foolish behavior*) payasadas *fpl* **2.** (*tricks*) travesuras *fpl*

antidepressant [ˌæn·tɪ·dɪ·'pres·ənt] I. *adj* antidepresivo, -a II. *n* antidepresivo *m*

antidote [æn·tɪ·doʊt] *n* antídoto *m*; **an ~ to sth** un antídoto contra algo

antiestablishment *adj* antisistema

antifreeze ['æn·tɪ·friz] *n* anticongelante *m*

antigen ['æn·tɪ·dʒən] *n* antígeno *m*

Antigua and Barbuda [æn·'ti·gə·ən·bar·'bu·də] *n* Antigua y Barbuda

Antiguan [æn·'ti·gən] I. *adj* antiguano, -a II. *n* antiguano, -a *m, f*

antihero [æn·tɪ·'hɪr·oʊ] <-es> *n* antihéroe *m*

antihistamine [ˌæn·tɪ·'hɪs·tə·ˌmin] *n* MED antihistamínico *m*

anti-inflammatory [ˌæn·ti·ɪn·'flæm·ə·tɔr·i] *adj* MED antiinflamatorio, -a

antiknock ['æn·tɪ·'nak] *adj* antidetonante

Antilles [æn·'tɪl·iz] *npl* **the ~** las Antillas

antilock braking system *n* AUTO sistema *m* antibloqueo de frenos

antimatter ['æn·tɪ·mæt̬·ər] *n* antimateria *f*

antimissile [ˌæn·tɪ·'mɪs·əl] *adj* antimisil

antioxidant [ˌæn·tɪ·'ak·sɪ·dənt] *n* antioxidante *m*

antipasto [ˌæn·t̬i·'pæs·ti] *n* entrada *f*; **antipasti** *pl* entremeses *mpl*

antipathy [æn·'tɪp·ə·θi] <-ies> *n* antipatía *f*

antiperspirant [ˌæn·tɪ·'pɜr·spər·ənt] *n* antitranspirante *m*

antipodes [æn·'tɪp·ə·diz] *npl* antípodas *fpl*

antipollution *adj* (*filter, law*) anticontaminante

antiquarian [ˌæn·tɪ·'kwer·i·ən] I. *n* (*dealer*) anticuario, -a *m, f*; (*collector*) coleccionista *mf* de antigüedades II. *adj* antiguo, -a

antiquary ['æn·tɪ·kwər·i] <-ies> *n s.* **antiquarian**

antiquated ['æn·tɪ·kwei·t̬ɪd] *adj* anticuado, -a

antique [æn·'tik] I. *n* (*object, piece of furni-*

ture) antigüedad *f*; (*old-fashioned*) antigualla *f* **II.** *adj* antiguo, -a; (*old-fashioned*) anticuado, -a

antique dealer *n* anticuario, -a *m, f*

antique shop *n* tienda *f* de antigüedades, anticuario *m*

antiquity [æn·'tɪk·wə·t̬i] <-ies> *n* **1.** (*ancient times*) antigüedad *f* **2.** *pl* (*relics*) antigüedades *fpl*

antirust [ˌæn·tɪ·'rʌst] *adj* antioxidante

anti-Semite [ˌæn·tɪ·'sem·aɪt] *n* antisemita *mf*

anti-Semitic [ˌæn·tɪ·sə·'mɪt̬·ɪk] *adj* antisemita

anti-Semitism [æn·tɪ·'sem·ə·t̬ɪz·əm] *n* antisemitismo *m*

antiseptic [ˌæn·tə·'sep·tɪk] **I.** *n* antiséptico *m* **II.** *adj* **1.** MED antiséptico, -a **2.** *fig, pej* aséptico, -a

antisocial [ˌæn·tɪ·'soʊ·ʃəl] *adj* antisocial

antistatic [ˌæn·tɪ·'stæt̬·ɪk] *adj* antiestático, -a

antitank [ˌæn·tɪ·'tæŋk] *adj* antitanque

antiterrorist *adj* (*measures*) antiterrorista

antithesis [æn·'tɪθ·ə·sɪs] <-ses> *n* antítesis *f inv*

antithetic [ˌæn·tɪ·'θet̬·ɪk] *adj*, **antithetical** [ˌæn·tɪ·'θet̬·ɪ·kəl] *adj* antitético, -a

antitoxin [ˌæn·tɪ·'tak·sɪn] *n* antitoxina *f*

antivirus [ˌæn·tɪ·'vaɪ·rəs] *adj* COMPUT antivirus *inv*; ~ **program** (programa *m*) antivirus *m inv*

antiwar [ˌæn·tɪ·'wɔr] *adj* antibelicista

antiwrinkle cream [ˌæn·tɪ·'rɪŋ·kəl·krim] *n* crema *f* antiarrugas

antler ['ænt·lər] *n* cuerno *m*; ~**s** cornamenta *f*

antonym ['æn·tə·nɪm] *n* antónimo *m*

Antwerp ['æn·twɜrp] *n* Amberes *m*

anus ['eɪ·nəs] *n* ano *m*

anvil ['æn·vɪl] *n a.* ANAT yunque *m*

anxiety [æŋ·'zaɪ·ə·t̬i] *n* **1.** (*concern*) inquietud *f*; PSYCH ansiedad *f*; **a source of ~** una fuente de preocupación **2.** (*desire*) ansia *f*; ~ **to do sth** ansias de hacer algo; ~ **for sth** ansia de [*o* por] algo

anxiety attack *n* ataque *m* de ansiedad

anxious ['æŋk·ʃəs] *adj* **1.** (*concerned*) preocupado, -a; (*look*) de inquietud; **to keep an ~ eye on sth** no quitar los ojos de encima a algo; **to be ~ about sth** estar preocupado por algo; **an ~ moment** un momento de preocupación **2.** *inf* (*eager*) ansioso, -a, chingo, -a *Ven*; **to be ~ to do sth** estar ansioso por hacer algo; **to be ~ for sth** estar ansioso por algo

any ['en·i] **I.** *adj* **1.** (*some*) algún, alguna; ~ **books** algunos libros; **do they have ~ money?** ¿tienen dinero?; **do you want ~ more soup?** ¿quieres más sopa? **2.** (*not important which*) cualquier; **come at ~ time** ven cuando quieras; **in ~ case** en cualquier caso **3.** (*in negatives*) ningún, ninguna; **I don't have ~ money** no tengo dinero; **there aren't ~ cars** no hay ningún coche **II.** *adv* **1.** (*not*) **more** no más; **she doesn't come here ~ more** ya no viene más **2.** (*at all*) **does she feel ~ better?** ¿se siente algo mejor?; **that doesn't help him ~** *inf* no le ayuda para nada

III. *pron* **1.** (*some*) alguno, alguna; ~ **of you** alguno de vosotros; ~ **but him would have gone** cualquier otro habría ido **2.** (*in negatives*) ninguno, ninguna; **not ~** ninguno; **he ate two pastries and I didn't eat ~** él se comió dos pasteles y yo ninguno

anybody ['en·i·bad·i] *pron indef* **1.** (*someone*) alguien, alguno **2.** (*not important which*) cualquiera; ~ **but him** cualquiera menos él; ~ **else would have done it** cualquier otro lo hubiese hecho; **she's not just ~** no es cualquiera **3.** (*no one*) nadie, ninguno; **I've never seen ~ like that** no he visto a nadie así; **more than ~** más que nadie

anyhow ['en·i·haʊ] *adv* **1.** (*in any case*) de todas maneras, de todos modos; (*nevertheless*) igual *inf* **2.** (*well*) bueno; ~**, as I was saying...** bueno, como iba diciendo... **3.** (*in a disorderly way*) de cualquier manera; **she dumped the tools into the box just ~** metió las herramientas en la caja de cualquier manera

anyone ['en·i·wʌn] *pron indef s.* **anybody**

anyplace ['en·i·pleɪs] *adv* **1.** (*interrogative*) en alguna parte; **have you seen my glasses ~?** ¿has visto mis gafas en alguna parte? **2.** (*in or at any location*) en cualquier parte [*o* sitio]; **I can sleep ~** puedo dormir en cualquier sitio **3.** (*in negatives*) en ninguna parte; **you won't see this ~** no verás esto en ningún sitio

anything ['en·i·θɪŋ] *pron indef* **1.** (*something*) algo; ~ **else?** ¿algo más?; **is there ~ new?** ¿alguna novedad? **2.** (*each thing*) cualquier cosa; **it is ~ but funny** es todo menos gracioso; ~ **and everything** cualquier cosa; **to be as fast as ~** *inf* ser rapidísimo **3.** (*nothing*) nada; **hardly ~** casi nada; **I didn't find ~ better** no encontré nada mejor; **I was afraid, if ~** estaba asustado, si acaso; **for ~** (*in the world*) por nada del mundo

anytime ['en·i·taɪm] *adv* a cualquier hora

anyway ['en·i·weɪ] *adv*, **anyways** ['en·i·weɪz] *adv sl* **1.** (*in any case*) de todas maneras, de todos modos **2.** (*well*) bueno; ~**, as I was saying...** bueno, como iba diciendo...

anywhere ['en·i·wer] *adv* **1.** (*interrogative*) en alguna parte; **have you seen my glasses ~?** ¿has visto mis gafas en alguna parte?; **are we ~ near finished yet?** *inf* ¿nos queda mucho para terminar? **2.** (*positive sense*) en cualquier parte [*o* sitio]; **I can sleep ~** puedo dormir en cualquier sitio; **its value is ~ between $25 and $30** vale entre los 25 y los 30 dólares; **to live miles from ~** *inf* vivir en el quinto pino; ~ **else** en cualquier otro sitio; (*in negatives*) en ningún otro sitio **3.** (*in negatives*) en ninguna parte; **you won't see this ~** no verás esto en ningún sitio; **he isn't ~ near as popular as he used to be** *inf* no es ni la mitad de popular de lo que era (antes)

aorta [eɪ·'ɔr·t̬ə] *n* <-s *o* -tae> aorta *f*

apace [ə·'peɪs] *adv* aprisa

apart [ə·'part] *adv* **1.** (*separated*) aparte; **to be 20 miles ~** estar a 20 millas de distancia; **far ~**

lejos; **to move** ~ apartarse **2.** (*aside*) **to be ~ from sth** estar apartado de algo; **to set sth ~** apartar algo; **to stand** ~ mantenerse apartado **3.** (*into pieces*) **to come** ~ desprenderse; **to take sth** ~ desmontar algo **4.** (*except for*) **you and me** ~ excepto [*o* salvo] tú y yo; **all joking** ~ bromas aparte

apart from *prep* **1.** (*except for*) excepto, salvo; ~ **that** excepto [*o* salvo] eso **2.** (*in addition to*) aparte de, además de **3.** (*separate from*) **to live ~ sb** vivir separado de alguien; **to live ~ each other** vivir separados el uno del otro

apartheid [ə·'part·heɪt] *n* apartheid *m*

apartment *n* apartamento *m*, piso *m*, departamento *m AmL*

apartment building *n*, **apartment house** *n* edificio *m* de apartamentos, bloque *m* de pisos, edificio *m* de departamentos *AmL*

apathetic [ˌæp·ə·'θeṭ·ɪk] *adj* apático, -a

apathy ['æp·ə·θi] *n* apatía *f*; ~ **about sth** apatía respecto a algo

ape [eɪp] **I.** *n* mono *m*, simio *m* ▶**to go** ~ *inf* volverse loco **II.** *vt* imitar

aperitif [ə·ˌper·ə·'tif] *n* aperitivo *m*

aperture ['æp·ər·tʃʊr] *n* **1.** (*crack*) rendija *f* **2.** PHOT abertura *f*

apex ['eɪ·peks] <-es *o* apices> *n* **1.** (*top*) ápice *m* **2.** *fig* cumbre *f*, cima *f* **3.** MATH vértice *m*

aphid ['eɪ·fɪd] *n* áfido *m*

aphorism ['æf·ə·rɪz·əm] *n* aforismo *m*

aphrodisiac [ˌæf·rə·'dɪ·zi·æk] **I.** *n* afrodisíaco *m*, afrodisiaco *m* **II.** *adj* afrodisíaco, -a, afrodisiaco, -a

apiarist ['eɪ·pɪ·ə·rɪst] *n* apicultor(a) *m(f)*

apiary ['eɪ·pɪ·er·i] <-ies> *n* colmenar *m*

apiculture ['æ·pɪ·ˌkʌl·tʃər] *n* apicultura *f*

apiece [ə·'pis] *adv* **1.** (*per item*) cada uno; **they cost $5** ~ cuestan 5 dólares cada uno **2.** (*per person*) por persona, por cabeza *inf*

aplenty [ə·'plen·ti] *adv* en abundancia

aplomb [ə·'plam] *n* aplomo *m*

apnea ['æp·ni·ə] *n* apnea *f*; **sleep** ~ apnea del sueño

APO *n abbr of* **Army Post Office** *servicio postal del ejército*

apocalypse [ə·'pak·ə·lɪps] *n* apocalipsis *m inv*; **the Apocalypse** REL el Apocalipsis

apocalyptic [ə·ˌpak·ə·'lɪp·tɪk] *adj* apocalíptico, -a

apocryphal [ə·'pak·rə·fəl] *adj* apócrifo, -a

apogee ['æp·ə·dʒi] *n a.* ASTR apogeo *m*

apologetic [ə·ˌpal·ə·'dʒeṭ·ɪk] *adj* (*tone, look, smile*) de disculpa; **to be ~ about sth** disculparse por algo

apologetically *adv* disculpándose, excusándose; **to say sth** ~ decir algo disculpándose

apologize [ə·'pal·ə·dʒaɪz] *vi* disculparse; **to ~ to sb for sth** pedir perdón a alguien por algo; **I (do)** ~ **if...** pido disculpas si...

apology [ə·'pal·ə·dʒi] <-ies> *n* disculpa *f*; **to make an** ~ disculparse; **please accept my apologies** le ruego (que) me disculpe

apoplectic [ˌæp·ə·'plek·tɪk] *adj* **1.** MED apopléjico, -a, apoplético, -a **2.** *fig* (*angry*) furioso, -a; **to be ~ about sth** estar hecho una furia por algo

apoplectic stroke *n* apoplejía *f*

apostle [ə·'pas·əl] *n* apóstol *m*

apostolic [ˌæp·ə·'stal·ɪk] *adj* apostólico, -a

apostrophe [ə·'pas·trə·fi] *n* apóstrofo *m*

Appalachia [ˌæp·ə·'leɪ·ʃə] *n* los Apalaches *mpl*

Appalachian Mountains [ˌæp·ə·'leɪ·ʃən maʊn·tənz] *npl* Montes *mpl* Apalaches

---

i Los **Appalachian Mountains** (Montes Apalaches) se extienden a lo largo de 1.600 millas (2.270 km) en la región oriental de Norteamérica, desde Quebec, en Canadá, hasta Alabama, en EE.UU. Más antiguos, y por lo tanto más erosionados que las Montañas Rocosas del oeste norteamericano, estos montes albergan hermosos bosques y carreteras escénicas como la Blue Ridge Parkway y la Skyline Drive, así como un sendero peatonal de 2.050 millas (3.299 km) de largo (the **Appalachian Trail** — la Senda Apalache), que se extiende desde el estado de Maine hasta el de Georgia.

---

appall [ə·'pɔl] *vt* horrorizar; **to be ~led at sth** estar horrorizado de [*o* por] algo

appalling *adj* **1.** (*shocking: behavior*) escandaloso, -a **2.** (*terrible: conditions*) horroroso, -a

apparatus [ˌæp·ə·'ræṭ·əs] *n* **1.** (*equipment*) equipo *m*; **a piece of** ~ un aparato **2.** (*organization*) aparato *m*

apparel [ə·'pær·əl] *n* FASHION indumentaria *f*; **sports** ~ ropa *f* deportiva

apparent [ə·'pær·ənt] *adj* **1.** (*clear*) evidente; **to become ~ that...** hacerse evidente que...; **it is ~ to me that...** me parece evidente que... +*subj* **2.** (*seeming*) aparente; **for no ~ reason** sin motivo aparente

apparition [ˌæp·ə·'rɪʃ·ən] *n* aparición *f*, espectro *m*, azoro *m AmC*

appeal [ə·'pil] **I.** *vi* **1.** (*attract*) atraer; **the idea doesn't ~ to me** no me atrae la idea **2.** LAW apelar **3.** (*plead*) ~ **to sb for sth** pedir algo a alguien; **to ~ for donations/help** solicitar donaciones/ayuda; **she ~ed to his sense of honor** apeló a su sentido del honor **II.** *n* **1.** (*attraction*) atractivo *m*; **to have** ~ tener gancho *inf* **2.** LAW apelación *f*; **court of ~s** tribunal *m* de apelación; **to file an** ~ (**against sth**) interponer una apelación (contra algo) **3.** (*request*) petición *f*; **an ~ to sb for sth** una solicitud de algo a alguien; **to launch an** ~ **to do sth** hacer un llamamiento para hacer algo **4.** (*authority of: to reason, justice, sense of humanity*) llamamiento *m*

appealing [ə·'pi·lɪŋ] *adj* **1.** (*attractive: smile*) atractivo, -a; (*idea*) tentador(a) **2.** (*beseeching*:

eyes) suplicante

appealingly *adv* **1.** (*dress*) con estilo **2.** (*look*) de manera suplicante; (*speak*) con tono suplicante

appear [ə·'pɪr] *vi* **1.** (*be seen*) aparecer **2.** (*newspaper*) salir; (*book*) publicarse, aparecer; (*film*) estrenarse **3.** LAW **to ~ in court/ before a judge** comparecer ante un tribunal/ ante un juez **4.** (*seem*) **to ~ to be...** parecer ser...; **it ~s to me that...** me parece que...; **it ~s so** eso parece; **it would ~ that...** parecería que...

appearance [ə·'pɪr·əns] *n* **1.** (*instance of appearing*) aparición *f*; **to make an ~** aparecer **2.** LAW comparecencia *f* **3.** (*looks*) aspecto *m* **4.** *pl* (*outward signs*) apariencias *fpl*; **from all ~s** según parece; **to keep up ~s** guardar las apariencias **5.** (*performance*) actuación *f*; **stage ~** aparición *f* en escena ▶ **~s can be deceptive** *prov* las apariencias engañan *prov*

appease [ə·'piz] *vt form* **1.** (*pacify: person*) apaciguar; POL contemporizar con **2.** (*relieve: hunger, suspicion*) aplacar; (*pain*) mitigar

appeasement *n* **1.** (*conciliation*) apaciguamiento *m*; **policy of ~** POL política *f* de contemporización **2.** (*relief: of anger*) aplacamiento *m*; (*of pain*) mitigación *f*

appellant [ə·'pel·ənt] *n* apelante *mf*

appellation [ˌæp·ə·'leɪ·ʃən] *n* título *m*; (*of wine*) denominación *f* de origen

append [ə·'pend] *vt* (*document, note*) adjuntar; (*signature*) añadir

appendage [ə·'pen·dɪdʒ] *n* apéndice *m*, añadidura *f*

appendicitis [ə·ˌpen·dɪ·'saɪ·tɪs] *n* MED apendicitis *f inv*

appendix [ə·'pen·dɪks] *n* **1.** <-es> ANAT apéndice *m* **2.** <-dices *o* -es> TYPO apéndice *m*

appertain [ˌæp·ər·'teɪn] *vi* **to ~ to** (*person*) relacionarse con; (*matter*) tener que ver con

appetite ['æp·ə·taɪt] *n* **1.** (*for food*) apetito *m*, antojo *m Méx* **2.** *fig* (*for gambling, adventure*) afán *m*

appetite suppressant *n* inhibidor *m* del apetito

appetizer ['æp·ə·taɪ·zər] *n* **1.** (*first course*) entrante *m* **2.** (*snack*) aperitivo *m*, botana *f Méx*, pasabocas *m inv Col*

appetizing ['æp·ə·taɪ·zɪŋ] *adj* apetitoso, -a

applaud [ə·'plɔd] **I.** *vi* aplaudir **II.** *vt a. fig* aplaudir

applause [ə·'plɔz] *n* aplauso *m*; **a round of ~ for the singer** un aplauso para el cantante; **loud ~** fuerte aplauso

apple ['æp·əl] *n* manzana *f* ▶ **to be the ~ of sb's eye** ser la niña de los ojos de alguien; **the Big Apple** *inf* la Gran Manzana (*Nueva York*)

applecart *n* **to upset the ~** desbaratar los planes

apple juice *n* zumo *m* de manzana

apple pie *n* pastel *m* de manzana; **to be as American as ~** ser tan estadounidense como el que más

apple polisher *n inf* pelota *mf*, regalado, -a *m, f Col*, barbero, -a *m, f Méx*

applesauce *n* compota *f* de manzana

apple tree *n* manzano *m*, manzanero *m Ecua*

appliance [ə·'plaɪ·əns] *n* aparato *m*; **electrical ~** electrodoméstico *m*

applicability [ˌæp·lɪ·kə·'bɪl·ə·ţi] *n* aplicabilidad *f*

applicable [ə·'plɪ·kə·bəl] *adj* aplicable; **delete where not ~** táchese lo que no proceda; **those rules are not ~ anymore** esas normas ya no están vigentes

applicant ['æp·lɪ·kənt] *n* **1.** (*for job*) candidato, -a *m, f* **2.** (*for money, support*) solicitante *mf*

application [ˌæp·lɪ·'keɪ·ʃən] *n* **1.** (*form: for job, credit card, loan*) (hoja *f* de) solicitud *f* **2.** (*coating*) aplicación *f* **3.** (*use*) uso *m*; A.COMPUT aplicación *f* **4.** (*perseverance*) diligencia *f*, aplicación *f* **5.** (*request*) solicitud *f*; **on ~** mediante solicitud

application form *n* (hoja *f* de) solicitud *f*

applied [ə·'plaɪd] *adj* aplicado, -a

appliqué [ˌæp·lɪ·'keɪ] *n* FASHION bordado *m* sobrepuesto

apply [ə·'plaɪ] **I.** *vi* **1.** (*request*) presentarse; **to ~ to a college/a company** solicitar plaza en una universidad/un puesto de trabajo; **to ~ to sb for sth** solicitar algo a alguien; **to ~ for a job** presentarse a [*o* solicitar] un puesto de trabajo; **to ~ in writing** dirigirse por escrito **2.** (*be relevant*) **to ~ to sb** concernir a alguien **II.** *vt* **1.** (*glue, paint*) aplicar **2.** (*use*) aplicar, usar; **to ~ force** hacer uso de la fuerza; **to ~ pressure to sth** ejercer presión sobre algo; **to ~ sanctions** aplicar sanciones; **to ~ common sense** usar el sentido común **3.** (*work hard*) **to ~ oneself to sth** dedicarse a algo

appoint [ə·'pɔɪnt] *vt* **1.** (*select*) nombrar; **to ~ sb as heir** nombrar a alguien heredero **2.** *form* (*designate*) **to ~ a date** fijar una fecha; **at the ~ed time** a la hora señalada

appointee [ə·pɔɪn·'ti] *n* persona *f* nombrada

appointment [ə·'pɔɪnt·mənt] *n* **1.** (*to office, position*) nombramiento *m* **2.** (*meeting*) cita *f*; **dentist's ~** cita *f* con el dentista; **to have an ~ at the hairdresser's** tener hora en la peluquería; **to keep an ~** acudir a una cita; **by ~ only** sólo con cita previa **3.** *pl* (*furniture*) mobiliario *m*

appointment book *n* libro *m* de visitas

apportion [ə·'pɔr·ʃən] *vt* repartir

apposite ['æp·ə·zɪt] *adj form* apropiado, -a; (*observation*) pertinente

apposition [ˌæp·ə·'zɪʃ·ən] *n* aposición *f*

appraisal [ə·'preɪ·zəl] *n* **1.** (*evaluation*) evaluación *f*; (*of performance, evidence*) valoración *f*; (*of property*) tasación *f* **2.** (*estimation*) estimación *f*

appraise [ə·'preɪz] *vt* **1.** (*evaluate*) evaluar; (*performance, evidence*) valorar; (*property*) tasar; **to ~ sb's needs** valorar las necesidades de alguien **2.** (*estimate*) estimar

appreciable [ə·'pri·ʃə·bəl] *adj* apreciable; (*change*) notorio, -a; (*progress*) considerable
appreciate [ə·'pri·ʃi·eɪt] I. *vt* 1. (*value*) apreciar 2. (*understand*) comprender 3. (*be grateful for*) agradecer II. *vi* FIN (*in price*) subir; (*in value: property, shares*) revalorizarse
appreciation [ə·ˌpri·ʃi·'eɪ·ʃən] *n* 1. (*gratitude*) agradecimiento *m* 2. (*understanding*) aprecio *m;* **she has no ~ of my work** no sabe apreciar mi trabajo 3. FIN (*in price*) subida *f;* (*in value: of property, shares*) revalorización *f*
appreciative [ə·'pri·ʃə·t̬ɪv] *adj* agradecido, -a; **an ~ audience** un público que sabe apreciar
apprehend [ˌæp·rɪ·'hend] *vt form* 1. (*arrest*) detener 2. (*comprehend*) entender; **to ~ the importance of doing sth** darse cuenta de la importancia de hacer algo
apprehensible [ˌæp·rɪ·'hen·sə·bəl] *adj form* aprehensible
apprehension [ˌæp·rɪ·'hen·ʃən] *n* 1. (*of a criminal*) detención *f* 2. (*fear*) aprensión *f;* **~ about sth** temor *m* por algo 3. *form* (*comprehension*) comprensión *f*
apprehensive [ˌæp·rɪ·'hen·sɪv] *adj* aprensivo, -a, flatoso, -a *AmL;* **to be ~ about sth** estar preocupado por algo; **to be ~ that** temer que +*subj*
apprentice [ə·'pren·t̬ɪs] *n* aprendiz(a) *m(f),* peón, -ona *m, f Méx*
apprenticeship [ə·'pren·t̬ɪs·ʃɪp] *n* aprendizaje *m*
approach [ə·'proʊtʃ] I. *vt* 1. (*get close to*) acercarse a 2. (*ask*) dirigirse a; **to ~ sb** (**about sth**) dirigirse a alguien (para pedir algo) 3. (*deal with*) abordar II. *vi* acercarse III. *n* 1. (*coming*) aproximación *f;* **at the ~ of winter** al acercarse el invierno 2. (*access: to highway, bridge*) acceso *m* 3. (*proposition*) propuesta *f;* (*for help*) petición *f;* **to make ~es to sb** dirigirse a alguien 4. (*methodology*) enfoque *m*
approachable [ə·'proʊ·tʃə·bəl] *adj* (*person, place*) accesible
appropriate¹ [ə·'proʊ·pri·ət] *adj* apropiado, -a, adecuado, -a; **~ to the occasion** apropiado [*o* adecuado] para la ocasión
appropriate² [ə·'proʊ·pri·eɪt] *vt form* 1. (*take*) apropiarse de 2. FIN asignar; **to ~ funds** (**for sth**) destinar fondos (a algo)
appropriation [ə·ˌproʊ·pri·'eɪ·ʃən] *n* 1. (*taking*) apropiación *f* 2. FIN asignación *f*
approval [ə·'pru·vəl] *n* aprobación *f;* **to meet with sb's ~** obtener la aprobación de alguien; **to nod one's ~** asentir con la cabeza; **on ~** ECON a prueba
approve [ə·'pruv] I. *vi* estar de acuerdo; **to ~ of sth** estar de acuerdo con [*o* aprobar] algo; **she doesn't ~ of smoking** no le parece bien que se fume II. *vt* aprobar
approved *adj* 1. (*agreed*) aprobado, -a 2. (*authorized*) autorizado, -a; **an ~ qualification** un título homologado
approving [ə·'pru·vɪŋ] *adj* de aprobación

approvingly [ə·'pru·vɪŋ·li] *adv* con aprobación; **to smile ~** sonreír en señal de aprobación
approx. [ə·'prak·sɪ·met·li] *n abbr of* **approximately** aprox.
approximate¹ [ə·'prak·sɪ·mət] *adj* aproximado, -a
approximate² [ə·'prak·sɪ·meɪt] I. *vt* aproximarse a II. *vi form* **to ~ to sth** aproximarse a algo
approximately *adv* aproximadamente
approximation [ə·ˌprak·sɪ·'meɪ·ʃən] *n* aproximación *f*
APR [ˌeɪ·pi·'ar] *n abbr of* **annual percentage rate** TAE *f*
Apr. [ˈeɪ·prəl] *n abbr of* **April** abr.
apricot [ˈeɪ·prɪ·kat] I. *n* 1. (*fruit*) albaricoque *m,* chabacano *m Méx,* damasco *m AmS* 2. (*tree*) albaricoquero *m,* chabacano *m Méx,* damasco *m AmS* 3. (*color*) (color *m*) albaricoque *m* II. *adj* (de color) albaricoque
April [ˈeɪ·prəl] *n* abril *m;* **in ~** en abril; **every ~** todos los meses de abril; **the month of ~** el mes de abril; **at the beginning/end of ~** a principios/finales de abril; **on ~ (the) fourth** el cuatro de abril
April Fools' Day *n* ≈ Día *m* de los Santos Inocentes (*en Estados Unidos, el 1 de abril*)
a priori [ˌeɪ·pri·'ɔr·i] *adv* a priori
apron [ˈeɪ·prən] *n* 1. (*clothing*) delantal *m* 2. AVIAT pista *f* de estacionamiento 3. THEAT proscenio *m*
apron strings *n pl* cordeles *mpl* del delantal ▶**to be** tied **to one's mother's ~** estar pegado a las faldas de la madre
apropos, a propos [ˌæp·rə·'poʊ] I. *prep* a propósito de II. *adv* a propósito III. *adj* apropiado, -a
apse [æps] *n* ARCHIT ábside *m*
apt [æpt] *adj* 1. (*appropriate*) apropiado, -a; (*comment*) oportuno, -a; (*description*) adecuado, -a 2. (*clever*) inteligente 3. (*likely*) **to be ~ to do sth** tener tendencia a hacer algo
apt. [ə·'part·mənt] *n abbr of* **apartment** apto.
aptitude [ˈæp·tɪ·tud] *n* aptitud *f*
aquacize [ˈæk·wə·saɪz] *n* SPORTS aeróbic *m* en el agua
aquaculture [ˈak·wə·ˌkʌl·tʃər] *n* acuicultura *f*
Aqua-Lung® [ˈæk·wə·lʌŋ] escafandra *f* autónoma
aquamarine [ˌak·wə·mə·'rin] I. *n* 1. (*stone*) aguamarina *f* 2. (*color*) color *m* verde mar II. *adj* de color verde mar
aquaplaning [ˌak·wə·'pleɪ·nɪŋ] *n* 1. SPORTS ≈ esquí *m* acuático 2. AUTO aquaplaning *m*
aquarium [ə·'kwer·i·əm] <-s *o* -ria> *n* (*at home*) acuario *m;* (*public*) acuárium *m*
Aquarius [ə·'kwer·i·əs] *n* Acuario *m*
aquatic [ə·'kwæt̬·ɪk] *adj* acuático, -a
aquatics *npl* SPORTS deportes *m* acuáticos *pl*
aqueduct [ˈæk·wɪ·dʌkt] *n* acueducto *m*
aquifer [ˈæk·wɪ·fər] *n* acuífero *m*
aquiline [ˈæk·wɪ·laɪn] *adj* aquilino, -a; **~ nose** nariz *f* aguileña

AR *abbr of* **Arkansas** Arkansas
Arab ['ær·əb] **I.** *adj* árabe; **the (United) ~ Emirates** los Emiratos Árabes (Unidos) **II.** *n* árabe *mf*
arabesque [ˌær·ə·'besk] *n* arabesco *m*
Arabia [ə·'reɪ·bi·ə] *n* Arabia *f*
Arabian *adj* árabe, arábigo, -a
Arabic ['ær·ə·bɪk] *n* LING árabe *m*
arable ['ær·ə·bəl] *adj* cultivable
arachnid [ə·'ræk·nɪd] *n* arácnido *m*
arbiter ['ar·bɪ·ţər] *n* árbitro, -a *m*, *f*
arbitrage ['ar·bɪ·traʒ] *n* arbitraje *m* (financiero)
arbitrariness ['ar·bɪ·trer·ɪ·nɪs] *n* arbitrariedad *f*
arbitrary ['ar·bɪ·trer·i] *adj* arbitrario, -a
arbitrate ['ar·bɪ·treɪt] **I.** *vt* arbitrar, mediar en; **to ~ an argument** mediar en una disputa **II.** *vi* arbitrar, mediar
arbitration [ˌar·bɪ·'treɪ·ʃən] *n* arbitraje *m*, mediación *f*; **to go to ~** recurrir al arbitraje
arbitrator ['ar·bɪ·treɪ·ţər] *n* árbitro, -a *m*, *f*
arbor ['ar·bər] *n* cenador *m*

> **i** En Estados Unidos, **Arbor Day** (el Día del Árbol) es un día especial en el que es costumbre reunirse para sembrar árboles. En algunos estados es un día festivo. No todos los estados celebran Arbor Day el mismo día, ya que la temporada apropiada para plantar árboles varía de acuerdo a la zona geográfica.

arboriculture ['ar·bər·ɪ·ˌkʌl·tʃər] *n* arboricultura *f*
arc [ark] **I.** *n* arco *m* **II.** *vi* arquearse
arcade [ær·'keɪd] *n* **1.** (*of shops*) galería *f* comercial **2.** (*around square*) soportales *mpl* **3.** (*with games*) sala *f* de juegos recreativos
arcane [ær·'keɪn] *adj* arcano, -a
arch[1] [artʃ] **I.** *n* arco *m* **II.** *vi* arquearse **III.** *vt* arquear; **to ~ one's eyebrows** arquear las cejas
arch[2] [artʃ] <-er, -est> *adj* burlón, -ona
archaeology [ˌar·ki·'al·ə·dʒi] *n* arqueología *f*
archaic [ar·'keɪ·ɪk] *adj* arcaico, -a
archangel ['ark·eɪn·dʒl] *n* arcángel *m*
archbishop [ˌartʃ·'bɪʃ·əp] *n* arzobispo *m*
archdeacon [ˌartʃ·'di·kən] *n* arcediano *m*
archdiocese [ˌartʃ·'daɪ·ə·sɪs] *n* archidiócesis *f inv*
archenemy <-ies> *n* archienemigo, -a *m*, *f*
archeological [ˌar·ki·ə·'ladʒ·ɪ·kəl] *adj* arqueológico, -a
archeologist [ˌar·ki·'al·ə·dʒɪst] *n* arqueólogo, -a *m*, *f*
archeology [ˌar·ki·'al·ə·dʒi] *n s.* **archaeology**
archer ['ar·tʃər] *n* arquero, -a *m*, *f*
archery ['ar·tʃə·ri] *n* tiro *m* con arco
archetype ['ar·kɪ·taɪp] *n* arquetipo *m*
archipelago [ˌar·kə·'pel·ə·goʊ] <-(e)s> *n*

archipiélago *m*
architect ['ar·kə·tekt] *n* **1.** (*of building*) arquitecto, -a *m*, *f* **2.** *fig* artífice *mf*
architecture ['ar·kə·tek·tʃər] *n* arquitectura *f*
archive ['ar·kaɪv] *n a.* COMPUT archivo *m*
archivist ['ar·kə·vɪst] *n* archivero, -a *m*, *f*, archivista *mf*
archway ['artʃ·weɪ] *n* (*entrance*) arco *m*; (*passageway*) pasadizo *m* abovedado
arc lamp *n*, **arc light** *n* arco *m* voltaico
Arctic ['ark·tɪk] **I.** *n* **the ~** el Ártico **II.** *adj* ártico, -a
arctic ['ark·tɪk] *adj* (*extremely cold*) glacial
Arctic Circle *n* círculo *m* polar ártico
Arctic Ocean *n* Océano *m* Glacial Ártico
arc welding *n* soldadura *f* por arco
ardent ['ar·dənt] *adj* ferviente; (*desire, plea*) vehemente
ardor ['ar·dər] *n* fervor *m*
arduous ['ar·dʒu·əs] *adj* arduo, -a; (*task*) trabajoso, -a
are [ər, *stressed:* ar] *vi s.* **be**
area ['er·i·ə] *n* **1.** *a.* MATH, SPORTS área *f*; **in the ~ of** alrededor de **2.** (*field*) campo *m*; **~ of competence/knowledge** ámbito *m* de competencia(s)/conocimiento(s)
area code *n* prefijo *m*
area rug *n* alfombra *f*
arena [ə·'ri·nə] *n a. fig* arena *f*
aren't [arnt] = **are not**
Argentina [ˌar·dʒən·'ti·nə] *n* Argentina *f*
Argentine ['ar·dʒən·tin], **Argentinean** [ˌar·dʒən·'tɪn·i·ən] **I.** *adj* argentino, -a **II.** *n* argentino, -a *m*, *f*
argon ['ar·gan] *n* CHEM argón *m*
arguable ['ar·gju·ə·bəl] *adj* discutible
arguably *adv* posiblemente
argue ['ar·gju] **I.** *vi* **1.** (*disagree*) discutir, alegar *AmL* **2.** (*reason*) razonar; **to ~ against/for sth** abogar contra/a favor de algo **II.** *vt* **1.** (*debate*) sostener; **to ~ that...** sostener que... **2.** (*persuade*) **to ~ sb into doing sth** persuadir a alguien de hacer algo; **to ~ sb out of doing sth** persuadir a alguien para que abandone la idea de hacer algo
argument ['ar·gjə·mənt] *n* **1.** (*disagreement*) discusión *f* **2.** (*reasoning*) argumento *m*; **for the sake of ~, suppose that...** pongamos por caso que... **3.** LAW alegato *m* **4.** MATH variable *f* independiente **5.** COMPUT, LING argumento *m*
argumentative [ˌar·gjə·'men·ţə·ţɪv] *adj* discutidor(a)
argyle ['ar·gaɪl] *n* diseño *m* de rombos
aria ['a·ri·ə] *n* MUS aria *f*
arid ['ær·ɪd] *adj* árido, -a
Aries ['er·iz] *n* Aries *m*
arise [ə·'raɪz] <arose, arisen> *vi* **1.** (*come about*) surgir; **to ~ from** surgir de; **should the need ~** si fuera necesario; **should doubt ~** en caso de presentarse la duda **2.** *form* (*rise up*) alzarse
arisen [ə·'rɪz·ən] *pp of* **arise**
aristocracy [ˌær·ɪ·'stak·rə·si] <-ies> *n* + *sing/*

A

pl vb aristocracia *f*
aristocrat [ə·'rɪs·tə·kræt] *n* aristócrata *mf*
aristocratic [e·ˌrɪs·tə·'kræt̬·ɪk] *adj* aristocrático, -a
arithmetic [ə·'rɪθ·mɪ·tɪk] **I.** *n* aritmética *f*
II. *adj* aritmético, -a
arithmetical [ˌær·ɪθ·'met̬·ɪ·kəl] *adj* aritmético,
-a
Ariz. [ˌær·ɪ·'zoʊ·nə] *n abbr of* **Arizona** Arizona
Arizona [ˌær·ɪ·'zoʊ·nə] *n* Arizona
ark [ark] *n* arca *f*; **Noah's ~** el Arca de Noé
Ark. *abbr of* **Arkansas** Arkansas
Arkansas ['ar·kən·sɔ] *n* Arkansas

i El **Arlington National Cemetery**
(Cementerio Nacional de Arlington), ubicado 2 millas (3,2 km) al sureste de Washington D.C., del otro lado del río Potomac,
ocupa cerca de una milla cuadrada (2,6 km²)
y en él se encuentran las tumbas de más de
60.000 soldados estadounidenses, así como
las de norteamericanos notables como el presidente William Howard Taft, el presidente
John F. Kennedy, el general John J. Pershing y
el almirante Robert E. Peary; también se
encuentra allí **the Tomb of the Unknown
Soldier** (la Tumba del Soldado Desconocido), custodiada 24 horas diarias los 365
días del año.

arm¹ [arm] *n* **1.** ANAT, GEO brazo *m;* **to put
one's ~s around sb** abrazar a alguien; **to
hold sb in one's ~s** tener a alguien en brazos;
~ in ~ (agarrados) del brazo **2.** (*sleeve*) manga
f **3.** (*division*) sección *f* ▸ **to welcome sb
with open ~s** recibir algo con los brazos abiertos; **the** (**long**) **~ of the law** el brazo de la ley;
to cost an ~ and a leg *inf* costar un ojo de la
cara; **to keep sb at ~'s length** *fig* mantener a
alguien a distancia
arm² [arm] MIL **I.** *vt* **1.** (*supply with weapons*)
armar; **to ~ oneself against sth** armarse
contra algo **2.** (*prepare for detonation*) activar;
(*rocket*) armar **II.** *n* (*weapon*) arma *f;* **under
~s** en armas; **to bear ~s** portar armas; **to lay
down one's ~s** rendir las armas; **to take up
~s** (**against sb/sth**) tomar las armas (contra
alguien/algo) ▸ **to be up in ~s about...** poner
el grito en el cielo contra...
armadillo [ar·ˌmə·'dɪl·oʊ] *n* ZOOL armadillo *m*
armaments ['ar·mə·mənts] *npl* armamento *m*
armature ['ar·mə·tʃər] *n* **1.** TECH, ZOOL, BOT
armadura *f* **2.** ELEC inducido *m*
armband ['arm·bænd] *n* brazalete *m*
armchair ['arm·tʃer] *n* sillón *m*
armed [armd] *adj* armado, -a
armed forces *npl* **the ~** las fuerzas armadas
Armenia [ar·'mi·ni·ə] *n* Armenia *f*
Armenian I. *n* **1.** (*person*) armenio, -a *m, f*
2. LING armenio *m* **II.** *adj* armenio, -a

armful ['arm·fʊl] *n* brazada *f*
armhole ['arm·hoʊl] *n* sisa *f*
arming ['ar·mɪŋ] *n* aprovisionamiento *m* de
armas
armistice ['ar·mə·stɪs] *n* armisticio *m*
armload *n* brazada *f*
armor ['ar·mər] *n* **1.** (*protective covering*) blindaje *m* **2.** *a.* MIL, ZOOL armadura *f* **3.** (*tanks*)
carros *mpl* blindados
armored *adj* (*car*) blindado, -a; (*train*) acorazado, -a
armor-plated *adj* blindado, -a
armpit ['arm·pɪt] *n* axila *f*, sobaco *m*
armrest ['arm·rest] *n* apoyabrazos *m inv*
arms control *n*, **arms limitation** *n* MIL control
m de armamentos
arms race *n* **the ~** la carrera armamentista
arms reduction *n* reducción *f* de armamentos
arm-wrestle *vi* echar [*o Col* hacer] un pulso,
jugar a las vencidas *Méx*
arm wrestling *n* pulso *m*, vencidas *fpl*
army ['ar·mi] <-ies> *n* **1.** MIL ejército *m;* **to
join the ~** alistarse **2.** *fig* multitud *f*
army brat *n inf* hijo de un miembro del ejército estadounidense
aroma [ə·'roʊ·mə] *n* aroma *m*
aromatherapy [ə·ˌroʊ·mə·'θer·ə·pi] *n* aro-
materapia *f*
aromatic [ˌær·ə·'mæt̬·ɪk] *adj* aromático, -a
arose [ə·'roʊz] *pt of* **arise**
around [ə·'raʊnd] **I.** *prep* **1.** (*surrounding*)
alrededor de; **all ~ sth** por todas partes; **the
earth goes ~ the sun** la tierra gira alrededor
del sol; **to go ~ the corner** doblar la esquina
2. (*move within sth*) por; **to drive ~ France**
viajar (en coche) por Francia; **to go ~ a
museum** visitar un museo; **to sit ~ the room**
sentarse en la habitación **3.** (*approximately*)
más o menos, alrededor de; **~ May 10th** sobre
el 10 de mayo; **somewhere ~ here** en algún
lugar por aquí **II.** *adv* **1.** (*all over*) alrededor; **all
~** en todas partes; **for 50 miles ~** en un radio
de 50 millas; **for miles ~** en millas a la
redonda; **to be the other way ~** ser exactamente al revés **2.** (*aimlessly*) **to walk ~** dar
una vuelta; **to stand/hang ~** estar/andar por
ahí; **to have been ~** haber visto mundo;
(*be experienced*) tener mucha experiencia
3. (*near by*) por ahí; **is he ~?** ¿está por ahí?; **to
be still ~** seguir todavía ahí
arouse [ə·'raʊz] *vt* **1.** (*stir*) suscitar; (*anger*)
provocar **2.** (*sexually excite*) excitar
arraign [ə·'reɪn] *vt* LAW hacer comparecer (ante
el tribunal)
arrange [ə·'reɪndʒ] **I.** *vt* **1.** (*organize*) organizar; **to ~ a date** acordar una cita **2.** (*put in
order*) *a.* MUS arreglar **II.** *vi* disponer; **to ~ for
sth** disponer algo; **to ~ to do sth** quedar en
hacer algo
arrangement *n* **1.** *pl* (*preparations*) preparativos *mpl;* **to make ~s** (**for sth**) hacer los preparativos (de algo) **2.** (*agreement*) acuerdo *m;*
to have an ~ with sb tener un acuerdo con al-

guien **3.** (*method of organizing sth*) *a.* MUS arreglo *m*

array [ə-'reɪ] I. *n* **1.** (*display*) colección *f* **2.** *form* (*clothes*) atavío *m* **3.** MIL formación *f* II. *vt* **1.** (*display*) colocar, exponer **2.** *form* (*dress finely*) ataviar **3.** MIL desplegar

arrears [ə-'rɪrz] *npl* FIN atraso *m;* **to be in ~ on sth** estar atrasado en el pago de algo; **to pay in ~** pagar con atraso

arrest [ə-'rest] I. *vt* **1.** LAW detener **2.** *form* (*put a stop to*) detener **3.** (*attract*) **to ~ sb's attention** captar la atención de alguien II. *n* detención *f;* **to be under ~** estar detenido; **to put sb under ~** detener a alguien

arresting *adj* llamativo, -a; (*account*) cautivador, -a; (*performance*) impresionante

arrival [ə-'raɪ-vəl] *n* **1.** (*at destination*) llegada *f;* **on his ~** a su llegada **2.** (*person*) persona *f* que llega; **new ~** recién llegado *m*

arrive [ə-'raɪv] *vi* **1.** (*come*) llegar; **to ~ at a conclusion** llegar a una conclusión **2.** *inf* (*establish one's reputation*) llegar a ser alguien **3.** (*be born*) nacer

arriviste [ˌæ·rɪ·'vist] *n* arribista *mf*

arrogance ['ær·ə·gəns] *n* arrogancia *f*

arrogant ['ær·ə·gənt] *adj* arrogante

arrow ['ær·oʊ] *n* flecha *f,* jara *f Guat, Méx*

arrowhead *n* punta *f* de flecha

arrowroot *n* BOT maranta *f,* arruruz *m*

arsenal ['ar·sə·nəl] *n* arsenal *m*

arsenic ['ar·sə·nɪk] *n* arsénico *m*

arson ['ar·sən] *n* incendio *m* provocado

art [art] *n* arte *m*

art collection *n* colección *f* de arte

art critic *n* crítico *m* de arte

art dealer *n* marchante *mf* de arte

arterial [ar·'tɪr·i·əl] *adj* **1.** ANAT arterial **2.** AUTO, RAIL principal

arteriosclerosis [ar·ˌtɪr·i·oʊ·sklə·'roʊ·səs] *n* MED arteriosclerosis *f inv*

artery ['ar·tə·ri] <-ies> *n* arteria *f*

artesian well [ar·'ti·ʒən·'wel] *n* pozo *m* artesiano

artful ['art·fəl] *adj* hábil, ingenioso, -a

art gallery *n* (*for exhibits*) museo *m* de arte; (*for selling*) galería *f* de arte

arthritic [ar·'θrɪt̬·ɪk] *adj* artrítico, -a

arthritis [ar·'θraɪ·t̬ɪs] *n* MED artritis *f inv*

artichoke ['ar·t̬ɪ·tʃoʊk] *n* CULIN alcachofa *f*

article ['ar·t̬ɪ·kəl] *n* **1.** (*object*) artículo *m,* objeto *m; ~* **of clothing** prenda *f* de vestir **2.** *a.* LAW, LING, TYPO artículo *m*

articulate¹ [ar·'tɪk·jə·lət] *adj* **1.** (*person*) que se expresa con claridad; (*speech*) claro, -a **2.** TECH, ANAT articulado, -a

articulate² [ar·'tɪk·jə·leɪt] *vt form* **1.** (*express*) expresar claramente; **to ~ an idea** articular una idea **2.** (*pronounce*) articular

articulation [ar·ˌtɪk·jə·'leɪ·ʃən] *n* (*pronunciation*) articulación *f;* (*of idea, feeling*) expresión *f*

artifact ['ar·t̬ə·fækt] *n* artefacto *m*

artifice ['ar·t̬ə·fɪs] *n form* artificio *m*

artificial [ˌar·tə·'fɪʃ·əl] *adj* artificial

artificial insemination *n* inseminación *f* artificial

artificial intelligence *n* inteligencia *f* artificial

artificial respiration *n* respiración *f* asistida

artillery [ar·'tɪl·ə·ri] *n* artillería *f*

artilleryman [ar·'tɪl·ə·ri·mən] *n* artillero *m*

artisan ['ar·t̬ɪ·zən] *n* artesano, -a *m, f*

artist ['ar·t̬ɪst] *n* artista *mf*

artiste [ar·'tist] *n* THEAT artista *mf*

artistic [ar·'tɪs·tɪk] *adj* artístico, -a

artistry ['ar·t̬ɪ·stri] *n* arte *m o f*

artless ['art·lɪs] *adj* **1.** (*natural*) sencillo, -a **2.** (*clumsy*) torpe

arts and crafts *n* trabajos *mpl* manuales

artsy ['art·si] *adj* **1.** *inf: relacionado con la creación de objetos decorativos o de obras de arte* **2.** *pej* pseudoartístico, a-

artwork ['art·wɜrk] *n* material *m* gráfico, ilustraciones *fpl*

arty ['ar·t̬i] <-ier, -iest> *adj inf* (*person*) pseudoartístico, -a; (*film*) pretencioso, -a

as [əz, *stressed:* æz] I. *prep* como; **dressed ~ a clown** vestido de payaso; **the king, ~ such** el Rey, como tal; **~ a baby, I was...** de bebé, yo era...; **to use sth ~ a lever** utilizar algo como palanca II. *conj* **1.** (*in comparison*) como; **the same name ~ sth/sb** el mismo nombre que algo/alguien; **~ fast ~ sth/sb** tan rápido como algo/alguien; **to eat ~ much ~ sb** comer tanto como alguien; **~ soon ~ possible** lo antes posible, tan pronto como sea posible **2.** (*like*) (tal) como; **~ it is** tal como es; **I came ~ promised** vine, como prometí; **she was dressed just ~ he was** llevaba la misma ropa que él; **~ if it were true** como si fuese verdad **3.** (*because*) como; **~ he is here, I'm going** como él está aquí, yo me voy **4.** (*while*) mientras **5.** (*although*) **~ nice ~ the day is...** aunque el día está bien,...; **try ~ I might, I couldn't** por más que me esforzara, no podía ►**~ far ~** (*to the extent that*) en la medida en que; (*concerning*) respecto a; **~ for her/him/me/them...** en lo que a ella/él/mí/ellos respecta... III. *adv* **~ well** también; **~ long as** mientras que +*subj;* **~ much as** tanto como; **~ soon as** en cuanto, tan pronto

ASAP [ˌeɪ·es·eɪ·'pi] *abbr of* **as soon as possible** lo antes posible, tan pronto como sea posible

asbestos [æs·'bes·təs] *n* asbesto *m*

asbestosis [ˌæs·bes·'toʊ·sɪs] *n* asbestosis *f inv*

ascend [ə-'send] I. *vt form* (*steps*) subir; (*mountain*) ascender; **to ~ the throne** subir al trono II. *vi* ascender; **in ~ing order** en orden ascendente

ascendancy [ə-'sen·dən·tsi] *n* ascendencia *f;* (*supremacy*) supremacía *f*

ascendant [ə-'sen·dənt] I. *n form* **1.** (*position of power*) **to be in the ~** estar en alza **2.** ASTR ascendente *m* II. *adj* ascendente

ascendency [ə-'sen·dən·tsi] *n s.* **ascendancy**

ascendent [ə-'sen·dənt] *n, adj s.* **ascendant**

ascension [ə·'sen·ʃən] *n* **1.** (*going up*) ascensión *f* **2.** REL **the Ascension** la Ascensión
Ascension Day *n* día *m* de la Ascensión
ascent [ə·'sent] *n* **1.** *form* (*climb*) ascensión *f* **2.** (*slope*) pendiente *f*
ascertain [ˌæs·ər·'teɪn] *vt* **1.** (*find out*) averiguar **2.** (*make sure*) comprobar
ascetic [ə·'seṭ·ɪk] **I.** *n* asceta *mf* **II.** *adj* ascético, -a
asceticism [ə·'seṭ·ə·sɪz·əm] *n* ascetismo *m*
ASCII ['æs·ki] *abbr of* **American Standard Code for Information Interchange** (código *m*) ASCII *m*
ascot ['æs·kət] *n* FASHION ≈ bufanda *f* ancha, fular *m*
ascribe [ə·'skraɪb] *vt* **to ~ sth to sb** atribuir algo a alguien
ascription [ə·'skrɪp·ʃən] *n* atribución *f*
ASE *n abbr of* **American Stock Exchange** *segunda bolsa de valores más grande de EEUU*
asexual [ˌeɪ·'sek·ʃu·əl] *adj* **1.** (*reproduction*) asexual **2.** (*person*) asexuado, -a
ash[1] [æʃ] *n* (*from fire*) ceniza *f*
ash[2] [æʃ] *n* **1.** BOT (*tree*) fresno *m* **2.** (*wood*) (madera *f* de) fresno *m*
ashamed [ə·'ʃeɪmd] *adj* avergonzado, -a; **to feel ~** estar avergonzado; **to be ~ of oneself** avergonzarse de uno mismo
ashore [ə·'ʃɔr] **I.** *adj* en tierra **II.** *adv* a tierra; **to go ~** desembarcar; **to run ~** encallar
ashtray ['æʃ·ˌtreɪ] *n* cenicero *m*
Ash Wednesday *n* Miércoles *m* de Ceniza
Asia ['eɪ·ʒə] *n* Asia *f*
Asia Minor *n* Asia *f* Menor
Asian ['eɪ·ʒən] **I.** *n* asiático, -a *m, f* **II.** *adj* asiático, -a
Asian American *n* ciudadano *o* residente en *EEUU de origen asiático*
Asiatic [ˌeɪ·ʒi·'æṭ·ɪk] **I.** *adj* asiático, -a **II.** *n offensive* asiático, -a *m, f*
aside [ə·'saɪd] **I.** *n* **1.** (*in a speech*) digresión *f;* (*in a conversation*) comentario *m* aparte **2.** THEAT aparte *m* **II.** *adv* a un lado; **to stand** [*o* **step**] **~** hacerse a un lado; **to leave sth ~** dejar algo a un lado
aside from *prep* aparte de
ask [æsk] **I.** *vt* **1.** (*request information*) preguntar; **to ~ sb sth** preguntar algo a alguien; **to ~** (**sb**) **a question about sth** hacer (a alguien) una pregunta acerca de algo; **don't ~ me** ni me preguntes; **if you ~ me...** en mi opinión... **2.** (*request*) pedir; **to ~ sb's advice/a favor** pedir consejo/un favor a alguien **3.** (*invite*) invitar; **to ~ sb to do sth** invitar a alguien a hacer algo **4.** (*demand a price*) pedir; **to ~ 100 dollars for sth** pedir 100 dólares por algo **5.** (*expect*) **to ~ too much of sb** pedir demasiado de alguien **II.** *vi* **1.** (*request information*) preguntar **2.** (*make a request*) pedir
♦ **ask for** *vt* **1.** (*request*) pedir **2.** (*inquire about*) preguntar por **3.** (*deserve*) **to ~ trouble** buscar complicaciones

askance [ə·'skæns] *adv* con recelo; **to look ~** (**at sb/sth**) mirar con recelo (a alguien/algo)
askew [ə·'skju] *adj* torcido, -a, ladeado, -a
asking ['æs·kɪŋ] *n* petición *f;* **it's yours for the ~** lo tienes a pedir de boca
asking price *n* precio *m* de venta
asleep [ə·'slip] *adj* dormido, -a; **to be ~** estar dormido; **to fall ~** quedarse dormido
asocial [eɪ·'soʊ·ʃəl] *adj* (*not sociable*) asocial; (*antisocial*) antisocial
asparagus [ə·'spær·ə·gəs] *n* **1.** CULIN (*vegetable*) espárrago *m* **2.** (*plant*) esparraguera *f*
aspartame ['æs·pər·teɪm] *n* aspartame *m*
ASPCA [ˌeɪ·es·pi·si·'eɪ] *n abbr of* **American Society for Prevention of Cruelty to Animals** *asociación estadounidense protectora de los animales*
aspect ['æs·pekt] *n* **1.** (*point of view*) punto *m* de vista **2.** (*feature*) faceta *f* **3.** (*direction*) orientación *f* **4.** (*appearance*) aspecto *m* **5.** ASTR aspecto *m* **6.** LING aspecto *m*
aspen ['æs·pən] *n* BOT álamo *m* temblón
aspersion [ə·'spɜr·ʒən] *n form* calumnia *f;* **to cast ~s on sb** calumniar a alguien
asphalt ['æs·fɔlt] **I.** *n* asfalto *m*, asfaltado *m* AmL **II.** *vt* asfaltar
asphalt jungle *n* jungla *f* de asfalto
asphyxia [æs·'fɪk·si·ə] *n* asfixia *f*
asphyxiate [əs·'fɪk·si·eɪt] **I.** *vi form* asfixiarse **II.** *vt* asfixiar
asphyxiation [əs·ˌfɪk·si·'eɪ·ʃən] *n* asfixia *f*
aspic ['æs·pɪk] *n* CULIN áspic *m*
aspirant ['æs·pər·ənt] *n form* aspirante *mf;* (*to job, position*) candidato, -a *m, f*
aspiration [ˌæs·pə·'reɪ·ʃən] *n* aspiración *f*
aspire [ə·'spaɪr] *vi* **to ~ to sth** aspirar a algo
aspirin ['æs·pə·rɪn] *n* aspirina *f*
aspiring [ə·'spaɪr·ɪŋ] *adj* en ciernes
ass [æs] *n* **1.** *vulg* (*bottom*) culo *m*, siete *m* AmS, Méx **2.** (*donkey*) asno *m* **3.** *inf* (*idiot*) burro, -a *m, f;* **to make an ~ of oneself** hacer el burro ▶ **get your ~ in gear!** ¡espabílate!; **move your ~!** ¡muévete!; **to work one's ~ off** trabajar como un burro
assail [ə·'seɪl] *vt* **1.** (*attack*) atacar; (*verbally*) insultar **2.** (*torment*) atormentar
assailant *n* asaltante *mf*, agresor(a) *m(f)*
assassin [ə·'sæs·ɪn] *n* asesino, -a *m, f;* **paid ~** asesino a sueldo
assassinate [ə·'sæs·ə·neɪt] *vt* asesinar (*a una persona importante*)
assassination [ə·ˌsæs·ɪ·'neɪ·ʃən] *n* asesinato *m* (*de una persona importante*)
assault [ə·'sɔlt] **I.** *n* (*attack*) ataque *m*, fajada *f* Ant; **to make an ~ on sth/sb** asaltar algo/a alguien **II.** *vt* atacar
assault and battery *n* lesiones *fpl*
assault course *n* pista *f* americana
assemble [ə·'sem·bəl] **I.** *vi* congregarse **II.** *vt* **1.** (*collect: people, things*) reunir **2.** (*put together*) armar
assembly [ə·'sem·bli] <-ies> *n* **1.** (*meeting*) reunión *f* **2.** TECH montaje *m;* (*on toy package*);

"~ **required**" "precisa montaje„, "de armar„
assembly line n línea f de montaje
assent [ə·'sent] I. n form consentimiento m
II. vi to ~ **to sth** asentir a algo
assert [ə·'sɜrt] vt afirmar; **to ~ oneself** imponerse
assertion [ə·'sɜr·ʃən] n afirmación f
assertive [ə·'sɜr·ʈɪv] adj confiado, -a
assertiveness n autoafirmación f
assess [ə·'ses] vt 1.(evaluate) evaluar 2.(tax) calcular
assessment n 1.(calculation) valoración f 2.(evaluation) evaluación f 3.(taxation) cálculo m de los ingresos imponibles
assessor [ə·'ses·ər] n 1.(tax evaluator) tasador(a) m(f) 2.(legal advisor) asesor(a) m(f); **legal ~** asesor jurídico 3.(evaluator) evaluador(a) m(f)
asset ['æs·et] n 1.(benefit) ventaja f; (person) persona f valiosa; **he is an ~ to the team** es una valiosa aportación al equipo 2. pl FIN activo m; **liquid ~s** activos mpl líquidos
assiduous [ə·'sɪdʒ·u·əs] adj 1.(hardworking) diligente 2.(keen) asiduo, -a
assign [ə·'saɪn] vt 1.(task, resources) asignar, apropiar AmL; **to ~ sb to a position** destinar a alguien a un puesto; **to ~ sb to do sth** asignar a alguien la tarea de hacer algo; **to ~ the blame for sth to sb** atribuir la culpa de algo a alguien 2. LAW ceder
assignment n 1.(task) tarea f; **foreign ~** cargo m en el extranjero; **diplomatic ~** misión f diplomática; **to send sb on an ~** mandar a alguien a una misión; **an ~ to do sth** un encargo de hacer algo 2.(attribution) asignación f
assimilate [ə·'sɪm·ə·leɪt] I. vt asimilar II. vi asimilarse
assimilation [ə·ˌsɪm·ə·'leɪ·ʃən] n asimilación f
assist [ə·'sɪst] I. vt ayudar; **to ~ sb with sth** ayudar a alguien con algo II. vi ayudar; **to ~ with sth** ayudar en algo
assistance [ə·'sɪs·təns] n asistencia f; **to be of ~** ser de ayuda; **can I be of any ~?** ¿puedo ayudar en algo?
assistant n 1.(helper) ayudante mf, suche m Chile 2. COMPUT asistente m
assistant manager n subdirector(a) m(f)
assn. [ə·ˌsou·si·'eɪ·ʃən] n abbr of **association** asoc.
associate[1] [ə·'sou·ʃi·ɪt] I. n asociado, -a m, f; **business ~** socio, -a m, f II. adj UNIV asociado, -a
associate[2] [ə·'sou·ʃi·eɪt] I. vt asociar; **to ~ oneself with sth** relacionarse con algo II. vi relacionarse
associate professor n profesor m asociado, profesora f asociada
associate's degree n UNIV ≈ primer ciclo m (título que se obtiene tras los dos primeros años de carrera)
association n 1.(organization) asociación f 2.(involvement) colaboración f 3.(mental connection) asociación f

assorted [ə·'sɔr·ʈɪd] adj (mixed) surtido, -a; (wares) variado, -a
assortment [ə·'sɔrt·mənt] n surtido m; **a rich ~** una rica variedad
asst. [ə·'sɪs·tənt] n abbr of **assistant** ayudante, asistente
assuage [ə·'sweɪdʒ] vt (pain) aliviar; (anger) aplacar
assume [ə·'sum] vt 1.(regard as true) suponer, asumir AmL; **let's ~ that...** supongamos que... 2.(adopt: alias, identity) adoptar 3.(undertake) asumir; (power) tomar
assumed [ə·'sumd] adj supuesto, -a; **under an ~d name** bajo un nombre falso
assumption [ə·'sʌmp·ʃən] n 1.(supposition) supuesto m; **on the ~ that...** en el supuesto de que...; **to act on the ~ that...** actuar suponiendo que... 2.(hypothesis) suposición f 3.(of office, power) toma f 4. REL **the Assumption** la Asunción
assurance [ə·'ʃur·əns] n 1.(self-confidence) seguridad f; **to have ~** tener confianza 2.(promise) garantía f; **to give an ~ of sth** dar garantías de algo
assure [ə·'ʃur] vt 1.(guarantee) asegurar 2.(promise) garantizar; **to ~ sb of sth** asegurar algo a alguien
assured adj seguro, -a
assuredly adv 1.(confidently) seguramente 2.(certainly) ciertamente
asterisk ['æs·tə·rɪsk] n TYPO asterisco m
astern [ə·'stɜrn] adv 1. NAUT hacia popa; **to go ~** ir hacia atrás 2.(behind) ~ **of** detrás de 3.(backwards) hacia atrás
asteroid ['æs·tə·rɔɪd] n asteroide m
asthma ['æz·mə] n MED asma m
asthma attack n ataque m de asma
asthmatic [æz·'mæt·ɪk] I. n asmático, -a m, f II. adj asmático, -a
astigmatism [ə·'stɪg·mə·tɪz·əm] n astigmatismo m
astonish [ə·'stan·ɪʃ] vt asombrar; **to be ~ed** asombrarse
astonishing adj asombroso, -a
astonishment n asombro m; **to her ~** para gran sorpresa suya
astound [ə·'staʊnd] vt asombrar; **to be ~ed** quedarse atónito
astounding adj asombroso, -a
astray [ə·'streɪ] adv **to go ~** (letter) extraviarse; (person) descarriarse fig; **to lead sb ~** llevar a alguien por mal camino
astride [ə·'straɪd] I. prep a horcajadas [o a caballo] sobre II. adv a horcajadas
astringent [ə·'strɪn·dʒənt] I. n astringente m II. adj 1. MED astringente 2. fig cáustico, -a
astrologer [ə·'stral·ə·dʒər] n astrólogo, -a m, f
astrological [ˌæs·trə·'ladʒ·ɪ·kəl] adj astrológico, -a
astrology [ə·'stral·ə·dʒi] n astrología f
astronaut ['æs·trə·nɔt] n astronauta mf
astronomer [ə·'stran·ə·mər] n astrónomo, -a m, f

astronomical [ˌæs·trə·'nam·ɪ·kəl] *adj a. fig* astronómico, -a

astronomy [ə·'stran·ə·mi] *n* astronomía *f*

AstroTurf® ['æs·troʊ·ˌtɜrf] *n* hierba *f* artificial

Asturian [ə·'stʊr·i·ən] I. *adj* asturiano, -a II. *n* (*person*) asturiano, -a *m, f*

astute [ə·'stut] *adj* astuto, -a

astuteness *n* astucia *f*

asylum [ə·'saɪ·ləm] *n* 1. (*protection*) asilo *m* 2. (*institution*) asilo *m;* **insane ~** manicomio *m*

asylum seeker *n* solicitante *mf* de asilo

asymmetrical [ˌeɪ·sɪ·'met·rɪ·kəl] *adj* asimétrico, -a

at[1] [ət, æt] *prep* 1. (*place*) en; **~ the dentist's** en el dentista; **~ home/school** en casa/la escuela; **~ the table/office** en la mesa/oficina; **~ the window** a la ventana 2. (*time*) **~ Christmas** en Navidad; **~ night** por la noche; **~ once** enseguida; **all ~ once** de repente; **~ present** en este momento; **~ the time** en el momento; **~ the same time** al mismo tiempo; **~ three o'clock** a las tres; **while I am ~ it** mientras lo estoy haciendo 3. (*towards*) **to laugh ~ sb** reírse de alguien; **to look/aim ~ sth/sb** mirar/apuntar a algo/alguien; **to point ~ sb** señalar a alguien; **to rush ~ sb/sth** abalanzarse sobre alguien/algo 4. (*in reaction to*) **~ sb's request** a petición de alguien; **to be astonished/annoyed ~ sth** estar asombrado/molesto por algo; **to be mad ~ sb** estar enfadado con alguien; **to be unhappy ~ sth** no estar feliz con algo 5. (*in amount of*) **~ all** para nada; **to sell sth ~ $10 a pound** vender algo a 10 dólares la libra; **~ 120 mph** a 120 m/h (*193 km/h*) 6. (*in state of*) **~ best/worst** en el mejor/peor de los casos; **~ first** al principio; **~ least** al menos; **~ war/peace** en guerra/paz; **~ 20** a los 20 (años); **I feel ~ ease** me siento tranquilo; **to be ~ a loss** estar sin saber qué hacer; **a child ~ play** un niño jugando 7. (*in ability to*) **to be good/bad ~ French** ser bueno/malo en francés; **to be ~ an advantage** estar en ventaja 8. (*repeatedly*) **to pull ~ sb's hair** tirar de los pelos a alguien; **to tug ~ the rope** tirar de la cuerda; **to wear ~ sb's nerves** poner los nervios de punta a alguien ▶ **~ all** en realidad; **did you know the film ~ all?** ¿conocías la película?; **not ~ all!** ¡para nada!, ¡en absoluto!; (*as answer to thanks*) ¡de nada!; **nobody ~ all** nadie en absoluto

at[2] [æt] (*in email address*) arroba *f*

at bat *n* (*in baseball*) turno *m* de bateo

ate [eɪt] *pt of* **eat**

atheism ['eɪ·θi·ɪz·əm] *n* ateísmo *m*

atheist ['eɪ·θi·ɪst] I. *n* ateo, -a *m, f* II. *adj* ateísta

Athens ['æθ·ənz] *n* Atenas *f*

athlete ['æθ·lit] *n* atleta *mf*

athletic [æθ·'let·ɪk] *adj* atlético, -a

athletics *npl* atletismo *m*

Atlanta [æt·'læn·tə] *n* Atlanta

Atlantic [ət·'læn·tɪk] I. *n* **the ~** (**Ocean**) el (Océano) Atlántico II. *adj* atlántico, -a

atlas ['æt·ləs] <-es> *n* atlas *m inv*

ATM [ˌeɪ·ti·'em] *n abbr of* **automated teller machine** cajero *m* automático

atmosphere ['æt·mə·sfɪr] *n* 1. *a.* PHYS atmósfera *f* 2. *fig* ambiente *m*

atmospheric [ˌæt·mə·'sfer·ɪk] *adj* 1. METEO atmosférico, -a 2. *fig* evocador(a)

atoll ['æt·ɔl] *n* atolón *m*

atom ['æt·əm] *n a. fig* átomo *m*

atom bomb *n* bomba *f* atómica

atomic [ə·'tam·ɪk] *adj* atómico, -a

atomic energy *n* energía *f* atómica

atomize ['æt·ə·maɪz] *vt* atomizar; *fig* pulverizar

atomizer ['æt·ə·maɪ·zər] *n* atomizador *m*

atone for [ə·'toʊn] *vt* (*sin*) expiar; (*mistake*) reparar

atonement *n* expiación *f*

atrocious [ə·'troʊ·ʃəs] *adj* atroz

atrocity [ə·'tras·ə·ţi] <-ies> *n* atrocidad *f*

atrophy ['æt·rə·fi] <-ies> I. *n* atrofia *f* II. *vi* atrofiarse

at sign *n* COMPUT arroba *f*

attach [ə·'tætʃ] I. *vt* 1. (*fix onto*) fijar; (*label*) pegar; **to ~ sth to sth** fijar [*o* pegar] una cosa a otra 2. (*connect*) ligar 3. COMPUT (*to email*) adjuntar 4. (*join*) unir; **to ~ oneself to sb** unirse a alguien; **to be** (**very**) **~ed to one's family/car** tener mucho apego a su familia/coche 5. (*assign*) destinar; **to be ~ed to sth** estar destinado a algo 6. (*associate*) vincular; **to ~ importance to sth** dar importancia a algo II. *vi form* acompañar; **no blame ~es to you** tú no tienes ninguna culpa

attaché [ˌæt·ə·'ʃeɪ] *n* agregado, -a *m, f*

attaché case *n* cartera *f*, maletín *m*, portafolio *m AmL*

attachment [ə·'tætʃ·mənt] *n* 1. (*fondness*) apego *m;* **to form an ~ to sb** coger cariño a alguien 2. (*support*) adhesión *f* 3. (*union*) fijación *f* 4. (*attached device*) accesorio *m* 5. LAW incautación *f* 6. COMPUT archivo *m* adjunto, anexo *m*

attack [ə·'tæk] I. *n* ataque *m;* **to be on the ~** emprender una ofensiva; **to come under ~** ser atacado II. *vt* 1. (*physically, verbally*) atacar, cachorrear *Col* 2. (*tackle: problem*) afrontar 3. (*eat greedily*) devorar III. *vi* atacar

attain [ə·'teɪn] *vt* alcanzar; (*independence*) lograr

attainable *adj* alcanzable

attainment *n* logro *m*

attempt [ə·'tempt] I. *n* 1. (*try*) intento *m;* **to make an ~ at doing sth** intentar hacer algo 2. (*attack*) atentado *m* II. *vt* intentar

attempted murder *n* intento *m* de asesinato

attend [ə·'tend] I. *vt* (*be present at*) asistir a II. *vi* 1. (*be present*) asistir 2. (*take care of*) **to ~ to sb/sth** atender a alguien/algo 3. *form* (*listen carefully*) atender

attendance [ə·'ten·dəns] *n* 1. (*presence*)

asistencia *f;* **to be in** ~ estar presente **2.** (*people present*) concurrencia *f*
attendant [ə·'ten·dənt] I. *n* **1.** (*helper*) asistente, -a *m, f* **2.** (*servant*) encargado, -a *m, f* II. *adj* relacionado, -a, asociado, -a
attention [ə·'ten·ʃən] *n* **1.** (*maintenance*) cuidado *m* **2.** (*care, notice*) atención *f;* **Attention: John Smith** (*on envelope*) a la atención de John Smith; **to pay** ~ prestar atención; **to turn one's** ~**s to sth** dirigir la atención hacia algo **3.** MIL **to stand at** ~ cuadrarse; ~**!** ¡firmes!
attention deficit disorder *n* trastorno *m* por déficit de atención
attention deficit hyperactivity disorder *n* trastorno *m* por déficit de atención con hiperactividad
attention span *n* capacidad *f* de concentración
attentive [ə·'ten·tɪv] *adj* atento, -a; **to be** ~ **to sb** ser atento con alguien; **to be** ~ **to sb's needs** preocuparse por las necesidades de alguien
attenuate [ə·'ten·ju·eɪt] *vt form* atenuar
attest [ə·'test] I. *vt* **1.** (*demonstrate*) testimoniar **2.** (*authenticate*) atestiguar II. *vi* testimoniar
Att. Gen. [ə·'tɜr·ni 'dʒen·ər·əl] *n abbr of* **Attorney General** fiscal *mf* general del Estado
attic ['æt·ɪk] *n* desván *m,* ático *m,* tabanco *m AmC,* entretecho *m CSur*
attire [ə·'taɪr] *n form* atavío *m*
attitude ['æt·ɪ·tud] *n* **1.** (*opinion*) actitud *f;* **a change of** ~ un cambio de actitud; **to have the** ~ **that...** ser de la opinión de que...; **an** ~ **towards sb/sth** una actitud hacia alguien/algo **2.** (*position*) postura *f;* **to adopt an** ~ adoptar una postura **3.** ART posición *f*
attorney [ə·'tɜr·ni] *n* abogado, -a *m, f;* **criminal** ~ abogado penalista; **legal** ~ apoderado *m* legal
attorney-at-law *n* <attorneys-at-law> abogado, -a *m, f*
attract [ə·'trækt] *vt* atraer, jalar *AmL;* **to** ~ **attention/support** atraer la atención/conseguir el apoyo; **to** ~ **sb's notice** atraer la atención de alguien; **to be** ~**ed by sb/sth** sentirse atraído por alguien/algo
attraction [ə·'træk·ʃən] *n* **1.** (*force, place of enjoyment*) atracción *f;* **tourist** ~ atracción turística **2.** (*appeal*) atractivo *m;* **to feel an** ~ **to sb** sentirse atraído por alguien
attractive [ə·'træk·tɪv] *adj* atractivo, -a
attribute[1] [ə·'trɪb·jut] *vt* **1.** (*ascribe*) atribuir; **to** ~ **the blame to sb** achacar la culpa a alguien; **to** ~ **importance to sth** dar importancia a algo **2.** (*give credit for*) **to** ~ **sth to sb** atribuir algo a alguien
attribute[2] ['æt·rɪ·bjut] *n* atributo *m*
attributive [ə·'trɪb·jə·tɪv] *adj* atributivo, -a
attrition [ə·'trɪʃ·ən] *n* **1.** (*wearing down*) desgaste *m;* **war of** ~ guerra *f* de desgaste **2.** ECON *práctica laboral que reduce personal al no reponer las bajas vegetativas* (*por jubilación, fallecimiento, etc.*) **3.** REL atrición *f*

ATV [ˌeɪ·ti·'vi] *n abbr of* **all terrain vehicle** vehículo *m* todoterreno
at-will *adj* LAW (*contract, basis*) que se puede rescindir sin previo aviso; (*employee, employment*) con un contrato que se puede rescindir sin previo aviso
auburn ['ɔ·bərn] *adj* castaño, -a
auction ['ɔk·ʃən] I. *n* subasta *f;* **to be sold at** ~ ser vendido en [*o* por] subasta; **to put sth up for** ~ subastar algo II. *vt* **to** ~ **sth** (**off**) subastar algo
auctioneer [ˌɔk·ʃə·'nɪr] *n* subastador(a) *m(f)*
audacious [ɔ·'deɪ·ʃəs] *adj* **1.** (*bold*) audaz **2.** (*impudent*) descarado, -a
audacity [ɔ·'dæs·ə·t̬i] *n* **1.** (*boldness*) audacia *f* **2.** (*impudence*) descaro *m*
audible ['ɔ·də·bəl] I. *adj* audible *m,* perceptible II. *n* (*in football*) *cambio que el quarterback o el linebacker hacen de la jugada estando ya en la formación*
audience ['ɔ·di·əns] *n* **1.** (*spectators*) público *m;* TV, RADIO audiencia *f;* (*of book*) lectores *mpl* **2.** (*formal interview*) audiencia *f*
audio ['ɔ·di·oʊ] I. *adj inv* de sonido; ~ **cassette** casete *m o f* II. *n* (*sound*) audio *m*
audio-visual *adj* audiovisual
audit[1] ['ɔ·dɪt] FIN I. *n* auditoría *f* contable II. *vt* auditar
audit[2] ['ɔ·dɪt] *vt* UNIV **to** ~ **a course** asistir de oyente a un curso
audition [ɔ·'dɪʃ·ən] THEAT I. *n* audición *f* II. *vi* hacer una prueba III. *vt* **to** ~ **sb** hacer una prueba a alguien
auditor ['ɔ·də·t̬ər] *n* **1.** COM auditor(a) *m(f)* **2.** UNIV oyente *mf*
auditorium [ˌɔ·də·'tɔr·i·əm] <-s *o* auditoria> *n* auditorio *m*
Aug. ['ɔ·gəst] *n abbr of* **August** ago. *m*
augment [ɔg·'ment] *vt form* aumentar; **to** ~ **one's income** aumentar sus ingresos
au gratin [oʊ·'gra·tən] *adj* gratinado, -a
augur ['ɔ·gər] I. *vi* **to** ~ **badly/well** ser de mal/buen agüero II. *vt* augurar
august [ɔ·'gʌst] *adj form* augusto, -a
August ['ɔ·gəst] *n* agosto *m; s.a.* **April**
aunt [ænt] *n* tía *f*
au pair [oʊ·'per] I. *n* au pair *mf* II. *adj* ~ **girl** chica au pair
aura ['ɔr·ə] *n* aura *f*
aural ['ɔr·əl] *adj* auditivo, -a
auricle ['ɔr·ɪ·kəl] *n* ANAT (*of ear*) pabellón *m* de la oreja; (*of heart*) aurícula *f*
auricular [ɔ·'rɪk·jə·lər] *adj* **1.** (*relating to hearing*) auditivo, -a **2.** (*concerning the heart*) auricular
aurora [ɔ·'rɔr·ə] *n* aurora *f*
aurora borealis [ɔ·'rɔr·ə·ˌbɔr·i·'æl·ɪs] <aurora borealises *o* aurorae borealis> *n* ASTR aurora *f* boreal
auspices ['ɔ·spɪ·sɪz] *n pl* auspicios *mpl;* **under the** ~ **of** bajo los auspicios de
auspicious [ɔ·'spɪʃ·əs] *adj form* propicio, -a
austere [ɔ·'stɪr] *adj* austero, -a

austerity [ɔ·'ster·ə·ți] <-ies> *n* austeridad *f;*
~ **program** ECON programa *m* de austeridad
Australia [ɔ·'streɪl·jə] *n* Australia *f*
Australian I. *n* australiano, -a *m, f* **II.** *adj* australiano, -a
Austria ['ɔ·stri·ə] *n* Austria *f*
Austrian I. *n* austriaco, -a *m, f* **II.** *adj* austriaco, -a
authentic [ɔ·'θen·țɪk] *adj* auténtico, -a;
~ **leather** cuero genuino; **an ~ Goya paint-**
ing un Goya auténtico
authenticate [ɔ·'θen·țɪ·keɪt] *vt* autentificar
authentication [ɔ·ˌθen·țɪ·'keɪ·ʃən] *n* autentifi-
cación *f*
authenticity [ˌɔ·θən·'tɪs·ə·ți] *n* autenticidad *f*
author ['ɔ·θər] **I.** *n* **1.** (*writer*) autor(a) *m(f)*
2. *fig* creador(a) *m(f)* **II.** *vt* escribir
authoritarian [ə·ˌθɔr·ə·'ter·i·ən] **I.** *n* autoritario, -a *m, f* **II.** *adj* autoritario, -a
authoritative [ə·'θɔr·ə·teɪ·țɪv] *adj* **1.** (*asser-*
tive) autoritario, -a **2.** (*reliable*) autorizado, -a
authority [ə·'θɔr·ə·ți] <-ies> *n* **1.** (*right to*
control) autoridad *f;* **to be in ~** tener autoridad **2.** (*permission*) autorización *f* **3.** (*control*)
control *m* **4.** (*knowledge*) **with ~** con conocimiento de causa; **to be an ~ on sth** ser una
autoridad en algo **5.** (*organization*) autoridad *f;*
the authorities las autoridades ▶ **to have sth**
on good ~ saber algo de buena tinta; **to have**
sth on sb's ~ saber algo a través de alguien
authorization [ɔ·θər·ɪ·'zeɪ·ʃən] *n* autorización *f*
authorize ['ɔ·θə·raɪz] *vt* autorizar; **to ~ sb to**
do sth autorizar a alguien para que haga algo
authorship ['ɔ·θər·ʃɪp] *n* autoría *f;* **the article**
is of unknown ~ el artículo es de autor desconocido
autistic [ɔ·'tɪs·țɪk] *adj* autista
auto ['ɔ·țoʊ] *n* coche *m*, carro *m AmL*
autobiographical [ˌɔ·țə·baɪ·ə·'græf·ɪ·kəl] *adj*
autobiográfico, -a
autobiography [ˌɔ·țə·baɪ·'ag·rə·fi] *n* autobiografía *f*
autocracy [ɔ·'tak·rə·si] *n* autocracia *f*
autocrat ['ɔ·țə·kræt] *n* autócrata *mf*
autocratic [ˌɔ·țə·'kræț·ɪk] *adj* autocrático, -a
autocross *n* autocross *m*
autograph ['ɔ·țə·græf] **I.** *n* autógrafo *m* **II.** *vt*
firmar
automate ['ɔ·țə·meɪt] *vt* automatizar
automated *adj* automatizado, -a
automated teller machine *n* cajero *m* automático
automatic [ˌɔ·țə·'mæț·ɪk] **I.** *n* **1.** (*machine*)
máquina *f* **2.** (*car*) coche *m* automático **3.** (*pis-*
tol) pistola *f* automática; (*rifle*) metralleta *f*
II. *adj* automático, -a
automatic pilot *n* piloto *m* automático
automation [ˌɔ·țə·'meɪ·ʃən] *n* automatiza-
ción *f*
automaton [ɔ·'tam·ə·țən] <automata> *n a. fig*
autómata *m*
automobile ['ɔ·țə·moʊ·bil] *n* automóvil *m;*

~ **accident** accidente de coche
automotive [ˌɔ·țə·'moʊ·țɪv] *adj inv* automovilístico, -a
autonomous [ɔ·'tan·ə·məs] *adj* autónomo, -a
autonomy [ɔ·'tan·ə·mi] *n* autonomía *f*
autopsy ['ɔ·tap·si] <-ies> *n* autopsia *f*
autumn ['ɔ·țəm] *n* otoño *m;* **in** (**the**) ~ en (el)
otoño; ~ **colors** colores *mpl* otoñales
autumnal [ɔ·'tʌm·nəl] *adj* otoñal
auxiliary [ɔg·'zɪl·jə·ri] <-ies> **I.** *n* **1.** (*aid in*
hospital) auxiliar *mf* **2.** LING auxiliar *m* **3.** HIST
(*soldier*) soldado *m* auxiliar **II.** *adj* auxiliar;
~ **staff** personal *m* auxiliar
AV *abbr of* **audiovisual** audiovisual
av. 1. *abbr of* **average** media *f* **2.** *abbr of*
avenue Avda.
avail [ə·'veɪl] **I.** *n* provecho *m;* **to no** ~ en vano
II. *vt* **to ~ oneself of sth** aprovecharse de algo
available [ə·'veɪ·lə·bəl] *adj* **1.** (*obtainable*) disponible; **to make sth ~ to sb** poner algo a disposición [*o* al alcance] de alguien **2.** (*free*) libre;
to be ~ to do sth tener tiempo para hacer algo
3. (*free for romantic involvement*) **to be ~**
estar libre y sin compromiso
avalanche ['æv·ə·læntʃ] *n* **1.** (*of snow*) alud *m,*
avalancha *f* **2.** *fig* torrente *m*
avant-garde [ˌa·vant·'gard] **I.** *n* vanguardia *f*
II. *adj* vanguardista, de vanguardia
avarice ['æv·ə·rɪs] *n form* avaricia *f*
avaricious [ˌæv·ə·'rɪʃ·əs] *adj form* avaro, -a
Ave. *n abbr of* **Avenue** Avda.
avenge [ə·'vendʒ] *vt* vengar; **to ~ oneself** vengarse
avenue ['æv·ə·nu] *n* **1.** (*street*) avenida *f*, carrera *f AmL* **2.** (*possibility*) camino *m;* **to**
explore an ~ explorar una vía
average ['æv·ər·ɪdʒ] **I.** *n* MATH promedio *m,*
media *f;* **above/below** ~ por encima/por
debajo de la media; **on** ~ por término medio
II. *adj* **1.** MATH medio, -a; ~ **rainfall** precipitación media **2.** (*mediocre*) mediocre **3.** (*ordi-*
nary) ~ **Joe** un tío [*o AmL* tipo] corriente *inf*
III. *vt* **1.** (*have mean value*) promediar **2.** (*cal-*
culate mean value of) sacar la media de
averse [ə·'vɜrs] *adj* **to be ~ to sth** ser contrario
a algo; **I'm not ~ to an occasional glass of**
wine no tengo nada en contra de tomar un
vino de vez en cuando
aversion [ə·'vɜr·ʒən] *n* **1.** (*dislike*) aversión *f;*
to have an ~ to sth/sb sentir aversión hacia
algo/alguien **2.** (*object of dislike*) fobia *f*
avert [ə·'vɜrt] *vt* **1.** (*prevent*) prevenir **2.** (*turn*
away) **to ~ one's eyes from sth** desviar la
mirada de algo; **to ~ one's thoughts from sth**
apartar sus pensamientos de algo
aviary ['eɪ·vi·er·i] *n* pajarera *f*
aviation [ˌeɪ·vi·'eɪ·ʃən] *n* aviación *f*
aviation industry *n* industria *f* aeronáutica
avid ['æv·ɪd] *adj* ávido, -a
avidity [ə·'vɪd·ə·ți] *n* avidez *f*
avocado [ˌæv·ə·'ka·doʊ] <-s *o* -es> *n* CULIN
aguacate *m*
avoid [ə·'vɔɪd] *vt* (*person, thing*) evitar; (*when*

moving) esquivar; **to ~ doing sth** evitar hacer algo

avoidable *adj* evitable

avoidance *n* evasión *f*

avow [ə·ˈvaʊ] *vt form* 1.(*admit*) admitir 2.(*declare*) declarar

avowal [ə·ˈvaʊ·əl] *n form* declaración *f*

avowedly [ə·ˈvaʊ·ɪd·li] *adv* abiertamente

AWACS [ˈeɪ·wæks] *n abbr of* **airborne warning and control system** sistema *m* AWACS

await [ə·ˈweɪt] *vt* aguardar; **eagerly ~ed** esperado con ansiedad

awake [ə·ˈweɪk] I.<awoke *o* awaked, awoken *o* awaked> *vi* despertarse; **to ~ to sth** *fig* darse cuenta de algo II. *vt* despertar III. *adj* 1.(*not sleeping*) despierto, -a; **to stay ~** mantenerse despierto; **to keep sb ~** mantener a alguien despierto; **to lie ~** quedarse despierto 2. *fig* alerta; **to be ~ to sth** estar alerta ante algo

awaken [ə·ˈweɪ·kən] I. *vt form* despertar; **to ~ sb to sth** *fig* abrir los ojos a alguien sobre algo II. *vi fig* darse cuenta

awakening [ə·ˈweɪ·kə·nɪŋ] *n* despertar *m;* **she's in for a rude ~** le espera una desagradable sorpresa

award [ə·ˈwɔrd] I. *n* 1.(*prize*) premio *m* 2.(*reward*) recompensa *f* 3. MIL condecoración *f* II. *vt* otorgar; **to ~ sth to sb** conferir algo a alguien; **to ~ damages** indemnizar por daños y perjuicios; **to ~ sb a grant** conceder a alguien una beca

aware [ə·ˈwer] *adj* 1.(*knowing*) **to be ~ that...** saber que...; **as far as I'm ~...** por lo que yo sé...; **not that I'm ~ of** no, que yo sepa 2.(*sense*) **to be ~ of sth** ser consciente de algo

awareness [ə·ˈwer·nɪs] *n* conciencia *f*

awash [ə·ˈwɑʃ] *adj* inundado, -a; **to be ~ with money** estar forrado de dinero

away [ə·ˈweɪ] *adv* 1.(*distant*) **10 miles ~** a 10 millas; **as far ~ as possible** lo más lejos posible; **to be miles ~** *fig* no prestar atención 2.(*absent*) fuera; **to be ~ on vacation** estar de vacaciones 3.(*in future time*) **to be only a week ~** no faltar más que una semana; **right ~!** ¡enseguida! 4.(*continuously*) **to read/eat/write ~** leer/comer/escribir sin cesar

away from *prep* 1.(*at distance from*) **~ the town** lejos del pueblo; **~ each other** alejados el uno del otro; **to stay ~ sth/sb** mantenerse alejado de algo/alguien 2.(*in other direction from*) **to go ~ sth** alejarse de algo

away game *n* partido *m* fuera de casa

awe [ɔ] *n* sobrecogimiento *m;* **to hold sb in ~** tener un gran respeto por alguien; **to stand in ~ of sb** imponer alguien respeto a uno

awe-inspiring *adj* imponente

awesome [ˈɔ·səm] *adj* 1.(*impressive*) imponente 2. *inf* (*very good*) estupendo, -a 3.(*fearsome*) temible 4.(*daunting*) intimidatorio, -a

awestricken [ˈɔ·strɪk·ən] *adj*, **awestruck** [ˈɔ·strʌk] *adj* atemorizado, -a

awful [ˈɔ·fəl] *adj* 1.(*bad*) terrible 2.(*as intensifier*) **an ~ lot** muchísimo

awfully [ˈɔ·fə·li] *adv* 1.(*badly*) terriblemente 2.(*very*) **~ smart/stupid** muy inteligente/tonto; **I'm ~ sorry** lo siento muchísimo; **not to be ~ good at sth** no ser muy bueno para algo

awhile [ə·ˈhwaɪl] *adv* **to wait ~** esperar un rato

awkward [ˈɔk·wərd] *adj* 1.(*difficult*) difícil; **an ~ customer** *inf* un tipo difícil; **to make things ~ for sb** crear problemas a alguien 2.(*embarrassed*) incómodo, -a; **an ~ silence** un silencio incómodo; **an ~ question** una pregunta delicada; **to feel ~** sentirse incómodo 3.(*inconvenient*) **an ~ time** una hora inoportuna 4.(*clumsy*) torpe

awl [ɔl] *n* punzón *m*, lezna *f*

awning [ˈɔ·nɪŋ] *n* toldo *m*

awoke [ə·ˈwoʊk] *pt of* **awake**

awoken [ə·ˈwoʊ·kən] *pp of* **awake**

AWOL [ˈeɪ·wɔl] MIL *abbr of* **absent without leave** ausente sin permiso; **to go ~** *inf* desaparecer así como así

awry [ə·ˈraɪ] *adj* **to go ~** salir mal

ax *n*, **axe** [æks] I. *n* hacha *f* ▶ **to get the ~** *inf* (*worker*) ser despedido; (*project*) ser anulado; **to have an ~ to grind** tener un interés personal II.<axing> *vt* recortar; **to ~ jobs** reducir puestos de trabajo

axiom [ˈæk·si·əm] *n* axioma *m*

axis [ˈæk·sɪs] *n a.* MATH, POL eje *m*

axle [ˈæk·səl] *n* eje *m*, cardán *m AmC, Ven, Col;* **back/front ~** eje trasero/delantero

ayatollah [ˌaɪ·ə·ˈtoʊ·lə] *n* ayatolá *m*

aye [aɪ] *n* POL **the ~s** los votos a favor

AZ [ær·ɪ·ˈzoʊ·nə] *n abbr of* **Arizona** Arizona

azalea [ə·ˈzeɪl·jə] *n* BOT azalea *f*

Azerbaijan [ˌæz·ər·baɪ·ˈdʒɑn] *n* Azerbaiyán *m*

Azerbaijani I. *adj* azerbaiyano, -a II. *n* azerbaiyano, -a *m, f*

Aztec [ˈæz·tek] I. *adj* azteca II. *n* azteca *mf*

azure [ˈæʒ·ər] I. *n* azul *m* celeste II. *adj* azul celeste

B

B, b [bi] *n* 1.(*letter*) B, b *f;* **~ as in Bravo** B de Barcelona 2. MUS si *m*

b & b *n*, **B & B** [ˌbi·ənd·ˈbi] *n abbr of* **bed and breakfast** pensión *f*

BA [ˌbi·ˈeɪ] *n abbr of* **Bachelor of Arts** Ldo. , -a *m, f* en Filosofía y Letras

baa [bæ] I. *n* be *m* II.<-ed> *vi* balar

babble [ˈbæb·əl] I. *n* 1.(*of a baby*) balbuceo *m* 2.(*of a stream*) murmullo *m* II. *vi* (*baby*) balbucear; (*adult*) parlotear

babe [beɪb] *n* 1.(*baby*) bebé *m inf* 2. *pej, sl* (*young woman*) tía *f* 3.(*term of endearment*)

ricura *f*, cariño *m*, mamita *Col*
baboon [bæ·'bun] *n* babuino *m*
baby ['beɪ·bi] **I.** *n* **1.** (*child*) bebé *m;* **to expect/have a ~** esperar/tener un bebé **2.** (*youngest person*) benjamín, -ina *m, f* **3.** *inf* (*term of endearment*) nene, -a *m, f* **4.** (*personal interest*) **that's her ~** está como loca con eso ▶ **to throw out the ~ with the bath-water** tirar las frutas frescas con las pochas **II.** *adj* **1.** (*person*) infantil **2.** (*carrots*) pequeño, -a **III.** *vt* mimar
baby carriage *n* cochecito *m* de bebé, carriola *f Méx*
baby food *n* comida *f* para bebés
babyhood ['beɪ·bɪ·hʊd] *n* niñez *f*
babyish ['beɪ·bi·ɪʃ] *adj* infantil
babysitter ['beɪ·bi·ˌsɪt̬·ər] *n* canguro *mf*, nana *f Méx*
bachelor ['bætʃ·ə·lər] *n* **1.** (*man*) soltero *m* **2.** UNIV licenciado, -a *m, f;* **Bachelor of Arts** Licenciado, -a *m, f* en Filosofía y Letras; **Bachelor of Science** Licenciado, -a *m, f* en Ciencias

i **Bachelor's degree** es el título que otorgan las universidades (**colleges**) a los estudiantes que han cursado una carrera (generalmente, de cuatro años). El título específico varía según el área de estudios. Los títulos más importantes son: **BA** (**Bachelor of Arts**) en Humanidades, **BSc** (**Bachelor of Science**) en las disciplinas científicas, **BEd** (**Bachelor of Education**) en Pedagogía, **LLB** (**Bachelor of Laws**) en Derecho y **BMus** (**Bachelor of Music**) en Musicología.

back [bæk] **I.** *n* **1.** (*opposite of front*) parte *f* trasera; (*of a hand*) dorso *m;* (*of a chair*) respaldo *m;* (*reverse side*) revés *m;* (*of a piece of paper, envelope*) dorso *m;* **~ to front** al revés; **to know sth ~ to front** saberse algo al derecho y al revés **2.** (*end: of a book*) final *m* **3.** ANAT espalda *f;* (*of an animal*) lomo *m;* **to be on one's ~** estar boca arriba; **to break one's ~** *inf* deslomarse; **to do sth behind sb's ~** *a. fig* hacer algo a espaldas de alguien; **to turn one's ~ on sb** *a. fig* dar la espalda a alguien **4.** SPORTS defensa *mf* ▶ **to know sth like the ~ of one's hand** conocer algo al dedillo *inf;* **to have one's ~ against the wall** estar entre la espada y la pared; **you scratch my ~ and I'll scratch yours** hoy por ti, mañana por mí; **to stab sb in the ~** dar a alguien una puñalada por la espalda **II.** *adj* **1.** (*rear*) trasero, -a **2.** MED dorsal **III.** *adv* **1. to be ~** estar de vuelta; **to come ~** volver; **to want sb ~** querer que alguien vuelva; **I want the money ~** quiero que me devuelvan el dinero; **to bring ~ memories** traer viejos recuerdos a la memoria **2.** (*to the rear, behind*) detrás, atrás; **~ and forth** atrás y adelante; **to look ~** mirar (hacia) atrás;

to sit ~ recostarse **3.** (*in return*) de vuelta **4.** (*into the past*) atrás **IV.** *vt* respaldar
◆ **back away** *vi* echarse atrás
◆ **back down** *vi* retirarse
◆ **back off** *vi* **1.** (*physically*) retroceder **2.** (*personally*) mantener [*o* guardar] las distancias
◆ **back out of** *vt* salir de; *fig* retirarse de
◆ **back up** *vt* **1.** (*reverse*) dar marcha atrás **2.** COMPUT **to ~ data/files** hacer copias de seguridad de datos/archivos **3.** (*support*) respaldar
backbone *n* **1.** (*spine*) columna *f* vertebral **2.** *fig* pilar *m* **3.** (*strength of character*) coraje *m*
back door *n* puerta *f* trasera
backdrop *n a. fig* telón *m* de fondo
backer ['bæk·ər] *n* partidario, -a *m, f;* **financial ~** refaccionador(a) *m(f)*
backfire ['bæk·faɪr] *vi* **1.** (*go wrong*) fallar; **his plans ~d** sus planes fracasaron **2.** AUTO petardear, detonar *AmL*
backgammon ['bæk·gæm·ən] *n* backgammon *m*
background ['bæk·graʊnd] *n* **1.** (*rear view*) fondo *m;* **in the ~** *fig* en segundo plano **2.** (*education, family*) educación *f* **3.** (*training*) formación *f;* **to have a ~ in mathematics** tener una formación en matemáticas **4.** (*circumstances*) antecedentes *mpl*
background music *n* música *f* de fondo
backhand ['bæk·hænd] *n* revés *m*
backing ['bæk·ɪŋ] *n* **1.** (*support, aid*) apoyo *m* **2.** FASHION refuerzo *m* **3.** MUS acompañamiento *m*
backlash *n* reacción *f* violenta
backlog *n* atraso *m*
backpack ['bæk·pæk] **I.** *n* mochila *f* **II.** *vi* viajar con mochila
backpacker *n* mochilero, -a *m, f*
back pay *n* atrasos *mpl* de sueldo
back seat *n* asiento *m* trasero
backside *n inf* trasero *m*
backslash *n* barra *f* inversa
backspace (**key**) *n* tecla *f* de retroceso
backstabbing ['bæk·ˌstæb·ɪŋ] *n* habladurías *fpl* a espaldas de alguien, viboreo *m Méx*
backstage [bæk·'steɪdʒ] **I.** *adj* **1.** THEAT de bastidores **2.** *fig* entre bastidores **II.** *adv* THEAT tras bambalinas, entre bastidores
backstory *n* historia *f* de fondo [*o* de trasfondo]
backstroke *n* (estilo *m*) espalda *f*, nado *m* de dorso *AmL*
back talk *n* réplicas *fpl*
backtrack ['bæk·træk] *vi* **1.** (*go back*) retroceder; (*to previous topic*) volver **2.** *fig* dar marcha atrás; **to ~ on one's statement** retirar lo dicho
backup ['bæk·ʌp] *n* **1.** COMPUT copia *f* de seguridad **2.** (*support*) apoyo *m*
backward ['bæk·wərd] **I.** *adj* **1.** (*to the rear*) hacia atrás **2.** (*slow in learning*) retrasado, -a **3.** (*underdeveloped*) atrasado, -a **II.** *adv* hacia

B

atrás

backward(s) ['bæk·wərdz] *adv* **1.** (*towards the back*) hacia atrás **2.** (*in reverse order*) al revés **3.** (*from better to worse*) a peor; (*step*) atrás **4.** (*into the past*) atrás en el tiempo

backwater *n* **1.** (*river*) remanso *m* **2.** *pej* lugar *m* atrasado

backwoods *npl* **the** ~ *zona atrasada y poco habitada*

backyard *n* jardín *m* trasero

bacon ['beɪ·kən] *n* beicon *m,* tocino *m AmL* ►**to bring** home **the** ~ *inf* ganarse los garbanzos

bacteria [bæk·'tɪr·i·ə] *n pl of* **bacterium**

bacteriologist [bæk·ˌtɪr·ɪ·'al·ə·dʒɪst] *n* bacteriólogo, -a *m, f*

bacterium [bæk·'tɪr·i·əm] *n* <-ria> bacteria *f*

bad [bæd] <worse, worst> **I.** *adj* **1.** (*not good*) malo, -a; **to have a** ~ **marriage** tener un matrimonio difícil; **to feel** ~ sentirse mal; **to look** ~ tener mal aspecto; **too** ~! ¡qué lástima!; ~ **habits** malas costumbres; **to use** ~ **language** decir palabrotas; ~ **luck** mala suerte; macacoa *f PRico;* **a** ~ **name** una mala reputación; **in** ~ **taste** de mal gusto; **to have a** ~ **temper** tener mal carácter; ~ **times** tiempos *mpl* difíciles **2.** (*harmful*) dañino, -a; **to be** ~ **for sth/sb** ser perjudicial para algo/alguien **3.** (*spoiled*) malo, -a; **to go** ~ echarse a perder **4.** (*unhealthy*) enfermo, -a; **to have a** ~ **heart/back** estar mal del corazón/de la espalda **5.** (*serious: accident, mistake*) grave **6.** (*severe: pain*) fuerte ►**to go from** ~ **to worse** ir de mal en peor **II.** *adv inf* mal **III.** *n* **the** ~ lo malo

bad dream *n* pesadilla *f*

badge [bædʒ] *n* insignia *f,* placa *f Méx*

badger ['bædʒ·ər] **I.** *n* tejón *m* **II.** *vt* importunar

badly ['bæd·li] <worse, worst> *adv* **1.** (*poorly*) mal **2.** (*in a negative way*) mal; **to think** ~ **of sb** pensar mal de alguien; **to come out of sth** ~ salir mal parado de algo; **to be** ~ **off** andar escaso de dinero **3.** (*very much*) desesperadamente; **to be** ~ **in need of sth** necesitar algo desesperadamente; **he was** ~ **defeated** fue derrotado estrepitosamente

badminton ['bæd·mɪn·tən] *n* bádminton *m*

baffle ['bæf·əl] **I.** *vt* **1.** (*confuse*) desconcertar **2.** (*hinder*) impedir **II.** *n* TECH deflector *m;* (*audio*) bafle *m,* bafle *m Méx*

baffling *adj* desconcertante

bag [bæg] **I.** *n* **1.** (*container*) bolsa *f,* busaca *f Col, Ven;* (*handbag*) bolso *m;* (*sack*) saco *m;* **to pack one's** ~**s** hacer las maletas; *fig* marcharse **2.** (*under eyes*) **to have** ~**s under one's eyes** tener ojeras **3.** *sl* (*unpleasant woman*) bruja *f* **4.** (*catch*) presa *f* ►**to be a** ~ **of bones** *inf* ser un saco de huesos; **the whole** ~ **of** tricks *inf* todas las mañas; **a mixed** ~ un grupo heterogéneo **II.** *vt* <-gg-> **1.** (*groceries*) meter en una bolsa **2.** *inf* (*obtain*) agenciarse **3.** (*capture*) cazar

bagel ['beɪ·gəl] *n tipo de rosca de pan*

baggage ['bæg·ɪdʒ] *n* **1.** (*luggage*) equipaje *m;* **excess** ~ exceso *m* de equipaje **2.** (*army equipment*) bagaje *m* **3.** *pej* (*unpleasant woman*) bruja *f*

baggage allowance *n* límite *m* de equipaje

baggage car *n* vagón *m* de equipaje, breque *m Ecua, Perú, RíoPl*

baggage check *n* documentación *f* del equipaje

baggage claim *n* recogida *f* del equipaje

baggy ['bæg·i] *adj* (*pants*) ancho, -a, holgado, -a

bag lady *n inf* vagabunda *f*

bagpipes *npl* gaita *f*

baguette [bæ·'get] *n* CULIN pan *m* francés

Bahamas [bə·'ha·məz] *npl* **the** ~ las (Islas) Bahamas

Bahamian [bə·'hæ·mi·ən] **I.** *adj* bahameño, -a **II.** *n* bahameño, -a *m, f*

Bahrain [ba·'reɪn] *n* Bahrein *m*

bail [beɪl] **I.** *n* fianza *f;* **on** ~ bajo fianza; **to post** ~ **for sb** pagar la fianza de alguien **II.** *vi* achicar **III.** *vt* **1.** (*remove: water*) achicar **2.** (*guarantee*) afianzar

◆**bail out** *vt* **to bail sb out** (**of trouble**) sacar a alguien de apuros

bailiff ['beɪ·lɪf] *n* alguacil *mf*

bait [beɪt] **I.** *n* **1.** (*for fish*) cebo *m* **2.** *fig* señuelo *m;* **to swallow the** ~ *inf* morder el anzuelo **II.** *vt* **1.** (*put bait on: hook*) cebar **2.** (*harass: person*) acosar

bake [beɪk] **I.** *vi* **1.** (*cook*) cocerse **2.** *inf* (*be hot: place*) ser un horno **II.** *vt* **1.** (*cook*) hornear **2.** (*harden*) tostar

baker ['beɪ·kər] *n* panadero, -a *m, f*

bakery ['beɪ·kə·ri] *n* panadería *f*

baking *adj* **it's** ~ **hot** hace un calor achicharrante

baking powder *n* levadura *f*

baking soda *n* bicarbonato *m* de sodio

balance ['bæl·ənts] **I.** *n* **1.** (*device*) balanza *f* **2.** *a. fig* equilibrio *m;* **to lose one's** ~ perder el equilibrio **3.** (*state of equality*) equidad *f* **4.** (*in bank account*) saldo *m* **5.** (*amount to be paid*) balance *m* **II.** *vi* mantener el equilibrio **III.** *vt* **1.** (*compare*) contrapesar; **to** ~ **sth against sth** comparar algo con algo **2.** (*keep in a position*) estabilizar **3.** (*achieve equilibrium*) equilibrar; **to** ~ **the books** hacer cuadrar las cuentas; *fig;* **to** ~ **working and having a family** compaginar el trabajo con la familia

balanced *adj* equilibrado, -a; **a** ~ **diet** una dieta equilibrada [*o* balanceada]

balance of trade *n* balanza *f* comercial

balance sheet *n* balance *m*

balcony ['bæl·kə·ni] *n* balcón *m*

bald [bɔld] *adj* **1.** (*lacking hair*) calvo, -a, pelón, -ona *Méx;* **to go** ~ quedarse calvo **2.** (*plain*) escueto, -a

baldness ['bɔld·nɪs] *n* calvicie *f,* pelada *f CSur*

bale [beɪl] **I.** *n* fardo *m* **II.** *vt* embalar

Balearic Islands *n* **the** ~ las Islas Baleares

Balearics [ˌbal·i·ˈær·ɪks] *n* the ~ las Baleares
baleen whale [bə·ˈlin·ˈhweɪl] *n* misticeto *m*
baleful [ˈbeɪl·fʊl] *adj* siniestro, -a
balk [bɔk] I. *n* viga *f* II. *vi* to ~ at sth resistirse
a algo
Balkans [ˈbɔl·kəns] *n* the ~ los Balcanes
ball [bɔl] *n* 1. (*for golf, tennis*) pelota *f;* (*for
soccer, basketball, football*) balón *m,* pelota *f;*
to play ~ jugar a la pelota; *fig* cooperar
2. (*round form*) bola *f* 3. (*dance*) baile *m* ▶ to
have a ~ divertirse; to get the ~ rolling
poner las cosas en marcha
ballad [ˈbæl·əd] *n* balada *f*
balladeer [ˌbæl·ə·ˈdɪr] *n* cantautor(a) *m(f)*
ballast [ˈbæl·əst] *n* 1. NAUT lastre *m* 2. (*gravel*)
balasto *m*
ball bearing *n* cojinete *m*
ballerina [ˌbæl·ə·ˈri·nə] *n* bailarina *f*
ballet dancer *n* bailarín, -ina *m, f*
ball game *n* partido *m* de béisbol ▶ it's a
whole new ~ es un panorama completamente
distinto
ballistic [bə·ˈlɪs·tɪk] *adj* balístico, -a ▶ to go ~
sl ponerse como loco
balloon [bə·ˈlun] I. *n* globo *m* ▶ to go over
like a lead ~ fracasar estrepitosamente II. *vi*
inflarse
balloonist *n* ascensionista *mf*
ballot [ˈbæl·ət] I. *n* 1. (*paper*) papeleta *f*
2. (*election*) sufragio *m* 3. (*process*) votación
f II. *vi* invitar a votar III. *vt* consultar por votación
ballot box *n* urna *f*
ballot paper *n* papeleta *f*
ballpark *n* 1. estadio *m* de béisbol 2. *fig* a ~ figure una cifra aproximada
ballplayer *n* jugador(a) *m(f)* de béisbol
ballpoint (pen) *n* bolígrafo *m,* birome *m RíoPl*
ballroom *n* salón *m* de baile
ballroom dancing *n* baile *m* de salón
balm [bam] *n* 1. (*ointment*) bálsamo *m* 2. *fig*
consuelo *m*
balmy [ˈba·mi] <-ier, -iest> *adj* (*weather*) templado, -a; (*breeze*) suave
Baltic [ˈbɔl·tɪk] *n* the ~ (Sea) el (Mar) Báltico
balustrade [ˈbæl·ə·streɪd] *n* balaustrada *f,* barandilla *f Méx*
bamboo [bæm·ˈbu] *n* bambú *m*
bamboozle [bæm·ˈbu·zəl] *vt inf* 1. (*confuse*)
enredar 2. (*trick*) engatusar
ban [bæn] I. *n* prohibición *f;* to put [*o* place] a
~ on sth prohibir algo II. *vt* <-nn-> prohibir;
she was ~ned from driving le prohibieron
conducir
banal [bə·ˈnal] *adj* banal
banality [bə·ˈnæl·ə·ṭi] *n* <-ies> banalidad *f*
banana [bə·ˈnæn·ə] *n* plátano *m,* banana *f*
AmL ▶ to go ~s *sl* ponerse como loco
banana republic *n pej* república *f* bananera
band¹ [bænd] *n* 1. (*strip: of cloth, metal*)
banda *f* 2. (*stripe*) franja *f* 3. (*ribbon*) cinta *f;*
head ~ cinta *f* del pelo; waist ~ faja *f*
4. (*range*) *a.* TEL banda *f* 5. (*ring*) anillo *m;*

wedding ~ alianza *f*
band² [bænd] *n* 1. MUS grupo *m;* brass ~ charanga *f* 2. (*of friends*) pandilla *f;* (*of robbers*)
banda *f*
  ◆ band together *vi* agruparse
bandage [ˈbæn·dɪdʒ] I. *n* vendaje *m* II. *vt* vendar
Band-Aid® *n* tirita *f*
bandit [ˈbæn·dɪt] *n* bandido, -a *m, f,* carrilano,
-a *m, f Chile*
bandsman [ˈbændz·mən] *n* <-men> músico
m (de banda)
bandstand *n* quiosco *m* (de música)
bandwagon *n* to jump on the ~ *fig* subirse al
carro
bandwidth *n* COMPUT ancho *m* de banda
bandy [ˈbæn·di] I. <-ier, -iest> *adj* (*bent*) patizambo, -a II. *vt* <-ies, -ied> (*insults, words*)
intercambiar
  ◆ bandy about *vt* it was bandied about
that... se rumoreaba que...
bang [bæŋ] I. *n* 1. (*noise, blow*) golpe *m;*
(*explosion*) detonación *f* 2. ~s (*hair*) flequillo
m, pollina *f PRico, Ven* ▶ to go over with a ~
inf (*idea, event*) salir a las mil maravillas II. *adv*
1. *inf* (*exactly*) exactamente; smack ~ in the
middle of the road en el mismísimo centro
de la carretera 2. (*make noise*) to go ~ estallar
III. *interj* bang IV. *vi* (*make noise*) dar golpes;
(*exploding noise*) estallar; (*slam*) cerrarse de
golpe; to ~ on sth dar golpes en algo V. *vt* (*hit*)
golpear; to ~ one's head against/on sth
darse un golpe en la cabeza contra/con algo
Bangladesh [bæŋ·glə·ˈdeʃ] *n* Bangladesh *m*
Bangladeshi [bæŋ·glə·ˈdeʃi] I. *n* bangladesí
mf II. *adj* bangladesí
bangle [ˈbæŋ·gəl] *n* ajorca *f*
banish [ˈbæn·ɪʃ] *vt a. fig* desterrar; to ~ sth
from one's mind apartar algo de la mente
banishment *n* destierro *m*
banister [ˈbæn·ə·stər] *n* pasamano *m*
banjo [ˈbæn·ʒoʊ] *n* <-(oe)s> banjo *m*
bank¹ [bæŋk] I. *n* 1. FIN banco *m;* (*in games*)
banca *f;* to break the ~ hacer saltar la banca
2. (*storage place*) depósito *m;* blood ~ banco
m de sangre; data ~ banco *m* de datos ▶ to be
laughing all the way to the ~ *inf* ganar
mucha pasta [*o* un platal] II. *vi* 1. (*do banking*)
to ~ with Nearbank tener una cuenta en
Nearbank 2. (*rely on*) to ~ on sb/sth for sth
contar con alguien/algo para algo III. *vt*
depositar
bank² [bæŋk] I. *n* (*edge: of river*) orilla *f,* ribera
f II. *vi* AVIAT ladearse
bank³ [bæŋk] *n* (*of earth*) terraplén *m;* (*of fog*)
banco *m;* (*of clouds, snow*) montón *m;* (*of
switches*) batería *f*
  ◆ bank up I. *vi* amontonarse II. *vt* amontonar
bank account *n* cuenta *f* bancaria
bank balance *n* balance *m* bancario
bankbook *n* libreta *f* bancaria
bank charges *n* gastos *mpl* bancarios
bank clerk *n* empleado, -a *m, f* de banco

banker ['bæŋ·kər] *n* banquero, -a *m, f*

bank holiday *n* día o días en que los bancos deben permanecer cerrados

banking *n* banca *f*

banking hours *npl* horario *m* bancario

bank manager *n* gerente *mf* de banco

bank note *n* billete *m* de banco

bank rate *n* tipo *m* bancario

bank robber *n* ladrón, -ona *m, f* de bancos

bankrupt ['bæŋk·rʌpt] I. *n* quebrado, -a *m, f* II. *vt* llevar a la bancarrota III. *adj* (*bust*) insolvente; **to be ~** estar en quiebra; **to go ~** quebrar

bankruptcy ['bæŋk·rəp·si] *n* <-ies> bancarrota *f*

bank statement *n* estado *m* de cuentas

bank transfer *n* transferencia *f* bancaria

banner ['bæn·ər] *n* **1.** (*flag*) bandera *f*; **under the ~ of...** bajo la bandera de... **2.** (*placard*) pancarta *f* **3.** (*in Internet*) anuncio *m*

banquet ['bæŋ·kwət] I. *n* banquete *m* II. *vi* banquetear

banter ['bæn·tər] I. *n* bromas *fpl* II. *vi* bromear

baptism ['bæp·tɪz·əm] *n* bautismo *m*; **~ of fire** bautismo de fuego

baptismal ['bæp·tɪz·məl] *adj* bautismal

baptismal font *n* pila *f* bautismal

Baptist ['bæp·tɪst] *n* bautista *mf*; **John the ~** Juan el Bautista; **the Baptist Church** la Iglesia Bautista

baptize ['bæp·taɪz] *vt* bautizar; **I was ~d Clara** me bautizaron con el nombre de Clara

bar¹ [bar] I. *n* **1.** (*of metal, wood*) barra *f*; (*of a cage, prison*) reja *f*; (*of chocolate*) tableta *f*; (*of gold*) lingote *m*; (*of soap*) pastilla *f*; **to be behind ~s** *inf* estar entre rejas **2.** (*band of color*) franja *f* **3.** MUS compás *m* **4.** MIL barra *f* **5.** (*sandbank*) banco *m* de arena **6.** (*restriction*) obstáculo *m* **7.** (*nightclub*) bar *m*; (*counter: in bar*) barra *f*; (*in store*) mostrador *m* **8.** COMPUT barra *f*; **task/scroll/space ~** barra de tareas/de desplazamiento/espaciadora II. *vt* <-rr-> **1.** (*fasten: door, window*) atrancar **2.** (*obstruct*) obstruir; **to ~ sb's way/path** obstaculizar el camino/paso a alguien **3.** (*prohibit*) prohibir; **to ~ sb from doing sth** prohibir a alguien hacer algo **4.** (*exclude*) excluir

bar² [bar] *prep* excepto; **~ none** sin excepción

Bar [bar] *n* **the ~** (*group of lawyers*) el Colegio de Abogados; (*profession*) el foro, la Barra *Méx*

barb [barb] *n* **1.** ZOOL barbilla *f* **2.** (*insult*) comentario *m* hiriente

Barbadian [bar·'beɪ·di·ən] I. *adj* barbadense II. *n* barbadense *mf*

Barbados [bar·'beɪ·dous] *n* Barbados *m*

barbarian [bar·'ber·i·ən] *n* bárbaro, -a *m, f*

barbaric [bar·'ber·ɪk] *adj* bárbaro, -a

barbarity [bar·'ber·ə·t̬i] *n* <-ies> crueldad *f*

barbarous ['barbər·əs] *adj* bárbaro, -a

barbecue ['bar·bɪ·kju] *n* **1.** (*grill*) parrilla *f* **2.** (*event*) barbacoa *f*, parrillada *f* *Col, Ven*,

asado *m* *Chile*

> **i** Los festejos, sobre todo los celebrados por iglesias, escuelas y asociaciones, suelen recibir su nombre del tipo de comida que se ofrece, como p. ej. una barbacoa (**barbecue** o **cook-out**). En un **clam bake** — que tiene lugar generalmente en la playa — se calientan piedras al fuego, se cubren con algas y se asan en ellas moluscos. En un **corn roast** se asan al fuego mazorcas o panochas de maíz y se comen calientes con mantequilla o manteca y sal. Los cuerpos de bomberos voluntarios suelen ofrecer un **pancake breakfast**, donde todos pagan dos o tres dólares y pueden comer tantos panqueques con mantequilla o manteca y jarabe de arce como quieran.

barbed [barbd] *adj* **1.** (*with barbs*) de púas **2.** *fig* (*comment, criticism*) mordaz

barbed wire *n* alambre *m* de púas

barber ['bar·bər] *n* barbero, -a *m, f*

barbershop *n* barbería *f*

barbiturate [bar·'bɪtʃ·ər·ət] *n* barbitúrico *m*

bar code *n* código *m* de barras

bard [bard] *n* bardo *m*; **the Bard** Shakespeare

bare [ber] I. *adj* **1.** (*without clothes*) desnudo, -a; (*uncovered*) descubierto, -a; **with one's ~ hands** con las propias manos; **to fight with one's ~ hands** luchar sin armas **2.** (*empty*) vacío, -a; (*without plants, leaves*) desnudo, -a; **to be ~ of sth** estar desprovisto de algo **3.** (*unadorned*) **to tell sb the ~ facts** [*o* **truth**] decir a alguien la pura verdad **4.** (*little*) **the ~ minimum** lo mínimo; **the ~ necessities** las necesidades básicas II. *vt* desnudar; **to ~ one's teeth** enseñar los dientes; **to ~ one's heart/soul to sb** abrir su corazón/alma a alguien

bareback ['ber·bæk] *adv* a pelo

barefaced ['ber·feɪst] *adj* descarado, -a

barefoot ['ber·fʊt] *adv*, **barefooted** [,ber·'fʊt·ɪd] *adv* descalzo, -a

barely ['ber·li] *adv* **1.** (*hardly*) apenas, agatas *Arg, Urug, Par* **2.** (*scantily*) escasamente

barf [barf] *vi sl* vomitar, guacarear *Méx, inf*

barf bag *n sl* bolsa *f* para vomitar [*o* guacarear *Méx*]

bargain ['bar·gɪn] I. *n* **1.** (*agreement*) trato *m*; **to drive a hard ~** saber regatear; **to strike a ~** cerrar un trato **2.** (*item*) ganga *f*, pichincha *f* *Arg, Bol, Par, Urug*, mamada *f* *AmC, Bol, Chile, Perú* ▶ **into the ~** por añadidura II. *vi* (*negotiate*) negociar; (*haggle*) regatear; **to ~ sth away** malvender algo

♦ **bargain for** *vi*, **bargain on** *vi* contar con; **to get more than one bargained for** *fig* recibir más de lo que uno se esperaba

bargain basement *n* sección *f* de ofertas

bargain sale *n* rebajas *fpl*

barge [bardʒ] **I.** *n* barcaza *f* **II.** *vt inf* empujar; **to ~ one's way through sth** abrirse paso por algo
♦ **barge in** *vi* **1.** (*intrude*) colarse **2.** *fig* (*interrupt*) **sorry to ~** disculpe si me entrometo
♦ **barge into** *vi* **to ~ sb** chocar con alguien
♦ **barge through** *vi* abrirse paso a empujones
bar graph *n* gráfico *m* de barras
baritone ['ber·ə·toʊn] **I.** *n* barítono *m* **II.** *adj* barítono, -a
bark¹ [bark] **I.** *n* (*of a dog*) ladrido *m* ► **his ~ is worse than his** bite perro ladrador poco mordedor *prov* **II.** *vi* ladrar; (*person*) gritar **III.** *vt* gritar
♦ **bark out** *vt* gritar
bark² [bark] *n* (*of a tree*) corteza *f*
barkeeper ['bar·ki·pər] *n* (*owner*) tabernero, -a *m, f*; (*bartender*) camarero, -a *m, f*
barley ['bar·li] *n* cebada *f*
barman ['bar·mən] *n* <-men> camarero *m*
barmy ['bar·mi] *adj inf* chiflado, -a
barn [barn] *n* granero *m*
barnacle ['bar·nə·kəl] *n* bálano *m*
barnyard *n* corral *m*
barometer [bə·'ram·ə·ṭər] *n* barómetro *m*
baron ['bær·ən] *n* **1.** (*aristocrat*) barón *m* **2.** *fig* magnate *m*
baroness ['bær·ə·nɪs] *n* baronesa *f*
baronet ['bær·ə·nɪt] *n* baronet *m*
baronial [bə·'roʊ·ni·əl] *adj* baronial
baroque [bə·'roʊk] *adj a. fig* barroco, -a
barracks ['bær·əks] *npl* cuartel *m*
barrage [bə·'raʒ] *n* **1.** MIL cortina *f* de fuego **2.** *fig* (*of questions, complaints*) aluvión *m*
barrel ['bær·əl] **I.** *n* **1.** (*container*) barril *m*, tonel *m* **2.** (*measure: of oil*) barril *m* **3.** (*of a gun*) cañón *m* ► **to be a ~ of** fun [*o* laughs] ser una panzada de reír, ser divertidísimo; **to** have **sb over a ~** tener a alguien en un puño; **to** scrape **(the bottom of) the ~** tener que recurrir a lo peor, valerse del último recurso **II.** *vi* <-l-> *inf* ir disparado; **to ~** along (*vehicle, person in vehicle*) ir a toda [*o* Col, Méx a mil] pastilla **III.** *vt* <-l-> embarrilar
barren ['bær·ən] *adj* **1.** (*infertile*) estéril; (*landscape*) árido, -a **2.** (*unproductive*) improductivo, -a; **~ years** años perdidos
barricade ['bær·ə·keɪd] **I.** *n* barricada *f* **II.** *vt* cerrar con barricadas; **she ~d herself into her room** se atrincheró en su habitación
barrier ['bær·i·ər] *n* barrera *f*; **language ~** barrera lingüística
barring ['bar·ɪŋ] *prep* (*except for*) excepto; (*if there are no*) a menos que +*subj*; **~ accidents** a menos que surja un imprevisto; **~ complications** a menos que se presenten complicaciones; **~ delays** a menos que se produzcan retrasos
barrow ['bær·oʊ] *n* (*wheelbarrow*) carretilla *f*; (*cart*) carreta *f*
bartender ['bar·ten·dər] *n* camarero, -a *m, f*
barter ['bar·ṭər] **I.** *n* trueque *m* **II.** *vi* comerciar **III.** *vt* **to ~ sth for sth** trocar [*o* cambiar] algo por algo
basalt [bə·'salt] *n* basalto *m*
base¹ [beɪs] **I.** *n* **1.** (*lower part*) base *f* **2.** (*bottom*) fondo *m* **3.** (*source of support*) apoyo *m* **4.** (*basis*) fundamento *m* **5.** MIL base **6.** (*of a company*) sede *f* ► **to** be **off ~** *inf* estar equivocado; **to** touch **~** tocar fondo **II.** *vt* **1.** (*found*) basar; **to be ~d on** basarse en **2.** MIL estacionar **3.** (*stay*) **to be ~d in Florida** (*company*) tener su sede en Florida; (*person*) trabajar en Florida; **which hotel are they ~d at?** ¿en qué hotel se alojan?
base² [beɪs] *adj* **1.** (*not honorable*) vil **2.** (*not pure: metal*) impuro, -a
baseball ['beɪs·bɔl] *n* béisbol *m*

> **i** El béisbol (**baseball**) es el deporte nacional estadounidense. Dos equipos se alternan en el **up**, es decir, en el ataque y la defensa, y tratan de conseguir **runs** (carreras), para lo cual los jugadores tienen que tocar sucesivamente cuatro **bases** (bases) de un cuadro. El **pitcher** (lanzador) de la parte contraria lanza la pelota y un jugador intenta golpear la bola con su bate, echando entonces a correr para alcanzar al menos la primera base antes de que el equipo contrario vuelva a hacerse con el control de la bola.

base camp *n* campamento *m* base
Basel ['ba·zəl] *n* Basilea *f*
baseless ['beɪs·lɪs] *adj* sin fundamento; (*accusation*) infundado, -a
base pay *n* salario *m* base
bash [bæʃ] **I.** *n* **1.** (*blow*) porrazo *m* **2.** *sl* (*party*) juerga *f* **II.** *vt* (*hit hard: thing*) golpear; (*person*) pegar
♦ **bash into** *vi insep* estrellarse contra
♦ **bash up** *vt inf* (*car*) estrellar
bashful ['bæʃ·fəl] *adj* tímido, -a
basic ['beɪ·sɪk] **I.** *adj* básico, -a; **~ idea** idea *f* principal; **~ requirements** requisitos mínimos; **to have a ~ command of sth** tener conocimientos básicos de algo **II.** *npl* **the ~s** lo básico
BASIC ['beɪ·sɪk] *n* COMPUT *abbr of* **Beginner's All-purpose Symbolic Instruction Code** BASIC *m*
basically *adv* básicamente
basil ['beɪ·zəl] *n* albahaca *f*
basilica [bə·'sɪl·ɪ·kə] *n* ARCHIT basílica *f*
basin ['beɪ·sɪn] *n* **1.** (*for washing*) lavadero *m* **2.** (*sink*) lavabo *m* **3.** (*large bowl*) cuenco *m* **4.** GEO cuenca *f*
basis ['beɪ·sɪs] *n* <bases> base *f*; **on a weekly ~** semanalmente; **to be the ~ for sth** ser el fundamento de algo; **on the ~ of sth** sobre la base de algo
bask [bæsk] *vi* **to ~ in the sun** tomar el sol; **to ~ in sb's favor** gozar del favor de alguien
basket ['bæs·kət] *n* **1.** (*container*) cesto *m*;

(*with two handles*) canasta *f* **2.**(*amount in basket*) canastada *f* **3.** SPORTS canasta *f*

basketball ['bæs·kət·bɔl] *n* baloncesto *m*

basket case *n sl* to be a ~ ser un fracaso

Basque [bæsk] I. *adj* vasco, -a; ~ **Country** País *m* Vasco II. *n* **1.** vasco, -a *m, f* **2.** LING euskera *m*

bass[1] [beɪs] *n* MUS **1.** (*voice*) bajo *m* **2.** (*instrument: classical*) contrabajo *m;* (*electric*) bajo *m*

bass[2] [bæs] *n* ZOOL lubina *f*

bass clef *n* clave *f* de fa

bass drum *n* bombo *m*

bassoon [bə·'sun] *n* fagot *m*

bastard ['bæs·tərd] *n* **1.** (*child*) bastardo, -a *m, f* **2.** *vulg* cabrón, -ona *m, f*

baste [beɪst] *vt* **1.** CULIN lardear **2.** (*sew loosely*) hilvanar

bastion ['bæs·tʃən] *n a. fig* baluarte *m*

bat[1] [bæt] *n* ZOOL murciélago *m* ▶ **to have ~s in the belfry** *inf* estar mal de la azotea; **to be as blind as a ~** no ver tres en un burro

bat[2] [bæt] *vt* (*blink*) **to ~ one's eyelashes** pestañear; **to ~ one's eyelashes at sb** guiñar un ojo a alguien; **he/she didn't ~ an eyelash when...** *fig* permaneció sin tan siquiera pestañear cuando...

bat[3] [bæt] I. *n* **1.** (*in baseball*) bate *m;* **to be up at ~** ser bateador **2.** (*blow*) golpe *m* ▶ **right off the ~** al instante II. *vt, vi* <-tt-> SPORTS batear

batch [bætʃ] *n* <-es> tanda *f;* COM, COMPUT lote *m;* (*of cookies*) hornada *f*

batch file *n* COMPUT fichero *m* por lotes

batch processing *n* COMPUT procesamiento *m* por lotes

bated ['beɪ·tɪd] *adj* **with ~ breath** conteniendo la respiración

bath [bæθ] *n* **1.** (*action*) baño *m*, bañada *f Méx;* **to give a child/dog a ~** bañar a un niño/perro; **to take a ~** bañarse **2.** (*bathtub*) bañera *f*, tina *f AmL*, bañadera *f Arg* **3.** (*bathroom*) baño *m* **4.** CHEM baño *m*

bathe [beɪð] I. *vi* bañarse II. *vt* (*person, animal*) bañar; (*wound, eyes*) lavar; **to be ~d in sweat/tears** estar bañado en sudor/lágrimas; **the living room was ~d in sunlight** la luz del día inundaba el salón

bathing *n* ~ **prohibited** prohibido bañarse

bathing cap *n* gorro *m* de baño

bathing suit *n* bañador *m*, malla *f* (de baño) *RíoPl*, vestido *m* de baño *Col*

bathing trunks *npl* bañador *m*

bath mat *n* alfombrilla *f* de baño

bathrobe *n* albornoz *m*, bata *f Col, Méx*

bathroom *n* **1.** (*room with bath*) (cuarto *m* de) baño *m* **2.** (*lavatory*) aseo *m;* (*public*) servicio *m;* **to go to the ~** ir al baño [*o* al servicio]

bath towel *n* toalla *f* de baño

bathtub *n* bañera *f*, tina *f AmL*, bañadera *f Arg*

baton [bə·'tan] *n* **1.** MUS batuta *f;* MIL bastón *m* **2.** (*of a policeman*) porra *f* **3.** SPORTS testigo *m;* ~ **change** relevo *m*

batsman ['bæts·mən] <-men> *n* SPORTS batea-

---

dor *m*

battalion [bə·'tæl·jən] *n* batallón *m*

batten ['bæt·ən] I. *n* NAUT (*for a sail*) sable *m;* (*for a hatch*) listón *m*, barra *f* de cierre II. *vt* reforzar con listones III. *vi* **to ~ on sb** vivir a costa de alguien

◆ **batten down** *vt* **to ~ the hatches** *fig* atarse los machos

batter[1] ['bæt·ər] I. *n* CULIN (*for fried food*) rebozado *m;* (*for pancakes, cake*) masa *f* II. *vt* CULIN rebozar

batter[2] ['bæt·ər] I. *n* SPORTS bateador(a) *m(f)* II. *vt* **1.** (*assault*) apalear; (*child, wife, pet*) maltratar **2.** (*hit*) golpear; **to ~ the door in** [*o* **down**] echar la puerta abajo III. *vi* **to ~ at the door** aporrear la puerta; **the waves ~ed against the rocks** las olas azotaban las rocas

battered ['bæt·ərd] *adj* **1.** (*injured*) maltratado, -a **2.** (*damaged: hat, clothes*) estropeado, -a; (*reputation, image*) maltrecho, -a **3.** CULIN rebozado, -a

battering ['bæt·ər·ɪŋ] *n* paliza *f;* **to give sb a ~** dar una paliza a alguien

battery ['bæt·ə·ri] <-ies> *n* **1.** (*for a radio, flashlight*) pila *f;* (*for a car*) batería *f* **2.** (*large number*) serie *f;* **a ~ of questions** una sarta de preguntas **3.** MIL batería *f* **4.** LAW agresión *f*

battery charger *n* cargador *m* de pilas; AUTO cargador *m* de baterías

battle ['bæt·əl] I. *n* **1.** MIL batalla *f* **2.** (*struggle*) lucha *f* ▶ **that's half the ~** esa es la clave de la victoria; **to fight a losing ~** luchar por una causa perdida II. *vi* (*fight*) pelear; (*nonviolently*) luchar III. *vt* combatir; **to ~ one's way to the top** abrirse paso hasta la cima

battle-ax(e) ['bæt·əl·æks] *n* **1.** HIST hacha *f* de guerra **2.** *pej, inf* (*woman*) sargenta *f*, sisebuta *f RíoPl*

battle cry *n* grito *m* de guerra

battlefield *n*, **battleground** *n* campo *m* de batalla

battlements ['bæt·əl·mənts] *npl* almenas *fpl*

battleship *n* acorazado *m*

batty ['bæt·i] *adj sl* grillado, -a, chalado, -a; **to go ~** volverse majara, chiflarse

baud [bɔd] *n* COMPUT baudio *m*

baud rate *n* COMPUT velocidad *f* de transmisión

bawdy ['bɔ·di] <-ier, -iest> *adj* (*scene*) subido, -a de tono; (*joke*) verde, colorado, -a *Méx*

bawl [bɔl] I. *vi* **1.** (*yell at*) vociferar **2.** (*weep*) berrear II. *vt* gritar; **to ~ sb out** echar la bronca a alguien; **to ~ one's eyes out** desgañitarse

bay[1] [beɪ] *n* GEO bahía *f*

bay[2] [beɪ] *n* BOT laurel *m*

bay[3] [beɪ] *n* ARCHIT (*between columns*) intercolu(m)nio *m;* (*in a house*) saliente *m;* (*for car*) plaza *f* [*o* cajón *m Méx*] de aparcamiento; (*for boat*) muelle *m;* (*for bus*) andén *m*

bay[4] [beɪ] *n* ZOOL caballo *m* zaino

bay[5] [beɪ] I. *vi* (*dog, wolf*) aullar II. *n* (*howling*) aullido *m* ▶ **to be at ~** estar acorralado; **to bring sth/sb to ~** acorralar algo/a alguien; **to**

hold sth/sb at ~ mantener algo/a alguien a raya
bay leaf *n* hoja *f* de laurel
Bay of Biscay *n* mar *m* Cantábrico, Golfo *m* de Vizcaya
bayonet [ˌbeɪ·ə·ˈnet] I. *n* bayoneta *f* II. *vt* (*wound*) herir con una bayoneta; (*kill*) matar con una bayoneta
bayou *n* pantano *m* (*en Luisiana*)
bay window *n* mirador *m*
bazaar [bə·ˈzar] *n* 1. (*market*) bazar *m* 2. (*event*) venta *f* benéfica, bazar *m Col*
BBQ [ˈbar·bɪ·kju] *n abbr of* **barbecue** (*event*) barbacoa *f, Col, Ven,* parrillada *f Col, Ven,* asado *m Chile*
BC [ˌbiˈsi] *abbr of* **British Columbia** Colombia *f* Británica
B.C. [ˌbiˈsi] *adv abbr of* **before Christ** a.C.
BCG (**vaccine**) *abbr of* **bacillus of Calmette and Guérin** vacuna *f* de la tuberculosis
be [bi] <was, been> I. *vi* 1. + *n/adj* (*permanent state, quality, identity*) ser; **she's a cook** es cocinera; **she's Spanish** es española; **to ~ good** ser bueno; **to ~ able to do sth** ser capaz de hacer algo; **what do you want to ~ when you grow up?** ¿qué quieres ser de mayor?; **to ~ married/single** estar [*o* ser *CSur*] casado/ soltero; **to ~ a widow** ser viuda 2. + *adj* (*mental and physical states*) estar; **to ~ fat/happy** estar gordo/contento; **to ~ hungry** tener hambre 3. (*age*) tener; **I'm 21 (years old)** tengo 21 años 4. (*indicates sb's opinion*) **to ~ for/against sth** estar a favor/en contra de algo 5. (*calculation, cost*) **two and two is four** dos y dos son cuatro; **these glasses are $2 each** estos vasos cuestan $2 cada uno; **how much is that?** ¿cuánto es? 6. (*measurement*) medir; (*weight*) pesar; **to ~ 2 feet long** medir 2 pies de largo 7. (*exist, live*) **there is/ are...** hay...; **to let sth/sb ~** dejar en paz algo/ a alguien; **I think, therefore I am** pienso, luego existo; **to ~ or not to ~** ser o no ser 8. (*location, situation*) estar; **to ~ in Rome** estar en Roma; **to ~ in a bad situation** estar en una mala situación 9. *pp* (*go, visit*) **I've never ~en to Mexico** nunca he estado en Méjico; **the plumber hasn't ~en here yet** el fontanero todavía no ha venido 10. (*take place*) ser, tener lugar; **the meeting is next Tuesday** la reunión es el próximo martes 11. (*circumstances*) **to ~ on the pill** tomar la píldora; **to ~ on vacation** estar de vacaciones; **to ~ on a diet** estar a régimen 12. (*in time expressions*) **don't ~ too long** no tardes mucho 13. (*expressing possibility*) **that...?** *form* ¿puede ser que... +*subj?*; **what are we to do?** ¿qué podemos hacer? ▶ **~ that as it may** sea como fuere; **so ~ it** así sea II. *impers vb* (*expressing conditions, circumstances*) **it's cloudy** está nublado; **it's sunny** hace sol; **it's two o'clock** son las dos; **it's ~en so long!** ¡cuánto tiempo!; **it's ten minutes by bus to the market** el mercado está a diez minutos en autobús; **it was Anne who drank**

it fue Anne quien se lo bebió III. *aux vb* 1. (*expressing continuation*) estar; **to ~ doing sth** estar haciendo algo; **don't sing while I'm reading** no cantes mientras estoy leyendo [*o* mientras leo]; **you're always complaining** siempre te estás quejando 2. (*expressing the passive*) ser; **to ~ discovered by sb** ser descubierto por alguien; **he was left speechless** lo dejaron sin palabras; **he was asked...** le preguntaron... 3. (*expressing future*) **we are to visit Peru in the winter** vamos a ir a Perú en invierno; **she's leaving tomorrow** se va mañana 4. (*expressing future in past*) **she was never to see her brother again** nunca más volvería a ver a su hermano 5. (*expressing the subjunctive in conditionals*) **if he was to work harder, he'd get better grades** si trabajara más, sacaría mejores notas; **were I to refuse, they'd ~ very annoyed** si me negara, se enfadarían mucho 6. (*expressing obligation*) **you are to come here right now** tienes que venir aquí ahora mismo 7. (*in tag questions*) **she is tall, isn't she?** es alta, ¿verdad?
beach [bitʃ] I. *n* playa *f* II. *vt* hacer embarrancar, varar
beach ball *n* balón *m* de playa
beachhead *n* cabeza *f* de playa
beachwear *n* ropa *f* playera
beacon [ˈbi·kən] *n* 1. (*signal*) baliza *f* 2. (*lighthouse*) faro *m* 3. (*fire*) almenara *f* 4. *fig* (*guide*) luz *f*
bead [bid] *n* 1. (*out of glass*) abalorio *m*, cuenta *f;* (*out of wood*) viruta *f* 2. (*drop*) gota *f;* **~s of sweat** gotas *fpl* de sudor 3. *pl* **~s** (*necklace*) collar *m* de cuentas 4. **~s** REL rosario *m* 5. (*on a gun*) punto *m* de mira; **to draw a ~ on sb/sth** apuntar a alguien/algo 6. (*on a tire*) talón *m*
beading [ˈbi·dɪŋ] *n* ARCHIT moldura *f*
beady [ˈbi·di] <-ier, -iest> *adj* **~ eyes** ojos redondos, pequeños y brillantes; **to have one's ~ eyes on sth** mirar algo con lupa
beak [bik] *n* 1. ZOOL pico *m* 2. *inf* (*nose*) napia *f,* naso *m RíoPl*
beaker [ˈbi·kər] *n* 1. CHEM vaso *m* de precipitados 2. (*cup*) jarra *f*
be all *n* **the ~ (and end all)** la única cosa que
beam [bim] I. *n* 1. (*ray*) rayo *m;* (*light*) haz *m* de luz; **high ~** AUTO luces *fpl* largas, luces *fpl* altas *Chile, Col;* **low ~** luces *fpl* cortas, luces *fpl* bajas *Chile, Col* 2. ARCHIT viga *f* 3. SPORTS barra *f* sueca 4. NAUT bao *m* II. *vt* (*broadcast*) transmitir; (*send*); **to ~ a smile at sb** dedicar una sonrisa a alguien III. *vi* brillar; (*smile*) sonreír (abiertamente)
beaming *adj* **to be ~** estar radiante
bean [bin] I. *n* 1. (*green*) judía *f* verde, habichuela *f Col,* ejote *m Méx,* chaucha *f RíoPl,* poroto *m* verde *Chile,* vainita *f Ven* 2. (*dried*) alubia *f;* **baked ~s** alubias *fpl* en salsa de tomate 3. (*seed, pod*) **coffee ~** grano *m* de

café; **vanilla** ~ vaina *f* de vainilla **4.** (*plant*) judía *f* ▶ **to be full of** ~**s** *inf* estar lleno de vida; **to not have a** ~ *inf* estar pelado; **to spill the** ~**s** *inf* descubrir el pastel, levantar la perdiz *RíoPl* II. *vt sl* **to** ~ **sb** (**on the head**) dar un porrazo en la cabeza a alguien

beanbag *n* (*toy*) bolsa rellena de alubias usada a modo de pelota; (*chair*) puf *m*

bean sprout *n* brote *m* de soja

bear¹ [ber] *n* **1.** ZOOL oso, -a *m, f* **2.** FIN bajista *mf* **3.** *sl* (*sth difficult*) (algo) muy chungo, -a [*o* tenaz *Col*]

bear² [ber] <bore, borne> I. *vt* **1.** (*carry*) llevar; **to** ~ **arms** *form* portar armas **2.** (*display*) **to** ~ **a resemblance to...** parecerse a... **3.** (*have, possess*) tener; **to** ~ **a scar** tener una cicatriz **4.** (*conduct*) **to** ~ **oneself** comportarse **5.** (*support: weight*) aguantar **6.** (*accept: cost*) correr con; (*responsibility*) cargar con **7.** (*endure: hardship, pain*) soportar; (*blame*) cargar con **8.** (*be fit for*) **what might have happened doesn't** ~ **thinking about** da miedo sólo de pensar lo que podía haber pasado; **he said something so awful that it doesn't** ~ **repeating** dijo algo tan horrible que no es como para repetirlo **9.** (*tolerate*) soportar, aguantar **10.** (*harbor*) **to** ~ **sb a grudge** tener [*o* guardar] rencor a alguien; **she** ~**s him no ill will** no le desea ningún mal **11.** (*keep*) **to** ~ **sth/sb in mind** tener algo/a alguien presente **12.** (*give birth to*) dar a luz a, tener; **she bore him a daughter** tuvo una hija con él **13.** AGR, BOT *a. fig* (*fruit*) dar **14.** FIN, ECON (*interest*) devengar **15.** (*give*) **to** ~ **testimony** [*o* **witness**] **to sth** atestiguar algo II. *vi* (*tend*) **to** ~ **east** dirigirse al este; **to** ~ **left/right** torcer a la izquierda/a la derecha

◆**bear down on** *vt* avanzar hacia; **the train was bearing down on her** el tren se le venía encima

◆**bear on** *vt* **1.** (*be relevant to*) tener que ver con **2.** (*have affect on*) afectar a **3.** (*pressurize*) hacer presión sobre

◆**bear up** *vi* aguantar

◆**bear with** *vi* tener paciencia con

bearable ['ber·ə·bəl] *adj* soportable

beard [bɪrd] I. *n* **1.** (*facial hair*) barba *f*; **to shave off one's** ~ afeitarse la barba **2.** ZOOL barbas *fpl* II. *vt* HIST desafiar

bearded *adj* barbudo, -a

beardless ['bɪrd·lɪs] *adj* lampiño, -a; **to be** ~ ser imberbe

bearer ['ber·ər] *n* portador(a) *m(f)*

bearing ['ber·ɪŋ] *n* **1.** NAUT rumbo *m;* **to get one's** ~**s** *a. fig* orientarse; **to lose one's** ~**s** *a. fig* desorientarse **2.** (*behavior*) comportamiento *m* **3.** (*posture*) porte *m* **4.** TECH cojinete *m* **5.** ARCHIT soporte *m* ▶ **to have some** ~ **on sth** tener que ver con algo

bearskin ['ber·skɪn] *n* **1.** (*bear fur*) piel *f* de oso **2.** (*military hat*) gorro *m* militar de piel de oso

beast [bist] *n* **1.** (*animal*) bestia *f*; ~ **of burden**

animal *m* de carga **2.** *inf* (*person*) animal *m;* **to be a** ~ **to sb** portarse como un animal con alguien

beastly ['bist·li] <-ier, -iest> *adj inf* horroroso, -a; **to be** ~ **to sb** portarse muy mal con alguien

beat [bit] <beat, beaten> I. *n* **1.** (*pulsation: of the heart*) latido *m;* (*of the pulse*) pulsación *f;* (*of a hammer*) martilleo *m* **2.** MUS (*stress*) tiempo *m;* (*stroke of the hand*) compás *m;* (*rhythm*) ritmo *m* **3.** (*of a police officer*) ronda *f;* **to walk one's** ~ hacer la ronda II. *adj inf* (*worn out*) reventado, -a III. *vt* **1.** (*strike*) golpear; (*metal*) batir; (*carpet*) sacudir, festejar *Méx;* **to** ~ **sb black and blue** dar una paliza soberana a alguien; **to** ~ **a confession out of sb** arrancar una confesión a palos a alguien; **to** ~ **sb to death** matar a alguien a golpes **2.** (*wings*) batir **3.** CULIN batir **4.** (*cut through*) **to** ~ **a path through sth** abrirse paso en [*o* a través de] algo **5.** (*defeat*) derrotar, ganar; **Mary always** ~**s me at chess** Mary siempre me gana al ajedrez **6.** (*surpass: record*) batir **7.** (*arrive before*) **she** ~ **me to the door** llegó antes que yo a la puerta **8.** (*be better than*) superar; **to** ~ **sb in** [*o* **at**] **sth** superar a alguien en algo; **taking the bus sure** ~**s walking there** *inf* es mucho mejor coger el autobús que ir caminando **9.** MUS (*drum*) tocar ▶ **if you can't** ~ **them, join them** *prov* si no puedes vencerlos, únete a ellos; **that** ~**s everything** *inf* ¡eso es el colmo!; ~ **it!** *sl* ¡lárgate!, ¡mándate mudar! *RíoPl;* **it** ~**s me how/why...** no llego a comprender cómo/por qué... IV. *vi* **1.** (*pound: rain*) caer; (*sea*) batir; (*person*) golpear **2.** (*pulsate, vibrate: heart, pulse*) latir; (*wings*) batir; (*drum*) redoblar; (*hammer*) martillear

◆**beat around** *vi* **to** ~ **the bush** andarse por las ramas, firuletear *Arg, Urug*

◆**beat back** *vt* rechazar

◆**beat down** I. *vi* (*hail, rain*) caer con fuerza; (*sun*) picar II. *vt* **1.** (*haggle*) **to beat the price down** bajar el precio; **I managed to beat him down to 50 cents** conseguí que me lo dejara a 50 centavos **2.** (*flatten: door*) derribar

◆**beat off** *vt* rechazar

◆**beat up** I. *vt* dar una paliza a II. *vi* **to** ~ **on sb** dar una paliza a alguien

beaten ['bit·ən] I. *pp of* **beat** II. *adj* **1.** (*metal*) batido, -a **2.** **to be off the** ~ **track** [*o* **path**] (*isolated*) estar en medio de la nada

beater ['bi·ţər] *n* **1.** CULIN batidora *f;* (*for carpets*) sacudidor *m* **2.** (*in hunting*) batidor(a) *m(f)*

beatify [bɪ·'æţ·ə·faɪ] *vt* beatificar

beating ['bi·ţɪŋ] *n* **1.** (*assault*) paliza *f*, cueriza *f AmL*, zumba *f AmL*, biaba *f Arg, Urug*, batida *f Perú, PRico*, fajada *f Arg;* **to give sb a** ~ dar una paliza a alguien **2.** (*defeat*) derrota *f;* **to take a** ~ recibir una paliza **3.** (*of the heart*) latido *m*

beautician [bju·'tɪʃ·ən] *n* esteticista *mf*

beautiful ['bju·ţə·fəl] *adj* hermoso, -a, precioso, -a; (*sight, weather*) estupendo, -a

beautify ['bju·tə·faɪ] *vt* embellecer
beauty ['bju·ti] <-ies> *n* **1.**(*property*) belleza *f* **2.**(*beautiful woman*) belleza *f* **3.** *inf*(*specimen*) preciosidad *f*, maravilla *f* **4.** *inf*(*advantage*) **the ~ of...** lo bueno de... ▶**~ is in the eye of the beholder** *prov* todo depende del color del cristal con que se mira; **~ is only skin-deep** *prov* la belleza está en el interior
beauty contest *n*, **beauty pageant** *n* concurso *m* de belleza
beauty parlor *n*, **beauty salon** *n*, **beauty shop** *n* salón *m* de belleza
beauty spot *n* **1.**(*location*) lugar *m* pintoresco **2.**(*on the skin*) lunar *m*
beaver ['bi·vər] **I.** *n* **1.** ZOOL castor *m* **2.**(*fur*) piel *f* de castor **3.** *fig, inf*(*person*) (*eager*) ~ persona *f* trabajadora **4.** *vulg*(*female genitals*) coño *m*, panocha *f Col, Méx*, cola *f RíoPl* **II.** *vi inf* **to ~ away** trabajar como una hormiguita
becalmed [bɪ·'kɑmd] *adj* **to be ~** estar inmóvil (a causa de la falta de viento)
became [bɪ·'keɪm] *pt of* **become**
because [bɪ·'kɔz] **I.** *conj* porque; **just ~ he's smiling doesn't mean he is in love** *inf* que sonría no significa que esté enamorado; **~ I said that, I had to leave** como dije eso, tuve que irme; **not ~ I am sad but...** no porque esté triste, sino... **II.** *prep* **~ of** a causa de; **~ of me** por mi culpa; **~ of illness** por enfermedad; **~ of the fine weather** debido al buen tiempo
beck [bek] *n* **to be at sb's ~ and call** estar siempre a entera disposición de alguien
beckon ['bek·ən] **I.** *vt* llamar por señas; **to ~ sb over** hacer señas a alguien para que se acerque; **I ~ed her to follow** (**me**) le hice señas para que me siguiera **II.** *vi* **to ~ to sb** hacer señas a alguien; **I have to go because work ~s** me tengo que ir porque el trabajo me llama
become [bɪ·'kʌm] <became, become> **I.** *vi* **1.**(+ *adj*) volverse; (+ *n*) llegar a ser; **to ~ angry** enfadarse; **to ~ famous/old** hacerse famoso/viejo; **to ~ sad/happy** ponerse triste/feliz; **to ~ convinced that...** convencerse de que...; **to ~ interested in sth/sb** interesarse por algo/alguien **2.**(*happen to*) **what ever became of her?** ¿qué fue de ella? **II.** *vt* **1.**(*look good*) favorecer **2.**(*be appropriate*) ser apropiado para
becoming [bɪ·'kʌm·ɪŋ] *adj* **1.**(*clothes, haircut*) favorecedor(a), sentador(a) *Arg, Chile* **2.**(*behavior*) apropiado, -a
becquerel [bə·'krel] *n* becquerel *m*
bed [bed] **I.** *n* **1.**(*furniture*) cama *f;* **to get out of ~** levantarse de la cama; **to go to ~** acostarse; **to go to ~ with sb** acostarse con alguien; **to make the ~** hacer la cama; **to put sb to ~** acostar a alguien; (*bedtime*) (hora *f* de) acostarse **2.**(*for vegetables, flowers*) arriate *m*, era *f*, cantero *m RíoPl*; (*of clams, oysters*) vivero *m*, banco *m* **3.**(*base*) base *f* **4.**(*bottom: of the ocean*) fondo *m*; (*of a river*) lecho *m* **5.**(*layer*) capa *f* ▶**a ~ of nails** un calvario; **a ~ of roses** un lecho de rosas; **to get**

up on the wrong side of the ~ levantarse con el pie izquierdo; **you have made your ~ and now you have to lie in it** quien mal cama hace en ella se yace *prov* **II.**<-dd-> *vt* **1.** *form* (*have sex with*) acostarse con **2.**(*embed*) asentar
◆**bed down** *vi* acostarse
BEd [bi·'ed] *abbr of* **Bachelor of Education** Ldo., -a *m, f* en Magisterio
bed and breakfast *n* pensión *f*
bedbug *n* chinche *m* o *f*
bedclothes *npl* ropa *f* de cama, cobijas *fpl AmL*
bedding ['bed·ɪŋ] *n* **1.**(*blankets and sheets*) ropa *f* de cama **2.**(*for an animal*) cama *f*
bedecked [bɪ·'dekt] *adj* **to be ~ with...** estar adornado con...
bedevil [bɪ·'dev·əl] <-l-> *vt* **to be ~ed with** [*o* **by**] **problems** estar plagado de problemas
bedfellow *n* **to make strange ~s** hacer una extraña pareja
bedlam ['bed·ləm] *n* alboroto *m*
bed linen *n* ropa *f* de cama
Bedouin ['bed·u·ɪn] **I.** *adj* beduino, -a **II.**<-(s)> *n* beduino, -a *m, f*
bedraggled [bɪ·'dræg·əld] *adj* **1.**(*wet*) empapado, -a **2.**(*disheveled: person, appearance*) desaliñado, -a; (*hair*) despeinado, -a
bedridden ['bed·ˌrɪd·ən] *adj* postrado, -a en cama
bedrock ['bed·rak] *n* **1.** GEO roca *f* firme **2.** *fig* cimientos *mpl*, base *f*
bedroom ['bed·rum] *n* dormitorio *m*, recámara *f Méx*
bedside ['bed·saɪd] *n* cabecera *f*
bedside lamp *n* lámpara *f* de noche
bedside rug *n* alfombrilla *f* de cama
bedside table *n* mesita *f* de noche, nochero *m Col, Chile, Urug*, buró *m Méx*
bedsore ['bed·sɔr] *n* escara *f*, úlcera *f* de decúbito
bedspread ['bed·spred] *n* cubrecama *m*, colcha *f*
bedspread ['bed·spred] *n* cubrecama *m*
bedtime ['bed·taɪm] *n* hora *f* de acostarse; **it's (way) past your ~** hace rato que deberías estar durmiendo
bee [bi] *n* **1.** ZOOL abeja *f* **2.**(*group*) círculo *m*; **sewing ~** círculo de costura; **spelling ~** concurso *m* de deletreo ▶**to have a ~ in one's bonnet about sth** tener algo metido entre ceja y ceja; **to be a busy ~** *iron* estar muy atareado
beech [bitʃ] *n* BOT haya *f*
beechnut ['bitʃ·nʌt] *n* hayuco *m*
beef [bif] **I.** *n* **1.** CULIN ternera *f*, res *f AmC, Méx;* **ground ~** carne *f* picada de ternera; **roast ~** rosbif *m* **2.** *sl*(*complaint*) queja *f* **II.** *vi sl* **to ~ about sth** refunfuñar por algo
◆**beef up** *vt* mejorar
beefcake *n inf* machote *m*, cachas *m inv*
beefsteak *n* bistec *m*, churrasco *m AmS*, bife *m RíoPl*

beefy ['bi·fi] <-ier, -iest> *adj inf* fornido, -a, cachas

beehive ['bi·haɪv] *n* colmena *f*

beekeeper ['bi·ki·pər] *n* apicultor(a) *m(f)*

beeline ['bi·laɪn] *n inf* **to make a ~ for sth/sb** ir derechito a algo/alguien

been [bɪn] *pp of* be

beep [bip] **I.** *n* pitido *m* **II.** *vi* pitar

beeper ['bi·pər] *n* localizador *m*, busca *m inf*

beer [bɪr] *n* cerveza *f*

beer belly *n* barriga *f* cervecera

beer garden *n* terraza *f* de verano

beery ['bɪr·i] *adj* de cerveza

beeswax ['biz·wæks] *n* cera *f* de abeja

beet [bit] *n* **1.** (*vegetable*) remolacha *f*, betabel *f Méx;* **to turn as red as a ~** ponerse rojo como un tomate **2.** (*sugar beet*) remolacha *f* (azucarera)

beetle ['bit̬·əl] *n* escarabajo *m*

beet sugar *n* azúcar *m* de remolacha

befit [bɪ·'fɪt] <-tt-> *vt form* corresponder a; **as ~ s a princess** como corresponde a una princesa

befitting *adj form* conveniente

before [bɪ·'fɔr] **I.** *prep* **1.** (*earlier*) antes de; **to leave ~ sb** salir antes que alguien; **~ doing sth** antes de hacer algo; **to wash one's hands ~ lunch** lavarse las manos antes de la comida **2.** (*in front of*) delante de; **~ my house** delante de mi casa; **to bow ~ sb** inclinarse ante alguien; **~ our (very) eyes** ante nuestros ojos **3.** (*preceding*) **C comes ~ D** la C va delante de la D; **just ~ the bus stop** justo antes de la parada del autobús **4.** (*having priority*) antes que; **~ everything** antes que nada; **to put sth ~ sth else** anteponer algo a algo **5.** (*as future task*) **to have sth ~ one** tener algo ante sí **II.** *adv* **1.** (*previously*) antes; **I've seen it ~** lo he visto anteriormente; **the day ~** el día anterior; **two days ~** dos días antes; **as ~** como antes **2.** (*in front*) **this word and the one ~** esta palabra y la anterior **III.** *conj* antes de que *+subj;* **he spoke ~ she went out** habló antes de que ella se fuera; **he had a glass ~ he went** se tomó una copa antes de irse; **it was a week ~ he came** pasó una semana antes de que llegara; **he'd die ~ he'd tell the truth** preferiría morir a decir la verdad

beforehand [bɪ·'fɔr·hænd] *adv* de antemano

befriend [bɪ·'frend] *vt* hacerse amigo de

beg [beg] <-gg-> **I.** *vt* (*request*) suplicar, rogar; **to ~ sb to do sth** suplicar a alguien que haga algo; **to ~ sb's pardon** pedir disculpas a alguien; **I ~ your pardon!** ¡discúlpe! **II.** *vi* **1.** (*seek charity*) pedir (limosna); **to ~ on the streets** mendigar por las calles; **to ~ for sth** pedir algo **2.** (*request*) implorar; **I ~ of you** ¡te lo imploro!; **to ~ for mercy** implorar clemencia; **I ~ to differ** *form* no estoy de acuerdo **3.** (*sit up and request: dog*) levantar las patitas ◆ **beg off** *vi* excusarse; **to ~ (from sth)** excusarse (de algo)

began [bɪ·'gæn] *pt of* begin

beget [bɪ·'get] <begot, begotten> *vt form* engendrar

beggar ['beg·ər] **I.** *vt* **to ~ belief** parecer absolutamente inverosímil; **to ~ description** resultar indescriptible **II.** *n* (*poor person*) mendigo, -a *m, f,* limosnero, -a *m, f AmL* ▶ **~ s can't be choosers** *prov* a buen hambre no hay pan duro *prov*

begin [bɪ·'gɪn] <began, begun> **I.** *vt* empezar, comenzar; **to ~ a conversation** entablar una conversación; **to ~ doing sth** empezar a hacer algo; **to ~ work** empezar a trabajar **II.** *vi* empezar, comenzar; **the film ~ s at eight** la película comienza a las ocho; **to ~ with...** en primer lugar...; (*enumeration*) primero...; **"well" he began...** "bueno", comenzó...

beginner [bɪ·'gɪn·ər] *n* principiante *mf;* **~ s' class** curso *m* para principiantes; **~ 's luck** la suerte del principiante

beginning **I.** *n* **1.** (*start*) principio *m*, comienzo *m*, empiezo *m Arg, Col, Ecua, Guat;* **at** [*o* **in**] **the ~** al principio; **from ~ to end** de principio a fin **2.** (*origin*) origen *m;* **the ~ s of humanity** los albores de la humanidad **II.** *adj* inicial; **~ stage** fase *f* inicial

begonia [bɪ·'goʊn·jə] *n* BOT begonia *f*

begot [bɪ·'gat] *pt, pp of* beget

begotten [bɪ·'gat·n] *pp of* beget

begrudge [bɪ·'grʌdʒ] *vt* **1.** (*envy*) tener envidia de **2.** (*resent*) **to ~ doing sth** hacer algo de mala gana

begun [bɪ·'gʌn] *pp of* begin

behalf [bɪ·'hæf] *n* **on ~ of sb/sth** (*for*) en beneficio de alguien/algo; (*from*) de parte de alguien/algo

behave [bɪ·'heɪv] *vi* **1.** (*act*) comportarse; (*in a proper manner*) conducirse; **to ~ badly/well** portarse mal/bien; **~ yourself!** ¡pórtate bien! **2.** (*function*) funcionar

behavior [bɪ·'heɪv·jər] *n* comportamiento *m;* **to be on one's best ~** portarse lo mejor posible

behavioral *adj* de la conducta

behaviorism [bɪ·'heɪv·jə·rɪz·əm] *n* conductismo *m*

behead [bɪ·'hed] *vt* decapitar

behind [bɪ·'haɪnd] **I.** *prep* **1.** (*to the rear of*) detrás de; **right ~ sb/sth** justo detrás de alguien/algo; **he's walking ~ me** camina detrás de mí; **~ the wheel** al volante; **a face ~ a mask** un rostro detrás de una máscara **2.** *fig* **who is ~ that plan?** ¿quién está detrás de ese plan?; **there is somebody ~ this** hay alguien detrás de todo esto; **~ the scenes** entre bastidores **3.** (*in support of*) **to be ~ sb/sth** (*all the way*) estar con alguien/algo (hasta el final) **4.** (*late for*) **~ time** retrasado; **to be ~ schedule** ir con retraso **5.** (*less advanced*) **to be ~ sb/the times** estar atrasado con respecto a alguien/la época **II.** *adv* **1.** (*at the back*) detrás; **to fall ~** (*be slower*) quedarse atrás; (*in work, studies*) atrasarse; **to come from ~** venir desde atrás; **a blow from ~** un golpe por detrás; **to leave sb** ~ dejar a alguien atrás; **to stay** ~ quedarse atrás **2.** (*overdue*) **to be** ~ retrasarse; **he is way** ~ está muy retrasado; **to be** ~ (**in sth**) estar atrasado (en algo) **III.** *n inf* trasero *m;* **to get off one's** ~ mover el culo

behindhand [bɪ·'haɪnd·hænd] *adv* atrasado, -a; **to be** ~ estar atrasado

behold [bɪ·'hoʊld] *vt* contemplar

beige [beɪʒ] *adj* beige

being ['bi·ɪŋ] **I.** *n* **1.** (*creature*) ser *m* **2.** (*life*) vida *f;* **to come into** ~ nacer **3.** (*soul*) alma *f* **II.** *pres p of* **be III.** *adj after n* **for the time** ~ por el momento

Belarus [bel·ə·'rus] *n* Bielorrusia *f*

Belarusian [bel·ə·'ru·si·ən] **I.** *adj* bielorruso, -a **II.** *n* **1.** (*person*) bielorruso, -a *m, f* **2.** LING bielorruso *m*

belated [bɪ·'leɪ·ɾɪd] *adj* tardío, -a

belch [beltʃ] **I.** *n inf* eructo *m* **II.** *vi inf* soltar un eructo **III.** *vt fig* **to** ~ **clouds of smoke** arrojar nubes de humo

beleaguered [bɪ·'li·gərd] *adj* (*city*) asediado, -a; (*person, government*) acosado, -a

belfry ['bel·fri] *n* campanario *m*

Belgian ['bel·dʒən] **I.** *adj* belga **II.** *n* belga *mf*

Belgium ['bel·dʒəm] *n* Bélgica *f*

belie [bɪ·'laɪ] *irr vt* **1.** (*conceal*) ocultar **2.** (*contradict*) contradecir; (*lie, rumors*) desmentir

belief [bɪ·'lif] *n* **1.** REL creencia *f* **2.** (*conviction*) opinión *f;* **it is my firm** ~ **that...** creo firmemente que...; **to be beyond** ~ ser increíble; **in the** ~ **that...** con la convicción de que...

believable [bɪ·'li·və·bəl] *adj* creíble

believe [bɪ·'liv] **I.** *vt* creer; ~ (**you**) **me!** ¡créeme!; **would you** ~ **it?** ¡no lo puedo creer!; **she couldn't** ~ **her eyes/ears** no podía dar crédito a sus ojos/oídos; **I can't** ~ **how...** me cuesta creer cómo...; **I'll** ~ **it when I see it!** ¡lo creeré cuando lo vea!; ~ **it or not,...** aunque parezca mentira... **II.** *vi* creer; **to** ~ **in sth/sb** (*reincarnation, ghosts*) creer en algo/alguien; (*support*) ser partidario de algo

believer [bɪ·'li·vər] *n* **1.** REL creyente *mf* **2.** (*supporter*) partidario, -a *m, f;* **to be a** ~ **in sth** ser partidario de algo

belittle [bɪ·'lɪt̬·əl] *vt* menospreciar

Belize [bə·'liz] *n* Belice *m*

Belizean [bə·'li·zi·ən] **I.** *adj* beliceño, -a **II.** *n* beliceño, -a *m, f*

bell [bel] *n* **1.** (*of a church*) campana *f;* (*hand bell*) campanilla *f;* (*on a hat, cat*) cascabel *m;* (*of a bicycle, door*) timbre *m* **2.** (*signal*) campanada *f* ▶ **as clear as a** ~ más claro que el agua; **his name/face rings a** ~ me suena su nombre/cara

belladonna ['bel·ə·dan·ə] *n* belladona *f*

bellboy *n* botones *m inv*

bellhop *n* botones *m inv*

bellicose ['bel·ɪ·koʊs] *adj* belicoso, -a; **to be in a** ~ **mood** tener ganas de pelear

belligerent [bɪ·'lɪdʒ·ər·ənt] *adj* beligerante

bellow ['bel·oʊ] **I.** *vt* gritar **II.** *vi* bramar **III.** *n* grito *m;* (*of animal*) bramido *m*

bellows ['bel·oʊz] *npl* fuelle *m;* **a pair of** ~ un fuelle

bell pepper *n* pimiento *m* [*o* pimentón *m Col*] dulce

belly ['bel·i] <-ies> *n* **1.** *inf* (*stomach*) panza *f,* guata *f Chile* **2.** (*of a ship*) seno *m* ▶ **to have fire in one's** ~ tener mucho celo idealista; **to go** ~ **up** *inf* quebrar

bellyache *inf* **I.** *n* dolor *m* de barriga; **to have a** ~ tener dolor(es) de barriga **II.** *vi* quejarse

bellybutton *n* ombligo *m*

belly dancer *n* bailarín , -ina *m, f* de la danza del vientre

belly flop *n inf* panzazo *m*

belong [bɪ·'laŋ] *vi* **1.** (*be property of, be from*) **to** ~ **to sb/sth** pertenecer a alguien/algo **2.** (*have a place*) **where do these spoons** ~? ¿dónde pongo estas cucharas?; **this doesn't** ~ **here** esto no va aquí; **I feel I don't** ~ **here** no me encuentro a gusto aquí **3.** (*be a member of*) **to** ~ **to** (*club*) ser socio de; (*political party*) estar afiliado a **4.** (*should be*) deber estar **5.** (*match*) **they** ~ **together** están hechos el uno para el otro

belongings *npl* pertenencias *fpl*

Belorussian [bel·ə·'rʌʃ·ən] *adj, n s.* **Belarusian**

beloved[1] [bɪ·'lʌv·ɪd] *n* amado, -a *m, f*

beloved[2] [bɪ·'lʌvd] *adj* amado, -a; **her** ~ **husband** su amado marido; **to be** ~ **by sb** ser amado por alguien

below [bɪ·'loʊ] **I.** *prep* **1.** (*lower than, underneath*) debajo de, bajo; ~ **the table/surface** debajo de la mesa/superficie; ~ **us** debajo de nosotros; ~ **sea level** por debajo del nivel del mar; **the sun sank** ~ **the horizon** el sol se iba perdiendo por detrás del horizonte **2.** GEO **San Diego is** ~ **Los Angeles** San Diego está debajo de Los Angeles; **the river** ~ **the town** el río más abajo del pueblo **3.** (*less than*) ~ **average** por debajo de la media; ~ **freezing** bajo cero; **it's 4 degrees** ~ **zero** estamos a 4 grados bajo cero; **children** ~ **the age of twelve** menores de doce años **4.** (*inferior to*) **to be** ~ **sb in rank** tener un rango por debajo de alguien; **to work** ~ **sb** trabajar bajo (las órdenes de) alguien **5.** (*of a lower standard than*) **to be** ~ **sb** no ser digno de alguien; **to marry** ~ **oneself** casarse por debajo de sus expectativas **II.** *adv* abajo; **the family** (**in the apartment**) ~ la familia (del apartamento) de abajo; **from** ~ desde abajo; **see** ~ (*in a text*) ver más adelante

belt [belt] **I.** *n* **1.** FASHION cinturón *m;* **to fasten one's** ~ abrocharse el cinturón **2.** TECH correa *f* **3.** (*area*) zona *f* **4.** *sl* (*punch*) golpe *m* ▶ **to tighten one's** ~ apretarse el cinturón; **to have some experience under one's** ~ tener algo de experiencia a sus espaldas **II.** *vt* **1.** (*secure with a belt*) ceñir **2.** *sl* (*hit*) zurrar **III.** *vi sl* correr a todo tren; **to** ~ **along** ir como una bala

◆**belt out** *vt sl* to ~ **a song** cantar una canción a pleno pulmón

◆**belt up** *vi* **1.** AUTO abrocharse el cinturón **2.** *inf* ~! ¡cierra el pico!

bemoan [bɪ·'moʊn] *vt form* lamentar; **to ~ one's fate** quejarse de su destino

bemused [bɪ·'mjuzd] *adj* desconcertado, -a; **a ~ look** una mirada de desconcierto

bench [bentʃ] *n* **1.** (*seat*) banco *m* **2.** SPORTS **the ~** el banquillo, la banca **3.** LAW **the ~** la judicatura; **to serve on the ~** actuar como juez **4.** (*worktable*) mesa *f* de trabajo

benchmark ['bentʃ·mark] *n* punto *m* de referencia

bend [bend] <bent, bent> I. *n* **1.** (*in a river, road*) curva *f*; (*in a pipe*) codo *m* **2.** ~**s** *inf* (*illness*) apoplejía *f* por descompresión ▶ **to go/ be around the ~** *sl* volverse/estar chiflado II. *vi* **1.** (*move*) doblarse **2.** (*change direction: road*) hacer una curva III. *vt* **1.** (*move: arms, legs*) doblar; (*head*) inclinar **2.** (*change*) **to ~ sb to one's will** someter a alguien a la voluntad de uno **3.** (*not follow strictly*) **to ~ the rules** interpretar las reglas a su manera ▶ **to ~ sb's ear** *inf* comerle la oreja a alguien

◆**bend back** *vt* doblar hacia atrás

◆**bend down** *vi* inclinarse

◆**bend over** *vi* inclinarse ▶ **to ~ backwards (to help sb)** mover cielo y tierra (por alguien)

bended ['ben·dɪd] *adj form* **on ~ knee** arrodillado; **to go down on ~ knee** arrodillarse

beneath [bɪ·'niθ] I. *prep* **1.** (*lower than, underneath*) debajo de, bajo; ~ **the table/surface** debajo de la mesa/superficie; ~ **us** debajo de nosotros; **the sun sank ~ the horizon** el sol se iba perdiendo por detrás del horizonte **2.** (*inferior to*) **to be ~ sb in rank** tener un rango por debajo de alguien **3.** (*lower standard than*) **to marry ~ oneself** casarse por debajo de sus expectativas; **to be ~ sb** no ser digno de alguien II. *adv* abajo

benediction [ˌben·ɪ·'dɪk·ʃən] *n form* bendición *f*

benefactor ['ben·ə·fæk·tər] *n* benefactor *m*

benefactress ['ben·ɪ·fæk·trɪs] *n* benefactora *f*

beneficence [bɪ·'nef·ɪ·səns] *n* beneficencia *f*

beneficent [bɪ·'nef·ɪ·sənt] *adj form* (*benign*) benigno, -a; (*charitable*) benéfico, -a

beneficiary [ˌben·ɪ·'fɪʃ·i·ər·i] *n* <-ies> beneficiario, -a *m, f*

benefit ['ben·ɪ·fɪt] I. *n* **1.** (*profit*) beneficio *m*; **to derive (much) ~ from sth** sacar (mucho) provecho a algo; **to be of ~ to sb** ser de utilidad a alguien; **for the ~ of sb** a beneficio de alguien; **to the ~ of sth/sb** para beneficio de algo/alguien; **to give sb the ~ of the doubt** darle a alguien el beneficio de la duda **2.** (*welfare payment*) subsidio *m* II. <-t- *o* -tt-> *vi* **to ~ from sth** beneficiarse de algo III. <-t- *o* -tt-> *vt* beneficiar

Benelux ['ben·ɪ·lʌks] *n* **the ~ countries** los países del Benelux

Bengali [beŋ·'gɔ·li] I. *adj* bengalí II. *n* bengalí

mf

Benin [be·'nin] *n* Benín *m*

Beninese [ben·i·'niz] I. *adj* beninés, -esa II. *n* beninés, -esa *m, f*

bent [bent] I. *pt, pp of* **bend** II. *n* **1.** (*tendency*) inclinación *f*; **to have a ~ for sth** tener aptitud para algo; **to follow one's ~** obrar de acuerdo con sus inclinaciones **2.** (*preference*) afición *f* III. *adj* **1.** (*not straight*) torcido, -a **2.** (*determined*) **to be ~ on (doing) sth** estar empeñado en (hacer) algo ▶ **to get all ~ out of shape** *sl* mosquearse, encabronarse *Méx*

bequeath [bɪ·'kwɪð] *vt form* legar

bequest [bɪ·'kwest] *n form* legado *m*

berate [bɪ·'reɪt] *vt form* amonestar

bereaved [bɪ·'rivd] *n* **the ~** la familia del difunto

bereavement [bɪ·'riv·mənt] *n* muerte *f* (de un familiar); **to suffer a ~** sufrir la pérdida de un familiar

bereft [bɪ·'reft] *adj form* **to be ~ of sth** verse privado de algo; **to feel ~** sentirse desolado

beret [bə·'reɪ] *n* boina *f*

Bermuda [bər·'mju·də] *n* las Bermudas

Bermuda shorts *n* bermudas *fpl*

berry ['ber·i] <-ies> *n* baya *f*

berserk [bər·'sɜrk] *adj* **1.** (*angry*) furioso, -a; **to go ~ (over sth)** enfurecerse (por algo); (*be enthusiastic*) loco, -a; **Mary goes ~ over chocolate** a Mary la vuelve loca el chocolate **2.** (*upset*) enloquecido, -a *inf*

berth [bɜrθ] I. *n* **1.** (*on a train*) litera *f* **2.** (*on a ship*) camarote *m* **3.** (*in a harbor*) amarradero *m* **4.** *fig* **to give sb a wide ~** evitar a alguien II. *vt, vi* NAUT atracar

beseech [bɪ·'sitʃ] <beseeched, besought> *vt form* **to ~ sb to do sth** suplicar a alguien que haga algo

beseeching *adj* suplicante

beset [bɪ·'set] <beset, beset> *vt* acosar; **to be ~ by sth** estar acosado por algo; ~ **by worries** atormentado por las preocupaciones

beside [bɪ·'saɪd] *prep* **1.** (*next to*) al lado de; **right ~ sb/sth** justo al lado de alguien/algo **2.** (*together with*) ~ **sb** junto a alguien **3.** (*in comparison to*) al lado de **4.** (*overwhelmed*) **to be ~ oneself** estar fuera de sí **5.** (*irrelevant to*) **to be ~ the point** no venir al caso

besides [bɪ·'saɪdz] I. *prep* **1.** (*in addition to*) además de **2.** (*except for*) excepto II. *adv* **1.** (*in addition*) además **2.** (*else*) **nothing ~** nada más

besiege [bɪ·'sidʒ] *vt* **1.** (*city*) sitiar **2.** *fig* (*with questions, complaints*) acosar

besmirch [bɪ·'smɜrtʃ] *vt liter* manchar; **to ~ sb's good name** mancillar el buen nombre de alguien

besotted [bɪ·'sa·tɪd] *adj* enamorado, -a; **to be ~ with sth** estar obsesionado con algo; **to be ~ with sb** estar chalado por alguien *inf*

besought [bɪ·'sɔt] *pt, pp of* **beseech**

best [best] I. *adj superl of* **good** mejor; **the ~** el/la mejor; **the ~ days of my life** los mejores días de mi vida; **the ~ part** (*the majority*) la mayor parte; **may the ~ man win** que gane el mejor; **~ wishes!** ¡felicidades! **II.** *adv superl of* **well** mejor; **the ~** lo mejor; **as ~ (as) you can** lo mejor que puedas; **do what you think is ~** haz lo que te parezca mejor; **at ~** como mucho, a lo mucho *Méx* **III.** *n* **1.** (*the finest*) **all the ~!** *inf* ¡felicidades!; **to be the ~ of friends** ser los mejores amigos; **to bring out the ~ in sb** sacar lo mejor de alguien; **to the ~ of my knowledge** que yo sepa **2.** SPORTS récord *m* **IV.** *vt form* vencer

bestial ['bes·tʃəl] *adj* bestial

bestiality [ˌbes·tʃi·'æl·ə·t̬i] *n* **1.** (*behavior*) bestialidad *f* **2.** LAW (*sexual*) zoofilia *f*

best man *n* padrino *m* (de boda)

bestow [bɪ·'stoʊ] *vt form* **to ~ sth on sb** otorgar algo a alguien; **to ~ a favor on sb** conceder un favor a alguien

bestowal [bɪ·'stoʊ·əl] *n form* concesión *f*

bestseller *n* éxito *m* de ventas

bet [bet] <bet *o* -ted, bet *o* -ted> **I.** *n* apuesta *f*; **it is a fair** [*o* **safe**] **~ that...** es casi seguro que... +*subj*; **to be the best ~** ser la mejor opción; **to make a ~ with sb** hacer una apuesta con alguien; **to place a ~ on sth** apostar por algo ▶ **to hedge one's ~s** cubrirse contra un riesgo **II.** *vt* apostar; **I ~ you don't!** ¡a que no lo haces! **III.** *vi* apostar; **to ~ on sth** apostar por algo; **I wouldn't ~ on it** yo no estaría tan seguro ▶ **I'll ~!** ¡seguro!; **you ~!** *inf* ¡ya lo creo!

beta ['beɪ·t̬ə] *n* beta *f*

beta-blocker ['beɪ·t̬ə·'blak·ər] *n* MED betabloqueador *m*, betabloqueante *m*

beta testing *n* COMPUT pruebas *fpl* beta

beta version *n* COMPUT versión *f* beta

betray [bɪ·'treɪ] *vt* **1.** (*be disloyal to*) traicionar; **to ~ a promise** romper una promesa; **to ~ sb's trust** defraudar la confianza de alguien; **to be ~ed by sb** ser traicionado por alguien; **he ~ed his wife** engañó a su esposa **2.** (*reveal*) delatar; **to ~ sth to sb** revelar algo a alguien; **to ~ one's ignorance** demostrar ignorancia

betrayal [bɪ·'treɪ·əl] *n* **1.** (*disloyalty*) traición *f*; **an act of ~** una traición **2.** (*revelation*) revelación *f*

better¹ ['bet̬·ər] **I.** *adj comp of* **good** mejor; **to be ~** MED estar mejor; **~ than nothing** mejor que nada; **to appeal to sb's ~ nature** apelar a la bondad de alguien; **~ luck next time** mejor suerte la próxima vez; **it's ~ that way** es mejor así **II.** *adv comp of* **well** mejor; **I like this ~** me gusta más esto; **there is nothing I like ~ than...** nada me gusta más que...; **we'd ~ stay here** lo mejor es quedarse aquí; **it would be ~ to tell her** más vale decírselo; **you had ~ go** mejor que te vayas; **to think ~ of sth** cambiar de opinión respecto a algo; **or ~ yet...** o mejor aún... **III.** *n* **1.** el/la mejor; **not to have seen ~** no haber visto nada mejor; **to change for the ~** cambiar para bien; **the sooner, the ~** cuanto antes, mejor; **so much the ~** tanto

mejor **2.** **~s, my ~s** mis superiores ▶ **for ~ or** (**for**) **worse** para bien o para mal; **to get the ~ of sth/sb** ganarle la batalla a algo/alguien **IV.** *vt* vencer; **to ~ oneself** prosperar; (*further one's knowledge*) superarse

better² ['bet̬·ər] *n s.* **bettor**

betterment ['bet̬·ər·mənt] *n* mejoramiento *m*

betting ['bet̬·ɪŋ] *n* apuestas *fpl*

betting office *n* agencia *f* de apuestas

bettor ['bet̬·ər] *n* apostador(a) *m(f)*

between [bɪ·'twin] **I.** *prep* entre; **to eat ~ meals** comer entre horas; **~ now and tomorrow** entre hoy y mañana; **~ the two of us** entre nosotros dos; **a misunderstanding ~ the couple** un malentendido entre la pareja; **nothing will come ~ them** nada se interpondrá entre ellos; **the 3 children have $10 ~ them** entre los 3 niños tienen 10 dólares **II.** *adv* (**in**) **~** en medio de; (*time*) a mitad de

bevel ['bev·əl] **I.** <-l-> *vt* biselar **II.** *n* bisel *m*

beverage ['bev·ər·ɪdʒ] *n* bebida *f*; **alcoholic ~s** bebidas alcohólicas

bevy ['bev·i] *n* (*of birds*) bandada *f*; *inf* (*of people*) grupo *m*

bewail [bɪ·'weɪl] *vt form* lamentar

beware [bɪ·'wer] *vi* tener cuidado; **~!** ¡ten cuidado!; **~ of pickpockets!** ¡cuidado con los carteristas!

bewilder [bɪ·'wɪl·dər] *vt* desconcertar

bewildered *adj* desconcertado, -a

bewildering *adj* desconcertante

bewilderment *n* desconcierto *m*, azoro *m* *Méx*, *Perú*, *PRico*

bewitch [bɪ·'wɪtʃ] *vt* **1.** (*place magic charm on*) hechizar **2.** (*fascinate*) fascinar

bewitching *adj* fascinante

beyond [bɪ·'jand] **I.** *prep* **1.** (*on the other side of*) más allá de; **~ the mountain** al otro lado de la montaña; **don't go ~ the line!** ¡no traspases la línea!; **~ the wall** más allá del muro; **from ~ the grave** desde el más allá **2.** (*after*) después de; (*more than*) más de; **~ 8:00** después de las 8:00; **to stay ~ a week** quedarse más de una semana; **~ lunchtime** después del almuerzo **3.** (*further than*) más allá de; **to see/go** (**way**) **~ sth** ver/ir (mucho) más allá de algo; **it goes ~ a joke** va más allá de una broma; **~ the reach of sb** fuera del alcance de alguien; **~ belief** increíble; **~ hope** más allá de toda esperanza; **he is ~ help** a. *iron* es un caso perdido; **~ the shadow of a doubt** sin lugar a dudas; **to go ~ the point of no return** entrar [*o* encontrarse] en un callejón sin salida **4.** (*too difficult for*) **to be ~ sb** (*theory, idea*) ser demasiado (difícil) para alguien; **that's ~ me** se me escapa; **this is ~ my abilities** esto sobrepasa mis capacidades **5.** (*more than*) por encima de; **to live ~ one's means** vivir por encima de sus posibilidades; **to value sth above and ~ all else** valorar algo por encima de todo **6.** *with neg or interrog* (*except for*) fuera de, excepto **II.** *adv* **1.** (*past*) **the house ~** la casa de más allá **2.** (*future*) **the next ten**

years and ~ los próximos diez años y más **III.** *n* **the** ~ REL el más allá

biannual [ˌbaɪ·'æn·ju·əl] *adj* semestral

bias ['baɪ·əs] **I.** *n* **1.** (*prejudice*) prejuicio *m;* **to have** ~**es against sb/sth** ser parcial contra alguien/algo **2.** (*one-sidedness*) parcialidad *f;* **without** ~ imparcialmente **3.** (*tendency*) tendencia *f;* **to have a** ~ **towards sth** sentir inclinación por algo **4.** (*in sewing, cooking*) sesgo *m;* **on the** ~ al sesgo **II.** <-s-> *vt* influir; **to** ~ **sb towards/against sb** predisponer a alguien a favor de/en contra de alguien

biased *adj* parcial; ~ **in sb's favor** predispuesto a favor de alguien; ~ **opinions** opiniones parciales

bib [bɪb] *n* babero *m*

Bible ['baɪ·bəl] *n* **the** ~ la Biblia

biblical ['bɪb·lɪ·kəl] *adj* bíblico, -a

bibliographer [ˌbɪb·lɪ·'ag·rə·fər] *n* bibliógrafo, -a *m, f*

bibliographic [ˌbɪb·lɪ·ə·'græf·ɪk] *adj*, **bibliographical** *adj* bibliográfico, -a

bibliography [ˌbɪb·li·'ag·rə·fi] <-ies> *n* bibliografía *f*

bibliophile ['bɪb·lɪ·ə·faɪl] *n form* bibliófilo, -a *m, f*

bicarbonate [ˌbaɪ·'kar·bə·nɪt] *n* bicarbonato *m*

bicarbonate of soda *n* bicarbonato *m* de soda

bicentenary [baɪ·'sen·ten·ə·ri] <-ies> *n*, **bicentennial** [baɪ·sen·'ten·ɪ·əl] **I.** *n* bicentenario *m* **II.** *adj* bicentenario, -a; ~ **celebration** celebración *f* del bicentenario

biceps ['baɪ·seps] *n inv* bíceps *m inv*

bicker ['bɪk·ər] *vi* reñir

bickering *n* riñas *fpl*

bicycle ['baɪ·sɪk·əl] *n* bicicleta *f;* **to ride a** ~ montar en bicicleta; **by** ~ en bicicleta

bicycle lane *n* carril *m* de bicicletas

bid¹ [bɪd] <bid *o* bade, bid *o* bidden> *vt form* **1.** (*greet*) **to** ~ **sb farewell** decir adiós a alguien; **to** ~ **sb good morning** desear buenos días a alguien; **to** ~ **sb welcome** dar la bienvenida a alguien **2.** (*command*) ordenar **3.** (*invite*) invitar

bid² [bɪd] **I.** *n* **1.** (*offer*) oferta *f;* **hostile takeover** ~ COM oferta hostil de adquisición; **to make a** ~ **to do sth** ofrecerse a/para hacer algo; **to make a** ~ **for sth** hacer una oferta sobre [*o* por] algo **2.** (*attempt*) intento *m* **II.** <bid, bid> *vi* **1.** (*at an auction*) pujar **2.** COM hacer una oferta; **to** ~ **for a contract** concursar por un contrato **III.** <bid, bid> *vt* pujar

bidden ['bɪd·ən] *pp of* **bid¹**

bidder ['bɪd·ər] *n* postor(a) *m(f);* **to the highest** ~ al mejor postor

bidding ['bɪd·ɪŋ] *n* **1.** FIN puja *f* **2.** (*command*) orden *f;* **to do sb's** ~ cumplir las órdenes de alguien; **at sb's** ~ a las órdenes de alguien

bide [baɪd] *vt* **to** ~ **one's time** esperar el momento oportuno

bidet [bɪ·'deɪ] *n* bidé *m*

biennial [baɪ·'en·i·əl] **I.** *adj a.* BOT bienal **II.** *n*

1. (*event*) bienal *f* **2.** ZOOL planta *f* bienal

bier [bɪr] *n* andas *fpl*

bifocal ['baɪ·fou·kəl] *adj* bifocal

bifocals ['baɪ·fou·kəlz] *npl* gafas *fpl* bifocales, anteojos *mpl* bifocales *AmL*

big [bɪg] <-ger, -gest> *adj* **1.** (*in size, amount*) grande; (*before singular nouns*) gran; **a** ~ **book** un libro grande; **a** ~ **budget film** una película de gran presupuesto; **a** ~ **house** una casa grande; ~ **letters** mayúsculas *fpl;* **to be a** ~ **spender** *inf* ser un derrochador; ~ **words** *inf* palabras *fpl* altisonantes; **the** ~**ger the better** cuanto más grande mejor **2.** (*older*) mayor; ~ **boy/girl** chico/chica mayor; ~ **sister/brother** hermana/hermano mayor **3.** (*significant*) gran(de); **a** ~ **day** *inf* un gran día; **a** ~ **decision** una decisión importante; **this group is** ~ **in Spain** este grupo es muy popular en España **4.** (*on a large scale*) a gran escala ▶**to have a** ~ **heart** tener un buen corazón; **to have a** ~ **mouth** *inf* ser un bocazas [*o* bocón]; **to make it** ~ *inf* triunfar a lo grande; **to think** ~ tener grandes aspiraciones

bigamist ['bɪg·ə·mɪst] *n* bígamo, -a *m, f*

bigamy ['bɪg·ə·mi] *n* bigamia *f*

Big Apple *n* **the** ~ Nueva York *f*

big business *n* el gran capital; **to be** ~ ser un gran negocio

Big Dipper *n* **the** ~ ASTR el Carro

Big Easy *n* **the** ~ Nueva Orleans *f*

big game *n* caza *f* mayor

bigot ['bɪg·ət] *n* intolerante *mf;* REL fanático, -a *m, f*

bigoted *adj* intolerante; REL fanático, -a

bigotry ['bɪg·ə·tri] *n* intolerancia *f*

big shot *n sl* pez *m* gordo

big toe *n* dedo *m* gordo del pie

big top *n* circo *m*

bigwig *n sl* pez *m* gordo

bike [baɪk] *n inf* **1.** (*bicycle*) bici *f* **2.** (*motorcycle*) moto *f*

biker ['baɪ·kər] *n inf* motero, -a *m, f*

bikini [bɪ·'ki·ni] *n* bikini *m*

bilateral [ˌbaɪ·'læt·ər·əl] *adj* bilateral

bile [baɪl] *n* **1.** ANAT bilis *f inv* **2.** *fig* mal genio *m*

bilingual [baɪ·'lɪŋ·gwəl] *adj* bilingüe

bilious ['bɪl·jəs] *adj* **1.** MED bilioso, -a **2.** *fig* (*angry*) bilioso, -a; (*unpleasant*) asqueroso, -a

bill¹ [bɪl] **I.** *n* **1.** (*invoice*) factura *f;* **phone** ~ factura del teléfono; **to foot the** ~ pagar la cuenta; **the** ~**, please** la cuenta, por favor **2.** (*bank note*) billete *m* **3.** POL, LAW proyecto *m* de ley; **to pass a** ~ aprobar un proyecto de ley **4.** (*poster*) cartel *m* ▶**to give sth/sb a clean** ~ **of health** dar a algo/alguien el visto bueno; **to fit the** ~ convenir **II.** *vt* **to** ~ **sb** pasar la cuenta a alguien; **to** ~ **sb for sth** facturar algo a alguien

bill² [bɪl] **I.** *n* (*of a bird*) pico *m* **II.** *vi* **to** ~ **and coo** *inf* estar como dos tortolitos

billboard *n* valla *f* publicitaria

bill collector *n* cobrador(a) *m(f)* (de deudas)

billet ['bɪl·ət] MIL **I.** *n* acantonamiento *m* **II.** *vt*

acantonar
billfold n cartera f
billiard ball n bola f de billar
billiards ['bɪl·jərdz] n billar m
billiard table n mesa f de billar
billing n **to be given top** ~ encabezar el reparto
billion ['bɪl·jən] n mil millones mpl
billow ['bɪl·oʊ] I. vi (clothes, sails) hincharse II. n a ~ **of smoke** una nube de humo
billowy adj (waves, clouds) ondulante; (sail) ondeante
billposter n cartelero m
billy club n porra f
billy goat n inf macho m cabrío
bimbo ['bɪm·boʊ] <-(e)s> n pej, sl: mujer joven y guapa, pero tonta
bimonthly [‚baɪ·'mʌnθ·li] I. adj **1.** (twice a month) quincenal **2.** (every two months) bimestral II. adv **1.** (twice a month) quincenalmente **2.** (once every two months) bimestralmente
bin [bɪn] n recipiente m; **trash** ~ cubo m de basura, basurero m Méx
binary ['baɪ·nə·ri] adj COMPUT binario, -a
binary code n COMPUT código m binario
bind [baɪnd] I. n inf lío m; **to be in a** ~ estar metido en un lío II. <bound, bound> vi unirse III. <bound, bound> vt **1.** (tie together) atar; **to be bound hand and foot** estar atado de pies y manos **2.** (unite) **to** ~ (**together**) unir; **to be bound to sb** estar ligado a alguien **3.** (commit) vincular **4.** (sew) ribetear **5.** (book) encuadernar **6.** (oblige) **to** ~ **sb to do sth** obligar a alguien a hacer algo; **to** ~ **sb to a contract** comprometer a alguien contractualmente
binder ['baɪn·dər] n (notebook) carpeta f
binding ['baɪn·dɪŋ] I. n **1.** TYPO encuadernación f **2.** FASHION ribete m II. adj vinculante
binge [bɪndʒ] inf I. n (of drinking) borrachera f, vacilada f Méx; (of eating) comilona f; **to go on a** ~ ir de farra, ir de parranda II. vi atiborrarse
bingo ['bɪŋ·goʊ] I. n bingo m II. interj inf bingo
binoculars [bɪ·'nak·jə·lərz] npl prismáticos mpl, binoculares mpl AmL; **a pair of** ~ unos prismáticos
binomial [baɪ·'noʊ·mi·əl] I. n MATH binomio m II. adj MATH binomial
biochemical [‚baɪ·oʊ·'kem·ɪ·kəl] adj bioquímico, -a
biochemist [‚baɪ·oʊ·'kem·ɪst] n bioquímico, -a m, f
biochemistry [‚baɪ·oʊ·'kem·ɪ·stri] n bioquímica f
biodegradable [‚baɪ·oʊ·dɪ·'greɪ·də·bəl] adj biodegradable
biodegrade [‚baɪ·oʊ·dɪ·'greɪd] vi biodegradarse
biodiversity [‚baɪ·oʊ·dɪ·'vɜr·sə·t̬i] n biodiversidad f

bioengineering [‚baɪ·oʊ·en·dʒɪ·'nɪr·ɪŋ] n ingeniería f biológica
biofeedback [‚baɪ·oʊ·'fid·bæk] n retroalimentación f biológica
biofuel ['baɪ·oʊ·ˌfjul] n combustible m biológico
biogas ['baɪ·oʊ·ˌgæs] n biogás m
biographer [baɪ·'ag·rə·fər] n biógrafo, -a m, f
biographical [‚baɪ·oʊ·'græf·ɪ·kəl] adj biográfico, -a
biography [baɪ·'ag·rə·fi] <-ies> n biografía f
biological [‚baɪ·ə·'ladʒ·ɪ·kəl] adj biológico, -a; ~ **cycle/rhythm** ciclo/ritmo biológico; ~ **parents** padres biológicos
biological clock n reloj m biológico
biological control n control m biológico
biological indicator n indicador m biológico
biologist [baɪ·'al·ə·dʒɪst] n biólogo, -a m, f
biology [baɪ·'al·ə·dʒi] n biología f
biomass ['baɪ·oʊ·ˌmæs] n BIO biomasa f
biopsy ['baɪ·ap·si] n MED biopsia f
biorhythm ['baɪ·oʊ·rɪð·əm] n biorritmo m
biosphere ['baɪ·ə·sfɪr] n biosfera f
biotechnology [‚baɪ·oʊ·tek·'nal·ə·dʒi] n biotecnología f
biotope ['baɪ·ə·toʊp] n biótopo m
bipartisan [‚baɪ·'par·t̬ə·zən] adj POL bipartidista
biped ['baɪ·ped] n BIO bípedo m
biplane ['baɪ·pleɪn] n biplano m
bipolar [‚baɪ·'poʊ·lər] adj ELEC, PHYS bipolar
birch [bɜrtʃ] n BOT abedul m
bird [bɜrd] n **1.** ZOOL pájaro m; (larger) ave f; **a flock of** ~**s** una bandada de pájaros **2.** inf (person) **a strange** [o **queer**] ~ un bicho raro ▶ ~**s of a** feather **flock together** prov Dios los cría y ellos se juntan prov; **to kill two** ~**s with one** stone matar dos pájaros de un mismo tiro fig; **the early** ~ **catches the** worm prov al que madruga, Dios le ayuda prov; **to** give **sb the** ~ inf abuchear a alguien, hacer pistola a alguien Col; for **the** ~**s** para nada
bird bath n alberquilla f, pila f
birdcage n pajarera f, jaula f
bird flue n gripe f aviar
birdie ['bɜr·di] n **1.** (in golf, badminton) birdie m **2.** childspeak pajarito m; **watch the** ~ PHOT ¡mira el pajarito!
birdseed n alpiste m
bird's-eye view n vista f panorámica
bird watching n observación f de aves
birth [bɜrθ] n **1.** nacimiento m, paritorio m Cuba, Ven; MED parto m; **at** ~ al nacer; **by** ~ de nacimiento; **from** ~ de nacimiento; **date/place of** ~ fecha/lugar de nacimiento; **to give** ~ **to a child** dar a luz a un bebé **2.** (descent, beginning) origen m; **to be of low/noble** ~ ser de origen humilde/noble
birth certificate n certificado m de nacimiento
birth control n control m de natalidad
birthday ['bɜrθ·deɪ] n cumpleaños m inv; **happy** ~! ¡feliz cumpleaños!
birthday cake n tarta f de cumpleaños, pastel

m de cumpleaños *AmL*
birthday card *n* tarjeta *f* de cumpleaños
birthday party *n* fiesta *f* de cumpleaños
birthday present *n* regalo *m* de cumpleaños
birthday suit *n* *inf* in one's ~ en cueros
birthmark *n* marca *f* de nacimiento
birthplace *n* lugar *m* de nacimiento
birthrate *n* tasa *f* de natalidad; **falling/rising ~** natalidad decreciente/creciente
birthright *n* derecho *m* de nacimiento; *fig* patrimonio *m*
Biscay ['bɪs·keɪ] *n* Vizcaya *f*
biscuit ['bɪs·kɪt] *n* CULIN bizcocho *m*

---

i El término **biscuits and gravy** describe un desayuno típico procedente del sur de EE.UU. Los **biscuits** son una especie de panecillos planos que se sirven con **gravy** (salsa hecha a partir de caldo de carne). En algunas zonas, este desayuno sólo se sirve en **truck stops** (locales frecuentados por camioneros).

---

bisect ['baɪ·sekt] *vt* MATH bisecar
bisection [baɪ·'sek·ʃən] *n* MATH bisección *f*
bisexual [ˌbaɪ·'sek·ʃʊ·əl] I. *n* bisexual *mf* II. *adj* bisexual
bishop ['bɪʃ·əp] *n* 1. REL obispo *m* 2. (*chess piece*) alfil *m*
bishopric ['bɪʃ·ə·prɪk] *n* obispado *m*
bison ['baɪ·sən] *n* bisonte *m*
bit[1] [bɪt] *n* 1. (*small piece*) trozo *m*, pedazo *m*; (*of glass*) fragmento *m*; **a ~ of paper** un trozo de papel; **little ~s** pedacitos *mpl*; **to smash sth to ~s** romper algo en pedazos 2. (*some*) **a ~ of** un poco de; **a ~ of news** una noticia; **a ~ of trouble** un problemilla 3. (*part*) parte *f*; **~ by ~** poco a poco; **to do one's ~** *inf* poner su granito de arena 4. *inf* (*short time*) momento *m*; **for a ~** por un momento; **hold on a ~** espera un momento 5. (*somewhat*) **a ~** algo; **a ~ stupid** un poco tonto; **quite a ~** bastante; **not a ~** en absoluto
bit[2] [bɪt] *n* 1. (*for horses*) bocado *m* 2. (*for drill*) broca *f* ▶ **to champ at the ~** impacientarse, comer ansias *Méx*
bit[3] [bɪt] *n* COMPUT bit *m*
bit[4] [bɪt] *pt of* bite
bitch [bɪtʃ] I. *n* 1. ZOOL perra *f* 2. *offensive, sl* (*woman*) zorra *f*, tusa *f* *AmL, Cuba;* **you ~!** ¡lagarta! 3. *sl* (*difficult matter*) putada *f*; **life's a ~** esta vida es una mierda II. *vi sl* quejarse; **to ~ about sb/sth** quejarse de alguien/algo
bitchy ['bɪtʃ·i] *adj sl* con mala leche
bite [baɪt] I. <bit, bitten> *vt* morder; (*insect*) picar; **to ~ one's nails/lips** morderse las uñas/los labios II. <bit, bitten> *vi* (*dog, person*) morder; (*insect, fish*) picar ▶ **once bitten twice shy** *prov* el gato escaldado del agua fría huye *prov* III. *n* 1. (*of a dog, person*) mordisco *m*; (*of an insect*) picadura *f*; **~ mark**

marca *f* de mordedura; (*of an insect*) picadura *f*; **a dog's ~** una mordedura de un perro; **to give sb a ~** dar un mordisco a alguien; **to take a ~ of sth** tomar un bocado de algo 2. (*mouthful*) bocado *m* 3. *fig* (*sharpness*) mordacidad *f*; **to have (real) ~** tener (verdadera) garra
biting ['baɪ·tɪŋ] *adj* (*wind*) cortante; (*criticism*) mordaz
bitten ['bɪt·ən] *pp of* bite
bitter ['bɪt̬·ər] I. *adj* <-er, -est> 1. (*in taste*) agrio, -a; (*fruit*) amargo, -a 2. (*painful*) amargo, -a; **to be ~ about sth** estar amargado por algo; **to carry on to the ~ end** seguir hasta el final 3. (*intense*) acérrimo, -a; (*dispute*) encarnizado, -a; (*disappointment*) amargo, -a; (*wind*) cortante II. *n* **~s** (*in cocktails*) licor *m* amargo
bitterly *adv* 1. (*resentfully*) con rencor; **to weep ~** llorar a lágrima viva 2. (*intensely*) intensamente; **to condemn sth ~** condenar algo firmemente
bitterness *n* 1. (*animosity*) amargura *f*; (*resentment*) resentimiento *m;* **~ towards sb** resentimiento contra alguien 2. (*taste*) amargor *m*
bitumen [bɪ·'tu·mən] *n* betún *m*
bituminous [bɪ·'tu·mɪ·nəs] *adj* bituminoso, -a
bivalve ['baɪ·vælv] *n* bivalvo *m*
bivouac ['bɪv·u·æk] I. *n* vivaque *m* II. <-k-> *vi* vivaquear
biweekly [ˌbaɪ·'wik·li] I. *adj* 1. (*every two weeks*) quincenal 2. (*twice a week*) bisemanal II. *adv* 1. (*every two weeks*) quincenalmente 2. (*twice a week*) bisemanalmente
bizarre [bɪ·'zar] *adj* (*behavior, person*) extraño, -a; (*clothes*) estrafalario, -a
blab [blæb] <-bb-> *vi inf* 1. (*reveal secret*) chivarse 2. (*talk too much*) irse de la lengua
blabber ['blæb·ər] *vi* irse de la lengua
blabbermouth *n* 1. (*revealer of secret*) chivato, -a *m, f*, chismoso, -a *m, f* 2. (*talkative person*) parlanchín, -ina *m, f*
black [blæk] I. *adj* 1. (*color*) negro, -a; **~ man** negro *m;* **~ woman** negra *f* 2. *fig* (*extreme*) negro, -a; **~ despair** negra desesperación 3. (*dark*) oscuro, -a; *fig;* **to give sb a ~ look** ponerle a alguien mala cara 4. (*very dirty: hands*) mugriento, -a, mugroso, -a *Méx* ▶ **to beat sb ~ and blue** *inf* moler a alguien a palos II. *vt* (*make black*) ennegrecer; **to ~ one's face** pintarse la cara de negro III. *n* 1. (*color*) negro *m;* **in ~** de negro; **in ~ and white** CINE, PHOT en blanco y negro 2. (*person*) negro, -a *m, f* 3. FIN **in the ~** en números negros
♦ **black out** I. *vi* perder el conocimiento, desmayarse II. *vt* 1. (*make illegible*) oscurecer, ennegrecer 2. (*censure*) censurar
blackball *vt* (*vote*) votar en contra de; (*reject*) dar bola negra a
blackberry ['blæk·ber·i] <-ies> *n* (*fruit*) zarzamora *f*; (*plant*) zarza *f*
blackbird *n* mirlo *m*
blackboard *n* pizarra *f*
black book *n* **to be in sb's ~(s)** figurar en la

lista negra de alguien

black box *n* AVIAT caja *f* negra

blacken ['blæk·ən] **I.** *vt* **1.** (*make black*) ennegrecer; **to ~ sb's eye** poner a alguien el ojo morado [*o* a la funerala] **2.** (*slander*) desacreditar; **to ~ sb's name** manchar la reputación de alguien **II.** *vi* ennegrecerse

black eye *n* ojo *m* morado

blackguard *n* sinvergüenza *m*

black hat *n* COMPUT sombrero *m* negro (*hacker que tiene la intención de cometer fraude*)

blackhead ['blæk·hed] *n* espinilla *f*

black hole *n* agujero *m* negro

black ice *n* hielo invisible en la carretera

blackish ['blæk·ɪʃ] *adj* negruzco, -a

blackjack *n* **1.** GAMES veintiuna *f* **2.** (*weapon*) (cachi)porra *f*

black light *n* luz *f* negra [*o* ultravioleta]

blacklist ['blæk·lɪst] **I.** *vt* poner en la lista negra **II.** *n* lista *f* negra

blackmail ['blæk·meɪl] **I.** *n* chantaje *m* **II.** *vt* chantajear; **to ~ sb into doing sth** chantajear a alguien para que haga algo

blackmailer ['blæk·meɪ·lər] *n* chantajista *mf*

black mark *n* punto *m* en contra

black market *n* mercado *m* negro

black markete(e)r *n* estraperlista *mf*

blackness ['blæk·nɪs] *n* (*color*) negrura *f*; (*darkness*) oscuridad *f*

blackout ['blæk·aʊt] *n* **1.** (*faint*) desmayo *m*; **to have a ~** sufrir un desmayo **2.** ELEC apagón *m* **3.** (*censorship*) bloqueo *m*; **news ~** bloqueo informativo

Black Sea *n* Mar *m* Negro

black sheep *n a. fig* oveja *f* negra

blacksmith *n* herrero *m*

bladder ['blæd·ər] *n* ANAT vejiga *f*

blade [bleɪd] **I.** *n* (*of a tool, weapon*) hoja *f*; (*of an oar*) pala *f*; (*of ice skate*) cuchilla *f*; **~ of grass** brizna *f* de hierba **II.** *vi inf* patinar (en línea)

blah [bla] **I.** *adj inf* (*boring*) pesado, -a, soso, -a **II.** *interj inf* **~, ~, (~)** blabla

blame [bleɪm] **I.** *vt* culpar; **to ~ sb for sth, to ~ sth on sb** echar a alguien la culpa de algo; **to be to ~ for sth** tener la culpa de algo; **I don't ~ you** te comprendo **II.** *n* culpa *f*; **to carry the ~** tener la culpa; **to lay the ~ for sth on sb** echar a alguien la culpa de algo; **to take the ~** declararse culpable

blameless ['bleɪm·lɪs] *adj* libre de culpa; **~ life** vida *f* intachable

blameworthy ['bleɪm·wɜr·ði] *adj form* censurable

blanch [blænʃ] **I.** *vi* (*become pale*) palidecer **II.** *vt* **1.** (*whiten*) blanquear **2.** CULIN escaldar; **~ed almonds** almendras peladas

bland [blænd] *adj* **1.** (*mild*) suave **2.** (*dull*) soso, -a

blandishments ['blæn·dɪʃ·mənts] *npl* halagos *mpl*

blank [blæŋk] **I.** *adj* **1.** (*empty*) en blanco; **~ page/space** página *f*/espacio *m* en blanco;

~ tape cinta *f* virgen; **~ check** cheque *m* en blanco; **to go ~** quedarse en blanco; **my mind went ~** me quedé con la mente en blanco; **the screen went ~** la pantalla se quedó negra **2.** (*without emotion: look*) sin expresión **3.** (*complete*) absoluto, -a; (*despair*) completo, -a; **to be met by a ~ refusal** encontrarse con un rechazo absoluto **II.** *n* **1.** (*space*) espacio *m*; (*on form*) hueco *m*, espacio *m* **2.** (*cartridge*) cartucho *m* de salvas ▶ **to draw a (complete) ~** no obtener ningún resultado

blanket ['blæŋ·kɪt] **I.** *n* **1.** (*cover*) manta *f*, frisa *f* RDom, PRico, cobija *f* Méx; *fig* cobertura *f* **2.** (*of snow*) capa *f* **II.** *vt* cubrir; **to ~ sth in sth** cubrir algo con algo **III.** *adj* general; LING (*term*) genérico, -a

blankly *adv* (*without expression*) inexpresivamente; (*without understanding*) sin comprender

blare [bler] **I.** *vi* resonar **II.** *n* estruendo *m*; (*of a trumpet*) trompetazo *m*

blaspheme ['blæs·fim] *vi* blasfemar

blasphemous ['blæs·fə·məs] *adj* blasfemo, -a

blasphemy ['blæs·fə·mi] *n* blasfemia *f*

blast [blæst] **I.** *vt* **1.** (*with an explosive*) volar **2.** *inf* (*criticize*) criticar duramente **II.** *n* **1.** (*detonation*) explosión *f* **2.** (*gust of wind*) ráfaga *f* **3.** (*noise*) toque *m*; (*of a trumpet*) trompetazo *m* **4.** *sl* (*party*) juerga *f*, tambarria *f* AmC, AmS, guateque *m*; (*lots of fun*) **to have a ~** pasarlo bomba [*o* Méx padre] ▶ **(at) full ~** (*volume*) al máximo (de volumen); (*speed*) a toda marcha **III.** *interj inf* maldición; **~ it!** ¡maldita sea!

blasted *adj inf* (*damned*) maldito, -a

blastoff ['blæst·af] *n* despegue *m*

blatant ['bleɪ·tənt] *adj* descarado, -a

blaze[1] [bleɪz] **I.** *vi* resplandecer, brillar; (*fire*) arder; **to ~ with anger** echar chispas **II.** *vt* **to ~ a trail** abrir camino **III.** *n* **1.** (*fire*) fuego *m*; (*flames*) llamarada *f* **2.** (*of light*) llamarada *f*; (*of color*) derroche *m* **3.** (*display*) **a ~ of glory** un rayo de gloria; **a ~ of publicity** una campaña de publicidad a bombo y platillo; **~ of anger** arranque *m* de ira

◆**blaze up** *vi* encenderse vivamente; (*temper*) caldearse

blaze[2] [bleɪz] *n* (*on horse*) mancha *f* blanca en la frente

blazer ['bleɪ·zər] *n* chaqueta *f*

blazing ['bleɪ·zɪŋ] *adj* resplandeciente; (*heat*) abrasador(a); (*sunshine*) esplendoroso, -a; (*light*) brillante; (*fire*) vivo, -a; **to have a ~ temper** tener muy mal carácter

bleach [blitʃ] **I.** *vt* blanquear **II.** *n* lejía *f*; (*for hair*) decolorante *m*

bleachers ['bli·tʃərz] *n pl* gradería *f*

bleak [blik] *adj* (*future*) sombrío, -a; (*weather*) gris; (*landscape*) desolador(a); (*smile*) triste

bleary ['blɪr·i] *adj* <-ier, -iest> (*person*) cansado, -a; (*eyes*) lagañoso, -a

bleary-eyed *adj* **to be ~** estar medio dormido

bleat [blit] **I.** *vi* **1.** (*sheep, goat*) balar; (*calf* mugir **2.**(*complain*) quejarse **II.** *n* **1.**(*of sheep*) balido *m* **2.**(*complaint*) quejido *m*

bled [bled] *pt, pp of* **bleed**

bleed [blid] <bled, bled> **I.** *vi* **1.**(*from a wound*) sangrar; **to ~ to death** morir desangrado; **my heart ~s for...** se me parte el alma por... **2.**(*colors: in the laundry*) desteñir, destintar **II.** *vt* **1.** hacer una sangría a; **to ~ sb dry** *inf* dejar seco a alguien **2.** TECH, AUTO (*drain*) purgar

bleep [blip] **I.** *n* (*sound*) pitido *m* **II.** *vi* (*emit sound*) pitar **III.** *vt* (*censor*) censurar las palabrotas con pitidos

blemish ['blem·ɪʃ] **I.** *n a. fig* mancha *f;* **a reputation without ~** una reputación intachable **II.** *vt a. fig* manchar

blemish-free *adj* sin defectos

blench [blentʃ] *vi* recular; **to ~ at a thought** retroceder ante un pensamiento

blend [blend] **I.** *n* mezcla *f* **II.** *vt* mezclar **III.** *vi* armonizar; **to ~ in** no desentonar

blender ['blen·dər] *n* licuadora *f*

bless [bles] *vt* bendecir ▶ ~ **him/her!** ¡bendito sea!; **(God) ~ you!** (*after a sneeze*) ¡Jesús!

blessed ['bles·ɪd] *adj* **1.**(*holy*) bendito, -a; (*ground*) santo, -a; **the Blessed Virgin** la Santísima Virgen; **~ are the meek...** bienaventurados los humildes... **2.** *inf* (*as intensifier*) dichoso, -a; **the whole ~ day** todo el santo día

blessing ['bles·ɪŋ] *n* **1.**(*benediction*) bendición *f;* **to give one's ~ to sth** dar su aprobación a algo **2.**(*benefit*) beneficio *m;* (*advantage*) ventaja *f* ▶ **it's a ~ in disguise** no hay mal que por bien no venga *prov;* **to count one's ~s** apreciar lo que uno tiene

blew [blu] *pt of* **blow**

blight [blaɪt] **I.** *vt* AGR *a.* arruinar **II.** *n* **1.** AGR añublo *m* **2.** *fig* ruina *f;* **to cast a ~ on sth** arruinar algo

blimp [blɪmp] *n* (*airship*) zepelín *m*, dirigible *m* (no rígido); (*obese person*) obeso, -a *m, f*

blind [blaɪnd] **I.** *n* **1.** *pl* (*person*) **the ~** los ciegos **2.**(*window shade*) persiana *f* **3.**(*for hunters, photographers*) escondite *m* **II.** *vt* **1.** ANAT, MED cegar **2.**(*dazzle*) deslumbrar **III.** *adj* **1.**(*unable to see*) ciego, -a; **to be ~ in one eye** ser tuerto; **to be ~ to sth** no (querer) ver algo **2.**(*hidden: corner*) de poca visibilidad **3.**(*with fury*) ciego, -a; (*acceptance, devotion*) ciego, -a **4.**(*without knowledge*) a tientas; **~ taste test** cata con los ojos vendados **IV.** *adv* **1.**(*without sight*) a ciegas **2.**(*as intensifier*) **to be ~ drunk** estar más borracho que una cuba

blind alley <-s> *n a. fig* callejón *m* sin salida

blind date *n* cita *f* a ciegas

blinders ['blaɪn·dərz] *n pl* SPORTS anteojeras *fpl*

blindfold ['blaɪnd·foʊld] **I.** *n* venda *f* **II.** *vt* vendar los ojos a **III.** *adj* con los ojos vendados; **to be able to do sth ~ed** poder hacer algo con los ojos cerrados

blinding *adj* (*dazzling: light*) cegador(a); (*color*) deslumbrante

blindman's buff *n* gallina *f* ciega

blindness *n* ceguera *f*

blind spot *n* punto *m* ciego

bling [blɪŋ] **I.** *n sl* joyas *fpl* llamativas y ostentosas **II.** *adj pred, sl* (*look, outfit*) recargado, -a; (*person*) emperifollado, -a

blink [blɪŋk] **I.** *vt* parpadear; **to ~ one's eyes** parpadear **II.** *vi* pestañear; **to ~ back one's tears** contener las lágrimas; **she didn't even ~** ni se inmutó **III.** *n* parpadeo *m* ▶ **in the ~ of an eye** en un abrir y cerrar de ojos; **to be on the ~** *inf* estar averiado

blinker ['blɪŋ·kər] *n* AUTO intermitente *m*, direccional *f* Col, Méx; **to turn on the ~** poner el intermitente

blinkered *adj* estrecho, -a de miras

bliss [blɪs] *n* dicha *f;* **marital ~** felicidad *f* conyugal

blissful ['blɪs·fəl] *adj* **1.**(*happy: childhood*) feliz **2.**(*enjoyable: holiday*) maravilloso, -a

blister ['blɪs·tər] **I.** *n* **1.** ANAT ampolla *f* **2.**(*bubble*) burbuja *f* **II.** *vt* ampollar **III.** *vi* ampollarse

blistering *adj* (*very hot*) abrasador(a)

blithering ['blɪð·ər·ɪŋ] *adj* **~ idiot!** ¡imbécil!

blizzard ['blɪz·ərd] *n* ventisca *f*

bloated ['bloʊ·t̬ɪd] *adj* **1.**(*swollen*) hinchado, -a **2.**(*excessive*) excesivo, -a

blob [blab] *n* goterón *m*

block [blak] **I.** *n* **1.**(*solid lump*) bloque *m;* (*of wood*) zoquete *m* **2.**(*city block*) manzana *f;* (*neighborhood*) barrio *m;* (*group of buildings*) manzana *f*, cuadra *f* AmL **3.**(*barrier*) barrera *f;* (*impediment*) obstáculo *m* **4.**(*child's toy*) cubo *m* **5.**(*for executions*) tajo *m;* **to be sent to the ~** ser condenado a ser decapitado **6.** *sl* (*head*) **to knock sb's ~ off** romperle la crisma a alguien; **he's a chip off the old ~** tiene tanto éxito como su padre **7.** SPORTS taco *m* de salida **8.** COMPUT bloque *m* **II.** *vt* **1.**(*road, pipe*) bloquear; (*sb's progress*) obstaculizar **2.** COMPUT **to ~ and copy** seleccionar y copiar

◆ **block off** *vt* cortar

◆ **block out** *vt* **1.**(*censor: name*) suprimir **2.**(*repress: memory*) borrar de su memoria

◆ **block up I.** *vt* cerrar, tapar **II.** *vi* atascarse, atorozarse *AmC;* MED taponarse

blockade [bla·'keɪd] **I.** *n* bloqueo *m* **II.** *vt* bloquear; (*block off*) cortar

blockage ['blak·ɪdʒ] *n* obstrucción *f*

blockhouse ['blak·haʊs] *n* blocao *m*

block letters *n* letras *fpl* mayúsculas de imprenta

blond(e) [bland] **I.** *adj* (*hair*) rubio, -a, güero, -a Méx, Guat, Ven **II.** *n* rubio, -a *m, f*, güero, -a Méx, Guat, Ven

blood [blʌd] *n* sangre *f;* **to be of the same ~** ser parientes ▶ **to have ~ on one's hands** tener las manos manchadas de sangre *fig;* **~ is thicker than water** la sangre siempre tira; **bad ~** mala sangre; **in cold ~** a sangre fría; **her ~ ran cold** se le heló la sangre; **it makes my ~ boil** hace que me hierva la sangre; **to make sb's ~ curdle** hacer que a alguien se le hiele la sangre; **to smell** ~ oler la sangre; **to sweat** ~ sudar tinta; **to be after sb's** ~ beber la sangre a alguien

blood bank n banco m de sangre

bloodbath n baño m de sangre

blood clot n coágulo m de sangre

bloodcurdling adj espeluznante

blood donor n donante mf de sangre

blood group n grupo m sanguíneo

bloodhound n a. fig sabueso m

bloodless ['blʌd·lɪs] adj **1.** (face, lips) con poca vitalidad **2.** (coup) incruento, -a **3.** (emotionless: film, style) soso, -a

blood poisoning n MED septicemia f

blood pressure n tensión f arterial

blood relation n, **blood relative** n pariente, -a m, f consanguíneo, -a

bloodshed n derramamiento m de sangre

bloodshot ['blʌd·ʃat] adj inyectado, -a en sangre; (eyes) rojo, -a

blood sport n (hunting) deporte m cinegético elev

bloodstained ['blʌd·steɪnd] adj manchado, -a de sangre

bloodstock n caballos mpl de raza

bloodstream n corriente f sanguínea

bloodsucker n sanguijuela f

blood sugar n azúcar m de la sangre

blood test n análisis m inv de sangre

bloodthirsty ['blʌd·θɜr·sti] adj sanguinario, -a

blood transfusion n transfusión f de sangre

blood type n grupo m sanguíneo

blood vessel n vaso m sanguíneo

bloody ['blʌd·i] <-ier, -iest> adj **1.** (with blood) ensangrentado, -a; **he has a ~ nose** le sangra la nariz **2.** (battle) sangriento, -a; **he gets a ~ nose** le sangra la nariz

bloom [blum] **I.** n a. fig flor f; **to come into ~** florecer; **in the full ~ of youth** en la flor de la juventud **II.** vi **1.** (produce flowers) florecer **2.** (peak) prosperar

blooming ['blu·mɪŋ] adj floreciente

blossom ['blas·əm] **I.** n flor f; **in ~** en flor; **orange ~** azahar m **II.** vi **1.** (flower) florecer **2.** (mature) madurar

blot [blat] **I.** n **1.** (mark) borrón m **2.** (on sb's reputation) mancha f **II.** vt **1.** (make mark on) emborronar **2.** (dry) secar

blotch [blatʃ] n borrón m; (on the skin) mancha f

blotchy ['blatʃ·i] <-ier, -iest> adj lleno, -a de manchas

blotter ['blat·ər] n hoja f de papel secante

blotting paper n papel m secante

blotto ['blat·oʊ] adj sl **to be ~** estar como una cuba

blouse [blaʊs] n blusa f

blow[1] [bloʊ] n **1.** (hit) golpe m, zuque m Col; (with the fist) puñetazo m; **to come to ~s** llegar a las manos **2.** fig (setback) disgusto m

blow[2] [bloʊ] **I.** <blew, blown> vi **1.** (expel air) soplar **2.** (fuse) fundirse **3.** (tire) reventar ▸ **to ~ hot and cold** cambiar de opinión constante-

mente **II.** vt **1.** (instrument) tocar (un instrumento de viento) **2.** (clear) **to ~ one's nose** sonarse la nariz **3.** (burst: tire) reventar **4.** sl (spend) despilfarrar **5.** (mess up, fail) echar a perder ▸ **it blew my mind!** sl ¡me dejó de piedra!; **to ~ one's top** [o lid] inf salirse de sus casillas

◆**blow away** vt **1.** (wind) arrancar, llevar **2.** sl (kill) liquidar

◆**blow down I.** vi (fall down) caerse **II.** vt (knock down) derribar

◆**blow off** vt quitar soplando; (wind) llevarse; **to ~ off steam** desfogarse

◆**blow out I.** vt (candle) apagar **II.** vi apagarse

◆**blow over** vi (scandal) pasar al olvido; (argument, dispute) calmarse

◆**blow up I.** vi **1.** (storm, gale) levantarse **2.** (bomb) explotar **II.** vt **1.** (fill with air: balloon) inflar **2.** PHOT (enlarge) ampliar **3.** (explode) volar

blow-by-blow adj **a ~ account** una descripción con todo lujo de detalles

blow-dry vt secar con secador

blow dryer n secador m [o secadora f Méx] (de pelo)

blowfly <-ies> n moscarda f

blowgun n (weapon) cerbatana f

blowhole n (in whale, dolphin) orificio m nasal

blowjob n vulg mamada f

blown [bloʊn] vt, vi pp of **blow**

blowout n **1.** (burst tire) reventón m, pinchazo m **2.** sl (party) fiestón m, pachangón m Méx, inf, rumba f Col, inf

blowtorch n soplete m

blowup n PHOT ampliación f

blubber[1] ['blʌb·ər] vi (cry) lloriquear

blubber[2] ['blʌb·ər] n (whale fat) grasa f (de ballena)

bludgeon ['blʌdʒ·ən] **I.** n porra f, tolete m AmC, AmS **II.** vt aporrear

blue [blu] **I.** adj **1.** (color) azul; **light/dark ~** azul claro/oscuro; **pale/deep ~** azul pálido/intenso **2.** (sad) triste; **to feel ~** sentirse triste **II.** n azul m; **sky ~** azul cielo; **the door is painted ~** la puerta está pintada de azul ▸ **out of the ~** cuando menos se espera

bluebell n BOT campánula f azul

blueberry ['blu·ber·i] <-ies> n arándano m

bluebottle n mosca f azul

blue chip adj puntero, -a

blue collar adj (union, background) obrero, -a; (job) manual

blueprint n plano m; (plan of action) programa m

blues [bluz] npl **1.** (sadness) melancolía f **2.** MUS blues m

blue whale n ballena f azul

bluff[1] [blʌf] **I.** vi tirarse un farol **II.** vt engañar **III.** n farol m, bluff m AmL; **to call sb's ~** descubrir a alguien el farol

bluff[2] [blʌf] n (steep bank) risco m; (cliff) acantilado m

bluff³ [blʌf] <-er, -est> *adj* (*in manner*) campechano, -a

bluffer ['blʌf·ər] *n* farolero, -a *m, f*

bluish ['blu·ɪʃ] *adj* azulado, -a

blunder ['blʌn·dər] **I.** *n* error *m* garrafal, embarrada *f AmL* **II.** *vi* **1.** (*make a mistake*) cometer un error garrafal **2.** (*move clumsily*) **to ~ into sth** tropezar con algo

blunt [blʌnt] **I.** *adj* **1.** (*not sharp*) desafilado, -a, pompo, -a *Ecua, Col* **2.** (*direct*) directo, -a **II.** *vt* despuntar; *fig* suavizar

bluntly *adv* sin rodeos; **to put it ~,...** para decirlo sin rodeos,...

bluntness *n* **1.** (*of a blade*) falta *f* de filo **2.** (*directness*) franqueza *f*

blur [blɜr] **I.** *vi* <-rr-> desdibujarse **II.** *vt* <-rr-> desdibujar; (*picture*) desenfocar **III.** *n* (*shape*) contorno *m* borroso; (*memory*) vago recuerdo *m*

blurb [blɜrb] *n* propaganda *f*

blurred [blɜrd] *adj* indistinto, -a; (*photograph, picture*) borroso, -a

blurt out [blɜrt·'aʊt] *vt* soltar

blush [blʌʃ] **I.** *vi* ruborizarse **II.** *n* **1.** (*natural color*) rubor *m* **2.** (*makeup*) colorete *m*, rouge *m Chile*

blusher ['blʌʃ·ər] *n* colorete *m*, rouge *m Chile*

blushing *adj* ruboroso, -a

bluster ['blʌs·tər] **I.** *vi* **1.** (*speak*) bravuconear **2.** (*blow*) rugir **II.** *n* bravuconería *f*

BO [ˌbiˈoʊ] *n abbr of* **body odor** olor *m* corporal

boa ['boʊ·ə] *n* ZOOL boa *f*

boar [bɔr] *n* (*male pig*) cerdo *m* macho; (**wild**) ~ jabalí *m*

board [bɔrd] **I.** *n* **1.** (*wood*) tabla *f* **2.** (*blackboard*) pizarra *f*; (*notice board*) tablero *m* **3.** GAMES tablero *m* **4.** ADMIN consejo *m* de administración, junta *f*; ~ (**of directors**) junta directiva; ~ **of trade/education** Cámara *f* de Comercio; ~ **of education** *organismo encargado de dirigir un distrito escolar* **5.** (*in a hotel*) **room and ~** pensión *f* completa **6.** NAUT **on ~** a bordo ▸ **to sweep the ~** llevarse todos los premios; (*in gambling*) limpiar la mesa; **to take sth on ~** adoptar algo; **to tread the ~s** THEAT salir a escena; **across the ~** en general **II.** *vt* (*get on: ship*) subir a bordo de; (*bus, train*) subir a; (*airplane*) embarcar **III.** *vi* (*stay*) alojarse; (*in school*) estar interno; **to ~ with sb** hospedarse en casa de alguien

◆**board up** *vt* entablar

boarder ['bɔr·dər] *n* (*in a rooming house*) huésped *mf*, inquilino, -a *m, f*; (*at a school*) interno, -a *m, f*

board game *n* juego *m* de mesa

boarding house *n* pensión *f*

boarding pass *n* tarjeta *f* de embarque

boarding school *n* internado *m*

board meeting *n* reunión *f* de la junta directiva

boardroom *n* sala *f* de juntas

boardwalk *n paseo marítimo entablado*

boast [boʊst] **I.** *vi* alardear; **to ~ about/of sth** vanagloriarse sobre/de algo **II.** *vt* (*be proud of*) enorgullecerse de; (*have*); **this house ~s 10 rooms** esta casa cuenta con 10 habitaciones **III.** *n* alarde *m*

boastful ['boʊst·fəl] *adj* fanfarrón, -ona, bocatero, -a *AmL*

boat [boʊt] *n* barco *m*; (*small*) barca *f*, bote *m*; (*large*) buque *m*; **to go by ~** ir en barco ▸ **to be in the same ~** estar en la misma situación; **to miss the ~** perder la oportunidad; **to rock the ~** *inf* hacer olas

boat hook *n* bichero *m*

boathouse *n* cobertizo *m*

boating ['boʊ·tɪŋ] *n* **to go ~** dar un paseo en barca

boatman *n* barquero *m*

boat people *npl* refugiados *mpl* del mar

boat race *n* regata *f*

boatswain ['boʊ·sən] *n* contramaestre *m*

boat train *n* tren *m* que enlaza con un barco

boat trip *n* viaje *m* en barco

bob [bab] <-bb-> **I.** *vi* **to ~ (up and down)** agitarse **II.** *n* **1.** (*hairstyle*) pelo *m* a lo garçon **2.** (*movement*) meneo *m*

bobbin ['bab·ɪn] *n* bobina *f*

bobby pin *n* horquilla *f*, pinza *f Col*

bobsled ['bab·sled] *n* SPORTS bobsleigh *m*

bobtail ['bab·teɪl] *n* **1.** (*docked tail*) cola *f* cortada **2.** (*animal*) animal *m* rabicorto

bode [boʊd] **I.** *vi* **to ~ well/ill** ser una buena/mala señal **II.** *vt* presagiar

bodice ['bad·ɪs] *n* (*of a dress*) canesú *m*

bodily ['bad·əl·i] **I.** *adj* corpóreo, -a; (*harm, injury*) corporal; (*functions, needs*) fisiológico, -a **II.** *adv* (*in person*) en persona; (*as a whole*) en conjunto

body ['bad·i] <-ies> *n* **1.** *a.* ANAT, ASTR, CHEM cuerpo *m*; (*dead*) cadáver *m*; *fig* (*person*); **a cheerful old ~** un tipo alegre **2.** ADMIN, POL unidad *f*; (*governing*) organismo *m*; (*group*) grupo *m*; **in a ~** en bloque **3.** (*amount*) cantidad *f*; (*of water*) masa *f* **4.** AUTO caja *f*, carrocería *f* **5.** MUS caja *f* **6.** (*of wine, sauce*) cuerpo *m* ▸ **to keep ~ and soul together** sobrevivir; **to throw oneself ~ and soul into sth** entregarse a algo en cuerpo y alma; **over my dead ~** ¡por encima de mi cadáver!; **to sell one's ~** prostituirse

body bag *n* bolsa *f* para cadáveres

bodybuilding *n* culturismo *m*

bodyguard *n* guardaespaldas *mf inv*, espaldero *m Ven*

body language *n* lenguaje *m* corporal

body lotion *n* loción *f* corporal

body politic *n* POL estado *m*

body search *n* cacheo *m*

body suit *n* body *m*

bodywork *n* AUTO carrocería *f*

bog [bag] *n* (*wet ground*) ciénaga *f Bol, Col, Ven*; **peat ~** turbera *f*

◆**bog down** <-gg-> *vt* **to get bogged down in sth** quedar atascado en algo; *fig* atrancarse en algo

bogey ['boʊ·gi] *n* (*golf score*) bogey *m*

boggle ['bag·əl] **I.** *vi* quedarse atónito **II.** *vt* **to ~ the mind** ser increíble

boggy ['bag·i] <-ier, -iest> *adj* pantanoso, -a

bogus ['boʊ·gəs] *adj* (*document*) falso, -a; (*argument*) falaz; (*person*) presuntuoso, -a

bohemian [boʊ·'hi·mi·ən] **I.** *n* bohemio, -a *m, f* **II.** *adj* bohemio, -a

boil [bɔɪl] **I.** *vi, vt a. fig* hervir; **a** (**hard/soft**) **~ed egg** un huevo duro/pasado por agua **II.** *n* **1. to bring sth to a ~** calentar algo hasta que hierva; **to be at a ~** estar hirviendo **2.** MED furúnculo *m*

◆ **boil away** *vi* evaporarse

◆ **boil down I.** *vi* reducirse por cocción; *fig;* **it all boils down to...** todo se reduce a... **II.** *vt* reducir

◆ **boil over** *vi* **1.** CULIN rebosarse por el fuego, irse **2.** (*person*) perder el control; (*situation*) estallar

◆ **boil up** *vt* hervir

boiler ['bɔɪ·lər] *n* caldera *f*

boiler room *n* sala *f* de calderas

boiling *adj* **1.** (*liquid*) hirviendo **2.** *fig* (*day, weather*) abrasador(a); (*angry: person*) enfadadísimo, -a; **to be ~ mad** estar furioso; **I am ~** (*feeling hot*) me estoy asando; **it's ~** (**hot**) **today** hace un calor achicharrante

boiling point *n* punto *m* de ebullición; **to reach the ~** *fig* ponerse al rojo vivo

boisterous ['bɔɪ·stər·əs] *adj* **1.** (*person, party*) bullicioso, -a **2.** (*sea*) enfurecido, -a

bold [boʊld] <-er, -est> *adj* **1.** (*brave, audacious*) audaz **2.** (*not shy*) atrevido, -a; (*cheeky*) descarado, -a **3.** (*strong: color*) llamativo, -a **4.** COMPUT, TYPO ~ (**type**) negrita *f;* **in ~** en negrita

boldness *n* audacia *f*

bole [boʊl] *n* (*of tree*) tronco *m*

bolero [bə·'ler·oʊ] <-s> *n* **1.** (*short jacket*) torera *f* **2.** MUS bolero *m*

Bolivia [bə·'lɪv·i·ə] *n* Bolivia *f*

Bolivian [bə·'lɪv·i·ən] **I.** *adj* boliviano, -a **II.** *n* boliviano, -a *m, f*

bolster ['boʊl·stər] **I.** *n* cabezal *m* **II.** *vt* **1.** (*support*) reafirmar **2.** (*encourage*) alentar **3.** (*increase*) levantar

bolt [boʊlt] **I.** *vi* (*run away*) huir **II.** *vt* **1.** (*lock*) echar el pestillo a **2.** (*fasten down*) atornillar **III.** *n* **1.** (*on a door*) pestillo *m* **2.** (*screw*) tornillo *m* **3.** (*of lightning*) rayo *m* **4.** (*roll: of cloth*) rollo *m* **5.** (*arrow*) flecha *f* ▶ **to make a ~ for it** correr hacia algo; **a ~ from the blue** un acontecimiento inesperado **IV.** *adv* **~ upright** rígido, derecho

◆ **bolt down** *vt* (*food*) engullir

bomb [bam] **I.** *n* **1.** (*explosive*) bomba *f;* (*for killing insects*) bote *m* de spray, bomba Col, Méx de spray; **the ~** la bomba *f* atómica **2.** *fig, sl* (*failure*) desastre *m* **II.** *vt* bombardear **III.** *vi sl* estrellarse

bombard [bam·'bard] *vt* bombardear; **to ~ sb**

with questions acribillar a alguien a preguntas

bombardment [bam·'bard·mənt] *n* bombardeo *m*

bombast ['bam·bæst] *n* grandilocuencia *f*

bombastic [bam·'bæs·tɪk] *adj* grandilocuente; (*style*) rimbombante

bomb crater *n* cráter *m* de bomba

bombed [bamd] *adj* **1.** bombardeado, -a **2.** *sl* (*with alcohol*) mamado, -a; (*with drugs*) colocado, -a

bomber ['bam·ər] *n* **1.** AVIAT bombardero *m* **2.** (*terrorist*) terrorista *mf* (que coloca bombas)

bombing *n* **1.** MIL bombardeo *m* **2.** (*by terrorists*) atentado *m* (con bomba)

bombproof *adj* a prueba de bombas

bomb scare *n* alerta *f* de bomba

bombshell ['bam·ʃel] *n* **1.** MIL obús *m* **2.** (*woman*) mujer *f* despampanante **3.** (*surprise*) bombazo *m inf*

bona fide [ˌboʊ·nə·'faɪd] *adj* **1.** (*genuine*) genuino, -a; (*agreement, alibi*) auténtico, -a **2.** (*serious*) serio, -a

bonanza [bə·'næn·zə] *n a. fig* bonanza *f*

bond [band] **I.** *n* **1.** (*connection*) vínculo *m;* (*of friendship, love*) lazo *m;* **to break one's ~** romper sus cadenas *fig* **2.** (*obligation*) obligación *f* **3.** FIN bono *m;* **to place goods in ~** poner mercancías en el depósito de aduanas **4.** LAW garantía *f;* (*bail*) fianza *f* **5.** ~ **s** *liter* (*chains*) cadenas *fpl* **6.** (*joint*) junta *f* **II.** *vt* **1.** (*stick*) pegar **2.** (*unite emotionally*) **to ~** (**together**) vincular **3.** COM depositar bajo fianza **III.** *vi* adherirse

bondage ['ban·dɪdʒ] *n* **1.** *liter* (*slavery*) esclavitud *f* **2.** (*sexual*) bondage *m*

bonded *adj* **1.** COM en depósito aduanero **2.** FIN garantizado, -a por obligación escrita

bonded debt *n* FIN deuda *f* consolidada

bonded warehouse *n* COM depósito *m* de aduana

bondholder *n* FIN titular *mf* de bonos

bone [boʊn] **I.** *n* ANAT hueso *m;* (*of a fish*) espina *f* ▶ ~ **of contention** manzana *f* de la discordia; **to work one's fingers to the ~** trabajar como un esclavo; **close to the ~** fuera de tono; **to cut sth to the ~** reducir algo a lo esencial; **to feel sth in one's ~s** tener un presentimiento de algo; **to make no ~s about sth** no ocultar algo; **to have a ~ to pick with sb** *inf* tener que ajustar cuentas con alguien **II.** *adj* de hueso **III.** *adv* (*as intensifier: dry, lazy, tired*) muy **IV.** *vt* (*chicken, meat*) deshuesar; (*fish*) quitar las espinas a

◆ **bone up for** *vt inf* (*exam*) empollar

bonehead *n inf* estúpido, -a *m, f*

bone marrow *n* médula *f* ósea

bone meal *n* harina *f* de huesos

bonfire ['ban·faɪr] *n* hoguera *f*

bonk [baŋk] *inf* **I.** *vt* (*hit on head*) dar un golpe en la cabeza **II.** *n* golpe *m* en la cabeza

bonkers ['baŋ·kərz] *adj inf* loco, -a; **to go ~** volverse loco

bonnet ['bɑn·ɪt] n (hat) sombrero m; (baby's) gorrito m

bonus ['boʊ·nəs] I. n 1. (money) prima f, abono m AmL; (for Christmas) paga f extraordinaria; **productivity ~ plus** m 2. (advantage) ventaja f II. adj (additional) de regalo

bony ['boʊ·ni] adj <-ier, -iest> 1. (with prominent bones) huesudo, -a; (fish) con muchas espinas 2. (like bones) óseo, -a

boo [bu] I. interj inf bu II. vi abuchear, pifiar Chile, Méx III. vt abuchear; **he was ~ed off the stage** lo abuchearon hasta que abandonó el escenario

boob [bub] n 1. vulg (breast) teta f 2. sl (fool) bobo, -a m, f

boob tube n sl caja f tonta

booby ['bu·bi] n bobo, -a m, f

booby prize n premio m al peor

booby trap n trampa f

booger ['bʊg·ər] n sl 1. (dried mucus) moco m seco 2. (person) desgraciado, -a m, f

book [bʊk] I. n 1. libro m; **the Good Book** la Biblia 2. (of stamps) taco m; (of tickets) talonario m; **~ of matches** ≈ caja f de cerillas [o fósforos] 3. COM, FIN **the ~s** las cuentas; **to cook the ~s** inf amañar las cuentas ▶ **to be a closed ~ (to sb)** ser un misterio (para alguien); **to bring sb to ~** pedir cuentas a alguien; **I know her like a ~** para mí ella es como un libro abierto; **to be able to read sb like a ~** conocer a alguien a fondo; **to throw the ~ at sb** castigar duramente a alguien, cantar las cuarenta [o la tabla] a alguien; **in my ~** en mi opinión; **by the ~** siguiendo las normas II. vt 1. (reserve) reservar 2. (register) fichar 3. (file charges against) **to ~ sb for robbery** levantar cargos contra alguien por robo III. vi reservar ◆ **book up** vt **to be booked up** estar completo

bookbinder n encuadernador(a) m(f)

bookbinding n encuadernación f

bookcase n estantería f de libros

book club n club m de lectores

bookend n sujetalibros m inv

bookie ['bʊk·i] n inf corredor(a) m(f) de apuestas

booking ['bʊk·ɪŋ] n reserva f; **to make/cancel a ~** hacer/cancelar una reserva

bookish ['bʊk·ɪʃ] adj libresco, -a; pej pedante

bookkeeper n contable mf

bookkeeping n contabilidad f

booklet ['bʊk·lɪt] n folleto m

bookmaker n corredor(a) m(f) de apuestas

bookmark n a. COMPUT marcador m

bookplate n ex libris m

book review n crítica f de libros

book reviewer n crítico, -a m, f de libros

bookseller n (person) librero, -a m, f; (shop) librería f

bookshelf <-shelves> n estante m

bookshop n librería f

bookstore n librería f

bookworm n ratón m de biblioteca

boom¹ [bum] ECON I. vi estar en auge II. n boom m III. adj en alza; **a ~ time** un período de prosperidad; **a ~ town** una ciudad próspera

boom² [bum] I. n (sound) estruendo m II. vi **to ~ (out)** tronar; (voice) resonar III. vt tronar

boom³ [bum] n 1. NAUT botavara f 2. (floating barrier) barrera f 3. (for a microphone) jirafa f

boom box n minicadena f, grabadora f Méx, Col

boomerang ['bu·mə·ræŋ] I. n bumerán m II. vi **it ~ed on her/him** le salió el tiro por la culata inf

boon [bun] n beneficio m; **to be a ~ (to sb)** ser de gran ayuda (para alguien); **~ companion** liter amigo, -a m, f del alma

boondocks n pl **the ~** el quinto pino, la conchinchina Col, la chingada Méx

boonies n pl, sl s. **boondocks**

boor [bʊr] n grosero, -a m, f

boorish ['bʊr·ɪʃ] adj grosero, -a

boost [bust] I. n 1. (lift) **to give sb a ~** subir a alguien, dar un impulso a alguien 2. (increase) **to give a ~ to sth, to give sth a ~** estimular algo; **a ~ in sales** un impulso m en las ventas; (incentive) incentivo m II. vt 1. (help go higher) subir, dar un impulso 2. (increase) aumentar, incrementar; (morale) reforzar; (process) estimular 3. inf (promote) promover; (image, ego) potenciar

booster ['bu·stər] n 1. (improvement) mejora f 2. MED vacuna f de recuerdo

booster rocket n TECH cohete m propulsor

booster seat n AUTO asiento m infantil de seguridad

boot [but] I. n 1. (footwear) bota f; **ankle ~** botín m; **rubber ~** bota f de caucho, katiuska f 2. inf (kick) patada f, puntapié m; fig (dismissal from job); **to get the ~** ser despedido; **to give sb the ~** echar a alguien 3. COMPUT arranque m, inicialización f; **warm/cold ~** arranque en frío/en caliente ▶ **to be too big for one's ~s** inf tener muchos humos; **to lick sb's ~s** hacer la pelota a alguien, lambonear a alguien Col; **to shake in one's ~s** inf temblar de miedo II. vt 1. (kick) dar un puntapié a 2. fig, sl (fire from job) echar 3. COMPUT arrancar ▶ **to ~** además, por si fuera poco ◆ **boot out** vt inf poner de patitas en la calle

bootblack ['but·blæk] n limpiabotas mf inv

boot-cut adj (jeans) de campana, de pata de elefante

bootee ['bu·ti] n patuco m

booth [buð] n 1. (cubicle) cubículo m; (telephone) cabina f; (polling) cabina f 2. (at a fair, market) caseta f

bootlace ['but·leɪs] n cordón m

bootleg ['but·leg] <-gg-> adj 1. (alcohol, cigarettes) de contrabando 2. (recording, software) pirata

bootlicker ['but·lɪk·ər] n inf lameculos mf inv, olfa mf Arg, Par, Urug

booty ['bu·ti] n botín m

booze [buz] I. n sl bebida f alcohólica; **to be**

on the ~ darle a la bebida **II.** *vi sl* empinar el codo, chupar *AmL*

boozer ['buˑzər] *n sl* borrachín, -ina *m, f*

boozy ['buˑzi] <-ier, -iest> *adj sl* borrachín, -ina

border ['bɔrˑdər] **I.** *n* **1.** (*between states, countries*) frontera *f* **2.** (*edge, boundary*) borde *m* **3.** FASHION cenefa *f* **4.** (*in a garden*) arriate *m* **II.** *adj* fronterizo, -a **III.** *vt* limitar con
 ◆ **border on** *vt* **1.** (*share border with*) limitar con **2.** *fig* rayar en

bordering *adj* limítrofe

borderland ['bɔrˑdərˑlænd] *n* zona *f* fronteriza

borderline ['bɔrˑdərˑlaɪn] **I.** *n* frontera *f* **II.** *adj* (*candidate, case*) dudoso, -a

bore¹ [bɔr] **I.** *n* **1.** (*thing*) aburrimiento *m;* (*task*) lata *f,* fastidio *m;* **what a ~!** ¡qué lata! **2.** (*person*) pesado, -a *m, f.* <bored> *vt* aburrir; **to ~ sb to death** *inf* aburrir a alguien como una ostra

bore² [bɔr] **I.** *n* (*of a pipe*) alma *f;* (*of a gun*) calibre *m* **II.** *vt* perforar; **to ~ a hole** abrir un agujero

bore³ [bɔr] *pp of* bear

bored *adj* aburrido, -a

boredom ['bɔrˑdəm] *n* aburrimiento *m*

boric ['bɔrˑɪk] *adj* bórico, -a; **~ acid** ácido bórico

boring ['bɔrˑɪŋ] *adj* aburrido, -a, cansador(a) *Arg, Chile, Urug,* fome *Arg, Chile;* **to find sth ~** encontrar algo pesado

born [bɔrn] *adj* **1.** (*brought into life*) nacido, -a; **to be ~** nacer; **where were you ~?** ¿dónde naciste?; **he was ~ in (the year)** 1975 nació en (el año) 1975; **he was ~ blind** es ciego de nacimiento **2.** (*ability*) nato, -a; (*quality, sympathy*) innato, -a; **to be ~ to do sth** haber nacido para hacer algo ► **I wasn't ~ yesterday** *inf* no nací ayer

born-again *adj* vuelto, -a a nacer; **~ Christian** cristiano convertido

borne [bɔrn] *pt of* bear

borough ['bɜrˑoʊ] *n* municipio *m*

borrow ['barˑoʊ] *vt* **1.** (*be given temporarily*) tomar prestado; (*ask for*) pedir prestado; **may I ~ your bag?** ¿me prestas tu bolso? **2.** MATH llevarse **3.** LING tomar

borrower *n* prestatario, -a *m, f*

borrowing *n* préstamo *m*

Bosnia ['bazˑniˑə] *n* Bosnia *f*

Bosnia-Herzegovina ['bazˑniˑəˌhertˑsəˑgoʊ·viˑnə] *n* Bosnia *f* Herzegovina

Bosnian ['bazˑniˑən] **I.** *adj* bosnio, -a **II.** *n* bosnio, -a *m, f*

bosom ['bʊzˑəm] *n* **1.** (*chest*) pecho *m* **2.** *fig* seno *m;* **in the ~ of one's family** en el seno de su familia

bosom buddy *n* amigo *m* del alma

boss [bas] **I.** *n* **1.** (*supervisor*) jefe, -a *m, f;* (*owner*) patrón, -ona *m, f;* **to be one's own ~** ser su propio jefe **2.** (*bossy person*) mandón, -ona *m, f* **II.** *vt inf* **to ~ sb around** mangonear a alguien

bossy ['baˑsi] <-ier, -iest> *adj* mandón, -ona

> **i** El **Boston Tea Party** (Motín del Té de Boston), ocurrido en 1773, fue un acto de desafío americano contra el control británico sobre las colonias en América. Varios colonos, entre ellos Samuel Adams y Paul Revere, se disfrazaron de nativos americanos, abordaron los barcos ingleses y arrojaron al agua cientos de cajas de té para protestar contra los impuestos cobrados por los ingleses a las colonias sin permitir representación americana en el gobierno. Éste fue uno de los sucesos cruciales que condujeron a la guerra revolucionaria de independencia en la que Estados Unidos se emancipó de Inglaterra.

botanical [bəˑ'tænˑɪˑkəl] *adj* botánico, -a

botanist ['batˑənˑɪst] *n* botánico, -a *m, f*

botany ['batˑənˑi] *n* botánica *f*

botch [batʃ] **I.** *n* chapuza *f;* **to make a ~ of sth** hacer una chapuza de algo **II.** *vt* **to ~ sth (up)** chapucear algo

botch-up *s.* botch I.

both [boʊθ] **I.** *adj, pron* los dos, las dos, ambos, ambas; **~ of them** ellos dos, ellas dos; **~ of us** nosotros dos, nosotras dos; **~ (the) brothers** los dos hermanos; **on ~ sides** en ambos lados **II.** *adv* **~ Cathy and Julie** tanto Cathy como Julie; **to be ~ sad and pleased** estar a la vez triste y satisfecho

bother ['baðˑər] **I.** *n* molestia *f,* friega *f AmL;* **not to want to be a ~** no querer molestar; **it is not worth the ~** no vale la pena **II.** *vi* molestarse; **to (not) ~ to do sth** (no) molestarse en hacer algo; **why ~?** ¿para qué molestarse? **III.** *vt* **1.** (*annoy*) molestar **2.** (*worry*) preocupar; **he doesn't seem to be ~ed by...** no parece que le preocupe...; **what ~s me is...** lo que me preocupa es... **3.** (*give pain: body part, organ*) doler

bothersome ['baðˑərˑsəm] *adj* molesto, -a, tequioso, -a *AmC,* espeso, -a *Perú, Ven*

Botswana [ˌbatˑ'swaˑnə] *n* Botsuana *f*

Botswanan [ˌbatˑ'swaˑnən] **I.** *adj* botsuano, -a **II.** *n* botsuano, -a *m, f*

bottle ['batˑəl] **I.** *n* **1.** (*container*) botella *f;* (*of ink, perfume*) frasco *m;* (*baby's*) biberón *m* **2.** *inf* (*alcohol*) **the ~** la bebida; **to hit the ~** empinar el codo **II.** *vt* embotellar; *fig* (*emotions*) reprimir

bottlebrush *n* limpiabotellas *m inv*

bottled ['batˑəld] *adj* embotellado, -a; (*beer, gas*) de botella

bottle-feeding *n* alimentación *f* con biberón

bottle green *adj* verde botella

bottleneck ['batˑəlˑnek] **I.** *n a. fig* cuello *m* de botella **II.** *vi* (*traffic*) embotellarse, trancarse *Col*

bottle opener *n* abrebotellas *m inv*

bottom ['baṭ·əm] I. *n* 1. (*of sea, street, glass*) fondo *m*; (*of chair*) asiento *m*; (*of stairs, page*) pie *m*; **to touch ~** (*reach bottom of water*) llegar al fondo; *fig* tocar fondo 2. (*lower part*) parte *f* inferior; **from top to ~** de arriba (a) abajo 3. (*buttocks*) trasero *m* ► **from the ~ of one's heart** de todo corazón; **~s up!** ¡al centro y pa'dentro! *inf*; **to get to the ~ of sth** llegar al fondo de algo; **at ~** en el fondo; **to be at the ~ of sth** ser el motivo de algo II. *adj* (*lower*) más bajo; **the ~ half of society** la clase media-baja; **the ~ end of the table** la mitad inferior de la mesa

bottomless ['baṭ·əm·lɪs] *adj* 1. (*without limit*) sin fondo 2. (*very deep*) infinito, -a; **a ~ pit** *fig* un pozo sin fondo

bottom line *n* **the ~** *fig* lo fundamental

botulism ['batʃ·ə·lɪz·əm] *n* botulismo *m*

bough [baʊ] *n liter* rama *f*

bought [bɔt] *vt pt of* **buy**

boulder ['boʊl·dər] *n* roca *f*

boulevard ['bʊl·ə·vard] *n* bulevar *m*

bounce [baʊnts] I. *vi* 1. (*rebound*) (re)botar; **to ~ against sth** botar contra algo 2. (*jump or spring up and down*) dar brincos 3. *inf* COM ser devuelto II. *vt* 1. (*cause to rebound*) hacer (re)botar; **to ~ a baby** hacer el caballito a un niño; **to ~ an idea off sb** pedir la opinión a alguien; **to ~ sb into doing sth** presionar a alguien para que haga algo 2. *inf* COM **to ~ a check** devolver un cheque III. *n* 1. (*rebound*) (re)bote *m* 2. (*spring*) bote *m* 3. (*vitality*) vitalidad *f*; (*energy*) energía *f* 4. *sl* **to give sb the ~** poner a alguien de patitas en la calle

◆ **bounce back** *vi* recuperarse

bouncer ['baʊn·tsər] *n sl* gorila *m*

bouncing *adj* robusto, -a

bouncy ['baʊn·tsi] *adj* 1. (*ball*) que rebota 2. (*lively*) animado, -a

bound[1] [baʊnd] I. *vi* 1. (*leap*) saltar 2. (*bounce: ball*) botar, rebotar *AmL* II. *n* salto *m*; **with one ~** de un salto; **in leaps and ~s** a pasos agigantados

bound[2] [baʊnd] *vt* (*confine*) **to be ~ed by sth** estar rodeado por algo

bound[3] [baʊnd] *adj* (*showing direction*) **to be ~ for...** ir rumbo a...; **where is this ship ~ for?** ¿adónde se dirige este barco?; **north/south-bound traffic** tráfico que va hacia el norte/sur

bound[4] [baʊnd] I. *pt, pp of* **bind** II. *adj* 1. (*sure*) **she's ~ to come** seguro que viene; **it's ~ to be cheap** seguro que es barato; **it was ~ to happen sooner or later** tarde o temprano tenía que suceder 2. (*obliged*) **to be ~ to do sth** estar obligado a hacer algo

boundary ['baʊn·dri] <-ies> *n* 1. *a. fig* (*line*) límite *m*; **to blur the boundaries** *fig* desdibujar los límites 2. (*border*) frontera *f*; **to cross a ~** cruzar una frontera; **to mark a ~ (between two places)** establecer una frontera (entre dos lugares) 3. SPORTS **boundaries** límites *mpl* del terreno de juego

boundless ['baʊnd·lɪs] *adj* (*love, patience*) sin límites; (*energy*) ilimitado, -a, inagotable; (*universe*) infinito, -a

bounds [baʊndz] *n pl a.* SPORTS límites *mpl*; **to know no ~** no conocer límites; **to be beyond the ~ of possibility** no ser posible; **to be outside the ~ of acceptable behavior** estar lejos de ser un comportamiento aceptable; **this area is out of ~ to civilians** los civiles tienen prohibido entrar en esta zona; **within ~** dentro de ciertos límites; **to be within the ~ of the law** estar dentro de los límites legales

bounty ['baʊn·ti] <-ies> *n* 1. (*reward*) recompensa *f* 2. (*gift*) regalo *m* 3. *liter* (*generosity*) munificencia *f*

bouquet [boʊ·'keɪ] *n* 1. (*of flowers*) ramo *m* 2. (*smell, aroma*) aroma *m*; (*of wine*) buqué *m*

bourbon ['bɜr·bən] *n* bourbon *m*

bourgeois ['bʊr·ʒwa] *adj* burgués, -esa

bout [baʊt] *n* 1. SPORTS (*in boxing, wrestling*) combate *m*; (*in fencing*) asalto *m* 2. (*of illness*) ataque *m*; **~ of coughing** ataque *m* de tos; **drinking ~** borrachera *f*

boutique [bu·'tik] *n* boutique *f*

boutonniere [bu·tə·'nir] *n* flor *f* de ojal

bovine ['boʊ·vaɪn] *adj* 1. (*of cows*) bovino, -a 2. *fig* (*stupid*) tonto, -a

bow[1] [boʊ] *n* 1. (*weapon*) *a.* MUS arco *m* 2. (*knot*) lazo *m*, moño *m AmL*, moña *f Urug*, rosa *f Chile*

bow[2] [baʊ] *n* NAUT proa *f*

bow[3] [baʊ] I. *vi* 1. (*as greeting*) hacer una reverencia; *fig* ceder; **to ~ to sb** hacer una reverencia ante alguien 2. (*yield*) **to ~ to sth** someterse a algo ► **to ~ and scrape** hacer la pelota, hacer la barba *Méx* II. *vt* (*one's head*) inclinar, agachar; (*body*) doblegar III. *n* reverencia *f*, venia *f CSur, Col*, caravana *f Méx*; **to take a ~** recibir un aplauso

◆ **bow out** *vi* retirarse

bowdlerize ['boʊd·lə·raɪz] *vt* expurgar

bowel ['baʊ·əl] *n* 1. MED intestino *m* grueso 2. **~s** (*of a ship*) las entrañas *fpl* (de un barco)

bowel movement *n* evacuación *f* (intestinal); **to have a ~** hacer de vientre, mover el vientre *RíoPl*

bowl[1] [boʊl] *n* 1. (*dish*) bol *m*; (*for soup*) plato *m* hondo; **fruit ~** frutero *m*, frutera *f CSur*; **salad ~** ensaladera *f* 2. (*of toilet*) taza *f* (*for washing*) palangana *f*; (*of pipe*) cazoleta *f*; (*of fountain*) pila *f* 3. (*stadium*) estadio *m* 4. GEO (*hollow*) hondonada *f*

bowl[2] [boʊl] SPORTS I. *vi* 1. (*go bowling*) jugar a los bolos 2. (*throw bowling ball*) lanzar la bola (de bolos) II. *vt* lanzar; **to ~ a strike/spare** conseguir un pleno/semipleno; **to ~ a 7** tirar 7 III. *n* (*throw of the ball*) bola *f*, bocha *f*

◆ **bowl out** *vt* eliminar

◆ **bowl over** *vt* 1. (*knock over*) tumbar 2. (*astonish*) dejar atónito; **to be bowled over** estar desconcertado

bow-legged [,boʊ·'legd] *adj* (*person*) patizambo, -a, cascorvo, -a *Col*; (*table*) de patas

arqueadas
bowler ['boʊ·lər] *n* **1.** (*in bowling*) jugador(a) *m(f)* de bolos **2.** (*hat*) bombín *m*
bowling *n* (*game*) bolos *mpl*
bowling alley *n* bolera *f*
bowling ball *n* bola *f* de bolos
bowman ['boʊ·mən] *n* arquero *m*
bowstring ['boʊ·strɪŋ] *n* MUS cuerda *f* del arco
bow tie *n* pajarita *f*, corbatín *m Col*, moñita *f Urug*
bow window *n* mirador *m*
box[1] [baks] **I.** *vi* SPORTS boxear **II.** *vt* **1.** SPORTS boxear con [*o* contra] **2.** to ~ sb's ears dar un sopapo a alguien **III.** *n* sopapo *m;* **to give sb a ~ on the ears** dar un sopapo a alguien
box[2] [baks] **I.** *n* **1.** (*container*) caja *f;* **card-board ~** caja de cartón; **tool ~** caja de herramientas **2.** (*rectangular space*) casilla *f;* (*in soccer, baseball*) área *f;* (**penalty**) ~ (*in soccer*) área (de castigo); (*in ice hockey*) banquillo *m* **3.** *pej* (*small space*) agujero *m;* **their new house is just a ~** su nueva casa es un agujero **4.** THEAT palco *m;* (*booth*) cabina *f* **5.** *inf* (*television*) **the ~** la caja tonta **6.** (*mailbox*) buzón *m* **7.** COMPUT **dialog ~** cuadro *m* de diálogo ▸ **to think outside of the ~** tener ideas innovadoras **II.** *vt* poner en una caja
◆ **box in** *vt* acorralar; **to ~ a car** cerrar el paso a un coche; **to feel boxed in** *fig* sentirse limitado
◆ **box off** *vt* compartimentar
◆ **box up** *vt* poner en una caja
boxer ['bak·sər] *n* **1.** (*person*) boxeador(a) *m(f)* **2.** (*dog*) bóxer *mf*
boxer shorts *npl* bóxer *m*
boxing ['bak·sɪŋ] *n* boxeo *m*, box *m AmL*
boxing glove *n* guante *m* de boxeo
boxing match *n* combate *m* de boxeo
boxing ring *n* cuadrilátero *m*
box lunch *n* comida *f* en una tartera [*o* en una lonchera *f Col, Méx*]
box office *n* taquilla *f*, boletería *f AmL*
boy [bɔɪ] **I.** *n* **1.** (*child*) niño *m* **2.** (*young man*) chico *m*, muchacho *m*, chamaco, -a *m, f Méx*, pibe *m Arg;* **country/city ~** chico *m* de campo/ciudad **3.** (*son*) hijo *m*, chico *m* **4.** *pej* (*servant*) criado *m*, mozo *m* **5.** (*boyfriend*) novio *m* ▸ **the old ~ network** el amiguismo, la rosca *Col;* **the ~s in blue** *inf* la poli; **~s will be ~s** así son los chicos [*o* niños] **II.** *interj* (oh) ~! ¡vaya!
boycott ['bɔɪ·kat] **I.** *vt* boicotear **II.** *n* boicot *m*
boyfriend ['bɔɪ·frend] *n* novio *m*
boyhood ['bɔɪ·hʊd] *n* niñez *f*
boyish ['bɔɪ·ɪʃ] *adj* (*woman*) de chico; (*enthusiasm*) de niño
Boy Scout *n* boy scout *m*
Bq PHYS *abbr of* **becquerel** Bq
bra [bra] *n* sujetador *m*, brasier *m Col, Méx*, corpiño *m RíoPl*
brace [breɪs] **I.** *vt* **1.** (*prepare*) to ~ oneself for sth prepararse para algo **2.** (*support: wall*) reforzar **II.** *n* **1.** ~s (*for teeth*) aparato(s) *m(pl)*

2. (*for the back*) aparato *m* ortopédico
3. (*clamp*) abrazadera *f;* (*for drilling*) refuerzo *m* **4.** TYPO (*curly brackets*) llave *f*
bracelet ['breɪs·lɪt] *n* pulsera *f*
bracket ['bræk·ɪt] **I.** *n* **1.** *pl* TYPO (*round*) paréntesis *m inv;* **angle ~** corchete *m;* **curly ~** llave *f;* **square ~** corchete *m* agudo; **in ~s** entre paréntesis **2.** (*category*) categoría *f;* **age ~** grupo *m* etario *elev;* **income ~** nivel *m* de ingresos; **tax ~** banda *f* impositiva **3.** (*for a shelf*) soporte *m* **II.** *vt* **1.** TYPO poner entre paréntesis **2.** (*include*) agrupar; **to ~ sb with sb else** equiparar a alguien con alguien
brackish ['bræk·ɪʃ] *adj* salobre
brag [bræg] <-gg-> **I.** *vi* fanfarronear; **to ~ about sth** alardear de algo **II.** *vt* **to ~ that...** jactarse de que... **III.** *n* **1.** (*instance*) chulería *f* **2.** (*person*) fanfarrón, -ona *m, f*
braid [breɪd] **I.** *n* **1.** (*in hair*) trenza *f*, chongo *m Méx*, chapeca *f Arg* **2.** FASHION galón *m* **II.** *vt*, *vi* (*hair*) trenzar
Braille [breɪl] *n* braille *m*
brain [breɪn] **I.** *n* **1.** (*organ*) cerebro *m* **2.** ~s (*substance*) sesos *mpl* **3.** (*intelligence*) cabeza *f;* **to have ~s** ser inteligente **4.** *inf* (*intelligent person*) cerebro *m*, lumbrera *f;* **the best ~s** los mejores cerebros ▸ **to beat one's ~s out** *inf* estrujarse el cerebro; **to blow sb's ~s out** *inf* levantar la tapa de los sesos a alguien; **to have sth on the ~** *inf* estar obsesionado con algo; **to pick sb's ~s** *inf* hacer preguntas a alguien; **to rack one's ~** devanarse los sesos **II.** *vt sl* romper la crisma a
brainchild *n* creación *f*
brain damage *n* lesión *f* cerebral
brain-dead *adj* **1.** MED clínicamente muerto, -a **2.** *fig* subnormal
brain death *n* muerte *f* clínica [*o* cerebral]
brain drain *n* fuga *f* de cerebros
brainless ['breɪn·lɪs] *adj* estúpido, -a
brain scan *n* exploración *f* cerebral mediante escáner
brainstorm ['breɪn·stɔrm] **I.** *vi* hacer un brainstorming **II.** *vt* hacer un brainstorming sobre [*o* de] **III.** *n* (*great idea*) idea *f* brillante
brainstorming ['breɪn·ˌstɔr·mɪŋ] *n* brainstorming *m*
brain trust *n* grupo *m* de peritos
brain tumor *n* tumor *m* cerebral
brainwash ['breɪn·waʃ] *vt* lavar el cerebro a
brainwashing ['breɪn·waʃ·ɪŋ] *n* lavado *m* de cerebro
brainwave ['breɪn·weɪv] *n* *inf* **1.** ANAT onda *f* cerebral **2.** *fig* idea *f* brillante, lamparazo *m Col;* **she had a ~** tuvo una idea genial, tuvo un lamparazo *Col*, se le prendió el foco *Méx*, se le prendió la lamparilla *RíoPl*
brainwork *n* trabajo *m* intelectual
brainy ['breɪ·ni] <-ier, -iest> *adj* inteligente
braise [breɪz] *vt* estofar
brake [breɪk] **I.** *n* freno *m;* **to put on the ~s** frenar; **to put a ~ on sth** *fig* poner freno a algo **II.** *vi* frenar

brake block *n* pastilla *f* del freno
brake fluid *n* AUTO líquido *m* de frenos
brake shoe *n* AUTO zapata *f* del freno
braking *n* frenado *m*
braking distance *n* distancia *f* de frenado
bramble ['bræm·bəl] *n* (*bush*) zarza *f*
bran [bræn] *n* salvado *m*
branch [bræntʃ] **I.** *n* **1.** (*of a tree*) rama *f* **2.** (*of a railroad, river, road*) ramal *m* **3.** (*office: of a company, bank, library*) sucursal *f*; (*of a union, government department*) delegación *f* **4.** (*subdivision*) rama *f*; **the ~es of learning** las ramas del saber **II.** *vi* **1.** (*tree*) echar ramas **2.** (*river, road*) bifurcarse
 ◆**branch off** *vi* **1.** (*start*) bifurcarse **2.** (*digress*) **to ~ from a subject** salirse de un tema
 ◆**branch out** *vi* diversificarse; **to ~ on one's own** establecerse por su cuenta
branch office *n* sucursal *f*
brand [brænd] **I.** *n* **1.** COM marca *f* **2.** *fig* clase *f*; **do you like his ~ of humor?** ¿te gusta su tipo de humor? **3.** (*mark*) hierro *m* **II.** *vt* **1.** (*label*) **to ~ sth/sb (as) sth** tachar algo/a alguien de algo; **to ~ sb a liar** tildar a alguien de mentiroso **2.** (*cattle, slave*) marcar con hierro candente
brandish ['bræn·dɪʃ] *vt* blandir
brand name *n* marca *f*
brand-new *adj inv* completamente nuevo, -a; **~ baby** recién nacido *m*
brandy ['bræn·di] <-ies> *n* brandy *m;* **French ~** coñac *m*
brash [bræʃ] *adj* **1.** (*cocky: attitude*) chulo, -a **2.** (*gaudy: colors*) chillón, -ona
brass [bræs] *n* **1.** (*metal*) latón *m* **2.** + *sing/pl vb* MUS **the ~** los metales **3.** (*plaque: in a church*) placa *f* conmemorativa (*de latón*)
brass band *n* banda *f* de música, orfeón *m Chile*
brass plate *n* placa *f* conmemorativa
brass section *n* MUS **the ~** los metales
brassware *n* latonería *f*
brassy ['bræs·i] <-ier, -iest> *adj* **1.** (*of brass*) de latón; **~ color** color *m* dorado **2.** (*voice*) estridente **3.** (*cocky*) ordinario, -a
brat [bræt] *n inf* mocoso, -a *m, f;* **he is a spoiled ~** es un niño mimado, es un sute *Col, Ven*
bravado [brə·'va·dou] *n* bravuconada *f*
brave [breɪv] **I.** *adj* valiente **II.** *vt* afrontar **III.** *n* (*Native American warrior*) guerrero , -a *m, f* piel roja
bravery ['breɪ·və·ri] *n* valentía *f*
brawl [brɔl] **I.** *n* pelea *f*, bulla *f AmL* **II.** *vi* pelearse
brawling *n* alboroto *m*
brawn [brɔn] *n* (*physical strength*) fuerza *f* muscular
brawny ['brɔ·ni] <-ier, -iest> *adj* musculoso, -a
bray [breɪ] **I.** *vi* (*donkey*) rebuznar; **~ing laugh** risa *f* estridente **II.** *n* rebuzno *m*
brazen ['breɪ·zən] *adj* descarado, -a; **~ lie** mentira *f* descarada
 ◆**brazen out** *vt* **to brazen it out** defenderse con argumentos descarados
brazier ['breɪ·zər] *n* brasero *m*
Brazil [brə·'zɪl] *n* Brasil *m*
Brazilian [brə·'zɪl·jən] **I.** *n* brasileño, -a *m, f* **II.** *adj* brasileño, -a
Brazil nut *n* coquito *m* del Brasil
breach [britʃ] **I.** *n* **1.** (*infraction: of a regulation*) infracción *f*, violación *f*; (*of an agreement*) ruptura *f*; (*of confidence*) abuso *m*; (*of a contract*) incumplimiento *m*; **to be in ~ of the law** infringir la ley **2.** (*opening*) brecha *f* **II.** *vt* **1.** (*break: law*) infringir, violar; (*agreement*) romper; (*contract*) incumplir; (*security*) poner en peligro **2.** (*infiltrate*) abrir una brecha en
breach of promise *n* incumplimiento *m* de una promesa
breach of the peace *n* alteración *f* del orden público
bread [bred] **I.** *n* **1.** pan *m;* **a loaf of ~** una barra *f* de pan, un pan *m* **2.** *sl* (*money*) pasta *f* ▸**to cast one's ~ upon the waters** *form* hacer el bien sin mirar a quién; **to earn one's (daily) ~** *form* ganarse el pan (de cada día) **II.** *vt* CULIN (*fish, chicken*) empanar, rebozar
bread and butter *n* sustento *m;* **~ issues** asuntos *mpl* básicos
breadbasket *n* **1.** (*container*) panera *f* **2.** (*region*) granero *m*
breadbox *n* panera *f*
breadcrumb *n* **1.** (*small fragment*) miga *f* (de pan) **2.** **~s** CULIN pan *m* rallado
breadth [bredθ] *n* **1.** anchura *f*; **to be 5 feet in ~** tener 5 pies de ancho **2.** *fig* amplitud *f*
breadwinner *n* sostén *m* de la familia
break [breɪk] **I.** *n* **1.** (*crack, gap*) grieta *f* **2.** (*escape*) fuga *f*; **to make a ~ for/towards sth** correr hacia algo **3.** (*interruption*) interrupción *f*; (*commercial*) descanso *m* **4.** (*rest period*) descanso *m;* **coffee/lunch ~** pausa del café/para comer **5.** (*vacation*) vacaciones *fpl;* **spring ~** SCHOOL semana *f* de vacaciones durante la evaluación de primavera en Estados Unidos **6.** (*first light*) **the ~ of day** [*o* **dawn**] el amanecer **7.** (*divergence*) ruptura *f;* **a ~ from sth** un descanso de algo **8.** (*opportunity*) oportunidad *f* **9.** SPORTS rotura *f* de servicio ▸**to make a clean ~** cortar por lo sano; **give me a ~!** ¡déjame en paz! **II.** <broke, broken> *vt* **1.** (*shatter, damage, fracture*) romper; **to ~ sth (in)to pieces** hacer algo añicos **2.** (*interrupt: circuit*) cortar; (*silence*) romper **3.** (*put an end to: deadlock, impasse*) salir de; (*peace, silence*) romper; (*strike*) poner fin a; (*give up: habit*) dejar; **to ~ sb of a habit** quitar a alguien una costumbre **4.** (*in tennis*) **to ~ sb's service** romper el servicio a alguien **5.** (*violate: agreement*) incumplir; (*date*) no acudir a; (*promise*) romper; (*treaty*) violar **6.** (*decipher: code*) descifrar **7.** (*make public*) revelar **8.** (*tell*) decir; **to ~ the news**

to **sb** dar la noticia a alguien; ~ **it to me gently!** *iron* ¡dímelo con tacto! **9.** (*make change for*) cambiar; **to ~ a bill** cambiar un billete **10.** **to ~ a sweat** romper a sudar; *fig* (*become nervous*) crisparse **11.** MIL **to ~ formation** romper filas **III.** <broke, broken> *vi* **1.** (*arm, leg*) romperse; (*chair, glass*) romperse; (*TV, toy*) estropearse; **to ~ into pieces** hacerse añicos **2.** (*interrupt*) **shall we ~ for lunch?** ¿paramos para comer? **3.** (*hit the shore: wave*) romper **4.** (*change of voice*) **the boy's voice is ~ing** la voz del niño está cambiando; (*under strain*); **her voice broke (with emotion)** se le quebró la voz (de la emoción) **5.** (*come to end: fever*) desaparecer **6.** METEO (*weather*) cambiar; (*dawn, day*) romper, despuntar **7.** (*in pool, snooker*) abrir el juego **8.** (*giving birth*) **her water broke on the way to hospital** rompió aguas de camino al hospital ▸ **to ~ even** salir sin ganar ni perder; **to ~ free** liberarse; **to ~ loose** soltarse
◆ **break away** *vi* (*piece, from friends*) desprenderse; (*boat*) soltarse; POL (*faction, region*) escindirse
◆ **break down I.** *vi* **1.** (*stop working*) dejar de funcionar; (*car, machine*) averiarse **2.** (*marriage*) romperse; (*negotiations*) fracasar **3.** (*physically, psychologically*) derrumbarse **4.** (*decompose*) descomponerse **II.** *vt* **1.** (*door*) echar abajo **2.** (*opposition, resistance*) acabar con **3.** CHEM descomponer **4.** (*separate into parts: sentence*) separar, dividir; (*process*) dividir
◆ **break in I.** *vi* **1.** (*enter: burglar*) entrar (para robar) **2.** (*interrupt*) interrumpir; **to ~ on sb** interrumpir a alguien **II.** *vt* **1.** (*make comfortable: shoes*) ablandar **2.** AUTO hacer el rodaje de **3.** (*tame: animal*) domar
◆ **break into** *vi* **1.** (*enter: car*) entrar (para robar) **2.** (*start doing*) **to ~ laughter/tears** echarse a reír/llorar; **to ~ song** ponerse a cantar **3.** (*get involved in: business*) introducirse en
◆ **break off I.** *vt* **1.** (*detach*) partir **2.** (*end: relationship*) romper **II.** *vi* **1.** (*become detached*) desprenderse **2.** (*stop speaking*) callarse
◆ **break out** *vi* **1.** (*escape*) escaparse; (*of a prison*) fugarse **2.** (*begin: war, storm, laughing*) estallar **3.** **to ~ in a sweat** empezar a sudar; **she broke out in a rash** le salió un sarpullido; **he broke out in spots** le salieron granos
◆ **break through I.** *vi* penetrar; (*sun*) salir **II.** *vt* atravesar; **to ~ a crowd** abrirse paso entre una multitud
◆ **break up I.** *vt* **1.** (*end: meeting, strike*) terminar; **break it up, you two!** *inf* ¡vosotros dos, basta ya! **2.** (*split up: coalition, union*) disolver; (*collection*) dividir; (*family*) separar; (*gang, monopoly, cartel*) desarticular **3.** (*make laugh*) **to break sb up** hacer reír a alguien **II.** *vi* **1.** (*end a relationship*) separarse

2. (*come to an end: marriage*) fracasar; (*meeting*) terminar **3.** (*fall apart: coalition*) fracasar; (*ship*) irse a pique
breakable ['breɪ·kə·bəl] *adj* frágil
breakage ['breɪ·kɪdʒ] *n* roturas *fpl*
breakaway ['breɪk·ə·weɪ] *adj* POL disidente
breakdown ['breɪk·daʊn] *n* **1.** (*collapse: in negotiations, relationship*) ruptura *f* **2.** TECH avería *f* **3.** (*division*) división *f;* **give me a ~ of the situation** detállame la situación **4.** (*decomposition*) descomposición *f* **5.** PSYCH (*nervous*) ~ crisis *f inv* nerviosa
breaker ['breɪ·kər] *n* **1.** (*wave*) gran ola *f* **2.** *inf* RADIO radioaficionado, -a *m, f*
breakfast ['brek·fəst] **I.** *n* desayuno *m;* **to have ~** desayunar **II.** *vi form* desayunar

> **i** En Norteamérica se aprecia mucho un desayuno (**breakfast**) fuerte. Además del desayuno habitual se sirven enormes cantidades de huevos revueltos, tocino y panceta o patatas salteadas con salchichas. Los fines de semana se comen también panqueques (**pancakes**), o **French toast** — pan de molde empapado en huevo y frito.

breaking and entering *n* allanamiento *m* de morada
breaking point *n* límite *m;* **to reach the ~** llegar al límite
breakneck ['breɪk·nek] *adj* vertiginoso, -a; **at ~ speed** a una velocidad vertiginosa
breakout ['breɪk·aʊt] *n* fuga *f*
breakthrough ['breɪk·θru] *n* **1.** (*in science*) adelanto *m* **2.** MIL avance *m*
breakup ['breɪk·ʌp] *n* (*of marriage*) separación *f;* (*of group, empire*) disolución *f;* (*of talks*) fracaso *m;* (*of family, physical structure*) desintegración *f*
breakwater ['breɪk·wɑ·tər] *n* rompeolas *m inv,* molo *m* Chile
breast [brest] *n* **1.** ANAT pecho *m* **2.** CULIN pechuga *f*
breastbone ['brest·boʊn] *n* **1.** ANAT esternón *m* **2.** CULIN hueso *m* de la pechuga
breast cancer *n* cáncer *m* de mama
breastfeed ['brest·fid] *vt* amamantar
breast pocket *n* bolsillo *m* superior
breaststroke ['brest·stroʊk] *n* (estilo *m*) braza *f;* **to do (the)** ~ nadar a braza
breath [breθ] *n* aliento *m;* **to be out of ~** estar sin aliento; **to be short of ~** ahogarse; **to catch one's ~** (*stop breathing*) quedarse sin respiración; (*return to normal breathing*) volver a respirar; **to draw ~** respirar; **to hold one's ~** *a. fig* contener la respiración; **to mutter sth under one's ~** decir algo entre dientes; **to take a deep ~** respirar hondo; **to go out for a ~ of fresh air** salir para que le dé a uno el aire ▸ **in the same ~** a continuación; **to take sb's ~ away** dejar a alguien sin habla

breathalyze ['breθ·ə·laɪz] *vt* hacer la prueba de la alcoholemia a

Breathalyzer® *n* alcoholímetro *m*

breathe [briɓ] **I.** *vi* respirar; **to ~ again** [*o easily*] respirar tranquilo; **to ~ through one's nose** respirar por la nariz; **to let a wine ~** dejar respirar un vino **II.** *vt* **1.** (*exhale*) **to ~ smoke on sb** echar el humo a alguien **2.** (*whisper*) musitar; **don't ~ a word of this to anyone!** ¡ni una palabra de esto a nadie! **3.** (*let out: sigh*) dejar escapar

breather ['bri·ðər] *n* descanso *m*, respiro *m*; **to take a ~** descansar

breathing *n* respiración *f*

breathing room *n*, **breathing space** *n* respiro *m*

breathless ['breθ·lɪs] *adj* (*person*) sin aliento; (*words*) entrecortado, -a

breathtaking *adj* imponente, impresionante

breath test *n* prueba *f* de la alcoholemia

bred [bred] *pt, pp of* **breed**

breech [britʃ] *n* recámara *f*

breeches ['brɪtʃ·ɪz] *npl* **1.** (*knee-length pants*) pantalones *mpl* bombachos; **riding ~** pantalones *mpl* de montar, zamarros *mpi Col, Ecua, Ven* **2.** *inf* (*pants*) pantalones *mpl*

breed [brid] **I.** *vt* <bred, bred> **1.** (*animals, plants*) criar **2.** (*disease, violence*) engendrar, generar **II.** *vi* <bred, bred> reproducirse; (*violence*) generarse **III.** *n* **1.** ZOOL raza *f*; BOT variedad *f* **2.** *inf* (*type of person*) tipo *m*; **a dying ~** una especie en vías de extinción

breeder ['bri·dər] *n* (*of animals*) criador(a) *m(f)*; (*of plants*) cultivador(a) *m(f)*

breeding *n* **1.** (*of animals*) cría *f* **2.** *fig* (*upbringing*) educación *f*

breeding ground *n fig* caldo *m* de cultivo

breeze [briz] **I.** *n* **1.** (*wind*) brisa *f* **2.** *inf* (*easy task*) **to be a ~** ser pan comido, ser un bollo *RíoPl* **3.** (*cinders*) cisco *m* de carbón y leña ► **to shoot the ~** estar de palique **II.** *vi* **to ~ into the room** entrar en la habitación como Pedro por su casa

breezy ['bri·zi] <-ier, -iest> *adj* **1.** (*windy*) ventoso, -a; **it is ~** hace viento **2.** (*lively*) alegre

breve [briv] *n* MUS breve *f*

brevity ['brev·ə·t̬i] *n* **1.** (*shortness*) brevedad *f* **2.** (*conciseness*) concisión *f*

brew [bru] **I.** *n* **1.** (*mixture*) brebaje *m* **2.** *inf* (*beer*) cerve *f* **II.** *vi* **1.** (*beer*) fermentar **2.** (*tea*) hacerse; **to let the tea ~** dejar reposar el té **3.** (*storm, trouble*) avecinarse; **there's something ~ing** se está cociendo algo **III.** *vt* (*beer*) elaborar; (*tea*) hacer

◆ **brew up I.** *vi* (*develop: storm, trouble*) avecinarse **II.** *vt inf* **to ~ a story/an excuse** inventarse una historia/excusa

brewer ['bru·ər] *n* cervecero, -a *m, f*

brewery ['bru·ə·ri] <-ies> *n* **1.** (*company*) cervecería *f*, cervecera *f Méx* **2.** (*place*) fábrica *f* de cerveza

brewski ['bru·ski] <-ies *o* -s> *n sl* birra *f*, bironga *f Méx*

briar ['braɪ·ər] *n* brezo *m*

bribe [braɪb] **I.** *vt* sobornar; **to ~ sb into doing sth** sobornar a alguien para que haga algo **II.** *n* soborno *m;* **to take a ~** dejarse sobornar, aceptar un soborno

bribery ['braɪ·bə·ri] *n* soborno *m*, coima *f Perú, CSur,* mordida *f Méx*

bric-a-brac ['brɪk·ə·bræk] *n* baratijas *fpl*

brick [brɪk] *n* ladrillo *m*

◆ **brick in** *vt* tapiar

◆ **brick up** *vt* tapiar

bricklayer *n* albañil *mf*

brick wall *n* pared *f* (de ladrillos) ► **to be banging one's head against a ~** *inf* llevar todas las de perder

brickwork *n* enladrillado *m*

brickyard *n* fábrica *f* de ladrillos

bridal ['braɪd·əl] *adj* (*suite*) nupcial; (*shop*) para novias; (*gown*) de novia

bridal shower *n* despedida *f* de soltera

bride [braɪd] *n* novia *f*

bridegroom ['braɪd·ˌgrum] *n* novio *m*

bridesmaid ['braɪdz·ˌmeɪd] *n* dama *f* de honor

bridge [brɪdʒ] **I.** *n* **1.** *a.* ARCHIT, MED, MUS puente *m* **2.** ANAT caballete *m* **3.** NAUT puente *m* (de mando) **4.** GAMES bridge *m* ► **to burn one's ~s** quemar las naves **II.** *vt* **1.** (*build a bridge over*) construir un puente sobre **2.** (*decrease the difference*) salvar

bridge loan *n* préstamo *m* puente, crédito *m* puente

bridle ['braɪd·əl] **I.** *n* brida *f* **II.** *vt* (*horse*) embridar **III.** *vi* **to ~ at sth** molestarse por algo

bridle path *n* camino *m* de herradura

brief [brif] **I.** *adj* **1.** (*short*) corto, -a **2.** (*concise*) conciso, -a, sucinto, -a; **be ~!** ¡sé breve!; **in ~** en resumen **II.** *n* **1.** (*instructions*) instrucciones *fpl* **2.** LAW escrito *m* **3.** ~**s** (*underwear: men's*) calzoncillos *mpl*, slip *m;* (*women's*) bragas *fpl* **III.** *vt* **1.** (*inform*) informar **2.** (*give instructions to*) dar instrucciones a

briefcase ['brif·ˌkeɪs] *n* maletín *m*

briefing *n* **1.** (*instructions*) instrucciones *fpl* **2.** (*information session*) reunión *f* informativa; (*for reporters*) rueda *f* de prensa

briefly *adv* **1.** (*for short time*) por poco tiempo **2.** (*concisely*) brevemente; ~**,...** en resumen,...

briefness *n* brevedad *f*

brigade [brɪ·ˈgeɪd] *n* MIL brigada *f*

brigadier general [ˌbrɪg·ə·dɪr·ˈdʒen·ər·əl] *n* MIL general *m* de brigada

bright [braɪt] **I.** *adj* **1.** (*light*) brillante, fuerte; (*room*) con mucha luz; (*star*) brillante; **a ~ day** un día soleado **2.** (*color*) vivo, -a, fuerte; **to go ~ red** ponerse rojo como un tomate **3.** (*intelligent: person*) inteligente; (*idea*) brillante **4.** (*cheerful, happy*) vivaracho, -a **5.** (*promising: future*) prometedor(a) ► **to look on the ~ side of sth** mirar [*o* ver] el lado bueno de algo; **to get up ~ and early** levantarse tempranito **II.** *n* ~**s** AUTO (luces *fpl*) largas

fpl, (luces *fpl*) altas *fpl And*
brighten ['braɪt·ən] I. *vt* **to ~ sth (up)**
1. (*make brighter*) iluminar 2. (*become cheerful*) alegrar, animar II. *vi* **to ~ (up)** 1. (*become brighter*) hacerse más brillante; (*weather*) mejorar 2. (*become cheerful*) animarse, alegrarse; (*eyes, face*) iluminarse 3. (*become more promising: future*) mejorar
brightness *n* 1. (*lightness*) brillo *m;* (*of sound*) claridad *f* 2. (*cheerfulness*) alegría *f* 3. (*cleverness*) inteligencia *f*
brilliance ['brɪl·jəns] *n* 1. (*cleverness*) brillantez *f* 2. (*brightness*) resplandor *m*
brilliant ['brɪl·jənt] *adj* 1. (*shining: color*) brillante; (*sunlight, smile*) radiante; (*water*) resplandeciente 2. (*clever*) brillante; (*idea*) genial 3. *inf* (*excellent*) fantástico, -a; **~ success** gran éxito
brim [brɪm] I. *n* 1. (*of a hat*) ala *f* 2. (*of a vessel*) borde *m;* **to fill sth to the ~** llenar algo hasta el borde II. *vi* <-mm-> **to ~ with happiness/energy** rebosar de felicidad/energía
♦ **brim over** *vi a. fig* rebosar
brimful [ˌbrɪm·'fʊl] *adj* repleto, -a; (*of life, confidence*) rebosante
brine [braɪn] *n* CULIN salmuera *f;* (*sea water*) agua *f* salada [*o* de mar]
bring [brɪŋ] <brought, brought> *vt* 1. (*come with, carry*) traer; **~ her here!** ¡tráela aquí!; **to ~ sb in** hacer pasar a alguien; **to ~ sth in** meter algo; **to ~ news** traer noticias 2. (*take*) llevar; **this subject ~s me to the second part** este tema me lleva a la segunda parte; **to ~ sth/sb with oneself** llevar algo/a alguien consigo 3. (*cause to come or happen*) causar, traer; **to ~ poverty/fame to a town** traer pobreza/fama a un pueblo; **to ~ sb luck** traer suerte a alguien 4. LAW interponer; **to ~ a lawsuit (against sb)** interponer una demanda (contra alguien); **to ~ a complaint against sb** formular un queja contra alguien 5. (*force*) **to ~ oneself to do sth** obligarse a hacer algo 6. FIN dar
♦ **bring about** *vt* 1. (*cause to happen*) provocar 2. (*achieve*) lograr
♦ **bring along** *vt* traer
♦ **bring around** *vt* 1. MED hacer volver en sí 2. (*persuade*) convencer
♦ **bring back** *vt* 1. (*reintroduce*) volver a introducir 2. (*call to mind*) recordar 3. (*return*) devolver
♦ **bring down** *vt* 1. (*reduce: benefits, level*) reducir; (*temperature*) hacer bajar 2. (*fell: tree*) talar; (*person*) derribar; (*dictator, government*) derrocar 3. (*knock down*) tirar, echar abajo 4. (*make sad*) deprimir
♦ **bring forth** *vt insep, form* procrear, dar a luz
♦ **bring forward** *vt* 1. (*reschedule for an earlier date*) adelantar 2. (*present for discussion*) presentar 3. FIN (*carry over*) transferir
♦ **bring in** *vt* 1. (*introduce*) introducir; (*bill*) presentar 2. (*call in*) llamar 3. FIN (*earn*) **to ~ a profit** reportar un beneficio 4. (*reap*) cosechar

5. LAW (*produce*) **to ~ a verdict of not guilty** pronunciar un veredicto de inocente
♦ **bring off** *vt inf* lograr
♦ **bring on** *vt* 1. (*cause to occur*) provocar; (*shame, dishonor, discredit*) causar, acarrear; **to bring sth on oneself** buscarse algo uno mismo 2. (*improve*) mejorar
♦ **bring out** *vt* 1. COM introducir (en el mercado); (*book*) publicar 2. (*reveal*) **to ~ the best/worst in sb** hace salir lo mejor/peor de alguien
♦ **bring over** *vt* 1. (*person*) convertir, convencer 2. (*take with*) traer
♦ **bring to** *vt always sep* reanimar
♦ **bring up** *vt* 1. (*child*) criar; **to bring sb up to be/to do sth** educar a alguien para que sea/haga algo 2. (*mention*) sacar 3. *inf* (*vomit*) vomitar
brink [brɪŋk] *n* borde *m;* **to drive sb to the ~ of sth** llevar a alguien al borde de algo; **to be on the ~ of bankruptcy/war** estar al borde de la bancarrota/la guerra
briny ['braɪ·ni] <-ier, -iest> *adj liter* salobre
briquet(te) [brɪ·'ket] *n* briqueta *f*
brisk [brɪsk] *adj* 1. (*fast: pace*) rápido, -a; (*walk*) a paso ligero 2. (*refreshing: breeze*) fresco, -a 3. (*manner, voice*) enérgico, -a
briskness *n* (*of pace*) brío *m;* (*of trading*) dinamismo *m;* (*of business*) eficiencia *f*
bristle ['brɪs·əl] I. *n* (*of an animal*) cerda *f;* (*on the face*) barba; (*of a brush*) cerda *f* II. *vi* 1. (*fur, hair*) erizarse, ponerse de punta 2. *fig* **to ~ with anger** enfurecerse
bristly ['brɪs·li] <-ier, -iest> *adj* hirsuto, -a
Brit [brɪt] *n inf* británico, -a *m, f*
Britain ['brɪt·ən] *n* Gran Bretaña *f*
British ['brɪt̬·ɪʃ] I. *adj* británico, -a; **~ English** inglés *m* británico II. *n pl* **the ~** los británicos
British Columbia *n* Columbia *f* Británica
British Isles *n* **the ~** las Islas Británicas
Briton ['brɪt·ən] *n* británico, -a *m, f*
Brittany ['brɪt·ən·i] *n* Bretaña *f*
brittle ['brɪt̬·əl] *adj* 1. (*fragile*) quebradizo, -a 2. (*irritable*) susceptible
broach [broʊtʃ] I. *vt* (*mention*) mencionar II. *n* (*pin*) broche *m*
broad [brɔd] I. *adj* 1. (*wide*) ancho, -a 2. (*spacious*) amplio, -a 3. (*obvious*) **a ~ hint** una clara indirecta 4. (*general*) general 5. (*wide-ranging*) amplio, -a; **~ interests** intereses diversos 6. (*liberal*) liberal; **a ~ mind** una mente abierta 7. (*strong: accent*) cerrado, -a II. *n offensive, sl* (*woman*) tía *f*
broadcast ['brɔd·kæst] I. *n* RADIO programa *m* (de radio); TV programa *m* (de televisión); (*of a concert*) emisión *f* II. *vi,vt* <broadcast *o* broadcasted, broadcast *o* broadcasted> transmitir, emitir III. *vt* <broadcast *o* broadcasted, broadcast *o* broadcasted> TV transmitir; RADIO emitir; (*rumor*) difundir
broadcaster *n* (*person*) locutor(a) *m(f);* (*station*) emisora *f*
broadcasting *n* TV transmisión *f;* RADIO radiodi-

B

fusión *f*

broadcasting station *n* emisora *f*

broaden ['brɔd·ən] I. *vi* (*interests*) ampliarse; (*valley*) ensancharse II. *vt* (*street*) ensanchar; (*horizons*) ampliar; **to ~ the mind** abrir la mente

broadly ['brɔd·li] *adv* 1. (*generally*) en líneas generales 2. (*widely: smile*) de oreja a oreja

broad-minded *adj* con mentalidad abierta

broadside ['brɔd·saɪd] *n* 1. NAUT, MIL andanada *f* 2. (*verbal attack*) ataque *m* verbal 3. (*paper*) periódico de formato grande

> **i** **Broadway** es el nombre de una larga calle de la ciudad de Nueva York. Esta calle es el eje de una intensa actividad teatral que incluye la representación de las principales obras de teatro de Estados Unidos. Las obras que — ya sea por su bajo presupuesto o por su carácter experimental — no se representan en Broadway reciben el nombre de **off-Broadway plays**.

brocade [brou·'keɪd] *n* brocado *m*

broccoli ['brak·ə·li] *n* brócoli *m*, brécol *m*

brochure [brou·'ʃur] *n* folleto *m*

brogue [broug] *n* LING acento *m* irlandés

broil [brɔɪl] I. *vt* asar a la parrilla II. *n* (*argument*) gresca *f*

broiler ['brɔɪ·lər] *n* 1. (*grill*) parrilla *f*, grill *m* 2. (*chicken*) pollo *m* para asar, pollo *m* parrillero *RíoPl*, broiler *m Chile*

broke [brouk] I. *pt of* **break** II. *adj inf* pelado, -a, planchado, -a *Chile* ▸ **to go ~** *inf* arruinarse; **to go for ~** *inf* jugarse el todo por el todo

broken ['brou·kən] I. *pp of* **break** II. *adj* 1. (*damaged: TV, radio, toy*) roto, -a; (*marriage, family, home*) roto, -a; (*heart, spirit*) destrozado 2. LING **in ~ English** en un inglés incorrecto 3. (*interrupted*) interrumpido, -a

broken-down *adj* 1. TECH averiado, -a, en pana *Chile*, varado, -a *Col* 2. (*dilapidated: building*) ruinoso, -a

broken-hearted *adj* destrozado, -a, deshecho, -a; **to die ~** morir de pena

broker ['brou·kər] I. *n* 1. FIN corredor(a) *m(f)* de bolsa 2. (*of an agreement, marriage*) agente *mf* II. *vt* 1. FIN hacer corretaje de 2. (*agreement*) negociar

brokerage ['brou·kər·ɪdʒ] *n* FIN 1. (*commission*) corretaje *m* 2. (*business*) agencia *f* de corredores de bolsa

bromide ['brou·maɪd] *n* 1. CHEM bromuro *m* 2. (*cliché*) lugar *m* común, tópico *m*

bromine ['brou·min] *n* bromo *m*

bronchial ['braŋ·ki·əl] *adj* bronquial

bronchial tubes *npl* bronquios *mpl*

bronchitis [braŋ·'kaɪ·tɪs] *n* bronquitis *f*

bronze [branz] I. *n* bronce *m* II. *adj* de bronce; (*hair*) dorado, -a; (*skin*) bronceado, -a

Bronze Age I. *n* **the ~** la Edad de Bronce

II. *adj* de la Edad de Bronce

bronze medal *n* medalla *f* de bronce

brooch [broutʃ] *n* broche *m*

brood [brud] I. *n* 1. (*of mammals*) camada *f*; (*of birds*) nidada *f* 2. *iron* (*children*) prole *f* II. *vi* 1. (*reflect at length, worry about*) **to ~ over sth** dar vueltas a algo 2. (*hatch*) empollar

broody ['bru·di] <-ier, -iest> *adj* 1. (*hen*) clueco, -a 2. (*gloomy*) melancólico, -a

brook[1] [bruk] *n* arroyo *m*

brook[2] [bruk] *vt form* (*tolerate*) tolerar

broom [brum] *n* 1. (*for sweeping*) escoba *f* 2. BOT retama *f*, hiniesta *f* ▸ **a new ~ sweeps clean** *prov* escoba nueva barre bien *prov*

broomstick ['brum·stɪk] *n* palo *m* de escoba

broth [brɔθ] *n* caldo *m*

brothel ['braθ·əl] *n* burdel *m*

brother ['brʌð·ər] *n* 1. hermano *m* 2. *inf* (*male friend*) colega *m*

brotherhood ['brʌð·ər·hud] *n* + *sing/pl vb* 1. (*fellowship*) fraternidad *f* 2. (*organization*) hermandad *f* 3. REL cofradía *f*

brother-in-law <brothers-in-law *o* brother-in-laws> *n* cuñado *m*, concuño *m AmL*

brotherly ['brʌð·ər·li] *adj* fraternal

brought [brɔt] *pp*, *pt of* **bring**

brow [brau] *n* 1. *liter* (*forehead*) frente 2. (*of a hill*) cima *f*

browbeat ['brau·bit] <browbeat, browbeaten> *vt* intimidar; **to ~ sb into doing sth** intimidar a alguien para que haga algo

brown [braun] I. *n* marrón *m* II. *adj* marrón; (*eyes, hair*) castaño, -a III. *vi* (*leaves*) amarillear; (*person*) broncearse; CULIN dorarse IV. *vt* broncear; CULIN dorar

brown bread *n* pan *m* integral

brownie ['brau·ni] *n* 1. (*sweet*) brownie *m* (*bizcocho de chocolate y nueces*) 2. (*young girl scout*) joven exploradora *f*

brownish ['brau·nɪʃ] *adj* pardusco, -a

brownnose ['braun·nouz] I. *vi inf* ser un pelota, ser un lambón *Col* II. *vt* hacer la pelota a, hacer la barba a *Méx*, echar cepillo a *Col*

brownout ['braun·aut] *n* ELEC apagón *m* (parcial)

brown rice *n* arroz *m* integral

brownstone ['braun·stoun] *n* 1. (*sandstone*) piedra *f* rojiza 2. (*house*) casa *f* de piedra rojiza

browse [brauz] I. *vi* 1. (*skim*) **to ~ through sth** echar un vistazo a algo; (*book, magazine*) hojear algo 2. (*look around*) mirar 3. (*graze*) pastar II. *n* 1. (*act of looking around*) **to go for a ~ around the shops** ir de tiendas 2. (*act of skimming*) ojeada *f*, vistazo *m*; **to have a ~ through sth** echar una ojeada [*o* un vistazo] a algo; (*book, magazine*) hojear algo

browser ['brau·zər] *n* COMPUT navegador *m*

bruise [bruz] I. *n* morado *m*, moretón *m*; (*on fruit*) golpe *m*; **to be covered in ~s** estar lleno de morados II. *vt* (*person*) contusionar; (*fruit*) magullar; *fig* (*hurt*) herir; **to ~ one's arm** hacerse morados [*o* un morado] en el brazo; **to ~ sb's feelings** herir los sentimientos de al-

guien **III.** *vi* (*fruit*) magullarse; **she ~s easily** le salen morados con mucha facilidad
bruiser ['bru·zər] *n inf* armario *m*
brunch [brʌntʃ] *n* desayuno-almuerzo *m*
Brunei [bru·'naɪ] *n* Brunei *m*
brunette [bru·'net] *n* morena *f*, morocha *f CSur*
brunt [brʌnt] *n* (*impact*) impacto *m;* **to bear the ~ of sth** aguantar lo más duro de algo
brush [brʌʃ] **I.** *n* **1.** (*for hair*) cepillo *m* **2.** (*broom*) escoba *f* **3.** (*for painting*) pincel *m;* (*bigger*) brocha *f* **4.** (*action*) cepilladura *f* **5.** (*stroke*) pincelada *f* **6.** (*encounter*) roce *m;* **a ~ with death/with the law** un encuentro con la muerte/con la ley **7.** (*brushwood*) maleza *f* **8.** (*fox's tail*) cola *f* **II.** *vt* **1.** (*hair*) cepillar; **to ~ one's teeth** lavarse los dientes **2.** (*remove*) **to ~ sth off** quitar algo con un cepillo **3.** (*graze, touch lightly*) rozar
◆**brush against** *vt* rozar
◆**brush aside** *vt* **1.** (*push to one side*) apartar **2.** (*disregard*) hacer caso omiso de; (*criticism*) pasar por alto
◆**brush away** *vt* quitar
◆**brush off** *vt* (*dust*) quitar; (*person*) no hacer caso a; (*criticism*) pasar por alto
◆**brush up I.** *vt* dar un repaso a **II.** *vi* **to ~ on sth** dar un repaso a algo
brush-off *n inf* **to give sb the ~** dar calabazas a alguien; **to get the ~ from sb** recibir calabazas de alguien
brushwood ['brʌʃ·wʊd] *n* maleza *f*
brusque [brʌsk] *adj* brusco, -a
brusqueness *n* brusquedad *f*
Brussels ['brʌs·əlz] *n* Bruselas *f*
Brussels sprout *n* col *f* de Bruselas
brutal ['bruṭ·əl] *adj* **1.** (*cruel, savage: attack*) brutal; (*words*) cruel **2.** (*harsh: honesty, truth*) crudo, -a
brutality [bru·'tæl·ə·ṭi] *n* (*cruelty: of an attack*) brutalidad *f;* (*of words*) crueldad *f;* (*harshness*) crudeza *f*
brutalize ['bruṭ·əl·aɪz] *vt* **1.** (*treat cruelly*) tratar con crueldad **2.** (*make brutal*) brutalizar
brute [brut] **I.** *n* **1.** (*person*) bestia *f*, bruto, -a *m, f* **2.** (*animal*) bestia *f* **II.** *adj* **~ force** fuerza *f* bruta
brutish ['bru·ṭɪʃ] *adj* **1.** (*cruel*) brutal, salvaje **2.** (*coarse*) bruto, -a **3.** (*like an animal*) animal
BSc [ˌbi·es·'si] *abbr of* **Bachelor of Science** Ldo., -a *m, f* (en Ciencias)
BSE [ˌbi·es·'i] *n abbr of* **bovine spongiform encephalopathy** encefalopatía *f* espongiforme bovina
bubble ['bʌb·əl] **I.** *n* **1.** burbuja *f;* (*in cartoons*) bocadillo *m;* **to blow a ~** hacer una pompa [*o* Col bomba] **2.** *fig, inf* (*protective environment*) **to live in a ~** vivir en una burbuja ▶**to burst sb's ~** desengañar a alguien; **the ~ has burst** se ha roto el encanto **II.** *vi* **1.** (*boil*) hervir **2.** (*make boiling sound*) borbotear
◆**bubble over with** *vi* **to ~ joy** no caber en sí de alegría

bubble bath *n* (*product*) espuma *f* de baño; (*bath*) baño *m* de espuma
bubblegum *n* chicle *m*
bubble-jet printer *n* COMPUT impresora *f* de inyección de burbujas
bubbly ['bʌb·li] **I.** *n inf* champán *m* **II.** *adj* **1.** (*full of bubbles*) burbujeante **2.** *fig* (*lively*) animado, -a
bubonic plague [bu·ˌban·ɪk·'pleɪg] *n* peste *f* bubónica
buccaneer [ˌbʌk·ə·'nɪr] *n* bucanero *m*
buck¹ [bʌk] <-(s)> **I.** *n* **1.** (*male: deer*) ciervo *m* (macho); (*rabbit*) conejo *m;* (*hare*) liebre *f* macho **2.** *liter* (*man*) galán *m* **II.** *vi* corcovear **III.** *vt* ir contra; **to ~ the trend** invertir la tendencia
buck² [bʌk] *n inf* (*dollar*) dólar *m;* **to make a fast ~** hacer dinero fácil
buck³ [bʌk] *n inf* **to pass the ~** escurrir el bulto; **the ~ stops here** *prov* yo soy el responsable
◆**buck up** *vt inf* **1.** (*cheer up*) **to buck up sb** levantar el ánimo a alguien **2. to ~ one's ideas** espabilarse
bucket ['bʌk·ɪt] *n* (*pail*) cubo *m* ▶**a drop in the ~** un grano de arena en el desierto; **to kick the ~** *inf* estirar la pata
bucketful ['bʌk·ɪt·fʊl] <-s *o* bucketsful> *n* cubo *m* (lleno)
bucket truck *n* camión *m* cesta
buckle ['bʌk·əl] **I.** *n* hebilla *f* **II.** *vt* **1.** (*fasten: belt, shoes*) abrochar **2.** (*bend*) torcer **III.** *vi* **1.** (*fasten*) abrocharse **2.** (*bend*) torcerse; (*knees*) doblarse; (*metal*) combarse
◆**buckle down** *vi* ponerse a hacer algo en serio
◆**buckle up** *vi* abrocharse el cinturón
buckshot *n* perdigón *m*
buckskin I. *n* gamuza *f* **II.** *adj* de gamuza
buckwheat *n* alforfón *m*, trigo *m* sarraceno
bud [bʌd] **I.** *n* (*of leaf, branch*) brote *m;* (*of a flower*) capullo *m;* **to be in ~** tener brotes **II.** *vi* <-dd-> echar brotes
Buddhism ['bu·dɪz·əm] *n* budismo *m*
Buddhist I. *n* budista *mf* **II.** *adj* budista
budding ['bʌd·ɪŋ] *adj* en ciernes; *fig* (*romance, relationship*) floreciente
buddy ['bʌd·i] *n inf* colega *m*, cuate *m Méx*
budge [bʌdʒ] **I.** *vi* **1.** (*move*) moverse **2.** (*change opinion*) **to not ~ (from sth)** no cambiar de opinión (en algo) **II.** *vt* **1.** (*move*) mover **2.** (*cause to change opinion*) hacer cambiar de opinión a
budgerigar ['bʌdʒ·ə·rɪ·gar] *n* periquito *m*
budget ['bʌdʒ·ɪt] **I.** *n* presupuesto *m* **II.** *vt* presupuestar; (*wages, time*) administrar **III.** *vi* **to ~ for sth** presupuestar algo **IV.** *adj* (*travel, prices*) económico, -a
budgetary ['bʌdʒ·ɪ·ter·i] *adj* presupuestario, -a
budget deficit *n* déficit *m inv* presupuestario
budgie ['bʌdʒ·i] *n inf* periquito *m*
buff [bʌf] **I.** *n* **1.** (*leather*) gamuza *f* **2.** *inf* (*person*) entusiasta *mf;* **film ~** cinéfilo, -a *m, f* ▶**in**

the ~ *inf*en cueros, en pelota *Col, Méx* **II.** *adj* **1.** color de ante **2.** *sl* (*muscular: athlete*) musculoso, -a, mazas *inv* **III.** *vt* (*metal*) pulir; (*shoes*) sacar brillo a

buffalo ['bʌf·ə·loʊ] <-(es)> *n* búfalo *m*

buffer ['bʌf·ər] **I.** *n* **1.** (*of a train*) tope *m;* (*absorbing impact*) barrera *f; fig* (*intermediary*) mediador(a) *m(f)* **2.** COMPUT búfer *m* **3.** CHEM regulador *m* **II.** *vt* proteger

buffer zone *n* zona *f* de protección

buffet¹ [bə·'feɪ] *n* **1.** (*meal*) buffet *m* **2.** (*bar*) cafetería *f*

buffet² ['bʌf·ɪt] *vt* (*hit repeatedly*) zarandear, sacudir

buffet lunch *n* buffet *m*

buffoon [bə·'fun] *n* bufón, -ona *m, f;* **to play the** ~ hacer el payaso, hacer payasadas

bug [bʌg] **I.** *n* **1.** ZOOL chinche *f;* (*any insect*) bicho *m* **2.** MED virus *m inv* **3.** COMPUT error *m* **4.** TEL micrófono *m* oculto **5.** *inf* (*enthusiasm*) fiebre *f,* entusiasmo *m;* **she's caught the travel ~** le ha picado el gusanillo de viajar ▸ **to be snug as a ~ in a rug** estar muy cómodo **II.** *vt* <-gg-> **1.** (*tap: telephone*) pinchar; (*conversation*) escuchar clandestinamente; (*room*) ocultar micrófonos en **2.** *inf* (*annoy*) fastidiar

bugaboo ['bʌg·ə·bu] *n* pesadilla *f*

bugger ['bʌg·ər] **I.** *n* **1.** *vulg* (*sodomite*) sodomita *mf* **2.** *sl* (*contemptible person*) gilipollas *mf inv;* **poor ~** pobre desgraciado **II.** *vt vulg* cometer sodomía con

buggery ['bʌg·ə·ri] *n* sodomía *f*

buggy ['bʌg·i] *n* <-ies> **1.** (*stroller*) cochecito *m* (de niño) **2.** (*carriage*) calesa *f*

bugle ['bju·gəl] *n* clarín *m*

bugler ['bju·glər] *n* corneta *mf*

build [bɪld] **I.** *vt* <built, built> **1.** (*make: house*) construir; (*fire*) hacer; (*car*) fabricar **2.** (*establish: trust*) cimentar; (*relationship*) establecer; (*support, a following*) hacerse con, conseguir **II.** *vi* <built, built> **1.** (*construct*) edificar, construir **2.** (*increase*) aumentar **III.** *n* complexión *f*

◆ **build in** *vt* incorporar

◆ **build on** *vt* tomar como base; **to build sth on sth** agregar algo a algo

◆ **build up I.** *vt* **1.** (*increase*) acrecentar **2.** (*accumulate*) acumular **3.** (*strengthen*) fortalecer **4.** (*develop*) desarrollar **5.** (*praise*) **build sb up** poner a alguien por las nubes **II.** *vi* **1.** (*increase*) ir en aumento **2.** (*accumulate*) acumularse

builder ['bɪl·dər] *n* (*company*) constructor(a) *m(f);* (*worker*) albañil *mf*

building *n* edificio *m*

building contractor *n* contratista *mf* (de obras)

building permit *n* permiso *m* de obras

building site *n* obra *f*

build-up *n* **1.** (*accumulation*) acumulación *f;* (*of pressure*) aumento *m* **2.** (*publicity*) propaganda *f*

built [bɪlt] **I.** *pp, pt of* **build II.** *adj* **1.** (*house*)

well ~ bien construido **2.** (*person*) **slightly** ~ menudo; **well** ~ de complexión robusta **3.** (*have nice body*) **he's/she's** (**really**) **built!** ¡vaya un cuerpazo que tiene!

built-in *adj* **1.** (*cabinets*) empotrado, -a **2.** (*feature*) incorporado, -a **3.** (*advantage*) intrínseco, -a

built-up *adj* **1.** (*area*) edificado, -a **2.** (*heels, shoes*) con alza

bulb [bʌlb] *n* **1.** BOT bulbo *m* **2.** (*of a thermometer*) cubeta *f* **3.** ELEC bombilla *f,* bombillo *m AmL*

bulbous ['bʌl·bəs] *adj* bulboso, -a; ~ **nose** nariz *f* protuberante

Bulgaria [bʌl·'ger·i·ə] *n* Bulgaria *f*

Bulgarian [bʌl·'ger·i·ən] **I.** *adj* búlgaro, -a **II.** *n* **1.** (*person*) búlgaro, -a *m, f* **2.** LING búlgaro *m*

bulge [bʌldʒ] **I.** *vi* sobresalir; **her eyes ~d in surprise** su sorpresa fue tal que los ojos se le salían de las órbitas; **to** ~ (**with sth**) estar repleto (de algo) **II.** *n* **1.** (*swelling*) bulto *m* **2.** (*a statistical trend*) alza *f*

bulging *adj* abultado, -a; (*bag, box*) repleto, -a; ~ **eyes** ojos *mpl* saltones

bulimia [bu·'li·mi·ə] *n* MED bulimia *f*

bulk [bʌlk] **I.** *n* **1.** (*magnitude*) volumen *m* **2.** (*mass*) mole *f* **3.** (*quantity*) **in** ~ a granel; ECON al por mayor; **to** ~ **buy sth, to buy** (**sth**) **in** ~ comprar (algo) en grandes cantidades; ECON comprar (algo) al por mayor **4.** (*largest part*) **the** ~ **of** la mayor parte de **II.** *vi* **to** ~ **large** ser importante **III.** *adj* (*large in quantity: mailing, order*) grande; (*goods*) en grandes cantidades

bulk buying *n* ECON compra *f* al por mayor

bulkhead ['bʌlk·hed] *n* NAUT mamparo *m*

bulky ['bʌl·ki] <-ier, iest> *adj* (*large*) voluminoso, -a; (*heavy*) pesado, -a; (*person*) corpulento, -a

bull [bʊl] *n* **1.** (*male bovine*) toro *m* **2.** (*male animal*) macho *m;* ~ **elephant** elefante *m;* ~ **whale** ballena *f* macho ▸ **to take the ~ by the horns** coger [*o* agarrar *AmL*] el toro por los cuernos; **to be like a red rag to a ~ to sb** poner furioso a alguien **4.** *sl* (*nonsense*) chorradas *fpl,* macanas *fpl RíoPl* **5.** FIN alcista *m;* ~ **market** mercado *m* alcista

bulldog ['bʊl·dɔg] *n* bulldog *m*

bulldoze ['bʊl·doʊz] *vt* **1.** ARCHIT demoler **2.** *fig* **to** ~ **sth through** conseguir algo a la fuerza; **to** ~ **sb into doing sth** forzar a alguien a hacer algo

bulldozer ['bʊl·doʊ·zər] *n* bulldozer *m,* topadora *f Arg, Méx, Urug*

bullet ['bʊl·ɪt] *n* MIL bala *f;* **to fire a** ~ disparar una bala ▸ **to bite the** ~ *inf*apretar los dientes, hacer de tripas corazón

bulletin ['bʊl·ə·tɪn] *n* boletín *m;* (**news**) ~ TV, CINE boletín (informativo)

bulletin board *n a.* COMPUT tablón *m* de anuncios

bulletproof ['bʊl·ɪt·pruf] *adj* a prueba de balas; ~ **glass** vidrio *m* antibalas

bulletproof vest *n* chaleco *m* antibalas
bullfight ['bʊl·faɪt] *n* corrida *f* de toros
bullfighter ['bʊl·faɪ·tər] *n* torero, -a *m, f*
bullfinch ['bʊl·fɪntʃ] *n* pinzón *m*
bullion ['bʊl·jən] *n* **gold/silver** ~ oro *m*/plata *f* en lingotes
bullock ['bʊl·ək] *n* (*castrated bull*) buey *m;* (*young bull*) novillo *m*
bullring ['bʊl·rɪŋ] *n* plaza *f* de toros
bull's-eye *n* blanco *m;* **to hit the** ~ *a. fig* dar en el blanco
bullshit ['bʊl·ʃɪt] I. *n sl* gilipolleces *fpl;* **don't give me that** ~! ¡no me vengas con hostias! *vulg* II. *interj sl* y una mierda *vulg* III. <-tt-> *vi sl* decir gilipolleces
bully ['bʊl·i] I. <-ies> *n* (*person*) matón, -ona *m, f* <-ie-> *vt* intimidar; **to** ~ **sb into doing sth** intimidar a alguien para que haga algo III. *interj inf* ~ **for you!** ¡qué bien!; *iron* ¡bravo!
bulrush ['bʊl·rʌʃ] <-es> *n* anea *f*
bulwark ['bʊl·wərk] *n* **1.** (*fortification*) baluarte *m* **2.** NAUT macarrón *m*
bum [bʌm] I. *n* **1.** (*lazy person*) vago, -a *m, f* **2.** (*homeless person*) vagabundo, -a *m, f* **3.** *Can* (*buttocks*) culo *m* ▶ **to give sb the** ~ **'s rush** *inf* echar a alguien a patadas II. *adj inf* (*bad, useless*) malo, -a; **a** ~ **job** una porquería de trabajo III. <-mm-> *vt sl* **to** ~ **sth off sb** gorronear [*o Col* lagartear] algo a alguien IV. *vi inf* **1.to** ~ **around** (*live as a bum*) vagabundear; (*laze around*) pasar el rato **2.** (*cadge*) **to** ~ **off sb** gorronear a alguien
bumble ['bʌm·bəl] *vi* andar a tropezones
bumblebee ['bʌm·bəl·bi] *n* abejorro *m*
bumbling *adj* torpe
bummed out *adj sl* depre
bump [bʌmp] I. *n* **1.** (*lump*) bulto *m;* (*on head*) chichón *m;* (*on road*) bache *m* **2.** *inf* (*blow*) porrazo *m* **3.** (*thud*) golpe *m* **4.** (*collision*) topetazo *m* II. *vt* chocar contra; **to** ~ **one's head on/against sth** darse un golpe en la cabeza con/contra algo
◆**bump into** *vt insep* **1.** (*collide with*) chocar contra **2.** (*meet accidentally*) topar con
◆**bump off** *vt sl* **to bump sb off** cargarse a alguien
bumper ['bʌm·pər] I. *n* AUTO parachoques *m inv,* paragolpes *m inv AmL,* defensa *f Méx;* **the traffic is** ~ **to** ~ hay un atasco II. *adj* **1.** (*crop*) abundante **2.** (*edition*) especial
bumper car *n* coche *m* de choque, carrito *m* chocón *Méx, Ven,* carro *m* loco *Col*
bumper sticker *n* pegatina *f* (para el coche)
bumpkin ['bʌmp·kɪn] *n inf* (**country**) ~ paleto, -a *m, f*
bumptious ['bʌmp·ʃəs] *adj* engreído, -a
bumpy ['bʌm·pi] <-ier, iest> *adj* (*surface*) desigual; (*road*) lleno, -a de baches; (*journey*) movidito *inf*
bun [bʌn] *n* **1.** (*pastry*) bollo *m* **2.** (*roll*) panecillo *m,* pancito *m CSur* **3.** (*knot of hair*) moño *m,* chongo *m Méx* **4.** ~ **s** *sl* (*buttocks*) culo,

pompis *m inv Méx,* cola *f Col, Csur*
bunch [bʌntʃ] <-es> I. *n* **1.** (*of bananas, grapes*) racimo *m;* (*of carrots, radishes, keys*) manojo *m;* (*of flowers*) ramo *m* **2.** (*group: of people*) grupo *m;* (*of friends*) pandilla *f* **3.** (*a lot*) **a** (**whole**) ~ **of problems** un montón de problemas ▶ **to be the best of the** ~ ser lo mejor II. *vt* agrupar III. *vi* **to** ~ (**together**) amontonarse
bundle ['bʌn·dəl] I. *n* (*of clothes*) fardo *m;* (*of money*) fajo *m;* (*of sticks*) haz *f* ▶ **to be a** ~ **of joy** *inf* ser un cascabel; **to be a** ~ **of laughs** ser muy divertido; **to be a** ~ **of nerves** ser un manojo de nervios II. *vt* **to** ~ **sb into a car** meter a alguien a empujones en un coche
◆**bundle up** I. *vt* atar, liar II. *vi* (*dress warmly*) abrigarse
bung [bʌŋ] I. *n* (*stopper*) tapón *m* II. *vt* (*close*) taponar
bungalow ['bʌŋ·gə·loʊ] *n* bungalow *m,* bóngalo *m AmL*
bungee jumping ['bʌn·dʒiˌdʒʌm·pɪŋ] *n* puenting *m*
bungle ['bʌŋ·gəl] *vt* chapucear
bungler *n* chapucero, -a *m, f*
bungling *adj* torpe
bunk [bʌŋk] *n a.* NAUT litera *f,* cucheta *f RíoPl*
◆**bunk down** *vi inf* irse a sobar
bunk bed *n* litera *f*
bunker ['bʌŋ·kər] *n* búnker *m*
bunkum ['bʌŋ·kəm] *n* chorradas *fpl*
bunny (**rabbit**) ['bʌn·iˌ('ræb·ɪt)] *n childspeak* conejito *m*
Bunsen burner ['bʌn·sɪnˌbɜr·nər] *n* mechero *m* Bunsen
bunting ['bʌn·tɪŋ] *n* banderitas *fpl*
buoy [bɔɪ] *n* boya *f*
◆**buoy up** *vt* **1.** (*cause to float*) mantener a flote **2.** *fig* (*cause to rise*) aumentar **3.** *fig* (*cheer up*) **to buoy sb up** animar a alguien
buoyancy ['bɔɪ·jən·si] *n* **1.** *a.* NAUT capacidad *f* para flotar **2.** (*cheerfulness*) optimismo *m*
buoyant ['bɔɪ·jənt] *adj* **1.** (*able to float*) flotante **2.** (*cheerful*) optimista; **to be in a** ~ **mood** estar de buen humor
burble ['bɜr·bəl] *vi* **1.** (*make burbling noise*) borbotar **2.** (*talk nonsense*) hablar atropelladamente
burden ['bɜr·dən] I. *n* **1.** (*load*) carga *f* **2.** *fig* carga *f;* (*responsibility*) responsabilidad *f;* **tax** ~ ECON gravamen *m;* **the** ~ **of proof** LAW la carga de la prueba; **to be a** ~ **on** [*o to*] **sb** ser una carga para alguien II. *vt* **1.** (*load*) cargar **2.** *fig* estorbar; **I don't want to** ~ **you with my problems** no quiero preocuparte con mis problemas
burdensome ['bɜr·dən·səm] *adj form* oneroso, -a
bureau ['bjʊr·oʊ] <-s> *n* **1.** (*government department*) departamento *m;* (*office*) agencia *f* **2.** (*chest of drawers*) cómoda *f*
bureaucracy [bjʊ·'rak·rə·si] *n* burocracia *f*
bureaucrat ['bjʊr·ə·kræt] *n* burócrata *mf*

bureaucratic [ˌbjʊr·ə·ˈkræt̬·ɪk] *adj* burocrático, -a

burgeoning [ˈbɜr·dʒə·nɪŋ] *adj* creciente

burger [ˈbɜr·gər] *n inf abbr of* **hamburger** hamburguesa *f*

burglar [ˈbɜr·glər] *n* ladrón, -ona *m, f*

burglar alarm *n* alarma *f* antirrobo

burglarize [ˈbɜr·glə·raɪz] *vt* robar; **five houses have been ~d** han entrado a robar en cinco casas

burglary [ˈbɜr·glə·ri] <-ies> *n* robo *m*

burgle [ˈbɜr·gəl] *vt s.* **burglarize**

burial [ˈber·i·əl] *n* entierro *m*

burial ground *n* cementerio *m*

burial service *n* funerales *mpl*

Burkinabe [ˈbɜr·ki·neɪb] I. *adj* de Burkina Faso II. *n* habitante *mf* de Burkina Faso

Burkina Faso [bɜrˌki·nə·ˈfa·soʊ] *n* Burkina *f* Faso

burlesque [bɜr·ˈlesk] I. *n* parodia *f* II. *adj* burlesco, -a

burly [ˈbɜr·li] <-ier, -iest> *adj* (*man*) fornido, -a

Burma [ˈbɜr·mə] *n* Birmania *f*

burn [bɜrn] I.<burnt *o* -ed, burnt *o* -ed> *vi* 1.(*be in flames: house, wood*) arder, quemarse; (*be black: food*) quemarse 2.(*be hot*) arder; **his forehead was ~ing** la frente le ardía 3.(*be switched on*) estar encendido, -a; **he left all the lights ~ing** dejó todas las luces encendidas 4.(*want*) **to be ~ing to do sth** estar deseando hacer algo 5.(*feel emotion strongly*) **to ~ with sth** arder de algo; **to ~ with desire** desear ardientemente 6.(*be red*) **his face ~ed with anger/shame** se puso rojo de furia/vergüenza II.<burnt *o* -ed, burnt *o* -ed> *vt* (*paper, garbage, food*) quemar; (*building*) incendiar; (*throat, tongue*) quemar, escaldar; **to be ~ed** (*by the sun*) quemarse; (*injured*) sufrir quemaduras; **to ~ calories/fat** quemar calorías/grasa; **this machine ~s electricity** esta máquina funciona con electricidad; **we ~ a lot of gas** consumimos mucho gas III. *n* quemadura *f,* quemada *f Méx;* **severe/minor ~s** quemaduras graves/leves

◆**burn away** I. *vi* (*forest*) quemarse; (*candle*) consumirse II. *vt* quemar

◆**burn down** I. *vt* incendiar II. *vi* (*house*) incendiarse; (*fire, candle*) apagarse

◆**burn out** I. *vi* (*engine*) quemarse; (*fire, candle*) apagarse; (*light bulb*) fundirse II. *vt* **to burn oneself out** agotarse, quemarse

◆**burn up** I. *vt* 1.(*fuel*) consumir; (*calories*) quemar 2. *inf* (*make angry*) reventar II. *vi* abrasarse; **you're burning up!** *inf* (*have fever*) ¡estás ardiendo!

burner [ˈbɜr·nər] *n* fogón *m;* TECH quemador *m*

burning [ˈbɜr·nɪŋ] *adj* 1.(*hot*) ardiente; (*sun*) abrasador; **to be ~ hot** estar ardiendo; **a ~ sensation** una quemazón 2.(*issue, question*) candente; (*desire, hatred*) ardiente

burnt [bɜrnt] I. *pt, pp of* **burn** II. *adj* quemado, -a; **a ~ smell/taste** un olor/sabor a quemado

burp [bɜrp] I. *n* eructo *m;* **to let out a ~** soltar

un eructo II. *vi* eructar III. *vt* **to ~ a baby** hacer eructar a un bebé

burr [bɜr] *n* 1. BOT abrojo *m* 2.(*sound*) zumbido *m*

burrow [ˈbɜr·oʊ] I. *n* madriguera *f;* **rabbit ~** conejera *f* II. *vi* (*dig a hole*) excavar un agujero; (*a tunnel*) excavar un túnel; (*a home*) excavar una madriguera; **to ~ into sth** horadar algo; *fig* hurgar en algo III. *vt* excavar

bursar [ˈbɜr·sər] *n* tesorero, -a *m, f* (*de un monasterio, colegio, universidad...*)

burst [bɜrst] I. *n* 1.(*explosion*) explosión *f* 2. MIL (*of fire*) ráfaga *f* 3.(*brief period*) **a ~ of laughter** una carcajada; **a ~ of applause** una salva de aplausos; **a ~ of anger** un arranque de cólera II.<burst, burst> *vi* 1.(*balloon, tire*) reventar; (*storm*) desatarse; **to ~ into tears** romper a llorar 2.(*move suddenly*) **to ~ into a place** irrumpir en un lugar; **to ~ open** abrir(se) de golpe 3. *fig* **to be ~ing to do sth** morirse de ganas de hacer algo; **to be ~ing with health** rebosar de salud; **to be ~ing with curiosity** morirse de curiosidad III.<burst, burst> *vt* reventar; **to ~ its banks** (*river*) desbordarse

◆**burst forth** *vi* brotar

◆**burst in** *vi* entrar de sopetón

◆**burst out** *vi* 1.(*exclaim*) saltar 2.(*break out*) **to ~ laughing/crying** echarse a reír/llorar

Burundi [bʊ·ˈrʊn·di] *n* Burundi *m*

bury [ˈber·i] <-ie-> *vt* 1.(*put underground*) enterrar 2.(*hide*) ocultar; **to ~ oneself in sth** enfrascarse en algo; **to be buried in thought** estar ensimismado; **to ~ one's head in one's hands** ocultar el rostro entre las manos

bus [bʌs] I.<-es> *n* autobús *m,* camión *m Méx,* colectivo *m Arg, Ven,* guagua *f Cuba,* ómnibus *m Perú, Urug;* **school ~** autobús escolar; **to catch/miss the ~** coger/perder el autobús; **to go by ~** [*o* **to take the ~**] ir en autobús ▶**to miss the ~** perder el autobús II.<-ss-> *vt* 1.(*travel by bus*) llevar en autobús 2.(*in restaurant*) **to ~ tables** limpiar mesas III.<-ss-> *vi* ir en autobús

busboy *n* ayudante *mf* de camarero

bus driver *n* conductor(a) *m(f)* de autobús

bush [bʊʃ] <-es> *n* 1. BOT arbusto *m;* **a ~ of hair** una mata de pelo 2.(*land*) **the ~** el monte ▶**to beat around the ~** andarse con rodeos; **to beat the ~es for sth** buscar algo por todas partes

bushel [ˈbʊʃ·əl] *n* fanega *f* (*en Gran Bretaña, esta medida equivale a 36,4 l; en Estados Unidos, a 35,2 l.*) ▶**to hide one's light under a ~** ocultar sus talentos

bushman [ˈbʊʃ·mən] <-men> *n* bosquimano *m*

bushy [ˈbʊʃ·i] <-ier, -iest> *adj* (*hair*) tupido, -a; (*beard, mustache*) espeso, -a; (*eyebrows*) poblado, -a

busily *adv* afanosamente

business [ˈbɪz·nɪs] *n* 1.(*trade, commerce*)

negocios *mpl;* **to be away on** ~ estar de viaje de negocios; **to do** ~ **with sb** hacer negocios con alguien; **to get down to** ~ ir al grano; **to go out of** ~ cerrar; **to set up a** ~ montar un negocio; **to set up** ~ **as a lawyer** establecerse como abogado; **to work in** ~ dedicarse a los negocios; ~ **is booming** el negocio va muy bien; **once we get the computer installed, we'll be in** ~ *inf* una vez que hayamos instalado el ordenador, podremos empezar **2.** <-es> (*sector*) industria *f;* **the frozen food** ~ la industria de los congelados; **what line of** ~ **are you in?** ¿en qué ramo trabajas? **3.** <-es> (*company*) empresa *f;* **to start up/run a** ~ poner/llevar un negocio **4.** (*matter*) asunto *m;* **an unfinished** ~ un asunto pendiente; **it's none of your** ~! *inf* ¡no es asunto tuyo!; **mind your own** ~! *inf* ¡no te metas donde no te llaman!; **to have no** ~ **doing sth** no tener derecho a hacer algo; **I make it my** ~ **to do that** me encargo de hacer eso; **it's a time-consuming** ~ requiere mucho tiempo ▶~ **before pleasure** *prov* antes es la obligación que el placer; ~ **as** usual *prov* todo sigue igual; **to** (**not**) be **in the** ~ **of doing sth** (no) tener por costumbre hacer algo; **to give sb the** ~ echar la bronca a alguien; **to mean** ~ hablar en serio; **like nobody's** ~ *inf* como un loco
business address *n* dirección *f* comercial
business card *n* tarjeta *f* comercial
business class *n* AVIAT clase *f* preferente
business expenses *npl* gastos *mpl* comerciales
business hours *n* horas *fpl* de oficina
business letter *n* carta *f* comercial
businesslike ['bɪz·nɪs·laɪk] *adj* **1.** (*serious*) formal **2.** (*efficient*) eficiente
businessman <-men> *n* hombre *m* de negocios
business park *n* parque *m* de negocios
business trip *n* viaje *m* de negocios
businesswoman <-women> *n* mujer *f* de negocios
busk [bʌsk] *vi* tocar un instrumento en la calle
busker ['bʌs·kər] *n* músico, -a *m, f* ambulante
busload ['bʌs·loʊd] *n* ~s **of tourists** autobuses *mpl* llenos de turistas
bus service *n* servicio *m* de autobuses
bus station *n* estación *f* de autobuses
bus stop *n* parada *f* de autobús
bust[1] [bʌst] *n* ART busto *m*
bust[2] [bʌst] **I.** *adj sl* **1.** (*broken*) destrozado, -a **2.** (*bankrupt*) en bancarrota; **to go** ~ quebrar **II.** *vt inf* **1.** (*break*) destrozar **2.** (*raid*) realizar una redada en ▶**to** ~ **one's** butt (**doing sth/to do sth**) partirse la espalda (haciendo algo)
bustle ['bʌs·əl] **I.** *vi* **to** ~ **around** ir y venir; **to** ~ **with activity** rebosar de actividad **II.** *n* **1.** ajetreo *m;* **hustle and** ~ bullicio *m* **2.** HIST (*dress part*) polisón *m*
bustling *adj* (*town, street*) animado, -a
busy ['bɪz·i] **I.** <-ier, -iest> *adj* **1.** (*occupied*) atareado, -a; **to be** ~ **doing sth** estar muy ocu-

pado haciendo algo; **to be** ~ **with sth** estar ocupado con algo; **to get** ~ empezar a trabajar **2.** (*full of activity*) activo, -a; (*exhausting*) agotador(a); ~ **street** calle *f* concurrida; ~ **seaport** puerto *m* marítimo de gran actividad; **a** ~ **time** un tiempo de actividad frenética; **I've had a** ~ **day** he tenido un día ajetreado **3.** TEL **to be** ~ (*phone line*) estar ocupado **4.** (*pattern, wallpaper*) recargado, -a **II.** <-ie-> *vt* **to** ~ **oneself with sth** ocuparse de algo
busybody ['bɪz·i·ˌbad·i] <-ies> *n inf* entrometido, -a *m, f;* **to be a** ~ ser un metomenttodo
but [bʌt] **I.** *prep* excepto; **all** ~ **one** todos excepto uno; **anything** ~... lo que sea menos...; **nothing** ~... nada más que...; **no one** ~ **him** nadie salvo él; ~ **for that I'd have had an accident** si no fuera por eso, habría tenido un accidente **II.** *conj* pero; **I'm not quitting** ~ **taking time off** no voy a dimitir, sino a tomarme tiempo libre; **he has paper** ~ **no pen** tiene papel pero no una pluma; **it is not red** ~ **pink** no es rojo sino rosa **III.** *adv* sólo; **he is** ~ **a baby** no es más que un bebé; **I can't help** ~ **cry** no puedo evitar llorar; **I can** ~ **hope she wins** solamente puedo esperar que gane **IV.** *n* pero *m;* **there are no** ~s **about it!** ¡no hay peros que valgan!
butane ['bju·teɪn] *n* butano *m*
butch [bʊtʃ] *adj* **1.** (*man*) macho **2.** (*woman*) marimacho
butcher ['bʊtʃ·ər] **I.** *n* carnicero, -a *m, f* **II.** *vt* **1.** (*meat*) matar **2.** (*murder*) asesinar (brutalmente), masacrar **3.** *fig* **to** ~ **a language** mutilar un idioma
butchery ['bʊtʃ·ə·ri] *n* **1.** (*of an animal*) matanza *f* **2.** (*killing*) carnicería *f*
butler ['bʌt·lər] *n* mayordomo *m*
butt [bʌt] **I.** *n* **1.** (*of rifle*) culata *f* **2.** (*of cigarette*) colilla *f* **3.** (*blow: with the head*) cabezazo *m* **4.** (*target*) **to be the** ~ **of sth** ser el blanco de algo **5.** (*container*) tonel *m* **6.** *inf* (*buttocks*) culo *m* **II.** *vt* (*with the horns*) topetar; (*with the head*) dar un cabezazo contra
butter ['bʌt·ər] **I.** *n* mantequilla *f* ▶**he/she looks as if** ~ **wouldn't melt in his/her** mouth parece que no haya roto un plato en su vida **II.** *vt* untar con mantequilla
◆**butter up** *vt* dar coba a, cepillar *AmL*
buttercup *n* BOT ranúnculo *m*
butter dish *n* recipiente *m* para mantequilla
butterfingers *n inv* manazas *mf inv*
butterfly ['bʌt·ər·flaɪ] <-ies> *n* **1.** ZOOL mariposa *f; fig* (*person*) persona *f* frívola **2.** TECH calón *m* **3.** SPORTS mariposa *f* ▶**to have butterflies in one's** stomach estar con los nervios a flor de piel
buttermilk ['bʌt·ər·mɪlk] *n* suero *m* de leche
buttery ['bʌt·ə·ri] <-ier, -iest> *adj* de mantequilla
butthead *n vulg sl* imbécil *mf,* chiflado, -a *m, f*
buttock ['bʌt·ək] *n* nalga *f*
button ['bʌt·ən] **I.** *n* (*on clothing*) botón *m;* (*with slogan*) chapa *f;* **start** ~ botón de inicio;

right/left mouse ~ botón derecho/izquierdo del ratón; **to push a** ~ apretar un botón; **at the push of a** ~ con sólo pulsar un botón ▸ **to be right on the** ~ estar en lo cierto **II.** *vi* abrocharse **III.** *vt* abrochar ▸ **to** ~ **it** [*o* one's lip] *inf* no decir ni esta boca es mía
◆ **button up** *vt* abrochar
buttonhole ['bʌt·ən·hoʊl] **I.** *n* FASHION ojal *m* **II.** *vt* obligar a escuchar
buttress ['bʌt·rɪs] <-es> *n* ARCHIT contrafuerte *m;* *fig* apoyo *m*
buxom ['bʌk·səm] *adj* pechugona
buy [baɪ] **I.** *n* compra *f;* **a good** ~ una ganga **II.**<bought, bought> *vt* **1.**(*purchase*) comprar; **to** ~ **sth from** [*o inf* **off**] **sb** comprar algo a alguien; **to** ~ **sb's silence** comprar el silencio de alguien **2.** *inf* (*believe*) creer; **did the teacher** ~ **your excuse?** ¿se tragó el profesor tu excusa? **3.**(*bribe*) sobornar
◆ **buy back** *vt* volver a comprar
◆ **buy into** *vt* (*in business*) comprar acciones de; *fig* (*accept as valid*) aceptar como válido
◆ **buy off** *vt always sep* sobornar
◆ **buy out** *vt* COM comprar la parte de
◆ **buy up** *vt insep* acaparar
buyer ['baɪ·ər] *n* **1.**(*in store*) comprador(a) *m(f)* **2.**(*as work*) encargado, -a *m, f* de compras
buyout ['baɪ·aʊt] *n* FIN compra *f* (*de la totalidad de las acciones*)*;* **management/worker** ~ compra de una empresa por los gerentes/empleados
buzz [bʌz] **I.** *vi* **1.**(*hum*) zumbar; (*bell*) sonar; **my ears were** ~**ing** me zumbaban los oídos; **the town was** ~**ing with rumors** el pueblo era un hervidero de rumores **2.** *sl* **to be** ~**ed** (*be tipsy*) ir borracho **II.** *vt inf* **1.** TEL llamar; (*signal to*) dar un toque a **2.** AVIAT (*fly low over*) sobrevolar a poca altura **III.** *n* **1.**(*humming noise*) zumbido *m;* (*low noise*) rumor *m;* (*of a doorbell*) llamada *f;* **the** ~ **of conversation** el rumor de la conversación **2.** *inf* (*telephone call*) llamada *f;* **to give sb a** ~ llamar a alguien **3.** *inf* (*feeling*) excitación *f;* (*from alcohol*) subidón *m;* **I get a** ~ **from** [*o* out of] **surfing** el surf me entusiasma; **sb gets a** ~ **from sth** algo excita a alguien; **I get a** ~ **from champagne** el champán se me sube a la cabeza
◆ **buzz off** *vi inf* largarse
buzzard ['bʌz·ərd] *n* (*turkey vulture*) gallinazo *m* común
buzzer ['bʌz·ər] *n* timbre *m*
buzz word *n* palabra *f* de moda
by [baɪ] **I.** *prep* **1.**(*near*) cerca de; **close** [*o* **near**] ~**...** cerca de...; **to be/lie/stand** ~ **...** estar/yacer/permanecer cerca de...; ~ **the sea** junto al mar **2.**(*at*) junto a; **to remain** ~ **sb for two days** quedarse junto a alguien durante

dos días **3.**(*during*) ~ **day/night** durante el día/la noche; ~ **moonlight** a la luz de la luna **4.**(*at the latest time*) para; ~ **tomorrow/midnight** para mañana/la medianoche; ~ **then/now** para entonces/ahora **5.**(*cause*) por; **a novel** ~ **Joyce** una novela de Joyce; **to be killed** ~ **sth/sb** ser matado por algo/alguien; **surrounded** ~ **dogs** rodeado de perros **6.**(*through means of*) ~ **train/plane/bus** en tren/avión/autobús; **made** ~ **hand** hecho a mano; **to hold sb** ~ **the arm** tomar a alguien por el brazo; ~ **doing sth** haciendo algo **7.**(*through*) ~ **chance/mistake** por suerte/error **8.**(*under*) **to call sb/sth** ~ **their/its name** llamar a alguien/algo por su nombre; **what does he mean** ~ **that?** ¿a qué se refiere con eso? **9.**(*alone*) **to be** ~ **oneself** estar solo; **to do sth** ~ **oneself** hacer algo solo **10.**(*as promise to*) **to swear** ~ **God/sth** jurar por Dios/algo **11.**(*in measurement, arithmetic*) **to buy** ~ **the pound/dozen** comprar por libra/docenas; **to divide** ~ **6** dividir entre 6; **to increase** ~ **10%** aumentar en un 10%; **to multiply** ~ **4** multiplicar por 4; **paid** ~ **the hour/day** pagado por hora/día; **4 feet** ~ **6** 4 por 6 pies; **one** ~ **one** uno a uno **12.**(*from the perspective of*) **to judge** ~ **appearances** juzgar por las apariencias; **all right** ~ **me** *inf* por mí, de acuerdo **II.** *adv* **1.**(*aside*) cerca; **to put/lay sth** ~ poner/dejar algo a mano **2.**(*in a while*) ~ **and** ~ dentro de poco **3.**(*past*) **to go/pass** ~ pasar ▸ ~ **and large** en general
bye [baɪ] *interj,* **bye-bye** [ˌbaɪ·'baɪ] *interj inf* adiós
by-election ['baɪ·ɪˌlek·ʃən] *n* elección *f* parcial
Byelorussian [ˌbjel·oʊ·'rʌʃ·ən] *adj, n s.* **Belarusian**
bygone ['baɪ·gɔn] **I.** *adj inv* pasado, -a **II.** *n* **let** ~ **s be** ~ **s** lo pasado pasado está
bylaw *n* **1.**(*regional law*) reglamento *m* local **2.**(*organization's rule*) estatuto *m*
bypass ['baɪ·pæs] **I.** *n* **1.** AUTO carretera *f* de circunvalación **2.** ELEC desviación *f* **3.** MED bypass *m* **II.** *vt* **1.**(*make a detour*) evitar **2.** *fig* (*act without permission of*) **to** ~ **sb** actuar sin el consentimiento de alguien **3.** *fig* (*avoid*) evitar
by-play *n* THEAT acción *f* de segundo plano
byproduct ['baɪ·prɑdˌəkt] *n* subproducto *m;* *fig* derivado *m*
byroad ['baɪ·roʊd] *n* carretera *f* secundaria
bystander ['baɪ·stænˌdər] *n* espectador(a) *m(f)*
byte [baɪt] *n* byte *m*
byway ['baɪ·weɪ] *n* carretera *f* secundaria
byword ['baɪ·wɜrd] *n* ejemplo *m;* **to be a** ~ **for sth** ser sinónimo de algo

C

C, c [si] *n* **1.** (*letter*) C, c *f;* ~ **as in Charlie** C de Carmen **2.** MUS do *m* **3.** SCHOOL ≈ suficiente *m*

C *after n abbr of* **Celsius, centigrade** C

C. *abbr of* **century** s.

c. 1. *abbr of* **circa** (*by numbers*) aprox.; (*by dates*) hacia **2.** *abbr of* **cent** cent **3.** *abbr of* **cup** taza *f* (*aprox. 250 ml*)

ca. *abbr of* **circa 1.** (*by numbers*) aprox. **2.** (*by dates*) hacia

CA [ˌkæl·ɪ·ˈfɔr·njə] *n abbr of* **California** California *f*

cab [kæb] *n* **1.** (*taxi*) taxi *m;* **by** ~ en taxi **2.** (*of truck, locomotive*) cabina *f* **3.** HIST (*horse-drawn*) carruaje *n*

cabaret [ˌkæb·ə·ˈreɪ] *n* cabaret *m*

cabbage [ˈkæb·ɪdʒ] *n* CULIN repollo *m*

cabbie *n*, **cabby** [ˈkæb·i] *n*, **cabdriver** *n* taxista *mf*

cabin [ˈkæb·ɪn] *n* **1.** (*house*) cabaña *f* **2.** (*in ship, airplane*) cabina *f*

cabin class *n* NAUT clase de camarote superior a la clase turista e inferior a la primera clase

cabin cruiser *n* yate *m* de motor

cabinet [ˈkæb·ɪ·nɪt] *n* **1.** (*storage place*) armario *m;* (*glass-fronted*) vitrina *f;* **filing** ~ archivador *m* **2.** + *sing/pl vb* POL gabinete *m*, consejo *m* de ministros

cabinetmaker *n* ebanista *mf*

cable [ˈkeɪ·bəl] *n* **1.** (*wire rope*) cable *m;* **coil of** ~ rollo *m* de cable **2.** TV televisión *f* por cable **3.** HIST (*electrically transmitted message*) cablegrama *m;* **to send sth by** ~ cablegrafiar algo II. *vt* HIST cablegrafiar

cable car *n* teleférico *m*

cable network *n* cableado *m*

cable railway *n* funicular *m*

cable stitch *n* punto *m* trenzado

cable television *n*, **cable TV** *n* televisión *f* por cable

caboodle [kə·ˈbud·əl] *n inf* **the whole** (**kit and**) ~ toda la pesca

cabriolet [ˌkæb·ri·ə·ˈleɪ] *n* descapotable *m*

cacao [kə·ˈkaʊ] *n* cacao *m;* ~ (**bean**) (semilla *f* de) cacao *m*

cache [kæʃ] *n* **1.** (*hiding place*) escondite *m;* (*secret stockpile*) alijo *m;* **weapons** ~ alijo de armas **2.** COMPUT caché *m;* ~ **memory** memoria *f* caché

cachet [kæ·ˈʃeɪ] *n* distinción *f*, prestigio *m*

cackle [ˈkæk·əl] I. *vi* **1.** (*hen*) cacarear **2.** *fig* (*laugh*) reírse escandalosamente **3.** (*talk*) cotorrear II. *n* **1.** (*of hen*) cacareo *m* **2.** (*laugh*) risotada *f*

cacophony [kə·ˈkaf·ə·ni] *n* (*loud discord*) cacofonía *f;* (*noise*) estrépito *m*

cactus [ˈkæk·təs] <-es *o* cacti> *n* cactus *m inv,* ulala *f Bol*

CAD [kæd] *n abbr of* **Computer-Aided Design** CAD *m*, DAC *m AmL*

cadaver [kə·ˈdæv·ər] *n* MED cadáver *m*

CAD/CAM [ˈkæd·kæm] *n abbr of* **computer-aided design/computer-aided manufacturing** CAD/CAM *m*

caddie, caddy [ˈkæd·i] <-ies> I. *n* caddie *mf*, caddy *mf* II. <caddied, caddied, caddying> *vi* **to** ~ **for sb** hacer de caddy de alguien

cadence [ˈkeɪd·əns] *n* cadencia *f*

cadet [kə·ˈdet] *n a.* MIL cadete *mf*

cadmium [ˈkæd·mi·əm] *n* cadmio *m*

cadre [ˈka·dreɪ] *n* **1.** (*elite trained group*) cuadro *m* **2.** (*group member*) (miembro *mf* del) cuadro *m*

Caesar [ˈsi·zər] *n* César *m;* **Julius** ~ HIST Julio César

caesarean [si·ˈzer·i·ən] *n* ~ (**section**) cesárea *f*

cafe *n*, **café** [kæ·ˈfeɪ] *n* cafetería *f*

cafeteria [ˌkæf·ɪ·ˈtɪr·i·ə] *n* restaurante *m* autoservicio, self-service *m*

caffeine [kæ·ˈfin] *n* cafeína *f*

cage [keɪdʒ] I. *n* jaula *f* II. *vt* enjaular

cagey [ˈkeɪ·dʒi] <-ier, -iest> *adj inf* reservado, -a; **to be** ~ **about sth** ocultar [*o* reservarse] información sobre algo

cahoots [kə·ˈhuts] *npl inf* **to be in** ~ (**with sb**) estar compinchado (con alguien)

cairn [kern] *n* mojón *m* (de piedras)

Cairo [ˈkaɪ·roʊ] *n* El Cairo

cajole [kə·ˈdʒoʊl] I. *vt* engatusar; **to** ~ **sb into/out of doing sth** engatusar a alguien para que haga/no haga algo II. *vi* engatusar, camelar *inf*

cake [keɪk] I. *n* **1.** CULIN pastel *m;* (*small*) pasta *f;* **frosted** ~ tarta *f* helada; **sponge** ~ bizcocho *m*, queque *m AmL* **2.** (*of soap*) pastilla *f;* (*of chocolate*) barra *f* ▶ **to sell like hot** ~**s** *inf* venderse como rosquillas [*o* como pan caliente *Col*]; **to want to have one's** ~ **and eat it, too** quererlo todo; **to take the** ~ (*positively and negatively*) llevarse la palma, ser el colmo *AmS* II. *vt* (*cover with*) **his boots were** ~**d with mud** sus botas estaban cubiertas de barro III. *vi* (*form into mass*) endurecerse

Cal. *abbr of* **California** California *f*

cal. *n abbr of* **calorie** cal *f*

calamity [kə·ˈlæm·ə·ti] <-ies> *n* calamidad *f*

calciferous [kæl·ˈsɪf·ər·əs] *adj* calizo, -a

calcify [ˈkæl·sɪ·faɪ] <-ie-> I. *vt* calcificar II. *vi* calcificarse

calcium [ˈkæl·si·əm] *n* calcio *m*

calculable [ˈkæl·kjə·lə·bəl] *adj* MATH, ECON calculable; **the total damage is** ~ **at $15,000** los daños totales se estiman en 15.000 dólares

calculate [ˈkæl·kjə·leɪt] I. *vt* calcular; **to** ~ **sth at...** calcular algo en... II. *vi* calcular

calculated *adj* **1.** (*likely*) probable **2.** MATH calculado, -a; **a** ~ **risk** un riesgo calculado **3.** (*deliberate*) deliberado, -a

calculating *adj* calculador(a)

calculation [ˌkæl·kjə·ˈleɪ·ʃən] *n* **1.** MATH cálculo *m;* (*figures*) cómputo *m* **2.** (*foreseeing*) cálculo *m* **3.** (*selfish planning*) premeditación *f*

calculator [ˈkæl·kjə·leɪ·tər] *n* calculadora *f*

calculus ['kæl·kjə·ləs] *n* cálculo *m*
calendar ['kæl·ən·dər] *n* calendario *m*, exfoliador *m Chile, Méx*
calendar month <-es> *n* mes *m*
calendar year *n* año *m* civil
calf[1] [kæf] <calves> *n* **1.** (*young cow or bull*) ternero, -a *m, f*; **to be in ~** estar preñada **2.** (*leather*) piel *f* de becerro ▶**to kill the** **fatted** ~ hacer una gran fiesta de bienvenida
calf[2] [kæf] <calves> *n* (*lower leg*) pantorrilla *f*
caliber ['kæl·ə·bər] *n* calibre *m*; **to be of (a)** **high** ~ ser de grueso calibre
calibrate ['kæl·ɪ·breɪt] *vt* calibrar
calico ['kæl·ɪ·koʊ] *n* calicó *m*, percal *m*
Calif. *abbr of* **California** California *f*
California [ˌkæl·ə·ˈfɔr·njə] *n* California *f*
call [kɔl] **I.** *n* **1.** (*telephone*) llamada *f*; **to give** **sb a** ~ llamar a alguien (por teléfono) **2.** (*visit*) visita *f*; **to be on a** ~ estar haciendo una visita; **to be on** ~ estar de guardia; **to pay a** ~ **on sb** hacer una visita a alguien **3.** (*shout*) grito *m* **4.** (*animal cry*) grito *m*; (*bird*) canto *m* **5.** *a.* POL llamamiento *m*; **a** ~ **for help** una llamada de socorro **6.** *a.* ECON requerimiento *m*; **money** **on** ~ dinero *m* a la vista; **there is not much** ~ **for sth** no hay demasiada demanda de algo **7.** *form* (*need*) **to have no** ~ **for sth** no tener ninguna necesidad de algo; **you had no** ~ **to** **say that** no tenías por qué decir eso **8.** (*decision*) decisión *f*; **you make the** ~ tú decides **9.** (*attraction*) llamada *f*; **the** ~ **of the wild** la llamada de la selva ▶**to have a close** ~ salvarse por los pelos [*o* por un pelo] **II.** *vt* **1.** (*name, address as*) llamar; **to** ~ **sb names** insultar a alguien; **what's that actor** ~**ed?** ¿cómo se llama ese actor?; **what's his new** **film** ~**ed?** ¿cómo se titula su nueva película?; **she's** ~**ed by her middle name, Jane** la llaman por su segundo nombre, Jane **2.** (*telephone*) llamar, telefonear *AmL;* **to** ~ **sb collect** llamar a alguien a cobro revertido **3.** (*make noise to attract*) **to** ~ **sb's attention** llamar la atención de alguien; **I** ~**ed you to** **come to eat ten minutes ago** te he llamado para que vinieras a comer hace diez minutos **4.** (*ask to come*) reclamar; **she was** ~**ed to a** **meeting in Denver** fue convocada a una reunión en Denver **5.** (*ask for quiet*) **to** ~ **for** **order** pedir orden **6.** (*reprimand*) amonestar; **to** ~ **sth to mind** (*recall*) acordarse de algo; (*remember*) recordar algo **7.** (*regard as*) **to** ~ **sth one's own** poder decir que algo es de uno; **you** ~ **this a party?** ¿a esto llamas fiesta?; **I'm** **not** ~**ing you a liar** no digo que seas un mentiroso; **I don't know exactly how much** **you owe me, but let's** ~ **it an even $10** no sé cuánto me debes exactamente, ¿lo dejamos en 10 dólares justos?; **he has very few ideas** **that he can genuinely** ~ **his own** tiene muy pocas ideas realmente propias **8.** (*decide to* *have*) **to** ~ **a meeting** (**to order**) convocar una reunión; **to** ~ **a halt to sth** suspender algo; **to** ~ **a strike** declarar una huelga **III.** *vi*

1. (*telephone*) llamar **2.** (*drop by*) pasar **3.** (*shout*) gritar
◆**call away** *vt* **he was called away** tuvo que salir; **he was called away on business** tuvo que irse por negocios
◆**call back I.** *vt* **1.** (*telephone*) devolver la llamada a **2.** (*ask to return*) hacer volver **3.** ECON requerir; **the company has called back a** **type of toy** la empresa ha pedido la devolución de un tipo de juguete **II.** *vi* (*phone* *again*) volver a llamar
◆**call for** *vt insep* **1.** (*come to get*) pasar a recoger **2.** (*ask*) pedir **3.** (*demand, require*) exigir; (*require*) requerir; **this calls for a cel**-**ebration** esto hay que celebrarlo
◆**call forth** *vt form* suscitar
◆**call in** *vt* **1.** (*ask to come*) llamar **2.** FIN **to** ~ **a loan** pedir la devolución de un préstamo
◆**call off** *vt* **1.** (*cancel*) suspender **2.** (*order* *back*) **he called off his dog** llamó a su perro
◆**call on** *vt insep* **1.** (*appeal to*) **to** ~ **sb** (**to do** **sth**) apelar a alguien (para que haga algo); **to** ~ **a witness** citar a un testigo; **I now** ~ **every**-**one to raise a glass to our friend** *form* propongo un brindis por nuestro amigo **2.** (*visit*) visitar
◆**call out I.** *vt* (*shout*) gritar **II.** *vi* **1.** (*shout*) gritar **2.** *fig* (*demand*) **to call out for sth** exigir algo
◆**call up** *vt* **1.** (*telephone*) llamar **2.** COMPUT **to** ~ **sth** sacar algo en pantalla **3.** (*order to join* *the military*) **to call up the reserves** llamar a filas a los reservistas **4.** (*conjure up*) conjurar
caller ['kɔ·lər] *n* **1.** (*on the telephone*) persona *f* que llama por teléfono **2.** (*at bingo game*) *persona que extrae las bolas del bingo y las lee* *en alto;* (*at square dance*) *persona que dirige* *un baile de grupo, diciendo los pasos que se* *deben realizar*
call girl *n* prostituta *f*
calligraphy [kə·ˈlɪg·rə·fi] *n* caligrafía *f*
call-in *n* RADIO, TV *programa con llamadas del* *público*
calling ['kɔ·lɪŋ] *n form* vocación *f*
calling card *n* tarjeta *f* telefónica
callous ['kæl·əs] *adj* (*heartless*) cruel; (*insensi*-*tive*) insensible
call sign ['kɔl·saɪn] *n* distintivo *m* de llamada
callus ['kæl·əs] <-es> *n* MED callo *m*
calm [kam] **I.** *adj* **1.** (*not nervous*) tranquilo, -a; **to keep** ~ mantener la calma **2.** (*peaceful*) pacífico, -a **3.** (*not windy*) sin viento **4.** (*not* *wavy*) sin olas **II.** *n* tranquilidad *f;* **the** ~ **before the storm** *fig* la calma que precede a la tormenta **III.** *vt* tranquilizar; **to** ~ **oneself** calmarse
calmness *n* **1.** (*lack of agitation*) tranquilidad *f* **2.** (*of the sea*) calma *f*
caloric [kə·ˈlɔr·ɪk] *adj* calórico, -a
calorie ['kæl·ə·ri] *n* caloría *f*
calorie-laden *adj* rico, -a en calorías
calorific [ˌkæl·ə·ˈrɪf·ɪk] *adj* calorífico, -a
calumny ['kæl·əm·ni] *n form* calumnia *f*

calve [kæv] *vi* parir

Calvinism ['kæl·vɪ·nɪz·əm] *n* REL calvinismo *m*

Calvinist ['kæl·vɪ·nɪst] REL **I.** *n* calvinista *mf* **II.** *adj* calvinista

CAM [kæm] *n abbr of* **computer assisted manufacturing** fabricación *f* asistida por ordenador

cam [kæm] *n* TECH leva *f*

camaraderie [ˌkæ·mə·'ra·də·ri] *n* camaradería *f*

camber ['kæm·bər] *n* (*of road*) peralte *m*

Cambodia [kæm·'bou·di·ə] *n* Camboya *f*

Cambodian [kæm·'bou·di·ən] **I.** *adj* camboyano, -a **II.** *n* camboyano, -a *m, f*

camcorder ['kæm·kɔr·dər] *n* videocámara *f*

came [keɪm] *vi pt of* **come**

camel ['kæm·əl] **I.** *n* **1.** ZOOL camello *m* **2.** (*color*) beige *m* **II.** *adj* **1.** (*camel-hair*) de pelo de camello **2.** (*color*) beige

camel-hair ['kæm·əl·her] *n* pelo *m* de camello

cameo ['kæm·i·ou] *n* **1.** (*jewelry*) camafeo *m* **2.** CINE, TV aparición *f* breve, papel *m* corto

camera ['kæm·ər·ə] *n* **1.** PHOT cámara *f* (de fotos); CINE cámara *f* (de vídeo); **to be on ~** estar en imagen **2.** LAW **in ~** a puerta cerrada; *fig* en secreto

camera angle *n* ángulo *m* de cámara

cameraman <-men> *n* cámara *m*

camera-ready *adj* TYPO preparado, -a para la cámara

camera shot *n* CINE toma *f*

camera-shy *adj* **to be ~** no ser muy amigo de las fotografías

camerawoman <-women> *n* cámara *f*

Cameroon [ˌkæm·ə·'run] *n* Camerún *m*

Cameroonian [ˌkæm·ə·'ru·ni·ən] **I.** *adj* camerunés, -esa **II.** *n* camerunés, -esa *m, f*

camomile *n s.* **chamomile**

camouflage ['kæm·ə·ˌflaʒ] **I.** *n* camuflaje *m* **II.** *vt* camuflar; **to ~ oneself** camuflarse

camp¹ [kæmp] **I.** *n* **1.** (*encampment*) campamento *m;* **army ~** campamento militar; **summer ~** campamento de verano; **to break ~** levantar el campamento; **to set up ~** establecer [o montar] el campamento **2.** (*group*) bando *m;* **to go over to the other ~** pasarse al otro bando; **to have a foot in both ~s** estar en ambos bandos, nadar entre dos aguas **II.** *vi* acampar; **to ~ out** acampar; **to go ~ing** ir de camping [o acampada], campear *AmL*

camp² [kæmp] **I.** *n* (**high**) **~** amaneramiento *m* **II.** *adj* (*affected*) afectado, -a; (*effeminate*) amanerado, -a **III.** *vt* **to ~ it up** actuar con afectación

campaign [kæm·'peɪn] **I.** *n* campaña *f;* **~ trail** campaña *f* electoral **II.** *vi* hacer campaña; **to ~ for sth/sb** hacer campaña a favor de algo/alguien

campaigner [kæm·'peɪ·nər] *n* **1.** (*election worker*) partidario, -a *m, f* **2.** (*person who campaigns*) defensor(a) *m(f);* **a ~ for sth** un luchador a favor de algo

camper ['kæm·pər] *n* **1.** (*person*) campista *mf*

2. AUTO caravana *f*

campfire *n* fogata *f;* **~ song** canción *f* de hoguera

camp follower *n* **1.** (*civilian worker*) trabajador(a) *m(f)* civil **2.** (*supporter*) simpatizante *mf*

campground *n* (zona *f* de) camping *m*, campamento *m Col, Méx*

camphor ['kæm·fər] *n* MED alcanfor *m*

camping ['kæm·pɪŋ] *n* camping *m;* **to go ~** ir de acampada

campsite ['kæmp·sait] *n* campamento *m*, camping *m;* (*for one tent*) parcela *f* de camping

campus ['kæm·pəs] <-es> *n* campus *m inv*

camshaft ['kæm·ʃæft] *n* TECH árbol *m* de levas

can¹ [kæn] **I.** *n* **1.** (*container*) lata *f;* (*of oil*) bidón *m* **2.** *sl* (*toilet*) trono *m* **3.** *inf* (*prison*) trullo *m* ▸ **a ~ of worms** un problema peligudo; **to open (up) a ~ of worms** abrir la caja de los truenos **II.** <-nn-> *vt* **1.** (*put in cans*) enlatar **2.** *sl* (*stop*) **~ it!** ¡basta ya!

can² [kən] <could, could> *aux* **1.** (*be able to*) poder; **if I could** si pudiera; **I think she ~ help you** creo que ella te puede ayudar; **I could have kissed her** habría podido besarla **2.** *inf* (*be permitted to*) poder; **you can't go** no puedes ir; **could I look at it?** ¿podría verlo? **3.** (*know how to*) saber; **~ you swim?** ¿sabes nadar?

Canada ['kæn·ə·də] *n* Canadá *m*

Canadian [kə·'neɪ·di·ən] **I.** *n* canadiense *mf* **II.** *adj* canadiense

canal [kə·'næl] *n* canal *m*

canalization [ˌkæn·ə·lɪ·'zeɪ·ʃən] *n* canalización *f*

canalize ['kæn·ə·laɪz] *vt* **1.** (*provide with canals*) *a. fig* encauzar **2.** (*convert into a canal*) canalizar

canary [kə·'ner·i] **I.** <-ies> *n* canario *m* **II.** *adj* **~ yellow** amarillo canario

Canary Islands *n* Islas *fpl* Canarias

canary seed *n* alpiste *m*

canasta [kə·'næs·tə] *n* GAMES canasta *f*

cancel ['kæn·səl] <-ll-, -l-> **I.** *vt* **1.** (*reservation, meeting*) cancelar; (*party, concert*) suspender; (*result, license*) anular; (*payment*) retirar **2.** MATH **to ~ each other out** anularse mutuamente **3.** COMPUT cancelar **II.** *vi* (*reservation*) cancelar una reserva; (*meeting*) cancelar una reunión

cancellation [ˌkæn·sə·'leɪ·ʃən] *n* (*of reservation, meeting*) cancelación *f;* (*of party, concert*) suspensión *f;* (*of license*) anulación *f;* (*of contract*) rescisión *f*

cancer ['kæn·sər] *n* MED cáncer *m*, cangro *m Col, Guat;* **~ specialist** oncólogo, -a *m, f;* **~ cell** célula *f* cancerígena

Cancer ['kæn·sər] *n* Cáncer *m*

cancer clinic *n* MED clínica *f* oncológica

cancerous ['kæn·sər·əs] *adj* MED canceroso, -a

cancer research *n* MED investigación *f* oncológica

candelabra [ˌkæn·dəl·'a·brə] <-(s)> *n* candelabro *m*, candil *m AmL*

candid ['kæn·dɪd] *adj* franco, -a; (*talk*) sincero, -a; (*picture*) natural

candidacy ['kæn·dɪ·də·si] *n* candidatura *f*

candidate ['kæn·dɪ·dət] *n* 1. POL (*competitor*) candidato, -a *m, f* 2. (*possible choice*) candidato, -a *m, f*

candidature ['kæn·də·də·tʃʊr] *n* candidatura *f*

candid camera *n* cámara *f* indiscreta

candied ['kæn·dɪd] *adj* confitado, -a

candle ['kæn·dəl] *n* 1. (*light*) vela *f* 2. BOT castaña *f* de Indias ►**to burn one's ~ at both ends** hacer de la noche día; **she can't hold a ~ to him** no le llega ni a la suela del zapato

candlelight ['kæn·dəl·laɪt] *n* luz *f* de una vela; **to do sth by ~** hacer algo a la luz de una vela

Candlemas ['kæn·dəl·məs] *n* REL Candelaria *f*

candlepower ['kæn·dəl·paʊ·ər] *n* candela *f*

candlestick ['kæn·dəl·stɪk] *n* candelero *m*

candlewick ['kæn·dəl·wɪk] *n* (*textile*) chenilla *f*

candor ['kæn·dər] *n form* franqueza *f*

candy ['kæn·di] I.<-ies> *n* (*sweets*) golosinas *fpl* II. *vt* escarchar

candy bar *n* tableta *f* de chocolate

candy store *n* tienda *f* de golosinas

cane [keɪn] I. *n* 1. (*dried plant stem*) caña *f* 2. (*furniture*) mimbre *m* 3. (*stick*) bastón *m;* (*for punishment*) palmeta *f* II. *vt* dar palmetazos

cane sugar *n* azúcar *m* de caña

canine ['keɪ·naɪn] I. *n* 1. ZOOL canino *m* 2. (*tooth*) colmillo *m*, canino *m* II. *adj* canino, -a

canister ['kæn·ɪ·stər] *n* (*metal*) lata *f;* (*plastic*) bote *m*

cannabis ['kæn·ə·bɪs] *n* (*plant*) cannabis *f;* (*drug*) marihuana *f*

canned [kænd] *adj* 1. (*in metal containers*) enlatado, -a; (*fruit, vegetables*) en conserva; (*food, meat, beer*) de lata 2. MUS, TV ~ **music** música *f* enlatada; ~ **laughter** risas *fpl* grabadas

cannery ['kæn·ə·ri] <-ies> *n* fábrica *f* de conservas

cannibal ['kæn·ɪ·bəl] *n* caníbal *mf*

cannibalism ['kæn·ɪ·bəl·ɪz·əm] *n* canibalismo *m*

cannibalize ['kæn·ɪ·bə·laɪz] *vt* AUTO desguazar

canning ['kæn·ɪŋ] *n* enlatado *m;* ~ **factory** fábrica *f* de conservas

cannon ['kæn·ən] *n* MIL cañón *m*

cannon ball *n* bala *f* de cañón

cannon fodder *n* carne *f* de cañón

cannot ['kæn·at] *aux* = **can not** *s.* **can²**

canny ['kæn·i] <-ier, -iest> *adj* (*clever*) astuto, -a

canoe [kə·'nu] *n* canoa *f* ►**to paddle one's own ~** arreglárselas solo

canoeing *n* piragüismo *m*

canoeist [kə·'nu·ɪst] *n* piragüista *mf*

canon ['kæn·ən] *n* 1. REL, MUS canon *m* 2. (*per-*son) canónigo *m* 3. LIT obra *f* (literaria)

canonization [ˌkæn·ə·nɪ·'zeɪ·ʃən] *n* canonización *f*

canonize ['kæn·ə·naɪz] *vt* canonizar

can opener ['kæn·ˌoʊ·pə·nər] *n* abrelatas *m inv*

canopy ['kæn·ə·pi] <-ies> *n* 1. (*roof-like covering*) toldo *m* 2. AVIAT cubierta *f* transparente 3. ARCHIT baldaquín *m* 4. *form* (*sky*) bóveda *f* celeste

cant¹ [kænt] *n* 1. (*insincere talk*) hipocresía *f* 2. LING jerga *f*

cant² [kænt] I. *n* inclinación *f* II. *vt* inclinar III. *vi* inclinarse, ladearse

can't [kænt] = **cannot**

cantankerous [kæn·'tæŋ·kər·əs] *adj* intratable

cantata [kən·'ta·tə] *n* MUS cantata *f*

canteen [kæn·'tin] *n* 1. (*cafeteria*) cantina *f* 2. MIL (*drink container*) cantimplora *f*

canter ['kæn·tər] I. *n* medio galope *m* II. *vi* ir a medio galope

cantilever ['kæn·tə̣l·i·vər] *n* viga *f* voladiza; ~ **bridge** puente *m* voladizo

Cantonese [ˌkæn·tə·'niz] I. *adj* cantonés, -esa II. *n* 1. (*language*) cantonés *m* 2. (*person*) cantonés, -esa *m, f*

canvas ['kæn·vəs] <-es> *n* 1. (*cloth*) lona *f;* NAUT velamen *m;* **under ~** (*in a tent*) en una tienda de campaña 2. ART lienzo *m*, holán *m AmC*

canvass ['kæn·vəs] I. *vt* 1. (*gather opinion*) sondear; **to ~ sth** hacer una encuesta de algo 2. POL (*votes*) escrutar II. *vi* POL hacer campaña

canvasser ['kæn·və·sər] *n* POL persona que va de puerta en puerta solicitando votos para un determinado partido político

canvassing *n* POL solicitación *f* de votos

canyon ['kæn·jən] *n* GEO cañón *m*

CAP [ˌsi·eɪ·'pi] *n abbr of* **Civil Air Patrol** Patrulla Civil Aérea

cap¹ [kæp] I. *n* 1. (*without peak*) gorro *m* 2. (*with peak*) gorra *f;* ~ **and gown** UNIV toga *f* y birrete *m* 3. (*cover*) tapón *m;* PHOT tapa *f;* **screw-on ~** casquete *m* 4. (*of tooth*) funda *f* 5. (*limit*) tope *m;* **salary ~** salario *m* máximo 6. (*contraceptive*) diafragma *m* 7. (*in toy gun*) fulminante *m* ►**to put on one's thinking ~** *inf* hacer uso de la materia gris *prov* II. <-pp-> *vt* 1. (*limit*) limitar 2. (*cover*) tapar; (*tooth*) enfundar 3. (*outdo*) coronar; **to ~ it all** para colmo

cap² [kæp] *n abbr of* **capital** (**letter**) mayúscula *f*

capability [ˌkeɪ·pə·'bɪl·ə·ti] <-ies> *n* 1. (*ability*) capacidad *f;* (*power*) poder *m* 2. (*skill*) aptitud *f*

capable ['keɪ·pə·bəl] *adj* 1. (*competent*) competente 2. (*able*) capaz; **to be ~ of doing sth** ser capaz de hacer algo

capacity [kə·'pæs·ə·ti] <-ies> *n* 1. (*volume*) cabida *f*, capacidad *f;* **to be full to ~** estar completamente lleno; **filled to ~** completamente lleno 2. (*ability*) capacidad *f;* (*mental*) aptitud *f*

3. (*amount*) capacidad *f;* **seating** ~ aforo *m*
4. (*output*) rendimiento *m;* **to work at full** ~
trabajar a pleno rendimiento **5.** (*role*) calidad *f*
cape¹ [keɪp] *n* GEO cabo *m*
cape² [keɪp] *n* (*cloak*) capa *f*
caper¹ ['keɪ·pər] I. *n* **1.** (*joyful leaping movement*) cabriola *f;* **to cut** ~**s** hacer cabriolas
2. (*dubious activity*) travesura *f* II. *vi* dar brincos
caper² ['keɪ·pər] *n* BOT alcaparra *f*
Cape Town ['keɪp·taʊn] *n* Ciudad *f* del Cabo
Cape Verde ['keɪp·vɜrd] *n* Cabo *m* Verde
capillary ['kæp·ə·ler·i] <-ies> *n* vaso *m* capilar
capital ['kæp·ə·təl] I. *n* **1.** (*principal city*) capital *f* **2.** TYPO mayúscula *f;* **small** ~**s** versalitas
fpl **3.** ARCHIT capitel *m* **4.** FIN capital *m;* **to
make** ~ (**out**) **of sth** *fig* sacar partido de algo
II. *adj* **1.** (*principal*) primordial; ~ **city** capital
f **2.** TYPO (*letter*) mayúscula *f* **3.** LAW capital;
~ **punishment** pena *f* capital [*o* de muerte]
capital assets *npl* FIN activo *m* fijo
capital crime *n* LAW crimen *m* capital
capital gains tax <-es> *n* impuesto *m* sobre la
plusvalía
capital investment *n* FIN inversión *f* de capital
capital investment company <-ies> *n* sociedad *f* inversora
capitalism ['kæp·ə·təl·ɪz·əm] *n* capitalismo *m*
capitalist ['kæp·ə·təl·ɪst] I. *n* capitalista *mf*
II. *adj* capitalista
capitalistic [ˌkæp·ə·tə·'lɪs·tɪk] *adj* capitalista
capitalization [ˌkæp·ə·təl·ɪ·'zeɪ·ʃən] *n* capitalización *f*
capitalize ['kæp·ə·tə·laɪz] *vt* **1.** TYPO escribir en
mayúsculas **2.** *a.* FIN capitalizar
capital letter ['kæp·ə·təl·'le·t̬ər] *n* mayúscula
f; **in** ~**s** en mayúsculas
capital punishment *n* pena *f* de muerte
capitulate [kə·'pɪtʃ·ə·leɪt] *vi* **1.** MIL **to** ~ **to
sth/sb** capitular ante algo/alguien **2.** (*give
way*) ceder
capitulation [kə·'pɪtʃ·ə·'leɪ·ʃən] *n* capitulación
f; ~ **to sb/sth** capitulación ante alguien/algo
cappuccino [ˌkæp·ə·'tʃi·noʊ] *n* capuchino *m*
caprice [kə·'pris] *n liter* capricho *m*
capricious [kə·'prɪʃ·əs] *adj* caprichoso, -a
Capricorn ['kæp·rɪ·kɔrn] *n* Capricornio *m*
caps. *n abbr of* **capital letters** mayúsc. *fpl*
capsize ['kæp·saɪz] I. *vt* NAUT hacer zozobrar;
fig volcar II. *vi* NAUT zozobrar; *fig* volcar
capstan ['kæp·stən] *n* NAUT cabrestante *m*
capsule ['kæp·səl] *n* cápsula *f*
captain ['kæp·tɪn] I. *n* capitán, -ana *m, f* II. *vt*
capitanear
captaincy ['kæp·tɪn·si] *n* capitanía *f*
caption ['kæp·ʃən] *n* **1.** TYPO, PUBL (*heading*)
título *m;* (*for cartoon*) leyenda *f* **2.** CINE subtítulo *m*
captivate ['kæp·tə·veɪt] *vt* cautivar
captive ['kæp·tɪv] I. *n* cautivo, -a *m, f* II. *adj*
cautivo, -a; **to hold sb** ~ tener prisionero a alguien
captivity [kæp·'tɪv·ə·ti] *n* cautiverio *m;* **to be**

in ~ estar en cautividad
capture ['kæp·tʃər] I. *vt* **1.** (*take prisoner*)
apresar **2.** (*take possession of*) capturar; (*city*)
conquistar; (*ship*) apresar; (*votes*) conseguir
3. (*gain*) captar; **to** ~ **the market** COM hacerse
con el mercado **4.** ART captar; **to** ~ **sth on film**
reproducir algo en una película **5.** COMPUT
recoger II. *n* captura *f;* (*of city*) conquista *f;* (*of
ship*) apresamiento *m*
car [kar] *n* **1.** AUTO coche *m*, carro *m* AmL, auto
m Arg, Chile, Urug **2.** RAIL vagón *m* **3.** (*in airship, balloon*) barquilla *f*
carafe [kə·'ræf] *n* garrafa *f*
caramel ['kar·məl] I. *n* **1.** (*burnt sugar*) caramelo *m* **2.** (*sweet*) caramelo *m* II. *adj* de caramelo; ~ **cream** crema *f* de caramelo
carat <-(s)> *n s.* **karat**
caravan ['kær·ə·væn] *n* (*group of travelers*)
caravana *f*
caravansary [ˌkær·ə·'væn·sə·ri] *n,* **caravanserai** [ˌkær·ə·'væn·sə·raɪ] *n* caravasar *m*
caraway ['kær·ə·weɪ] *n* alcaravea *f*
caraway seed *n* carvi *m*
carbide ['kar·baɪd] *n* carburo *m*
carbine ['kar·bin] *n* carabina *f*
car body ['kar·bad·i] <-ies> *n* chasis *m inv* del
automóvil
carbohydrate [ˌkar·boʊ·'haɪ·dreɪt] *n* hidrato
m de carbono; ~ **content** contenido *m* de carbohidratos
carbolic [kar·'bal·ɪk] *adj* ~ **acid** ácido *m* fénico
car bomb ['kar·bam] *n* coche *m* bomba
carbon ['kar·bən] I. *n* **1.** CHEM carbono *m*
2. (*copy*) copia *f* al carbón **3.** (*paper*) papel *m*
de calco, papel *m* carbón II. *adj* de carbono
carbon copy <-ies> *n* copia *f* en papel de
calco
carbon dating *n* datación *f* por C-14
carbon dioxide *n* dióxido *m* de carbono
carbonic [kar·'ban·ɪk] *adj* ~ **acid** ácido *m* carbónico
carbonize ['kar·bə·naɪz] I. *vt* carbonizar II. *vi*
carbonizarse
carbon monoxide *n* monóxido *m* de carbono
carbon paper *n* papel *m* de calco
carbuncle ['kar·bʌŋ·kəl] *n* **1.** MED furúnculo
m, carbunco *m* **2.** (*gem*) carbúnculo *m*
carburet ['kar·bə·reɪt] *vt* mezclar con carbono
carburetor ['kar·bə·rei·t̬ər] *n* carburador *m*
carcass ['kar·kəs] <-es> *n* **1.** (*of animal*)
cadáver *m* de animal **2.** (*of vehicle*) armazón
m **3.** (*of cooked chicken*) huesos *mpl*
carcinogen [kar·'sɪn·ə·dʒen] *n* MED (agente
m) carcinógeno *m*
carcinogenic [ˌkar·sɪn·ə·'dʒen·ɪk] *adj* MED
cancerígeno, -a
carcinoma [kar·sə·'noʊ·mə] *n* MED carcinoma *m*
card¹ [kard] I. *n* **1.** (*birthday, Christmas, etc.*)
tarjeta *f* **2.** GAMES carta *f*, naipe *m;* **pack of** ~**s**
baraja *f;* **to play** ~ jugar a las cartas **3.** (*proof
of identity*) carnet *m;* **membership** ~ carnet
de socio **4.** *a.* FIN, COMPUT tarjeta *f* **5.** SPORTS

(*program*) programa *m;* **boxing** ~ velada de boxeo **6.** (*index* ~) ficha *f* **7.** *inf* cómico, -a *m, f,* persona *f* chusca ▶ **to have a ~ up one's sleeve** tener un as en la manga; **to put one's ~s on the table** poner las cartas sobre la mesa; **to play one's ~s right** jugar bien sus cartas; **to be in the ~s** ser probable que ocurra, estar previsto **II.** *vt inf* pedir la documentación

card² [kard] **I.** *n* carda *f* **II.** *vt* cardar

cardboard ['kard·bɔrd] *n* cartón *m*

cardiac ['kar·di·æk] *adj* MED cardíaco, -a; (*disease*) cardiovascular

cardigan ['kar·di·gən] *n* cárdigan *m;* (*for women*) rebeca *f*

cardinal ['kar·din·əl] **I.** *n* **1.** REL, ZOOL cardenal *m* **2.** (*number*) cardinal *m* **II.** *adj* (*important: rule*) fundamental; (*error*) grave; (*sin*) capital

cardinal number *n* número *m* cardinal

cardinal points *npl* puntos *mpl* cardinales

card index ['kard·in·deks] <-es> *n* fichero *m*

cardiogram ['kar·di·ə·græm] *n* MED cardiograma *m*

card reader *n* lector *m* de tarjetas perforadas

card table *n* tapete *m* (verde)

care [ker] **I.** *n* **1.** (*attention*) cuidado *m;* **to take ~ of** cuidar de; (*object*) guardar; (*situation*) encargarse de; **take ~** (**of yourself**)! ¡cuídate!; **to do sth with ~** hacer algo con cuidado; **that takes ~ of that!** ¡eso ya está!; **handle with ~** frágil **2.** (*worry*) preocupación *f;* **to not have a ~ in the world** no tener ninguna preocupación **II.** *vi* **1.** (*be concerned*) preocuparse; **to ~ about sb/sth** preocuparse por alguien/algo; **as if I ~d!** ¿y a mí qué?; **for all I ~** (*as far as I'm concerned*) por mí; **who ~s?** ¿qué más da? **2.** (*feel affection*) importar **3.** (*want*) **to ~ to do sth** estar dispuesto a hacer algo

CARE [ker] *n abbr of* **Cooperative for American Relief Everywhere** *cooperativa de auxilio estadounidense en cualquier parte del mundo*

career [kə·'rir] *n* **1.** (*profession*) profesión *f* **2.** (*working life*) carrera *f* profesional

career counselor *n* consejero, -a *m, f* de orientación profesional

careerist [kə·'rir·ist] **I.** *n* ambicioso, -a *m, f,* arribista *mf* **II.** *adj* ambicioso, -a

career woman <-women> *n* mujer *f* dedicada por completo a su profesión

carefree ['ker·fri] *adj* despreocupado, -a

careful ['ker·fəl] *adj* **1.** (*cautious*) cuidadoso, -a; (*driver*) prudente; **to be ~ of sth** tener cuidado con algo; **to be ~ to do sth** procurar hacer algo **2.** (*painstaking, meticulous*) meticuloso, -a; (*worker*) esmerado, -a

carefulness *n* **1.** (*caution*) cuidado *m* **2.** (*meticulousness*) meticulosidad *f*

careless ['ker·lis] *adj* **1.** (*lacking attention*) distraído, -a **2.** (*unthinking*) irreflexivo, -a, despistado, -a **3.** (*not painstaking*) descuidado, -a, imprudente **4.** (*carefree*) despreocupado, -a

carelessness *n* **1.** (*lack of attention*) falta *f* de atención **2.** (*lack of concern*) despreocupación *f*

caress [kə·'res] **I.** <-es> *n* caricia *f* **II.** *vi, vt* acariciar, barbear *AmC*

caretaker ['ker·tei·kər] *n* (*of building, property*) conserje *mf,* vigilante *mf,* portero(a) *m(f),* guachimán *m Col, CRi, Chile, Pan, Gui-nEc, Nic*

careworn ['ker·wɔrn] *adj* agobiado, -a por las preocupaciones

car ferry <-ies> *n* NAUT transbordador *m*

cargo ['kar·gou] <-(e)s> *n* **1.** (*goods*) carga *f* **2.** (*load*) cargamento *m*

cargo aircraft *n* avión *m* de carga

cargo boat *n* carguero *m*

cargo plane *n* avión *m* de carga

cargo ship *n* barco *m* de carga

cargo vessel *n* carguero *m*

Caribbean [ˌker·i·'bi·ən] **I.** *n* **the ~** el Caribe **II.** *adj* caribeño, -a, caribe *AmL*

caricature ['ker·ə·kə·tʃur] **I.** *n a.* ART caricatura *f* **II.** *vt* LIT caricaturizar

caricaturist ['kær·ə·kə·tʃur·ist] *n* ART caricaturista *mf*

caries ['ker·iz] *n* MED caries *f inv*

caring *adj* compasivo, -a

car insurance *n* seguro *m* de vehículos

carjacking *n* robo *m* de coche (*por la fuerza o con intimidación*)

carnage ['kar·nidʒ] *n* matanza *f*

carnal ['kar·nəl] *adj* carnal

carnation [kar·'nei·ʃən] **I.** *n* **1.** BOT clavel *m* **2.** (*color*) rosa *m* vivo **II.** *adj* rosa vivo

carnival ['kar·nə·vəl] *n* carnaval *m,* chaya *f Arg, Bol, Chile*

carnivore ['kar·nə·vɔr] *n* carnívoro, -a *m, f*

carnivorous [kar·'niv·ər·əs] *adj* carnívoro, -a

carol ['ker·əl] *n* villancico *m*

carol singer *n* persona *f* que canta villancicos

carotene ['kær·ə·tin] *n* BIO caroteno *m*

carousel [ˌkær·ə·'sel] *n* **1.** (*merry-go-round*) tiovivo *m* **2.** (*baggage return*) cinta *f* transportadora

carp¹ [karp] <-(s)> *n* ZOOL carpa *f*

carp² [karp] *vi* criticar por criticar; **to ~ about sth/sb** quejarse de algo/alguien sin motivo

carpenter ['kar·pən·tər] *n* carpintero, -a *m, f*

carpentry ['kar·pən·tri] *n* carpintería *f*

carpet ['kar·pət] **I.** *n* (*fitted*) moqueta *f,* alfombra *f AmL;* (*not fitted*) alfombra *f* ▶ **to sweep sth under the ~** correr un velo sobre algo **II.** *vt* **1.** (*cover floor*) enmoquetar, alfombrar *AmL* **2.** *liter* (*cover sth*) cubrir con un manto

carpetbag ['kar·pət·bæg] *n* maletín *o* bolso *de tejido de alfombra*

carpetbagger ['kar·pət·bæg·ər] *n* persona *f* de fuera, *persona que intenta entrar en el mundo de la política lejos de su lugar de origen porque piensa que así tiene más posibilidades de triunfar*

carpeting ['kar·pi·tɪŋ] *n* alfombrado *m*

carpool ['kar·pul] *n grupo de personas que*

comparten el mismo coche para desplazarse al trabajo

car rental n alquiler m de coches

carriage ['ker·ɪdʒ] n 1.(horse-drawn vehicle) carruaje m 2.(part of typewriter) carro m

carriage return n TYPO retorno m de carro

carrier ['kær·i·ər] n 1.(person who carries) transportista mf; (messenger) mensajero, -a m, f 2.MIL (vehicle) vehículo m transportador; **aircraft** ~ portaaviones m inv 3.MED portador(a) m(f) 4.(transport company) empresa f de transportes

carrion ['ker·i·ən] n carroña f

carrion crow n corneja f

carrot ['ker·ət] n 1.(vegetable) zanahoria f 2.inf (reward) incentivo m; **the ~-and-stick approach** la política de incentivos y amenazas

carroty ['ker·ə·t̬i] <-ier, -iest> adj (de) color zanahoria

carry ['ker·i] <-ies, -ied> I.vt 1.(transport in hands or arms) llevar; (take) traer 2.(transport) transportar, acarrear 3.(have on one's person) llevar encima 4.MED (transmit) transmitir 5.(support) soportar 6.(sell) vender 7.(win: position) conquistar 8.(approve) aprobar 9.PUBL **to ~ an article** publicar un artículo 10.(develop) **to ~ consequences** tener consecuencias; **to ~ an argument to its (logical) conclusion** desarrollar un argumento hacia su conclusión (lógica) 11.(be pregnant) **to ~ a child** esperar un hijo II.vi 1.(be audible) oírse 2.(fly) volar

♦**carry along** vt llevar; (water) arrastrar

♦**carry away** vt 1.(remove) arrastrar 2.**to be carried away (by sth)** (be overcome by) dejarse llevar (por algo); (be enchanted by) entusiasmarse (con algo); **to get carried away** exaltarse

♦**carry forward** vt FIN transferir

♦**carry off** vt 1.(remove) **to carry sb off** llevarse 2.(succeed) **to carry sth off** salir airoso de algo

♦**carry on** I.vt insep continuar con; ~ **(with) the good work!** ¡sigue/seguid con el buen trabajo! II.vi 1.(continue) seguir; **to ~ doing sth** continuar haciendo algo 2.inf (make a fuss) montar un número

♦**carry out** vt (repairs) hacer; (plan, attack) llevar a cabo; (job) realizar; (order) cumplir

♦**carry over** I.vt 1.(bring forward) pasar a cuenta nueva; FIN transferir 2.(postpone) posponer II.vi 1.**to ~ into sth** (have an effect on) influir en algo 2.(remain) quedar

♦**carry through** vt 1.(support) sostener 2.(complete successfully) llevar a término

carryall ['kær·i·ɔl] n bolso m grande

carrying capacity <-ies> n capacidad f de carga

carrying-on <carryings-on> n inf 1.(dubious affair) enredos mpl 2.(dubious activity) líos mpl

carryover n 1.FIN pérdida trasladada al ejercicio siguiente 2.(remnant) remanente m

cart [kart] I.n 1.(vehicle) carreta f; carro m 2.(supermarket trolley) carro m (de la compra) ▶ **to put the ~ before the horse** poner el carro delante de los bueyes II.vt (transport) acarrear; (carry) cargar

carte blanche [ˌkart·'blanʃ] n carta f blanca

cartel [kar·'tel] n cártel m

cartilage ['kar·t̬əl·ɪdʒ] n cartílago m

cartload ['kart·loʊd] n carretada f; ~**s of garbage** montones mpl de basura

cartographer [kar·'tag·rə·fər] n cartógrafo, -a m, f

cartography [kar·'tag·rə·fi] n cartografía f

carton ['kar·tən] n (box) caja f de cartón; (of juice, milk) (envase m de) cartón m

cartoon [kar·'tun] n 1.ART viñeta f 2.CINE dibujos mpl animados

cartoonist n dibujante mf

cartridge ['kar·trɪdʒ] n 1.(for ink, ammunition, cassette) cartucho m, cachimba f AmL 2.(for record player) cápsula f

cartwheel ['kart·hwil] I.n rueda f; **to do a ~** hacer la rueda II.vi hacer ruedas

carve [karv] I.vt 1.(cut) cortar; **to ~ (out) a name for oneself** fig hacerse un nombre 2.(stone, wood) tallar 3.(cut meat) trinchar II.vi cortar

carver ['kar·vər] n 1.ART escultor(a) m(f) 2.~**s** CULIN trinchantes mpl

carving n ART 1.(art of cutting) arte m de esculpir 2.(ornamental figure) escultura f; **wood** ~ talla f

carving knife <knives> n cuchillo m de trinchar

car wash <-es> n tren m de lavado

cascade [kæs·'keɪd] I.n 1.(waterfall) cascada f 2.liter (flowing mass) torrente m II.vi **to ~ from sth** caer en cascada de algo

case[1] [keɪs] n 1.a. MED caso m; **in any ~** en cualquier caso; **just in ~** por si acaso; **in ~ it rains** en caso de que llueva; **as the ~ may be** tal como sea el caso 2.LING caso m 3.LAW caso m; **to close the ~** cerrar el caso; **to lose one's ~** perder el caso 4.(argument) **to make a ~ for sth** argumentar a favor de algo

case[2] [keɪs] n (container) caja f; (for jewels, eyeglasses) estuche m; (for camera, musical instrument) funda f; **a ~ of beer/soft drinks** una caja [o un guacal Col, Méx, Ven] de cerveza/de refrescos; **glass** ~ vitrina f

casebook n diario m; MED registro m

case law n LAW jurisprudencia f

case study <-ies> n monografía f

cash [kæʃ] I.n dinero m en efectivo; ~ **in advance** adelanto m; **to be strapped for** ~ inf andar corto de dinero II.vt cobrar; (check) cambiar; **to ~ sth in** canjear algo; **to ~ in (one's chips)** inf (die) palmarla

♦**cash in** I.vt insep canjear II.vi **to ~ on sth** sacar provecho de algo

cash-and-carry [ˌkæʃ·ənd·'ker·i] I.<-ies> n tienda f de venta al por mayor II.adj de venta al por mayor

cash cow *n sl* gallina *f* de los huevos de oro

cash crop *n* cultivo *m* comercial

cashew ['kæʃ·u] *n*, **cashew nut** *n* anacardo *m*, acajú *m Cuba, Méx, PRico, RDom*

cash flow ['kæʃ·ˌfloʊ] *n* FIN flujo *m* de caja

cashier [kæ·'ʃɪr] *n* cajero, -a *m, f*

cash machine *n* cajero *m* automático

cashmere ['kæʒ·mɪr] *n* cachemir *m*

cash register *n* caja *f* registradora

casing ['keɪ·sɪŋ] *n* cubierta *f; (of machine)* carcasa *f; (of cable)* tubo *m* de revestimiento

casino [kə·'si·noʊ] *n* casino *m*

cask [kæsk] *n* tonel *m; (of wine)* barril *m*

casket ['kæs·kɪt] *n* 1. *(box)* cofre *m; (for jewels)* joyero *m* 2. *(coffin)* ataúd *m*

Caspian Sea ['kæs·pi·ən] *n* Mar *m* Caspio

casserole ['kæs·ə·roʊl] *n* 1. *(cooking vessel)* cazuela *f; (of iron)* cacerola *f* 2. CULIN guiso *m*

cassette [kə·'set] *n* casete *m o f;* **video ~** cinta *f* (de vídeo)

cassette deck *n* pletina *f*

cassette player *n*, **cassette recorder** *n* casete *m*

cast [kæst] I. *n* 1. THEAT, CINE reparto *m;* **supporting ~** reparto secundario 2. *(mold)* molde *m* 3. MED escayola *f* 4. *(of worm)* rastro *m* II. <cast, cast> *vt* 1. *(throw)* lanzar; *(fishing line)* arrojar 2. *(direct)* **to ~ doubt on sth** poner algo en duda; **to ~ a shadow on sth** ensombrecer algo; **to ~ light on sth** proyectar luz sobre algo; *fig* echar luz sobre algo 3. *(allocate roles)* asignar; **to ~ sb as sb/sth** dar a alguien el papel de alguien/algo; **to ~ sb in a role** elegir a alguien para un papel 4. *(give)* dar; *(vote)* emitir 5. *(make in a mould)* vaciar

◆ **cast aside** *vt*, **cast away** *vt (rid oneself of)* dejar de lado; *(free oneself of)* desechar

◆ **cast off** I. *vt* 1. *(get rid of)* desechar 2. *(stitch)* cerrar II. *vi* 1. NAUT soltar amarras 2. *(in knitting)* terminar

◆ **cast on** I. *vt (in knitting: stitch)* echar II. *vi (in knitting)* montar los puntos

◆ **cast out** *vt* arrojar; *(demons, ideas)* echar fuera de sí; *form (person)* expulsar

castanets [ˌkæs·tə·'nets] *npl* castañuelas *fpl*

castaway ['kæst·ə·weɪ] *n* 1. *(survivor from a ship)* náufrago, -a *m, f* 2. *(discarded object)* trasto *m*

caste [kæst] *n (social class)* casta *f;* **~ system** sistema *m* de castas

caster ['kæs·tər] *n* ruedecita *f*

castigate ['kæs·tɪ·geɪt] *vt form* fustigar; **to ~ sb for sth** censurar a alguien por algo

castigation [ˌkæs·tɪ·'geɪ·ʃən] *n* censura *f; (rebuke)* reprobación *f*

casting ['kæs·tɪŋ] *n* 1. *(forming in a mold)* vaciado *m* 2. THEAT reparto *m* de papeles

cast iron [ˌkæst·'aɪ·ərn] *n* hierro *m* fundido

cast-iron *adj* 1. *(made of cast iron)* de hierro fundido 2. *fig (evidence)* irrefutable; *(alibi)* a toda prueba; *(promise)* firme

castle ['kæs·əl] I. *n* 1. *(building)* castillo *m* 2. *(chess piece)* torre *f* ▶ **to build ~s in the**

air construir castillos en el aire II. *vi (in chess)* enrocar

castoff ['kæst·af] I. *n (garment)* prenda *f* desechada [*o* vieja]; **~s** ropa *f* desechada [*o* vieja] II. *adj (clothes, shoes)* desechado, -a, viejo, -a

castor ['kæs·tər] *n* ruedecita *f*

castor oil *n* aceite *m* de ricino

castrate [kæs·'treɪt] *vt* castrar, componer *AmL*

casual ['kæʒ·u·əl] *adj* 1. *(relaxed)* relajado, -a 2. *(not permanent)* casual; *(sex)* ocasional 3. *(not serious)* despreocupado, -a; *(glance)* al azar; *(remark)* a la ligera; *(meeting)* fortuito, -a 4. *(not habitual)* de vez en cuando 5. *(informal)* informal; *(clothes)* informal

casually *adv* de forma relajada

casualty ['kæʒ·u·əl·ti] <-ies> *n* 1. *(accident victim)* víctima *f; (injured person)* herido, -a *m, f;* MIL *(dead person)* baja *f* 2. *(sth eliminated)* pérdidas *fpl*

cat [kæt] *n* gato, -a *m, f* ▶ **to let the ~ out of the bag** descubrir el pastel, irse de la lengua; **to fight like ~s and dogs** llevarse como (el) perro y (el) gato; **to rain ~s and dogs** llover a cántaros [*o* a chuzos]; **to play ~ and mouse with sb** jugar al gato y al ratón con alguien; **has the ~ got your tongue?** ¿te ha comido la lengua el gato?, ¿te comieron la lengua los ratones? *Col, Méx*

CAT [kæt] *n* 1. COMPUT *abbr of* **computer-assisted translation** TAO *f* 2. MED *abbr of* **computerized axial tomography** TAC *m o f;* **~ scan** (escáner *m*) TAC *m*

cataclysmic [ˌkæt·ə·'klɪz·mɪk] *adj* desastroso, -a

catacombs ['kæt·ə·koʊmz] *npl* catacumbas *fpl*

Catalan ['kæt·əl·æn] I. *adj* catalán, -ana II. *n* 1. *(habitant)* catalán, -ana *m, f* 2. *(language)* catalán *m*

catalog ['kæt·əl·ag] I. *n* catálogo *m; (repeated events)* serie *f;* **a ~ of mistakes** *fig* un error detrás de otro II. *vt* catalogar

Catalonia [ˌkæt·ə·'loʊ·ni·ə] *n* Cataluña *f*

Catalonian [ˌkæt·ə·'loʊ·ni·ən] *adj, n s.* **Catalan**

catalysis [kə·'tæl·ə·sɪs] *n* catálisis *f inv*

catalyst ['kæt·əl·ɪst] *n a. fig* catalizador *m*

catalytic [kæt·ə·'lɪt·ɪk] *adj* catalítico, -a; **~ converter** AUTO catalizador *m*

catamaran [ˌkæt·ə·mə·'ræn] *n* catamarán *m*

catapult ['kæt·ə·pʌlt] I. *n* tirachinas *m inv;* HIST catapulta *f* II. *vt* catapultar

cataract¹ ['kæt·ə·rækt] *n* MED catarata *f*

cataract² ['kæt·ə·rækt] *n liter (waterfall)* catarata *f*

catarrh [kə·'tar] *n* catarro *m*

catastrophe [kə·'tæs·trə·fi] *n* catástrofe *f*

catastrophic [ˌkæt·ə·'straf·ɪk] *adj* catastrófico, -a

catcall ['kæt·kɔl] *n (booing)* abucheo *m; (whistling)* silbido *m*

catch [kætʃ] <-es> I. *n* 1. *(fish caught)* pesca *f* 2. *(fastening device)* pestillo *m; (on window)*

cierre *m* **3.** *inf* (*suitable partner*) **he's a good ~** es un buen partido **4.** (*trick*) trampa *f* **II.** <caught, caught> *vt* **1.** (*object in motion*) agarrar; (*animal, person*) atrapar; **to ~ sb at a bad moment** pillar a alguien en un mal momento **2.** (*entangle*) involucrar; **to get caught in sth** quedar atrapado en algo; **to get caught up in sth** quedar involucrado en algo; **to get caught on sth** engancharse a algo **3.** (*collect*) acumular; (*liquid*) recoger **4.** (*capture an expression*) percibir; (*hear*) oír **5.** (*attract*) atraer **6.** (*get*) coger, tomar *AmL;* **to ~ the bus** coger el bus **7.** (*discover*) descubrir **8.** (*notice*) darse cuenta de; (*by chance*) pillar por casualidad **9.** (*discover by surprise*) **to ~ sb** (**doing sth**) sorprender [*o* pillar] a alguien (haciendo algo); **to ~ sb red-handed** *fig* coger [*o* pillar] a alguien con las manos en la masa; **to ~ sb with their pants down, to ~ sb napping** *fig* coger [*o* pillar] a alguien desprevenido **10.** MED (*become infected*) contagiarse de **11.** (*start burning: fire*) prender
♦ **catch on** *vi* **1.** (*become popular*) ponerse de moda **2.** *inf* (*understand*) entender
♦ **catch up I.** *vi* **to ~ with sb** alcanzar el nivel de alguien; **to ~ with sth** (*make up lost time*) ponerse al corriente de algo; (*equal the standard*) igualarse a algo **II.** *vt* **to catch sb up** poner al día [*o* al corriente] a alguien
catchall ['kætʃ·ɔl] *adj* comodín
catcher ['kætʃ·ər] *n* SPORTS catcher *mf*
catch phrase ['kætʃ·freɪz] *n* eslogan *m*
catchup ['kætʃ·əp] *n s.* **ketchup**
catchword ['kætʃ·wɜrd] *n* eslogan *m*
catchy ['kætʃ·i] <-ier, -iest> *adj* pegadizo, -a
catechism ['kæt·ɪ·kɪz·əm] *n* **1.** (*instruction*) catequesis *f inv* **2.** (*book*) catecismo *m*
categorical [ˌkæt·ə·ˈgɔr·ɪ·kəl] *adj* (*denial, refusal*) categórico, -a
categorize ['kæt·ə·gə·raɪz] *vt* clasificar
category ['kæt·ə·gɔr·i] <-ies> *n* categoría *f*
cater ['keɪ·tʃər] *vi* encargarse del servicio de comidas
caterer ['keɪ·tʃər·ər] *n* encargado, -a *m, f* del servicio de comidas
catering ['keɪ·tər·ɪŋ] *n* restauración *f;* (*service*) servicio *m* de comidas
Caterpillar® ['kæt·ər·pɪl·ər] *n* tractor *m* oruga
caterpillar ['kæt·ər·pɪl·ər] *n* ZOOL oruga *f*
caterwaul ['kæt·ər·wɔl] **I.** *n* aullido *m* **II.** *vi* aullar
catfish *n* siluro *m*, bagre *m Col, Méx*
catgut ['kæt·gʌt] *n* cuerda *f* de tripa; MED catgut *m*
cathartic [kə·ˈθɑr·tɪk] *adj* catártico, -a
cathedral [kə·ˈθi·drəl] *n* catedral *f;* **~ city** ciudad *f* episcopal
catheter ['kæθ·ə·tər] *n* MED catéter *m*
cathode ['kæθ·oʊd] *n* ELEC cátodo *m*
cathode ray *n* rayo *m* catódico
Catholic ['kæθ·ə·lɪk] REL **I.** *n* católico, -a *m, f* **II.** *adj* católico, -a
catholic ['kæθ·ə·lɪk] *adj* variado, -a

Catholicism [kə·ˈθɑl·ə·sɪz·əm] *n* catolicismo *m*
cat litter *n* arena *f* higiénica
catnap ['kæt·næp] **I.** *n inf* siestecita *f;* **to have a ~** echar una cabezada **II.** <-pp-> *vi inf* echar una siestecita
cat's cradle [ˌkæts·ˈkreɪ·dəl] *n* juego *m* de la cuna
catsup ['ketʃ·əp] *n s.* **ketchup**
cattle ['kæt·əl] *npl* (*bovines*) ganado *m;* **beef ~** ganado vacuno; **dairy ~** vacas *fpl* lecheras
cattle breeder *n* ganadero, -a *m, f*
cattle breeding *n* ganadería *f*
cattle car *n* RAIL vagón *m* de ganado
cattle thief <thieves> *n* ladrón, -ona *m, f* de ganado
catty ['kæt·i] <-ier, -iest> *adj* (*hurtful*) malicioso, -a; (*remark*) intencionado, -a
catwalk ['kæt·wɔk] *n* **1.** THEAT puente *m* de trabajo **2.** FASHION pasarela *f*
Caucasian [kɔ·ˈkeɪ·ʒən] *form* **I.** *n* **1.** (*white*) blanco, -a *m, f* **2.** (*European*) caucásico, -a *m, f* **3.** (*languages*) caucásico *m* **II.** *adj* **1.** (*white*) blanco, -a **2.** (*European*) caucásico, -a **3.** (*of the Caucasus*) caucasiano, -a; (*language*) caucásico, -a
caucus ['kɔ·kəs] **I.** *n* <-es> **1.** (*group*) comité *m* **2.** (*members*) camarilla *f* **3.** (*meeting*) reunión *f* del comité de un partido **II.** *vi* celebrar una reunión del comité del partido
caught [kɔt] *pt, pp of* **catch**
cauldron ['kɔl·drən] *n* caldero *m;* *fig* hervidero *m*
cauliflower ['kɔ·lɪ·flaʊ·ər] *n* coliflor *f*
caulk [kɔk] *vt* enmasillar; NAUT calafatear
causal ['kɔ·zəl] *adj a.* LING causal; (*relationship*) de causa-efecto
causality [kɔ·ˈzæl·ə·ti] *n form* causalidad *f*
causative ['kɔ·zə·tɪv] *adj form* **1.** (*acting as a cause*) causante **2.** LING causativo, -a
cause [kɔz] **I.** *n* **1.** (*a reason for*) causa *f*, motivo *m;* **he is the ~ of all her woes** él es el causante de todas sus penas; **this is no ~ for...** esto no justifica... **2.** (*objective*) causa *f* **3.** (*principle*) causa *f;* **to do sth in the ~ of sth** hacer algo en pro de algo **4.** LAW pleito *m* **II.** *vt* causar; (*an accident*) provocar; **to ~ sb/ sth to do sth** hacer que alguien/algo haga algo; **to ~ sb harm** ocasionar daños a alguien; **this medicine may ~ dizziness and nausea** este medicamento puede provocar mareos y náuseas
causeway ['kɔz·weɪ] *n* **1.** (*road bridge*) carretera *f* elevada **2.** (*pathway*) paso *m* elevado
caustic ['kɔ·stɪk] *adj a. fig* cáustico, -a; (*lime*) vivo, -a; (*remark*) mordaz; (*tongue*) viperino, -a
cauterize ['kɔ·tə·raɪz] *vt a. fig* cauterizar
caution ['kɔ·ʃən] *n* **1.** (*carefulness*) cautela *f;* **~ is advised** se recomienda prudencia; **to throw ~ to the winds** jugársela; **to treat sth with ~** tratar algo con cuidado **2.** (*warning*) advertencia *f;* **a note of ~** un aviso; **~!** ¡cui-

dado! **II.** *vt form* prevenir a; **to ~ sb to do sth**
aconsejar a alguien que haga algo; **to ~ sb
about sth** llamar la atención a alguien por algo
cautionary ['kɔ·ʃə·ner·i] *adj* aleccionador(a); **a
~ tale** un cuento con moraleja
cautious ['kɔ·ʃəs] *adj* cauto, -a; (*optimism*)
moderado, -a; **to be ~ about sth** ser prudente
en algo
cavalcade [ˌkæv·əl·'keɪd] *n* **1.** (*procession*)
cabalgata *f* **2.** (*succession*) desfile *m;* (*of memories*) sucesión *f*
cavalier [ˌkæv·ə·'lɪr] **I.** *n* HIST caballero *m* **II.** *adj*
arrogante; **a ~ attitude** una actitud desdeñosa
cavalry ['kæv·əl·ri] *n pl vb* MIL caballería *f*
cavalryman ['kæv·əl·ri·mən] <-men> *n* **1.** HIST
(*mounted*) caballero *m* **2.** MIL (*in armored
vehicles*) soldado *m* de caballería
cave [keɪv] **I.** *n* (*natural*) cueva *f;* (*man-made*)
caverna *f* **II.** *vi* **1.** (*hollow out*) cavar **2.** SPORTS
hacer espeleología
 ◆**cave in** *vi* ceder; (*fall in, fall down*) venirse
abajo, derrumbarse
caveat ['kæ·vi·æt] *n* **1.** (*warning*) advertencia *f*
2. LAW *anotación provisional para asegurar el
cumplimiento de la resolución judicial*
cave dweller *n* cavernícola *mf*
cave-in *n* derrumbamiento *m*
caveman ['keɪv·mæn] <-men> *n* **1.** (*prehistoric man*) hombre *m* de las cavernas **2.** *inf*
(*socially underdeveloped*) bruto *m inf*, troglodita *m*
cave painting *n* pintura *f* rupestre
caver ['keɪ·vər] *n* espeleólogo, -a *m, f*
cavern ['kæv·ərn] *n* caverna *f*
cavernous ['kæv·ər·nəs] *adj* cavernoso, -a;
(*hole, room*) oscuro, -a; (*pit*) profundo, -a;
(*eyes*) hundido, -a
caviar(e) ['kæv·i·ar] *n* caviar *m*
cavity ['kæv·ɪ·ti] <-ies> *n* **1.** *a.* ANAT cavidad *f;*
nasal ~ fosa *f* nasal **2.** MED caries *f inv*
caw [kɔ] **I.** *n* graznido *m* **II.** *vi* graznar
cayenne [kaɪ·'en] *n,* **cayenne pepper** *n*
(pimienta *f* de) cayena *f*
Cayman Islands ['keɪ·mən·ˌaɪ·ləndz] *n* Islas
fpl Caimán
CB [ˌsi·'bi] *n abbr of* **Citizen's Band** banda *f*
ciudadana
CBW *n abbr of* **chemical and biological warfare** guerra *f* bioquímica
cc [ˌsi·'si] *abbr of* **cubic centimeter** cc
CCTV [ˌsi·si·ti·'vi] *n abbr of* **closed-circuit
television** circuito *m* cerrado de televisión
ccw. *adj, adv abbr of* **counterclockwise** en
sentido contrario a las agujas del reloj
CD [ˌsi·'di] *n abbr of* **compact disc** CD *m*
CD-R *n abbr of* **compact disc-recordable**
CD-R *m*
CD-ROM [ˌsi·di·'ram] *n abbr of* **compact disc
read-only memory** CD-ROM *m;* **on ~** en CD-
ROM
CD-RW *n abbr of* **compact disc-rewritable**
CD *m* regrabable
cease [sis] *form* **I.** *vi* cesar; **to ~ to do sth** cesar

de (hacer) algo **II.** *vt* suspender; **it never ~s to
amaze me** nunca deja de sorprenderme;
~ fire! MIL ¡alto el fuego! **III.** *n* without ~ sin
cesar
cease-fire [ˌsis·'faɪr] *n* MIL alto *m* el fuego, cese
m del fuego *AmL*
ceaseless ['sis·lɪs] *adj* incesante
cedar ['si·dər] *n* **1.** (*tree*) cedro *m* **2.** (*wood*)
(madera *f* de) cedro *m*
cede [sid] *vt form* ceder
ceiling ['si·lɪŋ] *n* **1.** ARCHIT, AVIAT techo *m*
2. (*upper limit*) tope *m;* (*on prices*) límite *m;*
to impose a ~ on sth poner un tope a algo
3. METEO cielo *m* (raso) ▶**to hit the ~** *inf*
subirse por las paredes
celebrate ['sel·ɪ·breɪt] **I.** *vi* celebrar; **let's ~!**
¡vamos a celebrarlo! **II.** *vt* celebrar; **they ~d
him as a hero** lo agasajaron como a un héroe
celebrated *adj* célebre
celebration [ˌsel·ɪ·'breɪ·ʃən] *n* **1.** (*party*) fiesta
f **2.** (*of an occasion*) celebración *f;* (*of an
event*) conmemoración *f;* **to throw a party in
~ of sth** dar una fiesta para celebrar algo; **this
calls for (a) ~!** ¡esto hay que celebrarlo!
celebratory ['sel·ə·brə·tɔr·i] *adj* **we went for
a ~ dinner** fuimos a cenar para celebrarlo;
~ gunfire erupted hubo disparos al aire para
celebrar (algo)
celebrity [sə·'leb·rə·ti] *n* **1.** <-ies> (*person*)
famoso, -a *m, f,* celebridad *f* **2.** (*fame*) celebridad *f*
celeriac [sə·'ler·i·æk] *n* apio *m* nabo
celery ['sel·ə·ri] *n* apio *m*, panul *m CSur*
celery root *n* apio *m* nabo
celestial [sɪ·'les·tʃəl] *adj a. fig* celestial
celestial body <-ies> *n* cuerpo *m* celeste
celibacy ['sel·ɪ·bə·si] *n* **1.** *a.* REL celibato *m*
2. (*being single*) soltería *f*
celibate ['sel·ɪ·bət] **I.** *n* célibe *mf* **II.** *adj* **1.** *a.*
REL (*refraining from sex*) célibe **2.** (*unmarried*)
soltero, -a
cell [sel] *n* **1.** (*in prison*) celda *f,* separo *m Méx*
2. BIO, POL célula *f;* **a single-~ animal** un animal unicelular; **grey ~s** materia *f* gris *inf*
3. ELEC pila *f*
cellar ['sel·ər] *n* **1.** (*basement*) sótano *m;* (*for
wine*) bodega *f* **2.** SPORTS farolillo *m* rojo *inf*
cellist ['tʃel·ɪst] *n* MUS violonchelista *mf*
cell nucleus ['sel·ˌnu·kli·əs] <-clei *o* -es> *n*
núcleo *m* celular
cello ['tʃel·oʊ] <-s *o* -li> *n* MUS violonchelo *m*
cellophane ['sel·ə·feɪn] *n* celofán *m*
cell phone ['sel·foʊn] *n* (teléfono *m*) móvil,
(teléfono *m*) celular *Col*
cellular ['sel·ju·lər] *adj* **1.** BIO celular
2. (*porous*) poroso, -a
cellular phone *n* (teléfono *m*) móvil, (teléfono
m) celular *Col*
cellulite ['sel·jə·laɪt] *n* celulitis *f inv*
celluloid ['sel·ju·bɪd] **I.** *n* celuloide *m* **II.** *adj*
de celuloide
cellulose ['sel·ju·loʊs] *n* celulosa *f*
Celsius ['sel·si·əs] *adj* PHYS Celsius

Celt [kelt, selt] *n* HIST celta *mf*
Celtic ['kel·tɪk, 'sel·tɪk] I. *adj* céltico, -a; (*language*) celta II. *n* celta *m*
cement [sɪ'ment] I. *n* 1. ARCHIT cemento *m* 2. (*glue*) cola *f;* rubber ~ adhesivo de goma, resistol® *m Méx,* pegante bóxer *Col* 3. MED empaste *m* 4. (*uniting idea*) aglutinante *m* II. *vt* 1. (*cover with cement*) revestir de cemento; to ~ over sth revestir algo de cemento 2. (*stabilize*) fortalecer; (*a friendship*) consolidar 3. MED empastar
cemetery ['sem·ə·ter·i] <-ies> *n* cementerio *m,* panteón *m AmL*
censer ['sen·sər] *n* REL incensario *m*
censor ['sen·sər] I. *n* 1. (*official*) censor(a) *m(f)* 2. PSYCH censura *f* II. *vt* censurar
censorious [sen·'sɔr·i·əs] *adj* censurador(a); (*comments*) de reprobación; to be ~ about [*o* of] sth/sb censurar algo/a alguien
censorship ['sen·sər·ʃɪp] *n* censura *f*
censure ['sen·ʃər] *vt* censurar
census ['sen·səs] <-es> *n* censo *m*
cent [sent] *n* centavo *m* ▶ to not have a red ~ *inf* no tener ni un céntimo
centenarian [ˌsen·tə·'ner·i·ən] *n* centenario, -a *m, f*
centenary ['sen·tə·ner·i] I. <-ies> *n* centenario *m* II. *adj* (*once every century*) secular; ~ year año *m* del centenario
centennial [sen·'ten·i·əl] I. *n* centenario *m* II. *adj* centenario, -a
center ['sen·tər] I. *n* 1. (*focus*) *a.* PHYS, POL, SPORTS centro *m* 2. (*of population*) núcleo *m* 3. (*building*) centro *m* 4. SPORTS (*in football*) centro *m* II. *vt* 1. *a.* SPORTS, TYPO centrar 2. (*efforts*) concentrar
◆center around *vi* girar en torno a; his life centers around his family su vida se centra en su familia
◆center on *vi* concentrarse en
centerpiece ['sen·tər·pis] *n* eje *m;* racial integration was the ~ of the party's proposals la integración racial era el aspecto fundamental de las propuestas del partido
centigrade ['sen·tə·greɪd] *adj* centígrado, -a
centigram ['sen·tə·græm] *n* centigramo *m*
centimeter ['sen·tə·ˌmi·tər] *n* centímetro *m*
centipede ['sen·tə·pid] *n* ciempiés *m inv*
central ['sen·trəl] 1. (*at the middle*) central; in ~ Boston en el centro de Boston 2. (*important: issue*) fundamental; to be ~ to sth ser vital para algo; to be of ~ importance (to sb) ser de una importancia primordial (para alguien); the ~ character el protagonista 3. (*from a main point: bank, air conditioning*) central; ~ processing unit COMPUT unidad *f* central de proceso
Central African I. *adj* centroafricano, -a II. *n* centroafricano, -a *m, f*
Central African Republic *n* República *f* Centroafricana
centralization [ˌsen·trə·lɪ'zeɪ·ʃən] *n* centralización *f*

centralize ['sen·trə·laɪz] *vt* centralizar
centrifugal [sen·'trɪf·jə·gəl] *adj* PHYS centrífugo, -a
centrifuge ['sen·trə·fjudʒ] *n* MED, TECH centrifugadora *f*
centripetal [sen·'trɪp·ə·t̬əl] *adj* PHYS centrípeto, -a
century ['sen·tʃə·ri] <-ies> *n* (*100 years*) siglo *m;* the twentieth ~ el siglo XX; a centuries-old custom una costumbre secular
CEO [ˌsi·i·'oʊ] *n abbr of* chief executive officer director(a) *m(f)* general
ceramic [sə·'ræm·ɪk] *adj* de cerámica
ceramics *n pl* cerámica *f*
cereal ['sɪr·i·əl] I. *n* 1. (*cultivated grass*) cereal *m* 2. (*breakfast food*) cereales *mpl* II. *adj* cereal
cerebellum [ˌser·ə·'bel·əm] <-s *o* -la> *n* cerebelo *m*
cerebral ['ser·ə·brəl] *adj* cerebral; ~ palsy parálisis *f inv* cerebral
cerebrum ['ser·ə·brəm] <-(bra)> *n* cerebro *m*
ceremonial [ˌser·ə·'moʊ·ni·əl] I. *n form* ceremonial *m* II. *adj* ceremonial; (*event*) solemne; (*uniform*) de gala
ceremonious [ˌser·ə·'moʊ·ni·əs] *adj* ceremonioso, -a
ceremony ['ser·ə·moʊ·ni] <-ies> *n* ceremonia *f;* to go through the ~ of sth *fig* cumplir con todas las formalidades de algo
certain ['sɜr·tən] I. *adj* 1. (*sure*) seguro, -a; it is quite ~ (that)... es muy probable que... +*subj;* to be ~ about sb confiar en alguien; to be ~ about sth estar convencido de algo; to make ~ of sth asegurarse de algo; it is not yet ~ ... todavía no se sabe con certeza...; to feel ~ (that...) estar convencido (de que...); to make ~ (that...) asegurarse (de que...); please make ~ that he has answered por favor, asegúrate de que ha respondido; I don't know yet for ~ todavía no lo sé a ciencia cierta; one thing is (for) ~ ... de lo que no cabe duda es...; for ~ con certeza 2. (*undeniable*) cierto, -a; it is ~ that... es cierto que...; the disaster seemed ~ el desastre parecía inevitable 3. (*specified*) cierto, -a; a ~ Steve Rukus un tal Steve Rukus; to a ~ extent hasta cierto punto II. *pron* cierto, -a
certainly *adv* 1. (*surely*) por supuesto; she ~ is a looker, isn't she? es guapa, ¿verdad?; she ~ had a friend called Mark está claro que tenía un amigo que se llamaba Mark; he is ~ strong desde luego es fuerte 2. (*gladly*) desde luego; why, ~! ¡claro que sí!; ~, Sir! ¡por supuesto, señor!; ~ not! ¡desde luego que no!
certainty ['sɜr·tən·ti] <-ies> *n* certeza *f;* Joan is a ~ to win está claro que Joan ganará; with ~ a ciencia cierta
certifiable ['sɜr·t̬ə·ˌfaɪ·ə·bəl] *adj* 1. (*declared*) certificable 2. PSYCH (*mentally ill*) demente; he is ~! *inf* ¡está para que lo encierren!
certificate [sər·'tɪf·ɪ·kət] *n* 1. (*document*) certificado *m;* (*of baptism, birth, death*) partida *f;*

(*of ownership*) título *m* **2.** SCHOOL título *m*
certification [ˌsɜr·t̬ə·fɪ·'keɪ·ʃən] *n* **1.** (*process*) certificación *f* **2.** (*document*) certificado *m*
certify ['sɜr·t̬ə·faɪ] <-ie-> *vt* certificar; **certi-fied copy** copia *f* legalizada; **this is to ~ that...** *form* por la presente certifico que...; **he is certified to practice medicine** está habili-tado para ejercer la medicina
certitude ['sɜr·t̬ə·tud] *n* certidumbre *f*
cervical ['sɜr·vɪ·kəl] *adj* **1.** (*neck*) cervical; **~ collar** collarín *m;* **~ vertebra** (vértebra *f*) cervical *f* **2.** (*cervix*) del cuello del útero
cervix ['sɜr·vɪks] <-es *o* -vices> *n* **1.** (*neck*) cerviz *f* **2.** (*womb*) cuello *m* del útero
cesarean [sə·'zer·i·ən] *n* **a ~ section** una cesá-rea
cesium ['si·zi·əm] *n* cesio *m*
cessation [se·'seɪ·ʃən] *n* *form* (*end*) cesación *f;* (*of hostilities*) cese *m*
cesspit ['ses·pɪt] *n* pozo *m* séptico [*o* negro *Arg*]
cesspool ['ses·pul] *n* **1.** (*for excrements*) pozo *m* negro **2.** (*unpleasant area*) cloaca *f*
Ceylon [sɪ·'lan] *n* **1.** HIST (*Sri Lanka*) Ceilán *m* **2.** (*Ceylon tea*) té *m* de Ceilán
Ceylonese [ˌsi·lə·'niz] **I.** *n* ceilanés, -esa *m, f* **II.** *adj* HIST ceilanés, -esa
cf. *abbr of* **confer** (**compare**) cf.
CFC [ˌsi·ef·'si] *n* *abbr of* **chlorofluorocarbon** CFC *m*
Chad [tʃæd] *n* Chad *m*
Chadian I. *adj* chadiano, -a **II.** *n* chadiano, -a *m, f*
chador [tʃa·'dor] *n* chador *m* (*velo que utilizan las mujeres árabes para cubrirse*)
chafe [tʃeɪf] **I.** *vi* **1.** (*become sore*) rozar; (*become worn*) desgastarse **2.** *fig* (*feel irri-tated*) irritarse; **to ~ at sth** enfadarse por algo; **to ~ to do sth** estar impaciente por algo **II.** *vt* **1.** (*rub sore*) irritar **2.** (*rub*) rozar; (*rub for warmth*) frotar **3.** *fig* enfadar
chafer ['tʃeɪ·fər] *n* escarabajo *m*
chaff[1] [tʃæf] *n* AGR **1.** (*husks*) granza *f* **2.** (*cut grass*) forraje *m* **3.** (*worthless material*) paja *f*
chaff[2] [tʃæf] **I.** *n* broma *f* **II.** *vt* tomar el pelo a
chagrin [ʃə·'grɪn] **I.** *n* irritación *f* **II.** *vt* irritar
chain [tʃeɪn] **I.** *n* **1.** cadena *f;* **~ gang** cuerda *f* de presos; **to be in ~s** estar encadenado **2.** GEO cadena *f* montañosa, cordillera *f* **3.** (*series*) cadena *f;* (*of mishaps, events*) sucesión *f* **II.** *vt* encadenar; **to ~ sth/sb (up) to sth** encadenar algo/a alguien a algo; **to be ~ed to a desk** *fig* estar encerrado en un despacho
chain letter *n* carta *f* en cadena (*que debe ser copiada y remitida a varias personas*)
chain mail *n* cota *f* de malla
chain reaction *n* reacción *f* en cadena; **to set off a ~** provocar una reacción en cadena
chain saw *n* motosierra *f*
chain smoker *n* fumador(a) *m(f)* empeder-nido, -a
chain store *n* tienda *f* de una cadena
chair [tʃer] **I.** *n* **1.** (*seat*) silla *f* **2.** (*head*) presi-

dente, -a *m, f;* **to be ~ of a department** ser jefe de un departamento **3.** UNIV cátedra *f* **4.** *sl* (*electric chair*) silla *f* eléctrica **5.** MUS lugar *m* en la orquesta **II.** *vt* (*a meeting*) presidir
chairlift *n* telesilla *m*
chairman ['tʃer·mən] <-men> *n* presidente *m*
chairmanship ['tʃer·mən·ʃɪp] *n* presidencia *f*
chairperson ['tʃer·ˌpɜr·sən] *n* presidente, -a *m, f*
chairwoman <-women> *n* presidenta *f*
chalet [ʃæ·'leɪ] *n* chalet *m*
chalk [tʃɔk] **I.** *n* **1.** GEO (*stone*) caliza *f* **2.** (*stick*) tiza *f,* gis *m Méx* **II.** *vt* (*write*) escribir con tiza; (*draw*) dibujar con tiza

   ◆ **chalk up** *vt* **1.** (*ascribe*) atribuir; **to ~ sth to sb/sth** anotar algo en la cuenta de alguien/algo; **they won, and you can chalk that up to experience** ganaron, lo que se puede atri-buir a su experiencia **2.** (*achieve*) lograr, apun-tar
chalkboard ['tʃɔk·bɔrd] *n* pizarra *f*
chalky ['tʃɔk·i] <-ier, -iest> *adj* **1.** (*made of chalk*) calcáreo, -a; (*water*) calcáreo, -a **2.** (*dusty*) **to be all ~** estar lleno de tiza **3.** (*chalk-like*) terroso, -a **4.** (*pale*) apagado, -a
challenge ['tʃæl·ɪndʒ] **I.** *n* **1.** (*a call to com-petition*) desafío *m;* **to be faced with a ~** enfrentarse a un reto; **to present sb (with) a ~** enfrentar a alguien con un reto; **to pose a ~ to sth** poner algo en tela de juicio **2.** *a.* MIL alto *m* **3.** LAW recusación *f* **II.** *vt* **1.** (*ask to com-pete*) desafiar; **to ~ sb to a duel** retar a al-guien a duelo **2.** (*question*) cuestionar, poner en tela de juicio **3.** (*test*) poner a prueba; **that's a matter that ~s attention** es una cuestión que requiere atención **4.** *a.* MIL dar el alto; **I was ~d by the new security guard** me paró el nuevo guardia de seguridad **5.** LAW recusar
challenger ['tʃæl·ɪn·dʒər] *n* desafiador(a) *m(f);* (*for a title*) aspirante *mf*
challenging *adj* (*book*) que hace pensar; (*idea*) desafiante, estimulante; (*course, task*) exigente
chamber ['tʃeɪm·bər] *n* **1.** (*room*) cámara *f;* **torture ~** sala *f* de tortura **2.** ANAT, POL cámara *f* **3.** ECON **~ of commerce** cámara de comercio **4. ~s** LAW (*judge's office*) despacho *m* del juez **5.** TECH (*of a gun*) recámara *f;* **combustion ~** cámara de combustión
chambermaid ['tʃeɪm·bər·meɪd] *n* camarera *f*
chamber music *n* música *f* de cámara
chamber pot *n* orinal *m,* escupidera *f AmL,* tibor *m Cuba*
chameleon [kə·'mi·li·ən] *n* *a. fig* camaleón *m*
chamois ['ʃæm·i] <- *o* chamoix> *n* *inv* gamuza *f*
chamomile ['kæm·ə·mil] *n* camomila *f;* **~ tea** manzanilla *f*
champ [tʃæmp] **I.** *n* *inf* campeón, -ona *m, f* **II.** *vi* masticar **III.** *vt* masticar
champagne [ʃæm·'peɪn] **I.** *n* champán *m* **II.** *adj* **1.** (*color*) color champán **2.** (*expensive*) **he has ~ tastes** tiene gustos caros

champion ['tʃæm·pi·ən] I. *n* 1. SPORTS campeón, -ona *m*, *f* 2. (*supporter*) defensor(a) *m(f)*; **to be a ~ of sth** ser un paladín de algo II. *vt* defender; **to ~ a cause** abogar por una causa III. *adj* SPORTS campeón, -ona

championship ['tʃæm·pi·ən·ʃɪp] *n* 1. (*competition*) campeonato *m* 2. (*advocacy*) defensa *f*

chance [tʃæns] I. *n* 1. (*random force*) casualidad *f*; **a ~ encounter** un encuentro casual; **a game of ~** un juego de azar; **to leave nothing to ~** no dejar nada al azar; **by ~** por casualidad 2. (*likelihood*) probabilidad *f*; **there's not much of a ~ that I'll go to the party** no es muy probable que vaya a la fiesta; **the ~s are that she's already gone** lo más probable es que ya se haya marchado; **to do sth on the off ~ that...** hacer algo con la esperanza de que...; **to stand a ~ of doing sth** *inf* tener posibilidades de hacer algo; **to not stand a ~ with sb** tenerlo muy difícil con alguien; **not a ~!** *inf* ¡ni en broma! 3. (*opportunity*) oportunidad *f*; **the ~ of a lifetime** la oportunidad de su vida; **to give sb a ~ (to do sth)** dar a alguien una oportunidad (de hacer algo); **given half a ~...** a la menor ocasión...; **to have the ~ (to do sth)** tener la ocasión (de hacer algo); **to jump at the ~** no dejar escapar la oportunidad; **to miss one's ~ (to do sth)** desperdiciar la ocasión (de hacer algo); **to not have a ~ in hell** no tener ninguna posibilidad; **you have to take your ~s when they arise** cuando se presenta una oportunidad, debes aprovecharla 4. (*hazard*) riesgo *m*; **to take a ~** arriesgarse II. *vt* arriesgar; **to ~ it** arriesgarse III. *vi* ocurrir (por casualidad)

chancellery ['tʃæn·sə·lə·ri] <-ies> *n* cancillería *f*

chancellor ['tʃæn·sə·lər] *n* 1. POL (*head of state*) canciller *mf* 2. (*head of a university*) rector(a) *m(f)*

chancy ['tʃæn·si] <-ier, -iest> *adj* arriesgado, -a

chandelier [ˌʃæn·də·'lɪr] *n* (*lamp*) araña *f*

change ['tʃeɪndʒ] I. *n* 1. (*alteration*) cambio *m*; **a ~ of clothes** una muda, un cambio de ropa *Méx*; **for a ~** para variar; **that would be a nice ~** no estaría mal hacer eso para variar; **we could use a ~ of pace** no nos vendría mal un cambio de ritmo 2. (*coins*) cambio *m*, sencillo *m AmL*, feria *f Méx*; **small ~** calderilla *f inf*; **a dollar in ~** un dólar en monedas; **have you got ~ for a twenty-dollar bill?** ¿tienes cambio de 20 dólares?; **how much do you have in ~?** ¿cuánto dinero suelto llevas? 3. (*money returned*) vuelta *f*, vuelto *m AmL*; **no ~ given** no (se) devuelve cambio 4. (*exact amount*) **to have exact ~** tener el importe exacto II. *vt* 1. (*exchange*) cambiar; **to ~ places with sb** *fig* ponerse en el lugar de alguien; **to ~ sth/sb into sth/a** convertir algo/a alguien en algo 2. (*get off a train/plane and board another*) **to ~ trains** cambiar de tren, hacer transbordo 3. (*alter speed*) **to ~ gear(s)**

cambiar de marcha III. *vi* 1. (*alter*) cambiar; **to ~ into sth** convertirse en algo; **the traffic light ~d back to red** el semáforo se puso en rojo 2. (*get off a train/plane and board another*) hacer transbordo 3. (*put on different clothes*) cambiarse (de ropa)

changeable ['tʃeɪn·dʒə·bəl] *adj* cambiante

changeover ['tʃeɪndʒˌoʊ·vər] *n* 1. (*transition*) cambio *m* 2. (*in a race*) relevo *m*

changing ['tʃeɪn·dʒɪŋ] *adj* cambiante; **~ room** SPORTS vestuario *m*; (*in a shop*) probador *m*

channel ['tʃæn·əl] I. *n* 1. TV canal *m* 2. (*waterway*) canal *m*; **The English Channel** el Canal de la Mancha; **irrigation ~** acequia *f* 3. (*means*) conducto *m*; **distribution ~** canal de distribución; **through diplomatic ~s** por la vía diplomática II. <-ll-, -l-> *vt* canalizar; *fig* encauzar

Channel Islands *n* Islas *fpl* Normandas

chant [tʃænt] I. *n* 1. REL canto *m*; (*singing*) salmodia *f*; **Gregorian ~** canto gregoriano 2. (*utterance*) consigna *f* II. *vi* 1. REL (*intone*) salmodiar 2. (*repeat*) gritar al unísono III. *vt* 1. REL (*sing*) cantar; (*speak in a monotone*) salmodiar 2. (*repeat*) repetir al unísono

Chanukah ['ha·nə·kə] *n* REL Januká *m*

chaos ['keɪ·as] *n* caos *m inv*

Chaos Theory *n* PHYS teoría *f* del caos

chaotic [keɪ·'ɑ·ɪk] *adj* caótico, -a

chap [tʃæp] <-pp-> I. *vi* agrietarse, pasparse *RíoPl* II. *vt* agrietar

chap. *n abbr of* **chapter** cap. *m*

chapel ['tʃæp·əl] *n* 1. (*room*) capilla *f*; **funeral ~** capilla ardiente 2. (*small church*) templo *m* 3. (*religious service*) servicio *m* religioso

chaperon(e) ['ʃæp·ə·roʊn] *n* carabina *f*; (*supervisor*) acompañante *f*

chaplain ['tʃæp·lɪn] *n* REL capellán *m*

chapter ['tʃæp·tər] *n* 1. *a. fig* capítulo *m* 2. (*local branch*) sección *f*

chapter house *n* 1. (*fraternity*) sala *f* capitular 2. (*chapter*) sala *f* de reuniones

char [tʃar] <-rr-> I. *n* carbón *m* de leña II. *vi* (*be burned black*) carbonizarse III. <-rr-> *vt* (*burn black*) carbonizar

character ['ker·ək·tər] *n* 1. (*qualities*) carácter *m*; **to be in/out of ~ with sb/sth** ser/no ser típico de alguien/algo 2. (*moral integrity*) reputación *f*; **~ reference** referencias *fpl*; **to be a bad ~** tener mala reputación; **of dubious ~** de dudosa reputación; **of irreproachable ~** de una reputación intachable 3. (*unique person*) personaje *mf* 4. (*representation*) personaje *m*, carácter *m Col, Méx*; **in the ~ of...** en el papel de... 5. TYPO carácter *m*

character actor *n* actor *m* de carácter

characteristic [ˌker·ək·tə·'rɪs·tɪk] I. *n* característica *f* II. *adj* característico, -a; **with her ~ dignity** con la dignidad que la caracteriza

characteristically [ˌker·ək·tə·'rɪs·tɪk·li] *adv* de forma característica

characterization [ˌker·ək·tər·ɪ·'zeɪ·ʃən] *n* caracterización *f*

characterize ['ker·ək·tə·raɪz] *vt* **1.** *a.* CINE, THEAT caracterizar **2.** (*outline*) describir; **to ~ sth/sb as sth** calificar algo/a alguien de algo
charade [ʃə·'reɪd] *n* **1. ~s** GAMES charada *f* **2.** (*pretence*) farsa *f*
charcoal ['tʃar·koʊl] I. *n* **1.** (*fuel*) carbón *m* vegetal **2.** ART (*for drawing*) carboncillo *m*, carbonilla *f RíoPl;* **to draw in ~** dibujar al carboncillo II. *adj* **1.** (*of charcoal*) **~ drawing** dibujo *m* al carboncillo **2.** (*dark grey*) **~ grey** gris marengo
charge [tʃardʒ] I. *n* **1.** (*cost*) precio *m;* **admission ~** (precio de *m*) entrada *f;* **at no extra ~** sin cargo adicional; **free of ~** gratis **2.** LAW (*accusation*) cargo *m;* **to bring ~s against sb** presentar cargos contra alguien **3.** (*attack: of a bull*) embestida *f;* MIL carga *f;* SPORTS ofensiva *f* **4.** (*authority*) responsabilidad *f;* **in the ~ of sb** a cargo de alguien; **to be in ~ of sb/sth** tener algo/a alguien a su cargo; **who is in ~ here?** ¿quién es el responsable aquí? **5.** ELEC carga *f* **6.** (*load*) carga *f* II. *vi* **1.** FIN cobrar **2.** (*attack*) **to ~ at sb/sth** arremeter contra alguien/algo; MIL cargar contra alguien/algo; **~!** ¡al ataque! **3.** ELEC cargarse III. *vt* **1.** FIN (*ask a price*) cobrar; **to ~ sth to sb's account** cargar algo en la cuenta de alguien **2.** LAW (*accuse*) acusar; **she's been ~d with murder** se la acusa de asesinato; **the crimes with which he is ~d** los delitos que se le imputan *elev* **3.** MIL cargar contra **4.** ELEC cargar
chargeable ['tʃar·dʒə·bəl] *adj* FIN **~ to the customer** a cargo del cliente; **to be ~ to tax** estar sujeto a impuestos
charge account *n* cuenta *f* de crédito
charge card *n* tarjeta *f* de pago
charged *adj* cargado, -a
chargé d'affaires [ʃar·ʒeɪ·də·'fer] <chargés d'affaires> *n* encargado, -a *m, f* de negocios
chariot ['tʃær·i·ət] *n* HIST carro *m*
charisma [kə·'rɪz·mə] *n* carisma *m*
charitable ['tʃer·ɪ·tə·bəl] *adj* **1.** (*with money*) generoso, -a; (*with kindness*) bueno, -a **2.** (*concerning charity*) caritativo, -a; (*gifts, donation*) benéfico, -a; (*organization*) de beneficencia
charity ['tʃer·ə·ti] <-ies> *n* **1.** (*generosity of spirit*) caridad *f* **2.** (*compassion*) compasión *f;* **to depend on ~** depender de limosnas **3.** (*organization*) institución *f* benéfica
charlatan ['ʃar·lə·tən] *n* charlatán *m*
charm [tʃarm] I. *n* **1.** (*quality*) encanto *m* **2.** (*ornament*) colgante *m* **3.** (*talisman*) amuleto *m*, payé *m CSur* II. *vt* cautivar; **to ~ sb into doing sth** embelesar a alguien para que haga algo ▶ **to ~ the** pants **off** (**of**) **sb** *sl* llevarse a alguien de calle
charmed *adj* afortunado, -a; **to lead a ~ life** tener una vida afortunada
charmer ['tʃar·mər] *n* persona *f* encantadora
charming ['tʃar·mɪŋ] *adj* encantador(a); **oh, that's rather ~!** ¡es de lo más encantador!
charred *adj* carbonizado, -a

chart [tʃart] I. *n* **1.** (*display of information*) tabla *f;* **weather ~** mapa *m* meteorológico **2.** *pl* MUS **the ~s** la lista de éxitos; **to top the ~s** llegar al número uno de la lista II. *vt* **1.** *a. fig* trazar; **the map ~s the course of the river** el mapa reproduce gráficamente el curso del río **2.** (*observe*) seguir atentamente
charter ['tʃar·tər] I. *n* **1.** (*government statement*) estatutos *mpl* **2.** (*document stating aims*) carta *f* **3.** (*exclusive right*) privilegio *m* **4.** (*founding document*) escritura *f* de constitución **5.** COM fletamento *m* **6.** COM contrato *m* de fletamento II. *vt* **1.** (*sign founding papers*) estatuir **2.** COM fletar
charter company <-ies> *n* compañía *f* de vuelos chárter
chartered ['tʃar·tərd] *adj* COM fletado, -a
charter flight *n* vuelo *m* chárter
chase [tʃeɪs] I. *n* **1.** (*pursuit*) persecución *f;* **to give ~** salir en persecución **2.** (*hunt*) *a. fig* caza *f* II. *vi* (*rollick about*) **they ~ed after her** fueron tras ella III. *vt* **1.** (*pursue: dreams*) perseguir; (*women*) andar detrás de **2.** (*scare away*) **to ~ away sb/sth** ahuyentar a alguien/algo
chasm ['kæz·əm] *n* **1.** (*abyss*) abismo *m* **2.** (*omission*) hueco *m* **3.** *fig* (*great discrepancy*) diferencias *fpl;* **to bridge a ~** salvar las diferencias
chassis ['ʃæs·i] *n inv* chasis *m inv*
chaste [tʃerst] *adj form* casto, -a
chasten ['tʃer·sən] *vt* **1.** (*admonish*) reprender **2.** (*punish*) castigar
chastise ['tʃæs·taɪz] *vt* reprender
chastity ['tʃæs·tə·ti] *n* castidad *f;* **vow of ~** voto *m* de castidad
chat [tʃæt] I. *n* **1.** charla *f* **2.** COMPUT chat *m* II. *vi* <-tt-> **1.** (*informally*) charlar, versar *AmC;* (*animatedly*); **to ~ away** estar de [*o Col* echar] cháchara, echar la chorcha *Méx;* (*idly*) hablar sin ton ni son **2.** COMPUT chatear
chateau [ʃæt·'oʊ] *n* casa *f* señorial
chatroom *n* foro *m* de chat
chatter ['tʃæt·ər] I. *n* cháchara *f;* (*of birds*) cotorreo *m* II. *vi* **1.** (*converse superficially*) **to ~ about sth** charlar sobre algo; **they ~ed about everything and nothing** chacharearon de todo y de nada **2.** (*make clacking noises: machines*) tabletear; (*birds*) cotorrear; (*teeth*) castañear
chatty ['tʃæt·i] <-ier, -iest> *adj inf* **1.** (*friendly person*) hablador(a) **2.** LIT (*informal*) informal; (*style*) llano, -a
chauffeur ['ʃoʊ·'fər] I. *n* chófer *mf* II. *vt* **to ~ sb around** *a. fig* hacer de chófer de alguien
chauvinism ['ʃoʊ·vɪ·nɪz·əm] *n* chovinismo *m*
chauvinist *n* chovinista *mf*
chauvinistic [ʃoʊ·vɪ·'nɪs·tɪk] *adj* chovinista
cheap [tʃip] *adj* **1.** (*inexpensive*) barato, -a; (*ticket*) económico, -a; **dirt ~** tirado, -a de precio **2.** (*exploited*) **~ labor** mano *f* de obra barata **3.** (*worthless*) regalado, -a **4.** (*inexpensive but bad quality*) ordinario, -a **5.** (*miserly*) chapucero, -a

C

cheapen ['tʃiˑpən] *vt* **1.** (*lower price of*) rebajar **2.** (*reduce morally*) degradar
cheaply *adv* de forma barata
cheapness ['tʃipˑnɪs] *n* **1.** (*low price*) bajo precio *m* **2.** (*low quality*) pacotilla *f*
cheapskate ['tʃipˑˌskeɪt] *sl* **I.** *n* tacaño, -a *m, f* **II.** *adj* tacaño, -a, agarrado, -a
cheat [tʃit] **I.** *n* **1.** (*dishonest person*) estafador(a) *m(f)* **2.** (*trick*) trampa *f* **II.** *vi* to ~ **at sth** hacer trampa(s) en algo; **to** ~ **on a test** copiar en un examen **III.** *vt* engañar; **to** ~ **the taxman** estafar a Hacienda
check [tʃek] **I.** *n* **1.** (*inspection*) control *m*; **security** ~ control de seguridad **2.** (*restraint*) control *m*; **to keep sth in** ~ mantener algo bajo control **3.** (*a look*) vistazo *m* **4.** (*search for information*) verificación *f*; **to run a** ~ realizar una inspección **5.** (*deposit receipt*) resguardo *m*; **coat** ~ guardarropa *m* **6.** (*mark*) marca *f*, visto *m* **7.** (*paper money*) cheque *m*; **to make out a blank** ~ hacer un cheque en blanco; *fig* dar carta blanca; **to pay by** ~ pagar con cheque **8.** (*bill for food*) cuenta *f* **9.** (*textile*) tela *f* de cuadros **10.** GAMES jaque *m*; **to be in** ~ estar en jaque **II.** *adj* a cuadros **III.** *vt* **1.** (*inspect for problems*) comprobar, chequear *AmL* **2.** (*prevent*) frenar **3.** (*temporarily deposit*) dejar en consigna; AVIAT facturar **4.** (*make a mark*) marcar **5.** GAMES dar jaque a **IV.** *vi* **1.** (*examine*) revisar **2.** (*ask*) consultar **3.** (*be in accordance with*) coincidir
◆**check in** *vi* **1.** (*at airport*) facturar **2.** (*at hotel*) registrarse
◆**check off** *vt* verificar (haciendo marcas)
◆**check out I.** *vi* to ~ **of a room** dejar libre una habitación **II.** *vt* **1.** (*investigate*) investigar **2.** *sl* (*look at*) mirar
◆**check up on** *vt* controlar; (*person*) hacer averiguaciones sobre
checkbook ['tʃekˑˌbʊk] *n* talonario *m* de cheques
checked *adj* a cuadros
checkerboard ['tʃekˑərˑˌbɔrd] *n* (*chessboard for checkers*) tablero *m* de ajedrez
checkered ['tʃekˑərd] *adj* **1.** (*patterned with squares*) a cuadros **2.** (*inconsistent*) accidentado, -a; **to have a** ~ **past** tener un pasado con altibajos
checkers ['tʃekˑərz] *n* + *sing vb* GAMES damas *fpl*
check-in ['tʃekˑɪn] *n* facturación *f*
check-in counter *n*, **check-in desk** *n* mostrador *m* de facturación
checking account *n* cuenta *f* corriente
check-in time *n* hora *f* de facturación
checklist ['tʃekˑlɪst] *n* lista *f*
checkmate I. *n* **1.** GAMES (jaque *m*) mate *m* **2.** (*defeat*) fracaso *m* **II.** *vt* **1.** GAMES dar (jaque) mate a **2.** (*win a victory over*) ganar
checkout ['tʃekˑaʊt] *n* caja *f*
checkout counter *n* caja *f*
checkpoint ['tʃekˑpɔɪnt] *n* punto *m* de control
checkroom *n* **1.** (*for coats*) guardarropa *m*

2. (*for luggage*) consigna *f*
checkup ['tʃekˑʌp] *n* comprobación *f*; MED chequeo *m* médico
cheddar ['tʃedˑər] *n* queso *m* de cheddar
cheek [tʃik] *n* **1.** ANAT mejilla *f* **2.** (*impertinence*) descaro *m*, empaque *m AmL*; **to have the** ~ **to do sth** tener la caradura de hacer algo ▶**to turn the other** ~ poner la otra mejilla
cheekbone ['tʃikˑboʊn] *n* pómulo *m*
cheeky ['tʃiˑki] <-ier, -iest> *adj* descarado, -a, fregado, -a *AmL*; **to be** ~ **to sb** ser descarado con alguien
cheep [tʃip] **I.** *n* (*of bird*) pío *m*; **to not get a** ~ **out of sb** no sacarle ni una palabra a alguien; **to not hear a** ~ **out of sb** no decir alguien esta boca es mía **II.** *vi* piar
cheer [tʃɪr] **I.** *n* **1.** (*exuberant shout*) ovación *f*; **three** ~ **s for the champion!** ¡tres hurras por el campeón!; **to give a** ~ vitorear **2.** (*joy*) alegría *f*; **to be of good** ~ estar animado **II.** *interj* ~**s** (*said when drinking*) salud **III.** *vi* to ~ **for sb** animar a alguien
cheerful ['tʃɪrˑfʊl] *adj* **1.** (*happy*) alegre; (*with a positive attitude*) jovial **2.** (*color*) vivo, -a **3.** (*encouraging*) alentador(a)
cheerfulness *n* alegría *f*
cheeriness *n* **1.** (*happiness*) alegría *f* **2.** (*brightness*) jovialidad *f*
cheering I. *n* aplausos *mpl* **II.** *adj* alentador(a)
cheerleader ['tʃɪrˑˌliˑdər] *n* animadora *f*

---

i **Cheerleaders** es el nombre que se da en EE.UU. a las chicas jóvenes que animan a un equipo deportivo. Su labor consiste en dirigir las canciones y gritos de ánimo de los **fans** y entretener al público con pequeñas coreografías en las que utilizan los característicos **pompoms.** Suelen llevar vestido corto o falda y blusa, además de calcetines y zapatos de cuero, en los colores de su equipo o colegio.

---

cheery ['tʃɪrˑi] <-ier, -iest> *adj* alegre
cheese [tʃiz] *n* queso *m*; **hard** ~ queso curado; **melted** ~ queso fundido ▶**say** ~! ¡decid patata!
cheeseburger ['tʃizˑˌbɜrˑgər] *n* hamburguesa *f* con queso
cheesecake ['tʃizˑkeɪk] *n* tarta *f* de queso
cheesecloth ['tʃizˑklaθ] <-es> *n* estopilla *f*
cheese-paring ['tʃizˑˌperˑɪŋ] *n* tacaño, -a *m, f*
cheesy ['tʃiˑzi] <-ier, -iest> *adj* **1.** (*like cheese*) como queso **2.** *inf* (*cheap and shoddy*) chungo, -a
cheetah ['tʃɪˑtə] *n* guepardo *m*
chef [ʃef] *n* jefe, -a *m, f* de cocina, chef *mf*
chemical ['kemˑɪˑkəl] **I.** *n* (*atoms*) sustancia *f* química; (*additive*) aditivo *m* **II.** *adj* químico, -a
chemist ['kemˑɪst] *n* químico, -a *m, f*
chemistry ['kemˑɪˑstri] *n* química *f*

chemotherapy [ˌki·mou·'θer·ə·pi] n quimioterapia f; **to undergo** ~ seguir un tratamiento de quimioterapia

cherish ['tʃer·ɪʃ] vt (hold dear) apreciar; (remember fondly) recordar

cheroot [ʃə·'rut] n puro m (cortado por ambos extremos)

cherry ['tʃer·i] <-ies> I. n 1.(fruit) cereza f 2.(tree) cerezo m II. adj (de) color rojo cereza

cherry blossom n flor f de cerezo

cherry brandy n aguardiente m de cerezas

cherry tomato n tomate m cherry

cherub ['tʃer·əb] <-s o -im> n querubín m

chervil ['tʃɜr·vɪl] n perifollo m

chess [tʃes] n ajedrez m

chessboard ['tʃes·bɔrd] n tablero m de ajedrez

chessman n, chess piece <-men> n pieza f de ajedrez

chest [tʃest] n 1.(human torso) pecho m; ~ pains dolores mpl pectorales; **to fold one's arms across one's** ~ cruzarse de brazos 2.(breasts) senos mpl 3.(trunk) baúl m, petaca f AmL; **medicine** ~ botiquín m ▶**to get sth off one's** ~ desahogarse confesando algo

chestnut ['tʃes·nʌt] I. n 1.(fruit) castaña f 2.(tree) castaño m 3.(wood) (madera f de) castaño m 4.(color) (color m) castaño, marrón m 5.(horse) caballo m castaño II. adj castaño, -a

chesty ['tʃes·ti] <-ier, -iest> adj inf con mucho pecho, bustona Col, Méx

chew [tʃu] I. n 1.(tobacco plug) mascada f 2.(candy) mascada f II. vt masticar

◆chew out vt sl echar la bronca a

chewing gum ['tʃu·ɪŋ·gʌm] n chicle m

chewy ['tʃu·i] <-ier, -iest> adj masticable; (meat) duro, -a

chic [ʃik] I. n chic m II. adj chic, a la moda

chicane [ʃɪ·'keɪn] n chicane f

chicanery [ʃɪ·'keɪ·nə·ri] n artimaña f

Chicano [tʃɪ·'ka·nou] n, adj chicano, -a m, f

chick [tʃɪk] n 1.(baby chicken) pollito, -a m, f 2.(young bird) polluelo, -a m, f 3. sl (young woman) tía f

chicken ['tʃɪk·ən] n 1.(farm bird) pollo, -a m, f 2.(meat) (carne f de) pollo m; **fried/roasted** ~ pollo frito/asado; **grilled** ~ pollo a la brasa 3. inf(person) gallina m, rajado m, rajón, -ona m, f Cuba, Méx ▶it's a ~ **and egg situation** es como lo del huevo y la gallina; **to not be a** (**spring**) ~ ya no ser ningún crío

chicken broth n sopa f de pollo

chicken farm n granja f de pollos

chicken feed n 1.(food) pienso m 2.(small amount of money) calderilla f

chicken-hearted adj cobarde

chickenpox n varicela f

chicken run n gallinero m

chickpea ['tʃɪk·pi] n garbanzo m

chicory ['tʃɪk·ə·ri] n 1.BOT endivia f, endibia f 2.(in coffee) achicoria f, radicheta f Arg, Urug

chief [tʃif] I. n 1.(boss) jefe, -a m, f 2.(of a tribe) jefe, -a m, f II. adj 1.(top) primero, -a 2.(major) principal

chief executive n, chief executive officer n director(a) m(f) general

chief justice n presidente, -a m, f del Tribunal Supremo

chiefly adv principalmente

chieftain ['tʃif·tən] n cacique m

chiffon [ʃɪ·'fan] n chifón m, chiffon m

child [tʃaɪld] <children> pl n 1.(person who's not fully grown) niño, -a m, f; **unborn** ~ feto m 2.(offspring) hijo, -a m, f; **illegitimate** ~ hijo bastardo; **to be a** ~ **of the eighties** fig ser un producto de los (años) ochenta ▶**spare the rod and spoil the** ~ prov quien bien te quiere te hará llorar prov

child abuse ['tʃaɪld·ə·bjus] n maltrato m de un niño; (sexual) abuso m (sexual) de un niño

childbearing I. n maternidad f II. adj **women of** ~ **age** mujeres fpl en edad de tener hijos

childbirth n parto m, parición f AmL

child-care n cuidado m de los niños

childhood n infancia f

childish ['tʃaɪl·dɪʃ] adj pej infantil, achiquillado, -a Méx; **don't be** ~! ¡no seas niño!

childless ['tʃaɪld·lɪs] adj sin hijos

childlike ['tʃaɪld·laɪk] adj infantil

childproof adj a prueba de niños; ~ **lock** cerradura f de seguridad para niños

children ['tʃɪl·drən] n pl of child

child-resistant adj form a prueba de niños

child's play n fig juego m de niños

child support n subsidio m de maternidad

Chile ['tʃɪl·i] n Chile m

chile ['tʃɪl·i] n s. chili

Chilean [tʃɪ·'leɪ·ən] I. adj chileno, -a II. n chileno, -a m, f

chili ['tʃɪl·i] <-es> n chile m, ají m (picante) AmS, Ant

chill [tʃɪl] I. n 1.(coldness) frío m; **to catch a** ~ resfriarse; **to take the** ~ **off of something** calentar algo un poco 2.(shiver) escalofrío m; **to send a** ~ **down someone's spine** hacer entrar escalofríos a alguien II. adj (cold) frío, -a; (frightening) estremecedor(a) III. vt enfriar; **to be** ~ed **to the bone** estar como un témpano (de hielo)

chill(i)ness n frío m; fig frialdad f

chilling adj terrorífico, -a

chilly ['tʃɪl·i] <-ier, -iest> adj a. fig frío, -a; **to feel** ~ tener frío

chime [tʃaɪm] I. n repique m; **wind** ~s carillón m II. vi repicar III. vt to ~ **eleven** dar las once

chimney ['tʃɪm·ni] n 1.(in a building) chimenea f, tronera f Méx 2.(in rock) cañón m

chimney pot n cañón m de la chimenea

chimney sweep n, chimneysweeper n a. HIST deshollinador(a) m(f)

chimpanzee [tʃɪm·'pæn·zi] n chimpancé m

chin [tʃɪn] n barbilla f ▶**to keep one's** ~ **up** no desanimarse

china ['tʃaɪ·nə] n 1.(porcelain) porcelana f

2. (*crockery*) vajilla *f*

China ['tʃaɪ·nə] *n* China *f*

Chinatown ['tʃaɪ·nə·ˌtoʊn] *n* barrio *m* chino

chinchilla [tʃɪn·'tʃɪl·ə] *n* chinchilla *f*

Chinese [tʃaɪ·'niz] I. *adj* chino, -a II. *n* 1. (*person*) chino, -a *m, f* 2. LING chino *m*

Chinese cabbage *n* col *f* china

Chinese lantern *n* farolillo *m*

chink [tʃɪŋk] I. *n* 1. (*thin opening*) hendidura *f;* the ~ in sb's armor *fig* el punto débil de alguien 2. (*clinking noise*) tintineo *m* II. *vi* tintinear

chintz [tʃɪnts] *n* chintz *m*

chip [tʃɪp] I. *n* 1. (*flake*) pedazo *m; (stone*) lasca *f; (wood*) astilla *f* 2. COMPUT chip *m* 3. (*money token for gambling*) ficha *f;* bargaining ~ moneda *f* de cambio 4. CULIN chocolate ~ galleta con trocitos de chocolate ▶ he's a ~ off the old block *inf* de tal palo, tal astilla; to have a ~ on one's **shoulder** *inf* estar resentido; when the ~s are **down** *inf* a la hora de la verdad II. *vt* <-pp-> desportillar III. *vi* <-pp-> desportillarse

chipmunk ['tʃɪp·mʌŋk] *n* ardilla *f* listada

chipped [tʃɪpt] *adj* desportillado, -a

chiropractic ['kaɪ·rə·ˌpræk·tɪk] *n* quiropráctica *f*

chiropractor ['kaɪ·roʊ·ˌpræk·tər] *n* quiropráctico, -a *m, f*

chirp ['tʃɜrp] I. *n* gorjeo *m* II. *vi* gorjear III. *vt* decir alegremente

chirpy ['tʃɜr·pi] <-ier, -iest> *adj* animado, -a

chirrup ['tʃɪr·əp] *s.* chirp

chisel ['tʃɪz·əl] I. *n* cincel *m* II.<-ll-, -l-> *vt* 1. (*cut*) esculpir 2. *inf* (*get by trickery*) estafar

chit [tʃɪt] *n* 1. (*note*) nota *f* 2. (*voucher*) vale *m*

chitchat ['tʃɪt·ˌtʃæt] I. *n inf* cháchara *f* II. *vi inf* to ~ about sth estar de palique sobre algo

chivalrous ['ʃɪv·əl·rəs] *adj* caballeroso, -a

chivalry ['ʃɪv·əl·ri] *n* 1. (*gallant behavior*) caballerosidad *f* 2. HIST caballería *f*

chives [tʃaɪvz] *npl* cebollinos *mpl*

chloride ['klɔr·aɪd] *n* cloruro *m*

chlorinate ['klɔr·ɪ·ˌneɪt] *vt* clorar

chlorine ['klɔr·in] *n* cloro *m*

chlorofluorocarbon [ˌklɔr·oʊ·ˌflɔr·oʊ·'kar·bən] *n* clorofluorocarbono *m*

chloroform ['klɔr·ə·ˌfɔrm] I. *n* cloroformo *m* II. *vt* cloroformizar

chlorophyll ['klɔr·ə·fɪl] *n* clorofila *f*

chock [tʃak] *n* cuña *f*

chock-a-block [ˌtʃak·ə·'blak] *adj* ~ with people abarrotado de gente

chock-full *adj* to be ~ of sth estar abarrotado de algo; ~ of calories cargado de calorías

chocolate ['tʃak·lət] *n* 1. (*sweet*) chocolate *m;* dark ~ chocolate negro; a bar of ~ una tableta de chocolate 2. (*piece of chocolate candy*) bombón *m*

choice [tʃɔɪs] I. *n* 1. (*possibility of selection*) elección *f;* to make a ~ elegir; to have no ~ no tener alternativa; she didn't have much ~ no tenía muchas opciones 2. (*selection*) selec-

ción *f;* a wide ~ of sth un amplio surtido de algo 3. (*selected person or thing*) preferencia *f* II. *adj* 1. (*top quality*) selecto, -a 2. *fig* (*bitingly angry*) furioso, -a

choir ['kwaɪr] *n* coro *m*

choirmaster ['kwaɪr·ˌmæs·tər] *n* director(a) *m(f)* de coro

choke [tʃoʊk] I. *vi* sofocarse; to ~ to death morir asfixiado II. *n* AUTO estárter *m* III. *vt* 1. (*deprive of air*) estrangular 2. (*block*) obstruir; ~d with leaves atascado de hojas

◆**choke back** *vt* ahogar; to ~ tears contener las lágrimas

◆**choke off** *vt* (*bring to an end*) cortar

◆**choke up** *vt* obstruir

choker ['tʃoʊ·kər] *n* gargantilla *f*

cholera ['kal·ər·ə] *n* cólera *m*

choleric ['kal·ə·rɪk] *adj* colérico, -a

cholesterol [kə·'les·tə·ral] *n* colesterol *m*

choose [tʃuz] <chose, chosen> I. *vt* elegir; (*prefer*) preferir, decidirse por II. *vi* elegir; to have to ~ between tener que elegir entre

choos(e)y ['tʃu·zi] <-ier, -iest> *adj inf* quisquilloso, -a

chop [tʃap] I. *vt* <-pp-> cortar; (*wood*) partir; (*meat*) picar II. *vi* <-pp-> cortar III. *n* 1. CULIN chuleta *f* 2. (*blow*) golpe *m*

◆**chop away** *vt* cortar

◆**chop down** *vt* talar

◆**chop off** I. *vt* tronchar II. *vi* (*wind*) cambiar repentinamente de dirección

chop-chop [ˌtʃap·'tʃap] *interj inf* ¡vamos, deprisa!

chopper ['tʃap·ər] *n* 1. (*tool*) hacha *f* 2. *inf* AVIAT helicóptero *m*

choppy ['tʃap·i] <-ier, -iest> *adj* 1. NAUT agitado, -a 2. (*words, sentences*) entrecortado, -a

chopsticks ['tʃap·stɪks] *npl* palillos *mpl* (para comer comida oriental)

chop suey [ˌtʃap·'su·i] *n* chop suey *m*

choral ['kɔr·əl] *adj* coral; ~ society coral *f*

chord [kɔrd] *n* MUS acorde *m* ▶ to strike a ~ (with sb) tocar la fibra sensible (a alguien)

chore [tʃɔr] *n* 1. (*routine job*) tarea *f;* household ~s quehaceres *mpl* domésticos 2. (*tedious task*) lata *f*

choreograph ['kɔr·i·ə·ˌgræf] *vi, vt* coreografiar

choreographer [ˌkɔr·i·'ag·rə·fər] *n* coreógrafo, -a *m, f*

choreography [ˌkɔr·i·'ag·rə·fi] *n* coreografía *f*

chorus ['kɔr·əs] I. <-es> *n* 1. (*refrain*) estribillo *m;* to join in the ~ cantar el estribillo 2. + *sing/pl vb* (*group of singers*) coral *f* 3. + *sing/pl vb* (*supporting singers*) coro *m;* ~ girl corista *f;* in ~ a coro II. *vi, vt* corear

chose [tʃoʊz] *pt of* choose

chosen ['tʃoʊ·zən] *pp of* choose

chow [tʃaʊ] *n sl* (*food*) comida *f*, lata *f Col*, morfi *m CSur*

chow chow *n* (*dog*) chow-chow *mf*

chowder ['tʃaʊ·dər] *n* sopa espesa o guiso de pescado o verduras

Christ [kraɪst] I. *n* Cristo *m* II. *interj sl* ¡Dios!,

¡joder! *vulg;* **for ~'s sake** ¡por amor de Dios!
christen ['krɪs·ən] *vt* **1.** (*baptize*) bautizar **2.** (*give name to*) **they ~ed their second child Sarah** a su segundo bebé le pusieron Sara **3.** (*use for first time*) estrenar
Christendom ['krɪs·ən·dəm] *n* HIST cristiandad *f*
christening ['krɪs·ə·nɪŋ] *n,* **christening ceremony** *n* bautismo *m,* bautizo *m*
Christian ['krɪs·tʃən] **I.** *n* cristiano, -a *m, f* **II.** *adj* **1.** (*of Christ's teachings*) cristiano, -a **2.** (*kind*) amable **3.** (*decent*) honrado, -a
Christian burial *n* cristiana sepultura *f*
Christianity [ˌkrɪs·tʃi·'æn·ə·ţi] *n* cristianismo *m*
Christianize ['krɪs·tʃə·naɪz] *vt* cristianizar
Christian name *n* nombre *m* de pila
Christmas ['krɪs·məs] <-es *o* -ses> *n* Navidad *f;* **at ~** en Navidad; **Merry ~!** ¡Feliz Navidad!; **Father ~** Papá *m* Noel, viejo *m* Pascuero *Chile*
Christmas carol *n* villancico *m*
Christmas Day *n* día *m* de Navidad, día *m* de Pascua *Perú, Chile*
Christmas Eve *n* Nochebuena *f*
Christmas tree *n* árbol *m* de Navidad

---

i En Estados Unidos, el envío de **Christmas cards** (tarjetas de navidad) comienza a principios del mes de diciembre. Esta costumbre surgió a mediados del siglo XIX. Otra de las tradiciones navideñas estadounidenses consiste en colgar los **Christmas stockings** (medias de gran tamaño) para que aparezcan llenas de regalos a la mañana siguiente. Los niños acostumbran colgarlas durante **Christmas Eve** (Nochebuena). Los demás regalos se colocan debajo del árbol de navidad, para ser abiertos en la mañana del 25 de diciembre.

Christopher ['krɪs·tə·fər] *n* Cristóbal *m; ~* **Columbus** HIST Cristóbal Colón
chromatic [kroʊ·'mæţ·ɪk] *adj* cromático, -a
chrome [kroʊm] *n* cromo *m*
chrome-plated *adj* cromado, -a
chromosome ['kroʊ·mə·soʊm] *n* cromosoma *m*
chronic ['kran·ɪk] *adj* **1.** (*lasting a long time*) crónico, -a **2.** (*habitual: liar*) empedernido, -a
chronicle ['kran·ɪ·kəl] **I.** *vt* registrar **II.** *n* crónica *f*
chronicler ['kran·ɪ·klər] *n* cronista *mf*
chronological [ˌkran·ə·'ladʒ·ɪ·kəl] *adj* cronológico, -a; **in ~ order** en orden cronológico
chronology [krə·'nal·ə·dʒi] *n* cronología *f*
chrysalis ['krɪs·ə·lɪs] <-es> *n* crisálida *f*
chrysanthemum [krɪ·'sæn·θə·məm] *n* crisantemo *m*
chubby ['tʃʌb·i] <-ier, -iest> *adj* (*fingers, legs,*

face) regordete, -a; (*child*) gordinflón, -ona, rechoncho, -a, tacuaco, -a *Chile*
chuck¹ [tʃʌk] **I.** *vt* **1.** *inf* (*throw*) tirar **2.** *inf* (*discard*) dejar, tirar **II.** *n inf* tiro *m*
chuck² [tʃʌk] *n* **1.** (*cut of beef*) corte de carne vacuna del cuarto delantero **2.** (*device for holding tool*) portabrocas *m inv*
chuckhole *n* bache *m,* pozo *m Csur*
chuckle ['tʃʌk·əl] **I.** *n* risita *f* **II.** *vi* reírse
chug [tʃʌg] **I.** <-gg-> *vi* resoplar **II.** *n* resoplido *m*
chum¹ [tʃʌm] *n inf* amigo, -a *m, f,* colega *mf,* cuate *m Méx*
chum² [tʃʌm] *n* (*bait*) cebo *m*
chummy ['tʃʌm·i] <-ier, -iest> *adj inf* (*friendly*) simpático, -a; **to get ~ with sb** hacerse amigo de alguien
chump [tʃʌmp] *n inf* tontorrón, -ona *m, f*
chump change *n sl* calderilla *f*
chunk [tʃʌŋk] *n* **1.** (*thick lump: of cheese, bread, meat*) pedazo *m,* trozo *m,* troncho *m CSur* **2.** *inf* (*large part*) buena parte *f*
chunky ['tʃʌn·ki] <-ier, -iest> *adj* (*person*) fornido, -a, macizo, -a; (*peanut butter*) con trozos de cacahuete; (*soup*) con tropezones
church [tʃɜrtʃ] **I.** *n* iglesia *f;* **to go to ~** ir a misa; **to enter the ~** hacerse sacerdote; (*become a nun*) meterse a monja **II.** *adj* **1.** (*of the organization: parade, celebration*) religioso, -a **2.** (*of a building*) de iglesia
churchgoer ['tʃɜrtʃ·ˌgoʊ·ər] *n* practicante *mf*
churchyard ['tʃɜrtʃ·jard] *n* cementerio *m*
churlish ['tʃɜr·lɪʃ] *adj* grosero, -a, maleducado, -a
churn [tʃɜrn] **I.** *n* **1.** (*for milk*) lechera *f* **2.** (*for butter*) mantequera *f* **II.** *vt* batir; *fig* agitar **III.** *vi* (*liquid*) arremolinarse; (*wheels*) girar rápidamente; **my stomach was ~ing** tenía un nudo en el estómago
chute [ʃut] *n* **1.** (*sloping tube*) rampa *f;* **garbage ~** vertedero *m* de basuras **2.** (*swimming pool slide*) tobogán *m* (de agua) **3.** *inf* AVIAT paracaídas *m inv*
chutney ['tʃʌt·ni] *n* chutney *m* (*conserva agridulce que se come con carnes, queso, etc.*)
CIA [ˌsi·aɪ·'eɪ] *n abbr of* **Central Intelligence Agency** CIA *f*
cicada <-s *o* -dae> [sɪ'keɪdə] *n* cigarra *f*
cider ['saɪ·dər] *n* (*unfermented*) **sweet ~** zumo *m* de manzana
cigar [sɪ·'gar] *n* puro *m*
cigar box <-es> *n,* **cigar case** *n* cigarrera *f*
cigar cutter *n* cortapuros *m inv*
cigarette [ˌsɪg·ə·'ret] *n* cigarrillo *m;* **to light a ~** encender un cigarrillo
cigarette butt *n* colilla *f*
cigarette case *n* pitillera *f*
cigarette holder *n* boquilla *f*
cigarette paper *n* papel *m* de fumar, mortaja *f AmL*
cigarillo [sɪg·ə·'rɪl·oʊ] *n* purito *m*
cilantro [sɪ·'læn·troʊ] *n* cilantro *m*
cinch [sɪntʃ] <-es> *n* **it's a ~** *inf* está tirado [*o*

C

chupado|

cinder ['sɪn·dər] n **1.** (burnt residue) carbonilla f, carboncillo m; **to burn sth to a ~** carbonizar algo **2. ~s** (ashes) ceniza f

Cinderella [ˌsɪn·də·'rel·ə] n Cenicienta f

cinema ['sɪn·ə·mə] n cine m, biógrafo m Arg, Chile, Urug

cinemagoer ['sɪn·ə·mə·ˌgou·ər] n cinéfilo, -a m, f

cinematic [ˌsɪn·ə·'mæt̬·ɪk] adj cinematográfico, -a

cinnamon ['sɪn·ə·mən] n canela f; **a ~ stick** un trozo de canela en rama

CIO n abbr of **Congress of Industrial Organizations** Congreso m de Organizaciones Industriales

cipher ['saɪ·fər] n clave f; **in ~** en clave

circa ['sɜr·kə] prep hacia; **~ 1850** hacia (el año) 1850

circle ['sɜr·kəl] **I.** n **1.** a. MATH círculo m; **to go around in ~s** dar vueltas; **to run around in ~s** fig dar vueltas y más vueltas a algo; **to have ~s under one's eyes** tener ojeras **2.** THEAT anfiteatro m ▶ **to come full ~** volver al punto de partida; **to square the ~** buscar la cuadratura del círculo **II.** vt trazar un círculo alrededor de; (move in a circle around) dar vueltas alrededor de, rodear **III.** vi dar vueltas; (aircraft) volar en círculos

circuit ['sɜr·kɪt] n **1.** ELEC circuito m **2.** SPORTS **the senior ~** el circuito profesional **3.** (circular route) vuelta f **4.** (district under circuit judge) distrito m, territorio m jurisdiccional

circuit board n placa f base

circuit breaker n cortacircuitos m inv

circuitous [sər·'kju·ə·t̬əs] adj (route) tortuoso, -a

circular ['sɜr·kjə·lər] **I.** adj circular **II.** n circular f

circular saw n sierra f circular

circulate ['sɜr·kjə·leɪt] **I.** vt hacer circular, divulgar; (notice) enviar una circular a **II.** vi circular

circulating library <-ies> n biblioteca f

circulation [ˌsɜr·kjʊ·'leɪ·ʃən] n circulación f; **to be out of ~** estar fuera de circulación

circulatory ['sɜr·kjə·lə·tɔr·i] adj circulatorio, -a

circumcise ['sɜr·kəm·saɪz] vt circuncidar

circumcision [ˌsɜr·kəm·'sɪʒ·ən] n circuncisión f

circumference [sər·'kʌm·fər·əns] n **1.** (circle's boundary line) circunferencia f **2.** (perimeter) perímetro m

circumlocution [ˌsɜr·kəm·lou·'kju·ʃən] n form **1.** (expression) circunlocución f **2.** (way of speaking) circunloquio m

circumnavigate [ˌsɜr·kəm·'næv·ɪ·geɪt] vt form circunnavegar

circumnavigation [ˌsɜr·kəm·ˌnæv·ɪ·'geɪ·ʃən] n form circunnavegación f

circumscribe ['sɜr·kəm·skraɪb] vt form circunscribir

circumscription [ˌsɜr·kəm·'skrɪp·ʃən] n **1.** cir-

cunscripción f **2.** (on coin) grafila f

circumspect ['sɜr·kəm·spekt] adj form circunspecto, -a

circumstance ['sɜr·kəm·stæns] n circunstancia f; **under no ~s** bajo ningún concepto, bajo ninguna circunstancia

circumstantial [ˌsɜr·kəm·'stæn·ʃəl] adj circunstancial

circumvent [ˌsɜr·kəm·'vent] vt form (regulations) burlar; (obstacle) sortear, salvar

circus ['sɜr·kəs] **I.** <-es> n circo m **II.** adj de circo

cirrhosis [sə·'rou·sɪs] n cirrosis f inv; **~ of the liver** cirrosis hepática

cirrus ['sɪr·əs] n METEO cirro m, cirrus m inv

CIS [ˌsi·aɪ·'es] n abbr of **Commonwealth of Independent States** CEI f

cistern ['sɪs·tərn] n cisterna f, jagüel m AmL

citadel ['sɪt̬·ə·dəl] n ciudadela f

citation [saɪ·'teɪ·ʃən] n **1.** (written quotation) cita f **2.** MIL mención f **3.** (ticket) multa f

cite [saɪt] vt form **1.** (offer as proof) alegar **2.** (quote) citar **3.** MIL **to be ~d** recibir una mención

citizen ['sɪt̬·ɪ·zən] n **1.** (subject) ciudadano, -a m, f **2.** (resident of town) habitante mf

citizens' band n s. **CB** banda f ciudadana

citizenship ['sɪt̬·ɪ·zən·ʃɪp] n ciudadanía f

citric ['sɪt·rɪk] adj cítrico, -a

citrus ['sɪt·rəs] <citrus o citruses> **I.** n cítrico m **II.** adj cítrico, -a

city ['sɪt̬·i] <-ies> **I.** n ciudad f **II.** adj (landscape) urbano, -a; (life) de (la) ciudad

i Muchas **cities** (ciudades) de EE.UU. son conocidas por sus sobrenombres. Así, **New York** es conocida como **The Big Apple** o **Gotham**; **Los Angeles**, como **The Big Orange** o **City of the Angels**. De la misma manera, **Chicago** es conocida como **The Windy City**. El apelativo **The City of Brotherly Love** se usa para referirse a **Philadelphia**. **Denver**, debido a su situación geográfica, es conocida como **The Mile-High City** y **Detroit**, por su industria automovilística, como **Motor City**.

city hall n ayuntamiento m

civic ['sɪv·ɪk] <inv> adj (authorities) civil; (education) cívico, -a

civies ['sɪv·iz] npl sl s. **civvies**

civil ['sɪv·əl] adj **1.** civil **2.** (courteous) cortés; **to not have a ~ word to say about sb** hablar mal de alguien

civil action n procedimiento m civil

civil court n Sala f de lo Civil

civil defense n defensa f civil

civil disobedience n resistencia f pasiva

civil engineer n ingeniero, -a m, f de caminos

civilian [sɪ·'vɪl·jən] <inv> **I.** n civil mf **II.** adj (clothes) de paisano, -a; (population) civil

civility [sɪ·'vɪl·ə·ti] <-ies> *n* **1.** (*formality*) urbanidad *f* **2.** (*formal remarks*) cumplido *m*
civilization [ˌsɪv·ə·lɪ·'zeɪ·ʃən] *n* civilización *f*
civilize ['sɪv·ə·laɪz] *vt* civilizar
civil law ['sɪv·əl·'lɔ] *n* derecho *m* civil
civil liberties *npl* derechos *mpl* civiles
civil marriage *n* matrimonio *m* civil
civil rights *npl* derechos *mpl* civiles
civil servant *n* funcionario, -a *m, f*
civil service *n* Administración *f* Pública
civil war *n* guerra *f* civil

i La **Civil War** (Guerra Civil) (1861-1865) de Estados Unidos se libró entre 24 estados norteños en su mayoría industriales y antiesclavistas, y 11 estados sureños predominantemente agrícolas y esclavistas, que se separaron de la Unión y constituyeron los **Confederate States of America** (Estados Confederados de América). La guerra produjo más de 970.000 bajas, incluidos más de 560.300 muertos, siendo el conflicto con mayor pérdida de vidas en la historia de Estados Unidos.

civvies ['sɪv·iz] *npl sl* **in** ~ de paisano
clack [klæk] I. *vi* **1.** (*heels*) taconear; (*typewriter*) teclear **2.** (*talk rapidly*) parlotear II. *n* **1.** (*with heels*) taconeo *m* **2.** (*continual rapid talk*) parloteo *m*
clad [klæd] I. *adj a. iron* vestido, -a II. *vt pt, pp of* **clothe**
claim [kleɪm] I. *n* **1.** (*assertion*) afirmación *f* **2.** (*written demand*) demanda *f*; (*insurance*) reclamación *f*; **to put in a** ~ **(for sth)** presentar una demanda (por algo) **3.** (*right*) derecho *m*; **to lay** ~ **to sth** reivindicar algo II. *vt* **1.** (*assert*) asegurar, afirmar; (*right, responsibility*) reivindicar **2.** (*declare ownership*) reclamar; (*reward, title*) reivindicar; (*diplomatic immunity*) solicitar **3.** (*require: time*) llevar, requerir **4.** (*demand in writing*) reclamar; **to ~ damages** reclamar daños y perjuicios III. *vi* **to ~ for sth** reclamar algo
claimant ['kleɪ·mənt] *n* solicitante *mf*; (*to a throne*) pretendiente, -a *m, f*
clairvoyance [ˌkler·'vɔɪ·ənts] *n* clarividencia *f*
clairvoyant [ˌkler·'vɔɪ·ənt] I. *n* clarividente *mf* II. *adj* extrasensorial; **to be** ~ ser clarividente
clam [klæm] *n* **1.** almeja *f* **2.** *sl* (*dollar*) dólar *m* ▶**to be happy as a** ~ estar feliz como una lombriz [*o* perdiz]
◆**clam up** <-mm-> *vi* (*not say anything*) no abrir la boca
clamber ['klæm·bər] I. *vi* trepar II. *n* ascensión *f*
clam chowder ['klæm·ˌtʃaʊ·dər] *n* sopa *f* de almejas
clammy ['klæm·i] <-ier, -iest> *adj* (*feet*) sudoroso, -a; (*weather*) bochornoso, -a
clamor ['klæm·ər] I. *vi* (*demand loudly*) pedir a

gritos, clamar II. *n* clamor *m*
clamorous ['klæm·ər·əs] *adj* **1.** (*vociferous*) vociferante **2.** (*loud, noisy*) ruidoso, -a
clamp [klæmp] I. *n* **1.** ARCHIT abrazadera *f* **2.** TECH tornillo *m* de banco II. *vt* **1.** (*fasten together*) sujetar con abrazaderas **2.** (*impose forcefully*) imponer
◆**clamp down** *vi* **to** ~ **on sth** tomar medidas drásticas contra algo
clan [klæn] *n* clan *m*
clandestine [klæn·'des·tɪn] *adj form* clandestino, -a
clang [klæŋ] I. *vi* (*bells*) repicar II. *vt* **to ~ sth shut** cerrar algo con estruendo III. *n* sonido *m* metálico fuerte; **the ~ of the bell** el repiqueteo de la campana
clangor ['klæŋ·ər] *n* sonido *m* metálico fuerte
clank [klæŋk] I. *vi* hacer ruido II. *vt* hacer sonar III. *n* ruido *m* metálico
clap¹ [klæp] I. <-pp-> *vt* **1.** (*applaud*) aplaudir **2.** (*slap palms together*) **to ~ one's hands** (*together*) batir palmas, dar palmadas II. <-pp-> *vi* **1.** (*applaud*) aplaudir **2.** (*slap palms together*) dar palmadas III. *n* **1.** (*slap*) palmada *f* **2.** (*applause*) aplauso *m*; **to give sb a** ~ aplaudir a alguien **3.** (*noise*) ruido *m*; **a ~ of thunder** un trueno
clap² [klæp] *n sl* **the** ~ la gonorrea
clapper ['klæp·ər] *n* badajo *m*
claptrap ['klæp·træp] *n inf* tonterías *fpl*
claret ['kler·ət] *n* **1.** (*wine*) burdeos *m inv* **2.** (*color*) granate *m*
clarification [ˌkler·ɪ·fɪ·'keɪ·ʃən] *n* aclaración *f*
clarify ['kler·ɪ·faɪ] <-ie-> *vt* **1.** (*make clearer*) aclarar **2.** (*explain*) explicar **3.** (*purify*) clarificar
clarinet [ˌkler·ə·'net] *n* clarinete *m*
clarity ['kler·ə·ti] *n* claridad *f*
clash [klæʃ] I. *vi* **1.** (*fight*) tener un enfrentamiento; (*argue*) discutir; **to ~ over sth** discutir sobre algo **2.** (*compete against*) enfrentarse **3.** (*contradict: views*) contradecirse **4.** (*not match: colors*) desentonar, no pegar *inf* **5.** (*make loud noise*) sonar fuerte II. *vt* **1.** (*strike*) golpear con estruendo **2.** (*produce sound*) tocar III. <-es> *n* **1.** (*hostile encounter*) enfrentamiento *m* **2.** (*contest*) contienda *f* **3.** (*conflict*) conflicto *m* **4.** (*incompatibility*) choque *m* **5.** (*loud harsh noise*) estruendo *m*
clasp [klæsp] I. *n* **1.** (*firm grip: of hands*) apretón *m* **2.** (*fastening device*) broche *m*, cierre *m* II. *vt* **1.** (*grip*) agarrar, sujetar; **to ~ one's hands** darse un apretón de manos; **to ~ sb in one's arms** estrechar a alguien entre sus brazos **2.** (*fasten: belt*) apretar
clasp knife <-knives> *n* navaja *f*
class [klæs] I. <-es> *n* clase *f* II. *vt* catalogar; **to ~ sb as sth** catalogar a alguien de algo; **to ~ sb among sth** considerar a alguien como algo
class-conscious ['klæs·ˌkan·tʃəs] *adj* con conciencia de clase (social)
classic ['klæs·ɪk] I. *adj* **1.** clásico, -a; (*typical*)

típico, -a **2.** *inf* (*joke, story*) genial **II.** *n*
1. (*work*) clásico *m* **2.** (*garment*) prenda *f*
clásica
classical ['klæs·ɪ·kəl] *adj* clásico, -a
classicism ['klæs·ɪ·sɪz·əm] *n* clasicismo *m*
classicist ['klæs·ɪ·sɪst] *n* clasicista *mf*
classics ['klæs·ɪks] *n* **1.** *pl* the ~ (*great litera-*
ture) los clásicos **2.** + *sing vb* (*Greek and*
Roman studies) clásicas *fpl inf*
classification [ˌklæs·ə·fɪ·'keɪ·ʃən] *n* clasificación *f*
classified ['klæs·ɪ·faɪd] <inv> *adj* clasificado,
-a; (*confidential*) confidencial, secreto, -a
classified advertisement *n* anuncio *m* clasificado
classify ['klæs·ɪ·faɪ] <-ie-> *vt* clasificar; (*desig-*
nate as secret) clasificar como secreto
classless ['klæs·lɪs] *adj* (*society*) sin clases
classmate *n* compañero, -a *m, f* de clase
classroom *n* clase *f*, aula *f*
class struggle *n*, **class war** *n* lucha *f* de
clases
classy ['klæs·i] <-ier, -iest> *adj* con estilo, con
clase
clatter ['klæt̬·ər] **I.** *vi* hacer ruido **II.** *n*
estruendo *m*; (*of hooves*) chacoloteo *m*
clause [klɔz] *n* cláusula *f*; LING oración *f*
claustrophobia [ˌklɔ·strə·'foʊ·bi·ə] *n* claustrofobia *f*
claustrophobic *adj* claustrofóbico, -a
clavicle ['klæv·ɪ·kəl] *n* clavícula *f*
claw [klɔ] **I.** *n* garra *f*; (*of sea creatures*) pinza *f*;
to show one's ~s *fig* sacar [*o* enseñar] las
uñas **II.** *vt* arañar
clay [kleɪ] **I.** *n* **1.** arcilla *f*; *fig, liter* barro *m*
2. SPORTS tierra *f* batida **II.** *adj* de arcilla
clay pigeon *n* plato *m* de tiro
clean [klin] **I.** *adj* **1.** (*free of dirt*) limpio, -a;
(**as**) ~ **as a whistle** (tan) limpio como una
patena [*o* un espejo] [*o* una tacita de plata]
2. (*free from bacteria*) desinfectado, -a **3.** (*fair*)
honrado, -a **4.** (*morally acceptable*) decente;
(*reputation*) sin tacha; (*driving license*) sin
sanciones; ~ **police record** registro *m* de
antecedentes penales limpio **5.** (*smooth: cut*)
limpio, -a; (*design*) elegante **6.** (*complete*) **to**
make a ~ break with sth romper por completo con algo **7.** (*blank: piece of paper*) en
blanco **II.** *n* limpieza *f* **III.** *adv* completamente;
to ~ forget that... olvidarse por completo de
que... **IV.** *vt* limpiar **V.** *vi* hacer la limpieza; **the**
coffee stain ~ed off easily la mancha de café
salió fácilmente
◆ **clean out** *vt* **1.** (*clean thoroughly*) limpiar;
(*with water*) lavar **2.** *sl* (*make penniless*) dejar
sin blanca a
◆ **clean up I.** *vt* **1.** (*make clean*) limpiar; (*tidy*
up) ordenar; **to ~ the city** limpiar la ciudad; **to**
clean oneself up asearse **2.** (*eradicate*) acabar con **II.** *vi* **1.** (*make clean*) limpiar **2.** *sl*
(*make profit*) hacer un buen negocio
clean-cut [ˌklin·'kʌt] *adj* (*straight*) preciso, -a;
(*features*) perfilado, -a; (*person*) de buen

parecer
cleaner ['kli·nər] *n* **1.** (*person*) hombre , mujer
de la limpieza *m* **2.** (*substance*) producto *m* de
limpieza
cleaning ['kli·nɪŋ] *n* limpieza *f*
cleaning lady <-ies> *n*, **cleaning woman**
<women> *n* mujer *f* de la limpieza
cleanliness ['klen·lɪ·nɪs] *n* aseo *m*
cleanly ['klen·li] *adv* limpiamente
cleanse [klenz] *vt* **1.** (*make clean*) limpiar
2. (*make morally pure*) purificar
cleanser ['klen·zər] *n* leche *f* limpiadora
clean-shaven ['klin·'ʃeɪ·vən] *adj* bien afeitado, -a
cleansing cream *n* leche *f* limpiadora
cleansing tissue *n* toallita *f* desmaquilladora
cleanup ['klin·ʌp] *n* limpieza *f*
clear [klɪr] **I.** *n* **to be in the ~** estar fuera de
peligro **II.** *adv* claramente; **to get ~ of sth** deshacerse de algo; **to stand ~ (of sth)** mantenerse a distancia (de algo) **III.** *adj* **1.** (*transpar-*
ent) claro, -a; (*air*) transparente; (*picture*)
nítido, -a; **to make oneself ~** explicarse con
claridad; **as ~ as day** más claro que el agua
2. (*obvious*) evidente **3.** (*free from guilt: con-*
science) tranquilo, -a; **to be ~ of debt** estar
libre de deudas **4.** (*net*) neto, -a **IV.** *vt*
1. (*remove obstacles*) limpiar; (*empty*) desocupar **2.** (*remove blockage*) desatascar; **to ~ the**
way abrir el camino **3.** (*remove doubts*) aclarar; **to ~ one's head** despejar la cabeza
4. (*acquit*) absolver **5.** (*net*) sacar beneficio de
6. (*jump*) saltar por encima de **7.** (*give official*
permission) autorizar **V.** *vi* (*water*) aclararse;
(*weather*) despejarse
◆ **clear away I.** *vt* quitar **II.** *vi* irse
◆ **clear off I.** *vi inf* largarse, jalar *Bol, PRico,*
Urug **II.** *vt* liquidar
◆ **clear out I.** *vt* limpiar; (*throw away*) vaciar
II. *vi* irse
◆ **clear up I.** *vt* aclarar; (*tidy*) ordenar **II.** *vi*
despejarse
clearance ['klɪr·əns] *n* **1.** (*act of clearing*) despeje *m* **2.** (*space*) espacio *m* libre **3.** (*per-*
mission) autorización *f*
clearance sale *n* liquidación *f*
clear-cut [ˌklɪr·'kʌt] **I.** *adj* bien definido, -a; *fig*
claro, -a **II.** *vt* cortar de forma neta
clearheaded *adj* perspicaz
clearing ['klɪr·ɪŋ] *n* claro *m*
clearing-house *n* cámara *f* de compensación
clearly ['klɪr·li] *adv* **1.** (*distinctly*) claramente
2. (*obviously*) evidentemente; (*undoubtedly*)
sin duda
clearness ['klɪr·nɪs] *n* claridad *f*
clear-sighted [ˌklɪr·'saɪ·tɪd] *adj* clarividente
cleavage ['kli·vɪdʒ] *n* **1.** (*in a dress*) escote *m*
2. *form* (*division*) división *f*
cleave [kliv] <cleft *o* cleaved *o* clove, cleft *o*
cleaved *o* cloven> **I.** *vi liter* henderse **II.** *vt*
partir
cleaver ['kli·vər] *n* cuchillo *m* de carnicero
clef [klef] *n* MUS clave *f*

cleft [kleft] I.<inv> *adj* dividido, -a; (*lip*) partido, -a II. *n* grieta *f*

clematis ['klem·ə·ţəs] *n inv* clemátide *f*

clemency ['klem·ən·si] *n form* clemencia *f*

clement ['klem·ənt] *adj* 1. *form* (*mild*) benigno, -a 2. *form* (*merciful*) clemente

clench [klentʃ] *vt* presionar; (*one's fist*) apretar

clergy ['klɜr·dʒi] *n + sing/pl vb* clero *m*

clergyman ['klɜr·dʒɪ·mən] <-men> *n* sacerdote *m*; (*protestant*) pastor *m*

clergywoman ['klɜr·dʒɪ·wʊm·ən] <-women> *n* pastora *f*

cleric ['kler·ɪk] *n* clérigo *m*

clerical ['kler·ɪ·kəl] *adj* 1. (*of the clergy*) clerical 2. (*of offices*) de oficina; ~ **worker** oficinista *mf*

clerical error *n* error *m* administrativo

clerical staff *n* personal *m* de oficina

clerical work *n* trabajo *m* de oficina

clerk [klɜrk] *n* 1. (*in office*) oficinista *mf* 2. (*in hotel*) recepcionista *mf*; (*in shop*) dependiente *mf*; **sales** ~ vendedor(a) *m(f)*

clever ['klev·ər] *adj* 1. (*intelligent*) inteligente 2. (*skillful*) hábil; (*invention*) ingenioso, -a 3. *pej* astuto, -a; **to be too** ~ **by half** pasarse de listo

cleverness *n* 1. (*intelligence*) inteligencia *f* 2. (*skill*) habilidad *f*

cliché [kli·'ʃeɪ] *n* 1. cliché *m* 2. (*platitude*) tópico *m*

click [klɪk] I. *n* clic *m*; (*of one's heels*) taconeo *m*; (*of one's tongue*) chasquido *m* II. *vi* 1. (*make short, sharp sound*) chasquear 2. COMPUT hacer clic; **to** ~ **on a symbol** hacer clic en un símbolo 3. (*become friendly*) congeniar; (*become popular*) tener éxito 4. (*become clear*) caer en la cuenta III. *vt* 1. (*make short, sharp sound: tongue*) chasquear; (*heels*) taconear 2. (*press button on mouse*) pulsar

client ['klaɪ·ənt] *n* cliente *mf*

clientele [ˌklaɪ·ən·'tel] *n* clientela *f*

cliff [klɪf] *n* precipicio *m*; (*on coast*) acantilado *m*

cliffhanger *n* situación *f* de suspense

climacteric [klaɪ·'mæk·tər·ɪk] *n form* climaterio *m*

climactic [ˌklaɪ·'mæk·tɪk] *adj* culminante

climate ['klaɪ·mɪt] *n* 1. (*weather*) clima *m* 2. (*general conditions*) ambiente *m*; **the** ~ **of opinion** la opinión general

climatic [klaɪ·'mæţ·ɪk] *adj* climático, -a

climatologist [ˌklaɪ·mə·'tal·ə·dʒɪst] *n* climatólogo, -a *m, f*

climatology [ˌklaɪ·mə·'tal·ə·dʒi] *n* climatología *f*

climax ['klaɪ·mæks] I.<-es> *n a.* LIT clímax *m inv*; (*sexual*) orgasmo *m* II. *vi* llegar a un punto culminante; (*sexual*) llegar al orgasmo

climb [klaɪm] I. *n* subida *f*; (*to power*) ascenso *m* II. *vt* (*stairs*) subir; (*tree*) trepar a; (*mountain*) escalar III. *vi* subir; **to** ~ **to a height of...** AVIAT ascender a una altura de...

◆**climb down** *vi* bajar(se) de; *fig* volverse atrás

climb-down ['klaɪm·daʊn] *n* vuelta *f* atrás

climber ['klaɪ·mər] *n* 1. (*of mountains*) alpinista *mf*, andinista *mf AmL*; (*of rock faces*) escalador(a) *m(f)* 2. (*plant*) enredadera *f* 3. *inf* (*striver for higher status*) arribista *mf*

climbing ['klaɪ·mɪŋ] I. *n* 1. (*ascending mountains*) alpinismo *m*, andinismo *m AmL* 2. (*ascending rock faces*) escalada *f* II. *adj* (*plant*) trepador(a); (*boots*) de montaña

climbing iron *n s.* **crampon**

clinch [klɪntʃ] I.<-es> *n* abrazo *m* II. *vt* 1. (*settle decisively*) resolver; (*a deal*) cerrar 2. (*secure a nail*) remachar 3. (*in boxing*) SPORTS abrazarse a (*sujetar al púgil rival para evitar recibir golpes*)

clincher ['klɪn·tʃər] *n inf* argumento *m* decisivo

cling [klɪŋ] <clung, clung> *vi* 1. (*embrace*) abrazarse a 2. (*hold*) agarrarse a; *fig* aferrarse a 3. (*stick*) adherirse a 4. (*stay close*) pegarse a 5. (*follow closely*) no separarse de

clinging *adj* 1. (*clothes*) ajustado, -a, ceñido, -a 2. (*person*) pegajoso, -a

clingy ['klɪŋ·i] <-ier, -iest> *adj* pegajoso, -a

clinic ['klɪn·ɪk] *n* clínica *f*

clinical ['klɪn·ɪ·kəl] *adj* 1. clínico, -a 2. (*emotionless*) frío, -a

clinician [klɪ·'nɪʃ·ən] *n* médico, -a que practica la medicina clínica (*en oposición a los especializados en investigación*)

clink [klɪŋk] I. *vt* hacer tintinear; (*glasses*) chocar II. *vi* tintinear III. *n* 1. tintineo *m*; (*of glasses*) choque *m* 2. *sl* (*prison*) chirona *f*

clinker ['klɪn·kər] *n* escoria *f*

clip¹ [klɪp] I. *n* 1. (*fastener*) clip *m*; (*for paper*) sujetapapeles *m inv*, broche *m AmL*; (*for hair*) horquilla *f* 2. (*gun part*) cargador *m* 3. (*jewelry*) broche *m* II.<-pp-> *vt* sujetar

clip² [klɪp] <-pp-> I. *vt* 1. (*cut*) recortar; (*hair, nails*) cortar; (*sheep*) esquilar; (*ticket*) picar 2. (*reduce*) abreviar; (*words*) comerse 3. (*attach*) sujetar 4. (*hit*) dar una bofetada a II. *n* 1. (*trim*) recorte *m* 2. (*extract*) fragmento *m* 3. (*hit*) bofetada *f*

clipboard ['klɪp·bɔrd] *n* tablilla *f* con sujetapapeles; COMPUT portapapeles *m inv*

clipped *adj* cortado, -a

clipper ['klɪp·ər] *n* NAUT clíper *m*

clipping ['klɪp·ɪŋ] *n* recorte *m*

clique [klik] *n* pandilla *f*

cliquey ['kli·ki] <cliquier, cliquiest> *adj*, **cliquish** ['kli·kɪʃ] *adj* exclusivista

clitoris ['klɪţ·ər·əs] <-es> *n* clítoris *m inv*

cloak [kloʊk] I. *n* 1. *a. fig* capa *f* 2. (*covering*) manto *m*; **under the** ~ **of darkness** al amparo de la oscuridad II. *vt* encapotar; (*hide*) encubrir

cloakroom ['kloʊk·rum] *n* guardarropa *m*

clobber ['klab·ər] *vt sl* dar una paliza a

clock [klak] I. *n* 1. (*for time*) reloj *m*; **alarm** ~ despertador *m*; **around the** ~ las 24 horas; **to run against the** ~ correr contra reloj

2. (*speedometer*) velocímetro *m;* (*odometer*) cuentakilómetros *m inv* **II.** *vt* **1.** (*take amount of time*) cronometrar **2.** (*measure time*) registrar; **this car can ~ 150mph** este coche alcanza una velocidad de 150 millas por hora
♦**clock in** *vi* **1.** (*record time*) fichar (*al llegar al trabajo*) **2.** *inf* (*arrive*) llegar al trabajo
♦**clock out** *vi* **1.** (*record time*) fichar (*al salir del trabajo*) **2.** *inf* (*leave work*) salir del trabajo
♦**clock up** *vt insep* (*attain*) alcanzar; (*travel*) recorrer

clock face *n* esfera *f* del reloj

clock radio *n* despertador *m* con radio

clockwise *adj, adv* en el sentido de las agujas del reloj

clockwork *n* mecanismo *m* de relojería; **to go like ~** salir todo bien; **as regular as ~** como un reloj

clod [klad] *n* **1.** (*earth*) terrón *m* **2.** (*person*) zopenco, -a *m, f*

clog [klag] **I.** <-gg-> *vi* atascarse **II.** <-gg-> *vt* atascar
♦**clog up** *vt* atascar

cloister ['klɔɪ·stər] *n* claustro *m*

clone [kloʊn] **I.** *n* **1.** BIO clon *m* **2.** COMPUT clónico *m* **II.** *vt* clonar

cloning ['kloʊ·nɪŋ] *n* clonación *f*

close¹ [kloʊs] **I.** *adj* **1.** (*near in location*) cercano, -a; **~ combat** combate *m* cuerpo a cuerpo **2.** (*intimate*) íntimo, -a; **~ relatives** parientes *mpl* cercanos **3.** (*almost even*) exacto, -a **4.** (*similar*) parecido, -a **5.** (*unwilling to be frank*) reservado, -a **6.** (*airless*) sofocado, -a; (*stuffy*) cargado, -a **II.** *adv* **1.** (*near in location*) cerca; **to move ~** acercarse **2.** (*near in time*) casi

close² [kloʊz] **I.** *n* (*end*) fin *m;* (*finish*) final *m;* **to bring sth to a ~** terminar algo **II.** *vt* **1.** (*shut*) cerrar; **to ~ ranks** cerrar filas **2.** (*end*) terminar; (*bring to an end*) concluir; **to ~ a deal** cerrar un trato **III.** *vi* **1.** (*shut*) cerrarse **2.** (*end*) terminarse
♦**close down I.** *vi* cerrarse (definitivamente) **II.** *vt* cerrar (definitivamente)
♦**close in** *vi* **1.** (*surround*) rodear **2.** (*get shorter*) acortarse
♦**close off** *vt* cerrar
♦**close up I.** *vi* **1.** (*people*) arrimarse *inf* **2.** (*wound*) cicatrizar **II.** *vt* cerrar del todo

closed *adj* cerrado, -a; **behind ~ doors** a puerta cerrada

closed-door *adj* a puerta cerrada

closedown *n* cierre *m*

close-knit *adj* unido, -a

closely ['kloʊs·li] *adv* **1.** (*near*) de cerca **2.** (*intimately*) estrechamente **3.** (*carefully*) atentamente

closeness ['kloʊs·nɪs] *n* **1.** (*nearness*) proximidad *f* **2.** (*intimacy*) intimidad *f* **3.** (*airlessness*) bochorno *m*

closet ['klaz·ɪt] **I.** *n* (*cupboard*) armario *m;* (*for clothes*) (armario) *m* ropero *m;* (*for food*) alacena *f* ▶**to come out of the ~** salir del

armario *inf* **II.** *adj* secreto, -a **III.** *vt* **to be ~ed with sb** estar reunido con alguien a puerta cerrada

close to I. *prep* **1.** (*near*) cerca de; **to be ~ the beginning/end of sth** estar cerca del comienzo/final de algo; **to live ~ the airport** vivir cerca del aeropuerto **2.** (*almost*) **~ tears/death** a punto de llorar/morir; **~ doing sth** cerca de hacer algo; **~ three feet** cerca de tres pies **3.** (*in friendship with*) **to be ~ sb** estar unido a alguien **II.** *adv* (*almost*) **~ finished/complete** casi terminado/completo

close-up ['kloʊs·ʌp] *n* CINE primer plano *m*

closing I. *adj* último, -a; (*speech*) de clausura **II.** *n* **1.** (*ending*) conclusión *f;* (*act*) clausura *f* **2.** COM cierre *m*

closing date *n* fecha *f* límite

closing time *n* hora *f* de cierre

closure ['kloʊ·ʒər] *n* (*closing*) cierre *m;* (*end*) fin *m*

clot [klat] **I.** *n* coágulo *m;* **blood ~** coágulo *m* sanguíneo **II.** <-tt-> *vi* cuajar; (*blood*) coagularse

cloth [klɔθ] **I.** *n* **1.** (*material*) tela *f;* (*for cleaning*) trapo *m* **2.** (*clergy*) clero *m;* **a man of the ~** un clérigo **II.** *adj* de tela

clothe [kloʊð] *vt* vestir; *fig* revestir de

clothes [kloʊz] *npl* vestidos *mpl;* (*collectively*) ropa *f*

clothes hanger *n* percha *f*

clotheshorse *n* tendedero *m* plegable

clothesline *n* cuerda *f* para tender la ropa

clothespin *n* pinza *f* (para la ropa)

clothing ['kloʊ·ðɪŋ] *n* ropa *f;* **article of ~** prenda *f* de vestir [*o* de ropa]

clothing industry <-ies> *n* industria *f* textil

cloud [klaʊd] **I.** *n* nube *f* ▶**every ~ has a silver lining** *prov* no hay mal que por bien no venga *prov;* **to be on ~ nine** estar en el séptimo cielo; **to be under a ~** estar bajo sospecha **II.** *vt a. fig* nublar
♦**cloud over** *vi* **1.** METEO nublarse **2.** (*become gloomy*) ensombrecerse; (*face*) entristecerse **3.** (*become misty: eyes*) empañarse

cloud bank *n* banco *m* de nubes

cloudburst *n* chaparrón *m*

cloud-capped *adj* envuelto, -a en nubes

cloud chamber *n* PHYS cámara *f* de niebla

clouded ['klaʊ·dɪd] *adj* **1.** (*cloudy*) nublado, -a **2.** (*not transparent: liquid*) turbio, -a **3.** (*confused: mind*) confuso, -a

cloudless ['klaʊd·lɪs] *adj* despejado, -a

cloudy ['klaʊ·di] <-ier, -iest> *adj* **1.** (*overcast*) nublado, -a **2.** (*not transparent: liquid*) turbio, -a

clout [klaʊt] **I.** *n* **1.** *inf* (*hit*) tortazo *m* **2.** (*power*) influencia *f* **II.** *vt inf* dar un tortazo a

clove¹ [kloʊv] *n* CULIN clavo *m;* (*of garlic*) diente *m*

clove² [kloʊv] *pt of* **cleave**

cloven ['kloʊ·vən] **I.** *pp of* **cleave II.** *adj* hendido, -a

clover ['klou·vər] *n* trébol *m*
cloverleaf *n* <-leaves> hoja *f* de trébol
clown [klaun] I. *n* payaso, -a *m, f* II. *vi* **to ~ around** hacer el payaso
clownish ['klau·nɪʃ] *adj* torpe; (*behavior*) grosero, -a
cloying ['klɔɪ·ɪŋ] *adj* empalagoso, -a
cloyingly *adv* de manera empalagosa; **~ sweet** empalagoso, -a
club [klʌb] I. *n* 1. (*group*) asociación *f*, club *m* 2. (*team*) club *m* 3. SPORTS palo *m* de golf 4. (*weapon*) cachiporra *f* 5. (*playing card*) trébol *m;* (*in Spanish cards*) basto *m* 6. (*disco*) sala *f* de fiestas, club *m* II. <-bb-> *vt* aporrear
clubbing *vi* **to go ~** salir por la noche (a las discotecas)
club car *n* coche *m* salón
clubfoot <feet> *n* pie *m* zopo
clubhouse *n* sede *f* de un club
club sandwich <-es> *n* sándwich con carne, lechuga, tomate y mayonesa
club soda *n* soda *f*
cluck [klʌk] *vi* cloquear; *fig* parlotear
clue [klu] *n* 1. (*evidence*) indicio *m;* (*hint*) pista *f* 2. (*secret*) clave *f* 3. (*idea*) idea *f;* **I don't have a ~** *inf* no tengo ni idea
◆**clue in** *vt* **to clue sb in** (**on sth**) informar a alguien (de algo)
clueless ['klu·lɪs] *adj inf* despistado, -a
clump [klʌmp] I. *vt* **to ~ sth together** agrupar algo II. *vi* 1. (*group*) **to ~ together** agruparse 2. (*walk noisily*) caminar haciendo ruido III. *n* 1. (*thick group: of trees*) grupo *m;* (*of flowers*) macizo *m* 2. (*lump*) terrón *m*
clumsiness ['klʌm·zɪ·nɪs] *n* torpeza *f*
clumsy ['klʌm·zi] <-ier, -iest> *adj* sin gracia, desgarbado, -a; (*bungling*) torpe
clung [klʌŋ] *pp, pt of* **cling**
clunk [klʌŋk] *n* sonido *m* metálico
cluster ['klʌs·tər] I. *n* (*of people*) grupo *m;* (*of fruits*) racimo *m* II. *vi* agruparse
cluster bomb *n* bomba *f* de fragmentación
clutch [klʌtʃ] I. *vi* **to ~ at sth** agarrarse a algo II. *vt* agarrar III. *n* 1. AUTO embrague *m* 2. (*set: of eggs*) nidada *f* 3. (*control*) **to be in the ~es of sb/sth** estar en las garras de alguien/algo 4. (*crucial situation*) **to come through in the ~** salir airoso de una situación difícil
clutch bag *n* bolso *m* de mano
clutch hitter *n* (*in baseball*) *jugador que siempre consigue batear en los momentos cruciales del juego*
clutter ['klʌt̬·ər] I. *n* desorden *m* II. *vt* desordenar
◆**clutter up** *vt* atestar
cluttered *adj* desordenado, -a; *fig* confuso, -a; **to be ~ with** estar atestado de
cm *inv abbr of* **centimeter** cm
c'mon *inf* = **come on**
CO¹ [ˌkal·ə·'rad·ou] *n abbr of* **Colorado** Colorado *m*
CO² [ˌsi·'ou] *n*, **C.O.** [ˌsi·'ou] *n* 1. *abbr of* **Commanding Officer** oficial *mf* al mando 2. *abbr*

of **conscientious objector** objetor (a) *m(f)* de conciencia
Co *n abbr of* **cobalt** Co
co. [kou] 1. *abbr of* **company** cía. 2. GEO *abbr of* **county** condado *m*
c/o *abbr of* **care of** a/c
coach [koutʃ] I. <-es> *n* 1. (*private bus*) autocar *m* 2. (*horse-drawn carriage*) coche *m* de caballos, diligencia *f* 3. (*railway car*) vagón *m* 4. (*teacher*) profesor(a) *m(f)* particular; SPORTS entrenador(a) *m(f)* II. *vt* **to ~ sb** (**in sth**) enseñar (algo) a alguien III. *vi* dar clases particulares
coaching *n* preparación *f*
coaching staff *n* + *sing/pl vb* personal *m* de entrenamiento
coagulate [kou·'æg·jə·leɪt] I. *vi* (*blood*) coagularse; (*sauce*) ligarse II. *vt* (*blood*) coagular; (*sauce*) ligar
coagulation [kou·ˌæg·jə·'leɪ·ʃən] *n* coagulación *f*
coal [koul] *n* carbón *m;* **piece of ~** hulla *f*
coal black *adj* negro, -a como el carbón
coalesce [kou·ə·'les] *vi form* (*to merge*) fundirse; (*to unite in coalition*) unirse (en coalición)
coalescence [kou·ə·'les·ənts] *n form* (*merger*) fusión *f;* (*coalition*) unión *f*
coalfield *n* yacimiento *m* de carbón
coal-fired *adj* que quema carbón
coalition [ˌkou·ə·'lɪʃ·ən] *n* coalición *f*
coal mine *n* mina *f* de carbón
coal miner *n* minero, -a *m, f* de carbón
coal mining *n* explotación *f* hullera
coal tar *n* alquitrán *m* mineral
coarse [kɔrs] <-r, -st> *adj* 1. (*rough*) basto, -a; (*sand*) grueso, -a; (*skin*) áspero, -a 2. (*vulgar*) grosero, -a
coarsely *adv* toscamente
coarseness ['kɔrs·nɪs] *n* 1. (*roughness*) tosquedad *f* 2. (*rudeness*) grosería *f*
coast [koust] I. *n* costa *f* ► **the ~ is clear** *inf* no hay moros en la costa II. *vi* avanzar sin esfuerzo
coastal ['kou·stəl] *adj* costero, -a, abajeño, -a *AmL;* **~ traffic** cabotaje *m*
coaster ['kou·stər] *n* 1. (*for glasses*) posavasos *m inv* 2. *inf* (*roller coaster*) montaña *f* rusa
coast guard ['koust·gard] *n*, **Coast Guard** ['koust·gard] *n* guardacostas *mf inv,* guardia *mf* costero, -a
coastline *n* línea *f* de costa
coast-to-coast *adj* de costa a costa
coat [kout] I. *n* 1. (*overcoat*) abrigo *m*, tapado *m AmS;* (*jacket*) chaqueta *f* 2. (*animal's skin*) pelaje *m* 3. (*layer*) capa *f;* (*of paint*) mano *f;* (*of chocolate*) baño *m* ► **to cut one's ~ according to one's cloth** vivir según sus posibilidades II. *vt* **to ~ sth in sth** cubrir algo de algo
coated ['kou·tɪd] *adj* cubierto, -a
coat hanger *n* percha *f*
coat hook *n* colgador *m*
coati [kou·'a·ti] *n* coatí *m*

coating ['koʊ·t̬ɪŋ] *n s.* **coat I,3**
coat of arms <coats of arms> *n* escudo *m* de armas
coattails *npl* faldones *mpl* (*de un frac, etc.*)
▶ **to ride on sb's** ~ salir adelante gracias al favor de alguien
coauthor [koʊ·'ɔ·θər] **I.** *n* coautor(a) *m(f)* **II.** *vt* escribir conjuntamente
coax [koʊks] *vt* convencer; **to** ~ **sth out of sb** sonsacarle algo a alguien
coaxing I. *n* persuasión *f* **II.** *adj* persuasivo, -a
coaxingly *adv* persuasivamente
cob [kɔb] *n* (*of corn*) mazorca *f*, elote *m AmC, Méx*
cobalt ['koʊ·bɔlt] *n* cobalto *m*
cobalt blue *n* azul *m* cobalto
cobble¹ ['kab·əl] **I.** *n* adoquín *m* **II.** *vt* adoquinar
cobble² ['kab·əl] *vt* (*repair*) remendar
◆ **cobble together** *vt* improvisar
cobbled *adj* ~ **streets** calles *fpl* adoquinadas
cobbler ['kab·lər] *n* zapatero *m* remendón
cobblestone ['kab·əl·stoʊn] *n* adoquín *m*
cobnut ['kab·nʌt] *n* avellana *f*
Cobol *n*, **COBOL** ['koʊ·bɔl] *n* COMPUT *abbr of* **common business-oriented language** COBOL *m*
cobra ['koʊ·brə] *n* cobra *f*
cobweb ['kab·web] *n* telaraña *f*
coca ['koʊ·kə] *n* coca *f*
Coca-Cola® [‚koʊ·kə·'koʊ·lə] *n* Coca-Cola *f*
cocaine [koʊ·'keɪn] *n* cocaína *f*
coccyx ['kak·sɪks] <-es *o* coccyges> *n* coxis *m inv*
cochineal ['katʃ·ə·nil] *n* cochinilla *f*
cochlea ['kak·li·ə] <-e *o* -s> *n* cóclea *f*
cock [kak] **I.** *n* **1.** (*male chicken*) gallo *m* **2.** *vulg* (*penis*) polla *f*, pichula *f Arg, Chile, Perú* **II.** *vt* **1.** (*turn*) ladear **2.** (*ready gun*) amartillar **III.** *adj* (*in ornithology*) macho
cockade [ka·'keɪd] *n* escarapela *f*
cock-a-doodle-doo [‚kak·ə·‚du·dəl·'du] *n childspeak* quiquiriquí *m*
cock-a-leekie *n* CULIN caldo *m* de pollo y puerros
cock-and-bull story <-ies> *n* cuento *m* chino
cockatoo ['kak·ə·'tu] <-(s)> *n* cacatúa *f*
cockcrow ['kak·kroʊ] *n* canto *m* del gallo; **at** ~ al amanecer
cocked *adj* ~ **hat** sombrero *m* de tres picos
cockerel ['kak·ər·əl] *n* gallo *m* joven
cocker spaniel *n* cocker spaniel *mf*
cockeyed ['kak·aɪd] *adj* **1.** *inf* (*not straight*) torcido, -a **2.** (*ridiculous*) disparatado, -a
cockfight *n* pelea *f* de gallos
cockiness ['kak·ɪ·nɪs] *n* presunción *f*
cockle ['kak·əl] *n* berberecho *m*
cockpit ['kak·pɪt] *n* **1.** (*pilot's area*) cabina *f* **2.** (*area of fighting*) campo *m* de batalla
cockroach ['kak·roʊtʃ] <-es> *n* cucaracha *f*, surupa *f Ven*
cockscomb ['kaks·koʊm] *n* cresta *f* de gallo
cocksure [‚kak·'ʃʊr] *adj inf* engreído, -a

cocktail ['kak·teɪl] *n* **1.** (*drink*) cóctel *m*, copetín *m Arg* **2.** *inf* (*mixture*) mezcla *f*
cocktail dress <-es> *n* vestido *m* de cóctel
cocktail lounge *n* salón *m* de cóctel
cocky ['kak·i] <-ier, -iest> *adj inf* gallito, -a
cocoa ['koʊ·koʊ] *n* **1.** (*chocolate powder*) cacao *m* **2.** (*hot drink*) chocolate *m*
cocoa butter *n* manteca *f* de cacao
coconut ['koʊ·kə·nʌt] *n* coco *m*
coconut butter *n* manteca *f* de coco
coconut matting *n* estera *f* de (fibras de) coco
coconut milk *n* leche *f* de coco
coconut oil *n* aceite *m* de coco
coconut palm *n* cocotero *m*
cocoon [kə·'kun] **I.** *n* capullo *m* **II.** *vt a. fig* arropar
cod [kad] *n inv* bacalao *m*
COD [‚si·oʊ·'di] *abbr of* **cash on delivery** (pago *m*) contra reembolso
coda ['koʊ·də] *n* MUS coda *f*
coddle ['kad·əl] *vt* **1.** (*cook gently*) cocer a fuego lento **2.** (*treat tenderly*) mimar
code [koʊd] **I.** *n* **1.** (*ciphered language*) clave *f*, código *m* **2.** LAW código *m* **II.** *vt* cifrar
coded *adj* codificado, -a
codeine ['koʊ·din] *n* codeína *f*
code name *n* nombre *m* en clave
code-named *adj* **the mission is** ~ **'Dolores'** la misión tiene el nombre en clave de 'Dolores'
code number *n* prefijo *m*
code of conduct *n* código *m* de conducta
codetermination [‚koʊ·dɪ·tɜr·mɪ·'neɪ·ʃən] *n* codeterminación *f*
code word *n* palabra *f* en clave
codex ['koʊ·deks] <codices> *n* códice *m*
codger ['kadʒ·ər] *n iron* vejete *m*
codices ['koʊ·də·siz] *n pl of* **codex**
codicil ['kad·ɪ·sɪl] *n* codicilo *m*
codify ['kad·ɪ·faɪ] <-ie-> *vt* codificar
codling ['kad·lɪŋ] *n* bacalao *m* pequeño
codling moth *n* gusano *m* de la manzana
cod-liver oil *n* aceite *m* de hígado de bacalao
coed ['koʊ·ed] **I.** *adj inf* mixto, -a **II.** *n inf* alumna *f* de un colegio mixto
coeducation [‚koʊ·edʒ·ʊ·'keɪ·ʃən] *n* educación *f* mixta
coeducational [‚koʊ·edʒ·ə·'keɪ·ʃən·əl] *adj* mixto, -a
coefficient [‚koʊ·ɪ·'fɪʃ·ənt] *n* coeficiente *m*
coequal [‚koʊ·'i·kwəl] **I.** *n form* igual *mf* **II.** *adj form* igual
coerce [koʊ·'ɜrs] *vt form* coaccionar
coercion [koʊ·'ɜr·ʒən] *n* coacción *f*
coercive [koʊ·'ɜr·sɪv] *adj* coactivo, -a
coeval [koʊ·'i·vəl] *form* **I.** *n* coetáneo, -a *m, f* **II.** *adj* coetáneo, -a
coexist [‚koʊ·ɪg·'zɪst] *vi* coexistir
coexistence [‚koʊ·ɪg·'zɪs·təns] *n* coexistencia *f*
coexistent [‚koʊ·ɪg·'zɪs·tənt] *adj* coexistente
coffee ['kɔ·fi] *n* café *m*
coffee bean *n* grano *m* de café
coffee break *n* pausa *f* para tomar café

C

coffeecake *n* pastel *m* de café
coffee-colored *adj* de color café
coffee cup *n* taza *f* de café
coffee grinder *n* molinillo *m* de café
coffee grounds *n pl* posos *mpl*
coffeehouse *n* café *m*
coffee klatch <-es> *n* tertulia *f*
coffeemaker *n* máquina *f* de café, greca *f AmL*
coffee mill *n* molinillo *m* de café
coffeepot *n* cafetera *f*
coffee shop *n* cafetería *f*
coffee table *n* mesa *f* baja
coffee-table book *n* libro *m* de gran formato
coffer ['kɔ·fər] *n* **1.** (*storage place*) cofre *m* **2.** ~ s (*money reserves*) fondos *mpl*
coffin ['kɔ·fɪn] *n* ataúd *m*
cog [kag] *n* TECH diente *m;* (*wheel*) rueda *f* dentada; **to be a ~ in a machine** ser una pieza más del engranaje de una organización
cogency ['kou·dʒən·si] *n form* fuerza *f*
cogent ['kou·dʒənt] *adj form* fuerte; (*argument*) convincente
cogently *adv form* convincentemente
cogitate ['kadʒ·ə·teɪt] *vi* reflexionar
cogitation [ˌkadʒ·ə·'teɪ·ʃən] *n* reflexión *f*
cognac ['koʊn·jæk] *n* coñac *m*
cognate ['kag·neɪt] *adj* afín
cognition [kag·'nɪʃ·ən] *n form* **1.** (*thought*) percepción *f* **2.** (*mental processes*) cognición *f*
cognitive ['kag·nə·tɪv] *adj* cognitivo, -a
cognitive psychology *n* psicología *f* cognitiva
cognitive therapy <-ies> *n* terapia *f* cognitiva
cognizance ['kag·nə·zəns] *n* LAW competencia *f;* **to take ~ of sth** tener algo en cuenta
cognizant ['kag·nə·zənt] *adj* conocedor(a); LAW competente
cognomen [kag·'noʊ·mən] *n* **1.** (*nickname*) apodo *m* **2.** HIST apellido *m*
cognoscenti [ˌkag·nə·'ʃen·ti] *npl* expertos *mpl*
cogwheel ['kag·wil] *n* rueda *f* dentada
cohabit [kou·'hæb·ɪt] *vi* cohabitar
cohabitant [kou·'hæb·ɪ·tənt] *n* cohabitante *mf*
cohabitation [kou·ˌhæb·ɪ·'teɪ·ʃən] *n* cohabitación *f*
cohere [kou·'hɪr] *vi* ser coherente
coherence [kou·'hɪr·əns] *n* coherencia *f*
coherent [kou·'hɪr·ənt] *adj* coherente
coherently *adv* coherentemente
cohesion [kou·'hi·ʒən] *n* cohesión *f*
cohesive [kou·'hi·sɪv] *adj* cohesivo, -a
cohesiveness *n* cohesión *f*
cohort ['kou·hɔrt] *n* cohorte *f*
coil [kɔɪl] I. *n* **1.** (*spiral*) rollo *m* **2.** ELEC bobina *f* **3.** MED espiral *f* (intrauterina) II. *vi* enrollarse III. *vt* enrollar
coiled *adj* enrollado, -a
coin [kɔɪn] I. *n* moneda *f;* **to toss a ~** echar [*o* lanzar] una moneda al aire II. *vt* acuñar ▶ **to ~ a phrase...** como se suele decir...

---

i Las monedas (**coins**) tienen en EE.UU. nombres especiales. Mientras que un **dollar**

tiene 100 **cents**, una moneda de un centavo se llama **penny**. La siguiente moneda en tamaño es la de 5 centavos y se llama **nickel**. Una moneda de 10 centavos se llama **dime**, y la de 25 centavos se denomina **quarter** (cuarto de dólar). Hay también **half dollars** (monedas de medio dólar) y **dollar coins** (monedas de un dólar).

coinage ['kɔɪ·nɪdʒ] *n* **1.** (*system*) sistema *m* monetario **2.** (*act*) acuñación *f*
coincide [ˌkou·ɪn·'saɪd] *vi* coincidir; (*agree*) estar de acuerdo
coincidence [kou·'ɪn·sɪ·dəns] *n* coincidencia *f;* (*chance*) casualidad *f*
coincident [kou·'ɪn·sɪ·dənt] *adj* coincidente
coincidental [kou·ˌɪn·sɪ·'den·təl] *adj* coincidente
coincidentally *adv* por casualidad
coitus ['kou·ə·ṭəs] *n form* coito *m*
coitus interruptus *n* coitus *m inv* interruptus
coke [kouk] *n* **1.** (*fuel*) coque *m* **2.** *sl* coca *f,* pichicata *f Arg*
Coke® [kouk] *n* Coca-Cola® *f*
col. [kal] *n abbr of* **column** columna *f*
Col. *n abbr of* **colonel** coronel *m*
cola ['kou·lə] *n* Coca-Cola® *f*
colander ['kʌl·ən·dər] *n* colador *m*
cold [kould] I. *adj* frío, -a; **to be ~** tener frío; **to go ~** (*soup, coffee*) enfriarse; **to get ~** (*person*) tener frío; **it's bitterly ~** hace un frío que pela ▶ **to leave sb ~** dejar frío a alguien II. *n* **1.** METEO **the ~** el frío **2.** MED resfriado *m;* **to catch a ~** acatarrarse; **to have a ~** estar acatarrado ▶ **to leave sb out in the ~** dejar a alguien al margen
cold-blooded *adj* (*animal*) de sangre fría; (*person*) cruel
cold call *n* estilo de venta que consiste en llamar a la puerta del potencial cliente o llamarle por teléfono
cold comfort *n* poco consuelo *m*
cold cream *n* crema *f* para el cutis
cold cuts *npl* fiambres *mpl*
cold feet *n pl, sl* mieditis *f,* culillo *m Col, Nic, Ecua, Pan, ElSal*
cold frame *n* vivero *m* de plantas
cold front *n* frente *m* frío
cold-hearted *adj* insensible
coldish ['koul·dɪʃ] *adj* fresquito, -a
coldness ['koʊld·nɪs] *n* frialdad *f*
cold snap *n* ola *f* de frío
cold sore *n* MED herpes *m* simplex
cold start *n* AUTO, COMPUT arranque *m* en frío
cold storage *n* conservación *f* en cámara frigorífica
cold store *n* cámara *f* frigorífica
cold sweat *n* sudor *m* frío
cold truth *n* **the ~** la cruda verdad
cold turkey I. *n sl* mono *m* II. *adv* **to quit smoking ~** de golpe (y porrazo), de una vez

cold war *n* guerra *f* fría
cold wave *n* ola *f* de frío
coleslaw ['koʊl·slɔ] *n* ensalada *f* de col con salsa
colic ['kal·ɪk] *n* cólico *m*
collaborate [kə·'læb·ə·reɪt] *vi* colaborar
collaboration [kə·ˌlæb·ə·'reɪ·ʃən] *n* colaboración *f*
collaborationist [kə·ˌlæb·ə·'reɪ·ʃə·nɪst] *adj* colaboracionista *mf*
collaborative [kə·'læb·ə·rə·tɪv] *adj* de colaboración; (*effort*) común
collaborator [kə·'læb·ə·reɪ·tər] *n* **1.** colaborador(a) *m(f)* **2.** *pej* colaboracionista *mf*
collage [kə·'laʒ] *n* collage *m*
collagen ['kal·ə·dʒən] *n* colágeno *m*
collagen implant *n*, **collagen injection** *n* implante *m* de colágeno
collapse [kə·'læps] **I.** *vi* **1.** MED sufrir un colapso **2.** (*fall down: building*) derrumbarse; (*person*) hundirse **3.** (*fail*) fracasar **II.** *n* **1.** MED colapso *m* **2.** (*act of falling down*) derrumbamiento *m;* (*of people*) hundimiento *m* **3.** (*failure*) fracaso *m*
collapsible [kə·'læp·sɪ·bəl] *adj* plegable
collar ['kal·ər] **I.** *n* **1.** FASHION cuello *m* **2.** (*of a dog, cat*) collar *m* ▶**to get** (**all**) **hot under the ~** acalorarse **II.** *vt sl* (*seize*) agarrar, detener
collarbone *n* clavícula *f*
collate [kə·'leɪt] *vt* **1.** (*arrange in order*) ordenar **2.** (*analyze*) cotejar
collateral [kə·'læt̬·ər·əl] **I.** *n* FIN garantía *f* subsidiaria **II.** *adj* colateral
collateral damage *n* daño *m* colateral
collateral loan *n* FIN préstamo *m* pignoraticio
collaterally [kə·'læt̬·ər·ə·li] *adv* colateralmente
colleague ['kal·ig] *n* colega *mf*
collect[1] [kə·'lekt] **I.** *vt* **1.** (*gather*) reunir; (*money*) recaudar; (*stamps*) coleccionar **2.** (*pick up*) recoger **3.** *form* (*regain control*) **to ~ oneself** reponerse; **to ~ one's thoughts** poner en orden sus ideas **II.** *vi* **1.** (*gather*) reunirse **2.** (*money: contributions*) hacer una colecta [*o* una vaca *Col*]; (*money: payments due*) cobrar **III.** *adj* TEL (*call*) a cobro revertido **IV.** *adv* TEL (*call*) a cobro revertido, por cobrar
collect[2] [kə·'lekt] *n* REL colecta *f*
collectable [kə·'lek·tə·bəl] **I.** *adj* coleccionable **II.** *n* coleccionable *m*
collect call *n* llamada *f* a cobro revertido; **to place** [*o* **make**] **a ~** llamar [*o* por cobrar] a cobro revertido
collected [kə·'lek·tɪd] *adj* sosegado, -a
collectible [kə·'lek·tə·bəl] **I.** *adj* coleccionable **II.** *n* coleccionable *m*
collection [kə·'lek·ʃən] *n* **1.** (*money gathered*) recaudación *f*; REL colecta *f* **2.** (*objects collected*) colección *f* **3.** (*large number*) montón *m* **4.** (*act of getting*) recogida *f*
collective [kə·'lek·tɪv] **I.** *adj* colectivo, -a **II.** *n* colectivo *m*

collective bargaining *n* negociación *f* colectiva
collective farm *n* granja *f* colectiva
collectively *adv* colectivamente
collective noun *n* nombre *m* colectivo
collectivism [kə·'lek·tə·vɪz·əm] *n* colectivismo *m*
collector [kə·'lek·tər] *n* **1.** (*one who gathers objects*) coleccionista *mf* **2.** (*one who collects payments*) cobrador(a) *m(f)*
collector's item *n*, **collector's piece** *n* pieza *f* de coleccionista
college ['kal·ɪdʒ] *n* **1.** (*school*) colegio *m* **2.** (*university*) universidad *f*

ℹ️ El término **college** se refiere a aquellas instituciones de educación superior que ofrecen carreras de cuatro a cinco años de duración. Al final de la carrera, los estudiantes reciben el **bachelor's degree** (licenciatura). El término **university** se reserva a aquellas instituciones que ofrecen **higher degrees** (títulos superiores); por ejemplo, el **master's degree** y el **doctorate**. Los **junior colleges** ofrecen los dos primeros años de educación superior o la capacitación necesaria para ejercer una profesión técnica.

---

college graduate *n* licenciado, -a *m, f*
collegiate [kə·'li·dʒɪt] *adj* colegiado, -a, universitario, -a
collide [kə·'laɪd] *vi* chocar
collie ['kal·i] *n* collie *m*
collier ['kal·jər] *n form* **1.** MIN minero, -a *m, f* de carbón **2.** (*ship*) barco *m* carbonero
colliery ['kal·jə·ri] <-ies> *n* mina *f* de carbón
collision [kə·'lɪʒ·ən] *n* colisión *f*
collocate ['kal·ə·keɪt] **I.** *vi* LING **to ~ with sth** aparecer en combinación con algo **II.** *n* LING colocación *f*
collocation [ˌkal·ə·'keɪ·ʃən] *n* colocación *f*
colloquial [kə·'loʊ·kwi·əl] *adj* familiar; (*language*) coloquial
colloquialism *n* expresión *f* coloquial
colloquy ['kal·ə·kwi] *n* coloquio *m*
collude [kə·'lud] *vi form* confabularse
collusion [kə·'lu·ʒən] *n form* confabulación *f*
collusive [kə·'lu·sɪv] *adj form* colusorio, -a
Colo. *abbr of* **Colorado** Colorado *m*
cologne [kə·'loʊn] *n* (*perfume*) colonia *f*
Colombia [kə·'lʌm·bi·ə] *n* Colombia *f*
Colombian [kə·'lʌm·bi·ən] **I.** *adj* colombiano, -a **II.** *n* colombiano, -a *m, f*
colon ['koʊ·lən] *n* **1.** ANAT colon *m* **2.** LING dos puntos *mpl*
colon cancer *n* cáncer *m* de colon
colonel ['kɜr·nəl] *n* coronel *mf*
colonial [kə·'loʊ·ni·əl] **I.** *adj* colonial **II.** *n* colono, -a *m, f*
colonialism [kə·'loʊ·ni·ə·lɪz·əm] *n* colonialismo *m*

colonialist I. *n* colonialista *mf* II. *adj* colonialista

colonial mentality *n* mentalidad *f* colonial

colonist ['kal·ə·nɪst] *n* 1. (*foreigner*) colonizador(a) *m(f)* 2. (*former inhabitant*) colono, -a *m, f*

colonization [ˌkal·ə·nɪ·'zeɪ·ʃən] *n* colonización *f*

colonize ['kal·ə·naɪz] *vt* colonizar

colonizer ['kal·ə·naɪ·zər] *n* colonizador(a) *m(f)*

colony ['kal·ə·ni] <-ies> *n a.* ZOOL colonia *f*

color ['kʌl·ər] I. *n* 1. (*appearance*) color *m;* primary ~ color primario; what ~ is your dress? ¿de qué color es tu vestido?; to have ~ in one's cheeks tener las mejillas sonrosadas 2. (*vigor*) colorido *m* 3. (*dye*) tinte *m* 4. ~ s POL, MIL (*official flag*) bandera *f;* to present the ~ s mostrar [*o* izar] la bandera 5. (*character*) to show one's true ~ s quitárse la máscara, mostrar su verdadero rostro II. *vt* 1. (*change color of*) colorear, pintar; to ~ a room blue pintar una habitación de azul 2. (*dye*) teñir 3. (*distort*) alterar III. *vi* sonrojarse

Colorado [ˌkal·ə·'rad·oʊ] *n* Colorado *m*

Colorado beetle [ˌkal·ə·'rad·oʊ·'bi·ṯəl] *n*, Colorado potato beetle *n* escarabajo *m* de la patata

coloration [ˌkʌl·ə·'reɪ·ʃən] *n* coloración *f*

colorblind *adj* daltónico, -a

colorblindness *n* daltonismo *m*

colored *adj* coloreado, -a; (*pencil, people*) de color

colorfast ['kʌl·ər·fæst] *adj* no desteñible

color filter *n* PHOT filtro *m* de color

colorful ['kʌl·ər·fəl] *adj* 1. (*full of color: paintings, clothing*) lleno, -a de colorido 2. (*lively*) vivo, -a; (*countryside*) pintoresco, -a; ~ part of town zona *f* animada de la ciudad

coloring ['kʌl·ər·ɪŋ] *n* 1. (*complexion*) color *m* 2. (*chemical*) colorante *m*

colorless ['kʌl·ər·lɪs] *adj* 1. (*having no color*) incoloro, -a 2. (*bland*) soso, -a; a grey, ~ city una ciudad gris, apagada

color line *n* barrera *f* racial

color scheme *n* combinación *f* de colores

color slide *n* diapositiva *f* de color

color television *n* televisión *f* en color

colossal [kə·'las·əl] *adj* colosal

colossus [kə·'las·əs] *n* <-es *o* colossi> coloso *m*

colt [koʊlt] *n* potro *m,* potranco *m AmL*

Columbia [kə·'lʌm·bi·ə] *n* the District of ~ el Distrito de Columbia

Columbus Day [kə·'lʌm·bəs·deɪ] *n* día *m* de la Hispanidad, día *m* de la Raza *AmL*

---

i Columbus Day (que corresponde al Día de la Raza en América Latina) es el día en el que se conmemora el descubrimiento del Nuevo Mundo por Cristóbal Colón (Chris-topher Columbus) el 12 de octubre de 1492. Desde 1971, este día se celebra siempre el segundo lunes del mes de octubre.

---

column ['kal·əm] *n a.* ARCHIT, ANAT, TYPO columna *f;* spinal ~ columna vertebral; to march in ~ s MIL, NAUT marchar en filas

columnist ['kal·əm·nɪst] *n* columnista *mf*

coma ['koʊ·mə] *n* coma *m;* to go into a ~ entrar en coma; to wake up out of one's ~ salir del coma

comatose ['koʊ·mə·toʊs] *adj* comatoso, -a; ~ state estado *m* de coma

comb [koʊm] I. *n* 1. (*hair device*) peine *m* 2. ZOOL cresta *f* de gallo II. *vt* 1. (*tidy with a comb*) to ~ one's hair peinarse el pelo 2. (*search thoroughly*) to ~ an area peinar una zona; to ~ an apartment for clues registrar un apartamento en busca de pruebas

◆comb out *vt* (*a knot, tangles*) desenredar; (*lice*) quitar

combat ['kam·bæt] I. *n* 1. (*wartime fighting*) combate *m;* hand-to-hand ~ combate cuerpo a cuerpo 2. (*battle*) lucha *f* II. *vt* luchar contra; (*crime*) combatir; (*a desire*) resistirse a

combat aircraft *n* avión *m* de combate

combatant [kəm·'bæt·ənt] *n* combatiente *mf*

combative [kəm·'bæṯ·ɪv] *adj* combativo, -a

combination [ˌkam·bə·'neɪ·ʃən] *n* 1. (*mixture*) combinación *f* 2. (*sequence of numbers*) combinación *f;* in ~ (*together*) en combinación

combine [kəm·'baɪn] I. *vt* combinar; to ~ family life with a career compaginar la vida familiar con una carrera profesional; to ~ ingredients mezclar ingredientes; to ~ forces against sb/sth reunir fuerzas contra alguien/ algo II. *vi* asociarse

combined [kəm·'baɪnd] *adj* combinado, -a; (*efforts*) conjunto, -a

combine harvester *n* cosechadora *f*

combustible [kəm·'bʌs·tə·bəl] *adj form* 1. (*highly flammable*) combustible 2. (*easily angry*) excitable

combustion [kəm·'bʌs·tʃən] *n* combustión *f*

combustion chamber *n* cámara *f* de combustión

come [kʌm] <came, come, coming> *vi* 1. (*move towards*) venir; to ~ towards sb venir hacia alguien 2. (*go*) venirse; are you coming to the game with us? ¿te vienes al juego con nosotros? 3. (*arrive*) llegar; January ~ s before February enero precede a febrero; the year to ~ el próximo año; to ~ to an agreement llegar a un acuerdo; to ~ to a decision llegar a una decisión; to ~ home volver a casa; to ~ to sb's rescue socorrer a alguien; to ~ first/second/third ser primero/ segundo/tercero 4. (*happen*) pasar; to ~ to pass suceder, ocurrir; ~ what may pase lo que pase; how ~? *inf* ¿cómo es?; nothing came of it todo quedó en nada 5. (*become*) hacerse, llegar a; **my dream has ~ true** mi sueño se ha hecho realidad; **I like it as it ~s** me gusta tal cual; **to ~ open** abrirse; **to ~ in red** haberlo en rojo **6.** *vulg* (*have an orgasm*) correrse, acabar *AmL* ►~ **again?** *inf* ¿cómo?; **to ~ clean** (**about sth**) ser sincero (acerca de algo); **good things ~ to those who wait** *prov* con paciencia y esperar se gana el cielo *prov;* **to have it coming** tenerlo merecido

♦**come about** *vi* suceder

♦**come across** **I.** *vt insep* encontrarse con, dar con; **to ~ a problem** topar con un problema **II.** *vi* **1.** (*be evident*) ser entendido **2.** (*create an impression*) dar una imagen

♦**come along** *vi* **1.** (*hurry*) darse prisa; ~**!** ¡date prisa! **2.** (*go too*) venir también **3.** (*progressing*) progresar

♦**come apart** *vi* separarse

♦**come around** *vi* **1.** (*change one's mind*) cambiar de opinión; **to ~ to sb's point of view** adoptar el punto de vista de alguien **2.** MED volver en sí **3.** (*visit sb's home*) pasarse

♦**come at** *vt insep* atacar

♦**come away** *vi* **1.** (*leave*) irse **2.** (*become detached*) separarse; **to ~ from sth** desprenderse de algo

♦**come back** *vi* **1.** (*return*) regresar **2.** (*be remembered*) volver (a la memoria) **3.** (*return to fashion*) volver **4.** SPORTS contraatacar

♦**come by** **I.** *vt insep* conseguir **II.** *vi* visitar

♦**come down** *vi* **1.** (*move down*) bajar; (*move down in rank: people*) descender **2.** (*drop: roof*) venirse abajo **3.** (*land*) aterrizar **4.** (*fall: rain, snow*) caer **5.** (*visit southern place*) bajar (a) **6.** (*become less: prices, cost, inflation*) reducirse; (*lower one's price*) rebajarse

♦**come forward** *vi* **1.** (*advance*) avanzar **2.** (*offer assistance*) ofrecerse (voluntariamente); **to ~ to do sth** ofrecerse para hacer algo

♦**come from** *vt* ser de; (*a family*) descender de; **where do you ~?** ¿de dónde eres?; **to ~ a good family** ser de buena familia

♦**come in** *vi* **1.** (*enter*) entrar **2.** (*arrive*) llegar **3.** (*become fashionable*) ponerse de moda **4.** (*be useful*) servir **5.** (*be*) resultar **6.** (*participate in*) tomar parte en **7.** (*be positioned*) **to ~ first** situarse primero

♦**come into** *vt insep* **1.** (*enter*) entrar en; (*power*) tomar; **to ~ office** tomar posesión de un cargo; **to ~ fashion** ponerse de moda; **to ~ sb's life** entrar en la vida de alguien **2.** (*inherit*) heredar

♦**come off** **I.** *vi* **1.** *inf* (*succeed*) tener éxito **2.** (*end up*) terminar **3.** (*become detached*) desprenderse **4.** (*fall*) caerse **II.** *vt insep* (*complete*) terminar; **to ~ an injury** MED recuperarse de una herida ►~ **it!** *inf* ¡anda ya!

♦**come on** **I.** *vi* **1.** (*improve*) progresar **2.** THEAT, CINE (*actor, performer*) aparecer **3.** (*begin: film, program*) empezar; **what time does the news ~?** ¿a qué hora dan las noti-

cias? **4.** (*start gradually*) **I've got a headache coming on** me está empezando a dar dolor de cabeza **II.** *vt insep* encontrar (por casualidad) **III.** *interj* (*hurry*) ¡date prisa!, ¡ándale! *Méx;* (*encouragement*) ¡ánimo!, ¡órale! *Méx;* (*annoyance*) ¡venga ya!

♦**come out** *vi* **1.** (*express opinion*) **to ~ in favor of/against sth** pronunciarse a favor/en contra de algo **2.** (*end up*) **how did your painting ~?** ¿cómo quedó tu cuadro? **3.** + *n* **to ~ a mess** resultar un desastre **4.** + *adj* **to ~ wrong/right** salir mal/bien **5.** (*go out socially*) presentarse en sociedad **6.** (*become known*) darse a conocer; **to ~ that...** revelarse que... **7.** (*reveal one's homosexuality*) salir del armario **8.** (*be removed*) salir, quitarse **9.** (*become available: stamp, book, magazine*) publicarse **10.** (*appear in sky: moon, stars, sun*) aparecer **11.** (*open: flowers*) florecer

♦**come over** **I.** *vi* **1.** (*come nearer*) acercarse **2.** (*visit sb's home*) visitar **3.** (*feel*) sentir **II.** *vt* **to ~ sb** apoderarse de alguien

♦**come through** **I.** *vi* **1.** (*show: one's nervousness, excitement, charm*) mostrar **2.** (*arrive: results, visa, call*) llegar **3.** (*survive*) sobrevivir **II.** *vt insep* superar

♦**come to** **I.** *vt insep* **1.** (*reach*) llegar a; **to come down to sth** bajar a algo; **to come up to sth** subir a algo; **to ~ rest** irse a dormir; **to ~ nothing** quedarse en nada **2.** (*amount to*) ascender a **II.** *vi* MED volver en sí

♦**come under** *vt* **1.** (*be listed under*) aparecer bajo **2.** (*be dealt with*) ser competencia de **3.** (*be subjected to*) **to ~ criticism** ser objeto de crítica

♦**come up** *vi* **1.** (*be mentioned*) mencionarse **2.** (*happen*) suceder **3.** (*arrive: a holiday*) llegar

♦**come upon** *vt* encontrarse con

comeback ['kʌm·bæk] *n* **1.** vuelta *f;* SPORTS recuperación *f,* regreso *m* **2.** (*retort*) réplica *f*

comedian [kə·'mi·di·ən] *n* **1.** (*person telling jokes*) cómico, -a *m, f* **2.** (*funny person*) payaso, -a *m, f*

comedienne [kə·,mi·di·'ən] *n* **1.** (*female comedian*) cómica *f* **2.** (*funny female*) payasa *f*

comedown ['kʌm·daʊn] *n inf* **1.** (*anticlimax*) revés *m* **2.** (*decline in status*) humillación *f*

comedy ['kam·ə·di] <-ies> *n* **1.** CINE, THEAT, LIT comedia *f* **2.** (*funny situation*) comicidad *f*

comeliness ['kʌm·li·nɪs] *n* encanto *m*

comely ['kʌm·li] <-ier, -iest> *adj* (*woman*) atractiva

come-on ['kʌm·ɔn] *n* **1.** *sl* (*expression of sexual interest*) insinuación *f* **2.** (*enticement*) reclamo *m*

comet ['kam·ɪt] *n* cometa *m*

comeuppance [kʌm·'ʌp·ənts] *n* merecido *m;* **he got his ~ in the end** al final se llevó su merecido

comfort ['kʌm·fərt] **I.** *n* **1.** (*comfortable feeling*) comodidad *f,* confort *m* **2.** (*consolation*) consuelo *m;* **to be a ~ to sb** ser un consuelo para alguien **3.** (*pleasurable things in life*) bienestar *m;* **the ~s of life** las cosas agradables de la vida **II.** *vt* consolar

comfortable ['kʌm·fər·tə·bəl] *adj* **1.** (*offering comfort*) cómodo, -a, confortable; **to make oneself ~** ponerse cómodo **2.** (*financially stable*) acomodado, -a; **~ life** vida *f* holgada **3.** SPORTS (*substantial*) fácil

comfortably ['kʌm·fər·tə·bli] *adv* **1.** (*in a comfortable manner: sit, lie*) cómodamente, confortablemente **2.** (*easily*) fácilmente **3.** (*in financially stable manner*) **to live ~** vivir de forma acomodada

comforter ['kʌm·fər·ţər] *n* (*duvet*) edredón *m*

comforting ['kʌm·fər·ţɪŋ] *adj* (*thought, words*) reconfortante

comfortless ['kʌm·fərt·lɪs] *adj form* incómodo, -a

comfy ['kʌm·fi] <-ier, -iest> *adj inf* (*furniture, clothes*) cómodo, -a

comic ['kam·ɪk] **I.** *n* **1.** (*cartoon magazine*) cómic *m*, tebeo *m* **2.** (*person*) cómico, -a *m, f* **II.** *adj* cómico, -a; **~ play** comedia *f*

comical ['kam·ɪ·kəl] *adj* cómico, -a; (*idea*) divertido, -a

comic book *n* (*comic*) tebeo *m*

comic strip *n* tira *f* cómica

coming ['kʌm·ɪŋ] **I.** *adj* **1.** (*next*) próximo, -a; **the ~ year** el año que viene **2.** (*approaching*) venidero, -a **II.** *n* llegada *f;* **~s and goings** idas y venidas

comma ['kam·ə] *n* coma *f*

command [kə·'mænd] **I.** *vt* **1.** (*order*) **to ~ sb to do sth** ordenar a alguien que haga algo; **to ~ that** mandar que +*subj* **2.** (*have command over*) estar al mando de **3.** (*have at one's disposal*) disponer de **4.** (*overlook: view*) tener **5.** (*respect*) imponer; (*sympathy*) inspirar **II.** *n* **1.** (*order*) orden *f;* **to obey a ~** acatar una orden; **at sb's ~** a las órdenes de alguien; **under sb's ~** bajo las órdenes de alguien **2.** (*control*) mando *m;* **to be in ~ of sth** estar al mando de algo; **to take ~ of** asumir el mando de **3.** MIL comandancia *f* **4.** COMPUT comando *m* **5.** (*knowledge*) dominio *m*

commandant ['kam·ən·dænt] *n* MIL comandante *mf*

commandeer [ˌkam·ən·'dɪr] *vt* apropiarse de

commander [kə·'mæn·dər] *n* **1.** MIL (*officer in charge*) comandante *mf* **2.** MIL, NAUT (*naval officer*) capitán *m* de fragata

commanding [kə·'mæn·dɪŋ] *adj* **1.** (*authoritative*) dominante; (*voice*) imponente **2.** (*dominant: position*) dominante **3.** (*considerable*) abrumador(a)

command key *n* COMPUT tecla *f* de comando

commandment [kə·'mænd·mənt] *n* liter orden *f*

Commandment [kə·'mænd·mənt] *n* **the Ten ~s** REL los diez mandamientos

command module *n* AVIAT módulo *m* de maniobra y mando

commando [kə·'mæn·doʊ] <-s *o* -es> *n* MIL **1.** (*group of soldiers*) comando *m* **2.** (*member of commando*) miembro *mf* de un comando

command post *n* MIL puesto *m* de mando

command prompt *n* COMPUT línea *f* de comandos

commemorate [kə·'mem·ə·reɪt] *vt* conmemorar

commemoration [kə·ˌmem·ə·'reɪ·ʃən] *n* conmemoración *f;* **in ~ of...** en conmemoración de...

commemorative [kə·'mem·ər·ə·tɪv] *adj* conmemorativo, -a

commence [kə·'mens] *vi form* empezar; **to ~ speaking** comenzar un discurso

commencement [kə·'mens·mənt] *n* form **1.** (*beginning*) inicio *m* **2.** SCHOOL, UNIV (*ceremonia f de*) graduación *f*

commend [kə·'mend] *vt* **1.** (*praise*) elogiar; **to ~ sth/sb (on sth)** alabar algo/a alguien (por algo) **2.** (*entrust*) encomendar; **to ~ sth to sb** encomendar algo a alguien **3.** (*recommend*) recomendar

commendable [kə·'men·də·bəl] *adj* recomendable; **~ bravery** valor *m* loable

commendation [ˌkam·ən·'deɪ·ʃən] *n* **1.** (*praise*) elogio *m* **2.** (*award*) mención *f* de honor

commendatory [kə·'men·də·tɔr·i] *adj* loable

commensurable [kə·'men·sər·ə·bəl] *adj* conmensurable

commensurate [kə·'men·sər·ət] *adj form* proporcionado, -a

comment ['kam·ent] **I.** *n* comentario *m;* **no ~** sin comentarios; **to make a ~** hacer una observación **II.** *vi* comentar; **to ~ that...** observar que...

commentary ['kam·ən·ter·i] <-ies> *n* comentario *m;* **color ~** reportaje *m* en color; **literary ~** crítica *f* literaria

commentate ['kam·ən·teɪt] *vi* TV, RADIO **to ~ on sth** hacer un reportaje sobre algo

commentator ['kam·ən·teɪ·ţər] *n* TV, RADIO comentarista *mf*

commerce ['kam·ərs] *n* comercio *m*

commercial [kə·'mɜr·ʃəl] **I.** *adj* **1.** (*relating to commerce*) comercial **2.** RADIO, TV publicitario, -a **II.** *n* RADIO, TV anuncio *m*, comercial *m* AmL

commercialism [kə·'mɜr·ʃə·lɪz·əm] *n* comercialismo *m*

commercialization [kə·ˌmɜr·ʃə·lɪ·'zeɪ·ʃən] *n* comercialización *f*

commercialize [kə·'mɜr·ʃə·laɪz] *vt* comercializar

commercialized *adj* comercializado, -a

commiserate [kə·'mɪz·ə·reɪt] *vi* mostrar conmiseración

commiseration [kə·ˌmɪz·ə·'reɪ·ʃən] *n* conmiseración *f*

commission [kə·'mɪʃ·ən] **I.** *vt* **1.** (*order*) encargar **2.** MIL (*appoint*) **to ~ sb as sth** nombrar a alguien de algo; **~ed officer** oficial *mf* **II.** *n* **1.** (*order*) encargo *m* **2.** (*system of payment*) comisión *f;* **to be on ~** estar a comisión

3. (*investigative body*) comisión *f* **4.** MIL (*appointment*) nombramiento *m;* **to resign one's** ~ dimitir del cargo **5.** LAW (*perpetration*) perpetración *f* **6.** NAUT, AVIAT **out of** ~ fuera de servicio

commissioned officer *n* oficial *m*

commissioner [kə·'mɪʃ·ə·nər] *n* comisario, -a *m, f*

commit [kə·'mɪt] <-tt-> *vt* **1.** (*carry out*) cometer; **to** ~ **suicide** suicidarse; **to** ~ **an error** incurrir en un error **2.** (*bind*) **to** ~ **one-self (to sth)** comprometerse (a algo); **to** ~ **sol-diers to the defense of a region** enviar sol-dados a defender una región **3.** (*institutional-ize*) **to** ~ **sb to prison** encarcelar a alguien; **to** ~ **sb to a hospital** internar a alguien en un hospital **4.** (*entrust*) **to** ~ **sth to memory** memorizar algo; **to** ~ **sth to paper** poner algo por escrito

commitment [kə·'mɪt·mənt] *n* **1.** (*dedication*) dedicación *f* **2.** (*obligation*) obligación *f;* **family** ~**s** compromisos *mpl* familiares; **to make a** ~ hacer una promesa

committed *adj* comprometido, -a

committee [kə·'mɪt̬·i] *n* comité *m;* **to appoint a** ~ nombrar un comité; **to be** [*o* sit] **on a** ~ ser miembro de un comité

commode [kə·'moʊd] *n* **1.** (*chest of drawers*) cómoda *f* **2.** (*toilet*) taza *f*

commodious [kə·'moʊ·di·əs] *adj* amplio, -a, espacioso, -a

commodity [kə·'mad·ə·ti] <-ies> *n* **1.** (*prod-uct*) mercancía *f;* ~ **markets** mercados *mpl* de mercancías **2. commodities** (*raw material*) materia *f* prima

commodore ['kam·ə·dɔr] *n* comodoro *m*

common ['kam·ən] **I.** *adj* **1.** (*ordinary*) co-rriente; (*usual*) usual; (*widespread*) frecuente; **a** ~ **disease** una enfermedad común; **to be** ~ **knowledge** ser de dominio público; **a** ~ **name** un nombre común; **the** ~ **man** el hombre medio **2.** (*shared*) común; ~ **property** propiedad *f* comunal; **by** ~ **assent** por unani-midad; **for the** ~ **good** en beneficio de todos **3.** (*vulgar*) vulgar **II.** *n* **1.** (*land*) ejido *m* **2.** ~**s** UNIV comedor *m*

common denominator *n* denominador *m* común

commoner ['kam·ə·nər] *n* plebeyo, -a *m, f*

common ground *n* puntos *mpl* en común; **to be on** ~ **with sb** coincidir con alguien

common law *n* ≈ derecho *m* consuetudinario

common-law marriage *n* concubinato *m,* unión *f* libre *Col*

common-law wife <wives> *n* mujer *f* en una pareja de hecho

commonly *adv* (*often*) frecuentemente; (*usually*) normalmente

commonplace ['kam·ən·pleɪs] **I.** *adj* co-rriente; **it is** ~ **to see that...** es frecuente ver que... **II.** *n* lugar *m* común

common room *n* sala *f* de reuniones (de un colegio)

common sense *n* sentido *m* común; **a** ~ **solu-tion** una solución lógica

common stock *n* FIN acciones *fpl* ordinarias

Commonwealth ['kam·ən·welθ] *n* **the** ~ la Commonwealth

commotion [kə·'moʊ·ʃən] *n* alboroto *m,* con-moción *f*

communal [kə·'mju·nəl] *adj* comunal

commune ['kam·jun] *n* comuna *f*

communicable [kə·'mju·ni·kə·bəl] *adj* **1.** (*information*) comunicable **2.** MED transmi-sible

communicate [kə·'mju·nɪ·keɪt] **I.** *vt* **1.** (*information*) comunicar **2.** MED transmitir **II.** *vi* comunicar(se); **I'm afraid we just don't** ~ **well** me temo que simplemente no conecta-mos

communication [kə·ˌmju·nɪ·'keɪ·ʃən] *n* **1.** (*process*) comunicación *f* **2.** (*missive*) comunicación *f* **3.** ~**s** (*means*) comunica-ciones *fpl*

communicative [kə·'mju·nə·keɪ·tɪv] *adj* comunicativo, -a

communion [kə·'mjun·jən] *n* comunión *f;* **to take** ~ comulgar

communiqué [kə·ˌmju·nɪ·'keɪ] *n* comuni-cado *m*

communism ['kam·jə·nɪz·əm] *n* comu-nismo *m*

Communist ['kam·jə·nɪst] **I.** *n* comunista *mf* **II.** *adj* comunista

community [kə·'mju·nə·ti] <-ies> *n* **1.** (*of people*) comunidad *f;* **the local** ~ el vecin-dario **2.** (*of animals, plants*) colonia *f* **3.** (*togetherness*) colectividad *f*

community center *n* centro *m* social

community service *n* trabajo *m* social

commutable [kə·'mju·t̬ə·bəl] *adj* conmutable

commutation [ˌkam·jə·'teɪ·ʃən] *n* conmuta-ción *f*

commutation ticket *n* abono *m* de transporte

commute [kə·'mjut] **I.** *vi* viajar (diariamente) al lugar de trabajo **II.** *n inf* viaje *m* (diario) al tra-bajo **III.** *vt* **1.** (*change, convert*) convertir **2.** FIN, LAW conmutar

commuter [kə·'mju·t̬ər] *n persona que debe viajar diariamente para ir al trabajo*

commuter train *n* tren *m* de cercanías

compact¹ ['kam·pækt] **I.** *adj* (*small*) com-pacto, -a; (*material*) apretado, -a **II.** *n* conden-sar **III.** *n* **1.** AUTO utilitario *m* **2.** (*powder*) pol-vera *f*

compact² ['kam·pækt] *n* (*agreement*) acuerdo *m*

compact disk *n* compact *m,* disco *m* compacto

compact disk player *n* reproductor *m* de CD

compactness [kəm·'pækt·nɪs] *n* compresión *f*

companion [kəm·'pæn·jən] *n* **1.** (*person, ani-mal*) compañero, -a *m, f;* **traveling** ~ com-pañero de viaje **2.** (*guidebook*) guía *f*

companionable [kəm·'pæn·jə·nə·bəl] *adj* simpático, -a

companionship *n* compañerismo *m*

companionway [kəm·'pæn·jən·weɪ] *n* NAUT escalerilla *f*

company ['kʌm·pə·ni] <-ies> *n* **1.** (*firm, enterprise*) empresa *f;* **Duggan and Company** Duggan y Compañía; **~ union** sindicato *m* de empresa **2.** (*companionship*) compañía *f;* **you are in good ~** estás en buena compañía; **to keep sb ~** hacer compañía a alguien; **he's been keeping bad ~** va con malas compañías; **Mary stayed for a week as ~ for my mother** Mary se quedó una semana para hacer compañía a mi madre **3.** (*group*) *a.* MIL compañía *f* ► **two's ~ (three's a crowd)** *prov* dos son compañía, tres son multitud

comparable ['kam·pər·ə·bəl] *adj* comparable; **~ to** equiparable a

comparative [kəm·'per·ə·tɪv] **I.** *n* comparativo *m* **II.** *adj* comparativo, -a; **~ literature** literatura *f* comparada

comparatively *adv* (*by comparison*) comparativamente; (*relatively*) relativamente

compare [kəm·'per] **I.** *vt* comparar; **to ~ sth/sb to** [*o* **with**] **sth/sb** comparar algo/a alguien con algo/alguien; **instant coffee can't be ~d with an espresso** el café instantáneo no puede compararse con un expreso; **to ~ notes on sth** hacer un intercambio de impresiones sobre algo **II.** *vi* compararse; **to ~ favorably with sth** ser mejor que algo; **last year's weather just doesn't ~** el tiempo del año pasado no puede compararse

comparison [kəm·'per·ɪ·sən] *n* comparación *f;* **to make a ~** hacer una comparación; **by ~ with sb/sth** en comparación con alguien/algo; **there's no ~ between the two restaurants** no hay ni punto de comparación entre los dos restaurantes

compartment [kəm·'part·mənt] *n* **1.** RAIL compartimento *m* **2.** (*section*) departamento *m*

compass ['kʌm·pəs] <-es> *n* **1.** *a.* NAUT brújula *f* **2.** *form* (*range*) alcance *m;* (*area*) ámbito *m;* **to be beyond the ~ of sb's knowledge** sobrepasar los límites de los conocimientos de alguien

compassion [kəm·'pæʃ·ən] *n* compasión *f*

compassionate [kəm·'pæʃ·ə·nɪt] *adj* compasivo, -a

compatibility [kəm·ˌpæt·ə·'bɪl·ə·ti] *n* compatibilidad *f*

compatible [kəm·'pæt·ə·bəl] *adj* **1.** *a.* MED, COMPUT compatible **2.** (*consistent*) conciliable

compatriot [kəm·'peɪ·tri·ət] *n* **1.** (*countryman*) compatriota *mf* **2.** (*companion*) colega *mf*

compel [kəm·'pel] <-ll-> *vt* **1.** (*force*) obligar **2.** (*produce*) imponer

compelling *adj* (*reason*) imponente; (*film*) convincente

compendium [kəm·'pen·di·əm] <-s *o* -dia> *n* compendio *m*

compensate ['kam·pən·seɪt] **I.** *vt* (*make up for*) compensar; (*for loss, damage*) indemnizar **II.** *vi* **to ~ for sth** (*reward*) compensar algo

compensation [ˌkam·pen·'seɪ·ʃən] *n* **1.** (*award*) compensación *f;* (*for loss, damage*) indemnización *f;* **to claim ~** reclamar una indemnización; **in ~ for sth** en compensación por algo **2.** (*recompense*) recompensa *f;* **in ~** como recompensa

compete [kəm·'pit] *vi* **1.** (*strive*) competir; **to ~ for sth** competir por algo; **the new shop will have a tough time competing with the two supermarkets** la nueva tienda lo tendrá difícil si quiere competir con los dos supermercados; **turn the music down — I'm not competing with that noise** baja la música — no pienso gritar para que me puedas oír **2.** (*take part*) participar; **to ~ in an event** participar [*o* competir] en una prueba

competence ['kam·pɪ·təns] *n,* **competency** *n* competencia *f*

competent ['kam·pɪ·tənt] *adj* competente; **to be ~ at sth** ser competente en algo

competition [ˌkam·pə·'tɪʃ·ən] *n* **1.** (*state of competing*) competencia *f* **2.** (*rivalry*) rivalidad *f* **3.** (*contest*) concurso *m;* **beauty ~** concurso de belleza; **to enter a ~** presentarse a un concurso

competitive [kəm·'pet·ɪ·tɪv] *adj* competitivo, -a; **~ spirit** espíritu *m* competitivo; **~ sports** deportes *mpl* de competición; **their prices are very ~** sus precios son muy competitivos

competitiveness [kəm·'pet·ə·tɪv·nɪs] *n* competitividad *f*

competitor [kəm·'pet·ə·tər] *n* **1.** *a.* ECON competidor(a) *m(f)* **2.** SPORTS rival *mf;* (*participant*) participante *mf*

compilation [ˌkam·pə·'leɪ·ʃən] *n* **1.** (*act of compiling*) compilación *f* **2.** (*collection*) recopilación *f*

compile [kəm·'paɪl] *vt* **1.** *a.* COMPUT compilar **2.** (*collect*) recopilar

compiler [kəm·'pi·lər] *n* **1.** (*person*) recopilador(a) *m(f)* **2.** *a.* COMPUT compilador *m*

complacence [kəm·'pleɪ·səns] *n,* **complacency** *n* complacencia *f* (*excesiva*)

complacent [kəm·'pleɪ·sənt] *adj* satisfecho, -a de sí mismo, -a

complain [kəm·'pleɪn] *vi* quejarse; **to ~ about** [*o* **of**] **sth** quejarse de algo

complainant [kəm·'pleɪ·nənt] *n* LAW demandante *mf*

complaint [kəm·'pleɪnt] *n* **1.** (*expression of displeasure*) queja *f;* **to have cause for ~** tener motivos de queja; **to make a ~ about sb/sth** quejarse de alguien/algo; **to lodge a ~** formular una queja **2.** LAW querella *f* **3.** (*illness*) enfermedad *f*

complaisance [kəm·'pleɪ·səns] *n form* complacencia *f*

complaisant [kəm·'pleɪ·sənt] *adj form* compaciente

complement ['kam·plɪ·mənt] *vt* complementar

complementary [ˌkam·plə·'men·tə·ri] *adj* complementario, -a

complete [kəm·'plit] **I.** *vt* **1.** (*add what is missing*) completar **2.** (*finish*) terminar; **to ~ doing sth** terminar de hacer algo **3.** (*fill out entirely*) rellenar **II.** *adj* completo, -a, entero, -a; **~ coverage** cobertura *f* total; **in ~ darkness** en la más absoluta oscuridad; **~ paralysis** parálisis *f inv* total; **the man's a ~ fool!** ¡el hombre es un tonto de remate!

completely *adv* totalmente

completeness *n* totalidad *f*

completion [kəm·'pli·ʃən] *n* finalización *f;* **to be nearing ~** estar a punto de terminarse; **you'll be paid upon ~ of the project** cobrarás cuando se haya terminado el proyecto

complex ['kam·pleks] **I.** *adj* complejo, -a **II.** <-es> *n* **1.** PSYCH complejo *m;* **guilt/inferiority ~** complejo de culpabilidad/inferioridad; **to have a ~ about sth** estar acomplejado por algo; **to give sb a ~** acomplejar a alguien; **I've got a real ~ about spiders** tengo verdadera fobia a las arañas **2.** ARCHIT complejo

complexion [kəm·'plek·ʃən] *n* **1.** (*skin*) cutis *m inv;* (*color*) tez *f;* **a healthy ~** un cutis sano **2.** (*character*) cariz *m;* (*of people*) aspecto *m;* **that puts a different ~ on things** eso le da un cariz nuevo a las cosas

complexity [kəm·'plek·sə·ti] *n* complejidad *f*

compliance [kəm·'plaɪ·ənts] *n* obediencia *f;* (*agreement*) conformidad *f;* **in ~ with the law** conforme a la ley; **to act in ~ with sth** actuar de acuerdo con algo

compliant [kəm·'plaɪ·ənt] *adj form* (*obedient*) obediente; (*overly obedient*) sumiso, -a

complicate ['kam·plə·keɪt] *vt* complicar; (*make worse*) empeorar; **his breathing problem has been ~d by the flu** su problema respiratorio se ha visto agravado por una gripe

complicated *adj* complicado, -a

complication [ˌkam·plə·'keɪ·ʃən] *n* complicación *f;* **if any ~s arise, let me know and I'll help** si surge alguna dificultad, avísame y te ayudaré

complicity [kəm·'plɪs·ə·ti] *n* complicidad *f*

compliment ['kam·plə·mənt] **I.** *n* **1.** (*expression of approval*) cumplido *m;* (*flirt*) piropo *m;* **to pay sb a ~** hacer un cumplido a alguien; **to repay a ~** devolver un cumplido; **I take it as a ~ that...** me halaga que... **2.** **~s** saludos *mpl;* **to present one's ~s** *form* presentar sus respetos; **to send ~s** enviar saludos; **with ~s** con un atento saludo ▶ **to fish for ~s** buscar elogios **II.** *vt* **to ~ sb on sth** felicitar a alguien por algo

complimentary [ˌkam·plə·'men·tə·ri] *adj* **1.** (*praising*) positivo, -a; **to be ~ about sth** hablar en términos muy favorables de algo **2.** (*free*) gratuito, -a

comply [kəm·'plaɪ] <-ie-> *vi* cumplir; **to refuse to ~** negarse a obedecer; **to ~ with the law/the rules** acatar la ley/las normas

component [kəm·'pou·nənt] *n* componente *m;* **key ~** pieza *f* clave

compose [kəm·'pouz] **I.** *vi* (*write music, poetry*) componer **II.** *vt* **1.** (*music, poetry*) componer **2.** (*write*) redactar **3.** (*make up*) **to be ~d of sth** constar de algo; **the committee is ~d of experts** el comité está formado por expertos **4.** (*calm*) **to ~ oneself** calmarse; **to ~ one's thoughts** ordenar sus pensamientos **5.** TYPO componer

composed [kəm·'pouzd] *adj* tranquilo, -a

composer [kəm·'pou·zər] *n* compositor(a) *m(f)*

composite [kəm·'paz·ɪt] *adj* compuesto, -a

composition [ˌkam·pə·'zɪʃ·ən] *n* **1.** composición *f;* SCHOOL redacción *f* **2.** LAW arreglo *m* **3.** (*make-up: of a group*) formación *f*

compositor [kəm·'paz·ɪ·tər] *n* TYPO cajista *m, f*

compost ['kam·poust] **I.** *n* abono *m* orgánico **II.** *vt* **1.** (*turn into fertilizer*) convertir en abono **2.** (*fertilize*) abonar

composure [kəm·'pou·ʒər] *n* compostura *f;* **to lose/regain one's ~** perder/recobrar la compostura

compound¹ [ˌkəm·'paund] *vt* **1.** (*make worse*) agravar **2.** (*mix*) combinar **3.** (*make up*) **to be ~ed of sth** constar de algo

compound² ['kam·paund] *n* **1.** (*combination*) mezcla *f* **2.** CHEM compuesto *m* **3.** (*enclosure*) recinto *m*

compound fracture *n* fractura *f* múltiple

compound interest *n* interés *m* compuesto

comprehend [ˌkam·prɪ·'hend] *vi, vt* comprender

comprehensible [ˌkam·prɪ·'hen·sə·bəl] *adj* comprensible

comprehension [ˌkamprɪ'henʃən] *n* comprensión *f;* **beyond ~** incomprensible; **he has no ~ of the size of the problem** no es consciente de la envergadura del problema

comprehensive [ˌkam·prɪ·'hen·sɪv] *adj* exhaustivo, -a; (*global*) completo, -a; **~ coverage** cobertura *f* global; **~ list** lista *f* detallada

compress¹ [kəm·'pres] *vt* **1.** *a.* COMPUT comprimir **2.** (*make shorter*) condensar; **I had to ~ ten pages of notes into four paragraphs** tuve que resumir diez páginas de apuntes en cuatro párrafos

compress² ['kam·pres] <-es> *n* compresa *f*

compressed [kəm·'prest] *adj* comprimido, -a

compression [kəm·'preʃ·ən] *n a.* COMPUT compresión *f*

compressor [kəm·'pres·ər] *n* compresor *m*

comprise [kəm·'praɪz] *vt* **1.** (*consist of*) constar de, componerse de **2.** (*include*) comprender

compromise ['kam·prə·maɪz] **I.** *n* **1.** (*concession*) transigencia *f;* **to agree to a ~** consentir en transigir; **to make a ~** hacer una concesión **2.** (*agreement*) arreglo *m*, compromiso *m;* **to reach a ~** llegar a un acuerdo **II.** *vi* transigir **III.** *vt* **1.** (*betray*) comprometer; **to ~ one's beliefs/principles** dejar de lado sus creencias/principios **2.** (*endanger*) poner en peligro; **to ~ one's reputation** poner en entredicho su reputación

compromising *adj* comprometido, -a

comptroller [kən·'troʊ·lər] *n* interventor(a) *m(f)*, contralor(a) *m(f) AmL*

compulsion [kəm·'pʌl·ʃən] *n* obligación *f;* **to be under no ~ to do sth** no estar obligado a hacer algo; **he seems to have a constant ~ to eat** parece que tiene una obsesión constante por la comida

compulsive [kəm·'pʌl·sɪv] *adj* compulsivo, -a

compulsory [kəm·'pʌl·sə·ri] *adj* obligatorio, -a; **~ education** enseñanza *f* obligatoria; **~ by law** preceptivo por ley

compunction [kəm·'pʌŋk·ʃən] *n* remordimiento *m;* **to have no ~ about sth** no tener reparo en algo

computation [ˌkam·pjə·'teɪ·ʃən] *n* cómputo *m;* COMPUT computación *f*

compute [kəm·'pjut] *vt* computar

computer [kəm·'pju·tər] *n* ordenador *m*, computador(a) *m(f) AmL;* **to do sth by ~** hacer algo con el ordenador

computer-aided *adj* asistido, -a por ordenador

computer center *n* centro *m* de informática

computer game *n* videojuego *m*, juego *m* de ordenador

computer graphics *n* + *sing/pl vb* gráficos *mpl* por ordenador [*o* por computadora *AmL*]

computerization [kəm·ˌpju·tər·ɪ·'zeɪ·ʃən] *n* **1.** (*computer storage*) computerización *f* **2.** (*equipping with computers*) instalación *f* de equipo informático

computerize [kəm·'pju·tə·raɪz] **I.** *vt* **1.** (*store on computer*) informatizar, computerizar **2.** (*equip with computers*) instalar ordenadores [*o* computadoras *AmL*] en **II.** *vi* informatizarse

computer network *n* red *f* de ordenadores [*o* computadoras *AmL*]

computer program *n* programa *m* (de ordenador)

computer programmer *n* programador(a) *m(f)*

computer science *n* informática *f;* **~ course** curso *m* de informática

computer scientist *n* informático, -a *m, f*

computer search <-es> *n* búsqueda *f* por ordenador [*o* por computadora *AmL*]

computer virus <-es> *n* virus *m inv* (informático)

computer workstation *n* terminal *m* de trabajo

computing *n* informática *f*

comrade ['kam·ræd] *n* **1.** (*friend*) compañero, -a *m, f* **2.** POL camarada *mf*

comradeship ['kam·ræd·ʃɪp] *n* camaradería *f;* **there's a great sense of ~ in the group** hay mucho compañerismo en el grupo

Comsat ['kam·sæt] *n abbr of* **communications satellite** Comsat *m*

con¹ [kan] <-nn-> *vt inf* (*to swindle*) engañar; **to ~ sb** (**into doing sth**) engañar a alguien (para que haga algo); **to ~ sb into believing that...** hacer creer a alguien que...; **to ~ sb out of sth** estafar algo a alguien

con² [kan] *n* (*against*) contra *m;* **the pros and ~s of sth** los pros y los contras de algo

con³ [kan] *n sl* (*convict*) convicto, -a *m, f*

con artist [ˌkan·'ar·təst] *n inf* estafador(a) *m(f)*

concatenation [kən·ˌkæt·ə·'neɪ·ʃən] *n* concatenación *f*

concave ['kan·keɪv] *adj* cóncavo, -a

concavity [kan·'kæv·ə·ti] <-ies> *n* concavidad *f*

conceal [kən·'sil] *vt* esconder; (*a surprise*) contener; (*the truth*) encubrir

concealment [kən·'sil·mənt] *n* (*of information, evidence*) encubrimiento *m;* (*of feelings*) disimulación *f;* **to watch sth from a place of ~** ver algo desde un escondrijo

concede [kən·'sid] **I.** *vt* **1.** (*acknowledge*) conceder; (*defeat*) aceptar; **to ~ that...** admitir que... **2.** (*surrender*) ceder; **to ~ sth to sb** otorgar algo a alguien **3.** (*permit*) acceder a **4.** (*allow to score*) **to ~ a goal** conceder un gol **II.** *vi* darse por vencido

conceit [kən·'sit] *n* **1.** (*vanity*) vanidad *f;* **to be full of ~** tener muchas presunciones **2.** *liter* (*elaborate comparison*) concepto *m*

conceited [kən·'si·t̬ɪd] *adj* vanidoso, -a; **without wishing to sound ~** sin querer parecer presuntuoso

conceivable [kən·'siv·ə·bəl] *adj* concebible; **it's ~** es verosímil

conceive [kən·'siv] **I.** *vt* **1.** (*imagine, become pregnant with*) concebir **2.** (*devise*) idear; (*arrange*) preparar **II.** *vi* **1.** (*think*) **to ~ of sb/sth** formarse un concepto de alguien/algo; **other people may influence how we ~ of ourselves** los demás pueden influir en el concepto que tenemos de nosotros mismos **2.** (*devise*) imaginar(se) **3.** (*become pregnant*) concebir

concentrate ['kan·sən·treɪt] **I.** *vi* **1.** (*focus one's thoughts*) concentrarse; **to ~ on sth** concentrarse en algo **2.** (*gather*) reunirse **II.** *vt* **1.** (*focus*) concentrar; (*search*) centrar **2.** (*accumulate*) reunir; (*population*) concentrar **3.** (*not dilute*) concentrar **III.** *n* concentrado *m*

concentrated *adj a. fig* concentrado, -a; (*attack*) conciso, -a

concentration [ˌkan·sən·'treɪ·ʃən] *n* **1.** concentración *f;* **to lose (one's) ~** perder la concentración; **~ on sth** concentración en algo **2.** (*accumulation*) acumulación *f;* (*of troops*) concentración *f*

concentration camp *n* campo *m* de concentración

concentric [kən·'sen·trɪk] *adj* concéntrico, -a

concept ['kan·sept] *n* concepto *m;* **to grasp a ~** coger una idea

conception [kən·'sep·ʃən] *n* **1.** (*notion*) noción *f;* (*idea*) idea *f;* (*creation*) concepción *f* **2.** BIO concepción *f*

conceptual [kən·'sep·tʃu·əl] *adj* conceptual

conceptualize [kən·'sep·tʃu·ə·laɪz] I. *vi* formarse un concepto II. *vt* conceptualizar

concern [kən·'sɜrn] I. *vt* 1. (*apply to*) referirse a; **to ~ oneself about sth** interesarse por algo; **there's no need for you to ~ yourself with this matter** no tienes por qué meterte en este asunto 2. (*affect*) incumbir; **to whom it may ~** a quien corresponda 3. (*be about*) tener que ver con; **to be ~ed with sth** ocuparse de algo; **as far as I'm ~ed** por lo que a mí respecta; **I'd like to thank everyone ~ed** me gustaría dar las gracias a todos los que han colaborado; **I'm not very good where money is ~ed** no soy muy bueno en cuestiones de dinero; **her job is something ~ed with computers** su trabajo tiene que ver con ordenadores 4. (*worry*) preocuparse; **to be ~ed about sth** estar preocupado por algo II. *n* 1. (*matter of interest*) asunto *m;* **a major ~** una grave preocupación; **it's no ~ of mine** eso no es de mi incumbencia; **what's happening? — that's none of your ~** ¿qué ocurre? — no es asunto tuyo; **to be of ~ to sb** interesar a alguien 2. (*worry*) preocupación *f;* **a matter of ~** un asunto de interés; **the ~ for sth** la inquietud por algo 3. (*company*) empresa *f;* **a going ~** una empresa próspera

concerning *prep* acerca de

concert ['kan·sərt] *n* 1. (*musical performance*) concierto *m;* **~ hall** sala *f* de conciertos; **~ pianist** pianista *mf;* **~ tour** gira *f* de conciertos 2. **in ~** (*performing live*) en concierto; *form* (*all together*) conjuntamente; **in ~ with sb** conjuntamente con alguien; **to act in ~** actuar de común acuerdo

concerted [kən·'sɜr·tɪd] *adj* 1. (*joint*) concertado, -a; (*action*) conjunto, -a; (*exercise*) acordado, -a 2. (*resolute*) resuelto, -a; (*effort*) enérgico, -a

concert grand [ˌkan·sərt·'grænd] *n* piano *m* de cola

concertina [ˌkan·sər·'ti·nə] *n* concertina *f*

concertina wire *n* alambre *m* de espino [*o* de púas *Col, Méx*]

concertmaster [ˌkan·sərt·'mæs·tər] *n* concertino *m*

concerto [kən·'tʃer·toʊ] <-s *o* -ti> *n* concierto *m* (*de música clásica*)

concert pitch *n* MUS diapasón *m* ▶ **to be at ~** estar preparado

concession [kən·'sef·ən] *n* 1. (*tax compensation*) desgravación *f* 2. (*compromise*) concesión *f;* **~ to sell goods** licencia *f* para vender productos

conciliate [kən·'sɪl·i·eɪt] I. *vi* conciliarse II. *vt* 1. (*placate*) apaciguar 2. (*reconcile*) conciliar

conciliation [kən·ˌsɪl·i·'eɪ·ʃən] *n form* conciliación *f*

conciliatory [kən·'sɪl·i·ə·tɔr·i] *adj* conciliador(a)

concise [kən·'saɪs] *adj* conciso, -a

conciseness *n,* **concision** [kən·'sɪʒ·ən] *n* concisión *f*

conclave ['kan·kleɪv] *n form* 1. (*private meeting*) reunión *f* a puerta cerrada 2. REL (*gathering of cardinals*) cónclave *m*

conclude [kən·'klud] I. *vi* concluir; **to ~ by doing sth** terminar haciendo algo II. *vt* 1. (*finish*) finalizar 2. (*decide*) resolver; **we talked all night, but nothing was ~d** hablamos toda la noche, pero no llegamos a ninguna conclusión 3. (*infer*) **to ~ (from sth) that...** deducir (de algo) que... 4. (*ratify*) pactar; (*a contract*) firmar; (*a peace treaty*) ratificar

concluding *adj* final; (*chapter*) último, -a

conclusion [kən·'klu·ʒən] *n* 1. (*end*) conclusión *f;* (*of a story*) final *m* 2. (*decision*) decisión *f* 3. (*inference*) conclusión *f;* **to come to a ~** llegar a una conclusión 4. (*ratification*) ratificación *f;* (*of a contract*) firma *f* 5. (*lastly*) **in ~** en conclusión; **in ~, I would like to say that...** para terminar, me gustaría decir que...

conclusive [kən·'klu·sɪv] *adj* 1. (*convincing*) concluyente; **~ arguments** argumentos *mpl* irrefutables 2. (*decisive*) decisivo, -a

concoct [kən·'kakt] *vt* 1. (*create by mixing ingredients: a dish*) preparar 2. (*devise*) tramar; (*a plan*) maquinar 3. (*fabricate*) inventar

concoction [kən·'kak·ʃən] *n* (*dish*) mezcla *f;* (*drink*) brebaje *m;* **is this dish one of your ~s, Paul?** *iron* ¿este plato es invento tuyo, Paul?

concourse ['kan·kɔrs] *n* (gran) hall *m*

concrete ['kan·krit] I. *n* hormigón *m* II. *adj* de hormigón III. *vt* revestir de hormigón

concrete mixer *n* hormigonera *f*

concubine ['kaŋ·kju·baɪn] *n* HIST concubina *f*

concur [kən·'kɜr] <-rr-> *vi form* 1. (*agree*) coincidir; **to ~ with sb (in sth)** estar de acuerdo con alguien (en algo) 2. (*happen simultaneously*) concurrir

concurrence [kən·'kʌr·əns] *n form* 1. (*agreement*) conformidad *f* 2. (*simultaneous occurrence*) concurrencia *f*

concurrent [kən·'kʌr·ənt] *adj* concurrente

concuss [kən·'kʌs] *vt* **to be ~ed** tener una conmoción cerebral

concussed *adj* que padece una conmoción cerebral

concussion [kən·'kʌʃ·ən] *n* conmoción *f* cerebral; **to suffer (from) a ~** padecer una conmoción cerebral

condemn [kən·'dem] *vt* 1. (*reprove*) condenar; **to ~ sb for sth** censurar a alguien por algo 2. (*sentence*) **to be ~ed to death** ser condenado a muerte 3. (*pronounced unsafe: building*) declarar en ruina

condemnation [ˌkan·dem·'neɪ·ʃən] *n* 1. (*reproof*) condena *f* 2. (*reason to reprove*) motivo *m* de crítica

condensation [ˌkan·den·'seɪ·ʃən] *n* 1. CHEM, PHYS condensación *f* 2. (*reduction in size*) abreviación *f*

condense [kən·'dens] I. *vt* 1. (*shorten*) sintetizar 2. (*concentrate*) **to ~ a liquid** condensar un líquido 3. (*form droplets from*) **the air was**

~d into clouds el aire formó nubes por condensación **II.** *vi* condensarse

condenser [kən·'den·sər] *n* condensador *m*

condescend [ˌkan·dɪ·'send] *vi* **to ~ to do sth** rebajarse [*o* condescender] a hacer algo

condescending [ˌkan·dɪ·'sen·dɪŋ] *adj* con aires de superioridad

condescension [ˌkan·dɪ·'sen·ʃən] *n* aires *mpl* de superioridad

condiment ['kan·də·mənt] *n form* condimento *m;* **~ set** aliño *m*

condition [kən·'dɪʃ·ən] **I.** *n* **1.** (*state*) condición *f;* **in perfect ~** en perfecto estado; **in peak ~** en condiciones óptimas; **in terrible ~** en un estado deplorable; **to be out of ~** (*person*) estar en baja forma; (*thing*) estar en mal estado; **to be in no ~ to do sth** no estar en condiciones de hacer algo; **for a man of sixty-three, Jim's in pretty good ~** para tener sesenta y tres, Jim está en plena forma **2.** (*mental or physical state*) estado *m;* **heart ~** afección *f* cardíaca **3.** (*circumstances*) **~s** *pl* condiciones *fpl* **4.** (*stipulation*) condición *f;* **to make a ~** poner una condición; **on the ~ that** con la condición de que +*subj;* **under the ~s of sth** según los términos de algo **II.** *vt* **1.** (*train*) preparar; (*influence*) condicionar **2.** (*treat hair*) acondicionar

conditional [kən·'dɪʃ·ə·nəl] **I.** *adj* (*provisional*) condicional; **~ on sth** condicionado a algo **II.** *n* LING **the ~** el condicional

conditionally [kən·'dɪʃ·ə·nə·li] *adv* con reservas

conditioned [kən·'dɪʃ·ənd] *adj* (*trained*) preparado, -a; (*place, air*) acondicionado, -a; (*reflex*) condicionado, -a

conditioner [kən·'dɪʃ·ə·nər] *n* **1.** (*for hair*) acondicionador *m*, bálsamo *m Col, Méx* **2.** (*for soil*) acondicionador *m* de suelo

conditioning *n* condicionamiento *m*

condo ['kan·dou] *n inf s.* **condominium**

condolence [kən·'dou·ləns] *n* **~s** pésame *m*, condolencias *fpl;* **to offer one's ~s** (**to sb**) *form* dar el pésame (a alguien)

condom ['kan·dəm] *n* condón *m*

condominium [ˌkan·də·'mɪn·i·əm] *n* **1.** (*apartment building*) propiedad *f* horizontal, condominio *m AmL* **2.** (*unit*) piso *m* **3.** POL condominio *m*

condone [kən·'doun] *vt* **1.** (*approve*) aprobar **2.** (*forgive*) condonar

conducive [kən·'du·sɪv] *adj* propicio, -a; **to be ~ to sth** ser apropiado para algo

conduct¹ [ˌkan·'dʌkt] **I.** *vt* **1.** (*carry out*) llevar a cabo **2.** (*direct*) dirigir; **to ~ a business** conducir un negocio; **to ~ a religious service** dirigir un oficio religioso; (*guide*) guiar **3.** (*behave*) **to ~ oneself** comportarse **4.** ELEC, PHYS (*transmit*) conducir **II.** *vi* MUS llevar la batuta

conduct² ['kan·dʌkt] *n* **1.** (*management*) dirección *f* **2.** (*behavior*) conducta *f; sb's ~ towards sb* el comportamiento de alguien hacia alguien

conductive [kən·'dʌk·tɪv] *adj* ELEC, PHYS conductor(a)

conductor [kən·'dʌk·tər] *n* **1.** (*director*) director(a) *m(f)* **2.** PHYS, ELEC conductor *m* **3.** (*fare collector*) cobrador *m;* (*of train*) revisor *m*

conductress [kən·'dʌk·trɪs] <-es> *n* cobradora *f;* (*of train*) revisora *f*

conduit ['kan·du·ɪt] *n* conducto *m*

cone [koun] *n* **1.** *a.* MATH cono *m* **2.** (*for ice cream*) cucurucho *m* **3.** BOT piña *f*

confection [kən·'fek·ʃən] *n form* **1.** COM confección *f* **2.** CULIN dulce *m;* (*sweet*) golosina *f*

confectioner [kən·'fek·ʃə·nər] *n* confitero, -a *m, f*

confectionery [kən·'fek·ʃə·ner·i] *n* confitería *f*

confederacy [kən·'fed·ər·ə·si] <-ies> *n* **1.** + *sing/pl vb* (*union*) confederación *f;* **the Confederacy** HIST la Confederación **2.** (*plot*) complot *m*

confederate [kən·'fed·ər·ət] **I.** *n* cómplice *mf* **II.** *adj* POL, HIST confederado, -a

confederation [kən·ˌfed·ə·'rei·ʃən] *n + sing/pl vb* POL confederación *f*

> **i** El **Confederation Day** o **Canada Day** es la fiesta nacional de Canadá que se celebra el día 1 de julio.

confer [kən·'fɜr] <-rr-> **I.** *vi* consultar **II.** *vt* otorgar

conference ['kan·fər·əns] *n* **1.** (*meeting*) conferencia *f;* **to be in a ~** (**with sb**) estar reunido (con alguien) **2.** SPORTS conferencia *f*, liga *f*

confess [kən·'fes] **I.** *vi* confesarse; **to ~ to a crime** confesar (haber cometido) un crimen **II.** *vt* confesar; **I must ~ that I'm a little bit confused** tengo que admitir que estoy un poco confuso

confessedly *adv* con franqueza

confession [kən·'feʃ·ən] *n* **1.** (*admission*) confesión *f;* **I have a ~ to make** tengo que hacer una confesión **2.** (*profession*) profesión *f; ~ of faith* profesión de fe

confessional [kən·'feʃ·ə·nəl] *n* confesionario *m*

confessor [kən·'fes·ər] *n* confesor *m*

confetti [kən·'feţ·i] *n* confeti *m;* **to shower sb in ~** tirar confeti a alguien

confidant [ˌkan·fə·'dænt] *n* confidente *m*

confidante [ˌkan·fə·'dænt] *n* confidente *f*

confide [kən·'faɪd] *vt* confiar; **to ~ (to sb) that...** decir (a alguien) en confidencia que...

confidence ['kan·fə·dəns] *n* **1.** (*trust*) confianza *f;* **to have every ~ in sb** tener toda la confianza en alguien; **to place one's ~ in sb/sth** poner la confianza en alguien/algo; **to take sb into one's ~** confiar en alguien; **to win sb's ~** ganarse la confianza de alguien; **he certainly doesn't lack ~** desde luego no le falta confianza en sí mismo **2.** (*secrecy*) **~s** confidencia *f*

confident ['kɑn·fə·dənt] *adj* **1.** (*sure*) seguro, -a; **to be ~ about oneself** tener confianza en uno mismo; **to be ~ about sth** estar seguro de algo **2.** (*self-assured*) confiado, -a
confidential [ˌkɑn·fə·'den·ʃəl] *adj* confidencial
confidentially [ˌkɑn·fə·'den·ʃə·li] *adv* confidencialmente
confiding [kən·'faɪ·dɪŋ] *adj* confiado, -a
configuration [kən·ˌfɪg·jə·'reɪ·ʃən] *n a.* COMPUT configuración *f*
confine [kən·'faɪn] **I.** *vt* **1.** (*limit*) **to ~ sth to sth** restringir algo a algo; **to be ~d to doing sth** limitarse a hacer algo **2.** (*imprison*) confinar **3.** (*shut in: person*) recluir; (*animal*) encerrar; **to be ~d to quarters** MIL estar retenido en los barracones **II.** *n pl* **the ~s** los confines; **beyond the ~s of sth** más allá de los límites de algo
confined *adj* (*prisoner*) recluido, -a; (*space*) reducido, -a
confinement [kən·'faɪn·mənt] *n* (*act of being confined*) reclusión *f*; (*state of being confined*) confinamiento *m*; **his ~ to bed really annoyed him** le resultaba especialmente fastidioso tener que quedar en cama
confines *n pl* límites *mpl*, confines *mpl*
confirm [kən·'fɜrm] **I.** *vt* **1.** (*verify*) verificar **2.** REL **to ~ sb's faith** confirmar la fe de alguien **II.** *vi* confirmarse
confirmation [ˌkɑn·fər·'meɪ·ʃən] *n a.* REL confirmación *f*
confirmed [kən·'fɜrmd] *adj* **1.** (*established*) firme **2.** (*chronic*) **~ alcoholic** alcohólico *m* empedernido **3.** (*proved*) confirmado, -a
confiscate ['kɑn·fə·skeɪt] *vt* confiscar
conflict¹ ['kɑn·flɪkt] *n* **1.** (*clash*) conflicto *m*; **to come into ~ with sb** entrar en conflicto con alguien **2.** (*battle*) discrepancia *f*
conflict² [kən·'flɪkt] *vi* (*differ*) **to ~ with sth** chocar con algo
conflicting [kən·'flɪk·tɪŋ] *adj* opuesto, -a; (*evidence*) contradictorio, -a; (*interest*) encontrado, -a
confluence ['kɑn·flu·əns] *n* confluencia *f*
conform [kən·'fɔrm] *vi* conformarse; **to ~ to the law** ser conforme a la ley
conformist [kən·'fɔr·mɪst] **I.** *n* conformista *mf* **II.** *adj* conformista
conformity [kən·'fɔr·mə·t̬i] *n* conformidad *f*; **in ~ with sth** conforme con algo
confound [kən·'faʊnd] *vt* confundir
confounded *adj inf* maldito, -a
confront [kən·'frʌnt] *vt* (*a danger*) enfrentarse a; (*the enemy*) plantar cara a
confrontation [ˌkɑn·frən·'teɪ·ʃən] *n* confrontación *f*
confrontational [ˌkɑn·frən·'teɪ·ʃə·nəl] *adj* contencioso, -a; (*opinions*) polémico, -a
confuse [kən·'fjuz] *vt* **1.** (*perplex*) desconcertar **2.** (*put into disarray*) turbar **3.** (*mix up*) confundir
confused [kən·'fjuzd] *adj* (*perplexed*) confundido, -a; (*disordered*) confuso, -a

confusing [kən·'fju·zɪŋ] *adj* confuso, -a
confusion [kən·'fju·ʒən] *n* **1.** (*perplexity*) desconcierto *m* **2.** (*mix up*) confusión *f* **3.** (*disorder*) desorden *m*
congeal [kən·'dʒil] *vi* (*sauce*) espesarse; (*fat*) cuajar; (*blood*) coagularse
congenial [kən·'dʒin·jəl] *adj* placentero, -a; (*people*) agradable
congenital [kən·'dʒen·ə·t̬əl] *adj* congénito, -a
congested [kən·'dʒes·tɪd] *adj* **1.** (*overcrowded*) congestionado, -a; (*people*) abarrotado, -a **2.** MED (*blocked*) congestionado, -a
congestion [kən·'dʒes·tʃən] *n* **1.** (*overcrowding*) congestión *f*; (*on roads, freeways*) caravana *f* **2.** MED congestión *f*
conglomerate [kən·'glam·ə·rət] *n* conglomerado *m*
conglomeration [kən·ˌglam·ə·'reɪ·ʃən] *n* conglomeración *f*
Congo ['kɑŋ·goʊ] **I.** *n* **the ~** el Congo **II.** *adj* del Congo
Congolese [ˌkɑŋ·gə·'liz] **I.** *adj* congoleño, -a **II.** *n* congoleño, -a *m*, *f*
congratulate [kən·'grætʃ·ə·leɪt] *vt* felicitar; **to ~ sb (on sth)** felicitar a alguien (por algo)
congratulation [kən·ˌgrætʃ·ə·'leɪ·ʃən] *n* felicitación *f*; **~s!** ¡enhorabuena!; **a note of ~** una postal de felicitación
congregate ['kɑŋ·grɪ·geɪt] *vi* congregarse
congregation [ˌkɑŋ·grɪ·'geɪ·ʃən] *n* congregación *f*
congregational [ˌkɑŋ·grɪ·'geɪ·ʃə·nəl] *adj* congregacionalista
congress ['kɑŋ·gres] *n* congreso *m*
congressional [kən·'greʃ·ə·nəl] *adj* congresista
congressional candidate *n* candidato, -a *m*, *f* al Congreso
congressional debate *n* debate *m* en el Congreso
congressional election *n* elecciones *fpl* al Congreso
congressman ['kɑŋ·gres·mən] *n* <-men> congresista *m*
congresswoman *n* <-women> congresista *f*
congruence ['kɑŋ·gru·əns] *n a.* MATH congruencia *f*
congruent ['kɑŋ·gru·ənt] *adj a.* MATH congruente
conical ['kɑn·ɪ·kəl] *adj* cónico, -a
conifer ['kɑn·ə·fər] *n* conífera *f*
coniferous [koʊ·'nɪf·ər·əs] *adj* conífero, -a
conjectural [kən·'dʒek·tʃər·əl] *adj* conjetural
conjecture [kən·'dʒek·tʃər] **I.** *n* conjetura *f* **II.** *vi* conjeturar
conjugal ['kɑn·dʒə·gəl] *adj form* conyugal; **~ visit** visita *m* conyugal
conjugate ['kɑn·dʒə·geɪt] *vt* conjugar
conjugation [ˌkɑn·dʒə·'geɪ·ʃən] *n* conjugación *f*
conjunction [kən·'dʒʌŋk·ʃən] *n a.* LING conjunción *f*; **in ~ with** conjuntamente con
conjunctivitis [kən·ˌdʒʌŋk·tə·'vaɪ·t̬ɪs] *n* con-

juntivitis *f inv*

conjure ['kan·dʒər] **I.** *vi* hacer magia **II.** *vt* conjurar; *fig* evocar

◆**conjure up** *vt* hacer aparecer; **to ~ an image** evocar una imagen

conjurer ['kan·dʒər·ər] *n*, **conjuror** ['kan·dʒər·ər] *n* mago, -a *m, f*

conk [kaŋk] **I.** *n sl* (*blow*) coscorrón *m* **II.** *vt sl* **to ~ sb on the head** dar un coscorrón a alguien

◆**conk out** *vi sl* **1.** (*break down: machine, vehicle*) averiarse **2.** (*become exhausted*) quedar hecho polvo

con man ['kan·ˌmæn] *n abbr of* **confidence man** estafador *m*

Conn. *n abbr of* **Connecticut** Connecticut *m*

connect [kə·'nekt] **I.** *vi* conectar(se); **to ~ to the Internet** conectarse a Internet **II.** *vt* **1.** (*join*) conectar **2.** (*associate*) **to ~ sth/sb with sth** asociar algo/a alguien con algo **3.** (*join by telephone*) poner en contacto **4.** (*in tourism*) enlazar

connected *adj* **1.** (*joined together*) conectado, -a **2.** (*having ties*) **to be ~d to sb** tener relación con alguien

Connecticut [kə·'net̮·ɪ·kət] *n* Connecticut *m*

connecting *adj* comunicado, -a; **~ link** enlace *m* de conexión

connection [kə·'nek·ʃən] *n* **1.** *a.* ELEC, COMPUT conexión *f* **2.** (*relation*) relación *f*

connector *n* conector *m*

connivance [kə·'naɪ·vənts] *n* connivencia *f*

connive [kə·'naɪv] *vi* **to ~ with sb** confabularse con alguien

connoisseur [ˌkan·ə·'sɜr] *n* entendido, -a *m, f*; **art/wine ~** experto, -a *m, f* en arte/vino

connotation [ˌkan·ə·'teɪ·ʃən] *n* connotación *f*

conquer ['kaŋ·kər] *vt* **1.** *a.* HIST conquistar **2.** (*a problem*) acabar con

conqueror ['kaŋ·kər·ər] *n* **1.** *a.* HIST conquistador(a) *m(f)* **2.** (*in a competition*) vencedor(a) *m(f)*

conquest ['kan·kwest] *n a. iron* conquista *f*

conscience ['kan·ʃəns] *n* conciencia *f*; **a clear ~** una conciencia limpia; **a guilty ~** remordimientos *mpl* de conciencia; **to prey on sb's ~** *fig* pesar en la conciencia de alguien; **in all** [*o* **good**] **~** en conciencia

conscientious [ˌkan·tʃi·'en·tʃəs] *adj* concienzudo, -a

conscientiousness *n* escrupulosidad *f*

conscientious objector *n* objetor *m* de conciencia

conscious ['kan·ʃəs] *adj* **1.** (*deliberate*) expreso, -a **2.** (*aware*) consciente; **fashion ~** preocupado por la moda; **to be ~ of sth** ser consciente de algo; **to become ~ of sth** darse cuenta de algo

consciousness ['kan·ʃəs·nɪs] *n* **1.** MED (*state of being conscious*) conocimiento *m* **2.** (*awareness*) conciencia *f*; **political/social ~** conciencia política/social; **to raise one's ~** concienciarse

conscript¹ ['kan·skrɪpt] **I.** *n* MIL recluta *mf* **II.** *adj* MIL reclutado, -a

conscript² [kan·'skrɪpt] *vt* MIL reclutar

conscription [kən·'skrɪp·ʃən] *n* MIL servicio *m* militar, conscripción *f AmL*

consecrate ['kan·sə·kreɪt] *vt* consagrar

consecration [ˌkan·sə·'kreɪ·ʃən] *n* REL consagración *f*

consecutive [kən·'sek·jə·t̮ɪv] *adj* consecutivo, -a

consecutively *adv* consecutivamente

consensus [kən·'sen·səs] *n* consenso *m*

consent [kən·'sent] **I.** *n form* consentimiento *m*; **by common ~** de común acuerdo **II.** *vi* (*agree*) **to ~ to do sth** consentir en hacer algo

consequence ['kan·sɪ·kwənts] *n* consecuencia *f*; **as a ~** como consecuencia; **in ~** por consiguiente; **nothing of ~** nada importante

consequent ['kan·sɪ·kwənt] *adj*, **consequential** [ˌkan·sɪ·'kwen·tʃəl] *adj* consiguiente

consequently *adv* por consiguiente

conservation [ˌkan·sər·'veɪ·ʃən] *n* conservación *f*; **environmental ~** preservación *f* del medio ambiente

conservationist [ˌkan·sər·'veɪ·ʃə·nɪst] *n* conservacionista *mf*

conservatism [kən·'sɜr·və·tɪz·əm] *n* conservadurismo *m*

conservative [kən·'sɜr·və·t̮ɪv] *adj* **1.** *a.* POL (*opposed to change*) conservador(a) **2.** (*cautious*) cauteloso, -a; **~ estimate** estimación *f* prudente

conservatory [kən·'sɜr·və·tɔr·i] *n* conservatorio *m*

conserve [kən·'sɜrv] *vt* conservar; **to ~ energy** ahorrar energía; **to ~ strength** reservar energías

consider [kən·'sɪd·ər] *vt* **1.** (*contemplate*) considerar **2.** (*look attentively at*) examinar **3.** (*show regard for*) tener en cuenta **4.** (*regard as*) **to be ~ed to be the best** ser considerado el mejor; **to ~ that...** creer que...

considerable [kən·'sɪd·ər·ə·bəl] *adj* considerable

considerate [kən·'sɪd·ər·ət] *adj* considerado, -a

consideration [kən·ˌsɪd·ə·'reɪ·ʃən] *n* consideración *f*; **to take sth into ~** tener algo en cuenta; **the project is under ~** el proyecto se está estudiando; **for a small ~** *iron* por una módica cantidad

considered [kən·'sɪd·ərd] *adj* considerado, -a; **highly ~** muy bien considerado

considering [kən·'sɪd·ər·ɪŋ] **I.** *prep* teniendo en cuenta; **~ the weather** en vista del tiempo **II.** *adv* a pesar de todo **III.** *conj* **~ (that)...** ya que..., teniendo en cuenta que...

consignment [kən·'saɪn·mənt] *n* **1.** (*instance of consigning*) envío *m* **2.** ECON remesa *f*; **goods on ~** mercancías *fpl* en consignación

consist [kən·'sɪst] *vi* **to ~ of sth** consistir en algo

consistency [kən·'sɪs·tən·si] *n* **1.** (*degree of*

firmness) consistencia *f* **2.** (*being coherent*) coherencia *f*

consistent [kən·'sɪs·tənt] *adj* **1.** (*keeping to same principles*) consecuente; **to be ~ with sth** ser consecuente con algo **2.** (*not varying*) estable

consolation [ˌkan·sə·'leɪ·ʃən] *n* consuelo *m;* **it was no ~ to him to know that...** no le reconfortó saber que...; **if it's of any ~ ...** si te sirve de consuelo...

consolation prize *n* premio *m* de consolación

consolatory [kən·'sal·ə·tɔr·i] *adj* consolador(a); **~ words** palabras *fpl* reconfortantes

console[1] [kən·'soʊl] *vt* (*comfort*) consolar

console[2] ['kan·soʊl] *n* (*switch panel*) consola *f*

consolidate [kən·'sal·ə·deɪt] **I.** *vi* **1.** (*reinforce*) consolidarse **2.** (*unite*) fusionarse **II.** *vt* consolidar

consolidated *adj* consolidado, -a

consolidation [kən·ˌsal·ə·'deɪ·ʃən] *n* **1.** (*becoming stronger*) fortalecimiento *m* **2.** ECON consolidación *f*

consommé [ˌkan·sə·'meɪ] *n* consomé *m*

consonance ['kan·sə·nəns] *n* LING, MUS consonancia *f*

consonant ['kan·sə·nənt] *n* consonante *f*

consort [kən·'sɔrt] **I.** *vi* **to ~ with sb** tratar con alguien **II.** *n* consorte *mf*; **prince ~** príncipe *m* consorte

consortium [kən·'sɔr·ṭi·əm] *n* <consortiums *o* consortia> consorcio *m; ~* **of companies** grupo *m* de empresas

conspicuous [kən·'spɪk·ju·əs] *adj* conspicuo, -a; (*feature*) llamativo, -a; (*figure*) llamativo, -a; **to be ~ by one's absence** *iron* brillar por su ausencia

conspiracy [kən·'spɪr·ə·si] <-ies> *n* conspiración *f*; **a ~ against sb** un complot contra alguien

conspirator [kən·'spɪr·ə·ṭər] *n* conspirador(a) *m(f)*

conspire [kən·'spaɪr] *vi* conspirar; **to ~ to do sth** conspirar para hacer algo; **to ~ against sb** conspirar contra alguien

constancy ['kan·stən·si] *n form* constancia *f*

constant ['kan·stənt] **I.** *n* constante *f* **II.** *adj* **1.** (*continuous*) constante; (*noise*) continuo, -a; (*surveillance*) incesante **2.** (*unchanging*) inalterable; (*temperature*) constante **3.** (*frequent*) asiduo, -a; **~ use** uso *m* frecuente; **to be in ~ trouble** meterse en problemas constantemente

constantly *adv* constantemente

constellation [ˌkan·stə·'leɪ·ʃən] *n* constelación *f*

consternation [ˌkan·stər·'neɪ·ʃən] *n* consternación *f*

constipate ['kan·stə·peɪt] *vt* MED estreñir

constipated *adj* estreñido, -a

constipation ['kan·stə·'peɪ·ʃən] *n* MED estreñimiento *m*, prendimiento *m CSur*

constituency [kən·'stɪtʃ·u·ən·si] *n* **1.** (*electoral district*) distrito *m* electoral **2.** (*body of*

voters in this area) electorado *m* de un distrito electoral **3.** (*seat*) escaño *m*

constituent [kən·'stɪtʃ·u·ənt] **I.** *n* **1.** (*voter*) elector(a) *m(f)* **2.** CHEM, PHYS (*component*) constituyente *m* **II.** *adj* constituyente

constitute ['kan·stə·tut] *vt* constituir

constitution [ˌkan·stə·'tu·ʃən] *n* constitución *f*

> **i** La Constitución (**Constitution**) de Estados Unidos se redactó en 1787 y entró en vigor en 1789; estableció las tres ramas del gobierno estadounidense (legislativa, ejecutiva y judicial) y facultó a cada una de ellas de manera que se preservara un equilibrio de poder entre las tres. Es la legislación suprema de los Estados Unidos de América y es la constitución escrita todavía vigente más antigua que existe.

constitutional [ˌkan·stə·'tu·ʃə·nəl] **I.** *adj* constitucional; **~ law** derecho político **II.** *n iron* paseo *m*

constrain [kən·'streɪn] *vt* **1.** (*restrict*) constreñir **2.** (*oblige*) **to be** [*o* **feel**] **~ed to do sth** verse [*o* sentirse] obligado a hacer algo

constraint [kən·'streɪnt] *n* **1.** (*compulsion*) coacción *f*; **under ~** bajo coacción **2.** (*limit*) restricción *f*; **to impose ~s on sb/sth** imponer limitaciones a alguien/algo

constrict [kən·'strɪkt] *vt* constreñir

constriction [kən·'strɪk·ʃən] *n* constricción *f*

constrictor *n* constrictor(a) *m(f)*

construct [kən·'strʌkt] **I.** *n* construcción *f* **II.** *vt* construir

construction [kən·'strʌk·ʃən] *n* **1.** (*act of making or building*) construcción *f* **2.** (*building*) edificio *m* **3.** LING construcción *f* **4.** *form* (*interpretation*) interpretación *f*; **to put a ~ on sth** interpretar algo

constructional [kən·'strʌk·ʃə·nəl] *adj* estructural

constructive [kən·'strʌk·tɪv] *adj* constructivo, -a

constructor [kən·'strʌk·tər] *n* constructor(a) *m(f)*

construe [kən·'stru] *vt* interpretar

consul ['kan·səl] *n* cónsul *mf*

consular ['kan·sə·lər] *adj* consular

consulate ['kan·sə·lət] *n* consulado *m*

consulate general *n* consulado *m* general

consul general *n* cónsul *mf* general

consult [kən·'sʌlt] **I.** *vi* consultar **II.** *vt* **1.** (*seek information or advice*) consultar **2.** (*examine*) tener en cuenta; **to ~ one's feelings** considerar sus sentimientos

consultancy [kən·'sʌl·tən·si] <-ies> *n* asesoría *f*

consultant [kən·'sʌl·tənt] *n* ECON asesor(a) *m(f)*; **management ~** asesor de gestión; **tax ~** asesor fiscal

consultation [ˌkan·sʌl·'teɪ·ʃən] *n* consulta *f*

consultative [kən·'sʌl·tə·tɪv] *adj* consultivo, -a
consulting [kən·'sʌl·tɪŋ] *adj* ~ **fee** honorarios *mpl* (de asesoramiento o consultoría)
consume [kən·'sum] *vt* consumir; **to be ~d by sth** estar consumido por algo; **to be ~d by anger** estar corroído por la ira; **to be ~d by envy** estar muerto de envidia
consumer [kən·'su·mər] *n* consumidor(a) *m(f)*; ~ **credit** crédito *m* al consumidor; ~ **demand** demanda *f* de consumo; ~ **society** sociedad *f* de consumo
consumerism [kən·'su·mə·rɪz·əm] *n* **1.** (*protection*) defensa *f* del consumidor **2.** *pej* (*exaggerated purchasing*) consumismo *m*
consummate ['kan·sə·meɪt] **I.** *adj form* consumado, -a; ~ **happiness** felicidad *f* completa; ~ **skill** suma habilidad *f* **II.** *vt* **1.** (*complete*) **to ~ a marriage** consumar un matrimonio **2.** *form* (*conclude*) **to ~ a deal** cerrar un trato
consummation [ˌkan·sə·'meɪ·ʃən] *n form* consumación *f*
consumption [kən·'sʌmp·ʃən] *n* **1.** consumo *m* **2.** HIST, MED tisis *f inv*
consumptive [kən·'sʌmp·tɪv] *adj* HIST, MED tísico, -a
contact ['kan·tækt] **I.** *n* **1.** (*state of communication*) contacto *m* **2.** (*connection*) relación *f*; **to have ~s** tener contactos **3.** (*act of touching*) *a.* ELEC contacto *m*; **physical ~** contacto físico; **to come into ~ with sth** entrar en contacto con algo **II.** *vt* contactar con
contact lens *n* lentilla *f*
contact man *n* intermediario *m*
contact print *n* contacto *m*
contagion [kən·'teɪ·dʒən] *n form* contagio *m*
contagious [kən·'teɪ·dʒəs] *adj a. fig* contagioso, -a
contain [kən·'teɪn] *vt* contener
container [kən·'teɪ·nər] *n* **1.** (*vessel*) recipiente *m*; **unbreakable ~** envase *m* irrompible **2.** (*for transport*) contenedor *m*
containerize [kən·'teɪ·nə·raɪz] *vt* poner en contenedores
container ship *n* buque *m* contenedor
containment [kən·'teɪn·mənt] *n* contención *f*
contaminate [kən·'tæm·ə·neɪt] *vt* contaminar
contamination [kən·ˌtæm·ɪ·'neɪ·ʃən] *n* contaminación *f*
contemplate ['kan·tem·pleɪt] *vt* **1.** (*intend*) **to ~ doing sth** tener la intención de hacer algo; **to ~ suicide** pensar suicidarse **2.** (*consider*) reflexionar acerca de **3.** (*gaze at*) contemplar
contemplation [ˌkan·tem·'pleɪ·ʃən] *n* contemplación *f*
contemplative [kən·'tem·plə·tɪv] *adj* **1.** (*reflective*) contemplativo, -a **2.** (*meditative*) meditativo, -a
contemporary [kən·'tem·pə·rer·i] **I.** *n* contemporáneo, -a *m, f* **II.** *adj* contemporáneo, -a
contempt [kən·'tempt] *n* desprecio *m*; **to be beneath ~** ser despreciable; **to hold sth/sb in ~** despreciar algo/a alguien
contemptible [kən·'temp·tə·bəl] *adj* despreciable

contemptuous [kən·'temp·tʃu·əs] *adj* desdeñoso, -a; (*look*) de desprecio; **to be ~ of sb** menospreciar a alguien
contend [kən·'tend] **I.** *vi* **1.** (*compete*) competir; **to ~ for sth** competir por algo **2.** (*struggle*) luchar, contender; **to have sb/sth to ~ with** tener que enfrentarse a alguien/algo; **to ~ against sb/sth** contender contra alguien/algo **II.** *vi* **to ~ that...** afirmar que...
contender *n* aspirante *mf*
content[1] ['kan·tent] *n* contenido *m*
content[2] [kən·'tent] **I.** *vt* satisfacer; **to ~ oneself with sth** contentarse con algo **II.** *adj* contento, -a; **to be ~ with sth** estar satisfecho con algo; **to be ~ to do sth** estar contento de hacer algo **III.** *n* **to one's heart's ~** a más no poder
contented *adj* satisfecho, -a
contention [kən·'ten·ʃən] *n* **1.** (*disagreement*) controversia *f*; **teams in ~** grupos *mpl* rivales **2.** (*opinion*) opinión *f* **3.** (*competition*) **to be in ~ for sth** competir por algo; **to be out of ~ for sth** no tener posibilidades de algo
contentious [kən·'ten·ʃəs] *adj* conflictivo, -a
contentment [kən·'tent·mənt] *n* satisfacción *f*
contents ['kan·tents] *n pl* contenido *m*; (*index*) índice *m*
contest **I.** ['kan·test] *n* **1.** (*competition*) concurso *m*; **beauty ~** concurso *m* de belleza; **sports ~** competición *f* deportiva **2.** (*dispute*) controversia *f* **II.** [kən·'test] *vt* **1.** (*challenge*) rebatir; (*claims, a will*) impugnar; (*a decision*) cuestionar **2.** (*compete for*) presentarse como candidato a
contestant [kən·'tes·tənt] *n* (*in a match*) contrincante *mf*; (*in an election*) candidato, -a *m, f*; (*in a contest*) concursante *mf*
context ['kan·tekst] *n* contexto *m*
contextual [kən·'teks·tʃu·əl] *adj form* contextual
contextualize [kən·'teks·tʃu·ə·laɪz] *vt* contextualizar
continent[1] ['kan·tə·nənt] *n* GEO continente *m*
continent[2] ['kan·tə·nənt] *adj a.* MED continente
continental [ˌkan·tə·'nen·təl] **I.** *adj* **1.** (*relating to a continent*) continental; ~ **drift** deriva *f* continental; ~ **shelf** plataforma *f* continental **2.** (*of the mainland*) ~ **Europe** de Europa continental; **the ~ United States** Estados Unidos continental **II.** *n* europeo, -a *m, f* continental
continental breakfast *n* desayuno *m* continental
contingency [kən·'tɪn·dʒən·si] <-ies> *n form* (*possibility*) contingencia *f*; (*event*) acontecimiento *m* fortuito
contingent [kən·'tɪn·dʒənt] **I.** *n* **1.** (*part of a larger group*) representación *f* **2.** MIL contingente *m* **II.** *adj* **1.** (*liable to happen*) eventual **2.** (*dependent*) **to be ~ on** [*o* upon] **sth** depender de algo **3.** (*incidental*) **risks ~ to a profession** riesgos derivados de una profesión
continual [kən·'tɪn·ju·əl] *adj* continuo, -a

continually *adv* continuamente
continuation [kən·ˌtɪn·juˈeɪ·ʃən] *n* continuación *f*
continue [kənˈtɪn·ju] I. *vi* 1.(*persist*) continuar; **he ~d by saying that...** prosiguió diciendo que...; **to ~ to do** [*o* **doing**] **sth** seguir haciendo algo 2.(*remain unchanged*) seguir; **to ~ (on) one's way** seguir su camino; **to be ~d** continuará II. *vt* 1.(*go on*) seguir con 2.(*lengthen*) prolongar 3. LAW aplazar
continued *adj* **to be ~** continuará
continuity [ˌkan·tə·ˈnu·ə·ti] *n* 1.(*fact of continuing*) continuidad *f* 2. RADIO, TV (*between two programs*) contenido musical o hablado de transición entre un programa y otro 3. CINE, TV (*scenario*) guión *m*
continuous [kənˈtɪn·ju·əs] *adj* continuo, -a
contort [kənˈtɔrt] I. *vi* crisparse; **his face had ~ed with bitterness and rage** tenía el rostro desencajado por la amargura y la rabia II. *vt* torcer; **to ~ the truth** deformar la verdad
contortion [kənˈtɔr·ʃən] *n* contorsión *f;* **bodily ~s** contorsiones *fpl;* **a ~ of reality** una deformación de la realidad
contortionist [kənˈtɔr·ʃə·nɪst] *n a. fig* contorsionista *mf*
contour [ˈkan·tʊr] I. *n* contorno *m;* (*face*) perfil *m* II. *vt* perfilar
contour line *n* GEO curva *f* de nivel
contour map *n* GEO mapa *m* topográfico
contraband [ˈkan·trə·bænd] I. *n* contrabando *m* II. *adj* de contrabando
contraception [ˌkan·trə·ˈsep·ʃən] *n* anticoncepción *f,* contracepción *f*
contraceptive [ˌkan·trə·ˈsep·tɪv] *n* anticonceptivo *m,* contraceptivo *m*
contract¹ [kənˈtrækt] I. *vi* contraerse II. *vt* 1.(*make shorter*) contraer 2.(*catch*) **to ~ smallpox/AIDS/a cold** contraer la viruela/el SIDA/un resfriado
contract² [ˈkan·trækt] I. *n* contrato *m; ~ of* **employment** contrato laboral; **temporary ~** contrato temporal; **to sign/enter into a ~** firmar/celebrar un contrato II. *vi* **to ~ with sb** celebrar un contrato con alguien III. *vt* contratar
◆ **contract out** *vt* subcontratar
contraction [kənˈtræk·ʃən] *n* contracción *f*
contractor [ˈkan·træk·tər] *n* contratista *mf*
contractual [kənˈtræk·tʃu·əl] *adj* contractual; **~ conditions** condiciones *fpl* contractuales; **~ terms** términos *mpl* del contrato; **to be under a ~ obligation to sb** tener un contrato con alguien
contradict [ˌkan·trə·ˈdɪkt] I. *vi* contradecirse II. *vt* contradecir; **to ~ oneself** contradecirse; **everything I say you want to ~** quieres contradecir todo lo que digo; **don't ~ me!** ¡no me contradigas!
contradiction [ˌkan·trə·ˈdɪk·ʃən] *n* contradicción *f;* **a ~ in terms** un contrasentido
contradictory [ˌkan·trə·ˈdɪk·tə·ri] *adj* contradictorio, -a

contralto [kənˈtræl·toʊ] *n* MUS 1.(*voice*) contralto *m* 2.(*person*) contralto *mf*
contraption [kənˈtræp·ʃən] *n* artilugio *m; don't ask me how to use this ~* no me preguntes cómo funciona este chisme
contrary [ˈkan·trer·i] I. *n* **on the ~** al contrario; **quite the ~!** ¡todo lo contrario!; **to the ~** en contra II. *adj* contrario, -a; **to be ~ to...** ser contrario a...
contrary to *prep* al contrario de; **~ what he says** al contrario de lo que dice; **~ all our expectations** contra todo pronóstico
contrast¹ [kənˈtræst] *vt* contrastar
contrast² [ˈkan·træst] *n* contraste *m; to be quite a ~ to sb/sth* contrastar mucho con alguien/algo; **by** [*o* **in**] **~** por contraste; **in ~ to** [*o* **with**] **sb/sth** a diferencia de alguien/algo
contrast control *n* TV control *m* del contraste
contrasting *adj* contrastante
contravene [ˌkan·trə·ˈvin] *vt* contravenir
contravention [ˌkan·trə·ˈven·ʃən] *n* contravención *f; to act in ~ of the regulations* obrar en contravención de las normas
contribute [kənˈtrɪb·jut] I. *vi* 1.(*money, time*) contribuir; **to ~ towards sth** contribuir en algo; **to ~ to a fund** hacer aportaciones [*o* aportes *AmL*] a un fondo 2.(*participate*) intervenir 3. PUBL colaborar II. *vt* 1.(*money*) contribuir; **to ~ (sth) to sth** contribuir (con algo) a algo; **to ~ sth towards...** aportar algo a... 2.(*article*) escribir; (*information*) aportar
contribution [ˌkan·trɪ·ˈbju·ʃən] *n* 1.(*something contributed*) contribución *f* 2.(*money*) aportación *f;* **a ~ to a charitable organization** una contribución [*o* donación] a una institución benéfica 3.(*text or article for publication*) colaboración *f;* **a ~ for the Fall issue of a magazine** un artículo para el número de otoño de una revista
contributor [kənˈtrɪb·jə·tər] *n* contribuyente *mf*
contributory [kənˈtrɪb·jə·tɔr·i] *adj* contributivo, -a
contrite [kənˈtraɪt] *adj* contrito, -a; **~ expression** expresión *f* de arrepentimiento
contrition [kənˈtrɪʃ·ən] *n* contrición *f*
contrivance [kənˈtraɪ·vəns] *n* 1.(*act of contriving*) artimaña *f* 2.(*device*) artilugio *m* 3.(*inventive capacity*) ingenio *m*
contrive [kənˈtraɪv] *vt* 1.(*plan*) ingeniar; (*a meeting*) arreglar; (*a plan*) idear 2.(*manage*) **to ~ to do sth** ingeniárselas para hacer algo; **she ~d to make it happen** se las ingenió para que ocurriera
contrived *adj* artificial
control [kənˈtroʊl] I. *n* 1.control *m;* **to bring sth under ~** controlar algo; **to go out of ~** descontrolarse; **to have ~ over sb** tener el control sobre alguien; **to lose ~ over sth** perder el control de algo; **to lose ~ of oneself** perder el control de uno mismo 2.(*leadership*) mando *m;* **to be in ~** mandar; **to be under the ~ of sb** estar bajo el dominio de alguien

3. AVIAT estación *f* de control **4.** ~**s** TECH mandos *mpl;* **to be at the** ~**s** llevar los mandos **II.** *vt* <-ll-> **1.** (*have power over*) controlar; (*vehicle*) manejar **2.** (*restrain: anger*) dominar; (*temper, urge*) controlar **3.** (*stop: epidemic, disease*) controlar **4.** ECON, FIN controlar

control board *n* tablero *m* de mando

control center *n* centro *m* de control

control column *n* palanca *f* de mando

control desk *n* consola *f*

controllable *adj* controlable

controlled [kən-'trould] *adj* controlado, -a

controller [kən-'trou-lər] *n* **1.** FIN, ECON director(a) *m(f)* financiero, -a **2.** AVIAT **air traffic** ~ controlador(a) *m(f)* aéreo, -a

control panel *n* tablero *m* de control, panel *m* de control

control point *n* punto *m* de control

control tower *n* torre *f* de control

control unit *n* COMPUT unidad *f* de control

controversial [ˌkan-trə-'vɜr-ʃəl] *adj* polémico, -a, controvertido, -a

controversy ['kan-trə-vɜr-si] *n* <-ies> polémica *f*, controversia *f;* **to be beyond** ~ ser incuestionable

contusion [kən-'tu-ʒən] *n* contusión *f*

conundrum [kə-'nʌn-drəm] *n* acertijo *m*

conurbation [ˌkan-ɜr-'beɪ-ʃən] *n* conurbación *f*

convalesce [ˌkan-və-'les] *vi* convalecer; **to** ~ **from sth** convalecer [*o* recuperarse] de algo

convalescence [ˌkan-və-'les-əns] *n* convalecencia *f*

convalescent [ˌkan-və-'les-ənt] **I.** *n* convaleciente *mf* **II.** *adj* convaleciente; **a long** ~ **period** un largo período de convalecencia; ~ **hospital** clínica *f* de reposo

convection [kən-'vek-ʃən] *n* convección *f*

convection oven *n* horno *m* de convección

convector [kən-'vek-tər] *n,* **convector heater** *n* estufa *f* de convección

convene [kən-'vin] **I.** *vi form* reunirse **II.** *vt form* citar; (*meeting*) convocar

convener [kən-'vi-nər] *n* convocador(a) *m(f)*

convenience [kən-'vin-jəns] *n* **1.** conveniencia *f* **2.** (*practicality*) comodidad *f;* (*advantage*) ventaja *f;* **for the sake of** ~ por comodidad; **at your** ~ cuando le(s) venga bien

convenience store *n tienda que abre temprano y cierra tarde*

convenient [kən-'vin-jənt] *adj* **1.** (*handy*) útil **2.** (*suitable*) conveniente **3.** (*practical*) práctico, -a **4.** (*easily accessible*) bien situado, -a

convenor [kən-'vi-nər] *n s.* **convener**

convent ['kan-vənt] *n* convento *m*

convention [kən-'ven-ʃən] *n* **1.** (*custom*) convención *f;* ~ **dictates that** es costumbre que +*subj* **2.** (*general agreement*) convenio *m;* (*of human rights*) convención *f* **3.** (*large meeting*) congreso *m*

conventional [kən-'ven-ʃə-nəl] *adj* convencional; (*wisdom*) ortodoxo, -a; (*medicine*) tradicional

conventionally *adv* de manera convencional

converge [kən-'vɜrdʒ] *vi a. fig* converger; (*persons*) reunirse

convergence [kən-'vɜr-dʒəns] *n* convergencia *f*

convergent [kən-'vɜr-dʒent] *adj* convergente

conversant [kən-'vɜr-sənt] *adj* versado, -a; **to be** ~ **with sth** ser versado en algo

conversation [ˌkan-vər-'seɪ-ʃən] *n* (*word exchange*) conversación *f,* plática *f AmL;* **to strike up a** ~ **with sb** entablar conversación con alguien

conversational [ˌkan-vər-'seɪ-ʃə-nəl] *adj* familiar; (*tone*) coloquial; (*skills*) conversacional

conversationally *adv* en tono familiar

converse[1] [kən-'vɜrs] *vi form* **to** ~ **with sb** conversar con alguien, platicar con alguien *AmL*

converse[2] ['kan-vɜrs] **I.** *n* **the** ~ lo opuesto **II.** *adj form* inverso, -a

conversely *adv* a la inversa

conversion [kən-'vɜr-ʒən] *n* conversión *f*

conversion rate *n* precio *m* de conversión

convert[1] [kən-'vɜrt] **I.** *vi* convertirse **II.** *vt* convertir

convert[2] ['kan-vɜrt] *n* converso, -a *m, f*

converter [kən-'vɜr-tər] *n* **1.** (*person*) convertidor(a) *m(f)* **2.** ELEC transformador *m* **3.** TECH convertidor *m*

convertible [kən-'vɜr-tə-bəl] **I.** *n* AUTO descapotable *m* **II.** *adj a.* FIN, ECON convertible; ~ **sofa** sofá cama *m,* convertible *m AmL*

convex ['kan-veks] *adj* convexo, -a

convey [kən-'veɪ] *vt* **1.** (*transport*) transportar; (*electricity*) conducir **2.** (*communicate*) transmitir; **to** ~ **how...** expresar cómo...; **to** ~ **sth to sb** dar a entender algo a alguien

conveyance [kən-'veɪ-əns] *n* **1.** (*act of carrying*) transporte *m;* **these pipes are used for the** ~ **of water** estas tuberías sirven para conducir agua **2.** (*communication*) transmisión *f* **3.** (*vehicle*) vehículo *m;* **form of** ~ medio *m* de transporte **4.** LAW traspaso *m;* (*document*) escritura *f* de traspaso

conveyancing *n* LAW traspaso; (*document*) redacción *f* de una escritura de traspaso

conveyor [kən-'veɪ-ər] *n* transportador *m;* (*belt*) cinta *f* transportadora, banda *f* transportadora *Méx*

convict[1] ['kan-vɪkt] *n* presidiario, -a *m, f,* convicto, -a *m, f*

convict[2] [ˌkan-'vɪkt] *vt* condenar

conviction [kən-'vɪk-ʃən] *n* **1.** LAW condena *f* **2.** (*firm belief*) convicción *f;* **to have a** ~ **about sth** estar convencido de algo

convince [kən-'vɪns] *vt* convencer; **I'm not** ~**d** no estoy convencido

convincing [kən-'vɪn-sɪŋ] *adj* convincente

convoluted [ˌkan-və-'lutɪd] *adj* enrevesado, -a

convoy ['kan-vɔɪ] **I.** *n* convoy *m;* **in** ~ en caravana **II.** *vt* escoltar

convulse [kən-'vʌls] **I.** *vi* tener convulsiones; **to** ~ **in laughter** desternillarse de risa; **to** ~ **in pain** retorcerse de dolor **II.** *vt* convulsionar; **to**

be ~d with anger descomponerse de ira
convulsion [kən·'vʌl·ʃən] *n* **1.** (*violent
motion*) convulsión *f;* **she went into ~s** le dio
un ataque convulsivo; (*uncontrolled laughter*)
le dio un ataque de risa **2.** (*violent natural
occurrence*) conmoción *f*
convulsive [kən·'vʌl·sɪv] *adj* convulsivo, -a
coo [ku] **I.** *vi* arrullar **II.** *vt* susurrar
cook [kʊk] **I.** *n* cocinero, -a *m, f* ▸ **too many
~s spoil the** <u>broth</u> *prov* muchas manos en un
plato hacen mucho garabato *prov* **II.** *vi*
hacerse; **how long does pasta take to ~?**
¿cuánto tarda en hacerse la pasta? ▸ **what's
~ing?** *sl* ¿qué pasa? **III.** *vt* cocinar; (*meat*)
asar; **to ~ lunch** hacer la comida
cookbook ['kʊk·bʊk] *n* libro *m* de cocina
cooker ['kʊk·ər] *n* cocina *f;* **a slow ~** una olla
de cocción lenta
cookery ['kʊk·ə·ri] *n* cocina *f*
cookie ['kʊk·i] *n* **1.** (*biscuit*) galleta *f* **2.** *sl* (*person*) tipo *m;* **a tough ~** *sl* un tipo *m* duro, una
vieja *f* dura **3.** COMPUT cookie *m* ▸ **that's the
way the ~ crumbles** *inf* ¡así es la vida!
cooking ['kʊk·ɪŋ] *n* **to do the ~** hacer la
comida
cool [kul] **I.** *adj* **1.** (*slightly cold: drink, evening*) fresco, -a; (*color*) frío, -a **2.** (*calm*) tranquilo, -a; **keep ~** tómatelo con calma **3.** (*indifferent: greeting*) frío, -a **4.** *inf* (*fashionable*) **to
be ~** estar en la onda; **that outfit you have on
is really ~** la ropa que llevas mola mucho
II. *interj inf* ¡genial! **III.** *n* **1.** (*coolness*) fresco
m **2.** (*calm*) calma *f* **IV.** *vt* enfriar; **just ~ it** *inf*
¡calma! **V.** *vi* (*become colder*) enfriarse; **to ~
down** [*o* **off**] (*become cooler*) enfriarse;
(*become calmer*) calmarse
cooler ['ku·lər] *n* **1.** (*box*) refrigerador *m*
2. (*drink*) refresco *m*
cool-headed [ˌkul·'hed·ɪd] *adj* sereno, -a
cooling ['ku·lɪŋ] *adj* refrescante; (*breeze*)
fresco, -a
cooling tower *n* torre *f* de refrigeración
coolly ['ku·li] *adv* **1.** (*calmly*) con serenidad
2. (*coldly*) fríamente
coolness ['kul·nɪs] *n* **1.** METEO frescor *m*
2. (*unfriendliness*) frialdad *f*
coop [kup] **I.** *n* gallinero *m* **II.** *vt* encerrar
◆ **coop up** *vt* encerrar
co-op ['kou·ap] *n abbr of* **cooperative** cooperativa *f*
cooper ['ku·pər] **I.** *n* tonelero, -a *m, f* **II.** *vi*
(*make barrels*) fabricar barriles; (*repair barrels*) reparar barriles
cooperate [kou·'ap·ə·reɪt] *vi* cooperar; **to ~
with sb** colaborar con alguien
cooperation [kouˌap·ə·'reɪ·ʃən] *n* cooperación *f*
cooperative [kou·'ap·ər·ə·t̬ɪv] **I.** *n* ECON
cooperativa *f* **II.** *adj* cooperativo, -a; **~ society**
sociedad *f* cooperativa
co-opt [kou·'apt] *vt* **1.** (*adopt as own*) adoptar
como propio **2.** (*absorb into larger unit*) **to be
~ed into sth** ser incorporado a algo

coordinate [kouˌ'ɔr·dɪn·eɪt] **I.** *n* coordenada *f*
II. *vi* **1.** (*work together effectively*) coordi-
nar(se) **2.** (*match*) combinar **III.** *vt* coordinar
IV. *adj* **1.** (*equal*) igual (en rango/importancia)
2. (*involving coordination*) coordinado, -a
coordination [kouˌɔr·də·'neɪ·ʃən] *n* coordinación *f*
coordinator *n* coordinador(a) *m(f)*
coot [kut] *n* ZOOL fúlica *f*
cop [kap] **I.** *n inf* (*police officer*) poli *mf;* **to
play ~s and robbers** jugar a polis y cacos
II. <-pp-> *vt* **1.** (*grab*) coger; **to ~ a** (**quick**)
look at sth echar una ojeada a algo **2.** LAW **to ~
a plea** declararse culpable
copartner ['kou·ˌpart·nər] *n* copartícipe *mf*
copartnership ['kou·ˌpart·nər·ʃɪp] *n* coparti-
cipación *f*
cope [koup] *vi* **1.** (*master a situation*) aguantar
2. (*deal with*) poder con; (*situation*) enfrentarse; (*problem*) hacer frente; (*pain*) soportar
copier ['kap·i·ər] *n* copiadora *f*
copilot ['kouˌpaɪ·lət] *n* copiloto *mf*
copious ['kou·pi·əs] *adj* copioso, -a; (*amount*)
abundante
copper ['kap·ər] **I.** *n* (*metal*) cobre *m* **II.** *adj*
(*color*) cobrizo, -a
copper beech <-es> *n* haya *f* roja
copper ore *n* mineral *m* de cobre
copperplate **I.** *n* **1.** (*handwriting*) caligrafía *f*
2. (*metal plaque*) lámina *f* de cobre **II.** *adj* cali-
grafiado, -a
coppersmith *n* trabajador (a) del cobre *m*
coppice ['kap·ɪs] **I.** *n* bosquecillo *m* **II.** *vt* talar
copulate ['kap·jə·leɪt] *vi* copular
copulation [ˌkap·jə·'leɪ·ʃən] *n* cópula *f*
copy ['kap·i] **I.** <-ies> *n* **1.** (*facsimile*) copia *f;*
(*of a book*) ejemplar *m;* ART imitación *f;* **to be a
carbon ~ of sb** ser idéntico a alguien; **an
exact ~** una reproducción exacta **2.** COMPUT
copia *f;* **hard ~** copia impresa; **to make a ~**
hacer una copia **3.** (*text to be published*) original *m;* (*advertisement text*) texto *m* publicitario **4.** (*topics for articles*) tema *m* **II.** <-ie->
vt **1.** COMPUT, MUS copiar **2.** (*imitate*) imitar
III. *vi* SCHOOL copiar
copybook ['kap·i·bʊk] **I.** *adj* **1.** (*exemplary*)
modélico, -a **2.** (*unoriginal*) convencional **II.** *n*
cuaderno *m* de escritura
copycat ['kap·i·kæt] **I.** *n childspeak, inf* copión, -ona *m, f*
II. *adj* **~ version** imitación *f;* **a ~ crime** un
crimen inspirado en otro
copy desk *n* mesa *f* de redacción
copy editor *n* corrector(a) *m(f)* de originales
copy protection *n* COMPUT protección *f* contra
escritura
copyright *n* derechos *mpl* de autor; **to hold
the ~ of sth** tener los derechos de autor de
algo; **protected under ~** protegido según
los derechos de la propiedad intelectual;
~ reserved reservado el derecho de reproducción
copywriter *n* escritor(a) *m(f)* de textos publici-
tarios

coral ['kɔr·əl] **I.** *n* coral *m;* **made of** ~ de coral **II.** *adj* (*reddish color*) coralino, -a

coral island *n* isla *f* coralina

coral reef *n* arrecife *m* de coral

cord [kɔrd] *n* **1.** (*rope*) cuerda *f*, piola *f AmS;* ELEC cable *m;* **spinal** ~ médula *f* espinal; **umbilical** ~ cordón *m* umbilical **2.** (*unit of volume*) **a** ~ **of wood** carga de leña con un volumen de *128 pies cúbicos* (*unos 3,6 metros cúbicos*)

cordial ['kɔr·dʒəl] **I.** *adj* **1.** (*friendly*) cordial; (*relations*) amistoso, -a **2.** *form* (*strong*) de corazón **II.** *n* **1.** (*tonic*) cordial *m* **2.** (*liqueur*) licor *m*

cordiality [ˌkɔr·dʒɪ·'æl·ə·ti] <-ies> *n form* cordialidad *f*

cordless ['kɔrd·lɪs] *adj* inalámbrico, -a

cordon ['kɔr·dən] **I.** *n* **1.** (*line*) cordón *m;* **police** ~ cordón policial **2.** (*fruit tree*) enredadera *f* **II.** *vt* acordonar

cords *npl* pantalón *m* de pana

corduroy ['kɔr·də·rɔɪ] *n* pana *f*

core [kɔr] **I.** *n* **1.** (*center*) centro *m;* **to the** ~ *fig* hasta la médula; **to be rotten to the** ~ *fig* estar podrido hasta la médula, estar completamente corrompido; **to be at the** ~ **of a problem** llegar al quid de la cuestión **2.** (*sample of strata*) muestra *f* **3.** (*center with seeds*) corazón *m* **4.** PHYS núcleo *m* **5.** ELEC eje *m* **II.** *adj* **the** ~ **issue** la cuestión principal **III.** *vt* deshuesar

CORE [kɔr] *n abbr of* **Congress of Racial Equality** Congreso *m* de la Igualdad Racial

core subject *n* tema *m* central

coriander ['kɔr·i·æn·dər] *n* cilantro *m*

cork [kɔrk] **I.** *n* **1.** corcho *m* **2.** (*stopper*) tapón *m* **II.** *vt* **1.** (*put stopper in*) taponar **2.** (*restrain*) **to** ~ **one's anger** contener su enfado, tragarse la propia ira **3.** (*blacken*) **to** ~ **one's face** taparse la cara

corkage ['kɔr·kədʒ] *n*, **cork charge** *n* precio que algunos restaurantes hacen pagar por servir vino comprado en otro lugar

corkscrew ['kɔrk·skru] **I.** *n* sacacorchos *m inv* **II.** *adj* en espiral; ~ **curls** tirabuzones *mpl*

corn[1] [kɔrn] *n* **1.** (*crop*) maíz *m*, choclo *m AmS*, abatí *m Arg;* ~ **on the cob** mazorca *f* de maíz **2.** *sl* (*something trite*) sensiblería *f*

corn[2] [kɔrn] *n* MED callo *m* ▸ **to tread on sb's** ~ **s** herir los sentimientos de alguien

corn bread *n* pan *m* de maíz

corncob *n* mazorca *f* de maíz

cornea ['kɔr·ni·ə] *n* córnea *f*

corner ['kɔr·nər] **I.** *n* **1.** (*junction of two roads*) esquina *f;* **to cut a** ~ doblar una esquina; **to be around the** ~ estar a la vuelta de la esquina; **to turn the** ~ doblar la esquina; *fig* salir de un apuro **2.** (*of a room*) rincón *m* **3.** (*place*) **a distant** ~ **of the globe** un rincón remoto de la tierra; **the four** ~ **s of the world** todos los rincones del mundo **4.** (*kick or shot*) córner *m* **5.** (*difficult position*) **to be in a tight** ~ estar en un aprieto; **to drive sb into a (tight)** ~

poner a alguien entre la espada y la pared **6.** (*domination*) **to have a** ~ **of the market** controlar una parte del mercado **7.** (*periphery*) **out of the** ~ **of one's eye** con el rabillo del ojo; **out of the** ~ **of sb's mouth** en la comisura de los labios ▸ **to cut** ~ **s** ahorrar esfuerzos **II.** *vt* **1.** (*hinder escape*) acorralar; *iron* abordar; **to get sb** ~ **ed** *fig* acorralar a alguien **2.** ECON **to** ~ **the market** acaparar el mercado **III.** *vi* (*auto*) tomar una curva

cornered ['kɔr·nərd] *adj* acorralado, -a

corner house *n* casa *f* que hace esquina

corner seat *n* asiento *m* en la esquina

corner shop *n* tienda *f* de la esquina

cornerstone *n a. fig* piedra *f* angular

cornet [kɔr·'net] *n* **1.** (*brass instrument*) corneta *f* **2.** (*wafer cone*) cucurucho *m*

cornflakes ['kɔrn·fleɪks] *npl* copos *mpl* de maíz; **a bowl of** ~ un tazón de cereales

cornflower ['kɔrn·flaʊ·ər] **I.** *n* aciano *m* **II.** *adj* ~ **blue** azul aciano

cornice ['kɔr·nɪs] *n* ARCHIT cornisa *f*

corn poppy <-ies> *n* amapola *f*

cornstarch *n* maicena *f*, almidón *m* de maíz

corny ['kɔr·ni] <-ier, -iest> *adj* **1.** *inf* viejo, -a; (*joke*) gastado, -a **2.** (*emotive*) sensiblero, -a

corollary ['kɔr·ə·ler·i] <-ies> *n form* corolario *m*

coronary ['kɔr·ə·ner·i] **I.** *n* infarto *m* (de miocardio); **when he got the bill he nearly had a** ~ **iron** cuando le dieron la cuenta casi le da un infarto **II.** *adj* coronario, -a

coronation [ˌkɔr·ə·'neɪ·ʃən] **I.** *n* coronación *f* **II.** *adj* de coronación

coroner ['kɔr·ə·nər] *n funcionario encargado de investigar muertes no naturales*

corp. *abbr of* **corporation** sociedad *f* anónima

corporal ['kɔr·pər·əl] **I.** *n* MIL cabo *mf* **II.** *adj form* corporal; **a** ~ **oath** HIST juramento *m* a la corona

corporate ['kɔr·pər·ət] *adj* **1.** (*shared by group*) colectivo, -a **2.** (*of corporation*) corporativo, -a, empresarial; ~ **capital** capital *m* social; ~ **law** derecho *m* de sociedades; ~ **policy** política *f* empresarial

corporation [ˌkɔr·pə·'reɪ·ʃən] *n + sing/pl vb* **1.** (*business*) sociedad *f* anónima; **multinational** ~ empresa *f* multinacional, empresa transnacional *AmL;* **a public** ~ una empresa pública **2.** (*local council*) ayuntamiento *m;* **municipal** ~ corporación *f* municipal

corporation tax <-es> *n* impuesto *m* de sociedades

corps [kɔr] *n + sing/pl vb* **1.** MIL (*unit*) cuerpo *m* **2.** (*group*) equipo *m*

corps de ballet [ˌkɔr·də·bæ·'leɪ] *n* cuerpo *m* de baile

corpse [kɔrps] *n* cadáver *m*

corpus ['kɔr·pəs] <-pora *o* -es> *n* **1.** LIT (*collection*) colección *f* **2.** LING corpus *m inv* **3.** ECON capital *m*

Corpus Christi [ˌkɔr·pəs·'krɪs·ti] *n* REL Corpus *m inv*

corpuscle ['kɔr·pʌs·əl] *n* corpúsculo *m*

corral [kə·'ræl] **I.** *n* caballeriza *f* **II.**<-ll-> *vt* estabular

correct [kə·'rekt] **I.** *vt* (*put right*) corregir; ~ **me if I'm wrong, but...** corrígeme si me equivoco, pero... **II.** *adj* correcto, -a; **that is ~ form** así es

correction [kə·'rek·ʃən] *n* **1.** corrección *f;* **subject to ~** sujeto a enmienda **2.** (*improvememt*) rectificación *f*

correction fluid *n* líquido *m* corrector

corrective [kə·'rek·tɪv] **I.** *adj* correctivo, -a **II.** *n* medida *f* correctiva

correctly [kə·'rekt·li] *adv* correctamente

correctness [kə·'rekt·nɪs] *n* corrección *f*

correlate ['kɔr·ə·leɪt] **I.** *vt* correlacionar **II.** *vi* (*relate*) poner en correlación; *fig* estar en relación

correlation [ˌkɔr·ə·'leɪ·ʃən] *n* (*connection*) correlación *f;* (*relationship*) relación *f;* **there is a ~ between smoking and lung cancer** el tabaco y el cáncer de pulmón están relacionados entre sí

correspond [ˌkɔr·ə·'spand] *vi* **1.** (*be equal to*) corresponder a **2.** (*write*) cartearse

correspondence [ˌkɔr·ə·'span·dəns] *n* correspondencia *f;* **business ~** correspondencia comercial; **to enter into ~ with sb** *form* cartearse con alguien

correspondent [ˌkɔr·ə·'span·dənt] *n* **1.** (*writer of letters*) correspondiente *mf,* corresponsal *mf* **2.** (*journalist*) corresponsal *mf;* **special ~** enviado, -a *m, f* especial

corresponding [ˌkɔr·ə·'span·dɪŋ] *adj* correspondiente

corridor ['kɔr·ɪ·dər] *n* **1.** (*passage*) pasillo *m* **2.** (*land*) corredor *m*

corroborate [kə·'rab·ə·reɪt] *vt* corroborar

corroboration [kə·ˌrab·ə·'reɪ·ʃən] *n* corroboración *f;* **in ~ of sth** de conformidad con algo

corroborative [kə·'rab·ə·rə·tɪv] *adj* corroborativo, -a

corrode [kə·'roud] **I.** *vi* corroerse **II.** *vt* corroer; *fig* menoscabar

corrosion [kə·'rou·ʒən] *n* **1.** corrosión *f* **2.** *fig* (*deterioration*) deterioro *m*

corrosive [kə·'rou·sɪv] **I.** *adj* **1.** (*destructive*) corrosivo, -a **2.** *fig* (*harmful*) destructivo, -a; **~ attack** *fig* ataque *m* con malicia **II.** *n* corrosivo *m*

corrugated ['kɔr·ə·ger·ţɪd] *adj* (*cardboard*) ondulado, -a, corrugado, -a; (*iron*) corrugado, -a, acanalado, -a

corrupt [kə·'rʌpt] **I.** *vt* **1.** (*debase*) corromper **2.** (*influence by bribes*) sobornar **3.** (*document*) dañar **II.** *vi* corromper **III.** *adj* **1.** (*influenced by bribes*) corrupto, -a; **~ practices** prácticas *fpl* corruptas **2.** (*document*) dañado, -a

corruption [kə·'rʌp·ʃən] *n* **1.** (*debasement*) corrupción *f* **2.** (*bribery*) soborno *m*

corset ['kɔr·sɪt] *n* corsé *m*

cos [kas] MATH *abbr of* **cosine** cos

cosec ['kou·sek] MATH *abbr of* **cosecant** cosec

cosignatory [ˌkou·'sɪg·nə·tɔr·i] <-ies> *n* cosignatario, -a *m, f*

cosine ['kou·saɪn] *n* coseno *m*

cosmetic [kaz·'meţ·ɪk] **I.** *n* cosmético *m;* **~s** cosméticos *mpl* **II.** *adj* **1.** cosmético, -a; **~ cream** crema *f* cosmética **2.** (*superficial*) superficial

cosmetician [ˌkaz·mə·'tɪʃ·ən] *n* cosmetólogo, -a *m, f*

cosmic ['kaz·mɪk] *adj fig* cósmico, -a; **of ~ proportions** de proporciones astronómicas

cosmology [kaz·'mal·ə·dʒi] *n* cosmología *f*

cosmonaut ['kaz·mə·nɔt] *n* cosmonauta *mf*

cosmopolitan [ˌkaz·mə·'pal·ɪ·tən] **I.** *adj* cosmopolita **II.** *n* cosmopolita *mf*

cosmos ['kaz·mous] *n* cosmos *m inv*

cost [kɔst] **I.** *vt* **1.** <cost, cost> (*amount to*) valer; **to ~ a fortune** *inf* costar un ojo de la cara [*o* un riñón] **2.** <cost, cost> (*cause the loss of*) costar; **to ~ sb dearly** salir caro a alguien **3.** <costed, costed> (*calculate price*) calcular el precio de **II.** *n* **1.** (*price*) coste *m;* **at ~** a precio de coste; **at no extra ~** sin costes adicionales; **to cut the ~** recortar costes; **to defray the ~ of sth** *form* costear algo **2.** **~s** (*expense*) costes *mpl;* LAW costas *fpl;* **to cut ~s** recortar costes **3.** (*cost price*) **to purchase sth at ~** comprar a precio de coste **4.** *fig* (*sacrifice*) (**only**) **at the ~ of doing sth** (sólo) a costa de hacer algo; **at all ~(s)** a toda costa

co-star ['kou·star] **I.** *n* coprotagonista *mf* **II.**<-rr-> *vt* coprotagonizar **III.**<-rr-> *vi* **to ~ with sb** protagonizar con alguien

costly ['kɔst·li] <-ier, -iest> *adj* costoso, -a; (*mistake*) caro, -a; **to prove ~** *a. fig* resultar muy caro

costume ['kas·tum] *n* **1.** (*national dress*) traje *m;* **to dress in ~** ir trajeado **2.** (*decorative dress*) disfraz *m*

cot [kat] *n* (*camp bed*) cama *f* plegable

cot(an) MATH *abbr of* **cotangent** cot

cotangent [ˌkou·'tæn·dʒənt] *n* cotangente *f*

cottage ['kaţ·ɪdʒ] *n* **country ~** casa *f* de campo; **thatched ~** casa *f* con techo de paja

cottage cheese *n* requesón *m*

cottage industry <-ies> *n* industria *f* familiar

cotton ['kat·ən] *n* **1.** (*plant*) algodón *m* **2.** (*material*) algodón *m* **3.** (*thread*) hilo *m* de coser

cotton candy *n* algodón *m* de azúcar

cotton gin *n* almarrá *m,* desmotadora *f*

cotton-picking *adj inf* **~ fool** tonto, -a *m, f* de remate

cottonseed *n* semilla *f* de algodón

couch [kautʃ] <-es> **I.** *n* sofá *m;* **psychiatrist's ~** diván *m* **II.** *vt* expresar

couch potato <- -es> *n persona perezosa que está todo el día sentada o tumbada, normalmente viendo la televisión*

cough [kɔf] **I.** *n* tos *f* **II.** *vi* **1.** toser **2.** (*auto*) rugir **III.** *vt* **to ~ blood** escupir sangre

◆**cough up** *vt* **1.** (*bring up: blood*) escupir;

MED expectorar **2.** *sl* (*pay*) apoquinar; (*divulge reluctantly*) soltar prenda

cough drop *n* pastilla *f* para la tos

cough medicine *n* medicina *f* para la tos

could [kʊd] *pt, pp* **can²**

council ['kaʊn·səl] *n* ADMIN **city ~** ayuntamiento *m;* MIL consejo *m;* **local ~** consejo local; **the United Nations Security Council** el Consejo de Seguridad de las Naciones Unidas

council(l)or ['kaʊn·sə·lər] *n* concejal(a) *m(f)*

counsel ['kaʊn·səl] I.<-ll-, -l-> *vt* (*advise*) aconsejar; **to ~ sb against sth** *form* prevenir a alguien de algo II. *n* **1.** *form* (*advice*) consejo *m;* **to seek ~** buscar consejo **2.** (*lawyer*) abogado, -a *m, f;* **~ for the defense** abogado defensor; **~ for the prosecution** fiscal *mf* ▶ **to keep one's** <u>own</u> **~** guardar silencio

counsel(l)ing I. *n* asesoramiento *m* II. *adj* de orientación

counsel(l)or ['kaʊn·sə·lər] *n* **1.** (*adviser*) asesor(a) *m(f);* **marriage guidance ~** consejero, -a *m, f* matrimonial **2.** (*lawyer*) abogado, -a *m, f*

count¹ [kaʊnt] *n* conde *m*

count² [kaʊnt] I. *n* **1.** (*sum*) total *m;* **final ~** suma *f* final **2.** (*measured amount*) recuento *m* **3.** (*act of counting*) cuenta *f;* **to keep ~ of sth** contar algo; **to lose ~ of sth** perder la cuenta de algo **4.** LAW acusación *f* **5.** (*opinion*) opinión *f;* **to be angry with sb on several ~s** estar enfadado con alguien por varios motivos II. *vt* **1.** (*number*) contar; **to ~ one's change** contar el cambio; **to ~ heads** [*o* **noses**] contar uno por uno **2.** (*consider*) considerar; **to ~ sth a success/failure** considerar algo un éxito/fracaso; **to ~ sb as a friend** tener a alguien como amigo III. *vi* **1.** (*number*) contar; **that's what ~s** eso es lo que importa; **this doesn't ~ for anything** esto no cuenta para nada **2.** (*be considered*) **to not ~** no tener ni voz ni voto

◆**count down** *vi* hacer la cuenta atrás

◆**count on** *vt* (*depend on*) contar con, confiar en

◆**count out** *vt always sep* **1.** (*money*) contar **2.** *inf* (*leave out*) **to count sb out** no contar con alguien

countdown ['kaʊnt·daʊn] *n* cuenta *f* atrás

countenance ['kaʊn·tə·nəns] I. *n* **1.** *form* (*facial expression*) rostro *m;* **to be of noble ~** tener rasgos nobles **2.** (*approval*) aprobación *f;* **to give ~ to sth** dar el visto bueno a algo II. *vt form* aprobar

counter ['kaʊn·tər] I. *n* **1.** (*service point*) mostrador *m;* **over the ~** *fig* subrepticiamente **2.** (*person who counts*) cajero, -a *m, f* **3.** (*machine*) caja *f;* TECH contador *m* **4.** (*disc*) ficha *f* II. *vt* contrarrestar III. *vi* **1.** (*oppose*) oponerse **2.** (*react by scoring*) responder IV. *adv* en contra; **to act ~ to sth** actuar contrariamente a algo; **to run ~ to sth** oponerse a algo

counteract [ˌkaʊn·tər·'ækt] *vt* contrarrestar; **to ~ the effects of sth** neutralizar los efectos de

algo; **~ inflation** combatir la inflación

counteractive [ˌkaʊn·tər·'æk·tɪv] *adj* **1.** (*working against*) que contrarresta **2.** (*neutralizing*) neutralizador(a)

counterattack ['kaʊn·tər·ə·ˌtæk] I. *n* contraataque *m* II. *vt* contraatacar III. *vi* (*attack in return*) contraatacar

counterbalance ['kaʊn·tər·ˌbæl·əns] I. *n* contrapeso *m;* *fig* compensación *f* II. *vt* (*balance out*) contrapesar; *fig* compensar

countercharge ['kaʊn·tər·ˌtʃardʒ] I. *n* LAW reconvención *f* II. *vt* LAW reconvenir

countercheck ['kaʊn·tər·ˌtʃek] I. *n* **1.** (*restraint*) obstáculo *m;* **to put a ~ on sth** *fig* poner trabas a algo **2.** (*second check*) segunda comprobación *f* II. *vt* volver a comprobar

counterclockwise [ˌkaʊn·tər·'klak·waɪz] *adj* en sentido opuesto a las agujas del reloj

counterespionage [ˌkaʊn·tər·'es·pi·ə·naʒ] *n* contraespionaje *m*

counterfeit ['kaʊn·tər·fɪt] I. *adj* falsificado, -a; (*money*) falso, -a II. *vt* falsificar III. *n* falsificación *f*

counterintelligence [ˌkaʊn·tər·ɪn·'tel·ɪ·dʒəns] *n* contraespionaje *m*

countermand [ˌkaʊn·tər·'mænd] *vt* contramandar; MIL contradecir

countermeasure ['kaʊn·tər·ˌmeʒ·ər] *n* medida *f* en contra

counterpart ['kaʊn·tər·ˌpart] *n* contrapartida *f;* POL homólogo, -a *m, f*

counterpoint ['kaʊn·tər·ˌpɔɪnt] *n* MUS contrapunto *m*

counterpoise ['kaʊn·tər·ˌpɔɪz] *form* I. *n* contrapeso *m;* *fig* compensación *f* II. *vt* contrapesar; *fig* compensar

counterproductive [ˌkaʊn·tər·prə·'dʌk·tɪv] *adj* contraproducente

counterrevolution [ˌkaʊn·tər·ˌrev·ə·'lu·ʃən] *n* contrarrevolución *f*

countersign ['kaʊn·tər·ˌsaɪn] *vt* refrendar

countersink ['kaʊn·tər·ˌsɪŋk] *irr vt* avellanar

countersue *vt* reconvenir

counterterrorism [ˌkaʊn·tər·'ter·ər·ɪz·əm] *n* acción *f* contra el terrorismo

countless ['kaʊnt·lɪs] *adj* incontable

country ['kʌn·tri] I. *n* **1.** (*rural area*) campo *m* **2.**<-ies> (*political unit*) país *m;* (*native land*) patria *f* **3.** (*area of land*) territorio *m* **4.** MUS (música *f*) country *m* II. *adj* **1.** (*rural*) del campo; (*life, manners*) rural **2.** MUS (*music*) country

country bumpkin *n* pueblerino, -a *m, f*

country club *n* club *m* de campo

country-dance *n* danza *f* folclórica

country folk *n* + *pl vb* gente *f* de campo

country house *n* casa *f* solariega

countryman ['kʌn·tri·mən] <-men> *n* **1.** (*same nationality*) compatriota *m* **2.** (*from rural area*) campesino *m*

country music *n* música *f* country

country road *n* camino *m* rural

countryside ['kʌn·tri·saɪd] *n* campo *m*, verde *m AmC, Méx*

countrywide ['kʌn·tri·waɪd] *adj* a escala nacional

countrywoman ['kʌn·tri·wʊm·ən] <-women> *n* **1.** (*same nationality*) compatriota *f* **2.** (*from rural area*) campesina *f*

county ['kaʊn·ti] <-ies> *n* condado *m*

county fair *n* feria *f* del condado

county seat *n* capital *f* del condado

coup [ku] <coups> *n* golpe *m*

coup de grâce [ˌku·də·'gras] *n* golpe *m* de gracia

coup d'état <coups d'état> *n* golpe *m* de Estado

coupé ['ku·peɪ] *n* cupé *m*

couple ['kʌp·əl] **I.** *n* **1.** (*a few*) par *m;* **the first ~ of weeks** las primeras dos semanas **2.** + *sing/pl vb* (*two people*) pareja *f;* (*married*) matrimonio *m* **II.** *vt* **1.** RAIL, AUTO enganchar **2.** (*connect*) conectar **3.** (*link*) unir **III.** *vi* HIST aparearse

couplet ['kʌp·lɪt] *n* dístico *m;* (*rhyming*) pareado *m*

coupling ['kʌp·lɪŋ] *n* **1.** RAIL, AUTO enganche *m* **2.** (*linking*) combinación *f* **3.** (*sexual intercourse: of people*) cópula *f;* (*of animals*) apareamiento *m*

coupon ['ku·pan] *n* **1.** (*voucher*) vale *m* **2.** (*order form*) cupón *m*

courage ['kʌr·ɪdʒ] *n* coraje *m;* **to show great ~** mostrar gran valor; **to take one's ~ in both hands** hacer de tripas corazón

courageous [kə·'reɪ·dʒəs] *adj* (*person*) valiente; (*act*) valeroso, -a

courier ['kʊr·i·ər] **I.** *n* (*messenger*) mensajero, -a *m, f* **II.** *adj* **~ service** servicio *m* de mensajería

course [kɔrs] **I.** *n* **1.** (*direction*) recorrido *m;* (*of a river*) curso *m;* **to be off ~** *a. fig* desviarse; **to set ~ for sth** poner rumbo hacia algo; **your best ~ of action would be...** lo mejor que podrías hacer sería... **2.** (*development*) transcurso *m;* **over the ~ of time** con el tiempo **3.** (*treatment*) tratamiento *m* **4.** SPORTS (*area*) pista *f;* (*golf*) campo *m* **5.** (*part of meal*) plato *m* **6.** (*layer*) hilada *f* ▶ **to let sth run its ~** dejar que algo siga su curso; **to stay the ~** aguantar hasta el final; **of ~** claro, por supuesto; **of ~ not** desde luego que no **II.** *vi* correr

courseware *n* COMPUT material *m* de enseñanza informatizado

court [kɔrt] **I.** *n* **1.** (*room for trials*) juzgado *m* **2.** (*judicial body*) tribunal *m* **3.** (*playing area*) cancha *f;* (*for tennis*) pista *f;* (*for basketball*) cancha *f* **4.** (*road*) calle *f* **5.** HIST palacio *m* **6.** (*sovereign*) corte *f* ▶ **to hold ~** recibir en audiencia; **to laugh sb out of ~** reírse de alguien **II.** *vt* (*woman*) cortejar; (*danger*) exponerse a **III.** *vi* (*couple*) salir

courteous ['kɜr·ṭi·əs] *adj* cortés

courtesy ['kɜr·ṭə·si] <-ies> *n* **1.** (*politeness*) gentileza *f,* cortesía *f* **2.** (*decency*) decencia *f*

courtesy light *n* AUTO luz *f* interior

courtesy title *n* tratamiento *m* de cortesía

court hearing *n* vista *f* judicial

courthouse ['kɔrt·haʊs] *n* juzgado *m*

courtier ['kɔr·ti·ər] *n* cortesano, -a *m, f*

court-martial **I.** <courts-martial> *n* consejo *m* de guerra **II.** <-ll-, -l-> *vt* someter a consejo de guerra

court of appeals *n* tribunal *m* de apelación

court of law *n* tribunal *m* de justicia

courtroom ['kɔrt·rum] *n* sala *f* (de tribunal)

courtship *n* noviazgo *m; a.* ZOOL cortejo *m*

courtyard *n* patio *m*

cousin ['kʌz·ɪn] *n* primo, -a *m, f*

couture [ku·'tʊr] *n* FASHION costura *f;* **haute ~** alta costura

cove [koʊv] *n* GEO cala *f,* ensenada *f*

covenant ['kʌv·ə·nənt] **I.** *n* contrato *m* **II.** *vt* contratar

cover ['kʌv·ər] **I.** *n* **1.** (*top*) tapa *f* **2.** (*outer sheet: of a book*) cubierta *f;* (*of a magazine*) portada *f* **3.** (*bedding*) cubrecama *m* **4.** (*concealment*) abrigo *m;* **to break ~** salir al descubierto **5.** (*shelter*) refugio *m;* **to take ~** guarecerse **6.** (*insurance*) cobertura *f* **7.** (*provision*) suplencia *f* **8.** (*envelope*) sobre; **first day ~** sobre que lleva un sello franqueado y matasellado el primer día de su emisión **9.** MUS versión *f* **II.** *vt* **1.** (*hide: eyes, ears*) tapar; (*head*) cubrir **2.** (*put over*) tapar; (*book*) forrar **3.** (*keep warm*) abrigar **4.** (*travel*) recorrer **5.** (*deal with*) contemplar **6.** (*include*) incluir **7.** (*report on*) informar acerca de **8.** (*insure*) asegurar **9.** (*give armed protection*) cubrir **10.** MUS (*song*) versionar **11.** *sl* **to ~ one's ass** cubrirse las espaldas **III.** *vi* sustituir
 ◆ **cover over** *vt* cubrir
 ◆ **cover up** **I.** *vt* (*protect*) cubrir **II.** *vi* **to ~ for sb** encubrir a alguien

coverage ['kʌv·ər·ɪdʒ] *n* **1.** (*reporting*) cobertura *f* **2.** (*dealing with*) contemplación *f*

coveralls ['kʌv·ər·ɔlz] *npl* mono *m* (de trabajo)

cover charge ['kʌv·ər·tʃɑrdʒ] *n dinero extra que se paga en un restaurante o discoteca para cubrir algunos gastos de éstos*

covered *adj* **1.** (*roofed over*) cubierto, -a **2.** (*insured*) asegurado, -a

cover girl ['kʌv·ər·gɜrl] *n* modelo *f* de portada

covering *n* capa *f*

cover letter *n* carta *f* adjunta

covers ['kʌv·ərz] *n* mantas *fpl*

cover story <-ies> *n* noticia *f* de primera página

covert[1] ['koʊ·vɜrt] *adj* encubierto, -a

covert[2] ['kʌv·ərt] *n* (*thicket*) espesura *f*

cover-up ['kʌv·ər·ʌp] *n* encubrimiento *m*

covet ['kʌv·ɪt] *vt* desear

cow[1] [kaʊ] *n* **1.** (*female ox*) vaca *f* **2.** (*female mammal*) hembra *f* ▶ **until the ~s come home** hasta que las ranas críen pelo

cow[2] [kaʊ] *vt* intimidar

coward ['kaʊ·ərd] *n* cobarde *mf*

cowardice ['kaʊ·ər·dɪs] n cobardía f
cowardly ['kaʊ·ərd·li] adj 1.(fearful) cobarde
2.(nasty) mezquino, -a
cowboy ['kaʊ·bɔɪ] I. n 1.(cattle tender)
vaquero m, cowboy m, tropero m Arg 2. sl
(reckless driver) pirata mf II. adj vaquero, -a
cower ['kaʊ·ər] vi encogerse de miedo
cowherd ['kaʊ·hɜrd] n vaquero, -a m, f
cowhide I. n cuero m II. adj de cuero
cowl [kaʊl] n 1.(hood) capucha f 2.(hood on
chimney) sombrerete m 3.(engine hood)
cubierta f
cowling n cubierta f de proa
cowman ['kaʊ·mən] <-men> n vaquero m
co-worker ['koʊ·ˌwɜr·kər] n compañero , -a m,
f de trabajo, colaborador(a) m(f)
cowshed ['kaʊ·ʃed] n establo m
cowslip ['kaʊ·slɪp] n prímula f
cox [kaks] <-es> n, coxswain ['kak·sən] n
form timonel mf
coy [kɔɪ] <-er, -est> adj 1.(secretive) tímido,
-a 2.(flirtatiously shy) coqueto, -a
coyote [kaɪ·'oʊ·ṭi] n coyote m
coziness ['koʊ·zɪ·nɪs] n comodidad f
cozy ['koʊ·zi] I. <-ier, -iest> adj 1.(comfortable) cómodo, -a; (place) acogedor(a) 2. pej
(convenient) de conveniencia II. <-ies> n
tapadera f
CPA [ˌsi·pi·'eɪ] n abbr of certified public
accountant contable público con un certificado oficial
CPL n MIL abbr of corporal cabo m
CPR [ˌsi·pi·'ar] n abbr of cardiopulmonary
resuscitation reanimación f cardiopulmonar
CPU [ˌsi·pi·'ju] n COMPUT abbr of central processing unit CPU f, UCP f
crab¹ [kræb] n 1.(sea animal) cangrejo m,
jaiba f AmL 2. ASTR Cáncer m
crab² [kræb] <-bb-> vi rezongar
crab (apple) ['kræb·ˌæp·əl] n 1.(fruit) manzana f silvestre 2.(tree) manzano m silvestre
crabby ['kræb·i] <-ier, -iest> adj inf rezongón,
-ona
crab louse n ladilla f
crack [kræk] I. n 1.(fissure) grieta f 2.(sharp
sound: of a rifle) estallido m; (of a breaking
branch) crujido m; (of a whip) chasquido m
3. sl (drug) crack m 4. inf (attempt) intento m
▶the ~ of dawn el amanecer II. adj de
primera III. vt 1.(break) romper 2.(open: an
egg) cascar; (nuts) partir; (safe) forzar; (code)
descifrar 3.(resolve) resolver 4.(hit) pegar;
(knuckles) hacer crujir; (whip) hacer chasquear; to ~ a joke contar un chiste IV. vi
1.(break) romperse; (paintwork) agrietarse
2.(break down) sufrir una crisis nerviosa
3.(make a sharp noise) chasquear ▶to get
~ing poner manos a la obra
◆crack down vi to ~ on sb/sth tomar medidas enérgicas contra alguien/algo
◆crack up vi (laugh) reír a carcajadas
crackdown ['kræk·daʊn] n ofensiva f
cracked [krækt] adj (having fissures) rajado,

-a; (lips) agrietado, -a
cracker ['kræk·ər] n 1.(dry biscuit) galleta f
2. COMPUT crackeador(a) m(f)
crackle ['kræk·əl] I. vi (of paper) crujir; (telephone line) hacer ruido; (burning logs) crepitar II. vt hacer crujir III. n (of paper) crujido
m; (of a telephone line) ruido m; (of burning
wood) chisporroteo m
crackling ['kræk·lɪŋ] n 1.(sound: of a fire)
crujido m; (of a radio) ruido m 2.~s (pork
skin) chicharrón m
crackpot ['kræk·pat] I. n inf chiflado, -a m, f
II. adj inf chalado, -a
cradle ['kreɪ·dəl] I. n 1.(baby's bed) cuna f;
from the ~ to the grave durante toda la vida
2.(framework) andamio m II. vt acunar
craft [kræft] I. n 1.(means of transport) nave f
2.(special skill) arte m 3.(trade) oficio m
4.(ability) destreza f II. vt construir
craftiness n astucia f
craftsman ['kræfts·mən] <-men> n artesano m
craft store n tienda f de artesanía
crafty ['kræf·ti] <-ier, -iest> adj astuto, -a
crag [kræg] n peñasco m
craggy ['kræg·i] <-ier, -iest> adj escarpado, -a;
(features) marcado, -a
cram [kræm] <-mm-> I. vt meter; to ~ sth
with sth llenar algo de algo II. vi memorizar
cramp [kræmp] I. vt poner obstáculos a; to ~
sb's style cortar las alas a alguien II. n calambre m
cramped adj apretujado, -a
crampon ['kræm·pan] n crampón m
cranberry ['kræn·ˌber·i] <-ies> n arándano m
crane [kreɪn] I. n 1.(vehicle for lifting) grúa f
2. ZOOL grulla f II. vt to ~ one's neck estirar el
cuello III. vi to ~ forward inclinarse estirando
el cuello
crane fly <-ies> n típula f
cranium ['kreɪ·ni·əm] <craniums o crania> n
cráneo m
crank¹ [kræŋk] I. n inf maniático, -a m, f II. adj
a ~ call una broma [o pega] telefónica Col
crank² [kræŋk] n TECH cigüeñal m
crankcase ['kræŋk·keɪs] n cárter m (del cigüeñal)
crankshaft ['kræŋk·ʃæft] n eje m (del cigüeñal)
cranky ['kræŋ·ki] <-ier, -iest> adj inf maniático, -a
cranny ['kræn·i] <-ies> n ranura f; in every
nook and ~ en el último rincón
crap [kræp] I. <-pp-> vi vulg cagar II. n vulg
1.(excrement) mierda f 2.(nonsense) estupidez f III. adj de mierda
crape [kreɪp] n crespón m
crapper ['kræp·ər] n vulg cagatorio m, cagó-
dromo m ▶to go in the ~ sl irse a la mierda
crappy ['kræp·i] <-ier, -iest> adj sl malo, -a
crash [kræʃ] I. n <-es> 1.(accident) accidente
m; (of a car) choque m 2.(noise) estrépito m
3. COM crac m 4. COMPUT caída f (del sistema)
II. vi 1.(have an accident) chocar; (plane)

estrellarse **2.** (*make loud noise*) retumbar
3. (*break noisily*) derrumbarse **4.** com colap-
sarse **5.** comput colgarse **III.** *vt* **1.** (*damage in
accident*) chocar **2.** (*make noise*) hacer ruido
▶ **to ~ a party** colarse en una fiesta
crash barrier *n* barrera *f* de protección
crash course *n* curso *m* intensivo
crash diet *n* dieta *f* intensiva
crash helmet *n* casco *m* protector
crash-land ['kræʃ·lænd] *vi* hacer un aterrizaje
forzoso
crash landing *n* aterrizaje *m* forzoso
crash-test *vt* hacer pruebas de choque a
crass [kræs] *adj* **1.** (*gross*) flagrante **2.** (*coarse:
comment*) grosero, -a
crate [kreɪt] **I.** *n* cajón *m* **II.** *vt* embalar en
cajones
crater ['kreɪ·tər] *n* cráter *m*
cravat [krə·'væt] *n* fular *m*
crave [kreɪv] *vt* ansiar; (*attention*) reclamar
craving ['kreɪ·vɪŋ] *n* ansia *f*
crawl [krɔl] **I.** *vi* **1.** (*go on all fours*) gatear
2. (*move slowly*) arrastrarse **3.** *inf* (*be obsequious*) **to ~** (**up**) **to sb** hacer la pelota a alguien
4. *inf* (*become infested*) **to be ~ing with sth**
estar plagado de algo **II.** *n* **1.** (*go very slowly*)
arrastramiento *m* **2.** (*style of swimming*) crol
m; **to do the ~** nadar a crol
crawler ['krɔ·lər] *n* **1.** tech tractor *m* oruga
2. (*baby*) bebé *mf*
crayfish ['kreɪ·fɪʃ] *n inv* **1.** (*freshwater*) cangrejo *m* de río **2.** (*lobster*) langosta *f*
crayon ['kreɪ·an] **I.** *n* lápiz *m* de color **II.** *vt*
colorear **III.** *vi* dibujar
craze [kreɪz] *n* manía *f*
crazed [kreɪzd] *adj* de loco, -a; (*expression*)
enloquecido, -a
craziness *n* locura *f*
crazy ['kreɪ·zi] <-ier, -iest> *adj* loco, -a, tarado,
-a *AmL;* **to go ~** volverse loco
creak [krik] **I.** *vi* (*door*) chirriar; (*bones*) crujir
II. *n* (*of door*) chirrido *m;* (*of bones*) crujido *m*
creaky ['kri·ki] <-ier, -iest> *adj* **1.** (*squeaky*)
chirriante **2.** (*decrepit*) decrépito, -a
cream [krim] **I.** *n* **1.** (*milk fat*) nata *f* **2.** (*cosmetic product*) crema *f* **3.** (*the best*) flor y nata
f; **the ~ of the crop** la crème de la crème, la
crema y nata **II.** *adj* **1.** (*containing cream*) cremoso, -a **2.** (*off-white color*) de color crema
III. *vt* (*butter*) batir; (*milk*) desnatar; **to ~ coffee** añadir crema al café
cream cheese *n* queso *m* para untar
cream-colored *adj* de color crema
creamery ['kri·mə·ri] <-ies> *n* lechería *f*
creamy ['kri·mi] <-ier, -iest> *adj* **1.** (*smooth*)
cremoso, -a; (*skin*) hidratado, -a **2.** (*off-white*)
de color hueso
crease [kris] **I.** *n* **1.** (*fold*) arruga *f;* (*hat*)
pliegue *m* **2.** (*in ice hockey*) área *f* **II.** *vt* arrugar **III.** *vi* arrugarse
create [kri·'eɪt] *vt* **1.** (*produce new*) crear
2. (*produce skillfully*) posibilitar **3.** (*cause*)
causar; (*impression*) provocar; (*sensation*)

hacer; (*scandal*) motivar
creation [kri·'eɪ·ʃən] *n* **1.** (*making*) creación *f*
2. (*product*) producción *f* **3.** fashion modelo *m*
creative [kri·'eɪ·t̬ɪv] *adj* creativo, -a; (*imagination*) original
creator [kri·'eɪ·t̬ər] *n* creador(a) *m(f)*
creature ['kri·tʃər] *n* **1.** (*being*) criatura *f*
2. (*person being discussed*) individuo, -a *m, f;*
to be a ~ of habit ser un animal de costumbres; **poor ~!** ¡pobrecito! **3.** (*pawn*)
títere *m*
creature comforts *npl inf* bienestar *m*
material
crèche [kreɪʃ] *n* rel belén *m,* pesebre *m Col,
Méx*
credence ['krid·əns] *n form* crédito *m*
credentials [krɪ·'den·ʃəlz] *npl* credenciales *fpl*
credibility [ˌkred·ə·'bɪl·ə·t̬i] *n* credibilidad *f*
credible ['kred·ə·bəl] *adj* verosímil; (*witness*)
creíble
credit ['kred·ɪt] **I.** *n* **1.** (*belief*) crédito *m;* **to
give ~ to sth/sb** dar crédito a algo/alguien
2. (*honor*) honor *m;* (*recognition*) mérito *m;*
to be a ~ to sb ser un orgullo [*o* honor] para alguien; **to sb's ~** en favor de alguien; **to take
(the) ~ for sth** atribuirse el mérito de algo; **to
give ~ where ~'s due** dar el honor a quien le
corresponda **3.** fin crédito *m;* **to buy sth on ~**
comprar algo a plazos; **to give sb ~** abrir
crédito a alguien **4.** com haber *m* **5.** **~s** cine
títulos *mpl* de crédito, créditos *mpl* **II.** *vt*
1. (*believe*) creer **2.** fin **to ~ sb with 2000
dollars** abonar 2000 dólares en cuenta a alguien **3.** (*attribute*) **he is ~ed with...** se le
atribuye...
creditable ['kred·ɪ·t̬ə·bəl] *adj* **1.** (*believable*)
digno, -a de crédito **2.** (*commendable*) digno,
-a de elogio
credit card *n* tarjeta *f* de crédito
credit limit *n* límite *m* de crédito
creditor ['kred·ɪ·t̬ər] *n* acreedor(a) *m(f)*
credit rating *n* clasificación *f* de solvencia
credits *npl* cine créditos *mpl*
credit slip *n* nota *f* de crédito
credit terms *npl* condiciones *fpl* de un crédito
credit union *n* cooperativa *f* de crédito
creditworthy ['kred·ɪt̬·wɜr·ði] *adj* solvente
credulity [krə·'du·lə·t̬i] *n* credulidad *f*
credulous ['kredʒ·ə·ləs] *adj* crédulo, -a
creed [krid] *n* credo *m;* **the Creed** el Credo
creek [krik] *n* (*stream*) riachuelo *m* ▶ **to be up
the ~** (**without a paddle**) *inf* estar en un
aprieto
creep [krip] **I.** <crept, crept> *vi* **1.** (*crawl*)
arrastrarse; (*snake*) reptar; (*baby*) andar a
gatas; (*plant*) trepar **2.** (*move imperceptibly*)
deslizarse **3.** (*move slowly*) moverse lentamente **II.** *n* **1.** (*act of creeping*) deslizamiento
m **2.** *sl* (*sycophant*) pelotillero, -a *m, f,* lambis-
cón, -ona *m, f Méx,* lambón, -ona *m, f Col* **3.** *sl*
(*pervert*) pervertido, -a *m, f* ▶ **to give sb the
~s** *inf* poner a alguien la carne de gallina
◆ **creep into** *vt insep* entrar sigilosamente en

C

◆**creep up** *vi* **to ~ on sb** acercarse sigilosamente a alguien

creeper ['kri·pər] *n* **1.**(*rope*) trepador *m* **2.**BOT enredadera *f* **3.**ZOOL ave *f* trepadora

creeping *adj* progresivo, -a

creepy ['kri·pi] <-ier, -iest> *adj inf* espeluznante

creepy-crawly *n inf* bicho *m*

cremate ['kri·meɪt] *vt* incinerar

cremation [krɪ·'meɪ·ʃən] *n* incineración *f*, cremación *f*

crematorium [ˌkri·mə·'bri·i·əm] <-s *o* -ria> *n* crematorio *m*

crematory ['kri·mə·bri] **I.** *n* (*crematorium*) crematorio *m* **II.** *adj* crematorio, -a

crème de la crème [ˌkrem·də·la·'krem] *n* **the ~** la crème de la crème

crepe [kreɪp] *n* **1.**FASHION crepé *f* **2.**CULIN crêpe *f*

crept [krept] *pp, pt of* **creep**

crescendo [krɪ·'ʃen·dou] *n* crescendo *m*

crescent ['kres·ənt] **I.** *n* **1.**(*shape*) media luna *f* **2.**(*curved street*) calle en forma de media luna **II.** *adj* creciente

cress [kres] *n* berro *m*

crest [krest] **I.** *n* **1.**(*peak*) cima *f*; (*of wave, bird*) cresta *f* **2.**(*helmet decoration*) cimera *f* **3.**ARCHIT caballete *m* **II.** *vt* coronar **III.** *vi* (*wave*) encresparse

crestfallen ['krest·fɔ·lən] *adj* cabizbajo, -a

Crete [krit] *n* Creta *f*

cretin ['kri·tən] *n sl* (*idiot*) cretino, -a *m, f*

crevasse [krə·'væs] *n* grieta *f* en un glaciar

crevice ['krev·ɪs] *n a. fig* grieta *f*

crew [kru] **I.** *n* + *sing/pl vb* **1.**NAUT, AVIAT tripulación *f*; RAIL personal *m*; **ground/flight ~** personal de tierra/de vuelo **2.**(*sport of rowing*) tripulación *f* **3.** *inf* (*gang*) banda *f* **II.** *vt* **to ~ a boat** formar parte de la tripulación de una embarcación **III.** *vi* **to ~ for sb** formar parte de la tripulación del barco de alguien

crew cut *n* corte *m* de pelo al rape

crewman <-men> *n* miembro *m* de la tripulación

crewmember *n* miembro *mf* de la tripulación

crib [krɪb] *n* **1.**(*baby's bed*) cuna *f* **2.** *sl* (*home*) casa *f* **3.** *inf* SCHOOL chuleta *f* [*o* chancucho] *m Col*, acordeón *m Méx*, machete *m RíoPl*

cribbage ['krɪb·ɪdʒ] *n* GAMES juego de naipes

crick [krɪk] **I.** *n* (*in the neck*) tortícolis *f inv;* (*in the back*) lumbago *m;* **to have a ~ in one's neck/back** tener tortícolis/lumbago **II.** *vt* **I have ~ed my neck/back** me ha dado tortícolis/lumbago

cricket[1] ['krɪk·ɪt] *n* SPORTS cricket *m*

cricket[2] ['krɪk·ɪt] *n* ZOOL grillo *m*, siripita *f Bol*

cricket bat *n* bate *m* de cricket

cricketer ['krɪk·ɪt·ər] *n* jugador(a) *m(f)* de cricket

cricket field *n*, **cricket ground** *n* campo *m* de cricket

crier ['kraɪ·ər] *n* pregonero, -a *m, f*

crime [kraɪm] *n* **1.**LAW (*illegal act*) delito *m;*

(*more serious*) crimen *m;* **a ~ against humanity** un crimen contra la humanidad; **~ of passion** crimen pasional; **to accuse sb of a ~** imputar un delito a alguien; **to commit a ~** cometer un delito; **the scene of the ~** la escena del crimen; **it would be a ~** *inf* sería un pecado **2.**(*criminal activity*) delincuencia *f;* **~ rate** índice *m* de criminalidad; **organized ~** crimen organizado

crime prevention *n* prevención *f* de la delincuencia

crime-ridden *adj* con un alto índice de criminalidad

crime wave *n* ola *f* de delincuencia

criminal ['krɪm·ə·nəl] **I.** *n* (*offender*) delincuente *mf;* (*more serious*) criminal *mf* **II.** *adj* **1.**(*illegal*) delictivo, -a; (*more serious*) criminal **2.**LAW penal; **~ court** juzgado *m* de lo penal; **~ lawyer** abogado, -a *m, f* penalista; **~ record** antecedentes *mpl* penales **3.** *fig* (*shameful*) vergonzoso, -a; **to be ~ to do sth** ser un crimen hacer algo

criminality [ˌkrɪm·ə·'næl·ə·ti] *n* criminalidad *f*

criminologist [ˌkrɪm·ə·'nal·ə·dʒɪst] *n* criminólogo, -a *m, f*

criminology [ˌkrɪm·ə·'nal·ə·dʒi] *n* criminología *f*

crimp [krɪmp] *vt* **1.**(*press into folds, frill*) plisar **2.**(*make wavy*) ondular; (*make curly*) rizar

crimson ['krɪm·zən] **I.** *n* carmesí *m* **II.** *adj* **1.**(*color*) carmesí **2.**(*red-faced*) colorado, -a

cringe [krɪndʒ] *vi* **1.** *inf* (*shrink*) encogerse; **to ~ with embarrassment at sth** morirse de vergüenza por algo **2.**(*lower*) humillarse; **to ~ before sb** arrastrarse ante alguien

crinkle ['krɪŋ·kəl] **I.** *vt* (*wrinkle*) arrugar; (*wave*) ondular **II.** *vi* **to ~ (up)** (*wrinkle*) arrugarse; (*ripple*) ondularse **III.** *n* arruga *f;* (*in hair*) rizo *m*

crinkly ['krɪŋ·kli] <-ier, -iest> *adj* **1.**(*wrinkled*) arrugado, -a **2.**(*wavy*) ondulado, -a; (*curly*) rizado, -a

cripple ['krɪp·əl] **I.** *n* lisiado, -a *m, f* **II.** *vt* **1.**(*disable*) lisiar; (*machine, object*) inutilizar **2.**(*paralyze*) paralizar

crippling *adj fig* terrible

crisis ['kraɪ·sɪs] <crises> *n* crisis *f inv;* **a ~ over sth** una crisis provocada por algo; **to go through a ~** atravesar una crisis

crisis management *n* gestión *f* de crisis

crisp [krɪsp] **I.** <-er, -est> *adj* **1.**(*snow, bacon*) crujiente **2.**(*apple, lettuce*) fresco, -a **3.**(*shirt, pants*) recién planchado, -a; (*banknote*) nuevo, -a **4.**(*air*) vivificante **5.**(*sharp*) nítido, -a **6.**(*lively*) animado, -a **7.**(*quick and precise*) escueto, -a; (*manner*) seco, -a; (*style*) conciso, -a **II.** *vt* **1.**(*make crisp*) tostar ligeramente **2.**(*curl*) encrespar

crispy ['krɪs·pi] <-ier, -iest> *adj* crujiente

crisscross ['krɪs·kras] **I.** *vt* entrecruzar **II.** *vi* entrecruzarse **III.** *adj* entrecruzado, -a **IV.** <-es> *n* **1.**entramado *m* **2.** *fig* enredo *m*

criterion [kraɪ·'tɪr·i·ən] <-ria> *n* criterio *m*

critic ['krɪt̬·ɪk] *n* crítico, -a *m, f*
critical ['krɪt̬·ɪ·kəl] *adj* **1.**(*disapproving*) crítico, -a; to be ~ of sth/sb criticar algo/a alguien; **to be highly ~ of sth** criticar duramente algo **2.**(*decisive*) fundamental; **to be ~ to sth** ser de vital importancia para algo; **to be in ~ condition** *a.* MED estar en estado crítico
criticism ['krɪt̬·ɪ·sɪz·əm] *n* crítica *f*; to take ~ admitir la crítica; **I have a few ~s about what you said** tengo algunas críticas que hacer respecto a lo que dijiste
criticize ['krɪt̬·ɪ·saɪz] *vt, vi* criticar
critique [krɪ·'tik] *n* crítica *f*
croak [kroʊk] **I.** *vi* **1.**(*crow*) graznar; (*frog*) croar; (*person*) gruñir **2.** *sl* (*die*) estirar la pata **II.** *vt* decir con voz ronca **III.** *n* (*crow*) graznido *m*; (*frog*) croar *m*; (*person*) gruñido *m*
Croat ['kroʊ·æt] *n* croata *mf*
Croatia [kroʊ·'eɪ·ʃə] *n* Croacia *f*
Croatian [kroʊ·'eɪ·ʃən] **I.** *adj* croata **II.** *n* croata *mf*
crochet [kroʊ·'ʃeɪ] **I.** *n* ganchillo *m*, croché *m* **II.** *vi* hacer ganchillo **III.** *vt* hacer a ganchillo
crochet hook *n*, **crochet needle** *n* aguja *f* de ganchillo [o de croché]
crock [krak] *n* **1.**(*clay container*) vasija *f* de barro **2.** *sl* **a ~ of shit** (*nonsense*) una chorrada **3.** *iron old* ~ (*person*) carcamal *m inf*; (*thing*) cacharro *m inf*
crockery ['krak·ə·ri] *n* vajilla *f*
crocodile ['krak·ə·daɪl] <-(s)> *n* ZOOL cocodrilo *m*
crocodile tears *npl* lágrimas *fpl* de cocodrilo; **to shed** ~ llorar lágrimas de cocodrilo
crocus ['kroʊ·kəs] <-es> *n* azafrán *m*
croissant [krwa·'san] *n* croissant *m*, cruasán *m*
crony ['kroʊ·ni] <-ies> *n iron, inf* amigote *mf*
crook [krʊk] **I.** *n* **1.**(*criminal*) delincuente *mf* **2.** *inf* (*rogue*) sinvergüenza *mf* **3.**(*of elbow*) pliegue *m*; (*of leg*) corva *f* **4.**(*curve*) recodo *m* **5.**(*staff: of shepherd*) cayado *m*; (*of bishop*) báculo *m* **II.** *vt* doblar; **to ~ one's finger at sb** hacer señas con el dedo a alguien
crooked ['krʊk·ɪd] *adj* **1.**(*not straight: nose, legs*) torcido, -a; (*back*) encorvado, -a; (*path*) tortuoso, -a **2.** *inf* (*dishonest*) deshonesto, -a
croon [krun] **I.** *vt, vi* canturrear **II.** *n* canturreo *m*
crooner ['kru·nər] *n iron, inf* cantante *mf* melódico, -a
crop [krap] **I.** *n* **1.** AGR (*plant*) cultivo *m*; (*harvest*) cosecha *f* **2.**(*group: of people*) montón *m*; (*of things*) sarta *f*; **a ~ of lies** una sarta de mentiras **3.**(*haircut*) corte *m* de pelo muy corto; **to wear one's hair in a ~** llevar el pelo muy corto **4.**(*of bird*) buche *m* **5.**(*whip*) fusta *f* **II.** <-pp-> *vt* **1.** AGR cultivar **2.**(*cut*) recortar; (*tail*) cortar; (*hair*) cortar muy corto; (*plant*) podar **3.**(*graze*) pacer **III.** *vi* AGR darse; (*land*) rendir
♦**crop out** *vi* GEO aflorar
♦**crop up** *vi* surgir

crop-duster *n* avión *m* fumigador
cropper ['krap·ər] *n* agricultor(a) *m(f)*
crop rotation *n* rotación *f* de cultivos
croquet [kroʊ·'keɪ] *n* croquet *m*
cross [krɔs] **I.** *vt* **1.**(*go across: road, threshold*) cruzar; (*desert, river, sea*) atravesar **2.**(*lie across*) **the bridge ~es the river** el puente cruza el río **3.**(*place crosswise*) **to ~ one's legs** cruzar las piernas; **to ~ one's arms** cruzarse de brazos; **to ~ one's fingers** *a. fig* cruzar los dedos **4.** BIO (*crossbreed*) cruzar **5.** REL **to ~ oneself** santiguarse, persignarse **6.**(*oppose*) contrariar **7.**(*mark with a cross*) marcar con una cruz **8.**(*draw a line across*) cruzar, rayar ▶ **I'll ~ that bridge when I come to it** me ocuparé de ello cuando llegue el momento; ~ **my heart and hope to die** que me muera si no es verdad; **to ~ swords with sb** habérselas con alguien **II.** *vi* **1.**(*intersect*) cruzarse **2.**(*go across*) cruzar **III.** *n* **1.** *a.* REL cruz *f*; **the sign of the ~** la señal de la cruz; **to bear one's ~** cargar con su cruz; **Maltese ~** cruz de Malta **2.**(*crossing: of streets, roads*) cruce *m* **3.** BIO cruce *m*, cruza *f AmL* **4.**(*mixture*) mezcla *f* **IV.** *adj* enfadado, -a; **to be ~ about sth** estar enfadado por algo; **to get ~ with sb** enfadarse con alguien
♦**cross off** *vt*, **cross out** *vt* tachar
♦**cross over** *vi*, *vt* cruzar
crossbar ['krɔs·bar] *n* travesaño *m*; (*of goal*) larguero *m*; (*of bicycle*) barra *f*
crossbeam *n* viga *f* transversal
cross-border *adj* transfronterizo, -a
crossbow *n* ballesta *f*
crossbreed *n* BIO cruce *m*, cruza *f AmL*
crosscheck **I.** *n* **1.**(*verification*) comprobación *f* adicional **2.** SPORTS *en hockey o en lacrosse*, obstrucción a un rival con el stick **II.** *vt* **1.**(*verify*) volver a comprobar **2.** SPORTS *en hockey o en lacrosse*, obstruir a un rival con el stick
cross-country **I.** *adj* a campo traviesa; ~ **race** cross *m;* ~ **skiing** esquí *m* nórdico **II.** *adv* a campo traviesa **III.** *n* competición *f* a campo a través
cross-cultural *adj* intercultural
crosscurrent *n* contracorriente *f*
cross-dress *vi* travestirse
cross-dresser *n* travesti *mf*
cross-examination *n* LAW interrogatorio *m* cruzado
cross-examine *vt* contrainterrogar
cross-eyed *adj* bizco, -a
cross-fertilization *n* BIO fecundación *f* cruzada
crossfire *n* fuego *m* cruzado; **to be caught in the ~** *fig* estar entre dos fuegos
cross-grained *adj* (*wood*) de fibras cruzadas
crossing ['krɔ·sɪŋ] *n* **1.**(*place to cross*) paso *m;* **level** ~ RAIL paso *m* a nivel; **border** ~ paso fronterizo; **pedestrian** ~ paso de peatones **2.**(*crossroads*) cruce *m* **3.** ARCHIT crucero *m* **4.**(*journey*) paso *m;* (*across the sea*) travesía *f;*

the ~ **of the Alps** el paso de los Alpes

crossing guard *n persona que detiene el tráfico para permitir que los escolares crucen la calle*

cross-legged [ˌkrɔs·'leg·ɪd] *adj* con las piernas cruzadas

crossover *n* paso *m;* **a ~ of popular and classical music** una fusión de música popular y clásica

cross-purposes *npl* **to be talking at ~** estar hablando de cosas distintas

cross-reference *n* remisión *f*

crossroads *n inv* **1.** cruce *m* **2.** *fig* encrucijada *f;* **to be at a ~** estar en una encrucijada

cross section *n* **1.** sección *f* transversal **2.** *fig* muestra *f* representativa

crosswalk *n* (*pedestrian crossing*) paso *m* de peatones [*o* paso *m* de cebra]

crossways *adv* transversalmente

crosswind *n* viento *m* de costado

crosswise *adv* transversalmente

crossword (puzzle) *n* crucigrama *m*

crotch [kratʃ] <-es> *n* entrepierna *f*

crotchet ['kratʃ·ət] *n* MUS negra *f*

crotchety ['kratʃ·ə·ti] *adj inf* (*bad-tempered*) malhumorado, -a

crouch [kraʊtʃ] **I.** *vi* **to ~ (down)** agacharse; **to be ~ing** estar en cuclillas **II.** *n* **to lower oneself into a ~** agacharse

croup [krup] *n* **1.** (*rump*) grupa *f* **2.** MED crup *m,* garrotillo *m*

croupier ['kru·pi·ər] *n* crupier *mf*

crow[1] [kroʊ] *n* ZOOL cuervo *m* ▶ **to eat ~** *inf* tener que reconocer un error; **as the ~ flies** en línea recta

crow[2] [kroʊ] <crowed, crowed> **I.** *n* **1.** (*call of a cock*) cacareo *m* **2.** (*cry of pleasure*) grito *m* de alegría; (*of baby*) gorjeo *m* **II.** *vi* **1.** (*cock*) cacarear **2.** (*cry out happily*) gritar de entusiasmo; (*baby*) gorjear **3.** (*boast*) alardear; **to ~ over sth** jactarse de algo

crowbar ['kroʊ·bar] *n* palanca *f*

crowd [kraʊd] **I.** *n + sing/pl vb* **1.** (*throng*) multitud *f;* **there was quite a ~** había mucha gente **2.** *inf* (*group*) grupo *m;* **the usual ~** los de siempre **3.** *inf* (*large number*) montón *m;* **a ~ of things** un montón de cosas **4.** (*common people*) **the ~** el vulgo **5.** (*masses*) masas *fpl;* **to stand out from the ~** *fig* destacar(se); **to follow the ~** *fig* dejarse llevar por los demás **6.** (*audience*) público *m,* espectadores *mpl* **II.** *vi* aglomerarse; **to ~ into a place** entrar en tropel en un sitio; **to ~ around sb/sth** apiñarse alrededor de alguien/algo **III.** *vt* **1.** (*fill*) llenar; **to ~ the streets/a stadium** abarrotar las calles/un estadio **2.** (*cram*) amontonar **3.** *inf* (*pressure*) atosigar

◆ **crowd out** *vt* **1.** (*exclude*) excluir **2.** (*fill*) **to be crowded out** estar lleno de gente

crowded *adj* lleno, -a; **~ together** amontonados; **the bar was ~** había mucha gente en el bar

crowd-pleaser *n inf* de gusto popular; (*song*)

hit *m,* éxito *m* musical

crown [kraʊn] **I.** *n* **1.** corona *f;* **the Crown** (*monarchy*) la Corona **2.** (*top part: of hill, mountain*) cima *f;* (*of hat, tree*) copa *f;* (*of head*) coronilla *f;* (*of road*) centro *m;* (*of roof*) caballete *m* **3.** ZOOL (*of bird*) cresta *f* **4.** (*culmination*) culminación *f* **5.** (*of tooth*) funda *f* **II.** *vt* **1.** (*coronate*) coronar; **to ~ sb queen** coronar reina a alguien **2.** (*complete*) rematar; **the church is ~ed by a golden dome** una cúpula dorada corona la iglesia; **the prize ~ed his career** el premio fue la culminación de su carrera **3.** *inf* (*hit on head*) dar un golpe en la cabeza **4.** MED (*tooth*) poner una funda en

crown colony <-ies> *n* colonia *f* de la Corona

crowning *adj* supremo, -a

crown jewels *n a. fig, iron* joyas *fpl* de la Corona

crown prince *n* príncipe *m* heredero

crow's feet ['kroʊz·fit] *npl* patas *fpl* de gallo

crow's nest *n* NAUT torre *f* de vigía

CRT [ˌsi·ar·'ti] *n abbr of* **cathode-ray tube** TRC *m*

crucial ['kru·ʃəl] *adj* (*decisive*) decisivo, -a; (*moment*) crucial; **to be ~ to sth** ser decisivo para algo; **it is ~ that...** es de vital importancia que... +*subj*

crucible ['kru·sɪ·bəl] *n a. fig* crisol *m*

crucifix [ˌkru·sɪ·'fɪks] <-es> *n* crucifijo *m*

crucifixion [ˌkru·sɪ·'fɪk·ʃən] *n* crucifixión *f*

crucify ['kru·sɪ·faɪ] <-ie-> *vt* **1.** (*execute*) crucificar **2.** *fig* martirizar; **if she ever finds out, she'll ~ me** si alguna vez lo descubre, me matará

cruddy ['krʌd·i] <-ier, -iest> *adj sl* asqueroso, -a; **a ~ book** una porquería de libro

crude [krud] **I.** *adj* **1.** (*rudimentary*) rudimentario, -a; (*letter*) tosco, -a **2.** (*unrefined*) bruto, -a; (*oil*) crudo, -a **3.** (*unfinished, undeveloped*) mal acabado, -a **4.** (*vulgar*) basto, -a; (*manners*) grosero, -a **II.** *n* crudo *m*

cruel ['kru·əl] <-(l)ler, -(l)lest> *adj* cruel; **to be ~ to sb** ser cruel con alguien ▶ **to be ~ to be kind** *prov* hacer sufrir a alguien por su bien

cruelty ['kru·əl·ti] <-ies> *n* crueldad *f;* **~ to sb** crueldad con alguien; **society for the prevention of ~ to animals** sociedad *f* protectora de animales

cruise [kruz] **I.** *n* crucero *m;* **~ ship** transatlántico *m;* **to go on a ~** hacer un crucero **II.** *vi* **1.** NAUT (*take a cruise*) hacer un crucero **2.** (*travel at constant speed*) ir a una velocidad de crucero; (*airplane*) volar a una velocidad constante **3.** (*police car*) patrullar **4.** *inf* (*drive around aimlessly*) dar una vuelta en coche

cruise control *n* AUTO controlador *m* de velocidad de crucero

cruise missile *n* MIL misil *m* de crucero

cruiser ['kru·zər] *n* **1.** (*warship*) crucero *m* **2.** (*pleasure boat*) embarcación *f* de recreo **3.** (*squad car*) coche *m* patrulla

cruise ship *n* transatlántico *m*

cruising *adj* (*speed*) de crucero

crumb [krʌm] *n* 1. (*of bread*) miga *f* 2. (*small amount*) pizca *f*; **a small ~ of...** un poco de...; **a ~ of hope** algo de esperanza

crumble ['krʌm·bəl] I. *vt* 1. (*bread, biscuit*) desmigajar 2. (*stone, cheese*) desmenuzar II. *vi* (*cliff*) derrumbarse; (*plaster, stone*) desmenuzarse; (*empire*) desmoronarse; (*resistance, opposition*) venirse abajo

crumbly ['krʌm·bli] <-ier, -iest> *adj* (*bread, cake*) que se desmigaja; (*cheese*) desmenuzable; (*house, wall*) desmoronadizo, -a

crummy ['krʌm·i] <-ier, -iest> *adj sl* (*film, idea, car*) de pena; (*furniture, house*) cutre; (*place*) de mala muerte; **a ~ salary** un sueldo miserable

crumple ['krʌm·pəl] I. *vt* (*clothes, paper*) arrugar; (*metal*) abollar; **to ~ a piece of paper into a ball** hacer una pelota con un papel II. *vi* 1. (*become wrinkled: fabric, face*) arrugarse 2. (*collapse*) desplomarse

crunch [krʌntʃ] I. *vt* 1. (*in the mouth*) masticar (haciendo ruido) 2. (*grind*) hacer crujir II. *vi* crujir III. <-es> *n* 1. (*crushing sound*) crujido *m* 2. (*crisis*) momento *m* de la verdad 3. (*a sit-up*) (ejercicio *m*) abdominal *m*

crunchy ['krʌn·tʃi] <-ier, -iest> *adj* crujiente

crusade [kru·'seɪd] I. *n* 1. REL, HIST cruzada *f* 2. *fig* campaña *f*; **a ~ for/against sth** una campaña a favor/en contra de algo II. *vi* 1. HIST, REL participar en una cruzada 2. *fig* hacer una campaña; **to ~ for sth** hacer una cruzada en pro de algo

crusader [kru·'seɪ·dər] *n* 1. REL, HIST cruzado *m* 2. *fig* defensor(a) *m(f)*; **a ~ against sth** un detractor de algo

crush [krʌʃ] I. *vt* 1. (*compress*) aplastar; (*paper*) estrujar; (*dress*) arrugar; (*person*) apretujar; **to be ~ed to death** morir aplastado 2. (*grind: garlic*) machacar; (*grapes, olives*) prensar; (*stone*) triturar; (*ice*) picar 3. (*shock severely*) abatir 4. (*defeat, suppress*) aplastar; (*rebellion, revolution*) reprimir; (*opponent*) derrotar; (*one's hopes*) frustrar; (*rumor*) acallar II. <-es> *n* 1. (*act of crushing*) aplastamiento *m* 2. (*throng*) muchedumbre *f*; **there was a great ~** había una gran aglomeración 3. *inf* (*temporary infatuation*) enamoramiento *m*; **to have a ~ on sb** encapricharse de alguien

◆**crush up** *vt* triturar

crushing I. *n* aplastamiento *m* II. *adj* (*defeat*) aplastante; (*reply, argument*) contundente

crust [krʌst] I. *n* 1. CULIN, BOT corteza *f*; (*dry bread*) mendrugo *m*; **~ of the Earth** GEO corteza terrestre 2. (*hard external layer*) capa *f*; **a ~ of ice/dirt** una capa de hielo/suciedad 3. ZOOL caparazón *m* 4. MED costra *f* 5. (*deposit from wine*) poso *m* II. *vi* formar una costra III. *vt* **to be ~ed with mud** tener una capa de barro

crustacean [krʌ·'steɪ·ʃən] *n* crustáceo *m*

crusty ['krʌs·ti] <-ier, -iest> *adj* 1. CULIN crujiente 2. (*grumpy, surly*) malhumorado, -a

crutch [krʌtʃ] <-es> *n* 1. MED muleta *f*; **to be on ~es** andar con muletas 2. *fig* (*source of support*) apoyo *m*

crux [krʌks] *n* punto *m* clave; **the ~ of sth** lo esencial de algo; **the ~ of the matter** el quid de la cuestión

cry [kraɪ] I. <-ie-> *vi* 1. (*weep*) llorar; **to ~ for joy** llorar de alegría 2. (*shout*) gritar; (*animal*) aullar; **to ~ for help** pedir ayuda a gritos II. <-ie-> *vt* 1. (*shed tears*) llorar 2. (*shout*) gritar 3. (*announce publicly*) pregonar ▶ **to ~ one's eyes out** llorar a lágrima viva; **to ~ foul at sth** mostrarse indignado por algo; **to ~ wolf** dar una falsa alarma; **to ~ over spilled milk** llorar sobre la leche derramada III. *n* 1. (*weeping*) llanto *m*; **to have a ~** llorar 2. (*shout*) grito *m*; **to give a ~** dar un grito; **a ~ for help** una llamada de socorro 3. (*slogan*) lema *m* 4. ZOOL aullido *m* ▶ **to be a far ~ from sth** tener poco que ver con algo, ser muy distinto de algo

◆**cry down** *vt* 1. (*decry*) despreciar 2. (*disparage*) desacreditar

◆**cry for** *vt insep* pedir

◆**cry off** *vi inf* echarse atrás; **to ~ a deal** romper un trato

◆**cry out** I. *vi* gritar; **to ~ against sth** clamar contra algo; **to ~ for sth** pedir algo a gritos; **for crying out loud!** *inf* ¡por el amor de Dios! II. *vt* gritar

crying ['kraɪ·ɪŋ] I. *n* lloro *m* II. *adj* (*need*) apremiante; (*injustice*) que clama al cielo; **a ~ shame** *inf* una verdadera vergüenza

crypt [krɪpt] *n* cripta *f*

cryptic ['krɪp·tɪk] *adj* críptico, -a; (*comment, remark*) ambiguo, -a; (*smile*) enigmático, -a

crystal ['krɪs·təl] I. *n* cristal *m* II. *adj* 1. cristalino, -a 2. (*made of crystal*) de cristal

crystal ball *n* bola *f* de cristal

crystal clear *adj* 1. (*transparent: water*) cristalino, -a; (*image*) nítido, -a 2. (*obvious*) obvio, -a; **it is ~ (that)** está más claro que el agua (que)

crystalline ['krɪs·tə·laɪn] *adj* cristalino, -a

crystallization [ˌkrɪs·tə·lɪ·'zeɪ·ʃən] *n* cristalización *f*

crystallize ['krɪs·tə·laɪz] I. *vi* cristalizarse II. *vt* 1. cristalizar; (*plan, thought*) materializar 2. CULIN escarchar

ct. 1. *abbr of* **cent** centavo *m* 2. *abbr of* **carat** quilate *m*

CT *n* 1. GEO *abbr of* **Connecticut** Connecticut *m* 2. MED *abbr of* **computerized tomography** tomografía *f* computadorizada

cub [kʌb] *n* ZOOL cachorro *m*

Cuba ['kju·bə] *n* Cuba *f*

Cuban ['kju·bən] I. *adj* cubano, -a II. *n* cubano, -a *m, f*

cubbyhole ['kʌb·ɪ·hoʊl] *n* cuchitril *m*

cube [kjub] I. *n* 1. cubo *m*; (*of cheese*) taco *m*; (*of sugar*) terrón *m*; **ice ~** cubito *m* de hielo; **~ root** MATH raíz *f* cúbica II. *vt* 1. CULIN cortar en tacos 2. MATH elevar al cubo; **2 ~d** 2 (elevado) al cubo

cubic ['kju·bɪk] *adj* **1.**(*cube-shaped*) cúbico, -a; ~ **feet/yards** pies *mpl* cúbicos/yardas *fpl* cúbicas **2.** MATH de tercer grado; ~ **equation** ecuación *f* de tercer grado

cubicle ['kju·bɪ·kəl] *n* **1.**(*changing room*) probador *m* **2.**(*sleeping compartment*) cubículo *m*

Cub Scout *n* lobato, -a *m, f*

cuckoo ['ku·ku] **I.** *n* cuco *m* **II.** *adj inf* chiflado, -a

cuckoo clock *n* reloj *m* de cuco

cucumber ['kju·kʌm·bər] *n* pepino *m* ▸(**as**) **cool as a** ~ *inf* más fresco que una lechuga

cud [kʌd] *n* **to chew the** ~ *a. fig, inf* rumiar

cuddle ['kʌd·əl] **I.** *vt* abrazar **II.** *vi* abrazarse **III.** *n* abrazo *m;* **to give sb a** ~ abrazar a alguien

cuddly <-ier, -iest> *adj* mimoso, -a; ~ **toy** (juguete *m* de) peluche *m*

cudgel ['kʌdʒ·əl] **I.** *n* **1.**(*short thick stick*) garrote *m* **2.**(*weapon*) porra *f* **II.**<-ll-, -l-> *vt* (*with a cudgel*) dar garrotazos a; (*with a weapon*) golpear

cue [kju] *n* **1.** THEAT pie *m;* **to miss one's** ~ no salir a escena en el momento debido **2.** MUS entrada *f* **3.**(*billiards*) taco *m;* ~ **ball** bola *f* blanca ▸**to** **take** one's ~ **from sb** seguir el ejemplo de alguien; (**right**) **on** ~ en el momento justo

cuff [kʌf] **I.** *n* **1.**(*end of sleeve*) puño *m* **2.**(*turned-up trouser leg*) vuelta *f*, valenciana *f* *Méx* **3.** ~**s** *inf* (*handcuffs*) esposas *fpl* ▸**off** **the** ~ improvisado, -a **II.** *vt inf* esposar

cuff links *npl* gemelos *mpl*, mellizos *mpl AmL*, mancuernas *fpl AmC, Méx, Ven, Fili,* colleras *f Chile, Col*

cuisine [kwɪ·'zin] *n* cocina *f*

cul-de-sac ['kʌl·də·sæk] <-s *o* culs-de-sac> *n* *a. fig* callejón *m* sin salida

culinary ['kʌl·ə·ner·i] *adj* culinario, -a

cull [kʌl] **I.** *vt* **1.** ZOOL sacrificar (*de forma selectiva*) **2.**(*choose*) seleccionar; **to** ~ **sth from sth** entresacar algo de algo **II.** *n* matanza *f* (selectiva)

culminate ['kʌl·mɪ·neɪt] *vi* culminar; **to** ~ **in sth** culminar en algo

culmination [ˌkʌl·mɪ·'neɪ·ʃən] *n* culminación *f*

culottes ['ku·lats] *npl* falda *f* pantalón, pollera *f* pantalón *AmL;* **a pair of** ~ una falda pantalón

culpable ['kʌl·pə·bəl] *adj form* culpable; **to hold sb** ~ **for sth** considerar a alguien culpable de algo

culprit ['kʌl·prɪt] *n* culpable *mf*

cult [kʌlt] *n* **1.**(*sect*) secta *f* **2.**(*worship*) culto *m*

cult figure *n* ídolo *m*

cultivate ['kʌl·tə·veɪt] *vt a. fig* cultivar

cultivated *adj* **1.** AGR cultivado, -a **2.**(*person*) culto, -a

cultivation [ˌkʌl·tə·'veɪ·ʃən] *n* **1.** AGR cultivo *m;* **to be under** ~ estar en cultivo **2.**(*of a person*) cultura *f*

cultivator ['kʌl·tə·veɪ·tər] *n* AGR **1.**(*tool,*

machine) cultivadora *f* **2.**(*person*) cultivador(a) *m(f)*

cultural ['kʌl·tʃər·əl] *adj* cultural

culture ['kʌl·tʃər] **I.** *n* **1.**(*way of life*) cultura *f* **2.**(*arts*) cultura *f* **3.** AGR cultivo *m* **II.** *vt* cultivar

cultured ['kʌl·tʃərd] *adj* **1.** AGR cultivado, -a **2.**(*intellectual*) culto, -a; (*taste*) refinado, -a **3.** BIO de cultivo; ~ **pearls** perlas cultivadas

culture shock *n* shock [*o* choque] *m* cultural

cumbersome ['kʌm·bər·səm] *adj* **1.**(*unwieldy*) engorroso, -a; (*heavy*) pesado, -a; (*big*) voluminoso, -a **2.**(*awkward*) torpe

cumin ['kju·mɪn] *n* comino *m*

cumulative ['kju·mjə·lə·t̬ɪv] *adj* **1.**(*increasing*) acumulativo, -a **2.**(*accumulated*) acumulado, -a

cumulus ['kju·mjə·ləs] <-li> *n* cúmulo *m*

cunning ['kʌn·ɪŋ] **I.** *adj* **1.**(*ingenious: person*) astuto, -a; (*device, idea, plan*) ingenioso, -a **2.**(*sly*) taimado, -a **II.** *n* astucia *f*

cunt [kʌnt] *n* **1.** *vulg* coño *m* **2.** *offensive, vulg* (*despicable woman*) zorra *f*

cup [kʌp] **I.** *n* **1.**(*container*) taza *f;* **coffee/tea** ~ taza de café/té; **egg** ~ huevera *f;* **a** ~ **of flour/sugar** una taza de harina/azúcar **2.** SPORTS (*trophy*) copa *f;* **the World Cup** la copa del mundo, el mundial **3.** BOT, REL cáliz *m* **4.**(*part of bra*) copa *f;* **a C** ~ una copa de la talla 90-95 ▸**it's not my** ~ **of tea** no es plato de mi gusto **II.**<-pp-> *vt* **to** ~ **one's hands** ahuecar las manos; **to** ~ **one's hands to one's mouth** hacer bocina con las manos

cupboard ['kʌb·ərd] *n* armario *m;* **built-in** ~ armario empotrado; **kitchen** ~ armario de cocina

cupful ['kʌp·fʊl] *n* taza *f;* **a** ~ **of sugar** una taza de azúcar

cupola ['kju·pə·lə] *n* ARCHIT cúpula *f*

cur [kɜr] *n* **1.**(*dog*) perro *m* callejero **2.**(*person*) canalla *m*

curable ['kjʊr·ə·bəl] *adj* curable

curate ['kjʊr·ət] *n* coadjutor *m*

curator ['kjʊ·reɪ·tər] *n* director(a) *m(f)* (*de museo o galería*)

curb [kɜrb] **I.** *vt* (*anger, passion*) dominar; (*inflation, appetite*) controlar; (*expenditure*) frenar **II.** *n* **1.**(*control*) freno *m;* **to keep a** ~ **on sth** refrenar algo; **to put a** ~ **on sth** poner freno a algo **2.**(*obstacle*) estorbo *m* **3.**(*at roadside*) bordillo *m*, cordón *m CSur*

curb bit *n* freno *m* de las caballerías

curbstone ['kɜrb·stoʊn] *n* bordillo *m*

curd [kɜrd] *n* cuajada *f;* ~ **cheese** requesón *m;* ~**s and whey** cuajada y suero

curdle ['kɜr·dəl] **I.** *vi* cuajar(se); (*sauce*) cortarse **II.** *vt* cuajar; (*sauce*) cortar

cure [kjʊr] **I.** *vt* **1.** MED, CULIN curar **2.**(*problem*) remediar **3.**(*leather*) curtir **II.** *vi* curar; (*meat, fish*) curarse **III.** *n* **1.** MED, CULIN cura *f* **2.**(*return to health*) curación *f* **3.**(*solution*) remedio *m* **4.**(*of leather*) curtido *m*

cure-all ['kjʊr·ɔl] *n* curalotodo *m;* **a** ~ **for sth**

una panacea para algo

curfew ['kɜr·fju] *n* (toque *m* de) queda *f*

curiosity [ˌkjʊr·ɪ·'as·ə·ti] <-ies> *n* **1.** (*desire to know*) curiosidad *f* **2.** (*strange thing*) curiosidad *f* ▶ ~ **killed the cat** *prov* la curiosidad mató al gato

curious ['kjʊr·i·əs] *adj* curioso, -a; **to be ~ to see sth/sb** tener curiosidad por ver algo/a alguien; **to be ~ about sth** tener curiosidad por algo; **it is ~ that** es curioso que +*subj*

curl [kɜrl] **I.** *n* **1.** (*loop of hair*) rizo *m* **2.** (*sinuosity*) serpenteo *m* **3.** (*spiral*) espiral *f;* ~ **of smoke** voluta *f* de humo **4.** (*of the lips*) mueca *f* de desprecio **5.** (*weightlifting move*) curl *m* (*movimiento que se hace con los brazos al levantar pesas*) **II.** *vi* (*hair*) rizarse; (*paper*) ondularse; (*path*) serpentear; (*smoke*) hacer volutas **III.** *vt* (*hair*) rizar; **to ~ oneself up** acurrucarse ▶ **to ~ one's lip** hacer una mueca de desprecio

curler ['kɜr·lər] *n* rulo *m*

curling ['kɜr·lɪŋ] *n* **1.** (*of hair*) rizado *m* **2.** SPORTS curling *m*

curling iron *n* tenacilla *f* de rizar

curly ['kɜr·li] <-ier, -iest> *adj* (*hair*) rizado, -a, crespo, -a

currant ['kɜr·ənt] *n* **1.** (*dried grape*) pasa *f* de Corinto **2.** (*berry*) grosella *f*

currency ['kɜr·ən·si] <-ies> *n* **1.** FIN moneda *f;* **foreign ~** divisas *fpl;* ~ **conversion** conversión *f* de moneda; ~ **market** mercado *m* de divisas; ~ **unit** unidad *f* monetaria **2.** (*acceptance*) difusión *f;* **to enjoy wide ~** tener una amplia difusión; **to gain ~** extenderse

current ['kɜr·ənt] **I.** *adj* **1.** (*present*) actual; (*year, month*) en curso; **in ~ use** en uso **2.** (*latest*) último, -a; **the ~ issue** (*of magazine*) el último número; **the ~ craze** el último grito **3.** (*prevalent: use*) generalizado, -a; (*practice*) común **4.** (*valid*) vigente **II.** *n* **1.** *a.* ELEC corriente *f* **2.** (*tendency: of fashion*) tendencias *fpl* ▶ **to drift with the ~** dejarse llevar por la corriente; **to swim against the ~** nadar contra corriente

current affairs *npl,* **current events** *npl* sucesos *mpl* de actualidad

current expenses *npl* gastos *mpl* corrientes

currently *adv* **1.** (*at present*) actualmente **2.** (*commonly*) comúnmente

current opinion *n* opinión *f* generalizada

current rate *n* tipo *m* actual

curry[1] ['kɜr·i] **I.** <-ies> *n* curry *m;* **chicken ~** pollo *m* al curry; **vegetable ~** curry de verduras **II.** *vt* preparar con curry

curry[2] ['kɜr·i] *vt* **1.** (*groom: horse*) almohazar **2.** (*leather*) curtir ▶ **to ~ favor with sb** buscar el favor de alguien

curse [kɜrs] **I.** *n* **1.** (*bad word*) palabrota *f,* grosería *f* Col **2.** (*evil spell*) maldición *f;* **to put a ~ on sb** echar una maldición a alguien **3.** (*affliction*) **the ~ of racism** la lacra del racismo; **to be the ~ of sb's life** ser la cruz de alguien **II.** *vt* **1.** (*swear at*) insultar **2.** (*wish evil on*)

maldecir a **III.** *vi* (*swear*) soltar palabrotas; (*blaspheme*) blasfemar

cursed ['kɜr·sɪd] *adj* maldito, -a

cursor ['kɜr·sər] *n* COMPUT cursor *m*

cursory ['kɜr·sə·ri] *adj* (*glance, reading*) rápido, -a; (*check, examination*) superficial; (*remark*) somero, -a

curt [kɜrt] *adj* **1.** (*brief*) conciso, -a **2.** (*laconic*) lacónico, -a **3.** (*rudely brief*) seco, -a; (*refusal*) tajante

curtail [kər·'teɪl] *vt* **1.** (*limit, reduce: rights, freedom*) restringir; (*expenses*) reducir **2.** (*shorten*) abreviar

curtailment *n* **1.** (*of spending*) reducción *f;* (*of rights, freedom*) restricción *f* **2.** (*cutting short*) acortamiento *m*

curtain ['kɜr·tən] **I.** *n* **1.** *a. fig* cortina *f;* **lace ~** visillo *m;* **to draw the ~s** correr las cortinas **2.** THEAT telón *m;* **to raise/lower the ~** subir/bajar el telón ▶ **it's ~s for you** estás acabado **II.** *vt* poner cortinas en; **to ~ off** separar con una cortina

curtain call *n* THEAT salida *f* a escena para saludar; **to take a ~** salir al escenario a saludar

curtain raiser *n* THEAT pieza *f* preliminar

curtsey ['kɜrt·si] **I.** *vi* hacer una reverencia **II.** *n* reverencia *f;* **to make a ~ to sb** hacer una reverencia a alguien

curvature ['kɜr·və·tʃər] *n* curvatura *f;* MED desviación *f*

curve [kɜrv] **I.** *n* curva *f* **II.** *vi* estar curvado; (*path, road*) hacer una curva; **to ~ around to the left** (*path*) torcer a mano izquierda **III.** *vt* curvar

cushion ['kʊʃ·ən] **I.** *n* **1.** cojín *m* **2.** TECH colchón *m;* **a ~ of air** un colchón de aire **3.** (*in billiards*) banda *f* **II.** *vt* **1.** (*furnish with cushions*) poner cojines en **2.** (*pad*) almohadillar **3.** (*ease the effects of*) amortiguar **4.** (*protect*) proteger

cushy ['kʊʃ·i] <-ier, -iest> *adj inf* fácil; **a ~ job** un chollo

cuss [kʌs] *inf* **I.** *vi* **1.** (*swear*) decir palabrotas **2.** (*curse*) despotricar **II.** *n* palabrota *f*

custard ['kʌs·tərd] *n* ≈ natillas *fpl*

custodial [kʌs·'toʊ·di·əl] *adj* **1.** LAW carcelario, -a **2.** (*care*) protectivo, -a

custodian [kʌs·'toʊ·di·ən] *n* **1.** (*keeper, conservator*) custodio, -a *m, f;* (*of morals, of a castle*) guardián, -ana *m, f* **2.** (*of a building*) portero, -a *m, f* **3.** (*of a museum*) conservador(a) *m(f)*

custody ['kʌs·tə·di] *n* **1.** (*care*) cuidado *m;* **in the ~ of sb** al cuidado de alguien **2.** (*guardianship*) custodia *f;* **to award ~ of sb to sb** conceder a alguien la custodia de alguien **3.** LAW (*detention*) detención *f;* **to take sb into ~** detener a alguien

custom ['kʌs·təm] *n* **1.** (*tradition*) costumbre *f;* **an ancient ~** una antigua tradición; **according to ~** según la costumbre; **it is his ~ to do sth** tiene por costumbre hacer algo **2.** LAW derecho *m* consuetudinario **3.** ~**s** (*place*) aduana *f;* (*tax*) aranceles *mpl;* **to get through ~s** pasar por la aduana; **to pay ~s (on sth)** pagar derechos de aduana (por algo)

customary ['kʌs·tə·mer·i] *adj* **1.** (*traditional*) tradicional; **it is ~ to** +*infin* es costumbre +*infin* **2.** (*usual*) habitual

custom-built ['kʌs·təm·ˌbɪlt] *adj* (*car*) hecho, -a de encargo

custom clothes *npl* ropa *f* hecha a la medida

customer ['kʌs·tə·mər] *n* (*buyer, patron*) cliente, -a *m, f;* **regular ~** cliente habitual **2.** *inf* (*person*) tío, -a *m, f*

customer service *n* (servicio *m* de) atención *f* al cliente

customize ['kʌs·tə·maɪz] *vt* adaptar (según las necesidades del cliente); *a.* COMPUT personalizar

customized *adj* personalizado, -a

custom-made ['kʌs·təm·ˌmeɪd] *adj* (*clothes*) hecho, -a a medida; (*car, furniture*) hecho, -a de encargo

customs declaration *n* declaración *f* de aduana

custom(s)house *n* aduana *f*

customs officer *n*, **customs official** *n* oficial *mf* de aduana

customs union *n* unión *f* aduanera

cut [kʌt] **I.** *n* **1.** (*incision*) *a.* FASHION corte *m;* **to make a ~** hacer un corte; **the ~ of a shirt** el corte de una camisa **2.** (*gash, wound*) corte *m*, herida *f*, cortada *f AmL;* **a deep ~** un corte profundo; **to get a ~** cortarse **3.** (*action: with a knife*) cuchillada *f;* (*with a whip*) latigazo *m* **4.** (*portion*) parte *f;* (*slice*) tajada *f;* **to take one's ~ of sth** *inf* sacar tajada de algo **5.** (*part*) trozo *m;* **cold ~s** fiambres *mpl* **6.** (*decrease*) reducción *f;* **a ~ in production** una disminución de la producción; **a ~ in staff** una reducción de plantilla; **wage/budget ~** recorte *m* salarial/presupuestario **7.** CINE escenas *fpl* suprimidas; **to make a ~ in a film** cortar una secuencia de una película **8.** GAMES **who's ~ is it?** ¿quién corta? **9.** *inf* (*absence*) ausencia *f* **10.** (*swing in baseball*) bateo *m* ▶ **the ~ and thrust** el toma y daca; **to be a ~ above sb/sth** ser superior a alguien/algo **II.** *adj* cortado, -a; (*glass, diamond*) tallado, -a **III.** <cut, cut, -tt-> *vt* **1.** (*make an incision*) cortar; **to ~ one-self** cortarse; **to ~ sth open** abrir algo con un corte; **to ~ sth in half** partir algo por la mitad; **to ~ sth to pieces** trocear algo; **to have one's hair ~** cortarse el pelo; **to ~ the lawn** cortar el césped; **who's going to ~ the cards?** GAMES ¿quién corta? **2.** (*saw down: trees*) talar **3.** (*reap: corn*) segar **4.** (*cause moral pain*) herir **5.** (*decrease size, amount, length*) reducir; (*costs, budget*) recortar; (*prices*) rebajar; (*wages, workforce*) hacer recortes en **6.** (*divide: benefits*) repartir **7.** (*hollow out*) **to ~ a hole** hacer un agujero **8.** shorten; (*speech*) acortar; CINE, TV editar **9.** (*shape precisely: diamond*) tallar **10.** *inf* (*skip: school, class*) faltar a **11.** TECH (*turn off: motor, lights*) apagar **12.** MUS (*a record, CD*) grabar **IV.** <cut, cut, -tt-> *vi* **1.** (*slice*) cortar(se); **this knife ~s well**

este cuchillo corta bien; **this cheese ~s easily** este queso se corta con facilidad **2.** GAMES cortar; **let's ~ to see who starts** vamos a cortar para ver quién sale **3.** CINE **~!** ¡corten! **4.** (*change direction suddenly*) **to ~ to the right** torcer a mano derecha **5.** (*morally wound: remark, words*) herir ▶ **to ~ both ways** ser un arma de doble filo; **to ~ and run** salir pitando *inf*

◆ **cut across** *vt insep* **1.** (*take short cut*) atajar por **2.** (*transcend*) trascender

◆ **cut away** *vt* cortar

◆ **cut back I.** *vt* **1.** (*trim down*) recortar; (*bushes, branches*) podar **2.** (*reduce: production*) reducir; **to ~ (on) sth** hacer recortes en algo; **to ~ (on) costs** recortar costes **II.** *vi* CINE **to ~ to...** volver a..., retroceder a...

◆ **cut down I.** *vt* **1.** (*tree*) talar **2.** (*reduce: production*) reducir; **to ~ expenses** recortar gastos **3.** (*destroy, kill*) destruir; **he was ~ in his prime** murió en la flor de la vida **4.** (*remodel, shorten: garment*) acortar **II.** *vi* **to ~ on sth** reducir el consumo de algo; **to ~ on smoking** fumar menos

◆ **cut in I.** *vi* **1.** (*interrupt*) **to ~ (on sb)** interrumpir (a alguien); **to ~ on a conversation** interrumpir una conversación; **may I ~?** (*in dance*) ¿me permite? **2.** AUTO meterse delante; **to ~ on sb** meterse delante de alguien, cerrar el paso a alguien **II.** *vt* **1.** (*divide profits with*) **to cut sb in on sth** hacer partícipe a alguien en los beneficios de algo **2.** (*include when playing*) **to cut sb in on the game** dejar entrar a alguien en el juego

◆ **cut into** *vt insep* **1.** (*start cutting: cake*) empezar a cortar **2.** (*interrupt*) interrumpir **3.** AUTO meterse delante de

◆ **cut off** *vt* **1.** (*sever*) *a.* ELEC, TEL cortar **2.** (*amputate*) amputar **3.** (*stop talking*) interrumpir **4.** (*separate, isolate*) aislar; **to cut oneself off (from sb)** aislarse (de alguien); **to be ~ by the snow** estar incomunicado por la nieve **5.** AUTO cortar el paso a

◆ **cut out I.** *vt* **1.** (*slice out of*) cortar, recortar **2.** (*suppress: sugar, fatty food*) eliminar; **to cut a scene out of a film** suprimir una escena de una película; **to cut sb out of one's will** desheredar a alguien **3.** *inf* (*stop*) dejar; **to ~ smoking** dejar de fumar; **~ all this nonsense** ¡déjate de tonterías!; **cut it out!** ¡basta ya! **II.** *vi* TECH (*engine*) pararse; (*machine*) apagarse

◆ **cut short** *vt* acortar

◆ **cut up I.** *vt* **1.** (*slice into pieces*) cortar en pedazos; (*meat*) trinchar **2.** (*hurt*) herir; **to be badly ~** tener heridas graves **II.** *vi* (*to clown*) payasear

cut-and-dried [ˌkʌt·ən·ˈdraɪd] *adj* **1.** (*fixed in advance*) decidido, -a de antemano **2.** (*not original*) preparado, -a de antemano; (*idea*) preconcebido, -a

cut-and-paste [ˌkʌt·ənd·ˈpeɪst] *adj a.* COMPUT de cortar y pegar

cutback ['kʌt·bæk] *n* **1.** (*reduction*) reducción

f; ~ **in expenditures** recorte *m* de los gastos **2.** CINE flashback *m*

cute [kjut] *adj* **1.** (*sweet: baby*) mono, -a *inf* **2.** (*remark, idea*) ingenioso, -a

cutey ['kju·ţi] <-ies> *n inf s.* **cutie**

cuticle ['kju·ţə·kəl] *n* cutícula *f*

cutie ['kju·ţi] *n inf* (*woman*) bombón *m;* (*child*) monada *f*

cutlass ['kʌt·ləs] <-es> *n* MIL alfanje *m*

cutlery ['kʌt·lə·ri] *n* cubiertos *fpl*

cutlet ['kʌt·lɪt] *n* chuleta *f*

cutoff ['kʌţ·ɔf] *n* **1.** TECH corte *m,* cierre *m;* ~ **date** fecha *f* límite; ~ **point** tope *m* **2.** (*end of supply*) corte *m* del suministro **3.** (*baseball player*) **to hit the** ~ pasar la bola al cortador

cutout *n* **1.** (*design prepared for cutting*) recortable *m* **2.** ELEC cortacircuitos *m inv* **3.** TECH válvula *f* de escape

cut-rate *adj* rebajado, -a

cutter ['kʌt·ər] *n* **1.** (*tool which cuts*) cúter *m,* cuchilla *f;* (*for metal*) cizalla *f;* (*for glass*) diamante *m* **2.** (*person*) cortador(a) *m(f);* (*of precious stones*) tallista *mf* **3.** NAUT cúter *m*

cutthroat ['kʌt·θroʊt] I. *n* **1.** (*murderer*) asesino, -a *m, f* **2.** (*razor*) navaja *f* barbera II. *adj* salvaje; (*competition*) feroz

cutting ['kʌţ·ɪŋ] I. *n* **1.** (*act*) corte *m* **2.** (*piece*) recorte *m;* (*of cloth*) retal *m* **3.** BOT esqueje *m,* gajo *m* Arg **4.** (*for road, railway*) zanja *f* **5.** CINE montaje *m* II. *adj* (*blade*) cortante; *fig* (*remark, comment*) hiriente

cutting-edge *adj* puntero, -a

cuttlefish ['kʌţ·əl·fɪʃ] *n inv* sepia *f*

cyanide ['saɪ·ə·naɪd] *n* cianuro *m*

cybercafé ['saɪ·bər·kæˌfeɪ] *n* cibercafé *m*

cybercash ['saɪ·bərˌkæʃ] *n* dinero *m* electrónico

cybernaut [ˌsaɪ·bər·'nɔt] *n* cibernauta *mf*

cybernetics [ˌsaɪ·bər·'neţ·ɪks] *n* + *sing vb* cibernética *f*

cybersex ['saɪ·bər·seks] *n* cibersexo *m*

cyberspace *n* ciberespacio *m*

cyclamen ['saɪ·klə·mən] *n* BOT ciclamen *m*

cycle[1] ['saɪ·kəl] I. *n* bicicleta *f* II. *vi* ir en bicicleta

cycle[2] ['saɪ·kəl] *n* **1.** (*of life, seasons*) ciclo *m* **2.** ASTR órbita *f*

cyclic ['saɪ·klɪk] *adj,* **cyclical** *adj* cíclico, -a

cycling I. *n* SPORTS ciclismo *m* II. *adj* ~ **shorts** culotte *m*

cyclist ['saɪ·klɪst] *n* SPORTS ciclista *mf*

cyclone ['saɪ·kloʊn] *n* METEO ciclón *m*

cygnet ['sɪg·nɪt] *n* pollo *m* de cisne

cylinder ['sɪl·ɪn·dər] *n* **1.** MATH, AUTO, TECH cilindro *m* **2.** (*container: of gas*) bombona *f,* garrafa *f* Arg, Urug; (*of water*) tanque *m*

cylinder block *n* TECH bloque *m* de cilindros

cylinder capacity *n* TECH cilindrada *f*

cylinder head *n* TECH culata *f*

cylindrical [sɪ·'lɪn·drɪ·kəl] *adj* cilíndrico, -a

cymbal ['sɪm·bəl] *n* MUS platillo *m*

cynic ['sɪn·ɪk] I. *n* cínico -a *m, f,* valemadrista *mf* Méx II. *adj* cínico, -a, valemadrista *Méx*

cynical ['sɪn·ɪ·kəl] *adj* cínico, -a

cynicism ['sɪn·ɪ·sɪzˌəm] *n* cinismo *m*

cypress ['saɪ·prəs] <-es> *n* ciprés *m*

Cypriot ['sɪp·ri·ət] I. *adj* chipriota II. *n* chipriota *mf*

Cyprus ['saɪ·prəs] *n* GEO Chipre *m*

cyst [sɪst] *n* MED quiste *m*

cystitis [sɪ·'staɪ·ţɪs] *n* MED cistitis *f inv*

czar [zar] *n* zar *m*

czarina [za·'ri·nə] *n* zarina *f*

Czech [tʃek] I. *n* **1.** (*person*) checo, -a *m, f* **2.** (*language*) checo *m* II. *adj* checo, -a

Czech Republic *n* República *f* Checa

D

D, d [di] *n* **1.** (*letter*) D, d *f;* ~ **as in Delta** D de Dolores **2.** MUS re *m* **3.** *s.* **day** día *m*

d *abbr of* **diameter** d

d. **1.** *abbr of* **date** fecha *f* **2.** *abbr of* **died** m.

DA [ˌdi·'eɪ] *n abbr of* **District Attorney** fiscal *mf* del distrito

dab [dæb] I. <-bb-> *vt* tocar ligeramente II. <-bb-> *vi* to ~ **at sth** dar ligeros toques a algo III. *n* **1.** (*pat*) toque *m;* **to give sth a** ~ (**with sth**) dar a algo un toque (de algo) **2.** (*tiny bit*) pizca *f;* (*of liquid*) gota *f;* **a** ~ **of paint** un toque de pintura

dabble ['dæb·əl] I. <-ling> *vi* **1.** (*play in water*) chapotear **2.** (*work*) **to** ~ **in sth** interesarse superficialmente por algo II. <-ling> *vt* salpicar; **to** ~ **sth** (**in sth**) mojar algo (en algo)

dad [dæd] *n inf* papá *m*

daddy ['dæd·i] *n childspeak, inf* papaíto *m,* tata *m AmL*

daddy longlegs [ˌdæd·i·'lɔŋ·legz] *n* segador *m*

daemon ['di·mən] *n* COMPUT demonio *m*

daffodil ['dæf·ə·dɪl] *n* narciso *m*

dagger ['dægər] *n* puñal *m* ▶ **to look** ~**s at sb** fulminar a alguien con la mirada

dahlia ['dæl·jə] *n* dalia *f*

daily ['deɪ·li] I. *adj* diario, -a; **on a** ~ **basis** por días; **to earn one's** ~ **bread** *inf* ganarse el pan II. *adv* a diario; **twice** ~ dos veces al día III. <-ies> *n* PUBL diario *m*

daintiness *n* **1.** (*delicacy*) delicadeza *f* **2.** (*affectation*) remilgos *mpl*

dainty ['deɪn·ti] <-ier, -iest> *adj* **1.** (*delicate: flowers, painting*) delicado, -a; (*manners*) refinado, -a **2.** (*delicious*) exquisito, -a **3.** (*scrupulous*) escrupuloso, -a **4.** (*affected*) remilgado, -a

dairy ['der·i] I. *n* **1.** (*farm*) vaquería *f,* tambo *m* Arg **2.** (*shop*) lechería *f* II. *adj* **1.** (*made from milk*) lácteo, -a **2.** (*producing milk*) lechero, -a; (*farm, herd*) de vacas; ~ **industry** industria láctea

dairy cattle *npl* vacas *fpl* lecheras
dairy farm *n* vaquería *f*, tambo *m Arg*
dairyman *n* lechero *m*
dairy products *npl* productos *mpl* lácteos
dais ['deɪ·ɪs] *n* ARCHIT tarima *f*
daisy ['deɪ·zi] <-ies> *n* margarita *f* ▸ **to feel as fresh as a ~** sentirse tan fresco como una rosa; **to be pushing up daisies** *sl* criar malvas
daisy wheel *n* margarita *f;* **~ printer** impresora *f* de margarita
dally ['dæl·i] <-ie-> *vi* 1. (*dawdle*) perder el tiempo; **to ~ around** entretenerse; **to ~ over sth** perder el tiempo haciendo algo 2. (*play*) jugar; **to ~ with sb/sth** coquetear con alguien/algo; **to ~ with an idea** dar vueltas a una idea
dam [dæm] I. *n* 1. (*barrier*) presa *f* 2. (*reservoir*) embalse *m* II.<-mm-> *vt* (*river*) represar; *fig* (*emotions, feelings*) contener
damage ['dæm·ɪdʒ] I. *vt* 1. (*harm, hurt: building, objects, environment*) dañar; (*health, reputation*) perjudicar; **to be badly ~d** sufrir daños de consideración 2. (*ruin*) estropear II. *n* 1. (*harm: to objects*) daño *m;* (*to pride, reputation*) perjuicio *m;* **to do ~ to sb/sth** hacer daño a alguien/dañar algo; **to cause serious ~ to sb's reputation** perjudicar seriamente la reputación de alguien 2. *pl* LAW daños *mpl* y perjuicios ▸ **the ~ is done** *inf* el daño ya está hecho; **what's the ~?** *inf* ¿qué se debe?
damage control *n* POL *táctica para minimizar el impacto negativo de una decisión*
Damascus [də·'mæs·kəs] *n* Damasco *m*
damask ['dæm·əsk] I. *n* damasco *m* II. *adj* de damasco
dame [deɪm] *n pej, sl* (*woman*) tía *f*, tipa *f AmL*
damn [dæm] *sl* I. *interj* mierda II. *adj* (*expressing irritation*) maldito, -a; **to be a ~ fool** ser tonto de remate III. *vt* 1. (*expressing irritation*) (**God** *vulg*) **~ it!** ¡me cago en la puta!; **~ him! he took my bike without asking!** ¡ese idiota se ha llevado mi bicicleta sin pedirme permiso! 2. REL condenar ▸ **well, I'll be ~ed!** ¡mecachis!, ¡caramba!; **I'll be ~ed if I know** que me cuelguen si lo sé IV. *adv* muy; **to be ~ lucky** tener una suerte increíble; **you know ~ well that...** sabes perfectamente que... V. *n* **I don't give a ~ what he says!** ¡me importa un comino lo que diga!
damnable ['dæm·nə·bəl] *adj sl* maldito, -a, puto, -a *argot*
damnation [dæm·'neɪ·ʃən] I. *n* condenación *f* II. *interj* ¡maldición!
damned I. *adj sl* 1. (*expressing irritation*) maldito, -a 2. (*for emphasis*) puto, -a *vulg* II. *npl* REL **the ~** los condenados
damning *adj* **~ evidence** prueba *f* irrecusable
damp [dæmp] I. *adj* húmedo, -a II. *vt* 1. (*moisten*) humedecer 2. *a. fig* PHYS, TECH amortiguar; MUS (*sound*) apagar 3. (*extinguish*) **to ~** (**down**) (*flames, fire*) sofocar; (*enthusiasm*) enfriar; **to ~ down sb's spirits** desalen-

tar a alguien
dampen ['dæm·pən] *vt* 1. (*make wet*) humedecer 2. (*lessen*) desanimar; **to ~ sb's enthusiasm** apagar el entusiasmo de alguien; **to ~ sb's expectations** frustrar las esperanzas de alguien 3. *a. fig* PHYS, TECH amortiguar; MUS (*sound*) apagar
damper ['dæm·pər] *n* 1. (*on fireplace*) regulador *m* de tiro 2. *inf* gafe *m;* **to put a ~ on things** aguar la fiesta; **to put a ~ on sb's enthusiasm** apagar el entusiasmo de uno
dampness *n* humedad *f*
dance [dæns] I.<-cing> *vi* 1. (*move to music*) bailar; **to ~ to sth** bailar al compás de algo; **shall we ~?** ¿bailas?; **to go dancing** ir a bailar 2. (*move energetically*) saltar; **to ~ with joy** dar saltos de alegría 3. (*twinkle*) **his eyes ~d with pleasure** sus ojos brillaban de placer 4. (*bob*) agitarse; **the daffodils were dancing in the breeze** los narcisos se mecían con la brisa ▸ **to ~ to sb's tune** estar a las órdenes de alguien *fig* II.<-cing> *vt* bailar; **to ~ the night away** bailar toda la noche III. *n* baile *m;* **to have a ~ with sb** bailar con alguien; **the band played a slow ~** la orquesta tocaba una (canción) lenta
dance band *n* orquesta *f* de baile
dance music *n* música *f* de baile
dancer ['dæn·sər] *n* bailarín, -ina *m, f*
dancing *n* baile *m*
dancing partner *n* pareja *f* de baile
dancing shoes *npl* zapatillas *fpl* de baile
dandelion ['dæn·də·laɪ·ən] *n* BOT diente *m* de león
dandruff ['dæn·drəf] *n* caspa *f*
dandy ['dæn·di] I.<-ies> *n* dandi *m* II.<-ier, -iest> *adj* estupendo, -a
Dane [deɪn] *n* danés, -esa *m, f*
danger ['deɪn·dʒər] *n* 1. (*peril*) peligro *m;* **to be in ~** correr peligro; **to be out of ~** estar fuera de peligro; **a ~ to sth/sb** un peligro para algo/alguien; **there's no ~ of him knowing that** no hay peligro de que lo sepa 2. (*perilous aspect*) riesgo *m;* **the ~s of sth** los peligros de algo
dangerous ['deɪn·dʒər·əs] *adj* peligroso, -a, riesgoso, -a *AmL*
danger pay *n* plus *m* de peligrosidad
danger zone *n* zona *f* peligrosa
dangle ['dæn·gəl] I.<-ling> *vi* 1. (*hang down*) colgar; **to ~ from sth** colgar de algo 2. (*follow*) **to ~ after sb** ir detrás de alguien II.<-ling> *vt* 1. (*cause to hang down*) hacer oscilar 2. (*tempt with*) **to ~ sth in front of sb** tentar a alguien con algo
Danish ['deɪ·nɪʃ] I. *adj* danés, -esa II. *n* 1. (*person*) danés, -esa *m, f* 2. LING danés *m* 3. CULIN **~** (**pastry**) *pastelito cubierto de azúcar glaseado o fruta*
dank [dæŋk] *adj* (*air, building*) húmedo, -a
Danube ['dæn·jub] *n* GEO Danubio *m*
dapper ['dæp·ər] *adj* (*man*) atildado, -a; **a ~ appearance** un aspecto pulcro

dapple ['dæp·əl] *vt* motear

dare [der] I.<-ring> *vt* 1.(*risk doing*) atreverse a, intentar 2.(*challenge*) desafiar; **to ~ sb** (**to do sth**) retar a alguien (a hacer algo) II.<-ring> *vi* (*risk doing*) atreverse; **to ~ to do sth** atreverse a hacer algo; **I don't ~ go there** no me atrevo a ir; **just you ~!** ¡atrévete y verás!; **how ~ you...** ¿cómo te atreves a...?, ¿cómo osas...? ▶ **don't you ~!** ¡ni se te ocurra! III. *n* desafío *m;* **to take a ~** aceptar un reto

daredevil ['der·ˌdev·əl] *inf* I. *n* balarrasa *mf* II. *adj* temerario, -a

daresay ['der·seɪ] *vt* suponer; **I ~** (**you're right**) me lo imagino

daring ['der·ɪŋ] I. *adj* 1.(*courageous*) temerario, -a 2.(*provocative: dress*) atrevido, -a II. *n* osadía *f*

dark [dark] I. *adj* 1.(*without light, black*) oscuro, -a; (*coffee*) solo, negro; **~ blue** azul oscuro; **~ chocolate** chocolate *m* negro 2.(*not pale: complexion, hair*) moreno, -a 3.(*tragic, depressing*) sombrío, -a; **a ~ chapter** un capítulo oscuro; **to have a ~ side** tener un lado oscuro; **to look on the ~ side of things** ver el lado malo de las cosas 4.(*evil*) tenebroso, -a 5.(*unknown, secret*) oculto, -a; **the ~ side of sth** la cara oculta de algo II. *n* 1.(*darkness*) oscuridad *f;* **to be in the ~** estar a oscuras; **to be afraid of the ~** tener miedo a la oscuridad 2.(*time of day*) **at ~** al caer la noche; **to do sth before/after ~** hacer algo antes/después de que anochezca ▶ **to keep sb in the ~ about sth** ocultar algo a alguien

Dark Ages *npl* HIST **the ~** la Alta Edad Media; *fig* la prehistoria

darken ['dar·kən] I. *vi* oscurecerse; (*sky*) nublarse; *fig* ensombrecerse II. *vt* (*make darker*) oscurecer; *fig* ensombrecer

dark horse *n* POL ganador(a) *m(f)* sorpresa

darkly *adv* 1.(*mysteriously*) misteriosamente 2.(*gloomily*) tristemente; **to look at sb ~** mirar a alguien con aire sombrío

darkness *n* 1.(*dark*) oscuridad *f;* **to plunge sth into ~** sumir algo en la oscuridad 2.*fig* (*lack of knowledge*) tinieblas *fpl*

darkroom *n* PHOT cámara *f* oscura

dark-skinned *adj* de piel oscura

darling ['dar·lɪŋ] I. *n* 1.(*beloved person*) amor *m* 2.(*term of endearment*) cariño *mf* II. *adj* 1.(*beloved*) querido, -a 2.(*cute*) mono, -a; **a ~ little room** una monada de habitación

darn¹ [darn] I. *vt* (*sock*) zurcir II. *n* zurcido *m*

darn² [darn] *vt inf* **~ it!** ¡maldita sea!, ¡carajo!; **well, I'll be ~ed!** (*in surprise*) ¡mecachis!; **I'll be ~ed if I'll do it!** ¡no lo hago ni que me maten!

darning *n* zurcido *m*

darning needle *n* aguja *f* de zurcir

dart [dart] I. *n* 1.(*type of weapon*) dardo *m;* **to fire a ~ at sb/sth** disparar un dardo a alguien/algo 2.**~s** (*game*) dardos *mpl;* **to play ~s** jugar a los dardos; **a game of ~s** una partida de dardos 3.(*quick run*) movimiento *m* rápido 4.FASHION pinza *f* II. *vi* **to ~** (**for sth**) precipitarse (hacia algo); **to ~ away** salir disparado; **I ~ed behind the sofa** corrí a esconderme detrás del sofá III. *vt* 1.(*send quickly: look*) lanzar 2.(*move quickly*) lanzar; **the lizard ~ed out its tongue** la largatija disparó la lengua

dartboard ['dart·bɔrd] *n* diana *f*

dash [dæʃ] I.<-es> *n* 1.(*rush*) carrera *f;* **to make a ~ for** precipitarse hacia; **to make a ~ for it** huir precipitadamente 2.(*pinch*) poquito *m;* (*of salt*) pizca *f;* **a ~ of color** una nota de color [*o* un toque] 3.(*flair*) brío *m* 4.TYPO guión *m* 5.(*in Morse code*) raya *f* II. *vi* 1.(*hurry*) precipitarse 2.(*slam into*) **to ~ against sth** romperse contra algo III. *vt* 1.(*shatter*) romper 2.(*hopes*) defraudar 3.(*to ~ off a letter/note*) escribir a toda prisa una carta/nota

dashboard ['dæʃ·bɔrd] *n* AUTO salpicadero *m*

dashing ['dæʃ·ɪŋ] *adj* gallardo, -a

dastardly ['dæs·tərd·li] *adj liter* (*crime, act*) ruin

DAT [dæt] *n abbr of* **digital audio tape** DAT *m*

data ['deɪ·t̬ə] *npl* + *sing/pl vb a.* COMPUT datos *mpl*

data bank *n*, **databank** *n* banco *m* de datos

database *n* base *f* de datos

data file *n* fichero *m* de datos

data processing *n* procesamiento *m* de datos

date¹ [deɪt] I. *n* 1.(*calendar day*) fecha *f;* **expiration ~** fecha de vencimiento; **what ~ is it today?** ¿cuál es la fecha de hoy?; **to be out of ~** FASHION estar pasado de moda 2.FIN plazo *f* 3.(*appointment*) cita *f;* **to have a ~** tener una cita; **to make a ~ with sb** quedar con alguien 4.*inf* (*person*) novio, -a *m, f* II. *vt* 1.(*recognize age of*) fechar; **to ~ sth at...** fechar algo en... 2.(*give date to sth*) asignar una fecha a algo 3.*inf* (*have relationship with*) **to ~ sb** salir con alguien III. *vi* 1.(*go back to*) **to ~ back to** remontarse a 2.(*go out of fashion*) pasar de moda 3.(*go on dates*) salir con alguien

date² [deɪt] *n* 1.(*fruit*) dátil *m* 2.(*tree*) palmera *f* datilera

dated ['deɪ·t̬ɪd] *adj* anticuado, -a

dateline ['deɪt·laɪn] *n* línea *f* de cambio de fecha

date rape *n* violación *durante una cita* (*cometida por el acompañante*)

ℹ️ En el ámbito de las citas (**dating**) en EE.UU. hay diversos modos de expresar la relación entre dos personas. 'Seeing each other' significa que ambos salen a menudo pero no obstante son libres de salir con otras parejas. 'Going out' quiere decir que tienen una relación fija. Cuando un chico se interesa por una chica, le pregunta si quiere salir con él. La pregunta "Do you want to go out sometime?" significa solamente '¿Quieres que quedemos alguna vez?,

dative ['deɪ·t̬ɪv] I. *n* dativo; **to be in the ~** estar en dativo II. *adj* dativo, -a
daub [dɔb] I. *vt* 1.(*smear*) **to ~ sth with sth** manchar algo de algo 2.(*paint unskillfully*) pintarrajear II. *n* 1.(*smear*) mancha *f* 2.(*painting*) pintarrajo *m*
daughter ['dɔ·t̬ər] *n* hija *f*
daughter-in-law <daughters-in-law> *n* nuera *f*
daunt [dɔnt] *vt* 1.(*discourage*) desalentar 2.(*intimidate*) intimidar
daunting *adj* amedrentador(a)
dauntless ['dɔnt·lɪs] *adj* intrépido, -a
dawdle ['dɔd·əl] *vi* holgazanear
dawdler ['dɔd·lər] *n* persona *f* lenta
dawn [dɔn] I. *n* 1.(*time of day*) alba *m*, amanezca *f Méx;* **from ~ to dusk** de sol a sol; **at ~** al alba 2.*fig* (*beginning*) nacimiento *m* II. *vi* amanecer; *fig* (*era*) nacer; **it ~ed on him that...** cayó en la cuenta de que...
day [deɪ] *n* 1.día *m;* **~ after** día tras día; **~ by ~** día a día; **all ~ (long)** todo el día; **any ~ now** cualquier día de estos; **by ~** de día; **by the ~** diariamente; **for a few ~s** durante algunos días; **from that ~ on(wards)** desde ese día; **from this ~ forth** de aquí en adelante; **from one ~ to the next** de un día para otro; **one ~** algún día; **two ~s ago** hace dos días; **the ~ before yesterday** anteayer; **the ~ after tomorrow** pasado mañana; **in the (good) old ~s** en los buenos/viejos tiempos; **the exam is ten ~s from now** [*o* **in ten ~s**] el examen es dentro de diez días 2.(*working period*) jornada *f;* **to take a ~ off** tomarse un día de descanso ▶ **in this ~ and age** en los tiempos que corren; **to have seen** better **~s** haber conocido tiempos mejores; **to** call **it a ~** dejarlo para otro día; **to** carry **the ~** salir victorioso; **~ in ~ out** un día sí y otro también
day bed *n* cama *f* turca
daybreak ['deɪ·breɪk] *n* alba *m*
day camp *n* campamento *m* de verano (*abierto sólo de día y entre semana*)
daycare ['deɪ·ker] *n* 1.(*for children*) servicio *m* de guardería; (*place*) guardería *f* 2.(*for the elderly*) atención *f* geriátrica de día
daydream ['deɪ·drim] I. *vi* soñar despierto II. *n* ensueño *m*
daylight ['deɪ·laɪt] *n* luz *f* del día; **in broad ~** a plena luz del día ▶ **to scare the** living **~s out of sb** *inf* dar un susto de muerte a alguien
day shift *n* turno *m* de día
daytime ['deɪ·taɪm] *n* día *m;* **in the ~** de día
day-to-day *adj* cotidiano, -a
day trip *n* excursión *f* (*de un día*)
daze [deɪz] I. *n* aturdimiento *m;* **to be in a ~** estar aturdido II. *vt* aturdir
dazed *adj* aturdido, -a
dazzle ['dæz·əl] I. *vt* deslumbrar II. *n* deslum-

bramiento *m*
dazzled *adj* deslumbrado, -a
dB *n abbr of* **decibel** dB
DC [ˌdi·'si] *n* 1.*abbr of* **direct current** CC 2. *abbr of* **District of Columbia** Distrito *m* de Columbia
DD [ˌdi·'di] *n abbr of* **Doctor of Divinity** Dr. , Dra. *m*, *f* en Teología
D-Day ['di·deɪ] *n* el día D
DDT [ˌdi·di·'ti] *n abbr of* **dichlorodiphenyl-trichloroethane** DDT *m*
DE *n abbr of* **Delaware** Delaware *m*
deacon ['di·kən] *n* diácono *m*
deaconess ['di·kə·nɪs] *n* diaconisa *f*
dead [ded] I. *adj* 1.(*no longer alive*) muerto, -a; **to be ~ on arrival** ingresar cadáver (en el hospital); **she wouldn't be seen ~ wearing that** *inf* por nada del mundo se pondría eso 2. *inf* (*inactive*) parado, -a; (*fire*) apagado, -a; (*battery*) descargado, -a; ((*telephone*) *line*) cortado, -a 3. *inf* (*quiet, boring*) muerto, -a; (*town*) desierto, -a 4.(*numb*) dormido, -a 5.(*complete: silence*) profundo, -a; **to be a ~ loss** ser un desastre total; **to come to a ~ stop** pararse en seco ▶ **as ~ as a** doornail muerto y bien muerto; **~** men **tell no tales** *prov* los muertos no hablan II. *n* **the ~** los muertos ▶ **in the ~ of** night/winter en plena noche/pleno invierno III. *adv* 1. *inf* (*totally*) completamente; **to be ~ set against/on sth** estar completamente en contra de/decidido a algo 2.(*directly*) justo; **~ ahead** justo al frente
deadbeat [ˌded·'bit] *adj sl* rendido, -a, muerto, -a *inf;* **~ dad** padre que evita pagar la pensión *tras divorcio*
dead center *n* punta *f* fija
deaden ['ded·ən] *vt* (*pain*) aliviar; (*noise*) amortiguar
dead-end *n* callejón *m* sin salida
dead-end *adj* sin salida; **~ job** trabajo *m* sin porvenir
dead heat *n* empate *m*
deadline ['ded·laɪn] *n* fecha *f* límite; **to meet/miss the ~** cumplir/incumplir el plazo
deadlock ['ded·lak] *n* punto *m* muerto
deadly ['ded·li] I.<-ier, -iest> *adj* 1.(*capable of killing*) mortal; (*weapon*) mortífero, -a; (*silence*) sepulcral 2. *inf* (*boring*) aburridísimo, -a II.<-ier, -iest> *adv* extremadamente; **~ pale** blanco como la cera
deadpan *adj* inexpresivo, -a
Dead Sea *n* Mar *m* Muerto
deadwood ['ded·wʊd] *n* 1.(*branch, tree*) madera *f* seca 2. *inf* (*person*) persona *f* inútil; (*people*) gente *f* inútil; (*thing*) cosa *f* inútil
deaf [def] I. *adj* sordo, -a; **to go ~** quedarse sordo; **to be ~ to sth** *fig* hacer oídos sordos a algo II. *npl* **the ~** los sordos
deafen ['def·ən] *vt* ensordecer
deafening *adj* ensordecedor(a)
deaf-mute [ˌdef·'mjut] *n* sordomudo, -a *m, f*
deafness *n* sordera *f*
deal¹ [dil] *n* (*large amount*) cantidad *f;* **a great**

~ una gran cantidad; **a great ~ of effort** mucho esfuerzo

deal² [dil] <dealt, dealt> **I.** *n* **1.** COM negocio *m;* **a big ~** un negocio importante **2.** *(agreement)* pacto *m;* **to do a ~ (with sb)** hacer un trato (con alguien) **3.** GAMES *(of cards)* reparto *m;* **it's your ~** te toca dar a ti ▶ **big ~!** *iron, sl* ¡gran cosa!; **it's no big ~!** *sl* ¡no es para tanto! **II.** *vi* **1.** *(do business)* negociar; **to ~ with sb** hacer negocios con alguien; **to ~ in sth** comerciar con algo **2.** GAMES repartir **3.** *sl (accept situation, cope)* **to ~ (with sth)** arreglárselas (con algo) **III.** *vt* **1.** GAMES *(cards)* repartir **2.** *(give)* dar; **to ~ sb a blow** propinar un golpe a alguien

◆ **deal out** *vt* repartir

◆ **deal with** *vt* **1.** *(take care of: problem)* ocuparse de; *(person)* tratar con **2.** *(be about: book)* tratar de **3.** *(punish)* castigar

dealer ['di·lər] *n* **1.** COM negociante *mf;* **drug ~** traficante *mf* de drogas; **antique ~** marchante *mf* de antigüedades **2.** GAMES *(in cards)* persona *f* que reparte

dealership ['di·lər·ʃɪp] *n* COM concesión *f*

dealing ['di·lɪŋ] *n* **1.** COM comercio *m* **2. ~s** FIN transacciones *fpl* **3. ~s** *(relations)* relaciones *fpl;* **to have ~s with sb** tratar con alguien **4.** GAMES reparto *m*

dealt [delt] *pt, pp of* **deal**

dean [din] *n* **1.** UNIV decano, -a *m, f* **2.** REL deán *m*

dean's list *n* UNIV *lista honorífica de los mejores estudiantes una universidad (elaborada por el decano)*

dear [dɪr] **I.** *adj* **1.** *(much loved)* querido, -a; **it is ~ to me** le tengo mucho cariño **2.** *(in letters)* estimado, -a; **Dear Sarah** Querida Sarah; **Dear Sir** Muy señor mío **3.** *(expensive)* caro, -a **II.** *adv* caro **III.** *interj inf* **oh ~!** ¡Dios mío! **IV.** *n* encanto *m;* **she is a ~** es encantadora; **be a ~ and...** hazme el favor de..., ten la gentileza de...

dearly *adv* **1.** mucho; **I love her ~** la quiero mucho **2.** *fig* caro; **he paid ~ for his success** su éxito le costó caro

dearth [dɜrθ] *n* escasez *f;* **to suffer from a ~ of sth** sufrir escasez de algo

death [deθ] *n* muerte *f;* **to die a natural ~** morir de muerte natural; **to put sb to ~** matar a alguien; **to be bored to ~ with sth** *inf* morirse de aburrimiento con algo; **scared to ~** *inf* muerto de miedo; **to catch one's ~ of cold** coger una gripe de muerte ▶ **to be at ~'s door** estar a las puertas de la muerte; **to be the ~ of sb/sth** acabar con alguien/algo

deathbed ['deθ·bed] *n* lecho *m* de muerte

deathblow *n* golpe *m* mortal

death certificate *n* certificado *m* de defunción

deathly ['deθ·li] **I.** *adv* de muerte; **~ pale** pálido como la muerte **II.** *adj* de muerte, mortal

death penalty *n* pena *f* de muerte

death rate *n* tasa *f* de mortalidad

death row *n* corredor *m* de la muerte

death sentence *n* pena *f* de muerte

death squad *n* escuadrón *m* de la muerte

death trap *n* trampa *f* mortal

debacle [dɪ·'bɑ·kəl] *n* debacle *f*

debar [dɪ·'bar] <-rr-> *vt* excluir; **to ~ sb from doing sth** privar a alguien de hacer algo

debase [dɪ·'beɪs] *vt (degrade)* degradar; ECON devaluar

debatable [dɪ·'beɪ·ṭə·bəl] *adj* discutible

debate [dɪ·'beɪt] **I.** *n* debate *m;* **a ~ over sth** un debate sobre algo **II.** *vt* debatir **III.** *vi* debatir; **to ~ about sth** debatir acerca de algo

debater [dɪ·'beɪ·ṭər] *n* polemista *mf*

debauch [dɪ·'bɔtʃ] **I.** *vt* corromper **II.** *n* orgía *f*

debauchery [dɪ·'bɔ·tʃə·ri] *n* vicio *m*

debenture [dɪ·'ben·tʃər] *n* FIN obligación *f*

debilitate [dɪ·'bɪl·ɪ·teɪt] *vt* debilitar

debilitating *adj* debilitante

debility [dɪ·'bɪl·ə·ṭi] *n* debilidad *f*

debit ['deb·ɪt] **I.** *n* débito *m* **II.** *vt* **the bank ~ed my account for the rent** el banco cargó a [*o* debitó de] mi cuenta el alquiler

debit card *n* tarjeta *f* de débito

debit column *n* debe *m*

debonair(e) [ˌdeb·ə·'ner] *adj form* refinado, -a

debris [də·'bri] *n* desechos *mpl*

debt [det] *n* deuda *f;* **to be in ~** *(person)* tener deudas; *(business)* estar en números rojos; **to pay off a ~** pagar una deuda; **to be out of ~** estar libre de deudas

debt collector *n* cobrador(a) *m(f)* (de deudas)

debtor ['det·ər] *n* deudor(a) *m(f)*

debtor country *n*, **debtor nation** *n* país *m* deudor

debug [ˌdi·'bʌg] <-gg-> *vt* COMPUT depurar

debunk [di·'bʌŋk] *vt* desacreditar

debut [deɪ·'bju] **I.** *n* **1.** *(first public appearance)* debut *m;* **to make one's ~** debutar **2.** *(introduction into society)* presentación *f* en sociedad **II.** *vi* debutar; **to ~ in/as sth** debutar en/como algo

debutante ['deb·ju·tant] *n* debutante *mf*

Dec. *n abbr of* **December** dic.

decade ['dek·eɪd] *n* década *f*

decadence ['dek·ə·dəns] *n* decadencia *f*

decadent ['dek·ə·dənt] *adj* decadente

decaf ['di·kæf] *adj, n inf abbr of* **decaffeinated** descafeinado, -a

decaffeinated [ˌdi·'kæf·ɪ·ner·ṭɪd] *adj* descafeinado, -a

decamp [dɪ·'kæmp] *vi (leave)* irse; *(secretly)* fugarse, rajarse *AmL; (run away)* huir

decant [dɪ·'kænt] *vt* decantar

decanter [dɪ·'kæn·tər] *n* licorera *f*

decapitate [dɪ·'kæp·ɪ·teɪt] *vt* decapitar

decapitation [dɪ·ˌkæp·ɪ·'ter·ʃən] *n* decapitación *f*

decathlete [dɪ·'kæθ·lit] *n* decatleta *mf*

decathlon [dɪ·'kæθ·lan] *n* decatlón *m*

decay [dɪ·'keɪ] **I.** *n (of food)* descomposición *f; (of building, intellect)* deterioro *m; (dental)* caries *f inv; (of civilization)* decadencia *f* **II.** *vi* (*food*) pudrirse; (*building, intellect*) deteriorarse; (*teeth*) cariarse **III.** *vt* descomponer

decease [dɪ·'sis] *n* fallecimiento *m*

deceased [dɪ·'sist] **I.** *n* difunto, -a *m, f* **II.** *adj* difunto, -a

deceit [dɪ·'sit] *n* engaño *m*, transa *f Méx*

deceitful [dɪ·'sit·fəl] *adj* engañoso, -a

deceive [dɪ·'siv] *vt* engañar; **to ~ oneself** engañarse a sí mismo ▶ **appearances** can ~ *prov* las apariencias engañan *prov*

deceiver [dɪ·'si·vər] *n* impostor(a) *m(f)*

decelerate [di·'sel·ə·reɪt] **I.** *vi* desacelerarse; (*vehicle, driver*) reducir la velocidad **II.** *vt* desacelerar

December [dɪ·'sem·bər] *n* diciembre *m; s.a.* **April**

decency ['di·sən·si] *n* **1.** (*respectability*) decencia *f* **2. decencies** (*approved behavior*) buenas costumbres *fpl*

decent ['di·sənt] *adj* **1.** (*socially acceptable*) decente; **are you ~?** *fig* ¿estás presentable? **2.** *inf* (*kind*) amable **3.** *inf* (*adequate: salary, living, wage*) decente

decentralization [di·,sen·trə·lɪ·'zeɪ·ʃən] *n* descentralización *f*

decentralize [di·'sen·trə·laɪz] *vt* descentralizar

decentralized *adj* descentralizado, -a

deception [dɪ·'sep·ʃən] *n* engaño *m;* **to practice ~ on sb** engañar a alguien

deceptive [dɪ·'sep·tɪv] *adj* engañoso, -a

decibel ['des·ə·bəl] *n* decibel(io) *m*

decide [dɪ·'saɪd] **I.** *vi* decidirse; **to ~ on sth** decidirse [*o* optar] por algo **II.** *vt* decidir

decided [dɪ·'saɪ·dɪd] *adj* **1.** (*obvious: improvement, success*) indudable **2.** (*resolute: person, manner*) decidido, -a

deciduous [dɪ·'sɪdʒ·u·əs] *adj* caducifolio, -a

decimal ['des·ə·məl] **I.** *n* decimal *m* **II.** *adj* decimal

decimalize ['des·ə·mə·laɪz] *vt* aplicar el sistema decimal a

decimate ['des·ə·meɪt] *vt* diezmar

decipher [dɪ·'saɪ·fər] *vt* descifrar

decision [dɪ·'sɪʒ·ən] *n* **1.** (*choice, resolution*) decisión *f;* **to make a ~** tomar una decisión **2.** LAW fallo *m* **3.** (*resoluteness*) resolución *f*

decision-making *adj* ~ **process** proceso *m* decisorio

decisive [dɪ·'saɪ·sɪv] *adj* **1.** (*factor*) decisivo, -a **2.** (*resolute: manner*) categórico, -a **3.** (*beyond doubt: victory, defeat*) contundente; (*change*) rotundo, -a

deck [dek] **I.** *n* **1.** (*of ship*) cubierta *f;* **to go below ~** ir bajo cubierta **2.** (*back porch*) patio *m* trasero **3.** (*of cards*) baraja *f* **4.** MUS, ELEC platina *f* ▶ **to clear the ~** *inf* prepararse para algo; **to hit the ~** *sl* caerse al suelo **II.** *vt* **to ~ sth** adornar algo; **to ~ sb/oneself out** engalanar a alguien/engalanarse; **to be all ~ed out** ir de tiros largos

deck chair *n* tumbona *f*, reposera *f Arg*

declaim [dɪ·'kleɪm] *vi, vt* declamar

declamation [,de·klə·'meɪ·ʃən] *n* declamación *f*

declamatory [dɪ·'klæm·ə·tɔr·i] *adj form* declamatorio, -a

declaration [,de·klə·'reɪ·ʃən] *n* declaración *f;* **the D~ of Independence** la Declaración de Independencia de EE.UU.

declare [dɪ·'kler] **I.** *vt* declarar; **to ~ war on sb** declarar la guerra a alguien; **to ~ oneself (to be) bankrupt** declararse en bancarrota **II.** *vi* declararse

decline [dɪ·'klaɪn] **I.** *vi* **1.** (*price*) bajar; (*power, influence*) disminuir; (*civilization*) decaer; **to ~ in value** disminuir de valor **2.** MED debilitarse **3.** (*refuse*) rehusar **II.** *vt* **1.** (*refuse*) rehusar **2.** LING declinar **III.** *n* **1.** (*in price, power, influence*) disminución *f;* (*of civilization*) decadencia *f;* **to be in ~** estar en declive **2.** MED debilitación *f*

decode [,di·'koʊd] *vi, vt* descodificar

decoder *n* descodificador *m*

decolonization [,di·,kal·ə·nɪ·'zeɪ·ʃən] *n* descolonización *f*

decompose [,di·kəm·'poʊz] **I.** *vi* descomponerse **II.** *vt* descomponer

decomposition [,di·kam·pə·'zɪʃ·ən] *n* descomposición *f*

decompress [,di·kəm·'pres] *vt* descomprimir

decompression [,di·kəm·'preʃ·ən] *n* descompresión *f*

decompression chamber *n* cámara *f* de descompresión

decontaminate [,di·kən·'tæm·ɪ·neɪt] *vt* descontaminar

decontamination [,di·kən·,tæm·ɪ·'neɪ·ʃən] *n* descontaminación *f*

decontrol [,di·kən·'troʊl] <-ll-> *vt* liberalizar

decor ['deɪ·kɔr] *n* decorado *m*

decorate ['dek·ə·reɪt] **I.** *vt* **1.** (*adorn*) decorar; (*by painting*) pintar; (*by wallpapering*) empapelar **2.** (*honor*) condecorar **II.** *vi* **1.** (*paint*) pintar **2.** (*wallpaper*) empapelar

decoration [,dek·ə·'reɪ·ʃən] *n* **1.** (*ornament*) adorno *m* **2.** (*act of decorating*) decoración *f* **3.** (*medal*) condecoración *f*

decorative ['dek·ər·ə·t̬ɪv] *adj* decorativo, -a

decorator ['dek·ə·reɪ·t̬ər] *n* decorador(a) *m(f)*

decorous ['dek·ər·əs] *adj form* decoroso, -a

decorum [dɪ·'kɔr·əm] *n form* decoro *m*

decoy ['di·kɔɪ] **I.** *n a. fig* señuelo *m;* **to act as a ~** hacer de señuelo **II.** *vt* atraer con un señuelo

decrease¹ [dɪ·'kris] **I.** *vi* disminuir; (*prices*) bajar **II.** *vt* disminuir

decrease² ['di·kris] *n* disminución *f*

decree [dɪ·'kri] **I.** *n* **1.** (*command*) decreto *m;* **to issue a ~** promulgar un decreto **2.** LAW sentencia *f* **II.** *vt* decretar

decrepit [dɪ·'krep·ɪt] *adj* deteriorado, -a; (*house*) destartalado, -a; (*person*) decrépito, -a

decrepitude [dɪ·'krep·ɪ·tud] *n* deterioro *m;* (*of person*) decrepitud *f*

decriminalize [,di·'krɪm·ə·nə·laɪz] *vt* despenalizar

decry [dɪ·'kraɪ] *vt* censurar

dedicate ['ded·ɪ·keɪt] *vt* **1.** (*devote*) **to ~ one-self/one's life to sth** dedicarse/consagrar su vida a algo **2.** (*book, poem, song*) **to ~ sth to sb** dedicar algo a alguien **3.** (*formally open*) inaugurar; (*a church*) dedicar

dedicated *adj* dedicado, -a

dedication [,ded·ɪ·'keɪ·ʃən] *n* **1.** (*devotion*) dedicación *f* **2.** (*inscription*) dedicatoria *f* **3.** (*official opening*) inauguración *f;* (*of a church*) dedicación *f*

deduce [dɪ·'dus] *vt* deducir

deducible [dɪ·'du·sə·bəl] *adj* deducible

deduct [dɪ·'dʌkt] *vt* deducir

deductible *adj* deducible

deduction [dɪ·'dʌk·ʃən] *n* deducción *f;* **$1000 after ~s** 1000 dólares netos

deductive [dɪ·'dʌk·tɪv] *adj* deductivo, -a

deed [did] *n* **1.** (*act*) acto *m;* (*remarkable*) hazaña *f;* **in word and ~** de palabra y obra **2.** LAW escritura *f*

deejay ['di·dʒeɪ] *n inf* pincha *mf*

deem [dim] *vt form* considerar; **he was ~ed to be of sound mind** se juzgó que gozaba de plenas facultades mentales

deep [dip] **I.** *adj* **1.** (*not shallow*) profundo, -a **2.** (*full*) **to take a ~ breath** respirar hondo **3.** (*extending back*) **the dresser is 2 feet ~** la cómoda tiene 61 cm de fondo **4.** (*extreme: love, disappointment*) gran(de); **in ~ mourning** de luto riguroso; **to be in ~ trouble** estar metido en un buen lío *inf* **5.** (*absorbed by*) **to be in ~ thought** estar absorto en sus pensamientos **6.** *inf* (*hard to understand*) profundo, -a **7.** (*low in pitch*) grave **8.** (*dark*) oscuro, -a; **~ red** rojo intenso **II.** *adv* **1.** (*far down*) mucho más abajo; **~ in the forest** en lo más profundo del bosque **2.** (*extremely*) mucho; **to be ~ in debt** estar cargado de deudas ► **to dig ~** cavar hondo; **to go ~ into sth** ahondar en algo **III.** *n liter* **the ~** el piélago; **in the ~ of winter** en lo más crudo del invierno

deepen ['di·pən] **I.** *vt* **1.** (*make deeper*) hacer más profundo **2.** (*increase*) aumentar; (*knowledge*) ampliar **II.** *vi* **1.** (*become deeper*) hacerse más profundo **2.** (*increase*) aumentar **3.** (*become lower in pitch*) volverse grave **4.** (*color*) intensificarse

deep freeze *n* congelador *m*

deep-frozen *adj* ultracongelado, -a

deep-fry *vt* freír en abundante aceite

deeply *adv* profundamente; (*breathe*) hondo; **to be ~ interested in sth** sentir un profundo interés por algo

deepness *n* profundidad *f*

deep-rooted *adj* **1.** (*well-established*) profundamente arraigado, -a **2.** BOT de raíces profundas

deep-seated *adj* profundamente arraigado, -a; (*hatred*) de raíces profundas

deep space *n* AVIAT espacio *m* interplanetario

deer [dɪr] *n inv* ciervo *m*

deerstalker ['dɪr·ˌstɔ·kər] *n* gorra *f* de cazador

deface [dɪ·'feɪs] *vt* afear; (*a wall*) pintarrajear;

(*a stamp*) matar

defamation [,def·ə·'meɪ·ʃən] *n* difamación *f*

defamatory [dɪ·'fæm·ə·tɔr·i] *adj* difamatorio, -a

defame [dɪ·'feɪm] *vt* difamar

default [dɪ·'fɔlt] **I.** *vi* **1.** FIN no pagar; **to ~ on a loan** estar en mora en un préstamo **2.** LAW estar en rebeldía **3.** SPORTS no presentarse **II.** *n* **1.** (*failure to do sth*) omisión *f;* FIN mora *f* **2.** LAW **judgment by ~** sentencia *f* en rebeldía; **to win a case by ~** ganar un caso en rebeldía del adversario **3.** (*pre-selected option*) **by ~** por defecto **4.** *form* (*absence*) **in ~ of any better alternative...** a falta de una alternativa mejor...

default value *n* COMPUT valor *m* por defecto

defeat [dɪ·'fit] **I.** *vt* derrotar; (*hopes*) frustrar; (*a proposal*) rechazar **II.** *n* **1.** (*loss*) derrota *f;* **to admit ~** darse por vencido **2.** (*of plans*) fracaso *m*

defeatism [dɪ·'fi·ţɪ·zəm] *n* derrotismo *m*

defeatist *adj* derrotista

defecate ['def·ə·keɪt] *vi* MED defecar

defecation [,def·ə·'keɪ·ʃən] *n* MED defecación *f*

defect¹ ['di·fekt] *n a.* TECH, MED defecto *m*

defect² [dɪ·'fekt] *vi* POL (*from a country*) huir; (*from the army*) desertar

defection [dɪ·'fek·ʃən] *n* POL defección *f;* MIL deserción *f*

defective [dɪ·'fek·tɪv] *adj* defectuoso, -a

defend [dɪ·'fend] **I.** *vt* **1.** (*protect*) defender; **to ~ oneself (from sb/sth)** defenderse (de alguien/algo) **2.** *a.* LAW defender **3.** SPORTS (*a title*) defender **II.** *vi* **1.** LAW **who is ~ing in that case?** ¿quién actúa por la defensa en esa causa? **2.** SPORTS (*play defense*) defender

defendant [dɪ·'fen·dənt] *n* LAW (*in a civil case*) demandado, -a *m, f;* (*in a criminal case*) acusado, -a *m, f*

defense [dɪ·'fens] *n* **1.** (*against attack*) defensa *f;* **to rush to sb's ~** acudir en defensa de alguien; MED; **the body's ~s** las defensas del organismo **2.** LAW **the ~** la defensa; **counsel for the ~** abogado(a) *m(f)* defensor(a) **3.** SPORTS **to play ~** jugar en la defensa

defenseless [dɪ·'fens·lɪs] *adj* indefenso, -a

defense mechanism *n* PSYCH mecanismo *m* de defensa

defensible [dɪ·'fen·sə·bəl] *adj* **1.** (*against attack*) defendible **2.** (*justifiable*) justificable

defensive [dɪ·'fen·sɪv] **I.** *adj* defensivo, -a; **she's very ~ about her family background** se pone a la defensiva cuando se trata de su situación familiar **II.** *n* **to be/go on the ~** estar/ponerse a la defensiva

defer [dɪ·'fɜr] <-rr-> *vt* aplazar

deference ['def·ər·əns] *n* deferencia *f*

deferential [,def·ə·'ren·tʃəl] *adj* respetuoso, -a

deferred [dɪ·'fɜrd] *adj* aplazado, -a, diferido, -a; **~ payment** pago *m* aplazado

defiance [dɪ·'faɪ·əns] *n* desafío *m;* **in ~ of sth** a despecho de algo

defiant [dɪ·'faɪ·ənt] *adj* **1.** (*person*) rebelde

2. (*attitude*) desafiante

deficiency [dɪ·'fɪʃ·ən·si] *n* (*shortage*) escasez *f*; (*of funds*) déficit *m*; (*of nutrients*) deficiencia *f*

deficient [dɪ·'fɪʃ·ənt] *adj* deficiente; **to be ~ in sth** carecer de algo

deficit ['def·ɪ·sɪt] *n* déficit *m*

defile [dɪ·'faɪl] **I.** *vt form* **1.** (*spoil*) corromper; (*reputation*) mancillar **2.** (*desecrate*) profanar **II.** *n* desfiladero *m*

define [dɪ·'faɪn] *vt* **1.** (*give definition of*) definir **2.** (*explain*) determinar; (*rights*) formular **3.** (*characterize*) caracterizar **4.** (*clearly show*) **the outline of the skyscraper was clearly ~d against the sky** el contorno del rascacielos se recortaba nítidamente contra el cielo

definite ['def·ɪ·nɪt] *adj* **1.** (*certain*) seguro, -a; (*date*) confirmado, -a; (*opinion*) claro, -a; **to be ~ about sth** ser categórico respecto a algo; **it's ~ that...** no hay duda de que... **2.** (*clearly defined*) definitivo, -a

definite article *n* artículo *m* determinado

definitely *adv* definitivamente

definition [ˌdef·ɪ·'nɪʃ·ən] *n* **1.** definición *f* **2. to give ~ to sth** realzar algo; **her ideas lack ~** sus ideas no son muy claras

definitive [dɪ·'fɪn·ɪ·t̬ɪv] *adj* **1.** (*final*) definitivo, -a, rajante *Arg* **2.** (*best*) de mayor autoridad

definitively *adv* definitivamente

deflate [dɪ·'fleɪt] **I.** *vt* **1.** (*let air out of*) desinflar **2.** (*reduce*) reducir; (*hopes*) frustrar **3.** (*cause to lose confidence*) deprimir **4.** ECON, FIN deflactar **II.** *vi* desinflarse

deflation [dɪ·'fleɪ·ʃən] *n* **1.** (*act of deflating*) desinflamiento *m* **2.** ECON, FIN deflación *f* **3.** (*reduction*) caída *f*

deflationary *adj* deflacionario, -a

deflect [dɪ·'flekt] **I.** *vt* desviar **II.** *vi* (*change direction of*) **to ~ off sth** desviarse de algo

deflection [dɪ·'flek·ʃən] *n* desviación *f*

defog [ˌdi·'fɔg] *vt* (*window*) desempañar

defogger [ˌdi·'fɔ·gər] *n* AUTO dispositivo *m* antivaho

defoliant [ˌdi·'fou·li·ənt] *n* defoliante *m*

defoliate [ˌdi·'fou·li·eɪt] *vt* defoliar

deforest [ˌdi·'fɔr·ɪst] *vt* deforestar

deforestation [di·ˌfɔr·ɪ·'steɪ·ʃən] *n* deforestación *f*

deform [dɪ·'fɔrm] **I.** *vt* deformar; (*person*) desfigurar **II.** *vi* deformarse; (*person*) desfigurarse

deformation [ˌdi·fɔr·'meɪ·ʃən] *n* deformación *f*; (*of a person*) desfiguración *f*

deformed *adj* deformado, -a

deformity [dɪ·'fɔr·mə·t̬i] *n* deformidad *f*

defraud [dɪ·'frɔd] *vt* estafar; **to ~ sb (of sth)** estafar (algo) a alguien

defray [dɪ·'freɪ] *vt form* (*costs, expenses*) sufragar

defrost [ˌdi·'frɔst] **I.** *vt* deshelar; (*fridge, food*) descongelar; (*windshield*) desempañar **II.** *vi* deshelarse; (*fridge, food*) descongelarse

deft [deft] *adj* hábil; **to be ~ at sth** ser diestro

en algo

defunct [dɪ·'fʌŋkt] *adj* (*dead*) difunto, -a; (*idea*) caduco, -a; (*institution*) extinto, -a

defy [dɪ·'faɪ] *vt* **1.** (*challenge: authority, gravity*) desafiar, desafiar **2.** (*resist*) resistirse a; **it defies description** es indescriptible **3.** (*disobey*) desobedecer

deg. *abbr of* **degree** grado *m*

degenerate[1] [dɪ·'dʒen·ə·reɪt] *vi* (*lose quality*) degenerar; (*health*) deteriorarse; **to ~ into sth** degenerar en algo

degenerate[2] [dɪ·'dʒen·ər·ət] **I.** *adj* degenerado, -a **II.** *n* degenerado, -a *m, f*

degeneration [dɪ·ˌdʒen·ə·'reɪ·ʃən] *n* degeneración *f*

degrade [dɪ·'greɪd] **I.** *vt* **1.** *a.* CHEM degradar; **to ~ oneself** rebajarse **2.** (*decompose: leaves, garbage*) descomponer, degradar **II.** *vi* degradarse

degree [dɪ·'gri] *n* **1.** MATH, METEO grado *m*; **5 ~s below zero** 5 grados bajo cero; **first/second ~ murder** LAW homicidio *m* en primer/segundo grado; **first/second ~ burns** MED quemaduras *fpl* de primer/segundo grado **2.** (*amount*) nivel *m* **3.** (*extent*) **I agree with you to some ~** estoy de acuerdo contigo hasta cierto punto; **by ~s** gradualmente; **to the last ~** en grado sumo **4.** UNIV título *m*; **to have a ~ in sth** ser licenciado en algo; **she's got a physics ~ from UCLA** es licenciada en física por la UCLA; **to have a master's ~ in sth** tener un máster en algo; **to do a ~ in chemistry** estudiar (la carrera de) química

dehumanize [ˌdi·'hju·mə·naɪz] *vt* deshumanizar

dehydrate [ˌdi·haɪ·'dreɪt] **I.** *vt* deshidratar **II.** *vi* MED deshidratarse

dehydrated *adj* deshidratado, -a; (*milk*) en polvo; **to become ~** deshidratarse

dehydration [ˌdi·haɪ·'dreɪ·ʃən] *n* MED deshidratación *f*

deice [ˌdi·'aɪs] *vt* deshelar

deign [deɪn] *vi* **to ~ to do sth** dignarse a hacer algo

deism ['di·ɪz·əm] *n* deísmo *m*

deity ['di·ə·t̬i] *n* deidad *f*

deject [dɪ·'dʒekt] *vt* desanimar

dejected *adj* desanimado, -a

dejection [dɪ·'dʒek·ʃən] *n* desánimo *m*

Del. *n abbr of* **Delaware** Delaware *m*

Delaware [del·ə·'wer] *n* Delaware *m*

delay [dɪ·'leɪ] **I.** *vt* aplazar; **to be ~ed** retrasarse; **to ~ doing sth** posponer el momento de hacer algo **II.** *vi* tardar; **to ~ in doing sth** dejar algo para más tarde; **don't ~!** ¡no te entretengas! **III.** *n* tardanza *f*; **without ~** sin dilación; **a two-hour ~** un retraso de dos horas

delayed-action *adj* de efecto retardado

delaying tactics *npl* tácticas *fpl* dilatorias

delectable [dɪ·'lek·tə·bəl] *adj* deleitable, deleitoso, -a; (*food, taste*) delicioso, -a; (*person*) encantador, -a

delectation [ˌdi·lek·'teɪ·ʃən] *n form* deleite *m*;

for the public's ~ para deleite del público
delegate¹ ['del·ɪ·gət] *n a.* POL delegado, -a *m, f*
delegate² ['del·ɪ·geɪt] *vt* delegar
delegation [ˌdel·ɪ·'geɪ·ʃən] *n* delegación *f*
delete [dɪ·'lit] *vt* 1.(*erase*) borrar 2.COMPUT
suprimir; (*file*) eliminar
deletion [dɪ·'li·ʃən] *n* 1.(*act of erasing*) eliminación *f* 2.(*removal*) supresión *f*
deli ['del·i] *n inf* s. **delicatessen**
deliberate¹ [dɪ·'lɪb·ər·ət] *adj* 1.(*intentional*)
deliberado, -a 2.(*cautious: decision*) medi-
tado, -a 3.(*unhurried*) lento, -a; (*movement*)
pausado, -a
deliberate² [dɪ·'lɪb·ə·reɪt] I. *vi* to ~ on sth
reflexionar sobre algo; to ~ on a case deliberar
sobre una causa II. *vt* deliberar sobre
deliberately *adv* 1.(*intentionally*) adrede
2.(*unhurriedly*) pausadamente
deliberation [dɪ·ˌlɪb·ə·'reɪ·ʃən] *n* 1.(*formal
discussion*) deliberación *f* 2.(*consideration*)
reflexión *f*; after due ~ después de pensarlo
bien 3.(*unhurried manner*) parsimonia *f*
delicacy ['del·ɪ·kə·si] *n* 1.(*tact*) delicadeza *f*
2.(*trickiness*) the ~ of the situation lo delicado de la situación 3.(*food*) manjar *m*
delicate ['del·ɪ·kət] *adj* 1.(*fragile*) frágil; to be
in ~ health estar delicado (de salud) 2.(*fine*)
primoroso, -a; (*balance*) delicado, -a 3.(*soft*)
suave; (*aroma*) exquisito, -a 4.(*tricky: situation*) delicado, -a 5.(*highly sensitive*) muy
sensible
delicatessen [ˌdel·ɪ·kə·'tes·ən] *n* delicatessen
m o f inv
delicious [dɪ·'lɪʃ·əs] *adj* delicioso, -a,
exquisito, -a
delight [dɪ·'laɪt] I. *n* placer *m;* to do sth with
~ hacer algo con gusto; to take ~ in sth disfrutar con algo II. *vt* deleitar; to be ~ed with sth
estar encantado con algo
♦**delight in** *vi* to ~ doing sth deleitarse
haciendo algo
delighted *adj* encantado, -a
delightful [dɪ·'laɪt·fəl] *adj* delicioso, -a; (*person*) encantador(a)
delimit [dɪ·'lɪm·ɪt] *vt* delimitar
delineate [dɪ·'lɪn·i·eɪt] *vt* 1.(*draw*) delinear
2.(*describe: plan*) trazar; (*character*) perfilar
delinquency [dɪ·'lɪŋ·kwən·si] *n* delincuencia *f*
delinquent [dɪ·'lɪŋ·kwənt] I. *n* LAW delincuente *mf;* **juvenile** ~ delincuente juvenil
II. *adj* 1.(*behavior*) delictivo, -a 2.(*account*)
moroso, -a
delirious [dɪ·'lɪr·i·əs] *adj* to be ~ delirar; to be
~ with joy *fig, inf* estar delirante de alegría
deliriously *adv* 1.MED delirantemente; she
raves ~ desvaría en su delirio 2. *inf, fig* locamente; she was ~ happy estaba loca de alegría *inf*
delirium [dɪ·'lɪr·i·əm] *n* delirio *m*
deliver [dɪ·'lɪv·ər] I. *vt* 1.(*hand over*) entregar; (*letter, package*) repartir (a domicilio)
2.(*recite: lecture*) dar; (*speech, verdict*) pronunciar 3.(*direct*) to ~ a blow to sb's head

asestar a alguien un golpe en la cabeza; he
~ed a sharp rebuke to his son propinó una
severa reprimenda a su hijo; SPORTS (*throw*) lanzar 4.(*give birth to*) to ~ a baby (*mother*)
tener un bebé; (*doctor*) asistir a un parto
5.(*save*) librar 6.(*produce*) to ~ a promise
cumplir una promesa; to ~ the goods cumplir
lo prometido II. *vi* 1.COM we ~ se entrega a
domicilio 2. *inf* (*make good on*) to ~ on
(*promise*) cumplir 3.(*give birth*) dar a luz
♦**deliver of** *vt* to deliver oneself of sth
expresar algo
deliverance [dɪ·'lɪv·ər·əns] *n* liberación *f*
deliverer *n* libertador(a) *m(f)*
delivery [dɪ·'lɪv·ə·ri] *n* 1.(*distribution*) reparto
m; ~ charges gastos *mpl* de envío; ~ man repartidor *m;* ~ woman repartidora *f;* to pay on
~ pagar contra reembolso; to take ~ of sth
recibir algo 2.(*manner of speaking*) pronunciación *f* 3.SPORTS lanzamiento *m* 4.(*birth*)
parto *m*
delivery room *n* sala *f* de partos
delivery service *n* servicio *m* de reparto a
domicilio
delivery truck *n* furgoneta *f* de reparto
delta ['del·tə] *n* GEO delta *m*
delta wing *n* AVIAT ala *f* delta
delude [dɪ·'lud] *vt* engañar; to ~ sb into
believing sth hacer creer algo a alguien
deluge ['del·judʒ] I. *n* 1.(*downpour*) diluvio
m; (*flood*) inundación *f* 2. *a. fig* (*inundation*)
avalancha *f;* (*of complaints*) aluvión *m* II. *vt a.*
fig inundar; to be ~d with tears estar bañado
en lágrimas; she is ~d with offers le llueven
las ofertas
delusion [dɪ·'lu·ʒən] *n* 1.(*wrong idea*) error
m; to labor under a ~ estar equivocado
2.PSYCH alucinación *f;* ~ s of grandeur megalomanía *f* 3.(*deceit*) engaño *m*
deluxe [dɪ·'lʌks] *adj* de lujo
delve [delv] *vi* 1.(*explore*) to ~ into sth ahondar en algo 2.(*rummage*) hurgar
demagog *n s.* **demagogue**
demagogic [ˌdem·ə·'gadʒ·ɪk] *adj* demagógi-
co, -a
demagogue ['dem·ə·gɔg] *n* demagogo, -a *m, f*
demagoguery [ˌdem·ə·'gɔ·gə·ri] *n,* **dema-
gogy** ['dem·ə·gɔdʒ·i] *n* demagogia *f*
demand [dɪ·'mænd] I. *vt* 1.(*ask for forcefully*)
exigir; (*a right*) reclamar; to ~ that... exigir
que... +*subj;* she demanded to see the person in charge insistió en ver a la persona responsable 2.(*require*) requerir II. *n*
1.(*insistent request*) exigencia *f;* on ~ a petición; ~ for independence reivindicación *f* de
independencia; to make a ~ for sth exigir
algo; to make a ~ that... hacer una petición
de que... +*subj;* to make heavy ~s on sb's
time ocupar gran parte del tiempo de alguien;
to meet a ~ for sth satisfacer las exigencias de
algo; by popular ~ a petición del público
2.COM demanda *f;* payable on ~ pagadero, -a
a la vista; to be in ~ (*object*) tener mucha

D

demanda; (*person*) estar muy solicitado
demanding *adj* exigente
demand note *n* título *m* pagadero a la vista
demarcate [di·'mar·keɪt] *vt* demarcar
demarcation [ˌdi·mar·'keɪ·ʃən] *n* demarcación *f*
demarcation line *n* MIL, POL línea *f* de demarcación
demean [dɪ·'min] *vt* degradar; **to ~ oneself** rebajarse
demeaning *adj* degradante
demeanor [dɪ·'mi·nər] *n* (*behavior*) conducta *f*; (*bearing*) porte *m*
demented [dɪ·'men·tɪd] *adj* MED demente, loco, -a; *fig, inf* chalado, -a
dementia [dɪ·'men·ʃə] *n* MED demencia *f*
demerit [dɪ·'mer·ɪt] *n* **1.** SCHOOL punto *m* negativo **2.** (*fault*) desmerecimiento *m*
demesne [dɪ·'meɪn] *n* **1.** LAW propiedad *f* **2.** (*domain*) esfera *f* de actividad
demigod ['dem·i·gad] *n* semidiós *m*
demilitarize [ˌdi·'mɪl·ɪ·tə·raɪz] *vt* desmilitarizar
demise [dɪ·'maɪz] *n* **1.** (*death*) deceso *m* **2.** *fig* (*end*) desaparición *f*; (*of a company*) cierre *m*
demo ['dem·oʊ] *n* *inf s.* **demonstration** **1.** (*act of showing*) demo *f*; (*music*) maqueta *f*, demo *m* *Méx, Col* **2.** (*protest*) manifa *f*, manifestación *f*
demobilize [ˌdi·'moʊ·bə·laɪz] **I.** *vt* desmovilizar **II.** *vi* desmovilizarse
democracy [dɪ·'mak·rə·si] *n* democracia *f*
democrat ['dem·ə·kræt] *n* demócrata *mf*
democratic [ˌdem·ə·'kræt·ɪk] *adj* democrático, -a
democratization [dɪˌmak·rə·tɪ·'zeɪ·ʃən] *n* democratización *f*
democratize [dɪ·'mak·rə·taɪz] *vt* democratizar
demolish [dɪ·'mal·ɪʃ] *vt* (*a building*) demoler; (*a car*) destrozar; *fig* (*argument*) echar por tierra
demolition [ˌdem·ə·'lɪʃ·ən] *n* (*of a building*) demolición *f*; *fig* destrucción *f*
demon ['di·mən] *n* **1.** (*evil spirit*) demonio *m* **2.** (*destructive force*) demonio; **childhood ~s** fantasmas *mpl* de la infancia ▶ **to be a ~ at sth** *inf* ser un hacha [*o* monstruo] haciendo algo; **to work like a ~** trabajar como una fiera
demoniac [dɪ·'moʊ·ni·æk] *adj*, **demonic** [dɪ·'man·ɪk] *adj* **1.** (*devilish*) demoníaco, -a **2.** (*evil*) diabólico, -a
demonstrable [dɪ·'man·strə·bəl] *adj* demostrable
demonstrate ['dem·ən·streɪt] **I.** *vt* (*show clearly*) mostrar; (*prove*) demostrar; **to ~ that...** demostrar que... **II.** *vi* POL manifestarse
demonstration [ˌdem·ən·'streɪ·ʃən] *n* **1.** (*act of showing*) demostración *f*; **she gave him a kiss as a ~ of her affection** le dio un beso como muestra de su afecto **2.** (*march*) manifestación *f*; **to hold a ~** manifestarse
demonstrative [dɪ·'man·strə·tɪv] *adj* **1.** (*illustrative*) concluyente **2.** (*expressing feelings*)

efusivo, -a
demonstrator ['dem·ən·streɪ·tər] *n* **1.** (*of a product*) demostrador(a) *m(f)* **2.** (*protester*) manifestante *mf*
demoralize [dɪ·'mɔr·ə·laɪz] *vt* desmoralizar
demote [dɪ·'moʊt] *vt* bajar de categoría; MIL degradar
demure [dɪ·'mjʊr] *adj* **1.** (*modest, shy*) recatado, -a **2.** (*affectedly modest*) remilgado, -a
den [den] *n* **1.** (*animal habitation*) guarida *f* **2.** *a. iron* (*place for vice*) antro *m*; **a ~ of thieves** una guarida de ladrones **3.** (*small room*) salita *f* **4.** (*in cub scouts*) grupo *m*
denationalize [ˌdi·'næʃ·ə·nə·laɪz] *vt* privatizar
denial [dɪ·'naɪ·əl] *n* **1.** (*act of refuting*) negación *f* **2.** (*refusal*) negativa *f* **3.** (*of a right*) denegación *f* **4.** (*rejection*) desmentido *m*; **to issue a ~ of sth** desmentir algo
denigrate ['den·ɪ·greɪt] *vt* denigrar
denim ['den·ɪm] *n* **1.** (*cloth*) tela *f* vaquera **2. ~s** *inf* (*clothes*) mono *m*
denim jacket *n* chaqueta *f* vaquera
denim shirt *n* camisa *f* vaquera
Denmark ['den·mark] *n* Dinamarca *f*
denomination [dɪˌnam·ə·'neɪ·ʃən] *n* **1.** (*religious group*) confesión *f* **2.** (*unit of value*) denominación *f*
denominational [dɪˌnam·ə·'neɪ·ʃə·nəl] *adj* confesional
denominator [dɪ·'nam·ə·neɪ·tər] *n* denominador *m*
denotation [ˌdi·noʊ·'teɪ·ʃən] *n* denotación *f*
denote [dɪ·'noʊt] *vt* **1.** (*indicate*) denotar **2.** (*show: displeasure*) mostrar
denouement [deɪ·'nu·mãŋ] *n* desenlace *m*
denounce [dɪ·'naʊns] *vt* **1.** (*condemn*) censurar **2.** (*give information against*) denunciar
dense [dens] *adj* **1.** (*thick*) espeso, -a **2.** (*closely packed*) denso, -a; (*compact*) compacto, -a; (*print*) apiñado, -a **3.** (*complex*) difícil **4.** *inf* (*stupid*) duro, -a de mollera
densely *adv* densamente
density ['den·sə·ti] *n* **1.** (*compactness*) densidad *f*; **to be high/low in ~** ser de alta/baja densidad **2.** (*complexity*) impenetrabilidad *f*
dent [dent] **I.** *n* **1.** (*mark*) abolladura *f* **2.** (*adverse effect*) mella *f* **II.** *vt* **1.** (*put a dent in*) abollar **2.** (*have adverse effect on: confidence*) hacer mella en
dental ['den·təl] *adj* dental
dental floss *n* hilo *m* [*o* seda *f*] dental
dentist ['den·tɪst] *n* dentista *mf*
dentistry ['den·tɪ·stri] *n* odontología *f*
dentition [den·'tɪʃ·ən] *n* dentadura *f*; ZOOL dentición *f*
dentures ['den·tʃərz] *npl* dentadura *f* postiza
denude [dɪ·'nud] *vt* (*surface*) denudar
denunciation [dɪˌnʌn·si·'eɪ·ʃən] *n* **1.** (*condemnation*) censura *f* **2.** (*accusation*) denuncia *f*
deny [dɪ·'naɪ] *vt* **1.** (*declare untrue*) negar; (*report*) desmentir; **to ~ having done sth**

negar haber hecho algo; **she denies that she saw it** niega haberlo visto **2.** (*refuse*) denegar; **to ~ oneself sth** privarse de algo; **to ~ sb a privilege** negar a alguien un privilegio; **to ~ sb a right** privar a alguien de un derecho **3.** (*disown*) renegar de

deodorant [di·'oʊ·dər·ənt] *n* desodorante *m*

deodorize [di·'oʊ·də·raɪz] *vt* desodorizar

dep. 1. *abbr of* **department** dpto. **2.** *abbr of* **deputy** diputado, -a *m*, *f*

depart [dɪ·'part] **I.** *vi* (*person*) partir; (*plane*) despegar; (*train*) salir; (*ship*) zarpar **II.** *vt* **to ~ this life** dejar de existir
◆**depart from** *vi* desviarse de

departed I. *adj* **1.** (*dead*) difunto, -a **2.** (*past: era, triumph*) pasado, -a **II.** *n pl* **the ~** los difuntos; **to mourn the ~** llorar por las almas

department [dɪ·'part·mənt] *n* **1.** (*division: of a university, company*) departamento *m*; (*of a shop*) sección *f* **2.** ADMIN, POL ministerio *m*; **~ of Health and Human Services** Ministerio de Sanidad y Asuntos Sociales **3.** *inf* (*domain*) terreno *m*, cosa *f inf*

departmental [ˌdi·part·'men·təl] *adj* departamental

department store *n* grandes almacenes *mpl*, tienda *f* por departamentos *AmS*

departure [dɪ·'par·tʃər] *n* **1.** (*act of leaving*) partida *f*; (*of vehicle, train*) salida *f*; (*of plane*) despegue *m*; **~ from politics** alejamiento *m* de la política; **to make one's ~** marcharse **2.** (*deviation*) desviación *f*; (*new undertaking*) nuevo rumbo *m*; **to be a new ~ for sb/sth** ser una novedad para alguien/algo

departure gate *n* AVIAT puerta *f* de embarque

departure lounge *n* AVIAT sala *f* de embarque

departure time *n* hora *f* de salida

depend [dɪ·'pend] *vi* **1.** (*be determined by*) **to ~ on sb/sth** depender de alguien/algo; **~ing on the weather...** según el tiempo que haga... **2.** (*rely on for aid*) **she depends on her father for money** depende del dinero de su padre **3.** (*trust*) **to ~ on sb/sth** confiar en alguien/algo

dependability [dɪ·ˌpen·də·'bɪl·ə·t̪i] *n* seriedad *f*

dependable [dɪ·'pen·də·bəl] *adj* (*thing*) fiable; (*person*) serio, -a

dependence [dɪ·'pen·dəns] *n* dependencia *f*

dependency *n* **1.** (*dependence*) dependencia **2.** (*territory*) dependencia; **Puerto Rico is a U.S. ~** Puerto Rico es una dependencia de EE.UU.

dependent [dɪ·'pen·dənt] **I.** *adj* **1.** (*conditional*) **to be ~ on sb/sth** depender de alguien/algo **2.** (*in need of*) dependiente; **to be ~ on sth** depender de algo; **to be ~ on drugs** ser drogadicto; **she has two ~ children** tiene dos niños a su cargo **II.** *n* familiar *m* dependiente

depict [dɪ·'pɪkt] *vt* representar

depiction [dɪ·'pɪk·ʃən] *n* representación *f*

depilatory [dɪ·'pɪl·ə·tɔr·i] **I.** *n* depilatorio *m* **II.** *adj* depilatorio, -a

depilatory cream *n* crema *f* depilatoria

deplete [dɪ·'plit] *vt* agotar

depleted *adj* agotado, -a

depletion [dɪ·'pli·ʃən] *n* (*of resources*) agotamiento *m*; (*of money*) merma *f*; (*of nutrients*) pérdida *f*; **~ of the ozone layer** reducción *f* de la capa de ozono

deplorable [dɪ·'plɔr·ə·bəl] *adj* deplorable

deplore [dɪ·'plɔr] *vt* deplorar

deploy [dɪ·'plɔɪ] *vt* (*resources*) utilizar; (*troops*) desplegar; (*skills*) demostrar

deployment [dɪ·'plɔɪ·mənt] *n* utilización *f*; (*of troops*) despliegue *m*

depopulate [ˌdi·'pap·jə·leɪt] *vt* despoblar

deport [dɪ·'pɔrt] *vt* deportar

deportation [ˌdi·pɔr·'teɪ·ʃən] *n* deportación *f*

deportee [ˌdi·pɔr·'ti] *n* deportado, -a *m*, *f*

deportment [dɪ·'pɔrt·mənt] *n* porte *m*

depose [dɪ·'poʊz] *vt* destituir

deposit [dɪ·'paz·ɪt] **I.** *vt* **1.** (*leave*) depositar; (*eggs*) poner; (*luggage*) guardar en consigna; **the bus ~ed me in the middle of nowhere** el autobús me dejó en mitad de la nada **2.** FIN (*store, pay into account*) ingresar; **to ~ $1000** dejar 1000 dólares en depósito **II.** *n* **1.** (*sediment*) sedimento *m* **2.** GEO yacimiento *m* **3.** (*first payment*) depósito *m*; **to make a ~** efectuar un depósito; **to leave a ~** dejar un depósito; **to leave sth as a ~** dejar algo en garantía; **on ~** en depósito

deposition [ˌdep·ə·'zɪʃ·ən] *n* **1.** (*removal from power*) destitución *f*; (*of a dictator*) derrocamiento *m* **2.** LAW declaración *f*; **to file a ~** dar testimonio

depositor [dɪ·'paz·ə·tər] *n* cuentahabiente *mf*

depot ['di·poʊ] *n* **1.** (*station*) estación *f* **2.** (*storehouse*) almacén *m*; (*for vehicles*) cochera *f*

deprave [dɪ·'preɪv] *vt* pervertir

depraved *adj* depravado, -a

depravity [dɪ·'præv·ə·t̪i] *n* depravación *f*

deprecate ['dep·rɪ·keɪt] *vt* **1.** (*disapprove of*) reprobar **2.** (*belittle*) menospreciar

deprecating *adj* **1.** (*disapproving*) de desaprobación **2.** (*belittling*) de desprecio

deprecation [ˌdep·rɪ·'keɪ·ʃən] *n* **1.** (*disapproval*) desaprobación *f* **2.** (*belittlement*) menosprecio *m*

deprecatory ['dep·rɪ·kə·tɔr·i] *adj s.* **deprecating**

depreciate [dɪ·'pri·ʃi·eɪt] **I.** *vi* depreciarse **II.** *vt* depreciar

depreciation [dɪ·ˌpri·ʃi·'eɪ·ʃən] *n* depreciación *f*

depredation [ˌdep·rə·'deɪ·ʃən] *n* estragos *fpl*

depress [dɪ·'pres] *vt* **1.** (*sadden*) deprimir; **it ~es me that...** me deprime que... +*subj* **2.** (*reduce activity of*) disminuir; (*the economy*) paralizar; (*earnings*) reducir; (*prices*) bajar **3.** (*press down*) presionar; (*pedal, button*) apretar

depressant I. *n* sedante *m* **II.** *adj* deprimente

D

depressed *adj* **1.** (*sad*) deprimido, -a, apolismado, -a *Méx, Ven;* **to feel** ~ sentirse abatido **2.** (*impoverished: period*) de depresión; (*area*) deprimido, -a; (*economy*) en crisis

depressing *adj* deprimente

depression [dɪ'preʃ·ən] *n* **1.** PSYCH, FIN depresión *f;* METEO zona *f* de bajas presiones **2.** (*hollow*) hoyo *m*

depressive [dɪ'pres·ɪv] **I.** *n* depresivo, -a *m, f* **II.** *adj* depresivo, -a

deprivation [ˌdep·rɪ'veɪ·ʃən] *n* privación *f*

deprive [dɪ'praɪv] *vt* (*of dignity*) despojar; (*of sleep*) quitar; **to** ~ **sb of sth** privar a alguien de algo

deprived *adj* desvalido, -a

depth [depθ] *n* **1.** *a. fig* profundidad *f;* **in the** ~ **of despair** en lo más hondo de su desesperación; **in the** ~ **of winter** en pleno invierno; **in the** ~**s of the ocean** en las profundidades del océano; **in the** ~**s of the forest** en la espesura del bosque **2.** (*intensity*) intensidad *f* **3.** (*low sound*) gravedad *f* ▶ **in** ~ en detalle

depth charge *n* carga *f* de profundidad

deputation [ˌdep·jə'teɪ·ʃən] *n* + *sing/pl vb* delegación *f*

depute [dɪ'pjut] *vt* **1.** (*appoint*) comisionar **2.** (*delegate*) **to** ~ **sth to sb** delegar algo en alguien

deputize ['dep·jə·taɪz] *vi* **to** ~ **for sb** suplir a alguien

deputy ['dep·jə·ti] *n* delegado, -a *m, f;* (*assistant*) segundo, -a *m, f;* (*in police department*) ayudante *mf* del sheriff

derail [dɪ'reɪl] **I.** *vt* hacer descarrilar; *fig* (*stop*) desbaratar **II.** *vi* descarrilar; *fig* venirse abajo, fracasar

derailment [dɪ'reɪl·mənt] *n* descarrilamiento *m; fig* fracaso *m*

derange [dɪ'reɪndʒ] *vt* perturbar

deranged *adj* trastornado, -a

derangement *n* trastorno *m* mental

derby ['dɜr·bi] *n* **1.** Derby *m* **2.** (*hat*) (sombrero de) hongo *m*

deregulation [ˌdɪ·reg·jə'leɪ·ʃən] *n* liberalización *f*

derelict ['der·ə·lɪkt] **I.** *adj* (*building*) abandonado, -a; (*site*) baldío, -a **II.** *n* (*person*) desposeído, -a *m, f*

dereliction [ˌder·ə'lɪk·ʃən] *n* **1.** (*dilapidation*) abandono *m* **2.** (*deliberate neglect*) negligencia *f*

deride [dɪ'raɪd] *vt* burlarse de; **to** ~ **sb for doing sth** ridiculizar a alguien por hacer algo

derision [dɪ'rɪʒ·ən] *n* burla *f;* **to meet sth with** ~ hacer burla de algo

derisive [dɪ'raɪ·sɪv] *adj* burlón, -ona

derisory [dɪ'raɪ·sə·ri] *adj* (*amount*) irrisorio, -a

derivation [ˌder·ɪ'veɪ·ʃən] *n* **1.** (*origin*) origen *m* **2.** (*sth derived*) derivado *m* **3.** (*process of evolving*) derivación *f*

derivative [dɪ'rɪv·ə·tɪv] **I.** *adj* **1.** derivado, -a **2.** *pej* poco original **II.** *n* derivado *m*

derive [dɪ'raɪv] **I.** *vt* **to** ~ **sth from sth** obtener algo de algo; **I** ~ **a lot of pleasure from working with children** disfruto mucho trabajando con niños **II.** *vi* **to** ~ **from sth** derivar de algo

dermatitis [ˌdɜr·mə'taɪ·təs] *n* dermatitis *f inv*

dermatologist *n* dermatólogo, -a *m, f*

dermatology [ˌdɜr·mə'tal·ə·dʒi] *n* dermatología *f*

derogate ['der·ə·geɪt] *vi* **to** ~ **from sth** atentar contra algo

derogation [ˌder·ə'geɪ·ʃən] *n* menosprecio *m*

derogatory [dɪ'rag·ə·tɔr·i] *adj* desdeñoso, -a

derrick ['der·ɪk] *n* **1.** (*crane*) grúa *f* **2.** (*framework*) torre *f* de perforación

desalinate [ˌdi'sæl·ɪ·neɪt] *vt* desalinizar

desalination [di·ˌsæl·ɪ'neɪ·ʃən] *n* desalinización *f*

desalination plant *n* planta *f* desalinizadora

descale [ˌdi'skeɪl] *vt* desincrustar

descant ['des·kænt] *n* MUS contrapunto *m*

descend [dɪ'send] **I.** *vi* **1.** (*go down*) descender; (*fall*) caer **2.** (*lower oneself*) **to** ~ **to stealing** rebajarse a robar **3.** (*come from*) ~ **from sb/sth** provenir de alguien/algo **II.** *vt* descender; (*a ladder*) bajar

descendant [dɪ'sen·dənt] *n* descendiente *mf*

descent [dɪ'sent] *n* **1.** AVIAT descenso *m;* (*way down*) bajada *f* **2.** (*decline*) declive *m* **3.** (*ancestry*) origen *m;* **of Irish** ~ de ascendencia irlandesa

describe [dɪ'skraɪb] *vt* **1.** (*tell in words*) describir; (*an experience*) relatar; **to** ~ **sb as stupid** calificar a alguien de tonto **2.** (*draw*) trazar

description [dɪ'skrɪp·ʃən] *n* **1.** (*account*) descripción *f;* **to answer a** ~ **of sb/sth** encajar con [*o* en] una descripción de alguien/algo **2.** (*sort*) clase *f;* **of every** ~ de todo tipo

descriptive [dɪ'skrɪp·tɪv] *adj* descriptivo, -a

desecrate ['des·ɪ·kreɪt] *vt* profanar

desecration [ˌdes·ɪ'kreɪ·ʃən] *n* profanación *f*

desegregate [ˌdi'seg·rɪ·geɪt] *vt* desegregar

desegregation [di·ˌseg·rɪ'geɪ·ʃən] *n* desegregación *f*

desensitize [ˌdi'sen·sɪ·taɪz] *vt a.* MED insensibilizar

desert¹ [dɪ'zɜrt] **I.** *vi* MIL desertar **II.** *vt* **1.** MIL desertar de **2.** (*abandon*) abandonar; (*one's post*) retirarse de; **to** ~ **sb** (**for sb else**) dejar a alguien (por otra persona)

desert² ['dez·ərt] *n* desierto *m;* ~ **plant/animal** planta/animal del desierto

deserted *adj* **1.** (*place*) desierto, -a **2.** (*person*) abandonado, -a

deserter *n* MIL desertor(a) *m(f);* POL tránsfuga *mf*

desertification [dɪ·ˌzɜr·tə·fɪ'keɪ·ʃən] *n* desertificación *f*

desertion [dɪ'zɜr·ʃən] *n* MIL deserción *f;* (*act of leaving*) abandono *m*

deserts [dɪ'zɜrts] *npl* merecido *m;* **to get one's just** ~ tener su merecido

deserve [dɪ'zɜrv] *vt* merecer; **what have I done to ~ (all) this?** ¿qué he hecho yo para merecer (todo) esto?

deservedly *adv* merecidamente

deserving *adj* meritorio, -a; **to be ~ of sth** ser digno de algo

design [dɪ'zaɪn] **I.** *vt* **1.** (*plan*) **to ~ sth (for sb)** diseñar algo (para alguien) **2.** (*intend*) **to ~ sth for sb/sth** concebir algo para alguien/ algo; **this dictionary is ~ed for advanced learners** este diccionario está dirigido a estudiantes de nivel avanzado; **these measures are ~ed to reduce criminality** estas medidas buscan reducir la criminalidad **II.** *vi* hacer diseños **III.** *n* **1.** (*plan*) diseño *m* **2.** (*sketch*) bosquejo *m* **3.** (*pattern*) motivo *m* **4.** (*intention*) propósito *m;* **to do sth by ~** hacer algo adrede **5. ~ s** *inf* (*dishonest intentions*) malas intenciones *fpl;* **to have ~s on a championship title** pretender un campeonato **IV.** *adj* de diseño

designate¹ ['dez·ɪg·neɪt] *vt* **1.** (*appoint*) nombrar; **to ~ sb to do sth** designar a alguien para hacer algo **2.** (*indicate*) señalar

designate² ['dez·ɪg·nɪt] *adj* nombrado, -a; **the ambassador ~** quien ha sido nombrado embajador

designated driver *n persona que se abstiene de beber para conducir a la vuelta,* conductor *m* asignado *Méx*

designation [ˌdez·ɪg·'neɪ·ʃən] *n* **1.** (*appointment*) nombramiento *m* **2.** (*act of indicating*) señalamiento *m* **3.** (*title*) denominación *f*

designedly *adv* a propósito

designer [dɪ'zaɪ·nər] **I.** *n* diseñador(a) *m(f)* **II.** *adj* de marca

designing I. *n* (*art*) diseño *m* **II.** *adj pej* intrigante

desirable [dɪ'zaɪr·ə·bəl] *adj* **1.** (*necessary*) conveniente; **it is ~ that...** sería deseable que... +*subj* **2.** (*sexually attractive*) deseable **3.** (*popular or fashionable: area, job*) codiciado, -a

desire [dɪ'zaɪr] **I.** *vt* **1.** (*request*) **to ~ that...** desear que... +*subj* **2.** (*want*) desear; **I ~ you to leave** le ruego que se vaya **3.** (*be sexually attracted to*) **to ~ sb** desear a alguien **II.** *n* **1.** (*craving*) deseo *m* **2.** (*request*) petición *f* **3.** (*sensual appetite*) deseo *m* (sexual); **to be the object of sb's ~** ser el objeto de deseo de alguien

desired *adj* deseado, -a

desirous [dɪ'zaɪ·rəs] *adj* deseoso, -a

desist [dɪ'sɪst] *vi form* desistir

desk [desk] *n* **1.** (*table*) escritorio *m; (in school*) pupitre *m* **2.** (*service counter*) mostrador *m* **3.** (*department of a newspaper*) mesa *f*

desk lamp *n* lámpara *f* de escritorio

desktop *n* COMPUT **~** (**computer**) (ordenador *m*) portátil *m*

desktop publishing *n* autoedición *f*

desolate¹ ['des·ə·lət] *adj* **1.** (*barren*) yermo, -a; (*landscape*) desolado, -a; (*prospect*) desola-

dor, a **2.** (*sad*) desolado, -a; **to feel ~** sentirse desconsolado

desolate² ['des·ə·leɪt] *vt* desolar

desolation [ˌdes·ə·'leɪ·ʃən] *n* **1.** (*barrenness*) desolación *f* **2.** (*sadness*) aflicción *f*

despair [dɪ'sper] **I.** *n* desesperación *f;* **to be in ~ about sth** estar desesperado por algo; **to drive sb to ~** desesperar a alguien ▶ **to be the ~ of sb** traer de cabeza a alguien **II.** *vi* desesperarse; **to ~ of sb/sth** perder las esperanzas con alguien/algo

despairing *adj* desesperado, -a; (*glance*) de desesperación

despatch [dɪ'spætʃ] *n, vt s.* **dispatch**

desperado [ˌdes·pə·'ra·dou] <-(e)s> *n* forajido, -a *m, f*

desperate ['des·pər·ɪt] *adj* **1.** (*as last chance: measure, solution*) desesperado, -a; (*violent*) encarnizado, -a **2.** (*serious*) grave; (*poverty*) extremo, -a; (*situation*) desesperado, -a **3.** (*great*) extremo, -a; **to be in a ~ hurry** estar muy apurado **4.** (*having great need*) **to be ~ for sth** necesitar algo con suma urgencia

desperation [ˌdes·pə·'reɪ·ʃən] *n* desesperación *f;* **in ~** a la desesperación; **to drive sb to ~** desesperar a alguien

despicable [dɪ'spɪk·ə·bəl] *adj* despreciable

despise [dɪ'spaɪz] *vt* despreciar; **to ~ sb for sth** menospreciar a alguien por algo

despite [dɪ'spaɪt] *prep* a pesar de

despoil [dɪ'spɔɪl] *vt* saquear

despondent [dɪ'span·dənt] *adj* desalentado, -a; **to feel ~ about sth** sentirse desanimado por algo

despot ['des·pət] *n* déspota *mf*

despotic [des·'pat·ɪk] *adj* despótico, -a

despotism ['des·pə·tɪz·əm] *n* despotismo *m*

dessert [dɪ'zɜrt] *n* postre *m*

dessertspoon [dɪ'zɜrt·ˌspun] *n* **1.** (*spoon*) cuchara *f* de postre **2.** (*amount*) cucharadita *f*

destabilization [ˌdi·'steɪ·bə·lɪ·'zeɪ·ʃən] *n* desestabilización *f*

destabilize [di·'steɪ·bə·laɪz] *vt* desestabilizar

destination [ˌdes·tə·'neɪ·ʃən] *n* destino *m*

destine ['des·tɪn] *vt* **1.** (*be certain*) destinar; **to be ~d to fail/succeed** estar destinado al fracaso/éxito **2.** (*intend*) **to be ~d for sth** estar destinado a algo **3.** (*have as destination*) tener por destino; **we're ~d for Tennessee** nos dirigimos a Tennessee

destiny ['des·tə·ni] *n* destino *m;* **to fight one's ~** luchar contra el destino; **to shape one's ~** hacerse su propio destino

destitute ['des·tɪ·tut] **I.** *adj* necesitado, -a **II.** *n* **the ~** *pl* los indigentes

destitution [ˌdes·tɪ·'tu·ʃən] *n* miseria *f*

destroy [dɪ'strɔɪ] *vt* **1.** (*demolish*) destruir **2.** (*kill*) matar; (*animal*) sacrificar **3.** (*ruin*) arruinar

destroyer [dɪ'strɔɪ·ər] *n* NAUT destructor *m*

destructible [dɪ'strʌk·tə·bəl] *adj* destructible

destruction [dɪ'strʌk·ʃən] *n* destrucción *f;* **mass ~** destrucción en masa; **to leave a trail**

of ~ dejar una estela de destrucción

destructive [dɪ·'strʌk·tɪv] *adj* destructivo, -a

destructiveness *n* destructividad *f*

desulphurization [di·,sʌl·fər·ɪ·'zeɪ·ʃən] *n* desulfurización *f*

desultory ['des·əl·tɔr·i] *adj* (*disconnected*) inconexo, -a; (*lacking plan*) desordenado, -a

detach [dɪ·'tætʃ] *vt* separar

detachable *adj* separable

detached *adj* **1.** (*separated*) separado, -a **2.** (*aloof*) indiferente **3.** (*impartial*) imparcial

detachment [dɪ·'tætʃ·mənt] *n* **1.** (*separation*) separación *f* **2.** (*disinterest*) desinterés *m* **3.** (*of soldiers*) destacamento *m*

detail [dɪ·'teɪl] **I.** *n* **1.** (*item of information*) detalle *m;* **in** ~ en detalle; **to go into** ~ entrar en detalles **2.** (*unimportant item*) minucia *f;* **gory** ~**s** *iron* intimidades *fpl* **3.** (*small feature*) elemento *m* **4.** MIL (*group*) destacamento *m* **II.** *vt* **1.** (*explain fully*) detallar **2.** (*tell, mention*) pormenorizar **3.** (*assign a duty to*) **to** ~ **sb to do sth** destacar a alguien para que haga algo

detailed *adj* detallado, -a; (*report, study*) pormenorizado, -a

detain [dɪ·'teɪn] *vt* **1.** (*hold as prisoner*) retener **2.** (*delay*) entretener; (*keep waiting*) retener

detainee [,di·teɪ·'ni] *n* detenido, -a *m, f*

detect [dɪ·'tekt] *vt* **1.** (*note*) advertir; (*sense presence of*) percibir; (*a mine*) hallar **2.** (*discover*) descubrir

detectable [dɪ·'tek·tə·bəl] *adj* (*discernible*) perceptible; (*able to be found*) averiguable

detection [dɪ·'tek·ʃən] *n* descubrimiento *m*

detective [dɪ·'tek·tɪv] *n* **1.** (*private investigator*) detective *mf* **2.** (*police officer*) agente *mf*

detective novel *n*, **detective story** *n* novela *f* policíaca

detector [dɪ·'tek·tər] *n* detector *m*

detention [dɪ·'ten·ʃən] *n* **1.** (*act*) detención *f* **2.** (*as a prisoner*) arresto *m* **3.** SCHOOL castigo *f*

detention home *n* correccional *m*

deter [dɪ·'tɜr] <-rr-> *vt* disuadir

detergent [dɪ·'tɜr·dʒənt] *n* detergente *m*

deteriorate [dɪ·'tɪr·i·ə·reɪt] *vi* **1.** (*wear out*) deteriorarse **2.** (*become worse*) empeorar

deterioration [dɪ·,tɪr·i·ə·'reɪ·ʃən] *n* **1.** (*wearing out*) deterioro *m* **2.** (*worsening*) empeoramiento *m*

determinable [dɪ·'tɜr·mə·nə·bəl] *adj* determinable

determinant [dɪ·'tɜr·mə·nənt] **I.** *n* determinante *m* **II.** *adj* determinante

determinate [dɪ·'tɜr·mə·nɪt] *adj* **1.** (*limited*) definido, -a **2.** (*of specific scope*) determinado, -a

determination [dɪ·,tɜr·mɪ·'neɪ·ʃən] *n* **1.** (*firmness of purpose*) resolución *f* **2.** (*decision*) determinación *f*

determine [dɪ·'tɜr·mɪn] **I.** *vi* **1.** (*decide*) **to** ~ **on sth** decidirse por algo **2.** LAW expirar **II.** *vt*

1. (*decide*) decidir; (*settle*) establecer **2.** (*find out*) fijar **3.** (*influence*) influir **4.** LAW (*terminate*) rescindir

determined [dɪ·'tɜr·mɪnd] *adj* decidido, -a; **to be** ~ **to do sth** estar resuelto a hacer algo

deterrence [dɪ·'tɜr·əns] *n* disuasión *f*

deterrent [dɪ·'tɜr·ənt] **I.** *n* freno *m;* **to act as a** ~ **to sb** disuadir a alguien **II.** *adj* disuasivo, -a

detest [dɪ·'test] *vt* detestar

detestable [dɪ·'tes·tə·bəl] *adj* detestable

detestation [,di·te·'steɪ·ʃən] *n* aborrecimiento *m*

dethrone [dɪ·'θroʊn] *vt* destronar

detonate ['det·ə·neɪt] *vi, vt* detonar

detonation [,det·ə·'neɪ·ʃən] *n* detonación *f*

detonator ['det·ə·neɪ·tər] *n* detonador *m*

detour ['di·tʊr] *n* desvío *m;* **to make a** ~ dar un rodeo

detoxify [di·'tak·sɪ·faɪ] *vt* desintoxicar

detract [dɪ·'trækt] *vi* **1.** (*devalue*) **to** ~ **from sth** quitar mérito a algo **2.** (*take away*) apartar

detractor [dɪ·'træk·tər] *n* detractor(a) *m(f)*

detriment ['det·rə·mənt] *n* perjuicio *m;* **to the** ~ **of sth** en detrimento de algo; **without** ~ **to sth** sin perjuicio de algo

detrimental [,det·rɪ·'men·təl] *adj* nocivo, -a

detritus [dɪ·'traɪ·təs] *n* **1.** (*small fragments*) detrito *m* **2.** (*debris*) desechos *mpl*

deuce [dus] *n* **1.** (*in cards*) dos *m* **2.** (*in tennis*) empate *m*

devaluate [,di·'væl·u·eɪt] *vt s.* **devalue**

devaluation [,di·væl·ju·'eɪ·ʃən] *n* devaluación *f*

devalue [,di·'væl·ju] *vt* devaluar

devastate ['dev·ə·steɪt] *vt* devastar

devastating *adj* **1.** (*causing destruction*) desolador(a); (*powerful*) devastador(a) **2.** (*stunning*) abrumador(a); (*beauty*) arrollador(a); (*charm*) irresistible

devastation [,dev·ə·'steɪ·ʃən] *n* devastación *f*

develop [dɪ·'vel·əp] **I.** *vi* (*grow*) desarrollarse; (*become more advanced*) progresar; **to** ~ **into sth** transformarse en algo **II.** *vt* **1.** (*expand*) desarrollar; (*improve*) ampliar **2.** (*create*) crear **3.** (*begin to show*) revelar; (*catch*) empezar a tener; (*an illness*) contraer **4.** (*build*) construir; (*build on*) urbanizar **5.** PHOT revelar **6.** MUS elaborar

developed *adj* desarrollado, -a; ~ **countries** países desarrollados

developer [dɪ·'vel·ə·pər] *n* **1.** (*person*) promotor(a) *m(f)* inmobiliario, -a; (*company*) inmobiliaria *f* **2.** PHOT revelador *m*

developing *adj* de desarrollo; ~ **countries** países en vías de desarrollo

development [dɪ·'vel·əp·mənt] *n* **1.** (*process*) desarrollo *m;* (*growth*) crecimiento *m* **2.** (*growth stage*) avance *m;* (*of skills*) evolución *f* **3.** (*progress*) progreso *m;* (*of products*) explotación *f* **4.** (*event*) acontecimiento *m* **5.** (*building of*) construcción *f;* **housing** ~ construcción de viviendas **6.** (*building on: of land*) urbanización *f* **7.** (*industrialization*) industrialización *f* **8.** MUS (*elaboration*) elaboración *f*

deviant ['di·vi·ənt] *adj* (*behavior*) que se aparta de la norma, desviado, -a; (*sexually*) pervertido, -a

deviate ['di·vi·ert] *vi* apartarse; **to ~ from sth** desviarse de algo

deviation [ˌdi·vi·'er·ʃən] *n* desviación *f*

device [dɪ·'vaɪs] *n* **1.** (*mechanism*) dispositivo *m;* **input/output ~** COMPUT dispositivo de entrada/salida **2.** (*method*) estrategia *f;* **literary/rhetorical ~** recurso *m* literario/retórico **3.** (*bomb*) artefacto *m;* **nuclear ~** arma *f* nuclear ▶ **to leave sb to their own ~s** abandonar a alguien a su suerte

devil ['dev·əl] *n* **1.** (*Satan*) diablo *m,* demonio *m;* **to be possessed by the D~** estar poseído por el demonio **2.** (*evil spirit*) demonio **3.** *inf* (*wicked person*) diablo *m* **4.** (*mischievous person*) **to be a ~** ser malo; **lucky ~!** ¡qué suerte!; **the poor ~!** ¡pobre diablo! **5.** (*difficult thing*) **to have a ~ of a time doing sth** costar Dios y ayuda hacer algo, costar un huevo hacer algo *elev* **6.** (*feisty energy*) arrojo *m;* **to be full of the ~** estar lleno de coraje **7.** (*machine*) máquina *f* deshilachadora ▶ **~ take the hindmost** camarón que se duerme se lo lleva la corriente *prov;* **between the ~ and the deep blue sea** entre la espada y la pared; **to sell one's soul to the ~** vender el alma al diablo; **to go to the ~** irse al infierno; **there'll be the ~ to pay** se formará un lío de todos los diablos; **to play the ~ with sth** estropear algo; **speak of the ~** hablando del rey de Roma, por la puerta asoma; **how/who/what/where the ~...?** ¿cómo/quién/qué/dónde diablos...?; **like the ~** como el demonio

devilish ['dev·ə·lɪʃ] *adj* **1.** (*evil*) diabólico, -a **2.** (*mischievous*) malvado, -a **3.** (*extreme*) extremo, -a; (*terrible*) infernal **4.** (*very clever*) ingenioso, -a

devil-may-care *adj* irresponsable

devilment ['dev·əl·mənt] *n,* **devilry** ['dev·əl·ri] *n* diablura *f*

devil's advocate *n* **to play the ~** hacer de abogado del diablo

devil's food cake *n* pastel *m* de chocolate

devious ['di·vi·əs] *adj* **1.** (*dishonest*) taimado, -a **2.** (*winding*) tortuoso, -a; (*route*) intrincado, -a

devise [dɪ·'vaɪz] **I.** *n* legado *m* **II.** *vt* **1.** (*plan, think out*) idear; (*a plot*) diseñar; (*a scheme*) trazar **2.** LAW legar

devoid [dɪ·'vɔɪd] *adj* **to be ~ of sth** estar desprovisto de algo

devolution [ˌdev·ə·'lu·ʃən] *n* **1.** (*progression through stages*) transferencia *f* **2.** (*transference of wealth*) traspaso *m* **3.** POL (*decentralization of power*) delegación *f*

devolve [dɪ·'valv] **I.** *vi* recaer **II.** *vt* (*transfer*) transferir; (*powers*) delegar

devote [dɪ·'voʊt] *vt* dedicar; **to ~ oneself to sth** dedicarse a algo

devoted [dɪ·'voʊ·tɪd] *adj* dedicado, -a; (*husband, mother*) devoto, -a; **to be ~ to sb/sth** estar consagrado a alguien/algo

devotee [ˌdev·ə·'ti] *n* (*supporter*) partidario, -a *m, f;* (*admirer*) fanático, -a *m, f;* (*advocate*) devoto, -a *m, f*

devotion [dɪ·'voʊ·ʃən] *n* **1.** (*loyalty*) lealtad *f;* (*affection*) afecto *m;* (*admiration*) fervor *m;* (*great attachment*) dedicación *f;* **to inspire ~** inspirar devoción **2.** REL devoción *f* **3.** (*devoutness*) fervor

devotional [dɪ·'voʊ·ʃə·nəl] *adj* (*attitude*) devoto, -a; (*music, practices*) religioso, -a

devour [dɪ·'vaʊ·ər] *vt* **1.** (*eat eagerly*) tragar **2.** (*engulf*) devorar **3.** (*consume quickly*) consumir; (*feel strongly*); **to be ~ed by jealousy** estar consumido por los celos

devouring *adj* devorador(a)

devout [dɪ·'vaʊt] *adj* **1.** REL devoto, -a **2.** (*compulsive*) fervoroso, -a

dew [du] *n* rocío *m*

dewdrop ['du·drap] *n* gota *f* de rocío

dewy ['du·i] *adj* cubierto, -a de rocío

dexterity [ˌdek·'ster·ə·ti] *n* agilidad *f*

dexterous ['dek·stər·əs] *adj* diestro, -a

dextrose ['dek·stroʊs] *n* dextrosa *f*

dextrous ['dek·strəs] *adj s.* **dexterous**

diabetes [ˌdaɪ·ə·'bi·tɪz] *n* diabetes *f inv*

diabetic [ˌdaɪ·ə·'bet·ɪk] **I.** *n* diabético, -a *m, f* **II.** *adj* diabético, -a

diabolic [ˌdaɪ·ə·'bal·ɪk] *adj,* **diabolical** [ˌdaɪ·ə·'bal·ɪ·kəl] *adj* **1.** (*of the Devil*) diabólico, -a **2.** (*evil*) malvado, -a **3.** *inf* (*very bad*) maligno, -a

diadem ['daɪ·ə·dem] *n* diadema *f*

diagnose [ˌdaɪ·əg·'noʊs] **I.** *vi* hacer un diagnóstico **II.** *vt* diagnosticar

diagnosis [ˌdaɪ·əg·'noʊ·sɪs] <-ses> *n* **1.** (*process*) diagnosis *f inv* **2.** (*result*) diagnóstico *m*

diagnostic [ˌdaɪ·əg·'nas·tɪk] **I.** *n* diagnóstico *m* **II.** *adj* diagnóstico, -a

diagonal [daɪ·'æg·ə·nəl] **I.** *n* diagonal *f* **II.** *adj* diagonal

diagram ['daɪ·ə·græm] **I.** *n* **1.** (*drawing*) diagrama *m;* (*plan*) esquema *m* **2.** (*chart*) gráfico *m* **3.** (*figure*) figura *f* **II.** <-mm-> *vt* hacer un diagrama de

dial ['daɪ·əl] **I.** *n* **1.** (*face of clock*) esfera *f,* tablero *m Col,* carátula *f Guat* **2.** (*on telephone*) disco *m* **3.** (*on radio*) dial *m* **II.** <-l- *o* -ll-, -l- *o* -ll-> *vi* marcar, discar *Arg, Perú, Urug;* **to ~ direct** hacer una llamada directa **III.** *vt* **1.** (*phone number*) marcar **2.** (*radio station*) sintonizar

◆ **dial in** *vi* **to ~ (to sth)** (*conseguir*) conectar (con algo)

dialect ['daɪ·ə·lekt] *n* dialecto *m*

dialectal [ˌdaɪ·ə·'lek·təl] *adj* dialectal

dialectical [ˌdaɪ·ə·'lek·tɪ·kəl] *adj* dialéctico, -a

dialog *n,* **dialogue** ['daɪ·ə·lag] *n* **1.** (*conversation*) diálogo *m* **2.** POL diálogo; **to engage in ~** dialogar

dial tone *n* TEL tono *m* de marcado

dial-up service n COMPUT servicio m de marcado

dialysis [daɪ·'æl·ə·sɪs] n diálisis f inv

diameter [daɪ·'æm·ə·tər] n diámetro m

diametrically [ˌdaɪ·ə·'met·rɪ·kə·li] adv 1. (as a diameter) diametralmente 2. (completely) en su totalidad

diamond ['daɪ·ə·mənd] n 1. (gemstone) diamante m; the ace/king of ~s GAMES el as/rey de diamantes 2. (rhombus) rombo m 3. (for cutting glass) cortavidrios m inv 4. (baseball field) diamante; (infield) cuadro m ▶ a ~ in the rough un diamante en bruto

diamond cutter n diamantista mf

diaper ['daɪ·pər] n pañal m

diaphanous [daɪ·'æf·ə·nəs] adj liter diáfano, -a; (cloth) transparente

diaphragm ['daɪ·ə·fræm] n diafragma m

diarist ['daɪ·ə·rɪst] n diarista mf

diarrhea [ˌdaɪ·ə·'ri·ə] n diarrea f

diary ['daɪ·ə·ri] n diario m

diatonic [ˌdaɪ·ə·'tan·ɪk] adj MUS diatónico, -a

diatribe ['daɪ·ə·traɪb] n diatriba f

dice [daɪs] I. npl 1. (cubes) dados mpl; to roll the ~ tirar los dados 2. (game) juego m de dados 3. (food cut in cubes) tacos mpl ▶ no ~ sl ni de coña II. vi jugar a los dados III. vt cortar en tacos

dicey ['daɪ·si] <-ier, -iest> adj inf peligroso, -a

dichotomy [daɪ·'kat·ə·mi] n dicotomía f

dick [dɪk] n vulg 1. (penis) polla f, pija f AmL, paloma f Méx, Ven, pajarito m RíoPl 2. (stupid person) gilipollas mf inv

dickens ['dɪk·ɪnz] npl sl what the ~...? ¿qué hostias...?, ¿qué diablos...?; to scare the ~ out of sb dar mucho cague a alguien, hacer cagar del susto a alguien

dicky ['dɪk·i] n inf (weak) a ~ heart una debilidad cardiaca

Dictaphone® ['dɪk·tə·foʊn] n dictáfono® m

dictate ['dɪk·teɪt] I. n dictado m II. vi 1. (command) mandar 2. (to a typist) dictar; to ~ to sb dictar a alguien III. vt 1. (give orders) ordenar 2. (make necessary) influir; (state exactly) imponer 3. (to a typist) dictar

dictation [dɪk·'teɪ·ʃən] n SCHOOL dictado m

dictator ['dɪk·teɪ·tər] n POL dictador(a) m(f)

dictatorial [ˌdɪk·tə·'tɔr·i·əl] adj dictatorial

dictatorship [dɪk·'teɪ·tər·ʃɪp] n dictadura f

diction ['dɪk·ʃən] n dicción f

dictionary ['dɪk·ʃə·ner·i] n diccionario m

did [dɪd] pt of do

didactic [daɪ·'dæk·tɪk] adj didáctico, -a

diddle ['dɪd·əl] vt sl (swindle) timar; to ~ sb out of sth estafar algo a alguien
  ◆**diddle around** vi (hang around: aimlessly) pasar el tiempo; (hang around: unproductively) perder el tiempo

didn't ['dɪd·ənt] = did not s. do

die[1] [daɪ] <dice> n 1. dado m 2. TECH molde m ▶ the ~ is cast la suerte está echada

die[2] [daɪ] <dying, died> vi 1. (cease to live) morir; to ~ a violent/natural death morir de muerte violenta/natural; to ~ by one's own hand suicidarse 2. (end) desaparecer; the secret will ~ with her se llevará el secreto a la tumba 3. (stop functioning: appliance) estropearse; (battery) gastarse; the engine just ~d el motor se ha muerto 4. (go out, fade away) extinguirse ▶ to ~ hard persistir; never say ~! ¡nunca te rindas!; to do or ~ vencer o morir; to be dying to do sth tener muchas ganas de hacer algo; I'm dying for a cup of tea me muero por una taza de té
  ◆**die away** vi desaparecer; (sobs, anger) calmarse; (enthusiasm) decaer; (wind) amainar; (sound) apagarse
  ◆**die back** vi secarse
  ◆**die down** vi apagarse
  ◆**die off** vi (species) extinguirse; (customs) desaparecer
  ◆**die out** vi extinguirse

dieback ['daɪ·bæk] n muerte f de los bosques (a causa de la contaminación del medio ambiente)

die-hard n intransigente mf; a ~ conservative un conservador recalcitrante

diesel ['di·zəl] n diesel m

diesel engine n motor m diesel

diet[1] ['daɪ·ət] I. n dieta f; to be on a ~ estar a dieta; to put sb on a ~ poner a alguien a dieta; to go on a ~ seguir una dieta II. vi estar a dieta III. vt to ~ sb poner a alguien a dieta

diet[2] ['daɪ·ət] n (legislative body) asamblea f legislativa

dietary ['daɪ·ɪ·ter·i] adj (food) dietético, -a; (habit) de alimentación

dietary fiber n fibra f dietética

dietetic [ˌdaɪ·ə·'tet·ɪk] adj dietético, -a

dietetics n dietética f

dietician n, **dietitian** [ˌdaɪ·ə·'tɪʃ·ən] n dietista mf

differ ['dɪf·ər] vi 1. (be unlike) ser diferente; to ~ from sth ser distinto de algo 2. (disagree) no estar de acuerdo; to ~ about sth discrepar en algo

difference ['dɪf·ər·əns] n 1. (state of being different) dife rencia f 2. (distinction) distinción f; that makes all the ~ eso cambia todo; to make a ~ importar; to not make any ~ dar igual 3. (new feature) singularidad f 4. (remaining amount) to pay the ~ pagar la diferencia 5. (disagreement) discrepancia f; to put aside ~s dejar de lado las diferencias; to settle ~s resolver diferencias

different ['dɪf·ər·ənt] adj 1. (not the same) diferente 2. (distinct) distinto, -a 3. (unusual) raro, -a; to do something ~ romper la rutina ▶ to be as ~ as night and day ser la noche y el día

differential [ˌdɪf·ə·'ren·tʃəl] I. n 1. a. MATH diferencial m 2. (difference in pay) pay ~s diferencia f de sueldo II. adj 1. (different) diferente 2. MATH diferencial

differentiate [ˌdɪf·ə·'ren·tʃi·eɪt] vi, vt distinguir

differentiation [ˌdɪf·ə·ren·tʃi·'eɪ·ʃən] n diferenciación *f*

difficult ['dɪf·ɪ·kəlt] *adj* **1.** (*not easy*) difícil; **she is said to be a very ~ person** dicen que es una persona muy difícil **2.** (*troublesome*) duro, -a

difficulty ['dɪf·ɪ·kəl·ti] <-ies> *n* **1.** (*being difficult*) dificultad *f;* **with** ~ con dificultad **2.** (*problem*) obstáculo *m;* **to have difficulties with sb** tener problemas con alguien; **to have ~ doing sth** tener problemas para hacer algo; **to encounter difficulties** encontrar dificultades

diffident ['dɪf·ɪ·dənt] *adj* (*shy*) tímido, -a; (*modest*) modesto, -a

diffract [dɪ·'frækt] *vt* difractar

diffuse¹ [dɪ·'fjuz] I. *vi* difundirse II. *vt* difundir

diffuse² [dɪ·'fjus] *adj* **1.** (*spread out*) dilatado, -a **2.** (*verbose*) verboso, -a **3.** (*imprecise*) difuso, -a

diffusion [dɪ·'fju·ʒən] *n* **1.** (*process of diffusing*) difusión *f* **2.** CHEM, PHYS dispersión *f*

dig [dɪg] I. *n* **1.** (*poke*) empujón *m* **2.** (*excavation*) excavación *f* **3.** (*sarcastic remark*) pulla *f* II. <-gg-, dug, dug> *vi* **1.** (*turn over ground*) cavar, escarbar; **to ~ deeper** *fig* ahondar **2.** (*poke*) empujar III. *vt* **1.** (*move ground*) cavar; (*a well, canal*) abrir **2.** (*excavate*) excavar **3.** (*stab, poke*) clavar; **to ~ one's elbow into sb's ribs** dar un codazo en las costillas a alguien; **to ~ one's spurs into a horse** hincar las espuelas a un caballo **4.** *sl* (*like*) molar ▶ **to ~ one's own grave** cavarse su propia tumba

◆ **dig in** I. *vi inf* (*start eating*) atacar II. *vt* **1.** (*bury*) enterrar **2.** (*dig trenches*) atrincherarse **3.** (*establish oneself*) instalarse; (*settle in*) asentarse

◆ **dig into** I. *vi* clavar ▶ **to dig (deeper) into one's pockets** poner (más) dinero de su propio bolsillo II. *vt always sep inf* atacar ▶ **to dig oneself into a hole** meterse en un problema

◆ **dig out** *vt* (*hole*) excavar; (*buried object*) desenterrar, extraer

◆ **dig up** *vt* **1.** (*from ground*) desenterrar **2.** (*excavate*) excavar **3.** *fig* (*find out*) descubrir

digest¹ ['daɪ·dʒest] *n* **1.** (*of essays*) resumen *m* **2.** (*of laws*) digesto *m*

digest² [daɪ·'dʒest] I. *vi* (*food*) digerirse; (*person*) hacer la digestión II. *vt* **1.** (*break down: food*) digerir **2.** *inf* (*understand*) asimilar **3.** (*classify*) clasificar

digestible [daɪ·'dʒes·tə·bəl] *adj* digerible

digestion [daɪ·'dʒes·tʃən] *n* digestión *f*

digestive [daɪ·'dʒes·tɪv] *adj* digestivo, -a

digger ['dɪg·ər] *n* **1.** (*machine*) excavadora *f* **2.** (*person*) cavador(a) *m(f)*

digit ['dɪdʒ·ɪt] *n* **1.** (*number*) dígito *m* **2.** (*finger, toe*) dedo *m*

digital ['dɪdʒ·ɪ·təl] *adj* digital

digitalize ['dɪdʒ·ɪ·təl·aɪz] *vt* digitalizar

digitize ['dɪdʒ·ɪ·taɪz] *vt* COMPUT digitalizar

digitizer ['dɪdʒ·ɪtaɪ·zər] *n* COMPUT digitalizador *m*

dignified ['dɪg·nɪ·faɪd] *adj* **1.** (*honorable*) digno, -a **2.** (*solemn*) solemne

dignify ['dɪg·nɪ·faɪ] <-ie-> *vt* dignificar

dignitary ['dɪg·nə·ter·i] <-ies> *n* dignatario, -a *m, f*

dignity ['dɪg·nə·ti] *n* **1.** (*state worthy of respect*) dignidad *f* **2.** (*respect*) respeto *m;* **to be beneath sb's** ~ no ser digno de alguien **3.** (*composed style*) decoro *m*

digress [daɪ·'gres] *vi* **1.** (*wander from topic*) hacer una digresión **2.** (*deviate*) desviarse; **to ~ from sth** apartarse de algo

digressive [daɪ·'gres·ɪv] *adj* digresivo, -a

dike [daɪk] *n* **1.** a. *fig* dique *m* **2.** (*channel*) acequia *f*

dilapidated [dɪ·'læp·ɪ·deɪ·t̬ɪd] *adj* (*house*) derruido, -a; (*car*) destartalado, -a

dilate ['daɪ·leɪt] I. *vi* dilatarse II. *vt* dilatar

dilation [daɪ·'leɪ·ʃən] *n* dilatación *f*

dilatory ['dɪl·ə·tɔr·i] *adj* **1.** (*slow*) lento, -a **2.** LAW dilatorio, -a

dilemma [dɪ·'lem·ə] *n* dilema *m;* **to be in a ~** estar en un dilema; **to face a ~** enfrentarse a un dilema

dilettante [ˌdɪl·ə·'tant] *n* <-s *o* -ti> diletante *mf*

diligence ['dɪl·ɪ·dʒəns] *n* diligencia *f*

diligent ['dɪl·ɪ·dʒənt] *adj* (*careful*) concienzudo, -a; (*hard-working*) diligente

dill [dɪl] *n* eneldo *m*

dilly-dally ['dɪl·i·dæl·i] *vi inf* **1.** (*waste time*) perder el tiempo **2.** (*be indecisive*) vacilar

dilute [daɪ·'lut] I. *vt* diluir II. *vi* diluirse III. *adj* diluido, -a

dilution [daɪ·'lu·ʃən] *n* a. *fig* disolución *f*

dim [dɪm] I. <-mm-> *vi* (*lights*) apagarse II. *vt* apagar III. <-mm-> *adj* **1.** (*not bright*) tenue **2.** (*unclear, faint*) borroso, -a **3.** (*stupid*) lerdo, -a **4.** (*unfavorable*) sombrío, -a

dime [daɪm] *n* moneda *f* de diez centavos ▶ **they're a ~ a dozen** los hay a patadas

dimension [dɪ·'men·tʃən] I. *n* dimensión *f* II. *vt* dimensionar

dimensional [dɪ·'men·tʃə·nəl] *adj* dimensional

diminish [dɪ·'mɪn·ɪʃ] I. *vi* disminuir; **to (greatly) ~ in value** perder mucho valor II. *vt* **1.** (*make less*) disminuir **2.** (*damage sb's reputation*) rebajar

diminution [ˌdɪm·ə·'nu·ʃən] *n* disminución *f*

diminutive [dɪ·'mɪn·jə·t̬ɪv] I. *n* LING diminutivo *m* II. *adj* diminuto, -a

dimmer ['dɪm·ər] *n* potenciómetro *m*

dimness *n* penumbra *f*

dimple ['dɪm·pəl] I. *n* hoyuelo *m* II. *vt* formar hoyuelos en

din [dɪn] *n* estrépito *m*

dine [daɪn] *vi* cenar

diner ['daɪ·nər] *n* **1.** (*person*) comensal *mf* **2.** (*restaurant*) restaurante *m* de carretera

---

ℹ En EE.UU. se llama **diner** a un tipo de restaurante que en lugar de mesas tiene barra y

compartimentos con asientos. Original-
mente, en la carta de los diners se encon-
traba en los años cincuenta comida rápida
del tipo hamburguesas, patatas o papas fritas.
Hoy son conocidos por tener una carta larga
como una novela, ya que ofrecen tanto sánd-
wiches como platos de carne, pollo y huevos.
Puesto que muchos diners están en manos
de inmigrantes griegos, también es habitual
encontrar en ellos especialidades helénicas.

dinghy ['dɪŋ·i] *n* <-ies> bote *m*
dingy ['dɪn·dʒi] <-ier, -iest> *adj* deslustrado, -a
dining car *n* vagón *m* restaurante
dining room *n* comedor *m*
DINK [dɪŋk] *n abbr of* **dual income no kids**
pareja con dos sueldos y sin hijos
dinky ['dɪŋ·ki] *adj* 1. (*insignificant*) pobre
2. (*shabby*) destartalado, -a
dinner ['dɪn·ər] *n* cena *f,* comida *f AmS;* (**Sunday**) ~ merienda *f;* **to make** ~ hacer la cena [*o*
el almuerzo *AmS*]
dinner jacket *n* esmoquin *m*
dinner party *n* cena *f*
dinner service *n* vajilla *f*
dinner table *n* mesa *f* (*del comedor*)
dinnertime *n* hora *f* de cenar
dinnerware *n* vajilla *f*
dinosaur ['daɪ·nə·sɔr] *n* dinosaurio *m; fig* antigualla *f*
dint [dɪnt] *n* **by ~ of sth** a fuerza de algo
diocese ['daɪ·ə·sɪs] *n* diócesis *f inv*
dioxide [daɪ·'ak·saɪd] *n* dióxido *m*
dioxin [daɪ·'ak·sɪn] *n* dioxina *f*
dip [dɪp] I. *n* 1. (*dunking*) baño *m* 2. (*sudden
drop*) caída *f;* (*in the road*) hondonada *f*
3. (*cold sauce*) salsa *f* 4. (*brief swim*) chapuzón *m* 5. (*depression in horizon, ground*)
depresión *f* 6. (*magnetic*) inclinación *f* II. *vi*
1. (*drop down*) descender; (*prices*) caer;
(*road*) bajar 2. (*slope down*) inclinarse 3. (*into
a liquid*) zambullirse III. *vt* 1. (*immerse*)
sumergir; *a.* CULIN mojar 2. (*put into*) meter
3. (*dye*) teñir 4. (*wash*) desinfectar 5. (*lower*)
bajar
♦ **dip into** *vt* 1. *always sep* (*put*) meter 2. **to ~
one's savings/retirement account** echar
mano de los ahorros/la cuenta de jubilación
3. (*look casually*) **I'll just ~ this store** voy a
echar un vistazo en esta tienda
diphtheria [dɪf·'θɪr·i·ə] *n* MED difteria *f*
diphthong ['dɪf·θaŋ] *n* LING diptongo *m*
diploma [dɪ·'ploʊ·mə] *n* diploma *m*
diplomacy [dɪ·'ploʊ·mə·si] *n* 1. (*between
countries*) diplomacia *f* 2. (*tact*) tacto *m*
diplomat ['dɪp·lə·mæt] *n* 1. (*of country*) diplomático, -a *m, f* 2. (*tactful person*) persona *f*
diplomática
diplomatic [,dɪp·lə·'mæt̬·ɪk] *adj* diplomático,
-a

dippy ['dɪp·i] *adj sl* flipado, -a, ahuevado, -a
Col, Perú, Nic, Pan
dipsomania [,dɪp·sə·'meɪ·ni·ə] *n* MED dipso-
manía *f*
dipsomaniac [,dɪp·sə·'meɪ·ni·æk] *n* MED dip-
sómano, -a *m, f*
dipstick ['dɪp·stɪk] *n* varilla *f* de medir
dire ['daɪr] *adj* 1. (*terrible*) horrendo, -a
2. (*serious*) grave; **to be in ~ straits** estar en
grandes apuros 3. (*extreme*) extremo, -a
direct [dɪ·'rekt] I. *vi* MUS dirigir II. *vt* 1. (*point,
intend*) dirigir; **to ~ sth at sb** dirigir algo a alguien 2. (*command*) ordenar 3. (*indicate*) **to
~ sb to a place** indicar a alguien el camino
hacia un sitio III. *adj* 1. (*straight*) directo, -a
2. (*exact*) exacto, -a; **the ~ opposite of sth**
exactamente lo contrario de algo 3. (*frank*)
directo, -a, franco, -a IV. *adv* 1. (*with no intermediary*) directamente 2. (*by a direct way*)
recto
direct action *n* acción *f* directa
direct current *n* corriente *f* continua
direct deposit *n* (*banking*) depósito *m* directo
direct hit *n* blanco *m*
direction [dɪ·'rek·ʃən] *n* 1. (*supervision*) dirección *f* 2. (*movement*) **in the ~ of sth** hacia [*o*
en dirección a] algo; **sense of ~** sentido *m* de
la orientación 3. *pl* (*information*) instrucciones *fpl;* **can you give me ~s?** ¿me puedes
indicar el camino?
directional [dɪ·'rek·ʃə·nəl] *adj* direccional
directive [dɪ·'rek·tɪv] *n* directriz *f,* directiva *f*
AmL
directly [dɪ·'rekt·li] *adv* 1. (*without deviation*)
directamente 2. (*immediately*) inmediatamente; (*right after*) inmediatamente después
3. (*shortly*) pronto 4. (*exactly*) exactamente
5. (*frankly*) directamente, con franqueza
direct object *n* objeto *m* [*o* complemento] *m*
directo
director [dɪ·'rek·tər] *n* 1. ECON (*manager*)
director(a) *m(f)* 2. (*board member*) miembro
m del consejo; **board of ~s** junta *f* directiva
directorate [dɪ·'rek·tər·ət] *n* 1. (*board of directors*) junta directiva 2. (*department*) directiva *f*
directorship [dɪ·'rek·tər·ʃɪp] *n* dirección *f*
directory [dɪ·'rek·tə·ri] *n* 1. (*book*) guía *f,*
directorio *m Méx* 2. COMPUT directorio
directory assistance *n* (servicio *m* de)
información *f* telefónica
dirt [dɜrt] *n* 1. (*earth, soil*) tierra *f* 2. (*unclean
substance*) suciedad *f* 3. (*excrement*) excrementos *mpl* 4. *inf* (*worthless thing*) porquería
f, escoria *f;* (*person*); **don't bother with him,
he's ~** pasa de él, no es un mierda *inf;* **to
treat sb like ~** tratar a alguien como basura
5. (*foul language*) obscenidad *f* 6. *inf* (*scandal,
gossip*) trapos *mpl* sucios *fig;* **to get the ~ on
sb** enterarse de los trapos sucios de alguien
▶ **to eat ~** tragar quina [*o* mierda] *inf*
dirt cheap *adj inf* tirado, -a, botado, -a *Méx*
dirt road *n* carril *m* (de tierra), camino *m* de

terracería *Méx*

dirty ['dɜr·ţi] I. *vt* ensuciar; **to ~ one's hands** ensuciarse las manos II.<-ier, -iest> *adj* 1.(*not clean*) sucio, -a, chancho, -a *AmL* 2.(*mean, nasty*) bajo, -a; (*look*) asesino, -a 3.(*lewd*) obsceno, -a; (*joke*) verde; **~ old man** viejo *m* verde 4.(*unpleasant*) sucio, -a; **to do the ~ work** hacer el trabajo sucio III. *adv* suciamente; **to play ~** jugar sucio

disability [ˌdɪs·ə·'bɪl·ə·ţi] *n* 1.(*handicap*) discapacidad *f*, invalidez *f AmL* 2.(*condition of incapacity*) incapacidad *f*

disable [dɪs·'eɪ·bəl] *vt* 1.incapacitar 2.MED lisiar

disabled I. *npl* **the ~** los discapacitados II. *adj* incapacitado, -a

disablement *n* incapacitación *f*; MED minusvalía *f*

disabuse [ˌdɪs·ə·'bjuz] *vt* **to ~ sb of sth** desengañar a alguien de algo

disadvantage [ˌdɪs·əd'væn·tɪdʒ] I. *n* desventaja *f*; **to be at a ~** estar en desventaja II. *vt* perjudicar

disadvantaged *adj* desfavorecido, -a

disadvantageous [ˌdɪs·ˌæd·væn·'teɪ·dʒəs] *adj* desfavorable

disaffected [ˌdɪs·ə·'fek·tɪd] *adj* 1.(*disloyal*) desleal 2.(*estranged*) desafecto, -a

disaffection [ˌdɪs·ə·'fek·ʃən] *n* desafección *f*

disagree [ˌdɪs·ə·'gri] *vi* 1.(*not agree*) no estar de acuerdo, discrepar *elev;* **to ~ on sth** no estar de acuerdo en algo 2.(*differ*) diferir; **the answers ~** las respuestas no concuerdan 3.(*have bad effect*) sentar mal; **spicy food ~s with me** la comida picante me sienta mal

disagreeable [ˌdɪs·ə·'gri·ə·bəl] *adj* desagradable

disagreement [ˌdɪs·ə·'gri·mənt] *n* 1.(*lack of agreement*) desacuerdo *m* 2.(*argument*) discusión *f* 3.(*discrepancy*) discrepancia *f*

disallow [ˌdɪs·ə·'laʊ] *vt* rechazar; *a.* LAW, SPORTS anular

disappear [ˌdɪs·ə·'pɪr] *vi* desaparecer; **to ~ from sight** desaparecer de la vista; **to ~ without a trace** desaparecer sin dejar rastro; **to have all but ~ed** haber casi desaparecido

disappearance [ˌdɪs·ə·'pɪr·əns] *n* desaparición *f*

disappoint [ˌdɪs·ə·'pɔɪnt] *vt* decepcionar, enchilar *AmC*

disappointed *adj* decepcionado, -a; **to be ~ in sb** estar decepcionado con alguien

disappointing *adj* decepcionante

disappointment [ˌdɪs·ə·'pɔɪnt·mənt] *n* decepción *f*

disapprobation [ˌdɪs·ˌæp·rə·'beɪ·ʃən] *n* desaprobación *f*

disapproval [ˌdɪs·ə·'pru·vəl] *n* desaprobación *f*

disapprove [ˌdɪs·ə·'pruv] *vi* desaprobar; **to ~ of sth** desaprobar algo

disarm [dɪs·'arm] I. *vi* deponer las armas II. *vt* 1.(*take weapons away*) desarmar 2.(*remove fuse: bomb*) desactivar 3.(*win over*) apaciguar

disarmament [dɪs·'ar·mə·mənt] *n* desarme *m*

disarming [dɪs·'ar·mɪŋ] *adj* 1.MIL en desarme 2.(*person, smile*) encantador(a)

disarrange [ˌdɪs·ə·'reɪndʒ] *vt* desarreglar; (*untidy*) desordenar

disarray [ˌdɪs·ə·'reɪ] *n* (*disorder*) desorden *m;* (*confusion*) confusión *f*

disaster [dɪ·'zæs·tər] *n* 1.(*great misfortune*) desastre *m; ~* **area** zona *f* catastrófica 2.(*failure*) fiasco *m*

disastrous [dɪ·'zæs·trəs] *adj* 1.(*causing disaster*) desastroso, -a 2.(*unsuccessful*) catastrófico, -a

disband [dɪs·'bænd] *vt* disolver

disbelief [ˌdɪs·bɪ·'lif] *n* incredulidad *f*

disbelieve [ˌdɪs·bɪ·'liv] *vt* no creer

disbeliever *n* incrédulo, -a *m, f*

disburse [dɪs·'bɜrs] *vt* desembolsar

disbursement [dɪs·'bɜrs·mənt] *n* desembolso *m*

disc [dɪsk] *n* disco *m*

discard¹ ['dɪs·kard] *n* descarte *m*

discard² [dɪ·'skard] *vt* 1.(*get rid of*) desechar 2. *a.* GAMES descartar

disc brake *n* freno *m* de disco

discern [dɪ·'sɜrn] *vt* 1.(*perceive*) percibir; (*distinguish*) distinguir 2.(*make out*) discernir

discernible [dɪ·'sɜr·nə·bəl] *adj* (*with senses*) perceptible; (*mentally*) discernible

discerning [dɪ·'sɜr·nɪŋ] *adj* (*discriminating*) exigente; (*acute*) perspicaz

discernment [dɪ·'sɜrn·mənt] *n* (*good judgment*) criterio *m;* (*clear perception*) discernimiento *m*

discharge¹ ['dɪs·tʃardʒ] *n* 1.(*release*) liberación *f;* (*from hospital*) alta *f* 2.(*release papers*) alta 3.(*firing off*) disparo *m* 4.(*emission*) emisión *f;* (*of liquid*) secreción *f* 5.(*debt payment*) liquidación *f* 6.(*performing of a duty*) desempeño *m* 7.(*energy release*) descarga *f*

discharge² [dɪs·'tʃardʒ] I. *vi* 1.(*ship*) descargar 2.(*produce liquid*) segregar; (*wound*) supurar II. *vt* 1. *a.* LAW (*release*) liberar 2.MIL, ECON (*dismiss*) despedir 3.(*let out*) emitir 4.(*utter*) gritar 5.(*perform*) **to ~ one's duty** cumplir con sus obligaciones 6.(*pay: debt*) liquidar 7.(*cancel*) cancelar 8.(*shoot*) lanzar

disciple [dɪ·'saɪ·pəl] *n* 1.(*follower*) seguidor(a) *m(f)* 2. *a.* REL, PHILOS (*student*) discípulo, -a *m, f*

disciplinary ['dɪs·ə·plə·ner·i] *adj* disciplinario, -a

discipline ['dɪs·ə·plɪn] I. *n* 1.(*obedience, self-control*) disciplina *f* 2.(*punishment*) castigo *m* 3.(*field of study*) disciplina II. *vt* 1.(*punish*) castigar; **to ~ oneself to do sth** obligarse a hacer algo 2.(*train*) disciplinar

disciplined *adj* disciplinado, -a

disc jockey *n* disc jockey *mf*, pinchadiscos *mf inv*

disclaim [dɪs·'kleɪm] *vt* 1.(*deny*) negar 2.(*give up right to*) renunciar a

disclaimer [dɪs·'kleɪ·mər] *n* 1.(*denial*) desdecimiento *m*, rectificación *f* 2.(*repudiating a claim*) repudio *m* 3. LAW descargo *m* de responsabilidad

disclose [dɪs·'kloʊz] *vt* 1.(*make public*) divulgar 2.(*uncover*) desvelar

disclosure [dɪs·'kloʊ·ʒər] *n* 1.(*act of making public*) divulgación *f* 2.(*revelation*) revelación *f*

disco ['dɪs·koʊ] *n* 1.(*music*) música *f* disco 2.(*place*) discoteca *f*

discolor [dɪs·'kʌl·ər] I. *vi* desteñirse II. *vt* decolorar; **my blue shirt has ~d the curtains** mi camisa azul ha desteñido en las cortinas

discomfit [dɪs·'kʌm·fɪt] *vt* desconcertar

discomfiture [dɪs·'kʌm·fɪ·tʃər] *n* (*uneasiness*) turbación *f*; (*confusion*) desconcierto *m*

discomfort [dɪs·'kʌm·fərt] *n* 1.(*uneasiness*) malestar *m*; ~ **at sth** malestar respecto a algo 2.(*inconvenience*) molestia *f*

disconcert [ˌdɪs·kən·'sɜrt] *vt* desconcertar

disconnect [ˌdɪs·kə·'nekt] *vt* 1.(*phone*) desconectar; (*customer*) cortar el suministro a 2.(*unplug*) desenchufar 3.(*unfasten*) separar

disconnected *adj* 1.(*cut off*) desconectado, -a 2.(*incoherent*) inconexo, -a

disconsolate [dɪs·'san·sə·lət] *adj* desconsolado, -a

discontent [ˌdɪs·kən·'tent] I. *n* descontento *m* II. *adj* descontento, -a

discontented *adj* descontento, -a

discontentment *n* descontento

discontinue [ˌdɪs·kən·'tɪn·ju] I. *vi* desistir II. *vt* suspender

discontinuity [ˌdɪs·kan·tə·'nu·ə·t̬i] <-ies> *n* 1.(*lack of continuity*) discontinuidad *f* 2.(*gap*) laguna *f*

discontinuous [ˌdɪs·kən·'tɪn·ju·əs] *adj* (*without continuity*) discontinuo, -a; (*broken*) interrumpido, -a

discord ['dɪs·kɔrd] *n* 1.(*disagreement*) discordia *f* 2.(*clashing noise*) discordancia *f* 3.(*lack of harmony*) disonancia *f*

discordant [dɪ·'skɔr·dənt] *adj* 1.(*disagreeing*) discordante 2.(*not in harmony*) disonante

discotheque ['dɪs·kə·tek] *n* discoteca *f*

discount¹ ['dɪs·kaʊnt] *n* descuento *m*; **at a ~** con descuento

discount² [dɪs·'kaʊnt] *vt* 1.(*reduce price*) rebajar 2.(*disregard*) no hacer caso de 3.(*leave out*) dejar de lado

discount store *n* tienda *f* de descuento

discourage [dɪ·'skɜr·ɪdʒ] *vt* 1.(*dishearten*) desanimar 2.(*dissuade*) **to ~ sb from doing sth** disuadir a alguien de hacer algo 3.(*oppose*) desaprobar

discouragement [dɪ·'skɜr·ɪdʒ·mənt] *n* 1.(*feeling*) desaliento *m* 2.(*deterrent*) impedimento *m*

discouraging *adj* desalentador(a)

discourse¹ ['dɪs·kɔrs] *n* discurso *m*; (*written*) tratado *m*; **a ~ about** [*o* **on**] **sth** un discurso sobre algo; (*written*) un tratado sobre algo

discourse² [dɪ·'skɔrs] *vi* hablar; **to ~ on sth** conversar sobre algo, platicar sobre algo *AmL*

discourteous [dɪs·'kɜr·t̬i·əs] *adj* descortés

discourtesy [dɪs·'kɜr·t̬ə·si] <-ies> *n* 1.(*rudeness*) descortesía *f* 2.(*act of rudeness*) grosería *f*

discover [dɪ·'skʌv·ər] *vt* 1.(*find out*) descubrir 2.(*find*) hallar, descubrir

discoverer *n* descubridor(a) *m(f)*

discovery [dɪ·'skʌv·ə·ri] <-ies> *n* descubrimiento *m*

discredit [dɪs·'kred·ɪt] I. *n* 1.(*disrepute*) desprestigio *m* 2.(*disgrace*) vergüenza *f*; **she is a ~ to her school** es una vergüenza para su escuela 3.(*doubt*) duda *f* II. *vt* desacreditar

discreditable [dɪs·'kred·ɪ·t̬ə·bəl] *adj* deshonroso, -a

discreet [dɪ·'skrit] *adj* discreto, -a

discrepancy [dɪ·'skrep·ən·si] <-ies> *n* discrepancia *f*

discrete [dɪ·'skrit] *adj* diferenciado, -a

discretion [dɪ·'skreʃ·ən] *n* 1.(*discreet behavior*) discreción *f* 2.(*good judgment*) criterio *m*; **to leave sth to sb's ~** dejar algo a discreción de alguien 3. LAW (*of court*) arbitrio *m*

discriminate [dɪ·'skrɪm·ə·neɪt] I. *vi* 1.(*see a difference*) discernir 2.(*treat unfairly*) **to ~ against sb** discriminar a alguien II. *vt* distinguir

discriminating *adj* 1.(*able to discern*) discerniente 2.(*palate, taste*) exigente

discrimination [dɪ·ˌskrɪm·ɪ·'neɪ·ʃən] *n* 1.(*unfair treatment*) discriminación *f* 2.(*good judgment*) criterio *m* 3.(*ability to differentiate*) discernimiento *m*

discriminatory [dɪ·'skrɪm·ɪ·nə·bɔr·i] *adj* discriminatorio, -a

discursive [dɪ·'skɜr·sɪv] *adj* digresivo, -a

discus ['dɪs·kəs] *n* SPORTS disco *m*

discuss [dɪ·'skʌs] *vt* 1.(*exchange ideas about*) discutir 2.(*consider*) abordar

discussion [dɪ·'skʌʃ·ən] *n* discusión *f*, argumento *m* *AmL*; ~ **group** grupo *m* de discusión

disdain [dɪs·'deɪn] I. *n* desdén *m* II. *vt* desdeñar; **to ~ to do sth** no dignarse a hacer algo

disdainful [dɪs·'deɪn·fəl] *adj* desdeñoso, -a

disease [dɪ·'ziz] *n a. fig* enfermedad *f*

diseased *adj a. fig* enfermo, -a

disembark [ˌdɪs·ɪm·'bark] *vi* desembarcar

disembarkation [ˌdɪs·ɪm·bar·'keɪ·ʃən] *n* desembarque *m*

disembodied [ˌdɪs·ɪm·'bad·id] *adj* incorpóreo, -a

disenchant [ˌdɪs·ɪn·'tʃænt] *vt* desencantar

disenchanted *adj* desencantado, -a

disenfranchise [ˌdɪs·ɪn·'fræn·tʃaɪz] *vt* (*of vote, rights*) privar

disengage [ˌdɪs·ɪn·'geɪdʒ] I. *vi* 1.(*become detached*) separarse 2.(*in fencing*) fintar II. *vt* 1.(*uncouple*) separar 2.(*detach*) desconectar; (*a clutch*) quitar 3. MIL retirar

disengagement [ˌdɪs·ɪn·'geɪdʒ·mənt] *n* desconexión *f*

disentangle [ˌdɪs·ɪn·'tæŋ·gəl] **I.** *vi* desenredarse **II.** *vt* **1.** (*release*) librar, soltar; **to ~ oneself from sb/sth** librarse de algo/alguien **2.** (*untangle*) desenredar **3.** *fig* (*unravel*) desembrollar

disfavor [ˌdɪs·'feɪ·vər] **I.** *n* desaprobación *f;* **to fall into ~** caer en desgracia **II.** *vt* desfavorecer

disfigure [dɪs·'fɪg·jər] *vt* desfigurar

disfigurement *n* desfiguración *f*

disfranchise [dɪs·'fræn·tʃaɪz] *s.* **disenfranchise**

disgorge [dɪs·'gɔrdʒ] *vt* arrojar; *fig* vomitar

disgrace [dɪs·'greɪs] **I.** *n* **1.** (*loss of honor*) deshonra *f* **2.** (*sth or sb shameful*) vergüenza *f* **II.** *vt* deshonrar

disgraced *adj* deshonrado, -a

disgraceful [dɪs·'greɪs·fəl] *adj* vergonzoso, -a

disgruntled [dɪs·'grʌn·təld] *adj* contrariado, -a; **to be ~ at sth** estar descontento con algo

disguise [dɪs·'gaɪz] **I.** *n* disfraz *m;* **to be in ~** estar disfrazado **II.** *vt* **1.** (*change appearance*) disfrazar; **to ~ oneself as sth** disfrazarse de algo **2.** (*hide*) encubrir

disgust [dɪs·'gʌst] **I.** *n* **1.** (*repugnance*) asco *m;* **to turn away from sth in ~** alejarse con repugnancia de algo **2.** (*indignation*) indignación *f;* **~ at sth** indignación por algo **II.** *vt* **1.** (*sicken*) dar asco, repugnar, chocar *AmL* **2.** (*be offensive*) indignar

disgusted *adj* **1.** (*sickened*) asqueado, -a **2.** (*indignant*) indignado, -a

disgusting *adj* **1.** (*repulsive*) repugnante, chocante *AmL* **2.** (*unacceptable*) indignante

dish [dɪʃ] **I.** <-es> *n* **1.** (*for food*) plato *m;* **to do the ~es** fregar los platos [*o* lavar] **2.** TEL (antena *f*) parabólica *f* **3.** *sl* (*attractive person*) bombón *m* **II.** *vi inf* (*gossip*) cotillear, chismear

◆**dish out** *vt* **1.** (*give too liberally*) repartir a diestro y siniestro **2.** (*serve*) servir

◆**dish up** *vt inf* **1.** (*serve*) servir **2.** *inf* (*offer*) ofrecer

dish antenna *n* (antena *f*) parabólica *f*

disharmonious [ˌdɪs·har·'mou·ni·əs] *adj* discordante

disharmony [dɪs·'har·mə·ni] *n* falta *f* de armonía

dishcloth ['dɪʃ·klaθ] *n* paño *m* de cocina, repasador *m Arg, Urug*

dishearten [dɪs·'har·tən] *vt* descorazonar

disheveled *adj*, **dishevelled** [dɪ·'ʃev·əld] *adj* desaliñado, -a; **with ~ hair** despeinado, -a

dishonest [dɪs·'an·ɪst] *adj* deshonesto, -a; **to be ~ about sth** ser falso acerca de algo

dishonesty [dɪs·'an·əs·ti] *n* **1.** (*lack of honesty*) falta *f* de honestidad **2.** (*dishonest act*) fraude *m*

dishonor [dɪs·'an·ər] **I.** *n* deshonor *m;* **to bring ~ on sb** traer la deshonra a alguien **II.** *vt* **1.** (*disgrace*) deshonrar **2.** (*not keep: agreement*) incumplir **3.** (*not pay: a check, bill*) impagar

dishonorable [dɪs·'an·ər·ə·bəl] *adj* deshonroso, -a

dishtowel *n* paño *m* de cocina

dishwasher *n* **1.** (*machine*) lavaplatos *m inv,* lavavajillas *m inv;* **to run the ~** poner el lavaplatos **2.** (*person*) lavaplatos *mf inv*

dishwater *n* agua *f* de lavar platos

disillusion [ˌdɪs·ɪ·'lu·ʒən] **I.** *vt* desilusionar **II.** *n* desilusión *f*

disillusioned *adj* desilusionado, -a; **to be ~ with sth/sb** estar desilusionado con algo/alguien

disillusionment *n* desilusión *f*

disinclination [ˌdɪs·ɪn·klɪ·'neɪ·ʃən] *n* renuencia *f*

disinclined [ˌdɪs·ɪn·'klaɪnd] *adj* renuente; **to be ~ to do sth** tener pocas ganas de hacer algo

disinfect [ˌdɪs·ɪn·'fekt] *vt* desinfectar

disinfectant [ˌdɪs·ɪn·'fek·tənt] **I.** *n* desinfectante *m* **II.** *adj* desinfectante

disinfection [ˌdɪs·ɪn·'fek·ʃən] *n* desinfección *f*

disingenuous [ˌdɪs·ɪn·'dʒen·ju·əs] *adj* insincero, -a

disinherit [ˌdɪs·ɪn·'her·ɪt] *vt* desheredar

disintegrate [dɪs·'ɪn·tə·greɪt] **I.** *vi* desintegrarse **II.** *vt* desintegrar

disintegration [dɪs·ˌɪn·tə·'greɪ·ʃən] *n* desintegración *f*

disinterested [dɪs·'ɪn·trɪ·stɪd] *adj* **1.** (*impartial*) desinteresado, -a, imparcial **2.** (*not interested*) desinteresado, -a

disjointed [dɪs·'dʒɔɪn·tɪd] *adj* inconexo, -a

disk [dɪsk] *n* COMPUT disco *m;* **hard ~** disco duro; **floppy ~** disquete *m;* **start-up ~** disco de arranque; **high density ~** disquete de alta densidad; **compact laser ~** laserdisc *m*

disk drive *n* disquetera *f*

diskette [dɪs·'ket] *n* disquete *m*

dislike [dɪs·'laɪk] **I.** *vt* tener aversión a **II.** *n* aversión *f;* **to take a ~ to sb/sth** tomar aversión a alguien/algo

dislocate [dɪs·'lou·keɪt] *vt* **1.** (*place elsewhere*) desplazar **2.** MED (*shoulder, hip, jaw*) dislocarse **3.** *fig* (*disturb the working of*) trastornar

dislocation [ˌdɪs·lou·'keɪ·ʃən] *n* **1.** (*displacement*) desplazamiento *m* **2.** MED dislocación *f* **3.** *fig* (*disturbance*) trastorno *m*

dislodge [dɪs·'ladʒ] *vt* desalojar

disloyal [dɪs·'bɪ·əl] *adj* desleal; **to be ~ to sb/sth** ser desleal a alguien/algo

dismal ['dɪz·məl] *adj* **1.** (*depressing*) deprimente **2.** *inf* (*awful*) terrible; (*truth*) triste

dismantle [dɪs·'mæn·təl] *vt* desmontar; (*system*) desmantelar

dismay [dɪs·'meɪ] **I.** *n* consternación *f;* **to sb's (great) ~** para (gran) consternación de alguien **II.** *vt* consternar

dismayed *adj* consternado, -a

dismember [dɪs·'mem·bər] *vt a. fig* desmembrar

dismiss [dɪs·'mɪs] *vt* **1.** (*allow to leave*) dejar ir **2.** (*from job*) despedir; **to be ~ed from one's job** ser despedido (del trabajo) **3.** (*not consider*) descartar **4.** LAW desestimar

dismissal [dɪsˈmɪs·əl] *n* **1.**(*from school*) expulsión *f*; (*from job*) despido *m* **2.**(*disregarding*) descarte *m*

dismissive [dɪsˈmɪs·ɪv] *adj* **she was ~ of the idea** no daba crédito a la idea

dismount [dɪsˈmaʊnt] *vi* desmontar(se)

disobedience [ˌdɪs·ə·ˈbi·di·əns] *n* desobediencia *f*

disobedient [ˌdɪs·ə·ˈbi·di·ənt] *adj* desobediente

disobey [ˌdɪs·ə·ˈbeɪ] *vi, vt* desobedecer

disoblige [ˌdɪs·ə·ˈblaɪdʒ] *vt* **1.**(*act contrary to*) incumplir **2.**(*offend*) disgustar

disobliging *adj* desatento, -a

disorder [dɪsˈɔr·dər] *n* **1.**(*lack of order*) desorden *m*, desparramo *m CSur* **2.** MED trastorno *m*

disordered *adj* desordenado, -a

disorderly [dɪsˈɔr·dər·li] *adj* **1.**(*untidy*) desordenado, -a **2.**(*unruly*) escandaloso, -a; **~ conduct** alteración *f* del orden público

disorganized [dɪsˈɔr·gə·naɪzd] *adj* desorganizado, -a

disorient [dɪsˈɔr·i·ent] *vt* desorientar; **to become** [*o* get| **~ed** desorientarse

disoriented *adj* desorientado, -a

disown [dɪsˈoʊn] *vt* repudiar

disparage [dɪˈsper·ɪdʒ] *vt* menospreciar

disparagement *n* menosprecio *m*

disparaging *adj* (*disdainful*) despreciativo, -a; (*remark*) desdeñoso, -a

disparate [ˈdɪs·pər·ət] *adj* dispar

disparity [dɪˈsper·ə·ti] *n* disparidad *f*

dispassionate [dɪsˈpæʃ·ə·nɪt] *adj* desapasionado, -a

dispatch [dɪˈspætʃ] I.<-es> *n* **1.**(*message, news item*) despacho *m*; **the latest ~ from our war correspondent** el último despacho de nuestro corresponsal de guerra **2.**(*delivery*) envío *m* II. *vt a. fig* despachar

dispel [dɪˈspel] <-ll-> *vt* (*fears, doubts*) disipar; (*a rumor*) desmentir

dispensable [dɪˈspen·sə·bəl] *adj* prescindible

dispensary [dɪˈspen·sə·ri] *n* dispensario *m*

dispensation [ˌdɪs·pen·ˈseɪ·ʃən] *n* **1.**(*act of distributing*) administración *f* **2.**(*special permission*) dispensa *f*

dispense [dɪˈspens] *vt* **1.**(*give out*) repartir **2.** MED (*medicine*) administrar

◆**dispense with** *vt* prescindir de

dispenser [dɪˈspen·sər] *n* **1.**(*device*) máquina *f* expendedora **2.**(*one who distributes*) distribuidor(a) *m(f)*

dispersal [dɪˈspɜr·səl] *n* dispersión *f*

disperse [dɪˈspɜrs] I. *vt* dispersar II. *vi* dispersarse

dispersion [dɪˈspɜr·ʒən] *n* dispersión *f*

dispirited [dɪˈspɪr·ɪ·t̬ɪd] *adj* desanimado, -a

displace [dɪsˈpleɪs] *vt* **1.**(*force to leave*) desplazar **2.**(*take the place of*) reemplazar

displacement [dɪsˈpleɪs·mənt] *n* desplazamiento *m*

display [dɪˈspleɪ] I. *vt* **1.**(*arrange for showing*) exhibir; **to ~ sth in a store window** exhibir algo en un escaparate **2.**(*express*) demostrar II. *n* **1.**(*arrangement*) exposición *f*; **firework ~** exhibición *f* pirotécnica **2.**(*demonstration*) demostración *f* **3.** COMPUT pantalla *f*; **liquid crystal ~** pantalla de cristal líquido

display case *n* estuche *m*

display window *n* escaparate *m*

displease [dɪsˈpliz] *vt* disgustar; **to be ~d by sth** estar disgustado con algo

displeasing *adj* desagradable

displeasure [dɪsˈpleʒ·ər] *n* disgusto *m*

disposable [dɪˈspoʊ·zə·bəl] *adj* desechable

disposable income *n* renta *f* disponible

disposal [dɪˈspoʊ·zəl] *n* **1.**(*getting rid of*) eliminación *f* **2.**(*garbage disposal*) trituradora *f* ► **to be at sb's ~** estar a disposición de alguien

dispose [dɪˈspoʊz] I. *vt* **1.**(*place*) disponer **2.**(*incline*) predisponer II. *vi* **to ~ of sth** (*throw away*) desechar algo; (*get rid of*) deshacerse de algo; **to ~ of sb** *fig* cargarse a alguien [*o* liquidar]

disposed *adj* **to be well ~ towards sb** estar bien dispuesto hacia alguien

disposition [ˌdɪs·pə·ˈzɪʃ·ən] *n* disposición *f*; **to have a happy ~** mostrar una buena disposición

dispossess [ˌdɪs·pə·ˈzes] *vt* desposeer

disproportionate [ˌdɪs·prə·ˈpɔr·ʃə·nɪt] *adj* desproporcionado, -a

disprove [dɪsˈpruv] *vt* refutar

disputable [dɪˈspju·t̬ə·bəl] *adj* discutible

disputation [ˌdɪs·pju·ˈteɪ·ʃən] *n* debate *m*

disputatious [ˌdɪs·pju·ˈteɪ·ʃəs] *adj* disputador(a)

dispute [dɪˈspjut] I. *vt* **1.**(*argue*) discutir **2.**(*doubt*) poner en duda II. *vi* **to ~ over sth** discutir (con alguien) sobre algo III. *n* discusión *f*; **a ~ over sth** una discusión sobre algo

disqualification [dɪsˌkwal·ə·fɪ·ˈkeɪ·ʃən] *n* **1.** SPORTS descalificación *f* **2.**(*incapacity*) incapacidad *f*

disqualify [dɪsˈkwal·ə·faɪ] <-ie-> *vt* descalificar; **to ~ sb from an event** descalificar a alguien de un evento

disquiet [dɪsˈkwaɪ·ət] I. *n* inquietud *f*; **~ over sth** inquietud acerca de algo II. *vt* inquietar

disquieting *adj* inquietante

disregard [ˌdɪs·rɪ·ˈgard] I. *vt* desatender II. *n* despreocupación *f*

disrepair [ˌdɪs·rɪ·ˈper] *n* deterioro *m*; **to be in a state of ~** estar en mal estado

disreputable [dɪsˈrep·jə·t̬ə·bəl] *adj* de mala fama

disrepute [ˌdɪs·rɪ·ˈpjut] *n* desprestigio *m*

disrespect [ˌdɪs·rɪ·ˈspekt] *n* falta *f* de respeto; **to show ~** mostrar descortesía

disrespectful [ˌdɪs·rɪ·ˈspekt·fəl] *adj* descortés

disrupt [dɪsˈrʌpt] *vt* (*disturb*) trastornar; (*interrupt*) interrumpir

disruption [dɪsˈrʌp·ʃən] *n* (*disturbance*) perturbación *f; fig* (*disorder*) desorganización *f;* (*interruption*) interrupción *f*

disruptive [dɪs·'rʌp·tɪv] *adj* que trastorna

dissatisfaction [dɪs·ˌsæt̬·ɪs·'fæk·ʃən] *n* insatisfacción *f*

dissatisfied [dɪs·'sæt̬·ɪs·faɪd] *adj* insatisfecho, ·a

dissect [dɪ·'sekt] *vt* 1. (*cut open*) diseccionar 2. *fig* (*examine*) examinar

dissection [dɪ·'sek·ʃən] *n* disección *f*

dissemble [dɪ·'sem·bəl] *vi, vt* disimular

disseminate [dɪ·'sem·ɪ·neɪt] *vt* diseminar

dissemination [dɪ·ˌsem·ɪ·'neɪ·ʃən] *n* diseminación *f*

dissension [dɪ·'sen·ʃən] *n* disensión *f;* **to sow ~** sembrar (la) discordia

dissent [dɪ·'sent] I. *n* disidencia *f* II. *vi* 1. (*disagree with*) disentir; **to ~ from sth** disentir de algo 2. (*reject a doctrine*) disidir

dissenter *n* disidente *mf*

dissertation [ˌdɪs·ər·'teɪ·ʃən] *n* UNIV tesis *f inv*

disservice [dɪs·'sɜr·vɪs] *n* perjuicio *m;* **to do sth/sb a ~** perjudicar algo/a alguien

dissident ['dɪs·ɪ·dənt] I. *n* disidente *mf* II. *adj* disidente

dissimilar [ˌdɪ·'sɪm·ɪ·lər] *adj* diferente, disímbolo, ·a *Méx;* **to be ~ to sb/sth** ser distinto de alguien/algo

dissimilarity [ˌdɪ·sɪm·ɪ·'ler·ə·t̬i] <-ies> *n* desemejanza *f*

dissimulation [ˌdɪ·ˌsɪm·jə·'leɪ·ʃən] *n* disimulo *m*

dissipate ['dɪs·ɪ·peɪt] I. *vi* 1. (*disperse*) disiparse 2. *fig* (*indulge in pleasures*) llevar una vida disoluta II. *vt* disipar

dissipated *adj* disipado, ·a

dissipation [ˌdɪs·ɪ·'peɪ·ʃən] *n* 1. (*dispersion*) dispersión *f* 2. (*frivolous waste*) desperdicio *m;* (*of money*) derroche *m* 3. (*indulgence in pleasure*) disipación *f*

dissociate [dɪ·'soʊ·ʃi·eɪt] *vt* **to ~ carbon from sth** disociar el carbono de algo; **to ~ oneself from sb/sth** disociarse de alguien/algo

dissociation [dɪ·ˌsoʊ·ʃi·'eɪ·ʃən] *n* disociación *f*

dissolute ['dɪs·ə·lut] *adj liter* disoluto, ·a

dissolution [ˌdɪs·ə·'lu·ʃən] *n* disolución *f*

dissolve [dɪ·'zalv] I. *vi* 1. (*in a liquid*) disolverse 2. *fig* (*collapse*) deshacerse; **to ~ into tears/laughter** deshacerse en lágrimas/carcajadas 3. *fig* (*disappear*) desvanecerse II. *vt* disolver; **to ~ a business** disolver un negocio

dissonance ['dɪs·ə·nəns] *n* disonancia *f*

dissonant ['dɪs·ə·nənt] *adj* disonante; *fig* discordante

dissuade [dɪ·'sweɪd] *vt* disuadir

distance ['dɪs·təns] I. *n* 1. (*space*) distancia *f*; **his house is within walking ~** se puede ir andando a su casa; **to keep one's ~** guardar las distancias 2. (*space far away*) lejanía *f*; **in the ~** de lejos II. *vt* **to ~ oneself from sb/sth** distanciarse de alguien/algo

distant ['dɪs·tənt] *adj* 1. (*far away*) distante 2. (*relative, cousin*) lejano, ·a

distantly *adv* 1. (*in the distance*) de lejos 2. *fig* (*in unfriendly manner*) distantemente

distaste [dɪs·'teɪst] *n* aversión *f*

distasteful [dɪs·'teɪst·fəl] *adj* desagradable

distemper [dɪs·'tem·pər] *n* 1. (*animal disease*) moquillo *m* 2. (*bad temper*) mal humor *m*

distend [dɪ·'stend] *vi* distenderse

distension [dɪ·'sten·ʃən] *n* distensión *f*

distill [dɪ·'stɪl] *vt* destilar

distillation [ˌdɪs·tə·'leɪ·ʃən] *n* destilación *f*

distiller [dɪ·'stɪl·ər] *n* 1. (*company*) destilería *f* 2. (*person*) destilador(a) *m(f)*

distillery [dɪ·'stɪl·ə·ri] *n* destilería

distinct [dɪ·'stɪŋkt] *adj* 1. (*separate*) distinto, ·a 2. (*marked*) definido, ·a 3. (*noticeable*) nítido, ·a

distinction [dɪ·'stɪŋk·ʃən] *n* 1. (*difference*) distinción *f* 2. (*eminence*) distinción; **of great ~** de gran renombre 3. (*honors*) sobresaliente *m*

distinctive [dɪ·'stɪŋk·tɪv] *adj* característico, ·a

distinguish [dɪ·'stɪŋ·gwɪʃ] I. *vi* distinguir II. *vt* 1. (*tell apart*) distinguir 2. (*be excellent in*) **to ~ oneself in sth** destacar en algo

distinguishable *adj* distinguible

distinguished *adj* 1. (*celebrated*) eminente 2. (*stylish*) distinguido, ·a

distort [dɪ·'stɔrt] *vt* torcer; (*facts, the truth*) tergiversar

distortion [dɪ·'stɔr·ʃən] *n* (*of the truth, facts*) distorsión *f*; (*of a face*) contorsión *f*

distract [dɪ·'strækt] *vt* distraer

distracted *adj* distraído, ·a

distraction [dɪ·'stræk·ʃən] *n* 1. (*disturbance*) distracción *f* 2. (*confused agitation*) aturdimiento *m* 3. (*pastime*) entretenimiento *m*

distraught [dɪ·'strɔt] *adj* turbado, ·a

distress [dɪ·'stres] I. *n* 1. (*emotional*) congoja *f* 2. (*extreme pain*) aflicción *f* 3. (*state of danger*) apuro *m* II. *vt* afligir

distressed *adj* 1. (*unhappy*) afligido, ·a 2. (*in difficulties*) apurado, ·a 3. FASHION (*jeans*) desteñido, ·a, deslavado, ·a *Méx*

distressful *adj*, **distressing** *adj* 1. (*causing worry*) angustioso, ·a 2. (*painful*) doloroso, ·a

distribute [dɪ·'strɪb·jut] *vt* 1. (*share*) repartir 2. (*spread over space*) distribuir; **to be widely ~d** estar ampliamente repartido 3. (*supply goods*) distribuir

distribution [ˌdɪs·trɪ·'bju·ʃən] *n* 1. (*giving out*) reparto *m* 2. (*spread*) distribución

distribution area *n* ECON área *f* de distribución

distribution channel *n* ECON canal *m* de distribución

distribution rights *npl* derechos *mpl* de distribución

distributive [dɪ·'strɪb·jə·t̬ɪv] *adj* distributivo, ·a

distributor [dɪ·'strɪb·jə·t̬ər] *n* 1. (*person*) distribuidor(a) *m(f)* 2. AUTO distribuidor *m*

district ['dɪs·trɪkt] *n* 1. (*defined area*) distrito

m, intendencia *f CSur* **2.** (*region*) región *f*
district attorney *n* fiscal *m* del distrito
district court *n* tribunal *m* federal
distrust [dɪs·ˈtrʌst] **I.** *vt* desconfiar de **II.** *n* desconfianza *f*
distrustful [dɪs·ˈtrʌst·fəl] *adj* desconfiado, -a
disturb [dɪ·ˈstɜrb] *vt* **1.** (*interrupt*) molestar **2.** (*worry*) preocupar **3.** (*move around*) perturbar
disturbance [dɪ·ˈstɜr·bəns] *n* **1.** (*interruption*) molestia *f* **2.** (*public incident*) disturbio *m*
disturbed *adj* **1.** (*mentally ill*) trastornado, -a, perturbado, -a **2.** (*restless*) inquieto, -a **3.** (*moved around*) perturbado, -a
disturbing *adj* **1.** (*annoying*) molesto, -a **2.** (*worrying*) preocupante
disunite [ˌdɪs·ju·ˈnaɪt] *vt* desunir
disunity [dɪs·ˈju·nə·t̮i] *n* desunión *f*
disuse [dɪs·ˈjus] *n* desuso *m*
disused [dɪs·ˈjuzd] *adj* en desuso
ditch [dɪtʃ] **I.** <-es> *n* **1.** (*trench*) zanja *f*; (*by a road*) cuneta *f*; **irrigation ~** acequia *f* **2.** (*for defense*) foso *m* **II.** *vt* **1.** *sl* (*discard*) deshacerse de; (*car*) abandonar; (*idea*) descartar **2.** *sl* (*escape from*) zafarse de **3.** *sl* (*end a relationship*) cortar con **4.** (*land in water*) **to ~ a plane** hacer un amaraje forzoso **III.** *vi* abrir zanjas
dither [ˈdɪð·ər] **I.** *n* **to be in a ~** estar hecho un flan **II.** *vi* *inf* **1.** (*be indecisive*) vacilar **2.** (*behave nervously*) ponerse nervioso
ditsy [ˈdɪt·si] *adj sl* empanado, -a, elevado, -a *Col*
ditto [ˈdɪt̮·oʊ] **I.** *n* (*mark indicating repetition*) comillas *fpl* **II.** *adv* (*so do I*) ídem; (*same for me*) lo mismo digo
ditty [ˈdɪt̮·i] <-ies> *n* cancioncilla *f*
diurnal [daɪ·ˈɜr·nəl] *adj* diurno, -a
divan [dɪ·ˈvan] *n* diván *m*
dive [daɪv] **I.** *n* **1.** (*in swimming*) salto *m* [*o AmL* clavado *m*] de cabeza **2.** (*submerge*) inmersión *f* **3.** *a. fig* (*sudden decline*) caída *f* en picado [*o* picada *Col*]; **to take a ~** caer en picado **4.** (*leap*) brinco; **to make a ~ for...** precipitarse hacia... **5.** *sl* (*undesirable establishment*) antro *m* **II.** *vi* <dived *o* dove, dived *o* dove> **1.** (*in swimming*) tirarse de cabeza **2.** (*submerge*) zambullirse; **to ~ under sth** bucear por debajo de algo; **to ~ to a depth of...** sumergirse a una profundidad de... **3.** (*go sharply downwards*) bajar en picado **4.** (*move towards*) precipitarse; **to ~ for cover** buscar abrigo precipitadamente
diver [ˈdaɪ·vər] *n* **1.** (*sb who dives*) buceador(a) *m(f)* **2.** (*sb working under water*) buzo *mf*, submarinista *mf*
diverge [dɪ·ˈvɜrdʒ] *vi* divergir; **to ~ from sth** apartarse de algo
divergence [dɪ·ˈvɜr·dʒəns] *n* divergencia *f*
divergent [dɪ·ˈvɜr·dʒənt] *adj* **1.** (*differing*) divergente **2.** (*different*) distinto, -a
diverse [dɪ·ˈvɜrs] *adj* **1.** (*varied*) diverso, -a, variado, -a **2.** (*not alike*) diferente

diversification [dɪ·ˌvɜr·sɪ·fɪ·ˈkeɪ·ʃən] *n* diversificación *f*
diversify [dɪ·ˈvɜr·sɪ·faɪ] <-ie-> **I.** *vi* diversificarse **II.** *vt* diversificar
diversion [dɪ·ˈvɜr·ʃən] *n* **1.** (*changing of direction*) desviación *f*; (*of traffic, river*) desvío *m* **2.** (*distraction*) entretenimiento *m* **3.** (*activity*) diversión *f*
diversity [dɪ·ˈvɜr·sə·t̮i] *n* diversidad *f*
divert [dɪ·ˈvɜrt] *vt* **1.** (*change direction*) desviar **2.** (*distract*) distraer **3.** (*amuse*) divertir
diverting [dɪ·ˈvɜr·t̮ɪŋ] *adj* divertido, -a
divest [dɪ·ˈvest] **I.** *vt* despojar de **II.** *vi* **1.** ECON (*sell off*) vender **2.** (*renounce*) **to ~ from sth** renunciar a algo
  ◆**divest of** *vt fig* **to divest oneself of sth** despojarse de algo
divide [dɪ·ˈvaɪd] **I.** *n* **1.** (*separating line*) línea *f* divisoria **2.** (*watershed*) punto *m* de inflexión **II.** *vt* **1.** *a.* MATH dividir; **to ~ sth into three groups** dividir algo en tres grupos; **the party is ~d** *fig* el partido está dividido **2.** (*allot*) repartir **III.** *vi* (*split*) dividirse; **their paths ~d** sus caminos se separaron ▸ **~ and conquer** divide y vencerás
  ◆**divide off** *vt always sep* dividir
  ◆**divide out, divide up** *vt always sep* (re)partir
divided *adj* **1.** (*not in agreement*) dividido, -a **2.** (*separated*) separado, -a **3.** (*undecided*) **to be ~ between two options** encontrarse en un dilema entre dos opciones
dividend [ˈdɪv·ɪ·dend] *n* MATH, FIN dividendo *m*
dividing line *n* línea *f* divisoria
divination [ˌdɪv·ɪ·ˈneɪ·ʃən] *n* adivinación *f*
divine [dɪ·ˈvaɪn] **I.** *adj* **1.** (*of or from God*) divino, -a **2.** (*wonderful*) sublime **II.** *vt* (*guess correctly*) adivinar; (*the future*) predecir **III.** *vi* hacer pronósticos
diviner [dɪ·ˈvaɪ·nər] *n* adivinador(a) *m(f)*; (*of future events*) vidente *mf*
diving *n* **1.** (*jumping*) zambullida *f* **2.** (*swimming*) buceo *m*
diving bell *n* campana *f* de buzo
diving board *n* trampolín *m*
diving suit *n* escafandra *f*
divining rod *n* varilla *f* de zahorí
divinity [dɪ·ˈvɪn·ə·t̮i] <-ies> *n* **1.** (*state*) divinidad *f* **2. the D~** (*God*) la divinidad **3.** (*study*) teología *f*
divisible [dɪ·ˈvɪz·ə·bəl] *adj* divisible
division [dɪ·ˈvɪʒ·ən] *n* **1.** *a.* MIL, MATH, SPORTS división *f* **2.** (*splitting up*) repartimiento *m* **3.** (*disagreement*) discordia *f* **4.** (*separating point*) división *f* **5.** COM sección *f*
divisive [dɪ·ˈvaɪ·sɪv] *adj* divisivo, -a
divorce [dɪ·ˈvɔrs] **I.** *n* divorcio *m*; *fig* separación *f* **II.** *vt* **1.** (*break marriage*) **to get ~d (from sb)** divorciarse (de alguien); **he ~d her for infidelity** se divorció de ella por infidelidad **2.** *fig* (*separate*) separar **III.** *vi* divorciarse
divorcé [dɪ·ˈvɔr·seɪ] *n* divorciado *m*
divorced *adj* divorciado, -a

divorcée [dɪˌvɔrˈseɪ] *n* divorciada *f*
divulge [dɪˈvʌldʒ] *vt* divulgar
DIY [ˌdiˑaɪˈwaɪ] *abbr of* **do-it-yourself** bricolaje *m*
dizziness *n* mareo *m;* (*because of height*) vértigo *m*
dizzy [ˈdɪzˑi] <-ier, -iest> *adj* **1.** (*having vertigo*) mareado, -a **2.** (*causing vertigo*) vertiginoso, -a **3.** *sl* (*silly*) lelo, -a
DJ [ˈdiːdʒeɪ] *n abbr of* **disc jockey** DJ *mf*
Djibouti [dʒɪˈbuˑti] *n* Yibuti *m*
Djiboutian [dʒɪˈbuˑti·ən] **I.** *adj* de Yibuti **II.** *n* habitante *mf* de Yibuti
DMV [ˌdiˑemˈvi] *n abbr of* **Department of Motor Vehicles** ≈ DGT *f*
DNA [ˌdiˑenˈeɪ] *n abbr of* **deoxyribonucleic acid** ADN *m*
do [du] **I.** *n* **1.** the ~s and don'ts el conjunto de normas **2.** *inf* (*party*) fiesta *f* **3.** *sl* (*hairdo*) peinado *m* **4.** *sl* (*excrement*) popó *m;* **dog** ~ caca *f* de perro; **cow** ~ boñiga *f* **II.** <does, did, done> *aux* **1.** (*in questions*) ~ **you own a dog?** ¿tienes (un) perro? **2.** (*in negatives*) **Frida** ~**esn't like olives** a Frida no le gustan las aceitunas **3.** (*in imperatives*) ~ **your homework!** ¡haz los deberes! [*o* las tareas]; ~ **come in!** pero pasa, por favor **4.** (*for emphasis*) ~ **go to the party!** ¡anda y ve a la fiesta!; **he** ~**es get on my nerves** me saca de quicio, de verdad; **he did** ~ **it** sí que lo hizo **5.** (*replacing a repeated verb*) **so** ~ **I** yo también; **neither** ~ **I** yo tampoco; **she speaks more fluently than he** ~**es** ella habla con mayor fluidez que él **6.** (*requesting affirmation*) ¿verdad?; **you** ~**n't want to answer,** ~ **you?** no quieres contestar, ¿verdad? **III.** <does, did, done> *vt* **1.** (*carry out*) hacer; **to** ~ **nothing but...** hacer sólo...; **to** ~ **one's best** emplearse a fondo; **to** ~ **justice** hacer justicia; **to** ~ **everything possible** hacer todo lo posible; **what on earth are you** ~**ing** (**there**)? ¿que diablos haces (ahí)?; **what is to be** ~**ne about that?** ¿qué se puede hacer al respecto?; ~**n't just stand there,** ~ **something!** ¡no te quedes ahí plantado, haz algo! **2.** (*undertake*) realizar **3.** (*help*) **to** ~ **something for sb/sth** hacer algo por alguien/algo **4.** (*act*) actuar; **to** ~ **as others** ~ hacer como hacen los demás **5.** (*deal with*) encargarse de; **if you** ~ **the washing up, I'll** ~ **the drying** si tú lavas los platos yo los secaré **6.** (*learn: math, English*) estudiar **7.** (*figure out: puzzle, math problem*) resolver **8.** (*finish*) terminar **9.** (*put in order*) ordenar; (*clean*) limpiar; **to** ~ **one's nails** (*with nail polish*) pintarse las uñas; (*cut*) cortarse las uñas; **to do one's hair** peinarse **10.** (*make neat: the bathroom, one's room*) arreglar **11.** (*tour: Europe, California*) visitar **12.** (*go at a speed of*) **to** ~ **Barcelona to Geneva in seven hours** cubrir el trayecto de Barcelona a Ginebra en siete horas **13.** (*be satisfactory*) **I only have beer, will that** ~ **you?** sólo tengo cerveza, ¿te va bien? **14.** (*sell*)

vender; **the shop does fancy kitchen equipment** la tienda ofrece artículos selectos de cocina; (*offer*) servir **15.** (*cook*) cocer, cocinar *AmL;* **to** ~ **sth for sb** cocinar algo para alguien **16.** (*cause*) **to** ~ **sb credit** decir mucho a favor de alguien; **to** ~ **sb a good turn** echar una mano a alguien; **to** ~ **sb good** sentar bien a alguien **17.** (*perform: a play, song*) interpretar; (*imitate: an accent, bird call*) imitar **18.** *inf* (*serve prison sentence: time, life, 10 years*) cumplir condena **19.** *inf* (*burglarize*) allanar **20.** *inf* (*swindle*) estafar **21.** *sl* (*drugs*) meterse **22.** *sl* (*have sex*) **to** ~ **it** hacerlo ▸ **just** ~ **it!** ¡hazlo!; **what's** ~**ne is** ~**ne** a lo hecho, pecho; **that** ~**es it** eso es el colmo **IV.** <does, did, done> *vi* **1.** (*behave, act*) hacer, actuar; ~ **as I say** ¡simplemente haz lo que te digo! **2.** (*manage*) salir adelante; **to** ~ **well in school** ir bien en la escuela; **mother and baby are** ~**ing well** la madre y el bebé se encuentran bien; **many stores are** ~**ing well** muchas tiendas van prosperando; **how are you** ~**ing?** ¿qué tal estás?; **to** ~ **well for oneself** darse una buena vida **3.** (*finish with*) **to be** ~**ne with sb/sth** haber terminado con alguien/algo **4.** (*be satisfactory*) **this behavior just won't** ~! ¡no se puede tolerar este comportamiento! **5.** (*function as*) **it'll** ~ **for a spoon** servirá de cuchara **6.** *inf* (*going on*) **to be** ~**ing** pasar **7.** (*treat*) **to** ~ **badly/well by sb** tratar mal/bien a alguien ▸ **that will never** ~ eso no sirve; ~ **unto others as you would have them** ~ **unto you** *prov* no quieras para los otros lo que no quieras para ti; **that will** ~! ¡ya basta!
◆ **do away with** *vi* **1.** (*dispose of*) suprimir **2.** *inf* (*kill*) **to** ~ **sb** liquidar a alguien
◆ **do in** *vt always sep, sl* **1.** (*murder*) **to do sb in** acabar con alguien **2.** (*ruin*) arruinar **3.** *fig* (*make exhausted*) agotar
◆ **do out** *vt always sep* **1.** (*adorn*) decorar **2.** (*cheat*) **to do sb out of sth** quitar una cosa a alguien por engaño, sacar algo a alguien *inf*
◆ **do over** *vt always sep* **1.** *inf* (*redo*) **to do sth over again** volver a hacer algo **2.** *inf* (*redecorate*) redecorar **3.** *inf* (*beat up*) **to do sb over** dar una paliza a alguien
◆ **do up** *vt* **1.** (*fasten: button*) abrochar; (*tie*) hacer el nudo; (*shoes*) atarse; (*zipper*) cerrar **2.** (*make attractive: one's hair*) arreglarse; **to do oneself up** acicalarse **3.** (*wrap*) envolver
◆ **do with** *vi* **1.** (*be related to*) **to have to** ~ **with sth** (*book*) tratar de algo; (*person*) tener que ver con algo; **to not have anything to** ~ **with sb** no tener tratos con alguien **2.** *inf* (*need*) **I could** ~ **with a drink** me hace falta tomar algo
◆ **do without** *vi* apañarse sin
DOA [ˌdiˑouˈeɪ] *abbr of* **dead on arrival** ingresó cadáver
doable [ˈduˑəˑbəl] *n inf* factible, realizable
docile [ˈdasˑəl] *adj* dócil
docility [daˈsɪlˑəˑti] *n* docilidad *f*
dock[1] [dak] **I.** *n* **1.** (*wharf*) desembarcadero *m;*

(*pier*) dique *m* **2.** (*enclosed part of port*) dársena *f* **II.** *vi* **1.** NAUT atracar **2.** (*spacecraft*) acoplarse **III.** *vt* NAUT atracar

dock² [dak] *n* **to be in the ~** estar en el banquillo (de los acusados); *fig* estar en apuros

dock³ [dak] *vt* **1.** (*take away: sb's pay, salary*) deducir **2.** (*cut off*) descolar; (*tail*) cortar

dock⁴ [dak] *n* BOT romaza *f*

docker ['dak·ər] *n* inf estibador(a) *m(f)*

docket ['dak·ɪt] **I.** *n* **1.** LAW (*list of cases*) registro *m* de sumarios de causas **2.** (*business agenda*) agenda *f* **3.** (*documentation*) cédula *f* **II.** *vt* LAW registrar

docking ['dak·ɪŋ] *n* **1.** NAUT amarra *f* **2.** (*joining of spacecraft*) acoplamiento *m* **3.** (*cutting*) reducción *f*; (*of wages*) reajuste *m*

dockyard ['dak·jard] *n* astillero *m*

doctor ['dak·tər] **I.** *n* **1.** (*physician*) médico, -a *m, f*; **D~ Smith** (el) doctor Smith; **to be at the ~'s** estar en la consulta; **to go to the ~'s** ir al médico; **this hot bath is just what the ~ ordered** *fig* este baño caliente es justo lo que necesitaba **2.** UNIV doctor(a) *m(f)* **II.** *vt* **1.** (*fix temporarily*) **to ~ sth (up)** hacer un apaño a algo *inf* **2.** (*change*) hacer unos arreglos, ajustar; (*illegally*) falsear **3.** (*improve taste of*) aderezar

doctorate ['dak·tər·ət] *n* doctorado *m*

> ℹ️ El **doctorate** o **doctor's degree** en una disciplina es el título académico más alto que se puede obtener en una universidad. En las universidades anglosajonas, los doctorados reciben diversas denominaciones, de acuerdo a la carrera cursada. El doctorado más común es el **PhD**, también llamado **DPhil (Doctor of Philosophy)**. Este título se concede tras la presentación y defensa de una tesis doctoral en cualquier área de estudios, exceptuando Derecho y Medicina. Otros títulos de doctorado son: **DMus (Doctor of Music)**, **MD (Doctor of Medicine)**, **LLD (Doctor of Laws,** doctor en Derecho) y **DD (Doctor of Divinity,** doctor en Teología). Las universidades también pueden conceder el título de doctor a aquellas personalidades que se han destacado por su contribución a la investigación científica, por su trabajo o por sus publicaciones. Este tipo de doctorado se denomina doctorado Honoris Causa. A esta modalidad pertenecen el **DLitt (Doctor of Letters)** y el **DSc (Doctor of Science)**.

doctrinaire [ˌdak·trə·'ner] *adj* doctrinario, -a

doctrine ['dak·trɪn] *n* doctrina *f*; **military ~** credo *m* militar

docudrama *n* docudrama *m*

document ['dak·jə·mənt] **I.** *n* documento *m*

II. *vt* documentar

documentary [ˌdak·jə·'men·tə·ri] **I.** <-ies> *n* documental *m* **II.** *adj* documental

documentation [ˌdak·jə·men·'teɪ·ʃən] *n* documentación *f*

DOD *n* abbr of **Department of Defense** Ministerio *m* de Defensa

dodge [dadʒ] **I.** *vt* esquivar; *fig* (*a question, the press*) eludir; **to ~ doing sth** escaquearse de hacer algo *inf* **II.** *vi* SPORTS regatear **III.** *n* *inf* treta *f*

dodger ['dadʒ·ər] *n* granuja *mf*

doe [doʊ] *n* **1.** (*female deer*) cierva *f*, venada *f* AmL **2.** (*female rabbit*) coneja *f*

DOE *n* abbr of **Department of Energy** Ministerio de Medio Ambiente y Recursos Naturales

doer ['du·ər] *n* **1.** (*person acting*) hacedor(a) *m(f)* **2.** (*active person*) persona *f* dinámica

does [dʌz] *vt, vi, aux* **3.** *pers sing of* **do**

doeskin ['doʊ·skɪn] *n* ante *m*

doesn't ['dʌz·ənt] = **does not** *s.* **do**

dog [dɔg] **I.** *n* **1.** perro, -a *m, f*; **hunting ~** perro de caza; **pet ~** perro mascota **2.** *sl* (*unattractive person*) callo *m*, coco *m*; (*mean person*); **the (dirty) ~!** ¡el muy canalla!; (*failure: movie, product*) fiasco *m* ▸ **he doesn't have a ~'s chance** *inf* no tiene la más remota posibilidad; **every ~ has its day** *prov* a cada uno le llega su momento de gloria, a cada cerdo le llega su san Martín; **to lead a ~'s life** llevar una vida de perros; **to be a ~ in the manger** ser como el perro del hortelano; **to give a ~ a bad name** *prov* por un perro que maté, mataperros me llamaron *prov*; **it's a ~ eat ~ world** este mundo es un lugar despiadado; **to go to the ~s** ir de capa caída **II.** <-gg-> *vt* (*pursue*) perseguir; *fig* acosar

dog biscuit *n* canil *m*

dog collar *n* collar *m* de perro; *iron* alzacuello *m*

dog days *n pl* canícula *f*

dog-eared *adj* (*book*) **to be ~** tener las esquinas dobladas

dogged ['dɔ·gɪd] *adj* obstinado, -a

doggerel ['dɔ·gər·əl] *n* poesía *f* barata

doggy bag *n* *inf*: bolsa que ofrecen en el restaurante para que el cliente se lleve a casa las sobras

doghouse *n* perrera *f*; **to be in the ~** haber caído en desgracia

dogma ['dɔg·mə] *n* dogma *m*

dogmatic [dɔg·'mæt̬·ɪk] *adj* dogmático, -a

dogmatism ['dɔg·mə·tɪz·əm] *n* dogmatismo *m*

do-gooder *n* *inf* tonto , -a de tan bueno, -a *m*

dog-tired *adj* *inf* hecho, -a polvo

doing ['du·ɪŋ] *n* **1.** **~s** (*activities*) actividades *fpl* **2.** (*action*) **to be (of) sb's ~** ser cosa de alguien; **to take some ~** requerir esfuerzo

do-it-yourself *n* bricolaje *m*

doldrums ['doʊl·drəmz] *npl* GEO zona *f* de las calmas ecuatoriales; **to be in the ~** (*person*) estar deprimido; (*business*) estar estancado

dole (out) vt (money, food) repartir

doleful ['doʊl·fəl] adj (person) triste; (expression) compungido, -a; (cry) lastimero, -a

doll [dal] n 1. (toy) muñeco, -a m, f 2. sl (nice person) encanto m 3. sl (term of address) guapo, -a m, f
◆**doll up** vt emperifollar; **to doll oneself up** ponerse de punta en blanco

dollar ['dal·ər] n dólar m ▸**to feel like a million** ~s sentirse a las mil maravillas; **to look like a million** ~s estar despampanante; **to earn a quick** ~ ganar dinero fácil

dollhouse n casa f de muñecas

dollop ['dal·əp] n (amount) porción f; (spoonful) cucharada f

dolly ['dal·i] <-ies> n 1. childspeak (doll) muñequita f 2. (for transporting) plataforma f rodante

dolphin ['dal·fɪn] n delfín m, bufeo m Perú

dolt [doʊlt] n imbécil mf

domain [doʊ·'meɪn] n 1. POL, COMPUT dominio m; (lands) propiedad f 2. (sphere of activity) ámbito m; **to be in the public** ~ ser de dominio público; **that is outside my** ~ eso está fuera de mi campo

dome [doʊm] n 1. (rounded roof) cúpula f 2. (rounded ceiling) bóveda f 3. sl (head) cabeza f

domestic [də·'mes·tɪk] I. adj 1. (of the house) doméstico, -a 2. (home-loving) casero, -a 3. a. ECON, FIN, POL (produce, flight, news) nacional; (market, trade, policy) interior; **gross ~ product** producto m interior bruto II. n doméstico m

domestic appliance n electrodoméstico m

domesticate [də·'mes·tɪ·keɪt] vt (animal) domesticar; (plant) aclimatar; (person) volver casero; **he is a very ~d man** es un hombre muy de su casa

domesticated adj domesticado, -a

domesticity [ˌdoʊ·me·'stɪs·ə·t̬i] n domesticidad f

domestic market n mercado m nacional

domestic science n economía f doméstica

domicile ['dam·ə·saɪl] I. n domicilio m II. vt domiciliar; **to be ~d in** residir en

dominance ['dam·ə·nəns] n 1. (rule) predominio m 2. MIL supremacía f

dominant ['dam·ə·nənt] adj dominante

dominate ['dam·ə·neɪt] vi, vt dominar

domination [ˌdam·ə·'neɪ·ʃən] n dominación f

domineer [ˌdam·ə·'nɪr] vi avasallar; **to ~ over sb** tiranizar a alguien

domineering adj dominante; **a ~ management style** una forma de dirigir muy tiránica

Dominica [ˌdam·ɪ·'ni·kə] n Dominica f

Dominican [də·'mɪn·ɪ·kən] I. adj dominicano, -a II. n 1. (nationality) dominicano, -a m, f 2. REL dominico, -a m, f

Dominican Republic n República f Dominicana

dominion [də·'mɪn·jən] n dominio m; **to have**

~ **over sb/sth** tener a alguien/algo bajo su dominio

domino ['dam·ə·noʊ] <-es> n 1. ~es (game) dominó m; **to play ~es** jugar al dominó 2. (piece) ficha f de dominó

domino effect n efecto m dominó

don [dan] vt (clothing) ponerse

donate ['doʊ·neɪt] vt donar

donation [doʊ·'neɪ·ʃən] n 1. (contribution) donativo m 2. (act) donación f

done [dʌn] pp of **do**

donkey ['daŋ·ki] n burro m; a. fig burro, -a m, f

donkeywork n sl trabajo m pesado

donor ['doʊ·nər] n donante mf

don't [doʊnt] = **do not** s. **do**

donut ['doʊ·nʌt] n s. **doughnut**

doodad ['du·dæd] n inf la cosa f esa

doodle ['du·dəl] I. vi garabatear II. n garabato m

doom [dum] I. n 1. (destiny) suerte f 2. (death) muerte f II. vt condenar

doomed adj condenado, -a; **to be ~ to failure** estar condenado al fracaso; ~ **to die** condenado a muerte

doomsday ['dumz·deɪ] n día m del juicio final

door [dɔr] n 1. puerta f; **front/back** ~ puerta principal/trasera; **revolving/sliding** ~ puerta giratoria/corredera; **to knock at** [o on] **the** ~ llamar a la puerta; **there's someone at the** ~ llaman a la puerta; **to answer the** ~ abrir la puerta; **to see sb to the** ~ acompañar a alguien hasta la puerta; **to live next** ~ (**to sb**) vivir al lado (de alguien); **to show sb the** ~ echar a alguien; **out of** ~s al aire libre; **behind closed** ~s a puerta cerrada; **to close the** ~ **on sb** cerrar la puerta a alguien; **to leave the** ~ **open to sb** dejar la puerta abierta a alguien 2. (doorway) entrada f ▸**to slam the** ~ **in sb's face** dar a alguien con la puerta en las narices; **to never darken sb's** ~s **again** liter no volver a poner los pies en casa de alguien; **to lay sth at sb's** ~ echar a alguien la culpa de algo

doorbell n timbre m

doorjamb n marco m de la puerta

doorkeeper n s. **doorman**

doorknob n pomo m (de la puerta)

doorman <-men> n portero m

doormat n felpudo m

doornail n inf **dead as a** ~ muerto y bien muerto

doorstep n peldaño m (de la puerta de entrada) ▸**to be right on sb's** ~ estar a la vuelta de la esquina

door-to-door I. adj de puerta a [o en] puerta; ~ **selling** venta f a domicilio II. adv de puerta a [o en] puerta

doorway n entrada f

dope [doʊp] I. n inf 1. (drugs) drogas fpl; (marijuana) maría f 2. SPORTS dopaje m; ~ **test** control m antidopaje 3. (stupid person) capullo m, pava f 4. (information) información f; **to give sb the** ~ **on** [o about] **sth** pasar informes a alguien sobre algo **II.** *vt* (*drug*) drogar; SPORTS dopar

dope dealer *n*, **dope pusher** *n inf* camello, -a *m, f*

dopey *adj*, **dopy** ['doʊ·pi] *adj* <-ier, -iest> *sl* **1.** (*drowsy*) grogui, abombado, -a *AmS* **2.** (*stupid*) lelo, -a

dormant ['dɔr·mənt] *adj* (*volcano*) inactivo, -a; (*animal*) aletargado, -a; (*law*) inaplicado, -a; (*idea*) latente; **to lie ~** permanecer latente

dormer *n* buhardilla *f*

dormitory ['dɔr·mə·tɔr·i] <-ies> *n* **1.** (*room*) dormitorio *m;* **~ town** ciudad *f* dormitorio **2.** UNIV residencia *f* de estudiantes

dormouse ['dɔr·maʊs] <-mice> *n* lirón *m*

dorsal ['dɔr·səl] *adj* dorsal

DOS [das] *n abbr of* **disk operating system** DOS *m*

dosage ['doʊ·sɪdʒ] *n* dosis *f inv*

dose [doʊs] **I.** *n a. fig* dosis; **a ~ of bad news** una mala noticia; **a nasty ~ of the flu** una gripe muy fuerte **II.** *vt* administrar una dosis a; **to ~ oneself with** medicarse con

dossier ['das·i·eɪ] *n* expediente *m;* **to keep a ~ on sb/sth** llevar un expediente sobre alguien/algo

dot [dat] **I.** *n* **1.** punto *m;* **on the ~** en punto; **she arrived at half past three on the ~** llegó a las tres y media en punto **2.** **~s** TYPO puntos *mpl* suspensivos; **120 ~s per inch** 120 píxeles [*o* píxeles] por pulgada **II.** <-tt-> *vt* **1.** (*mark with a dot*) dejar un punto en **2.** (*put a dot on*) poner el punto a [*o* en] **3.** (*scatter*) esparcir ▶ **to ~ one's i's and** cross **one's t's** poner los puntos sobre las íes

dote on [ˌdoʊt·ˈɔn] *vt* adorar

doting *adj* muy cariñoso, -a; **we saw photos of the ~ father with the baby** le vimos en unas fotos, hecho todo un padrazo con el bebé

dot-matrix printer *n* impresora *f* matricial

dotty ['dat·i] *adj* <-ier, -iest> (*person*) chiflado, -a; (*idea*) descabellado, -a

double ['dʌb·əl] **I.** *adj* **1.** (*twice as much/ many*) doble; **a ~ door** una puerta de dos hojas; **a ~ whiskey** un whisky doble; **it is ~ that** es el doble de eso; **to have a ~ meaning** tener un doble sentido; **to lead a ~ life** llevar una doble vida **2.** (*composed of two*) **in ~ digits** de varias cifras; **the number of deaths has now reached ~ digits** la cifra de muertos ya ha pasado de diez; **a ~ 's'** dos eses **3.** (*for two*) **~ mattress** colchón *m* de matrimonio; **~ room** habitación *f* doble **II.** *adv* doble; **to see ~** ver doble; **to fold sth ~** doblar algo por la mitad; **he's ~ your age** te dobla la edad; **to be bent ~** estar encorvado **III.** *vt* (*increase*) doblar; (*efforts*) redoblar; **we have ~d our profits** hemos duplicado los beneficios **IV.** *vi* duplicarse; **to ~ for sb** CINE, THEAT doblar a alguien; **to ~ as sth** (*person*) hacer también de algo, fungir; (*object*) servir también de algo **V.** *n* **1.** (*double quantity*) doble *m* **2.** (*person*) doble *mf;* **sb's ~** el/la doble de alguien **3.** **~s**

SPORTS dobles *mpl;* **to play ~s** jugar una partida de dobles ▶ **on** [*o* at] **the ~** inmediatamente

◆**double back** *vi* (*person, animal*) volver sobre sus pasos; (*path, river*) describir una curva

◆**double up** *vi* **1.** (*bend over*) retorcerse; **to ~ with laughter** troncharse de risa; **to ~ with pain** retorcerse de dolor **2.** (*share room*) compartir habitación

double-barreled *adj* **1.** (*shotgun*) de dos cañones **2.** (*having two purposes*) de doble efecto

double bass <-es> *n* contrabajo *m*

double bed *n* cama *f* de matrimonio

double-breasted *adj* (*jacket*) cruzado, -a

double-check *vi, vt* comprobar dos veces; **to ~ that...** volver a comprobar que...; **to ~ sth** (*verify again*) verificar algo por segunda vez; (*verify in two ways*) comprobar de dos formas diferentes que...

double chin *n* papada *f*

double-click *vi* COMPUT hacer doble clic; **to ~ on the left mouse button** hacer doble clic con el botón izquierdo

double-cross I. *vt* traicionar **II.** <-es> *n* traición *f*

double-crosser *n* traidor(a) *m(f)*

double-dealer *n* embustero, -a *m, f*

double-dealing *n* engaño *m*

double-decker *n* **1.** (*bus*) autobús *m* de dos pisos **2.** (*sandwich*) **~** (**sandwich**) sandwich *m* doble (*compuesto de 3 rebanadas de pan*)

double-edged *adj a. fig* de doble filo

double-entry bookkeeping *n* contabilidad *f* por partida doble

double feature *n* programa *m* doble

double-glaze *vt* **to ~ a window** instalar doble aislamiento en una ventana

double-jointed *adj* con articulaciones dobles

double-park *vi, vt* aparcar en doble fila

double-quick I. *adv* a paso ligero; **to get home ~** llegar a casa en un momento **II.** *adj* (*step*) ligero, -a; **in ~ time** volando

doublespeak ['dʌb·əl·spik] *n s.* **double-talk**

double standard *n* **to have ~s** no medir con el mismo rasero

double take *n* reacción *f* tardía; **to do a ~** tardar en reaccionar

double talk *n* palabras *fpl* ambiguas

doublethink *n* aceptación *f* de principios contradictorios

double time *n* **1.** COM, ECON paga *f* doble **2.** MIL paso *m* ligero

double vision *n* visión *f* doble

doubly ['dʌb·li] *adv* doblemente; **to make ~ sure that...** asegurarse bien de que... +*subj*

doubt [daʊt] **I.** *n* duda *f;* **to be in ~ whether to...** dudar si...; **without a shadow of a ~** sin lugar a dudas; **no ~** sin duda; **without a ~** sin duda alguna; **he will no ~ come at Christmas** seguro que vendrá en Navidad; **there is no ~ about it** no cabe la menor duda; **to have one's ~s about sth** tener sus dudas respecto a algo; **the future of the project is in** ~ no se sabe si el proyecto seguirá adelante; **beyond all reasonable** ~ más allá de toda duda fundada; **to raise ~s about sth** hacer dudar de algo; **to cast ~ on sth** poner algo en tela de juicio II. *vt* **1.**(*be unwilling to believe*) dudar de; **to ~ sb's word** dudar de la palabra de alguien **2.**(*call into question: abilities, sincerity*) poner en duda **3.**(*feel uncertain*) dudar; **to ~ that** dudar que +*subj;* **to ~ if** [*o* **whether**]... dudar si...; **I ~ it very much** lo dudo mucho III. *vi* dudar

doubtful ['daʊt·fəl] *adj* **1.**(*uncertain, undecided*) indeciso, -a; **to be ~ whether to...** dudar si...; **to be ~ about going** estar indeciso respecto a si ir o no **2.**(*unlikely*) incierto, -a **3.**(*questionable*) dudoso, -a

doubtless ['daʊt·lɪs] *adv* sin duda

dough [doʊ] *n* **1.** CULIN masa *f* **2.** *sl* (*money*) pasta *f,* plata *f AmS*

doughnut ['doʊ·nʌt] *n* donut *m*

doughy ['doʊ·i] *adj* pastoso, -a

dour [dʊr] *adj* (*manner*) adusto, -a; (*appearance*) austero, -a

douse [daʊs] *vt* **1.**(*throw liquid on*) mojar; **to ~ sth in gas** mojar algo con gasolina **2.**(*extinguish: light, candle*) apagar

dove[1] [dʌv] *n* ZOOL paloma *f*

dove[2] [doʊv] *pt of* **dive**

dovecot(e) ['dʌv·koʊt] *n* palomar *m*

dovetail ['dʌv·teɪl] I. *n* TECH cola *f* de milano II. *vi* encajar III. *vt* **1.** TECH ensamblar a cola de milano **2.**(*fit*) **to ~ sth into/with sth** encajar algo en/con algo

dowager ['daʊ·ə·dʒər] *n* viuda *f* de un noble

dowdy ['daʊ·di] *adj* <-ier, -iest> poco atractivo, -a; **to wear ~ clothes** vestir con poca gracia

dowel ['daʊ·əl] *n* TECH espiga *f*

down[1] [daʊn] *n* (*feathers*) plumón *m;* (*hairs*) pelusa *f;* (*on body*) vello *m;* (*on face*) bozo *m*

down[2] [daʊn] I. *adv* **1.**(*movement*) abajo; **to fall ~** caerse; **to lie ~** acostarse **2.**(*from another point*) **to go ~ to Washington/the lake** bajar a Washington/al lago; **~ South** hacia el sur **3.**(*less in volume or intensity*) **to be worn ~** estar gastado; **the wind died ~** el viento se calmó [*o* amainó]; **the sun is ~** se ha puesto el sol; **the fire is burning ~** el fuego se está consumiendo; **the price is ~** el precio ha bajado **4.**(*temporal*) **from 1900 ~ to the present** desde 1900 hasta el presente; **~ through the ages** a través de la historia **5.**(*in writing*) **to write/get sth ~** escribir/ anotar/apuntar algo **6.**(*not functioning*) **to be ~** (*computer*) no funcionar; (*server*) estar caído; (*telephone lines*) estar cortado **7.**(*as deposit*) **to put $100/10% ~ on sth** pagar 100 dólares/el 10% de entrada para algo, abonar 100 dólares/un abono del 10% para algo ▶ **to be ~ on sb** tener manía a alguien; **~ with the dictator!** ¡abajo el dictador! II. *prep* **1.**(*lower*) **to go ~ the stairs** bajar las

escaleras; **to run ~ the slope** correr cuesta abajo **2.**(*along*) **to go ~ the street** ir por la calle

down and out, down-and-out I. *adj* **to be ~** no tener donde caerse muerto II. *n* vagabundo, -a *m, f*

downcast ['daʊn·kæst] *adj* alicaído, -a

downfall ['daʊn·fɔl] *n* (*of government*) caída *f;* (*of organization, firm*) derrumbamiento *m;* (*of person*) perdición *f;* **that will be his ~** eso será su ruina

downgrade [ˌdaʊn·'greɪd] I. *vt* **1.**(*lower category of*) bajar de categoría **2.**(*disparage*) minimizar; **to ~ the importance of sth** minimizar la importancia de algo II. *n* bajada; **to be on the ~** *fig* ir cuesta abajo

downhearted [ˌdaʊn·'har·ţɪd] *adj* descorazonado, -a

downhill [ˌdaʊn·'hɪl] I. *adv* cuesta abajo; **to go ~** ir cuesta abajo; *fig* ir de mal en peor II. *adj* (*path*) cuesta abajo; **it's all ~ from now on** *fig* ya lo tenemos chupado *inf*

download ['daʊn·loʊd] *vt* COMPUT bajar(se)

down-market I. *adj* (*neighborhood, newspaper*) popular; (*shop, store*) barato, -a; (*program*) de masas II. *adv* **to move ~** perder prestigio; (*intentionally*) dirigirse a un sector popular del público

down payment *n* entrada *f,* cuota *f* inicial *AmL;* **to make a ~ on sth** dar la entrada para comprar algo

downplay ['daʊn·pleɪ] *vt* restar importancia a

downpour ['daʊn·pɔr] *n* chaparrón *m*

downright ['daʊn·raɪt] I. *adj* (*refusal*) rotundo, -a; (*disobedience*) completo, -a; (*lie*) abierto, -a; (*liar*) redomado, -a; (*fool*) de remate; **it is a ~ disgrace** es una auténtica vergüenza; **that's ~ stupid** eso es una solemne tontería II. *adv* completamente; **to be ~ difficult** ser dificilísimo; **to refuse ~** negarse rotundamente

downside ['daʊn·saɪd] *n* desventaja *f;* **on the ~, it's far from town** tiene el inconveniente de que está lejos del pueblo

downsize ['daʊn·saɪz] *vt* reducir

downsizing *n* reducción *f*

downstairs [ˌdaʊn·'sterz] I. *adv* abajo; **to go ~** bajar (las escaleras); **to run ~** bajar corriendo (las escaleras) II. *adj* (*del piso*) de abajo III. *n* planta *f* baja

downstream [ˌdaʊn·'strim] *adv* río abajo; **it is another few miles ~ from here** eso está a unas cuantas millas río abajo

Down syndrome *n* síndrome *m* de Down

downtime ['daʊn·taɪm] *n* **1.** COMPUT, TECH tiempo *m* improductivo **2.**(*rest*) descanso *m*

down-to-earth *adj* (*explanation*) realista; (*person*) práctico, -a

downtown [ˌdaʊn·'taʊn] I. *n* centro *m* (de la ciudad) II. *adv* **to go ~** ir al centro; **to live ~** vivir en el centro III. *adj* (*in the city center*) céntrico, -a; (*related to the city center*) del centro (de la ciudad); **~ Los Angeles** el centro de Los Ángeles

downtrodden ['daʊn·trad·ən] *adj* (*grass*) pisoteado, -a; (*person*) oprimido, -a

downturn ['daʊn·tɜrn] *n* empeoramiento *m;* **a ~ in sth** un giro negativo en algo; **to take a ~** dar un bajón; **an economic ~** un empeoramiento de la situación económica

downward ['daʊn·wərd] **I.** *adj* (*movement*) descendente; (*direction*) hacia abajo; (*path*) cuesta abajo; (*tendency, prices*) a la baja; **inflation is on a ~ trend** la inflación está disminuyendo **II.** *adv* hacia abajo

downwards ['daʊn·wərdz] *adv* hacia abajo

downy ['daʊ·ni] *adj* aterciopelado, -a

dowry ['daʊ·ri] <-ies> *n* dote *f*

dowse[1] [daʊz] *vi* buscar con una varilla de zahorí; **to ~ for water** buscar agua con una varilla de zahorí

dowse[2] [daʊs] *vt s.* **douse**

dowser *n* **1.** (*rod*) varilla *f* de zahorí **2.** (*person*) zahorí *mf*

dowsing *n* búsqueda *f de agua o metales con una varilla de zahorí*

dowsing rod *n* varilla *f* de zahorí

doyen ['dɔɪ·ən] *n* decano *m*

doyenne [dɔɪ·'en] *n* decana *f*

doz. *abbr of* **dozen** docena *f*

doze [doʊz] **I.** *vi* dormitar; **to ~ off** dormirse **II.** *n* cabezada *f;* **to have a ~** echar un sueño

dozen ['dʌz·ən] *n* **1.** (*twelve*) docena *f;* **half a ~** media docena; **two ~ eggs** dos docenas de huevos **2.** (*many*) **~s of times** montones de veces; **by the ~** por docenas ▶ **it's six of one and half a ~ of the other** lo mismo da que da lo mismo

dozy ['doʊ·zi] *adj* <-ier, -iest> soñoliento, -a

DP 1. *abbr of* **data processing** PD *m* **2.** *abbr of* **displaced person** desplazado, -a *m, f*

DPh *n*, **DPhil** *n abbr of* **Doctor of Philosophy** doctor(a) *m(f)* en Filosofía

Dr. 1. *abbr of* **Doctor** Dr. *m*, Dra. *f* **2.** *abbr of* **Drive** C/ *f*

drab [dræb] *adj* <drabber, drabbest> **1.** (*dull: food*) soso, -a; (*color*) apagado, -a, pardo, -a; (*existence*) monótono, -a **2.** (*khaki colored*) (de color) kaki [*o* caqui]

draconian [drə·'koʊ·ni·ən] *adj* draconiano, -a

draft [dræft] **I.** *n* **1.** (*current of air*) corriente *f* de aire **2.** (*drawing*) boceto *m* **3.** (*preliminary version*) borrador *m;* (*of novel, speech*) primera versión *f;* (*of contract*) minuta *f;* **~ bill** LAW anteproyecto *m* de ley **4. the ~** MIL el reclutamiento (*en caso de guerra*), destacamento *m* **5.** NAUT calado *m* **6.** MED dosis *f inv* **7.** (*drink*) trago *m* **8.** (*beer from tap*) cerveza de barril *f* [*o* a presión]; **on ~** de barril **II.** *vt* **1.** (*prepare first version*) hacer un borrador de; (*novel*) redactar la primera versión de; (*plan*) trazar; (*contract*) redactar la minuta de **2.** MIL llamar a filas **III.** *adj* **1.** (*beer*) de barril **2.** (*horse*) de tiro

draft board *n junta encargada de seleccionar a los que serán llamados a filas*

draft dodger *n* MIL prófugo, -a *m, f*

draftee [dræf·'ti] *n* MIL recluta *mf*

draftsman ['dræfts·mən] <-men> *n* TECH delineante *m*

drafty ['dræf·ti] *adj* <-ier, -iest> lleno, -a de corrientes de aire; **it's ~ here with the door open** hace [*o* hay] corriente con la puerta abierta

drag [dræg] **I.** <-gg-> *vt* **1.** (*pull*) arrastrar; **to ~ oneself somewhere** arrastrarse hasta un sitio; **to ~ one's heels** [*o* **feet**] arrastrar los pies; *fig* dar largas a un asunto; **to ~ sb's name through the mud** dejar a alguien por los suelos **2.** (*in water*) dragar **3.** COMPUT arrastrar **II.** <-gg-> *vi* **1.** (*trail along*) arrastrarse por el suelo **2.** (*time*) pasar lentamente; (*meeting, conversation*) hacerse interminable **3.** (*lag behind*) rezagarse **III.** *n* **1.** (*device*) draga *f* **2.** PHYS resistencia *f* al avance; AVIAT resistencia *f* aerodinámica **3.** (*hindrance*) estorbo *m;* **to be a ~ on sb** ser una carga para alguien **4.** *sl* (*boring person*) pelmazo, -a *m, f;* (*boring experience*) lata *f;* **what a ~!** ¡qué rollo! **5.** *inf* (*women's clothes*) disfraz *m* de mujer; **to be in ~** ir vestido de mujer **6.** *inf* (*inhalation*) calada *f;* **to take a ~** dar una calada ▶ **the main ~** *sl* la calle principal

♦drag along *vt* arrastrar con dificultad

♦drag away *vt* arrancar

♦drag behind *vi* seguir con atraso

♦drag down *vt* **1.** (*lower forcefully*) arrastrar hacia abajo **2.** (*make depressed*) hundir; (*make weak*) debilitar

♦drag in *vt* (*person*) involucrar; (*subject*) traer por los pelos

♦drag on *vi* (*meeting, film*) hacerse interminable

♦drag out *vt* (*meeting, conversation*) alargar

♦drag up *vt* sacar a relucir

draglift *n* telearrastre *m*

dragon ['dræg·ən] *n* **1.** (*mythical creature*) dragón *m* **2.** *fig* (*fierce woman*) arpía *f*

dragonfly ['dræg·ən·flaɪ] <-ies> *n* libélula *f*, alguacil *m RíoPl*

dragoon [drə·'gun] *n* MIL dragón *m*

drain [dreɪn] **I.** *vt* **1.** AGR, MED drenar; (*pond*) vaciar; (*river*) desaguar; (*food*) escurrir; (*machine*) purgar **2.** (*empty by drinking: glass, cup*) apurar; (*bottle*) acabar(se) **3.** (*exhaust, tire out: person*) dejar agotado; (*resources*) agotar; **to ~ sb's energy** agotar las energías de alguien; **war ~s the nation of its youth and its wealth** la guerra mina la juventud y la riqueza de una nación **II.** *vi* (*dishes*) escurrir **III.** *n* **1.** (*channel*) canal *m* de desagüe; (*pipe*) tubo *m* de desagüe **2.** (*sewer*) alcantarilla *f*, resumidero *m AmL* **3.** (*in sink*) desagüe *m*, sifón *m; fig;* **to throw sth down the ~** tirar algo por la borda; **to throw** [*o* **pour**] **money down the ~** tirar el dinero por la ventana; **to go down the ~** *fig* irse al garete [*o* al traste] **4.** (*constant outflow*) fuga *f;* **brain ~** fuga de cerebros; **to be a ~ on sb's resources** consu-

mir los recursos de alguien
◆**drain away** *vi* (*water*) irse; (*energy*) agotarse; (*tension*) disiparse
◆**drain off** *vt* (*liquid*) extraer
drainage ['dreɪ·nɪdʒ] *n* **1.** AGR, MED drenaje *m* **2.** TECH desagüe *m;* ~ **system** alcantarillado *m*
drainage basin *n* cuenca *f* hidrográfica
drainboard *n* escurridero *m*
drainpipe *n* tubo *m* de desagüe
drake [dreɪk] *n* pato *m* (macho)
dram [dræm] *n* (*of whiskey, brandy*) copita *f*
drama ['dra·mə] *n* **1.** LIT, CINE drama *m* **2.** THEAT arte *m* dramático; ~ **teacher** profesor(a) *m(f)* de arte dramático **3.** *inf* (*emotional situation*) drama *m;* **high** ~ follón padre
drama school *n* escuela *f* de arte dramático
dramatic [drə·'mæt̬·ɪk] *adj* **1.** THEAT dramático, -a; (*artist, production*) teatral; (*rescue, events, escape*) dramático, -a **2.** (*very noticeable: rise, discovery*) espectacular; (*effect*) notable
dramatics [drə·'mæt̬·ɪks] *npl* **1.** + *sing vb* THEAT teatro *m;* **amateur** ~ teatro amateur **2.** *pej* (*behavior*) teatralidad *f*
dramatis personae [ˌdræm·ə·t̬ɪs·pər·'soʊ·ni] *npl* THEAT personajes *mpl* (*de una obra de teatro*)
dramatist ['dræm·ə·t̬ɪst] *n* THEAT dramaturgo, -a *m, f*
dramatization [ˌdræm·ə·t̬ɪ·'zeɪ·ʃən] *n* dramatización *f*
dramatize ['dræm·ə·taɪz] *vt* **1.** THEAT adaptar al teatro **2.** (*exaggerate*) dramatizar
drank [dræŋk] *pt of* **drink**
drape [dreɪp] **I.** *vt* **1.** (*hang*) cubrir; **to** ~ **sth** (**in a flag**) cubrir algo (con una bandera) **2.** (*place*) colocar; **she** ~**d the scarf around her shoulders** se puso el chal sobre los hombros; **to** ~ **one's arms/legs over sth** apoyar los brazos/las piernas en algo **II.** *vi* colgar; **to** ~ **well** (*clothes*) tener caída **III.** *n* **1.** ~**s** (*curtains*) cortinas *fpl* **2.** MED talla *f* **3.** (*how sth hangs*) caída *f*
drapery ['dreɪ·pə·ri] <-ies> *n* **1.** (*hangings*) ropaje *m* **2. draperies** (*curtains*) cortinas *fpl* **3.** (*cloths, fabrics*) pañería *f*
drastic ['dræs·tɪk] *adj* (*measure*) drástico, -a; (*change*) radical
drat [dræt] *interj* ¡maldita sea!
draw [drɔ] **I.** <drew, drawn> *vt* **1.** ART dibujar; (*line*) trazar; (*character*) perfilar; (*diagram, map*) representar; **to** ~ **sth to scale** reproducir algo a escala **2.** (*pull, haul: cart, wagon*) arrastrar; **to** ~ **the curtains** correr las cortinas; **to** ~ **sb aside** llevarse a alguien aparte; **to** ~ **sb into a trap** conducir a alguien a una trampa; **I was soon** ~**n into the argument** pronto me vi envuelto en la discusión **3.** (*attract*) atraer; **to** ~ **applause** arrancar aplausos; **to be** ~**n toward(s) sb** sentirse atraído por alguien; **to** ~ **attention to** llamar la atención sobre; **to** ~ **criticism** suscitar críticas **4.** (*elicit, evoke*) **to** ~ **sth** (**from sb/sth**) conseguir algo (de alguien/algo); **to** ~ **a confession from sb** sacar

una confesión a alguien; **to** ~ **a reply** obtener una respuesta; **to** ~ **laughter** provocar risa **5.** (*formulate, perceive*) **to** ~ **an analogy** establecer una analogía; **to** ~ **a conclusion** sacar una conclusión; **to** ~ **an inference** inferir **6.** (*take out: gun*) sacar; **to** ~ **a card** (**from the deck**) GAMES elegir [*o* escoger] una carta (de la baraja); **to** ~ **blood** *fig* sacar sangre **7.** (*obtain*) obtener; (*salary*) ganar; (*pension*) cobrar **8.** (*pay with*) **to** ~ **a check** extender [*o* librar] un cheque; (*withdraw: money*) retirar [*o* sacar] **9.** (*lottery*) sortear; **to** ~ **straws** echarlo a suertes **10.** SPORTS, GAMES empatar **11.** CULIN **to** ~ **a beer** poner una cerveza de barril **12.** NAUT **the boat** ~**s 24 inches** el barco tiene un calado de 61 metros **13.** SPORTS **to** ~ **a bow** tensar un arco **II.** <drew, drawn> *vi* **1.** ART dibujar **2.** (*move, proceed*) **to** ~ **ahead** adelantarse; **to** ~ **away** apartarse; ~ **up here and he'll get into the car** para aquí para que se suba al coche **3.** (*approach*) acercarse; **to** ~ **to a close** finalizar; **to** ~ **to an end** concluir **4.** (*chimney*) tirar (bien) **5.** (*draw lots*) echar a suertes **6.** SPORTS, GAMES empatar **III.** *n* **1.** (*attraction*) atracción *f* **2.** SPORTS, GAMES empate *m* **3.** (*drawing of lots*) sorteo *m* **4.** (*act of drawing a gun*) **to be quick on the** ~ ser rápido en sacar la pistola; *fig* pescarlas al vuelo **5.** (*of a chimney*) tiro *m*
◆**draw apart** *vi* distanciarse
◆**draw aside** *vt always sep* (*person*) apartar; (*curtain*) correr
◆**draw away** **I.** *vi* **1.** (*move off*) alejarse **2.** (*move ahead*) **to** ~ **from sb** dejar atrás a alguien **3.** (*move away*) apartarse **II.** *vt* apartar
◆**draw down** *vt* bajar; **to wear a hat drawn down over one's ears** llevar un gorro calado hasta las orejas
◆**draw in** **I.** *vi* **1.** (*car, bus, train*) llegar **2.** (*days*) acortarse **II.** *vt* **1.** (*breath*) tomar **2.** (*attract*) atraer
◆**draw off** *vt* (*boots*) quitarse; (*liquid*) vaciar
◆**draw on** **I.** *vt* **1.** (*make use of*) usar; **to** ~ **sb's own resources** utilizar sus propios recursos; **to** ~ **the stocks** tirar de existencias **2.** (*put on*) ponerse **II.** *vi* **1.** (*continue: time, day*) seguir su curso **2.** (*approach*) acercarse
◆**draw out** **I.** *vt* **1.** (*prolong*) alargar **2.** (*elicit*) sacar; **to** ~ **information from sb** sonsacar información a alguien; **to** ~ **feelings and memories** hacer aflorar sentimientos y recuerdos; **to draw sb out** (**of himself**) hacer que alguien se desinhiba **3.** FIN, ECON, COM retirar **II.** *vi* **1.** (*car, bus, train*) salir **2.** (*day*) hacerse más largo
◆**draw together** **I.** *vt* juntar **II.** *vi* acercarse
◆**draw up** **I.** *vt* **1.** (*draft*) redactar; (*list*) hacer; (*guidelines, plan*) trazar; **to** ~ **a constitution** LAW redactar una constitución **2.** (*pull toward one*) arrimar **3.** (*raise*) levantar; **to draw oneself up** erguirse **II.** *vi* (*vehicle*) pararse
drawback *n* inconveniente *m*, desventaja *f*
drawbridge *n* puente *m* levadizo

drawer [drɔr] *n* cajón *m*

drawing *n* ART dibujo *m*

drawing board *n* mesa *f* [*o* tablero] *m* de dibujo; **back to the ~!** ¡vuelta a empezar!

drawing room *n* salón *m*

drawl [drɔl] **I.** *n* habla *f* lenta **II.** *vi* hablar arrastrando las vocales

drawn [drɔn] **I.** *pp of* **draw II.** *adj* **1.** (*face*) demacrado, -a; **you look tired and ~** se te ve cansado y ojeroso **2.** (*butter*) derretido, -a

dread [dred] **I.** *vt* temer; **I ~ to think...** me da miedo pensar... **II.** *n* terror *m;* **to fill sb with ~** aterrorizar a alguien **III.** *adj* aterrador(a)

dreadful ['dred·fəl] *adj* **1.** (*terrible*) espantoso, -a; (*mistake*) terrible; (*disease*) atroz; **I feel ~ about it** me da mucha pena **2.** (*of bad quality*) fatal **3.** (*very great*) horroroso, -a; (*atrocity*) espantoso, -a

dreadfully ['dred·fə·li] *adv* **1.** (*in a terrible manner*) terriblemente **2.** (*very poorly*) fatal **3.** (*extremely*) enormemente

dream [drim] **I.** *n* **1.** sueño *m;* **a bad ~** una pesadilla **2.** (*daydream*) ensueño *m;* (*fantasy*) ilusión *f;* **to be in a ~** estar en las nubes; **like a ~** como un sueño; **he cooks like a ~** cocina de maravilla; **to go like a ~** ir como la seda; **a ~ come true** un sueño hecho realidad; **in your ~s!** *inf* ¡ni lo sueñes! **II.** <dreamed *o* dreamt, dreamed *o* dreamt> *vi* soñar; **to ~ of** (**doing**) **sth** soñar con (hacer) algo; **~ on!** *inf* ¡ni de coña!; **I wouldn't ~ of** (**doing**) **that** no se me pasaría por la cabeza (hacer) eso **III.** <dreamed *o* dreamt, dreamed *o* dreamt> *vt* soñar; **I never ~ed that...** nunca se me había ocurrido que... +*condicional* **IV.** *adj* ideal; **his ~ house** la casa de sus sueños; **to be** (**living**) **in a ~ world** vivir en las nubes ◆ **dream away** *vt* **to ~ the day** pasarse el día soñando ◆ **dream up** *vt* idear

dreamer ['dri·mər] *n* soñador(a) *m(f); pej* iluso, -a *m, f*

dreamland *n* país *m* de los sueños

dreamless *adj* sin sueños

dreamlike *adj* de ensueño

dreamt [dremt] *pt, pp of* **dream**

dreamy ['dri·mi] *adj* <-ier, -iest> **1.** (*dreamlike*) de ensueño **2.** (*as in daydream*) soñador(a) **3.** *inf* (*wonderful*) maravilloso, -a

dreary ['drɪr·i] *adj* <-ier, -iest> (*life*) deprimente; (*place*) lóbrego, -a; (*weather*) gris

dredge¹ [dredʒ] **I.** *n* TECH red *f* de arrastre **II.** *vt* TECH dragar

dredge² [dredʒ] *vt* CULIN espolvorear

dredger¹ ['dredʒ·ər] *n* TECH draga *f*

dredger² ['dredʒ·ər] *n* CULIN espolvoreador *m*

dregs [dregz] *npl* **1.** (*sediment*) posos *mpl* **2.** (*undesirable part*) **the ~ of society** la escoria de la sociedad

drench [drentʃ] *vt* empapar; **to be ~ed in** estar calado de

dress [dres] **I.** *n* <-es> vestido *m;* **strapless/ sleeveless ~** vestido sin tirantes/con los hombros destapados/sin mangas **II.** *vi* vestirse; **to ~ in blue** ir [*o* vestir] de azul; **to ~ for sth** vestirse para algo **III.** *vt* **1.** (*put clothes on*) vestir **2.** CULIN (*greens, salad*) aliñar **3.** MED (*wound*) vendar **4.** (*decorate*) adornar; (*hair*) peinar; **to ~ shop windows** decorar escaparates **IV.** *adj* de gala; **a ~ suit** traje *m* de gala ◆ **dress down I.** *vi* vestir informal **II.** *vt* **to dress sb down** regañar a alguien ◆ **dress up I.** *vi* ponerse elegante; **to ~ as** disfrazarse de **II.** *vt* **1.** (*put on formal clothes*) poner elegante **2.** (*disguise*) disfrazar; **to dress sb up as** disfrazar a alguien de **3.** (*embellish*) adornar

dress circle *n* THEAT piso *m* principal

dresser ['dres·ər] *n* **1.** FASHION **to be a very stylish ~** vestir con mucho estilo **2.** THEAT encargado, -a *m, f* de vestuario **3.** (*chest of drawers*) tocador *m;* (*sideboard*) aparador *m*

dressing ['dres·ɪŋ] *n* **1.** FASHION el vestir **2.** CULIN aliño *m* **3.** MED vendaje *m*

dressing-down *n* reprimenda *f*

dressing gown *n* bata *f;* (*bathrobe*) albornoz *m*

dressing room *n* vestidor *m;* THEAT camerino *m*

dressing table *n* tocador *m*

dressmaker ['dres·ˌmeɪ·kər] *n* modisto, -a *m, f*

dress rehearsal *n* ensayo *m* general

dress shirt *n* camisa *f* de etiqueta

dress suit *n* vestido *m* de gala

dress uniform *n* uniforme *m* de gala

dressy ['dres·i] *adj* <-ier, -iest> (*clothing*) elegante

drew [dru] *pt of* **draw**

dribble ['drɪb·əl] **I.** *vi* **1.** (*person*) babear **2.** (*water*) gotear **3.** SPORTS regatear; **to ~ past a defender** driblar a un defensa **II.** *vt* **1.** (*water*) dejar caer gota a gota **2.** SPORTS regatear con **III.** *n* **1.** (*saliva*) baba *f* **2.** (*water*) chorrito *m* **3.** SPORTS drible *m*

driblet ['drɪb·lɪt] *n* trocito *m;* **in ~s** en pequeñas cantidades

dried [draɪd] **I.** *pt, pp of* **dry II.** *adj* seco, -a; **~ meat** cecina *f;* **~ milk** leche *f* en polvo

dried-up *adj*, **dried up** *adj* seco, -a

drier ['draɪ·ər] *adj comp of* **dry**

drift [drɪft] **I.** *vi* **1.** (*on water*) dejarse llevar por la corriente; **to ~ out to sea** ir a la deriva; (*in air*) dejarse llevar por el viento **2.** (*move aimlessly*) dejarse llevar **3.** (*progress aimlessly*) vivir sin rumbo **4.** METEO (*sand, snow*) amontonarse **II.** *n* **1.** NAUT deriva *f* **2.** *fig* (*movement*) movimiento *m* **3.** (*trend*) tendencia *f* **4.** METEO montón *m;* **a sand ~** un montón de arena **5.** *inf* (*sense*) onda *f;* **to catch sb's ~** captar a alguien ◆ **drift apart** *vi* (*people*) distanciarse (progresivamente) ◆ **drift off** *vi* dormirse lentamente

drifter ['drɪf·tər] *n* vagabundo, -a *m, f*

drift ice *n* hielo *m* flotante

driftwood *n madera que flota en el mar arras-*

trada por la corriente
drill [drɪl] **I.** *n* **1.** TECH taladro *m;* (*dentist's*) fresa *f;* ~ **bit** broca *f* **2.** MIL, SCHOOL ejercicios *fpl;* **spelling** ~ ejercicios de ortografía **II.** *vt* **1.** TECH perforar; **to** ~ **a hole** hacer un agujero **2.** SCHOOL instruir; **to** ~ **sth into sb** inculcar algo a alguien **3.** MIL enseñar la instrucción a **III.** *vi* **1.** TECH perforar **2.** (*go through exercise*) hacer ejercicios **3.** MIL hacer la instrucción **IV.** *adj* MIL de instrucción
drilling rig *n* torre *f* de perforación
drink [drɪŋk] **I.** <drank, drunk> *vi* beber; **to** ~ **heavily/in moderation** beber en exceso/con moderación; **to** ~ **to sb** brindar por alguien **II.** <drank, drunk> *vt* beber; **to** ~ **a toast** (to **sb/sth**) brindar (por alguien/algo); **to** ~ **sb under the table** tener mucho más aguante que alguien; **to** ~ **one's troubles away** ahogar sus problemas en alcohol **III.** *n* bebida *f;* (*alcoholic beverage*) copa *f;* **to have a** ~ tomar algo; **to drive sb to** ~ llevar a alguien a la bebida; **the** ~ *sl* el agua
◆**drink in** *vt* beber; (*words*) estar pendiente de
drinkable ['drɪŋ·kə·bəl] *adj* potable
drinker *n* bebedor(a) *m(f)*
drinking *n* (*act*) bebida *f;* (*drunkenness*) alcoholismo *m;* **no** ~ **allowed on these premises** se prohíbe el consumo de bebidas alcohólicas
drinking fountain *n* fuente *f* (*de agua potable*)
drinking song *n* canción *f* de taberna
drinking water *n* agua *f* potable
drip [drɪp] **I.** <-pp-> *vi* gotear **II.** <-pp-> *vt* chorrear; (*drop by drop*) echar a gotas; **to** ~ **water on the floor** salpicar [*o* chorrear] agua en el suelo **III.** *n* **1.** (*act of dripping*) goteo *m* **2.** (*drop*) gota *f* **3.** MED gota a gota *m* **4.** *sl* (*person*) pánfilo, -a *m, f*
drip-dry <-ie-> *adj* de lava y pon
dripping ['drɪp·ɪŋ] **I.** *adj* **1.** (*faucet, pipe*) que gotea **2.** (*extremely wet*) empapado, -a **II.** *adv* **to be** ~ **wet** estar chorreando **III.** *n* ~ **s** pringue *m o f*
drive [draɪv] **I.** <drove, driven> *vt* **1.** AUTO conducir, manejar *AmL;* (*race car*) pilotar; **to** ~ **a sports car** tener un (coche) deportivo; **to** ~ **sb home** llevar a alguien a casa (*en un vehículo*) **2.** (*urge*) empujar; **to** ~ **sb to** (**do**) **sth** forzar a alguien a (hacer) algo **3.** (*cattle*) guiar **4.** (*render, make*) volver; **to** ~ **sb crazy** sacar a alguien de quicio **5.** (*ball*) golpear; (*tunnel*) abrir, perforar; (*nail, stake*) clavar **6.** TECH mover **II.** <drove, driven> *vi* AUTO **1.** (*operate vehicle*) conducir, manejar *AmL;* **the car** ~**s well/smoothly** es un coche muy manejable **2.** (*travel*) ir (*en un vehículo*) **3.** (*function*) funcionar **III.** *n* **1.** AUTO paseo *m*, vuelta *f;* (*journey*) viaje *m;* **to go for a** ~ ir a dar una vuelta en coche **2.** (*in street names*) **Broadview D~** calle Broadview **3.** (*driveway*) entrada *f* **4.** TECH transmisión *f;* **front-wheel** ~ tracción *f* delantera; **all-wheel** [*o* **four-wheel**] ~ tracción a

las cuatro ruedas **5.** PSYCH impulso *m;* **to have** ~ ser emprendedor; **sex** ~ apetito *m* sexual **6.** (*campaign*) campaña *f;* **a fund-raising** ~ campaña para recaudar fondos **7.** SPORTS golpe *m* fuerte **8.** COMPUT unidad *f* de disco
◆**drive at** *vt inf* querer decir, insinuar
◆**drive in I.** *vi* entrar (*en un vehículo*) **II.** *vt* (*nail*) clavar
◆**drive off I.** *vt always sep* ahuyentar **II.** *vi* irse (*en un vehículo*)
◆**drive out** *vt* expulsar
◆**drive up** *vi* **to** ~ (**somewhere**) acercarse (a algún sitio)
drive-in ['draɪv·ɪn] *n* (*restaurant*) restaurante donde se sirve a los clientes en el coche; (*cinema*) autocine *m*
drive-in bank *n* autobanco *m*
drive-in movie *n*, **drive-in theater** *n* autocine *m*
drivel ['drɪv·əl] *n* tonterías *fpl*
driven ['drɪv·ən] *pp of* **drive**
driver ['draɪ·vər] *n* **1.** AUTO conductor(a) *m(f);* **truck** ~ camionero, -a *m, f;* **taxi** ~ taxista *mf;* **to be in the** ~**'s seat** *fig* llevar las riendas de algo **2.** COMPUT driver *m*
driver's license *n* carné *m* de conducir, brevete *m Perú*
drive-through *adj*, **drive-thru** *adj* (*pharmacy, restaurant, bank*) donde se atiende a los clientes en el coche
driveway ['draɪv·weɪ] *n* camino *m* de entrada
driving I. *n* conducción *f*, manejo *m AmL* **II.** *adj* **1.** AUTO, TECH de conducir **2.** METEO (*rain*) torrencial **3.** (*powerful: ambition, force*) impulsor(a)
driving force *n* fuerza *f* motriz
driving instructor *n* profesor(a) *m(f)* de autoescuela
driving lessons *npl* prácticas *fpl* de conducir
driving school *n* autoescuela *f*
driving test *n* examen *m* de conducir
drizzle ['drɪz·əl] METEO **I.** *n* llovizna *f*, garúa *f AmL*, chipichipi *m Méx* **II.** *vi* lloviznar, garuar *AmL*
drizzly ['drɪz·li] *adj* **it was a grey** ~ **afternoon** era una tarde gris de llovizna
droll [droʊl] *adj* divertido, -a
dromedary ['drɑm·ɪ·der·i] <-ies> *n* dromedario *m*
drone [droʊn] **I.** *n* **1.** ZOOL zángano *m* **2.** (*sb who does no work*) vago, -a *m, f;* (*sb who does menial work*) azacán, -ana *m, f* **3.** (*sound: of bees, aircraft, machinery*) zumbido *m;* (*of people, voices*) murmullo *m* **4.** AVIAT avión *m* teledirigido **II.** *vi* **1.** (*hum*) zumbar **2.** (*speak in monotonous tone*) hablar con monotonía
drool [drul] **I.** *vi* babear; **to** ~ **over sth/sb** *fig* caérsele la baba con algo/alguien **II.** *n* baba *f*
droop [drup] **I.** *vi* **1.** (*fall*) colgar **2.** (*flowers*) marchitarse **3.** (*person*) desanimarse; (*mood, spirits*) decaer **II.** *vt* inclinar
drop [drɑp] **I.** *n* **1.** (*of liquid*) gota *f;* ~ **by** ~ gota a gota **2.** *inf* (*small amount: of drink*) sorbo *m;* **just a** ~ sólo un poco; **to have had a**

~ **too much** (**to drink**) llevar una copa de más **3.** *fig* (*trace*) pizca *f* **4.** (*vertical distance*) declive *m;* **a sheer** ~ un profundo precipicio **5.** (*decrease*) disminución *f;* (*in temperature*) descenso *m* **6.** (*fall*) caída *f;* (*distribution by aircraft*) lanzamiento *m;* ~ **of medical supplies** aprovisionamiento *m* aéreo de suministros médicos **7.** (*secret collection point*) escondrijo *m* **8.** (*sweet*) **lemon/peppermint** ~s grageas *fpl* de limón/menta ▶ **it's a** ~ **in the** <u>bucket</u> es una gota de agua en el mar; **at the** ~ **of a** <u>hat</u> en un abrir y cerrar de ojos **II.** <-pp-> *vt* **1.** (*allow to fall*) dejar caer; **to** ~ **anchor** echar el ancla; **to** ~ **a bomb** lanzar una bomba **2.** (*lower*) bajar; **to** ~ **prices** bajar [*o* reducir] los precios; **to** ~ **one's voice** bajar la voz **3.** *inf* (*send*) enviar; **to** ~ **a letter into a mailbox** echar una carta al correo; **to** ~ **sb a line** [*o* **note**] escribir [*o* dedicar] a alguien unas líneas **4.** *inf* (*express*) soltar; **to** ~ **a hint** soltar [*o* tirar] una indirecta; **to** ~ **names** mencionar nombres de famosos (*para impresionar*) **5.** (*dismiss*) despedir **6.** (*abandon, give up*) renunciar a; **to** ~ **a demand** retirar una demanda; **to** ~ **a class** darse de baja de un curso; **to** ~ **sb** romper con alguien **7.** (*leave out*) omitir; **let's** ~ **the subject** dejemos de lado [*o* cambiemos] ese tema **III.** <-pp-> *vi* **1.** (*descend*) bajar **2.** (*go to*) **to** ~ **into a bar/a store** pasarse por un bar/una tienda **3.** (*go lower: prices*) bajar **4.** *inf* (*become exhausted*) estar agotado, -a; **to** ~ **with exhaustion** caer rendido; **he is ready to** ~ está que no se tiene; **to** ~ **dead** caerse muerto; ~ **dead!** *inf* ¡muérete! ▶ **to** <u>let</u> **it** ~ dejarlo caer; **to** <u>let</u> **it** ~ **that...** dar a entender que...

◆ **drop behind** *vi* quedarse atrás; **to** ~ **in sth** rezagarse en algo

◆ **drop by** *vi* pasarse; **I just thought I'd** ~ **and say hello** he pensado en pasarme y saludar

◆ **drop down** *vi* caer

◆ **drop in** *vi inf* entrar un momento; **to** ~ **on sb** ir a ver a alguien; (*unexpectedly*) pasarse por casa de alguien

◆ **drop off I.** *vt inf* (*passenger*) dejar **II.** *vi* **1.** (*decrease*) disminuir **2.** *inf* (*fall asleep*) quedarse dormido **3.** (*become separated*) desprenderse

◆ **drop out** *vi* (*person*) darse de baja; **to** ~ **of college/a club** darse de baja en la universidad/un club

drop-down menu *n* COMPUT menú *m* desplegable

drop kick *n* SPORTS botepronto *m*

droplet ['drap·lət] *n* gotita *f*

dropout ['drap·aʊt] *n* **1.** UNIV, SCHOOL persona *f* que ha abandonado los estudios **2.** (*from society*) automarginado, -a *m, f*

dropper ['drap·ər] *n* cuentagotas *m inv*, gotero *m AmL*

droppings ['drap·ɪŋz] *npl* excremento *m*

drop shot *n* SPORTS dejada *f*

dross [dras] *n* escoria *f*

drought [draʊt] *n* sequía *f*

drove¹ [droʊv] *n* **1.** (*of animals*) rebaño *m* **2.** ~s *inf* (*of people*) manada *f;* **in** ~s a montones **3.** (*chisel*) cincel *m*

drove² [droʊv] *pt of* **drive**

drover ['droʊ·vər] *n* pastor(a) *m(f)*

drown [draʊn] **I.** *vt* **1.** (*kill in water*) ahogar; **to look like a** ~**ed rat** *inf* estar calado hasta los huesos **2.** (*engulf in water*) anegar **3.** (*make inaudible*) ahogar; **to** ~ **sth out** ahogar algo ▶ **to** ~ **one's sorrows in** <u>drink</u> ahogar las penas en alcohol **II.** *vi* **1.** (*die*) ahogarse **2.** *fig, inf* (*have too much*) **to be** ~**ing in work** estar hasta arriba de trabajo

drowning *n* ahogo *m*

drowse [draʊz] *vi* dormitar

drowsy ['draʊ·zi] <-ier, -iest> *adj* soñoliento, -a

drudge [drʌdʒ] **I.** *n* esclavo, -a *m, f* del trabajo **II.** *vi* trabajar como un esclavo

drudgery ['drʌdʒ·ə·ri] *n* trabajo *m* penoso

drug [drʌg] **I.** *n* **1.** MED fármaco *m* **2.** (*narcotic*) droga *f;* **to take** ~s tomar drogas **II.** <-gg-> *vt* drogar

drug abuse *n* toxicomanía *f*

drug addict *n* toxicómano, -a *m, f*, drogadicto, -a *m, f*

drug addiction *n* drogadicción *f*

drug bust *n* incautación *f* de droga

drug dealer *n* camello, -a *m, f inf*, jíbaro *m Col*, burro *m Méx*

drug manufacturer *n* fabricante *mf* de drogas sintéticas

drug pusher *n inf* camello, -a *m, f*

drugstore *n* farmacia *f* (*donde suelen venderse otros artículos, además de productos farmacéuticos*)

drug traffic *n* narcotráfico *m*

drug trafficker *n* narcotraficante *mf*

drug trafficking *n* narcotráfico

druid ['dru·ɪd] *n* druida *m*

drum [drʌm] **I.** *n* **1.** MUS, TECH tambor *m* **2.** ~s (*in a band*) batería *f* **3.** (*for oil*) bidón *m* **4.** ANAT tímpano *m* **II.** <-mm-> *vi* (*play percussion*) tocar la percusión; (*with fingers*) tamborilear con los dedos; **to** ~ **on sth** tamborilear con los dedos sobre algo **III.** <-mm-> *vt inf* **to** ~ **sth into sb** meter a alguien algo en la cabeza

drumbeat *n* redoble *m*

drum brake *n* freno *m* de tambor

drumhead *n* parche *m* de tambor

drum major *n* tambor *m* mayor

drummer ['drʌm·ər] *n* (*in a band*) tambor *m;* (*in a group*) batería *f*

drumstick *n* **1.** MUS palillo *m* **2.** CULIN muslito *m*

drunk [drʌŋk] **I.** *vt, vi pp of* **drink II.** *adj* **1.** (*inebriated*) borracho, -a, jumo, -a *AmL*, ido, -a *AmC*, bota *Méx;* **to be** ~ estar borracho; **to get** ~ emborracharse; ~ **driving** conducción *f* en estado de embriaguez **2.** *fig* (*very much affected*) **to be** ~ **with joy** estar ebrio de alegría III. *n* borracho, -a *m, f*

drunkard ['drʌŋ·kərd] *n* borracho, -a *m, f*

drunken ['drʌŋ·kən] *adj* borracho, -a; **a ~ brawl** una reyerta de borrachos; **~ driving** conducción *f* en estado de embriaguez

drunkenness ['drʌŋ·kən·nɪs] *n* borrachera *f,* embriaguez *f elev,* bomba *f AmL*

dry [draɪ] I. <-ier *o* -er, -iest *o* -est> *adj* 1. (*not wet*) seco, -a; **to go ~** secarse; **~ red wine** vino tinto seco 2. (*climate, soil*) árido, -a 3. (*bread, toast*) sin mantequilla 4. (*without alcohol: state, county*) prohibicionista 5. (*uninteresting*) aburrido, -a 6. (*brief*) lacónico, -a; **~ (sense of) humor** (sentido *m* del) humor *m* agudo ▶**to run ~** agotarse II. <-ie-> *vt* secar; (*tears*) enjugarse III. <-ie-> *vi* secarse; **to put sth out to ~** sacar algo para que se seque

◆**dry up** I. *vi* 1. (*become dry*) secarse 2. (*dry the dishes*) secar los platos 3. *inf* (*become silent*) quedarse en silencio; (*stop talking*) cerrar el pico; (*on stage*) quedarse en blanco 4. (*run out*) agotarse II. *vt* secar

dryad ['draɪ·æd] *n* dríade *f*

dry cell *n* ELEC pila *f* seca

dry cell battery *n* batería *f* de pila(s) seca(s)

dry-clean *vt* limpiar en seco

dry cleaner's *n* tintorería *f*

dry cleaning *n* limpieza *f* en seco

dry dock *n* dique *m* seco

dryer ['draɪ·ər] *n* 1. (*for hair*) secador *m* 2. (*for clothes*) secadora *f*

dry goods *npl* mercería *f*

dry ice *n* hielo *m* seco

dry land *n* (*not sea*) tierra *f* firme

dry measure *n* medida *f* para áridos

dryness ['draɪ·nɪs] *n a. fig* sequedad *f*

dry rot *n* putrefacción *f* de la madera

dry run *n* prueba *f;* (*tryout*) ensayo *m*

dry wall *n* muro *m* de mampostería en seco

DSc *abbr of* **Doctor of Science** doctor(a) *m(f)* en Ciencias

DTP [ˌdi·ti·'pi] *n abbr of* **desktop publishing** DTP *m*

dual ['du·əl] *adj inv* doble; **~ ownership** ECON condominio *m*

dual citizenship *n* doble nacionalidad *f*

dualism ['du·ə·lɪz·əm] *n* dualismo *m*

dub¹ [dʌb] <-bb-> *vt* 1. (*confer knighthood*) armar caballero 2. (*give sb/sth a nickname*) apodar

dub² [dʌb] <-bb-> *vt* (*film*) doblar; **to be ~bed into English/French** estar doblado en inglés/francés

dubbing ['dʌb·ɪŋ] *n* doblaje *m*

dubious ['du·bi·əs] *adj* 1. (*doubtful*) dubitativo, -a 2. (*untrustworthy*) dudoso, -a

duchess ['dʌtʃ·ɪs] *n* duquesa *f*

duchy ['dʌtʃ·i] *n* ducado *m*

duck [dʌk] I. *n* 1. (*bird*) pato *m* 2. (*lowering of head*) inclinación *f* de cabeza ▶**to take to sth like a ~ to water** *inf* sentirse como pez en el agua con/en algo II. *vi* 1. (*dip head*) agachar

la cabeza 2. (*go under water*) chapuzarse 3. (*hide*) agacharse; **to ~ out of sth** *inf* escaquearse de algo III. *vt* 1. (*lower suddenly*) **to ~ one's head** agachar la cabeza; **to ~ one's head under water** sumergir la cabeza dentro del agua 2. (*avoid*) esquivar; *fig* eludir; **to ~ an issue** eludir un tema

duckboards ['dʌk·bɔrdz] *npl* pasadera *f*

duckling ['dʌk·lɪŋ] *n* patito *m*

ducky ['dʌk·i] *n sl* a pedir de boca

duct [dʌkt] *n* 1. (*pipe*) conducto *m;* **air ~** conducto del aire 2. ANAT canal *m;* **ear ~** canal auditivo

dud [dʌd] *n* 1. (*person*) inútil *mf* 2. (*bomb*) bomba *f* que no llega a estallar 3. (*failure*) fiasco *m* 4. **~s** (*clothing*) trapos *mpl*

dude [dud] *n* 1. *sl* (*guy*) tío, -a *m, f* 2. *inf* (*smartly dressed*) figurín *m*

due [du] I. *adj* 1. (*payable*) pagadero, -a; (*owing*) debido, -a; **~ date** fecha *f* límite; ECON fecha de vencimiento; **the loan is now ~ (for repayment)** hay que devolver el préstamo; **to fall ~** vencer 2. (*appropriate*) conveniente; **in ~ course** a su debido tiempo; **with all ~ respect** con el debido respeto; **to treat sb with the respect ~ to him/her** tratar a alguien con el respeto que se merece 3. (*expected*) esperado, -a; **I'm ~ in Mexico City this evening** esta noche me esperan en la Ciudad de México 4. (*owing to, because of*) **~ to** debido a; **~ to circumstances beyond our control...** por circunstancias ajenas a nuestra voluntad... II. *n* 1. (*fair treatment*) merecido *m;* **to give sb his/her ~** dar a alguien lo que se merece 2. **~s** (*debts*) deudas *f;* (*obligations*) deberes *mpl;* **to pay one's ~s** (*meet obligations/duties*) cumplir con sus obligaciones/deberes; (*meet debts*) pagar las deudas 3. **~s** (*regular payment*) cuota *f* III. *adv* *before adv* exactamente; **~ north/south** derecho hacia el norte/sur

duel ['du·əl] I. *n* duelo *m;* **to fight a ~** batirse en duelo II. *vi* <-l- *o* -ll-, -l- *o* -ll-> batirse en duelo

duet [du·'et] *n* dúo *m;* **to play a ~** interpretar un dueto

duffer ['dʌf·ər] *n* zoquete *m*

duffle bag ['dʌf·ə·l·ˌbæg] *n* talego *m*

duffle coat *n* trenca *f*

dug¹ [dʌg] *pt, pp of* **dig**

dug² [dʌg] *n* (*of mammal*) teta *f;* (*of cow*) ubre *f*

dugout ['dʌg·aʊt] *n* 1. MIL refugio *m* subterráneo 2. SPORTS banquillo *m* 3. NAUT piragua *f* (*hecha de un tronco*)

duke [duk] *n* duque *m*

dull [dʌl] I. *adj* 1. (*boring*) aburrido, -a; (*life*) monótono, -a 2. (*not bright: surface*) deslustrado, -a; (*sky*) gris; (*weather*) desapacible; (*color*) apagado, -a; (*light*) pálido, -a 3. (*muffled, muted*) callado, -a; (*ache, thud*) sordo, -a 4. (*not sharp: knife, ax*) desafilado, -a II. *vt* 1. (*alleviate*) aliviar 2. (*desensitize*) insensibilizar **3.** (*make blunt*) desafilar, embotar

dullard ['dʌl·ərd] *n* zoquete *m*

dullness ['dʌl·nɪs] *n* **1.** (*lack of excitement*) aburrimiento *m* **2.** (*tediousness*) pesadez *f*

duly ['du·li] *adv* **1.** (*appropriately*) debidamente **2.** (*on time*) a su debido tiempo

dumb [dʌm] *adj* **1.** *often offensive* (*mute*) mudo, -a; **deaf and ~** sordomudo, -a; **to be struck ~** quedarse mudo de asombro **2.** *inf* (*stupid*) estúpido, -a; **to play ~** hacerse el tonto

dumbbell ['dʌm·bel] *n* **1.** (*weight*) pesa *f* **2.** *sl* (*person*) capullo, -a *m, f*

dumbfound ['dʌm·faʊnd] *vt* dejar mudo (de asombro)

dumbfounded *adj* mudo, -a de asombro

dumbstruck ['dʌm·strʌk] *adj* mudo, -a (de asombro)

dumb waiter *n* montaplatos *m*

dumfound *vt s.* **dumbfound**

dummy ['dʌm·i] **I.** <-ies> *n* **1.** (*mannequin*) maniquí *mf* **2.** (*duplicate*) imitación *f* **3.** (*fool*) tonto *m* **II.** *adj* (*duplicate*) copiado, -a; (*false*) falso, -a **III.** *vi sl* **to ~ up** callarse como un muerto

dump [dʌmp] **I.** *n* **1.** (*for waste*) vertedero *m*, basurero *m*, botadero *m* *Ven* **2.** *fig, sl* (*dirty place*) tugurio *m* **3.** MIL depósito *m;* **ammunition ~** almacén *m* de municiones **II.** *vt* **1.** (*drop carelessly*) verter; (*get rid of*) deshacerse de **2.** (*abandon*) abandonar **3.** *inf* (*end relationship with*) plantar **4.** COMPUT volcar **III.** *vi sl* **to ~ on sb** pagarla con alguien

dumper ['dʌm·pər] *n* dumper *m*

dumping *n* dumping *m*

dumping ground *n* vertedero *m*, basurero *m*

dumpling ['dʌmp·lɪŋ] *n bolita de masa rellena de carne o fruta*

dumpy ['dʌm·pi] <-ier, -iest> *adj* regordete, -a

dun¹ [dʌn] *adj* pardo, -a

dun² [dʌn] **I.** <-nn-> *vt* **to ~ sb** apremiar a alguien para que pague lo que debe **II.** *n* petición *f* de reembolso

dunce [dʌns] *n* burro, -a *m, f fig*

dune [dun] *n* duna *f*

dung [dʌŋ] *n* excrementos *mpl*, estiércol *m*

dungarees [ˌdʌŋ·gə·'riz] *npl* mono *m*

dungeon ['dʌn·dʒən] *n* mazmorra *f*

dunghill ['dʌŋ·hɪl] *n* estercolero *m*

dunk [dʌŋk] *vt* mojar

duo ['du·oʊ] *n* dúo *m;* **comedy ~** pareja cómica

duodenum [ˌdu·ə·'di·nəm] <-na *o* -s> *n* duodeno *m*

dup. *n abbr of* **duplicate** dup.

dupe [dup] **I.** *n* inocentón, -ona *m, f* **II.** *vt* **to be ~d** ser engañado

duplex ['du·pleks] **I.** *n* **1.** (*house*) casa *f* adosada **2.** (*apartment*) dúplex *m* **II.** *adj* doble

duplicate¹ ['du·plɪ·kət] **I.** *adj inv* duplicado, -a; **~ key** duplicado *m* de una llave **II.** *n* duplicado

duplicate² ['du·plɪ·keɪt] *vt* **1.** (*replicate*) duplicar; (*repeat*) repetir **2.** (*copy*) copiar; **to ~ a device** hacer una réplica de un dispositivo

duplicator ['du·plɪ·keɪ·tər] *n* multicopista *f*

duplicity [du·'plɪs·ə·ti] *n* duplicidad *f*

durability [ˌdʊr·ə·'bɪl·ə·ti] *n* **1.** (*permanence*) permanencia *f;* (*persistence*) persistencia *f* **2.** (*life of a product*) durabilidad *f*

durable ['dʊr·ə·bəl] *adj* **1.** (*hard-wearing*) resistente **2.** (*long-lasting*) duradero, -a

duration [dʊ·'reɪ·ʃən] *n* duración *f;* **for the ~** hasta que se acabe

duress [dʊ·'res] *n* coacción *f;* **under ~** bajo coacción

during ['dʊr·ɪŋ] *prep* durante; **~ work/the week** durante el trabajo/la semana

dusk [dʌsk] *n* crepúsculo *m;* **at ~** al atardecer

dusky ['dʌs·ki] <-ier, iest> *adj* **1.** (*almost dark*) oscuro, -a **2.** *a. pej* (*dark-skinned*) moreno, -a

dust [dʌst] **I.** *n* polvo *m;* **coal ~** cisco *m* ▶ **to bite the ~** morder el polvo; **to leave sb in the ~** avanzar mucho más que alguien, dejar alguien atrás; **to wait till the ~ has settled** dejar que se aclare la atmósfera; **to turn to ~** *liter* convertirse en polvo **II.** *vt* **1.** (*clean*) quitar el polvo a **2.** (*spread over*) salpicar; **to ~ sth with insecticide** espolvorear insecticida sobre algo **III.** *vi* quitar el polvo

dust bunny *n inf* pelusa *f*

dust cover *n* **1.** (*for furniture*) guardapolvo *m* **2.** (*on book*) forro *m*

duster ['dʌs·tər] *n* trapo *m*

dust jacket *n* (*on book*) sobrecubierta *f*

dust mite *n* ácaro *m* del polvo

dustpan *n* recogedor *m;* **~ and brush** recogedor y cepillo [*o* escoba]

dust storm *n* tormenta *f* de polvo

dustup *n sl* (*fistfight*) pelea *f;* (*argument*) enfrentamiento *m*

dusty ['dʌs·ti] <-ier, -iest> *adj* **1.** (*covered in dust*) polvoriento, -a **2.** (*grayish*) ceniciento, -a; **~ brown** marrón grisáceo

Dutch [dʌtʃ] **I.** *adj* holandés, -esa **II.** *n* **1.** *pl* (*people*) **the ~** los holandeses **2.** LING holandés ▶ **to go ~** pagar a escote

Dutchman ['dʌtʃ·mən] <-men> *n* holandés *m*

Dutchwoman ['dʌtʃ·wʊm·ən] <-women> *n* holandesa *f*

dutiable ['du·ti·ə·bəl] *adj* sujeto, -a a derechos de aduana

dutiful ['du·ti·fəl] *adj* obediente

duty ['du·ti] <-ies> *n* **1.** (*moral*) deber *m;* (*obligation*) obligación *f;* **it's my ~** es mi deber; **to do sth out of ~** hacer algo por compromiso; **to do one's ~** cumplir con su obligación **2.** (*task, function*) función *f* **3.** (*work*) tarea *f;* **to do ~ for sb** sustituir a alguien; **to be suspended from ~** ser suspendido del servicio; **to be on/off ~** estar/no estar de servicio **4.** (*tax*) impuesto *m;* (*revenue on imports*) derechos *mpl* de aduana; **customs duties** arancel *m;* **to pay ~ on sth** pagar derechos de aduana por algo

duty call *n* visita *f* de cumplido
duty-free *adj* libre de impuestos
duty roster *n* lista *f* de guardias
duvet [du·'veɪ] *n* edredón *m* nórdico
DVD [ˌdi·vi·'di] *n inv* COMPUT *abbr of* **Digital Video Disk** DVD *m*
dwarf [dwɔrf] I.<-s *o* -ves> *n* enano, -a *m, f* II. *vt* empequeñecer
dwell [dwel] <dwelt *o* -ed, dwelt *o* -ed> *vi* 1.(*live*) morar 2.(*give attention to*) **to ~ on sth** insistir en algo; **to ~ on a subject** explayarse en un tema
dweller *n* morador(a) *m(f)*
dwelling ['dwel·ɪŋ] *n* morada *f*
dwelt [dwelt] *pp, pt of* **dwell**
dwindle ['dwɪn·dəl] *vi* menguar
dye [daɪ] I. *vt* teñir II. *n* tinte *m*
dyed-in-the-wool *adj* convencido, -a; **~ opinions** opiniones *fpl* firmes
dye-works ['daɪ·wɜrks] *n* tintorería *f*
dying ['daɪ·ɪŋ] *adj* 1.(*approaching death*) moribundo, -a 2.(*words, wishes*) último, -a
dyke¹ [daɪk] *n s.* **dike**
dyke² [daɪk] *n offensive, sl* (*lesbian*) tortillera *f pey*
dynamic [daɪ·'næm·ɪk] *adj* dinámico, -a
dynamics [daɪ·'næm·ɪks] *n* 1. PHYS dinámica *f*; (*development*) desarrollo *m* 2. MUS (*alterations of volume*) crecimiento *m*
dynamite ['daɪ·nə·maɪt] I. *n* dinamita *f* II. *vt* dinamitar
dynamo ['daɪ·nə·moʊ] <-s> *n* dinamo *f*
dynasty ['daɪ·nə·sti] <-ies> *n* dinastía *f*
dysentery ['dɪs·ən·ter·i] *n* MED disentería *f*
dysfunctional [dɪs·'fʌŋk·ʃə·nəl] *adj* disfuncional
dyslexia [dɪ·'sleksiə] *n* dislexia *f*
dyslexic [dɪs·'lek·sɪk] *adj* disléxico, -a
dyspepsia [dɪs·'pep·si·ə] *n* MED dispepsia *f*

E

E, e [i] *n* 1.(*letter*) E, e *f*; **~ as in Echo** E de España 2. MUS mi *m*
E *abbr of* **east** E
each [itʃ] I. *adj* cada; **~ one of you** cada uno de vosotros; **~ and every house** cada casa sin excepción II. *pron* cada uno, cada una; **~ of them could beat you** cada uno de ellos podría ganarte; **$70 ~** 70$ cada uno; **he gave us $10 ~** nos dio a cada uno 10$; **I'll take a pound of ~** tomaré una libra de cada (uno)
each other *pron* uno a otro, una a la otra; **they are always arguing with ~** siempre discuten entre ellos; **to help ~** ayudarse mutuamente; **to be made for ~** estar hechos el uno para el otro
eager ['i·gər] *adj* ansioso, -a, ávido, -a; **to be ~**

for sth ansiar algo; **to be ~ for revenge** tener sed de venganza; **to be ~ to start** estar ansioso por empezar; **to be ~ to please** estar ansioso por agradar
eager beaver *n inf* **he is an ~** se esmera mucho en su trabajo
eagerness *n* entusiasmo *m*
eagle ['i·gəl] *n* águila *f*
eagle eye *n* 1.(*keen eyesight*) ojo *m* de lince, vista *f* de águila 2.(*observe attentively*) **he/she monitors the expenses with an ~** controla los gastos minuciosamente
eagle-eyed ['i·gəl·aɪd] *adj* **to be ~** tener ojos de lince
ear¹ [ɪr] *n* ANAT oído *m;* (*outer part*) oreja *f*; **~, nose and throat specialist** otorrinolaringólogo, -a *m, f*; **to have a good ~** tener buen oído; **to have an ~ for music** tener buen oído para la música; **to smile from ~ to ~** sonreír de oreja a oreja ▶**to be up to one's ~s in debt** *inf* estar endeudado hasta la camisa; **to have** [*o* **keep**] **an** [*o* **one's**] **~ to the ground** *inf* mantenerse al corriente; **to be all ~s** *inf* ser todo oídos; **to keep one's (eyes and) ~s open** *inf* abrir bien (los ojos y) los oídos; **to fall on deaf ~s** caer en oídos sordos [*o* en saco roto]; **to turn a deaf ~ (to sth)** hacer oídos sordos (a algo); **he'll be out on his ~** *inf* lo van a poner de patitas en la calle; **to be wet behind the ~s** estar verde; **it goes in one ~ and out the other** *inf* por un oído le entra y por el otro le sale; **to lend sb an ~** prestar atención a alguien; **to play it by ~** *inf* tocarlo de oído, improvisar sobre la marcha
ear² [ɪr] *n* BOT espiga *f*
earache ['ɪr·eɪk] *n* dolor *m* de oído
eardrum *n* tímpano *m*
ear infection *n* infección *f* de oído
earl [ɜrl] *n* conde *m*
earlobe ['ɪr·loʊb] *n* lóbulo *m* de la oreja
early ['ɜr·li] I.<-ier, -iest> *adj* 1.(*ahead of time, near the beginning*) temprano, -a; **to be ~** llegar temprano; **~ retirement** jubilación *f* anticipada; **to take ~ retirement** jubilarse anticipadamente; **an ~ death** una muerte prematura; **the ~ hours** la madrugada; **in the ~ morning** de madrugada; **in the ~ afternoon** a primera hora de la tarde; **at an ~ age** a una edad temprana; **he is in his ~ twenties** tiene poco más de veinte años; **in the ~ 15th century** a principios del siglo XV; **~ education** primera enseñanza *f*; **to make it an ~ night** acostarse temprano; **the ~ stages** las primeras fases; **the ~ days/years of sth** los primeros tiempos de algo; **to die an ~ death** morir prematuramente [*o* joven] 2. *form* (*prompt: reply*) rápido, -a; **at your earliest (possible) convenience** tan pronto como le sea posible 3.(*first*) primero, -a II. *adv* 1.(*ahead of time*) temprano; **to get up ~** madrugar; **~ in the morning** por la mañana temprano; **~ in the year** a principios de año; **to be half an hour ~** llegar media hora antes 2.(*soon*) pronto; **as ~**

as possible tan pronto como sea posible; **reply** ~ respondan cuanto antes; **book your tickets** ~ compren sus entradas con tiempo **3.** (*prematurely*) prematuramente; **to die** ~ morir joven

earmark ['ɪr·mɑrk] **I.** *vt* **1.** (*animal*) marcar en la oreja; (*document*) marcar **2.** (*put aside*) reservar; (*funds*) destinar **II.** *n* marca *f* en la oreja; *fig* marca *f* distintiva

earmuffs ['ɪr·mʌfs] *npl* orejeras *fpl*

earn [ɜrn] **I.** *vt* **1.** (*be paid*) ganar; **to ~ one's daily bread** ganarse el pan; **to ~ a living** ganarse la vida **2.** (*bring in*) dar; (*interest*) devengar **3.** (*obtain*) **to ~ money from sth** obtener dinero de algo; **coffee exports ~ Brazil millions of dollars** Brasil obtiene muchos millones de dólares de la exportación de café **4.** (*deserve*) merecer, ganarse; **his decision ~ed him the confidence/respect of his boss** su decisión le valió la confianza/el respeto de su jefe **II.** *vi* trabajar

earned income ['ɜrnd·'ɪn·kʌm] *n* ingresos *mpl* en concepto de salario

earner *n* asalariado, -a *m, f*

earnest ['ɜr·nɪst] **I.** *adj* **1.** (*serious*) serio, -a **2.** (*sincere*) sincero, -a; (*attempt*) concienzudo, -a; (*desire*) ferviente **II.** *n* seriedad *f*; **in ~** en serio; **school has now begun in ~** ahora ha empezado de verdad el colegio

earnestly *adv* **1.** (*speak*) seriamente **2.** (*desire*) de todo corazón

earning power *n* potencial *m* de ingresos

earnings ['ɜr·nɪŋz] *npl* **1.** (*of a person*) ingresos *mpl* **2.** (*of a company*) beneficios *mpl*, utilidades *fpl AmL*

earnings-related *adj* proporcional al sueldo

earphones ['ɪr·foʊnz] *npl* auriculares *mpl*

earpiece ['ɪr·pis] *n* **1.** (*of a phone*) auricular *m* **2.** (*of glasses*) patilla *f*

earplug ['ɪr·plʌg] *n* tapón *m* para el oído

earring ['ɪr·rɪŋ] *n* pendiente *m*, caravana *f CSur*, candonga *f Col*; **a pair of ~s** unos pendientes

earshot ['ɪr·ʃɑt] *n* alcance *m* del oído; **in/out of** ~ al alcance/fuera del alcance del oído; **within** ~ al alcance del oído

earth [ɜrθ] *n* **1.** (*planet*) Tierra *f*; **on** ~ en el mundo **2.** (*soil*) tierra *f* ▶ **to bring sb back (down) to** ~ hacer bajar de las nubes a alguien; **to come back (down) to** ~ bajar de las nubes; **what/who/where/why on** ~ ...? *inf* ¿qué/quién/dónde/por qué diablos...?

earthbound ['ɜrθ·baʊnd] *adj* **1.** terrestre; (*aircraft, spacecraft*) que no puede despegar **2.** *fig* (*ordinary*) prosaico, -a

earthenware ['ɜrθ·ən·wer] **I.** *n* objetos *mpl* de barro **II.** *adj* de barro

earthiness ['ɜr·θi·nɪs] *n* **1.** (*directness*) llaneza *f* **2.** (*coarseness*) grosería *f*

earthling ['ɜrθ·lɪŋ] *n* terrícola *mf*

earthly ['ɜrθ·li] *adj* **1.** (*concerning life on earth*) terreno, -a; (*existence, paradise*) terrenal; **her ~ belongings** *form* todo lo que posee

en este mundo; ~ **remains** restos *mpl* mortales **2.** *inf* (*possible*) **to be of no ~ use** no servir absolutamente para nada

earthquake ['ɜrθ·kweɪk] *n* **1.** terremoto *m*, temblor *m AmL* **2.** *fig* conmoción *f*

earth-shattering *adj* que causa conmoción

earthwork *n* **1.** *pl* MIL terraplén *m* **2.** (*work*) trabajos *mpl* de preparación del terreno

earthworm *n* lombriz *f*

earthy ['ɜr·θi] <-ier, -iest> *adj* **1.** (*soil-like: color, smell*) terroso, -a **2.** (*coarse: joke, person*) burdo, -a, basto, -a **3.** (*simple*) **an ~ homemade stew** un guiso casero puro y duro

earwax ['ɪr·wæks] *n* cerumen *m*

earwig ['ɪr·wɪg] *n* tijereta *f*

ease [iz] **I.** *n* **1.** (*without much effort*) facilidad *f*; **for ~ of access** para facilitar el acceso; **to do sth with** ~ hacer algo con facilidad **2.** (*comfort*) comodidad *f*; **to live a life of** ~ vivir con desahogo; **to feel at** ~ sentirse cómodo; **to be ill at** ~ estar molesto; **to be at** ~ estar a sus anchas; **to put sb at** (**his/her**) ~ hacer que alguien se relaje; (**stand**) **at ~!** MIL ¡descansen! **II.** *vt* **1.** (*relieve: pain*) aliviar; (*tension*) hacer disminuir; **to ~ one's conscience** descargarse la conciencia; **to ~ sb's mind** tranquilizar a alguien **2.** (*burden*) aligerar **III.** *vi* (*pain*) aliviarse; (*tension, prices*) disminuir

◆**ease off** *vi*, **ease up** *vi* (*pain*) aliviarse; (*fever, sales*) bajar; (*tension*) disminuir; (*person*) relajarse; ~ **or you will have a nervous breakdown** si no te relajas, tendrás una crisis nerviosa; (*wind*) amainar; (*rain*) pasar

easel ['i·zəl] *n* caballete *m*

easily ['i·zə·li] *adv* **1.** (*without difficulty*) fácilmente; **to be ~ impressed** ser fácil de impresionar; **to win ~** ganar sin dificultades; **I get tired very** ~ me canso en seguida **2.** + *superl* (*clearly*) **to be ~ the best** ser con mucho el mejor **3.** (*probably*) perfectamente; **his guess could ~ be wrong** es fácil que se equivoque

easiness ['i·zɪ·nɪs] *n* facilidad *f*

east [ist] **I.** *n* este *m*; **to lie 5 miles to the ~ of Boston** quedar a 5 millas al este de Boston; **to go/drive to the** ~ ir/conducir hacia el este; **further** ~ más hacia el este; **in the ~ of France** en el este de Francia; **Far East** Extremo *m* Oriente; **Middle East** Oriente *m* Medio **II.** *adj* del este; ~ **wind** viento *m* de Levante; ~ **coast** costa *f* este; **East Indies** Indias *fpl* Orientales

eastbound ['ist·baʊnd] *adj* que va en dirección este

Easter ['i·stər] *n* **1.** (*holiday*) Pascua *f* **2.** (*season*) Semana *f* Santa; **during ~** en Semana Santa

---

i En Semana Santa (**Easter Week**) es costumbre en Estados Unidos decorar huevos duros, que son escondidos por los adultos y buscados posteriormente por los niños para el desayuno del domingo de Pascua. Hoy en día, el término **Easter egg** (huevo de Pascua) se usa también para denominar el huevo de chocolate que se suele regalar durante esta temporada festiva.

Easter Bunny *n* conejo *m* de Pascua
Easter Day *n* Domingo *m* de Pascua
Easter egg *n* huevo *m* de Pascua
Easter holidays *npl* vacaciones *fpl* de Semana Santa
Easter Island *npl* Isla *f* de Pascua
easterly ['i·stər·li] I. *adj* (*wind*) del este; **in an ~ direction** en dirección este II. *adv* 1. (*towards the east*) hacia el este 2. (*from the east*) del este III. *n* viento *m* del este
Easter Monday *n* lunes *m* de Pascua
eastern ['i·stərn] *adj* del este, oriental
easterner ['i·stər·nər] *n* habitante *mf* del nordeste de los Estados Unidos
easternmost ['i·stərn·moʊst] *adj* más oriental; **the ~ time zone** la zona horaria más oriental
Easter Sunday *n* Domingo *m* de Pascua
East Germany [ˌist·'dʒɜr·mə·ni] *n* HIST Alemania *f* oriental
eastward ['ist·wərd] I. *adj* **in an ~ direction** en dirección este II. *adv* hacia el este
eastwards ['ist·wərdz] *adv* hacia el este
easy ['i·zi] <-ier, -iest> I. *adj* 1. (*simple*) fácil; **~ money** *inf* dinero *m* fácil; **the hotel is within ~ reach of the beach** el hotel está muy cerca de la playa; **to be far from ~** no ser fácil en absoluto; **~ to get along with** de trato fácil; **to take the ~ way out** optar por el camino más fácil; **to be as ~ as anything** [*o* **can be**] *inf* estar tirado [*o* regalado]; **to be the easiest thing in the world** ser lo más fácil del mundo; **that's easier said than done** *inf* es más fácil decirlo que hacerlo 2. (*relaxed*) natural; **to have an ~ manner** comportarse de forma natural; **at an ~ pace** sin prisa; **to be on ~ terms with sb** estar en confianza con alguien 3. (*pleasant*) **~ on the ear/eye** agradable al oído/a la vista; **an ~ disposition** una buena disposición 4. (*undemanding*) indulgente; **to be ~ on sb** ser poco severo con alguien 5. (*exploitable*) **an ~ target** un blanco fácil 6. (*financially secure*) seguro, -a, acomodado, -a; **to live the ~ life** vivir una vida fácil 7. *pej, sl* (*sexually promiscuous*) fácil; **she's an ~ lay** es una tía fácil (de llevar al huerto) ▶**to be (as) ~ as pie** ser pan comido II. *adv* 1. (*cautiously*) con cuidado; **~ does it** *inf* despacito y buena letra 2. (*lenient*) **to go ~ on sb** *inf* no ser demasiado severo con alguien 3. *inf* (*less actively*) **to take things ~** tomarse las cosas con calma; **take it ~!** ¡cálmate! ▶**~ come, ~ go** *inf* tan fácil como viene, se va
easy-care *adj* que no necesita plancha
easy chair *n* poltrona *f*
easy-going *adj* (*person*) de trato fácil; (*attitude*) tolerante

eat [it] I. <ate, eaten> *vt* comer; **to ~ breakfast** tomar el desayuno, desayunar; **to ~ lunch/dinner** comer/cenar, almorzar/comer *AmL;* **to ~ one's fill** comer hasta saciarse ▶**~ your heart out!** ¡muérete de envidia!; **to ~ one's words** comerse sus propias palabras; **what is ~ing him?** *inf* ¿qué mosca le ha picado? II. *vi* comer
◆**eat away** *vt* (*acid*) corroer; (*termites*) carcomer
◆**eat away at** *vt*, **eat into** *vt* corroer
◆**eat in** *vi* comer en casa
◆**eat out** I. *vi* comer fuera II. *vt vulg* comer el coño
◆**eat up** *vt* comerse, terminar
eaten ['i·t̬ən] *pp of* **eat**
eater ['i·t̬ər] *n* **to be a big ~** ser un comilón; **to be a small ~** no ser de mucho comer
eatery ['i·t̬ə·ri] *n inf* restaurante *m*
eating disorder *n* trastorno *m* alimenticio
eating habits *npl* hábitos *mpl* alimenticios
eats *npl sl* papeo *m;* **good ~** buena comida
eau de Cologne [ˌoʊ·də·kə·'loʊn] *n* (agua *f* de) colonia *f*
eaves [ivz] *npl* ARCHIT alero *m*, tejaván *m AmL*
eavesdrop ['ivz·drɑp] <-pp-> *vi* **to ~ on sth/sb** escuchar algo/a alguien a escondidas
eavesdropper ['ivz·drɑp·ər] *n* escuchón, -ona *m, f*
eaves spout *n reg*, **eaves trough** *n reg* (*gutter*) canalón *m*, canal *mf*
ebb [eb] I. *vi* 1. (*tide*) bajar 2. *fig* decaer II. *n* 1. (*tide*) reflujo *m;* **the tide is on the ~** la marea está bajando 2. *fig* **the ~ and flow of sth** los altibajos de algo; **to be at a low ~** estar en un punto bajo; (*person*) estar deprimido
ebb tide *n* reflujo *m*
ebony ['eb·ə·ni] *n* ébano *m*
ebullient [ɪ·'bʊl·jənt] *adj* vivaz; **to be in an ~ mood** estar exaltado
EC [ˌi·'si] *n abbr of* **European Community** CE *f*
eccentric [ɪk·'sen·trɪk] I. *n* excéntrico, -a *m, f* II. *adj* excéntrico, -a
eccentricity [ˌek·sen·'trɪs·ə·t̬i] *n* <-ies> excentricidad *f*
ecclesiastic [ɪ·ˌkli·zi·'æs·tɪk] I. *n form* eclesiástico *m* II. *adj form* eclesiástico, -a
ecclesiastical [ɪ·ˌkli·zi·'æs·tɪ·kəl] *adj form* eclesiástico, -a
ECG [ˌi·si·'dʒi] *n abbr of* **electrocardiogram** electrocardiograma *m*, electro *m inf*
echelon ['eʃ·ə·lɑn] *n* 1. (*strata*) nivel *m;* (*of society*) capa *f;* **the highest ~s of sth** el más alto grado de algo 2. MIL escalón *m*
echo ['ek·oʊ] I. <-es> *n* eco *m* II. <-es, -ing, -ed> *vi* resonar III. <-es, -ing, -ed> *vt* 1. (*reflect*) repetir; **the mountains ~ed his howls** las montañas le devolvían el eco de sus alaridos 2. (*repeat*) repetir 3. (*imitate*) parecerse a
echo chamber *n* cámara *f* de resonancia
echo sounder *n* sonda *f* acústica

eclectic [ek·'lek·tɪk] **I.** *n form* ecléctico, -a *m, f* **II.** *adj form* ecléctico

eclipse [ɪ·'klɪps] **I.** *n* eclipse *m;* **solar/lunar ~** eclipse solar/de luna; **total/partial ~ of the sun** eclipse solar total/parcial; **to be in ~** *a. fig* estar eclipsado **II.** *vt* eclipsar

ecological [ˌi·kə·'lɑdʒ·ɪ·kəl] *adj* ecológico, -a

ecologically [ˌi·kə·'lɑdʒ·ɪk·li] *adv* ecológicamente; **~ friendly** ecológico, -a; **~ harmful** perjudicial para el medio ambiente

ecologist [i·'kal·ə·dʒɪst] *n* **1.** (*expert*) ecólogo, -a *m, f* **2.** POL ecologista *mf*

ecology [i·'kal·ə·dʒi] *n* ecología *f*

ecology movement *n* movimiento *m* ecologista

e-commerce ['i·kam·ɜrs] *n* comercio *m* electrónico

economic [ˌi·kə·'nam·ɪk] *adj* **1.** POL, ECON económico, -a **2.** (*profitable*) rentable

economical [ˌi·kə·'nam·ɪ·kəl] *adj* económico, -a

economics [ˌi·kə·'nam·ɪks] *npl* **1.** + *sing vb* (*discipline*) economía *f;* **School of Economics** Facultad *f* de Ciencias Económicas **2.** + *pl vb* (*matter*) aspecto *m* económico; **the ~ of the agreement** la rentabilidad del acuerdo

economist [ɪ·'kan·ə·mɪst] *n* economista *mf*

economize [ɪ·'kan·ə·maɪz] *vi* ahorrar; **to ~ on sth** economizar en algo

economy [ɪ·'kan·ə·mi] <-ies> *n* **1.** (*frugality*) ahorro *m;* **for the purposes of ~** por ahorro; **to make economies, to practice ~** ahorrar **2.** (*monetary assets*) economía *f;* **the state of the ~** la situación económica; **capitalist/market/planned ~** economía capitalista/de mercado/planificada

economy class *n* AVIAT clase *f* turista

economy size *n* tamaño *m* familiar

ecosystem *n* ecosistema *m*

ecotourism *n* ecoturismo *m*

ecotourist *n* ecoturista *mf*

eco-warrior *n* ecologista *mf* militante

ecstasy ['ek·stə·si] <-ies> *n* **1.** (*psychological state*) éxtasis *m inv* **2.** (*drug*) éxtasis *m*

ecstatic [ek·'stæt̮·ɪk] *adj* extático, -a; (*rapturous*) eufórico, -a; **to be ~ about sth** estar entusiasmado con algo

ECT [ˌi·si·'ti] *n abbr of* **electroconvulsive therapy** terapia *f* de electroshock

Ecuador ['ek·wə·dɔr] *n* Ecuador *m*

Ecuadorian [ˌek·wə·'dɔr·i·ən] **I.** *n* ecuatoriano, -a *m, f* **II.** *adj* ecuatoriano, -a

ecumenical [ˌek·ju·'men·ɪ·kəl] *adj* ecuménico, -a

eczema ['ek·sə·mə] *n* eczema *m*

ed. 1. *abbr of* **editor** editor(a) *m(f)* **2.** *abbr of* **edition** ed. **3.** *abbr of* **edited** editado, -a

eddy ['ed·i] **I.** <-ie-> *vi* arremolinarse **II.** <-ies> *n* remolino *m*

Eden ['i·dən] *n* Edén *m;* **the garden of ~** el jardín del Edén

edge [edʒ] **I.** *n sing* **1.** (*limit*) borde *m;* (*of a*

lake, pond) orilla *f;* (*of a mountain*) cresta *f;* (*of a page*) margen *m;* (*of a table, coin*) canto *m;* **to bring sth to the ~ of disaster** llevar algo hasta el límite del desastre; **to take the ~ off one's appetite/hunger** calmar el apetito/hambre; **to take the ~ off an argument** quitar hierro [*o* fuerza] a una discusión **2.** (*cutting part*) filo *m;* **to put an ~ on sth** afilar algo **3.** (*anger*) **to be on ~** tener los nervios a flor de piel; **there's a definite ~ in her voice** hay un tono áspero en su voz **4.** SPORTS ventaja *f;* **to have the ~ over sb** tener ventaja sobre alguien ▶ **to be (balanced) on a razor's ~** pender de un hilo; **to set sb's teeth on ~** sacar de quicio a alguien; **to live on the ~** vivir en el filo (de la navaja) **II.** *vt* **1.** (*border*) bordear **2.** (*in sewing*) ribetear **3.** (*move slowly*) **to ~ one's way through sth** ir abriéndose paso por algo; **she's edging her party towards extremism** está acercando su partido hacia el extremismo **4.** (*skis*) angular **III.** *vi* **to ~ closer to sth** ir acercándose a algo; **to ~ away from danger** ir alejándose del peligro; **to ~ forward** ir avanzando

edgeways ['edʒ·weɪz] *adv*, **edgewise** *adv* de lado

edging ['edʒ·ɪŋ] *n* borde *m;* (*of a ribbon*) ribete *m*

edgy ['edʒ·i] <-ier, -iest> *adj inf* nervioso

edible ['ed·ɪ·bəl] **I.** *adj* comestible **II.** *n* **~s** (*food*) víveres *mpl*, comestibles *mpl*

edict ['i·dɪkt] *n* **1.** HIST edicto *m* **2.** (*order*) mandato *m*

edification [ˌed·ɪ·fɪ·'keɪ·ʃən] *n form* edificación *f*

edifice ['ed·ɪ·fɪs] *n* **1.** *form* (*building*) edificio *m* **2.** *fig* (*of ideas*) estructura *f*

edify ['ed·ɪ·faɪ] <-ie-> *vt form* edificar

edifying *adj form* edificante

edit ['ed·ɪt] *vt* **1.** (*correct*) corregir; (*articles*) editar **2.** (*newspaper*) dirigir **3.** CINE montar **4.** COMPUT editar

◆ **edit out** *vt* suprimir

edition [ɪ·'dɪ·ʃən] *n* edición *f;* (*set of books*) tirada *f;* **paperback ~** encuadernación *f* en pasta blanda [*o* en rústica]; **limited ~** edición limitada; **collector's ~** edición para coleccionistas

editor ['ed·ɪ·tər] *n* **1.** (*of book*) editor(a) *m(f);* (*of article*) redactor(a) *m(f);* (*of newspaper*) director(a) *m(f);* **chief ~** redactor(a) *m(f)* jefe; **sports ~** redactor(a) *m(f)* de deportes **2.** CINE montador(a) *m(f)* **3.** COMPUT editor *m*

editorial [ˌed·ə·'tɔr·i·əl] **I.** *n* editorial *m* **II.** *adj* editorial; **~ staff** redacción *f*

editor-in-chief [ˌed·ɪ·tər·ɪn·'tʃif] *n* redactor(a) *m(f)* jefe

EDP [ˌi·di·'pi] *n abbr of* **electronic data processing** PED *m*

EDT [ˌi·di·'ti] *n abbr of* **Eastern Daylight Time** *Tiempo Oriental* (*4 horas menos que el Tiempo Universal Coordinado*)

educate ['edʒ·ə·keɪt] *vt* **1.** (*bring up*) educar

2. (*teach*) instruir; **to ~ the ear** educar el oído
3. (*inform*) concienciar; **to ~ sb in sth** concienciar a alguien de algo

educated ['edʒ·ə·keɪ·ţɪd] *adj* culto, -a; **highly ~** cultivado, -a

education [ˌedʒ·ʊ·'keɪ·ʃən] *n* **1.** SCHOOL educación *f*; **primary/secondary ~** enseñanza *f* primaria/secundaria; **Education Secretary** [*o* **Secretary of Education**] Ministerio *m* de Educación **2.** (*training*) formación *f*; **science/literary ~** formación científica/literaria **3.** (*teaching*) enseñanza *f*; (*study of teaching*) pedagogía *f* **4.** (*culture*) cultura *f*

educational [ˌedʒ·ʊ·'keɪ·ʃə·nəl] *adj* **1.** SCHOOL (*system*) educativo, -a; (*establishment*) docente; (*method*) pedagógico, -a; **for ~ purposes** con fines educativos **2.** (*instructive*) instructivo, -a **3.** (*raising awareness*) de concienciación

educationalist, educationist *n* pedagogo, -a *m, f*

educator ['edʒ·ə·keɪ·ţər] *n* educador(a) *m(f)*

EEC [ˌi·i·'si] *n abbr of* **European Economic Community** CEE

EEG [ˌi·i·'dʒi] *n abbr of* **electroencephalogram** electroencefalograma *m*

eel [il] *n* anguila *f* ▶ **to be as slippery as an ~** ser igual de escurridizo que una anguila

eerie ['ɪr·i] *adj*, **eery** <-ier, -iest> *adj* espeluznante

efface [ɪ·'feɪs] *vt* **1.** *a. fig* borrar **2.** (*be humble*) **to ~ oneself** intentar pasar inadvertido

effect [ɪ·'fekt] **I.** *n* **1.** (*consequence*) efecto *m*; **to have an ~ on sth** afectar a algo; **to have a disastrous ~ on** [*o* **upon**] **sth** tener consecuencias nefastas para algo; **to have no ~ on sb** no hacer ningún efecto a alguien **2.** (*result*) resultado *m*; **to have little/no ~** dar poco/no dar resultado; **to take ~** surtir efecto; (*medicine, alcohol*) hacer efecto; **to the ~ that...** con el propósito de...; **to no ~** en vano **3.** LAW vigencia *f*; **to come into** [*o* **to take**] **~** entrar en vigor; **to remain/be in ~** permanecer/estar vigente **4.** (*gist*) **to the same ~** por el estilo; **he disapproved of our idea and wrote to us to that ~** no estaba de acuerdo con nuestra idea y nos escribió para manifestarlo **5.** (*impression*) impresión *f*; **the overall ~** la impresión general; **for ~** para llamar la atención **6. ~s** (*belongings*) efectos *mpl*; **personal ~s** efectos personales ▶ **in ~** en efecto **II.** *vt* realizar; (*payment*) efectuar; (*cure*) lograr

effective [ɪ·'fek·tɪv] *adj* **1.** (*giving result*) efectivo, -a; (*medicine*) eficaz; **he was an ~ speaker** tenía grandes dotes de orador **2.** (*real*) real; **~ control** control efectivo **3.** (*operative*) vigente; **to become ~** entrar en vigor **4.** (*striking*) impresionante

effectively *adv* **1.** (*giving result*) eficazmente **2.** (*really*) realmente **3.** (*strikingly*) de manera impresionante

effectiveness *n* **1.** (*efficiency*) efectividad *f*; (*of a plan*) eficacia *f* **2.** (*of a rule*) vigencia *f*

effectual [ɪ·'fek·tʃu·əl] *adj* **1.** (*efficient*) efectivo, -a **2.** (*operative*) válido, -a

effectuate [ɪ·'fek·tʃu·eɪt] *vt form* efectuar

effeminacy [ɪ·'fem·ɪ·nə·si] *n* afeminación *f*, afeminamiento *m*

effeminate [ɪ·'fem·ə·nɪt] **I.** *adj* afeminado, -a **II.** *n* afeminado *m*

effervesce [ˌef·ər·'ves] *vi* **1.** (*bubble*) burbujear **2.** *fig* (*person*) estar eufórico, -a

effervescence [ˌef·ər·'ves·əns] *n* efervescencia *f*

effervescent [ˌef·ər·'ves·ənt] *adj* **1.** efervescente **2.** *fig* eufórico, -a

effete [ɪ·'fit] *adj* **1.** (*enfeebled*) debilitado, -a **2.** (*decadent*) decadente **3.** (*effeminate*) amanerado, -a

efficacious [ˌef·ɪ·'keɪ·ʃəs] *adj form* (*solution, suggestion*) eficaz; **an ~ medicine** un medicamento efectivo

efficacy ['ef·ɪ·kə·si] *n form* eficacia *f*

efficiency [ɪ·'fɪʃ·ən·si] *n* **1.** (*of a person*) eficiencia *f*; (*of a method*) eficacia *f* **2.** (*of a machine*) rendimiento *m*

efficient [ɪ·'fɪʃ·ənt] *adj* (*person*) eficiente; (*machine, system*) de buen rendimiento

effigy ['ef·ɪ·dʒi] *n* efigie *f*

effluent ['ef·lu·ənt] *n* **1.** efluente *m* **2.** (*liquid waste*) vertidos *mpl*

effort ['ef·ərt] *n* **1.** *a.* PHYS esfuerzo *m*; **to be worth the ~** valer la pena; **to make an ~ to do sth** esforzarse [*o* hacer un esfuerzo] para hacer algo; **to spare no ~** no escatimar esfuerzos; **without ~** sin esfuerzo **2.** (*attempt*) tentativa *f*; **please make an ~ to...** por favor, intenten... **3.** (*work*) obra *f*

effortless ['ef·ərt·lɪs] *adj* fácil; **an ~ movement** un movimiento sin esfuerzo aparente; **an ~ grace** una gracia natural

effrontery [e·'frʌn·tə·ri] *n form* descaro *m*; **to have the ~ to do sth** tener la desfachatez de hacer algo

effusion [ɪ·'fju·ʒən] *n a. fig* efusión *f*

effusive [ɪ·'fju·sɪv] *adj form* efusivo, -a

e-file *vt abbr of* **electronically file to ~ one's tax return** realizar la declaración de la renta online

eft [eft] *n* tritón *m*

EFTS *abbr of* **electronic funds transfer system** servicio *m* de pagos electrónico

e.g. [ˌi·'dʒi] *abbr of* **exempli gratia** (= **for example**) p.ej.

egalitarian [ɪ·ˌgæl·ɪ·'ter·i·ən] *adj* igualitario, -a

e-generation [i·ˌdʒen·ə·'reɪ·ʃən] *n* generación *f* de internet

egg [eg] *n* huevo *m*; **fried/boiled ~s** huevos fritos/pasados por agua; **hard-boiled ~** huevo duro; **scrambled ~s** huevos revueltos ▶ **to put all one's ~s in one basket** poner todos los huevos en un mismo cesto; **they had ~ on their faces** *inf* quedaron en ridículo; **to be a bad ~** *sl* ser un sinvergüenza

◆ **egg on** *vt* incitar

egg cell *n* óvulo *m*

eggcup *n* huevera *f*
egghead *n inf* cerebro *m*
eggnog *n* ponche *m* de huevo
eggplant *n* berenjena *f*
egg roll *n* rollito *m* de primavera
eggshell *n* cáscara *f* de huevo
egg timer *n* temporizador *m* para huevos (*en forma de reloj de arena*)
egg yolk *n* yema *f* de huevo
ego ['i·goʊ] *n* <-s> 1. PSYCH ego *m;* **to bolster sb's ~** reforzar el ego de alguien 2. (*self-esteem*) amor *m* propio
egocentric [ˌi·goʊ·'sen·trɪk] *adj* egocéntrico, -a
egoism ['i·goʊ·ɪz·əm] *n* egoísmo *m*
egoist ['i·goʊ·ɪst] *n* egoísta *mf*
egoistic [ˌi·goʊ·'ɪs·tɪk] *adj*, **egoistical** [ˌi·goʊ·'ɪs·tɪ·kəl] *adj* egoísta
ego surfing *n* COMPUT introducir en un buscador de Internet el propio nombre
egotism ['i·goʊ·tɪz·əm] *n* egotismo *m*
egotist ['i·goʊ·tɪst] *n* egotista *mf*
egotistic [ˌi·goʊ·'tɪs·tɪk] *adj*, **egotistical** [ˌi·goʊ·'tɪs·tɪ·kəl] *adj* 1. (*selfish*) egoísta 2. (*self-important*) egotista
ego trip ['i·goʊ·trɪp] *n* **to be on an ~** darse autobombo
egregious [ɪ·'gri·dʒəs] *adj* escandaloso, -a
Egypt ['i·dʒɪpt] *n* Egipto *m*
Egyptian [ɪ·'dʒɪp·ʃən] I. *n* egipcio, -a *m, f* II. *adj* egipcio, -a
eh [eɪ] *interj* 1. (*what did you say?*) ¿qué? 2. *Can* (*isn't it; aren't you/they/we?*) ¿verdad?
eider ['aɪ·dər] *n* eider *m*
eiderdown ['aɪ·dər·daʊn] *n* edredón *m*
eight [eɪt] I. *adj* ocho *inv;* **there are ~ of us** somos ocho; **~ and a quarter/half** ocho y cuarto/medio; **~ o'clock** las ocho; **it's ~ o'clock** son las ocho; **it's half past ~** son las ocho y media; **at ~ twenty/thirty** a las ocho y veinte/media II. *n* ocho *m*
eighteen [ˌeɪ·'tin] I. *adj* dieciocho II. *n* dieciocho *m; s.a.* **eight**
eighteenth [ˌeɪ·'tinθ] I. *adj* decimoctavo, -a II. *n* 1. (*order*) decimoctavo, -a *m, f* 2. (*date*) ocho *m* 3. (*fraction*) dieciochoavo *m;* (*part*) decimoctava parte *f; s.a.* **eighth**
eighth [eɪtθ] I. *adj* octavo, -a; **~ note** corchea *f* II. *n* 1. (*order*) octavo, -a *m, f;* **to be ~ in a race** quedar de octavo en una carrera 2. (*date*) ocho *m;* **the ~** el día ocho; **the ~ of December** [*o* December (the) ~] el ocho de diciembre 3. (*fraction*) octavo *m;* (*part*) octava parte *f* III. *adv* (*in lists*) octavo
eight-hour day *n* jornada *f* de ocho horas
eightieth ['eɪ·tɪ·əθ] I. *adj* octogésimo, -a II. *n* (*order*) octogésimo, -a *m, f;* (*fraction*) octogésimo *m;* (*part*) octogésima parte *f; s.a.* **eighth**
eighty ['eɪ·ti] I. *adj* ochenta *inv;* **he is ~ (years old)** tiene ochenta años; **a man of about ~ years of age** un hombre de unos ochenta años

II. *n* <-ies> 1. (*number*) ochenta *m;* **to do ~** *inf* ir a 80 millas (125 km) por hora 2. (*age*) **a woman in her eighties** una mujer en sus ochenta 3. (*decade*) **the eighties** los (años) ochenta
either ['i·ðər] I. *adj* 1. (*one of two*) **I'll do it ~ way** lo hará de una manera u otra; **I don't like ~ dress** no me gusta ninguno de los dos vestidos 2. (*each*) cada; **on ~ side of the river** a cada lado del río II. *pron* cualquiera (de los dos); **which one? — ~** ¿cuál? — cualquiera III. *adv* tampoco; **if he doesn't go, I won't go ~** si él no va, yo tampoco IV. *conj* **~ ... or...** o... o...; **~ buy it or rent it** cómpralo o alquílalo; **I can ~ stay or leave** puedo quedarme o irme
ejaculate[1] [ɪ·'dʒæk·jʊ·leɪt] I. *vt* 1. (*semen*) eyacular 2. *liter* (*blurt out*) exclamar II. *vi* ANAT eyacular
ejaculate[2] [ɪ·'dʒæk·jʊ·lət] *n* eyaculación *f*
ejaculation [ɪ·ˌdʒæk·jʊ·'leɪ·ʃən] *n* 1. (*of semen*) eyaculación *f* 2. *liter* (*sudden outburst*) exclamación *f*
eject [ɪ·'dʒekt] I. *vt* echar, expulsar; (*liquid, gas*) expeler II. *vi* eyectarse
ejector seat [ɪ·'dʒek·tər·sit] *n* asiento *m* de eyección
eke out ['ik·ˌaʊt] *vt* (*money, food*) hacer durar; **to ~ one's salary** estirar su sueldo *inf;* **to ~ a living** ganarse la vida a duras penas
EKG [ˌi·keɪ·'dʒi] *n abbr of* **electrocardiogram** electrocardiograma *m*, electro *m*
elaborate[1] [ɪ·'læb·ər·ət] *adj* (*complicated*) complicado, -a; (*very detailed: plan*) minucioso, -a; (*style*) trabajado, -a; (*excuse*) rebuscado, -a; (*meal*) de muchos platos
elaborate[2] [ɪ·'læb·ə·reɪt] I. *vt* elaborar; (*plan*) idear II. *vi* entrar en detalles; **to refuse to ~** negarse a dar más detalles; **to ~ on an idea** explicar una idea con más detalle
elaboration [ɪ·ˌlæb·ə·'reɪ·ʃən] <-(s)> *n* 1. (*of a theory*) elaboración *f;* (*of texts*) explicación *f;* **without ~** sin entrar en demasiados detalles 2. (*complexity*) complicación *f*
elapse [ɪ·'læps] *vi form* transcurrir
elastic [ɪ·'læs·tɪk] I. *adj* elástico, -a II. *n* 1. (*material*) elástico *m* 2. (*garter*) liga *f*
elasticity [ˌe·læ·'stɪs·ə·ti] *n a. fig* elasticidad *f*
elate [ɪ·'leɪt] *vt* regocijar; **to be ~d about sth** estar eufórico por algo
elated *adj* eufórico, -a
elation [ɪ·'leɪ·ʃən] *n* regocijo *m*
elbow ['el·boʊ] I. *n* 1. (*of people*) codo *m;* (*of animals*) codillo *m* 2. (*in a pipe*) codo *m;* (*in a road, river*) recodo *m* ▸ **to rub ~s with sb** codearse con alguien II. *vt* dar un codazo a; **to ~ one's way through the crowd** abrirse paso a codazos entre la multitud
elbow grease *n inf* fuerza *f;* **to put some ~ into sth** poner empeño en algo
elbow room *n* 1. (*space*) espacio *m* 2. (*freedom*) libertad *f* de acción
elder[1] ['el·dər] I. *n* 1. (*older person*) mayor *mf;* **she is my ~ by three years** es tres años

mayor que yo **2.** (*senior person*) anciano, -a *m,*
f **3.** (*in Mormon Church*) miembro *m* del consejo **II.** *adj* mayor; **~ statesman/states-**
woman POL veterano, -a *m*, *f* de la política
elder² ['el·dər] *n* BOT saúco *m*
elderberry ['el·dər·ber·i] <-ies> *n* **1.** (*berry*)
baya *f* del saúco **2.** BOT saúco *m*
elderly ['el·dər·li] **I.** *adj* anciano, -a; **an ~**
woman una señora mayor **II.** *n* **the ~** los
ancianos
eldest ['el·dɪst] *adj superl of* **old** mayor; **the ~**
el/la mayor; **her ~** (*child*) **is nearly 14** su hijo
mayor tiene casi 14 años
elect [ɪ·'lekt] **I.** *vt* **1.** (*by vote*) elegir **2.** (*not by*
vote) decidir; **to ~ to resign** optar por dimitir
II. *n* REL **the ~** los elegidos **III.** *adj* **the presi-**
dent ~ el presidente *m* electo, la presidenta *f*
electa
election [ɪ·'lek·ʃən] *n* **1.** (*event*) elecciones *fpl*;
to call/hold an ~ convocar/celebrar elec-
ciones; **to run for ~** presentarse a las elecciones **2.** (*action*) elección *f*
election campaign *n* campaña *f* electoral
Election Day *n* jornada *f* electoral
election defeat *n* derrota *f* electoral
electioneer [ɪ·ˌlek·ʃə·'nɪr] *vi* hacer campaña
electoral
electioneering [ɪ·ˌlek·ʃə·'nɪr·ɪŋ] *n* campaña *f*
electoral; *pej* promesas *fpl* electoralistas
election platform *n*, **election program** *n*
programa *m* electoral
election results *npl*, **election returns** *npl*
resultados *mpl* electorales
election speech *n* discurso *m* electoral
elective [ɪ·'lek·tɪv] **I.** *adj* **1.** *form* (*appointed by*
election) electivo, -a; (*based on voting*) electoral **2.** (*optional*) optativo, -a **3.** (*selective*) **~**
affinity afinidad electiva **II.** *n* SCHOOL, UNIV
optativa *f*
elector [ɪ·'lek·tər] *n* **1.** (*voter*) elector(a) *m(f)*
2. (*member of Electoral College*) miembro *mf*
de un colegio electoral
electoral [ɪ·'lek·tər·əl] *adj* electoral; **Electoral**
College Colegio *m* Electoral; **~ register** [*o*
roll] censo *m* electoral
electorate [ɪ·'lek·tər·ət] *n* electorado *m*
electric [ɪ·'lek·trɪk] *adj* **1.** ELEC eléctrico, -a;
(*fence*) electrificado, -a; **~ blanket** manta eléctrica; **~ stove** estufa *f* eléctrica; **~ current** corriente *f* eléctrica; **~ heater** estufa *f* eléctrica;
~ shock descarga *f* eléctrica **2.** *fig* electrizante;
(*atmosphere*) cargado, -a de electricidad
electrical [ɪ·'lek·trɪ·kəl] *adj* eléctrico, -a;
~ tape cinta *f* aislante; **~ engineering** ingeniería *f* eléctrica, electrotecnia *f*
electric chair *n* silla *f* eléctrica; **he was sen-**
tenced to death in the ~ fue condenado a
morir en la silla eléctrica
electric guitar *n* guitarra *f* eléctrica
electrician [ɪ·ˌlek·'trɪʃ·ən] *n* electricista *mf*
electricity [ɪ·ˌlek·'trɪs·ə·ti] *n* electricidad *f*;
powered by ~ eléctrico, -a; **to run on ~** funcionar con electricidad

electrification [ɪ·ˌlek·trɪ·fɪ·'keɪ·ʃən] *n* electrifi-
cación *f*
electrify [ɪ·'lek·trɪ·faɪ] *vt* electrificar; *fig* electrizar
electroanalysis [ɪ·ˌlek·trou·ə·'næl·ɪ·sɪs] *n*
electroanálisis *m*
electrocardiogram [ɪ·ˌlek·trou·'kar·dɪ·ə·
græm] *n* electrocardiograma *m*
electroconvulsive therapy [ɪ·ˌlek·trou·kən-
'vʌl·sɪv·'θer·ə·pi] *adj* electroterapia *f*
electrocute [ɪ·'lek·trə·kjut] *vt* electrocutar
electrocution [ɪ·ˌlek·trə·'kju·ʃən] *n* electrocución *f*
electrode [ɪ·'lek·troud] *n* electrodo *m*
electroencephalogram [ɪ·ˌlek·trou·en·'sef·ə·
lou·ˌgræm] *n* electroencefalograma *m*
electrolysis [ɪ·ˌlek·'tral·ə·sɪs] *n* electrólisis *f*
electromagnet [ɪ·'lek·trou·'mæg·nɪt] *n* elec-
troimán *m*
electromagnetic [ɪ·ˌlek·trou·mæg·'neṭ·ɪk]
adj electromagnético, -a
electron [ɪ·'lek·tran] *n* electrón *m*
electronic [ɪ·ˌlek·'tran·ɪk] *adj* electrónico, -a
electronic data processing *n* procesamiento
m electrónico de datos
electronic fund transfer *n* transferencia *f*
electrónica de fondos
electronic mail *n* correo *m* electrónico
electronic music *n* música *f* electrónica
electronics [ɪ·ˌlek·'tran·ɪks] *n + sing vb* electrónica *f*; **the ~ industry** la industria electrónica
electron microscope *n* microscopio *m* electrónico
electroplate [ɪ·'lek·trou·pleɪt] *vt* galvanizar
electroscope [ɪ·'lek·trou·ˌskoup] *n* electrosco-
pio *m*
electrotherapy *n* electroterapia *f*
elegance ['el·ɪ·gəns] *n* elegancia *f*
elegant ['el·ɪ·gənt] *adj* elegante
elegiac [ˌel·ɪ·'dʒaɪ·ək] **I.** *adj* elegíaco, -a **II.** *n*
~ s versos *mpl* elegíacos
elegy ['el·ə·dʒi] *n* elegía *f*
element ['el·ə·mənt] *n* **1.** *a.* CHEM, MATH
elemento *m;* **the four ~s** los cuatro
elementos; **he's in his ~** está en su elemento
2. (*factor*) factor *m;* **an ~ of luck** algo de
suerte; **the ~ of surprise** el factor sorpresa;
there's an ~ of truth in what they say hay
algo de verdad en lo que dicen **3.** ELEC resistencia *f* **4. ~ s** (*rudiments*) rudimentos *mpl*
5. METEO **the ~s** los elementos
elemental [ˌel·ə·'men·təl] *adj* elemental;
(*forces*) de la naturaleza; (*feelings, needs*) primario, -a
elementary [ˌel·ə·'men·tə·ri] *adj* elemental;
(*course*) básico, -a
elementary school *n* escuela *f* (de enseñanza)
primaria
elephant ['el·ə·fənt] *n* elefante *m*
elephantiasis [ˌel·ə·fən·'taɪ·ə·sɪs] *n* MED ele-
fantiasis *f inv*
elephantine [ˌel·ɪ·'fæn·taɪn] *adj* **1.** (*huge*)

colosal 2. (*clumsy*) torpe

elevate ['el·ə·veɪt] *vt* **1.** (*raise*) elevar; (*prices*) aumentar; **to ~ the mind** ser edificante **2.** REL alzar **3.** (*in rank*) ascender

elevated ['el·ə·veɪ·t̬ɪd] *adj* **1.** (*raised: part*) elevado, -a **2.** (*important*) alto, -a; (*position*) importante

elevation [ˌel·ɪ·'veɪ·ʃən] *n* **1.** (*rise*) elevación *f*; (*of person*) ascenso *m* **2.** (*height*) altura *f* **3.** GEO elevación *f* (del terreno) **4.** ARCHIT alzado *m*

elevator ['el·ə·veɪ·t̬ər] *n* (*for people*) ascensor *m*, elevador *m* AmL; (*for goods*) montacargas *m inv*

eleven [ɪ·'lev·ən] **I.** *adj* once **II.** *n* once *m; s.a.* **eight**

eleventh [ɪ·'lev·ənθ] **I.** *adj* undécimo, -a **II.** *n* **1.** (*order*) undécimo, -a *m, f* **2.** (*date*) once *m* **3.** (*fraction*) onceavo *m;* (*part*) onceava parte *f; s.a.* **eighth**

elf [elf] <**elves**> *n* (*folklore*) duende *m;* (*mythology*) elfo *m*

elicit [ɪ·'lɪs·ɪt] *vt* **1.** (*obtain*) obtener **2.** (*provoke: criticism, response*) suscitar

eligibility [ˌel·ɪ·dʒə·'bɪl·ə·t̬i] *n* elegibilidad *f*

eligible ['el·ɪ·dʒə·bəl] *adj* **1.** elegible; **~ to vote** con derecho a voto **2.** (*desirable*) deseable; **to be ~ for the job** reunir los requisitos necesarios para el puesto; **an ~ bachelor** un soltero codiciado; **an ~ young man/woman** un buen partido

eliminate [ɪ·'lɪm·ɪ·neɪt] *vt* **1.** (*eradicate*) eliminar **2.** (*exclude from consideration*) descartar

elimination [ɪ·ˌlɪm·ɪ·'neɪ·ʃən] *n* eliminación *f;* **by (a) process of ~** por eliminación

elite [ɪ·'lit] **I.** *n* elite *f* **II.** *adj* de elite

elitism [ɪ·'li·t̬ɪz·əm] *n* elitismo *m*

elitist [ɪ·'li·t̬ɪst] *adj* elitista

elixir [ɪ·'lɪk·sər] *n* elixir *m*

elk [elk] <-(s)> *n* (*European*) alce *m;* (*American*) uapití *m*

ellipse [ɪ·'lɪps] *n* elipse *f*

elliptical [ɪ·'lɪp·t̬ɪk] *adj*, **elliptical** [ɪ·'lɪp·t̬ɪ·kəl] *adj* elíptico, -a

elm [elm] *n* olmo *m*

elocution [ˌel·ə·'kju·ʃən] *n* dicción *f;* (*art*) elocución *f*

elongate [ɪ·'laŋ·geɪt] **I.** *vt* alargar **II.** *vi* alargarse

elongated *adj* alargado, -a

elope [ɪ·'loʊp] *vi* fugarse (*para casarse en secreto*)

elopement [ɪ·'loʊp·mənt] *n* fuga *f* (*para casarse en secreto*)

eloquent ['el·ə·kwənt] *adj* elocuente

El Salvador *n* El Salvador *m*

El Salvadorian I. *adj* salvadoreño, -a **II.** *n* salvadoreño, -a *m, f*

else [els] *adv* **1.** (*in addition*) más; **anyone/ anything ~** cualquier otra persona/cosa; **anywhere ~** en cualquier otro lugar; **anyone ~?** ¿alguien más?; **anything ~?** ¿algo más?; **everybody ~** (todos) los demás; **I can't**

remember anything/anybody ~ no puedo recordar nada/a nadie más; **everything ~** todo lo demás; **if all ~ fails** como último recurso; **someone/something ~** otra persona/cosa; **it's something ~!** ¡es algo fuera de serie!; **how ~?** ¿de qué otra forma?; **what/ who ~?** ¿qué/quién más? **2.** (*otherwise*) **or ~** si no; **come here or ~!** ¡ven, o ya verás!; **shut up, or else!** ¡como no te calles...!

elsewhere ['els·wer] *adv* en otro sitio; **let's go ~!** ¡vamos a otra parte!

elucidate [ɪ·'lus·ɪ·deɪt] *form* **I.** *vt* dilucidar; (*mystery*) esclarecer **II. I don't understand, you'll have to ~** no lo entiendo, tendrás que aclarármelo

elude [ɪ·'lud] *vt* eludir; (*blow*) esquivar

elusive [ɪ·'lu·sɪv] *adj* **1.** (*evasive*) evasivo, -a; (*personality*) esquivo, -a; **memory** fugaz **2.** (*slippery*) escurridizo, -a **3.** (*difficult to obtain*) difícil de conseguir

elves [elvz] *n pl of* **elf**

emaciated [ɪ·'meɪ·ʃi·eɪ·t̬ɪd] *adj form* demacrado, -a, jalado, -a AmL

e-mail ['i·meɪl] **I.** *n abbr of* **electronic mail** (mensaje de) correo *m* electrónico, e-mail *m* **II.** *vt* mandar por correo electrónico

e-mail address *n* dirección *f* de correo electrónico

emanate ['em·ə·neɪt] **I.** *vi form* (*originate*) proceder; (*radiate*) emanar **II.** *vt* emanar

emancipate [ɪ·'mæn·sɪ·peɪt] *vt* emancipar

emancipated *adj* emancipado, -a; (*not constrained by tradition*) liberado, -a; (*ideas*) progresista

emancipation [ɪ·ˌmæn·sɪ·'peɪ·ʃən] *n* emancipación *f*

embalm [em·'bam] *vt* embalsamar

embankment [em·'bæŋk·mənt] *n* (*of a road*) terraplén *m;* (*by river*) dique *m*

embargo [em·'bar·goʊ] **I.** <-**goes**> *n* embargo *m;* **trade ~** embargo comercial; **to be under ~** estar sujeto a embargo; **to put an ~ on a country** imponer un embargo sobre un país **II.** *vt* prohibir; LAW embargar

embark [em·'bark] **I.** *vi* embarcar(se); **to ~ on** [*o* **upon**] **a journey** embarcarse en un viaje **II.** *vt* embarcar

embarkation [ˌem·bar·'keɪ·ʃən] *n* embarque *m*

embarrass [em·'bær·əs] *vt* **1.** (*make feel uncomfortable*) avergonzar **2.** (*disconcert*) desconcertar

embarrassed *adj* avergonzado, -a; **to be ~** pasar vergüenza; **I felt ~ about saying that** me daba vergüenza decir eso

embarrassing *adj* embarazoso, -a, penoso, -a *Méx, Col, Pan, Ven, CRi;* (*silence*) incómodo, -a

embarrassment [em·'bær·əs·mənt] *n* **1.** (*shame*) vergüenza *f*, pena *f Méx, Col, Pan, Ven, CRi* **2.** (*trouble, nuisance*) molestia *f;* **to be an ~ (to sb)** ser un estorbo (para alguien)

embassy ['em·bə·si] <-**ies**> *n* embajada *f*

embed [em·'bed] <-dd-> *vt* **1.** (*fix*) hincar; (*in rock*) incrustar; (*in memory*) grabar **2.** (*integrate*) integrar, *a un periodista en una unidad militar*

embellish [em·'bel·ɪʃ] *vt* adornar

embers ['em·bərz] *npl* ascuas *fpl*

embezzle [ɪm·'bez·əl] <-ing> *vt* desfalcar

embezzlement [ɪm·'bez·əl·mənt] *n* desfalco *m;* ~ **of public funds** malversación *f* de fondos públicos

embezzler [em·'bez·lər] *n* desfalcador(a) *m(f)*

embitter [em·'bɪt·ər] *vt* amargar

emblem ['em·bləm] *n* emblema *m*

embodiment [em·'bad·ɪ·mənt] *n* **1.** (*personification*) encarnación *f;* **the ~ of virtue** la virtud personificada **2.** (*inclusion*) incorporación *f*

embody [em·'bad·i] <-ied> *vt* **1.** (*convey: theory, idea*) expresar **2.** (*personify*) personificar **3.** (*include*) incorporar

embolism ['em·bə·lɪz·əm] *n* MED embolia *f*

emboss [em·'bas] *vt* **1.** (*design, letters*) grabar en relieve **2.** (*leather, metal*) repujar; **~ed writing paper** papel *m* de carta con membrete en relieve

embrace [em·'breɪs] **I.** *vt* **1.** (*hug*) abrazar **2.** (*accept: offer*) aceptar; (*ideas, religion*) adoptar **3.** (*include*) abarcar **II.** *vi* abrazarse **III.** *n* abrazo *m*

embrocation [ˌem·brou·'keɪ·ʃən] *n* cataplasma *f*

embroider [em·'brɔɪ·dər] **I.** *vi* bordar **II.** *vt* bordar; *fig* adornar

embroidery [em·'brɔɪ·də·ri] *n* **1.** bordado *m;* ~ **frame** bastidor *m* **2.** *fig* florituras *fpl*

embroil [ɪm·'brɔɪl] *vt* embrollar

embryo ['em·bri·ou] *n* embrión *m*

embryonic [ˌem·brɪ·'an·ɪk] *adj* embrionario, -a; *fig* en estado embrionario

emcee [em·'si] **I.** *n* presentador(a) *m(f)*, maestro (a) de ceremonias *m* **II.** *vt* presentar **III.** *vi* ser el presentador

emend [ɪ·'mend] *vt form* enmendar

emerald ['em·ər·əld] **I.** *n* esmeralda *f* **II.** *adj* de esmeraldas; (*color*) esmeralda

emerge [ɪ·'mɜrdʒ] *vi* (*come out*) salir; (*secret*) revelarse; (*ideas*) surgir; **they ~d from the bushes** salieron de entre los arbustos; **new ideas ~d from the meeting** a partir de la reunión surgieron nuevas ideas

emergence [ɪ·'mɜr·dʒəns] *n* salida *f;* (*of a secret*) revelación *f;* (*appearance*) aparición *f*

emergency [ɪ·'mɜr·dʒən·si] **I.** <-ies> *n* **1.** (*dangerous situation*) emergencia *f;* **in an** [*o* **in case of**] ~ en caso de emergencia; **to be ready for an** ~ estar preparado para cualquier eventualidad **2.** MED urgencia *f;* ~ **room** sala *f* de urgencias **3.** POL crisis *f inv;* **national** ~ crisis nacional; **to declare a state of** ~ declarar el estado de excepción **II.** *adj* (*exit*) de emergencia; (*services*) de urgencia; (*brake*) de mano; (*landing*) forzoso, -a; (*rations*) de reserva; ~ **exit** salida de emergencia; ~ **landing** aterrizaje forzoso; ~ **services** servicio de urgencia

emergency room *n* sala *f* de urgencias

emergent [ɪ·'mɜr·dʒənt] *adj* emergente; (*democracy, nation*) joven

emerging *adj* emergente

emery ['em·ə·ri] *n* esmeril *m*

emery board *n* lima *f* de uñas (de esmeril)

emetic [ɪ·'meṭ·ɪk] **I.** *adj* MED emético, -a, vomitivo, -a **II.** *n* emético *m,* vomitivo *m*

emigrant ['em·ɪ·grənt] *n* emigrante *mf*

emigrate ['em·ɪ·greɪt] *vi* emigrar

emigration [ˌem·ɪ·'greɪ·ʃən] *n* emigración *f*

eminence ['em·ɪ·nəns] *n* eminencia *f;* **Your Eminence** REL Vuestra Eminencia

eminent ['em·ɪ·nənt] *adj* eminente

eminently *adv* sumamente

emissary ['em·ɪ·ser·i] <-ies> *n* emisario, -a *m, f*

emission [ɪ·'mɪʃ·ən] *n* emisión *f*

emit [ɪ·'mɪt] <-tt-> *vt* (*radiation, light*) emitir; (*heat*) desprender; (*odor*) despedir; (*smoke*) echar; (*cry*) dar

emoticon *n* COMPUT emoticón *m*

emotion [ɪ·'mou·ʃən] *n* **1.** (*feeling*) sentimiento *m* **2.** (*affective state*) emoción *f*

emotional [ɪ·'mou·ʃə·nəl] *adj* **1.** (*relating to the emotions*) emocional; (*involvement, link*) afectivo, -a **2.** (*moving*) conmovedor(a) **3.** (*governed by emotion*) emocionado, -a; **to get ~** emocionarse **4.** (*determined by emotion: decision*) impulsivo, -a

emotionless *adj* impasible

emotive [ɪ·'mou·ṭɪv] *adj* emotivo, -a

empathy ['em·pə·θi] *n* empatía *f*

emperor ['em·pər·ər] *n* emperador *m*

emphasis ['em·fə·sɪs] <emphases> *n* **1.** (*importance*) énfasis *m inv;* **to put** [*o* **place**] **great ~ on punctuality** hacer especial hincapié en la puntualidad **2.** LING acento *m*

emphasize ['em·fə·saɪz] *vt* **1.** (*insist on*) poner énfasis en, enfatizar *AmL;* (*fact*) hacer hincapié en **2.** LING acentuar

emphatic [em·'fæṭ·ɪk] *adj* (*forcibly expressive*) enfático, -a; (*strong*) enérgico, -a; (*assertion*) categórico, -a; (*refusal*) rotundo, -a; **to be ~ about sth** hacer hincapié en algo

emphatically *adv* (*expressively*) con énfasis; (*strongly*) enérgicamente; (*forcefully*) categóricamente

empire ['em·paɪr] *n* imperio *m*

empirical [em·'pɪr·ɪ·kəl] *adj* empírico, -a

employ [em·'plɔɪ] *vt* **1.** (*give a job to*) emplear; **to ~ sb to do sth** contratar a alguien para hacer algo **2.** (*put to use*) utilizar

employee ['em·plɔɪ·'i] *n* empleado, -a *m, f*

employer [em·'plɔɪ·ər] *n* empresario, -a *m, f*

employment ['em·plɔɪ·mənt] *n* **1.** (*of a person*) empleo *m* **2.** (*of an object*) utilización *f*

employment agency *n* agencia *f* de empleo

employment equity *n Can* paridad *f* (en el trabajo)

emporium [em·'pɔr·i·əm] <-s *o* emporia> *n* emporio *m*

empower [em·'pau·ər] *vt* **to ~ sb to do sth**

(*give ability to*) capacitar a alguien para hacer algo; (*authorize*) autorizar a alguien a hacer algo

empowerment [em·'pau·ər·mənt] *n* autorización *f*

empress ['em·prɪs] *n* emperatriz *f*

emptiness ['emp·tɪ·nɪs] *n* vacío *m; fig* vacuidad *f elev*

empty ['emp·ti] I. <-ier, -iest> *adj* 1. (*with nothing inside*) vacío, -a; (*truck, ship, train*) sin carga; (*house*) desocupado, -a 2. (*insincere: promise*) vacío, -a; (*threat*) vano, -a 3. (*useless*) inútil; (*words*) vano, -a; ~ **phrase** frase vacía II. <-ie-> *vt* (*pour*) verter; (*deprive of contents*) vaciar III. <-ie-> *vi* vaciarse; (*river*) desembocar; **to ~ into the Mississippi** desembocar en el Misisipí IV. <-ies> *n* **empties** envases *mpl* (vacíos)

◆ **empty out** *vt* vaciar

empty-handed [‚emp·tɪ·'hæn·dɪd] *adj* con las manos vacías

empty-headed *adj* cabeza hueca

empty nester *n* padre cuyos hijos son ya mayores y han abandonado la vivienda familiar

empty-nest syndrome *n* síndrome *m* del nido vacío

EMT [‚i·em·'ti] *n abbr of* **emergency medical technician** técnico *m* médico de emergencia

emu ['i·mju] *n* emú *m*

emulate ['em·jʊ·leɪt] *vt* emular

emulation [‚em·jʊ·'leɪ·ʃən] *n* emulación *f;* ~ **of sb** imitación *f* de alguien

emulsifier [ɪ·'mʌl·sɪ·faɪ·ər] *n* emulsionante *m*

emulsify [ɪ·'mʌl·sɪ·faɪ] <-ie-> I. *vt* emulsionar II. *vi* emulsionarse

emulsion [ɪ·'mʌl·ʃən] *n* 1. *a.* PHOT emulsión *f* 2. (*paint*) pintura *f* emulsionada

enable [ɪ·'neɪ·bəl] *vt* 1. **to ~ sb to do sth** permitir a alguien que haga algo 2. COMPUT activar

enact [ɪ·'nækt] *vt* 1. (*carry out*) llevar a cabo 2. THEAT representar 3. (*law*) promulgar; **to ~ that...** decretar que...

enactment *n* 1. (*carrying out*) puesta *f* en práctica; (*of legislation*) promulgación *f* 2. THEAT representación *f*

enamel [ɪ·'næm·əl] I. *n* esmalte *m* II. <-ll-, -l-> *vt* esmaltar

enamored [ɪ·'næm·ərd] *adj* **to be ~ of sb** estar enamorado de alguien; **to be ~ with sth** estar entusiasmado con algo

enc. *s.* enc(l).

encamp [en·'kæmp] *vi* acampar

encampment *n* campamento *m*

encapsulate [ɪn·'kæp·sə·leɪt] *vt* encapsular; *fig* resumir

encase [en·'keɪs] *vt* encerrar

encephalitis [en·‚sef·ə·'laɪ·t̬ɪs] *n* encefalitis *f inv*

enchant [en·'tʃænt] *vt* 1. (*charm*) encantar 2. (*bewitch*) hechizar

enchanted *adj* 1. (*charmed*) encantado, -a 2. (*bewitched*) hechizado, -a

enchanter *n* (*sorcerer*) hechicero *m*

enchanting *adj* encantador(a)

enchantment *n* 1. (*charm*) encanto *m* 2. (*spell*) hechizo *m*

enchantress *n* (*charming woman*) mujer *f* encantadora; (*witch*) hechicera *f*

enchilada [‚en·tʃɪ·'la·də] *n* enchilada *f;* **the whole ~** *fig* todo el pastel

encipher [en·'saɪ·fər] *vt* codificar

encircle [en·'sɜr·kəl] *vt* rodear; **to ~ the enemy** rodear al enemigo

encirclement *n* cerco *m;* MIL envolvimiento *m*

enc(l). *abbr of* **enclosure** recinto *m*

enclave ['en·kleɪv] *n* enclave *m*

enclose [en·'kloʊz] *vt* 1. (*surround*) cercar; (*field*) rodear; **to ~ sth in brackets** poner algo entre paréntesis 2. (*include*) adjuntar, adosar *AmL*

enclosed [en·'kloʊzd] *adj* 1. (*confined*) cerrado, -a; (*garden*) vallado, -a 2. (*included*) adjunto, -a

enclosure [en·'kloʊ·ʒər] *n* 1. (*enclosed area*) recinto *m;* (*for animals*) corral *m* 2. (*action*) cercamiento *m* 3. (*letter*) documento *m* adjunto

encode [en·'koʊd] *vt a.* COMPUT codificar; LING cifrar

encompass [en·'kʌm·pəs] *vt* 1. (*surround*) rodear 2. (*include*) abarcar

encore ['an·kɔr] I. *n* repetición *f;* **as** [*o* **for**] **an ~** como bis II. *interj* otra

encore marriage *n* segundo matrimonio *m*

encore performance *n* bis *m,* ¡otra! *f*

encounter [en·'kaʊn·tər] I. *vt* encontrar; **to ~ sb** encontrarse con alguien (por casualidad) II. *n* encuentro *m;* **a close ~** avistamiento *m*

encourage [en·'kɜr·ɪdʒ] *vt* 1. (*give confidence*) alentar; (*give hope*) dar ánimos a; **to ~ sb to do sth** animar a alguien a hacer algo 2. (*support*) fomentar

encouragement [en·'kɜr·ɪdʒ·mənt] *n* estímulo *m;* **to give ~ to sth** fomentar algo; **to give ~ to sb** animar a alguien

encouraging *adj* alentador(a); **an ~ prospect** una perspectiva de futuro halagüeña

encroach [en·'kroʊtʃ] *vi* **to ~ on** [*o* **upon**] **sth** (*intrude*) invadir algo; *fig* usurpar algo

encroachment *n* 1. (*intrusion*) invasión *f* 2. *fig* usurpación *f;* **an ~ on human rights** una violación de los derechos humanos

encryption [ɪn·'krɪp·ʃən] *n* COMPUT codificación *f*

encumber [en·'kʌm·bər] *vt* **to be ~ed with sth** tener que cargar con algo; (*impede*) ser estorbado por algo

encyclopedia [en·‚saɪ·klə·'pi·di·ə] *n* enciclopedia *f*

encyclopedic [en·‚saɪ·klə·'pi·dɪk] *adj* enciclopédico, -a

end [end] I. *n* 1. (*finish*) fin *m* 2. (*extremity*) extremo *m* 3. (*boundary*) límite *m* 4. (*stop*) fin *m* 5. ~**s** (*goal*) fin *m;* (*purpose*) intención *f;* **to achieve one's ~s** conseguir los propios

objetivos **6.** (*phone line*) **who is on the other ~?** ¿quién está al otro lado de la línea? **7.** (*death*) muerte *f;* **he is nearing his ~** está a punto de morir **8.** (*piece remaining*) resto *m* **9.** (*obligation*) **to uphold one's ~ of the deal** [*o* **bargain**] cumplir su parte del trato **10.** SPORTS lado *m* **11.** COMPUT tecla *f* de fin ▶ **to reach the ~ of the** line [*o* **road**] llegar al final; **the ~s justify the** means *prov* el fin justifica los medios *prov;* **~ of** story punto y final, se acabó; **you deserved to be punished, ~ of story** merecías ser castigado, y punto; **to be at the ~ of one's** rope no poder más; **it's not the ~ of the** world no es el fin del mundo; **to be the ~** *sl* ser la leche [*o* la machera]; **to go off the** deep **~** *inf* subirse por las paredes; **to** make **~s meet** llegar a fin de mes; **to** meet **one's ~** encontrar la muerte; **to play both ~s against the** middle oponer a dos contrincantes en beneficio propio; **to put an ~ to oneself** [*o* **it all**] acabar con su vida; **in the ~** a fin de cuentas; **to** this **~** para ello **II.** *vt* **1.** (*finish*) acabar **2.** (*bring to a stop: reign, war*) poner fin a **III.** *vi* acabar; **to ~ in sth** terminar en algo
◆ **end up** *vi* terminar; **to ~ in love with sb** acabar enamorándose de alguien; **to ~ a rich man** acabar siendo un hombre rico; **to ~ penniless** acabar sin dinero; **to ~ in prison** acabar en la cárcel; **to ~ doing sth** terminar haciendo algo

endanger [en·'deɪn·dʒər] *vt* poner en peligro; **an ~ed species** una especie en peligro de extinción

endear [en·'dɪr] *vt* **to ~ oneself to sb** hacerse querer por alguien

endearing *adj* entrañable; **an ~ smile** una sonrisa agradable

endearment *n* ternura *f;* **terms of ~** palabras *fpl* cariñosas

endeavor [en·'dev·ər] **I.** *vi* **to ~ to do sth** esforzarse por hacer algo **II.** *n* esfuerzo *m;* **to make every ~ to do sth** hacer todo lo posible para conseguir algo

endemic [en·'dem·ɪk] *adj* endémico, -a

ending ['en·dɪŋ] *n* fin *m;* LING terminación *f*

endive ['en·daɪv] *n* CULIN endibia *f*

endless ['end·lɪs] *adj* interminable, inacabable

endorse [en·'dɔrs] *vt* **1.** (*declare approval for*) aprobar; (*product*) promocionar; (*candidate*) respaldar, apoyar **2.** FIN endosar

endorsee [ɪn‚dɔr·'si] *n* endosatario, -a *m, f*

endorsement *n* **1.** (*support: of a plan*) aprobación *f;* (*of a candidate*) respaldo, apoyo *m;* (*recommendation*) recomendación *f* **2.** FIN endoso *m*

endorser *n* endosante *mf*

endow [en·'daʊ] *vt* dotar; **to be ~ed with sth** estar dotado de algo

endowment *n* **1.** FIN dotación *f* **2.** (*talent*) talento *m* **3.** BIO **genetic ~** dotación *f* genética

endpaper ['end·peɪ·pər] *n* guarda *f*

end product *n* producto *m* final

end result *n* resultado *m* final

end table *n* mesa *f* auxiliar

endurable [en·'dʊr·ə·rəbl] *adj* soportable

endurance [en·'dʊr·əns] *n* resistencia *f*

endurance athlete *n* atleta *mf* de resistencia

endurance sports *n* deportes *m* de resistencia *pl*

endure [en·'dʊr] **I.** *vt* **1.** (*tolerate*) soportar, aguantar **2.** (*suffer*) resistir **II.** *vi form* durar

enduring *adj* duradero, -a

ENE *abbr of* **east-northeast** ENE

enema ['en·ə·mə] <-s *o* enemata> *n* enema *m*

enemy ['en·ə·mi] **I.** *n* enemigo, -a *m, f* **II.** *adj* enemigo, -a

energetic [‚en·ər·'dʒeṭ·ɪk] *adj* enérgico, -a; (*active*) activo, -a

energize ['en·ər·dʒaɪz] *vt* **1.** ELEC activar **2.** *fig* dar energía a

energy ['en·ər·dʒi] <-ies> *n* energía *f;* **to be full of ~** estar lleno de energía; **to have the ~ to do sth** tener energías para hacer algo

energy crisis *n* crisis *f inv* energética

energy resources *npl* fuentes *fpl* energéticas [*o* de energía]

energy-saving *adj* que ahorra energía

enervate ['en·ər·veɪt] *vt liter* enervar

enervating *adj liter* enervante

enfeeble [en·'fi·bəl] *vt form* debilitar

enforce [en·'fɔrs] *vt* aplicar; (*law*) hacer cumplir; (*regulation*) poner en vigor

enforceable *adj* ejecutable; (*law*) que se puede hacer cumplir

enforcement [en·'fɔrs·mənt] *n* (*of a law*) aplicación *f;* (*of a regulation*) ejecución *f*

enfranchise [en·'fræn·tʃaɪz] *vt form* conceder el derecho a voto a

engage [en·'geɪdʒ] **I.** *vt* **1.** *form* (*hold interest*) atraer; **to ~ sb's attention** llamar la atención de alguien **2.** (*put into use*) activar **3.** TECH (*cogs*) engranar; **to ~ the clutch** embragar, enclochar *Col, Méx* **4.** MIL (*the enemy*) entablar combate con **II.** *vi* **1.** MIL trabar [*o* librar] batalla **2.** TECH engranar

engaged *adj* **1.** (*to be married*) prometido, -a; **to get ~** (**to sb**) prometerse (con alguien) **2.** (*occupied*) ocupado, -a **3.** (*in battle*) enzarzado, -a

engagement [en·'geɪdʒ·mənt] *n* **1.** (*appointment*) compromiso *m* **2.** (*marriage*) compromiso *m* **3.** MIL combate *m*

engagement ring *n* anillo *m* de compromiso

engaging *adj* atractivo, -a

engender [en·'dʒen·dər] *vt form* engendrar

engine ['en·dʒɪn] *n* **1.** (*motor*) motor *m;* **diesel/gasoline ~** motor diesel/de gasolina; **jet ~** motor a reacción **2.** RAIL máquina *f*

engineer [‚en·dʒɪ·'nɪr] **I.** *n* **1.** (*with a degree*) ingeniero, -a *m, f;* **civil ~** ingeniero de caminos **2.** (*technician*) técnico, -a *m, f* **3.** RAIL maquinista *mf* **II.** *vt* construir; *fig* maquinar

engineering [‚en·dʒɪ·'nɪr·ɪŋ] *n* ingeniería *f*

England ['ɪŋ·glənd] *n* Inglaterra *f*

English ['ɪŋ·glɪʃ] **I.** *n inv* **1.** (*language*) inglés

m **2.** *pl* (*people*) **the** ~ los ingleses **II.** *adj* inglés, -esa; **a movie in** ~ una película en inglés; **an** ~ **class** una clase de inglés
English breakfast *n* desayuno *m* inglés
English Canada *n* Canadá *m* de habla inglesa
English Canadian *n* canadiense *mf* anglófono, -a
English Channel *n* Canal *m* de la Mancha
Englishman <-men> *n* inglés *m*
English muffin *n* *bollo de pan que se corta en dos y se toma tostado y untado en mantequilla*
English speaker *n* persona *f* de habla inglesa
English-speaking *adj* de habla inglesa
Englishwoman <-women> *n* inglesa *f*
engrave [en·'greɪv] *vt* grabar; **to be ~d in the memory** estar grabado en la memoria
engraver [en·'greɪ·vər] *n* grabador(a) *m(f)*
engraving [en·'greɪ·vɪŋ] *n* grabado *m*
engross [en·'groʊs] *vt* absorber; **to be ~ed in sth** estar absorto en algo
engulf [en·'gʌlf] *vt* hundir
enhance [ɪn·'hæns] *vt* realzar; (*improve or intensify: chances*) aumentar; (*memory*) refrescar; (*photo*) retocar
enigma [ɪ·'nɪg·mə] *n* enigma *m*
enigmatic [ˌen·ɪg·'mæt̬·ɪk] *adj*, **enigmatical** [ˌen·ɪg·'mæt̬·ɪ·kəl] *adj* enigmático, -a
enjoy [en·'dʒɔɪ] **I.** *vt* **1.** (*get pleasure from*) disfrutar de; **to** ~ **doing sth** disfrutar haciendo algo; ~ **yourselves!** ¡que lo paséis bien! **2.** (*have: health*) poseer; **to** ~ **sb's confidence** tener la confianza de alguien; **to** ~ **good health** gozar de buena salud **II.** *vi* pasarlo bien
enjoyable [en·'dʒɔɪ·ə·bəl] *adj* agradable; (*film, book, play*) divertido, -a
enjoyment [en·'dʒɔɪ·mənt] *n* disfrute *m;* **to get real** ~ **out of doing sth** disfrutar realmente haciendo algo
enlarge [en·'lardʒ] **I.** *vt* **1.** (*make bigger*) agrandar; (*expand*) extender; **to** ~ **one's vocabulary** ampliar su léxico **2.** PHOT ampliar **II.** *vi* extenderse
enlargement *n* aumento *m;* (*expanding*) extensión *f;* PHOT ampliación *f*
enlighten [en·'laɪ·tən] *vt* **1.** REL iluminar **2.** (*explain*) instruir; **to** ~ **the public about sth** informar al público de algo
enlightened *adj* (*person*) progresista; REL iluminado, -a; (*age*) ilustrado, -a
enlightenment [en·'laɪ·tən·mənt] *n* **1.** REL iluminación *f* **2.** PHILOS **the** (**Age of**) **Enlightenment** el Siglo de las Luces **3.** (*explanation*) aclaración *f;* **to give sb** ~ **about sth** hacer una aclaración a alguien sobre algo
enlist [en·'lɪst] **I.** *vi* alistarse **II.** *vt* **1.** MIL alistar, reclutar **2.** (*support*) conseguir; **to** ~ **sb's help** conseguir la ayuda de alguien
enliven [en·'laɪ·vən] *vt* avivar; (*person*) animar
en masse [an·'mæs] *adv* en masa
enmesh [en·'meʃ] *vt* coger en una red; **to be ~ed in sth** *a. fig* estar enredado en algo; **to get ~ed in sth** *a. fig* enredarse en algo

enmity ['en·mə·ti] <-ies> *n* enemistad *f*
ennoble [e·'noʊ·bəl] *vt* ennoblecer
enormity [ɪ·'nɔr·mə·ti] <-ies> *n* (*of damage*) magnitud *f;* (*of a task, mistake*) enormidad *f;* (*of a crime*) atrocidad *f*
enormous [ɪ·'nɔr·məs] *adj* enorme; ~ **difficulties** grandes dificultades *fpl*
enough [ɪ·'nʌf] **I.** *adj* (*sufficient*) suficiente, bastante **II.** *adv* bastante; **to be experienced** ~ (**to do sth**) tener la suficiente experiencia (para hacer algo); **to have seen** ~ haber visto demasiado; **she was kind** [*o* **friendly**] ~ **to help me** tuvo la amabilidad de ayudarme; **oddly** [*o* **strangely**] ~ por extraño que parezca **III.** *interj* basta **IV.** *pron* bastante; **to have** ~ **to eat and drink** tener lo suficiente para comer y beber; **I know** ~ **about it** sé lo suficiente acerca de ello; **that should be** ~ eso debería ser suficiente; **more than** ~ más que suficiente; **it is** ~ **for me to know ...** me basta con saber...; **to have had** ~ (**of sb/sth**) estar harto (de alguien/algo); **as if that weren't** ~ por si fuera poco; **that's** (**quite**) ~**!** ¡basta ya!; ~ **is** ~ basta y sobra
enquire [en·'kwaɪr] *vi*, *vt* *s.* **inquire**
enquiry [en·'kwaɪr·i] <-ies> *n* **1.** (*question*) pregunta *f;* **to make an** ~ **into sth** indagar en algo **2.** (*investigation*) investigación *f;* **an** ~ **into sth** una investigación sobre algo; **to hold an** ~ llevar a cabo una investigación
enrage [en·'reɪdʒ] *vt* enfurecer
enraged [en·'reɪdʒd] *adj* enfurecido, -a
enrapture [en·'ræp·tʃər] *vt* embelesar
enrich [en·'rɪtʃ] *vt* enriquecer
enroll <-ll-> *vt*, **enrol** [en·'roʊl] **I.** *vi* inscribirse; **to** ~ **for/in a course** matricularse para/ en un curso **II.** *vt* inscribir; (*in a course*) matricular
enrollment *n*, **enrolment** [en·'roʊl·mənt] *n* inscripción *f;* (*in a course*) matriculación *f*
en route [ˌan·'rut] *adv* en el camino
ensemble [an·'sam·bəl] *n* **1.** MUS, THEAT grupo *m* **2.** FASHION conjunto *m*
ensign ['en·sən] *n* MIL **1.** enseña *f* **2.** (*standard-bearer*) abanderado *m*
enslave [en·'sleɪv] *vt* esclavizar; **to be ~d by sb/sth** ser dominado por alguien/algo
ensnare [en·'sner] *vt liter* atrapar, coger en una trampa; **to be ~d in sth** estar atrapado en algo
ensue [en·'su] *vi form* seguir; **to** ~ **from sth** resultar de algo
ensuing *adj* siguiente
en suite bathroom [ˌan·swit·'bæθ·rum] *n* baño *m* incorporado
ensure [en·'ʃʊr] *vt* asegurar; (*guarantee*) garantizar
ENT *abbr of* **ear, nose and throat** otorrinolaringología *f*
entail [en·'teɪl] *vt* **1.** (*involve*) acarrear; **to** ~ **some risk** entrañar algún riesgo **2.** (*necessitate*) **to** ~ **doing sth** implicar hacer algo
entangle [en·'tæŋ·gəl] *vt* enredar; **to** ~ **oneself** enredarse; **to get ~d in sth** quedar enre-

dado en algo; *fig* verse envuelto en algo; **to get ~d with sb** meterse en un lío con alguien

entanglement *n* enredo *m;* (*situation*) embrollo *m;* **emotional ~s** aventuras *fpl* amorosas

enter ['en·tər] I. *vt* 1. (*go into*) entrar en; (*penetrate*) penetrar 2. (*insert*) introducir; (*into a register*) inscribir; COMPUT: **to ~ data** introducir datos 3. (*compete in*) inscribirse en; **to ~ a competition** presentarse a un concurso 4. (*begin*) entrar en; **to ~ politics** meterse en el mundo de la política; **to ~ adulthood** alcanzar la mayoría de edad 5. (*make known*) anotar; (*claim*) presentar; (*plea*) formular II. *vi* THEAT entrar

◆**enter into** *vi* (*form part of*) tomar parte en; **to ~ marriage** contraer matrimonio; **to ~ conversation** entablar una conversación; **to ~ discussion** meterse en una discusión; **to ~ negotiations** iniciar negociaciones

enter key *n* COMPUT tecla *f* intro

enterprise ['en·tər·praɪz] *n* 1. (*business firm*) empresa *f;* **to start an ~** abrir un negocio 2. (*initiative*) iniciativa *f*

enterprising *adj* emprendedor(a)

entertain [ˌen·tər·'teɪn] I. *vt* 1. (*amuse*) entretener 2. (*guests*) recibir 3. (*consider*) considerar; **to ~ doubts** abrigar dudas; **to ~ an idea/a plan** estudiar una idea/un proyecto II. *vi* (*invite guests*) recibir en casa

entertainer [ˌen·tər·'teɪ·nər] *n* artista *mf*

entertaining *adj* entretenido, -a; (*person*) divertido, -a

entertainment [ˌen·tər·'teɪn·mənt] *n* 1. (*amusement*) diversión *f;* **to provide some ~** proporcionar entretenimiento 2. (*show*) espectáculo *m*

enthrall [en·'θrɔl] *vt* cautivar

enthrone [en·'θroʊn] *vt form* entronizar

enthuse [en·'θuz] I. <-sing> *vi* **to ~ about sth** entusiasmarse muchísimo con algo II. <-sing> *vt* **to ~ sb (with sth)** entusiasmar a alguien (con algo)

enthusiasm [en·'θu·zɪ·æz·əm] *n* entusiasmo *m;* **~ for sth** entusiasmo por algo

enthusiast [ɪn·'θu·zɪ·æst] *n* entusiasta *mf*

enthusiastic [en·ˌθu·zɪ·'æs·tɪk] *adj* entusiasta; **to be ~ about sth** estar entusiasmado con algo

entice [en·'taɪs] *vt* tentar; **to ~ sb to do sth** tentar a alguien a hacer algo; **to ~ sb away from sth** inducir con maña a alguien para que deje algo

enticement *n* tentación *f*

enticing *adj* tentador(a); (*smile*) atractivo, -a

entire [en·'taɪr] *adj* 1. (*whole: life*) todo, -a; **the ~ day** todo el día; **the ~ world** el mundo entero 2. (*total: commitment, devotion*) total 3. (*complete*) entero, -a

entirely *adv* enteramente; **she's/he's ~ to blame** la culpa es entera suya; **to agree ~** estar completamente de acuerdo; **to disagree ~** estar del todo en desacuerdo

entirety [en·'taɪ·rə·ți] *n* **in its ~** en su totalidad

entitle [en·'taɪ· țəl] *vt* 1. (*give right*) autorizar; **to ~ sb to act** autorizar a alguien para actuar; **to ~ sb to a holiday** dar a alguien derecho a vacaciones 2. (*book*) titular

entitled *adj* 1. (*person*) autorizado, -a 2. (*book*) titulado, -a

entitlement [en·'taɪ·țəl·mənt] *n* autorización *f;* (*claim*) derecho *m*

entity ['en·tə·ti] <-ies> *n form* entidad *f;* **legal ~** persona *f* jurídica; **a single/separate ~** un ente único/separado

entomology [ˌen·tə·'mal·ə·dʒi] *n* entomología *f*

entourage [ˌan·tʊ·'raʒ] *n* séquito *m elev*

entrails ['en·treɪlz] *npl* entrañas *fpl*

entrance[1] ['en·trəns] *n* 1. (*act of entering*) entrada *f* 2. (*way in*) entrada *f;* (*door*) puerta *f;* **front ~** entrada *f* principal; **the ~ to sth** la entrada de algo; **to refuse sb ~** [*o* **to refuse ~ to sb**] negar el acceso a alguien 3. THEAT entrada *f* en escena

entrance[2] [en·'træns] *vt* (*cast spell*) encantar

entrance exam(ination) *n* examen *m* de ingreso

entrance fee *n* cuota *f* de entrada [*o* de inscripción]

entrance hall *n* vestíbulo *m*

entrance requirement *n* requisito *m* de entrada

entrant ['en·trənt] *n* participante *mf*

entreat [en·'trit] *vt* **to ~ sb to do sth** suplicar a alguien que haga algo

entreaty [en·'tri·ți] <-ies> *n* ruego *m*

entrée ['an·treɪ] *n* plato [*o* fuerte] principal *m,* principio *m Col*

entrench [en·'trentʃ] *vt passive* 1. **to become ~ed** (*idea*) arraigarse 2. **to ~ oneself** MIL atrincherarse

entrenched *adj* 1. (*idea*) arraigado, -a 2. MIL atrincherado, -a

entrepreneur [ˌan·trə·prə·'nɜr] *n* empresario, -a *m, f*

entrepreneurial spirit [ˌan·trə·prə·'nɜr·i·əl·'spɪr·ɪt] *n* espíritu *m* empresarial

entrust [en·'trʌst] *vt* confiar; **to ~ sth to sb** [*o* **to ~ sb with sth**] confiar algo a alguien; **to ~ sth into sb's care** dejar algo al cuidado de alguien

entry ['en·tri] <-ies> *n* 1. (*act of entering*) entrada *f;* (*joining an organization*) ingreso *m* 2. (*right to enter*) acceso *m;* **to refuse sb ~** negar el acceso a alguien 3. (*entrance*) acceso *m* 4. (*in dictionary*) entrada *f*

entry fee *n* cuota *f* de entrada

entry-level job *n* empleo *m* raso (*empleo en el nivel más bajo de la jerarquía de una empresa*)

entwine [en·'twaɪn] *vt* (*weave*) entretejer; (*twist*) entrelazar; (*plants*) enredar; **to be ~d** (*together*) *fig* estar entrelazados

enumerate [ɪ·'nu·mə·reɪt] *vt* enumerar

enumeration [ɪ·ˌnu·mə·'reɪ·ʃən] *n* enumeración *f*

enunciate [ɪ·'nʌn·si·eɪt] *vt* **1.** (*sound*) pronunciar, articular **2.** (*theory*) enunciar

envelop [en·'vel·əp] *vt* envolver

envelope ['en·və·loʊp] *n* sobre *m,* cierro *m Chile*

enviable ['en·vɪ·ə·bəl] *adj* envidiable

envious ['en·vi·əs] *adj* envidioso, -a; **to be ~ of sb/sth** tener envidia de alguien/algo

environment [en·'vaɪ·ərn·mənt] *n* entorno *m;* **the ~** ECOL el medio ambiente; **home/professional ~** entorno familiar/profesional; **working ~** ambiente *m* de trabajo

environmental [en·,vaɪ·ərn·'men·təl] *adj* ambiental; ECOL medioambiental; **~ damage** daños *mpl* ecológicos; **~ impact** impacto *m* sobre el medio ambiente; **~ pollution** contaminación *f* ambiental; **~ stress** electrosmog *m*

environmentalist [en·,vaɪ·ərn·'men·təl·ɪst] *n* ecologista *mf*

environmentally-friendly [en·,vaɪ·ərn·'men·tə·li·'frend·li] *adj* ecológico, -a

environs [en·'vaɪ·rənz] *npl form* alrededores *mpl*

envisage [en·'vɪz·ɪdʒ] *vt,* **envision** [en·'vɪʒ·ən] *vt* **1.** (*expect*) prever **2.** (*imagine*) formarse una idea de; **to ~ that...** prever [o calcular] que...

envoy ['an·vɔɪ] *n* enviado, -a *m, f*

envy ['en·vi] **I.** *n* envidia *f;* **this car is the ~ of my brother** mi hermano me envidia este coche; **she feels ~ towards her sister** le tiene envidia a su hermana ▸ **to be green with ~** reconcomerse de envidia **II.** <-ie-> *vt* envidiar

enzyme ['en·zaɪm] *n* enzima *f*

EOF *n* COMPUT *abbr of* **end of file** fin *m* de archivo

eon ['i·an] *n* **1.** (*period of time*) eón *m* **2.** *fig* eternidad *f*

EP [,i·'pi] **1.** *abbr of* **extended play** EP *m* **2.** *abbr of* **European plan** sólo alojamiento

EPA [,i·pi·'eɪ] *abbr of* **Environmental Protection Agency** Agencia *f* del Medio Ambiente

ephemeral [ɪ·'fem·ər·əl] *adj a.* BIO efímero, -a

epic ['ep·ɪk] **I.** *n* epopeya *f* **II.** *adj* épico, -a; **~ poetry** poesía épica; **an ~ journey** una odisea *fig*

epicenter ['ep·ɪ·sen·tər] *n* epicentro *m*

epicycle ['ep·ɪ·saɪ·kəl] *n* MATH, ASTR epiciclo *m*

epidemic [,ep·ɪ·'dem·ɪk] **I.** *n* epidemia *f* **II.** *adj* epidémico, -a; **~ proportions** proporciones gigantescas

epidermis [,ep·ɪ·'dɜr·mɪs] <-mes> *n* epidermis *f inv*

epidural *n* MED epidural *f*

epigram ['ep·ɪ·græm] *n* epigrama *m*

epilepsy ['ep·ɪ·lep·si] *n* epilepsia *f*

epileptic [,ep·ɪ·'lep·tɪk] **I.** *n* epiléptico, -a *m, f* **II.** *adj* epiléptico, -a; **~ seizure** ataque epiléptico

epilog ['ep·ɪ·lag] *n* epílogo *m*

Epiphany [ɪ·'pɪf·ə·ni] <-ies> *n* epifanía *f*

episcopacy [ɪ·'pɪs·kə·pə·si] <-ies> *n* episcopado *m*

episcopal [ɪ·'pɪs·kə·pəl] *adj* episcopal

Episcopalian [ɪ·,pɪs·kə·'peɪ·li·ən] **I.** *adj* episcopaliano, -a **II.** *n* episcopaliano, -a *m, f*

episiotomy [ɪ·,pɪz·i·'aṭ·ə·mi] *n* MED episiotomía *f*

episode ['ep·ɪ·soʊd] *n* episodio *m*

episodic [,ep·ɪ·'sad·ɪk] *adj* **1.** (*occasional*) episódico, -a **2.** LIT (*consisting of episodes*) por episodios [o capítulos]

epistle [ɪ·'pɪs·əl] *n* epístola *f*

epistolary [ɪ·'pɪs·tə·ler·i] *adj* epistolar

epitaph ['ep·ɪ·tæf] *n* epitafio *m*

epithet ['ep·ɪ·θet] *n* LING epíteto *m*

epitome [ɪ·'pɪt̬·ə·mi] *n* **1.** (*embodiment*) personificación *f* **2.** (*example*) arquetipo *m;* **the ~ of poor taste** el colmo del mal gusto

epitomize [ɪ·'pɪt̬·ə·maɪz] *vt* personificar

epoch ['ep·ək] *n form* era *f;* **historical ~** época *f* histórica

epoch-making ['ep·ək·,meɪ·kɪŋ] *adj* **it was an ~ discovery** fue un descubrimiento *m* que hizo época

eponymous [ɪ·'pan·ə·məs] *adj* epónimo, -a

epoxy [ɪ·'pak·si] *n* epoxi *m*

equable ['ek·wə·bəl] *adj* (*temperament*) ecuánime; (*climate*) constante; **to have an ~ disposition** ser de talante tranquilo

equal ['i·kwəl] **I.** *adj* **1.** (*the same*) igual; (*treatment*) equitativo, -a; **to have ~ reason to do sth** tener las mismas razones para hacer algo; **of ~ size** de la misma medida; **on ~ terms** en igualdad de condiciones **2.** (*able to do*) **to be ~ to a task** ser capaz de realizar una tarea **II.** *n* igual *mf;* **it has no ~** no hay nada parecido **III.** *vt* **1.** **~s** MATH ser igual a **2.** (*match*) igualar

equality [ɪ·'kwal·ə·ti] *n* igualdad *f*

equalization [,i·kwə·lɪ·'zeɪ·ʃən] *n* equiparación *f*

equalize ['i·kwə·laɪz] *vt* nivelar

equalizer ['i·kwə·laɪ·zər] *n* **1.** MUS ecualizador *m* **2.** SPORTS tanto *m* del empate; (*in soccer*) gol *m* del empate

equally ['i·kwə·li] *adv* igualmente; **to contribute ~ to sth** contribuir por igual a algo; **to divide sth ~** dividir algo equitativamente

equal opportunity *n* igualdad *f* de oportunidades

equal(s) sign *n* MATH signo *m* de igual

equanimity [,ek·wə·'nɪm·ə·ti] *n* ecuanimidad *f;* **to receive sth with ~** recibir algo serenamente

equate [ɪ·'kweɪt] **I.** *vt* equiparar **II.** *vi* **to ~ to sth** ser equivalente [o igual] a algo

equation [ɪ·'kweɪ·ʒən] *n* ecuación *f*

equator [ɪ·'kweɪ·ţər] *n* ecuador *m*

equatorial [,ek·wə·'tɔr·i·əl] *adj* ecuatorial

Equatorial Guinea *n* Guinea *f* Ecuatorial

equestrian [ɪ·'kwes·tri·ən] **I.** *adj* ecuestre; **~ events** pruebas hípicas; **~ statue** estatua *f* ecuestre **II.** *n* (*man*) jinete *m;* (*woman*) amazona *f*

equidistant [ˌiˌkwɪˈdɪsˌtənt] *adj* equidistante
equilateral [ˌiˌkwɪˈlætˌərˌəl] *adj* MATH equilátero, -a
equilibrium [ˌiˌkwɪˈlɪbˌriˌəm] *n* equilibrio *m*
equinoctial [ˌiˌkwɪˈnakˌʃəl] *adj* equinoccial
equinox [ˈiˌkwɪˌnaks] <-es> *n* equinoccio *m;* **fall** ~ equinoccio de otoño; **spring** ~ equinoccio de primavera
equip [ɪˈkwɪp] <-pp-> *vt* **1.** (*fit out*) equipar; **to** ~ **sth/sb with sth** proveer algo/a alguien de algo **2.** (*prepare*) preparar
equipment [ɪˈkwɪpˌmənt] *n* equipo *m;* **camping** ~ accesorios *mpl* de cámping; **office** ~ *mobiliario, máquinas y material de oficina*
equitable [ˈekˌwɪˌtəˌbəl] *adj* equitativo, -a
equity [ˈekˌwəˌti] <-ies> *n* **1.** (*fairness*) equidad *f* **2. equities** FIN acciones *fpl* ordinarias
eq(uiv). *abbr of* **equivalent** equivalente
equivalence [ɪˈkwɪvˌəˌləns] *n* equivalencia *f*
equivalent [ɪˈkwɪvˌəˌlənt] **I.** *adj* equivalente; **to be** ~ **to sth** equivaler a algo **II.** *n* equivalente *m*
equivocal [ɪˈkwɪvˌəˌkəl] *adj* equívoco, -a
equivocate [ɪˈkwɪvˌəˌkeɪt] *vi form* hablar de forma equívoca
equivocation [ɪˌkwɪvˌəˈkeɪˌʃən] *n* ambigüedad *f*
ER *n abbr of* **emergency room** urgencias *fpl*
era [ˈɪrˌə] *n* era *f;* **communist** ~ era comunista; **postwar** ~ época *f* de la posguerra; **to usher in a new** ~ marcar el cominezo de una nueva era
eradicate [ɪˈrædˌɪˌkeɪt] *vt* erradicar
erase [ɪˈreɪs] *vt a.* COMPUT borrar; **to** ~ **a deficit** eliminar un déficit
eraser [ɪˈreɪˌsər] *n* goma *f* de borrar
erasure [ɪˈreɪˌʃər] *n* borradura *f*
ere [er] *prep liter* antes de; ~ **long** dentro de poco **II.** *conj liter* antes de que
erect [ɪˈrekt] **I.** *adj* erguido, -a; ANAT erecto, -a **II.** *vt* erigir; (*construct*) construir; (*put up*) levantar
erectile [ɪˈrekˌtəl] *adj* ANAT eréctil
erectile dysfunction *n* disfunción *f* eréctil
erection [ɪˈrekˌʃən] *n* **1.** ANAT erección *f* **2.** ARCHIT construcción *f*
erg [ɜrg] *n* PHYS ergio *m*
ergo [ˈerˌgoʊ] *adv* por lo tanto
ergonomic [ˌɜrˌgəˈnamˌɪk] *adj* ergonómico, -a
ergonomics *n* ergonomía *f*
ermine [ˈɜrˌmɪn] *n* armiño *m*
erode [ɪˈroʊd] **I.** *vt* erosionar **II.** *vi* erosionarse
erogenous [ɪˈradʒˌəˌnəs] *adj* erógeno, -a
erogenous zone *n* zona *f* erógena
erosion [ɪˈroʊˌʒən] *n* erosión *f*
erotic [ɪˈraˌtɪk] *adj* erótico, -a
eroticism [ɪˈraˌtəˌsɪzˌəm] *n* erotismo *m*
err [ɜr] *vi* errar; **to** ~ **on the side of sth** pecar (por exceso) de algo; **to** ~ **on the side of caution** pecar de cauteloso ▸ **to** ~ **is human** *prov* errar es humano *prov*
errand [ˈerˌənd] *n* recado *m;* **to run an** ~ (salir a) hacer un recado; **an** ~ **of mercy** *form* una

misión de caridad
errand boy *n* chico *m* de los recados
errant [ˈerˌənt] *adj* (*off course*) fallido, -a; (*deviant: youngster*) descarriado, -a; (*ways*) poco ortodoxo, -a
erratic [ɪˈrætˌɪk] *adj* **1.** (*inconsistent: heartbeat*) irregular; (*behavior*) imprevisible **2.** (*offline*) desconectado, -a; (*course*) errático, -a **3.** GEO errático, -a
erratum [ɪˈraˌtəm] <-ta> *n form* errata *f*
erroneous [ɪˈroʊˌniˌəs] *adj* erróneo, -a; ~ **assumption** suposición equivocada
error [ˈerˌər] *n* error *m;* **to do sth in** ~ hacer algo por equivocación; **human** ~ error humano ▸ **to see the** ~ **of one's ways** darse cuenta de lo mal que uno ha actuado; **to show sb the** ~ **of his/her ways** demostrar a alguien lo equivocado de su actuación
error message *n* COMPUT mensaje *m* de error
error-prone *adj* propenso, -a a errores
ersatz [ˈerˌzats] *adj* ~ **coffee** sucedáneo m del café
erudite [ˈerˌjəˌdaɪt] *adj* erudito, -a
erudition [ˌerˌjuˈdɪʃˌən] *n* erudición *f*
erupt [ɪˈrʌpt] *vi* **1.** (*explode: volcano*) entrar en erupción; *fig* estallar **2.** MED salir
eruption [ɪˈrʌpˌʃən] *n* erupción *f;* *fig* estallido *m*
escalate [ˈesˌkəˌleɪt] **I.** *vi* (*increase*) aumentar; (*incidents*) intensificarse; **to** ~ **into sth** terminar en algo **II.** *vt* intensificar
escalation [ˌesˌkəˈleɪˌʃən] *n* escalada *f;* ~ **of tension** escalada de la tensión
escalator [ˈesˌkəˌleɪˌtər] *n* escalera *f* mecánica
escalope [ˌesˌkəˈloʊp] *n* escalope *m*
escapade [ˌesˌkəˈpeɪd] *n* aventura *f;* (*mischievous*) travesura *f*
escape [ɪˈskeɪp] **I.** *vi* escaparse; (*person*) huir de; **to** ~ **from** escaparse de; **to** ~ **from a program** COMPUT salir de un programa **II.** *vt* escapar a; (*avoid*) evitar; **to** ~ **sb('s attention)** pasar desapercibido a alguien; **nothing** ~**s his attention** no se le escapa ni una; **the word** ~**s me** se me ha ido la palabra (de la cabeza); **a cry** ~**d him** se le escapó un grito **III.** *n* **1.** (*act*) fuga *f;* **to make a narrow** ~ salvarse por muy poco **2.** (*outflow*) escape *m* **3.** LAW ~ **clause** cláusula *f* de excepción
escapee [ɪˈskeɪˈpi] *n* fugitivo, -a *m, f*
escapism [ɪˈskeɪˌpɪzˌəm] *n* escapismo *m*
escapist I. *n* escapista *mf* **II.** *adj* escapista; ~ **literature** literatura *f* de evasión
escarole [ˈesˌkəˌroʊl] *n* escarola *f*
escarpment [ɪˈskarpˌmənt] *n* escarpa *f*
eschew [esˈtʃu] *vt form* evitar
escort [ˈesˌkɔrt] **I.** *vt* acompañar; (*politician*) escoltar **II.** *n* **1.** (*companion*) acompañante *mf* **2.** (*paid companion*) chico, -a *m, f* de compañía **3.** (*guard*) escolta *f*
ESE *n abbr of* **east-southeast** ESE *m*
Eskimo [ˈesˌkəˌmoʊ] <Eskimo o -s> *n* **1.** (*person*) esquimal *mf* **2.** LING esquimal *m*
Eskimo pie® *n* barra de helado de vainilla

bañado en chocolate

ESL [ˌiˑesˑ'el] *n abbr of* **English as a second language** inglés *m* como segunda lengua

ESOL ['iˑsal] *n abbr of* **English for speakers of other languages** inglés para extranjeros

esophagus [ɪ'safˑəˑgəs] *n* esófago *m*

esoteric [ˌesˑəˑ'terˑɪk] *adj* esotérico, -a

ESP [ˌiˑesˑ'pi] *n abbr of* **extrasensory perception** percepción *f* extrasensorial

esp. *abbr of* **especially** especialmente

espadrille ['esˑpəˑdrɪl] *n* alpargata *f*

especial [ɪ'speʃˑəl] *adj* especial

especially [ɪ'speʃˑəˑli] *adv* **1.** (*particularly*) especialmente; **I bought this ~ for you** lo compré expresamente para ti **2.** (*in particular*) en particular

espionage ['esˑpiˑəˑnaʒ] *n* espionaje *m;* **industrial ~** espionaje industrial

esplanade ['esˑpləˑnad] *n* paseo *m* marítimo

espousal [ɪ'spaʊˑzəl] *n form* apoyo *m*

espouse [ɪ'spaʊz] *vt* apoyar

espresso [ɪ'spresˑoʊ] <-s> *n* café *m* exprés

Esq. *abbr of* **Esquire** Sr.

essay¹ ['esˑeɪ] *n* **1.** LIT ensayo *m* **2.** SCHOOL redacción *f;* **an ~ about sth** una redacción sobre algo

essay² [eˑ'seɪ] *vt* **1.** (*try*) intentar hacer **2.** (*test*) probar

essayist *n* ensayista *mf*

essence ['esˑəns] *n* **1.** esencia *f;* **in ~** en resumidas cuentas; **time is of the ~** el tiempo es de vital importancia **2.** (*in food*) esencia *f*, extracto *m*

essential [ɪ'senˑʃəl] **I.** *adj* esencial; (*difference*) fundamental; **to be ~ to sb/sth** ser esencial para alguien/algo **II.** *n* **the ~s** los elementos básicos [*o* esenciales]; **the bare ~s** lo justamente necesario

essentially [ɪ'senˑʃəˑli] *adv* esencialmente

essential oil *n* aceite *m* esencial

est. 1. *abbr of* **estimated** est. **2.** *abbr of* **established** fundado, -a

establish [ɪ'stæbˑlɪʃ] **I.** *vt* **1.** (*found*) fundar; (*commission, hospital*) crear; (*dictatorship*) instaurar **2.** (*begin: relationship*) entablar **3.** (*set: precedent*) sentar; (*priorities, norm*) establecer **4.** (*secure*) asegurar; (*order*) imponer; **he ~ed his authority over the workers** afirmó su autoridad sobre los obreros; **to ~ a reputation as a pianist** hacerse un nombre como pianista **5.** (*demonstrate*) **to ~ sb as sth** acreditar a alguien como algo **6.** (*determine*) determinar, establecer; (*facts*) verificar; (*truth*) comprobar; **to ~ whether/ where...** determinar si/dónde...; **to ~ that...** comprobar que... **7.** ADMIN **to ~ residence** fijar la residencia **II.** *vi* establecerse

established [ɪ'stæbˑlɪʃt] *adj* **1.** (*founded*) fundado, -a **2.** (*fact*) comprobado, -a; (*procedures*) establecido, -a

establishment [ɪ'stæbˑlɪʃˑmənt] *n* **1.** (*business*) empresa *f;* **family ~** empresa *f* familiar **2.** (*organization*) establecimiento *m;* **edu-**

cational ~ centro *m* educativo; **financial ~** institución *f* financiera; **the Establishment** POL la clase dirigente

estate [ɪ'steɪt] *n* **1.** (*piece of land*) finca *f;* **country ~** finca *f*, hacienda *f* AmL **2.** LAW (*possessions after death*) patrimonio *m;* **industrial ~** polígono *m* industrial

estate tax *n* impuesto *m* sobre sucesiones

esteem [ɪ'stim] **I.** *n* estima *f;* **to fall/rise in sb's ~** perder/ganarse la estima de alguien; **to hold sb in high/low ~** tener a alguien en gran/poca estima **II.** *vt* **1.** (*respect*) apreciar, valorar **2.** (*consider*) considerar, estimar; **to ~ it an honor to do sth** considerar un honor (poder) hacer algo

esteemed *adj* apreciado, -a, valorado, -a; **highly ~** muy apreciado

esthetic [es·'θetˑɪk] *adj* estético, -a

esthetics *n* estética *f*

estimable ['esˑtɪˑməˑbəl] *adj form* estimable

estimate¹ ['esˑtɪˑmeɪt] *vt* calcular; **to ~ that...** calcular que...

estimate² ['esˑtɪˑmɪt] *n* cálculo *m* (aproximado); **a rough ~** *inf* un cálculo aproximado

estimated ['esˑtɪˑmeɪˑtɪd] *adj* estimado, -a

estimation [ˌesˑtɪˑ'meɪˑʃən] *n* opinión *f;* **in my ~** a mi juicio

Estonia [es·'toʊˑniˑə] *n* Estonia *f*

Estonian [es·'toʊˑniˑən] **I.** *adj* estonio, -a **II.** *n* **1.** (*person*) estonio, -a *m, f* **2.** LING estonio *m*

estrange [ɪ'streɪndʒ] *vt* **to ~ sb from sb/sth** distanciar a alguien de alguien/algo

estranged *adj* (*distance*) distanciado, -a; (*state*) separado, -a

estrangement [ɪ'streɪndʒˑmənt] *n* distanciamiento *m*

estrogen ['esˑtrəˑdʒən] *n* estrógeno *m*

estuary ['esˑtʃuˑerˑi] <-ies> *n* estuario *m*

ETA [ˌiˑtiˑ'eɪ] *abbr of* **estimated time of arrival** hora *f* prevista de llegada

et al. [et·'æl] *abbr of* **et alii** (= **and others**) et al.

etc. *abbr of* **et cetera** etc.

etcetera [ɪtˑ'setˑərˑə] *adv* etcétera

etch [etʃ] *vt* **1.** grabar (al agua fuerte) **2.** *fig* **to be ~ed in sb's memory** estar grabado en la memoria de alguien

etcher *n* aguafuertista *mf*

etching *n* aguafuerte *m*

ETD *abbr of* **estimated time of departure** hora *f* prevista de salida

eternal [ɪ'tɜrˑnəl] *adj* **1.** (*lasting forever: life*) eterno, -a **2.** (*constant: complaints*) constante, incesante

eternally [ɪ'tɜrˑnəˑli] *adv* **1.** (*forever*) eternamente **2.** (*constantly*) constantemente, incesantemente

eternity [ɪ'tɜrˑnəˑt̬i] *n* eternidad *f;* **to seem like an ~** parecer una eternidad; **to wait an ~ for sb** esperar una eternidad a alguien

ether ['iˑθər] *n* éter *m*

ethereal [ɪ'θɪrˑiˑəl] *adj* etéreo, -a

ethic ['eθˑɪk] *n* **work ~** ética *f* del trabajo

ethical *adj* ético, -a
ethics *n* + *sing vb* ética *f*
Ethiopia [ˌiˈθiˈouˈpiˈə] *n* Etiopía *f*
Ethiopian [ˌiˈθiˈouˈpiˈən] **I.** *n* etíope *mf*
II. *adj* etíope
ethnic [ˈeθˈnɪk] *adj* étnico, -a; **~ cleansing** limpieza étnica; **~ costumes** trajes *mpl* tradicionales
ethnology [eθˈnalˈəˈdʒi] *n* etnología *f*
ethos [ˈiˈθas] *n* espíritu *m;* **the working-class ~** los valores de la clase trabajadora
ethyl alcohol [ˈeθˈəlˈælˈkəˈhɔl] *n* alcohol *m* etílico
etiquette [ˈeţˈiˈkɪt] *n* etiqueta *f;* **court ~** etiqueta de palacio
etymological [ˌeţˈəˈməˈladʒˈiˈkəl] *adj* etimológico, -a
etymology [ˌeţˈiˈmalˈəˈdʒi] *n* etimología *f*
EU [ˌiˈju] *n abbr of* **European Union** UE *f*
eucalyptus [ˌjuˈkəˈlɪpˈtəs] <-es *o* -ti> *n* eucalipto *m*
eucalyptus oil *n* bálsamo *m* de eucalipto
Eucharist [ˈjuˈkərˈɪst] *n* REL **the ~** la Eucaristía
euchre [ˈjuˈkər] *n juego de cartas*
eulogize [ˈjuˈləˈdʒaɪz] **I.** *vt form* elogiar **II.** *vi form* **to ~ over sth/sb** elogiar algo/a alguien
eulogy [ˈjuˈləˈdʒi] <-ies> *n form* **1.** (*high praise*) elogio *m* **2.** LIT panegírico *m;* **to deliver a ~** dedicar un panegírico
eunuch [ˈjuˈnək] *n* eunuco *m*
euphemism [ˈjuˈfəˈmɪzˈəm] *n* eufemismo *m*
euphemistic [ˌjuˈfəˈmɪsˈtɪk] *adj* eufemístico, -a
euphony [ˈjuˈfəˈni] *n form* eufonía *f*
euphoria [juˈfɔrˈiˈə] *n* euforia *f*
euphoric [juˈfɔrˈɪk] *adj* eufórico, -a
EUR *n abbr of* **Euro** EUR *m*
Eurasia [juˈreɪˈʒə] *n* Eurasia *f*
Eurasian [juˈreɪˈʒən] **I.** *adj* euroasiático, -a **II.** *n* euroasiático, -a *m, f*
eurhythmics [juˈrɪðˈmɪks] *n* + *sing vb* gimnasia *f* rítmica
euro [ˈjurˈou] *n* euro *m*
Eurocrat [ˈjurˈəˈkræt] *n* eurócrata *mf*
Europe [ˈjurˈəp] *n* Europa *f*
European [ˌjurˈəˈpiˈən] **I.** *adj* europeo, -a **II.** *n* europeo, -a *m, f*
European Union *n* Unión *f* Europea
euthanasia [ˌjuˈθəˈneɪˈʒə] *n* eutanasia *f*
evacuate [ɪˈvækˈjuˈeɪt] *vt* (*people*) evacuar; (*building*) desocupar
evacuation [ɪˌvækˈjuˈeɪˈʃən] *n* evacuación *f;* **~ of the bowels** MED evacuación *f*
evacuee [ɪˌvækˈjuˈi] *n* evacuado, -a *m, f*
evade [ɪˈveɪd] *vt* (*responsibility, person*) eludir; (*police*) escaparse de; (*taxes*) evadir; **to ~ doing sth** evitar hacer algo
evaluate [ɪˈvælˈjuˈeɪt] *vt* (*value*) tasar; (*result*) evaluar; (*person*) examinar
evaluation [ɪˌvælˈjuˈeɪˈʃən] *n* evaluación *f;* (*of an experience*) valoración *f;* (*of a book*) crítica *f*
evangelical [ˌiˈvænˈdʒelˈiˈkəl] **I.** *n* evangélico, -a *m, f* **II.** *adj* evangélico, -a
evangelist [ɪˈvænˈdʒəˈlɪst] *n* evangelista *mf*
evangelize [ɪˈvænˈdʒəˈlaɪz] **I.** *vt* evangelizar **II.** *vi* evangelizar
evaporate [ɪˈvæpˈəˈreɪt] **I.** *vt* evaporar **II.** *vi* evaporarse; *fig* desaparecer
evaporated milk *n* leche evaporada
evaporation [ɪˌvæpˈəˈreɪˈʃən] *n* evaporación *f*
evasion [ɪˈveɪˈʒən] *n* **1.** (*of tax, responsibility*) evasión *f* **2.** (*avoidance*) evasiva *f*
evasive [ɪˈveɪˈsɪv] *adj* evasivo, -a
eve [iv] *n* víspera *f;* **on the ~ of** en vísperas de; **Christmas Eve** Nochebuena *f;* **New Year's Eve** Nochevieja *f*
Eve [iv] *n* Eva *f*
even [ˈiˈvən] **I.** *adj* **1.** (*level*) llano, -a; (*surface*) liso, -a **2.** (*equalized*) igualado, -a; **the chances are about ~** hay casi las mismas posibilidades; **to be on ~ terms** estar en las mismas condiciones; **to get ~ with sb** ajustar cuentas con alguien **3.** (*of same size, amount*) igual **4.** (*constant, regular*) uniforme; (*rate*) constante **5.** (*fair*) ecuánime **6.** MATH par **II.** *vt* **1.** (*make level*) nivelar; (*surface*) allanar **2.** (*equalize*) igualar **III.** *adv* **1.** (*indicates the unexpected*) incluso; **not ~** ni siquiera **2.** (*despite*) **~ if...** aunque... +*subj;* **~ so...** aun así...; **~ though...** aunque... +*subj* **3.** (*used to intensify*) hasta **4.** + *comp* (*all the more*) aún; **it will be ~ colder** hará incluso más frío
◆ **even out I.** *vi* (*prices*) nivelarse **II.** *vt* igualar
◆ **even up** *vt* igualar
evening [ˈivˈnɪŋ] *n* (*early*) tarde *f;* (*late*) noche *f;* **good ~!** ¡buenas tardes/noches!; **in the ~** por la tarde/noche; **that ~** esa noche; **the previous ~** la noche anterior; **every Monday ~** cada lunes por la noche; **on Monday ~** el lunes por la noche; **during the ~** durante la tarde; **one July ~** una noche de julio; **8 o'clock in the ~** las 8 de la tarde; **at the end of the ~** al final de la tarde; **all ~ (long)** toda la tarde
evening class *n* clase *f* nocturna
evening dress *n* (*for woman*) vestido *m* [*o* traje *m*] de noche; (*for man*) traje *m* de etiqueta; **to wear ~** ir de etiqueta
evening edition *n* edición *f* vespertina
evening gown *n* traje *m* de noche
evening (news)paper *n* periódico *m* de la tarde
evening prayer *n* oración *f* de la tarde
evening star *n* estrella *f* vespertina
evenly [ˈiˈvənˈli] *adv* **1.** (*calmly*) apaciblemente; **to state sth ~** decir algo sin alterarse **2.** (*equally*) igualmente; **to divide sth ~** dividir algo de forma equitativa
evenness [ˈiˈvənˈnɪs] *n* **1.** uniformidad *f* **2.** (*calmness*) serenidad *f*
even-steven *adj,* **even-Steven** *adj inf* **1.** (*settled up: transaction*) en paz; **to be ~** estar en paz **2.** SPORTS (*game*) empatado, -a; **to be ~** estar a mano

event [ɪ·'vent] *n* **1.** (*happening*) aconteci-miento *m,* evento *m;* **sports** ~ acontecimiento *m* deportivo; **to be swept along by the tide of** ~**s** dejarse llevar por los acontecimientos **2.** (*case*) caso *m;* **in any** [*o* **either**] ~ en cualquier caso; **in the** ~ (**that**) **it rains** en caso de que llueva

even-tempered ['i·vən·'tem·pərd] *adj* ecuá-nime

eventful [ɪ·'vent·fəl] *adj* (*journey, week*) muy movido, -a; (*decision*) memorable

eventual [ɪ·'ven·tʃʊ·əl] *adj* final

eventuality [ɪ·ˌven·tʃʊ·'æl·ə·ti] <-ies> *n inv* eventualidad *f*

eventually [ɪ·'ven·tʃʊ·ə·li] *adv* **1.** (*finally*) final-mente **2.** (*some day*) con el tiempo

ever ['ev·ər] *adv* **1.** (*on any occasion*) alguna vez; **have you** ~ **been to Hawaii?** ¿has estado alguna vez en Hawai?; **for the first time** ~ por primera vez; **the hottest day** ~ el día mas caluroso; **better than** ~ mejor que nunca; **have you** ~ **seen such a thing!** ¡habráse visto semejante cosa!; **would you** ~ **dye your hair?** ¿te teñirías el pelo? **2.** (*in negative statements*) nunca, jamás; **nobody has** ~ **heard of him** nadie ha oído nunca ha-blar de él; **never** ~ nunca jamás; **hardly** ~ casi nunca; **nothing** ~ **happens** nunca pasa nada; **don't you** ~ **do that again!** ¡no se te ocurra volver a hacerlo! **3.** (*always*) ~ **after** desde entonces; **as** ~ como siempre; ~ **since...** desde que...; ~ **since** (*since then*) desde entonces **4.** (*used to intensify*) **who** ~ **was that woman?** ¿quién demonios era esa mujer?; **all he** ~ **does is** +*infin* lo único que hace es +*infin;* **don't you** ~ **come here again!** ¡no se te ocurra volver por aquí!

everglade ['ev·ər·gleɪd] *n tierra baja panta-nosa cubierta de altas hierbas*

evergreen ['ev·ər·grin] **I.** *n* planta *f* de hoja perenne **II.** *adj* de hoja perenne; *fig* impe-recedero, -a

everlasting [ˌev·ər·'læs·tɪŋ] *adj* **1.** (*undying*) imperecedero, -a; (*gratitude, love*) eterno, -a *f* **2.** (*incessant*) interminable

evermore [ˌev·ər·'mɔr] *adv liter* eternamente; **for** ~ por siempre jamás

every ['ev·ri] *adj* **1.** (*each*) cada; ~ **time** cada vez; **her** ~ **wish** su más mínimo deseo; **not** ~ **book can be borrowed** no se prestan todos los libros **2.** (*all*) todo, -a; ~ **one of them** todos y cada uno de ellos; **in** ~ **way** de todas las maneras **3.** (*repeated*) ~ **other week** una semana sí y otra no; ~ **now and then** [*o* **again**] de vez en cuando ▶~ **little bit helps** *prov* cualquier ayuda es buena

everybody ['ev·ri·ˌbad·i] *pron indef, sing* todos, todo el mundo; ~ **but Paul** todos menos Paul; ~ **who agrees** todos los que están de acuerdo

everybody else *pron* todos los demás

everyday ['ev·ri·deɪ] *adj* diario, -a; (*clothes*) de diario; (*event*) ordinario, -a; (*language*) co-

rriente; (*life*) cotidiano, -a

everyone ['ev·ri·wʌn] *pron s.* **everybody**

everything ['ev·ri·θɪŋ] *pron indef, sing* todo; **is** ~ **all right?** ¿está todo bien?; ~ **they drink** todo lo que beben; **to be** ~ **to sb** serlo todo para alguien; **to do** ~ **necessary/one can** hacer todo lo necesario/lo posible; **time is** ~ el tiempo lo es todo; **money isn't** ~ la riqueza no lo es todo

everywhere ['ev·ri·wer] *adv* en todas partes; ~ **else** en cualquier otro sitio; **to look** ~ **for sth** buscar algo por todas partes; **to travel** ~ viajar a todas partes

evict [ɪ·'vɪkt] *vt* desahuciar

eviction [ɪ·'vɪk·ʃən] *n* desahucio *m*

evidence ['ev·ɪ·dəns] *n* **1.** (*sign*) indicios *mpl* **2.** (*proof*) prueba *f* **3.** (*testimony*) testimonio *m;* **based on the** ~ basado en el testimonio; **to turn state's** ~ **against sb** testificar en contra **4.** (*view*) evidencia *f;* **to be in** ~ ser manifiesto

evident ['ev·ɪ·dənt] *adj* evidente; **to be** ~ ser evidente; **to be** ~ **to sb** ser evidente para al-guien; **to be** ~ **in sth** manifestarse en algo; **it is** ~ **that...** está claro que...

evidently *adv* evidentemente

evil ['i·vəl] **I.** *adj* malo, -a; ~ **spirit** espíritu maligno; **to have an** ~ **tongue** tener una len-gua afilada **II.** *n* mal *m;* **social** ~ lacra *f* social; **an aura of** ~ un aura de maldad; **good and** ~ el bien y el mal; **the lesser of two** ~**s** el menor de dos males

evildoer [ˌi·vəl·'du·ər] *n* malhechor(a) *m(f)*

evil eye *n* mal *m* de ojo; **to give sb the** ~ **eye** echar a alguien mal de ojo

evil-minded *adj* malintencionado, -a

evil-tempered *adj* de muy mal genio; **to be** ~ tener muy mal genio

evince [ɪ·'vɪns] *vt form* dar señales de; **to** ~ **interest** mostrar interés

evocation [ˌev·ə·'keɪ·ʃən] *n form* evocación *f*

evocative [ɪ·'vak·ə·tɪv] *adj* evocador(a); **an** ~ **image** una imagen sugerente; **to be** ~ **of sth** evocar algo

evoke [ɪ·'vouk] *vt* evocar

evolution [ˌev·ə·'lu·ʃən] *n* evolución *f; fig* des-arrollo *m*

evolutionary theory *n* teoría *f* evolucionista

evolve [ɪ·'valv] **I.** *vi* (*gradually develop*) desa-rrollarse; (*animals*) evolucionar; **to** ~ **into sth** convertirse en algo **II.** *vt* desarrollar; **to** ~ **new forms of life** crear nuevas formas de vida

ewe [ju] *n* oveja *f*

ewer ['ju·ər] *n* aguamanil *m*

ex [eks] <-es> *n inf* ex *mf*

exacerbate [ɪg·'zæs·ər·beɪt] *vt* exacerbar

exact [ɪg·'zækt] **I.** *adj* exacto, -a; **to be** ~ **in one's reporting** ser muy preciso al informar; **the** ~ **opposite** justo lo contrario **II.** *vt* exigir; **to** ~ **sth from sb** exigir algo a alguien

exacting *adj* exigente

exactitude [ɪg·'zæk·tə·tud] *n* exactitud *f*

exactly [ɪg·'zækt·li] *adv* exactamente; ~ **like...** justo como...; **how/what/where** ~**...** cómo/

qué/dónde exactamente...; **I don't ~ agree with that** no estoy del todo de acuerdo en eso; **not ~** no precisamente; **~!** ¡exacto!

exactness [ɪg·'zækt·nɪs] *n* exactitud *f*

exaggerate [ɪg·'zædʒ·ə·reɪt] *vi, vt* exagerar; **let's not ~!** ¡no exageremos!

exaggerated [ɪg·'zædʒ·ə·reɪ·tɪd] *adj* exagerado, -a; **greatly ~** muy exagerado

exaggeration [ɪg·,zædʒ·ə·'reɪ·ʃən] *n* exageración *f;* **it's no ~ to say that...** no es exagerado decir que...

exalt [ɪg·'zɔlt] *vt* **1.** (*praise*) exaltar; (*honor*) ensalzar; **to ~ sth as a virtue** elevar algo a la categoría de virtud **2.** (*raise rank*) ascender

exaltation [,eg·zɔl·'teɪ·ʃən] *n* exaltación *f*

exalted [ɪg·'zɔl·tɪd] *adj* **1.** (*elevated*) elevado, ·a; **~ rank** alto rango **2.** (*jubilant*) exaltado, -a

exam [ɪg·'zæm] *n* examen *m*

examination [ɪg·,zæm·ɪ·'neɪ·ʃən] *n* **1.** (*exam*) examen *m* **2.** (*investigation*) investigación *f;* **medical ~** reconocimiento *m* médico **3.** LAW interrogatorio *m*

examine [ɪg·'zæm·ɪn] *vt* **1.** (*study*) estudiar; **to ~ the effects of sth** estudiar los efectos de algo **2.** MED hacer un reconocimiento médico de **3.** LAW interrogar

examinee [ɪg·,zæm·ɪ·'ni] *n* examinando, -a *m, f*

examiner [ɪg·'zæm·ɪn·ər] *n* examinador(a) *m(f)*

example [ɪg·'zæm·pəl] *n* **1.** (*sample, model*) ejemplo *m;* **for ~** por ejemplo; **to be a shining ~ of sth** ser un ejemplo magnífico de algo; **to follow sb's ~** seguir el ejemplo de alguien; **to give (sb) an ~ (of sth)** dar (a alguien) un ejemplo (de algo); **to set a good ~** dar (un) buen ejemplo **2.** (*copy*) ejemplar *m*

exasperate [ɪg·'zæs·pə·reɪt] *vt* exasperar; **he ~s me** me saca de quicio

exasperating [ɪg·'zæs·pə·reɪ·tɪŋ] *adj* irritante

exasperation [ɪg·,zæs·pə·'reɪ·ʃən] *n* exasperación *f*

ex-boyfriend *n* ex novio *m*

excavate ['ek·skə·veɪt] I. *vt* **1.** (*expose*) desenterrar **2.** (*hollow*) excavar II. *vi* excavar

excavation [,ek·skə·'veɪ·ʃən] *n* excavación *f*

excavator ['ek·skə·veɪ·tər] *n* excavadora *f*

exceed [ɪk·'sid] *vt* exceder; (*outshine*) sobrepasar

exceedingly *adv* excesivamente

excel [ɪk·'sel] <-ll-> I. *vi* sobresalir; **to ~ at** [*o* **in**] **sth** destacar en algo II. *vt* **to ~ oneself** lucirse; **to ~ all others** superar a todos los demás

excellence ['ek·sə·ləns] *n* excelencia *f*

Excellency ['ek·sə·lən·si] *n* Excelencia *f;* **His ~** Su Excelencia; **(Your) ~** (Su/Vuestra) Excelencia

excellent ['ek·sə·lənt] *adj* excelente

except [ɪk·'sept] I. *prep* **~ (for)** excepto, salvo, zafo *AmL;* **to do nothing ~ wait** no hacer nada más que esperar II. *vt form* exceptuar; **to ~ sth/sb from sth** excluir algo/a alguien de

algo; **children under the age of 14 are ~ed** a excepción de los niños menores de 14 años

excepting *prep* excepto, salvo

exception [ɪk·'sep·ʃən] *n* excepción *f;* **to be an ~** ser una excepción; **to make an ~** hacer una excepción; **with the ~ of...** con excepción de...; **to take ~ (to sth)** ofenderse (por algo); **I take great ~ to your last comment** me ha molestado mucho tu último comentario ▸ **the ~ proves the rule** *prov* la excepción confirma la regla *prov*

exceptional [ɪk·'sep·ʃə·nəl] *adj* excepcional

exceptionally [ɪk·'sep·ʃə·nə·li] *adv* excepcionalmente; **to be ~ clever** ser especialmente listo

excerpt ['ek·sɜrpt] *n* extracto *m*

excess [ɪk·'ses] <-es> *n* exceso *m;* **to eat to ~** comer en exceso; **to carry sth to ~** llevar algo al exceso; **in ~ of** superior a

excess baggage *n s.* **excess luggage**

excessive [ɪk·'ses·ɪv] *adj* excesivo, -a; (*claim*) exagerado, -a; (*violence*) gratuito, -a

excess luggage *n* exceso *m* de equipaje

excess supply *n* exceso *m* de oferta

exchange [ɪks·'tʃeɪndʒ] I. *vt* **1.** (*trade for the equivalent*) cambiar **2.** (*interchange*) intercambiar; **to ~ blows** pegarse; **to ~ words** discutir II. *n* **1.** (*interchange, trade*) intercambio *m;* **in ~ for sth** a cambio de algo; **~ of (gun)fire** tiroteo *m* **2.** FIN, ECON cambio *m;* **foreign ~** divisas *fpl* **3.** (*verbal interchange*) **~ of threats** intercambio *m* de amenazas

exchangeable *adj* cambiable; (*goods*) canjeable; **~ currency** divisa *f;* **to be ~ for sth** ser intercambiable por algo

exchange rate *n* tipo *m* de cambio

exchange student *n* estudiante *mf* de intercambio

exchange teacher *n* profesor(a) *m(f)* de intercambio

excise [ek·'saɪz] *vt form* **1.** quitar; (*tumor*) extirpar **2.** *fig* eliminar, suprimir

excise tax *n* impuesto *m* a las transacciones [*o* indirectos]

excitable [ɪk·'saɪ·ţə·bəl] *adj* excitable

excite [ɪk·'saɪt] *vt* **1.** (*move*) emocionar; **to ~ an audience** entusiasmar al público; **to be ~d about an idea** estar entusiasmado ante una idea **2.** (*stimulate*) estimular; **to ~ sb's curiosity** despertar la curiosidad de alguien

excited [ɪk·'saɪ·tɪd] *adj* emocionado, -a

excitement [ɪk·'saɪt·mənt] *n* emoción *f;* **to be in a state of ~** estar emocionado; **what ~!** ¡qué emoción!

exciting [ɪk·'saɪ·tɪŋ] *adj* emocionante

excl. 1. *abbr of* **excluding** excepto, salvo **2.** *abbr of* **exclusive** exclusive

exclaim [ɪk·'skleɪm] *vi, vt* exclamar; **to ~ in delight** exclamar de placer

exclamation [,ek·sklə·'meɪ·ʃən] *n* exclamación *f*

exclamation mark *n,* **exclamation point** *n* signo *m* de exclamación

exclude [ɪk·'sklud] *vt* **1.** (*keep out*) excluir; **to ~ sb from a group** excluir a alguien de un grupo **2.** (*possibility*) descartar

excluding [ɪk·'sklu·dɪŋ] *prep* excepto, salvo

exclusion [ɪk·'sklu·ʒən] *n* exclusión *f*

exclusive [ɪk·'sklu·sɪv] **I.** *adj* exclusivo, -a; **~ interview** entrevista *f* en exclusiva; **in ~ circles** en círculos selectos; **to be ~ to sb** ser exclusivo de alguien; **~ of** sin; **to be ~ of** no incluir **II.** *n* exclusiva *f*

exclusively *adv* exclusivamente

excommunicate [ˌeks·kə·'mju·nɪ·keɪt] *vt* excomulgar

excommunication [ˌeks·kə·ˌmju·nɪ·'keɪ·ʃən] *n* excomunión *f*

excrement ['ek·skrə·mənt] *n* excremento *m*

excreta [ɪk·'skri·ţə] *n form* excrementos *mpl*

excrete [ɪk·'skrit] *vi, vt form* excretar

excretion [ɪk·'skri·ʃən] *n form* excreción *f*

excruciating [ɪk·'skru·ʃi·eɪ·ţɪŋ] *adj* **1.** agudísimo, -a; (*pain*) atroz, insoportable **2.** (*intense: accuracy*) extenuante

excursion [ɪk·'skɜr·ʒən] *n* excursión *f;* **to go on an ~** ir de excursión

excusable [ɪk·'skju·zə·bəl] *adj* perdonable

excuse¹ [ɪk·'skjuz] *vt* **1.** (*justify: behavior*) justificar; (*lateness*) disculpar; **to ~ sb for sth** excusar a alguien por algo **2.** (*forgive*) perdonar; **~ me!** ¡perdón! **3.** (*allow not to attend*) **to ~ sb from sth** dispensar a alguien de algo **4.** (*leave*) **after an hour she ~d herself** después de una hora se disculpó y se fue

excuse² [ɪk·'skjus] *n* **1.** (*explanation*) excusa *f,* disculpa *f,* agarradera *f AmL* **2.** (*pretext*) pretexto *m;* **poor ~** mal pretexto; **to make ~s for sb** justificar a alguien; **be there on time — no ~s!** ¡sé puntual, nada de excusas!

exec *n inf abbr of* **executive** ejecutivo, -a *m, f*

execute ['ek·sɪ·kjut] *vt* **1.** (*carry out*) realizar; (*maneuver*) efectuar; (*plan*) llevar a cabo; (*order*) cumplir; **to ~ sb's will** ejecutar el testamento de alguien **2.** (*put to death*) ejecutar

execution [ˌek·sɪ·'kju·ʃən] *n* **1.** (*carrying out*) realización *f;* **to put a plan into ~** llevar a cabo un plan **2.** (*putting to death*) ejecución *f*

executioner [ˌek·sɪ·'kju·ʃə·nər] *n* verdugo *m*

executive [ɪg·'zek·ju·ţɪv] **I.** *n* **1.** (*senior manager*) ejecutivo, -a *m, f* **2.** + *sing/pl vb* POL poder *m* ejecutivo; ECON órgano *m* ejecutivo **II.** *adj* ejecutivo, -a; **~ branch** poder ejecutivo

executive assistant *n* asistente *mf* ejecutivo, -a

executive order *n* ≈ real decreto *m,* orden *f* ejecutiva

executive producer *n* productor (a) ejecutivo, -a *m*

executor [ɪg·'zek·ju·ţər] *n* albacea *mf*

exemplary [ɪg·'zem·plə·ri] *adj* ejemplar

exemplification [ɪg·ˌzem·plə·fɪ·'keɪ·ʃən] *n* ejemplificación *f;* (*of an idea*) ilustración *f*

exemplify [ɪg·'zem·plɪ·faɪ] <-ie-> *vt* ejemplificar; (*strategy*) mostrar

exempt [ɪg·'zempt] **I.** *vt* eximir **II.** *adj* exento,

-a; **to be ~ from** (**doing**) **sth** estar exento de (hacer) algo

exemption [ɪg·'zemp·ʃən] *n* exención *f*

exercise ['ek·sər·saɪz] **I.** *vt* **1.** (*muscles*) ejercitar; (*dog*) llevar de paseo; (*horse*) entrenar; **to ~ one's muscles/memory** ejercitar los músculos/la memoria **2.** (*apply: authority, control*) ejercer; **to ~ caution** proceder con cautela; **to ~ common sense** hacer uso del sentido común; **to ~ discretion** actuar con discreción; **to ~ self-discipline** imponerse autodisciplina **II.** *vi* hacer ejercicio **III.** *n* **1.** (*physical training*) ejercicio *m;* **physical ~** gimnasia *f;* **to do ~s** hacer ejercicios **2.** SCHOOL, UNIV ejercicio *m;* **written ~s** ejercicios *mpl* escritos **3.** MIL maniobras *fpl* **4.** (*action, achievement*) acción *f* **5.** (*use*) uso *m* **6.** **~s** ceremonia *f;* **graduation ~s** ceremonia *f* de graduación

exercise bike *n* bicicleta *f* de ejercicio [*o* estática]

exercise book *n* cuaderno *m*

exerciser ['ek·sər·saɪ·zər] *n* máquina *f* de ejercicios

exert [ɪg·'zɜrt] *vt* ejercer; (*apply*) emplear; **to ~ oneself** esforzarse

exertion [ɪg·'zɜr·ʃən] *n* **1.** (*application: of authority, influence*) ejercicio *m;* (*of strength*) empleo *m* **2.** (*physical effort*) esfuerzo *m*

exfoliant [eks·'foʊ·li·ənt] *n* exfoliante *m*

exfoliating cream [eks·ˌfoʊ·lɪ·'eɪ·ţɪŋ·krim] *n* crema *f* exfoliante

exfoliation [eks·ˌfoʊ·li·'eɪ·ʃən] *n* exfoliación *f*

ex-girlfriend *n* ex novia *f*

exhalation [eks·hə·'leɪ·ʃən] *n* exhalación *f*

exhale [eks·'heɪl] **I.** *vt* espirar; (*gases, scents*) despedir **II.** *vi* espirar

exhaust [ɪg·'zɔst] **I.** *vt a. fig* agotar; **to ~ oneself** agotarse **II.** *n* **1.** AUTO (*gas*) gases *mpl* de escape **2.** (*pipe*) tubo *m* de escape

exhausted *adj* agotado, -a

exhaust fumes *npl* gases *mpl* de escape

exhausting *adj* agotador(a)

exhaustion [ɪg·'zɔs·tʃən] *n* agotamiento *m;* **to suffer from ~** estar agotado

exhaustive [ɪg·'zɔs·tɪv] *adj* exhaustivo, -a

exhaust pipe *n* tubo *m* de escape

exhaust system *n* sistema *m* de escape

exhibit [ɪg·'zɪb·ɪt] **I.** *n* **1.** (*display*) objeto *m* expuesto **2.** LAW prueba *f* presentada en juicio **II.** *vt* **1.** (*show*) enseñar; (*work*) presentar **2.** (*display character traits*) mostrar; (*rudeness, confidence*) demostrar

exhibition [ˌek·sɪ·'bɪʃ·ən] *n* (*display*) exposición *f;* (*performance*) exhibición *f* ▶ **to make an ~ of oneself** ponerse en ridículo

exhibitionism [ˌek·sɪ·'bɪʃ·ə·nɪz·əm] *n* exhibicionismo *m*

exhibitionist [ˌek·sɪ·'bɪʃ·ə·nɪst] *n* exhibicionista *mf*

exhibitor [ɪg·'zɪb·ɪ·tər] *n* expositor(a) *m(f)*

exhilarating [ɪg·'zɪl·ə·reɪ·ţɪŋ] *adj* estimulante; **an ~ performance** un espectáculo emocionante

exhilaration [ɪg·'zɪl·ə·reɪ·ʃən] *n* regocijo *m;* **the ~ of liberty/speed** la sensación estimulante de la libertad/velocidad; **the ~ of doing sth** la alegría de hacer algo

exhort [ɪg·'zɔrt] *vt form* **to ~ sb to do sth** exhortar a alguien a hacer algo; **she ~ed him to keep working** le exhortó a que siguiera trabajando

exhortation [ˌeg·zɔr·'teɪ·ʃən] *n* exhortación *f*

exhumation [ˌeg·zju·'meɪ·ʃən] *n* exhumación *f*

exhume [ɪg·'zum] *vt* exhumar

ex-husband *n* ex marido *m*

exigence ['ek·sɪ·dʒəns] *n,* **exigency** ['ek·sɪ·dʒən·si] <-ies> *n* **1.**(*extreme urgency*) emergencia *f* **2. ~ s** (*urgent demands*) exigencias *fpl*

exigent ['ek·sɪ·dʒənt] *adj form* **1.**(*urgent*) apremiante; **an ~ issue** una cuestión urgente; **an ~ environmental problem** un problema medioambiental inaplazable **2.**(*demanding*) exigente

exiguous [ɪg·'zɪg·ju·əs] *adj form* exiguo, -a

exile ['ek·saɪl] **I.** *n* **1.**(*banishment*) exilio *m;* **political ~** exilio político; **to be in ~** estar en el exilio; **to go into ~** exiliarse **2.**(*person*) exiliado, -a *m, f* **II.** *vt* exiliar; **to ~ sb to Siberia** exiliar a alguien a Siberia

exist [ɪg·'zɪst] *vi* **1.**(*be*) existir **2.**(*live*) vivir; **to ~ on sth** vivir de algo; **to ~ without sth** sobrevivir sin algo

existence [ɪg·'zɪs·təns] *n* **1.**(*being*) existencia *f;* **to be in ~** existir; **to come into ~** venir al mundo **2.**(*life*) vida *f*

existent [ɪg·'zɪs·tent] *adj* existente

existential [ˌeg·zɪ·'sten·ʃəl] *adj* existencial

existentialism [ˌeg·zɪ·'sten·ʃə·lɪz·əm] *n* existencialismo *m*

existing [ɪg·'zɪs·tɪŋ] *adj* existente; **the ~ laws** la actual legislación

exit ['eg·sɪt] **I.** *n* salida *f;* (*of road*) desvío *m;* **to make an ~** salir **II.** *vt* salir de **III.** *vi* **1.** *a.* COMPUT (*leave*) salir **2.** THEAT hacer mutis

exit visa *n* visado *m* de salida

exodus ['ek·sə·dəs] *n* éxodo *m*

ex officio [ˌeks·ə·'fɪʃ·i·oʊ] **I.** *adv* ADMIN oficialmente; **to act ~** actuar de oficio **II.** *adj* ADMIN de oficio

exonerate [ɪg·'zan·ə·reɪt] *vt form* exonerar; **to ~ sb from sth** exonerar a alguien de algo

exoneration [ɪg·ˌzan·ə·'reɪ·ʃən] *n form* exoneración *f*

exorbitance [ɪg·'zɔr·bə·təns] *n* exorbitancia *f*

exorbitant [ɪg·'zɔr·bə·tənt] *adj* exorbitante; (*demand*) excesivo, -a; (*price*) desorbitado, -a

exorcism ['ek·sɔr·sɪz·əm] *n* exorcismo *m*

exorcist ['ek·sɔr·sɪst] *n* exorcista *mf*

exorcize ['ek·sɔr·saɪz] *vt* exorcizar

exotic [ɪg·'zat·ɪk] *adj* exótico, -a; **~ fruit** frutas *fpl* exóticas

expand [ɪk·'spænd] **I.** *vi* **1.**(*increase*) expandirse; (*trade*) desarrollarse **2.**(*spread*) extenderse **3.** PHYS dilatarse **II.** *vt* **1.**(*make larger*) ampliar; (*wings*) extender; (*trade*) desarrollar **2.** PHYS dilatar **3.**(*elaborate*) desarrollar

expandable [ɪk·'spæn·də·bəl] *adj* expansible

expanse [ɪk·'spæns] *n* **1.**(*large area*) extensión *f* **2.**(*expansion*) expansión *f*

expansion [ɪk·'spæn·ʃən] *n* **1.**(*spreading out*) expansión *f;* (*of a metal*) dilatación *f* **2.**(*elaboration*) desarrollo *m*

expansionism [ɪk·'spæn·ʃə·nɪz·əm] *n* expansionismo *m;* **policy of ~** política *f* expansionista

expansive [ɪk·'spæn·sɪv] *adj* **1.**(*sociable*) expansivo, -a **2.**(*broad, vast*) amplio, -a **3.**(*elaborated*) extenso, -a

ex-partner *n* (*intimate*) ex compañero , -a sentimental *m;* (*business*) ex socio, -a *m, f*

expat [ˌeks·'pæt] *n esp. Can abbr of* **expatriate** expatriado, -a *m, f*

expatriate[1] [eks·'peɪ·tri·ət] *n* expatriado, -a *m, f*

expatriate[2] [eks·'peɪ·tri·eɪt] *vt* expatriar

expect [ɪk·'spekt] *vt* esperar; (*imagine*) imaginarse; **to ~ to do sth** esperar hacer algo; **to ~ sb to do sth** esperar que alguien haga algo; **you are ~ed to return books on time** debes devolver los libros puntualmente; **to ~ sth of sb** esperar algo de alguien; **to be ~ing (a baby)** esperar un bebé; **I ~ed as much** ya me lo esperaba; **I ~ed better of you than that** esperaba algo más de ti que eso; **I ~ you are hungry** supongo que estaréis hambrientos; **I ~ so** me lo imagino; **to ~ that** esperar que +*subj*

expectancy [ɪk·'spek·tən·si] *n* esperanza *f;* **life ~** esperanza *f* de vida

expectant [ɪk·'spek·tənt] *adj* expectante; (*look*) de esperanza; **~ mother** futura madre

expectation [ˌek·spek·'teɪ·ʃən] *n* **1.**(*hope*) esperanza *f* **2.**(*anticipation*) expectativa *f;* **in ~ of sth** en espera de algo

expectorate [ɪk·'spek·tə·reɪt] *vi form* expectorar

expedience *n,* **expediency** [ɪk·'spi·di·ən·si] *n* **1.**(*advisability*) conveniencia *f;* **as a matter of ~, we will not be hiring any new staff members this year** no nos conviene contratar a más personal este año **2.**(*self-interest*) oportunismo *m;* **to operate on the basis of ~** actuar por conveniencia

expedient [ɪk·'spi·di·ənt] **I.** *adj* **1.**(*advantageous*) conveniente; **it is ~ to do sth** es oportuno hacer algo *elev* **2.**(*necessary*) necesario, -a; (*measure*) oportuno, -a; **to be ~ that** ser conveniente que +*subj* **II.** *n* recurso *m;* **they took the ~ of asking advice** tomaron la precaución de consejo

expedite ['ek·spɪ·daɪt] *vt form* acelerar

expedition [ˌek·spɪ·'dɪʃ·ən] *n* expedición *f;* **to be on an ~** estar de expedición; **to go on an ~** ir de expedición; **to go on a shopping ~** *iron* ir de compras

expeditious [ˌek·spɪ·'dɪʃ·əs] *adj form* expeditivo, -a

expel [ɪk·'spel] <-ll-> *vt* expeler, arrojar; (*per-*

son) expulsar; **to ~ sb from school** expulsar a alguien del colegio

expend [ɪk·'spend] *vt form* dedicar; (*money*) gastar; **to ~ time on sth** dedicar tiempo a algo

expenditure [ɪk·'spen·dɪ·tʃər] *n* (*money*) gasto *m;* **public ~s** gasto público; **cleaning ~s** gastos de limpieza

expense [ɪk·'spens] *n* gasto(s) *m(pl);* **all ~(s) paid** con todos los gastos pagados; **at great ~** por un precio muy elevado; **at sb's ~** *a. fig* a costa de alguien; **at the ~ of sth** *a. fig* a costa de algo; **to go to ~** meterse en gastos; **to go to the ~ of** meterse en gastos para; **to spare no ~** no reparar en gastos

expense account *n* cuenta *f* de gastos de representación

expensive [ɪk·'spen·sɪv] *adj* caro, -a; **that was an ~ mistake for him to make** el error le ha salido bien caro

experience [ɪk·'spɪr·i·əns] **I.** *n* experiencia *f;* **to have translating ~** tener experiencia en traducción; **from ~** por experiencia; **to know sth from ~** saber algo por experiencia; **to learn by ~** aprender a través de la experiencia **II.** *vt* experimentar; **to ~ happiness/pain** sentir alegría/dolor; **please do not adjust your television set — we're experiencing technical difficulties** por favor, no intente ajustar su televisor — estamos teniendo dificultades técnicas; **to ~ a loss** sufrir una pérdida

experienced [ɪk·'spɪr·i·ənst] *adj* experimentado, -a; **to be ~ at organizing large events** tener experiencia en la organización de grandes espectáculos

experiment [ɪk·'sper·ɪ·mənt] **I.** *n* experimento *m;* **as an ~** como experimento; **by ~** experimentando **II.** *vi* experimentar; **to ~ on a patient** hacer experimentos con un paciente; **to ~ with mice** hacer experimentos con ratones

experimental [ɪk·ˌsper·ɪ·'men·təl] *adj* experimental; **~ psychology** psicología *f* experimental; **to be still at the ~ stage** estar todavía en fase experimental

experimentation [ɪk·ˌsper·ɪ·men·'teɪ·ʃən] *n* experimentación *f*

expert ['ek·spɜrt] **I.** *n* experto, -a *m, f;* **to be a computer ~** ser un experto en ordenadores **II.** *adj* **1.** (*skilful*) experto, -a; **she's an ~ swimmer** es una experta nadadora **2.** LAW pericial; **~ report** informe *m* pericial

expert advice *n* **to seek ~** asesorarse con un experto

expertise [ˌek·spɜr·'tiz] *n* pericia *f;* (*knowledge*) conocimientos *mpl*

expert knowledge *n* conocimientos *mpl* de experto

expert opinion *n* dictamen *m* pericial

expert witness *n* perito, -a *m, f*

expiate ['ek·spi·eɪt] *vt form* expiar

expiation [ˌek·spi·'eɪ·ʃən] *n form* expiación *f*

expiration [ˌek·spə·'reɪ·ʃən] *n* terminación *f;* COM vencimiento *f*, caducidad *f*

expiration date *n* (*of a contract*) fecha *f* de vencimiento; (*of food or medicine*) fecha *f* de caducidad

expire [ɪk·'spaɪr] **I.** *vi* **1.** (*terminate*) finalizar; (*contract, license*) expirar; (*passport, food*) caducar **2.** (*die*) expirar **II.** *vt* espirar

expiry [ɪk·'spaɪ·ri] *n s.* **expiration**

explain [ɪk·'spleɪn] **I.** *vt* explicar; **to ~ how/what/where/why...** explicar cómo/qué/dónde/por qué...; **to ~ oneself** explicarse; **that ~s everything!** ¡eso lo aclara todo! **II.** *vi* explicar

◆**explain away** *vt* justificar

explanation [ˌek·splə·'neɪ·ʃən] *n* explicación *f;* **to give an ~ for an incident** dar una explicación de [*o* sobre] un incidente; **to offer no ~ for the delay** no dar explicaciones sobre el retraso; **by way of ~** como explicación

explanatory [ɪk·'splæn·ə·tɔr·i] *adj* explicativo, -a

expletive ['ək·splɪ·t̬ɪv] *n* palabrota *f;* **to unleash a string of ~s** soltar una sarta de tacos

explicable [ek·'splɪk·ə·bəl] *adj* explicable

explicate ['ek·splɪ·keɪt] *vt form* explicar

explicit [ɪk·'splɪs·ɪt] *adj* **1.** (*exact*) explícito, -a; **~ directions** instrucciones explícitas; **he was very ~ about the plans** era muy categórico en cuanto a los planes **2.** (*vulgar*) vulgar; **~ language** lenguaje *m* vulgar

explode [ɪk·'sploʊd] **I.** *vi* **1.** (*blow up*) explotar; (*bomb*) estallar; (*tire*) reventar; **to ~ with anger** montar en cólera **2.** (*grow rapidly*) dispararse **II.** *vt* **1.** (*blow up: bomb*) hacer explotar; (*ball*) reventar **2.** (*discredit: theory*) refutar; (*myth*) destruir

exploit ['ek·splɔɪt] **I.** *vt* explotar, pilotear *Chile* **II.** *n* hazaña *f*

exploitation [ˌek·splɔɪ·'teɪ·ʃən] *n* explotación *f*

exploration [ˌek·splɔ·'reɪ·ʃən] *n* **1.** *a.* exploración *f;* **voyage of ~** viaje *m* de exploración; **to make an ~ of sth** explorar algo **2.** (*examination*) estudio *m*

exploratory [ɪk·'splɔr·ə·tɔr·i] *adj* (*voyage*) de exploración; (*test*) de sondeo; (*meeting*) preliminar; **~ foreign language class** clase preparatoria de lengua extranjera

explore [ɪk·'splɔr] **I.** *vt* **1.** *a.* MED, COMPUT explorar **2.** (*examine*) analizar; **to ~ sb's past** investigar sobre el pasado de alguien **II.** *vi* explorar

explorer [ɪk·'splɔr·ər] *n* explorador(a) *m(f)*

explosion [ɪk·'sploʊ·ʒən] *n* explosión *f;* **gas ~** explosión de gas; **population ~** explosión demográfica; **there has been an ~ in demand for computers in the last few years** la demanda de ordenadores se ha disparado en los últimos años

explosive [ɪk·'sploʊ·sɪv] **I.** *adj* explosivo, -a; **~ device** artefacto explosivo; **an ~ situation** una situación delicada; **an ~ issue** un asunto espinoso; **to have an ~ temper** tener un genio muy vivo **II.** *n* explosivo *m*

exponent [ɪk·'spoʊ·nənt] *n* **1.** (*person*) exponente *mf;* **a leading ~ of neoclassicism** un máximo exponente del neoclasicismo **2.** MATH exponente *m*

export I. [ɪkˈspɔrt] *vt* exportar **II.** [ˈekˈspɔrt] *n* **1.** (*product*) artículo *m* de exportación **2.** (*selling*) exportación *f;* **~ taxes** aranceles *mpl* de exportación

exportable [ɪkˈspɔrˈṭəˈbəl] *adj* exportable

exportation [ˌekˈspɔrˈteɪˈʃən] *n* exportación *f*

export business *n* **1.** (*business which sells abroad*) negocio *m* de exportación **2.** (*special branch*) exportación *f;* **to be in the ~** dedicarse a la exportación

exporter [ɪkˈspɔrˈtər] *n* exportador(a) *m(f)*

export goods *npl* productos *mpl* de exportación

export license *n* licencia *f* de exportación

export regulations *npl* normativa *f* de exportación

export surplus *n* excedente *m* de exportación

export trade *n* comercio *m* de exportación

expose [ɪkˈspoʊz] *vt* **1.** (*uncover*) enseñar **2.** (*leave vulnerable to*) exponer; **to ~ sb to ridicule** poner a alguien en ridículo **3.** (*reveal: person*) descubrir; (*plot*) desvelar; (*secret*) sacar a la luz; **to ~ a business as a fraud** desvelar un negocio fraudulento

exposé [ˌekˈspoʊˈzeɪ] *n* revelación *f*

exposed [ɪkˈspoʊzd] *adj* **1.** (*vulnerable*) expuesto, -a **2.** (*uncovered*) descubierto, -a **3.** (*unprotected*) desprotegido, -a

exposition [ˌekˈspəˈzɪʃˈən] *n* exposición *f*

expostulate [ɪkˈspasˈtʃəˈleɪt] *vi form* protestar; **to ~ with the waiter about the bill** reconvenir al camarero sobre la factura

exposure [ɪkˈspoʊˈʒər] *n* **1.** (*contact*) exposición *f;* **~ to the sun** exposición al sol; **~ to new ideas** contacto *m* con nuevas ideas **2.** MED hipotermia *f;* **to die of ~** morir de frío **3.** *a.* PHOT exposición *f* **4.** (*revelation*) descubrimiento *m* **5.** (*media coverage*) publicidad *f*

exposure meter *n* PHOT exposímetro *m*

expound [ɪkˈspaʊnd] **I.** *vi form* hablar; **to ~ (at length) on** [*o* about] **sth** hablar (largo y tendido) sobre algo **II.** *vt form* exponer

express [ɪkˈspres] **I.** *vt* **1.** (*convey: thoughts, feelings*) expresar; **to ~ oneself** expresarse; **to ~ oneself through music** expresarse a través de la música; **I would like to ~ my thanks for...** querría expresar mi gratitud por... **2.** *inf* (*send quickly*) enviar por correo urgente; **to ~ sth to sb** enviar algo a alguien por correo urgente **3.** *form* (*squeeze out*) exprimir **II.** *adj* **1.** (*rapid*) rápido, -a; **by ~ delivery** por correo urgente; **~ train** tren expreso; **~ mail** correo urgente **2.** (*precise*) explícito, -a; **by ~ order** por orden expresa; **these are his/her ~ wishes** estos son sus deseos expresos **III.** *n* (*train*) expreso *m* **IV.** *adv* **to send sth ~** enviar algo por correo urgente

expression [ɪkˈspreʃˈən] *n* expresión *f;* (*of love, solidarity*) demostración *f;* **as an ~ of thanks** en señal de agradecimiento; **to give ~**

to sth expresar algo; **to find ~ in music** expresarse a través de la música

expressionism [ɪkˈspreʃˈəˈnɪzˈəm] *n* expresionismo *m*

expressionist [ɪkˈspreʃˈəˈnɪst] *n* expresionista *mf*

expressionless [ɪkˈspreʃˈənˈlɪs] *adj* inexpresivo, -a

expressive [ɪkˈspresˈɪv] *adj* expresivo, -a; **to be ~ of sadness** *form* denotar tristeza

expressly [ɪkˈspresˈli] *adv* **1.** (*clearly*) claramente **2.** (*especially*) expresamente

expressway [ɪkˈspresˈweɪ] *n* autopista *f*

ex-prisoner *n* ex prisionero, -a *m, f*

expropriate [eksˈproʊˈpriˈeɪt] *vt* expropiar

expropriation [eksˈproʊˈpriˈeɪˈʃən] *n* expropiación *f*

expulsion [ɪkˈspʌlˈʃən] *n* expulsión *f*

exquisite [ˈekˈskwɪˈzɪt] *adj* **1.** (*delicate*) exquisito, -a; **an ~ piece of china** una delicada pieza de porcelana **2.** (*intense*) intenso, -a

ex-serviceman [ˌeksˈsɜrˈvɪsˈmən] <-men> *n* excombatiente *m*

ext. TEL *abbr of* **extension** Ext.

extant [ˈekˈstənt] *adj form* (todavía) existente; **to be still ~** existir todavía

extemporaneous [ɪkˌstemˈpəˈreɪˈniˈəs] *adj form* improvisado, -a

extempore [ɪkˈstemˈpəˈri] *form* **I.** *adj* improvisado, -a **II.** *adv* improvisadamente; **to perform ~** improvisar; **to speak ~** improvisar un discurso

extemporize [ɪkˈstemˈpəˈraɪz] *vi form* improvisar

extend [ɪkˈstend] **I.** *vt* **1.** (*enlarge: house*) ampliar; (*street*) alargar **2.** (*prolong: deadline*) prorrogar; (*holiday*) prolongar **3.** (*offer*) ofrecer; **to ~ an invitation to sb** cursar una invitación a alguien; **to ~ one's hand as a greeting** tender la mano para saludar; **to ~ one's thanks to sb** dar las gracias a alguien; **to ~ a warm welcome to sb** dar una calurosa bienvenida a alguien **4.** FIN (*credit*) conceder **II.** *vi* extenderse; **to ~ beyond the river** extenderse más allá del río; **to ~ to a discussion** llegar a una discusión

extended *adj* extenso, -a; **~ family** clan *m* familiar; **an ~ holiday** unas vacaciones prolongadas

extension [ɪkˈstenˈʃən] *n* **1.** (*increase*) extensión *f;* (*of rights*) ampliación *f;* **by ~** por extensión **2.** (*of a deadline*) prórroga *f* **3.** (*appendage*) apéndice *m* **4.** TEL extensión *f,* supletorio *m AmL,* anexo *m Chile*

extension cord *n* alargador *m,* alargue *m RíoPl*

extension ladder *n* escalera *f* extensible

extensive [ɪkˈstenˈsɪv] *adj* **1.** *a. fig* extenso, -a; (*knowledge*) exhaustivo, -a; (*experience*) amplio, -a **2.** (*large: repair*) importante; **~ damage** daños *mpl* de consideración **3.** AGR (*farming*) extensivo, -a

extensively *adv* intensamente

extent [ɪkˈstent] *n* **1.** (*size*) extensión *f;* **to its**

fullest ~ en toda su extensión **2.** (*degree*) alcance *m;* **to go to the ~ of hitting sb** llegar al extremo de golpear a alguien; **to a great ~** en gran parte; **to the same ~ as...** en la misma medida que...; **to some ~** hasta cierto punto; **to such an ~ that...** hasta tal punto que...; **to that ~** hasta ese punto; **to what ~...?** ¿hasta qué punto...?

extenuate [ɪk·'sten·jʊ·eɪt] *vt form* atenuar

extenuating *adj form* atenuante; **~ circumstances** circunstancias *fpl* atenuantes

extenuation [ɪk·ˌsten·jʊ·'eɪ·ʃən] *n form* atenuación *f;* **in ~ of sth** como atenuante de algo

exterior [ɪk·'stɪr·i·ər] **I.** *adj* exterior **II.** *n* **1.** (*outside surface*) exterior *m* **2.** (*outward appearance*) aspecto *m* **3.** CINE exteriores *mpl*

exterminate [ɪk·'stɜr·mɪ·neɪt] *vt* exterminar

extermination [ɪk·ˌstɜr·mɪ·'neɪ·ʃən] *n* exterminio *m,* exterminación *f*

external [ɪk·'stɜr·nəl] **I.** *adj* **1.** (*exterior*) externo, -a; (*influence*) del exterior; (*wall*) exterior; **to be ~ to the problem** ser ajeno al problema **2.** (*foreign*) exterior **3.** MED tópico, -a **II.** *npl* las apariencias

externalize [ɪk·'stɜr·nə·laɪz] *vt* exteriorizar

external world *n* mundo *m* exterior

exterritorial [ˌeks·ˌter·ɪ·'tɔr·i·əl] *adj* extraterritorial

extinct [ɪk·'stɪŋkt] *adj* (*practice*) extinto, -a; (*volcano*) inactivo, -a; **to become ~** extinguirse

extinction [ɪk·'stɪŋk·ʃən] *n* extinción *f*

extinguish [ɪk·'stɪŋ·gwɪʃ] *vt* (*candle, cigar*) apagar; (*love, passion*) extinguir; (*life, memory*) apagar; (*debt*) amortizar

extinguisher [ɪk·'stɪŋ·gwɪʃ·ər] *n* extintor *m*

extol <-ll-> *vt,* **extoll** [ɪk·'stoʊl] *vt* alabar; **to ~ (upon) the virtues of yoga** ensalzar las virtudes del yoga

extort [ɪk·'stɔrt] *vt* extorsionar; (*confession*) arrancar

extortion [ɪk·'stɔr·ʃən] *n* extorsión *f;* **that's sheer ~!** ¡esto es un robo!

extortionate [ɪk·'stɔr·ʃə·nɪt] *adj* abusivo, -a; **~ demands** peticiones desmesuradas; **~ prices** precios *mpl* exorbitantes

extra ['ek·strə] **I.** *adj* adicional; **to work an ~ two hours** trabajar dos horas más; **~ clothes** ropa *f* de repuesto; **it costs an ~ $2** cuesta dos dólares más; **meals are ~** el precio no incluye las comidas **II.** *adv* (*more*) más; (*extraordinarily*) extraordinariamente; **they pay her ~ to work nights** le pagan más por trabajar por la noche; **I'll try ~ hard this time** esta vez voy a poner más empeño; **$10 ~** diez dólares más; **to charge ~ for sth** cobrar algo aparte **III.** *n* **1.** ECON suplemento *m;* AUTO extra *m* **2.** CINE extra *mf*

extract [ɪk·'strækt] **I.** *vt* **1.** (*remove*) extraer **2.** (*obtain: information*) sacar **3.** MATH (*square root*) sacar **II.** *n* **1.** (*concentrate*) extracto *m* **2.** (*excerpt*) fragmento *m*

extraction [ɪk·'stræk·ʃən] *n* **1.** (*removal*) extracción *f* **2.** (*descent*) origen *m;* **he's of Irish ~** es de origen irlandés

extracurricular [ˌek·strə·kə·'rɪk·jə·lər] *adj* extraescolar, extracurricular; **~ activities** actividades extraescolares; **are you involved in any ~ activities?** *a. fig* ¿participas en alguna actividad extraescolar?

extradite ['ek·strə·daɪt] *vt* extraditar

extradition [ˌek·strə·'dɪʃ·ən] *n* extradición *f*

extramarital [ˌek·strə·'mer·ɪ·ţəl] *adj* extramatrimonial

extraneous [ɪk·'streɪ·ni·əs] *adj* extraño, -a; **to be ~ to sth** no tener relación con algo

extranet ['ek·strə·net] *n* COMPUT extranet *f*

extraordinary [ɪk·'strɔr·də·ner·i] *adj* **1.** *a.* POL extraordinario, -a **2.** (*astonishing*) asombroso, -a

extrapolate [ek·'stræp·ə·leɪt] **I.** *vt form* extrapolar **II.** *vi form* **to ~ from sth** hacer una extrapolación de algo

extrasensory [ˌek·strə·'sen·sə·ri] *adj* extrasensorial; **~ perception** percepción *f* extrasensorial

extraterrestrial ['ek·strə·tə·'res·tri·əl] *adj* extraterrestre

extraterritorial [ˌek·strə·ˌter·ɪ·'tɔr·i·əl] *adj* extraterritorial

extravagance [ɪk·'stræv·ə·gəns] *n* **1.** (*wastefulness*) derroche *m* **2.** (*luxury*) lujo *m* **3.** (*elaborateness*) extravagancia *f*

extravagant [ɪk·'stræv·ə·gənt] *adj* **1.** (*wasteful*) despilfarrador(a) **2.** (*luxurious*) lujoso, -a; **an ~ lifestyle** un tren de vida lujoso **3.** (*exaggerated: praise*) excesivo, -a; **~ price** precio *m* exorbitante **4.** (*elaborate*) extravagante

extravaganza [ɪk·ˌstræv·ə·'gæn·zə] *n* (*spectacle*) **a film ~** una película espectacular

extreme [ɪk·'strim] **I.** *adj* extremo, -a; **an ~ case** un caso extremo; **with ~ caution** con sumo cuidado; **~ difficulties** grandes dificultades; **~ pain** dolor agudo; **in the ~ north** en la zona más septentrional; **~ sport** deporte de alto riesgo; **to be ~ in sth** ser extremista en algo **II.** *n* extremo *m;* **a man of ~s** un extremista; **at the ~** *fig* en el peor de los casos; **in the ~** sumamente; **to go from one ~ to the other** pasar de un extremo a otro; **to go to ~s** llegar a extremos

extremely *adv* extremadamente; **to be ~ sorry** estar muy arrepentido

---

[i] Los deportes poco corrientes como bungee-jumping (puenting), skate boarding (monopatín) o snowboarding se denominan en EE.UU. **extreme sports** o **alternative sports**. También heliskiing, cave-diving (espeleobuceo), wakeboarding y street-luge se cuentan entre estos extreme sports. Su popularidad se debe precisamente a que la velocidad y el peligro son mayores, por lo

que poseen más atractivo que otros deportes como pueda ser el tenis.

extremism [ɪk·'stri·mɪz·əm] *n* extremismo *m*
extremist [ɪk·'stri·mɪst] **I.** *adj* extremista; ~ **tendencies** tendencias extremistas **II.** *n* extremista *mf*
extremity [ɪk·'strem·ə·t̬i] *n* **1.** (*furthest point*) extremo *m* **2.** (*greatest degree*) extremo *m;* **at the** ~ **of his endurance** al extremo de su resistencia **3.** (*situation*) situación *f* extrema **4. extremities** ANAT extremidades *fpl*
extricate ['ek·strɪ·keɪt] *vt form* sacar; **to** ~ **one-self from sth** lograr salir de algo
extrovert ['ek·strə·vərt] *n* extrovertido, -a *m, f*
extroverted *adj* extrovertido, -a
extrude [ek·'strud] **I.** *vt* **1.** TECH extrudir **2.** (*force out*) expulsar **II.** *vi* sobresalir
exuberance [ɪg·'zu·bər·əns] *n* **1.** (*abundance*) exuberancia *f* **2.** (*liveliness*) exaltación *f*
exuberant [ɪg·'zu·bər·ənt] *adj* **1.** (*luxuriant*) exuberante **2.** (*energetic*) desbordante; **young and** ~ joven y lleno de energía
exude [ɪg·'zud] **I.** *vt* **1.** exudar; **to** ~ **pus** supurar **2.** *fig* rezumar; **to** ~ **confidence** irradiar confianza **II.** *vi* exudar
exult [ɪg·'zʌlt] *vi form* regocijarse; **to** ~ **at** [*o* **in**] **the prize** regocijarse con [*o* de] [*o* en] el premio
exultant [ɪg·'zʌl·tənt] *adj form* regocijado, -a, exultante; ~ **shout** grito *m* de júbilo
exultation [ˌek·sʌl·'teɪ·ʃən] *n form* regocijo *m*, exultación *f;* ~ **at sth** regocijo *m* por algo
ex-wife *n* ex mujer *f*, ex esposa *f*
eye [aɪ] **I.** *n* **1.** ANAT ojo *m; to* **blink one's ~s** parpadear; **to keep an** ~ **on sth/sb** *inf* echar un ojo a algo/alguien; **to roll one's ~s** tener los ojos en blanco; **to rub one's ~s** restregarse los ojos; **to set ~s on sb/sth** poner los ojos en alguien/algo; **visible to the naked** ~ visible a simple vista; **her ~s flashed with anger** sus ojos echaban chispas; **his ~s** (**nearly**) **popped** (**out of his head**) (casi) se le salieron los ojos de las órbitas; **he couldn't take his ~s off the girl** *inf* no le quitaba ojo a la chica **2.** BOT yema *f* ▶ **to have ~s in the back of one's** head *inf* tener ojos en la nuca; **an** ~ **for an** ~, **a** tooth **for a tooth** *prov* ojo por ojo y diente por diente; **to be** all **~s** ser todo ojos; **to give sb a** black ~ poner a alguien un ojo a la funerala [*o* negro]; **to turn a** blind ~ (**to sth**) hacer la vista gorda (a algo); **as** far **as the** ~ **can see** hasta donde alcanza la vista; **to have a** good ~ **for sth** tener (buen) ojo para algo; **there's** more **to this than meets the** ~ las apariencias engañan; **to keep one's ~s** open mantener los ojos bien abiertos; **to do sth with one's ~s** open *inf* hacer algo a sabiendas; **to keep one's ~s** peeled **for sth** *inf* estar ojo avizor; **to go around with one's ~s** closed *inf* andar siempre distraído; **to be able to do sth with**

one's ~s closed *inf* poder hacer algo con los ojos cerrados; (**right**) **before** [*o* **under**] **my** very **~s** delante de mis propios ojos; **to not** believe **one's ~s** no dar crédito a sus ojos; **to** catch **sb's** ~ llamar la atención de alguien; **to** give **sb the** ~ *inf,* **to** make **~s at sb** *inf* echar miraditas a alguien; **to** open **sb's ~s** abrir los ojos a alguien; **to** run **one's ~s** ~ **over sth** dar una ojeada a algo; **to** (**not**) see ~ **to** ~ **with sb** (no) estar de acuerdo con alguien; **in my ~s** en mi opinión; **in the** public ~ a la luz pública **II.** <-ing> *vt* mirar; (*observe*) observar; **to** ~ **sb up and down** mirar a alguien de arriba abajo
eyeball ['aɪ·bɔl] **I.** *n* globo *m* ocular ▶ **to meet** ~ to **~ with sb** *inf* enfrentarse cara a cara con alguien **II.** *vt inf* mirar de arriba abajo
eyebrow *n* ceja *f;* **bushy ~s** cejas pobladas; **to raise one's ~s at sth** asombrarse ante algo
eyebrow pencil *n* lápiz *m* de cejas
eye-catching ['aɪ·ˌkætʃ·ɪŋ] *adj* llamativo, -a
eye contact *n* contacto *m* visual; **to establish** ~ establecer contacto visual
eyedrops *npl* gotas *f* para los ojos *pl*
eyeful *n* **to be an** ~ *inf* estar de buen ver; **get an** ~ **of this!** *inf* ¡echa un vistazo a esto!; **I got an** ~ **of dust** me ha entrado polvo en el ojo
eyeglass *n* **1.** monóculo *m* **2.** *pl* gafas *fpl*
eyelash <-es> *n* pestaña *f;* **false ~es** pestañas *fpl* postizas
eyelet *n* ojete *m*
eyelid *n* párpado *m*
eyeliner ['aɪ·laɪ·nər] *n* delineador *m* de ojos; (*pencil a.*) lápiz *m* de ojos
eye opener *n inf* revelación *f;* **it was quite an** ~ **for me** me hizo abrir los ojos
eyepiece *n* ocular *m*
eye-popping *adj inf* impresionante
eye shadow *n* sombra *f* de ojos
eyesight *n* vista *f;* **keen** ~ vista aguda; **his ~ is failing** le está fallando la vista
eyesore *n* **to be an** ~ ofender a la vista
eyestrain *n* vista *f* cansada; **to cause** ~ cansar la vista
eyewitness <-es> *n* testigo *mf* ocular
e-zine ['i·zin] *n* revista *f* electrónica

F

F, f [ef] *n* **1.** (*letter*) F, f *f;* ~ **as in Foxtrot** F de Francia **2.** MUS fa *m*
f *abbr of* **feminine** f
f. *abbr of* **folio** f
F *abbr of* **Fahrenheit** F
fable ['feɪ·bəl] *n* **1.** (*story*) fábula *f* **2.** (*lie*) cuento *m*
fabled ['feɪ·bld] *adj* legendario, -a
fabric ['fæb·rɪk] *n* **1.** (*cloth, textile*) tejido *m; cotton* ~ tela *f* de algodón; **woolen** ~ género

m de lana **2.**(*of building*) estructura *f;* **the ~ of society** el tejido social

fabricate ['fæb·rɪ·keɪt] *vt* **1.**(*manufacture*) fabricar **2.** *fig* (*invent*) **to ~ an excuse** inventar(se) una excusa **3.** (*forge*) falsificar

fabulous ['fæb·jə·ləs] *adj* fabuloso, -a; **to look absolutely ~** estar estupendo

façade [fə·'sɑd] *n a. fig* fachada *f*

face [feɪs] **I.** *n* **1.** *a.* ANAT cara *f*; **a happy/sad ~** una cara de felicidad/de tristeza; **a smiling ~** un rostro sonriente; **to dare (to) show one's ~** atreverse a dar la cara; **to have a puzzled expression on one's ~** tener un semblante preocupado; **to keep a smile on one's ~** no perder la sonrisa; **to keep a straight ~** mantenerse impávido; **to laugh in sb's ~** reírse en la cara de alguien; **to make a ~ (at sb)** hacer una mueca (a alguien); **to tell sth to sb's ~** decir algo a la cara de alguien; **you should have seen her ~** tenías que haber visto la cara que puso **2.** (*front: of building*) fachada *f;* (*of coin*) cara *f;* (*of clock*) esfera *f,* carátula *f Méx;* (*of mountain*) pared *f* **3.**(*respect, honor*) prestigio *m;* **to lose ~** desprestigiarse; **to save ~** guardar las apariencias ▶ **to put a brave ~ on sth** poner al mal tiempo buena cara; **to be brought ~ to ~ with sth** tener que enfrentarse a algo; **to make a long ~** poner cara larga; **his ~ fell when he opened the letter** le mudó el semblante cuando abrió la carta; **to fly in the ~ of logic/reason** oponerse abiertamente a la lógica/razón; **on the ~ of it** a primera vista **II.** *vt* **1.**(*turn towards*) mirar hacia; **to ~ the audience** volverse hacia el público; **please ~ me when I'm talking to you** por favor, mírame cuando te hablo **2.**(*confront*) hacer frente a; **the two teams will ~ each other next week** los dos equipos se enfrentarán la próxima semana; **to ~ the facts** enfrentarse a los hechos; **to ~ one's fears/problems** afrontar los miedos/problemas de uno; **to be ~d with sth** verse frente a algo; **I can't ~ doing that** no me atrevo a hacer eso; **we are ~d with financial problems** estamos pasando por problemas financieros; **she can't ~ seeing him so soon after their breakup** no podría soportar verlo tan poco tiempo después de romper **3.**ARCHIT recubrir **4.** FASHION forrar ▶ **to ~ the music** *inf* afrontar las consecuencias **III.** *vi* **to ~ towards the street** dar a la calle; **about ~!** ¡media vuelta!
◆ **face up to** *vt* **to ~ sth** hacer frente a algo; **you must ~ the fact that ...** debes aceptar que...

facecloth *n* toallita *f*

face cream *n* crema *f* facial

facelift *n* lifting *m*

face pack *n* mascarilla *f*

face powder *n* polvos *mpl* (para la cara)

facet ['fæs·ɪt] *n a. fig* faceta *f*

facetious [fə·'si·ʃəs] *adj* chistoso, -a, faceto, -a *Méx;* **stop being so ~** deja de hacerte el gracioso

face to face [ˌfeɪs·tə·'feɪs] *adv* cara a cara; **to come ~ with sth/sb** encontrarse frente a frente con algo/alguien; **to discuss sth ~ with sb** discutir algo con alguien cara a cara

face value *n* **1.** ECON valor *m* nominal **2.** *fig* **to take sth at ~** creer algo a pie juntillas; **to take sb at ~** fiarse de alguien

facial ['feɪ·ʃəl] **I.** *adj* facial **II.** *n* mascarilla *f* facial

facile ['fæs·ɪl] *adj* **1.**(*remark, argument*) simplista **2.**(*victory*) fácil

facilitate [fə·'sɪl·ɪ·teɪt] *vt* facilitar

facilitator [fə·'sɪl·ɪ·teɪ·tər] *n* promotor(a) *m(f)*

facility [fə·'sɪl·ə·t̬i] *n* <-ies> **1.**(*services*) servicio *m;* **transport facilities** medios *mpl* de transporte **2.**(*ability, feature*) facilidad *f;* **~ for doing sth** facilidad para hacer algo **3.**(*building for a special purpose*) complejo *m;* **research ~** centro *m* de investigación; **sports ~** complejo *m* deportivo

facing ['feɪ·sɪŋ] *n* **1.**ARCHIT revestimiento *m* **2.**(*cloth strip*) vuelta *f*

facsimile [fæk·'sɪm·ə·li] *n* **1.**(*exact copy*) facsímil *m* **2.**(*fax*) fax *m*

facsimile machine *n* máquina *f* de fax

fact [fækt] *n* hecho *m;* **the bare ~s** los hechos concretos; **to stick to the ~s** atenerse a los hechos ▶ **~s and figures** *inf* información *f* detallada; **a ~ of life** ley de vida; **the ~s of life** los detalles de la reproducción; **as a matter of ~ ...** de hecho...; **the ~ of the matter is that ...** la verdad es que...; **in ~** de hecho

fact-check *vt* (*in journalism: article*) **to ~ sth** controlar que algo esté correctamente escrito

fact-checker *n* (*in journalism*) corrector(a) *m(f)* (en un periódico)

fact-finding ['fækt·faɪn·dɪŋ] *adj* investigador(a); **~ committee** comisión *f* de investigación

faction ['fæk·ʃən] *n* POL facción *f*

factor ['fæk·tər] *n* factor *m;* **to be a contributing ~ in sth** contribuir a algo; **to be a crucial ~ in sth** ser de vital importancia para algo; **rhesus ~** factor *m* rhesus

factory ['fæk·tə·ri] *n* <-ies> *n* fábrica *f;* **car ~** fábrica de coches

factory worker *n* obrero, -a *m, f* de fábrica

factotum [fæk·'toʊ·təm] *n form* factótum *m*

factual ['fæk·tʃu·əl] *adj* basado, -a en hechos reales; **~ error** un error de hecho

faculty ['fæk·əl·ti] *n* <-ies> *n* **1.**(*teachers*) cuerpo *m* docente **2.** UNIV facultad *f* **3.**(*ability*) facultad *f;* **to have a ~ for sth** tener facilidad para algo

fad [fæd] *n inf* **1.**(*fashion*) moda *f;* **a passing ~** una moda pasajera **2.**(*obsession*) manía *f*

faddish ['fæd·ɪʃ] *adj,* **faddy** ['fæd·i] *adj* maniático, -a, mañoso, -a *AmL*

fade [feɪd] **I.** *vi* **1.**(*lose color*) desteñirse **2.**(*lose intensity: light*) apagarse; (*sound*) debilitarse; (*smile*) borrarse; (*interest*) decaer; (*hope, optimism, memory*) desvanecerse; (*plant, beauty*) marchitarse; (*life*) apagarse

3. (*disappear*) desaparecer; **to ~ from sight/ view** perderse de vista; **to ~ from the scene** desaparecer del mapa **4.** CINE, TV fundirse **II.** *vt* desteñir

◆**fade away** *vi* (*hope, memory*) desvanecerse; (*sound, love, grief*) apagarse; (*beauty*) marchitarse; (*person*) consumirse

◆**fade in I.** *vi* (*picture*) aparecer progresivamente; (*sound*) subir gradualmente **II.** *vt* (*picture*) hacer aparecer progresivamente; (*sound*) subir gradualmente

◆**fade out** *vi* (*picture*) desaparecer gradualmente; (*sound*) desvanecerse

fag [fæg] *n offensive, sl* (*homosexual*) marica *m*

faggot ['fæg·ət] *n offensive, sl* (*homosexual*) marica *m*

fagot ['fæg·ət] *n* (*bundle of sticks*) haz *m* de leña

Fahrenheit ['fær·ən·haɪt] *n* Fahrenheit *m*

fail [feɪl] **I.** *vi* **1.** (*not succeed: person*) fracasar; (*attempt, plan, operation*) fallar; **if all else ~s** como último recurso; **to ~ to do sth** no conseguir hacer algo; **to never ~ to do sth** siempre salirse con la suya; **to ~ to appreciate sth** no saber apreciar algo; **to ~ in one's duty** no cumplir con las obligaciones de uno; **I ~ to see why that matters** no veo qué importancia tiene **2.** SCHOOL, UNIV suspender, ser reprobado *AmL* **3.** TECH, AUTO (*brakes, steering*) fallar; (*engine*) averiarse; (*eyesight, hearing, heart*) fallar **4.** FIN, COM (*go bankrupt*) quebrar **5.** (*crops*) perderse **II.** *vt* **1.** (*not pass: exam, subject, pupil*) suspender **2.** (*not help*) **her courage ~ed her** le abandonó el coraje; **his nerve ~ed him** perdió el valor **III.** *n* SCHOOL, UNIV suspenso *m*, reprobado *m AmL* ▶ **without ~** (*definitely*) sin falta; (*always*) sin excepción

failing ['feɪ·lɪŋ] **I.** *adj* (*health*) débil **II.** *n* (*of mechanism*) defecto *m*; (*of person*) debilidad *f* **III.** *prep* a falta de

fail-safe ['feɪl·seɪf] *adj* infalible

fail-safe device *n* mecanismo *m* de seguridad

failure ['feɪl·jər] *n* **1.** (*lack of success*) fracaso *m*; **crop ~** AGR pérdida *f* de la cosecha; **to be doomed to ~** estar destinado al fracaso; **the ~ to answer** el no responder **2.** TECH, ELEC (*breakdown*) fallo *m* **3.** COM quiebra *f*

faint [feɪnt] **I.** *adj* **1.** (*scent, odor, taste*) leve; (*sound, murmur*) apenas perceptible; (*light, glow*) tenue; (*line, outline, scratch*) apenas visible; (*memory*) confuso, -a; (*smile*) ligero, -a **2.** (*slight: resemblance, sign, suspicion*) vago, -a; (*chance, hope, possibility*) ligero, -a; **not to make the ~est attempt to do sth** no mostrar la menor intención de hacer algo; **not to have the ~est idea** *inf* no tener ni idea **3.** (*weak*) **to be ~ with hunger** estar desfallecido por el hambre; **to feel ~** sentirse mareado **II.** *vi* desmayarse **III.** *n* desmayo *m*; **to fall down in a faint** caer desmayado

faint-hearted [ˌfeɪnt·'har·t̬ɪd] *adj* (*person*) pusilánime

faintly *adv* (*barely perceptibly*) débilmente; **the light shone ~** la luz brillaba tenue; (*remember*) vagamente; (*smile*) ligeramente

fair¹ [fer] **I.** *adj* **1.** (*just: society, trial, wage*) justo, -a; (*price*) razonable; **a ~ share** una parte equitativa; **~ enough** está bien; **it's only ~ that she should be told** lo justo es decírselo **2.** *inf* (*quite large: amount*) bastante; **it's a ~ size** es bastante grande **3.** (*reasonably good: chance, prospect*) bueno, -a **4.** (*not bad*) aceptable **5.** (*light in color: skin*) blanco, -a, güero, -a *AmL;* (*hair*) rubio, -a **6.** METEO **~ weather** tiempo *m* agradable ▶ **by ~ means or foul** con métodos ortodoxos o sin ellos; **~'s ~** *inf* lo justo es justo **II.** *adv* **to play ~** jugar limpio ▶ **~ and square** (*following the rules*) con todas las de la ley; (*directly*) de lleno

fair² [fer] *n* feria *f*; **trade ~** feria comercial

fair game *n* caza *f* legal; *fig* objeto *m* legítimo

fairground ['fer·graʊnd] *n* parque *m* de atracciones

fair-haired [ˌfer·'herd] *adj* rubio, -a

fairly ['fer·li] *adv* **1.** (*quite*) bastante **2.** (*justly*) con imparcialidad **3.** *liter* (*almost*) prácticamente

fair-minded [ˌfer·'maɪn·dɪd] *adj* imparcial

fairness *n* **1.** (*justice*) justicia *f*; **in (all) ~ ...** para ser justos... **2.** (*of skin*) blancura *f*; (*of hair*) lo rubio

fair play *n* juego *m* limpio

fair trade *n* comercio *m* justo

fairway ['fer·weɪ] *n* **1.** (*in golf*) calle *f* **2.** NAUT canal *m* navegable

fairy ['fer·i] <-ies> *n* **1.** (*creature*) hada *f* **2.** *offensive, sl* (*homosexual*) mariquita *m*

fairy tale *n* cuento *m* de hadas; *fig* cuento *m* chino; **a ~ ending** un final feliz

faith [feɪθ] *n* fe *f*; **to have/lose ~ in sb/sth** tener fe/perder la fe en alguien/algo; **to put one's ~ in sb/sth** confiar en alguien/algo; **to renounce one's ~** renunciar a sus creencias; **to keep the ~** mantener la fe

faithful ['feɪθ·fəl] **I.** *adj* fiel **II.** *n* **the ~** los fieles

faithfully *adv* **1.** (*loyally: serve*) lealmente; **to promise ~ to do sth** prometer sinceramente hacer algo **2.** (*exactly: copy, translate*) fielmente

faith healer *n* curandero, -a *m, f*

faithless ['feɪθ·lɪs] *adj* REL infiel; (*disloyal*) desleal

fake [feɪk] **I.** *n* **1.** (*painting, jewel*) falsificación *f* **2.** (*person*) impostor(a) *m(f)* **II.** *adj* **~ fur** piel sintética; **~ jewel** joya falsa; **a ~ tan** un bronceado artificial **III.** *vt* **1.** (*counterfeit*) falsificar **2.** (*pretend to feel*) fingir **IV.** *vi* fingir

falcon ['fæl·kən] *n* halcón *m*

Falkland Islands ['fɔk·lənd·ˌaɪ·ləndz] *npl* **the ~** las (Islas) Malvinas

fall [fɔl] <fell, fallen> **I.** *vi* **1.** (*drop down*) caerse; (*rain, snow*) caer; (*tree*) venirse abajo; THEAT (*curtain*) caer; **to ~ flat** (*joke*) no tener gracia; (*plan, suggestion*) no tener éxito; **to ~ down the stairs** caerse por las escaleras; **to ~**

(**down**) **dead** caer muerto; **to ~ flat on one's face** caerse de morros *inf* **2.** **to ~ to one's knees** caer de rodillas **3.** (*land: bomb, missile*) caer **4.** (*decrease: prices*) bajar; (*demand*) descender; **to ~ sharply** caer de forma acusada **5.** (*temperature*) descender **6.** (*accent, stress*) recaer **7.** (*in rank, on charts*) bajar **8.** (*be defeated*) caer; **to ~ under sb's power** caer bajo el dominio de alguien; **the prize fell to him** le tocó el premio **9.** *liter* (*die in battle*) caer **10.** REL pecar **11.** (*occur*) **to ~ on a Monday** caer en lunes **12.** (*happen: darkness, silence*) caer; **night was ~ing** anochecía **13.** (*belong*) **to ~ into a category** pertenecer a una categoría **14.** (*hang down: hair, cloth*) colgar **15.** (*go down: cliff, ground, road*) descender **16.** + *adj* (*become*) **to ~ asleep** dormirse; **to ~ due** tocar (pagar); **to ~ afoul of the law** infringir la ley; **to ~ ill** caer enfermo **17.** (*enter a particular state*) **to ~ madly in love** (**with sb/sth**) enamorarse perdidamente (de alguien/algo); **to ~ out of favor** perder popularidad; **to ~ under the influence of sb/sth** caer bajo la influencia de alguien/algo; **to ~ to pieces** *fig* (*person*) venirse abajo; (*plan, relationship*) terminar en nada **II.** *n* **1.** (*drop from a height*) caída *f* **2.** (*decrease*) disminución *f*; **~ in temperature** descenso *m* de la temperatura **3.** (*defeat*) caída *f* **4.** (*autumn*) otoño *m* **5.** **~s** (*waterfall*) cascada *f*; **Niagara Falls** las cataratas del Niágara **6.** REL **the Fall** la Caída **III.** *adj* (*occurring in autumn: festival, sale*) en otoño; (*of autumn: colors, temperatures, weather*) otoñal

◆**fall apart** *vi* (*thing*) romperse; (*emotionally: person*) desmoronarse

◆**fall away** *vi* **1.** (*become detached: plaster, rock*) desprenderse **2.** (*slope downward*) caer en declive **3.** (*decrease: attendance, support*) decaer; **to ~ sharply** irse a pique **4.** (*disappear: feeling*) desvanecerse

◆**fall back** *vi* **1.** (*move backwards: crowd*) quedarse atrás **2.** (*retreat: army*) replegarse **3.** SPORTS (*runner*) perder posiciones **4.** (*decrease: production, prices*) reducirse

◆**fall back on** *vt*, **fall back upon** *vt* echar mano de

◆**fall behind** *vi* **1.** (*become slower*) quedarse atrás **2.** (*achieve less: team, country*) quedarse rezagado **3.** (*fail to do sth on time*) retrasarse **4.** SPORTS quedarse atrás

◆**fall down** *vi* **1.** (*person*) caerse; (*building*) derrumbarse; **to be falling down** estar viniéndose abajo **2.** (*be unsatisfactory: person, plan*) fallar

◆**fall for** *vt* **to ~ sb** enamorarse de alguien; **to ~ a trick** caer en una trampa

◆**fall in** *vi* **1.** (*into water, hole*) caerse **2.** (*collapse: roof, ceiling*) venirse abajo **3.** MIL formar filas

◆**fall in with** *vt insep* **1.** (*agree to*) aceptar **2.** (*become friendly with*) **to ~ sb** juntarse con alguien

◆**fall off** *vi* **1.** (*become detached*) desprenderse **2.** (*decrease*) reducirse

◆**fall on** *vt insep* **1.** (*day or date*) caer en **2.** (*attack*) caer sobre; **they fell on the food** se abalanzaron sobre la comida; **to ~ sb** (*cuts*) recaer sobre alguien ▸**to ~ hard times** pasar por malos tiempos

◆**fall out** *vi* **1.** (*drop out: of container*) caer; (*teeth, hair*) caerse **2.** *inf* (*argue*) pelearse **3.** MIL romper filas

◆**fall over** **I.** *vi insep* caerse **II.** *vt* tropezarse con; **to ~ oneself to do sth** *inf* desvivirse por hacer algo

◆**fall through** *vi* fracasar

◆**fall to** *vt insep* (*be responsibility of*) tocar a *inf*

◆**fall upon** *vt s.* **fall on**

fallacious [fə·'leɪ·ʃəs] *adj form* falaz

fallacy ['fæl·ə·si] <-ies> *n form* falacia *f*

fallen ['fɔ·lən] *adj* caído, -a; **~ arches** MED pies *mpl* planos; **a ~ dictator** un dictador derrocado; **a ~ woman** una mujer perdida

fall guy *n sl* cabeza *f* de turco

fallible ['fæl·ə·bəl] *adj* falible; **we are all ~** errar es humano

falling star *n* estrella *f* fugaz

falloff ['fɔl·af] *n* COM baja *f*; (*lessening*) disminución *m*

fallopian tube [fə·'loʊ·pi·ən·'tub] *n* trompa *f* de Falopio

fallout ['fɔl·aʊt] *n* **1.** PHYS lluvia *f* radiactiva **2.** *fig* secuelas *fpl*

fallout shelter *n* refugio *m* antinuclear

fallow ['fæl·oʊ] **I.** *adj* **1.** (*ground, field*) en barbecho **2.** (*period, time*) improductivo, -a **II.** *adv* **to lie ~** estar en barbecho

fallow deer *n inv* gamo *m*

false [fɔls] **I.** *adj* **1.** (*untrue: idea, information*) falso, -a; **a ~ dawn** una señal errónea; **~ economy** falso ahorro *m*; **~ move** movimiento *m* en falso; **to take a ~ step** dar un paso en falso; **a ~ pregnancy** MED, PSYCH embarazo *m* psicológico; **to give a ~ impression** dar una impresión equivocada; **to raise ~ hopes** crear falsas esperanzas **2.** (*artificial: beard, eyelashes*) postizo, -a; **a ~ bottom** un doble fondo **3.** (*name, address, identity*) falso, -a; **to give ~ evidence in court** LAW dar falso testimonio en un juicio; **~ accounting** LAW, FIN falsificación *f* de la contabilidad; **under ~ colors** *liter* aparentando lo que no es; **under ~ pretenses** con engaños **4.** (*insincere: smile, laugh, manner*) falso, -a; **to put on a ~ front** ser hipócrita; **~ modesty** falsa modestia *f* **5.** *liter* (*disloyal*) **a ~ friend** un amigo traicionero **II.** *adv* **to play sb ~** traicionar a alguien

false alarm *n* falsa alarma *f*

false friend *n* LING falso amigo *m*

falsehood ['fɔls·hʊd] *n* **1.** (*untruth*) falsedad *f* **2.** (*lie*) mentira *f*

false imprisonment *n* detención *f* ilegal

falseness *n* **1.** (*inaccuracy*) inexactitud *f* **2.** (*insincerity*) falsedad *f*

false start *n* SPORTS salida *f* nula
false teeth *npl* dientes *mpl* postizos
falsetto [fɔl·'seṭ·oʊ] I. *n* falsete *m;* ~ **voice** voz *f* de falsete II. *adv* **to sing** ~ cantar en falsete
falsification [ˌfɔl·sɪ·fɪ·'keɪ·ʃən] *n* falsificación *f;* ~ **of evidence** falseamiento *m* de las pruebas
falsify ['fɔl·sɪ·faɪ] *vt* falsificar
falsity ['fɔl·sə·ṭi] *n* 1.(*inaccuracy*) inexactitud *f* 2.(*insincerity*) falsedad *f*
falter ['fɔl·tər] *vi* (*person*) vacilar; (*conversation*) decaer; (*courage, negotiations*) tambalearse
faltering ['fɔl·tər·ɪŋ] *adj* (*voice, speech*) entrecortado, -a; (*steps*) indeciso, -a
fame [feɪm] *n* fama *f;* **to rise to** ~ hacerse famoso
famed *adj* famoso, -a
familiar [fə·'mɪl·jər] *adj* 1.(*well-known*) familiar; (*face*) conocido, -a 2.(*acquainted*) familiarizado, -a; **to be** ~ **with sth** estar familiarizado con algo 3.(*friendly*) de familiaridad; ~ **form of address** LING forma *f* de trato informal; **to be on** ~ **terms** (**with sb**) tener un trato de confianza (con alguien)
familiarity [fə·ˌmɪl·i·'er·ə·ṭi] *n* 1.(*intimacy*) familiaridad *f;* (*inappropriate friendliness*) confianza *f* excesiva 2.(*knowledge*) conocimiento *m*
familiarize [fə·'mɪl·jə·raɪz] *vt* acostumbrar; **to** ~ **oneself with sth** familiarizarse con algo
family ['fæm·ə·li] <-ies> I. *n* familia *f;* **to be** ~ ser familia; **to be** (**like**) **one of the** ~ ser como uno más de la familia; **to run in the** ~ venir de familia; **to start a** ~ formar una familia II. *adj* familiar
family allowance *n* Can subsidio *m* familiar
family doctor *n* médico *m* de cabecera
family man *n* (*enjoying family life*) hombre *m* casero; (*with wife and family*) padre *m* de familia
family name *n* apellido *m*
family planning *n* planificación *f* familiar
family tree *n* árbol *m* genealógico
famine ['fæm·ɪn] *n* hambruna *f*
famished ['fæm·ɪʃt] *adj* inf **to be** ~ estar muerto de hambre
famous ['feɪ·məs] *adj* famoso, -a; **to become** ~ **for sth** hacerse célebre por algo
famously *adv* **to get on** ~ llevarse divinamente
fan[1] [fæn] I. *n* 1.(*hand-held*) abanico *m* 2.(*electrical*) ventilador *m* II.<-nn-> *vt* 1.(*cool with fan*) abanicar; **to** ~ **oneself** abanicarse 2.*fig* (*heighten: passion, interest*) avivar; **to** ~ **the flames** *fig* echar leña al fuego
fan[2] [fæn] *n* (*admirer: of person*) admirador(a) *m(f);* (*of team*) hincha *mf;* (*of music*) fan *mf*
fanatic [fə·'næṭ·ɪk] *n* 1.entusiasta *mf* 2.*pej* fanático, -a *m, f*
fanatical *adj* fanático, -a; **to be** ~ **about sth** estar ciego por algo
fanaticism [fə·'næṭ·ɪ·sɪz·əm] *n* fanatismo *m*
fan belt *n* AUTO correa *f* del ventilador
fancier ['fæn·tsɪ·ər] *n* **pigeon** ~ criador(a)

m(f) de palomas
fanciful ['fæn·tsɪ·fəl] *adj* 1.(*idea, notion*) descabellado, -a 2.(*design, style*) imaginativo, -a
fan club *n* club *m* de fans
fancy ['fæn·tsi] I. *adj* <-ier, -iest> 1.(*elaborate: decoration, frills*) de adorno; **the speech was all** ~ **phrases** el discurso estaba lleno de florituras 2.*inf* (*expensive*) carísimo, -a; ~ **hotel** hotel *m* de lujo; ~ **prices** precios *mpl* exorbitantes 3.(*whimsical: ideas, notions*) extravagante II. *n* <-ies> 1.(*liking*) **to take a** ~ **to sth/sb** quedarse prendado de algo/alguien; **to take sb's** ~ dejar fascinado a alguien; **it tickled his** ~ le hizo gracia 2.(*imagination*) fantasía *f* 3.(*whimsical idea*) capricho *m;* **whenever the** ~ **takes you** cuando se te antoje *inf* III.<-ie-> *vt* 1.(*want, like*) **to** ~ **doing sth** tener ganas de hacer algo; **he fancies you** le gustas; **to** ~ **oneself** ser un creído *inf* 2.(*imagine*) **to** ~ **oneself as sth** dárselas de algo; **to** ~ (**that**)... imaginarse (que)...; ~ (**that**)! ¡lo que son las cosas! ~ **meeting you here!** ¡qué casualidad encontrarnos aquí!
fancy-free [ˌfæn·tsi·'fri] *adj* libre
fancy goods *npl* artículos *mpl* de regalo
fanfare ['fæn·fer] *n* fanfarria *f*
fang [fæŋ] *n* (*of dog, lion*) colmillo *m;* (*of snake*) diente *m*
fan mail *n* cartas *fpl* de admiradores
fanny ['fæn·i] *n* sl culo *m*
fantasize ['fæn·tə·saɪz] *vi* **to** ~ **about sth** fantasear sobre algo
fantastic [fæn·'tæs·tɪk] *adj* 1.(*excellent*) fantástico, -a 2.(*unbelievable: coincidence*) increíble; (*notion, plan*) absurdo, -a
fantasy ['fæn·tə·si] <-ies> *n* fantasía *f*
fanzine ['fæn·zin] *n* fanzine *m*
FAQ *n* COMPUT *abbr of* **frequently asked question** FAQ *m*
far [far] <farther, farthest *o* further, furthest> I. *adv* 1.(*a long distance*) lejos; **how** ~ **is it from Boston to Maine?** ¿qué distancia hay entre Boston y Maine?; ~ **away** muy lejos; ~ **from doing sth** lejos de hacer algo; ~ **from it** todo lo contrario 2.(*distant in time*) **as** ~ **back as I remember...** hasta donde me alcanza la memoria...; **to be not** ~ **off sth** faltar poco para algo; **as** ~ hasta ahora 3.(*in progress*) **to not get very** ~ **with sb/sth** no llegar muy lejos con alguien/algo; **he will go** ~ llegará lejos; **to go too** ~ ir demasiado lejos 4.(*much*) ~ **better** mucho mejor; ~ **nicer** mucho más bonito; **to be the best by** ~ ser el/la mejor con diferencia; **to be** ~ **too expensive** ser demasiado caro 5.(*connecting adverbial phrase*) **as** ~ **as I know...** que yo sepa...; **as** ~ **as you can** en (todo) lo que puedas; **as** ~ **as possible** en lo posible; **as** ~ **as I'm concerned** ... en lo que a mí se refiere...; **the essay is OK as** ~ **as it goes** la redacción es aceptable ▶ **so** ~ **so good** hasta ahora todo va bien; ~ **and wide** por todas partes II. *adj* 1.(*distant*) lejano, -a; **in the** ~ **distance** a lo

lejos; **a ~ country** *liter* un país lejano
2. (*further away*) **the ~ bank of the river** la
otra orilla del río; **the ~ left/right (of a political party)** la extrema izquierda/derecha (de
un partido)
faraway ['far·ə·weɪ] *adj* **a ~ land** una tierra
lejana; **to have a ~ expression** estar abstraído
farce [fars] *n* **1.** THEAT farsa *f* **2.** *fig* follón *m*
farcical ['far·sɪ·kəl] *adj* absurdo, -a
fare [fer] **I.** *n* **1.** (*for journey*) tarifa *f*; **one way
~** billete *m* [*o* pasaje *m*] sencillo; **round trip ~**
billete *m* [*o* pasaje *m*] de ida y vuelta **2.** (*taxi
passenger*) pasajero, -a *m, f* **3.** CULIN comida *f*;
simple home-style ~ comida *f* casera **II.** *vi* **to
~ badly/well** salir mal/bien parado; **how did
she ~ at the interview?** ¿qué tal le fue la
entrevista?
Far East *n* **the ~** el Lejano Oriente
farewell [ˌfer·'wel] **I.** *interj form* adiós; **to bid ~
to sb/sth** despedirse de alguien/algo **II.** *n* despedida *f* **III.** *adj* de despedida
far-fetched [ˌfar·'fetʃt] *adj* inverosímil
far-flung [ˌfar·'flʌŋ] *adj liter* **1.** (*spread over
wide area*) extenso, -a **2.** (*remote*) lejano, -a
farm [farm] **I.** *n* (*small*) granja *f*, hacienda *f
AmL,* chacra *f CSur, Perú;* (*large*) hacienda *f*
II. *vt* cultivar **III.** *vi* cultivar la tierra
◆ **farm out** *vt* **to ~ work** subcontratar
farmer ['far·mər] *n* granjero, -a *m, f*, hacendado, -a *m, f*, chacarero, -a *m, f CSur, Perú*
farm hand *n* mozo *m* de labranza
farmhouse *n* <-s> casa *f* de labranza
farmland *n* terreno *m* agrícola
farmstead *n* edificios de una granja
farmyard *n* corral *m*
far-off [ˌfar·'af] *adj* (*place, country*) lejano, -a;
(*time*) remoto, -a
far-reaching [ˌfar·'ri·tʃɪŋ] *adj* de grandes reper-
cusiones
farseeing [ˌfar·'si·ɪŋ] *adj* (*decision, policy*) con
visión de futuro; (*person*) previsor(a)
farsighted [ˌfar·'saɪ·ṭɪd] *adj* (*decision, policy*)
con visión de futuro; (*person*) previsor(a)
far-sighted *adj* MED hipermétrope
fart [fart] *sl* **I.** *n* pedo *m;* **to do** [*o* lay] **a ~** tirarse un pedo **II.** *vi* tirarse un pedo
farther ['far·ðər] **I.** *adv comp of* **far 1.** (*distance*) más allá; **~ away from...** más lejos
de...; **~ down/up** más abajo/arriba **2.** (*time*)
~ back in time más atrás en el tiempo **II.** *adj
comp of* **far** más lejano, -a
farthest ['far·ðɪst] **I.** *adv superl of* **far** más lejos
II. *adj superl of* **far** (*distance*) más lejano, -a;
(*time*) más remoto, -a
fascia ['fæ·ʃi·ə] <fasciae> *n* **1.** ANAT fascia *f*
2. (*board above shop window*) letrero *m*
3. ARCHIT faja *f*
fascinate ['fæs·ə·neɪt] *vt* fascinar
fascinating ['fæs·ə·neɪ·ṭɪŋ] *adj* fascinante
fascination [ˌfæs·ə·'neɪ·ʃən] *n* fascinación *f;* **to
listen in ~** escuchar fascinado
fascism *n*, **Fascism** ['fæʃ·ɪz·əm] *n* fascismo *m*
fascist, Fascist ['fæʃ·ɪst] **I.** *n* fascista *mf*

II. *adj* fascista
fashion ['fæʃ·ən] **I.** *n* **1.** (*popular style*) moda *f;*
to be in ~ estar de moda; **to be out of ~** estar
pasado de moda; **to come into ~** ponerse de
moda; **to be all the ~** estar muy de moda; **the
latest ~** la última moda **2.** (*manner*) manera *f;*
in the usual ~ como de costumbre; **after a ~**
si se le puede llamar así **II.** *vt* dar forma a; (*create*) crear
fashionable ['fæʃ·ə·nə·bəl] *adj* (*clothes, style*)
moderno, -a; (*nightclub, restaurant*) de moda;
(*person, set*) a la moda
fashion designer *n* diseñador(a) *m(f)* de
moda
fashion show *n* desfile *m* de moda
fast[1] [fæst] **I.** <-er, -est> *adj* **1.** (*quick*) rápido,
-a; **the ~ lane** el carril de adelantamiento;
~ train tren *m* expreso; **to be a ~ worker** trabajar rápido **2.** (*clock*) **to be ~** ir adelantado
3. (*firmly fixed*) fijo, -a; **to make ~** NAUT amarrar firmemente; **to make sth ~ (to sth)** fijar
algo (a algo) **4.** (*immoral*) **~ woman** mujer *f*
lanzada **II.** *adv* **1.** (*quickly*) rápidamente; **not
so ~!** ¡no tan rápido! **2.** (*firmly*) firmemente;
to hold ~ to sth agarrarse bien a algo; **to
stand ~** mantenerse firme **3.** (*deeply*) profundamente; **to be ~ asleep** estar profundamente
dormido
fast[2] [fæst] **I.** *vi* (*go without food*) ayunar **II.** *n*
(*period without food*) ayuno *m*
fasten ['fæs·ən] *vt* **1.** (*do up*) atar **2.** (*fix
securely*) fijar, sujetar; **to ~ one's seatbelt**
abrocharse el cinturón **3. to ~ sth onto sth**
atar firmemente algo a algo; **to ~ one's eyes
on sth** fijar la mirada en algo; **to ~ sth
together** (*with paper clip*) unir algo; (*with
string*) atar algo
◆ **fasten down** *vt* sujetar
◆ **fasten on I.** *vt* fijarse en; **to ~ an idea** aferrarse a una idea **II.** *vi* **to ~ to sb** pegarse a alguien
◆ **fasten up** *vt* (*dress*) abrochar
fastener ['fæs·ə·nər] *n* cierre *m; snap ~* cierre
m automático
fast food *n* comida *f* rápida
fast-forward [ˌfæst·'fɔr·wərd] **I.** *vt* hacer avanzar rápidamente **II.** *vi* avanzar rápidamente
III. *n* botón *m* de avance
fastidious [fə·'stɪd·i·əs] *adj* escrupuloso, -a
fastness ['fæst·nɪs] <-es> *n* **1.** (*of color*)
solidez *f* **2.** MIL fortaleza *f* **3.** *liter* (*stronghold*)
refugio *m*
fat [fæt] **I.** *adj* **1.** gordo, -a; **to get ~** engordar
2. (*thick*) grueso, -a **3.** (*large*) grande; **a ~
check** un cheque sustancioso ▶ **~ chance!** *inf*
¡para nada!, ¡ni soñarlo! **II.** *n* grasa *f; animal/
vegetable ~* grasa animal/vegetal ▶ **the ~ is
in the fire** aquí se va a armar la gorda; **to live
off the ~ of the land** vivir a cuerpo de rey; **to
chew the ~ with sb** *inf* estar de palique [*o* de
cháchara] con alguien
fatal ['feɪṭ·əl] *adj* **1.** (*causing death*) mortal
2. (*disastrous*) desastroso, -a **3.** *liter* (*conse-*

quences) funesto, -a

fatalism ['feɪt̬·əl·ɪz·əm] *n* fatalismo *m*

fatalist *n* fatalista *mf*

fatality [feɪ·'tæl·ə·t̬i] <-ies> *n* fatalidad *f*

fatally *adv* **1.** (*causing death*) mortalmente; ~ **ill** enfermo de muerte **2.** (*disastrously*) desastrosamente; ~ **damaged** dañado de forma irreparable

fate [feɪt] *n* (*destiny*) destino *m;* (*one's end*) suerte *f;* **to leave sb to his** ~ dejar a alguien a su suerte; **to meet one's** ~ hallar su destino; **to seal sb's** ~ determinar el destino de alguien; **to share the same** ~ compartir la misma suerte; **to tempt** ~ tentar a la suerte; **a** ~ **worse than death** un destino peor que la muerte; **it must be** ~ debe ser el destino

fated ['feɪ·t̬ɪd] *adj* predestinado, -a; **to be** ~ **to do sth** estar predestinado a hacer algo; **it was** ~ **that...** estaba escrito que...

fateful ['feɪt·fəl] *adj* fatídico, -a

fat-free *adj* sin grasas

fathead ['fæt̬·ˌhed] *n sl* imbécil *mf inf*

father ['fɑ·ðər] **I.** *n* **1.** (*parent*) padre *m;* **from** ~ **to son** de padre a hijo; **to be like a** ~ **to sb** ser como un padre para alguien; **on your** ~**'s side** por parte paterna **2.** (*founder*) fundador *m* **3.** ~**s** *liter* (*ancestors*) antepasados *mpl* ▶ **like** ~, **like son** de tal palo, tal astilla **II.** *vt* (*child*) engendrar; (*idea*) crear

Father Christmas *n* Papá *m* Noel

father figure *n* figura *f* paterna

fatherhood ['fɑ·ðər·hʊd] *n* paternidad *f*

father-in-law ['fɑ·ðər·ɪn·lɔ] <fathers-in-law *o* father-in-laws> *n* suegro *m*

fatherland ['fɑ·ðər·lænd] *n* patria *f*

fatherless ['fɑ·ðər·lɪs] *adj* huérfano, -a de padre

fatherly ['fɑ·ðər·li] *adj* paternal

Father's Day *n* Día *m* del Padre

fathom ['fæð·əm] **I.** *n* NAUT braza *f* **II.** *vt* (*mystery*) desentrañar

fathomless *adj liter* **1.** (*too deep to measure*) insondable **2.** (*impossible to understand*) incomprensible

fatigue [fə·'tig] **I.** *n* **1.** (*tiredness*) cansancio *m,* fatiga *f;* **to suffer from** ~ estar cansado **2.** TECH fatiga *f* **3.** MIL faena *f;* (*uniform*) uniforme *m* de faena **II.** *vt* **1.** *form* (*tire*) cansar **2.** TECH (*weaken*) debilitar

fatigues *npl* MIL traje *m* de faena

fatten ['fæt̬·ən] *vt* engordar

fattening *adj* que hace engordar

fatty ['fæt̬·i] **I.** *adj* **1.** (*food*) graso, -a **2.** (*tissue*) adiposo, -a **II.** <-ies> *n inf* gordinflón, -ona *m, f*

fatuous ['fætʃ·u·əs] *adj* fatuo, -a

faucet ['fɔ·sɪt] *n* grifo *m,* bitoque *m Chile, Col, Méx,* canilla *f RíoPl;* **to turn the** ~ **on/off** abrir/cerrar el grifo

fault [fɔlt] **I.** *n* **1.** (*responsibility*) culpa *f;* **it's not my** ~ yo no tengo la culpa; **to be sb's** ~ (**that...**) ser culpa de alguien (que...); **to be at** ~ tener la culpa; **to find** ~ **with sb** criticar a alguien **2.** (*character weakness*) debilidad *f;* **to**

have its ~**s** tener sus defectos; **to be generous to a** ~ ser demasiado generoso **3.** (*defect*) fallo *m;* **electrical/technical** ~ fallo eléctrico/técnico **4.** GEO falla *f* **5.** SPORTS falta *f;* **double** ~ doble falta; **foot** ~ falta de pie; **to call a** ~ pitar una falta **II.** *vt* encontrar defectos en

faultfinding ['fɔlt·ˌfaɪn·dɪŋ] **I.** *n* (*criticism*) crítica *f* **II.** *adj* criticón, -ona

faultless ['fɔlt·lɪs] *adj* impecable

faulty ['fɔl·t̬i] *adj* defectuoso, -a; ~ **logic** lógica *f* imperfecta

faun [fɔn] *n* fauno *m*

fauna ['fɔ·nə] *n* fauna *f*

favor ['feɪ·vər] **I.** *n* **1.** (*approval*) favor *m,* aprobación *f;* **to be in** ~ **of sb/sth** estar a favor de alguien/algo; **to decide/vote in** ~ **of** (**doing**) **sth** decidir/votar a favor de (hacer) algo; **to come down in** ~ **of** (**doing**) **sth** ponerse a favor de (hacer) algo; **to be in** ~ tener mucha aceptación; **to be in** ~ **with sb** tener el apoyo de alguien; **to be out of** ~ no tener aceptación; **to reject sth in** ~ **of sth else** rechazar algo por otra cosa; **to find in** ~ **of sb** LAW fallar a favor de alguien; **to find** ~ **with sb** caer en gracia a alguien; **to gain** [*o* **win**] **sb's** ~ ganarse la simpatía de alguien; **to show** ~ **to sb** *form* favorecer a alguien **2.** (*advantage*) **to be in sb's** ~ apoyar a alguien; **to have sth in one's** ~ tener algo a favor; **to have the wind in one's** ~ tener el viento a favor **3.** (*helpful act*) favor *m,* valedura *f Méx;* **to ask sb a** ~ pedir un favor a alguien; **to do sb a** ~ hacer un favor a alguien; **do me a** ~! *inf* ¡hazme el favor! **4.** (*small gift*) detalle *m* **II.** *vt* **1.** (*prefer*) preferir **2.** (*give advantage to*) favorecer **3.** (*show partiality towards*) mostrar parcialidad por **4.** *form* (*graciously give*) **to** ~ **sb with sth** dar algo a alguien

favorable ['feɪ·vər·ə·bəl] *adj* **1.** (*approving*) favorable; **to make a** ~ **impression** (**on sb**) causar una impresión favorable (a alguien) **2.** (*advantageous*) ventajoso, -a; ~ **to sth/sb** ventajoso para algo/alguien

favored ['feɪ·vərd] *adj* predilecto, -a

favorite ['feɪ·vər·ɪt] **I.** *adj* (*most liked*) favorito, -a; ~ **son** POL hijo *m* predilecto **II.** *n* favorito, -a *m, f*

favoritism *n* favoritismo *m*

fawn[1] [fɔn] **I.** *n* **1.** (*young deer*) cervato *m* **2.** (*color*) beige *m* **II.** *adj* beige

fawn[2] [fɔn] *vi* (*be eager to please*) **to** ~ **on sb** adular a alguien

fawning ['fɔ·nɪŋ] *adj* adulador(a)

fax [fæks] **I.** *n* fax *m;* **to send something by** ~ enviar algo por fax **II.** *vt* mandar por fax; **to** ~ **sth through to sb** pasar algo por fax a alguien

fax machine *n* fax *m*

FBI [ˌef·bi·'aɪ] *n abbr of* **Federal Bureau of Investigation** FBI *m*

ℹ️ El **FBI** (Federal Bureau of Investigation) es la policía criminal estadounidense. Los funcionarios de dicha institución se conocen también como 'federales' (**feds**). La Central Intelligence Agency (**CIA**) es el servicio secreto exterior de EE.UU. Aparte hay otros diversos servicios secretos.

FDA [ˌef·di·'eɪ] *n abbr of* **Food and Drug Administration** *Administración de Drogas y Alimentos de los Estados Unidos*
fear [fɪr] I. *n* miedo *m;* **to have a ~ of sth** tener miedo de algo; **~ of heights** miedo a las alturas; **for ~ of doing sth** por miedo a hacer algo; **for ~ that** por temor a que; **to be in ~ of sth** temer algo; **to go in ~ of sth** temer por algo; **to put the ~ of God into sb** dar un susto de muerte a alguien; **without ~ or favor** imparcialmente II. *vt* **1.** (*be afraid of*) tener miedo de; **to have nothing to ~** no tener nada que temer; **to ~ to do sth** tener miedo de hacer algo **2.** *form* (*feel concern*) **to ~** (**that...**) temer (que...) III. *vi liter* tener miedo; **to ~ for one's life** temer por la vida de uno; **never ~!** ¡pierde cuidado!
fearful ['fɪr·fəl] *adj* **1.** (*anxious*) temeroso, -a; **~ of doing sth** temeroso de hacer algo **2.** (*terrible: pain, accident*) terrible **3.** *inf* (*very bad: noise, mess*) horrendo, -a
fearless ['fɪr·ləs] *adj* intrépido, -a
fearsome ['fɪr·səm] *adj* temible
feasibility [ˌfi·zə·'bɪl·ə·t̬i] *n* viabilidad *f*
feasibility study *n* estudio *m* de viabilidad
feasible ['fi·zə·bəl] *adj* **1.** (*plan*) factible **2.** (*story*) plausible
feast [fist] I. *n* **1.** (*meal*) banquete *m;* **a ~ for the eye** una fiesta para los ojos; **a ~ for the ear** un deleite para el oído **2.** REL festividad *f* II. *vi* **to ~ on sth** darse un banquete con algo III. *vt* preparar un banquete para ▶**to ~ one's eyes on sth** regalarse la vista con algo
feat [fit] *n* hazaña *f;* **~ of agility** proeza *f* de agilidad; **~ of engineering** logro *m* de la ingeniería
feather ['feð·ər] I. *n* pluma *f* ▶**to be a ~ in sb's cap** ser un triunfo para alguien; **as light as a ~** tan ligero como una pluma; **to ruffle sb's ~s** buscar las cosquillas a alguien II. *vt* **to ~ one's own nest** barrer para dentro
featherbed ['feð·ər·bed] *vt, vi práctica laboral mediante la que se limita la producción o se contratan más empleados de los necesarios para realizar un trabajo con el fin de evitar despidos*
featherbrained ['feð·ər·breɪnd] *adj* (*idea*) disparatado, -a; **to be ~** (*person*) ser un cabeza hueca *inf*
featherweight ['feð·ər·weɪt] *n* SPORTS peso *m* pluma
feathery ['feð·ə·ri] *adj* (*clouds, leaves*) ligero, -a (como una pluma); (*feel, texture*) plumoso, -a
feature ['fi·tʃər] I. *n* **1.** (*distinguishing*

attribute) característica *f;* (*specialty*) peculiaridad *f;* **sb's/sth's best ~** lo mejor de alguien/ algo; **a distinguishing ~** un rasgo distintivo; **a physical ~** un rasgo físico; **to make a ~ of sth** hacer de algo un rasgo distintivo **2.** **~s** (*of face*) facciones *fpl;* **to have regular/strong ~s** tener las facciones normales/muy marcadas **3.** (*in newspaper, magazine*) reportaje *m* **4.** CINE largometraje *m* II. *vt* **1.** (*have as performer, star*) presentar; **a film featuring sb as...** una película que presenta a alguien en el papel de... **2.** (*give special prominence to*) ofrecer (como atracción principal); **to ~ sth** (*article, report*) destacar algo; (*product*) ofrecer la prestación de algo **3.** (*include*) incluir III. *vi* **1.** (*appear*) constar; **to ~ in...** constar en... **2.** (*be an actor in*) **to ~ in a movie** aparecer en una película; **the movie ~s him as...** figura en la película como...
feature film *n* largometraje *m*
featureless *adj* sin rasgos distintivos
feature story *n* reportaje *m*
Feb. *n abbr of* **February** feb.
febrile ['fi·brɪl] *adj liter* febril
February ['feb·ru·er·i] *n* febrero *m; s.a.* **April**
feces ['fi·siz] *npl* heces *fpl*
feckless ['fek·lɪs] *adj form* **1.** (*lacking vitality: person*) apático, -a **2.** (*futile*) inútil **3.** (*unthinking*) irresponsable
fed [fed] *pt, pp of* **feed**
fed. *abbr of* **federal** fed.
federal ['fed·ər·əl] *adj* federal; **~ republic** república *f* federal
federalism ['fed·ər·ə·lɪz·əm] *n* federalismo *m*
federalist ['fed·ər·ə·lɪst] *n* federalista *mf*
federate ['fed·ə·reɪt] *vi, vt* federar(se)
federation [ˌfed·ə·'reɪ·ʃən] *n* federación *f*
fed up *adj inf* harto, -a; **to be ~ with sth/sb** estar harto de algo/alguien
fee [fi] *n* (*for doctor, lawyer*) honorarios *mpl;* (*for membership*) cuota *f* de miembro; (*for school, university*) tasas *fpl* de matrícula; **to charge/receive a ~ for sth** cobrar/recibir unos honorarios por algo
feeble ['fi·bəl] *adj* (*person, attempt*) débil; (*performance*) flojo, -a
feeble-minded [ˌfi·bl·'maɪn·dɪd] *adj* lelo, -a
feebleness *n* debilidad *f*
feed [fid] <fed> I. *vt* **1.** (*give food to: person, animal*) alimentar; (*plant*) nutrir; (*baby*) amamantar; **to ~ the fire** avivar el fuego **2.** (*provide food for: family, country*) dar de comer a **3.** (*supply*) proporcionar; **to ~ the data from a scanner into the computer** introducir datos de un escáner al ordenador; **to ~ sb a line** THEAT apuntar a alguien II. *vi* alimentarse; (*baby*) mamar III. *n* **1.** (*for farm animals*) pienso *m;* **cattle ~** pienso para ganado; **to be off its ~** no tener apetito **2.** *inf* (*meal*) comida *f* **3.** TECH tubo *m* de alimentación
◆**feed back** *vt* proporcionar
◆**feed in** *vt* alimentar; (*information*) introducir

◆**feed on** vt insep, a. fig alimentarse de

◆**feed up** vt (person) alimentar; (animal) cebar

feedback ['fid·bæk] n **1.** (evaluation) reacción f; **positive/negative** ~ reacción f positiva/negativa **2.** ELEC realimentación f

feeder n **1.** TECH alimentador m **2.** (river) afluente m; ~ **road** carretera f de acceso

feel [fil] <felt> I. vi **1.** + adj/n (sensation or emotion) sentir; **to** ~ **well** sentirse bien; **to** ~ **hot/cold** tener calor/frío; **to** ~ **hungry/thirsty** tener hambre/sed; **to** ~ **certain/convinced** estar seguro/convencido; **to** ~ **as if...** sentirse como si... +subj; **to** ~ **like a cup of coffee/something sweet** tener ganas de tomar un café/comer algo dulce; **to** ~ **like a walk** tener ganas de dar un paseo; **to** ~ **free to do sth** sentirse libre para hacer algo; **to** ~ **one's age** notar el peso de los años; **it** ~**s wonderful/awful** me parece maravilloso/fatal; **how do you** ~ **about him?** ¿qué opinas de él?; **how would you** ~ **if...?** ¿qué te parece si...? **2.** + adj (seem) parecer **3.** (search) **to** ~ **for sth** buscar algo; **to** ~ (**around**) **somewhere** buscar palpando por algún sitio II. vt **1.** (experience) experimentar; **not to** ~ **a thing** no sentir nada; **to** ~ **the cold/heat** sentir frío/calor; **to** ~ **something/nothing for sb** sentir algo/no sentir nada por alguien; **to** ~ **it in one's bones** (**that...**) sentir en la propia piel (que...) **2.** (think, believe) **to** ~ (**that**)... creer (que)...; **to** ~ **it appropriate/necessary to do sth** considerar adecuado/necesario hacer algo **3.** (touch) tocar; (pulse) tomar III. n **1.** (texture) textura f; **the** ~ **of sth** el tacto de algo **2.** (act of touching) tacto m; **to have a** ~ **of sth** tocar algo **3.** (character, atmosphere) ambiente m; **a** ~ **of mystery** una atmósfera de misterio **4.** (natural talent) talento m natural; **to have a** ~ **for sth** tener talento natural para algo; **to get the** ~ **of sth** acostumbrarse a algo

◆**feel around** vi buscar palpando; **to** ~ **for sth** buscar algo a tientas

◆**feel for** vt **to** ~ **sb** sentirlo por alguien, compadecer a alguien

feeler ['fi·lər] n ZOOL antena f ▶**to put out one's** ~**s** tantear el terreno

feel-good ['fil·ɡʊd] adj que hace sentir bien; ~ **factor** sensación f de bienestar

feeling ['fi·lɪŋ] n **1.** (emotion) sentimiento m; **mixed** ~**s** sentimientos entremezclados [o encontrados]; **to hurt sb's** ~**s** herir los sentimientos de alguien **2.** (sensation) sensación f; **a dizzy** ~ una sensación de vértigo **3.** (impression) impresión f; **to have the** ~ (**that**)... tener la impresión (de que)...; **to have a bad** ~ **about sth/sb** tener un mal presentimiento acerca de algo/alguien **4.** (opinion) opinión f; **to have strong** ~**s about sth** tener firmes convicciones sobre algo **5.** (strong emotion) sentimiento m; **to say sth with** ~ decir algo con emoción **6.** (physical sensation) sensibilidad f; **to lose the** ~ **in one's leg** perder la sen-

sibilidad de la pierna **7.** (natural talent) **to have a** ~ **for sth** tener un talento innato para algo

feet [fit] n pl of **foot**

feign [feɪn] vt liter fingir; **to** ~ **madness** fingir estar loco

feigned [feɪnd] adj liter fingido, -a

feint [feɪnt] I. vi hacer una finta; **to** ~ **left** fintar a la izquierda; **to** ~ **to do sth** simular la intención de hacer algo II. n SPORTS finta f

felicitous [fə·'lɪs·ɪ·t̬əs] adj form (suitable) oportuno, -a

felicity [fə·'lɪs·ə·t̬i] <-ies> n liter felicidad f

feline ['fi·laɪn] I. adj **1.** ZOOL felino, -a **2.** (cat-like) de gato II. n felino m

fell¹ [fel] pt of **fall**

fell² [fel] vt **1.** (cut down) talar **2.** (knock down: boxer) derribar

fell³ [fel] adj HIST feroz, terrible ▶**at** [o **in**] **one** ~ **swoop** de un solo golpe

fellow ['fel·oʊ] I. n **1.** inf (man) tío m; **an odd** ~ un tipo raro **2.** UNIV profesor(a) m(f) **3.** form (colleague) compañero, -a m, f II. adj ~ **student** compañero, -a m, f de clase

fellow citizen n conciudadano, -a m, f

fellow countryman n compatriota m

fellow feeling n compañerismo m

fellow member n consocio mf

fellowship ['fel·oʊ·ʃɪp] n **1.** (comradely feeling) compañerismo m **2.** form (group) asociación f, sociedad f **3.** UNIV **research** ~ beca f de investigación

fellow traveler n compañero, -a m, f de viaje

fellow worker n compañero, -a m, f de trabajo

felon ['fel·ən] n criminal mf

felonious [fə·'loʊ·ni·əs] adj criminal

felony ['fel·ə·ni] <-ies> n crimen m

felt¹ [felt] pt, pp of **feel**

felt² [felt] I. n (material) fieltro m II. adj de fieltro

felt-tip (**pen**) [ˌfelt·'tɪp·(pen)] n rotulador m

female ['fi·meɪl] I. adj femenino, -a; ZOOL, TECH hembra II. n (woman) mujer f; ZOOL hembra f

feminine ['fem·ə·nɪn] I. adj femenino, -a II. n LING **the** ~ el femenino

femininity [ˌfem·ə·'nɪn·ə·t̬i] n feminidad f

feminism ['fem·ɪ·nɪz·əm] n feminismo m

feminist ['fem·ɪ·nɪst] I. n feminista mf II. adj feminista

femur ['fi·mər] <-s o -mora> n fémur m

fence [fens] I. n **1.** (barrier) cerca f **2.** inf (person) perista mf ▶**to mend one's** ~**s** mejorar su reputación; **to sit on the** ~ nadar entre dos aguas II. vi **1.** SPORTS practicar esgrima **2.** form **to** ~ (**with sb**) enfrentarse (a alguien) III. vt (enclose) cercar

fencer n esgrimista mf

fencing n esgrima f

fend for vt (go without help) **to** ~ **oneself** arreglárselas solo

◆**fend off** vt (defend against: attacker) rechazar; **to** ~ **a question** esquivar una pregunta

fender ['fen·dər] n **1.** AUTO parachoques m inv,

bómper *m AmL*, defensa *f Méx* **2.** (*around fireplace*) guardafuegos *m* **3.** NAUT defensa *f*
fennel ['fen·l] *n* hinojo *m*
ferment¹ [fər·'ment] **I.** *vt* **1.** CHEM hacer fermentar **2.** *form* (*stir up*) agitar **II.** *vi* **1.** CHEM fermentar **2.** *form* (*develop*) desarrollarse
ferment² ['fɜr·ment] *n* **1.** *form* (*state of excitement*) agitación *f;* **to be in ~** estar conmocionado **2.** (*fermentation*) fermentación *f*
fermentation [ˌfɜr·men·'teɪ·ʃən] *n* fermentación *f*
fern [fɜrn] *n* helecho *m*
ferocious [fə·'roʊ·ʃəs] *adj* (*battle, criticism*) feroz; (*competition*) duro, -a; (*heat*) tremendo, -a; (*temper*) violento, -a
ferocity [fə·'ras·ə·t̬i] *n* (*of animal, person*) ferocidad *f;* (*of attack*) violencia *f;* (*of storm, wind*) gran intensidad *f*
ferret ['fer·ɪt] **I.** *n* hurón *m* **II.** *vi* **1.** (*search*) **to ~ around for sth** husmear en algo **2.** (*hunt with ferrets*) **to go ~ing** ir a cazar con hurones
Ferris wheel ['fer·ɪs·ˌhwil] *n* noria *f*
ferrous ['fer·əs] *adj* ferroso, -a
ferry ['fer·i] <-ies> **I.** *n* (*ship*) ferry *m;* (*smaller*) balsa *f;* **car ~** ferry de coches **II.** *vt* **1.** (*in boat*) llevar en barca **2.** *inf* (*by car*) llevar en coche
ferryboat *n* ferry *m*
ferryman <-men> *n* barquero *m*
fertile ['fɜr·t̬əl] *adj a. fig* fértil; **to be ~ ground for sth** *fig* ser terreno propicio para algo
fertility [fər·'tɪl·ə·t̬i] *n* fertilidad *f*
fertilization [ˌfɜr·t̬əl·ɪ·'zeɪ·ʃən] *n* fertilización *f*
fertilize ['fɜr·t̬əl·aɪz] *vt* **1.** BIO fertilizar **2.** AGR abonar
fertilizer ['fɜr·t̬əl·aɪ·zər] *n* fertilizante *m*
fervent ['fɜr·vənt] *adj,* **fervid** ['fɜr·vɪd] *adj form* ferviente
fervor ['fɜr·vər] *n* fervor *m*
fester ['fes·tər] *vi* (*wound, anger*) enconarse
festival ['fes·tɪ·vəl] *n* **1.** (*special event*) festival *m;* **a film/music ~** un festival de cine/música **2.** REL festividad *f,* fiesta *f*
festive ['fes·tɪv] *adj* festivo, -a; **to be in ~ mood** estar muy alegre
festivity [fes·'tɪv·ə·t̬i] <-ies> *n* **1. festivities** (*festive activities*) festejos *mpl* **2.** (*festival*) fiesta *f*
festoon [fe·'stun] **I.** *n* guirnalda *f* **II.** *vt* adornar
fetal ['fiː·t̬l] *adj* BIO fetal
fetch [fetʃ] *vt* **1.** (*bring back*) traer; **to ~ the police** ir por la policía; **to ~ sb sth** (*from somewhere*) traer algo a alguien (de algún sitio) **2.** (*be sold for*) venderse por
fetching ['fetʃ·ɪŋ] *adj* atractivo, -a
fête [feɪt] **I.** *n* (*festival, party*) fiesta *f* **II.** *vt* festejar
fetid ['fet̬·ɪd] *adj form* fétido, -a
fetish ['fet̬·ɪʃ] *n* fetiche *m;* **to make a ~ of sth** hacer que algo se convierta en una obsesión
fetishism ['fet̬·ɪ·ʃɪz·əm] *n* fetichismo *m*
fetter ['fet̬·ər] *vt* **1.** (*chain up*) **to ~ sb** (**to sth**) encadenar a alguien (a algo); **to ~ a horse** atar

a un caballo **2.** *liter* (*restrict freedom*) atar
fetus ['fi·t̬əs] *n* feto *m*
feud [fjud] **I.** *n* enemistad *f* (heredada); **a ~ between sb and sb** una enemistad de sangre entre alguien y alguien; **a ~ over sth** un odio de sangre por algo; **a family ~** una enemistad entre familias **II.** *vi* pelearse
feudal ['fjud·əl] *adj* HIST feudal
feudalism ['fjud·əl·ɪz·əm] *n* feudalismo *m*
fever ['fi·vər] *n* **1.** MED fiebre *f;* **to have** [*o* **run**] **a ~** tener fiebre **2.** (*excited state*) emoción *f;* **a ~ of excitement** un estado de emoción; **baseball ~** fiebre del béisbol
feverish ['fi·vər·ɪʃ] *adj* **1.** MED con fiebre **2.** (*frantic*) febril
few [fju] <-er, -est> **I.** *adj det* **1.** (*small number*) pocos, pocas; **there are ~ things that please him** hay pocas cosas que le agradan; **one of her ~ friends** uno de sus pocos amigos; **quite a ~ people** bastante gente; **not ~er than 100 people** no menos de 100 personas; **the pickings are ~** las ganancias son pocas; **to be ~ and far between** ser poquísimos, ser contadísimos **2.** (*some*) algunos, algunas; **they left a ~ boxes** dejaron algunas cajas **II.** *pron* pocos, pocas; **a ~** unos pocos; **I'd like a ~ more** quisiera unos pocos más; **the ~ who have the book** los pocos que tienen el libro; **the happy/lucky ~** los pocos felices/afortunados
fewer ['fju·ər] *adj, pron* menos; **no ~ than** nada menos que
fewest ['fju·ɪst] *adj, pron* los menos, las menos
ff. *abbr of* **the following** ss.
fiancé [ˌfi·an·'seɪ] *n* prometido *m*
fiancée [ˌfi·an·'seɪ] *n* prometida *f*
fiasco [fi·'æs·koʊ] <-cos *o* -coes> *n* fiasco *m*
fib [fɪb] <-bb-> *inf* **I.** *vi* decir mentirijillas; **to ~** (**to sb**) **about sth** decir mentirijillas (a alguien) sobre algo **II.** *n* mentirijilla *f,* pepa *f And;* **to tell a ~** (**about sth/sb**) decir una mentirijilla (sobre algo/alguien)
fibber ['fɪb·ər] *n* mentirosillo, -a *m, f*
fiber ['faɪ·bər] *n* **1.** fibra *f* **2.** *fig* carácter *m*
fiberglass ['faɪ·bər·ˌglæs] *n* fibra *f* de vidrio
fiber optic cable *n* cable *m* de fibra óptica
fiber optics *n + sing vb* transmisión *f* por fibra óptica
fibula ['fɪb·jə·lə] <-s *o* -ae> *n* peroné *m*
fickle ['fɪk·l] *adj* inconstante
fiction ['fɪk·ʃən] *n* **1. a.** LIT ficción *f;* **~ writer** escritor(a) *m(f)* de novelas de ficción **2.** (*false statement*) invención *f*
fictional ['fɪk·ʃə·nəl] *adj* ficticio, -a
fictitious [fɪk·'tɪʃ·əs] *adj* **1.** (*false, untrue*) falso, -a **2.** (*imaginary*) ficticio, -a; **~ character** personaje *m* de ficción
fiddle ['fɪd·l] **I.** *vi* **1.** (*play the violin*) tocar el violín *Fam* **2. to ~** (**around**) **with sth** (*fidget with*) juguetear con algo; (*try to repair*) intentar arreglar algo **II.** *vt* (*falsify*) falsificar **III.** *n* **1.** (*violin*) violín *m;* **to play the ~** tocar el violín **2.** (*fraud*) trampa *f;* **to be on the ~** trapi-

chear ▶**to be** (**as**) <u>fit</u> **as a** ~ *inf* estar en plena forma; **to play** <u>second</u> ~ desempeñar un papel secundario

fiddler ['fɪd·lər] *n* 1.(*violinist*) violinista *mf* 2.(*swindler*) tramposo, -a *m, f*

fiddling ['fɪd·lɪŋ] I. *adj* trivial; ~ **restrictions** restricciones *fpl* insignificantes II. *n* trampas *fpl*

fidelity [fɪ·'del·ə·t̬i] *n* fidelidad *f*

fidget ['fɪdʒ·ɪt] I. *vi* no parar quieto *inf* II. *n* persona *f* inquieta; **to have the** ~**s** ponerse inquieto

fidgety ['fɪdʒ·ɪ·t̬i] *adj* inquieto, -a

fiefdom ['fif·dəm] *n* feudo *m*

field [fild] I. *n* 1. a. ELEC, AGR, SPORTS campo *m*; (*meadow*) prado *m* 2.+ *sing/pl vb* (*contestants*) competidores *mpl;* **to lead the** ~ ir en cabeza; **to play the** ~ *fig* tantear el terreno 3.(*sphere of activity*) esfera *f;* **to be outside sb's** ~ estar fuera del ámbito de alguien; **it's not my** ~ no es mi campo 4. COMPUT campo *m* II. *vt* 1.(*return*) ~ **the ball** recoger la pelota; **to** ~ **a question** sortear una pregunta 2.(*candidate*) presentar

field day *n* 1. SPORTS día *m* de competición 2. MIL día de maniobras *fpl* ▶**to have a** ~ divertirse muchísimo

fielder ['fil·dər] *n* SPORTS fildeador(a) *m(f)* (*una de las posiciones en béisbol*)

field event *n* SPORTS prueba *f* de atletismo

field glasses *n* prismáticos *mpl*

field mouse *n* ratón *m* de campo

fieldwork ['fild·ˌwɜrk] *n* trabajo *m* de campo

fieldworker *n* investigador(a) *m(f)* de campo

fiend [find] *n* 1.(*brute*) demonio *m* 2. *inf* (*enthusiast*) entusiasta *mf;* **a chess** ~ un fanático del ajedrez

fiendish ['fin·dɪʃ] *adj* (*cruel*) diabólico, -a

fierce [fɪrs] *adj* <-er, -est> 1.(*animal*) salvaje 2.(*love, jealousy*) ardiente; (*hate*) profundo, -a; (*competition, opposition*) intenso, -a; (*debate, discussion*) acalorado, -a; (*fighting*) encarnizado, -a; (*wind*) fuerte 3. *inf* (*hard*) difícil

fierceness ['fɪrs·nɪs] *n* 1.(*wildness*) furia *f* 2.(*of competition, opposition*) intensidad *f;* (*of emotions*) fogosidad *f* 3.(*of wind*) ferocidad *f*

fiery ['faɪr·i] <-ier, -iest> *adj* 1.(*heat*) abrasador(a) 2.(*passionate*) apasionado, -a 3.(*very spicy*) muy picante

FIFA ['fi·fə] *n abbr of* **Fédération Internationale de Football Association** FIFA *f*

fife [faɪf] *n* pífano *m*

fifteen [ˌfɪf·'tin] I. *adj* quince II. *n* quince *m;* *s.a.* **eight**

fifteenth I. *adj* decimoquinto, -a II. *n* 1.(*order*) decimoquinto, -a *m, f* 2.(*date*) quince *m* 3.(*fraction*) quinceavo *m;* (*part*) decimoquinta parte *f; s.a.* **eighth**

fifth [fɪfθ] I. *adj* quinto, -a II. *n* 1.(*order*) quinto, -a *m, f* 2.(*date*) cinco *m* 3.(*fraction*) quinto *m;* (*part*) quinta parte *f; s.a.* **eighth**

fiftieth ['fɪf·ti·əθ] I. *adj* quincuagésimo, -a II. *n* (*order*) quincuagésimo, -a *m, f;* (*fraction*) quincuagésimo *m;* (*part*) quincuagésima parte *f; s.a.* **eighth**

fifty ['fɪf·ti] I. *adj* cincuenta II.<-ies> *n* cincuenta *m; s.a.* **eighty**

fig [fɪg] *n* 1.(*fruit*) higo *m* 2.(*tree*) higuera *f* ▶**I don't** <u>give</u> [*o* <u>care</u>] **a** ~ **about it!** ¡me importa un comino!; **to be not** <u>worth</u> **a** ~ no valer nada

fig. I. *n abbr of* **figure** fig. II. *adj abbr of* **figurative** fig.

fight [faɪt] I. *n* 1.(*physical*) pelea *f;* (*argument*) disputa *f;* **to put up a** ~ defenderse bien 2. MIL combate *m* 3.(*struggle*) lucha *f;* **the** ~ **against AIDS** la lucha contra el SIDA 4.(*spirit*) combatividad *f;* **to show some** ~ enseñar los dientes II.<fought, fought> *vi* 1.(*exchange blows*) pelear; MIL combatir; **to** ~ **with each other** pelearse; **to** ~ **with sb** (*against*) luchar contra alguien; (*on same side*) luchar junto a alguien 2.(*dispute*) discutir; **to** ~ **over sth** discutir por algo; **to** ~ **about sth** discutir sobre algo 3.(*struggle to overcome*) luchar; **to** ~ **for/against sth** luchar por/contra algo III. *vt* 1.(*exchange blows with, argue with*) pelearse con 2.(*wage war, do battle*) luchar con; **to** ~ **a battle** librar una batalla; **to** ~ **a duel** batirse en duelo 3.(*struggle to overcome*) combatir; **to** ~ **a case** LAW llevar un caso a los tribunales 4.(*struggle to obtain*) **to** ~ **one's way through the crowd** hacerse paso entre la multitud; **to** ~ **one's way to the top** hacerse camino luchando hasta la cima

◆**fight back** I. *vi* (*defend oneself*) defenderse; (*counterattack*) contraatacar II. *vt* **to** ~ **one's tears** contener las lágrimas

◆**fight off** *vt* (*repel*) rechazar; (*master, resist*) resistir; **to** ~ **the cold/depression** luchar por no sucumbir ante el frío/la depresión

◆**fight on** *vi* seguir luchando

fighter ['faɪ·t̬ər] *n* 1.(*person*) luchador(a) *m(f)* 2. AVIAT caza *m*

fighting ['faɪ·t̬ɪŋ] I. *n* lucha *f;* (*battle*) combate *m* II. *adj* combativo, -a; ~ **spirit** espíritu *m* de lucha ▶**there's a** ~ <u>chance</u> **that...** existen grandes posibilidades de que... +*subj*

figment ['fɪg·mənt] *n* **a** ~ **of the imagination** un producto de la imaginación

figurative ['fɪg·jər·ə·t̬ɪv] *adj* 1. LING figurado, -a 2. ART figurativo, -a

figuratively *adv* en sentido figurado

figure ['fɪg·jər] I. *n* 1.(*shape*) figura *f;* **mother** ~ figura materna; **a fine** ~ **of a man** un hombre de físico imponente; **to cut a fine** ~ causar buena impresión; **to cut a sorry** ~ parecer ridículo; **to keep one's** ~ guardar la línea 2. ART estatua *f;* (*human being*) figura *f* 3.(*digit*) dígito *m;* (*numeral*) cifra *f;* **column of** ~**s** columna *f* de números; **to have a head for** ~**s** ser bueno para los números; **to be good at** ~**s** saber de aritmética; **in round** ~**s** en cifras redondas 4.(*price*) precio *m;* **a high**

~ una gran suma de dinero **5.** (*diagram*) figura *f;* (*illustration*) ilustración *f* **II.** *vt* **1.** (*think*) figurarse; **to ~ that...** figurarse que... **2.** (*in diagram*) representar **3.** (*calculate*) calcular **III.** *vi* (*feature*) figurar; **to ~ in sth** figurar en algo; **to ~ as sth/sb** figurar como algo/alguien; **that ~s!** es natural

◆**figure out** *vt* (*comprehend*) entender; (*work out*) resolver; **to ~ why...** explicarse por qué...

figurehead [ˈfɪɡ·jər·hed] *n* **1.** NAUT mascarón *m* de proa **2.** *fig* testaferro *m*

figure skater *n* patinador(a) *m(f)* artístico, -a

figure skating *n* patinaje *m* artístico

Fiji [ˈfiː·dʒi] *n* **the ~ Islands** las Islas Fiji

Fijian [fɪˈdʒiː·ən] **I.** *adj* de Fiji **II.** *n* habitante *mf* de (las Islas) Fiji

filament [ˈfɪl·ə·mənt] *n* filamento *m*

filch [fɪltʃ] *vt inf* birlar

file¹ [faɪl] **I.** *n* **1.** (*folder*) carpeta *f* **2.** (*record*) expediente *m;* **to open a ~** abrir un expediente; **to keep sth on ~** guardar algo archivado **3.** COMPUT fichero *m*, archivo *m* **4.** (*row*) fila *f;* **in single ~** en fila india **II.** *vt* **1.** (*record*) archivar, failear *AmC, RíoPl* **2.** (*present: claim, complaint*) presentar; **to ~ a petition** interponer una demanda **III.** *vi* **1.** LAW **to ~ for bankruptcy** declararse en quiebra; **to ~ for divorce** presentar una demanda de divorcio **2.** (*move in line*) desfilar

◆**file away** *vt* archivar

◆**file in** *vi* entrar en fila

◆**file out** *vi* salir en fila

file² [faɪl] **I.** *n* (*tool*) lima *f* **II.** *vt* limar; **to ~ one's nails** limarse las uñas **III.** *vi* **to ~ sth down** limar algo; **to ~ through sth** partir algo con una lima

file manager *n* administrador *m* de archivos [*o* ficheros]

file name *n* nombre *m* de archivo [*o* fichero]

filial [ˈfɪl·i·əl] *adj form* filial

filibuster [ˈfɪl·ɪ·bʌs·tər] *vi* POL usar maniobras obstruccionistas

filigree [ˈfɪl·ɪ·ɡri] *n* filigrana *f*

filing [ˈfaɪ·lɪŋ] *n* **1.** (*archiving*) clasificación *f* **2.** LAW presentación *f* **3. ~s** (*bits of metal*) limaduras *fpl*

filing cabinet *n* archivador *m*

Filipino [fɪl·ɪˈpiː·noʊ] **I.** *adj* filipino, -a **II.** *n* filipino, -a *m, f*

fill [fɪl] **I.** *vt* **1.** (*make full*) llenar; (*space*) ocupar; **to ~ a vacancy** cubrir una vacante; **to ~ a vacuum** llenar un vacío; **to ~ a need** satisfacer una necesidad; **to ~ a need in the market** satisfacer una demanda del mercado **2.** (*seal*) empastar, emplomar *AmL* **3.** CULIN rellenar **4.** (*fulfill: order, requirement*) cumplir **II.** *vi* llenarse **III.** *n* **1. to drink/eat one's ~** hartarse de beber/comer; **to have one's ~ of sth** estar harto de algo **2.** (*dirt*) relleno *m*

◆**fill in I.** *vt* **1.** (*seal opening*) llenar; **to ~ a hole** tapar un agujero **2.** (*document*) rellenar **3.** (*color in*) colorear **4.** (*inform*) informar; **to**

fill sb in on the details poner a alguien al corriente de los detalles **5.** (*time*) ocupar **II.** *vi* **to ~ (for sb)** hacer las veces (de alguien)

◆**fill out I.** *vt* (*document*) rellenar **II.** *vi* (*put on weight*) engordar

◆**fill up I.** *vt* llenar; (*completely*) colmar; **to fill oneself up** llenarse el estómago **II.** *vi* llenarse

filler [ˈfɪl·ər] *n* **1.** (*sealing material*) masilla *f* **2.** TV relleno *m*

fillet [ˈfɪl·ɪt] **I.** *n* filete *m* **II.** *vt* cortar en filetes; **to ~ a fish** cortar un pescado en filetes

fillet steak *n* solomillo *m*

filling I. *n* **1.** (*substance*) relleno *m* **2.** (*in tooth*) empaste *m*, emplomadura *f AmL* **II.** *adj* sólido, -a; **to be ~** que llena (el estómago)

filling station *n* gasolinera *f*, bencinera *f Chile*, grifo *m Perú*

fillip [ˈfɪl·ɪp] *n* estímulo *m;* **to provide a ~ to sb** estimular a alguien; **to give sb a (big) ~** dar un (gran) estímulo a alguien

film [fɪlm] **I.** *n* **1.** PHOT, CINE película *f;* **to make a ~** hacer una película; **to see** [*o* **watch**] **a ~** ver una película **2.** (*fine coating*) capa *f;* **a ~ of oil** una película de aceite **II.** *vt* filmar **III.** *vi* rodar

film buff *n* cinéfilo, -a *m, f*

film camera *n* cámara *f* cinematográfica

film director *n* director(a) *m(f)* de cine

film star *n* estrella *f* de cine

film studio *n* estudio *m* de cine

filter [ˈfɪl·tər] **I.** *n* filtro *m* **II.** *vt* filtrar **III.** *vi* filtrarse

◆**filter out I.** *vi* llegar a saberse **II.** *vt* quitar filtrando

◆**filter through** *vi* filtrarse

filter bed *n* lecho *m* de filtración

filter paper *n* papel *m* de filtro

filter tip *n* filtro *m*

filth [fɪlθ] *n* **1.** (*dirt*) mugre *f;* (*excrement*) excrementos *mpl* **2.** (*obscenity*) obscenidad *f*

filthy [ˈfɪl·θi] **I.** *adj* **1.** (*very dirty*) inmundo, -a; (*weather*) asqueroso, -a *inf* **2.** (*obscene*) obsceno, -a **II.** *adv inf* **to be ~ rich** estar forrado

filtration [fɪlˈtreɪ·ʃən] *n* filtración *f*

fin [fɪn] *n* aleta *f*

final [ˈfaɪ·nəl] **I.** *adj* **1.** (*last*) final; **~ installment** último plazo *m* **2.** (*irrevocable*) definitivo, -a; **to have the ~ say (on sth)** tener la última palabra (sobre algo); **and that's ~** *inf* y sanseacabó **II.** *n* **1.** SPORTS final *f;* **to get (through) to the ~s** llegar a la final **2.** *pl* UNIV exámenes *m* de fin de carrera *pl;* **to take one's ~s** hacer los exámenes de fin de carrera

finale [fɪˈnæl·i] *n* final *m;* **grand ~** gran escena final

finalist [ˈfaɪ·nə·lɪst] *n* finalista *mf*

finality [faɪˈnæl·ə·ṭi] *n* **1.** (*irreversibility*) carácter *m* definitivo **2.** (*determination*) resolución *f*

finalize [ˈfaɪ·nə·laɪz] *vt* ultimar

finally [ˈfaɪ·nə·li] *adv* **1.** (*at long last*) final-

mente; (*expressing impatience*) por fin **2.**(*in conclusion*) en conclusión **3.**(*irrevocably*) definitivamente; (*decisively*) de forma decisiva
finance ['faɪ·nænts] *vt* financiar
finance company *n*, **finance house** *n* sociedad *f* financiera
finances ['faɪ·næn·tsɪz] *npl* finanzas *fpl*
financial [faɪ·'næn·tʃəl] *adj* financiero, -a; (*problem*) monetario, -a; **sb's ~ affairs** los asuntos financieros de alguien
financial adviser *n* asesor(a) *m(f)* financiero
financial year *n* año *m* fiscal
financier [ˌfɪn·ən·'sɪr] *n* financiero, -a *m, f,* financista *mf AmL*
finch [fɪntʃ] *n* ZOOL pinzón *m*
find [faɪnd] **I.**<found, found> *vt* **1.**(*lost object, person*) encontrar **2.**(*locate*) localizar, hallar; **to ~ support** encontrar apoyo; **to ~ happiness with sb** descubrir la felicidad con alguien; **to ~ oneself somewhere** encontrarse en algún sitio; **to be nowhere to be found** no encontrarse por ningún sitio; **to ~ no reason why...** no hallar razón alguna por la que...; **to ~ (the) time** sacar tiempo *inf;* **to ~ excuses** buscar pretextos; **to ~ the strength (to do sth)** hallar las fuerzas (para hacer algo); **to ~ (enough) money** conseguir (suficiente) dinero **3.**(*experience*) sentir; **to ~ oneself alone** sentirse solo **4.**(*conclude*) **to ~ sb guilty/innocent** declarar a alguien culpable/inocente **5.**(*discover*) descubrir **II.** *n* hallazgo *m*
◆**find out I.** *vt* descubrir; (*dishonesty*) desenmascarar; **to ~ when/where/who...** averiguar cuándo/dónde/quién... **II.** *vi* **to ~ about sth/sb** informarse sobre algo/alguien
finder ['faɪn·dər] *n* (*of sth unknown*) descubridor(a) *m(f);* (*of sth lost*) persona *f* que encuentra (algo)
finding ['faɪn·dɪŋ] *n* **1.** LAW fallo *m* **2.**(*recommendation*) recomendación *f* **3.**(*discovery*) descubrimiento *m*
fine[1] [faɪn] **I.** *adj* **1.**(*slender, light*) fino, -a; (*feature*) delicado, -a; (*nuance*) sutil **2.**(*good*) bueno, -a; (*satisfactory*) satisfactorio, -a; **~ weather** buen tiempo *m;* **how are you? — I'm ~, thanks** ¿qué tal estás? — bien, gracias; **to be ~ by sb** estar bien para alguien; **that's all very ~, but...** está todo muy bien, pero... **3.**(*excellent*) excelente; **the ~st wines in the world** los vinos más selectos del mundo; **to have a ~ time doing sth** pasarlo bien haciendo algo; **to appeal to sb's ~r feelings** apelar a los mejores sentimientos de alguien **4.**(*deep*) profundo, -a **II.** *adv* **1.**(*all right*) muy bien; **to feel ~** sentirse bien; **to work ~** funcionar bien **2.**(*fine-grained*) fino, -a
fine[2] [faɪn] **I.** *n* (*penalty*) multa *f,* boleta *f AmS* **II.** *vt* (*order to pay penalty*) multar
fine arts *n* bellas artes *fpl*
fineness *n* (*lightness*) fineza *f;* (*delicacy, ornateness*) delicadeza *f*
finery ['faɪ·nə·ri] *n* **in all one's ~** con las mejores galas

finesse [fɪ·'nes] *n* **1.**(*elegance*) fineza *f* **2.**(*skill*) habilidad *f*
fine-tooth comb [ˌfaɪn·tuθ·'koʊm] *n* **to go through sth with a ~** revisar algo a fondo
finger ['fɪŋ·gər] **I.** *n* dedo *m;* **little/middle ~** dedo meñique/corazón ▶**to be able to be counted on the ~s of one hand** poderse contar con los dedos de una mano; **to have a ~ in every pie** meter baza en todo; **to have one's ~ on the pulse** estar al tanto de lo que pasa; **to put one's ~ on the spot** poner el dedo en la llaga; **to catch sb with their ~s in the till** pillar a alguien robando (en la empresa); **to get/have one's ~s burned** pillarse los dedos *fig;* **to have sb wrapped around one's little ~** hacer que alguien baile al son que le tocan; **to keep one's ~s crossed** tener los dedos cruzados; **to lay a ~ on sb** poner la mano encima a alguien; **to not lift a ~** no mover ni un dedo **II.** *vt* **1.**(*touch*) manosear **2.** *sl* (*reveal*) delatar; **to ~ sb to the police** denunciar a alguien a la policía
fingering ['fɪŋ·gər·ɪŋ] *n* MUS digitación *f*
finger mark ['fɪŋ·gər·mark] *n* huella *f* (dactilar)
fingernail *n* uña *f*
fingerprint **I.** *n* huella *f* dactilar **II.** *vt* **to ~ sb** tomar las huellas dactilares a alguien
fingertip *n* punta *f* del dedo; **to have sth at one's ~s** tener algo a mano; *fig* saber(se) algo al dedillo
finicky ['fɪn·ɪ·ki] *adj* **1.**(*person*) melindroso, -a **2.**(*job*) delicado, -a
finish ['fɪn·ɪʃ] **I.** *n* **1.**(*end*) final *m,* fin *m;* SPORTS meta *f;* **to be in at the ~** estar presente en la conclusión **2.**(*sealing, varnishing: of fabric*) acabado *m;* (*of furniture*) pulido *m* **II.** *vi* terminar(se), acabar(se); **to ~ doing sth** terminar de hacer algo; **to ~ by saying that...** concluir diciendo que... **III.** *vt* **1.**(*bring to end*) terminar, acabar; **to ~ school** terminar los estudios; **to ~ a sentence** completar una oración **2.**(*make final touches to*) acabar
◆**finish off I.** *vt* **1.**(*end*) terminar, acabar, rematar; (*use up*) terminar **2.**(*defeat*) acabar con **3.** *inf* (*murder*) liquidar **II.** *vi* concluir
◆**finish up I.** *vi* **to ~ at** ir a parar a **II.** *vt* (*food, drink*) terminar
◆**finish with** *vt* terminar con; **to ~ sb** romper con alguien; **to ~ politics** abandonar la política
finished *adj* (*product*) terminado, -a, acabado, -a
finishing line *n*, **finishing post** *n* línea *f* de meta
finite ['faɪ·naɪt] *adj a.* LING finito, -a
Finland ['fɪn·lənd] *n* Finlandia *f*
Finn [fɪn] *n* finlandés, -esa *m, f*
Finnish ['fɪn·ɪʃ] **I.** *adj* finlandés, -esa **II.** *n* finlandés *m*
fiord [fjɔrd] *n* fiordo *m*
fir [fɜr] *n* abeto *m*
fire ['faɪr] **I.** *n* **1.**(*flames*) fuego *m;* (*in fire-*

place) lumbre *f;* (*accidental*) incendio *m;* **to set sth on** ~ prender fuego a algo; **to catch** ~ encenderse; **forest** ~ incendio forestal **2.** TECH calefacción *f;* (*stove*) hornillo *m* **3.** MIL **to open** ~ **on sb** abrir fuego contra alguien; **to be under** ~ MIL estar en la línea de fuego; *fig* ser criticado **4.** (*passion*) pasión *f* ▶**there's no smoke without** ~ *prov* cuando el río suena, agua lleva *prov;* **to go through** ~ **and** <u>water</u> afrontar todos los peligros; **to set the** <u>world</u> **on** ~ hacerse famoso; **to** <u>hang</u> ~ suspender operaciones; **to** <u>play</u> **with** ~ jugar con fuego **II.** *vt* **1.** (*burn*) encender; (*ceramics*) cocer **2.** (*weapon*) disparar; **to** ~ **questions at sb** bombardear a alguien con preguntas **3.** *inf* (*dismiss*) despedir, botar *AmL,* fletar *Arg* **4.** (*inspire*) inspirar **III.** *vi* **1.** (*with gun*) disparar; **to** ~ **at sb** disparar contra alguien **2.** AUTO encenderse

◆**fire away** *vi inf* seguir adelante
◆**fire off** *vt* (*letter, reply*) despachar enseguida
fire alarm *n* alarma *f* contra incendios
firearm *n* arma *f* de fuego
fireball *n* bola *f* de fuego
firebrand *n* **1.** (*torch*) tea *f* **2.** *fig* agitador(a) *m(f)*
firebreak *n* cortafuegos *m inv*
firebrick *n* ladrillo *m* refractario
firecracker *n* petardo *m*
fire department *n* cuerpo *m* de bomberos
fire-eater *n* tragafuegos *mf inv*
fire engine *n* coche *m* de bomberos
fire escape *n* escalera *f* de incendios
fire exit *n* salida *f* de incendios
fire extinguisher *n* extintor *m*
firefighter *n* bombero *mf*
firefly *n* luciérnaga *f*, cocuyo *m AmL*
fireguard *n* pantalla *f*
fire house *n* parque *m* de bomberos
fire insurance *n* seguro *m* contra incendios
fire irons *npl* utensilios *mpl* de chimenea
fireman <-men> *n* bombero *m*
fireplace *n* chimenea *f,* hogar *m*
fireproof *adj* a prueba de incendios
fireside *n* hogar *m*
fire station *n* parque *m* de bomberos
firewall *n* muro *m* cortafuegos
firewater *n sl* aguardiente *m*
firewoman <-women> *n* mujer *f* bombero
firewood *n* leña *f*
fireworks *npl* **1.** fuegos *m* artificiales *pl* **2.** *pl, fig* explosión *f* (de cólera)
firing ['faɪr·ɪŋ] *n* **1.** MIL disparo *m* **2.** (*of ceramic*) cocción *f*
firing line *n* línea *f* de fuego
firing squad *n* pelotón *m* de fusilamiento
firm[1] [fɜrm] **I.** *adj* **1.** (*secure*) firme; (*strong*) fuerte; **a** ~ **offer** una oferta en firme **2.** (*dense, solid*) duro, -a **3.** (*resolute*) decidido, -a **4.** (*strict*) estricto, -a **II.** *adv* firmemente; **to stand** ~ mantenerse firme
firm[2] [fɜrm] *n* (*company*) empresa *f;* ~ **of law-yers** bufete *m* de abogados

firmament ['fɜr·mə·mənt] *n* firmamento *m*
firmness ['fɜrm·nɪs] *n* **1.** (*hardness*) dureza *f* **2.** (*strictness*) firmeza *f*
first [fɜrst] **I.** *adj* (*earliest*) primero, -a; **for the** ~ **time** por primera vez; **at** ~ **sight** a primera vista; **the** ~ **of December/December** ~ el primero de diciembre, el uno de diciembre *inf* ▶~ **and foremost** ante todo **II.** *adv* primero; (*firstly*) en primer lugar; ~ **of all** ante todo; **at** ~ al principio; **to go head** ~ meterse de cabeza ▶~ **come** ~ <u>served</u> *inf* por orden de llegada **III.** *n* **the** ~ el primero, la primera; **from the** (**very**) ~ desde el principio
first aid *n* primeros auxilios *mpl*
first aid box *n* botiquín *m* de primeros auxilios
firstborn ['fɜrst·ˌbɔrn] **I.** *adj* primogénito, -a **II.** *n* primogénito, -a *m, f*
first class I. *n* primera clase *f* **II.** *adv* **to travel** ~ viajar en primera
first-class *adj* de primera clase
first cousin *n* primo, -a *m, f* hermano
first floor *n* planta *f* baja
firsthand [ˌfɜrst·'hænd] **I.** *adj* de primera mano **II.** *adv* directamente
first lady, First Lady *n* **the** ~ la Primera Dama
firstly ['fɜrst·li] *adv* en primer lugar
first name *n* nombre *m* (de pila)
first night *n* noche *f* de estreno
first offender *n* persona que comete un delito *por primera vez*
first person *n* LING primera persona *f*
first-rate [ˌfɜrst·'reɪt] *adj* de primer orden
first strike *n* primer golpe *m*
fiscal ['fɪs·kəl] *adj* fiscal
fish [fɪʃ] **I.** <-(es)> *n* **1.** ZOOL pez *m* **2.** CULIN pescado *m* ▶**to be a big** ~ **in a small** <u>pond</u> ser un pez gordo (en un sitio pequeño); **there are plenty more** ~ **in the** <u>sea</u> hay mucho más dónde elegir; (**like**) **a** ~ **out of** <u>water</u> como pez fuera del agua; **to have** <u>bigger</u> ~ **to fry** tener cosas más importantes que hacer; **an** <u>odd</u> ~ un tipo raro **II.** *vi* pescar; **to** ~ **for information** ir a la caza de información; **to** ~ **for compliments** andar a la caza de cumplidos **III.** *vt* pescar
fishbone ['fɪʃ·boʊn] *n* espina *f* (de pescado)
fishcake ['fɪʃ·keɪk] *n* croqueta *f* de pescado
fisherman ['fɪʃ·ər·mən] <-men> *n* pescador *m*
fishery ['fɪʃ·ə·ri] *n* pesquería *f*
fishhook *n* anzuelo *m*
fishing I. *n* pesca *f* **II.** *adj* pesquero, -a
fishing grounds *npl* zona *f* de pesca
fishing line *n* sedal *m*
fishing pole *n*, **fishing rod** *n* caña *f* de pescar
fishing tackle *n* aparejo *m* de pesca
fishnet *n* red *f* de pesca
fishpond ['fɪʃ·pand] *n* estanque *m* para peces
fish stick *n* palito *m* de merluza
fishy ['fɪʃ·i] <-ier, -iest> *adj* **1.** (*taste*) que sabe a pescado; (*smell*) que huele a pescado **2.** *inf* (*dubious*) dudoso, -a ▶**to smell** ~ oler a cha-musquina
fissile ['fɪs·ɪl] *adj* físil

fission ['fɪʃ·ən] n PHYS fisión f; BIO escisión f
fissure ['fɪʃ·ər] n fisura f
fist [fɪst] n puño m; **to clench one's ~s** cerrar los puños; **to shake one's ~ at sb** amenazar a alguien con el puño
fistfight n pelea f; **to have a ~** liarse a golpes inf
fit¹ [fɪt] I. <-tt-> adj 1. (apt, suitable) apto, -a, apropiado, -a; (competent) capaz; **~ to eat** bueno para comer; **it's not ~ to eat** no se puede comer 2. (ready) listo, -a 3. SPORTS en forma 4. MED sano, -a ▶**to be ~ to be tied** estar fuera de sí II. <-tt-> vt 1. (adapt) ajustar; **to ~ the key in the lock** meter la llave en la cerradura 2. (clothes) quedar bien 3. (facts) corresponder con 4. TECH caber en, encajar en III. vi <-tt-> 1. (be correct size) ir bien 2. (correspond) corresponder IV. n ajuste m
◆**fit in** I. vi 1. (conform) encajar 2. (get along well) llevarse bien II. vt tener tiempo para
◆**fit out** vt equipar
◆**fit together** vi encajar
◆**fit up** vt equipar
fit² [fɪt] n 1. MED ataque m; **coughing ~** acceso m de tos 2. (outburst of rage) arranque m; **they were in ~s of laughter** se morían de (la) risa; **in ~s and starts** a trancas y barrancas inf, a tirones inf
fitful ['fɪt·fəl] adj espasmódico, -a; (breath) entrecortado, -a; (gusts) intermitente; (sleep) irregular
fitness ['fɪt·nɪs] n 1. (good condition) (buena) condición f física; (health) (buena) salud f; **physical ~** ejercicio físico 2. (competence, suitability) conveniencia f
fitted ['fɪt·ɪd] adj (adapted, suitable) idóneo, -a; (tailor-made) a medida
fitter ['fɪt·ər] n técnico mf
fitting ['fɪt·ɪŋ] I. n 1. ~s (fixtures) accesorios mpl 2. (of clothes) prueba f II. adj apropiado, -a
five [faɪv] I. adj cinco II. n cinco m; **gimme ~!** sl ¡choca esos cinco!; s.a. **eight**
fivefold adj quíntuple
fiver ['faɪ·vər] n inf billete m de cinco dólares
fix [fɪks] I. vt 1. (repair) arreglar 2. (fasten) sujetar; **to ~ sth in one's mind** grabar algo en la memoria; **to ~ one's eyes on sb** fijar los ojos en alguien 3. (determine) fijar; **to ~ a date** fijar una fecha 4. (arrange) arreglar; **to ~ one's face** inf maquillarse 5. inf (lunch, dinner) preparar 6. inf (manipulate: election, result) amañar 7. inf (take revenge on) ajustar las cuentas con; **I'll ~ him** me las pagará 8. PHYS, PHOT (color) fijar II. vi **to be ~ing to do sth** reg; esp. Southern estar planeando hacer algo III. n 1. inf (dilemma) aprieto m; **to be in a ~** estar en un aprieto 2. sl (dose of heroin) chute m, pichicata f Arg 3. AVIAT, AUTO posición f
◆**fix on** vt 1. (choose) escoger 2. (make definite) fijar
◆**fix up** vt 1. (supply with) **to fix sb up (with**

sth) proveer a alguien (de algo) 2. inf (arrange a date) **to fix sb up (with sb)** arreglárselo a alguien (con alguien) 3. (arrange) organizar 4. (repair) arreglar
fixation [fɪk·'seɪ·ʃən] n fijación f
fixed adj fijo, -a; **to be of no ~ abode** LAW no tener domicilio permanente
fixedly ['fɪk·sɪd·li] adv fijamente
fixer n inf chanchullero, -a m, f
fixings npl inf guarnición f
fixity ['fɪk·sə·t̬i] n form fijeza f
fixture ['fɪkst·ʃər] n (in bathroom and kitchen) instalación f fija; **light ~s** iluminación f
fizz [fɪz] I. vi burbujear II. n 1. (bubble, frothiness) efervescencia f 2. inf (champagne) champán m 3. (soda) gaseosa f
fizzle ['fɪz·l] vi chisporrotear
fizzy ['fɪz·i] <-ier, -iest> adj (bubbly) efervescente; (carbonated) gaseoso, -a
fjord [fjɔrd] n fiordo m
FL n, **Fla.** n abbr of **Florida** Florida f
flabbergast ['flæb·ər·gæst] vt inf dejar sin habla
flabby ['flæb·i] <-ier, -iest> adj pej 1. (body) fofo, -a 2. (weak) débil
flaccid ['flæs·ɪd] adj flácido, -a; fig flojo, -a
flag¹ [flæg] I. n 1. (national) bandera f; (pennant) estandarte m; **to raise a ~** izar una bandera; **to fly the ~** fig hacer acto de presencia; **to keep the ~ flying** fig resistir 2. (marker) señalizador m II. <-gg-> vt (mark) señalar; (label computer data) etiquetar III. <-gg-> vi flaquear
flag² [flæg] n (stone) losa f

ℹ️ El Día de la Bandera (**Flag Day**) recuerda el 14 de junio de 1777, cuando el Congreso Continental (Continental Congress) eligió las barras y estrellas (**Stars and Stripes**) como bandera nacional. Sin embargo, no es fiesta oficial. Para los estadounidenses, la bandera es un importante símbolo de su país.

---

flagellate ['flædʒ·ə·leɪt] vt flagelar
flagon ['flæg·ən] n jarro m
flagpole ['flæg·ˌpoʊl] n asta f (de una bandera)
flagrant ['fleɪ·grənt] adj flagrante
flagship ['flæg·ʃɪp] n buque m insignia
flagstaff ['flæg·stæf] n s. **flagpole**
flail [fleɪl] I. vt 1. (beat) golpear, azotar 2. (one's arms) agitar II. vi (arms) agitarse
flair [fler] n 1. (genius) don m, talento m; **to have a ~ for sth** tener olfato para algo 2. (style) estilo m
flak [flæk] n 1. MIL fuego m antiaéreo 2. inf (criticism) críticas fpl; **to give sb ~** echar la bronca a alguien
flake [fleɪk] I. vi (skin) pelarse; (paint) descroncharse; (wood) astillarse; (plaster) descascararse II. n (shaving, sliver) viruta f; (of paint, wood) lámina f; (of plaster) placa f; (of skin) escama f; (of snow) copo m

◆**flake out** *vi sl* caer rendido

flaky ['fleɪ·ki] <-ier, -iest> *adj* 1.(*skin*) escamoso, -a; (*paint*) de láminas 2. *sl* (*strange*) chiflado, -a

flaky pastry *n* hojaldre *m*

flamboyant [flæm·'bɔɪ·ənt] *adj* (*manner, person*) exuberante; (*air, clothes*) vistoso, -a

flame [fleɪm] I. *n* 1. llama *f;* **to be in ~s** arder en llamas; **to go up in ~s** ser presa de las llamas; **to burst into ~** estallar en llamas 2.(*lover*) (**old**) **~** antiguo amor *m* II. *vi* (*blaze, burn*) llamear; (*glare*) brillar

flaming ['fleɪ·mɪŋ] *adj* 1.(*burning*) en llamas 2.*fig* (*quarrel*) acalorado, -a

flamingo [flə·'mɪŋ·goʊ] <-(e)s> *n* flamenco *m*

flammable ['flæm·ə·bəl] *adj* inflamable

flan [flæn] *n* tarta *f*

Flanders ['flæn·dərz] *n* Flandes *m*

flange [flændʒ] *n* TECH pestaña *f*

flank [flæŋk] I. *n* (*of person*) costado *m;* (*of animal*) ijada *f,* verija *f AmL;* (*of hill*) lado *m;* MIL flanco *m* II. *vt* flanquear

flannel ['flæn·l] *n* 1.(*material*) franela *f* 2.**~s** (*trousers*) pantalones *mpl* de franela

flap [flæp] I. <-pp-> *vt* (*wings*) batir; (*shake*) sacudir II. <-pp-> *vi* 1.(*wings*) aletear; (*flag*) ondear 2. *inf* (*become nervous*) agitarse; **don't ~!** ¡con calma! III. *n* 1.(*of cloth*) faldón *m;* (*of skin*) colgajo *m;* (*of pocket, envelope*) solapa *f;* (*of table*) hoja *f* 2. AVIAT flap *m* 3.(*of wing*) aleteo *m* 4. *inf* (*commotion*) jaleo *m;* **to cause a ~** armar un lío

flapjack ['flæp·dʒæk] *n* (*pancake*) torta *f,* panqueque *m AmL*

flare [fler] I. *n* 1.(*blaze*) llamarada *f;* (*of light*) resplandor *m* 2.(*signal*) cohete *m* de señales 3. MIL bengala *f* 4.(*of clothes*) vuelo *m* II. *vi* 1.(*blaze*) llamear; (*light*) resplandecer 2.(*trouble*) estallar 3.(*skirt*) acampanarse III. *vt* **to ~ one's nostrils** resoplar

flare-up *n* estallido *m fig*

flash [flæʃ] I. *vt* 1.(*shine: light*) enfocar; **to ~ a light in sb's eyes** dirigir un rayo de luz a los ojos de alguien 2.(*show quickly*) mostrar (rápidamente); **to ~ sth on the screen** proyectar algo en la pantalla muy rápidamente 3.(*communicate*) transmitir; (*smile, look*) lanzar II. *vi* 1.(*lightning*) relampaguear; *fig* (*eyes*) brillar 2. *sl* (*expose oneself in public*) exhibirse 3.(*move swiftly*) **to ~ by** pasar como un rayo III. *n* 1.(*of light*) destello *m;* **~ of inspiration** momento *m* de inspiración; **~ of lightning** relámpago *m* 2. PHOT flash *m* ▶**a ~ in the pan** flor de un día; **like a ~** como un relámpago; **in a ~** en un instante IV. <-er, -est> *adj sl* llamativo, -a

flashback ['flæʃ·bæk] *n* CINE, LIT, THEAT escena *f* retrospectiva, flashback *m*

flashbulb ['flæʃ·bʌlb] *n* bombilla *f* de flash

flasher ['flæʃ·ər] *n sl* exhibicionista *m*

flashgun ['flæʃ·gʌn] *n* disparador *m* de flash

flashlight ['flæʃ·laɪt] *n* linterna *f* eléctrica

flash point *n* 1. CHEM punto *m* de inflamación

2. *fig* punto *m* crucial

flashy ['flæʃ·i] <-ier, -iest> *adj* ostentoso, -a, llamativo, -a

flask [flæsk] *n* CHEM matraz *m;* (*thermos*) termo *m;* **hip ~** petaca *f*

flat¹ [flæt] I. *adj* <-tt-> 1.(*surface*) llano, -a, plano, -a; **~ as a pancake** *inf* liso como la palma de la mano 2.(*unexciting*) soso, -a *inf* 3.(*drink*) sin gas 4.(*tire*) desinflado, -a 5.(*absolute: refusal, rejection*) categórico, -a; **and that's ~** y no hay más que hablar 6. COM (*not changing*) fijo, -a 7. MUS desafinado, -a II. <-tt-> *adv* 1.(*level*) horizontalmente; **to lie ~ on one's back** estar boca arriba 2. *inf* (*absolutely*) completamente ▶**to be ~ broke** no tener ni un duro; **to fall ~** resultar un fracaso; **in five minutes ~** *inf* en sólo cinco minutos III. *n* 1.(*level surface: of sword, knife*) plano *m;* **the ~ of one's hand** la palma de la mano 2.(*low level ground*) llanura *f;* **salt ~s** salinas *fpl* 3.(*flat tire*) pinchazo *m* 4. MUS bemol *m*

flat² [flæt] *n* (*apartment*) piso *m,* apartamento *m Ven, Col,* departamento *m Méx, CSur*

flat feet *npl* pies *mpl* planos

flatfish ['flæt·fɪʃ] <-(e)s> *n* pez *m* pleuronecto

flat-footed [‚flæt·'fʊt·ɪd] *adj* de pies planos

flatly *adv* (*deny, refuse*) rotundamente

flatness *n* 1.(*of surface*) llanura *f* 2.(*lack of excitement*) aburrimiento *m*

flatten ['flæt·n] *vt* 1.(*make level*) allanar; **to ~ oneself against sth** pegarse contra algo 2. MUS bajar el tono

flatter ['flæt·ər] *vt* 1.(*gratify vanity*) adular 2.(*make attractive*) favorecer 3.(*be proud of*) **to ~ oneself on sth** enorgullecerse de algo

flatterer *n* adulador(a) *m(f)*

flattering *adj* 1.(*clothes, portrait*) que favorece 2.(*remark, description*) halagador(a)

flattery ['flæt·ə·ri] *n* adulación *f;* **~ will get you nowhere** adulando no conseguirás tu propósito

flatulence ['flætʃ·ə·ləns] *n form* flatulencia *f*

flaunt [flɔnt] *vt* hacer alarde de

flautist ['flɔ·tɪst] *n* flautista *mf*

flavor ['fleɪ·vər] I. *n* 1.(*taste*) gusto *m;* (*ice cream, fizzy drink*) sabor *m* 2. *fig* sabor *m;* **a novel with a romantic ~** una novela con sabor romántico II. *vt* sazonar

flavoring ['fleɪ·vər·ɪŋ] *n* condimento *m;* (*in industry*) aromatizante *m*

flaw [flɔ] I. *n* (*in machine*) defecto *m;* (*in argument, character*) fallo *m;* (*in cloth*) imperfección *f* II. *vt* dañar

flawless ['flɔ·lɪs] *adj* intachable; **~ performance** actuación *f* impecable

flax [flæks] *n* lino *m*

flaxen ['flæk·sn] *adj liter* muy rubio, -a

flay [fleɪ] *vt* 1.(*animal*) desollar 2. *fig* despellejar

flea [fli] *n* pulga *f* ▶**to send sb away with a ~ in his/her ear** echar un buen rapapolvo a alguien

fleabite ['fli·baɪt] *n* picadura *f* de pulga

flea-bitten *adj* **1.** (*with fleas*) pulgoso, -a **2.** *inf* (*seedy*) de mala muerte

flea market *n* rastro *m*

fleck [flek] **I.** *n* (*of color*) mota *f;* (*of paint*) salpicadura *f* **II.** *vt* salpicar

fled [fled] *pp of* **flee**

fledged [fledʒd] *adj* plumado, -a, con plumas

fledgeling, fledgling ['fledʒ·lɪŋ] **I.** *n* (*young bird*) polluelo *m* **II.** *adj* (*inexperienced*) inexperto, -a

flee [fli] <fled> **I.** *vt* (*run away from*) huir de **II.** *vi* (*run away*) escaparse; *liter* desaparecer

fleece [flis] **I.** *n* **1.** (*of sheep*) vellón *m* **2.** (*clothing*) borreguillo *m* **II.** *vt* **1.** (*a sheep*) esquilar **2.** *inf* (*cheat*) despojar

fleet¹ [flit] *n* **1.** NAUT flota *f* **2.** (*of airplanes*) escuadrón *m;* **car** ~ parque *m* móvil

fleet² [flit] <-er, -est> *adj* (*quick*) veloz

fleeting ['fli·tɪŋ] *adj* (*encounter, romance*) pasajero, -a; (*glance, impression, smile*) efímero, -a; (*moment, opportunity, time*) breve; (*idea*) fugaz

Flemish ['flem·ɪʃ] *adj* flamenco, -a

flesh [fleʃ] *n* (*body tissue*) carne *f;* (*pulp*) pulpa *f;* **to put** ~ **on an argument/idea** dar cuerpo a un argumento/idea ►**to be** (**only**) ~ **and blood** ser (sólo) de carne y hueso; **it made my** ~ **crawl** se me puso la piel de gallina; **in the** ~ en persona

fleshpot ['fleʃ·pat] *n* antro *m* de placer

flesh wound *n* herida *f* superficial

fleshy ['fleʃ·i] <-ier, -iest> *adj* (*voluminous: person, limb*) rechoncho, -a; (*fruit*) carnoso, -a

flew [flu] *pp, pt of* **fly**

flex [fleks] **I.** *vt* flexionar ►**to** ~ **one's muscles** medir sus fuerzas **II.** *n* ELEC cable *m*

flexibility [ˌflek·sə·ˈbɪl·ə·t̬i] *n* **1.** (*of material*) elasticidad *f* **2.** (*of person, approach*) flexibilidad *f*

flexible ['flek·sə·bəl] *adj* **1.** (*pliable: material, tubing*) flexible **2.** (*arrangement, policy, schedule*) flexible

flexitarian [flek·sɪ·ˈte·ri·ən] *n* vegetariano que ocasionalmente come carne o pescado

flextime ['fleks·taɪm] *n* horario *m* flexible

flick [flɪk] **I.** *vt* chasquear; **to** ~ **the light switch on/off** encender/apagar la luz; **to** ~ **channels** cambiar los canales **II.** *n* **1.** (*sudden movement, strike*) golpecito *m* (rápido) **2.** *sl* (*movie*) peli *f;* **the** ~**s** (*cinema*) el cine

flicker ['flɪk·ər] **I.** *vi* parpadear **II.** *n* parpadeo *m*

flier ['flaɪ·ər] *n* **1.** (*leaflet*) folleto *m* **2.** (*in airplane*) aviador(a) *m(f)*

flight [flaɪt] *n* **1.** (*movement through air*) vuelo *m;* **the** ~ **of time** el paso del tiempo **2.** (*group: of birds*) bandada *f;* (*of aircraft*) escuadrilla *f* **3.** (*retreat*) huida *f;* ~ **of investment** fuga *f* de inversión; **to take** ~ darse a la fuga; **to put sb to** ~ poner a alguien en fuga **4.** (*series: of stairs*) tramo *m* ►**a** ~ **of fancy** una fantasía

flight attendant *n* auxiliar *mf* de vuelo

flight controller *n* controlador(a) *m(f)* aéreo, -a

flight deck *n* **1.** (*cockpit*) cabina *f* de pilotaje **2.** (*on aircraft carrier*) cubierta *f* de aterrizaje

flight engineer *n* mecánico *m* de vuelo

flight instructor *n* instructor(a) *m(f)* de vuelo

flightless *adj* incapaz de volar

flight number *n* número *m* de vuelo

flight path *n* trayectoria *f* de vuelo

flight recorder *n* caja *f* negra

flighty ['flaɪ·t̬i] <-ier, -iest> *adj pej* (*woman*) frívolo, -a

flimsiness ['flɪm·zi·nɪs] *n* debilidad *f*

flimsy ['flɪm·zi] <-ier, -iest> *adj* **1.** (*light: dress, blouse*) ligero, -a **2.** (*construction*) débil **3.** (*argument, excuse*) poco sólido, -a

flinch [flɪntʃ] *vi* (*from pain*) rechistar; (*from the truth*) no dejar de hacer/decir algo, vacilar

fling [flɪŋ] <flung> **I.** *vt* (*throw*) lanzar; **to** ~ **oneself in front of a train** tirarse al tren; **to** ~ **sb into prison** meter a alguien a la cárcel; **to** ~ **accusations at sb** lanzar acusaciones a alguien **II.** *n* **1.** (*short pleasant time*) rato *m* de juerga **2.** (*relationship*) aventura *f* (amorosa) **3.** *inf* (*try*) **to have a** ~ **at sth** intentar algo

◆**fling away** *vt* desechar

◆**fling off** *vt* **to** ~ **one's clothes** desvestirse con prisa

◆**fling on** *vt inf* **to** ~ **one's clothes** vestirse deprisa

◆**fling open** *vt* abrir de golpe

◆**fling out** *vt inf* (*throw out*) tirar

flint [flɪnt] *n* pedernal *m*

flip [flɪp] <-pp-> **I.** *vt* (*turn over quickly*) dar la vuelta a; **to** ~ **a coin** echar a cara o cruz ►**to** ~ **one's lid** poner el grito en el cielo **II.** *vi* **1.** (*turn quickly*) **to** ~ **over** dar una vuelta de campana **2.** *sl* (*go crazy*) perder la chaveta **III.** *n* (*toss in the air*) ~ **of a coin** lanzamiento *m* de una moneda

flip chart *n* rotafolio *m*

flip-flop ['flɪp·flap] *n* chancla *f*

flippancy ['flɪp·ənt·si] *n* falta *f* de seriedad

flippant ['flɪp·ənt] *adj* poco serio, -a

flipper ['flɪp·ər] *n* (*for diving*) a. ZOOL aleta *f*

flip side *n* **1.** MUS (*of record*) cara *f* B **2.** (*of policy, situation*) **the** ~ la otra cara de la moneda

flirt [flɜrt] **I.** *n* (*woman*) coqueta *f;* (*man*) galanteador *m* **II.** *vi* **1.** (*be sexually attracted*) flirtear **2.** (*toy with*) **to** ~ **with sth** jugar con algo

flirtation [flɜr·ˈteɪ·ʃən] *n* flirteo *m*

flirtatious [flɜr·ˈteɪ·ʃəs] *adj* (*woman*) coqueta; (*man*) galanteador

flit [flɪt] <-tt-> *vi* **to** ~ (**around**) (*bats*) revolotear; (*bees*) volar; (*people*) moverse

float [floʊt] **I.** *vi* **1.** (*in liquid, air*) flotar, boyar *AmL;* **to** ~ **to the surface** salir a la superficie **2.** (*move aimlessly*) moverse sin rumbo **3.** ECON fluctuar **II.** *vt* **1.** (*keep afloat*) poner a flote **2.** ECON, FIN **to** ~ **a business/company** lanzar una empresa/compañía a bolsa **3.** (*suggest*) **to** ~ **an idea/a plan** sugerir una idea/un plan **III.** *n* **1.** NAUT flotador *m;* (*for people*) salvavidas *m inv* **2.** (*vehicle*) carroza *f*

◆**float around** *vi inf* (*circulate*) circular;

(*people*) moverse sin rumbo; (*rumor*) correr ◆ **float off** *vi* irse a la deriva

floatation [floʊ·'teɪ·ʃən] *n s.* **flotation**

floating ['floʊ·t̬ɪŋ] *adj* flotante

flock [flɑk] I. *n* 1. (*group: of goats, sheep*) rebaño *m;* (*of birds*) bandada *f,* parvada *f AmL;* (*of people*) multitud *f* 2. REL grey *f* II. *vi* congregarse

floe [floʊ] *n* témpano *m* de hielo

flog [flɑg] <-gg-> *vt* 1. (*punish*) azotar; *fig* flagelar 2. *inf* (*sell*) vender ▶ **to ~ sth to death** *inf* repetir algo hasta la saciedad

flogging *n* azotaina *f*

flood [flʌd] I. *vt* inundar; **the calls for tickets ~ed the switchboard** el aluvión de peticiones de entradas colapsó la centralita; **to ~ an engine** AUTO ahogar un motor II. *vi* METEO (*town*) inundarse; (*river*) desbordarse; *fig:* **refugees have been ~ing in** ha estado llegando un aluvión de refugiados III. *n* 1. METEO inundación *f* 2. REL **the Flood** el Diluvio 3. *fig* (*outpouring*) torrente *m;* **~ of tears** mar *m* de lágrimas; **~ of products** productos *mpl* a raudales; **~ of abuse** aluvión *m* de insultos; **to let out a ~ of abuse** soltar una retahíla de insultos; **~ of complaints** lluvia *f* de quejas

floodgate ['flʌd·geɪt] *n* esclusa *f; fig;* **to open the ~s to sth** abrir las puertas a algo

floodlight ['flʌd·laɪt] I. *n* foco *m* II. *vt irr* iluminar (con focos)

floor [flɔr] I. *n* 1. (*of room*) suelo *m;* **dance ~** pista *f* de baile; **to take the ~** (*in debate*) tomar la palabra; (*start dancing*) salir a bailar 2. (*level in building*) piso *m;* **sea ~** fondo *m* [*o* lecho] del mar *m* 3. FIN (*lowest limit*) mínimo *m* ▶ **to wipe the ~ with sb** hacer trizas a alguien; **to go through the ~** (*prices*) estar por los suelos II. *vt* (*knock down*) tumbar; **the question ~ed her** la pregunta la dejó sin respuesta

floorboard ['flɔr·bɔrd] *n* tabla *f* del suelo

flooring *n* solado *m;* **wooden ~** entablado *m*

floor lamp *n* lámpara *f* de pie

floor model *n* modelo *m* de muestra

floor polish *n* cera *f* para el suelo

floorshow *n* espectáculo *m* de cabaret

floorwalker *n* encargado *m*

flop [flɑp] <-pp-> I. *vi* 1. (*fall*) dejarse caer 2. *inf* (*fail*) fracasar II. *n inf* (*failure*) fracaso *m*

floppy ['flɑp·i] I. <-ier, -iest> *adj* (*ears*) caído, -a; (*hat*) flexible II. <-ies> *n* diskette *m*

floppy disk *n* diskette *m*

flora ['flɔr·ə] *n* flora *f;* **~ and fauna** flora y fauna

floral ['flɔr·əl] *adj* floral

florid ['flɔr·ɪd] *adj* 1. (*style*) florido, -a; (*prose, rhetoric*) ornamentado, -a 2. *form* (*ruddy*) rojizo, -a

Florida ['flɔr·ɪ·də] *n* Florida *f*

florist ['flɔr·ɪst] *n* florista *mf;* **the ~'s** la floristería

flotation [floʊ·'teɪ·ʃən] *n* ECON, FIN salida *f* a Bolsa

flotilla [floʊ·'tɪl·ə] *n* MIL, NAUT flotilla *f*

flotsam ['flɑt·səm] *n* restos *mpl* flotantes; **~ and jetsam** desechos *mpl*

flounce[1] [flaʊnts] *vi* (*in lively manner*) **to ~ around** moverse violentamente; (*emotionally*); **to ~ in/out** entrar/salir indignado

flounce[2] [flaʊnts] *n* (*decoration*) volante *m,* arandela *f Méx, Perú*

flounder[1] ['flaʊn·dər] *vi* 1. (*struggle*) sufrir 2. (*fail*) ir(se) a pique

flounder[2] ['flaʊn·dər] *n* (*flatfish*) platija *f*

flour ['flaʊ·ər] I. *n* harina *f* II. *vt* enharinar

flourish ['flɜr·ɪʃ] I. *vi* florecer II. *vt* hacer gala de III. *n* **with a ~** con un gesto ceremonioso

flourishing *adj* (*place*) esplendoroso, -a; (*business, market, trade*) próspero, -a

flour mill *n* molino *m* de harina

floury ['flaʊ·ə·ri] <-ier, -iest> *adj* harinoso, -a

flout [flaʊt] *vt* **to ~ a law/rule** incumplir una ley/regla; **to ~ tradition** no hacer caso de la tradición

flow [floʊ] I. *vi* fluir, correr II. *n* (*of water, ideas*) flujo *m;* (*of goods*) circulación *f;* **~ of oil/water** chorro *m* de aceite/agua; **~ of blood** derrame *m* de sangre ▶ **in full ~** en pleno discurso; **to go against the ~** ir contra la corriente; **to go with the ~** seguir la corriente

flowchart *n,* **flow diagram** *n* organigrama *m*

flower ['flaʊ·ər] I. *n* 1. (*plant, bloom*) flor *f;* **to be in ~** estar en flor 2. *liter* (*best*) **the ~** la flor y nata II. *vi* florecer, florear *AmL; fig* desarrollarse

flower arrangement *n* arreglo *m* floral

flowerbed *n* arriate *m* de flores

flower garden *n* jardín *m* de flores

flower girl *n* niña *f* de las flores

flowerpot *n* maceta *f*

flowery ['flaʊ·ə·ri] <-ier, -iest> *adj* 1. (*material*) floreado, -a 2. (*style, language*) florido, -a

flowing *adj* (*hair, robes*) suelto, -a

flown [floʊn] *pp of* **fly**[1]

flu [flu] *n* gripe *f,* gripa *f Col*

fluctuate ['flʌk·tʃu·eɪt] *vi* fluctuar

fluctuation [ˌflʌk·tʃu·'eɪ·ʃən] *n* fluctuación *f*

flue [flu] *n* cañón *m* de chimenea

fluency ['flu·ənt·si] *n* fluidez *f*

fluent ['flu·ənt] *adj* (*style, movement*) con fluidez; **to speak ~ English** hablar inglés con soltura

fluff [flʌf] I. *n* 1. (*furry piece*) lanilla *f;* (*dust*) pelusa *f* 2. (*unimportant matter*) nimiedad *f* II. *vt* 1. **to ~ (up) a pillow** mullir una almohada 2. *inf* (*fail*) hacer mal

fluffy ['flʌf·i] <-ier, -iest> *adj* (*furry: animal*) peludo, -a; (*toy*) de peluche; (*clothes*) lanudo, -a; CULIN (*light*) esponjoso, -a

fluid ['flu·ɪd] I. *n* fluido *m* II. *adj* 1. (*liquid*) líquido, -a 2. (*situation*) inestable

fluid ounce *n* onza *f* líquida (*unidad de capacidad equivalente a 29,57 mililitros*)

flung [flʌŋ] *pp, pt of* **fling**

flunk [flʌŋk] *vt inf* (*student*) catear, tronar *Méx,* *argot,* rajarse *Col;* (*subject: math, history*) caer a alguien

fluorescence [flɔ·'res·ns] *n* fluorescencia *f*

fluorescent [flɔ·'res·nt] *adj* fluorescente; ~ **tube** tubo *m* fluorescente

fluoride ['flɔr·aɪd] *n* fluoruro *m*

fluorine ['flɔr·in] *n* flúor *m*

fluorocarbon [,flɔr·ə·'kar·bən] *n* fluorocarburo *m*

flurry ['flɜr·i] <-ies> *n* agitación *f;* (*of snow*) ráfaga *f;* **a ~ of excitement** un frenesí; **a ~ of speculation** una ola de especulación

flush¹ [flʌʃ] **I.** *vi* (*blush*) ruborizarse **II.** *vt* **to ~ the toilet** tirar de la cadena **III.** *n* **1.** (*blush*) rubor *m;* ~ **of anger** sonrojo *m* de rabia **2.** (*toilet*) cisterna *f*
♦ **flush out** *vt* hacer salir

flush² [flʌʃ] *adj* **1.** (*level*) llano, -a **2.** *inf* (*rich*) **to be ~ with money** andar bien de dinero

flushed [flʌʃt] *adj* emocionado, -a; ~ **with anger** rojo de rabia; ~ **with joy** pletórico de alegría; ~ **with success** emocionado con el éxito

fluster ['flʌs·tər] **I.** *vt* **to ~ sb** poner nervioso a alguien **II.** *n* **to be in a ~** estar nervioso

flute [flut] *n* MUS flauta *f*

fluting *n* acanalado *m*

flutist ['flu·tɪst] *n s.* **flautist**

flutter ['flʌt̬·ər] **I.** *n* **1.** (*sound*) revoleteo *m* **2.** *fig* (*nervousness*) agitación *f;* **to put sb in a ~** poner nervioso a alguien; **to be all in a ~** ser un manojo de nervios **II.** *vi* **1.** (*quiver*) temblar; **to make hearts ~** *fig* hacer palpitar los corazones **2.** (*flap*) agitarse **III.** *vt* (*flap*) agitar; **to ~ one's wings** aletear; **to ~ one's eyelashes** pestañear

fluvial ['flu·vi·əl] *adj* fluvial

flux [flʌks] *n* **1.** (*change*) cambio *m* continuo; **to be in a state of ~** estar continuamente cambiando **2.** MED flujo *m*

fly¹ [flaɪ] <flew, flown> **I.** *vi* **1.** (*through air*) volar; (*travel by aircraft*) viajar en avión **2.** (*move rapidly*) lanzarse; **to ~ at sb** precipitarse sobre alguien **3.** *inf* (*leave*) salir corriendo ▸ **to ~ high** volar muy alto **II.** *vt* **1.** (*aircraft*) pilotar **2.** (*make move through air*) hacer volar; **to ~ a flag** enarbolar una bandera; **to ~ a kite** hacer volar una cometa
♦ **fly away** *vi* irse volando
♦ **fly in** *vi* **to ~ from somewhere** llegar (en avión) desde algún sitio
♦ **fly off** *vi* irse volando

fly² [flaɪ] *n* (*insect*) mosca *f* ▸ **he wouldn't harm a ~** sería incapaz de matar una mosca; **to drop (off)** [*o* **die**] **like flies** *inf* caer como moscas; **a ~ in the ointment** la única pega

flyaway ['flaɪ·ə·weɪ] *adj* suelto, -a

flyby *n* AVIAT, ASTR acercamiento *m*

fly-by-night ['flaɪ·baɪ·naɪt] *adj inf* nada serio, -a

flycatcher ['flaɪ·kætʃ·ər] *n* papamoscas *m*

flyer ['flaɪ·ər] *n* **1.** (*leaflet*) folleto *m* **2.** (*in airplane*) aviador(a) *m(f)*

flying ['flaɪ·ɪŋ] **I.** *n* el volar **II.** *adj* **to pass an exam with ~ colors** aprobar un examen sin problemas

flying boat *n* hidroavión *m*

flying fish *n* pez *m* volador

flying fox *n* panique *m*

flying saucer *n* platillo *m* volante

flying start *n* SPORTS salida *f* lanzada; **to get off to a ~** entrar con buen pie

flying time *n* horas *fpl* de vuelo

flyleaf ['flaɪ·lif] <flyleaves> *n* guarda *f*

flyover ['flaɪ·ou·vər] *n* desfile *m* aéreo

flypaper ['flaɪ·peɪ·pər] *n* papel *m* matamoscas

flysheet *n* doble techo *m* (*de una tienda de campaña*)

fly swatter *n* matamoscas *m*

flytrap *n* atrapamoscas *m*

flyweight ['flaɪ·weɪt] *n* SPORTS peso *m* mosca

flywheel ['flaɪ·hwil] *n* TECH volante *m*

FM [,ef·'em] PHYS *abbr of* **frequency modulation** FM

foal [foul] **I.** *n* potro, -a *m, f;* **to be in ~** estar preñada **II.** *vi* parir

foam [foum] **I.** *n* (*bubbles, foam rubber*) espuma *f* **II.** *vi* **to ~ with rage** echar espuma de (pura) rabia

foam rubber *n* goma espuma *f*

foamy ['fou·mi] <-ier, -iest> *adj* espumoso, -a

focal ['fou·kəl] *adj* focal; ~ **point** foco *m*

focus ['fou·kəs] <-es *o* foci> **I.** *n* **1.** foco *m;* **to be in/out of ~** estar enfocado/desenfocado **2.** (*center*) centro *m;* ~ **of interest** centro de interés; **the ~ of a program** el enfoque de un programa; **to bring sth into ~** *fig* destacar algo **II.** <-s- *o* -ss-> *vi* enfocar; **to ~ on sth** (*concentrate*) concentrarse en algo **III.** *vt* enfocar; **to ~ one's attention on sth** centrar la atención en algo

fodder ['fad·ər] *n* **1.** (*animal food*) forraje *m;* ~ **crop** cereal-pienso *m* **2.** *fig, inf* pasto *m*

foe [fou] *n* enemigo, -a *m, f*

fog [fag] *n* niebla *f;* **to be in a ~** *fig* estar confundido
♦ **fog up** *vi* (*eyeglasses, window*) empañarse

fog bank *n* banco *m* de niebla

fogbound ['fag·baund] *adj* inmovilizado, -a por la niebla

fogey ['fou·gi] <-ies> *n pej, inf s.* **fogy**

foggy ['fa·gi] <-ier, -iest> *adj* **1.** (*weather*) nebuloso, -a **2.** (*unclear: memory*) vago, -a ▸ **to not have the foggiest** (idea) no tener la más remota idea

foghorn ['fag·hɔrn] *n* sirena *f* de niebla; **to have a voice like a ~** tener una voz chillona

fog light *n* faro *m* antiniebla

fogy ['fou·gi] <-ies> *n pej, inf* persona *f* chapada a la antigua; **old ~** carroza *mf;* **young ~** joven *mf* de ideas anticuadas

foible ['fɔɪ·bəl] *n* debilidad *f*

foil¹ [fɔɪl] *n* **1.** (*metal sheet*) papel *m* de aluminio **2.** (*sword*) florete *m* **3.** *fig* **to act as a ~ to sth** servir de contraste con algo

foil² [fɔɪl] *vt* (*cause to fail*) frustrar

F

foist (up)on [ˌfɔɪst·(ə·ˈp)an] *vt* **to foist sth (up)on sb** hacer que alguien se encargue de algo

fold¹ [fould] **I.** *vt* **1.** (*bend*) plegar; **to ~ sth back/down** plegar algo **2.** (*wrap*) **to ~ sth (in sth)** envolver algo (en algo) **II.** *vi* **1.** (*bend over*) doblarse **2.** (*fail, go bankrupt*) fracasar **III.** *n* pliegue *m*
◆**fold up** *vt* doblar

fold² [fould] *n* (*sheep pen*) redil *m;* **to return to the ~** *fig* volver al hogar

folder [ˈfoul·dər] *n a.* COMPUT carpeta *f,* fólder *m Col, Méx*

folding [ˈfoul·dɪŋ] *adj* plegable; **~ door** puerta *f* plegadiza; **~ money** billetes *mpl* de banco

foliage [ˈfou·lɪ·ɪdʒ] *n* follaje *m*

folio [ˈfou·li·ou] *n* folio *m*

folk [fouk] *n* **1.** *pl* pueblo *m;* **farming ~** gente *f* de campo; **the old ~** los viejos; **ordinary ~** gente *f* corriente; (*~ memory*) memoria *f* colectiva; **~ wisdom** sabiduría *f* popular **2. ~s** (*parents*) viejos *mpl*

folk dance *n* baile *m* popular

folklore [ˈfouk·lɔr] *n* folklore *m*

folk music *n* música *f* folk

folk song *n* canción *f* popular

folksy [ˈfouk·si] <-ier, -iest> *adj* (*friendly*) amigable

folktale *n* cuento *m* popular

follow [ˈfal·ou] **I.** *vt* **1.** (*take same route as*) seguir **2.** (*happen next*) **to ~ sth** suceder a algo **3. to ~ sb's example/advice** seguir el ejemplo/consejo de alguien **4.** (*understand*) **to ~ sb/sth** seguir a alguien/algo **5.** (*have an interest in*) **to ~ sth** interesarse por algo **II.** *vi* **1.** (*take same route as*) seguir **2.** (*happen next*) suceder **3.** (*result*) resultar; **to ~ from sth** ser consecuencia de algo
◆**follow on** *vi* seguir
◆**follow through I.** *vt* **1.** (*study*) investigar **2.** (*see through to end*) terminar **II.** *vi* SPORTS acompañar (un golpe)
◆**follow up I.** *vt* **1.** (*consider, investigate*) investigar **2.** (*do next*) **to ~ sth by** [*o* with]... hacer algo después de...

follower *n* seguidor(a) *m(f)*

following I. *n inv* **1. I'd say the ~** diría lo siguiente; **my idea was the ~** mi idea era la siguiente **2.** (*supporters: of idea*) partidarios, -as *m, f pl;* (*of doctrine*) seguidores, -as *m, f pl* **II.** *adj* **1.** (*next*) siguiente; **the ~ ideas** las siguientes ideas **2.** (*from behind*) **~ wind** viento de cola [*o* de popa] **III.** *prep* después de; **~ dinner/your letter** después de la cena/tu carta

follow-up *n* seguimiento *m*

folly [ˈfal·i] *n* (*foolishness*) locura *f;* **it's sheer ~!** ¡es una locura!

fond [fand] <-er, -est> *adj* **1.** (*with liking for*) **to be ~ of sb** tener cariño a alguien; **he is ~ of...** le gusta... **2.** (*loving*) cariñoso, -a; **~ memories** tiernos recuerdos *mpl* **3.** (*hope*) vano, -a

fondle [ˈfan·dl] <-ling> *vt* acariciar

fondness [ˈfand·nɪs] *n* cariño *m;* **to have a ~ for sth** tener una afición por algo

font [fant] *n* **1.** TYPO fuente *f* **2.** (*receptacle*) pila *f* (bautismal)

food [fud] *n* comida *f* ▶**to give sb ~ for thought** dar a alguien algo en que pensar; **to be off one's ~** estar desganado

food chain *n* cadena *f* alimentaria

food poisoning *n* intoxicación *f* por alimentos

food processor *n* procesador *m* de alimentos

food stamps *n* vales emitidos por el gobierno estadounidense para la compra de comida

foodstuff *n* artículo *m* alimenticio

fool [ful] **I.** *n* idiota *mf;* **to be a big enough ~ to do sth** ser bastante idiota como para hacer algo; **to act like a ~** hacer el tonto; **to make a ~ of sb** poner a alguien en ridículo; **any ~** cualquiera **II.** *vt* engañar; **you could have ~ed me!** *inf* ¡no me lo puedo creer! **III.** *vi* (*joke around*) bromear **IV.** *adj inf* (*silly*) tonto, -a
◆**fool around** *vi* hacer payasadas

foolhardy [ˈful·har·di] *adj* temerario, -a

foolish [ˈfu·lɪʃ] *adj* tonto, -a

foolproof [ˈful·pruf] *adj* a prueba de tontos

fool's cap *n* papel *m* tamaño folio

foot [fut] **I.** <feet> *n* **1.** (*of person*) pie *m;* (*of animal*) pata *f* **2.** (*unit of measurement*) pie *m* (*30,48 cm*) **3.** (*bottom or lowest part*) **at the ~ of one's bed** al pie de la cama; **at the ~ of the page** a pie de página ▶**to get a ~ in the door** abrirse una brecha, introducirse; **to have one ~ in the grave** estar con un pie en la tumba; **to have both feet on the ground** ser realista; **to set ~ on dry land** poner los pies en tierra firme; **to be back on one's feet** haberse recuperado; **to have/get cold feet** estar/ponerse nervioso; **to get off on the wrong ~** empezar con mal pie; **to fall on one's feet** caer de pie; **to find one's feet** acostumbrarse al ambiente; **to put one's ~ down** no ceder; **to put one's ~ in it** [*o* in one's mouth] meter la pata; **to set ~ in sth** pisar algo; **I'll never set ~ in his house again** no volveré a pisar su casa; **to be under sb's feet** estar siempre pegado a alguien **II.** *vt inf* **to ~ the bill** pagar

footage [ˈfut·ɪdʒ] *n* CINE, TV secuencias *fpl,* imágenes *fpl*

foot-and-mouth disease *n* fiebre *f* aftosa

football [ˈfut·bɔl] *n* **1.** (*sport*) fútbol *m* americano **2.** (*ball*) balón *m* de fútbol americano

i El **football** americano es muy diferente al fútbol europeo, que en EE.UU. se conoce como **soccer**. El balón tiene dos extremos en punta y no sólo se puede impulsar con el pie sino que también se lanza con la mano. Cada tiempo comienza con un **kickoff**, es decir, un jugador da una patada al balón y los demás de su equipo intentan atraparlo con las manos para correr con él a la portería. Los contrarios frenan al jugador que lleva el balón mediante **tackling**, para lo cual lo sujetan con los brazos y lo empujan contra el suelo.

football player *n* jugador (a) *m(f)* de fútbol americano
footboard *n* AUTO estribo *m*
footbridge ['fʊt·brɪdʒ] *n* puente *m* peatonal
footer ['fʊt·ər] *n* pie *m* de página
foothills ['fʊt·hɪlz] *n* estribaciones *fpl*
foothold ['fʊt·hoʊld] *n* punto *m* de apoyo para el pie; **to gain a ~** *fig* lograr establecerse
footing ['fʊt·ɪŋ] *n* **1.** **to lose one's ~** resbalar **2.** (*basis*) posición *f*; **on an equal ~** en una situación de igualdad
footlights ['fʊt·laɪts] *npl* candilejas *fpl*
footling ['fut·lɪŋ] *adj* trivial
footloose ['fʊt·lus] *adj* libre ▶**to be ~ and fancy-free** estar soltero y sin compromiso
footman ['fʊt·mən] <-men> *n* lacayo *m*
footnote ['fʊt·noʊt] *n* nota *f* a pie de página
footpath ['fʊt·pæθ] *n* sendero *m*
footprint ['fʊt·prɪnt] *n* huella *f*
footrest ['fʊt·rest] *n* reposapiés *m inv*
footsie ['fʊt·si] *n inf* **to play ~ with sb** acariciar a alguien con el pie
footslog ['fʊt·slag] <-gg-> *vi inf* andar hasta acabar rendido
footsore ['fʊt·sɔr] *adj liter* **to be ~** tener los pies cansados
footstep ['fʊt·step] *n* paso *m*
footstool ['fʊt·stul] *n* reposapiés *m inv*
footwear ['fʊt·wer] *n* calzado *m*
footwork ['fʊt·wɜrk] *n* juego *m* de piernas
for [fɔr] **I.** *prep* **1.** (*destined for*) para; **this is ~ you** esto es para ti; **a present ~ my mother** un regalo para mi madre **2.** (*in order to help*) por; **to do sth ~ sb** hacer algo por alguien **3.** (*intention, purpose*) **~ sale/rent** en venta/alquiler; **sth ~ a headache** algo para el dolor de cabeza; **it's time ~ lunch** es hora del almuerzo; **to invite sb ~ dinner** invitar a alguien a cenar; **to wait ~ sb** esperar a alguien; **to go ~ a walk** ir a dar un paseo; **fit ~ nothing** bueno para nada; **what ~?** ¿para qué?; **what's that ~?** ¿para qué es eso?; **it's ~ cutting cheese** es para cortar queso; **~ this to be possible** para que esto sea posible; **to look ~ a way to do sth** buscar una manera de hacer algo **4.** (*to acquire*) **eager ~ power** ávido de poder; **to search ~ sth** buscar algo; **to ask/hope ~ news** pedir/esperar noticias; **to apply ~ a job** solicitar un trabajo; **to shout ~ help** gritar pidiendo ayuda **5.** (*towards*) **the train ~ Boston** el tren hacia Boston; **to make ~ home** dirigirse hacia casa; **to run ~ safety** correr a ponerse a salvo **6.** (*distance*) **to walk ~ 8 miles** caminar durante 8 millas **7.** (*time*) **~ now** por ahora; **~ a while/a time** por un rato/un momento; **to last ~ hours** durar horas y horas; **I'm going to be here ~ three

weeks** voy a estar aquí durante tres semanas; **I haven't been there ~ three years** hace tres años que no estoy allí; **I have known her ~ three years** la conozco desde hace tres años **8.** (*on date of*) **to have sth finished ~ Sunday** acabar algo para el domingo; **to set the wedding ~ May 4th** fijar la boda para el 4 de mayo **9.** (*in support of*) **is he ~ or against it?** ¿está a favor o en contra?; **to fight ~ sth** luchar por algo **10.** (*employed by*) **to work ~ a company** trabajar para una empresa **11.** (*the task of*) **it's ~ him to say/do...** le toca a él decir/hacer... **12.** (*in substitution*) **the substitute ~ the teacher** el substituto del maestro; **say hello ~ me** dile hola de mi parte **13.** (*price*) **a check ~ $100** un cheque por valor de cien dólares; **I paid $10 ~ it** pagué diez dólares por ello **14.** (*concerning*) **as ~ me/that** en cuanto a mí/eso; **two are enough ~ me** dos son suficientes para mí; **sorry ~ doing that** perdón por hacer eso; **the best would be ~ me to go** lo mejor sería que me fuese **15.** (*in reference to*) **what's Chinese ~ 'book'?** ¿cómo se dice 'libro' en chino? **16.** (*cause*) **excuse me ~ being late** siento llegar tarde; **as the reason ~ one's behavior** como razón por su comportamiento **17.** (*because of*) **to do sth ~ love** hacer algo por amor; **~ fear of doing sth** por miedo a hacer algo; **to cry ~ joy** gritar de alegría; **he can't talk ~ laughing** no puede hablar de la risa **18.** (*despite*) **~ all that/her money** a pesar de todo eso/de su dinero; **~ all I know** que yo sepa **19.** (*as*) **~ example** por ejemplo; **he ~ one** empezando por él ▶**she's ~ it!** ¡se la va a cargar!; **that's kids ~ you!** ¡así son los niños! **II.** *conj form* pues
forage ['fɔr·ɪdʒ] **I.** *vi* **to ~ for sth** buscar algo **II.** *n* (*fodder*) forraje *m*
foray ['fɔr·eɪ] *n* (*raid*) correría *f*; **to make a ~ (into sth)** hacer una incursión (en algo)
forbad(e) [fər·'bæd] *pt of* forbid
forbear [fɔr·'ber] <forbore, forborne> *vi form* (*abstain, refrain*) contenerse; **to ~ from doing sth** abstenerse de hacer algo
forbearance [fɔr·'ber·əns] *n form* **1.** (*patience*) paciencia *f* **2.** (*self-control*) dominio *m* de sí mismo
forbid [fər·'bɪd] <forbade, forbidden> *vt* prohibir; **to ~ sb from doing sth** prohibir a alguien hacer algo; **to ~ sb sth** *form* prohibir algo a alguien
forbidden [fər·'bɪd·ən] *pp of* forbid
forbidding [fər·'bɪd·ɪŋ] *adj* **1.** (*threatening*) que intimida **2.** (*disapproving: frown, look*) severo, -a; (*bearing rain: sky, clouds*) amenazador, a
forbore [fɔr·'bɔr] *pt of* forbear
forborne [fɔr·'bɔrn] *pp of* forbear
force [fɔrs] **I.** *n* **1.** (*power*) fuerza *f*; **by sheer ~ of numbers** por superioridad numérica; **~ of gravity** PHYS fuerza de la gravedad; **to combine ~s** unir esfuerzos **2.** (*large numbers*) **in ~** en grandes cantidades **3.** (*influence*) influen-

cia *f;* **by ~ of circumstance** debido a las circunstancias; **by ~ of habit** por costumbre; **the ~s of nature** las fuerzas de la naturaleza **4.** (*validity*) validez *f;* **to come into ~** entrar en vigor **5.** MIL **police ~** cuerpo *m* de policía; **Air Force** Fuerzas *f* Aéreas; **the armed ~s** fuerzas *fpl* armadas **II.** *vt* **1.** (*use power*) forzar; **to ~ a door** forzar una puerta **2.** (*oblige to do*) obligar; **to ~ sb to do sth** obligar a alguien a hacer algo; **to ~ sb into** (**doing**) **sth** forzar a alguien a (hacer) algo; **to ~ sth on sb** imponer algo a alguien; **to ~ a smile** sonreír forzadamente; **to ~ words out of sb** hacer hablar a alguien **3.** (*cause to grow faster*) hacer madurar temprano
 ◆ **force off** *vt* quitar por la fuerza
 ◆ **force out** *vt* hacer salir
forced *adj* (*smile, friendliness*) forzado, -a; **~ landing** aterrizaje *m* forzoso
force-feed ['fɔrs·fid] *vt* dar de comer a la fuerza
forceful ['fɔrs·fəl] *adj* enérgico, -a
forceps ['fɔr·seps] *npl* MED fórceps *m inv;* **a pair of ~** unos fórceps
forcible ['fɔr·sə·bəl] *adj* a la fuerza
forcibly *adv* a la fuerza
ford [fɔrd] **I.** *n* vado *m,* botadero *m Méx* **II.** *vt* vadear
fore [fɔr] **I.** *adj* anterior, delantero, -a; **~ and aft** de popa a proa **II.** *n* **to be to the ~** ir delante; **to come to the ~** destacar **III.** *interj* (*in golf*) **~!** ¡bola!
forearm¹ ['fɔr·arm] *n* (*body part*) antebrazo *m*
forearm² [,fɔr·'arm] *vt liter* (*prepare for battle*) **to ~ oneself** (**against sth**) prevenirse (contra algo)
forebears ['fɔr·berz] *npl form* antepasados *mpl*
forebode [fɔr·'boʊd] *vt liter* presagiar
foreboding [fɔr·'boʊ·dɪŋ] *n liter* presentimiento *m;* **to have a ~** (**that**)... tener una corazonada (de que)...
forecast ['fɔr·kæst] <forecast *o* forecasted> **I.** *n* predicción *f;* **weather ~** previsión *f* meteorológica **II.** *vt* pronosticar
forecaster *n* ECON pronosticador(a) *m(f);* **weather ~** meteorólogo, -a *m, f*
foreclose [fɔr·'kloʊz] **I.** *vt* **to ~ a possibility** descartar una posibilidad **II.** *vi* FIN extinguir; **to ~ on a loan** liquidar un préstamo
forecourt ['fɔr·kɔrt] *n* patio *m* delantero
forefathers ['fɔr·,fa·ðərz] *npl liter* antepasados *mpl*
forefinger ['fɔr·fɪŋ·gər] *n* índice *m*
forefront ['fɔr·frʌnt] *n* primer plano *m;* **to be at the ~ of sth** estar en la vanguardia de algo
forego [fɔr·'goʊ] <forewent, foregone> *vt s.* **forgo**
foregoing ['fɔr·goʊ·ɪŋ] **I.** *adj form* anterior **II.** *n* **the ~** *form* el anterior
foregone [fɔr·'gan] *pp of* **forego**
foreground ['fɔr·graʊnd] **I.** *n* **1.** ART **the ~** el primer plano *m;* **in the ~** en primer término **2.** (*prominent position*) **to put oneself in the**

~ ponerse al frente **II.** *vt* destacar
forehand ['fɔr·hænd] *n* (*tennis shot*) golpe *m* de derechas
forehead ['fɔr·hed] *n* frente *f*
foreign ['fɔr·ɪn] *adj* **1.** (*from another country*) extranjero, -a; **~ soil** *form* suelo *m* extranjero **2.** (*involving other countries*) exterior; **~ relations** relaciones *fpl* exteriores; **~ trade** comercio *m* exterior **3.** (*unknown*) extraño, -a; (*uncharacteristic*) impropio, -a; **to be ~ to sb** ser extraño para alguien; **to be ~ to one's nature** no ser propio de la naturaleza de uno **4.** (*not belonging*) ajeno, -a; **a ~ body** un cuerpo extraño
foreign affairs *npl* asuntos *mpl* exteriores
foreign aid *n* ayuda *f* extranjera
foreign correspondent *n* corresponsal *mf* en el extranjero
foreign currency *n* divisa *f*
foreigner ['fɔr·ɪ·nər] *n* extranjero, -a *m, f*
foreign exchange *n* **1.** (*system*) cambio *m* de divisas **2.** (*currency*) divisa *f*
foreign minister *n* ministro, -a *m, f* de Asuntos Exteriores, canciller *mf AmL*
foreign policy *n* política *f* exterior
foreknowledge [,fɔr·'nal·ɪdʒ] *n* presciencia *f elev;* **to have ~ of sth** saber algo de antemano
foreman ['fɔr·mən] <-men> *n* **1.** (*in factory*) capataz *m* **2.** LAW (*head of jury*) presidente *m* (del jurado)
foremost ['fɔr·moʊst] *adj* **1.** (*most important*) principal; **to be ~ among...** ser el más importante entre... **2.** (*furthest forward*) delantero, -a
forename ['fɔr·neɪm] *n form* nombre *m* (de pila)
forensic [fə·'ren·sɪk] *adj* forense; **~ medicine** medicina *f* forense
foreordain [,fɔr·ɔr·'deɪn] *vt form* predeterminar; **to be ~ed** (**to do sth**) estar predestinado (a hacer algo)
foreplay ['fɔr·pleɪ] *n* juegos *mpl* eróticos preliminares
forerunner ['fɔr·,rʌn·ər] *n* precursor(a) *m(f)*
foresail ['fɔr·seɪl] *n* NAUT trinquete *m*
foresee [fɔr·'si] *irr vt* prever
foreseeable *adj* previsible; **in the ~ future** en el futuro inmediato
foreshadow [fɔr·'ʃæd·oʊ] *vt* anunciar
foresight ['fɔr·saɪt] *n* previsión *f;* **lack of ~** falta *f* de previsión
foreskin ['fɔr·skɪn] *n* prepucio *m*
forest ['fɔr·ɪst] **I.** *n* (*woods*) bosque *m;* (*tropical*) selva *f* **II.** *adj* forestal
forestall [fɔr·'stɔl] *vt* anticiparse a; **to ~ criticism** adelantarse a las críticas
forester ['fɔr·ɪ·stər] *n* guardabosques *mf inv*
forest fire *n* incendio *m* forestal
forest ranger *n* guarda *mf* forestal
forestry ['fɔr·ɪ·stri] *n* silvicultura *f*
foretaste ['fɔr·teɪst] *n* anticipo *m*
foretell [fɔr·'tel] <foretold> *vt* predecir
forever [fɔr·'ev·ər] *adv* **1.** (*for all time*) para siempre **2.** *inf* (*continually*) continuamente; **to**

be ~ **doing sth** estar haciendo algo sin cesar

forewarn [fɔr·'wɔrn] *vt* prevenir ▶~**ed is forearmed** *prov* hombre prevenido vale por dos

forewent [fɔr·'went] *pp of* **forego**

foreword ['fɔr·wɜrd] *n* prefacio *m*

forfeit ['fɔr·fɪt] **I.** *vt* **1.** (*lose*) perder **2.** (*renounce*) perder el derecho a **II.** *n* **1.** (*fine*) multa *f;* **to pay a ~** pagar una multa **2.** *pl* (*game*) **to play ~s** jugar a las prendas **3.** *form* (*penalty*) pena *f* **III.** *adj* **her property was ~** sus bienes fueron confiscados

forfeiture ['fɔr·fə·tʃər] *n* pérdida *f*

forgather [fɔr·'gæð·ər] *vi form* reunirse

forgave [fər·'geɪv] *n pt of* **forgive**

forge [fɔrdʒ] **I.** *vt* **1.** (*make illegal copy*) falsificar **2.** (*metal*) forjar **3.** *fig* **to ~ a bond** forjar un vínculo; **to ~ a career** forjarse un porvenir **II.** *vi* **to ~ into the lead** adelantarse mucho **III.** *n* **1.** (*furnace*) fragua *f* **2.** (*smithy*) herrería *f*

♦**forge ahead** *vi* **1.** (*make progress*) avanzar rápidamente **2.** (*move into lead*) ponerse en cabeza

forger ['fɔr·dʒər] *n* falsificador(a) *m(f)*

forgery ['fɔr·dʒə·ri] <-ies> *n* falsificación *f*

forget [fər·'get] <forgot, forgotten> **I.** *vt* **1.** (*not remember*) olvidar; **to ~ to do sth** olvidarse de hacer algo; **to ~ (that)...** olvidar (que)... **2.** (*leave behind*) **to ~ sth** dejarse algo; **to ~ one's keys** dejarse las llaves **3.** (*stop thinking about*) **to ~ sth/sb** dejar de pensar en algo/alguien; **to ~ one's dignity** dejar la dignidad de uno a un lado; **it's best forgotten** sería mejor olvidarlo **4.** (*give up*) **to ~ sth** dejar algo; **~ it** olvídalo **5.** **to ~ oneself** (*behave badly*) propasarse **II.** *vi* **1.** (*not remember*) olvidarse; **to ~ about sth/sb** olvidarse de algo/alguien; **to ~ about doing sth** olvidarse de hacer algo **2.** (*stop thinking about*) **to ~ about sth/sb** dejar de pensar en algo/alguien; **to ~ about a plan** desistir de un plan; **let's ~ about it!** ¡pelillos a la mar! **3.** **~ it!** (*no*) ¡ni lo sueñes!

forgetful [fər·'get·fəl] *adj* olvidadizo, -a

forget-me-not *n* nomeolvides *f inv*

forgive [fər·'gɪv] <forgave, forgiven> **I.** *vt* **1.** (*pardon*) perdonar; **to ~ sb for sth** perdonar algo a alguien; **to ~ sb for doing sth** perdonar a alguien por hacer algo **2.** (*pardon*) **~ me** discúlpeme; **~ my ignorance/language** disculpe mi ignorancia/lenguaje; **~ me for mentioning it** perdone que lo mencione **II.** *vi* perdonar; **to ~ and forget** perdonar y olvidar

forgiven *pp of* **forgive**

forgiveness *n* perdón *m*

forgiving *adj* misericordioso, -a

forgo [fɔr·'goʊ] *irr vt* privarse de

forgot [fər·'gat] *pt of* **forget**

forgotten [fər·'gatn] **I.** *pp of* **forget II.** *adj* olvidado, -a

fork [fɔrk] **I.** *n* **1.** (*cutlery*) tenedor *m* **2.** (*tool*)

horca *f* **3.** (*in road*) bifurcación *f* **4.** *pl* (*on bicycle*) horquilla *f* **II.** *vt* coger con tenedor, agarrar con tenedor *AmL* **III.** *vi* (*road*) bifurcarse

forked *adj* bifurcado, -a

forklift [,fɔrk·'lɪft] *n* carretilla *f* elevadora

forlorn [fɔr·'lɔrn] *adj* (*person*) triste; (*place*) abandonado, -a; (*hope*) vano, -a

form [fɔrm] **I.** *n* **1.** (*type, variety*) tipo *m;* **~ of exercise** tipo de ejercicio; **~ of government** sistema *m* de gobierno; **~ of transportation** medio *m* de transporte; **~ of persuasion** medida *f* de persuasión; **a ~ of disease** un tipo de enfermedad; **in any way, shape or ~** de cualquier modo; **in the ~ of sth** en forma de algo; **to take the ~ of sth** adoptar la forma de algo **2.** (*outward shape*) forma *f;* (*of an object*) bulto *m;* **to take ~** tomar forma; **in liquid/solid ~** en estado líquido/sólido **3.** LING (*of word*) forma *f;* **the singular ~** LING el singular **4.** (*document*) formulario *m;* **an application/entry ~** un formulario de solicitud/admisión; **to fill in a ~** rellenar un formulario **5.** SPORTS forma *f;* **to be in ~** estar en forma; **to be out of ~** estar en baja forma **6.** (*correct procedure*) **in due ~** de la debida forma; **a matter of ~** una cuestión de forma; **for ~'s sake** para salvar las apariencias; **to be bad ~** ser de mal gusto **7.** (*mol, a. for baking*) molde *m* **II.** *vt* **1.** (*make*) formar; **to ~ part of sth** formar parte de algo; **to ~ the basis of sth** constituir la base de algo; **to ~ a line** formar una cola; **to ~ the impression that...** tener la impresión de que...; **to ~ an opinion** formarse una opinión; **to ~ a habit** adquirir un hábito **2.** (*shape*) moldear **3.** (*set up*) establecer; **to ~ a committee/government** formar un comité/gobierno; **to ~ a relationship** iniciar una relación; **to ~ an alliance with sb** establecer una alianza con alguien **III.** *vi* formarse

formal ['fɔr·məl] *adj* (*official, ceremonious*) formal; **~ dress** traje *m* de etiqueta; **~ procedures** procedimientos *mpl* oficiales; **~ interest** interés *m* sólo de palabra

formaldehyde [fɔr·'mæl·dɪ·haɪd] *n* formaldehído *m*

formality [fɔr·'mæl·ə·ți] <-ies> *n* formalidad *f;* **to be merely a ~** ser una pura formalidad

formalize ['fɔr·mə·laɪz] *vt* formalizar; **to ~ one's thoughts** dar forma a los pensamientos de uno

formally *adv* formalmente

format ['fɔr·mæt] **I.** *n* formato *m* **II.** <-tt-> *vt* COMPUT formatear

formation [fɔr·'meɪ·ʃən] *n* formación *f;* **rock ~** formación *f* rocosa; **in ~** en formación; **in battle ~** en orden de batalla

formation flying *n* vuelo *m* en formación

formative ['fɔr·mə·țɪv] *adj* formativo, -a; **the ~ years** los años de formación

formatting *n* COMPUT formateo *m*

former ['fɔr·mər] *adj* **1.** (*previous*) anterior; **in a ~ life** en una vida anterior **2.** (*first of two*)

F

primero, -a
formerly *adv* antes; ~ **known as** anteriormente conocido como
form feed *n* COMPUT avance *m* de página
formic acid [ˌfɔr·mɪk·ˈæs·ɪd] *n* ácido *m* fórmico
formidable [ˈfɔr·mə·də·bəl] *adj* (*person*) extraordinario, -a; (*opponent, task*) difícil
formless [ˈfɔrm·lɪs] *adj* amorfo, -a
formula [ˈfɔr·mjʊ·lə] <-s *o* -lae> *n* **1.** MATH *a. fig* fórmula *f* **2.** COM (*recipe for product*) receta *f;* **the ~ for success** la fórmula del éxito **3.** (*form of words*) expresión *f* **4.** (*baby milk*) leche *f* para lactantes
formulate [ˈfɔr·mjʊ·leɪt] *vt* **1.** (*draw up*) formular **2.** (*express in words*) formular
formulation [ˌfɔr·mjʊ·ˈleɪ·ʃən] *n* formulación *f*
fornicate [ˈfɔr·nɪ·keɪt] *vi* fornicar
forsake [fɔr·ˈseɪk] <forsook, forsaken> *vt* (*abandon*) abandonar; (*give up*) renunciar a
forsaken [fɔr·ˈseɪ·kən] I. *pp of* forsake II. *adj* abandonado, -a
forsook [fɔr·ˈsʊk] *pt of* forsake
forswear [fɔr·ˈswer] <forswore, forsworn> *vt liter* renunciar a
fort [fɔrt] *n* fuerte *m*
forte¹ [ˈfɔr·teɪ, fɔrt] *n* (*strong point*) fuerte *m*
forte² [ˈfɔr·teɪ] *adv* MUS forte *m*
forth [fɔrθ] *adv* **to go ~** irse; **back and ~** de acá para allá; **from that day ~** de ese día en adelante
forthcoming [ˌfɔrθ·ˈkʌm·ɪŋ] *adj* **1.** (*happening soon*) venidero, -a; (*book*) de próxima aparición; (*film*) de próximo estreno **2.** (*available*) **to be ~** (**from sb**) venir (de alguien) **3.** (*informative*) **to be ~** (**about sth**) estar dispuesto a hablar (de algo)
forthright [ˈfɔrθ·raɪt] *adj* directo, -a
forthwith [ˌfɔrθ·ˈwɪθ] *adv form* en el acto
fortieth [ˈfɔr·tɪ·əθ] I. *adj* cuadragésimo, -a II. *n* (*order*) cuadragésimo, -a *m, f;* (*fraction*) cuadragésimo *m;* (*part*) cuadragésima parte *f; s.a.* **eighth**
fortification [ˌfɔr·tə·fɪ·ˈkeɪ·ʃən] *n* fortificación *f*
fortify [ˈfɔr·tə·faɪ] <-ie-> *vt* **1.** MIL fortificar **2. to ~ oneself** (**with sth**) fortalecerse (con algo); **fortified with vitamins and minerals** enriquecido con vitaminas y minerales
fortitude [ˈfɔr·tə·tud] *n form* fortaleza *f*
fortnight [ˈfɔrt·naɪt] *n* quince días *mpl;* (*business*) quincena *f*
fortress [ˈfɔr·trɪs] *n* fortaleza *f*
fortuitous [fɔr·ˈtu·ə·təs] *adj form* fortuito, -a
fortunate [ˈfɔr·tʃə·nɪt] *adj* afortunado, -a; **to be ~ to do sth** tener la suerte de hacer algo; **to be ~ in sth** tener suerte en algo; **it is ~ for her that...** tiene la suerte de que...
fortunately *adv* afortunadamente
fortune [ˈfɔr·tʃən] *n* **1.** (*money*) fortuna *f;* **a small ~** una pequeña fortuna; **to be worth a ~** valer una fortuna; **to cost a ~** costar un dineral; **to make a ~** hacer una fortuna **2.** *form* (*luck, destiny*) suerte *f;* **good/ill ~** buena/

mala suerte; **to have the good ~ to do sth** tener la suerte de hacer algo; **to tell sb's ~** decir la buenaventura a alguien **3.** *liter* (*luck personified*) ~ **smiled on him** la fortuna le sonrió **4.** *pl* (*fate*) peripecias *fpl*
fortune cookie *n* galleta *f* de la fortuna
fortune hunter *n* cazafortunas *mf*
fortune teller *n* adivino, -a *m, f*
forty [ˈfɔr·ti] I. *adj* cuarenta II. <-ies> *n* cuarenta *m; s.a.* **eighty**
forum [ˈfɔr·əm] *n* foro *m*
forward [ˈfɔr·wərd] I. *adv* **1.** (*towards the front*) hacia adelante; **to lean ~** inclinarse hacia adelante; **a step ~** *fig* un paso hacia adelante **2.** (*in time*) en adelante; **from that day/ time ~** de ese día/momento en adelante; **to set one's watch/the clock ~** adelantar el reloj; **to look ~ to sth** esperar algo (con ansia) II. *adj* **1.** (*towards the front*) hacia adelante; ~ **movement** movimiento *m* hacia adelante; ~ **gear** AUTO marcha *f* adelante **2.** (*in a position close to front*) en la parte delantera; **to be ~ of sth** estar en la parte de delante de algo **3.** (*near front of plane*) delantero, -a; (*ship*) de proa **4.** (*relating to the future*) ~ **buying** compra *f* a plazos; ~ **look** mirada *f* hacia el futuro; ~ **planning** planes *mpl* de futuro **5.** (*bold, not modest*) descarado, -a III. *n* SPORTS delantero, -a *m, f;* **center ~** delantero centro IV. *vt* **1.** (*letter, e-mail*) remitir; (*e-mail*) reenviar; **please ~** por favor, hacer seguir **2.** (*help to progress*) promover
forwarding address *n* dirección *f* (*para enviar el correo*)
forward-looking *adj* con miras al futuro
forwardness *n* precocidad *f*
forwards [ˈfɔr·wərdz] *adv* **1.** (*towards the front*) hacia adelante **2.** (*in time*) en adelante
forwent [fɔr·ˈwent] *pt of* forgo
fossil [ˈfas·əl] *n* **1.** GEO fósil *m* **2.** *fig, inf* (*person*) carca *mf*
fossil fuel *n* combustible *m* fósil
fossilized [ˈfas·ə·laɪzd] *adj* **1.** GEO fosilizado, -a **2.** *fig, inf* (*outdated*) anticuado, -a
foster [ˈfa·stər] *vt* **1.** (*look after*) acoger **2.** (*encourage*) fomentar
foster child *n* hijo, -a *m, f* acogido, -a
foster father *n* padre *m* de acogida
foster home *n* casa *f* de acogida
foster mother *n* madre *f* de acogida
fought [fɔt] *pt, pp of* fight
foul [faʊl] I. *adj* **1.** (*disagreeable: mood, temper*) insoportable; (*air*) sucio, -a; (*weather*) pésimo, -a **2.** (*rotten: taste*) asqueroso, -a; (*smell*) fétido, -a **3.** (*vulgar: language*) ordinario, -a II. *n* SPORTS falta *f,* penal *m AmL* III. *vt* **1.** (*pollute*) ensuciar; (*dog*) hacer sus necesidades en **2.** SPORTS **to ~ sb** hacer una falta a alguien **3.** (*tangle*) liar
◆**foul up** *vt inf* arruinar
foulmouthed *adj* malhablado, -a
foulness [ˈfaʊl·nɪs] *n* **1.** (*dirtiness*) suciedad *f* **2.** (*unpleasantness*) lo desagradable

3. (*coarseness*) ordinariez *f*

foul play *n* **1.** SPORTS juego *m* sucio **2.** (*crime*) delito *m*

found¹ [faʊnd] *pt, pp of* **find**

found² [faʊnd] *vt* **1.** (*establish*) fundar **2.** (*base*) basar; **to ~ a statement/a case on sth** basar una declaración/un caso en algo **3.** (*build*) **to be ~ed on sth** estar construido sobre algo

found³ [faʊnd] *vt* MIN fundir

foundation [faʊn·'deɪ·ʃən] *n* **1.** *pl* (*of building*) cimientos *mpl;* **to lay the ~(s) (of sth)** poner los cimientos (de algo) **2.** *fig* (*basis*) base *f;* **to lay the ~(s) of sth** establecer la(s)base(s) de algo **3.** (*evidence*) fundamento *m;* **to have no ~** no tener fundamento alguno **4.** (*act of establishing*) establecimiento *m* **5.** (*organization*) fundación *f* **6.** (*make-up*) maquillaje *m* de base

foundation cream *n* maquillaje *m* de base

foundation stone *n* piedra *f* fundamental

founder¹ ['faʊn·dər] *n* (*of organization*) fundador(a) *m(f)*

founder² ['faʊn·dər] *vi* **1.** (*sink*) hundirse **2.** *fig* (*fail*) fracasar; **to ~ on sth** fracasar en algo

Founding Fathers *npl* **the ~** *los fundadores de la nación americana*

foundry ['faʊn·dri] <-ries> *n* fundición *f,* fundidora *f AmS*

fount [faʊnt] *n a. fig, form* fuente *f;* **to be the ~ of all knowledge/wisdom** ser la fuente del conocimiento/de la sabiduría

fountain ['faʊn·tən] *n* fuente *f*

fountain pen *n* pluma *f* estilográfica

four [fɔr] **I.** *adj* cuatro **II.** *n* **1.** cuatro *m* **2.** (*group of four*) cuarteto *m* ▶ **to go on all ~s** andar a gatas; *s.a.* **eight**

four-by-four *n* AUTO cuatro por cuatro *m*

four-door car *n* coche *m* de cuatro puertas

fourfold ['fɔr·foʊld] **I.** *adj* cuádruple **II.** *adv* **to increase ~** aumentar en cuatro veces

four-footed *adj* cuadrúpedo, -a

fourhanded *adj* **1.** (*involving four people: bridge, checkers, poker*) de cuatro jugadores **2.** (*for two pianists*) a cuatro manos

four-leaf clover *n* trébol *m* de cuatro hojas

four-letter word *n* palabrota *f*

foursome ['fɔr·səm] *n* grupo *m* de cuatro personas; **to make up a ~** hacer un grupo de cuatro

foursquare [ˌfɔr·'skwer] *adj* **1.** (*building*) firme **2.** (*person*) resoluto, -a; **to stand ~ behind sb** apoyar decididamente a alguien

fourteen [ˌfɔr·'tin] **I.** *adj* catorce **II.** *n* catorce *m; s.a.* **eight**

fourteenth **I.** *adj* decimocuarto, -a **II.** *n* **1.** (*order*) decimocuarto, -a *m, f* **2.** (*date*) catorce *m* **3.** (*fraction*) catorceavo *m;* (*part*) catorceava parte *f; s.a.* **eighth**

fourth [fɔrθ] **I.** *adj* cuarto, -a **II.** *n* **1.** (*order*) cuarto, -a *m, f* **2.** (*date*) cuatro *m* **3.** (*fraction*) cuarto *m;* (*part*) cuarta parte *f* **4.** MUS cuarta *f; s.a.* **eighth**

fourth gear *n* AUTO cuarta marcha *f*

Fourth of July *n* Día *m* de la Independencia de Estados Unidos

i **Fourth of July** o **Independence Day** es el día festivo no confesional más importante de EE.UU. En este día se conmemora la **Declaration of Independence** (declaración de independencia), mediante la cual las colonias británicas situadas en el actual territorio estadounidense se declararon independientes de Gran Bretaña. Este documento fue firmado el 4 de julio de 1776. El día se celebra con meriendas campestres, fiestas familiares y partidos de béisbol (baseball) y culmina con vistosos fuegos artificiales.

four-wheel drive *n* tracción *f* a las cuatro ruedas

fowl [faʊl] <-(s)> *n* ave *f* de corral

fox [faks] **I.** *n* **1.** (*animal*) zorro *m* **2.** (*fur*) piel *f* de zorro **3.** *inf* (*cunning person*) **an old ~** un viejo zorro **4.** *sl* (*sexy woman*) tía *f* buena **II.** *vt* **1.** (*mystify*) mistificar **2.** (*trick*) engañar

foxglove ['faks·glʌv] *n* BOT dedalera *f*

foxhunt ['faks·hʌnt] *n* cacería *f* del zorro

fox terrier *n* fox terrier *mf*

foxtrot ['faks·trat] <-tt-> **I.** *n* foxtrot *m* **II.** *vi* bailar un foxtrot

foxy ['fak·si] <-ier, -iest> *adj* **1.** (*crafty*) taimado, -a **2.** *sl* (*sexy*) sexy

foyer ['fɔɪ·ər] *n* **1.** (*in house*) vestíbulo *m,* hall *m* **2.** (*in hotel, theater*) vestíbulo *m*

fracas ['freɪ·kəs] <-(ses)> *n* gresca *f*

fractal ['fræk·təl] *n* MATH fractal *m*

fraction ['fræk·ʃən] *n* fracción *f;* **at a ~ of the cost** por parte del costo

fractional ['fræk·ʃə·nəl] *adj* **1.** MATH fraccionario, -a **2.** (*difference*) mínimo, -a

fractious ['fræk·ʃəs] *adj* díscolo, -a

fracture ['fræk·tʃər] **I.** *vt* **1.** MED fracturar; **to ~ one's leg** fracturarse la pierna **2.** (*break*) romper; **to ~ an agreement** romper un acuerdo **II.** *vi* (*leg*) fracturarse **III.** *n* MED fractura *f*

fragile ['fræd·ʒ·əl] *adj* delicado, -a; (*object, peace*) frágil; **to feel ~** sentirse débil

fragility [frə·'dʒɪl·ə·t̬i] *n* fragilidad *f*

fragment ['fræg·ment] **I.** *n* fragmento *m* **II.** *vi* **1.** (*break into pieces*) fragmentarse **2.** *fig* (*break up*) romperse **III.** *vt* **1.** (*break into pieces*) fragmentar **2.** *fig* (*break up*) romper

fragmentary ['fræg·mən·ter·i] *adj* fragmentario, -a

fragrance ['freɪ·grəns] *n* fragancia *f*

fragrant ['freɪ·grənt] *adj* fragante

frail [freɪl] *adj* (*person*) endeble; (*thing*) frágil

frailty ['freɪl·ti] <-ies> *n* **1.** (*weakness: of person*) flaqueza *f;* (*of thing*) fragilidad *f* **2.** (*moral flaw*) defecto *m* moral

frame [freɪm] **I.** *n* **1.** (*for door, picture*) *a.* COM-

PUT marco *m* **2.** *pl* (*spectacles*) montura *f* **3.** (*of building*) armazón *m o f* **4.** (*body*) cuerpo *m;* **a slight/sturdy ~** un cuerpo esbelto/robusto **5.** CINE, TV fotograma *m* **II.** *vt* **1.** (*picture*) enmarcar; (*form an attractive border to*) servir de marco **2.** (*conceive: proposal*) elaborar; (*put into words: reply*) formular **3.** *inf* (*falsely incriminate*) incriminar dolosamente

frame-up ['freɪm·ʌp] *n inf* montaje *m* (*para inculpar a alguien*)

framework ['freɪm·wɜrk] *n* **1.** (*supporting structure*) armazón *m o f* **2.** *fig* (*set of rules, principles*) sistema *m*

franc [fræŋk] *n* franco *m*

France [fræns] *n* Francia *f*

franchise ['fræn·tʃaɪz] **I.** *n* franquicia *f* **II.** *vt* conceder en franquicia

Franciscan [fræn·'sɪs·kən] **I.** *n* REL franciscano, -a *m, f* **II.** *adj* REL franciscano, -a

francophone ['fræŋ·kə·ˌfoʊn] *n, adj* francófono, -a *m, f*

frank [fræŋk] **I.** *adj* franco, -a; **to be ~,...** sinceramente,... **II.** *vt* franquear

frankfurter ['fræŋk·fɜr·ˌtər] *n* salchicha *f* de Frankfurt

frankincense ['fræŋ·kɪn·sents] *n* REL incienso *m*

frankly *adv* sinceramente

frantic ['fræn·tɪk] *adj* (*hurry, activity*) frenético, -a; **to be ~ with rage** estar furioso; **to be ~ with worry** andar loco de inquietud; **to drive sb ~** sacar a alguien de quicio

fraternal [frə·'tɜr·nəl] *adj* **1.** (*brotherly*) fraternal **2.** *fig* (*friendly*) cordial

fraternity [frə·'tɜr·nə·ˌti] <-ies> *n* **1.** (*brotherly feeling*) fraternidad *f* **2.** (*group of people*) cofradía *f* **3.** UNIV hermandad *f* (de estudiantes)

fraternize ['fræt·ər·naɪz] *vi* fraternizar

fratricide ['fræt·rə·saɪd] *n* (*crime*) fratricidio *m*

fraud [frɔd] *n* **1.** *a.* LAW fraude *m* **2.** (*trick*) trampa *f* **3.** (*person*) impostor(a) *m(f)*

fraudulence ['frɔ·dʒə·ləns] *n* **1.** (*financial dishonesty*) fraude *m* **2.** (*of claim, behavior*) fraudulencia *f*

fraudulent ['frɔ·dʒə·lənt] *adj* fraudulento, -a

fraught [frɔt] *adj* tenso, -a; **to be ~ with difficulties/problems** estar lleno de dificultades/problemas

fray[1] [freɪ] *vi* (*rope, cloth*) deshilacharse; **tempers were beginning to ~** la gente estaba perdiendo la paciencia

fray[2] [freɪ] *n* (*fight*) lucha *f;* **to enter the ~** entrar en la refriega

freak [frik] **I.** *n* **1.** (*abnormal person, thing*) monstruo *m;* **a ~ of nature** un fenómeno de la naturaleza **2.** (*enthusiast*) fanático, -a *m, f* **II.** *adj* anormal **III.** *vi s.* **freak out I**

◆**freak out I.** *vi* flipar **II.** *vt* **to freak sb out** alucinar a alguien

freckle ['frek·l] *n* peca *f*

freckled ['frek·ld] *adj* pecoso, -a

free [fri] **I.** <-r, -est> *adj* **1.** (*not constrained:*

person, country, elections) libre; **to break ~** (*of sth*) soltarse (de algo); **to break ~ of sb** despegarse de alguien; **to go ~** salir en libertad; **to set sb ~** poner en libertad a alguien; **to be ~ to do sth** no tener reparos en hacer algo **2.** (*not affected by*) **to be ~ of sth** no estar afectado por algo; **to be ~ of a disease** no estar afectado por una enfermedad **3.** (*not attached*) **to get sth ~** liberar algo **4.** (*not busy*) **to be ~ to do sth** estar libre para hacer algo; **to leave sb ~ to do sth** dejar a alguien que haga algo **5.** (*not occupied*) libre; **to leave sth ~** dejar algo libre **6.** (*costing nothing*) gratis; **~ ticket** entrada *f* gratis; **~ of charge** gratis; **~ sample** muestra *f* gratuita; **to be ~ of customs/tax** estar libre de aranceles/impuestos; **to be ~ to sb** ser gratis para alguien **7.** (*generous*) **to be ~ with sth** dar algo en abundancia; **to make ~ with sth** *pej* usar algo como si fuera cosa propia **8.** (*translation, verse*) libre ▸ **~ and easy** despreocupado **II.** *adv* gratis; **~ of charge** gratis; **for ~** *inf* gratis **III.** *vt* **1.** (*release: person*) poner en libertad **2.** (*make available*) permitir; **to ~ sb to do sth** dar libertad a alguien para que haga algo

freebie ['fri·bi] *n* obsequio *m*

freebooter ['fri·bu·ˌtər] *n* filibustero *m*

freedom ['fri·dəm] *n* **1.** (*of person, country*) libertad *f;* **to have the ~ to do sth** tener libertad para hacer algo; **~ of action/movement** libertad *f* de acción/movimiento; **~ of the press** libertad *f* de prensa; **~ of speech/thought** libertad *f* de expresión/pensamiento; **to have ~ from interference** no sufrir intromisiones **2.** (*right*) derecho *m* **3.** (*room for movement*) libertad *f* **4.** (*unrestricted use*) usufructo *m;* **to have the ~ of sb's house** tener el usufructo de la casa de alguien

free enterprise *n* libre empresa *f*

free fall *n* caída *f* libre; **to go into ~** FIN caer en picado

free-for-all *n* gresca *f*

freehold ['fri·hould] **I.** *n* plena propiedad *f* **II.** *adj* de plena propiedad **III.** *adv* en propiedad absoluta

freeholder *n* propietario, -a *m, f* absoluto, -a

free kick *n* SPORTS tiro *m* libre

freelance ['fri·læns] **I.** *n* freelance *mf* **II.** *adj* autónomo, -a **III.** *adv* por cuenta propia **IV.** *vi* trabajar por cuenta propia

freeload ['fri·loud] *vi pej* gorronear; **to ~ off sb** gorronear a alguien

freeloader *vi pej* gorrón, -ona *m, f*

freely *adv* **1.** (*unrestrictedly*) sin límite; **to be ~ available** poder obtenerse sin trabas **2.** (*without obstruction*) libremente **3.** (*frankly: speak, criticize*) francamente **4.** (*generously*) generosamente

freeman ['fri·mən] <-men> *n* **1.** HIST (*not slave*) hombre *m* libre **2.** (*honorary citizen*) ciudadano *m* de honor

free market *n* mercado *m* libre

Freemason ['fri·ˌmeɪ·sən] *n* masón, -ona *m, f*

free port *n* puerto *m* franco
free press *n* prensa *f* independiente
free-range [ˌfriˈreɪndʒ] *adj* de granja
free-range chicken *n* pollo *m* de corral
free-range egg *n* huevo *m* de granja
free speech *n* libertad *f* de expresión
free-spoken [ˌfriˈspoʊˌkən] *adj* que habla sin reservas
freestanding [ˌfriˈstænˌdɪŋ] *adj* independiente
freestyle [ˈfriˌstaɪl] *n* estilo *m* libre
freethinker [ˌfriˈθɪŋˌkər] *n* librepensador(a) *m(f)*
freethinking *adj* librepensador(a)
free trade *n* librecambio *m*
freeware *n* COMPUT programa *m* de libre distribución
freeway *n* autopista *f*
freewheel [ˈfriˌhwil] *vi* ir en punto muerto
free will *n* libre albedrío *m*
freeze [friz] <froze, frozen> **I.** *vi* **1.** (*liquid*) helarse; (*food*) congelarse **2.** (*become totally still*) quedarse completamente quieto, -a **II.** *vt* (*liquid*) helar; (*food, prices*) congelar **III.** *n* **1.** METEO ola *f* de frío **2.** ECON congelación *f*; **to place a ~ on prices/hiring** congelar los precios/la contratación
  ◆ **freeze up** *vi* helarse
freezer *n* congelador *m*, congeladora *f* AmS
freezing I. *adj* glacial; **it's ~** hiela; **I'm ~** estoy helado **II.** *n* congelación *f*
freezing point *n* punto *m* de congelación
freight [freɪt] **I.** *n* **1.** (*type of transportation*) flete *m* **2.** (*goods*) mercancías *fpl* **3.** (*charge*) porte *m* **II.** *adv* por flete **III.** *vt* fletar
freight car *n* RAIL vagón *m* de mercancías
freighter [ˈfreɪˌtər] *n* **1.** (*ship*) buque *m* de carga **2.** (*plane*) avión *m* de mercancías **3.** RAIL tren *m* de mercancías
freight train *n* tren *m* de mercancías
French [frentʃ] **I.** *adj* francés, -esa; **~ speaker** francófono, -a *m, f* **II.** *n* **1.** (*person*) francés, -esa *m, f* **2.** (*language*) francés *m*
French bread *n* pan *m* francés
French Canadian I. *n* canadiense francófono, -a *m, f* **II.** *adj* francocanadiense
French chalk *n* jabón *m* de sastre
French doors *npl* puertaventana *f*
French dressing *n* vinagreta *f*
French fried potatoes *npl*, **French fries** *npl* patatas *fpl* fritas
French horn *n* trompa *f* de llaves
French kiss *n* beso *m* francés [o de tornillo], morreo *m inf*
Frenchman <-men> *n* francés *m*
French toast *n* torrija *f*
French windows *npl s.* **French doors**
Frenchwoman <-women> *n* francesa *f*
frenetic [frəˈneˌɪk] *adj* frenético, -a
frenzied *adj* frenético, -a
frenzy [ˈfrenˌzi] *n* frenesí *m*
frequency [ˈfriˌkwənˌtsi] <-cies> *n* frecuencia *f*

frequency band *n* banda *f* de frecuencia
frequency modulation *n* frecuencia *f* modulada
frequent[1] [ˈfriˌkwənt] *adj* (*occurring often*) frecuente, tupido, -a *Méx*
frequent[2] [frɪˈkwent] *vt* (*visit regularly*) frecuentar
frequently [ˈfriˌkwəntˌli] *adv* con frecuencia
fresco [ˈfresˌkoʊ] <-s *o* -es> *n* fresco *m*
fresh [freʃ] *adj* **1.** (*not stale: air, water, food*) fresco, -a; (*bread*) recién hecho, -a **2.** (*new*) nuevo, -a; (*snow*) virgen; **to make a ~ start** volver a empezar; **~ from the oven/the factory** recién salido del horno/de fábrica **3.** (*cool: breeze*) fresco, -a **4.** (*not tired*) como nuevo, -a **5.** *inf* (*disrespectful*) descarado, -a
freshen [ˈfreʃˌən] *vt* refrescar; (*one's breath*) refrescarse el aliento; **can I ~ your drink?** ¿quieres que te refresque la bebida?
freshman [ˈfreʃˌmən] <-men> *n* **1.** UNIV novato *m*, estudiante *mf* del primer año **2.** (*high school*) estudiante *m* del noveno grado

> **i**   Con el nombre de **freshman** se conoce en EE.UU. a un alumno del noveno grado, con el de **sophomore** a uno del décimo, con el de **junior** al alumno del undécimo grado y con el de **senior** al del duodécimo. Los términos citados se utilizan incluso en aquellas **high schools** (escuelas secundarias) en las que los alumnos sólo se incorporan a partir del décimo grado. También se emplean para hacer referencia a los cuatro años de **college** (primer ciclo de enseñanza superior).

freshness *n* **1.** (*of air, water, food*) frescura *f* **2.** (*of ideas, approach*) novedad *f*
fresh water *n* agua *f* dulce
fret[1] [fret] **I.** <-tt-> *vi* (*worry*) inquietarse **II.** *n* **to be in a ~** estar muy inquieto
fret[2] [fret] *n* MUS traste *m*
fretful [ˈfretˌfəl] *adj* (*person, tone*) quejoso, -a
fret saw [ˈfretˌsɔ] *n* sierra *f* de calados
fretwork [ˈfretˌwɜrk] *n* calado *m*
Fri. *n abbr of* **Friday** viern.
friar [ˈfraɪˌər] *n* fraile *m*
fricative [ˈfrɪkˌəˌtɪv] LING **I.** *adj* fricativo, -a **II.** *n* fricativa *f*
friction [ˈfrɪkˌʃən] *n* **1.** (*rubbing*) fricción *f* **2.** *fig* (*disagreement*) desavenencia *f*
Friday [ˈfraɪˌdi] *n* viernes *m inv*; **on ~s** los viernes; **every ~** todos los viernes; **this (coming) ~** este (próximo) viernes; **on ~ mornings** los viernes por la mañana; **on ~ night** el viernes por la noche; **last/next ~** el viernes pasado/que viene; **every other ~** un viernes sí y otro no; **on ~ we are going on vacation** el viernes nos vamos de vacaciones
fridge [frɪdʒ] *n* nevera *f*, refrigeradora *f* AmS
fried [fraɪd] *adj* frito, -a

fried chicken *n* pollo *m* frito
fried egg *n* huevo *m* frito
friend [frend] *n* **1.** amigo, -a *m, f;* **to be ~s** ser amigos; **to make ~s** (**with sb**) hacerse amigo (de alguien); **a ~ of mine/yours/his/hers** un amigo mío/tuyo/suyo **2.** (*supporter*) defensor *m* (a), amigo *m* , -a
friendless ['frend·lɪs] *adj* sin amigos
friendly ['frend·li] <-ier, -iest> *adj* (*person*) simpático, -a, entrador(a) *Arg;* (*house, environment*) acogedor(a); (*nation*) cordial; **to be on ~ terms with sb** estar a bien con alguien; **to be ~ towards sb** mostrarse amable con alguien; **to be ~ with sb** llevarse bien con alguien
friendly fire *n* fuego *m* amigo [*o* no hostil]
friendship ['frend·ʃɪp] *n* amistad *f*
fries [fraɪz] *npl inf* patatas *fpl* fritas
frigate ['frɪg·ət] *n* fragata *f*
fright [fraɪt] *n* **1.** (*feeling of fear*) terror *m;* **to take ~** (**at sth**) asustarse (por algo) **2.** (*frightening experience*) susto *m,* jabón *m Arg, Méx, PRico;* **to get a ~** llevarse un susto; **to give sb a ~** dar un susto a alguien **3.** *inf* (*unattractive sight*) adefesio *m;* **to look a ~** tener un aspecto horrible
frighten ['fraɪt·ən] I. *vt* asustar II. *vi* asustarse
♦ **frighten away** *vt* espantar
frightened *adj* asustado, -a
frightening *adj* aterrador(a)
frightful ['fraɪt·fəl] *adj* espantoso, -a
frigid ['frɪdʒ·ɪd] *adj* **1.** (*very cold*) glacial **2.** (*sexually*) frígido, -a **3.** (*unfriendly*) frío, -a
frigidity [frɪ'dʒɪd·ə· t̬i] *n* **1.** (*sexual*) frigidez *f* **2.** (*unfriendliness*) frialdad *f*
frill [frɪl] *n* **1.** (*cloth*) volante *m* **2. no ~s** sin excesos
frilly ['frɪl·i] *adj* (*dress*) de volantes; (*style*) recargado, -a
fringe [frɪndʒ] I. *n* **1.** (*decorative edging*) flecos *mpl,* barbitas *f Méx* **2.** (*edge*) margen *m; fig;* **on the ~ of society** al margen de la sociedad; **the lunatic ~** facción *f* extremista (de un grupo) **3.** (*fringe benefit*) extra *m* II. *vt* rodear III. *adj* secundario, -a
fringe benefits *npl* ECON beneficios *mpl* complementarios
fringe group *n* grupo *m* marginal
frippery ['frɪp·ə·ri] <-ies> *n pl* perifollos *mpl*
frisk [frɪsk] I. *vi* juguetear II. *vt* cachear
frisky ['frɪs·ki] <-ier, -iest> *adj* **1.** (*lively, energetic*) retozón, -ona; (*horse*) fogoso, -a **2.** *inf* (*sexually*) juguetón, -ona
fritter[1] ['frɪt̬·ər] *n* CULIN buñuelo *m,* picarón *m AmL*
fritter[2] ['frɪt̬·ər] *vt* (*reduce*) **to ~** (**away**) desperdiciar
frivolity [frɪ·'val·ə·t̬i] <-ties> *n* frivolidad *f*
frivolous ['frɪv·ə·ləs] *adj* frívolo, -a; (*not serious*) poco formal
frizzy ['frɪz·i] *adj* (*hair*) encrespado, -a
fro [froʊ] *adv* **to and ~** de un lado a otro
frock [frak] *n* vestido *m*

frog[1] [frag] *n* ZOOL rana *f* ▶ **to have a ~ in one's throat** tener carraspera
frog[2] [frag] *n offensive, sl* (*French person*) gabacho, -a *m, f*
frogman ['frag·mən] <-men> *n* hombre rana *m*
frog-march ['frag·martʃ] *vt* llevar a la fuerza
frolic ['fral·ɪk] I. <-ck-> *vi* juguetear II. *n* jolgorio *m*
frolicsome ['fral·ɪk·səm] *adj* juguetón, -ona
from [fram] *prep* **1.** (*as starting point*) de; **where is he ~?** ¿de dónde es?; **the flight ~ Boston** el vuelo procedente de Boston; **to fly ~ New York to Tokyo** volar de Nueva York a Tokio; **to appear ~ among the trees** aparecer de entre los árboles; **shirts ~ $10** camisas desde 10$; **~ inside** desde dentro; **to drink ~ a cup/the bottle** beber de una taza/la botella **2.** (*temporal*) **~ day to day** día tras día; **~ time to time** de vez en cuando; **~ his childhood** desde su infancia; **~ that date on(wards)** desde esa fecha **3.** (*at distance to*) **100 miles ~ the river** a 100 millas del río; **far ~ doing sth** lejos de hacer algo **4.** (*one to another*) **to go ~ door to door** ir de puerta en puerta; **to tell good ~ evil** distinguir el bien del mal **5.** (*originating in*) **a card ~ Paul/Corsica** una tarjeta de Paul/Córcega; **~ my point of view** en mi opinión **6.** (*in reference to*) **~ what I heard** según lo que he escuchado; **translated ~ English** traducido del inglés; **quotations ~ Joyce** citas de Joyce; **~ 'War and Peace'** de 'Guerra y Paz'; **to judge ~ appearances** juzgar según las apariencias; **different ~ the others** diferente de los demás **7.** (*caused by*) **~ experience** por experiencia; **weak ~ hunger** débil por el hambre; **to die ~ thirst** morirse de sed **8.** (*removed*) **to steal/take sth ~ sb** robar/quitar algo a alguien; **to prevent sb ~ doing sth** evitar que alguien haga algo; **to keep sth ~ sb** mantener algo alejado de alguien; **to protect ~ the sun** protegerse del sol; **4 ~ 7 equals 3** 7 menos 4 es igual a 3
front [frʌnt] I. *n* **1.** (*forward-facing part*) frente *f;* (*of building*) fachada *f* **2.** PUBL (*outside cover*) cubierta *f* exterior; (*first pages*) principio *m* **3.** (*front area*) parte *f* delantera; **in ~** delante; **in ~ of** delante de **4.** THEAT auditorio *m* **5.** (*deceptive appearance*) apariencias *fpl;* **he's/she's putting on a bold ~** la procesión va por dentro **6.** MIL frente *m; fig;* **on the domestic/work ~** en el terreno doméstico/laboral **7.** POL frente *m;* **a united ~** un frente común **8.** (*promenade*) paseo *m* marítimo **9.** METEO frente *m* II. *adj* **1.** (*at the front*) delantero, -a **2.** (*first*) primero, -a III. *vt* **1.** (*be head of*) liderar **2.** TV presentar IV. *vi* estar enfrente de; **the apartment ~s north** el piso da al norte; **to ~ for** servir de fachada [*o* tapadera]
frontage ['frʌn·tɪdʒ] *n* fachada *f*
frontal ['frʌn·təl] *adj* ANAT, METEO frontal;

(*attack*) de frente
front door *n* puerta *f* principal
front-end *n* COMPUT frontal *m*
frontier [frʌn·'tɪr] *n* **1.** (*border*) *a. fig* frontera *f* **2.** (*outlying areas*) **the ~** los límites
frontiersman <-men> *n* HIST hombre *m* de la frontera
frontier station *n* puesto *m* fronterizo
frontispiece ['frʌn·tɪ·spis] *n* frontispicio *m*
front line *n* primera línea *f*
front page *n* primera página *f*
front-page *adj* de primera plana
front-runner *n* líder *mf*
front-wheel drive *n* tracción *f* delantera
front yard *n* patio *m* delantero, antejardín *m* Col, Chil
frost [frast] **I.** *n* (*crystals*) escarcha *f*; (*on ground*) helada *f* **II.** *vt* **1.** (*cover with frost*) cubrir de escarcha **2.** (*cover with icing: cake*) escarchar
frostbite ['frast·baɪt] *n* congelación *f*
frostbitten *adj* congelado, -a
frost-bound *adj* helado, -a
frosted *adj* **1.** (*covered with icing*) escarchado, -a **2.** (*opaque: glass*) esmerilado, -a
frosting *n* (*on cake*) (azúcar *m*) glaseado
frosty ['fra·sti] <-ier, -iest> *adj* **1.** (*with frost*) escarchado, -a **2.** (*unfriendly*) frío, -a
froth [fraθ] **I.** *n* **1.** (*bubbles*) espuma *f* **2.** *fig* banalidad *f* **II.** *vi* echar espuma **III.** *vt* espumar
frothy ['fra·θi] <-ier, -iest> *adj* espumoso, -a
frown [fraʊn] **I.** *vi* **1.** fruncir el ceño; **to ~ at sb/sth** mirar con el ceño fruncido a alguien/algo **2.** *fig* (*disapprove of*) **to ~ on sth** no ver algo con buenos ojos **II.** *n* ceño *m* fruncido
frowsy *adj*, **frowzy** ['fraʊ·zi] <-ier, -iest> *adj inf* desaliñado, -a
froze [froʊz] *pt of* **freeze**
frozen ['froʊ·zn] **I.** *pp of* **freeze II.** *adj* congelado, -a
frugal ['fru·gəl] *adj* frugal
frugality [fru·'gæl·ə·t̮i] *n* frugalidad *f*
fruit [frut] **I.** *n* **1.** (*for eating*) fruta *f*; (*on tree, product*) fruto *m* **2.** (*results*) fruto *m* ► **to bear ~** dar fruto; *fig* dar resultado **II.** *vi* dar fruto
fruitcake ['frut·keɪk] *n* **1.** (*cake*) tarta *f* de frutas **2.** *sl* (*crazy person*) chiflado, -a *m, f*
fruitful ['frut·fəl] *adj* **1.** (*productive*) provechoso, -a; (*discussion*) productivo, -a **2.** *liter* (*fertile*) fructuoso, -a
fruition [fru·'ɪʃ·ən] *n* **to bring sth to ~** llevar algo a buen término; **to come to ~** realizarse
fruit knife *n* cuchillo *m* de la fruta
fruitless ['frut·lɪs] *adj* infructuoso, -a
fruit salad *n* macedonia *f*
fruity ['fru·t̮i] <-ier, -iest> *adj* **1.** afrutado, -a **2.** *sl* (*crazy*) loco, -a, chiflado, -a
frumpish ['frʌm·pɪʃ] *adj pej* anticuado, -a
frustrate ['frʌs·treɪt] <-ting> *vt* frustrar
frustrated *adj* frustrado, -a
frustrating *adj* frustrante
frustration [frʌ·'streɪ·ʃən] *n* frustración *f*

fry¹ [fraɪ] <-ie-> **I.** *vt* freír **II.** *vi* **1.** (*be cooked*) freírse **2.** *inf* (*get burned*) quemarse **III.** *n* **fish ~** ≈sardinada *f*
fry² [fraɪ] *n* **small ~** (*unimportant person*) don nadie *mf*; (*young person*) renacuajo, -a *m, f inf*
frying pan *n* sartén *f*, paila *f AmL* ► **to jump out of the ~ into the fire** salir de Guatemala y meterse en Guatepeor
ft. *abbr of* **foot, feet** pie
FT [ˌef·'ti] *abbr of* **full-time** a [*o* de] tiempo completo
fuchsia ['fju·ʃə] **I.** *n* fucsia *m* **II.** *adj* fucsia
fuck [fʌk] *vulg* **I.** *vt* follarse, coger *AmL*; **~ you!** ¡jódete!; **~ that idea** ¡a la mierda esa idea! **II.** *vi* follar, coger *AmL* **III.** *n* polvo *m* **IV.** *interj* joder
  ♦ **fuck off** *vi* **~!** ¡vete a la mierda!
fucked up *adj vulg* (*drunk*) pedo *mf*, rascado, -a Col; (*messed up*) jodido, -a
fucker ['fʌk·ər] *n vulg* gilipollas *mf inv*
fuddled ['fʌd·ld] *adj* **1.** (*confused*) aturdido, -a **2.** (*drunk*) borracho, -a
fuddy-duddy ['fʌd·i·ˌdʌd·i] **I.** <-ies> *n pej, inf* persona *f* chapada a la antigua **II.** *adj pej, inf* chapado, -a a la antigua
fudge [fʌdʒ] **I.** *n* **1.** (*candy*) dulce *m* de azúcar **2.** (*nonsense*) chorradas *fpl vulg*, pendejadas *m Méx, Col* **II.** <-ging> *vt* (*issue*) esquivar; (*numbers, figures*) falsear **III.** <-ging> *vi* quedar indeciso, -a
fuel ['fju·əl] **I.** *n* combustible *m* **II.** <-l-> *vt* **1.** (*provide with fuel*) aprovisionar de combustible **2.** (*increase: tension, controversy*) avivar
fuel consumption *n* AUTO consumo *m* de gasolina
fuel gauge *n* indicador *m* del nivel de gasolina
fuel injection *n* inyección *f* (de gasolina)
fuel pump *n* bomba *f* de combustible
fuel rod *n* varilla *f* del combustible
fug [fʌg] *n* aire *m* viciado
fuggy ['fʌg·i] <-ier, -iest> *adj* cargado, -a
fugitive ['fju·dʒɪ·t̮ɪv] **I.** *n* fugitivo, -a *m, f* **II.** *adj* (*escaping*) fugitivo, -a
fugue [fjug] *n* MUS fuga *f*
fulfil <-ll-> *vt*, **fulfill** [fʊl·'fɪl] *vt* (*ambition, task*) realizar; (*condition, requirement*) cumplir; (*need*) satisfacer; (*function, role*) desempeñar; **to ~ oneself** realizarse
fulfilment *n*, **fulfillment** *n* (*of condition, requirement*) cumplimiento *m*; (*of function, role*) desempeño *m*; (*satisfaction*) realización *f*
full [fʊl] **I.** <-er, -est> *adj* **1.** (*container, space*) lleno, -a; (*vehicle*) completo, -a **2.** (*total: support*) total; (*recovery*) completo, -a; (*member*) de pleno derecho; **to be in ~ dress** estar de gala; **to be in ~ flow** estar en pleno discurso; **to be in ~ swing** estar en pleno apogeo **3.** (*maximum: employment*) pleno, -a; **~ of mistakes** lleno de errores; **at ~ speed** a toda velocidad; **at ~ stretch** al máximo **4.** (*busy and active*) ocupado, -a **5.** (*rounded*) redondo, -a **6.** (*wide*) amplio, -a; (*skirt*) holgado, -a **7.** (*wine*) con cuerpo **8.** (*not hungry*) **to be ~**

estar lleno 9. (*conceited*) **to be ~ of oneself** ser un creído **II.** *adv* **1.** (*completely*) completamente **2.** (*directly*) directamente **3.** (*very*) muy; **to know ~ well** (**that...**) saber muy bien (que...) **III.** *n* **in ~** sin abreviar; **to the ~** al máximo

fullback ['fʊl·bæk] *n* SPORTS defensa *mf*

full-blooded [ˌfʊl·'blʌd·ɪd] *adj* **1.** (*wholehearted*) entusiasta **2.** (*animal*) de raza

full-blown [ˌfʊl·'bloʊn] *adj* (*disaster, scandal*) auténtico, -a

full board *n* pensión *f* completa

full-bodied [ˌfʊl·'bad·ɪd] *adj* (*taste*) fuerte; (*wine*) con mucho cuerpo

full-fledged [ˌfʊl·'fledʒd] *adj* **1.** (*person*) hecho, -a y derecho, -a **2.** (*bird*) plumado

full-frontal I. *adj* desenfrenado, -a **II.** *n* desnudo *m* integral

full-grown *adj* crecido, -a

full-length *adj* **1.** (*for entire body*) de cuerpo entero **2.** (*not short*) extenso, -a

full moon *n* luna *f* llena

fullness *n* **1.** (*being full*) plenitud *f*; **in the ~ of time** a su debido tiempo **2.** (*roundedness*) redondez *f* **3.** (*richness*) riqueza *f*

full-page *adj* de página entera

full-scale *adj* **1.** (*original size*) de tamaño natural **2.** (*all-out*) a gran escala

full stop I. *n* punto *m*; **to come to a ~** *fig* paralizarse **II.** *adv* y punto

full-time *adj* de horario completo

fully ['fʊl·i] *adv* **1.** (*completely*) completamente **2.** (*in detail*) detalladamente **3.** (*at least*) al menos

fulminate ['fʌl·mɪ·neɪt] *vi* **to ~** (**against sth**) tronar (contra algo)

fulsome ['fʊl·səm] *adj pej* (*praise*) exagerado, -a; (*person, manner*) servil

fumble ['fʌm·bəl] **I.** *vi* **to ~ around for sth** buscar algo a tientas; **to ~ for words** titubear buscando las palabras **II.** *vt* SPORTS **to ~ the ball** dejar caer la pelota

fumbler ['fʌmb·lər] *n* torpe *mf*

fume [fjum] *vi* **1.** (*be angry*) estar furioso, -a; **to ~ at sb** echar pestes de alguien **2.** (*emit gases*) humear

fumigate ['fju·mɪ·geɪt] *vt* fumigar

fun [fʌn] **I.** *n* diversión *f*; **it was a lot of ~** fue muy agradable; **full of ~** pletórico de alegría; **to do sth for ~** hacer algo por placer; **to do sth in ~** hacer algo en broma; **to have (a lot of) ~** divertirse (mucho); **have ~ on your weekend!** ¡pásalo bien el fin de semana!; **have ~!** ¡diviértete!; **to have ~ at sb's expense** reírse a costa de alguien; **to get a lot of ~ out of** [*o* from] **sth** pasarlo bien con algo; **to make ~ of sb, to poke ~ at sb** reírse de alguien; **what ~!** ¡qué divertido! ▸ **~ and games** *pej* odisea *f*; **it's not all ~ and games** no todo el monte es orégano **II.** *adj* **1.** (*enjoyable*) agradable **2.** (*funny*) divertido, -a; **she's a real ~ person** *inf* es una persona divertidísima

function ['fʌŋk·ʃən] **I.** *n* **1.** *a.* MATH función *f*; **in my ~ as mayor,...** como alcalde,... **2.** (*formal ceremony*) ceremonia *f*; (*formal social event*) acto *m* **II.** *vi* funcionar

functional ['fʌŋk·ʃə·nəl] *adj* **1.** *a.* LING funcional **2.** (*operational, working*) práctico, -a

functionary ['fʌŋk·ʃə·ner·i] <-ies> *n* funcionario, -a *m, f*

function key *n* COMPUT tecla *f* de función

fund [fʌnd] **I.** *n* fondo *m*; **to be short of ~s** ir mal de fondos; **to have a ~ of knowledge about sth** saber mucho de algo **II.** *vt* financiar

fundamental [ˌfʌn·də·'men·təl] **I.** *adj* fundamental; (*difference*) esencial; (*principles*) básico, -a; **to be of ~ importance** ser de vital importancia **II.** *n* the **~s** los principios básicos

fundamentalism [ˌfʌn·də·'men·təl·ɪz·əm] *n* fundamentalismo *m*

fundamentalist I. *n* integrista *mf* **II.** *adj* integrista

fundamentally *adv* **1.** (*basically*) fundamentalmente **2.** (*in the most important sense*) esencialmente

funding *n* (*act*) financiación *f*; (*resources*) fondos *mpl*

fund-raising *n* recaudación *f* de fondos

funeral ['fju·nər·əl] *n* entierro *m*; **to attend a ~** asistir a un funeral ▸ **that's your/his ~** *inf* eso es tu/su problema

funeral director *n* director(a) *m(f)* de funeraria

funeral home *n* funeraria *f*

funeral march <-es> *n* marcha *f* fúnebre

funeral parlor *n* funeraria *f*

funeral pyre *n* pira *f*

funereal [fju·'nɪr·i·əl] *adj* fúnebre

fungicide ['fʌn·dʒɪ·saɪd] *n* fungicida *m*

fungus ['fʌn·gəs] *n* (*wild mushroom*) hongo *m*; (*mold*) moho *m*

fun house *n* casa *f* del terror

funicular [fju·'nɪk·ju·lər] *n*, **funicular railway** *n* funicular *m*

funk [fʌŋk] *n* **1.** (*depression*) abatimiento *m fig* **2.** *inf* (*fear*) mieditis *f*, canguelo *m*, culillo *m* PRico, Ecua, Nic, Pan, Col **3.** (*music*) funk *m*

funky ['fʌŋ·ki] <-ier, -iest> *adj* **1.** (*musty*) **a ~ taste/smell** un sabor/olor raro **2.** *sl* (*cool*) genial **3.** (*music*) funky

fun-loving *adj* marchoso, -a

funnel ['fʌn·əl] **I.** *n* **1.** (*tool*) embudo *m* **2.** NAUT chimenea *f* **II.** <-l-> *vt* canalizar

funnies ['fʌn·iz] *npl* the **~** las tiras cómicas

funny ['fʌn·i] <-ier, -iest> *adj* **1.** (*amusing*) divertido, -a; **to see the ~ side of a situation** observar lo curioso de una situación **2.** *inf* (*witty*) gracioso, -a; **to try to be ~** *inf* hacerse el gracioso **3.** (*odd, peculiar*) raro, -a; **to have a ~ feeling that...** tener la extraña sensación de que...; **to have ~ ideas** tener ideas de bombero **4.** (*slightly ill*) **to feel ~** no encontrarse bien

funny bone *n inf* hueso *m* de la alegría

fur [fɜr] *n* **1.** (*animal hair*) piel *f* **2.** (*garment*)

F

prenda *f* de pieles
fur coat *n* abrigo *m* de pieles
furious ['fjʊr·i·əs] *adj* **1.** (*very angry*) furioso,
-a, enchilado, -a *Méx,* caribe *Ant;* **to be ~
about sth** estar furioso por algo; **a ~ outburst**
un acceso de furia **2.** (*intense, violent*) violento, -a; **at a ~ pace** a un ritmo vertiginoso
furl [fɜrl] *vt* (*flag, sail*) recoger
furlong ['fɜr·lɑŋ] *n* estadio *m* (*medida de longitud equivalente a 200 metros aproxima-
damente*)
furlough ['fɜr·loʊ] *n* MIL permiso *m;* **to be on ~**
estar de permiso
furnace ['fɜr·nɪs] *n a. fig* horno *m*
furnish ['fɜr·nɪʃ] *vt* **1.** (*supply*) proporcionar; **to
~ sb with sth** suministrar algo a alguien; **to be
~ed with sth** estar provisto de algo **2.** (*provide furniture for*) amueblar
furnished ['fɜr·nɪʃt] *adj* amueblado, -a
furnishings ['fɜr·nɪ·ʃɪŋz] *npl* muebles *mpl*
furniture ['fɜr·nɪ·tʃər] *n* mobiliario *m;* **piece of
~** mueble *m*
furniture van *n* camión *m* de mudanzas
furor ['fjʊr·ɔr] *n* furor *m*
furrier ['fɜr·i·ər] *n* peletero, -a *m, f*
furrow ['fɜr·oʊ] **I.** *n* **1.** (*groove*) ranura *f*
2. (*wrinkle*) arruga *f* **II.** *vt* arrugar; **to ~ one's
brow** fruncir el ceño
furry ['fɜr·i] <-ier, -iest> *adj* **1.** peludo, -a
2. (*looking like fur*) peloso, -a; **~ toy** peluche *m*
further ['fɜr·ðər] **I.** *adj comp of* **far 1.** (*greater
distance*) más lejano; **nothing could be ~
from his mind** estará pensando en cualquier
cosa menos en eso **2.** (*additional*) otro, -a; **if
you have any ~ problems...** si tienes más
problemas...; **until ~ notice** hasta nuevo aviso
II. *adv comp of* **far 1.** (*greater distance*) más
lejos; **we didn't get much ~** no llegamos
mucho más allá; **~ on** más adelante; **~ and ~**
cada vez más lejos; **to go ~ with sth** hacer
progresos con algo **2.** (*more*) más; **I have
nothing ~ to say** no tengo (nada) más que
decir ►**to not go any ~** no ir más allá; **this
can't go on any ~** esto debe quedar entre
nosotros **III.** *vt* fomentar; **to ~ sb's interests**
favorecer los intereses de alguien
furtherance ['fɜr·ðər·əns] *n form* fomento *m*
furthermore ['fɜr·ðər·mɔr] *adv* además
furthermost ['fɜr·ðər·moʊst] *adj* más lejano, -a
furthest ['fɜr·ðɪst] **I.** *adj* **1.** *superl of* **far
2.** (*greatest*) mayor; **prices have fallen/risen
~ in the south** los precios han bajado/subido
más en el sur **3.** (*at the greatest distance*) más
lejano, -a; **the ~ island from the mainland** la
isla más apartada de tierra firme **II.** *adv*
1. *superl of* **far 2.** (*greatest distance*) más
lejos; **that's the ~ I can go** eso es lo más lejos

que puedo ir
furtive ['fɜr·tɪv] *adj* furtivo, -a
furtiveness *n* furtivismo *m*
fury ['fjʊr·i] *n* furor *m;* **fit of ~** ataque *m* de
furia
fuse [fjuz] **I.** *n* **1.** ELEC fusible *m;* **the ~ has
blown** han saltado los plomos **2.** (*ignition
device, detonator*) espoleta *f;* (*string*) mecha *f*
►**to have a short ~** tener mucho genio; **to
light the ~** encender la mecha **II.** *vi* **1.** ELEC
fundirse **2.** (*join together*) fusionarse **III.** *vt*
1. ELEC fundir **2.** (*join*) fusionar
fuse box <-es> *n* caja *f* de fusibles
fuselage ['fju·sə·lɑʒ] *n* AVIAT fuselaje *m*
fusion ['fju·ʒən] *n* **1.** (*joining together*) fusión
f **2.** PHYS fusión *f;* **nuclear ~** fusión nuclear
fusion bomb *n* bomba *f* termonuclear
fusion reactor *n* reactor *m* nuclear
fuss [fʌs] **I.** *n* alboroto *m;* **it's a lot of ~ about
nothing** mucho ruido y pocas nueces; **to
make a ~** armar un escándalo **II.** *vi* preocuparse; **to ~ over sth/sb** preocuparse en
exceso por algo/alguien
fusspot ['fʌs·pɑt] *n inf* quisquilloso, -a *m, f*
fussy ['fʌs·i] <-ier, -iest> *adj* **1.** (*overly particular*) puntilloso, -a **2.** (*quick to criticize*) quisquilloso, -a **3.** (*overdone, overdecorated*)
recargado, -a **4.** (*baby*) llorón, -ona
fusty ['fʌs·ti] <-ier, -iest> *adj pej* **1.** (*smelling
musty*) rancio, -a; (*room*) que huele a cerrado
2. (*old-fashioned*) anticuado, -a
futile ['fju·təl] *adj* inútil; **~ attempt** intento *m*
en vano
futility [fju·'tɪl·ə·ti] *n* inutilidad *f*
future ['fju·tʃər] **I.** *n* **1.** *a.* LING futuro *m;* **to
have plans for the ~** tener planes de futuro;
in the ~ tense en futuro; **the distant/near ~**
el futuro lejano/próximo; **what the ~ will
bring** lo que depara el futuro **2.** (*prospects*)
porvenir *m;* **she has a great ~ ahead of her**
tiene un gran porvenir **II.** *adj* futuro, -a
future perfect *n* LING futuro *m* perfecto
futures market *n* mercado *m* de futuros
futuristic [ˌfju·tʃə·'rɪs·tɪk] *adj* futurista
fuze [fjuz] **I.** *n* (*ignition device, detonator*)
espoleta *f;* (*string*) mecha *f* **II.** *vt* poner mecha
(a algo)
fuzz [fʌz] *n* **1.** (*fluff*) pelusa *f* **2.** (*fluffy hair*)
pelo *m* crespo **3.** (*short growing hair*) vello *m;*
peach ~ *fig* piel *f* de melocotón **4.** *sl* (*police*)
the ~ la pasma
fuzzy ['fʌz·i] *adj* **1.** (*unclear*) borroso, -a
2. (*short, soft: hair*) velloso, -a; (*curly*)
rizado, -a
fuzzy logic *n* lógica *f* difusa
f-word ['ef·wɜrd] *n forma de evitar el uso de la
palabra 'fuck'*

G

G, g [dʒi] *n* G, g *f;* ~ **as in Golf** G de Granada
g *abbr of* **gram** g
GA ['dʒɔr·dʒə], **Ga.** *n abbr of* **Georgia** Georgia *f*
gab [gæb] I. <-bb-> *vi sl* estar de palique II. *n* cháchara *f;* **to have the gift of** ~ tener mucha labia
gabardine ['gæb·ər·din] *n* gabardina *f*
gabble ['gæb·əl] I. *vi* (*talk inarticulately*) farfullar; (*talk quickly*) hablar atropelladamente II. *vt* (*utter too quickly*) decir atropelladamente; (*utter indistinctly*) pronunciar de modo ininteligible III. *n* (*inarticulate speech*) farfulla *f;* (*quick speech*) habla *f* atropellada
gable ['geɪ·bəl] *n* ARCHIT aguilón *m;* ~ **roof** tejado *m* de dos aguas
Gabon [gæ·'boʊn] *n* Gabón *m*
Gabonese [ˌgæb·oʊ·'niz] I. *adj* gabonés, -esa II. *n* gabonés, -esa *m, f*
gad [gæd] <-dd-> *vi inf* **to ~ about** callejear
gadabout ['gæd·ə·baʊt] *n* trotacalles *mf inv*
gadfly ['gæd·flaɪ] <-flies> *n* **1.** (*nuisance*) latoso, -a *m, f* **2.** (*insect*) tábano *m*
gadget ['gædʒ·ɪt] *n* artilugio *m;* ~**s** chismes *mpl*
gadgetry ['gædʒ·ɪ·tri] *n* chismes *mpl*
Gaelic ['geɪ·lɪk] I. *n* gaélico *m* II. *adj* gaélico, -a
gaff[1] [gæf] *n* arpón *m*
gaff[2] [gæf] *n s.* **gaffe**
gaffe [gæf] *n* metedura *f* de pata
gaffer ['gæf·ər] *n* iluminista *mf*
gag [gæg] I. *n* **1.** (*cloth*) mordaza *f* **2.** (*joke*) broma *f* **3.** THEAT morcilla *f* II. <-gg-> *vt* amordazar; (*silence*) hacer callar III. <-gg-> *vi inf* (*to joke*) contar chistes; THEAT meter morcillas
gaga ['ga·ga] *adj inf* chocho, -a; **to go** ~ chochear
gage [geɪdʒ] *n, vt s.* **gauge**
gaggle ['gæg·əl] *n a. iron* manada *f*
gag order *n* LAW bloqueo *m* informativo
gaiety ['geɪ·ə·ṭi] *n* alegría *f*
gaily ['geɪ·li] *adv* alegremente
gain [geɪn] I. *n* **1.** (*increase*) aumento *m;* ~ **in weight** aumento de peso **2.** ECON, FIN (*profit*) beneficio *m;* **net** ~ beneficio neto **3.** *fig* (*advantage*) ventaja *f* II. *vt* **1.** (*obtain*) ganar **2.** (*acquire*) adquirir; **to ~ success** cosechar el éxito **3.** (*increase: velocity*) adquirir; **to ~ weight** ganar peso ▶ **to ~ the upper hand** llevar ventaja; **to ~ ground** ganar terreno III. *vi* **1.** (*benefit*) beneficiarse de, sacar provecho de **2.** (*increase*) aumentar; (*experience, confidence*) adquirir **3.** (*put on weight*) engordar; **when he/she quit his/her diet, he/she started ~ing again** cuando dejó la dieta volvió a engordar **4.** (*clock, watch*) adelantarse
◆ **gain on** *vt* ir alcanzando; **hurry up! they're ~ing on us!** ¡apúrate! Nos están ganando terreno!

gainful ['geɪn·fəl] *adj* lucrativo, -a; ~ **employment** trabajo *m* remunerado
gait [geɪt] *n a.* SPORTS paso *m*
gaiter ['geɪ·ṭər] *n* polaina *f*
gal [gæl] *n inf* tía *f,* chica *f*
gal. *abbr of* **gallon** gal.
gala ['geɪ·lə] I. *n* gala *f* II. *adj* (*festive*) de gala; ~ **night** noche *f* de gala
galactic [gə·'læk·tɪk] *adj* galáctico, -a
Galapagos Islands [gə·'læp·ə·gəs·'aɪ·ləndz] *npl* Islas *fpl* Galápagos
galaxy ['gæl·ək·si] <-ies> *n* **1.** (*space*) galaxia *f* **2.** *fig* **a** ~ **of performers** una constelación de estrellas *f*
gale [geɪl] *n* temporal *m;* **a** ~**-force wind** un vendaval
gale warning *n* aviso *m* de temporal
gall [gɔl] I. *n* **1.** (*bile*) hiel *f inv* **2.** (*impertinence*) impertinencia *f;* **to have the** ~ **to do sth** tener agallas para hacer algo; *pej* tener la cara de hacer algo II. *vt* irritar
gallant ['gæl·ənt] I. *adj* **1.** (*chivalrous*) galante **2.** (*brave*) valiente II. *n* HIST galán *m*
gallantry ['gæl·ən·tri] *n* **1.** (*chivalry*) cortesía *f* **2.** (*courage*) valentía *f* **3.** <-tries> (*act of courtly politeness*) galanterías *fpl*
gall bladder *n* vesícula *f* biliar
galleon ['gæl·i·ən] *n* galeón *m*
gallery ['gæl·ə·ri] <-ries> *n* **1.** (*for displaying art*) museo *m;* (*for paintings*) galería *f* **2.** ARCHIT, THEAT tribuna *f*
galley ['gæl·i] *n* **1.** NAUT, AVIAT (*kitchen*) cocina *f* **2.** HIST (*ship*) galera *f*
galley proof *n* galerada *f*
gallivant [ˌgæl·ə·'vænt] *vi* **to ~ around** callejear
gallon ['gæl·ən] *n* galón *m* (*3,79 l*)
gallop ['gæl·əp] I. *vi* galopar II. *vt* (*cause to gallop*) hacer galopar III. *n* galope *m;* **to break into a** ~ echar a galopar; **at a** ~ *fig* al galope
gallows ['gæl·oʊz] *npl* **the** ~ la horca; **to send sb to the** ~ mandar a alguien al patíbulo
gallstone ['gɔl·stoʊn] *n* cálculo *m* biliar
Gallup poll ['gæl·əp·poʊl] *n* sondeo *m* de la opinión pública
galore [gə·'lɔr] *adj* en cantidad
galoshes [gə·'laʃ·ɪz] *npl* chanclos *mpl*
galvanize ['gæl·və·naɪz] *vt a. fig* impulsar
Gambia ['gæm·bi·ə] *n* Gambia *f*
Gambian I. *adj* gambiano, -a II. *n* gambiano, -a *m, f*
gambit ['gæm·bɪt] *n* **1.** (*tactic*) táctica *f;* **opening** ~ estrategia *f* inicial **2.** (*chess move*) gambito *m*
gamble ['gæm·bəl] I. *n* apuesta *f;* **business** ~ riesgo *m* comercial II. *vi* jugar; **to ~ on sth** confiar en algo; **to ~ on the stock market** jugar a la bolsa III. *vt* (*money*) jugarse; (*one's life*) arriesgar; **to ~ one's fortune/future** jugarse la fortuna/el futuro
gambler ['gæm·blər] *n* jugador(a) *m(f)*
gambling *n* juego *m*
gambol ['gæm·bəl] <-ll-, -l-> *vi liter* retozar

game¹ [geɪm] I. *n* **1.** (*in sports*) partido *m;* **the Olympic Games** los Juegos Olímpicos **2.** (*in games*) partida *f;* **board ~** juego de mesa; **~ of chance** juego de azar; **a ~ of chess** una partida de ajedrez **3.** SPORTS (*skill level*) **to be off one's ~** *a. fig* estar en baja forma **4.** (*tactic*) **the ~ is up** se acabó el juego; **what's your ~?** ¿a qué juegas? ▶**to give the ~ away** descubrir las cartas; **two can play at that ~** donde las dan las toman; **to beat sb at his/her own ~** ganar a alguien con sus propias armas II. *adj* (*willing*) animoso, -a; **to be ~** (**to do sth**) animarse (a hacer algo); **to be ~ for anything** apuntarse a un bombardeo

game² [geɪm] *n* (*in hunting*) caza *f;* **big ~** caza mayor

gamecock ['geɪm·kak] *n* gallo *m* de pelea

gamekeeper *n* guardabosque *mf*

game show *n* concurso *m* de televisión

gaming ['geɪ·mɪŋ] *n* **1.** (*gambling*) juego *m* **2.** COMPUT videojuegos *mpl*

gamma radiation *n,* **gamma rays** *npl* rayos *mpl* gamma

gammon ['gæm·ən] *n* jamón *m*

gamut ['gæm·ət] *n* gama *f*

gander ['gæn·dər] *n* **1.** (*male goose*) ganso *m* **2.** *inf* (*look*) **to take a ~** echar una ojeada

gang [gæŋ] *n* **1.** (*criminal group*) banda *f* **2.** (*organized group*) cuadrilla *f;* **chain ~** grupo *m* de presidiarios encadenados **3.** *inf* (*group of friends*) pandilla *f,* barra *f AmL,* trinca *f And, CSur*

♦ **gang up on** *vt* unirse contra

gangling ['gæŋ·glɪŋ] *adj* larguirucho, -a

gangly ['gæŋ·gli] <-ier, -iest> *adj* larguirucho, -a

gangplank ['gæŋ·plæŋk] *n* plancha *f*

gangrene ['gæŋ·grin] *n* gangrena *f*

gangrenous ['gæŋ·grə·nəs] *adj* gangrenoso, -a

gangster ['gæŋ·stər] *n* gángster *mf*

gang warfare *n* guerra *f* entre bandas

gangway ['gæŋ·weɪ] I. *n* (*gangplank*) pasarela *f;* (*ladder*) escalerilla *f* II. *interj inf* ¡paso!

gantry ['gæn·tri] <-ies> *n* caballete *m;* (*crane*) pórtico *m;* AVIAT torre *f* de lanzamiento

gap [gæp] *n* **1.** (*opening*) abertura *f;* (*empty space*) hueco *m;* (*in text, memory*) laguna *f;* **to fill a ~** llenar un vacío **2.** (*break in time*) intervalo *m* **3.** (*difference*) diferencia *f;* **age ~** diferencia de edad

gape [geɪp] I. *vi* abrirse; (*person*) quedarse boquiabierto II. *n* (*look*) mirada *f* pasmada; (*yawn*) bostezo *m*

gaping *adj* (*hole*) enorme; (*wound*) abierto, -a

garage [gə·'raʒ] I. *n* **1.** (*of house*) garaje *m,* cochera *f* **2.** (*for repair*) taller *m* II. *vt* **to ~ a car** dejar un coche en el garaje

garage sale *n* venta *f* de objetos usados en casa de un particular; venta *f* de garaje *Col*

garb [garb] I. *n* atuendo *m* II. *vt* **to be ~ed as** ir vestido de

garbage ['gar·bɪdʒ] *n* basura *f;* **to take** [o throw] **out the ~** sacar la basura

garbage can *n* cubo *m* de la basura, tacho *m AmL*

garbage disposal *n* triturador *m* de basura

garbage dump *n* vertedero *m*

garbage man *n* basurero *m,* recogedor *Col* de basura

garbage truck *n* camión *m* de la basura

garble ['gar·bəl] *vt* **1.** (*confuse: facts*) confundir **2.** (*distort: message*) distorsionar

garbled *adj* **1.** (*confused: facts*) confuso, -a **2.** (*distorted: message*) distorsionado, -a

garden ['gar·dən] I. *n* **1.** jardín *m;* **vegetable ~** huerto *m;* **~ furniture** muebles *mpl* de jardín **2. ~s** (*ornamental grounds*) parque *m;* **botanical ~** jardín *m* botánico II. *vi* (*with flowers*) trabajar en el jardín; (*with vegetables*) cultivar el huerto

gardener ['gard·nər] *n* **1.** (*of flowers*) jardinero, -a *m, f* **2.** (*of vegetables*) hortelano, -a *m, f*

gardenia [gar·'di·ni·ə] *n* gardenia *f*

gardening ['gard·nɪŋ] *n* (*of flowers*) jardinería *f;* (*of vegetables*) horticultura *f*

garden party <-ies> *n* fiesta *f* al aire libre

gargantuan [gar·'gæn·tʃu·ən] *adj liter* colosal

gargle ['gar·gəl] I. *vi* hacer gárgaras II. *n* gárgaras *fpl*

gargoyle ['gar·gɔɪl] *n* gárgola *f*

garish ['ger·ɪʃ] *adj* excesivo, -a; (*color, clothes*) chillón, -ona

garland ['gar·lənd] I. *n* guirnalda *f* II. *vt* adornar con guirnaldas

garlic ['gar·lɪk] *n* ajo *m;* **clove of ~** diente *m* de ajo; **~ sauce** ajiaceite *m*

garlic press <-es> *n* triturador *m* de ajos

garment ['gar·mənt] *n* prenda *f* de vestir

garnet ['gar·nɪt] *n* granate *m*

garnish ['gar·nɪʃ] I. *vt* adornar; CULIN aderezar II. <-es> *n* adorno *m;* CULIN aderezo *m*

garrison ['ger·ə·sən] I. *n* guarnición *f* II. *vt* (*troops*) poner en guarnición, acuartelar; (*place*) guarnecer

garrulous ['ger·ə·ləs] *adj* gárrulo, -a

garter ['gar·tər] *n* liga *f*

garter belt *n* liguero *m*

garter stitch <-es> *n* punto *m* de media

gas [gæs] I. <-s(s)es> *n* **1.** *a.* MED, CHEM gas *m;* **natural ~** gas natural; **to cut off the ~** cerrar el gas **2.** (*fuel*) gasolina *f;* **leaded/unleaded ~** gasolina con plomo/sin plomo; **to step on the ~** acelerar **3.** (*flatulence*) gases *fpl,* ventosidad *f* II. <-ss-> *vt* asfixiar con gas

gas can *n* bidón *m* de gasolina

gas chamber *n* cámara *f* de gas

gaseous ['gæs·i·əs] *adj* gaseoso, -a

gas field *n* yacimiento *m* de gas

gas gauge *n* medidor *m* del nivel de gasolina

gas-guzzler *n inf* (*vehicle*) esponja *f,* vehículo *m* de alta consumición

gash [gæʃ] I. <-es> *n* (*deep cut*) tajo *m;* (*wound*) cuchillada *f* II. *vt* rajar; (*wound*) acuchillar

gas heater *n* estufa *f* de gas
gas heating *n* calefacción *f* de gas
gasholder *n* gasómetro *m*
gasket ['gæs·kɪt] *n* junta *f*
gas lamp *n* lámpara *f* de gas
gas lighter *n* mechero *m* de gas
gas mask *n* máscara *f* antigás
gas meter *n* contador *m* del gas
gasoline ['gæs·ə·lin] *n* gasolina *f*, nafta *f CSur*
gasoline tank *n* depósito *m* de gasolina
gasometer *n* gasómetro *m*
gas oven *n* horno *m* de gas
gasp [gæsp] **I.** *vi* **1.** (*breathe with difficulty*) jadear; **to ~ for air** [*o* **breath**] hacer esfuerzos para respirar **2.** (*in shock*) dar un grito ahogado; **I ~ed in amazement** di un grito ahogado de asombro **II.** *vt* **to ~ sth out** decir algo con voz entrecortada **III.** *n* jadeo *m;* **he gave a ~ of astonishment** dio un grito ahogado de asombro ▶ **to be at one's last ~** estar en las últimas; **to do sth at the last ~** hacer algo en el último segundo
gas pedal *n* acelerador *m*
gas pipe *n* tubería *f* de gas
gas pump *n* surtidor *m* de gasolina
gas station *n* gasolinera *f*, bomba *f And, Ven*, estación *f* de nafta *RíoPl*, bencinera *f Chile*, grifo *m Perú*
gas station attendant *n* gasolinero, -a *m, f*
gas stove *n* cocina *f* de gas
gassy ['gæs·i] <-ier, -iest> *adj* **1.** (*full of gas*) lleno, -a de gas **2.** (*gas-like*) gaseoso, -a
gas tank *n* depósito *m* de gasolina
gastric ['gæs·trɪk] *adj* gástrico, -a
gastritis [gæs·'straɪ·t̮əs] *n* gastritis *f inv*
gastroenteritis [ˌgæs·troʊ·ˌen·t̮ə·'raɪ·t̮əs] *n* gastroenteritis *f inv*
gastronomic [ˌgæs·trə·'nam·ɪk] *adj* gastronómico, -a
gastronomy [gæ·'stran·ə·mi] *n* gastronomía *f*
gastroscopy [ˌgæs·'tras·kə·pi] <-ies> *n* MED endoscopia *f*
gate [geɪt] *n* **1.** (*entrance barrier*) puerta *f*; RAIL barrera *f* **2.** SPORTS entrada *f* **3.** AVIAT puerta *f* de embarque **4.** NAUT compuerta *f*
gatecrash ['geɪt·kræʃ] **I.** *vt* colarse en **II.** *vi* colarse
gatecrasher *n sl* (*at party, concert*) intruso, -a *m, f* (*que se cuela sin pagar o sin haber sido invitado*), colado, -a *m, f Col*
gatehouse *n* casa *f* del guarda
gatekeeper *n* portero, -a *m, f;* RAIL guardabarrera *mf*
gatepost *n* poste *m* ▶ **between you and me and the ~** que no salga de estas cuatro paredes
gate receipts *n pl* taquilla *f*
gateway *n* **1.** (*entrance*) entrada *f* **2.** (*means of access*) puerta *f*
gateway drug *n* droga *f* trampolín
gather ['gæð·ər] **I.** *vt* **1.** (*convene: people*) reunir, juntar **2.** (*harvest*) cosechar; (*flowers*) recoger **3.** (*accumulate*) acumular; (*information*) reunir **4.** (*increase*) **to ~ speed**

ganar velocidad **5.** (*muster*) **to ~ one's strength** cobrar fuerzas; **to ~ one's courage** armarse de valor **6.** (*infer*) deducir; **to ~ that...** sacar la conclusión de que... **II.** *vi* **1.** (*convene*) reunirse **2.** (*accumulate: things*) amontonarse; (*storm*) amenazar
gathering *n* reunión *f*
GATT [gæt] *n abbr of* **General Agreement on Tariffs and Trade** GATT *m*
gaudy ['gɔ·di] <-ier, -iest> *adj* llamativo, -a
gauge [geɪdʒ] **I.** *n* **1.** (*measure*) medida *f* **2.** (*instrument*) indicador *m* **3.** RAIL ancho *m* de vía **4.** *fig* indicio *m*, indicador *m* **II.** *vt* **1.** (*measure*) medir **2.** (*assess*) determinar; **it's difficult to ~ what his response will be** resulta difícil determinar qué responderá
gaunt [gɔnt] *adj* **1.** (*very thin*) flaco, -a; (*too thin*) demacrado, -a **2.** (*desolate*) desolado, -a
gauntlet ['gɔnt·lɪt] *n* guante *m;* HIST guantelete *m;* **to take up/throw down the ~** *fig* recoger/arrojar el guante ▶ **to run the ~** MIL, HIST correr baquetas
gauze [gɔz] *n a.* MED gasa *f*
gauzy ['gɔ·zi] <-ier, -iest> *adj* diáfano, -a
gave [geɪv] *pt of* **give**
gavel ['gæv·əl] **I.** *n* mazo *m* **II.** <-ll-, -l-> *vt* dar con el mazo (*llamando al orden*)
gawk [gɔk] *vi* papar moscas; **to ~ at** mirar embobado
gawky ['gɔ·ki] *adj* torpe; (*tall, awkward*) desgarbado, -a
gay [geɪ] **I.** *adj* **1.** (*homosexual*) gay **2.** (*cheerful*) alegre **II.** *n* (*man*) gay *m;* (*woman*) lesbiana *f*
gaze [geɪz] **I.** *vi* mirar fijamente; **to ~ at sth** mirar algo fijamente **II.** *n* mirada *f* fija; **to be exposed to the public ~** estar expuesto para contemplación del público
gazelle [gə·'zel] *n* gacela *f*
gazette [gə·'zet] *n* gaceta *f*
gazetteer [ˌgæz·ə·'tɪr] *n* índice *m* geográfico
GB [ˌdʒi·'bi] *n* **1.** COMPUT *abbr of* **gigabyte** GB **2.** *abbr of* **Great Britain** GB
GDP [ˌdʒi·di·'pi] *n abbr of* **gross domestic product** PIB *m*
gear [gɪr] *n* **1.** TECH engranaje *m* **2.** AUTO marcha *f* **3.** (*equipment*) equipo *m*
gearbox ['gɪr·baks] <-es> *n* caja *f* de cambios
gearshift ['gɪr·ʃɪft] *n* palanca *f* de cambio
gearwheel *n* rueda *f* dentada
gee whiz ['dʒi·ˌwɪz] *interj inf* caramba
geez [dʒiz] *interj inf* vaya
geezer ['gi·zər] *n sl* tío *m;* **old ~** vejestorio *m*
geisha (girl) ['geɪ·ʃə] *n* geisha *f*
gel [dʒel] *n* gel *m*
gelatin(e) ['dʒel·ə·tɪn] *n* gelatina *f*
gelatinous [dʒɪ·'læt̮·ə·nəs] *adj* gelatinoso, -a
geld [geld] *vt* castrar
gelding ['gel·dɪŋ] *n* caballo *m* castrado
gem [dʒem] *n* **1.** (*jewel*) piedra *f* preciosa **2.** (*person*) joya *f fig*
Gemini ['dʒem·ɪ·naɪ] *n* Géminis *mf*
gen. *n* **1.** *abbr of* **general** Gral. *mf* **2.** *abbr of*

generation generación *f*

gender ['dʒen·dər] *n* **1.** (*sexual identity*) sexo *m* **2.** LING género *m*

gene [dʒin] *n* gen *m*

genealogical [ˌdʒi·ni·ə·'ladʒ·ɪ·kəl] *adj* genealógico, -a

genealogist [ˌdʒi·nɪ·'æl·ə·dʒɪst] *n* genealogista *mf*

genealogy [ˌdʒi·nɪ·'æl·ə·dʒi] *n* genealogía *f*

gene bank *n* banco *m* genético

general ['dʒen·ər·əl] **I.** *adj* general; **to be of ~ interest** ser de interés general; **as a ~ rule** por regla general; **to talk in ~ terms** hablar en términos generales **II.** *n* MIL general *mf*; **major ~** general *mf* de división; **lieutenant ~** teniente *mf* general; **four-star ~** capitán , -ana *m*, *f* general

general admission *n* admisión *f* general

general anesthetic *n* anestesia *f* general

general assembly <-ies> *n* asamblea *f* general

general director *n* director(a) *m(f)* general

general election *n* elecciones *fpl* generales

general hospital *n* centro *m* hospitalario

generality [ˌdʒen·ə·'ræl·ə·ți] <-ies> *n* generalidad *f*

generalization [ˌdʒen·ər·ə·lɪ·'zeɪ·ʃən] *n* generalización *f*

generalize ['dʒen·ər·ə·laɪz] *vi*, *vt* generalizar

generally ['dʒen·ər·ə·li] *adv* **1.** (*usually*) generalmente **2.** (*mostly*) en general **3.** (*widely, extensively*) por lo general; **~ speaking** hablando en términos generales

general management *n* dirección *f* general

general manager *n* director(a) *m(f)* general

general partnership *n* sociedad *f* regular colectiva

general practitioner *n* médico , -a *m*, *f* de cabecera

general store *n* tienda *f*

general view *n* opinión *f* general; **I do not subscribe to the ~ that...** no estoy de acuerdo con la opinión general de que...

generate ['dʒen·ə·reɪt] *vt* generar

generating station ['dʒen·ə·reɪ·țɪŋ·ˌsteɪ·ʃən] *n* central *f* generadora

generation [ˌdʒen·ə·'reɪ·ʃən] *n* generación *f;* **for ~s** durante generaciones

generative ['dʒen·ər·ə·țɪv] *adj* generativo, -a

generator ['dʒen·ə·reɪ·țər] *n a.* ELEC generador *m*

generic [dʒɪ·'ner·ɪk] **I.** *adj* genérico, -a **II.** *n* producto *m* no de marca

generosity [ˌdʒen·ə·'ras·ə·ți] *n* generosidad *f*

generous ['dʒen·ər·əs] *adj* **1.** (*magnanimous: person*) generoso, -a, rangoso, -a *AmS* **2.** (*ample: serving*) abundante; (*slice*) grande **3.** (*better than deserved*) espléndido, -a

genesis ['dʒen·ə·sɪs] *n* génesis *f inv*

gene therapy [ˌdʒin·'θer·ə·pi] *n* terapia *f* génica

genetic [dʒɪ·'neț·ɪk] *adj* genético, -a; **~ disease** enfermedad *f* genética

geneticist [dʒɪ·'neț·ə·sɪst] *n* genetista *mf*

genetics *n + sing vb* genética *f*

genial ['dʒi·ni·əl] *adj* afable

geniality [ˌdʒi·nɪ·'æl·ə·ți] *n* afabilidad *f*

genie ['dʒi·ni] <-nii *o* -ies> *n* genio *m*

genitalia [dʒen·ɪ·'teɪ·li·ə] *npl form*, **genitals** ['dʒen·ə·təlz] *npl* genitales *mpl*

genitive ['dʒen·ɪ·țɪv] **I.** *adj* genitivo, -a **II.** *n* genitivo *m*

genius ['dʒin·jəs] *n* <-ses> genio *mf*

genocide ['dʒen·ə·saɪd] *n* genocidio *m*

genre ['dʒɑn·rə] *n a.* LIT género *m*

genre painting *n* pintura *f* de género

gent [dʒent] *n inf abbr of* **gentleman** caballero *m*

genteel [dʒen·'til] *adj* distinguido, -a

Gentile ['dʒen·taɪl] **I.** *adj* gentil **II.** *n* gentil *mf*

gentle ['dʒen·təl] *adj* **1.** (*kind*) amable; (*calm*) suave; **to be as ~ as a lamb** ser manso como un cordero **2.** (*moderate*) moderado, -a; (*slight: nudge, breeze, slope*) suave; (*tap on the door*) suave, pasito *Col*, quedito *Méx* **3.** (*upper-class*) **to be of ~ birth** ser de alcurnia

gentlefolk ['dʒen·təl·foʊk] *npl* gente *f* de buena familia

gentleman ['dʒen·təl·mən] <-men> *n* **1.** (*man*) señor *m;* **ladies and gentlemen** señoras y señores **2.** (*well-behaved man*) caballero *m;* **he is a true ~** es todo un caballero

gentlemanly ['dʒen·təl·mən·li] *adj* caballeroso, -a

gentleman's agreement *n* pacto *m* de caballeros

gentleness ['dʒen·təl·nɪs] *n* delicadeza *f*

gentlewoman ['dʒen·təl·wʊm·ən] <-women> *n* dama *f*

gentry ['dʒen·tri] *n* clase *f* acomodada

genuine ['dʒen·ju·ɪn] *adj* **1.** (*not fake*) genuino, -a **2.** (*real, sincere*) verdadero, -a

genus ['dʒi·nəs] <-nera> *n* BIO género *m*

geocentric [ˌdʒi·oʊ·'sen·trɪk] *adj* geocéntrico, -a

geodesic [ˌdʒ·ə·'des·ɪk] *adj* geodésico, -a

geographer [dʒi·'ag·rə·fər] *n* geógrafo, -a *m*, *f*

geographic [ˌdʒi·ə·'græf·ɪk] *adj*, **geographical** [ˌdʒi·ə·'græf·ɪ·kəl] *adj* geográfico, -a

geography [dʒi·'ag·rə·fi] *n* geografía *f*

geological [ˌdʒi·ə·'ladʒ·ɪ·kəl] *adj* geológico, -a

geologist [dʒi·'al·ə·dʒɪst] *n* geólogo, -a *m*, *f*

geology [dʒi·'al·ə·dʒi] *n* geología *f*

geometric [ˌdʒi·ə·'met·rɪk] *adj*, **geometrical** [ˌdʒi·ə·'met·rɪ·kəl] *adj* geométrico, -a

geometry [dʒi·'am·ə·tri] *n* geometría *f*

geophysical [ˌdʒi·oʊ·'fɪz·ɪ·kəl] *adj* geofísico, -a

geophysics [ˌdʒi·oʊ·'fɪz·ɪks] *n + sing vb* geofísica *f*

Georgia ['dʒɔr·dʒə] *n* Georgia *f*

geothermal [ˌdʒi·oʊ·'θɜr·məl] *adj* geotérmico, -a

geranium [dʒɪ·'reɪ·ni·əm] *n* geranio *m*, malvón *m Arg, Méx, Par, Urug*

G

geriatric [ˌdʒerˑiˑˈætˑrɪk] *adj* anciano, -a
geriatrician [ˌdʒerˑiˑəˈtrɪʃˑən] *n* geriatra *mf*
geriatrics *n* + *sing vb* geriatría *f*
germ [dʒɜrm] *n* germen *m*
German [ˈdʒɜrˑmən] I. *n* 1. (*person*) alemán, -ana *m, f* 2. (*language*) alemán *m* II. *adj* alemán, -ana
germane [dʒɜrˈmeɪn] *adj form* relacionado, -a
Germanic [dʒɜrˈmænˑɪk] *adj* germánico, -a
German measles *n* + *sing vb* rubeola *f*
German shepherd *n* pastor *m* alemán
Germany [ˈdʒɜrˑməˑni] *n* Alemania *f*
germfree *adj* esterilizado, -a
germicidal [ˌdʒɜrˑməˈsaɪˑdəl] *adj* germicida
germicide [ˈdʒɜrˑməˑsaɪd] *n* germicida *m*
germinal [ˈdʒɜrˑməˑnəl] *adj* germinal
germinate [ˈdʒɜrˑməˑneɪt] *vi, vt* germinar
germination [ˌdʒɜrˑməˈneɪˑʃən] *n* germinación *f*
germ warfare *n* guerra *f* bacteriológica
gerontologist [ˌdʒerˑənˈtalˑəˑdʒɪst] *n* gerontólogo, -a *m, f*
gerontology [ˌdʒerˑənˈtalˑəˑdʒi] *n* gerontología *f*
gerund [ˈdʒerˑənd] *n* gerundio *m*
gestation [dʒeˈsteɪˑʃən] *n* gestación *f*
gesticulate [dʒeˈstɪkˑjəˑleɪt] *vi form* gesticular
gesticulation [dʒeˌstɪkˑjəˈleɪˑʃən] *n form* gesticulación *f*
gesture [ˈdʒesˑtʃər] I. *n* 1. (*body movement*) gesto *m* 2. (*act*) muestra *f;* a ~ towards sb un detalle con alguien II. *vi* hacer un ademán III. *vt* indicar con un ademán
get [get] I. <got, gotten> *vt* 1. (*obtain*) obtener; (*a massage*) recibir; (*a manicure*) hacerse; to ~ the impression that... dar a alguien la impresión de que... 2. (*receive: letter, present*) recibir; to ~ sth from sb recibir algo de alguien; to ~ a surprise llevarse una sorpresa; to ~ pleasure out of sth disfrutar con algo 3. (*catch: plane, train*) coger; (*the flu*) pillar, pescar *Col;* do you ~ channel 4? ¿pillas el canal 4?, ¿te entra el canal 4? *Col* 4. (*hear, understand*) comprender; (*message*) captar; (*picture*) entender; to ~ sth/sb wrong entender algo/a alguien mal; I don't ~ it no lo pillo, no agarro la onda 5. (*answer*) to ~ the door *inf* abrir la puerta; to ~ the phone *inf* coger el teléfono 6. (*buy: groceries*) comprar; to ~ food/drinks *inf* pillar algo de comer/beber 7. (*cause to be done*) to ~ sth done hacer algo; to ~ sb to do sth hacer que alguien haga algo 8. (*start*) to ~ sb to do sth conseguir que alguien haga algo; to ~ the ball rolling poner las cosas en marcha, echar a rodar algo 9. *inf* (*irk*) repatear; (*make emotional*) afectar; that really ~s me eso me afecta realmente 10. *inf* (*start*) to ~ going poner en marcha; to ~ cracking poner manos a la obra II. *vi* 1. + *n*/*adj* (*become*) volverse; to ~ married casarse; to ~ upset enfadarse; to ~ used to sth acostumbrarse a algo; to ~ to be sth llegar a ser algo; to ~ to like sth coger

afición a algo 2. (*have opportunity*) to ~ to do sth llegar a hacer algo; to ~ to see sb lograr ver a alguien 3. (*travel*) llegar; to ~ home llegar a casa
◆get across *vt* hacer llegar; to get a point across to sb hacer llegar una idea a alguien
◆get after *vt* regañar
◆get along *vi* 1. (*have a good relationship*) llevarse bien 2. (*manage*) arreglárselas
◆get around I. *vt insep* (*avoid*) evitar II. *vi* 1. (*spread*) llegar a; word eventually got around that... con el tiempo se difundió [o regó la ola de *Col*] que... 2. (*travel*) viajar mucho
◆get at *vt insep* 1. (*reach*) llegar a 2. (*suggest*) apuntar a
◆get away *vi* irse
◆get away with *vt* to ~ sth salirse con la suya; *a. fig;* to ~ murder quedar impune de un asesinato
◆get back *vt* recuperar
◆get back at *vt* vengarse de
◆get back to *vt* (*letter*) contestar; (*call*) devolver
◆get behind I. *vi* atrasarse II. *vt insep* respaldar
◆get by *vi* (*manage*) arreglárselas
◆get down I. *vt always sep* (*disturb*) deprimir II. *vi* 1. (*descend*) bajar 2. *inf* (*enjoy oneself*) pachanguear *Méx,* rumbear *Col*
◆get down to *vt* ponerse con; to ~ doing sth ponerse a hacer algo
◆get in I. *vi* 1. (*arrive*) llegar a casa; what time does your flight ~? ¿a qué hora llega tu avión? 2. (*enter*) entrar 3. (*become member*) ser aceptado II. *vt* 1. (*say*) (lograr) decir 2. (*bring inside*) llevar dentro 3. (*accomplish*) lograr
◆get into *vt insep* 1. (*become interested in*) interesarse por 2. (*involve*) meter; to get sb into trouble meter a alguien en problemas
◆get off I. *vi* 1. (*avoid punishment*) librarse 2. (*leave work*) salir 3. (*have audacity*) atreverse 4. *sl* (*have orgasm*) correrse, venirse *Col, Méx* II. *vt always sep* 1. (*shot*) disparar 2. (*help avoid punishment*) librar de 3. (*work*) acabar 4. (*send*) enviar
◆get on I. *vi* 1. (*manage*) arreglárselas 2. (*age*) envejecer II. *vt sl* let's get it on (*enthusiastically begin*) ¡pogamos manos a la obra!; (*have sex*) hagámoslo
◆get out I. *vi* 1. (*leave home*) salir 2. (*spread*) correr la voz 3. (*escape*) escaparse, volarse *Col, Méx* II. *vt* 1. (*make leave*) echar 2. (*make spread*) anunciar
◆get over *vt insep* 1. (*recover from*) recuperarse de; (*illness*) reponerse de; (*difficulty*) superar 2. (*forget about*) to ~ sb/sth olvidarse de alguien/algo
◆get through I. *vt* 1. (*survive*) pasar; (*exam*) aprobar 2. (*finish*) terminar 3. (*make understood*) to get it through to sb that... hacer que alguien entienda que... II. *vi* to ~ to sth/

sb comunicarse con algo/alguien
◆**get together I.** *vi* reunirse **II.** *vt* **1.** (*meet*) juntarse **2.** (*gather*) reunir **3.** (*organize*) preparar
◆**get up I.** *vt* **1.** *always sep* (*wake*) levantarse **2.** (*muster: courage*) conseguir **3.** *insep* (*climb*) subir **4.** *inf* (*dress*) ataviar **II.** *vi* **1.** (*get out of bed*) levantarse **2.** (*rise*) subir
◆**get up to** *vt* llegar a
get-at-able [,get·'æt·ə·bəl] *adj inf* a mano
getaway ['get·ə·weɪ] *n* fuga *f;* **to make a** (**clean**) ~ fugarse (sin dejar ni rastro)
get-together ['get·tə·'geð·ər] *n inf* reunión *f*
get-up ['get·ʌp] *n inf* atuendo *m*
geyser ['gi·zər] *n* géiser *m*
Ghana ['ga·nə] *n* Ghana *f*
Ghanaian [ga·'ni·ən] **I.** *adj* ghanés, -esa **II.** *n* ghanés, -esa *m, f*
ghastly ['gæst·li] <-ier, -iest> *adj* **1.** (*frightful*) horroroso, -a **2.** (*unpleasant*) muy desagradable **3.** *liter* (*pallid*) ~ **white/pale** blanco, -a/pálido, -a (como la cera)
gherkin ['gɜr·kɪn] *n* pepinillo *m*
ghetto ['get·oʊ] **I.** <-s *o* -es> *n* gueto *m* **II.** *adj sl* (*lame*) **that's so ~, dude!** ¡qué cutre, tío!, ¡qué ordinariez, hombre!
ghetto blaster *n sl* loro *m* portátil, grabadora *f Col, Méx*
ghost [goʊst] **I.** *n a. fig* (*spirit*) fantasma *m*, espanto *m AmL*, azoro *m AmC;* **to believe in ~s** creer en fantasmas; **to be haunted by ~s** (*house*) tener fantasmas; (*person*) ser perseguido por fantasmas; **the ~ of the past** los fantasmas del pasado ▶**not to have a ~ of a chance** no tener ni la más mínima oportunidad; **to give up the ~** *liter* (*to die*) exhalar el último suspiro; *inf* (*to stop working*) escacharrarse **II.** *vt inf* escribir para otro; **his autobiography was ~ed** un negro escribió su autobiografía **III.** *vi* hacer de negro
ghostly ['goʊst·li] <-ier, -iest> *adj* **1.** (*ghost-like*) fantasmal **2.** (*spooky*) escalofriante
ghost story *n* historia *f* de fantasmas
ghost town *n* pueblo *m* fantasma
ghost-write *vt* escribir para otro
ghost-writer *n* negro, -a *m, f* (*persona que escribe para otra*)
ghoul [gul] *n* (*evil spirit*) espíritu *m* necrófago
GHz *n s.* **gigahertz** GHz *m*
GI [,dʒi·'aɪ] *n* soldado *m* norteamericano (*especialmente en la II Guerra Mundial*)
GI *abbr of* **government issue** reglamentario, -a
giant ['dʒaɪ·ənt] **I.** *n* gigante *m;* **a political ~** un coloso de la política **II.** *adj* gigantesco, -a
giantess ['dʒaɪ·ən·tɪs] *n* **1.** (*woman giant*) giganta *f* **2.** (*influential woman*) colosa *f*
gibberish ['dʒɪb·ər·ɪʃ] *n* galimatías *m inv*
gibbon ['gɪb·ən] *n* gibón *m*
gibe [dʒaɪb] **I.** *vi* **to ~ at sb/sth** burlarse de alguien/algo **II.** *vt* burlarse de **III.** *n* burla *f*
giblets ['dʒɪb·lɪts] *npl* menudillos *mpl*
giddy ['gɪd·i] <-ier, -iest> *adj* mareado, -a
gift [gɪft] *n* **1.** (*present*) regalo *m;* **to bear ~s**

traer [*o* llevar] regalos; **to be a ~ from the Gods** ser un regalo caído del cielo **2.** *inf* (*bargain*) **$100 for this bicycle? it's a ~!** ¿100 dólares por esta bicicleta? ¡Es una ganga! **3.** (*talent*) don *m;* **to have a ~ for languages** tener talento para los idiomas; **to have the ~ of gab** *inf* tener mucha labia
gift certificate *n* vale *m* de [*o* por un] regalo
gifted *adj* **1.** (*talented: musician*) de (gran) talento **2.** (*intelligent*) brillante; **~ child** niño *m* superdotado
gift horse *n* **never look a ~ in the** <u>mouth</u> *prov* a caballo regalado, no le mires el dentado *prov*
gift shop *n* tienda *f* de regalos
gig¹ [gɪg] **I.** *n sl* (*musical performance*) concierto *m;* **to do a ~** dar un concierto **II.** *vi* <-gg-> (*do a gig*) dar un concierto
gig² [gɪg] *n* COMPUT *abbr of* **gigabyte** giga *m*
gigabyte ['gɪg·ə·baɪt] *n* gigabyte *m*
gigantic [dʒaɪ·'gæn·tɪk] *adj* gigantesco, -a
giggle ['gɪg·əl] **I.** *vi* reír(se) tontamente **II.** *n* **1.** (*laugh*) risita *f* **2.** *pl* **the ~s** la risa floja; **to get the ~s** tener un ataque de risa
gild [gɪld] *vt* **1.** (*cover with gold*) dorar **2.** (*light up*) iluminar ▶**to ~ the <u>lily</u>** rizar el rizo
gilded *adj* dorado, -a
gill [gɪl] *n* (*of a fish*) agalla *f* ▶**to be green around** [*o* about] **the ~s** *inf* estar pálido como la cera; **to the ~s** *inf* a tope; **to be <u>stuffed</u> to the ~s** *inf* estar para reventar
gilt [gɪlt] **I.** *adj* dorado, -a **II.** *n* dorado *m*
gilt-edged [,gɪlt·'edʒd] *adj* (*securities, stocks*) de máxima garantía
gimcrack ['dʒɪm·kræk] *n* baratija *f*, chuchería *f Col, Méx*
gimlet ['gɪm·lɪt] *n* **1.** (*alcoholic drink*) cóctel *m* de lima con vodka o ginebra **2.** (*tool*) barrena *f*
gimlet-eyed *adj* penetrante; **to be ~** tener una mirada penetrante
gimmick ['gɪm·ɪk] *n* **1.** (*trick*) truco *m* (*para vender más*); **sales ~** truco publicitario **2.** (*attention-getter*) truco *m* efectista (*para atraer la atención*)
gimmicky ['gɪm·ɪk·i] *adj* efectista
gin¹ [dʒɪn] *n* ginebra *f;* **~ and tonic** gin tonic *m*
gin² [dʒɪn] *n* AGR **cotton ~** desmotadora *f* de algodón
gin³ [dʒɪn] *n* (*card game*) juego de cartas parecido al rummy
ginger ['dʒɪn·dʒər] **I.** *n* **1.** (*root spice*) jengibre *m* **2.** (*color*) rojo *m* anaranjado **II.** *adj* rojizo, -a
ginger ale *n* ginger ale *m*, refresco *m* de jengibre
gingerbread ['dʒɪn·dʒər·bred] *n* pan *m* de jengibre
gingerly ['dʒɪn·dʒər·li] *adv* con cautela
ginger snap *n* galleta *f* de jengibre
gingivitis [,dʒɪn·dʒə·'vaɪ·ţəs] *n* gingivitis *f inv*
ginseng ['dʒɪn·seŋ] *n* ginseng *m*
gip [dʒɪp] *vt, n sl s.* **gyp**
gipsy ['dʒɪp·si] *n s.* **gypsy**

giraffe [dʒə·'ræf] *n* <-(s)> jirafa *f*
girder ['gɜr·dər] *n* viga *f* (*de metal u hormigón*)
girdle ['gɜr·dəl] I. *n* 1. *a. fig* (*belt*) cinturón *m* 2. (*corset*) faja *f* II. *vt a. fig* (*surround*) rodear
girl [gɜrl] *n* 1. (*child*) niña *f*; (*young woman*) chica *f*, piba *f Arg* 2. (*daughter*) hija *f* 3. **the ~s** *pl* (*at work*) las compañeras; (*friends*) las amigas
girl Friday *n* chica *f* para todo
girlfriend ['gɜrl·frend] *n* 1. (*of man*) novia *f*, polola *f And* 2. (*of woman*) amiga *f*
girlhood ['gɜrl·hʊd] *n* juventud *f*
girlie ['gɜr·li] *adj* de destape
girlie magazine *n* revista *f* de chicas desnudas
girlish ['gɜr·lɪʃ] *adj* de [*o* como una] niña
Girl Scout *n* exploradora *f*
girth [gɜrθ] *n* 1. (*circumference*) circunferencia *f* 2. *iron* (*obesity*) sebo *m* 3. (*strap around horse*) cincha *f*
gist [dʒɪst] *n* **the ~** lo esencial; **to give sb the ~** (**of sth**) contar a alguien lo fundamental (sobre algo); **to get the ~ of sth** entender lo básico de algo
give [gɪv] I. *vt* <gave, given> 1. (*offer*) dar, ofrecer; (*kiss, signal*) dar; (*a seat*) ceder; **to ~ sb an excuse for sth** dar una excusa a alguien para algo; **given the choice...** si pudiera elegir...; **to ~ sb something to eat/drink** dar a alguien algo de comer/beber; **to not ~ much for sth** *fig* no importar mucho algo a alguien; **to ~ sb life in prison** condenar a alguien a cadena perpetua; **don't ~ me that!** *inf* ¡venga ya, tú me la quieres dar con queso!; **~ me a break!** ¡dame un respiro!; **I don't ~ a damn** *inf* me importa un bledo; **to ~ notice** avisar, hacer saber; **to ~ sb the creeps** producir a alguien escalofríos; **to ~ (it) one's all** [*o* best] dar todo de sí mismo; **to ~ anything for sth/ to do sth** dar cualquier cosa por algo/por hacer algo; **to ~ one's life to sth** dedicar la vida a algo 2. (*lecture, performance*) dar; (*speech*) pronunciar; (*strange look*) echar; (*headache, trouble*) producir, dar; **to ~ sb a call** llamar a alguien (por teléfono); **to ~ sth a go** intentar algo; **to ~ sb to understand sth** *form* dar a entender algo a alguien 3. (*organize*) dar, organizar 4. (*pass on*) contagiar II. *vi* <gave, given> 1. (*offer*) dar, ofrecer; **to ~ as good as one gets** devolver golpe por golpe; **to ~ of one's money** hacer una aportación (económica); **to ~ of one's best** dar todo de sí 2. (*stretch*) estirarse, dar de sí; **something will have to ~** *fig* algo tendrá que cambiar 3. **what ~s?** *inf* ¿qué hay? ▸ **it is better to ~ than to receive** *prov* es mejor dar que recibir *prov* III. *n* elasticidad *f*
◆ **give away** *vt* 1. (*for free*) regalar 2. (*reveal*) revelar 3. (*betray*) **to give sb away** delatar a alguien 4. *form* (*bride*) entregar en matrimonio 5. SPORTS regalar al (equipo) contrario
◆ **give back** *vt* devolver, regresar *Méx*
◆ **give in** I. *vi* rendirse; **to ~ to sth** acceder

(finalmente) a algo II. *vt* entregar
◆ **give off** *vt* emitir; (*odor*) despedir; (*heat*) producir
◆ **give out** I. *vt* 1. (*distribute*) repartir 2. (*announce*) anunciar 3. (*emit*) producir; (*noise*) emitir II. *vi* 1. (*run out*) acabar(se) 2. (*machine*) estropearse; (*legs*) ceder
◆ **give up** I. *vt* 1. (*renounce*) renunciar; **to ~ candy for a month** renunciar a los dulces por un mes; **to ~ doing sth** dejar de hacer algo; **to ~ smoking** dejar de fumar 2. (*hand over*) ceder; **please give these seats up to senior citizens** hagan el favor de ceder sus asientos a las personas mayores 3. (*lose hope*) **to give sb up for dead** dar a alguien por muerto; **to give sb up as lost** dar a alguien por desaparecido 4. (*surrender*) entregar; **to give oneself up (to the police)** entregarse (a la policía) II. *vi* 1. (*quit*) abandonar 2. (*cease trying to guess*) rendirse
give-and-take [,gɪv·ən·'teɪk] *n* (*compromise*) toma y daca *m*
giveaway ['gɪv·ə·weɪ] *n* 1. *inf* (*free gift*) regalo *m* 2. *inf* (*exposure*) prueba *f* (que delata algo); **the way he dresses is a dead ~** su forma de vestir lo delata
given ['gɪv·ən] I. *pp of* give II. *adj* 1. (*specified*) determinado, -a, dado, -a; **at a ~ time and place** a una hora y en un lugar determinados 2. **to be ~ to (doing) sth** ser dado a (hacer) algo III. *prep* **~ that** dado que +*subj*, en el caso de que +*subj*; **~ the chance, I would go to Japan** si tuviese la oportunidad, iría a Japón IV. *n* dato *m* conocido; **to take sth as a ~** dar algo por sentado; **that's a ~** eso se sobreentiende
giver ['gɪv·ər] *n* donante *mf*
glacé [gla·'seɪ] *adj inv* glaseado, -a; **~ fruit** fruta *f* confitada
glacial ['gleɪ·ʃəl] *adj* GEO glacial; **~ epoch/ look** era *f*/mirada *f* glacial
glacier ['gleɪ·ʃər] *n* glaciar *m*
glad [glæd] <gladder, gladdest> *adj* contento, -a; **to be ~ about sth** alegrarse de algo; **I'd be ~ to go with you** me encantaría ir contigo; **I'm ~ you can help** agradezco tu ayuda
gladden ['glæd·ən] *vt* alegrar
glade [gleɪd] *n* claro *m* (de un bosque)
gladiator ['glæd·i·eɪ·tər] *n* gladiador *m*
gladiolus [,glæd·i·'oʊ·ləs] <-es *o* -li> *n* gladiolo *m*
gladly ['glæd·li] *adv* con mucho gusto
gladness ['glæd·nɪs] *n* alegría *f*
glad rags *n pl, sl* **to put on one's ~** emperifollarse
glamor ['glæm·ər] *n s.* glamour
glamorize ['glæm·ə·raɪz] *vt* hacer más atractivo; **this film ~s violence** esta película exalta la violencia
glamorous ['glæm·ə·rəs] *adj* glamoroso, -a, atractivo, -a; (*outfit*) sofisticado, -a
glamour ['glæm·ər] *n* glamour *m*, encanto *m*, atractivo *m*

glamour-puss n (woman) bombón m
glance [glæns] I. n mirada f; **to take a ~ at sth** echar una mirada [o un vistazo] a algo; **at first ~ a** primera vista; **at a ~** de un vistazo II. vi 1. (look cursorily) **to ~ up (from sth)** levantar la mirada (de algo); **to ~ around sth** mirar alrededor de algo; **to ~ over sth** echar un vistazo a algo 2. (shine) brillar
♦ **glance off** vi (chocar y) rebotar
gland [glænd] n glándula f
glandular ['glæn·dʒə·lər] adj glandular
glare [gler] I. n 1. (mean look) mirada f (feroz); **to give sb a ~** fulminar a alguien con la mirada 2. (reflection) resplandor m; **to give off ~** deslumbrar; **to be dazzled by the ~ of sth** quedar deslumbrado por el resplandor de algo II. vi 1. (look) fulminar con la mirada 2. (shine) resplandecer; **the sun ~s down on my eyes** el sol me da directamente en los ojos
glaring adj 1. (obvious: error) que salta a la vista; **~ weakness** debilidad f manifiesta; **~ injustice** injusticia f que clama al cielo 2. (sun) deslumbrante 3. (hostile: eyes) desafiante
glass [glæs] <-es> n 1. (material) vidrio m, cristal m; **pane of ~** hoja f de vidrio 2. (for drinks) vaso m; **a ~ of milk** un vaso de leche 3. (drink) copa f 4. **~s** gafas fpl, lentes fpl AmL 5. (glassware) cristalería f
glass blower ['glæs·blou·ər] n soplador(a) m(f) de vidrio
glass cutter n cortador(a) m(f) de vidrio
glassful ['glæs·fʊl] n vaso m; **a ~ of orange juice** un vaso (lleno) de zumo de naranja
glasshouse ['glæs·haʊs] n invernadero m
glassware n cristalería f
glassworks npl fábrica f de vidrio
glassy ['glæs·i] <-ier, -iest> adj 1. liter (as glass) vítreo, -a 2. (eyes) vidrioso, -a
glaucoma [glaʊ·'koʊ·mə] n glaucoma m
glaucous ['glɔ·kəs] adj 1. (greenish-blue) glauco, -a 2. BOT (with bloom) cubierto, -a de una pelusilla verdosa
glaze [gleɪz] I. n a. CULIN glaseado m; (painting) barniz m; (pottery) vidriado m II. vt 1. (pottery) vidriar 2. (donut) glasear 3. (window) poner vidrios a
glazier ['gleɪ·zi·ər] n vidriero, -a m, f, cristalero, -a m, f
gleam [glim] I. n reflejo m, destello m; **~ of hope** rayo m de esperanza II. vi brillar, relucir
glean [glin] vt **to ~ sth from sb** deducir algo (de las palabras) de alguien
gleanings npl información f recogida
glee [gli] n júbilo m; **to do sth with ~** hacer algo con gran alegría
gleeful ['gli·fəl] adj eufórico, -a
glen [glen] n cañada f
glib [glɪb] <glibber, glibbest> adj simplista
glide [glaɪd] I. vi 1. (move smoothly) deslizarse 2. AVIAT planear; **to take sb gliding** llevar a alguien a volar con planeador II. n 1. (sliding movement) deslizamiento m 2. AVIAT planeo

m; **with a ~** con un movimiento deslizante
glider ['glaɪ·dər] n planeador m
glider pilot n piloto mf de planeador
gliding ['glaɪ·dɪŋ] n vuelo m sin motor
glimmer ['glɪm·ər] I. vi brillar tenuemente II. n (light) luz f tenue; **~ of hope** atisbo m de esperanza
glimpse [glɪmps] I. vt (signs) vislumbrar II. n **to catch a ~ of** vislumbrar
glint [glɪnt] I. vi destellar; **to ~ with sth** brillar a causa de algo II. n destello m
glisten ['glɪs·ən] vi brillar, relucir
glitch [glɪtʃ] <-es> n fallo m
glitter ['glɪt̬·ər] I. vi brillar, relucir II. n 1. (sparkling) brillo m, destello m 2. (excitement) esplendor m 3. (shiny material) purpurina f
glittering adj 1. (sparkling, impressive) brillante 2. (exciting) esplendoroso, -a
glitz [glɪts] n ostentosidad f
glitzy ['glɪt·si] <-ier, -iest> adj inf ostentoso, -a; (party) esplendoroso, -a, suntuoso, -a
gloat [gloʊt] I. vi disfrutar con regocijo; **to ~ over sth** manifestar (gran) satisfacción por algo; **to ~ at sth** regodearse con algo II. n regocijo m
global ['gloʊ·bəl] adj 1. (worldwide) (a nivel) mundial, global 2. (complete) global, total, general; COMPUT **~ search and replace** buscar y reemplazar en todo el documento
global warming n calentamiento m global
globe [gloʊb] n 1. (map of world) globo m terráqueo 2. (object) globo m
globetrotter ['gloʊb·trɑt̬·ər] n trotamundos mf inv
globule ['glɑb·jul] n glóbulo m
gloom [glum] n 1. (hopelessness) pesimismo m, melancolía f; **~ and doom** profunda desesperación; **~ and despondency** pesimismo y abatimiento 2. (darkness) oscuridad f
gloominess ['glu·mi·nəs] n 1. (hopelessness) pesimismo m 2. (darkness) oscuridad f
gloomy ['glu·mi] <-ier, -iest> adj 1. (dismal) lúgubre; (thoughts) melancólico, -a; **to be ~ about sth** ser pesimista respecto a algo; **to turn ~** abatirse 2. (dark: corner, day) oscuro, -a
glorification [ˌglɔr·ə·fə·'keɪ·ʃən] n 1. (honoring, praising) alabanza f 2. (seem more splendid) glorificación f
glorify ['glɔr·ə·faɪ] <-ie-> vt 1. (make seem better) glorificar 2. (honor) alabar; **to ~ God** REL alabar a Dios
glorious ['glɔr·i·əs] adj 1. (honorable, illustrious) glorioso, -a 2. (splendid: day, weather) espléndido, -a 3. iron (extreme) enorme; **this bedroom is one ~ mess** esta habitación es un completo desastre
glory ['glɔr·i] n 1. (honor) gloria f; **to bathe in ~** bañarse de gloria; **to cover oneself in ~** cubrirse de gloria; **to deserve/get all the ~ for sth** merecer/conseguir toda la gloria por algo 2. (splendor) esplendor m; **in all her ~** en todo su esplendor 3. (state of delight) **to be in**

G

one's ~ estar en la gloria **4.** (*adoration, praise*) adoración *f* ► ~ **be!** (*thank God!*) ¡gracias a Dios! **II.** <-ie-> *vi* vanagloriarse; **to** ~ **in sth** vanagloriarse de algo

gloss¹ [glas] *n* **1.** (*shine*) brillo *m*, lustre *m*; **high** ~ mucho brillo *m* **2.** (*shiny substance*) abrillantador *m* **3.** (*shiny finish*) acabado *m* brillante **4.** (*shiny paint*) esmalte *m* **5.** (*lip moisturizer*) brillo *m* para labios

gloss² [glas] **I.** <-es> *n* glosa *f* **II.** *vt* glosar ◆ **gloss over** *vt* pasar por alto

glossary ['glas·ə·ri] <-ies> *n* PUBL, LIT glosario *m*

glossy ['glas·i] **I.** <-ier, -iest> *adj* **1.** (*shiny*) brillante, lustroso, -a; (*paper*) satinado, -a **2.** *inf* (*superficially attractive*) bambollero, -a **II.** <-ies> *n* PHOT fotografía *f* brillante

glottal stop ['glaṭ·əl·'stap] *n* LING oclusión *f* glotal

glottis ['glaṭ·əs] <-es> *n* ANAT, MED glotis *f inv*

glove [glʌv] **I.** *n* guante *m*; **leather/wool** ~**s** guantes *mpl* de piel/lana; **a pair of** ~**s** unos guantes; **to put on/take off one's** ~**s** ponerse/sacarse los guantes ► **to** fit **(sb) like a** ~ venir a alguien como anillo al dedo, quedar a alguien como un guante **II.** *vt* **1.** (*dress in gloves*) **to** ~ **one's hands** ponerse los guantes **2.** (*catch*) atrapar

glove box *n*, **glove compartment** *n* AUTO guantera *f*

glow [gloʊ] **I.** *n* **1.** (*light*) luz *f* **2.** (*warmth and redness*) ardor *m* **3.** (*good feeling*) sensación *f* grata; ~ **of happiness/pride/satisfaction** oleada *f* de felicidad/orgullo/satisfacción **II.** *vi* **1.** (*illuminate*) brillar **2.** (*be red and hot*) arder **3.** (*look radiant*) estar radiante

glower ['glaʊ·ər] **I.** *vi* mirar con el ceño fruncido; **to** ~ **at sb** mirar con el ceño fruncido a alguien **II.** *n* mirada *f* furiosa

glowing *adj* (*embers*) ardiente; (*report, praise*) efusivo, -a

glow-worm *n* luciérnaga *f*, candelilla *f* CRi, Chile, Hond

glucose ['glu·koʊs] *n* glucosa *f*; ~ **syrup** jarabe *m* de glucosa

glue [glu] **I.** *n* cola *f*, pegamento *m*; **to fix sth with** ~ fijar algo con cola; **to sniff** ~ esnifar pegamento **II.** *vt* encolar; **to** ~ **sth together** pegar algo; **to** ~ **sth on** encolar algo; **to be** ~**d to sth** *fig* estar pegado a algo; **to keep one's eyes** ~**d to sth/sb** *fig* mantener los ojos pegados a algo/alguien

glue stick *n* pegamento *m* en barra

glum [glʌm] <glummer, glummest> *adj* **1.** (*morose, downcast*) taciturno, -a; **to be/feel** ~ (**about sth**) estar/sentirse melancólico (por algo) **2.** (*drab*) monótono, -a

glut [glʌt] **I.** *n* ECON exceso *m* de oferta; **a** ~ **of sth** una superabundancia de algo **II.** <-tt-> *vt* ECON saturar

gluten ['glu·tən] *n* gluten *m*

gluten intolerance *n* intolerancia *f* al gluten, enfermedad *f* celíaca

gluten-intolerant *adj inv* celíaco, -a, alérgico, -a al gluten

glutinous ['glut·ən·əs] *adj* glutinoso, -a

glutton ['glʌt·ən] *n* **1.** (*overeater*) glotón, -ona *m, f* **2.** (*enthusiast*) entusiasta *mf*

gluttonous ['glʌt·ən·əs] *adj* glotón, -ona, angurriento, -a *AmL*

gluttony ['glʌt·ən·i] *n* glotonería *f*

glycerin ['glɪs·ər·ɪn] *n*, **glycerine** ['glɪs·ər·in] *n*, **glycerol** ['glɪs·ə·ral] *n* glicerina *f*

glycol ['glaɪ·kal] *n* glicol *m*

gnarled [narld] *adj* (*knobby and twisted*) retorcido, -a; (*knotted*) nudoso, -a

gnash [næʃ] *vt* hacer rechinar; **to** ~ **one's teeth about sth** rechinar los dientes por algo

gnat [næt] *n* BIO mosquito *m*, jején *m AmS*

gnaw [nɔ] **I.** *vi* **1.** (*chew*) **to** ~ **at** [*o* **on**] **sth** roer algo **2.** *fig* (*deplete*) reducir; **to** ~ **away at sth** agotar algo **3.** (*bother*) atormentar; **to** ~ **at sb** atormentar a alguien **II.** *vt* **1.** (*chew*) roer **2.** *fig* (*pursue*) **to be** ~**ed by doubt/fear/guilt** ser asaltado por las dudas/el miedo/el sentimiento de culpa

gnawing *adj* persistente; (*pain*) punzante; (*doubt*) que atormenta

gnome [noʊm] *n* gnomo, -a *m, f*

GNP [,dʒi·en·'pi] *abbr of* **Gross National Product** PNB

gnu [nu] <-(s)> *n* ZOOL ñu *m*

go [goʊ] **I.** <went, gone> *vi* **1.** (*proceed*) ir; **to** ~ (**and**) **do sth** ir a hacer algo; **to** ~ **home** irse a casa **2.** (*travel*) viajar; **to** ~ **on a cruise** ir de crucero; **to** ~ **on a holiday** irse de vacaciones; **to** ~ **on a trip** irse de viaje; **to** ~ **abroad** viajar al extranjero **3.** (*adopt position*) **when I** ~ **like this, my back hurts** cuando hago esto, me duele la espalda **4.** (*leave*) marcharse; **to have to** ~ tener que irse; **when does the bus** ~**?** ¿a qué hora sale el autobús? **5.** (*do*) hacer; **to** ~ **biking** salir en bicicleta; **to** ~ **camping/fishing/shopping** ir de camping/pesca/compras; **to** ~ **jogging** hacer footing; **to** ~ **swimming** ir a nadar **6.** (*attend*) asistir; **to** ~ **to a concert** ir a un concierto; **to** ~ **to a movie** ir a ver una película; **to** ~ **to a party** ir a una fiesta **7.** + *adj or n* (*become*) volverse; **to** ~ **senile** volverse viejo; **to** ~ **bankrupt** caer en bancarrota; **to** ~ **public** hacerse público; **to** ~ **communist** volverse comunista; **to** ~ **adrift** fallar; **to** ~ **bald** quedarse calvo; **to** ~ **haywire** volverse loco; **to** ~ **to sleep** dormirse; **to** ~ **wrong** salir mal **8.** + *adj* (*exist*) **to** ~ **hungry/thirsty** pasar hambre/sed; **to** ~ **unmentioned/unsolved** no ser mencionado/no solucionarse; **to** ~ **unnoticed** pasar desapercibido; **as prices** ~**...** considerando los precios actuales... **9.** (*happen*) **to** ~ **badly/well** ir mal/bien; **to** ~ **from bad to worse** ir de mal en peor; **the way things are** ~**ing** tal como van las cosas **10.** (*pass*) pasar; **time seems to** ~ **faster as you get older** parece que pasa el tiempo más rápido a medida que envejeces **11.** (*begin*) empezar; **ready, set,** ~ preparados, listos, ya **12.** (*fail*) **to ~ downhill** ir de capa caída **13.** (*belong*) pertenecer; **where does this ~?** ¿dónde va esto? **14.** (*fit*) quedar bien; **that old picture would ~ well on that wall** ese viejo cuadro quedaría bien en aquella pared; **two ~es into eight four times** MATH ocho entre dos da cuatro **15.** (*lead*) conducir; **this highway ~es all the way from here to California** esta carretera llega hasta California **16.** (*extend*) extenderse; **those numbers ~ from 1 to 10** esos números van del 1 al 10 **17.** (*function*) funcionar; **to ~ slow** ir despacio; **to get sth to ~** hacer que algo funcione; **to keep a conversation ~ing** mantener una conversación **18.** (*be sold*) venderse; **the painting went for a lot more than was expected** el cuadro se vendió mucho más caro de lo esperado; **to ~ for $50** venderse por 50 dólares; **to ~ like hot cakes** *fig* venderse como rosquillas **19.** (*contribute*) contribuir; **love and friendship ~ to make a lasting relationship** el amor y la amistad contribuyen a hacer duradera una relación **20.** (*sound*) sonar; **the ambulance had sirens ~ing** la ambulancia hacía sonar las sirenas **21.** (*be told*) **as the saying ~es** como dice el refrán **22.** GAMES tocar; **I ~ now** ahora me toca a mí **23.** *inf* (*use the toilet*) **do any of the kids have to ~?** ¿alguno de los niños tiene que ir al lavabo? **24.** (*express annoyance*) **~ climb a rock!** *inf* ¡vete a freír espárragos! ▶**what he says ~es** lo que él dice va a misa; **anything ~es** cualquier cosa vale; **here ~es!** ¡vamos allá! **II.** <went, gone> *vt* **1.** *inf* (*say*) decir; **and then he goes, "Knock it off!"** y entonces es cuando dice: "¡Ya basta!"; **ducks ~ 'quack'** los patos hacen 'cuac' **2.** (*make*) hacer; **to ~ it alone** hacerlo solo **III.** <-es> *n* **1.** (*attempt*) intento *m;* **all in one ~** todo de un tirón; **to have a ~ at sth** intentar algo; **to have a ~ at sb about sth** tomarla con alguien por algo **2.** (*a success*) éxito *m;* **to be no ~** ser imposible; **to make a ~ of sth** tener éxito en algo **3.** (*activity*) actividad *f;* **to be on the ~** trajinar; **to keep sb on the ~** hacer que alguien siga trabajando ▶**from the word ~** desde el principio **IV.** *adj* AVIAT listo, -a

◆**go about I.** *vt insep* **1.** (*proceed with*) ocuparse de; **to ~ one's business** ocuparse de sus asuntos **2.** (*perform a task*) llevar a cabo **II.** *vi* andar (por ahí)

◆**go after** *vt insep* **1.** (*follow*) seguir; **to ~ sb** ir detrás de alguien **2.** (*chase*) perseguir **3.** (*try to get*) andar tras

◆**go against** *vt insep* **1.** (*contradict*) contradecir **2.** (*oppose*) ir en contra de, oponerse a **3.** (*disobey*) desobedecer

◆**go ahead** *vi* **1.** (*begin*) empezar **2.** (*go before*) ir delante **3.** (*proceed*) seguir adelante; **~!** ¡sigue!; **all preparations have finished but they can't ~** todos los preparativos están listos pero no pueden sacarlo adelante

◆**go along** *vi* **1.** (*move onward*) ir hacia de-

lante **2.** (*proceed*) proceder a

◆**go around** *vi* **1.** (*move around*) andar (de acá para allá) **2.** (*move in a curve*) girar **3.** (*visit*) **to ~ to sb's** visitar a alguien; **to ~ and see sb** ir a ver a alguien **4.** (*rotate*) rotar **5.** (*be in circulation*) estar circulando; **it's going around that...** se dice que...

◆**go at** *vt insep* **1.** (*attack*) acometer, lanzarse sobre **2.** (*work hard*) **to ~ it** trabajar mucho

◆**go away** *vi* **1.** (*travel*) viajar **2.** (*leave*) marcharse **3.** (*disappear*) desaparecer

◆**go back** *vi* **1.** (*move backwards*) retroceder **2.** (*return*) volver, regresarse *AmL* **3.** (*date back*) remontarse

◆**go between** *vi* interponerse

◆**go beyond** *vt* **1.** (*proceed past*) sobrepasar **2.** (*exceed*) superar

◆**go by** *vi* **1.** (*move past*) pasar (junto a) **2.** (*pass*) transcurrir; **in days gone by** *form* en tiempos pasados; **to let sth ~** no aprovechar algo

◆**go down I.** *vt insep* bajar, descender; **to ~ a mine** MIN bajar a una mina **II.** *vi* **1.** (*set*) caer; (*sun*) ponerse; (*ship*) hundirse; (*plane*) estrellarse; **to ~ on all fours** ponerse [o en cuatro patas] a gatas **2.** (*medicine*) tragar **3.** (*decrease*) disminuir; FIN ir a la baja; (*decrease in quality*) empeorar; **to ~ in sb's estimation** bajar en la estima de alguien; (*decrease in size*) empequeñecer **4.** *sl* (*happen*) pasar; **what's going down, my man?** ¿qué pasa, tío? **5.** (*lose*) perder; **to ~ to sb/sth** ser derrotado por alguien/algo; SPORTS perder frente a alguien/algo; **to ~ without a fight** rendirse sin luchar **6.** (*travel southward*) ir hacia el sur; **we're going down to Los Angeles for the weekend** vamos a bajar a Los Ángeles por el fin de semana **7.** (*extend*) extenderse **8.** (*be received*) ser recibido; **to ~ well/badly (with sb)** ser bien/mal recibido (por alguien) **9.** (*be recorded*) quedar registrado; **to ~ in writing** quedar registrado por escrito **10.** *vulg* (*give oral sex to*) **to ~ on sb** hacer una mamada [o mamárselo] a alguien

◆**go far** *vi* **1.** (*have success*) llegar lejos **2.** (*contribute*) **to ~ towards sth** contribuir de forma significativa a algo; **not to ~** no estirarse

◆**go for** *vt insep* **1.** (*fetch*) ir a por, ir a buscar; **could you ~ oranges?** ¿puedes ir a por naranjas? **2.** (*try to achieve*) intentar conseguir; (*try to grasp*) intentar alcanzar; **~ it!** ¡a por ello! **3.** (*choose*) elegir **4.** (*attack*) atacar; **to ~ sb with sth** atacar a alguien con algo **5.** (*sell for*) venderse por **6.** *inf* (*like*) molar; (*believe*) creer en

◆**go in** *vi* **1.** (*enter*) entrar; (*go to work*) empezar a trabajar **2.** (*belong in*) ir en; **those forks ~ the drawer** esos tenedores van en el cajón

◆**go into** *vt insep* **1.** (*enter*) entrar en **2.** (*fit into*) encajar en; **does two ~ six?** ¿seis es divisible por dos? **3.** (*begin*) empezar; **to ~ a coma/trance** MED entrar en coma/en trance;

G

to ~ **action** pasar a la acción; **to ~ effect** entrar en vigor **4.** (*begin*) **to ~ politics** dedicarse a la política; **to ~ production** empezar a producirse **5.** (*examine and discuss*) examinar; **to ~ detail** entrar en detalles **6.** (*be used in*) ser utilizado en **7.** (*join*) unirse; **to ~ the military** enrolarse en el ejército **8.** (*crash into*) dar de lleno contra

◆**go off** *vi* **1.** (*explode: bomb*) estallar **2.** (*make sound: alarm clock, siren*) (empezar a) sonar **3.** (*proceed*) pasar; **to ~ badly/well** salir mal/bien **4.** (*leave*) irse **5.** (*digress*) salirse; **to ~ the subject** salirse del tema ▶ **to ~ the deep end** perder los estribos

◆**go on I.** *vi* **1.** (*move on*) seguir su camino, seguir adelante **2.** (*continue*) seguir; (*continue speaking*) continuar **3.** (*go further*) ir más allá; **to ~ ahead** seguir adelante **4.** (*extend*) extenderse **5.** (*pass*) pasar **6.** (*happen*) suceder **7.** (*start*) empezar; (*begin functioning*) empezar a funcionar; THEAT, MUS salir (a escena); **the show must ~** el espectáculo debe continuar **II.** *vt insep* basarse en **III.** *interj* (*as encouragement*) vamos; (*express disbelief*) anda ya

◆**go out** *vi* **1.** (*leave*) salir; **to ~ to dinner** salir a cenar **2.** (*on a date*) salir; **to ~ with sb** salir con alguien **3.** (*stop working*) estropearse, dañarse; (*light*) apagarse; (*fire*) extinguirse **4.** (*recede*) retirarse **5.** (*become unfashionable*) pasarse de moda

◆**go over I.** *vt insep* **1.** (*examine*) examinar **2.** (*cross*) atravesar; **to ~ a mountain** subir y bajar una montaña; **to ~ a border/river/ street** cruzar una frontera/un río/una calle **3.** (*exceed*) exceder; **to ~ a budget/limit** exceder un presupuesto/límite **II.** *vi* **to ~ to** (*visit*) visitar; (*change party*) pasarse a

◆**go through** *vt insep* **1.** (*pass*) pasar por **2.** (*experience*) vivir; (*operation*) sufrir **3.** (*practice, perform*) practicar; (*review, discuss*) repasar **4.** (*be approved*) aprobarse **5.** (*use up*) gastar **6.** (*look through*) examinar

◆**go to** *vt insep* visitar; **to ~ the country** ir a elecciones generales; **to ~ court** acudir a los tribunales

◆**go together** *vi* **1.** (*harmonize*) **to ~ (with sth)** pegar (con algo) **2.** (*go with*) ir juntos

◆**go under** *vi* **1.** NAUT (*sink*) hundirse **2.** (*move below*) ir por debajo de **3.** (*fail*) fracasar; (*be defeated*) ser derrotado

◆**go up** *vi* **1.** (*move higher*) subir **2.** (*increase*) aumentar; FIN, ECON ascender **3.** (*approach*) **to ~ to sb/sth** acercarse a alguien/algo **4.** (*travel*) subir, viajar hacia el norte; **to ~ to Baltimore** subir a Baltimore **5.** (*be built*) ser construido **6.** (*burn up*) arder; **to ~ in flames** ser presa de las llamas

◆**go with** *vt insep* **1.** (*accompany*) ir con **2.** (*match: clothing, food and drink*) pegar con **3.** (*agree with*) estar de acuerdo con; **to ~ sb on sth** coincidir con alguien en algo **4.** (*follow*) seguir **5.** (*date*) salir con

◆**go without** *vt insep* pasar sin, prescindir de

goad [goʊd] **I.** *vt* **1.** (*spur*) incitar; (*curiosity*) despertar **2.** (*tease*) fastidiar **II.** *n* **1.** (*motivating factor*) estímulo *m* **2.** AGR aguijada *f*

go-ahead ['goʊ·ə·hed] *n* (*permission*) luz *f* verde; **to give/receive the ~** dar/recibir luz verde

goal [goʊl] *n* **1.** (*aim*) objetivo *m*, meta *f*; **to achieve a ~** conseguir un objetivo; **to pursue a ~** perseguir un fin; **to set a ~** fijar un objetivo **2.** SPORTS (*scoring area*) portería *f*; **to play in ~** ser portero **3.** SPORTS (*point*) gol *m*; **to score a ~** marcar un gol; **to give up a ~** un gol de penalty

goalie ['goʊ·li] *n inf*, **goalkeeper** ['goʊl·ki· pər] *n* SPORTS portero, -a *m, f*

goal line *n* SPORTS línea *f* de gol

goalpost *n* SPORTS poste *m* de la portería

goat [goʊt] *n* **1.** ZOOL cabra *f*; **~'s milk** leche *f* de cabra; **~'s cheese** queso *m* de cabra; **mountain ~** cabra montés **2.** *inf* (*man*) viejo *m* verde **3.** (*scapegoat*) chivo *m* expiatorio ▶ **to get sb's ~** *inf* sacar de quicio a alguien

goatee [goʊ·'ti] *n* perilla *f*

gobble ['gab·əl] **I.** *vi* **1.** (*devour*) jalar **2.** (*turkey*) gluglutear **II.** *vt inf* (*devour*) jalar **III.** *n* (*of turkey*) gluglú *m*

gobbledegook, gobbledygook ['gab·əl·di· ˌguk] *n inf* galimatías *m; inv*

go-between ['goʊ·bə·ˌtwin] *n* mediador(a) *m(f)*; **to act as a ~** hacer de intermediario

goblet ['gab·lət] *n* cáliz *m*

goblin ['gab·lɪn] *n* duende *m*

go-cart ['goʊ·kart] *n* AUTO, SPORTS kart *m*

god [gad] *n* **1.** REL God Dios; **God bless** que Dios te/le... bendiga; **God bless America** Dios bendiga a los EEUU; **God forbid** no lo permita Dios; **God (only) knows** sólo Dios lo sabe; **please God!** ¡Dios lo quiera!; **for God's sake!** ¡por el amor de Dios! **2.** REL **Greek/ Roman ~s** dioses *mpl* griegos/romanos **3.** (*idolized person*) ídolo *m*

God-awful *adj sl* horrible; **the ~ truth** la horrible verdad

godchild *n* ahijado, -a *m, f*

goddamn(ed) *adj sl* maldito, -a

goddaughter *n* ahijada *f*

goddess ['gad·ɪs] <-es> *n* **1.** REL diosa *f* **2.** (*idolized woman*) musa *f*

godfather *n* padrino *m*

God-fearing *adj* temeroso, -a de Dios

godforsaken *adj* dejado, -a de la mano de Dios

godless ['gad·lɪs] *adj* **1.** REL impío, -a; (*without God*) sin Dios **2.** (*evil*) demoníaco, -a

godlike ['gad·laɪk] *adj* divino, -a

godly ['gad·li] *adj* piadoso, -a; **to lead a ~ life** llevar una vida piadosa

godmother *n* madrina *f*

godparents *npl* padrinos *mpl*

godsend *n* cosa *f* llovida del cielo; **to be a ~ (to sb)** ser un regalo celestial (para alguien)

godson *n* ahijado *m*

goes [goʊz] *3rd pers sing of* **go**

go-getter [ˌgoʊ·'get·ər] *n inf* persona *f* emprendedora

goggle ['gag·əl] I. *n* ~s (*glasses*) gafas *fpl;* **safety** ~s gafas de protección; **ski/swim** ~s gafas de esquí/natación II. *vi* **to** ~ **at sb/sth** mirar con ojos desorbitados a alguien/algo
goggle-eyed ['gag·əl·aɪd] *adj* con ojos desorbitados; (*person*) con [*o* de] ojos saltones
go-go dancer ['gou·gou·'dæn·sər] *n* gogó *mf*
go-go dancing *n* baile *m* de gogós
going ['gou·ɪŋ] I. *n* 1. (*act of leaving*) ida *f;* (*departure*) salida *f* 2. (*conditions*) **easy/ rough** ~ condiciones *fpl* favorables/adversas; **while the** ~ **is good** mientras las condiciones lo permitan 3. (*progress*) progreso *m* ▶ **when the** ~ **gets** <u>tough</u> (**the tough get** ~) cuando las cosas se ponen feas (los fuertes entran en acción) II. *adj* 1. (*available*) disponible 2. (*in action*) en funcionamiento; **to get sth** ~ poner algo en funcionamiento 3. (*current*) actual; ~ **price** precio *m* actual, precio *m* de mercado III. *vi aux* **to be** ~ **to do sth** ir a hacer algo
going-away party *n* fiesta *f* de despedida
goings-on [,gou·ɪŋz·'ɒn] *npl* 1. (*events*) sucesos *mpl* 2. (*activities*) tejemanejes *mpl*
goiter ['gɔɪ·t̬ər] *n* MED bocio *m*
go-kart ['gou·kart] *n s.* **go-cart**
gold [gould] I. *n* 1. (*metal*) oro *m;* **to pan for** ~ lavar oro; **to strike** ~ encontrar oro; **to be dripping with** ~ *fig* llevar muchos oros 2. SPORTS (medalla *f* de) oro; **to win the** ~ llevarse el oro; **to go for** ~ ir a por el oro ▶ **to be worth one's** <u>weight</u> **in** ~ valer su peso en oro; **to be** <u>good</u> **as** ~ portarse como un ángel; **all that** <u>glitters</u> **is not** ~ *prov* no es oro todo lo que reluce *prov* II. *adj* de oro; **a** ~ **ring** un anillo de oro
gold bullion *n* oro *m* en lingotes
gold digger *n* 1. (*gold miner*) buscador(a) *m(f)* de oro 2. (*money-seeker*) cazafortunas *mf inv*
gold dust *n* oro *m* en polvo; **to be like** ~ *fig* ser muy cotizado
golden ['goul·dən] *adj* 1. de oro; ~ **anniversary** bodas *fpl* de oro 2. (*color*) dorado, -a; ~ **brown** tostado, -a; (*skin*) bronceado, -a 3. (*very good*) excelente; ~ **oldies** MUS melodías *fpl* de ayer; *iron* viejas cantinelas *fpl*
golden age *n* edad *f* de oro
golden goose *n* gallina *f* de los huevos de oro
golden mean *n* punto *m* medio
golden triangle *n* **the** ~ el Triángulo Dorado
golden wedding *n* bodas *fpl* de oro
goldfinch ['gould·fɪntʃ] <-es> *n* jilguero *m*
goldfish *n inv* pez *m* de colores
gold leaf *n* pan *m* de oro
gold medal *n* SPORTS medalla *f* de oro
goldmine *n* 1. (*mine*) mina *f* de oro 2. FIN filón *m*
gold nugget *n* pepita *f* de oro
gold plating *n* 1. (*layer*) baño *m* de oro 2. (*production process*) chapado *m* de oro
gold reserve *n* reserva *f* de oro
goldsmith *n* orfebre *mf*
gold standard *n* FIN patrón *m* oro

golf [galf] I. *n* golf *m;* **to play** ~ jugar al golf; **miniature** ~ minigolf *m* II. *vi* jugar al golf
golf ball *n* pelota *f* de golf
golf club *n* 1. (*stick*) palo *m* de golf 2. (*sports association*) club *m* de golf
golf course *n* campo *m* de golf
golfer ['gal·fər] *n* golfista *mf*
Goliath [gə·'laɪ·əθ] *n* Goliat *m;* **a David and** ~ **battle** *fig* una batalla entre David y Goliat
golliwog *n*, **golliwogg** ['gal·ɪ·wɔg] *n* muñeco negro de trapo (*puede considerarse ofensivo*)
golly ['gal·i] *interj inf* caramba; **by** ~ ¡vaya!
gondola ['gan·də·lə] *n* góndola *f*
gondolier [,gan·də·'lɪr] *n* gondolero, -a *m, f*
gone [gɒn] I. *pp of* **go** II. *adj* 1. (*absent*) ausente 2. (*used up*) acabado, -a 3. *inf* (*dead*) muerto, -a 4. (*lost: hope*) perdido, -a
goner ['gɔ·nər] *n sl* **to be a** ~ (*bound to die*) ser hombre muerto; (*broken*) estar para tirar
gong [gaŋ] *n* gong *m*
gonorrhea [,gan·ə·'ri·ə] *n* gonorrea *f*
goo [gu] *n inf* 1. (*substance*) sustancia *f* viscosa 2. (*sentimentality*) sensiblería *f*
goober ['gu·bər] *n reg: Southern* (*peanut*) cacahuete *m*, maní *AmS*
good [gʊd] I. <better, best> *adj* 1. (*of high quality*) bueno, -a; ~ **ears** buen oído; ~ **eyes** buena vista; ~ **thinking!** ¡buena idea!; **to be a** ~ **catch** un buen partido; **to do a** ~ **job** hacer un buen trabajo; **to have the** ~ **sense to do sth** tener el sentido común para hacer algo; **to be in** ~ **shape** estar en buena forma; **to be/to be not** ~ **enough** ser/no ser lo suficientemente bueno 2. (*skilled*) capacitado, -a; **to be** ~ **at** [*o* **in**] **sth/doing sth** estar capacitado para algo/hacer algo; **to be** ~ **at sth** dársele bien algo; **to be** ~ **with one's hands** ser bueno con las manos 3. (*pleasant*) placentero, -a; **to have a** ~ **day/evening** tener un buen día/pasar una velada placentera; **to have a** ~ **time** pasarlo/pasárselo bien 4. (*appealing to senses*) **to feel** ~ sentirse bien; **to have** ~ **looks** ser guapo; **to look** ~ tener buen aspecto; **to smell** ~ oler bien 5. (*favorable*) **the** ~ **life** la buena vida; ~ **luck** (**in sth**) buena suerte (en algo); **a** ~ **omen** un buen presagio; ~ **times** buenos tiempos; **to be a** ~ **thing that...** ser bueno que... +*subj;* **to be/sound too** ~ **to be true** ser demasiado bueno/sonar demasiado bien para ser verdad 6. (*beneficial*) beneficioso, -a; **a** ~ **habit** una buena costumbre; **to be** ~ **for sb/sth** ser bueno para alguien/algo; **to be** ~ **for business** ser bueno para el negocio 7. (*useful*) útil 8. (*appropriate*) adecuado, -a; (*choice, decision*) correcto, -a; **to be in a** ~ **position to do sth** estar en buena posición para hacer algo; **a** ~ **time to do sth** un buen momento para hacer algo 9. (*kind*) amable; ~ **deeds/work** buenas obras/buen trabajo 10. (*moral*) **the Good Book** la Biblia; **a** ~ **name/reputation** un buen nombre/una buena reputación; **to be only as** ~ **as one's word** cumplir su palabra 11. (*well-behaved*)

de buenos modales; **a ~ loser** un buen perdedor; **to be on ~ behavior** comportarse bien **12.** (*thorough*) completo, -a; **a ~ beating** una buena paliza **13.** (*valid*) válido, -a; (*not forged*) auténtico, -a; (*useable*) útil, provechoso, -a; **to make sth ~** (*pay for*) pagar por algo; (*do successfully*) cumplir algo; **to be ~ for nothing** ser completamente inútil **14.** (*substantial*) sustancial; **a ~ many/few** muchos/unos pocos **15.** CULIN en su punto **16.** (*almost, virtually*) it's as **~ as done** está prácticamente terminado; **to be as ~ as new** estar como nuevo **17.** (*said to emphasize*) **to be ~ and ready** estar listo **18.** (*said to express affection*) **the ~ old days** los buenos tiempos ▶ **to give as ~ as one gets** devolver golpe por golpe **II.** *n* **1.** (*moral force, not evil*) bien *m;* **to be no ~** ser inútil; **to be up to no ~** estar tramando algo **2.** (*profit, benefit*) beneficio *m;* **this soup will do you ~** esta sopa te sentará bien; **for one's own ~** en beneficio propio; **to do ~** hacer bien; **to do more harm than ~** hacer más daño que bien; **to be not much ~** no valer mucho **3.** *pl* (*moral people*) **the ~** la gente buena ▶ **for ~** definitivamente **III.** *adv inf* (*well*) bien **IV.** *interj* **1.** (*to express approval*) bien **2.** (*to express surprise, shock*) ~ **God!** ¡Dios mío!; ~ **grief!** ¡madre mía! **3.** (*said as greeting*) ~ **afternoon/evening** buenas tardes; ~ **morning** buenos días; ~ **night** buenas noches

goodbye **I.** *interj* adiós **II.** *n* **1.** (*departing word*) adiós *m;* **to say ~** (**to sb**) decir adiós (a alguien); **to say ~** despedirse **2.** *inf* (*loss*) **to say ~ to sth** olvidarse definitivamente de algo; **to kiss sth ~** despedirse de algo

good-for-nothing ['gʊd·fər·ˌnʌθ·ɪŋ] **I.** *n* inútil *mf* **II.** *adj* inútil

Good Friday *n* Viernes *m* Santo

good-humored [ˌgʊd·'hju·mərd] *adj* afable

Good Humor man *n* hombre *m* modelo

good-looking [ˌgʊd·'lʊk·ɪŋ] <better-looking, best-looking> *adj* guapo, -a

good looks *n* atractivo *m*

goodly ['gʊd·li] <-ier, -iest> *adj* agradable

good-natured <better-natured, best-natured> *adj* **1.** (*pleasant*) afable **2.** (*inherently good*) bonachón, -ona

goodness ['gʊd·nɪs] **I.** *n* **1.** (*moral virtue*) bondad *f* **2.** (*kindness*) amabilidad *f* **3.** (*quality*) buena calidad *f* **4.** (*said for emphasis*) **my ~!** ¡madre mía!; **for ~' sake** ¡por Dios!; **thank ~!** ¡gracias a Dios!; **to wish** [*o* **to hope**] **to ~** rogar a Dios **II.** *interj* ~ **gracious!** (*surprise*) ¡Dios mío!; (*annoyance*) ¡vaya por Dios!

goods [gʊdz] *npl* **1.** (*wares*) productos *mpl;* **manufactured ~** bienes *mpl* elaborados **2.** (*personal belongings*) pertenencias *fpl* **3.** (*desired things*) artículos *mpl* pedidos; **to deliver the ~** entregar la mercancía; *fig* dar la talla

good-sized [ˌgʊd·'saɪzd] <better-sized, best-sized> *adj* bastante grande

good-tempered [ˌgʊd·'tem·pərd] <better-tempered, best-tempered> *adj irr* afable

goodwill [ˌgʊd·'wɪl] *n* buena voluntad *f;* ~ **towards sb** buenas intenciones con alguien; **a gesture of ~** un gesto de buena voluntad

goody ['gʊd·i] **I.** <-ies> *n* CULIN golosina *f* **II.** *interj childspeak* qué bien

goody two-shoes *n inf* santurrón, -ona *m, f*

gooey ['gu·i] <gooier, gooiest> *adj* (*sticky*) pegajoso, -a; CULIN (*dessert*) empalagoso, -a

goof [guf] **I.** *vi sl* pifiarla **II.** *n sl* **1.** (*mistake*) pifia *f* **2.** (*silly person*) bobo, -a *m, f*

goofball *n sl* memo, -a *m, f,* tontarrón, -ona *m, f*

goofy ['gu·fi] <-ier, -iest> *adj sl* bobo, -a

goon [gun] *n sl* **1.** (*stupid person*) imbécil *mf* **2.** (*thug*) gángster *mf* a sueldo

goose [gus] <geese> *n* ganso, -a *m, f* ▶ **to kill the ~ that lays the golden eggs** matar la gallina de los huevos de oro; **to cook someone's ~** *inf* hacer la pascua a alguien

gooseberry ['gus·ber·i] <-ies> *n* grosella *f* espinosa

goose bumps *npl* carne *f* de gallina

goose step *n* paso *m* de oca

goose-step <-pp-> *vi* marchar a paso de oca

gore[1] [gɔr] *n* (*blood*) sangre *f* derramada; **blood and ~** sangre y vísceras

gore[2] [gɔr] *vt* (*pierce*) cornear

gorge [gɔrdʒ] **I.** *n* **1.** GEO cañón *m* **2.** ANAT garganta *f;* **my ~ rises** me dan arcadas **II.** *vt* **to ~ oneself on sth** atiborrarse de algo **III.** *vi* engullir

gorgeous ['gɔr·dʒəs] **I.** *adj* **1.** (*attractive: woman, man*) atractivo, -a; (*dress*) precioso, -a **2.** *inf* (*pleasant: weather*) formidable **II.** *n* **hello, ~!** ¡hola, ricura!

gorilla [gə·'rɪl·ə] *n* gorila *m*

gory ['gɔr·i] <-ier, -iest> *adj* (*bloody*) sangriento, -a **2.** *fig* **the ~ details about sth** los detalles morbosos de algo

gosh [gaʃ] *interj inf* dios mío

gosling ['gaz·lɪŋ] *n* ansarino *m*

gospel ['gas·pəl] *n* **1.** REL evangelio *m;* **to spread/preach the ~** extender/predicar el evangelio; ~ **singer** cantante *mf* de gospel **2.** (*principle*) doctrina *f*

gossamer ['gas·ə·mər] **I.** *n* hilo *m* de telaraña **II.** *adj* sutil

gossip ['gas·əp] **I.** *n* **1.** (*rumor*) chismorreo *m;* **idle ~** rumor *m* infundado; **the latest ~** los últimos chismes; ~ **columnist** periodista *mf* de prensa rosa **2.** (*person*) chismoso, -a *m, f* **II.** *vi* **1.** (*spread rumors*) chismorrear; **to ~ about sb** cotillear acerca de alguien **2.** (*chatter*) contar chismes

gossip column *n* columna *f* de cotilleo

gossipy ['gas·ə·pi] *adj* **1.** (*rumor-spreading: neighbor*) chismoso, -a, lenguón, -ona *AmL* **2.** (*containing gossip: article*) de cotilleo

got [gat] *pt of* **get**

Gothic ['gaθ·ɪk] **I.** *adj* **1.** ARCHIT, LIT gótico, -a; ~ **architecture** arquitectura *f* gótica **2.** (*of*

Goths) godo, -a **3.** TYPO ~ **script** escritura *f* gótica **II.** *n* **1.** LING gótico *m* **2.** TYPO letra *f* gótica

gotten ['gɑt·ən] *pp of* **get**

gouge [gaʊdʒ] **I.** *vt* **1.** (*pierce*) excavar; **to ~ a hole into sth** hacer un agujero en algo **2.** *inf* (*overcharge*) cobrar de más **II.** *n* gubia *f*

goulash ['gu·lɑʃ] *n* puchero *m* (húngaro)

gourd [gɔrd] *n* calabaza *f* (*para beber*)

gourmand ['gʊr·mɑnd] *n* glotón, -ona *m, f*

gourmet ['gʊr·meɪ] CULIN **I.** *n* gastrónomo, -a *m, f* **II.** *adj* gastronómico, -a

gout [gaʊt] *n* gota *f*

Gov. *abbr of* **Governor** gobernador(a) *m(f)*

govern ['gʌv·ərn] **I.** *vt* **1.** POL, ADMIN (*country*) gobernar; (*organization*) dirigir **2.** (*regulate*) regular; **to ~ how/when/what...** regular cómo/cuándo/qué... **3.** LAW (*contract*) regir **4.** (*control*) controlar **5.** BIO **to be ~ed by sth** ser determinado por algo **6.** LING regir **II.** *vi* POL, ADMIN gobernar; **to be fit/unfit to ~** tener/no tener las cualidades para gobernar

governess ['gʌv·ər·nɪs] <-es> *n* institutriz *f*, gobernanta *f AmL*

governing *adj* directivo, -a

government ['gʌv·ərn·mənt] *n* **1.** (*ruling body*) gobierno *m*, administración *f Arg*; **~ organization** organización *f* gubernamental; **~ policy** política *f* estatal; **~ securities** FIN valores *mpl* del Estado **2.** (*administration*) administración *f*; **to form a ~** formar gobierno **3.** (*governing*) **to be in ~** estar en el gobierno

governmental [ˌgʌv·ərn·ˈmen·təl] *adj* gubernamental

governor ['gʌv·ər·nər] *n* **1.** POL gobernador(a) *m(f)* **2.** (*of organization*) director(a) *m(f)*; **the board of ~s** el consejo de dirección **3.** TECH regulador *m*

govt. *abbr of* **government** gobno.

gown [gaʊn] *n* **1.** (*evening dress*) traje *m*; **ball ~** vestido *m* de baile **2.** MED bata *f*; **surgical ~** bata de cirujano **3.** UNIV toga *f*; **cap and ~** toga y birrete

grab [græb] **I.** <-bb-> *vt* **1.** (*snatch*) quitar; **to ~ sth (away) from sb** arrebatar algo a alguien; **to ~ sth out of sb's hands** quitar algo a alguien de las manos **2.** (*take hold of*) agarrar, hacerse con; **to ~ hold of sth** hacerse con algo **3.** (*arrest*) detener **4.** *inf* (*get, acquire*) conseguir; **to ~ some sleep** dormir un rato; **to ~ a chance** aprovechar una oportunidad; **to ~ sb's attention** captar la atención de alguien; **how does this ~ you?** *inf* ¿qué te parece esto? **II.** <-bb-> *vi* **1.** (*snatch*) arrebatar **2.** (*hold on*) asir **III.** *n* **to make a ~ for sth** hacerse con algo; **to be up for ~s** *sl* estar libre

grace [greɪs] **I.** *n* **1.** (*movement*) elegancia *f*, gracia *f* **2.** (*elegant proportions*) elegancia *f* **3.** REL gracia *f*; **divine ~** gracia divina; **by the ~ of God** por la gracia de Dios; **to be in a state of ~** estar en estado de gracia; **the year of ~** *form* el año de gracia **4.** (*favor*) favor *m*; **to be in/get into sb's good ~s** congraciarse con al-

guien; **to fall from ~** caer en desgracia **5.** (*politeness*) cortesía *f*; **to do sth with good/bad ~** hacer algo de buen grado/a regañadientes; **to have the (good) ~ to do sth** tener la cortesía de hacer algo **6.** (*prayer*) bendición *f* (de la mesa); **to say ~** bendecir la mesa **7.** (*leeway*) demora *f* **8.** (*Highness*) **Your/His/Her Grace** su Excelencia **9.** (*sister goddesses*) **the Graces** las Gracias **II.** *vt* **1.** (*honor*) honrar **2.** (*make beautiful*) embellecer

graceful ['greɪs·fəl] *adj* **1.** (*move*) grácil; **~ movements** movimientos *mpl* garbosos **2.** (*elegant*) elegante **3.** (*polite*) educado, -a

graceless ['greɪs·lɪs] *adj* **1.** (*lacking elegance*) desgarbado, -a **2.** (*impolite*) descortés

grace period *n* FIN periodo *m* [*o* período] de gracia

gracious ['greɪ·ʃəs] **I.** *adj* **1.** (*kind: host*) hospitalario, -a **2.** (*comfortable: living*) acomodado, -a **3.** (*tactful: humor*) sutil **4.** (*merciful*) clemente **II.** *interj* **goodness ~** ¡Dios mío!

gradation [grəɪ·ˈdeɪ·ʃən] *n* gradación *f*

grade [greɪd] **I.** *n* **1.** SCHOOL curso *m*; **to skip a ~** perder un curso **2.** (*mark*) nota *f*; **good/bad ~s** buenas/malas notas **3.** (*level of quality*) clase *f*, calidad *f*; **high/low ~** alta/baja calidad **4.** GEO pendiente *f*; **gentle/steep ~** pendiente suave/pronunciada **5.** (*rank*) rango *m* ▶ **to make the ~** dar la talla **II.** *vt* **1.** SCHOOL, UNIV (*evaluate*) evaluar; **to ~ up/down** subir/bajar la nota **2.** (*categorize*) clasificar

grade school *n* SCHOOL escuela *f* primaria

gradient ['greɪ·di·ənt] *n* GEO, AUTO pendiente *f*

grading ['greɪ·dɪŋ] *n* **1.** (*gradation*) gradación *f* **2.** (*classification*) clasificación *f*

> **i** El sistema de calificación que se utiliza en EE.UU. recibe el nombre de **grading system**. En él se emplean las siguientes letras para expresar las distintas calificaciones: A, B, C, D, E y F. La letra E, sin embargo, no se suele utilizar. La A es la máxima calificación, mientras que la F **(Fail)** significa 'no aprobado'. Las notas, además, pueden ir matizadas por un más o un menos. Quien obtiene una A+ ha demostrado un nivel de rendimiento sobresaliente.

gradual ['grædʒ·u·əl] *adj* **1.** (*not sudden: erosion, improvement*) gradual **2.** (*not steep: slope*) suave

gradually ['grædʒ·u·ə·li] *adv* **1.** (*not suddenly: improve*) progresivamente, paulatinamente **2.** (*not steeply*) suavemente

graduate¹ ['grædʒ·u·ət] *n* **1.** UNIV licenciado, -a *m, f*; **university ~** licenciado *m* universitario **2.** SCHOOL graduado, -a *m, f* **3.** (*postgraduate*) pos(t)graduado, -a *m, f*

graduate² ['grædʒ·u·eɪt] **I.** *vi* **1.** UNIV licenciarse; SCHOOL graduarse; **to ~ cum laude** graduarse cum laude **2.** (*move to a higher* *level*) subir de categoría; **to ~ to...** ascender a... **3.** (*calibrate*) calibrar **II.** *vt* graduar

graduated *adj* graduado, -a

graduate school *n* escuela *f* de pos(t)grado

graduation [,grædʒ·u·'eɪ·ʃən] *n* **1.** SCHOOL, UNIV graduación *f*, egreso *m Arg, Chile* **2.** (*promotion*) ascenso *m* **3.** (*marks of calibration*) calibrado *m*

graduation ceremony *n* ceremonia *f* de graduación

graffiti [grə·'fi·ţi] *npl* graffiti *m*

graffiti artist *n* artista *mf* del graffiti

graft [græft] **I.** *n* **1.** BOT, AGR, MED injerto *m;* **a skin ~** un injerto de piel **2.** POL corrupción *f* **II.** *vt* **1.** BOT, AGR, MED injertar **2.** (*add on*) añadir **III.** *vi* POL sobornar

grafter ['græf·tər] *n* injertador(a) *m(f)*

Grail [greɪl] *n* **the Holy ~** el Santo Grial

grain [greɪn] **I.** *n* **1.** (*cereal*) cereal *m* **2.** (*smallest piece*) grano *m;* **~ of sand/salt** grano de arena/sal **3.** (*smallest quantity*) pizca *f;* **a ~ of hope** una brizna de esperanza; **a ~ of truth** una pizca de verdad **4.** (*direction of fibers*) fibra *f;* **wood ~** hebra *f* de madera ▶**to take sth with a ~ of <u>salt</u>** no creerse algo del todo; **to go against the ~** no ser propio (de alguien o algo) **II.** *vt* **1.** (*granulate*) granular **2.** (*remove hair from*) pelar

grain elevator *n* elevador *m* de granos

gram [græm] *n* gramo *m*

grammar ['græm·ər] *n* gramática *f*

grammar book *n* libro *m* de gramática

grammarian [grə·'mer·i·ən] *n* gramático, -a *m, f*

grammar school *n* colegio *m*

grammatical [grə·'mæţ·ɪ·kəl] *adj* gramatical

gramophone ['græm·ə·foʊn] *n* gramófono *m*, vitrola *f AmL*

granary ['græn·ə·ri] AGR **I.** <-ies> *n* **1.** (*silo*) granero *m* **2.** (*grain region*) granero *m* **II.** *adj* del grano

grand [grænd] **I.** *adj* **1.** (*splendid*) magnífico, -a; **in ~ style** de estilo sublime; **a ~ opening** una gran apertura; **to make a ~ entrance** hacer una entrada triunfal; **the Grand Canyon** el Cañón del Colorado **2.** (*excellent*) sublime **3.** (*far-reaching*) importante; **~ ambitions/ideas** grandes ambiciones/ideas **4.** (*large*) grande; **on a ~ scale** a gran escala **5.** (*overall*) **the ~ total** el importe total **6.** (*of upper class*) **~ duke** gran duque *m* **II.** *n* **1.** *inv, sl* (*money*) mil dólares *mpl* **2.** MUS piano *m* de cola; **baby ~** piano *m* de cola

grandchild <-children> *n* nieto, -a *m, f*

granddad *n* **1.** *inf* (*grandfather*) abuelito *m* **2.** (*old man*) abuelo *m*

granddaughter *n* nieta *f*

grandeur ['græn·dʒər] *n* **1.** (*imposing splendor*) magnificencia *f* **2.** (*nobility*) nobleza *f*

grandfather *n* abuelo *m*

grandiloquent [græn·'dɪl·ə·kwənt] *adj* grandilocuente

grandiose ['græn·di·oʊs] *adj* **1.** (*ideas, plans*) grandioso, -a **2.** (*façade of building*) pomposo, -a

grand jury <- -ies> *n* LAW gran jurado *m*

grand larceny *n* hurto *m* mayor

grandly *adv* majestuosamente

grandma *n inf* abuelita *f*

grandmaster *n* GAMES (*chess pro*) gran maestro *m*

grandmother *n* abuela *f*

grandpa *n inf* abuelito *m*

grandparents *npl* abuelos *mpl*

grand piano *n* piano *m* de cola

grandson *n* nieto *m*

grandstand *n* tribuna *f;* **~ seat** asiento *m* de tribuna; **~ ticket** entrada *f* de tribuna; **a ~ view** *fig* una vista panorámica

granite ['græn·ɪt] *n* granito *m*

grannie, granny ['græn·i] *n* **1.** *inf* abuelita *f* **2.** *inf* (*fussy person*) cascarrabias *mf inv* **3.** *reg: esp. Southern* (*midwife*) matrona *f*

grant [grænt] **I.** *n* **1.** UNIV beca *f;* **research ~** subvención *f* a una investigación; **to be on a ~** disfrutar de una beca; **to give sb a ~** conceder una beca a alguien **2.** (*a government grant*) subvención *f* **3.** (*from authority*) concesión *f;* **federal ~** ayuda *f* estatal; **to apply for a ~** solicitar una subvención **4.** LAW cesión *f* **II.** *vt* **1.** (*allow*) otorgar; **to ~ sb a permit/visa** conceder a alguien un permiso/visado **2.** (*transfer legally*) ceder; (*asylum*) dar; **to ~ sb a pardon** conceder un indulto a alguien **3.** *form* (*consent to fulfill*) **to ~ sb sth** conceder algo a alguien; **to ~ sb a favor** hacer un favor a alguien; **to ~ sb a request** acceder a la petición de alguien; **to ~ sb a wish** conceder un deseo a alguien **4.** (*admit to*) reconocer, admitir; **~ed** de acuerdo; **~ed, it's not easy...** de acuerdo, no es fácil...; **I ~ you,...** estoy de acuerdo contigo,...; **to ~ that...** estar de acuerdo en que... ▶ +*subj* ▶**to <u>take</u> sth for ~ed** dar algo por sentado; **to <u>take</u> sb for ~ed** no valorar a alguien como se merece

granular ['græn·jə·lər] *adj* granular

granulated ['græn·jə·leɪ·ţɪd] *adj* **1.** (*in grains*) granulado, -a; **~ sugar** azúcar *m* cristalizado **2.** (*grainy*) rugoso, -a

granule ['græn·jul] *n* gránulo *m;* **~s** granos *mpl;* **instant coffee ~s** granos de café instantáneo

grape [greɪp] *n* **1.** (*fruit*) uva *f;* **a bunch of ~s** un racimo de uvas **2.** *iron* (*wine*) **the ~** el vino ▶**it's just <u>sour</u> ~s** es pura envidia

grapefruit ['greɪp·frut] *n inv* pomelo *m*

grape juice *n* mosto *m*

grapevine *n* vid *f;* (*climbing plant*) parra *f* ▶**to <u>hear</u> sth on the ~** saber algo por los rumores que corren

graph[1] [græf] *n* gráfica *f;* (*diagram*) gráfico *m;* **temperature ~** gráfico de temperaturas

graph[2] [græf] *n* LING grafía *f*

graphic ['græf·ɪk] *adj* gráfico, -a; **to describe sth in ~ detail** describir algo de forma gráfica; **~ works** (**of an artist**) trabajos gráficos (de un

artista)
graphic design *n* diseño *m* gráfico
graphics *n* + *sing vb* **1.** (*drawings*) artes *fpl*
gráficas **2.** COMPUT gráficos *mpl;* **computer ~**
gráficos de ordenador
graphics card *n* tarjeta *f* gráfica
graphite ['græf·aɪt] *n* grafito *m*
graphologist [grə·'fal·ə·dʒɪst] *n* grafólogo, -a
m, f
graphology [grə·'fal·ə·dʒi] *n* grafología *f*
grapple ['græp·əl] *vi* **to ~ for/with sth** luchar
a brazo partido por/con algo
grappling hook *n*, **grappling iron** *n* arpeo *m*
grasp [græsp] I. *n* **1.** (*grip*) agarre *m* **2.** (*attain-
ability*) alcance *m;* **to be beyond sb's ~** estar
fuera del alcance de alguien **3.** (*understanding*) comprensión *f;* (*knowledge*) conocimiento *m* ▶**his reach exceeds his ~** alarga
más el brazo que la manga II. *vt* **1.** (*take firm
hold*) agarrar; **to ~ sb by the arm/hand** agarrar a alguien del brazo/de la mano **2.** (*understand*) entender III. *vi* **1.** (*try to hold*) intentar
coger **2.** *fig* (*take advantage*) **to ~ at** sacar
provecho de; **to ~ at the chance** aprovechar
la oportunidad
grasping *adj* avaro, -a
grass [græs] I. <-es> *n* **1.** hierba *f;* **wild ~es**
hierbas silvestres **2.** (*area of grass*) prado *m;*
(*lawn*) césped *m;* **to cut the ~** cortar el césped
3. *sl* (*marijuana*) hierba *f inf,* traba *f AmL, inf*
▶**to let the ~ grow under one's feet** perder
el tiempo; **the ~ is** (**always**) **greener on the
other side** (**of the fence**) *prov* las manzanas
siempre parecen mejores en el huerto del
vecino *prov* II. *vt* cubrir de hierba
grasshopper ['græs·hap·ər] *n* saltamontes *m
inv,* chapulín *m AmC, Méx,* saltagatos *m inv
AmC, Méx*
grassland *n* pastos *mpl;* (*savannah*) sabana *f*
grassroots I. *npl* (*ordinary people*) pueblo *m;*
(*of a party, organization*) base *f* popular II. *adj*
básico, -a; **~ opinion** opinión *f* del pueblo;
~ politics política *f* que trata los problemas
cotidianos
grass snake *n* culebra *f* de collar
grass widow *n mujer cuyo marido está
ausente*
grass widower *n ≈* Rodríguez *m inf* (*marido
cuya mujer está ausente*)
grassy ['græs·i] <-ier, -iest> *adj* cubierto, -a de
hierba, pastoso, -a *AmL*
grate¹ [greɪt] *n* **1.** (*covering an opening*) rejilla
f **2.** (*in fireplace, furnace*) hogar *m,* parrilla *f
AmS*
grate² [greɪt] I. *vi* **1.** (*annoy: noise*) rechinar;
to ~ on sb irritar a alguien **2.** (*rub together*)
rozar; **to ~ against each other** rozar uno con
otro II. *vt* **1.** CULIN rallar **2.** (*one's teeth*) rechinar
grateful ['greɪt·fəl] *adj* agradecido, -a; **to be ~**
(**to sb**) **for sth** agradecer algo (a alguien); **I'd
be most ~ if you...** *form* le agradecería
mucho que... +*subj*

grater ['greɪ·ţər] *n* rallador *m*
gratification [ˌgræţ·ə·fɪ·'keɪ·ʃən] *n* gratificación *f;* (*of a wish*) satisfacción *f;* **sexual ~**
placer *m* sexual; **with** (**some**) **~** con (cierta)
satisfacción
gratify ['græţ·ə·faɪ] <-ie-> *vt* **1.** (*please*) gratificar; **to be gratified at sth** estar complacido
por algo **2.** (*satisfy*) satisfacer
gratifying *adj* gratificante
grating ['greɪ·ţɪŋ] I. *n* rejilla *f* II. *adj*
1. (*scraping*) que rasca; (*squeaking*) chirriante
2. (*annoyingly harsh*) áspero, -a; **~ voice** voz *f*
rasgada
gratis ['græţ·əs] I. *adj* gratuito, -a II. *adv* gratis
gratitude ['græţ·ə·tud] *n form* gratitud *f,* reconocimiento *m;* **as a token of my ~** como
muestra de mi gratitud
gratuitous [grə·'tu·ə·ţəs] *adj* **1.** (*unnecessary:
criticism, violence*) innecesario, -a, gratuito, -a
2. (*free*) gratuito, -a
gratuity [grə·'tu·ə·ţi] <-ies> *n form* propina *f*
grave¹ [greɪv] *n* tumba *f,* sepultura *f;* **mass ~**
fosa *f* común; **to go to one's ~** irse a la tumba;
beyond the ~ más allá de la sepultura; **from
beyond the ~** desde el más allá
grave² [greɪv] *adj* **1.** (*serious: crisis, wound*)
grave; **a ~ mistake/risk** un grave error/
riesgo; **~ news** noticias *fpl* alarmantes
2. (*worrying: problem*) grave **3.** (*solemn: face,
person*) serio, -a; **a ~ ceremony** una ceremonia solemne **4.** (*quite important: decision*)
importante; (*momentous*) trascendental
gravedigger ['greɪv·ˌdɪg·ər] *n* sepulturero, -a
m, f
gravel ['græv·əl] *n* **1.** (*small stones*) gravilla *f;*
GEO grava *f;* **a ~ path** un camino de grava
2. MED arenilla *f*
gravel pit *n* gravera *f*
grave robber *n* ladrón, -ona *m, f* de tumbas
gravestone *n* lápida *f*
graveyard *n* cementerio *m*
graving dock ['greɪ·vɪŋ·ˌdak] *n* dique *m* seco
[*o de carena*]
gravitate ['græv·ɪ·teɪt] *vi* gravitar; **to ~
towards sth/sb** tender hacia algo/alguien
gravitation [ˌgræv·ɪ·'teɪ·ʃən] *n* **1.** (*movement*)
gravitación *f;* (*tendency*) tendencia *f;* **the ~ of
people to/towards the cities** la emigración
de la gente a/hacia las ciudades **2.** (*attracting
force*) atracción *f*
gravitational [ˌgræv·ɪ·'teɪ·ʃə·nəl] *adj* gravita-
cional; **~ force** fuerza *f* gravitatoria
gravity ['græv·ə·ţi] *n* gravedad *f;* **the law of ~**
la ley de la gravedad
gravure [grə·'vjʊr] *n* fotograbado *m*
gravy ['greɪ·vi] *n* **1.** CULIN *salsa hecha con el
jugo de la carne* **2.** *sl* (*easy money*) ganga *f;* **to
make some ~** conseguir un chollo
gravy boat *n* salsera *f*
gravy train *n* chollo *m*
gray [greɪ] I. *adj* **1.** (*colored gray*) gris; **to be
dressed in ~** ir de gris **2. ~ weather** tiempo
m gris **3.** *fig* (*gloomy: mood*) triste **4.** (*grey-*

haired) canoso, -a; **to go ~** encanecer; **he has started to go ~** empieza a tener canas **5.** (*color of horse*) rucio, -a **6.** (*pale*) pálido, -a **II.** *n* **1.** (*color*) gris *m* **2.** (*horse*) rucio *m* **III.** *vi* (*become old*) envejecer

graybeard ['greɪˌbɪrd] *n* anciano *m*

graying *adj* con canas

grayish ['greɪ·ɪʃ] *adj* grisáceo, -a; (*hair*) entrecano, -a

gray matter *n inf* materia *f* gris

graze¹ [greɪz] **I.** *n* roce *m* **II.** *vt* rozar; **the bullet just ~d his arm** la bala sólo le rozó el brazo

graze² [greɪz] AGR **I.** *vi* pastar **II.** *vt* apacentar

grease [gris] **I.** *n* **1.** (*fat*) grasa *f* **2.** (*lubricant*) lubricante *m* **II.** *vt* engrasar; (*in mechanics*) lubricar

grease gun *n* pistola *f* de engrase

grease monkey *n sl* mecánico, -a *m, f*

greasepaint *n* maquillaje *m* teatral

grease pencil *n* lápiz *m* vidriográfico

greasy ['gri·si] <-ier, -iest> *adj* (*food*) grasiento, -a; (*hair, skin*) graso, -a

greasy spoon *n sl* freiduría *f*, fritanguería *f Col*

great [greɪt] **I.** *n* grande *mf*; **Alexander the ~** Alejandro *m* Magno **II.** *adj* **1.** (*very big*) enorme; **a ~ amount** una gran cantidad; **a ~ deal of time/money** muchísimo tiempo/ dinero; **a ~ joy/sadness** una gran alegría/ pena; **a ~ many people** muchísima gente; **the ~ majority of people** la gran mayoría (de la gente); **it gives me ~ pleasure to announce...** *form* es un gran placer para mí anunciar...; **it is with ~ sorrow that I tell you of...** lamento mucho comunicarles que... **2.** (*famous and important*) famoso, -a; **the ~est boxer** el boxeador más destacado; **~ minds think alike** las mentes más prestigiosas piensan parecido **3.** (*wonderful*) magnífico, -a; **to be ~ at doing sth** *inf* ser muy bueno en algo; **she's ~ at playing tennis** *inf* se le da muy bien el tenis; **to be a ~ one for doing sth** encantar a uno hacer algo; **it's ~ to be back home again** es maravilloso estar de nuevo en casa; **the ~ thing about sth/sb is** (that) lo mejor de algo/alguien es (que); **I had a ~ time with you** lo he pasado fenomenal contigo; **~!** ¡estupendo! **4.** (*very healthy*) sano, -a; **to feel ~** estar estupendamente **5.** (*for emphasis*) **they're ~ friends** son muy amigos; **he's a ~ big... friends** es un gran(dísimo)... **6.** (*good*) excelente; **Peter is a ~ organizer** Peter es un magnífico organizador

great-aunt *n* tía *f* abuela

greatcoat *n* sobretodo *m*

Great Depression *n* Gran Depresión *f*

great-grandchild *n* bisnieto, -a *m, f*

great-grandparents *npl* bisabuelos *mpl*

great-great-grandparents *npl* tatarabuelos *mpl*

Great Lakes *n* Grandes Lagos *mpl*

> ℹ️ Los **Great Lakes** (Grandes Lagos), que se ubican en la frontera entre Estados Unidos y Canadá, conforman la agrupación de lagos de agua dulce más grande de la Tierra y, en combinación con el Estuario del río San Lorenzo, constituyen el mayor sistema hídrico dulce del mundo. Desde el occidente hasta el oriente, los cinco lagos que forman este mar interior son Superior, Michigan, Huron, Erie y Ontario. Entre el Lago Ontario y el Lago Erie se encuentran las magníficas **Niagara Falls** (Cataratas del Niágara), un extremo de las cuales se ubica en Estados Unidos y el otro en Canadá.

greatly ['greɪt·li] *adv form* sumamente; **to improve ~** mejorar mucho; **to ~ regret sth** lamentar algo muchísimo; **to be ~ impressed** estar muy impresionado

great-nephew *n* sobrino *m* nieto

greatness ['greɪt·nɪs] *n* grandeza *f*

great-niece *n* sobrina *f* nieta

> ℹ️ Las Grandes Llanuras (**Great Plains**), situadas en las provincias occidentales canadienses de Alberta, Saskatchewan y Manitoba se extienden hasta Tejas. En el pasado estas fueron amplias praderas cubiertas de hierba (**prairies**). El cultivo las convirtió en una de las regiones cerealistas más productivas del mundo.

great-uncle *n* tío *m* abuelo

Greece [gris] *n* Grecia *f*

greed [grid] *n* codicia *f*; (*for food*) gula *f*; (*for money*) avaricia *f*; (*for power*) ambición *f*

greediness ['gri·dɪ·nɪs] *n s.* greed

greedy ['gri·di] <-ier, -iest> *adj* (*wanting too much*) codicioso, -a; (*wanting food*) glotón, -ona; (*wanting money, things*) avaricioso, -a; **~ for success/victory** ávido de éxito/victoria

Greek [grik] **I.** *n* **1.** (*person*) griego, -a *m, f* **2.** (*language*) griego *m* **II.** *adj* griego, -a ▶ **it's all ~ to me** eso me suena a chino

green [grin] **I.** *n* **1.** (*color*) verde *m* **2.** **~s** (*green vegetables*) verduras *fpl* **3.** (*lawn*) césped *m* **4.** SPORTS pista *f*; **bowling ~** pista de bolos; **putting ~** putting green *m* **5.** ECOL, POL **Green** verde *mf* **II.** *adj* **1.** (*green-colored*) verde; **to turn ~** (*traffic lights*) ponerse en verde **2.** (*not ripe*) verde, tierno, -a *Chile, Ecua, Guat* **3.** (*inexperienced*) novato, -a, verde; (*naive*) ingenuo, -a **4.** (*covered with plants*) cubierto, -a de vegetación **5.** *fig* (*jealous*) **~ with envy** verde de envidia **6.** ECOL, POL verde

greenback *n inf* billete *m* de un dólar

green belt *n* cinturón *m* verde

green card *n* permiso *m* de residencia y de trabajo

greenery ['gri·nə·ri] *n* vegetación *f*
green-eyed ['grin·aɪd] *adj* **1.** (*with green eyes*) de ojos verdes **2.** *fig* (*jealous*) celoso, -a
greenhorn *n* novato, -a *m, f*
greenhouse *n* invernadero *m*
greenhouse effect *n* **the** ~ el efecto invernadero
greenish ['gri·nɪʃ] *adj* verdoso, -a
Greenland ['grin·lənd] *n* Groenlandia *f*
greenness ['grin·nɪs] *n* verdor *m*
green pepper [ˌgrin·'pep·ər] *n* pimiento *m* verde
green politics *n* + *sing vb* política *f* del medioambiente
green tea *n* té *m* verde
green thumb *n* **to have a** ~ tener habilidad para la jardinería
greet [grit] *vt* **1.** (*welcome*) saludar; (*receive*) recibir; **to** ~ **each other** saludarse; **to** ~ **sb by shaking hands/with a smile** saludar a alguien con un apretón de manos/con una sonrisa **2.** (*react*) **to** ~ **sth** acoger algo; **to** ~ **sth with anger/applause** recibir algo con enfado/un aplauso; **to** ~ **sth with delight** sentir gran placer ante algo **3.** *fig* (*make itself noticeable*) presentarse; **a scene of joy** ~**ed us** se mostró ante nosotros una escena de alegría
greeting *n* saludo *m;* (*receiving*) recibimiento *m*
gregarious [grɪ·'ger·i·əs] *adj* **1.** (*liking company*) sociable **2.** ZOOL (*living in groups*) gregario, -a
grenade [grɪ·'neɪd] *n* granada *f;* **hand** ~ granada de mano
grenadier [ˌgren·ə·'dɪr] *n* **1.** (*soldier*) granadero *m* **2.** (*fish*) granadero *m*
grew [gru] *pt of* **grow**
grey [greɪ] *adj, n, vi, vt s.* **gray**
greyhound *n* galgo *m*
grid [grɪd] *n* parrilla *f;* SPORTS parrilla de salida
griddle ['grɪd·əl] **I.** *n* CULIN plancha *f*, burén *m* Cuba, PRico **II.** *vt* **to** ~ **food** asar comida a la plancha
gridiron ['grɪd·aɪ·ərn] *n* **1.** (*American football field*) campo *m* de fútbol americano **2.** (*metal grid*) parrilla *f* **3.** THEAT peine *m*
gridlock *n* paralización *f* del tráfico; *fig* inactividad *f*
grid square *n* cuadrícula *f*
grief [grif] *n* (*extreme sadness*) aflicción *f;* (*individual mournful feelings*) pesar *m;* (*pain*) dolor *m;* **to cause** ~ *inf* dar pena; **to cause sb** ~ causar aflicción a alguien; **to give sb (a lot of)** ~ hacer sentir (muy) mal a alguien ▸ **to come to** ~ (*fail*) fracasar; (*have an accident*) sufrir un percance; **good** ~! *inf* ¡caramba!
grievance ['gri·vəns] *n* **1.** (*complaint*) queja *f*, reivindicación *f;* **to harbor a** ~ **against sb** presentar una queja contra alguien **2.** (*sense of injustice*) injusticia *f*
grieve [griv] **I.** *vi* sufrir; **to** ~ **for sth/sb** llorar por algo/alguien **II.** *vt* **1.** (*distress*) causar

dolor; (*make sad*) afligir; **it** ~**s me to see your situation** me apena ver tu situación **2.** (*mourn*) llorar; **to** ~ **the death of...** llorar la pérdida de...
grievous ['gri·vəs] *adj form* **1.** (*causing grief: loss*) doloroso, -a; (*news*) lamentable **2.** (*causing pain: pain*) fuerte; (*wound*) de extrema gravedad **3.** (*extreme: danger*) serio, -a; (*error*) craso, -a **4.** (*serious*) grave; **a** ~ **crime** un crimen grave
grievous bodily harm *n* graves daños *mpl* corporales
griffin ['grɪf·ən] *n*, **griffon** *n* grifo *m*
grill [grɪl] **I.** *n* **1.** (*part of oven*) parrilla *f;* (*for barbecue*) parrilla *f*, grill *m* **2.** (*informal restaurant*) asador *m* **II.** *vt* (*cook*) asar a la parrilla
grille [grɪl] *n* rejilla *f;* (*of windows*) reja *f;* (*of doors*) verja *f;* (*of car*) calandra *f*, parrilla *f* AmS (*rejilla del radiador*)
grilling ['grɪl·ɪŋ] *n inf* interrogatorio *m;* **to give sb a (good)** ~ interrogar a alguien (muy) intensamente
grim [grɪm] *adj* **1.** (*very serious: expression*) severo, -a **2.** (*unpleasant*) desagradable; (*horrible*) horrible; **to feel** ~ sentirse muy mal **3.** (*without hope*) ~ **outlook** mirada *f* inexorable; **the future looks** ~ el futuro parece muy desalentador ▸ **to hang on like** ~ **death** (*dog*) no soltar la presa; (*person*) no cejar en el empeño
grimace ['grɪm·əs] **I.** *n* (*facial expression*) mueca *f;* **to make a** ~ **of disgust/pain/ hatred** hacer una mueca de asco/dolor/odio **II.** *vi* hacer muecas; **to** ~ **with pain** hacer muecas de dolor
grime [graɪm] **I.** *n* (*ingrained dirt*) mugre *f;* (*soot*) hollín *m* **II.** *vt* **to be** ~**d with soot** estar manchado de hollín
Grim Reaper *n liter* ≈ la dama de la guadaña
grimy ['graɪ·mi] <-ier, -iest> *adj* (*face, hands*) mugriento, -a; (*sooty*) sucio, -a
grin [grɪn] **I.** *n* amplia sonrisa *f* **II.** *vi* (*with amusement*) sonreír de oreja a oreja; (*with glee*) sonreír alegremente; (*with embarrassment*) sonreír nerviosamente; **to** ~ **impishly at sb** dirigir una sonrisa traviesa a alguien ▸ **to** ~ **and bear it** poner al mal tiempo buena cara
grind [graɪnd] **I.** *n inf* **1.** (*tiring work*) trabajo *m* pesado; **to be a real** ~ ser un trabajo durísimo **2.** (*boring work*) rutina *f;* **the daily** ~ la rutina diaria **II.** <ground, ground> *vt* **1.** (*crush*) aplastar; (*mill*) moler; **to** ~ **sth (in)to flour/a powder** reducir algo a harina/ polvo **2.** (*chop finely: meat*) picar **3.** (*press firmly and twist*) **to** ~ **a cigarette into an ashtray** apagar un cigarrillo en un cenicero **4.** (*sharpen*) afilar **III.** *vi* **1.** (*pulverize*) pulverizar **2.** *inf* (*devote oneself*) emplearse a fondo; **to** ~ **away at sth** emplearse a fondo en algo **3.** *inf* (*dance seductively*) bailar meneando la cadera; **to bump and** ~ bailar meneando la cadera de forma seductiva **4.** (*in skateboarding*) girar

◆**grind down** vt 1. (*file*) pulir 2. (*mill*) moler 3. (*wear*) desgastar 4. (*oppress*) oprimir; (*treat cruelly*) maltratar; **to grind sb down** destrozar a alguien

◆**grind out** vt (*produce continuously*) producir mecánicamente

grinder ['graɪn·dər] n 1. (*crushing machine*) molinillo m; (*for meat*) picadora f; **a hand/electric ~** una picadora manual/eléctrica 2. (*sharpener*) afilador m 3. (*person who sharpens things*) afilador(a) m(f); **knife/scissor ~** afilador(a) m(f) de cuchillos/tijeras

grindstone ['graɪnd·stoʊn] n muela f, afiladora f ▶ **to keep one's nose to the ~** *inf* trabajar como un enano

gringo ['grɪŋ·goʊ] n offensive, sl gringo, -a m, f

grip [grɪp] I. n 1. (*hold*) agarre m; fig control m; **to keep a firm ~ on sth** agarrar algo fuertemente; **to be in the ~(s) of sth** estar en poder de algo; **the economy is in the ~(s) of a crisis** la economía está atravesando una crisis 2. (*way of holding*) asidero m 3. (*bag*) maletín m ▶ **to get up to ~s with sth** enfrentarse a algo; **to get a ~ on oneself** controlarse II. <-pp-> vt 1. (*hold firmly*) agarrar 2. (*overwhelm*) **to be ~ped by emotion** estar embargado por la emoción; **he was ~ped by fear** el miedo lo invadió 3. (*interest deeply*) absorber la atención de III. vi agarrarse

gripe [graɪp] I. n inf queja f II. vi inf quejarse

gripping ['grɪp·ɪŋ] adj (*exciting: story*) apasionante

grisly ['grɪz·li] <-ier, -iest> adj (*repellant: murder*) espeluznante; fig que pone los pelos de punta; **a ~ discovery** un descubrimiento espeluznante

grist [grɪst] n **it's all ~ for one's** [o **the**] **mill** se puede sacar provecho de todo

gristle ['grɪs·əl] n cartílago m

grit [grɪt] I. n 1. (*small stones*) arenilla f 2. inf (*courage*) valor m II. <-tt-> vt 1. (*press together*) **to ~ one's teeth** a. fig apretar los dientes 2. **to ~ a road** echar grava a un camino

grits [grɪts] n pl ≈ sémola f de maíz sin pl

gritty ['grɪt̬·i] <-ier, -iest> adj (*sandy*) con arenilla; (*brave: decision*) valiente

grizzly ['grɪz·li] I. <-ier, iest> adj gris II. <-ies> n oso m pardo americano

groan [groʊn] I. n gemido m II. vi 1. (*make a noise*) gemir; **to ~ in pain** gemir de dolor 2. (*express dissatisfaction*) gruñir; **to ~ inwardly** lamentarse para sus adentros 3. (*complain*) quejarse; **to ~ about sth** quejarse de algo; **why are you moaning and ~ing about that?** ¿por qué te quejas tanto de eso?

grocer ['groʊ·sər] n 1. (*store owner*) tendero, -a m, f 2. (*food store*) tienda f de comestibles

groceries ['groʊ·sə·riz] n pl provisiones fpl, víveres mpl

grocery store n tienda f de comestibles

grog [grag] n grog m, ponche m

groggy ['grag·i] <-ier -iest> adj grogui

groin [grɔɪn] n ingle f; (*male sex organs*) entrepierna f (del hombre)

groom [grum] I. n 1. (*for horses*) mozo m de cuadra 2. (*bridegroom*) novio m II. vt 1. (*clean: an animal*) cepillar; (*a horse*) almohazar 2. (*prepare: a person*) acicalar

groove [gruv] n ranura f; MUS surco m; fig onda f ▶ **to be in a ~** estar estancado en la rutina

groovy ['gru·vi] <-ier, -iest> adj sl guay

grope [groʊp] I. vi ir a tientas; **to ~ for sth** buscar algo a tientas; **to ~ for the right words** buscar las palabras adecuadas II. vt 1. sl (*touch sexually*) sobar 2. **to ~ one's way** ir a tientas

gropingly ['groʊ·pɪŋ·li] adv a tientas

gross [groʊs] I. adj 1. (*vulgar*) grosero, -a 2. LAW grave; (*neglect*) serio, -a; (*negligence*) grave 3. (*revolting*) asqueroso, -a 4. (*total*) total; (*without deductions*) bruto, -a II. n <-es> gruesa f; **by the ~** al por mayor III. vt FIN (*earn before taxes*) ganar en bruto

gross domestic product n producto m interior bruto

gross income n ingreso m bruto

grossly adv (*in a gross manner*) groseramente; (*extremely*) enormemente; **to be ~ unfair** ser completamente injusto

gross national product n producto m nacional bruto

gross negligence n imprudencia f temeraria

gross pay n paga f íntegra

gross profit n ganancia f bruta

gross tonnage n tonelaje m bruto

gross weight n peso m total

grotesque [groʊ·'tesk] n a. ART, LIT grotesco, -a

grotto ['grat̬·oʊ] <-oes o -os> n gruta f

grouch [graʊtʃ] I. n (*grumpy person*) refunfuñón, -ona m, f, cascarrabias mf inv II. vi refunfuñar; **to ~ about sth/sb** quejarse de algo/alguien; **stop your ~ing and get on with the work!** ¡deja de quejarte y ponte a trabajar!

grouchy ['graʊ·tʃi] <-ier, -iest> adj malhumorado, -a

ground¹ [graʊnd] I. n 1. (*the Earth's surface*) tierra f; **above/below ~** sobre el nivel del suelo/bajo tierra 2. (*soil*) suelo m 3. (*area of land*) terreno m; **breeding ~** zona f de cría; **fishing ~s** pesquería f; **waste ~** tierra f baldía 4. (*reason*) motivo m; **to have ~s to do sth** tener motivos para hacer algo; **on the ~s that...** porque... 5. (*area of knowledge*) tema m; **to be on one's own ~** estar en su propio terreno; **to give ~** ceder terreno; **to stand one's ~** mantenerse firme II. vt 1. AVIAT no dejar despegar; **to be ~ed** no poder despegar 2. (*unable to move*) **to be ~ed** estar encallado, -a 3. fig, inf no dejar salir

ground² [graʊnd] I. vt pt of grind II. adj (*crystal*) deslustrado, -a III. n ~s sedimentos mpl; **coffee ~s** poso m de café

ground ball n (*in baseball*) roletazo m

groundbreaking ['graʊnd·ˌbreɪ·kɪŋ] adj pionero, -a

ground control n control m de [o desde] tierra

ground crew *n* personal *m* de tierra
ground floor *n* planta *f* baja; **on the ~** en la planta baja, en el primer piso *AmS;* **~ apartment** entresuelo *m* ▶**to get in on the ~** empezar desde abajo
ground forces *npl* MIL ejército *m* de tierra

---

i El 2 de febrero se conoce en EE.UU como Día de la Marmota (**Groundhog Day**). Al parecer, este día sale el groundhog (la marmota canadiense) de su madriguera, donde ha hibernado. La tradición popular afirma que, si ve su propia sombra, regresa a su agujero porque el invierno va a durar otras seis semanas. Pero si no la puede ver porque está nublado, entonces se queda en el exterior porque llega la primavera.

---

groundless ['graʊnd·lɪs] *adj* infundado, -a
ground rule double *n* SPORTS doble *m* de campo
ground rules *npl* **1.** (*guidelines*) directrices *fpl* **2.** (*in baseball*) normativa *f,* reglas *fpl*
grounds crew *n* personal *m* de mantenimiento
groundskeeper *n* cuidador(a) *m(f)* del terreno de juego
ground speed *n* velocidad *f* respecto a la tierra
groundswell ['graʊnd·swel] *n* **1.** (*opinion*) oleada *f* **2.** NAUT (*heavy sea*) mar *m o f* de fondo
ground-to-air missile *n* misil *m* tierra-aire
ground water *n* aguas *fpl* subterráneas
groundwork ['graʊnd·wɜrk] *n* trabajo *m* preliminar; (*for further study*) trabajo *m* preparatorio; **to lay the ~ for sth** *fig* establecer las bases de algo
group [grup] **I.** *n* **1.** *a.* CHEM grupo *m;* **~ photo** foto *f* de grupo; **~ of trees** arboleda *f;* **in ~s** en grupos; **to get into ~s** formar grupos **2.** (*specially assembled*) colectivo *m* **3.** (*business association*) agrupación *f* **4.** (*musicians*) conjunto *m* musical **II.** *vt* agrupar **III.** *vi* agruparse; **to ~ together around sb** agruparse en torno a alguien
group discount *n* descuento *m* de grupo
group dynamics *npl* dinámica *f* de grupo
groupie ['gru·pi] *n sl* groupie *mf*
grouping ['gru·pɪŋ] *n* agrupación *f*
group rate *n* tarifa *f* de grupo
group therapy <-ies> *n* terapia *f* de grupo
grouse¹ [graʊs] *n* **black ~** gallo *m* lira; **red ~** urogallo *m* escocés
grouse² [graʊs] **I.** *n* **1.** (*complaint*) queja *f* **2.** (*complaining person*) cascarrabias *mf inv* **II.** *vi* quejarse; **to ~ at sb** quejarse de alguien
grove [groʊv] *n* (*group of trees*) arboleda *f;* (*orchard*) plantación *f;* **olive ~** olivar *m;* **orange ~** naranjal *m*
grow [groʊ] <grew, grown> **I.** *vi* **1.** (*increase in size*) crecer; (*flourish*) florecer; **to ~ taller** crecer en estatura **2.** (*increase*) aumentar; **to ~ by 2%** aumentar un 2% **3.** (*develop*) desarrollarse **4.** (*become*) volverse; **to ~ old** hacerse viejo; **to ~ to like sth** llegar a gustarle algo **II.** *vt* **1.** (*cultivate*) cultivar **2.** (*let grow*) dejar crecer; **to ~ a beard** dejarse (crecer la) barba; **some animals ~ a thicker coat in winter** algunos animales adquieren un pelaje más grueso en invierno
◆**grow into** *vt insep* llegar a ser; *fig* acostumbrarse a
◆**grow on** *vt* **1.** (*become pleasing: a taste*) gustar cada vez más **2.** (*become apparent: feeling*) crecer, apoderarse de alguien o algo
◆**grow out of** *vt insep* **1.** (*become too big*) **she has grown out of her clothes** se le ha quedado la ropa pequeña **2.** (*habit*) perder
◆**grow up** *vi* **1.** (*become adult*) crecer; (*behave like an adult*) madurar; **oh, ~! stop your whining!** ¡a ver si creces de una vez! ¡deja de lloriquear!; **when I grow up I'd like to...** cuando sea mayor me gustaría... **2.** (*develop*) desarrollarse
grower ['groʊ·ər] *n* **1.** (*gardener*) cultivador(a) *m(f)* **2.** (*plant*) **this plant is a good ~** esta planta crece rápido
growing ['groʊ·ɪŋ] **I.** *n* crecimiento *m* **II.** *adj* **1.** (*developing*) **a ~ boy/girl** un chico/una chica en edad de crecimiento **2.** ECON que se expande **3.** (*increasing*) que aumenta
growing pains *npl* **1.** (*pains in the joints*) dolores *mpl* del crecimiento **2.** (*adolescent emotional problems*) problemas *mpl* de la adolescencia
growl [graʊl] **I.** *n* **1.** (*low throaty sound: of a dog*) gruñido *m;* (*of a person*) refunfuño *m* **2.** (*rumble*) ruido *m* sordo **II.** *vi* (*dog*) gruñir; (*person*) refunfuñar
grown [groʊn] **I.** *adj* adulto, -a **II.** *pp of* **grow**
grown-up ['groʊn·ʌp] *n* adulto, -a *m, f*
growth [groʊθ] *n* **1.** (*increase in size*) crecimiento *m* **2.** (*stage of growing*) madurez *f;* **to reach full ~** alcanzar su plenitud **3.** (*increase*) aumento *m;* **rate of ~** tasa *f* de crecimiento **4.** (*development*) desarrollo *m* **5.** (*growing part of plant*) brote *m* **6.** (*beard*) crecimiento *m;* **three days ~ of beard** una barba de tres días **7.** MED bulto *m*
growth hormone *n* hormona *f* del crecimiento
growth industry *n* sector *m* en expansión
growth rate *n* ECON tasa *f* de crecimiento
growth stock *n* ECON acciones *fpl* con perspectivas de valorización
grub [grʌb] **I.** *n* **1.** *sl* (*food*) manduca *f,* mandado *m Méx* **2.** (*larva*) larva *f* **II.**<-bb-> *vi* cavar; **to ~ about** (**for sth**) remover la tierra (buscando algo) **III.** *vt* **to ~ up** arrancar
grubby ['grʌb·i] <-ier, -iest> *adj inf* roñoso, -a
grudge [grʌdʒ] **I.** *n* rencor *m,* roña *f Cuba, Méx, PRico;* **to have** [*o* **hold**] **a ~ against sb** guardar rencor a alguien **II.** *vt* **to ~ sb sth** envidiar algo a alguien
grudge match *n* duelo *m fig*

G

grudging *adj* mezquino, -a
grudgingly ['grʌdʒ·ɪŋ·li] *adv* de mala gana
gruel ['gru·əl] *n* gachas *fpl*
grueling ['gru·lɪŋ] *adj* duro, -a, penoso, -a
gruesome ['gru·səm] *adj* horripilante
gruff [grʌf] *adj* (*reply*) brusco, -a; **a ~ voice** una voz bronca
grumble ['grʌm·bəl] **I.** *n* (*complaint*) queja *f* **II.** *vi* (*person*) quejarse; (*stomach*) sonar; **to ~ about sth/sb** quejarse de algo/alguien
grumpy ['grʌm·pi] <-ier, -iest> *adj inf* (*bad tempered*) gruñón, -ona; (*annoyed*) cabreado, -a
grunt [grʌnt] **I.** *n* **1.** (*snort*) gruñido *m;* (*groan*) resoplido *m* **2.** *sl* (*soldier*) soldado *mf* **3.** *sl* (*laborer*) currante *mf* [*o* cargaladrillos] *mf* Col **II.** *vi* **1.** (*snort*) gruñir **2.** (*groan*) resoplar
gryphon *n s.* **griffin**
G-string ['dʒi·strɪŋ] *n* tanga *m*
GU *n abbr of* **Guam** Guam *m*
Guam [gwam] *n* Guam *m*
Guamanian [ˌgwə·'meɪ·ni·ən] **I.** *adj* guamaniano, -a **II.** *n* guamaniano, -a *m, f*
guarantee [ˌger·ən·'ti] **I.** *n* **1.** (*certainty*) garantía *f;* **there's no ~ that...** no hay ninguna garantía de que... +*subj* **2.** (*for repair or replacement*) garantía *f* **3.** (*a promise*) promesa *f;* **to give sb one's ~** garantizar algo a alguien **4.** (*responsibility for debt*) aval *m* **5.** (*document*) certificado *m* de garantía **6.** (*security*) prenda *f* **II.** *vt* **1.** (*promise*) prometer **2.** (*promise to correct faults*) ofrecer una garantía; **to be ~d for three years** tener una garantía de tres años **3.** (*make certain*) **to ~ that** asegurar que **4.** (*another's debt*) avalar
guarantor [ˌger·ən·'tɔr] *n* garante *mf*
guaranty ['ger·ən·ti] <-ies> *n* **1.** (*acceptance of debt*) garantía *f* **2.** (*thing offered as security*) prenda *f*
guard [gard] **I.** *n* **1.** (*person*) guardia *mf;* **prison ~** carcelero, -a *m, f;* **security ~** guardia de seguridad; **to post ~s** designar las guardias; **to be on ~** estar en guardia; (*soldier*) estar de guardia; **to be on one's ~** (*against sth/sb*) estar en alerta (contra algo/alguien); **to be under ~** estar bajo guardia y custodia; **to drop one's ~** bajar la guardia; **to keep ~ over sth/sb** vigilar algo/a alguien **2.** (*in basketball*) base *mf* **3.** (*in football*) escolta *mf* **4.** (*protective device*) resguardo *m* **5.** MIL **the National Guard** la Guardia Nacional **II.** *vt* **1.** (*protect*) proteger; (*prevent from escaping*) vigilar **2.** (*keep secret*) guardar **3.** SPORTS defender
♦ **guard against** *vt always sep* (*protect from*) **to guard sth/sb against sth/sb** proteger algo/a alguien de algo/alguien
guard dog *n* perro *m* guardián
guard duty <-ies> *n* guardia *f*
guarded ['gar·dɪd] *adj* cauteloso, -a
guardhouse *n* cuartel *m* de la guardia
guardian ['gar·di·ən] *n* **1.** (*responsible person*) guardián, -ana *m, f* **2.** *form* (*protector*) protector(a) *m(f)*

guardian angel *n a. fig* ángel *m* de la guarda
guardianship *n* **1.** (*being a guardian*) custodia *f* **2.** *form* (*care*) cuidado *m;* **to be in the ~ of sb** estar bajo la tutela de alguien
guardrail ['gard·reɪl] *n* (*in bridge*) pretil *m;* (*in staircase*) barandilla *f*
guardroom *n* cuarto *m* de guardia
guardsman <-men> *n* guardia *m*
Guatemala [ˌgwa·tə·'ma·lə] *n* Guatemala *f*
Guatemalan [ˌgwa·tə·'ma·lən] **I.** *adj* guatemalteco, -a **II.** *n* guatemalteco, -a *m, f*
guerilla *n,* **guerrilla** [gə·'rɪl·ə] *n* guerrilla *f*
guerrilla warfare *n* guerra *f* de guerrillas
guess [ges] **I.** *n* conjetura *f;* **a lucky ~** un acierto por casualidad; **to take a ~** adivinar; **to take a wild ~** hacer una conjetura al azar; **your ~ is as good as mine!** ¡vaya Vd. a saber!
▶ **it's anybody's ~** ¿quién sabe? **II.** *vi* **1.** (*conjecture*) conjeturar; **to ~ right/wrong** adivinar/equivocarse; **~ what I'm doing now?** ¿adivinas qué estoy haciendo ahora?; **to ~ that...** imaginar que...; **how did you ~?** ¿cómo lo has adivinado? **2.** (*believe, suppose*) suponer; (*suspect*) sospechar; **I ~ you're right** supongo que estás en lo cierto **III.** *vt* adivinar
▶ **to keep sb ~ing** tener a alguien en suspense; **~ what?** ¿sabes qué?
guessing game ['ges·ɪŋ·geɪm] *n a. fig* adivinanza *f*
guesstimate ['ges·tɪ·mət] **I.** *n inf* estimación *f,* cálculo *m* a grandes rasgos **II.** *vt inf* **to ~ sth** calcular algo grosso modo
guesswork ['ges·wɜrk] *n* conjeturas *fpl*
guest [gest] **I.** *n* **1.** (*invited person*) invitado, -a *m, f;* **paying ~** (*person renting*) inquilino, -a *m, f;* (*lodger*) huésped *mf* **2.** (*hotel customer*) cliente *mf* ▶ **be my ~** *inf* ¡adelante! **II.** *vi a.* TV aparecer como invitado
guesthouse *n* casa *f* de huéspedes
guestroom *n* habitación *f* de invitados
guffaw [gə·'fɔ] **I.** *n* carcajada *f* **II.** *vi* reírse a carcajadas
GUI *n* COMPUT *abbr of* **graphical user interface** GUI
guidance ['gaɪ·dəns] *n* (*help and advice*) consejo *m;* (*direction*) orientación *f;* **~ system** *a.* MIL sistema *m* de dirección
guide [gaɪd] **I.** *n* **1.** (*person*) guía *mf;* **tour/ mountain ~** guía turístico/de montaña **2.** (*book*) guía *f* **3.** (*help*) orientación *f* **4.** (*indication*) indicación *f* **II.** *vt* **1.** (*show*) guiar **2.** (*instruct*) orientar; **the manual will ~ you to...** el manual te dará instrucciones para... **3.** (*steer, influence*) dirigir; **to be ~d by one's emotions** dejarse llevar por los sentimientos
guidebook *n* guía *f*
guided ['gaɪ·dɪd] *adj* **1.** (*led by a guide*) dirigido, -a; **~ed tour** excursión *f* con guía **2.** (*automatically steered*) teledirigido, -a; **~ missile** MIL misil *m* teledirigido
guide dog *n* perro-guía *m*
guideline *n* directriz *f;* (*figure*) pauta *f*
guiding hand ['gaɪ·dɪŋ·'hænd] *n fig* mano *f*

amiga
guiding light n norte m
guiding principle n principio m rector
guild [gɪld] n (of merchants) corporación f; (of craftsmen) gremio m; **Writers' Guild** asociación f de escritores
guilder ['gɪl·dər] n florín m holandés
guile [gaɪl] n form astucia f
guileful ['gaɪl·fəl] adj form astuto, -a
guileless ['gaɪl·lɪs] adj inocente
guillotine ['gɪl·ə·tin] n guillotina f
guilt [gɪlt] n 1. (shame for wrongdoing) culpabilidad f 2. (responsibility for crime) culpa f; **to admit one's ~** confesarse culpable; **to establish sb's ~** determinar la culpabilidad de alguien
guiltless ['gɪlt·lɪs] adj inocente
guilt-ridden adj atormentado, -a por un sentido de culpabilidad
guilty ['gɪl·ti] <-ier, -iest> adj culpable; **to be ~ of a crime/murder** ser culpable de un delito/asesinato; **to have a ~ conscience** tener un sentimiento de culpabilidad; **to feel ~ about sth** sentirse culpable por algo; **to plead ~ to a crime** declararse culpable de un crimen; **to prove sb ~** demostrar la culpabilidad de alguien
Guinea ['gɪn·i] n Guinea f
guinea fowl n gallina f de Guinea
Guinean I. adj guineano, -a **II.** n guineano, -a m, f
guinea pig n conejillo m de Indias, cuy m AmS
guise [gaɪz] n 1. (pretense) pretensión f; **under the ~ of sth** bajo el disfraz de algo 2. (appearance) apariencia f; **it's an old idea in a new ~** se trata de una antigua idea pero con un nuevo aspecto
guitar [gɪ·'tar] n guitarra f; **to play the ~** tocar la guitarra
guitarist [gɪ·'tar·ɪst] n guitarrista mf
gulf [gʌlf] n 1. (area of sea) golfo m; **the Gulf of Mexico** el Golfo de Méjico; **the Persian Gulf** el Golfo Pérsico; **the Gulf of Suez** el Golfo de Suez 2. (chasm) abismo m 3. (difference of opinion) diferencias fpl; **to bridge a ~** llenar un vacío
gull¹ [gʌl] n zool gaviota f
gull² [gʌl] vt **to ~ sb** estafar a alguien; **I was ~ed into believing that it was a great chance** me hicieron creer que era una gran oportunidad
gullet ['gʌl·ɪt] n 1. (food pipe) esófago m 2. (throat) garganta f
gullible ['gʌl·ə·bəl] adj crédulo, -a
gully ['gʌl·i] <-ies> n (narrow gorge) barranco m; (channel) hondonada f
gulp [gʌlp] **I.** n trago m; **in one ~** de un trago; **a ~ of water** un trago de agua; **a ~ of air** una bocanada de aire **II.** vt tragar; (liquid) beber **III.** vi 1. (swallow with emotion) tragar saliva 2. (breath) **to ~ for air** respirar hondo
gum¹ [gʌm] **I.** n 1. (soft sticky substance) goma f; bot resina f 2. (adhesive) pegamento

m; (on envelope flap) cola f 3. **chewing ~** chicle m; **fruit gum** gominola f **II.** vt pegar
gum² [gʌm] n anat encía f
◆**gum up** vt estropear ▸**to ~ the works** (stop operation) paralizar los trabajos; (interfere) estropearlo todo
gumball n bola f de chicle
gumbo ['gʌm·boʊ] n reg: Southern (okra) quingombó m; (soup) sopa f de quingombó
gum disease n inflamación f de la encía
gumdrop ['gʌm·drap] n pastilla f de goma
gummed adj engomado, -a
gummy ['gʌm·i] <-ier, -iest> adj (sticky) pegajoso, -a
gumption ['gʌmp·ʃən] n inf 1. (courage) valor m; **to have the ~ to do sth** tener valor para hacer algo 2. (intelligence) seso m
gumshoe ['gʌm·ʃu] n sl (investigator) detective mf
gum tree ['gʌm·tri] n árbol m de caucho, gomero m AmL
gun [gʌn] **I.** n 1. (weapon) arma f de fuego; (cannon) cañón m; (pistol) pistola f; (revolver) revólver m; (rifle) fusil m; **to carry a ~** llevar pistola 2. sports pistoletazo m; **to jump the ~** salir antes de tiempo 3. (device) pistola f inyectora; **grease ~** pistola de engrase 4. (person) pistolero, -a m, f; **a hired ~** un pistolero a sueldo ▸**to stick to one's ~s** mantenerse en sus trece **II.** <-nn-> vi (vehicle) salir disparado
◆**gun down** vt derribar (a tiros), abalear
gunboat n cañonera f
gunboat diplomacy n diplomacia f de cañón
gun control n regulación f sobre armas de fuego
gunfight n tiroteo m
gunfire n 1. (gunfight) tiroteo m; (shots) disparos mpl 2. (cannon fire) cañoneo m
gung-ho ['gʊŋ·hoʊ], **gung ho** adj sl entusiasmado, -a
gunk [gʊŋk] n inf porquería f
gunman <-men> n pistolero m
gunner ['gʌn·ər] n artillero, -a m, f
gunpoint n **at ~** a punta de pistola
gunpowder n pólvora f
gunrunner n traficante mf de armas
gunrunning n contrabando m de armas
gunship n helicóptero m de combate
gunshot ['gʌn·ʃat] n disparo m
gunshot wound n herida f de bala
gunslinger ['gʌn·slɪŋ·ər] n hist pistolero, -a m, f
gurgle ['gɜr·gəl] **I.** n (noise of water) borboteo m; (of baby) gorjeo m **II.** vi 1. (water) borbotear 2. (baby) gorjear; **to ~ with pleasure/ with delight** gorjear de felicidad/regocijo
guru ['gu·ru] n gurú mf
gush [gʌʃ] **I.** <-es> n chorro m; fig efusión f; **a ~ of water** un chorro de agua **II.** vi 1. (any liquid) chorrear 2. inf (praise excessively) deshacerse en elogios **III.** vt derramar a borbollones
gusher ['gʌʃ·ər] n pozo m petrolífero

G

gushing *adj* (excesivamente) efusivo, -a

gushy ['gʌʃ·i] <-ier, -iest> *adj* (*manner, praise*) sentimental, efusivo, -a

gusset ['gʌs·ɪt] *n* escudete *m*

gust [gʌst] **I.** *n* (*of wind*) ráfaga *f;* (*of rain*) chaparrón *m* **II.** *vi* soplar

gusto ['gʌs·toʊ] *n* entusiasmo *m*

gusty ['gʌs·ti] <-ier -iest> *adj* borrascoso, -a

gut [gʌt] **I.** *n* **1.** (*intestine*) intestino *m;* **a ~ reaction/feeling** una reacción visceral/un instinto **2.** (*string from animal intestine*) tripa *f* **3. ~ s** *sl* (*bowels*) entrañas *fpl* **4. ~ s** (*courage*) valor *m;* (*strength of character*) determinación *f;* **it takes ~ s** se necesita valor ▶ **to bust a ~** *sl* echar los bofes **II.** <-tt-> *vt* **1.** (*remove the innards*) destripar **2.** (*destroy by fire*) **to be ~ ed** estar destruido **3.** (*emotional suffering*) destrozar

gutless ['gʌt·lɪs] *adj sl* (*lacking courage*) cobarde; (*lacking enthusiasm*) apático, -a

gutsy ['gʌt·si] <-ier, -iest> *adj* **1.** (*brave*) valiente; (*adventurous*) atrevido, -a **2.** (*powerful*) vigoroso, -a

gutter ['gʌt·ər] *n* (*on the roadside*) alcantarilla *f;* (*on the roof*) canalón *m; fig* barrio *m* marginal

guttural ['gʌt·ər·əl] *adj a.* LING gutural

guy [gaɪ] *n* **1.** *inf* (*man*) tío *m;* **hi ~ s** ¿qué hay, colegas? **2.** (*for tent: guy rope*) viento *m*

Guyana [gaɪ·'æn·ə] *n* Guyana *f*

Guyanese [ˌgaɪ·ə·'niz] **I.** *adj* guyanés, -esa **II.** *n* guyanés, -esa *m, f*

guzzle ['gʌz·əl] **I.** *vt* (*of person: alcohol*) beber como si fuera agua; (*of car: gas*) chupar **II.** *vi* zampar

gym [dʒɪm] *n* **1.** (*gymnasium*) gimnasio *m* **2.** (*school subject*) gimnasia *f,* educación *f* física

gymnasium [dʒɪm·'neɪ·zi·əm] *n* gimnasio *m*

gymnast ['dʒɪm·næst] *n* gimnasta *mf*

gymnastic [dʒɪm·'næs·tɪk] *adj* gimnástico, -a

gymnastics [dʒɪm·'næs·tɪks] *npl* gimnasia *f*

gym shoes *n* zapatillas *fpl* de deporte

gynecological [ˌgaɪ·nə·kə·'ladʒ·ɪ·kəl] *adj* ginecológico, -a

gynecologist *n* ginecólogo, -a *m, f*

gynecology [ˌgaɪ·nə·'kal·ə·dʒi] *n* ginecología *f*

gyp [dʒɪp] *sl* **I.** *vt* birlar **II.** *n* **1.** (*swindler*) estafador(a) *m(f)* **2.** (*swindle*) timo *m*

gypsum ['dʒɪp·səm] *n* yeso *m*

gypsy ['dʒɪp·si] <-ies> **I.** *n* gitano, -a *m, f* **II.** *adj* gitano, -a; **~ encampment** campamento *m* de gitanos

gyrate [ˌdʒaɪ·'reɪt] *vi* girar

gyration [ˌdʒaɪ·'reɪ·ʃən] *n* giro *m; fig* vuelco *m*

gyrocompass ['dʒaɪ·roʊ·ˌkʌm·pəs] *n* brújula *f* giroscópica

gyroscope ['dʒaɪ·rə·skoʊp] *n* NAUT, AVIAT giroscopio *m*

H

H, h [eɪtʃ] *n* H, h *f;* **~ as in Hotel** H de Huelva

ha [ha] *interj a. iron* ¡ajá!

habeas corpus [ˌheɪ·bi·əs·'kɔr·pəs] *n* LAW hábeas corpus *m*

haberdasher ['hæb·ər·dæʃ·ər] *n* mercero, -a *m, f,* camisero, -a *m, f*

haberdashery ['hæb·ər·dæʃ·ə·ri] <-ies> *n* **1.** (*clothing*) ropa *f* de caballero **2.** (*shop*) mercería *f*

habit ['hæb·ɪt] *n* **1.** (*customary practice*) hábito *m,* costumbre *f;* **to be in the ~ of doing sth** tener por costumbre hacer algo; **by (sheer) force of ~** por pura costumbre; **to do sth out of ~** hacer algo por costumbre; **to get into the ~ (of doing sth)** acostumbrarse (a hacer algo); **to get out of the ~ of doing sth** perder la costumbre de hacer algo; **a bad ~** una mala costumbre; **to break a ~** quitarse una costumbre; **don't make a ~ of it** no lo vuelvas una costumbre **2.** (*dress*) hábito *m;* **riding ~** traje *m* de montar **3.** (*addiction*) adicción *f;* **to have a heroin ~** ser adicto a la heroína

habitable ['hæb·ɪ·tə·bəl] *adj* habitable

habitat ['hæb·ɪ·tæt] *n* hábitat *m*

habitation [ˌhæb·ɪ·'teɪ·ʃən] *n* **1.** (*occupancy*) **unfit for human ~** inhabitable **2.** (*dwelling*) vivienda *f,* morada *f* **3.** (*settlement*) asentamiento *m*

habitual [hə·'bɪtʃ·u·əl] *adj* **1.** (*usual*) habitual; **~ drug use** consumo frecuente de drogas **2.** (*describing person*) empedernido, -a; (*liar, drug user*) empedernido, -a

habituate [hə·'bɪtʃ·u·eɪt] *vt* habituar; **to be ~ d to doing sth** estar acostumbrado a hacer algo

hack¹ [hæk] **I.** *vt* **1.** (*chop violently*) cortar a tajos; **to ~ sth to pieces** hacer algo trizas **2.** *sl* (*cope with*) aguantar; **I can't ~ this job** este trabajo me la puede **II.** *vi* **1.** (*chop*) hacer tajos; **to ~ at sth** cortar algo a tajos **2.** (*cough*) toser (con tos seca) **III.** *n* (*writer*) escritorzuelo, -a *m, f;* (*journalist*) periodista *mf* de pacotilla

hack² [hæk] *vt* COMPUT **to ~ (into) a system** introducirse ilegalmente en un sistema

hack³ [hæk] **I.** *vi* montar a caballo **II.** *n* **1.** (*horse*) caballo [*o* de silla] de alquiler *m;* (*worn out*) jamelgo *m,* penco *m* **2.** *inf* (*taxi cab*) taxi *m*

hacker ['hæk·ər] *n* COMPUT hacker *mf,* pirata *mf* informático, -a

hackles ['hæk·əlz] *npl* (*on back of dog*) pelo *m* erizado; (*on neck of bird*) collar *m* ▶ **to get one's ~ up** enfurecerse; **to make sb's ~ rise** poner furioso a alguien; **to raise ~** levantar ampollas

hackney ['hæk·ni] *n,* **hackney carriage** *n* **1.** (*horse*) caballo *m* de alquiler, cuartago *m* **2.** (*carriage*) coche *m* de alquiler

hackneyed ['hæk·nɪd] *adj* (*argument, theme*)

trillado, -a

hacksaw ['hæk·sɔ] *n* sierra *f* para metales

had [hæd, *unstressed:* həd] *pt, pp of* **have**

haddock ['hæd·ək] *n* abadejo *m*

hadn't ['hæd·ənt] = **had not** *s.* **have**

haft [hæft] *n* (*of a knife*) mango *m;* (*of a sword*) empuñadura *f*

hag [hæg] *n* (*woman*) bruja *f*

haggard ['hæg·ərd] *adj* macilento, -a, ojeroso, -a

haggle ['hæg·əl] *vi* regatear; **to ~ over sth** regatear el precio de algo

Hague [heɪɡ] *n* **the ~** la Haya

ha-ha ['ha·ha] *interj iron* ¡ja, ja!

hail¹ [heɪl] **I.** *n* METEO granizo *m;* (*of stones, insults*) lluvia *f* **II.** *vi* granizar; **criticism hailed down on him** le llovieron las críticas

hail² [heɪl] **I.** *vt* **1.** (*call*) llamar; **to ~ a taxi** parar un taxi **2.** (*acclaim*) aclamar **3.** (*welcome*) acoger; **she ~ed the news with joy** recibió la noticia con alegría **II.** *vi* **to ~ from** (*person*) ser de; (*thing*) proceder de

hail-fellow(-well-met) *n* (demasiado) campechano, -a

hair [her] *n* **1.** (*on head*) cabello *m,* pelo *m Col;* (*on chest, a. head*) pelo *m;* (*on armpits, legs, pubic*) vello *m;* **to do one's ~** arreglarse el pelo; **to have one's ~ cut** cortarse el pelo; **to wash one's ~** lavarse el pelo; **to wear one's ~ up/down** llevar el pelo recogido/suelto **2.** (*on animal*) pelo *m* **3.** (*on plant*) pelusa *f* ▶ **that'll put ~ on your chest** *inf* eso te dejará como nuevo; **to make sb's ~ curl** *inf* poner los pelos de punta a alguien; **to get in sb's ~** poner a alguien nervioso; **to not harm a ~ on sb's head** no tocarle ni un pelo a alguien; **to split ~s** buscarle tres pies al gato

hairbrush <-es> *n* cepillo *m* (del pelo)

hairclip *n* pasador *m,* clip *m* para el pelo

hair conditioner *n* acondicionador *m* del cabello, bálsamo *m*

haircut *n* corte *m* de pelo; **to get a ~** cortarse el pelo

hairdo *n inf* peinado *m*

hairdresser *n* peluquero, -a *m, f;* **the ~'s** la peluquería

hairdressing *n* **1.** (*profession*) peluquería *f* **2.** (*activity*) peinado *m*

hair dryer *n* secador *m* (de pelo)

hairless ['her·lɪs] *adj* (*head*) calvo, -a, pelado, -a *AmS;* (*body*) sin vello; (*face*) lampiño, -a; (*animal*) sin pelo

hairline *n* **1.** (*edge of the hair*) nacimiento *m* del pelo; **he has a receding ~** tiene entradas **2.** (*fine line*) línea *f* muy fina

hairline crack *n,* **hairline fracture** *n* grieta *f* fina

hairnet *n* redecilla *f*

hairpiece *n* postizo *m*

hairpin *n* horquilla *f,* gancho *m AmL,* pinza *f Col*

hairpin curve *n,* **hairpin turn** *n* curva *f* muy cerrada

hair-raising *adj* espeluznante

hair remover *n* crema *f* depilatoria

hair restorer *n* tónico *m* capilar

hairsplitting **I.** *n* sutilezas *fpl* **II.** *adj* (*argument, remark*) demasiado sutil; (*person*) quisquilloso, -a

hair spray *n* laca *f* (para el pelo)

hairstyle *n* peinado *m*

hairy ['her·i] <-ier, -iest> *adj* **1.** (*having much hair*) peludo, -a **2.** *sl* (*difficult, dangerous: escape, problem*) peliagudo, -a

Haiti ['heɪ·ti] *n* Haití *m*

Haitian ['heɪ·ʃən] **I.** *n* haitiano, -a *m, f* **II.** *adj* haitiano, -a

hake [heɪk] <-(s)> *n* merluza *f*

hale [heɪl] *adj* robusto, -a

half [hæf] **I.** <halves> *n* (*equal part*) mitad *f;* **~ an apple** media manzana; **in ~** por la mitad; **to cut sth into halves** partir algo por la mitad; **a pound and a ~** una libra y media; **to go halves (on sth)** *inf* pagar (algo) por mitades; **to go halves with sb** ir a medias con alguien; **my better ~** *fig* mi media naranja; **first/second ~** SPORTS primer/segundo tiempo; **the first/second ~ of a century** la primera/segunda mitad de un siglo **II.** *adj* medio, -a; **~ a pint** media pinta; **~ an hour** [o **a ~ hour**] media hora; **she's ~ the player she used to be** esta jugadora no es ni sombra de lo que era **III.** *adv* **1.** (*almost*) casi; **to be ~ sure** estar casi seguro **2.** (*partially*) a medias; **~ asleep** medio dormido; **~ cooked** medio crudo; **~ dead** medio muerto; *fig* (*exhausted*) medio muerto; **~ done** a medio hacer; **~ naked** medio desnudo; **~ empty/full** medio vacío/lleno **3.** (*by fifty percent*) **~ as many/much** la mitad; **~ as much again** la mitad más **4.** *inf* (*most*) la mayor parte; **~ (of) the time** la mayor parte del tiempo **5.** (*thirty minutes after*) **~ past three** las tres y media; (**at**) **~ past nine** a las nueve y media; **at ~ past** a y media **IV.** *pron* la mitad; **only ~ of them came** sólo vino la mitad de ellos

half and half *adj* **to split sth ~** dividir algo mitad y mitad

half-and-half *n* leche *f* con crema

halfback *n* (*in rugby*) medio *m* de melé y medio de apertura; (*in football*) corredor *m*

half-baked *adj* **1.** (*food*) medio cocido, -a **2.** *inf* (*plan*) sin sentido, estúpido, -a

half boot *n* botín *m,* bota *f* corta

half-breed *n* mestizo, -a

half brother *n* hermanastro *m*

half-caste *n offensive* mestizo, -a *m, f*

half-dollar *n* moneda *f* de cincuenta centavos de dólar estadounidense

half-dozen *adj* media docena *f*

half-empty *adj* (*glass*) medio vacío, -a

halfhearted *adj* poco entusiasta; **a ~ attempt** un intento desganado

half-life *n* PHYS media *f* vida, tiempo *m* para reducción a la mitad

half-mast *n* **at ~** a media asta

half-moon *n* media luna *f;* ~ **shaped** en forma de media luna
half note *n* MUS blanca *f*
half-price *n* at ~ a mitad de precio
half sister *n* hermanastra *f*
half-timbered *adj* con entramado de madera
halftime *n* SPORTS descanso *m;* **at** ~ en el descanso
half title *n* **1.**(*first printed page*) portadilla *f* **2.**(*title*) titulillo *m*
halftone *n* **1.** MUS semitono **2.** TYPO medio tono *m*
half-truth *n* verdad *f* a medias
halfway ['hæf·weɪ] **I.** *adj* **1.**(*midway*) medio, -a; ~ **point** punto medio; ~ **stage** etapa *f* intermedia **2.**(*partial*) parcial **II.** *adv* **1.**(*half the distance*) a mitad de camino; **to be** ~ **between ... and ...** estar entre... y...; **to be** ~ **through sth** ir por la mitad de algo; ~ **through the year** a mediados de año; ~ **up** a media cuesta; **to meet sb** ~ *fig* llegar a un acuerdo con alguien **2.**(*nearly, partly*) **to go** ~ **toward (doing)** sth hacer algo en parte; **the proposals only went** ~ **toward meeting their demands** las propuestas sólo satisfacían en parte sus exigencias
halfway house . *n* centro *m* de reinserción
half-wit *n* imbécil *mf*
halibut ['hæl·ə·bət] <-(s)> *n* halibut *m*
Haligonian [ˌhæl·ɪ·'goʊ·ni·ən] **I.** *n* natural de *Halifax* **II.** *adj* de Halifax
halitosis [ˌhæl·ɪ·'toʊ·sɪs] *n* halitosis *f inv*
hall [hɔl] *n* **1.**(*corridor*) pasillo *m*, corredor *m* **2.**(*entrance room*) vestíbulo *m* **3.**(*large public room*) sala *f;* (*in schools*) comedor *m;* **concert** ~ sala *f* de conciertos; **town** [*o* **city**] ~ ayuntamiento *m* **4.** UNIV colegio *m* mayor; **residence** ~ residencia *f* universitaria
hallelujah [ˌhæl·ɪ·'lu·jə] **I.** *interj* ¡aleluya! **II.** *n* aleluya *m*
hallmark ['hɔl·mark] **I.** *n* **1.**(*identifying symbol*) distintivo *m;* **her** ~ su sello personal; **to bear all the ~s of...** *fig* tener todas las características de... **2.**(*engraved mark*) contraste *m* **II.** *vt* contrastar
hallow ['hæl·oʊ] *vt* **1.**(*sanctify*) santificar; (*consecrate*) consagrar; **to be ~ed** ser sagrado **2.**(*venerate*) venerar
hallowed *adj* sagrado, -a
Halloween *n*, **Hallowe'en** [ˌhæl·ə·'win] *n* víspera *f* de Todos los Santos, Día *f* de las Brujas

---

[i] La fiesta de **Halloween** se celebra el 31 de octubre, en la víspera de **All Saints' Day** (Todos los Santos), conocido también como **All Hallows**. Tradicionalmente, los espíritus y las brujas desempeñan un papel importante en esta fiesta. Los niños confeccionan faroles con calabazas vaciadas en forma de cabezas. Al atardecer se disfrazan y van de puerta en puerta con una bolsa en la mano, pidiendo

golosinas. Cuando el dueño de la casa abre la puerta, los niños gritan: '**Trick or treat!**'; el dueño puede darles una golosina **(treat)** o arriesgarse a que le gasten una broma **(trick)**. Entre los niños pequeños, estas bromas prácticamente han desaparecido, pues sólo se acercan a aquellas casas en las que las luces externas han sido encendidas en señal de bienvenida. Los jóvenes, en cambio, aprovechan la ocasión para escribir con jabón en las ventanas de los vecinos y 'decorar' sus jardines con papel higiénico, lanzando rollos de este material por encima de los árboles de manera que el papel se desenrolle en ellos.

---

hallucinate [hə·'lu·sɪ·neɪt] *vi a. fig* alucinar
hallucination [hə·ˌlu·sɪ·'neɪ·ʃən] *n* alucinación *f*
hallucinogen [hə·'lu·sɪ·nə·'dʒen] *n* alucinógeno *m*
hallucinogenic *adj* alucinógeno, -a
halo ['heɪ·loʊ] <-s *o* -es> *n* **1.** *a. fig* REL aureola *f* **2.** *a. fig* ASTR halo *m*
halogen ['hæl·ə·dʒen] *n* halógeno *m*
halogen bulb *n* bombilla *f* halógena
halogen lamp *n* lámpara *f* halógena
halt [hɔlt] **I.** *n* **1.**(*standstill, stop*) parada *f;* **to bring sth/sb to a** ~ detener algo/a alguien; **to call a** ~ **to sth** poner coto a algo; **to come** [*o* **grind**] **to a** ~ pararse **2.**(*interruption*) interrupción *f* **3.** RAIL apeadero *m* **II.** *vt* (*stop permanently*) parar; (*stop temporarily*) interrumpir **III.** *vi* (*permanently*) parar; (*temporarily*) interrumpirse **IV.** *interj* ~! ¡alto!
halter ['hɔl·tər] *n* **1.**(*on animal*) ronzal *m*, cabestro *m* **2.**(*for criminal*) soga *f* **3.**(*top*) top *m* con tiras que se atan al cuello
halter-top *n* top *m* con tiras que se atan al cuello
halting *adj* (*speech, movement*) vacilante
halve [hæv] **I.** *vt* **1.**(*lessen*) reducir a la mitad; (*number*) dividir por dos **2.**(*cut in half*) partir por la mitad **II.** *vi* reducirse a la mitad
ham [hæm] **I.** *n* **1.**(*cured*) jamón *m* (serrano); (*cooked*) jamón *m* (cocido); **a slice of** ~ una loncha *f* [*o* tajada *Col f*] de jamón **2.**(*actor*) histrión *m* **3.**(*radio*) radioaficionado, -a *m, f* **II.** *vi* actuar con histrionismo
◆**ham up** *vt* interpretar con afectación; **to ham it up** actuar histriónicamente
hamburger ['hæm·bɜr·gər] *n* **1.**(*patty*) hamburguesa *f* **2.**(*meat*) carne *f* picada
ham-fisted *adj*, **ham-handed** *adj* torpe
hamlet ['hæm·lət] *n* aldea *f*
hammer ['hæm·ər] **I.** *n* **1.**(*tool*) martillo *m;* ~ **blow** *a. fig* martillazo *m;* **the** ~ **and sickle** POL, HIST la hoz y el martillo; **to go under the** ~ *a. fig* (*painting*) salir a subasta **2.**(*of gun*) percutor *m* ▶ **to go at it** ~ **and tongs** *inf* (*do energetically*) echar el resto; (*fight*) luchar a

brazo partido **II.** *vt* **1.** (*hit with tool: metal*) martillear; (*nail*) clavar; **to ~ sth** (**into sth**) clavar algo (en algo); **to ~ sth into sb** *fig* meter algo en la cabeza a alguien **2.** *inf* SPORTS (*beat easily*) dar una paliza **3.** (*criticize: book, film*) machacar; **to ~ sb for sth** criticar duramente a alguien por algo **4.** *inf* (*become very drunk*) **to get ~ed** (**on sth**) emborracharse (de algo) **III.** *vi* **1.** (*use a hammer*) martillear; **to ~ at sth** dar martillazos a algo **2.** (*beat heavily*) golpear; (*heart*) latir con fuerza; (*head*) estar a punto de estallar; **to ~ on sth** aporrear algo
◆ **hammer in** *vt* clavar
◆ **hammer out** . *vt* **1.** (*correct: dent*) alisar a martillazos **2.** (*find solution*) negociar; **to ~ a settlement** llegar a un arreglo
hammer drill *n* taladro *m* de percusión
hammerhead *n* **1.** (*on hammer*) cabeza *f* de martillo **2.** ZOOL **~ shark** pez *m* martillo
hammock ['hæm·ək] *n* hamaca *f*
hamper[1] ['hæm·pər] *vt* (*hinder*) dificultar; **to ~ sb/sth** poner trabas a alguien/algo
hamper[2] ['hæm·pər] *n* **1.** (*picnic basket*) cesta *f* (*con tapa*) **2.** (*for dirty laundry*) cesto *m* de la ropa
hamster ['hæm·stər] *n* hámster *m*
hamstring ['hæm·strɪŋ] **I.** *n* ANAT tendón *m* de la corva; ZOOL tendón *m* del corvejón **II.** *vt irr* **1.** (*cut the hamstring*) desjarretar **2.** (*render powerless: thing*) paralizar; (*person*) incapacitar; **to be hamstrung** estar atado de pies y manos
hand [hænd] **I.** *n* **1.** ANAT mano *f;* **to be good with one's ~s** tener habilidad manual; **to deliver a letter by ~** entregar una carta en mano; **to do sth by ~** hacer algo a mano; **to keep one's ~s off** no tocar; **to shake ~s with sb** estrechar la mano a alguien; **to take sb by the ~** llevar a alguien de la mano; **to tie ~ and foot** *a. fig* atar de pies y manos; **sword in ~** espada en ristre; **~ in ~** de la mano; **get your ~s off!** ¡no toques!; **~s up!** ¡manos arriba!; **to ask for sb's ~** (**in marriage**) pedir la mano de alguien **2.** (*handy, within reach*) **at ~** muy cerca; **to keep sth close at ~** tener algo a mano; **to be at ~** acercarse; **on ~** (*available to use*) disponible; **to be on ~** (*object*) estar a mano; (*person*) estar ahí **3.** (*what needs doing now*) **the problem at ~** el problema que nos ocupa; **in ~** (*being arranged*) entre manos; **preparations are in ~** los preparativos están en marcha **4. ~s** (*responsibility, authority, care*), **to be in good ~s** estar en buenas manos; **to fall into the ~s of sb** caer en manos de alguien; **to put sth into sb's ~s** poner algo en manos de alguien; **at the ~s of sb** (*because of*) a manos de alguien **5.** (*assistance*) **to give** (**sb**) **a ~** (**with sth**) echar (a alguien) una mano (con algo); **to keep one's ~ in** no perder la práctica **6.** (*control*) **to get out of ~** (*things, situation*) irse de las manos; (*person*) descontrolarse; **to have sth in ~** tener algo entre manos; **to have sth well in ~** tener

algo bajo control; **to have a ~ in sth** intervenir en algo; **to take sb in ~** apretar las clavijas a alguien **7.** GAMES **to have a good/poor ~** tener una buena/mala mano; **to show one's ~** *a. fig* enseñar las cartas; **a ~ of poker** una mano de póquer **8.** (*on clock*) manecilla *f;* **the hour ~** la aguja de las horas; **the minute ~** el minutero; **the second ~** el segundero **9.** (*manual worker*) obrero, -a *m, f;* (*sailor*) marinero, -a *m, f;* **farm ~** peón, -a *m, f* **10.** (*skillful person*) **old ~** veterano, -a *m, f;* **to be an old ~ at sth** tener mucha experiencia en algo; **to try one's ~ at sth** intentar algo alguna vez; **to be able to turn one's ~ to anything** saber hacer cualquier cosa **11.** (*applause*) aplauso *m;* **let's have a big ~ for ...** un gran aplauso para... **12.** (*measurement for horses*) palmo *m* de alzada **13.** (*handwriting*) letra *f;* **in his own ~** de su puño y letra ▶ **to make money ~ over fist** hacer dinero a espuertas [*o* a lo loco]; **to lose money ~ over fist** perder dinero rápidamente; **to be ~ in glove with sb** ser uña y carne con alguien; **to put one's ~ in one's pocket** contribuir con dinero, meterse la mano al bolsillo; **with a firm ~** con mano dura; **at first ~** de primera mano; **to have one's ~s full** estar muy ocupado; **with a heavy** [*o* **an iron**] **~** con mano dura; **to play a lone ~** actuar solo; **on the one ~ ... on the other** (**~**)... por un lado..., por otro (lado)...; **to have one's ~s tied** tener las manos atadas; **to have sb eat out of one's ~** meterse a alguien en el bolsillo, poner a alguien a comer de la mano de otro; **to force sb's ~** forzar la mano a alguien; **to get one's ~s on sb** atrapar a alguien, ponerle la mano encima a alguien; **to lay one's ~s on sth** hacerse con algo; **to not soil one's ~s with sth** no mancharse las manos con algo; **to throw in one's ~** darse por vencido **II.** *vt* **1.** (*give*) dar; **will you ~ me my bag?** ¿puedes pasarme mi bolso? **2.** (*give credit to*) **you've got to ~ it to him** hay que reconocer que lo hace muy bien
◆ **hand around** *vt* hacer circular
◆ **hand back** *vt* devolver
◆ **hand down** *vt* **1.** (*knowledge, tradition*) transmitir; (*objects*) pasar **2.** LAW (*judgment*) pronunciar, dictar
◆ **hand in** *vt* (*task, document*) entregar; **to ~ one's resignation** presentar la dimisión
◆ **hand on** *vt* (*knowledge*) transmitir; (*object*) pasar; **to hand sth on to sb** pasar algo a alguien
◆ **hand out** *vt* **1.** (*distribute*) repartir **2.** (*give: advice*) dar; (*punishment*) aplicar
◆ **hand over I.** *vt* **1.** (*give, submit: money, prisoner*) entregar; (*check*) extender **2.** (*pass: power, authority*) transferir; (*property*) ceder **3.** TEL pasar; **to hand sb over to sb** pasar a alguien con alguien **II.** *vi* **to ~ to sb** delegar en alguien; TV pasar la conexión a alguien
handbag *n* bolso *m,* cartera *f AmL*
handball *n* SPORTS balonmano *m*

handbill *n* folleto *m*, volante *m*
handbook *n* manual *m*
hand brake *n* AUTO freno *m* de mano
handcart *n* carretilla *f*
handcuff *vt* esposar
handcuffs *npl* esposas *fpl;* **a pair of** ~ unas esposas
handful ['hænd·fʊl] *n* **1.** *a. fig* (*small amount*) puñado *m;* **a** ~ **of people** un puñado de gente **2.** (*person*) **to be a real** ~ (*child*) ser un bicho [*o* terremoto]; (*adult*) ser una buena pieza
hand grenade *n* granada *f* de mano
handgun *n* pistola *f*
handicap ['hæn·dɪ·kæp] I. *n* **1.** (*disability*) discapacidad *f;* **mental** ~ discapacidad *f* mental; **physical** ~ invalidez *f* **2.** (*disadvantage*) desventaja *f* **3.** SPORTS hándicap *m* II.<-pp-> *vt* perjudicar; **to be** ~**ped** estar en una situación de desventaja
handicapped I. *adj* **physically** ~ minusválido, -a; **mentally** ~ discapacitado psíquico II. *n* **the** ~ los minusválidos
handicraft ['hæn·dɪ·kræft] *n* **1.** (*work*) trabajo *m* artesanal **2.** (*product*) artesanía *f*
handiwork ['hæn·dɪ·wɜrk] *n* **1.** (*work*) trabajo *m* artesanal **2.** (*product*) trabajo *m* manual; **this must be Peter's** ~ *iron* esto debe ser obra de Peter
handkerchief ['hæn·kər·tʃɪf] *n* pañuelo *m*
handle ['hæn·dəl] I. *n* **1.** (*of pot, basket, bag*) asa *f;* (*of drawer*) tirador *m;* (*of knife*) mango *m* **2.** (*knob*) pomo *m;* (*lever*) palanca *f* **3.** *sl* RADIO (*name*) código *m* ▶ **to fly off the** ~ *inf* perder los estribos; **to get a** ~ **on sth** dar con el clavo [*o* truco] de algo II. *vt* **1.** (*touch*) tocar **2.** (*move, transport*) llevar; ~ **with care** frágil **3.** (*machine, tool, weapon*) manejar; (*chemicals*) manipular; **to** ~ **a situation well** manejar bien una situación; **she** ~**s light expertly in her paintings** en sus cuadros maneja la luz con maestría; **I don't know how to** ~ **her** no sé cómo tratarla **4.** (*direct*) ocuparse de; (*case*) llevar; **I'll** ~ **this** yo me encargo de esto; **he** ~**s the marketing** es el responsable de marketing; **he doesn't know how to** ~ **other people** (*business*) no sabe dirigir; (*socially*) no tiene don de gentes **5.** (*control*) dominar; (*work, difficult situation*) poder con; **to** ~ **an increase in prices** hacer frente a un aumento de precios **6.** (*discuss, portray: subject*) tratar **7.** (*operate: car*) conducir, manejar *AmL;* (*boat*) dirigir III. *vi* + *adv/prep* responder; **to** ~ **poorly** no responder bien
handlebar moustache *n* bigote *m* afilado
handlebars *npl* manillar *m*
handler *n* adiestrador(a) *m(f)*, contacto *m*
handling *n* **1.** (*management*) manejo *m;* (*of goods*) manipulación *f;* (*of subject*) tratamiento *m;* (*of person*) trato *m;* (*of car*) conducción, manejo *m AmL* **2.** COM (*fee*) porte *m*
hand luggage *n* equipaje *m* de mano
handmade *adj* hecho, -a a mano
hand-me-down *n* prenda *f* heredada

hand-operated *adj* manual
handout ['hænd·aʊt] *n* **1.** (*money*) limosna *f* **2.** (*leaflet*) folleto *m* **3.** (*press release*) comunicado *m* de prensa **4.** (*written information*) apuntes *mpl*, hojas *fpl*
hand-picked *adj* cuidadosamente seleccionado, -a
handrail *n* (*on stairs*) pasamanos *m inv;* (*on bridge*) barandilla *f*
handsaw *n* serrucho *m*
handshake *n* apretón *m* de manos
handsome ['hæn·səm] *adj* **1.** (*man*) guapo; (*animal, thing*) bello, -a; **the most** ~ **man** el hombre más apuesto **2.** (*impressive*) magnífico, -a **3.** (*large*) considerable; (*price, salary*) elevado, -a; (*donation*) generoso, -a; **by a** ~ **margin** por un amplio margen **4.** (*gracious: gesture*) noble
hands-on *adj* **1.** (*practical*) práctico, -a; ~ **approach** enfoque práctico **2.** COMPUT manual
handspring *n* salto *m* mortal; **backward** ~ salto mortal hacia atrás
handstand *n* pino *m;* **to do a** ~ hacer el pino, pararse en las manos *Col*
hand-to-mouth *adj* (*salary*) precario, -a; **to lead a** ~ **existence** tener lo justo para vivir
handwork *n* trabajo *m* hecho a mano
handwriting *n* letra *f*
handwritten *adj* manuscrito, -a
handy ['hæn·di] <-ier, -iest> *adj* **1.** (*convenient, available*) a mano; (*nearby*) cercano, -a; **to keep sth** ~ tener algo a mano; **to be** ~ **for sth** quedar cerca de algo **2.** (*user-friendly*) manejable; (*form, guide*) sencillo, -a **3.** (*skillful*) hábil; **to be** ~ **with sth** ser mañoso [*o* habilidoso] para algo; **to be** ~ **around the house** ser un manitas **4.** (*convenient*) práctico, -a; (*useful*) útil, venir bien; **to come in** ~ (*for sth*) venir muy bien (a alguien)
handyman ['hæn·dɪ·mæn] <-men> *n* manitas *m inv*

hang [hæŋ] I. <hung, hung> *vi* **1.** (*be suspended*) colgar; (*picture*) estar colgado; **to** ~ **by/on/from sth** colgar de algo; **to** ~ **in a gallery** estar expuesto en una galería **2.** (*lean over or forward*) inclinarse **3.** (*float: smoke, fog*) flotar; (*bird*) planear; **to** ~ **above sb/sth** cernirse sobre alguien/algo; **to leave a question** ~**ing** dejar una pregunta en el aire **4.** (*die*) morir en la horca **5.** (*fit, drape: clothes, fabrics*) caer; **to** ~ **well** tener buena caída **6.** *sl* (*be friendly with*) **to** ~ **with sb** mantenerse con alguien; (*spend time at*) pasársela con alguien ▶ ~ **in there!** ¡aguanta! II. <hung, hung> *vt* **1.** (*attach*) colgar; (*laundry*) tender; (*door*) colocar; **to** ~ **wallpaper** (**on a wall**) empapelar (una pared); **to** ~ **the curtains** colgar las cortinas; **the gallery will** ~ **many of his paintings** muchas de sus obras se expondrán en la galería **2.** (*lights, ornaments, decorations*) adornar **3.** (*one's head*) bajar **4.** (*execute*) ahorcar ▶ **to** ~ **it up** acabar con algo **III.** *n* FASHION caída *f* ▶ **to get the ~ of sth** *inf* coger el truquillo a algo; **I don't give a ~** *inf* me importa un bledo

hang around I. *vi* **1.** *sl* (*waste time*) perder el tiempo **2.** (*wait*) esperar **3.** (*idle*) no hacer nada; **a couple of kids are hanging around on the street** dos niños andan vagabundeando por la calle **4.** (*be friendly with*) **to ~ with sb** andar por ahí con alguien **II.** *vt insep* rondar; **I had to ~ the bus station for an hour** tuve que estar una hora de plantón en la estación de autobuses; **to ~ a place** andar rondando por un sitio
◆**hang back** *vi* **1.** (*be reluctant to move forward*) quedarse atrás **2.** (*hesitate*) vacilar
◆**hang behind** *vi* rezagarse
◆**hang on I.** *vi* **1.** (*wait briefly*) esperar; **to keep sb hanging on** hacer esperar a alguien; **~!** *inf* ¡espera un momento!; **she's on the other phone — would you like to ~?** está hablando por la otra línea, ¿quiere esperar? **2.** (*hold on to*) **to ~ to sth** agarrarse a algo; **~ tight** agárrate fuerte **3.** (*persevere*) mantenerse firme; (*resist*) aguantar **II.** *vt insep* **1.** (*depend upon*) depender de **2.** (*give attention*) estar pendiente de; **to ~ sb's every word** estar pendiente de lo que dice alguien **3.** (*depend on*) depender de
◆**hang out I.** *vt* (*laundry*) tender; (*tongue*) sacar; (*flag*) izar **II.** *vi* **1.** **let it all ~!** *sl* (*be relaxed*) ¡suéltate la melena! *fig* **2.** *sl* (*spend time at*) andar; **where does he ~ these days?** ¿por dónde anda estos días?
◆**hang over** *vt insep* estar suspendido sobre; *fig* cernirse sobre
◆**hang together** *vi* **1.** (*make sense*) ser coherente **2.** (*remain associated*) permanecer unidos
◆**hang up I.** *vi* **1.** colgar; **to ~ on sb** colgar a alguien **2.** *inf* **to get hung up on sth** (*have trouble with*) quedar varado **II.** *vt* **1.** (*curtains, receiver*) colgar **2.** (*give up*) **to ~ one's cleats/boxing gloves** *fig* colgar las botas/los guantes **3.** (*delay*) causar un retraso a

hangar ['hæŋ·ər] *n* hangar *m*
hangdog ['hæŋ·dɔg] *adj* **1.** (*defeated*) abatido, -a **2.** (*ashamed*) avergonzado, -a
hanger ['hæŋ·ər] *n* (*clothes*) percha *f*, gancho *m* de colgar ropa
hanger-on *n a. fig* lapa *f*, parásito *m*
hang glider *n* SPORTS ala *f* delta
hang-gliding *n* SPORTS vuelo *m* con ala delta
hanging ['hæŋ·ɪŋ] **I.** *n* **1.** (*act of execution*) ejecución *f* (en la horca) **2.** (*system of execution*) horca *f* **II.** *adj* **1.** (*bridge*) colgante **2.** (*crime*) condenado, -a a la horca
hangman <-men> *n* **1.** (*person*) verdugo *m* **2.** GAMES ahorcado *m*
hangnail *n* padrastro *m*
hangout *n sl* guarida *f*; **a favorite ~ of artists** un lugar frecuentado por artistas
hangover *n* **1.** (*after drinking*) resaca *f*, goma *f* AmL, guayabo *m* Col **2.** (*left-over*) vestigio *m*

hang-up *n inf* complejo *m*; **to have a ~ about sth** estar acomplejado por algo
hank [hæŋk] *n* madeja *f*
◆**hanker after** ['hæŋ·kər] *vt*, **hanker for** *vt* ansiar; **to ~ the past** sentir nostalgia del pasado
hankering ['hæŋ·kər·ɪŋ] *n* anhelo *m;* **to have a ~ for sth** ansiar algo
hankie *n*, **hanky** ['hæŋ·ki] *n inf abbr of* **handkerchief** pañuelo *m*
hanky-panky [ˌhæŋ·ki·'pæŋ·ki] *n sl* (*dishonest behavior*) tejemanejes *mpl*, chanchullo *m;* (*involving sex*) asunto *m*
Hanukkah ['ha·nə·kə] *n* Hanukah *m*
haphazard [hæp·'hæz·ərd] *adj* **1.** (*random, arbitrary*) caprichoso, -a **2.** (*badly planned*) hecho, -a de cualquier manera
hapless ['hæp·lɪs] *adj* desafortunado, -a
happen ['hæp·ən] *vi* **1.** (*occur*) pasar; **if anything ~s to me...** si me ocurre algo...; **these things ~** [*o sl* **shit ~s**] son cosas que pasan; **whatever ~s** pase lo que pase; **what ~ed to your hand?** ¿qué te ha pasado en la mano?; **something amazing ~ed to her that day** aquel día le sucedió una cosa asombrosa **2.** (*chance*) **I ~ed to be at home** dio la casualidad de que estaba en casa; **it ~ed (that)...** resultó que...; **as it ~s...** da la casualidad de que...; **how does it ~ that...?** ¿cómo puede ser que...?; **he ~s to be my best friend** pues resulta que es mi mejor amigo
happening ['hæp·ə·nɪŋ] *n* **1.** (*events*) suceso *m* **2.** (*performance*) happening *m*
happily ['hæp·ɪ·li] *adv* **1.** (*contentedly*) felizmente; **they lived ~ ever after** fueron felices y comieron perdices **2.** (*willingly*) con mucho gusto **3.** (*fortunately*) afortunadamente
happiness ['hæp·ɪ·nɪs] *n* felicidad *f;* **I wish you every ~** que seas muy feliz
happy ['hæp·i] <-ier, -iest> *adj* **1.** (*feeling very good*) feliz; **to be ~ that...** estar contento de que...; **to be ~ to know that...** alegrarse de saber que...; **I'm so ~ for you** me alegro mucho por ti; **to be ~ to do sth** estar encantado de hacer algo; **I'll be ~ to see you tomorrow morning** les recibiré con mucho gusto mañana por la mañana; **~ birthday!** ¡feliz cumpleaños!; **many ~ returns (of the day)!** ¡que cumplas muchos más! **2.** (*satisfied*) contento, -a; **to be ~ about sb/sth** estar contento con alguien/algo; **to be ~ doing sth** estar contento de hacer algo; **are you ~ with the idea?** ¿te parece bien la idea? **3.** (*fortunate*) afortunado, -a; **a ~ coincidence** una feliz coincidencia **4.** (*suitable: phrase, behavior*) acertado, -a; **a ~ thought** una feliz idea
happy-go-lucky *adj* despreocupado, -a
happy medium *n* justo [*o* término] medio *m*
harass [hə·'ræs] *vt* **1.** (*persistently annoy*) acosar; (*with cares*) abrumar; (*with troubles*) agobiar; **to ~ sb with questions** acosar a alguien a preguntas **2.** (*torment*) atormentar **3.** (*attack continually*) hostigar

harassed [hə·'ræst] *adj* agobiado, -a

harassment [hə·'ræs·mənt] *n* **1.**(*pestering*) acoso *m;* **sexual ~** acoso sexual **2.**(*attack*) hostigamiento *m*

harbinger ['har·bɪn·dʒər] *n liter* (*person*) precursor(a) *m(f);* (*thing*) presagio *m;* **a ~ of doom** un mal presagio

harbor ['har·bər] **I.** *n* **1.**(*port*) puerto *m;* **fishing ~** puerto pesquero **2.** *fig* (*shelter*) refugio *m* **II.** *vt* **1.**(*give shelter to*) dar cobijo a **2.**(*keep: feelings*) albergar; (*hopes*) abrigar; **to ~ suspicions** tener sospechas; **to ~ a grudge** (**against sb**) guardar rencor (a alguien) **3.**(*keep in hiding*) esconder; (*criminal*) encubrir **4.**(*contain*) contener

hard [hard] **I.** *adj* **1.**(*firm, rigid*) duro, -a; (*rule*) estricto, -a; (*fate*) cruel; **~ times** malos tiempos; **to have a ~ time** pasarlo mal; **to give sb a ~ time** hacérselo pasar mal a alguien; **to have ~ luck** tener mala suerte **2.**(*intense, concentrated*) **to take a** (**good**) **~ look at sth** analizar algo detenidamente; **a ~ fight** una lucha encarnizada; **to be a ~ worker** ser muy trabajador **3.**(*forceful*) fuerte **4.**(*difficult, complex*) difícil; **~ landing** AVIAT aterrizaje forzado, -a; **to be ~ work for sb to do sth** ser muy difícil para alguien hacer algo; **to be ~ to please** ser difícil de contentar; **to get ~** complicarse; **a ~ bargain** un trato poco ventajoso; **to learn the ~ way** *fig* aprender a base de errores [*o* palos] **5.**(*severe*) severo, -a **6.**(*hostile, unkind*) **a ~ heart** un corazón de piedra; **to be ~ on sb/sth** ser duro con alguien/algo **7.**(*extremely cold*) riguroso, -a **8.**(*solid: evidence*) concluyente; (*fact*) innegable; **~ and fast information** información veraz **9.**(*with alcohol*) **~ cider/punch** sidra/ ponche fuerte [*o* cargado, -a] **10.** CHEM (*water*) duro, -a **II.** *adv* **1.**(*forcefully*) fuerte; **to hit sb ~** pegar fuerte a alguien; **to press/pull ~** apretar/estirar con fuerza **2.**(*rigid*) **frozen ~** helado, -a **3.**(*energetically, vigorously*) mucho; **to fight ~** *fig* luchar con todas sus fuerzas; **to study/work ~** estudiar/trabajar mucho; **to try ~ to do sth** esforzarse en hacer algo; **to be ~ at it** trabajar con ahínco; **think ~** concéntrate; **to die ~** *fig* tardar en desaparecer **4.**(*intently*) detenidamente; **to look ~ at sth** estudiar algo con detenimiento **5.**(*closely*) muy cerca; **to be ~ up** no tener ni un céntimo **6.**(*heavy*) mucho; **it rained ~** llovió fuerte; **to take sth ~** tomarse algo muy mal; **I would be ~ pressed to choose one** me costaría mucho decidirme por uno

hardback ['hard·bæk] **I.** *n* (*book*) libro *m* de tapa dura; **in ~** con tapa dura **II.** *adj* con tapa [*o* pasta] dura

hardball *n* **1.**(*baseball*) béisbol *m* **2.** *inf* **to ~ sb** ponerse duro con alguien

hard-bitten *adj* endurecido, -a

hardboard *n* chapa *m* de madera

hard-boiled *adj* (*egg*) duro, -a; (*person*) endurecido, -a

hard cash *n* dinero *m* contante y sonante

hard copy <-ies> *n* COMPUT impresión *f*

hard core *n* **1.**(*inner circle within group*) núcleo *m* duro **2.**(*pornography*) pornografía *f* dura

hard court *n* pista *f* (de tenis) dura

hardcover *n* (*book*) tapa [*o* pasta]*f* dura

hard currency <-ies> *n* FIN moneda *f* fuerte

hard disk *n* COMPUT disco *m* duro

hard drive *n* COMPUT disco *m* duro

hard drug *n* droga *f* dura

hard-earned *adj* (*money*) ganado, -a con el sudor de la frente; (*rest, vacation*) merecido, -a

harden ['har·dən] **I.** *vt* **1.**(*make more solid, firmer*) endurecer; (*steel*) templar **2.**(*make tougher*) curtir; **to ~ oneself to sth** insensibilizarse a algo; **to become ~ed** curtirse; **life has ~ed his personality** la vida lo ha endurecido; **to ~ one's heart** *fig* mostrarse inflexible **3.**(*opinions, feelings*) afianzar; (*character*) confirmar **II.** *vi* **1.**(*become firmer: character*) endurecerse **2.**(*become accustomed to*) **to ~ to sth** acostumbrarse a algo **3.**(*attitude*) volverse inflexible **4.**(*become confirmed: idea*) confirmarse; (*feeling, intention*) afianzarse

hardening *n* **~ of the arteries** arterioesclerosis *f*

hard feelings *npl* resentimiento *m;* **no ~!** ¡olvidémoslo!

hard-fought *adj* reñido, -a

hardhat *n* casco *m*

hardheaded *adj* **1.**(*stubborn*) terco, -a, testarudo, -a **2.**(*realistic*) realista

hardhearted *adj* duro, -a de corazón

hard-hit *adj* muy afectado, -a; **to be ~ by sth** ser azotado por algo

hard-hitting *adj* impactante

hard labor *n* LAW trabajos *mpl* forzados

hard line *n* POL línea *f* dura

hard-liner *n* POL radical

hard liquor *n* bebida *f* fuerte

hardly ['hard·li] *adv* **1.**(*barely*) apenas; **~ anything** casi nada; **~ ever** casi nunca; **she can ~...** apenas puede...; **she can ~ wait until tomorrow** tiene unas ganas locas de que llegue mañana **2.**(*certainly not*) **it's ~ my fault that it's raining** ¿qué culpa tengo de que llueva?; **you can ~ expect him to do that** no puedes esperar que haga eso; **~!** ¡qué va! *inf*

hardness ['hard·nɪs] *n* **1.**(*solidity*) dureza *f;* (*lack of feeling*) insensibilidad *f;* **~ of heart** dureza de corazón **2.**(*difficulty*) dificultad *f* **3.**(*of winter*) rigor *m*

hard-nosed *adj* duro, -a

hard-pressed *adj* apurado, -a

hard rock *n* MUS rock *m* pesado

hard sell *n* venta *f* agresiva

hardship ['hard·ʃɪp] *n* (*suffering*) penas *fpl;* (*adversity*) adversidad *f;* (*deprivation*) penuria *f;* **to suffer great ~** pasar muchos apuros; **to live in ~** pasar privaciones

hardtop *n* AUTO coche *m* no descapotable

hardware n 1. (*household articles*) ferretería f; ~ **store** ferretero, -a m, f; (*home improvement center*) centro m de mejoramiento para el hogar 2. (*articles of metal*) quincallería f 3. COMPUT hardware m; **computer** ~ soporte m físico del ordenador 4. MIL armamento m

hard-wearing adj resistente

hardwood n madera f noble

hard-working adj trabajador(a)

hardy ['har·di] <-ier, -iest> adj (*person*) valeroso, -a; (*animal*) fuerte; (*plant*) resistente

hare [her] n BIO liebre f

harebrained ['her·breɪnd] adj disparatado, -a

harelip n MED labio m leporino

harem ['her·əm] n harén m

hark [hark] vi ~! ¡escucha!; **to ~ back to sth** fig evocar algo

harm [harm] I. n daño m; **to do ~ to sb/sth** hacer daño a alguien/algo; **to do more ~ than good** hacer más mal que bien; (**to put**) **out of ~'s way** (poner) a salvo; **to see no ~ in sth** no ver nada malo en algo; **I meant no ~** no pretendía hacer daño; **you will come to no ~** no te va a pasar nada; **there's no ~ in trying** no se pierde nada con intentarlo II. vt 1. (*hurt, ruin*) hacer daño; (*reputation*) perjudicar; **it wouldn't ~ you to stay at home** no te morirás por quedarte en casa 2. (*spoil*) estropear

harmful ['harm·fəl] adj dañino, -a; (*thing*) nocivo, -a; **to be ~ to sth** ser perjudicial para algo

harmless ['harm·lɪs] adj (*animal, person*) inofensivo, -a; (*thing*) inocuo, -a; (*fun, joke*) inocente

harmonic [har·'man·ɪk] adj armónico, -a

harmonica [har·'man·ɪ·kə] n MUS armónica f, rondín m Bol, Ecua, Perú

harmonious [har·'moʊ·ni·əs] adj armonioso, -a

harmonium [har·'moʊ·ni·əm] n MUS armonio m

harmonization [ˌhar·mə·nɪ·'zeɪ·ʃən] n armonización f

harmonize ['har·mə·naɪz] I. vt armonizar II. vi **to ~** (**with sb/sth**) armonizar (con alguien/algo)

harmony ['har·mə·ni] <-ies> n armonía f; **in ~** (**with sb/sth**) en armonía (con alguien/algo)

harness ['har·nɪs] I. n 1. (*for animals*) arnés m; (*for children*) correas fpl 2. (*cooperation*) **to work in ~** trabajar en equipo 3. (*everyday life*) **to get back in ~** fig volver a la rutina II. vt 1. (*secure: horse*) poner los arreos a; **to ~ a horse/donkey to a carriage** enganchar un caballo/burro a un carro 2. (*exploit: resources*) aprovechar

harp [harp] I. n MUS arpa f II. vi **to ~ on about sth** (*talk about*) insistir sobre algo; (*complain*) quejarse de algo

harpoon [har·'pun] I. n arpón m II. vt arponear

harpsichord ['harp·sɪ·kɔrd] n MUS clavicém-

balo m

harrow ['hær·oʊ] I. n grada f II. vt 1. AGR gradar 2. (*distress*) atormentar

harrowing adj (*story, experience*) desgarrador(a); (*prospect*) angustioso, -a

harsh [harʃ] adj 1. (*severe: parents*) severo, -a; (*punishment*) duro, -a 2. (*unfair: criticism*) cruel; (*words, reality*) duro, -a 3. (*unfriendly*) desabrido, -a 4. (*uncomfortable: light*) fuerte; (*climate, winter*) riguroso, -a; (*terrain*) desolado, -a; (*contrast*) violento, -a 5. (*rough*) áspero, -a 6. (*unaesthetic: color*) chillón, -ona 7. (*unpleasant to the ear: sound*) discordante; (*voice*) estridente

harum-scarum [ˌher·əm·'sker·əm] I. adv alocadamente II. adj atolondrado, -a

harvest ['har·vɪst] I. n (*of crops*) cosecha f; (*of grapes*) vendimia f; (*of vegetables*) recolección f; **the apple ~** la cosecha de la manzana; **a good ~ of potatoes** una buena cosecha de patatas [o papas] II. vt a. fig cosechar; (*grapes*) vendimiar; (*vegetables*) recolectar; **to ~ a field** hacer la cosecha en un campo III. vi cosechar

harvester n 1. (*machine*) **combine ~** cosechadora f 2. (*person*) recolector(a) m(f); (*of grain*) segador(a) m(f); (*of grapes*) vendimiador(a) m(f)

harvest moon n luna f llena de otoño

has [hæz, *unstressed:* həz] *3rd pers sing of* **have**

has-been n inf vieja gloria f; **to be a ~** ser alguien que ya ha pasado a la historia

hash¹ [hæʃ] I. vt CULIN picar II. n 1. CULIN picadillo m 2. inf lío m; **to make a ~ of sth** armarse un lío con algo

◆**hash up** vt echar a perder

hash² [hæʃ] n sl (*hashish*) chocolate m inf

hash browns npl patatas hervidas y después fritas

hashish ['hæʃ·iʃ] n hachís m inv

hasn't ['hæz·ənt] = **has not** s. **have**

hassle ['hæs·əl] I. n inf (*trouble*) lío m; **to give sb a ~** fastidiar a alguien; **it's such a ~** es un jaleo II. vt inf fastidiar; **to ~ sb to do sth** estar encima a alguien para que haga algo

hassock ['hæs·ək] n 1. (*for kneeling*) cojín m (para arrodillarse) 2. (*tuft of grass*) mata f de hierba

haste [heɪst] n prisa f; **to make ~** apresurarse; **in ~** de prisa

hasten ['heɪ·sən] I. vt acelerar; **to ~ sb along** dar prisa a alguien; **to ~ one's steps** apresurar el paso II. vi apresurarse; **to ~ to do sth** apresurarse a hacer algo

hasty ['heɪ·sti] <-ier, -iest> adj 1. (*fast*) rápido, -a; **to beat a ~ retreat** a. fig retirarse a toda prisa 2. (*not thought out*) precipitado, -a; **to make ~ decisions** tomar decisiones irreflexivamente; **to leap to ~ conclusions** sacar conclusiones precipitadas; **to be ~ in doing sth** precipitarse en algo

hat [hæt] n sombrero m; **to pass around the ~**

pasar la gorra ▶ **at the** drop **of a ~** con nada;
I'll eat **my ~ if...** que me maten [o ahorquen]
si...; **to** hang **one's ~ somewhere** quedarse a
vivir en algún sitio; **to** keep **sth under one's
~** no decir ni una palabra sobre algo; **to** talk
through one's ~ inf decir bobadas

hatch¹ [hætʃ] I. vi salir del cascarón II. vt
1. (chick) incubar, empollar **2.** (devise in
secret) tramar; **to ~ a plan** urdir un plan

hatch² [hætʃ] <-es> n trampilla f; NAUT escotilla ▶ down **the ~!** ¡salud!

hatch³ [hætʃ] vt ART sombrear

hatchback ['hætʃ·bæk] n AUTO coche m con
puerta trasera

hatchet ['hætʃ·ɪt] n hacha f (pequeña) ▶ **to**
bury **the ~** enterrar el hacha de guerra, hacer
la paz

hatchet-faced adj de cara chupada

hatchet man n sl **1.** (hired) encargado de los
trabajos sucios **2.** (thug) matón m

hatching ['hætʃ·ɪŋ] n salida f del huevo

hate [heɪt] I. n odio m; **to feel ~ for sth/sb**
odiar algo o a alguien II. vt odiar; **to ~ sb's**
guts sl odiar a alguien a muerte

hate crime n delito de carácter xenófobo, racista, antihomosexual, etc.

hateful ['heɪt·fəl] adj odioso, -a

hatpin ['hæt·pɪn] n alfiler m de sombrero

hatred ['heɪ·trɪd] n odio m

hat trick n SPORTS tres goles marcados por un
mismo jugador; **to score a ~** marcar tres tantos

haughty ['hɔ·t̬i] <-ier, iest> adj altivo, -a

haul [hɔl] I. vt **1.** (pull with effort) arrastrar; **to
~ up the sail** izar la vela; **to ~ a boat out of
the water** sacar una barca del agua **2.** inf
(force to go) forzar, jalar **3.** (transport goods)
transportar II. n **1.** (distance) trayecto m; **long
~ flight** vuelo m intercontinental; **in** [o over]
the long ~ fig a la larga **2.** (quantity caught: of
fish, shrimp) redada f; (of stolen goods) botín
m **3.** (tug) tirón m, jalón m CSur

◆**haul down** vt (flag, sail) arriar

◆**haul off** vi NAUT cambiar de rumbo

◆**haul up** vt inf to haul sb up before sb
hacer que alguien dé explicaciones a alguien

haulage ['hɔ·lɪdʒ] n **1.** (transportation) transporte m **2.** (costs) gastos mpl de transporte

hauler ['hɔ·lər] n (business) empresa f de
transportes; (person) transportista mf

haunch [hɔntʃ] <-es> n **1.** ANAT cadera f; **to sit
on one's ~es** ponerse de [o en] cuclillas **2.** (of
meat) pierna f

haunt [hɔnt] I. vt **1.** (ghost) aparecerse
2. (bother, torment) perseguir; **to be ~ed by
memories of an unhappy childhood** perseguir (a alguien) los recuerdos de una infancia
infeliz; **to be ~ed by sth** estar obsesionado
por algo **3.** (frequent) frecuentar; **to ~ a place**
rondar un lugar II. n lugar m preferido; **a student ~** un lugar frecuentado por los estudiantes

haunted adj **1.** (by ghosts) embrujado, -a

2. (troubled: look) angustiado, -a, preocupado, -a

haunting adj **1.** (disturbing) **a ~ fear/mem-
ory** un miedo/recuerdo recurrente e inquietante **2.** (memorable) **to have a ~ beauty**
tener una belleza fascinante; **a ~ melody** una
melodía inolvidable

Havana [hə·'væn·ə] n La Habana

have [hæv, unstressed: həv] I.<has, had,
had> vt **1.** (own) tener, poseer; **I have two
brothers** tengo dos hermanos; **~ you got a
cold? — no, I ~ a headache** ¿estás resfriado?
— no, me duele la cabeza; **to ~ sth to do**
tener algo que hacer **2.** (engage in) **to ~ a talk
with sb** hablar con alguien; **to ~ a game of
sth** echar una partida de un juego **3.** (eat) **to ~
breakfast/a snack** desayunar/merendar; **to
~ lunch** comer, almorzar Col; **to ~ dinner**
cenar, comer Col; **I ~n't had shrimp in ages!**
¡hace años que no como gambas!; **to ~ some
coffee** tomar un poco de café **4.** (give birth to)
to ~ a child tener un hijo **5.** (receive) tener,
recibir; **to ~ news about sb/sth** tener [o reci-
bir] noticias de alguien o algo; **to ~ visitors**
tener visita **6.** (show trait) **to ~ patience/
mercy** tener paciencia/compasión; **to ~
doubts/second thoughts** tener dudas/reser-
vas **7.** (cause to occur) **to ~ dinner ready**
tener la cena preparada; **I'll ~ Bob give you a
ride home** le pediré [o diré] a Bob que te lleve
a casa; **I won't ~ him doing that** no dejo que
haga esto ▶ **to ~ it** in **for sb** inf tenerla tomada
con alguien; **to ~ it** in **one to do sth** ser capaz
de hacer algo; **I didn't think she had it in
her!** ¡no pensaba que fuera capaz de eso!; **to ~
had it with sb/sth** inf haber tenido más que
suficiente de alguien/algo II.<has, had, had>
aux **1.** (indicates perfect tense) **he has never
been to California** nunca ha estado en California; **we had been swimming** habíamos
estado nadando; **had I known you were
coming,...** form si hubiera sabido que ibas a
venir,... **2.** (must) **to ~ (got) to do sth** tener
que hacer algo; **what time ~ we got to be
there?** ¿a qué hora tenemos que estar allí?; **do
we ~ to finish this today?** ¿tenemos que acabar esto hoy? III. n pl **the ~s and the have-
nots** los ricos y los pobres

◆**have around** vt always sep (gadget) tener a
mano

◆**have back** vt always sep **can I have it
back?** ¿me lo devuelves?; **they solved their
problems and she had him back** resolvie-
ron sus diferencias y ella le abrió las puertas de
casa de nuevo

◆**have in** vt always sep invitar; **they had
some experts in** llamaron a algunos expertos

◆**have on** vt always sep **1.** (wear: clothes) llevar (puesto); **he didn't have any clothes on**
estaba desnudo **2.** (carry) **to have sth on oneself** llevar algo encima; **have you got any
money on you?** ¿llevas dinero contigo?

◆**have out** vt always sep **1.** (remove) sacar

2. *inf*(*argue*) **to have it out with sb** poner las cosas en claro

◆**have over** *vt always sep* invitar

◆**have up** *vt always sep* invitar

haven ['heɪ·vən] *n* refugio *m*

have-nots *npl* **the ~** los pobres

haven't ['hæv·ənt] = **have not** *s.* **have**

havoc ['hæv·ək] *n* estragos *mpl;* **the ~ of the fire/the storm** los estragos del fuego/de la tormenta; **to play ~ with sth** hacer estragos de algo; **to wreak ~ on sth** desbaratar algo

haw [hɔ] **I.** *interj* (*to horse*) ¡ria! **II.** *vi* **to hem and ~** vacilar

Hawaii [hə·'waɪ·i] *n* Hawai *m*

Hawaiian [hə·'waɪ·jən] **I.** *n* **1.** (*person*) hawaiano, -a *m, f* **2.** LING hawaiano *m* **II.** *adj* hawaiano, -a

hawk [hɔk] **I.** *n* halcón *m* **II.** *vt* (*wares*) pregonar **III.** *vi* carraspear

hawker *n* vendedor (a) *m(f)* ambulante

hawk-eyed *adj* **to be ~** tener ojos de lince

hawkmoth *n* esfinge *m*

hawser ['hɔ·zər] *n* NAUT guindaleza *f*

hawthorn ['hɔ·θɔrn] *n* BOT espino *m*

hay [heɪ] *n* heno *m* ▸ **to hit the ~** *inf* acostarse

hay fever *n* fiebre *f* del heno

haystack *n* almiar *m*

haywire *adj inf* **to go/be ~** (*person*) volverse/ estar loco; (*machine*) estropearse

hazard ['hæz·ərd] **I.** *n* **1.** (*danger*) peligro *m* **2.** (*risk*) riesgo *m;* **fire ~** peligro de incendio; **health ~** riesgo para la salud **II.** *vt* **1.** (*dare*) aventurar; **to ~ a guess at sth** aventurar una respuesta a algo **2.** (*endanger*) arriesgar

hazard lights *npl* AUTO luces *fpl* de emergencia

hazardous ['hæz·ər·dəs] *adj* (*dangerous*) peligroso, -a; (*risky*) arriesgado, -a

haze [heɪz] **I.** *n* **1.** (*mist*) neblina *f;* (*smog*) calima *f* **2.** (*mental*) aturdimiento *m* **II.** *vt* ESP. UNIV hacer novatadas a

hazel ['heɪ·zəl] **I.** *adj* (*eyes*) color avellana **II.** *n* BOT avellano *m*

hazelnut ['heɪ·zəl·nʌt] *n* BOT avellana *f*

hazy ['heɪ·zi] <-ier, -iest> *adj* **1.** (*with bad visibility*) neblinoso, -a **2.** (*confused, unclear*) vago, -a

HDTV [ˌeɪtʃ·di·ti·'vi] *n* TV *abbr of* **high-definition television** televisión *f* de alta definición

he [hi] **I.** *pron pers* **1.** (*male person or animal*) él; **~ 's** [*o* ~ **is**] **my father** (él) es mi padre; **~ 's gone away but ~ 'll be back soon** se ha ido, pero volverá pronto; **here ~ comes** ahí viene **2.** (*unspecified sex*) **if somebody comes, ~ will buy it** si alguien viene, lo comprará; **~ who...** *form* aquél que... **II.** *n* (*of baby*) varón *m;* (*of animal*) macho *m*

head [hed] **I.** *n* **1.** ANAT cabeza *f;* **to nod one's ~** asentir con la cabeza; **to go straight to sb's ~** (*alcohol, wine*) subírse a la cabeza a alguien **2.** (*unit*) cabeza *f;* **a** [*o* **per**] **~** por cabeza; **a hundred ~ of cattle** cien cabezas de ganado; **to be a ~ taller than sb** sacar una cabeza a alguien **3.** (*mind*) **to clear one's ~** aclararse las

ideas; **to get sth/sb out of one's ~** sacarse algo/a alguien de la cabeza; **to have a good ~ for numbers** tener cabeza para los números; **to need a clear ~ to do sth** necesitar tener la cabeza clara [*o* fría] para hacer algo **4.** (*top: of line*) cabeza *f;* (*of bed, table*) cabecera; (*of a page, column*) parte *f* superior **5.** BOT cabeza *f;* **a ~ of lettuce** una lechuga **6.** **~s** FIN (*face of coin*) cara *f;* **~s or tails?** ¿cara o cruz? **7.** (*beer foam*) espuma *f* **8.** GEO (*of river*) nacimiento *m* **9.** (*boss*) jefe, -a *m, f* **10.** TECH (*device*) cabezal *m* **11.** COMPUT **read/write ~** cabeza *f* de lectura/escritura **12.** NAUT (*toilet*) baño *m* ▸ **to have one's ~ in the clouds** tener la cabeza [*o* en las nubes] llena de pájaros; **to be ~ over heels in love** estar locamente enamorado; **to fall ~ over heels in love with sb** enamorarse locamente de alguien; **to bury one's ~ in the sand** hacer como el avestruz; **to not be able to make ~ (n)or tail of sth** no entender ni jota de algo, no encontrarle pies ni cabeza a algo; **~s I win, tails you lose** o gano yo o gano yo; **to bang one's ~ against a wall** darse de cabeza contra la pared; **to keep one's ~ above water** mantenerse a flote; **to keep one's ~ down** (*avoid attention*) mantenerse al margen; (*work hard*) no levantar la cabeza; **to hold one's ~ high** mantener la cabeza alta; **~s up!** ¡cuidado!, ¡pilas! *Col,* ¡aguas! *Méx;* **to be soft in the ~** estar un poco tocado; **to have one's ~ screwed on right** tener la cabeza bien puesta; **to bite sb's ~ off** echar una bronca a alguien; **to bring sth to a ~** llevar algo a un punto crítico; **to give sb his/her ~** dejar a alguien obrar a su antojo; **to laugh one's ~ off** desternillarse de risa; **~s will roll** van a rodar cabezas **II.** *vt* **1.** (*lead*) encabezar; (*a company, organization*) dirigir; (*team*) capitanear **2.** PUBL encabezar **3.** SPORTS (*ball*) cabecear **III.** *vi* **to ~ (for) home** dirigirse hacia casa

◆**head back** *vi* volver, regresar

◆**head for** *vt insep* ir rumbo a; **to ~ the exit** dirigirse hacia la salida; **to ~ disaster** ir camino del desastre

◆**head off I.** *vt* cortar el paso a **II.** *vi* **to ~ toward** salir hacia

◆**head up** *vt* dirigir

headache ['hed·eɪk] *n* dolor *m* de cabeza

headband *n* cinta *f* de pelo

headbanger *n sl: aficionado a la musica heavy*

headboard *n* cabecera *f*

head cold *n* resfriado *m*

head cook *n* jefe, -a *m, f* de cocina

headdress <-es> *n* tocado *m*

header ['hed·ər] *n* **1.** SPORTS cabezazo *m* **2.** COMPUT cabecera *f*

headfirst ['hed·'fɜrst] *adv* de cabeza; **to dive/ fall ~** clavar/caer de cabeza

headhunt *vt* ECON cazar talentos

headhunter *n* **1.** ECON cazatalentos *mf inv* **2.** (*warrior*) cazador *m* de cabezas

heading ['hed·ɪŋ] *n* (*of chapter*) encabezamiento *m;* (*letterhead*) membrete *m*

headland ['hed·lænd] *n* cabo *m*
headless *adj* descabezado
headlamp *n,* **headlight** *n* faro *m*
headline I. *n* titular *m* ▶ **to hit the ~s** salir en primera plana II. *vt* titular
headlong I. *adv* precipitadamente; **to rush ~ into sth** hacer algo de forma precipitada II. *adj* precipitado, -a
headmaster *n* director *m* de colegio
headmistress <-es> *n* directora *f* de colegio
head of state <heads of state> *n* jefe , -a *m, f* de Estado
head-on I. *adj* (*collision*) frontal II. *adv* frontalmente, de frente
headphones *npl* auriculares *mpl,* audífonos *mpl AmL*
headquarters *n* + *sing/pl vb* MIL cuartel *m* general; (*of company*) oficina *f* central; (*of political party*) sede *f;* (*of the police*) jefatura *f* de policía
headrest *n* reposacabezas *m inv*
headroom *n* altura *f*
headscarf <-scarves> *n* pañuelo *m* para la cabeza
headset *n* auriculares *mpl,* audífonos *mpl AmL*
headship *n* ADMIN dirección *f*
headshrinker *n* *sl* (*psychiatrist*) loquero, -a *m, f*
head start *n* ventaja *f;* **to give sb a ~** dar ventaja a alguien
headstone *n* lápida *f*
headstrong *adj* testarudo, -a
heads-up *adj* (*baseball, player, technology*) atento, -a, alerta
headwaiter *n* jefe *m* de comedor, maître *m*
headwaters *npl* GEO cabecera *f* (de un río)
headway *n* progreso *m;* **to make ~** hacer progresos
headwind *n* viento *m* contrario [*o* en contra]; NAUT viento *f* de proa
headword *n* encabezamiento *m*
heady ['hed·i] <-ier, -iest> *adj* **1.** (*intoxicating*) embriagador(a) **2.** (*exciting*) emocionante
heal [hil] I. *vt* (*wound*) curar; (*differences*) salvar II. *vi* (*wound, injury*) cicatrizar
health [helθ] *n* salud *f;* **to be in good/bad ~** estar bien/mal de salud; **to drink to sb's ~** beber a la salud de alguien
health care *n* asistencia *f* sanitaria [*o* médica]
health center *n* centro *m* médico
health certificate *n* certificado *m* médico
health club *n* gimnasio *m*
health food *n* alimentos *mpl* naturales
health food shop *n,* **health food store** *n* tienda *f* de productos naturales
health hazard *n* riesgo *m* para la salud
health insurance *n* seguro *m* médico
health resort *n,* **health spa** *n* balneario *m,* centro *m* de reposo
healthy ['hel·θi] <-ier, -iest> *adj* **1.** MED sano, -a **2.** FIN (*strong*) próspero, -a; (*profit*) sustancial **3.** (*positive: attitude*) positivo, -a
heap [hip] I. *n* (*pile*) pila *f,* montón *m;* **to col-**

lapse in a ~ *fig* (*person*) caer desplomado; **a** (**whole**) ~ **of work** *inf* un montón de trabajo II. *vt* amontonar, apilar
hear [hɪr] <heard, heard> I. *vt* **1.** (*perceive*) oír **2.** (*be told*) enterarse de; **to ~ that...** enterarse de que..., oír que... **3.** (*listen*) escuchar; **Lord, ~ our prayers** REL escúchanos, Señor **4.** LAW **to ~ a case** ver un caso; **to ~ a witness** oír a un testigo II. *vi* **1.** (*perceive*) oír **2.** (*get news*) enterarse; **to ~ of** [*o* about] **sth** enterarse de algo ▶ **~, ~!** ¡muy bien!
heard [hɜrd] *pt, pp of* **hear**
hearing ['hɪr·ɪŋ] *n* **1.** (*sense*) oído *m;* **to be hard of ~** ser duro de oído, no oír bien **2.** (*act*) audición *f* **3.** (*range*) **in sb's ~** en presencia de alguien **4.** LAW vista *f*
hearing aid *n* audífono *m*
hearsay ['hɪr·seɪ] *n* habladurías *fpl;* **by ~** de oídas
hearse [hɜrs] *n* coche [*o* carro] *m* fúnebre
heart [hart] *n* **1.** ANAT corazón *m* **2.** (*center of emotions*) **to break sb's ~** partir el corazón a alguien; **to have a cold ~** ser duro de corazón; **to have a change of ~** cambiar de opinión; **to have a good** [*o* kind] **~** tener buen corazón; **to lose ~** desanimarse; **to lose one's ~** (**to sb/sth**) enamorarse (de alguien/algo); **to pour one's ~ out to sb** desahogarse con alguien; **to take ~** animarse; **her ~ sank** se le cayó el alma a los pies **3.** (*core*) centro *m;* **to get to the ~ of the matter** llegar al fondo de la cuestión **4.** CULIN (*of lettuce*) cogollo *m;* **artichoke ~s** corazones *mpl* de alcachofa **5.** *pl* (*card suit*) corazones *mpl;* (*in Spanish pack*) copas *fpl* ▶ **to one's ~'s content** hasta quedarse satisfecho; **to have a ~ of gold/stone** tener un corazón de oro/piedra, ser todo corazón; **to have one's ~ in the right place** tener buen corazón; **to wear one's ~ on one's sleeve** ir con el corazón en la mano; **with all one's ~** con toda su alma; **she is a girl after my own ~** es una chica de las que a mí me gustan; **to not have the ~ to do sth** no tener el valor para hacer algo; **by ~** de memoria; **in one's ~ of ~s** en lo más recóndito de su corazón
heartache ['hart·eɪk] *n* pena *f*
heart attack *n* ataque *m* al corazón
heartbeat *n* latido *m* (del corazón)
heartbreak *n* pena *f,* aflicción *f*
heartbreaking *adj* desgarrador(a)
heartbroken *adj* con el corazón partido
heartburn *n* MED acidez *f* de estómago
heart disease *n* enfermedad *f* coronaria
heartening ['har·tə·nɪŋ] *adj* alentador(a)
heart failure *n* insuficiencia *f* cardíaca
heartfelt *adj* sincero, -a; **my ~ condolences** mi más sentido pésame; **~ relief** gran alivio
hearth [harθ] *n* **1.** (*of fire place*) chimenea *f* **2.** *liter* (*home*) hogar *m;* **to leave ~ and home** abandonar el hogar
hearth rug *n* alfombrilla *f* (de la chimenea)
heartily ['har·ṭɪ·li] *adv* con efusividad; **to dis-**

like sth/sb ~ detestar algo/a alguien; **to eat ~** comer con ganas
heartland ['hart·lænd] *n* centro *m;* **the economic ~** el corazón económico
heartless ['hart·lɪs] *adj* sin corazón
heart murmur *n* MED soplo *m* cardíaco
heart rate *n* frecuencia *f* cardiaca
heart-rending *adj* desgarrador(a)
heart-searching *n* examen *m* de conciencia
heartstrings *npl* **to pull at sb's ~** *fig* tocar la fibra sensible a alguien
heartthrob *n* *inf* ídolo *m*
heart-to-heart I. *n* conversación *f* franca y abierta II. *adj* franco, -a y abierto, -a
heart transplant *n* trasplante *m* de corazón
heartwarming *adj* reconfortante
hearty ['har·t̬i] *adj* <-ier, -iest> 1. (*enthusiastic*) entusiasta; ~ **congratulations** felicidades de todo corazón; ~ **welcome** bienvenida calurosa 2. (*large, strong*) fuerte; ~ **appetite** buen apetito; **a ~ breakfast** un desayuno opíparo; **to have a ~ dislike for sth** tener manía a algo
heat [hit] I. *n* 1. (*warmth, high temperature*) calor; **in the ~ of the day** cuando más calor hace; **to cook sth on a high/low ~** cocinar algo a fuego alto/bajo 2. (*heating system*) calefacción *f;* **to turn down/up the ~** bajar/subir la calefacción 3. (*emotional state*) acaloramiento *m;* **in the ~ of the argument** en el momento más acalorado de la discusión 4. (*sports race*) eliminatoria *f* 5. ZOOL celo *m;* **to be in ~** estar en celo ▶ **if you can't take the ~, get out of the kitchen** *prov* quien no aguante la presión, que no se meta en la olla *prov;* **to put the ~ on sb** presionar a alguien; **to take the ~ off sb** dar un respiro a alguien II. *vt* 1. (*make hot*) calentar 2. (*excite*) acalorar III. *vi* (*become hot*) calentarse; *fig* (*inflame*) acalorarse
◆ **heat up** I. *vi* calentarse II. *vt* calentar
heated *adj* 1. (*window*) térmico, -a; (*pool*) climatizado, -a; (*room*) caldeado, -a 2. (*argument*) acalorado, -a
heatedly *adv* acaloradamente; **to ~ deny sth** negar algo con vehemencia
heater ['hi·t̬ər] *n* calefactor *m;* **water ~** calentador *m* de agua, radiador *m*
heat exchanger *n* (inter)cambiador *m* térmico
heat exhaustion *n* MED colapso *m* por exceso de calor
heat gauge *n* termostato *m*
heath [hiθ] *n* BOT brezal *m*
heathen ['hi·ðən] I. *n* pagano, -a *m, f;* **the ~** los infieles II. *adj* pagano, -a
heather ['heð·ər] *n* BOT brezo *m*
heating *n* calefacción *f*
heating system *n* sistema *m* de calefacción
heat pump *n* bomba *f* de calor [*o* térmica]
heat rash <-es> *n* sarpullido *m*
heat-resistant *adj*, **heat-resisting** *adj* resistente al calor
heat-seeking *adj* MIL termodirigido, -a

heat shield *n* blindaje *m* térmico
heat stroke *n* MED insolación *f*
heat treatment *n* termoterapia *f*
heat wave *n* ola *f* de calor
heave [hiv] I. *vi* 1. (*pull*) tirar; (*push*) empujar 2. (*move up and down*) subir y bajar; **to ~ into view** [*o* **sight**] NAUT aparecer 3. (*vomit*) tener bascas II. *vt* 1. (*pull*) tirar; (*push*) empujar; **he ~d the door open** abrió la puerta de un empujón; **to ~ a sigh (of relief)** dar un suspiro (de alivio); **to ~ sth at sb** lanzar algo a alguien 2. (*lift*) levantar III. *n* 1. (*push*) empujón *m;* (*pull*) tirón *m* 2. (*great effort*) gran esfuerzo *m*
◆ **heave to** *vi* <hove to, hoved to> NAUT ponerse al pairo
◆ **heave up** *vt* vomitar
heaven ['hev·ən] *n* cielo *m;* **to go to ~** ir al cielo; **it's ~** *fig, inf* es divino, es fantástico; **to be ~ on earth** *fig* (*place*) ser paradisiaco; **to be in (seventh) ~** *a. fig* estar en el (séptimo) cielo; **the ~s** (*sky*) el cielo ▶ **to move ~ and earth** remover Roma con Santiago, mover cielo y tierra; **what/where/when/who/why in ~'s name...?** ¿qué/dónde/cuándo/quién/por qué demonios...?; **for ~s sake!** ¡por Dios!; **good ~s!** ¡santo cielo!; **to stink to high ~** oler a perro muerto; **~ only knows** sólo Dios lo sabe; ~ **help us** que Dios nos ayude; **thank ~s** gracias a Dios
heavenly ['hev·ən·li] *adj* <-ier, -iest> 1. (*of heaven*) celestial; ~ **body** cuerpo *m* celeste 2. (*wonderful*) divino, -a
heavens *npl liter* firmamento *m*
heaven-sent *adj* caído, -a del cielo
heavy ['hev·i] I. *adj* <-ier, -iest> 1. (*weighing a lot*) pesado, -a; ~ **food** comida pesada 2. (*difficult*) difícil; (*schedule*) apretado, -a; **the book was rather ~ going** la lectura del libro era bastante pesada 3. (*strong*) fuerte; ~ **fall** *a.* ECON fuerte descenso 4. (*not delicate, coarse*) poco delicado, -a; (*features*) basto, -a 5. (*severe*) severo, -a; (*responsibility*) fuerte; (*sea*) grueso, -a; ~ **casualties** muchas bajas 6. (*abundant*) abundante; (*investment*) cuantioso, -a; ~ **frost/rain** helada/chubasco fuerte; **to go ~ on sth** consumir mucho de algo; **the tree was ~ with fruit** el árbol estaba cargado de frutas 7. (*excessive*) ~ **drinker/smoker** bebedor/fumador empedernido 8. (*thick*) grueso, -a; (*beard*) denso, -a; (*sky*) encapotado, -a II. *n* <-ies> *sl* matón *m*
heavy drinker *n* gran bebedor(a) *m(f)*
heavy-duty *adj* resistente; (*machine*) resistente; (*vehicle*) (muy) resistente
heavy going *adj* dificultoso, -a
heavy-handed *adj* 1. (*clumsy*) torpe 2. (*harsh*) duro, -a
heavy-hearted *adj* afligido, -a
heavy hitter *n* autoridad *mf,* duro *m* Col
heavy industry *n* industria *f* pesada
heavy metal *n* 1. (*lead, cadmium*) metal *m* pesado 2. MUS heavy *m* (metal)
heavy water *n* agua *f* pesada

heavyweight I. *adj* **1.** SPORTS (de la categoría) de los pesos pesados **2.** (*cloth*) resistente **3.** (*important*) serio, -a e importante II. *n a. fig* peso pesado *m*

Hebrew ['hi·bru] I. *n* **1.** (*person*) hebreo, -a *m, f* **2.** LING hebreo *m* II. *adj* hebreo, -a

Hebrides ['heb·rɪ·diz] *n* **the** ~ las Hébridas

heck [hek] *interj sl* caramba; **where the** ~ **have you been?** ¿dónde demonios habéis estado?; **what the** ~? ¿qué más da?

heckle ['hek·əl] *vi, vt* interrumpir con preguntas [*o* comentarios]

heckler ['hek·lər] *n* persona *f* que interrumpe

hectare ['hek·ter] *n* hectárea *f*

hectic ['hek·tɪk] *adj* ajetreado, -a; ~ **fever** fiebre hé(c)tica; ~ **pace** ritmo intenso

he'd [hid] = **he had, he would** *s.* **have, will**

hedge [hedʒ] I. *n* **1.** (*row of bushes*) seto *m* vivo **2.** FIN (*protection*) cobertura *f* II. *vi* (*avoid action*) dar rodeos; FIN cubrirse III. *vt* cercar (con un seto vivo)

hedge fund *n* FIN un grupo inversionista, por lo general en forma de una sociedad limitada, que emplea técnicas especulativas con la intención de obtener cuantiosas ganancias de capital

hedgehog ['hedʒ·hɔg] *n* erizo *m*

hedgerow *n* seto *m* vivo

hedging ['hedʒ·ɪŋ] *n* FIN cobertura *f* de riesgos

heebie-jeebies ['hi·bɪ·'dʒi·biz] *npl sl* **to give sb the** ~ poner a alguien la carne de gallina

heed [hid] I. *vt form* hacer caso de; **to** ~ **advice** seguir los consejos II. *n* **to pay** (**no**) ~ **to sth, to take** (**no**) ~ **of sth** (no) prestar atención a algo, hacer caso omiso de algo

heedful ['hid·fəl] *adj* **to be** ~ **of sb's advice** prestar atención a los consejos de alguien

heedless ['hid·lɪs] *adj* irresponsable; ~ **of sth** sin hacer caso a algo; **to be** ~ **of the risk** no preocuparse del riesgo

hee-haw ['hi·hɔ] I. *n* rebuzno *m* II. *vi* (*donkey*) rebuznar

heel [hil] I. *n* **1.** (*of foot*) talón *m;* **to be at sb's** ~**s** pisar los talones a alguien **2.** (*of shoe*) tacón *m,* taco *m AmL* **3.** (*of the hand*) base *f* de la mano **4.** (*of loaf of bread*) cuscurro *m,* punta *f* **5.** *inf* (*cad*) canalla *m* ▶ **to be down** at the ~**s** estar en mal estado; **to follow close on the** ~**s of sth** seguir inmediatamente a algo; **to be hard on sb's** ~**s** pisar los talones a alguien; **under** the ~ **of sb/sth** sometido a alguien/algo; **to bring sb to** ~ meter a alguien en cintura; **to come to** ~ acceder a obedecer, acudir; **to dig one's** ~**s in** mantenerse en sus trece; **to take to one's** ~**s** *inf* poner pies en polvorosa; **to turn on one's** ~ dar media vuelta; **to walk to** ~ andar pegado a alguien II. *interj* (*to dogs*) ven aquí

hefty ['hef·ti] *adj* <-ier, -iest> (*person*) corpulento, -a; (*profit, amount*) cuantioso, -a; (*book*) gordo, -a; (*price increase*) alto, -a

heifer ['hef·ər] *n* vaquilla *f*

height [haɪt] *n* **1.** (*of person*) estatura *f;* (*of thing*) altura *f* **2.** ~**s** (*high places*) alturas *fpl;*

to be afraid of ~**s** tener vértigo; **to attain great** ~**s** *fig* alcanzar el punto (más) alto; **to scale** (**new**) ~**s** *fig* alcanzar (nuevas) cotas **3.** ~**s** (*hill*) cerros *mpl* **4.** (*strongest point*) cima *f;* **to be at the** ~ **of one's career** estar en la cima de su carrera; **the** ~ **of fashion** el último grito **5.** (*the greatest degree*) cumbre; **the** ~ **of stupidity** el colmo de la estupidez; **the** ~ **of kindness/patience** el súmmum de la amabilidad/la paciencia

heighten ['haɪ·tən] I. *vi* aumentar II. *vt* **1.** (*elevate*) elevar **2.** (*increase*) aumentar; **to** ~ **the effect of sth** acentuar el efecto de algo

heinous ['heɪ·nəs] *adj form* atroz

heir [er] *n* heredero *m;* **to be** (**the**) ~ **to sth** ser el heredero de algo; ~ **apparent** heredero forzoso; ~ **to the throne** heredero del trono

heiress ['er·ɪs] *n* heredera *f*

heirloom ['er·lum] *n* reliquia *f;* **family** ~ reliquia familiar

heist [haɪst] *n* *inf* robo *m* a mano armada

held [held] *pt, pp of* **hold**

Helgoland ['hel·ɪ·gou·lænd] *n* Hel(i)goland *f*

helicopter ['hel·ɪ·kap·tər] *n* helicóptero *m*

helipad ['hel·ɪ·pæd helipuerto] *n* plataforma *f* de aterrizaje de los helicópteros

heliport ['hel·ɪ·pɔrt] *n* helipuerto *m*

helium ['hi·li·əm] *n* helio *m*

hell [hel] I. *n* **1.** (*place of punishment*) infierno *m;* ~ **on earth** infierno en vida; **to be** (**pure**) ~ ser un (auténtico) infierno; **to go to** ~ ir al infierno; **to go through** ~ pasar un calvario; **to make sb's life** ~ *inf* hacer la vida imposible a alguien **2.** *inf* (*as intensifier*) un frío de mil demonios; **as hot as** ~ un calor infernal; **as hard as** ~ duro a más no poder; **to annoy the** ~ **out of sb** molestar horrores a alguien; **to beat the** ~ **out of sb** dar a alguien una paliza de padre y muy señor mío; **to frighten the** ~ **out of sb** dar a alguien un susto de miedo; **to hurt like** ~ hacer un daño de mil demonios; **to run like** ~ correr (uno) que se las pela; **a** ~ **of a decision** una decisión muy importante; **that's a** ~ **of a way to treat your mother!** ¡qué manera de tratar a tu madre! ▶ **the road to** ~ **is paved with good intentions** *prov* el camino que lleva al infierno está lleno de buenas intenciones; **come** ~ **or high water** contra viento y marea; **to have been to** ~ **and back** haber pasado un calvario; **all** ~ **broke loose** se armó la gorda; **to catch** ~ recibir una bronca; **to do sth for the** ~ **of it** hacer algo porque sí; **to give sb** ~ (**for sth**) echar un rapapolvo a alguien (por algo), hacérselas pasar negras a alguien *AmL;* **go to** ~! *inf* (*leave me alone*) ¡déjame en paz!; (*stronger*) ¡vete a la mierda! *vulg;* **to hope to** ~ *inf* esperar fervientemente; **to have** ~ **to pay** *inf* armarse la gorda; **like** ~ *inf* y un cuerno; **what the** ~ *inf* qué más da II. *interj* (*emphasis*) ¡demonios! ▶ ~**'s bells!** ¡por Dios!; **what the** ~...! ¡qué diablos...!

he'll [hil] = **he will** *s.* **will**

hellacious [he·'leɪ·ʃəs] *adj* (*awful*) terrible
hell-bent *adj* **to be ~ on** (**doing**) **sth** estar completamente decidido a (hacer) algo
hellfire *n* fuego *m* del infierno
hellhole *n inf* antro *m*, hueco *m Col*
hellish ['hel·ɪʃ] *adj* infernal; (*experience*) horroroso, -a
hellishly *adv* endemoniadamente
hello [hə·'loʊ] I.<hellos> *n* hola *m;* **a big ~** un gran saludo II. *interj* **1.** (*greeting*) hola; **to say ~ to sb** saludar a alguien **2.** (*beginning of phone call*) diga, dígame, aló *AmC, AmS* **3.** (*to attract attention*) oiga **4.** (*surprise*) anda, ¡ey!; **~,~** pero bueno
helm [helm] *n* timón *m;* **to be at the ~** llevar el timón; *fig* (*lead*) llevar el mando; **to take the ~** (*control*) tomar el mando; *fig* llevar las riendas
helmet ['hel·mɪt] *n* casco *m;* **crash ~** casco protector
helmsman ['helmz·mən] *n* <-men> timonel *m*
help [help] I. *vi* **1.** (*assist*) ayudar **2.** (*make easier*) facilitar **3.** (*improve situation*) mejorar II. *vt* **1.** (*assist*) ayudar; **nothing can ~ him now** ya no se puede hacer nada por él; **can I ~ you?** (*in shop*) ¿en qué puedo servirle?; **to ~ sb with sth** ayudar a alguien con algo; **to ~ sb with his homework** ayudar a alguien a hacer sus deberes [*o* tareas] **2.** (*improve*) (ayudar a) mejorar; **this medicine will ~ your headache** esta medicina te aliviará el dolor de cabeza **3.** (*contribute to a condition*) contribuir [*o* ayudar] a **4.** (*prevent*) evitar; **it can't be ~ed** es así y no hay más remedio; **to not be able to ~ doing sth** no poder dejar de hacer algo; **I can't ~ it** no puedo remediarlo; **he can't ~ the way he is** él es así, ¿qué se le va hacer?; **to not be able to ~ but...** no poder menos de... **5.** (*take sth*) **to ~ oneself to sth** (*at table*) servirse algo; (*steal*) llevarse III. *n* **1.** (*assistance*) ayuda *f;* **to be a ~** ser una ayuda **2.** (*servant*) mujer *f* de la limpieza; (*in a shop*) ayudante *mf* IV. *interj* **~!** ¡socorro!; **so ~ me God** y que Dios me asista
◆**help out** *vt* ayudar
helper ['hel·pər] *n* ayudante *mf*
helpful ['help·fəl] *adj* **1.** (*willing to help*) servicial **2.** (*useful*) útil
helping ['hel·pɪŋ] I. *n* (*food*) ración *f*, porción *f AmL* II. *adj* **to give sb a ~ hand** echar una mano a alguien
helpless ['help·lɪs] *adj* indefenso, -a
helpline ['help·laɪn] *n* teléfono *m* de asistencia
helter-skelter [ˌhel·tər·'skel·tər] I. *adj* caótico, -a II. *adv* a la desbandada
hem [hem] I. *n* dobladillo *m*, basta *f AmL;* **to take the ~ up/down** meter/sacar [*o* subir/bajar] el dobladillo II. *vt* hacer el dobladillo [*o* la bastilla] a III. *vi* <-mm-> **to ~ and haw** titubear IV. *interj* ejem
◆**hem in** *vt* (*surround*) encerrar; (*constrain*) constreñir

he-man ['hi·mæn] <-men> *n inf* machote *m*
hematite ['hi·mə·taɪt] *n* MIN hematites *f inv*
hemisphere ['hem·ɪ·sfɪr] *n* hemisferio *m*
hemline ['hem·laɪn] *n* bajo(s) *m(pl)* (del vestido o la falda)
hemlock ['hem·lak] *n* cicuta *f*
hemoglobin ['hi·mə·gloʊ·bɪn] *n* hemoglobina *f*
hemophilia [ˌhi·moʊ·'fɪl·i·ə] *n* hemofilia *f*
hemophiliac [ˌhi·moʊ·'fɪl·i·æk] *n* hemofílico, -a *m, f*
hemorrhage ['hem·ər·ɪdʒ] I. *n* hemorragia *f;* **brain ~** derrame *m* cerebral II. *vi* MED tener una hemorragia
hemorrhoids ['hem·ər·ɔɪdz] *npl* hemorroides *fpl*
hemp [hemp] *n* cáñamo *m*
hen [hen] *n* (*female chicken*) gallina *f;* (*female bird*) hembra *f*
hence [hens] *adv* **1.** (*therefore*) de ahí **2.** *after n* (*from now*) dentro de; **two years ~** de aquí a dos años
henceforth [ˌhens·'fɔrθ] *adv*, **henceforward** [ˌhens·'fɔr·wərd] *adv* de ahora en adelante
henchman ['hentʃ·mən] <-men> *n* secuaz *m*
hencoop ['hen·kup] *n*, **henhouse** ['hen·haʊs] *n* gallinero *m*
henna ['hen·ə] I. *n* gena *f*, jena *f* II. *vt* tintar con gena [*o* jena]
hennery ['hen·ə·ri] *n* <-ies> gallinero *m*
henpecked ['hen·pekt] *adj* **a ~ husband** un calzonazos
HEPA ['hep·ə] *abbr of* **high-efficiency particulate arresting ~ filter** (*in vacuum cleaner*) filtro hepa
hepatitis [ˌhep·ə·'taɪ·t̬ɪs] *n* hepatitis *f inv*
heptathlon [hep·'tæθ·lan] *n* heptatlón *m*
her [hɜr] I. *adj pos* su; **~ dress/house** su vestido/casa; **~ children** sus hijos II. *pron pers* **1.** (*she*) ella; **it's ~** es ella; **older than ~** mayor que ella; **if I were ~** si yo fuese ella **2.** *direct object* la; *indirect object* le; **look at ~** mírala; **I saw ~** la vi; **he told ~ that...** le dijo que...; **he gave ~ the pencil** le dio el lápiz (a ella) **3.** *after prep* ella; **it's for/from ~** es para/de ella
herald ['her·əld] I. *vt* presagiar; **to ~ a new era** anunciar una nueva era; **the much ~ed** el tan anunciado II. *n* **1.** (*sign*) presagio *m;* **to be a ~ of sth** ser una señal de algo **2.** HIST (*bringer of news*) heraldo *m*
heraldic [hə·'ræl·dɪk] *adj* heráldico, -a
heraldry ['her·əl·dri] *n* heráldica *f*
herb [ɜrb] *n* hierba *f*
herbaceous [hər·'beɪ·ʃəs] *adj* herbáceo, -a
herbalism ['ɜr·bə·lɪz·əm] *n* fitoterapia *f*
herbalist ['ɜr·bə·lɪst] *n* herbolario, -a *m, f*, yerbatero, -a *m, f AmS*
herbal medicine *n* fitoterapia *f*, medicina *f* a base de hierbas
herbicide ['hɜr·bɪ·saɪd] *n* herbicida *m*
herbivore ['hɜr·bɪ·vɔr] *n* herbívoro *m*
herbivorous [hɜr·'bɪv·ər·əs] *adj* herbívoro, -a

Herculean [ˌhɜr·kjuˈliˑən] *adj* hercúleo, -a; ~ **task** tarea [o titánica] de romanos *f*

Hercules [ˈhɜr·kjə·liz] *n* Hércules *m inv*

herd [hɜrd] **I.** *n* + *sing/pl vb* **1.** (*of animals*) manada *f*; (*of sheep*) rebaño *f*; (*of pigs*) piara *f* **2.** (*of people*) multitud *f*; **to follow the ~** seguir a la masa **II.** *vt* (*animals*) llevar en manada; (*sheep*) guardar; **they ~ed us into the press room** nos reunieron en la sala de prensa **III.** *vi* ir en manada [o rebaño]
◆ **herd together** *vt* (*animals*) reunir en una manada [o en un rebaño]

herd instinct *n* instinto *m* gregario

herdsman [ˈhɜrdz·mən] *n* <-men> (*of cattle*) vaquero *m*; (*of sheep*) pastor *m*

here [hɪr] **I.** *adv* **1.** (*in, at, to this place*) aquí; **over ~** acá; **give it ~** *inf* dámelo; **~ and there** aquí y allá **2.** (*in introductions*) **here is...** aquí está... **3.** (*show arrival*) **they are ~** ya han llegado **4.** (*next to*) **my colleague ~** mi colega que está aquí **5.** (*now*) **where do we go from ~?** ¿dónde vamos ahora?; **~ you are, ~ you go** (*giving sth*) aquí tienes; **the ~ and now** el presente; **~ goes** *inf* allá voy; **~ we go** ya estamos otra vez **II.** *interj* (*in roll call*) ¡presente!, ¡aquí!

hereabouts [ˌhɪr·əˈbaʊts] *adv* por aquí

hereafter [hɪrˈæf·tər] **I.** *adv* en lo sucesivo **II.** *n* **the ~** el más allá

hereby [hɪrˈbaɪ] *adv form* por la presente

hereditary [həˈred·ɪ·ter·i] *adj* hereditario, -a

heredity [həˈred·ɪ·t̬i] *n* herencia *f*

herein [ˌhɪrˈɪn] *adv form* en esto

hereof [hɪrˈʌv] *adv form* de esto

heresy [ˈher·ə·si] <-ies> *n* herejía *f*

heretic [ˈher·ə·tɪk] *n* hereje *mf*

heretical [həˈret̬·ɪ·kəl] *adj* herético, -a

hereupon [ˌhɪr·əˈpan] *adv form* en ese momento

herewith [ˌhɪrˈwɪθ] *adv form* adjunto, -a

heritage [ˈher·ɪ·t̬ɪdʒ] *n* **1.** (*objects*) patrimonio *m* histórico **2.** (*tradition*) ...: patrimonio *m* cultural

hermaphrodite [hərˈmæf·roʊ·daɪt] **I.** *n* hermafrodita *mf* **II.** *adj* hermafrodita

hermetic [hərˈmet̬·ɪk] *adj* hermético, -a; ~ **seal** cierre hermético

hermit [ˈhɜr·mɪt] *n* eremita *mf*

hermitage [ˈhɜr·mɪ·t̬ɪdʒ] *n* ermita *f*

hermit crab *n* cangrejo *m* ermitaño

hernia [ˈhɜr·ni·ə] *n* MED hernia *f*

hero [ˈhɪr·oʊ] <heroes> *n* **1.** (*brave man*) héroe *m* **2.** (*main character*) protagonista *m*; **the ~ of a film** el protagonista de una película **3.** (*idol*) ídolo *m* **4.** (*sandwich*) sándwich de carne fría, queso y lechuga

heroic [hɪˈroʊ·ɪk] *adj* **1.** (*brave, bold*) heroico, -a; ~ **attempt** intento heroico; ~ **deed** hazaña *f* **2.** (*epic*) heroico, -a; ~ **verse** verso heroico

heroics *n pl* **1.** (*action*) acción *f* arriesgada **2.** (*language*) lenguaje *m* grandilocuente

heroin [ˈher·oʊ·ɪn] *n* heroína *f*

heroin addict *n* MED heroinómano, -a *m, f*

heroine [ˈher·oʊ·ɪn] *n* (*brave woman*) heroína *f*; (*of film*) protagonista *f*

heroism [ˈher·oʊ·ɪz·əm] *n* heroísmo *m*

heron [ˈher·ən] <-(s)> *n* garza *f* (real)

herpes [ˈhɜr·piz] *n* herpes *m inv*

herring [ˈher·ɪŋ] <-(s)> *n* arenque *m*

herringbone [ˈher·ɪŋ·boʊn] FASHION **I.** *n* espiga *f* **II.** *adj* de espiga

herring gull *n* gaviota *f* argéntea

hers [hɜrz] *pron pos* (el) suyo, (la) suya, (los) suyos, (las) suyas; **it's not my bag, it's ~** no es mi bolsa, es la de ella; **this house is ~** esta casa es suya; **this glass is ~** este vaso es suyo; **a book of ~** un libro suyo

herself [hɜrˈself] *pron* **1.** *reflexive* se; *after prep* sí (misma); **she lives by ~** vive sola **2.** *emphatic* ella misma; **she hurt ~** se hizo daño

hertz [hɜrts] *n inv* hercio *m*

he's [hiz] **1.** = **he is** *s.* **be 2.** = **he has** *s.* **have**

hesitant [ˈhez·ɪ·tənt] *adj* **1.** (*indecisive*) indeciso, -a; **to be ~ about doing sth** no estar decidido a hacer algo **2.** (*shy, uncertain*) vacilante

hesitantly *adv* con indecisión

hesitate [ˈhez·ɪ·teɪt] *vi* **1.** (*be indecisive*) vacilar, trepidar *AmL*; **to (not) ~ to do sth** (no) dudar en hacer algo **2.** (*be shy, uncertain*) dudar

hesitation [ˌhez·ɪˈteɪ·ʃən] *n* vacilación *f*; **without ~** sin titubear; **to have no ~ in doing sth** no tener ninguna duda en hacer algo

heterogeneous [ˌhet̬·ər·əˈdʒi·ni·əs] *adj* heterogéneo, -a

heterosexual [ˌhet̬·ə·roʊˈsek·ʃu·əl] **I.** *n* heterosexual *mf* **II.** *adj* heterosexual

hew [hju] <hewed, hewed *o* hewn> **I.** *vt* **1.** (*cut away*) extraer **2.** (*cut into shape*) to ~ **stone/wood** tallar piedra/madera **II.** *vi* (*conform*) **to ~ to sth** atenerse a algo

hewn [hjun] *pp of* **hew**

hex [heks] *n* maleficio *m*; **to put a ~ on sb/sth** hacer un maleficio a alguien/algo

hexagon [ˈhek·sə·gan] *n* hexágono *m*

hexagonal [hekˈsæg·ə·nəl] *adv* hexagonal

hexameter [hekˈsæm·ɪ·t̬ər] *n* hexámetro *m*

hey [heɪ] *interj inf* eh, oye, órale *Méx*

heyday [ˈheɪ·deɪ] *n* apogeo *m*; **in his/her/its ~** en su apogeo

hi [haɪ] *interj* hola

HI *n abbr of* **Hawaii** Hawai *m*

hiatus [haɪˈeɪ·t̬əs] <-es> *n* **1.** LING hiato *m* **2.** (*pause*) pausa *f*

hibernate [ˈhaɪ·bər·neɪt] *vi* hibernar

hibernation [ˌhaɪ·bərˈneɪ·ʃən] *n* hibernación *f*

hibiscus [hɪˈbɪs·kəs] <-es> *n* BOT hibisco *m*

hiccup, hiccough [ˈhɪk·ʌp] **I.** *n* hipo *m*; **to have the ~s** tener hipo **II.** *vi* <-p(p)-> tener hipo

hid [hɪd] *pt of* **hide**[2]

hidden [ˈhɪd·ən] **I.** *pp of* **hide**[2] **II.** *adj* (*person, thing*) escondido, -a; (*emotion, information*) oculto, -a; ~ **assets** ECON activos encubiertos; ~ **economy** economía sumergida

hide¹ [haɪd] *n* (*of an animal*) piel *f* ▶ **to see neither ~ nor** hair **of sb** no verle el pelo a alguien

hide² [haɪd] <hid, hidden> I. *vi* (*be out of sight*) esconderse, escorarse *Cuba, Hond* II. *vt* (*conceal: person, thing*) esconder; (*emotion, information*) ocultar; **to ~ one's face** taparse la cara

◆ **hide away** *vt* esconder

◆ **hide out** *vi*, **hide up** *vi* esconderse

hide-and-seek *n* escondite *m;* **to play ~** jugar al escondite

hideaway ['haɪd·ə·weɪ] *n* escondite *m*

hideous ['hɪd·i·əs] *adj* **1.** (*very unpleasant, ugly*) espantoso, -a **2.** (*terrible*) terrible

hideout ['haɪd·aʊt] *n* escondrijo *m;* **secret ~** guarida *f* secreta

hiding¹ ['haɪ·dɪŋ] *n a. fig* paliza *f;* **to get a real ~** (*defeat*) sufrir una fuerte derrota

hiding² ['haɪ·dɪŋ] *n* **to be in ~** estar escondido; **to go into ~** ocultarse

hierarchic [ˌhaɪ·'rar·kɪk] *adj*, **hierarchical** [ˌhaɪ·'rar·kɪ·kəl] *adj* jerárquico, -a

hierarchy ['haɪ·rar·ki] <-ies> *n* **1.** (*system*) jerarquía *f* **2.** (*upper levels of organization*) cúpula *f*

hieroglyph [ˌhaɪ·roʊ·'glɪf] *n* jeroglífico *m*

hieroglyphics *npl* jeroglíficos *mpl*

hi-fi ['haɪ·faɪ] I. *n abbr of* **high-fidelity** alta fidelidad *f* II. *adj abbr of* **high-fidelity** de alta fidelidad; **~ equipment** equipo *m* de alta fidelidad

higgledy-piggledy [ˌhɪg·əl·dɪ·'pɪg·əl·di] *adj inf* revuelto, -a

high [haɪ] I. *adj* **1.** (*elevated*) alto, -a; **one yard ~ and three yards wide** una yarda de alto y tres yardas de ancho; **knee/waist-~** hasta la rodilla/cintura; **to fly at ~ altitude** volar a gran altitud; **~ cheekbones** pómulos elevados; **to do a ~ dive** lanzarse desde una altura considerable **2.** (*above average*) superior; **to have ~ hopes** (**for sb/sth**) tener grandes esperanzas (puestas en alguien/algo); **to have a ~ opinion of sb** estimar mucho a alguien; **to have ~ praise** (**for sb/sth**) elogiar mucho (a alguien/algo); **of the ~est caliber** de lo mejor; **~ blood-pressure/fever** presión/ fiebre alta; **a ~ caliber gun** un arma de gran calibre **3.** (*important, eminent*) elevado, -a; **of ~ rank** de alto rango; **to have friends in ~ places** tener amigos en las altas esferas; (*regarding job*) tener enchufe; **an order from on ~** una orden que viene de arriba; **to be ~ and mighty** ser un engreído **4.** (*under influence of drugs*) colocado, -a **5.** (*of high frequency, shrill: voice*) agudo, -a; **a ~ note** una nota alta **6.** FASHION **with a ~ neckline/waistline** con escote a (la) caja **7.** (*at peak, maximum*) máximo, -a; **~ noon** mediodía *m;* **~ priority** alta prioridad ▶ **to leave sb ~ and dry** dejar a alguien colgado II. *adv* **1.** (*at or to a*

great point or height) a gran altura **2.** (*rough or strong*) con fuerza; **the sea runs ~** la mar está brava ▶ **to search for sth ~ and low** buscar algo por todas partes III. *n* **1.** (*high(est) point*) punto *m* máximo; **an all-time ~** un récord de todos los tiempos; **to reach a ~** alcanzar un nivel récord **2.** *sl* (*from drugs*) **to be on a ~** estar colocado, estar drogado **3.** (*heaven*) **on ~** en el cielo

highball *n* whisky *m* con soda

high beam *n* luces *fpl* largas

highboy *n* cómoda *f* alta

highbrow I. *adj* culto, -a II. *n* intelectual *mf*

highchair *n* silla *f* alta

high-class *adj* de clase alta

high court *n* tribunal *m* superior de justicia

high-definition television *n* televisión *f* de alta definición

high-density *adj a.* COMPUT de alta densidad; **~ disk** disco *m* de alta densidad

high-end *adj* sofisticado, -a

higher education *n* enseñanza *f* superior

higher-up *n inf* superior *m*

highfalutin [ˌhaɪ·fə·'lu·tɪn] *adj inf* presuntuoso, -a

high-fiber [ˌhaɪ·'faɪ·bər] *adj* rico, -a en fibra

high fidelity *n* alta fidelidad *f*

highflier *n* persona *f* de mucho talento

high-flown *adj* exagerado, -a; **~ ideas** ideas *fpl* altisonantes

high frequency *adj* de alta frecuencia

high-grade *adj* (*fruit, beef*) de primera calidad; (*minerals*) de alto grado (de pureza)

highhanded *adj* arbitrario, -a; (*treatment*) despótico, -a

highhandedness *n* arbitrariedad *f*

high heels *npl* tacones *mpl* altos

high horse *n* **to get** (**down**) **off one's ~** bajarse del pedestal

highjack *vt s.* **hijack**

high jinks *npl* jolgorio *m*

high jump *n* salto *m* de altura

Highlands *npl* región *f* montañosa

high-level *adj* de alto nivel

highlife *n* vida *f* de la alta sociedad; **to live the ~** vivir la buena vida

highlight I. *n* **1.** (*most interesting part*) aspecto *m* más interesante **2. ~s** (*in hair*) mechas *fpl* II. *vt* **1.** (*draw attention to*) destacar; (*a problem*) señalar **2.** (*with marker*) subrayar

highlighter *n* rotulador *m*

highly ['haɪ·li] *adv* **1.** (*very*) muy **2.** (*very well*) **to speak ~ of sb** hablar muy bien de alguien; **to think ~ of sb** tener muy buen concepto de alguien

highly-educated *adj* de nivel cultural alto

highly-skilled *adj* con grandes habilidades

High Mass [ˌhaɪ·'mæs] *n* REL misa *f* mayor

highness ['haɪ·nɪs] <-es> *n* **1.** (*level*) altura *f* **2.** (*prince or princess*) **His/Her/Your Highness** Su Alteza

high noon *n* mediodía *m*

high-octane *n* **~ gasoline** gasolina de alto

octanaje
high-performance *adj a.* AUTO de gran rendimiento
high-pitched *adj* 1.(*sloping steeply*) escarpado, -a; ~ **roof** tejado *m* pendiente 2.(*sound*) agudo, -a; **a ~ voice** una voz aguda
high point *n* **the ~** (*most successful state*) el clímax; (*of career*) la cima, la cúspide; (*most enjoyable state*) súmmum *m*
high-powered *adj* 1.(*powerful*) de gran potencia 2.(*influential, important*) poderoso, -a 3.(*advanced*) avanzado, -a
high pressure *n* METEO presión *f* alta
high-pressure I. *adj* 1.METEO **a ~ area** una zona de altas presiones 2.(*aggressive*) enérgico, -a; ~ **sales techniques** ECON técnicas de venta agresivas 3.(*stressful: job*) de mucha responsabilidad, estresante II. *vt* presionar
high priest *n* REL sumo sacerdote *m*
high priestess *n* REL sacerdotisa *f*
high-profile *adj* ilustre, prominente
high-protein *adj* rico, -a en proteínas
high-ranking *adj* de categoría
high-resolution *adj* COMPUT (*image, screen, shot*) de alta resolución
high-rise I. *adj* elevado, -a; ~ **building** edificio *m* elevado II. *n* edificio *m* elevado
high-risk *adj* de alto riesgo; (*investment*) arriesgado, -a
high school *n* instituto *m* de enseñanza secundaria (grados 9 a 12); **junior ~** instituto de enseñanza secundaria (grados 7 a 8)

> **i** El término **high school** se utilizaba antiguamente en Gran Bretaña para designar una **grammar school** (escuela secundaria de nivel superior). En EE.UU., se emplea actualmente con el significado de **secondary school** (escuela secundaria).

high seas *npl* alta mar *f*
high-security *adj* de alta seguridad
high sign *n* *inf* señal *m* convenida
high society *n* alta sociedad *f*
high-sounding *adj* altisonante
high-speed *adj* de alta velocidad
high-spirited *adj* (*cheerful, lively*) animoso, -a; (*fiery: horse*) fogoso, -a
high spirits *npl* buen humor *m*
high-strung *adj* muy excitable
high summer *n* canícula *f* del verano
hightail *sl* I. *vi* darse el piro II. *vt* **to ~ it home** largarse a casa
high-tech *adj* de alta tecnología
high technology *n* alta tecnología *f*
high-tension *adj* ELEC de alta tensión
high tide *n* 1.(*of ocean*) marea *f* alta 2.*fig* (*most successful point*) apogeo *m*
high-tops *npl* zapatos de tenis tipo bota, con suela alta de caucho
high treason *n* alta traición *f*
high-up I. *adj* importante II. *n* alto cargo *m*

high water *n* marea *f* alta
high-water mark *n* 1.(*showing water level*) línea *f* de pleamar 2.(*most successful point*) punto *m* culminante
highway ['haɪ·weɪ] *n* carretera *f*
highway patrol *n* policía *mf* de carreteras
highway robbery <-ies> *n* 1.HIST asalto *m* 2.*fig, inf* (*too expensive*) atraco *m;* **that's ~!** ¡eso es un atraco!
hijack ['haɪ·dʒæk] I. *vt* 1.(*take over by force: plane*) secuestrar un avión 2.*fig* (*adopt as one's own*) **to ~ sb's ideas/plans** hacer propias las ideas/los planes de alguien II. *n* secuestro *m*
hijacker ['haɪ·dʒæk·ər] *n* secuestrador (a) *m(f)* (aéreo)
hijacking ['haɪ·dʒæk·ɪŋ] *n* secuestro *m* (aéreo)
hike [haɪk] I. *n* 1.(*long walk*) caminata *f;* **to go on a ~** dar una caminata; **take a ~!** *sl* ¡vete al diablo! 2.(*increase*) aumento *m* II. *vi* ir de excursión (a pie) III. *vt* (*increase: prices, taxes*) aumentar
hiker ['haɪ·kər] *n* excursionista *mf*
hiking ['haɪ·kɪŋ] *n* excursionismo *m*
hilarious [hɪ·'ler·i·əs] *adj* 1.(*very funny*) divertidísimo, -a 2.(*high-spirited*) alegre
hilarity [hɪ·'ler·ə·t̬i] *n* hilaridad *f*
hill [hɪl] *n* 1.(*in landscape*) colina *f;* **the ~s** sierra 2.(*in road*) cuesta *f* 3.(*small heap*) montoncito *m* 4.POL **The Hill** Capitolio *m*, Congreso *m* ▶ **it ain't** [*o* **it's not**] **worth a ~ of beans** *sl* no merece la pena; **as old as the ~s** tan viejo como el mundo; **to be over the ~** *inf* ser demasiado viejo
hillbilly ['hɪl·bɪl·i] <-ies> *n* palurdo, -a *m, f,* montañés *m*
hillock ['hɪl·ək] *n* montículo *m*
hillside ['hɪl·saɪd] *n* ladera *f*
hilltop ['hɪl·tap] I. *n* cumbre *f* II. *adj* de la cima
hilly ['hɪl·i] <-ier, -iest> *adj* montañoso, -a
hilt [hɪlt] *n* (*of a weapon*) empuñadura *f* ▶ **to the ~** totalmente, hasta el cuello *inf;* **to be mortgaged to the ~** estar completamente hipotecado
him [hɪm] *pron pers* 1.(*he*) él; **it's ~** es él; **older than ~** mayor que él; **if I were ~** yo en su lugar 2. *direct object* lo, le; *indirect object* le; **she gave ~ the pencil** le dio el lápiz (a él) 3. *after prep* él; **it's for/from ~** es para/de él 4.(*unspecified sex*) **if somebody comes, tell ~ that...** si viene alguien, dile que...
Himalayas [ˌhɪm·ə·'leɪ·əz] *npl* el Himalaya
himself [hɪm·'self] *pron* 1. *reflexive* se; *after prep* sí (mismo); **for ~** para sí (mismo); **he lives by ~** vive solo 2. *emphatic* él mismo; **he hurt ~** se hizo daño
hind [haɪnd] I. *adj* trasero, -a II. <-(s)> *n* cierva *f*
hinder ['hɪn·dər] *vt* 1.(*obstruct*) estorbar; **to ~ progress** frenar el progreso 2.(*prevent*) **to ~ sb from doing sth** impedir a alguien hacer algo
Hindi ['hɪn·di] *n* hindi *m*

hind legs *npl* patas *fpl* traseras ▶ **to talk the ~ off a** <u>donkey</u> *inf* hablar por los codos

hindmost ['haɪnd·moʊst] *adj* **1.** (*last*) último, -a **2.** (*rear*) trasero

hindquarters ['haɪnd·ˌkwɔr·tərz] *npl* ZOOL cuartos *mpl* traseros

hindrance ['hɪn·drəns] *n* **1.** (*obstruction*) estorbo *m* **2.** (*obstacle*) obstáculo *m*; **to allow sb to enter without ~** dejar que alguien entre sin poner obstáculos

hindsight ['haɪnd·saɪt] *n* percepción *f* retrospectiva; **in ~** en retrospectiva; **with the benefit of ~** con la perspectiva del tiempo

Hindu ['hɪn·du] I. *n* hindú *mf* II. *adj* hindú

Hinduism ['hɪn·du·ɪz·əm] *n* REL hinduismo *m*

hinge [hɪndʒ] I. *n* bisagra *f* II. *vi* **to ~ on/ upon sb/sth** depender de alguien/algo

hint [hɪnt] I. *n* **1.** (*trace: of anger, suspicion*) asomo *m*, atisbo *m* **2.** (*allusion*) indirecta *f*; **to drop a ~** lanzar una indirecta; **to take a ~** pillarse una indirecta **3.** (*practical tip*) consejo *m*; **a handy ~** una indicación útil **4.** (*slight amount: of salt, curry*) pizca *f* II. *vt* **to ~ sth to sb** insinuar algo a alguien III. *vi* soltar indirectas; **to ~ at sth** hacer alusión a algo

hip [hɪp] I. *n* **1.** ANAT cadera *f*; **to stand with one's hands on (one's) ~s** ponerse en jarras **2.** BOT escaramujo *m* II. *adj sl* (*fashionable*) moderno, -a

hipbone ['hɪp·ˌboʊn] *n* hueso *m* de la cadera

hip flask *n* petaca *m*

hippie ['hɪp·i] *n* hippy *mf*

hippo ['hɪp·oʊ] *n inf abbr of* **hippopotamus** hipopótamo *m*

hippopotamus [ˌhɪp·ə·'paṭ·ə·məs] <-es *o* -mi> *n* hipopótamo *m*

hippy ['hɪp·i] <-ies> *n* hippy *mf*

hire [haɪr] I. *n* **1.** (*rental*) alquiler *m* **2.** *inf* (*hired person*) contratación *f*; **a new ~** un nuevo empleado II. *vt* **1.** (*rent*) alquilar, fletar *AmL*; **to ~ sth by the hour/day/week** alquilar algo por horas/días/semanas **2.** (*employ*) contratar, conchabar *AmL*; **to ~ more staff** ampliar la plantilla

◆**hire out** *vt* alquilar; **to ~ sth by the hour/ day/week** alquilar algo por horas/días/semanas; **to ~ oneself out as sth** trabajar de algo

hired hand *n* (*on ranch, farm*) jornalero, -a *m, f*

his [hɪz] I. *adj pos* su (de él); **~ car/house** su coche/casa; **~ children** sus hijos II. *pron pos* (el) suyo, (la) suya, (los) suyos, (las) suyas, de él; **it's not my bag, it's ~** no es mi bolsa, es la suya; **this house is ~** esta casa es suya; **this glass is ~** este vaso es suyo; **a book of ~** un libro suyo

Hispanic [hɪs·'pæn·ɪk] I. *adj* hispánico, -a II. *n* hispano, -a *m, f*

hiss [hɪs] I. *vi* **1.** (*tea kettle, crowd*) silbar; **to ~ at sb** silbar a alguien; (*theatre*) abuchear **2.** (*cat*) bufar II. *vt* silbar III. *n* silbido *m*

histamine ['hɪs·tə·min] *n* MED histamina *f*

historian [hɪ·'stɔr·i·ən] *n* historiador(a) *m(f)*

historic [hɪ·'stɔr·ɪk] *adj* histórico, -a; **this is a ~ moment...** es un momento clave...

historical *adj* histórico, -a; **the ~ present** el presente histórico

history ['hɪs·tə·ri] *n* historia *f*; **a ~ book** un libro de historia; **sb's life ~** la vida de alguien; **to make ~** hacer época; **sb's medical ~** historia médica de alguien; **to have a ~ of doing sth** tener una larga trayectora haciendo algo

histrionic [ˌhɪs·trɪ·'an·ɪk] *adj* histriónico, -a

hit [hɪt] I. *n* **1.** (*blow, stroke*) golpe *m* **2.** *inf* (*shot*) tiro *m* certero **3.** (*bomb*) impacto *m* **4.** SPORTS punto *m*; **to score a ~** marcar un tanto [*o* punto] **5.** (*success*) éxito *m* **6.** *sl* (*murder*) golpe, ataque II. <-tt-, hit, hit> *vt* **1.** (*strike*) golpear, pepenar *Méx*; **to ~ sb hard** *a. fig* pegar a alguien con fuerza **2.** (*crash into*) chocar contra; **to ~ a reef/a sandbank** dar contra un arrecife/banco de arena; **to ~ one's head on a shelf** dar con la cabeza contra un estante **3.** (*arrive at, reach target*) alcanzar **4.** (*wound*) herir; *inf* (*kill*) matar **5.** (*affect*) afectar; **to ~ sb where it hurts** dar a alguien donde más le duele **6.** (*reach*) tocar; **to ~ rock bottom** *fig* tocar fondo **7.** (*encounter*) tropezar con; **to ~ a lot of resistance/a traffic jam** encontrar mucha resistencia/un atasco **8.** *inf* (*arrive in or at*) llegar a; **to ~ 100 mph** alcanzar las 100 m/h III. *vi* **1.** (*strike*) **to ~ against sth** chocar con algo; **to ~ at sb/sth** asestar un golpe a alguien/algo **2.** (*attack*) **to ~ at sth** atacar algo

◆**hit back** *vi* devolver el golpe; **to ~ at sb** defenderse de alguien

◆**hit off** *vt* **to hit it off (with sb)** hacer buenas migas (con alguien)

◆**hit on** *vt* **1.** (*show sexual interest*) ligar con **2.** (*think of*) dar con

◆**hit out** *vi* lanzar un ataque; **to ~ at sb** asestar un golpe a alguien; *fig* tirar pullas a alguien

◆**hit up** *vi always sep* **to hit sb up for sth** sacarle algo a alguien

hit-and-run *adj* **~ accident** accidente de carretera en el que el conductor se da a la fuga; **~ attack** MIL ataque relámpago; **~ driver** conductor que se da a la fuga tras atropellar a alguien

hitch [hɪtʃ] I. <-es> *n* **1.** (*obstacle*) obstáculo *m*; **technical ~** problema *m* técnico; **to go off without a ~** salir a pedir de boca **2.** (*sudden pull*) tirón *m* **3.** (*for a trailer*) enganche *m* II. *vt* **1.** (*fasten*) atar; **to ~ sth to sth** atar algo a algo; **to ~ an animal to sth** amarrar un animal a algo **2.** *inf* (*hitchhike*) **to ~ a lift** [*o* **ride**] hacer dedo [*o* autostop] III. *vi inf* hacer dedo

◆**hitch up** *vt* **1.** (*fasten*) **to hitch sth up to sth** atar algo a algo; **to ~ an animal to sth** amarrar un animal a algo **2.** (*pull up quickly: clothes*) levantar

hitcher ['hɪtʃ·ər] *n* autostopista *mf*

hitchhike ['hɪtʃ·haɪk] *vi* hacer autostop, hacer colita *AmS*, pedir aventón *Méx*, echar dedo *Col*

H

hitchhiker ['hɪtʃ·haɪ·kər] *n* autostopista *mf*
hitch-hiking *n* autostop *m*
hi-tech [ˌhaɪ·'tek] *adj* de alta tecnología
hither ['hɪð·ər] *adv form* acá; **~ and thither** [*o* **yon**] acá y allá
hitherto [ˌhɪð·ər·'tu] *adv form* hasta ahora; **~ unpublished** no publicado por ahora
hit list *n* (*of target, murder victim*) lista *f* negra
hit man ['hɪt·mæn] <-men> *n* asesino *m* a sueldo
hit-or-miss *adj* a la buena de Dios
hit parade *n* HIST (*top forty*) lista *f* de éxitos; **to be at the top of the ~** estar en lo más alto de la lista de éxitos
HIV [ˌeɪtʃ·aɪ·'vi] *abbr of* **human immunodeficiency virus** VIH *m*
hive [haɪv] **I.** *n* **1.** (*beehive*) colmena *f* **2.** + *sing/pl vb* (*swarm of bees*) enjambre *m* **3.** (*busy place*) **to be a ~ of business** ser un punto neurálgico de negocios **II.** *vt* **to ~ sth off** (*separate*) separar algo
◆ **hive off** *vi* separarse
hives [haɪvz] *n* MED urticaria *f*
ho [hoʊ] *interj inf* (*expressing scorn, surprise*) oh; (*attracting attention*) oiga; **land ~!** NAUT ¡tierra a la vista!
hoagie ['hoʊ·gi] *n* sándwich de carne fría, queso y lechuga
hoard [hɔrd] **I.** *n* acumulación *f* **II.** *vt* acumular; (*food*) amontonar
hoarding ['hɔr·dɪŋ] *n* valla *f* de construcción
hoarfrost [ˌhɔr·'frɔst] *n* escarcha *f*
hoarse [hɔrs] *adj* ronco, -a
hoarseness *n* MED ronquera *f*; (*quality*) ronquedad *f*
hoary ['hɔr·i] <-ier, -iest> *adj* **1.** *liter* (*hair*) cano, -a **2.** *fig* (*old*) **~ old joke** chiste *m* viejo; **~ old excuse** excusa *f* de siempre
hoax [hoʊks] **I.** <-es> *n* (*joke*) broma *f* de mal gusto; (*fraud*) engaño *m* **II.** *vt* engañar
hoaxer *n* (*joker*) gracioso, -a *m, f*; (*fraudster*) embaucador(a) *m(f)*
hobble ['hab·əl] **I.** *vi* cojear; **to ~ around** ir cojeando **II.** *vt* **1.** *liter* (*hinder*) obstaculizar **2.** (*tie legs: animal*) manear
hobby ['hab·i] <-ies> *n* hobby *m*
hobbyhorse *n* **1.** (*toy*) caballito *m* **2.** (*topic*) tema *m* preferido (de conversación)
hobgoblin ['hab·gab·lɪn] *n* duende *m*
hobnailed ['hab·neɪld] *adj* con clavos; **~ boots** botas de suela claveteada
hobnob ['hab·nab] <-bb-> *vi* alternar; **to ~ with the rich and famous** codearse con los ricos y famosos
hobo ['hoʊ·boʊ] <-s *o* -es> *n* **1.** (*tramp*) vagabundo, -a *m, f* **2.** (*migrant worker*) temporero, -a *m, f*, peón *m*
hock[1] [hak] *inf* **I.** *vt* (*pawn off*) empeñar **II.** *n* **to be in ~** (*object*) estar empeñado; **my car is in ~** tengo el coche empeñado; **to be in ~** (**to sb**) (*person*) estar endeudado (con alguien)
hock[2] [hak] *n* ANAT corvejón *m*
hockey ['hak·i] *n* hockey *m;* **field ~** hockey *m*

sobre hierba; **ice ~** hockey sobre hielo
hockey stick *n* SPORTS stick *m*, palo *m* de hockey
hocus-pocus [ˌhoʊ·kəs·'poʊ·kəs] *n* camelo *m*
hodgepodge ['hadʒ·padʒ] *n* batiburrillo *m*
hoe [hoʊ] **I.** *n* azada *f* **II.** *vt* azadonar
hoedown *n* contradanza *f*
hog [hɔg] **I.** *n* **1.** (*pig*) puerco *m*, chancho *m* AmS **2.** *inf* (*person*) egoísta *mf* ▶ **to live high on the ~** *sl* vivir como un rajá **II.** <-gg-> *vt inf* (*keep for oneself*) acaparar; (*food*) devorar; **to ~ sb/sth** (**all to oneself**) acaparar a alguien/algo (para uno mismo)
hog heaven *n sl* **to be in ~** estar más contento que unas castañuelas
hogshead ['hɔgz·hed] *n* **1.** (*barrel*) pipa *f* **2.** (*measurement*) medida de capacidad de aprox. 240 litros
hogwash ['hɔg·waʃ] *n inf* (*nonsense*) monserga *f*
ho-hum ['hoʊ·hʌm] *adj inf* vano, -a, ocioso, -a
hoi polloi [ˌhɔɪ·pə·'lɔɪ] *npl* **the ~** las masas, el vulgo, el populacho
hoist [hɔɪst] *vt* (*raise up*) alzar; (*flag*) enarbolar
hoity-toity [ˌhɔɪ·t̬i·'tɔɪ·t̬i] *adj* repipi
hold [hoʊld] **I.** *n* **1.** (*grasp, grip*) agarre *m;* **to take ~ of sb/sth** asirse de [*o* a] alguien/algo; **to catch ~ of sb/sth** agarrar a alguien/algo; **to keep ~ of sth** seguir agarrado a algo **2.** (*thing to hold by*) asidero *m* **3.** (*wrestling*) presa *f*; **no ~s barred** *fig* sin restricciones **4.** (*control*) dominio *m;* **to have a** (**strong/ powerful**) **~ over sb** tener (mucha/gran) influencia sobre alguien **5.** NAUT, AVIAT bodega *f* **6.** (*delayed*) **to be on ~** estar en espera; TEL; **to put sb on** ~ poner alguien en espera **7.** (*understand*) **to get ~ of sth** comprender algo; **to have a ~ of sth** tener idea de algo; **to get ~ of the wrong idea** hacerse una idea equivocada; **I don't know where you got ~ of that idea** no sé de dónde has sacado esa idea **8.** (*prison cell*) prisión **II.** <held, held> *vt* **1.** (*keep*) tener; (*grasp*) agarrar; **to ~ a gun** sostener un arma; **to ~ hands** agarrarse de la mano; **to ~ sth in one's hand** sostener algo en la mano; **to ~ sb in one's arms** estrechar a alguien entre los brazos; **to ~ sb/sth** (**tight**) sujetar a alguien/algo (con fuerza); **to ~ the door open for sb** aguantar la puerta abierta a alguien **2.** (*support*) soportar; **to ~ one's head high** mantener la cabeza alta **3.** (*cover up*) **to ~ one's ears/nose** taparse los oídos/la nariz **4.** (*keep, retain*) mantener; **to ~ sb's attention/interest** mantener la atención/el interés de alguien; **to ~ sb in custody** LAW mantener detenido a alguien; **to ~ sb hostage** retener a alguien como rehén; **to ~ (on to) the lead** llevar la antorcha, seguir por delante **5.** (*maintain*) **to ~ oneself in readiness** estar listo; **to ~ oneself well** mantenerse en forma **6.** (*make keep to*) **to ~ sb to his/her word** [*o* **promise**] hacer cumplir a alguien su palabra **7.** (*control*) **to ~ sth at the present/last year's**

level mantener algo al nivel actual/del año pasado; **to ~ a note** MUS sostener una nota **8.** (*delay, stop*) detener; **~ it!** ¡para!; **to ~ one's breath** contener la respiración; **to ~ one's fire** MIL detener el fuego; **to ~ sb's phone calls** TEL retener las llamadas de alguien **9.** (*contain*) contener; **it ~s many surprises** conlleva muchas sorpresas; **what the future ~s** lo que depara el futuro **10.** (*possess, own*) poseer; (*land, town*) ocupar; **to ~ an account** (**with a bank**) tener una cuenta (en un banco); **to ~ the** (**absolute**) **majority** contar con la mayoría (absoluta); **to ~ a position** (**as sth**) mantener un puesto (como algo); **to ~** (**down**) **the fort** MIL quedarse al cargo; *fig* hacerse cargo de **11.** (*make happen*) **to ~ a conversation** (**with sb**) mantener una conversación (con alguien); **to ~ an election/a meeting/a news conference** convocar elecciones/una reunión/una rueda de prensa; **to ~ maneuvers** MIL estar de maniobras; **to ~ talks** dar charlas **12.** (*believe*) creer; **to be held in great respect** ser muy respetado; **to ~ sb responsible for sth** considerar a alguien responsable de algo; **to ~ sb/sth in contempt** despreciar alguien/algo **III.** *vi* **1.** (*continue*) seguir; **to ~ still** pararse; **to ~ true** seguir siendo válido; **~ tight!** ¡quieto! **2.** (*stick*) pegarse **3.** (*believe*) sostener
♦**hold against** *vt always sep* **to hold sth against sb** hacerse una mala idea de alguien por algo
♦**hold back I.** *vt* (*keep*) retener; **to ~ information** ocultar información; (*stop*) detener; (*impede development*) parar; **to ~ tears** contener las lágrimas ▸ **there's no holding me back** nada me retiene **II.** *vi* **1.** (*be unforthcoming*) refrenarse **2.** (*refrain*) **to ~ from doing sth** abstenerse de hacer algo
♦**hold down** *vt* sujetar; (*control, suppress*) oprimir; **to ~ a job** mantener un trabajo
♦**hold forth** *vi* **to ~** (**about sth**) explayarse acerca de algo
♦**hold in** *vt* (*emotion*) contener
♦**hold off I.** *vt* (*enemy*) detener; (*reporters*) dar largas a **II.** *vi* mantenerse a distancia; (*wait*) esperar, posponer
♦**hold on** *vi* **1.** (*attach*) agarrarse bien; **to be held on by/with sth** estar sujeto a/con algo **2.** (*manage to keep going*) **to ~** (**tight**) aguantar **3.** (*wait*) esperar
♦**hold onto** *vt insep* **1.** (*grasp*) agarrarse bien a **2.** (*keep*) guardar
♦**hold out I.** *vt* extender **II.** *vi* **1.** (*offer, chance*) ofrecer **2.** (*manage to resist*) resistir; **to be unable to ~** no poder aguantar; **to ~ for sth** resistir hasta conseguir algo **3.** (*refuse to give sth*) **to ~ on sb** no acceder a los deseos de alguien
♦**hold over** *vt* **1.** (*defer*) aplazar **2.** (*extend*) alargar
♦**hold to** *vt insep* atenerse a
♦**hold together I.** *vi* mantenerse unidos; **to**

be held together with glue mantenerse pegados **II.** *vt* mantener unidos
♦**hold up I.** *vt* **1.** (*raise*) levantar; **to ~ one's hand** levantar la mano; **to be held up by** (**means of**)/**with sth** ser sostenido por (mediante)/con algo; **to hold one's head up high** *fig* mantener la cabeza alta **2.** (*delay*) atrasar **3.** (*rob with violence*) atracar **4.** (*offer as example*) **to hold sb up as an example of sth** mostrar a alguien como ejemplo de algo **II.** *vi* (*weather*) seguir bueno; (*material*) durar
♦**hold with** *vt insep* estar de acuerdo con
holdall ['hoʊld·ɔl] *n* bolsa *f* de viaje
holder ['hoʊl·dər] *n* **1.** (*device*) soporte *m*; **cigarette ~** boquilla *f* **2.** (*person: of shares, of account*) titular *mf*; (*of title*) poseedor(a) *m(f)*; **world record ~** plusmarquista *mf* mundial
holding *n* **1.** (*property*) propiedades *fpl*. **~s** (*tenure*) tenencia *f* **3.** ECON participación *f*; **~s** valores *mpl* en cartera
holding company *n* holding *m*
holdup ['hoʊld·ʌp] *n* **1.** (*robbery*) atraco *m* **2.** (*delay*) retraso *m*
hole [hoʊl] **I.** *n* **1.** (*hollow space*) agujero *m*; *fig* (*in an argument, sb's reasoning*) laguna *f*; vacío *m* **2.** (*in golf*) hoyo *m* **3.** (*of mouse*) ratonera *f*; (*of rabbit*) madriguera *f* **4.** *inf* (*jam*) apuro *m*; **to be in a ~** estar en un apuro [o aprieto] ▸ **to be a round peg in a square ~** estar fuera de lugar; **to be in the ~** estar endeudado **II.** *vt* **1.** (*perforate*) agujerear **2.** (*in golf*) embocar, hacer un hoyo
♦**hole up** *vi inf* esconderse
holiday ['hɑl·ɪ·deɪ] *n* (*public day off*) día *m* festivo ▸ **a busman's ~** día de fiesta que uno pasa trabajando
holiday resort *n* centro *m* turístico
holiness ['hoʊ·lɪ·nɪs] *n* santidad *f*; **His/Your Holiness** Su Santidad
holism ['hoʊ·lɪz·əm] *n* holismo *m*
holistic [hoʊ·'lɪs·tɪk] *adj* holístico, -a
Holland ['hɑl·ənd] *n* Holanda *f*
holler ['hɑl·ər] **I.** *vi* (*yell*) gritar, chillar **II.** *n inf* chillido *m*
hollow ['hɑl·oʊ] **I.** *adj* **1.** (*empty*) hueco, -a **2.** (*worthless, empty: promise*) vano, -a; (*victory*) vacío, -a; (*laughter*) falso, -a **3.** (*sound*) sordo, -a **II.** *n* hueco *m*; (*valley*) hondonada *f* **III.** *vt* **to ~** (**out**) (*pumpkin*) vaciar; (*tree trunk*) ahuecar **IV.** *vi* (*become hollow: tree*) ahuecarse
holly ['hɑl·i] *n* BOT acebo *m*
hollyhock ['hɑl·ɪ·hɑk] *n* BOT malvarrosa *f*
holocaust ['hɑl·ə·kɔst] *n* holocausto *m*
hologram ['hɑl·ə·græm] *n* holograma *m*
holster ['hoʊl·stər] *n* pistolera *f*, cañonera *f* AmL
holy ['hoʊ·li] <-ier, -iest> *adj* **1.** (*sacred*) santo, -a; (*water*) bendito, -a **2.** *fig* **to be a ~ terror** ser el mismísimo demonio
Holy Communion *n* Sagrada Comunión *f*
Holy Father *n* Santo Padre *m*
Holy Ghost *n* Espíritu *m* Santo

Holy Scripture *n* the ~ las Sagradas Escrituras
Holy See *n* Santa Sede *f*
Holy Spirit *n* Espíritu *m* Santo
Holy Week *n* Semana *f* Santa
homage ['ham·ɪdʒ] *n* homenaje *m;* **to pay ~ to sb** rendir homenaje a alguien
home [hoʊm] **I.** *n* **1.** (*residence*) casa *f;* **at ~** en casa; **to leave ~** salir [*o* irse] de casa; **away from ~** fuera de casa; **I live in Seattle but my ~ is in Vera Cruz** vivo en Seattle pero soy de Vera Cruz; **make yourself at ~** ponte cómodo, estás en tu casa **2.** (*family*) hogar *m* **3.** (*institution*) asilo *m;* (*for old people*) residencia *f;* **children's ~** orfanato *m* **II.** *adv* **1.** (*one's place of residence*) **to be ~** estar en casa; **to go/come ~** ir/venir a casa; **to take work ~** llevarse trabajo a casa **2.** (*understanding*) **to bring sth ~ to sb** conseguir que alguien se dé cuenta de algo; **to hit ~** causar impacto, dar en el blanco ▸ **to be ~ free** tener la victoria asegurada; **this is nothing to write ~ about** esto no es nada del otro mundo **III.** *adj* **1.** (*from own country*) nacional **2.** (*from own area*) local; (*team*) de casa; (*game*) en casa; **the ~ ground** el campo de casa
◆**home in on** *vt insep, inf* **1.** MIL apuntar **2.** (*locate*) localizar y dirigirse hacia
home address *n* dirección *f* particular, domicilio *m*
home banking *n* telebanking *m*
homebody *n* persona *f* hogareña
homeboy *n sl* (*from same neighborhood*) paisano *m;* (*from same gang*) compinche *mf*
homebrew *n* cerveza hecha en casa
homecoming *n* regreso *m* (a casa)

> ℹ️ El término **Homecoming** se utiliza en EE.UU. para referirse a una importante fiesta que se celebra en la **high school** (escuela secundaria) y en la universidad. Con ocasión de las festividades, el equipo de **football** local juega en su propio campo. Por la noche se celebra una fiesta formal, presidida por la **Homecoming queen** y el **Homecoming king** (reyes de la simpatía).

home computer *n* ordenador [*o* computador]*m* doméstico
home cooking *n* cocina *f* casera
home ec *n inf,* **home economics** *n + sing vb* economía *f* doméstica
home-equity loan *n* FIN crédito *m* hipotecario
home fries *npl* CULIN papas *fpl* fritas
homegirl *n sl* (*from same neighborhood*) paisana *f;* (*from same gang*) compinche *mf*
homegrown *adj* **1.** (*vegetables*) de cosecha propia **2.** (*not foreign*) del país **3.** (*local*) local
home-helper *n* asistente, -a *m, f* (para las tareas domésticas)
homeland *n* (*country of birth*) tierra *f* natal; (*of*

cultural heritage) patria *f*
Homeland Security *n* Departamento *m* de Seguridad
homeless I. *adj* sin hogar **II.** *n + pl vb* **the ~** los sin techo
homelike *adj* hogareño, -a
homely ['hoʊm·li] <-ier, -iest> *adj* **1.** (*ugly*) feúcho, -a **2.** (*simple*) sencillo, -a **3.** (*domestic*) casero, -a, doméstico, -a
homemade *adj* casero, -a
homemaker *n* ama *f* de casa
homeopath ['hoʊ·mi·oʊ·pæθ] *n* homeópata *mf*
homeopathic [ˌhoʊ·mi·oʊ·'pæθ·ɪk] *adj* homeopático, -a
homeopathy [ˌhoʊ·mi·'ap·ə·θi] *n* homeopatía *f*
homeowner ['hoʊm·ˌoʊ·nər] *n* propietario, -a *m, f*
homepage *n* página *f* inicial, portal *m*
home plate *n* SPORTS base *f* del bateador
homeroom *n* SCHOOL (*in high school*) salón donde cada alumno debe presentarse todas las mañanas
home rule *n* gobierno *m* autónomo
homeschool *vt* impartir enseñanza doméstica
homesick ['hoʊm·sɪk] *adj* nostálgico, -a; **to feel ~** (**for**) tener morriña (de)
homesickness *n* morriña *f*
homespun ['hoʊm·spʌn] *adj* de entrecasa; (*wisdom*) popular
homestead *n* finca *f*
homestretch <-es> *n* recta *f* final
home team *n* equipo *m* local [*o* de casa]
hometown *n* ciudad *f* natal, pueblo *m* natal
home truth *n* **to tell sb a few ~s** decir a alguien unas cuantas verdades
home video *n* video *m* doméstico [*o* casero]
homeward ['hoʊm·wərd] **I.** *adv* de camino a casa **II.** *adj* (*journey*) de regreso
homewards *adv s.* **homeward I.**
homework ['hoʊm·wɜrk] *n* SCHOOL deberes *mpl,* tareas *fpl* Col
homey ['hoʊ·mi] <-ier, -iest> *adj* **1.** (*cozy*) casero, -a **2.** *sl* (*home boy or girl*) paisano, -a
homicidal [ˌham·ə·'saɪ·dəl] *adj* LAW homicida
homicide ['ham·ə·saɪd] **I.** *n* **1.** (*crime*) homicidio *m* **2.** (*criminal*) homicida *mf* **II.** *adj* **~ squad** brigada *f* de homicidios
homing ['hoʊ·mɪŋ] *adj* (*instinct*) de volver al hogar; (*device*) buscador(a)
homing pigeon *n* paloma *f* mensajera
hominy grits [ˌham·ə·ni·'grɪts] *npl* gachas *f* de sémola de maíz
homogeneous *adj,* **homogenous** [ˌhoʊ·moʊ·'dʒi·ni·əs] *adj* homogéneo, -a
homogenize [hə·'madʒ·ə·naɪz] *vt* homogeneizar
homograph ['ham·ə·græf] *n* homógrafo *m*
homonym ['ham·ə·nɪm] *n* homónimo *m*
homophobia [ˌhoʊ·mə·'foʊ·bi·ə] *n* homofobia *f*
homophone ['ham·ə·foʊn] *n* homófono *m*

homosexual [ˌhoʊ·mə·ˈsek·ʃu·əl] I. *adj* homosexual II. *n* homosexual *mf*

homosexuality [ˌhoʊ·moʊ·sek·ʃu·ˈæl·ə·t̬i] *n* homosexualidad *f*

Hon. 1. *abbr of* **Honorable** (*title for high government officials*) Honorable, el señor(ora)... **2.** *abbr of* **Honorary** Hon.

Honduran [han·ˈdʊr·ən] I. *adj* hondureño, -a II. *n* hondureño, -a *m, f*

Honduras [han·ˈdʊr·əs] *n* Honduras *f*

hone [hoʊn] *vt* (*sharpen*) afilar; *fig* (*refine*) afinar

◆**hone in on** *vt* **1.** (*move toward target*) dirigirse a **2.** (*focus on*) concentrarse en

honest [ˈan·ɪst] *adj* **1.** (*trustworthy*) honesto, -a **2.** (*truthful*) sincero, -a; **to be ~ with oneself** ser sincero consigo mismo; **~** (**to God**) *inf* como Dios manda **3.** (*fair: wages, day's work*) justo, -a, equitativo, -a

honestly *adv* (*truthfully*) sinceramente; (*with honesty*) honradamente

honest-to-goodness *adj* como Dios manda

honesty [ˈan·ɪ·sti] *n* **1.** (*trustworthiness*) honestidad *f* **2.** (*sincerity*) sinceridad *f;* **in all ~** para ser sincero

honey [ˈhʌn·i] *n* **1.** CULIN miel *f* **2.** (*term of endearment*) cariño *m* **3.** (*sweet person*) encanto *m;* (*sweet thing*) preciosidad *f*

honeybee *n* abeja *f*

honeycomb I. *n* panal *m* II. *adj* (*pattern*) de panal

honeydew (**melon**) *n* melón *m* dulce

honeymoon I. *n* luna *f* de miel II. *vi* pasar la luna de miel

honeysuckle *n* BOT madreselva *f*

honk [haŋk] I. *vi* **1.** ZOOL graznar **2.** AUTO tocar la bocina [*o* el pito *Col*] II. *n* **1.** ZOOL graznido *m* **2.** AUTO bocinazo *m* [*o* pitazo] *m Col*

honor [ˈan·ər] I. *n* **1.** (*respect*) honor *m;* **in ~ of sb/sth** en honor de alguien/algo; **to be** (**in**) **~ bound to...** estar moralmente obligado a... **2.** LAW **Her/His/Your Honor** Su Señoría **3. ~s** (*distinction*) honores *mpl;* **final ~s** honras *fpl* fúnebres; **to graduate with ~s** licenciarse [*o* graduarse] con matrícula de honor II. *vt* **1.** (*fulfill: promise, contract*) cumplir (con) **2.** (*confer honor*) honrar; **to be ~ed** sentirse honrado

honorable *adj* **1.** (*worthy of respect: person*) honorable; (*agreement*) honroso, -a **2.** (*honest*) honrado, -a **3.** LAW **the Honorable John Thompson, Judge of the District Court** el Honorable Juez Thompson, juez de la Corte del Distrito

honorary [ˈan·ə·rer·i] *adj* **1.** (*conferred as an honor: title*) honorario, -a; (*president*) de honor **2.** (*without pay*) no remunerado, -a

honor roll *n* UNIV, SCHOOL lista *f* de honor académica

⎢**i**⎥ Los nombres de los escolares y estudiantes que obtienen notas especialmente buenas aparecen en las publicaciones de los centros

de estudio y a veces también en la prensa local. Esta lista se conoce como **honor roll** o, especialmente en las universidades, como **dean's list**. Quienes aparecen en dichas listas reciben a menudo un trato preferente por parte de las universidades cuando solicitan un puesto de estudios o por las empresas a la hora de buscar trabajo.

hood¹ [hʊd] *n* **1.** (*covering for head*) capucha *f* **2.** AUTO capó *m* **3.** (*on machine*) cubierta *f;* (*on cooker*) campana *f*

hood² [hʊd] *n* **1.** *sl* (*gangster*) matón, -ona *m, f* **2.** *sl* (*urban neighborhood*) barrio *m*

hoodlum [ˈhʊd·ləm] *n* matón, -ona *m, f*

hoodwink [ˈhʊd·wɪŋk] *vt* (*deceive*) engañar, emplumar *Guat, Cuba*

hoof [hʊf] I.<hooves *o* hoofs> *n* casco *m,* pezuña *f;* **on the ~** (*cattle*) en pie II. *vt sl* **to ~ it** ir a pata

hoo-ha [ˈhu·ha] *n sl* jaleo *m*

hook [hʊk] I. *n* **1.** (*for holding sth*) gancho *m;* (*for clothes*) percha *f;* (*fish*) anzuelo *m;* **to leave the phone off the ~** dejar el teléfono descolgado **2.** (*in boxing*) gancho *m* ▸ **by ~ or by crook** por las buenas o por las malas; **to fall for sth ~, line and sinker** tragárselo [*o* creérselo] todo; **to be off the ~** librarse; **to get one's ~ into sb** tener a alguien en las garras (de uno) II. *vt* **1.** (*fasten*) enganchar **2.** (*fish*) pescar **3.** (*capture attention*) atraer, atrapar III. *vi* (*clothes*) abrocharse (con corchetes o ganchitos); (*parts*) engancharse

◆**hook on** I. *vi* conectarse II. *vt* enganchar

◆**hook up** I. *vt* **1.** (*hang: curtains*) poner **2.** (*link up*) enganchar; (*connect*) conectar; **to hook sb up with sb** *sl* (*arrange date*) reunirse con alguien II. *vi* **1.** (*connect*) conectarse **2.** (*clothes*) abrocharse

hooked [hʊkt] *adj* **1.** (*nose*) ganchudo, -a **2.** (*fascinated*) atrapado, -a **3.** (*addicted*) enganchado, -a

hooker [ˈhʊk·ər] *n sl* (*prostitute*) prostituta *f,* puta *f*

hooky [ˈhʊk·i] *n inf* **to play ~** hacer novillos, capar clase *Col*

hooligan [ˈhu·lɪ·gən] *n* hooligan *mf,* vándalo *m*

hooliganism *n* hooliganismo *m,* gamberrismo *m*

hoop [hup] *n* aro *m; sl* (*in basketball*); **to shoot some ~s** echar unos tiros ▸ **to put sb through the ~s** hacérselas pasar negras a alguien

hoot [hut] I. *vi* (*owl*) ulular; (*with horn*) tocar la bocina [*o* el pito]; **to ~ with laughter** desternillarse de risa II. *vt* **to ~ sb** tocar la bocina [*o* pitar] a alguien III. *n* (*of owl*) ululato *m;* (*factory whistle*) sirena *f;* (*of horn*) bocinazo *m;* (*of train*) pitido *m;* **to give a ~ of laughter** soltar una carcajada; **to give a ~ of disgust** dar

H

un grito de repugnancia; **to not give a ~ (about sth)** importar algo un pito a alguien ▶**to be a [real]** ~ *inf*ser para morirse de risa ◆**hoot down** *vt* abuchear

hop¹ [hap] *n* BOT lúpulo *m*

hop² [hap] <-pp-> **I.** *vi* **1.** (*on 1 foot*) saltar; *fig;* **to ~ to it** ponerse manos a la obra **2.** *inf* (*be busy*) **to be ~ping** (*city streets, restaurant*) tener mucho ajetreo [*o* movimiento] **II.** *vt inf* (*bus, train*) subir a **III.** *n* **1.** (*leap*) salto *m;* (*using only one leg*) salto *m* a la pata coja, brinco *m* de cojito *Méx* **2.** *inf* (*informal dance*) baile *m* **3.** (*short flight*) vuelo *m* corto ▶**a ~, skip and a jump** *inf*un salto, estar a un paso ◆**hop around** *vi* saltar; **to ~ from one subject to another** saltar de un tema a otro ◆**hop in** *vt insep* pillar; **to ~ a taxi** *inf*pillar un taxi ◆**hop out** *vi* bajar (de un salto); **to ~ of bed** saltar de la cama

hope [houp] **I.** *n* esperanza *f;* **to give up ~** perder la(s) esperanza(s); **to pin all one's ~s on sb/sth** poner todas las esperanzas en alguien/algo; **there is still ~** todavía hay esperanzas ▶**to not have a ~ in hell** no tener ni la más remota posibilidad; **to hope against ~** perder la esperanza **II.** *vi* (*wish*) esperar; **to ~ for the best** esperar que la suerte lo acompañe a uno

hopeful ['houp·fəl] **I.** *adj* **1.** (*person*) esperanzado, -a; **to be ~** ser optimista **2.** (*promising*) esperanzador(a) **II.** *n* candidato, -a *m, f;* **young ~s** jóvenes aspirantes *mfpl*

hopefully *adv* **1.** (*in a hopeful manner*) con ilusión **2.** (*one hopes*) **~!** ¡ojalá!; **~ we'll be in Sweden at 6.00 P.M.** si todo sale bien estaremos en Suecia a las 6 de la tarde

hopeless ['houp·lɪs] *adj* (*situation*) desesperado, -a; (*effort*) imposible; **to be ~** *inf* (*person*) ser inútil; (*service*) ser un desastre; **to be ~ at sth** ser negado para algo

hopelessly *adv* **1.** (*without hope*) sin esperanzas **2.** (*totally, completely*) **~ lost** totalmente perdido

hopper ['hap·ər] *n* tolva *f*

hopping mad *adj* furioso, -a; **he is ~** está que trina

hopscotch ['hap·skatʃ] *n* **to play ~** jugar a la rayuela

horde [hɔrd] *n* multitud *f*, horda *f*

horizon [hə·'raɪ·zən] *n a. fig* horizonte *m*

horizontal [ˌhɔr·ɪ·'zan·təl] **I.** *adj* horizontal **II.** *n* horizontal *f*

hormone ['hɔr·moun] *n* hormona *f*

horn [hɔrn] *n* **1.** ZOOL cuerno *m* **2.** MUS trompa *f* **3.** AUTO bocina *f* **4.** (*material*) cuerno *m* ▶**to be on the ~s of a dilemma** estar entre la espada y la pared; **to draw in one's ~s** apretarse el cinturón; **to lock ~s** (*over sth*) tener un enfrentamiento (por algo); **to toot** [*o* **blow**] **one's own ~** echarse flores ◆**horn in** *vi* **to ~ on sth** entrometerse en algo

hornet ['hɔr·nɪt] *n* avispón *m*

horn-rimmed *adj* (*glasses*) de concha

horny ['hɔr·ni] <-ier, -iest> *adj* **1.** (*made of horn*) córneo, -a **2.** *vulg* (*sexually aroused*) cachondo, -a, arrecho, -a *Col*

horoscope ['hɔr·ə·skoup] *n* horóscopo *m*

horrendous [hə·'ren·dəs] *adj* **1.** (*crime*) horrendo, -a **2.** (*losses*) terrible

horrible ['hɔr·ə·bəl] *adj* horrible

horrid ['hɔr·ɪd] *adj* (*unpleasant*) horrible; (*unkind*) antipático, -a

horrific [hə·'rɪf·ɪk] *adj* horroroso, -a

horrify ['hɔr·ə·faɪ] <-ie-> *vt* horrorizar

horror ['hɔr·ər] *n* horror *m*, espantosidad *f AmC, Col, PRico;* **~ film** película *f* de terror

horror-stricken *adj*, **horror-struck** *adj* horrorizado, -a

hors d'œuvre [ɔr·'dɜrv] <hors d'œuvre *o* hors d'œvres> *n* CULIN entremés *m*, entremeses *mpl*

horse [hɔrs] *n* **1.** ZOOL caballo *m; to ride a ~** montar a caballo; **to eat like a ~** comer como una lima [*o* un caballo] **2.** SPORTS potro *m* ▶**to change ~s** (**in**) **midstream** cambiar de parecer a mitad de camino; **to get sth straight from the ~'s mouth** saber algo de buena tinta; **don't look a gift ~ in the mouth** *prov*a caballo regalado, no le mires el dentado *prov;* **you can take a ~ to water but you can't make him drink** *prov* puedes darle un consejo a alguien, pero no puedes obligarlo a que lo siga; **to flog a dead ~** perder el tiempo (intentando algo), arar en el mar; **to be on one's high ~** *inf* tener muchos humos; **to hold one's ~s** *inf* parar el carro; **hold your ~s!** *inf*¡espera un minuto!, ¡no te aceleres! ◆**horse around** *vi* hacer el tonto

horseback ['hɔrs·bæk] **I.** *n* **on ~** a caballo **II.** *adj* **~ riding** equitación *f*

horse chestnut *n* (*tree*) castaño *m* de Indias; (*nut*) castaña *f* de Indias

horse-drawn *adj* tirado, -a por caballos

horsefly <-ies> *n* tábano *m*

horsehair *n* crin *f*

horseman ['hɔrs·mən] <-men> *n* jinete *m*

horsemanship *n* equitación *f*

horseplay ['hɔrs·pleɪ] *n* jugueteo(s) *m(pl)*

horsepower *inv n* caballo (*m* de vapor)

horserace *n* carrera *f* de caballos

horseracing *n* carreras *fpl* de caballos

horseradish *n* rábano *m* picante

horse sense *n inf*sentido *m* común

horseshoe *n* herradura *f*

horse-trading *n* tira *m* y afloja

horse van *n* remolque *m* para transportar caballos

horsewhip ['hɔrs·wɪp] **I.** <-pp-> *vt* dar latigazos a **II.** *n* látigo *m*

horsewoman ['hɔrs·wʊm·ən] <-women> *n* amazona *f*

hors(e)y ['hɔr·si] <-ier, -iest> *adj* **1.** (*interested in horses*) aficionado, -a a los caballos **2.** (*like a horse: face*) de caballo

horticultural [ˌhɔr·tə·'kʌl·tʃər·əl] *adj* hortícola

horticulture ['hɔr·tə·ˌkʌl·tʃər] *n* horticultura *f*
hose [hoʊz] *n* **1.** (*in garden*) manguera *f* **2.** (*in motor*) manguera *f* **3.** (*pantyhose*) medias *fpl* pantalón [*o* de nylon *Méx*] [*o* veladas *Col*]
hosiery ['hoʊ·zə·ri] *n* (*shop*) calcetería *f;* (*goods*) medias *fpl* y calcetines
hospice ['has·pɪs] *n* **1.** (*hospital*) residencia *f* para enfermos terminales **2.** (*house of shelter*) hospicio *m*
hospitable ['has·pɪ·tə·bəl] *adj* hospitalario, -a
hospital ['has·pɪ·təl] *n* hospital *m*
hospitality [ˌhas·pɪ·'tæl·ə·ti] *n* hospitalidad *f*
hospitalization [ˌhas·pɪ·tə·lɪ·'zeɪ·ʃən] *n* hospitalización *f*
hospitalize ['has·pɪ·tə·laɪz] *vt* hospitalizar
host¹ [hoʊst] **I.** *n* **1.** (*person who receives guests*) anfitrión, -ona *m, f* **2.** (*presenter*) presentador(a) *m(f)* **3.** BIO huésped *m* **4.** COMPUT servidor *m* **II.** *vt* **1.** (*party*) dar; (*event*) ser la sede de **2.** TV, RADIO (*program*) presentar
host² [hoʊst] *n* multitud *f;* **a whole ~ of reasons** muchas razones
Host [hoʊst] *n* REL hostia *f*
hostage ['has·tɪdʒ] *n* rehén *mf;* **to take/hold sb ~** tomar/tener a alguien como rehén
host country <-ies> *n* país *m* anfitrión
hostel ['has·təl] *n* (*inexpensive hotel*) hostal *m;* **student ~** residencia *f* de estudiantes; **youth ~** albergue *m* juvenil
hosteler ['has·tə·lər] *n* alberguista *mf*
hostess ['hoʊ·stɪs] <-es> *n* **1.** (*woman who receives guests*) anfitriona *f* **2.** (*presenter*) presentadora *f* **3.** (*in restaurant*) mesonera *f*
hostile ['has·təl] *adj* hostil; **~ aircraft** avión enemigo
hostility [ha·'stɪl·ə·ti] <-ies> *n* hostilidad *f*
hot [hat] **I.** *adj* **1.** (*very warm: food, water*) caliente; (*day, weather*) caluroso, -a; (*climate*) cálido, -a; **it's ~** hace calor **2.** (*spicy*) picante, bravo, -a *AmL* **3.** *inf* (*skillful*) hábil; **to be ~ stuff** ser cosa fina **4.** *inf* (*demanding*) estricto, -a; **to be ~ for sth** dar mucha importancia a algo **5.** (*dangerous*) peligroso, -a; **to be too ~ to handle** *fig* ser demasiado difícil de manejar **6.** *sl* (*sexually attractive*) **to be ~** estar bueno **7.** (*exciting: music, party*) animado, -a; **~ news** noticias frescas **8.** *sl* (*stolen*) robado, -a ▸ **to be all ~ and bothered** estar sulfurado **II.** *n* **to have the ~s for sb** estar interesado (sentimentalmente) en alguien
◆ **hot up** <-tt-> *vi sl* (*situation*) calentarse
hot air *n fig* palabras *fpl* huecas; **to be full of ~** ser sólo palabrería
hot-air balloon *n* globo *m* de aire caliente
hotbed ['hat·bed] *n fig* (*of vice, disease, crime*) caldo *m* de cultivo
hot-blooded *n* (*easy to anger*) irascible; (*passionate*) apasionado, -a
hotcake *n* panqueque *m;* **to sell like ~s** se vende como pan caliente
hot dog *n* CULIN perrito *m* caliente, pancho *m* *Arg*
hotel [hoʊ·'tel] *n* hotel *m*

hotel accommodations *npl* alojamiento *m*
hotel bill *n* factura *f* del hotel
hotelier [ˌhoʊ·tel·'jeɪ] *n* (*owner*) hotelero, -a *m, f;* (*manager*) director (a) *m(f)* del hotel
hotel industry *n* industria *f* hotelera
hotel staff *n* personal *m* del hotel
hotfoot ['hat·fʊt] **I.** *adv* a toda prisa **II.** *vt* **to ~ it somewhere** *inf* ir volando a algún sitio
hothead ['hat·hed] *n* persona *f* alocada
hotheaded *adj* impulsivo, -a
hothouse ['hat·haʊs] **I.** *n* invernadero *m* **II.** *adj* de invernadero
hot line *n* TEL línea *f* directa
hotly *adv* apasionadamente
hot metal *n* TYPO fundición *f*
hot plate *n* hornillo *m*
hot potato <-oes> *n fig* patata *f* caliente
hot rod *n sl* AUTO coche *m* trucado
hot seat *n* **1.** (*difficult position*) **to be in the ~** estar en la línea de fuego **2.** (*electric chair*) silla *f* eléctrica
hotshot *n sl* hacha *f;* **to be a (real) ~ at sth** *fig* ser un as en algo
hot spot *n inf* **1.** (*popular place*) lugar *m* concurrido **2.** (*nightclub*) club *m* nocturno
hot stuff *n* **1.** (*good*) **to be ~ at sth** ser un as en algo **2.** (*sexy*) **to be ~** estar bueno
hot-tempered *adj* irascible
hot-water bottle *n* bolsa *f* de agua caliente
hound [haʊnd] **I.** *n* perro *m* de caza **II.** *vt* perseguir
hour [aʊr] *n* **1.** (*60 minutes*) hora *f;* **to be paid by the ~** cobrar por horas **2.** (*time of day*) **at all ~s of the day and night** noche y día; **ten minutes to the ~** diez minutos para en punto; **till all ~s** hasta [*o* las tantas] muy tarde; **after ~s** fuera del horario establecido **3.** (*time for an activity*) **lunch ~** hora de comer [*o* almorzar]; **at the agreed ~** a la hora convenida; **opening ~s** horario *m* (comercial) **4.** (*period of time*) momento *m;* **at any ~** en cualquier momento; **to spend long ~s doing sth** pasarse mucho tiempo haciendo algo; **to change from ~ to ~** cambiar cada hora; **to keep irregular/regular ~s** llevar un horario variable/regular; **to work long ~s** trabajar hasta muy tarde; **~ after ~** hora tras hora; **sb's ~ of need** la hora de la necesidad de alguien
hour hand *n* manecilla *f*
hourly *adv* (*every hour*) cada hora; (*pay*) por horas
house¹ [haʊs] *n* **1.** (*inhabitation*) casa *f;* **to set one's ~ in order** *fig* poner sus cosas en orden **2.** (*family*) familia *f* **3.** (*business*) empresa *f;* **it's on the ~** invita la casa **4.** UNIV (*fraternity*) colegio *m* mayor **5.** (*legislative body*) cámara *f* **6.** (*audience*) público *m;* **full ~** (teatro *m*) lleno *m;* **to bring the ~ down** *inf* ser todo un éxito
house² [haʊz] *vt* **1.** (*give place to live*) alojar **2.** (*contain*) albergar
house arrest *n* arresto *m* domiciliario
houseboat *n* casa *f* flotante

housebreaker ['haʊs-ˌbreɪ-kər] *n* ladrón , -ona *m*, *f* (que desvalija viviendas)

housebreaking *n* allanamiento *m* de morada con robo

housebroken *adj* adiestrado, -a

housecleaning *n* limpieza *f* de la casa

housecoat ['haʊs-koʊt] *n* bata *f*

housefly <-ies> *n* mosca *f* común

household ['haʊs-hoʊld] **I.** *n* hogar *m* **II.** *adj* doméstico, -a

householder *n* (*owner*) propietario , -a *m*, *f* de una casa; (*head*) cabeza *m* de familia

house-hunt *vi inf* buscar casa

househusband *n* amo *m* de casa

housekeeper ['haʊs-ˌki-pər] *n* ama *f* de llaves

housekeeping *n* organización *f* doméstica

housekeeping money *n* dinero *m* para los gastos de la casa

housemaid ['haʊs-meɪd] *n* criada *f*, la muchacha *f Col*

housemate *n* compañero , -a de casa *m*

House of Representatives *n* POL *cámara baja del Congreso de Estados Unidos*

house physician *n* médico , -a *m*, *f* residente

houseplant *n* planta *f* de interior

house rules *npl* normas *fpl* de la casa

house sitter *n* cuidandero *m Col*, vigilante *m*

house-to-house *adj* puerta a puerta

housewarming *n*, **house-warming party** *n* fiesta *f* de inauguración (de una nueva vivienda)

housewife <-wives> *n* ama *f* de casa

housework *n* tareas *fpl* del hogar, el oficio *m*

housing ['haʊ-zɪŋ] *n* **1.** (*for living*) vivienda *f* **2.** (*for machinery*) cubierta *f* protectora

housing association *n* cooperativa *f* inmobiliaria

housing conditions *npl* condiciones *fpl* de habitabilidad

housing development *n* urbanización *f*, condominio *m*

housing project *n* vivienda *f* de interés social

hove [hoʊv] *vi* NAUT *pp of* **heave**

hovel ['hʌv-əl] *n* tugurio *m*, sucucho *m AmL*

hover ['hʌv-ər] *vi* **1.** (*stay in air*) cernerse **2.** (*wait near*) rondar **3.** (*be in an uncertain state*) estar vacilante **4.** (*hesitate*) dudar; **to ~ on the brink of accepting sth** estar casi a punto de aceptar algo

hovercraft ['hʌv-ər-kræft] <-(s)> *n* aerodeslizador *m*

HOV lane *n abbr of* **High Occupancy Vehicle lane** carril para vehículos de alta ocupación

how [haʊ] **I.** *adv* **1.** (*in this way*) como; (*in which way?*) cómo **2.** (*in what condition?*) ~ **are you?** ¿qué tal?; ~ **do you do?** encantado de conocerle **3.** (*for what reason?*) ~ **come...?** *inf* ¿cómo es que...? **4.** (*suggestion*) ~ **about...?** ¿qué tal si...? **?; ~ about that!** ¡mira por dónde!; **~'s that for an offer?** ¿trato hecho? **5.** (*intensifier*) ~ **pretty she looked!** ¡qué guapa estaba!; **and ~!** ¡ni que lo digas!; **well, ~ about that!** (*expressing surprise,*

approval) ¡caramba! **II.** *n* modo *m;* **to know the ~(s) and why(s) of sth** saber el cómo y el porqué de algo

howdy *interj inf* hola, ¿qué hay?, ¡quiubo! *Méx, Col*

however [haʊ-'ev-ər] **I.** *adv* **1.** (*no matter how*) por más que +*subj*; ~ **hard she tries...** por mucho que lo intente... **2.** (*in whichever way*) como; **do it ~ you like** hazlo como quieras **II.** *conj* (*nevertheless*) sin embargo

howl [haʊl] **I.** *vi* **1.** (*person, animal*) aullar; (*wind*) silbar; **to ~ in** [*o* **with**] **pain** dar alaridos de dolor **2.** (*cry*) chillar; (*child*) berrear **3.** *sl* (*laugh*) morirse de risa **II.** *n* **1.** (*person, animal*) aullido *m* **2.** (*cry*) chillido *m;* (*of child*) berrido *m;* **to give a ~ of pain** soltar un alarido de dolor

◆ **howl down** *vt* hacer callar a gritos

howler ['haʊ-lər] *n sl* error *m* garrafal; **to make a ~** meter la pata hasta el fondo

howling *adj* aullador(a)

hp [ˌeɪtʃ-'pi] *abbr of* **horsepower** CV

HP [ˌeɪtʃ-'pi] *abbr of* **high pressure** alta presión

HQ [ˌeɪtʃ-'kju] *abbr of* **headquarters** sede *f* central

HRT [ˌeɪtʃ-ɑr-'ti] *abbr of* **hormone replacement therapy** terapia *f* hormonal sustitutiva

ht *abbr of* **height** a

HTML [ˌeɪtʃ-ti-em-'el] COMPUT *abbr of* **Hypertext Markup Language** HTML

http, HTTP COMPUT *abbr of* **hypertext transfer protocol** http

hub [hʌb] *n* **1.** (*of wheel*) cubo *m* **2.** *fig* (*center*) centro *m*

hubbub ['hʌb-ʌb] *n* barullo *m*

hubcap ['hʌb-kæp] *n* tapacubos *m inv*, copa *f* del carro *Col*

huckleberry ['hʌk-əl-ber-i] <-ies> *n* BOT arándano *m*

huckster ['hʌk-stər] *n* **1.** (*salesman*) charlatán, -ana *m*, *f* **2.** *inf* (*writer*) publicista *mf* de pacotilla

HUD [hʌd] *abbr of* **Department of Housing and Urban Development** Departamento para el Desarrollo Urbano y la Vivienda

huddle ['hʌd-əl] **I.** *vi* apiñarse **II.** *n* (*close group*) piña *f;* **to go into a ~** hacer grupo aparte

◆ **huddle down** *vi* acurrucarse

◆ **huddle together** *vi* amontonarse

◆ **huddle up** *vi* acurrucarse

hue [hju] *n* **1.** (*shade*) tonalidad *f;* **all ~s of...** *fig* todo tipo de... **2.** (*disapproval*) ~ **and cry** protesta *f*

huff [hʌf] **I.** *vi* **to ~ and puff** (*breathe loudly*) jadear; *inf* (*complain*) quejarse **II.** *vt* vociferar **III.** *n inf* enfado *m;* **to be in a ~** estar de morros, estar enfurruñado; **to get into a ~** enfadarse; **to go off in a ~** irse ofendido

huffy ['hʌf-i] <-ier, -iest> *adj* **1.** (*offended*) ofendido, -a **2.** (*touchy*) susceptible

hug [hʌg] **I.** <-gg-> *vt* **1.** (*embrace*) abrazar **2.** *fig* (*idea, belief*) aferrarse a **3.** (*not slide on*)

these tires ~ the road estos neumáticos se agarran a la carretera **II.** *n* abrazo *m*

huge [hjudʒ] *adj* (*extremely big*) enorme; (*impressive*) imponente

hugely *adv* enormemente

hugeness *n* enormidad *f*

hulk [hʌlk] *n* **1.** (*old, large body*) carraca *f;* (*of ship*) casco *m* **2.** (*mass*) mole *f*

hulking *adj* grandote, -a

hull [hʌl] **I.** *n* **1.** NAUT casco *m* **2.** (*shell*) cáscara *f;* (*of peas*) vaina *f;* (*of strawberry*) cabito *m* **II.** *vt* pelar

hullabaloo [ˌhʌl·ə·bə·ˈlu] *n* barullo *m;* **to make a ~** armar un follón [*o* alboroto]

hum [hʌm] <-mm-> **I.** *vi* **1.** (*bee*) zumbar **2.** (*sing*) tararear **3.** (*be full of activity*) bullir de animación **II.** *vt* tararear **III.** *n* zumbido *m;* (*of traffic*) murmullo *m*

human [ˈhju·mən] **I.** *n* humano *m* **II.** *adj* humano, -a

human being *n* ser *m* humano

humane [hju·ˈmeɪn] *adj* humanitario, -a

humanism [ˈhju·mə·nɪz·əm] *n* humanismo *m*

humanistic [ˌhju·mə·ˈnɪs·tɪk] *adj* humanista

humanitarian [hju·ˌmæn·ə·ˈter·i·ən] **I.** *n* humanitario, -a *m, f* **II.** *adj* humanitario, -a; **~ aid** ayuda humanitaria

humanities [hju·ˈmæn·ə·tiz] *npl* ESP. UNIV humanidades *fpl*

humanity [hju·ˈmæn·ə·t̮i] *n* humanidad *f*

humanize [ˈhju·mə·naɪz] *vt* humanizar

humanly *adv* humanamente

human nature *n* naturaleza *f* humana

human race *n* raza *f* humana

human resources *npl* recursos *mpl* humanos

human rights *npl* derechos *mpl* humanos

humble [ˈhʌm·bəl] **I.** *adj* **1.** (*meek*) humilde; **in my ~ opinion,...** en mi modesta opinión,... **2.** (*lowly: cottage, furnishings, abode*) modesto, -a **II.** *vt* humillar; (*beat*) derrotar

humbleness *n* modestia *f;* (*humility*) humildad *f*

humbug [ˈhʌm·bʌg] *n* (*fraud*) engaño *m;* (*nonsense*) patrañas *fpl;* ~! ¡paparruchas!

humdrum [ˈhʌm·drʌm] *adj* (*dull*) aburrido, -a; (*lacking excitement*) rutinario, -a

humid [ˈhju·mɪd] *adj* húmedo, -a

humidifier [hju·ˈmɪd·ɪ·faɪ·ər] *n* humidificador *m*

humidify [hju·ˈmɪd·ɪ·faɪ] *vt* humidificar

humidity [hju·ˈmɪd·ə·t̮i] *n* humedad *f*

humiliate [hju·ˈmɪl·i·eɪt] *vt* **1.** (*shame*) avergonzar, achunchar *AmC;* (*humble*) humillar **2.** (*defeat*) derrotar

humiliating *adj* humillante

humiliation [hju·ˌmɪl·i·ˈeɪ·ʃən] *n* humillación *f*

humility [hju·ˈmɪl·ə·t̮i] *n* humildad *f*

hummingbird [ˈhʌm·ɪŋ·bɜrd] *n* colibrí *m,* chupaflor *m AmC*

humor [ˈhju·mər] *n* **1.** (*capacity for amusement*) humor *m;* **sense of ~** sentido *m* del humor **2.** *form* (*mood*) talante *m;* **in (a) good/bad ~** de buen/mal humor

humorist [ˈhju·mər·ɪst] *n* **1.** (*writer*) humorista *mf* **2.** (*funny person*) cómico, -a *m, f*

humorless [ˈhju·mər·lɪs] *adj* sin sentido del humor; **a ~ smile** una sonrisa forzada

humorous [ˈhju·mər·əs] *adj* (*speech*) humorístico, -a; (*situation*) divertido, -a; **~ story** historia graciosa

hump [hʌmp] **I.** *n* joroba *f,* petaca *f AmC* ▶ **to be over the ~** haber pasado lo más difícil **II.** *vt* **1.** *sl* (*lug, carry*) acarrear **2.** *vulg* (*have sex*) follar, coger *AmL,* pichar *Col*

humpback [ˈhʌmp·bæk] *n* joroba *f*

humpbacked [ˈhʌmp·bækt] *adj* jorobado, -a; **~ bridge** ARCHIT puente peraltado

humph [hʌmpf, mm] *interj* ¡ja!

hunch [hʌntʃ] **I.** <-es> *n* presentimiento *m;* **to have a ~ that...** tener la corazonada de que...; **to act on a ~** actuar por intuición **II.** *vi* encorvarse **III.** *vt* curvar

hunchback [ˈhʌntʃ·bæk] *n* (*person*) jorobado, -a *m, f*

hundred [ˈhʌn·drəd] <-(s)> **I.** *n* cien *m;* **~s of times** cientos de veces **II.** *adj* ciento; (*before a noun*) cien

hundredfold [ˈhʌn·drəd·foʊld] *n* cien veces *fpl*

hundredth [ˈhʌn·drədθ] **I.** *n* centésimo *m* **II.** *adj* centésimo, -a

hundredweight [ˈhʌn·drəd·weɪt] <-(s)> *n* unidad de peso equivalente a 50,80 kg en Gran Bretaña y 45,36 en los EE.UU.

hung [hʌŋ] **I.** *pt, pp of* **hang II.** *adj* colgado, -a; **~ jury** LAW jurado que se disuelve porque no se llega a ningún acuerdo

Hungarian [hʌŋ·ˈger·i·ən] **I.** *adj* húngaro, -a **II.** *n* **1.** (*person*) húngaro, -a *m, f* **2.** LING húngaro *m*

Hungary [ˈhʌŋ·gə·ri] *n* Hungría *f*

hunger [ˈhʌŋ·gər] **I.** *n* **1.** hambre *f,* filo *m AmC* **2.** *fig* (*desire*) ansia *f;* **to have a ~ for sth** estar sediento de algo **II.** *vi fig* **to ~ after** [*o* **for**] ansiar

hungry [ˈhʌŋ·gri] <-ier, -iest> *adj* **1.** (*desiring food*) hambriento, -a; **to go ~** pasar hambre **2.** *fig* (*wanting badly*) ansioso, -a; **to be ~ for sth** estar ávido de algo

hung up *adj* **1.** (*delayed*) varado **2.** (*unable to continue*) trancado **3.** (*obsessed with*) obsesionado con

hunk [hʌŋk] *n* **1.** (*piece*) trozo *m* **2.** *sl* (*man*) cachas *m inv*

hunky [ˈhʌŋki] *adj inf* (*man*) atractivo

hunky dory [ˌhʌŋ·ki·ˈdɔr·i] *adj sl* guay, muy bien

hunt [hʌnt] **I.** *vt* **1.** (*chase to kill*) cazar **2.** (*search for*) buscar **II.** *vi* **1.** (*chase to kill*) cazar; **to go ~ing** ir de caza **2.** (*search*) **to ~ for** buscar **III.** *n* **1.** (*chase*) cacería *f;* **to go on a ~** ir de caza **2.** (*search*) búsqueda *f*

hunter *n* **1.** (*person*) cazador(a) *m(f)* **2.** (*dog*) perro *m* de caza **3.** (*horse*) caballo *m* de caza

hunting *n* caza *f*

hunting ground *n* coto *m* de caza

hunting license *n* licencia *f* de caza
hunting season *n* temporada *f* de caza
huntress ['hʌn·trɪs] *n* cazadora *f*
huntsman ['hʌnts·mən] <-men> *n* cazador *m*
hurdle ['hɜr·dəl] I. *n* 1. *a.* SPORTS (*fence*) valla *f*, obstáculo *m* 2.(*difficulty*) obstáculo *m* II. *vi* SPORTS saltar vallas [*o* obstáculos] III. *vt* SPORTS saltar
hurdler *n* SPORTS vallista *mf*
hurdle race *n* SPORTS carrera [*o* obstáculos] de vallas *f*
hurdy-gurdy [ˌhɜr·di·'gɜr·di] <-ies> *n* organillo *m*
hurl [hɜrl] *vt* 1.(*throw*) lanzar 2.*fig* (*utter: insults*) soltar
hurly-burly ['hɜr·li·bɜr·li] *n* alboroto *m*
hurrah [hə·'ra] *interj*, **hurray** [hə·'reɪ] *interj* hurra
hurricane ['hɜr·ɪ·keɪn] *n* huracán *m*
hurricane lamp *n* farol *m*
hurried ['hɜr·id] *adj* apresurado, -a, apurado, -a *AmL*
hurry ['hɜr·i] <-ie-> I. *vi* darse prisa, apurarse *AmL* II. *vt* 1.(*rush*) meter prisas, apurar *AmL* 2.(*take quickly*) **he was hurried to the hospital** lo llevaron en seguida al hospital III. *n* prisa *f*, apuro *m* *AmL;* **to leave in a ~** irse disparado; **to do sth in a ~** hacer algo de prisa; **what's (all) the ~?** ¿a qué viene tanta prisa?
◆**hurry along** I. *vi* apresurarse II. *vt* *always sep* meter prisas
◆**hurry away, hurry off** I. *vi* marcharse de prisa II. *vt* (*person*) hacer marchar de prisa; (*object*) hacer llevar de prisa
◆**hurry on** *vi* continuar rápidamente
◆**hurry up** I. *vi* darse prisa II. *vt* meter prisa
hurt [hɜrt] I. <hurt, hurt> *vi* (*physically, emotionally*) doler II. *vt* 1.(*wound*) herir 2.(*cause pain*) lastimar; **it ~s me** me duele 3.(*offend*) ofender 4.(*damage*) dañar III. *adj* (*in pain, injured*) dañado, -a; (*grieved, distressed*) dolido, -a IV. *n* 1.(*pain*) dolor *m* 2.(*injury*) herida *f* 3.(*offence*) ofensa *f* 4.(*damage*) daño *m*
hurtful ['hɜrt·fəl] *adj* perjudicial
hurtle ['hɜr·təl] I. *vi* lanzarse; **to ~ along** ir como un rayo II. *vt* lanzar
husband ['hʌz·bənd] I. *n* marido *m*, esposo *m* II. *vt* economizar
husbandry ['hʌz·bən·dri] *n* 1.(*care, management*) cuidado *m* 2. AGR agricultura *f;* **animal ~** cría *f* de animales
hush [hʌʃ] I. *n* silencio *m* II. *interj* ~! ¡chitón! III. *vi* callarse IV. *vt* (*make silent*) hacer callar; (*soothe*) acallar
◆**hush up** *vt* encubrir
hush-hush *adj* *inf* secreto, -a
hush money *n* *inf* unto *m* (*que se utiliza para comprar el silencio de alguien*)
husk [hʌsk] I. *n* (*outside covering*) cáscara *f;* (*of corn*) farfolla *f* II. *vt* descascarillar, destusar *AmC,* despancar *AmS*
husky[1] ['hʌs·ki] <-ier, -iest> *adj* 1.(*low,*

rough: voice) ronco, -a 2.(*big, strong*) fornido, -a; *euph* (*well-built*) robusto, -a
husky[2] ['hʌs·ki] <-ies> *n* perro *m* esquimal
hussy ['hʌs·i] *n* desvergonzada *f*
hustings ['hʌs·tɪŋz] *npl* campaña *f* electoral
hustle ['hʌs·əl] I. *vt* 1.(*hurry*) dar prisa a; (*push*) empujar 2.(*achieve*) hacerse con II. *vi* 1.(*push for*) moverse *inf* 2.(*practice prostitution*) prostituirse III. *n* ajetreo *m*
hustler ['hʌs·lər] *n* 1.(*persuader*) camelador(a) *m(f)* 2.(*swindler*) estafador(a) *m(f)* 3.(*prostitute*) puto, -a *m, f*
hustling ['hʌs·lɪŋ] *n* ajetreo *m*
hut [hʌt] *n* cabaña *f*
hutch [hʌtʃ] <-es> *n* 1.(*box for animals*) jaula *f;* (*for rabbits*) conejera *f* 2.(*cupboard*) aparador *m*
hyacinth ['haɪ·ə·sɪnθ] *n* BOT jacinto *m*
hybrid ['haɪ·brɪd] *n* híbrido, -a *m, f*
hydrangea [haɪ·'dreɪn·dʒə] *n* BOT hortensia *f*
hydrant ['haɪ·drənt] *n* boca *f* de riego, hidrante *m*
hydrate ['haɪ·dreɪt] *n* hidrato *m*
hydraulic [haɪ·'drɔ·lɪk] *adj* hidráulico, -a
hydraulics [haɪ·'drɔ·lɪks] *n* hidráulica *f*
hydrocarbon [ˌhaɪ·droʊ·'kar·bən] I. *n* hidrocarburo *m* II. *adj* de hidrocarburo
hydrochloric acid [ˌhaɪ·droʊ·klɔr·ɪk·'æs·ɪd] *n* ácido *m* clorhídrico
hydroelectric [ˌhaɪ·droʊ·ɪ·'lek·trɪk] *adj* hidroeléctrico, -a
hydrofoil ['haɪ·drə·fɔɪl] *n* hidroala *m*
hydrogen ['haɪ·drə·dʒən] *n* hidrógeno *m*
hydrogen bomb *n* bomba *f* de hidrógeno
hydrophobia [ˌhaɪ·drə·'foʊ·bi·ə] *n* hidrofobia *f*
hydroponics [ˌhaɪ·drə·'pan·ɪks] *n* + *sing vb* hidroponía *f*
hyena [haɪ·'i·nə] *n* hiena *f*
hygiene ['haɪ·dʒin] *n* higiene *f*, salubridad *f* *AmL*
hygienic [ˌhaɪ·dʒi·'en·ɪk] *adj* higiénico, -a
hygroscope ['haɪ·grə·skoʊp] *n* higroscopio *m*
hymn [hɪm] *n* himno *m*
hymnal ['hɪm·nəl] *n*, **hymnbook** *n* himnario *m*
hype [haɪp] I. *n* COM bombo publicitario II. *vt* dar bombo publicitario a
hyperactive [ˌhaɪ·pər·'æk·tɪv] *adj* hiperactivo, -a
hyperbola [haɪ·'pɜr·bə·lə] *n* MATH hipérbola *f*
hyperbole [haɪ·'pɜr·bə·li] *n* LIT hipérbole *f*
hyperbolic [haɪ·pər·'bal·ɪk] *adj* LIT hiperbólico, -a
hyperlink [ˌhaɪ·pər·'lɪŋk] *n* COMPUT hiperenlace *m*, hipervínculo *m*
hypermarket ['haɪ·pər·mar·kɪt] *n* hipermercado *m*
hypersensitive [ˌhaɪ·pər·'sen·sɪ·tɪv] *adj* hipersensible
hypertension *n* hipertensión *f*
hypertext [ˌhaɪ·pər·'tekst] *n* COMPUT hipertexto *m*

hyphen ['haɪ·fən] *n* TYPO guión *m*
hyphenate ['haɪ·fə·neɪt] *vt* separar con guiones
hypnosis [hɪp·'noʊ·sɪs] *n* hipnosis *f inv;* **to be under ~** estar hipnotizado
hypnotherapy [ˌhɪp·noʊ·'θer·ə·pi] *n* hipnoterapia *f*
hypnotic [hɪp·'naʈ·ɪk] *adj* hipnótico, -a
hypnotist ['hɪp·nə·tɪst] *n* hipnotizador(a) *m(f)*
hypnotize ['hɪp·nə·taɪz] *vt* hipnotizar
hypochondria [ˌhaɪ·pə·'kan·dri·ə] *n* hipocondría *f*
hypochondriac [ˌhaɪ·pə·'kan·drɪ·æk] **I.** *n* hipocondríaco, -a *m, f* **II.** *adj* hipocondríaco, -a
hypocrisy [hɪ·'pak·rə·si] *n* hipocresía *f*
hypocrite ['hɪp·ə·krɪt] *n* hipócrita *mf*
hypocritical [ˌhɪp·ə·'krɪʈ·ɪ·kəl] *adj* hipócrita
hypodermic [ˌhaɪ·pə·'dɜr·mɪk] *adj* hipodérmico, -a
hypotenuse [ˌhaɪ·'pat·ə·nus] *n* MATH hipotenusa *f*
hypothermia [ˌhaɪ·poʊ·'θɜr·mi·ə] *n* hipotermia *f*
hypothesis [haɪ·'paθ·ɪ·sɪs] *n* <-es> hipótesis *f inv*
hypothetical [ˌhaɪ·pə·'θeʈ·ɪ·kəl] *adj* hipotético, -a
hysterectomy [ˌhɪs·tə·'rek·tə·mi] *n* MED histerectomía *f*
hysteria [hɪ·'ster·i·ə] *n* histeria *f*
hysteric [hɪ·'ster·ɪk] **I.** *adj* histérico, -a **II.** *n* histérico, -a *m, f*
hysterical *adj* histérico, -a

I

I, i [aɪ] *n* I, i *f; ~* **as in India** I de Italia
I [aɪ] *pron pers* (*1st person sing*) yo; *~***'m coming** ya voy; *~***'ll do it** (yo) lo haré; **am ~ late?** ¿llego tarde?; **she and ~** ella y yo; **it was *~* who did that** fui yo quien lo hizo
IA ['aɪ·ə·wə] *n*, la. *n abbr of* **Iowa** Iowa *f*
IAEA *n abbr of* **International Atomic Energy Agency** OIEA *f*
IATA [ˌaɪ·ˌeɪ·ti·'eɪ] *n abbr of* **International Air Transport Association** IATA *f*
ibex ['aɪ·beks] <-es> *n* íbice *m*, cabra *f* montesa
ibid. [ɪ·'bɪd] *adv abbr of* **ibidem** ibid.
IC [ˌaɪ·'si] *n abbr of* **integrated circuit** CI *m*
ICBM [ˌaɪ·si·bi·'em] *n abbr of* **intercontinental ballistic missile** ICBM *m*
ice [aɪs] **I.** *n* (*frozen water*) hielo *m* ▶**to be skating on thin ~** andar sobre terreno peligroso; **to break the ~** *inf* romper el hielo; **to put sth on ~** posponer algo **II.** *vt* **1.** (*chill a drink*) enfriar con hielo **2.** (*put icing on*) escarchar

◆**ice over** *vi* helarse
Ice Age *n* era *f* glacial
ice ax <-es> *n* piolet *m*
iceberg *n* iceberg *m;* **the tip of the ~** *fig* la punta del iceberg
iceberg lettuce *n* lechuga *f* repollada
icebound *adj* bloqueado, -a por el hielo
icebox <-es> *n* **1.** (*freezer*) congelador *m* **2.** (*fridge*) nevera *f,* refrigeradora *f AmL*
icebreaker *n* rompehielos *m inv*
ice cap *n* casquete *m* de hielo
ice-cold *adj* helado, -a
ice cream *n* helado *m*, nieve *f AmC*
ice-cream cone *n* **1.** (*only wafer*) cucurucho *m* **2.** (*with ice-cream*) cucurucho *m* de helado [*o* cono *m Méx, Col*]
ice-cream parlor *n* heladería *f*
ice cube ['aɪs·kjub] *n* cubito *m* de hielo
iced [aɪst] *adj* **1.** (*drink*) con hielo **2.** (*covered with icing*) escarchado, -a
ice floe ['aɪs·floʊ] *n* témpano *m* de hielo
ice hockey *n* hockey *m* sobre hielo
Iceland ['aɪs·lənd] *n* Islandia *f*
Icelander ['aɪs·lən·dər] *n* islandés, -esa *m, f*
Icelandic [aɪs·'læn·dɪk] **I.** *adj* islandés, -esa **II.** *n* islandés *m*
ice pack *n* bolsa *f* de hielo
ice rink *n* pista *f* de patinaje
ice skate *n* patín *m* de cuchilla [*o* de hielo]
ice-skate *vi* patinar sobre hielo
ice skater *n* patinador(a) *m(f)* sobre hielo
ice-skating *n* patinaje *m* sobre hielo
icicle ['aɪ·sɪ·kəl] *n* carámbano *m*
icing ['aɪ·sɪŋ] *n* **1.** glaseado *m* **2.** (*in ice hockey*) pista *f* de hockey sobre hielo ▶**to be the ~ on the cake** ser la guinda del pastel [*o* ser la frutilla de la torta]
icon ['aɪ·kan] *n* icono *m*
iconoclast [aɪ·'kan·ə·klæst] *n* iconoclasta *mf*
iconoclastic [aɪ·ˌkan·ə·'klæs·tɪk] *adj* iconoclasta
ICU [ˌaɪ·si·'ju] *n abbr of* **intensive care unit** UCI *f*
icy ['aɪ·si] <-ier, -iest> *adj* **1.** (*with ice*) helado, -a; (*very cold*) glacial **2.** (*unfriendly*) frío, -a
Id. *n abbr of* **Idaho** Idaho *m*
ID¹ [ˌaɪ·'di] **I.** *n abbr of* **identification** identificación *f* **II.** *vt inf abbr of* **identify** identificar; **to positively ~ sb** identificar positivamente a alguien
ID² [ˌaɪ·'di] *n abbr of* **Idaho** Idaho *m*
I'd [aɪd] **1.** = I would *s.* would **2.** = I had *s.* have
Idaho ['aɪ·də·hoʊ] *n* Idaho *m*
ID card [aɪ·'di·kard] *n s.* **identity card** carné *m* de identidad
idea [aɪ·'di·ə] *n* **1.** (*opinion*) idea *f* **2.** (*conception*) noción *f;* **to get an ~ of sth** hacerse una idea de algo
ideal [aɪ·'di·əl] **I.** *adj* ideal **II.** *n* ideal *m*
idealism [aɪ·'di·ə·lɪz·əm] *n* idealismo *m*
idealist [aɪ·'di·ə·lɪst] *n* idealista *mf*
idealistic [ˌaɪ·di·ə·'lɪs·tɪk] *adj* idealista

I

idealize [aɪˈdiːəˌlaɪz] *vt* idealizar

ideally [aɪˈdiːli] *adv* **1.** (*in an ideal way*) inmejorablemente **2.** ~, **we could catch the train** lo ideal sería coger el tren

identical [aɪˈdentɪkəl] *adj* idéntico, -a, individual *CSur*

identifiable [aɪˌdentəˈfaɪəbəl] *adj* identificable

identification [aɪˌdentəfɪˈkeɪʃən] *n* identificación *f*

identification papers *npl* documentación *f*

identifier [aɪˈdentəˌfaɪər] *n* COMPUT identificador *m*

identify [aɪˈdentəfaɪ] <-ie-> *vt* identificar

identity [aɪˈdentəti] <-ies> *n* identidad *f*

identity card *n* carné *m* de identidad

ideological [ˌaɪdiːəˈlɑdʒɪkəl] *adj* ideológico, -a

ideologist [ˌaɪdiːˈɑlədʒɪst] *n* ideólogo, -a *m, f*

ideology [ˌaɪdiːˈɑlədʒi] <-ies> *n* ideología *f*

idiocy [ˈɪdiːəsi] <-ies> *n* idiotez *f,* imbecilidad *f*

idiom [ˈɪdiːəm] *n* LING **1.** (*phrase*) modismo *m* **2.** (*style of expression*) lenguaje *m*

idiomatic [ˌɪdiːəˈmætɪk] *adj* idiomático, -a

idiosyncrasy [ˌɪdiːoʊˈsɪŋkrəsi] <-ies> *n* idiosincrasia *f*

idiosyncratic [ˌɪdiːoʊsɪŋˈkrætɪk] *adj* idiosincrático, -a

idiot [ˈɪdiːət] *n* idiota *mf*

idiotic [ˌɪdiːˈɑtɪk] *adj* tonto, -a

idle [ˈaɪdəl] **I.** *adj* **1.** (*lazy*) holgazán, -ana **2.** (*not busy*) desocupado, -a; (*machine*) parado, -a, desocupado, -a **3.** (*frivolous: pleasures*) frívolo, -a **4.** (*unfounded*) vano, -a; (*gossip*) insustancial; (*fear*) infundado, -a **5.** (*ineffective: threat*) inútil **6.** FIN de paro; (*capital*) improductivo, -a **II.** *n* AUTO ralentí *m* **III.** *vi* (*engine*) marchar al ralentí, funcionar en vacío; (*person*) haraganear

idleness [ˈaɪdəlnɪs] *n* holgazanería *f*

idler [ˈaɪdlər] *n* vago, -a *m, f*

idol [ˈaɪdəl] *n* ídolo *m*

idolatrous [aɪˈdɑlətrəs] *adj* REL idólatra

idolatry [aɪˈdɑlətri] *n* idolatría *f*

idolize [ˈaɪdəˌlaɪz] *vt* idolatrar

idyll [ˈaɪdəl] *n* idilio *m*

idyllic [aɪˈdɪlɪk] *adj* idílico, -a

i.e. [ˌaɪˈi] *abbr of* **id est** i.e.

if [ɪf] **I.** *conj* **1.** (*supposing that*) si; ~ **it snows** si nieva; ~ **not** si no; **as** ~ **it were true** como si fuera verdad; ~ **they exist at all** si es que en realidad existen; ~ **A is right, then B is wrong** si A es verdadero, entonces B es falso; **I'll stay,** ~ **only for a day** me quedaré, aunque sea sólo un día **2.** (*every time that*) ~ **he needs me, I'll help him** si me necesita, le ayudaré **3.** (*whether*) **I wonder** ~ **he'll come** me pregunto si vendrá **4.** (*although*) aunque; **cold** ~ **sunny weather** clima soleado aunque frío **II.** *n* pero *m;* **no** ~**s, ands, or buts!** ¡no hay peros que valgan!

iffy [ˈɪfi] <-ier, -iest> *adj inf* dudoso, -a; (*per-*

son) sospechoso, -a

igloo [ˈɪɡlu] *n* iglú *m*

igneous [ˈɪɡniːəs] *adj* ígneo, -a

ignite [ɪɡˈnaɪt] **I.** *vi* incendiarse **II.** *vt form* incendiar

ignition [ɪɡˈnɪʃən] *n* **1.** AUTO encendido *m;* **to switch on the** ~ dar al contacto **2.** *form* (*causing to burn*) ignición *f*

ignition coil *n* bobina *f* de encendido

ignition key *n* llave *f* de contacto, suiche *m Méx*

ignition switch <-es> *n* interruptor *m* de encendido

ignoble [ɪɡˈnoʊbəl] *adj liter* innoble

ignominious [ˌɪɡnəˈmɪniːəs] *adj liter* ignominioso, -a

ignominy [ˈɪɡnəˌmɪni] *n* ignominia *f*

ignoramus [ˌɪɡnəˈreɪməs] *n* ignorante *mf*

ignorance [ˈɪɡnərəns] *n* ignorancia *f;* **to be left in** ~ **of sth** quedarse sin saber algo ► ~ **is bliss** ojos que no ven, corazón que no siente

ignorant [ˈɪɡnərənt] *adj* ignorante; **to be** ~ **about sth** desconocer algo

ignore [ɪɡˈnɔr] *vt* no hacer caso de, ignorar

iguana [ɪˈɡwanə] *n* iguana *f,* basilisco *m Méx*

IL *n*, **III.** *n abbr of* **Illinois** Illinois *m*

ilk [ɪlk] *n liter* calaña *f*

ill [ɪl] **I.** *adj* **1.** (*sick*) enfermo, -a; **to fall** ~ caer enfermo **2.** (*bad*) malo, -a; (*harmful*) nocivo, -a; (*unfavorable*) perjudicial; **an** ~ **omen** un mal presagio **II.** *adv form* (*badly*) mal; **to bode** ~ ser de mal agüero; **to speak** ~ **of sb** hablar mal de alguien

I'll [aɪl] = **I will** *s.* **will**

ill-advised [ˌɪləɑdˈvaɪzd] *adj* imprudente

ill at ease *adj* incómodo, -a

ill-bred *adj* mal educado, -a

ill-conceived *adj* desacertado, -a

illegal [ɪˈliɡəl] *adj* ilegal

illegal immigrant *n* inmigrante *mf* ilegal

illegality [ˌɪlɪˈɡæləti] <-ies> *n* ilegalidad *f*

illegible [ɪˈledʒəbəl] *adj* ilegible

illegitimate [ˌɪlɪˈdʒɪtəmət] *adj* ilegítimo, -a

ill-equipped [ˌɪlɪˈkwɪpt] *adj* mal equipado, -a

ill-fated *adj* (*having bad luck*) desafortunado, -a; (*bringing bad luck*) gafe; **an** ~ **hour** una hora funesta

ill-favored *adj* feo, -a, poco agraciado, -a

ill-fitting *adj* ~ **clothes** ropa *f* que no queda bien

ill-gotten *adj* mal habido, -a

illiberal [ɪˈlɪbərəl] *adj* intolerante

illicit [ɪˈlɪsɪt] *adj* ilícito, -a

illimitable [ɪˈlɪmɪtəbəl] *adj* ilimitado, -a

ill-informed [ˈɪlɪnˌfɔrmd] *adj* **1.** (*wrongly informed*) mal informado, -a **2.** (*ignorant*) ignorante

Illinois [ˌɪləˈnɔɪ] *n* Illinois *m*

illiteracy [ɪˈlɪtərəsi] *n* analfabetismo *m*

illiterate [ɪˈlɪtərət] **I.** *adj* analfabeto, -a; *pej, fig* inculto, -a **II.** *n* analfabeto, -a *m, f*

ill-mannered [ˌɪlˈmænərd] *adj* mal educado, -a

ill-natured *adj* malicioso, -a
illness ['ɪl·nɪs] <-es> *n* enfermedad *f*
illogical [ɪ·'lɑdʒ·ɪ·kəl] *adj* ilógico, -a
illogicality [ɪ·ˌlɑdʒ·ɪ·'kæl·ə·ţi] *n* incongruencia *f*
ill-omened [ˌɪl·'oʊ·mənd] *adj* aciago, -a
ill-starred *adj* desdichado, -a
ill-tempered *adj* de mal genio
ill-timed *adj* inoportuno, -a
ill-treat [ˌɪl·'trit] *vt* maltratar
ill-treatment [ˌɪl·'trit·mənt] *n* maltrato *m*
illuminate [ɪ·'lu·mə·neɪt] *vt* iluminar; *fig* aclarar
illuminating [ɪ·'lu·mɪ·neɪ·ţɪŋ] *adj form* aclaratorio, -a
illumination [ɪ·ˌlu·mɪ·'neɪ·ʃən] *n a.* ART iluminación *f*
illus. *abbr of* **illustrated, illustration** ilus.
illusion [ɪ·'lu·ʒən] *n* (*misleading appearance*) apariencia *f*; (*false impression*) ilusión *f*; **to have no ~s** (*about sth*) no tener esperanzas (en algo); **to be under the ~ that...** estar equivocado creyendo que...
illusionist [ɪ·'lu·ʒə·nɪst] *n* ilusionista *mf*
illusive [ɪ·'lu·sɪv] *adj,* **illusory** [ɪ·'lu·sə·ri] *adj* ilusorio, -a
illustrate ['ɪl·ə·streɪt] *vt* ilustrar; *fig* ejemplificar
illustration [ˌɪl·ə·'streɪ·ʃən] *n* 1. (*drawing*) ilustración *f* 2. (*example*) ejemplo *m;* **by way of ~** a modo de ejemplo
illustrative [ɪ·'lʌs·trə·ţɪv, 'ɪl·ə·streɪ·ţɪv] *adj form* ilustrativo, -a
illustrator ['ɪl·ə·streɪ·ţər] *n* ilustrador(a) *m(f)*
illustrious [ɪ·'lʌs·tri·əs] *adj form* ilustre
ill will *n* animadversión *f*
I'm [aɪm] = **I am** *s.* **am**
image ['ɪm·ɪdʒ] *n* 1. (*likeness*) imagen *f;* **to be the living ~ of sb** ser el vivo retrato de alguien 2. (*picture*) retrato *m* 3. (*reputation*) reputación *f*
imagery ['ɪm·ɪdʒ·ri] *n* LIT imágenes *fpl*
imaginable [ɪ·'mædʒ·ə·nə·bəl] *adj* imaginable
imaginary [ɪ·'mædʒ·ə·ner·i] *adj* imaginario, -a
imagination [ɪ·ˌmædʒ·ə·'neɪ·ʃən] *n* imaginación *f;* (*inventiveness*) inventiva *f*
imaginative [ɪ·'mædʒ·ə·nə·ţɪv] *adj* imaginativo, -a
imagine [ɪ·'mædʒ·ɪn] *vt* 1. (*form mental image*) imaginar 2. (*suppose*) figurarse; **~ that!** ¡figúratelo!
imaging *n* COMPUT tratamiento *m* de imágenes
imbalance [ˌɪm·'bæl·əns] *n* desequilibrio *m*
imbecile ['ɪm·bə·sɪl] *n* imbécil *mf*
imbecility [ˌɪm·bə·'sɪl·ə·ţi] *n form* imbecilidad *f*
imbibe [ɪm·'baɪb] *vt* beber; *fig* empaparse de
imbroglio [ɪm·'broʊl·joʊ] *n liter* embrollo *m*
imbue [ɪm·'bju] *vt form* 1. (*fill, inspire*) **to ~ sb with sth** imbuir a alguien de algo; **to be ~d with** estar empapado de 2. (*soak*) empapar
IMF [ˌaɪ·em·'ef] *n abbr of* **International Monetary Fund** FMI *m*

imitate ['ɪm·ɪ·teɪt] *vt* imitar; (*copy*) copiar
imitation [ˌɪm·ɪ·'teɪ·ʃən] **I.** *n* 1. (*mimicry*) imitación *f;* **in ~ of sb/sth** a imitación de alguien/algo 2. (*copy*) reproducción *f* **II.** *adj* de imitación; (*silk*) sintético, -a; **~ jewels** bisutería *f*
imitative ['ɪm·ɪ·teɪ·ţɪv] *adj* imitativo, -a
imitator ['ɪm·ɪ·teɪ·ţər] *n* imitador(a) *m(f)*
immaculate [ɪ·'mæk·jʊ·lət] *adj* 1. (*spotless, neat*) inmaculado, -a 2. (*flawless*) impecable
immanence ['ɪm·ə·nəns] *n* PHILOS inmanencia *f*
immanent ['ɪm·ə·nənt] *adj* inmanente
immaterial [ˌɪm·ə·'tɪr·i·əl] *adj* 1. (*not important*) irrelevante 2. (*intangible*) inmaterial
immature [ˌɪm·ə·'tʃʊr] *adj* 1. (*young*) inmaduro, -a; (*people, animals*) joven 2. (*childish: behavior*) infantil
immaturity [ˌɪm·ə·'tʃʊr·ə·ţi] *n* inmadurez *f*
immeasurable [ɪ·'meʒ·ər·ə·bəl] *adj* 1. (*boundless*) inconmensurable 2. (*vast*) inmenso, -a; (*effect*) incalculable
immediacy [ɪ·'mi·di·ə·si] *n* inmediatez *f;* (*nearness*) proximidad *f*
immediate [ɪ·'mi·di·ɪt] *adj* inmediato, -a; **the ~ family** los familiares directos; **in the ~ area** en las inmediaciones; **in the ~ future** en un futuro inmediato
immediately *adv* 1. (*time*) inmediatamente; **~ after...** justo después de... 2. (*place*) **my flat is the one ~ above yours** mi piso está justo encima del tuyo
immemorial [ˌɪm·ə·'mɔr·i·əl] *adj liter* inmemorial, inmemorable
immense [ɪ·'mens] *adj* inmenso, -a; (*importance*) extremo, -a
immensely *adv* enormemente
immensity [ɪ·'men·sə·ţi] *n* inmensidad *f*
immerse [ɪ·'mɜrs] *vt* sumergir; **to be ~d in sth** *fig* estar absorto en algo; **to ~ oneself in sth** *fig* sumirse en algo
immersion [ɪ·'mɜr·ʃən] *n* 1. (*putting under water*) inmersión *f* 2. (*absorption*) sumersión *f*
immersion heater *n* calentador *m* de inmersión
immigrant ['ɪm·ɪ·grənt] *n* inmigrante *mf*
immigrate ['ɪm·ɪ·greɪt] *vi* inmigrar
immigration [ˌɪm·ɪ·'greɪ·ʃən] *n* inmigración *f*
imminence ['ɪm·ɪ·nəns] *n* inminencia *f*
imminent ['ɪm·ɪ·nənt] *adj* inminente
immobile [ɪ·'moʊ·bəl] *adj* 1. (*not moving*) inmóvil 2. (*rigid*) entumecido, -a
immobility [ˌɪm·oʊ·'bɪl·ə·ţi] *n* inmovilidad *f;* (*being still*) entumecimiento *m*
immobilize [ɪ·'moʊ·bə·laɪz] *vt* inmovilizar
immoderate [ɪ·'mad·ər·ət] *adj* excesivo, -a
immodest [ɪ·'mad·ɪst] *adj* 1. (*conceited*) creído, -a 2. (*slightly indecent*) descarado, -a
immolate ['ɪm·ə·leɪt] *vt form* inmolar
immoral [ɪ·'mɔr·əl] *adj* inmoral
immortal [ɪ·'mɔr·ţəl] **I.** *adj* 1. (*undying*) inmortal 2. (*remembered forever*) imperecedero, -a **II.** *n* inmortal *mf*

immortality [ˌɪ·mɔr·'tæl·ə·t̬i] *n* inmortalidad *f*
immortalize [ɪ·'mɔr·t̬ə·laɪz] *vt* inmortalizar
immovable [ɪ·'mu·və·bəl] *adj* **1.**(*not moveable*) inamovible **2.**(*not changeable*) inalterable; (*belief*) inquebrantable
immune [ɪ·'mjun] *adj* **1.**MED inmune **2.**POL, LAW exento, -a
immune system *n* sistema *m* inmunológico
immunity [ɪ·'mju·nə·t̬i] *n* **1.**MED inmunidad *f* **2.**(*lack of susceptibility*) insensibilidad *f* **3.**LAW exención *f*; **diplomatic ~** inmunidad *f* diplomática
immunize ['ɪm·jə·naɪz] *vt* inmunizar
immunological [ˌɪm·jə·noʊ·'ladʒ·ɪ·kəl] *adj* inmunológico, -a
immunologist [ˌɪm·jʊ·'nal·ə·dʒɪst] *n* inmunólogo, -a *m, f*
immure [ɪ·'mjʊr] *vt liter* enclaustrar
immutable [ɪ·'mju·t̬ə·bəl] *adj form* **1.**(*unchangeable: fact, set of rules*) inmutable **2.**COMPUT (*file, image*) inalterable
imp [ɪmp] *n* **1.**(*mischievous child*) pillín, -ina *m, f* **2.**(*small devil*) diablillo, -a *m, f*
impact ['ɪm·pækt] **I.** *n* **1.**(*striking contact*) choque *m*; (*force of striking contact*) impacto *m*; **on ~** por impacto **2.**(*effect*) impacto *m* **II.** *vt* incidir en **III.** *vi* **to ~ on** sb/sth impactar en alguien/algo
impacted [ɪm·'pæk·tɪd] *adj* impactado, -a
impair [ɪm·'per] *vt* (*hearing*) dañar; (*health*) perjudicar; (*one's performance, chances*) debilitar; (*communications*) deteriorar
impaired *adj* (*speech, vision, hearing*) dañado, -a; (*health*) perjudicado, -a; **~ driving** conducción bajo los efectos del alcohol o narcóticos; **to be visually ~** estar impedido visualmente
impale [ɪm·'peɪl] *vt* **to ~** sb/oneself **on** atravesar a alguien/atravesarse con
impalpable [ɪm·'pæl·pə·bəl] *adj liter* impalpable; (*change*) imperceptible
impart [ɪm·'part] *vt form* impartir; (*bestow*) conferir; (*secret*) divulgar
impartial [ɪm·'par·ʃəl] *adj* imparcial
impartiality [ˌɪm·ˌpar·ʃɪ·'æl·ə·t̬i] *n* imparcialidad *f*
impassable [ɪm·'pæs·ə·bəl] *adj* intransitable; *fig* infranqueable
impasse ['ɪm·pæs] *n a. fig* callejón *m* sin salida; **to have reached an ~** haber llegado a un punto muerto [*o* a un atolladero]
impassioned [ɪm·'pæʃ·ənd] *adj form* apasionado, -a; **an ~ appeal for help** una encarecida petición de ayuda
impassive [ɪm·'pæs·ɪv] *adj* impasible
impatience [ɪm·'peɪ·ʃəns] *n* impaciencia *f*
impatient [ɪm·'peɪ·ʃənt] *adj* impaciente; **to be ~ to do sth** estar impaciente por hacer algo
impeach [ɪm·'pitʃ] *vt* acusar, (someter a un proceso de incapacitación presidencial)
impeachment [ɪm·'pitʃ·mənt] *n* acusación *f* (*proceso de incapacitación presidencial*)
impeccable [ɪm·'pek·ə·bəl] *adj* impecable; (*manners*) intachable

impecunious [ˌɪm·pɪ·'kju·ni·əs] *adj form* sin peculio
impede [ɪm·'pid] *vt* impedir
impediment [ɪm·'ped·ɪ·mənt] *n* **1.**(*hindrance*) impedimento *m* **2.**MED defecto *m;* **a speech ~** un defecto del habla
impel [ɪm·'pel] <-ll-> *vt* impeler
impend [ɪm·'pend] *vi* avecinarse
impending *adj* inminente
impenetrable [ɪm·'pen·ɪ·trə·bəl] *adj* **1.**impenetrable **2.**(*incomprehensible*) incomprensible
impenitent [ɪm·'pen·ɪ·tənt] *adj form* impenitente
imperative [ɪm·'per·ə·t̬ɪv] **I.** *adj* **1.**(*urgently essential*) imprescindible **2.**LING imperativo, -a **II.** *n a.* LING imperativo *m*
imperceptible [ˌɪm·pər·'sep·tə·bəl] *adj* imperceptible
imperfect [ɪm·'pɜr·fɪkt] **I.** *adj* imperfecto, -a; (*flawed*) defectuoso, -a **II.** *n* LING (pretérito *m*) imperfecto *m*
imperfection [ˌɪm·pər·'fek·ʃən] *n* imperfección *f*
imperial [ɪm·'pɪr·i·əl] *adj* imperial
imperialism [ɪm·'pɪr·i·ə·lɪz·əm] *n* imperialismo *m*
imperialist [ɪm·'pɪr·i·ə·lɪst] **I.** *n* imperialista *mf* **II.** *adj* imperialista
imperil [ɪm·'per·əl] <-ll-, -l-> *vt form* poner en peligro
imperious [ɪm·'pɪr·i·əs] *adj* **1.**(*bossy*) imperioso, -a **2.**(*arrogant*) arrogante
imperishable [ɪm·'per·ɪʃ·ə·bəl] *adj* imperecedero, -a
impermanent [ɪm·'pɜr·mə·nənt] *adj* pasajero, -a
impermeable [ɪm·'pɜr·mi·ə·bəl] *adj* impermeable
impersonal [ˌɪm·'pɜr·sə·nəl] *adj a.* LING impersonal
impersonate [ɪm·'pɜr·sə·neɪt] *vt* hacerse pasar por; (*imitate*) imitar
impersonator *n* imitador(a) *m(f)*
impertinent [ɪm·'pɜr·t̬ə·nənt] *adj* impertinente
imperturbable [ˌɪm·pər·'tɜr·bə·bəl] *adj form* imperturbable
impervious [ɪm·'pɜr·vi·əs] *adj* impermeable; (*not affected*) inmune
impetuous [ɪm·'petʃ·u·əs] *adj* impetuoso, -a; (*action*) precipitado, -a
impetus ['ɪm·pɪ·t̬əs] *n* **1.**(*push*) impulso *m* **2.**(*driving force*) ímpetu *m*
impiety [ɪm·'paɪ·ə·t̬i] *n* impiedad *f*
impinge [ɪm·'pɪndʒ] *form* **I.** *vt* afectar **II.** *vi* **to ~ on** sb/sth afectar a alguien/algo
impious ['ɪm·pi·əs] *adj* impío, -a
impish ['ɪm·pɪʃ] *adj* **1.**(*mischievous*) malicioso, -a **2.**(*impudent*) pillín, -ina; (*grin*) pícaro, -a
implacable [ɪm·'plæk·ə·bəl] *adj form* implacable

implacably *adv form* implacablemente

implant [ɪm·'plænt] **I.** *n* implante *m* **II.** *vt* **1.** (*add surgically*) implantar **2.** (*put in the mind*) inculcar

implausible [ɪm·'plɔ·zə·bəl] *adj* inverosímil

implement ['ɪm·plɪ·mənt] **I.** *n* (*tool*) instrumento *m;* (*small tool*) utensilio *m* **II.** *vt* implementar

implementation [ˌɪm·plɪ·men·'teɪ·ʃən] *n* (*of tools, devices*) puesta *f* en práctica; (*of measures, policies*) implementación *f*

implicate ['ɪm·plɪ·keɪt] *vt* **1.** (*show sb's involvement*) implicar **2.** (*involve*) involucrar

implication [ˌɪm·plɪ·'keɪ·ʃən] *n* **1.** (*hinting at*) insinuación *f;* **by ~** implícitamente **2.** (*effect*) consecuencia *f* **3.** (*showing of involvement*) implicación *f*

implicit [ɪm·'plɪs·ɪt] *adj* **1.** (*suggested*) implícito, -a **2.** (*total*) absoluto, -a; (*faith*) incondicional

implied [ɪm·'plaɪd] *adj* tácito, -a; (*criticism*) implícito, -a

implode [ɪm·'ploʊd] *vi* implosionar

implore [ɪm·'plɔr] *vt* implorar; **to ~ sb to do sth** suplicar a alguien que haga algo

imploring [ɪm·'plɔr·ɪŋ] *adj* implorante; (*voice*) suplicante

implosion [ɪm·'ploʊ·ʒən] *n* implosión *f*

imply [ɪm·'plaɪ] <-ie-> *vt* **1.** (*suggest*) sugerir **2.** *form* (*involve*) implicar

impolite [ˌɪm·pə·'laɪt] *adj* descortés; (*rude*) grosero, -a

impoliteness *n* descortesía *f*

impolitic [ɪm·'pal·ə·tɪk] *adj form* imprudente

imponderable [ɪm·'pan·də·rə·bəl] **I.** *adj* imponderable **II.** *n* imponderable *m*

import I. [ɪm·'pɔrt] *vt* **1.** ECON, COMPUT importar **2.** *form* (*signify*) significar **II.** ['ɪm·pɔrt] *n* **1.** (*product*) producto *m* de importación **2.** *form* (*significance*) importancia *f*

importance [ɪm·'pɔr·təns] *n* importancia *f*

important [ɪm·'pɔr·tənt] *adj* importante

importantly *adv* significativamente

importation [ˌɪm·pɔr·'teɪ·ʃən] *n* ECON importación *f*

import duty <-ies> *n* derecho *m* de aduana

importunate [ɪm·'pɔr·tʃə·nɪt] *adj form* inoportuno, -a, molesto, -a

importune [ˌɪm·pɔr·'tun] *vt form* importunar

impose [ɪm·'poʊz] **I.** *vt* **1.** (*implement*) imponer **2.** (*force on*) obligar **II.** *vi* aprovecharse; **to ~ on sb** aprovecharse de alguien; **I don't want to ~** no quiero molestar

imposing [ɪm·'poʊ·zɪŋ] *adj* imponente

imposition [ˌɪm·pə·'zɪʃ·ən] *n* **1.** (*forcing, application*) imposición *f* **2.** (*inconvenience*) molestia *f*

impossibility [ɪm·ˌpas·ə·'bɪl·ə·t̬i] *n* imposibilidad *f*

impossible [ɪm·'pas·ə·bəl] **I.** *adj* **1.** (*not possible*) imposible **2.** (*not resolvable*) irresoluble **3.** (*difficult to deal with*) insoportable **II.** *n* **the ~** lo imposible

impossibly *adv* extremadamente

imposter *n*, **impostor** [ɪm·'pas·tər] *n* impostor(a) *m(f)*

imposture [ɪm·'pas·tʃər] *n* impostura *f*

impotence ['ɪm·pə·təns] *n* impotencia *f*

impotent ['ɪm·pə·tənt] *adj* impotente

impound [ɪm·'paʊnd] *vt* incautar

impoverish [ɪm·'pav·ər·ɪʃ] *vt* **1.** (*make poor*) empobrecer **2.** (*deplete*) menguar

impoverished *adj* **1.** (*made poor*) empobrecido, -a **2.** (*depleted*) menguado, -a

impracticable [ɪm·'præk·tɪ·kə·bəl] *adj* impracticable; (*person*) intratable

impractical [ɪm·'præk·tɪ·kəl] *adj* poco práctico, -a

imprecation [ˌɪm·prɪ·'keɪ·ʃən] *n form* imprecación *f*

imprecise [ˌɪm·prɪ·'saɪs] *adj* impreciso, -a

impregnable [ɪm·'preg·nə·bəl] *adj* **1.** (*unable to be taken*) inexpugnable **2.** (*undefeatable*) imbatible

impregnate [ɪm·'preg·neɪt] *vt* **1.** (*inseminate*) fecundar **2.** (*saturate*) impregnar

impresario [ˌɪm·prə·'sar·i·oʊ] *n* empresario, -a *m, f*

impress [ɪm·'pres] **I.** *vt* **1.** (*affect*) impresionar **2.** (*stamp*) estampar; **to ~ sth on** [*o* **upon**] **sb** (*make realize*) inculcar algo a alguien; (*make remember*) recalcar algo a alguien **II.** *vi* impresionar

impression [ɪm·'preʃ·ən] *n* **1.** (*general opinion*) impresión *f;* **to be of** [*o* **under**] **the ~ that...** tener la impresión de que... **2.** (*feeling*) sensación *f;* **to make an ~ on sb** causar impresión a alguien **3.** (*imitation*) imitación *f* **4.** (*imprint*) impresión *f; fig* huella *f*

impressionable [ɪm·'preʃ·ə·nə·bəl] *adj* impresionable

impressionism [ɪm·'preʃ·ə·nɪz·əm] *n* impresionismo *m*

impressionist [ɪm·'preʃ·ə·nɪst] **I.** *n* **1.** ART impresionista *mf* **2.** (*imitator*) imitador(a) *m(f)* **II.** *adj* impresionista

impressionistic [ɪm·ˌpreʃ·ə·'nɪs·tɪk] *adj* impresionista

impressive [ɪm·'pres·ɪv] *adj* impresionante

imprint I. [ɪm·'prɪnt] *vt* **1.** (*stamp*) estampar; (*paper*) imprimir; (*coins*) acuñar; (*leather*) grabar **2.** (*in memory*) grabar **II.** ['ɪm·prɪnt] *n* **1.** (*mark*) marca *f; fig* huella *f* **2.** TYPO pie *m* de imprenta

imprison [ɪm·'prɪz·ən] *vt* encarcelar

imprisonment [ɪm·'prɪz·ən·mənt] *n* encarcelamiento *m;* **life ~** cadena *f* perpetua

improbability [ˌɪm·prab·ə·'bɪl·ə·t̬i] *n* improbabilidad *f*

improbable [ɪm·'prab·ə·bəl] *adj* improbable

impromptu [ɪm·'pramp·tu] *adj* de improviso

improper [ɪm·'prap·ər] *adj* **1.** (*incorrect*) incorrecto, -a; (*showing bad judgment*) injusto, -a **2.** (*not socially decent*) indecoroso, -a; (*immoral*) indecente **3.** (*dishonest*) deshonesto, -a

impropriety [ˌɪm·prə·ˈpraɪ·ə·t̬i] <-ies> *n*
1. (*improper doings*) incongruencia *f;* (*language*) impropiedad *f* **2.** (*indecency*) indecoro *m*

improve [ɪm·ˈpruv] **I.** *vt* mejorar **II.** *vi* **1.** mejorar; (*progress*) hacer progresos **2.** (*price*) subir
♦ **improve on** *vi* superar

improvement [ɪm·ˈpruv·mənt] *n* **1.** (*betterment*) mejora *f;* (*progress*) progreso *m* **2.** (*of illness*) mejoría *f* **3.** (*increase in value*) revalorización *f*

improvident [ɪm·ˈprɑv·ə·dənt] *adj form*
1. (*not planning*) imprevisor(a) **2.** (*imprudent*) imprudente

improvisation [ɪm·ˌprɑv·ɪ·ˈzeɪ·ʃən] *n* improvisación *f*

improvise [ˈɪm·prə·vaɪz] *vi, vt* improvisar

imprudent [ɪm·ˈpru·dənt] *adj form* imprudente

impudence [ˈɪm·pjʊ·dəns] *n* descaro *m*

impudent [ˈɪm·pjʊ·dənt] *adj* impertinente

impugn [ɪm·ˈpjun] *vt form* impugnar

impulse [ˈɪm·pʌls] *n* **1.** *a.* ELEC, PHYS, BIO impulso *m;* **to do sth on (an)** ~ hacer algo por impulso **2.** (*motive*) incentivo *m*

impulsion [ɪm·ˈpʌl·ʃən] *n* **1.** (*urge*) impulso *m;* **to have** [*o* feel] **the** ~ **to do sth** sentirse impulsado a hacer algo **2.** (*force*) empuje *m*

impulsive [ɪm·ˈpʌl·sɪv] *adj* impulsivo, -a

impunity [ɪm·ˈpju·nə·t̬i] *n* impunidad *f*

impure [ɪm·ˈpjʊr] *adj* impuro, -a

impurity [ɪm·ˈpjʊr·ə·t̬i] <-ies> *n* impureza *f*

imputation [ˌɪm·pjʊ·ˈteɪ·ʃən] *n form* imputación *f*

impute [ɪm·ˈpjut] *vt* imputar

in [ɪn] **I.** *prep* **1.** (*inside, into*) en, dentro de; **to be** ~ **bed** estar en la cama; **gun** ~ **hand** pistola en mano; **there is sth** ~ **the drawer** hay algo dentro del cajón; **to put sth** ~ **sb's hands** poner algo en manos de alguien; ~ **town/jail** en la ciudad/cárcel; ~ **the country/hospital** en el país/hospital; ~ **Canada/Mexico** en Canadá/México **2.** (*within*) ~ **sb's face/the picture** en el rostro de alguien/la fotografía; ~ **the snow/sun** en la nieve/el sol; **the best** ~ **New England/town** lo mejor de Nueva Inglaterra/de la ciudad; **to find a friend** ~ **sb** encontrar un amigo en alguien **3.** (*position of*) ~ **the beginning/end** al principio/final; **right** ~ **the middle** justo en medio **4.** (*during*) ~ **the twenties** en los (años) veinte; **to be** ~ **one's thirties** estar en los treinta; ~ **May/the spring** en mayo/primavera; ~ **the afternoon** por la tarde **5.** (*at later time*) ~ **a week/three hours** dentro de una semana/tres horas; ~ (**the**) **future** en el futuro **6.** (*in less than*) **to do sth** ~ **4 hours** hacer algo en 4 horas **7.** (*for*) **he hasn't done that** ~ **years/a week** no ha hecho eso desde hace años/una semana **8.** (*in situation, state of*) ~ **fashion** de moda; ~ **search of sth/sb** en busca de algo/alguien; ~ **this way** de esta manera; **when** ~ **doubt** en caso de duda; ~ **anger** enfurecido, alebrestado

Col, Ven; ~ **fun** de broma, en chanza; ~ **earnest** sinceramente; **to be** ~ **a hurry** tener prisa; **to be** ~ **love (with sb)** estar enamorado (de alguien); ~ **alphabetical order** en orden alfabético; **written** ~ **black and white** *fig* claramente escrito; **dressed** ~ **red** vestido de rojo **9.** (*concerning*) **deaf** ~ **one ear** sordo de un oído; **to be interested** ~ **sth** estar interesado en algo; **to have faith** ~ **God** tener fe en Dios; **to have confidence** ~ **sb** tener confianza en alguien; **to have a say** ~ **the matter** tener algo que decir al respecto; **a change** ~ **attitude** un cambio de actitud; **a rise** ~ **prices** un aumento de los precios **10.** (*by*) ~ **saying sth** al decir algo; **to spend one's time** ~ **doing sth** dedicar su tiempo a hacer algo **11.** (*taking the form of*) **to speak** ~ **French** hablar en francés; ~ **the form of a request** en forma de petición **12.** (*made of*) ~ **wood/stone** de madera/piedra **13.** (*sound of*) ~ **a whisper** en un murmullo; **to speak** ~ **a loud/low voice** hablar en voz alta/baja **14.** (*aspect of*) **6 feet** ~ **length/height** 2 metros de largo/alto; ~ **every respect** en todos los sentidos **15.** (*ratio*) **two** ~ **six** dos de cada seis; **to buy sth** ~ **twos** comprar algo de dos en dos; **10** ~ **number** 10 en número; ~ **part** en parte; ~ **tens** en grupos de diez **16.** (*substitution of*) ~ **your place** en tu lugar; ~ **lieu of sth** *form* en lugar de algo **17.** (*as consequence of*) ~ **return** a cambio; ~ **reply** como respuesta ▸~ **all** con todo; **all** ~ **all** en resumen **II.** *adv* **1.** (*inside, into*) dentro, adentro; **to go** ~ entrar; **to put sth** ~ meter algo **2.** (*to a place*) **to be** ~ *inf* estar en casa; **to hand sth** ~ entregar algo **3.** (*popular*) **to be** ~ estar de moda **4.** (*up*) **the tide is coming** ~ la marea está entrando ▸ **to be** ~ **for sth** *inf* estar a punto de recibir algo; **to be** ~ **on sth** estar enterado de algo **III.** *adj* de moda **IV.** *n* **the** ~**s and outs** los pormenores

IN [ɪn·di·ˈæn·ə] *n abbr of* **Indiana** Indiana *f*

in. *abbr of* **inch** pulgada *f*

inability [ˌɪn·ə·ˈbɪl·ə·t̬i] *n* incapacidad *f,* ineptitud *f pey*

inaccessible [ˌɪn·æk·ˈses·ə·bəl] *adj* inaccesible

inaccuracy [ɪn·ˈæk·jər·ə·si] <-ies> *n* **1.** (*fact*) error *m* **2.** (*quality*) imprecisión *f,* inexactitud *f*

inaccurate [ɪn·ˈæk·jər·ət] *adj* **1.** (*inexact*) inexacto, -a **2.** (*wrong*) equivocado, -a

inaction [ɪn·ˈæk·ʃən] *n* inacción *f*

inactive [ɪn·ˈæk·tɪv] *adj* inactivo, -a

inactivity [ˌɪn·æk·ˈtɪv·ə·t̬i] *n* inactividad *f*

inadequacy [ɪn·ˈæd·ɪ·kwə·si] <-ies> *n*
1. (*insufficiency*) insuficiencia *f* **2.** (*quality of being inadequate*) falta *f* de adecuación

inadequate [ɪn·ˈæd·ɪ·kwət] *adj* inadecuado, -a; (*inept*) inepto, -a

inadmissible [ˌɪn·əd·ˈmɪs·ə·bəl] *adj* inadmisible

inadvertent [ˌɪn·əd·ˈvɜr·tənt] *adj* involuntario, -a

inadvisable [ˌɪn·əd·'vaɪ·zə·bəl] *adj* desaconsejable

inalienable [ɪn·'eɪ·li·ə·nə·bəl] *adj form* inalienable

inane [ɪn·'eɪn] *adj* estúpido, -a

inanimate [ɪn·'æn·ɪ·mət] *adj* inanimado, -a

inanity [ɪ·'næn·ə·ti] <-ies> *n* necedad *f*

inapplicable [ɪn·'æp·lɪ·kə·bəl] *adj* inaplicable

inappropriate [ˌɪn·ə·'proʊ·pri·ət] *adj* inapropiado, -a; (*not suitable*) inadecuado, -a

inapt [ɪn·'æpt] *adj* inadecuado, -a; (*not skillful*) inhábil, no capacitado, -a

inaptitude [ɪn·'æp·tə·tud] *n* inhabilidad *f*

inarticulate [ˌɪn·ar·'tɪk·ju·lət] *adj* **1.** (*unable to express*) incapaz de expresarse **2.** (*unclear*) inarticulado, -a

inartistic [ˌɪn·ar·'tɪs·tɪk] *adj* poco artístico, -a

inasmuch as [ˌɪn·əz·'mʌtʃ·əz] *conj form* **1.** (*because*) dado que **2.** (*to the extent that*) en tanto que +*subj*

inattention [ˌɪn·ə·'ten·ʃən] *n* inatención *f*

inattentive [ˌɪn·ə·'ten·tɪv] *adj* distraído, -a; **to be ~ to sb/sth** no prestar atención a alguien/algo

inaudible [ɪn·'ɔ·də·bəl] *adj* inaudible

inaugural [ɪn·'ɔ·gju·rəl] *adj* inaugural; (*speech*) de apertura

inaugurate [ɪn·'ɔ·gju·reɪt] *vt* inaugurar

inauguration [ɪn·ˌɔ·gju·'reɪ·ʃən] *n* inauguración *f*

inauspicious [ˌɪn·ɔ·'spɪʃ·əs] *adj* poco propicio, -a

in-between *adj* intermedio, -a

inboard ['ɪn·bɔrd] *adj* interno, -a

inborn ['ɪn·bɔrn] *adj* innato, -a

inbred ['ɪn·bred] *adj* **1.** (*too closely related*) endogámico, -a **2.** (*inherent*) innato, -a

inbreeding ['ɪn·bri·dɪŋ] *n* endogamia *f*

inbuilt ['ɪn·bɪlt] *adj* integrado, -a; *fig* inherente, innato, -a

Inc. [ɪŋk] *abbr of* **incorporated** Inc.

incalculable [ɪn·'kæl·kju·lə·bəl] *adj* incalculable

incandescent [ˌɪn·ken·'des·ənt] *adj* incandescente

incantation [ˌɪn·kæn·'teɪ·ʃən] *n* conjuro *m*, ensalmo *m*

incapability [ɪn·ˌkeɪ·pə·'bɪl·ə·ti] *n* incapacidad *f*

incapable [ɪn·'keɪ·pə·bəl] *adj* incapaz; **to be ~ of doing sth** ser incapaz de hacer algo

incapacitate [ˌɪn·kə·'pæs·ɪ·teɪt] *vt* incapacitar

incapacity [ˌɪn·kə·'pæs·ə·ti] *n* incapacidad *f*

incarcerate [ɪn·'kar·sə·reɪt] *vt* encarcelar

incarnate [ɪn·'kar·nɪt] *adj* encarnado, -a; **the devil ~** el mismo diablo

incarnation [ˌɪn·kar·'neɪ·ʃən] *n* encarnación *f*; **to be the ~ of sth** ser la personificación de algo

incautious [ɪn·'kɔ·ʃəs] *adj form* imprudente

incendiary [ɪn·'sen·di·er·i] *adj a. fig* incendiario, -a

incense[1] ['ɪn·sents] *n* incienso *m*

incense[2] [ɪn·'sents] *vt* indignar

incensed *adj* indignado, -a

incentive [ɪn·'sen·tɪv] *n* incentivo *m*

incentive plan *n* plan *m* de incentivos

inception [ɪn·'sep·ʃən] *n* inicio *m*

incertitude [ɪn·'sɜr·t̬ɪ·tud] *n* incertidumbre *f*

incessant [ɪn·'ses·ənt] *adj* incesante

incest ['ɪn·sest] *n* incesto *m*

incestuous [ɪn·'ses·tʃu·əs] *adj a. fig* incestuoso, -a

inch [ɪntʃ] **I.** <-es> *n* pulgada *f*; **she knows every ~ of Miami** conoce cada centímetro de Miami ▶ **give someone an ~ and they'll take a mile** *prov* les das la mano y te cogen el brazo *prov*; **to do sth ~ by ~** hacer algo paso a paso **II.** *vi* moverse lentamente

◆ **inch forward** *vi* avanzar lentamente

incidence ['ɪn·sɪ·dənts] *n* incidencia *f*; **there is a higher ~ of left-handedness amongst girls than boys** existe un índice mayor de zurdas que de zurdos

incident [ɪn·'sɪ·dənt] *n* incidente *m*; **an isolated ~** un incidente aislado

incidental [ˌɪn·sɪ·'den·təl] *adj* **1.** (*related, of lesser importance*) secundario, -a **2.** (*occurring by chance*) imprevisto, -a

incidentally *adv* por cierto, a propósito

incinerate [ɪn·'sɪn·ə·reɪt] *vt* incinerar

incinerator [ɪn·'sɪn·ə·reɪ·t̬ər] *n* incinerador *m*

incipient [ɪn·'sɪp·i·ənt] *adj* incipiente; **at an ~ stage** en una etapa naciente

incise [ɪn·'saɪz] *vt* cortar; (*in wood*) grabar

incision [ɪn·'sɪʒ·ən] *n* MED incisión *f*

incisive [ɪn·'saɪ·sɪv] *adj* **1.** (*clear*) incisivo, -a; (*penetrating*) penetrante **2.** (*keen, acute*) agudo, -a; (*mind*) perspicaz

incisor [ɪn·'saɪ·zər] *n* incisivo *m*

incite [ɪn·'saɪt] *vt* instigar

incitement [ɪn·'saɪt·mənt] *n* incitación *f*

incivility [ˌɪn·sɪ·'vɪl·ə·ti] *n form* descortesía *f*

inclement [ɪn·'klem·ənt] *adj* inclemente

inclination [ˌɪn·klɪ·'neɪ·ʃən] *n* **1.** (*tendency*) propensión *f*; **to have an ~ to do sth** tener inclinación a hacer algo **2.** (*slope*) inclinación *f*

incline[1] ['ɪn·klaɪn] *n* inclinación *f*; (*of hill, mountain*) pendiente *f*

incline[2] [ɪn·'klaɪn] **I.** *vi* **1.** (*tend*) tender **2.** (*lean*) inclinarse **II.** *vt* **1.** (*make sth tend*) predisponer; **to ~ (sb) to do sth** influir (a alguien) para que haga algo **2.** (*make lean*) inclinar

inclined [ɪn·'klaɪnd] *adj* predispuesto, -a; **to be ~ to do sth** estar dispuesto a hacer algo

inclose [ɪn·'kloʊz] *vt s.* **enclose**

include [ɪn·'klud] *vt* incluir; (*in a letter*) adjuntar; **do you ~ that in the service?** ¿está incluido en el servicio?

including [ɪn·'klu·dɪŋ] *prep* incluso; **(not) ~ tax** impuesto (no) incluido; **up to and ~ June 6th** hasta el 6 de junio inclusive

inclusion [ɪn·'klu·ʒən] *n* inclusión *f*

inclusive [ɪn·'klu·sɪv] *adj* incluido, -a

incognito [ˌɪn·kag·'ni·toʊ] *adv* de incógnito, -a

incoherent [ˌɪn·koʊ·'hɪr·ənt] *adj* incoherente
income ['ɪn·kʌm] *n* ingresos *mpl*
income tax *n* impuesto *m* sobre la renta; **graduated** ~ impuesto *m* proporcional
incoming ['ɪn·ˌkʌm·ɪŋ] I. *adj* entrante II. *interj* MIL se presenta
incommensurate [ˌɪn·kə·'men·sər·ət] *adj* desproporcionado, -a; **to be** ~ **to** no guardar relación con
incommunicado [ˌɪn·kə·mju·nɪ·'kad·oʊ] *adj* incomunicado, -a; **we wanted to invite you to the party, but you were** ~ queríamos invitarte a la fiesta pero estabas ilocalizable
incomparable [ɪn·'kam·pər·ə·bəl] *adj* incomparable
incompatibility [ˌɪn·kəm·ˌpæt·ə·'bɪl·ə·t̬i] <-ies> *n* incompatibilidad *f;* ~ **with sth** falta de compatibilidad con algo; **Laura left the firm because of her** ~ **with her colleagues** Laura dejó la empresa por falta de entendimiento con sus compañeros
incompatible [ˌɪn·kəm·'pæt̬·ə·bəl] *adj* incompatible
incompetence [ɪn·'kam·pə·təns] *n,* **incompetency** *n* incompetencia *f*
incompetent [ɪn·'kam·pə·tənt] I. *adj* incompetente; **mentally** ~ deficiente mental; **she was mentally** ~ **when she wrote the will** no contaba con plenas facultades mentales cuando redactó el testamento II. *n* incompetente *mf*
incomplete [ˌɪn·kəm·'plit] *adj* incompleto, -a; (*not finished*) inacabado, -a
incomprehensible [ˌɪn·kam·prɪ·'hen·sə·bəl] *adj* incomprensible
inconceivable [ˌɪn·kən·'si·və·bəl] *adj* inconcebible
inconclusive [ˌɪn·kən·'klu·sɪv] *adj* 1.(*not convincing*) inconcluyente 2.(*without definite results*) no fructífero, -a
incongruous [ɪn·'kaŋ·gru·əs] *adj* 1.(*unsuitable*) inapropiado, -a 2.(*strange*) fuera de lugar
inconsequent [ɪn·'kan·sɪ·kwənt] *adj form* intrascendente
inconsequential [ɪn·ˌkan·sɪ·'kwen·ʃəl] *adj* 1.(*illogical*) inconsecuente 2.(*unimportant*) intrascendente
inconsiderable [ˌɪn·kən·'sɪd·ər·ə·bəl] *adj* **a not** ~ **amount** una suma nada desdeñable
inconsiderate [ˌɪn·kən·'sɪd·ər·ət] *adj* desconsiderado, -a; (*insensitive*) insensible
inconsistency [ˌɪn·kən·'sɪs·tən·si] <-ies> *n* 1.(*lack of consistency*) falta *f* de coherencia 2.(*discrepancy*) contradicción *f*
inconsistent [ˌɪn·kən·'sɪs·tənt] *adj* 1.(*changeable*) incoherente 2.(*lacking agreement*) contradictorio, -a
inconsolable [ˌɪn·kən·'soʊ·lə·bəl] *adj* inconsolable
inconspicuous [ˌɪn·kən·'spɪk·ju·əs] *adj* desapercibido, -a; **highly** ~ imperceptible; **to try to look** ~ tratar de pasar inadvertido

inconstant [ɪn·'kan·stənt] *adj* 1.(*changing*) inconstante; (*unpredictable*) imprevisible 2.(*unfaithful*) infiel
incontestable [ˌɪn·kən·'tes·tə·bəl] *adj form* incontestable; **it is** ~ **that...** es irrefutable que...
incontinent [ɪn·'kan·tə·nənt] *adj* MED incontinente
incontrovertible [ɪn·ˌkan·trə·'vɜr·t̬ə·bəl] *adj* incontrovertible; **her logic is** ~ su lógica es indiscutible; ~ **proof** prueba *f* irrefutable; **it is** ~ **that...** es incuestionable que...
inconvenience [ˌɪn·kən·'vin·jəns] I. *n* inconveniencia *f* II. *vt* causar molestias
inconvenient [ˌɪn·kən·'vin·jənt] *adj* inconveniente; (*time*) inoportuno, -a; **it's a very** ~ **place to hold the party** es un lugar muy poco adecuado para hacer la fiesta
incorporate [ɪn·'kɔr·pə·reɪt] *vt* 1.(*integrate*) incorporar; (*work into*) integrar; (*add*) añadir 2.(*include*) incluir 3. LAW, ECON constituir; **to** ~ **a company** formar una empresa
incorporation [ɪn·ˌkɔr·pə·'reɪ·ʃən] *n* 1.(*integration*) incorporación *f;* (*working into*) integración *f* 2. LAW, ECON constitución *f*
incorrect [ˌɪn·kə·'rekt] *adj* 1.(*wrong, untrue*) incorrecto, -a; (*diagnosis*) erróneo, -a; **it is** ~ **that...** no es cierto que... 2.(*improper*) inapropiado, -a
incorrigible [ɪn·'kɔr·ə·dʒə·bəl] *adj* incorregible
incorruptible [ˌɪn·kə·'rʌp·tə·bəl] *adj* 1.(*not able to be corrupted*) incorruptible; (*morally incorruptible*) íntegro, -a 2.(*not subject to decay*) inalterable
increase[1] ['ɪn·kris] *n* 1.(*raised amount*) incremento *m;* (*willful*) subida *f* 2.(*act of getting higher and higher*) crecimiento *m;* **to be on the** ~ ir en aumento
increase[2] [ɪn·'kris] I. *vi* (*become more*) incrementarse; (*grow*) crecer; **to** ~ **dramatically** aumentar espectacularmente; **to** ~ **tenfold/ threefold** multiplicarse por diez/tres II. *vt* (*make more*) incrementar; (*make stronger*) intensificar; (*make larger*) aumentar
increasing *adj* creciente
increasingly *adv* cada vez más
incredible [ɪn·'kred·ə·bəl] *adj* increíble
incredibly *adv* 1.(*in an incredible way*) increíblemente 2. ~, **nobody was hurt** parece increíble, pero no hubo heridos
incredulity [ˌɪn·krɪ·'du·lə·t̬i] *n* incredulidad *f;* (*bewilderment*) desconcierto *m*
incredulous [ɪn·'kredʒ·ə·ləs] *adj* incrédulo, -a
increment ['ɪŋ·krə·mənt] *n* incremento *m;* (*willful*) subida *f;* **salary** ~ aumento *m* salarial
incremental [ˌɪŋ·krə·'mən·təl] *adj* ECON en aumento
incriminate [ɪn·'krɪm·ɪ·neɪt] *vt* incriminar; **to** ~ **oneself** autoinculparse
incriminating *adj* comprometedor(a)
incubate ['ɪn·kju·beɪt] I. *vt* incubar II. *vi* incubarse

incubation [ˌɪn·kjʊ·'beɪ·ʃən] *n* incubación *f*
incubation period *n* período *m* de incubación
incubator ['ɪŋ·kjʊ·beɪ·t̬ər] *n* incubadora *f*
inculcate ['ɪn·kʌl·keɪt] *vt* inculcar
incumbent [ɪŋ·'kʌm·bənt] I. *adj* **it is ~ on sb to do sth** incumbe a alguien hacer algo II. *n* titular *mf*
incur [ɪn·'kɜr] <-rr-> *vt* **1.** FIN, ECON (*debt*) contraer; (*costs*) incurrir en; (*losses*) sufrir **2.**(*bring upon oneself*) acarrear; **to ~ the anger of sb** provocar el enfado de alguien
incurable [ɪn·'kjʊr·ə·bəl] *adj* incurable; *fig* incorregible; **he is an ~ romantic** es un romántico empedernido
incursion [ɪn·'kɜr·ʃən] *n* **1.** MIL incursión *f* **2.**(*intrusion*) intrusión *f*
Ind. *n abbr of* **Indiana** Indiana *f*
indebted [ɪn·'det̬·ɪd] *adj* **1.**(*obliged*) en deuda; **to be ~ to sb** (**for sth**) estar en deuda con alguien (por algo) **2.**(*having debt*) endeudado, -a
indebtedness *n* **1.**(*state of obligation*) deuda *f* **2.**(*state of debt*) endeudamiento *m*
indecency [ɪn·'di·sən·si] *n* **1.**(*impropriety*) indecencia *f* **2.** LAW indecencia *f*; **public ~** escándalo público
indecent [ɪn·'di·sənt] *adj* indecente, indecoroso, -a
indecipherable [ˌɪn·dɪ·'saɪ·frə·bəl] *adj* indescifrable
indecision [ˌɪn·dɪ·'sɪʒ·ən] *n* indecisión *f*, irresolución *f elev*
indecisive [ˌɪn·dɪ·'saɪ·sɪv] *adj* **1.**(*unable to make decisions*) indeciso, -a **2.**(*not clear*) irresoluto, -a
indeclinable [ɪn·dɪ·'klaɪ·nə·bəl] *adj* LING indeclinable
indecorous [ɪn·'dek·ər·əs] *adj form* (*unsuitable*) indecoroso, -a; (*undignified*) indigno, -a
indeed [ɪn·'did] I. *adv* **1.**(*really*) realmente; **this is good news ~!** ¡eso sí que es una buena noticia!; **many people here are very rich ~** mucha gente de aquí es verdaderamente rica **2.**(*expresses affirmation*) en efecto; **yes, he did ~ say that** sí, en efecto dijo eso II. *interj* ya lo creo; **he's a lovely boy! — ~!** es un chico encantador — ¡ya lo creo!
indefatigable [ˌɪn·dɪ·'fæt̬·ɪ·gə·bəl] *adj form* infatigable
indefensible [ˌɪn·dɪ·'fen·sə·bəl] *adj* insostenible; MIL indefendible
indefinable [ˌɪn·dɪ·'faɪ·nə·bəl] *adj* indefinible
indefinite [ɪn·'def·ə·nɪt] *adj* indefinido, -a; **for an ~ period** por un tiempo indeterminado
indefinite article *n* LING artículo *m* indefinido
indefinitely *adv* indefinidamente
indelible [ɪn·'del·ə·bəl] *adj* imborrable; (*colors, stains, ink*) indeleble
indemnify [ɪn·'dem·nɪ·faɪ] <-ie-> *vt* **1.**(*insure against damage*) asegurar **2.**(*compensate for damage*) indemnizar
indemnity [ɪn·'dem·nə·t̬i] <-ies> *n form* **1.**(*insurance for damage*) indemnidad

f **2.**(*compensation*) indemnización *f* **3.**(*exemption*) inmunidad *f*
indent [ɪn·'dent] I. *vi* TYPO (*make a space*) sangrar II. *vt* marcar; TYPO sangrar; **his footsteps ~ed the sand** sus pasos dejaron marcas en la arena III. *n* TYPO sangrado *m*
indentation [ˌɪn·den·'teɪ·ʃən] *n* **1.** TYPO sangría *f* **2.**(*notch*) hendidura *f*; (*cut*) mella *f*
independence [ˌɪn·dɪ·'pen·dəns] *n* independencia *f*
Independence Day *n* día *m* de la Independencia

> ⓘ En la **Declaración de Independencia**, las trece colonias en Norteamérica proclamaron su independencia de Gran Bretaña, bautizaron el país como **the thirteen United States of America** (los trece Estados Unidos de América) y explicaron su justificación para hacerlo. La Declaración fue ratificada por el Congreso Continental el 4 de julio de 1776 y este evento se conmemora todos los años en EE.UU. como el Día de la Independencia (**Independence Day**).

independent [ˌɪn·dɪ·'pen·dənt] I. *adj* independiente; **to be financially ~** ser económicamente independiente II. *n* POL diputado, -a *m*, *f* independiente
in-depth ['ɪn·depθ] *adj* exhaustivo, -a, a fondo
indescribable [ˌɪn·dɪ·'skraɪ·bə·bəl] *adj* indescriptible
indestructible [ˌɪn·dɪ·'strʌk·tə·bəl] *adj* indestructible; **~ waste products** productos *mpl* no desechables
indeterminable [ˌɪndɪ·'tɜrmɪnə·bəl] *adj* indeterminable
indeterminate [ˌɪn·dɪ·'tɜr·mə·nɪt] *adj* indeterminado, -a; **to take an ~ stance** adoptar una postura ecléctica
index ['ɪn·deks] I. *n* **1.** <-es> (*alphabetical list*) índice *m* **2.** <-ices *o* -es> ECON índice *m*; **the Dow Jones Index** el índice Dow Jones; **consumer price ~** índice de precios al consumo **3.** <-ices *o* -es> (*indication*) indicador *m* **4.** <-ices> MATH exponente *m* II. *vt* **1.**(*provide with a list*) poner índice a **2.**(*enter in a list*) indexar **3.** ECON **to ~ wages to inflation** equilibrar los sueldos a la inflación
indexation [ˌɪn·dek·'seɪ·ʃən] *n* ECON indexación *f*
index card *n* ficha *f*
indexer ['ɪn·dek·sər] *n* clasificador *m*
index finger *n* dedo *m* índice
India ['ɪn·di·ə] *n* la India *f*
India ink *n* tinta *f* china
Indian ['ɪn·di·ən] I. *adj* **1.**(*of India*) indio, -a, hindú **2.**(*of America*) indio, -a, indígena II. *n* **1.**(*of India*) indio, -a *m*, *f*, hindú *mf* **2.**(*of America*) indio, -a *m*, *f*, indígena *mf*
Indiana [ɪn·ˌdi·'æn·ə] *n* Indiana *f*

Indian Ocean n Océano m Índico
Indian summer n veranillo m de San Martín
India rubber n (substance) caucho m
indicate ['ɪn·dɪ·keɪt] vt indicar; **to ~ (to sb) that...** señalar (a alguien) que...
indication [ˌɪn·dɪ·'keɪ·ʃən] n **1.** (evidence) indicio m; **an ~ of willingness** una muestra de voluntad **2.** a. MED indicación f
indicative [ɪn·'dɪk·ə·tɪv] **I.** adj indicativo, -a **II.** n indicativo m
indicator ['ɪn·dɪ·keɪ·t̬ər] n indicador m
indices ['ɪn·dɪ·siz] n pl of **index**
indict [ɪn·'daɪt] vt **to ~ sb for sth** LAW acusar a alguien de algo
indictment [ɪn·'daɪt·mənt] n **1.** LAW acusación f **2.** fig crítica f
indie ['ɪn·di] adj inf (album, record company) independiente
Indies ['ɪn·diz] npl Indias fpl; **the West ~** las Antillas
indifference [ɪn·'dɪf·rəns] n indiferencia f
indifferent [ɪn·'dɪf·rənt] adj **1.** (not interested) indiferente, valemadrista inv Méx **2.** (neither good nor bad) mediocre
indigenous [ɪn·'dɪdʒ·ə·nəs] adj indígena
indigestible [ˌɪn·dɪ·'dʒəs·tə·bəl] adj **1.** (food) indigesto, -a **2.** fig indigerible
indigestion [ˌɪn·dɪ·'dʒəs·tʃən] n indigestión f; **to give oneself ~** empacharse
indignant [ɪn·'dɪg·nənt] adj indignado, -a; **to become ~** indignarse; **to be/feel ~ about sth** estar/sentirse indignado por algo
indignation [ˌɪn·dɪg·'neɪ·ʃən] n indignación f
indignity [ɪn·'dɪg·nə·t̬i] <-ies> n **1.** (humiliation) indignidad f **2.** (sth that humiliates) afrenta f
indirect [ˌɪn·dɪ·'rekt] adj indirecto, -a
indirect object n LING objeto m [o complemento] m indirecto
indiscernible [ˌɪn·dɪ·'sɜr·nə·bəl] adj indiscernible; (not visible) imperceptible; **~ to the naked eye** imperceptible a simple vista
indiscreet [ˌɪn·dɪ·'skrit] adj indiscreto, -a; (tactless) falto, -a de tacto
indiscretion [ˌɪn·dɪ·'skreʃ·ən] n (lack of discretion) indiscreción f; (lack of tactfulness) falta f de tacto
indiscriminate [ˌɪn·dɪ·'skrɪm·ə·nɪt] adj **1.** (uncritical) sin criterio **2.** (random) indiscriminado, -a
indispensable [ˌɪn·dɪ·'spen·sə·bəl] adj indispensable
indisposed [ˌɪn·dɪ·'spoʊzd] adj indispuesto, -a; **to be/feel ~ to do sth** estar/sentirse indispuesto para hacer algo
indisposition [ˌɪn·dɪs·pə·'zɪʃ·ən] n form **1.** (illness) indisposición f **2.** (disinclination) reticencia f
indisputable [ˌɪn·dɪ·'spju·t̬ə·bəl] adj indiscutible; (evidence) incuestionable
indistinct [ˌɪn·dɪ·'stɪŋkt] adj indistinto, -a; (blurred) borroso, -a
indistinguishable [ˌɪn·dɪ·'stɪŋ·gwɪ·ʃə·bəl]

adj indistinguible; (not perceptible) imperceptible
individual [ˌɪn·dɪ·'vɪdʒ·u·əl] **I.** n individuo, -a m, f **II.** adj individual; (particular) particular; **an ~ style** un estilo propio
individualism [ˌɪn·dɪ·'vɪdʒ·u·ə·lɪz·əm] n individualismo m
individualist n individualista mf
individualistic [ˌɪn·dɪ·ˌvɪdʒ·u·ə·'lɪs·tɪk] adj individualista
individuality [ˌɪn·dɪ·ˌvɪdʒ·u·'æl·ə·t̬i] n individualidad f
individualize [ˌɪn·dɪ·'vɪdʒ·u·ə·laɪz] vt individualizar
individually adv individualmente
indivisible [ˌɪn·dɪ·'vɪz·ə·bəl] adj indivisible
Indochina [ˌɪn·doʊ·'tʃaɪ·nə] n Indochina f
indoctrinate [ɪn·'dak·trɪ·neɪt] vt adoctrinar; **to ~ children in sth** adoctrinar a los niños en algo
indoctrination [ɪn·ˌdak·trɪ·'neɪ·ʃən] n adoctrinamiento m
indolent ['ɪn·də·lənt] adj indolente
indomitable [ɪn·'dam·ə·t̬ə·bəl] adj indómito, -a; **an ~ strength of character** una fuerza de carácter indomable
Indonesia [ˌɪn·də·'ni·ʒə] n Indonesia f
Indonesian I. adj indonesio, -a **II.** n indonesio, -a m, f
indoor [ˌɪn·'dɔr] adj interior; (pool) cubierto, -a; **~ plant** planta f de interior
indoors [ˌɪn·'dɔrz] adv dentro
indubitable [ɪn·'du·bɪ·t̬ə·bəl] adj form indubable
indubitably [ɪn·'du·bɪ·t̬ə·bli] adv form indubablemente
induce [ɪn·'dus] vt **1.** (persuade) a. ELEC, PHYS inducir **2.** (cause) provocar
inducement [ɪn·'dus·mənt] n incentivo m
induct [ɪn·'dʌkt] vt **1.** (install) investir **2.** (initiate) iniciar **3.** (recruit) reclutar
induction [ɪn·'dʌk·ʃən] n **1.** (installation) instalación f; (into organization) ingreso m **2.** (initiation) iniciación f **3.** a. MED inducción f **4.** PHILOS, ELEC inducción f
inductive [ɪn·'dʌk·tɪv] adj inductivo, -a
indulge [ɪn·'dʌldʒ] vt (allow) consentir; (desire) satisfacer; **to ~ oneself in...** darse el lujo de..., permitirse...
indulgence [ɪn·'dʌl·dʒəns] n **1.** (treat) placer m; (satisfaction) satisfacción f; **~ in** abandono a **2.** (tolerance) tolerancia f **3.** REL indulgencia f
indulgent [ɪn·'dʌl·dʒənt] adj **1.** (lenient) indulgente **2.** (tolerant) tolerante
industrial [ɪn·'dʌs·tri·əl] **I.** adj industrial; (dispute) laboral; **for ~ use** para uso industrial **II.** npl FIN acciones fpl industriales
industrialism [ɪn·'dʌs·tri·ə·lɪz·əm] n industrialismo m
industrialist n industrial mf
industrialization [ɪn·ˌdʌs·tri·ə·lɪ·'zeɪ·ʃən] n industrialización f
industrialize [ɪn·'dʌs·tri·ə·laɪz] **I.** vi industria-

lizarse **II.** *vt* industrializar

industrial park *n* polígono *m* industrial

Industrial Revolution *n* Revolución *f* Industrial

industrious [ɪn·'dʌs·tri·əs] *adj* trabajador(a)

industry ['ɪn·dəs·tri] *n* **1.** (*manufacturing production*) industria *f*; **heavy/light ~** industria pesada/ligera **2.** <-ies> (*branch*) sector *m* **3.** (*diligence*) laboriosidad *f*

inebriate [ɪ·'ni·bri·eɪt] *vt form* embriagar

inedible [ɪn·'ed·ə·bəl] *adj* **1.** (*unsuitable as food*) no comestible **2.** (*extremely unpalatable*) incomible

ineducable [ɪn·'edʒ·ə·kə·bəl] *adj* ineducable

ineffable [ɪn·'ef·ə·bəl] *adj* inefable

ineffective [ˌɪn·ɪ·'fek·tɪv] *adj* ineficaz

ineffectual [ˌɪn·ɪ·'fek·tʃʊ·əl] *adj* ineficaz, inútil

inefficiency [ˌɪn·ɪ·'fɪʃ·ən·si] *n* ineficiencia *f*

inefficient [ˌɪn·ɪ·'fɪʃ·ənt] *adj* ineficiente

inelegant [ˌɪn·'el·ɪ·gənt] *adj* **1.** (*unattractive*) poco elegante **2.** (*unrefined*) tosco, -a; (*gesture, movement*) basto, -a

ineligible [ɪn·'el·ɪdʒ·ə·bəl] *adj* inelegible; **to be ~ for sth** no reunir los requisitos para algo; **to be ~ to do sth** no tener derecho a hacer algo

inept [ɪn·'ept] *adj* (*unskilled*) inepto, -a; (*inappropriate*) inoportuno, -a; **to be ~ at sth** ser inepto para algo; **to be socially ~** no tener don de gentes

inequality [ˌɪn·ɪ·'kwal·ə·ti] <-ies> *n* desigualdad *f*

inequitable [ɪn·'ek·wə·tə·bəl] *adj* injusto, -a

inequity [ɪn·'ek·wə·ti] <-ies> *n* injusticia *f*

ineradicable [ˌɪn·ɪ·'ræd·ɪ·kə·bəl] *adj* (*disease*) incurable; (*feeling, memory*) indeleble

inert [ɪn·'ɜrt] *adj* **1.** (*not moving*) inerte; *fig* inmóvil **2.** PHYS inactivo, -a

inertia [ɪn·'ɜr·ʃə] *n* inercia *f*; *fig* pereza *f*

inescapable [ˌɪn·ɪ·'skeɪ·pə·bəl] *adj* ineludible

inessential [ˌɪn·ɪ·'sen·ʃəl] **I.** *adj* no esencial **II.** *n* cosa *f* no esencial

inestimable [ɪn·'es·tɪ·mə·bəl] *adj* inestimable; **to be of ~ value** tener un valor incalculable

inevitable [ɪn·'ev·ɪ·tə·bəl] **I.** *adj* inevitable; (*conclusion, consequence*) inexorable **II.** *n* **the ~** lo inevitable

inexact [ˌɪn·ɪg·'zækt] *adj* inexacto, -a

inexcusable [ˌɪn·ɪk·'skju·zə·bəl] *adj* imperdonable

inexhaustible [ˌɪn·ɪg·'zɔs·tə·bəl] *adj* inagotable

inexorable [ˌɪn·'ek·sər·ə·bəl] *adj form* inexorable

inexpedient [ˌɪn·ɪk·'spi·di·ənt] *adj form* inapropiado, -a

inexpensive [ˌɪn·ɪk·'spen·sɪv] *adj* económico, -a; **to be ~ to do sth** ser asequible hacer algo

inexperience [ˌɪn·ɪk·'spɪr·i·ənts] *n* falta *f* de experiencia

inexperienced [ˌɪn·ɪk·'spɪr·i·ənst] *adj* inexperto, -a; **to be ~ with relationships** no tener experiencia con los hombres/las mujeres

inexpert [ɪn·'ek·spɜrt] *adj* inexperto, -a; (*unskilled*) torpe

inexplicable [ˌɪn·ɪk·'splɪk·ə·bəl] **I.** *adj* inexplicable **II.** *n* **the ~** lo inexplicable

inextricable [ˌɪn·ɪk·'strɪk·ə·bəl] *adj* inextricable

infallible [ɪn·'fæl·ə·bəl] *adj* indefectible; (*incapable of being wrong*) infalible

infamous ['ɪn·fə·məs] *adj* **1.** (*shocking*) infame **2.** (*notorious*) de mala fama

infamy ['ɪn·fə·mi] *n* **1.** <-ies> (*shocking act*) infamia *f* **2.** (*notoriety*) mala fama *f*

infancy ['ɪn·fən·si] *n* infancia *f*; **from ~** desde niño; **to be in its ~** *fig* estar aún en pañales

infant ['ɪn·fənt] *n* (*very young child*) bebé *m*; **a newborn ~** un recién nacido

infanticide [ɪn·'fæn·tə·saɪd] *n* infanticidio *m*

infantile ['ɪn·fən·taɪl] *adj* infantil

infant mortality *n* mortalidad *f* infantil

infantry ['ɪn·fən·tri] *n + sing/pl vb* MIL infantería *f*

infantryman <-men> *n* MIL soldado *m* de infantería

infatuated [ɪn·'fætʃ·u·eɪ·tɪd] *adj* encaprichado, -a; **to become ~ with sb/sth** encapricharse con alguien/algo

infect [ɪn·'fekt] *vt* infectar; *a. fig* (*person*) contagiar

infection [ɪn·'fek·ʃən] *n* infección *f*; *fig* contagio *m*; **risk of ~** riesgo *m* de contagio

infectious [ɪn·'fek·ʃəs] *adj* infeccioso, -a; *a. fig* contagioso, -a

infelicitous [ˌɪn·fɪ·'lɪs·ə·təs] *adj iron* desafortunado, -a

infer [ɪn·'fɜr] <-rr-> *vt* inferir

inference ['ɪn·fər·əns] *n form* **1.** (*conclusion*) conclusión *f*; **to draw the ~ that...** sacar la conclusión de que... **2.** (*process of inferring*) inferencia *f*; **by ~** por inferencia

inferior [ɪn·'fɪr·i·ər] **I.** *adj* inferior **II.** *n* inferior *mf*

inferiority [ɪn·ˌfɪr·i·'ɔr·ə·ti] *n* inferioridad *f*

inferiority complex <-es> *n* complejo *m* de inferioridad

infernal [ɪn·'fɜr·nəl] *adj* infernal

inferno [ɪn·'fɜr·noʊ] *n* infierno *m*; **the building was an ~** el edificio ardía en llamas

infertile [ɪn·'fɜr·təl] *adj* estéril

infertility [ˌɪn·fər·'tɪl·ə·ti] *n* esterilidad *f*

infest [ɪn·'fest] *vt* infestar

infestation [ˌɪn·fes·'teɪ·ʃən] *n* plaga *f*, infestación *f*

infidel ['ɪn·fə·del] *n* REL infiel *mf*

infidelity [ˌɪn·fə·'del·ə·ti] *n* infidelidad *f*

infighting ['ɪn·faɪ·tɪŋ] *n* lucha *f* interna

infiltrate [ɪn·'fɪl·treɪt] *vt* infiltrarse en

infiltration [ˌɪn·fɪl·'treɪ·ʃən] *n* infiltración *f*

infiltrator *n* infiltrado, -a *m, f*

infinite ['ɪn·fə·nɪt] *adj* infinito, -a; **with ~ patience** con una paciencia infinita; **to take ~ care** poner sumo cuidado

infinitely *adv* infinitamente

infinitesimal [ˌɪn·fɪn·ɪ·'tes·ɪ·məl] *adj form*

infinitesimal

infinitive [ɪn·'fɪn·ə·tɪv] LING **I.** *n* infinitivo *m* **II.** *adj* infinitivo, -a

infinity [ɪn·'fɪn·ə·ti] <-ies> *n* **1.** MATH infinito *m;* **to** ~ hasta el infinito **2.** (*huge amount*) infinidad *f*

infirm [ɪn·'fɜrm] *adj* enfermizo, -a; (*weak*) débil

infirmary [ɪn·'fɜr·mə·ri] <-ies> *n* **1.** (*hospital*) hospital *m* **2.** (*room*) enfermería *f*

infirmity [ɪn·'fɜr·mə·ti] <-ies> *n* **1.** (*illness*) enfermedad *f* **2.** (*weakness*) debilidad *f*

inflame [ɪn·'fleɪm] *vt* **1.** *a.* MED inflamar **2.** (*stir up*) encender; **to** ~ **sb with passion** desatar la pasión de alguien

inflammable [ɪn·'flæm·ə·bəl] *adj* inflamable; (*situation*) explosivo, -a

inflammation [ˌɪn·flə·'meɪ·ʃən] *n* MED inflamación *f*

inflammatory [ɪn·'flæm·ə·tɔr·i] *adj* **1.** MED inflamatorio, -a **2.** (*speech*) incendiario, -a

inflatable [ɪn·'fleɪ·tə·bəl] **I.** *adj* hinchable **II.** *n* bote *m* hinchable

inflate [ɪn·'fleɪt] **I.** *vt* **1.** (*fill with air*) hinchar, inflar **2.** (*exaggerate*) exagerar **3.** ECON (*prices*) disparar **II.** *vi* hincharse

inflated [ɪn·'fleɪ·tɪd] *adj* **1.** (*filled with air*) hinchado, -a **2.** (*exaggerated*) exagerado, -a **3.** ECON (*price*) excesivo, -a

inflation [ɪn·'fleɪ·ʃən] *n* inflación *f*

inflationary *adj* FIN inflacionario, -a

inflect [ɪn·'flekt] *vt* (*verb*) conjugar; (*noun*) declinar; **to** ~ **one's voice** modular la voz

inflection [ɪn·'flek·ʃən] *n* inflexión *f*

inflexibility [ɪm·'paɪ·ə·ti] *n* inflexibilidad *f;* (*rigidity*) rigidez *f*

inflexible [ɪn·'flek·sə·bəl] *adj* inflexible

inflict [ɪn·'flɪkt] *vt* infligir

infliction [ɪn·'flɪk·ʃən] *n* imposición *f*

influence ['ɪn·flu·əns] **I.** *n* influencia *f;* **to exert one's** ~ ejercer su influencia; **to bring one's** ~ **to bear on sb** ejercer presión sobre alguien; **to be under the** ~ *fig* estar borracho; **to drive under the** ~ *fig* conducir bajo los efectos del alcohol **II.** *vt* influir

influential [ˌɪn·flu·'en·ʃəl] *adj* influyente

influenza [ˌɪn·flu·'en·zə] *n* gripe *f*

influx ['ɪn·flʌks] *n* influjo *m*

inform [ɪn·'fɔrm] **I.** *vt* informar; **I'm happy to** ~ **you that...** tengo el placer de comunicarle que...; **to be ~ed about sth** estar enterado de algo **II.** *vi* **to** ~ **against sb** delatar a alguien

informal [ɪn·'fɔr·məl] *adj* informal; (*tone, manner*) familiar; (*person*) afable

informality [ˌɪn·fɔr·'mæl·ə·ti] *n* **1.** (*lack of formality*) informalidad *f* **2.** (*unofficial character*) falta *f* de ceremonia

informant [ɪn·'fɔr·mənt] *n* informante *mf;* **a reliable** ~ una fuente fiable

information [ˌɪn·fər·'meɪ·ʃən] *n* **1.** (*data*) información *f;* **a lot of/a little** ~ mucha/poca información; **to ask for** ~ pedir información; **for further** ~ para más información **2.** COMPUT datos *mpl* **3.** (*knowledge*) conocimientos *mpl*

4. (*inquiry desk*) información *f* **5.** LAW denuncia *f*

information age *n* era *f* de la información

information science *n* ciencias *fpl* de la información

information superhighway *n* autopista *f* de la información

information technology *n* tecnologías *fpl* de la información

informative [ɪn·'fɔr·mə·tɪv] *adj* informativo, -a

informed *adj* informado, -a

informer [ɪn·'fɔr·mər] *n* informante *mf,* informador(a) *m(f)*

infotainment ['ɪn·fou·teɪn·mənt] *n* infotainment *m*

infraction [ɪn·'fræk·ʃən] *n* infracción *f*

infrared ['ɪn·frə·'red] *adj* infrarrojo, -a

infrastructure ['ɪn·frə·ˌstrʌk·tʃər] *n* infraestructura *f*

infrequent [ɪn·'fri·kwənt] *adj* poco frecuente

infringe [ɪn·'frɪndʒ] **I.** *vt* LAW infringir; **to** ~ **sb's right** violar un derecho ajeno **II.** *vi* **to** ~ **on** [*o* **upon**] **sth** usurpar

infringement [ɪn·'frɪndʒ·mənt] *n* LAW infracción *f;* (*of a rule*) violación *f,* vulneración *f;* **copyright** ~ violación de los derechos de autor; ~ **of a law** violación de una ley

infuriate [ɪn·'fjʊr·i·eɪt] *vt* enfurecer

infuse [ɪn·'fjuz] *vt* **1.** (*fill*) infundir; **to** ~ **sb with courage** infundir ánimo a alguien **2.** (*tea, herbs*) hacer una infusión de

infusion [ɪn·'fju·ʒən] *n a.* MED infusión *f;* ECON inyección *f*

ingenious [ɪn·'dʒin·jəs] *adj* **1.** (*creatively inventive*) inventivo, -a; (*idea, method, plan*) ingenioso, -a **2.** (*innovative*) innovador(a)

ingenuity [ˌɪn·dʒɪ·'nu·ə·ti] *n* ingenuidad *f;* **to use one's** ~ utilizar el ingenio

ingenuous [ɪn·'dʒen·ju·əs] *adj form* **1.** (*naive*) ingenuo, -a **2.** (*openly honest*) candoroso, -a

ingest [in·'dʒest] *vt form* ingerir

inglenook ['ɪŋ·gəl·nʊk] *n* ARCHIT rincón *m* de la chimenea

inglorious [ɪn·'glɔr·i·əs] *adj* ignominioso, -a; (*dishonorable*) deshonroso, -a

ingoing ['ɪn·gou·ɪŋ] *adj* entrante

ingot ['ɪŋ·gət] *n* barra *f;* (*of gold, silver*) lingote *m*

ingrained [ˌɪn·'greɪnd] *adj* **1.** (*embedded: dirt*) incrustado, -a; **to be/become** ~ **in sth** estar/quedarse incrustado en algo **2.** (*deep-seated*) arraigado, -a

ingratiate [ɪn·'greɪ·ʃi·eɪt] *vt* **to** ~ **oneself** (**with sb**) congraciarse (con alguien)

ingratitude [ɪn·'græt·ə·tud] *n* ingratitud *f*

ingredient [ɪn·'gri·di·ənt] *n* **1.** CULIN ingrediente *m* **2.** (*component*) *a.* MED componente *m*

ingrowing ['ɪn·grou·ɪŋ] *adj* que crece hacia dentro (de la piel); ~ **toenail** uñero *m*

ingrown ['ɪn·groun] *adj* que crece hacia dentro (de la piel); ~ **toenail** uñero *m;* (*innate*); ~ **habits** hábitos *mpl* instintivos

inhabit [ɪn·ˈhæb·ɪt] *vt* habitar
inhabitable *adj* habitable
inhabitant [ɪn·ˈhæb·ɪ·tənt] *n* habitante *mf*
inhale [ɪn·ˈheɪl] **I.** *vt* aspirar; MED inhalar **II.** *vi* inhalar
inhaler [ɪn·ˈheɪ·lər] *n* inhalador *m*
inharmonious [ˌɪn·har·ˈmoʊ·ni·əs] *adj* **1.** (*not peaceful*) poco armonioso, -a **2.** MUS disonante **3.** (*not blending well*) discorde
inhere [ɪn·ˈhɪr] *vi form* **to ~ in** sth/sb ser inherente a algo/en alguien
inherent [ɪn·ˈhɪr·ənt] *adj* inherente; PHILOS intrínseco, -a; **to be ~ in** sth ser inherente a algo
inherit [ɪn·ˈher·ɪt] **I.** *vt* heredar **II.** *vi* recibir una herencia
inheritable *adj* heredable
inheritance [ɪn·ˈher·ɪ·təns] *n* herencia *f*; *fig* legado *m*; **to come into an ~** recibir una herencia
inhibit [ɪn·ˈhɪb·ɪt] *vt* (*hinder*) impedir; (*impair*) inhibir; **to ~ sb from doing sth** impedir a alguien hacer algo
inhibition [ˌɪn·ɪ·ˈbɪʃ·ən] *n* inhibición *f*
inhospitable [ɪn·ˈhas·pɪ·ṭə·bəl] *adj* inhospitalario, -a; (*attitude*) poco amistoso, -a; (*place*) inhóspito, -a
in-house [ˈɪn·haʊs] COM **I.** *adj* interno, -a **II.** *adv* dentro de la empresa
inhuman [ɪn·ˈhju·mən] *adj* (*not human*) inhumano, -a
inhumane [ˌɪn·hju·ˈmeɪn] *adj* (*cruel*) inhumano, -a, cruel
inhumanity [ˌɪn·hju·ˈmæn·ə·ṭi] *n* inhumanidad *f*
inimical [ɪ·ˈnɪm·ɪ·kəl] *adj form* **1.** (*hostile*) contrario, -a; **to be ~ to** sth ser contrario a algo **2.** (*harmful*) perjudicial
inimitable [ɪ·ˈnɪm·ɪ·ṭə·bəl] *adj* inimitable
iniquitous [ɪ·ˈnɪk·wɪ·ṭəs] *adj* inicuo, -a
iniquity [ɪ·ˈnɪk·wə·ṭi] <-ies> *n* **1.** (*wickedness*) iniquidad *f*; (*sinfulness*) perversidad *f*; (*unfairness*) injusticia *f* **2.** (*act of wickedness*) iniquidades *fpl*; (*act of unfairness*) injusticias *fpl*
initial [ɪ·ˈnɪʃ·əl] **I.** *n* inicial *f*; **one's ~s** las iniciales de uno **II.** *adj* inicial; (*first*) primero, -a; **in the ~ phases** en las primeras etapas **III.** <-ll-, -l-> *vt* marcar con las iniciales
initialize [ɪ·ˈnɪʃ·ə·laɪz] *vt* COMPUT inicializar
initially [ɪ·ˈnɪʃ·ə·li] *adv* en un principio
initiate [ɪ·ˈnɪʃ·i·eɪt] **I.** *vt* **1.** (*start*) iniciar, dar comienzo a; (*proceedings*) entablar **2.** (*admit to group*) admitir (como miembro) **II.** *n* iniciado, -a *m, f*
initiation [ɪ·ˌnɪʃ·i·ˈeɪ·ʃən] *n* **1.** (*starting*) inicio *m* **2.** (*introducing*) iniciación *f*; (*as a member*) admisión *f*
initiative [ɪ·ˈnɪʃ·ə·ṭɪv] *n* iniciativa *f*; **to take the ~ in** sth tomar la iniciativa en algo; **to show ~** demostrar iniciativa; **to use one's ~** obrar por cuenta propia
inject [ɪn·ˈdʒekt] *vt* **1.** *a.* MED inyectar **2.** (*intro-*

duce) introducir; (*funds, money*) inyectar; (*invest*) invertir
injection [ɪn·ˈdʒek·ʃən] *n* inyección *f*
injudicious [ˌɪn·dʒu·ˈdɪʃ·əs] *adj* imprudente
injunction [ɪn·ˈdʒʌŋk·ʃən] *n* mandato *m*; LAW mandato *m* judicial
injure [ˈɪn·dʒər] *vt* **1.** (*wound*) herir, victimar *AmL* **2.** (*damage*) dañar **3.** (*do wrong to*) perjudicar
injured *adj* **1.** (*wounded*) herido, -a, victimado, -a *AmL* **2.** (*damaged*) dañado, -a **3.** (*wronged*) perjudicado, -a
injury [ˈɪn·dʒə·ri] <-ies> *n* **1.** (*physical*) lesión *f*, herida *f*; **a knee/back ~** una lesión de rodilla/espalda; **to receive an ~** ser herido **2.** (*psychological*) daño *m*
injustice [ɪn·ˈdʒʌs·tɪs] *n* injusticia *f*; **you do me an ~** no eres justo conmigo
ink [ɪŋk] **I.** *n* tinta *f*; **to write in ~** escribir con tinta **II.** *vt* **1.** TYPO entintar **2.** *inf* (*to sign*) echar un autógrafo, firmar
ink-jet printer *n* impresora *f* de chorro de tinta
inkling [ˈɪŋk·lɪŋ] *n* **1.** (*suspicion*) sospecha *f*; **to have an ~ that...** tener la sospecha de que... **2.** (*hint*) indicio *m*
inkpad [ˈɪŋk·pad] *n* almohadilla *f*
inky [ˈɪŋ·ki] <-ier, -iest> *adj* **1.** (*stained*) manchado, -a de tinta **2.** (*black*) negro, -a como la tinta
inlaid [ˈɪn·leɪd] **I.** *vt pt, pp of* inlay **II.** *adj* de marquetería; **~ work** taracea *f*
inland [ˈɪn·lənd] **I.** *adj* (*not coastal: sea, shipping*) interior; (*town, village*) del interior *m* **II.** *adv* **1.** (*direction*) tierra adentro **2.** (*place*) hacia el interior
in-laws [ˈɪn·lɔz] *npl* suegros *mpl*
inlay [ˌɪn·ˈleɪ] **I.** *n* **1.** (*embedded pattern*) incrustación *f* **2.** MED empaste *m* **II.** <inlaid, inlaid> *vt* taracear
inlet [ˈɪn·let] *n* **1.** GEO ensenada *f*; (*of sea*) cala *f* **2.** TECH entrada *f*; (*pipe*) tubo *m* de admisión
in-line skate *n* patín *m* en línea
inmate [ˈɪn·meɪt] *n* residente *mf*; (*prison*) preso, -a *m, f*
inn [ɪn] *n* posada *f*
innards [ˈɪn·ərdz] *npl inf* **1.** (*entrails*) tripas *fpl* **2.** TECH engranajes *mpl*
innate [ɪ·ˈneɪt] *adj* innato, -a
inner [ˈɪn·ər] *adj* **1.** (*located in the interior*) interno, -a, interior **2.** (*deep*) íntimo, -a; (*secret*) secreto, -a; **one's ~ feelings** los sentimientos más íntimos de uno
inner city *n* parte céntrica de la ciudad, *habitada con frecuencia por gente pobre y marginada*
innermost [ˈɪn·ər·moʊst] *adj* más íntimo, -a; **in his/her ~ being** en lo más profundo de su ser
inner tube *n* cámara *f* de aire
inning [ˈɪn·ɪŋ] *n* SPORTS (*part of baseball game*) inning *m*
innocence [ˈɪn·ə·səns] *n* inocencia *f*; **to plead one's ~** declararse inocente; **in all ~** inocente-

innocent ['ɪn·ə·sənt] I. *adj* inocente; **to be ~ of sth** ser inocente de algo; **an ~ bystander** un testigo casual II. *n* inocente *mf;* **to be an ~** ser un inocente
innocuous [ɪ·'nak·jʊ·əs] *adj* inocuo, -a
innovate ['ɪn·ə·veɪt] *vi* innovar; (*introduce changes*) introducir novedades
innovation [ˌɪn·ə·'veɪ·ʃən] *n* novedad *f,* innovación *f*
innovative ['ɪn·ə·veɪ·ţɪv] *adj* (*model, product*) novedoso, -a; (*person*) innovador(a)
innovator *n* innovador(a) *m(f)*
innuendo [ˌɪn·ju·'en·doʊ] <-(e)s> *n* 1.(*insinuation*) insinuación *f;* **to make an ~** (**about sth**) hacer una insinuación (sobre algo) 2.(*suggestive remark*) indirecta *f*
innumerable [ɪ·'nu·mər·ə·bəl] *adj* innumerable
innumerate [ɪ·'nu·mər·ət] *adj* **to be ~** ser incapaz de realizar cálculos
inoculate [ɪ·'nak·jə·leɪt] *vt* **to ~ sb** (**against sth**) inocular a alguien (contra algo)
inoculation [ɪ·ˌnak·jə·'leɪ·ʃən] *n* inoculación *f*
inoffensive [ˌɪn·ə·'fen·sɪv] *adj* inofensivo, -a
inoperable [ˌɪn·'ap·ər·ə·bəl] *adj* inoperable
inoperative [ˌɪn·'ap·ər·ə·ţɪv] *adj* inoperante
inopportune [ˌɪn·ˌap·ər·'tun] *adj* inoportuno, -a; (*inconvenient*) inconveniente
inordinate [ɪn·'ɔr·dɪn·ɪt] *adj* desmesurado, -a; **an ~ amount of sth** una cantidad excesiva de algo
inorganic [ˌɪn·ɔr·'gæn·ɪk] *adj* inorgánico, -a
inpatient ['ɪn·peɪ·ʃənt] *n* paciente *mf* interno, -a
input ['ɪn·pʊt] I. *n* 1.(*contribution*) contribución *f,* aportación *f;* COMPUT entrada *f;* **power ~** entrada (de potencia) 2. *a.* FIN inversión *f* II.<-tt-> *vt* COMPUT introducir; (*with a scanner*) escanear
inquest ['ɪn·kwest] *n* 1.LAW pesquisa *f* judicial; **to hold an ~** (**into sth**) llevar a cabo una investigación (sobre algo) 2. *fig* indagación *f;* **to hold an ~** realizar un análisis
inquire [ɪn·'kwaɪr] I. *vi* 1.(*ask*) preguntar; **to ~ about sb** preguntar por alguien; **to ~ about sth** pedir información sobre algo 2.(*investigate*) investigar; **to ~ into a matter** indagar en un asunto II. *vt* preguntar; **to ~ the reason** preguntar por qué
inquiry [ɪn·'kwaɪ·ri] *n* 1.(*question*) pregunta *f* 2.(*investigation*) investigación *f*
inquisition [ˌɪn·kwɪ·'zɪʃ·ən] *n* 1.(*questioning*) investigación *f;* **to subject sb to an ~** someter a alguien a una investigación 2.HIST **the Inquisition** la Inquisición
inquisitive [ɪn·'kwɪz·ɪ·ţɪv] *adj* 1.(*curious*) curioso, -a; (*look, expression*) interrogante; (*child*) preguntón, -ona; **to be ~ about sth/sb** sentir curiosidad sobre algo/alguien 2.(*prying*) fisgón, -ona
inroad ['ɪn·roʊd] *n* MIL incursión *f; fig* invasión *f;* **to make ~s into sth** abrirse camino en algo

inrush ['ɪn·rʌʃ] <-es> *n* irrupción *f;* (*of people*) afluencia *f*
insalubrious [ˌɪn·sə·'lu·bri·əs] *adj* (*unpleasant*) poco recomendable; (*unhealthy*) malsano, -a; (*dirty*) sucio, -a; **an ~ climate** un clima perjudicial para la salud
ins and outs *npl* pormenores *mpl*
insane [ɪn·'seɪn] *adj* demente; *a. fig* (*crazy*) loco, -a; **to be/go ~** estar/volverse loco
insanitary [ɪn·'sæn·ɪ·ter·i] *adj* antihigiénico, -a
insanity [ɪn·'sæn·ə·ţi] *n* 1.(*mental illness*) demencia *f* 2. *a. fig* (*craziness*) locura *f*
insatiable [ɪn·'seɪ·ʃə·bəl] *adj* insaciable
inscribe [ɪn·'skraɪb] *vt* inscribir; (*engrave*) grabar
inscription [ɪn·'skrɪp·ʃən] *n* inscripción *f;* (*dedication*) dedicatoria *f*
inscrutable [ɪn·'skru·ţə·bəl] *adj* (*look, smile*) enigmático, -a; (*person*) inescrutable
insect ['ɪn·sekt] *n* insecto *m; ~* **bite** picadura *f* de insecto
insecticide [ɪn·'sek·tɪ·saɪd] *n* insecticida *m*
insecure [ˌɪn·sɪ·'kjʊr] *adj* inseguro, -a; (*future*) incierto, -a
insecurity [ˌɪn·sɪ·'kjʊr·ə·ţi] <-ies> *n* inseguridad *f*
inseminate [ɪn·'sem·ɪ·neɪt] *vt* inseminar
insemination [ɪn·ˌsem·ɪ·'neɪ·ʃən] *n* inseminación *f*
insensible [ɪn·'sen·sə·bəl] *adj form* 1.(*unfeeling*) insensible; (*indifferent*) indiferente; **to be ~ to sth** ser indiferente a algo 2.(*unaware*) no consciente; **to be ~ of sth** no ser consciente de algo
insensitive [ɪn·'sen·sɪ·ţɪv] *adj* insensible; (*indifferent*) indiferente
inseparable [ɪn·'sep·rə·bəl] *adj* inseparable, indisoluble
insert[1] ['ɪn·sɜrt] *n* 1.(*page*) encarte *m* 2.(*piece of material*) añadido *m*
insert[2] [ɪn·'sɜrt] *vt* 1.(*put into*) insertar; (*coins*) introducir 2.(*add within a text*) intercalar; (*fill in*) añadir
insertion [ɪn·'sɜr·ʃən] *n* 1.(*act of inserting*) inserción *f;* (*of coins*) introducción *f* 2.(*thing inserted*) añadido *m* 3.(*in a newspaper*) inserción *f*
in-service ['ɪn·sɜr·vɪs] *adj* en funcionamiento
inshore [ˌɪn·'ʃɔr] I. *adj* cerca de la orilla; **~ waters** aguas *fpl* costeras II. *adv* hacia la costa
inside [ɪn·'saɪd] I. *adj* 1.(*internal*) interno, -a; **the ~ door** la puerta interior 2.(*from within: information*) confidencial; **the robbery was an ~ job** realizaron el robo con ayuda de alguien de dentro II. *n* 1.(*internal part or side*) interior *m;* **on the ~** por dentro; **to turn sth ~ out** volver algo del revés; **to turn the whole room ~ out** *fig* revolver toda la habitación; **to know a place ~ out** conocer muy bien un lugar; **to know the ~ of sth** conocer los entresijos de algo 2.~s *inf* (*entrails*) tripas *fpl* III. *prep* (*within*) ~ (**of**) dentro de; **to play ~**

the house jugar dentro de casa; **to go ~ the house** entrar en casa **IV.** *adv* **1.** (*within something*) dentro; **to go ~** entrar **2.** (*internally*) interiormente

insider ['ɪn·ˌsaɪ·dər] *n* persona *f* de la casa; (*with special knowledge*) persona *f* enterada

insidious [ɪn·'sɪd·i·əs] *adj* insidioso, -a; (*subversive*) subversivo, -a; **~ disease** enfermedad *f* maligna

insight ['ɪn·saɪt] *n* **1.** (*capacity*) perspicacia *f* **2.** (*instance*) nueva percepción *f;* **to gain ~ into sth/sb** entender mejor algo/a alguien; **the exhibition gave us ~ into the 19th century** la exposición ha sido una revelación del siglo XIX

insignia [ɪn·'sɪg·ni·ə] *n* insignia *f*

insignificance [ˌɪn·sɪg·'nɪf·ɪ·kəns] *n* insignificancia *f;* **to fade into ~** hacerse insignificante

insignificant [ˌɪn·sɪg·'nɪf·ɪ·kənt] *adj* insignificante; (*trivial*) trivial

insincere [ˌɪn·sɪn·'sɪr] *adj* poco sincero, -a

insinuate [ɪn·'sɪn·ju·eɪt] **I.** *vt* **1.** (*imply sth unpleasant*) insinuar **2.** (*maneuver*) introducir **II.** *vr* **to ~ oneself into** introducirse en

insinuation [ɪn·ˌsɪn·ju·'eɪ·ʃən] *n* **1.** insinuación *f* **2.** (*hint*) indirecta *f*

insipid [ɪn·'sɪp·ɪd] *adj* **1.** (*food, drink, entertainment*) insípido, -a **2.** (*person*) soso, -a

insist [ɪn·'sɪst] **I.** *vi* insistir; **to ~ on doing sth** obstinarse en hacer algo; **if you ~** si insistes **II.** *vt* **1.** (*state*) insistir **2.** (*demand*) exigir

insistence [ɪn·'sɪs·təns] *n* insistencia *f;* **her ~ on...** su insistencia en..; **to do sth at sb's ~** hacer algo por insistencia de alguien

insistent [ɪn·'sɪs·tənt] *adj* insistente; **to be ~ (that)...** insistir (en que)...

insofar as [ˌɪn·sou·'far·əz] *adv form* en tanto que +*subj*

insole ['ɪn·soul] *n* plantilla *f*

insolence ['ɪn·sə·ləns] *n* insolencia *f*

insolent ['ɪn·sə·lənt] *adj* insolente

insoluble [ɪn·'sal·jə·bəl] *adj* insoluble

insolvency [ɪn·'sal·vən·si] *n* insolvencia *f*

insolvent [ɪn·'sal·vənt] **I.** *adj* insolvente **II.** *n* insolvente *mf*

insomnia [ɪn·'sam·ni·ə] *n* insomnio *m;* **to suffer from ~** padecer insomnio

insomniac [ɪn·'sam·ni·æk] *n* insomne *mf*

insomuch as [ˌɪn·sou·'mʌtʃ] *conj form* **1.** (*because*) ya que **2.** (*to the extent that*) en tanto que +*subj*

inspect [ɪn·'spekt] *vt* **1.** (*examine carefully*) inspeccionar **2.** (*examine officially*) registrar; **to ~ the books** examinar los libros (de contabilidad) **3.** MIL **to ~ the troops** pasar revista

inspection [ɪn·'spek·ʃən] *n* inspección *f;* MIL revista *f*

inspector [ɪn·'spek·tər] *n* inspector(a) *m(f);* **ticket ~** revisor(a) *m(f)*

inspiration [ˌɪn·spə·'reɪ·ʃən] *n* **1.** a. MED inspiración *f* **2.** (*source*) fuente *f* de inspiración; **to provide the ~ for sth** servir de inspiración para algo; **to lack ~** no tener inspiración

inspire [ɪn·'spaɪr] *vt* **1.** (*stimulate*) inspirar; **to ~ sb with hope** infundir esperanza a alguien **2.** (*cause, lead to*) llevar a

inspired *adj* inspirado, -a

instability [ˌɪn·stə·'bɪl·ə·ti] *n* inestabilidad *f*

instal <-ll->, **install** [ɪn·'stɔl] **I.** *vt* **1.** a. TECH, COMPUT instalar **2.** (*place*) colocar; **to ~ sb** colocar a alguien (en un cargo) **II.** *vr* **to ~ oneself** instalarse

installation [ˌɪn·stə·'leɪ·ʃən] *n* instalación *f*

installment *n*, **instalment** [ɪn·'stɔl·mənt] *n* **1.** RADIO, TV entrega *f* **2.** COM plazo *m;* **to pay (for sth) in ~s** pagar (algo) a plazos; **to be payable in monthly ~s** ser pagadero a plazos mensuales

installment plan *n* compra *f* a plazos

instance ['ɪn·stəns] **I.** *n* **1.** (*case*) caso *m;* **in this ~** en este caso; **for ~** por ejemplo; **in the first/second ~** en primer/segundo lugar **2.** *form* (*request*) petición *f;* (*order*) pedido *m;* **to do sth at sb's ~** hacer algo a petición de alguien **II.** *vt* poner por caso

instant [ɪn·'stənt] **I.** *n* instante *m*, momento *m;* **at the same ~** al mismo tiempo; **for an ~** por un momento; **in an ~** al instante; **to do sth this ~** hacer algo inmediatamente **II.** *adj* **1.** (*immediate*) inmediato, -a **2.** CULIN instantáneo, -a; **~ coffee** café *m* instantáneo; **~ soup** (*in packets*) sopa *f* de sobre; (*in cans*) sopa *f* de lata **3.** *liter* (*urgent*) urgente

instantaneous [ˌɪn·stən·'teɪ·ni·əs] *adj* instantáneo, -a; (*effect, reaction*) inmediato, -a; (*spontaneous*) espontáneo, -a

instantaneously *adv* instantáneamente; (*spontaneously*) espontáneamente

instantly ['ɪn·stənt·li] *adv* al instante

instant replay *n* (*action replay*) repetición *f*

instead [ɪn·'sted] **I.** *adv* en cambio, en lugar de eso **II.** *prep* **~ of** en vez de, en lugar de; **~ of him** en su lugar; **~ of doing sth** en lugar de hacer algo

instep ['ɪn·step] *n* **1.** (*part of foot*) empeine *m* **2.** (*part of shoe*) lengüeta *f*

instigate [ɪn·'stɪ·geɪt] *vt* **1.** (*initiate*) instigar **2.** (*incite*) incitar

instigation [ˌɪn·stɪ·'geɪ·ʃən] *n* instigación *f;* **to do sth at the ~ of sb** hacer algo a instigación de alguien

instil [ɪn·'stɪl] <-ll-> *vt*, **instill** *vt* **to ~ sth (into sb)** infundir algo (a alguien); (*teach*) inculcar algo (a alguien)

instinct ['ɪn·stɪŋkt] *n* instinto *m;* **to do sth by ~** hacer algo por instinto; **a business/political ~** visión para los negocios/la política

instinctive [ɪn·'stɪŋk·tɪv] *adj* instintivo, -a; (*innate*) innato, -a; (*without reflection*) irreflexivo, -a

institute ['ɪn·stɪ·tut] **I.** *n* academia *f;* (*of education*) instituto *m* **II.** *vt form* (*establish: system, reform*) instituir **2.** (*initiate: steps, measures*) iniciar; (*legal action*) emprender

institution [ˌɪn·stɪ·'tu·ʃən] *n* **1.** (*act*) institución *f*, establecimiento *m* **2.** (*society*) asocia-

I

ción *f* **3.** (*home*) asilo *m* **4.** *inf* (*person*)
mito *m*

institutional [ˌɪn·stɪˈtu·ʃə·nəl] *adj* institucional

institutionalize [ˌɪn·stɪˈtuˈʃə·nə·laɪz] *vt* institucionalizar; (*person*) ingresar

in-store [ˌɪnˈstɔr] *adj* en el establecimiento; ~ **detective** detective *mf* del establecimiento

instruct [ɪnˈstrʌkt] *vt* **1.** (*teach*) instruir **2.** (*order*) ordenar; (*give instructions*) dar instrucciones; **to ~ sb** (**to do sth**) ordenar a alguien (hacer algo) **3.** LAW dar instrucciones

instruction [ɪnˈstrʌkˈʃən] *n* **1.** (*teaching*) instrucción *f;* **to give sb ~ in sth** enseñar algo a alguien **2.** (*order*) orden *f;* **to give sb ~s** dar órdenes a alguien; **to act on ~s** actuar cumpliendo órdenes; **to carry out ~s** cumplir órdenes **3. ~s** (*information on method*) instrucciones *fpl*

instruction manual *n* manual *m* de instrucciones

instructive [ɪnˈstrʌkˈtɪv] *adj* instructivo, -a

instructor [ɪnˈstrʌkˈtər] *n* **1.** (*teacher*) instructor(a) *m(f);* **driving ~** profesor(a) *m(f)* de autoescuela; **ski ~** profesor(a) *m(f)* de esquí **2.** UNIV profesor(a) *m(f)*

instrument [ˈɪn·strə·mənt] *n* **1.** MUS instrumento *m* **2.** (*tool*) herramienta *f* **3.** LAW (*document*) instrumento *m*

instrumental [ˌɪn·strəˈmen·təl] **I.** *adj* **1.** MUS instrumental **2.** (*greatly influential*) **to be ~ to sth** contribuir sustancialmente a algo; **to be ~ in doing sth** jugar un papel decisivo en algo **3.** (*relating to tools*) instrumental **II.** *n* MUS pieza *f* instrumental

instrumentation [ˌɪn·strə·men·ˈteɪ·ʃən] *n* MUS instrumentación *f*

instrument board *n,* **instrument panel** *n* AUTO salpicadero *m;* AVIAT, NAUT cuadro *m* de mandos

insubordinate [ˌɪn·səˈbɔr·dən·ɪt] *adj* insubordinado, -a; ~ **behavior** comportamiento *m* insubordinado

insubstantial [ˌɪn·səbˈstæn·ʃəl] *adj* **1.** (*lacking substance*) insustancial **2.** (*lacking significance*) insignificante **3.** (*not real*) irreal

insufferable [ɪnˈsʌf·rə·bəl] *adj* insufrible; (*person*) insoportable; **to be ~** ser inaguantable

insufficiency [ˌɪn·səˈfɪʃ·ən·si] <-ies> *n* insuficiencia *f*

insufficient [ˌɪn·səˈfɪʃ·ənt] *adj* insuficiente

insular [ˈɪn·sə·lər] *adj* **1.** GEO insular **2.** (*person*) estrecho, -a de miras

insularity [ˌɪn·səˈler·ə·ţi] *n* **1.** GEO insularidad *f* **2.** (*of person*) estrechez *f* de miras

insulate [ˈɪn·sə·leɪt] *vt* aislar; **to ~ sth** (**against sth**) aislar algo (de algo)

insulating [ˈɪn·sə·leɪ·ţɪŋ] *adj* aislante; (*protective*) protector(a)

insulation [ˌɪn·sə·ˈleɪ·ʃən] *n* aislamiento *m*

insulin [ˈɪn·sə·lɪn] *n* insulina *f*

insult I. [ɪnˈsʌlt] *vt* insultar **II.** [ˈɪn·sʌlt] *n*

insulto *m,* insultada *f AmL* ▶**to add ~ to injury...** y por si fuera poco...

insuperable [ɪnˈsu·prə·bəl] *adj* insuperable

insupportable [ˌɪn·səˈpɔr·ţə·bəl] *adj form* insoportable

insurance [ɪnˈʃʊr·əns] *n* **1.** (*financial protection*) seguro *m;* **life ~** seguro de vida; **to have ~** (**against sth**) tener un seguro (contra algo); **to take out ~** (**against sth**) hacerse un seguro (contra algo) **2.** (*payment*) indemnización *f;* (*premium*) prima *f* de seguro **3.** (*measure*) medida *f* preventiva

insurance policy <-ies> *n* póliza *f* de seguros

insure [ɪnˈʃʊr] *vt* asegurar

insured [ɪnˈʃʊrd] **I.** *adj* asegurado, -a **II.** *n* **the ~** el asegurado

insurer [ɪnˈʃʊr·ər] *n* **1.** (*agent*) asegurador(a) *m(f)* **2.** (*company*) aseguradora *f*

insurmountable [ˌɪn·sərˈmaʊn·ţə·bəl] *adj* insuperable

insurrection [ˌɪn·səˈrek·ʃən] *n* insurrección *f;* **to crush the ~** acabar con la sublevación

intact [ɪnˈtækt] *adj* intacto, -a

intake [ˈɪn·teɪk] *n* **1.** TECH (*mechanical aperture*) toma *f;* **fuel ~** toma de combustible **2.** (*action of taking in*) toma *f;* (*of air, water*) entrada *f* **3.** (*amount taken in*) consumo *m;* **the recommended daily ~ of fiber** la cantidad diaria recomendada de fibra; **food ~** ración *f*

intangible [ɪnˈtæn·dʒə·bəl] **I.** *adj* intangible; ~ **assets** activos *mpl* inmateriales **II.** *n* imponderable *m*

integer [ˈɪn·tɪ·dʒər] *n* MATH número *m* entero

integral [ˈɪn·tə·grəl] *adj* **1.** (*central, essential*) esencial; **to be ~ to sth/sb** ser de vital importancia para algo/alguien **2.** (*part of the whole*) integrante **3.** (*complete*) integral **4.** MATH ~ **calculus** cálculo *m* integral

integrate [ˈɪn·tə·greɪt] **I.** *vt* (*cause to merge socially*) **to ~ sb/sth into sth** integrar a alguien/algo en algo; **to ~ oneself into sth** integrarse en algo; **to ~ learning with playing** combinar el aprendizaje y los juegos **II.** *vi* integrarse

integrated [ˈɪn·tɪ·greɪ·ţɪd] *adj* **1.** (*coordinating different elements*) integrado, -a **2.** (*with different ethnic groups*) ~ **school** escuela *f* no segregacionista

integration [ˌɪn·tə·ˈgreɪ·ʃən] *n* **1.** *a.* MATH integración *f* **2.** (*unification, fusion*) unificación *f*

integrity [ɪnˈteg·rə·ţi] *n* **1.** (*incorruptibility, uprightness*) integridad *f;* **a man of ~** un hombre íntegro; **artistic/professional ~** coherencia *f* artística/profesional **2.** *form* (*unity, wholeness*) totalidad *f*

intellect [ˈɪn·təl·ekt] *n* **1.** (*faculty*) intelecto *m;* **a man/woman of ~** un hombre/una mujer de gran inteligencia; **powers of ~** capacidad *f* intelectual **2.** (*thinker, intellectual*) intelectual *mf*

intellectual [ˌɪn·tə·ˈlek·tʃʊ·əl] **I.** *n* intelectual *mf* **II.** *adj* intelectual

intelligence [ɪn·'tel·ə·dʒəns] *n* inteligencia *f;* **artificial** ~ inteligencia artificial; **the** ~ **community** los agentes de los servicios secretos; ~ **sources** fuentes *fpl* del servicio de inteligencia

intelligence quotient *n* coeficiente *m* intelectual

intelligence test *n* test *m* de inteligencia

intelligent [ɪn·'tel·ə·dʒənt] *adj* inteligente

intelligentsia [ɪn·ˌtel·ɪ·'dʒen·si·ə] *n* **the** ~ la intelectualidad

intelligible [ɪn·'tel·ɪ·dʒə·bəl] *adj* inteligible; **this text is hardly** ~ este texto es muy difícil de entender

intend [ɪn·'tend] *vt* 1. (*aim for, plan*) pretender; **to** ~ **to do sth** tener la intención de hacer algo; **I'm sure that remark was** ~**ed for me** estoy convencido de que el comentario iba dirigido a mí; **I** ~**ed no harm** no quería hacer daño 2. (*mean*) querer decir 3. (*earmark, destine*) **to be** ~**ed for sth** estar destinado a algo; **to be** ~**ed to do sth** estar destinado a hacer algo; **this film is not** ~**ed for children** esta película no es para niños

intended [ɪn·'ten·dɪd] I. *adj* 1. (*planned, intentional*) intencional; (*sought*) deseado, -a 2. (*husband, wife*) futuro, -a II. *n inf* prometido, -a *m, f*

intense [ɪn·'tens] *adj* 1. (*acute, concentrated, forceful*) intenso, -a; (*desire*) ardiente; (*feeling, hatred, friendship*) profundo, -a; (*interest*) sumo, -a; (*love*) apasionado, -a; (*pain, pressure, wind*) fuerte 2. (*demanding*) agotador(a)

intensify [ɪn·'ten·sɪ·faɪ] <-ie-> I. *vt* intensificar; (*joy, sadness*) aumentar; (*pain*) agudizar II. *vi* intensificarse; (*joy, sadness*) aumentar; (*pain*) agudizarse

intensity [ɪn·'ten·sə·t̪i] *n* intensidad *f*

intensive [ɪn·'ten·sɪv] *adj* intensivo, -a

intensive care *n* cuidados *mpl* intensivos

intent [ɪn·'tent] I. *n* propósito *m;* **a declaration of** ~ una declaración de intenciones; **to all** ~**s and purposes** a efectos prácticos; **with** ~ **to** con el objeto de; **with good/evil** ~ con buenas/malas intenciones II. *adj* 1. (*absorbed, concentrated, occupied*) abstraído, -a; (*look*) atento, -a; **to be** ~ **on sth** estar concentrado en algo 2. (*decided, set*) decidido, -a; **to be/seem** ~ **on doing sth** estar/parecer resuelto a hacer algo

intention [ɪn·'ten·tʃən] *n* intención *f;* **it is my** ~ **to...** tengo la intención de...; **to have no** ~ **of doing sth** no tener ninguna intención de hacer algo; **with the best of** ~**s** con la mejor intención

intentional [ɪn·'ten·tʃə·nəl] *adj* intencional; (*insult*) deliberado, -a

interact [ɪn·tər·'ækt] *vi* interaccionar

interaction [ɪn·tər·'æk·ʃən] *n* interacción *f;* **nonverbal** ~ comunicación *f* no verbal

interactive [ɪn·tər·'æk·tɪv] *adj* interactivo, -a

interactive TV *n* televisión *f* interactiva

interbreed [ɪn·tər·'brid] *irr* I. *vt* cruzar II. *vi* cruzarse

intercede [ɪn·tər·'sid] *vi* interceder; **to** ~ **for/on behalf of sb** interceder por/en nombre de alguien

intercept [ɪn·tər·'sept] *vt* interceptar; MATH cortar; **to** ~ **sb** cerrar el paso a alguien

interception [ɪn·tər·'sep·ʃən] *n* 1. (*act of intercepting*) interceptación *f;* MATH intersección *f* 2. SPORTS (*football play*) intercepción *f*

interceptor [ɪn·tər·'sep·tər] *n* MIL interceptador(a) *m(f)*

intercession [ɪn·tər·'seʃ·ən] *n* intercesión *f;* **through the** ~ **of sb/sth** gracias a la intercesión de alguien/algo; **the** ~ **of human rights organizations** la mediación de organizaciones pro derechos humanos

interchange [ɪn·tər·'tʃeɪndʒ] I. *n* 1. intercambio *m;* ~ **of ideas** intercambio de ideas 2. (*of roads*) enlace *m,* periférico *m Méx* II. *vt* 1. (*exchange: ideas, knowledge*) intercambiar; COMPUT (*data*) intercambiar 2. (*switch one for another*) sustituir 3. (*alternate*) alternar

interchangeable [ɪn·tər·'tʃeɪn·dʒə·bəl] *adj* intercambiable

interchangeably *adv* de manera intercambiable

intercom ['ɪn·tər·kam] *n* (*on a plane or ship*) intercomunicador *m;* (*in a building*) portero *m* automático; **through** (**an**) ~ por el interfono; **to speak over the** ~ hablar por el portero automático

intercommunicate [ɪn·tər·kə·'mju·nɪ·keɪt] *vi* comunicarse

intercontinental [ɪn·tər·ˌkan·tə·'nen·təl] *adj* intercontinental; ~ **flight** vuelo *m* intercontinental

intercourse ['ɪn·tər·kɔrs] *n* 1. **sexual** ~ contacto *m* sexual; **to have sexual** ~ **with sb** tener relaciones sexuales con alguien 2. *form* **social** ~ trato *m* social; **commercial** ~ relaciones *fpl* comerciales

interdenominational [ɪn·tər·dɪ·ˌnam·ə·'neɪ·ʃə·nəl] *adj* interconfesional

interdepartmental ['ɪn·tər·ˌdi·part·'men·təl] *adj* interdepartamental

interdependence [ɪn·tər·di·'pen·dəns] *n* interdependencia *f*

interdependent [ɪn·tər·di·'pen·dənt] *adj* interdependiente

interdict [ɪn·tər·'dɪkt] *n* LAW interdicto *m*

interest ['ɪn·trɪst] I. *n* 1. (*hobby*) interés *m;* **to take an** ~ **in sth** interesarse por algo 2. (*curiosity*) **just out of** ~ *inf* por curiosidad; **to lose** ~ **in sb/sth** perder el interés por alguien/algo; **to take no further** ~ **in sth** dejar de interesarse por algo 3. ~**s** (*profit, advantage*) interés *m;* **a conflict of** ~**s** un conflicto de intereses; **to look after the** ~**s of sb** velar por los intereses de alguien; **to pursue one's own** ~**s** perseguir los propios intereses; **in the** ~ **of liberty** en pro de la libertad; **it's in your own** ~ **to do it** te conviene hacerlo por tu propio interés **4.**(*power to excite attentiveness*) interés *m;* **to be of ~ for sb** interesar a alguien; **this might be of ~ to you** esto puede interesarte; **this is of no ~ to me** eso no me interesa **5.** FIN interés *m;* **~ rate** tipo *m* de interés; **at 5% ~** con un interés del 5%; **to bear ~** devengar interés; **to earn/pay ~ on sth** percibir/pagar intereses por algo; **to pay back with ~** pagar con intereses; *fig* pagar con creces **6.**(*legal right*) participación *f;* **to have an ~ in sth** tener una participación en algo; **to have a controlling ~ in a firm** tener una participación mayoritaria en una empresa; **business ~s** negocios *mpl;* **crude oil ~s** la industria petrolífera; **vested ~s** intereses *mpl* creados **II.** *vt* interesar; **may I ~ you in this encyclopedia?** ¿puedo mostrarle esta enciclopedia?

interested ['ɪn·trɪ·stɪd] *adj* interesado, -a; **to be ~ in sth/sb** estar interesado en algo/alguien; **I am ~ to know more about it** me interesaría saber más sobre eso; **the ~ parties** las partes interesadas

interest-free *adj* FIN sin intereses

interesting ['ɪn·trɪ·stɪŋ] *adj* interesante; **it is ~ to do sth** resulta interesante hacer algo

interface ['ɪn·tər·feɪs] **I.** *n* **1.**(*point of contact*) punto *m* de contacto **2.** PHYS superficie *f* de contacto **3.** COMPUT interfaz *f;* **user ~** interfaz de usuario; **graphic/parallel/serial ~** interfaz gráfica/en paralelo/en serie **II.** *vi* COMPUT **to ~ with sth** funcionar conjuntamente con algo **III.** *vt* COMPUT conectar

interfere [ˌɪn·tər·'fɪr] *vi* **1.**(*become involved*) interferir; **to ~ between two people** entrometerse entre dos personas; **to ~ in sth** inmiscuirse en algo **2.**(*disturb*) molestar **3.**(*touch*) tocar; **someone has been interfering with my papers** alguien ha estado revolviendo mis papeles **4.** RADIO, TECH (*hamper signals*) producir interferencias **5.** SPORTS (*get in way*) obstaculizar

interference [ˌɪn·tər·'fɪr·əns] *n* **1.**(*hindrance*) intromisión *f* **2.** RADIO, TECH, SPORTS interferencia *f*

interim ['ɪn·tər·ɪm] **I.** *n* ínterin *m* **II.** *adj* provisional; (*payment*) a cuenta; **~ dividend** FIN dividendo *m* a cuenta; **~ coach/manager** entrenador/manager interino

interior [ɪn·'tɪr·i·ər] **I.** *adj* **1.**(*inner, inside, internal*) interno, -a; (*lighting*) interior **2.**(*central, inland, remote*) del interior **II.** *n* **1.**(*inside*) interior *m;* **the ~ of the country** el interior del país **2.** POL (*home affairs*) **the U.S. Department of the Interior** el departamento del Interior de EE.UU.

interior decoration *n* interiorismo *m*

interior designer *n* interiorista *mf*

interject [ˌɪn·tər·'dʒekt] *vt form* interponer; **to ~ a few remarks** agregar algunos comentarios

interjection [ɪn·tər·'dʒek·ʃən] *n* **1.** *form* (*verbal interruption*) exclamación *f;* **~s from the audience** interrupciones *fpl* del público

2. LING interjección *f*

interlace [ˌɪn·tər·'leɪs] **I.** *vt* entrelazar **II.** *vi* entrelazarse

interlibrary loan [ɪn·tər·'laɪ·brər·ɪ·ˌloʊn] *n* préstamo *m* interbibliotecario

interlocutor [ˌɪn·tər·'lak·jə·tər] *n form* interlocutor(a) *m(f)*

interloper ['ɪn·tər·loʊ·pər] *n* intruso, -a *m, f*

interlude ['ɪn·tər·lud] *n* **1.**(*interval*) intervalo *m;* **a romantic ~** un paréntesis amoroso **2.** THEAT (*intermission*) entreacto *m;* (*short play*) entremés *m* **3.** MUS interludio *m*

intermarry ['ɪn·tər·ˌmær·i] <-ie-> *vi* (*marry between groups*) casarse personas de diferentes razas, grupos, clases, etc.; (*marry within family*) casarse entre sí

intermediary [ˌɪn·tər·'mi·di·er·i] **I.** *adj* (*between persons*) intermediario, -a; (*intermediate*) intermedio, -a **II.** <-ies> *n* intermediario, -a *m, f*

intermediate [ˌɪn·tər·'mi·di·ət] **I.** *adj* intermedio, -a; **~ course** curso *m* de nivel intermedio; **~ students** estudiantes *mpl* de ciclo medio; **~ memory** COMPUT memoria *f* intermedia **II.** *n* intermediario, -a *m, f*

intermezzo [ˌɪn·tər·'met·soʊ] <-s *o* -zi> *n* MUS intermezzo *m*

interminable [ɪn·'tɜr·mɪ·nə·bəl] *adj* interminable

intermission [ˌɪn·tər·'mɪʃ·ən] *n* **1.** intermedio *m;* **without ~** sin pausa **2.** CINE, THEAT descanso *m*

intermittent [ˌɪn·tər·'mɪt·ənt] *adj* intermitente; **~ fever** fiebre *f* recurrente

intern[1] ['ɪn·tɜrn] *n* estudiante *mf* en prácticas; **hospital ~** médico *m* asistente; **she worked for the Washington Post as a summer ~** durante el verano estuvo haciendo prácticas en el Washington Post

intern[2] [ɪn·'tɜrn] **I.** *vt* recluir **II.** *vi* MED trabajar como interno, -a; SCHOOL hacer (las) prácticas

internal [ɪn·'tɜr·nəl] *adj a.* MED interno, -a; **for ~ use only** sólo para uso interno; **Internal Revenue Service** Hacienda

internal affairs *n* POL asuntos *mpl* interiores

international [ˌɪn·tər·'næʃ·ə·nəl] **I.** *adj a.* LAW internacional; (*trade*) exterior **II.** *n* POL Internacional *f*

international date line *n* línea *f* (de cambio) de fecha

internationalize [ˌɪn·tər·'næʃ·ə·nə·laɪz] *vt* internacionalizar

International Monetary Fund *n* Fondo *m* Monetario Internacional

International Olympic Committee *n* Comité *m* Olímpico Internacional

internee [ˌɪn·tɜr·'ni] *n* interno, -a *m, f*

Internet ['ɪn·tər·net] *n* COMPUT internet *m o f;* **to access the ~** entrar en internet; **to do business over the ~** hacer negocios a través de internet

Internet café *n* ciber (café) *m*

Internet service provider *n* proveedor *m* de

internet
internist [ɪn·'tɜr·nɪst] *n* internista *mf*
internment [ɪn·'tɜrn·mənt] *n* internamiento *m*
internment camp *n* campo *m* de internamiento
internship *n* prácticas *fpl* como interno, -a *m, f,* pasantía *f Col*
interoffice *adj* de régimen interno; ~ **memo** comunicado *m* de régimen interno, memo *m* interno
interpersonal *adj* interpersonal
interplanetary [ˌɪn·tər·'plæn·ə·ter·i] *adj* interplanetario, -a
interplay ['ɪn·tər·pleɪ] *n* interacción *f*
Interpol ['ɪn·tər·pal] *n abbr of* **International Criminal Police Organization** Interpol *f*
interpret [ɪn·'tɜr·prɪt] **I.** *vt* interpretar **II.** *vi* interpretar; **to ~ from English into Spanish** interpretar del inglés al español
interpretation [ɪn·ˌtɜr·prɪ·'teɪ·ʃən] *n* interpretación *f;* **to give an ~ of sth** interpretar algo; **the rules are open to ~** las normas pueden interpretarse de varias formas
interpreter [ɪn·'tɜr·prɪ·tər] *n* intérprete *mf*
interpreting [ɪn·'tɜr·prɪ·tɪŋ] *n* interpretación *f*
interrelate [ˌɪn·tər·rɪ·'leɪt] *vi* interrelacionarse; **to ~ with each other** relacionarse entre sí
interrogate [ɪn·'ter·ə·geɪt] *vt* interrogar
interrogation [ɪn·ˌter·ə·'geɪ·ʃən] *n* **1.** *a.* COMPUT interrogación *f* **2.** LAW interrogatorio *m;* **police ~** interrogatorio policial; **~ room** sala *f* de interrogatorios
interrogative [ˌɪn·tə·'rag·ə·tɪv] **I.** *n* LING (*word*) palabra *f* interrogativa; (*sentence*) oración *f* interrogativa **II.** *adj* **1.** *liter* (*having questioning form*) interrogador(a) **2.** LING interrogativo, -a
interrogator [ɪn·'ter·ə·geɪ·tər] *n* interrogador(a) *m(f)*
interrogatory [ˌɪn·tə·'rag·ə·tɔr·i] **I.** *adj* interrogador(a) **II.** <-ies> *n* interrogatorio *m*
interrupt [ˌɪn·tə·'rʌpt] *vi, vt* interrumpir
interrupter [ˌɪn·tə·'rʌp·tər] *n* ELEC interruptor *m*
interruption [ˌɪn·tə·'rʌp·ʃən] *n* interrupción *f;* **without ~** sin interrupciones
intersect [ˌɪn·tər·'sekt] **I.** *vt* (*cross at a junction*) cruzar; (*lines*) cortar **II.** *vi* **1.** (*cut, divide*) cortarse; (*cross at a junction*) cruzarse; **~ing roads** carreteras *fpl* que se cruzan **2.** MATH (*sets*) formar intersección
intersection [ˌɪn·tər·'sek·ʃən] *n* **1.** (*crossing of lines*) intersección *f* **2.** AUTO cruce *m*
intersession [ˌɪn·tər·'seʃ·ən] *n* UNIV vacaciones *fpl* entre trimestres
intersperse [ˌɪn·tər·'spɜrs] *vt* intercalar; **to ~ sth with sth** intercalar algo en algo; **to ~ sth between sth** esparcir algo entre algo; **to ~ anecdotes throughout a speech** salpicar un discurso de anécdotas
interstate ['ɪn·tər·'steɪt] *adj* interestatal; **~ trade** comercio *m* entre estados
interstate (**highway**) *n* autopista *f* interestatal

interstellar [ˌɪn·tər·'stel·ər] *adj form* interestelar
interstice [ɪn·'tɜr·stɪs] *n form* intersticio *m*
intertwine [ˌɪn·tər·'twaɪn] **I.** *vt* entrelazar **II.** *vi* (*flowers, hands*) entrelazarse; (*paths*) entrecruzarse
interurban [ˌɪn·tər·'ɜr·bən] *adj* interurbano, -a
interval ['ɪn·tər·vəl] *n a.* MUS intervalo *m;* **at ~s of five minutes** a intervalos de cinco minutos; **at two-inch ~s** con espacios de cinco centímetros; **at regular ~s** a intervalos regulares; **sunny ~s** *Can* METEO claros *mpl*
intervene [ɪn·tər·'vin] *vi* **1.** (*involve oneself to help*) intervenir; **to ~ militarily/personally** intervenir militarmente/personalmente; **to ~ on sb's behalf** interceder por alguien **2.** (*meddle unhelpfully*) **to ~ in sth** mezclarse en algo **3.** (*elapse*) sobrevenir; **six months ~d before the opening of the swimming pool** transcurrieron seis meses antes de la inauguración de la piscina
intervening *adj* **in the ~ period** en el ínterin; **in the ~ days** en los días intermedios
intervention [ɪn·tər·'ven·ʃən] *n* intervención *f;* **military ~** MIL intervención militar; **~ price** ECON precio *m* de intervención
interventionist [ɪn·tər·'ven·ʃə·nɪst] **I.** *n* POL, ECON intervencionista *mf* **II.** *adj* intervencionista
interview ['ɪn·tər·vju] **I.** *n* **1.** (*formal conversation*) entrevista *f;* **telephone ~** encuesta *f* telefónica; **to have a job ~** tener una entrevista de trabajo; **to give an ~** conceder una entrevista **2.** *inf* (*person being interviewed*) entrevistado, -a *m, f* **II.** *vt* entrevistar; **to ~ sb about sth** encuestar a alguien sobre algo
interviewee [ˌɪn·tər·vju·'i] *n* entrevistado, -a *m, f*
interviewer ['ɪn·tər·vju·ər] *n* entrevistador(a) *m(f)*
interweave [ˌɪn·tər·'wiv] *irr* **I.** *vt* entretejer; **to be interwoven with sth** estar estrechamente unido a algo **II.** *vi* (*threads*) entretejerse; (*paths*) entrecruzarse
intestate [ɪn·'tes·teɪt] *adj* intestado, -a
intestine [ɪn·'tes·tɪn] *n* intestino *m*
intimacy ['ɪn·tə·mə·si] <-ies> *n* **1.** (*familiarity*) intimidad *f;* **to be on terms of ~ with sb** tener confianza con alguien **2.** (*sexual relations*) relaciones *fpl* íntimas
intimate[1] ['ɪn·tə·mət] **I.** *adj* **1.** (*close, sexual*) íntimo, -a; **~ relationship** relaciones *fpl* íntimas; **to be on ~ terms with sb** tener confianza con alguien; **to become ~ with sb** intimar con alguien; **to be ~ with sb** tener relaciones íntimas con alguien **2.** (*personal: letter*) personal **3.** (*very detailed: knowledge*) profundo, -a **4.** (*link*) estrecho, -a **II.** *n* amigo, -a *m, f* íntimo, -a
intimate[2] ['ɪn·tə·meɪt] *vt form* insinuar; **to ~ to sb (that)...** dar a entender a alguien (que)...
intimation [ˌɪn·tə·'meɪ·ʃən] *n form* (*hint*) insinuación *f;* (*sign*) indicación *f;* **~s** indicios *mpl*

intimidate [ɪn·'tɪm·ɪ·deɪt] *vt* intimidar; **to ~ sb into doing sth** coaccionar a alguien para que haga algo

intimidating *adj* intimidante

intimidation [ɪn·ˌtɪm·ɪ·'deɪ·ʃən] *n* intimidación *f*

into ['ɪn·tə] *prep* **1.** (*to the inside of*) en; (*towards*) hacia; **to walk ~ a place** entrar en un sitio; **to get ~ bed** meterse en la cama; **shall we walk ~ the park?** ¿vamos dar un paseo por el parque?; **~ the future** hacia el futuro **2.** (*indicating an extent in time or space*) **deep ~ the forest** en lo más profundo del bosque; **to work late ~ the evening** trabajar hasta tarde **3.** (*against*) contra; **to drive ~ a tree** chocar contra un árbol; **to bump ~ a friend** tropezar con un amigo **4.** (*to the state or condition of*) **to burst ~ tears** echarse a llorar; **to grow ~ a woman** hacerse una mujer; **to translate from Spanish ~ English** traducir del español al inglés; **to turn sth ~ sth** convertir algo en algo **5.** *inf* (*interested in*) **she's really ~ her new job** está entusiasmada con su nuevo trabajo; **I think they are ~ drugs** creo que andan metidos en drogas **6.** MATH **two goes ~ five two and a half times** cinco dividido entre dos es igual a dos y medio

intolerable [ɪn·'tal·ər·ə·bəl] *adj* intolerable

intolerance [ɪn·'tal·ər·əns] *n* intolerancia *f*

intolerant [ɪn·'tal·ər·ənt] *adj* intolerante; **to be ~ of different opinions** ser intolerante con las opiniones diferentes; **to be ~ of sb** ser intransigente con alguien; **to be ~ of alcohol** MED no tolerar el alcohol

intonation [ɪn·toʊ·'neɪ·ʃən] *n* LING, MUS entonación *f*

intone [ɪn·'toʊn] *vt form* **1.** (*sing*) entonar **2.** (*say solemnly*) recitar

intoxicant [ɪn·'tak·sɪ·kənt] *n* MED (*alcohol*) bebida *f* alcohólica; (*drug*) estupefaciente *m*

intoxicate [ɪn·'tak·sɪ·keɪt] **I.** *vt* **1.** *a. fig* (*induce inebriation*) embriagar **2.** MED intoxicar **II.** *vi* **1.** *a. fig* (*cause intoxication*) embriagar **2.** MED intoxicar

intoxicating [ɪn·'tak·sɪ·keɪ·tɪŋ] *adj* **1.** (*exhilarating, stimulating*) embriagador(a) **2.** (*substance*) estupefaciente; (*causing drunkenness*) alcohólico, -a; **~ drink** bebida *f* alcohólica

intoxication [ɪn·ˌtak·sɪ·'keɪ·ʃən] *n* **1.** *a. fig* (*drunkenness*) embriaguez *f;* **in a state of ~** en estado de embriaguez **2.** MED intoxicación *f*

intractable [ˌɪn·'træk·tə·bəl] *adj form* **1.** (*temperament*) obstinado, -a **2.** (*problem*) insoluble; **an ~ situation** una situación difícil de resolver **3.** MED incurable

intramural [ɪn·trə·'mjʊr·əl] *adj* **1.** (*city*) intramuros *inv;* (*institution*) interno, -a **2.** SCHOOL dentro de la escuela; UNIV dentro de la universidad; **~ sports** deportes *m* dentro de la universidad *pl*

Intranet [ˌɪn·trə·'net] *n* intranet *f*

intransigence [ɪn·'træn·sə·dʒəns] *n form* intransigencia *f*

intransigent [ɪn·'træn·sə·dʒənt] *adj form* intransigente

intransitive [ɪn·'træn·sɪ·t̬ɪv] *adj* LING, MATH intransitivo, -a

intrauterine [ˌɪn·trə·'ju·t̬ər·ɪn] *adj* MED intrauterino, -a; **~ device** dispositivo *m* intrauterino

intravenous [ˌɪn·trə·'vi·nəs] *adj* MED intravenoso, -a; **~ feeding** alimentación *f* por vía intravenosa

intrepid [ɪn·'trep·ɪd] *adj* intrépido, -a

intricacy ['ɪn·trɪ·kə·si] <-ies> *n* complejidad *f*

intricate ['ɪn·trɪ·kət] *adj* **1.** (*detailed*) intrincado, -a; (*knowledge*) exhaustivo, -a **2.** (*complicated: mechanism*) complejo, -a; (*problem*) complicado, -a

intrigue I. [ɪn·'trig] *vt* intrigar; **to be ~d by sth** estar intrigado con algo II. *vi* (*plot*) intrigar III. ['ɪn·trig] *n* intriga *f*

intriguing [ɪn·'tri·gɪŋ] *adj* **1.** (*mysterious*) intrigante **2.** (*fascinating*) fascinante; (*smile*) enigmático, -a

intrinsic [ɪn·'trɪn·sɪk] *adj* intrínseco, -a; **the ~ value of a coin** el valor real de una moneda; **this is ~ to...** eso es esencial para...

introduce [ˌɪn·trə·'dus] *vt* **1.** (*acquaint*) presentar; **allow me to ~ myself** permítame que me presente; **may I ~ you to my husband?** ¿le puedo presentar a mi marido?; **they were ~d to each other** los presentaron **2.** (*raise interest in subject*) **to ~ sb to sth** iniciar a alguien en algo **3.** (*bring in*) introducir; (*question*) formular; (*subject*) abordar; (*bill*) presentar; **to ~ a product into the market** lanzar un producto al mercado **4.** (*insert*) **to ~ sth into sth** introducir algo en algo **5.** (*begin, present: book*) prologar; **the second movement is ~d by...** el segundo movimiento está introducido por...; **the director will ~ the film personally** el director presentará personalmente la película

introduction [ˌɪn·trə·'dʌk·ʃən] *n* **1.** (*making first acquaintance*) presentación *f;* **letter of ~** carta *f* de presentación; **to do the ~s** hacer las presentaciones **2.** (*first contact with sth*) iniciación *f;* **my holidays served as an ~ to sailing** mis vacaciones fueron una primera toma de contacto con la navegación **3.** (*establishment*) introducción *f;* (*of a bill*) presentación *f;* **~ into the market** lanzamiento *m* al mercado **4.** (*insertion*) introducción *f* **5.** (*preface*) prólogo *m;* MUS introducción *f*

introductory [ˌɪn·trə·'dʌk·tə·ri] *adj* **1.** (*elementary, preparatory*) de introducción; (*course*) de iniciación **2.** COM (*price*) de lanzamiento **3.** (*beginning*) introductorio, -a; **~ chapter** introducción *f;* **~ remarks** aclaraciones *fpl* preliminares

introspection [ˌɪn·troʊ·'spek·ʃən] *n* introspección *f*

introspective [ˌɪn·troʊ·'spek·tɪv] *adj* introspectivo, -a

introvert [ˌɪn·troʊ·'vɜrt] *n* introvertido, -a *m, f*

introverted *adj* introvertido, -a
intrude [ɪn·'trud] I. *vi* **1.** (*meddle*) entrometerse; **to ~ into sth** inmiscuirse en algo; **to ~ upon sb's privacy** meterse en la vida privada de alguien **2.** (*disturb*) estorbar; **to ~ on sb** importunar a alguien; **am I intruding?** ¿molesto? II. *vt* **to ~ sth on sb** importunar a alguien con algo
intruder [ɪn·'tru·dər] *n* intruso, -a *m, f*
intrusion [ɪn·'tru·ʒən] *n* **1.** (*encroachment, infringement*) intrusión *f* **2.** (*meddling*) intromisión *f*
intrusive [ɪn·'tru·sɪv] *adj* (*noise*) molesto, -a; (*question*) indiscreto, -a; (*person*) entrometido, -a
intuition [ˌɪn·tu·'ɪʃ·ən] *n* intuición *f*; **to have an ~ (that)...** tener la intuición (de que)...
intuitive [ɪn·'tu·ɪ·tɪv] *adj* intuitivo, -a; **an ~ feeling** una intuición
inundate ['ɪn·ən·deɪt] *vt a. fig* inundar; **to ~ sb with sth** inundar a alguien de algo; **to be ~d with letters** recibir un aluvión de cartas; **to be ~d with presents** verse inundado de regalos
inundation [ˌɪn·ən·'deɪ·ʃən] *n a. fig* inundación *f*
inure [ɪn·'jʊr] *vt form* (*become familiar with*) habituar; (*harden*) curtir, endurecer; **to ~ sb to sth** acostumbrar a alguien a algo; **to ~ oneself against sth** hacerse inmune a algo
invade [ɪn·'veɪd] I. *vt* invadir; **to ~ sb's privacy** invadir la intimidad de alguien II. *vi* invadir
invader [ɪn·'veɪ·dər] *n* invasor(a) *m(f)*
invalid[1] ['ɪn·və·lɪd] I. *n* (*incapacitated person*) inválido, -a *m, f*; (*sick person*) enfermo, -a *m, f* II. *adj* (*disabled*) inválido, -a; (*sick*) enfermo, -a *f* III. *vt* (*disable*) dejar inválido, -a; (*make sick*) poner enfermo, -a
invalid[2] [ɪn·'væl·ɪd] *adj* **1.** LAW (*not legally binding*) nulo, -a; **legally ~** sin validez legal; **to become ~** caducar **2.** (*unsound*) no válido, -a; **technically ~** técnicamente incorrecto
invalidate [ɪn·'væl·ɪdeɪt] *vt* **1.** (*argument, decision*) invalidar; (*results*) anular **2.** LAW anular; **to ~ a judgment** revocar una sentencia
invalidism [ˌɪn·və·'lɪ·dɪz·əm] *n* invalidez *f*
invalidity [ˌɪn·və·'lɪd·ə·ţi] *n* **1.** (*inadmissibility: of a contract*) nulidad *f*; (*of evidence*) invalidez *f* **2.** (*faultiness: of a theory*) invalidez *f*
invaluable [ɪn·'væl·ju·ə·bəl] *adj* inestimable; **to be ~ to sb** tener un valor inestimable para alguien
invariable [ɪn·'ver·i·ə·bəl] *adj form* (*custom*) invariable; (*smile, attitude*) eterno, -a
invariably *adv* invariablemente; **he would ~ be sitting at the bar** siempre se le veía sentado en la barra
invasion [ɪn·'veɪ·ʒən] *n* **1.** MIL invasión *f*; **~ by enemy forces** invasión de las tropas enemigas **2.** (*interference*) violación *f*; **~ of privacy/of a right** violación de la intimidad/de un derecho
invective [ɪn·'vek·tɪv] *n form* invectiva *f*; **a stream of ~** un aluvión de invectivas

inveigle [ɪn·'veɪ·gəl] *vt* **to ~ sb into (doing) sth** embaucar a alguien para (que haga) algo
invent [ɪn·'vent] *vt* inventar
invention [ɪn·'ven·ʃən] *n* **1.** (*gadget*) invento *m* **2.** (*creativity*) inventiva *f* **3.** (*falsehood*) invención *f*
inventive [ɪn·'ven·tɪv] *adj* inventivo, -a
inventiveness [ɪn·'ven·tɪv·nɪs] *n* inventiva *f*
inventor [ɪn·'ven·tər] *n* inventor(a) *m(f)*
inventory ['ɪn·vən·tɔr·i] <-ies> I. *n* **1.** (*catalog*) inventario *m*; **to draw up an ~** levantar un inventario **2.** (*stock*) stock *m* II. *vt* inventariar III. *adj* (*audit, level, number*) de inventario
inverse [ɪn·'vɜrs] I. *adj* inverso, -a II. *n* **the ~** lo inverso; **the ~ of sth** lo contrario de algo
inversion [ɪn·'vɜr·ʒən] *n* inversión *f*
invert [ɪn·'vɜrt] *vt* invertir
invertebrate [ɪn·'vɜr·ţə·brɪt] I. *n* invertebrado *m* II. *adj* invertebrado, -a
invest [ɪn·'vest] I. *vt* **1.** (*put in*) invertir; **to ~ time and effort in sth** invertir tiempo y dinero en algo **2.** (*bestow attributes*) investir; **to ~ sb with sth** investir a alguien de algo II. *vi* invertir; **to ~ in sth** invertir en algo
investigate [ɪn·'ves·tɪ·geɪt] *vt* investigar
investigation [ɪn·ˌves·tɪ·'geɪ·ʃən] *n* investigación *f*
investigative [ɪn·'ves·tɪ·geɪ·ţɪv] *adj* investigador(a); **~ journalism** periodismo *m* de investigación
investigator [ɪn·'ves·tɪ·geɪ·ţər] *n* investigador(a) *m(f)*
investment [ɪn·'vest·mənt] I. *n a. fig* inversión *f*; **to be a good ~** ser una buena inversión; **long-term ~s** inversiones *fpl* a largo plazo II. *adj* de inversión
investor [ɪn·'ves·tər] *n* inversor(a) *m(f)*
inveterate [ɪn·'veţ·ər·ət] *adj* inveterado, -a; (*smoker*) empedernido, -a; (*liar*) compulsivo, -a
invidious [ɪn·'vɪd·i·əs] *adj* odioso, -a; (*unfair*) injusto, -a; **to be in an ~ position** estar en una posición poco envidiable
invigorate [ɪn·'vɪg·ə·reɪt] *vt* vigorizar; (*stimulate*) estimular
invigorating [ɪn·'vɪg·ə·reɪ·ţɪŋ] *adj* vigorizante
invincible [ɪn·'vɪn·sə·bəl] *adj* invencible
invisible [ɪn·'vɪz·ə·bəl] *adj* invisible; **~ to sth** invisible a algo
invitation [ˌɪn·vɪ·'teɪ·ʃən] *n* invitación *f*; **an ~ to sth** una invitación a algo
invite[1] ['ɪn·vaɪt] *n inf* invitación *f*
invite[2] [ɪn·'vaɪt] *vt* **1.** (*request to attend*) invitar; **to ~ sb for/to sth** invitar a alguien a algo **2.** (*request*) pedir; **to ~ offers** solicitar ofertas; **they ~d readers to send in their views** pidieron a los lectores sus opiniones; **to ~ questions** abrirse a preguntas **3.** (*provoke*) buscarse; **to ~ trouble** buscar(se) problemas
inviting [ɪn·'vaɪ·ţɪŋ] *adj* **1.** (*attractive*) atractivo, -a, atrayente **2.** (*tempting*) tentador(a)
in vitro [ɪn·'vi·troʊ] *adj, adv* in vitro

in vitro fertilization n fecundación f in vitro

invocation [ˌɪn·və·ˈkeɪ·ʃən] n invocación f

invoice [ˈɪn·vɔɪs] I. vt facturar II. n factura f; ~ **for sth** factura de algo

invoke [ɪn·ˈvoʊk] vt invocar

involuntary [ɪn·ˈval·ən·ter·i] adj involuntario, -a

involve [ɪn·ˈvalv] vt **1.** (implicate) implicar, involucrar; **to be ~d in sth** estar metido [o envuelto] en algo; **to get ~d in sth** meterse en algo; **to ~ sb in an argument** mezclar a alguien en una disputa **2.** (entail) implicar; **to ~ great expense** suponer muchos gastos

involved [ɪn·ˈvalvd] adj **1.** (implicated) involucrado, -a **2.** (complicated) complicado, -a

involvement [ɪn·ˈvalv·mənt] n implicación f

invulnerable [ɪn·ˈvʌl·nər·ə·bəl] adj invulnerable; **to be ~ to sth** ser inmune a algo

inward [ˈɪn·wərd] adj **1.** (inner) interior, íntimo, -a **2.** (moving in: flow) hacia adentro **3.** (in the mind: doubts) interior, interno, -a

inwardly adv interiormente

inwardness n interioridad f

inwards [ˈɪn·wərds] adv hacia adentro, para dentro

I/O COMPUT abbr of **input/output** E/S

IOC n abbr of **International Olympic Committee** COI m

iodine [ˈaɪ·ə·daɪn] n yodo m

ion [ˈaɪ·ən] n ión m

Ionic [aɪ·ˈan·ɪk] adj jónico, -a

iota [aɪ·ˈoʊ·t̬ə] n **1.** ápice m; **there is not one ~ of truth in that** no hay ni una pizca de verdad en eso **2.** (letter) iota f

IOU [ˌaɪ·oʊ·ˈju] n inf abbr of **I owe you** pagaré m

Iowa [ˈaɪ·ə·wə] n Iowa f

IQ [ˌaɪ·ˈkju] n abbr of **intelligence quotient** CI m

IRA [ˌaɪ·ar·ˈeɪ] n abbr of **Irish Republican Army** IRA m

Iran [ɪ·ˈræn] n Irán m

Iranian [ɪ·ˈreɪ·ni·ən] I. n iraní mf II. adj iraní

Iraq [ɪ·ˈrak] n Irak m

Iraqi [ɪ·ˈrak·i] I. n iraquí mf II. adj iraquí

irascible [ɪ·ˈræs·ə·bəl] adj irascible

irate [aɪ·ˈreɪt] adj airado, -a

Ireland [ˈaɪr·lənd] n Irlanda f; **Republic of ~** República f de Irlanda; **Northern ~** Irlanda del Norte

iridescent [ˌɪr·ɪ·ˈdes·ənt] adj iridiscente

iris [ˈaɪ·rɪs] <-es> n **1.** BOT lirio m **2.** ANAT iris m

Irish [ˈaɪ·rɪʃ] I. adj irlandés, -esa II. n **1.** pl (people) **the ~** los irlandeses **2.** LING irlandés m; **~ Gaelic** gaélico m irlandés

Irishman [ˈaɪ·rɪʃ·mən] <-men> n irlandés m

Irishwoman [ˈaɪ·rɪʃ·wʊm·ən] <-women> n irlandesa f

irk [ɜrk] vt fastidiar

irksome [ˈɜrk·səm] adj fastidioso, -a

iron [ˈaɪ·ərn] I. n **1.** (metal) hierro m, fierro m AmL **2.** (for pressing clothes) plancha f; **steam ~** plancha de vapor **3.** SPORTS (golf club) hierro

m **4.** pl (shackles) cadenas fpl ►**to have many ~s in the fire** tener muchos asuntos entre manos II. vt planchar; fig allanar III. vi planchar IV. adj de hierro; (discipline) férreo, -a

Iron Age I. n edad f del hierro II. adj de la edad del hierro

ironclad [ˈaɪ·ərn·ˌklæd] adj **1.** (solid: rule, job security) férreo, -a **2.** (covered with iron) acorazado, -a

Iron Curtain n HIST, POL Telón m de Acero, Cortina f de Hierro

iron fist n puño m de hierro; **to rule with an ~** gobernar con puño de hierro

ironic [aɪ·ˈran·ɪk] adj, **ironical** [aɪ·ˈran·ɪ·kəl] adj irónico, -a

ironing [ˈaɪ·ər·nɪŋ] n planchado m; **to do the ~** planchar

ironing board n tabla f de planchar, burro m de planchar Méx

iron lung n pulmón m de acero

ironman n SPORTS hombre m de hierro

ironman triathlon n ironman triathlon m

ironwork n herraje m

ironworks n inv fundición f, herrería f AmL

irony [ˈaɪ·rə·ni] <-ies> n ironía f; **~ of fate** ironía del destino

irradiate [ɪ·ˈreɪ·di·eɪt] vt irradiar

irrational [ɪ·ˈræʃ·ə·nəl] adj irracional

irrational number n MATH número m irracional

irreconcilable [ɪ·ˌrek·ən·ˈsaɪ·lə·bəl] adj (positions) inconciliable; (differences) irreconciliable

irrecoverable [ˌɪr·ɪ·ˈkʌv·ər·ə·bəl] adj irrecuperable

irredeemable [ˌɪr·ɪ·ˈdi·mə·bəl] adj irredimible

irrefutable [ɪ·ˈref·jə·tə·bəl] adj (evidence) irrefutable; (argument, fact, logic) irrebatible

irregular [ɪ·ˈreg·jə·lər] adj irregular; (surface) desigual; (behavior) anómalo, -a; (life) desordenado, -a; **~ soldiers** tropas fpl irregulares

irregularity [ɪ·ˌreg·jə·ˈler·ə·t̬i] <-ies> n irregularidad f; (of surface) desigualdad f; (of behavior) anormalidad f

irrelevance [ɪr·ˈrel·ə·vənts] n, **irrelevancy** <-ies> n irrelevancia f; **to fade into ~** volverse irrelevante

irrelevant [ɪr·ˈrel·ə·vənt] adj irrelevante; **to be ~ to sth** no ser relevante para algo

irremediable [ˌɪr·ɪ·ˈmi·di·ə·bəl] adj irremediable; (damage, loss) irreparable

irreparable [ɪ·ˈrep·ər·ə·bəl] adj irreparable

irreplaceable [ˌɪr·ɪ·ˈpleɪ·sə·bəl] adj irreemplazable

irrepressible [ˌɪr·ɪ·ˈpres·ə·bəl] adj irrefrenable, incontrolable

irreproachable [ˌɪr·ɪ·ˈproʊ·tʃə·bəl] adj irreprochable; (past) intachable

irresistible [ˌɪr·ɪ·ˈzɪs·tə·bəl] adj irresistible

irresolute [ɪ·ˈrez·ə·lut] adj irresoluto, -a; (reply) indeciso, -a

irrespective [ˌɪr·ɪ·ˈspek·tɪv] prep ~ **of** aparte de; ~ **of whether he agrees or not** con independencia de si está de acuerdo; ~ **of sth/sb** sin tener en cuenta algo/a alguien

irresponsible [ˌɪr·ɪ·ˈspan·sə·bəl] *adj* irresponsable

irretrievable [ˌɪr·ɪ·ˈtri·və·bəl] *adj* irrecuperable; (*mistake*) irreparable

irreverence [ɪ·ˈrev·ər·əns] *n* irreverencia *f*

irreverent [ɪ·ˈrev·ər·ənt] *adj* irreverente

irreversible [ˌɪr·ɪ·ˈvɜr·sə·bəl] *adj* irreversible; (*decision*) irrevocable

irrevocable [ɪ·ˈrev·ə·kə·bəl] *adj* irrevocable

irrigate [ˈɪr·ɪ·geɪt] *vt* **1.** AGR regar; **to ~ land** regar la tierra **2.** MED irrigar

irrigation [ˌɪr·ɪ·ˈgeɪ·ʃən] **I.** *n* **1.** AGR riego *m* **2.** MED irrigación *f* **II.** *adj* de riego; **~ canal** acequia *f*

irrigation plant *n* planta *f* de riego

irritable [ˈɪr·ɪ·tə·bəl] *adj* irritable

irritant [ˈɪr·ɪ·tənt] *n* irritante *m*

irritate [ˈɪr·ɪ·teɪt] *vt* **1.** (*aggravate*) irritar, molestar **2.** MED irritar

irritated *adj* irritado, -a

irritating *adj* irritante

irritation [ˌɪr·ɪ·ˈteɪ·ʃən] *n* irritación *f*

IRS [ˌaɪ·arˈes] *n abbr of* **Internal Revenue Service** *Oficina de la Renta de EE.UU*

is [ɪz] *vt, vi 3rd pers sing of* **to be**

ISBN [ˌaɪ·es·bi·ˈen] *n abbr of* **International Standard Book Number** ISBN *m*

ISDN *n abbr of* **integrated services digital network** RDSI *f*

Islam [ɪz·ˈlam] *n* islam *m*

Islamic [ɪz·ˈlam·ɪk] *adj* islámico, -a; **~ law** ley islámica

island [ˈaɪ·lənd] *n* isla *f*; **~ of calm** *fig* refugio *m* de paz

islander [ˈaɪ·lən·dər] *n* isleño, -a *m, f*

isle *n*, **Isle** [aɪl] *n* isla *f* (pequeña)

islet [ˈaɪ·lɪt] *n liter* ínsula *f*

isn't [ˈɪz·ənt] = **is not**

isobar [ˈaɪ·sou·bar] *n* METEO isobara *f*

isolate [ˈaɪ·sə·leɪt] *vt* aislar

isolated [ˈaɪ·sə·leɪ·tɪd] *adj* **1.** (*outlying, disconnected*) aislado, -a **2.** (*lonely*) apartado, -a

isolation [ˌaɪ·sə·ˈleɪ·ʃən] *n* **1.** (*separation*) aislamiento *m* **2.** (*loneliness*) soledad *f*

isolationism [ˌaɪ·sə·ˈleɪ·ʃə·nɪz·əm] *n* aislacionismo *m*

isosceles triangle [aɪ·ˈsas·ə·liz·ˌtraɪ·æŋ·gəl] *n* MATH triángulo *m* isósceles

isotherm [ˈaɪ·sou·θɜrm] *n* METEO, PHYS isotermo *m*

isotope [ˈaɪ·sə·toup] *n* PHYS, ELEC isótopo *m*

Israel [ˈɪz·ri·əl] *n* Israel *m*

Israeli [ɪz·ˈreɪ·li] **I.** *n* israelí *mf* **II.** *adj* israelí

Israelite [ˈɪz·ri·ə·laɪt] *n* israelita *mf*

issue [ˈɪʃ·u] **I.** *n* **1.** (*problem, topic*) cuestión *f*; **family ~s** asuntos *mpl* familiares; **side ~** asunto *m* menor; **a burning ~** *fig* un asunto caliente; **the real ~s** las cuestiones de fondo; **the point at ~** el punto en cuestión; **to force an ~** forzar una decisión; **to make an ~ of sth** convertir algo en un problema; **at ~** a debate

2. PUBL (*copy*) número *m;* **latest ~** último número **3.** FIN, ECON (*of shares, stamps*) emisión *f;* (*of checks*) expedición *f* **4.** *form* (*offspring, children*) descendencia *f* **II.** *vt* **1.** (*supply*) emitir; (*passport*) expedir; (*patent*) conceder **2.** (*announce*) **to ~ a statement** hacer una declaración; **to ~ a call for sth** hacer un llamamiento a algo; (*ultimatum*) presentar **3.** (*publish*) publicar **III.** *vi* **to ~ from** (*be born out of*) surgir de; (*come out of*) provenir de

isthmus [ˈɪs·məs] <-es> *n* istmo *m*

it [ɪt] **I.** *pron dem* la, le, lo (*in many cases, 'it' is omitted when referring to information already known*); **who was ~?** ¿quién era?; **~'s in my bag** está en mi bolso; **~'s Paul who did that** fue Paul quien lo hizo; **~ was in Chicago that...** fue en Chicago donde... **II.** *pron pers* **1.** él, ella, ello; *direct object:* lo, la; *indirect object:* le, se; **where is your pencil/notebook? ~ is on my desk** ¿dónde está tu lápiz/cuaderno? está encima de mi escritorio; **~ went off badly** aquello fue mal; **your purse? I took ~** ¿tu monedero? lo cogí yo; **~'s your cat, give ~ something to eat** es tu gato, dale algo de comer; **I'm afraid of ~** le tengo miedo; **I fell into ~** me caí dentro **2.** (*time*) **what time is ~?** ¿qué hora es? **3.** (*weather*) **~'s cold** hace frío; **~'s snowing** está nevando **4.** (*distance*) **~'s 5 miles to town from here** hay 8 km hasta el pueblo **5.** (*empty subject*) **~ seems that...** parece que... **6.** (*passive subject*) **~ is said/hoped that...** se dice/espera que...

IT [ˌaɪ·ˈti] *n* COMPUT *abbr of* **Information Technology** informática *f*

Italian [ɪ·ˈtæl·jən] **I.** *adj* italiano, -a **II.** *n* **1.** (*person*) italiano, -a *m, f* **2.** LING italiano *m*

italicize [ɪ·ˈtæl·ɪ·saɪz] *vt* poner en cursiva

italics [ɪ·ˈtæl·ɪks] *npl* cursiva *f;* **in ~** en cursiva

Italy [ˈɪt·ə·li] *n* Italia *f*

itch [ɪtʃ] **I.** *vi* **1.** MED picar **2.** *fig, inf* **to be ~ing to do sth** morirse por hacer algo *fig* **II.** *n* **1.** MED comezón *f*, rasquiña *f* *Arg* **2.** *fig, inf* ganas *fpl* locas

itchy [ˈɪtʃ·i] <-ier, -iest> *adj* que pica; **my arm feels ~** siento picazón en el brazo; **I've got an ~ feeling** tengo un sentimiento inquietante

item [ˈaɪ·təm] *n* **1.** (*thing*) artículo *m*, objeto *m;* **luxury ~** artículo de lujo; **~ of clothing** prenda *f* de vestir **2.** (*topic*) asunto *m;* **~ on the agenda** asunto a tratar; **~ by ~** punto por punto **3.** COM partida *f;* **~ of expenditure** partida de gasto **4.** PUBL noticia *f;* **news ~** noticia *f* **5.** *inf* (*couple*) pareja *f*

itemize [ˈaɪ·tə·maɪz] *vt* detallar

itinerant [aɪ·ˈtɪn·ər·ənt] **I.** *n* viajante *mf* **II.** *adj* itinerante; (*merchant*) ambulante

itinerary [aɪ·ˈtɪn·ə·rer·i] <-ies> *n* itinerario *m*

it'll [ˈɪt·əl] = **it will**

its [ɪts] *adj pos* su; **~ color/weight** su color/peso; **~ mountains** sus montañas; **the cat hurt ~ head** el gato se lastimó la cabeza

I

it's [ɪts] **1.** = **it is 2.** = **it has**

itself [ɪt·'self] *pron reflexive* él mismo, ella misma, ello mismo; *direct, indirect object:* se; *after prep:* sí mismo, -a; **the place** ~ el sitio en sí; **by** ~ solo

IUD [ˌaɪ·ju·'di] *n abbr of* **intrauterine device** DIU *m*

IV [ˌaɪ·'vi] <IVs> *abbr of* **intravenous** i.v.

I've [aɪv] = **I have** *s.* **have**

IVF [ˌaɪ·vi·'ef] *n* MED *abbr of* **in vitro fertilization** fecundación *f* in vitro

ivory ['aɪ·və·ri] <-ies> *n* **1.** marfil *m* **2. ivories** *inf* MUS teclas *fpl* (del piano); **to tickle the ivories** *fig* tocar el piano **3. ivories** *sl* ANAT piños *mpl*

Ivory Coast *n* Costa *f* de Marfil

ivory tower *n fig* torre *f* de marfil

ivy ['aɪ·vi] <-ies> *n* hiedra *f*

Ivy League *n* UNIV *grupo formado por ocho prestigiosas universidades de EE.UU.*

J

J, j [dʒeɪ] *n* J, j *f;* ~ **as in Juliet** J de Juan

J *n* PHYS *abbr of* **joule** J

jab [dʒæb] **I.** *n* **1.** (*with a pin*) pinchazo *m;* (*with an elbow*) codazo *m* **2.** (*in boxing*) (*golpe m*) corto *m* **II.** <-bb-> *vt* **to** ~ **a needle into sth** pinchar algo con una aguja; **to** ~ **a finger at sth** señalar algo con el dedo; **to** ~ **sb in the eye with sth** meter algo a alguien en el ojo **III.** <-bb-> *vi* **to** ~ **at sb/sth** (**with sth**) dar a alguien/algo (con algo)

jabber ['dʒæb·ər] *vi, vt* farfullar

jabbering *n* farfulla *f*

jack [dʒæk] *n* **1.** AUTO gato *m* **2.** (*in cards*) jota *f;* (*in a Spanish pack*) sota *f* **3.** *sl* (*anything*) **you don't know** ~! ¡tú no sabes un carajo!

♦ **jack off** *vi vulg* cascársela, hacerse la paja Col [o una puñeta Méx]

♦ **jack up** *vt* **1.** (*object*) levantar **2.** *sl* (*prices*) subir

jackal ['dʒæk·əl] *n* **1.** ZOOL chacal *m* **2.** *pej, inf* (*person*) carroñero, -a *m, f*

jackass ['dʒæk·æs] *n* **1.** ZOOL asno *m* **2.** *pej, inf* (*idiot*) burro, -a *m, f*

jackboot ['dʒæk·but] *n* bota *f* alta

jackdaw ['dʒæk·dɔ] *n* grajilla *f*

jacket ['dʒæk·ɪt] *n* **1.** (*short coat*) chaqueta *f*, percha *f* AmC, chapona *f* RíoPl, cuácara *f* Chile **2.** (*of a book*) sobrecubierta *f;* (*of a record*) funda *f*

jacket potato *n* patata *f* asada (*con piel*)

jack-in-the-box ['dʒæk·ɪn·ðə·baks] <-xes> *n* caja *f* de sorpresas

jackknife ['dʒæk·naɪf] **I.** *n* **1.** (*knife*) navaja *f* **2.** (*dive*) salto *m* de carpa **II.** *vi* plegarse

jack-o'-lantern ['dʒæk·ə·ˌlæn·tərn] *n* lámpara

hecha con una calabaza ahuecada

jackpot ['dʒæk·pat] *n* (premio *m*) gordo *m* ▶ **to hit the** ~ *inf* llevarse el gordo

Jacuzzi® [dʒə·'ku·zi] *n* jacuzzi® *m*

jade [dʒeɪd] *n* **1.** (*precious green stone*) jade *m* **2.** (*color*) verde *m* jade

jaded ['dʒeɪ·dɪd] *adj* **to be** ~ **with sth** estar harto de algo

jagged ['dʒæg·ɪd] *adj* irregular; (*coastline, rocks*) recortado, -a; (*cut, tear*) desigual

jaggy ['dʒæg·i] <-ier, -iest> *adj* irregular

jaguar ['dʒæg·war] *n* jaguar *m*

jail [dʒeɪl] **I.** *n* cárcel *f*, prisión *f;* **to be in** ~ (**for sth**) estar en la cárcel (por algo); **to put sb in** ~ encarcelar a alguien **II.** *vt* encarcelar; **she was** ~**ed for life** la condenaron a cadena perpetua

jailbird ['dʒeɪl·bɜrd] *n inf* carne *f* de cárcel

jailbreak *n* fuga *f*

jailer *n*, **jailor** ['dʒeɪ·lər] *n* carcelero, -a *m, f*

jalopy [dʒə·'lap·i] *n inf* cacharro *m*

jam¹ [dʒæm] *n* CULIN mermelada *f*

jam² [dʒæm] **I.** *n* **1.** *inf* (*awkward situation*) aprieto *m;* **to get into a** ~ meterse en un lío **2.** (*blockage*) **traffic** ~ atasco *m;* **paper** ~ COMPUT atasco de papel **II.** <-mm-> *vt* **1.** (*cause to become stuck*) atascar; (*door*) obstruir; **to** ~ **sth into sth** embutir algo en algo **2.** (*a wheel*) trabar **3.** RADIO interferir **III.** <-mm-> *vi* **1.** (*become stuck*) atrancarse; (*brakes*) bloquearse; (*rifle*) encasquillarse **2.** (*play music*) tocar, improvisar

Jamaica [dʒə·'meɪ·kə] *n* Jamaica *f*

Jamaican I. *adj* jamaicano, -a **II.** *n* jamaicano, -a *m, f*

jamb [dʒæm] *n* jamba *f*

jamboree [ˌdʒæm·bə·'ri] *n* **1.** (*celebration*) juerga *f* **2.** (*scouts' meeting*) congreso *m* de exploradores

jammies ['dʒæm·iz] *npl inf* pijama *m*

jammy ['dʒæm·i] <-ier, -iest> *adj* cubierto, -a de mermelada

jam-packed [ˌdʒæm·'pækt] *adj inf* **to be** ~ (**with sth**) estar repleto (de algo); **the streets were** ~ **with people** las calles estaban atestadas de gente

jam session *n inf* jam session *f*

Jan. *n abbr of* **January** en.

Jane Doe *n* Pepita Pérez

jangle ['dʒæŋ·gəl] **I.** *vt* (*coins, keys*) hacer tintinear; **to** ~ **sb's nerves** poner a alguien los nervios de punta **II.** *vi* tintinear; **to make sb's nerves** ~ crispar los nervios a alguien **III.** *n* sonido *m* metálico

janitor ['dʒæn·ɪ·tər] *n* conserje *mf*

January ['dʒæn·ju·er·i] <-ies> *n* enero *m; s.a.* **April**

Jap [dʒæp] *abbr of* **Japanese I.** *n offensive, sl* japo *m* **II.** *adj offensive, sl* japonés, -esa

japan [dʒə·'pæn] *n* laca *f* japonesa

Japan [dʒə·'pæn] *n* Japón *m*

Japanese [ˌdʒæp·ə·'niz] **I.** *adj* japonés, -esa **II.** *n* **1.** (*person*) japonés, -esa *m, f* **2.** LING japonés *m*

jar¹ [dʒar] *n* **1.**(*container*) tarro *m* **2.**(*amount*) (contenido *m* del) tarro *m*

jar² [dʒar] **I.**<-rr-> *vt* (*shake*) sacudir **II.**<-rr-> *vi* **1.**(*cause unpleasant feelings*) **to ~ on sb's nerves** crispar los nervios a alguien **2.**(*make unpleasant sound*) chirriar **3.**(*clash: colors, design*) desentonar; **to ~ on the eye** hacer daño a la vista **III.** *n* **1.**(*shake*) sacudida *f* **2.**(*shock*) golpe *m*

jargon ['dʒar·gən] *n* jerga *f*

jasmine ['dʒæs·mɪn] *n* jazmín *m*

jaundice ['dʒɔn·dɪs] *n* MED ictericia *f*

jaundiced ['dʒɔn·dɪst] *adj* **1.**MED ictérico, -a **2.**(*bitter*) negativo, -a; **to look on sth with a ~ eye** ver algo con cierta dosis de cinismo

jaunt [dʒɔnt] *n* excursión *f;* **to go on a ~** salir de excursión

jaunty ['dʒɔn·ti] <-ier, -iest> *adj* desenfadado, -a; **~ step** paso *m* desenvuelto

Java ['dʒa·və] *n* Java *f*

java ['dʒa·və] *n inf* cafecito *m*

javelin ['dʒæv·lɪn] *n* **1.**(*spear*) jabalina *f* **2.**(*competition*) lanzamiento *m* de jabalina

jaw [dʒɔ] **I.** *n* **1.**ANAT mandíbula *f* **2.~s** (*mouth*) boca *f; fig* fauces *fpl* **3.~s** TECH mordazas *fpl* **II.** *vi sl* darle a la sinhueso; **to ~ away at sb** cotorrear con alguien

jawbone ['dʒɔ·boʊn] *n* maxilar *m*

jawbreaker ['dʒɔ·breɪ·kər] *n* **1.**(*sweet*) caramelo *m* duro **2.**sl (*tongue twister*) trabalenguas *m inv*

jay [dʒeɪ] *n* arrendajo *m*

jaywalk ['dʒeɪ·wɔk] *vi* cruzar la calzada imprudentemente

jaywalker ['dʒeɪ·wɔ·kər] *n* peatón, -ona *m, f* imprudente

jaywalking *n* cruce *m* imprudente de calzada

jazz [dʒæz] *n* jazz *m; ~* **band/club** grupo *m/* club *m* de jazz ▶**and all that ~** *sl* y todo ese rollo

◆**jazz up** *vt sl* crear ambiente

jazzy ['dʒæz·i] <-ier, -iest> *adj* **1.**MUS de jazz **2.** *sl* (*flashy*) llamativo, -a

jealous ['dʒel·əs] *adj* **1.**(*envious*) envidioso, -a; **to be ~ of sb** tener celos de alguien; **to feel/be ~** sentir/tener envidia **2.**(*fiercely protective*) celoso, -a; **to be ~ of sth** ser celoso de algo

jealousy ['dʒel·ə·si] <-ies> *n* **1.**(*possessiveness*) celos *mpl;* **to be consumed by ~** estar consumido por los celos **2.**(*envy*) envidia *f*

jeans [dʒinz] *npl* vaqueros *mpl;* **a pair of ~** unos vaqueros

jeep [dʒip] *n* jeep *m*

jeer [dʒɪr] **I.** *vt* abuchear **II.** *vi* mofarse; **to ~ at sb** burlarse [*o* mofarse] de alguien **III.** *n* burla *f*

jeez [dʒiz] *interj inf* (*expressing surprise*) ¡hala!; (*expressing annoyance*) ¡vaya, hombre!

Jehovah [dʒɪ·'hoʊ·və] *n* Jehová; **~'s Witness** testigo, -a *m, f* de Jehová

jell [dʒel] *vi s.* **gel**

jellied ['dʒel·id] *adj* en gelatina

Jell-O® ['dʒel·oʊ] *n* gelatina *f* (de frutas)

jelly ['dʒel·i] <-ies> *n* **1.**(*soft transparent substance*) gelatina *f* **2.**(*jam*) mermelada *f* ▶**my legs turned to ~** *inf* se me pusieron las piernas como un flan

jellybean *n* gominola *f* (*en forma de judía*)

jellyfish <-es> *n* medusa *f*

jeopardize ['dʒep·ər·daɪz] *vt* poner en peligro

jeopardy ['dʒep·ər·di] *n* peligro *m;* **to put sth in ~** poner algo en peligro

jerk [dʒɜrk] **I.** *n* **1.**(*jolt*) sacudida *f;* **with a ~** con un sobresalto **2.**(*movement*) tirón *m;* **to give sth a ~** dar un tirón a [*o* de] algo **3.** *pej, sl* (*person*) gilipollas *mf;* **to feel like such a ~** sentirse un gilipollas **II.** *vi* sacudirse; **to ~ to a halt** detenerse con una sacudida **III.** *vt* **1.**(*shake*) sacudir **2.**(*pull*) tirar bruscamente de

◆**jerk off** *vi vulg* hacerse una paja

jerkin ['dʒɜr·kɪn] *n* chaleco *m*

jerky¹ ['dʒɜr·ki] <-ier, -iest> *adj* (*not smooth: ride*) dando botes [*o* tumbos], a tirones *Méx*

jerky² ['dʒɜr·ki] *n beef* ~ cecina *f*

jersey ['dʒɜr·zi] *n* **1.**(*garment*) jersey *m* **2.**(*sports shirt*) camiseta *f* **3.**(*cloth*) tejido *m* de punto **4.**(*type of cow*) Jersey *f* (*raza de ganado vacuno*)

jest [dʒest] **I.** *n form* chanza *f;* **to say sth in ~** decir algo en broma ▶**many a true word is spoken in ~** *prov* bromeando, bromeando, amargas verdades se van soltando *prov* **II.** *vi form* bromear; **to ~ about sth** burlarse de algo

jester ['dʒes·tər] *n* HIST bufón *m*

jesting *I.* *n* gracia *f* **II.** *adj* gracioso, -a

Jesuit ['dʒez·u·ɪt] **I.** *n* jesuita *m* **II.** *adj* jesuita

Jesus ['dʒi·zəs] **I.**Jesús **II.** *interj inf* ¡por Dios!, ¡híjole! *AmL*

Jesus Christ I. *n* Jesucristo *m* **II.** *interj inf* ¡Dios mío!

jet¹ [dʒet] **I.** *n* **1.**(*aircraft*) avión *m* a reacción, jet *m* **2.**(*stream*) chorro *m* **3.**(*nozzle*) surtidor *m* **II.**<-tt-> *vi* volar; **to ~ off** viajar en avión

jet² [dʒet] *n* (*stone*) azabache *m*

jet-black *adj* negro azabache; **~ eyes/hair** ojos/pelo de azabache

jet engine *n* motor *m* a reacción

jet fighter *n* caza *m* a reacción

jetfoil *n* hidroala *f* a reacción

jet lag *n* desfase *m* horario, jet lag *m*

jetliner *n* jetliner *m*, reactor *m*

jet plane *n* avión *m* a reacción

jet-propelled *adj* a reacción

jet propulsion *n* propulsión *m* a reacción

jetsam ['dʒet·səm] *n s.* **flotsam**

jet set *n inf* **the ~** la jet-set

Jet Ski® **I.** *n* moto *f* acuática **II.** *vi* ir en moto acuática

jet stream *n* GEO corriente *f* en chorro

jettison ['dʒet·ɪ·sən] *vt* **1.**NAUT tirar por la borda **2.**(*get rid of: person*) deshacerse de; (*plan*) echar por la borda

jetty ['dʒet·i] *n* embarcadero *m*

Jew [dʒu] *n* judío, -a *m, f*

jewel ['dʒu·əl] *n* **1.**(*piece of jewelry*) *a. fig* joya *f; (precious stone)* piedra *f* preciosa **2.** *(watch part)* rubí *m*

jeweler ['dʒu·ə·lər] *n,* **jeweller** ['dʒu·ə·lər] *n* joyero, -a *m, f*

jewelry ['dʒu·əl·ri] *n* joyas *fpl;* **a piece of ~** una joya

Jewess ['dʒu·ɪs] *n offensive* judía *f*

Jewish ['dʒu·ɪʃ] *adj* judío, -a

Jewry ['dʒu·ri] *n form* los judíos

Jew's harp *n* birimbao *m*

jib¹ [dʒɪb] *n (sail)* foque *m*

jib² [dʒɪb] *n (of a crane)* brazo *m*

jibe [dʒaɪb] *vi inf (agree)* cuadrar

jiffy ['dʒɪf·i] *n inf* **in a ~** en un santiamén

jig [dʒɪg] **I.** <-gg-> *vi* **1.** *(dance a jig)* bailar la giga **2.** *(move around)* brincar **II.** *n* **1.** *(dance)* giga *f* **2.** TECH *(device)* plantilla *f* de guía

jigger ['dʒɪg·ər] *n* medida *f (para bebidas alcohólicas)*

jiggle ['dʒɪg·əl] **I.** *vt* mover; **to ~ sth about** menear algo **II.** *vi* moverse **III.** *n* meneo *m*

jigsaw ['dʒɪg·sɔ] *n* sierra *f* de vaivén

jigsaw puzzle *n* puzzle *m,* rompecabezas *m inv*

jilt [dʒɪlt] *vt* dejar plantado

Jim Crow [,dʒɪm·'kroʊ] *n pej* racista *mf*

jimmy ['dʒɪm·i] **I.** *n* palanqueta *f,* ganzúa *f* **II.** *vt* abrir haciendo palanca [o con ganzúa]

jingle ['dʒɪŋ·gəl] **I.** *vt* hacer tintinear **II.** *vi* tintinear **III.** *n* **1.** *(noise)* tintineo *m* **2.** *(in advertisements)* jingle *m*

jingoism ['dʒɪŋ·goʊ·ɪz·əm] *n pej* patriotería *f*

jingoistic [,dʒɪŋ·goʊ·'ɪs·tɪk] *adj pej* patriotero, -a

jinx [dʒɪŋks] **I.** *vt* gafar **II.** *n* gafe *f;* **to put a ~ on sb/sth** echar una maldición a alguien/algo

jitterbug ['dʒɪt̬·ər·bʌg] **I.** *n* **1.** *(dance)* jitterbug *m (baile muy movido)* **2.** *(nervous person)* manojo *m* de nervios **II.** <-gg-> *vi* bailar el jitterbug

jitters ['dʒɪt̬·ərz] *npl inf (nervousness)* nervios *mpl;* **he got the ~** le entró el canguelo

jittery ['dʒɪt̬·ər·i] <-ier, -iest> *adj inf* nervioso, -a; **he felt ~** le dió el tembleque; **he got ~** le entró el canguelo

jiujitsu [,dʒu·'dʒɪt·su] *n s.* **jujitsu**

jive [dʒaɪv] **I.** *n* swing *m* **II.** *vi* bailar el swing

job [dʒab] *n* **1.** *(piece of work, employment)* trabajo *m;* **to apply for a ~** presentarse para un trabajo **2.** *(duty)* deber *m;* **to do one's ~** cumplir con su deber; **it's not her ~** no es asunto suyo **3.** *inf (robbery)* **do a bank ~** dar un golpe en un banco

job description *n* descripción *f* del puesto

jobholder *n* trabajador, -a *m, f* (fijo, -a), empleado, -a *m, f*

job interview *n* entrevista *f* de trabajo

jobless ['dʒab·lɪs] **I.** *adj* desocupado, -a **II.** *npl* **the ~** los parados *mpl;* **~ figures** cifras *fpl* de paro

job market *n* mercado *m* laboral

job rating *n* evaluación *f* del lugar de trabajo

jobseeker *n* demandante *mf* de empleo

jock [dʒak] *n* **1.** *sl (athlete)* atleta *m; pej* musculitos *m inv* cabezahueca **2.** *(jockstrap)* suspensorio *m*

jockey ['dʒak·i] **I.** *n* jockey *mf* **II.** *vi* **to ~ for sth** competir por algo; **to ~ for position** disputarse un puesto

jockstrap *n* suspensorio *m*

jocose [dʒoʊ·'koʊs] *adj form* jocoso, -a

jocular ['dʒak·jə·lər] *adj* jocoso, -a

jocund ['dʒak·ənd] *adj* jocundo, -a

jodhpurs ['dʒad·pərz] *npl* pantalones *mpl* de montar

Joe Blow *n inf* Perico *m* de los Palotes

jog [dʒag] **I.** *n* **1.** *(run)* trote *m;* **to go for a ~** hacer footing **2.** *(nudge)* golpe *m;* **to give sth a ~** empujar algo **II.** <-gg-> *vi* correr **III.** <-gg-> *vt* **to ~ sb's memory** refrescar la memoria a alguien

◆**jog along** *vi inf* ir tirando

jogger ['dʒag·ər] *n* persona *f* que hace footing

jogging ['dʒag·ɪŋ] *n* footing *m;* **to go (out) ~** hacer footing

joggle ['dʒag·əl] **I.** *vt* mover **II.** *n* meneo *m*

john [dʒan] *n sl (toilet)* váter *m*

John Bull *n inf* John Bull *m (personificación de todo lo inglés)*

John Doe *n* Pepito Pérez

John Hancock *n inf* autógrafo *m fig,* firma *f*

join [dʒɔɪn] **I.** *vt* **1.** *(connect)* juntar, unir; **to ~ hands** cogerse de la mano; **to ~ sb (together) in marriage** *form* unir a alguien en matrimonio **2.** *(come together with sb)* reunirse [o juntarse] con; **they'll ~ us after dinner** vendrán después de cenar **3.** *(become member of: club)* unirse a; *(society)* ingresar en; *(army)* alistarse en **4.** *(begin to work with)* incorporarse a **II.** *vi* **1.** *(unite)* unirse **2.** *(become member)* hacerse socio **3.** *(participate)* **to ~ in sth** tomar parte en algo **III.** *n* unión *f,* juntura *f*

joiner ['dʒɔɪ·nər] *n* carpintero, -a *m, f*

joinery ['dʒɔɪ·nə·ri] *n* carpintería *f*

joint [dʒɔɪnt] **I.** *adj* conjunto, -a **II.** *n* **1.** ANAT articulación *f;* **out of ~** dislocado; **to come out of ~** dislocarse **2.** *(connection)* unión *f,* juntura *f* **3.** TECH conexión **4.** *sl (nightclub)* garito *m* **5.** *sl (jail)* chirona *f,* cana *f Col, Chile, Perú, Urug* **6.** *sl (marijuana)* porro *m*

jointed *adj* articulado, -a

joint effort *n* trabajo *m* de equipo

jointly *adv* conjuntamente

joint ownership *n* copropiedad *f*

joint stock *n* capital *m* social

joint-stock company *n* sociedad *f* anónima

joint venture *n* empresa *f* conjunta

joist [dʒɔɪst] *n* viga *f*

joke [dʒoʊk] **I.** *n* **1.** *(amusing story)* chiste *m;* *(trick, remark)* broma *f;* **to play a ~ on sb** gastar una broma a alguien; **to not be able to take a ~** no aceptar una broma; **to do sth as a ~** hacer algo en broma **2.** *inf (easy thing)* **to be no ~** no ser cosa de broma **3.** *inf (ridiculous thing or person)* ridiculez *f;* **what a ~!** ¡qué farsa! ▶ **the ~ was on me** me salió el tiro por la culata *inf* **II.** *vi* bromear; **to ~ about sth** hacer bromas sobre algo; **you must be joking!** ¿lo dices en serio?

joker ['dʒoʊ·kər] *n* **1.** (*one who jokes*) bromista *mf* **2.** *inf* (*annoying person*) idiota *m* **3.** (*playing card*) comodín *m* ▸ **to be the ~ in the pack** ser la gran incógnita

joking I. *adj* jocoso, -a **II.** *n* bromas *fpl*

jokingly *adv* en broma

jolly ['dʒal·i] <-ier, -iest> *adj* **1.** (*happy: tune*) alegre **2.** (*enjoyable*) agradable; **to have a ~ time** pasarla en grande

jolt [dʒoʊlt] **I.** *n* **1.** (*sudden jerk*) sacudida *f* **2.** (*shock*) impresión *f* **II.** *vt* **1.** (*jerk*) sacudir **2.** (*shock*) sobresaltar **III.** *vi* dar una sacudida; (*vehicle*) traquetear

Jordan ['dʒɔr·dən] *n* **1.** (*country*) Jordania *f* **2.** (*river*) Jordán *m*

Jordanian [dʒɔr·'deɪ·ni·ən] **I.** *adj* jordano, -a **II.** *n* jordano, -a *m, f*

josh [dʒaʃ] *vt, vi inf* tomar el pelo

jostle ['dʒas·əl] **I.** *vt* empujar **II.** *vi* **1.** (*push*) empujarse **2.** (*compete*) disputarse; **to ~ for position** luchar por hacerse un hueco

jot [dʒat] **I.** <-tt-> *vt* **to ~ sth down** apuntar algo **II.** *n* **there's not a ~ of truth in it** eso no tiene ni pizca de verdad

jottings *npl* apuntes *mpl*

joule [dʒul] *n* PHYS julio *m*

journal ['dʒɜr·nəl] *n* **1.** (*periodical*) revista *f* especializada **2.** (*diary*) diario *m*

journalism ['dʒɜr·nə·lɪz·əm] *n* periodismo *m*, diarismo *m AmL*

journalist ['dʒɜr·nə·lɪst] *n* periodista *mf*

journalistic [ˌdʒɜr·nə·'lɪs·tɪk] *adj* periodístico, -a

journey ['dʒɜr·ni] **I.** *n* viaje *m* **II.** *vi liter* viajar

journeyman ['dʒɜr·ni·mən] <-men> *n* trabajador *m* cualificado

joust [dʒaʊst] **I.** *vi* justar **II.** *n* justa *f*

jovial ['dʒoʊ·vi·əl] *adj* jovial

joviality [ˌdʒoʊ·vi·'æl·ə·t̬i] *n* jovialidad *f*

jowl [dʒaʊl] *n* quijada *f*

joy [dʒɔɪ] *n* **1.** (*gladness*) alegría *f;* **to jump for ~** saltar de alegría **2.** (*cause of joy*) placer *m*

joyful ['dʒɔɪ·fəl] *adj* feliz

joyless ['dʒɔɪ·lɪs] *adj* falto, -a de alegría; (*expression*) triste

joyous ['dʒɔɪ·əs] *adj liter* de júbilo

joy ride ['dʒɔɪ·raɪd] *n paseo en un coche robado*

joystick ['dʒɔɪ·stɪk] *n* **1.** AVIAT palanca *f* de mando **2.** COMPUT joystick *m*

JPEG ['dʒeɪ·ˌpeg] *n* COMPUT JPEG *m*

Jr., jr. *abbr of* **Junior** Jr.

jubilant ['dʒu·bɪ·lənt] *adj* jubiloso, -a; (*crowd*) exultante

jubilation [ˌdʒu·bɪ·'leɪ·ʃən] *n* júbilo *m*

jubilee ['dʒu·bə·li] *n* **1.** (*anniversary*) aniversario *m* **2.** REL jubileo *m*

Judaism ['dʒu·di·ɪz·əm] *n* judaísmo *m*

Judas ['dʒu·dəs] *n* judas *m*

judge [dʒʌdʒ] **I.** *n* **1.** LAW juez *mf* **2.** (*referee*)

árbitro *m;* (*in a jury*) miembro *m* del jurado; **panel of ~s** jurado *m* **II.** *vi a.* LAW juzgar; (*give one's opinion*) opinar **III.** *vt* **1.** *a.* LAW juzgar; (*question*) decidir; (*assess*) valorar; (*consider*) considerar; **to ~ that...** opinar que... **2.** (*as a referee*) arbitrar; (*in a jury*) actuar como miembro del jurado de

judg(e)ment ['dʒʌdʒ·mənt] *n* **1.** LAW fallo *m* **2.** (*opinion*) opinión *f* **3.** (*discernment*) criterio *m*

judgmental [dʒʌdʒ·'men·təl] *adj* sentencioso, -a

judicature ['dʒu·dɪ·kə·tʃər] *n* judicatura *f*

judicial [dʒu·'dɪʃ·əl] *adj* judicial

judiciary [dʒu·'dɪʃ·i·er·i] *n form* poder *m* judicial

judicious [dʒu·'dɪʃ·əs] *adj form* acertado, -a

judo ['dʒu·doʊ] *n* judo *m*

jug [dʒʌg] *n* **1.** (*container*) jarra; (*small: for milk, cream*) jarrita *f* **2.** *pl vulg* (*breasts*) melones *mpl*, tetas *fpl*

juggernaut ['dʒʌg·ər·nɔt] *n* fuerza *f* irresistible

juggle ['dʒʌg·əl] **I.** *vi a. fig* hacer juegos malabares **II.** *vt a. fig* hacer juegos malabares con

juggler ['dʒʌg·lər] *n* malabarista *mf*

jugular ['dʒʌg·jə·lər] *n* yugular *f* ▸ **to go for the ~** *inf* entrar a degüello

jugular vein *n* vena *f* yugular

juice [dʒus] *n* **1.** (*drink*) zumo *m* **2.** (*of meat*) jugo *m* **3.** *sl* (*electricity*) luz *f;* (*fuel*) sopa *f* ▸ **to stew in one's own ~** cocerse en su propia salsa

juiced *adj sl* (*drunk*) bolinga, rascado *Col;* **to be ~** tener una peda *Méx*

juicy ['dʒu·si] <-ier, -iest> *adj* **1.** (*fruit, steak*) jugoso, -a **2.** *inf* (*profit*) sustancioso, -a; (*role*) suculento, -a **3.** *inf* (*scandalous*) jugoso, -a; (*details*) picante

jujitsu [ˌdʒu·'dʒɪt·su] *n* jiu-jitsu *m*

jukebox ['dʒuk·baks] *n* máquina *f* de discos

Jul. *n abbr of* **July** jul.

julep ['dʒu·ləp] *n* (*drink*) julepe *m;* **mint ~** julepe de menta

July [dʒu·'laɪ] *n* julio *m; s.a.* **April**

jumble ['dʒʌm·bəl] **I.** *n* revoltijo *m* **II.** *vt* mezclar

jumbo ['dʒʌm·boʊ] **I.** *adj* gigante *m* **II.** *n inf* gigante, -a *m, f*

jumbo jet *n* AVIAT jumbo *m*

jump [dʒʌmp] **I.** *vi* **1.** (*leap*) saltar; **to ~ up and down** pegar saltos **2.** (*skip*) brincar; **to ~ for joy** brincar de alegría **3.** (*jerk*) sobresaltarse **4.** (*increase suddenly*) subir de golpe ▸ **go ~ in the lake!** *inf* ¡vete a freír espárragos! **II.** *vt* **1.** (*leap across or over*) saltar **2.** (*attack*) atacar **3.** (*disregard*) saltarse ▸ **to ~ the gun** precipitarse **III.** *n* **1.** (*leap*) salto *m* **2.** (*hurdle*) obstáculo *m*

◆ **jump about** *vi* dar saltos

◆ **jump at** *vt* (*an opportunity*) no dejar escapar; (*an offer*) aceptar con entusiasmo

◆ **jump down** *vi* bajar de un salto

J

◆**jump in** *vi* entrar deprisa
◆**jump on** *vt* (*criticize*) poner verde
◆**jump up** *vi* levantarse de un salto
jumper ['dʒʌm·pər] *n* **1.** (*person, animal*) saltador(a) *m(f)* **2.** (*dress*) pichi *m*
jumper cables *npl* AUTO cables *mpl* de arranque
jump jet *n* avión *m* de despegue vertical
jump-start *vt* **1.** AUTO hacer arrancar (*empujando o haciendo un puente*) **2.** *inf* (*reinvigorate: a career*) dar nuevo ímpetu a
jumpsuit *n* FASHION mono
jumpy ['dʒʌm·pi] <-ier, -iest> *adj inf* nervioso, -a
Jun. *n abbr of* **June** jun.
junction ['dʒʌŋk·ʃən] *n* cruce *m*
juncture ['dʒʌŋk·tʃər] *n form* coyuntura *f*; **at this ~** en este momento
June [dʒun] *n* junio *m*; *s.a.* **April**
jungle ['dʒʌŋ·gəl] *n* **1.** (*forest*) selva *f* **2.** *fig* (*tangled mass*) maraña *f*; (*of laws*) laberinto *m*
junior ['dʒun·jər] **I.** *adj* **1.** (*younger*) más joven **2.** SPORTS juvenil **3.** (*lower in rank*) subalterno, -a; (*partner*) comanditario, -a **II.** *n* **1.** (*younger person*) **he is five years my ~** es cinco años menor que yo **2.** (*low-ranking person*) subalterno, -a *m, f* **3.** UNIV, SCHOOL estudiante *mf* de tercer año
junior college *n* *colegio que comprende los dos primeros años universitarios*
junior high school *n* instituto *m* de enseñanza media
juniper ['dʒu·nɪ·pər] *n* enebro *m*
junk[1] [dʒʌŋk] **I.** *n* **1.** (*objects of no value*) trastos *mpl*, tiliches *mpl* *AmC, Méx* **2.** *sl* (*heroin*) caballo *m* **II.** *vt inf* tirar a la basura
junk[2] [dʒʌŋk] *n* (*boat*) junco *m*
junk bond *n* FIN bono *m* de alto rendimiento, bono basura *inf*
junk food *n* comida *f* basura
junkie ['dʒʌŋ·ki] *n* **1.** *sl* (*addict*) yonqui *mf* **2.** *sl* (*fanatic*) fanático, -a *m, f*
junk mail *n* propaganda *f* postal
junkyard *n* chatarrería *f*
junta ['hʊn·tə] *n* gobierno *f* dictatorial; (**military**) ~ junta *f* militar
Jupiter ['dʒu·pɪ·tər] *n* Júpiter *m*
juridical [dʒʊ·'rɪd·ɪ·kəl] *adj* jurídico, -a
jurisdiction [ˌdʒʊr·ɪs·'dɪk·ʃən] *n* jurisdicción *f*; **to have ~ in sth** tener competencia en algo
jurisprudence [ˌdʒʊr·ɪs·'pru·dəns] *n* jurisprudencia *f*
jurist ['dʒʊr·ɪst] *n* jurista *mf*
juror ['dʒʊr·ər] *n* miembro *mf* del jurado
jury ['dʒʊr·i] *n* jurado *m*
jury-rig *vt* improvisar
just [dʒʌst] **I.** *adv* **1.** (*very soon*) enseguida; **we're ~ about to leave** estamos a punto de salir **2.** (*now*) precisamente; **to be ~ doing sth** estar justamente haciendo algo **3.** (*very recently*) ~ **after 10 o'clock** justo después de las 10; **she's ~ turned 15** acaba de cumplir 15 años **4.** (*exactly, equally*) exactamente, justo;

~ **like that** justo así; ~ **as I expected** tal y como yo esperaba; ~ **now** ahora mismo; **not ~ yet** todavía no **5.** (*only*) solamente; ~ **a minute** espera un momento **6.** (*simply*) simplemente; ~ **in case it rains** por si llueve **7.** (*barely*) ~ (**about**), (**only**) ~ apenas; ~ **in time** justo a tiempo **8.** (*very*) muy; **you look ~ wonderful!** ¡estás maravillosa! **9.** ~ **about** (*nearly*) casi **10.** **it's ~ as well that...** menos mal que... ▶ ~ **my luck!** ¡me tenía que pasar a mí! **II.** *adj* (*fair*) justo, -a ▶ **to get one's ~ deserts** llevarse su merecido
justice ['dʒʌs·tɪs] *n* **1.** justicia *f*; **to bring sb to ~** llevar a alguien a los tribunales **2.** (*judge*) juez *mf*
Justice of the Peace *n* juez *mf* de paz
justifiable [ˌdʒʌs·tə·'faɪ·ə·bəl] *adj* justificable
justification [ˌdʒʌs·tə·fɪ·'keɪ·ʃən] *n* justificación *f*
justify ['dʒʌs·tɪ·faɪ] *vt* justificar; **to ~ oneself** disculparse; **to ~ oneself to sb** dar explicaciones a alguien
justly ['dʒʌst·li] *adv* justamente
jut [dʒʌt] <-tt-> *vi* **to ~ out** sobresalir
jute [dʒut] *n* yute *m*
juvenile ['dʒu·və·naɪl] *adj* **1.** *form* (*young*) juvenil **2.** *pej* (*childish*) infantil
juvenile court *n* tribunal *m* de menores
juvenile delinquency *n* delincuencia *f* juvenil
juvenile delinquent *n* delincuente *mf* juvenil
juxtapose ['dʒʌk·stə·poʊz] *vt* yuxtaponer
juxtaposition [ˌdʒʌk·stə·pə·'zɪʃ·ən] *n* yuxtaposición *f*

K

K, k [keɪ] *n* K, k *f*; ~ **as in Kilo** K de kilo
K 1. COMPUT *abbr of* **kilobyte** K *m* **2.** (*thousand*) **$30~** 30.000 dólares
kaiser roll ['kaɪ·zər·ˌroʊl] *n* panecillo con semillas de amapola
kale [keɪl] *n, n* col *f* rizada
kaleidoscope [kə·'laɪ·də·skoʊp] *n* caleidoscopio *m*
kamik ['kam·ɪk] *n* *Can: bota usada por los esquimales*
kamikaze [ˌka·mɪ·'ka·zi] *adj* kamikaze *m* [*o* camicace] *m*
kamikaze attack *n* ataque *m* kamikaze
Kampuchea [ˌkæm·pu·'tʃi·ə] *n* Camboya *f*
Kampuchean I. *adj* camboyano, -a **II.** *n* camboyano, -a *m, f*
kangaroo [ˌkæŋ·gə·'ru] <-(s)> *n* canguro *m*
kangaroo court *n* tribunal *m* desautorizado
Kans. *n abbr of* **Kansas** Kansas *f*
Kansas ['kæn·zəs] *n* Kansas *f*
kaolin ['keɪ·ə·lɪn] *n, n* MIN caolín *m*
Kaposi's sarcoma [kə·'poʊ·zɪz·sar·'koʊ·mə]

n MED sarcoma *m* de Kaposi

kaput [kə·'pʌt] *adj inf* (*appliance, car, etc.*) escacharrado, -a, dañado, -a; (*relationship*) finito, -a, acabado, -a; **to go ~** (*appliance, car, etc.*) escacharrarse; (*relationship*) irse al traste

karaoke [kær·i·'oʊ·ki] *n* karaoke *m*

karat ['ker·ət] <-(s)> *n* quilate *m*

karate [kə·'ra·ţi] *n* kárate *m*

karate chop *n* golpe *m* de kárate

karma ['kar·mə] *n* karma *m*

katydid ['keɪ·ţi·dɪd] *n* saltamontes *m inv* nocturno

kayak ['kaɪ·æk] *n* kayak *m*

kayaking *n* **I love ~** me encanta ir en kayak

kazoo [kə·'zu] *n* MUS pito *m* de feria

Kb, KB [ˌkeɪ·'bi] COMPUT *abbr of* **kilobyte** Kb

kbyte COMPUT *abbr of* **kilobyte** kbyte

kc *abbr of* **kilocycle** kc

kebab [kə·'bab] *n* kebab *m*

keel [kil] *n* NAUT quilla *f*

◆**keel over** *vi* volcarse; (*person*) desplomarse

keen [kin] **I.** *adj* **1.** (*intent, eager*) entusiasta; (*student*) aplicado, -a; **to be ~ to do sth** tener ganas de hacer algo; **to be ~ on sth** ser aficionado, -a a algo **2.** (*perceptive: intelligence*) agudo, -a; (*ear*) fino, -a; **to have ~ eyesight** tener muy buena vista; **to have a ~ sense of smell** tener un agudo sentido del olfato **3.** (*extreme*) fuerte; **a ~ interest** un vivo interés; **to have a ~ appetite** tener buen apetito **4.** *liter* (*sharp*) afilado, -a; (*wind*) cortante **5.** (*shrill, piercing*) penetrante **II.** *n* lamento *m* fúnebre **III.** *vi* lamentar; **to ~ for sb** llorar la muerte de alguien

keep [kip] **I.** *n* **1.** (*livelihood*) subsistencia *f*; **to earn one's ~** ganarse el sustento **2.** HIST (*castle tower*) torre *f* del homenaje ▶**for ~s** para siempre **II.**<kept, kept> *vt* **1.** (*have: shop*) tener; (*guesthouse*) dirigir; (*animals*) criar; (*children*) cuidar **2.** (*store: silence, secret*) guardar; **~ my seat** guárdame el sitio; **~ the change** quédese con el cambio **3.** (*maintain*) mantener; **to ~ sb under observation** tener a alguien en observación; **to ~ one's eyes fixed on sth/sb** no apartar los ojos de algo/alguien; **to ~ sb awake** no dejar dormir a alguien; **to ~ sth going** mantener algo a flote *fig* **4.** (*detain*) **to ~ sb waiting** hacer esperar a alguien; **to ~ sb in prison** tener a alguien en la cárcel; **he was kept at the hospital** se quedó ingresado en el hospital; **what kept you?** ¿qué es lo que te ha entretenido? **5.** (*guard*) guardar; **to ~ one's temper** contener el genio **6.** (*fulfill*) cumplir; **to ~ an appointment** acudir a una cita; **to ~ one's word** cumplir su palabra **7.** (*record: diary*) escribir; (*accounts*) llevar **8.** (*person's expenses*) mantener; **to earn enough to ~ oneself** ganar lo bastante para mantenerse; **to ~ a mistress** mantener a una amante **9.** (*obey, respect*) obedecer; (*law*) observar **10.** (*remain involved*) **to ~ one's hand in** no perder la práctica ▶**to ~ one's balance** mantener el equilibrio; **to ~ time**

marcar la hora **III.**<kept, kept> *vi* **1.** *a. fig* (*stay fresh*) conservarse **2.** (*stay*) mantenerse; **to ~ fit** mantenerse en forma; **to ~ silent** (**about sth**) guardar silencio (sobre algo); **to ~ to the left** circular por la izquierda; **~ quiet!** ¡cállate!; **~ still!** ¡estate quieto! **3.** (*continue*) **to ~ going** (*person*) ir tirando; (*machine*) seguir funcionando; **to ~ doing sth** seguir haciendo algo; **he ~s losing his keys** siempre pierde las llaves

◆**keep ahead** *vi* seguir en cabeza; **to ~ of the others** seguir por delante de los demás

◆**keep at** **I.** *vi* perseverar; **to ~ work** seguir con el trabajo; **~ it!** ¡ánimo! **II.** *vt* **to keep sb at sth** tener a alguien haciendo algo

◆**keep away** **I.** *vi* mantenerse alejado, -a; **keep medicines away from children** mantenga los medicamentos fuera del alcance de los niños; **he can't ~ from it** no puede dejarlo; **~!** ¡no te acerques! **II.** *vt always sep* mantener alejado, -a

◆**keep back** **I.** *vi* (*stay away*) **to ~ from sth/sb** mantenerse alejado de algo/alguien **II.** *vt* **1.** **to ~ one's tears** contener las lágrimas **2.** (*hide*) ocultar; **to keep the truth back from sb** ocultar la verdad a alguien **3.** (*retain sth*) **to keep sth back** quedarse con algo; (*slow down*) retrasar algo

◆**keep down** *vt* **1.** **to keep one's voice down** no levantar la voz; **to keep prices down** controlar los precios **2.** (*suppress*) **to keep sb down** oprimir a alguien **3.** (*not vomit*) retener

◆**keep from** **I.** *vt always sep* **1.** (*prevent*) impedir; **to keep sb from doing sth** impedir que alguien haga algo **2.** (*retain information*) **to keep sth from sb** ocultar algo a alguien **II.** *vi* evitar; **I couldn't ~ laughing** no me podía aguantar la risa

◆**keep in** **I.** *vt* (*person*) no dejar salir; (*emotions*) contener; **to keep a pupil in** retener a un alumno como castigo **II.** *vi* **to ~ line** comportarse bien; **to ~ with sb** llevarse bien con alguien

◆**keep off** **I.** *vi* (*stay off*) mantenerse alejado, -a; **'~'** 'prohibido el paso'; **'~ the grass'** 'prohibido pisar el césped' **II.** *vt* **1.** mantener alejado, -a; **to keep the rain off sth/sb** resguardar algo/a alguien de la lluvia; **keep your hands off!** ¡no lo toques! **2.** (*avoid*) evitar; **to ~ a subject** no mencionar un tema

◆**keep on** **I.** *vi* **1.** (*continue*) seguir; **to ~ doing sth** seguir haciendo algo **2.** (*pester*) **to ~ about sb/sth** no parar de hablar de alguien/algo; **to ~ at sb** estar siempre encima de alguien **II.** *vt always sep* **1.** seguir teniendo; (*not to dismiss*) no despedir **2.** (*not to get rid of*) no deshacerse de, quedarse con

◆**keep out** **I.** *vi* no entrar; **~!** ¡prohibido el paso!; **to ~ of sth** no meterse en algo; **to ~ of trouble** no meterse en líos **II.** *vt* **to keep sth/sb out** (**of sth**) no dejar que entre algo/alguien (en algo); **to keep the rain/cold out** resguardar de la lluvia/del frío

◆ **keep to** I. *vt always sep* (*remain private*) to **keep sth to oneself** guardarse algo para sí; **to ~ oneself** ser poco sociable II. *vi* 1. (*stay in*) ~ **the right** seguir hacia la derecha; **to ~ one's bed** quedarse en la cama 2. (*respect*) **to ~ sth** ceñirse a algo; **to keep sb to his/her word** tomar la palabra a alguien

◆ **keep together** I. *vt* mantener juntos, -as II. *vi* mantenerse unidos, -as; **please, ~** por favor, no se separen

◆ **keep up** I. *vt* 1. (*trousers*) sujetar; (*ceiling*) sostener; (*prices*) mantener alto, -a 2. (*continue*) seguir; **to ~ the payments** estar al corriente de los pagos; **~ the good work!** ¡sigue así!; **keep it up!** ¡sigue! 3. (*maintain*) **to ~ appearances** guardar las apariencias; **to ~ traditions** mantener las tradiciones 4. (*stop sb sleeping*) tener en vela II. *vi* 1. (*prices*) mantenerse estable; (*moral*) no decaer 2. (*continue*) seguir; **the rain kept up all night** siguió lloviendo durante toda la noche 3. (*to stay level with*) **to ~** (**with sb/sth**) seguir el ritmo (de alguien/algo); **wages are failing to ~ with inflation** los sueldos no aumentan a la par que la inflación; **I cannot ~ with their conversations** no puedo seguir sus conversaciones; **to ~ with the Joneses** *fig* no ser menos que los demás 4. (*maintain contact with*) **to ~ with sb** mantener el contacto con alguien 5. (*remain informed*) **to ~ with sth** mantenerse al tanto de algo; **to ~ with the times** estar al día

keeper ['ki·pər] *n* 1. (*in charge*) guarda *mf;* (*museum*) conservador(a) *m(f);* (*jail*) carcelero, -a *m, f* 2. SPORTS portero, -a *m, f,* arquero, -a *m, f Arg,* golero, -a *m, f Urug*

keeping ['ki·pɪŋ] *n* 1. (*guarding*) cargo *m;* **to leave sth/sb in sb's ~** dejar algo/a alguien al cuidado de alguien; **to leave sth/sb in safe ~** dejar algo/a alguien en buenas manos 2. **in ~ with sth** de acuerdo con algo; **to be out of ~ with sth** desentonar con algo

keepsake ['kip·seɪk] *n* recuerdo *m*

kefir [ke·'fir] *n* kéfir *m*

keg [keg] *n* barril *m*

keister ['ki·stər] *n sl* (*buttocks*) culo *m,* trasero *m;* (*anus*) ojete *m*

kelp [kelp] *n tipo de alga marrón usada en comidas*

ken [ken] *n* **to be beyond sb's ~** ser desconocido para alguien

Ken. *n abbr of* **Kentucky** Kentucky *m*

kennel ['ken·əl] *n* 1. (*doghouse*) perrera *f* 2. **~s** (*boarding*) residencia *f* canina; (*breeding*) criadero *m* de perros

Kentucky [kən·'tʌk·i] *n* Kentucky *m*

Kenya ['ken·jə] *n* Kenia *f*

Kenyan ['ken·jən] I. *n* keniata *mf* II. *adj* keniata

Keogh plan ['ki·ou·plæn] *n plan de jubilación para personas con negocio propio y para sus empleados*

kept [kept] I. *pt, pp of* **keep** II. *adj* mantenido, -a; **a ~ woman** una amante; **a ~ man** un gigoló

kerchief ['kɜr·tʃɪf] *n* pañuelo *m*

kernel ['kɜr·nəl] *n* 1. (*center of fruit*) almendra *f* 2. **corn ~** grano *m* de maíz 3. (*essential part*) núcleo *m;* **a ~ of truth** una pizca de verdad

kerosene ['ker·ə·sin] *n* queroseno *m*

kerosene heater *n* estufa *f* de queroseno

ketchup ['ketʃ·əp] *n* ketchup *m*

kettle ['ket·əl] *n* tetera *f,* pava *f AmL;* **to put the ~ on** poner agua a hervir ▶ **that's a different ~ of fish** eso es harina de otro costal; **to get into a pretty ~ of fish** meterse en un buen berenjenal *inf*

kettledrum ['ket·əl·drʌm] *n* MUS timbal *m*

key¹ [ki] I. *n* 1. (*doors*) llave *f;* **master ~** llave maestra 2. *a.* COMPUT tecla *f;* **caps lock ~** tecla de bloqueo de mayúsculas; **to hit a ~** pulsar una tecla 3. (*essential point*) clave *f;* **the ~ to a mystery** la clave de un misterio; **a ~ factor/role** un factor/papel clave [*o* decisivo] 4. (*list*) clave *f;* (*map*) lista *f* de símbolos convencionales; (*exercises*) soluciones *fpl* 5. MUS tono *m;* **change of ~** cambio *m* de tono; **in the ~ of C major** en (tono de) do mayor; **to go off ~** desafinar ▶ **to hold the ~ to sth** tener la clave de algo II. *adj* (*factor, figure, role*) clave; **~ decision** decisión *f* clave [*o* fundamental] III. *vt* 1. (*type*) **to ~** (**in**) teclear 2. (*make appropriate*) adaptar

◆ **key in** *vt* COMPUT picar, teclear

◆ **key up** *vt* emocionar; **to be keyed up** estar emocionado, -a; **to be keyed up for sth** estar listo para algo

key² [ki] *n* (*island*) cayo *m*

keyboard ['ki·bɔrd] I. *n* teclado *m* II. *vi, vt* teclear

keyboarding *n* introducción *f* desde teclado

keyboard instrument *n* instrumento *m* de teclado

keycard *n* tarjeta *f* magnética [*o* electrónica]

keyhole ['ki·houl] *n* ojo *m* de la cerradura

Key Largo *n* Cayo *m* Largo

key money *n* adelanto *m; as ~* en concepto de adelanto

keynote ['ki·nout] *n* 1. MUS nota *f* tónica 2. (*central idea*) idea *f* fundamental; **to be the ~ of sth** ser la piedra angular de algo *fig*

keynote address *n* discurso *m* central

keynoter *n* ponente *mf* del discurso central

keynote speech *n* discurso *m* central

keypad ['ki·pæd] *n* COMPUT teclado *m* numérico

key ring *n* llavero *m*

keystone *n* 1. ARCHIT (*center stone*) dovela *f* 2. (*crucial part*) piedra *f* angular

keystroke *n* pulsación *f*

Key West *n* Cayo Hueso *m*

keyword *n* palabra *f* clave

kg *abbr of* **kilogram** kg

khaki ['kæk·i] I. *n* (*color, cloth*) caqui *m;* **~s** pantalones *mpl* caqui II. *adj* caqui

kHz *n abbr of* **kilohertz** KHz
KIA *adj abbr of* **killed in action** fallecido, -a en acto de servicio
kibble ['kɪb·əl] *n* pienso *m* para gatos/perros
kibbutz [kɪ·'bʊts] *n* kibbutz *m*
kibosh ['kaɪ·baʃ] *n inf* **to put the ~ on sth** dar al traste con algo
kick [kɪk] **I.** *n* **1.** (*person*) patada *f;* (*horse*) coz *f;* (*in football*) tiro *m;* (*in swimming*) movimiento *m* de las piernas **2.** (*exciting feeling*) placer *m;* **to do sth for ~s** hacer algo para divertirse; **to get a ~ out of sth** encontrar placer en algo; **this drink has a ~ to it** esta bebida es fuerte **3.** (*craze*) **he is on an exercise ~ at the moment** ahora le ha dado por hacer ejercicio **4.** (*gun jerk*) culatazo *m* ►**to be a ~ in the** <u>teeth</u> ser como un jarro de agua fría **II.** *vt* **1.** dar una patada; **to ~ sth open** abrir algo de una patada; **to ~ a ball** chutar una pelota; **to ~ oneself** *fig* darse con la cabeza en la pared *fig* **2.** (*stop*) dejar; **to ~ a habit** dejar un vicio **III.** *vi* **1.** (*person*) dar patadas a; (*horse*) dar coces a; SPORTS chutar **2.** (*gun*) dar culatazo **3.** (*complain*) protestar; **to ~ about sth** quejarse de algo; **to ~ against sth** oponerse a algo **4. to be alive and ~ing** *inf* estar vivito y coleando
◆**kick about, kick around I.** *vi inf* (*hang about*) andar por ahí; (*thing*) andar rodando **II.** *vt* **1.** (*a ball*) dar patadas a **2.** (*treat badly*) maltratar
◆**kick against** *vt insep* protestar contra
◆**kick around** *vt inf* **1.** (*treat badly*) tratar a patadas **2.** (*ponder: idea*) plantearse, dar vueltas a **3.** *insep* (*person*) andar (dando vueltas) por; (*lost item*) andar por
◆**kick at** *vt* golpear
◆**kick away** *vt* apartar de un golpe
◆**kick back I.** *vt* (*football*) devolver **II.** *vi inf* **1.** (*recoil*) retroceder; (*gun*) dar culatazo **2.** *inf* (*relax*) ponerse cómodo **3.** *sl* (*give a kickback*) sobornar
◆**kick in** *vt* derribar a patadas; **to kick sb's teeth in** romper la cara a alguien
◆**kick off I.** *vi* (*begin*) empezar, arrancar *inf;* (*in football*) hacer el saque de centro **II.** *vt* quitar de un puntapié
◆**kick out I.** *vt* **to kick sb out** poner a alguien de patitas en la calle *inf;* **he was kicked out of the party** lo echaron de la fiesta **II.** *vi* (*person*) dar patadas; (*horse*) dar coces
◆**kick over** *vi* **to ~ the traces** desmandarse
◆**kick up** *vt* **to ~ dust** *a. fig* levantar polvo; **to ~ a fuss/row** armar un escándalo/una bronca ►**to ~ one's** <u>heels</u> echar una cana al aire
kickback ['kɪk·bæk] *n sl* soborno *m*
kicker ['kɪk·ər] *n* **1.** (*person who kicks*) pateador(a) *m(f)* **2.** *fig* **to be a ~** tener agallas **3.** (*surprise*) **it was a real ~ for me** me dejó de piedra *inf* **4.** (*sth disadvantageous*) pega *f*
kickoff ['kɪk·ɔf] *n* **1.** SPORTS saque *m* inicial **2.** *inf* (*beginning*) arranque *m*
kick starter *n* AUTO pedal *m* de arranque

kid [kɪd] **I.** *n* **1.** (*child*) niño, -a *m, f,* chavito, -a *m, f Méx,* pelado, -a *m, f Col, Ecua;* **~ brother** hermano *m* pequeño; **as a ~ ...** de niño... **2.** (*young person*) chico, -a *m, f,* muchacho, -a *m, f* **3.** *sl* (*term of address*) nene, -a *m, f* **4.** ZOOL cría *f;* (*young goat*) cabrito *m* **5.** (*goat leather*) cabritilla *f* ►**to treat sb with ~** <u>gloves</u> tratar a alguien con guante blanco; **that's ~'s** <u>stuff</u> eso está tirado [*o* regalado] *inf* **II.** <-dd-> *vi* bromear; **are you ~ding?** ¿bromeas?; **just ~ding** es broma; **no ~ding!** ¡te lo juro! **III.** *vt* **to ~ sb** (**about sth**) tomar el pelo a alguien (con algo) **IV.** *vr* **to ~ oneself that...** hacerse la ilusión de que...; **stop ~ding yourself!** ¡desengáñate!
kiddie *n,* **kiddy** ['kɪd·i] *n sl* crío, -a *m, f*
kiddie pool *n* piscina *f* hinchable para niños
kidnap ['kɪd·næp] **I.** <-pp-> *vt* secuestrar, plagiar *AmL* **II.** *n* secuestro *m,* plagio *m AmL*
kidnapper ['kɪd·næp·ər] *n* secuestrador(a) *m(f)*
kidnapping *n* secuestro *m*
kidney ['kɪd·ni] *n* riñón *m;* **~ disease** enfermedad *f* renal
kidney bean *n* judía *f,* poroto *m CSur*
kidney donor *n* donante *mf* de riñón
kidney failure *n* MED fracaso *m* renal
kidney machine *n* MED riñón *m* artificial
kidney stone *n* MED cálculo *m* renal
kill [kɪl] **I.** *n* **1.** (*slaughter*) matanza *f* **2.** (*hunting*) pieza *f* ►**to be** <u>in</u> **at the ~** estar presente en el momento crucial; **to go** <u>in</u> **for the ~** entrar a matar **II.** *vi* matar; **thou shalt not ~** (*Bible*) no matarás ►**to be** <u>dressed</u> **to ~** ir despampanante **III.** *vt* **1.** (*cause to die*) matar; **to ~ oneself** suicidarse; **to ~ oneself with laughter** *fig* morirse de risa; **this will ~ you!** *fig* ¡con esto te vas a morir de risa!; **not to ~ oneself trying** *fig, inf* no matarse *fig* **2.** (*destroy*) acabar con; **to ~ the flavor of sth** quitar el gusto a algo; **my feet are ~ing me!** ¡los pies me están matando!; **to ~ sb with kindness** abrumar a alguien con atenciones
◆**kill off** *vt* exterminar; (*a disease*) erradicar
killer ['kɪl·ər] *n* **1.** (*sb who kills*) asesino, -a *m, f;* **to be a ~** (*person*) ser un asesino; (*disease*) cobrar muchas víctimas; **the test was a real ~** *fig, sl* el examen ha sido mortal **2.** *sl* (*amusing, talented*) **to be a ~** ser genial; **this joke is a ~** este chiste es para morirse de risa
killer disease *n* enfermedad *f* mortal
killer whale *n* orca *f*
killing ['kɪl·ɪŋ] **I.** *n* (*of a person*) asesinato *m;* (*of an animal*) matanza *f* ►**to make a ~** *inf* hacer su agosto **II.** *adj* **1.** (*murderous*) asesino, -a **2.** (*exhausting*) mortal **3.** (*funny*) para morirse de risa
killjoy ['kɪl·dʒɔɪ] *n* aguafiestas *mf inv*
kiln [kɪln] *n* horno *m*
kilo ['ki·lʊ] *n* kilo *m*
kilobyte ['kɪl·ə·baɪt] *n* COMPUT kilobyte *m*
kilocycle ['kɪl·ə·ˌsaɪ·kəl] *n* kilociclo *m*
kilogram ['kɪl·ə·græm] *n* kilogramo *m*

K

kilohertz [ˈkɪl·ə·hɜrts] *n* kilohercio *m*
kilojoule [ˈkɪl·ə·dʒul] *n* kilojulio *m*
kilometer [kɪˈlam·ɪ·tər] *n* kilómetro *m*
kilowatt [ˈkɪl·ə·wat] *n* kilovatio *m*
kilowatt-hour *n* kilovatio hora *m*
kilt [kɪlt] *n* falda *f* escocesa, pollera *f* escocesa *CSur*
kimono [kəˈmou·nə] *n* kimono *m*
kin [kɪn] *n* **next of ~** parientes *mpl* más cercanos
kind¹ [kaɪnd] *adj* amable; **to be ~ to sb** ser amable con alguien; **he was ~ enough to...** tuvo la amabilidad de...; **would you be ~ enough/so ~ as to...?** ¿me haría usted el favor de...?; **with ~ regards** (*in a letter*) muchos recuerdos
kind² [kaɪnd] **I.** *n* **1.** (*type*) clase *f;* **sth of the ~** algo por el estilo; **he is not that ~** (*of person*) no es de esa clase (de personas); **what ~ of...?** ¿qué clase de...?; **all ~s of...** todo tipo de...; **the first of its ~** el primero en su especie; **to hear/say nothing of the ~** no haber oído/dicho nada parecido; **they are two of a ~** son tal para cual **2.** (*sth similar to*) especie *f;* **a ~ of soup** una especie de sopa **3.** (*sth equal to*) **to do sth in ~** hacer algo de la misma manera; **he swore at me so I answered in ~** me insultó, así que le respondí de igual manera; **he repaid her betrayal in ~** pagó su traición con la misma moneda **4.** (*limited*) **in a ~ of way** en cierta manera; **she has found happiness of a ~ with him** ha encontrado una cierta felicidad junto a él **5.** (*payment*) **to pay sb in ~** pagar a alguien en especias **II.** *adv inf* **I ~ of like it** bueno, no está mal; **he was ~ of sad** estaba como triste; **"do you like it?" — "~ of"** "¿te gusta?" — "no está mal"
kindergarten [ˈkɪn·dər·gar·dən] *n* guardería *f,* jardín *m* infantil *Chile,* jardín *m* de infantes *RíoPl*
kindhearted [ˌkaɪnd·ˈhar·tɪd] *adj* bondadoso, -a; **he is very ~** tiene muy buen corazón
kindle [ˈkɪn·dəl] **I.** *vt a. fig* encender; **to ~ sb's interest** despertar el interés de alguien; **to ~ sb's desire** provocar el deseo en alguien **II.** *vi a. fig* encenderse
kindling [ˈkɪnd·lɪŋ] *n* **1.** (*firewood*) leña *f* **2.** *a. fig* (*act of lighting*) despertar *m*
kindly [ˈkaɪnd·li] **I.** <-ier, -iest> *adj* amable; (*person*) bondadoso, -a **II.** *adv* **1.** (*in a kind manner*) amablemente **2.** (*please*) **you are ~ requested to leave the building** se ruega abandonen el edificio; **~ put that book away!** ¡haz el favor de guardar ese libro! **3.** (*favorably*) **to take ~ to sth** aceptar algo de buen grado
kindness [ˈkaɪnd·nɪs] <-es> *n* **1.** (*act of being kind*) amabilidad *f* **2.** (*kind act*) favor *m;* **to do sb a ~** hacer un favor a alguien
kindred [ˈkɪn·drɪd] **I.** *n* + *pl vb* parientes *mpl* **II.** *adj* afín; **~ spirits** almas *fpl* gemelas
kinetic [kɪˈnet̮·ɪk] *adj* PHYS cinético, -a
kinfolk [ˈkɪn·fouk] *n* + *pl vb* parientes *mpl*
king [kɪŋ] *n* **1.** *a.* GAMES rey *m;* **the ~ of beasts** el rey de la selva **2.** (*in checkers*) dama *f*
kingdom [ˈkɪŋ·dəm] *n* reino *m;* **animal/plant ~** reino animal/vegetal; **the ~ of God** REL el Reino de Dios ▶ **to blow sth to ~ come** hacer saltar algo en pedazos; **(un)til ~ come** hasta el Día del Juicio Final
kingfisher [ˈkɪŋˌfɪʃ·ər] *n* martín *m* pescador
kingly [ˈkɪŋ·li] *adj* regio, -a
kingpin [ˈkɪŋ·pɪn] *n* **1.** (*in bowling*) bolo *m* central **2.** TECH pivote *m* central; **to be the ~** (*person*) ser el cerebro; (*thing*) ser la piedra angular
king-size [ˈkɪŋ·saɪz] *adj* gigante; **~ bed** cama *f* de matrimonio extragrande; **~ cigarettes** cigarros *mpl* extralargos
kink [kɪŋk] *n* **1.** (*twist: in a pipe, rope*) retorcimiento *m;* (*in hair*) rizo *m* **2.** (*sore muscle*) tortícolis *f inv;* **to have a ~ in one's neck** tener tortícolis **3.** (*problem*) fallo *m;* **to iron out (a few) ~s** pulir algunos defectos **4.** (*strange habit*) manía *f*
kinky [ˈkɪŋ·ki] <-ier, -iest> *adj* **1.** (*twisted*) retorcido, -a **2.** (*with tight curls*) ensortijado, -a **3.** (*unusual*) raro, -a; (*involving unusual sexual acts*) pervertido, -a
kinsfolk [ˈkɪnz·fouk] *n* HIST + *pl vb* parientes *mpl*
kinship *n* (*family relationship*) parentesco *m;* (*similarity*) afinidad *f;* **to feel a ~ with sb** tener afinidad con alguien
kinsman <-men> *n* HIST pariente *m*
kinswoman <-women> *n* HIST parienta *f*
kiosk [ˈki·ask] *n* (*stand, pavilion*) quiosco *m*
kipper [ˈkɪp·ər] *n* arenque *m* ahumado
kiss [kɪs] **I.** <-es> *n* beso *m;* **~ of life** respiración *f* boca a boca; **~ of death** *fig* beso de la muerte; **to blow sb a ~** lanzar un beso a alguien; **love and ~es** (*at the end of a letter*) muchos besos **II.** *vi* besarse **III.** *vt* besar; **to ~ sb goodnight/goodbye** dar un beso de buenas noches/despedida a alguien; **to ~ sth goodbye** despedirse de algo
kisser [ˈkɪs·ər] *n* **1.** (*person*) **he's a wonderful ~!** ¡besa muy bien! **2.** *sl* (*mouth*) morro *m,* trompa *f;* (*face*) jeta *f*
kiss-off [ˈkɪs·ɔf] *n sl* **to give the ~** dar calabazas
kissproof *adj* indeleble
kit [kɪt] *n* **1.** (*set*) utensilios *mpl;* **first aid ~** botiquín *m* de primeros auxilios; **sewing ~** costurero *m;* **tool ~** caja *f* de herramientas **2.** (*parts to put together*) kit *m*
kitchen [ˈkɪtʃ·ɪn] *n* cocina *f*
kitchen cabinet *n* POL camarilla *f*
kitchenette [ˌkɪtʃ·ɪ·ˈnet] *n* cocinita *f,* rincón *m* cocina
kitchen foil *n* papel *m* de aluminio
kitchen garden *n* huerto *m*
kitchen paper *n* papel *m* de cocina
kitchen range *n* cocina *f* económica
kitchen sink *n* fregadero *m,* lavaplatos *m inv And,* pileta *f RíoPl* ▶ **to take everything but the ~** irse con la casa a cuestas

kitchen stove *n* cocina *f* económica
kitchen towel *n* (*dishtowel*) paño *m* de cocina
kitchen unit *n* módulo *m* de cocina
kitchenware *n* utensilios *m* de cocina *pl* [*o* batería] *f*
kite [kaɪt] *n* **1.** ZOOL milano *m* **2.** FIN cheque *m* sin fondos *f*, (*toy*) cometa *f*, volantón *m* *AmL*; **to fly a ~** hacer volar una cometa; *fig* tantear el terreno ▸ **go fly a ~!** *inf* ¡vete a freír espárragos!
kitsch [kɪtʃ] **I.** *n* kitsch *m inv* **II.** *adj* kitsch *inv*
kitten ['kɪt-ən] *n* gatito, -a *m, f* ▸ **I nearly had ~s** casi me da un ataque
kittenish ['kɪt-ən-ɪʃ] *adj* coquetón, -ona
kitty ['kɪt̬-i] <-ies> *n* **1.** (*kitten or cat*) minino *m* **2.** (*money*) fondo *m*
kiwi ['ki-wi] *n* **1.** ZOOL, BOT kiwi *m* **2.** *inf* (*New Zealander*) neozelandés, -esa *m, f*
kJ *abbr of* **kilojoule** kJ
KKK [ˌkeɪ-keɪ-'keɪ] *n abbr of* **Ku Klux Klan** KKK *m*
Klaxon® ['klæk-sən] *n* sirena *f*
Kleenex® ['kli-neks] *n* kleenex® *m*
kleptomania [ˌklep-toʊ-'meɪ-ni-ə] *n* cleptomanía *f*
kleptomaniac [ˌklep-toʊ-'meɪ-ni-æk] *n* cleptómano, -a *m, f*
klick [klɪk] *n sl* (*kilometer*) kilómetro *m;* **the speed limit is 100 ~s** el límite de velocidad es de 100 km/h
klutz [klʌts] *n sl* patoso, -a *m, f*
km *abbr of* **kilometer** km
km/h, kmph *abbr of* **kilometers per hour** km/h
knack [næk] *n* habilidad *f;* **to have a ~ for sth** tener facilidad para algo; **to get the ~ of sth** coger el tranquillo a algo, tomar la mano a algo *AmL*
knapsack ['næp-sæk] *n* mochila *f*, tamuga *f* *AmC*
knead [nid] *vt* **1.** CULIN amasar; (*clay*) modelar **2.** (*massage*) masajear
knee [ni] **I.** *n* rodilla *f;* **to be on one's ~s** *a. fig* estar de rodillas; **to get down on one's ~s** ponerse de rodillas; **on your ~s!** ¡de rodillas! ▸ **to bring sb to their ~s** derrotar a alguien **II.** *vt* **to ~ sb** dar un rodillazo a alguien
kneecap ['ni-ˌkæp] **I.** *n* rótula *f* **II.** <-pp-> *vt* disparar en la rodilla o en las piernas
knee-deep *adj* **to be ~ in sth** estar metido hasta las rodillas en algo
knee-high *adj* **to be ~** llegar hasta las rodillas
knee-jerk ['ni-dʒɜrk] *adj sl* (*predictable*) previsible; (*spontaneous*) impulsivo, -a
kneel [nil] <knelt *o* kneeled, knelt *o* kneeled> *vi* arrodillarse
knee pad *n* SPORTS rodillera *f*
knee sock *n* media *f*, calcetín *m*
knell [nel] *n* toque *m* de difuntos; **to sound the ~ for sth** *fig* anunciar el fin de algo
knelt [nelt] *pt of* **kneel**
knew [nu] *pt of* **know**
knickers ['nɪk-ərz] *npl* bombachos *mpl*

knickknack ['nɪk-næk] *n inf* cachivache *m*
knife [naɪf] <knives> **I.** *n* **1.** cuchillo *m* **2.** (*dagger*) puñal *m;* **to wield a ~** blandir un puñal *elev* **3.** (*in a machine*) cuchilla *f* ▸ **to turn the ~ (in the wound)** poner el dedo en la llaga; **to be under the ~** MED estar en la mesa de operaciones **II.** *vt* apuñalar
knife-edge *n* filo *m;* **to be (balanced) on a ~** *fig* pender de un hilo
knife sharpener *n* afilador *m*
knifing ['naɪ-fɪŋ] *n* pelea *f* con navajas
knight [naɪt] **I.** *n* **1.** (*man given honorable rank*) sir *m* **2.** HIST (*man of high social position*) caballero *m* **3.** (*chess figure*) caballo *m* ▸ **~ in shining armor** príncipe *m* azul **II.** *vt* HIST armar caballero; (*give honorable title*) conceder el título de 'sir,
knight-errant [ˌnaɪt-'er-ənt] <knights-errant> *n* caballero *m* andante
knighthood *n* título *m* de 'sir,; **to give sb a ~** conceder a alguien el título de 'sir,
knightly ['naɪt-li] *adj liter* caballeresco, -a
knit [nɪt] **I.** *vi* (*wool*) hacer punto; (*with a machine*) tejer **II.** *vt* (*wool*) tejer ▸ **to ~ one's brows** fruncir el ceño
◆ **knit together I.** *vi* **1.** (*combine or join*) unirse **2.** (*mend*) soldarse **II.** *vt* **1.** (*bones*) soldar **2.** *fig* (*join*) unir
knitter ['nɪt̬-ər] *n* **Paula is a wonderful ~** a Paula se le da muy bien hacer punto
knitting *n* **1.** (*the product of knitting*) tejido *m* de punto **2.** (*material being knitted*) labor *f* de punto **3.** (*action of knitting*) **she likes ~** le gusta hacer punto
knitting needle *n* aguja *f* de hacer punto, aguja *f* de tejer *AmL*
knitting yarn *n* lana *f* de tejer
knitwear ['nɪt-wer] *n* géneros *mpl* de punto
knives *n pl of* **knife**
knob [nab] *n* **1.** (*round handle: of a door*) pomo *m;* (*of switch*) botón *m;* (*of a drawer*) tirador *m* **2.** (*small amount*) pedazo *m;* (*of butter*) trocito *m* **3.** (*lump*) bulto *m*
knobby ['nab-i] <-ier, -iest> *adj* nudoso, -a; (*knees*) huesudo, -a
knock [nak] **I.** *n* **1.** (*blow*) golpe *m* **2.** (*sound*) llamada *f;* **to give a ~ at the door** llamar a la puerta **3.** *fig, inf* crítica *f;* **to take a ~** aguantar un revés **IV.** *vi* **1.** (*hit*) golpear; **to ~ on the window/at the door** llamar a la ventana/ puerta **2.** TECH (*engine, pipes*) martillear **III.** *vt* **1.** (*hit*) golpear; **to ~ sb** dar un golpe a alguien; **to ~ a hole into the wall** abrir un agujero en la pared; **to ~ the bottom out of sth** *a. fig* echar por tierra algo **2.** *inf* (*criticize*) criticar
◆ **knock about** *vi, vt s.* **knock around**
◆ **knock around I.** *vi inf* andar vagando, vagabundear; **to ~ in town** rular por la ciudad **II.** *vt* (*person*) pegar; (*ball*) golpear
◆ **knock back** *vt inf* **1.** (*drink quickly*) pimplar rápidamente; **to knock a beer back** pimplarse una cerveza de golpe **2.** (*surprise*) pasmar

◆**knock down** vt **1.** (*cause to fall*) derribar; (*with a car*) llevarse por delante **2.** (*demolish*) demoler; **to ~ every argument** *fig* rebatir todos los argumentos **3.** (*reduce*) rebajar **4.** (*sell at auction*) adjudicar; **the picture was knocked down to Peter** se adjudicó el cuadro a Peter **5.** (*reduce*) **to knock the price down** bajar el precio
◆**knock into** vt (*make understand*) inculcar; **to knock some sense into sb** hacer entrar en razón a alguien
◆**knock off** I. vt **1.** (*cause to fall off*) hacer caer; **to knock sb off his pedestal** *fig* hacer bajar a alguien de su pedestal **2.** (*reduce*) rebajar; **to knock $5 off the price** rebajar 5 dólares el precio **3.** *sl* (*steal*) choricear **4.** *sl* (*murder*) cargarse **5.** (*produce easily*) hacer (fácilmente); **to ~ some copies** hacer algunas copias **6.** (*stop*) **to knock it off** dejarlo; **knock it off!** ¡déjalo! II. *vi inf* terminar; **to ~ work at 3 p.m.** soltar a las 3 de la tarde; **to ~ for lunch** salir para comer
◆**knock on** vi **to be knocking on 40** estar acercándose a los 40
◆**knock out** vt **1.** (*render unconscious*) dejar sin sentido; SPORTS dejar K.O.; (*cause to sleep*) hacer dormir; (*exhaust*) agotar **2.** (*remove*) quitar; (*contents in text*) suprimir **3.** (*eliminate*) eliminar; **to be knocked out of a competition** ser eliminado de una competición **4.** (*produce quickly*) hacer (en un momento), producir **5.** *inf* (*astonish*) pasmar; **to knock sb out** dejar pasmado a alguien
◆**knock over** vt atropellar; (*an object*) volcar
◆**knock together** vt construir deprisa, improvisar; **to ~ something to eat** hacer algo rápido para comer
◆**knock up** I. vt *sl* (*impregnate*) dejar preñada; **to get knocked up** quedarse preñada II. *vi* SPORTS pelotear
knockabout ['nak·ə·baʊt] adj **1.** (*rowdy*) bullicioso, -a **2.** (*sturdy: overcoat, toy*) resistente
knockdown adj **1.** (*very cheap*) baratísimo, -a; **~ price** precio m de saldo; (*at auction*) precio m inicial **2.** (*violent: blow*) duro, -a; (*argument*) arrollador(a); (*fight*) violento, -a
knockdown-dragout adj (*fight*) salvaje
knocker ['nak·ər] n (*on door*) aldaba f
knock-kneed ['nak·nid] adj patizambo, -a; *fig* débil
knockoff n FASHION *inf* imitación f
knockout I. n **1.** (*competition*) eliminatoria f **2.** SPORTS (*boxing*) K.O. m; **to win sth by a ~** ganar algo por K.O. **3.** *sl* (*person*) puntazo m; (*attractive*) bombón m II. adj **1.** (*competition*) eliminatorio, -a **2.** (*boxing*) **~ blow** golpe m duro; *fig* duro revés m; **to deal sb's hopes a ~ blow** pulverizar las esperanzas de alguien **3.** *sl* (*attractive*) macizo, -a
knoll [noʊl] n montículo m
knot [nat] I. n **1.** (*tied join*) a. NAUT nudo m; **to tie/untie a ~** hacer/deshacer un nudo **2.** (*bow*) lazo m **3.** (*chignon*) moño m, chongo

m Méx **4.** (*small group*) corrillo m **5.** (*in a wooden board*) nudo m ▶**to tie the ~** *inf* prometerse II. <-tt-> vt anudar; **to ~ sth together** atar algo III. <-tt-> vi anudarse
knotty ['nat̬·i] <-ier, -iest> adj **1.** (*full of knots: lumber, wood*) nudoso, -a; (*hair*) enredado, -a **2.** (*difficult*) difícil
knotty pine n pino m nudoso
know [noʊ] I. <knew, known> vt **1.** (*have information*) saber; **to ~ a bit of English** saber un poco de inglés; **she ~s all of their names** se sabe los nombres de todos; **to ~ how to do sth** saber hacer algo; **to ~ all there is to ~ about sth** saber todo lo que hay que saber sobre algo; **to ~ what one is talking about** saber de lo que uno habla; **to ~ sth by heart** saberse algo de memoria; **not to ~ the first thing about sth/sb** no saber nada de algo/alguien; **to ~ all the answers** tener todas las respuestas; **if you ~ what I mean** si sabes a lo que me refiero; **do you ~ what I mean?** ¿entiendes?; **to ~ that...** saber que...; **to want to ~ sth** querer saber algo; **do you ~...?** ¿sabes...?; **you ~ what?** *inf* ¿sabes qué? **2.** (*be acquainted with*) conocer; **to ~ sb by sight/by name/personally** conocer a alguien de vista/por el nombre/personalmente; **(not) to ~ sb to speak to** (no) conocer a alguien como para entablar una conversación; **~ing Mary,...** conociendo a Mary,...; **to get to ~ sb** llegar a conocer a alguien; **to get to ~ each other** llegar a conocerse (bien); **to have ~n sth** haber experimentado algo; **to ~ sth like the back of one's hand** *fig* conocer algo como la palma de su mano **3.** (*recognize*) conocer, reconocer; **to ~ sb/sth by sth** reconocer a alguien/algo por algo; **to ~ sb for sth** reconocer a alguien por algo II. <knew, known> vi **1.** (*be informed*) saber; **as far as I ~** por lo que sé; **to ~ better (than sb)** saber más (que alguien); **to ~ of [o about] sth** saber de algo, estar enterado de algo; **you ~** (*you remember*) ya sabes; (*you understand*) tú ya me entiendes; **(well) what do you ~!** *iron* ¡no me digas!; **I ~!** (*I've got an idea!*) ¡ya la tengo!; (*said to agree with sb*) lo sé **2.** (*be certain*) estar seguro; **there's no ~ing** no es seguro; **one never ~s** nunca se sabe **3.** *inf* (*understand*) entender III. n **to be in the ~** estar en el ajo; **to be in the ~ about sth** estar al tanto de algo
know-how n know-how m; **to have ~ about sth** tener el know-how de algo, *tener conocimientos y experiencia en algo*
knowing ['noʊ·ɪŋ] I. adj astuto, -a; (*grins, look, smile*) de complicidad II. n **there's no ~** no hay forma de saberlo
knowingly adv **1.** (*meaningfully*) con conocimiento **2.** (*with full awareness*) a sabiendas
know-it-all ['noʊ·ɪt̬·ɔl] n *inf* sabelotodo mf
knowledge ['nal·ɪdʒ] n **1.** (*body of learning*) conocimiento m; **to have (some) ~ of sth** tener (algún) conocimiento de algo; **to have a**

thorough ~ of sth conocer algo a fondo **2.** (*acquired information*) saber *m;* **to have (no) ~ about sth/sb** (no) saber de algo/alguien; **to my ~** que yo sepa; **to be common ~** ser de dominio público **3.** (*awareness*) conocimiento *m;* **to bring sth to sb's ~** poner a alguien en conocimiento de algo; **to do sth without sb's ~** hacer algo sin que alguien lo sepa; **to deny all ~ (of sth)** negar cualquier conocimiento (de algo)

knowledgeable ['nɑl·ɪdʒ·ə·bəl] *adj* entendido, -a; **to be ~ about sth** ser un erudito en algo

known [noʊn] **I.** *vt, vi pp of* **know II.** *adj* (*expert*) reconocido, -a; (*criminal*) conocido, -a; **no ~ reason** sin razón aparente; **to make sth ~** dar a conocer algo; **to make oneself ~ to sb** darse a conocer a alguien

knuckle ['nʌk·əl] *n* nudillo *m* ▶ **to rap sb's ~s** *inf* echar un rapapolvo a alguien

♦**knuckle down** *vi* ponerse a hacer algo con ahínco; **to ~ to work** ponerse a trabajar concienzudamente

♦**knuckle under** *vi* darse por vencido, -a

knuckle-duster ['nʌk·əl·dʌs·tər] *n sl* (*weapon*) puño *m* de hierro

knucklehead *n inf* cabeza *mf* de chorlito

knuckle sandwich *n sl* puñetazo *m* en toda la boca

KO [ˌkeɪ·'oʊ] *abbr of* **knockout** K.O.

koala [koʊ·'al·ə] *n*, **koala bear** *n* koala *m*

kooky ['ku·ki] <-ier, -iest> *adj sl* majareta

Koran [kə·'ræn] *n* **the ~** el Corán

Korea [kə·'ri·ə] *n* Corea *f;* **North/South ~** Corea del Norte/Sur

Korean [kə·'ri·ən] **I.** *adj* coreano, -a **II.** *n* **1.** (*person*) coreano, -a *m, f* **2.** LING coreano *m*

kosher ['koʊ·ʃər] *adj* autorizado, -a por la ley judía

kowtow [ˌkaʊ·'taʊ] *vi* saludar humildemente; **to ~ to sb** humillarse ante alguien

kraft (paper) *n* papel *m* de estraza

Kremlin ['krem·lɪn] *n* **the ~** el Kremlin

KS *n abbr of* **Kansas** Kansas *f*

kudos ['ku·doʊz] *n* gloria *f;* **to get ~ for sth** conseguir prestigio por algo

kudzu ['kud·zu] *n* viña *f* kudzu

Ku Klux Klan ['ku·'klʌks·'klæn] *n* **the ~** el Ku Klux Klan

kumquat ['kʌm·kwat] *n* quinoto *m,* naranja *f* china

kung fu [ˌkʊŋ·'fu] *n* kung fu *m*

Kurd [kɜrd] *n* kurdo, -a *m, f*

Kurdish I. *adj* kurdo, -a **II.** *n* **1.** (*person*) kurdo, -a *m, f* **2.** LING kurdo *m*

Kurdistan [ˌkɜr·dɪ·'stæn] *n* Kurdistán *m*

Kuwait [kʊ·'weɪt] *n* Kuwait *m*

Kuwaiti I. *adj* kuwaití **II.** *n* **1.** (*person*) kuwaití *mf* **2.** LING kuwaití *m*

kW *abbr of* **kilowatt** KW

Kwanzaa ['kwan·zə] *n* kwanzaa *m, festival cultural afroamericano*

kWh *abbr of* **kilowatt hour** kWh

KWIC [kwɪk] COMPUT *abbr of* **key word in context** KWIC

KWOC COMPUT *abbr of* **key word out of context** KWOC

Ky. *n abbr of* **Kentucky** Kentucky *m*

KY *n abbr of* **Kentucky** Kentucky *m*

L

L, l [el] *n* L, l *f;* **~ as in Lima** L de Lisboa

l *abbr of* **liter** l.

L. *abbr of* **lake** lago *m*

LA [ˌel·'eɪ] *n* **1.** *abbr of* **Los Angeles** Los Ángeles **2.** *abbr of* **Louisiana** Luisiana *f*

La. *n abbr of* **Louisiana** Luisiana *f*

lab [læb] *n abbr of* **laboratory** laboratorio *m*

lab coat *n* bata *f* blanca

label ['leɪ·bəl] **I.** *n* **1.** (*on bottle, clothing*) etiqueta *f* **2.** (*brand name*) marca *f* **3.** (*description*) descripción *f* **II.** <-l- *o* -ll-, -l- *o* -ll-> *vt* **1.** (*affix label*) etiquetar **2.** (*categorize*) clasificar

labelling *n,* **labeling** *n* etiquetado *m*

labor ['leɪ·bər] **I.** *n* **1.** (*work*) trabajo *m;* **manual ~** trabajo manual; **to be a ~ of love** ser una tarea muy grata **2.** ECON (*workers*) mano *f* de obra; **skilled ~** mano de obra cualificada **3.** MED (*childbirth*) parto *m;* **to be in ~** estar de parto **II.** *vi* **1.** (*work*) trabajar **2.** (*do sth with effort*) esforzarse; **to ~ over sth** esforzarse en algo **3.** (*move*) moverse penosamente **4.** (*act at a disadvantage*) **to ~ under a delusion** estar equivocado **III.** *vt* insistir en; **to ~ a point** insistir (demasiado) en un punto

laboratory ['læb·rə·ˌtɔr·i] <-ies> *n* laboratorio *m*

laboratory assistant *n* auxiliar *mf* de laboratorio

laboratory test *n* prueba *f* de laboratorio

labor camp *n* campo *m* de trabajos forzados

labor costs *npl* costes *mpl* de la mano de obra

Labor Day *n* Día *m* del Trabajo (*primer lunes de septiembre*)

i El **Labor Day**, el Día del Trabajo estadounidense, no se celebra el 1 de mayo, sino el primer lunes de septiembre, y es fiesta oficial en todo el país.

labor dispute *n* conflicto *m* laboral

laborer *n* peón *m*

labor force *n* (*of country*) mano *f* de obra; (*of company*) plantilla *f*

labor-intensive *adj* que requiere mucha mano de obra

laborious [lə·'bɔr·i·əs] *adj* **1.** (*task*) laborioso, -a **2.** (*style*) farragoso, -a

labor pains *npl* MED dolores *mpl* de parto

labor relations *npl* relaciones *fpl* laborales

laborsaving *adj* que ahorra trabajo

labor shortage *n* escasez *f* de mano de obra

labor union *n* sindicato *m*

Labrador (**retriever**) ['læb·rə·dɔr·(rɪ·'tri·vər)] *n* ZOOL labrador *m*

labyrinth ['læb·ə·rɪnθ] *n* laberinto *m*

lace [leɪs] **I.** *n* **1.** (*cloth*) encaje *m*, cinta *f;* (*edging*) puntilla *f* **2.** (*cord*) cordón *m; shoe ~s* cordones *mpl* (de zapatos) **II.** *vt* **1.** (*fasten*) atar **2.** (*add alcohol to*) echar licor a **3.** *she ~d her speech with humorous remarks* aderezó su discurso con comentarios humorísticos
  ◆ **lace into** *vt* **to ~ sb** dar una paliza a alguien
  ◆ **lace up** *vt* atar

lacerate ['læs·ə·reɪt] *vt* lacerar

laceration [ˌlæs·ə·'reɪ·ʃən] *n* laceración *f*

lachrymose ['læk·rə·moʊs] *adj liter* **1.** (*given to crying*) llorón, -ona **2.** (*sad*) lacrimógeno, -a

lack [læk] **I.** *n* falta *f; ~ of funds* escasez *f* de fondos; *for ~ of ...* por falta de... **II.** *vt* carecer de; *she ~s talent/experience* le falta talento/experiencia; *to ~ the energy to do sth* no tener la fuerza para hacer algo

lackadaisical [ˌlæk·ə·'deɪ·zɪ·kəl] *adj* apático, -a

lackey ['læk·i] *n a. fig* lacayo, -a *m, f*

lacking ['læk·ɪŋ] *adj he is ~ in talent/experience* le falta talento/experiencia

lackluster ['læk·ˌlʌs·tər] *adj* **1.** (*not shiny*) deslustrado, -a **2.** (*dull*) gris

laconic [lə·'kɑn·ɪk] *adj* lacónico, -a

lacquer ['læk·ər] **I.** *n* (*for wood*) laca *f* **II.** *vt* lacar

lacrosse [lə·'krɑs] *n* SPORTS lacrosse *m*

lactose ['læk·toʊs] *n* lactosa *f; to be ~ intolerant* no tolerar la lactosa

lad [læd] *n inf* chico *m*

ladder ['læd·ər] *n* **1.** (*for climbing*) escalera *f* (de mano) **2.** (*hierarchy*) escala *f; to move up the ~* ascender de categoría; (*in company*) ascender en la empresa; *to climb the social ~* subir en la escala social

laden ['leɪ·dən] *adj* cargado, -a; *to be ~ with...* estar cargado de...

la-di-da [ˌla·di·'da] *adj inf* repipi

ladies' room *n* servicio *f* [o baño *m*] de señoras

lading ['leɪ·dɪŋ] *n* NAUT cargamento *m*

ladle ['leɪ·dəl] **I.** *n* cucharón *m*, ramillón *m* Col, Ven; *soup ~* cucharón para la sopa **II.** *vt* **1.** (*soup*) servir (*con cucharón*) **2.** (*advice*) repartir generosamente

lady ['leɪ·di] <-ies> *n* señora *f;* (*aristocratic*) dama *f; young ~* señorita *f; the ~ of the house* la señora de la casa; *to be a real ~* ser toda una señora; *cleaning ~* mujer de la limpieza; *ladies and gentlemen!* ¡señoras y señores!

ladybug ['leɪ·di·bʌg] *n* mariquita *f*

lady in waiting <-ies> *n* dama *f* de honor

lady-killer *n sl* casanova *m*

ladylike *adj* femenino, -a

ladyship *n form* **her/your Ladyship** Su Señoría

lady's maid *n* doncella *f*

lady's man *n* casanova *m*, donjuán *m*

LAFTA *n abbr of* **Latin American Free Trade Association** ALALC *f*

lag [læg] **I.** *n* (*lapse*) lapso *m* **II.** <-gg-> *vi* rezagarse; *to ~ behind* (*sb/sth*) quedarse atrás (con respecto a alguien/algo)

lager ['la·gər] *n* cerveza *f* rubia

lagging ['læg·ɪŋ] *n* revestimiento *m*

lagoon [lə·'gun] *n* laguna *f*, cocha *f* AmS

laid [leɪd] *pt, pp of* **lay**[1]

laid-back *adj inf* relajado, -a

lain [leɪn] *pp of* **lie**[2]

lair [ler] *n* **1.** (*of animal*) cubil *m*, guarida *f* **2.** (*of criminal*) guarida *f*

laissez faire ['les·eɪ·'fer] *n* laissez-faire *m;* ECON, POL liberalismo *mf; ~ attitude* actitud *f* permisiva

laity ['leɪ·ə·ṭi] *n the ~* el laicado

lake [leɪk] *n* lago *m*

lam [læm] **I.** *n sl to be on the ~* ser fugitivo de la justicia **II.** <-mm-> *vt sl* (*strike*) pegar

lama ['la·mə] *n* REL lama *m*

lamb [læm] **I.** *n* **1.** (*animal*) cordero *m* **2.** (*meat*) (carne *f* de) cordero *m* **II.** *vi* parir (*una oveja*)

lambaste [læm·'beɪst] *vt inf* vapulear

lamb chop *n* chuleta *f* de cordero

lambskin *n* piel *f* de cordero

lamb's wool *n* lana *f* de cordero

lame [leɪm] *adj* **1.** (*person, horse*) cojo, -a; *to go ~* quedarse cojo **2.** *inf* (*argument*) flojo, -a; (*excuse*) débil, poco convincente; (*effort*) débil

lameness *n* **1.** (*of person, horse*) cojera *f* **2.** *inf* (*of argument*) flojedad *f;* (*of excuse*) debilidad *f*

lament [lə·'ment] **I.** *n* MUS, LIT elegía *f* **II.** *vt* lamentar; *to ~ sb* llorar a alguien **III.** *vi to ~ over sth* lamentarse de algo

lamentable [lə·'mən·tə·bəl] *adj* lamentable

lamentation [ˌlæm·ən·'teɪ·ʃən] *n* **1.** (*mourning*) lamentación *f* **2.** (*regrets*) lamentos *mpl*

laminate[1] ['læm·ɪ·nɪt] *n* TECH laminado *m*

laminate[2] ['læm·ɪ·neɪt] *vt* (*document*) plastificar; (*glass, wood*) laminar

laminated ['læm·ɪ·neɪ·ṭɪd] *adj* (*document*) plastificado, -a; (*glass, wood*) laminado, -a

lamp [læmp] *n* lámpara *f; bedside ~* lamparilla *f* de mesita de noche; *street ~* farola *f*

lampoon [læm·'pun] **I.** *n* sátira *f* **II.** *vt* satirizar

lamppost ['læmp·poʊst] *n* farola *f*

lamprey ['læm·pri] *n* lamprea *f*

lampshade ['læmp·ʃeɪd] *n* pantalla *f* (de lámpara)

LAN [læn] *n* COMPUT *abbr of* **local area network** (red *f*) LAN *f*

lance [læns] **I.** *n* MIL lanza *f* **II.** *vt* MED abrir con lanceta

lancet ['læn·sɪt] *n* MED lanceta *f*

land [lænd] **I.** *n* **1.** GEO, AGR tierra *f;* **on ~** en tierra; **to travel by ~** viajar por tierra; **to work (on) the ~** trabajar (en) el campo; **to have dry ~ under one's feet** pisar tierra firme **2.** (*for building*) terreno *m* **3.** (*country*) país *m* ►**to see how the ~ lies** tantear el terreno **II.** *vi* **1.** (*plane, bird*) aterrizar; **to ~ on the moon** alunizar; **to come in to ~** aterrizar **2.** (*arrive by boat*) arribar **3.** (*set down, fall on: bird, fly*) posarse; (*object*) aterrizar **4.** (*person, ball*) caer; **if they catch you, you'll ~ in trouble** si te pillan, te meterás en un buen lío *inf* **III.** *vt* **1.** (*bring onto land: aircraft*) (hacer) aterrizar; (*boat*) amarrar **2.** (*unload*) desembarcar **3.** (*obtain*) conseguir; (*fish*) pescar; **to ~ a job** conseguir un trabajo **4.** (*cause*) **to ~ sb with a problem** endosar un problema a alguien; **to ~ sb in trouble** meter a alguien en un lío

landed ['læn·dɪd] *adj* que posee tierras; **a ~ family** una familia hacendada; **the ~ gentry** los terratenientes

landfall ['lænd·fɔl] *n* vista *f* de tierra; **to make ~** avistar tierra

landfill ['lænd·fɪl] *n* vertedero *m* de basuras

landholder *n* terrateniente *mf*

landing ['læn·dɪŋ] *n* **1.** AVIAT aterrizaje *m;* **to make a ~** realizar un aterrizaje **2.** NAUT desembarco *m* **3.** (*on staircase*) rellano *m*

landing card *n* tarjeta *f* de desembarque

landing craft *n* MIL lancha *f* de desembarco

landing field *n* campo *m* de aterrizaje

landing gear *n* AVIAT tren *m* de aterrizaje

landing net *n* salabardo *m*

landing strip *n* pista *f* de aterrizaje

landlady ['lænd·leɪ·di] <-ies> *n* (*of house*) propietaria *f;* (*of boarding house*) patrona *f*

landless *adj* sin tierra

landlocked *adj* cercado, -a de tierra; **a ~ country** un país sin acceso al mar

landlord *n* (*of house*) propietario *m;* (*of boarding house*) patrón *m*

landlubber *n* marinero *m* de agua dulce

landmark **I.** *n* **1.** (*object serving as a guide*) mojón *m;* (*point of recognition*) punto *m* destacado, marca *f* **2.** (*monument*) monumento *m* histórico **3.** (*event*) hito *m* **II.** *adj* (*significant: decision, ruling*) que marca un hito

land mine *n* mina *f* terrestre

land office *n* HIST oficina *f* del catastro; **to do a land-office business** *inf* hacer un buen negocio

landowner *n* terrateniente *mf*

land reform *n* reforma *f* agraria

landscape ['lænd·skeɪp] **I.** *n* **1.** (*scenery, painting*) paisaje *m;* **urban ~** paisaje urbano **2.** *fig* panorama *m;* **the political ~** el panorama político **3.** COMPUT impresión *f* apaisada **II.** *vt* ajardinar

landscape architect *n* arquitecto, -a *m, f* de jardines

landscape architecture *n* arquitectura *f* de jardines

landscape gardener *n* paisajista *mf*

landscape gardening *n* paisajismo *m*

landscape painter *n* paisajista *mf*

landslide ['lænd·slaɪd] *n* **1.** GEO corrimiento *m* de tierras **2.** POL victoria *f* arrolladora; **to win by a ~** ganar por mayoría abrumadora

land speculation *n* ECON especulación *f* inmobiliaria

landward **I.** *adj* de la parte de la tierra; **the ~ side** el lado de la tierra **II.** *adv* hacia (la) tierra

lane [leɪn] *n* **1.** (*marked strip: on highway*) carril *m;* SPORTS calle *f;* **bus/bike ~** carril bus/de bicicleta; **to change ~s** cambiar de carril **2.** (*small road*) vereda *f* **3.** AVIAT vía *f* aérea; NAUT ruta *f* marítima

language ['læŋ·gwɪdʒ] *n* **1.** (*system of communication*) lenguaje *m;* **bad ~** palabrotas *fpl;* **formal/spoken/written ~** lengua formal/oral/escrita **2.** (*of particular community*) idioma *m;* **native ~** lengua *f* materna; **the English ~** la lengua inglesa **3.** (*jargon*) lenguaje *m;* **computer programming ~** lenguaje de programación (de ordenadores); **legal ~** lenguaje jurídico ►**to speak the same ~** hablar el mismo idioma

language arts *n* SCHOOL lengua *f*

language lab *n*, **language laboratory** *n* laboratorio *m* de idiomas

language learning *n* aprendizaje *m* de una lengua

languid ['læŋ·gwɪd] *adj* lánguido, -a

languish ['læŋ·gwɪʃ] *vi* languidecer; **he ~ed in bed for weeks** estuvo postrado en cama durante semanas

languor ['læŋ·gər] *n liter* languidez *f*

languorous ['læŋ·gər·əs] *adj liter* lánguido, -a

lank [læŋk] *adj* **1.** (*hair*) lacio, -a **2.** (*person*) larguirucho, -a

lanky ['læŋ·ki] *adj* desgarbado, -a

lanolin ['læn·ə·lɪn] *n* lanolina *f*

lantern ['læn·tərn] *n* linterna *f;* (*light*) farol *m*

lanyard ['læn·jərd] *n* **1.** (*short rope or cord*) cordel *m* **2.** NAUT acollador *m*

Laos [laʊs] *n* Laos *m*

lap¹ [læp] *n* falda *f* ►**to live in the ~ of luxury** vivir a cuerpo de rey

lap² [læp] SPORTS **I.** *n* vuelta *f;* **~ of honor** vuelta de honor **II.** <-pp-> *vt* SPORTS doblar

lap³ [læp] <-pp-> **I.** *vt* **1.** (*drink*) beber dando lengüetazos **2.** (*waves*) acariciar **II.** *vi* (*hit gently*) **to ~ against sth** chocar suavemente contra algo

◆ **lap up** *vt* **1.** (*drink*) beber dando lengüetazos **2.** *fig* aceptar entusiasmado; **he lapped up the praise** saboreaba las alabanzas

lap dog *n* perro *m* faldero

lapel [lə·'pel] *n* solapa *f;* **to grab sb by the ~s** agarrar a alguien por las solapas

lapis lazuli [ˌlæp·ɪs·'læz·ə·li] *n* **1.** (*blue gemstone*) lapislázuli *m* **2.** (*blue color*) azul *m* de ultramar

Lapland ['læp·lænd] *n* Laponia *f*

Laplander ['læp·læn·dər] *n*, **Lapp** [læp] *n* lapón, -ona *m, f*

lapse [læps] I. *n* 1. (*failure*) lapsus *m inv;* ~ **in judgment** desacierto *m;* ~ **of memory** lapsus de memoria 2. (*period*) lapso *m* II. *vi* 1. (*deteriorate*) deteriorarse 2. (*end*) terminar; (*contract*) vencer; (*subscription*) caducar 3. (*revert to*) **to** ~ **into sth** reincidir en algo; **to** ~ **into one's native dialect** recurrir al dialecto nativo; **to** ~ **into silence** quedar(se) en silencio

lapsed [læpst] *adj* (*membership, subscription*) caducado, -a; (*Catholic*) no practicante

laptop (**computer**) ['læp·tap] *n* (ordenador *m*) portátil *m*

larceny ['lar·sə·ni] <-ies> *n* hurto *m;* **petty/grand** ~ hurto menor/mayor

larch [lartʃ] *n* BOT alerce *m*

lard [lard] I. *n* manteca *f* de cerdo II. *vt* untar (con manteca de cerdo); **to** ~ **sth with sth** *fig* (*text*) salpicar de algo

larder ['lar·dər] *n* despensa *f*

large [lardʒ] *adj* grande; **a** ~ **number of people** un gran número de gente; **a** ~ **family** una familia numerosa ▸**to be at** ~ andar suelto; **by and** ~ por lo general

largely ['lardʒ·li] *adv* en gran parte

largeness *n* (gran) tamaño *m*

large-scale *adj* a gran escala

largess(e) [lar·'dʒes] *n* generosidad *f*

lariat ['ler·i·ət] *n* lazo *m*

lark¹ [lark] *n* (*bird*) alondra *f* ▸**to be up with the** ~ levantarse con las gallinas

lark² [lark] *n* 1. (*joke*) broma *f;* **for a** ~ de broma 2. (*adventure*) **to go on a** ~ irse a la aventura

larkspur ['lark·spɜr] *n* BOT espuela *f* de caballero

larva ['lar·və] <-vae> *n* larva *f*

laryngitis [ˌler·ɪn·'dʒaɪ·ţɪs] *n* laringitis *f inv*

larynx ['ler·ɪŋks] <-ynxes *o* -ynges> *n* ANAT laringe *f*

lasagna [lə·'zan·jə] *n* lasaña *f*

lascivious [lə·'sɪv·i·əs] *adj* lascivo, -a

laser ['leɪ·zər] *n* láser *m*

laser beam *n* rayo *m* láser

laser printer *n* impresora *f* láser

laser show *n* espectáculo *m* con láser

lash¹ [læʃ] <-es> *n* (*eyelash*) pestaña *f*

lash² [læʃ] I. <-es> *n* 1. (*whip*) látigo *m;* (*flexible part of a whip*) tralla *f* 2. (*stroke of whip*) latigazo *m;* (*of tail*) coletazo *m; fig;* **he felt a** ~ **of despair/conscience** tuvo un momento de desesperación/conciencia ▸**to feel the** ~ **of sb's tongue** ser fustigado verbalmente por alguien II. *vt* 1. (*whip*) azotar; (*rain*) golpear; (*tail*) sacudir 2. (*criticize*) vituperar

◆**lash about** *vi,* **lash around** *vi* golpear a diestro y siniestro

◆**lash down** *vt* atar firmemente

◆**lash out** *vi* **to** ~ **at sb** atacar a alguien; (*verbally*) arremeter contra alguien

lashing ['læʃ·ɪŋ] *n* azotaina *f;* **to give sb a tongue** ~ echar un rapapolvo a alguien

lass [læs] <-es> *n* (*girl*) chica *f*

lassitude ['læs·ɪ·tud] *n form* lasitud *f*

lasso ['læs·oʊ] I. <-os *o* -oes> *n* lazo *m* II. *vt* echar el lazo a

last¹ [læst] *n* (*for shoes*) horma *f*

last² [læst] I. *adj* 1. (*final: time, opportunity*) último, -a; **to have the** ~ **word** tener la última palabra; **to wait till the** ~ **minute** (**to do sth**) esperar hasta el último minuto (para hacer algo); **this will be the** ~ **time** esta será la última vez 2. (*most recent*) último, -a; ~ **week** la semana pasada; ~ **night** anoche II. *adv* 1. (*at the end*) por último; ~ **but not least** por último, pero no por eso menos importante 2. (*most recently*) por última vez III. *n* **the** ~ **to do sth** el último en hacer algo; **the second to** ~ el penúltimo; **that was the** ~ **of the cake** era todo lo que quedaba del pastel ▸**at** (*long*) ~ al fin; **to the** ~ *form* hasta el final

last³ [læst] I. *vi* durar II. *vt* **this coat has** ~**ed me five years** hace cinco años que tengo este abrigo

last-ditch *adj* desesperado, -a

lasting ['læs·tɪŋ] *adj* duradero, -a

lastly ['læst·li] *adv* por último

last minute *adj* de última hora

last name *n* apellido *m*

latch [lætʃ] <-es> *n* pestillo *m*

◆**latch on** *vi inf* 1. (*attach oneself*) **to** ~ **to sb/sth** agarrarse a alguien/algo 2. (*obtain*) **to** ~ **to sth** (*idea*) tener

latchkey ['lætʃ·ki] *n* llave *f* (de casa)

latchkey child *n* niño que está solo en casa después del colegio porque sus padres trabajan

late [leɪt] I. *adj* 1. (*after appointed time*) retrasado, -a; **you're** ~! ¡llegas tarde!; **the train was an hour** ~ el tren llegó con una hora de retraso 2. (*after the usual time*) tardío, -a; ~ **developer** (persona) que tarda en espabilar 3. (*towards end of*) ~ **night TV show** programa *m* de televisión de noche; **in the** ~ **nineteenth century** a finales del siglo XIX; **in** ~ **summer** a finales del verano 4. (*recent: development*) reciente; ~**est news** noticias *fpl* de última hora 5. (*deceased*) fallecido, -a, difunto, -a II. *adv* 1. (*after usual time*) tarde; **too little, too** ~ poco y tarde *inf;* **to work** ~ trabajar hasta (muy) tarde; **it's kind of** ~ **in the day to do sth** es tarde para hacer algo 2. (*towards end of*) ~ **in the day** a última hora del día; ~ **at night** (muy) entrada la noche; **he got his driver's license** ~ **in life** se sacó el carnet de conducir de mayor 3. (*recently*) **as** ~ **as the 1980s** aún en los años ochenta; **of** ~ últimamente ▸**better** ~ **than never** *prov* más vale tarde que nunca *prov*

late-breaking *adj* de gran actualidad

latecomer ['leɪtˌkʌm·ər] *n persona o cosa que llega tarde*

lately ['leɪt·li] *adv* (*recently*) últimamente, ultimadamente *Méx;* **until** ~ hasta hace poco

lateness ['leɪt·nɪs] *n* retraso *m*

late-night *adj* nocturno, -a

latent ['leɪ·tənt] *adj* latente

later ['leɪ·tər] I. *adj comp of* late posterior; (*version*) más reciente II. *adv comp of* late más tarde; **no ~ than nine o'clock** no más tarde de las nueve; **~ on** después; **see you ~!** ¡hasta luego!

lateral ['læt·ə·rəl] *adj* lateral; **~ thinking** pensamiento *m* lateral

latest ['leɪ·t͜ɪst] I. *adj superl of* late último, -a; **the ~...** el más reciente...; **his ~ movie** su última película; **at the ~** a más tardar II. *n* **the ~ las últimas noticias; have you heard the ~ about them?** ¿te has enterado de lo suyo?; **the ~ in art/physics** lo último en arte/física; **at the (very) ~** a más tardar

latex ['leɪ·teks] *n* látex *m*

lath [læθ] <-es> *n* listón *m*

lathe [leɪð] *n* torno *m*

lathe operator *n* tornero, -a *m, f*

lather ['læð·ər] I. *n* **1.** (*fine bubbles*) espuma *f* **2.** (*sweat*) sudor *m;* **to be in a ~ over sth** *fig* estar histérico por algo II. *vi* hacer espuma III. *vt* enjabonar

Latin ['læt·ən] I. *adj* latino, -a II. *n* **1.** LING latín *m* **2.** (*person*) latino, -a *m, f*

Latina [lə·'ti·nə] *n* (*person*) latina *f*

Latin America *n* Latinoamérica *f,* América *f* Latina

Latin American I. *adj* latinoamericano, -a II. *n* (*person*) latinoamericano, -a *m, f*

Latino [lə·'ti·noʊ] *n* (*person*) latino, -a *m, f*

latish ['leɪ·t͜ɪʃ] I. *adj* (algo) tardío, -a II. *adv* algo tarde

latitude ['læt̬·ɪ·tud] *n* **1.** GEO latitud *f* **2.** (*freedom*) libertad *f*

latrine [lə·'trin] *n* letrina *f*

latter ['læt̬·ər] *adj* **1.** (*second of two*) **the ~** el último; **in the ~ half of the year** en la segunda mitad del año **2.** (*near the end*) hacia el final

Latter-day Saint *n* mormón, -ona *m, f*

latterly *adv* últimamente

lattice ['læt̬·ɪs] *n* (*framework*) enrejado *m;* (*window*) celosía *f*

Latvia ['læt·vi·ə] *n* Letonia *f*

Latvian I. *adj* letón, -ona II. *n* **1.** (*person*) letón, -ona *m, f* **2.** LING letón *m*

laudable ['lɔ·də·bəl] *adj form* loable

laudanum ['lɔ·də·nəm] *n* láudano *m*

laudatory ['lɔ·də·tɔr·i] *adj form* laudatorio, -a

laugh [læf] I. *n* **1.** (*sound*) risa *f;* **to get a ~** hacer reír; **to do sth for a ~** [*o* for ~s] hacer algo para divertirse **2.** *inf* (*activity*) actividad *f* divertida **3.** *inf* (*funny thing*) risas *mpl;* (*sth absurd*) ridículo, -a; **his answer was a ~** su respuesta fue ridícula II. *vi* reír(se); **to ~ aloud** reírse a carcajadas; **to make sb ~** hacer reír a alguien; **to ~ at sb/sth** *a. fig* reírse de alguien/algo; **to ~ until one cries** llorar de la risa; **don't make me ~** ¡no me hagas reír! ► **he who ~s last ~s best** *prov* quien ríe el último, ríe mejor *prov*

♦ **laugh off** *vt* tomar a risa

laughable ['læf·ə·bəl] *adj* de risa

laughing I. *n* risas *fpl* II. *adj* de risa; **this is no ~ matter** no es cosa de risa

laughing gas *n* gas de la risa *m* [*o* hilarante]

laughingstock *n* hazmerreír *m*

laughter ['læf·tər] *n* risa(s) *f(pl); to roar with ~* echarse a reír ► **~ is the best medicine** *prov* quien canta, sus males espanta *prov*

launch [lɔntʃ] I. <-ches> *n* **1.** (*boat*) lancha *f* **2.** (*of a boat*) botadura *f* **3.** (*of a missile*) lanzamiento *m* **4.** (*introduction: of exhibition*) inauguración *f;* (*of book*) presentación *f* II. *vt* **1.** (*set in the water*) botar **2.** (*set in motion: missile*) lanzar **3.** (*introduce: book*) presentar **4.** (*start: investigation*) emprender; (*exhibition*) inaugurar **5. to ~ oneself at sb** lanzarse sobre alguien

♦ **launch into** *vt* emprender

♦ **launch out** *vi* lanzarse

launching ['lɔn·tʃɪŋ] *n* **1.** (*of boat*) botadura *f* **2.** (*of missile*) lanzamiento *m* **3.** (*of exhibition, campaign*) inauguración *f* **4.** (*of book*) presentación *f*

launching pad *n,* **launch pad** *n* rampa *f* de lanzamiento

launder ['lɔn·dər] *vt* **1.** (*clothing*) lavar y planchar **2.** *fig* (*money*) blanquear, lavar *AmL*

launderette [lɔn·də·'ret] *n,* **Laundromat** ['lɔn·drə·mæt] *n* lavandería *f* (automática)

laundry ['lɔn·dri] *n* **1.** (*dirty clothes*) ropa *f* sucia; **to do the ~** hacer la colada **2.** (*washed clothes*) ropa *f* lavada **3.** <-ies> (*place*) lavandería *f* ► **to wash one's dirty ~ in public** sacar los trapos sucios a relucir

laundry basket *n* cesto *m* de la ropa sucia

laundry service *n* servicio *m* de lavandería

laureate ['lɔr·i·ɪt] *n* galardonado, -a *m, f;* **Nobel ~** premio *mf* Nobel

laurel ['lɔr·əl] *n* laurel *m* ► **to rest on one's ~s** dormirse en los laureles

lava ['la·və] *n* lava *f*

lavatory ['læv·ə·tɔr·i] <-ies> *n* lavabo *m,* lavatorio *m AmL*

lavender ['læv·ən·dər] I. *n* BOT lavanda *f* II. *adj* (de) lavanda

lavish ['læv·ɪʃ] I. *adj* (*banquet*) opíparo, -a; (*party*) espléndido, -a; (*reception*) fastuoso, -a; (*praise*) abundante II. *vt* **to ~ sth on sb** [*o* **to ~ sb with sth**] prodigar algo a alguien

law [lɔ] *n* **1.** *a.* PHYS ley *f;* **the ~ of supply and demand** la ley de la oferta y la demanda; **the ~ of averages** (lo que dicen) las estadísticas; **the ~s governing the export of paintings** las leyes que regulan la exportación de cuadros; **his word is ~** lo que él dice va a misa; **the first ~ of sth** el principio básico de algo **2.** (*legal system*) derecho *m;* (*body of laws*) ley *f;* **~-and-order** la ley y el orden; **to be against the ~** ser ilegal; **to take the ~ into one's own hands** tomarse la justicia por su mano **3.** (*the police*) policía *f* **4.** (*trial*) **to go to ~** recurrir a los tribunales ► **the ~ of the jungle** la ley de la selva

law-abiding *adj* observante de la ley
lawbreaker *n* transgresor(a) *m(f)* de la ley
law enforcement *n* aplicación *f* de la ley
lawful ['lɔ·fəl] *adj* **1.** (*legal*) legal; (*demands*) legítimo, -a; ~ **owner** propietario, -a *m, f* legítimo **2.** (*law-abiding*) observante de la ley
lawgiver ['lɔ·ˌgɪv·ər] *n* legislador(a) *m(f)*
lawless ['lɔ·lɪs] *adj* sin ley; (*country*) anárquico, -a
lawmaker ['lɔ·ˌmeɪ·kər] *n* legislador(a) *m(f)*
lawn [lɔn] *n* césped *m*, pasto *m AmL*
lawn mower *n* cortacésped *m*
lawn tractor *n* tractor *m* cortacésped
law school *n* facultad *f* de derecho
law student *n* estudiante *mf* de derecho
lawsuit *n* proceso *m* (judicial); **to bring a ~ against sb** presentar una demanda contra alguien
lawyer ['lɔ·jər] *n* abogado, -a *m, f*
lax [læks] *adj* **1.** (*lacking care*) descuidado, -a; ~ **security** seguridad *f* poco rigurosa; **to be ~ in doing sth** hacer algo de manera negligente **2.** (*not tense*) flojo, -a **3.** (*lenient*) indulgente; (*rules*) poco severo, -a, laxo, -a
laxative ['læk·sə·ţɪv] **I.** *n* laxante *m* **II.** *adj* laxante
laxity ['læk·sə·ţi] *n*, **laxness** *n* dejadez *f*
lay¹ [leɪ] **I.** *n* **1.** (*situation*) situación *f*; **the ~ of the land** la configuración del terreno; *fig* situación actual **2.** *vulg* **to be a good ~** tener buen polvo **II.** <laid, laid> *vt* **1.** (*place*) poner; **to ~ sth on/over sth** poner algo en/encima de algo; **to ~ sth flat** derribar algo; **to ~ stress on sth** poner énfasis en algo; **to ~ the blame on sb** echar la culpa a alguien **2.** (*install*) colocar; (*cable*) tender; (*carpet*) poner, extender; (*pipes*) instalar; **to ~ the foundation for sth** a. *fig* poner los cimientos de algo **3.** (*prepare*) preparar; **to ~ a plan** idear un plan **4.** (*egg*) poner **5.** *vulg* (*have sex with*) follar **6.** (*gamble*) apostar; **to ~ an amount on sth** apostar una cantidad en algo **7.** (*state*) presentar; **to ~ sth before sb** poner algo frente a alguien; **to ~ one's case before sb/sth** presentar su caso ante alguien/algo; **to ~ a charge against sb** formular una acusación contra alguien; **to ~ claim to sth** reclamar algo **III.** <laid, laid> *vi* poner huevos
◆**lay about** *vt* **to ~ sb** emprenderla a golpes con alguien
◆**lay aside** *vt* **1.** (*put away*) guardar **2.** (*save: food*) guardar; (*money*) ahorrar
◆**lay away** *vt* **1.** (*save: food*) guardar; (*money*) ahorrar **2.** (*at department store*) reservar (mediante el pago de un depósito)
◆**lay back** *vt* reposar
◆**lay by** *vt* reservar
◆**lay down** *vt* **1.** (*put down*) poner a un lado; (*arms*) deponer; (*life*) sacrificar **2.** (*establish*) estipular; (*law*) dictar; **it is laid down that...** está estipulado que...
◆**lay in** *vt* proveerse de
◆**lay into** *vt sl* **1.** (*assault*) atacar **2.** (*criticize*)

arremeter contra **3.** (*eat*) lanzarse sobre
◆**lay off I.** *vt* despedir (temporalmente) **II.** *vi sl* dejar; **to ~ sb** dejar en paz a alguien; **to ~ smoking** dejar de fumar
◆**lay on** *vt* **1.** (*provide: food, drink*) proveer de **2.** *sl* (*reveal*) **to ~ sth on sb** contarle algo a alguien
◆**lay open** *vt* **1.** (*uncover*) descubrir **2.** (*expose*) exponer; **to lay oneself open** exponerse
◆**lay out** *vt* **1.** (*organize*) organizar **2.** (*explain*) presentar **3.** (*spread out*) extender **4.** (*prepare for burial*) amortajar **5.** *inf* (*knock unconscious*) dejar fuera de combate **6.** *inf* (*money*) gastar
◆**lay over** *vi* hacer un alto [*o* una escala] (en el camino)
◆**lay to** *vi* NAUT ponerse al pairo
◆**lay up** *vt* **1.** (*store*) guardar; (*money*) ahorrar **2.** (*ship*) desarmar; (*car*) dejar en el garaje **3.** *inf* (*in bed*) **to be laid up** guardar cama
lay² [leɪ] *adj* **1.** (*not professional*) lego, -a; **in ~ terms** en términos profanos **2.** REL laico, -a
lay³ [leɪ] *pt of* **lie²**
layabout ['leɪ·ə·ˌbaʊt] *n inf* vago, -a *m, f*
layaway ['leɪ·ə·weɪ] *n* **to buy/put on ~** comprar/reservar (mediante el pago de un depósito)
layer¹ ['leɪ·ər] **I.** *n* **1.** (*of dust, paint*) capa *f*; **ozone ~** capa de ozono **2.** (*level*) estrato *m*, capa *f* **II.** *vt* acodar
layer² ['leɪ·ər] *n* ZOOL (*hen*) gallina *f* ponedora
layer cake *n* pastel *m* en capas
layered *adj* en capas
layette [leɪ·'et] *n* canastilla *f*
layman ['leɪ·mən] <-men> *n* lego *m*
layoff ['leɪ·ɔf] *n* despido *m* (*por falta de trabajo*)
layout ['leɪ·aʊt] *n* **1.** (*of letter, magazine*) diseño *m*; (*of town*) trazado *m*; (*of building, factory*) distribución *f* **2.** TYPO maquetación *f*
layover ['leɪ·oʊ·vər] *n* (*on journey*) parada *f*; AVIAT escala *f*
laywoman ['leɪ·wʊm·ən] <-women> *n* lega *f*
laze [leɪz] <-zing> *vi* holgazanear
laziness ['leɪ·zɪ·nɪs] *n* holgazanería *f*
lazy ['leɪ·zi] <-ier, -iest> *adj* (*person*) vago, -a; (*day*) en el/la que no se hace nada, sin hacer nada
lb. *abbr of* **pound** libra *f* (≈ *0,45 kg*)
LCD [ˌel·si·'di] *n abbr of* **liquid crystal display** pantalla *f* de cristal líquido
lead¹ [lid] **I.** *n* **1.** (*front position*) delantera *f*; **to be in the ~** estar en cabeza; **to hold the ~** llevar la delantera; **to lose one's ~** perder la delantera; **to move into the ~** ponerse en cabeza; **to take the ~** tomar la delantera **2.** (*example*) ejemplo *m*; (*guiding*) iniciativa *f*; **to follow sb's ~** seguir el ejemplo de alguien **3.** THEAT papel *m* principal; **to play the ~** representar el papel principal **4.** (*clue, tip*) pista *f*; **to get a ~ on sth** recibir una pista acerca de algo; **to give a ~** dar una indicación **5.** (*connecting*

wire) cable *m,* conductor *m* **6.**(*dog leash*) correa *f* **II.** <led, led> *vt* **1.**(*be in charge of*) dirigir; (*discussion, inquiry*) conducir **2.**(*conduct*) conducir, llevar; **to ~ the way** ir primero; *fig* mostrar el camino **3.**(*induce*) inducir; **to ~ sb to do sth** llevar a alguien a hacer algo; **to ~ sb to believe that...** hacer creer a alguien que... **4.** COM, SPORTS (*be ahead of*) liderar; **to ~ the field** *fig* ir en cabeza **5.**(*live a particular way: life*) llevar; **to ~ a life of luxury** llevar una vida de lujo; **to ~ a quiet/hectic life** llevar una vida tranquila/ajetreada ▸ **to ~ sb (around) by the nose** *inf* manejar a alguien fácilmente **III.** <led, led> *vi* **1.**(*be in charge*) dirigir **2.**(*guide followers*) guiar **3.**(*conduct*) llevar; **to ~ to/into sth** *a. fig* conducir a/hacia algo **4.**(*be ahead*) ser líder; **to ~ by 2 laps** tener una ventaja de 2 vueltas

◆ **lead along** *vt* llevar (de la mano)
◆ **lead aside** *vt* llevar a un lado
◆ **lead astray** *vt* llevar por mal camino
◆ **lead away** *vt* llevar; **he was led away by the police** fue arrestado por la policía
◆ **lead back** *vt* hacer volver
◆ **lead off I.** *vt* (*person*) llevar afuera; (*room*) comunicar con **II.** *vi* empezar
◆ **lead on** *vt* (*trick, fool*) engañar; (*encourage*) incitar a; **she doesn't want to lead him on** no quiere darle falsas expectativas
◆ **lead to** *vt* llevar a
◆ **lead up to** *vi* **1.**(*cause*) conducir a **2.**(*slowly introduce*) preparar **3.**(*precede*) preceder a

lead² [led] *n* **1.**(*metal*) plomo *m* **2.**(*in pencil*) mina *f* **3.** NAUT sonda *f*

leaded ['led·əd] **I.** *adj* emplomado, -a; **~ fuel** gasolina *f* con plomo **II.** *n* gasolina *f* con plomo

leaden ['led·ən] *adj* **1.**(*heavy*) pesado, -a; **~ limbs** pies *mpl* de plomo **2.**(*dull*) apagado, -a **3.**(*dark*) plomizo, -a

leader ['li·dər] *n* **1.**(*of group*) líder *mf* **2.**(*guide*) guía *mf* **3.** MUS (*conductor*) director(a) *m(f)* **4.** MUS (*in section of orchestra*) intérprete *mf* principal

leadership ['li·dər·ʃɪp] *n* **1.**(*ability to lead*) liderazgo *m;* **~ qualities** dotes *fpl* de mando **2.**(*leaders*) dirección *f* **3.**(*guidance*) mando *m;* **to be under sb's ~** estar bajo el mando de alguien

lead-free ['led·fri] *adj* sin plomo

lead guitar *n* **to play ~** ser el guitarrista principal

leading ['li·dɪŋ] **I.** *adj* (*main, principle*) principal **II.** *n* mando *m*

leading-edge *adj* puntero, -a; **~ technology** tecnología *f* punta

leading lady *n* actriz *f* principal

leading light *n* *inf* **to be a ~ in sth** ser una figura de referencia en algo

leading man *n* actor *m* principal

leading question *n* pregunta *f* capciosa

lead pencil *n* lápiz *m* de mina

lead poisoning *n* saturnismo *m*

lead singer *n* cantante *mf* principal

lead story *n* PUBL artículo *m* principal

lead-time *n* tiempo *m* de entrega

lead-up *n* tiempo *m* preparatorio

leaf [lif] <leaves> *n* **1.**(*of plant*) hoja *f* **2.**(*foliage*) follaje *m;* **to be in** [*o* **come into**] **~** echar hojas **3.**(*piece of paper*) hoja *f;* **~ of paper** hoja de papel **4.**(*thin layer*) **gold/silver ~** baño *m* en oro/plata **5.**(*of table*) tablero *m* ▸ **to take a ~ from sb's book** seguir el ejemplo de alguien; **to shake like a ~** temblar como una pluma; **to turn over a new ~** hacer borrón y cuenta nueva

◆ **leaf through** *vt* hojear

leafless ['lif·lɪs] *adj* deshojado, -a

leaflet ['lif·lɪt] *n* folleto *m*

leafy ['li·fi] <-ier, -iest> *adj* frondoso, -a

league [lig] *n* **1.** *a.* SPORTS liga *f;* **soccer ~** liga de fútbol; **to be/to not be in the same ~ as sb/sth** *fig* estar/no estar a la altura de alguien/algo; **to be out of sb's ~** no tener comparación con alguien **2.**(*measurement*) legua *f* ▸ **to be in ~ with sb** estar confabulado con alguien

leak [lik] **I.** *n* (*of gas, water*) fuga *f;* (*of information*) filtración *f;* (*in roof*) gotera *f* **II.** *vi* **1.**(*let sth escape*) tener una fuga; (*tire*) perder aire; (*hose, bucket*) perder (agua); (*pen*) perder (tinta); (*faucet*) gotear **2.**(*information*) filtrarse **III.** *vt* **1.**(*let escape*) derramar; **to ~ water** perder (agua) **2.**(*information*) filtrar

leakage ['li·kɪdʒ] *n* **1.**(*leak*) fuga *f* **2.**(*of information*) filtración *f*

leaky ['li·ki] <-ier, -iest> *adj* que tiene fugas

lean¹ [lin] **I.** <-ed, -ed> *vi* inclinarse; **to ~ against sth** apoyarse en algo **II.** <-ed, -ed> *vt* apoyar; **to ~ sth against sth** apoyar algo contra algo

◆ **lean back** *vi* reclinar(se)
◆ **lean forward** *vi* inclinarse hacia adelante
◆ **lean on** *vt* **1.**(*rely on*) apoyarse en **2.** *sl* (*pressure*) ejercer presión sobre
◆ **lean out** *vi* asomarse
◆ **lean over I.** *vt* inclinarse sobre **II.** *vi* inclinarse

lean² [lin] *adj* **1.**(*thin*) flaco, -a; (*face*) enjuto, -a; (*with little fat: meat*) magro, -a **2.**(*efficient: company*) eficiente

leaning ['li·nɪŋ] *n* inclinación *f;* **political ~s** tendencias *fpl* políticas

lean-to ['lin·tu] *n* **1.**(*building extension*) anexo *m* **2.**(*shack*) cobertizo *m*

leap [lip] **I.** <leaped *o* leapt, leaped *o* leapt> *vi* saltar; **to ~ forward** saltar hacia adelante; **to ~ with joy** saltar de alegría; **to ~ to do sth** abalanzarse a hacer algo; **to ~ to sb's defense** saltar en defensa de alguien; **his heart ~ed** le dio un vuelco el corazón; **to ~ to mind** venir a la mente **II.** <leaped *o* leapt, leaped *o* leapt> *vt* saltar **III.** *n* salto *m;* **to take a ~** dar un salto ▸ **by ~s and bounds** a pasos de gigante; **a ~**

in the <u>dark</u> un salto al vacío

◆**leap at** vt **1.** (*jump*) saltar hacia **2.** *inf* (*accept*) no dejar pasar; **to ~ the chance to do sth** no dejar escapar la oportunidad de hacer algo

◆**leap out** vi saltar

◆**leap up** vi **1.** (*jump up*) ponerse en pie de un salto; **to ~ to do sth** apresurarse a hacer algo **2.** (*rise quickly*) subir de pronto

leapfrog ['lip·ˌfrɔg] **I.** n potro m, pídola f; **to play a game of ~** jugar a saltar al potro, jugar a la pídola, saltar el burro *Méx* **II.** <-gg-> vt pasar por encima de

leapt [lept] vt, vi pt, pp of **leap**

leap year n año m bisiesto

learn [lɜrn] **I.** <learned, learned> vt aprender; **to ~ that** enterarse de que **II.** <learned, learned> vi aprender; **to ~ to do sth** aprender a hacer algo; **to ~ from one's mistakes** aprender de los propios errores

learned ['lɜr·nɪd] adj erudito, -a

learner ['lɜr·nər] n aprendiz mf; **to be a quick ~** aprender rápido

learner's permit n permiso m de conducción provisional

learning ['lɜr·nɪŋ] n **1.** (*acquisition of knowledge*) aprendizaje m **2.** (*extensive knowledge*) saber m

learning disability n <-ies> dificultad f de aprendizaje

lease [lis] **I.** vt alquilar **II.** n (*act*) arrendamiento m; (*contract*) contrato m de arrendamiento; **to take sth on ~** tomar algo en arriendo ▶ **a new ~ on life** el comienzo de una nueva vida

leasehold ['lis·hoʊld] COM, FIN, ECON **I.** n bien m arrendado **II.** adj **1.** (*kept by lease*) en arrendamiento **2.** (*dealing with leases*) de arrendamiento

leaseholder ['lis·hoʊl·dər] n arrendatario, -a m, f

leash [liʃ] n correa f ▶ **to keep sb on a <u>tight</u> ~** atar corto a alguien

leasing ['li·sɪŋ] n leasing m

least [list] **I.** adj mínimo, -a; (*age*) menor **II.** adv menos; **the ~ possible** lo menos posible **III.** n lo menos; **at (the very) ~** por lo menos, al menos; **not in the ~!** ¡en absoluto!; **to say the ~** para no decir más

leather ['leð·ər] n cuero m

leatherneck ['leð·ər·nek] n sl soldado m de infantería (*de la marina estadounidense*)

leathery ['leð·ə·ri] adj (*skin*) curtido, -a; (*meat*) correoso, -a

leave[1] [liv] **I.** <left, left> vt **1.** (*depart from*) salir de; (*school, college*) abandonar; (*work*) dejar; **to ~ home** irse de casa **2.** (*not take away with*) dejar; (*forget*) olvidar(se); **to ~ sth to sb** dejar algo a alguien; **to ~ sth at home** dejar(se) algo en casa; **to ~ a note/message (for sb)** dejar una nota/un mensaje (para alguien); **to ~ stains** dejar mancha(s) **3.** (*put in a situation*) **to ~ sb alone** dejar a alguien en

paz; **to be left homeless** quedarse sin hogar; **to ~ sth open** dejar algo abierto ▶ **to ~ a <u>lot</u> to be desired** dejar mucho que desear; **to ~ it <u>at</u> that** dejarlo **II.** <left, left> vi marcharse, despabilarse *AmL* **III.** n partida f; **to take (one's) ~ (of sb)** despedirse (de alguien); **to take (complete) ~ of one's senses** perder la cabeza (completamente)

◆**leave behind** vt **1.** (*not take along*) dejar **2.** (*forget*) olvidar **3.** (*progress beyond*) dejar atrás

◆**leave off I.** vt **1.** (*give up*) dejar de **2.** (*omit*) omitir **II.** vi acabar

◆**leave on** vt dejar(se) puesto; (*light*) dejar encendido

◆**leave out** vt **1.** (*omit*) omitir **2.** (*exclude*) excluir

◆**leave over** vt dejar; **there's nothing left over** no queda nada

leave[2] [liv] n permiso m; **to have/get sb's ~ (to do sth)** tener/obtener el permiso de alguien (para hacer algo); **with/without sb's ~** con/sin el permiso de alguien; **to go/be on ~** MIL salir/estar de permiso

leaven ['lev·ən] **I.** n levadura f **II.** vt (a)leudar; *fig* impregnar; **to ~ a speech with jokes** aligerar un discurso con bromas

leaves [livz] n pl of **leaf**

leave-taking n despedida f

leaving ['li·vɪŋ] n **1.** (*departure*) partida f **2.** **~s** (*leftovers*) sobras fpl

Lebanese [ˌleb·ə·'niz] **I.** adj libanés, -esa **II.** n libanés, -esa m, f

Lebanon ['leb·ə·nan] n (**the**) **~** el Líbano

lech [letʃ] n sl, **lecher** ['letʃ·ər] n (hombre m) lascivo m

lecherous ['letʃ·ər·əs] adj lascivo, -a

lechery ['letʃ·ə·ri] n lascivia f, lujuria f

lectern ['lek·tərn] n atril m; REL facistol m

lecture ['lek·tʃər] **I.** n a. UNIV conferencia f, clase f; **a ~ on sth** una conferencia acerca de algo; **to give sb a ~** *fig* sermonear a alguien **II.** vi (*give a lecture*) dar una conferencia; (*teach*) dar clases **III.** vt **1.** (*give a lecture*) dar una conferencia a; (*teach*) dar clases a **2.** *fig* (*criticize*) sermonear

lecture hall n auditorio m

lecture notes npl apuntes mpl (de clase)

lecturer ['lek·tʃər·ər] n conferenciante mf; UNIV profesor(a) m(f) universitario, -a

lecture tour n gira f de conferencias

led [led] pt, pp of **lead**[1]

LED [ˌel·i·'di] n abbr of **light-emitting diode** LED m

ledge [ledʒ] n (*shelf*) repisa f; (*on building*) cornisa f; (*on cliff*) saliente m; **window ~** alféizar m

ledger ['ledʒ·ər] n COM libro m mayor

lee [li] n sotavento m

leech [litʃ] n <-es> n sanguijuela f, saguaipé m *Arg*; **he <u>stuck</u> to her like a ~** se pegó a ella como una lapa

leek [lik] n CULIN puerro m

leer [lɪr] **I.** *vi* mirar lascivamente **II.** *n* mirada *f* lasciva

leery ['lɪr·i] *adj* desconfiado, -a, receloso, -a; **to be ~ of sb/sth** desconfiar de alguien/algo

leeward ['li·wərd] METEO **I.** *adj* de sotavento **II.** *adv* a sotavento

Leeward Islands *n* Islas *f* de Sotavento *pl*

leeway ['li·weɪ] *n* flexibilidad *f*

left¹ [left] *pt, pp of* **leave¹**

left² [left] **I.** *n* **1.** (*direction, sight*) izquierda *f;* **the ~** la izquierda; **to turn to the ~** girar a la izquierda; **on/to the/her ~** en/a la/su izquierda **2.** POL izquierda *f;* **on the ~ de** izquierda(s) **II.** *adj* izquierdo, -a **III.** *adv* a [*o* hacia] la izquierda; **to turn ~** girar hacia la izquierda

left field *n* (*in baseball*) jardín *m* izquierdo; *fig, sl;* **to be out in ~** irse la olla a uno, estar fuera de onda

left hand *n* (mano *f*) izquierda *f;* **on the ~** a la izquierda

left-hand *adj* a la izquierda; **~ side** lado *m* izquierdo; **~ turn** curva *f* a la izquierda

left-handed *adj* zurdo, -a; **~ scissors** tijeras *fpl* para zurdos

left-hander *n* zurdo, -a *m, f*

leftist ['lef·tɪst] POL **I.** *adj* izquierdista **II.** *n* izquierdista *mf*

leftovers ['left·ou·vərz] *npl* **1.** (*food*) sobras *fpl* **2.** (*remaining things*) restos *mpl*

left wing *n* POL izquierda *f*

left-wing *adj* POL de izquierda

left-winger *n* POL izquierdista *mf*

lefty *n* zurdo, -a *m, f*

leg [leg] **I.** *n* **1.** (*of person*) pierna *f;* (*of animal, furniture*) pata *f* **2.** (*of pants*) pernera *f* **3.** CULIN (*of lamb, pork*) pierna *f;* (*of chicken*) muslo *m* **4.** (*segment of journey*) etapa *f* ▸ **to be on one's last ~s** estar para el arrastre; **to give sb a ~ up** *inf* echar una mano a alguien; **break a ~!** ¡mucha suerte!; **to pull sb's ~** *inf* tomar el pelo a alguien; **to shake a ~** *inf* darse prisa **II.** *vt* <-gg-> *inf* **to ~ it** (*go by foot*) ir a pie; (*run fast*) echar a correr

legacy ['leg·ə·si] <-ies> *n* legado *m;* (*inheritance*) herencia *f*

legal ['li·gəl] *adj* **1.** (*in accordance with law*) legal **2.** (*concerning the law*) jurídico, -a

legal advice *n* consejo *m* jurídico

legal age *n* mayoría *f* de edad

legal aid *n* derecho a tener un abogado de oficio

legal fee *n* honorarios *mpl* de los abogados

legality [li·'gæl·ə·ti] *n* legalidad *f*

legalization [ˌli·gə·lɪ·'zeɪ·ʃən] *n* legalización *f*

legalize ['li·gə·laɪz] *vt* legalizar

legally ['li·gə·li] *adv* legalmente

legal system *n* sistema *m* judicial

legate ['leg·ɪt] *n* legado *m*

legation [lɪ·'geɪ·ʃən] *n* legación *f*

legend ['ledʒ·ənd] *n* leyenda *f;* **~ has it that...** dice la leyenda que...; **he was a ~ in his own time** era una leyenda viva

legendary ['ledʒ·ən·der·i] *adj* legendario, -a

legerdemain [ˌledʒ·ər·də·'meɪn] *n* juego *m* de manos

leggings ['leg·ɪŋz] *npl* mallas *fpl*

leggy ['leg·i] <-ier, -iest> *adj* patilargo, -a

legible ['ledʒ·ə·bəl] *adj* legible

legion ['li·dʒən] **I.** *n* **1.** (*national organization*) legión *f* **2.** (*many*) multitud *f* **II.** *adj form* **the difficulties are ~** las dificultades son innumerables

legionary ['li·dʒə·ner·i] **I.** *adj* legionario, -a **II.** *n* <-ies> legionario, -a *m, f*

legionnaire [ˌli·dʒə·'ner] *n* legionario *m*

Legionnaires' disease *n* MED enfermedad *f* del legionario, legionelosis *f*

legislate ['ledʒ·ɪ·sleɪt] *vi* legislar

legislation [ˌledʒ·ɪ·'sleɪ·ʃən] *n* legislación *f*

legislative ['ledʒ·ɪ·sleɪ·tɪv] *adj* legislativo, -a

legislator ['ledʒ·ɪ·sleɪ·tər] *n* legislador(a) *m(f)*

legislature ['ledʒ·ɪ·sleɪ·tʃər] *n* cuerpo *m* legislativo

legit [lə·'dʒɪt] *adj sl* válido, -a

legitimacy [lə·'dʒɪt·ə·mə·si] *n* legitimidad *f*

legitimate¹ [lə·'dʒɪt·ə·mɪt] *adj* **1.** (*legal*) legal; **a ~ government** un gobierno legítimo **2.** (*reasonable*) válido, -a **3.** (*born in wedlock*) legítimo, -a

legitimate² [lə·'dʒɪt·ə·meɪt] *vt* legitimar

legitimize [lə·'dʒɪt·ə·maɪz] *vt* **1.** (*make legal*) legitimar **2.** (*justify*) justificar

legroom ['leg·rum] *n* espacio *m* para las piernas

legume [lə·'gjum] *n* CULIN legumbre *f*

leguminous [lə·'gju·mə·nəs] *adj* leguminoso, -a

leisure ['li·ʒər] *n* ocio *m* ▸ **at one's ~** cuando uno quiera; **call me at your ~** llámame cuando tengas tiempo

leisure activities *n* actividades *fpl* recreativas

leisured *adj* (*comfortable*) acomodado, -a

leisurely **I.** *adj* pausado, -a **II.** *adv* pausadamente

leisure time *n* tiempo *m* libre

leisure wear *n* ropa *f* deportiva

lemming ['lem·ɪŋ] ZOOL lemming *m*

lemon ['lem·ən] *n* **1.** (*fruit*) limón *m;* **a slice of ~** una rodaja de limón **2.** (*color*) amarillo *m* limón **3.** *inf* (*defective object*) patata *f*

lemonade [ˌlem·ə·'neɪd] *n* limonada *f*

lemon juice *n* zumo *m* de limón

lemon peel *n* corteza *f* de limón

lend [lend] <lent, lent> **I.** *vt* **1.** (*give temporarily*) prestar; **to ~ money to sb** prestar dinero a alguien **2.** (*impart, provide*) dar; **to ~ color to sth** dar color a algo; **to ~ support to a view** apoyar una opinión ▸ **to ~ an ear** prestar atención; **to ~ an ear to sb** prestar oído a alguien; **to ~ a hand to sb** echar una mano a alguien; **to ~ one's name to sth** ofrecer su nombre para algo; **to ~ wings to sb/sth** dar alas a alguien/algo **II.** *vi* prestar dinero

lender ['len·dər] *n* FIN prestamista *mf*

lending ['len·dɪŋ] *n* préstamo *m*

lending library *n* biblioteca *f* pública
length [leŋkθ] *n* 1. (*measurement*) longitud *f;*
it's 3 yards in ~ tiene 3 yardas de largo;
(*along*) the ~ of sth a lo largo de algo
2. (*piece: of pipe, rope*) trozo *m* 3. (*of swimming pool*) largo *m* 4. (*duration*) duración *f;*
(for) any ~ of time (por) cualquier lapso de
tiempo; at ~ al fin, finalmente; to speak at ~
hablar largamente; at great ~ detalladamente
▶to go to great ~s to do sth dar el máximo
para hacer algo
lengthen ['leŋk·θən] I. *vt* 1. (*in time*) prolongar 2. (*physically*) alargar II. *vi* 1. (*in time*) prolongarse 2. (*physically*) alargarse
lengthways ['leŋkθ·weɪz] *adv, adj*, **lengthwise** ['leŋkθ·waɪz] *adv, adj* a lo largo
lengthy ['leŋk·θi] <-ier, -iest> *adj* prolongado,
-a; (*speech*) prolijo, -a; a ~ wait una larga
espera
lenience ['li·ni·ənts] *n*, **leniency** *n* indulgencia *f*
lenient ['li·ni·ənt] *adj* (*judge*) indulgente;
(*punishment*) poco severo, -a
lens [lenz] <-es> *n* 1. (*of glasses*) lente *m o f;*
contact ~es lentes *fpl* de contacto, lentillas
fpl 2. (*of camera*) objetivo *m;* zoom ~ lente de
acercamiento 3. ANAT cristalino *m*
lent [lent] *pt, pp of* lend
Lent [lent] *n* Cuaresma *f*
lentil ['len·təl] *n* lenteja *f*
Leo ['li·oʊ] *n* Leo *m*
leonine ['li·ə·naɪn] *adj form* leonino, -a
leopard ['lep·ərd] *n* leopardo *m* ▶a ~ can't
change its spots *prov* el árbol que nace torcido jamás sus ramas endereza *prov*, el que
nace barrigón ni que lo fajen chiquito *Ven,
prov*
leotard ['li·ə·tard] *n* malla *f*
leper ['lep·ər] *n* 1. MED leproso, -a *m, f* 2. *fig*
marginado, -a *m, f*
leprosy ['lep·rə·si] *n* lepra *f*
leprous ['lep·rəs] *adj* leproso, -a
lesbian ['lez·bi·ən] I. *n* lesbiana *f* II. *adj* lésbico, -a
lesbianism *n* lesbianismo *m*
lesion ['li·ʒən] *n* lesión *f*
Lesotho [lə·'soʊ·toʊ] *n* Lesoto *m*
less [les] *comp of* **little** I. *adj* (*in degree, size*)
menor; (*in quantity*) menos; sth of ~ value
algo de menor valor; ~ wine/fat menos vino/
grasa II. *adv* menos; to drink ~ beber menos;
to see sb ~ ver menos a alguien; ~ than 10
menos de [*o* que] 10; to grow [*o* become] ~
disminuir; not him, much ~ her él no, y
mucho menos ella III. *pron* menos; ~ than...
menos que...; ~ and ~ cada vez menos; to
cost ~ than... costar menos que...; the ~ you
eat, the ~ you get fat cuanto menos comas,
menos gordo estarás IV. *prep* menos; a
month, ~ two days un mes menos dos días
lessen ['les·ən] I. *vi* (*danger*) reducirse; (*fever*)
bajar; (*pain*) aliviarse II. *vt* (*diminish*) disminuir; (*risk*) reducir; (*pain*) aliviar

lesser ['les·ər] *adj comp of* **less** menor; to a ~
extent en menor grado
lesson ['les·ən] *n* 1. SCHOOL clase *f;* ~s lecciones *fpl* 2. *fig* lección *f;* to draw a ~ (from
sth) aprender una lección (de algo); to learn
one's ~ aprenderse la lección; to teach sb a ~
dar a alguien una lección
lest [lest] *conj liter* 1. (*for fear that*) no sea que
+*subj;* I didn't do it ~ he should come no lo
hice por si venía 2. (*if*) en caso de que +*subj*
let¹ [let] *n* SPORTS let *m* ▶without ~ or hindrance LAW sin estorbo ni obstáculo
let² [let] *vt* <let, let> 1. (*allow*) dejar; to ~ sb
do sth dejar a alguien hacer algo; to ~ sb
know sth hacer saber algo a alguien; to ~ sth
pass pasar algo por alto; to ~ sb alone dejar a
alguien en paz; ~ him be! ¡déjalo en paz!
2. (*in suggestions*) ~ 's go! ¡vámonos!; ~ 's
say... digamos...; ~ us pray oremos 3. *inf* (*filler while thinking*) ~ 's see veamos; ~ me
think déjame pensar 4. MATH ~ x be y supongamos que x sea igual a y ▶~ alone... (y)
menos aún...; to ~ sb have it decir cuatro verdades a alguien; to ~ sth lie dejar algo como
está; to ~ rip desatarse; to ~ it rip correr
◆let by *vt* dejar pasar
◆let down *vt* 1. (*disappoint*) decepcionar
2. (*lower*) bajar; (*hair*) soltar; to let one's hair
down *a. fig* soltarse el pelo 3. FASHION alargar
◆let in *vt* (*person*) dejar entrar; (*light*) dejar
pasar ▶to let oneself in for sth meterse en
algo; to let sb in on sth revelar un secreto a
alguien
◆let off *vt* 1. (*forgive*) perdonar; to let sb off
with a fine poner sólo una multa a alguien
2. (*fire: gun*) disparar; (*bomb, firework*) hacer
explotar
◆let on *vi inf* (*divulge*) to ~ about sth revelar
algo; to not ~ about sth callarse algo
◆let out I. *vi* culminar II. *vt* 1. (*release*) dejar
salir; (*prisoner*) poner en libertad; (*laugh*) soltar; to ~ a scream pegar un grito *inf* 2. FASHION
ensanchar 3. (*reveal: secret*) revelar
◆let up *vi* 1. (*become weaker, stop*) debilitarse; (*rain*) amainar; (*cold*) suavizarse; (*fog*)
desvanecerse 2. (*relent*) aflojar; to ~ on sb ser
menos duro con alguien; to ~ on the gas soltar el acelerador
lethal ['li·θəl] *adj* letal; (*poison*) mortífero, -a;
(*weapon*) mortal; this brandy's ~! *inf* ¡este
brandy es mortal!
lethargic [lɪ·'θar·dʒɪk] *adj* 1. (*lacking energy*)
letárgico, -a 2. (*drowsy*) somnoliento, -a
lethargy ['leθ·ər·dʒi] *n* 1. (*lack of energy*) letargo *m* 2. (*drowsiness*) sopor *m*
letter ['leţ·ər] *n* 1. (*message*) carta *f;* ~ of recommendation carta de recomendación; ~ of
credit letra de crédito 2. (*symbol*) letra *f* ▶to
stick to the ~ of the law aplicar la ley en
sentido estricto; to the ~ al pie de la letra
letter bomb *n* carta *f* bomba
letterbox *n* buzón *m* (de correos)
letterhead *n* (*logo*) membrete *m;* (*paper*)

papel *m* membreteado
lettering ['leţ·ər·ɪŋ] *n* caracteres *mpl*
letterpress *n* TYPO tipografía *f*
lettuce ['leţ·ɪs] *n* lechuga *f*
leucocyte *n s.* **leukocyte**
leukemia [lu·'ki·mi·ə] *n* leucemia *f*
leukocyte ['lu·kou·saɪt] *n* MED leucocito *m*
level ['lev·əl] **I.** *adj* **1.** (*horizontal*) horizontal; (*flat*) plano, -a; (*spoonful*) raso, -a **2.** (*having same height*) **to be ~ with sth** estar a la misma altura que algo **3.** (*in same position*) **to be ~ with sb/sth** estar a la par de alguien/algo **4.** (*of same amount*) igual **5.** (*calm*) sereno, -a; (*look*) sincero, -a; (*tone*) tranquilo, -a; (*voice*) mesurado, -a; **to keep a ~ head** no perder la cabeza **6.** (*uniform*) uniforme ▶ **to do one's ~ best** *inf* hacer todo lo posible **II.** *adv* a nivel **III.** *n* **1.** (*position, amount*) nivel *m* **2.** (*height*) altura *f*; **above sea ~** sobre el nivel del mar; **at ground ~** a ras de tierra **3.** (*position in hierarchy*) categoría *f*; **at a higher ~** en una categoría superior; **at the (very) highest ~** en el nivel más alto; **to be on a ~ with sb/sth** estar a la misma altura que alguien/algo; **to find one's (own) ~** *inf* encontrar su sitio en la sociedad **4.** (*quality of performance*) nivel *m*; **intermediate ~ students** estudiantes *mfpl* de nivel intermedio **5.** (*meaning*) **on another ~** en otro sentido; **on a serious ~** en un plano serio ▶ **to be on the ~** (*business, person*) ser serio **IV.** <-l- *o* -ll-> *vt* **1.** (*smoothen, flatten*) nivelar **2.** (*demolish completely*) arrasar **3.** (*point*) **to ~ sth at sb** apuntar con algo a alguien
◆ **level down** *vt* nivelar (por abajo)
◆ **level off** *vi*, **level out** *vi* (*aircraft*) nivelarse; (*inflation*) equilibrarse
◆ **level up** *vt* igualar
◆ **level with** *vt inf* sincerarse con
levelheaded *adj* sensato, -a
lever ['lev·ər] **I.** *n* palanca *f* **II.** *vt* apalancar, palanquear *AmL;* **to ~ sth open** abrir algo con una palanca
leverage ['lev·ər·ɪdʒ] *n* **1.** (*using lever*) apalancamiento *m* **2.** *fig* influencia *f*
leviathan [lɪ·'vaɪ·ə·θən] *n* **1.** *liter* (*machine, organization*) gigante *mf* **2.** REL leviatán *m*
levitate ['lev·ɪ·teɪt] **I.** *vt* hacer levitar **II.** *vi* levitar
levity ['lev·ə·ţi] *n* ligereza *f*
levy ['lev·i] **I.** <-ies> *n* tasa *f* **II.** <-ie-> *vt* imponer; **to ~ a tax on sth** gravar algo con un impuesto
lewd [lud] *adj* (*person*) lascivo, -a; (*gesture, remark*) obsceno, -a
lewdness *n* (*behavior*) lascivia *f*; (*of gesture, remark*) obscenidad *f*
lexical ['lek·sɪ·kəl] *adj* léxico, -a
lexicographer [ˌlek·sɪ·'kag·rə·fər] *n* lexicógrafo, -a *m, f*
lexicography [ˌlek·sɪ·'kag·rə·fi] *n* lexicografía *f*
lexicology [ˌlek·sɪ·'kal·ə·dʒi] *n* lexicología *f*
lexicon ['lek·sɪ·kan] *n* **1.** (*vocabulary: of person, subject*) vocabulario *m;* (*of language*) léxico *m*, lexicón *m* **2.** (*dictionary*) diccionario *m*
lexis ['lek·sɪs] *n* LING léxico *m*, vocabulario *m*
LF *abbr of* **low frequency** BF
liability [ˌlaɪ·ə·'bɪl·ə·ţi] *n* **1.** FIN, LAW responsabilidad *f*; **to accept ~ for sth** hacerse responsable de algo *f* **2.** FIN **liabilities** deudas *fpl*
liable ['laɪ·ə·bəl] *adj* **1.** (*prone*) propenso, -a; **to be ~ to do sth** ser propenso a hacer algo **2.** LAW responsable; **to be ~ for sth** ser responsable de algo
liaise ['laɪ·eɪz] *vi* **to ~ with sb/sth** servir de enlace con alguien/algo
liaison ['li·eɪ·zan] *n* **1.** *a.* LING (*contact*) enlace *m;* (*coordination*) coordinación *f* **2.** (*person*) enlace *mf*, oficial *mf* de enlace **3.** (*sexual affair*) aventura *f*
liar ['laɪ·ər] *n* mentiroso, -a *m, f*
lib [lɪb] *n inf abbr of* **liberation** liberación *f*
libel ['laɪ·bəl] **I.** *n* LAW libelo *m;* PUBL difamación *f;* **to sue sb for ~** demandar a alguien por difamación **II.** <-l- *o* -ll-> *vt* LAW, PUBL difamar
libelous ['laɪ·bə·ləs] *adj* LAW, PUBL difamatorio, -a
liberal ['lɪb·ər·əl] **I.** *adj* **1.** (*tolerant*) *a.* POL liberal **2.** (*generous*) generoso, -a **3.** (*plentiful*) copioso, -a **4.** (*not strict: interpretation*) amplio, -a **II.** *n* liberal *mf*
liberal arts *n* humanidades *fpl*
liberalism ['lɪb·ər·ə·lɪz·əm] *n* liberalismo *m*
liberality [ˌlɪb·ə·'ræl·ə·ţi] *n* **1.** (*tolerance*) liberalidad *f* **2.** (*generosity*) generosidad *f*
liberalization [ˌlɪb·ər·ə·lɪ·'zeɪ·ʃən] *n* liberalización *f*
liberalize ['lɪb·ər·ə·laɪz] *vt* liberalizar
liberate ['lɪb·ə·reɪt] *vt* **1.** (*free*) liberar; (*slaves*) manumitir *elev;* **to ~ oneself from sth/sb** librarse de algo/alguien **2.** *fig, iron, sl* (*steal*) levantar
liberation [ˌlɪb·ə·'reɪ·ʃən] *n* liberación *f*
liberator ['lɪb·ər·eɪ·ţər] *n* liberador(a) *m(f)*
Liberia [laɪ·'bɪr·i·ə] *n* Liberia *f*
Liberian **I.** *adj* liberiano, -a **II.** *n* liberiano, -a *m, f*
libertine ['lɪb·ər·tin] *n* libertino, -a *m, f*
liberty ['lɪb·ər·ţi] *n form* **1.** (*freedom*) libertad *f*; **to be at ~** estar en libertad; **to be at ~ to do sth** tener el derecho de hacer algo; **to take the ~ of doing sth** tomarse la libertad de hacer algo; **to take liberties with sb** tomarse libertades con alguien **2.** **liberties** *pl* (*rights*) derechos *mpl*
libidinous [lə·'bɪd·ən·əs] *adj form* libidinoso, -a
libido [lɪ·'bi·dou] *n* libido *f*
Libra ['li·brə] *n* Libra *m*
librarian [laɪ·'brer·i·ən] *n* bibliotecario, -a *m, f*
library ['laɪ·brer·i] *n* <-ies> **1.** (*place*) biblioteca *f;* **film ~** filmoteca *f;* **newspaper ~** hemeroteca *f* **2.** (*collection*) archivo *m*
libretto [lɪ·'breţ·ou] *n* MUS libreto *m*
Libya ['lɪb·i·ə] *n* Libia *f*

L

Libyan I. *adj* libio, -a **II.** *n* libio, -a *m, f*
lice [laɪs] *npl* s. **louse**
license ['laɪ·səns] **I.** *n* **1.** (*document*) licencia *f*, permiso *m;* **driver's** ~ carnet *m* [*o* permiso *m*] de conducir; **gun** ~ permiso *m* de armas **2.** (*freedom*) libertad *f;* **artistic** ~ libertad artística **II.** *vt* autorizar
licensed *adj* autorizado, -a; **to be** ~ **to do sth** tener la autorización para hacer algo
licensed practical nurse *n* enfermera *f* con un título oficial
licensee [ˌlaɪ·sən·'si] *n* beneficiario , -a *m, f* de una licencia
license plate *n* AUTO matrícula *f*
license plate number *n* AUTO número *m* de matrícula
licensing ['laɪ·sən·sɪŋ] *n* autorización *f*
licentious [laɪ·'sen·ʃəs] *adj* licencioso, -a
lichen ['laɪ·kən] *n* liquen *m*
lick [lɪk] **I.** *n* **1.** (*with tongue*) lamedura *f* **2.** (*light coating*) **a** ~ **of paint** una mano de pintura **3.** *inf* (*try*) **to give sth a** ~ intentar algo **4.** MUS frase *f* **5.** (*salt stick*) bloque *m* de sal (para el ganado) ▸ **a** ~ **and a promise** *inf* un lavoteo, un baño de vaquero *Ven* **II.** *vt* **1.** (*with tongue*) lamer **2.** (*lightly touch*) rozar **3.** *sl* (*defeat*) derrotar **4.** *sl* (*beat up*) dar una paliza a
licking *n* **1.** *sl* (*physical beating*) paliza *f* **2.** SPORTS (*defeat*) derrota *f*
licorice ['lɪk·ər·ɪʃ] *n* regaliz *f*
lid [lɪd] *n* **1.** (*for container*) tapa *f*, tape *m Cuba, PRico* **2.** *fig* (*limit*) tope *m* **3.** (*eyelid*) párpado *m* ▸ **to keep the** ~ **on sth** ocultar algo; **that puts the** ~ **on it** se acabó
lie¹ [laɪ] **I.** <-y-> *vi* mentir; **to** ~ **about sth** mentir sobre algo **II.** <-y-> *vt* **to** ~ **oneself out of sth** salvarse de algo por una mentira **III.** *n* mentira *f*, guayaba *f AmL*, boleto *m Arg;* **to be an outright** ~ ser de una falsedad total; **to live a** ~ vivir en la mentira; **don't tell me** ~**s!** ¡no me mientas!, ¡no me caigas a cuentos! *Col, Ven*
lie² [laɪ] **I.** <lay, lain> *vi* **1.** (*be lying down: person*) estar tumbado; **to** ~ **in bed** estar acostado en la cama; **to** ~ **on the ground** estar tumbado en el suelo; **to** ~ **awake** estar despierto; **to** ~ **still** quedarse inmóvil **2.** (*be positioned*) hallarse; **to** ~ **off the coast** (*boat*) hallarse lejos de la costa; **to** ~ **on the route to...** encontrarse en la ruta de...; **to** ~ **to the east of...** quedar al este de...; **to** ~ **in ruins** estar en ruinas; **to** ~ **in wait** estar a la espera **3.** *form* (*be buried*) estar enterrado, -a **4. to** ~ **with sb/sth** (*be responsibility of*) corresponder a alguien/algo; (*be the reason for sth*) ser culpa de alguien/algo **5.** SPORTS ubicarse **II.** *n* posición *f*
◆**lie around** *vi* **1.** (*be somewhere*) estar por ahí tirado **2.** (*be lazy*) holgazanear
◆**lie back** *vi* recostarse
◆**lie down** *vi* **1.** (*act*) acostarse **2.** *inf* (*do nothing*) **to** ~ **on the job** no hacer su trabajo; **to take sth lying down** aceptar algo sin protestar

◆**lie to** *vi* NAUT estar a la capa
lie detector *n* detector *m* de mentiras
lien [lin] *n* derecho *m* de retención
lieu [lu] *n* **in** ~ **of** en lugar de
lieutenant [lu·'ten·ənt] *n* **1.** MIL teniente *mf* **2.** (*assistant*) lugarteniente *mf*
life [laɪf] <lives> *n* **1.** vida *f;* ~ **after death** vida después de la muerte; **intelligent** ~ vida inteligente; **plant** ~ vida vegetal; **private** ~ vida privada; **a sign of** ~ una señal de vida; **to be full of** ~ estar lleno de vida; **to lose one's** ~ perder la vida; **to take sb's** ~ matar a alguien; **to take one's** (**own**) ~ quitarse la vida, suicidarse **2.** (*existence*) existencia *f;* **to want sth out of** ~ querer algo de la vida; **to be sb's** (**whole**) ~ ser la vida (entera) de alguien **3.** (*duration*) vida *f* (útil), duración *f* **4.** *sl* (*prison sentence*) cadena *f* perpetua; **to get** ~ ser condenado a cadena perpetua ▸ **a** ~ **and death struggle** una lucha a vida o muerte; **to be a matter of** ~ **and death** ser un asunto de vida o muerte; **to take one's** ~ **in one's hands** jugarse la vida; **to risk** ~ **and limb** (**to do sth**) jugarse la vida (para hacer algo); **to lay one's** ~ **on the line** poner la vida en peligro; **to be the** ~ **of the party** ser el alma de la fiesta; **to do sth for dear** ~ hacer algo desesperadamente; **to live the good** ~ darse la buena vida; ~ **is hard!** *iron, inf* ¡qué le vamos a hacer!; **as large as** ~ en carne y hueso; **to breathe** (**new**) ~ **into sth** infundir (nueva) vida a algo; **to bring sth to** ~ animar algo; **to come to** ~ volver a la vida; **to frighten the** ~ **out of sb** dar un susto de muerte a alguien; **to give one's** ~ **for sb/ sth** dar la vida por alguien/algo; **to make a new** ~ empezar una nueva vida; **for** ~ de por vida; **I'm not able for** the ~ **of me to...** por mucho que lo intente no puedo...; **not on your** ~! *inf* ¡ni hablar!; **that's** ~! ¡así es la vida!; **this is the** ~ (for me)! ¡esto sí es vida!
life annuity <-ies> *n* pensión *f* vitalicia
life belt *n* salvavidas *m inv*
lifeboat *n* bote *m* salvavidas
life buoy *n* salvavidas *m inv*
life cycle *n* ciclo *m* vital
life expectancy <-ies> *n* esperanza *f* de vida
life form *n* forma *f* de vida
lifeguard *n* socorrista *mf*, salvavidas *mf inv AmL*
life insurance *n* seguro *m* de vida
life jacket *n* chaleco *m* salvavidas
lifeless ['laɪf·lɪs] *adj* **1.** (*dead*) sin vida **2.** *fig* flojo, -a
lifelike ['laɪf·laɪk] *adj* natural
lifeline *n* **1.** NAUT cuerda *f* salvavidas **2.** *fig* cordón *m* umbilical; **to throw sb a** ~ dar una oportunidad a alguien
lifelong [ˌlaɪf·'lɑŋ] *adj* de toda la vida
life preserver *n* salvavidas *m inv*
lifer ['laɪ·fər] *n sl* condenado, -a *m, f* a cadena perpetua
life raft *n* bote *m* salvavidas

lifesaver *n* socorrista *mf*

life sentence *n* condena *f* a cadena perpetua

life-size *adj*, **life-sized** *adj* de tamaño natural

life span *n* (*of animals*) tiempo *m* de vida; (*of people*) longevidad *f;* **the average ~** el promedio de vida; (*of machines*) la vida útil

lifestyle *n* estilo *m* de vida

life-support system *n* sistema *m* de respiración artificial

life-threatening *adj* mortífero, -a

lifetime *n* **1.** (*of person*) vida *f;* **in my ~** durante mi vida; **the chance of a ~** (*for sb*) la oportunidad de su vida; **to happen once in a ~** suceder una vez en la vida; **to see sth during one's ~** ver algo en vida; **~ guarantee** garantía *f* de por vida **2.** *inf* (*eternity*) eternidad *f;* **to seem like a ~** parecer toda una vida

lifework *n* trabajo *m* de toda una vida

lift [lɪft] **I.** *n* **1.** (*upward motion*) elevación *f;* **to give sth a ~** levantar algo **2.** AVIAT fuerza *f* de ascensión **3.** *fig* (*positive feeling*) ánimos *mpl;* **to give sb a ~** levantar la moral a alguien **4.** (*hoisting device*) montacargas *m inv* **5.** *inf* (*help*) ayuda *f* **6.** *inf* (*car ride*) viaje *m* en coche (*gratuito*), aventón *m Méx;* **to give sb a ~** llevar (en coche) a alguien **II.** *vi* levantarse **III.** *vt* **1.** (*move upwards*) levantar; (*slightly*) alzar; **to ~ fingerprints from sth** sacar las huellas dactilares de algo; **to ~ one's eyes** alzar los ojos; **to ~ one's head** levantar la cabeza; **to ~ one's voice** levantar la voz; **to ~ one's voice to sb** (*yell at*) levantar la voz a alguien; (*argue with*) discutir con alguien **2.** (*stop*) suprimir; **to ~ restrictions** levantar las restricciones **3.** (*encourage*) animar; **to ~ sb's spirits** levantar los ánimos de alguien **4.** (*move by air*) transportar (en avión) **5.** *inf* (*steal*) mangar; (*plagiarize*) plagiar; **to ~ a tune** copiar una melodía

◆ **lift down** *vt* bajar con cuidado

◆ **lift off** *vi* AVIAT despegar

◆ **lift up** *vt* alzar; **to ~ one's head** levantar la cabeza; **to ~ one's voice** alzar la voz

liftoff *n* AVIAT, TECH despegue *m*

ligament ['lɪg·ə·mənt] *n* ligamento *m*

ligature ['lɪg·ə·tʃər] *n* **1.** (*cord*) *a.* MED ligadura *f* **2.** MUS, TYPO ligado *m*

light [laɪt] **I.** *n* **1.** (*energy, brightness*) luz *f;* **by the ~ of the moon** a la luz de la luna **2.** (*daytime*) luz *f* (de día); **first ~** primera luz del día **3.** (*source of brightness*) luz *f;* (*lamp*) lámpara *f;* **to turn a ~ off/on** apagar/encender una luz; **~s out** *inf* (*bedtime*) hora *f* de apagar la luz **4.** (*traffic light*) semáforo *m* **5.** (*flame*) fuego *m;* **to catch ~** incendiarse; **to set ~ to sth** prender fuego a algo; **do you have a ~?** ¿tienes fuego? **6.** (*clarification, insight*) comprensión *f;* **to bring sth to ~** sacar algo a la luz; **to cast** [*o* **shed**] **~ on sth** arrojar luz sobre algo; **to come to ~** salir a la luz **7.** (*perspective*) perspectiva *f;* **to see things in a new ~** ver las cosas desde otra perspectiva **8.** *fig* (*joy, inspiration*) sol *m;* **you are the ~ of my life**

eres mi sol **9.** **~s** (*person's abilities*) conocimientos *mpl;* **to do sth according to one's ~s** hacer algo como Dios le da a entender a uno ▶ **to see the ~ at the end of the tunnel** ver la luz al final del túnel; **to go out like a ~** *inf* (*fall asleep quickly*) quedarse dormido enseguida; (*faint suddenly*) perder el conocimiento **II.** *adj* **1.** (*not heavy*) ligero, -a; **a ~ touch** un pequeño toque **2.** (*not dark: color*) claro, -a; (*skin*) blanco, -a; (*room*) luminoso, -a **3.** (*not serious*) ligero, -a; **~ opera** opereta *f* **4.** (*not intense: breeze, rain*) leve; **to be a ~ sleeper** tener el sueño ligero; **to be ~ on sth** carecer de algo **5.** CULIN frugal; **a ~ meal** una comida ligera **6.** (*with few calories*) bajo, -a en calorías, dietético, -a, light **III.** *adv* ligeramente ▶ **to get off ~** salir bien parado; **to make ~ of sth** no dar importancia a algo **IV.** *vt* <lit *o* lighted> **1.** (*illuminate*) iluminar; **to ~ the way** mostrar el camino **2.** (*start burning*) encender, prender *AmL;* **to ~ a cigarette** encender un cigarrillo **V.** *vi* <lit *o* lighted> (*catch fire*) encenderse

◆ **light into** *vt inf* echar la bronca a

◆ **light up I.** *vt* **1.** alumbrar, iluminar **2.** (*cigarette*) encender **II.** *vi* **1.** (*become bright*) iluminarse **2.** (*become animated*) animarse; **his face lit up** se le iluminó la cara **3.** (*start smoking*) encender un cigarrillo

◆ **light upon** *vi* caer en la cuenta de; (*suddenly see*) dar con

light bulb *n* bombilla *f*, foco *m AmL*

lighten ['laɪ·tən] **I.** *vt* **1.** (*become brighter*) clarear **2.** (*become less heavy*) aligerarse; (*mood*) alegrarse **II.** *vt* **1.** (*make less heavy*) aligerar; **to ~ sb's burden** [*o* **load**] aligerar la carga a alguien **2.** (*bleach, make paler*) aclarar

◆ **lighten up** *vi* relajarse

lighter ['laɪ·tər] *n* mechero *m*, encendedor *m AmL*

light-fingered *adj* de manos largas

light-footed *adj* ligero, -a de pies

lightheaded *adj* **1.** (*faint*) mareado, -a **2.** (*excited*) delirante

lighthearted *adj* (*carefree*) despreocupado, -a; (*happy*) alegre; **a ~ look at sth** una mirada alegre a algo

lighthouse *n* faro *m*

lighting ['laɪ·t̮ɪŋ] *n* iluminación *f*

lightly ['laɪt·li] *adv* ligeramente; (*to rest, touch*) levemente; **to sleep ~** dormir ligeramente; **to take sth ~** tomar algo a la ligera; **to get off ~** salir bien parado

light meter *n* fotómetro *m;* PHOT exposímetro *m*

lightness ['laɪt·nɪs] *n* **1.** (*of thing, touch*) ligereza *f* **2.** (*brightness*) claridad *f*

lightning ['laɪt·nɪŋ] *n* relámpago *m;* **a bolt of ~** un relámpago; **thunder and ~** rayos y centellas; **quick as ~** rápido como un relámpago

lightning bug *n* luciérnaga *f*, cocuyo *m*, AmL

lightning rod *n* pararrayos *m inv*

light pen *n* lápiz *m* óptico

L

light pollution *n* contaminación *f* luminosa
lightship *n* buque faro *m*
lightweight I. *adj* (*clothing, material*) ligero, -a
II. *n* **1.** SPORTS peso *m* ligero **2.** *sl* (*unimpressive person*) persona *f* de poco peso
light-year *n* año *m* luz; **to be ~s away** *inf* estar a años luz de distancia
likable ['laɪ·kə·bəl] *adj* simpático, -a
like¹ [laɪk] **I.** *vt* **1.** (*find good*) **I ~ it** (esto) me gusta; **she ~s apples** le gustan las manzanas; **I ~ swimming** me gusta nadar; **I ~ her** (ella) me cae bien; **he ~s classical music** le gusta la música clásica; **I ~ it when/how...** me gusta cuando/cómo...; **well, how do you ~ that?** (*expressing surprise*) ¿quién lo diría? **2.** (*desire, wish*) querer; **I would ~ to go to...** me gustaría ir a...; **would you ~ a cup of tea?** ¿quieres un té?; **I would ~ a little bit more time** quisiera tener un poquito más de tiempo; **I'd ~ to know...** quisiera saber...; **I'd ~ a steak** querría un filete **II.** *n* **~s** gustos *mpl;* **sb's ~s and dislikes** las preferencias de alguien
like² [laɪk] **I.** *adj* semejante; **to be of ~ mind** pensar de la misma manera **II.** *prep* **1. to be ~ sb/sth** ser como alguien/algo; **what was it ~?** ¿cómo fue?; **what does it look ~?** ¿cómo es?, ¿qué aspecto tiene?; **to work ~ crazy** *inf* trabajar como un burro; **there's nothing ~...** no hay nada que se parezca a... **2.** *sl* **to be ~...** (*say*) decir ►**~ anything** a más no poder **III.** *conj inf* como si +*subj;* **he speaks ~ he was drunk** habla como si estuviera borracho; **he doesn't do it ~ I do** él no lo hace como yo **IV.** *n* **1.** (*similar things*) **toys, games and the ~** juguetes, juegos y cosas por el estilo **2.** *inf* **the ~s of sth/sb** algo/gente como algo/alguien
likeable *adj s.* **likable**
likelihood ['laɪk·li·hʊd] *n* probabilidad *f;* **in all ~** con toda probabilidad; **there is every/little ~ that...** hay muchas/pocas probabilidades de que... +*subj*
likely ['laɪk·li] **I.** <-ier, -iest> *adj* probable; **it is ~ (that...)** es probable (que... +*subj*); **to be quite/very ~** ser bastante/muy probable; **to be a ~ story** *iron* ser un cuento chino, ser puro cuento *AmL;* **not ~!** *inf* ¡ni hablar! **II.** *adv* probablemente; **as ~ as not** a lo mejor; **most/very ~** muy probablemente
like-minded *adj* del mismo parecer
liken ['laɪ·kən] *vt* comparar; **to ~ sb to sb** comparar alguien con alguien
likeness ['laɪk·nɪs] <-es> *n* **1.** (*similarity*) semejanza *f;* **to bear a ~ to sb** tener parecido con alguien **2.** (*painting*) retrato *m*
likewise ['laɪk·waɪz] *adv* de la misma forma, asimismo; **to do ~** hacer lo mismo; **thank you for your help — ~** igualmente, lo mismo digo
liking ['laɪ·kɪŋ] *n* afición *f;* (*for particular person*) simpatía *f;* **to develop a ~ for sb/sth** tomar cariño a alguien/algo; **to be to sb's ~** ser del agrado de alguien; **it's too sweet**

for my ~ es demasiado dulce para mi gusto
lilac ['laɪ·læk] **I.** *n* **1.** (*bush*) lila *f* **2.** (*color*) lila *m* **II.** *adj* lila
lilt [lɪlt] *n* cadencia *f*
lily ['lɪl·i] <-ies> *n* lirio *m;* **water ~** nenúfar *m*
lily-livered *adj liter* cobarde
lily pad *n* hoja *f* de nenúfar
lima bean ['laɪ·mə·bin] *n* judía *f* blanca, poroto *m Arg,* fríjol *m* verde *Col*
limb [lɪm] *n* **1.** BOT rama *f* **2.** ANAT extremidad *f* ►**to be/go out on a ~** (*to do sth*) estar/ponerse en una situación arriesgada (para hacer algo); **to tear sb ~ from ~** despedazar a alguien
limber ['lɪm·bər] *adj* (*person*) ágil; (*material*) flexible
♦**limber up** *vi* hacer ejercicios de precalentamiento
limbo ['lɪm·boʊ] *n* **1.** *a. fig* limbo *m;* **to be in ~** estar en el limbo **2.** (*dance*) limbo *m;* **to do the ~** bailar el limbo
lime¹ [laɪm] **I.** *n* **1.** (*fruit*) lima *f* **2.** (*tree*) limero *m* **3.** (*juice*) zumo *m* de lima **4.** (*color*) verde *m* lima **II.** *adj* de color verde lima
lime² [laɪm] **I.** *n* CHEM cal *f* **II.** *vt* abonar con cal
lime³ [laɪm] *n* (*linden tree*) tilo *m*
limelight ['laɪm·laɪt] *n* foco *m* proyector; **to be in the ~** estar en el candelero; **to steal the ~** acaparar la atención del público
limerick ['lɪm·ər·ɪk] *n* quintilla *f* humorística
limestone ['laɪm·stoʊn] *n* (piedra *f*) caliza *f*
limit ['lɪm·ɪt] **I.** *n* límite *m;* **speed ~** AUTO límite *m* de velocidad; **to put a ~ on sth** poner un límite a algo; **to overstep the ~** pasarse del límite; **to know one's ~s** conocer los propios límites; **to know no ~s** no tener límites; **within ~s** dentro de ciertos límites; **to be off ~s** (**to sb**) quedar prohibido el acceso (a alguien) **II.** *vt* limitar; **to ~ oneself to sth** limitarse a algo
limitation [ˌlɪm·ɪ·'teɪ·ʃən] *n* **1.** (*lessening*) restricción *f;* (*of pollution, weapons*) limitación *f* **2. ~s** limitaciones *fpl;* **she knows her ~s** ella sabe sus limitaciones **3.** LAW prescripción *f*
limited ['lɪm·ɪ·t̬ɪd] *adj* limitado, -a; **to be ~ to sth** estar limitado a algo
limitless ['lɪm·ɪt·lɪs] *adj* ilimitado, -a
limousine ['lɪm·ə·zin] *n* limusina *f*
limp¹ [lɪmp] **I.** *vi* cojear **II.** *n* cojera *f;* **to walk with a ~** cojear
limp² [lɪmp] *adj* flojo, -a; (*lettuce*) mustio, -a; **to have a ~ handshake** dar la mano de forma poco enérgica
limpet ['lɪm·pɪt] *n* lapa *f*
limpid ['lɪm·pɪd] *adj liter* límpido, -a; (*air*) diáfano, -a; (*eyes*) claro, -a
limy ['laɪ·mi] *adj* calizo, -a
linchpin ['lɪntʃ·pɪn] *n* **1.** TECH pezonera *f* **2.** *fig* eje *m*
linden ['lɪn·dən] *n* BOT tilo *m*
line¹ [laɪn] <-ning> *vt* revestir; (*clothes*) forrar
line² [laɪn] **I.** *n* **1.** (*mark*) *a.* MATH línea *f;* **divid-**

ing ~ línea divisoria; **to be in a ~** estar en línea; **to form a ~** formar una línea **2.** (*for waiting*) fila *f*, cola *f AmL;* **to get in ~** ponerse en fila; **to stand in ~** hacer cola; **to wait in ~** esperar en la cola **3.** (*chronological succession*) linaje *m;* **a** (**long**) **~ of disasters/ kings** una (larga) sucesión de desastres/reyes **4.** (*cord*) cuerda *f;* **clothes ~** cuerda para colgar la ropa **5.** TEL línea *f;* **~s will be open from...** las líneas estarán abiertas a partir de...; **to be/stay on the ~** estar/seguir al habla; **hold the ~!** no cuelgue(s) **6.** COMPUT **on ~** en línea; **off ~** desconectado **7.** (*defense*) frente *m;* **front ~** línea del frente; **to be the last ~ of defense** *fig* ser la última línea de defensa; **to be behind enemy ~s** estar detrás de las líneas enemigas **8.** (*set of tracks*) vía *f;* (*train route*) línea *f;* **the end of the ~** el final de la línea; **to be at** [*o* **to reach**] **the end of the ~** *fig* tocar fondo **9.** (*transport company*) línea *f;* **cruise ~** línea de cruceros **10.** (*of text, poem*) línea *f*, renglón *m;* **to drop sb a ~** *inf* escribir a alguien **11.** MUS melodía *f* **12.** (*comment*) comentario *m; sl* (*indicating sexual interest*) *frase utilizada para ligar;* **to come up with a ~ about sb/sth** salir con un comentario acerca de alguien/algo **13.** (*position, attitude*) línea *f;* **~ of reasoning** razonamiento *m;* **to be divided along ethnic ~s** estar dividido según criterios étnicos; **the official ~** (**on sth**) la línea oficial (acerca de algo); **to take a ~ on sth** tomar posición sobre algo **14.** (*field, pursuit, interest*) especialidad *f;* **what ~ are you in?** ¿a qué se dedica? **15.** (*product type*) línea *f;* FASHION línea *f* de moda; **to come out with a new ~** sacar una nueva línea **16.** *sl* (*of cocaine*) raya *f;* **to do a ~ of cocaine, to do ~s** esnifar una raya (de coca) ► **somewhere along the ~** en algún momento; **right down the ~** hasta el último momento; **to cross the ~** pasarse de la raya; **to get a ~ on sb** obtener información acerca de alguien; **to give sb a ~ on sb** dar a alguien información sobre alguien; **to be in ~ for sth** tener muchas posibilidades de ascender; **to be in ~ with sb/sth** estar de acuerdo con alguien/algo; **to be out of ~** estar fuera de lugar; **to be out of ~ with sb/sth** no estar de acuerdo con alguien/algo **II.** <-ning> *vt* **to ~ the streets** ocupar las calles ◆ **line up I.** *vt* alinear **II.** *vi* **1.** (*stand in row*) alinearse **2.** (*wait for sth*) ponerse en fila, hacer cola **3.** (*oppose*) **to ~ against sb/sth** alinearse en contra de alguien/algo

lineage ['lɪn·i·ɪdʒ] *n* linaje *m*

lineal ['lɪn·i·əl] *adj* en línea directa

linear ['lɪn·i·ər] *adj* lineal

linear equation *n* ecuación *f* lineal

line backer *n* (*in football*) line backer *m*

line dancing *n* baile *m* en línea

linen ['lɪn·ɪn] *n* lino *m;* **bed ~s** sábanas *fpl;* **table ~s** mantelería *f*

liner ['laɪ·nər] *n* **1.** (*lining*) forro *m;* (*garbage bag*) bolsa *f* de basura **2.** (*ship*) transat-

lántico *m*

linesman ['laɪnz·mən] <-men> *n* SPORTS juez *mf* de línea

line-up ['laɪn·ʌp] *n* **1.** SPORTS (*team*) alineación *f;* (*of baseball players*) orden *m* de los bateadores **2.** (*for identifying criminals*) rueda *f* de identificación

linger ['lɪŋ·gər] *vi* **1.** entretenerse; (*film*) hacerse largo; **to ~ in one's memory** perdurar en la memoria; **to ~ over sth** tomarse tiempo para (hacer) algo **2.** (*die slowly*) **to ~ on** permanecer, perdurar

lingerie [ˌlan·ʒə·'reɪ] *n* lencería *f*

lingering ['lɪŋ·gər·ɪŋ] *adj* prolongado, -a; (*doubt*) persistente

lingo ['lɪŋ·goʊ] <-es> *n inf* **1.** (*unfamiliar language*) idioma *m* (extranjero) **2.** (*jargon*) jerga *f*

linguist ['lɪŋ·gwɪst] *n* lingüista *mf*

linguistic [lɪŋ·'gwɪs·tɪk] *adj* lingüístico, -a

linguistics [lɪŋ·'gwɪs·tɪks] *n* lingüística *f*

liniment ['lɪn·ə·mənt] *n* linimento *m*

lining ['laɪ·nɪŋ] *n* **1.** (*of coat, jacket*) forro *m;* (*of boiler, pipes*) revestimiento *m* **2.** ANAT pared *f*

link [lɪŋk] **I.** *n* **1.** (*in chain*) eslabón *m* **2.** (*connection*) conexión *f;* **rail ~** enlace *m* ferroviario **3.** COMPUT vínculo *m*, enlace *m* **II.** *vt* **1.** (*connect*) conectar; **to ~ arms** cogerse del brazo **2.** (*be related to*) relacionar; **to be ~ed** (**together**) estar relacionados

links [lɪŋks] *n* SPORTS campo *m* de golf

linkup *n* conexión *f;* (*of spacecraft*) acoplamiento *m;* **satellite ~** conexión vía satélite

linnet ['lɪn·ɪt] *n* pardillo *m*

linoleum [lɪ·'noʊ·li·əm] *n* linóleo *m*

Linotype® ['laɪ·nə·taɪp] *n* linotipia *f*

linseed ['lɪn·sid] *n* linaza *f*

linseed oil *n* aceite *m* de linaza

lint [lɪnt] *n* pelusa *f*

lintel ['lɪn·təl] *n* dintel *m*

lion ['laɪ·ən] *n* león *m* ► **the ~'s share** la parte del león

lioness [laɪ·ə·'nes] <-sses> *n* leona *f*

lionhearted *adj* valiente

lionize ['laɪ·ə·naɪz] *vt* tratar como a un personaje importante

lip [lɪp] *n* **1.** ANAT labio *m;* **my ~s are sealed** mis labios están sellados **2.** (*rim: of cup, bowl*) borde *m;* (*of jug*) pico *m* **3.** *sl* (*impudence*) insolencia *f*

lip balm *n* bálsamo *m* labial

lip-gloss *n* brillo *m* de labios

liposuction ['lɪp·oʊ·ˌsak·ʃən] *n* liposucción *f*

lip-read I. *vi* leer los labios **II.** *vt* leer los labios a

lip service *n inf* jarabe *m* de pico; **to pay ~ to sth** apoyar algo sólo de boquilla

lipstick *n* barra *f* de labios

liquefy ['lɪk·wə·faɪ] <-ie-> **I.** *vt* licuar **II.** *vi* licuarse

liqueur [lɪ·'kɜr] *n* licor *m*

liquid ['lɪk·wɪd] **I.** *n* líquido *m* **II.** *adj* líquido, -a

liquidate ['lɪk·wɪ·deɪt] *vt a. fig* liquidar

liquidation [ˌlɪk·wɪ·'deɪ·ʃən] *n* liquidación *f;* **to go into** ~ ECON entrar en liquidación

liquidity [lɪ·'kwɪd·ə·t̮i] *n* liquidez *f*

liquidize ['lɪk·wɪ·daɪz] *vt* licuar

liquidizer ['lɪk·wɪ·daɪ·zər] *n* licuadora *f*

liquor ['lɪk·ər] *n* licor *m*

liquor laws *n* leyes *fpl* de control de licores

liquor license *n* licencia *f* de licores

Lisbon ['lɪz·bən] *n* Lisboa *f*

lisp [lɪsp] I. *n* ceceo *m* II. *vi* cecear III. *vt* pronunciar ceceando

lissom(e) ['lɪs·əm] *adj liter* grácil

list[1] [lɪst] I. *n* lista *f;* ~ **price** precio *m* según catálogo; **shopping** ~ lista de la compra; **to make a** ~ **(of sth)** hacer un listado (de algo) II. *vt* 1. (*make a list*) listar 2. (*enumerate*) enumerar 3. (*have list price*) **to** ~ **at $100** tener un precio de catálogo [*o* de lista] de 100$

list[2] [lɪst] NAUT I. *vi* escorar II. *n* escora *f*

listen ['lɪs·ən] I. *n inf* **to have a** ~ **(to sth)** *inf* escuchar (algo) II. *vi* 1. (*hear*) escuchar; **to** ~ **to sth/sb** escuchar algo/a alguien; **to** ~ **to reason** atender a razones 2. (*pay attention*) estar atento; **to** ~ **for sth** estar atento para oír algo
♦ **listen in** *vi* escuchar (a escondidas); **to** ~ **on sth** escuchar algo (a escondidas)

listener ['lɪs·nər] *n* oyente *mf*

listeria [lɪ·'stɪr·i·ə] *npl* listeria *f*

listing ['lɪs·tɪŋ] *n* 1. (*list*) lista *f,* listado *m* 2. (*entry in list*) entrada *f*

listless ['lɪst·lɪs] *adj* 1. (*lacking energy: person*) apagado, -a; (*economy*) débil 2. (*lacking enthusiasm*) apático, -a; (*performance*) deslucido, -a

lit [lɪt] *pt, pp of* **light**

litany ['lɪt·ə·ni] <-ies> *n* letanía *f*

litchi ['li·tʃi] *n* BOT lichi *m*

liter ['li·tər] *n* litro *m*

literacy ['lɪt̮·ər·ə·si] *n* alfabetización *f;* ~ **rate** índice *m* de alfabetización

literal ['lɪt̮·ər·əl] *adj* literal; **to take sth in the** ~ **sense of the word** tomar algo al pie de la letra

literally ['lɪt̮·ər·ə·li] *adv* literalmente; **to take sth/sb** ~ tomar algo/a alguien al pie de la letra; **quite** ~ literalmente

literary ['lɪt̮·ə·rer·i] *adj* literario, -a

literary criticism *n* crítica *f* literaria

literate ['lɪt̮·ər·ɪt] *adj* 1. (*able to read and write*) que sabe leer y escribir; **to be** ~ saber leer y escribir 2. (*well-educated*) culto, -a

literature ['lɪt̮·ər·ə·tʃər] *n* 1. (*novels, poems*) literatura *f;* **nineteenth-century** ~ literatura del siglo XIX 2. (*promotional material*) material *m* informativo

lithe [laɪð] *adj* ágil

lithium ['lɪθ·i·əm] *n* litio *m*

lithograph ['lɪθ·ə·græf] I. *n* litografía *f* II. *vi* litografiar

lithography [lɪ·'θag·rə·fi] *n* litografía *f*

Lithuania [ˌlɪθ·u·'eɪ·ni·ə] *n* Lituania *f*

Lithuanian I. *n* 1. (*person*) lituano, -a *m, f*

2. LING lituano *m* II. *adj* lituano, -a

litigant ['lɪt̮·ɪ·gənt] *n* litigante *mf*

litigate ['lɪt̮·ɪ·geɪt] *vi* litigar

litigation [ˌlɪt̮·ɪ·'geɪ·ʃən] *n* litigio *m*

litigious [lɪ·'tɪdʒ·əs] *adj* pleiteador(a)

litmus ['lɪt·məs] *n* tornasol *m*

litmus paper *n* papel *m* de tornasol

litmus test *n* prueba *m* de tornasol; *fig* prueba *f* de fuego

litter ['lɪt̮·ər] I. *n* 1. (*refuse*) basura *f* 2. ZOOL camada *f* 3. (*bedding for animals*) lecho *m* de paja 4. MED camilla *f* II. *vt* 1. (*make untidy*) ensuciar (tirando basura) 2. *inf* (*scatter*) esparcir; **the floor was** ~**ed with clothes** el suelo estaba cubierto de ropa

litter box *n* bandeja *f* para la arena del gato

litterbug *n inf: persona que tira basura en un lugar público*

little ['lɪt̮·əl] I. *adj* 1. (*in size, age*) pequeño, -a; **a** ~ **old man/woman** un viejecito/una viejecita; **the** ~ **ones** *inf* los niños; **my** ~ **brother/sister** mi hermanito, -a, mi hermano pequeño/mi hermana pequeña 2. (*in amount*) poco, -a; **a** ~ **bit (of sth)** un poco (de algo); **a** ~ **something** alguna cosita; (*to eat or drink*) algo (de comer o de beber); ~ **hope** pocas esperanzas; ~ **by** ~ poco a poco 3. (*in distance*) corto, -a; **a** ~ **way** un camino corto 4. (*in duration*) breve; **for a** ~ **while** durante un ratito; **to have a** ~ **word with sb** cruzar algunas palabras con alguien II. *n* poco *m;* **a** ~ un poco; **to know** ~ saber poco; **we see** ~ **of him** lo vemos poco; **to have** ~ **to say** tener poco que decir III. *adv* poco; ~ **less than...** poco menos que...; ~ **more than an hour** poco más de una hora; **to make** ~ **of sth** sacar poco en claro de algo

liturgical [lɪ·'tɜr·dʒɪ·kəl] *adj* litúrgico, -a

liturgy ['lɪt̮·ər·dʒi] <-ies> *n* REL liturgia *f*

live[1] [laɪv] I. *adj* 1. (*living*) vivo, -a 2. RADIO, TV en directo; THEAT, MUS en vivo 3. ELEC que lleva corriente; (*wire*) conectado, -a; **to be a** (**real**) ~ **wire** *fig* rebosar energía 4. (*cartridge*) cargado, -a; (*bomb*) con carga explosiva II. *adv* RADIO, TV en directo; THEAT, MUS en vivo

live[2] [lɪv] I. *vi* vivir; **to** ~ **above one's means** vivir por encima de las posibilidades de uno; **to** ~ **in sb's memory** perdurar en la memoria de alguien; **long** ~ **the king!** ¡viva el rey!; **to** ~ **off sth/sb** vivir de algo/alguien; **to** ~ **on sth** (*eat*) alimentarse de algo ▸ **to** ~ **and let** ~ vivir y dejar vivir II. *vt* vivir; **to** ~ **a happy life** llevar una vida feliz
♦ **live down** *vt* lograr superar
♦ **live in** *vi* vivir en el lugar donde uno trabaja
♦ **live on** *vi* vivir; (*tradition*) seguir vivo
♦ **live out** *vt* vivir; (*dreams*) realizar
♦ **live through** *vt* (*experience*) vivir
♦ **live together** *vi* vivir juntos
♦ **live up** *vt* **to live it up** vivir a lo grande
♦ **live up to** *vt* vivir conforme a; **to** ~ **expectations** estar a la altura de lo esperado
♦ **live with** *vt* 1. (*share home*) vivir con

2. (*accept*) vivir con

livelihood ['laɪv·li·hʊd] *n* sustento *m;* **to earn one's ~** ganarse la vida

liveliness ['laɪv·li·rɪn] *n* viveza *f*

lively ['laɪv·li] *adj* (*person, conversation*) animado, -a; (*imagination, interest*) vivo, -a

liven up ['laɪ·vən·ʌp] **I.** *vi* animarse **II.** *vt* animar

liver ['lɪv·ər] *n* hígado *m*

liverish ['lɪv·ər·ɪʃ] *adj* **1.** (*ill*) enfermo, -a del hígado **2.** (*grumpy*) malhumorado, -a

liverwurst ['lɪv·ər·wɜrst] *n* (embutido *m* de) paté *m* de hígado

livery ['lɪv·ə·ri] *n* **1.** FASHION librea *f* **2.** (*for horses*) servicio de cuidado y alimentación de caballos

livestock ['laɪv·stak] *n* ganado *m*

livid ['lɪv·ɪd] *adj* **1.** (*discolored*) lívido, -a **2.** (*furious*) furioso, -a

living ['lɪv·ɪŋ] **I.** *n* **1.** (*livelihood*) vida *f;* **to work for one's ~** trabajar para ganarse la vida; **to make a ~** ganarse la vida **2.** (*way of life*) (modo *m* de) vida *f* **3.** *pl* (*people*) **the ~** los vivos **II.** *adj* vivo, -a; (*creature*) viviente

living conditions *npl* condiciones *fpl* de vida

living quarters *npl* alojamiento *m*

living room *n* cuarto *m* de estar, living *m AmL*

living space *n a. fig* espacio *m* vital

living wage *n* salario *m* digno

lizard ['lɪz·ərd] *n* lagarto *m;* (*small*) lagartija *f*

llama ['la·mə] *n* llama *f*

load [loʊd] **I.** *n* **1.** ELEC *a. fig* carga *f;* **take a ~ off** (*your feet*) *inf* (*sit down*) sentarse; *inf;* **that took a ~ off my mind!** eso me quitó un (gran) peso de encima **2.** (*amount of work*) cantidad *f* (de trabajo); **a heavy/light ~** mucho/poco trabajo **3.** *inf* (*lots*) montón *m;* **~s** [*o* **a ~**] **of...** un montón de... ▶ **to get a ~ of** sth *sl* fijarse en algo **II.** *vt a.* AUTO, PHOT, COMPUT cargar **III.** *vi* cargarse

◆ **load down** *vt* recargar; *fig* agobiar

◆ **load up I.** *vt* cargar **II.** *vi* cargarse

loaded ['loʊ·dɪd] *adj* **1.** (*filled*) cargado, -a **2.** (*unfair: question*) tendencioso, -a; **~ dice** dados *mpl* cargados **3.** *sl* (*rich*) forrado, -a **4.** *sl* (*drunk*) mamado, -a

loadstone *n s.* **lodestone**

loaf[1] [loʊf] <loaves> *n* pan *m;* **a ~ of bread** una barra *f* de pan, un pan ▶ **half a ~ is better than none** *prov* algo es algo

loaf[2] [loʊf] *vi* gandulear; **to ~ around** hacer el vago

loafer ['loʊ·fər] *n* **1.** (*lazy person*) holgazán, -ana *m, f* **2.** (*shoe*) mocasín *m*

loam [loʊm] *n* marga *f*

loan [loʊn] **I.** *vt* prestar **II.** *n* préstamo *m*, avío *m AmS*

loan shark *n* usurero, -a *m, f*

loan-word ['loʊn·wɜrd] *n* LING préstamo *m* (lingüístico)

loath [loʊθ] *adj form* reacio, -a; **to be ~ to do sth** resistirse a hacer algo

loathe [loʊð] *vt* (*thing*) detestar; (*person*) aborrecer

loathing *n* odio *m;* **to have a ~ for sb** aborrecer a alguien; **to have a ~ for sth** tener aversión a algo

loathsome ['loʊð·səm] *adj* (*thing*) asqueroso, -a; (*person*) odioso, -a

loaves [loʊvz] *n pl of* **loaf[1]**

lob [lab] **I.** <-bb-> *vt* lanzar; SPORTS hacer un globo a **II.** *n* SPORTS globo *m*

lobby ['lab·i] **I.** <-ies> *n* **1.** ARCHIT vestíbulo *m* **2.** POL grupo *m* de presión **II.** <-ie-> *vi* **to ~ to have sth done** hacer presión para que se haga algo; **to ~ against/for sth** presionar en contra de/en pro de algo **III.** <-ie-> *vt* presionar

lobbyist ['lab·i·ɪst] *n* miembro *m* de un grupo de presión

lobe [loʊb] *n* lóbulo *m*

lobster ['lab·stər] *n* (*with claws*) bogavante *m;* (*spiny*) langosta *f*

lobster pot *n* nasa *f*

local ['loʊ·kəl] **I.** *adj* local; (*people*) del lugar; (*official, police*) municipal; TEL urbano, -a; **~ color** color *m* local **II.** *n* **1.** (*inhabitant*) lugareño, -a *m, f* **2.** (*bus*) autobús *m* de línea; (*train*) tren *m* de cercanías

local anesthetic *n* anestesia *f* local

local authority *n* municipio *m*, ayuntamiento *m*

local call *n* llamada *f* local

locale [loʊ·'kæl] *n* escenario *m*

local elections *npl* elecciones *fpl* municipales

local government *n* administración *f* municipal

locality [loʊ·'kæl·ə·t̬i] <-ies> *n* localidad *f*

localization [ˌloʊ·kə·lɪ·'zeɪ·ʃən] *n a.* COMPUT localización *f*

localize ['loʊ·kə·laɪz] *vt a.* COMPUT localizar

local paper *n* periódico *m* local

local time *n* hora *f* local

local train *n* tren *m* de cercanías

locate ['loʊ·keɪt] *vt* **1.** (*find*) localizar **2.** (*situate*) situar; **to be ~d near sth** estar situado cerca de algo

location [loʊ·'keɪ·ʃən] *n* **1.** (*place*) posición *f* **2.** (*act of locating*) localización *f* **3.** CINE exteriores *mpl;* **to film sth on ~** rodar algo en exteriores

loc. cit. [ˌlak·'sɪt] *abbr of* **loco citato** loc. cit.

loch [lak] *n Scot* **1.** (*lake*) lago *m* **2.** (*inlet*) brazo *m* de mar

lock[1] [lak] *n* (*of hair*) mechón *m*

lock[2] [lak] **I.** *n* **1.** (*fastening device*) cerradura *f*, chapa *f Arg, Méx* **2.** (*on canal*) esclusa *f* **3.** (*in wrestling*) llave *f* ▶ **~, stock and barrel** completamente, por completo; **to be under ~ and key** estar cerrado bajo llave **II.** *vt* **1.** (*fasten with lock*) cerrar con llave; (*confine safely: thing*) guardar bajo llave; (*person*) encerrar; **to be ~ed** (*be held fast*) estar sujeto **2.** (*make immovable*) bloquear; **be ~ed** estar bloqueado; **to be ~ed in(to) discussions** enredarse en discusiones **III.** *vi* cerrarse con llave

◆**lock away** vt (jewels, document) guardar bajo llave; (person) encerrar

◆**lock in** vt encerrar

◆**lock on** vi, **lock onto** vi MIL localizar y seguir

◆**lock out** vt impedir la entrada a; **to lock oneself out** dejarse las llaves dentro

◆**lock up** vt (jewels, document) guardar bajo llave; (person) encerrar

locker ['lak·ər] n (at train station) consigna f automática; (at school) taquilla f

locker room n vestuario m, desvestidero m Col, vestidor m Méx

locket ['lak·ɪt] n guardapelo m

lockjaw ['lak·dʒɔ] n MED trismo m

lockout ['lak·aʊt] n cierre m patronal

locksmith ['lak·smɪθ] n cerrajero, -a m, f

lockup ['lak·ʌp] n inf 1. (cell) calabozo m 2. (storage space) garaje m

locomotion [ˌloʊ·kə·'moʊ·ʃən] n locomoción f

locomotive [ˌloʊ·kə·'moʊ·tɪv] I. n locomotora f II. adj locomotor(a); (force) locomotriz

locus ['loʊ·kəs] <-ci> n 1. (exact place) lugar m 2. MATH lugar m geométrico 3. BIO locus m

locust ['loʊ·kəst] n langosta f, chapulín m Méx

locution [loʊ·'kju·ʃən] n locución f

lode [loʊd] n MIN filón m

lodestar ['loʊd·star] n estrella f polar

lodestone ['loʊd·stoʊn] n piedra f imán

lodge [ladʒ] I. vi 1. (stay in rented room) alojarse 2. (become fixed) quedarse clavado, -a II. vt 1. (accommodate) alojar 2. (place) colocar 3. (insert) meter 4. (deposit) depositar 5. (register officially: appeal) interponer; (complaint, protest) presentar III. n 1. (for hunters) refugio m; (inn) albergue m 2. (gatekeeper's house) casa f del guarda 3. (for organizations) logia f 4. (of beaver) madriguera f

lodger ['ladʒ·ər] n inquilino, -a m, f; **to take in ~s** alquilar habitaciones

lodging ['ladʒ·ɪŋ] n 1. (accommodations) alojamiento m 2. ~**s** (room to rent) habitación f de alquiler

loft [laft] I. n 1. (space under roof) buhardilla f; **hay ~** pajar m 2. (upstairs living space) loft m II. vt (ball) lanzar por lo alto

lofty ['laf·ti] <-ier, -iest> adj 1. (tall) altísimo, -a 2. (noble: aims, ideals) noble 3. (haughty) altivo, -a

log¹ [lɔg] I. n 1. (tree trunk) tronco m 2. (firewood) leño m ▶**to sleep like a ~** dormir como un tronco II. <-gg-> vt talar III. <-gg-> vi talar árboles

log² [lɔg] inf abbr of **logarithm** log.

log³ [lɔg] I. n registro m; **ship's ~** cuaderno m de bitácora II. vt 1. (record) registrar 2. (achieve, attain) alcanzar

◆**log in** vi COMPUT iniciar sesión

◆**log off** vi COMPUT terminar sesión

◆**log on** vi s. **log in**

◆**log out** vi s. **log off**

loganberry ['loʊ·gən·ber·i] <-ies> n fram-buesa f de Logan

logarithm ['lɔ·gə·rɪð·əm] n logaritmo m

logarithmic [ˌlɔ·gə·'rɪð·mɪk] adj logarítmico, -a

log book n NAUT diario m de navegación; AVIAT diario m de vuelo

log cabin n cabaña f de troncos

logger ['lɔ·gər] n leñador(a) m(f)

loggerheads ['lɔ·gər·hedz] npl inf **to be at ~ (with sb/over sth)** estar en desacuerdo (con alguien/sobre algo)

logic ['ladʒ·ɪk] n lógica f

logical ['ladʒ·ɪ·kəl] adj lógico, -a

login ['lɔg·ɪn] n COMPUT inicio m de sesión

logistics [loʊ·'dʒɪs·tɪks] n logística f

logjam n atolladero m

logo ['loʊ·goʊ] n logo(tipo) m

logoff ['lɔg·ɔf] n COMPUT fin m de sesión

logon ['lɔg·ɔn] n s. **login**

logrolling ['lɔg·roʊ·lɪŋ] n amiguismo m

loin [lɔɪn] I. n 1. ~**s** (body area) bajo vientre m 2. ~**s** liter, **the fruit of his ~s** el hijo/la hija de sus entrañas 3. CULIN lomo m II. adj de lomo

loincloth ['lɔɪn·klɔθ] n taparrabos m inv

loiter ['lɔɪ·tər] vi 1. (linger) pasar el rato 2. a. LAW merodear

loiterer ['lɔɪ·tər·ər] n 1. inf holgazán, -ana m, f 2. LAW merodeador(a) m(f)

loll [lal] vi colgar; **to ~ about** holgazanear

lollipop ['lal·i·pap] n chupachups® m inv

lollop ['lal·əp] vi moverse torpemente

London ['lʌn·dən] n Londres m

lone [loʊn] adj solitario, -a

loneliness ['loʊn·li·nɪs] n soledad f

lonely ['loʊn·li] <-ier, -iest> adj **to feel ~** sentirse solo, -a; (life) solitario, -a; (place) aislado, -a

loner ['loʊ·nər] n solitario, -a m, f

lonesome ['loʊn·səm] adj (person) solo, -a; (place) aislado, -a

long¹ [lɔŋ] I. adj (distance, time, shape) largo, -a; **to have a ~ way to go** tener mucho camino por recorrer; **it's been a ~ time since...** hace mucho tiempo desde que...; **~ time no see!** inf ¡cuánto tiempo (sin verte)! II. adv 1. (a long time) mucho (tiempo); **~ after/before** mucho después/antes; **~ ago** hace mucho (tiempo); **to take ~ (to do sth)** tardar mucho (en hacer algo); **to be not ~ in doing sth** form no tardar en hacer algo; **~ live the king!** ¡viva el rey! 2. (for the whole duration) **all day ~** todo el día; **as ~ as I live** mientras viva; **so ~ as** mientras 3. in comparisons **as ~ as** mientras +subj; **to no ~er do sth** ya no hacer algo ▶**so ~** inf ¡hasta luego! III. n mucho tiempo m ▶**the ~ and the short of it is that...** en resumidas cuentas...

long² [lɔŋ] vi **to ~ for sb** echar de menos a alguien; **to ~ for sth** estar deseando algo; **to ~ to do sth** anhelar hacer algo

long. abbr of **longitude** long.

longboat n bote m

long-distance I. adj (flight) de largo recorrido;

(*race, runner*) de fondo; (*negotiations, relationship*) a distancia; ~ **call** llamada *f* de larga distancia **II.** *adv* **to phone** ~ hacer una llamada interurbana

longevity [lanˈdʒevˑəˑt̬i] *n* longevidad *f*

longhaired *adj* (*person, animal*) de pelo largo

longhand *n* escritura *f* normal (*donde las palabras tienen todas sus letras*)

long-haul *adj* AVIAT de larga distancia

longing [ˈlɒŋˑɪŋ] **I.** *n* **1.** (*nostalgia*) nostalgia *f;* **to feel a** ~ **for sb** echar de menos a alguien **2.** (*strong desire*) anhelo *m;* **to have a** ~ **to do sth** anhelar hacer algo **II.** *adj* anhelante

longish [ˈlɒŋˑɪʃ] *adj inf* tirando a largo, -a

longitude [ˈlanˑdʒəˑtud] *n* longitud *f*

longitudinal [ˌlanˑdʒəˑˈtuˑdənˑəl] *adj* longitudinal

long johns *npl inf* calzoncillos *mpl* largos

long jump *n* salto *m* de longitud, salto *m* largo *AmL*

long-lived *adj* **1.** (*person*) longevo, -a **2.** (*feud, rumor*) que viene de lejos

long-lost *adj* perdido, -a hace mucho tiempo

long-range *adj* (*missile*) de largo alcance; (*aircraft*) transcontinental; (*policy*) a largo plazo

longship *n* barco *m* vikingo

long shot *n* **1.** (*not likely*) **to be a** ~ ser una posibilidad muy remota **2.** (*at all*) **not by a** ~ ni de lejos

long-sighted *adj* **1.** (*far-sighted*) hipermétrope **2.** (*having foresight*) previsor(a)

long-standing *adj* antiguo, -a

long-suffering *adj* sufrido, -a

long-term *adj* (*care*) prolongado, -a; (*loan, memory, strategy*) a largo plazo

long wave *n* onda *f* larga

long-wave *adj* de onda larga

long-winded *adj* prolijo, -a

longwise *adv s.* **lengthwise**

loofa(h) [ˈluˑfə] *n* esponja *f* vegetal

look [lʊk] **I.** *n* **1.** (*act of looking: at person, thing*) mirada *f;* (*examination: of book, face*) ojeada *f;* **to take** [*o* **have**] **a** ~ **at sth** echar un vistazo a algo; **to take a** ~ **for sth/sb** buscar algo/a alguien **2.** (*appearance*) aspecto *m;* **good** ~**s** guapura *f;* **to have the** ~ **of sb/sth** parecerse a alguien/algo; **by the** ~ **of things** según parece **3.** (*style*) look *m* **II.** *vi* **1.** (*use sight*) mirar; **to** ~ **at sth/sb** mirar algo/a alguien; **to** ~ **at a book** echar una ojeada a un libro; **to** ~ **out** (**of**) **the window** mirar por la ventana; **oh,** ~**!** ¡mira!; ~ **here** ¡oye, tú! **2.** (*search*) buscar; **to** ~ **for sth/sb** buscar algo/a alguien **3.** (*appear, seem*) parecer; **to** ~ **like sb/sth** parecerse a alguien/algo; **to** ~ **bad/good** tener mala/buena cara; **to** ~ **tired** parecer cansado; **to** ~ **as if...** parecer como si... +*subj;* ~ **alive!** ¡espabila! **4. to** ~ **on** (*face*) dar a; **to** ~ **north** mirar [*o* dar] al norte ▶ ~ **before you leap** *prov* mira lo que haces *prov* **III.** *vt* **1.** (*examine*) mirar; **to** ~ **sb in the eye** mirar a alguien a los ojos [*o* a la cara] **2.** (*seem*) parecer; **to** ~ **one's age** aparentar su edad; **to**

~ **the part** THEAT encajar muy bien en el papel ▶ **to** ~ **the other way** hacer la vista gorda

◆ **look about** *vi* mirar alrededor

◆ **look after** *vi* **1.** (*take care of*) cuidar **2.** (*take responsibility for*) encargarse de

◆ **look ahead** *vi* mirar hacia adelante; **looking ahead to...** de cara a...

◆ **look around I.** *vi* **1.** (*look behind oneself*) girarse **2.** (*look in all directions*) mirar alrededor **3.** (*search*) **to** ~ **for** buscar **II.** *vt* (*inspect*) inspeccionar

◆ **look away** *vi* apartar la mirada

◆ **look back** *vi* **1.** (*look behind oneself*) mirar (hacia) atrás **2.** (*remember*) recordar

◆ **look down** *vi* **1.** (*from above*) mirar hacia abajo; (*lower eyes*) bajar la vista **2.** (*feel superior*) **to** ~ **on sth/sb** menospreciar algo/a alguien

◆ **look for** *vt* **1.** (*search for*) buscar **2.** (*expect*) esperar

◆ **look forward** *vi* **to** ~ **to sth** tener muchas ganas de algo; **I** ~ **to hearing from you** espero tener pronto noticias suyas

◆ **look in** *vi* **to** ~ **on sb** ir a ver a alguien; **to** ~ **at the office** pasar por la oficina

◆ **look into** *vi* investigar

◆ **look on** *vi* **1.** (*watch*) mirar **2.** (*view*) ver

◆ **look onto** *vi* dar a

◆ **look out** *vi* **1.** (*face a particular direction*) **to** ~ **on** (*window*) dar a **2.** (*watch out*) tener cuidado; ~**!** ¡cuidado!; **to** ~ **for** tener cuidado con; (*look for*) buscar

◆ **look over** *vt* (*report*) revisar; (*house*) inspeccionar

◆ **look through** *vt* **1.** (*look*) mirar por **2.** (*examine*) revisar **3.** (*peruse*) **to** ~ **sth** echar un vistazo a algo

◆ **look to** *vi* **1.** (*attend to*) mirar por **2.** (*depend on*) depender de **3.** (*count on*) contar con

◆ **look up I.** *vt* **1.** (*consult*) buscar **2.** (*visit*) ir a ver **II.** *vi* **1.** (*raise one's eyes upward*) mirar hacia arriba; **to** ~ **to sb** *fig* tener a alguien de [*o* como] ejemplo **2.** (*improve*) mejorar; **things are looking up!** ¡las cosas van mejorando!

◆ **look upon** *vi s.* **look on**

look-alike [ˈlʊkˑəˑlaɪk] *n* (*person*) doble *mf;* (*thing*) imitación *f*

looker [ˈlʊkˑər] *n sl* **to be a** (**real**) ~ ser muy guapo, -a

looking glass <-es> *n* espejo *m*

lookout [ˈlʊkˑaʊt] *n* **1.** (*observation post*) puesto *m* de observación **2.** (*person*) centinela *mf;* **to be on the** ~ estar alerta **3.** *reg: Southern* (*panorama view*) vista *f* **4.** (*concern*) asunto *m;* **that's his/your** ~ eso es asunto suyo/tuyo

lookover [ˈlʊkˑoʊˑvər] *n* vistazo *m;* **to give sth a** ~ echar un vistazo a algo

loom[1] [lum] *n* (*for weaving*) telar *m*

loom[2] [lum] *vi* **1.** (*come into view*) surgir **2.** (*threaten*) amenazar; **to** ~ **large** cobrar mucha importancia

L

loony ['luˑni] sl I. <-ier, -iest> adj (person) chiflado, -a; (idea) disparatado, -a II. <-ies> n loco, -a m, f, chiflado, -a m, f

loop [lup] I. n 1. (bend) curva f; (of string) lazada f; (of river) meandro m 2. ELEC circuito m cerrado 3. COMPUT bucle m 4. (contraceptive coil) espiral f ▸ to **throw** sb for a ~ sl dejar a alguien de piedra II. vi serpentear III. vt atar con un lazo; to ~ sth **around...** pasar algo alrededor de... ▸to ~ **the** loop AVIAT rizar el rizo

loophole ['lupˑhoʊl] n fig escapatoria f; **legal** ~ laguna legal

loose [lus] I. adj 1. (not tight: clothing) holgado, -a; (knot, rope, screw) flojo, -a; (skin) fláccido, -a 2. (not confined) suelto, -a; ~ **change** (dinero m) suelto m, sencillo m AmS 3. (not exact: instructions) poco preciso, -a; (translation) libre 4. (not strict or controlled: discipline) relajado, -a; ~ **tongue** lengua f desatada 5. (sexually immoral) disoluto, -a II. n to be on the ~ estar en libertad III. vt soltar

loose cannon n sl he is a ~ es un peligro

loose-leaf notebook n cuaderno m de anillas [o de argollas Col, Méx]

loosely ['lusˑli] adv 1. (not tightly) sin apretar 2. (not exactly: translate) libremente; (speak) en términos generales 3. (not strictly: organized) de forma flexible

loosen ['luˑsən] I. vt (belt, knot) aflojar; (tongue) desatar II. vi aflojarse

loot [lut] I. n 1. (plunder) botín m 2. sl (money) pasta f, lana f AmL II. vt, vi saquear

looting n saqueo m

lop [lɑp] vt s. **lop off**
◆**lop off** <-pp-> vt 1. (branch) podar; (limb) amputar 2. (pages) eliminar

lope [loʊp] vi (person, animal) andar con paso largo

lopsided [ˌlɑpˈsaɪˑdɪd] adj 1. (leaning to one side) torcido, -a, chueco, -a AmL 2. (biased) parcial

loquacious [loʊˈkweɪˑfəs] adj locuaz

lord [lɔrd] n señor m

lordly ['lɔrdˑli] <-ier, -iest> adj 1. (suitable to a lord) señorial 2. (arrogant) arrogante

lordship ['lɔrdˑfɪp] n form His **Lordship** Su Señoría

lore [lɔr] n sabiduría f

lose [luz] <lost, lost> I. vt perder; to **get lost** (person) perderse; (object) extraviarse II. vi perder

loser ['luˑzər] n perdedor(a) m(f)

losing ['luˑzɪŋ] adj perdedor(a)

loss [lɔs] <-es> n pérdida f; to **be at a** ~ no saber cómo reaccionar; to **be at a** ~ **for words** no encontrar palabras con que expresarse

loss leader n artículo m de gancho

loss-making adj deficitario, -a

lost [lɔst] I. pt, pp of **lose** II. adj 1. perdido, -a; to **get** ~ perderse; to **give** sth/sb up for ~ dar algo/a alguien por perdido; to **be** ~ **in a book**

estar enfrascado en la lectura de un libro 2. (preoccupied) perplejo, -a; to **be** ~ **in thought** estar ensimismado

lost and found n oficina f de objetos perdidos

lot [lɑt] n 1. (for deciding) to **cast** ~s echar a suertes 2. (destiny) destino m; (fate) suerte f 3. (plot of land) terreno m 4. (in auction) lote m 5. inf (large quantity) **a** ~ **of,** lots **of** mucho(s); **a** ~ **of wine** mucho vino; ~s **of houses** muchas casas; I **like it a** ~ me gusta mucho; **the whole** ~ todo

loth [loʊθ] adj s. **loath**

lotion ['loʊˑfən] n loción f

lottery ['lɑtˑəˑri] <-ies> n lotería f, quiniela f CSur

lottery number n número m de lotería

lotus ['loʊˑtəs] <-es> n loto m

lotus position n posición f del loto (en yoga)

loud [laʊd] I. adj 1. (voice) alto, -a; (shout) fuerte 2. (noisy) ruidoso, -a 3. (vigorous: complaint) enérgico, -a 4. fig (color) chillón, -ona II. adv alto; to **laugh out** ~ reír a carcajadas

loudmouth ['laʊdˑmaʊθ] n inf escandaloso, -a m, f

loudness n 1. (volume) volumen m; (of explosion) estruendo m 2. (of color) lo chillón

loudspeaker [ˌlaʊdˈspiˑkər] n altavoz m

Louisiana [luˌiˑziˈænˑə] n Luisiana f

lounge [laʊndʒ] I. n 1. (room) salón m 2. (bar) bar m II. vi 1. (recline) repanchi(n)garse 2. (be idle) hacer el vago
◆**lounge around** vt holgazanear

lounge chair n tumbona f, reposera f RíoPl

lounge lizard n parásito mf social

loungewear n ropa f cómoda

louse [laʊs] n 1. <lice> (insect) piojo m 2. <-es> sl (person) canalla mf
◆**louse up** vt sl echar a perder

lousy ['laʊˑzi] <-ier, -iest> adj 1. (infested with lice) piojoso, -a 2. (of poor quality) pésimo, -a; to **feel** ~ sentirse fatal 3. (nasty) asqueroso, -a ▸to **be** ~ **with** money sl estar podrido de dinero

lout [laʊt] n patán m, jallán m AmC

loutish ['laʊˑtɪf] adj patán

louver ['luˑvər] n persiana f de listones

louvered door n puerta f de persiana

lovable ['lʌvˑəˑbəl] adj adorable

love [lʌv] I. vt querer, amar; I ~ **swimming,** I ~ **to swim** me encanta nadar ▸~ **me,** ~ **my dog** prov quien quiere a Beltrán, quiere a su can prov II. n 1. (affection) amor m; to **be in** ~ (**with sb**) estar enamorado (de alguien); to **fall in** ~ (**with sb**) enamorarse (de alguien); to **make** ~ **to sb** hacer el amor con alguien 2. inf (darling) cariño m 3. (in tennis) cero m ▸**not for** ~ **or** money por nada del mundo; **there is no** ~ **lost between the two** no se pueden ver III. vt querer, amar

love affair n aventura f (amorosa), romance m

lovebird n periquito m; fig tortolito m

love handles npl sl michelines mpl, llantas fpl Col, lonjas fpl Méx

love-hate relationship *n* relación *f* de amor y odio

loveless ['lʌv·lɪs] *adj* sin amor

love letter *n* carta *f* de amor

love life *n* vida *f* amorosa [*o* sentimental]

loveliness ['lʌv·lɪ·nɪs] *n* (*of scenery*) belleza *f*; (*of person*) encanto *m*

lovely ['lʌv·li] <-ier, -iest> *adj* (*house, present*) bonito, -a; (*weather*) precioso, -a; (*person*) encantador(a); **to have a ~ time** pasarlo estupendamente

lovemaking *n* relaciones *fpl* sexuales

lover ['lʌv·ər] *n* amante *mf*

love seat *n* sofá *m* para dos

lovesick ['lʌv·sɪk] *adj* locamente enamorado, -a, volado, -a *AmL*

love song *n* canción *f* de amor

love story *n* historia *f* de amor

loving ['lʌv·ɪŋ] *adj* cariñoso, -a

low¹ [loʊ] I. *adj* 1.(*not high, not loud*) bajo, -a; **to be ~ on sth** (*coffee, gas*) tener poco de algo; **to cook sth on ~ heat** hacer algo a fuego lento 2.(*poor: opinion, quality*) malo, -a; (*self-esteem*) bajo, -a; (*visibility*) poco, -a; **a ~ trick** una mala jugada II. *adv* bajo, -a; **to feel ~** estar deprimido; **stocks are running ~** las existencias están casi agotadas; **the batteries are running ~** se están gastando las pilas III. *n* 1. METEO borrasca *f* 2.(*minimum*) mínimo *m*; **an all-time ~** un mínimo histórico

low² [loʊ] I. *vi* (*cow*) mugir II. *n* mugido *m*

low-alcohol *adj* bajo, -a en alcohol

lowborn *adj* de casa pobre

lowbrow *adj* poco intelectual

low-cal *adj*, **low-calorie** *adj* bajo, -a en calorías

low-cost *adj* de bajo coste

low-cut *adj* escotado, -a

lowdown *n sl* **to give sb the ~ on sth** poner a alguien al tanto de algo

low-down *adj inf* bajo, -a; **a ~ trick** una mala jugada

lower¹ ['loʊ·ər] I. *vt* bajar; (*flag, sails*) arriar; (*lifeboat*) echar al agua; **to ~ one's eyes** bajar la vista; **to ~ oneself to do sth** rebajarse a hacer algo II. *vi* bajar III. *adj* inferior

lower² [laʊr] *vi* 1.(*person*) fruncir el ceño 2.(*sky*) encapotarse

lower-case *adj* minúsculo, -a; **in ~ letters** en minúsculas

low-fat *adj* bajo, -a en calorías; (*milk*) desnatado, -a

low frequency *n* baja frecuencia *f*

low-grade *adj* de baja calidad

low-key *adj* (*affair*) discreto, -a; (*debate, discussion*) mesurado, -a

lowlands *npl* tierras *fpl* bajas, bajío *m AmL*

low-level *adj* 1.(*discussion*) a bajo nivel 2.(*radiation*) de baja intensidad

lowly ['loʊ·li] <-ier, -iest> *adj* humilde

low-minded *adj* vulgar

lowness *n* 1.(*state of being low*) lo bajo 2. MUS gravedad *f* 3.(*baseness*) bajeza *f*, vileza *f*

4.(*humbleness*) humildad *f*

low-pitched *adj* (*voice*) grave

low profile *n* **to keep a ~** tratar de pasar desapercibido

low season *n* temporada *f* baja

low-spirited *adj* deprimido, -a

low-tech *adj* de baja tecnología

low tide *n*, **low water** *n* marea *f* baja, bajamar *f*

lox [laks] *n* CULIN salmón *m* ahumado

loyal ['lɔɪ·əl] *adj* leal; **to remain ~ (to sb/sth)** permanecer fiel (a alguien/algo)

loyalist ['lɔɪ·ə·lɪst] *n* partidario, -a *m*, *f* del régimen

loyalty ['lɔɪ·əl·ti] <-ies> *n* lealtad *f*

lozenge ['laz·əndʒ] *n* pastilla *f*

LP [ˌel·'pi] *n abbr of* **long-playing record** LP *m*

LPG *n abbr of* **liquefied petroleum gas** GLP *m*

LPN *n abbr of* **licensed practical nurse** enfermera con un título oficial

LSD [ˌel·es·'di] *n abbr of* **lysergic acid diethylamide** LSD *f*

LT *n*, **Lt.** *n abbr of* **Lieutenant** 1. MIL teniente *mf* 2.(*assistant*) lugarteniente *mf*

Ltd. ['lɪm·ɪ·tɪd] *abbr of* **Limited** ≈SA

lubricant ['lu·brɪ·kənt] *n* lubricante *m*

lubricate ['lu·brɪ·keɪt] *vt* lubricar

lubrication [ˌlu·brɪ·'keɪ·ʃən] *n* lubricación *f*

lubricator ['lu·brɪˌkeɪ·tər] *n* lubricador *m*

lucid ['lu·sɪd] *adj* 1.(*rational*) lúcido, -a 2.(*easily understood*) claro, -a

luck [lʌk] *n* suerte *f*; **good/bad ~** buena/mala suerte; **a stroke of ~** un golpe de suerte; **to bring sb ~** traer suerte a alguien; **to wish sb (good) ~** desear a alguien (buena) suerte; **with any ~** con un poco de suerte; **with no ~** sin éxito; **as ~ would have it...** quiso la suerte que... +*subj*; **to be down on one's ~** tener una mala racha ▶ **to be the ~ of the** draw ser cuestión de suerte; **no** such **~!** *inf* ¡qué va!; **to** press one's **~** tentar a la suerte

luckless ['lʌk·lɪs] *adj* desafortunado, -a

lucky ['lʌk·i] <-ier, -iest> *adj* afortunado, -a; **to be ~ in love** tener suerte en el amor; **to be ~ (in that...)** tener la suerte (de que...) +*subj*; **to make a ~ guess** acertar por (pura) casualidad; **~ day** día *m* de suerte; **~ number** número *m* de la suerte

lucrative ['lu·krə·tɪv] *adj* lucrativo, -a

lucre ['lu·kər] *n* lucro *m*; (filthy) **~** *iron* (cochino) dinero *m*

ludicrous ['lu·dɪ·krəs] *adj* absurdo, -a

lug [lʌg] I. *vt* <-gg-> *inf* arrastrar II. *n sl* bruto, -a *m*, *f*

luggage ['lʌg·ɪdʒ] *n* equipaje *m*

luggage rack *n* baca *f*

lugger ['lʌg·ər] *n* NAUT lugre *m*

lug nut *n* AUTO tuerca *f* (de una rueda)

lugubrious [lə·'gu·bri·əs] *adj* lúgubre

lukewarm [ˌluk·'wɔrm] *adj* 1.(*liquid*) tibio, -a 2. *fig* (*unenthusiastic*) poco entusiasta

lull [lʌl] I. *vt* 1.(*soothe*) calmar; **to ~ sb to sleep** dormir a alguien 2.(*deceive*) **to ~ sb**

L

into believing that... hacer creer a alguien que... II. *n* 1.(*temporary stillness*) período *m* de calma 2.(*in conversation*) pausa *f* 3.(*in fighting*) tregua *f*

lullaby ['lʌl·ə·baɪ] <-ies> *n* nana *f*

lumbago [lʌm·'beɪ·goʊ] *n* lumbago *m*

lumbar ['lʌm·bər] *adj* ANAT lumbar

lumbar puncture *n* MED punción *f* lumbar

lumber¹ ['lʌm·bər] *vi* moverse pesadamente

lumber² ['lʌm·bər] I. *n* madera *f* II. *vi* aserrar

lumberjack *n* leñador *m*

lumber room *n* trastero *m*

lumber trade *n* industria *f* maderera

lumberyard *n* almacén *m* de maderas

luminary ['lu·mə·ner·i] <-ies> *n fig* lumbrera *f*

luminosity [ˌlu·mə·'nas·ə·t̬i] *n* luminosidad *f*

luminous ['lu·mə·nəs] *adj* luminoso, -a

lump [lʌmp] I. *n* 1.(*solid mass*) masa *f;* (*of coal*) trozo *m;* (*of sugar*) terrón *m;* ~ **sum** cantidad *f* única 2.(*swelling: in breast, on head*) bulto *m* 3. *inf* (*person*) zoquete *mf* ▶ **to have a ~ in one's throat** tener un nudo en la garganta II. *vt* <to ~ (together)> agrupar

lump-sum payment *n* pago *m* único

lumpy ['lʌm·pi] <-ier, -iest> *adj* (*custard, sauce*) grumoso, -a; (*surface*) desigual

lunacy ['lu·nə·si] *n* locura *f*

lunar ['lu·nər] *adj* lunar

lunatic ['lu·nə·t̬ɪk] I. *n* loco, -a *m, f* II. *adj* lunático, -a

lunatic fringe *n* facción *f* extremista (de un grupo)

lunch [lʌntʃ] I. *n* comida *f;* **to have ~** comer ▶ **to be out to ~** *sl* estar en Babia II. *vi* comer

lunch break *n* descanso *m* para comer

luncheon ['lʌn·tʃən] *n form* almuerzo *m*

luncheon meat *n fiambre de cerdo en conserva*

lunch hour *n* hora *f* de comer

lunchtime I. *n* hora *f* de comer II. *adj* (*concert*) de mediodía

lung [lʌŋ] *n* pulmón *m;* **to shout at the top of one's ~s** decir a voz en grito

lung cancer *n* cáncer *m* de pulmón

lunge [lʌndʒ] I. *vi* **to ~ at sb** arremeter contra alguien II. *n* arremetida *f*

lupin(e) ['lu·pɪn] *n* BOT lupino *m,* altramuz *m*

lurch [lɜrtʃ] I. *vi* (*people*) tambalearse; (*car, train*) dar sacudidas II. <-es> *n* sacudida *f* ▶ **to leave sb in the ~** *inf* dejar a alguien colgado

lure [lʊr] I. *n* 1.(*attraction*) atractivo *m* 2.(*bait*) cebo *m;* (*decoy*) señuelo *m* II. *vt* atraer; **to ~ sb into a trap** hacer que alguien caiga en una trampa

lurid ['lʊr·ɪd] *adj* 1.(*gruesome: details*) escabroso, -a; (*language*) morboso, -a 2.(*sensationalist*) sensacionalista 3.(*extremely bright*) chillón, -ona

lurk [lɜrk] *vi* merodear, esconderse

luscious ['lʌʃ·əs] *adj* 1.(*fruit*) jugoso, -a 2. *inf* (*girl, curves*) voluptuoso, -a; (*lips*) carnoso, -a

lush [lʌʃ] I. *adj* 1.(*vegetation*) exuberante

2.(*luxurious*) opulento, -a II. *n* <-es> *sl* borracho, -a *m, f*

lust [lʌst] *n* 1.(*sexual desire*) lujuria *f* 2.(*strong desire*) anhelo *m;* ~ **for sth** ansia de algo; ~ **for life** ansias de vivir

luster ['lʌs·tər] *n* lustre *m*

lustful ['lʌst·fəl] *adj* lujurioso, -a

lusty ['lʌs·ti] <-ier, -iest> *adj* (*person*) sano, -a; (*voice*) potente

lute [lut] *n* MUS laúd *m*

Lutheran ['lu·θər·ən] I. *adj* luterano, -a II. *n* luterano, -a *m, f*

Luxembourg ['lʌk·səm·bɜrg] *n* Luxemburgo *m*

Luxembourger *n* luxemburgués, -esa *m, f*

luxuriant [lʌg·'ʒʊr·i·ənt] *adj* (*hair*) abundante; (*vegetation*) exuberante

luxuriate [lʌg·'ʒʊr·i·eɪt] *vi* 1.(*person*) deleitarse; **to ~ in sth** disfrutar con algo 2.(*plant*) crecer de manera exuberante

luxurious [lʌg·'ʒʊr·i·əs] *adj* lujoso, -a

luxury ['lʌk·ʃər·i] <-ies> *n* lujo *m;* ~ **apartment** piso *m* de lujo

LW *n abbr of* **long wave** OL *f*

lychee ['li·tʃi] *n* BOT *s.* **litchi**

Lycra® ['laɪ·krə] *n* licra® *f*

lye [laɪ] *n* lejía *f*

lying ['laɪ·ɪŋ] I. *n* mentiras *fpl* II. *adj* mentiroso, -a

Lyme disease ['laɪm·dɪ·ˌziz] *n* enfermedad *f* de Lyme

lymph [lɪmpf] *n* linfa *f*

lymphatic [lɪm·'fæt̬·ɪk] *adj* linfático, -a

lymph node *n* ganglio *m* linfático

lynch [lɪntʃ] *vt* linchar

lynx [lɪŋks] <-(es)> *n* lince *m*

lynx-eyed *adj* con ojos de lince

lyre [laɪr] *n* lira *f*

lyric ['lɪr·ɪk] I. *adj* lírico, -a II. *n* 1.(*poem*) poema *m* lírico 2.~ **s** (*words for song*) letra *f*

lyrical ['lɪr·ɪ·kəl] *adj* lírico, -a; **to get ~ about sth** *fig* entusiasmarse por algo

lyricism ['lɪr·ɪ·ˌsɪz·əm] *n* LIT, MUS lirismo *m*

lyricist ['lɪr·ɪ·sɪst] *n* letrista *mf*

M

M, m [em] *n* M, m *f;* ~ **as in Mike** M de María

M *n* 1. *abbr of* **male** H 2. *abbr of* **medium** M

m 1. *abbr of* **million** millón *m* 2. *abbr of* **minutes** min. 3. *abbr of* **meter** m

m. *n* 1. *abbr of* **mile** milla *f* 2. *abbr of* **married** casado, -a

MA [ˌem·'eɪ] *n* 1. *abbr of* **Master of Arts** máster *m* (*de Humanidades o de Filosofía y Letras);* **Louie Sanders, MA** Louie Sanders, licenciado con máster 2. *abbr of* **Massachusetts** Massachusetts *m*

ma [ma] *n inf* mamá *f*

ma'am [mæm] = **madam** (*form of address*) señora *f*

Mac [mæk] *n* COMPUT *abbr of* **Macintosh** Mac *m,* Mac *f AmL*

macabre [mə·'kab·rə] *adj* macabro, -a

macadam [mə·'kæd·əm] *n* macadán *m*

macaroni [ˌmæk·ə·'rou·ni] *n* macarrones *mpl*

macaroni and cheese *n* macarrones *mpl* con queso

mace¹ [meɪs] *n* (*club*) maza *f*

mace² [meɪs] *n* (*spice*) macis *f*

Mace® [meɪs] *n* spray *m* antivioladores

Macedonia [ˌmæs·ə·'dou·ni·ə] *n* Macedonia *f*

Macedonian I. *adj* macedonio, -a **II.** *n* 1.(*person*) macedonio, -a *m, f* 2. LING macedonio *m*

Mach [mak] *n* PHYS Mach *m*

machete [mə·'ʃeṭ·i] *n* machete *m*

machine [mə·'ʃin] *n* 1.(*mechanical device*) máquina *f* 2.(*system*) aparato *m*

machine gun *n* ametralladora *f*

machine-made *adj* hecho, -a a máquina

machine-readable *adj* COMPUT legible por máquina

machinery [mə·'ʃi·nə·ri] *n* 1. *a. fig* (*machines*) maquinaria *f* 2.(*mechanism*) mecanismo *m*

machine tool *n* máquina *f* herramienta

machine-wash *vt* lavar a máquina

machine-washable *adj* lavable a máquina

machinist [mə·'ʃi·nɪst] *n* maquinista *mf*

macho ['matʃ·ou] **I.** *n* machista *m* **II.** *adj* machista

mackerel ['mæk·rəl] <-(s)> *n* caballa *f*

macro ['mæk·rou] *n* COMPUT macro *f*

macrobiotic [ˌmæk·rou·baɪ·'aṭ·ɪk] *adj* macrobiótico, -a

macrocosm ['mæk·rou·kaz·əm] *n* macrocosmos *m inv*

macroeconomics [ˌmæk·rou·ˌek·ə·'nam·ɪks] *n* macroeconomía *f*

mad [mæd] *adj* 1.(*upset*) furioso, -a 2.(*frantic*) frenético, -a 3.(*insane: person*) loco, -a; **to go** ~ volverse loco; **to drive sb** ~ volver loco a alguien 4.(*enthusiastic*) **to be** ~ **about sb** estar loco por alguien; **she's** ~ **about chocolate** le encanta el chocolate

Madagascar [ˌmæd·ə·'gæs·kər] *n* Madagascar *m*

madam ['mæd·əm] *n* señora *f*

mad cow disease *n* mal *m* de las vacas locas

madden ['mæd·ən] *vt* enfurecer

maddening *adj* exasperante

made [meɪd] *pp, pt of* **make**

made-to-order [ˌmeɪd·tə·'ɔr·dər] *adj* 1.(*custom-made*) hecho, -a de encargo [*o* a la medida] 2.(*perfect*) plantado, -a

made-up ['meɪd·ʌp] *adj* 1.(*wearing make-up*) maquillado, -a 2.(*invented*) inventado, -a

madhouse ['mæd·haʊs] *n inf* loquero *m*

madly ['mæd·li] *adv* 1.(*frantically*) frenéticamente 2.(*intensely*) terriblemente; **she's** ~ **in love with him** está locamente enamorada de él

madman ['mæd·mən] <-men> *n* loco *m*

madness ['mæd·nɪs] *n* locura *f*, loquera *f AmL*

madwoman ['mæd·ˌwʊm·ən] <-women> *n* loca *f*

maelstrom ['meɪl·strəm] *n a. fig* vorágine *f*

maestro ['maɪ·strou] *n* maestro *m*

Mafia ['maf·i·ə] *n* mafia *f*

mag [mæg] *n sl abbr of* **magazine** revista *f*

magazine ['mæg·ə·zin] *n* 1.(*periodical publication*) revista *f* 2. MIL (*of gun*) recámara *f* 3. MIL (*storage place*) polvorín *m*

maggot ['mæg·ət] *n* gusano *m*

Magi ['meɪ·dʒaɪ] *npl* **the** ~ los Reyes Magos

magic ['mædʒ·ɪk] **I.** *n* magia *f*; **as if by** ~ como por arte de magia **II.** *adj* mágico, -a

magical *adj* 1.(*power*) mágico, -a 2.(*extraordinary, wonderful*) fabuloso, -a

magically *adv* por arte de magia

magic carpet *n* alfombra *f* mágica

magician [mə·'dʒɪʃ·ən] *n* mago, -a *m, f*

magisterial [ˌmædʒ·ɪ·'stɪr·i·əl] *adj* form 1.(*having complete authority*) magistral 2.(*imperious: tone, way*) autoritario, -a

magistrate ['mædʒ·ɪ·streɪt] *n juez que se ocupa de los delitos menores*

magnanimity [ˌmæg·nə·'nɪm·ə·ṭi] *n form* magnanimidad *f*

magnanimous [mæg·'næn·ə·məs] *adj form* magnánimo, -a

magnate ['mæg·neɪt] *n* magnate *mf*

magnesia [mæg·'ni·ʒə] *n* magnesia *f*

magnesium [mæg·'ni·zi·əm] *n* magnesio *m*

magnet ['mæg·nɪt] *n* imán *m*; **to act as a** ~ **for sth** *fig* atraer como un imán a algo

magnetic [mæg·'neṭ·ɪk] *adj* 1.(*force*) magnético, -a 2.(*personality*) atrayente

magnetic field *n* campo *m* magnético

magnetic pole *n* polo *m* magnético

magnetism ['mæg·nə·tɪz·əm] *n* magnetismo *m*

magnetize ['mæg·nə·taɪz] *vt* magnetizar; **to** ~ **sb** cautivar a alguien

magneto [mæg·'ni·ṭou] *n* TECH, AUTO magneto *m f*

magnification [ˌmæg·nɪ·fɪ·'keɪ·ʃən] *n* (*lens*) aumento *m*; (*photograph*) ampliación *f*

magnificence [mæg·'nɪf·ɪ·səns] *n* magnificencia *f*

magnificent [mæg·'nɪf·ɪ·sənt] *adj* magnífico, -a

magnify ['mæg·nɪ·faɪ] <-ie-> *vt* 1.(*make larger*) ampliar; (*voice*) amplificar 2.(*make worse: problem*) exagerar

magnifying glass *n* lupa *f*

magnitude ['mæg·nɪ·tud] *n* 1.(*importance*) magnitud *f* 2.(*large size*) envergadura *f*

magnolia [mæg·'noʊl·jə] *n* magnolia *f*

magnum opus [ˌmæg·nəm·'oʊ·pəs] *n form* obra *f* maestra

magpie ['mæg·paɪ] *n* (*bird*) urraca *f*

maharajah *n*, **maharaja** [ˌma·hə·'ra·dʒə] *n* HIST maharajá *m*

mahogany [mə·'hag·ə·ni] **I.** *n* caoba *f* **II.** *adj*

M

de caoba

maid [meɪd] *n* **1.**(*female servant*) criada *f,* mucama *f AmL;* (*in hotel*) camarera *f* **2.** *liter* (*girl, young woman*) doncella *f*

maiden ['meɪ·dən] **I.** *n liter* doncella *f* **II.** *adj* **1.**(*unmarried*) soltera **2.**(*first: voyage*) primero, -a

maidenhair fern [ˌmeɪ·dən·her·'fɜrn] *n* cabellos *mpl* de Venus

maiden name *n* apellido *m* de soltera

maid of honor *n* dama *f* de honor

mail[1] [meɪl] **I.** *n a.* COMPUT correo *m;* **electronic ~** COMPUT correo electrónico; **incoming/outgoing ~** COMPUT correo entrante/saliente; **by ~** por correo; **by return ~** a vuelta de correo; **to open the ~** abrir el correo; **to send sth through the ~** mandar [*o* enviar] algo por correo; **is there any ~?** ¿ha llegado alguna carta? **II.** *vt* mandar [*o* enviar] por correo

mail[2] [meɪl] *n* (*armor*) malla *f*

mailbox *n* **1.**(*for postal deliveries*) buzón *m* **2.** COMPUT (**electronic**) ~ buzón *m* electrónico

mailing list *n* lista *f* de direcciones (*a las que se envía publicidad o información*)

mailman *n* cartero *m*

mail order *n* venta *f* por correo

maim [meɪm] *vt* lisiar

main [meɪn] **I.** *adj* (*problem, reason, street*) principal **II.** *n* **1.**(*pipe*) cañería *f* principal; **the water ~** la cañería maestra; **the gas ~** la cañería principal de gas **2.**(*cable*) cable *m* principal

▶ **in the ~** en general

Maine [meɪn] *n* Maine *m*

mainframe ['meɪn·freɪm] *n* COMPUT ordenador *m* central, computadora *f* central *AmL*

mainland ['meɪn·lənd] **I.** *n* continente *m* **II.** *adj* ~ **China** China continental; ~ **Spain** España peninsular

mainline ['meɪn·laɪn] *sl* **I.** *vt* chutar **II.** *vi* chutarse

mainly ['meɪn·li] *adv* principalmente

main office *n* oficina *f* central

main road *n* carretera *f* general [*o* nacional]

mainsail *n* vela *f* mayor

mainspring *n* motivo *m* principal

mainstay *n* pilar *m*

mainstream **I.** *n* corriente *f* dominante **II.** *adj* **1.**(*ideology*) dominante **2.**(*film, novel*) comercial

maintain [meɪn·'teɪn] *vt* **1.**(*preserve, provide for*) mantener **2.**(*claim*) sostener

maintenance ['meɪn·tə·nəns] *n* **1.**(*repair work*) mantenimiento *m,* arreglos *mpl* **2.**(*keeping, preservation*) mantenimiento

Maj. *abbr of* **Major** comandante *mf*

majestic [mə·'dʒes·tɪk] *adj* majestuoso, -a

majesty ['mædʒ·ɪ·sti] <-ies> *n* majestuosidad *f;* **Her/His/Your Majesty** su Majestad

major ['meɪ·dʒər] **I.** *adj* **1.**(*important, significant*) muy importante, fundamental; **a ~ problem** un gran problema **2.**(*serious: illness*) grave **3.** MUS mayor; **in C ~** en do mayor

II. *n* **1.** MIL comandante *mf* **2.** UNIV especialidad *f*

Majorca [mə·'jɔr·kə] *n* Mallorca *f*

Majorcan **I.** *adj* mallorquín, -ina **II.** *n* mallorquín, -ina *m, f*

majorette [ˌmeɪ·dʒər·'et] *n* batonista *f*

major general [ˌmeɪ·dʒər·'dʒen·ər·əl] *n* general *m* de división

majority [mə·'dʒɔr·ə·ti] <-ies> *n* **1.**(*greater part/number*) mayoría *f;* **a narrow/large ~** POL un margen estrecho/amplio **2.**(*most powerful group*) grupo *m* mayoritario **3.**(*full legal age*) mayoría *f* de edad; **to reach the age of ~** alcanzar la mayoría de edad

make [meɪk] **I.** *vt* <made, made> **1.**(*produce: coffee, soup, dinner*) hacer; (*product*) fabricar; (*clothes*) confeccionar; (*record*) grabar; (*film*) rodar; **to make sth out of sth** hacer algo con algo; **to ~ time** hacer tiempo **2.**(*cause: trouble*) causar; **to ~ noise** hacer ruido; **to ~ a scene** montar una escena; **to ~ oneself look ridiculous** ponerse en ridículo; **to ~ a wonderful combination** ser una combinación fabulosa **3.**(*cause to be*) **to ~ sb sad** poner triste a alguien; **to ~ sb happy** hacer feliz a alguien; **to ~ oneself heard** hacerse oír; **to ~ oneself understood** hacerse entender; **to ~ sth easy** hacer que algo sea fácil; **to ~ something of oneself** llegar a ser algo **4.**(*perform, carry out*) **to ~ a call** hacer una llamada; **to ~ a decision** tomar una decision; **to ~ a reservation** hacer [*o* efectuar] una reserva **5.**(*force*) obligar; **to ~ sb do sth** hacer que alguien haga algo **6.**(*amount to, total*) ser; **two plus two ~s four** dos y dos son cuatro **7.**(*earn, get*) **to ~ friends** hacer amigos; **to ~ money** hacer [*o* ganar] dinero; **to ~ a profit/loss** tener beneficios/pérdidas; **to ~ a living** ganarse la vida **8.** *inf*(*get to, reach*) **to ~ it to somewhere** llegar a un sitio; **to ~ it** alcanzar el éxito **9.**(*make perfect*) **that made my day!** ¡eso me alegró el día! ▶ **to ~ or break sth** ser el éxito o la ruina de algo; **to ~ do (with sth)** arreglárselas (con algo) **II.** *vi* (*amount to, total*) **today's earthquake ~s five since the beginning of the year** el terremoto de hoy es el quinto de este año ▶ **to ~ as if to do sth** fingir hacer algo **III.** *n* **1.**(*brand*) marca *f* **2.**(*identification*) **to get a ~ on sb** identificar [*o* tener] a alguien ▶ **to be on the ~** *sl* (*for money, power*) intentar sacar tajada; (*sexually*) intentar ligar

◆ **make for** *vt insep* **1.**(*head for*) dirigirse a **2.**(*lead to*) **to ~ sth** contribuir a algo

◆ **make of** *vt* **what do you ~ this book?** ¿qué te parece este libro?

◆ **make off with** *vt* **to ~ sth** largarse con algo

◆ **make out I.** *vi* **1.**(*succeed, cope: person*) arreglárselas **2.** *sl* (*kiss passionately*) **to ~ with sb** darse el lote con alguien **II.** *vt* **1.**(*discern: writing, numbers*) distinguir; (*sth in the distance*) divisar, visualizar *AmL* **2.**(*pretend*) **he made himself out to be rich** se hizo pasar

por rico **3.** (*write out*) **to ~ a check for $100** extender un cheque por valor de 100 dólares
◆ **make over** *vt* **1.** LAW (*transfer: ownership*) transmitir **2.** (*alter, convert*) **to make sth over into sth** convertir algo en algo
◆ **make up** I. *vt* **1.** (*invent*) inventar **2.** (*prepare*) preparar **3.** (*compensate*) **to ~ for sth** compensar algo **4.** (*constitute*) constituir **5.** (*decide*) **to ~ one's mind** decidirse **6.** SCHOOL **to ~ an exam** cambiar (la fecha de) un examen II. *vi* reconciliarse
◆ **make up** *vt* **to make it up to sb** compensar a alguien

make-believe ['meɪk·bɪ·ˌliv] I. *n* (*pretence*) fingimiento *m;* **a world of ~** un mundo de fantasía [*o* de ensueño] II. *adj* imaginario, -a; (*weapon*) de mentira; **a ~ world** un mundo de fantasía

make-or-break *adj* (*plan*) clave, crucial

maker ['meɪ·kər] *n* **1.** (*manufacturer*) fabricante *mf* **2.** (*God*) **to meet one's Maker** entregar el alma a Dios

makeshift ['meɪk·ʃɪft] *adj* provisional

make-up ['meɪk·ʌp] *n* **1.** (*cosmetics*) maquillaje *m;* **to put on ~** maquillarse; **to wear ~** ir maquillado **2.** (*structure*) estructura *f* **3.** (*character*) carácter *m*

make-up artist *n* maquillador(a) *m(f)*

making ['meɪ·kɪŋ] *n* **1.** (*production*) producción *m;* (*of clothes*) confección *f;* (*of meals*) preparación *f* **2. ~s** (*essential qualities*), **to have the ~s of sth** tener madera de algo ▸ **to be the ~ of sb** ser decisivo para alguien

maladjusted [ˌmæl·ə·'dʒʌs·tɪd] *adj* PSYCH inadaptado, -a

maladroit ['mæl·ə·drɔɪt] *adj form* torpe

Malagasy [ˌmæl·ə·'gæs·i] I. *adj* malgache II. *n a.* LING malgache *m*

malaise [mæ·'leɪz] *n* malestar *m*

malapropism ['mæl·ə·prap·ɪz·əm] *n* LING equivocación *f* de palabras

malaria [mə·'ler·i·ə] *n* malaria *f*

Malawi [mə·'la·wi] *n* Malaui *m*

Malawian I. *adj* malauiano, -a II. *n* malauiano, -a *m, f*

Malaysia [mə·'leɪ·ʒə] *n* Malaisia *f*

Malaysian [mə·'leɪ·ʒən] I. *adj* malaisio, -a II. *n* malaisio, -a *m, f*

malcontent ['mæl·kən·ˌtənt] *n form* descontento, -a *m, f*

Maldives ['mæl·daɪvz] *npl* Maldivas *fpl*

male [meɪl] I. *adj* (*hormone, sex*) masculino, -a; (*animal*) macho; **~ chauvinism** machismo *m* II. *n* (*person*) varón *m;* (*animal*) macho *m*

malediction [ˌmæl·ə·'dɪk·ʃən] *n* maldición *f*

malevolent [mə·'lev·ə·lənt] *adj liter* (*malicious*) malévolo, -a; (*deity, powers*) maligno, -a

malformation [ˌmæl·fɔr·'meɪ·ʃən] *n* MED deformación *f*

malfunction [ˌmæl·'fʌŋk·ʃən] I. *vi* **1.** (*not work properly*) funcionar mal **2.** (*stop functioning*) fallar II. *n* **1.** (*defective functioning*) mal fun-

cionamiento *m* **2.** (*sudden stop*) fallo *m*

Mali ['ma·li] *n* Mali *m*

Malian I. *adj* malinés, -esa II. *n* malinés, -esa *m, f*

malice ['mæl·ɪs] *n* malicia *f;* **with ~ aforethought** con premeditación

malicious [mə·'lɪʃ·əs] *adj* malicioso, -a

malign [mə·'laɪn] I. *adj form* maligno, -a II. *vt* calumniar

malignancy [mə·'lɪg·nən·si] <-ies> *n a.* MED malignidad *f*

malignant [mə·'lɪg·nənt] *adj* maligno, -a

malinger [mə·'lɪŋ·gər] *vi* fingir estar enfermo

malingerer [mə·'lɪŋ·gər·ər] *n persona que finge estar enferma*

mall [mɔl] *n* centro *m* comercial

mallard ['mæl·ərd] <-(s)> *n* ánade *m* real

malleable ['mæl·i·ə·bəl] *adj* (*material*) maleable; (*person*) dócil

mallet ['mæl·ɪt] *n* mazo *m*

mallow ['mæl·ou] *n* malva *f*

malnutrition [ˌmæl·nu·'trɪʃ·ən] *n* desnutrición *f*

malodorous [ˌmæl·'ou·dər·əs] *adj form* maloliente

malpractice [ˌmæl·'præk·tɪs] *n* conducta *f* incorrecta; **medical ~** negligencia *f* médica

malt [mɔlt] I. *n* malta *f* II. *vt* maltear

Malta ['mɔl·tə] *n* Malta *f; s.a.* **Republic of Malta**

Maltese [ˌmɔl·'tiz] I. *adj* maltés, -esa; **~ cross** cruz *f* de Malta II. *n* maltés, -esa *m, f*

maltreat [ˌmæl·'trit] *vt form* maltratar

maltreatment *n* malos tratos *mpl*

mamma [mə·'ma] *n* mamá *f*

mammal ['mæm·əl] *n* mamífero *m*

mammary gland ['mæm·ə·ri·ˌglænd] *n* glándula *f* mamaria

mammography [mə·'mag·rə·fi] <-ies> *n* mamografía *f*

mammoth ['mæm·əθ] I. *adj* gigantesco, -a II. *n* mamut *m*

man [mæn] I. *n* <men> **1.** (*male human*) hombre *m* **2.** (*the human race*) ser *m* humano **3.** (*in games*) ficha *f* ▸ **to talk (as) ~ to ~** hablar de hombre a hombre; **as one ~** unánimemente II. *vt* <-nn-> (*operate*) encargarse de; (*ship*) tripular; **to ~ a factory** contratar personal para una fábrica; **some volunteers ~ the phones** algunos voluntarios cogen el teléfono III. *interj* ¡hombre!; **~, was that cake good!** ¡pues sí que estaba bueno el pastel!

manage ['mæn·ɪdʒ] I. *vt* **1.** *a.* ECON (*control, be in charge of*) dirigir; (*money, time*) administrar; (*a sports team*) dirigir **2.** (*accomplish*) lograr; **to ~ to do sth** conseguir hacer algo **3.** (*fit into one's schedule*) **to not ~ the time** no tener tiempo II. *vi* **to ~ on a few dollars a day** arreglárselas con un par de dólares al día

manageable ['mæn·ɪ·dʒə·bəl] *adj* (*vehicle*) manejable; (*person, animal*) dócil; (*amount*) razonable

management ['mæn·ɪdʒ·mənt] *n* **1.** (*direc-*

tion) manejo *m* **2.** *a.* ECON dirección *f;* **to study business** ~ estudiar administración de empresas

management consultant *n* consultor(a) *m(f)* gerencial

management information system *n* sistema *m* de información de gestión

manager ['mæn·ɪ·dʒər] *n* **1.** COM (*administrator*) administrador(a) *m(f); (of business unit*) gerente *mf* **2.** (*of performer, artist*) representante *mf* artístico, -a; (*of a sports team*) manager *mf*

managerial [ˌmæn·ə·'dʒɪr·i·əl] *adj* (*relating to a manager*) gerencial; (*directorial*) directivo, -a; ~ **position** posición directiva; ~ **skills** dotes *fpl* de mando

managing director *n* director(a) *m(f)* general

mandarin ['mæn·də·rɪn] *n* mandarín *m*

Mandarin *n* LING mandarín *m*

mandarin orange *n* mandarina *f*

mandate ['mæn·deɪt] I. *n* **1.** *a.* POL mandato *m* **2.** (*territory*) territorio *m* bajo mandato II. *vt* aprobar oficialmente

mandatory ['mæn·də·tɔr·i] *adj form* obligatorio, -a; **to make sth** ~ imponer algo

mandible ['mæn·dɪ·bəl] *n* mandíbula *f*

mandolin ['mæn·də·lɪn] *n* MUS mandolina *f,* bandolina *f AmL*

mandrake ['mæn·dreɪk] *n* mandrágora *f*

mandrill ['mæn·drɪl] *n* mandril *m*

mane [meɪn] *n* (*of horse*) crin *f;* (*of person, lion*) melena *f*

man-eater ['mæn·i·t̬ər] *n sl* devorador(a) *m(f)* de hombres

maneuver [mə·'nu·vər] I. *n a.* MIL maniobra *f;* **army** ~ **s** maniobras militares II. *vt* hacer maniobrar; **to** ~ **sb into doing sth** embaucar a alguien para que haga algo III. *vi* maniobrar

maneuverability [mə·ˌnu·vər·ə·'bɪl·ə·t̬i] *n* maniobrabilidad *f*

maneuverable [mə·'nu·vər·ə·bəl] *adj* maniobrable

manfully ['mæn·fʊl·i] *adv* valientemente

manganese ['mæn·gə·niz] *n* manganeso *m*

manger ['meɪn·dʒər] *n* pesebre *m*

mangle ['mæŋ·gəl] *vt* (*body, text*) mutilar

mango ['mæŋ·goʊ] *n* <-(e)s> mango *m*

mangrove ['mæn·groʊv] *n* mangle *m*

manhandle ['mæn·hæn·dəl] *vt* **1.** (*treat roughly: person*) maltratar **2.** (*move by hand: heavy object*) empujar

manhole ['mæn·hoʊl] *n* registro *m,* boca *f* de visita *Ven*

manhole cover *n* tapa *f* de registro

manhood ['mæn·hʊd] *n* **1.** (*adulthood*) edad *f* adulta **2.** (*masculinity*) virilidad *f*

man-hour ['mæn·aʊ·ər] *n* ECON hora-hombre *f*

manhunt ['mæn·hʌnt] *n* persecución *f*

mania ['meɪ·ni·ə] *n* (*obsession*) obsesión *f;* PSYCH manía *f*

maniac ['meɪ·ni·æk] *n* maníaco, -a *m, f*

maniacal [mə·'naɪ·ə·kəl] *adj inf* maníaco, -a

manic ['mæn·ɪk] *adj* maníaco, -a

manic depression *n* manía *f* depresiva

manic depressive *adj* maníaco, -a depresivo, -a

manic psychosis *n* PSYCH psicosis *f inv* maníaca

manicure ['mæn·ɪ·kjʊr] I. *n* manicura *f* II. *vt* **to** ~ **one's fingernails** hacerse la manicura

manicurist ['mæn·ɪ·kjʊr·ɪst] *n* manicuro, -a *m, f,* manicurista *mf AmL*

manifest ['mæn·ɪ·fest] I. *adj form* manifiesto, -a; **to make sth** ~ poner algo de manifiesto II. *vt form* declarar; **to** ~ **symptoms of sth** manifestar síntomas de algo

manifestation [ˌmæn·ɪ·fe·'steɪ·ʃən] *n form* manifestación *f*

manifestly ['mæn·ɪ·fest·li] *adv form* evidentemente

manifesto [ˌmæn·ɪ·'fes·toʊ] <-stos *o* -stoes> *n* manifiesto *m*

manifold ['mæn·ɪ·foʊld] I. *adj liter* múltiple II. *n* TECH, AUTO colector *m;* **exhaust** ~ colector de gases

manikin ['mæn·ɪ·kɪn] *n* **1.** (*model*) maniquí *mf* **2.** (*dwarf*) enano, -a *m, f*

manila envelope [mə·'nɪl·ə·'en·və·loʊp] *n* sobre *m* manila

manioc ['mæn·i·ak] *n* **1.** (*cassava*) yuca *f* **2.** (*flour*) tapioca *f*

manipulate [mə·'nɪp·jə·leɪt] *vt* manipular

manipulation [mə·ˌnɪp·jə·'leɪ·ʃən] *n* manipulación *f*

manipulative [mə·ˌnɪp·jə·'lə·t̬ɪv] *adj* manipulador(a)

manipulator [mə·'nɪp·jə·leɪ·t̬ər] *n* manipulador(a) *m(f)*

mankind [ˌmæn·'kaɪnd] *n* humanidad *f*

manliness ['mæn·li·nɪs] *n* hombría *f*

manly ['mæn·li] <-ier, -iest> *adj* varonil

man-made ['mæn·meɪd] *adj* (*lake*) artificial; (*fiber*) sintético, -a

manna ['mæn·ə] *n* maná *m*

manned [mænd] *adj* AVIAT tripulado, -a

mannequin ['mæn·ɪ·kɪn] *n* **1.** (*dummy*) maniquí *mf* **2.** (*person*) modelo *mf*

manner ['mæn·ər] *n* **1.** (*way, fashion*) manera *f;* **in the** ~ **of sb** al estilo de alguien; **in a** ~ **of speaking** por así decirlo; **a** ~ **of speech** una forma de hablar **2.** (*behavior*) ~ **s** modales *mpl;* **to teach sb** ~ **s** enseñar a alguien a comportarse; **it's bad** ~ **s to...** es de mala educación... **3.** *form* (*kind, type*) clase *f;* **what** ~ **of man is he?** ¿qué tipo de hombre es?; **all** ~ **of...** toda clase de... ▶ **as if to the** ~ **born** como si hubiera nacido para ello

mannered *adj* amanerado, -a

mannerism ['mæn·ə·rɪz·əm] *n* amaneramiento *m*

mannikin ['mæn·ɪ·kɪn] *n s.* **manikin**

mannish ['mæn·ɪʃ] *adj* hombruno, -a

manometer [mə·'nam·ə·t̬ər] *n* manómetro *m*

manor ['mæn·ər] *n* **1.** (*house*) casa *f* solariega **2.** HIST (*territory*) feudo *m*

manpower ['mæn·ˌpaʊ·ər] *n* mano *f* de obra

manservant ['mæn·ˌsɜr·vənt] *n* criado *m*
mansion ['mæn·ʃən] *n* mansión *f*
man-sized *adj* muy grande
manslaughter ['mæn·slɔ·ţər] *n* homicidio *m* involuntario
mantelpiece ['mæn·təl·pis] *n* repisa *f* de la chimenea
mantis ['mæn·ţɪs] *n* mantis *f* religiosa
mantle ['mæn·təl] *n* **1.** *liter* (*cloak, layer*) manto *m;* **a ~ of snow** un manto de nieve **2.** (*of gas lamp*) camisa *f*
man-to-man *adj* franco, -a
mantra ['mæn·trə] *n* mantra *m*
manual ['mæn·ju·əl] **I.** *adj* manual; **~ dexterity** habilidad manual **II.** *n* manual *m;* **instruction ~** manual de instrucciones
manual labor *n* trabajo *m* manual
manually ['mæn·ju·ə·li] *adv* manualmente, con las manos
manual transmission *n* AUTO transmisión *f* manual
manufacture [ˌmæn·ju·'fæk·tʃər] **I.** *vt* **1.** (*produce*) fabricar; **~d goods** artículos manufacturados **2.** (*invent*) inventar; **to ~ an excuse/a story** inventar una excusa/un cuento **II.** *n* **1.** (*production*) manufactura *f* **2.** (*product*) producto *m* manufacturado
manufacturer [ˌmæn·ju·'fæk·ʃər·ər] *n* fabricante *mf;* **~'s label** etiqueta *f* de fábrica; **to send sth back to the ~** devolver algo a la fábrica
manufacturing [ˌmæn·jə·'fæk·tʃər·ɪŋ] *adj* (*region, company*) industrial; **~ industry** industria *f* manufacturera
manure [mə·'nʊr] *n* abono *m*
manuscript ['mæn·ju·skrɪpt] *n* manuscrito *m*
many ['men·i] <more, most> **I.** *adj* muchos, muchas; **how ~ bottles?** ¿cuántas botellas?; **too/so ~ people** demasiada/tanta gente; **one too ~** uno de más; **~ times** muchas veces; **as ~ as...** tantos como... **II.** *pron* muchos, muchas; **~ think that...** muchos piensan que...; **so ~** tantos/tantas; **too ~** demasiados/demasiadas **III.** *n* **a good ~** un gran número
many-sided [ˌmen·i·'saɪ·dɪd] *adj* polifacético, -a
Maoism ['maʊ·ɪz·əm] *n* maoísmo *m*
Maoist ['maʊ·ɪst] **I.** *n* maoísta *mf* **II.** *adj* maoísta
Maori ['maʊ·ri] **I.** *n* maorí *mf* **II.** *adj* maorí
map [mæp] **I.** *n* **1.** (*of region, stars*) mapa *m;* (*of town*) plano *m;* **~ of the world** mapamundi *m;* **road ~** mapa de carreteras **2.** (*simple diagram*) plano *m* ▶ **to blow** [*o* **wipe**] **sth off the ~** borrar algo del mapa; **to put a town on the ~** dar a conocer un pueblo **II.** <-pp-> *vt* trazar un mapa de
◆ **map out** *vt* planear, proyectar; **to ~ a route** planear una ruta; **to ~ a course/a plan/a strategy** proyectar un curso/un plan/una estrategia; **his future is all mapped out for him** tiene la vida planificada
maple ['meɪ·pəl] *n* **1.** (*tree*) arce *m* **2.** (*wood*)

madera *f* de arce
maple leaf *n* hoja *f* de arce
maple sugar *n* azúcar *m* de arce
maple syrup *n* jarabe *m* de arce
map maker *n* cartógrafo, -a *m, f*
map making *n* cartografía *f*
mar [mar] <-rr-> *vt* (*ruin*) echar a perder; (*the fun, the day*) aguar
Mar. *n abbr of* **March** mar.
maraschino cherry [ˌmær·ə·'ʃi·nou·ˌtʃer·i] *n* guinda *f* confitada
marathon ['mær·ə·θən] *n a. fig* maratón *m o f*
marathon runner *n* maratonista *mf*
maraud [mə·'rɔd] *vi* merodear
marauder *n* merodeador(a) *m(f)*
marauding *adj* merodeador(a)
marble ['mar·bəl] *n* **1.** (*stone*) mármol *m;* **~ table** mesa *f* de mármol **2.** (*glass ball*) canica *f*, bolita *f CSur*, metra *f Ven;* **to play ~s** jugar a las canicas ▶ **to lose one's ~s** *inf* perder la cabeza
marble cake *n* pastel de molde con chocolate
march [martʃ] **I.** <-es> *n a.* MIL marcha *f;* **funeral ~** marcha fúnebre; **a 20 mile ~** una marcha de 32 km; **to be on the ~** estar en marcha; **to be within a day's ~** estar a un día de camino **II.** *vi a.* MIL marchar; (*parade*) desfilar; **to ~ into a country** invadir un país **III.** *vt* (*compel to walk*) **to ~ sb off** hacer marchar a alguien
March [martʃ] *n* marzo *m; s.a.* **April**
marching orders ['mar·tʃɪŋ·ˌɔr·dərz] *n* **1.** MIL **to get one's ~** ser despedido **2.** *inf* **to give sb his ~** echar a alguien (del trabajo)
Mardi Gras ['mar·di·ˌgra] *n* **1.** (*Shrove Tuesday*) martes *m* de carnaval **2.** (*carnival*) carnaval *m*

> **i** **Mardi Gras** es el equivalente norteamericano del carnaval. Esta fiesta fue traída por los colonizadores franceses a Nueva Orleans (en lo que posteriormente sería el estado de Luisiana). Aunque la mayoría de las personas piensan en Nueva Orleans cuando oyen la expresión **Mardi Gras**, lo cierto es que esta fiesta también se celebra en otros lugares como Biloxi (Misisipí) y Mobile (Alabama). En Nueva Orleans, los **krewes** (agrupaciones de carnaval) organizan muchas fiestas y bailes durante estos días, y el martes de carnaval se disfrazan y desfilan por las calles a pie, en carrozas o a caballo.

mare [mer] *n* yegua *f*
mare's nest *n* hallazgo *m* ilusorio
margarine ['mar·dʒər·ɪn] *n* margarina *f*
margin ['mar·dʒɪn] *n a.* TYPO margen *m;* **profit ~** margen de ganancia; **narrow** [*o* **tight**] **~** margen reducido; **~ of error** margen de error
marginal ['mar·dʒə·nəl] *adj* marginal; **to be of**

M

~ **interest** ser de interés secundario; ~ **land** tierra *f* marginal

marginalize ['mar·dʒɪ·nə·laɪz] *vt* marginar

marigold ['mær·ɪ·goʊld] *n* caléndula *f*

marihuana *n*, **marijuana** [ˌmær·ɪ·'wa·nə] *n* marihuana *f*

marina [mə·'ri·nə] *n* puerto *m* deportivo

marinade [ˌmær·ɪ·'neɪd] *n* escabeche *m*

marinate ['mær·ɪ·neɪt] *vt* marinar

marine [mə·'rin] I. *adj* (*of the sea*) marino, -a; NAUT marítimo, -a; MIL naval II. *n* infante *m* de marina

marine biologist *n* biólogo, -a *m*, *f* marino, -a

Marine Corps *n* Infantería *f* de Marina de EE.UU.

mariner ['mær·ə·nər] *n liter* marinero, -a *m*, *f*

marionette [ˌmær·i·ə·'net] *n* marioneta *f*

marital ['mær·ɪ·ţəl] *adj* marital; ~ **bliss** felicidad *f* marital; ~ **problems** problemas *mpl* conyugales

marital status *n form* estado *m* civil

maritime ['mær·ɪ·taɪm] *adj form* marítimo, -a

maritime law *n* código *m* marítimo

marjoram ['mar·dʒər·əm] *n* mejorana *f*

mark¹ [mark] I. *n* 1. (*spot, stain*) mancha *f*; (*scratch*) marca *f*; (*trace*) huella *f*; **to leave one's ~ on sth/sb** *fig* dejar sus huellas en algo/alguien 2. (*written sign*) raya *f* 3. (*required standard*) norma *f*; **to be up to the ~** ser satisfactorio; **to not feel up to the ~** no sentirse a la altura de las circunstancias 4. (*target*) blanco *m*; **to hit the ~** dar en el blanco 5. (*starting line*) línea *f* de partida; **on your ~, get set, go!** ¡preparados, listos, ya! 6. LING signo *m*; **punctuation ~** signo de puntuación ▶**to be wide of the ~** fallar por mucho, estar lejos de la verdad II. *vt* 1. (*make a spot, stain*) manchar 2. (*make written sign, indicate*) marcar; **I've ~ed the route on the map** he señalado la ruta en el mapa; **the bottle was ~ed 'poison'** la botella llevaba la etiqueta 'veneno' 3. (*characterize*) distinguir; **to ~ sb as sth** distinguir a alguien como algo 4. (*commemorate*) conmemorar; **to ~ the beginning/end of sth** conmemorar el principio/final de algo; **to ~ the 10th anniversary** celebrar el 10° aniversario

◆**mark down** *vt* 1. (*reduce prices*) rebajar 2. (*jot down*) apuntar 3. SCHOOL **to mark sb down** bajar las calificaciones de alguien 4. *fig* (*assess*) **to mark sb down as sth** catalogar a alguien como algo

◆**mark off** *vt* 1. (*divide land*) demarcar 2. (*cross off*) tachar

◆**mark out** *vt* trazar

◆**mark up** *vt* aumentar

mark² [mark] *n* FIN marco *m*

marked [markt] *adj* 1. (*improvement, difference*) marcado, -a; (*contrast*) acusado, -a 2. (*with distinguishing marks*) marcado, -a 3. (*liable to be attacked*) **to be a ~ man/woman** estar en el punto de mira

markedly ['mar·kəd·li] *adv* notablemente

marker ['mar·kər] *n* 1. (*sign, symbol*) señal *f* 2. (*pen*) rotulador *m*, marcador *m Arg* 3. SPORTS (*indicator*) marcador *m;* **the first-down ~** línea que se encuentra a 10 yardas en los campos de fútbol americano 4. *sl* (*IOU*) pagaré *m*

market ['mar·kɪt] I. *n* mercado *m*, recova *f And, Urug;* **the coffee ~** el mercado del café; **the housing ~** el mercado inmobiliario; **the job ~** el mercado de trabajo; **the stock ~** la bolsa de valores; **to put sth on the ~** poner algo a la venta; **on the ~** a la venta II. *vt* comercializar

marketable *adj* comercial; ~ **commodities** productos *mpl* comerciales

market forces *npl* fuerzas *fpl* del mercado

marketing *n* 1. (*discipline*) marketing *m* 2. (*commercialization*) comercialización *f*

marketing strategy *n* estrategia *f* de mercado

market leader *n* líder *mf* del mercado

marketplace *n* 1. ECON mercado *m* 2. (*square*) plaza *f* (del mercado)

market price *n* precio *m* de mercado

market research *n* estudio *m* de mercado

market researcher *n* investigador(a) *m(f)* de mercado

market trader *n* comerciante *mf*

marking *n* (*identification*) señal *f*; (*on animal*) pinta *f*

marksman ['marks·mən] <-men> *n* tirador *m*

marksmanship ['marks·mən·ʃɪp] *n* puntería *f*

markswoman ['marks·wʊm·ən] <-women> *n* tiradora *f*

markup ['mark·ʌp] *n* margen *m* de ganancia

marmalade ['mar·mə·leɪd] *n* mermelada *f* (*de cítricos*); **orange ~** mermelada de naranja

marmoset ['mar·mə·set] *n* tití *m*

maroon¹ [mə·'run] I. *n* granate *m* II. *adj* granate

maroon² [mə·'run] *vt* abandonar

marquee [mar·'ki] I. *n* 1. (*rooflike structure*) marquesina *f* 2. (*scrolling text*) letrero con el nombre de los artistas en la fachada de un teatro u otro local II. *adj* (*exceptional*) excepcional

marriage ['mær·ɪdʒ] *n* 1. (*wedding*) boda *f* 2. (*relationship, state*) matrimonio *m;* **arranged ~** matrimonio arreglado; **related by ~** emparentado por matrimonio; **he is a relative by ~** es pariente político 3. *fig* (*of organizations*) unión *f*

marriageable *adj* casadero, -a

marriage license *n* licencia *f* matrimonial

marriage of convenience *n* matrimonio *m* de conveniencia

married *adj* (*person*) casado, -a; ~ **couple** matrimonio *m;* ~ **life** vida *f* conyugal; **to be ~ to sth** *fig* estar atado a algo

married name *n* apellido *m* de casada

marrow ['mær·oʊ] *n* MED médula *f*

marrowbone *n* hueso *m* medular

marry ['mær·i] <-ie-> I. *vt* 1. (*become husband or wife*) **to ~ sb** casarse con alguien; **to get married (to sb)** casarse (con alguien)

2. (*priest*) casar **II.** *vi* casarse; **to ~ above/ beneath oneself** casarse con alguien de clase superior/inferior; **to ~ into a wealthy family** emparentar con una familia rica

Mars [marz] *n* Marte *m*

marsh [marʃ] <-es> *n* ciénaga *f*

marshal ['mar·ʃəl] **I.** <-ll-, -l-> *vt* ordenar **II.** *n* **1.** LAW alguacil *mf* **2.** (*police or fire officer*) comisario, -a *m, f* **3.** MIL mariscal(a) *m(f)*; **field ~** mariscal de campo **4.** (*honoree*) **the grand ~** el gran mariscal

marshland ['marʃ·lænd] *n* pantanal *m*

marshmallow ['marʃ·mel·oʊ] *n* **1.** (*sweet*) dulce *m* de malvavisco, carlotina *f* Ven **2.** (*plant*) malvavisco *m*

marshy ['mar·ʃi] <-ier, -iest> *adj* pantanoso, -a

marsupial [mar·'su·pi·əl] **I.** *n* marsupial *m* **II.** *adj* marsupial

marten ['mar·tən] *n* marta *f*

martial ['mar·ʃəl] *adj* marcial

martial arts *n* SPORTS artes *mpl* marciales

martial law *n* ley *f* marcial; **to impose ~ on a country** imponer la ley marcial en un país

Martian ['mar·ʃən] **I.** *adj* marciano, -a **II.** *n* marciano, -a *m, f*

martin ['mar·tən] *n* avión *m*

martinet [ˌmar·tə·'net] *n form* rigorista *mf*

Martinique [ˌmar·tən·'ik] *n* Martinica *f*

martyr ['mar·tər] **I.** *n* mártir *mf*; **to be a ~ to disease** *fig* estar martirizado por la enfermedad **II.** *vt* martirizar; **~ed saint** santo *m* mártir

martyrdom ['mar·tər·dəm] *n* martirio *m*; **to suffer ~** sufrir pena de martirio

marvel ['mar·vəl] **I.** *n* **1.** (*thing*) maravilla *f*; **it's a ~ to me how...** me maravilla cómo... **2.** (*person*) joya *f* **II.** <-ll-, -l-> *vi* **to ~ that...** maravillarse de que... +*subj*; **to ~ at sb/sth** maravillarse de alguien/algo

marvellous *adj*, **marvelous** ['mar·və·ləs] *adj* maravilloso, -a; **to feel ~** sentirse espléndido

Marxism ['mark·sɪz·əm] *n* marxismo *m*

Marxist ['mark·sɪst] **I.** *n* marxista *mf* **II.** *adj* marxista

marzipan ['mar·zɪ·pæn] *n* mazapán *m*

masc. *adj abbr of* **masculine**

mascara [mæ·'skær·ə] *n* rímel *m*

mascot ['mæs·kat] *n* mascota *f*

masculine ['mæs·kjə·lɪn] *adj a.* LING masculino, -a

masculinity [ˌmæs·kjə·'lɪn·ə·t̬i] *n* masculinidad *f*

MASH [mæʃ] *n abbr of* **mobile army surgical hospital** hospital *m* móvil quirúrgico del ejército

mash [mæʃ] **I.** *n* **1.** AGR (*animal feed*) afrecho *m*, salvado *m* **2.** (*fermentable mixture*) malta *f* **II.** *vt* machacar; **to ~ potatoes** hacer puré de patatas

♦**mash up** *vt* CULIN triturar

mask [mæsk] **I.** *n a. fig* máscara *f*; (*only covering eyes*) antifaz *m*; **oxygen ~** máscara de oxígeno **II.** *vt* enmascarar; **to ~ sth with sth** encubrir algo con algo; **to ~ the statistics** ocultar las estadísticas

♦**mask out** *vt* PHOT, TYPO ocultar

masked *adj* enmascarado, -a

masked ball *n* baile *m* de máscaras

masking tape *n* cinta *f* adhesiva protectora

masochism ['mæs·ə·kɪz·əm] *n* masoquismo *m*

masochist ['mæs·ə·kɪst] *n* masoquista *mf*

masochistic [ˌmæs·ə·'kɪs·tɪk] *adj* masoquista

mason ['meɪ·sən] *n* **1.** (*stonecutter*) cantero *m* **2.** (*bricklayer*) albañil *m* **3.** (*Freemason*) masón, -ona *m, f*

Masonic [mə·'san·ɪk] *adj* masónico, -a

masonic [mə·'san·ɪk] *adj* masónico, -a

Masonic Temple *n* templo *m* masónico

masonry ['meɪ·sən·ri] *n* **1.** (*occupation*) albañilería *f* **2.** (*stonework*) mampostería *f* **3.** (*Freemasonry*) masonería *f*

masquerade [ˌmæs·kə·'reɪd] **I.** *n* mascarada *f* **II.** *vi* **to ~ as sth** hacerse pasar por algo

masquerade ball *n* baile *m* de máscaras

mass [mæs] **I.** *n* **1.** *a.* PHYS masa *f* **2.** (*formless substance*) bulto *m* **3.** (*large quantity*) montón *m*; **to be a ~ of contradictions** estar lleno de contradicciones; **the ~ of the people** la muchedumbre; **the ~ of the population** la mayoría de la población **II.** *vi* (*gather*) juntarse; (*troops*) concentrarse **III.** *adj* de masas

Mass [mæs] *n* misa *f*; **to attend ~** ir a misa; **to celebrate a ~** oficiar una misa

Mass. *n abbr of* **Massachusetts** Massachusetts *m*

Massachusetts [ˌmæs·ə·'tʃu·sɪts] *n* Massachusetts *m*

massacre ['mæs·ə·kər] **I.** *n* **1.** (*killing*) masacre *f* **2.** *fig* (*defeat*) aniquilamiento *m* **II.** *vt* **1.** (*kill*) masacrar **2.** *fig* (*defeat*) aniquilar

massage [mə·'sadʒ] **I.** *n* masaje *m*; **to give sb a ~** dar a alguien un masaje; **water ~** hidromasaje *m* **II.** *vt* **1.** dar masajes a **2.** *fig* manipular

massage parlor *n* salón *m* de relax

masseur [mæ·'sɜr] *n* masajista *m*

masseuse [mæ·'sɜz] *n* masajista *f*

mass grave *n* fosa *f* común

massif ['mæs·ɪv] *n* GEO macizo *m*

massive ['mæs·ɪv] *adj* masivo, -a, enorme; **~ amounts of money** grandes cantidades de dinero

mass market *n* mercado *m* de masas

mass-market *adj* de alto consumo

mass media *n* **the ~** los medios de comunicación de masas

mass murder *n* asesinato *m* múltiple

mass murderer *n* asesino, -a *m, f* múltiple

mass-produce *vt* fabricar en serie

mass production *n* fabricación *f* en serie

mass tourism *n* turismo *m* de masas

mass unemployment *n* paro *m* masivo

mast [mæst] *n* **1.** NAUT mástil *m* **2.** (*flag pole*) asta *m*; **at half ~** a media asta **3.** RADIO, TV antena *f*

mastectomy [ˌmæs·'tek·tə·mi] <-ies> *n* mastectomía *f*

M

master ['mæs·tər] I. n 1. (of house) señor m; (of slave) amo m; (of dog) dueño m 2. (one who excels) maestro m; ~ **craftsman** maestro; **to be a ~ of sth** ser experto en algo 3. (instructor) instructor m; **dancing/singing** ~ instructor de baile/canto; **fencing** ~ maestro de esgrima 4. (master copy) original m ▶ **to be one's own** ~ no depender de nadie; **jack of all** trades, ~ **of none** aprendiz de todo, oficial de nada prov II. vt 1. (cope with) vencer; **to ~ one's fear of flying** superar el miedo a volar 2. (become proficient at) dominar

master bedroom n dormitorio m principal

master copy <-ies> n original m

masterful ['mæs·tər·fəl] adj 1. (authoritative) autoritario, -a 2. (skillful) magistral

master key n llave f maestra

masterly ['mæs·tər·li] adj magistral

mastermind ['mæs·tər·maɪnd] I. n cerebro m II. vt (activity) planear; (crime) ser el cerebro de

Master of Arts n licenciado, -a m, f con máster (en Humanidades o en Filosofía y Letras)

Master of Ceremonies n maestro m de ceremonias

masterpiece n obra f maestra

master plan n plan m maestro

master race n raza f superior

Master's n, **Master's degree** n máster m

ℹ️ En Estados Unidos se llama **Master's degree** al grado académico que se obtiene al finalizar una carrera universitaria, tras la defensa de una tesina (**Master's thesis** o **dissertation**). El **Master's degree** le sigue al **Bachelor's degree** (licenciatura) y recibe distintos nombres, según las disciplinas: MA (Master of Arts), MSc (Master of Science) y MPhil (Master of Philosophy).

---

masterstroke n toque m magistral

master switch <-es> n interruptor m principal

masterwork n s. **masterpiece**

mastery ['mæs·tə·ri] n (skill) maestría f; (sway) dominio m

masticate ['mæs·tɪ·keɪt] vt masticar

mastication [ˌmæs·tɪ·ˈkeɪ·ʃən] n masticación m

mastitis [mæ·ˈstaɪ·ṭɪs] n mastitis f

masturbate ['mæs·tər·beɪt] I. vi masturbarse II. vt masturbar

masturbation [ˌmæs·tər·ˈbeɪ·ʃən] n masturbación f, pascuala f Méx

mat¹ [mæt] n 1. (on floor) estera f; (decorative) tapiz m; **bath** ~ alfombra f de baño 2. (on table) salvamanteles m inv 3. SPORTS (in gymnastics) colchoneta f 4. (thick layer: of grass, hair) maraña f

mat² adj, **matte** [mæt] adj mate

matador ['mæṭ·ə·dɔr] n matador m

match¹ [mætʃ] <-es> n (for making fire) cerilla f, fósforo m, cerillo m Méx; **box of** ~**es** caja de fósforos

match² [mætʃ] I. n 1. (competitor) contrincante mf; **to be a good** ~ **for sb** poder competir con alguien; **to be no** ~ **for sb** no poder competir con alguien; **to meet one's** ~ encontrar la horma de su zapato 2. (similarity) **to be a good** ~ combinar bien 3. (in marriage) **to make a good** ~ casarse bien 4. SPORTS partido m; **wrestling** ~ combate m de lucha libre II. vi (harmonize: design, color) armonizar, pegar; (description) coincidir III. vt 1. (have same color) hacer juego con 2. (equal) igualar

◆**match against** vt always sep enfrentar

◆**match up** I. vi 1. (make sense) concordar 2. (align) alinear 3. **to ~ to sth** estar a la altura de algo II. vt (put together) emparejar

matchbox ['mætʃ·baks] <-es> n caja f de cerillas, cerillero m AmL

matching ['mætʃ·ɪŋ] adj que hace juego

matchless ['mætʃ·lɪs] adv incomparable

matchmaker ['mætʃ·meɪ·kər] n casamentero, -a m, f

match point n SPORTS bola f de partido

matchstick ['mætʃ·stɪk] n cerilla f, fósforo m, cerillo m Méx

mate¹ [meɪt] I. n 1. (spouse) cónyuge mf 2. ZOOL (male) macho m; (female) hembra f 3. NAUT oficial m de a bordo; **first/second** ~ primer/segundo oficial 4. (one of a pair) compañero, -a m, f II. vi aparearse III. vt aparear

mate² [meɪt] I. n GAMES mate m II. vt dar el mate a

material [mə·ˈtɪr·i·əl] I. n 1. PHILOS, PHYS materia f 2. (physical substance) material m; **raw** ~ materia f prima 3. (information) **publicity** ~ material m publicitario 4. (cloth) tela f 5. (textile) tejido m 6. ~**s** (equipment) materiales mpl; **writing** ~(**s**) útiles mpl de escritura II. adj 1. (physical) material; ~ **damage** daño m material 2. (important) importante; **to be ~ to sth** ser importante para algo

materialism [mə·ˈtɪr·i·ə·lɪz·əm] n materialismo m

materialist n materialista mf

materialistic [mə·ˌtɪr·i·ə·ˈlɪs·tɪk] adj materialista

materialize [mə·ˈtɪr·i·ə·laɪz] vi 1. (take physical form) materializarse 2. (hope, idea) realizarse 3. (appear) aparecer

material witness <-es> n testigo mf presencial

maternal [mə·ˈtɜr·nəl] adj 1. (feeling) maternal 2. (relative) materno, -a

maternity [mə·ˈtɜr·nə·ṭi] n maternidad f

maternity clothes npl ropa f premamá

maternity leave n baja f por maternidad

maternity ward n sala f de maternidad

math [mæθ] n inf abbr of **mathematics** mates fpl

mathematical [ˌmæθ·ə·ˈmæṭ·ɪ·kəl] adj matemático, -a

mathematician [ˌmæθ·ə·mə·'tɪʃ·ən] *n* matemático, -a *m, f*

mathematics [ˌmæθ·ə·'mæt̬·ɪks] *n* matemáticas *fpl*

matinee ['mæt̬·ə·neɪ] *n* CINE primera sesión *f;* THEAT función *f* de tarde

mating ['meɪ·t̬ɪŋ] *n* apareamiento *m*

mating season *n* época *f* de celo

matriarch ['meɪ·tri·ɑrk] *n* matriarca *f*

matrices ['meɪ·trɪ·siz] *n pl of* **matrix**

matriculate [mə·'trɪk·jə·leɪt] I. *vi* matricularse II. *vt* matricular

matriculation [mə·ˌtrɪk·jə·'leɪ·ʃən] *n* matrícula *f*

matrimonial [ˌmæt·rə·'moʊ·ni·əl] *adj form* matrimonial

matrimony ['mæt·rə·moʊ·ni] *n* matrimonio *m*

matrix ['meɪ·trɪks] <-ices> *n a.* MATH matriz *f*

matrix printer *n* COMPUT impresora *f* de matriz de punto

matron ['meɪ·trən] *n* 1.(*middle-aged woman*) matrona *f* 2.(*prison guard*) carcelera *f*

matronly ['meɪ·trən·li] *adj iron* de matrona; **a ~ figure** una persona madura y corpulenta

matron of honor *n* dama *f* de honor (*casada*)

matted *adj* enmarañado, -a

matter ['mæt̬·ər] I. *n* 1.(*subject*) materia *f;* (*question, affair*) asunto *m;* **that's another ~ altogether** eso es harina de otro costal *fig;* **that's no laughing ~** no es cosa de risa; **to do sth as a ~ of course** hacer algo como parte del procedimiento habitual; **the ~ at hand** el asunto a tratar; **it's a ~ of life or death** es una cuestión de vida o muerte; **money ~s** asuntos financieros; **a ~ of opinion** una cuestión de opinión; **the truth of the ~** la verdad de las cosas; **personal ~** asunto privado 2.**~s** (*situation*) situación *f;* **to make ~s worse** por si eso fuera poco; **to help ~s** mejorar las cosas 3.(*wrong*) problema *m;* **what's the ~ with you?** ¿qué te pasa?; **what's the ~ with asking for a pay raise?** ¿qué problema hay en pedir un aumento de sueldo? 4.(*material*) material *m;* **advertising ~** material publicitario 5.(*amount*) **a ~ of...** cosa de...; **in a ~ of seconds** en cuestión de segundos 6.(*substance*) materia *f* II. *vi* importar; **it really ~s to me** me importa mucho; **no ~ what they say** no importa lo que digan, digan lo que digan; **it doesn't ~ if...** no importa si...; **it ~s that...** importa que... +*subj;* **what ~s now is that...** lo que importa ahora es que...

matter-of-fact [ˌmæt̬·ər·əv·'fækt] *adj* 1.(*practical*) práctico, -a 2.(*emotionless*) prosaico, -a

matter-of-factly *adv* 1.(*practically*) prácticamente 2.(*emotionlessly*) prosaicamente

matting ['mæt̬·ɪŋ] *n* 1.(*floor covering*) estera *f* 2.(*tangling*) enmarañamiento *m*

mattress ['mæt·rɪs] *n* colchón *m*

mature [mə·'tʃʊr] I. *adj* 1.(*person, attitude*) maduro, -a; (*animal*) adulto, -a; **to be ~ beyond one's years** ser muy maduro para su

edad; **after ~ reflection** después de una larga reflexión 2.(*wine*) añejo, -a; (*cheese*) curado, -a; (*fruit*) maduro, -a 3. FIN vencido, -a II. *vi* 1.*a. fig* madurar 2. FIN vencer III. *vt* 1.(*cheese, ham*) curar; (*wine*) añejar 2.(*person*) hacer madurar

maturity [mə·'tʃʊr·ə·t̬i] *n* <-ies> 1.(*of person, attitude*) madurez *f;* **to come to ~** llegar a la madurez 2. FIN vencimiento *m;* **to reach ~** alcanzar la madurez

maudlin ['mɔd·lɪn] *adj* 1.(*sentimental*) sensiblero, -a 2.(*tearful*) llorón, -ona

maul [mɔl] *vt* 1.(*wound*) herir 2.(*criticize*) vapulear

Mauritania [ˌmɔr·ɪ·'ter·ni·ə] *n* Mauritania *f*

Mauritanian I. *n* mauritano, -a *m, f* II. *adj* mauritano, -a

Mauritian I. *n* mauriciano, -a *m, f* II. *adj* mauriciano, -a

Mauritius [mɔ·'rɪʃ·i·əs] *n* Mauricio *m*

mausoleum [ˌmɔ·sə·'li·əm] *n* mausoleo *m*

mauve [moʊv] *adj* malva

maverick ['mæv·ər·ɪk] *n* 1. ZOOL res *f* sin marcar 2.(*person*) inconformista *mf*

mawkish ['mɔ·kɪʃ] *adj* (*sentimental*) empalagoso, -a *fig*

max. *inf abbr of* **maximum** máx.

maxim ['mæk·sɪm] *n* máxima *f*

maximal ['mæk·sɪ·məl] *adj form* máximo, -a

maximize ['mæk·sɪ·maɪz] *vt* maximizar

maximum ['mæk·sɪ·məm] I. *n* máximo *m;* **to do sth to the ~** hacer algo al máximo; **to reach a ~** llegar al máximo II. *adj* máximo, -a; **this car has a ~ speed of 100 mph** este coche alcanza una velocidad máxima de 160 km/h

maximum security prison *n* prisión *f* de máxima seguridad

may¹ [meɪ] <might, might> *aux* 1.*form* (*be allowed*) poder; **~ I come in?** ¿puedo pasar?; **~ I ask you a question?** ¿puedo hacerte una pregunta? 2.(*possibility*) ser posible; **it ~ rain** puede que llueva; **be that as it ~** en cualquier caso 3.(*hope, wish*) **~ she rest in peace** que en paz descanse

may² [meɪ] *n* (*bush*) espino *m;* (*flower*) flor *f* de espino

May [meɪ] *n* mayo *m; s.a.* **April**

maybe ['meɪ·bi] I. *adv* 1.(*perhaps*) quizás 2.(*approximately*) probablemente; **~ as many as two hundred people** unas doscientas personas II. *n* quizás *m;* **a definite ~** un quizás definitivo

mayday ['meɪ·deɪ] *n* S.O.S. *m*

May Day *n* primero *m* de mayo

mayfly ['meɪ·flaɪ] *n* <-ies> cachipolla *f*

mayhem ['meɪ·hem] *n* caos *m inv;* **it was utter ~** era un caos total

mayo ['meɪ·oʊ] *n inf abbr of* **mayonnaise** mayonesa *f*

mayonnaise [ˌmeɪ·ə·'neɪz] *n* mayonesa *f*

mayor ['meɪ·ər] *n* alcalde(sa) *m(f)*

maypole ['meɪ·poʊl] *n* mayo *m* (*palo*)

M

may've *inf* = **may have** *s*. **may**

maze [meɪz] *n* laberinto *m*

MB [ˌemˈbi] *abbr of* **megabyte** MB

MBA [ˌemˈbiˈeɪ] *n abbr of* **Master of Business Administration** máster *m* en administración de empresas

MC [ˌemˈsi] *n* 1. *abbr of* **Master of Ceremonies** maestro, -a *m, f* de ceremonias 2. *abbr of* **Member of Congress** diputado, -a *m, f* del Congreso (de EE.UU.)

MD [ˌemˈdi] *n* 1. *abbr of* **Doctor of Medicine** Dr. *m*, Dra. *f* 2. *abbr of* **Maryland** Maryland *m* 3. *abbr of* **muscular dystrophy** distrofia *f* muscular

Md. *n abbr of* **Maryland** Maryland *m*

Me. *n abbr of* **Maine** Maine *m*

ME [meɪn] *n abbr of* **Maine** Maine *m*

me [mi] *pron* 1. me; **look at ~** mírame; **she saw ~** me vio; **he told ~ that...** me dijo que...; **he gave ~ the pencil** me dio el lápiz 2. *(after verb 'to be')* yo; **it's ~** soy yo; **she is older than ~** ella es mayor que yo 3. *(after prep)* mí; **is this for ~?** ¿es para mí esto?

meadow [ˈmedˈoʊ] *n* pradera *f*

meager *adj*, **meagre** [ˈmiˈgər] *adj* escaso, -a

meal[1] [mil] *n* comida *f*; **a heavy/light ~** una comida pesada/ligera; **to go out for a ~** comer/cenar fuera; **~s on wheels** distribución de comida a domicilio para gente necesitada o imposibilitada ► **to make a ~ of sth** hacer una montaña de algo

meal[2] [mil] *n* *(flour)* harina *f*

meal ticket *n* 1. *(lunch voucher)* vale *m* de comida 2. *fig (means of living)* fuente *f* de ingresos; **he's her latest ~** es el que la mantiene últimamente

mealtime [ˈmilˈtaɪm] *n* hora *f* de comer

mean[1] [min] *adj* 1. *(unkind)* vil; **to be ~ to sb** tratar mal a alguien; **to have a ~ streak** tener muy mala uva *inf* 2. *sl (excellent)* de la hostia; **he is one ~ cook** es un cocinero de la hostia

mean[2] [min] <meant, meant> *vt* 1. *(signify: word, event)* significar; **does that name ~ anything to you?** ¿te suena ese nombre? 2. *(express, indicate: person)* querer decir; **what do you ~?** ¿a qué te refieres?; **what do you ~ it was my fault?** ¿quieres decir que fue culpa mía?; **I ~ what I say** digo lo que pienso 3. *(intend for particular purpose)* destinar; **to be meant for sth** estar destinado a algo; **to be meant for each other** estar hechos el uno para el otro; **it was meant to be...** se suponía que iba a ser... 4. *(intend)* pretender; **to ~ to do sth** tener la intención de hacer algo; **to ~ well** tener buenas intenciones; **I ~ to say...** quiero decir...; **what do you ~ by arriving so late?** ¿qué te propones al llegar tan tarde? ► **to ~ business** *inf* hablar muy en serio

meander [mɪˈænˈdər] **I.** *n* meandro *m* **II.** *vi* 1. *(flow)* serpentear 2. *fig (wander)* vagar; *(digress)* divagar

meandering [mɪˈænˈdərˈɪŋ] *adj* 1. *(river)* sinuoso, -a 2. *(explanation)* confuso, -a

meanie [ˈmiˈni] *n* *inf* malo, -a *m, f*

meaning [ˈmiˈnɪŋ] *n* significado *m*; **to give sth a whole new ~** dar a algo un significado completamente nuevo; **what is the ~ of this?** ¿qué significa esto?; **the full ~ of sth** el sentido completo de algo; **to have ~ for sb** tener significado para alguien

meaningful [ˈmiˈnɪŋˈfəl] *adj* 1. *(difference, change)* significativo, -a 2. *(look, smile)* expresivo, -a 3. *(relationship)* importante

meaningless [ˈmiˈnɪŋˈlɪs] *adj* sin sentido

meanness [ˈminˈnɪs] *n* bajeza *f*

means [minz] *npl* 1. *(instrument, method)* medio *m*; **~ of communication/transport** medio de comunicación/transporte 2. *pl* *(resources)* medios *mpl*; **~ of support** medios de subsistencia; **ways and ~** medios y arbitrios; **by ~ of sth** por medio de algo; **to try by all (possible) ~ to do sth** intentar hacer algo por todos los medios; **to use all the ~ at one's disposal** usar todos los medios a su alcance 3. *pl (income)* recursos *mpl*; **a person of ~** una persona acaudalada; **private ~** fondos *mpl* privados; **to be without ~** form estar sin recursos; **to live beyond one's ~** vivir por encima de sus posibilidades ► **by all ~!** ¡por supuesto!; **by no ~** de ninguna manera

meant [ment] *pt, pp of* **mean**

meantime [ˈminˈtaɪm] **I.** *adv* mientras tanto **II.** *n* **in the ~** mientras tanto

meanwhile [ˈminˈhwaɪl] *adv* mientras tanto

meany [ˈmiˈni] *n inf* s. **meanie**

measles [ˈmiˈzəlz] *n* sarampión *m*

measly [ˈmiˈzli] *adj* <-ier, -iest> miserable

measurable [ˈmeʒˈərˈəˈbəl] *adj* 1. *(quantifiable)* medible 2. *(perceptible)* apreciable

measure [ˈmeʒˈər] **I.** *vt* medir; **to ~ sth in feet and inches** calcular algo en pies/pulgadas **II.** *vi* medir; **the box ~s 4 in. by 4 in. by 6 in.** la caja mide 10 cm por 10 cm por 15 cm **III.** *n* 1. *(size)* medida *f* 2. *(measuring instrument)* metro *m*; *(ruler)* regla *f* 3. *(proof)* medición *f* 4. **~s** *(action)* medidas *fpl;* **to take ~s to do sth** tomar medidas para hacer algo 5. *(degree, amount)* grado *m;* **there was some ~ of truth in what he said** hubo algo de cierto en lo que él dijo; **in some ~** hasta cierto punto 6. LIT metro *m* 7. MUS compás *m* ► **for good ~** por añadidura; **beyond ~** excesivamente

◆ **measure off** *vt* 1. *(for cutting)* medir 2. *(mark limits of)* delimitar

◆ **measure up** *vi* dar la talla; **to not ~ to sth** no estar a la altura de algo

measured *adj* *(response)* moderado, -a; *(voice, tone)* comedido, -a

measurement [ˈmeʒˈərˈmənt] *n* 1. *(size)* medida *f* 2. *(dimension of body)* medida; **to take sb's ~s** tomar a alguien las medidas 3. *(act of measuring)* medición *f*

measuring cup *n* vaso *m* medidor

measuring spoon *n* cuchara *f* medidora

meat [mit] *n* 1. carne *f* 2. *fig (essence)* sustancia *f* **3.** *fig* (*target*) this guy is fresh ~ ese tío es carne fresca ▶ one man's ~ is another man's poison *prov* lo que a uno cura a otro mata *prov*

meat-and-potatoes [ˌmit·ənd·pə·'teɪ·ţouz] *n inf* lo básico

meatball *n* albóndiga *f*

meat cleaver *n* cuchillo *m* de carnicero

meat grinder *n* picadora *f* de carne

meat hook *n* gancho *m* de carnicería

meat loaf *n* pastel *m* de carne

meat market *n sl* bar *m* de ligue

Mecca ['mek·ə] *n* REL La Meca

mecca ['mek·ə] *n* (*center*) meca *f*

mechanic [mɪ·'kæn·ɪk] *n* mecánico, -a *m, f*

mechanical *adj* **1.** (*relating to machines*) mecánico, -a **2.** (*without thinking*) maquinal

mechanical engineer *n* ingeniero, -a *m, f* mecánico, -a

mechanical engineering *n* ingeniería *f* mecánica

mechanical pencil *n* portaminas *m inv*

mechanics [mɪ·'kæn·ɪks] *npl* **1.** AUTO, TECH mecánica *f* **2.** *inf* (*how things are organized*) mecanismo *m*

mechanism ['mek·ə·nɪz·əm] *n* mecanismo *m*

mechanize ['mek·ə·naɪz] *vt* mecanizar

MEd [ˌem·'ed] *n abbr of* **Master of Education** diplomado , -a en pedagogía

med. *adj abbr of* **medium** mediano, -a

medal ['med·əl] *n* medalla *f*

medalist ['med·əl·ɪst] *n* medallista *mf*

medallion [mə·'dæl·jən] *n* medallón *m*

meddle ['med·əl] *vi* to ~ in sth entrometerse en algo

meddlesome ['med·əl·səm] *adj* entrometido, -a, metiche *Méx*, toposo, -a *Ven*

media ['mi·di·ə] *n* **1.** *pl of* **medium 2.** the ~ los medios; the mass ~ los medios de comunicación de masas; a ~ event un acontecimiento mediático

media campaign *n* campaña *f* de prensa

mediaeval [ˌmi·di·'i·vəl] *adj s.* **medieval**

media magnate *n*, **media mogul** *n* magnate *m* de la prensa

median ['mi·di·ən] *adj* mediano, -a

median strip *n* AUTO raya *f* divisoria

mediate ['mi·di·eɪt] I. *vi* mediar; to ~ between two groups/in sth mediar entre dos grupos/en algo II. *vt* to ~ a settlement hacer de intermediario en un acuerdo

mediation [ˌmi·di·'eɪ·ʃən] *n* mediación *f*

mediator ['mi·di·eɪ·ţər] *n* mediador(a) *m(f)*

medic ['med·ɪk] *n* médico, -a *m, f*

Medicaid ['med·ɪ·keɪd] *n* programa de asistencia sanitaria gratuita para personas con pocos ingresos

medical ['med·ɪ·kəl] I. *adj* médico, -a II. *n inf* reconocimiento *m* médico

medical examination *n* reconocimiento *m* médico

medical history *n* historial *m* clínico

medicament [mɪ·'dɪk·ə·mənt] *n* medi-

camento *m*

Medicare ['med·ɪ·ker] *n* programa de asistencia sanitaria para personas mayores de 65 años

medicate ['med·ɪ·keɪt] *vt* (*treat medically*) medicar

medicated *adj* (*soap, shampoo*) medicinal

medication [ˌmed·ɪ·'keɪ·ʃən] <-(s)> *n* medicamento *m*

medicinal [mə·'dɪs·ə·nəl] *adj* medicinal

medicine ['med·ɪ·sɪn] *n* **1.** (*substance*) medicamento *m;* to take (one's) ~ tomarse su medicina **2.** (*medical knowledge*) medicina *f* **3.** (*remedy*) remedio *m* ▶ to give sb a taste of his/her own ~ pagar a alguien con su misma moneda

medicine ball *n* balón *m* medicinal

medicine cabinet *n*, **medicine chest** *n* botiquín *m*

medicine man *n* <-men> hechicero *m*

medieval [ˌmi·di·'i·vəl] *adj* medieval

mediocre [ˌmi·di·'ou·kər] *adj* mediocre

mediocrity [ˌmi·di·'ak·rə·ţi] *n* **1.** (*quality*) mediocridad *f* **2.** (*person*) mediocre *mf*

meditate ['med·ɪ·teɪt] I. *vi* **1.** (*engage in contemplation*) meditar **2.** (*think deeply*) reflexionar; to ~ on sth reflexionar sobre algo II. *vt* (*plan: revenge*) planear

meditation [ˌmed·ɪ·'teɪ·ʃən] *n* meditación *f*

Mediterranean [ˌmed·ɪ·tə·'reɪ·ni·ən] I. *n* Mediterráneo *m* II. *adj* mediterráneo, -a

Mediterranean Sea *n* mar *m* Mediterráneo

medium ['mi·di·əm] I. *adj* **1.** (*not big or small*) mediano, -a **2.** CULIN a punto, término medio, medio hecho II. *n* **1.** <media *o* -s> (*method*) medio *m;* through the ~ of por medio de **2.** COMPUT soporte *m;* data ~ soporte de datos **3.** <-s> (*spiritualist*) médium *mf*

medium-dry *adj* semi seco, -a

medium-rare *adj* CULIN poco hecho, -a

medium-sized *adj* mediano, -a

medley ['med·li] *n* **1.** (*mixture*) mezcla *f* **2.** MUS popurrí *m*

meek [mik] *adj* manso, -a

meet [mit] <met, met> I. *vt* **1.** (*encounter*) encontrarse con; (*intentionally*) reunirse con; (*for first time*) conocer a; to arrange to ~ sb quedar con alguien **2.** (*wait for: at train station, airport*) ir a buscar a alguien **3.** (*confront: opponent*) enfrentarse con; (*problem*) tropezar con **4.** (*fulfill*) reunir; (*cost*) correr con; (*demand*) atender; (*obligation*) cumplir II. *vi* **1.** (*encounter*) encontrarse; (*intentionally*) reunirse; (*for first time*) conocerse; to arrange to ~ quedar **2.** (*join: lines*) unirse; (*rivers*) confluir **3.** SPORTS enfrentarse III. *n* (*sporting event*) encuentro *m;* a track ~ pruebas de atletismo

◆ **meet with** *vt insep* reunirse con; to ~ success tener éxito; to meet force with force combatir la fuerza con la fuerza

meeting ['mi·ţɪŋ] *n* **1.** (*gathering*) reunión *f;* to call a ~ convocar una reunión **2.** POL mitin

m **3.** (*casual*) encuentro *m*
meeting point *n* punto *m* de encuentro
megabyte ['meg·ə·baɪt] *n* COMPUT megabyte *m*
megahertz ['meg·ə·hɜrts] *n* ELEC megahercio *m*
megalomania [ˌmeg·ə·loʊ·'meɪ·ni·ə] *n* megalomanía *f*
megalomaniac [ˌmeg·ə·loʊ·'meɪ·ni·æk] *n* megalómano, -a *m, f*
megaphone ['meg·ə·foʊn] *n* megáfono *m*
megastore ['meg·ə·stɔr] *n* gran almacén *m*
megawatt ['meg·ə·wat] *n* megavatio *m*
melancholic [ˌmel·ən·'kal·ɪk] *adj* melancólico, -a
melancholy ['mel·ən·kal·i] **I.** *n* melancolía *f* **II.** *adj* melancólico, -a
melee ['meɪ·leɪ] *n* **1.** (*fight*) riña *f* **2.** (*crowd*) enjambre *m*
mellow ['mel·oʊ] **I.** *adj* <-er, -est> **1.** (*light: voice*) suave; (*flavor*) dulce **2.** (*mature: wine*) añejo, -a **3.** (*relaxed*) tranquilo, -a **II.** *vi* (*person, fruit*) madurar; (*voice, color*) suavizarse **III.** *vt* **1.** (*wine*) añejar **2.** (*make less severe*) suavizar
melodic [mə·'lad·ɪk] *adj* melódico, -a
melodious [mə·'loʊ·di·əs] *adj* melodioso, -a
melodrama ['mel·oʊ·dra·mə] *n* melodrama *m*
melodramatic [ˌmel·oʊ·drə·'mæt̬·ɪk] *adj* melodramático, -a
melody ['mel·ə·di] <-ies> *n* melodía *f*
melon ['mel·ən] *n* melón *m*; (*watermelon*) sandía *f*
melt [melt] **I.** *vt* (*metal*) fundir; (*ice, chocolate*) derretir **II.** *vi* **1.** (*metal*) fundirse; (*ice, chocolate*) derretirse **2.** *fig* enternecerse
meltdown ['melt·daʊn] *n* fusión *f*
melting point *n* punto *m* de fusión
melting pot *n a. fig* crisol *m*
member ['mem·bər] *n* miembro *mf*; (*of society, club*) socio, -a *m, f*
membership *n* **1.** (*state of belonging*) calidad *f* de miembro; (*to society, club*) calidad *f* de socio; **to apply for ~ to a club** solicitar ingreso en un club; **~ dues** cuotas *fpl* de socio **2.** (*number of members*) número *m* de socios
membership card *n* carnet *m* de socio
membrane ['mem·breɪn] *n* membrana *f*
memento [mə·'men·toʊ] <-s *o* -es> *n* recuerdo *m*
memo ['mem·oʊ] *n abbr of* **memorandum** **1.** (*message*) memorándum *m* **2.** (*note*) nota *f*
memoir ['mem·war] *n* **1.** (*record of events*) memoria *f* **2.** *pl* (*autobiography*) memorias *fpl*
memorabilia [ˌmem·ər·ə·'bɪl·i·ə] *npl* recuerdos *mpl*
memorable ['mem·ər·ə·bəl] *adj* memorable
memorandum [ˌmem·ə·'ræn·dəm] <-s *o* -anda> *n form* **1.** (*message*) memorándum *m* **2.** (*note*) nota *f*
memorial [mə·'mɔr·i·əl] **I.** *n* monumento *m* conmemorativo **II.** *adj* conmemorativo, -a
Memorial Day *n* Día *m* de los Caídos

ⓘ El **Memorial Day** se celebra el último lunes de mayo y es fiesta oficial en EE.UU. Este día se recuerda a los caídos en todas las guerras en las que han participado EE.UU.

memorize ['mem·ə·raɪz] *vt* memorizar
memory ['mem·ə·ri] <-ies> *n* **1.** (*ability to remember*) memoria *f*; **to recite sth from ~** recitar algo de memoria; **if my ~ serves me correctly** si la memoria no me falla **2.** (*remembered event*) recuerdo *m*; **to bring back memories** evocar recuerdos **3.** COMPUT memoria *f*; **internal/external/core ~** memoria interna/externa/del núcleo; **cache ~** memoria (intermedia) del caché; **read only ~** memoria de sólo lectura; **random access ~** memoria de acceso aleatorio
memory lane *n* **to take a walk down ~** rememorar el pasado
men [men] *n pl of* **man**
menace ['men·əs] **I.** *n* **1.** (*threat*) amenaza *f* **2.** (*child*) demonio *m*, peligro *m* **II.** *vt* amenazar
menacing *adj* amenazador(a)
menacingly *adv* de modo amenazador
ménage à trois [meɪˌnaʒ·a·'trwa] *n* <ménages à trois> ménage à trois *m*
menagerie [mə·'næʒ·ə·ri] *n* colección *f* de animales salvajes, casa *f* de fieras
mend [mend] **I.** *n* **1.** (*repair*) reparación *f* **2.** (*patch*) remiendo *m* **3.** *inf* **to be on the ~** ir mejorando **II.** *vt* **1.** (*repair*) reparar **2.** (*darn: socks*) zurcir **III.** *vi* (*improve*) mejorar; (*broken bone*) soldarse
mending ['men·dɪŋ] *n* **1.** (*repair work*) reparación *f* **2.** (*darning*) zurcido *m* **3.** (*clothes*) ropa *f* por remendar
menial ['mi·ni·əl] *adj* de baja categoría; **~ labor** trabajo *m* degradante
meningitis [ˌmen·ɪn·'dʒaɪ·t̬ɪs] *n* meningitis *f inv*
menopause ['men·ə·pɔz] *n* menopausia *f*
men's room ['menz·ˌrum] *n* lavabo *m* de hombres
menstrual ['men·stru·əl] *adj* menstrual
menstruate ['men·stru·eɪt] *vi* menstruar
menstruation [ˌmen·stru·'eɪ·ʃən] *n* menstruación *f*
mental ['men·t̬əl] *adj* **1.** (*of the mind*) mental **2.** *offensive, sl* (*crazy*) chiflado, -a
mental arithmetic *n* cálculo *m* mental
mental hospital *n* hospital *m* psiquiátrico
mental illness *n* <-es> enfermedad *f* mental
mentality [men·'tæl·ə·t̬i] <-ies> *n* mentalidad *f*
mentally *adv* mentalmente; **~ disturbed** trastornado, -a
mentally handicapped *adj* **to be ~** tener una minusvalía psíquica
menthol ['men·θəl] *n* mentol *m*
mention ['men·ʃən] **I.** *n* mención *f*; **to receive a (special) ~** obtener una mención (especial);

to make ~ of sth mencionar algo; **honorable ~** mención de honor **II.** *vt* mencionar; **don't ~ it!** ¡no hay de qué!; **not to ~...** sin contar...

mentor ['men·tər] *n* mentor(a) *m(f)*

menu ['men·ju] *n* **1.** (*list of dishes*) carta *f;* (*fixed meal*) menú *m* **2.** COMPUT menú; **context/pull-down ~** menú contextual/desplegable

menu bar *n* barra *f* de menús

menu-driven *adj* COMPUT guiado, -a por menús

meow [mi·'aʊ] **I.** *n* miau *m* **II.** *vi* maullar

mercenary ['mɜr·sə·ner·i] **I.** *n* <-ies> mercenario, -a *m, f* **II.** *adj* mercenario, -a

merchandise ['mɜr·tʃən·daɪz] *n* mercancía *f*

merchant ['mɜr·tʃənt] *n* comerciante *mf*

merchantman <-men> *n* buque *m* mercante

merchant marine *n* marina *f* mercante

merchant ship *n* mercante *m*

merciful ['mɜr·sɪ·fəl] *adj* misericordioso, -a

merciless ['mɜr·sɪ·lɪs] *adj* despiadado, -a

mercurial [mɜr·'kjʊr·i·əl] *adj* **1.** CHEM mercurial **2.** (*changeable*) voluble **3.** (*lively*) vivo, -a

mercury ['mɜr·kjə·ri] *n* mercurio *m*

Mercury ['mɜr·kjə·ri] *n* Mercurio *m*

mercy ['mɜr·si] *n* **1.** (*compassion*) compasión *f;* **to have ~ on sb** tener compasión de alguien **2.** (*forgiveness*) misericordia *f;* **to be at the ~ of sb** estar a merced de alguien; **to throw oneself upon sb's ~** abandonarse a la merced de alguien; **to plead for ~** pedir clemencia

mere [mɪr] *adj* mero, -a; **a ~ formality** una simple formalidad

merely ['mɪr·li] *adv* solamente

merge [mɜrdʒ] **I.** *vi* unirse; ECON, POL fusionarse; **to ~ into sth** fundirse con algo **II.** *vt* unir; ECON, POL, COMPUT fusionar

merger ['mɜr·dʒər] *n* ECON fusión *f*

meridian [mə·'rɪd·i·ən] *n* meridiano *m*

meringue [mə·'ræŋ] *n* merengue *m,* espumilla *f Ecua, Guat, Hond*

merit ['mer·ɪt] **I.** *n* **1.** (*virtue*) cualidad *f* **2.** (*advantage*) ventaja *f* **3.** *pl* (*commendable quality or act*) mérito *m;* **to achieve sth on one's own ~s** conseguir algo por mérito propio **II.** *vt* merecer; **this ~s another look** esto merece una reconsideración

meritocracy [ˌmer·ɪ·'tak·rə·si] <-ies> *n* meritocracia *f*

mermaid ['mɜr·meɪd] *n* sirena *f*

merriment ['mer·ɪ·mənt] *n* **1.** (*laughter and joy*) regocijo *m* **2.** (*amusement*) alegría *f*

merry ['mer·i] <-ier, -iest> *adj* alegre

merry-go-round ['mer·i·goʊ·ˌraʊnd] *n* tiovivo *m*

mesh [meʃ] **I.** *n* malla *f;* **wire ~** red *f* de alambrado **II.** *vi* engranar **III.** *vt* hacer engranar

mesmerism ['mez·mə·rɪz·əm] *n* hipnosis *f inv*

mesmerize ['mez·mə·raɪz] *vt* hipnotizar

mesmerizing [mez·'mer·ɪk] *adj* hipnótico, -a

mess [mes] <-es> *n* **1.** (*confusion*) confusión *f;* (*disorganized state*) desorden *m;* **to be in a ~** estar revuelto; **to make a ~ of sth** echar a perder algo; (*things*) caos *m inv* **2.** (*trouble*) lío

m, merengue *m Arg;* **this is a fine ~ you've gotten me into!** ¡vaya lío en el que me has metido! **3.** (*disheveled person*) desastre *m; just look at him — he's a ~!* ¡míralo — ¡va hecho un desastre! **4.** (*dining hall*) comedor *m*
◆ **mess around** *vi* **1.** (*joke*) hacer el tonto; **to ~ with sb** tontear a alguien, enredarse con alguien **2.** (*waste time*) pasar el rato **3.** *sl* (*have sex*) **to ~ with sb** montárselo con alguien
◆ **mess up I.** *vt inf* **1.** (*make untidy*) desordenar **2.** (*dirty*) ensuciar **3.** (*screw up*) echar a perder **II.** *vi* cagarla *inf*
◆ **mess with** *vi inf* **to ~ sb** meterse con alguien; **to ~ sth** interferir en algo

message ['mes·ɪdʒ] *n* mensaje *m;* **error ~** COMPUT mensaje *m* de error; **a ~ in a bottle** un mensaje en una botella

messenger ['mes·ɪn·dʒər] *n* mensajero, -a *m, f*

messenger boy *n* recadero *m*

messiah [mə·'saɪ·ə] *n* mesías *m inv*

mess-up ['mes·ʌp] *n inf* follón *m*

messy ['mes·i] <-ier, -iest> *adj* **1.** (*untidy*) desordenado, -a **2.** (*dirty*) sucio, -a **3.** (*unpleasant*) desagradable; **~ business** asunto *m* turbio

Met [met] *n* **1.** *s.* Metropolitan Museum of Art (**in New York**) Museo Metropolitano de Arte de Nueva York **2.** *s.* Metropolitan Opera House (**in New York**) Ópera Metropolitana de Nueva York

met [met] *vi, vt pt of* **meet**

metabolic [ˌmet·ə·'bal·ɪk] *adj* metabólico, -a

metabolism [mɪ·'tæb·ə·lɪz·əm] *n* metabolismo *m*

metal ['met·əl] **I.** *n* (*element*) metal *m* **II.** *adj* metálico, -a

metal detector *n* detector *m* de metales

metallic [mə·'tæl·ɪk] *adj* metálico, -a

metallurgy ['met·əl·ɜr·dʒi] *n* metalurgia *f*

metalwork ['met·əl·wɜrk] *n* metalistería *f*

metalworker *n* metalista *mf*

metamorphosis [ˌmet·ə·'mɔr·fə·sɪs] <-es> *n* metamorfosis *f inv*

metaphor ['met·ə·fɔr] *n* metáfora *f*

metaphorical [ˌmet·ə·'fɔr·ɪ·kəl] *adj* metafórico, -a

metaphysical [ˌmet·ə·'fɪz·ɪ·kəl] *adj* metafísico, -a

metaphysics [ˌmet·ə·'fɪz·ɪks] *n* metafísica *f*

metastasis [mə·'tæs·tə·sɪs] <-ses> *n* metástasis *f inv*

mete [mit] *vt* **to ~ out** (*punishment*) imponer

meteor ['mi·ti·ər] *n* meteoro *m*

meteoric [ˌmi·ti·'ɔr·ɪk] *adj a. fig* meteórico, -a

meteorite ['mi·ti·ə·raɪt] *n* meteorito *m*

meteorological [ˌmi·ti·ər·ə·'ladʒ·ɪ·kəl] *adj* meteorológico, -a

meteorologist [ˌmi·ti·ə·'ral·ə·dʒɪst] *n* meteorólogo, -a *m, f*

meteorology [ˌmi·ti·ə·'ral·ə·dʒi] *n* meteorología *f*

meter[1] ['mi·tər] *n* contador *m,* medidor *m*

M

AmL; (**parking**) ~ parquímetro *m;* (**taxi**) ~ taxímetro *m*

meter² ['mi· țər] *n* metro *m*

methane ['meθ·eɪn] *n* metano *m*

methanol ['meθ·ə·nɔl] *n* metanol *m*

method ['meθ·əd] *n* método *m;* **there's a ~ to his madness** no está tan loco como parece

methodical [mə·'θad·ɪ·kəl] *adj* metódico, -a

Methodism ['meθ·ə·dɪz·əm] *n* metodismo *m*

Methodist I. *n* metodista *mf* II. *adj* metodista

methodology [,meθ·ə·'dal·ə·dʒi] *n* metodología *f*

Methuselah [mə·'θu·zə·lə] *n* Matusalén ▶ **as old as** ~ más viejo que Matusalén

meticulous [mɪ·'tɪk·jʊ·ləs] *adj* meticuloso, -a, niquitoso, -a *Arg*

metric ['met·rɪk] *adj* métrico, -a

metrical ['met·rɪ·kəl] *adj* métrico, -a

metro¹ ['met·roʊ] *n* RAIL (*subway*) metro *m*

metro² ['met·roʊ] *adj abbr of* **metropolitan** metropolitano, -a; **the ~ area** el área metropolitana, la ciudad y sus alrededores

metronome ['met·rə·noʊm] *n* metrónomo *m*

metropolis [mə·'trap·ə·lɪs] <-es> *n* metrópoli *f*

metropolitan [,met·rə·'pal·ə·tən] *adj* metropolitano, -a

mettle ['met·əl] *n form* temple *m;* **to show one's ~** demostrar su brío; **to be on one's ~** mostrar todo lo que uno vale

mew [mju] I. *n* maullido *m* II. *vi* maullar

Mexican ['mek·sɪ·kən] I. *n* mexicano, -a *m, f* II. *adj* mexicano, -a

Mexico ['mek·sɪ·koʊ] *n* México *m;* **New ~** Nuevo México

Mexico City *n* Ciudad *f* de México

Mg *abbr of* **magnesium** Mg

mg *n abbr of* **milligram** mg

MH [,mar·ʃəl·'aɪ·ləndz] *abbr of* **Marshall Islands** Islas *fpl* Marshall

MHz *abbr of* **megahertz** MHz

MI ['mɪf·ɪ·gən] *n abbr of* **Michigan** Míchigan *m*

MIA [,em·aɪ·'eɪ] *abbr of* **missing in action** desaparecido, -a en combate

mic [maɪk] *n inf abbr of* **microphone** *s.* **mike**

mica ['maɪ·kə] *n* mica *f*

mice [maɪs] *n pl of* **mouse**

Mich. *n abbr of* **Michigan** Michigan *m*

mickey ['mɪk·i] *n sl:* bebida alcohólica con somníferos u otra droga; **to slip sb a ~** echar a alguien somníferos u otra droga en la copa

Mickey Mouse [,mɪk·i·'maʊs] *n* ratoncito *m* Mickey, ratón *m* Miguelito *Méx*

microbe ['maɪ·kroʊb] *n* microbio *m*

microbiology [,maɪ·kroʊ·baɪ·'al·ə·dʒi] *n* microbiología *f*

microbrewery *n* microcervecería *f,* pequeña fábrica de cerveza artesana para venta local

microchip ['maɪ·kroʊ·ˌtʃɪp] *n* microchip *m*

microclimate ['maɪ·kroʊ·ˌklaɪ·mɪt] *n* microclima *m*

microcomputer ['maɪ·kroʊ·kəm·ˌpju·țər] *n* microordenador *m,* microcomputadora *f AmL*

microcosm ['maɪ·kroʊ·kaz·əm] *n* microcosmos *m inv*

microeconomics *n* microeconomía *f*

microelectronics [,maɪ·kroʊ·ɪ·ˌlek·'tran·ɪks] *n* microelectrónica *f*

microfiche ['maɪ·kroʊ·fiʃ] *n* microficha *f*

microfilm ['maɪ·kroʊ·fɪlm] *n* microfilm *m*

Micronesia [,maɪ·kroʊ·'ni·ʒə] *n* Micronesia *f*

microorganism [,maɪ·kroʊ·'ɔr·gə·nɪz·əm] *n* microorganismo *m*

microphone ['maɪ·krə·foʊn] *n* micrófono *m;* **to speak into a ~** hablar por micrófono

microprocessor ['maɪ·kroʊ·ˌpras·es·ər] *n* microprocesador *m*

microscope ['maɪ·krə·skoʊp] *n* microscopio *m*

microscopic [,maɪ·krə·'skap·ɪk] *adj* microscópico, -a

microwave ['maɪ·kroʊ·weɪv] I. *n* 1. (*wave*) microonda *f* 2. (*oven*) microondas *m inv* II. *vt* poner en el microondas

microwave oven *n* microondas *m inv*

mid [mɪd] *prep* en medio de

midday [,mɪd·'deɪ] I. *n* mediodía *m;* **at ~** al mediodía; **~ meal** almuerzo *m,* comida *f* II. *adj* de mediodía

middle ['mɪd·əl] I. *n* 1. (*center*) medio *m;* **in the ~ of sth** en medio de algo; **in the ~ of the night** en plena noche; **to be in the ~ of doing sth** estar ocupado haciendo algo; (**in**) **the ~ of nowhere** donde da la vuelta el viento *fig* 2. *inf* (*waist*) cintura *f* II. *adj* 1. (*equidistant*) central 2. (*medium*) medio, -a

middle age *n* mediana edad *f*

middle-aged *adj* de mediana edad

Middle Ages *npl* Edad *f* Media

middle class *n* clase *f* media

middle-class *adj* de la clase media

Middle East *n* Oriente *m* Medio

middleman ['mɪd·əl·mæn] <-men> *n* intermediario *m*

middle name *n* segundo nombre *m*

middle-of-the-road *adj* moderado, -a

middleweight ['mɪd·əl·weɪt] *n* SPORTS peso *m* medio

middling ['mɪd·lɪŋ] I. *adj inf* 1. (*average*) mediano, -a 2. (*not very good*) regular, flojo, -a II. *adv* regular, pichí pichá *inf*

Mideast *n* Oriente *m* Medio

midget ['mɪdʒ·ɪt] I. *n* enano, -a *m, f* II. *adj* en miniatura

midlife crisis [,mɪd·'laɪf·'kraɪ·sɪs] *n* crisis *f inv* de los cuarenta

midnight ['mɪd·naɪt] I. *n* medianoche *f* II. *adj* de medianoche

midpoint ['mɪd·pɔɪnt] *n a.* MATH punto *m* medio

midpriced *adj* de gama media

midriff ['mɪd·rɪf] *n* ANAT diafragma *m*

midshipman ['mɪd·ʃɪp·mən] <-men> *n* aspirante *m* a oficial de marina

midst [mɪdst] *n* **in the ~ of** en medio de

midsummer [,mɪd·'sʌm·ər] *n* pleno verano *m*

midterm [ˌmɪd·'tɜrm] I. *n* UNIV (*exam*) parcial *m*; ~s exámenes *mpl* de mitad de trimestre II. *adj* de mitad del trimestre; ~ **vacation** vacaciones *fpl* de mitad de trimestre

midway [ˌmɪd·'weɪ] I. *adv* a medio camino II. *n* feria *f* (*con juegos de azar, espectáculos...*)

midweek [ˌmɪd·'wik] *adv* entre semana

midwife ['mɪd·waɪf] <-wives> *n* comadrona *f*

miffed [mɪft] *adj* ofendido, -a; **to be ~ at sb** estar picado [*o* mosqueado] con alguien *inf*

might¹ [maɪt] *pt of* **may it ~ be that...** podría ser que... +*subj*; **how old ~ she be?** ¿qué edad tendrá?

might² [maɪt] *n* 1. (*power*) poder *m* 2. (*strength*) fuerza *f*; **military ~** poderío *m* militar; **with all one's ~** con todas sus fuerzas

mightily ['maɪ·t̬ɪ·li] *adv liter* fuertemente

mighty ['maɪ·t̬i] I. <-ier, -iest> *adj* 1. (*powerful*) fuerte 2. (*great*) enorme II. *adv inf* tope; **that's ~ fine, indeed** está mogollón de bien

migraine ['maɪ·greɪn] <-(s)> *n* migraña *f*

migrant ['maɪ·grənt] I. *n* 1. (*person*) emigrante *mf* 2. ZOOL ave *f* migratoria II. *adj* migratorio, -a

migrant worker *n* trabajador(a) *m(f)* extranjero, -a

migrate ['maɪ·greɪt] *vi* emigrar

migration [maɪ·'greɪ·ʃən] <-(s)> *n* (*person*) emigración *f*; (*animal*) migración *f*

migratory ['maɪ·grə·tɔr·i] *adj* migratorio, -a

mike [maɪk] *n inf* micro *m*

mild [maɪld] <-er, -est> *adj* 1. (*not severe*) apacible; (*criticism*) moderado, -a; (*penalty*) leve 2. (*not strong tasting*) suave 3. METEO templado, -a 4. MED (*not serious*) benigno, -a

mildew ['mɪl·du] *n* moho *m*

mildly ['maɪld·li] *adv* 1. (*gently*) suavemente; **to punish sb ~** castigar a alguien de forma poco severa 2. (*slightly*) ligeramente ▶ **to put it ~, that's putting it ~** por no decir algo peor

mildness ['maɪld·nɪs] *n* 1. (*placidity*) tranquilidad *f* 2. (*softness*) suavidad *f*

mile [maɪl] *n* milla *f* (*1,61 km*); **to walk for ~s (and ~s)** andar kilómetros y kilómetros; **to be ~s away** *fig* estar fuera de onda ▶ **to smell sth a ~ away** ver algo a la legua

mileage ['maɪ·lɪdʒ] *n* AUTO kilometraje *m*

milepost ['maɪl·poʊst] *n* mojón *m*

milestone ['maɪl·stoʊn] *n* 1. (*marker*) mojón *m* 2. *fig* hito *m*

militant ['mɪl·ɪ·tənt] I. *adj* militante II. *n* militante *mf*

militarism ['mɪl·ɪ·tə·rɪz·əm] *n* militarismo *m*

militarist ['mɪl·ɪ·tə·rɪst] *n* militarista *mf*

militaristic [ˌmɪl·ɪ·tə·'rɪs·tɪk] *adj* militarista

militarize ['mɪl·ɪ·tə·raɪz] *vt* militarizar

military ['mɪl·ɪ·ter·i] I. **the ~** los militares II. *adj* militar

military academy *n* academia *f* militar

military police *n* policía *f* militar

military service *n* servicio *m* militar

militia [mɪ·'lɪʃ·ə] *n* milicia *f*

milk [mɪlk] I. *n* leche *f* ▶ **there's no use crying over spilt ~** a lo hecho pecho II. *vt* 1. **to ~ a cow** ordeñar una vaca 2. *fig, inf* (*exploit*) **to ~ sb dry** chupar la sangre a alguien

milk chocolate *n* chocolate *m* con leche

milkmaid *n* lechera *f*

milkman <-men> *n* lechero *m*

milkshake *n* batido *m*, malteada *f Méx*

milk tooth *n* diente *m* de leche

milky ['mɪl·ki] <-ier, -iest> *adj* 1. (*color, skin*) lechoso, -a 2. (*tea, coffee*) con mucha leche

Milky Way *n* **the ~** la Vía Láctea

mill [mɪl] I. *n* 1. (*machine: for grain*) molino *m*; (*for coffee*) molinillo *m* 2. (*factory*) fábrica *f* (de tejidos) II. *vt* 1. (*grain, coffee*) moler 2. (*metal*) fresar

♦ **mill about** *vi*, **mill around** *vi* arremolinarse

millennium [mɪ·'len·i·əm] <-s *o* -ennia> *n* milenio *m*

miller ['mɪl·ər] *n* molinero, -a *m, f*

millet ['mɪl·ət] *n* mijo *m*

millibar ['mɪl·ɪ·bar] *n* milibar *m*

milligram ['mɪl·ɪ·græm] *n* miligramo *m*

milliliter ['mɪl·ɪˌli·t̬ər] *n* mililitro *m*

millimeter ['mɪl·ɪˌmi·t̬ər] *n* milímetro *m*

milliner ['mɪl·ɪ·nər] *n* sombrerera *f*

millinery ['mɪl·ɪ·ner·i] *n* sombrerería *f*

million ['mɪl·jən] <-(s)> *n* millón *m*; **two ~ people** dos millones de personas; **a ~ times** *inf* un millón de veces; **to be one in a ~** ser único

millionaire [ˌmɪl·jə·'ner] *n* millonario, -a *m, f*

millipede ['mɪl·ɪ·pid] *n* milpiés *m inv*

mill wheel *n* rueda *f* de molino

milt [mɪlt] *n* lecha *f*

mime [maɪm] I. *n* THEAT pantomima *f*; (*person*) mimo *mf* II. *vi* actuar de mimo III. *vt* imitar

mimic ['mɪm·ɪk] I. *vt* <-ck-> imitar II. *n* imitador(a) *m(f)*

mimicry ['mɪm·ɪk·ri] *n* 1. (*art*) mímica *f*; (*imitation*) imitación *f* 2. BIO mimetismo *m*

mimosa [mɪ·'moʊ·sə] *n* mimosa *f*

min. 1. *abbr of* **minute** min. 2. *abbr of* **minimum** mín.

minaret [ˌmɪn·ə·'ret] *n* alminar *m*

mince [mɪns] I. *vt* 1. (*shred*) picar 2. (*use tact*) **to not ~ words** no andarse con rodeos II. *vi* andar con pasos muy cortos III. *n* carne *f* picada

mincemeat *n* 1. (*meat*) carne *f* picada 2. (*fruit*) picadillo *m* de fruta ▶ **to make ~ of sb/sth** *sl* hacer picadillo [*o* trizas] a alguien/algo

mince pie *n* pastel *m* de frutas picadas

mind [maɪnd] I. *n* 1. (*brain*) mente *f*; **to be in one's right ~** estar en sus cabales; **to be out of one's ~** estar fuera de juicio 2. (*thought*) pensamiento *m*; **to bear sth in ~** tener algo presente; **to bring sth to ~** recordar algo 3. (*intention*) intención *f*; **to change one's ~** cambiar de parecer; **to have sth in ~** tener pensado algo; **to have half a ~ to...** estar casi por...; **to know one's own ~** saber lo que uno quiere; **to make up one's ~** decidirse; **to set one's ~ on sth** desear algo con vehemencia; **to set one's ~ to sth** estar resuelto a algo; **to set one's ~ at ease** tranquilizarse **4.** (*consciousness*) conciencia *f;* **her mother is on her ~** está preocupada por su madre; **this will take your ~ off** (**of**) **it** esto te distraerá **5.** (*opinion*) opinión *f;* **to be of the same ~** ser de la misma opinión; **to give sb a piece of one's ~** cantar las cuarenta a alguien; **to be in two ~s** dudar entre dos cosas, estar en un dilema ▶ **in my ~'s** eye en mi imaginación; **it's a question of ~ over** matter es una cuestión que requiere fuerza de voluntad; **to have a ~ like a** sewer tener una mente cochambrosa **II.** *vt* **1.** (*be careful of*) tener cuidado con; **~ what you're doing!** ¡cuidado con lo que haces!; **~ the step!** ¡cuidado con el escalón! **2.** (*look after*) estar al cuidado de; **don't ~ me** no te preocupes por mí **3.** (*bother*) sentirse molesto por; **I don't ~ the cold** el frío no me molesta; **do you ~ my smoking?** ¿te molesta si fumo?; **would you ~ opening the window?** ¿haces el favor de abrir la ventana?; **I wouldn't ~ a beer** no me vendría mal una cerveza ▶ **to ~ one's** Ps **and** Qs tener sumo cuidado en lo que uno dice **III.** *vi* **never ~!** ¡no importa!; **I don't ~** me es igual; **if you don't ~, I prefer...** si no te importa, prefiero...; **would you ~ if...** ¿te importa si...?

mind-bending ['maɪnd·ben·dɪŋ] *adj* increíble

mind-blowing *adj inf* alucinante

mind-boggling *adj* increíble; **it's ~** no me entra en la cabeza

mindful ['maɪnd·fəl] *adj form* cuidadoso, -a; **to be ~ of sth** tener presente algo

mind game *n* juego *m* psicológico; **to play ~s** usar estratagemas

mindless ['maɪnd·lɪs] *adj* **1.** (*job*) mecánico, -a **2.** (*violence*) gratuito, -a **3.** (*heedless*) descuidado, -a

mind reader *n* adivinador(a) *m(f)* de pensamientos

mine[1] [maɪn] *pron pos* (el) mío, (la) mía, (los) míos, (las) mías; **it's not his bag, it's ~** no es su bolsa, es la mía; **this glass is ~** este vaso es (el) mío; **these are his shoes and those are ~** estos zapatos son suyos y estos (son) míos

mine[2] [maɪn] **I.** *n* MIN, MIL mina *f;* **a ~ of information** *fig* una fuente abundante de información **II.** *vt* **1.** MIN extraer **2.** MIL minar **III.** *vi* MIN explotar minas; **to ~ for silver/gold** buscar plata/oro

mine detector *n* detector *m* de minas

minefield ['maɪn·fild] *n* **1.** campo *m* de minas **2.** *fig* terreno *m* minado

miner ['maɪ·nər] *n* minero, -a *m, f*

mineral ['mɪn·ər·əl] **I.** *n* mineral *m* **II.** *adj* mineral

mineralogical [ˌmɪn·ər·ə·'ladʒ·ɪ·kəl] *adj* mineralógico, -a

mineralogist [ˌmɪn·ə·'ral·ə·dʒɪst] *n* mineralogista *mf*

mineralogy [ˌmɪn·ə·'ral·ə·dʒi] *n* mineralogía *f*

mineral water *n* agua *f* mineral

minestrone [ˌmɪn·ɪ·'strou·ni] *n* (sopa) minestrone *f,* sopa *f* de verduras

minesweeper ['maɪn·ˌswi·pər] *n* dragaminas *m inv*

mingle ['mɪŋ·gəl] **I.** *vi* mezclarse; **to ~ with the crowd/guests** mezclarse con la multitud/los invitados **II.** *vt* mezclar

miniature ['mɪn·i·ə·tʃər] **I.** *adj* de miniatura **II.** *n* miniatura *f*

miniature golf *n* minigolf *m*

minibus ['mɪn·i·bʌs] *n* microbús *m*

minimal ['mɪn·ɪ·məl] *adj* mínimo, -a

minimize ['mɪn·ɪ·maɪz] *vt* minimizar; *fig* menospreciar

minimum ['mɪn·ɪ·məm] **I.** <-s *o* minima> *n* mínimo *m;* **to reduce sth to a ~** reducir algo al mínimo **II.** *adj* mínimo, -a; **~ requirements** requisitos *mpl* básicos

mining ['maɪ·nɪŋ] *n* minería *f*

mining engineer *n* ingeniero, -a *m, f* de minas

minion ['mɪn·jən] *n* secuaz *mf*

miniskirt ['mɪn·i·skɜrt] *n* minifalda *f*

minister ['mɪn·ɪ·stər] *n* **1.** POL ministro, -a *m, f* **2.** REL pastor *m*

ministerial [ˌmɪn·ɪ·'stɪr·i·əl] *adj* ministerial

ministrations [ˌmɪn·ɪ·'streɪ·ʃən] *n pl, liter* atenciones *fpl*

ministry ['mɪn·ɪ·stri] <-ies> *n* **1.** REL sacerdocio *m;* **to enter the ~** (*Catholic*) hacerse sacerdote; (*Protestant*) hacerse pastor **2.** POL ministerio *m*

minivan ['mɪn·i·væn] *n* vehículo *m* mixto, minivan *m Col, Méx*

mink [mɪŋk] *n* visón *m*

Minn. *n abbr of* **Minnesota** Minnesota *f*

Minnesota [ˌmɪn·ɪ·'sou·t̬ə] *n* Minnesota *f*

minor ['maɪ·nər] **I.** *adj* (*not great*) pequeño, -a; (*role*) secundario, -a; (*detail*) sin importancia; **~ offense** delito *m* de menor cuantía; **B ~** MUS si *m* menor **II.** *n* **1.** (*person*) menor *mf* de edad **2.** UNIV asignatura *f* secundaria

Minorca [mɪ·'nɔr·kə] *n* Menorca *f*

Minorcan I. *adj* menorquín, -ina **II.** *n* menorquín, -ina *m, f*

minority [maɪ·'nɔr·ə·t̬i] **I.** <-ies> *n* minoría *f;* **to be in the ~** estar en minoría; **to be a ~ of one** ser el único que piensa así **II.** *adj* minoritario, -a; **~ sport** deporte de minorías

mint[1] [mɪnt] *n* **1.** (*herb*) hierbabuena *f* **2.** (*sweet*) caramelo *m* de menta

mint[2] [mɪnt] **I.** *n* (*coin factory*) casa *f* de la moneda **II.** *vt* acuñar **III.** *adj* (*coin*) de reciente acuñación; (*stamp*) nuevo, -a; **in ~ condition** en perfecto estado

mint julep *n* julepe *m* de menta

minuet [ˌmɪn·ju·'et] *n* minué *m*

minus ['maɪ·nəs] **I.** *prep* **1.** *a.* MATH menos; **5 ~ 2 equals 3** 5 menos 2 igual a 3; **~ ten degrees Celsius** diez grados bajo cero **2.** *inf* (*without*) sin **II.** *adj* MATH menos; **to be in ~ figures** estar en números rojos **III.** *n* **1.** MATH (signo *m* de) menos *m* **2.** (*negative amount*) cantidad *f* negativa

minuscule ['mɪn·ɪ·skjul] *adj* minúsculo, -a

minute[1] ['mɪn·ɪt] *n* **1.** (*sixty seconds*) minuto *m* **2.** (*moment*) momento *m;* **any** ~ de un momento a otro; **at the last** ~ a última hora; **in a** ~ en seguida; **this very** ~ ahora mismo; **to the** ~ puntual; **wait a** ~ espera un segundo **3.** ~ **s** (*of meeting*) acta(s) *f(pl)*

minute[2] [maɪ·'nut] *adj* diminuto, -a

minute hand *n* minutero *m*

minutely *adv* minuciosamente

minuteman *n miliciano de la Guerra de Independencia de EE.UU.*

minutiae [mɪ·'nu·ʃi·ə] *npl* minucias *fpl*

miracle ['mɪr·ə·kəl] *n* milagro *m;* **by a** ~ de milagro

miracle drug *n* cura *f* milagrosa

miraculous [mɪ·'ræk·jə·ləs] *adj* milagroso, -a

mirage [mə·'raʒ] *n* espejismo *m*

mire [maɪr] **I.** *vt* **to become** ~ **d in sth** quedar atascado en algo **II.** *n* **1.** (*swamp*) fango *m* **2.** *fig* berenjenal *m*

mirror ['mɪr·ər] **I.** *n* espejo *m* **II.** *vt* reflejar

mirror image *n* **1.** imagen *f* especular **2.** *fig* viva imagen *f*

mirth [mɜrθ] *n* regocijo *m*

mirthful ['mɜrθ·fəl] *adj* alegre

mirthless ['mɜrθ·lɪs] *adj* **1.** (*joyless*) triste **2.** (*unhappy*) infeliz

misadventure [ˌmɪs·əd·'ven·tʃər] *n* desgracia *f*

misalliance [ˌmɪs·ə·'laɪ·əns] *n* **1.** (*alliance*) alianza *f* inconveniente **2.** (*marriage*) matrimonio *m* desigual

misanthrope ['mɪs·ən·θroʊp] *n* misántropo, -a *m, f*

misanthropic [ˌmɪs·ən·'θrap·ɪk] *adj* misantrópico, -a

misanthropy [mɪs·'æn·θrə·pi] *n* misantropía *f*

misapply [ˌmɪs·ə·'plaɪ] <-ie-> *vt* **to** ~ **sth** hacer un uso indebido de algo

misapprehend [ˌmɪs·æprɪ·'hend] *vt* comprender mal

misapprehension [ˌmɪs·æprɪ·'hen·ʃən] *n* mala interpretación *f;* **to be under a** ~ estar equivocado

misappropriate [ˌmɪs·ə·'proʊ·pri·eɪt] *vt* FIN malversar

misappropriation [ˌmɪs·ə·ˌproʊ·prɪ·'eɪ·ʃən] *n* FIN malversación *f*

misbehave [ˌmɪs·bɪ·'heɪv] *vi* portarse mal

misbehavior [ˌmɪs·bɪ·'heɪv·jər] *n* mala conducta *f*

misc. *adj abbr of* **miscellaneous** diverso, -a

miscalculate [ˌmɪs·'kæl·kjə·leɪt] *vt, vi* calcular mal

miscalculation [ˌmɪs·ˌkæl·kjə·'leɪ·ʃən] *n* error *m* de cálculo

miscarriage ['mɪs·ˌkær·ɪdʒ] *n* **1.** MED aborto *m* (espontáneo) **2.** *form* (*failure*) fracaso *m;* **a** ~ **of justice** un error judicial

miscarry ['mɪs·ˌkær·i] <-ied, -ying> *vi* **1.** MED abortar **2.** *fig* fracasar

miscellaneous [ˌmɪs·ə·'leɪ·ni·əs] *adj* diverso, -a; ~ **expenses** gastos *mpl* varios

miscellany ['mɪs·ə·leɪ·ni] <-ies> *n* miscelánea *f*

mischance [ˌmɪs·'tʃæns] *n* (*bad luck*) mala suerte *f;* (*unlucky event*) infortunio *m;* **by some** ~ por desgracia

mischief ['mɪs·tʃɪf] *n* **1.** (*naughtiness*) travesura *f;* **to keep sb out of** ~ impedir a alguien hacer travesuras **2. to get** (**oneself**) **into** ~ meterse en problemas; **to make** ~ **for sb** amargar la vida a alguien **3.** (*wickedness*) malicia *f*

mischievous ['mɪs·tʃə·vəs] *adj* **1.** (*naughty*) travieso, -a **2.** (*malicious*) malicioso, -a; ~ **rumors** rumores *mpl* malintencionados

misconceive [ˌmɪs·kən·'siv] *vt form* malinterpretar

misconceived *adj* mal concebido, -a

misconception [ˌmɪs·kən·'sep·ʃən] *n* idea *f* equivocada; **a popular** ~ un error común

misconduct [ˌmɪs·'kan·dʌkt] **I.** *n* **1.** (*misbehavior*) mala conducta *f* **2.** (*mismanage*) mala gestión *f* **II.** [ˌmɪs·kən·'dʌkt] *vt* **1.** (*behave badly*) **to** ~ **oneself** comportarse mal **2.** (*organize badly*) gestionar mal

misconstruction [ˌmɪs·kən·'strʌk·ʃən] *n form* mala interpretación *f*

misconstrue [ˌmɪs·kən·'stru] *vt* malinterpretar

misdeed [ˌmɪs·'did] *n form* fechoría *f*

misdemeanor [ˌmɪs·dɪ·'mi·nər] *n* **1.** LAW falta *f* **2.** (*bad behavior*) mala conducta *f*

misdirect [ˌmɪs·də·'rekt] *vt* **1.** (*letter*) mandar a una dirección equivocada; (*person*) dar indicaciones equivocadas **2.** LAW instruir mal

miser ['maɪ·zər] *n* avaro, -a *m, f*

miserable ['mɪz·rə·bəl] *adj* **1.** (*unhappy*) triste; **to make life** ~ **for sb** hacer insoportable la vida a alguien **2.** (*unpleasant*) lamentable **3.** (*inadequate*) mísero, -a; **a** ~ **amount** una miseria

miserably *adv* **1.** (*unhappily*) tristemente; **to feel** ~ sentirse abatido **2.** (*completely*) **to fail** ~ fallar miserablemente

miserly *adj* avaricioso, -a

misery ['mɪz·ə·ri] *n* **1.** (*unhappiness*) infelicidad *f* **2.** (*suffering*) sufrimiento *m;* **to make sb's life a** ~ amargar la vida a alguien **3.** (*extreme poverty*) miseria *f,* lipidia *f AmC;* **to be born into** ~ nacer en la miseria

misfire [ˌmɪs·'faɪr] *vi* **1.** (*weapon*) encasquillarse **2.** *fig* (*joke*) no tener éxito **3.** (*engine*) fallar

misfit ['mɪs·fɪt] *n* inadaptado, -a *m, f*

misfortune [ˌmɪs·'fɔr·tʃən] *n* infortunio *m;* **to suffer** ~ sufrir una desgracia

misgiving [ˌmɪs·'gɪv·ɪŋ] *n* recelo *m;* **to express** ~**s** recelar; **to be filled with** ~ estar lleno de dudas

misgovern [mɪs·'gʌv·ərn] *vt* (*country*) gobernar mal; (*business*) gestionar mal

misgovernment *n* (*of country*) mal gobierno *m;* (*of company*) mala gestión *f*

M

misguided [mɪsˈgaɪ·dɪd] *adj* desencaminado, -a; ~ **idea** desacierto *m*

mishandle [ˌmɪsˈhæn·dəl] *vt* **1.** (*handle without care*) manejar mal **2.** (*maltreat*) maltratar **3.** (*deal badly with*) llevar mal

mishap [ˈmɪs·hæp] *n form* percance *m;* **he had a** ~ **iron** tuvo un percance; **a series of** ~**s** una serie de contratiempos

mishear [ˌmɪsˈhɪr] *vt irr* oír mal

mishmash [ˈmɪʃ·mæʃ] *n* revoltijo *m;* **a** ~ **of sth** una mezcolanza de algo

misinform [ˌmɪs·ɪnˈfɔrm] *vt* informar mal, desinformar *Méx*

misinformation *n* información *f* errónea; (*news*) desinformación *m*

misinterpret [ˌmɪs·ɪnˈtɜr·prɪt] *vt* malinterpretar

misinterpretation [ˌmɪs·ɪn·tɜr·prɪˈteɪ·ʃən] *n* interpretación *f* errónea

misjudge [ˌmɪsˈdʒʌdʒ] *vt* juzgar mal

misjudgment [mɪsˈdʒʌdʒ·mənt] *n* mal cálculo *m*

mislay [ˌmɪsˈleɪ] *vt irr, form* extraviar

mislead [ˌmɪsˈlid] *vt irr* **1.** (*deceive*) engañar; **to** ~ **sb about sth** engañar a alguien acerca de algo; **to** ~ **sb into doing sth** engañar a alguien para que haga algo **2.** (*lead into error*) hacer caer en un error; **to let oneself be misled** dejarse engañar **3.** (*corrupt*) corromper

misleading *adj* engañoso, -a

mismanage [ˌmɪsˈmæn·ɪdʒ] *vt* administrar mal; **to** ~ **a business** gestionar mal una empresa

mismanagement *n* mala gestión *f*

misname [ˌmɪsˈneɪm] *vt* **to** ~ **sth** dar un nombre equivocado a algo

misnomer [ˌmɪsˈnou·mər] *n* nombre *m* equivocado

misogynist [mɪˈsadʒ·ə·nɪst] **I.** *n* misógino *m* **II.** *adj* misógino, -a

misogynistic [mɪˌsadʒ·ɪˈnɪs·tɪk] *adj* misógino, -a

misplace [ˌmɪsˈpleɪs] *vt* **1.** (*lose*) extraviar **2.** *fig* (*confidence*) depositar en quien no lo merece

misprint [ˈmɪs·ˌprɪnt] *n* errata *f*

mispronounce [ˌmɪs·prəˈnaʊns] *vt* pronunciar mal

mispronunciation [ˌmɪs·prə·nʌn·siˈeɪ·ʃən] *n* mala pronunciación *f*

misread [ˌmɪsˈrid] *vt irr* **1.** (*read badly*) leer mal **2.** (*interpret badly*) malinterpretar

misrepresent [ˌmɪs·ˌrep·rɪˈzent] *vt* tergiversar

misrepresentation [ˌmɪs·rep·rɪ·zenˈteɪ·ʃən] *n* tergiversación *f*

miss[1] [mɪs] *n* (*form of address*) señorita *f;* **Miss America** Miss EE.UU.

Miss. *n abbr of* **Mississippi** Misisipí *m*

miss[2] [mɪs] **I.** <-es> *n* fallo *m* **II.** *vi* fallar **III.** *vt* **1.** (*not hit*) fallar **2.** (*not catch*) perder; **to** ~ **the bus/train** perder el bus/tren; **to** ~ **a deadline** no cumplir con una fecha límite **3.** (*avoid*) evitar **4.** (*not notice*) no fijarse en;

to ~ **sb** no encontrar a alguien; **you didn't** ~ **much** no te has perdido nada; **you can't** ~ **it** no te lo puedes perder **5.** (*not hear*) no oír **6.** (*overlook*) saltarse; **to** ~ **a meeting** faltar a una reunión **7.** (*not take advantage*) dejar pasar; **to** ~ **an opportunity** perder una oportunidad **8.** (*regret absence*) echar de menos **9.** (*notice loss*) echar en falta

◆ **miss out** *vi* perdérselo

◆ **miss out on** *vt* **to** ~ **sth** perderse algo

misshapen [ˌmɪsˈʃeɪ·pən] *adj* (*malformed*) deformado, -a

missile [ˈmɪs·əl] *n* (*rocket*) misil *m;* (*projectile*) proyectil *m*

missile base *n* base *f* de misiles

missile defense system *n* sistema *m* defensivo de misiles

missile launcher *n* lanzamisiles *m inv*

missing [ˈmɪs·ɪŋ] *adj* **1.** (*lost: person*) desaparecido, -a; (*thing or object*) perdido, -a; ~ **in action** desaparecido en combate; **to report sth** ~ dar parte de la pérdida de algo **2.** (*absent*) ausente

missing link *n* eslabón *m* perdido

missing person *n* desaparecido, -a *m, f*

mission [ˈmɪʃ·ən] *n* **1.** *a.* REL (*task*) misión *f;* **peace** ~ misión de paz; **rescue** ~ operación *f* de rescate; **his** ~ **in life** su misión en la vida; ~ **accomplished** misión cumplida **2.** (*space project*) misión *f* espacial **3.** POL delegación *f* **4.** (*building*) embajada *f*

missionary [ˈmɪʃ·ə·ner·i] **I.** <-ies> *n* misionero, -a *m, f* **II.** *adj* misionero, -a

missionary position *n iron* postura *f* del misionero

mission control *n* centro *m* de control

missis [ˈmɪs·ɪz] *n inf s.* **missus**

Mississippi [ˌmɪs·ɪˈsɪ·pi] *n* Misisipí *m*

I El río Misisipí (**Mississippi River**) es la tercera cuenca fluvial más grande del mundo después de las cuencas del río Amazonas y el río Congo, y se extiende a lo largo de 2.320 millas (3.733 km) desde su nacimiento en el Lago Itasca, en Minnesota, hasta su desembocadura en el Golfo de México, cerca de Nueva Orleans, Luisiana. Irriga una superficie de más de 1.245.000 millas cuadradas (3.225.000 km^2) en 31 estados y dos provincias canadienses. Una gota de lluvia que cae en el Lago Itasca tarda tres meses en llegar al Golfo de México.

Missouri [mɪˈzʊr·i] *n* Misuri *m*

misspell [ˌmɪsˈspel] *vt irr* escribir mal

misspelling *n* falta *f* de ortografía

misspent [ˌmɪsˈspent] *adj* desperdiciado, -a; **a** ~ **youth** una juventud malgastada

misstate [ˌmɪsˈsteɪt] *vt* sostener erróneamente

missus [ˈmɪs·ɪz] *n inf* (*wife*) parienta *f*

mist [mɪst] *n* **1.** (*light fog*) neblina *f;* **to be shrouded in** ~ estar cubierto por la neblina **2.** (*condensation*) vaho *m* ◆**mist up** *vi* empañarse
mistakable [mɪ·'steɪ·kə·bəl] *adj* confundible
mistake [mɪ·'steɪk] **I.** *n* error *m;* **typing** ~ errata *f;* **to learn from one's** ~**s** aprender de los propios errores; **to make a** ~ cometer un error; **make no** ~ **about it** no te equivoques; **to repeat past** ~**s** repetir los errores del pasado; **there must be some** ~ tiene que haber un error; **by** ~ por error **II.** *vt irr* confundir
mistaken [mɪ·'steɪ·kən] **I.** *pp of* **mistake II.** *adj* (*belief*) equivocado, -a; (*identity*) confundido, -a; **to be** (**very much**) ~ estar (muy) equivocado; **unless I'm very much** ~... si no me equivoco...
Mister ['mɪs·tər] *n* señor *m*
mistime [ˌmɪs·'taɪm] *vt* hacer algo a destiempo
mistletoe ['mɪs·əl·toʊ] *n* muérdago *m*
mistook [mɪ·'stʊk] *pt of* **mistake**
mistranslate [ˌmɪs·'træn·zleɪt] *vt* traducir mal
mistreat [ˌmɪs·'trit] *vt* maltratar
mistress ['mɪs·trɪs] *n* **1.** (*sexual partner*) amante *f* **2.** (*woman in charge*) ama *f;* **the** ~ **of the house** la dueña de la casa **3.** (*owner*) dueña *f*
mistrial ['mɪs·ˌtraɪ·əl] *n* juicio *m* invalidado
mistrust [ˌmɪs·'trʌst] **I.** *n* desconfianza *f;* **to have a** ~ **of sb/sth** recelar de alguien/algo **II.** *vt* **to** ~ **sb/sth** recelar de alguien/algo
mistrustful [ˌmɪs·'trʌst·fəl] *adj* receloso, -a; **to be** ~ **of sb/sth** recelar de alguien/algo
misty ['mɪs·ti] <-ier, -iest> *adj* **1.** (*foggy*) neblinoso, -a; (*window, glasses*) empañado, -a **2.** *fig* borroso, -a
misunderstand [ˌmɪs·ˌʌn·dər·'stænd] *vt irr* entender mal
misunderstanding *n* **1.** (*failure to understand*) malentendido *m;* **there must be some** ~ debe haber un malentendido **2.** (*disagreement*) desacuerdo *m*
misuse[1] [ˌmɪs·'jus] *n* **1.** (*wrong use*) mal uso *m* **2.** (*excessive consumption*) abuso *m*
misuse[2] [ˌmɪs·'juz] *vt* **1.** (*handle wrongly*) manejar mal **2.** (*consume to excess*) abusar de
mite[1] [maɪt] *n* (*insect*) ácaro *m*
mite[2] [maɪt] *n* (*small amount*) pizca *f*
miter ['maɪ·tər] *n* mitra *f*
mitigate ['mɪt̬·ɪ·geɪt] *vt form* mitigar
mitigation [ˌmɪt̬·ɪ·'geɪ·ʃən] *n* atenuación *f;* **in** ~ como atenuante
mitten ['mɪt·ən] *n* manopla *f*
mix [mɪks] **I.** *n* mezcla *f;* **a** ~ **of people** una mezcla de gente **II.** *vt* **1.** CULIN (*ingredients*) mezclar; (*cocktails*) preparar **2.** (*combine*) combinar; **to** ~ **business with pleasure** combinar los negocios con el placer; **religion and politics don't** ~ la religión y la política no hacen buena combinación **III.** *vi* **1.** (*combine*) mezclarse **2.** (*socially*) **to** ~ **with sb** frecuentar a alguien; **to** ~ **well** llevarse bien

◆**mix in I.** *vi* convivir **II.** *vt* **to mix sth in with sth** mezclar algo con algo
◆**mix up** *vt* **1.** (*confuse*) confundir **2.** (*put in wrong order*) revolver **3.** CULIN mezclar ▶**to mix it up with sb** *sl* enzarzarse con alguien
◆**mix up** *vi* **to be mixed up in sth** estar involucrado en algo
◆**mix up with** *vt* **to mix up sth with sth** mezclar algo con algo; **to be mixed up with sth** estar involucrado en algo
mixed *adj* **1.** (*containing various elements*) mezclado, -a; ~ **marriage** matrimonio mixto; **person of** ~ **race** mestizo, -a *m, f* **2.** (*contradictory*) contradictorio, -a; **to be a** ~ **blessing** tener ventajas e inconvenientes
mixed doubles *npl* SPORTS dobles *mpl* mixtos
mixed-gender *adj* mixto, -a
mixed marriage *n* matrimonio *m* mixto
mixed message *n* mensaje *m* poco claro; **to send** ~**s** enviar mensajes ambiguos
mixer ['mɪk·sər] *n* **1.** (*machine*) batidora *f* **2.** (*drink*) bebida que se mezcla con alcohol en cócteles y combinados
mixologist *n inf* barman *m* experimentado
mixture ['mɪks·tʃər] *n* mezcla *f*
mix-up ['mɪks·ʌp] *n* confusión *f*
ml *n abbr of* **milliliter** ml
mm *abbr of* **millimeter** mm
MMR [ˌemem'ar] *n* MED *abbr of* **measles, mumps and rubella** SPR *f*
MN [ˌmɪn·ɪ·'soʊ·t̬ə] *n abbr of* **Minnesota** Minnesota *f*
mnemonic [nɪ·'man·ɪk] *adj* mnemotécnico, -a
mo. [moʊ] *n abbr of* **month** mes *m*
Mo. *n abbr of* **Missouri** Misuri *m*
MO *n* **1.** *abbr of* **modus operandi** procedimiento *m* **2.** *abbr of* **Missouri** Misuri *m* **3.** *abbr of* **money order** giro *m*
moan [moʊn] **I.** *n* **1.** (*sound*) gemido *m* **2.** (*complaint*) quejido *m* **II.** *vi* **1.** (*make a sound*) gemir; **to** ~ **with pain** gemir de dolor **2.** (*complain*) lamentarse; **to** ~ **about sth** lamentarse de algo; **to** ~ **that...** lamentarse de que... +*subj*
moat [moʊt] *n* foso *m*
mob [mab] **I.** *n* + *sing/pl vb* **1.** (*crowd*) muchedumbre *f;* **angry** ~ turba *f* **2.** *inf* **the Mob** la mafia **II.** <-bb-> *vt* acosar; **he was** ~**bed by his fans** sus fans se aglomeraron en torno a él
mobile ['moʊ·bəl] **I.** *n a.* TEL móvil *m* **II.** *adj* **1.** (*able to move*) móvil; (*shop, canteen*) ambulante; **to be** ~ *inf* tener coche, estar motorizado *inf* **2.** (*movable*) movible
mobile home *n* caravana *f*
mobility [moʊ·'bɪl·ə·t̬i] *n* movilidad *f;* **social** ~ movilidad social
mobilization [ˌmoʊ·bə·lɪ·'zeɪ·ʃən] *n a.* MIL movilización *f*
mobilize ['moʊ·bə·laɪz] *vt* movilizar
mobster ['mab·stər] *n* gángster *mf*
moccasin ['mak·ə·sən] *n* mocasín *m*
mocha ['moʊ·kə] *n* moca *f;* ~ **ice cream**

M

helado *m* de moca
mock [mak] I. *adj* 1.(*imitation*) artificial;
~ **baroque** que imita el barroco 2.(*fake*) ficticio, -a; ~ **battle** simulacro *m* de batalla;
~ **approval/disapproval** aprobación/desa-
probación simulada 3.(*practice*) ~ **jury** jurado
de prueba *m* II. *vi* burlarse; **to** ~ **at sb/sth**
burlarse de alguien III. *vt* 1.(*ridicule*) mofarse
de 2.(*imitate*) remedar
mockery ['mak·ə·ri] *n* 1.(*ridicule*) mofa *f*
2.(*subject of derision*) hazmerreír *mf;* **to**
make a ~ **of sb/sth** ridiculizar a alguien/algo
3.(*ridiculous imitation*) parodia *f*
mocking *n* burla *f*
mockingbird ['mak·ɪŋ·bɜrd] *n* sinsonte *m,*
cenzontle *m Méx*
mock-up ['mak·ʌp] *n* réplica *f*
modal ['mou·dəl] *adj* modal
modal verb *n* verbo *m* modal
mode [moud] *n* 1. *a.* LING, PHILOS (*manner*)
modo *m;* ~ **of transportation** medio *m* de
transporte; ~ **of travel** medio de transporte
para viajar; ~ **of operation** forma *f* de operar;
~ **of expression** medio de expresión 2.*form*
(*fashion*) moda *f;* **to be all the** ~ estar de
moda; **in** ~ de moda
model ['mad·əl] I. *n* (*version, example*) *a.* ART
modelo *m;* (*of car, house*) maqueta *f;* **to be**
the very ~ **of sth** ser la viva imagen de algo
II. *adj* modélico, -a; **a** ~ **student** un alumno
modelo III. <-ll-> *vt* 1.(*make figure, representation*) modelar; **to** ~ **sth in clay** modelar algo
en barro 2.(*show clothes*) desfilar 3.**to** ~
oneself on sb tomar a alguien como modelo
IV. *vi* hacer de modelo
modem ['mou·dəm] *n* COMPUT módem *m*
moderate[1] ['mad·ər·ət] I. *adj* 1.(*neither large
nor small*) mediano, -a 2. *a.* POL (*not extreme:
speed*) moderado, -a; (*increase, means*) mesurado, -a; (*price*) módico, -a II. *n* POL moderado,
-a *m, f*
moderate[2] ['mad·ə·reɪt] I. *vt* moderar; **to** ~ **a**
debate moderar un debate II. *vi* 1.(*act as
moderator*) hacer de moderador 2.(*become
less extreme*) moderarse
moderation [ˌmad·ə·'reɪ·ʃən] *n* moderación *f;*
to drink in ~ beber con moderación
moderator ['mad·ə·reɪ·tər] *n form* 1.(*mediator*) mediador(a) *m(f)* 2.(*of discussion*) mo-
derador(a) *m(f)*
modern ['mad·ərn] *adj* moderno, -a
modernization [ˌmad·ər·nɪ·'zeɪ·ʃən] *n* modernización *f*
modernize ['mad·ər·naɪz] *vt* modernizar
modest ['mad·ɪst] *adj* 1.(*not boastful*) modesto, -a; **to be** ~ **about sth** ser modesto en
algo 2.(*moderate*) moderado, -a; **a** ~ **wage**
increase una modesta subida de sueldo
modesty ['mad·ɪ·sti] *n* modestia *f*
modicum ['mad·ɪ·kəm] *n* pizca *f,* pisca *f Méx;*
a ~ **of truth** una pizca de verdad
modifiable ['mad·ɪ·faɪ·ə·bəl] *adj* modificable
modification [ˌmad·ɪ·fɪ·'keɪ·ʃən] *n* modifica-

ción *f*
modifier ['mad·ɪ·faɪ·ər] *n* LING modificador *m*
modify ['mad·ɪ·faɪ] <-ie-> *vt a.* LING modificar
modular ['madʒ·ə·lər] *adj* modular; (*construction, degree*) por módulos
modulate ['madʒ·ə·leɪt] *vt a.* ELEC, RADIO, TV
modular
modulation [ˌmadʒ·ə·'leɪ·ʃən] *n* modulación *f*
module ['madʒ·ul] *n* módulo *m*
mohair ['mou·her] *n* mohair *m*
moist [mɔɪst] *adj* húmedo, -a
moisten ['mɔɪ·sən] I. *vt* humedecer II. *vi*
humedecerse
moisture ['mɔɪs·tʃər] *n* humedad *f*
moisturize ['mɔɪs·tʃə·raɪz] *vt* hidratar
moisturizer *n* hidratante *m*
molar[1] ['mou·lər] *n* muela *f*
molar[2] ['mou·lər] *adj* CHEM molar
molasses [mou·'læs·ɪz] *n* melaza *f*
mold[1] [mould] I. *n* (*for metal, clay, jelly*)
molde *m* ▶ **to be cast in the same** ~ estar
cortado por el mismo patrón II. *vt* moldear
mold[2] [mould] *n* BOT moho *m*
Moldavia [mal·'deɪ·vi·ə] *n s.* **Moldova**
Moldavian I. *adj* moldavo, -a II. *n* 1.(*person*)
moldavo, -a *m, f* 2. LING moldavo *m*
molder ['moul·dər] *vi* echarse a perder; *fig* desmoronarse
molding ['moul·dɪŋ] *n* ARCHIT moldura *f*
Moldova [mal·'dou·və] *n* Moldavia *f*
Moldovan I. *adj* moldavo, -a II. *n* moldavo, -a
m, f
moldy ['moul·di] <-ier, -iest> *adj* 1.CULIN
(*food*) mohoso, -a 2.(*stale*) a moho, rancio, -a
mole[1] [moul] *n* ANAT lunar *m*
mole[2] [moul] *n* 1.ZOOL topo *m* 2.(*spy*) topo *mf*
mole[3] [moul] *n* CHEM mol *m*
molecular [mə·'lek·jə·lər] *adj* molecular
molecule ['mal·ɪ·kjul] *n* molécula *f*
molehill ['moul·hɪl] *n* topera *f*
molest [mə·'lest] *vt* 1.(*pester*) importunar
2.(*sexually*) abusar (sexualmente) de
moll [mal] *n sl* amiga *f* de un gángster
mollify ['mal·ə·faɪ] <-ie-> *vt* 1.(*pacify*) apaciguar 2.(*reduce effect*) aplacar
mollusc *n,* **mollusk** ['mal·əsk] *n* molusco *m*
mollycoddle ['mal·ɪ·kad·əl] *vt* mimar, apapa-
char *Cuba, Méx, inf*
Molotov cocktail [ˌmal·ə·tɔf·'kak·teɪl] *n* cóctel
m molotov
molt [moult] ZOOL I. *vi* mudar II. *vt* mudar
III. *n* muda *f,* cambio *m Méx*
molten ['moul·tən] *adj* fundido, -a
mom [mam] *n inf* mamá *f*
moment ['mou·mənt] *n* momento *m; at the* ~
por el momento; **at any** ~ en cualquier
momento; **at the last** ~ en el último
momento; **in a** ~ enseguida; **not for a** ~ ni por
un momento; **the** ~ **that...** en cuanto... +*subj;*
the ~ **of truth** la hora de la verdad; **at the**
(**precise**) ~ **when...** en el (preciso) momento
en que...; **to choose one's** ~ escoger el
momento; **to leave sth until the last** ~ dejar

algo hasta el último momento

momentarily [ˌmoʊ·mən·'ter·ɪ·li] *adv* **1.** (*very briefly*) por un momento **2.** (*very soon*) en un momento

momentary ['moʊ·mən·ter·i] *adj* momentáneo, -a

momentous [moʊ·'men·təs] *adj* (*fact*) trascendental; (*day*) memorable

momentum [moʊ·'men·təm] *n* PHYS momento *m;* *fig* impulso *m;* **to gather ~** coger velocidad

momma ['ma·mə] *n*, **mommy** ['mam·i] *n inf* mamá *f*

Mon. *n abbr of* **Monday** lun.

Monaco ['man·ə·koʊ] *n* Mónaco *m*

monarch ['man·ərk] *n* monarca *mf*

monarchic [mə·'nar·kɪk] *adj*, **monarchical** [mə·'nar·kɪ·kəl] *adj* monárquico, -a

monarchism ['man·ər·kɪz·əm] *n* monarquismo *m*

monarchist ['man·ər·kɪst] *n* monárquico, -a *m, f*

monarchy ['man·ər·ki] <-ies> *n* monarquía *f*

monastery ['man·ə·ster·i] <-ies> *n* monasterio *m*

monastic [mə·'næs·tɪk] *adj* **1.** REL monástico, -a **2.** (*ascetic*) monacal

Monday ['mʌn·di] *n* lunes *m inv;* **Easter** [*o* **Whit**] **~** lunes de Pascua; *s.a.* **Friday**

monetary ['man·ə·ter·i] *adj* monetario, -a

monetary fund *n* fondo *m* monetario

monetary policy *n* política *f* monetaria

Monetary Union *n* Unión *f* Monetaria

money ['mʌn·i] *n* dinero *m;* **to be short of ~** ir escaso de dinero; **to change ~** cambiar dinero; **to make ~** hacer dinero; **to raise ~** recolectar fondos; **to throw ~ at sth** malgastar dinero en algo ▶ **~ is the root of all evil** *prov* el dinero es la fuente de todos los males *prov;* **put your ~ where your mouth is** predica con el ejemplo; **~ doesn't grow on trees** *prov* el dinero no cae del cielo *prov;* **to be made of ~** nadar en la abundancia; **he has ~ to burn** le sale el dinero por las orejas; **to marry into ~** casarse con alguien rico; **~ talks** *prov* poderoso caballero es don Dinero *prov;* **to be in the ~** estar forrado; **for my ~** en mi opinión

moneybags ['mʌn·i·bægz] *npl inf* ricachón, -ona *m, f*

moneychanger *n* cambista *mf*

moneyed *adj form* adinerado, -a

moneymaker *n* mina *f* (de dinero) *fig*

moneymaking **I.** *adj* muy lucrativo, -a **II.** *n* ganancia *f*

money market *n* mercado *m* monetario

money market account *n* cuenta *f* de depósitos a plazo

money order *n* giro *m* postal

Mongol ['maŋ·gəl] **I.** *adj* mongol(a) **II.** *n* **1.** (*person*) mongol(a) *m(f)* **2.** LING mongol *m*

Mongolia [maŋ·'goʊ·li·ə] *n* Mongolia *f*

Mongolian [maŋ·'goʊ·li·ən] **I.** *adj* mongol(a) **II.** *n* **1.** (*person*) mongol(a) *m(f)* **2.** LING mongol *m*

mongolism ['maŋ·gə·lɪz·əm] *n* mongolismo *m*

mongrel ['maŋ·grəl] **I.** *n* perro *m* cruzado, chucho *m pey* **II.** *adj* mestizo, -a

monitor ['man·ɪ·ţər] **I.** *n* **1.** COMPUT monitor *m;* **15-inch ~** monitor de 15 pulgadas **2.** (*person*) supervisor(a) *m(f)* **II.** *vt* controlar; **to ~ sb/sth closely** seguir a alguien/algo de muy cerca

monk [mʌŋk] *n* monje *m*

monkey ['mʌŋ·ki] *n* mono, -a *m, f* ▶ **to have a ~ on your back** tener un problemón
♦ **monkey around** *vi inf* hacer el indio

monkey bars *n pl* columpio *m* de barras

monkey business *n* **1.** (*improper conduct*) tejemaneje *m* **2.** (*mischief*) travesura *f*

monkey wrench *n* <-es> llave *f* inglesa

monkfish *n* rape *m*

mono[1] ['man·oʊ] **I.** *n* monofonía *f* **II.** *adj* mono *inv*

mono[2] ['man·oʊ] *n inf* MED *abbr of* (**infectious**) **mononucleosis** mononucleosis *f*

monochrome ['man·oʊ·kroʊm] *adj* monocromo, -a

monocle ['man·ə·kəl] *n* monóculo *m*

monogamous [mə·'nag·ə·məs] *adj* monógamo, -a

monogamy [mə·'nag·ə·mi] *n* monogamia *f*

monogram ['man·ə·græm] *n* monograma *m*

monolingual [ˌman·oʊ·'lɪŋ·gwəl] *adj* monolingüe

monolith ['man·ə·lɪθ] *n* monolito *m*

monolithic [ˌman·ə·'lɪθ·ɪk] *adj* monolítico, -a

monolog *n*, **monologue** ['man·ə·lag] *n* monólogo *m*

monopolize [mə·'nap·ə·laɪz] *vt* monopolizar

monopoly [mə·'nap·ə·li] <-ies> *n* monopolio *m*

monorail ['man·oʊ·reɪl] *n* monorraíl *m*

monosyllabic [ˌman·ə·sɪ·'læb·ɪk] *adj* monosilábico, -a

monotone ['man·ə·toʊn] *n* tono *m* monocorde

monotonous [mə·'nat·ən·əs] *adj* monótono, -a

monotony [mə·'nat·ən·i] *n* monotonía *f*

monoxide [mə·'nak·saɪd] *n* monóxido *m*

monsoon [man·'sun] *n* monzón *m;* **~s** lluvias *fpl* monzónicas

monster ['man·stər] **I.** *n* monstruo *m* **II.** *adj inf* pedazo de

monstrosity [man·'stras·ə·ţi] <-ies> *n* monstruosidad *f*

monstrous ['man·strəs] *adj* **1.** (*very big*) enorme **2.** (*awful*) monstruoso, -a **3.** (*outrageous*) escandaloso, -a

montage ['man·taʒ] *n* montaje *m*

Mont. *n abbr of* **Montana** Montana *f*

Montana [man·'tæn·ə] *n* Montana *f*

month [mʌnθ] *n* mes *m*

monthly ['mʌnθ·li] **I.** *adj* mensual **II.** *adv* mensualmente **III.** *n* publicación *f* mensual

monument ['man·jə·mənt] *n* monumento *m*

monumental [ˌman·jə·'men·təl] *adj* (*very big*)

M

monumental; (*error*) garrafal

moo [mu] I.<-s> *n* mugido *m* II. *vi* mugir

mood¹ [mud] *n* humor *m;* **in a good/bad ~** de buen/mal humor; **the public ~** el ánimo general; **to be in a talkative ~** estar hablador; **to not be in the ~ to do sth** no tener ganas de hacer algo

mood² [mud] *n* LING modo *m*

moodiness ['mu·dɪ·nɪs] *n* mal humor *m*

moody ['mu·di] <-ier, -iest> *adj* **1.** (*change-able*) voluble **2.** (*bad-tempered*) malhumorado, -a

moon [mun] I. *n* luna *f;* **full/new ~** luna llena/nueva ▶ **once in a blue ~** de higos a brevas, de Pascuas a Ramos; **to be over the ~** estar como un niño con zapatos nuevos II. *vt sl* **to ~ sb** hacer un calvo a alguien, mostrar el trasero a alguien

moonbeam ['mun·bim] *n* rayo *m* de luna

moonboots *npl* botas *fpl* de après-ski

moonlight I. *n* luz *f* de la luna II. *vi inf* estar pluriempleado

moonlit *adj* iluminado, -a por la luna

moonshine *n* **1.** *inf* (*alcoholic drink*) bebida alcohólica destilada ilegalmente **2.** (*moonlight*) claro *m* de luna

moonwalk I. *n* **1.** (*on moon*) paseo *m* por la luna **2.** (*glide*) moonwalk *m, paso de baile* II. *vi* **1.** (*on moon*) andar en la luna **2.** (*glide*) bailar el moonwalk

moor¹ [mʊr] *n* (*area*) páramo *m*

moor² [mʊr] *vt* NAUT amarrar

moorhen ['mʊr·hen] *n* polla *f* de agua

mooring ['mʊr·ɪŋ] *n* amarra *f*

moose [mus] *n* alce *m* americano

moot [mut] I. *adj* discutible; **the point is ~** eso es discutible II. *vt* **it has been ~ed that...** se ha sugerido que...

mop [map] I. *n* **1.** (*cleaning device*) fregona *f*, trapeador *Chile, Méx* **2.** (*mass*) **a ~ of hair** una mata de pelo II. <-pp-> *vt* fregar

mope [moʊp] *vi* estar deprimido

◆**mope about** *vi*, **mope around** *vi* andar deprimido

moped ['moʊ·ped] *n* ciclomotor *m*

moral ['mɔr·əl] I. *adj* moral; **to give sb ~ support** dar apoyo moral a alguien II. *n* **1.** (*message*) moraleja *f;* **the ~ of the story** la moraleja del cuento **2. ~s** (*standards*) moralidad *f*

morale [mə·'ræl] *n* moral *f*

moralist ['mɔr·ə·lɪst] *n* moralista *mf*

morality [mɔ·'ræl·ə·t̬i] <-ies> *n* moralidad *f*

moralize ['mɔr·ə·laɪz] *vi* moralizar

morass [mə·'ræs] *n* **1.** (*boggy area*) cenagal *m* **2.** *fig* (*complicated situation*) laberinto *m*

moratorium [ˌmɔr·ə·'tɔr·i·əm] <-s *o* -ria> *n form* moratoria *f*

morbid ['mɔr·bɪd] *adj* **1.** MED mórbido, -a **2.** (*person, interest*) morboso, -a

morbidity [mɔr·'bɪd·ə·t̬i] *n* morbosidad *f*

more [mɔr] *comp of* **much, many** I. *adj* más; **~ money/coins** más dinero/monedas; **a few ~ coins** unas pocas monedas más; **no ~**

money at all nada más de dinero; **some ~ money** un poco más de dinero II. *adv* más; **~ beautiful than me** más guapo que yo; **to drink (a bit/much) ~** beber (un poco/mucho) más; **once ~** una vez más; **never ~** nunca más; **to see ~ of sb** volver a ver a alguien; **~ than 10** más de 10 III. *pron* más; **~ and ~** más y más; **to have ~ than sb** tener más que alguien; **to cost ~ than sth** costar más que algo; **the ~ you try it, the ~ you'll like it** cuanto más lo tomas, más te gusta; **what ~ does he want?** ¿qué más quiere?; **many do it but ~ don't** muchos lo hacen, pero la mayoría no ▶ **all the ~** tanto más

moreover [mɔr·'oʊ·vər] *adv form* además

morgue [mɔrg] *n* depósito *m* de cadáveres, afanaduaría *f Méx*

moribund ['mɔr·ə·bʌnd] *adj form* moribundo, -a

Mormon ['mɔr·mən] I. *n* mormón, -ona *m, f* II. *adj* mormónico, -a

morning ['mɔr·nɪŋ] I. *n* mañana *f;* **good ~!** ¡buenos días!; **in the ~** por la mañana; **that ~** esa mañana; **the ~ after** la mañana siguiente; **every ~** cada mañana; **every Monday ~** cada lunes por la mañana; **to come in the ~** venir por la mañana; **one July ~** una mañana de julio; **early in the ~** por la mañana temprano; **6 o'clock in the ~** las 6 de la mañana; **from ~ until night** de la mañana a la noche II. *interj inf* ¡buenas!

morning-after pill [ˌmɔr·nɪŋ·'æf·tər·ˌpɪl] *n* píldora *f* del día después

Morning Prayer *n* maitines *mpl*

morning sickness *n* náuseas *fpl* matutinas

morning star *n* lucero *m* del alba

Moroccan [mə·'rak·ən] I. *n* marroquí *mf* II. *adj* marroquí

Morocco [mə·'rak·oʊ] *n* Marruecos *m*

moron ['mɔr·an] *n* capullo, -a *m, f*

moronic [mɔ·'ran·ɪk] *adj* capullo, -a

morose [mə·'roʊs] *adj* (*person, mood*) taciturno, -a; (*expression*) sombrío, -a

morpheme ['mɔr·fim] *n* LING morfema *m*

morphia ['mɔr·fi·ə] *n*, **morphine** ['mɔr·fin] *n* morfina *f*

morphological [ˌmɔr·fə·'ladʒ·ɪ·kəl] *adj* morfológico, -a

morphology [mɔr·'fal·ə·dʒi] *n* morfología *f*

Morse (code) [mɔrs] *n* morse *m*

morsel ['mɔr·səl] *n* (*of food*) bocado *m;* (*of hope*) brizna *f*

mortal ['mɔr·t̬əl] I. *adj* mortal; **~ danger** peligro *m* de muerte; **to be in ~ fear** estar aterrado II. *n liter* mortal *mf*

mortality [mɔr·'tæl·ə·t̬i] *n form* mortalidad *f*

mortar ['mɔr·tər] *n a.* MIL, TECH mortero *m*

mortarboard ['mɔr·tər·bɔrd] *n* birrete *m*, capelo *m Cuba, PRico, Ven*

mortgage ['mɔr·gɪdʒ] I. *n* hipoteca *f* II. *vt* hipotecar

mortician [mɔr·'tɪʃ·ən] *n* director(a) *m(f)* de funeraria

mortification [ˌmɔr·tə·fɪ·'keɪ·ʃən] *n* **1.** (*embarrassment*) humillación *f* **2.** REL mortificación *f*
mortify ['mɔr·tə·faɪ] *vt* <-ie-> **1.** (*embarrass*) avergonzar **2.** REL mortificar
mortuary ['mɔr·tʃu·er·i] *n* tanatorio *m*
mosaic [mou·'zeɪ·ɪk] *n* mosaico *m*
Moscow ['mas·kaʊ] *n* Moscú *m*
Moses ['mou·zɪz] *n* Moisés *m*
Moslem ['maz·ləm] **I.** *adj* musulmán, -ana **II.** *n* musulmán, -ana *m, f*
mosque [mask] *n* mezquita *f*
mosquito [mə·'ski·tou] <-(e)s> *n* mosquito *m*, zancudo *m AmL*
mosquito net *n* mosquitera *f*
moss [mas] <-es> *n* musgo *m*
mossy ['mas·i] <-ier, -iest> *adj* musgoso, -a
most [moust] *superl of* **many, much I.** *adj* la mayoría de; ~ **people** la mayoría de la gente; **to have the ~ friends** tener más amigos que nadie; **for the ~ part** en su mayor parte **II.** *adv* más; **the ~ beautiful** el más bello, la más bella; **a ~ beautiful evening** una tarde de lo más bella; **what I want ~** lo que más quiero; ~ **of all** más que nada; ~ **likely** muy probablemente **III.** *pron* la mayoría; **at the (very) ~** a lo sumo; ~ **of them** la mayoría de ellos; ~ **of the time** la mayor parte del tiempo; **to make the ~ of sth/of oneself** sacar el máximo partido a [*o* de] algo/sí mismo; **the ~ you can have is...** lo máximo que puedes tener es...
mostly ['moust·li] *adv* **1.** (*mainly*) sobre todo **2.** (*usually*) en general
motel [mou·'tel] *n* motel *m*, hotel-garaje *m AmL*
moth [mɔθ] *n* polilla *f*
mothball ['mɔθ·bɔl] **I.** *n* bola *f* de naftalina **II.** *vt* (*idea, plan*) aparcar *fig*
moth-eaten ['mɔθ·ˌi·tən] *adj* apolillado, -a
mother ['mʌð·ər] **I.** *n* **1.** (*woman*) madre *f* **2.** (*biggest thing*) madre; **that was the ~ of all wars** esa fue la madre de todas las guerras **II.** *vt* mimar
mother country *n* madre patria *f*
motherhood *n* maternidad *f*
mother-in-law *n* suegra *f*
motherly ['mʌð·ər·li] *adj* maternal
mother-of-pearl *n* nácar *m*
Mother's Day *n* día m de la madre
mother tongue *n* lengua *f* materna
motif [mou·'tif] *n* ART motivo *m*
motion ['mou·ʃən] **I.** *n* **1.** (*movement*) movimiento *m;* **in slow ~** a cámara lenta; **to put sth in ~** poner algo en marcha **2.** (*proposal*) moción *f* ▶ **to go through the ~s** cumplir con las formalidades **II.** *vt* indicar con un gesto; **to ~ sb to do sth** indicar a alguien que haga algo **III.** *vi* hacer señas
motionless *adj* inmóvil
motion picture *n* película *f*
motivate ['mou·tə·veɪt] *vt* **1.** (*cause*) motivar **2.** (*arouse interest of*) animar
motivation [ˌmou·tə·'veɪ·ʃən] *n* **1.** (*reason*) motivo *m* **2.** (*ambition, drive*) motivación *f*

motive ['mou·tɪv] **I.** *n* motivo *m* **II.** *adj* PHYS, TECH motriz
motley ['mat·li] <-ier, -iest> *adj pej* variopinto, -a
motor ['mou·tər] **I.** *n a. fig* motor *m* **II.** *adj a.* PHYS motor, motriz **III.** *vi form* (*drive*) ir en coche
motorbike *n* moto *f*
motorboat *n* lancha *f* motora
motorcycle *n* motocicleta *f*
motorcycling *n* motociclismo *m*
motorcyclist *n* motociclista *mf*
motor home *n* autocaravana *f*, casa *f* rodante *Méx*, carro-casa *m Col;* (*van*) furgoneta *f* convertida
motorist ['mou·tər·ɪst] *n* conductor(a) *m(f)*
motorize ['mou·tə·raɪz] *vt* motorizar
motor racing *n* automovilismo *m*
motor scooter *n* scooter *f*
motor vehicle *n form* automóvil *m*
mottled ['mat·əld] *adj* (*leaf, marble*) jaspeado, -a; (*skin*) manchado, -a
motto ['mat·ou] <-(e)s> *n* lema *m*
mound [maʊnd] *n* **1.** (*elevation*) montículo *m* **2.** (*heap*) montón *m* **3.** (*in baseball*) **the pitcher's** ~ el montículo del lanzador
mount [maʊnt] **I.** *n* **1.** (*horse*) montura *f* **2.** (*frame*) marco *m* **II.** *vt* **1.** (*get on: horse*) montar; **to ~ a ladder** subirse a una escalera; **to ~ the throne** *form* ascender al trono **2.** (*organize*) organizar; **to ~ a rescue/an attack** organizar un rescate/ataque **3.** (*fix for display*) fijar; (*stamps*) pegar **4.** ZOOL montar **III.** *vi* montarse
mountain ['maʊn·tən] *n* **1.** GEO montaña *f* **2.** *inf* (*amount*) montón *m* ▶ **to make a ~ out of a molehill** ahogarse en un vaso de agua, hacer de la camisa un trapo *Col, Ven;* **to move** ~s mover cielo y tierra
mountain bike *n* bicicleta *f* de montaña
mountain chain *n* GEO cordillera *f*
mountaineer [ˌmaʊn·tə·'nɪr] *n* montañero, -a *m, f*
mountaineering *n* montañismo *m*
mountainous ['maʊn·tə·nəs] *adj* **1.** GEO montañoso, -a **2.** (*large and high*) gigantesco, -a
mountain range *n* GEO sierra *f*
mounted ['maʊn·tɪd] *adj* montado, -a; ~ **police** policía *f* montada
mounting *n* (*of machine*) base *f;* (*in frame*) montaje *m*
mourn [mɔrn] **I.** *vi* lamentarse; **to ~ for sb** llorar la muerte de alguien **II.** *vt* llorar la muerte de
mourner ['mɔr·nər] *n* doliente *mf*
mournful ['mɔrn·fəl] *adj* **1.** (*grieving*) afligido, -a **2.** (*gloomy*) triste
mourning ['mɔr·nɪŋ] *n* luto *m;* **to be in** ~ estar de luto
mouse [maʊs] <mice> *n* ZOOL, COMPUT ratón *m* ▶ **to be as poor as a church** ~ ser más pobre que las ratas
mouse pad *n* COMPUT alfombrilla *f* del ratón

M

mousetrap *n* ratonera *f*
mousse [mus] *n* mousse *mf*
moustache ['mʌs·tæʃ] *n* bigote *m*
mousy ['maʊ·si] *adj* 1.(*shy*) apocado, -a; **she is very ~** es muy poquita cosa 2.(*brown*) pardo, -a
mouth¹ [maʊθ] *n* 1.(*of person, animal*) boca *f;* **to shut one's ~** *inf* cerrar el pico 2.(*opening*) abertura *f;* (*of bottle, jar, well*) boca *f;* (*of cave*) entrada *f;* (*of river*) desembocadura *f* ▶ **to be born with a silver spoon in one's ~** nacer con un pan debajo del brazo; **it made her ~ water** se le hizo la boca agua con eso; **to be down in the ~** estar de capa caída; **to shoot off one's ~ about sth** *inf* irse de la lengua sobre algo
mouth² [maʊð] *vt* 1.(*form words silently*) articular 2.(*say insincerely*) soltar; **to ~ an excuse** soltar la excusa de rigor
◆**mouth off** *vi sl* 1.(*rant*) despotricar 2.(*talk back*) protestar, revirar
mouthful ['maʊθ·fʊl] *n* (*of food*) bocado *m;* (*of drink*) sorbo *m*
mouthpiece *n* 1. TEL micrófono *m* 2.(*of pipe, instrument*) boquilla *f* 3.(*person*) portavoz *mf*
mouth-to-mouth resuscitation *n* reanimación *f* boca a boca
mouthwash *n* enjuague *m* bucal
mouthwatering *adj* apetitoso, -a
movable ['mu·və·bəl] *adj* móvil
move [muv] I. *n* 1.(*movement*) movimiento *m;* **to be on the ~** (*traveling*) estar de viaje; (*very busy*) no parar; **to get a ~ on** darse prisa 2.(*change of abode*) mudanza *f;* (*change of job*) traslado *m* 3. GAMES jugada *f;* **it's your ~** te toca (a ti) 4.(*action*) paso *m;* **to make the first ~** dar el primer paso II. *vi* 1.(*change position*) moverse; (*advance fast*) avanzar; (*make progress*) hacer progresos 2.(*in games*) mover 3.(*change abode*) mudarse; (*change job*) cambiar de trabajo ▶ **~ it!** *inf* ¡apúrate! III. *vt* 1.(*change position*) mover; (*make sb change their mind*) hacer cambiar de idea; (*reschedule*) cambiar la fecha de 2.(*cause emotions*) conmover; **to be ~d by sth** estar conmovido por algo 3.(*propose*) proponer
◆**move along** I. *vt* hacer circular II. *vi* circular
◆**move away** I. *vi* mudarse II. *vt* apartar
◆**move back** I. *vi* retirarse II. *vt* colocar más atrás
◆**move down** *vi, vt* bajar
◆**move forward** I. *vi* avanzar II. *vt* mover hacia adelante; (*date*) adelantar
◆**move in** I. *vi* 1.(*move into abode*) instalarse 2.(*intervene*) intervenir 3.(*advance to attack*) avanzar; **to ~ on enemy territory** invadir territorio enemigo II. *vt* instalar
◆**move on** *vi* 1.(*leave*) partir 2.(*continue to move*) seguir adelante; **to ~ to another subject** pasar a otro tema
◆**move out** *vi* 1.(*stop inhabiting*) dejar la casa 2.(*depart*) irse

◆**move over** I. *vi* 1.(*make room*) dejar sitio; (*on seat*) correrse hacia un lado 2.(*switch*) **to ~ towards sth** cambiar a algo II. *vt* mover a un lado
◆**move up** I. *vi* 1.(*make room*) hacer sitio; (*on seat*) correrse hacia un lado 2.(*increase*) subir 3.(*advance*) ascender; **he's slowly but surely moving up in the company** está ascendiendo en la empresa de forma lenta, pero segura II. *vt* subir
movement ['muv·mənt] *n* 1. a. MUS (*act*) movimiento *m* 2. FIN, COM actividad *f* 3.(*tendency*) tendencia *f*
movie ['mu·vi] *n* película *f;* **the ~s** el cine
movie camera *n* cámara *f* cinematográfica
moviegoer *n* cinéfilo, -a *m, f,* aficionado, -a *m,* al cine
movie star *n* estrella *f* de cine
movie theater *n* cine *m*
moving ['mu·vɪŋ] I. *adj* 1.(*that moves*) móvil; **~ stairs** escaleras mecánicas 2.(*motivating*) motor, motriz; **the ~ force** la fuerza motriz 3.(*causing emotion*) conmovedor(a) II. *n* mudanza *f*
moving box *n* caja *f* de embalaje
mow [moʊ] <mowed, mown *o* mowed> *vt* (*grass*) cortar; (*hay*) segar
◆**mow down** *vt* 1.(*kill*) acribillar 2.(*overwhelm*) aplastar
mower ['moʊ·ər] *n* (*for lawn*) cortacésped *m*
mown [moʊn] *pp of* **mow**
moxie ['mak·si] *n sl* (*courage*) huevos *mpl vulg*
MP [ˌem·'pi] *n abbr of* **Military Police** policía *f* militar
mpg *n abbr of* **miles per gallon** millas *fpl* por galón
mph [ˌem·pi·'eɪtʃ] *abbr of* **miles per hour** m/h
Mr. ['mɪs·tər] *n abbr of* **Mister** Sr.
Mrs. ['mɪs·ɪz] *n* Sra.
Ms. [mɪz] *n forma de tratamiento que se aplica tanto a mujeres solteras como casadas*
MS [ˌem·'es] 1. *abbr of* **multiple sclerosis** esclerosis *f inv* múltiple 2. *abbr of* **Mississippi** Misisipí *m* 3. *abbr of* **Master of Science** máster *m;* **Louie Sanders, MS** Louie Sanders, licenciado con máster
MSG [ˌem·es·'dʒi] *abbr of* **monosodium glutamate** glutamato *m* monosódico
MT *n* 1. *abbr of* **Montana** Montana *f* 2. *abbr of* **Mountain Time** Mountain Time (*zona horaria*)
Mt. *abbr of* **Mount** mte.
much [mʌtʃ] <more, most> I. *adj* mucho, mucha; **too ~ wine** demasiado vino; **how ~ milk?** ¿cuánta leche?; **too/so ~ water** demasiada/tanta agua; **as ~ as** tanto como; **three times as ~** tres veces más II. *adv* mucho; **~ better** mucho mejor; **thank you very ~** muchas gracias; **to be very ~ surprised** estar muy sorprendido; **~ to my astonishment** para gran sorpresa mía; **not him, ~ less her** él no, y mucho menos ella III. *pron* mucho; **~ of the day** la mayor parte del día; **I don't think**

~ **of it** no le doy mucha importancia; **to make**
~ **of sb/sth** dar importancia a alguien/algo
muck [mʌk] n 1.(*dirt*) suciedad f 2.(*manure*)
estiércol m ▶ **to be stuck in the** ~ estar estancado
◆ **muck up** vt inf cagarla
muckheap n estercolero, -a m, f
muckraker ['mʌk·reɪ·kər] n revelador(a) m(f)
de escándalos
mucky ['mʌk·i] <-ier, -iest> adj inf guarro, -a
mucous ['mju·kəs] adj MED mucoso, -a
mucous membrane n membrana f mucosa
mucus ['mju·kəs] n MED mucosidad m
mud [mʌd] n 1.(*wet earth*) barro m; **to wallow in** ~ revolcarse en el fango 2.(*insult*) **to
hurl** ~ **at sb** insultar a alguien ▶ **to drag sb's
name through the** ~ ensuciar el nombre de
alguien
muddle ['mʌd·əl] I. vt 1.(*mix up*) desordenar
2.(*confuse*) confundir II. vi **to** ~ **along** ir tirando III. n desorden m, desparpajo m AmL;
to get into a ~ liarse
muddle-headed ['mʌd·əl·ˌhed·ɪd] adj atontado, -a
muddy ['mʌd·i] I. <-ier, -iest> adj (*dirty*)
lleno, -a de barro; (*water*) turbio, -a; (*ground*)
fangoso, -a II. vt 1.(*make dirty*) manchar de
barro 2.(*confuse*) confundir ▶ **to** ~ **the
waters** complicar las cosas, crear confusión
mud flap n, **mudguard** ['mʌd·gard] n guardabarros m inv, salpicadera f Méx
mudslide n 1.(*flow*) avalancha f de lodo
2.(*alcoholic drink*) mudslide m (*cóctel que
contiene crema de whisky*)
mudslinging n inf insulto f
muff[1] [mʌf] I. vt 1.(*screw up: opportunity*)
echar a perder; THEAT (*one's lines*) decir mal
2. SPORTS perder [o botar] (un pase) II. n inepto,
-a m, f
muff[2] [mʌf] n FASHION manguito m
muffin ['mʌf·ɪn] n especie de magdalena
muffle ['mʌf·əl] vt amortiguar
muffler ['mʌf·lər] n AUTO silenciador m
mug[1] [mʌg] n (*for tea, coffee*) tazón m; (*for
beer*) jarra m
mug[2] [mʌg] I. n inf jeta f, escracho m RíoPl
II. <-gg-> vt atracar
mugger ['mʌg·ər] n atracador(a) m(f)
mugging ['mʌg·ɪŋ] n atraco m
muggy ['mʌg·i] <-ier, -iest> adj bochornoso, -a
mulberry ['mʌl·ber·i] n 1.(*fruit*) mora f
2.(*tree*) morera f
mule [mjul] n (*animal*) mulo, -a m, f ▶ **as
stubborn as a** ~ terco como una mula
mull [mʌl] vt **to** ~ **sth over** meditar algo
mulled wine [ˌmʌld·'waɪn] n vino tinto
caliente aromatizado con especias
mullet ['mʌl·ɪt] n 1.(*fish*) mújol m 2. inf (*hairstyle*) peinado por delante corto, por detrás
largo
mullion ['mʌl·jən] n ARCHIT parteluz m
multicolored [ˌmʌl·ti·'kʌl·ərd] adj multicolor

multicultural [ˌmʌl·ti·'kʌl·tʃər·əl] adj multicultural
multifarious [ˌmʌl·tə·'fer·i·əs] adj form
diverso, -a
multifunctional [ˌmʌl·ti·'fʌnk·ʃə·nəl] adj
multifuncional
multilateral [ˌmʌl·ti·'læt̬·ər·əl] adj POL multilateral
multilingual [ˌmʌl·ti·'lɪŋ·gwəl] adj plurilingüe
multilingualism [ˌmʌl·ti·'lɪŋ·gwəl·ɪz·əm] n
plurilingüismo m
multimedia [ˌmʌl·ti·'mi·di·ə] adj multimedia
inv
multimillionaire [ˌmʌl·ti·mil·jə·'ner] n multimillonario, -a m, f
multinational [ˌmʌl·ti·'næʃ·ə·nəl] I. n multinacional f II. adj multinacional
multiplayer ['mʌl·ti·pleɪ·ər] adj (*computer
game*) juego m multijudador
multiple ['mʌl·tə·pəl] adj múltiple
multiplex ['mʌl·tə·pleks] n multicines mpl
multiplication [ˌmʌl·tə·plɪ·'keɪ·ʃən] n multiplicación f
multiplicity [ˌmʌl·tə·'plɪs·ə·t̬i] n form multiplicidad f
multiplier ['mʌl·tə·plaɪ·ər] n MATH multiplicador m
multiply ['mʌl·tə·plaɪ] <-ie-> I. vt multiplicar
II. vi multiplicarse
multipurpose [ˌmʌl·ti·'pɜr·pəs] adj multiuso
multiracial [ˌmʌl·ti·'reɪ·ʃəl] adj multirracial
multistage [ˌmʌl·ti·'steɪdʒ] adj de varios escalones
multistory [ˌmʌl·ti·'stɔr·i] adj de varios pisos [o
plantas]
multitasking [ˌmʌl·ti·'tæs·kɪŋ] n COMPUT multitarea f
multitude ['mʌl·tə·tud] n 1.(*of things, problems*) multitud f 2.(*crowd*) muchedumbre f;
the ~**s** *liter* las masas
multitudinous [ˌmʌl·tə·'tu·də·nəs] adj multitudinario, -a
mum [mʌm] adj **to keep** ~ inf guardar silencio
▶ ~'**s the word** chitón
mumble ['mʌm·bəl] vi hablar entre dientes
mumbo jumbo [ˌmʌm·bou·'dʒʌm·bou] n inf
galimatías m inv
mummify ['mʌm·ə·faɪ] <-ie-> vt momificar
mummy ['mʌm·i] <-ies> n momia f
mumps [mʌmps] n MED paperas fpl; **he's got
the** ~ tiene paperas
munch [mʌntʃ] vi, vt masticar
mundane [mʌn·'deɪn] adj prosaico, -a
municipal [mju·'nɪs·ə·pəl] adj municipal
municipality [mju·ˌnɪs·ə·'pæl·ə·t̬i] n <-ies>
1.(*city, town*) municipio m, comuna f AmL
2.(*local government*) municipalidad f
munitions [mju·'nɪʃ·ənz] npl municiones fpl
mural ['mjur·əl] n mural m
murder ['mɜr·dər] I. n (*killing*) asesinato m;
LAW homicidio m; **to commit** ~ cometer un
asesinato; **this job is** ~ fig este trabajo es matador; **he gets away with** ~ fig se le consiente

M

cualquier cosa ▶ **to scream bloody** ~ poner el grito en el cielo **II.** *vt* (*kill*) asesinar, ultimar *AmL;* *fig* (*music, play*) destrozar

murderer ['mɜr·dər·ər] *n* (*killer*) asesino, -a *m, f;* LAW homicida *mf,* victimario, -a *m, f AmL*

murderous ['mɜr·dər·əs] *adj* **1.** (*capable of murder*) mortífero, -a **2.** (*capable of causing death: instinct, look*) asesino, -a; (*plan*) criminal **3.** *inf* (*difficult: heat*) insufrible

murky ['mɜr·ki] <-ier, -iest> *adj* (*water, past*) turbio, -a; (*night*) nublado, -a

murmur ['mɜr·mər] **I.** *vi, vt* murmurar **II.** *n* murmullo *m*

muscle ['mʌs·əl] *n* **1.** ANAT músculo *m* **2.** *fig* poder *m*
◆ **muscle in** *vi* to ~ (**on sth**) entrometerse (en algo)

muscle-bound ['mʌs·əl·ˌbaʊnd] *adj* demasiado musculoso, -a

muscle car *n* cochazo *m,* carrazo *m AmS*

muscleman ['mʌs·əl·mæn] <-men> *n* forzudo *m*

muscular ['mʌs·kjə·lər] *adj* **1.** (*pain, contraction*) muscular **2.** (*arms, legs*) musculoso, -a

muse [mjuz] **I.** *vi* to ~ (**on sth**) cavilar [*o* reflexionar] (sobre algo) **II.** *vt* to ~ that... pensar que... **III.** *n* musa *f*

museum [mju·'zi·əm] *n* museo *m;* ~ **piece** pieza *f* de museo

mush[1] [mʌʃ] *n* **1.** *inf* (*food*) papilla *f* **2.** (*in a film, book*) cursilada *f*

mush[2] [mʌʃ] **I.** *interj* ¡vamos!, ¡arre! **II.** *vt* azuzar **III.** *vi* viajar en trineo **IV.** *n* viaje *m* en trineo

mushroom ['mʌʃ·rum] **I.** *n* (*wild*) seta *f,* callampa *f Col, Chile, Perú;* (*button mushroom*) champiñón *m* **II.** *vi* (*population, prices*) dispararse; (*town*) crecer de la noche a la mañana

mushy ['mʌʃ·i] *adj* <-ier, -iest> **1.** (*soft: food*) blando, -a **2.** (*film, book*) sensiblero, -a

music ['mju·zɪk] *n* **1.** (*art*) música *f;* **it was ~ to her ears** le sonó a música celestial **2.** (*notes*) partitura *f;* **to read** ~ leer música

musical ['mju·zɪ·kəl] **I.** *adj* musical **II.** *n* musical *m*

music box *n* caja *f* de música

music hall *n* music hall *m*

musician [mju·'zɪʃ·ən] *n* músico, -a *m, f*

music stand *n* atril *m*

musk [mʌsk] *n* almizcle *m*

musket ['mʌs·kɪt] *n* mosquete *m*

musketeer [ˌmʌs·kə·'tɪr] *n* mosquetero *m*

muskrat ['mʌs·kræt] *n* almizclera *f,* rata *f* almizclada

Muslim ['mʌz·ləm] **I.** *adj* musulmán, -ana **II.** *n* musulmán, -ana *m, f*

muslin ['mʌz·lɪn] *n* muselina *f*

muss [mʌs] *vt* desordenar

mussel ['mʌs·əl] *n* mejillón *m*

must [mʌst] **I.** *aux* **1.** (*obligation*) deber; ~ **you leave so soon?** ¿tienes que irte tan pronto?; **you ~n't do that** no debes hacer eso **2.** (*probability*) deber de; **I ~ have lost it** debo de

haberlo perdido; **you ~ be hungry** supongo que tendrás hambre; **you ~ be joking!** ¡estarás bromeando! **II.** *n* cosa *f* imprescindible; **this book is an absolute ~** este es un libro de lectura obligada

mustache ['mʌs·tæʃ] *n* bigote *m*

mustang ['mʌs·tæn] *n* mustang *m*

mustard ['mʌs·tərd] *n* mostaza *f*

muster ['mʌs·tər] **I.** *vt* **1.** (*gather*) reunir; **to ~ the courage to do sth** armarse de valor para hacer algo **2.** MIL alistar **II.** *vi* congregarse **III.** *n* **to pass** ~ ser aceptable

mustn't ['mʌs·ənt] *must not* **must**

must-see *adj inf* que hay que ver; **this is the ~ movie of the year** no puedes dejar de ver esta película (porque es muy buena)

musty ['mʌs·ti] <-ier, -iest> *adj* (*room*) que huele a humedad; (*book*) que huele a rancio [*o* a viejo]

mutant ['mju·tənt] **I.** *adj* mutante **II.** *n* mutante *mf*

mutation [mju·'ter·ʃən] *n* mutación *f*

mute [mjut] **I.** *n* **1.** (*person*) mudo, -a *m, f* **2.** MUS sordina *f* **II.** *vt* MUS poner sordina a **III.** *adj* mudo, -a; **to remain ~** permanecer mudo

muted *adj* apagado, -a

mutilate ['mju·tə·leɪt] *vt* mutilar

mutilation [ˌmju·tə·'leɪ·ʃən] *n* mutilación *f*

mutineer [ˌmju·tən·'ɪr] *n* amotinador(a) *m(f)*

mutinous ['mju·tə·nəs] *adj* amotinado, -a

mutiny ['mju·tɪ·ni] **I.** *n* <-ies> motín *m* **II.** *vi* <-ie-> amotinarse

mutter ['mʌt̬·ər] **I.** *vi* **1.** (*talk*) murmurar **2.** (*complain*) refunfuñar; **to ~ about sth** refunfuñar por algo **II.** *vt* murmurar **III.** *n* protesta *f* en voz baja

mutton ['mʌt̬·ən] *n* carne *f* de oveja

muttonchops *n pl* (*whiskers*) patillas *fpl* de boca de hacha

mutual ['mju·tʃu·əl] *adj* (*understanding*) mutuo, -a; (*friend, interest*) común

mutual fund *n* fondo *m* de inversión mobiliaria

mutually *adv* mutuamente; **it was ~ agreed** se decidió de común acuerdo

Muzak® ['mju·zæk] *n* hilo *m* musical

muzzle ['mʌz·əl] **I.** *n* **1.** (*of horse, dog*) hocico *m* **2.** (*for dog*) bozal *m* **3.** (*of gun*) boca *f* **II.** *vt* **1.** (*dog*) poner un bozal a **2.** *fig* (*person, newspaper*) amordazar

MVP *n abbr of* **most valuable player** premio *m* MVP

MW ['meg·ə·wat] *abbr of* **megawatt** OM

my [maɪ] **I.** *adj pos* mi; ~ **dog/house** mi perro/casa; ~ **children** mis hijos; **this car is ~ own** este coche es mío; **I hurt ~ foot/head** me he hecho daño en el pie/la cabeza **II.** *interj* ¡madre mía!

myopia [maɪ·'oʊ·pi·ə] *n* miopía *f*

myopic [maɪ·'ap·ɪk] *adj form* **1.** (*shortsighted*) miope **2.** *fig* corto, -a de miras

myriad ['mɪr·i·əd] *n* miríada *f*

myrrh [mɜr] *n* mirra *f*

myrtle ['mɜr·təl] *n* mirto *m*
myself [maɪ·'self] *pron reflexive* **1.** (*direct, indirect object*) me; **I hurt ~** me hice daño; **I deceived ~** me engañé a mí mismo; **when I express/exert ~** cuando me expreso/ esfuerzo; **I bought ~ a bag** me compré un bolso **2.** *emphatic* yo (mismo, misma); **my brother and ~** mi hermano y yo; **I'll do it ~** lo haré yo mismo; **I did it (all) by ~** lo hice (todo) yo solo **3.** *after prep* mí (mismo, misma); **I said to ~** me dije (a mí mismo); **I am ashamed of ~** estoy avergonzado de mí mismo; **I live by ~** vivo solo
mysterious [mɪ·'stɪr·i·əs] *adj* misterioso, -a
mystery ['mɪs·tə·ri] <-ies> *n* misterio *m*
mystic ['mɪs·tɪk] **I.** *n* místico, -a *m, f* **II.** *adj* místico, -a
mystical ['mɪs·tɪ·kəl] *adj* místico, -a
mysticism ['mɪs·tɪ·sɪz·əm] *n* misticismo *m*
mystification [ˌmɪs·tɪ·fɪ·'keɪ·ʃən] *n* **1.** (*mystery*) misterio *m* **2.** (*confusion*) confusión *f*, perplejidad *f*
mystify ['mɪs·tə·faɪ] *vt* <-ie-> desconcertar
mystique [mɪs·'tik] *n* mística *f*
myth [mɪθ] *n* mito *m*
mythical ['mɪθ·ɪ·kəl] *adj* **1.** (*legendary*) mítico, -a **2.** (*supposed*) supuesto, -a
mythological [ˌmɪθ·ə·'lɑdʒ·ɪ·kəl] *adj* mitológico, -a
mythology [mɪ·'θɑl·ə·dʒi] *n* <-ies> mitología *f*

N

N, n [en] *n* N, n *f;* **~ as in November** N de Navarra
n *abbr of* **noun** n *m*
N *abbr of* **north** N *m*
nab [næb] <-bb-> *vt inf* (*person*) pillar, pescar; (*thing*) agarrar
nadir ['neɪ·dər] *n* nadir *m*
nag¹ [næg] *n* (*horse*) jamelgo *m*
nag² [næg] **I.** <-gg-> *vi* **1.** (*pester*) fastidiar; **to ~ at sb** dar la lata a alguien *inf* **2.** (*scold*) regañar **3.** (*complain*) quejarse **II.** <-gg-> *vt* **1.** (*pester*) fastidiar **2.** (*scold*) regañar, dar la lata a *inf* **III.** *n inf* quejica *mf*
nagging ['næg·ɪŋ] **I.** *n* quejas *fpl* **II.** *adj* **1.** (*pain, ache*) persistente **2.** (*pestering: husband, wife*) refunfuñón, -ona
nail [neɪl] **I.** *n* **1.** (*tool*) clavo *m* **2.** ANAT uña *f* ▶ **to hit the ~ on the head** dar en el clavo **II.** *vt* **1.** (*fasten*) clavar **2.** *sl* (*catch: police*) trincar; (*lie*) poner al descubierto
nail-biting *adj fig* angustioso, -a
nail brush <-es> *n* cepillo *m* de uñas
nail clippers *npl* cortaúñas *m inv*
nail file *n* lima *f* de uñas

nail polish *n* esmalte *m* de uñas
nail polish remover *n* quitaesmalte *m*
nail scissors *npl* tijeras *fpl* para uñas
naive, naïve [na·'iv] *adj* ingenuo, -a
naïveté [ˌna·iv·'teɪ], **naivety** [na·'i·və·t̬i] *n* ingenuidad *f*
naked ['neɪ·kɪd] *adj* **1.** (*unclothed*) desnudo, -a, encuerado, -a *Cuba, Méx* **2.** (*uncovered: blade*) desenvainado, -a; (*aggression*) manifiesto, -a; (*ambition*) puro, -a; **to the ~ eye** a simple vista
nakedness *n* desnudez *f*
namby-pamby [ˌnæm·bi·'pæm·bi] *adj inf* (*person*) ñoño, -a; (*poem*) cursi
name [neɪm] **I.** *n* **1.** nombre *m;* (*surname*) apellido *m;* **by ~** de nombre; **to know sb by ~** conocer a alguien de oídas; **to go by the ~ of...** *form* hacerse llamar...; **in ~ only** sólo de nombre; **under the ~ of...** bajo el seudónimo de...; **in God's ~** en nombre de Dios; **in the ~ of freedom and justice** en nombre de la libertad y la justicia; **to call sb ~s** llamar a alguien de todo; **in all but ~** en la práctica **2.** (*reputation*) fama *f;* **to give sb/sth a good ~** dar buena fama a alguien/algo; **his ~ is mud** *fig* es persona non grata; **to make a ~ for oneself** hacerse un nombre ▶ **the ~ of the game** lo fundamental; **not to have a penny to one's ~** no tener ni un duro, no tener donde caerse muerto **II.** *vt* **1.** (*call*) poner nombre a **2.** (*list*) nombrar **3.** (*choose*) **to ~ the time and the place** fijar la hora y el lugar
name day *n* santo *m;* **today is my ~** hoy es mi santo
name-dropping ['neɪm·drap·ɪŋ] *n* práctica de mencionar gente importante para impresionar
nameless ['neɪm·lɪs] *adj* indescriptible; (*author*) anónimo, -a
namely ['neɪm·li] *adv* a saber
nameplate ['neɪm·pleɪt] *n* placa *f* con el nombre
namesake ['neɪm·seɪk] *n* tocayo, -a *m, f*
Namibia [nə·'mɪb·i·ə] *n* Namibia *f*
Namibian **I.** *adj* namibio, -a **II.** *n* namibio, -a *m, f*
nanny ['næn·i] <-ies> *n* niñera *f*, nurse *f AmL*
nanny goat ['næn·i·goʊt] *n* cabra *f* (hembra)
nanosecond ['nan·ə·ˌsek·ənd] *n* nanosegundo *m*
nap¹ [næp] (*sleep*) **I.** *n* cabezadita *f;* (*after lunch*) siesta *f;* **to take a ~** echarse un sueñecito [*o* una siesta] **II.** <-pp-> *vi* echar una cabezadita
nap² [næp] *n* (*on fabric*) pelo *m*
napalm ['neɪ·pam] *n* napalm *m*
nape [neɪp] *n* nuca *f*, cogote *m*
napkin ['næp·kɪn] *n* servilleta *f*
narc [nark] *n sl abbr of* **narcotics agent** estupa *mf*
narcissism ['nar·sɪ·sɪz·əm] *n* narcisismo *m*
narcissus [nar·'sɪs·əs] <-es *o* narcissi> *n* narciso *m*
narcosis [nar·'koʊ·sɪs] *n* narcosis *f inv*

N

narcotic [nar·'kaṭ·ɪk] I. *n* narcótico *m* II. *adj* narcótico, -a
narrate ['nær·eɪt] *vt* **1.** (*tale, story*) narrar, relatar **2.** TV (*documentary*) hacer de comentarista de
narration [næ·'reɪ·ʃən] *n* (*tale*) narración *f*, relato *m;* TV comentario *m*
narrative ['nær·ə·ṭɪv] *n* relato *m;* LIT narrativa *f*
narrator ['nær·eɪ·ṭər] *n* narrador(a) *m(f);* TV comentarista *mf*
narrow ['nær·oʊ] I.<-er, -est> *adj* **1.** (*thin*) estrecho, -a **2.** (*limited*) limitado, -a **3.** (*small: margin*) escaso, -a, reducido, -a II. *vi* **1.** estrecharse; (*gap*) reducirse **2.** (*field*) limitarse, restringirse III. *vt* **1.** (*reduce width of*) estrechar; (*gap*) reducir **2.** (*restrict: field*) limitar, restringir
narrowly *adv* **1.** (*barely*) por poco, por un escaso margen **2.** (*meticulously*) meticulosamente
narrow-minded [ˌnær·oʊ·'maɪn·dɪd] *adj* de mentalidad cerrada; (*opinions, views*) cerrado, -a
NASA ['næs·ə] *n abbr of* **National Aeronautics and Space Administration** NASA *f*
nasal ['neɪ·zəl] *adj* nasal; (*voice*) gangoso, -a
nascent ['næs·ənt] *adj* naciente
nastiness ['næs·tɪ·nɪs] *n* **1.** (*wickedness*) maldad *f* **2.** (*of accident*) gravedad *f;* (*of odor*) peste *f* **3.** (*dirtiness*) suciedad *f*
nasturtium [nə·'stɜr·ʃəm] *n* BOT capuchina *f*
nasty ['næs·ti] <-ier, -iest> *adj* **1.** (*bad: person*) malvado, -a; (*habit*) feo, -a; (*smell, taste*) asqueroso, -a, repugnante; (*surprise*) desagradable **2.** (*dangerous*) peligroso, -a **3.** (*serious*) serio, -a; (*accident*) grave
natal ['neɪ·ṭəl] *adj* natal
natality [nə·'tæl·ə·ṭi] *n* tasa *f* de natalidad
nation ['neɪ·ʃən] *n* **1.** (*country*) nación *f*, país *m;* **to serve the ~** servir a la nación **2.** (*people living in a state*) **the Jewish ~** la nación judía
national ['næʃ·ə·nəl] I. *adj* nacional; **at the ~ level** a nivel nacional II. *n* ciudadano, -a *m, f;* **foreign ~** extranjero, -a *m, f*
national anthem *n* himno *m* nacional
national assembly <-ies> *n* asamblea *f* nacional
national bank *n* banco *m* nacional
national costume *n* traje *m* nacional
national currency <-ies> *n* moneda *f* nacional
national debt *n* deuda *f* nacional
National Guard *n* Guardia *f* Nacional
national holiday *n* fiesta *f* nacional
national income *n* renta *f* nacional
nationalism ['næʃ·ə·nə·lɪz·əm] *n* nacionalismo *m*
nationalist ['næʃ·ə·nə·lɪst] I. *adj* nacionalista II. *n* nacionalista *mf*
nationalistic [ˌnæʃ·ə·nə·'lɪs·tɪk] *adj* nacionalista
nationality [ˌnæʃ·ə·'næl·ə·ṭi] <-ies> *n* nacionalidad *f;* **to adopt American/Spanish ~** adoptar la nacionalidad estadounidense/española

nationalization [ˌnæʃ·ə·nə·lɪ·'zeɪ·ʃən] *n* nacionalización *f*
nationalize ['næʃ·ə·nə·laɪz] *vt* nacionalizar
national park *n* parque *m* nacional
national product *n* producto *m* interior
national security *n* seguridad *f* nacional
national service *n* (*community service*) servicio voluntario a la comunidad
national socialism *n* nacionalsocialismo *m*
national unity *n* unidad *f* nacional
nation state *n* estado-nación *m*
nationwide [ˌneɪ·ʃən·'waɪd] I. *adv* (*operate*) a nivel nacional II. *adj* (*chain of stores, survey*) nacional
native ['neɪ·ṭɪv] I. *adj* **1.** (*indigenous*) nativo, -a; (*plant, animal*) autóctono, -a, originario, -a; **to be ~ to the United States** (*person, plant, animal*) ser originario de Estados Unidos **2.** (*of place of origin*) nativo, -a, natural; **~ country** país *m* natal **3.** (*indigenous, aboriginal, primitive*) indígena **4.** (*original*) nativo, -a; (*innate*) innato, -a; (*language*) materno, -a II. *n* (*indigenous inhabitant*) nativo, -a *m, f*, natural *mf;* **a ~ of Mexico** un nativo de México; **to speak English like a ~** hablar el inglés como un nativo
native American I. *n* indígena *mf* americano, -a, amerindio, -a *m, f* II. *adj* indígena, amerindio, -a

native-born *adj* nativo, -a; **is he a ~ person or did he move there?** ¿es natural de allí o viene de fuera?; **~ citizen of New York** natural de Nueva York
native speaker *n* hablante *mf* nativo, -a
nativity [nə·'tɪv·ə·ṭi] <-ies> *n* natividad *f;* **the Nativity** la Navidad
nativity play *n* auto *m* de Navidad
NATO ['neɪ·ṭoʊ] *n abbr of* **North Atlantic Treaty Organization** OTAN *f*
natter ['næṭ·ər] *vi inf* charlar; **to ~ away** parlotear
natural ['nætʃ·ər·əl] I. *adj* **1.** (*not artificial, inherent*) natural; **~ causes** causas *fpl* naturales; **to die of ~ causes** morir de causas naturales; **~ disaster** desastre *m* natural; **to be a ~**

blonde ser rubio natural; ~ **father** padre *m* natural **2.** (*usual, to be expected*) normal; **I'm sure there's a ~ explanation for it** estoy seguro de que tiene una explicación razonable **II.** *n* **1.** *inf* **to be a ~ for sth** tener un talento innato para algo **2.** MUS nota *f* natural

natural childbirth *n* parto *m* natural

natural gas *n* gas *m* natural

natural history *n* historia *f* natural; ~ **museum** museo *m* de historia natural

naturalism ['nætʃ·ər·ə·lɪz·əm] *n* naturalismo *m*

naturalist ['nætʃ·ər·ə·lɪst] **I.** *n* naturalista *mf* **II.** *adj* naturalista

naturalistic [ˌnætʃ·ər·ə·'lɪs·tɪk] *adj* naturalista

naturalization [ˌnætʃ·ər·ə·lɪ·'zeɪ·ʃən] *n* naturalización *f*

naturalize ['nætʃ·ər·ə·laɪz] *vt* naturalizar

naturalized *adj* naturalizado, -a; ~ **citizen** ciudadano, -a *m, f* naturalizado, -a

natural language *n* lengua *f* natural

naturally *adv* naturalmente

natural resources *npl* recursos *mpl* naturales; **to be rich/poor in ~** ser rico/pobre en recursos naturales

natural science *n*, **natural sciences** *npl* ciencias *fpl* naturales

natural selection *n* selección *f* natural

nature ['neɪ·tʃər] *n* **1.** (*the environment, natural forces*) naturaleza *f*; **to get back to ~** volver a la naturaleza; **to let ~ take its course** dejar que la naturaleza siga su curso **2.** (*essential or innate qualities*) naturaleza *f*; **things of this ~** cosas de esta índole; **it's in the ~ of things** es natural; **to be in sb's ~** estar en la naturaleza de alguien ▶ **second ~** hábito muy arraigado en una persona

nature conservation *n* conservación *f* natural

nature lover *n* amante *mf* de la naturaleza

nature reserve *n* reserva *f* natural

nature study *n* historia *f* natural

nature trail *n* ruta *f* ecológica

nature worship *n* culto *m* a la naturaleza

naturism ['neɪ·tʃə·rɪz·əm] *n* naturismo *m*

naturist ['neɪ·tʃə·rɪst] *n form* naturista *mf*

naught [nɔt] *pron liter* nada *f*; **to be all for ~** quedarse en nada, en balde

naughty ['nɔ·ti] <-ier, -iest> *adj* **1.** (*badly behaved: children*) desobediente, travieso, -a **2.** *iron* (*adults*) pícaro, -a

nausea ['nɔ·zi·ə] *n* **1.** náusea *f*; **feeling of ~** sensación *f* de náusea; **to suffer from ~** tener náuseas **2.** *fig* repugnancia *f*

nauseate ['nɔ·zi·eɪt] *vt form* **1.** (*cause nausea*) **to be ~d by sth** tener náuseas por algo **2.** (*cause disgust*) asquear

nauseating ['nɔ·zi·eɪ·t̬ɪŋ] *adj* nauseabundo, -a

nauseous ['nɔ·ʃəs] *adj* mareado, -a; (*smell*) nauseabundo, -a; **she is ~** tiene náuseas

nautical ['nɔ·t̬ɪ·kəl] *adj* náutico, -a; ~ **chart** carta *f* náutica

nautical mile *n* milla *f* marina

naval ['neɪ·vəl] *adj* naval; ~ **commander** comandante *mf* naval; ~ **battle/engagement/force** batalla *f*/combate *m*/fuerza *f* naval

naval academy <-ies> *n* academia *f* naval

naval base *n* base *f* naval

naval power *n* potencia *f* naval

naval warfare *n* guerra *f* naval

nave [neɪv] *n* nave *f*

navel ['neɪ·vəl] *n* ombligo *m* ▶ **to contemplate one's ~** rascarse el ombligo

navel orange *n* naranja *f* nável, naranja *f* ombligona *Col, Méx*

navigable ['næv·ɪ·gə·bəl] *adj* navegable; ~ **waters** aguas *fpl* navegables

navigate ['næv·ɪ·geɪt] **I.** *vt* **1.** (*steer*) llevar; AUTO guiar **2.** (*sail*) navegar por; **to ~ the ocean/a river** navegar por el océano/un río **3.** (*cross*) atravesar **4.** COMPUT **to ~ the Internet** navegar por la red, surfear **II.** *vi* NAUT, AVIAT navegar; AUTO guiar, hacer de copiloto

navigation [ˌnæv·ɪ·'geɪ·ʃən] *n* navegación *f*

navigational [ˌnæv·ɪ·'geɪ·ʃə·nəl] *adj* de navegación; ~ **error** error *m* de navegación

navigator ['næv·ɪ·geɪ·t̬ər] *n* navegante *mf*; AUTO copiloto *mf*

navy ['neɪ·vi] **I.** <-ies> *n* (*military*) **the Navy** la Marina; **to be in the Navy** estar en la Marina; **to serve in the ~** servir en la Marina **II.** *adj* (*dark blue*) azul marino

navy bean *n* BOT judía *f* blanca, blanquillo *m Col*, frijol *m* bayo *Méx*

nay [neɪ] **I.** *adv form* no **II.** *n* (*negative vote*) voto *m* en contra

Nazi ['nat·si] *n* nazi *mf*

Naziism ['nat·si·ɪz·əm] *n*, **Nazism** ['nat·sɪz·əm] *n* nazismo *m*

NB [ˌen·'bi] **1.** *abbr of* **nota bene** N.B. **2.** *abbr of* **New Brunswick** Nueva Brunswick *m*

NBA [ˌen·bi·'eɪ] *n abbr of* **National Basketball Association** NBA

NC [ˌnɔrθ·ˌkær·ə·'laɪ·nə] *n abbr of* **North Carolina** Carolina *f* del Norte

NCO [ˌen·si·'oʊ] *n abbr of* **noncommissioned officer** suboficial *mf*

ND [ˌnɔrθ·də·'koʊ·də] *n abbr of* **North Dakota** Dakota *f* del Norte

NE 1. *abbr of* **Nebraska** Nebraska *f* **2.** *abbr of* **New England** Nueva Inglaterra *f* **3.** *abbr of* **northeast** NE *m*

neap tide ['nip·ˌtaɪd] *n* marea *f* muerta

near [nɪr] **I.** *adj* **1.** (*spatial*) cercano, -a **2.** (*temporal*) próximo, -a; **in the ~ future** en un futuro próximo **3.** (*dear*) **a ~ and dear friend** un amigo íntimo **4.** (*similar: portrait*) parecido, -a; **the ~est thing to sth** lo más parecido a algo **5.** (*almost true*) **to have a ~ accident** tener por poco un accidente; **that was a ~ miss** [*o* **thing**] faltó poco **II.** *adv* **1.** (*spatial or temporal*) cerca; **to be ~** estar cerca; **to come ~** aproximarse, acercarse; **to live quite ~** vivir bastante cerca; ~ **at hand** a mano; **to come ~er to sb/sth** acercarse más a alguien/algo **2.** (*almost*) ~ **to tears** a punto de llorar; **as ~ as I can guess** que yo sepa **III.** *prep* **1.** (*in* *proximity to*) ~ (to) cerca de; ~ (to) the house cerca de la casa; ~ the end of the film hacia el final de la película 2.(*almost*) it's ~ midnight es casi medianoche; it's nowhere ~ enough no basta ni con mucho 3.(*about ready to*) to be ~ to doing sth estar a punto de hacer algo 4.(*like*) the copy is ~ to the original la copia es parecida al original IV. *vt* acercarse a; it is ~ing completion está casi terminado; he is ~ing his goal está alcanzando su meta

nearby [ˌnɪr-ˈbaɪ] I. *adj* cercano, -a II. *adv* cerca; is it ~? ¿está cerca?

Near East *n* Oriente *m* Próximo

nearly [ˈnɪr-li] *adv* casi; ~ certain casi seguro; to be not ~ as bad no estar tan mal; to be ~ there estar casi ahí; to very ~ do sth estar a punto de hacer algo; that wall is ~ ten feet high esa pared mide casi tres metros; she's ~ as tall as her father es casi tan alta como su padre

near-sighted [ˌnɪr-ˈsaɪ-t̬ɪd] *adj a. fig* miope

nearsightedness [ˌnɪr-ˈsaɪ-t̬ɪd-nɪs] *n a. fig* miopía *f*

neat [nit] *adj* 1.(*orderly, well-ordered*) cuidado, -a, ordenado, -a; ~ appearance/beard apariencia *f*/barba *f* cuidada; to be ~ in one's habits ser de hábitos ordenados; ~ and tidy ordenado 2.(*deft*) cuidadoso, -a; ~ solution solución *f* exacta 3.(*undiluted, pure*) puro, -a; I'll have a ~ gin please un gin solo, por favor 4.*sl* (*fine, good, excellent*) guay *inf;* a ~ guy un tío guay

neaten [ˈni-tən] *vt* ordenar; to ~ sth up poner orden en algo

neatly *adv* 1.(*with care*) cuidadosamente 2.(*in orderly fashion*) de forma ordenada 3.(*deftly*) con estilo

neatness [ˈnit-nɪs] *n* pulcritud *f*, limpieza *f*

Nebr. *n abbr of* Nebraska Nebraska *f*

Nebraska [nə-ˈbræs-kə] *n* Nebraska *f*

nebula [ˈneb-jə-lə] <-lae *o* -las> *n* ASTR nebulosa *f*

nebulae *n pl of* nebula

nebular *adj* nebular

nebulous [ˈneb-jə-ləs] *adj* nebuloso, -a; ~ promise promesa *f* vaga

necessarily [ˌnes-ɪ-ˈser-ə-li] *adv* necesariamente; not ~ no necesariamente

necessary [ˈnes-ɪ-ser-i] *adj* necesario, -a; to make the ~ arrangements hacer los preparativos necesarios; a ~ evil un mal necesario; strictly ~ estrictamente necesario; to be ~ ser necesario; that won't be ~ no será necesario; was it really ~ for you to say that? ¿tenías que decir eso?; to do what is ~ hacer lo que es necesario; if ~ si es necesario

necessitate [nə-ˈses-ɪ-teɪt] *vt form* requerir; to ~ doing sth requerir [*o* necesitar] hacer algo

necessity [nə-ˈses-ə-t̬i] <-ies> *n* (*need*) necesidad *f;* in case of ~ en caso de necesidad; when the ~ arises cuando surja la necesidad; ~ of doing sth necesidad de hacer algo; ~ for sb to do sth necesidad de que alguien haga

algo; there's no ~ to pay in advance no hay necesidad de pagar por adelantado; by ~ por necesidad; bare ~ primera necesidad ▸ ~ is the mother of <u>invention</u> *prov* no hay mejor maestra que el hambre *prov*

neck [nek] I. *n* 1. ANAT cuello *m;* (*nape*) nuca *f;* to fling one's arms around sb's ~ abrazar a alguien por el cuello 2. FASHION cuello *m;* round ~ cuello redondo 3.(*of bottle, violin*) cuello *m* ▸ to be up to one's ~ in sth *inf* estar (metido) hasta el cuello en algo; to be breathing down sb's ~ estar encima de alguien *fig* II. *vi inf* besuquearse

neckerchief [ˈnek-ər-tʃɪf] <neckerchieves> *n* pañuelo *m* atado al cuello

necklace [ˈnek-lɪs] *n* collar *m*

neckline [ˈnek-laɪn] *n* escote *m*

necktie *n* corbata *f*

nectar [ˈnek-tər] *n* néctar *m*

nectarine [ˌnek-tə-ˈrin] *n* nectarina *f*

née [neɪ] *adj* de soltera

need [nid] I. *n* necesidad *f;* in ~ necesitado, -a; basic ~s necesidades básicas; ~ for sb/sth necesidad de alguien/algo; to be in ~ of sth necesitar (de) algo; to have no ~ of sth no necesitar (de) algo; as the ~ arises según se sienta la necesidad; if ~(s) be si es necesario; no ~ to be sth ninguna necesidad de ser algo; there's no ~ to shout so loud no hace falta gritar tanto; in sb's hour of ~ (*emergency, crisis*) en un momento de necesidad II. *vt* 1.(*require*) necesitar; to ~ sb to do sth necesitar que alguien haga algo 2.(*ought to have*) to ~ necesitar; to not ~ sth no necesitar (de) algo; to ~ (doing) sth necesitar (hacer) algo; I ~ it like (I ~) a hole in my head *iron* me hace tanta falta como un agujero en la cabeza 3.(*must, have*) to ~ to do sth tener que hacer algo; ~ we/I/you? ¿nos/me/te hace falta?; there was no ~ to do sth no había necesidad de hacer algo

needed *adj* necesario, -a

needle [ˈni-dəl] I. *n* aguja *f;* hypodermic ~ jeringa *f;* knitting ~ aguja *f* de hacer punto; ~ and thread aguja e hilo; to thread a ~ enhebrar una aguja ▸ it's like looking for a ~ in a <u>haystack</u> es como buscar una aguja en un pajar II. *vt* (*prick*) pinchar; (*annoy*) provocar

needless [ˈnid-lɪs] *adj* innecesario, -a; ~ to say... no hace falta decir...; ~ to say, I didn't reply ni que decir tiene que no respondí

needlework [ˈni-dəl-wɜrk] *n* labor *f* de aguja

needn't [ˈni-dənt] = need not *s.* need

needy [ˈni-di] I. <-ier, -iest> *adj* necesitado, -a II. *npl* the ~ los necesitados

nefarious [nə-ˈfer-i-əs] *adj pej, form* infame

negate [nɪ-ˈgeɪt] *vt* negar

negation [nɪ-ˈgeɪ-ʃən] *n* negación *f*

negative [ˈneg-ə-t̬ɪv] I. *adj* 1.(*not positive*) negativo, -a; ~ answer respuesta *f* negativa; ~ clause/form cláusula *f* negativa; to be ~ about sth/sb ser negativo respecto a algo/alguien 2. *a.* MED negativo, -a; ~ pole polo *m* negativo; ~ **number** número *m* negativo **II.** *n* **1.** (*rejection*) negativa *f* **2.** (*making use of negation*) negación *f* **3.** PHOT negativo *m* **III.** *vt* negar

negatively *adv* negativamente

negativity [ˌneg·ə·ˈtɪv·ə·t̬i] *n* negatividad *f*

neglect [nɪ·ˈglekt] **I.** *vt* desatender; **to ~ one's duties** descuidar los propios deberes; **to ~ to do sth** descuidar hacer algo; **I'd ~ed to write to him** me olvidé de escribirle **II.** *n* negligencia *f*; (*poor state, unrepaired state*) deterioro *m*; **to be in a state of ~** estar en un estado de deterioro; **to fall into a state of ~** deteriorarse

neglected *adj* descuidado, -a; (*undervalued, underappreciated*) infravalorado, -a; **~ child** niño, -a *m*, *f* abandonado, -a

neglectful [nɪ·ˈglekt·fəl] *adj* negligente; **~ parents** padres *mpl* negligentes; **to be ~ of sth/sb** ser negligente respecto a algo/alguien

negligée *n*, **negligee** [ˌneg·lə·ˈʒeɪ] *n* salto *m* de cama

negligence [ˈneg·lɪ·dʒəns] *n a.* LAW negligencia *f*; **gross ~** negligencia grave

negligible [ˈneg·lɪ·dʒə·bəl] *adj* insignificante

negotiable [nɪ·ˈgoʊ·ʃi·ə·bəl] *adj* negociable; **~ securities** FIN títulos *mpl* negociables; **non~** no negociable

negotiate [nɪ·ˈgoʊ·ʃi·eɪt] **I.** *vt* **1.** (*discuss*) negociar; **to ~ a loan/treaty** negociar un préstamo/tratado **2.** (*convert into money*) **to ~ a check** cobrar un cheque; **to ~ securities** negociar títulos **II.** *vi* negociar; **to ~ on sth** negociar algo; **to ~ with sb** negociar con alguien

negotiating committee *n* comité *m* de negociación

negotiating table *n fig* mesa *f* de negociaciones

negotiation [nɪ·ˌgoʊ·ʃi·ˈeɪ·ʃən] *n* negociación *f*; **~ for sth** negociación de algo

negotiator [nɪ·ˈgoʊ·ʃi·eɪ·t̬ər] *n* negociador(a) *m(f)*

Negress [ˈni·grɪs] *n offensive* negra *f*

Negro [ˈni·groʊ] <-es> *n* **1.** HIST (*league, people, spirituals*) negro, -a **2.** *offensive* negro, -a *m*, *f*

Negroid [ˈni·grɔɪd] *adj* negroide

neigh [neɪ] **I.** *n* relincho *m* **II.** *vi* relinchar

neighbor [ˈneɪ·bər] **I.** *n* vecino, -a *m*, *f*; (*fellow human*) prójimo, -a *m*, *f* ▸ **love your ~ as you love yourself** *prov* ama a tu prójimo como a ti mismo *prov* **II.** *vi* **to ~ on sth** lindar con algo

neighborhood [ˈneɪ·bər·hʊd] *n* **1.** (*smallish localized community*) vecindario *m*; (*people*) vecinos *mpl*; **a closed/friendly ~** un vecindario cerrado/agradable; **the whole ~ is talking about it** todo el vecindario habla de ello; **in the ~** en el vecindario **2.** (*vicinity*) alrededores *mpl*, cercanías *fpl*; **I wouldn't like to live in the ~ of the airport** no me gustaría vivir en los alrededores del aeropuerto **3.** **in the ~ of** alrededor de; **we're hoping to get something in the ~ of $125,000 for the house**

esperamos obtener alrededor de 125.000 dólares por la casa

neighborhood watch *n* vigilancia *f* vecinal

neighboring [ˈneɪ·bər·ɪŋ] *adj* (*nearby*) cercano, -a; (*bordering*) adyacente; **~ house** casa *f* adyacente; **~ country** país *m* vecino

neighborliness *n* convivencia *f*; **an act of ~** un acto de convivencia; **good ~** buena vecindad

neighborly [ˈneɪ·bər·li] *adj* amable

neither [ˈni·ðər] **I.** *pron* ninguno, -a; **which one? — ~ (of them)** ¿cuál? — ninguno (de los dos) **II.** *adv* ni; **~... nor...** ni... ni...; **he is ~ wounded nor dead** no está ni herido ni muerto **III.** *conj* tampoco; **if he won't eat, ~ will I** si él no come, yo tampoco **IV.** *adj* ningún, -una; **in ~ case** en ningún caso; **~ book is good** ninguno de los dos libros es bueno

nemesis [ˈnem·ə·sɪs] <-ses> *n a. fig* justo castigo *m*

neoclassical [ˌni·oʊ·ˈklæs·ɪ·kəl] *adj* neoclásico, -a

neocolonialist [ˌni·oʊ·kə·ˈloʊ·ni·ə·lɪst] *adj* neocolonialista

Neolithic [ˌni·oʊ·ˈlɪθ·ɪk] *adj* neolítico, -a; **~ Period** período *m* neolítico

neologism [ni·ˈal·ə·dʒɪz·əm] *n form* neologismo *m*

neon [ˈni·an] *n* neón *m*

neo-Nazi [ˌni·oʊ·ˈnat·si] **I.** *n* neonazi *mf* **II.** *adj* neonazi

neon lamp *n*, **neon light** *n* tubo *m* de neón

neon sign *n* letrero *m* de neón

nephew [ˈnef·ju] *n* sobrino *m*

nephritis [nɪ·ˈfraɪ·t̬əs] *n* MED nefritis *f inv*

nepotism [ˈnep·ə·tɪz·əm] *n* nepotismo *m*

Neptune [ˈnep·tun] *n* Neptuno *m*

nerd [nɜrd] *n pej, sl* **1.** (*awkward person*) repelente *m*; **computer ~** informático, -a *m*, *f* repelente **2.** (*foolish person*) pardillo, -a *m*, *f*

nerdy <-ier, -iest> *adj sl* pardillo, -a

nerve [nɜrv] *n* **1.** ANAT nervio *m* **2.** (*high nervousness*) **~s** nerviosismo *m*; **to be in a state of ~s** estar nervioso; **to be a bundle of ~s** *fig* ser un puñado de nervios; **to calm one's ~s** calmarse; **to get on sb's ~s** *inf* poner los nervios de punta a alguien **3.** (*courage, bravery*) valor *m*; **to lose one's ~** perder el valor **4.** (*apprehension*) **~s** ansiedad *f* **5.** (*temerity*) temeridad *f*; **to have the ~ to do sth** *inf* tener el morro de hacer algo; **of all the ~!** *inf* ¡qué morro! ▸ **~s of steel** nervios *mpl* de acero; **to expose** [*o* **to hit**] **a (raw) ~** tocar un tema sensible

nerve cell *n* célula *f* nerviosa

nerve center *n* **1.** ANAT centro *m* nervioso **2.** *fig* (*center of control*) centro *m* neurálgico

nerve gas <-es> *n* gas *m* nervioso

nerveless [ˈnɜrv·lɪs] *adj* **1.** (*calm*) imperturbable **2.** (*lacking courage*) cobarde

nerve-racking [ˈnɜrv·ræk·ɪŋ] *adj* perturbador(a)

nervous [ˈnɜr·vəs] *adj* (*jumpy*) nervioso, -a;

N

(*edgy*) ansioso, -a; **of a ~ disposition** de disposición nerviosa; **to be ~ in sb's presence** estar nervioso en presencia de alguien; **you look like a ~ wreck!** ¡pareces un manojo de nervios!; **to make sb ~** poner nervioso a alguien; **to be ~ about sth** estar nervioso por algo

nervous breakdown *n* ataque *m* de nervios; **to have a ~** sufrir un ataque de nervios

nervously *adv* nerviosamente

nervousness *n* (*nervous condition or state*) nerviosismo *m;* (*fearfulness*) ansiedad *f;* **~ about sth** nerviosismo por algo

nervous system *n* sistema *m* nervioso

nervy ['nɜr·vi] <-ier, -iest> *adj* **1.** (*rude*) descarado, -a **2.** (*courageous*) atrevido, -a

nest [nest] **I.** *n* **1.** (*of animal, insect*) nido *m;* (*of hen*) nidal *m* **2.** (*cozy domicile*) nido *m;* **to leave the ~** dejar el nido **3.** (*hotbed: of spies, rebels*) guarida *f,* cueva *f;* **a ~ of fanaticism** un foco fanático **4.** (*set, cluster, assemblage*) juego *m* **II.** *vi* anidar

nest egg *n* **1.** (*egg in a nest*) huevo *m* en un nido **2.** (*money saved*) ahorros *mpl*

nesting *adj* **1.** (*of sets fitting together*) que encaja **2.** (*concerning nests*) **~ time** tiempo *m* de anidar

nestle ['nes·əl] **I.** *vt* apoyar; **to ~ sth on sth** apoyar algo en algo **II.** *vi* **1.** (*snuggle up*) acomodarse; **to ~ up to sb** arrimarse a alguien **2.** (*be in sheltered position*) cobijarse

nestling ['nest·lɪŋ] *n* pichón *m* (*pájaro que aún no vuela*)

net¹ [net] **I.** *n* **1.** (*material with spaces*) malla *f;* (*fine netted fabric*) tul *m;* **mosquito ~** mosquitera *f* **2.** (*device for trapping fish*) red *f;* **to haul in a ~** pescar con redes; **to fall** [*o* **slip**] **through the ~** *fig* zafarse de las redes de alguien **3.** SPORTS red *f* **II.** <-tt-> *vt* (*catch: fish*) pescar; (*criminals*) capturar

net² [net] **I.** *adj* **1.** ECON neto, -a; **~ assets** activo *m* neto; **~ income** (*from work, services*) ingreso *m* neto; (*from sales, as profit*) beneficio *m* neto **2.** (*excluding package: weight*) neto, -a; **~ tonnage** tonelaje *m* neto **II.** *vt* **to ~ sth** ganar algo en neto

Net [net] *n* COMPUT **the ~** la red; **~ surfer** navegador(a) *m(f)* de la red

nether ['neθ·ər] *adj iron, liter* inferior

Netherlands ['neð·ər·ləndz] *n* **the ~** los Países Bajos, Holanda *f*

netiquette ['net·ɪ·ket] *n* COMPUT etiqueta *f* de red

Netspeak ['net·spik] *n* COMPUT lenguaje *m* de internet [*o* de la red]

nett [net] *adj, vt s.* **net¹** II., **net²**

netting ['net·ɪŋ] *n* **1.** (*net*) malla *f* **2.** SPORTS red *f*

nettle ['net·əl] **I.** *n* ortiga *f* **II.** *vt* irritar; **to be ~d by sth** estar irritado por algo

nettle rash <-es> *n* urticaria *f*

net weight *n* peso *m* neto

network ['net·wɜrk] **I.** *n* **1.** COMPUT, TEL red *f;*

cable ~ cableado *m;* **computer ~** red informática; **telephone ~** red telefónica **2.** TV cadena *f* **II.** *vt* **1.** (*link together*) conectar **2.** (*broadcast*) retransmitir **III.** *vi* interconectar

networking *n* COMPUT interconexión *f*

neural ['nʊr·əl] *adj* neural, del sistema nervioso

neuralgia [nʊ·'ræl·dʒə] *n* neuralgia *f*

neuralgic [nʊ·'ræl·dʒɪk] *adj* neurálgico, -a

neural network *n* COMPUT red *f* nerviosa

neurasthenia [ˌnʊr·æs·'θi·ni·ə] *n* neurastenia *f*

neuritis [nʊ·'raɪ·təs] *n* MED neuritis *f inv*

neurological [ˌnʊr·ə·'ladʒ·ɪ·kəl] *adj* neurológico, -a; **~ disorder** trastorno *m* neurológico

neurologist [nʊ·'ral·ə·dʒɪst] *n* neurólogo, -a *m, f*

neurology [nʊ·'ral·ə·dʒi] *n* neurología *f*

neuron ['nʊr·an] *n* neurona *f*

neuroscience [ˌnʊr·oʊ·'saɪ·əns] *n* neurología *f*

neurosis [nʊ·'roʊ·sɪs] <-es> *n* neurosis *f inv*

neurosurgeon [ˌnʊr·oʊ·'sɜr·dʒən] *n* neurocirujano, -a *m, f*

neurosurgery [ˌnʊr·oʊ·'sɜr·dʒə·ri] *n* neurocirugía *f*

neurotic [nʊ·'raṭ·ɪk] **I.** *n* neurótico, -a *m, f* **II.** *adj* neurótico, -a

neurotransmitter [ˌnʊr·oʊ·ˌtræns·'mɪt·ər] *n* MED neurotransmisor *m*

neuter ['nu·tər] **I.** *adj* neutro, -a; **~ noun** LING sustantivo *m* neutro **II.** *vt* **1.** (*castrate: male*) castrar **2.** (*sterilize: female*) esterilizar **3.** (*neutralize*) neutralizar

neutral ['nu·trəl] **I.** *adj* **1.** (*uninvolved*) neutral; **~ country** POL país *m* neutral; **to remain ~** mantenerse al margen **2.** *a.* CHEM, ELEC neutro, -a **3.** (*unemotional*) objetivo, -a **II.** *n* **1.** (*noncombatant in war*) territorio *m* neutral **2.** (*part of gear system*) punto *m* muerto; **in ~** en punto muerto

neutrality [nu·'træl·ə·ți] *n* neutralidad *f*

neutralization [ˌnu·trə·lɪ·'zeɪ·ʃən] *n* neutralización *f*

neutralize ['nu·trə·laɪz] *vt* neutralizar; **the bomb was ~d by the specialists** los especialistas desactivaron la bomba

neutron ['nu·tran] *n* neutrón *m*

neutron bomb *n* bomba *f* de neutrones

Nevada [nə·'vad·ə] *n* Nevada *f*

never ['nev·ər] *adv* **1.** (*at no time, on no occasion*) nunca, jamás; **I ~ forget a face** nunca olvido una cara **2.** (*under no circumstances*) jamás; **~ again!** ¡nunca más!; **~ fear!** ¡no te preocupes!; **well I ~ (did)** ¡no me digas!; **it's ~ too late to do sth** nunca es demasiado tarde para hacer algo; **~ before** nunca antes; **~ before had I had so much money** jamás había tenido tanto dinero; **as ~ before** como nunca; **~ ever** nunca jamás; **~ mind** qué más da; **~ say die** *fig* nunca tires la toalla

never-ending ['nev·ər·'en·dɪŋ] *adj* interminable

never-failing *adj* infalible

nevermore *adv* nunca más
never-never land *n fig, inf* país *m* de nunca jamás
nevertheless [ˌnev·ər·ðə·'les] *adv* sin embargo, no obstante
new [nu] **I.** *adj* **1.** (*latest, recent*) nuevo, -a, reciente; (*word*) de nuevo cuño; ~ **technology** tecnología *f* punta; **to be the ~est fad** [*o* **craze**] *inf* ser la última moda **2.** (*changed*) nuevo, -a; ~ **boy/girl** SCHOOL novato, -a *m, f;* **the ~ kid on the block** el chico nuevo **3.** (*inexperienced*) nuevo, -a, novato, -a; **to be a ~ one on sb** ser nuevo para alguien; **she's ~ to the job** es nueva en el trabajo **4.** (*in new condition*) nuevo, -a; **brand ~** nuevo flamante **5.** (*fresh*) fresco, -a; ~ **blood** *fig* sangre *f* fresca; **to feel like a ~ man/woman** sentirse un hombre nuevo/una mujer nueva **6.** (*freshly found or made public*) fresco, -a, reciente **II.** *n* **the ~** lo nuevo
New Age *n* **1.** (*movement*) New Age *m* **2.** (*music*) new age *f*
New Ager *n* seguidor(a) *m(f)* del New Age
New-Agey *adj* del New Age, de la Nueva Era
newbie ['nu·bi] *n* COMPUT novato, -a *m, f* (*en la red*)
newborn **I.** *adj* reciente; ~ **democracy/ science** democracia *f* /ciencia *f* reciente; ~ **baby** recién nacido, -a *m, f* **II.** *n* **the ~** los recién nacidos
New Brunswick *n* Nueva Brunswick *f*
New Caledonia *n* Nueva Caledonia *f*
newcomer *n* **1.** (*person who has just arrived*) recién llegado, -a *m, f* **2.** (*stranger*) nuevo, -a *m, f* **3.** (*beginner*) principiante *mf,* novato, -a *m, f;* **I'm a ~ to Phoenix** soy nuevo en Phoenix
newel ['nu·əl] *n* **1.** (*of a circular staircase*) espigón *m* **2.** (*supporting banister*) poste *m*
New England *n* Nueva Inglaterra *f*
newfangled *adj* novedoso, -a
new-fashioned *adj* moderno, -a, a la última (moda)
new-found [ˌnu·'faʊnd] *adj* recién descubierto, -a; **a ~ friend** un amigo nuevo
Newfoundland ['nu·fən·lənd] *n* Terranova *f*
Newfoundland (**dog**) *n* ZOOL (perro *m* de) Terranova
New Hampshire [ˌnu·'hæmp·ʃər] *n* Nueva Hampshire *f,* Nuevo Hampshire *m*
newish ['nu·ɪʃ] *adj inf* bastante nuevo, -a
New Jersey [ˌnu·'dʒɜr·zi] *n* Nueva Jersey *f*
new-laid ['nu·'leɪd] *adj* ~ **eggs** huevos *mpl* frescos
newly ['nu·li] *adv* **1.** (*recently: discovered, diagnosed, released*) recientemente; ~ **baked/painted** recién horneado/pintado; ~ **married** recién casados **2.** (*differently than before: named, phrased*) de otra manera
newly-wed ['nu·li·wed] **I.** *npl* recién casados *mpl* **II.** *adj* recién casado, -a
New Mexico [ˌnu·'mek·sɪ·koʊ] *n* Nuevo México *m*

new moon *n* luna *f* nueva
New Orleans [ˌnu·'ɔr·li·ənz] *n* Nueva Orleans *f*
new potatoes *npl* patatas *fpl* tiernas
New Right *n* Nueva Derecha *f*
news [nuz] *n + sing vb* **1.** (*fresh information*) noticias *fpl;* **the ~ media** los medios de comunicación; **bad/good ~** malas/buenas noticias; **he's bad ~ for the company** es pájaro de mal agüero para la empresa; **to break the ~ to sb** dar la noticia a alguien; **when the ~ broke** cuando se supo la noticia; **really! that's ~ to me** ¿de veras? no lo sabía **2.** (*broadcast*) noticias *fpl,* informativo *m;* **to be ~** ser noticia ▶ **no ~ is good ~** *prov* si no hay noticias, buena señal
news agency <-ies> *n* agencia *f* de noticias
newsboy *n* **1.** (*seller*) vendedor *m* de periódicos **2.** (*deliverer*) repartidor *m* de periódicos
newscast *n* informativo *m*
newscaster *n* (*on TV*) presentador(a) *m(f)* de un informativo; (*on radio*) locutor(a) *m(f)* de un informativo
news conference *n* rueda *f* de prensa
news dealer *n* vendedor(a) *m(f)* de periódicos
newsflash <-es> *n* noticia *f* de última hora
newsgirl *n* **1.** (*seller*) vendedora *f* de periódicos **2.** (*deliverer*) repartidora *f* de periódicos
newsgroup *n* COMPUT foro *m* de discusión
newshound *n fig, inf* cazanoticias *mf inv*
news item *n* noticia *f*
newsletter *n* nota *f* de prensa
newsmonger *n pej* chismoso, -a *m, f*
newspaper *n* periódico *m*
newspaper clipping *n* recorte *m* de periódico [*o* de prensa]
newspaper report *n* reportaje *m*
newspeak *n pej* lenguaje *m* de los políticos
newsprint *n* papel *m* de periódico
newsreel *n* noticiario *m* documental
news release *n* comunicado *m* de prensa
news report *n* reportaje *m* informativo
newsroom *n* sala *f* de redacción
newsstand *n* quiosco *m*
newsvendor *n* vendedor(a) *m(f)* de periódicos
newsworthy *adj* de interés periodístico
newsy ['nu·zi] <-ier, -iest> *adj* lleno, -a de noticias; **a ~ letter** una carta cargada de noticias
newt [nut] *n* tritón *m*
New Testament *n* REL Nuevo Testamento *m*
new town *n* ciudad creada para redistribuir la población
new wave *n fig* **1.** (*movement*) New Wave *f* **2.** (*fresh outbreak*) nueva ola *f;* **a ~ of layoffs/ violence** una nueva ola de despidos/violencia
new world order *n,* **New World Order** *n* nuevo orden *m* mundial
New Year *n* **1.** año *m* nuevo; **Happy ~** feliz año nuevo; **to celebrate ~** celebrar el año nuevo **2.** (*opening weeks of year*) principios *mpl* de año
New Year's *n inf* (*New Year's Day*) día *f* de año nuevo; (*New Year's Eve*) nochevieja *f*

N

New Year's Day *n* día *m* de año nuevo
New Year's Eve *n* nochevieja *f*
New York [ˌnu·ˈjɔrk] **I.** *n* Nueva York *f* **II.** *adj* neoyorquino, -a
New Yorker *n* neoyorquino, -a *m, f*
New Zealand [ˌnu·ˈzi·lənd] **I.** *n* Nueva Zelanda *f* **II.** *adj* neozelandés, -esa
New Zealander *n* neozelandés, -esa *m, f*
next [nekst] **I.** *adj* **1.** (*nearest in location*) siguiente **2.** (*following in time*) próximo, -a, que viene; **the ~ day** el día siguiente; **~ month** el mes que viene; **the ~ thing** el siguiente paso; **(the) ~ time** la próxima vez **3.** (*following in order*) siguiente; **to be ~** ser el siguiente; **to be (the) ~ to do sth** ser el próximo en hacer algo; **~ to sth/sb** cerca de algo/alguien **II.** *adv* **1.** (*afterwards, subsequently*) después, luego; **when are you going to New York ~?** ¿cuando vuelves a ir a Nueva York? **2.** (*almost as much*) **~ to** después de; **~ to cheese I like chocolate best** después del queso es el chocolate el que más me gusta **3.** (*again, once more*) de nuevo; **when I saw him ~ he had transformed** cuando volví a verlo estaba desconocido **4.** (*almost*) casi; **~ to impossible** casi imposible; **~ to nothing** casi nada **5.** (*second*) **the ~ best thing** lo segundo mejor **III.** *prep* **1.** (*beside*) **~ to** junto a; **~ to the skin** junto a la piel; **my room is ~ to yours** mi habitación está al lado de la tuya **2.** (*almost*) casi; **to cost ~ to nothing** no valer casi nada **3.** (*second to*) **~ to last** penúltimo; **~ to Bach, I like Mozart best** después de Bach, Mozart es el que me gusta más
next door [ˌnekst·ˈdɔr] *adv* al lado; **we live ~ to the airport** vivimos al lado del aeropuerto
next-door neighbor *n* vecino, -a *m, f* de al lado
next of kin *n* pariente *mf* cercano, -a
nexus [ˈnek·səs] *n inv* nexo *m*
NF *n abbr of* **Newfoundland** Terranova *f*
NFL [ˌen·ef·ˈel] *n abbr of* **National Football League** Liga Nacional de Fútbol Americano
NH [ˌnu·ˈhæmp·ʃər] *n abbr of* **New Hampshire** Nueva Hampshire *f* [*o* Nuevo Hampshire] *m*
NHL [ˌen·eɪtʃ·ˈel] *n abbr of* **National Hockey League** Liga Nacional de Hockey
Niagara Falls [naɪ·æg·ˌrə·ˈfɔlz] *n* **(the) ~** las cataratas del Niágara
nib [nɪb] *n* punta *f;* (*of a pen*) plumilla *f*
nibble [ˈnɪb·əl] **I.** *n* (*a small bite/peck*) mordisco *m,* bocado *m;* **to take a ~ (at sth)** dar un mordisco (a algo) **II.** *vt* **1.** (*bite*) mordisquear; (*rat*) roer **2.** (*pick at*) picar **III.** *vi* **1.** *a. fig* picar **2.** (*deplete slowly*) **to ~ away at sth** desgastar algo
Nicaragua [ˌnɪk·ə·ˈrag·wə] *n* Nicaragua *f*
Nicaraguan I. *n* nicaragüense *mf* **II.** *adj* nicaragüense
nice [naɪs] **I.** *adj* **1.** (*pleasant, agreeable*) bueno, -a; **~ one!, ~ work!** *inf* ¡bien hecho!; **~ weather** buen tiempo *m;* **~ work** *inf* buen trabajo *m;* **far ~r** mucho más bonito; **it is ~ to do sth** es agradable hacer algo **2.** (*amiable*) simpático, -a; (*kind*) amable; **to be ~ to sb** ser amable con alguien; **it is/was ~ of sb to do sth** es/fue un detalle por parte de alguien hacer algo; **~ boys** chicos majos **3.** *iron, inf* (*unpleasant*) **that's a ~ thing to say to your brother** ¡vaya cosa bonita para decirle a un hermano! **4.** (*subtle*) sutil, delicado, -a; (*fine*) fino, -a **II.** *adv* bien
nice-looking *adj* atractivo, -a
nicely [ˈnaɪs·li] *adv* **1.** (*well, satisfactorily*) bien; **to do very ~** quedar muy bonito **2.** (*having success*) espléndidamente **3.** (*in healthy state*) **the princess and the baby were both doing ~** la princesa y el bebé gozaban de buena salud **4.** (*pleasantly, politely*) amablemente
nicety [ˈnaɪ·sə·t̬i] <-ies> *n* **1.** (*subtle distinction*) sutileza *f* **2.** (*precision*) precisión *f;* **~ of an argument** pormenores *mpl* de una discusión **3.** (*precise differentiations*) **niceties** matices *mpl;* (*in negative sense*) nimiedades *fpl*
niche [nɪtʃ] *n* **1.** (*alcove*) nicho *m* **2.** (*desired job*) buen puesto *m;* (*suitable position*) buena posición *f* **3.** (*place suiting a particular group*) refugio *m*
niche market *n* ECON mercado *m* alternativo (especializado)
nick [nɪk] **I.** *n* (*chip in surface*) mella *f* ►**in the ~ of time** por los pelos **II.** *vt* **1.** (*chip*) mellar; (*cut*) cortar **2.** *sl* (*cheat*) engañar
nickel [ˈnɪk·əl] *n* **1.** CHEM níquel *m* **2.** (*coin*) moneda *f* de cinco centavos
nickel-plated *adj* niquelado, -a
nicknack [ˈnɪk·næk] *n s.* **knickknack**
nickname [ˈnɪk·neɪm] **I.** *n* apodo *m* **II.** *vt* apodar
nicotine [ˈnɪk·ə·t̬in] *n* nicotina *f*
nicotine patch <-es> *n* parche *m* de nicotina
niece [nis] *n* sobrina *f*
nifty [ˈnɪf·ti] <-ier, -iest> *adj sl* (*stylish, smart*) chulo, -a; (*skilful*) hábil
Niger [ˈnaɪ·dʒər] *n* Níger *m*
Nigeria [naɪ·ˈdʒɪr·i·ə] *n* Nigeria *f*
Nigerian I. *adj* nigeriano, -a **II.** *n* nigeriano, -a *m, f*
niggardly [ˈnɪg·ərd·li] *adj* (*stingy*) tacaño, -a; (*meager*) miserable
nigger [ˈnɪg·ər] *n offensive, sl* negraco, -a *m, f*
niggle [ˈnɪg·əl] **I.** *vi* fastidiar; **to ~ at sth** preocuparse por algo **II.** *vt* **1.** (*nag pettily*) reparar en minucias **2.** (*irritate*) enfurecer, irritar
niggling [ˈnɪg·lɪŋ] *adj* **1.** (*irritating, troubling*) molesto, -a **2.** (*needing very precise work*) meticuloso, -a
nigh [naɪ] *adj liter* inminente
night [naɪt] *n* noche *f;* **good ~!** ¡buenas noches!; **last ~** anoche; **10 (o'clock) at ~** las 10 de la noche; **the ~ before** la noche anterior; **open at ~** abierto por la noche; **~ and day** día y noche; **during the ~** durante la

noche; **during Tuesday** ~ durante la noche del martes; **far into the** ~ a altas horas de la noche; **in the dead of (the)** ~ en mitad de la noche; **wedding** ~ noche de bodas; **the Arabian Nights** las mil y una noches; **Twelfth Night** Noche *f* de Reyes; **to work** ~**s** trabajar de noche

night bird ['naɪt·bɜrd] *n* **1.** ZOOL pájaro *m* nocturno **2.** (*person*) noctámbulo, -a *m, f*, trasnochador(a) *m(f)*

night blindness *n* ceguera *f* nocturna

nightcap *n* **1.** (*cap*) gorro *m* de dormir **2.** (*drink*) bebida *f* (*que se toma antes de acostarse*)

nightclothes *npl* ropa *f* de dormir

nightclub *n* club *m* (nocturno)

nightdress <-es> *n* camisón *m*

nightfall *n* atardecer *m*

nightgown *n* camisón *m*

nightie ['naɪ·ţi] *n inf* camisón *m*

nightingale ['naɪ·ţɪŋ·geɪl] *n* ruiseñor *m*

night life *n* vida *f* nocturna

nightlight *n* lamparilla *f*

nightlong **I.** *adv* durante toda la noche **II.** *adj* (*vigil*) (durante) toda la noche

nightly ['naɪt·li] **I.** *adv* cada noche **II.** *adj* **1.** (*each night or evening: visits, TV program*) de todas las noches **2.** (*at night*) de noche

nightmare ['naɪt·mer] *n* pesadilla *f*

nightmarish ['naɪt·mer·ɪʃ] *adj* **1.** (*like a horrible dream*) espeluznante **2.** (*very distressing*) inquietante

night-night ['naɪt·ˌnaɪt] *interj inf* hasta mañanita

night-nurse *n* enfermera *f* de noche

night owl *n* (*person*) noctámbulo, -a *m, f*, trasnochador(a) *m(f)*

night porter *n* portero, -a *m, f* nocturno, -a

nights *adv* por la noche, de noche

night school *n* escuela *f* nocturna

night shift *n* turno *m* de noche

nightshirt *n* camisa *f* de dormir

nightspot *n inf* club *m* (nocturno)

nightstand *n* mesita *f* de noche

nightstick *n* porra *f*

night table *n* mesita *f* de noche

nighttime *n* noche *f*

night watch <-es> *n* vigilancia *f* nocturna

night watchman *n* vigilante *m* nocturno, nochero *m CSur*

nightwear *n* ropa *f* de dormir

nihilism ['naɪ·ə·lɪz·əm] *n* nihilismo *m*

nihilist ['naɪ·ə·lɪst] *n* nihilista *mf*

nihilistic [ˌnaɪ·ə·'lɪs·tɪk] *adj* nihilista

Nikkei ['ni·keɪ] *n*, **Nikkei Index** *n* FIN Nikkei *m*

nil [nɪl] *n* (*nothing, zero*) nada *f*, cero *m*

Nile [naɪl] *n* **the** ~ el Nilo

nimble ['nɪm·bəl] *adj* (*agile*) ágil; (*quick and light in movement*) diestro, -a; (*quick-thinking*) listo, -a; ~ **mind** mente *f* despierta

nimbus ['nɪm·bəs] *n* nimbo *m*

NIMBY, nimby ['nɪm·bi] *n abbr of* **not in my back yard** *persona que se opone a que en la*

zona donde vive se realice cualquier destrozo urbanístico o medioambiental

nincompoop ['nɪn·kəm·ˌpup] *n inf* zoquete *m no f*

nine [naɪn] **I.** *adj* nueve *inv* ►**a** ~ **days' wonder** la flor de un día; ~ **times** out of ten casi siempre **II.** *n* nueve *m* ► **to be** dressed **to the** ~**s** *inf* ir de punta en blanco; *s.a.* **eight**

9-11, 9/11 [naɪn·ɪ·'lev·ən] *n* el 11-S *m*, el 11-9 *m*

nineteen [ˌnaɪn·'tin] **I.** *adj* diecinueve **II.** *n* diecinueve *m; s.a.* **eight**

nineteenth **I.** *adj* decimonoveno, -a **II.** *n* **1.** (*order*) decimonoveno, -a *m, f* **2.** (*date*) diecinueve *m* **3.** (*fraction*) diecinueveavo *m*; (*part*) diecinueveava parte *f; s.a.* **eighth**

nineteenth hole *n inf* garito *m* (*en club de golf*)

nineties *npl* **the** ~ los noventa

ninetieth ['naɪn·ţi·əθ] **I.** *adj* nonagésimo, -a **II.** *n* (*order*) nonagésimo, -a *m, f*; (*fraction*) noventavo *m*; (*part*) noventava parte *f; s.a.* **eighth**

nine-to-five **I.** *adv* de nueve a cinco, en horario de oficina **II.** *adj* de nueve a cinco; ~ **schedule** horario *m* de nueve a cinco

ninety ['naɪn·ţi] **I.** *adj* noventa **II.** <-ies> *n* noventa *m; s.a.* **eighty**

ninja ['nɪn·dʒə] *n* ninja *mf*

ninny ['nɪn·i] <-ies> *n inf* bobo, -a *m, f*

ninth [naɪnθ] **I.** *adj* noveno, -a **II.** *n* **1.** (*order*) noveno, -a *m, f* **2.** (*date*) nueve *m* **3.** (*fraction*) noveno *m*; (*part*) novena parte *f; s.a.* **eighth**

nip¹ [nɪp] **I.** <-pp-> *vt* **1.** (*bite*) mordisquear **2.** (*pinch, squeeze: pliers*) pellizcar **3.** (*remove: dead leaves*) arrancar ►**to** ~ **sth in the** bud *fig* cortar algo de raíz **II.** *n* **1.** (*sip*) traguito *m* **2.** (*pinch, tight squeeze*) pellizco *m* **3.** (*bite*) mordisquito *m* **4.** (*coldness*) helada *f*

nip² [nɪp] *n inf* (*alcohol*) chupito *m*

nipple ['nɪp·əl] *n* ANAT pezón *m*; (*teat*) tetilla *f*, tetera *f AmL*

nippy ['nɪp·i] <-ier, -iest> *adj inf* helado, -a

nirvana [nɪr·'va·nə] *n* nirvana *m; fig* perfección *f*

Nissen hut ['nɪs·ən·hʌt] *n* barraca *f* prefabricada (*hecha de metal y cemento*)

nit [nɪt] *n* ZOOL liendre *f*

niter ['naɪ·ţər] *n* nitro *m*

nitpick ['nɪt·pɪk] *vi* buscarle los tres pies al gato *fig*

nitpicker ['nɪt·pɪk·ər] *n* (*quibbler*) quisquilloso, -a *m, f*; (*petty fault-finder*) criticón, -ona *m, f*

nitpicking ['nɪt·pɪk·ɪŋ] **I.** *adj inf* criticón, -ona; ~ **criticism** crítica *f* gratuita **II.** *n inf* pega *f*

nitrate ['naɪ·treɪt] *n* nitrato *m*

nitric ['naɪ·trɪk] *adj* nítrico, -a

nitric acid *n* ácido *m* nítrico

nitrite ['naɪ·traɪt] *n* nitrito *m*

nitrogen ['naɪ·trə·dʒən] *n* nitrógeno *m*

nitroglycerin(e) [ˌnaɪ·troʊ·'glɪs·ər·ɪn] *n* nitroglicerina *f*

N

nitrous ['naɪ·trəs] *adj* nitroso, -a; ~ **acid** ácido *m* nitroso

nitty-gritty [ˌnɪt̬·i·'grɪt̬·i] *n inf* the ~ el meollo; **to get down to the** ~ ir al grano

nitwit ['nɪt·wɪt] *n inf* idiota *mf*

nix [nɪks] I. *vt sl* rehusar II. *adv sl* ¡ni hablar! III. *n sl* na de na *f*

NJ [ˌnu·'dʒɜr·zi] *n abbr of* **New Jersey** Nueva Jersey *f*

NLP [ˌen·el·'pi] *n abbr of* **Neuro-Linguistic Programming** programación *f* neurolingüística

NM [ˌnu·'mek·sɪ·koʊ] *n abbr of* **New Mexico** Nuevo México *m*

NNE *abbr of* **north-northeast** NNE *m*

NNW *abbr of* **north-northwest** NNO *m*

no [noʊ] I. *adj* 1. (*not to any degree*) no; ~ **parking** prohibido estacionar; ~ **way** de ninguna manera; ~ **can do** *inf* no se puede; ~ **less than sth/sb** nada menos que algo/alguien 2. (*equivalent to a negative sentence*) no; (*emphasizes previous statement's falsity*) no II. *n* <-(e)s>, *n* (*denial, refusal*) no *m;* **to not take** ~ **for an answer** no admitir un no por respuesta III. *interj* (*word used to deny*) no; (*emphasizes distress*) qué me dices

no., No. *abbr of* **number** núm., nº

Noah's ark [ˌnoʊ·əz·'ark] *n* arca *f* de Noé

Nobel prize [ˌnoʊ·bel·'praɪz] *n* premio *m* nobel

Nobel prize winner *n* (premio) nobel *mf*

nobility [noʊ·'bɪl·ə·t̬i] *n* 1. + *sing/pl vb* (*aristocracy*) nobleza *f;* **the** ~ la aristocracia 2. (*nobleness of character*) generosidad *f;* (*selflessness*) altruismo *m*

noble ['noʊ·bəl] I. *adj* 1. (*of aristocratic or birth*) noble 2. (*honorable: person*) noble; (*action*) generoso, -a; (*ideas*) grande; ~ **act** acto *m* noble 3. (*splendid*) majestuoso, -a 4. (*excellent*) magnífico, -a; (*horse*) noble II. *n* noble *mf*

nobleman ['noʊ·bəl·mən] <-men> *n* aristócrata *m*

noble-minded *adj* honesto, -a

noblewoman <-women> *n* aristócrata *f*

nobly ['noʊ·bli] *adv* noblemente

nobody ['noʊ·bad·i] I. *pron indef, sing* nadie; ~ **speaks** nadie habla; **we saw** ~ (**else**) no vimos a nadie (más); **he told** ~ no se lo dijo a nadie II. *n inf* don nadie *m;* **those people are nobodies** esas personas son un cero a la izquierda

nocturnal [nak·'tɜr·nəl] *adj form* nocturno, -a

nocturnally *adv* por la noche

nod [nad] I. *n* cabezada *f,* inclinación *f* de cabeza II. <-dd-> *vt* **to** ~ **one's head** asentir con la cabeza; **to** ~ **one's head to do sth** dar el visto bueno para hacer algo; **to** ~ **one's head at sth** indicar algo con la cabeza; **to** ~ **farewell to sb** saludar a alguien con una inclinación de cabeza III. <-dd-> *vi* 1. (*incline head in agreement*) asentir con la cabeza; **to** ~ **to sb** saludar a alguien con una inclinación de

cabeza; **to** ~ **at sth** indicar algo con la cabeza 2. *inf* (*when sleepy*) dar cabezadas
♦ **nod off** *vi* quedarse dormido

nodding ['nad·ɪŋ] *adj* ~ **acquaintance** conocimiento *f* superficial; **to have only a** ~ **acquaintance with sth** conocer algo sólo por encima

node [noʊd] *n* 1. ANAT (*tissue*) ganglio *m* 2. BOT (*on a stem*) nódulo *m* 3. COMPUT nodo *m*

nodule ['nad·ʒ·ul] *n a.* ANAT, BOT nódulo *m*

no-fault ['noʊ·fɔlt] *adj* (*insurance*) con indemnización garantizada

noggin ['nag·ɪn] *n* 1. (*small measure*) vaso *m* pequeño 2. *sl* (*head, mind*) coco *m*

no-go area [noʊ·goʊ·'er·i·ə] *n* MIL zona *f* prohibida

nohow ['noʊ·haʊ] *adv sl* de ninguna manera

noise [nɔɪz] I. *n* 1. (*sound*) ruido *m;* **to make a** ~ hacer ruido 2. (*loud, unpleasant sounds*) estruendo *m* 3. ELEC interferencia *f* ▶ **to make** ~ **about sth** *inf* quejarse mucho de algo; **to make** (**the right**) ~**s** (*to go along with*) seguir la corriente; (*be polite*) ser muy cortés II. *adj* del ruido, ruidoso, -a

noise barrier *n* barrera *f* del sonido

noiseless ['nɔɪz·lɪs] *adj* silencioso, -a

noise pollution *n* contaminación *f* acústica

noise prevention *n* prevención *f* del ruido

noisome ['nɔɪ·səm] *adj form* (*offensive*) repulsivo, -a; (*odor*) fétido, -a

noisy ['nɔɪ·zi] <-ier, -iest> *adj* 1. (*making noise: crowd*) ruidoso, -a; (*very loud, unpleasant*) estrepitoso, -a; (*protest*) escandaloso, -a; **to be** ~ ser ruidoso 2. (*full of noise: restaurant, street*) bullicioso, -a 3. ELEC (*signal*) acústico, -a

no-jump [ˌnoʊ·'dʒʌmp] *n* SPORTS salto *m* nulo

nomad ['noʊ·mæd] *n* nómada *mf*

nomadic [noʊ·'mæd·ɪk] *adj* nómada

no man's land ['noʊ·mænz·lænd] *n* tierra *f* de nadie

nomenclature ['noʊ·mən·kleɪ·tʃər] *n* nomenclatura *f*

nominal ['nam·ə·nəl] *adj* 1. (*in name*) nominal 2. (*small: sum*) pequeño, -a

nominally ['nam·ə·nə·li] *adv* nominalmente

nominate ['nam·ə·neɪt] *vt* 1. (*propose*) proponer; (*for an award*) nominar 2. (*appoint*) nombrar

nomination [ˌnam·ə·'neɪ·ʃən] *n* 1. (*proposal*) propuesta *f* 2. (*appointment*) nombramiento *m;* (*for an award*) nominación *f* 3. (*action of proposing*) proposición *f*

nominative ['nam·ə·nə·t̬ɪv] I. *n* nominativo *m* II. *adj* nominativo, -a

nominee [ˌnam·ə·'ni] *n* candidato, -a *m, f;* (*for an award*) nominado, -a *m, f*

nonacceptance [ˌnan·ək·'sep·təns] *n* 1. (*failure to accept*) rechazo *m* 2. FIN no aceptación *f*

nonagenarian [ˌnan·ə·dʒə·'ner·i·ən] I. *n* nonagenario, -a *m, f* II. *adj* nonagenario, -a

nonaggression [ˌnan·ə·'greʃ·ən] *n* no agresión *f*

nonaggression pact, **nonaggression**

treaty <-ies> *n* pacto *m* de no agresión
nonalcoholic [ˌnan·æl·kə·ˈhal·ɪk] *adj* sin alcohol
nonaligned [ˌnan·ə·ˈlaɪnd] *adj* no alineado, -a
nonalignment [ˌnan·ə·ˈlaɪn·mənt] *n* no alineamiento *m*
nonappearance [ˌnan·ə·ˈpɪr·əns] *n* LAW incomparecencia *f*
nonattendance [ˌnan·ə·ˈten·dəns] *n* ausencia *f*
nonbelligerent [ˌnan·bə·ˈlɪdʒ·ər·ənt] *adj* no beligerante
nonce word [ˈnans·wɜrd] *n* palabra *f* ad hoc
nonchalant [ˌnan·ʃə·ˈlant] *adj* despreocupado, -a; **to appear** ~ mostrarse indiferente; **to be** ~ **about sth** estar indiferente ante algo
noncom [ˈnan·kam] *adj inf abbr of* **noncommissioned officer** suboficial *mf*
noncombatant [ˌnan·kəm·ˈbæt·ənt] *n* MIL no combatiente *mf*
noncombustible [ˌnan·kəm·ˈbʌs·tə·bəl] *adj* incombustible
noncommissioned officer [ˌnan·kə·ˌmɪʃ·ənd·ˈɔ·fɪ·sər] *n* MIL suboficial *mf*
noncommittal [ˌnan·kə·ˈmɪt̬·əl] *adj* evasivo, -a
noncompliance [ˌnan·kəm·ˈplaɪ·əns] *n* incumplimiento *m*
non compos mentis [ˌnan·ˌkam·poʊs·ˈmen·tɪs] *adj* LAW sin plenas facultades mentales
nonconformist [ˌnan·kən·ˈfɔr·mɪst] I. *adj* inconformista II. *n* inconformista *mf*
nonconformity [ˌnan·kən·ˈfɔr·mə·t̬i] *n* inconformidad *f*
noncontributory [ˌnan·kən·ˈtrɪb·ju·tɔr·i] *adj* sin contribución; ~ **pension plan** plan *m* de pensiones no contributivo
noncooperation [ˌnan·koʊ·ap·ə·ˈreɪ·ʃən] *n* no cooperación *f*
non-deposit bottle [ˌnan·dɪ·ˌpaz·ɪt·ˈbat̬·əl] *n* envase *m* no retornable
nondescript [ˌnan·dɪ·ˈskrɪpt] *adj* sin nada de particular; (*person*) anodino, -a; (*color*) indefinido, -a
nondurables [ˌnan·ˈdʊr·ə·bəlz] *npl* productos *mpl* perecederos
none [nʌn] I. *pron* 1. (*nobody*) nadie, ninguno, -a; ~ **of them** ninguno de ellos; ~ **but he saw it** sólo lo vio él; ~ **of you helped me** ninguno de vosotros me ayudó 2. (*not any*) ninguno, -a; ~ **of my letters arrived** ninguna de mis cartas llegó 3. (*not any*) nada; **nuts/wine? I've** ~ (**at all**) ¿frutos secos/vino? no tengo nada; ~ **of your speeches!** ¡nada de sermones!; ~ **of that!** ¡déjate de eso! II. *adv* 1. (*not*) ~ **the less** sin embargo; **to be** ~ **the wiser** seguir sin entender nada 2. (*not very*) **it's** ~ **too soon** ya era hora; **it's** ~ **too warm** no hace mucho calor
nonentity [nan·ˈen·tə·t̬i] <-ies> *n* 1. (*person*) cero *m* a la izquierda 2. (*insignificance*) insignificancia *f*
nonessential [ˌnan·ɪ·ˈsen·tʃəl] I. *adj* secundario, -a II. *n* cosa *f* sin importancia

nonevent [ˌnan·ɪ·ˈvent] *n inf* fiasco *m*
nonexistence *n* inexistencia *f*
nonexistent [ˌnan·ɪg·ˈzɪs·tənt] *adj* inexistente
nonfiction [ˌnan·ˈfɪk·ʃən] *n* no ficción *m*
nonflammable [ˌnan·ˈflæm·ə·bəl] *adj* no inflamable
noninfectious [ˌnan·ɪn·ˈfek·ʃəs] *adj* no infeccioso, -a
non-iron [ˌnan·ˈaɪ·ərn] *adj* que no necesita plancha
nonlocal *adj* no local
nonmember country [ˌnan·ˌmem·bər·ˈkʌn·tri] <-ies> *n* POL país *m* no miembro
nonnegotiable [ˌnan·nɪ·ˈgoʊ·ʃi·ə·bəl] *adj* LAW, FIN no negociable
nonpareil [ˌnan·pə·ˈrel] I. *adj liter* sin par II. *n liter* cosa *f* sin par
nonplus [ˌnan·ˈplʌs] <-ss-> *vt* dejar perplejo; **to be** ~**sed** quedarse perplejo
nonpolluting [ˌnan·pə·ˈlu·t̬ɪŋ] *adj* no contaminante
nonproductive [ˌnan·prə·ˈdʌk·tɪv] *adj* improductivo, -a
nonprofit [ˌnan·ˈpraf·ɪt], **non-profit-making** *adj* no lucrativo, -a
nonproliferation [ˌnan·prə·ˌlɪf·ə·ˈreɪ·ʃən] I. *n* POL no proliferación *f* II. *adj* POL de no proliferación
nonproliferation treaty <-ies> *n* POL tratado *m* de no proliferación
nonrefundable [ˌnan·rɪ·ˈfʌn·də·bəl] *adj* no reembolsable; ~ **down payment** pago *m* a fondo perdido
nonresident [ˌnan·ˈrez·ɪ·dənt] I. *adj* no residente II. *n* transeúnte *mf*
nonreturnable [ˌnan·rɪ·ˈtɜr·nə·bəl] *adj* no retornable
nonscheduled [ˌnan·ˈskedʒ·uld] *adj* no programado, -a
nonsense [ˈnan·sens] I. *n* tonterías *fpl*; **to make** ~ **of sth** ridiculizar algo; **to talk** ~ *inf* decir tonterías II. *adj* 1. LIT (*invented for amusement*) disparatado, -a 2. (*without meaning*) absurdo, -a III. *interj* tonterías
nonsensical [ˌnan·ˈsen·sɪ·kəl] *adj* absurdo, -a
nonshrink [ˌnan·ˈʃrɪŋk] *adj* que no encoge
nonskid [ˌnan·ˈskɪd] *adj* antideslizante
nonsmoker [ˌnan·ˈsmoʊ·kər] *n* no fumador(a) *m(f)*
nonsmoking *adj* para no fumadores; ~ **section** zona *f* para no fumadores
nonstarter [ˌnan·ˈstar·t̬ər] *n inf* **that proposal is a** ~ esa propuesta es imposible
nonstick [ˌnan·ˈstɪk] *adj* antiadherente
nonstop [ˌnan·ˈstap] I. *adj* 1. (*without stopping, direct*) sin parar; (*flight*) directo, -a 2. (*uninterrupted*) incesante II. *adv* sin pausa
nonswimmer [ˌnan·ˈswɪm·ər] *n* no nadador(a) *m(f)*
nontaxable [ˌnan·ˈtæk·sə·bəl] *adj* no gravable
nontoxic [ˌnan·ˈtak·sɪk] *adj* no tóxico, -a
nonverbal [ˌnan·ˈvɜr·bəl] *adj* no verbal
nonviolent [ˌnan·ˈvaɪ·ə·lənt] *adj* pacífico, -a

N

nonvoting [ˌnan·'vou·t̬ɪŋ] *adj* sin derecho a voto

noodle¹ ['nu·dəl] I. *n* fideo *m* II. *adj* de fideos

noodle² ['nu·dəl] *n sl* 1. (*head*) coco *m* 2. (*person*) tontolaba *mf*

noodle (**around**) *vi inf* MUS (*on an instrument*) tocarse algo

nook [nʊk] *n liter* rincón *m;* **I looked in every ~ and crannies** busqué en todos los rincones

noon [nun] *n* mediodía *m;* **at ~ a** mediodía; **about ~** alrededor de mediodía

no one ['nou·wʌn] *pron s.* **nobody**

noose [nus] *n* 1. (*loop of rope*) soga *f* 2. (*for catching*) lazo *m* 3. *fig* (*problem*) aprieto *m* ▶ **to have a ~ around one's neck** tener la soga al cuello

nope [noup] *adv inf* no

nor [nɔr] *conj* 1. (*and also not*) tampoco; **~** (**do**) **I** ni yo tampoco 2. (*not either*) ni

Nordic ['nɔr·dɪk] *adj* nórdico, -a

norm [nɔrm] *n* norma *f*

normal ['nɔr·məl] *adj* 1. (*within the ordinary*) normal 2. (*usual*) corriente; **as** (**is**) **~** como es normal

normalcy ['nɔr·məl·si], **normality** [nɔr·'mæl·ə·t̬i] *n* normalidad *f*

normalize ['nɔr·mə·laɪz] *a.* COMPUT I. *vt* normalizar II. *vi* normalizarse

normally ['nɔr·mə·li] *adv* normalmente

Normandy ['nɔr·mən·di] *n* Normandía *f*

north [nɔrθ] I. *n* 1. (*cardinal point*) norte *m;* **to lie 3 miles to the ~ of sth** estar a 5 km al norte de algo; **to go/drive to the ~** ir/viajar hacia el norte; **further ~** más al norte 2. GEO norte *m;* **in the ~ of France** en el norte de Francia; **the Far North** el extremo norte II. *adj* del norte, septentrional; **~ wind** viento *m* del norte; **~ coast** costa *f* norte; **the North Sea** El Mar del Norte; **North Star** Estrella *f* Polar; **the North Pole** el Polo Norte

North Africa *n* África *f* del Norte

North African I. *n* norteafricano, -a *m, f* II. *adj* norteafricano, -a

North America *n* América *f* del Norte

North American I. *n* norteamericano, -a *m, f* II. *adj* norteamericano, -a

North Carolina [ˌnɔrθ·ˌkær·ə·'laɪ·nə] *n* Carolina *f* del Norte

North Dakota [ˌnɔrθ·də·'kou·də] *n* Dakota *f* del Norte

northeast [ˌnɔrθ·'ist] I. *n* nordeste *m* II. *adj* del nordeste

northeastern [ˌnɔrθ·'i·stərn] *adj* nororiental

northerly ['nɔr·ðər·li] *adj* del norte; **~ direction** dirección *f* norte

northern ['nɔr·ðərn] *adj* del norte, norteño, -a, nortino, -a *Chile, Perú;* **~ hemisphere** hemisferio *m* norte; **the ~ part of the country** la parte norte del país; **~ lights** aurora *f* boreal

northerner ['nɔr·ðər·nər] *n* norteño, -a *m, f*

Northern Marianas *n* Marianas *fpl* del Norte

northernmost *adj* más septentrional

Northern Territory *n* territorio *m* norte

North Pole ['nɔrθ·poʊl] *n* **the ~** el Polo Norte

North Sea I. *n* Mar *m* del Norte II. *adj* del Mar del Norte

North-South divide *n* ECON división *f* Norte-Sur

northward ['nɔrθ·wərd] *adv* hacia el norte

northwest [ˌnɔrθ·'west] I. *n* noroeste *m;* **to the ~** (**of**) al noroeste (de) II. *adj* del noroeste; **~ Texas** el noroeste de Texas III. *adv* en dirección noroeste

northwesterly [ˌnɔrθ·'wes·tər·li] *adj* en dirección noroeste; (*from the northwest*) del noroeste; **~ part** parte *f* noroeste

Northwest Territories *n pl* territorios *mpl* del noroeste

Norway ['nɔr·weɪ] *n* Noruega *f*

Norwegian [nɔr·'wi·dʒən] I. *adj* noruego, -a II. *n* 1. (*person*) noruego, -a *m, f* 2. LING noruego *m*

nose [noʊz] I. *n* 1. ANAT nariz *f;* (*of animal*) hocico *m;* **to blow one's ~** sonarse la nariz 2. AVIAT (*front*) morro *m* 3. (*smell of wine*) bouquet *m* ▶ **with one's ~ in the air** mirando por encima del hombro; **to put one's ~ to the grindstone** *inf* trabajar duro; **to put sb's ~ out of joint** *inf* tocar las narices a alguien; **to keep one's ~ clean** *inf* no meterse en líos; **to follow one's ~** *inf* (*trust instincts*) guiarse por su olfato; (*go straight ahead*) seguir adelante; **to have a** (**good**) **~ for sth** tener buen olfato para algo; **to keep one's ~ out of sth** *inf* no meterse en algo; **to poke one's ~ into sth** *inf* meter las narices en algo; **to rub sb's ~ in it** restregar algo a alguien por las narices; **to thumb one's ~ at sb** tomar el pelo a alguien; (**from**) **under sb's** (**very**) **~** *inf,* **right out from under sb's ~** *inf* delante de las narices de alguien II. *vi* fisgonear III. *vt* **to ~ one's way in/out/up** entrar/salir/pasar lentamente; **to ~** (**its way**) **through sth** avanzar con precaución a través de algo

◆ **nose around** *vi inf* fisgonear

◆ **nose out** I. *vt* descubrir II. *vi* apartarse

nosebag ['noʊz·bæg] *n* morral *m*

nosebleed *n* hemorragia *f* nasal

nose cone *n* AVIAT cabeza *f*

nosedive I. *n* 1. AVIAT descenso *m* en picado 2. FIN caída *f* en picado II. *vi* 1. AVIAT descender en picado 2. FIN caer en picado

nosegay *n* ramillete *m* de flores

nose job *n inf* arreglo *m* de nariz

nose wheel *n* rueda *f* de proa

nosey ['noʊ·zi] <-ier, -iest> *adj s.* **nosy**

nosh [naʃ] I. *n inf* papeo *m* II. *vi* papear

nostalgia [na·'stæl·dʒə] *n* nostalgia *f*

nostalgic [na·'stæl·dʒɪk] *adj* nostálgico, -a

no-strike agreement [ˌnoʊ·straɪk·ə·'griˑmənt] *n* acuerdo *m* de no convocar huelgas

nostril ['nas·trəl] *n* ventana *f* de la nariz

nosy ['noʊ·zi] <-ier, -iest> *adj* fisgón, -ona; **to be ~** *pej* ser un cotilla

Nosy Parker ['noʊ·zi·'par·kər] *n inf* cotilla *mf*

not [nat] *adv* no; **it's a woman, ~ a man** es

una mujer, no un hombre; **he's asked me ~ to do it** me ha pedido que no lo haga; **~ all the children like singing** no les gusta cantar a todos los niños; **~ me!** ¡yo no!; **why ~?** ¿por qué no?; **he is ~ ugly** no es feo; **or ~ o** no; **~ at all** (*nothing*) en absoluto; (*no need to thank*) de nada; **~ only... but also...** no sólo... sino también; **~ just** [*o* **simply**] no sólo; **~ much** no mucho

notable ['nou·ṭə·bəl] **I.** *adj* **1.** (*remarkable*) notable **2.** (*eminent*) eminente **II.** *n* persona *f* importante

notably ['nou·ṭə·bli] *adv* notablemente

notary ['nou·ṭə·ri] <-ies> *n* ~ (**public**) notario, -a *m, f*

notation [nou·'teɪ·ʃən] *n* MATH, MUS notación *f*

notch [natʃ] <-es> **I.** *vt* **1.** (*cut*) hacer una muesca **2.** *inf* (*achieve*) conseguir **II.** *n* **1.** (*cut*) muesca *f;* (*hole*) agujero *m* **2.** (*degree*) punto *m* **3.** (*narrow valley*) valle *m*

note [nout] **I.** *n* **1.** (*annotation*) nota *f;* **to take ~** tomar nota **2.** LIT apunte *m* **3.** MUS nota *f;* (*sound*) tono *m;* **to strike the right ~** *fig* dar con el tono apropiado **4.** (*piece of paper money*) billete *m* **5.** (*importance*) **of ~** form notable; **nothing of ~** nada importante **II.** *vt* form anotar; (*mention*) observar; **to ~** (**that**)... hacer notar (que)...

notebook ['nout·bʊk] *n* cuaderno *m*

noted ['nou·ṭɪd] *adj* célebre; **to be ~ for sth** ser conocido por algo

notepad ['nout·pæd] *n* bloc *m*

notepaper ['nout·ˌpeɪ·pər] *n* papel *m* de carta

noteworthy ['nout·ˌwɜr·ði] *adj form* de interés; **nothing/something ~** nada/algo digno de atención

nothing ['nʌθ·ɪŋ] **I.** *pron indef, sing* **1.** (*no objects*) nada; **~ happens** no pasa nada; **we saw ~** (**else/more**) no vimos nada (más); **~ new** nada nuevo; **next to ~** casi nada **2.** (*not anything*) **~ came of it** no salió nada (de ahí); **~ doing!** *inf* ¡para nada!; **fit for ~** bueno para nada; **to make ~ of it** no darle importancia; **there is ~ to laugh at** no tiene ninguna gracia **3.** (*not important*) **that's ~!** ¡no es nada!; **time is ~ to me** el tiempo no es importante para mí **4.** (*only*) **~ but** tan sólo; **she is ~ if not patient** es paciente por encima de todo; **~ much** poca cosa **II.** *adv* **~ less than** ni más ni menos que; **~ daunted, I went on** sin flaquear, seguí adelante **III.** *n* **1.** nada *f* **2.** MATH, SPORTS cero *m;* **three to ~** tres a cero **3.** (*person*) don nadie *m*

nothingness ['nʌθ·ɪŋ·nɪs] *n* (*emptiness*) vacío *m;* (*worthlessness*) nada *f*

notice ['nou·ṭɪs] **I.** *vt* **1.** (*see*) ver; (*perceive*) fijarse en; **to ~** (**that**)... darse cuenta de (que)... **2.** (*recognize*) reconocer **II.** *vi* darse cuenta **III.** *n* **1.** (*attention*) interés *m;* **to take ~ of sb/sth** prestar atención a alguien/algo; **it came to my ~** (**that...**) me enteré que...; **that escaped my ~** se me pasó por alto; **it escaped my ~ that...** se me pasó por alto que... **2.** (*dis-*

play) letrero *m;* (*in a newspaper, magazine*) anuncio *m* **3.** (*warning*) aviso *m;* **to give sb ~** (**of sth**) avisar a alguien (de algo); **at short ~** a corto plazo; **at a moment's ~** al momento; **until further ~** hasta nuevo aviso **4.** LAW preaviso *m;* **to give** (**in**) **one's ~** presentar la dimisión; **to give sb their ~** despedir a alguien

noticeable ['nou·ṭɪs·ə·bəl] *adj* (*change, improvement*) evidente; (*difference, increase, lack of friendliness*) notable

notifiable ['nou·ṭə·faɪ·ə·bəl] *adj* (*disease*) que hay que notificar

notification [ˌnou·ṭə·fɪ·'keɪ·ʃən] *n* notificación *f*

notify ['nou·ṭə·faɪ] <-ie-> *vt* informar; **to ~ sb of sth** notificar algo a alguien

notion ['nou·ʃən] *n* **1.** (*idea*) noción *f;* **to have some ~ of sth** tener algunas nociones de algo; **to have no ~ of sth** no tener ni idea de algo **2.** (*silly idea*) burrada *f;* **to have a ~ to do sth** tener la intención de hacer algo

notional ['nou·ʃə·nəl] *adj form* teórico, -a

notoriety [ˌnou·ṭə·'raɪ·ə·ṭi] *n* mala fama *f*

notorious [nou·'tɔr·i·əs] *adj* de mala reputación; (*thief*) bien conocido, -a; **she's a ~ liar** tiene fama de mentirosa; **to be ~ for sth** tener mala fama por algo

notwithstanding [ˌnat·wɪθ·'stæn·dɪŋ] *form* **I.** *prep* a pesar de **II.** *adv* no obstante

nougat ['nu·gət] *n* ≈ turrón *m*

nought [nɔt] *pron s.* **naught**

noun [naʊn] **I.** *n* nombre *m;* LING sustantivo *m* **II.** *adj* nominal

nourish ['nɜr·ɪʃ] *vt* **1.** (*provide with food*) alimentar; **to ~ oneself on sth** alimentarse de algo **2.** *fig, form* (*cherish*) fomentar

nourishing ['nɜr·ɪʃ·ɪŋ] *adj* nutritivo, -a; (*rich*) rico, -a

nourishment *n* **1.** (*food*) alimento *m* **2.** (*providing with food*) alimentación *m*

Nov. *n abbr of* **November** nov.

Nova Scotia [ˌnou·və·'skou·ʃə] *n* Nueva Escocia *f*

novel[1] ['nav·əl] *n* LIT novela *f*

novel[2] ['nav·əl] *adj* (*new*) novedoso, -a

novelette [ˌnav·ə·'let] *n* novela *f* rosa

novelist ['nav·ə·lɪst] *n* novelista *mf*

novelty ['nav·əl·ti] **I.** <-ies> *n* **1.** (*newness*) novedad *f* **2.** (*innovation*) innovación *f* **3.** (*cheap trinket*) baratija *f* **II.** *adj* **1.** (*new*) novedoso, -a **2.** (*cheap*) barato, -a

November [nou·'vem·bər] *n* noviembre *m;* *s.a.* **April**

novice ['nav·ɪs] *n* novato, -a *m, f;* REL novicio, -a *m, f*

now [naʊ] **I.** *adv* **1.** (*at the present time*) ahora; **just ~** ahora mismo **2.** (*currently*) actualmente **3.** (*then*) entonces; **any time ~** en cualquier momento; (**every**) **~ and then** de vez en cuando **4.** (*give emphasis*) **~, where did I put her book?** ¿se puede saber dónde he puesto su libro?; **~ we're talking!** ¡parece que empezamos a entendernos!; **~ then** ¡vamos a

ver! ▶ (it's) ~ or **never** (es) ahora o nunca **II.** *n*
(*present*) presente *m;* **before** ~ antes; **by** ~
ahora ya; **for** ~ por ahora; **as of** ~ a partir de
ahora **III.** *conj* ~ (**that**)... ahora que...

nowadays ['nau·ə·deɪz] *adv* hoy en día

nowhere ['nou·hwer] *adv* en ninguna parte; **to
appear out of** ~ aparecer de la nada; **to be
going** ~ *a. fig* no llevar a ninguna parte

noxious ['nak·ʃəs] *adj form* nocivo, -a; (*very
unpleasant*) desagradable

nozzle ['naz·əl] *n* tobera *f;* (*of a gas pump*)
inyector *m;* (*of a gun*) boquilla *f*

NT 1. *abbr of* **New Testament** N.T. *m* **2.** *abbr
of* **Northwest Territories** Northwest Territories (Canadá)

nuance ['nu·ans] *n* matiz *m*

nub [nʌb] *n* **1.** (*point*) quid *m* **2.** (*piece*)
trozo *m*

nubile ['nu·bɪl] *adj* núbil

nuclear ['nu·kli·ər] *adj* nuclear

nuclear medicine *n* medicina *f* nuclear

nuclear nonproliferation treaty <-ies> *n*
POL, MIL tratado *m* de no proliferación de armas
nucleares

nuclear power station *n* central *f* nuclear

nuclear reactor *n* reactor *m* nuclear

nucleic acid [nu·'kli·ɪk·'æs·ɪd] *n* ácido *m*
nucleico

nucleus ['nu·kli·əs] <-ei *o* -es> *n* núcleo *m*

nude [nud] **I.** *adj* desnudo, -a **II.** *n* **1.** ART, PHOT
desnudo *m* **2.** (*naked*) **in the** ~ desnudo

nude beach *n* playa *f* nudista

nudge [nʌdʒ] **I.** *vt* dar un codazo a; *fig* empujar; **to** ~ **sb into doing sth** empujar a alguien a
hacer algo **II.** *n* **1.** (*push*) codazo *m* **2.** (*encouragement*) valor *m*

nudism ['nu·dɪz·əm] *n* nudismo *m*

nudist ['nu·dɪst] **I.** *n* nudista *mf* **II.** *adj* nudista

nudist camp *n* campamento *m* de nudistas

nudity ['nu·də·t̬i] *n* desnudez *f*

nugatory ['nu·gə·tɔr·i] *adj form* insignificante

nugget ['nʌg·ɪt] *n* MIN pepita *f*

nuisance ['nu·səns] *n* **1.** molestia *f,* camote *m*
AmL; **to make a** ~ **of oneself** dar la lata
2. LAW perjuicio *m*

nuke [nuk, njuk] *vt sl* **1.** MIL bombardear con
armas atómicas **2.** (*cook*) cocinar en el microondas

null [nʌl] *adj* nulo, -a; ~ **and void** sin efecto

nullification [ˌnʌl·ɪ·fɪ·'keɪ·ʃən] *n* anulación *f*

nullify ['nʌl·ɪ·faɪ] <-ie-> *vt* anular

nullity ['nʌl·ə·t̬i] *n* nulidad *f*

numb [nʌm] **I.** *adj* entumecido, -a; **to go** ~
entumecerse **II.** *vt* entumecer; (*desensitize*)
insensibilizar

number ['nʌm·bər] **I.** *n* **1.** MATH número *m;*
(*symbol*) cifra *f;* **house** ~ número de casa;
telephone ~ número de teléfono **2.** (*amount*)
cantidad *f;* (a) **small/large** ~(s) (of children)
(una) pequeña/gran cantidad (de niños); **for a**
~ **of reasons** por una serie de razones; **to be 3
in** ~ ser 3; **to be few in** ~ ser pocos **3.** PUBL,
MUS, THEAT número *m* ▶ ~ **one** uno *m* mismo;

to look after ~ **one** cuidar de uno mismo; **to
be** (**the**) ~ **one** ser el mejor; **to have sb's** ~
tener calado a alguien; **to be beyond** ~ ser
tantos que no se pueden contar **II.** *vt* **1.** (*assign
a number to*) poner número a; **to** ~ **sth
from... to...** numerar algo del... al... **2.** (*count*)
contar **3.** (*amount to*) sumar; **each group** ~**s
10 members** cada grupo tiene 10 miembros

numbering *n* numeración *f*

numberless *adj* innumerable

numbness ['nʌm·nɪs] *n* **1.** (*on part of body*)
entumecimiento *m* **2.** (*lack of feeling*) insensibilidad *f*

numeracy ['nu·mər·ə·si] *n* capacidad *f* para la
aritmética

numeral ['nu·mər·əl] *n* número *m*

numerate ['nu·mər·ət] *adj* MATH competente
en matemáticas

numeration [ˌnu·mə·'reɪ·ʃən] *n form* numeración *f*

numerical [nu·'mer·ɪ·kəl] *adj* numérico, -a; **in**
~ **order** por orden numérico

numeric keypad [nu·ˌmer·ɪk·'ki·pæd] *n* COM-
PUT teclado *m* numérico

numerous ['nu·mər·əs] *adj* numeroso, -a

numismatics [ˌnu·mɪz·'mæt̬·ɪks] *n + sing vb*
numismática *f*

numskull ['nʌm·skʌl] *n* idiota *mf*

nun [nʌn] *n* monja *f*

nuncio ['nʌn·si·ou] *n* REL nuncio *m*

nunnery ['nʌn·ə·ri] <-ies> *n* convento *m* de
monjas

nuptial ['nʌp·ʃəl] *adj* nupcial

nurse [nɜrs] **I.** *n* **1.** MED enfermero, -a *m, f*
2. (*nanny*) niñera *f;* (*wet nurse*) nodriza *f* **II.** *vt*
1. (*care for*) cuidar **2.** (*nurture*) nutrir **3.** (*harbor*) abrigar **4.** (*hold carefully*) sostener con
cuidado **5.** (*breastfeed*) amamantar **III.** *vi* dar
de mamar

nursery ['nɜr·sə·ri] **I.** <-ies> *n* **1.** (*school*)
guardería *f* **2.** (*bedroom*) cuarto *m* de los niños
3. BOT vivero *m* **II.** *adj* ~ **education** educación
f preescolar

nursery rhyme *n* canción *f* infantil

nursery school *n* parvulario *m,* jardín *m* de
infancia

nursing I. *n* enfermería *f* **II.** *adj* de enfermería

nursing home *n* asilo *m* de ancianos

nurture ['nɜr·tʃər] **I.** *vt* alimentar; (*a plant*) cuidar **II.** *n* nutrición *f*

nut [nʌt] *n* **1.** BOT nuez *f* **2.** TECH tuerca *f* **3.** *sl*
(*madman*) chiflado, -a *m, f;* (*enthusiast*) entu-
siasta *mf* **4.** *sl* (*person's head*) coco *m;* **to be
off one's** ~ estar grillado ▶ **the** ~**s and bolts
of sth** los aspectos prácticos de algo; **a hard** ~
to crack (*situation*) una situación difícil; (*person*) un hueso duro de roer

nutcracker ['nʌt·ˌkræk·ər] *n* cascanueces *m inv*

nuthatch <-es> *n* trepatroncos *m inv*

nuthouse <-s> *n sl* manicomio *m*

nutmeg *n* nuez *f* moscada

nutrient ['nu·tri·ənt] **I.** *n* nutriente *m* **II.** *adj*
nutritivo, -a

nutrition [nu·'trɪʃ·ən] I. *n* nutrición *f* II. *adj* nutricional

nutritionist [nu·'trɪʃ·ə·nɪst] *n* nutricionista *mf*

nutritious [nu·'trɪʃ·əs] *adj*, **nutritive** ['nu·trɪ·t̬ɪv] *adj* nutritivo, -a

nuts [nʌts] I. *npl vulg* cojones *mpl* II. *adj* **to be ~** estar chiflado; **to go ~** volverse loco; **to be ~ about sb** estar loquito por alguien; **to be ~ about sth** ser un flipado de algo

nutshell ['nʌt·ʃel] *n* cáscara *f* de nuez ▶ **to put sth in a ~** decir algo con gran concisión; **in a ~** en resumidas cuentas

nutty ['nʌt̬·i] <-ier, -iest> *adj* 1. (*cake*) con nueces; (*flavor*) de nuez; (*taste*) a nueces 2. *sl* (*crazy*) chiflado, -a, revirado, -a *Arg, Urug;* **to be (as) ~ as a fruitcake** estar más loco que una cabra

nuzzle ['nʌz·əl] I. *vt* acariciar con el hocico II. *vi* acurrucarse; **to ~ closer** arrimarse; **to ~ (up) against sb/sth** apretarse contra alguien/algo

NV [nə·'va·də] *abbr of* **Nevada** Nevada *f*

NW *abbr of* **northwest** NO *m*

NY [,nu·'jɔrk] *abbr of* **New York** Nueva York *f*

nylon ['naɪ·lan] I. *n* nailon *m* II. *adj* de nailon

nymph [nɪmf] *n* ninfa *f*

nymphomania [,nɪm·foʊ·'meɪ·ni·ə] *n* ninfomanía *f*

nymphomaniac [,nɪm·foʊ·'meɪ·ni·æk] *n* ninfómana *f*

NZ *abbr of* **New Zealand** Nueva Zelanda *f*

O

O, o [oʊ] *n* 1. (*letter*) O, o *f;* **~ as in Oscar** O de Oviedo 2. (*zero*) cero *m*

O. *n abbr of* **Ohio** Ohio *m*

oaf [oʊf] *n inf* (*uncultured*) cazurro, -a *m, f;* (*clumsy*) zopenco, -a *m, f*

oafish ['oʊ·fɪʃ] *adj inf* (*uncultured*) cazurro, -a; (*clumsy*) lerdo, -a

oak [oʊk] *n* (*tree, wood*) roble *m* ▶ **mighty ~s from little acorns grow** *prov* los grandes logros nacen de pequeñas cosas *prov*

oar [ɔr] *n* remo *m*

oarsman ['ɔrz·mən] <-men> *n* remero *m*

oarswoman ['ɔrz·wʊm·ən] <-women> *n* remera *f*

OAS [,oʊ·eɪ·'es] *n abbr of* **Organization of American States** OEA *f*

oasis [oʊ·'eɪ·sɪs] <-es> *n* oasis *m inv*

oatcake ['oʊt·keɪk] *n* torta *f* de avena

oath [oʊθ] *n* juramento *m;* **to take an ~** prestar juramento; **under ~** bajo juramento; **~ of allegiance** juramento de lealtad

oatmeal ['oʊt·mil] *n* harina *f* de avena

oats [oʊts] *n pl* avena *f* ▶ **to sow one's wild ~** andar de picos pardos *inf;* **to feel one's ~** sen-

tirse en plena forma

obduracy ['ab·dʊr·ə·si] *n* obstinación *f*

obdurate ['ab·dʊr·ɪt] *adj form* obstinado, -a

obedience [oʊ·'bi·di·əns] *n* obediencia *f;* **in ~ to** conforme a

obedient [oʊ·'bi·di·ənt] *adj* obediente; **to be ~ to sb/sth** obedecer a alguien/algo

obelisk ['ab·ə·lɪsk] *n* obelisco *m*

obese [oʊ·'bis] *adj* obeso, -a

obesity [oʊ·'bi·sə·t̬i] *n* obesidad *f*

obey [oʊ·'beɪ] *vt* (*person*) obedecer; (*instincts, advice*) hacer caso a; (*order, the law*) cumplir

obituary [oʊ·'bɪtʃ·u·er·i] <-ies> *n*, **obituary notice** *n* necrología *f,* obituario *m AmL*

object[1] ['ab·dʒɪkt] *n* 1. (*unspecified thing*) objeto *m* 2. (*purpose, goal*) propósito *m,* objetivo *m;* **the ~ of the exercise is...** el objeto del ejercicio es... 3. (*obstacle*) **money is no ~** el dinero no importa 4. LING complemento *m*

object[2] [əb·'dʒekt] I. *vi* oponerse II. *vt* objetar; **to ~ that...** objetar que...

objection [əb·'dʒek·ʃən] *n* objeción *f;* **to raise ~s** poner reparos; **to raise ~s to sth** protestar contra algo; **if there is no ~...** si no hay inconveniente...

objectionable [əb·'dʒek·ʃə·nə·bəl] *adj form* desagradable; (*person*) molesto, -a; (*conduct*) reprensible

objective [əb·'dʒek·tɪv] I. *n* objetivo *m* II. *adj* objetivo, -a

objectivity [,ab·dʒek·'tɪv·ə·t̬i] *n* objetividad *f*

object lesson *n* lección *f* práctica

objector *n* objetor(a) *m(f)*

obligate ['ab·lɪ·geɪt] *vt* obligar; **to ~ sb to do sth** obligar a alguien a hacer algo

obligation [,ab·lə·'geɪ·ʃən] *n* obligación *f;* **to be under an ~ to do sth** tener la obligación de hacer algo; **to have an ~ to sb** deber favores a alguien

obligatory [ə·'blɪg·ə·tɔr·i] *adj* obligatorio, -a

oblige [ə·'blaɪdʒ] I. *vt* 1. (*force*) obligar 2. (*perform service for*) hacer un favor a; **to ~ sb with sth** hacer a alguien el favor de algo II. *vi* **to be happy to ~** estar encantado de ayudar

obliging [ə·'blaɪ·dʒɪŋ] *adj* servicial, comedido, -a *AmL*

oblique [oʊ·'blik] I. *adj* 1. (*indirect*) indirecto, -a 2. (*slanting*) oblicuo, -a II. *n* 1. (*symbol*) barra *f* oblicua 2. (*muscle*) músculo *m* oblicuo

obliterate [ə·'blɪt̬·ə·reɪt] *vt* eliminar; (*town*) arrasar; (*writing*) borrar

obliteration [ə·,blɪt̬·ə·'reɪ·ʃən] *n* eliminación *f;* (*of town*) destrucción *f;* (*of writing*) borradura *f*

oblivion [ə·'blɪv·i·ən] *n* olvido *m;* **to fall into ~** caer en el olvido

oblivious [ə·'blɪv·i·əs] *adj* inconsciente; **~ of sth** inconsciente de algo

oblong ['ab·lan] I. *n* rectángulo *m,* oblongo *m* II. *adj* rectangular, oblongo, -a

obnoxious [əb·'nak·ʃəs] *adj* detestable

O

OBO [ˌoʊ·biˈoʊ] *adv abbr of* **or best offer** negociable

oboe [ˈoʊ·boʊ] *n* oboe *m*

oboist [ˈoʊ·boʊ·ɪst] *n* oboe *mf*

obscene [əbˈsin] *adj* **1.** (*indecent*) obsceno, -a, bascoso, -a *Col, Ecua* **2.** (*scandalous*) indecente

obscenity [əbˈsen·ə·t̬i] <-ies> *n* obscenidad *f*, indecencia *f*, bascosidad *f Col, Ecua*

obscure [əbˈskjʊr] **I.** *adj* oscuro, -a **II.** *vt* **1.** (*make difficult to see*) oscurecer **2.** (*make difficult to understand*) complicar **3.** (*hide*) ocultar

obscurity [əbˈskjʊr·ə·t̬i] *n* oscuridad *f*

obsequious [əbˈsi·kwi·əs] *adj* servil

observable [əbˈzɜr·və·bəl] *adj* observable

observance [əbˈzɜr·vəns] *n* **1.** (*of laws, rules*) observancia *f*; (*of customs*) cumplimiento *m* **2.** REL (*practice*) práctica *f*

observant [əbˈzɜr·vənt] *adj* **1.** (*quick to notice things*) observador(a) **2.** (*respectful: of rules, laws*) respetuoso, -a; (*of one's duty*) cumplidor(a)

observation [ˌab·zər·ˈveɪ·ʃən] *n* **1.** (*act of seeing*) observación *f*; LAW vigilancia *f*; **to keep sth/sb under** ~ vigilar algo/a alguien; **under** ~ MED en observación; **to escape** ~ pasar inadvertido **2.** (*remark*) comentario *m*, observación *f*; **to make an** ~ (**about sb/sth**) hacer una observación (sobre alguien/algo)

observation car *n* RAIL vagón *m* panorámico

observation post *n* MIL puesto *m* de observación

observation tower *n* atalaya *f*

observatory [əbˈzɜr·və·bɔr·i] *n* observatorio *m*

observe [əbˈzɜrv] **I.** *vt* **1.** (*watch closely*) observar; (*notice*) fijarse en; **to** ~ **sb doing sth** ver a alguien haciendo algo **2.** (*remark*) comentar **3.** (*obey: rules*) observar; (*silence, religious holiday*) guardar; **to** ~ **a minute of silence** guardar un minuto de silencio; **to** ~ **Passover** celebrar la Pascua **II.** *vi* **1.** (*watch*) observar **2.** (*remark*) **to** ~ (**up**)**on sth** hacer una observación sobre algo

observer [əbˈzɜr·vər] *n* observador(a) *m(f)*

obsess [əbˈses] *vt* obsesionar; **to be** ~**ed by sb/sth** obsesionarse por alguien/algo; **he is** ~**ed with being the best** está obsesionado con ser el mejor

obsession [əbˈseʃ·ən] *n* obsesión *f*; **to have an** ~ **with sb/sth** estar obsesionado con alguien/algo

obsessive [əbˈses·ɪv] *adj* **1.** (*person, jealousy*) obsesivo, -a; **to be** ~ **about sth** estar obsesionado con algo; **to become** ~ (**about sth**) empezar a obsesionarse (con algo) **2.** (*game*) obsesionante

obsolescence [ˌab·sə·ˈles·əns] *n* obsolescencia *f*

obsolescent [ˌab·sə·ˈles·ənt] *adj* que está quedando obsoleto, -a

obsolete [ˌab·sə·ˈlit] *adj* (*method, design*) obsoleto, -a; (*word, spelling*) caído, -a en desuso

obstacle [ˈab·stə·kəl] *n* obstáculo *m*; **an insurmountable** ~ un obstáculo insalvable; **to overcome an** ~ superar un obstáculo; **to put** ~**s in the way of sb/sth** poner dificultades a alguien/algo; **to be an** ~ **to sth** ser un obstáculo para algo

obstacle course *n* carrera *f* de obstáculos

obstetrician [ˌab·stə·ˈtrɪʃ·ən] *n* MED obstetra *mf*

obstetrics [əbˈstet·rɪks] **I.** *npl* MED obstetricia *f* **II.** *adj* MED obstétrico, -a

obstinacy [ˈab·stə·nə·si] *n* obstinación *f*

obstinate [ˈab·stə·nɪt] *adj* **1.** (*person, attitude*) obstinado, -a; **to be** ~ **about sth** ser terco en algo; **an** ~ **refusal** una negativa rotunda **2.** (*disease*) rebelde; (*problem*) persistente

obstreperous [əbˈstrep·ər·əs] *adj form* **1.** (*unruly*) rebelde **2.** (*noisy*) ruidoso, -a

obstruct [əbˈstrʌkt] *vt* **1.** (*block*) obstruir; (*traffic*) bloquear; (*view*) tapar **2.** (*hinder*) dificultar; (*passage*) impedir; (*progress*) obstaculizar; **to** ~ **the traffic** obstruir el tráfico

obstruction [əbˈstrʌk·ʃən] *n* **1.** (*action*) *a.* MED, POL obstrucción *f* **2.** (*impediment*) obstáculo *m*; **an** ~ **to sth** un obstáculo para algo; **to cause an** ~ estorbar; AUTO obstruir el paso

obstructive [əbˈstrʌk·tɪv] *adj* (*tactic, attitude*) obstruccionista; (*person*) que pone obstáculos; **don't be so** ~ no pongas tantos impedimentos

obtain [əbˈteɪn] **I.** *vt* obtener; **to** ~ **sth from sb/sth** obtener algo de alguien/algo; **to** ~ **sth for sb** conseguir algo a alguien **II.** *vi form* prevalecer

obtainable [əbˈteɪ·nə·bəl] *adj* que se puede conseguir; **it is not** ~ **in this country** no se puede adquirir en este país

obtrude [əbˈtrud] **I.** *vt form* (*force*) imponer; **to** ~ **one's opinion**(**s**) (**up**)**on sb** imponer su opinión/sus opiniones a alguien **II.** *vi form* **to** ~ **upon sth** entrometerse en algo

obtrusive [əbˈtru·sɪv] *adj form* (*question, presence*) inoportuno, -a; (*noise*) molesto, -a; (*smell*) (demasiado) penetrante; (*color, design*) (demasiado) llamativo, -a

obtuse [abˈtus] *adj* obtuso, -a

obviate [ˈab·vi·eɪt] *vt* (*necessity, difficulty*) obviar; (*danger*) evitar

obvious [ˈab·vi·əs] *adj* obvio, -a; **a sign of** ~ **displeasure** un signo de evidente disgusto; **for** ~ **reasons** por razones obvias; **it is** ~ **what/where...** está claro qué/dónde...; **it is** ~ **to me that...** me doy perfecta cuenta de que...; **to make sth** ~ **to sb** hacer algo patente a alguien; **the** ~ **thing to do** lo que hay que hacer

obviously *adv* obviamente, claramente; ~,... como es lógico,...

occasion [ə·ˈkeɪ·ʒən] **I.** *n* **1.** (*particular time*) ocasión *f;* on ~ de vez en cuando; on one ~ en una ocasión; on several ~s en varias ocasiones 2. (*event*) acontecimiento *m;* on the ~ of... con motivo de...; to dress to suit the ~ vestirse para la ocasión; to rise to the ~ estar a la altura de las circunstancias 3. (*reason*) motivo *m;* to give ~ to sth dar lugar a algo 4. (*opportunity*) ocasión; should the ~ arise si se presenta la ocasión; to have ~ to do sth tener ocasión de hacer algo **II.** *vt* ocasionar

occasional [ə·'keɪ·ʒə·nəl] *adj* ocasional; to pay sb an ~ visit visitar a alguien esporádicamente; I smoke an ~ cigarette fumo un cigarrillo de vez en cuando

occasionally *adv* ocasionalmente, de vez en cuando

Occident ['ak·sə·dənt] *n* the ~ Occidente

occidental [ˌak·sə·'den·təl] *adj* occidental

occult [ə·'kʌlt] **I.** *adj* oculto, -a **II.** *n* the ~ las ciencias ocultas

occultism [ə·'kʌl·tɪz·əm] *n* ocultismo *m*

occupancy ['ak·jə·pən·si] *n* (*of building*) ocupación *f;* (*of post*) tenencia *f*

occupancy rate *n* tasa *f* de ocupación

occupant ['ak·jə·pənt] *n form* **1.** (*of building, vehicle*) ocupante *mf;* (*tenant*) inquilino, -a *m, f* **2.** (*of post*) titular *mf*

occupation ['ak·jə·'peɪ·ʃən] *n* **1.** a. MIL ocupación *f;* ~ forces fuerzas *f* de ocupación *pl* **2.** (*profession*) profesión *f* **3.** (*pastime*) pasatiempo *m;* what's your favorite ~? ¿a qué prefieres dedicar tu tiempo libre?

occupational [ˌak·jə·'peɪ·ʃə·nəl] *adj* profesional

occupational disease *n* enfermedad *f* profesional

occupational hazard *n* riesgo *m* laboral

occupational therapy *n* terapia *f* ocupacional

occupier ['ak·jə·paɪ·ər] *n* (*of territory, building*) ocupante *mf;* (*tenant*) inquilino, -a *m, f*

occupy ['ak·ju·paɪ] <-ie-> *vt* **1.** (*room, position*) a. MIL ocupar; to ~ space ocupar espacio; the bathroom's occupied el lavabo está ocupado; ~ing forces fuerzas *fpl* de ocupación **2.** (*engage*) to be occupied with sth estar ocupado con algo; to keep sb occupied mantener a alguien ocupado; to keep one's mind occupied mantener la mente ocupada; to ~ oneself entretenerse **3.** (*hold*) to ~ a post ocupar un cargo **4.** (*dwell in*) the house hasn't been occupied for a long time nadie ha vivido en la casa durante mucho tiempo **5.** (*employ*) dar trabajo

occur [ə·'kɜr] <-rr-> *vi* **1.** (*happen*) ocurrir; (*change, problem*) producirse; don't let it ~ again! ¡que no vuelva a suceder!; consult your doctor if any of these symptoms ~ si se presenta alguno de estos síntomas consulte a su médico; to ~ once every two years tener lugar una vez cada dos años **2.** (*exist*) encontrarse; the disease does not ~ in this area la enfermedad no se da en esta zona **3.** (*come into mind*) to ~ to sb ocurrírsele a alguien; it

~d to me that... se me ocurrió que...; did it ever ~ to you that...? ¿no se te ha ocurrido nunca que...?

occurrence [ə·'kɜr·əns] *n* **1.** (*event*) acontecimiento *m;* an unexpected ~ un suceso inesperado; to be an everyday ~ ser cosa de todos los días; to be of frequent/rare ~ ser/no ser frecuente **2.** (*case*) caso *m* **3.** (*incidence: of disease*) incidencia *f*

ocean ['ou·ʃən] *n* océano *m* ► ~s of... un montón de... *inf*

oceangoing ['ou·ʃən·ˌgou·ɪŋ] *adj* transatlántico, -a

Oceania [ˌou·ʃi·'eɪ·ni·ə] *n* Oceanía *f*

oceanic [ˌou·ʃi·'æn·ɪk] *adj* oceánico, -a

ocean liner *n* NAUT transatlántico *m*

oceanography [ˌou·ʃə·'nag·rə·fi] *n* oceanografía *f*

ocelot ['as·ə·lat] *n* ocelote *m,* manigordo *m* CRi

ocher, ochre ['ou·kər] **I.** *n* ocre *m* **II.** *adj* ocre

o'clock [ə·'klak] *adv* it's one ~ es la una; it's two/seven ~ son las dos/las siete

Oct. *n abbr of* **October** oct.

octagon ['ak·tə·gan] *n* octógono *m,* octágono *m*

octagonal [ak·'tæg·ə·nəl] *adj* octogonal, octagonal

octane ['ak·teɪn] *n* octano *m*

octave ['ak·tɪv] *n* LIT, MUS octava *f*

octet [ak·'tet] *n* MUS octeto *m*

October [ak·'tou·bər] *n* octubre *m; s.a.* **April**

octogenarian [ˌak·tou·dʒɪ·'ner·i·ən] **I.** *adj* octogenario, -a **II.** *n* octogenario, -a *m, f*

octopus ['ak·tə·pəs] <-es *o* -pi> *n* pulpo *m*

oculist ['ak·jə·lɪst] *n* oculista *mf*

OD [ˌou·'di] **I.** *n abbr of* **overdose** sobredosis *f inv* **II.** *vi* to ~ on sth tomar una sobredosis de algo; *fig* abusar de algo

odd [ad] *adj* **1.** (*strange*) extraño, -a; an ~ person/thing una persona/cosa rara; how (very) ~! ¡qué raro!; it is ~ that... es raro que +*subj;* to look ~ tener un aspecto extraño **2.** (*not even: number*) impar **3.** (*approximately*) 30 ~ people 30 y pico personas **4.** (*occasional*) ocasional; at ~ times algunas veces; she does the ~ teaching job da alguna que otra clase **5.** (*unmatched: glove, sock*) suelto, -a **6.** (*left over*) sobrante; to be the ~ one out quedar excluido

oddball ['ad·bɔl] **I.** *n inf* bicho *m* raro **II.** *adj inf* (*sense of humor, idea*) descabellado, -a

oddity ['ad·ə·ţi] <-ies> *n* (*person*) excéntrico, -a *m, f;* (*thing*) cosa *f* rara; (*characteristic*) rareza *f*

odd-job man ['ad·dʒab·mæn] *n* chapuzas *m inv*

oddly *adv* **1.** (*in a strange manner*) de forma extraña **2.** (*curiously*) curiosamente; ~ enough por extraño que parezca

odds [adz] *npl* (*probability*) probabilidades *fpl;* the ~ against/in favor of sth las probabilidades en contra/a favor de algo; to shorten/

lengthen the ~ disminuir/aumentar las posibilidades; **the ~ are against us** tenemos las de perder; **the ~ are in his favor** tiene todas las de ganar; **the ~ are that...** lo más seguro es que *+subj* ▶~ **and** __ends__ *inf* (*bits*) cosas *fpl* sueltas; __against__ all (the) ~ contra todo pronóstico, aunque parezca increíble; **to be** __at__ ~ **with sb** estar en desacuerdo con alguien

odds-on [ˌadz·'an] *adj* seguro, -a; **it's ~ that...** lo más probable es que *+subj;* **the ~ favorite to win the race** el gran favorito de la carrera

ode [oʊd] *n* oda *f*

odious ['oʊ·di·əs] *adj* odioso, -a

odometer [oʊ·'dam·ə·tər] *n* cuentakilómetros *m inv*

odor ['oʊ·dər] *n* (*smell*) olor *m;* (*fragrance*) aroma *m*

odorless *adj form* inodoro, -a

odyssey ['ad·ɪ·si] *n* odisea *f*

OECD [ˌoʊ·i·si·'di] *n abbr of* **Organization for Economic Cooperation and Development** OCDE *f*

of [əv, *stressed:* ʌv] *prep* **1.** de **2.** (*belonging to*) de; **the works ~ Twain** las obras de Twain; **a friend ~ mine/theirs** un amigo mío/de ellos **3.** (*done by*) de; **it's kind ~ him** es amable de su parte **4.** (*representing*) de; **a drawing ~ Paul** un dibujo de Paul **5.** (*without*) **a tree bare ~ leaves** un árbol sin hojas; **free ~ charge** sin cargo; **free ~ tax** libre de impuestos; **to cure sb ~ a disease** curar a alguien de una enfermedad **6.** (*with*) **a man ~ courage** un hombre de valor; **a man ~ no importance** un hombre sin importancia; **a city ~ wide avenues** una ciudad con amplias avenidas **7.** (*away from*) **to be north ~ Atlanta** estar al norte de Atlanta **8.** (*temporal*) **the 4th ~ May** el 4 de mayo; **in May ~ 2006** en mayo de(l) 2006 **9.** (*to*) **it is ten/(a) quarter ~ two** son las dos menos diez/cuarto **10.** (*consisting of*) de; **a ring ~ gold** un anillo de oro; **to smell/ to taste ~ cheese** oler/saber a queso; **to consist ~ six parts** constar de seis partes **11.** (*characteristic*) **with the patience ~ a saint** con la paciencia de un santo; **this idiot ~ a plumber** el idiota del fontanero; **doctor ~ medicine** doctor en medicina **12.** (*concerning*) **his love ~ jazz** su amor por el jazz; **to know sth ~ sb's past** saber algo del pasado de alguien; **to approve ~ sb's idea** estar de acuerdo con la idea de alguien; **what has become ~ him?** ¿qué ha sido de él?; **what do you think ~ him?** ¿qué piensas de él? **13.** (*cause*) **because ~ sth/sb** a causa de algo/alguien; **to die ~ grief** morir de pena; **it happened ~ itself** sucedió de por sí **14.** (*a portion of*) **there's a lot ~ it** hay mucho de eso; **one ~ the best** uno de los mejores; **the best ~ friends** los mejores amigos; **many ~ them came** muchos de ellos vinieron; **there are five ~ them** hay cinco de ellos; **he knows the five ~ them** los conoce a los cinco; **two ~ the five** dos de los cinco; **he ~ all people**

knows that él lo sabe mejor que nadie; **today ~ all days** precisamente hoy **15.** (*to amount of*) **80 years ~ age** 80 años de edad

off [ɔf] **I.** *prep* **1.** (*near*) **to be just ~ the main road** estar muy cerca de la carretera principal **2.** (*away from*) **to take sth ~ the shelf** coger algo del estante; **keep ~ the grass** prohibido pisar el césped **3.** (*down from*) **to fall/jump ~ a ladder** caer/saltar de una escalera; **to get ~ the train** bajarse del tren **4.** (*from*) **to eat ~ a plate** comer de un plato; **to cut a piece ~ the cheese** cortar un pedazo del queso; **to take 10 dollars ~ the price** rebajar 10 dólares del precio **5.** (*stop using*) **to be ~ caffeine/drugs** dejar la cafeína/las drogas **6.** (*as source of*) **to run ~ batteries** funcionar con pilas **II.** *adv* **1.** (*not on*) **to switch/turn sth ~** apagar algo; **it's ~ between them** *fig* lo han dejado **2.** (*away*) **the town is 5 miles ~ to the east** el pueblo está 8 km más al este; **not far ~** no lejos (de); **a way's ~** a bastante distancia; **to drive/run ~** irse en coche/corriendo; **~ with him** fuera con él; **it's time I was ~** ya debería haber salido **3.** (*removed*) **the lid is ~** la tapa está fuera; **with one's coat ~** con el abrigo quitado; **~ with that hat!** ¡quítate el sombrero! **4.** (*free from work*) **to get ~ at 4:00 p.m.** salir (del trabajo) a las cuatro; **to get a day ~** tener un día libre **5.** (*completely*) **to kill ~** exterminar; **to pay sth ~** acabar de pagar **6.** COM **5% ~** 5% de descuento **7.** (*until gone*) **to walk ~** caminar para bajar la comida; **to sleep ~ the wine** dormir el vino **8.** (*separating*) **to fence sth ~** cercar algo ▶ **straight** [*o* **right**] **~ the bat** enseguida; **~ and on, on and ~** de cuando en cuando; **it rained ~ and on** llovió intermitentemente **III.** *adj* **1.** (*not on: light*) apagado, -a; (*faucet*) cerrado, -a; (*water*) cortado, -a **2.** (*canceled: engagement, wedding, deal*) suspendido, -a **3.** (*free from work*) **to be ~ at 5:00 p.m.** salir (del trabajo) a las cinco; **I'm ~ on Mondays** los lunes estoy libre **4.** (*provided for*) **to be well ~** tener dinero; **to be not well ~** andar mal de dinero **5.** (*substandard*) **to be ~ one's game** SPORTS estar en mala forma **6.** *inf* **to go ~ on sb** echar la bronca a alguien **IV.** *vt sl* **to ~ sb** cargarse a alguien

offal ['ɔ·fəl] *n* (*of animal*) despojos *mpl*, achura *f AmS*

offbeat [ˌɔf·'bit] *adj* poco convencional

off-Broadway *adj s.* **Broadway**

off-center *adj* **1.** (*diverging from the center*) descentrado, -a **2.** (*unconventional*) poco convencional

off chance ['ɔf·tʃæns] *n* **on the ~** por si acaso

off-color [ˌɔf·'kʌl·ər] *adj* **1.** (*unwell*) indispuesto, -a; **to feel ~** encontrarse mal; **to look ~** tener mala cara **2.** (*in bad taste: joke*) subido, -a de tono

off day *n* **to have an ~** tener un mal día

off-duty *adj* fuera de servicio

offend [ə·'fend] **I.** *vi* **1.** (*cause displeasure*) ofender **2.** (*violate*) **to ~ against sth** atentar contra algo; **his remarks ~ against common sense** sus comentarios atentan contra el sentido común **3.** LAW infringir la ley; (*commit a crime*) cometer un delito **II.** *vt* **1.** (*upset sb's feelings*) ofender; **to be ~ed by sth** ofenderse por algo; **to be easily ~ed** ser muy susceptible; **she was ~ed that she had not been invited** se ofendió por no haber sido invitada **2.** (*affect disagreeably*) **to ~ the eye** hacer daño a la vista; **to ~ good taste** atentar contra el buen gusto

offender [ə·'fen·dər] *n* infractor(a) *m(f)*; (*guilty of crime*) delincuente *mf;* **first ~** delincuente sin antecedentes; **previous** [*o* **repeat**] **~** reincidente *mf;* **young ~** delincuente juvenil

offense [ə·'fens] *n* **1.** (*crime*) delito *m;* **minor ~** infracción *f;* **second ~** reincidencia *f;* **traffic ~** infracción de tráfico **2.** (*affront*) atentado *m;* **an ~ against sth** un atentado contra algo; **it is an ~ to the eye** *fig* hace daño a la vista **3.** (*upset feeling*) ofensa *f;* **to cause ~** (**to sb**) ofender (a alguien); **to take ~** (**at sth**) ofenderse (por algo); **no ~** (**intended**) *inf* sin ánimo de ofender **4.** REL pecado *m* **5.** SPORTS ofensiva *f*

offensive [ə·'fen·sɪv] **I.** *adj* **1.** (*remark, joke*) ofensivo, -a; (*language, word*) grosero, -a; (*tone*) desagradable; **to be ~ to sb** insultar a alguien **2.** (*disagreeable: smell*) repugnante **3.** MIL **~ weapon** arma *f* ofensiva **II.** *n* MIL ofensiva *f;* **to go on the ~** pasar a la ofensiva; **to launch an ~** (**against sth**) lanzar una ofensiva (contra algo); **to take the ~** tomar la ofensiva

offer ['ɔ·fər] **I.** *vt* **1.** (*proffer: help, advice, money*) ofrecer; (*chance*) brindar; **to ~ sb sth** ofrecer algo a alguien; **to ~ an apology** pedir disculpas; **to ~ congratulations to sb** felicitar a alguien; **can I ~ you a drink?** ¿quiere tomar algo?; **to ~ a good price for sth** ofrecer un buen precio por algo; **to ~ information/advice** dar información/consejo; **to ~ a reward** ofrecer una recompensa; **to ~ an explanation** dar una explicación; **to ~ shelter** dar cobijo; **to have much to ~** tener mucho que ofrecer; **to ~ oneself for a position** presentarse para un puesto **2.** (*give: gift*) dar **3.** (*volunteer*) **to ~ to do sth** ofrecerse para [*o* a] hacer algo **4.** (*propose: plan*) proponer; (*excuse*) presentar; (*opinion*) expresar; **to ~ a suggestion** hacer una sugerencia **5.** (*show*) **to ~ resistance** oponer resistencia **II.** *vi* (*present itself: opportunity*) presentarse **III.** *n* (*proposal*) propuesta *f;* (*of help*) ofrecimiento *m;* (*of a job*) oferta *f;* **an ~ of marriage** una proposición de matrimonio; **to make sb an ~ they can't refuse** hacer a alguien una oferta muy tentadora; **that's my last ~** es mi última oferta; **to make** [*o* **put in**] **an ~ of $1000 for sth** ofrecer 1000 dólares por algo

offering ['ɔ·fər·ɪŋ] *n* **1.** (*thing given*) ofrecimiento *m;* **as an ~ of thanks** en señal de agradecimiento **2.** (*contribution*) donativo *m* **3.** REL (*sacrifice*) ofrenda *f*

offhand [ɔf·'hænd] **I.** *adj* **1.** (*without previous thought*) improvisado, -a; **an ~ remark** una respuesta de buenas a primeras [*o* improvisada o sin pensar]; **an ~ remark** una observación que no viene al caso **2.** (*uninterested*) brusco, -a; **to be ~ about sth** pasar (de algo), serle indiferente algo a uno *inf* **II.** *adv* de improviso; **to judge sb/sth ~** juzgar algo/a alguien a la ligera; **offhand, I'd say...** así de pronto [*o* de buenas a primeras], yo diría...

office ['ɔ·fɪs] *n* **1.** (*of a company*) oficina *f;* (*room in house*) despacho *m,* archivo *m Col;* **they've got ~s in Los Angeles and Miami** tienen oficinas en Los Ángeles y Miami; **to stay at the ~** quedarse en la oficina; **architect's ~** estudio *m* (de arquitecto); **doctor's ~** consultorio *m;* **lawyer's ~** bufete *m* **2.** POL (*authoritative position*) cargo *m;* **to hold ~** ocupar un cargo; **to be in ~** (*person*) estar en funciones; (*party*) estar en el poder; **to be out of ~** haber dejado el cargo; **to take ~** entrar en funciones **3. ~s** (*assistance*) mediación *f;* **through the ~s of** gracias a la mediación de **4.** REL oficio *m*

office building *n* bloque *m* de oficinas

office hours *npl* horas *fpl* de oficina; **to do sth after ~** hacer algo fuera del horario de oficina

officer ['ɔ·fɪ·sər] *n* **1.** MIL oficial *mf;* **naval ~** oficial de marina **2.** (*policeman*) policía *mf;* **police ~** agente *mf* de policía **3.** (*in organization*) directivo, -a *m, f;* (*in political party*) dirigente *mf* **4.** (*official*) funcionario, -a *m, f*

office staff *n* personal *m* de oficina

office supplies *npl* artículos *mpl* de oficina

office worker *n* oficinista *mf*

official [ə·'fɪʃ·əl] **I.** *n* **1.** POL oficial *mf* **2.** (*civil servant*) funcionario, -a *m, f* **II.** *adj* oficial

officialdom [ə·'fɪʃ·əl·dəm] *n pej* burocracia *f*

officialese [ə·fɪʃ·ə·'liz] *n* jerga *f* burocrática

officially [ə·'fɪʃ·ə·li] *adv* oficialmente

officiate [ə·'fɪʃ·i·eɪt] *vi form* oficiar; **to ~ at a ceremony** oficiar (en) una ceremonia

officious [ə·'fɪʃ·əs] *adj pej* oficioso, -a

offing ['ɔ·fɪŋ] *n* **to be in the ~** NAUT estar a la vista; *fig* estar en perspectiva; **good news is in the ~** pronto habrá buenas noticias

off-key MUS **I.** *adv* desafinadamente; **to play/sing ~** desafinar **II.** *adj* desafinado, -a

off-limits *adj* fuera de los límites (permitidos)

offline [ɔf·'laɪn] *adj* COMPUT desconectado, -a, fuera de línea

offload [ɔf·'loʊd] *vt* **1.** (*unload*) descargar **2.** (*get rid of*) **to ~ sth** deshacerse de algo; **to ~ sth onto sb** endosar algo a alguien; **to ~ work onto sb** descargar trabajo en alguien

off-peak [ɔf·'pik] *adj* (*fare, rate*) fuera de las horas punta; (*phone call*) de tarifa reducida

off-piste [ɔf·'pist] *adj* SPORTS fuera de pista; **~ skiing** esquí fuera de pista [*o* a campo traviesa]

off-putting ['ɔf·pʊt·ɪŋ] *adj* **1.** (*smell, manner, appearance, person*) desagradable **2.** (*experience*) desalentador(a)

O

off-ramp *n* carril *m* de salida (*cuesta abajo*)
off-road vehicle *n* vehículo todoterreno *m*
off-season ['ɔf·ˌsi·zən] I. *n* temporada *f* baja II. *adj* de temporada baja
offset ['ɔf·set] I. *n* 1. (*compensation*) compensación *f* 2. BOT vástago *m* 3. TYPO offset *m* II.<offset, offset> *vt* 1. (*compensate*) compensar; **in order to ~ the cost/loss...** a fin de compensar los costes/las pérdidas... 2. TYPO imprimir en offset
offset printing *n* impresión *f* en offset
offshore [ˌɔf·'ʃɔr] I. *adj* 1. (*from the shore: breeze, wind*) terral 2. (*at sea*) a poca distancia de la costa; **~ fishing** pesca de bajura; **~ oilfield** yacimiento *m* petrolífero marítimo 3. (*in foreign country*) en el exterior II. *adv* mar adentro; **to anchor ~** anclar a cierta distancia de la costa
offside [ˌɔf·'saɪd], **offsides** [ˌɔf·'saɪdz] SPORTS I. *adv* fuera de juego II. *adj* en fuera de juego III. *n* fuera de juego *m;* **to be called for an ~** ser penalizado por una falta
offspring ['ɔf·sprɪŋ] *n inv* 1. (*animal young*) cría *f* 2. *pl* (*children*) prole *f*
offstage [ˌɔf·'steɪdʒ] I. *adj* de entre bastidores II. *adv* entre bastidores
off-street parking [ˌɔf·strit·'par·kɪŋ] *n* aparcamiento *m* fuera de la vía pública, estacionamiento *m* fuera de la vía pública *AmL*
off-the-cuff [ˌɔf·ðə·'kʌf] I. *adj* espontáneo, -a II. *adv* espontáneamente
off-the-rack [ˌɔf·ðə·'ræk] *adj* prêt à porter
off-white [ˌɔf·'hwaɪt] *adj* de color hueso
often ['ɔ·fən] *adv* a menudo; **we ~ go there** solemos ir allí; **as ~ as** siempre que; **as ~ as not** la mitad de las veces; **every so ~** alguna que otra vez; **how ~?** ¿cuántas veces?; **it's not ~ that...** no es frecuente que +*subj;* **more ~ than not** la mayoría de las veces
ogle ['oʊ·gəl] *vt* **to ~ sb** comerse a alguien con los ojos
ogre ['oʊ·gər] *n* ogro *m*
ogress ['oʊ·gres] *n* ogra *f;* LIT ogresa *f*
oh [oʊ] *interj* 1. (*expressing surprise, disappointment, pleasure*) oh; **~ dear!** ¡Dios mío!; **~ no!** ¡ay, no!; **~ well** bueno; **~ yes?** ¿ah, sí? 2. (*by the way*) ah
OH [oʊ·'haɪ·oʊ] *n abbr of* **Ohio** Ohio *m*
Ohio [oʊ·'haɪ·oʊ] *n* Ohio *m*
oil [ɔɪl] I. *n* 1. (*lubricant*) aceite *m;* **sunflower ~** aceite de girasol 2. (*petroleum*) petróleo *m;* **to strike ~** encontrar petróleo; *fig* encontrar una mina de oro 3. (*grease*) grasa *f* 4. **~s** (*oil-based paint*) óleo *m;* **to paint in ~s** pintar al óleo ▶ **to burn the midnight ~** quemarse las pestañas; **to pour ~ on troubled waters** calmar los ánimos, poner paz II. *vt* engrasar
oilcan *n* aceitera *f*
oilcloth *n* hule *m*
oil consumption *n* consumo *m* de petróleo
oil crisis *n* crisis *f inv* del petróleo
oil-exporting *adj* exportador(a) de petróleo
oil field *n* yacimiento *m* petrolífero

oil-fired *adj* alimentado, -a a petróleo; **~ heating system** calefacción *f* a petróleo
oiliness ['ɔɪ·lɪ·nɪs] *n* 1. (*greasiness: of food*) lo aceitoso; (*of material, skin*) lo grasiento 2. *fig* lo empalagoso
oil lamp *n* quinqué *m*
oil level *n* TECH nivel *m* de aceite
oil painting *n* óleo *m*
oil pipeline *n* oleoducto *m*
oil-producing *adj* productor(a) de petróleo
oil-producing country *n* país *m* productor de petróleo
oil production *n* producción *f* de petróleo
oil rig *n* plataforma *f* petrolífera
oil sheik *n* magnate *mf* del petróleo
oilskin *n* 1. (*cloth*) hule *m* 2. **~s** (*clothing*) impermeable *m*
oil slick *n* marea *f* negra
oil tanker *n* NAUT petrolero *m*
oil well *n* pozo *m* de petróleo
oily ['ɔɪ·li] <-ier, -iest> *adj* 1. (*oil-like*) oleoso, -a 2. (*greasy: hands*) grasiento, -a; (*food*) aceitoso, -a; (*skin, hair*) graso, -a 3. (*manner*) empalagoso, -a
ointment ['ɔɪnt·mənt] *n* MED pomada *f*
OK[1] [oʊ·'keɪ] *inf* I. *adj* 1. (*acceptable*) **is it ~ with you if...?** ¿te importa si...?; **it's ~ with me** por mí no hay problema; **to be ~ for money/work** tener suficiente dinero/trabajo 2. (*not bad*) **to be ~** no estar mal; **her voice is ~, but it's nothing special** no tiene mala voz, pero tampoco es nada del otro mundo II. *interj* vale *inf*, okey *AmL, inf*, órale *Méx* III. <OKed, okayed> *vt* **to ~ sth** dar el visto bueno a algo IV. *n* visto bueno *m;* **to give (sb/sth) the ~** dar a alguien/algo) el visto bueno V. *adv* bastante bien
OK[2] [oʊ·klə·'hoʊ·mə] *n abbr of* **Oklahoma** Oklahoma *f*
Okla. *n abbr of* **Oklahoma** Oklahoma *f*
Oklahoma [oʊ·klə·'hoʊ·mə] *n* Oklahoma *f*
okra ['oʊk·rə] *n* quingombó *m*
old [oʊld] I. *adj* 1. (*not young*) viejo, -a; **~ people** la gente mayor; **to be a bit ~ to be doing sth** ser ya mayorcito para hacer algo; **to grow ~er** envejecer 2. (*not new*) viejo, -a; (*food*) pasado, -a; (*wine*) añejo, -a; (*furniture, house*) antiguo, -a 3. (*denoting an age*) **how ~ are you?** ¿cuántos años tienes?; **he's five years ~** tiene cinco años; **she's three years ~er than I** me lleva tres años; **to be ~ enough to do sth** tener edad suficiente para hacer algo 4. (*former: job*) antiguo, -a; **~ boyfriend** antiguo novio *m;* **Old English** inglés *m* antiguo 5. (*long known*) de siempre; **~ friend** viejo amigo; **the same ~ faces** las mismas caras de siempre 6. *inf* (*expression of affection*) **I heard poor ~ Frank has lost his job** he oído que el pobre Frank se ha quedado sin trabajo II. *n* 1. (*elderly people*) **the ~** los viejos, los ancianos *AmL;* **young and ~** grandes y chicos 2. *liter* (*past*) **of ~** antiguamente; **to know sb of ~** conocer a alguien desde hace

tiempo

old age *n* vejez *f;* **to reach ~** llegar a viejo

old-fashioned [ˌoʊld·'fæʃ·ənd] *adj pej* **1.** (*not modern: clothes*) pasado, -a de moda; (*views*) anticuado, -a; **to be ~** estar chapado a la antigua **2.** (*traditional*) tradicional; **it has an ~ charm** tiene el encanto de lo antiguo

oldie ['oʊl·di] *n* clásico *m;* **an ~ but a goodie** antiguo, pero mítico

old lady *n sl* **my ~** (*mother*) mi vieja; (*wife*) mi parienta

old man *n sl* **my ~** (*father*) mi viejo; (*husband*) mi marido

old master *n* ART **1.** (*artist*) gran maestro *m* de la pintura clásica **2.** (*painting*) obra *f* maestra de la pintura clásica

old school **I.** *adj* de la vieja escuela **II.** *n fig* vieja escuela *f*

Old Testament *n* Antiguo Testamento *m*

old-timer ['oʊld·ˌtaɪ·mər] *n inf* **1.** (*old man*) viejales *m inv* **2.** (*long-time worker, resident*) veterano, -a *m, f*

old wives' tale [ˌoʊld·'waɪvz·ˌteɪl] *n* cuento *m* de viejas

oleander [ˌoʊ·li·'æn·dər] *n* adelfa *f*

olfactory [al·'fæk·tə·ri] *adj* olfativo, -a

olive ['al·ɪv] *n* **1.** (*fruit*) oliva *f,* aceituna *f* **2.** (*tree*) olivo *m* **3.** (*color*) aceituna *m*

olive branch *n* rama *f* de olivo ▸ **to hold out the ~ to sb** tender a alguien la mano en son de paz

olive grove *n* olivar *m*

olive oil *n* aceite *m* de oliva

Olympiad [oʊ·'lɪm·pi·æd] *n* SPORTS olimpiada *f*

Olympian [oʊ·'lɪm·pi·ən] *adj* olímpico, -a

Olympic [oʊ·'lɪm·pɪk] *adj* olímpico, -a; **the Olympic Games** SPORTS los Juegos Olímpicos

Oman [oʊ·'man] *n* Omán *m*

Omani [oʊ·'ma·ni] **I.** *adj* omaní **II.** *n* omaní *mf*

ombudsman ['am·bədz·mən] <-men> *n* POL defensor *m* del pueblo

omelet(te) ['am·lət] *n* tortilla *f*

omen ['oʊ·men] *n* indicio *m,* augurio *m;* **to be a good/bad ~ for sth** ser un buen/mal augurio para algo

ominous ['am·ə·nəs] *adj* (*news*) ominoso, -a; (*implications*) funesto, -a; (*silence*) inquietante

omission [oʊ·'mɪʃ·ən] *n* omisión *f*

omit [oʊ·'mɪt] <-tt-> *vt* (*person, information*) omitir; (*paragraph, passage*) suprimir; **to ~ any reference to sb/sth** evitar toda referencia a alguien/algo; **to ~ to do sth** (*neglect*) dejar de hacer algo; (*forget*) olvidarse de hacer algo

omnibus ['am·nɪ·bʌs] **I.** <-es> *n* **1.** (*bus*) ómnibus *m* **2.** (*anthology*) antología *f* **II.** *adj* **~ edition** antología *f*

omnipotence [am·'nɪp·ə·təns] *n* omnipotencia *f*

omnipotent [am·'nɪp·ə·tənt] *adj* omnipotente

omnipresent [ˌam·nɪ·'prez·ənt] *adj form* omnipresente

omniscient [am·'nɪʃ·ənt] *adj form* omnisciente

omnivorous [am·'nɪv·ər·əs] *adj* omnívoro, -a; **to be an ~ reader** *fig* ser un lector insaciable

on [an] **I.** *prep* **1.** (*place*) sobre, en; **~ the table** sobre la mesa; **~ the wall** en la pared; **to put sth ~ sb's shoulder/finger** poner algo sobre el hombro/en el dedo de alguien; **to be ~ the plane** estar en el avión; **to hang ~ a branch** colgar de una rama; **to have sth ~ one's mind** *fig* tener algo en mente **2.** (*by means of*) **to go ~ the train** ir en tren; **to go ~ foot** ir a pie; **to keep a dog ~ a leash** llevar (a) un perro con correa **3.** (*source of*) con; **to run ~ gas** funcionar con gasolina; **to live ~ $2,000 a month** vivir con 2.000 dólares al mes **4.** MED **to be ~ drugs** tomar medicamentos **5.** (*spatial*) **~ the right/left** a la derecha/izquierda; **~ the corner/back of sth** en la esquina/la parte posterior de algo; **a house ~ the river** una casa junto al río **6.** (*temporal*) **~ Sunday** el domingo; **~ Sundays** los domingos; **~ the evening of May the 4th** el cuatro de mayo por la tarde; **at 2:00 p.m. ~ the dot** a las dos en punto de la tarde **7.** (*at time of*) **to leave ~ time** salir a tiempo; **~ her arrival** a su llegada; **~ arriving there** al llegar allí; **to finish ~ schedule** acabar puntualmente **8.** (*about*) sobre; **a lecture ~ Shakespeare** una conferencia sobre Shakespeare; **to compliment sb ~ sth** felicitar a alguien por algo; **to be there ~ business** estar ahí por negocios **9.** (*through medium of*) **~ TV/video/CD** en televisión/vídeo/CD; **to speak ~ the radio/the phone** hablar en la radio/por teléfono; **to work ~ a computer** trabajar con un ordenador; **to play sth ~ the flute** tocar algo con la flauta **10.** (*with basis in*) **~ the principle that** en el supuesto de que; **to do sth ~ purpose** hacer algo a propósito **11.** (*in state of*) **~ sale** en venta; **to set sth ~ fire** prender fuego a algo; **to go ~ vacation/a trip** ir de vacaciones/de viaje; **~ the whole** en general **12.** (*involved in*) **to be ~ the committee** estar en el comité; **to work ~ a project** trabajar en un proyecto; **to be ~ page 10** estar en la página 10; **two ~ each side** dos en [*o a*] cada lado **13.** (*because of*) **~ account of sth/sb** a causa de algo/alguien; **to depend ~ sb/sth** depender de alguien/algo **14.** (*against*) **to turn ~ sb** volverse contra alguien; **an attack ~ sb** un ataque contra alguien; **to cheat ~ sb** hacer trampa [*o* engañar] a alguien **15.** (*paid by*) **to buy sth ~ credit** comprar algo a crédito; **this is ~ me** *inf* esto corre por mi cuenta **II.** *adv* **1.** (*covering one's body*) **to put a hat ~** ponerse un sombrero; **to have sth ~** llevar algo (puesto); **to try ~ sth** probarse algo **2.** (*connected to sth*) **make sure the top's ~ properly** asegúrate de que esté bien tapado; **to screw sth ~** enroscar algo **3.** (*aboard*) **to get ~ a train** subir a un tren; **to get ~ a horse** montarse en un caballo **4.** (*not stopping*) **to keep ~ doing sth** seguir haciendo algo; **to get** ~ **with sth** ponerse a hacer algo **5.** (*in forward direction*) hacia adelante; **to move** ~ avanzar; **to urge sb** ~ *fig* animar a alguien; **from that day** ~ desde aquel día; **later** ~ más tarde; **and so** ~ y así sucesivamente **6.** (*in operation*) **to turn** ~ encender; (*tap*) abrir **7.** (*performing*) en escena; **to go** ~ salir a escena ▶~ **and off** de vez en cuando; ~ **and** ~ sin parar; **well** ~ **into the night** muy entrada la noche **III.** *adj* **1.** (*functioning: light*) encendido, -a; (*faucet*) abierto, -a; (*brake*) puesto, -a; **to leave the light** ~ dejar la luz encendida **2.** (*scheduled*) **what's** ~ **at the movies this week?** ¿qué dan en el cine esta semana? **the show will be** ~ **in Seattle very soon** el espectáculo estará muy pronto en Seattle; **have you got anything** ~ **for tomorrow?** ¿tienes algún plan para mañana? **3.** THEAT (*performing*) **to be** ~ estar en escena; (*performing well*) hacerlo muy bien **4.** (*job*) **to be** ~ **duty** estar de servicio; (*doctor*) estar de guardia **5.** (*good: day*) bueno, -a **6.** (*acceptable*) **you're** ~! ¡de acuerdo!

once [wʌns] **I.** *adv* **1.** (*one time*) una vez; ~ **a week** una vez por [o a la] semana; ~ **in a life-time** una vez en la vida; (*every*) ~ **in a while** de vez en cuando; ~ **again** de nuevo; ~ **and for all** de una vez por todas; **just for** ~ sólo una vez; ~ **more** (*one more time*) otra vez; (*again, as before*) una vez más; ~ **or twice** una o dos veces; **at** ~ (*simultaneously*) al mismo tiempo; (*immediately*) en seguida **2.** *liter* (*at one time past*) hace tiempo; ~ **upon a time there was...** *liter* érase una vez... **II.** *conj* una vez que +*subj*; **but** ~ **I'd arrived,...** pero una vez que llegué... ▶**all at** ~ todos a la vez; **at** ~ en seguida

once-over ['wʌns·oʊ·vər] *n inf* ojeada *f*; **to give sth/sb a** ~ echar un vistazo a algo/alguien; **to give sth/sb the** ~ mirar algo/a alguien de arriba a abajo

oncoming ['an·kʌm·ɪŋ] *adj* que se aproxima; (*traffic, vehicle*) que viene en dirección contraria

one [wʌn] **I.** *n* (*number*) uno *m* ▶**to land sb** ~ *inf* dar un puñetazo a alguien; (**all**) **in** ~ todo en uno; **as** ~ *form* a la vez; **in** ~ de una sola pieza **II.** *adj* **1.** *numeral* un, uno, -a; ~ **hundred** cien; **it's** ~ **o'clock** es la una; **as** ~ **man** todos a una; ~ **man out of** [o **in**] **two** uno de cada dos hombres **2.** *indef* un, uno, -a; **we'll meet** ~ **day** nos veremos un día de estos; ~ **winter night** una noche de invierno **3.** (*sole*) único, -a; **her** ~ **and only hope** su única esperanza **4.** (*single*) mismo, -a, único, -a; **all files on the** ~ **disk** todos los archivos en un único disco **III.** *pron pers* **1.** *impers, no pl* **what can** ~ **do?** ¿qué puede hacer uno?; **to wash** ~'**s face** lavarse la cara **2.** (*person*) **no** ~ nadie; **every** ~ cada uno; **the little** ~**s** los pequeños; **the** ~ **who...** el que...; **I for** ~ al menos yo **3.** (*particular thing or person*) **any** ~ cualquiera; **this** ~ éste; **which** ~? ¿cuál (de

ellos)?; **the** ~ **on the table** el que está en la mesa; **the thinner** ~ el más fino

one-armed [ˌwʌn·'armd] *adj* manco, -a, sunco, -a *Chile*

one-armed bandit *n* máquina *f* tragaperras, máquina *f* tragamonedas *AmL*

one-eyed [ˌwʌn·'aɪd] *adj* tuerto, -a

one-handed I. *adv* con una sola mano **II.** *adj* manco, -a

one-horse *adj* **1.** (*using one horse*) de un caballo **2.** (*second-rate*) de poca monta; **a** ~ **town** un pueblucho

one-legged *adj* cojo, -a

one-liner [ˌwʌn·'laɪ·nər] *n* frase *f* ingeniosa

one-man [ˌwʌn·'mæn] *adj* **1.** (*consisting of one person*) de un solo hombre; ~ **band** hombre *m* orquesta **2.** (*designed for one person*) individual

one-night stand [ˌwʌn·naɪt·'stænd] *n* **1.** *sl* (*relationship*) ligue *m* de una noche **2.** MUS, THEAT función *f* única

one-piece (**swimsuit**) ['wʌn·pis] *n* bañador *m*

onerous ['an·ər·əs] *adj* oneroso, -a

oneself [wʌn·'self] *pron reflexive* **1.** se; *emphatic* sí (mismo, misma); **to deceive** ~ engañarse a sí mismo; **to express** ~ expresarse **2.** (*same person*) uno mismo

one-sided [ˌwʌn·'saɪ·dɪd] *adj* (*contest*) desigual; (*decision*) unilateral; (*view, account*) parcial

one-time ['wʌn·taɪm] *adj* **1.** antiguo, -a; ~ **president** ex-presidente **2.** (*happening only once*) único, -a

one-track mind [ˌwʌn·træk·'maɪnd] *n* **to have a** ~ no pensar más que en una cosa

one-upmanship [ˌwʌn·'ʌp·mən·ʃɪp] *n inf*: arte de estar por encima de los demás

one-way street [ˌwʌn·weɪ·'strit] *n* calle *f* de sentido único

one-way ticket *n* billete *m* sencillo

ongoing ['an·goʊ·ɪŋ] *adj* en curso; ~ **state of affairs** situación que sigue en curso

onion ['ʌn·jən] *n* cebolla *f*

online, on-line COMPUT **I.** *adj* en línea; ~ **data service** servicio *m* de datos en línea; ~ **information service** servicio *m* de información en línea; ~ **shop** comercio *m* en línea **II.** *adv* en línea

onlooker ['an·lʊk·ər] *n* espectador(a) *m(f);* **there were many** ~**s at the accident site** había muchos curiosos en el lugar del accidente

only ['oʊn·li] **I.** *adj* único, -a; **the** ~ **glass he had** el único vaso que tenía; **the** ~ **way of doing sth** la única manera de hacer algo; **I'm not the** ~ **one** no soy el único; **the** ~ **thing is...** la única cosa es... **II.** *adv* sólo, nomás *AmL;* **not** ~... **but also** no sólo... sino también; **I can** ~ **say...** sólo puedo decir...; **he has** ~ **two** sólo tiene dos; ~ **Paul can do it** sólo Paul puede hacerlo; **I've** ~ **just eaten** acabo de comer ahora mismo **III.** *conj inf* sólo que

onrush ['an·rʌʃ] <-es> *n* **1.** (*of waves*) embate

871

m **2.** (*of people*) avalancha *f fig*
onset ['an·set] *n* comienzo *m;* (*of winter*) llegada *f;* (*of illness*) aparición *f*
onshore ['an·ʃɔr] **I.** *adj* (*wind*) del mar **II.** *adv* tierra adentro
onside ['an·'saɪd] SPORTS **I.** *adj* **to be ~** (*player*) estar en posición correcta **II.** *adv* en posición correcta
onside kick *n* onside kick *m*
onslaught ['an·slɔt] *n* ataque *m* violento; *fig* crítica *f* violenta
on-the-job training *n* formación *f* en el puesto de trabajo
onto ['an·tu] *prep,* **on to** *prep* **1.** (*in direction of*) sobre; **to put sth ~ the chair** poner algo sobre la silla; **to step ~ the road** pisar la calzada; **to come ~ a subject** tocar un tema **2.** (*connected to*) **to hold ~ sb's arm** aferrarse al brazo de alguien; **to be ~ sb** ver a alguien su juego
onus ['oʊ·nəs] *n* responsabilidad *f*
onward ['an·wərd] **I.** *adj* hacia adelante; **the ~ march of time** el avance inexorable del tiempo **II.** *adv* hacia adelante; **from today ~** de hoy en adelante
onyx ['an·ɪks] *n* GEO ónice *f,* ónix *f*
oodles ['u·dəlz] *npl inf* montones *mpl;* **~ of money** cantidad *f* de dinero
oomph [ʊmf] *n sl* **1.** (*energy, vitality*) brío *m;* **to have a lot of ~** estar lleno de vida **2.** (*sex appeal*) atractivo *m*
oops [ups] *interj inf* ¡huy!
ooze [uz] **I.** *vi* **1.** (*seep out*) exudar; **to ~ from sth** rezumar(se) de algo; **to ~ with sth** rezumar algo; **to ~ away** acabarse **2.** *fig* (*be full of*) rebosar; **to ~ with confidence** irradiar seguridad **II.** *vt* rezumar; **to ~ pus** supurar; **to ~ charisma** irradiar simpatía **III.** *n* cieno *m*
opacity [oʊ·'pæs·ə·t̬i] *n* **1.** (*non-transparency*) opacidad *f* **2.** (*incomprehensibility*) oscuridad *f*
opal ['oʊ·pəl] *n* GEO ópalo *m*
opalescent [,oʊ·pə·'les·ənt] *adj* opalescente
opaque [oʊ·'peɪk] *adj* **1.** (*not transparent*) opaco, -a **2.** (*unintelligible*) oscuro, -a
OPEC ['oʊ·pek] *n abbr of* **Organization of Petroleum Exporting Countries** OPEP *f*
open ['oʊ·pən] **I.** *adj* **1.** (*not closed*) abierto, -a; **wide ~** completamente abierto; **to push sth ~** abrir algo de un empujón **2.** (*undecided*) sin concretar; **to keep one's options ~** dejar abiertas todas las alternativas **3.** (*not secret, public: scandal*) público, -a; (*hostility*) abierto, -a, manifiesto, -a; **to be an ~ book** *fig* ser un libro abierto; **an ~ secret** una cosa sabida **4.** (*unfolded: map*) desplegado, -a **5.** (*frank: person*) abierto, -a; **to welcome sb with ~ arms** recibir a alguien con los brazos abiertos **6.** (*accessible to all*) abierto, -a; (*discussion*) abierto, -a al público; (*session*) a puertas abiertas; (*trial*) público, -a **7.** (*willing to listen to new ideas*) abierto, -a de mente; **to have an ~ mind** tener una actitud abierta **8.** (*still avail-*

able: job) vacante **9.** LING (*vowel*) abierto, -a **II.** *n* **1.** (*outdoors, outside*) (**out**) **in the ~** al aire libre **2.** (*not secret*) **to get sth** (**out**) **in the ~** sacar algo a la luz **III.** *vi* **1.** (*door, window, box*) abrirse **2.** (*shop*) abrir **3.** (*start*) comenzar, empezar **IV.** *vt* **1.** (*door, box, shop*) abrir; **to ~ the door to sth** *fig* abrir la puerta a algo; **to ~ sb's eyes** (**to sb/sth**) *fig* abrir a alguien los ojos (sobre alguien/algo); **to ~ fire** (**on sb**) abrir fuego (contra alguien) **2.** (*reveal feelings*) **to ~ one's heart to sb** abrir su corazón a alguien **3.** (*inaugurate*) inaugurar
◆**open onto** *vi* dar a
◆**open up I.** *vi* **1.** (*unfold*) abrirse **2.** (*shop*) abrir **3.** (*shoot*) abrir fuego **4.** (*become wider*) ensancharse **II.** *vt* abrir; (*map*) desplegar
open-air [,oʊ·pən·'er] *adj* al aire libre; **~ swimming pool** piscina *f* descubierta
open-ended [,oʊ·pən·'en·dɪd] *adj* (*contract*) de duración indefinida; (*question*) abierto, -a
opener ['oʊ·pə·nər] *n* abridor *m,* destapador *m AmL;* **bottle ~** abrebotellas *m inv;* **can ~** abrelatas *m inv*
open-heart surgery [,oʊ·pən·hart·'sɜr·dʒə·ri] *n* cirugía *f* a corazón abierto
opening ['oʊ·pə·nɪŋ] *n* **1.** (*gap, hole*) abertura *f;* (*in forest*) claro *m* **2.** (*job opportunity*) vacante *f* **3.** (*beginning*) apertura *f;* (*of book, film*) principio *m,* comienzo *m* **4.** (*ceremony*) inauguración *f;* (*new play, film*) estreno *m*
opening balance *n* FIN saldo *m* de apertura
opening bid *n* oferta *f* inicial
opening night *n* THEAT noche *f* del estreno
openly ['oʊ·pən·li] *adv* **1.** (*frankly*) honestamente **2.** (*publicly*) abiertamente
open market *n* mercado *m* abierto
open-minded [,oʊ·pən·'maɪn·dɪd] *adj* (*accessible to new ideas*) de actitud abierta; (*unprejudiced*) sin prejuicios
open-mouthed *adj* boquiabierto, -a
openness ['oʊ·pən·nəs] *n* franqueza *f*
open-source *adj* de software libre
open ticket *n* billete *m* abierto
opera ['ap·rə] *n* ópera *f*
operable ['ap·ər·ə·bəl] *adj* **1.** (*workable: plan*) factible **2.** MED operable
opera glasses *n* gemelos *mpl* de teatro
opera house *n* ópera *f*
operate ['ap·ə·reɪt] **I.** *vi* **1.** (*work, run*) funcionar **2.** (*have or produce an effect*) actuar, surtir efecto **3.** (*perform surgery*) operar; **to ~ on sb** operar a alguien **4.** (*do or be in business*) operar **II.** *vt* **1.** (*work*) manejar **2.** (*run, manage*) llevar, tener
operating ['ap·ə·reɪ·t̬ɪŋ] *adj* **1.** ECON (*profit, costs*) de explotación **2.** TECH (*speed*) de funcionamiento **3.** MED de operaciones; **~ room, ~ theater** quirófano *m*
operation [,ap·ə·'reɪ·ʃən] *n* **1.** (*way of working*) funcionamiento *m;* **to be in ~** estar en funcionamiento; **to come into ~** (*machines*) entrar en funcionamiento **2.** *a.* MED, MIL, MATH operación *f;* **rescue ~** operación de rescate

3. (*financial transaction*) operación *f* comercial

operational [ˌap·ə·'reɪ·ʃə·nəl] *adj* **1.** (*relating to operations*) operativo, -a; ~ **commander** MIL jefe, -a *m*, *f* de operaciones **2.** (*working*) **to be** ~ estar en funcionamiento

operative ['ap·ər·ə·t̬ɪv] **I.** *n* **1.** (*worker*) operario, -a *m*, *f* **2.** (*detective*) agente *mf* **II.** *adj* **1.** (*rules*) en vigor **2.** MED quirúrgico, -a

operator ['ap·ə·reɪ·t̬ər] *n* **1.** (*person*) operador(a) *m(f)*; TEL telefonista *mf*; **machine** ~ maquinista *mf*; **he's a smooth** ~ *inf* sabe conseguir lo que quiere **2.** (*company*) empresa *f*; **a tour** ~ un(a) agente de viajes

operetta [ˌap·ə·'ret̬·ə] *n* opereta *f*

ophthalmic [af·'θæl·mɪk] *adj* (*clinic*) oftalmológico, -a, de oftalmología; (*surgeon*) oftalmólogo, -a; (*vein*) oftálmico, -a

ophthalmologist [ˌaf·θəl·'mal·ə·dʒɪst] *n* oftalmólogo, -a *m*, *f*

opiate ['oʊ·pi·ɪt] *n* opiáceo *m*

opinion [ə·'pɪn·jən] *n* opinión *f*

opinionated [ə·'pɪn·jə·neɪ·t̬ɪd] *adj pej* dogmático, -a

opinion poll *n* encuesta *f* de opinión

opium ['oʊ·pi·əm] *n* opio *m*

opossum [ə·'pas·əm] *n* zarigüeya *f*, zorro *m Méx*

opponent [ə·'poʊ·nənt] *n* **1.** POL opositor(a) *m(f)* **2.** SPORTS contrincante *mf*, rival *mf*

opportune [ˌap·ər·'tun] *adj* oportuno, -a

opportunism [ˌap·ər·'tu·nɪz·əm] *n* oportunismo *m*

opportunist [ˌap·ər·'tu·nɪst] **I.** *n* oportunista *mf* **II.** *adj* oportunista

opportunity [ˌap·ər·'tu·nə·t̬i] <-ies> *n* oportunidad *f*; ~ **to do** [*o* **of doing**] **sth** oportunidad de hacer algo; **at the earliest** (**possible**) ~ lo antes posible

oppose [ə·'poʊz] *vt* **1.** (*be against*) oponerse a, estar en contra de **2.** (*resist*) combatir **3.** (*be on other team, play against*) enfrentarse a

opposed *adj* opuesto, -a; **to be** ~ **to sth** oponerse a algo, estar en contra de algo

opposing *adj* (*opinion, forces*) opuesto, -a, contrario, -a; (*team*) contrario, -a

opposite ['ap·ə·zɪt] **I.** *n* contrario *m*; **quite the** ~! ¡todo lo contrario! ►~**s attract** los extremos se atraen **II.** *adj* **1.** (*absolutely different*) contrario, -a; **the** ~ **sex** el sexo opuesto **2.** (*facing*) de enfrente; ~ **to/from sth** enfrente de algo; **his** ~ **number** su homólogo **III.** *adv* (*facing*) enfrente; **they live** ~ viven enfrente **IV.** *prep* enfrente de, frente a; ~ **to sth** enfrente de algo; ~ **me** frente a mí; **to sit** ~ **one another** estar sentados uno frente al otro

opposition [ˌap·ə·'zɪʃ·ən] *n* **1.** POL oposición *f* **2.** (*contrast*) contraposición *f*; **in** ~ **to sth** en contraposición a algo **3.** (*opponent*) adversario, -a *m*, *f*; ECON competencia *f*

oppress [ə·'pres] *vt* oprimir

oppression [ə·'preʃ·ən] *n* **1.** (*submission*) opresión *f* **2.** (*feeling*) agobio *m*

oppressive [ə·'pres·ɪv] *adj* **1.** (*harsh: regime, measures*) opresivo, -a **2.** (*burdensome*) agobiante; (*heat*) sofocante

oppressor [ə·'pres·ər] *n* opresor(a) *m(f)*

opt [apt] *vi* optar; **to** ~ **to do sth** optar por hacer algo; **to** ~ **for sth** optar por algo

◆ **opt in** *vi* **to** ~ (**to sth**) apuntarse (a algo)

◆ **opt out** *vi* **to** ~ (**of sth**) borrarse (de algo)

optic ['ap·tɪk] **I.** *n inf* ojo *m* **II.** *adj* óptico, -a

optical ['ap·tɪ·kəl] *adj* óptico, -a

optician [ap·'tɪʃ·ən] *n* MED óptico, -a *m*, *f*

optic nerve *n* ANAT nervio *m* óptico

optics ['ap·tɪks] *n* óptica *f*

optimal ['ap·tɪ·məl] *adj* óptimo, -a

optimism ['ap·tə·mɪz·əm] *n* optimismo *m*

optimist ['ap·tə·mɪst] *n* optimista *mf*

optimistic [ˌap·tə·'mɪs·tɪk] *adj* optimista

optimize ['ap·tə·maɪz] *vt* optimizar

optimum ['ap·tə·məm] **I.** *n* <-ma> **the** ~ lo ideal **II.** *adj* óptimo, -a

option ['ap·ʃən] *n* **1.** (*choice*) *a.* ECON opción *f*; **to have no** ~ **but to do sth** no tener más remedio que hacer algo; **call** ~ opción de compra **2.** (*possibility*) posibilidad *f*

optional ['ap·ʃə·nəl] *adj* opcional; (*subject*) optativo, -a

opulence ['ap·jə·ləns] *n* opulencia *f*

opulent ['ap·jə·lənt] *adj* opulento, -a

or [ɔr] *conj* o; (*before o, ho*) u; (*between numbers*) ó; **seven** ~ **eight** siete u ocho; **6** ~ **7** 6 ó 7; **either...** ~ **...** o... o...; **to ask whether** ~ **not sb is coming** preguntar si alguien viene o no; **I can't read** ~ **write** no sé leer ni escribir

OR *n* **1.** *abbr of* **operating room** quirófano *m*, sala *f* de operaciones **2.** *abbr of* **Oregon** Oregón *m*

oracle ['ɔr·ə·kəl] *n* oráculo *m*

oracular [ɔ·'ræk·ju·lər] *adj* del oráculo

oral ['ɔr·əl] *adj* **1.** (*tradition, exam, statement*) oral **2.** (*medication*) por vía oral; (*contraceptive, sex*) oral

orange ['ɔr·ɪndʒ] **I.** *n* naranja *f*; ~ **drink** naranjada *f* **II.** *adj* naranja

orangeade [ɔr·ɪndʒ·'eɪd] *n* naranjada *f*

orange grove *n* naranjal *m*

orange juice *n* zumo *m* de naranja

orange peel *n* cáscara *f* de naranja

orange tree *n* naranjo *m*

orangutan [ɔ·'ræŋ·ə·tæn] *n*, **orangutang** [ɔ·'ræŋ·ə·tæŋ] *n* orangután *m*

oration [ɔ·'reɪ·ʃən] *n* discurso *m*; **funeral** ~ oración *f* fúnebre

orator ['ɔr·ə·t̬ər] *n* orador(a) *m(f)*

oratorical [ɔr·ə·'tɔr·ɪ·kəl] *adj* oratorio, -a

oratorio [ɔr·ə·'tɔr·i·oʊ] *n* MUS oratorio *m*

orb [ɔrb] *n liter* esfera *f*

orbit ['ɔr·bɪt] **I.** *n* **1.** ASTR órbita *f*; **to go into** ~ entrar en órbita **2.** (*range of action, field*) campo *m* de influencia **II.** *vi* orbitar **III.** *vt* orbitar alrededor de

orbital ['ɔr·bɪ·t̬əl] *adj* orbital; ~ **path/trajectory** trayectoria *f* orbital

orchard ['ɔr·tʃərd] *n* huerto *m*; **cherry** ~ ce-

rezal *m*
orchestra ['ɔr·kɪ·strə] *n* orquesta *f*
orchestral [ɔr·'kes·trəl] *adj* orquestal
orchestra pit *n* foso *m* orquestal
orchestrate ['ɔr·kɪ·streɪt] *vt* **1.** MUS orquestar
2. *fig* (*arrange*) organizar
orchestration [ɔr·kɪ·'streɪ·ʃən] *n* **1.** MUS
orquestación *f* **2.** *fig* (*arrangement*) organización *f*
orchid ['ɔr·kɪd] *n* orquídea *f*
ordain [ɔr·'deɪn] *vt* **1.** REL ordenar; **to ~ sb as
(a) priest/minister** ordenar sacerdote/pastor
a alguien **2.** (*decree, order*) **to ~ that ...** decretar que + *subj*
ordeal [ɔr·'dil] *n* calvario *m*
order ['ɔr·dər] **I.** *n* **1.** (*sequence*) orden *m;* **to
put sth in ~** poner en orden algo; **to leave sth
in ~** dejar ordenado algo; **in alphabetical ~**
por orden alfabético **2.** (*instruction*) *a.* LAW, REL
orden *f;* **to give/receive an ~** dar/recibir una
orden; **by ~ of sb** por orden de alguien
3. (*working condition, satisfactory arrangement*) orden *m;* **to keep ~** mantener el orden;
a new world ~ un nuevo orden mundial; **the
car is in perfect working ~** el coche funciona perfectamente bien; **to be out of ~** no
funcionar; (*toilet*) estar fuera de servicio; **are
your immigration papers in ~?** ¿tienes los
papeles de inmigración en regla? **4.** (*appropriate behavior*) **out of ~** improcedente **5.** (*purpose*) **in ~ (not)** to *+infin;* **in ~ for,
in ~ that** para que + *subj* **6.** (*social class, rank,
kind*) clase *f* **7.** (*request to supply goods or
service*) pedido *m;* **to put in an ~ for sth**
hacer un pedido de [*o* encargar] algo; **made to
~** hecho por encargo **8.** (*architectural style*)
orden *m;* **Doric ~** orden dórico **II.** *vi* pedir; **are
you ready to ~?** ¿ya han decidido qué van a
tomar [*o* pedir]? **III.** *vt* **1.** (*command*) **to ~ sb
to do sth** ordenar a alguien que haga algo; **to
~ sb out** echar a alguien **2.** (*request goods or
service*) encargar **3.** (*arrange*) ordenar, poner
en orden; **to ~ one's thoughts** ordenar sus
pensamientos **4.** (*arrange according to procedure*) organizar
order book *n* libro *m* de pedidos
order form *n* hoja *f* de pedidos
orderly ['ɔr·dər·li] <-ies> **I.** *n* **1.** (*hospital
attendant*) celador(a) *m(f)* **2.** MIL ordenanza
mf **II.** *adj* **1.** (*tidy*) ordenado, -a **2.** (*well-behaved*) disciplinado, -a
ordinal ['ɔr·də·nəl] *n,* **ordinal number** *n* ordinal *m*
ordinance ['ɔr·də·nəns] *n* ordenanza *f*
ordinary ['ɔr·də·ner·i] **I.** *n* **out of the ~** fuera
de lo común; **nothing out of the ~** nada
excepcional **II.** *adj* normal, corriente; **in the ~
way...** normalmente...
ordinary share *n* acción *f* ordinaria
ordnance ['ɔrd·nəns] *n* artillería *f*
ordure ['ɔr·dʒər] *n* inmundicia *f*
ore [ɔr] *n* mena *f;* **iron/copper ~** mineral *m* de
hierro/cobre

Ore. *abbr of* **Oregon** Oregón *m*
oregano [ə·'reg·ə·noʊ] *n* orégano *m*
Oregon ['ɔr·ɪ·gən] *n* Oregón *m*
organ ['ɔr·gən] *n* órgano *m*
organ donor *n* donante *mf* de órganos
organ grinder *n* organillero, -a *m, f*
organic [ɔr·'gæn·ɪk] *adj* **1.** (*disease, substance, compound*) orgánico, -a **2.** (*produce,
farming method*) biológico, -a **3.** (*fundamental: part*) inherente **4.** (*systematic: change*) sistemático, -a
organism ['ɔr·gə·nɪz·əm] *n* organismo *m*
organist ['ɔr·gə·nɪst] *n* organista *mf*
organization [ɔr·gə·nɪ·'zeɪ·ʃən] *n* organización *f*
organizational [ɔr·gə·nɪ·'zeɪ·ʃə·nəl] *adj*
organizativo, -a
organization chart *n* ECON organigrama *m*
**Organization for Economic Cooperation
and Development** *n* Organización *f* para la
Cooperación y el Desarrollo Económico
**Organization of Petroleum Exporting
Countries** *n* Organización *f* de Países Exportadores de Petróleo
organize ['ɔr·gə·naɪz] **I.** *vt* organizar **II.** *vi*
organizarse; (*form trade union*) sindicarse
organized *adj* **1.** (*systemized*) ordenado, -a
2. (*arranged, brought together in a trade
union*) organizado, -a
organizer *n* **1.** (*person*) organizador(a) *m(f)*
2. COMPUT agenda *f* electrónica
orgasm ['ɔr·gæz·əm] **I.** *n* orgasmo *m* **II.** *vi*
tener un orgasmo
orgasmic [ɔr·'gæs·mɪk] *adj* orgásmico, -a
orgy ['ɔr·dʒi] <-ies> *n* orgía *f*
orient ['ɔr·i·ənt] *vt* **to ~ oneself** orientarse
Orient ['ɔr·i·ənt] *n* **the ~** (el) Oriente
oriental [ɔr·i·'en·təl] *adj* oriental
orientate ['ɔr·i·en·teɪt] *vt* **to ~ oneself** orientarse
orientation [ɔr·i·en·'teɪ·ʃən] *n* orientación *f*
orienteering [ɔr·i·en·'tɪr·ɪŋ] *n* orientación *f*
orifice ['ɔr·ə·fɪs] *n form* orificio *m*
origin ['ɔr·ə·dʒɪn] *n* origen *m*
original [ə·'rɪdʒ·ɪ·nəl] **I.** *n* original *m* **II.** *adj*
1. (*new, unusual*) original **2.** (*first*) originario, -a
originality [ə·ˌrɪdʒ·ɪ·'næl·ə·t̬i] *n* originalidad *f*
originally [ə·'rɪdʒ·ɪ·nə·li] *adv* **1.** (*initially*) originariamente **2.** (*unusually*) con originalidad
original sin *n* pecado *m* original
originate [ə·'rɪdʒ·ɪ·neɪt] **I.** *vi* originarse **II.** *vt*
crear
ornament ['ɔr·nə·mənt] **I.** *n* adorno *m* **II.** *vt*
adornar
ornamental [ɔr·nə·'men·təl] *adj* ornamental,
decorativo, -a
ornamentation [ɔr·nə·men·'teɪ·ʃən] *n form*
ornamentación *f,* decoración *f*
ornate [ɔr·'neɪt] *adj* **1.** (*elaborately decorated*)
ornamentado, -a **2.** (*language, style*) florido, -a
ornithologist [ɔr·nə·'θɑl·ə·dʒɪst] *n* ornitólogo, -a *m, f*

O

ornithology [ɔr·nə·'θal·ə·dʒi] *n* ornitología *f*

orphan ['ɔr·fən] **I.** *n* huérfano, -a *m, f,* guacho, -a *m, f Arg, Chile* **II.** *vt* **to be ~ed** quedar huérfano

orphanage ['ɔr·fə·nɪdʒ] *n* orfanato *m,* orfelinato *m*

orthodontist [ɔr·θə·'dan·tɪst] *n* ortodoncista *mf*

orthodox ['ɔr·θə·daks] *adj* ortodoxo, -a

orthodoxy ['ɔr·θə·dak·si] <-ies> *n* ortodoxia *f*

orthogonal [ɔr·'θag·ə·nəl] *adj* MATH ortogonal

orthographic [ɔr·θə·'græf·ɪk] *adj,* **orthographical** [ɔr·θə·'græf·ɪ·kəl] *adj* ortográfico, -a

orthography [ɔr·'θag·rə·fi] *n* ortografía *f*

orthopedic [ɔr·θə·'pi·dɪk] *adj* ortopédico, -a; **~ surgery** ortopedia *f*

orthopedics [ɔr·θə·'pi·dɪks] *npl* ortopedia *f*

orthopedist [ɔr·θə·'pi·dɪst] *n* ortopedista *mf*

OS [ou·'es] COMPUT *abbr of* **operating system** sistema *m* operativo

oscillate ['as·ə·leɪt] *vi a.* PHYS oscilar; **to ~ between hope and despair** moverse entre la esperanza y la resignación

oscillation [as·ə·'leɪ·ʃən] *n a.* PHYS oscilación *f*

oscilloscope [ə·'sɪl·ə·skoʊp] *n* osciloscopio *m*

osmosis [az·'moʊ·sɪs] *n* ósmosis *f inv*

osprey ['as·pri] *n* águila *f* pescadora

ossify ['as·ə·faɪ] <-ie-> **I.** *vi* 1. (*turn into bone*) osificarse 2. *fig* (*become rigid*) anquilosarse **II.** *vt* 1. (*turn into bone*) osificar 2. *fig* (*cause to be rigid*) anquilosar

ostensible [a·'sten·sə·bəl] *adj* aparente, pretendido, -a

ostentation [as·tən·'teɪ·ʃən] *n pej* ostentación *f*

ostentatious [as·tən·'teɪ·ʃəs] *adj pej* ostentoso, -a

osteoarthritis [as·ti·oʊ·ar·'θraɪ·tɪs] *n* osteoartritis *f inv*

osteopath ['as·ti·oʊ·pæθ] *n* MED osteópata *mf*

osteoporosis [as·ti·oʊ·pə·'roʊ·sɪs] *n* osteoporosis *f inv*

ostracism ['as·trə·sɪz·əm] *n* ostracismo *m*

ostracize ['as·trə·saɪz] *vt* hacer el vacío a, aislar

ostrich ['as·trɪtʃ] *n* avestruz *f*

OT 1. *abbr of* **Old Testament** A. T. 2. *abbr of* **overtime** horas *fpl* extras

other ['ʌð·ər] **I.** *adj* 1. (*different*) otro, -a; **some ~ way of doing sth** alguna otra forma de hacer algo 2. (*remaining*) **the ~ one** el otro; **the ~ three** los otros tres; **any ~ questions?** ¿alguna otra pregunta? 3. (*being vague*) **some ~ time** en algún otro momento; **the ~ day** el otro día; **every ~ day** un día sí y otro no **II.** *pron* 1. (*people*) **the ~s** los otros, los demás; **no ~ than he** *form* nadie excepto él 2. (*different ones*) **each ~** uno a(l) otro, mutuamente; **some eat, ~s drink** algunos comen, otros beben; **there might be ~s** puede haber otros 3. *sing* (*either/or*) **to choose one or the ~** escoger uno u otro; **not**

to have one without the ~ no tener uno sin el otro 4. (*being vague*) **someone or ~** alguien **III.** *adv* de otra manera; **somehow or ~** de una manera u otra

otherwise ['ʌð·ər·waɪz] **I.** *adj form* distinto, -a **II.** *adv* 1. (*differently: behave, act*) de otro modo 2. (*in other ways*) **~,...** por lo demás,... **III.** *conj* si no

otolaryngologist *n* MED otorrinolaringólogo, -a *m, f*

otter ['at·ər] *n* nutria *f*

ouch [aʊtʃ] *interj* ay

ought [ɔt] *aux* 1. (*have as duty*) deber; **you ~ to do it** deberías [*o* tendrías que] hacerlo 2. (*be likely*) tener que; **he ~ to be here** tendría que [*o* debería] estar aquí; **they ~ to win** merecerían ganar 3. (*probability*) **she ~ to have arrived by now** debe de haber llegado ya

ounce [aʊns] *n* 1. (*weight*) onza *f* (*28,4 g*) 2. (*of decency, common sense*) pizca *f*

our [aʊr] *adj pos* nuestro, -a; **~ house** nuestra casa; **~ children** nuestros hijos

ours [aʊrz] *pron pos* el nuestro, la nuestra; **it's not their bag, it's ~** no es su bolsa, es la nuestra; **this house is ~** esta casa es nuestra; **a book of ~** un libro nuestro; **~ is bigger** el nuestro es mayor

ourselves [aʊr·'selvz] *pron reflexive* 1. nos; *emphatic* nosotros mismos, nosotras mismas; **we hurt ~** nos lastimamos 2. *after prep* nosotros, -as (mismos, mismas)

oust [aʊst] *vt* (*rival*) desbancar; (*president*) derrocar

out [aʊt] **I.** *vt* revelar la homosexualidad de **II.** *adj* 1. (*absent: person*) fuera 2. (*released: book, news*) publicado, en 3. (*in blossom*) en flor 4. (*visible*) **the sun/the moon is ~** ha salido el sol/la luna 5. (*finished*) **before the week is ~** antes de que acabe la semana 6. (*not functioning: fire, light*) apagado, -a 7. SPORTS (*out of bounds*) fuera 8. (*unfashionable*) pasado, de moda 9. (*not possible*) **to be ~** estar descartado, ser imposible 10. (*in baseball*) fuera **III.** *adv* 1. (*not inside*) fuera, afuera; **to go ~** salir fuera; **get ~!** ¡fuera! 2. (*outside*) afuera; **keep ~!** prohibido el paso; **to eat ~** comer fuera 3. (*remove*) **to cross ~ words** tachar palabras; **to get a stain ~** sacar una mancha; **to put ~ a fire** apagar un fuego 4. (*available*) **the best one ~ right now** el mejor disponible en este momento 5. (*away*) **to be ~** (*person*) no estar; **to go ~ to the West Coast** salir para la costa oeste (de EE.UU); **to be ~ at sea** estar mar adentro; **the tide is going ~** la marea está bajando 6. (*unconscious*) **to pass ~** perder el conocimiento; **to be ~ cold** estar fuera de combate ▶ **to be ~ and about** (*on the road*) estar en camino; (*healthy*) estar repuesto; **~ with it!** ¡desembucha! **IV.** *prep* 1. (*towards outside*) **~ of** fuera de; **to go ~ of the room** salir de la habitación; **to jump ~ of bed** saltar de la cama; **to take sth ~ of a box** sacar algo de una caja; **to look/lean ~ of the window** mirar por/apoyarse en la ventana **2.** (*outside from*) **~ of sight/of reach** fuera de vista/de alcance; **to drink ~ of a glass** beber de un vaso; **to be ~ of it** estar en otra onda *inf* **3.** (*away from*) **to be ~ of town/the country** estar fuera de la ciudad/del país; **to get ~ of the rain** resguardarse de la lluvia; **~ of the way!** ¡quita de en medio! **4.** (*without*) **to be ~ of money/work** estar sin dinero/trabajo; **~ of breath** sin aliento; **~ of order** averiado, -a **5.** (*not included in*) **to get ~ of the habit of doing sth** quitarse el hábito de hacer algo; **his dog is ~ of control** su perro está fuera de control **6.** (*from*) **made ~ of wood/steel** hecho de madera/acero; **to copy sth ~ of a file** copiar algo de un archivo; **to get sth ~ of sb** sacar algo a alguien; **to read ~ of a novel** leer en una novela; **in 3 cases ~ of 10** en 3 de cada 10 casos **7.** (*because of*) **to do sth ~ of politeness** hacer algo por cortesía

out-and-out [ˌaʊt·ənd·ˈaʊt] *adj* (*liar, idiot*) consumado, -a, redomado, -a; (*lie*) como una casa; (*disaster*) total, absoluto, -a

outback [ˈaʊt·bæk] *n* **the ~** el interior (*zona despoblada de Australia*)

outbid [ˌaʊt·ˈbɪd] *vt irr* **to ~ sb** (**for sth**) pujar más que alguien (por algo)

outboard [ˈaʊt·bɔrd] *n*, **outboard motor** *n* fueraborda *m*

outbreak [ˈaʊt·breɪk] *n* (*of the flu, violence*) brote *m*; (*of war*) estallido *m*

outburst [ˈaʊt·bɜrst] *n* arrebato *m*

outcast [ˈaʊt·kæst] **I.** *n* paria *mf*; **social ~** marginado, -a *m, f* de la sociedad **II.** *adj* marginado, -a

outclass [ˌaʊt·ˈklæs] *vt* superar, aventajar

outcome [ˈaʊt·kʌm] *n* **1.** (*result*) resultado *m* **2.** (*consequence*) consecuencia *f*

outcrop [ˈaʊt·krap] **I.** *n* afloramiento *m* **II.** *vi* aflorar

outcry [ˈaʊt·kraɪ] <-ies> *n* gran protesta *f*

outdated [aʊt·ˈdeɪ·t̬ɪd] *adj* anticuado, -a, pasado, -a de moda

outdistance [aʊt·ˈdɪs·təns] *vt* dejar atrás

outdo [aʊt·ˈdu] *vt irr* superar, mejorar; **to ~ sb in sth** superar a alguien en algo; **to ~ oneself** mejorarse

outdoor [ˌaʊt·ˈdɔr] *adj* al aire libre; (*clothing*) de calle; (*plants*) de exterior

outdoors [ˌaʊt·ˈdɔrz] *n* **the great ~** el aire libre

outer [ˈaʊ·t̬ər] *adj* exterior; **~ ear** oído *m* externo

outermost [ˈaʊ·t̬ər·moʊst] *n* más exterior

outfield [ˈaʊt·fild] *n* (*in cricket, baseball*) parte *f* exterior del campo

outfielder [ˈaʊt·fil·dər] *n* (*baseball, softball*) jardinero, -a *m, f*

outfit [ˈaʊt·fɪt] *n* **1.** (*set of clothes*) conjunto *m* **2.** (*team, organization*) equipo *m*; **research ~** unidad *f* de investigación

outfitter [ˈaʊt·fɪt̬·ər] *n* **sports ~s** tienda *f* de

artículos de deporte

outflow [ˈaʊt·floʊ] *n* (*of liquid*) desagüe *m;* (*of capital*) fuga *f*

outfox [ˌaʊt·ˈfaks] *vt* burlar con astucia

outgoing [ˈaʊt·goʊ·ɪŋ] *adj* **1.** (*sociable, extroverted*) sociable, extrovertido, -a **2.** (*retiring: president*) saliente **3.** (*ship*) que sale; **~ call** llamada *f* al exterior

outgrow [ˌaʊt·ˈgroʊ] *vt irr* **1.** (*become bigger than*) crecer más que; **she's ~n her pants** se le han quedado pequeños los pantalones **2.** (*habit*) pasar de la edad de; **to ~ an illness** superar una enfermedad con la edad

outgrowth [ˈaʊt·groʊθ] *n* **1.** BOT brote *m* **2.** (*result*) resultado *m*

outhouse [ˈaʊt·haʊs] *n* retrete *m* exterior

outing [ˈaʊ·t̬ɪŋ] *n* excursión *f;* **to go on an ~** ir de excursión

outlandish [aʊt·ˈlæn·dɪʃ] *adj* (*clothes*) estrafalario, -a, extravagante; (*idea*) descabellado, -a

outlast [ˌaʊt·ˈlæst] *vt* **to ~ sth** durar más que algo; **to ~ sb** sobrevivir a alguien

outlaw [ˈaʊt·lɔ] **I.** *n* forajido, -a *m, f* **II.** *vt* (*product, practice*) prohibir; (*person*) proscribir

outlay [ˈaʊt·leɪ] *n* desembolso *m*

outlet [ˈaʊt·let] *n* **1.** ECON punto *m* de venta; **retail ~** tienda *f* al por menor **2.** (*means of expression*) válvula *f* de escape **3.** (*vent: for air*) respiradero *m;* (*for water*) desagüe *m* **4.** ELEC toma *f* de corriente

outline [ˈaʊt·laɪn] **I.** *n* **1.** (*draft*) esbozo *m* **2.** (*shape*) perfil *m* **3.** (*general description*) resumen *m* **II.** *vt* **1.** (*draw outer line of*) perfilar **2.** (*describe*) describir a grandes trazos; (*summarize*) resumir

outlive [ˌaʊt·ˈlɪv] *vt* sobrevivir a

outlook [ˈaʊt·lʊk] *n* **1.** (*prospects*) perspectivas *fpl* **2.** (*attitude*) punto *m* de vista **3.** (*view*) vista *f*

outlying [ˈaʊt·laɪ·ɪŋ] *adj* distante, alejado, -a

outmaneuver [ˌaʊt·mə·ˈnu·vər] *vt* (*person*) mostrarse más hábil que; (*car*) ser más maniobrable que

outmoded [ˌaʊt·ˈmoʊ·dɪd] *adj pej* anticuado, -a, pasado, -a de moda

outmost [ˈaʊt·moʊst] *adj* más remoto, -a

outnumber [ˌaʊt·ˈnʌm·bər] *vt* superar en número a

out-of-court settlement *n* arreglo *m* extrajudicial

out-of-date [ˌaʊt·əv·ˈdeɪt] *adj* (*clothing*) anticuado, -a, pasado, -a de moda; (*version*) antiguo, -a

out-of-the-way [ˌaʊt·əv·ðə·ˈweɪ] *adj* apartado, -a

outpatient [ˈaʊt·ˌpeɪ·ʃənt] *n* paciente *mf* externo, -a

outplay [ˌaʊt·ˈpleɪ] *vt* jugar mejor que

outpost [ˈaʊt·poʊst] *n* **1.** MIL puesto *m* de avanzada **2.** *fig* reducto *m*

outpouring [ˈaʊt·ˌpɔr·ɪŋ] *n* desahogo *m;* **~ of grief** lamento *m* de dolor

output [ˈaʊt·pʊt] *n* ECON producción *f;* (*of*

machine) rendimiento *m*

output device *n* COMPUT dispositivo *m* de salida

outrage ['aʊt·reɪdʒ] I. *n* 1. (*atrocity*) atrocidad *f;* (*terrorist act*) atentado *m* 2. (*scandal*) escándalo *m;* **to express ~** (**at sth**) mostrar indignación (ante algo); **to feel a strong sense of ~ at sth** sentirse ultrajado por algo II. *vt* (*offend*) ultrajar

outrageous [aʊt·'reɪ·dʒəs] *adj* 1. (*shocking: behavior*) escandaloso, -a; (*clothing*) extravagante, estrafalario, -a; (*person*) atrevido, -a 2. (*cruel, violent*) atroz

outré [u·'treɪ] *adj form* extravagante, estrafalario, -a

outrigger ['aʊt·rɪg·ər] *n* 1. (*stabilizer*) balancín *m* 2. (*boat*) canoa *f* con balancines

outright ['aʊt·raɪt] I. *adj* (*disaster, defeat*) total; (*winner*) indiscutible; (*hostilities*) declarado, -a II. *adv* 1. (*defeat, ignore*) totalmente; (*win*) indiscutiblemente 2. (*declare, ask*) descaradamente

outrun [aʊt·'rʌn] *vt irr* **to ~ sb** dejar atrás a alguien

outset ['aʊt·set] *n* principio *m;* **from the ~** de entrada

outshine [aʊt·'ʃaɪn] *vt irr* eclipsar

outside [ˌaʊt·'saɪd] I. *adj* 1. (*external*) externo, -a, exterior; (*world*) exterior; (*influence, help*) externo, -a; **the ~ door** la puerta exterior; **~ influences** influencias *fpl* exteriores 2. (*not likely*) **an ~ chance that...** una posibilidad remota de que... +*subj* 3. (*extreme*) extremo, -a II. *n* 1. (*external part or side*) exterior *m;* **judging from the ~** a juzgar por el aspecto exterior 2. (*at most*) **at the ~** a lo más III. *prep* 1. (*not within*) fuera de; **to wait ~ the door** esperar en la puerta; **~ business hours** fuera de horas de oficina 2. (*besides*) además de IV. *adv* 1. (*outdoors*) fuera, afuera; **to go ~** salir fuera; **to go ~ the house** salir de casa; **to live an hour ~ Detroit** vivir a una hora de Detroit; **to play ~** jugar fuera 2. (*beyond*) **to be ~ the perimeter** estar afuera del perímetro

outsider [aʊt·'saɪ·dər] *n* 1. (*person not from a group*) persona *f* de fuera 2. (*in race, competition*) **to be an ~** ser un desconocido

outsize [aʊt·'saɪz] *adj* muy grande

outskirts ['aʊt·skɜrts] *npl* afueras *fpl;* **on the ~** en las afueras

outsourcing ['aʊt·ˌsɔr·sɪŋ] *n* externalización *f*

outspoken [ˌaʊt·'spoʊ·kən] *adj* directo, -a; **to be ~** no tener pelos en la lengua

outstanding [ˌaʊt·'stæn·dɪŋ] *adj* 1. (*excellent*) destacado, -a 2. FIN (*account*) por pagar; (*debt*) pendiente (de pago) 3. (*unsolved*) por resolver

outstay [aʊt·'steɪ] *vt* **to ~ one's welcome** abusar de la hospitalidad

outstretched [ˌaʊt·'stretʃt] *adj* extendido, -a

outstrip [ˌaʊt·'strɪp] *vt irr* 1. (*go faster than*) aventajar 2. (*be greater than, exceed*) sobrepasar

outtake ['aʊt·ˌteɪk] *n* escena *f* eliminada

outthink [ˌaʊt·'θɪŋk] *irr vt* ser más listo que

outvote [ˌaʊt·'voʊt] *vt* vencer en unas elecciones; **to be ~d** perder las elecciones

outward ['aʊt·wərd] I. *adj* 1. (*visible: indication*) externo, -a 2. (*exterior: appearance, beauty*) exterior 3. (*apparent: similarities, differences*) aparente 4. (*voyage*) de ida II. *adv* hacia afuera, hacia el exterior III. *n liter* exterior *m*

outwardly ['aʊt·wərd·li] *adv* aparentemente

outwards ['aʊt·wərdz] *adv* hacia afuera, hacia el exterior

outweigh [ˌaʊt·'weɪ] *vt* 1. (*weight*) pesar más que 2. (*in importance or influence*) tener más peso que

outwit [ˌaʊt·'wɪt] <-tt-> *vt* burlar

outwork ['aʊt·wɜrk] I. *vt* trabajar mejor que II. *n* MIL defensa *f* (fuera de los límites de la fortificación principal)

oval ['oʊ·vəl] I. *n* óvalo *m* II. *adj* ovalado, -a, oval

Oval Office *n* **the ~** el despacho oval

ovary ['oʊ·və·ri] <-ies> *n* ovario *m*

ovation [oʊ·'veɪ·ʃən] *n* ovación *f;* **to get an ~** ser ovacionado; **a standing ~** una ovación de [*o* en] pie

oven ['ʌv·ən] *n* horno *m*

ovenproof ['ʌv·ən·pruf] *adj* refractario, -a

oven-ready [ʌv·ən·'red·i] *adj* listo, -a para hornear

ovenware ['ʌv·ən·ˌwer] *n* vajilla *f* refractaria

over ['oʊ·vər] I. *prep* 1. (*above*) encima de, por encima de; **the bridge ~ the freeway** el puente sobre la autopista; **to fly ~ the sea** volar sobre el mar 2. (*on*) **to hit sb ~ the head** golpear a alguien en la cabeza; **to drive ~ sth** arrollar algo; **to spread a cloth ~ the table** extender un mantel sobre la mesa 3. (*across*) **to go ~ the bridge** cruzar el puente; **the house ~ the road** la casa de enfrente; **it rained all ~ New England** llovió por toda Nueva Inglaterra; **famous all ~ the world** famoso en todo el mundo 4. (*behind*) **to look ~ sb's shoulder** mirar por encima del hombro de alguien; **~ the dune** detrás de la duna 5. (*during*) durante; **~ the winter** durante el invierno; **~ time** con el tiempo; **~ a two-year period** durante un período de dos años; **to stay ~ the weekend** quedarse a pasar el fin de semana 6. (*more than*) **to speak for ~ an hour** hablar más de una hora; **~ 150** más de 150; **children ~ 14** niños mayores de 14 (años); **~ and above that** además de eso 7. (*through*) **I heard it ~ the radio** lo oí por la radio; **to hear sth ~ the noise** escuchar algo a pesar del ruido; **what came ~ him?** ¿qué le picó? *inf* 8. (*in superiority to*) **to rule ~ the Romans** gobernar sobre los romanos; **to have command ~ sth** tener mando sobre algo; **to have an advantage ~ sb** tener ventaja sobre alguien 9. (*about*) **~ sth** acerca de algo; **to puzzle ~ a problem** romperse la cabeza por un problema **10.**(*for checking*) **to go ~ a text** revisar un texto; **to watch ~ a child** cuidar a un niño **11.**(*past*) **to be ~ the worst** haber pasado lo peor **12.** MATH **4 ~ 12 equals a third** 4 entre 12 es igual a un tercio **II.** *adv* **1.**(*moving above: go, jump*) por encima; **to fly ~ the city** sobrevolar la ciudad **2.**(*at a distance*) **to move sth ~** apartar algo; **~ here** acá; **~ there** allá; **~ the road** cruzando la calle **3.**(*moving across*) **to come ~ here** venir para acá; **to go ~ there** ir para allá; **he has flown ~ to Europe** se ha ido a Europa; **he swam ~ to me** nadó hacia mí; **he went ~ to the enemy** *fig* se cambió al bando enemigo **4.**(*on a visit*) **come ~ tonight** pásate por aquí esta noche **5.**(*changing hands*) **to pass/hand sth ~** pasar/dar algo **6.**(*downwards*) **to fall ~** caerse; **to knock sth ~** tirar algo **7.**(*another way up*) **to turn the page ~** pasar la página; **to turn the pancake ~** dar la vuelta al crep **8.**(*in exchange*) **to change ~** intercambiar; **to change ~** (**from sth**) **to sth else** cambiar (de algo) a otra cosa **9.**(*completely*) **to look for sb all ~** buscar a alguien por todos lados; **to turn sth ~ and ~ in one's mind** dar vueltas y vueltas a algo; **to think sth ~** pensar algo (detalladamente) **10.**(*again*) **to count them ~ again** contarlos otra vez; **I repeated it ~ and ~** lo repetí una y otra vez; **to do sth all ~** hacer algo desde el principio **11.**(*more*) **children 14 and ~** niños de 14 años en adelante **12.** RADIO, AVIAT **~** cambio; **~ and out** cambio y corto **III.** *adj* **1.**(*finished*) acabado, -a; **it's all ~** se acabó; **the snow is ~** se acabó la nieve **2.**(*remaining*) restante; **there are three left ~** quedan tres

overabundance [ˌoʊ·vər·ə·ˈbʌn·dəns] *n* superabundancia *f*
overabundant [ˌoʊ·vər·ə·ˈbʌn·dənt] *adj* superabundante
overachiever [ˌoʊ·vər·ə·ˈtʃi·vər] *n persona que rinde más de lo esperado*
overall [ˈoʊ·vər·ɔl] **I.** *adj* **1.**(*general*) global **2.**(*above all others*) total; **~ winner** campeón absoluto **II.** *adv* en conjunto **III.** *n* **~s** mono *m;* **a pair of ~s** un peto
overanxious [ˌoʊ·vər·ˈæŋk·ʃəs] *adj* demasiado preocupado, -a
overbearing [ˌoʊ·vər·ˈber·ɪŋ] *adj pej* despótico, -a
overblown [ˌoʊ·vər·ˈbloʊn] *adj* ampuloso, -a
overboard [ˈoʊ·vər·bɔrd] *adv* al agua; **to fall ~** caer al agua; **man ~!** ¡hombre al agua!; **to go ~** *inf* exagerar; **to go ~ for sth** *inf* entusiasmarse locamente por algo
overbook [ˌoʊ·vər·ˈbʊk] *vt* sobrecontratar, sobrevender *Col*
overbooking *n* sobrecontratación *f*
overburden [ˌoʊ·vər·ˈbɜr·dən] *vt* sobrecargar
overcapacity <-ies> *n* sobrecapacidad *f*
overcast [ˈoʊ·vər·kæst] *adj* nublado, -a
overcautious [ˌoʊ·vər·ˈkɔ·ʃəs] *adj* demasiado cauto, -a

overcharge [ˌoʊ·vər·ˈtʃardʒ] **I.** *vt* **to ~ sb** cobrar de más a alguien **II.** *vi* cobrar de más
overcoat [ˈoʊ·vər·koʊt] *n* abrigo *m*
overcome [ˌoʊ·vər·ˈkʌm] *irr* **I.** *vt* **1.**(*defeat*) vencer **2.**(*cope with*) superar; (*difficulty*) salvar; (*adversity*) vencer; **to ~ temptation** no sucumbir a la tentación **II.** *vi irr* vencer; **we shall ~** venceremos
overconfident [ˌoʊ·vər·ˈkan·fə·dənt] *adj* demasiado seguro, -a de sí mismo, -a
overcooked [ˌoʊ·vər·ˈkʊkt] *adj* recocido, -a
overcrowded [ˌoʊ·vər·ˈkraʊ·dɪd] *adj* abarrotado, -a
overdeveloped [ˌoʊ·vər·dɪ·ˈvel·əpt] *adj* superdesarrollado, -a; PHOT sobrerrevelado, -a
overdo [ˌoʊ·vər·ˈdu] *vt* **1.** **to ~ things** pasarse; (*work too hard*) trabajar demasiado **2.** *inf* (*exaggerate*) exagerar **3.**(*cook too long*) recocer
overdone [ˌoʊ·vər·ˈdʌn] *adj* **1.**(*overexaggerated*) exagerado, -a **2.**(*overcooked*) recocido, -a
overdose [ˈoʊ·vər·doʊs] **I.** *n* sobredosis *f inv* **II.** *vi* **to ~ on sth** tomar una sobredosis de algo
overdraft [ˈoʊ·vər·dræft] *n* FIN descubierto *m;* **to have an ~** tener un saldo deudor
overdraft protection *n* FIN protección *f* contra sobregiros
overdraw [ˌoʊ·vər·ˈdrɔ] *irr vi, vt* girar en descubierto
overdress [ˌoʊ·vər·ˈdres] *vi* vestirse con demasiada elegancia
overdrive [ˈoʊ·vər·draɪv] *n fig* **to go into ~** ir a toda marcha
overdue [ˌoʊ·vər·ˈdu] *adj* **1.**(*late*) atrasado, -a; **to be ~** llevar retraso **2.** FIN (*account*) por pagar; (*debt*) pendiente (de pago)
overeat [ˌoʊ·vər·ˈit] *irr vi* comer demasiado
overemphasize [ˌoʊ·vər·ˈem·fə·saɪz] *vt* sobreenfatizar
overestimate[1] [ˌoʊ·vər·ˈes·tɪ·mɪt] *n* sobreestimación *f*
overestimate[2] [ˌoʊ·vər·ˈes·tə·meɪt] *vt* sobreestimar
overexcited [ˌoʊ·vər·ɪk·ˈsaɪ·t̬ɪd] *adj* sobreexcitado, -a
overexert [ˌoʊ·vər·ɪg·ˈzɜrt] *vt* **to ~ oneself** hacer un esfuerzo excesivo
overexpose [ˌoʊ·vər·ɪk·ˈspoʊz] *vt* PHOT sobreexponer
overexposure [ˌoʊ·vər·ɪk·ˈspoʊ·ʒər] *n* **1.** PHOT sobreexposición *f* **2.** *fig* aparición *f* excesiva en los medios de comunicación
overextend [ˌoʊ·vər·ɪk·ˈstend] *vt* **to ~ oneself** contraer demasiadas obligaciones financieras
overflow [ˌoʊ·vər·ˈfloʊ] **I.** *n* **1.**(*excess: of liquid, people*) exceso *m* **2.**(*outlet*) rebosadero *m* **II.** *vi* rebosar; (*river*) desbordarse
overfly [ˌoʊ·vər·ˈflaɪ] <-ie-> *irr vt* sobrevolar
overgrown [ˌoʊ·vər·ˈɡroʊn] *adj* (*garden*) abandonado, -a; **to be ~ with sth** estar cubierto de algo
overhang [ˌoʊ·vər·ˈhæŋ] *irr* **I.** *n* (*cliff*) saliente

O

m; ARCHIT alero *m* **II.** *vt* **to ~ sth** sobresalir por encima de algo

overhaul [ˌoʊ·vər·ˈhɔl] **I.** *n* puesta *f* a punto, revisión *f* **II.** *vt* **1.** (*machine*) poner a punto; (*policy, system*) revisar **2.** (*overtake*) superar

overhead [ˌoʊ·vər·ˈhed] **I.** *n* gastos *mpl* generales **II.** *adj* de arriba, encima de la cabeza; **~ cable** cable *m* aéreo; **~ light** luz *f* de techo **III.** *adv* en lo alto, por encima de la cabeza

overhear [ˌoʊ·vər·ˈhɪr] *irr vt* oír por casualidad

overheat [ˌoʊ·vər·ˈhit] **I.** *vt* sobrecalentar **II.** *vi* recalentarse

overindulge [ˌoʊ·vər·ɪn·ˈdʌldʒ] **I.** *vt* consentir **II.** *vi* **to ~ in sth** abusar de algo

overjoyed [ˌoʊ·vər·ˈdʒɔɪd] *adj* encantado, -a

overkill [ˈoʊ·vər·kɪl] *n* **1.** MIL sobrecapacidad *f* de exterminación **2.** *fig* exceso *m* de medios

overland [ˈoʊ·vər·lænd] **I.** *adj* terrestre; **~ vehicle** vehículo *m* todoterreno; **by ~ mail** por vía terrestre **II.** *adv* por tierra

overlap¹ [ˈoʊ·vər·læp] *n* (*between tiles, planks*) superposición *f*; *fig* (*between knowledge, authority*) coincidencia *f* parcial

overlap² [ˌoʊ·vər·ˈlæp] <-pp-> **I.** *vi* (*between tiles, planks*) superponerse; *fig* (*between knowledge, authority*) coincidir en parte **II.** *vt* solapar

overleaf [ˈoʊ·vər·lif] *adv* al dorso

overload¹ [ˈoʊ·vər·loʊd] *n* **1.** ELEC sobrecarga *f* **2.** (*of work*) exceso *m*

overload² [ˌoʊ·vər·ˈloʊd] *vt* ELEC sobrecargar; **to be ~ed with sth** *fig* estar agobiado de algo

overlook [ˌoʊ·vər·ˈlʊk] *n* vista *f* **II.** *vt* **1.** (*look out onto*) tener vistas a **2.** (*not notice*) pasar por alto; (*deliberately*) no hacer caso de **3.** (*forget*) olvidar

overly [ˈoʊ·vər·li] *adv* demasiado

overmuch [ˌoʊ·vər·ˈmʌtʃ] **I.** *adj* excesivo, -a **II.** *adv* en exceso

overnight [ˌoʊ·vər·ˈnaɪt] **I.** *adj* de noche; **~ bag** bolsa *f* de fin de semana; **~ stay** estancia *f* de una noche; **~ delivery** envío *m* para la mañana siguiente **II.** *adv* durante la noche; **to stay ~** pasar la noche

overpass [ˈoʊ·vər·pæs] *n* paso *m* elevado

overpay [ˌoʊ·vər·ˈpeɪ] *irr vt* pagar de más

overpopulated [ˌoʊ·vər·ˈpɑp·jə·leɪ·ţɪd] *adj* superpoblado, -a

overpopulation [ˌoʊ·vər·ˌpɑp·jə·ˈleɪ·ʃən] *n* superpoblación *f*

overpower [ˌoʊ·vər·ˈpaʊ·ər] *vt* dominar

overpowering [ˌoʊ·vər·ˈpaʊ·ər·ɪŋ] *adj* (*person, attack*) abrumador(a); (*taste, smell*) muy fuerte

overproduce [ˌoʊ·vər·prə·ˈdus] **I.** *vi* sobreproducir **II.** *vt* producir en exceso

overrate [ˌoʊ·vər·ˈreɪt] *vt* sobrevalorar

overreach [ˌoʊ·vər·ˈritʃ] *vt* **to ~ oneself** extralimitarse

overreact [ˌoʊ·vər·ri·ˈækt] *vi* reaccionar de forma exagerada

overreaction [ˌoʊ·vər·ri·ˈæk·ʃən] *n* reacción *f* exagerada

override [ˌoʊ·vər·ˈraɪd] **I.** *n* anulación *f* de automatismo **II.** *vt* **1.** (*not accept*) anular **2.** (*interrupt*) cancelar

overriding [ˌoʊ·vər·ˈraɪ·dɪŋ] *adj* primordial

overrule [ˌoʊ·vər·ˈrul] *vt* anular; **to ~ an objection** LAW rechazar una objeción

overrun [ˌoʊ·vər·ˈrʌn] **I.** *n* sobrecoste *m* **II.** *vt irr* **1.** (*invade*) invadir; **to be ~ with sth** estar plagado de algo **2.** (*budget*) exceder **III.** *vi irr* prolongarse más de lo previsto; **to ~ on costs** excederse en los costes

overseas [ˌoʊ·vər·ˈsiz] **I.** *adj* extranjero, -a; (*trade*) exterior **II.** *adv* **to go/travel ~** ir/viajar al extranjero

oversee [ˌoʊ·vər·ˈsi] *irr vt* supervisar

overseer [ˈoʊ·vər·ˌsi·ər] *n* supervisor(a) *m(f)*

oversell [ˌoʊ·vər·ˈsel] *irr vt* insistir demasiado en

overshadow [ˌoʊ·vər·ˈʃæd·oʊ] *vt* **1.** (*cast shadow over*) ensombrecer **2.** (*make insignificant*) eclipsar

overshoe [ˈoʊ·vər·ʃu] *n* chanclo *m*

overshoot [ˌoʊ·vər·ˈʃut] *irr vt* pasar de, ir más allá de; AVIAT aterrizar más allá de ► **to ~ the mark** pasarse de la raya

oversight [ˈoʊ·vər·saɪt] *n* **1.** (*omission*) descuido *m*; **by an ~** por equivocación **2.** (*supervision*) supervisión *f*

oversimplify [ˌoʊ·vər·ˈsɪm·plə·faɪ] <-ie-> *vt* simplificar excesivamente

oversize [ˌoʊ·vər·ˈsaɪz] *adj*, **oversized** *adj* **1.** (*too big*) demasiado grande **2.** (*clothing*) de talla grande

oversleep [ˌoʊ·vər·ˈslip] *irr vi* quedarse dormido

overspend [ˌoʊ·vər·ˈspend] **I.** *vi* gastar demasiado **II.** *vt* **to ~ one's allowance** gastar más de la cuenta

overstaffed [ˌoʊ·vər·ˈstæft] *adj* con exceso de personal

overstate [ˌoʊ·vər·ˈsteɪt] *vt* exagerar

overstay [ˌoʊ·vər·ˈsteɪ] *vt* **to ~ one's welcome** quedarse más de lo conveniente, abusar de la hospitalidad

overstep [ˌoʊ·vər·ˈstep] *irr vt* sobrepasar ► **to ~ the mark** pasarse de la raya

oversupply [ˌoʊ·vər·sə·ˈplaɪ] *n* excedente *m*

overt [ˈoʊ·vɜrt] *adj* (*criticism*) abierto, -a; (*hostility*) declarado, -a

overtake [ˌoʊ·vər·ˈteɪk] *irr* **I.** *vt* **1.** AUTO adelantar; **events have ~n us** los acontecimientos se nos han adelantado **2.** (*in contest*) superar **II.** *vi* adelantar

overtax [ˌoʊ·vər·ˈtæks] *vt* **1.** FIN gravar en exceso (*con impuestos*) **2.** *fig* poner a prueba

over-the-counter [ˌoʊ·vər·ðə·ˈkaʊn·tər] *adj* sin receta

overthrow [ˌoʊ·vər·ˈθroʊ] **I.** *n* **1.** POL derrocamiento *m* **2.** (*in baseball*) tiro *m* desviado **II.** *vt irr* **1.** POL derrocar **2.** (*in baseball*) **to ~ a base/the cutoff man** tirar desviado sobre una base/el hombre de relevo **III.** *vi* (*in baseball*) lanzar demasiado fuerte

overtime ['oʊ·vər·taɪm] *n* **1.**(*work*) horas *fpl* extra **2.** SPORTS prórroga *f*
overtone ['oʊ·vər·toʊn] *n* **1.**(*implication*) trasfondo *m* **2.** MUS armónico *m*
overture ['oʊ·vər·tʃər] *n* **1.** MUS obertura *f* **2.**(*show of friendliness*) acercamiento *m;* **to make ~s towards sb** intentar acercarse a alguien
overturn [,oʊ·vər·'tɜrn] **I.** *vi* volcar, voltearse *AmL* **II.** *vt* volcar; POL derrumbar
overvalue [,oʊ·vər·'væl·ju] *vt* sobrevalorar
overview ['oʊ·vər·vju] *n* perspectiva *f* general
overweight [,oʊ·vər·'weɪt] *adj* demasiado pesado, -a; (*person*) demasiado gordo, -a; **to be ~** pesar más de la cuenta; **to be ~ by several pounds** pesar varios kilos de más
overwhelm [,oʊ·vər·'welm] *vt* **1.**(*overcome by force*) abrumar, sobrecoger; **to be ~ed by sth** estar agobiado por algo **2.**(*swamp*) inundar
overwhelming [,oʊ·vər·'wel·mɪŋ] *adj* abrumador(a); **~ grief** dolor inconsolable; **to feel an ~ need to do sth** sentir una urgente necesidad de hacer algo
overwork [,oʊ·vər·'wɜrk] **I.** *n* agotamiento *m* **II.** *vi* trabajar demasiado **III.** *vt* hacer trabajar demasiado; **to be ~ed and underpaid** ser explotado
overwrought [,oʊ·vər·'rɔt] *adj* **1.**(*person*) alterado, -a **2.**(*style*) recargado, -a
ovulate ['av·ju·leɪt] *vi* ovular
ovulation [,av·ju·'leɪ·ʃən] *n* ovulación *f*
ovum ['oʊ·vəm] <ova> *n* óvulo *m*
owe [oʊ] **I.** *vt* deber **II.** *vi* tener deudas
owing ['oʊ·ɪŋ] *adj* por pagar
owing to *prep* debido a
owl [aʊl] *n* búho *m,* tecolote *m AmC, Méx;* **barn ~** lechuza *f;* **little ~** mochuelo *m*
owlish ['aʊ·lɪʃ] *adj* sabiondo, -a
own [oʊn] **I.** *adj* propio, -a; **to see sth with one's ~ eyes** ver algo con sus propios ojos ▶ **to be one's own man/person/woman** ser dueño de sí mismo; **in one's ~ right** por derecho propio; **to do one's ~ thing** ir a su aire; **in one's ~ time** en su tiempo libre; **to hold one's ~** mantenerse firme **II.** *vt* poseer ▶ **as if one ~ed the place** como Pedro por su casa **III.** *vt* **to ~ that...** confesar que...
♦ **own up** *vi* confesar; **to ~ to sth** confesar algo
owner ['oʊ·nər] *n* propietario, -a *m, f;* **to be the ~ of sth** ser el dueño de algo
owner-occupied *adj* ocupado, -a por el dueño
owner-occupier [,oʊ·nər·'ak·ju·paɪ·ər] *n* ocupante *mf* propietario, -a
ownership ['oʊ·nər·ʃɪp] *n* posesión *f;* **to claim ~** reclamar la propiedad; **to be under private/public ~** ser de propiedad privada/pública
own goal *n* autogol *m*
ox [aks] <-en> *n* buey *m*
ox cart *n* carro *m* de bueyes
oxidation [,ak·sɪ·'deɪ·ʃən] *n* oxidación *f*

oxide ['ak·saɪd] *n* óxido *m*
oxidize ['ak·sɪ·daɪz] **I.** *vi* oxidarse **II.** *vt* oxidar
oxtail ['aks·teɪl] *n* rabo *m* de buey
oxtail soup *n* sopa *f* de rabo de buey
oxyacetylene [,ak·si·ə·'seṭ·ə·lin] *n* oxiacetileno *m*
oxygen ['ak·sɪ·dʒən] *n* oxígeno *m*
oxygen mask *n* máscara *f* de oxígeno
oxygen tent *n* cámara *f* de oxígeno
oxymoron [,ak·sɪ·'mɔr·ən] *n* oxímoron *m*
oyster ['ɔɪ·stər] *n* ostra *f*
oyster bank *n,* **oyster bed** *n* banco *m* de ostras
oz *n,* **oz.** *n abbr of* **ounce** onza *f* (*28,4 g*)
ozone ['oʊ·zoʊn] *n* ozono *m*
ozone layer *n* capa *f* de ozono

P

P, p [pi] <-'s> *n* P, p *f;* **~ as in Papa** P de París ▶ **to mind one's ~s and Qs** cuidarse de no meter la pata
p *abbr of* **page** pág. *f*
pa [pa] *n inf* papá *m*
PA *n* **1.** *abbr of* **public-address system** sistema *m* de megafonía **2.** *abbr of* **Pennsylvania** Pensilvania *f*
Pa. *n abbr of* **Pennsylvania** Pensilvania *f*
p.a. [,pi·'eɪ] *abbr of* **per annum** por año
pace [peɪs] **I.** *n* **1.**(*speed*) velocidad *f;* **to set the ~** marcar el ritmo; **to keep ~ with sb** llevar el mismo paso que alguien; **to keep ~ with sth** avanzar al mismo ritmo que algo; **to keep up/stand the ~** llevar/mantener el ritmo **2.**(*step*) paso *m;* **to quicken one's ~** acelerar el paso ▶ **a change of ~** (*sth different than the usual*) algo nuevo; **to put sb through his/her ~s** poner a alguien a prueba, entrenar a alguien **II.** <pacing> *vt* **1.**(*walk up and down*) pasearse por **2.**(*measure in strides*) medir a pasos **3.** SPORTS (*set a speed*) marcar el paso para; **to ~ oneself** controlarse el tiempo **III.** <pacing> *vi* **to ~ up and down** pasearse de un lado para otro
pacemaker ['peɪs·,meɪ·kər] *n* **1.** MED marcapasos *m inv* **2.** SPORTS liebre *f*
pacesetter ['peɪs·,seṭ·ər] *n* SPORTS liebre *f*
pachyderm ['pæk·ə·dɜrm] *n* paquidermo *m*
pacific [pə·'sɪf·ɪk] *adj* pacífico, -a
Pacific [pə·'sɪf·ɪk] **I.** *n* **the ~** el Pacífico; **the ~ Ocean** el Océano Pacífico **II.** *adj* del Pacífico
pacification [,pæs·ə·fɪ·'keɪ·ʃən] *n* pacificación *f*
pacifier ['pæs·ə·faɪ·ər] *n* **1.**(*for baby*) chupete *m* **2.**(*person*) pacificador(a) *m(f)*
pacifism ['pæs·ə·fɪz·əm] *n* pacifismo *m*
pacifist ['pæs·ə·fɪst] **I.** *n* pacifista *mf* **II.** *adj* pacifista

pacify ['pæs·ə·faɪ] <-ie-> vt 1.(*establish peace*) pacificar 2.(*calm*) calmar

pack [pæk] I. n 1.(*bundle*) fardo m; (*backpack*) mochila f, morral m; (*packet*) paquete m; (*of cigarettes*) cajetilla f; **ice ~** bolsa f de hielo 2.(*group*) grupo m; (*of wolves, hounds*) manada f; inf (*of lies*) montón m, sarta f II. vi (*prepare luggage*) hacer las maletas ▸ **to send sb ~ing** largar a alguien con viento fresco III. vt 1.(*fill: box, train*) llenar; **~ed with information** repleto de información 2.(*wrap*) envasar; (*put in packages*) empaquetar; **to ~ one's suitcase** hacer la maleta 3.(*compress*) comprimir
◆**pack away** vt 1.(*put back in place*) guardar 2.*inf* (*eat*) engullir
◆**pack in** I. vt 1.(*put in*) meter 2.*inf* (*stop*) dejar; **pack it in!** ¡déjalo! 3.(*attract audience*) captar II. vi apiñar
◆**pack off** vt *inf* **to pack sb off** deshacerse de alguien
◆**pack up** I. vt 1.(*put away*) guardar 2.*inf* (*finish*) terminar II. vi *inf* (*stop work*) dejar de trabajar

package ['pæk·ɪdʒ] I. n paquete m; (*of cookies*) caja f; **software ~** paquete de software II. vt 1.(*pack*) empaquetar 2.*fig* echar

package bomb n paquete m bomba

package deal n acuerdo m global con concesiones mutuas

package store n licorería f

packaging n 1.(*wrapping*) embalaje m 2.(*action*) envasado m

packer ['pæk·ər] n empaquetador(a) m(f), embalador(a) m(f)

packet ['pæk·ɪt] n 1.(*parcel*) paquete m; (*of cigarettes*) cajetilla f 2.*inf* (*money*) dineral m 3.COMPUT paquete m

packing n (*action, material*) embalaje m

packing routine n COMPUT rutina f de empaquetado

pact [pækt] n pacto m

pad¹ [pæd] I. n 1.(*cushion*) almohadilla f; **knee ~** rodillera f; **mouse ~** COMPUT alfombrilla f (del ratón); **shin ~** espinillera f; **shoulder ~** hombrera f 2.(*of paper*) bloc m 3.(*of animal's foot*) almohadilla f (de la pata) 4.AVIAT plataforma f 5.*sl* (*house, flat*) choza f, rancho m 6.(*of water lily*) hoja f de nenúfar II. <-dd-> vt 1.(*with wrapping material*) acolchar 2.*inf* (*inflate: a bill, costs, the budget*) inflar

pad² [pæd] <-dd-> vi (*walk*) andar silenciosamente
◆**pad out** vt meter paja en; **to ~ a speech/ text** inflar un discurso/texto con paja

padded adj acolchado, -a; **~ cell** celda f de aislamiento

padding n a. *fig* relleno m

paddle ['pæd·əl] I. n 1.(*type of oar*) canalete m 2.(*act of paddling*) chapoteo m; **to go for a ~** ir a mojarse los pies 3.*inf* (*spank*) zurra f II. vt 1.(*row*) impulsar con canalete 2.*inf*

(*spank*) zurrar III. vi 1.(*row*) remar (con canalete) 2.(*walk, swim*) chapotear

paddle boat n vapor m de paletas

paddle steamer n vapor m de ruedas

paddock ['pæd·ək] n corral m; (*at racecourse*) paddock m

Paddy ['pæd·i] <-ies> n *offensive, sl* irlandés, -esa m, f

paddy (**field**) ['pæd·i] n arrozal m

paddy wagon n *sl* furgón m policial

padlock ['pæd·lak] I. n candado m II. vt cerrar con candado

pagan ['peɪ·gən] I. n pagano, -a m, f II. adj pagano, -a

paganism ['peɪ·gə·nɪz·əm] n paganismo m

page¹ [peɪdʒ] n (*in book, newspaper*) a. COMPUT página f; (*sheet of paper*) hoja f; **front ~** primera plana f

page² [peɪdʒ] I. n 1.(*knight's attendant*) paje m 2.(*in hotel*) botones m inv II. vt (*over loudspeaker*) llamar por el altavoz; (*by pager*) llamar (a alguien) al busca

pageant ['pædʒ·ənt] n (*show, ceremony*) festividades fpl; **beauty ~** concurso m de belleza

pageantry ['pædʒ·ən·tri] n pompa f

pageboy ['peɪdʒ·bɔɪ] n 1.(*in hotel*) botones m inv 2.(*hairstyle*) peinado m de paje

page layout n diseño m de página

page proof n prueba f de plana

pager ['peɪ·dʒər] n busca m

page-turner n *inf* libro m apasionante

pagination [ˌpædʒ·ə·'neɪ·ʃən] n COMPUT, TYPO paginación f

pagoda [pə·'goʊ·də] n pagoda f

paid [peɪd] I. pt, pp of **pay** II. adj pagado, -a; **~ vacation** vacaciones fpl remuneradas

paid-up adj (*member*) que ha pagado una cuota

pail [peɪl] n (*container*) cubo m

pain [peɪn] I. n 1.(*physical suffering*) dolor m; **to be in ~** estar sufriendo; **I have a ~ in my foot** me duele el pie 2.**~s** (*great care*) gran cuidado m; **to be at ~s to do sth** esmerarse en hacer algo; **to spare no ~s** no escatimar esfuerzos 3. *inf* **to be a ~ in the backside** [o *vulg* **ass**] ser un plomo; **to be a ~ in the neck** *inf* ser un coñazo; **on** [o *under*] **~ of sth** so pena de algo II. vt doler; **it ~s me...** me da lástima (que)...

pain barrier n umbral m de protección

pained adj afligido, -a; **a ~ expression** una cara de disgusto

painful ['peɪn·fəl] adj 1.(*physically*) doloroso, -a 2.(*emotionally*) angustioso, -a 3.(*embarrassing*) desagradable

painfully adv 1.(*with pain*) dolorosamente 2.(*shy, obvious*) totalmente

painkiller ['peɪn·ˌkɪl·ər] n analgésico m

painless ['peɪn·lɪs] adj 1.(*not painful*) indoloro, -a 2.*fig* (*easy*) fácil

painstaking ['peɪnz·ˌteɪ·kɪŋ] adj (*research*) laborioso, -a; (*search*) exhaustivo, -a; (*effort*) grande

paint [peɪnt] **I.** *n* pintura *f* **II.** *vi* pintar **III.** *vt*
1. (*room, picture*) pintar; **to ~ a picture of**
sth *fig* describir algo **2.** (*apply makeup*) **to ~**
oneself maquillarse
paintball *n* GAMES paintball *m*
paint box *n* caja *f* de pinturas
paintbrush <-es> *n* (*for pictures*) pincel *m*;
(*for walls*) brocha *f*
painted ['peɪn·tɪd] *adj* pintado, -a
painter[1] ['peɪn·tər] *n* **1.** (*artist*) pintor(a) *m(f)*
2. (*decorator*) pintor(a) *m(f)* (de brocha gorda)
painter[2] ['peɪn·tər] *n* NAUT (*rope*) amarra *f*
painting *n* **1.** (*painted picture*) cuadro *m*
2. (*art*) pintura *f*; **19th century French ~** pintura francesa del siglo XIX
paint roller *n* rodillo *m*
paint stripper *n* quitapintura *m*
pair [per] **I.** *n* **1.** (*two matching items*) par *m*; **a**
~ of gloves/socks un par de guantes/calce-
tines; **a ~ of glasses** unas gafas; **a ~ of scis-**
sors unas tijeras; **a ~ of pants** un pantalón; **a**
~ of tweezers unas pinzas **2.** (*group of two*
people, animals) pareja *f*; **in ~s** de dos en dos
II. *vi* aparearse
◆**pair off I.** *vi* aparearse **II.** *vt* **to pair sb off**
(**with sb**) emparejar a alguien (con alguien)
pairing *n* apareamiento *m*
pajamas [pə·'dʒa·məz] *npl* pijama *m*; **in**
(**one's**) **~** en pijama; **a pair of ~** un pijama
Pakistan ['pæk·ɪ·stæn] *n* Paquistán *m*
Pakistani I. *n* paquistaní *mf* **II.** *adj* paquistaní
pal [pæl] *n inf* **1.** (*friend*) amigo, -a *m, f*
2. (*form of address*) tío, -a *m, f*, colega *mf*
◆**pal around** *vi inf* hacerse amigos; **to ~ with**
sb hacerse amigo de alguien
palace ['pæl·əs] *n* palacio *m*
palatable ['pæl·ə·ʈə·bəl] *adj* **1.** (*food*) sabroso,
-a **2.** (*suggestion*) aceptable
palate ['pæl·ət] *n* paladar *m*
palatial [pə·'leɪ·ʃəl] *adj* suntuoso, -a
palaver [pə·'læv·ər] *n inf* cháchara *f*, palabrería *f*
pale[1] [peɪl] **I.** *adj* **1.** (*lacking color*) pálido, -a;
to look ~ tener mal color **2.** (*not dark*) claro,
-a **II.** *vi* palidecer; **to ~ in comparison with**
sth perder en comparación con algo; **to ~ into**
insignificance verse insignificante
pale[2] [peɪl] *n* (*fence post*) estaca *f* ▶**to be**
beyond the ~ ser inaceptable
paleness ['peɪl·nɪs] *n* palidez *f*
paleography [ˌpeɪ·lɪ·'ag·rə·fi] *n* paleografía *f*
Paleolithic [ˌpeɪ·li·ə·'lɪθ·ɪk] **I.** *adj* paleolítico,
-a **II.** *n* **the Paleolithic** el Paleolítico
paleontologist [ˌpeɪ·li·an·'tal·ə·dʒɪst] *n* pale-
ontólogo, -a *m, f*
paleontology [ˌpeɪ·li·an·'tal·ə·dʒi] *n* paleontología *f*
Palestine ['pæl·ə·staɪn] *n* Palestina *f*
Palestinian I. *n* palestino, -a *m, f* **II.** *adj* palestino, -a
palette ['pæl·ɪt] *n* ART paleta *f*
palisade [ˌpæl·ə·'seɪd] *n* **1.** (*fence*) empalizada
f **2. ~s** (*cliffs*) acantilados *mpl*

pall[1] [pɔl] *vi* perder su interés
pall[2] [pɔl] *n* **1.** (*cloth*) paño *m* mortuorio; **a ~**
of smoke una capa de humo **2.** (*coffin*)
féretro *m*
pallbearer ['pɔl·ˌber·ər] *n* portador(a) *m(f)* del
féretro
pallet ['pæl·ɪt] *n* **1.** (*for transporting goods*)
palé *m* **2.** (*bed*) jergón *m*
palliative ['pæl·i·ə·ʈɪv] **I.** *n* paliativo *m* **II.** *adj*
paliativo, -a
pallid ['pæl·ɪd] *adj* **1.** (*very pale*) pálido, -a
2. (*lacking energy*) flojo, -a
pallor ['pæl·ər] *n* palidez *f*
pally ['pæl·i] <-ier, -iest> *adj inf* afable; **to be ~**
with sb ser muy amigo de alguien
palm[1] [pam] **I.** *n* (*of hand*) palma *f*; **to read**
sb's ~ leer la mano a alguien ▶**to have sb in**
the ~ of one's hand tener a alguien en la
palma de la mano; **to have sb eating out of**
the ~ of one's hand tener a alguien comiendo
de su mano **II.** *vt* **1.** (*hide*) escamotear
2. (*steal*) robar
palm[2] [pam] *n* (*tree*) palmera *f*
◆**palm off** *vt* **to palm sth off on sb** encajar
algo a alguien; **to palm sb off with sth** apartar
a alguien con algo
palmist ['pa·mɪst] *n* quiromántico, -a *m, f*
palm leaf <leaves> *n* hoja *f* de palmera
Palm Sunday *n* Domingo *m* de Ramos
palmtop *n* COMPUT palmtop *m* (*ordenador por-*
tátil que cabe en la palma de la mano)
palpable ['pæl·pə·bəl] *adj* palpable
palpitate ['pæl·pə·teɪt] *vi* (*heart*) palpitar
palpitations [ˌpæl·pə·'teɪ·ʃənz] *npl* MED palpi-
taciones *fpl*; **to have ~** tener vahídos
palsy ['pɔl·zi] *n* MED parálisis *f*; **cerebral ~**
parálisis *f* cerebral
paltry ['pɔl·tri] <-ier, -iest> *adj* insignificante;
(*wage*) miserable
Pampas ['pæm·pəz] *n + sing/pl vb* la Pampa *f*
pamper ['pæm·pər] *vt* mimar; **to ~ oneself**
mimarse
pamphlet ['pæm·flɪt] *n* (*leaflet*) folleto *m*; POL
panfleto *m*
pan[1] [pæn] **I.** *n* **1.** (*for cooking*) cazuela *f*; **fry-**
ing ~ sartén *f* **2.** (*of scales*) platillo *m* **II.** *vt*
(*gold*) separar en la batea
pan[2] [pæn] *vi* CINE panoramizar
pan[3] [pæn] *vt inf* dar un palo a; **to ~ a book/a**
film dejar por los suelos un libro/una película
◆**pan out** *vi inf* (*develop*) resultar; **to ~ well**
salir bien
panacea [ˌpæn·ə·'si·ə] *n* panacea *f*
panache [pə·'næʃ] *n* brío *m*
Panama ['pæn·ə·ma] *n* Panamá *m*
Panama Canal *n* Canal *m* de Panamá
Panama City *n* Ciudad *f* de Panamá
Panamanian [ˌpæn·ə·'mer·ni·ən] **I.** *adj*
panameño, -a **II.** *n* panameño, -a *m, f*
Pan-American ['pæn·ə·'mer·ɪ·kən] *adj* pana-
mericano, -a
pancake ['pæn·keɪk] *n* crep *m*, panqueque *m*
AmL

P

pancreas ['pæŋ·kri·əs] *n* páncreas *m inv*
pancreatic [ˌpæn·kri·'æt̪·ɪk] *adj* pancreático, -a
panda ['pæn·də] *n* panda *m;* **red** ~ panda rojo
pandemonium [ˌpæn·də·'moʊ·ni·əm] *n* **1.** (*confusion*) pandemonio *m* **2.** (*noise*) alboroto *m*
pander to ['pæn·dər·tə] *vt* consentir
P and H [ˌpi·ən·'eɪtʃ] *n abbr of* **postage and handling** correo *m* y embalaje *m*
P and L [ˌpi·ən·'el] *n abbr of* **profit and loss** pérdidas *fpl* y ganancias *fpl*
pane [peɪn] *n* cristal *m;* **window** ~ hoja *f* de cristal de una ventana
panel ['pæn·əl] **I.** *n* **1.** (*wooden*) tabla *f;* (*metal*) placa *f* **2.** FASHION paño *m* **3.** (*of cartoon strip*) tabla *f* **4.** (*team*) panel *m;* (*in exam*) tribunal *m* **5.** (*instrument board*) panel *m;* **control** ~ panel de control; **instrument** ~ AUTO, AVIAT cuadro *m* de mandos **II.** *vt* poner paneles a
panel discussion *n* mesa *f* redonda
paneling *n* paneles *mpl*
panelist ['pæn·ə·lɪst] *n* (*in discussion*) miembro *mf* de una mesa redonda; (*in quiz game*) miembro *mf* de un equipo (de un concurso)
pang [pæŋ] *n* punzada *f;* ~**s of remorse** remordimientos *mpl;* ~**s of guilt** sentimiento *m* de culpa
panhandle ['pæn·hæn·dəl] **I.** *n* GEO *faja angosta de territorio de un estado que entra en el de otro* **II.** *vi inf* mendigar **III.** *vt inf* **to** ~ **money** pedir dinero
panhandler ['pæn·hænd·lər] *n inf* pordiosero, -a *m, f*
panic ['pæn·ɪk] **I.** *n* pánico *m;* **to get into a** ~ ponerse nervioso; **to be in a** ~ estar nervioso **II.** <-ck-> *vi* ponerse nervioso
panic attack *n* PSYCH ataque *m* de pánico
panicky ['pæn·ɪ·ki] <-ier, iest> *adj* (*person*) inquieto, -a; (*feeling*) de pánico
panic-stricken *adj* preso, -a del pánico
pannier ['pæn·jər] *n* **1.** (*for bicycle*) cesto *m* **2.** (*for horse*) alforja *f*
panorama [ˌpæn·ə·'ræm·ə] *n* panorama *m*
panoramic [ˌpæn·ə·'ræm·ɪk] *adj* panorámico, -a; ~ **view** vista *f* panorámica
panpipes ['pæn·paɪps] *npl* MUS flauta *f* de pan
pansy ['pæn·zi] <-ies> *n* **1.** (*flower*) pensamiento *m* **2.** *offensive, sl* (*wimp*) nenaza *f;* (*homosexual*) maricón *m*
pant [pænt] **I.** *vi* (*person, dog*) jadear; **to be** ~**ing for** [*o* **after**] **sth** suspirar de [*o* por] algo **II.** *vt* decir jadeando
pantheism ['pæn·θi·ɪz·əm] *n* panteísmo *m*
pantheistic [ˌpæn·θi·'ɪs·tɪk] *adj* panteístico, -a
pantheon ['pæn·θi·an] *n* panteón *m*
panther ['pæn·θər] *n* **1.** (*black leopard*) pantera *f* **2.** (*puma*) puma *m*
panties ['pæn·tiz] *npl* bragas *fpl*
pantomime ['pæn·tə·maɪm] *n* **1.** (*gestures*) gestos *mpl* **2.** (*mime*) pantomima *f* **3.** (*performer*) mimo *mf*

pantry ['pæn·tri] <-ies> *n* despensa *f*
pants [pænts] *npl* **1.** (*trousers*) pantalones *mpl* **2.** (*underpants*) calzoncillos *mpl* ▶ **to be caught with one's** ~ **down** *inf* ser cogido en fuera de juego
pantsuit *n* traje *m* pantalón (de mujer)
pantyhose *npl* medias *fpl*
panty liner *n* punta *f* del calzón
pap [pæp] *n* **1.** (*food*) papilla *f* **2.** *inf* (*worthless entertainment*) chorrada *f*
papa ['pa·pə] *n* papá *m*
papacy ['peɪ·pə·si] *n* **1.** (*office*) pontificado *m* **2.** (*tenure of pope*) papado *m*
papal ['peɪ·pəl] *adj* papal
paparazzo [pa·pə·'rat·soʊ] <paparazzi> *n* paparazzi *m; inv*
papaya [pə·'paɪ·ə] *n* papaya *f*, lechosa *f Col, PRico, Ven*
paper ['peɪ·pər] **I.** *n* **1.** (*for writing*) papel *m;* **a sheet of** ~ una hoja de papel; **to put sth down on** ~ poner algo por escrito; **on** ~ (*in writing*) sobre papel; (*in theory*) sobre el papel **2.** (*newspaper*) periódico *m* **3.** (*wallpaper*) papel *m* para empapelar **4.** (*official document*) documentación *f;* ~**s** papeles *mpl* **5.** (*essay*) trabajo *m* (escrito) **6.** (*academic discourse*) conferencia *f;* **to give a** ~ dar un discurso **II.** *vt* **to** ~ **the walls** empapelar las paredes
◆ **paper over** *vt fig* disimular
paperback ['peɪ·pər·bæk] *n* libro *m* de bolsillo; **in** ~ en rústica
paperback edition *n* edición *f* de bolsillo
paper bag *n* bolsa *f* de papel
paperboy *n* repartidor *m* de periódicos
paper chase *n* papeleo *m*
paper clip *n* sujetapapeles *m inv*, clip *m*
paper cup *n* vaso *m* de papel
paper cutter *n* guillotina *f*
paper doll *n* muñeca *f* de papel
papergirl *n* repartidora *f* de periódicos
paperknife <knives> *n* abrecartas *m inv*
paper mill *n* fábrica *f* de papel
paper money *n* papel *m* moneda
paper napkin *n* servilleta *f* de papel
paper profit *n* beneficio *m* ficticio
paper route *n* ruta *f* del repartidor de periódicos
paper-thin *adj* fino, -a como el papel
paper tiger *n* **he's only a** ~ no es tan bravo el león como lo pintan
paper towel *n* toallita *f* de papel
paper trail *n inf* rastro *m* de documentos
paperweight *n* pisapapeles *m inv*
paperwork *n* trabajo *m* administrativo, papeleo *m inf*
papery ['peɪ·pə·ri] *adj* de papel
papier-mâché [ˌpeɪ·pər·mə·'ʃeɪ] *n* cartón *m* piedra
papist ['peɪ·pɪst] *offensive* **I.** *n* papista *mf* **II.** *adj* papista
papoose [pæ·'pus] *n* niño indio americano
pappy[1] ['pæp·i] <-ier, -iest> *adj* **1.** (*heavy*) como papilla **2.** *inf* (*of poor quality*) mediocre

pappy² ['pæp·i] *n* papá *m*

paprika [pæ·'pri·kə] *n* pimentón *m* dulce

Pap smear *n* MED prueba *f* de Papanicolau

Papua New Guinea [ˌpæp·ju·ə·nu·'gɪn·i] *n* Papúa-Nueva Guinea *f*

papyrus [pə·'paɪ·rəs] <-es *o* -ri> *n* papiro *m*

par [par] *n* **1.** (*standard*) **to be on a ~ with sb** estar al mismo nivel que alguien; **below ~** por debajo de la media; **to feel below ~** no sentirse del todo bien; **to not be up to ~** no llegar a la media **2.** (*in golf*) par *m* **3.** FIN (*face value*) valor *m* nominal; **at/above/below ~** a/sobre/bajo la par ►**to be ~ for the course** *inf* ser lo que uno se esperaba

par. *abbr of* **paragraph** párrafo *m*

parable ['pær·ə·bəl] *n* parábola *f*

parabola [pə·'ræb·ə·lə] *n* parábola *f*

parabolic [ˌpær·ə·'bal·ɪk] *adj* parabólico, -a

parachute ['pær·ə·ʃut] **I.** *n* paracaídas *m inv;* **~ pack** equipo *m* de paracaídas **II.** *vi* lanzarse en paracaídas **III.** *vt* lanzar en paracaídas

parachute jump *n* salto *m* en paracaídas

parachuting *n* paracaidismo *m*

parachutist ['pær·ə·ʃu·tɪst] *n* paracaidista *mf*

parade [pə·'reɪd] **I.** *n* **1.** (*festive procession*) desfile *m* **2.** MIL desfile *m;* (*inspection*) revista *f* de tropas **3.** *fig* (*series*) retahíla *f* **II.** *vi* **1.** (*walk in procession*) *a.* MIL desfilar **2.** (*show off*) **to ~ around** jactarse **III.** *vt* **1.** (*exhibit*) lucir **2.** *fig* (*show off*) ostentar; **to ~ one's knowledge/wealth/talents** hacer alarde de erudición/riqueza/talento

paradigm ['pær·ə·daɪm] *n* paradigma *m*

paradigmatic [ˌpær·ə·dɪg·'mæt·ɪk] *adj* paradigmático, -a

paradigm shift *n* cambio *m* de paradigma

paradise ['pær·ə·daɪs] *n* paraíso *m*

paradisiac [ˌpær·ə·'dɪ·si·æk] *adj,* **paradisiacal** [ˌpær·ə·'dɪ·si·ə·kəl] *adj* paradisíaco, -a

paradox ['pær·ə·daks] <-es> *n* paradoja *f*

paradoxical [ˌpær·ə·'dak·sɪ·kəl] *adj* paradójico, -a

paradoxically *adv* paradójicamente

paraffin ['pær·ə·fɪn] *n,* **paraffin wax** *n* parafina *f*

paragliding ['pær·ə·ˌglaɪ·dɪŋ] *n* parapente *m*

paragon ['pær·ə·gan] *n* arquetipo *m;* **a ~ of democracy** un modelo de democracia; **a ~ of virtue** *iron* un ejemplo de virtud

paragraph ['pær·ə·græf] *n* **1.** LING párrafo *m* **2.** PUBL (*short article*) breve *m*

Paraguay ['pær·ə·gwaɪ] *n* Paraguay *m*

Paraguayan [ˌpær·ə·'gwaɪ·ən] **I.** *adj* paraguayo, -a **II.** *n* paraguayo, -a *m, f*

parakeet ['pær·ə·kit] *n* periquito *m*

parallel ['pær·ə·lel] **I.** *adj* **1.** MATH paralelo, -a; **to run ~ to sth** correr paralelo a algo **2.** (*similar: lives, ideas*) paralelo, -a **II.** *n* **1.** MATH paralela *f* **2.** GEO paralelo *m* **3.** ELEC **in ~** en paralelo **4.** (*similarity*) similitud *f* **5. to draw a ~** (*make a comparison*) establecer un paralelismo; **to have no ~** no tener igual; **without ~** sin igual **III.** *vt* ser paralelo a

parallel bars *npl* SPORTS barras *fpl* paralelas

parallel line *n* línea *f* paralela

paralysis [pə·'ræl·ə·sɪs] <-ses> *n* parálisis *f inv*

paralytic [ˌpær·ə·'lɪt·ɪk] **I.** *adj* MED paralítico, -a **II.** *n* paralítico, -a *m, f*

paralyze ['pær·ə·laɪz] *vt* **1.** (*render immobile, powerless*) paralizar **2.** (*stupefy*) dejar estupefacto, -a; **to be ~d with fear** estar paralizado de miedo

paralyzed *adj* **1.** (*incapable of movement*) paralizado, -a **2.** *fig* inmovilizado, -a, paralizado, -a

paramedic [ˌpær·ə·'med·ɪk] *n* paramédico, -a *m, f*

parameter [pə·'ræm·ə·tər] *n* parámetro *m*

paramilitary [ˌpær·ə·'mɪl·ɪ·ter·i] **I.** *adj* paramilitar **II.** *n* paramilitar *m*

paramount ['pær·ə·maunt] *adj form* supremo, -a; **of ~ importance** de extrema importancia; **to be ~ to sth** ser vital para algo

paranoia [ˌpær·ə·'nɔɪ·ə] *n* paranoia *f*

paranoiac [ˌpær·ə·'nɔɪ·æk] **I.** *adj* paranoico, -a **II.** *n* paranoico, -a *m, f*

paranoid ['pær·ə·nɔɪd] *adj* **1.** PSYCH paranoico, -a **2.** (*very worried*) **to be ~ about sth** estar obsesionado por algo

paranoid schizophrenia *n* esquizofrenia *f* paranoide

paranormal [pær·ə·'nɔr·məl] **I.** *adj* paranormal; **~ powers** poderes *mpl* paranormales **II.** *n* **the ~** lo paranormal

parapet ['pær·ə·pɪt] *n* parapeto *m*

paraphernalia [ˌpær·ə·fə·'neɪl·jə] *npl* parafernalia *f*

paraphrase ['pær·ə·freɪz] **I.** *vt* parafrasear **II.** *n* (*reformulation*) paráfrasis *f inv;* **she gave us a quick ~ of what had been said** nos hizo un rápido resumen de lo que se había dicho

paraplegia [ˌpær·ə·'pli·dʒə] *n* paraplejía *f*

paraplegic [ˌpær·ə·'pli·dʒɪk] **I.** *adj* parapléjico, -a **II.** *n* parapléjico, -a *m, f*

parapsychology [ˌpær·ə·saɪ·'kal·ə·dʒi] *n* parapsicología *f*

parasite ['pær·ə·saɪt] *n a. fig* parásito *m*

parasitic [ˌpær·ə·'sɪt·ɪk] *adj a. fig* parásito, -a; **~ disease** enfermedad *f* parasitaria

parasol ['pær·ə·sɔl] *n* sombrilla *f*

parathyroid gland [pær·ə·'θaɪ·rɔɪd·glænd] *n* paratiroides *f inv*

paratrooper ['pær·ə·ˌtru·pər] *n* MIL paracaidista *mf*

paratroops ['pær·ə·trups] *npl* MIL paracaidistas *mpl*

paratyphoid [ˌpær·ə·'taɪ·fɔɪd] *n* MED paratifoidea *f*

parboil ['par·bɔɪl] *vt* CULIN sancochar

parcel ['par·səl] **I.** *n* **1.** (*package*) paquete *m* **2.** (*of land*) terreno *m,* parcela *f* **II.** <-I- *o* -ll-, -I- *o* -ll-> *vt* dividir; (*land*) parcelar

◆**parcel out** *vt* repartir en porciones; (*land*) parcelar

◆**parcel up** *vt* empaquetar

P

parcel bomb n paquete m bomba
parcel post n servicio m de paquetería
parch [partʃ] vt agostar
parched adj **1.** (dried-out) seco, -a; **to be ~ with heat** estar agostado por el calor **2.** fig, inf (very thirsty) **to be ~** estar muerto de sed
parchment ['partʃ·mənt] n pergamino m
pardon ['par·dən] **I.** vt (forgive) disculpar; (prisoner) indultar; **to ~** (**sb**) **sth** perdonar algo (a alguien); **to ~ sb for sth** perdonar a alguien por algo; **~ me for interrupting** siento interrumpir; **if you'll ~ the expression** si me permite la expresión; (**I beg your**) **~?** (requesting repetition) ¿cómo dice?; **~ me!** (after interrupting) ¡perdone!; (after burping) ¡perdón!; (requesting to pass) ¡disculpe!; (expressing indignation) ¡usted perdone!; **~ me for breathing!** ¡no hace falta que te pongas así! **II.** n indulto m
pardonable ['par·dən·ə·bəl] adj perdonable
pare [per] vt **1.** (peel: fruit) pelar **2.** (cut) **to ~ one's nails** cortarse las uñas **3.** fig (costs) recortar
 ◆ **pare down** vt reducir; **to pare sth down to the minimum** reducir algo al mínimo
 ◆ **pare off** vt pelar
parent ['per·ənt] n (father) padre m; (mother) madre f; **~s** padres mpl
parentage ['per·ən·tɪdʒ] n familia f
parental [pə·'ren·təl] adj de los padres
parental authority n patria f potestad
parental consent n consentimiento m de los padres
parent company <-ies> n sociedad f matriz
parenthesis [pə·'ren·θə·sɪs] <-ses> n **1.** TYPO paréntesis m inv; **in parentheses** en [o entre] paréntesis **2.** (remark) paréntesis m
parenthetical [ˌpær·ən·'θet·ɪ·kəl] adj parentético, -a; **~ remark** nota f explicativa
parenthetically adv a modo explicativo
parenthood ['per·ənt·hʊd] n (of man) paternidad f; (of woman) maternidad f
parenting ['per·ən·tɪŋ] n cuidado m de los hijos; **~ skills** habilidades fpl en el cuidado de los hijos
parentless ['per·ənt·lɪs] adj huérfano, -a
Parent Teacher Association n, **Parent Teacher Organization** n asociación f de padres y maestros
pariah [pə·'raɪ·ə] n paria mf
paring ['per·ɪŋ] n mondadura f
paring knife <knives> n cuchillo m para pelar fruta y verdura
Paris ['pær·ɪs] n París m
parish ['pær·ɪʃ] <-es> n **1.** REL parroquia f **2.** (in Louisiana) condado m
parish church <-es> n iglesia f parroquial
parish clerk n sacristán m
parishioner [pə·'rɪʃ·ə·nər] n feligrés, -esa m, f
parish priest n párroco m
parish register n registro m parroquial
Parisian [pə·'ri·ʒən] n parisino, -a m, f
parity ['pær·ɪ·t̬i] <-ies> n **1.** (equality) igual-

dad f, paridad f **2.** FIN paridad f
park [park] **I.** n **1.** parque m; (at country house) jardines mpl **2.** (stadium) **baseball ~** estadio m de béisbol **3.** AUTO (posición f de) estacionamiento **II.** vt **1.** (leave vehicle) aparcar, estacionar AmL; **to ~ a satellite** AVIAT estacionar un satélite **2.** fig **to ~ oneself somewhere** arrellanarse en algún sitio; **he ~ed himself in front of the TV** se arrepanchingó delante de la tele **III.** vi aparcar, estacionar AmL, parquear Col
parka ['par·kə] n parka f
park bench n banco m de un parque
parked adj aparcado, -a, estacionado, -a AmL
parking n aparcamiento m, estacionamiento m AmL
parking attendant n guarda mf del parking
parking brake n freno m de mano
parking fine n multa f de aparcamiento
parking garage n parking m
parking lights n luces fpl de estacionamiento
parking lot n aparcamiento m
parking meter n parquímetro m
parking offense n infracción f de aparcamiento
parking permit n permiso m de aparcamiento
parking space n, **parking spot** n sitio m (de aparcamiento), estacionamiento m AmL
parking ticket n multa f de aparcamiento
Parkinson's (**disease**) ['par·kɪn·sənz·(dɪ·ˌziz)] n enfermedad f de Parkinson
parkland ['park·lænd] n zona f verde
parkway ['park·weɪ] n avenida f ajardinada
Parl. abbr of **Parliament** Parlamento m
parlance ['par·ləns] n form lenguaje m; **in common ~** en lenguaje corriente; **as it is known in common ~** como se conoce popularmente; **in medical ~** en jerga médica
parley ['par·li] **I.** n parlamento m **II.** vi parlamentar
parliament ['par·lə·mənt] n parlamento m
parliamentarian [ˌpar·lə·mən·'ter·i·ən] n (member of parliament) parlamentario, -a m, f
parliamentary [ˌpar·lə·'men·tə·ri] adj parlamentario, -a
parliamentary democracy <-ies> n democracia f parlamentaria
parliamentary government n gobierno m parlamentario
parlor ['par·lər] n **1.** (store) **beauty ~** salón m de belleza; **ice-cream ~** heladería f; **pizza ~** pizzería f **2.** (in house) salón m
parlor car n RAIL vagón m de primera (con asientos individuales)
parlor game n juego m de salón
parlormaid n camarera f
parlous ['par·ləs] adj alarmante; **to be in a ~ state** estar en un estado deplorable
Parmesan (**cheese**) ['par·mə·zan·(tʃiz)] n queso m parmesano
parochial [pə·'roʊ·ki·əl] adj **1.** REL parroquial **2.** (narrow-minded) de miras estrechas
parochialism n provincialismo m

parochial school *n* escuela *f* religiosa

parodist ['pær·ə·dɪst] *n* parodista *mf*

parody ['pær·ə·di] I.<-ies> *n* **1.** (*humorous*) parodia *f* **2.** (*poor imitation*) burda imitación *f* II.<-ie-> *vt* parodiar

parole [pə·'roʊl] I. *n* LAW libertad *f* condicional; **to be out on** ~ estar en libertad condicional II. *vt* **to be ~d** ser puesto en libertad condicional

paroxysm ['pær·ək·sɪz·əm] *n* paroxismo *m;* ~ **of joy** exaltación *f* de júbilo; ~ **of rage** paroxismo de rabia

parquet [par·'keɪ] *n* parqué *m;* ~ **floor** suelo *m* de parqué

parricide ['pær·ɪ·saɪd] *n* form **1.** (*murder*) parricidio *m* **2.** (*murderer*) parricida *mf*

parrot ['pær·ət] I. *n* loro *m*, papagayo *m* II. *vt pej* repetir como un loro

parry ['pær·i] <-ie-> *vt* **1.** (*blow*) desviar **2.** (*question*) eludir

parse [pars] *vt* **to ~ a sentence** analizar una frase sintácticamente

parsimonious [ˌpar·sə·'moʊ·ni·əs] *adj form* parco, -a; **to be ~ with the truth** decir medias verdades

parsimoniously *adv form* escasamente

parsimoniousness *n*, **parsimony** ['par·sə·moʊ·ni] *n form* tacañería *f*

parsley ['pars·li] *n* perejil *m*

parsnip ['pars·nɪp] *n* CULIN chirivía *f*

parson ['par·sən] *n* cura *m;* (*protestant*) pastor *m*

parsonage ['par·sə·nɪdʒ] *n* REL rectoría *f*

part [part] I. *n* **1.** (*not the whole*) parte *f;* **the movie was good in ~s** la película tenía trozos buenos; ~ **of the body/family** parte del cuerpo/de la familia; **the easy/hard ~** la parte fácil/difícil; **essential/important/integral ~** parte esencial/importante/integrante; **in ~** en parte; **for the most ~** en la mayor parte **2.** (*component*) componente *m;* **spare ~s** piezas *fpl* sueltas **3.** (*area, region*) zona *f;* **in these ~s** *inf* por aquí **4.** (*in ratios, measure*) parte *f* **5.** (*role, involvement*) papel *m;* **to want no ~ in sth** no querer tener nada que ver en algo; **to do one's ~** cumplir con su obligación **6.** (*episode, chapter*) capítulo *m* **7.** (*character in movie*) papel *m;* **to play the ~ of the King** desempeñar el papel del rey **8.** (*in hair*) raya *f;* **a ~ in the middle/on the side** raya al medio/a un lado **9.** MUS (*score of an instrument*) parte *f* ▶ **to be ~ and parcel of sth** ser parte esencial de algo; **for my ~** por mi parte; **to take sb's ~** tomar partido por alguien; **on sb's ~** de parte de alguien; **it was a mistake on Julia's ~** fue un error por parte de Julia II. *adv* parcialmente; **to be ~ African** ser en parte africano III. *vt* **1.** (*detach, split*) separar; **to ~ sb from sb/sth** separar a alguien de alguien/algo; **to ~ company** tomar direcciones distintas **2.** (*divide*) partir, dividir; **to ~ sth in two** partir algo en dos; **to ~ sb's hair** hacer la raya (del pelo) a alguien IV. *vi* **1.** (*sep-*

arate) separarse; **to ~ from sb** separarse de alguien; *fig, inf;* **to ~ with one's cash** desprenderse de su dinero **2.** (*say goodbye*) despedirse **3.** (*curtains*) correr

partake [par·'teɪk] *vi irr* **1.** (*participate*) **to ~ in sth** tomar parte en algo **2.** **to ~ of sth** (*eat*) comer algo; (*drink*) beber algo

parted *adj* **1.** (*slightly opened*) ~ **lips** labios *mpl* entreabiertos **2.** (*unwillingly separated*) **to be ~ from sb** estar separado de alguien

partial ['par·ʃəl] *adj* **1.** (*incomplete*) parcial; ~ **recovery** recuperación *f* parcial **2.** (*biased*) parcial **3.** (*fond*) **she is ~ to...** tiene debilidad por...

partial eclipse *n* eclipse *m* parcial

partiality [ˌpar·ʃi·'æl·ə·t̬i] *n* **1.** (*bias*) parcialidad *f* **2.** (*liking*) afición *f*

partially *adv* parcialmente, en parte; ~ **cooked** medio hecho

participant [par·'tɪs·ə·pənt] *n* participante *mf;* (*in contest*) concursante *mf*

participate [par·'tɪs·ə·peɪt] *vi* participar; (*in contest*) concursar

participation [par·ˌtɪs·ə·'peɪ·ʃən] *n* participación *f*

participator [par·'tɪs·ə·peɪ·t̬ər] *n* participante *mf*

participatory [par·'tɪs·ə·pə·ˌtɔr·i] *adj* participativo, -a

participatory democracy <-ies> *n* democracia *f* participativa

participle ['par·tɪ·sɪ·pəl] *n* participio *m*

particle ['par·tɪ·kəl] *n* PHYS, LING partícula *f*

particle accelerator *n* acelerador *m* de partículas

particle physics *n* física *f* de partículas

particular [par·'tɪk·jə·lər] I. *adj* **1.** (*special*) particular, especial; (*specific*) concreto, -a, específico, -a; **to be of ~ concern to sb** ser de particular interés para alguien; **no ~ reason** ninguna razón en concreto; **in ~** en especial; **nothing in ~** nada en particular **2.** (*fussy, meticulous*) quisquilloso, -a; (*demanding*) exigente; **he is very ~ about his appearance** es muy maniático con su imagen II. *n* detalle *m;* **the ~** lo particular

particularity [pər·'tɪk·jə·'lær·ɪ·t̬i] *n* particularidad *f*

particularize [pər·'tɪk·ju·lə·raɪz] *vt* especificar, particularizar

particularly [pər·'tɪk·jə·lər·li] *adv* especialmente, particularmente; **I didn't ~ want to go but I had to** de hecho no tenía muchas ganas de ir, pero no tuve más remedio

parting ['par·t̬ɪŋ] I. *n* **1.** (*separation*) separación *f* **2.** (*saying goodbye*) despedida *f* II. *adj* de despedida; ~ **words** palabras *fpl* de despedida

parting shot *n* última palabra *f* (antes de irse)

partisan ['par·tɪ·zən] I. *adj* partidista; ~ **spirit** partidismo *m* II. *n* **1.** (*supporter*) partidario, -a *m, f* MIL partisano, -a *m, f*

partisanship *n* partidismo *m*

partition [par·'tɪʃ·ən] I. *n* 1.(*wall*) tabique *m* 2.(*of country*) división *f* 3.COMPUT partición *f* II. *vt* 1.(*room*) dividir con un tabique; **to ~ sth off** tabicar algo 2.(*country*) dividir

partly ['part·li] *adv* en parte, en cierto modo

partner ['part·nər] I. *n* 1.(*companion*) compañero *m* 2.COM socio, -a *m, f* 3.(*in relationship*) pareja *f* 4.(*in tennis, dancing*) pareja *f* 5.(*accomplice*) ~ **in crime** cómplice *mf* II. *vi* **to ~ with sb** asociarse con alguien

partnership ['part·nər·ʃɪp] *n* 1.(*association*) asociación *f* 2.COM sociedad *f* (colectiva); (*of lawyers*) bufete *m;* **to go into ~ with sb** asociarse con alguien

partnership agreement *n* contrato *m* de sociedad

part of speech *n* LING parte *f* de la oración

part-owner *n* copropietario, -a *m, f*

part ownership *n* copropiedad *f*

partridge ['par·trɪdʒ] *n* perdiz *f*

part song *n* canción *f* a diferentes voces

part-time [,part·'taɪm] I. *adj* a tiempo parcial; ~ **worker** trabajador(a) *m(f)* a tiempo parcial II. *adv* **to work ~** trabajar a tiempo parcial

part-time job *n* empleo *m* a tiempo parcial

part-timer *n* (*worker*) empleado, -a *m, f* a tiempo parcial; (*student*) estudiante *mf* a tiempo parcial

part-time staff *n* personal *m* a tiempo parcial

part-time student *n* estudiante *mf* a tiempo parcial

party ['par·ṭi] I. *n* <-ies> 1.(*social gathering*) fiesta *f;* **to have** [*o* **throw**] **a ~** hacer una fiesta 2. + *sing/pl vb* POL partido *m;* **opposition/ruling ~** partido en la oposición/en el poder 3. + *sing/pl vb* (*group*) grupo *m;* ~ **of students** grupo de escolares; **to make a reservation for a ~ of two/eight** reservar una mesa para dos/ocho 4. *a.* LAW parte *f;* **the guilty ~** la parte inculpada; **to be a ~ to sth** ser partícipe en algo; **to be ~ to an arrangement** ser parte implicada en un acuerdo; **to be a ~ to a crime** ser cómplice de un delito 5. *inf*(*person*) individuo *m* II. <-ie-> *vi* ir de fiesta

party convention *n* congreso *m* del partido

party headquarters *n* sede *f* del partido

party leader *n* líder *mf* del partido

party line *n* 1.TEL línea *f* de varios abonados 2.POL línea *f* política del partido; **to follow the ~** seguir la política del partido

party politics *npl* política *f* de partidos

party pooper *n sl* aguafiestas *mf inv*

parvenu ['par·və·nu] *n pej* advenedizo, -a *m, f*

pass [pæs] I. <-es> *n* 1.(*mountain road*) paso *m;* **mountain ~** puerto *m* [*o* paso *m*] de montaña 2.(*in football, soccer*) pase *m* 3.(*sexual advances*) **to make a ~ at (at sb)** insinuarse (a alguien) 4.(*in exam, class*) aprobado *m* 5.(*authorization*) pase *m;* (*for festival, concert*) entrada *f* 6.(*for bus, train*) abono *m* (de transportes) 7.SCHOOL (*permit to leave class*) permiso *m* ▶**to come to a pretty ~** llegar a una situación crítica; **things have come to a**

pretty ~ las cosas se han puesto feas II. *vt* 1.(*go past*) pasar; (*cross*) cruzar 2.(*exceed*) sobrepasar; **to ~ a limit** sobrepasar un límite 3.(*hand to*) **to ~ sth to sb** pasar algo a alguien 4.(*in football, soccer*) pasar 5.(*exam, class*) aprobar 6.(*avoid boredom*) **to ~ the time** pasar el rato 7.POL (*officially approve*) aprobar; **to ~ a bill/law** aprobar un proyecto de ley/una ley 8.(*utter, pronounce*) pronunciar; **to ~ a comment** hacer un comentario; **to ~ the news** correr la voz; **to ~ judgment** dictar sentencia; **to ~ sentence** LAW dictar sentencia 9.MED excretar; **to ~ urine** orinar III. *vi* 1.(*move by*) pasar; **we often ~ed on the stairs** a menudo nos cruzábamos en la escalera; **to ~ unnoticed** pasar desapercibido 2.(*come to an end*) desaparecer; **it'll soon ~** se olvidará pronto 3.(*in football*) pasar la pelota; (*in soccer*) pasar el balón 4.(*in exam*) aprobar 5.(*elapse: time*) pasar, transcurrir 6.(*not know answer*) pasar; **~!** ¡paso!

◆**pass away** *vi euph* (*die*) fallecer *elev*

◆**pass by** I. *vi* 1.(*elapse*) pasar 2.(*go past*) pasar de largo II. *vt* pasar algo por alto

◆**pass down** *vt* (*knowledge, beliefs*) transmitir; (*clothes, possessions*) pasar a

◆**pass off** I. *vt* 1.(*treat as unimportant*) disimular 2.(*sell fake*) **to ~ sth off as sth** vender algo como si fuera algo; (*give appearance of*); **he tried to pass himself off as an expert** intentó hacerse pasar por experto II. *vi* 1.(*take place successfully*) tener lugar 2.(*fade away, wear off*) desaparecer

◆**pass on** I. *vi* 1.(*continue moving*) seguir su camino; **to ~ to a different topic** pasar a un tema diferente 2.(*die*) fallecer *elev* II. *vt* 1.BIO (*transmit*) contagiar 2.(*information, advice*) pasar 3.(*refer*) **to pass sb on to sb** poner a alguien con alguien

◆**pass out** I. *vi* (*faint*) perder el conocimiento II. *vt* (*distribute*) repartir

◆**pass over** *vt* pasar por alto

◆**pass through** *vt* pasar por

◆**pass up** *vt* desperdiciar

passable ['pæs·ə·bəl] *adj* 1.(*unobstructed*) transitable 2.(*average, fair*) aceptable, pasable

passage ['pæs·ɪdʒ] *n* 1.(*corridor*) pasillo *m;* (*path*) pasadizo *m* 2.LIT, MUS pasaje *m* 3.(*onward journey*) viaje *m* 4.(*sea voyage*) travesía *f;* **bird of ~** ave *f* de paso 5. **with the ~ of time** con el transcurso del tiempo

passageway ['pæs·ɪdʒ·weɪ] *n* pasillo *m*

passbook ['pæs·bʊk] *n* libreta *f* de ahorros

passenger ['pæs·ən·dʒər] *n* pasajero, -a *m, f*

passenger list *n* lista *f* de pasajeros

passerby [,pæs·ər·'baɪ] <passersby> *n* transeúnte *mf*

passing I. *adj* 1.(*going past*) que pasa 2.(*brief: fad, infatuation*) pasajero, -a; (*glance*) rápido, -a; (*remark*) de pasada; ~ **fancy** capricho *m* II. *n euph* (*death*) fallecimiento *m elev* ▶**in ~** al pasar

passing grade *n*, **passing mark** *n* nota *f*

mínima para aprobar

passion ['pæʃ·ən] *n* (*emotion*) pasión *f;* (*anger*) cólera *f;* **crime of ~** crimen *m* pasional

passionate ['pæʃ·ə·nɪt] *adj* (*emotional*) apasionado, -a; (*angry*) colérico, -a

passionflower ['pæʃ·ən·ˌflaʊ·ər] *n* pasionaria *f*

passion fruit *n* fruta *f* de la pasión

passionless ['pæʃ·ən·lɪs] *adj* sin pasión

Passion play *n* drama *m* de La Pasión

Passion Week *n* Semana *f* Santa

passive ['pæs·ɪv] I. *n* LING voz *f* pasiva II. *adj* pasivo, -a

passiveness *n,* **passivity** [pæ·'sɪv·ɪ·ti] *n* pasividad *f*

passkey ['pæs·ki] *n* llave *f* maestra

Passover ['pæs·ˌoʊ·vər] *n* Pascua *f* judía

passport ['pæs·pɔrt] *n* pasaporte *m; fig;* **sb's ~ to success** su llave hacia el éxito

passport control *n* control *m* de pasaportes

passport holder *n* titular *mf* del pasaporte

password ['pæs·wɜrd] *n* COMPUT contraseña *f*

past [pæst] I. *n* pasado *m;* **to be a thing of the ~** ser una cosa del pasado; **sb with a ~** alguien con historia; **simple ~** LING pasado *m* simple; **to write in the ~** escribir en pasado II. *adj* pasado, -a; **the ~ week** la semana pasada; **in times ~** en otros tiempos; **that's ~ history** eso pertenece a la historia III. *prep* 1. (*temporal*) después de; **ten/quarter/half ~ two** dos y diez/cuarto/media; **it's ~ 2** son las 2 pasadas 2. (*spatial*) después de 3. (*beyond*) **to be ~ thirty** pasar de los treinta; ~ **belief** increíble; ~ **description** indescriptible; **I'm ~ caring** ya me trae sin cuidado; **I'm ~ that now** *iron* ya he superado eso IV. *adv* por delante; **to go/ run/march ~** (**sb/sth**) ir/correr/pasar por delante (de alguien/algo)

pasta ['pas·tə] *n* CULIN pasta *f*

past continuous *n* LING pasado *m* continuo

paste [peɪst] I. *n* pasta *f;* **almond ~** pasta *f* de almendras; **meat/fish ~** paté *m* de carne/pescado; **tomato ~** concentrado *m* de tomate II. *vt* 1. *a.* COMPUT (*stick*) pegar 2. *sl* (*beat*) dar una paliza a

pasteboard ['peɪst·bɔrd] *n* cartón *m*

pastel [pæ·'stel] I. *n* 1. ART (*drawing material*) pastel *m;* (*type of drawing*) pintura *f* al pastel 2. (*color*) tono *m* pastel II. *adj* pastel

paste-up ['peɪst·ʌp] *n* maqueta *f*

pasteurization [ˌpæs·tʃər·ɪ·'zeɪ·ʃən] *n* pasteurización *f*

pasteurize ['pæs·tʃə·raɪz] *vt* pasteurizar

pastime ['pæs·taɪm] *n* pasatiempo *m*

pastor ['pæs·tər] *n* pastor *m*

pastoral ['pæs·tər·əl] *adj* 1. REL pastoral 2. LIT, ART pastoril; ~ **scene** escena *f* bucólica

past participle *n* LING participio *m* pasado

past perfect *n* LING pretérito *m* perfecto

pastry ['peɪ·stri] <-ies> *n* 1. (*dough*) masa *f;* ~ **brush** pincel *m* de repostería 2. (*sweet bun*) pastel *m*

pastry chef *n,* **pastry cook** *n* pastelero, -a *m, f*

past tense *n* LING tiempo *m* pasado

pasture ['pæs·tʃər] I. *n* 1. AGR pasto *m* 2. *fig* **new ~s** nuevos horizontes *mpl;* **to put sb out to ~** *inf* jubilar a alguien II. *vt* apacentar III. *vi* pacer

pastureland *n* prado *m*

pasty[1] ['pæs·ti] <-ies> *n* **Cornish ~** empanada de patata, cebolla y carne

pasty[2] ['peɪ·sti] <-ier, -iest> *adj* (*texture*) pastoso, -a; (*complexion*) pálido, -a

pat[1] [pæt] I. <-tt-> *vt* (*touch softly*) dar palmaditas a; **to ~ sb on the back** *fig* felicitar a alguien II. *n* 1. (*tap*) palmadita; **to give sb a ~ on the back** *fig* felicitar a alguien *f* 2. (*of butter*) porción *f*

pat[2] [pæt] I. *adj pej* (*answer*) fácil II. *adv* **to have sth down ~** saberse algo de memoria [*o* al dedillo]

patch [pætʃ] I. *n* 1. (*piece of cloth*) parche *m;* (*for mending clothes*) remiendo *m;* (*on knee*) rodillera *f;* (*on elbow*) codera *f* 2. (*of land*) parcela *f* de tierra; (*of fog*) zona *f;* **vegetable ~** huerto *m* 3. *inf* (*phase*) fase *f* 4. COMPUT parche *m* 5. TEL conexión *f* (temporal) II. *vt* (*hole, clothes*) remendar
♦ **patch up** *vt* 1. (*mend*) hacer un arreglo provisional a 2. *fig* (*friendship*) arreglar; **to patch things up** hacer las paces

patchwork ['pætʃ·wɜrk] I. *n* 1. (*needlework*) labor *f* de retazos 2. *fig* (*mix*) mosaico *m* II. *adj* de retazos; **a ~ quilt** un edredón de retazos

patchy ['pætʃ·i] <-ier, -iest> *adj* (*performance, novel*) desigual; (*weather*) variable; (*results*) irregular

pâté [pa·'teɪ] *n* paté *m*

patella [pə·'tel·ə] <-e> *n* rótula *f*

patent ['pæt·ənt] I. *n* LAW patente *f;* **to take out a ~ on sth** patentar algo II. *adj* 1. LAW patentado, -a 2. (*unconcealed*) evidente, patente III. *vt* LAW patentar

patented *adj* LAW patentado, -a

patentee [ˌpæt·ən·'ti] *n* titular *mf* de una patente

patent leather I. *n* charol *m* II. *adj* (*handbag, jacket*) de charol

patent medicine *n* medicamento *m* patentado

patent office *n* oficina *f* de patentes

paternal [pə·'tɜr·nəl] *adj* paternal; ~ **grandfather** abuelo paterno; ~ **grandmother** abuela paterna

paternalism [pə·'tɜr·nə·lɪz·əm] *n* paternalismo *m*

paternalistic [pə·ˌtɜr·nəl·'ɪs·tɪk] *adj* paternalista

paternity [pə·'tɜr·nə·ti] *n* paternidad *f*

paternity leave *n* permiso *m* de paternidad

paternity suit *n* litigio *m* por paternidad

path [pæθ] *n* 1. (*footway, trail*) camino *m;* **bike ~** carril *m* bicicleta; **to clear a ~** abrir un sendero; **to follow a ~** seguir una senda 2. (*way*) trayecto *m;* (*of bullet*) trayectoria *f;* **to cross sb's ~** tropezar con alguien 3. COMPUT

P

ruta *f*, localización *f*

pathetic [pə·'θeṭ·ɪk] *adj* **1.** (*arousing sympathy*) conmovedor(a); **a ~ sight** una escena lastimosa **2.** (*arousing scorn*) patético, -a; **a ~ performance** una pésima actuación

pathfinder ['pæθ·ˌfaɪn·dər] *n* explorador(a) *m(f)*; **to be a ~** ser un pionero

pathological [ˌpæθ·ə·'ladʒ·ɪ·kəl] *adj* patológico, -a

pathologist [pə·'θal·ə·dʒɪst] *n* patólogo, -a *m, f*

pathology [pə·'θal·ə·dʒi] *n* MED patología *f*

pathos ['peɪ·θas] *n* patetismo *m*

pathway ['pæθ·weɪ] *n* camino *m*, sendero *m*

patience ['peɪ·ʃəns] *n* paciencia *f*; **to have the ~ of a saint** tener más paciencia que un santo

patient ['peɪ·ʃənt] **I.** *adj* paciente; **to be ~ with sb** tener paciencia con alguien; **just be ~!** ¡ten paciencia! **II.** *n* **1.** MED paciente *mf* **2.** LING paciente *m*

patina ['pæt·ən·ə] *n* pátina *f*

patio ['pæṭ·i·oʊ] <-s> *n* **1.** (*paved area*) área pavimentada contigua a una casa; **~ door** puerta *f* que da al patio **2.** (*courtyard*) patio *m*

patriarch ['peɪ·tri·ark] *n* patriarca *m*

patriarchal [ˌpeɪ·trɪ·'ar·kəl] *adj* patriarcal

patriarchy ['peɪ·tri·ar·ki] <-ies> *n* patriarcado *m*

patrician [pə·'trɪʃ·ən] **I.** *n* patricio *mf* **II.** *adj* patricio, -a

patricide ['pæt·rə·saɪd] *n* (*murderer*) parricida *mf*; (*crime*) parricidio *m*

patriot ['peɪ·tri·ət] *n* patriota *mf*

patriotic [ˌpeɪ·tri·'aṭ·ɪk] *adj* patriótico, -a

patriotism ['peɪ·tri·ə·tɪz·əm] *n* patriotismo *m*

patrol [pə·'troʊl] **I.** <-ll-> *vi* patrullar **II.** <-ll-> *vt* patrullar por **III.** *n* patrulla *f*; **to be on ~** patrullar

patrol car *n* coche *m* patrulla

patrol duty *n* servicio *m* de patrulla

patrolman *n* policía *m*

patrol wagon *n* furgón *m* policial

patron ['peɪ·trən] *n* **1.** (*benefactor*) patrocinador(a) *m(f)*; (*arts*) mecenas *mf* **2.** (*customer*) cliente, -a *m, f* **3.** REL patrón, -ona *m, f*

patronage ['peɪ·trə·nɪdʒ] *n* **1.** (*support*) patrocinio *m*; ART mecenazgo *m* **2.** ECON clientela *f*

patroness ['peɪ·trə·nɪs] *n* **1.** (*benefactor*) patrocinadora *f*; ART mecenas *f* **2.** REL patrona *f*

patronize ['peɪ·trə·naɪz] *vt* **1.** (*be customer*) ser cliente de **2.** (*treat condescendingly*) tratar con condescendencia

patronizing ['peɪ·trə·naɪ·zɪŋ] *adj* condescendiente

patter ['pæṭ·ər] **I.** *n* **1.** (*tapping: of rain*) golpeteo *m*; (*of feet*) pasitos *mpl* **2.** (*talk*) labia *f* **II.** *vi* **1.** (*make sound*) golpetear **2.** (*walk lightly*) corretear; **to ~ about** andar con pasos ligeros

pattern ['pæṭ·ərn] **I.** *n* **1.** (*model*) modelo *m* **2.** ART (*design, motif*) diseño *m*; **floral ~** motivo *m* floral **3.** FASHION (*paper guide*) patrón *m*; ECON (*sample*) muestra *f* **II.** *vt* (*emulate,*

follow, imitate) seguir el modelo

pattern book *n* muestrario *m*

patterned *adj* estampado, -a

paunch [pɔntʃ] *n* barriga *f*, tripa *f*

paunchy <-ier, -iest> *adj* barrigudo, -a

pauper ['pɔ·pər] *n* indigente *mf*

pause [pɔz] **I.** *n* pausa *f* ▸ **to give sb ~ for thought** *form* dar que pensar a alguien **II.** *vi* hacer una pausa

pave [peɪv] *vt* pavimentar; **to ~ the way for sth** *fig* preparar el terreno para algo

pavement ['peɪv·mənt] *n* calzada *f*

pavilion [pə·'vɪl·jən] *n* pabellón *m*

paving *n* **1.** (*space*) pavimento *m* **2.** (*material*) losas *fpl*

paw [pɔ] **I.** *n* pata *f*; (*of cat, lion*) garra *f*, zarpa *f*; *fig, inf* (*of person*) manaza *f* **II.** *vt* tocar con la pata; **to ~ sb** manosear a alguien **III.** *vi* **to ~ at sth** tocar algo con la pata

pawn[1] [pɔn] *n* GAMES peón *m*; *fig* títere *m*

pawn[2] [pɔn] **I.** *vt* empeñar **II.** *n* **to be in ~** estar en prenda

◆**pawn off** *vt* **to ~ sth off on sb** colocarle algo a alguien; **to ~ sth off as sth** vender algo como si fuera algo

pawnbroker ['pɔn·ˌbroʊ·kər] *n* prestamista *mf* (*sobre prenda*), agenciero, -a *m, f Chile*; **the ~'s** la casa de empeños

pawnbroking *n* empeño *m*

pawn shop *n* casa *f* de empeños

pay [peɪ] **I.** *n* paga *f*; **to be in sb's ~** estar a sueldo de alguien **II.** <paid, paid> *vt* **1.** (*redeem with money*) pagar; **to ~ cash** pagar al contado; **to ~ one's debts** liquidar las deudas de uno **2.** (*be worthwhile for*) ser provechoso, -a **3.** (*give, render*) **to ~ attention (to sb/sth)** prestar atención (a alguien/algo); **to ~ a call (on sb), to ~ (sb) a call** hacer una visita (a alguien); **to ~ sb a compliment** hacer un cumplido a alguien; **to ~ homage to sb** rendir homenaje a alguien; **to ~ respects to sb** presentar los respetos a alguien **III.** <paid, paid> *vi* **1.** (*settle, recompense*) pagar; **to ~ through the nose** pagar un precio muy alto (*por algo*) **2.** (*benefit*) ser provechoso, -a

◆**pay back** *vt* devolver; **I'll pay you back!** ¡me las vas a pagar!; **to pay sb back in the same coin** pagar a alguien con la misma moneda

◆**pay in** *vt* ingresar

◆**pay off I.** *vt* **1.** (*debt*) liquidar **2.** *inf* (*bribe*) sobornar **II.** *vi fig* merecer la pena

◆**pay out I.** *vt* **1.** (*money*) desembolsar **2.** **to ~ the rope** soltar cuerda **II.** *vi* pagar

◆**pay up** *vi* pagar (lo que se debe)

payable ['peɪ·ə·bəl] *adj* pagadero, -a; **to make a check ~ to sb** extender un cheque a favor de alguien

pay agreement *n* acuerdo *m* salarial

pay-as-you-go *n* **1.** (*for cell phone*) prepago *m* **2.** (*for debts*) política financiera por la cual no se acumulan deudas, sino que éstas se van liquidando en cuanto se originan

payback ['peɪ·bæk] *n* **1.** FIN (*return on investment*) restitución *f*, retorno *m* de la inversión; (*equaling the sum invested*) amortización *f*; **we're expecting ~ within 5 years** esperamos amortizar los gastos en 5 años **2.** (*benefit from action*) **I've helped you out and now it's time for ~** te he ayudado, y ahora me puedes devolver el favor

payback period *n* período *m* de restitución

paycheck *n* cheque *m* del salario

payday *n* día *m* de paga

pay deal *n* acuerdo *m* salarial

pay desk *n* caja *f*

pay differential *n* diferencia *f* de salarios

payee [peɪ·'i] *n* beneficiario, -a *m, f*

pay envelope *n* sobre *m* de la paga

payer ['peɪ·ər] *n* pagador(a) *m(f)*; **bad ~** moroso, -a *m, f*

pay freeze *n* congelación *f* salarial

pay hike *n* aumento *m* de sueldo

paying *adj* rentable

payload ['peɪ·loʊd] *n* **1.** AVIAT carga *f* útil **2.** MIL carga *f* explosiva

paymaster ['peɪ·mæs·tər] *n* pagador(a) *m(f)*

payment ['peɪ·mənt] *n* **1.** (*sum of cash*) pago *m* **2.** (*installment*) plazo *m*; (*reward*) recompensa *f*

pay negotiations *npl* negociaciones *fpl* salariales

payoff ['peɪ·ɔf] *n* **1.** (*payment*) pago *m*; (*debt payment*) liquidación *f* **2.** *inf* (*bribe*) soborno *m*, coima *f CSur*; mordida *f Méx*; **to make a ~ to sb** sobornar a alguien **3.** *inf* (*positive result*) beneficios *mpl*; (*on bet*) ganancias *fpl* **4.** *inf* (*climax of events*) clímax *m*

payout *n* FIN desembolso *m*

pay-per-click *n* base *o* referencia para determinar las tarifas de publicidad en Internet

pay-per-view *n* pago *m* por visión, pay-per-view *m*

pay phone *n* teléfono *m* público

pay raise *n* aumento *m* de sueldo

payroll *n* nómina *f*; **~ tax** impuesto *m* sobre salarios

payslip *n* nómina *f*

pay-TV *n* televisión *f* de pago

PBS [ˌpi·bi·'es] *n abbr of* **Public Broadcasting System** *organismo americano de producción audiovisual*

PC [ˌpi·'si] I. *n abbr of* **personal computer** PC *m*, pecé *m* II. *adj abbr of* **politically correct** políticamente correcto, -a

p.c. *abbr of* **percent** p.c.

PDT *n abbr of* **Pacific Daylight Time** Hora *f* del Pacífico

PE [ˌpi·'i] *abbr of* **physical education** educación *f* física

pea [pi] *n* guisante *m*, arveja *f Col, Chile* ▶ **to be like two ~s in a pod** ser como dos gotas de agua

peace [pis] *n* **1.** (*absence of war*) paz *f* **2.** (*social order*) orden *m* público; **to keep the ~** mantener el orden; **to make ~** hacer las paces; **to make one's ~ with sb** hacer las paces con alguien **3.** (*tranquility*) tranquilidad *f*; **~ of mind** tranquilidad de ánimo; **to be at ~ with** [*o* about] **one's situation** estar satisfecho de la propia situación; **~ and quiet** paz y tranquilidad; **to be at ~** estar en paz; **to give sb no ~** no dejar a alguien en paz; **to leave sb in ~** dejar a alguien en paz **4.** REL **~ be with you** que la paz sea contigo/con vosotros; (**may he) rest in ~** que en paz descanse ▶ **to be at ~ with the world** estar satisfecho de la vida; **to hold one's ~** guardar silencio; **speak now or forever hold your ~** que hable ahora o que calle para siempre

peaceable ['pi·sə·bəl] *adj* pacífico, -a

peace activist *n* pacifista *mf*

peace agreement *n* acuerdo *m* de paz

peace conference *n* conferencia *f* de paz

Peace Corps *n* Cuerpo *m* de Paz de EE.UU.

peaceful ['pis·fəl] *adj* **1.** (*calm, quiet: animal*) manso, -a; (*place, person*) tranquilo, -a **2.** (*non-violent*) pacífico, -a

peace initiative *n* iniciativa *f* de paz

peacekeeper *n* **1.** (*in family*) conciliador(a) *m(f)* **2.** (*soldier*) soldado *mf* en misión de paz

peacekeeping ['pis·ki·pɪŋ] *n* mantenimiento *m* de la paz

peacekeeping forces *npl* fuerzas *fpl* de paz

peace-loving *adj* amante de la paz

peacemaker ['pis·meɪ·kər] *n* (*between countries*) pacificador(a) *m(f)*; (*between friends*) conciliador(a) *m(f)*

peacemaking ['pis·meɪ·kɪŋ] I. *n* (*between countries*) pacificación *f*; (*between friends*) conciliación *f* II. *adj* (*between countries*) de pacificación; (*between friends*) de conciliación

peace march <-es> *n* marcha *f* por la paz

peace movement *n* movimiento *m* pacifista

peace negotiations *npl* negociaciones *fpl* de paz

peace offer *n* oferta *f* de paz

peace offering *n* prenda *f* de paz

peace pipe *n* pipa *f* de la paz

peace sign *n* señal *f* de paz

peacetime I. *n* tiempo *m* de paz II. *adj* de tiempo de paz

peace treaty <-ies> *n* tratado *m* de paz

peach [pitʃ] I. <-es> *n* **1.** (*fruit*) melocotón *m*, durazno *m Arg, Chile*; **~ orchard** melocotonar *m* **2.** (*tree*) melocotonero *m*, duraznero *m Arg, Chile* **3.** *fig, inf* (*nice person*) monada *f*; **a ~ of a day** un día encantador II. *adj* de color melocotón

peach tree *n* melocotonero *m*, duraznero *m Arg, Chile*

peachy ['pi·tʃi] *adj* **1.** (*like peaches*) de melocotón, aterciopelado, -a **2.** *inf* (*fine*) **to be (just) ~** ir como la seda

peacock ['pi·kak] *n* **1.** ZOOL pavo *m* real **2.** (*vain person*) engreído, -a *m, f* ▶ **to strut like a ~** pavonearse

pea green I. *n* verde *m* claro II. *adj* verde claro

peahen ['pi·hen] *n* pava *f* real

peak [pik] **I.** *n* **1.** (*mountain top*) cima *f;* **beat the egg whites to stiff** [*o* **firm**] **~s** bata las claras de huevo a punto de nieve **2.** (*highest point, summit*) punto *m* máximo; (*of a roof*) pico *m;* **to be at the ~ of one's career/ power** estar en la cúspide de su carrera/poder **II.** *vi* (*career*) alcanzar el apogeo; (*athlete*) alcanzar el mejor rendimiento; (*skill*) alcanzar el nivel más alto; (*figures, rates, production*) alcanzar el máximo **III.** *adj* máximo, -a

peak capacity <-ies> *n* capacidad *f* óptima

peak demand *n* demanda *f* máxima

peaked *adj* (*tired or sick*) enfermizo, -a; (*pale*) pálido, -a

peak hours *npl* horas *fpl* punta

peak level *n* nivel *m* máximo

peak load *n* **1.** (*full capacity*) capacidad *f* máxima **2.** ELEC carga *f* máxima

peak period *n* período *m* de máxima actividad

peak power *n* rendimiento *m* máximo

peak season *n* temporada *f* alta; **at ~** en temporada alta

peak speed *n* velocidad *f* máxima

peal [pil] **I.** *n* **1.** (*sound: of bell*) repique *m;* (*of thunder*) trueno *m;* **a ~ of laughter** una carcajada **2.** (*set*) **~ of bells** carillón *m* **II.** *vi* (*thunder, thunderstorm*) tronar; (*bell*) repiquetear
♦ **peal out** *vi* resonar; (*thunder*) tronar

peanut ['pi·nʌt] *n* **1.** (*nut*) cacahuete *m,* maní *m AmL,* cacahuate *m Méx* **2.** *inf* (*little money*) **to pay ~s** pagar una miseria

peanut butter *n* manteca *f* de cacahuete

pear [per] *n* **1.** (*fruit*) pera *f* **2.** (*tree*) peral *m*

pearl [pɜrl] *n* **1.** perla *f;* **to wear ~s** llevar perlas; **a string of ~s** un collar de perlas **2.** *fig* (*a drop*) gota *f;* **~ of dew** gota de rocío; **~s of sweat** gotas de sudor **3.** *fig* (*a fine example*) joya *f;* **a ~ of a...** una joya de... ▶ **to cast one's ~s before the swine** *prov* echar margaritas a los cerdos *prov*

pearl barley *n* cebada *f* perlada

pearl diver *n* pescador(a) *m(f)* de perlas

pearl diving I. *n* pesca *f* de perlas **II.** *adj* de pesca de perlas

pearl onion *n* cebolleta *f,* cebollina *f Col, Méx*

pearly ['pɜr·li] <-ier, -iest> *adj* perlino, -a, nacarado, -a; **~ whites** *inf* dientes de perlas; **the ~ gates** *fig* las puertas del cielo

pear tree *n* peral *m*

peasant ['pez·ənt] **I.** *n* **1.** (*poor farmer*) campesino, -a *m, f* **2.** *pej, inf* (*crude person*) paleto, -a *m, f* **II.** *adj* campesino, -a, rural

peasantry ['pez·ən·tri] *n* campesinado *m*

pea-souper ['pi·ˌsu·pər] *n Can, pej* (*French Canadian*) canadiense *mf* francófono, -a

peat [pit] *n* turba *f*

peat bog *n* turbera *f*

peat moss *n* BOT turba *f* de Sphagnum

pebble ['peb·əl] *n* guijarro *m*

pebbly ['peb·li] <-ier- iest> *adj* guijarroso, -a

pecan [pɪ·'kan] *n* BOT pacana *f*

peccadillo [ˌpek·ə·'dɪl·oʊ] <-(oe)s> *n* desliz *m*

peck [pek] **I.** *n* **1.** (*of bird*) picotazo *m* **2.** *inf* (*quick kiss*) besito *m* **II.** *vt* **1.** (*bird*) picar, picotear **2.** (*kiss quickly*) dar un besito **III.** *vi* **1.** picar **2.** (*nag*) **to ~ at sb** fastidiar a alguien

pecker ['pek·ər] *n vulg* (*penis*) polla *f,* verga *f AmL,* pija *f Arg, Urug*

pecking order *n inf* orden *m* de picoteo de las gallinas; *fig* jerarquía *f*

peckish ['pek·ɪʃ] *adj* irritable

pectin ['pek·tɪn] *n* pectina *f*

pectoral ['pek·tər·əl] *adj* pectoral

peculiar [pɪ·'kjul·jər] *adj* **1.** (*strange*) extraño, -a, raro, -a **2.** (*belonging to*) propio, -a, peculiar; **to be ~ to sb/sth** ser propio de alguien/ algo

peculiarity [pɪ·ˌkju·li·'ær·ɪ·ti] <-ies> *n* **1.** (*strangeness*) singularidad *f* **2.** (*strange habit*) rareza *f* **3.** (*idiosyncrasy*) peculiaridad *f*

peculiarly [pɪ·'kjul·jər·li] *adv* **1.** (*strangely*) de forma rara **2.** (*especially*) particularmente **3.** (*belonging to*) típicamente

pecuniary [pɪ·'kju·ni·er·i] *adj form* **1.** (*motives*) pecuniario, -a **2.** (*problems*) financiero, -a

pedagogic [ˌped·ə·'gadʒ·ɪk] *adj* pedagógico, -a

pedagogue ['ped·ə·gag] *n* pedagogo, -a *m, f*

pedagogy ['ped·ə·gadʒ·i] *n* pedagogía *f*

pedal ['ped·əl] **I.** *n* pedal *m* **II.** <-l- *o* -ll-, -l- *o* -ll-> *vt* **to ~ a bicycle** impulsar una bicicleta pedaleando **III.** <-l- *o* -ll-, -l- *o* -ll-> *vi* pedalear

pedal bin *n* cubo *m* de la basura (con pedal)

pedal boat *n* pedaleta *f*

pedant ['ped·ənt] *n pej* pedante *mf*

pedantic [pə·'dæn·tɪk] *adj pej* pedante

pedantry ['ped·ən·tri] <-ies> *n* pedantería *f*

peddle ['ped·əl] *vt* **1.** (*sell*) vender (de puerta en puerta); **to ~ drugs** traficar con drogas **2.** *pej* (*idea, lies*) difundir

peddler ['ped·lər] *n* vendedor(a) *m(f)* ambulante

pederast ['ped·ə·ræst] *n* pederasta *m*

pederasty ['ped·ə·ræs·ti] *n* pederastia *f*

pedestal ['ped·ɪ·stəl] *n* pedestal *m* ▶ **to knock sb off their ~** bajar los humos a alguien; **to put sb on a ~** poner a alguien en un pedestal

pedestrian [pə·'des·tri·ən] **I.** *n* peatón, -ona *m, f* **II.** *adj* **1.** (*for walkers*) peatonal **2.** *form* (*uninteresting*) pedestre

pedestrianize [pə·'des·tri·ə·naɪz] *vt* convertir en zona peatonal

pedestrian mall *n,* **pedestrian zone** *n* zona *f* peatonal

pediatric [ˌpi·di·'æt·rɪk] *adj* MED pediátrico, -a

pediatrician [ˌpi·di·ə·'trɪʃ·ən] *n* MED pediatra *mf*

pediatrics [ˌpi·dɪ·'æt·rɪks] *n* MED pediatría *f*

pedicure ['ped·ɪ·kjʊr] *n* pedicura *f*

pedicurist ['ped·ɪ·kjʊr·ɪst] *n* pedicuro, -a *m, f*

pedigree ['ped·ɪ·gri] **I.** *n* **1.** (*genealogy: of animal*) pedigrí *m;* (*of person*) genealogía *f*

2. (*background*) expediente *m* **II.** *adj* (*animal*) de raza

pedometer [pɪ·'dɑm·ə·ʈər] *n* podómetro *m*

pedophile ['ped·ə·faɪl] *n* pederasta *m*, pedófilo *m*

pee [pi] *sl* **I.** *n* pis *m;* **to take a ~, to go ~** hacer pis **II.** *vi* hacer pis; **to ~ in one's pants** mearse encima **III.** *vt* **to ~ oneself** mearse encima

peek [pik] **I.** *n* mirada *f* rápida; **to have a ~ at sth** echar una mirada furtiva a algo **II.** *vi* **1.** (*look*) mirar furtivamente; **to ~ at sth** echar una mirada furtiva a algo **2.** (*become visible*) asomar

◆**peek out** *vi* asomar; (*person*) asomarse

peel [pil] **I.** *n* piel *f;* (*of fruit*) cáscara *f;* (*peelings*) mondas *fpl* **II.** *vt* (*fruit*) pelar; (*paper*) despegar; (*bark*) descortezar; (*skin*) levantar **III.** *vi* (*person*) pelarse; (*paint*) desconcharse; (*layer of paper*) despegarse; (*bark*) descortezarse

◆**peel off I.** *vt* (*paper*) despegar; (*paint*) quitar; (*bark*) descortezar; (*clothes*) quitarse **II.** *vi* **1.** (*come off: paper*) despegarse; (*paint*) desconcharse; (*skin*) pelarse **2.** (*veer away: car, motorbike*) desviarse

◆**peel out** *vi sl* salir disparado, -a

peeler ['pi·lər] *n* pelapatatas *m inv*

peelings ['pi·lɪŋz] *npl* (*of fruit*) peladuras *fpl*

peep¹ [pip] **I.** *n* (*sound: of bird*) pío *m;* **to not say a ~** no decir ni pío **II.** *vi* piar

peep² [pip] **I.** *n* (*furtive look*) vistazo *m;* **to have a ~ at sth** echar una ojeada a algo **II.** *vi* **1.** (*look quickly*) mirar rápidamente, vichar *Arg;* **to ~ at sth** echar un vistazo a algo; **to ~ through sth** atisbar a través de algo **2.** (*become visible*) asomar **III.** *vt* asomar

◆**peep out** *vi* asomar

peephole ['pip·hoʊl] *n* mirilla *f*

peeping Tom *n* mirón, -ona *m, f*

peepshow ['pip·ʃoʊ] *n* espectáculo de strip-tease que funciona con monedas

peer¹ [pɪr] *vi* **to ~ at sth** escudriñar algo; **to ~ into the distance** fijar la mirada en la distancia; **to ~ over one's glasses** atisbar por encima de sus gafas

peer² [pɪr] *n* **1.** (*equal*) igual *mf*, par *mf;* **to have no ~s** no tener par; LAW; **to be tried by a jury of one's ~s** ser juzgado por los iguales de uno **2.** (*lord*) noble *mf*

peerage ['pɪr·ɪdʒ] *n* **1.** (*title*) **to be given a ~** recibir un título nobiliario **2.** (*aristocracy*) nobleza *f* **3.** (*book*) guía *f* nobiliaria

peeress ['pɪr·ɪs] <-es> *n* paresa *f*

peerless ['pɪr·lɪs] *adj* sin par, incomparable

peeve [piv] *vt inf* fastidiar

peeved [pivd] *adj inf* mosqueado, -a; **to be ~ at sb for sth** estar mosqueado con alguien por algo

peevish ['pi·vɪʃ] *adj* malhumorado, -a

peg [peg] **I.** *n* **1.** (*for coat*) colgador *m*, percha *f;* **to buy clothes off the ~** comprarse ropa de confección **2.** (*in furniture, for tent*) estaquilla *f;* (*in mountain climbing, on guitar*) clavija *f*

▶**to take sb down a ~ or two** bajar los humos a alguien; **to feel like a square ~ in a round hole** sentirse fuera de lugar [*o* estar como pez fuera del agua] **II.** <-gg-> *vt* **1.** (*hold down with pegs*) enclavijar **2.** ECON fijar; **to ~ prices** congelar precios **3.** (*link*) **to ~ sth to sth** [*o* **sb with sth**] vincular algo a algo **4.** *inf* (*throw*) lanzar **5.** *fig, inf* (*guess correctly*) acertar; **to ~ sb as sth** colocar a alguien la etiqueta de algo, encasillar a alguien como algo

◆**peg away** *vi inf* darle duro; **to ~ at sth** persistir en algo

◆**peg out** *vt* señalar con estacas

peg leg *n inf* pata *f* de palo

pejorative [pɪ·'dʒɔr·ə·ʈɪv] **I.** *adj* peyorativo, -a **II.** *n* palabra *f* despectiva

Pekinese [ˌpi·kə·'niz] **I.** *n* **1.** (*person*) pequinés, -esa *m, f* **2.** (*dog*) pequinés *m* **II.** *adj* pequinés, -esa

pelican ['pel·ɪ·kən] *n* pelícano *m*

pellet ['pel·ɪt] *n* **1.** (*small ball*) bolita *f* **2.** *inf* (*animal excrement*) cagadita *f*, bollito *m Col* **3.** (*gunshot*) perdigón *m*

pellet gun *n* pistola *f* de perdigones

pell-mell [ˌpel·'mel] *adv* (*hurriedly*) atropelladamente; (*confusedly*) desordenadamente

pelt¹ [pelt] *n* (*animal skin*) pellejo *m;* (*fur*) piel *f*

pelt² [pelt] **I.** *vt* (*throw*) lanzar; **to ~ sb with stones** tirar piedras a alguien **II.** *vi* **1.** (*rain*) llover a cántaros **2.** (*run, hurry*) apresurarse; **to ~ after sb** salir disparado tras alguien **III.** *n* **1.** (*smack*) golpe *m* **2.** (*quick pace*) paso *m* ligero; **at full ~** a todo correr

pelvic ['pel·vɪk] *adj* pélvico, -a

pelvis ['pel·vɪs] <-es> *n* pelvis *f inv*

pen¹ [pen] **I.** *n* (*fountain pen*) pluma *f* (*estilográfica*), pluma *f* fuente *AmL;* (*ballpoint pen*) bolígrafo *m*, birome *f Arg*, pluma *f* atómica *Méx*, lápiz *m* de pasta *Chile;* **felt-tip ~** rotulador *m;* **to put ~ to paper** ponerse a escribir

▶**the ~ is mightier than the sword** *prov* más puede la pluma que la espada *prov* **II.** <-nn-> *vt* escribir

pen² [pen] **I.** *n* **1.** (*enclosure*) corral *m;* **pig ~** pocilga *f* **2.** *inf* (*jail*) **the ~** el talego *m*, tanque *m Méx* **II.** *vt* **to ~ sb/sth in** cercar a alguien/algo

penal ['pi·nəl] *adj* penal

penal code *n* código *m* penal

penal institution *n* penitenciaría *f*

penalize ['pi·nə·laɪz] *vt* penalizar

penal offense *n* delito *m* penal

penalty ['pen·əl·ti] <-ies> *n* **1.** LAW pena *f;* **death ~** pena de muerte; **to pay a ~ for sth** ser penalizado por algo **2.** (*punishment*) castigo *m* **3.** SPORTS castigo *m;* (*in soccer*) penalti *m*

penalty area *n* SPORTS área *f* (de penalti)

penalty box <-es> *n* (*in ice hockey*) banquillo *m*

penalty clause *n* cláusula *f* penal

penalty kick *n* SPORTS (tiro *m* de) penalti *m;* **to**

award a ~ señalar un penalti
penance ['pen·əns] *n* REL penitencia *f;* **to do ~ for sth** hacer penitencia por algo
penchant ['pen·tʃənt] *n* inclinación *f;* **to have a ~ for sth** tener inclinación por algo
pencil ['pen·səl] I. *n* lápiz *m;* **colored ~** lápiz de color; **a ~ of light** un haz de luz II. <-l- *o* -ll-, -l- *o* -ll-> *vt* dibujar a lápiz
♦**pencil in** *vt* apuntar (de forma provisional)
pencil box <-es> *n* estuche *m* (para lápices), cartuchera *f Arg,* alcancía *f Urug*
pencil case *n* estuche *m* (para lápices), chuspa *f Col,* cartuchera *f Arg*
pencil pusher *n sl* chupatintas *mf inv,* suche *mf Chile*
pencil sharpener *n* sacapuntas *m inv,* tajalápiz *m Col*
pencil skirt *n* falda *f* de tubo, falda *f* ajustada
pendant ['pen·dənt] I. *n* colgante *m* II. *adj* colgante
pendant lamp *n* lámpara *f* de techo
pendent ['pen·dənt] *adj* LAW pendiente
pending ['pen·dɪŋ] I. *adj* pendiente; **~ deal** negocio *m* pendiente; **~ law suit** litigio *m* pendiente; **patent ~** patente en trámite II. *prep* hasta; **~ further instructions** hasta nuevo aviso
pendulous ['pen·dʒə·ləs] *adj form* colgante
pendulum ['pen·dʒə·ləm] *n* péndulo *m*
penetrate ['pen·ɪ·treɪt] *vt* **1.** (*move into or through*) penetrar; **to ~ a market** introducirse en un mercado **2.** (*spread through, permeate*) impregnar, calar en **3.** *fig* (*see through*) entender
penetrating *adj* (*voice, gaze, insight*) penetrante; (*rain*) que cala; (*heat, cold*) agudo, -a
penetration [ˌpen·ɪ·treɪ·ʃən] *n a. fig* penetración *f*
penguin ['peŋ·gwɪn] *n* pingüino *m*
penholder ['pen·ˌhoʊl·dər] *n* portalápices *m inv*
penicillin [ˌpen·ɪ·sɪl·ɪn] *n* penicilina *f*
peninsula [pə·ˈnɪn·sə·lə] *n* península *f*
peninsular [pə·ˈnɪn·sə·lər] *adj* peninsular
Peninsular War *n* **the ~** la Guerra de la Independencia
penis ['pi·nɪs] <-nises *o* -nes> *n* pene *m*
penitence ['pen·ɪ·təns] *n* REL penitencia *f*
penitent ['pen·ɪ·tənt] REL I. *n* penitente *mf* II. *adj* penitente
penitential [ˌpen·ɪ·ˈten·tʃəl] *adj* penitencial
penitentiary [ˌpen·ɪ·ˈten·tʃə·ri] *n* prisión *f* penitenciaria
penknife ['pen·naɪf] <-knives> *n* navaja *f*
penmanship *n* caligrafía *f*
pen name *n* seudónimo *m*
pennant ['pen·ənt] *n* **1.** SPORTS banderín *m* **2.** NAUT gallardete *m*
penniless ['pen·i·lɪs] *adj* **to be ~** no tener un duro; **to leave sb ~** dejar a alguien en la miseria
pennon ['pen·ən] *n* pendón *m;* (*on lance*) banderola *f*

Pennsylvania [ˌpen·sɪl·ˈveɪ·ni·ə] *n* Pensilvania *f*
penny ['pen·i] *n* centavo *m* ►**a ~ for your thoughts** ¿en qué piensas?; **to earn/cost a pretty ~** ganar/costar un dineral; **a ~ saved is a ~ earned** *prov* muchos pocos hacen un montón, de cinco en cinco se llega a mil, de poquito en poquito se hace muchito *prov;* **to pinch pennies** apretarse el cinturón
penny-pinching ['pen·i·ˌpɪn·tʃɪŋ] I. *n* tacañería *f* II. *adj* tacaño, -a
pennywhistle *n* flautín *m*
penny-wise *adj* **to be ~ and pound-foolish** gastar a manos llenas y hacer economías en nimiedades
pen pal *n* amigo, -a *m, f,* por correspondencia
pension¹ ['pen·ʃən] I. *n* FIN pensión *f;* **to draw a ~** cobrar una pensión II. *vt* **to ~ sb off** jubilar a alguien
pension² [pɑŋ·ˈsjoŋ] *n* (*boarding house*) pensión *f*
pensionable ['pen·ʃə·nə·bəl] *adj* de jubilación
pensioner ['pen·ʃə·nər] *n* pensionista *mf*
pension fund *n* fondo *m* de pensiones
pension plan *n* plan *m* de pensiones
pensive ['pen·sɪv] *adj* pensativo, -a; **to be in a ~ mood** estar meditabundo, -a
pentagon ['pen·tə·gan] *n* pentágono *m*
pentameter [pen·ˈtæm·ə·tər] *n* LIT pentámetro *m*
pentathlete [pen·ˈtæθ·lit] *n* pentatleta *mf*
pentathlon [pen·ˈtæθ·lan] *n* pentatlón *m*
Pentecost ['pen·tɪ·kɔst] *n* REL Pentecostés *m*
penthouse ['pent·haʊs] *n* ático *m* de lujo
pent-up [ˌpent·ˈʌp] *adj* **1.** (*emotion*) contenido, -a, reprimido, -a **2.** (*energy*) acumulado, -a
penultimate [pɪ·ˈnʌl·tə·mət] I. *n* **the ~** el penúltimo, la penúltima II. *adj* penúltimo, -a
penurious [pə·ˈnʊr·i·əs] *adj form* **1.** (*stingy*) miserable **2.** (*poor*) paupérrimo, -a
penury ['pen·ju·ri] *n form* penuria *f,* miseria *f*
peony ['pi·ə·ni] <-ies> *n* BOT peonía *f*
people ['pi·pəl] I. *n* **1.** *pl* (*plural of person*) gente *f;* **city/country ~** gente de ciudad/de campo; **the beautiful ~** la gente guapa, la gente linda *AmL* **2.** (*nation, ethnic group*) pueblo *m;* **~'s democracy** democracia *f* popular; **~'s republic** república *f* popular; **the chosen ~** REL el pueblo elegido **3.** *pl* (*ordinary citizens*) ciudadanos, -as *m, f pl;* **of/by/for the ~** del/por/para el pueblo II. *vt* **~d by** poblado de
people mover *n* (*moving sidewalk*) cinta *f* mecánica, banda *f* eléctrica; (*rail vehicle*) tren *m* eléctrico rápido
pep [pep] I. *n inf* empuje *m,* energía *f;* **to be full of ~** estar lleno de vitalidad II. <-pp-> *vt* **to ~ sb up** animar a alguien, levantar el ánimo a alguien
pepper ['pep·ər] I. *n* **1.** (*spice*) pimienta *f;* **black/white ~** pimienta negra/blanca **2.** (*vegetable*) pimiento *m* II. *vt* **1.** (*add*

pepper) poner [*o* echar] pimienta a **2.** (*pelt*) **to ~ sb with bullets** acribillar a alguien a balas; *fig;* **to ~ sb with questions** acribillar a alguien a preguntas **3.** (*contain*) **to be ~ed with sth** (*speech, comments*) estar acribillado de algo; **to be ~ed with mistakes** estar lleno de errores

peppercorn ['pep·ər·kɔrn] *n* grano *m* de pimienta

pepper mill *n* molinillo *m* de pimienta

peppermint ['pep·ər·mɪnt] *n* **1.** (*mint plant*) menta *f* **2.** (*sweet*) caramelo *m* de menta

peppermint tea *n* té *m* de menta

pepperoni [pe,·pə·'roʊ·ni] *n* CULIN chorizo *m* picante

peppershaker *n* pimentero *m*

peppery ['pep·ə·ri] *adj* **1.** CULIN picante **2.** *fig* (*irritable*) cascarrabias *inv*

pep pill *n inf* estimulante *m,* anfeta *f*

pep talk *n inf* **to give sb a ~** dar ánimos a alguien

peptic ['pep·tɪk] *adj* péptico, -a

peptic ulcer *n* úlcera *f* péptica

per [pɜr] *prep* **1.** (*for a*) por; **$5 ~ pound/hour** $5 por libra; **$5 ~ hour** $5 la hora **2.** (*in a*) por, a; **100 miles ~ hour** 100 millas por hora **3.** *form* **as ~...** (*as stated in*) de acuerdo con...; (**as**) **~ account** según consta; **as ~ usual** como siempre

per annum *adv* al año, por año

per capita I. *adv* per cápita II. *adj* **~ consumption** consumo *m* per cápita; **~ income** ingresos *mpl* per cápita

perceivable [pər·'si·və·bəl] *adj* perceptible

perceive [pər·'siv] *vt* **1.** (*see*) ver; (*sense*) percibir, notar; **to ~ that...** percibir que... **2.** (*view, regard*) considerar; **how do the young ~ the old?** ¿qué piensan los jovenes de los viejos? **3.** (*understand*) comprender

percent [pər·'sent] *n* porcentaje *m;* **25 ~** 25 por ciento; **what ~...** ¿qué porcentaje...?

percentage [pər·'sen·tɪdʒ] *n* **1.** (*proportion*) porcentaje *m;* **what ~...?** ¿qué porcentaje...?; **to get a ~ of sth** recibir un tanto por ciento de algo **2.** (*advantage*) tajada *f inf* ▶ **to play the ~s** sopesar las posibilidades

percentage point *n* punto *m* porcentual

perceptible [pər·'sep·tə·bəl] *adj* perceptible

perception [pər·'sep·ʃən] *n* **1.** percepción *f* **2.** (*idea*) idea *f* **3.** (*insight*) perspicacia *f,* agudeza *f*

perceptive [pər·'sep·tɪv] *adj* perspicaz, agudo, -a

perch[1] [pɜrtʃ] I. <-es> *n* **1.** (*for birds*) percha *f* **2.** (*high location or position*) posición *f* privilegiada ▶ **to knock sb off his ~** bajar los humos a alguien II. *vi* (*person*) sentarse; (*bird*) posarse

perch[2] [pɜrtʃ] *n* perca *f*

percolate ['pɜr·kə·leɪt] I. *vt* filtrar, colar; (*coffee*) preparar (en una cafetera eléctrica) II. *vi* **1.** (*filter through*) filtrarse **2.** *fig* (*spread*) difundirse

percolator ['pɜr·kə·leɪ·ţər] *n* cafetera *f* eléctrica

percussion [pər·'kʌʃ·ən] I. *n* MUS percusión *f;* **to play ~** ser percusionista II. *adj* MUS de percusión

percussionist *n* MUS percusionista *mf*

perdition [pər·'dɪʃ·ən] *n* **1.** *liter* (*hell*) perdición *f* **2.** *fig* (*state of ruin*) desastre *m*

peregrine ['per·ɪ·grɪn] *n* peregrino, -a *m, f*

peregrine falcon *n* halcón *m* peregrino

peremptorily *adv* en tono perentorio, imperiosamente

peremptory [pə·'remp·tə·ri] *adj* **1.** (*person*) autoritario, -a; (*order, tone*) perentorio, -a, imperioso, -a **2.** LAW perentorio, -a

perennial [pə·'ren·i·əl] I. *n* planta *f* perenne II. *adj* **1.** BOT perenne **2.** (*constant*) constante

perfect[1] ['pɜr·fɪkt] I. *adj* perfecto, -a; (*calm*) total; (*opportunity*) ideal; (*silence*) absoluto, -a; **in ~ condition** en perfecto estado; **the ~ crime** el crimen perfecto; **a ~ gentleman** todo un señor; **to be a ~ stranger** ser un completo desconocido; **to have the ~ right to do sth** tener todo el derecho a hacer algo; **to be far from ~** estar (muy) lejos de ser perfecto; **to be a ~ match for sth** ir de maravilla con algo; **to be a ~ match for sb** ser la pareja perfecta para alguien II. *n* LING perfecto *m*

perfect[2] [pɜr·'fekt] *vt* perfeccionar

perfectible [pər·'fek·tə·bəl] *adj form* perfectible

perfection [pər·'fek·ʃən] *n* perfección *f;* **to do sth to ~** hacer algo a la perfección

perfectionist *n* perfeccionista *mf*

perfectly *adv* perfectamente; **~ clear** completamente claro; **~ happy** absolutamente contento; **to be ~ honest,...** para serte sincero,...; **to be ~ right** tener toda la razón

perfidious [pər·'fɪd·i·əs] *adj liter* pérfido, -a; **~ attack** ataque *m* a traición

perforate ['pɜr·fə·reɪt] *vt* perforar; (*ticket*) picar

perforated *adj* perforado, -a; **to have a ~ eardrum** tener una perforación de tímpano

perforation [,pɜr·fə·'reɪ·ʃən] *n* perforación *f*

perform [pər·'fɔrm] I. *vt* **1.** MUS, THEAT, TV interpretar **2.** (*do, accomplish*) realizar; **to ~ one's duty/a function** cumplir con su deber/una función; **to ~ miracles/wonders** hacer milagros/maravillas; **to ~ a task** llevar a cabo una tarea; **to ~ a trick** hacer un truco **3.** COMPUT ejecutar **4.** MED, SPORTS practicar II. *vi* **1.** THEAT actuar; MUS tocar **2.** (*operate*) funcionar

performance [pər·'fɔr·məns] *n* **1.** (*of play*) representación *f;* (*by individual actor*) actuación *f;* **to give a ~** hacer una representación; **to put on a ~ of a play** poner en escena la representación de una obra **2.** SPORTS actuación *f;* **high/low ~** AUTO alto/bajo rendimiento *m*

performance art *n* arte *m* performativo

performance level *n* **1.** (*degree of success*) nivel *m* de rendimiento **2.** ECON (*output*) rendimiento *m*

P

performance report *n* informe *m* de rendimiento

performer [pər·'fɔr·mər] *n* **1.** THEAT artista *mf;* **star** ~ estrella *f* **2.** (*achiever*) **top** ~ (*at work*) empleado, -a *m, f* modelo; **bad** ~ (*at school*) mal(a) estudiante *mf;* (*at work*) mal(a) trabajador(a) *m(f)*

perfume ['pɜr·fjum] I. *n* **1.** (*scented liquid*) perfume *m;* ~ **maker** perfumista *mf;* **to put on** ~ ponerse perfume **2.** (*fragrance*) fragancia *f* II. *vt* perfumar

perfunctory [pər·'fʌŋk·tə·ri] *adj* (*inspection*) superficial; (*reading*) por encima; (*mention*) de pasada; (*greeting, smile*) forzado, -a; (*examination*) rutinario, -a

pergola ['pɜr·gə·lə] *n* pérgola *f*

perhaps [pər·'hæps] *adv* quizá(s), tal vez

peril ['per·əl] *n form* peligro *m;* **to be in** ~ correr peligro; **at one's** ~ por su cuenta y riesgo; **at** [*o* **in**] ~ **of sth** en peligro por algo; **the** ~**s of sth** el peligro de algo

perilous ['per·ə·ləs] *adj form* peligroso, -a

perimeter [pə·'rɪm·ə·tər] *n* perímetro *m*

perimeter fence *n* cercado *m*

period ['pɪr·i·əd] I. *n* **1. a.** GEO período *m;* **in/over a** ~ **of sth** en/durante un período de algo **2.** ECON plazo *m;* **a fixed** ~ un plazo fijo; ~ **of grace** [*o* **grace** ~] plazo *m* de gracia **3.** SCHOOL (*lesson*) hora *f* **4.** (*distinct stage*) época *f* **5.** (*menstruation*) período *m,* regla *f;* **to have one's** ~ tener la regla **6.** LING punto *m* final II. *interj* ¡y punto! *inf*

period furniture *n* mobiliario *m* de época

periodic [ˌpɪr·i·'ad·ɪk] *adj* periódico, -a

periodical [ˌpɪr·i·'ad·ɪ·kəl] I. *n* (*general*) publicación *f* periódica; (*specific*) boletín *m* II. *adj* periódico, -a

periodic table *n* tabla *f* periódica (de los elementos)

peripheral [pə·'rɪf·ər·əl] I. *adj* **1.** (*importance, role*) secundario, -a **2. a.** ANAT, COMPUT periférico, -a II. *n* COMPUT periférico *m*

periphery [pə·'rɪf·ə·ri] <-ies> *n* periferia *f;* (*of society*) margen *m*

periscope ['per·ɪ·skoup] *n* periscopio *m*

perish ['per·ɪʃ] *vi liter* **1.** (*die*) perecer **2.** (*disappear: motivation, hope*) desaparecer; ~ **the thought!** ¡Dios nos libre!

perishable ['per·ɪʃ·ə·bəl] *adj* perecedero, -a *elev*

peritonitis [ˌper·ɪ·tə·'naɪ·t̬ɪs] *n* MED peritonitis *f inv*

perjure ['pɜr·dʒər] *vt* **to** ~ **oneself** perjurar(se)

perjurer ['pɜr·dʒər·ər] *n* perjuro, -a *m, f*

perjury ['pɜr·dʒə·ri] *n* perjurio *m*

perk [pɜrk] *n inf abbr of* **perquisite 1.** (*advantage*) ventaja *f* **2.** (beneficio *m*) extra *m*

◆ **perk up** I. *vi* **1.** (*cheer up*) alegrarse; **to** ~ **at sth** alegrarse por algo **2.** (*improve*) mejorar II. *vt* **1.** (*cheer up*) alegrar; (*make more lively*) animar **2.** (*raise*) **to** ~ **one's ears** aguzar las orejas

perky ['pɜr·ki] <-ier, -iest> *adj* alegre

perm [pɜrm] I. *n inf* (*permanent wave*) permanente *f,* permanente *m Méx* II. *vt* **to** ~ **one's hair, to have one's hair** ~**ed** hacerse la permanente

permafrost ['pɜr·mə·frɔst] *n* permafrost *m*

permanence ['pɜr·mə·nəns] *n,* **permanency** *n* permanencia *f*

permanent ['pɜr·mə·nənt] *adj* (*job*) fijo, -a; (*damage*) irreparable; (*exhibition, situation, position*) permanente; (*ink*) indeleble; (*relationship*) estable; (*tooth*) definitivo, -a

permanent wave *n* permanente *f,* permanente *m Méx*

permanganate [pər·'mæŋ·gə·neɪt] *n* CHEM permanganato *m*

permeable ['pɜr·mi·ə·bəl] *adj* permeable

permeate ['pɜr·mi·eɪt] I. *vt* (*liquid, smoke, smell*) impregnar II. *vi* **to** ~ **into/through sth** penetrar en/a través de algo

permissible [pər·'mɪs·ə·bəl] *adj* (*permitted*) permisible; (*acceptable*) tolerable

permission [pər·'mɪʃ·ən] *n* permiso *m*

permission slip *n* SCHOOL autorización por escrito que los padres firman para que su hijo no tome parte en una actividad escolar

permissive [pər·'mɪs·ɪv] *adj* permisivo, -a

permissiveness *n* permisividad *f*

permit¹ ['pɜr·mɪt] *n* **1.** permiso *m* (por escrito); **parking/building** ~ permiso *m* de aparcamiento/obras; **learner's** ~ *permiso que autoriza a aprendices a conducir acompañados de una persona con carnet;* **to hold a** ~ tener un permiso **2. fishing/gun/building** ~ licencia *f* de pesca/armas/construcción

permit² [pər·'mɪt] <-tt-> I. *vt* permitir; **I will not** ~ **you to go there** no te permito que vayas allí; **to** ~ **oneself sth** permitirse algo II. *vi* **weather** ~**ing** si hace buen tiempo, si el tiempo no lo impide; **if time** ~**s** si hay tiempo; **the law** ~**s no other interpretation** *form* la ley no acepta otra interpretación

permitted [pər·'mɪt̬·ɪd] *adj* permitido, -a

permutation [ˌpɜrm·ju·'teɪ·ʃən] *n form* MATH permutación *f*

pernicious [pər·'nɪʃ·əs] *adj* **1.** *form* (*harmful*) perjudicial **2.** MED pernicioso, -a

pernicious anemia *n* anemia *f* perniciosa

peroxide [pə·'rak·saɪd] I. *n* peróxido *m;* **hydrogen** ~ agua *f* oxigenada II. *vt* oxigenar

peroxide blonde *n* rubia *f* de bote

perp [pɜrp] *n sl abbr of* **perpetrator** autor (a) (de un crimen) *m*

perpendicular [ˌpɜr·pən·'dɪk·ju·lər] I. *adj* perpendicular II. *n* perpendicular *f*

perpetrate ['pɜr·pə·treɪt] *vt* (*crime*) perpetrar, cometer; (*error*) cometer

perpetration [ˌpɜr·pə·'treɪ·ʃən] *n form* perpetración *f*

perpetrator ['pɜr·pə·treɪ·tər] *n* autor (a) (de un crimen) *m*

perpetual [pər·'petʃ·u·əl] *adj* **1.** (*lasting forever*) perpetuo, -a **2.** (*repeated*) continuo, -a

perpetuate [pər·'petʃ·u·eɪt] *vt* perpetuar

perpetuity [ˌpɜr·pə·'tu·ə·t̬i] *n form* perpetuidad *f*; **in ~** *a.* LAW a perpetuidad
perplex [pər·'pleks] *vt* desconcertar
perplexed [pər·'plekst] *adj* perplejo, -a
perplexity [pər·'plek·sə·t̬i] <-ies> *n* perplejidad *f*
perquisite ['pɜr·kwɪ·zɪt] *n* (beneficio *m*) extra *m*
persecute ['pɜr·sɪ·kjut] *vt* **1.** *a.* POL perseguir **2.** (*harass*) molestar
persecution [ˌpɜr·sɪ·'kju·ʃən] *n* persecución *f*; **~ complex** manía *f* persecutoria
persecutor *n* perseguidor(a) *m(f)*
perseverance [ˌpɜr·sə·'vɪr·əns] *n* perseverancia *f*
persevere [ˌpɜr·sə·'vɪr] *vi* perseverar
persevering *adj* perseverante
Persia ['pɜr·ʒə] *n* Persia *f*
Persian **I.** *adj* persa **II.** *n* **1.** (*person*) persa *mf* **2.** LING persa *m*
Persian Gulf *n* Golfo *m* Pérsico
persist [pər·'sɪst] *vi* **1.** (*continue: cold, heat, rain*) continuar; (*habit, belief, doubts*) persistir **2.** (*person*) insistir
persistence [pər·'sɪs·təns] *n* **1.** (*of cold, belief*) persistencia *f* **2.** (*of person*) insistencia *f*
persistent [pər·'sɪs·tənt] *adj* **1.** (*cold, belief*) persistente **2.** (*person*) insistente
persnickety [pər·'snɪk·ə·t̬i] *adj pej* **1.** (*exacting*) puntilloso, -a; **to be ~ about sth** ser puntilloso con algo **2.** (*difficult*) que requiere minuciosidad
person ['pɜr·sən] <people *o form* -s> *n* **1.** (*human*) persona *f*; **as a ~** como persona; **per ~** por persona **2.** LING persona *f*; **first/second ~** primera/segunda persona
persona [pər·'soʊ·nə] *n* **1.** <-s *o* -nae> (*character*) personaje *m* **2.** <-s> (*image*) imagen *f*
personable ['pɜr·sə·nə·bəl] *adj* agradable
personage ['pɜr·sə·nɪdʒ] *n form* personaje *m*
personal ['pɜr·sə·nəl] *adj* **1.** (*property*) privado, -a; (*data, belongings, account*) personal **2.** (*direct, done in person*) en persona **3.** (*private: letter*) personal; (*question*) indiscreto, -a; (*matter*) privado, -a, personal; (*life*) privado, -a **4.** (*offensive: comment, remark*) ofensivo, -a; **to get ~** llevar las cosas al plano personal; **it's nothing ~** no es nada personal **5.** (*bodily, physical: appearance*) personal; (*hygiene*) íntimo, -a **6.** (*human*) **~ quality** calidad *f* humana
personal assistant *n* ayudante *mf* personal
personal computer *n* ordenador *m* personal, computadora *f* personal *AmL*
personality [ˌpɜr·sə·'næl·ə·t̬i] *n* <-ies> **1.** (*character*) personalidad *f* **2.** (*famous person*) personalidad *f*, figura *f*
personally *adv* **1.** (*in person*) personalmente **2.** (*as offensive*) **to take sth ~** ofenderse con [*o* por] algo **3.** (*referring to oneself*) **~...** personalmente... **4.** (*referring to sb's character*)

como persona; **I don't like him ~** no me gusta como persona; **she's not involved with him ~** no tiene una relación personal con él
personal pronoun *n* pronombre *m* personal
personalty ['pɜr·sə·nəl·t̬i] <-ies> *n* LAW bienes *mpl* muebles
personification [pər·ˌsan·ə·fɪ·'keɪ·ʃən] *n* personificación *f*; **he is the ~ of kindness** es la amabilidad personificada
personify [pər·'san·ə·faɪ] *vt* personificar
personnel [ˌpɜr·sə·'nel] *n* **1.** *pl* (*staff, employees*) personal *m* **2.** (*department*) departamento *m* de personal
personnel department *n* departamento *m* de personal
personnel director *n* director(a) *m(f)* de personal
personnel manager *n* jefe, -a *m, f* de personal
perspective [pər·'spek·tɪv] *n* perspectiva *f*; **you have to keep things in ~** no tienes que perder de vista la verdadera dimensión de las cosas; **to put a different ~ on things** cambiar el cariz de las cosas
perspicacious [ˌpɜr·spɪ·'keɪ·ʃəs] *adj form* perspicaz
perspicacity [ˌpɜr·spɪ·'kæs·ə·t̬i] *n form* perspicacia *f*
perspicuity [ˌpɜr·spɪ·'kju·ə·t̬i] *n form* perspicuidad *f*
perspicuous [pər·'spɪk·ju·əs] *adj form* perspicuo, -a
perspiration [ˌpɜr·spə·'reɪ·ʃən] *n* transpiración *f*; **beads of ~** gotas *fpl* de sudor
perspire [pər·'spaɪr] *vi* transpirar
persuade [pər·'sweɪd] *vt* convencer; **to ~ sb into sth** convencer a alguien de algo; **to ~ sb out of sth** disuadir a alguien de algo; **to ~ sb to do sth** convencer a alguien de que haga algo; **to ~ sb that...** convencer a alguien de que...
persuasion [pər·'sweɪ·ʒən] *n* **1.** (*act*) persuasión *f* **2.** (*conviction*) creencia *f*
persuasive [pər·'sweɪ·sɪv] *adj* (*person, manner*) persuasivo, -a; (*argument*) convincente
pert [pɜrt] *adj* **1.** (*nose, breasts*) respingón, -ona **2.** (*reply*) descarado, -a **3.** (*hat*) chic
pertain [pər·'teɪn] *vi* **to ~ to sth** concernir algo
pertinent ['pɜr·tən·ənt] *adj* pertinente; **to be ~ to sth** guardar relación con algo
perturb [pər·'tɜrb] *vt* perturbar
perturbation [ˌpɜr·tər·'beɪ·ʃən] *n form* perturbación *f*
Peru [pə·'ru] *n* Perú *m*
perusal [pə·'ru·zəl] *n form* lectura *f*; **he sent a copy of the report for their ~** envió una copia del informe para que lo examinaran
peruse [pə·'ruz] *vt form* (*read*) leer detenidamente; (*examine*) examinar
Peruvian [pə·'ru·vi·ən] **I.** *adj* peruano, -a **II.** *n* peruano, -a *m, f*
pervade [pər·'veɪd] *vt* (*attitude, idea*) dominar; (*smell, smoke*) invadir

pervasive [pər·'veɪ·sɪv] *adj* (*attitude, idea*) dominante; (*influence*) omnipresente; (*smell*) penetrante

perverse [pər·'vɜrs] *adj* **1.**(*deviant, perverted*) perverso, -a **2.**(*stubborn*) obstinado, -a **3.**(*contrary*) con tendencia a contradecir

perverseness *n* **1.**(*deviancy*) perversidad *f* **2.**(*stubbornness*) obstinación *f* **3.**(*contrariness*) tendencia *f* a contradecir

perversion [pər·'vɜr·ʒən] *n* **1.**(*sexual deviance*) perversión *f* **2.**(*corruption*) ~ **of justice** deformación *f* de la justicia; ~ **of the truth** distorsión *f* de la verdad

perversity [pər·'vɜr·sə·ti] <-ies> *n* **1.**(*wickedness*) perversidad *f* **2.**(*stubbornness*) obstinación *f*

pervert¹ ['pɜr·vɜrt] *n* (*sexual deviant*) pervertido, -a *m, f*

pervert² [pər·'vɜrt] *vt* pervertir; **to ~ the truth** distorsionar la verdad

perverted *adj* (*person, practice*) pervertido, -a

peseta [pə·'seɪ·tə] *n* (*currency*) peseta *f*

peso ['peɪ·soʊ] *n* (*currency*) peso *m*

pessary ['pes·ə·ri] <-ies> *n* **1.** MED (*contraceptive*) pesario *m* **2.**(*suppository*) supositorio *m* vaginal

pessimism ['pes·ə·mɪz·əm] *n* pesimismo *m*

pessimist *n* pesimista *mf*

pessimistic [,pes·ə·'mɪs·tɪk] *adj* pesimista; **to be ~ about sth** ser pesimista con respecto a algo

pest [pest] *n* **1.**(*destructive insect, animal*) plaga *f* **2.** *inf*(*annoying person*) pesado, -a *m, f*

pest control *n* (*of insects*) fumigación *f*; (*of rats*) desratización *f*

pester ['pes·tər] *vt* molestar

pesticide ['pes·tə·saɪd] *n* pesticida *m*

pestiferous [pe·'stɪf·ər·əs] *adj* pestilente

pestilent ['pes·tə·lənt] *adj*, **pestilential** [,pes·tə·'len·tʃəl] *adj* **1.**(*deadly*) mortal **2.**(*troublesome*) pesado, -a

pestle ['pes·əl] *n* mano *f* de mortero

pet [pet] **I.** *n* **1.**(*house animal*) animal *m* doméstico, mascota *f* **2.** *pej* (*favorite person*) mimado, -a *m, f*; **he's the teacher's ~** es el mimado del profesor **II.** *adj* **1. my ~ cat** el gato que tengo de mascota, mi gato **2.**(*favorite: project, theory*) favorito, -a **III.** <-tt-> *vi* besarse y acariciarse **IV.** <-tt-> *vt* **1.**(*caress*) acariciar **2.**(*pamper*) mimar

petal ['peʈ·əl] *n* BOT pétalo *m*

peter ['pi·tər] *vi* **to ~ out** (*trail, track, path*) desaparecer; (*conversation, interest*) decaer

Peter ['pi·tər] **to rob ~ to pay Paul** *prov* desnudar a un santo para vestir a otro *prov*

petite [pə·'tit] *adj* (*of woman*) menuda

petition [pə·'tɪʃ·ən] **I.** *n* **1.** POL petición *f* **2.** LAW demanda *f* **II.** *vi* **1.** POL **to ~ for sth** elevar una petición solicitando algo **2.** LAW **to ~ for divorce** presentar una demanda de divorcio **III.** *vt* POL elevar una petición a, peticionar *AmL*

petitioner *n* **1.** POL peticionario, -a *m, f* **2.** LAW demandante *mf*

pet peeve *n* tema *m* favorito (*del que uno se queja*)

petrel ['pet·rəl] *n* ZOOL petrel *m*

petri dish ['pi·tri·,dɪʃ] *n* plato *m* de Petri

petrifaction [,pet·rɪ·'fæk·ʃən] *n*, **petrification** [,pet·rɪ·fɪ·'keɪ·ʃən] *n* **1.** GEO petrificación *f* **2.**(*terror*) terror *m*

petrified *adj* **1.** GEO petrificado, -a **2.**(*terrified*) aterrorizado, -a

petrify ['pet·rɪ·faɪ] <-ies> **I.** *vi* GEO petrificarse **II.** *vt* **1.** GEO petrificar **2.**(*terrify*) aterrorizar

petrochemical [,pet·roʊ·'kem·ɪ·kəl] **I.** *n* producto *m* petroquímico **II.** *adj* petroquímico, -a

petrodollar ['pet·roʊ·,dal·ər] *n* petrodólar *m*

petroleum [pə·'troʊ·li·əm] *n* petróleo *m*, canfín *m AmC*

pet shop *n* ≈ pajarería *f*

petticoat ['peʈ·i·koʊt] *n* enagua *f*, combinación *f*, fondo *m Méx*

pettifogging ['peʈ·i·fag·ɪŋ] *adj pej* (*person*) puntilloso, -a; (*paperwork*) farragoso, -a; (*details*) insignificante

pettiness ['peʈ·i·nɪs] *n* **1.**(*small-mindedness*) mezquindad *f* **2.**(*triviality, insignificance*) nimiedad *f*

petting ['peʈ·ɪŋ] *n* (*stroking*) caricias *fpl*; (*sexual*) manoseo *m*

petting zoo *n* ≈ granja *f* de animales

petty ['peʈ·i] <-ier, -iest> *adj* **1.** *pej* (*detail, amount*) trivial, insignificante; (*person, attitude*) mezquino, -a **2.** LAW menor

petty cash *n* fondo *m* disponible para gastos menores

petty larceny *n* LAW hurto *m* menor

petty officer *n* NAUT suboficial *mf* de marina

petulant ['petʃ·ə·lənt] *adj* enfurruñado, -a *inf*

petunia [pə·'tun·jə] *n* petunia *f*

pew [pju] *n* banco *m* (de iglesia)

pewit ['pi·wɪt] *n* avefría *f*

pewter ['pju·tər] *n* peltre *m*

PG [,pi·'dʒi] *n abbr of* **parental guidance** película para menores acompañados

pg. *abbr of* **page** pág. *f*

pH [,pi·'eɪtʃ] pH

phalanx ['feɪ·læŋks] <-es *o* phalanges> *n form* falange *f*

phallic ['fæl·ɪk] *adj* fálico, -a

phallus ['fæl·əs] <-es *o* phalli> *n* falo *m*

phantasmal [fæn·'tæz·məl] *adj liter* **1.**(*imaginary*) ilusorio, -a **2.**(*ghost-like*) fantasmal

phantom ['fæn·təm] **I.** *n* fantasma *m* **II.** *adj* **1.**(*ghostly*) fantasmal **2.**(*imaginary*) ilusorio, -a

Pharaoh ['fer·oʊ] *n* faraón *m*

pharisaic [,fer·ɪ·'seɪ·ɪk] *adj*, **pharisaical** [,fer·ɪ·'seɪ·ɪ·kəl] *adj* farisaico, -a

pharisee ['fer·ɪ·si] *n* fariseo, -a *m, f*

pharmaceutic(al) [,far·mə·'su·ʈɪk] *adj* farmacéutico, -a

pharmaceutical I. *adj* farmacéutico, -a **II.** *n* ~ **s** fármacos *mpl*

pharmaceutics *n* farmacia *f*
pharmaceutics industry *n* industria *f* farmacéutica
pharmacist ['far·mə·sɪst] *n* farmacéutico, -a *m, f,* farmaceuta *mf Col, Ven*
pharmacology [ˌfar·mə·'kal·ə·dʒi] *n* farmacología *f*
pharmacopoeia [ˌfar·mə·'koʊ·'pi·ə] *n* farmacopea *f*
pharmacy ['far·mə·si] <-ies> *n* farmacia *f*
pharyngitis [ˌfær·ɪn·'dʒaɪ·tɪs] *n* faringitis *f*
pharynx ['fær·ɪŋks] <pharynges> *n* faringe *f*
phase [feɪz] I. *n* (*stage*) fase *f;* (*period*) etapa *f;* **to go through a** ~ pasar por una etapa; **to be in** ~ estar sincronizado; **to be out of** ~ estar desfasado II. *vt* 1. (*do in stages*) realizar por etapas 2. (*coordinate*) sincronizar
◆**phase in** *vt* introducir paulatinamente
◆**phase out** *vt* (*service*) retirar progresivamente; (*product*) dejar de producir paulatinamente
PhD [ˌpi·eɪtʃ·'di] *n abbr of* **Doctor of Philosophy** 1. (*award*) doctorado *m* 2. (*person*) Dr. *m,* Dra. *f*
pheasant ['fez·ənt] <-(s)> *n* faisán *m*
phenomena *n pl of* **phenomenon**
phenomenal *adj* (*success, achievement*) espectacular; (*strength*) increíble
phenomenon [fə·'nam·ə·nan] <phenomena *o* -s> *n* fenómeno *m*
phew [fju] *interj inf* ¡uf!
philander [fɪ·'læn·dər] *vi* 1. (*one affair*) tener una aventura (*especialmente extramarital*) con una mujer 2. (*several affairs*) ser un mujeriego
philanderer *n* mujeriego *m*
philanthropic [ˌfɪl·ən·'θrap·ɪk] *adj* filantrópico, -a
philanthropist [fə·'læn·θrə·pɪst] *n* filántropo, -a *m, f*
philanthropy [fə·'læn·θrə·pi] *n* filantropía *f*
philatelic [fɪl·ə·'tel·ɪk] *adj* filatélico, -a
philatelist [fɪ·'læt̬·ə·lɪst] *n* filatelista *mf*
philately [fɪ·'læt̬·ə·li] *n* filatelia *f*
philharmonic [ˌfɪl·har·'man·ɪk] *adj* filarmónico, -a
Philippines ['fɪl·ə·pinz] *npl* **the** ~ las Filipinas
Philistine ['fɪl·ɪ·stin] *pej* I. *n* filisteo, -a *m, f elev* II. *adj* filisteo, -a *elev*
philological [ˌfɪl·ə·'ladʒ·ɪ·kəl] *adj* filológico, -a
philologist [fɪ·'lal·ə·dʒɪst] *n* filólogo, -a *m, f*
philology [fɪ·'lal·ə·dʒi] *n* filología *f*
philosopher [fɪ·'las·ə·fər] *n* filósofo, -a *m, f*
philosophic [ˌfɪl·ə·'saf·ɪk] *adj,* **philosophical** [ˌfɪl·ə·'saf·ɪ·kəl] *adj* filosófico, -a
philosophize [fɪ·'las·ə·faɪz] *vi* filosofar
philosophy [fɪ·'las·ə·fi] *n* filosofía *f*
philter *n,* **philtre** ['fɪl·tər] *n* filtro *m*
phlebitis [flɪ·'baɪ·tɪs] *n* MED flebitis *f inv*
phlegm [flem] *n* flema *f*
phlegmatic [fleg·'mæt̬·ɪk] *adj* flemático, -a
phobia ['foʊ·bi·ə] *n* PSYCH fobia *f*
phoenix ['fi·nɪks] *n* fénix *m*

phone [foʊn] I. *n* teléfono *m;* **to hang up the** ~ colgar el teléfono; **to pick up the** ~ coger el teléfono; **by** ~ por teléfono; **to be on the** ~ estar hablando por teléfono II. *vt* llamar (por teléfono), telefonear III. *vi* llamar (por teléfono), telefonear
◆**phone around** *vi* hacer llamadas
◆**phone back** *vt* volver a llamar (por teléfono), volver a telefonear
◆**phone in** I. *vi* llamar (por teléfono), telefonear; **to** ~ **sick** llamar (por teléfono) para dar parte de enfermo II. *vt* llamar por teléfono, telefonear
◆**phone up** *vt* llamar (por teléfono), telefonear
phone book *n* guía *f* (telefónica), directorio *m Col, Méx*
phone booth <-es> *n* cabina *f* (telefónica)
phone call *n* llamada *f* (telefónica)
phone card *n* tarjeta *f* telefónica
phone-in *n* programa de radio o televisión en el que el público participa por teléfono
phoneme ['foʊ·nim] *n* LING fonema *m*
phone number *n* número *m* (de teléfono), teléfono *m*
phonetic [fə·'net̬·ɪk] *adj* fonético, -a; **the International Phonetic Alphabet** el Alfabeto Fonético Internacional; ~ **transcription** transcripción *f* fonética
phonetician [ˌfoʊ·nə·'tɪʃ·ən] *n* fonetista *mf*
phonetics [fə·'net̬·ɪks] *n* fonética *f*
phoney ['foʊ·ni] *adj, n s.* **phony**
phonic ['fan·ɪk] *adj* LING fónico, -a
phonology [fə·'nal·ə·dʒi] *n* fonología *f*
phony ['foʊ·ni] I. <-ier, -iest> *adj inf* (*person, address*) falso, -a; (*documents*) falsificado, -a II. *n* (*person*) farsante *mf*
phooey ['fu·i] *interj inf* ¡bobadas!
phosphate ['fas·feɪt] *n* fosfato *m*
phosphorescence [ˌfas·fə·'res·əns] *n* fosforescencia *f*
phosphorescent [ˌfas·fə·'res·ənt] *adj* fosforescente
phosphoric [fas·'fɔr·ɪk] *adj,* **phosphorous** ['fas·fər·əs] *adj* fosfórico, -a
phosphorus ['fas·fər·əs] *n* fósforo *m*
photo ['foʊ·t̬oʊ] <-s> *n inf abbr of* **photograph** foto *f*
photo album *n* álbum *m* de fotos
photo call *n* sesión *f* (protocolaria) de fotos
photocell ['foʊ·t̬oʊ·sel] *n* célula *f* fotoeléctrica
photocopier [ˌfoʊ·t̬oʊ·'kap·i·ər] *n* fotocopiadora *f*
photocopy ['foʊ·t̬oʊ·ˌkap·i] I. <-ies> *n* fotocopia *f;* **to make a** ~ **of sth** hacer una fotocopia de algo II. *vt* fotocopiar
photocopying store *n* fotocopistería *f*
photoelectric [ˌfoʊ·t̬oʊ·ɪ·'lek·trɪk] *adj* fotoeléctrico, -a; ~ **cell** célula *f* fotoeléctrica
photo finish *n* SPORTS foto *f* finish
photoflash *n* flash *m*
photogenic [ˌfoʊ·t̬oʊ·'dʒen·ɪk] *adj* fotogénico, -a

P

photograph ['foʊ·toʊ·græf] I. n fotografía f;
aerial ~ fotografía aérea; color/black-and-
white ~ fotografía en color/blanco y negro; to
take a ~ of sb sacar una fotografía de alguien
II. vt fotografiar III. vi to ~ well ser fotogénico, salir bien en las fotos inf
photograph album n álbum m de fotos
photographer [fə·'tag·rə·fər] n fotógrafo, -a
m, f; amateur ~ fotógrafo aficionado; ~'s
model modelo mf fotográfico, -a
photographic [,foʊ·tə·'græf·ɪk] adj fotográfico, -a
photography [fə·'tag·rə·fi] n fotografía f
photojournalism [,foʊ·toʊ·'dʒɜr·nə·lɪz·əm] n
fotoperiodismo m, periodismo m gráfico
photojournalist n reportero, -a m, f gráfico, -a
photometer [foʊ·'tam·ɪ·tər] n fotómetro m
photomontage [,foʊ·toʊ·man·'taʒ] n fotomontaje m
photon ['foʊ·tan] n fotón m
photo opportunity n breve momento reservado a la prensa para fotografiar a los participantes de un acontecimiento relevante
photo reporter n reportero, -a m, f fotográfico, -a
photosensitive [,foʊ·toʊ·'sen·sɪ·tɪv] adj foto-
sensible
photosetting ['foʊ·toʊ·,seṭ·ɪŋ] n ART fotocom-
posición f
Photostat ['foʊ·toʊ·stæt] <-tt-> vt hacer
copias de material gráfico con una Photostat
photosynthesis [,foʊ·toʊ·'sɪn·θɪ·sɪs] n fotosíntesis f
phrasal verb [,freɪ·zəl·'vɜrb] n LING verbo m
con partícula
phrase [freɪz] I. n frase f; (idiomatic
expression) expresión f; verb/noun phrase
sintagma verbal/nominal; to have a good
turn of ~ ser muy elocuente II. vt to ~ sth
well/badly expresar algo bien/mal
phrase book n libro m de frases
phraseology [,freɪ·zi·'al·ə·dʒi] n fraseología f
pH factor n valor m del pH
phrenetic [frɪ·'neṭ·ɪk] adj s. frenetic
phys ed [,fɪz·'ed] n abbr of physical education educación f física
physical ['fɪz·ɪ·kəl] I. adj físico, -a; ~ attraction atracción f física; to be in poor ~ condition estar en bajo estado de forma; to have a
~ disability sufrir una discapacidad física;
~ exercise ejercicio m físico II. n MED reconocimiento m médico
physical education n educación f física
physically adv (attractive) físicamente; (dangerous) desde el punto de vista físico
physical therapist n fisioterapeuta mf
physical therapy n fisioterapia f
physician [fɪ·'zɪʃ·ən] n médico, -a m, f
physicist ['fɪz·ɪ·sɪst] n físico, -a m, f; (student)
estudiante mf de física
physics ['fɪz·ɪks] I. n física f II. adj físico, -a
physiognomy [,fɪz·i·'an·ə·mi] n fisonomía f
physiological [,fɪz·i·ə·'ladʒ·ɪ·kəl] adj fisio-

lógico, -a
physiologist n fisiólogo, -a m, f; (student)
estudiante mf de fisiología
physiology [,fɪz·i·'al·ə·dʒi] n fisiología f
physique [fɪ·'zik] n físico m
pianist ['pi·æn·ɪst] n pianista mf
piano [pi·'æn·oʊ] <-s> n piano m; to play the
~ tocar el piano
piazza [pɪ·'at·sə] n plaza f
picaresque [,pɪk·ə·'resk] adj LIT picaresco, -a
piccolo ['pɪk·ə·loʊ] <-s> n flautín m
pick [pɪk] I. vt 1. (select) elegir; to ~ sb for sth
elegir a alguien para algo; to ~ sth at random
elegir algo al azar; to ~ a fine time to do sth
iron escoger un buen momento para hacer
algo; to ~ one's way moverse con cuidado 2. (harvest: fruit, vegetables) recoger
3. (touch) tocar; to ~ one's nose hurgarse la
nariz; to ~ one's teeth limpiarse los dientes
con un palillo; to ~ holes in sth fig encontrar
fallos a algo 4. MUS (guitar) tocar 5. (steal)
robar; to ~ a lock forzar una cerradura; to ~
sb's pocket robar algo del bolsillo de alguien;
to ~ sb's brains fig aprovecharse de los
conocimientos de alguien 6. (provoke) to ~ a
fight (with sb) buscar camorra (con alguien)
II. vi to ~ and choose tardar en escoger,
escoger con sumo cuidado III. n 1. (selection)
elección f; (of people) selección f; to take
one's ~ elegir; to have one's ~ poder elegir;
the ~ of the bunch el mejor del grupo
2. (pickax) pico m; with ~s and shovels con
pico y pala 3. (for teeth) palillo m (de dientes)
◆ pick at vt insep 1. (toy with: food) juguetear
con 2. (handle) manosear; (scratch) rascar
3. (criticize) to ~ sb/sth fastidiar a alguien/
algo
◆ pick off vt 1. (shoot) abatir (a tiros) 2. fig
(take the best) escoger lo mejor 3. (pull off)
separar; to pick an apple off the tree coger
una manzana del árbol
◆ pick on vt insep 1. (victimize) meterse con
2. (select) to ~ sb for sth escoger a alguien
para algo
◆ pick out vt 1. (choose) elegir 2. (recognize)
distinguir
◆ pick over vt ir revolviendo y examinando
◆ pick up I. vt 1. (lift) levantar; to ~ the
phone coger el teléfono; to pick oneself up
ponerse de pie; to pick oneself up off the
floor levantarse del suelo; to ~ the pieces fig
empezar de nuevo 2. (get) conseguir; (conversation) captar; to ~ a bargain conseguir una
ganga; to ~ an illness contagiarse con una
enfermedad, pillar una enfermedad inf; to ~
speed coger velocidad; to ~ the bill [o tab]
inf pagar la cuenta 3. (collect) recoger; to pick
sb up recoger a alguien 4. (clean: one's room,
the living room) ordenar 5. (buy) ordenar
6. (detect: noise, signal) detectar 7. (learn)
aprender 8. sl (sexually) to pick sb up ligarse
a alguien 9. inf (halt) detener; (arrest) arrestar;
the police picked him up for speeding la

policía le detuvo por exceso de velocidad
10. *inf* (*earn*) ganar II. *vi* 1. (*improve*) mejorar; (*numbers*) ir a mejor; MED reponerse
2. (*continue*) continuar; **to ~ where one left
off** reanudar donde uno lo dejó 3. **she picked
up and left** cogió y se fue

pickax *n*, **pickaxe** ['pɪk·æks] *n* (*tool*) pico *m*,
azadón *m* de pico

picker *n* recolector(a) *m(f)*

picket ['pɪk·ɪt] I. *n* 1. (*stake*) estaca *f*
2. (*striker*) *a*. MIL piquete *m* II. *vt* (*in strike*)
formar piquete en

picket fence *n* valla *f*

picket line *n* piquete *m;* **to be on the ~** participar en un piquete; **to cross the ~** no hacer
caso de un piquete

picking *n* selección *f*

pickings ['pɪk·ɪŋz] *npl* sobras *fpl*

pickle ['pɪk·əl] I. *n* 1. (*pickled item*) encurtido
m 2. (*pickled cucumber*) pepinillo *m* en vinagre al eneldo ▶ **to be in a** (**pretty**) **~** *inf*
estar en un (buen) berenjenal II. *vt* (*vegetables*) conservar en vinagre; (*fish*) conservar
en escabeche

pickled *adj* 1. (*vegetables*) encurtido, -a; (*fish*)
en escabeche 2. *fig, sl* (*drunk*) borracho, -a; **to
get ~** emborracharse

picklock ['pɪk·lak] *n* 1. (*thief*) ladrón, -ona *m*,
f 2. (*instrument*) ganzúa *f*

pick-me-up *n inf* tónico *m;* (*drink*) bebida *f*
estimulante

pickpocket ['pɪk·pak·ɪt] *n* carterista *mf*, bolsista *mf* AmC, Méx

pickup *n* 1. *inf* (*collection*) recogida *f*, recolección *f* 2. (*increase*) aumento *m* 3. (*pickup
truck*) camioneta *f* con plataforma 4. (*part of
record player*) brazo *m* del tocadiscos 5. *sl*
(*partner for sex*) ligue *m*

pickup point *n* punto *m* de recogida

pickup truck *n* camioneta *f* con plataforma

picky ['pɪk·i] <-ier, -iest> *adj inf* criticón, -ona;
to be a ~ eater ser caprichoso para comer

picnic ['pɪk·nɪk] I. *n* picnic *m;* **to take a ~**
hacer un picnic; **to go on a ~** ir de picnic; **to
be a ~** parecer agradable; **to be no ~** *fig* no ser
nada agradable II. <-ck-> *vi* ir de picnic

picnicker *n* excursionista *mf*

picnic lunch *n* (comida *f* para un) picnic *m*

picnic site *n* lugar *m* para hacer picnics

pictogram ['pɪk·tə·græm] *n* pictograma *m*

pictorial [pɪk·'tɔr·i·əl] *adj* (*form, method*) pictórico, -a; (*book, brochure*) ilustrado, -a

picture ['pɪk·tʃər] I. *n* 1. (*image*) imagen *f;*
(*painting*) pintura *f;* (*drawing*) ilustración *f;* **to
draw a ~** hacer un dibujo; **to paint a ~** pintar
un cuadro; **as pretty as a ~** muy bonito
2. (*photo*) fotografía, foto *f;* **to take a ~** sacar
una foto; **satellite ~** fotografía por satélite
3. (*film*) película *f;* **to make a ~** hacer una
película; **to go to the ~s** ir al cine 4. (*mental
image*) imagen *f* 5. *fig* (*description*) representación *f;* **to paint a ~ of sth** representar algo;
to paint a very black ~ pintar un panorama

muy negro ▶ **a ~ is worth a thousand words**
prov una imagen vale más que mil palabras; **to
be in the ~** estar al corriente; **to get the ~**
entender; **to keep sb in the ~** mantener a alguien al tanto; **to put sb in the ~** poner a alguien en antecedentes II. *vt* imaginarse;
(*depict*) representar; **to ~ oneself...** imaginarse...

picture book *n* libro *m* ilustrado

picture frame *n* marco *m* (para cuadro)

picture gallery *n* galería *f* de arte

picture library *n* pinacoteca *f*

picture postcard *n* (tarjeta *f*) postal *f*

picture puzzle *n* rompecabezas *m inv*

picturesque [ˌpɪk·tʃə·'resk] *adj* 1. (*scenic*) pintoresco, -a 2. (*language*) vívido, -a

picture tube *n* tubo *m* de imagen

picture window *n* ventanal *m*

piddle ['pɪd·əl] *vi* 1. *inf* (*urinate*) mear, orinar
2. (*waste time*) **to ~ around** perder el tiempo

piddling ['pɪd·lɪŋ] *adj* de poca monta; **the ~
sum of $5** la insignificante suma de 5$

pidgin ['pɪdʒ·ɪn] *n* LING pidgin *m*

pie [paɪ] *n* tarta *f*, pay *m AmS* ▶ **it's ~ in the
sky** es como prometer la luna; (**as**) **easy as ~**
pan comido; **to eat humble ~** tragarse las
palabras

piebald ['paɪ·bɔld] *adj* (*horse*) pío, -a

piece [pis] *n* 1. (*small unit: of wood, metal,
food*) trozo *m;* (*of text*) sección *f;* (*of land*) terreno *m;* (*of broken glass*) fragmento *m;* **a ~ of
paper** (*scrap*) un trozo de papel; (*sheet*) una
hoja; **in one ~** en una sola pieza; **in ~s** en
pedazos; **to break sth to/in ~s** hacer algo
pedazos; **to tear sth into ~s** desgarrar algo;
(**all**) **in one ~** (todo) de una pieza; **~ by ~**
pieza por pieza; **to go** (**all**) **to ~s** (*suffer
trauma*) sufrir un ataque de nervios; (*collapse,
break*) venirse abajo 2. (*item, one of set*) unidad *f;* **~ of luggage** bulto *m;* **~ of clothing**
prenda *f* de vestir; **~ of equipment** aparato *m*
3. (*in games*) pieza *f* 4. (*with mass nouns*) **a ~
of advice** un consejo; **a ~ of evidence** una
prueba; **a ~ of information** una información;
a ~ of news una noticia 5. ART, MUS pieza *f;*
PUBL anuncio *m;* **a ~ of writing** un texto
6. (*coin*) moneda *f;* **a 50 cent ~** una moneda
de 50 centavos 7. *sl* (*gun*) **to carry a ~** llevar
una pipa ▶ **to get a ~ of the action** (*profits*)
obtener una parte del beneficio; (*excitement*)
pasarlo bien; **to be a ~ of cake** *inf* ser pan
comido; **to want a ~ of the pie** querer parte
del pastel; **to give sb a ~ of one's mind** *inf*
decir cuatro verdades a alguien; **to say one's ~**
decir lo que uno quiere decir

◆**piece together** *vt* (*reconstruct*)
reconstruir; **to ~ evidence** atar cabos

piecemeal ['pis·mil] I. *adv* poco a poco II. *adj*
que va poco a poco

piece number *n* número *m* de pieza

piece price *n* precio *m* por unidad

piece rate *n* precio *m* por unidad

piecework ['pis·wɜrk] *n* trabajo *m* a destajo; **to**

do ~ trabajar a destajo
pieceworker *n* trabajador(a) *m(f)* a destajo
pied [paɪd] *adj* (*patchy*) pío, -a
pie-eyed [ˌpaɪ·'aɪd] *adj sl* (*drunk*) **to be** ~ estar como una cuba
pier [pɪr] *n* **1.** (*at the water*) muelle *m*, malecón *m* **2.** ARCHIT (*pillar*) columna *f*, pilar *f*; (*buttress*) contrafuerte *m*
pierce [pɪrs] **I.** *vt* (*perforate*) perforar; **to** ~ **a hole in sth** agujerear algo; **to have one's ears** ~**d** hacerse agujeros en las orejas **II.** *vi* (*drill*) **to** ~ **into sth** penetrar en algo; **to** ~ **through sth** atravesar algo
piercing I. *adj* **1.** (*wind*) cortante; **it's** ~ **cold** hace un frío que pela **2.** (*eyes, gaze, look*) penetrante; (*question, reply, wit*) punzante; (*sarcasm*) agudo, -a **3.** (*cry*) desgarrador(a) **II.** *n* piercing *m*
piety ['paɪ·ə·ti] *n* piedad *f*
piffle ['pɪf·əl] *n* disparates *mpl*
piffling ['pɪf·lɪŋ] *adj* insignificante
pig [pɪg] *n* **1.** ZOOL cerdo *m*, cochino *m*, puerco *m*, marrano *m* **2.** *inf* (*person*) cochino, -a *m, f*; **to be a** ~ ser un cerdo; **to be a** ~ **to sb** portarse mal con alguien **3.** *offensive, sl* (*policeman*) madero *m*; **the** ~**s** la pasma, la chota *Méx* ▸ **to buy a** ~ **in a poke** cerrar un trato a ciegas; **to sell a** ~ **in a poke** dar gato por liebre; **to make a** ~ **of oneself** ponerse como un cerdo
◆ **pig out** <-gg-> *vi sl* ponerse morado; **to** ~ **out on sth** comer demasiado de algo
pigeon ['pɪdʒ·ən] *n* **1.** (*bird*) paloma *f* **2.** *fig* (*easy prey*) presa *f* fácil
pigeonhole ['pɪdʒ·ən·hoʊl] **I.** *n* casilla *f*; **to put sb in a** ~ encasillar a alguien **II.** *vt* **to** ~ **sb/sth** encasillar a alguien/algo; **to** ~ **sb as sth** poner la etiqueta de algo a alguien
pigeon-toed ['pɪdʒ·ən·toʊd] *adj* **to be** ~ tener los pies torcidos hacia dentro
piggery ['pɪg·ə·ri] <-ies> *n* **1.** AGR pocilga *f* **2.** (*gluttony*) glotonería *f*
piggish ['pɪg·ɪʃ] *adj* puerco, -a
piggy ['pɪg·i] <-ies> *n inf* cerdito *m*
piggyback ['pɪg·i·bæk] *n* **to carry sb/ride** ~ llevar/montar a caballito; **to give a child a** ~ **ride** llevar a un niño a caballito
piggy bank *n* alcancía *f*, *en forma de cerdito*
pigheaded [ˌpɪg·'hed·ɪd] *adj* testarudo, -a
pig iron *n* hierro *m* bruto
pig Latin *n juegos de palabras que consisten en tomar la inicial de cada palabra y colocarla al final, seguida de una vocal*
piglet ['pɪg·lɪt] *n* cochinillo *m*
pigment ['pɪg·mənt] *n* pigmento *m*
pigmentation [ˌpɪg·men·'teɪ·ʃən] *n* pigmentación *f*
Pigmy ['pɪg·mi] **I.** <-ies> *n* **1.** (*short person*) pigmeo, -a *m, f* **2.** (*unimportant person*) enano, -a *m, f* **II.** *adj* ZOOL enano, -a
pigskin ['pɪg·skɪn] *n* **1.** (*leather*) piel *f* de cerdo **2.** *inf* (*a football*) balón *m* de fútbol americano; **the** ~ el cuero

pigsty ['pɪg·staɪ] *n a. fig, pej* pocilga *f*
pigswill ['pɪg·swɪl] *n* bazofia *f*
pigtail ['pɪg·teɪl] *n* (*one of two braids*) trenza *f*; **to have one's hair in** ~**s** llevar el pelo trenzado
pike[1] [paɪk] *n* (*fish*) lucio *m*
pike[2] [paɪk] *n* (*weapon*) pica *f*
pike[3] [paɪk] *n* (*highway*) autopista *f*
pilaster [pɪ·'læs·tər] *n* pilastra *f*
pilchard ['pɪl·tʃərd] *n* sardina *f*
pile [paɪl] **I.** *n* **1.** (*stack*) pila *f* **2.** (*heap*) montón *m*; **to have** ~**s of sth** *inf* tener montones de algo; **to make a** ~ *fig, inf* hacer una fortuna **3.** ELEC pila *f* **4.** ARCHIT pila *f* **5.** (*of carpet*) pelo *m* **II.** *vt* amontonar; **to** ~ **sth high** apilar algo
◆ **pile in** *vi* ~! ¡todos dentro, que nos vamos!
◆ **pile on** *vt* **1.** (*enter*) entrar desordenadamente **2.** (*heap*) amontonar; **to pile sth on sth** amontonar algo encima de algo **3.** *inf* (*exaggerate*) **to** (**really**) **pile it on** exagerar (mucho)
◆ **pile up I.** *vi* **1.** (*accumulate*) acumularse **2.** (*form a pile*) apilarse **II.** *vt* amontonar
pile driver *n* martinete *m*
piles *npl inf* almorranas *fpl*
pileup ['paɪl·ʌp] *n* accidente *m* múltiple
pilfer ['pɪl·fər] *vt* ratear
pilfering *n* hurtos *mpl*
pilgrim ['pɪl·grɪm] *n* peregrino, -a *m, f*
pilgrimage ['pɪl·grə·mɪdʒ] *n* peregrinación *f*
pill [pɪl] *n* **1.** pastilla *f*, píldora *f*; **the** ~ (*contraception*) la píldora; **to be on the** ~ estar tomando la píldora; **to pop** ~**s** drogarse con pastillas **2.** *inf* (*pesky person*) pesado, -a *m, f* ▸ **to be a bitter** ~ **to swallow** ser un trago amargo; **to sweeten** [*o* **sugar**] **the** ~ dorar la píldora
pillage ['pɪl·ɪdʒ] **I.** *vt* saquear **II.** *vi* realizar un saqueo **III.** *n* saqueo *m*
pillar ['pɪl·ər] *n* **1.** ARCHIT pilar *m*, columna *f*; **a** ~ **of flame/smoke** una columna de fuego/humo **2.** *fig* (*of support*) sostén *m*, puntal *m*; **to be a** ~ **of strength** ser firme como una roca; **a** ~ **of society** un pilar de la sociedad ▸ **to chase sb from** ~ **to post** seguir a alguien por todas partes
pillbox ['pɪl·baks] *n* **1.** (*for tablets*) pastillero *m* **2.** MIL fortín *m*
pillion ['pɪl·jən] **I.** *n* (*on motorcycle*) asiento *m* de atrás **II.** *adv* **to ride/sit** ~ montarse/sentarse en el asiento de atrás
pillory ['pɪl·ə·ri] **I.** <-ie-> *vt* **to** ~ **sb/sth** poner en ridículo a alguien/algo **II.** *n* picota *f*
pillow ['pɪl·oʊ] *n* **1.** (*for bed*) almohada *f* **2.** (*cushion*) cojín *m*
pillowcase *n*, **pillow cover** *n*, **pillowslip** *n* funda *f* de almohada
pilot ['paɪ·lət] **I.** *n* **1.** AVIAT piloto *mf* **2.** NAUT práctico *mf* **3.** TV programa *m* piloto **4.** TECH (*flame*) piloto *m* **II.** *vt* **1.** (*plane*) pilotar **2.** (*boat*) guiar **3.** COM (*product*) desarrollar; **to** ~ **a bill** encargarse de un proyecto de ley
pilot boat *n* bote *m* del práctico
pilot burner *n* **1.** (*on boiler*) piloto *m* (de una

caldera) **2.** (*flame*) piloto *m*
pilot fish *n* pez *m* piloto
pilothouse *n* NAUT cabina *f* del timón
pilotless *adj* sin piloto
pilot light *n* piloto *m*
pilot plant *n* planta *f* piloto
pilot program *n* programa *m* piloto
pilot's license *n* licencia *f* de vuelo
pilot study *n* estudio *m* piloto
pilot survey *n* estudio *m* experimental
pilot test *n* prueba *f* piloto
pimento [pɪˈmen·toʊ] <-s> *n* pimiento *m*
pimp [pɪmp] **I.** *n* proxeneta *mf,* chulo *m* (de putas), *inf* **II.** *vi* hacer de chulo
pimple [ˈpɪm·pəl] *n* grano *m*
pimply [ˈpɪm·pli] <-ier, -iest> *adj* lleno, -a de granos
pin [pɪn] **I.** *n* **1.** (*needle*) alfiler *m*; MIL (*on grenade*) arandela *f*; **tie ~** alfiler *m* de corbata **2.** (*brooch*) prendedor *m* **3.** *pl, fig* (*legs*) patas *fpl* ▶ **to have ~s and needles** sentir un hormigueo; **you could have heard a ~ drop** se podía oír hasta el vuelo de una mosca **II.** <-nn-> *vt* **1.** (*attach using pin*) **to ~ sth on** prender algo con un alfiler; **to ~ back one's ears** *fig* escuchar atentamente **2.** (*associate with: crime*) **to ~ sth on sb** atribuir algo a alguien
◆ **pin down** *vt* **1.** (*define*) precisar **2.** (*locate*) concretar **3.** (*pressure to decide*) presionar (a alguien) para que se defina **4.** (*restrict movement*) inmovilizar
◆ **pin together** *vt* unir; **to pin papers together** grapar papeles
◆ **pin up** *vt* (*attach using pins*) recoger con alfileres; (*on the wall*) fijar con chinchetas; **to ~ one's hair** recogerse el pelo con horquillas
PIN [pɪn] *n abbr of* **personal identification number** PIN *m* (*número de identificación personal*)
pinafore [ˈpɪn·ə·fɔr] *n* **1.** (*apron*) delantal *m* **2.** (*dress*) pichi *m*
pinafore dress *n* pichi *m*
pinball [ˈpɪn·bɔl] *n* **to play ~** jugar a los petacos
pinball machine *n* (máquina *f* de) petacos *mpl*
pincers [ˈpɪn·sərz] *npl* **1.** ZOOL pinzas *fpl* **2.** (*tool*) tenazas *fpl*
pinch [pɪntʃ] **I.** *vt* **1.** (*with fingers*) pellizcar; **to ~ oneself** *fig* pellizcarse para ver si no se está soñando **2.** (*be too tight*) apretar; **the shoes ~ my feet** los zapatos me aprietan **3.** *inf* (*steal*) birlar **II.** *vi* **1.** (*with fingers*) estrujar **2.** (*boots, shoes, slippers*) apretar **III.** *n* **1.** (*nip*) pellizco *m*; **to give sb a ~** dar un pellizco a alguien; **in a ~** si realmente es necesario; **to feel the ~** pasar apuros **2.** (*small quantity*) pizca *f*
pinched [pɪntʃt] *adj* demacrado, -a
pincushion [ˈpɪn·ˌkʊʃ·ən] *n* acerico *m*
pine¹ [paɪn] *n* (*tree, wood*) pino *m*
pine² [paɪn] *vi* **1.** (*waste away*) **to ~ (away)** languidecer **2.** (*long for*) **to ~ for sb** suspirar por alguien

pineal [ˈpɪn·i·əl] *adj* pineal
pineal gland *n* glándula *f* pineal
pineapple [ˈpaɪn·æp·əl] *n* (*fruit*) piña *f*
pinecone *n* (*from pine tree*) piña *f*
pine forest *n* pinar *f*
pine grove *n* pinar *m*
pine needle *n* aguja *f* de pino
pine nut *n* piñón *m*
pine tree *n* pino *m*
pinfeather *n* cañón *m* (*pluma del plumaje natal*)
ping [pɪŋ] **I.** *n* (*sound: of bell*) tintín *m*; (*of glass, metal*) sonido *m* metálico **II.** *vi* tintinear; (*click*) hacer clic
Ping-Pong® [ˈpɪŋ·ˌpɑŋ] *n inf* ping-pong *m*
pinhead [ˈpɪn·hed] *n* **1.** (*part of pin*) cabeza *f* de alfiler **2.** *sl* (*simpleton*) cabeza *f* de chorlito
pinhole *n* agujero *m* muy pequeño
pinion¹ [ˈpɪn·jən] *vt* **1.** (*bird*) ala *f* **2.** (*hold down*) inmovilizar, maniatar; **she was ~ed against the wall** estaba contra la pared sin poderse mover
pinion² [ˈpɪn·jən] *n* TECH piñón *m*
pink [pɪŋk] **I.** *n* **1.** (*color*) rosa *m* **2.** BOT clavelina *f* ▶ **to be in the ~** rebosar de salud **II.** *adj* rosado, -a
pinkie [ˈpɪŋ·ki] *n inf* dedo *m* meñique
pinking shears *npl* tijeras *fpl* dentadas
pinko [ˈpɪŋ·koʊ] <-s *o* -es> *n pej, sl* POL rojo, -a *m, f*
pink slip *n* aviso *m* de la terminación de un contrato de trabajo
pinnacle [ˈpɪn·ə·kəl] *n* **1.** ARCHIT (*tower*) pináculo *m* **2.** (*of mountain*) pico *m* **3.** *fig* cúspide *f*
pinpoint [ˈpɪn·pɔɪnt] **I.** *vt* (*location, reason*) indicar con toda precisión; **to ~ the cause of sth** señalar la causa de algo **II.** *adj* exacto, -a; **~ accuracy** gran precisión *f*
pinprick [ˈpɪn·prɪk] *n* pinchazo *m*
pinstripe [ˈpɪn·straɪp] **I.** *adj* de raya diplomática **II.** *n* (*stripe*) raya *f* fina; (*suit*) traje *m* de raya diplomática
pint [paɪnt] *n* pinta *f* (*0,47 l*); **a ~ of beer/milk** una pinta de cerveza/leche
pintsize(d) [ˈpaɪnt·saɪz(d)] *adj inf* pequeño, -a
pinup [ˈpɪn·ʌp] *n* **1.** (*poster*) póster *m* (*de una persona atractiva*) **2.** (*man*) chico *m* de póster; (*girl*) pin-up *f*
pioneer [ˌpaɪ·əˈnɪr] **I.** *n* pionero, -a *m, f; fig* pionero, -a *m, f* **II.** *vt* ser pionero en
pioneering *adj* innovador(a), pionero, -a
pious [ˈpaɪ·əs] *adj* **1.** REL piadoso, -a **2.** *iron* piadoso, -a; **~ intentions** intenciones *fpl* piadosas; **~ fraud** fraude piadoso
pip¹ [pɪp] *n* BOT pepita *f*
pip² [pɪp] **I.** *n* (*sound*) pitido *m* **II.** <-pp-> *vi* (*hatch*) romper el cascarón
pipe [paɪp] **I.** *n* **1.** TECH (*tube*) tubo *m*; (*smaller*) caño *m*; (*for gas, water*) cañería *f*, tubería *f* **2.** (*for smoking*) pipa *f*, cachimba *f* AmL; **to light one's ~** encenderse la pipa; **put that in your ~ and smoke it** *fig* ¡chúpate eso!

3. MUS (*wind instrument*) caramillo *m;* (*in organ*) cañón *m;* ~ **s** gaita *f* **II.** *vt* **1.** (*transport*) transportar por tuberías; **to ~ music in** poner música en (algún lugar) **2.** (*speak shrilly*) decir con voz estridente **III.** *vi* trinar; (*very loudly*) hablar muy alto

◆ **pipe down** *vi inf* (*be quiet*) callarse; (*become quieter*) calmarse

◆ **pipe up** *vi* decir inesperadamente

pipe cleaner *n* limpiapipas *m inv*

pipe dream *n* sueño *m* imposible

pipe fitter *n* fontanero, -a *m, f*

pipeline ['paɪp·laɪn] *n* tubería *f;* **oil** ~ oleoducto *m;* **gas** ~ gasoducto *m;* **to be in the** ~ *fig* estar tramitándose

piper ['paɪ·pər] *n* gaitero, -a *m, f* ► **he who pays the** ~ **calls the** <u>tune</u> *prov* quien paga, manda

piping ['paɪ·pɪŋ] *n* **1.** FASHION ribete *m* **2.** (*pipes*) tubería *f*

piping hot *adv* bien caliente

pip-squeak ['pɪp·skwik] *n inf* fantoche *m*

piquant ['pi·kənt] *adj* **1.** (*food*) picante **2.** (*intriguing*) intrigante

pique [pik] **I.** *n* resentimiento *m* **II.** *vt* **1.** (*annoy*) ofender **2.** (*arouse*) **to ~ sb's curiosity/interest** despertar la curiosidad/el interés de alguien

piracy ['paɪ·rə·si] *n* NAUT, COM piratería *f;* **software** ~ piratería *f* de software

pirate ['paɪ·rət] **I.** *n* pirata *m* **II.** *adj* pirata; ~ **copy** copia *f* pirata; ~ **video** vídeo *m* pirata **III.** *vt* piratear

pirouette [ˌpɪr·u·'et] **I.** *n* pirueta *f* **II.** *vi* hacer piruetas

Pisces ['paɪ·siz] *n* Piscis *m*

piss [pɪs] *vulg* **I.** *n* meada *f;* **to take a** ~ mear; **to have to take a** ~ tener ganas de mear **II.** *vi* mear **III.** *vt* **to ~ one's pants** mearse encima

◆ **piss off** *vulg sl* **I.** *vi* ~ **!** (*go away!*) ¡largo! **II.** *vt* **to piss sb off** (*make angry*) cabrear a alguien, emputar a alguien *Méx*

pissed [pɪst] *adj vulg sl,* **pissed off** *adj sl* **to be** ~ (*angry*) estar de mala leche [*o* emputado *Col*]

pistachio [pɪ·'stæʃ·i·ou] <-s> *n* pistacho *m,* pistache *m Méx*

pistil ['pɪs·tɪl] *n* pistilo *m*

pistol ['pɪs·təl] *n* pistola *f;* **to hold a** ~ **to sb's head** *fig* poner a alguien entre la espada y la pared

pistol shot *n* pistoletazo *m*

piston ['pɪs·tən] *n* TECH pistón *m*

piston engine *n* motor *m* de pistón

piston ring *n* aro *m* de pistón

pit¹ [pɪt] **I.** *n* **1.** (*in ground*) hoyo *m;* (*on metal*) muesca *f;* (*on face*) marca *f;* **in the** ~ **of one's stomach** en la boca del estómago **2.** (*mine*) mina *f;* **to go down the** ~ bajar a la mina; **to work in the** ~ **s** trabajar en la mina; *fig* REL; **the** ~ el infierno **3. the** ~ **s** *pl, fig, inf* lo peor **4.** *inf* (*messy place*) lobera *f* **5.** THEAT (*seating area*) patio *m* de asientos; (*orchestral area*)

platea *f* **6. the** ~ **s** *pl* SPORTS los boxes **II.** <-tt-> *vt* **to be** ~ **ted** (**with sth**) tener marcas (formadas por algo)

pit² [pɪt] <-tt-> **I.** *n* (*of fruit*) hueso *m* **II.** *vt* CULIN deshuesar

pita (**bread**) ['pi·tə] *n* pan *m* de pita

pitapat ['pɪt·ə·pæt] *adv, n s.* **pitterpatter**

pitch¹ [pɪtʃ] **I.** *n* **1.** (*in baseball*) lanzamiento *m* **2.** (*in cricket*) área *f* **3.** (*movement of ship*) cabezada *f* **4.** (*slope*) grado *m* de inclinación; **low/steep** ~ pendiente *f* suave/pronunciada **5.** (*volume*) volumen *m;* **to be at fever** ~ estar muy emocionado **6.** MUS, LING tono *m* **7.** (*spiel*) rollo *m;* **sales** ~ labia *f* para vender; **to make a** ~ soltar un rollo **II.** *vt* **1.** (*throw*) lanzar; **to ~ sb into a situation** meter a alguien en una situación; **to be** ~ **ed** (**headlong**) **into despair** estar sumido en la desesperación **2.** SPORTS (*throw*) tirar **3.** (*fix level of sound*) **this tune is** ~ **ed** (**too**) **high/low** esta afinación es (demasiado) alta/baja **4.** (*direct at: speech, advertisement*) **to ~ sth at sb** diseñar algo para alguien **5.** (*set up*) **to ~ camp/a tent** montar el campamento/una tienda (de campaña) **6.** (*sell forcefully: product*) vender (de forma agresiva) **III.** *vi* **1.** (*fall headlong*) caerse de morros *inf* **2.** (*boat*) cabecear **3.** SPORTS (*throw baseball*) lanzar **4.** (*slope*) inclinarse

◆ **pitch in** *vi inf* contribuir

◆ **pitch into** *vt* **1.** (*attack verbally*) arremeter contra **2.** (*begin enthusiastically*) emprender enérgicamente

◆ **pitch out** *vt* tirar

pitch² [pɪtʃ] *n* (*bitumen*) brea *f*

pitch-black [ˌpɪtʃ·'blæk] *adj* (*extremely dark*) negro, -a [*o* oscuro, -a] como la boca de un lobo; (*very black*) muy negro, -a

pitched battle *n* batalla *f* campal

pitched roof *n* tejado *m* a dos aguas

pitcher¹ ['pɪtʃ·ər] *n* (*large jug*) cántaro *m;* (*smaller*) jarra *f*

pitcher² ['pɪtʃ·ər] *n* SPORTS (*in baseball*) lanzador(a) *m(f)*

pitchfork ['pɪtʃ·fɔrk] *n* (*farming tool*) horca *f*

pitch pine *n* pino *m* tea

piteous ['pɪt·i·əs] *adj* patético, -a; **a ~ sight** una escena patética

pitfall ['pɪt·fɔl] *n* escollo *m*

pith [pɪθ] *n* **1.** BOT médula *f* **2.** *fig* (*main point*) meollo *m;* (*substance of speech*) esencia *f*

pith helmet *n* salacot *m*

pithy ['pɪθ·i] <-ier, -iest> *adj* (*remark, summary, phrase*) sucinto, -a

pitiable ['pɪt·i·ə·bəl] *adj s.* **pitiful**

pitiful ['pɪt·ɪ·fəl] *adj* **1.** (*terrible*) lamentable; ~ **conditions** condiciones *fpl* lamentables; **a ~ sight** una escena patética **2.** (*unsatisfactory*) insatisfactorio, -a; ~ **excuse** excusa *f* pobre

pitiless ['pɪt·ɪ·lɪs] *adj* despiadado, -a

piton ['pi·tan] *n* (*in mountain climbing*) pitón *m*

pit stop *n* **1.** (*in racing*) parada *f* en boxes **2.** *fig* (*quick stop*) parada *f* rápida

pittance ['pɪt·əns] *n* miseria *f;* pavada *f CSur;*
to live on a ~ vivir de una renta miserable
pitter-patter ['pɪt̬·ər·pæt̬·ər] I. *adv* **his heart
went ~** su corazón empezó a palpitar a gran
velocidad II. *n* (*of feet*) paso *m* ligero; (*of
heart*) latido *m;* (*of rain*) golpeteo *m*
pituitary (**gland**) [pɪ·'tu·ə·ter·i] *n* glándula *f*
pituitaria
pity ['pɪt̬·i] I. *n* 1. (*compassion*) compasión *f;*
in ~ por piedad; **to feel ~ for sb** compadecerse de alguien; **to take ~ on sb** apiadarse de
alguien; **for ~'s sake** ¡por piedad! 2. (*shame*)
to be a ~ ser una pena; (**it's a**) **~ that...** (es
una) lástima que...; **what a ~!** ¡qué pena!
II. <-ies, -ied> *vt* compadecerse de
pitying *adj* compasivo, -a
pivot ['pɪv·ət] I. *n* 1. TECH eje *m* 2. (*focal point*)
punto *m* central, pivote *m;* **to be the ~ of sth**
ser el eje de algo; (*person*) ser el centro de algo
II. *vi* pivotar; **to ~ around** girar; **to ~ around
sth** *a. fig* girar en torno a algo; **to ~ 90
degrees** dar un giro de 90 grados; **to ~ on sth**
(*depend on*) depender de
pivotal ['pɪv·ə·t̬əl] *adj* fundamental
pixel ['pɪk·səl] *n* COMPUT pixel *m,* píxel *m*
pixie *n*, **pixy** ['pɪk·si] <-ies> *n* LIT duende *m*
pizza ['pit·sə] *n* pizza *f*
placard ['plæk·ard] *n* pancarta *f*
placate ['pleɪ·keɪt] *vt* 1. (*soothe*) aplacar
2. (*appease*) apaciguar
placatory ['pleɪ·kə·tɔr·i] *adj form* 1. (*calming*)
apaciguador(a) 2. (*appeasing, conciliatory*)
conciliador(a)
place [pleɪs] I. *n* 1. (*location, area*) lugar *m;*
~ of birth lugar de nacimiento; **~s of interest**
lugares de interés; **~ of refuge** refugio *m;*
people in high ~s gente *f* bien situada; **to be
in ~** estar en su sitio; *fig* estar listo; **to do sth
in ~** hacer algo en el acto; **if I were in your
~,...** yo en tu lugar...; **in ~ of sb/sth** en vez de
alguien/algo; **to not be the ~ to do sth** no ser
el lugar apropiado para hacer algo; **this is no ~
to bring up your children** éste no es un lugar
apropiado para criar a tus hijos; **it is not your
~ to say that** no eres quién para decir eso
2. *inf* (*house*) casa *f;* **at my ~** en mi
casa 3. (*building*) edificio *m* 4. (*commercial
location*) local *m* 5. (*position*) posición *f;* **to
lose one's ~** (*in book*) perder la página; **to
take first/second ~** quedar en primer/
segundo lugar; **in the first ~** primero; **in the
second ~** segundo; **a ~ among the best
directors** un lugar entre los mejores directores
6. (*seat*) sitio *m;* (*in theater*) localidad *f;* **is this
~ taken?** ¿está ocupado este sitio?; **to change
~s with sb** cambiar el sitio con alguien; **to
save sb a ~** guardar un sitio a alguien; **to set a
~ at the table** poner un cubierto en la mesa
7. (*in organization*) plaza *f;* **she has got a ~ at
the university** ha obtenido una plaza en la
universidad 8. MATH **decimal ~** decimal *m*
9. *inf* (*in location*) **any ~** en/a cualquier sitio;
every ~ en todas partes; **some ~** (a) algún

sitio; **no ~** en ningún sitio ▸ **a ~ in the sun**
una situación ventajosa; **to fall into ~** encajar;
to go ~s *inf* (*become successful*) llegar lejos;
to know one's ~ saber cuál es el lugar de uno;
to put sb in his/her ~ poner a alguien en su
sitio; **all over the ~** por todas partes; **to feel
out of ~** sentirse fuera de lugar; **a ~ for everything and everything in its ~** un sitio para
cada cosa y cada cosa en su sitio II. *vt* 1. (*position, put*) colocar; **to ~ sth somewhere** colocar algo en un sitio; **to ~ an advertisement in
the newspaper** poner un anuncio en el periódico; **to ~ a comma/period** poner una
coma/un punto; **to ~ sth on the agenda**
apuntar algo en la agenda; **we are well ~d to
see the match** estamos en un buen sitio para
ver el partido 2. (*impose*) imponer; **to ~ an
embargo on sth** prohibir algo; **to ~ a limit on
sth** poner un límite a algo; **to ~ sb under
arrest** arrestar a alguien; **to ~ sb under surveillance** poner a alguien bajo vigilancia
3. (*ascribe*) poner; **to ~ the blame on sb**
echar la culpa a alguien; **to ~ one's hopes on
sb/sth** poner sus esperanzas en alguien/algo;
to ~ importance on sb/sth conceder importancia a alguien/algo; **to ~ emphasis on sth**
hacer énfasis en algo; **to ~ one's faith in sb**
depositar su confianza en alguien 4. (*arrange
for*) hacer; **to ~ an order for sth** hacer un
pedido de algo; **to ~ a bet** hacer una apuesta;
to ~ sth at sb's disposal poner algo a disposición de alguien 5. (*appoint to a position*) **to ~
sb in charge** (**of sth**) poner a alguien a cargo
(de algo); **to ~ sth under the control of sb**
poner algo bajo el control de alguien; **to ~ sb
in jeopardy** poner a alguien en peligro; **to ~
sb under pressure** someter alguien a presión;
to ~ sb on (**the**) **alert** alertar a alguien; **to ~
sth above sth** poner algo por encima de algo;
to be ~d first/second SPORTS quedar en
primer/segundo lugar 6. (*employ*) colocar
7. (*identify*) reconocer; **I can't ~ him** [*o his
face*] su cara me suena, pero no la puedo situar
III. *vi* SPORTS clasificarse
placebo [plə·'si·bou] <-s> *n a. fig* placebo *m*
place card *n* tarjeta *f* (indicadora del puesto
que se ocupa)
place kick *n* SPORTS tiro *m* libre
place mat *n* salvamanteles *m inv*
placement ['pleɪs·mənt] *n* colocación *f*
place name *n* topónimo *m*
placenta [plə·'sen·tə] <-s *o* -ae> *n* MED placenta *f*
placid ['plæs·ɪd] *adj* plácido, -a
plagiarism ['pleɪ·dʒə·rɪz·əm] *n* plagio *m*
plagiarist ['pleɪ·dʒə·rɪst] *n* plagiario, -a *m, f*
plagiarize ['pleɪ·dʒə·raɪz] I. *vt* plagiar; **to ~
sth from sth** plagiar algo de algo II. *vi* hacer
un plagio; **to ~ from sth** hacer un plagio de
algo
plague [pleɪg] I. *n* peste *f;* (*infestation of
insects*) plaga *f;* (*source of annoyance*) pesadez *f;* **the ~** (*bubonic plague*) la peste; **to**

P

avoid sb like the ~ huir de alguien como de la peste II. *vt* fastidiar; **to** ~ **sb for sth** acosar a alguien por algo
plaice [pleɪs] *inv n* platija *f*
plaid [plæd] I. *n* tela *f* a cuadros II. *adj* de tartán; ~ **skirt** falda *f* escocesa
plain [pleɪn] I. *adj* 1.sencillo, -a; (*one color*) de un solo color; (*without additions*) sin aditivos; ~ **yogurt** yogur *m* natural 2.(*uncomplicated*) fácil; **the** ~ **folks** el pueblo llano; ~ **and simple** liso y llano 3.(*clear, obvious*) evidente; **it is** ~ **that...** es evidente que...; **to be** ~ **enough** estar lo suficientemente claro; **to make sth** ~ dejar algo claro; **to make oneself** ~ (**to sb**) hacerse entender (por alguien); **to be** ~ **with sb** ser franco con alguien; **to be as** ~ **as the nose on your face** estar más claro que el agua 4.(*mere, pure*) puro, -a; **the** ~ **truth** la pura verdad 5.(*not pretty*) sin atractivo; **a** ~ **girl** una chica más bien fea II. *adv inf* (*downright*) y punto; ~ **awful** horrible III. *n* 1. GEO llanura *f*; **the** ~**s** *pl* las llanuras; **the great Plains** las grandes llanuras (norteamericanas) 2.(*knitting stitch*) punto *m* de media
plainclothes LAW I. *n* (*of policeman*) ropa *f* de paisano II. *adj* (*policeman*) de paisano
plainclothesman *n* LAW policía *mf* vestido, -a de paisano [*o* de civil]
plainly [ˈpleɪn·li] *adv* 1.(*simply*) simplemente 2.(*clearly*) claramente; (*obviously*) evidentemente; **to be** ~ **visible** ser muy visible 3.(*undeniably*) sin duda
plainness [ˈpleɪn·nɪs] *n* 1.(*unattractiveness*) falta *f* de atractivo 2.(*simplicity*) sencillez *f* 3.(*obviousness*) evidencia *f*
plain sailing *n fig* **to be** ~ ser cosa de coser y cantar
plainspoken [ˌpleɪnˈspoʊ·kən] *adj* franco, -a
plaintiff [ˈpleɪn·tɪf] *n* LAW demandante *mf*
plaintive [ˈpleɪn·tɪv] *adj* lastimero, -a
plait [plæt] I. *n* trenza *f* II. *vt* trenzar III. *vi* hacer trenzas
plan [plæn] I. *n* 1.(*scheme, program*) plan *m*; **to draw up a** ~ elaborar un plan; **to go according to** ~ ir de acuerdo con lo previsto; **to change** ~**s** cambiar de planes; **to have** ~**s** tener planes; **do you have any** ~**s for this weekend?** ¿tienes planes para este fin de semana?; **to make** ~**s for sth** hacer planes para algo 2. FIN, ECON (*policy*) seguro *m*; **healthcare** ~ seguro *m* médico; **savings** ~ plan *m* de ahorro 3.(*diagram*) plano *m*; **street** ~ callejero *m* II.<-nn-> *vt* 1.(*work out in detail*) planificar; (*prepare*) preparar; ~**ned economy** economía *f* planificada; **to** ~ **sth for sb** preparar algo para alguien 2.(*intend*) proponerse; **to** ~ **to do sth** proponerse hacer algo III.<-nn-> *vi* 1.(*prepare*) hacer proyectos; **to** ~ **carefully** hacer proyectos detallados 2.(*reckon with*) **to** ~ **on sth** tener pensado algo; **can I** ~ **on your being there?** ¿puedo contar con que estarás allí?
plane¹ [pleɪn] I. *n* 1.(*level surface*) nivel *m*;

MATH plano *m* 2.(*level of thought*) nivel *m* (intelectual) II. *vi* planear III. *adj* plano, -a; MATH llano, -a; ~ **angle** ángulo *m* plano
plane² [pleɪn] *n* (*airplane*) avión *m*; **by** ~ en avión
plane³ [pleɪn] I. *n* (*tool*) cepillo *m* (de carpintero) II. *vt* cepillar
plane⁴ [pleɪn] *n* (*tree*) plátano *m*
plane crash *n* accidente *m* de avión
planet [ˈplæn·ɪt] *n* planeta *m*; ~ **Earth** la Tierra; ~ **Jupiter/Venus** el planeta Júpiter/Venus; **to be on a different** ~ *fig* estar en otro mundo
planetarium [ˌplæn·ɪˈter·i·əm] <-s *o* -ria> *n* planetario *m*
planetary [ˈplæn·ɪ·ter·i] *adj* planetario, -a; ~ **motion** movimiento *m* planetario
plane ticket *n* billete *m* de avión
plane tree *n* plátano *m*
plank [plæŋk] *n* 1.(*long board*) tabla *f*; NAUT tablazón *m* 2.(*of policy, ideology*) puntal *m*
planking *n* tablas *fpl*
plankton [ˈplæŋk·tən] *n* plancton *m*
planner *n* planificador(a) *m(f)*; **city** ~ urbanista *mf*
planning *n* planificación *f*; **city** ~ planificación urbanística; **environmental** ~ proyectos *mpl* medioambientales; **at the** ~ **stage** en la etapa de planificación
planning board *n* comisión *f* planificadora
plant [plænt] I. *n* 1. BOT planta *f* 2.(*factory*) fábrica *f* 3.(*machinery*) maquinaria *f* 4.(*misleading evidence*) **the drugs were a** ~ habían colocado las drogas para inculparlo; (*spy*) infiltrado, -a *m, f* II. *vt* 1. AGR (*put in earth*) plantar; **to** ~ **sth with sth** sembrar algo de algo 2.(*put*) colocar; **to** ~ **oneself somewhere** *inf* meterse en algún sitio; **to** ~ **one's feet on the ground** plantar los pies en el suelo, poner los pies sobre la tierra; **to** ~ **a bomb** poner una bomba; **to** ~ **a secret agent** introducir a un agente secreto 3. *inf* (*incriminate*) **to** ~ **evidence on sb** colocar pruebas para incriminar a alguien III. *adj* vegetal; **the** ~ **kingdom** el reino vegetal; ~ **life** vida *f* vegetal
plantain [ˈplæn·tɪn] *n* (*fruit, tree*) plátano *m*
plantation [plænˈteɪ·ʃən] *n* plantación *f*; (*of trees*) arboleda *f*
planter [ˈplæn·tər] *n* 1.(*plantation owner*) hacendado, -a *m, f* 2.(*plant holder*) maceta *f*
plaque [plæk] *n* 1.(*on building*) placa *f* 2. MED sarro *m*
plash [plæʃ] I. *n* (*splash*) salpicadura *f*; (*sound*) chapoteo *m* II. *vi* **to** ~ **about** (*play*) chapotear
plasma [ˈplæz·mə] *n* plasma *m*
plaster [ˈplæs·tər] I. *n a.* MED yeso *m* II. *vt* 1.(*wall, ceiling*) enyesar 2. *fig, inf* (*put all over*) llenar
plasterboard [ˈplæs·tər·bɔrd] *n* cartón *m* de yeso (y fieltro)
plaster cast *n* 1. MED escayola *f* 2. ART vaciado *m*

plastered *adj sl* (*drunk*) borracho, -a; **to get ~** emborracharse
plasterer *n* yesero, -a *m, f*
plaster of Paris *n* escayola *f*
plastic ['plæs·tık] I. *n* 1. (*material*) plástico *m* 2. ~s *pl* (*manufacturing sector*) sector *m* de los plásticos 3. *inf* (*credit card*) tarjeta *f* (de crédito) II. *adj* 1. (*made from plastic*) de plástico 2. *pej* (*artificial*) artificial 3. ART (*malleable*) ~ **arts** artes *fpl* plásticas 4. *fig* (*impressionable*) influenciable
plastic bag *n* bolsa *f* de plástico
plastic bomb *n* bomba *f* plástica
plastic bullet *n* bala *f* de goma
plastic explosive *n* explosivo *m* plástico
plasticity [plæ·'stıs·ə·ţi] *n* plasticidad *f*
plastic money *n* dinero *m* plástico
plastics industry *n* sector *m* de los plásticos
plastic surgery *n* cirugía *f* plástica
plate [pleıt] I. *n* 1. (*dinner plate*) plato *m* 2. (*panel, sheet*) lámina *f;* **steel ~** lámina de acero 3. AUTO **license ~** (placa *f* de la) matrícula *f* 4. TYPO lámina *f* 5. (*layer of metal*) capa *f;* **gold ~** capa de oro 6. (*picture in book*) ilustración *f* ▶ **to have a lot on one's ~** tener muchos asuntos entre manos II. *vt* **to ~ sth with gold/silver** chapar algo en oro/plata
plateau [plæ·'toʊ] <-x *o* -s> *n* meseta *f*
plated *adj* (*coated in metal*) chapeado, -a; (*jewelry*) chapado, -a
plateful ['pleıt·fʊl] *n* plato *m*
plate glass *n* vidrio *m*
platelet ['pleıt·lət] *n* plaqueta *f*
plate rack *n* portaplatos *m inv*
plate warmer *n* calentador *m* de platos
platform ['plæt·fɔrm] *n* 1. *a.* COMPUT plataforma *f* 2. RAIL andén *m;* **railroad ~** andén de estación de trenes 3. (*stage*) escenario *m* 4. (*means for expressing view*) medio *m* 5. POL (*policy*) programa *m* electoral 6. ~**s** (*shoes*) plataformas *fpl*
platform shoes *npl* zapatos *mpl* de plataforma
plating *n* enchapado *m;* **gold/silver ~** chapado *m* de oro/de plata
platinum ['plæt·nəm] *n* platino *m*
platitude ['plæţ·ə·tud] *n* perogrullada *f*
platonic [plə·'tan·ık] *adj* platónico, -a; **~ love** amor *m* platónico
platoon [plə·'tun] *n* MIL pelotón *m*
platter ['plæţ·ər] *n* 1. (*large dish*) fuente *f* 2. (*food*) plato *m* fuerte ▶ **to give sth to sb on a ~** servir algo a alguien en bandeja
platypus ['plæţ·ı·pəs] <-es> *n* ornitorrinco *m*
plausibility [ˌplɔ·zə·'bıl·ə·ţi] *n* plausibilidad *f*
plausible ['plɔ·zə·bəl] *adj* plausible
play [pleı] I. *n* 1. (*recreation*) juego *m;* **to be at ~** estar en juego; **to do sth in ~** hacer algo en broma; **it's only in ~** sólo es broma 2. SPORTS juego *m;* **to be in/out of ~** estar en/fuera de juego 3. SPORTS (*move*) jugada *f;* **foul ~** juego sucio; **to make a bad/good ~** hacer una mala/buena jugada 4. THEAT obra *f* de teatro; **one-act ~** obra de un acto; **radio ~**

emisión *f* dramática 5. (*free movement*) juego *m;* **to allow** [*o* **give**] **sth full ~** dar rienda suelta a algo 6. (*interaction*) juego *m;* **to bring sth into ~** poner algo en juego; **to come into ~** entrar en juego; **the police suspect foul ~** la policía sospecha que se ha cometido un delito ▶ **to make a ~ for sth** intentar conseguir algo II. *vi* 1. *a.* SPORTS jugar; **to ~ for a team** jugar en un equipo; **to ~ fair/rough** jugar limpio/sucio 2. (*perform*) actuar; **to ~ to a full house** llenar un teatro 3. MUS tocar 4. *inf* (*be received*) **to ~/not ~ well with sb** tener una buena/mala acogida en/entre alguien III. *vt* 1. (*participate in game, sport*) jugar; **to ~ bridge/soccer** jugar al bridge/al fútbol; **to ~ a card** jugar una carta; **to ~ a match/a round** jugar un partido/una ronda 2. (*perform a role*) interpretar, hacer el papel de; **to ~ the clown** [*o* **fool**] hacer el payaso 3. MUS (*piano, guitar, saxophone*) tocar 4. (*CD, tape, video, DVD*) poner; **do you have to ~ the music so loud?** ¿es necesario que pongas la música tan alta? 5. (*perpetrate: joke*) gastar ▶ **to ~ it safe** ir a lo seguro [*o* a la fija]
◆ **play along** *vi* **to ~ with sb** seguir la corriente a alguien
◆ **play around** *vi* 1. (*play*) jugar 2. (*commit adultery*) **to ~ with sb** tener un lío con alguien 3. (*experiment*) **to ~ with sth** ensayar algo de varias maneras 4. (*tamper*) **to ~ with sth** manosear algo
◆ **play at** *vt* 1. (*pretend*) **to ~** (**being**) **sth** jugar a (ser) algo 2. (*do for amusement*) **to ~** (**being**) **sth** hacer como que (se es) algo; **she is playing at being a student** hace como que estudia 3. *pej* (*do*) **what are you playing at?** ¿a qué viene esto?
◆ **play back** *vt* poner
◆ **play down** *vt* quitar importancia a
◆ **play off** I. *vi* jugar un partido de desempate II. *vt* **to play sb off against sb** oponer a dos personas
◆ **play on** I. *vt* 1. (*exploit*) **to ~ sb's feelings/weakness** aprovecharse de los sentimientos/la debilidad de alguien 2. (*phrase, word*) jugar con II. *vi* (*keep playing*) SPORTS, GAMES seguir jugando; MUS seguir tocando
◆ **play out** *vt* representar; **to ~ one's fantasies** convertir sus fantasías en realidad
◆ **play through** *vt* tocar
◆ **play up** I. *vt* (*exaggerate: problem, difficulty*) exagerar II. *vi inf* **to ~ to sb** (*flatter*) dar coba a alguien, echar cepillo a alguien, hacer la barba a alguien
◆ **play upon** *vt* **to ~ sb's feelings/weakness** aprovecharse de los sentimientos/la debilidad de alguien
◆ **play with** *vt* 1. *a. fig* (*play*) jugar 2. (*manipulate nervously*) juguetear; **to ~ one's food** jugar con la comida 3. (*consider*) **to ~ an idea** dar vueltas a una idea
playable ['pleı·ə·bəl] *adj* (*pitch*) que se puede jugar

P

play-act ['pleɪ·ækt] *vi* **1.** THEAT actuar **2.** *fig* hacer teatro

playback ['pleɪ·bæk] *n* (*of tape*) reproducción *f*

playbill *n* THEAT **1.** (*poster*) cartel *m* **2.** (*program*) programa *m*

playboy ['pleɪ·bɔɪ] *n* playboy *m*

play date *n* **to have a ~** quedar para jugar

Play-Doh® ['pleɪ·doʊ] *n* plastilina *f*

player ['pleɪ·ər] *n* **1.** SPORTS jugador(a) *m(f)*; **card ~** jugador(a) *m(f)* de cartas; **soccer ~** futbolista *mf*; **tennis ~** tenista *mf* **2.** MUS instrumentista *mf*; **cello ~** violoncelista *mf*; **flute ~** flautista *mf*; **oboe ~** oboísta *mf* **3.** THEAT actor *m*, actriz *f* **4.** (*playback machine*) **cassette ~** casete *m*; **CD ~** reproductor *m* de CD; **record ~** tocadiscos *m inv* **5.** *sl* (*important person*) peso *m* pesado

playful ['pleɪ·fəl] *adj* **1.** (*full of fun*) juguetón, -ona; **the children were in a ~ mood** los niños tenían ganas de jugar **2.** (*comment, tone*) de guasa; **he's only being ~** sólo está bromeando

playground ['pleɪ·graʊnd] *n* **1.** (*at school*) patio *m*; (*in park*) campo *m* de recreo **2.** *fig* (*resort*) lugar *m* de recreo

playgroup ['pleɪ·grup] *n* guardería *f*

playhouse ['pleɪ·haʊs] *n* **1.** (*theater*) teatro *m* **2.** (*miniature house*) casa *f* de muñecas

playing card *n* carta *f*, naipe *m*

playing field *n* terreno *m* de juego

playmate ['pleɪ·meɪt] *n* compañero, -a *m, f* de juegos

playoff ['pleɪ·ɔf] *n* desempate *m*; **~ match** partido *m* de desempate; **the ~s** las eliminatorias *fpl*, los playoffs *mpl*

playpen ['pleɪ·pen] *n* parque *m*

playroom ['pleɪ·rum] *n* cuarto *m* de jugar

playsuit ['pleɪ·sut] *n* (*for baby*) pelele *m*

plaything ['pleɪ·θɪŋ] *n a. fig* juguete *m*

playtime ['pleɪ·taɪm] *n* SCHOOL recreo *m*

playwright ['pleɪ·raɪt] *n* dramaturgo, -a *m, f*

plaza ['pla·zə] *n* **1.** (*open square*) plaza *f* **2.** (*shopping center*) (**shopping**) **~** centro *m* comercial

plea [pli] *n* **1.** (*appeal*) petición *f*, súplica *f*; **to make a ~ for help/mercy** pedir ayuda/clemencia **2.** LAW alegato *m*; **to enter a ~ of guilty/not guilty** declararse culpable/inocente **3.** *form* (*excuse*) pretexto *m*

plea-bargaining *n acuerdo táctico entre fiscal y defensa para agilizar los trámites judiciales y reducir la pena*

plead [plid] <-ed *o* pled, -ed *o* pled> I. *vi* **1.** (*implore, beg*) implorar, suplicar; **to ~ for forgiveness/justice** suplicar perdón/justicia; **to ~ with sb** (**to do sth**) suplicar a alguien (que haga algo) **2.** LAW **to ~ guilty/innocent** (**to a charge**) declararse culpable/inocente (de un cargo) II. *vt* **1.** LAW **to ~ sb's case** defender el caso de alguien; **to ~ insanity** alegar enajenación mental **2.** (*claim as pretext*) pretextar; **to ~ ignorance of sth** pretextar su ignorancia

en algo **3.** (*argue for*) **to ~ sb's cause** defender la causa de alguien; **to ~ one's suit** *form* pedir la mano de alguien

pleading ['pli·dɪŋ] I. *n* **1.** (*entreaty, appeal*) súplicas *fpl* **2.** LAW alegato *m* II. *adj* (*look, tone*) suplicante

pleasant ['plez·ənt] *adj* **1.** (*pleasing*) agradable; **what a ~ surprise!** ¡qué agradable sorpresa!; **have a ~ journey!** ¡buen viaje!; **~ weather** buen tiempo **2.** (*friendly*) amable; **to be ~** (**to sb**) ser amable (con alguien)

pleasantry ['plez·ən·tri] <-ies> *n* **1.** (*joke*) broma *f* **2.** *pl* (*remarks*) cumplidos *mpl*; **an exchange of pleasantries** un intercambio de cumplidos

please [pliz] I. *vt* **1.** (*make happy*) complacer; **to be hard to ~** ser difícil de contentar; **she's notoriously hard to ~** es muy difícil complacerla **2.** *inf* (*do as one wishes*) **~ yourself** haz lo que te parezca II. *vi* **1.** (*be agreeable*) **eager to ~** deseoso de agradar **2.** (*think fit, wish*) **to do as one ~s** hacer lo que uno quiera; **you can do as you ~** como usted quiera; **to do whatever one ~s** hacer todo lo que se quiera III. *interj* por favor; **if you ~** *form* con su permiso; **more potatoes? — (yes) ~** ¿más patatas? — sí, por favor; **oh, ~!** (*in annoyance*) ¡oh, por favor!

pleased *adj* **1.** (*satisfied, contented*) satisfecho, -a; **to be ~ about sth** estar contento de algo; **to be ~ that...** estar contento de que +*subj*; **to be ~ with oneself** estar satisfecho de uno mismo **2.** (*happy, glad*) contento, -a; **I'm ~ to inform you/to report that ...** me complace comunicarle/informarle de que...; **(I'm very) ~ to meet you** encantado de conocerle **3.** (*willing*) **to be ~ to do sth** estar encantado de hacer algo ▶ **to be as ~ as Punch** (**about sth**) estar más contento que unas pascuas (con algo)

pleasing *adj* agradable; **~ news** buenas noticias *fpl*

pleasurable ['pleʒ·ər·ə·bəl] *adj* grato, -a; **a ~ sensation** una agradable sensación

pleasure ['pleʒ·ər] *n* **1.** (*feeling of enjoyment*) placer *m*; **it was such a ~ to meet you** ha sido un placer conocerle; **to take ~ in sth/in doing sth** disfrutar de algo/haciendo algo; **with ~** con mucho gusto **2.** (*source of enjoyment*) placer *m*; **the ~s and pains of camping** los pros y los contras de la acampada; **are you here for business or ~?** ¿está aquí por negocios o por placer? **3.** *form* (*will, desire*) **what is your ~, Madame?** ¿en qué puedo servirle, señora?

pleasure principle *n* PSYCH principio *m* del placer

pleasure trip *n* viaje *m* de recreo

pleat [plit] *n* pliegue *m*

pleb [pleb] *n inf abbr of* **plebian** plebeyo, -a *m, f*

plebeian [plɪ·'bi·ən] I. *adj form* plebeyo, -a II. *n* HIST plebeyo, -a *m, f*

plebiscite ['pleb·ə·saɪt] *n* plebiscito *m;* **to hold a ~ (on sth)** someter (algo) a plebiscito

pled [pled] *pt, pp of* **plead**

pledge [pledʒ] I. *n* 1. (*solemn promise*) promesa *f* solemne; **to fulfill a ~** cumplir un compromiso; **to make a ~ that...** prometer solemnemente que... 2. (*symbolic sign of promise*) **as a ~ of sth** en señal de algo; **a ~ of good faith** una garantía de buena fe 3. (*promised donation*) donativo *m* prometido 4. (*pawned item*) prenda *f* 5. (*in fraternity*) *estudiante que ha sido aceptado por una fraternidad y que ha prometido unirse a ella pero que todavía no ha sido iniciado* II. *vt* 1. (*promise*) prometer; **to ~ loyalty** jurar lealtad; **to ~ to do sth** prometer hacer algo; **to ~ that...** prometer que...; **we've ~d ourselves to fight for justice** nos hemos comprometido a luchar por la justicia; **I've been ~d to secrecy** he jurado guardar secreto 2. (*give as security*) **to ~ money** dar dinero como garantía

plenary ['pli·nə·ri] *adj* plenario, -a

plenary meeting *n* reunión *f* plenaria

plenary powers *npl* plenos poderes *mpl*

plenary session *n* sesión *f* plenaria

plenipotentiary [ˌplen·ə·pə·'ten·ʃi·er·i] I. <-ries> *n* ADMIN, POL plenipotenciario, -a *m, f* II. *adj* ADMIN, POL plenipotenciario, -a; **~ power** plenipotencia *f*

plentiful ['plen·tɪ·fəl] *adj* abundante; **strawberries are ~ in the summer** en verano hay abundancia de fresas

plenty ['plen·ti] I. *n* 1. (*abundance*) abundancia *f;* **land of ~** tierra *f* de abundancia; **food in ~** comida *f* en abundancia 2. (*a lot*) **~ of money/time** dinero/tiempo de sobra II. *adv* suficientemente; **~ more** mucho más; **there's ~ more beer in the fridge** hay mucha más cerveza en la nevera

plenum ['pli·nəm] *n* pleno *m*

plethora ['pleθ·ər·ə] *n* plétora *f*

pleurisy ['plʊr·ə·si] *n* MED pleuresía *f*

plexus ['plek·səs] <-(es)> *n* plexo *m;* **solar ~** plexo solar

pliable ['plaɪ·ə·bəl] *adj* 1. (*supple*) flexible 2. *fig* (*easily influenced*) dócil

pliers ['plaɪ·ərz] *npl* alicates *mpl;* **a pair of ~** unos alicates

plight [plaɪt] I. *n* apuro *m;* **a dreadful ~** una terrible situación II. *vt form* **to ~ one's troth** prometerse

PLO [ˌpi·el·'oʊ] *n abbr of* **Palestine Liberation Organization** OLP *f*

plod [plad] I. *n* paso *m* lento II. <-dd-> *vi* 1. (*walk heavily*) andar con paso pesado; **to ~ through the mud** andar con dificultad por el barro 2. (*do without enthusiasm*) **to ~ through one's work** trabajar sin ganas; **to ~ through a book** leer un libro lentamente

◆**plod away** *vi* **to ~ at sth** ir tirando con algo

◆**plod on** *vi* caminar penosamente

plonk [plɑŋk] *n, vt s.* **plunk**

plop [plɑp] I. *n* plaf *m;* **to fall with a ~** caerse

haciendo plaf II. <-pp-> *vi* (*fall*) **to ~ into a chair/onto the bed** dejarse caer sobre la silla/la cama

plot [plɑt] I. *n* 1. (*conspiracy, secret plan*) conspiración *f;* **to foil a ~** hacer fracasar una conspiración; **to hatch a ~** tramar una intriga; **the ~ thickens** *iron* el asunto se complica 2. (*story line*) argumento *m* 3. (*small piece of land*) terreno *m;* **a ~ of land** un terreno; **building ~** solar *m* II. <-tt-> *vt* 1. (*conspire*) tramar 2. (*create*) **to ~ a story line** idear un argumento; **to ~ a play/novel** idear el argumento de una obra de teatro/novela 3. (*graph, line*) trazar; (*mark on map*) señalar; **to ~ a course** planear una ruta III. <-tt-> *vi* **to ~ against sb** conspirar contra alguien; **to ~ to do sth** planear hacer algo

◆**plot out** *vt* trazar

plotter ['plɑt·ər] *n* 1. (*person*) conspirador(a) *m(f)* 2. COMPUT plotter *m*, tabla *f* trazadora

plough [plaʊ] *n, vt, vi s.* **plow**

plow [plaʊ] I. *n* arado *m* ▶ **to put one's hand to the ~** ponerse manos a la obra II. *vt* 1. AGR arar 2. (*move through*) **to ~ one's way through sth** abrirse paso por algo; (*work through*) hacer algo sin ganas 3. (*invest*) **to ~ money into a project** invertir mucho dinero en un proyecto III. *vi* 1. AGR arar 2. **to ~ through sth** (*move through*) abrirse paso por algo; (*work through*) terminar algo a duras penas

◆**plow back** *vt* **to plow sth back (into sth)** reinvertir algo (en algo); **to plow profits back** reinvertir los beneficios

◆**plow into** *vt insep* chocar contra

◆**plow up** *vt* (*fields, land*) roturar

Plow [plaʊ] *n s.* **Big Dipper**

ploy [plɔɪ] *n* 1. (*activity*) aventura *f* 2. (*tactics*) estratagema *f*

pluck [plʌk] I. *n* 1. (*sharp pull*) tirón *m* 2. (*courage*) valor *m;* **to have a lot of ~** tener agallas; **it takes a lot of ~** hace falta mucho valor II. *vt* 1. (*remove quickly*) arrancar 2. (*remove hair, feathers*) **to ~ a chicken** desplumar un pollo; **to ~ one's eyebrows** depilarse las cejas 3. MUS puntear III. *vi* **to ~ at sb's sleeve** tirar a alguien de la manga

◆**pluck out** *vt* arrancar

◆**pluck up** *vt* **to ~ one's courage** armarse de valor; **to ~ the courage to do sth** armarse de valor para hacer algo

plucky ['plʌk·i] <-ier, -iest> *adj* valiente

plug [plʌg] I. *n* 1. ELEC (*connector*) enchufe *m;* (*socket*) toma *f* de corriente 2. (*stopper*) tapón *m* 3. *inf* (*publicity*) **to give sth a ~** dar publicidad a algo 4. (*spark plug*) bujía *f* 5. (*chunk*) **~ of tobacco** tableta *f* de tabaco de mascar II. <-gg-> *vt* 1. (*connect*) conectar; ELEC enchufar 2. (*stop up, close*) **to ~ a hole** tapar un agujero; **to ~ a leak** taponar un escape 3. (*publicize*) anunciar 4. *sl* (*shoot*) pegar un tiro a

◆**plug away** *vi* **to ~ (at sth)** perseverar (en

algo)
◆**plug in** I. *vt* conectar; ELEC enchufar II. *vi*
conectar; ELEC enchufar
◆**plug up** *vt* tapar
plug-in *n* COMPUT plug-in *m*, enchufe *m*
plum [plʌm] I. *n* 1. (*fruit*) ciruela *f*; (*tree*)
ciruelo *m* 2. (*opportunity, reward*) chollo *m*
3. (*color*) color *m* ciruela II. *adj* 1. (*color*)
de color ciruela 2. (*exceptionally good*)
inmejorable; **a ~ job** un trabajo fantástico
plumage ['plu·mɪdʒ] *n* plumaje *m*
plumb [plʌm] I. *vt* 1. *a. fig* sondar; **to ~ the
depth** sondar la profundidad; **to ~ the depths**
fig estar muy deprimido; **to ~ the mystery of
the universe** plantearse los misterios del universo 2. (*straighten, make vertical: wall,
frame, mast*) aplomar II. *adv inf* 1. (*exactly*)
exactamente; **he hit me ~ on the nose** me
dio de lleno en la nariz 2. (*completely*) **to be
~ wrong/right/tired/crazy** estar completamente equivocado/en lo cierto/cansado/loco
III. *n* plomada *f*; **to be out of** [*o* off] **~** no estar
a plomo
plumber ['plʌm·ər] *n* fontanero, -a *m, f*,
plomero, -a *m, f AmL*, gasfitero, -a *m, f Chile,
Perú*
plumbing ['plʌm·ɪŋ] I. *n* fontanería *f* II. *adj ~*
fixture instalación *f* sanitaria; **~ work** obra *f*
de fontanería
plume [plum] I. *n* 1. (*feather*) pluma *f*
2. (*cloud: of smoke, gas*) nube *f* II. *vt* **to ~
oneself on sth** vanagloriarse de algo
plummet ['plʌm·ɪt] *vi* caer en picado
plummy ['plʌm·i] <-ier, -iest> *adj* (*voice,
tone*) pijo, -a *inf*, popoff *Méx*
plump [plʌmp] *adj* (*person*) rollizo, -a; (*animal*) gordo, -a
◆**plump down** *inf* I. *vt* dejar caer II. *vi* dejarse
caer
◆**plump for** *vt inf* optar por
◆**plump up** *vt* 1. (*pillow*) sacudir
2. (*chicken*) cebar
plumpness ['plʌmp·nɪs] *n* gordura *f*
plum pudding *n* pudin *m* de pasas
plum tree *n* ciruelo *m*
plunder ['plʌn·dər] I. *n* 1. (*stolen goods*) botín
m 2. (*act of plundering*) saqueo *m* II. *vt* 1. (*village, city*) saquear 2. (*goods, gold, treasures*)
robar III. *vi* robar
plunderer ['plʌn·dər·ər] *n* saqueador(a) *m(f)*
plunge [plʌndʒ] I. *n* 1. (*sharp decline*) caída *f*
2. (*dive*) zambullida *f* de cabeza ▶ **to take the
~** dar el paso decisivo; (*get married*) casarse
II. *vi* 1. (*fall suddenly*) precipitarse; **to ~ to
one's death** tener una caída mortal 2. (*leap,
enter*) **we ~d into the sea** nos zambullimos
en el mar; **he ~d into the forest** se precipitó
hacia el bosque 3. (*begin abruptly*) **to ~ into
sth** emprender algo III. *vt* hundir; **to ~ a knife
into sth** clavar un cuchillo en algo; **we've ~d
ourselves into debt** nos hemos metido en
deudas
◆**plunge in** *vi* lanzarse

plunger ['plʌn·dʒər] *n* (*of syringe*) émbolo *m*;
(*for drain, toilet*) desatascador *m*
plunk [plʌŋk] I. *n inf* (*sound*) ruido *m* sordo
II. *vt inf* (*set down heavily*) dejar caer pesadamente; **she ~ed the books onto the table**
dejó caer pesadamente los libros sobre la mesa
◆**plunk down** *vt inf* dejar caer pesadamente;
to plunk oneself down on a chair dejarse
caer en una silla
pluperfect ['plu·ˌpɜr·fɪkt] *n* LING pluscuamperfecto *m*
plural ['plʊr·əl] I. *n* plural *m*; **in the ~** en plural; **second person ~** segunda persona del
plural II. *adj* 1. *a.* LING plural 2. (*multiple*)
múltiple
pluralism ['plʊr·ə·ˌlɪz·əm] *n* PHILOS pluralis-
mo *m*
pluralistic [ˌplʊr·ə·'lɪs·tɪk] *adj* pluralista
plurality [plʊ·'ræl·ə·t̬i] <-ies> *n* 1. (*variety*)
pluralidad *f*; **~ of opinions** diversidad *f* de
opiniones 2. (*share of votes*) mayoría *f* relativa; **to have a ~** ganar por mayoría relativa
plus [plʌs] I. *prep* más; **5 ~ 2 equals 7** 5 más 2
igual a 7 II. *conj* además III. <-es> *n* 1. (*mathematical symbol*) signo *m* más 2. (*advantage*)
punto *m* a favor IV. *adj* 1. (*above zero*) positivo, -a; **~ 8** más 8; **~ two degrees** dos grados
positivos 2. (*more than*) algo más de; **200 ~**
más de 200 3. (*advantageous*) **the ~ side** (of
sth) el lado positivo (de algo)
plus fours *npl* pantalones *mpl* de golf
plush [plʌʃ] I. *adj* 1. (*luxurious*) lujoso, -a,
elegante 2. (*fabric, carpet*) de felpa II. <-es> *n*
felpa *f*
plus sign *n* signo *m* más
Pluto ['plu·t̬oʊ] *n* Plutón *m*
plutocracy [plu·'tak·rə·si] <-ies> *n* plutocra-
cia *f*
plutocrat ['plu·t̬ə·kræt] *n* plutócrata *mf*
plutocratic [ˌplu·t̬ə·'kræt̬·ɪk] *adj* plutocráti-
co, -a
plutonium [plu·'toʊ·ni·əm] *n* plutonio *m*
ply[1] [plaɪ] *n* 1. (*thickness: of cloth, wood*) capa
f 2. (*strand of rope*) **two-~ rope** cuerda *f* de
dos cabos
ply[2] [plaɪ] <-ie-> I. *vt* 1. (*utilize: needle, tool*)
usar, manejar; **to ~ one's trade** ejercer su
profesión 2. **to ~ sb with questions** acosar a
alguien a preguntas; **to ~ sb with wine** no
parar de servir vino a alguien 3. (*sell*) **to ~
drugs** traficar con drogas; **to ~ one's wares**
vender su mercancía 4. (*travel: ship*) navegar
por; **to ~ a route** hacer un trayecto II. *vi* **to ~
between Paris and Lyon** hacer regularmente
el trayecto entre París y Lyon
plywood ['plaɪ·wʊd] *n* contrachapado *m*
P.M. [ˌpiˈem] *abbr of* **post meridiem** p.m.;
one ~ la una de la tarde; **ten ~** las diez de la
noche
PM [ˌpiˈem] *n* 1. *abbr of* **postmortem** autopsia
f 2. *abbr of* **prime minister** primer ministro
m, primera ministra *f*
PMS [ˌpi·em·ˈes] *n abbr of* **premenstrual syn-**

drome SPM *m*
pneumatic [nu·'mæt̬·ɪk] *adj* neumático, -a
pneumatic brakes *npl* frenos *mpl* neumáticos
pneumatic tire *n* neumático *m*
pneumonia [nu·'moʊn·jə] *n* neumonía *f*
PO [ˌpi·'oʊ] *n abbr of* **Post Office** Correos *m*
poach[1] [poʊtʃ] *vt* (*eggs*) escalfar; (*fish*) cocer
poach[2] [poʊtʃ] I. *vt* 1. (*hunt illegally*) cazar furtivamente; (*fish*) pescar furtivamente 2. (*take unfairly*) robar; **to ~ someone's ideas** birlar las ideas de alguien II. *vi* cazar furtivamente; (*fish*) pescar furtivamente; **to ~ on sb's territory** *fig* pisar el terreno a alguien
poacher ['poʊ·tʃər] *n* (*hunter*) cazador(a) *m(f)* furtivo, -a; (*fisherman*) pescador(a) *m(f)* furtivo, -a
poaching ['poʊ·tʃɪŋ] *n* (*hunting*) caza *f* furtiva; (*fishing*) pesca *f* furtiva
POB *n abbr of* **post office box** apdo. *m* de correos
PO Box [ˌpi·'oʊ·baks] <-es> *n abbr of* **post office box** apartado *m* de correos
pock [pak] *n* (*scar*) picadura *f*; (*pimple*) pústula *f*
pocket ['pak·ɪt] I. *n* 1. (*in pants, jacket*) bolsillo *m*, bolsa *f AmC, Méx;* **back/breast ~** bolsillo trasero/de pecho; **inside ~** bolsillo interior; **to be in ~/out of ~** salir ganando/perdiendo; **to pay for sth out of one's own ~** pagar algo de su bolsillo 2. (*isolated group, area*) **~ of green** [*o* **greenery**] zona *f* verde; **a ~ of resistance** un foco de resistencia; **~ of turbulence** AVIAT, METEO racha *f* de turbulencias 3. (*in pool table*) tronera *f* ▶ **to have sth/sb in one's ~** tener algo/a alguien en el bolsillo; **to line one's ~s** forrarse (de dinero) II. *vt* 1. (*put in pocket*) **to ~ sth** meterse algo en el bolsillo 2. (*keep for oneself*) apropiarse de 3. (*in billiards*) **to ~ a ball** meter una bola ▶ **to ~ one's pride** tragarse el orgullo III. *adj* **~ dictionary** diccionario *m* de bolsillo; **~ edition** edición *f* de bolsillo
pocketbook ['pak·ɪt·bʊk] *n* 1. (*woman's handbag*) bolso *m*, cartera *f AmL* 2. (*billfold*) monedero *m;* **to vote with one's ~** votar con el bolsillo 3. (*book*) libro *m* de bolsillo
pocket bread *n* pan *m* de pita
pocket calculator *n* calculadora *f* de bolsillo
pocket camera *n* cámara *f* de bolsillo
pocketful ['pak·ɪt·fʊl] *n* **a ~ of sth** un puñado de algo
pocket handkerchief *n* pañuelo *m* de bolsillo
pocketknife <-knives> *n* navaja *f*
pocket money *n* 1. (*for small expenses*) dinero *m* para gastos personales 2. (*from one's parents*) paga *f*
pocket-sized *adj* de bolsillo
pockmarks *npl* marcas *f* (de la viruela) *pl*
pod [pad] *n* 1. BOT vaina *f* 2. AVIAT tanque *m*
podcast I. *n* podcast *m* II. *vt* crear y difundir archivos de audio para que se puedan reproducir en un iPod
podcasting *n* podcasting *m, realización difu-*

sión de podcasts
podiatrist [pə·'daɪ·ə·trɪst] *n* podólogo, -a *m, f*
podium ['poʊ·di·əm] <-s *o* -dia> *n* podio *m*
poem ['poʊ·əm] *n* poema *m*
poet ['poʊ·ət] *n* poeta *mf*
poetic [poʊ·'et̬·ɪk] *adj* poético, -a
poetry ['poʊ·ə·tri] *n a. fig* poesía *f*
pogrom [pə·'gram] *n* pogromo *m elev*
poignant ['pɔɪn·jənt] *adj* conmovedor(a)
poinsettia [pɔɪnt·'set̬·i·ə] *n* flor *f* de Pascua
point [pɔɪnt] I. *n* 1. (*sharp end*) punta *f*; **knifepoint** punta de un cuchillo; **pencil ~** punta de un lápiz 2. GEO cabo *m* 3. (*particular place*) punto *m;* **boiling/freezing ~** punto *m* de ebullición/congelación; **starting ~** punto de partida; **New Haven and ~s north** New Haven y los lugares situados al norte 4. (*particular time*) momento *m;* **to do sth up to a ~** hacer algo hasta cierto punto; **to get to the ~ that...** llegar al extremo de...; **at that ~** en ese instante; **at this ~ in time** en este momento 5. (*significant idea*) cuestión *f;* **that's just the ~!** ¡eso es lo importante!; **to be to the ~** venir al caso; **to be beside the ~** no venir al caso; **to get to the ~** ir al grano; **to get the ~ (of sth)** entender (algo); **to make one's ~** expresar su opinión; **to miss the ~** no captar lo relevante; **to see sb's ~** aceptar la opinión de alguien; **to take sb's ~** aceptar el argumento de alguien; **~ taken** de acuerdo; **~ by ~** punto por punto 6. (*purpose*) finalidad *f;* **what's the ~?** ¿qué sentido tiene? 7. (*characteristic*) **sb's strong/weak ~s** los puntos fuertes/débiles de alguien 8. (*in score, result*) punto *m;* **percentage ~** puntos *mpl* porcentuales; **to win (sth) on ~s** (*in boxing*) ganar (algo) por puntos 9. MATH **decimal ~** coma *f*, punto *m* decimal *AmL* 10. *a.* TYPO punto *m;* **join ~s A and B together** unir los puntos A y B 11. **~s** AUTO (*electrical contacts*) platinos *mpl* ▶ **to make a ~ of doing sth** procurar de hacer algo II. *vi* (*with finger*) señalar; (*indicate*); **to ~ to sth** indicar algo; **to ~ to an icon** COMPUT señalar un icono III. *vt* 1. (*aim*) **to ~ sth at sb** apuntar con algo a alguien; **the man had ~ed a knife at him** el hombre le había amenazado con un cuchillo; **to ~ a finger at sb** *a. fig* señalar con el dedo a alguien 2. (*direct, show position or direction*) señalar; **to ~ sth toward sth/sb** dirigir algo hacia algo/alguien; **to ~ sb toward sth** indicar a alguien el camino hacia algo
◆ **point out** *vt* 1. (*show*) indicar; **if you see her, please point her out to me** si la ves, por favor indícame quién es 2. (*inform of*) **to point sth out to sb** advertir a alguien de algo; **to ~ that...** señalar que...
point-blank [ˌpɔɪnt·'blæŋk] I. *adv* 1. (*fire*) a quemarropa 2. (*ask*) a bocajarro; **to refuse ~** negarse rotundamente II. *adj* 1. (*very close, not far away*) **to shoot sb at ~ range** disparar a alguien a quemarropa 2. (*blunt, direct*) directo, -a

pointed ['pɔɪn·tɪd] *adj* **1.** (*implement, stick*) puntiagudo, -a **2.** *fig* (*criticism*) mordaz; (*question*) directo, -a; (*remark*) intencionado, -a

pointer ['pɔɪn·tər] *n* **1.** (*for blackboard*) puntero *m;* (*of clock*) aguja *f*, manecilla *f;* (*of scale*) fiel *m* **2.** COMPUT puntero *m;* **mouse ~** puntero del ratón **3.** (*advice, tip*) consejo *m* **4.** (*dog*) perro *m* de muestra, pointer *m*

pointless ['pɔɪnt·lɪs] *adj* inútil; **arguing with him is ~** no sirve de nada discutir con él

point of no return *n inf* punto *m* sin retorno, punto *m* de no retorno *Col, Méx*

point of view <points of view> *n* punto *m* de vista; **from a purely practical ~** desde una perspectiva puramente práctica

poise [pɔɪz] **I.** *n* **1.** (*composure*) aplomo *m;* **to lose/regain one's ~** perder/recobrar la serenidad **2.** (*elegance*) porte *m* **II.** *vt* **to be ~d to do sth** estar a punto de hacer algo

poised *adj* **1.** (*suspended*) suspendido, -a; **~ in the air** suspendido, -a en el aire **2.** (*ready*) preparado, -a **3.** (*calm*) sereno, -a

poison ['pɔɪ·zən] **I.** *n* veneno *m;* **rat ~** matarratas *m inv;* **to lace sth with ~** rociar algo con veneno; **to take ~** envenenarse ▸ **what's your ~?** *fig* ¿qué tomas? **II.** *vt* **1.** (*give poison to*) envenenar **2.** (*spoil, corrupt*) emponzoñar; **the long dispute has ~ed relations between the two countries** el largo conflicto ha enturbiado las relaciones entre ambos países; **to ~ sb's mind (against sb/sth)** predisponer a alguien (contra alguien)

poison gas *n* gas *m* tóxico

poisoning *n* envenenamiento *m*

poison ivy *n* BOT hiedra *f* venenosa

poisonous ['pɔɪ·zə·nəs] *adj* venenoso, -a; *fig;* **~ atmosphere** ambiente *m* pernicioso; **~ remark** comentario *m* malicioso

poke¹ [poʊk] *n reg: esp. Southern* (*bag*) bolsa *f*, saco *m*

poke² [poʊk] **I.** *n* (*push*) empujón *m;* (*with elbow*) codazo *m;* **to give sb a ~** dar un codazo a alguien **II.** *vt* **1.** (*with finger*) dar con la punta del dedo en, tocar con la punta del dedo; (*with elbow*) dar un codazo a; **to ~ a hole in sth** hacer un agujero en algo; **to ~ holes in an argument** echar un argumento por tierra; **to ~ one's nose into sb's business** meter las narices en los asuntos de alguien **2.** (*emerge*) asomar **3. to ~ fun at sb/sth** burlarse de alguien/algo **III.** *vi* **to ~ at sth/sb** dar a algo/alguien; **to ~ through (sth)** salirse (de algo)

◆ **poke around** *vi* curiosear

◆ **poke out I.** *vi* **to ~ (of sth)** salirse (de algo) **II.** *vt* **1.** (*stick out*) **to poke one's head out** asomar la cabeza **2.** (*push out*) **to poke sth out** sacar algo; **to poke sb's eye(s) out** saltarle los ojos a alguien

◆ **poke up** *vi* asomar

poker¹ ['poʊ·kər] *n* (*card game*) póquer *m*

poker² ['poʊ·kər] *n* (*fireplace tool*) atizador *m*

pokey ['poʊ·ki] **I.** *n sl* (*prison*) trullo *m;* **he'll get three years in the ~** le caerán tres años en chirona **II.** *adj s.* **poky**

poky ['poʊ·ki] **I.** <-ier, -iest> *adj inf* **1.** (*slow*) lerdo, -a **2.** (*small*) diminuto, -a; **a ~ little room** un cuartucho **II.** *n s.* **pokey**

Poland ['poʊ·lənd] *n* Polonia *f*

polar ['poʊ·lər] *adj* GEO, MATH polar; **~ opposites** polos *mpl* opuestos

polar bear *n* oso *m* polar

polar circle *n* círculo *m* polar

polar front *n* METEO frente *m* polar

polar icecap *n* casquete *m* polar

polarity [poʊ·'lær·ə·ti] *n* polaridad *f*

polarization [ˌpoʊ·lər·ɪ·'zeɪ·ʃən] *n* polarización *f*

polarize ['poʊ·lə·raɪz] **I.** *vt* polarizar; **to ~ sth into two groups** polarizar algo en dos grupos **II.** *vi* polarizarse

polar lights *npl* aurora *f* boreal

polar region *n* región *f* polar

polar zone *n* región *f* polar

pole¹ [poʊl] *n* palo *m;* **power ~** poste *m* de electricidad; **flagpole** asta *f* de bandera; **fishing ~** caña *f* de pescar; **telephone ~** poste *m* de teléfonos ▸ **to not touch sth with a 10-foot ~** no querer ver algo ni de lejos

pole² [poʊl] *n* **1.** GEO, ELEC polo *m;* **the magnetic ~s** los polos magnéticos; **the negative/positive ~** el polo negativo/positivo **2.** *fig* bando *m;* **to be ~s apart** ser polos opuestos; **political ~s** extremos *mpl* políticos

Pole¹ [poʊl] *n* (*person*) polaco, -a *m, f*

Pole² [poʊl] *n* GEO **the North/South ~** el Polo Norte/Sur

poleax(e) ['poʊl·æks] **I.** *n* **1.** (*medieval weapon*) hacha *f* de guerra **2.** (*axe in naval warfare*) hacha *f* de abordaje **II.** *vt* (*strike powerfully*) tumbar, noquear; **he was completely ~d when his wife left him** se quedó de una pieza cuando su mujer le dejó

pole dancer *n* go-go *f*, bailarina *f* de barra

pole dancing *n baile erótico de barra*

polemic [pə·'lem·ɪk] **I.** *n* polémica *f* **II.** *adj* polémico, -a

polemical *adj* polémico, -a

pole position *n* (*in auto racing*) pole position *f;* **to be in ~** tener la pole position

polestar *n* estrella *f* polar

pole vault *n* salto *m* con pértiga

pole vaulter *n* saltador(a) *m(f)* de pértiga

police [pə·'lis] **I.** *n* policía *f* **II.** *vt* **to ~ an area** vigilar una zona; **to ~ a process** supervisar un proceso; **to ~ oneself** controlarse; **to ~ the frontier** patrullar la frontera

police car *n* coche *m* de policía

police court *n* juzgado *m* de guardia

police department *n* departamento *m* de policía

police dog *n* perro *m* policía

police escort *n* escolta *f* policial; **under ~** con escolta policial

police force *n* cuerpo *m* de policía

police informer *n* confidente *mf* de la policía

policeman [pə·'lis·mən] <-men> *n* policía *m*, guardia *m*
police officer *n* policía *mf*, guardia *m*
police patrol *n* patrulla *f* policial
police raid *n* redada *f*, arreada *f Arg*
police record *n* **1.** (*file*) expediente *m* **2.** (*history of convictions*) antecedentes *mpl* penales; **to have a long** ~ tener un largo historial delictivo
police reporter *n* reportero, -a *m, f* de asuntos policiales
police state *n* estado *m* policíaco
police station *n* comisaría *f* (de policía)
policewoman [pə·'lis·ˌwʊm·ən] <-women> *n* (mujer *f*) policía *f*
policy¹ ['pal·ə·si] <-ies> *n* **1.** POL, ECON política *f*; **a change in** ~ un cambio de política; **domestic/economic** ~ política interior/económica; **company** ~ política de empresa; **to set** ~ (**on sth**) establecer una política (en materia de algo) **2.** (*principle*) principio *m;* **my** ~ **is to tell the truth whenever possible** tengo por norma decir la verdad siempre que sea posible
policy² ['pal·ə·si] <-ies> *n* FIN póliza *f;* **insurance** ~ póliza de seguros; **to take out a** ~ hacerse un seguro
policyholder ['pal·ə·si·ˌhoʊl·dər] *n* asegurado, -a *m, f*
policy maker *n* responsable *mf* de los principios políticos de un partido
policymaking *n* formulación *f* de principios políticos
policy number *n* número *m* de póliza
policy owner *n* titular *mf* de una póliza
polio [ˌpoʊ·li·oʊ] *n*, **poliomyelitis** [ˌpoʊ·li·oʊ·ˌmai·ə·'lai·təs] *n* MED polio *f*, poliomielitis *f*
polio vaccine *n* vacuna *f* contra la polio
polish ['pal·ɪʃ] **I.** *n* **1.** (*substance: for furniture*) cera *f;* (*for shoes*) betún *m;* (*for silver*) abrillantador *m;* (*for nails*) esmalte *m* **2.** (*action*) pulimento *m;* **to give sth a** ~ dar brillo a algo **3.** (*sophisticated, refined style*) refinamiento *m* **II.** *vt* **1.** (*make shine*) sacar brillo a; (*shoes, silver*) limpiar **2.** *fig* (*refine*) pulir
◆ **polish off** *vt* (*food*) despacharse; (*work, opponent*) liquidar
◆ **polish up** *vt* **1.** (*polish to a shine*) dar brillo a **2.** (*improve, brush up*) perfeccionar
Polish ['poʊ·lɪʃ] **I.** *adj* polaco, -a **II.** *n* LING polaco *m*
polished *adj* **1.** (*shiny*) pulido, -a **2.** *fig* (*sophisticated*) distinguido, -a; ~ **manners** modales *mpl* refinados; **a** ~ **performance** una actuación impecable
polite [pə·'lait] *adj* **1.** (*courteous*) atento, -a; ~ **refusal** declinación *f* cortés **2.** (*cultured*) educado, -a; (*refined*) fino, -a; ~ **society** buena sociedad *f* **3.** (*superficially courteous*) correcto, -a; **to keep a** ~ **conversation going** mantener una conversación por cortesía
politeness *n* **1.** (*good manners*) cortesía *f*, educación *f* **2.** (*consideration*) atenciones *fpl*

politic ['pal·ə·tɪk] *adj* **1.** (*judicious, prudent*) prudente **2.** POL **the body** ~ el cuerpo político
political [pə·'lɪt·ɪ·kəl] *adj* político, -a; ~ **pundit** experto, -a *m, f* en política; **to make** ~ **capital** (**out**) **of sth** sacar provecho político de algo
politically correct *adj* políticamente correcto, -a (*actitud que refleja una ideología progresista*)
politician [ˌpal·ə·'tɪʃ·ən] *n* político, -a *m, f*
politicize [pe·'lɪt·ə·saiz] *vt* politizar
politics *n pl* **1.** (*activities of government*) política *f;* **to go into** ~ dedicarse a la política; **to talk** ~ hablar de política **2.** (*political science*) ciencias *fpl* políticas **3.** (*intrigue*) **company/office/party** ~ intrigas en la empresa/la oficina/el partido; (*complex relationship*) **the** ~ **of stem cell research** la dimensión política de la investigación con células madre
polka ['poʊl·kə] **I.** *n* polca *f* **II.** *vi* bailar la polca
poll [poʊl] **I.** *n* **1.** (*public survey*) encuesta *f;* **opinion** ~ sondeo *m* de la opinión pública; **to conduct a** ~ hacer una encuesta **2.** *pl* (*elections*) **to go to the** ~**s** acudir a las urnas **3.** (*results of a vote*) **to head the** ~ obtener la mayoría de votos **4.** (*number of votes cast*) votos *mpl;* **there was a heavy/light** ~ ha habido una alta/baja participación (en las elecciones) **II.** *vt* **1.** (*record the opinion*) sondear; **half the people** ~**ed** la mitad de los encuestados **2.** (*receive*) **to** ~ **votes** obtener votos
pollard ['pal·ərd] *vt* desmochar
pollen ['pal·ən] *n* polen *m*
pollen count *n* índice *m* de polen en el aire
pollinate ['pal·ə·neit] *vt* polinizar
polling *n* votación *f*
polling place *n* colegio *m* electoral
pollster ['poʊl·stər] *n* encuestador(a) *m(f)*
pollutant [pə·'lu·tənt] *n* contaminante *m*, agente *m* contaminador
pollute [pə·'lut] *vt* **1.** (*river, atmosphere, environment*) contaminar **2.** *fig* (*corrupt*) corromper; **to** ~ **sb's mind** corromper la mente de alguien
polluter [pə·'lu·tər] *n* contaminador(a) *m(f)*
pollution [pə·'lu·ʃən] *n* contaminación *f*
polo ['poʊ·loʊ] *n* SPORTS polo *m*
polo shirt *n* polo *m*
polyamide ['pal·i·'æm·aid] *n* poliamida *f*
polychrome [ˌpal·ɪ·'kroʊm] *adj* polícromo, -a
polyclinic ['pal·ɪ·klɪn·ɪk] *n* policlínica *f*, policlínico *m AmL*
polyester ['pal·i·'es·tər] *n* poliéster *m*
polyethylene ['pal·i·ˌeθ·ə·lin] *n* polietileno *m*
polygamist [pə·'lɪg·ə·mist] *n* polígamo, -a *m, f*
polygamous [pə·'lɪg·ə·məs] *adj* polígamo, -a
polygamy [pə·'lɪg·ə·mi] *n* poligamia *f*
polyglot ['pal·i·glat] **I.** *adj* políglota **II.** *n* políglota *mf*
polygon ['pal·i·gan] *n* polígono *m*
polygonal [pə·'lɪg·ə·nəl] *adj* poligonal
polygraph ['pal·i·græf] *n* polígrafo *m*, detector

P

m de mentiras

polymeric [,pal·ɪ·'mer·ɪk] *adj* polimérico, -a

polymorphous [,pal·i·'mɔr·fəs] *adj* polimorfo, -a

Polynesia [,pal·ə·'ni·ʒə] *n* Polinesia *f*

Polynesian I. *adj* polinesio, -a **II.** *n* polinesio, -a *m, f*

polyp ['pal·ɪp] *n* MED, ZOOL pólipo *m*

polyphonic [,pal·i·'fan·ɪk] *adj* MUS polifónico, -a

polyphony [pə·'lɪf·ə·ni] *n* MUS polifonía *f*

polystyrene [,pal·i·'staɪ·rin] *n* (espuma *f* de) poliestireno *m*

polysyllabic [,pal·i·sɪ·'læb·ɪk] *adj* LING polisílabo, -a

polysyllable [,pal·i·'sɪl·ə·bəl] *n* LING polisílabo *m*

polytechnic [,pal·i·'tek·nɪk] *n* escuela *f* politécnica

polytheism ['pal·i·θi·ɪz·əm] *n* politeísmo *m*

polytheistic [,pal·i·θi·'ɪs·tɪk] *adj* politeísta

polyunsaturated [,pal·i·ʌn·'sætʃ·ə·rei·t̬ɪd] *adj* poliinsaturado, -a

polyunsaturated fats *npl*, **polyunsaturates** [,pal·i·ʌn·'sætʃ·ə·rəts] *npl* grasas *fpl* poliinsaturadas

polyurethane [,pal·i·'jʊr·ə·θeɪn] *n* poliuretano *m*

polyvalent [,pal·i·'vei·lənt] *adj* polivalente

pomade [poʊ·'meɪd] *n* pomada *f*

pomegranate ['pam·græn·ɪt] *n* 1. (*fruit*) granada *f* 2. (*tree*) granado *m*

pomp [pamp] *n* pompa *f;* **~ and circumstance** pompa y solemnidad

pomposity [pam·'pas·ə·t̬i] *n* pomposidad *f*

pompous ['pam·pəs] *adj* 1. pomposo, -a 2. (*pretentious*) ostentoso, -a; **~ language** lenguaje *m* ampuloso

poncho ['pan·tʃoʊ] *n* poncho *m*, ruana *f Col, Ven,* zarape *m Guat, Méx*

pond [pand] *n* 1. (*natural*) charca *f;* (*man-made*) estanque *m;* **duck ~** estanque de patos; **fish ~** vivero *m* 2. *fig* (*Atlantic ocean*) **the Pond** el charco

ponder ['pan·dər] **I.** *vt* considerar, sopesar; **to ~ whether/why...** preguntarse si/por qué... **II.** *vi* reflexionar; **to ~ on sth** meditar sobre algo

ponderous ['pan·dər·əs] *adj* 1. (*movement*) pesado, -a 2. (*style*) laborioso, -a

pone [poʊn] *n reg: Southern* borona *f;* **corn ~** pan *m* de maíz

pontiff ['pan·tɪf] *n* REL **the ~** el pontífice

pontifical [pan·'tɪf·ɪ·kəl] *adj* pontifical

pontificate¹ [pan·'tɪf·ɪ·keɪt] *vi* pontificar

pontificate² [pan·'tɪf·ɪ·kət] *n* (*office of pontiff*) pontificado *m*

pontoon [pan·'tun] *n* (*floating device*) pontón *m*

pontoon bridge *n* puente *m* de pontones

pony ['poʊ·ni] <-ies> *n* poni *m*

ponytail ['poʊ·ni·teɪl] *n* coleta *f*

poo [pu] *sl* **I.** *n* caca *f;* **to do ~** hacer caca **II.** *vi*

hacer caca

pooch [putʃ] *n sl* (*dog*) chucho *m*

poodle ['pu·dəl] *n* caniche *m,* perro *m* de lanas

poof [puf] *interj inf* ¡chas!

pooh [pu] *interj inf* 1. (*indicating disgust*) ~! **what a ghastly smell!** ¡puf, qué peste! 2. (*indicating impatience*) ¡bah!

pooh-pooh [,pu·'pu] *vt inf* **to ~ a plan/a proposal** desdeñar un plan/una propuesta

pool¹ [pul] *n* 1. (*of water*) charca *f;* (*of oil, blood*) charco *f;* **rock ~** piscina *f* de roca; **a ~ of light** un foco de luz 2. (*man-made*) estanque *m;* **swimming ~** piscina *f,* pileta *f RíoPl*

pool² [pul] **I.** *n* 1. (*common fund*) fondo *m* común 2. (*common supply*) reserva *f;* **car ~** parque *m* de automóviles; **gene ~** acervo *m* genético; **typing ~** servicio *m* de mecanografía 3. SPORTS billar *m* americano; **to play** [*o inf* **shoot**] (**a game of**) **~** jugar al [*o un*] billar; **to be dirty ~** *inf* ser un juego sucio **II.** *vt* (*money, resources*) hacer un fondo común; (*information*) compartir

pool hall *n,* **poolroom** *n* sala *f* de billar

pool table *n* mesa *f* de billar

poop¹ [pup] *n* NAUT popa *f;* **~ deck** castillo *m* de popa

poop² [pup] *n sl* (*information*) **to get the ~ on sth/sb** ponerse al tanto de algo/alguien

poop³ [pup] *sl* **I.** *n* caca *f;* **dog ~** caca de perro **II.** *vi* hacerse caca

♦**poop out** *vi inf* quedar hecho polvo

pooper-scooper ['pu·pər·,sku·pər] *n* pala *f* para recoger excrementos

poop sheet *n sl* folleto *m*

poor [pʊr] **I.** *adj* 1. (*lacking money*) pobre 2. (*attendance, harvest*) escaso, -a; (*memory, performance*) malo, -a; **~ soil** terreno *m* pobre; **~ visibility** visibilidad *f* escasa; **to be ~ at sth** no estar fuerte en algo; **to be in ~ health** estar mal de salud; **to be a ~ loser** no saber perder; **to give a ~ account of oneself** causar mala impresión; **to cut a ~ figure** (as sth) hacer un mal papel (como algo); **to be a ~ excuse for sth** ser una mala versión de algo; **to have ~ eyesight** tener mala vista; **to have ~ hearing** ser duro de oído; **to do a ~ job of** (**doing**) **sth** hacer algo mal 3. (*deserving of pity*) pobre; **you ~ thing!** ¡pobrecito! **II.** *n* **the ~ los pobres

poor box <-es> *n* cepillo *m* de los pobres

poorhouse *n* asilo *m* de los pobres

poorly ['pʊr·li] **I.** *adv* 1. (*resulting from poverty*) pobremente 2. (*inadequately*) mal; **~ dressed** mal vestido; **to think ~ of sb** tener mala opinión de alguien **II.** *adj* **to feel ~** encontrarse mal

poorness ['pʊr·nɪs] *n* 1. (*inadequacy*) impropiedad *f;* **the ~ of his judgment** lo inadecuado de su opinión 2. (*poverty*) pobreza *f*

poor relative *n* pariente *mf* pobre

pop¹ [pap] **I.** *adj* popular; **~ culture** cultura *f* pop **II.** *n* MUS (música *f*) pop *m*

pop² [pap] *n inf* (*father*) papá *m*

pop³ [pap] I. *n* **1.** (*small explosive noise*) pequeña explosión *f;* **the ~ of a champagne cork** el taponazo de una botella de champán **2.** (*soda pop*) gaseosa *f;* **orange ~** naranjada *f* II. <-pp-> *vi* **1.** (*explode*) estallar; (*burst*) reventar; **to let the cork ~** hacer saltar el tapón **2.** (*come, go quickly*) **to ~ upstairs** subir un momento; **to ~ out for sth** salir un momento a por algo III. <-pp-> *vt* **1.** (*make burst*) hacer estallar; **to ~ popcorn** hacer palomitas **2.** (*put quickly*) meter; **to ~ sth on/ off** ponerse/quitarse algo
◆ **pop in** *vi* entrar un momento en; **we popped in at my brother's on our way home** de vuelta a casa, pasamos por casa de mi hermano
◆ **pop for** *vi sl* **1.** (*pay for*) pagar **2.** (*get caught at*) **to get popped for sth** (*fine*) ser multado por algo; (*prison*) ser detenido por algo
◆ **pop out** *vi* salir; **to ~ from somewhere** salir de pronto de un sitio; **to ~ for sth** salir un momento a hacer algo
◆ **pop up** *vi* (*appear*) aparecer; **to ~ out of nowhere** surgir de la nada
pop. *n abbr of* **population** hab. *mf*
pop art *n* pop art *m*
pop concert *n* concierto *m* pop
popcorn ['pap·kɔrn] *n* palomitas *fpl* (de maíz), pororó *m CSur,* cacalote *m AmC, Méx*
pope [poup] *n* REL **1.** (*Catholic*) papa *m* **2.** (*Orthodox patriarch*) pope *m*
pope's nose *n* rabadilla *f*
popeyed ['pap·,aɪd] *adj* de ojos saltones; **he looked at me ~** me miró con los ojos desorbitados
pop group *n* grupo *m* pop
popgun *n* pistola *f* de juguete
poplar ['pap·lər] *n* álamo *m*
poplin ['pap·lɪn] *n* popelín *m*
pop music *n* música *f* pop
popper ['pap·ər] *n* **1.** (*for making popcorn*) *recipiente para hacer palomitas* **2.** *inf* (*drug*) popper *m*
poppy ['pap·i] <-ies> *n* amapola *f*
poppycock ['pap·i·kak] *n inf* tonterías *fpl*
poppy seeds *npl* semillas *fpl* de amapola
Popsicle® ['pap·sɪ·kəl] *n* polo *m,* paleta *f Amc, Méx*
pop singer *n* cantante *mf* pop
pop song *n* canción *f* pop
pop star *n* estrella *f* del pop
populace ['pap·jə·lɪs] *n* **the ~** el pueblo
popular ['pap·jə·lər] *adj* **1.** (*liked*) popular; **she is very ~ among her co-workers** es muy apreciada entre sus compañeros; **he is ~ with girls** tiene éxito con las chicas **2.** (*by the people*) popular; **~ elections** elecciones *fpl* democráticas; **~ front** frente *m* popular; **~ support** el apoyo del pueblo; **by ~ request** a petición del público **3.** (*widespread*) generalizado, -a
popularity [,pap·jə·'lær·ə·t̬i] *n* popularidad *f*
popularize ['pap·jə·lə·raɪz] *vt* **1.** (*make known*

or liked) popularizar **2.** (*make understood*) divulgar
popularly ['pap·jə·lər·li] *adv* generalmente; **to be ~ known as...** ser vulgarmente conocido como...
populate ['pap·jə·leɪt] *vt* poblar
population [,pap·jə·'leɪ·ʃən] *n* población *f;* **the working ~** la población activa; **the dolphin ~** la población de delfines
population density *n* densidad *f* de población
population explosion *n* explosión *f* demográfica
populism ['pap·jə·lɪz·əm] *n* populismo *m*
populist ['pap·jə·lɪst] *n* populista *mf*
populous ['pap·ju·ləs] *adj* populoso, -a
pop-up ['pap·ʌp] *n* COMPUT ventana *f* emergente
porcelain ['pɔr·sə·lɪn] *n* porcelana *f*
porch [pɔrtʃ] *n* **1.** (*over entrance*) porche *m;* (*church*) pórtico *m* **2.** (*verandah*) veranda *f*
porcupine ['pɔr·kju·paɪn] *n* puercoespín *m*
pore [pɔr] *n* poro *m*
◆ **pore over** *vi* reflexionar sobre; **to ~ a book/map** estudiar detenidamente un libro/ mapa
pork [pɔrk] *n* (carne *f* de) cerdo *m,* (carne *f* de) puerco *m Méx,* (carne *f* de) chancho *m Chile, Perú*
pork chop *n* chuleta *f* de cerdo
porker *n* cebón *m*
porky <-ier, -iest> *adj pej, sl* gordinflón, -ona
porn [pɔrn] *n abbr of* **pornography** porno *m*
pornographic [,pɔr·nə·'græf·ɪk] *adj* pornográfico, -a
pornography [pɔr·'nag·rə·fi] *n* pornografía *f;* **hard-core ~** pornografía dura
porous ['pɔr·əs] *adj* poroso, -a
porpoise ['pɔr·pəs] *n* marsopa *f*
porridge ['pɔr·ɪdʒ] *n* ≈ gachas *fpl* de avena
port¹ [pɔrt] *n* **1.** NAUT (*harbor*) puerto *m;* **~ of call** puerto de escala; **~ of entry** puerto de entrada; **fishing/trading ~** puerto pesquero/ comercial; **to come into ~** tomar puerto; **to leave ~** zarpar **2.** COMPUT puerto *m;* **parallel/ serial/printer/game ~** puerto paralelo/serial/de impresora/de juegos ▶ **any ~ in a storm** en tiempos de guerrra cualquier hoyo es trinchera
port² [pɔrt] I. *n* AVIAT, NAUT (*left side*) babor *m;* **to ~** a babor II. *adj* NAUT, AVIAT de babor; **on the ~ side** a babor
port³ [pɔrt] *n* (*wine*) oporto *m*
portable ['pɔr·t̬ə·bəl] *adj* portátil
portage ['pɔr·t̬ɪdʒ] *n* porte *m*
portal ['pɔr·t̬əl] *n a.* COMPUT (*gateway*) portal *m*
port authority *n* autoridad *f* portuaria
port charges *npl* derechos *mpl* portuarios
portcullis [,pɔrt·'kʌl·ɪs] <-es> *n* (*in gateway*) rastrillo *m*
port dues *npl* derechos *mpl* portuarios
portentous [pɔr·'ten·t̬əs] *adj* **1.** *form* (*signifying something to come*) profético, -a; (*ominous*) de mal agüero **2.** (*too serious*) solemne

P

porter ['pɔr·ʧər] *n* **1.** (*person who carries luggage*) mozo *m* de equipajes; (*on expedition*) porteador *m* **2.** (*attendant on a train*) camarero *m*

portfolio [pɔrt·'fou·li·ou] *n* **1.** (*case*) portafolio(s) *m* (*inv*) **2.** (*of drawings, designs*) carpeta *f* de trabajos **3.** FIN, POL cartera *f*; **minister without** ~ *Can* ministro, -a *m, f* sin cartera

porthole ['pɔrt·houl] *n* portilla *f*

portico ['pɔr·ʧi·kou] <-es *o* -s> *n* pórtico *m*

portion ['pɔr·ʃən] **I.** *n* **1.** (*part*) parte *f*; **to accept one's ~ of the blame** aceptar su parte de culpa **2.** (*serving*) ración *f*; (*of cake, cheese*) trozo *m* **II.** *vt* **to ~ out sth** repartir algo

portly ['pɔrt·li] <-ier, -iest> *adj* corpulento, -a

portrait ['pɔr·trɪt] **I.** *n* ART, LIT retrato *m*; **to paint a ~ of sb** retratar a alguien **II.** *adj* TYPO de formato vertical

portraitist *n*, **portrait painter** *n* retratista *mf*

portraiture ['pɔr·trɪ·ʧər] *n* ART, LIT retrato *m*

portray [pɔr·'treɪ] *vt* **1.** ART (*person*) retratar; (*object*) pintar; (*scene, environment*) representar **2.** *fig* describir **3.** THEAT interpretar

portrayal [pɔr·'treɪ·əl] *n* **1.** ART retrato *m* **2.** *fig* descripción *f* **3.** THEAT interpretación *f*

Portugal ['pɔr·ʧə·gəl] *n* Portugal *m*

Portuguese [ˌpɔr·ʧə·'giz] **I.** *adj* portugués, -esa **II.** *n* **1.** (*person*) portugués, -esa *m, f* **2.** LING portugués *m*

POS [ˌpi·ou·'es] *abbr of* **point-of-sale** punto *m* de venta

pose[1] [pouz] *vt* (*difficulty, problem*) plantear; (*question*) formular; **to ~ a threat to sb** representar una amenaza para alguien

pose[2] [pouz] **I.** *vi* **1.** ART, PHOT posar **2.** (*affected behavior*) darse aires **3.** (*pretend to be*) **to ~ as sb/sth** hacerse pasar por alguien/algo **II.** *n* **1.** (*body position*) pose *f*; **to adopt a ~** adoptar una pose **2.** (*pretence*) afectación *f*; **it's all a ~** es todo fachada

poser ['pou·zər] *n* **1.** *inf* (*question*) pregunta *f* difícil; (*problem*) dilema *m* **2.** *s.* **poseur**

poseur ['pou·zər] *n pej* (*person*) **he's a ~** se hace el interesante

posh [paʃ] *adj inf* (*stylish: area*) elegante; (*car, hotel, restaurant*) de lujo, pijo, -a *pey*

posit ['paz·ɪt] *vt form* postular

position [pə·'zɪʃ·ən] **I.** *n* **1.** *a.* MIL, SPORTS posición *f*; **from this ~ you can see the whole beach** desde este lugar se puede ver toda la playa; **the ~ of a house** la ubicación de una casa; **they took up their ~s** ocuparon sus puestos; **to be in ~** estar en su sitio; **to be out of ~** estar fuera de lugar; **yoga ~** postura *f* de yoga **2.** (*rank*) posición *f*, puesto *m*; (*social*) rango *m*; (*job*) puesto *m* (de trabajo); **the ~ of director** el cargo de director; **a ~ of responsibility/trust** un puesto de responsabilidad/confianza **3.** (*opinion*) postura *f*; **to take a ~ on sth** adoptar una postura sobre algo **4.** (*situation*) situación *f*; **financial ~** situación económica; **to be in the fortunate ~ of...** tener la suerte de...; **to be in a ~ to do sth** estar en

condiciones de hacer algo; **to be in no ~ to do sth** no estar en condiciones de hacer algo; **to put sb in a difficult ~** poner a alguien en un aprieto **II.** *vt* (*place*) colocar; MIL apostar

positive ['paz·ɪ·ʧɪv] *adj* **1.** *a.* ELEC, MATH positivo, -a; ~ **criticism** crítica *f* constructiva **2.** MED HIV ~ seropositivo, -a **3.** (*certain*) definitivo, -a; (*proof*) concluyente; **to be ~ about sth** estar seguro de algo; (*absolutely*) ~! ¡segurísimo! **4.** (*complete*) auténtico, -a; **a ~ miracle** un verdadero milagro

positively *adv* **1.** (*think*) positivamente; **to answer ~** contestar afirmativamente; **to think ~** pensar en positivo **2.** (*completely*) totalmente; **to ~ refuse to do sth** negarse rotundamente a hacer algo

poss. *abbr of* **possessive** posesivo *m*

posse ['pas·i] *n inf* banda *f*; **a whole ~ of reporters** una legión de reporteros

possess [pə·'zes] *vt* **1.** (*own, have*) poseer **2.** **to ~ sb** (*anger, fear*) apoderarse de alguien; (*evil spirit*) poseer a alguien; **what ~ed you to do that?** ¿cómo se te ocurrió hacer eso?

possessed [pə·'zest] *adj* poseso, -a, poseído, -a; **to be ~ with sth** estar obsesionado con algo; **to behave like sb ~** comportarse como un poseso

possession [pə·'zeʃ·ən] *n* **1.** (*having*) posesión *f*; **illegal ~ of arms** tenencia *f* ilícita de armas; **to take ~ of sth** tomar posesión de algo; **to come into ~ of sth** hacerse con algo; **to gain ~ of sth** apoderarse de algo; **to be in sb's ~** estar en poder de alguien; **to have sth in one's ~** *form* tener algo en su poder **2.** (*item of property*) bien *m* **3.** POL dominio *m* **4.** SPORTS **to be in ~ of the ball** llevar la bola ▶ ~ **is nine tenths of the law** la posesión es lo que cuenta

possessive [pə·'zes·ɪv] *adj* posesivo, -a; **to be ~ about sb** comportarse de manera posesiva con alguien

possessor [pə·'zes·ər] *n* poseedor(a) *m(f)*

possibility [ˌpas·ə·'bɪl·ə·ʧi] *n* <-ies> **1.** (*sth feasible*) posibilidad *f* **2.** (*likelihood*) perspectiva *f*; **within the realm of ~** dentro de lo posible; **if by any ~...** si por casualidad...; **is there any ~ (that)...?** ¿hay alguna posibilidad de que +*subj*...? **3.** (*potential*) **to have possibilities** tener posibilidades

possible ['pas·ə·bəl] *adj* posible; **as clean/good as ~** lo más limpio/lo mejor posible; **as far as ~** en lo posible; **as soon as ~** lo antes posible; **if ~** si es posible

possibly ['pas·ə·bli] *adv* **1.** (*perhaps*) quizás, posiblemente; **could you ~ help me?** ¿sería tan amable de ayudarme? **2.** (*by any means*) **we did all that we ~ could** hicimos todo lo posible; **I couldn't ~ do it** me es totalmente imposible hacerlo

possum ['pas·əm] <-(s)> *n* zarigüeya *f* ▶ **to play ~** (*pretend to be asleep*) hacerse el dormido; (*pretend to be ignorant*) hacerse el sueco [*o* tonto]

post¹ [poʊst] **I.** *n* correo *m* **II.** *vt* **1.** (*letter, package*) echar (al correo); **to ~ sth to sb** enviar algo por correo a alguien **2.** (*inform*) **to keep sb ~ed on sth** tener a alguien al corriente de algo **3.** (*in bookkeeping*) registrar

post² [poʊst] **I.** *n* (*job*) puesto *m* (de trabajo); **to apply for a teaching ~** solicitar un empleo de profesor; **to take up a ~** entrar en funciones; **to desert one's ~** MIL desertar del puesto **II.** *vt* **1.** (*send to work*) destinar **2.** MIL (*position*) apostar

post³ [poʊst] **I.** *n* **1. a.** SPORTS poste *m;* **starting/finishing ~** línea *f* de salida/de meta **2.** *inf* (*goalpost*) poste *m* (de la portería) **II.** *vt* **to ~ sth (on sth)** publicar algo (en algo); **to ~ sth on the bulletin board** poner algo en el tablón de anuncios; **~ no bills** prohibido fijar carteles

postage ['poʊ·stɪdʒ] *n* franqueo *m; ~ and handling* gastos *mpl* de envío

postage meter *n* (máquina *f*) franqueadora, estampilladora *f AmL*

postage paid *adj* con [o de] franqueo pagado

postage rate *n* tarifa *f* postal

postage stamp *n form* sello *m,* estampilla *f AmL*

postal ['poʊ·stəl] *adj* postal

postal worker *n* empleado, -a *m, f* de correos

post card *n* (tarjeta *f*) postal *f*

postdate [ˌpoʊst·'deɪt] *vt* **1.** (*write a later date on*) posfechar **2.** (*happen after*) ocurrir después de

postdoctoral [ˌpoʊst·'dak·tər·əl] *adj* postdoctoral

poster ['poʊ·stər] *n* **1.** (*picture*) póster *m* **2.** (*notice*) cartel *m*

posterior [pɑ·'stɪr·i·ər] **I.** *adj form* posterior **II.** *n fig* trasero *m inf*

posterity [pɑ·'ster·ə·ti] *n form* posteridad *f;* **to preserve sth for ~** guardar algo para la posteridad

postern ['poʊ·stərn] *n* postigo *m;* MIL poterna *f*

postgraduate [ˌpoʊst·'grædʒ·u·ɪt] **I.** *n* postgraduado, -a *m, f* **II.** *adj* de postgrado; **~ studies** (estudios *mpl* de) postgrado *m*

posthaste [ˌpoʊst·'heɪst] *adv form* con presteza

posthumous ['pɑs·tʃə·məs] *adj form* póstumo, -a

posting ['poʊ·stɪŋ] *n* destino *m*

Post-It® *n* post-it *m*

postman ['poʊst·mən] <-men> *n* cartero *m*

postmark ['poʊst·mɑrk] **I.** *n* matasellos *m inv* **II.** *vt* matasellar; **the letter is ~ed Rome** la carta lleva matasellos de Roma

postmaster ['poʊst·ˌmæs·tər] *n* jefe *m* de la oficina de correos; **~ general** director general de correos

post meridiem *adv s.* **P.M.**

postmodern [ˌpoʊst·'mad·ərn] *adj* posmoderno, -a

postmodernism *n* posmodernismo *m*

postmortem [ˌpoʊst·'mɔr·təm] *n* autopsia *f;* **to carry out a ~** realizar una autopsia

postnatal [ˌpoʊst·'neɪ·təl] *adj* postnatal; **~ depression** depresión *f* posparto

post office *n* (oficina *f* de) correos *m;* **to take sth to the ~** llevar algo a correos

post office box *n* apartado *m* de correos, casilla *f* postal *CSur*

post-op [ˌpoʊst·'ap] *adj inf* MED *abbr of* **post-operative** postoperatorio, -a

postoperative [ˌpoʊst·'ap·ər·ə·ṭɪv] *adj* MED postoperatorio, -a

postpaid [ˌpoʊst·'peɪd] **I.** *adj* (*letter*) con franqueo pagado; (*package*) sin gastos de franqueo **II.** *adv* (*send: letter*) con franqueo pagado; (*parcel*) con porte pagado

postpone [poʊst·'poʊn] *vt* aplazar, posponer, postergar *AmL*

postponement *n* aplazamiento *m,* postergación *f AmL*

postscript ['poʊst·skrɪp] *n* **1.** (*at end of letter*) pos(t)data *f* **2.** *fig* epílogo *m;* **as a ~ to sth** como colofón de algo

postulate¹ ['pɑs·tʃə·leɪt] *vt form* **1.** (*hypothesize*) postular **2.** (*assume*) presuponer

postulate² ['pɑs·tʃə·lɪt] *n form* postulado *m*

posture ['pɑs·tʃər] **I.** *n* postura *f,* actitud *f* **II.** *vi* tomar una postura, adoptar una actitud; **to ~ as sth** *pej* dárselas de algo

postwar [ˌpoʊst·'wɔr] *adj* de la posguerra; **the ~ years** la posguerra, los años de posguerra

posy ['poʊ·zi] <-ies> *n* ramillete *m*

pot¹ [pat] *n* **1.** (*container*) bote *m* **2.** (*for cooking*) olla *f; ~s and pans* cacharros *mpl* **3.** (*of food*) tarro *m;* (*of drink*) jarro *m;* (*for coffee*) cafetera *f;* (*for tea*) tetera *f* **4.** maceta *f,* tiesto *m* **5.** *inf* GAMES **to win the ~** llevarse el bote **6.** (*common fund*) fondo *m* común **7.** *inf* (*a lot*) montón *m; ~s of money* montones de dinero **8.** *fig* (*beer belly*) barriga *f inf* ▶ **it's like the ~ calling the kettle black** dijo la sartén al cazo, apártate que me tiznas; **to go to ~** *inf* echarse a perder; (*business, plan*) irse al garete **II.** <-tt-> *vt* **1.** (*put in a pot: food*) conservar en un tarro; **to ~ (up)** (*plants*) plantar **2.** (*shoot*) cazar **3.** SPORTS (*ball*) meter (en la tronera)

pot² [pat] *n sl* (*marijuana*) hierba *f,* maría *f,* mota *f Méx;* **to smoke ~** fumar maría

potash ['pat·æʃ] *n* potasa *f*

potassium [pə·'tæs·i·əm] *n* potasio *m*

potassium chloride *n* cloruro *m* potásico

potassium cyanide *n* cianuro *m* potásico

potassium permanganate *n* permanganato *m* potásico

potato [pə·'teɪ·toʊ] <-es> *n* patata *f,* papa *f AmL;* **sweet ~** batata *f;* **baked ~** patata al horno; **mashed ~es** puré *m* de patatas; **fried/roast(ed) ~s** patatas fritas/asadas

potato beetle *n,* **potato bug** *n* escarabajo *m* de la patata

potato chips *npl* patatas *fpl* fritas (en bolsa), papas *fpl* chip *AmL*

potato masher *n* pasapurés *m inv*

potato peeler *n* pelapatatas *m inv,* pelapapas *m*

P

inv AmL
potbellied *adj* barrigudo, -a
potbelly [pat·'bel·i] <-ies> *n* barriga *f*, guata *f* Chile
potbelly stove *n* estufa *f* de leña
potboiler ['pat·ˌbɔɪ·lər] *n pej: libro escrito rápidamente para ganar dinero*
potency ['poʊ·tən·si] *n* potencia *f*; (*of drink, evil, temptation*) fuerza *f*; (*of spell*) poder *m*
potent ['poʊ·tənt] *adj* potente; (*drink, poison, symbol*) fuerte; (*motive*) poderoso, -a; (*remedy*) eficaz; (*argument*) convincente
potentate ['poʊ·tən·teɪt] *n liter* potentado, -a *m, f*
potential [pə·'ten·ʃəl] I. *adj* 1. posible 2. LING, PHYS potencial II. *n* potencial *m;* **to have (a lot of)** ~ tener (un gran) potencial
potentiality [pə·ˌten·ʃi·'æl·ə·ti] *n form* posibilidad *f*
potentially [pə·'ten·ʃə·li] *adv* potencialmente
potholder ['pat·ˌhoʊl·dər] *n* agarrador *m*
pothole ['pat·ˌhoʊl] *n* 1. (*in road*) bache *m*, pozo *m CSur* 2. (*underground hole*) sima *f*
potion ['poʊ·ʃən] *n* poción *f*, pócima *f*
potluck *n* 1. (*sth left over*) **to take** ~ tomar lo que haya 2. *s.* **potluck dinner**
potluck dinner *n* cena a la que cada invitado lleva un plato para compartir con los demás, cena *f* de traje *Méx*

> ⓘ Un **potluck** es en EE.UU. una fiesta a la que cada invitado lleva una ensalada, un plato principal o un postre. Siempre se espera que de todo ello resulte una comida completa, pero puede ocurrir que al final, por ejemplo, no haya para comer más que postres.

potpourri [ˌpoʊ·pʊ·'ri] *n* popurrí *m*
pot roast *n* estofado *m*
potshot ['pat·ʃat] *n* tiro *m* al azar; **to take a** ~ **at sb** disparar al azar contra alguien; *fig* (*criticize*) arremeter contra alguien
potted ['pat·ɪd] *adj* 1. (*plant*) en tiesto, en maceta 2. (*food*) en conserva; ~ **shrimps** pasta *f* de camarones
potter ['pat·ər] *n* alfarero, -a *m, f*; ~'**s wheel** torno *m* de alfarero
pottery ['pat·ə·ri] *n* 1. (*art*) cerámica *f* 2. <-ies> (*workshop*) alfarería *f*
potty ['pat·i] <-ies> *n* (*for baby*) orinal *m;* **to go (to the)** ~ (*small child*) (ir a) hacer pis
pouch [paʊtʃ] *n* 1. a. ANAT, ZOOL bolsa *f* 2. (*handbag*) bolso *m*; (*for mail*) valija *f*; **tobacco** ~ petaca *f*
pouf [puf] *n* puf *m*
pouffy ['pu·fi] *adj* (*hair*) abultado, -a
poultice ['poʊl·tɪs] *n* cataplasma *f*
poultry ['poʊl·tri] *n* 1. (*birds*) aves *fpl* de corral 2. (*meat*) carne *f* de ave
poultry farm *n* granja *f* avícola
poultry farming *n* avicultura *f*

pounce [paʊns] I. *n* (*spring*) salto *m* II. *vi* 1. (*jump*) saltar; **to** ~ **on sth** abalanzarse sobre algo; (*cat*) lanzarse sobre algo; (*bird of prey*) precipitarse sobre algo 2. *fig* **to** ~ **on an opportunity** no dejar escapar una oportunidad
pound¹ [paʊnd] *n* 1. (*weight*) libra *f* (*454 g*); **by the** ~ por libras 2. (*currency*) libra *f;* ~ **sterling** libra esterlina
pound² [paʊnd] *n* (*for cars*) depósito *m*; (*for dogs*) perrera *f*; (*for sheep*) redil *m*
pound³ [paʊnd] I. *vt* 1. (*hit repeatedly*) aporrear; (*beat*) golpear; (*with a hammer*) martillear; **the waves** ~**ed the ship** las olas batían contra el barco 2. (*walk heavily*) patear; **I could hear him** ~**ing the floor upstairs** podía oír sus pasos en el piso de arriba 3. (*crush*) machacar; (*meat*) golpear, ablandar *Méx*, machacar *Col* 4. MIL batir; **to** ~ **sth to rubble** reducir algo a escombros II. *vi* 1. (*beat*) dar golpes; (*on a door, table*) aporrear; (*heart, pulse*) latir con fuerza; (*music*) retumbar; **to** ~ **away on a piano** aporrear un piano; **the waves** ~**ed against the shore** las olas azotaban la orilla; **my head is** ~**ing!** ¡la cabeza me va a estallar! 2. (*run*) **to** ~ **downstairs** bajar corriendo 3. *fig* **to** ~ **away at sth** insistir en algo
pounding *n* 1. (*noise*) golpeteo *m*; (*of heart*) fuerte latido *m;* (*of sea*) embate *m;* (*in head*) martilleo *m* 2. (*crushing*) trituración *f*; (*grinding*) molienda *f* 3. (*attack*) ataque *m; a. fig* (*beating*) paliza *f inf;* **to take a** ~ *a. fig* llevarse una paliza; **the film took a heavy** ~ la película tuvo muy malas críticas
pour [pɔr] I. *vt* 1. (*cause to flow*) verter; **to** ~ **coffee/wine** echar café/vino; **to** ~ **sb sth** servir algo a alguien; **to** ~ **oneself a glass of wine** echarse un vaso de vino 2. (*give in large amounts*) verter; (*money, resources*) invertir; **to** ~ **time into sth** dedicar tiempo a algo; **to** ~ **energy into sth** volcarse en algo II. *vi* 1. (*flow in large amounts: water*) fluir; (*letters, messages*) llegar en grandes cantidades; **to** ~ **into sth** (*sunshine*) entrar a raudales en algo; (*people*) entrar en tropel en algo; **refugees are** ~**ing into the country** no cesan de llegar refugiados al país; **to be** ~**ing with sweat** estar empapado en sudor 2. *impers* **it's** ~**ing** llueve a cántaros
♦**pour in** *vi* llegar en abundancia
♦**pour out** I. *vt* 1. (*from container*) verter 2. (*cause to flow quickly: smoke, water*) echar; **to** ~ **one's thanks** dar las gracias efusivamente 3. (*tell*) **to** ~ **sth to sb** revelar algo a alguien II. *vi* (*liquid*) salir; (*people*) salir en tropel
pout [paʊt] I. *vi* hacer un mohín II. *vt* **to** ~ **one's lips** hacer un mohín III. *n* mohín *m*
poverty ['pav·ər·ti] *n* 1. (*lack of money*) pobreza *f*; **extreme** ~ miseria *f* 2. *fig* (*lack of ideas, imagination*) escasez *f*
poverty level *n* umbral *m* de la pobreza; **to live below the** ~ vivir por debajo del umbral

de la pobreza

poverty-stricken ['pav·ər·ţi·ˌstrɪk·ən] *adj* muy pobre

POW [ˌpi·ou·'dʌb·əl·ju] *n abbr of* **prisoner of war** prisionero, -a *m, f* de guerra

powder ['pau·dər] **I.** *n* **1.** (*dust*) polvo *m;* **to crush** [*o* **reduce**] **sth to a ~** reducir algo a polvo **2.** (*makeup*) polvos *mpl;* **talcum ~** polvos (de) talco **3.** (*snow*) nieve *f* en polvo **II.** *vt* **1.** (*cover with powder*) empolvar; **to ~ one's face** empolvarse; **to ~ one's nose** *fig* ir al servicio **2.** (*sprinkle*) espolvorear **3.** *sl* (*win easily*) dar una paliza a

powder blue *n* azul *m* pastel

powdered *adj* en polvo; **~ sugar** azúcar *m* glas

powder keg *n fig* polvorín *m*

powder puff *n* borla *f,* cisne *m RíoPl*

powder room *n* tocador *m*

powdery ['pau·də·ri] *adj* como de polvo

power ['pau·ər] **I.** *n* **1.** (*ability to control*) poder *m;* **to be within one's ~ to do sth** estar en manos de alguien hacer algo **2.** (*country, organization, person*) potencia *f* **3.** (*right*) derecho *m* **4.** (*ability*) capacidad *f;* **sb's ~s of concentration/persuasion/observation** la capacidad de concentración/persuasión/ observación de alguien **5.** (*strength*) fuerza *f* **6.** (*electricity*) electricidad *f;* **to cut** (**off**) **the ~** cortar la corriente **7.** (*energy*) energía *f* **8.** MATH potencia *f;* **two to the ~ of five** dos elevado a la quinta potencia ▶ **more ~ to you!** ¡que tengas suerte!; **to be the ~ behind sb** ser el poder en la sombra; **the ~s that be** las autoridades **II.** *vi* **to ~ along the track** ir disparado por el camino **III.** *vt* impulsar

powerboat *n* lancha *f* fuera borda

power brakes *npl* AUTO frenos *mpl* asistidos, servofrenos *mpl*

power cable *n* cable *m* de energía eléctrica

power-driven *adj* eléctrico, -a

powerful ['pau·ər·fəl] *adj* **1.** (*influential, mighty*) poderoso, -a **2.** (*physically strong*) fuerte **3.** (*having a great effect*) convincente **4.** (*anger, jealousy*) intenso, -a; **~ emotions** emociones *fpl* fuertes **5.** (*able to perform well*) potente

powerfully ['pau·ər·fə·li] *adv* **1.** (*using great force*) con potencia **2.** (*argue, speak*) de forma convincente

powerhouse ['pau·ər·ˌhaus] *n* fuente *f* de energía; **to be a ~ of ideas** *fig* ser una fuente inagotable de ideas

powerless ['pau·ər·lɪs] *adj* impotente; **to be ~ against sb** no poder hacer nada contra alguien

power line *n* línea *f* eléctrica

power mower *n* segadora *f* eléctrica

power outage *n* apagón *m*

power plant *n* central *f* eléctrica; **nuclear ~** central *f* nuclear

power politics *n* política *f* de fuerza

power station *n* central *f* eléctrica

power steering *n* dirección *f* asistida

power tool *n* herramienta *f* mecánica

powwow ['pau·wau] *n* **1.** asamblea *f* (*de indígenas norteamericanos*) **2.** *fig, inf* discusión *f*

pox [paks] *n* MED (*chickenpox*) varicela *f;* (*smallpox*) viruela *f;* (*syphilis*) sífilis *f inv*

pp. *abbr of* **pages** págs.

PR [pi·'ar] *n* **1.** *abbr of* **public relations** relaciones *fpl* públicas **2.** POL *abbr of* **proportional representation** representación *f* proporcional **3.** GEO *abbr of* **Puerto Rico** Puerto Rico *m*

practicable ['præk·tɪ·kə·bəl] *adj form* factible

practical ['præk·tɪ·kəl] **I.** *adj* práctico, -a **II.** *n* examen *m* práctico

practicality [ˌpræk·tɪ·'kæl·ə·ţi] *n* <-ies> **1.** (*feasibility*) viabilidad *f* **2.** (*practical detail*) **the practicalities of sth** los detalles prácticos de algo

practical joke *n* broma *f* pesada, trastada *f*

practically ['præk·tɪk·li] *adv* **1.** (*almost*) casi **2.** (*of a practical nature*) **to be ~ based** basarse en la práctica; **to be ~ minded** tener sentido práctico

practice ['præk·tɪs] **I.** *n* **1.** (*act of practicing*) práctica *f;* **to be out of ~** estar desentrenado; **~ makes perfect** se aprende con la práctica **2.** (*custom, regular activity*) costumbre *f;* **traditional religious ~s** tradiciones *fpl* religiosas; **standard ~** práctica *f* habitual; **to make a ~ of sth** tener algo como norma **3.** (*training session*) entrenamiento *m* **4.** (*of a profession*) ejercicio *m* **5.** (*business, office*) bufete *m;* (*medical*) consulta *f* **II.** *vt* **1.** (*do, carry out*) practicar **2.** (*improve skill*) hacer ejercicios de; **to ~ the piano** estudiar el piano **3.** (*work in: medicine, law*) ejercer ▶ **to ~ what one preaches** predicar con el ejemplo **III.** *vi* **1.** (*improve skill*) practicar; SPORTS entrenarse **2.** (*work in profession*) ejercer; **to ~ as a doctor** ejercer de médico

practiced ['præk·tɪst] *adj* (*experienced, skilled*) experto, -a; **to be ~ in sth** tener experiencia en algo; **a ~ liar** un mentiroso consumado

practicing ['præk·tɪs·ɪŋ] *adj* (*doctor, lawyer*) en ejercicio; (*Catholic, Jew*) practicante

practitioner [præk·'tɪʃ·ə·nər] *n* (*of a skill*) profesional *mf;* (*doctor*) médico, -a *m, f;* **legal ~** abogado, -a *m, f*

pragmatic [præg·'mæţ·ɪk] *adj* pragmático, -a

pragmatism ['præg·mə·tɪz·əm] *n* pragmatismo *m*

prairie ['prer·i] *n* pradera *f*

praise [preɪz] **I.** *vt* **1.** (*express approval*) elogiar; **to ~ sb to the skies** [*o* **to no end**] poner a alguien por las nubes **2.** (*worship*) alabar **II.** *n* **1.** (*expression of approval*) elogio *m;* **to heap ~ on sb, to shower sb with ~** cubrir a alguien de alabanzas **2.** (*worship*) alabanza *f;* **~ be** (**to God**)! ¡alabado sea (Dios)!

praiseworthy ['preɪz·ˌwɜr·ði] *adj* loable

prance [præns] *vi* (*horse*) hacer cabriolas; (*person*) pavonearse

prank [præŋk] *n* broma *f;* **to play a ~ on sb** gastar una broma a alguien

P

prate [preɪt] *vi form* parlotear
prattle ['præt̬·əl] I. *vi* parlotear; (*child*) balbucear II. *n* parloteo *m;* (*of child*) balbuceo *m*
prawn [prɔn] *n* gamba *f*
prawn cocktail *n* cóctel *m* de gambas
pray [preɪ] I. *vi* 1. REL rezar; **to ~ to sb (that)** rogar a alguien (que +*subj*) 2. (*hope*) **to ~ for sth** rezar para obtener [*o* que ocurra] algo II. *vt* suplicar; **and what, ~ tell, are you doing?** ¿qué estás haciendo, si se puede saber?
prayer [prer] *n* 1. REL oración *f;* **to say a ~** [*o* **one's ~s**] rezar 2. (*action of praying*) rezo *m* 3. ~ **s** (*church service*), **morning/evening ~s** misa matinal/vespertina 4. *fig* (*hope*) súplica *f;* **to not have a ~ of doing sth** *inf* no tener ninguna posibilidad de hacer algo
prayer book *n* devocionario *m*
prayer meeting *n* reunión *f* de fieles para rezar
prayer rug *n* alfombra *f* de oración
praying mantis ['preɪ·ɪŋ·'mæn·tɪs] *n* mantis *f inv* religiosa
preach [pritʃ] I. *vi* predicar; **to ~ at sb** *pej* sermonear a alguien II. *vt* 1. REL (*a sermon, the Gospel*) predicar 2. (*advocate*) abogar por ▶ **to practice what you ~** predicar con el ejemplo
preacher ['pri·tʃər] *n* predicador(a) *m(f)*
preamble [pri·'æm·bəl] *n* preámbulo *m*
prearrange [ˌpri·ə·'reɪndʒ] *vt* organizar de antemano
precalculus [pri·'kæl·kjə·ləs] *n* precálculo *m*
precarious [prɪ·'ker·i·əs] *adj* precario, -a
precast ['pri·kæst] *adj* prefabricado, -a
precaution [prɪ·'kɔ·ʃən] *n* precaución *f*
precautionary [ˌprɪ·'kɔ·ʃə·ner·i] *adj* de precaución; ~ **measure** medida *f* preventiva
precede [prɪ·'sid] *vt* preceder; **to ~ the report with an introduction** empezar el informe con una introducción
precedence ['pres·ə·dəns] *n* 1. (*priority*) prioridad *f;* **to take ~ over sb** tener prioridad sobre alguien 2. (*order of priority*) preferencia *f*
precedent ['pres·ə·dent] *n* precedente *m;* **to set a ~ (for sth/doing sth)** sentar un precedente (para algo/hacer algo)
preceding [prɪ·'si·dɪŋ] *adj* precedente; **the ~ day** el día anterior
precept ['pri·sept] *n form* 1. (*rule*) precepto *m* 2. (*principle*) principio *m*
precinct ['pri·sɪŋkt] *n* 1. (*police district*) distrito *m* policial; (*police station*) comisaría *f* (de policía) 2. (*electoral district*) distrito *m*, circunscripción *f* 3. *form* (*environs*) alrededores *mpl*
precious ['preʃ·əs] I. *adj* 1. (*valuable: stone, metal*) precioso, -a; **you can keep your ~ ring!** *iron* ¡guárdate tu maldito anillo! 2. (*beloved: child, pet*) querido, -a 3. (*affected*) afectado, -a; (*person*) amanerado, -a II. *adv inf* (*very*) muy; ~ **few** muy pocos; **to be ~ little help** ser de muy poca ayuda
precipice ['pres·ə·pɪs] *n* precipicio *m*
precipitate¹ [prɪ·'sɪp·ɪ·teɪt] I. *vt* 1. *form* (*throw*) arrojar 2. *form* (*provoke*) precipitar 3. CHEM precipitar II. *vi* METEO precipitar

precipitate² [prɪ·'sɪp·ɪ·tɪt] I. *adj form* precipitado, -a II. *n* precipitado *m*
precipitation [prɪˌsɪp·ɪ·'teɪ·ʃən] *n* precipitación *f*
precipitous [prɪ·'sɪp·ɪ·t̬əs] *adj* 1. (*very steep*) empinado, -a 2. (*having many precipices*) escarpado, -a 3. (*rapid*) apresurado, -a 4. *form* (*precipitate*) precipitado, -a
précis [preɪ·'si] I. *n* resumen *m* II. *vt form* resumir
precise [prɪ·'saɪs] *adj* 1. (*moment, measurement*) preciso, -a 2. (*person*) meticuloso, -a
precisely *adv* 1. (*exactly*) precisamente; ~ **!** ¡eso es!; **to do ~ the opposite** hacer justamente [*o* justo] lo contrario 2. (*carefully*) meticulosamente
precision [prɪ·'sɪʒ·ən] I. *n* 1. (*accuracy*) precisión *f* 2. (*meticulous care*) exactitud *f* II. *adj* (*tool, equipment*) de precisión
preclude [prɪ·'klud] *vt form* excluir
precocious [prɪ·'kou·ʃəs] *adj* precoz
precociousness *n*, **precocity** [prɪ·'kas·ə·t̬i] *n form* precocidad *f*
preconceived [ˌpri·kən·'sivd] *adj* preconcebido, -a
preconception [ˌpri·kən·'sep·ʃən] *n* idea *f* preconcebida
precondition [ˌpri·kən·'dɪʃ·ən] *n* condición *f* previa
preconfigured *adj* **a ~ computer** una computadora *f* preconfigurada
precook [pri·'kʊk] *vt* precocinar
precursor [prɪ·'kɜr·sər] *n* precursor(a) *m(f)*
predate [pri·'deɪt] *vt* preceder
predator ['pred·ə·t̬ər] *n* depredador *m*
predatory ['pred·ə·tɔr·i] *adj* depredador(a)
predecessor ['pred·ə·ses·ər] *n* predecesor(a) *m(f);* (*ancestor*) antepasado, -a *m, f*
predestination [ˌpri·des·tɪ·'neɪ·ʃən] *n* predestinación *f*
predestine [ˌpri·'des·tɪn] *vt* predestinar
predetermine [ˌpri·dɪ·'tɜr·mən] *vt* predeterminar; **to ~ the consequences** determinar de antemano las consecuencias
predicament [prɪ·'dɪk·ə·mənt] *n* apuro *m*
predicate¹ ['pred·ɪ·kɪt] *n* LING predicado *m*
predicate² ['pred·ɪ·keɪt] *vt form* 1. (*be based on*) **to be ~d on sth** estar basado en algo 2. (*state, assert*) afirmar
predicative [prɪ·'dɪk·ə·t̬ɪv] *adj* LING predicativo, -a
predict [prɪ·'dɪkt] *vt* predecir
predictable [prɪ·'dɪk·tə·bəl] *adj* previsible
prediction [prɪ·'dɪk·ʃən] *n* 1. (*forecast*) pronóstico *m* 2. (*act of predicting*) predicción *f*
predilection [ˌpred·əl·'ek·ʃən] *n form* predilección *f*
predispose [ˌpri·dɪ·'spouz] *vt* predisponer
predisposition [ˌpri·dɪs·pə·'zɪʃ·ən] *n* 1. *form* (*tendency*) predisposición *f* 2. MED propensión *f*
predominance [prɪ·'dam·ə·nəns] *n* predominio *m*

predominant [prɪ·'dam·ə·nənt] *adj* predominante

predominate [prɪ·'dam·ə·neɪt] *vi* predominar

preemie ['pri·mi] *n inf* (*premature baby*) bebé *m* prematuro

preeminence [ˌpri·'em·ɪ·nəns] *n form* preeminencia *f*

preeminent [ˌpri·'em·ɪ·nənt] *adj form* preeminente

preempt [ˌpri·'empt] *vt* adelantarse a

preemption [ˌpri·'emp·ʃən] *n* apropiación *f* (por derecho preferente)

preemptive [pri·'emp·tɪv] *adj* 1. (*right*) prioritario, -a 2. (*attack*) preventivo, -a

preen [prin] I. *vi* 1. (*bird*) arreglarse 2. *fig* (*congratulate oneself*) pavonearse II. *vt* 1. (*cat, bird*) arreglar 2. (*groom*) **to ~ oneself** atildarse; **to ~ oneself on sth** (*congratulate*) enorgullecerse de algo

preexisting [ˌpri·ɪg·'zɪs·tɪŋ] *adj* preexistente

prefab ['pri·fæb] *inf* I. *n abbr of* **prefabricated house** casa *f* prefabricada II. *adj abbr of* **prefabricated** prefabricado, -a

prefabricate [ˌpri·'fæb·rɪ·keɪt] *vt* prefabricar

prefabricated *adj* prefabricado, -a

prefabricated house *n* casa *f* prefabricada

preface ['pref·ɪs] I. *n* prefacio *m* II. *vt* introducir

prefatory ['pref·ə·tɔr·i] *adj form* preliminar

prefect ['pri·fekt] *n* prefecto *m*

prefer [pri·'fɜr] <-rr-> *vt* preferir

preferable ['pref·rə·bəl] *adj* preferible

preferably ['pref·rə·bli] *adv* preferentemente, preferiblemente

preference ['pref·rəns] *n* 1. (*liking better*) preferencia *f* 2. (*priority*) preferencia *f*

preferential [ˌpref·ə·'ren·ʃəl] *adj* preferente, ECON preferencial

preferred [pri·'fɜrd] *adj* preferido, -a

prefigure [ˌpri·'fɪg·jər] *vt form* prefigurar

prefix ['pri·fɪks] <-es> *n* prefijo *m*

pregnancy ['preg·nən·si] *n* 1. (*condition: woman*) embarazo *m*; ZOOL preñez *f* 2. (*period of time*) embarazo *m*

pregnancy test *n* prueba *f* de embarazo

pregnant ['preg·nənt] *adj* 1. (*woman*) embarazada; (*animal*) preñado; **to be ~ by sb** estar embarazada de alguien; **to become ~** (*woman*) quedarse embarazada; (*animal*) quedarse preñado; **to get sb ~** dejar embarazada a alguien 2. *fig* (*silence, pause*) muy significativo, -a; **to be ~ with possibilities for sth** tener muchas posibilidades para algo

prehensile [pri·'hen·sɪl] *adj* prensil

prehistoric [ˌpri·hɪ·'stɔr·ɪk] *adj* prehistórico, -a

prehistory [ˌpri·'hɪs·tə·ri] *n* prehistoria *f*

prejudge [ˌpri·'dʒʌdʒ] *vt* prejuzgar

prejudice ['predʒ·ə·dɪs] I. *n* 1. (*preconceived opinion*) prejuicio *m* 2. (*bias*) parcialidad *f*; LAW perjuicio *m*; **without ~** sin detrimento de sus propios derechos; **without ~ to sth** LAW sin perjuicio de algo II. *vt* 1. (*bias*) **to ~ sb against sth** predisponer a alguien contra algo 2. (*dam-*

age: sb's case, a defendant, a candidate) perjudicar

prejudiced ['predʒ·ə·dɪst] *adj* (*person*) lleno, -a de prejuicios; (*attitude, judgment, opinion*) parcial; **to be ~ in favor of/against sb** estar predispuesto a favor de/contra alguien

prejudicial [ˌpredʒ·ə·'dɪʃ·əl] *adj form* perjudicial

preliminary [prɪ·'lɪm·ə·ner·i] I. *adj* preliminar II. <-ies> *n* 1. (*introduction*) preparativos *mpl* 2. SPORTS (*heat*) rondas *fpl* previas 3. *form* (*preliminary exam*) examen *m* preliminar

prelims ['pri·lɪms] *npl inf* 1. (*exams*) *abbr of* **preliminary exams** exámenes *mpl* preliminares 2. SPORTS rondas *fpl* previas 3. *abbr of* **preliminary pages** páginas *fpl* preliminares

prelude ['prel·jud] *n* preludio *m*

premarital [ˌpri·'mær·ɪ·təl] *adj* prematrimonial

premature [ˌpri·mə·'tʃʊr] *adj* prematuro, -a

premature ejaculation *n* eyaculación *f* precoz

premeditated [ˌpri·'med·ɪ·teɪ·tɪd] *adj* premeditado, -a

premeditation [ˌpri·med·ɪ·'teɪ·ʃən] *n* premeditación *f*

premenstrual [ˌpri·'men·strəl] *adj* premenstrual

premenstrual syndrome *n* síndrome *m* premenstrual

premier [prɪ·'mɪr] I. *n* POL primer ministro *m*, primera ministra *f* II. *adj* primero, -a

première [prɪ·'mɪr] I. *n* estreno *m* II. *vt, vi* estrenar

premise ['prem·ɪs] I. *n* 1. (*of argument*) premisa *f*; **on** [*o* **under**] **the ~ that...** en el supuesto de que... 2. *pl* (*land and building on it*) recinto *m* II. *vt form* 1. (*be based on*) basarse en 2. (*preface*) empezar

premium ['pri·mi·əm] I. *n* 1. (*insurance payment*) prima *f* 2. (*extra charge*) recargo *m*; (*high price*) precio *m* con prima [*o* inflado] 3. (*bonus*) prima *f* 4. (*importance*) **to put a ~ on sth** darle (gran) importancia a algo; **to be at a ~** (*very valuable*) ser muy importante 5. (*gasoline*) súper *f* II. *adj* de primera calidad

premium price *n* precio *m* con prima

premium quality *n* máxima calidad *f*

premonition [ˌpri·mə·'nɪʃ·ən] *n* premonición *f*; **to have a ~ that...** tener el presentimiento de que...

prenatal [ˌpri·'neɪ·təl] *adj* prenatal

preoccupation [ˌpri·ak·jə·'peɪ·ʃən] *n* preocupación *f*

preoccupied [pri·'ak·ju·paɪd] *adj* preocupado, -a; **to be ~ with sth** estar absorto en algo

preoccupy [pri·'ak·ju·paɪ] <-ie-> *vt* preocupar

preordain [ˌpri·ɔr·'deɪn] *vt* predeterminar

preowned [pri·'oʊnd] *adj* (*vehicle, home, electronics*) de segunda mano

prep [prep] I. *adj abbr of* **preparatory** preparatorio, -a II. *n inf abbr of* **preparation** preparación *f*

prepackage [ˌpri·'pæk·ɪdʒ] *vt* preempaquetar

prepaid [ˌpriˈpeɪd] *adj* pagado, -a por adelantado; ~ **phone** [*o* **calling**] **card** tarjeta (telefónica) de prepago

prepaid postcard *n* postal *f* franqueada

prepaid reply *n* sobre *m* con el franqueo pagado

preparation [ˌprepəˈreɪʃən] I. *n* 1.(*getting ready*) preparación *f* 2.(*substance*) preparado *m* 3. *pl* (*measures*) preparativos *mpl* II. *adj* de preparación

preparatory [prɪˈpærəˌtɔri] *adj* preliminar, preparatorio, -a

preparatory course *n* curso *m* preparatorio

preparatory school *n* colegio *m* privado (*de enseñanza secundaria*)

prepare [prɪˈper] I. *vt* preparar; **to ~ sb for sth** preparar a alguien para algo II. *vi* prepararse; **to ~ for action** prepararse para actuar

prepared [prɪˈperd] *adj* 1.(*ready*) listo, -a 2.(*willing*) dispuesto, -a; **to be ~ to do sth** estar preparado para hacer algo 3.(*food, speech*) preparado, -a de antemano

preparedness [prɪˈperˌɪdˌnɪs] *n* preparación *f*

prepay [ˌpriˈpeɪ] *vt irr* pagar por anticipado [*o* adelantado]

prepayment [ˌpriˈpeɪmənt] *n* pago *m* por adelantado

preponderance [prɪˈpanˌdərəns] *n form* predominio *m*, preponderancia *f*

preponderant [prɪˈpanˌdərənt] *adj form* predominante, preponderante

preposition [ˌprepəˈzɪʃən] *n* preposición *f*

prepossessing [ˌpripəˈzesˌɪŋ] *adj* agradable, atractivo, -a

preposterous [prɪˈpastərəs] *adj* ridículo, -a

preppie, preppy [ˈprepˌi] *pej* I.<-ies> *n inf* pijo, -a *m*, *f* II. *adj* <preppier, preppiest> *inf* pijo, -a

prepuce [ˈpriˌpjus] *n* (*foreskin*) prepucio *m*; (*clitoral foreskin*) prepucio del clítoris

prerequisite [ˌpriˈrekˌwɪˌzɪt] I. *adj* fundamental II. *n* requisito *m* esencial; **to be a ~ for sth** ser una condición sine qua non para algo

prerogative [prɪˈragəˌtɪv] *n* (*right, privilege*) prerrogativa *f*; **that's your ~** estás en tu derecho; **skiing used to be the ~ of the rich** antes, esquiar era patrimonio exclusivo de los ricos

pres. [prez] *n abbr of* **president** Pte.

presage [ˈpresˌɪdʒ] I. *n liter* 1.(*sign, omen*) presagio *m* 2.(*intuition*) presentimiento *m* II. *vt liter* (*warn*) presagiar III. *vi liter* **to ~ well/ill** ser buen/mal presagio

Presbyterian [ˌprezbɪˈtɪrˌiˌən] I. *n* presbiteriano, -a *m*, *f* II. *adj* presbiteriano, -a

presbytery [ˈprezbɪˌterˌi] *n* REL 1. ARCHIT (*part of church*) presbiterio *m* 2.(*priest's residence*) casa *f* del cura

preschool [ˈpriˌskul] I. *n* jardín *m* de infancia II. *adj* preescolar; (*child*) en edad preescolar

prescribe [prɪˈskraɪb] I. *vt* 1. MED recetar; (*rest, diet*) recomendar 2.*form* (*order*) prescribir; ~**d by law** establecido por la ley II. *vi* MED hacer una receta

prescribed [prɪˈskraɪbd] *adj* prescrito, -a; **in the ~ way** de conformidad con lo prescrito; **at the ~ time** en el plazo prescrito

prescription [prɪˈskrɪpʃən] *n* 1. MED receta *f*, fórmula *f* médica; **only available with a ~** sólo con receta médica; **to make out a ~** extender una receta; **to fill a ~** preparar una receta 2.*form* (*act of prescribing*) prescripción *f*

prescriptive [prɪˈskrɪpˌtɪv] *adj* preceptivo, -a

prescriptive grammar *n* LING gramática *f* normativa

presence [ˈprezˌəns] *n* 1.(*attendance*) presencia *f*; **military/police ~** presencia militar/policial; ~ **of mind** presencia de ánimo; **in sb's ~** en presencia de alguien; **in my ~** delante de mí; **in the ~ of two witnesses** ante dos testigos; **your ~ is requested** se ruega su asistencia; **to feel sb's ~** sentir la presencia de alguien; **to make one's ~ felt** hacerse notar 2.(*personality*) carisma *m*

present¹ [ˈprezˌənt] I. *n* presente *m* ▶ **at ~** en este momento; **for the ~** por ahora II. *adj* 1.(*current: address, generation*) actual; **at the ~ moment** [*o* **time**] en este momento; **the ~ year** el año en curso; **in the ~ case** en este caso; **up to the ~ time** hasta la fecha; **the ~ writer** quien esto escribe 2.(*in attendance*) presente; **to be ~ at sth** asistir a algo; **all those ~** todos los presentes; ~ **company excepted** exceptuando a los presentes

present² [ˈprezˌənt] *n* (*gift*) regalo *m*; **to give sb a ~** hacer un regalo a alguien; **I got it as a ~** me lo regalaron; **to make sb a ~ of sth** regalar algo a alguien

present³ [prɪˈzent] *vt* 1.(*give*) presentar; **to ~ one's apologies to sb** *form* presentar sus disculpas a alguien; **to ~ one's credentials** presentar sus credenciales; **to ~ sth (to sb)** entregar algo (a alguien); **to ~ sb with sth** obsequiar a alguien con algo, obsequiar algo a alguien *AmL* 2.(*introduce*) presentar; **to ~ sb to sb** presentar alguien a alguien; **may I ~ my wife?** permítame presentarle a mi esposa; **to ~ a bill** presentar un proyecto de ley 3.(*to an audience: play, musical, concert*) presentar; ~**ing X as Julius Caesar** con X en el papel de Julio César; **to ~ a paper at a conference** presentar una ponencia en un congreso 4.(*confront*) **to ~ sb with sth** enfrentar a alguien con algo; **to be ~ed with a complicated situation** verse frente a una situación complicada; **to ~ sb with a problem** plantear un problema a alguien 5.(*constitute*) constituir; **to ~ a problem for sb** significar [*o* suponer] un problema para alguien; **to ~ difficulties for sb** plantear dificultades a alguien 6.(*offer*) ofrecer; (*view, atmosphere*) presentar 7.(*exhibit: argument, plan, theory*) exponer; (*check, passport, ticket*) presentar; **to ~ a petition to sb** elevar una petición a al-

guien *elev* **8.** MIL **to ~ arms** presentar armas
9. (*appear*) **to ~ oneself for sth** presentarse a
algo
presentable [prɪ·'zen·tə·bəl] *adj* presentable;
to make oneself ~ arreglarse
presentation [ˌpre·zən·'teɪ·ʃən] *n* **1.** (*act*) presentación *f;* (*of theory, dissertation*) exposición
f; (*of thesis*) lectura *f;* **to make** [*o* **give**] **a ~**
hacer una exposición; **on ~ of this voucher** al
presentar este vale **2.** (*of prize, award*)
entrega *f*
presentation copy *n* ejemplar *m* de cortesía
present-day [ˌprez·ənt·deɪ] *adj* actual; **~ Boston** el Boston de hoy (en) día
presenter [prɪ·'zen·tər] *n* presentador(a) *m(f)*
presentiment [prɪ·'zen·tɪ·mənt] *n form* presentimiento *m;* **to have a ~ of sth** presentir
algo; **to have the ~ that...** tener el presentimiento de que...
presently ['prez·ənt·li] *adv* **1.** (*soon*) pronto;
I'll be there ~ voy enseguida **2.** (*now*) ahora
present participle *n* LING participio *m* presente
present tense *n* LING tiempo *m* presente
preservation [ˌprez·ər·'veɪ·ʃən] *n* **1.** (*of building*) conservación *f;* **to be in a poor/good
state of ~** estar en mal/buen estado de conservación **2.** (*of species, custom*) preservación *f*
preservative [prɪ·'zɜr·və·tɪv] **I.** *adj* preservativo, -a **II.** *n* conservante *m;* **without artificial ~s** sin conservantes (artificiales)
preserve [prɪ·'zɜrv] **I.** *vt* **1.** (*maintain: customs, peace*) mantener; (*dignity, sense of
humor, building*) conservar; (*appearance,
silence*) guardar **2.** (*food*) conservar **3.** (*protect*) proteger; **to ~ sb from sth** proteger a alguien de algo; **heaven ~ us!** ¡que Dios nos
ampare! **II.** *n* **1. ~s** (*jam*) confitura *f*
2. (*reserve*) coto *m*, vedado *m;* **game ~** coto
de caza; **wildlife ~** reserva *f* de animales **3.** *fig*
(*domain*) terreno *m;* **to be the ~ of the rich**
ser dominio exclusivo de los ricos; **to be a
male ~** estar vedado a las mujeres
preserved *adj* **1.** (*maintained*) conservado, -a;
to be badly ~ estar mal conservado **2.** (*food*)
en conserva; **~ food** conservas *fpl*
preshrunk [ˌpri·'ʃrʌŋk] *adj* (*fabric, jeans*) pre-
encogido, -a
preside [prɪ·'zaɪd] *vi* presidir; **to ~ at/over
sth** presidir algo; **to ~ at a table** presidir la
mesa
presidency ['prez·ɪ·dən·si] *n* **1.** (*office of
president*) POL presidencia *f;* (*of company*)
dirección *f;* (*of university*) rectoría *f* **2.** (*tenure
as president*) mandato *m* (presidencial)
president ['prez·ɪ·dənt] *n* POL presidente, -a *m,
f;* (*of company*) director(a) *m(f);* (*of university*) rector(a) *m(f)*
presidential [ˌprez·ɪ·'den·tʃəl] *adj* presidencial
presidential address *n* discurso *m* presidencial
presidential candidate *n* candidato, -a *m, f* a
la presidencia
presidential election *n* elecciones *fpl* presi-

denciales
President's Day *n* Día *m* del Presidente
press [pres] **I.** *vt* **1.** (*push: button, switch*) pulsar; (*doorbell*) tocar; (*trigger*) apretar; **to ~ sth
down** apretar algo **2.** (*squeeze*) apretar; **the
crowd ~ed us against the locked door** la
multitud nos apretujaba contra la puerta cerrada **3.** (*flatten: flowers, grapes, olives*) prensar **4.** (*extract juice*) exprimir **5.** (*iron: shirt,
dress*) planchar **6.** MUS (*album, disk*) imprimir
7. (*try to force*) presionar; **to ~ sb to do sth**
presionar a alguien para que haga algo; **to ~ sb
for sth** exigir algo de alguien; **to ~ sb for payment** acosar a alguien para que pague; **to ~
sth on sb** imponer algo a alguien **8.** (*find difficult*) **to be** (**hard**) **~ed to do sth** tener dificultad para hacer algo **9.** (*be short of*) **to be ~ed
for money/time** andar escaso [*o* justo] de
dinero/tiempo **10.** (*pursue*) insistir; **to ~ a
claim/one's case** insistir en una petición/sus
argumentos; **to ~ a point** insistir en algo
11. LAW **to ~ charges** presentar cargos **II.** *vi*
1. (*push*) apretar; **to ~ hard** apretar fuerte; **to
~ on the brakes** pisar el freno **2.** (*crowd*)
apiñarse; **to ~ through the crowd** abrirse
paso entre el gentío; **to ~ down** (**on sth**) hacer
presión (sobre algo) **3.** (*be urgent*) urgir; **time
is ~ing** el tiempo apremia **4.** (*put under pressure*) hacer presión; **to ~ for sth** insistir para
conseguir algo **III.** *n* **1.** (*push*) presión *f;* (*with
hand*) apretón *m;* **at the ~ of a button** apretando un botón **2.** (*ironing*) planchado *m;* **to
give sth a ~** planchar algo **3.** (*crush*) apiñamiento *m* **4.** (*machine*) prensa *f;* **printing ~**
imprenta *f;* **to be in ~** estar en prensa; **to go to
~** (*newspaper, book*) ir a imprenta; **hot off the
~** (*news*) de última hora **5.** PUBL **the ~** la
prensa; **to have bad/good ~** (*publicity*) tener
mala/buena prensa **6.** (*for tennis racket*) ten-
sor *m* **7.** (*cupboard*) ropero *m*
◆ **press ahead** *vi s.* **press on**
◆ **press down on** *vt* **1.** (*force down*) apretar
2. (*lean on*) apoyarse en
◆ **press forward** *vi s.* **press on**
◆ **press in** *vt* clavar
◆ **press on** *vi* seguir adelante
◆ **press upon** *vt* apretar
press agency *n* agencia *f* de prensa
press box *n* tribuna *f* de la prensa
press card *n* acreditación *f* de prensa
press conference *n* rueda *f* de prensa; **to
hold a ~** dar una rueda de prensa
press coverage *n* cobertura *f* periodística
press-gang ['pres·gæn] *vt* **to ~ sb into doing
sth** forzar a alguien a hacer algo
pressing I. *adj* (*issue, matter*) urgente; (*need*)
apremiante **II.** *n* (*of clothes*) planchado *m;* (*of
records, fruits*) prensado *m*
pressman ['pres·mən] *n* tipógrafo *m*
press office *n* oficina *f* de prensa
press release *n* comunicado *m* de prensa; **to
issue a ~** emitir un comunicado
pressure ['preʃ·ər] **I.** *n* **1.** *a.* PHYS presión *f;*

P

high/low ~ presión alta/baja; **to put** ~ **on** sth hacer presión sobre algo; **at full** ~ a toda presión; **to be under** ~ a. *fig* estar bajo presión **2.** (*influence*) **to put** ~ **on** sb (**to do** sth) presionar a alguien (para que haga algo); **to do** sth **under** ~ **from** sb hacer algo presionado por alguien; **under the** ~ **of circumstances** presionado por las circunstancias **3.** ~**s** (*stressful circumstances*), **the** ~**s of life/work** tensiones en la vida/el trabajo **4.** MED tensión *f;* **blood** ~ tensión arterial **5.** PHYS (*force*) presión *f* II. *vt* **to** ~ sb **to do** sth presionar a alguien para que haga algo

pressure cabin *n* AVIAT cabina *f* presurizada

pressure cooker *n* olla *f* a presión, olla *f* presto *Méx*

pressure gauge *n* manómetro *m*

pressure group *n* POL grupo *m* de presión

pressure washer *n* manguera a presión *f*

pressurize ['preʃ·ə·raɪz] *vt* **1.** (*control air pressure*) presurizar **2.** *inf* (*person, government*) presionar; **to** ~ sb **into doing** sth forzar a alguien a hacer algo

prestige [pre·'stiʒ] *n* prestigio *m*

prestigious [pre·'stɪdʒ·əs] *adj* prestigioso, -a

pre-stressed concrete [,pri·'strest·'kaŋ·krit] *n* hormigón *m* pretensado

presumably [prɪ·'zu·mə·bli] *adv* presumiblemente

presume [prɪ·'zum] I. *vt* **1.** (*suppose*) suponer; **to** ~ **that...** imaginarse que...; ~**d dead** dado por muerto; **to be** ~**d innocent** ser presuntamente inocente **2.** (*dare*) **to** ~ **to do** sth atreverse a hacer algo II. *vi* **1.** (*be presumptuous*) presumir; **I don't wish to** ~, **but...** no quisiera parecer impertinente, pero... **2.** (*assume*) **Dr Smith, I** ~**?** usted debe de ser el Dr. Smith **3.** (*take advantage of*) **to** ~ **on** sb abusar de alguien

presumption [prɪ·'zʌmp·ʃən] *n* **1.** (*assumption*) suposición *f;* **the** ~ **is that...** se supone que...; **the** ~ **of innocence** LAW la presunción de inocencia **2.** *form* (*arrogance*) presunción *f* **3.** (*daring*) atrevimiento *m*

presumptive [prɪ·'zʌmp·tɪv] *adj* presunto, -a

presumptuous [prɪ·'zʌmp·tʃu·əs] *adj* **1.** (*arrogant*) impertinente **2.** (*forward*) osado, -a

presuppose [,pri·sə·'poʊz] *vt form* presuponer

presupposition [,pri·sʌp·ə·'zɪʃ·ən] *n* presuposición *f;* **to be based on false** ~**s** basarse en suposiciones falsas

pretax [,pri·'tæks] *adj* antes de impuestos, bruto, -a

pretend [prɪ·'tend] I. *vt* **1.** (*make believe*) fingir; **to** ~ **to be interested** fingir interés; **to** ~ **to be dead** hacerse el muerto; **to** ~ **to be sb** hacerse pasar por alguien; **the children** ~**ed that they were dinosaurs** los niños imaginaban que eran dinosaurios **2.** (*claim*) pretender; **I don't** ~ **to know** no pretendo saber II. *vi* fingir; **he's just** ~**ing** sólo está fingiendo

pretended *adj* fingido, -a

pretender *n* pretendiente *mf;* **a** ~ **to the**

throne un pretendiente al trono

pretense ['pri·tens] *n* **1.** (*simulation*) fingimiento *m,* apariencia *f;* **to make a** ~ **of** sth fingir algo; **to make no** ~ **of** sth no disimular algo **2.** (*pretext*) pretexto *m;* **under** (**the**) ~ **of...** con el pretexto de..., so pretexto de...; **to do** sth **under false** ~**s** hacer algo bajo un falso pretexto **3.** (*claim*) pretensión *f;* **to make no** ~ **to objectivity/innocence** no pretender ser totalmente objetivo/inocente

pretension [prɪ·'ten·ʃən] *n* **1.** (*claim*) pretensión *f;* **to have** ~**s to** (**being/doing**) sth tener pretensiones de (ser/hacer) algo **2.** *s.* **pretentiousness**

pretentious [prɪ·'ten·ʃəs] *adj* pretencioso, -a; (*in bad taste*) cursi *inf*

pretentiousness *n* pretensión *f;* (*in bad taste*) cursilería *f*

preterit(e) ['preṭ·ər·ɪt] LING I. *n* pretérito *m* II. *adj* pretérito, -a *elev*

preternatural [,pri·ṭər·'nætʃ·ər·əl] *adj form* (*exceptional*) prodigioso, -a

pretext ['pri·tekst] *n* pretexto *m;* **a** ~ **for doing** sth un pretexto para hacer algo; **on the** ~ **that...** con el pretexto de que...; **under the** ~ **of doing** sth so pretexto de hacer algo *elev*

prettify ['prɪṭ·ɪ·faɪ] *vt inf* (*room, street*) engalanar; (*account, report*) adornar *fig*

pretty ['prɪṭ·i] I. *adj* <-ier, -iest> **1.** (*beautiful: thing*) bonito, -a, lindo, -a *AmL;* (*child, woman*) guapo, -a, lindo, -a *AmL;* **not a** ~ **sight** nada agradable de ver **2.** *inf* (*considerable*) menudo, -a; ~ **mess** menudo lío *m* II. *adv* (*quite*) bastante **2.** ~ **much** más o menos; **to be** ~ **much the same** ser prácticamente lo mismo; **I'm** ~ **nearly finished** ya casi he terminado; ~ **well everything** casi todo

pretzel ['pret·səl] *n* galleta *f* salada

prevail [prɪ·'veɪl] *vi* **1.** (*triumph*) prevalecer; **to** ~ **over/against** sth prevalecer sobre/contra algo; **to** ~ **over/against** sb triunfar sobre/contra alguien **2.** (*predominate*) predominar; (*conditions, situation*) imperar **3.** (*convince*) **to** ~ (**up**)**on** sb (**to do** sth) *form* convencer a alguien (para que haga algo)

prevailing *adj* predominante; (*atmosphere, feelings*) reinante; **under the** ~ **circumstances** en las circunstancias actuales

prevalence ['prev·ə·ləns] *n* **1.** (*common occurrence*) preponderancia *f;* **the** ~ **of drugs in some neighborhoods** la presencia habitual de drogas en algunos barrios **2.** (*predominance*) predominio *m*

prevalent ['prev·ə·lənt] *adj* **1.** (*common*) corriente; (*disease, opinion*) extendido, -a **2.** (*present-day*) actual **3.** (*predominant*) predominante

prevaricate [prɪ·'vær·ɪ·keɪt] *vi form* andarse con rodeos; **to** ~ **over** sth dar vueltas a algo

prevarication [prɪ·,vær·ɪ·'keɪ·ʃən] *n form* evasivas *fpl*

prevent [prɪ·'vent] *vt* **1.** (*hamper*) impedir; **to**

~ sb from doing sth impedir que alguien haga algo; **the news ~ed his coming** la noticia impidió que viniera **2.** (*avoid*) prevenir; (*confusion, panic, crime*) evitar

preventative [prɪ·'ven·tə·t̬ɪv] *adj s.* **preventive**

prevention [prɪ·'ven·ʃən] *n* prevención *f;* **for the ~ of crime** para evitar la delincuencia ▸~ **is better than cure** *prov,* **an ounce of ~ is worth a pound of cure** *prov* más vale prevenir que curar *prov*

preventive [prɪ·'ven·t̬ɪv] *adj* preventivo, -a

preview ['pri·vju] **I.** *n* CINE, THEAT preestreno *m;* (*film extract*) tráiler *m;* (*of TV program, exhibition*) adelanto *m* **II.** *vt* CINE, THEAT preestrenar

previous ['pri·vi·əs] *adj* **1.** (*former*) anterior; **on the ~ day/week** el día/la semana anterior; **no ~ experience required** no se necesita experiencia **2.** (*prior*) previo, -a

previous convictions *npl* antecedentes *mpl* penales

previously *adv* **1.** (*beforehand*) previamente **2.** (*formerly*) anteriormente; **to have met sb ~** haber visto a alguien antes

previous to *adv* **~ to doing sth** antes de hacer algo

prewar [ˌpri·'wɔr] *adj* de antes de la guerra, de preguerra; **the ~ years** la preguerra

prey [preɪ] *n* **1.** (*animal*) presa *f;* **bird of ~** ave *f* de presa **2.** (*person*) víctima *f;* **to be easy ~ for sb** ser presa [o blanco] fácil para alguien; **to fall ~ to** (*animal*) ser presa de; (*person*) ser víctima de

◆ **prey on** *vt,* **prey upon** *vt* **1.** (*feed on*) alimentarse de; **fear preyed on me** *fig* el miedo hizo presa de mí **2.** (*exploit*) aprovecharse de

price [praɪs] **I.** *n* **1.** COM precio *m;* **oil ~s, the ~ of oil** el precio del petróleo; **to ask a high/low ~** pedir un precio alto/bajo; **to be the same ~** valer [o costar] lo mismo; **to go up/down in ~** subir/bajar de precio; **to name a ~** pedir un precio; **what ~ are apples?** ¿a cuánto están las manzanas? **2.** FIN (*of stocks*) cotización *f,* precio *m* **3.** *fig* (*disadvantage*) precio *m;* **the ~ one has to pay for fame, the ~ of fame** el precio de la fama; **beyond** [o **without**] **~** sin precio; **to set a high ~ on sth** valorar mucho algo ▸**to set a ~ on one's head** poner precio a la cabeza de alguien; **at any ~** a toda costa; **not at any ~** por nada del mundo; **to pay a heavy ~** pagarlo caro; **to pay the ~** pagar caro; **at a ~** a un precio muy alto **II.** *vt* **1.** (*mark with price tag*) poner el precio a **2.** (*fix price*) poner precio a, valorar; **to be reasonably ~d** tener un precio razonable ▸**to be ~d out of the market** no poder competir en el mercado por su alto precio

price bracket *n* gama *f* de precios

price control *n* control *m* de precios

price-cutting *n* recorte *m* de precios

price fixing *n* fijación *f* de precios

price freeze *n* congelación *f* de precios

price index *n* índice *m* de precios

priceless ['praɪs·lɪs] *adj* **1.** (*invaluable*) incalculable; **to be ~** no tener precio **2.** *fig* (*funny*) divertidísimo, -a; **that's ~!** ¡eso es para partirse de risa! *inf,* ¡eso es un plato! *AmL, inf*

price level *n* nivel *m* de precios

price list *n* lista *f* de precios

price raise *n* aumento *m* de precios

price range *n* gama *f* de precios

price stability *n* estabilidad *f* de precios

price tag *n* **1.** (*label*) etiqueta *f* (del precio) **2.** *inf* (*cost*) precio *m*

price war *n* guerra *f* de precios

pricey ['praɪ·si] *adj* <pricier, priciest> *inf* (*object*) carillo, -a; (*shop*) carero, -a

pricing ['praɪ·sɪŋ] *n* fijación *f* de precios; **~ policy** política *f* de precios

prick [prɪk] **I.** *vt* **1.** (*jab*) pinchar, picar; **to ~ one's finger with** [o **on**] **a needle** pincharse el dedo con una aguja; **to ~ sb's conscience** hacer que a alguien le remuerda la conciencia **2.** (*mark with holes*) agujerear **3.** (*listen: animal*) **to ~ one's ears** levantar las orejas; (*person*) aguzar el oído **II.** *vi* **1.** (*pin*) pinchar **2.** (*hurt: eyes, skin*) escocer, arder *CSur* **III.** *n* **1.** (*act, pain*) pinchazo *m;* **to feel the ~ of conscience** tener remordimientos de conciencia **2.** (*mark*) agujero *m* **3.** *vulg* (*penis*) polla *f,* pija *f RíoPl* **4.** *vulg* (*idiot*) gilipollas *m inv*

◆ **prick out** *vt* (*flowers*) repicar

◆ **prick up** *vt* **to ~ one's ears** (*animal*) levantar las orejas; (*person*) aguzar el oído

prickle ['prɪk·əl] **I.** *n* **1.** (*thorn: of plant*) pincho *m;* (*of animal*) púa *f* **2.** (*tingle*) picor *m;* **to feel a ~ of excitement** sentir un cosquilleo de emoción **II.** *vi* **1.** (*cause prickling sensation*) picar **2.** (*tingle*) sentir picor **3.** (*prick*) pinchar **III.** *vt* (*prick*) pinchar, picar

prickly ['prɪk·li] <-ier, -iest> *adj* **1.** (*thorny: plant*) espinoso, -a; (*animal*) con púas **2.** (*tingling*) que pica; (*beard*) que pincha; **~ sensation** picor *m* **3.** *inf* (*easily offended*) irritable

prickly heat *n* fiebre *f* miliar

prickly pear *n* **1.** (*fruit*) higo *m* chumbo **2.** (*plant*) chumbera *f*

pride [praɪd] **I.** *n* **1.** (*proud feeling*) orgullo *m;* **to feel great ~** estar muy orgulloso; **to take ~ in sth** enorgullecerse de algo; (*one's work*) esmerarse en algo; **to be sb's ~ and joy** ser el orgullo de alguien **2.** (*self-respect*) amor *m* propio; **to hurt sb's ~** herir el orgullo de alguien; **to swallow one's ~** tragarse el orgullo; **false ~** vanidad *f* **3.** (*arrogance*) soberbia *f* **4.** (*group of lions*) manada *f* ▸**~ comes** [o **goes**] **before a fall** *prov* más dura será la caída; **to have ~ of place** ocupar el lugar de honor **II.** *vt* **to ~ oneself on** (**doing**) **sth** enorgullecerse de (hacer) algo; **to ~ oneself that...** preciarse de que...

priest [prist] *n* REL cura *m,* sacerdote *m*

priestess ['pri·stɪs] *n* REL sacerdotisa *f*

priesthood ['prist·hʊd] *n* REL **1.** (*position, office*) sacerdocio *m;* **to enter the ~** ser orde-

P

nado sacerdote **2.** (*priests in general*) clero *m*
priestly ['prist·li] *adj* sacerdotal
prig [prɪg] *n pej* mojigato, -a *m, f*
priggish ['prɪg·ɪʃ] *adj* mojigato, -a
prim [prɪm] <-mmer, -mmest> *adj* **1.** *pej* remilgado, -a; ~ **and proper** remilgado **2.** (*appearance*) escrupuloso, -a
primacy ['praɪ·mə·si] *n form* primacía *f*
prima donna [pri·mə·'dan·ə] *n* **1.** (*opera singer*) prima donna *f* **2.** (*arrogant person*) diva *f*
primal ['praɪ·məl] *adj* **1.** (*primitive*) primario, -a **2.** (*most important*) primordial
primarily [praɪ·'mer·ə·li] *adv* principalmente, ante todo
primary ['praɪ·mer·i] **I.** *adj* **1.** (*principal*) fundamental; (*aim*) prioritario, -a; **to be of** ~ **importance** ser de una importancia primordial **2.** (*basic*) primario, -a; (*industry*) de base, primario, -a; ~ **meaning of a word** primer sentido de una palabra; ~ **stress** LING acento *m* primario **II.** <-ies> *n* POL elecciones *fpl* primarias
primary color *n* color *m* primario
primary education *n* enseñanza *f* primaria
primary school *n* escuela *f* (de enseñanza) primaria
primate ['praɪ·meɪt] *n* **1.** ZOOL primate *m* **2.** REL primado *m*
prime [praɪm] **I.** *adj* **1.** (*main*) principal; (*objective*) prioritario, -a; **of** ~ **importance** de importancia primordial **2.** (*first-rate*) excelente; (*beef*) de primera calidad; **of** ~ **quality** de primera calidad; **in** ~ **condition** en perfecto estado **II.** *n* **1.** (*best stage*) apogeo *m elev;* **to be in one's** ~, **to be in the** ~ **of life** estar en la flor de la vida; **to be past one's** ~ no ser ya ningún jovencito; **to be cut off in one's** ~ morir en la flor de la vida **2.** (*prime number*) número *m* primo **III.** *vt* **1.** (*apply undercoat: surface*) aplicar una capa de base sobre; (*canvas*) aprestar **2.** (*prepare for exploding: gun, pump, motor*) cebar **3.** (*brief*) informar; (*prepare*); **to** ~ **sb for doing sth** preparar a alguien para hacer algo; **to be well** ~**d for an interview** ir bien preparado para una entrevista **4.** (*make drunk*) emborrachar; **to be well** ~**d** estar contentillo
prime cost *n* ECON coste *m* de producción
prime interest rate *n* FIN tipo *m* de interés preferente
prime meridian *n* GEO primer meridiano *m*
prime minister *n* POL primer(a) ministro, -a *m, f*
prime mover *n* fuerza *f* motriz; (*person*) promotor(a) *m(f)*
prime number *n* MATH número *m* primo
primer ['praɪ·mər] *n* **1.** (*paint*) (pintura *f* de) imprimación *f;* **a** ~ **coat** una primera mano **2.** (*explosive*) cebo *m* **3.** (*textbook*) manual *m;* (*for learning to read*) cartilla *f*
prime rate *n* FIN tipo *m* preferente
prime ribs *n* CULIN costillas *fpl* de primera calidad

prime time *n* RADIO, TV horas *fpl* de máxima audiencia
primeval [praɪ·'mi·vəl] *adj* primigenio, -a; (*forest*) virgen
primitive ['prɪm·ɪ·t̬ɪv] **I.** *adj a.* ART, HIST, ZOOL primitivo, -a; (*method, weapon*) rudimentario, -a **II.** *n* ART, HIST, SOCIOL primitivo, -a *m, f*
primogeniture [ˌpraɪ·mou·'dʒen·ɪ·t̬ʃər] *n form* primogenitura *f*
primordial [praɪ·'mɔr·di·əl] *adj form* **1.** (*from beginning*) primigenio, -a **2.** (*basic*) primario, -a
primrose ['prɪm·rouz] *n,* **primula** ['prɪm·jə·lə] *n* BOT prímula *f,* primavera *f*
prince [prɪns] *n* príncipe *m;* **crown** ~ príncipe heredero; **Prince Charming** príncipe azul; **Prince of Wales** Príncipe de Gales; **the Prince of Darkness** el príncipe de las tinieblas
prince consort *n* príncipe *m* consorte
princely ['prɪns·li] *adj* principesco, -a; *fig* magnífico, -a; **a** ~ **sum** una bonita suma
princess ['prɪn·sɪs] *n* princesa *f*
principal ['prɪn·sə·pəl] **I.** *adj* principal **II.** *n* **1.** (*head of a school*) director(a) *m(f)* **2.** FIN capital *m*
principality [ˌprɪn·sə·'pæl·ə·t̬i] *n* principado *m*
principally *adv* principalmente
principle ['prɪn·sə·pəl] *n* principio *m;* **in** ~ en principio; **on** ~ por principio
principle clause *n* cláusula *f* principal
print [prɪnt] **I.** *n* **1.** (*handwriting*) texto *m* impreso; (*type*); **bold** ~ negrita *f* **2.** (*printed form*) **to rush sth into** ~ publicar algo precipitadamente; **to appear in** ~ publicarse; **to go out of** ~ agotarse **3.** (*of artwork*) copia *f;* (*engraving*) grabado *m;* PHOT positivo *m* **4.** (*printed pattern*) estampado *m* **5.** ~**s** *inf* (*fingerprints*) huella *f* **II.** *vt* **1.** (*publish*) publicar **2.** (*put into printed form*) imprimir **3.** COMPUT (*make printout of*) imprimir **4.** PHOT positivar **5.** (*mark fabric*) estampar **6.** (*write in unjoined letters*) escribir con letra de imprenta **III.** *vi* **1.** (*appear in printed form*) imprimirse **2.** (*write in unjoined letters*) escribir con letra de imprenta
printable ['prɪn·t̬ə·bəl] *adj* imprimible
printed circuit (**board**) *n* ELEC circuito *m* impreso
printed material *n,* **printed matter** *n* material *m* impreso
printer ['prɪn·t̬ər] *n* **1.** COMPUT impresora *f;* **ink-jet/laser** ~ impresora de chorro de tinta/láser **2.** (*person*) impresor(a) *m(f)*
printer driver *n* COMPUT controlador *m* de impresora
printing *n* **1.** (*art*) imprenta *f* **2.** (*action*) impresión *f*
printing ink *n* tinta *f* de imprenta
printing office *n* imprenta *f*
printing press *n* prensa *f,* imprenta *f*
printout ['prɪnt·aʊt] *n* COMPUT impresión *f,* listado *m*

print run *n* tirada *f*

print shop *n* imprenta *f*

prior ['praɪ·ər] I. *adv form* (*before*) antes; ~ **to doing sth** antes de hacer algo II. *adj form* 1. (*earlier*) previo, -a; **without ~ notice** sin previo aviso 2. (*preferred*) preferente III. *n* REL prior *m*

prioritize [praɪ·'ɔr·ɪ·taɪz] *vt* priorizar

priority [praɪ·'ɔr·ə·t̬i] I. <-ies> *n* 1. (*being most important*) prioridad *f*; (*in time*) anterioridad *f* 2. *pl* (*order of importance*) prioridades *fpl*; **to get one's priorities right** establecer un orden de prioridades; **to set priorities** establecer un orden de prioridades II. *adj* 1. (*of utmost importance*) prioritario, -a 2. (*claim, right*) a. FIN preferente

priory ['praɪ·ə·ri] *n* priorato *m*

prism ['prɪz·əm] *n* prisma *m*

prismatic [prɪz·'mæt̬·ɪk] *adj* prismático, -a

prison ['prɪz·ən] *n* prisión *f*; **to go to ~** ir a la cárcel; **to put sb in ~** encarcelar a alguien

prison camp *n* campo *m* de prisioneros

prison cell *n* celda *f*

prisoner ['prɪz·ə·nər] *n* preso, -a *m, f*; MIL prisionero, -a *m, f*; **to hold sb ~** detener a alguien; **to take sb ~** hacer prisionero a alguien

prisoner of war *n* prisionero, -a *m, f* de guerra

prison inmate *n* recluso, -a *m, f*

prison riot *n* motín *m* carcelero

prison yard *n* patio *m* de la cárcel

pristine ['prɪs·tin] *adj form* prístino, -a

privacy ['praɪ·və·si] *n* intimidad *f*; **I'd like some ~** me gustaría estar a solas

private ['praɪ·vət] I. *adj* 1. (*not public*) privado, -a 2. (*confidential*) confidencial; **sb's ~ opinion** la opinión personal de alguien; **he's a very private person** es una persona muy reservada 3. (*intimate*) íntimo, -a; **~ parts** partes *fpl* pudendas II. *n* 1. **~s** *inf* (*genitals*) partes *fpl* 2. MIL soldado *m* raso

privateer [,praɪ·və·'tɪr] *n* NAUT (*vessel*) corsario *m*; (*commander*) comandante *mf* (de navío)

private eye *n inf*, **private investigator** *n* investigador(a) *m(f)* privado, -a

privately ['praɪ·vət·li] *adv* 1. (*in private*) en privado; **to celebrate ~** celebrar a puerta cerrada 2. (*secretly*) en secreto 3. (*personally*) personalmente

private property *n* propiedad privada

privation [praɪ·'veɪ·ʃən] *n form* privación *f*; **to live in ~** vivir en la miseria; **to suffer ~** pasar apuros

privatization [,praɪ·və·t̬ɪ·'zeɪ·ʃən] *n* privatización *f*

privatize ['praɪ·və·taɪz] *vt* privatizar

privet ['prɪv·ɪt] *n* BOT alheña *f*

privilege ['prɪv·ə·lɪdʒ] I. *n* 1. (*special right*) privilegio *m* 2. (*honor*) honor *m* II. *vt* **to be ~d to do sth** tener el privilegio de hacer algo

privileged *adj* 1. (*special*) privilegiado, -a 2. (*confidential*) confidencial

privy[1] ['prɪv·i] *adj form* **to be ~ to sth** estar al tanto de algo

privy[2] ['prɪv·i] *n* (*toilet*) retrete *m*

prize[1] [praɪz] I. *n* 1. (*in competition*) premio *m*; **to take home a ~** ganar un premio 2. (*reward*) recompensa *f* II. *adj* 1. *inf* (*first-rate*) de primera 2. (*prizewinning*) premiado, -a III. *vt* apreciar; **to ~ sth highly** estimar algo mucho

prize[2] [praɪz] *vt s.* **pry**[2]

prizefight ['praɪz·faɪt] *n* combate *m* de boxeo profesional

prizefighter *n* boxeador(a) *m(f)* profesional

prizefighting *n* boxeo *m* profesional

prize list *n* lista *f* de premiados

prize money *n* SPORTS premio *m* en metálico

prizewinning ['praɪz·,wɪn·ɪŋ] *adj* premiado, -a

pro[1] [proʊ] *inf* I. *n abbr of* **professional** profesional *mf* II. *adj abbr of* **professional** profesional

pro[2] [proʊ] I. *adv* a favor II. *n inf* pro *m*; **the ~s and cons of sth** los pros y los contras de algo III. *prep* pro IV. *adj* favorable

proactive [,proʊ·'æk·tɪv] *adj* con iniciativa

probability [,prab·ə·'bɪl·ə·t̬i] *n* probabilidad *f*; **in all ~** sin duda

probable ['prab·ə·bəl] *adj* 1. (*likely*) probable 2. (*credible*) verosímil 3. LAW **~ cause** motivo razonable, justificación *f*

probably *adv* probablemente

probate ['proʊ·beɪt] *n* LAW legalización *f* de un testamento

probation [proʊ·'beɪ·ʃən] *n* 1. (*at work*) período *m* de prueba; **to be on ~** estar a prueba 2. LAW libertad *f* condicional

probationary [proʊ·'beɪ·ʃə·ner·i] *adj* de prueba; **~ period** período *m* de prueba

probationer [proʊ·'beɪ·ʃə·nər] *n* 1. LAW persona *f* en libertad condicional 2. (*at work*) trabajador(a) *m(f)* en período de prueba

probation officer *n* funcionario que hace el seguimiento de personas en libertad condicional

probe [proʊb] I. *vi* (*examine*) investigar; **to ~ into the possibilities** tantear las posibilidades; **to ~ into sb's private life** indagar en la vida privada de alguien II. *vt* 1. (*examine*) investigar 2. MED sondar III. *n* 1. (*examination, investigation*) investigación *f* 2. MED, AVIAT sonda *f*

probity ['proʊ·bə·t̬i] *n form* probidad *f*

problem ['prab·ləm] *n* problema *m*

problematic [,prab·lə·'mæt̬·ɪk] *adj*, **problematical** [,prab·lə·'mæt̬·ɪ·kəl] *adj* 1. (*creating difficulty*) problemático, -a 2. (*questionable, disputable*) dudoso, -a

problem child *n* niño, -a *m, f* difícil [*o* problemático, -a]

proboscis [proʊ·'bas·ɪs] *n* 1. ZOOL probóscide *f* 2. *fig, hum* (*person's nose*) napia *f*

procedural [prə·'si·dʒər·əl] *adj* de procedimiento; LAW procesal

procedure [prə·'si·dʒər] *n* procedimiento *m*

proceed [proʊ·'sid] *vi* 1. (*move along*) seguir; (*continue*) continuar; (*continue driving*) seguir adelante; **to ~ with sth** avanzar con algo; **to ~ against sb** proceder contra alguien; AVIAT (*to a gate*) dirigirse a **2.** (*come from*) **to ~ from** provenir de, proceder de **3.** (*start, begin*) **to ~ with sth** empezar con algo; **to ~ to do sth** ponerse a hacer algo

proceedings [prou·'si·dɪŋz] *npl* **1.** LAW proceso *m* **2.** *form* (*events*) actos *mpl* **3.** *form* (*minutes of meeting*) actas *fpl*

proceeds ['prou·sidz] *n* ingresos *mpl*

process¹ ['pras·es] I. *n* proceso *m;* **in the ~** mientras tanto; **to be in the ~ of doing sth** estar en vías de hacer algo II. *vt* **1.** *a.* TECH, COMPUT procesar; (*raw materials, waste*) tratar **2.** PHOT revelar

process² [prə·'ses] *vi form* desfilar

process chart *n* diagrama *m* del proceso

process engineering *n* ingeniería *f* de procesos

processing ['pras·es·ɪŋ] *n* **1.** *a.* TECH, COMPUT procesamiento *m;* (*of raw materials, waste*) tratamiento *m;* **data ~** procesamiento de datos; **batch ~** procesamiento por lotes **2.** PHOT revelado *m*

procession [prə·'seʃ·ən] *n* **1.** desfile *m;* **funeral ~** cortejo *m* fúnebre; **to go in ~** desfilar **2.** REL procesión *f* **3.** *fig* serie *f*

processor [pra·'ses·ər] *n* COMPUT procesador *m*

pro-choice *adj* proabortista

proclaim [prou·'kleɪm] *vt form* proclamar; **to ~ war** declarar la guerra

proclamation [ˌprak·lə·'meɪ·ʃən] *n form* proclamación *f;* **a ~ of war** una declaración de guerra

proclivity [prou·'klɪv·ə·t̬i] *n form* propensión *f;* **sexual ~** tendencia *f* sexual; **to have a ~ for sth** ser proclive a algo

procrastinate [prou·'kræs·tə·neɪt] *vi* dejar para más tarde

procrastination [prou·ˌkræs·tə·'neɪ·ʃən] *n* dilación *f*

procreate ['prou·kri·eɪt] *vi form* procrearse

procreation [ˌprou·krɪ·'eɪ·ʃən] *n form* procreación *f*

proctor ['prak·tər] *n* UNIV vigilante *mf* (*durante un examen*)

procurable [prou·'kjur·ə·bəl] *adj* asequible

procurator ['prak·jə·reɪ·t̬ər] *n* LAW procurador(a) *m(f)*

procure [prou·'kjur] *form* I. *vt* (*obtain*) obtener; **to ~ sth for sb, to ~ sb sth** obtener algo para alguien II. *vi* LAW dedicarse al proxenetismo

procurement [prou·'kjur·mənt] *n* adquisición *f*

prod [prad] I. *n* (*poke*) golpe *m;* (*with elbow*) codazo *m;* (*with sharp object*) pinchazo *m;* **to give sb a ~** *fig* dar un empujón a alguien II.<-dd-> *vt* **1.** (*poke*) golpear; (*with elbow*) dar un codazo; (*with sharp object*) pinchar **2.** (*encourage, urge on*) **to ~ sb** (**into doing sth**) estimular a alguien (para que haga algo)

prodigal ['prad·ɪ·gəl] *adj form* pródigo, -a

prodigious [prə·'dɪdʒ·əs] *adj form* (*size, height*) ingente; (*achievement, talent*) prodigioso, -a

prodigy ['prad·ə·dʒi] *n* prodigio *m;* **child ~** niño, -a *m, f* prodigio

produce¹ [prə·'dus] I. *vt* **1.** (*create*) producir; (*manufacture*) fabricar **2.** (*give birth to*) dar a luz **3.** CINE, THEAT, TV realizar, producir; (*music, recording*) dirigir **4.** (*show*) mostrar; **to ~ a knife** sacar un cuchillo; **to ~ one's passport** enseñar el pasaporte; **to ~ an alibi** presentar una coartada **5.** (*cause*) causar; **to ~ results** producir resultados II. *vi* BOT (*bear fruit*) dar frutos

produce² ['prou·dus] *n* AGR productos *mpl* agrícolas; **the ~ section** (*in grocery store*) la sección de frutas y verduras

producer [prə·'du·sər] *n* productor(a) *m(f)*

product ['prad·əkt] *n* **1.** *a.* MATH producto *m* **2.** (*result*) resultado *m*

production [prə·'dʌk·ʃən] *n* **1.** (*of goods*) fabricación *f;* (*output of factory*) producción *f* **2.** CINE, THEAT, TV producción *f* **3.** *form* (*presentation: of ticket, passport*) presentación *f*

production capacity *n* capacidad *f* de producción

production costs *npl* costes *mpl* de producción

production director *n* director(a) *m(f)* de producción

production line *n* cadena *f* de montaje

production manager *n* encargado, -a *m, f* de producción

production time *n* tiempo *m* de producción

production volume *n* volumen *m* de producción

productive [prə·'dʌk·tɪv] *adj* productivo, -a; (*land, soil*) fértil; (*writer*) prolífico, -a

productivity [ˌprou·dək·'tɪv·ə·t̬i] *n* productividad *f*

productivity bonus *n* prima *f* de productividad

prof [praf] *abbr of* **professor** prof. *m,* profa. *f*

profane [prou·'feɪn] *adj* **1.** (*blasphemous*) blasfemo, -a **2.** *form* (*secular*) profano, -a

profanity [prou·'fæn·ə·t̬i] *n* **1.** (*blasphemy*) blasfemia *f* **2.** (*obscene language*) blasfemia *f* **3.** (*obscene word*) palabrota *f;* **to utter a ~** soltar un taco, decir una grosería

profess [prə·'fes] *vt* **1.** (*declare*) profesar; **to ~ little enthusiasm** manifestar poco entusiasmo; **to ~ oneself satisfied** (**with sth**) declararse satisfecho (con algo) **2.** (*pretend*) **to ~ to be sth** pretender ser algo **3.** (*religion, Catholicism*) profesar

professed [prə·'fest] *adj* **1.** (*self-acknowledged*) declarado, -a **2.** (*alleged*) supuesto, -a

profession [prə·'feʃ·ən] *n* **1.** (*occupation*) profesión *f;* **the teaching ~** la docencia **2.** (*declaration*) declaración *f*

professional [prə·'feʃ·ə·nəl] I. *adj* **1.** (*related to profession*) profesional **2.** (*competent*)

profesional **II.** *n* profesional *mf*
professionalism [prə·'feʃ·ə·nə·lɪz·əm] *n*
1. (*attitude*) profesionalidad *f* **2.** SPORTS profesionalismo *m*
professionally *adv* **1.** (*by a professional*) profesionalmente **2.** (*in professional manner*) con profesionalidad
professor [prə·'fes·ər] *n* UNIV profesor(a) *m(f)*
professorial [ˌprou·fə·'sɔr·i·əl] *adj* profesoral
professorship [prə·'fes·ər·ʃɪp] *n* cátedra *f*
proffer ['praf·ər] *vt form* ofrecer
proficiency [prə·'fɪʃ·ən·si] *n* competencia *f*
proficient [prə·'fɪʃ·ənt] *adj* competente
profile ['prou·faɪl] **I.** *n* **1.** (*side view*) perfil *m*; **in** ~ de perfil **2.** (*description*) descripción *f*; **user** ~ COMPUT perfil *m* de usuario ▸ **to keep a low** ~ tratar de pasar inadvertido **II.** *vt* **1.** (*describe*) describir **2.** (*police practice*) parar en un control policial (*a personas con un perfil determinado*)
profit ['praf·ɪt] **I.** *n* **1.** FIN beneficio *m* **2.** (*advantage*) provecho *m* **II.** *vi* **1.** (*benefit*) beneficiarse; **to** ~ **by sth** sacar provecho de algo **2.** (*make a profit*) ganar
profitability [ˌpraf·ɪ·t̬ə·'bɪl·ə·t̬i] *n* rentabilidad *f*
profitable ['praf·ɪ·t̬ə·bəl] *adj* **1.** FIN rentable; **a** ~ **investment** una inversión lucrativa **2.** (*advantageous*) provechoso, -a
profit and loss *n* FIN pérdidas *fpl* y ganancias *fpl*
profiteer [ˌpraf·ɪ·'tɪr] *n pej* especulador(a) *m(f)*
profiteering *n pej* especulación *f*
profit-making *adj* lucrativo, -a; ~ **movie** película *f* taquillera
profit margin *n* margen *m* de beneficio
profit maximization *n* maximización *f* del beneficio
profit-oriented *adj* orientado, -a a la obtención de beneficios
profit-related *adj* que depende de los beneficios
profit sharing *n* participación *f* en los beneficios
profit taking *n* FIN realización *f* de beneficios
profligate ['praf·lɪ·gɪt] *adj form* derrochador(a)
profound [prə·'faund] *adj* profundo, -a
profundity [prə·'fʌn·dɪ·t̬i] *n form* profundidad *f*
profuse [prə·'fjus] *adj* profuso, -a; **to be** ~ **in one's praise of sth** alabar algo con efusión
profusion [prə·'fju·ʒən] *n form* profusión *f*; **in** ~ en abundancia
prog. *n abbr of* **program** progr.
progenitor [prou·'dʒen·ə·t̬ər] *n form* progenitor(a) *m(f)*
progeny ['pradʒ·ə·ni] *n pl, form* progenie *f*
prognosis [prag·'nou·sɪs] *n* pronóstico *m*
prognosticate [prag·'nas·tɪ·keɪt] *vt form* pronosticar
program ['prou·græm] **I.** *n a.* COMPUT programa *m* **II.** <-mm-> *vt a.* COMPUT programar
programmable ['prou·græm·ə·bəl] *adj* programable

programmer *n a.* COMPUT programador(a) *m(f)*
programming *n a.* COMPUT programación *f*
programming language *n* COMPUT lenguaje *m* de programación
progress[1] ['prag·res] *n* progreso *m*; **to make** ~ avanzar; **to be in** ~ estar en curso
progress[2] [prou·'gres] *vi* **1.** (*improve*) progresar **2.** (*continue onward*) avanzar; **to** ~ **to sth** evolucionar hacia algo
progression [prə·'greʃ·ən] *n* **1.** (*development*) desarrollo *m*; (*of disease*) evolución *f* **2.** MATH (*series*) progresión *f*
progressive [prə·'gres·ɪv] **I.** *adj* **1.** (*by successive stages*) progresivo, -a; (*disease*) degenerativo, -a **2.** POL progresista **3.** (*modern*) moderno, -a **4.** MUS progresivo, -a; (*jazz*) experimental **5.** LING continuo, -a **II.** *n* **1.** POL progresista *mf* **2.** LING (*verb form*) tiempo *m* continuo
prohibit [prou·'hɪb·ɪt] *vt* **1.** (*forbid*) prohibir; **to be** ~**ed by law** estar prohibido por la ley **2.** (*prevent*) impedir
prohibition [ˌprou·ə·'bɪʃ·ən] *n* **1.** (*ban*) prohibición *f* **2.** HIST **Prohibition** la Ley Seca
prohibitive [prou·'hɪb·ɪ·t̬ɪv] *adj* prohibitivo, -a
project[1] ['pradʒ·ekt] *n* **1.** (*undertaking, plan*) proyecto *m* **2.** SCHOOL, UNIV (*essay*) trabajo *m* **3.** (*social housing*) ≈viviendas *fpl* de protección oficial [*o* de interés social *Col*]
project[2] [prə·'dʒekt] **I.** *vt* **1.** (*forecast*) pronosticar; **to be** ~**ed to do sth** estar previsto para hacer algo **2.** (*propel*) impulsar **3.** PSYCH proyectar; **to** ~ **sth onto sb** proyectar algo en alguien **4.** (*promote*) promover; **to** ~ **oneself** promocionarse **II.** *vi* **1.** (*extend out*) sobresalir **2.** (*speak loudly and clearly*) proyectar la voz
projectile [prə·'dʒek·t̬əl] *n* proyectil *m*
projection [prə·'dʒek·ʃən] *n* **1.** (*forecast*) pronóstico *m* **2.** (*protrusion*) saliente *m*; (*of rock*) prominencia *f* **3.** PSYCH proyección *f*
projectionist *n* proyeccionista *mf*
project management *n* coordinación *f* de proyectos, gestión *f* de proyectos
project manager *n* coordinador(a) *m(f)* de proyectos, gestor(a) *m(f)* de proyectos
projector [prə·'dʒek·tər] *n* proyector *m*
prolapse [prou·'læps] *n* MED prolapso *m*
prole [proul] *adj, n pej, inf abbr of* **proletarian** proletario, -a *m, f*; **the** ~**s** el proletariado
proletarian [ˌprou·lə·'ter·i·ən] **I.** *adj* proletario, -a **II.** *n* proletario, -a *m, f*
proletariat [ˌprou·lə·'ter·i·ət] *n* proletariado *m*
proliferate [prou·'lɪf·ə·reɪt] *vi* proliferar
proliferation [prou·ˌlɪf·ə·'reɪ·ʃən] *n* proliferación *f*
prolific [prou·'lɪf·ɪk] *adj* **1.** (*producing a lot*) prolífico, -a **2.** (*having many offspring*) prolífico, -a
prolix [prou·'lɪks] *adj pej, form* prolijo, -a
prolog(ue) ['prou·lag] *n* **1.** (*introduction*) prólogo *m*; (*in play*) presentación *f* **2.** *fig, inf* (*preliminary event*) preludio *m*; **to be a** ~ **to sth**

P

ser un preámbulo de algo
prolong [proʊˈlaŋ] *vt* prolongar; (*agony*) alargar
prolongation [ˌproʊˈlaŋˈgeɪˈʃən] *n* prolongación *f*
prom [pram] *n* (*school dance*) baile *m*

ℹ️ Un **prom** es un baile en una escuela secundaria norteamericana (**high school**). El **senior prom** es el baile para todos los **seniors**. Normalmente, los asistentes acuden con un acompañante (**date**) y una pareja es elegida reina y rey del baile (prom queen and king). Este acto constituye el punto culminante del año escolar. A menudo hay también un **junior prom** para los más jóvenes (juniors).

promenade [ˌpram·ə·ˈneɪd] I. *n form* (*walk*) paseo *m* II. *vi* pasearse
promenade deck *n* cubierta *f* de paseo
prominence [ˈpram·ə·nəns] *n* 1.(*conspicuousness*) prominencia *f*; **to give ~ to sth** hacer resaltar algo 2.(*importance*) importancia *f*; **to gain ~** ganar trascendencia
prominent [ˈpram·ə·nənt] *adj* 1.(*conspicuous*) prominente; **to put sth in a ~ position** poner algo en una buena posición 2.(*teeth, chin*) saliente 3.(*distinguished, well-known*) importante; (*position*) destacado, -a; **to be ~ in sth** desempeñar un papel importante en algo
promiscuity [ˌpram·ɪ·ˈskju·ə·t̬i] *n* promiscuidad *f*
promiscuous [prəˈmɪs·kju·əs] *adj* promiscuo, -a
promise [ˈpram·ɪs] I. *vt* (*pledge, have potential*) prometer; **to ~ to do sth** prometer hacer algo II. *vi* (*pledge*) prometer; **I ~!** ¡lo prometo! III. *n* 1.(*pledge*) promesa *f*; **to make a ~** prometer; **~s, ~s!** *iron* ¡promesas, promesas! 2.(*potential*) posibilidad *f*; **a young person of ~** un joven con porvenir; **to show ~** demostrar aptitudes; **to fulfill one's ~** satisfacer las esperanzas
promising *adj* prometedor(a)
promissory note [ˈpram·ɪ·sɔr·i·ˌnoʊt] *n* pagaré *m*
promo [ˈproʊ·moʊ] *n inf s.* **promotion** promoción *f*
promontory [ˈpram·ən·tɔr·i] <-ies> *n* GEO promontorio *m*
promote [prəˈmoʊt] *vt* 1.(*in army, company, organization*) ascender; (*soccer team*) subir 2.(*encourage*) promover 3.(*advertise*) promocionar
promoter *n* promotor(a) *m(f)*
promotion [prəˈmoʊ·ʃən] *n* 1.(*in army, company, organization*) ascenso *m*; **to get a ~** ser ascendido 2.(*encouragement, advertising*) promoción *f*; **sales ~** promoción de ventas

promotional material *n* material *m* de promoción
prompt [prampt] I. *vt* 1.(*spur*) provocar; **to ~ sb to do sth** estimular a alguien para que haga algo 2. THEAT apuntar II. *adj* (*quick*) rápido, -a; (*action*) inmediato, -a; (*delivery*) sin demora; **to be ~** ser puntual III. *adv* puntualmente IV. *n* 1. COMPUT línea *f* de comandos 2. THEAT (*prompter*) apuntador(a) *m(f)*; **to give sb a ~** apuntar a alguien
prompt box <-es> *n* THEAT concha *f* del apuntador
prompter [ˈpramp·tər] *n* THEAT apuntador(a) *m(f)*
promptitude [ˈpramp·tɪ·tud] *n form* prontitud *f*
promptly [ˈprampt·li] *adv* 1.(*quickly*) rápidamente 2. *inf* (*immediately afterward*) de inmediato
promptness [ˈprampt·nɪs] *n s.* **promptitude**
promulgate [ˈpram·əl·geɪt] *vt form* 1.(*theory, belief*) divulgar 2. LAW promulgar
promulgation [ˌpram·əl·ˈgeɪ·ʃən] *n form* 1.(*of theory, belief*) divulgación *f* 2. LAW promulgación *f*
prone [proʊn] I. *adj* **to be ~ to doing sth** ser propenso a hacer algo II. *adv* boca abajo; **to lie ~ on the floor/table** estar tumbado boca abajo sobre el suelo/la mesa
prong [praŋ] *n* (*of fork*) diente *m*; (*of antler*) punta *f*
pronominal [proʊˈnam·ə·nəl] *adj* LING pronominal
pronoun [ˈproʊ·naʊn] *n* LING pronombre *m*
pronounce [prəˈnaʊns] *vt* 1.(*speak*) pronunciar 2.(*declare*) declarar; (*judgment*) dictaminar; **to ~ that...** afirmar que...
pronounceable *adj* pronunciable
pronounced *adj* pronunciado, -a; (*accent*) marcado, -a
pronouncement [prəˈnaʊns·mənt] *n* declaración *f*; **to make a ~** pronunciarse; (*pass judgment*) hacer un dictamen
pronto [ˈpran·toʊ] *adv inf* enseguida
pronunciation [prəˌnʌn·si·ˈeɪ·ʃən] *n* LING pronunciación *f*
proof [pruf] I. *n* 1. *a.* LAW prueba *f*; **~ of sth** comprobación *f* de algo; **the burden of ~** el peso de la evidencia 2. TYPO prueba *f* de imprenta 3. MATH prueba *f* matemática 4.(*coin*) moneda *f* de coleccionista ► **the ~ of the pudding is in the eating** *prov* no se sabe si algo es bueno hasta que se prueba, por la muestra se conoce el paño II. *adj* (*alcoholic strength*) de graduación III. *vt* impermeabilizar
proofread [ˈpruf·rid] *irr* TYPO, PUBL I. *vt* corregir, revisar II. *vi* corregir pruebas
proofreader *n* corrector(a) *m(f)* de pruebas
proofreading *n* corrección *f* de pruebas
prop¹ [prap] I. *n* 1.(*support*) apoyo *m* 2. THEAT objeto *m* de atrezzo, utilería *f* II. <-pp-> *vt* sostener, apuntalar; **to ~ sth up with sth**

aguantar algo con [o contra] algo

prop² [prap] *n inf* AVIAT *abbr of* **propeller** hélice *f*

propaganda [ˌprap·ə·'gæn·də] *n* propaganda *f*

propagandist [ˌprap·ə·'gæn·dɪst] **I.** *n* propagandista *mf* **II.** *adj* propagandístico, -a

propagate ['prap·ə·geɪt] **I.** *vt* **1.** BOT propagar **2.** (*make known: lie, rumor*) difundir **II.** *vi* propagarse

propagation [ˌprap·ə·'geɪ·ʃən] *n* **1.** BOT, PHYS propagación *f* **2.** (*of lies, rumors*) difusión *f*

propane ['proʊ·peɪn] *n* propano *m*

propel [prə·'pel] <-ll-> *vt* propulsar

propellant [prə·'pel·ənt] *n* propelente *m*

propeller [prə·'pel·ər] *n* hélice *f*

propeller shaft *n* TECH árbol *m* de transmisión

propensity [prə·'pen·sə·ţi] *n form* propensión *f*; **to have a ~ for sth/to do sth** ser propenso a algo/a hacer algo

proper ['prap·ər] *adj* **1.** (*appropriate: time, place, method*) apropiado, -a; (*use*) correcto, -a; **~ meaning** sentido *m* exacto **2.** (*socially respectable*) **to be ~ to do sth** ser apropiado hacer algo **3.** (*itself*) verdadero, -a; **it's not in Boston ~** no está en Boston propiamente dicho **4.** (*real*) verdadero, -a; **a ~ job** un trabajo de verdad

proper fraction *n* MATH fracción *f* propia

properly ['prap·ər·li] *adv* **1.** (*correctly*) correctamente; **~ speaking** hablando como es debido; **~ dressed** vestido apropiadamente **2.** (*behave*) como es debido **3.** (*politely*) educadamente

proper name *n*, **proper noun** *n* nombre *m* propio

propertied *adj* ECON adinerado, -a

property ['prap·ər·ţi] *n* **1.** (*possession*) propiedad *f*; LAW (*house, land*) bien *m* inmueble; **a man of ~** un hombre adinerado **2.** (*house*) inmueble *m*; (*land*) terreno *m* **3.** *a.* COMPUT (*attribute*) propiedad *f*

property damage insurance *n* seguro *m* de la propiedad

property developer *n* ECON promotor(a) *m(f)* inmobiliario

property development *n* ECON promoción *f* inmobiliaria

property market *n* mercado *m* inmobiliario

property owner *n* propietario, -a *m, f*

property tax <-es> *n* impuesto *m* sobre la propiedad [o sobre los bienes inmuebles]

prophecy ['praf·ə·si] <-ies> *pl n* profecía *f*

prophesy ['praf·ə·saɪ] <-ie-> **I.** *vt* (*predict*) predecir; REL profetizar **II.** *vi* profetizar

prophet ['praf·ɪt] *n* adivino, -a *m, f*; REL profeta, -isa *m, f*; **~ of doom, doomsday ~** catastrofista *mf*

prophetess ['praf·ɪ·ţəs] *n* profetisa *f*

prophetic [prə·'feţ·ɪk] *adj* profético, -a

prophylactic [ˌproʊ·fə·'læk·tɪk] **I.** *adj* MED profiláctico, -a **II.** *n* **1.** MED (*preventive medicine*) (fármaco *m*) profiláctico *m* **2.** (*condom*) preservativo *m*

prophylaxis [ˌproʊ·fə·'læk·sɪs] *n* MED profilaxis *f*

propinquity [proʊ·'pɪŋ·kwə·ţi] *n form* **1.** (*proximity*) proximidad *f* **2.** (*kinship*) parentesco *m*

propitious [prə·'pɪʃ·əs] *adj form* propicio, -a

propjet *n* turbohélice *m*

propman *n* THEAT encargado *m* del atrezzo

proponent [prə·'poʊ·nənt] *n* defensor(a) *m(f)*

proportion [prə·'pɔr·ʃən] *n* **1.** (*relationship*) proporción *f*; **the ~ of A to B** el porcentaje entre A y B; **to be out of ~ to sth** estar desproporcionado con algo; **to be in ~ to sth** estar en proporción con algo; **to keep a sense of ~** mantener un sentido de la medida [o de la proporción]; **to blow sth (all) out of ~** exagerar algo desmesuradamente **2.** (*part*) parte *f* proporcional **3. ~s** (*size*) dimensiones *fpl*; **a building of gigantic ~s** un edificio de proporciones gigantes

proportional [prə·'pɔr·ʃə·nəl] *adj* proporcional; **inversely ~** inversamente proporcional

proportionality [prə·ˌpɔr·ʃə·'næl·ə·ţi] *n* proporcionalidad *f*

proportional representation *n* POL representación *f* proporcional

proportionate [prə·'pɔr·ʃə·nɪt] *adj s.* **proportional**

proportioned *adj* **well-~** bien proporcionado; **to be generously ~** *fig* estar muy bien hecho

proposal [prə·'poʊ·zəl] *n* **1.** (*suggestion*) propuesta *f*; **to put forward a ~** presentar una proposición; **peace ~** propuesta *f* de paz **2.** (*offer of marriage*) proposición *f*; **to make a marriage ~** hacer una petición de mano

propose [prə·'poʊz] **I.** *vt* **1.** (*put forward*) proponer; **to ~ a toast** proponer un brindis **2.** (*intend*) **to ~ to do sth** tener la intención de hacer algo **3.** (*nominate*) nombrar **II.** *vi* (*offer marriage*) **to ~** (**to sb**) declararse (a alguien) ▶ **man ~s, God disposes** *prov* el hombre propone y Dios dispone *prov*

proposer [prə·'poʊ·zər] *n* **1.** (*suggestor*) autor(a) *m(f)* de una moción **2.** (*nominator*) proponente *mf*

proposition [ˌprap·ə·'zɪʃ·ən] **I.** *n* **1.** (*theory, argument*) proposición *f* **2.** (*business*) ofrecimiento *m* **3.** (*suggestion*) sugerencia *f* **II.** *vt* hacer proposiciones deshonestas a

propound [prə·'paʊnd] *vt form* proponer

proprietary [prə·'praɪ·ə·ter·i] *adj* **1.** (*owning property*) propietario, -a **2.** ECON (*name, brand*) registrado, -a; (*article*) patentado, -a

proprietor [prə·'praɪ·ə·ţər] *n* propietario, -a *m, f*; (*of business*) dueño, -a *m, f*

proprietorship *n* propiedad *f*

proprietress [prə·'praɪ·ə·trɪs] *n* propietaria *f*

propriety [prə·'praɪ·ə·ţi] <-ies> *n* **1.** (*correctness*) corrección *f*, propiedad *f* **2. proprieties** (*standard of conduct*) convenciones *fpl* sociales; **to observe the proprieties** atenerse al decoro

prop room *n* THEAT habitación *f* del atrezzo

propulsion [prə·'pʌl·ʃən] n propulsión f
pro rata [ˌprou·'reɪ·tə] I. adj prorrateado, -a
II. adv proporcionalmente
prorate vt prorratear
prorogation [ˌprou·rou·'geɪ·ʃən] n POL prorrogación f
prorogue [prou·'roug] vt prorrogar
prosaic [prou·'zeɪ·ɪk] adj form prosaico, -a
proscenium [prou·'si·ni·əm] <-s o proscenia> n THEAT proscenio m
proscribe [prou·'skraɪb] vt proscribir
proscription [prou·'skrɪp·ʃən] n form proscripción f
prose [prouz] n prosa f
prosecutable [ˌpras·ɪ·'kju·tə·bəl] adj LAW procesable
prosecute ['pras·ɪ·kjut] I. vt 1. LAW to ~ sb
(for sth) procesar a alguien (por algo) 2. form
(pursue, follow up) proseguir; (studies) sacar
adelante II. vi interponer
prosecuting adj acusador(a)
prosecuting attorney n fiscal mf
prosecution [ˌpras·ɪ·'kju·ʃən] n 1. LAW (proceedings) proceso m 2. LAW (the prosecuting
party) the ~ la acusación; witness for the ~
testigo mf de cargo 3. form (of campaign,
inquiry) seguimiento m
prosecutor ['pras·ɪ·kju·tər] n LAW fiscal mf
proselyte ['pras·ə·laɪt] n REL prosélito, -a m, f
proselytize ['pras·ə·lɪ·taɪz] vi hacer proselitismo
prosody ['pras·ə·di] n prosodia f
prospect ['pras·pekt] I. n 1. (possibility) posibilidad f; the ~ of sth la probabilidad de algo
2. ~s (chances) perspectivas fpl 3. ECON
(potential customer) posible cliente mf;
(potential employee) candidato, -a m, f 4. liter
(view) panorama m; a ~ of/over sth una vista
de/sobre algo II. vi MIN buscar
prospective [prə·'spek·tɪv] adj posible; (candidate, student) futuro, -a
prospector ['pras·pek·tər] n MIN prospector(a)
m(f)
prospectus [prə·'spek·təs] n prospecto m;
UNIV folleto m informativo
prosper ['pras·pər] vi prosperar
prosperity [pra·'sper·ə·ţi] n prosperidad f
prosperous ['pras·pər·əs] adj próspero, -a;
(business) exitoso, -a
prostate (gland) ['pras·teɪt] n próstata f
prostitute ['pras·tə·tut] I. n prostituta f II. vt a.
fig to ~ oneself prostituirse; to ~ one's talents prostituir su talento
prostitution [ˌpras·tɪ·'tu·ʃən] n prostitución f
prostrate ['pras·treɪt] I. adj a. fig postrado, -a;
to be ~ with grief estar abatido por el dolor
II. vt to ~ oneself postrarse
protagonist [prou·'tæg·ə·nɪst] n 1. (main
character) protagonista mf 2. (advocate)
defensor(a) m(f); to be a ~ of sth luchar por
algo
protect [prə·'tekt] vt proteger; (one's interests) salvaguardar; to ~ oneself resguardarse

protection [prə·'tek·ʃən] n 1. (defense) protección f; to be under sb's ~ estar bajo la protección de alguien 2. (blackmail) chantaje m
(practicado a propietarios de comercios)
protection factor n factor m de protección
protectionism [prə·'tek·ʃə·nɪz·əm] n proteccionismo m
protectionist adj proteccionista
protective [prə·'tek·tɪv] adj 1. (giving protection) proteccionista; ~ custody detención f
preventiva 2. (wishing to protect: instinct)
protector(a)
protector [prə·'tek·tər] n 1. (person) protector(a) m(f) 2. (device) (aparato m) protector m
protectorate [prə·'tek·tər·ɪt] n protectorado m
protégé(e) ['prou·tə·ʒeɪ] n m(f) protegido, -a
m, f
protein ['prou·tin] n proteína f; ~ deficiency
deficiencia f proteínica
protest[1] ['prou·test] n 1. (complaint) protesta
f; in ~ en señal de protesta; to do sth under ~
hacer algo que conste como protesta 2. (demonstration) manifestación f de protesta
protest[2] [prou·'test] I. vi protestar; to ~
about/against sth protestar por/en contra de
algo II. vt 1. (solemnly affirm) to ~ that...
declarar que...; to ~ one's innocence afirmar
su inocencia 2. (show dissent) protestar en
contra de
Protestant ['praţ·ɪ·stənt] n protestante mf
Protestantism n protestantismo m
protestation [ˌpraţ·es·'teɪ·ʃən] n 1. (strong
objection) protesta f 2. (strong affirmation)
afirmación f
protester n manifestante mf
protest march n marcha f de protesta
protest vote n voto m de protesta
protocol ['prou·tə·kɔl] n a. COMPUT protocolo m
proton ['prou·tan] n protón m
protoplasm ['prou·tə·plæz·əm] n protoplasma m
prototype ['prou·tə·taɪp] n prototipo m
protozoan [ˌprou·tə·'zou·ən] <-s o -zoa> n
protozoo m
protract [prou·'trækt] vt prolongar
protracted [prou·'træk·tɪd] adj prolongado, -a
protraction [prou·'træk·ʃən] n 1. (prolonging)
prolongación f 2. ANAT (muscle action) extensión f
protractor [prou·'træk·tər] n (for measuring
angles) transportador m (de grados)
protrude [prou·'trud] vi sobresalir
protruding adj prominente; (ears) que sobresale
protrusion [prou·'tru·ʒən] n protuberancia f
protuberance [prou·'tu·bər·əns] n form protuberancia f
protuberant [prou·'tu·bər·ənt] adj form protuberante; (eyes) saltón, -ona
proud [praud] adj 1. (pleased) orgulloso, -a; to
be ~ of sth/sb enorgullecerse de algo/alguien; to be ~ to do sth tener el honor de

hacer algo; **to be ~ that...** estar orgulloso de que... **2.** (*having self-respect*) digno, -a **3.** (*arrogant*) arrogante

proudly *adv* orgullosamente

provable ['pruˑvəˑbəl] *adj* demostrable

prove [pruv] <proved, proved *o* proven> **I.** *vt* (*verify: theory*) probar; (*innocence, loyalty*) demostrar; **to ~ oneself** (**to be**) **sth** demostrarse (ser) algo; **to ~ sb innocent** probar la inocencia de alguien **II.** *vi* (*be established*) resultar; **to ~ to be sth** resultar ser algo

proven ['pruˑvən] **I.** *vi, vt pp of* **prove II.** *adj* (*verified*) comprobado, -a, probado, -a

provenance ['pravˑəˑnəns] *n form* procedencia *f*

provender ['pravˑənˑdər] *n* **1.** AGR forraje *m* **2.** *fig, inf* (*sustenance*) provisiones *fpl*

proverb ['pravˑɜrb] *n* refrán *m*, proverbio *m*; **as the ~ goes...** como dice el refrán...

proverbial [prəˑ'vɜrˑbiˑəl] *adj* proverbial

provide [prəˑ'vaɪd] **I.** *vt* **1.** proveer; **to ~ sb with sth** proveer a alguien de algo **2.** *form* LAW estipular **II.** *vi* **1.** (*prepare*) **to ~ for sth** tener algo preparado, hacerse cargo de algo **2.** (*support*) **to ~ for one's family/children** mantener a su familia/hijos **3.** (*mandate*) prever

provided *conj* **~ that...** con tal (de) que... +*subj*

providence ['pravˑəˑdəns] *n* providencia *f*; **divine ~** REL Divina Providencia

providential [ˌpravˑəˑ'denˑtʃəl] *adj form* providencial

provider *n* **1.** (*person*) proveedor(a) *m(f)* **2.** COMPUT (*for Internet services*) proveedor *m* (de Internet)

providing *conj* **~** (**that**)... con tal (de) que... +*subj*

province ['pravˑɪns] *n* **1.** POL, ADMIN provincia *f* **2.** (*branch of a subject*) campo *m*

provincial [prəˑ'vɪnˑtʃəl] **I.** *adj* **1.** POL, ADMIN provincial **2.** (*unsophisticated*) provinciano, -a **II.** *n* (*sb from provinces*) provinciano, -a *m, f*

proving ground *n* terreno *m* de pruebas

provision [prəˑ'vɪʒˑən] **I.** *n* **1.** (*act of providing*) suministro *m* **2.** (*thing provided*) provisión *f* **3.** (*preparation*) previsiones *fpl*; **to make ~s for sth** tomar medidas de previsión para algo **4.** LAW (*in will, contract*) disposición *f* **II.** *vt* abastecer

provisional [prəˑ'vɪʒˑəˑnəl] *adj* provisional

proviso [prəˑ'vaɪˑzoʊ] <-s> *n* condición *f*; **with the ~ that...** con la condición de que +*subj*

provocation [ˌpravˑəˑ'keɪˑʃən] *n* provocación *f*

provocative [prəˑ'vakˑəˑtɪv] *adj* **1.** (*sexually*) provocativo, -a **2.** (*thought-provoking: idea, question*) estimulante, provocador, -a **3.** (*causing anger*) provocador(a)

provoke [prəˑ'voʊk] *vt* **1.** (*make angry*) provocar; **to ~ sb into doing sth** provocar a alguien para que haga algo **2.** (*discussion*) motivar; (*interest*) despertar; (*crisis*) causar

provoking *adj* (*irritating*) irritante

provost ['proʊˑvoʊst] *n* UNIV rector(a) *m(f)*

prow [praʊ] *n* NAUT proa *f*

prowess ['praʊˑɪs] *n form* destreza *f*; (*sexual, sporting*) proeza *f*

prowl [praʊl] **I.** *n inf* **to be on the ~** estar merodeando **II.** *vt* vagar por; **to ~ the streets for victims** merodear por las calles en busca de víctimas **III.** *vi* **to ~** (**around**) rondar (por)

prowl car *n* coche *m* patrulla

prowler *n* merodeador(a) *m(f)*

prowling *n* merodeo *m*

proximity [prakˑ'sɪmˑəˑt̬i] *n form* proximidad *f*; **to be in** (**close**) **~ to sth** estar (muy) cerca de algo

proxy ['prakˑsi] <-ies> *n* apoderado, -a *m, f*; **to do sth by ~** hacer algo por poderes

prude [prud] *n* mojigato, -a *m, f*

prudence ['pruˑdəns] *n* prudencia *f*

prudent ['pruˑdənt] *adj* prudente

prudery ['pruˑdəˑri] <-ies> *n* mojigatería *f*

prudish ['pruˑdɪʃ] *adj* mojigato, -a

prune¹ [prun] *vt* podar; **to ~** (**back**) **costs** reducir gastos

prune² [prun] *n* (*dried plum*) ciruela *f* pasa

pruning *n* poda *f*

pruning hook *n* podadera *f*

pruning saw *n* serrucho *m* de podar

pruning shears *npl* BOT tijeras *fpl* de podar

prurience ['prʊrˑiˑəns] *n pej, form* lascivia *f*

prurient ['prʊrˑiˑənt] *adj pej, form* lascivo, -a

Prussia ['prʌʃˑə] *n* HIST, POL, GEO Prusia *f*

Prussian ['prʌʃˑən] **I.** *n* HIST prusiano, -a *m, f* **II.** *adj* prusiano, -a

pry¹ [praɪ] <pries, pried> *vi* (*be nosy*) husmear; **to ~ into sth** entrometerse en algo; **to ~ around** curiosear

pry² [praɪ] *vt* **to ~ sth off** arrancar algo; **to ~ sth open** abrir algo por la fuerza

prying *adj* fisgón, -ona; **~ eyes** miradas *fpl* indiscretas

PS [ˌpiˑ'es] *abbr of* **postscript** P.D.

psalm [sam] *n* REL salmo *m*

psephology [siˑ'falˑəˑdʒi] *n* análisis *m* electoral

pseudo ['suˑdoʊ] *adj* falso, -a

pseudointellectual I. *n* pseudointelectual *mf* **II.** *adj* pseudointelectual

pseudonym ['suˑdəˑnɪm] *n* seudónimo *m*

psittacosis [ˌsɪtˑəˑ'koʊˑsɪs] *n* MED psitacosis *f inv*

PST *n abbr of* **Pacific Standard Time** Hora *f* del Pacífico

psych(**e**) **up** ['saɪkˑʌp] *vt sl* **to psych**(**e**) **one-self up** mentalizarse; **to psych**(**e**) **sb up** mentalizar a alguien

psyche ['saɪˑki] *n* psique *f*

psychedelic [ˌsaɪˑkəˑ'delˑɪk] *adj* psicodélico, -a

psychiatric [ˌsaɪˑkiˑ'ætˑrɪk] *adj* psiquiátrico, -a

psychiatrist [saɪˑ'kaɪˑəˑtrɪst] *n* psiquiatra *mf*

psychiatry [saɪˑ'kaɪˑəˑtri] *n* psiquiatría *f*

psychic ['saɪˑkɪk] **I.** *adj* **1.** (*with occult powers*) parapsicológico, -a **2.** (*of the mind*) psíquico, -a **II.** *n* vidente *mf*

psycho ['saɪ·koʊ] *n sl* (*crazy person*) psicópata *mf*

psychoanalysis [ˌsaɪ·koʊ·ə·'næl·ə·sɪs] *n* psicoanálisis *m inv*

psychoanalyst [ˌsaɪ·koʊ·'æn·ə·lɪst] *n* psicoanalista *mf*

psychoanalytic [ˌsaɪ·koʊ·ˌæn·ə·'lɪt̬·ɪk] *adj*, **psychoanalytical** [ˌsaɪ·koʊ·ˌæn·ə·'lɪt̬·ɪ·kəl] *adj* psicoanalítico, -a

psychoanalyze [ˌsaɪ·koʊ·'æn·ə·laɪz] *vt* psicoanalizar

psychological [ˌsaɪ·kə·'ladʒ·ɪ·kəl] *adj* psicológico, -a

psychologist [saɪ·'kal·ə·dʒɪst] *n* psicólogo, -a *m, f*

psychology <-ies> *n* (*science, mentality*) psicología *f*

psychopath ['saɪ·kə·pæθ] *n* psicópata *mf*

psychopathic [ˌsaɪ·kə·'pæθ·ɪk] *adj* psicopático, -a

psychosis [saɪ·'koʊ·sɪs] <-ses> *n* psicosis *f inv*

psychosomatic [ˌsaɪ·koʊ·soʊ·'mæt̬·ɪk] *adj* psicosomático, -a

psychotherapist [ˌsaɪ·koʊ·'θer·ə·pɪst] *n* psicoterapeuta *mf*

psychotherapy [ˌsaɪ·koʊ·'θer·ə·pi] *n* psicoterapia *f*

psychotic [saɪ·'kat̬·ɪk] I. *adj* psicótico, -a II. *n* psicótico, -a *m, f*

PT [ˌpi·'ti] 1. *abbr of* **physical therapy** fisioterapia *f* 2. *abbr of* **physical training** educación *f* física 3. *abbr of* **part-time** a tiempo parcial

pt. *n* 1. *abbr of* **part** parte *f* 2. *abbr of* **pint** pinta *f* (≈ *0,47 litros*) 3. *abbr of* **point** punto *m*

PTA [ˌpi·ti·'eɪ] *n abbr of* **Parent Teacher Association** asociación *f* de padres y maestros

ptarmigan ['tar·mɪ·gən] *n* perdiz *f* blanca

p.t.o. *abbr of* **please turn over** ver al dorso

PTO [ˌpi·ti·'oʊ] *n abbr of* **Parent Teacher Organization** asociación *f* de padres y maestros

pub [pʌb] *n* pub *m*

puberty ['pju·bər·t̬i] *n* pubertad *f*

pubic ['pju·bɪk] *adj* pubiano, -a, púbico, -a

pubis ['pju·bɪs] <-es> *n* pubis *m inv*

public ['pʌb·lɪk] I. *adj* 1. (*of/for the people, provided by state*) público, -a 2. (*done openly*) abierto, -a; **to go ~ with sth** revelar algo II. *n* 1. (*people collectively, audience*) público *m*; **in ~** en público 2. (*ordinary people*) gente *f* de la calle

public accountant *n* contable *mf* público, -a, contador(a) *m(f)* público, -a

public-address system *n* sistema *m* de megafonía

public affairs *npl* asuntos *mpl* públicos

public appearance *n* aparición *f* pública

public appointment *n* designación *f* pública

public assistance *n* ayuda *f* estatal

publication [ˌpʌb·lɪ·'keɪ·ʃən] *n* publicación *f*

public authority *n* 1. (*state authority*) autoridad *f* estatal 2. (*department, authority*) departamento *m* público

Public Broadcasting System *n* organismo americano de producción audiovisual

public defender *n* LAW defensor(a) *m(f)* de oficio

public domain *n* dominio *m* público

public enemy *n* enemigo, -a *m, f* público, -a

public expenditure *n*, **public expense** *n* ADMIN, POL, ECON gasto *m* público

public funds *npl* POL, ADMIN, FIN, ECON fondos *mpl* públicos

public health *n* MED, ADMIN sanidad *f* pública

public health service *n* servicio *m* sanitario

public holiday *n* fiesta *f* oficial

public interest *n* interés *m* público

publicist ['pʌb·lɪ·sɪst] *n* publicista *mf*

publicity [pʌb·'lɪs·ə·t̬i] *n* 1. publicidad *f* 2. (*attention*) **to attract ~** atraer la atención ► **any ~ is good** ~ toda publicidad es buena

publicity agent *n* agente *mf* de publicidad

publicity campaign *n* ECON campaña *f* de promoción, campaña *f* publicitaria

publicity department *n* departamento *m* de promoción

publicity material *n* material *m* publicitario

publicize ['pʌb·lɪ·saɪz] *vt* promocionar

public law *n* LAW derecho *m* público

public library <-ies> *n* biblioteca *f* pública

publicly *adv* 1. (*openly*) en público 2. **~ owned** de propiedad pública

public nuisance *n* daño *m* público

public opinion *n* opinión *f* pública

public property *n* bienes *mpl* públicos

public prosecutor *n* fiscal *mf*

public records *npl* documentos *mpl* públicos

public relations *npl* relaciones *fpl* públicas

public-relations officer *n* secretario, -a *m, f* de relaciones públicas

public restroom *n* aseos *mpl* públicos

public school *n* escuela *f* pública

public sector *n* sector *m* público

public servant *n* funcionario, -a *m, f*

public service *n* funcionariado *m*

public-spirited [ˌpʌb·lɪk·'spɪr·ɪ·t̬ɪd] *adj* solidario, -a

public transportation *n* transporte *m* público

public utility *n* empresa *f* de servicios públicos

public works *npl* ADMIN, POL obras *fpl* públicas

publish ['pʌb·lɪʃ] *vt* (*book, author, result*) publicar; (*information*) divulgar

publisher *n* 1. (*company*) editorial *f* 2. (*person*) editor(a) *m(f)*

publishing *n* industria *f* editorial

publishing house *n* editorial *f*

puck [pʌk] *n* SPORTS disco *m*

pucker ['pʌk·ər] *vt* **to ~ one's lips** fruncir la boca

pudding ['pʊd·ɪŋ] *n* pudding *mpl*

puddle ['pʌd·əl] *n* charco *m*

pudenda [pju·'den·də] *npl form* partes *fpl* pudendas

pudgy ['pʊdʒ·i] <-ier, -iest> *adj* rechoncho, -a

puerile ['pju·ər·əl] *adj form* pueril

puerility [ˌpjuˈə·ˈrɪl·ə·t̬i] *n* puerilidad *f*
Puerto Rican [ˌpwer·t̬əˈri·kən] **I.** *n* portorriqueño, -a *m, f* **II.** *adj* portorriqueño, -a
Puerto Rico [ˌpwer·t̬əˈri·koʊ] *n* Puerto Rico *m*
puff [pʌf] **I.** *vi* **1.** (*blow*) soplar **2.** (*be out of breath*) jadear **3. to ~ on a pipe/cigar/cigarette** dar una calada [*o* chupada] a una pipa/un cigarro/un cigarrillo [*o* pipiada] **II.** *vt* **1.** (*smoke*) soplar; (*cigarette smoke*) echar **2.** (*praise: product, book*) dar bombo a **3.** (*say while panting*) resoplar **III.** *n* **1.** *inf* (*breath, wind*) soplo *m;* (*vapor*) soplido *m;* (*of dust, smoke*) bocanada *f;* (*of air*) ráfaga *f* **2.** (*drag, breathing-in*) calada *f,* pipiada *f Col,* chupada *f;* **to take ~s on a cigarette** dar caladas a un cigarrillo **3.** (*quilt*) edredón *m* **4.** *inf* (*speech, praise*) bombo *m*
 ◆**puff out** *vt* **1.** (*expand*) inflar **2.** (*exhaust*) dejar sin aliento
 ◆**puff up I.** *vt* inflar **II.** *vi* hincharse
puff adder *n* víbora *f* bufadora
puffin [ˈpʌf·ɪn] *n* (*bird*) frailecillo *m*
puff pastry *n* hojaldre *m*
puffy [ˈpʌf·i] <-ier, -iest> *adj* hinchado, -a
pug [pʌg] *n* doguillo *m*
pugilism [ˈpju·dʒɪ·lɪz·əm] *n* pugilismo *m,* boxeo *m*
pugilist [ˈpju·dʒɪ·lɪst] *n* púgil *m,* boxeador *m*
pugnacious [pʌgˈnei·ʃəs] *adj form* agresivo, -a
pugnacity [pʌgˈnæs·ə·t̬i] *n form* belicosidad *f*
pug nose *n* nariz *f* chata
puke [pjuk] *sl* **I.** *vt* vomitar, potar *inf,* guacarear *Méx, inf* **II.** *vi* vomitar, echar la pota, guacarear *Méx;* **he makes me (want to) ~!** ¡me da asco!
 ◆**puke up** *sl* **I.** *vt* **to puke sth up** vomitar algo, guacarear algo *Méx, inf,* potar algo *inf* **II.** *vi* vomitar, guacarear *Méx, inf,* echar la pota *inf*
pukka [ˈpʌk·ə] *adj* **1.** (*genuine*) genuino, -a **2.** (*of good quality*) auténtico, -a
pull [pʊl] **I.** *vt* **1.** (*draw*) tirar de, jalar *AmL;* (*trigger*) apretar **2.** *inf* (*take out: gun, knife*) sacar **3.** MED (*extract*) sacar; (*tooth*) extraer **4.** SPORTS, MED (*strain: muscle*) forzar **5.** (*attract: business, customers*) atraer ▶ **to ~ a fast one (on sb)** *inf* hacer una jugarreta (a alguien) **II.** *vi* **1.** (*exert force*) tirar **2. to ~ on a beer** dar un trago a una cerveza; **to ~ on a cigarette** dar una calada [*o* chupada] a un cigarrillo **3.** *inf* (*hope for success*) **to be ~ing for sb/sth** estar con alguien/algo **III.** *n* **1.** (*act of pulling*) tirón *m;* (*stronger*) jalón *m* **2.** *inf* (*influence*) influencia *f* **3.** (*on knob, handle*) cuerda *f;* (*of a curtain*) tirador *m* **4.** (*attraction*) atracción *f;* (*power to attract*) atractivo *m,* tirón *m* **5.** (*of cigarette*) chupada *f;* (*of drink*) trago *m*
 ◆**pull ahead** *vi* tomar la delantera
 ◆**pull apart** *vt insep* **1.** (*break into pieces*) separar **2.** (*separate using force*) hacer pedazos **3.** (*criticize*) poner por los suelos
 ◆**pull away I.** *vi* (*vehicle*) alejarse **II.** *vt* arrancar; **to pull sth away from sth** arrancar algo a algo
 ◆**pull back I.** *vi* **1.** (*move out of the way*) retirarse **2.** (*not proceed, back out*) dar marcha atrás **II.** *vt* retener
 ◆**pull down** *vt* **1.** (*move down*) bajar **2.** (*demolish*) tirar [*o* echar] abajo **3.** (*drag down, hold back*) **to pull sb down** arrastrar a alguien **4.** *inf* (*earn wages*) ganar
 ◆**pull in I.** *vi* (*vehicle*) llegar **II.** *vt* **1.** (*attract*) atraer **2.** (*arrest*) detener
 ◆**pull off I.** *vt inf* (*succeed*) lograr; **to pull it off** lograrlo, vencer **II.** *vi* (*leave*) arrancar
pull out I. *vi* **1.** (*move out to pass*) salirse; (*drive onto road*) meterse **2.** (*leave*) dejar **3.** (*withdraw*) retirarse **II.** *vt* (*take out*) sacar
 ◆**pull over I.** *vt* **1.** (*cause to fall*) volcar **2.** (*police*) parar **II.** *vi* hacerse a un lado
 ◆**pull through I.** *vi* reponerse **II.** *vt* **to pull sth through** ayudar a algo a reponerse
 ◆**pull together I.** *vt* **1.** (*regain composure*) **to pull oneself together** recobrar la compostura **2.** (*organize, set up*) organizar **II.** *vi* trabajar conjuntamente
 ◆**pull up I.** *vt* **1.** (*raise*) levantar; (*blinds*) subir **2.** (*plant*) arrancar **II.** *vi* parar
pull-down menu *n* COMPUT menú *m* desplegable
pullet [ˈpʊl·ɪt] *n* polla *f* (*gallina de menos de un año*)
pulley [ˈpʊl·i] <-s> *n* TECH polea *f*
Pullman (car) [ˈpʊl·mən] *n* RAIL coche *m* cama
pullout I. *n* **1.** MIL retirada *f* **2.** PUBL (*part of magazine*) desplegable *m* **II.** *adj* desplegable
pullover [ˈpʊl·oʊ·vər] *n* jersey *m,* suéter *m*
pull-up *n* (*exercise*) flexión *f,* en una barra horizontal
pulmonary [ˈpʌl·mə·ner·i] *adj* pulmonar
pulp [pʌlp] **I.** *n* **1.** (*soft wet mass*) pasta *f;* (*for making paper*) pulpa *f* de papel; **~ mill** fábrica *f* de pasta; **to beat sb to a ~** *inf* hacer papilla a alguien **2.** (*of fruit*) pulpa *f* **3.** (*literature*) literatura *f* barata **II.** *vt* hacer pulpa
pulpit [ˈpʊl·pɪt] *n* REL púlpito *m*
pulsar [ˈpʌl·sar] *n* ASTR púlsar *m*
pulsate [ˈpʌl·seɪt] *vi* palpitar
pulsation [pʌlˈseɪ·ʃən] *n* pulsación *f*
pulse[1] [pʌls] **I.** *n* **1.** ANAT pulso *m;* (*heartbeat*) latido *m;* **to take sb's ~** tomar el pulso a alguien **2.** (*single vibration*) pulsación *f* **II.** *vi* latir
pulse[2] [pʌls] *n* CULIN legumbre *f*
pulverize [ˈpʌl·və·raɪz] *vt* pulverizar
puma [ˈpu·mə] *n* puma *m*
pumice [ˈpʌm·ɪs] *n* ~ (**stone**) piedra *f* pómez
pummel [ˈpʌm·əl] <-l- *o* -ll-, -l- *o* -ll-> *vt* aporrear
pump [pʌmp] **I.** *n* bomba *f;* (*for fuel*) surtidor *m* **II.** *vt* bombear
pumpernickel [ˈpʌm·pər·nɪk·əl] *n* pan *m* integral de centeno

pumping *n* bombeo *m*
pumpkin ['pʌmp·kɪn] *n* calabaza *f,* zapallo *m* *CSur, Perú*

> **i** **Pumpkin pie** significa pastel de calabaza o zapallo. Este apreciado pie estadounidense se sirve principalmente en los días de Acción de Gracias (**Thanksgiving**) y Navidad (**Christmas**).

pun [pʌn] **I.** *n* juego *m* de palabras, albur *m* *Méx* **II.** <-nn-> *vi* hacer juegos de palabras, alburear *Méx*
punch¹ [pʌntʃ] **I.** *vt* **1.** (*hit*) pegar; **to ~ sb out** *sl* dar una paliza a alguien **2.** (*push: button, key*) pulsar, hundir **3.** (*pierce*) perforar, ponchar *Méx;* (*ticket*) picar; **to ~ holes in sth** hacer agujeros a algo, perforar; **to ~ the clock** [*o* **card**] fichar, marcar **4.** AGR (*cattle*) aguijonear, picanear *AmL* **II.** *vi* **1.** (*hit*) pegar **2.** (*employee*) **to ~ in/out** fichar (*al entrar/al salir*), checar la entrada y la salida **III.** <-es> *n* **1.** (*hit*) puñetazo *m;* (*in boxing*) golpe *m;* **to give sb a ~** dar un puñetazo a alguien **2.** (*tool for puncturing*) punzón *m;* (*for metal, leather*) sacabocados *m inv;* (**hole**) ~ perforadora *f;* (**ticket**) ~ máquina *f* de picar billetes **3.** *fig* (*strong effect*) fuerza *f;* **with** ~ con nervio ▶ **to beat** sb **to the** ~ ganar a alguien por la mano; **to pull one's** ~**es** no emplear toda su fuerza; **to roll with the** ~**es** saber arreglárselas
punch² [pʌntʃ] *n* (*beverage*) ponche *m*
punch bowl *n* ponchera *f*
punch card *n* tarjeta *f* perforada
punch-drunk ['pʌntʃ·drʌŋk] *adj a. fig* atontado, -a; **to be** ~ estar grogui *inf*
punching bag *n* (*in boxing*) saco *m* de arena
punch line *n* gracia *f* (de un chiste)
punctilious [pʌŋk·'tɪl·i·əs] *adj form* (*attentive to detail*) puntilloso, -a; (*with correct behavior*) formalista
punctual ['pʌŋk·tʃu·əl] *adj* puntual
punctuality [,pʌŋk·tʃu·'æl·ə·t̬i] *n* puntualidad *f*
punctuate ['pʌŋk·tʃu·eɪt] *vt* **1.** LING puntuar **2.** (*appear intermittently*) salpicar *fig;* (*interrupt*) interrumpir
punctuation [,pʌŋk·tʃu·'eɪ·ʃən] *n* LING puntuación *f*
punctuation mark *n* signo *m* de puntuación
puncture ['pʌŋk·tʃər] **I.** *vt* **1.** (*pierce*) pinchar, ponchar *Méx;* (*abscess*) reventar; (*lung*) perforar; **to ~ a hole in sth** hacer un agujero a algo **2.** *fig* (*sb's confidence, self-esteem, ego*) minar **II.** *vi* (*tire, ball*) pincharse, poncharse *Méx;* (*car*) pinchar **III.** *n* **1.** (*in tire, ball*) pinchazo *m,* ponchadura *f Méx;* **to have a** ~ (*driver*) pinchar **2.** MED (*in skin*) punción *f*
pundit ['pʌn·dɪt] *n* supuesto, -a experto, -a *m, f*
pungent ['pʌn·dʒənt] *adj* **1.** (*sharp*) punzante; (*smell*) acre; (*taste*) fuerte **2.** (*criticism*) cáustico, -a
punish ['pʌn·ɪʃ] *vt* castigar; **to ~ oneself** castigarse

punishable *adj liter* punible; ~ **by death** penado con la muerte
punishing **I.** *adj* (*difficult*) duro, -a; (*trying*) agotador(a) **II.** *n* **to take a** ~ llevarse una paliza; **this car has taken a real** ~ este coche está muy castigado
punishment ['pʌn·ɪʃ·mənt] *n* **1.** (*for misbehavior or crime*) castigo *m;* **capital** ~ pena *f* capital; **to inflict a** ~ **on sb** castigar a alguien **2.** (*rough use*) maltrato *m;* **to take a lot of** ~ estar muy baqueteado
punitive ['pju·nɪ·t̬ɪv] *adj form* punitivo, -a; ~ **damages** LAW daños *mpl* ejemplares; ~ **expedition** MIL expedición *f* punitiva; ~ **sanctions** sanciones *fpl*
punk [pʌŋk] **I.** *n* **1.** (*punk rocker*) punk *mf* **2.** (*troublemaker*) gamberro, -a *m, f* **II.** *adj* **1.** (*music, style*) punk **2.** (*poor quality*) de pacotilla
punt¹ [pʌnt] SPORTS **I.** *vt* (*in football*) despejar **II.** *vi* (*in football*) despejar **III.** *n* (*kick*) patada *f* de despeje
punt² [pʌnt] **I.** *vt* (*in boat*) **to ~ sb** llevar a alguien en batea **II.** *vi* (*in boat*) ir en batea **III.** *n* (*boat*) batea *f*
punt³ [pʌnt] *vi* GAMES jugar contra la banca
puny ['pju·ni] <-ier, -iest> *adj* (*person*) enclenque; (*argument*) endeble; (*attempt*) lastimoso, -a
pup [pʌp] **I.** *n* **1.** (*baby dog*) cachorro, -a *m, f* **2.** (*baby animal*) cría *f* **3.** (*young person*) niño, -a *m, f* **II.** <-pp-> *vi* parir
pupa ['pju·pə] <pupas *o* pupae> *n* BIO crisálida *f,* pupa *f*
pupate ['pju·peɪt] *vi* BIO convertirse en crisálida
pupil¹ ['pju·pəl] *n* SCHOOL alumno, -a *m, f*
pupil² ['pju·pəl] *n* ANAT pupila *f*
puppet ['pʌp·ɪt] *n a. fig* títere *m;* **hand** ~ muñeco *m* de guiñol
puppeteer [pʌp·ə·'tɪr] *n* titiritero, -a *m, f*
puppet government *n* gobierno *m* títere
puppet show *n* THEAT función *f* de marionetas
puppet theater *n* teatro *m* de polichinelas
puppy ['pʌp·i] <-ies> *n* cachorro, -a *m, f*
purchase ['pɜr·tʃəs] **I.** *vt* **1.** (*buy*) comprar, adquirir **2.** NAUT **to ~ the anchor** levar el ancla **II.** *n* **1.** (*act of buying*) compra *f,* adquisición *f;* **to make a** ~ hacer una adquisición **2.** (*hold*) agarre *m;* **to get a** ~ **on sth** agarrarse a [*o* del algo
purchase price *n* precio *m* de compra
purchaser *n* **1.** (*buyer*) comprador(a) *m(f)* **2.** (*at auction*) adjudicatario, -a *m, f*
purchasing *n* compras *fpl*
purchasing department *n* departamento *m* de compras
purchasing manager *n* director(a) *m(f)* de compras
purchasing power *n* poder *m* adquisitivo
pure [pjʊr] *adj* puro, -a; ~ **air** aire *m* puro; ~ **gold** oro *m* puro; ~ **mathematics** mate-

máticas *fpl* puras; ~ **and simple** simple y llano; **to be ~ in heart** ser limpio de corazón

purebred ['pjʊr·bred] I. *n* animal *m* de pura raza II. *adj* de pura raza; **a ~ horse** un purasangre

purée [pju·'reɪ] I. *vt* hacer puré de II. *n* puré *m*

purely ['pjʊr·li] *adv* **1.** (*completely*) puramente; **~ by chance** por pura casualidad **2.** (*simply*) meramente; **~ and simply** simple y llanamente

purgative ['pɜr·gə·t̬ɪv] I. *n* purga *f* II. *adj* MED purgante, purgativo, -a

purgatory ['pɜr·gə·tɔr·i] *n* **1.** REL Purgatorio *m;* **to be in ~** estar en el Purgatorio **2.** *fig* (*unpleasant experience*) calvario *m*

purge [pɜrdʒ] I. *vt* **1.** MED, POL purgar; **to ~ a group of extremist elements** purgar a un grupo de elementos extremistas; **to ~ sb from a party** expulsar a alguien de un partido **2.** *a.* REL (*crime, sin*) expiar II. *n* MED, POL purga *f*

purification [ˌpjʊr·ə·fɪ·'keɪ·ʃən] *n a.* REL purificación *f*; (*of water*) depuración *f*

purify ['pjʊr·ə·faɪ] *vt* (*cleanse*) purificar; (*language, water*) depurar; (*soul, body*) limpiar; **to ~ oneself of sth** purificarse de algo

purist ['pjʊr·ɪst] *n* purista *mf*

puritan ['pjʊr·ɪ·tən] *n a. fig* puritano, -a *m, f*

puritanical [ˌpjʊr·ɪ·'tæn·ɪ·kəl] *adj* puritano, -a

Puritanism *n* puritanismo *m*

purity ['pjʊr·ɪ·t̬i] *n* pureza *f*

purl [pɜrl] I. *n* punto *m* al revés II. *adj* ~ **stitch** punto *m* al revés III. *vt* hacer con puntos al revés; (*stitches*) hacer al revés; **knit one, ~ one** uno al derecho, otro al revés IV. *vi* tejer al revés

purloin [pər·'bɪn] *vt form* hurtar

purple ['pɜr·pəl] I. *adj* (*reddish*) púrpura; (*bluish*) morado, -a; **to be ~ with rage** estar lívido de rabia II. *n* (*reddish*) púrpura *m;* (*bluish*) morado *m*

purport [pɜr·'pɔrt] I. *vi form* (*claim*) **to ~ to be sth** pretender ser algo II. *n* **1.** (*meaning*) sentido *m* **2.** (*purpose*) intención *f*

purpose ['pɜr·pəs] *n* **1.** (*goal*) intención *f;* **for the ~** al efecto; **I did that for a ~** hice eso por algo; **for that very ~** precisamente por eso; **for practical ~s** a efectos prácticos; **for humanitarian ~s** con fines humanitarios; **for future ~s** para las necesidades futuras; **the sole ~ of sth** el único objetivo de algo; **not to the ~** que no viene al caso; **to have a ~ in life** tener una meta en la vida **2.** (*motivation*) (**strength of**) ~ resolución *f* **3.** (*use*) utilidad *f;* **to no ~** inútilmente; **to serve a ~** servir de algo; **what's the ~ of...?** ¿para qué sirve...? ▶ **on ~** a propósito

purposeful ['pɜr·pəs·fəl] *adj* **1.** (*determined*) decidido, -a **2.** (*meaningful*) con sentido **3.** (*intentional*) intencionado, -a

purposeless ['pɜr·pəs·lɪs] *adj* **1.** (*aimless*) sin sentido; (*utterance, violence*) gratuito, -a **2.** (*useless*) inútil **3.** (*character, person*) irresoluto, -a

purposely ['pɜr·pəs·li] *adv* a propósito

purr [pɜr] I. *vi* (*cat*) ronronear; (*engine*) zumbar II. *n* (*of cat*) ronroneo *m;* (*of engine*) zumbido *m*

purse [pɜrs] I. *n* **1.** (*handbag*) bolso *m*, cartera *f AmL*, bolsa *f Méx* **2.** (*wallet*) monedero *m* **3.** (*funds*) **to be beyond one's ~** estar por encima de las posibilidades de uno **4.** (*prize*) premio *m* en efectivo II. *vt* (*lips*) apretar

purser ['pɜr·sər] *n* AVIAT, NAUT contable *mf*

purse strings *npl fig* **to hold the ~** administrar el dinero; **to loosen the ~** aflojar la bolsa

pursuance [pər·'su·əns] *n form* ejecución *f;* **in ~ of sth** (*in accordance with*) de conformidad con algo; **in ~ of her duty** en cumplimiento de su deber

pursuant [pər·'su·ənt] *adv* LAW **~ to** conforme a, de acuerdo con

pursue [pər·'su] *vt* **1.** (*chase*) perseguir **2.** (*seek to find*) buscar; (*dreams, goals*) luchar por; (*rights, peace*) reivindicar **3.** (*follow: plan*) seguir; **to ~ a matter** seguir un caso **4.** (*work towards*) **to ~ a career** dedicarse a una carrera profesional; **to ~ a degree in sth** seguir estudios de algo

pursuer [pər·'su·ər] *n* perseguidor(a) *m(f)*

pursuit [pər·'sut] *n* **1.** (*chase*) persecución *f;* **police ~** persecución policial; **to be in ~ of sth** ir tras algo; (*knowledge, happiness*) ir en busca de algo; (*hunt*) ir a la caza de algo; **to be in hot ~ of sb** pisar los talones a alguien *fig* **2.** (*activity*) actividad *f;* **outdoor ~s** actividades al aire libre

purulent ['pjʊr·ə·lənt] *adj* purulento, -a

purvey [pər·'veɪ] *vt* proveer, suministrar; **to ~ sth to sb** proveer a alguien de algo

purveyor [pər·'veɪ·ər] *n* ECON proveedor(a) *m(f)*

pus [pʌs] *n* MED pus *m*, postema *f Méx*

push [pʊʃ] I. *vt* **1.** (*shove*) empujar; **to ~ one's way through sth** abrirse paso a empujones por algo; **to ~ sth to the back of one's mind** intentar no pensar en algo; **to ~ the door open** abrir la puerta de un empujón; **to ~ sb out of sth** echar a alguien de algo a empujones; **to ~ sb out of the way** apartar a alguien a empujones **2.** (*force*) **to ~ one's luck** tentar a la suerte; **to ~ sb too far** sacar a alguien de quicio **3.** (*coerce*) obligar; **to ~ sb to do** [*o* **into doing**] **sth** presionar a alguien para que haga algo; **to ~ oneself** exigirse demasiado **4.** (*insist*) insistir en; **to ~ sb for sth** apremiar a alguien para algo **5.** (*press: button*) apretar; (*the brakes, gas pedal*) pisar; **to ~ the doorbell** tocar el timbre **6.** *inf* (*promote*) promover; ECON fomentar **7. to be ~ing 30** rondar los 30 (años) II. *vi* **1.** (*force movement*) empujar **2.** (*press*) apretar **3.** (*insist*) presionar; **to ~ for sth** presionar para (conseguir) algo III. <-es> *n* **1.** (*shove*) empujón *m;* (*slight push*) empujoncito *m;* **to give sb a ~** *fig* dar un empujón a alguien **2.** (*press*) **at the ~ of a button** apretando un botón **3.** (*strong action*) impulso *m;* (*will to succeed*) empuje *m*

4. (*strong effort*) esfuerzo *m;* **to make a ~ for sth** hacer un esfuerzo para algo; **at a ~ ...** si me apuras... **5.** *inf* (*publicity*) campaña *f;* **to make a ~** hacer una campaña **6.** MIL (*military attack*) ofensiva *f* ▶ **if/when ~ comes to shove** en caso de apuro
◆ **push along** *vi inf* largarse
◆ **push around** *vt inf* mangonear *inf*
◆ **push away** *vt* apartar
◆ **push back** *vt* (*move backwards*) hacer retroceder; (*person*) empujar hacia atrás; (*hair*) echar hacia atrás
◆ **push down** *vt* **1.** (*knock down*) derribar **2.** (*press down*) apretar **3.** ECON (*price, interest rate*) hacer bajar
◆ **push forward I.** *vt* **1.** (*force forward*) empujar hacia adelante **2.** (*promote*) promocionar **II.** *vi* **1.** (*advance*) avanzar **2.** (*continue*) **to ~** (**with sth**) seguir (con algo)
◆ **push in I.** *vt* **1.** (*nail*) empujar (hacia adentro) **2.** (*force in*) **to push one's way in** colarse *inf* **II.** *vi* (*force way in*) entrar a empujones
◆ **push off I.** *vi inf* largarse **II.** *vt* NAUT (*boat*) desatracar
◆ **push on I.** *vi* **1.** (*continue despite problems*) **to ~** (**with sth**) seguir adelante (con algo) **2.** (*continue traveling*) **we pushed on to Veracruz** seguimos hasta Veracruz **II.** *vt* **1.** (*activate*) apresurar **2.** (*urge on*) **to push sb on to do sth** empujar a alguien a hacer algo
◆ **push out** *vt* **1.** (*force out*) **to push sb out** (**of sth**) echar a alguien (de algo) **2.** (*get rid of*) eliminar; **to push competitors out of the market** eliminar a los competidores del mercado **3.** (*produce: roots, blossoms*) echar **4.** NAUT (*boat*) echar al agua
◆ **push over** *vt always sep* (*thing*) volcar; (*person*) hacer caer
◆ **push through I.** *vi* abrirse paso entre **II.** *vt* **1.** (*legislation, proposal*) hacer aceptar **2.** (*help to succeed*) llevar a buen término
◆ **push up** *vt* **1.** (*move higher*) levantar; *fig* (*help*) dar un empujón **2.** (*price, interest rate*) hacer subir
pushbutton ['pʊʃˌbʌt·ən] **I.** *adj* de botones **II.** *n* botón *m*, botón *m* de control
push-button telephone *n* teléfono *m* de botones
pushcart ['pʊʃ·kart] *n* carretilla *f* de mano
pusher *n sl* camello *mf*
pushover ['pʊʃ·ou·vər] *n* **1.** (*easy success*) **to be a ~** ser pan comido **2.** (*easily influenced*) **to be a ~** ser muy fácil de convencer
pushpin ['pʊʃ·pɪn] *n* chincheta *f*
push start *n* AUTO **to give sb a ~** ayudar a alguien a arrancar empujando el coche
push-start *vi* AUTO arrancar empujando el coche
pushup ['pʊʃ·ʌp] *n* SPORTS flexión *f* de brazos; **to do ~s** hacer flexiones
pushy ['pʊʃ·i] *adj* avasallador(a), insistente
puss [pʊs] <-es> *n* (*cat*) minino, -a *m, f;* **Puss in Boots** el gato con botas

pussy ['pʊs·i] <-ies> *n* **1.** (*cat*) ~ (**cat**) minino, -a *m, f* **2.** *vulg* conejo *m,* concha *f AmL*
pussyfoot ['pʊs·i·fʊt] **to ~ around an issue** dar largas a un asunto
pussy willow *n* sauce *m* blanco
pustule ['pʌs·tʃul] *n* pústula *f*
put [pʊt] <-tt-, put, put> **I.** *vt* **1.** (*place*) poner; (*in box, hole*) meter; **~ the spoons next to the knives** pon las cucharas junto a los cuchillos; **to ~ sth to one's lips** llevarse algo a los labios; **~ it there!** (*shake hands*) ¡chócala!; **to ~ sth in the oven** meter algo en el horno **2.** (*add*) echar; **to ~ sugar/salt in sth** echar azúcar/sal a algo; **to ~ the date on sth** poner la fecha en algo; **to ~ sth on a list** apuntar algo en una lista **3.** (*direct*) **to ~ pressure on sb** presionar a alguien; **to ~ a spell on sb** echar una maldición a alguien; **to ~ one's heart into sth** poner todo el afán de uno en algo; **to ~ one's mind to sth** poner los cinco sentidos en algo; **to ~ one's trust in sb** depositar la confianza de uno en alguien; **to ~ one's faith in sb** tener fe en alguien; **to ~ one's hope in sb** poner las esperanzas de uno en alguien **4.** (*invest*) **to ~ sth into sth** invertir algo en algo; **to ~ energy/time into sth** dedicar energía/tiempo a algo **5.** (*bet*) apostar; **to ~ money on sth** jugarse dinero a algo; **to ~ sth toward sth** contribuir con algo para algo **6.** (*cause to be*) **to ~ sb in a good mood** poner a alguien de buen humor; **to ~ sb in danger** poner a alguien en peligro; **to ~ one-self in sb's place** [*o* **shoes**] ponerse en el lugar de alguien; **to ~ sb in prison** meter a alguien en la cárcel; **to ~ into practice** poner en práctica; **to ~ sb on the train** acompañar a alguien hasta el tren; **to ~ sth right** arreglar algo; **to ~ sb to bed** acostar a alguien; **to ~ sb to death** ejecutar a alguien; **to ~ sth to good use** hacer buen uso de algo; **to ~ sb to shame** avergonzar a alguien; **to ~ sb under oath** tomar juramento a alguien; **to ~ sb to expense** ocasionar gastos a alguien; **to ~ to flight** poner en fuga; **to ~ a stop to sth** poner fin a algo; **to ~ sb to work** poner a alguien a trabajar **7.** (*impose*) **to ~ an idea in sb's head** meter una idea en la cabeza a alguien; **to ~ a tax on sth** gravar algo con un impuesto **8.** (*attribute*) **to ~ a high value on sth** valorar mucho algo; **to ~ the blame on sb** echar la culpa a alguien; **to ~ emphasis on sth** conceder especial importancia a algo **9.** (*present*) **to ~ one's point of view** exponer el punto de vista de uno; **to ~ a question** plantear una pregunta; **to ~ sth to discussion** someter algo a debate; **to ~ sth to a vote** someter algo a votación; **to ~ a proposal before a committee** presentar una propuesta ante un comité; **I ~ it to you that...** mi opinión es que... **10.** (*express*) decir; **as John ~ it** como dijo John; **to ~ one's feelings into words** expresar sus sentimientos con palabras; **to ~ sth into Spanish** traducir algo al español; **to ~ sth in writing** poner algo

por escrito **11.**(*judge, estimate*) **I ~ the number of visitors at 2,000** calculo que el número de visitantes ronde los 2.000; **I'd ~ her at about 35** calculo que tiene unos 35 años; **to ~ sb on a level with sb** poner a alguien al mismo nivel que alguien **12.**SPORTS (*throw*) **to ~ the shot** lanzar el peso **II.** *vi* NAUT **to ~ to sea** zarpar
◆**put about** <-tt-> *irr* **I.** *vt* NAUT hacer virar **II.** *vi* NAUT virar
◆**put across** <-tt-> *irr vt* (*make understood*) comunicar; **to put sth across to sb** hacer entender algo a alguien; **to put oneself across well** causar buena impresión
◆**put aside** <-tt-> *irr vt* **1.**(*place to one side*) dejar a un lado **2.**(*save*) ahorrar; (*time*) reservar **3.**(*give up*) **to put sth aside** dejar algo **4.**(*reject*) rechazar **5.**(*ignore: fears, differences*) dejar de lado
◆**put away** <-tt-> *irr vt* **1.**(*save*) ahorrar **2.** *inf* (*eat a lot*) zamparse **3.**(*remove*) guardar **4.** *inf* (*imprison*) **to put sb away** encerrar a alguien **5.** *sl* (*kill*) matar
◆**put back** <-tt-> *irr vt* **1.**(*return*) volver a poner en su sitio **2.**(*postpone*) posponer **3.**SCHOOL (*not be promoted*) **to put sb back a year** hacer repetir curso a alguien **4.**(*set earlier: watch*) atrasar
◆**put by** <-tt-> *irr vt* ahorrar
◆**put down** <-tt-> *irr vt* **1.**(*set down*) dejar; **to not be able to put a book down** no poder parar de leer un libro **2.**(*lower*) bajar; **to put one's arm/feet down** bajar el brazo/los pies; **to put sb/sth down somewhere** dejar a alguien/algo en un sitio **3.**(*attribute*) **to put sth down to sb** atribuir algo a alguien **4.**(*write*) escribir; **to put sth down on paper** poner algo por escrito **5.**(*assess*) catalogar; **I put her down as 30** le echo 30 años **6.**(*register*) **to put sb down for sth** inscribir a alguien en algo **7.**FIN (*prices*) disminuir **8.**ECON (*leave as deposit*) dejar en depósito **9.**(*stop: rebellion, opposition*) reprimir **10.** *sl* (*humiliate*) menospreciar **11.**(*have killed: animal*) sacrificar
◆**put forward** <-tt-> *irr vt* **1.**(*offer for discussion: subject*) proponer; (*idea, plan*) exponer; (*suggestion*) hacer; **to ~ a proposal** hacer una propuesta **2.**(*advance: event*) adelantar; **to put the clock forward** adelantar el reloj
◆**put in** <-tt-> *irr* **I.** *vt* **1.**(*place inside*) meter **2.**(*add*) poner; **to ~ a comma/a period** añadir una coma/un punto **3.**(*say*) decir; (*remark*) hacer; **to put a word in** intervenir en la conversación; **to ~ a good word for sb** hablar bien de alguien **4.**AGR (*plant: vegetables, trees*) plantar; (*seeds*) sembrar **5.**TECH (*install*) instalar; **to ~ a shower** poner una ducha **6.**(*invest: money*) poner; (*time*) dedicar; **to ~ a lot of effort on sth** dedicar mucho esfuerzo a algo; **to ~ overtime** hacer horas extra **7.**(*submit: claim, request*) presentar; (*candidate*) presentarse; **to put oneself in for**

sth inscribirse para algo **8.**(*make*) **to ~ an appearance** hacer acto de presencia **II.** *vi* **1.**(*apply*) **to ~ for sth** solicitar algo **2.**NAUT (*dock*) hacer escala
◆**put into** <-tt-> *irr vt* **1.**(*place inside*) meter **2. to put sth into sth** (*add*) añadir algo a algo; CULIN echar algo a algo; (*include*) incluir algo en algo **3.**(*dress in*) **to put sb into sth** vestir a alguien de algo **4.**TECH (*install*) instalar **5.**FIN (*deposit*) **to put money into a bank** ingresar dinero en un banco **6.**(*invest*) **to put sth into sth** (*money*) invertir algo en algo; (*time, effort*) dedicar algo a algo **7.**(*cause to be*) **to put a plan into operation** [*o inf* **action**] poner un plan en marcha **8.**(*institutionalize*) **to put sb into sth** meter a alguien en algo; **to put sb into prison** meter a alguien en la cárcel
◆**put off** <-tt-> *irr vt* **1.**(*turn off: lights, TV*) apagar; (*take off: sweater, jacket*) quitarse **2.**(*delay*) posponer; **to put sth off for a week** aplazar algo una semana **3.** *inf* (*make wait*) entretener; **to put sb off with excuses** dar largas a alguien *inf* **4.**(*repel*) alejar; (*food, smell*) dar asco a **5.**(*disconcert*) desconcertar **6.**(*distract*) distraer; **to put sb off sth** distraer a alguien de algo; **to put sb off the scent** despistar a alguien
◆**put on** <-tt-> *irr vt* **1.**(*place upon*) **to put sth on sth** poner algo sobre algo **2.**(*attach*) **to put sth on sth** poner algo a algo **3.**(*wear: shirt, shoes*) ponerse; **to ~ make-up** maquillarse **4.**(*turn on*) encender; **to ~ Mozart** poner (música de) Mozart **5.**(*use*) **to ~ the brakes** frenar; **to put the handbrake on** poner el freno de mano **6.**(*perform: film*) dar; (*show*) presentar; (*play*) poner en escena **7.**(*provide: dish*) servir; **to ~ a party** dar una fiesta **8.**(*begin boiling: water, soup, potatoes*) calentar **9.**(*assume: expression*) adoptar; **to ~ a frown** fruncir el ceño; **to ~ airs** darse aires **10.**(*pretend*) fingir; (*accent*) afectar **11.**(*be joking with*) **to put sb on** tomar el pelo a alguien **12.**(*gain: weight*) engordar; **to ~ 10 years** envejecer 10 años **13.**TEL **to put sb on the (tele)phone** pasar el teléfono a alguien; **to put sb on to sb** poner a alguien con alguien; **I'll put him on** le paso con él **14.**(*inform*) **to put sb on to sb** hablar a alguien de alguien; **to put sb on to sth** dar a alguien información sobre algo
◆**put out** <-tt-> *irr* **I.** *vt* **1.**(*take outside*) **to put the dog out** sacar al perro **2.**(*extend*) extender; **to ~ one's hand** tender la mano **3.**(*extinguish: fire*) extinguir; **to ~ a cigarette** apagar un cigarrillo **4.**(*turn off: lights, TV*) apagar **5.**(*eject*) expulsar; (*dismiss*) echar **6.**(*publish: newsletter, magazine*) publicar; (*announcement*) hacer público **7.**(*spread: rumor*) hacer circular; **to put it out that...** hacer correr la voz de que... **8.**(*produce industrially*) producir **9.**(*sprout: leaves*) echar **10.**(*contract out*) **to put sth out to subcon-**

tract subcontratar; **to put sth out to bid** subcontratar algo con una empresa **11.** (*inconvenience*) molestar a; **to put oneself out for sb**
molestarse por alguien **12.** (*offend*) **to be ~**
ofenderse **13.** (*dislocate*) dislocar, zafar *AmL;*
to ~ one's shoulder dislocarse [*o* zafarse *AmL*]
el hombro **14.** NAUT botar **II.** *vi* NAUT zarpar
♦ **put over** <-tt-> *irr vt* **1.** (*place higher*) **to
put sth over sth** poner algo por encima de
algo **2.** (*make understood: idea, plan*) comunicar **3.** (*fool*) **to put sth over on sb** engañar a
alguien
♦ **put through** <-tt-> *irr vt* **1.** (*insert through*)
to put sth through sth hacer pasar algo por
algo **2.** (*complete, implement*) llevar a cabo;
(*proposal*) hacer aceptar; (*bill*) hacer aprobar
3. (*send*) mandar; **to put sb through college**
mandar a alguien a la universidad **4.** TEL poner;
to ~ a telephone call to Montreal contactar
con un número de Montreal; **to put a call
through** pasar una llamada; **to put sb
through** (**to sb**) pasar a alguien (con alguien)
5. *inf* (*make endure*) **to put sb through sth**
someter a alguien a algo; **to put sb through it**
hacer pasar un mal rato a alguien
♦ **put together** <-tt-> *irr vt* **1.** (*join*) juntar;
(*collection*) reunir; (*assemble*) ensamblar;
(*machine, model, radio*) montar; (*pieces*) acoplar **2.** *fig* (*connect: facts, clues*) relacionar
3. (*create*) crear; (*list*) hacer; (*team*) formar;
(*meal*) preparar; (*dress*) confeccionar **4.** MATH
sumar
♦ **put up** <-tt-> *irr* **I.** *vt* **1.** (*hang up*) colgar;
(*notice*) fijar **2.** (*raise*) levantar; (*one's collar*)
subirse; (*flag*) izar; (*umbrella*) abrir; **to put
one's hair up** recogerse el pelo **3.** (*build*)
construir; (*tent*) montar **4.** (*increase: prices*)
subir **5.** (*make available*) **to put sth up for
sale** poner algo a la [*o* en] venta; **to put sth up
for auction** sacar algo a subasta pública
6. (*give shelter*) alojar; **I can put you up for a
week** te puedes quedar una semana en casa
7. (*provide: funds*) aportar; **to ~ the money
for sth** poner el dinero para algo **8.** (*show
opposition*) **to ~ opposition** oponerse; **to ~ a
struggle** [*o* **fight**] oponer resistencia **9.** (*submit: candidate, proposal*) presentar **II.** *vi*
1. (*sleep at*) alojarse; **to ~ at a hotel** hospedarse en un hotel; **to ~ at sb's place for the
night** pasar la noche en casa de alguien
2. (*tolerate unwillingly*) **to ~ with sb/sth**
soportar a alguien/algo
putative ['pju·tə·ṭɪv] *adj form* (*reputed*)
supuesto, -a; (*father*) putativo, -a
putoff *n inf* aplazamiento *m;* **to give sb a ~** dar
largas a alguien
put-on *n sl* burla *f;* (*joke*) broma *f*
put option *n* ECON opción *f* de venta
putrefaction [ˌpju·trə·'fæk·ʃən] *n* putrefacción *f*
putrefy ['pju·trə·faɪ] <-ie-> *vi* pudrirse
putrid ['pju·trɪd] *adj* **1.** (*decayed*) podrido, -a,
putrefacto, -a; (*smell*) pútrido, -a **2.** (*very bad*)

pésimo, -a
putsch [pʊtʃ] <-es> *n* golpe *m* de Estado
putt [pʌt] SPORTS **I.** *vi* patear **II.** *n* golpe *m* corto
(al hoyo), put *m AmL*
puttee [pʌ·'ti] *n* polaina *f*
putter¹ ['pʌṭ·ər] *n* (*golf club*) putter *m*
putter² ['pʌṭ·ər] *vi* entretenerse; **to ~ around
the house** pasearse por la casa
putty ['pʌṭ·i] *n* masilla *f* ▶ **to be like ~ in sb's
hands** ser completamente manejable
putty knife <-knives> *n* española *f*
put-up *adj inf* **a ~ job** un asunto fraudulento
put-upon *adj inf* explotado, -a
puzzle ['pʌz·əl] **I.** *vt* dejar perplejo, -a **II.** *vi* **to ~
over sth** dar vueltas a algo **III.** *n* **1.** (*game*)
rompecabezas *m inv;* **jigsaw ~** puzzle *m;*
crossword ~ crucigrama *m* **2.** (*mystery*) misterio *m*, enigma *m;* **to be a ~ to sb** ser un misterio para alguien; **to solve a ~** resolver un
enigma
puzzled *adj* perplejo, -a; **to be ~ about sth**
estar desconcertado por algo
puzzler ['pʌz·lər] *n* (*mystery*) enigma *m*
puzzling *adj* desconcertante
PVC [ˌpi·vi·'si] *n abbr of* **polyvinyl chloride**
PVC *m*
pygmy ['pɪɡ·mi] **I.** *n* <-ies> **1.** (*short person*)
pigmeo, -a *m, f* **2.** *fig* enano, -a *m, f* **II.** *adj* ZOOL
enano, -a
pylon ['paɪ·lɑn] *n* ELEC torre *f* de alta tensión
pyramid ['pɪr·ə·mɪd] *n* pirámide *f*
pyre [paɪr] *n* pira *f*
Pyrenees ['pɪr·ə·ˌniz] *npl* **the ~** los Pirineos
Pyrex® ['paɪ·reks] **I.** *n* pyrex *m* **II.** *adj* de pyrex
pyrites [ˌpaɪ·'raɪ·tiz] <-tae> *n* pirita *f;* **iron ~**
pirita de hierro
pyromania [ˌpaɪ·roʊ·'meɪ·ni·ə] *n* piromanía *f*
pyromaniac *n* pirómano, -a *m, f*
pyrotechnic [ˌpaɪ·roʊ·'tek·nɪk] *adj* **1.** piroté-
nico, -a; **~ display** espectáculo pirotécnico
2. *fig* (*brilliant*) espectacular
python ['paɪ·θɑn] <-(ons)> *n* pitón *f*

Q

Q, q [kju] *n* Q, q *f;* **~ as in Quebec** Q de Queso
Q *abbr of* **Queen** reina *f*
Qatar ['ka·ṭar] *n* Qatar *m*
QED [ˌkju·i·'di] *abbr of* **quod erat demon-
strandum** Q.E.D.
qt. *n abbr of* **quart** cuarto *m* de galón
Q-Tip® *n* bastoncillo *m,* hisopo *m AmL,* coto-
nete *m Méx*
qtr. *abbr of* **quarter** cuarto *m*
qty. *abbr of* **quantity** cantidad *m*
quack¹ [kwæk] **I.** *n* (*duck's sound*) graznido *m*
II. *vi* graznar
quack² [kwæk] *pej* **I.** *n* **1.** (*doctor*) matasanos

m inv **2.** (*charlatan*) fantasmón, -ona *m, f inf* **II.** *adj* falso, -a

quad¹ [kwad] *n inf* (*quadriceps*) cuádriceps *m inv*

quad² [kwad] *n inf* (*quadrangle*) cuadrángulo *m*

quad³ [kwad] *inf* **I.** *n* (*quadruplet*) cuatrillizo, -a *m, f* **II.** *adj* (*quadruple*) cuádruple

quadrangle ['kwad·ræŋ·gəl] *n form* cuadrángulo *m*

quadrangular [kwa·'dræŋ·gjə·lər] *adj* cuadrangular

quadrant ['kwad·rənt] *n* cuadrante *m*

quadraphonic [ˌkwad·rə·'fan·ɪk] *adj* MUS cuadrafónico, -a

quadratic [kwa·'dræt̬·ɪk] *adj* cuadrático, -a

quadrilateral [ˌkwad·rɪ·'læt̬·ər·əl] *n* cuadrilátero *m*

quadripartite ['kwad·rɪ·'par·taɪt] *adj form* cuatripartito, -a

quadruped ['kwad·rə·ped] *n* cuadrúpedo *m*

quadruple [kwa·'dru·pəl] **I.** *vt* cuadruplicar **II.** *vi* cuadruplicarse **III.** *adj* cuádruple

quadruplet [kwa·'dru·plɪt] *n* cuatrillizo, -a *m, f*

quaff [kwaf] *vt liter* beber; **to ~ one's sorrows away** *fig* ahogar las penas

quagmire ['kwæg·maɪr] *n* **1.** (*area*) cenagal *m* **2.** (*situation*) atolladero *m*

quail¹ [kweɪl] <-(s)> *n* (*bird*) codorniz *f*

quail² [kweɪl] *vi* (*feel fear*) acobardarse; **to ~ before sb/sth** acobardarse ante alguien/algo

quaint [kweɪnt] *adj* **1.** (*charming*) pintoresco, -a **2.** *pej* (*strange*) raro, -a **3.** (*pleasantly unusual*) singular

quaintness ['kweɪnt·nɪs] *n* lo pintoresco *m;* (*strangeness*) lo raro *m*

quake [kweɪk] **I.** *n* **1.** (*shaking*) temblor *m* **2.** *inf* (*earthquake*) terremoto *m* **II.** *vi* **1.** (*move*) estremecerse **2.** (*shake*) temblar; **to ~ with fear** temblar de miedo; **to ~ at sth** temblar ante algo

Quaker ['kweɪ·kər] **I.** *n* cuáquero, -a *m, f;* **the ~s** los cuáqueros **II.** *adj* cuáquero, -a

qualification [ˌkwal·ə·fɪ·'keɪ·ʃən] *n* **1.** (*document*) título *m;* (*exam*) calificación *f;* **academic ~** título académico; **her ~s are very good** está muy cualificada **2.** (*limiting criterion*) restricción *f;* (*condition*) reserva *f;* (*change*) matización *f;* **without ~** sin reservas

qualified ['kwal·ɪ·faɪd] *adj* **1.** (*trained*) titulado, -a; (*certified*) certificado, -a; (*by the state*) homologado, -a **2.** (*competent*) capacitado, -a **3.** (*limited*) limitado, -a; **to be a ~ success** tener cierto éxito

qualify ['kwal·ɪ·faɪ] <-ie-> **I.** *vi* **1.** (*meet standards*) **to ~ for sth** estar habilitado para algo; (*be eligible*) tener derecho a algo; (*have qualifications*) estar acreditado para algo **2.** (*complete training*) titularse, recibirse *AmL* **3.** SPORTS clasificarse **II.** *vt* **1.** (*give credentials*) acreditar **2.** (*make eligible*) habilitar; **to ~ sb to do sth** dar derecho a alguien para hacer algo **3.** (*explain and limit*) limitar; **to ~ a remark**

matizar un comentario **4.** LING (*modify*) calificar

qualifying ['kwal·ɪ·faɪ·ɪŋ] *adj* **1.** (*limiting*) matizador(a) **2.** SPORTS (*testing standard*) clasificatorio, -a; **~ round** eliminatoria *f* **3.** LING (*modifying*) calificativo, -a

qualitative ['kwal·ɪ·ter·t̬ɪv] *adj* cualitativo, -a; **~ difference** diferencia cualitativa

quality ['kwal·ɪ·t̬i] **I.** <-ies> *n* **1.** (*degree of goodness*) calidad *f;* **~ of life** calidad de vida **2.** (*characteristic*) cualidad *f;* **artistic ~** cualidades *fpl* artísticas **II.** *adj* de calidad

quality control *n* control *m* de calidad

quality time *n* tiempo *m* para relacionarse, *en especial los momentos, escasos pero intensos, que una persona dedica a sus hijos*

qualm [kwam] *n* escrúpulo *m*, reparo *m;* **to feel/have ~s** (*about sth*) sentir/tener escrúpulos (respecto a algo); **to have no ~s about doing sth** no tener escrúpulos para hacer algo; **without the slightest ~** sin el menor remordimiento

quandary ['kwan·də·ri] <-ies> *n* dilema *m;* **to be in a ~** estar en un dilema

quantifiable ['kwan·tə·faɪ·ə·bəl] *adj* cuantificable

quantification [ˌkwan·tə·fɪ·'keɪ·ʃən] *n* cuantificación *f*

quantify ['kwan·tə·faɪ] <-ie-> *vt* cuantificar

quantitative ['kwan·tə·ter·t̬ɪv] *adj* cuantitativo, -a

quantity ['kwan·tə·t̬i] **I.** <-ies> *n* **1.** (*amount*) cantidad *f;* **a large/small ~ of sth** una gran/pequeña cantidad de algo **2.** (*large amounts*) cantidades *fpl;* **to buy in ~** comprar al por mayor **II.** *adj* en cantidad

quantity discount *n* descuento *m* por grandes cantidades

quantum ['kwan·təm] <quanta> *n* **1.** *form* (*quantity*) cuantía *f* **2.** PHYS (*unit of radiant energy*) cuanto *m*

quantum mechanics *n* + *sing vb* mecánica *f* cuántica

quarantine ['kwɔr·ən·ˌtin] **I.** *n* cuarentena *f;* **to be/place under ~** estar/poner en cuarentena **II.** *vt* **to ~ sb/an animal** poner en cuarentena a alguien/a un animal

quark [kwark] *n* PHYS quark *m*

quarrel ['kwɔr·əl] **I.** *n* disputa *f* **II.** <-ll-> *vi* reñir, pelearse; **to ~ about sth** pelearse por algo

quarrelsome ['kwɔr·əl·səm] *adj* **1.** (*belligerent*) pendenciero, -a, peleonero, -a *Méx* **2.** (*grumbly*) enojadizo, -a, enojón, -ona *Méx*

quarry¹ ['kwɔr·i] **I.** <-ies> *n* (*rock pit*) cantera *f* **II.** <-ie-> *vt* extraer

quarry² ['kwɔr·i] <-ies> *n* presa *f*

quart [kwɔrt] *n* cuarto *m* de galón

quarter ['kwɔr·t̬ər] **I.** *n* **1.** (*one fourth*) cuarto *m;* **three ~s** tres cuartos; **a ~ of the Mexicans** una cuarta parte de los mexicanos; **a ~ of a century/an hour** un cuarto de siglo/de hora; **(a) ~ to three** las tres menos cuarto, un cuarto para las tres *AmL;* (**a**) **~ past three** las tres y cuarto **2.** (*25 cents*) un cuarto de dólar **3.** *a.* FIN, SCHOOL trimestre *m* **4.** (*neighborhood*) barrio *m;* **the French Quarter** el Barrio Francés de Nueva Orleans; (*area*) zona *f;* **at close ~s** de cerca; **all ~s of the earth** en todos los confines de la tierra **5.** **~s** (*unspecified group or person*) círculos *mpl;* **in certain ~s** en ciertos círculos; **in high ~s** en altas esferas **6.** (*area of compass*) cuadrante *m;* **from the north/west ~** desde el cuadrante norte/oeste **7.** SPORTS cuarto *m* **8.** (*mercy*) cuartel *m;* **to give ~** dar cuartel; **to ask for ~** pedir cuartel **II.** *vt* **1.** (*cut into four*) cuartear; **to ~ sb** descuartizar a alguien **2.** (*give housing*) alojar; **to be ~ed with sb** estar alojado en casa de alguien; MIL acuartelar **III.** *adj* cuarto; **~ hour** un cuarto de hora

quarterdeck *n* NAUT alcázar *m*
quarterfinal *n* SPORTS cuarto *m* de final
quartering *n* **1.** (*dividing into fourths*) corte *m* en cuatro **2.** MIL (*housing*) acuartelamiento *m* **3.** (*emblems on shield*) cuartel *m*
quarterly ['kwɔr·ṭər·li] **I.** *adv* trimestralmente **II.** *adj* trimestral **III.** *n* publicación *f* trimestral
quartermaster ['kwɔr·ṭər·ˌmæs·tər] *n* **1.** MIL oficial *mf* de intendencia **2.** NAUT cabo *mf* de la marina
quartertone *n* MUS cuarto *m* de tono
quartet *n*, **quartette** [kwɔr·'tet] *n* MUS cuarteto *m*
quartz [kwɔrts] **I.** *n* cuarzo *m* **II.** *adj* de cuarzo; **~ crystal** cristal de cuarzo
quartz clock *n* reloj *m* de cuarzo
quasar ['kwei·zar] *n* quásar *m*
quash [kwaʃ] *vt* **1.** (*suppress*) suprimir; (*rebellion*) sofocar; (*rumor*) acallar; **to ~ sb's dreams/plans** aplastar los sueños/planes de alguien **2.** LAW (*annul: conviction, verdict, sentence*) anular; (*indictment, decision*) invalidar; (*law, bill, writ*) derogar
quasi- ['kwa·zi] cuasi-
quatrain ['kwat·rein] *n* LIT cuarteto *m*
quaver ['kwei·vər] **I.** *vi* temblar **II.** *n* temblor *m;* **with a ~ in one's voice** con voz trémula
quay [ki] *n* muelle *m*
queasy ['kwi·zi] <-ier, -iest> *adj* **1.** (*nauseous*) mareado, -a; **to have a ~ feeling** sentir náuseas **2.** *fig* (*unsettled*) intranquilo, -a; **with a ~ conscience** con la conciencia intranquila; **to feel ~ about sth** sentir desasosiego acerca de algo
Quebec [kwi·'bek] *n* Quebec *m*
queen [kwin] **I.** *n* **1.** (*monarch*) reina *f;* **~ of hearts/diamonds** (*cards*) reina de corazones/diamantes **2.** *offensive, sl* (*gay man*) loca *f;* **drag ~** drag queen *f* **II.** *vt* **1.** (*make queen*) **to ~ sb** coronar reina a alguien **2.** (*in chess*) coronar
queen bee *n* ZOOL abeja *f* reina
queen dowager *n* reina *f* viuda
queenly ['kwin·li] <-ier, iest> *adj* regio, -a
queen-size *adj* XL

queer [kwɪr] **I.** <-er, -est> *adj* **1.** (*strange*) extraño, -a; **to have ~ ideas** tener ideas raras **2.** *offensive, sl* (*homosexual*) maricón **II.** *n offensive, sl* maricón *m*
quell [kwel] *vt* (*unrest, rebellion, protest*) sofocar; (*doubts, fears, anxieties*) disipar; **to ~ sb's anger** calmar la rabia de alguien
quench [kwentʃ] *vt* **1.** (*satisfy*) satisfacer; (*thirst*) saciar; **to ~ sb's thirst for knowledge** *fig* saciar la curiosidad de alguien **2.** (*put out*) sofocar; **to ~ a fire** apagar un incendio **3.** (*supress*) suprimir; **to ~ sb's desire** el deseo de alguien; **to ~ sb's enthusiasm** contener el entusiasmo de alguien
querulous ['kwer·ə·ləs] *adj* (*person*) quejoso, -a; (*voice*) quejumbroso, -a
query ['kwɪr·i] **I.** <-ies> *n* pregunta *f;* **a ~ about sth** una pregunta sobre algo **II.** <-ie-> *vt* **1.** *form* (*dispute*) cuestionar; (*doubt*) poner en duda **2.** (*ask*) preguntar; **to ~ whether...** preguntar si...
quesadilla ['kei·sə·ˌdi·jə] *n* quesadilla *f* mexicana
quest [kwest] *n* búsqueda *f;* **the ~ for the truth/an answer** la búsqueda de la verdad/una respuesta
question ['kwes·tʃən] **I.** *n* **1.** (*inquiry*) pregunta *f;* **frequently asked ~s** *a.* COMPUT preguntas frecuentes; **to put a ~ to sb** hacer una pregunta a alguien; **to pop the ~ to sb** proponer matrimonio a alguien, declararse a alguien *Méx* **2.** (*doubt*) duda *f;* **without ~** sin duda; **to be beyond ~** estar fuera de duda **3.** (*issue*) cuestión *f;* **it's a ~ of life or death** *a. fig* es (una) cuestión de vida o muerte; **to be a ~ of time/money** ser una cuestión de tiempo/dinero; **to raise a ~** plantear un problema; **to be out of the ~** ser totalmente imposible; **there's no ~ of sb doing sth** sería imposible que alguien hiciera algo **4.** SCHOOL, UNIV (*test problem*) pregunta *f;* **to do a ~** resolver una pregunta **II.** *vt* **1.** (*ask*) preguntar **2.** (*interrogate*) interrogar **3.** (*doubt*) cuestionar; (*facts, findings*) poner en duda
questionable ['kwes·tʃə·nə·bəl] *adj* discutible
questioner *n* interrogador(a) *m(f)*
questioning **I.** *n* interrogatorio *m;* **to be taken in for ~** ser detenido para ser interrogado **II.** *adj* inquisidor(a); **to have a ~ mind** ser inquisitivo
question mark *n* signo *m* de interrogación; **a ~ hangs over sth** *fig* un interrogante se cierne sobre algo
questionnaire [ˌkwes·tʃə·'ner] *n* cuestionario *m*
queue [kju] *n* COMPUT cola *f*
quibble ['kwɪb·əl] **I.** *n* **1.** (*petty argument*) sutileza *f;* **a ~ over sth** una objeción acerca de algo **2.** (*criticism*) pega *f* **II.** *vi* poner peros a; **to ~ over sth** quejarse por algo
quibbler ['kwɪb·lər] *n* polemizador(a) *m(f)*
quibbling ['kwɪb·lɪŋ] **I.** *n* sutilezas *fpl* **II.** *adj* quisquilloso, -a

quiche [kiʃ] *n* quiche *f,* quiche *m AmL*
quick [kwɪk] I. <-er, -est> *adj* **1.** (*fast*) rápido,
-a, veloz; **~ as lightning** (veloz) como un rayo;
in ~ succession uno detrás del otro; **to be ~
to do sth** hacer algo con rapidez; **to have a ~
one** tomarse una copa rápida; **to have a ~
meal** hacer una comida rápida **2.** (*short*)
corto, -a; **the ~est way** el camino más corto;
to give sb a ~ call hacer una llamada corta a
alguien **3.** (*hurried*) apresurado, -a; **to say a ~
good-bye/hello** decir un adiós/hola apresurado **4.** (*smart*) vivo, -a; **~ thinking** pensamiento ágil; **to have a ~ mind** tener una
mente vivaz; **to have a ~ temper** tener mal
genio II. <-er, -est> *adv* rápidamente; **~!**
¡rápido!; **as ~ as possible** tan pronto como sea
posible; **to get rich ~** *inf* enriquecerse rápidamente III. *n* carne *f* viva; **to bite/cut nails to
the ~** dejar las uñas en carne viva ▶ **to cut sb
to the ~** herir a alguien en lo más vivo
quick-acting [ˌkwɪk·'æk·tɪŋ] *adj* de efecto
rápido; **to be ~** actuar rápidamente
quick-change artist *n* transformista *mf*
quicken ['kwɪk·ən] I. *vt* **1.** (*make faster*) apresurar; **to ~ the pace** acelerar el paso **2.** (*stimulate*) estimular II. *vi* **1.** (*increase speed*) acelerarse **2.** (*become more active*) avivarse
quick-freeze ['kwɪk·friz] *vt irr* congelar rápidamente
quickie ['kwɪk·i] *n inf* **1.** (*quick sex*) quiqui *m,*
palito *m Méx* **2.** (*fast drink*) copa *f* rápida
quickly ['kwɪk·li] *adv* rápidamente
quickness ['kwɪk·nɪs] *n* **1.** (*speed*) rapidez *f;*
~ of temper mal carácter *m* **2.** (*liveliness*)
viveza *f; ~* **of mind** mente *f* rápida
quicksand ['kwɪk·sænd] *n* arenas *fpl* movedizas; **moral ~** *fig* moral *f* de doble filo
quicksilver *n s.* **mercury** mercurio *m*
quickstep *n* quickstep *m* (*baile formal a ritmo
rápido*)
quick-tempered *adj* irascible
quick-witted *adj* perspicaz; **a ~ reply** una
respuesta aguda
quid pro quo ['kwɪd·proʊ·'kwoʊ] *n form* compensación *f*
quiescent [kwaɪ·'es·ənt] *adj form* inactivo, -a
quiet ['kwaɪ·ət] I. *n* **1.** (*silence*) silencio *m*
2. (*lack of activity*) sosiego *m;* **peace and ~**
paz y tranquilidad II. <-er, -est> *adj* **1.** (*not
loud*) silencioso, -a; **to speak in a ~ voice**
hablar en voz baja **2.** (*not talkative*) callado, -a;
to keep ~ mantenerse callado **3.** (*secret*)
secreto, -a; **to have a ~ word with sb** hablar
en privado con alguien; **to keep ~ about sth**
mantenerse callado respecto a algo **4.** (*unos-
tentatious*) discreto, -a **5.** (*unexciting*) tranquilo, -a
  ◆ **quiet down** I. *vi* **1.** (*quiet*) callarse **2.** (*calm*)
calmarse II. *vt* **1.** (*silence*) hacer callar **2.** (*calm
(down*)) calmar
quietly ['kwaɪət·li] *adv* **1.** (*not loudly*) silenciosamente; **to speak ~** hablar en voz baja
2. (*peacefully*) tranquilamente

quietness ['kwaɪ·ət·nɪs] *n* tranquilidad *f*
quietude ['kwaɪ·ə·tud] *n form* quietud *f*
quill [kwɪl] *n* **1.** (*feather, pen*) pluma *f; liter*
(*pen*) cálamo *m* **2.** (*of porcupine*) púa *f*
quilt [kwɪlt] I. *n* edredón *m* II. *vt* acolchar
quince [kwɪns] *n* membrillo *m*
quinine ['kwaɪ·naɪn] *n* quinina *f*
quintessence [kwɪn·'tes·əns] *n* quintaesen-
cia *f*
quintessential [ˌkwɪn·te·'sen·ʃəl] *adj form* por
antonomasia
quintet(te) [kwɪn·'tet] *n* quinteto *m*
quintuple [kwɪn·'tup·əl] *form* I. *adj* quíntuplo,
-a II. *vt* quintuplicar III. *vi* quintuplicarse
quintuplet [kwɪn·'tʌp·lɪt] *n* quintillizo, -a *m, f*
quip [kwɪp] I. *n* ocurrencia *f* II. *vi* decir
humorísticamente
quirk [kwɜrk] *n* **1.** (*habit*) excentricidad *f*
2. (*oddity*) rareza *f* **3.** (*sudden twist or turn*) **a
~ of fate** un capricho del destino
quirky ['kwɜr·ki] <-ier, -iest> *adj* **1.** (*original*)
original **2.** (*odd*) excéntrico, -a
quit [kwɪt] <quit *o* quitted, quit *o* quitted> I. *vi*
parar; (*job*) dimitir II. *vt* **1.** (*resign*) dejar
2. (*stop*) parar; (*smoking*) dejar de **3.** COMPUT
salir de
quite [kwaɪt] *adv* **1.** (*fairly*) bastante; **~ a bit**
mucho, bastantito *Méx; ~* **a distance** una distancia considerable; **~ something** una
cosa notable **2.** (*completely*) completamente;
~ wrong totalmente equivocado; **not ~** no
tanto; **not ~ as clever/rich as ...** no tan inteli-
gente/rico como...
quits [kwɪts] *adj inf* en paz; **to be ~ (with sb)**
estar en paz con alguien; **to call it ~** hacer las
paces
quittance ['kwɪt·əns] *n form* descargo *m*
quitter *n* desertor, -a *m, f,* rajado, -a *Méx*
quiver[1] ['kwɪv·ər] I. *n* (*shiver*) estremecimiento *m* II. *vi* temblar
quiver[2] ['kwɪv·ər] *n* aljaba *f*
quixotic [kwɪk·'sat̬·ɪk] *adj liter* quijotesco, -a
quiz [kwɪz] I. <-es> *n* encuesta *f* II. *vt* interrogar
quizmaster ['kwɪz·ˌmæs·tər] *n* moderador(a)
m(f)
quiz show *n* concurso *m* (de TV)
quizzical ['kwɪz·ɪ·kəl] *adj* interrogante
quorum ['kwɔr·əm] *n form* quórum *m*
quota ['kwoʊ·t̬ə] *n* **1.** (*fixed amount allowed*)
cuota *f;* **export ~** cupo *m* de exportación
2. (*proportion*) parte *f*
quotable ['kwoʊ·t̬ə·bəl] *adj* citable
quotation [kwoʊ·'teɪ·ʃən] *n* **1.** (*repeated
words*) cita *f* **2.** FIN cotización *f*
quotation marks *npl* comillas *fpl*
quote [kwoʊt] I. *n* **1.** *inf* (*quotation*) cita *f*
2. ~s (*quotation marks*) comillas *fpl* **3.** (*estimate*) presupuesto *m* **4.** FIN cotización *f* II. *vt*
1. citar **2.** (*name*) nombrar **3.** FIN cotizar; **a ~d
company** una empresa que cotiza en bolsa
III. *vi* (*repeat exact words*) citar; **to ~ from sb**
citar a alguien; **to ~ from memory** citar de

Q

memoria
quotidian [kwoʊˈtɪd·i·ən] *adj form* cotidiano, -a
quotient [ˈkwoʊ·ʃənt] *n* **1.** MATH cociente *m* **2.** (*factor*) coeficiente *m;* **intelligence** ~ coeficiente de inteligencia
QWERTY keyboard [ˌkwɜr·t̬i·ˈki·bɔrd] *n* teclado *m* QWERTY

R

r, R [ar] r, R *f;* ~ **as in Romeo** R de Ramón
R 1. CINE *abbr of* **restricted** *clasificación de cine para mayores de 17 años* **2.** *abbr of* **Republican** republicano, -a
R. *abbr of* **River** r.
rabbi [ˈræb·aɪ] *n* rabino *m*
rabbit [ˈræb·ɪt] **I.** *n* conejo, -a *m, f* **II.** *vi* cazar conejos
rabbit hole *n* conejera *f*
rabble [ˈræb·bəl] *n* muchedumbre *f;* **the** ~ el populacho
rabble-rouser [ˈræb·əlˌraʊ·zər] *n* agitador(a) *m(f)*
rabble-rousing *adj* agitador(a)
rabid [ˈræb·ɪd] *adj* **1.** (*furious*) furibundo, -a **2.** (*fanatical*) fanático, -a **3.** (*suffering from rabies*) rabioso, -a
rabies [ˈreɪ·biz] *n* rabia *f;* **to carry** ~ tener la rabia
raccoon [ræˈkun] *n* mapache *m*
race¹ [reɪs] **I.** *n* carrera *f;* **a** ~ **against time** una carrera contra reloj; **100-meter** ~ carrera de cien metros lisos [*o* planos] [*o* llanos]; **to run a** ~ participar en una carrera ▶ **slow and steady wins the** ~ *prov* despacito y buena letra **II.** *vi* **1.** (*move quickly*) correr; SPORTS competir; **to** ~ **through one's work** hacer el trabajo a toda prisa **2.** (*engine*) acelerarse **III.** *vt* **1.** (*compete against*) competir con; **to** ~ **sb home** echar una carrera hasta casa a alguien **2.** (*enter for race: horse*) hacer correr
race² [reɪs] *n* **1.** (*ethnic grouping*) raza *f* **2.** (*species*) especie *f* **3.** (*lineage*) estirpe *f*
racecar *n* coche *m* de carreras, carro *m* de carreras *Col*
racecar driver *n* piloto *mf* de carreras
race conflict *n* conflicto *m* racial
race hatred *n* odio *m* racial
racehorse [ˈreɪs·hɔrs] *n* caballo *m* de carreras
race meet *n,* **race meeting** *n* concurso *m* hípico
racer [ˈreɪ·sər] *n* **1.** (*person*) corredor(a) *m(f)* **2.** (*bicycle*) bicicleta *f* de carreras
race relations *npl* relaciones *fpl* interraciales
race riot *n* disturbio *m* racial
racetrack [ˈreɪs·træk] *n* (*for cars*) circuito *m;* (*for runners*) estadio *m;* (*for bicycles*) veló-

dromo *m;* (*for horses*) hipódromo *m*
racewalking *n* marcha *f* atlética
racial [ˈreɪ·ʃəl] *adj* racial
racial profiling *n* práctica policial que toma como base un perfil racial determinado para realizar sus controles
racing I. *n* carreras *fpl* **II.** *adj* de carreras
racing bicycle *n,* **racing bike** *n inf* bicicleta *f* de carreras
racing yacht *n* yate *m* de regata
racism [ˈreɪ·sɪz·əm] *n* racismo *m*
racist [ˈreɪ·sɪst] **I.** *n* racista *mf* **II.** *adj* racista
rack [ræk] **I.** *n* **1.** (*framework, shelf*) estante *m;* **luggage** ~ portaequipajes *m inv;* **dish** ~ escurreplatos *m inv* **2.** (*bar for hanging things on*) barra *f;* **towel** ~ portatoallas *m inv* **3.** CULIN ~ **of lamb/beef** costillar *m* de cordero/ternera **4.** (*torture instrument*) potro *m;* **to be on the** ~ *fig* estar en ascuas **II.** *vt* atormentar
racket [ˈræk·ɪt] *n* **1.** SPORTS raqueta *f* **2.** *inf* (*loud noise*) barullo *m,* balumba *f AmS;* **to make a** ~ armar un alboroto **3.** (*scheme*) chanchullo *m,* transa *f Méx*
racketeer [ˌræk·əˈtɪr] *n* timador(a) *m(f)*
racoon [ræˈkun] *n s.* **raccoon**
racy [ˈreɪ·si] <-ier, -iest> *adj* (*film, novel*) atrevido, -a
radar [ˈreɪ·dar] *n* radar *m*
radar screen *n* pantalla *f* de radar
radar trap *n* detector *m* de velocidad
radial [ˈreɪ·di·əl] *adj* radial; TECH en estrella
radiant [ˈreɪ·di·ənt] *adj* radiante
radiant (floor) heating *n* calefacción *f* por suelo radiante
radiate [ˈreɪ·di·eɪt] **I.** *vi* irradiar **II.** *vt* **1.** (*emit*) irradiar **2.** (*display: happiness, enthusiasm*) mostrar
radiation [ˌreɪ·diˈeɪ·ʃən] *n* radiación *f*
radiation sickness *n* radiotoxemia *f*
radiation therapy *n* radioterapia *f*
radiator [ˈreɪ·di·eɪ·t̬ər] *n* radiador *m*
radiator cap *n* tapón *m* del radiador
radical [ˈræd·ɪ·kəl] **I.** *n* **1.** *a.* CHEM, MATH radical *m* **2.** POL radical *mf* **II.** *adj* (*change, idea*) radical; (*measures*) drástico, -a
radicalism [ˈræd·ɪ·kəˌlɪz·əm] *n* radicalismo *m*
radicchio [rəˈdi·ki·oʊ] *n* tipo de achicoria
radii [ˈreɪ·di·aɪ] *n pl of* **radius**
radio [ˈreɪ·di·oʊ] **I.** *n* radio *f,* radio *m AmC* **II.** *vt* (*information*) radiar; (*person*) llamar por radio
radioactive [ˌreɪ·di·oʊˈæk·tɪv] *adj* radioactivo, -a
radioactivity [ˌreɪ·di·oʊ·æk·ˈtɪv·ə·t̬i] *n* radiactividad *f*
radio alarm (clock) *n* radio *f* despertador
radio beacon *n* radiofaro *m*
radiocarbon dating [ˌreɪ·di·oʊ·kar·bənˈdeɪ·tɪŋ] *n* fechado *m* por radiocarbono
radio cassette (recorder) *n* radiocasete *m*
radiogram [ˈreɪ·di·oʊgræm] *n* radiograma *m*
radiograph [ˈreɪ·di·oʊ·græf] *n* radiografía *f*
radiographer *n* radiógrafo, -a *m, f*

radiography [ˌreɪ·di·'ag·rə·fi] *n* radiografía *f*
radio ham *n* radioaficionado, -a *m, f*
radiologist [ˌreɪ·di·'al·ə·dʒɪst] *n* radiólogo, -a *m, f*
radiology [ˌreɪ·di·'al·ə·dʒi] *n* radiología *f*
radio operator *n* radioperador(a) *m(f)*
radio program *n* programa *m* de radio
radioscopy [ˌreɪ·di·'as·kə·pi] *n* MED radioscopia *f*
radio station *n* emisora *f* de radio, estación *f* de radio *AmL;* **pirate ~** emisora *f* pirata, estación *f* pirata *AmL*
radiotelephony [ˌreɪ·di·oʊ·tɪ·'lef·ə·ni] *n* radiotelefonía *f*
radio telescope *n* radiotelescopio *m*
radiotherapy [ˌreɪ·di·oʊ·'θer·ə·pi] *n* radioterapia *f*
radio wave *n* onda *f* de radio
radish ['ræd·ɪʃ] <-es> *n* rábano *m*
radium ['reɪ·di·əm] *n* radio *m*
radium treatment *n* radioterapia *f*
radius ['reɪ·di·əs] <-dii> *n* radio *m*
raffle ['ræf·əl] **I.** *n* rifa *f* **II.** *vt* rifar
raft[1] [ræft] **I.** *n* balsa *f* **II.** *vt* transportar en balsa **III.** *vi* ir en balsa
raft[2] [ræft] *n inf* montón *m;* **a ~ of options** un montón de opciones
rafter[1] ['ræf·tər] *n* ARCHIT viga *f*
rafter[2] ['ræf·tər] *n* (*person*) balsero, -a *m, f*
rafting *n* rafting *m*
rag [ræg] **I.** *n* **1.** (*old cloth*) trapo *m* **2.** *pl* (*worn-out clothes*) harapos *mpl* **3.** *pej, sl* (*newspaper*) periodicucho *m* **4.** MUS ragtime *m* **II.** <-gg-> *vt sl* tomar el pelo a
ragamuffin ['ræg·ə·mʌf·ɪn] *n* golfo, -a *m, f*
ragbag ['ræg·bæg] *n fig* mezcolanza *f*
rage [reɪdʒ] **I.** *n* **1.** (*anger*) furia *f;* **to be in a ~** estar hecho una furia **2.** (*fashion*) **to be all the ~** ser el último grito, estar en furor **II.** *vi* **1.** (*express fury*) enfurecerse; **to ~ at sb/sth** enfurecerse con alguien/algo **2.** (*continue: battle*) continuar con pleno vigor; (*epidemic*) hacer estragos; (*wind, storm*) bramar; (*fire*) arder furiosamente
ragged ['ræg·ɪd] *adj* **1.** (*torn: clothes*) hecho, -a jirones **2.** (*wearing worn clothes*) andrajoso, -a **3.** (*rough*) recortado, -a **4.** (*irregular*) irregular ▶ **to run sb ~** agotar a alguien
raging ['reɪ·dʒɪŋ] *adj* (*gale*) furioso, -a; (*fire*) incontenible; (*blizzard*) violento, -a; (*sea*) embravecido, -a
ragout [ræg·'u] *n* ragú *m*
ragtag ['ræg·tæg] *adj* (*unkempt*) desarreglado, -a
ragtag and bobtail *n* chusma *f*
ragtime ['ræg·taɪm] *n* ragtime *m*
rag trade *n sl* gremio *m* de la aguja
ragweed *n* ambrosía *f*
raid [reɪd] **I.** *n* **1.** MIL incursión *f* **2.** (*attack*) ataque *m* **3.** (*robbery*) asalto *m* **4.** (*by police*) redada *f* **II.** *vt* **1.** MIL invadir **2.** (*attack*) atacar **3.** (*by police*) hacer una redada en
rail [reɪl] **I.** *n* **1.** (*of fence*) valla *f;* (*of balcony,*

stairs) barandilla *f* **2.** (*railway system*) ferrocarril; **by ~** en tren, por ferrocarril; **~ ticket** billete *m* de ferrocarril, boleto *m* de tren *Méx* **3.** (*track*) raíl [*o* rail] *m,* riel *m AmL* **II.** *vt* **to ~ sth in** [*o* off] cercar algo
◆ **rail against** *vt* clamar contra
railhead ['reɪl·hed] *n* cabeza *f* de línea
railing ['reɪ·lɪŋ] *n* **1.** (*post*) valla *f;* **iron ~** verja *f;* **wooden ~** cerco *m* **2.** (*of stairs*) pasamanos *m inv*
rail network *n* red *f* ferroviaria
railroad ['reɪl·roʊd] **I.** *n* **1.** (*system*) ferrocarril *m* **2.** (*track*) línea *f* de ferrocarril **II.** *vt fig* **to ~ sb into doing sth** obligar a alguien a hacer algo
railroad bridge *n* puente *m* ferroviario
railroad crossing *n* paso *m* a nivel
railroad engine *n* locomotora *f*
railroader *n* ferroviario *m,* ferrocarrilero *m Méx*
railroad line *n* vía *f* del tren
railroad station *n* estación *f* del ferrocarril
railroad strike *n* huelga *f* de ferrocarril
railway ['reɪl·weɪ] *n* ferrocarril *m;* **commuter ~** tren *m* de cercanías
rain [reɪn] **I.** *n* lluvia *f;* **~ shower** chubasco *m;* **the ~s** la temporada de lluvias ▶ **come ~ or shine** pase lo que pase, llueva o truene; **to be as right as ~** *inf* estar perfectamente **II.** *vi* llover **III.** *vt* llover
◆ **rain out** *vt* **to be rained out** cancelarse por lluvia
rainbow *n* METEO arco *m* iris
rain cloud *n* nube *f* de lluvia
raincoat *n* gabardina *f,* piloto *m Arg*
raindrop *n* gota *f* de lluvia
rainfall *n* precipitación *f*
rain forest *n* selva *f* tropical
rain gauge *n* pluviómetro *m*
rainproof **I.** *adj* impermeable **II.** *vt* impermeabilizar
rainstorm *n* tormenta *f* de lluvia
rainwater *n* agua *f* de lluvia
rainy ['reɪ·ni] *adj* <-ier, -iest> lluvioso, -a; **the ~ season** la estación de las lluvias
raise [reɪz] **I.** *n* (*of wages, prices*) aumento *m* **II.** *vt* **1.** (*lift*) levantar; (*periscope, window*) subir; (*arm, hand, leg*) levantar; (*flag*) izar; (*anchor*) levar; (*ship*) poner a flote **2.** (*stir up*) provocar; (*doubts*) suscitar **3.** (*increase: wages, awareness*) aumentar; (*bet*) subir; MATH elevar; (*standards*) mejorar **4.** (*promote*) ascender **5.** (*introduce: subject, problem*) plantear **6.** FIN recaudar **7.** (*build*) erigir; (*monument*) levantar **8.** (*bring up, cultivate*) cultivar **9.** (*end: embargo*) levantar **10.** (*contact*) llamar, contactar *Méx, Col;* **to ~ the alarm** dar la voz de alarma ▶ **to ~ hell** [*o* **Cain**] poner el grito en el cielo
raisin ['reɪ·zən] *n* pasa *f*
rake[1] [reɪk] **I.** *n* (*tool*) rastrillo *m* **II.** *vt* rastrillar
rake[2] [reɪk] *n* (*dissolute man*) vividor *m*
◆ **rake in** *vt sl* (*money*) amasar; **to be raking**

R

it in estar forrándose
◆**rake up** *vt* **1.** (*gather*) reunir **2.** *fig* (*refer to*) sacar a relucir; (*quarrel*) atizar
rake-off ['reɪk·ɔf] *n inf* tajada *f*
rakish¹ ['reɪ·kɪʃ] *adj* (*jaunty*) desenvuelto, -a; **at a ~ angle** de medio lado
rakish² ['reɪ·kɪʃ] *adj* (*dissolute*) disoluto, -a
rally ['ræl·i] <-ies> **I.** *n* **1.** (*race*) rally *m* **2.** (*in tennis*) peloteo *m* **3.** POL mitin *m* **II.** *vi* **1.** MED mejorar; FIN repuntar **2.** MIL agruparse; **to ~ behind sb** apoyar a alguien **III.** *vt* **1.** MIL reagruparse **2.** (*support*) apoyar
◆**rally around I.** *vt* apoyar **II.** *vi* agruparse
ram [ræm] **I.** *n* **1.** (*male sheep*) carnero *m*; (*astrology*) Aries *m* **2.** (*implement*) maza *f*; MIL ariete *m* **II.** *vt* <-mm-> **1.** (*hit*) embestir contra **2.** (*push*) **to ~ sth into sth** embutir algo en algo
RAM [ræm] *n* COMPUT *abbr of* **Random Access Memory** RAM *f*
Ramadan [ˌræm·ə·'dan] *n* Ramadán *m*
ramble ['ræm·bəl] **I.** *n* (*walk*) caminata *f*; **to go for a ~** ir de excursión **II.** *vi* **1.** (*person*) pasear; (*river*) serpentear; (*plant*) trepar **2.** (*in speech*) divagar
rambler ['ræm·blər] *n* **1.** (*walker*) excursionista *mf* **2.** BOT rosa *f* trepadora
rambling ['ræm·blɪŋ] **I.** *n* **1.** (*wandering*) ambulación *f* **2. ~s** (*speech*) divagaciones *fpl* **II.** *adj* **1.** (*estate, house*) laberíntico, -a **2.** (*speech*) divagante **3.** (*rose*) trepador(a) **4.** (*roaming*) errante
ramification [ˌræm·ɪ·fɪ·'keɪ·ʃən] *n* ramificación *f*
ramify ['ræm·ɪ·faɪ] *vi* ramificarse
ramp [ræmp] *n* **1.** (*sloping way*) rampa *f*; AVIAT escalerilla *f* **2.** AUTO (*on-ramp*) carril *m* de incorporación; (*off-ramp*) carril *m* de salida
rampage ['ræm·peɪdʒ] **I.** *n* destrozos *mpl*; **to be on the ~** ir arrasando todo **II.** *vi* arrasar
rampant ['ræm·pənt] *adj* (*disease, growth*) exuberante; (*inflation*) galopante
rampart ['ræm·part] *n* muralla *f*
ramrod ['ræm·rad] *n* baqueta *f* ▶ **as stiff as a ~** más tieso que un ajo
ramshackle ['ræm·ʃæk·əl] *adj* **1.** (*dilapidated*) desvencijado, -a **2.** (*disorganized*) improvisado, -a
ran [ræn] *pt of* **run**
ranch [ræntʃ] **I.** <-es> *n* granja *f*, rancho *m* *Méx*, estancia *f RíoPl* **II.** *adj* de granja **III.** *vi* (*run a ranch*) llevar una granja
rancher ['ræn·tʃər] *n* **1.** (*owner*) hacendado, -a *m, f*, ranchero, -a *m, f Méx* **2.** (*worker*) granjero, -a *m, f*
rancid ['ræn·sɪd] *adj* rancio, -a
rancor ['ræŋ·kər] *n* rencor *m*
rancorous ['ræŋ·kər·əs] *adj* rencoroso, -a
R & B [ˌar·ænd·'bi] *abbr of* **rhythm and blues** rhythm *m* and blues
R & D [ˌar·ənd·'di] *abbr of* **Research and Development** I+D
random ['ræn·dəm] **I.** *n* **at ~** al azar **II.** *adj*

aleatorio, -a
R and R [ˌar·ən(d)·'ar] *abbr of* **rest and recreation/relaxation** descanso y recreación
rang [ræŋ] *pt of* **ring²**
range [reɪndʒ] **I.** *n* **1.** (*variety*) variedad *f*; **a ~ of interests** un cúmulo de intereses **2.** (*scale*) gama *f*; **the full ~ of sth** la gama completa de algo **3.** (*extent*) distancia *f*; **price ~** rango *m* **4.** (*maximum capability*) alcance *m*; **out of ~** fuera del alcance; **within ~** al alcance **5.** (*field*) ámbito *m*, campo *m*; **driving ~** (*in golf*) campo de práctica; **shooting ~** campo *m* de tiro **6.** (*pasture*) pradera *f* **7.** MUS extensión *f* **8.** GEO cadena *f*; **mountain ~** cordillera *f*; (*shorter*) sierra *f* **9.** (*for kitchen*) cocina *f* económica **II.** *vi* **1.** (*vary*) variar **2.** (*extend*) extenderse **3.** (*rove*) deambular **III.** *vt* alinear; **to ~ oneself** alinearse
range finder *n* telémetro *m*
ranger ['reɪn·dʒər] *n* guardabosque *mf*
rangy ['reɪn·dʒi] *adj* <-ier, -iest> larguirucho, -a
rank¹ [ræŋk] **I.** *n* **1.** (*status*) rango *m* **2.** MIL graduación *f*; **the ~s** las tropas; **to break ~s** romper filas **II.** *vi* clasificarse; **to ~ as sth** figurar como algo; **to ~ above sb** estar por encima de alguien **III.** *vt* **1.** (*classify*) clasificar **2.** (*arrange*) situar
rank² [ræŋk] *adj* **1.** (*smelling unpleasant*) fétido, -a **2.** (*absolute*) total; (*beginner*) absoluto, -a
◆**rank among** *vi* situarse entre
ranking ['ræŋ·kɪŋ] *n* clasificación *f*
rankle ['ræŋ·kəl] *vi* doler; **to ~ with sb** estar resentido con alguien; **it ~s that...** duele que... +*subj*
ransack ['ræn·sæk] *vt* **1.** (*search*) registrar **2.** (*plunder*) saquear
ransom ['ræn·səm] **I.** *n* rescate *m*; **to hold sb (for) ~** secuestrar a alguien y pedir rescate; *fig* chantajear a alguien **II.** *vt* rescatar
rant [rænt] **I.** *n* despotrique *m* **II.** *vi* despotricar; **to ~ and rave** despotricar
rap [ræp] **I.** *n* **1.** (*knock*) golpe *m* seco **2.** MUS rap *m* **II.** *vt* golpear **III.** *vi* **1.** (*talk*) charlar **2.** MUS rapear
rapacious [rə·'peɪ·ʃəs] *adj form* codicioso, -a; (*appetite*) voraz
rapacity [rə·'pæs·ə·t̬i] *n* rapacidad *f*
rape¹ [reɪp] **I.** *n* **1.** (*of person*) violación *f* **2.** (*of city*) saqueo *m* **II.** *vt* **1.** (*person*) violar **2.** (*city*) saquear
rape² [reɪp] *n* BOT, AGR colza *f*
rapeseed oil *n* aceite *m* de colza
rapid ['ræp·ɪd] *adj* (*quick*) rápido, -a
rapidity [rə·'pɪd·ə·t̬i] *n* rapidez *f*
rapids ['ræp·ɪdz] *n* rápidos *mpl*
rapid transit *n* transporte público rápido urbano, con trenes elevados o subterráneos
rapier ['reɪ·pi·ər] *n* estoque *m*
rapist ['reɪ·pɪst] *n* violador(a) *m(f)*
rappel [ræ·'pel] *vi* hacer rappel
rapport [ræ·'pɔr] *n* compenetración *f*

rapprochement [ˌraˌprɔʃ'maɳ] *n* acercamiento *m*

rapt [ræpt] *adj* (*person*) absorto, -a; (*attention*) completo, -a

rapture ['ræp·tʃər] *n* éxtasis *m inv*

rapturous ['ræp·tʃər·əs] *adj* (*expression*) extasiado, -a; (*applause*) entusiasta; (*welcome*) desbordante

rare[1] [rer] *adj* 1. (*uncommon: animal, coin, disease*) raro, -a 2. (*exceptional: genius, sense of honor*) único, -a

rare[2] [rer] *adj* CULIN poco hecho, -a

rarebit ['rer·bɪt] *n* **Welsh** ~ pan *m* tostado con queso derretido, mollete *m Méx*

rarefy ['rer·ə·faɪ] *vt* enrarecer

rarely ['rer·li] *adv* raramente, raras veces

raring ['rer·ɪɳ] *adj inf* **to be** ~ **to do sth** tener muchas ganas de hacer algo

rarity ['rer·ə·ti] <-ies> *n* rareza *f*

rascal ['ræs·kəl] *n* granuja *mf*

rash[1] [ræʃ] *n* 1. MED sarpullido *m* 2. (*outbreak: of burglaries, etc*) racha *f*

rash[2] [ræʃ] *adj* (*decision*) precipitado, -a; (*move*) impulsivo, -a

rasher ['ræʃ·ər] *n* loncha *f* (de beicon), rebanada *f* (de tocino) *AmC*

rashness ['ræʃ·nɪs] *n* precipitación *f*

rasp [ræsp] I. *n* 1. (*tool*) escofina *f* 2. (*sound*) chirrido *m* II. *vt* 1. (*file*) escofinar 2. (*rub roughly*) raspar 3. (*say roughly*) espetar III. *vi* (*make grating sound*) chirriar

raspberry ['ræz·ˌber·i] <-ies> *n* 1. (*fruit*) frambuesa *f* 2. *sl* (*sound*) pedorreta *f*, trompetilla *f AmL* 3. *sl* SPORTS (*wound*) rasponazo *m*

rasping ['ræs·pɪɳ] *adj* áspero, -a

Rastafarian [ˌras·tə·'far·i·ən] I. *n* rastafari *mf* II. *adj* rastafariano, -a

rat [ræt] I. *n* 1. (*animal*) rata *f* 2. (*person*) canalla *mf* ▶ I **smell a** ~ aquí hay gato encerrado II. *vi* (*betray*) delatar; **to** ~ **on sb** chivatear a alguien *Col, Cuba, PRico*

ratable ['reɪ·tə·bəl] *adj* imponible

ratatouille [ˌræt·ə·'tu·i] *n guiso de verduras*

ratchet ['rætʃ·ɪt] *n* TECH trinquete *m*

♦**ratchet up** *vt* incrementar

rate [reɪt] I. *n* 1. (*speed*) velocidad *f*; **at this** ~ a este ritmo; **at one's own** ~ a su propio ritmo 2. (*proportion*) índice *m*, tasa *f*; **birth** ~ tasa *f* de natalidad; **death** ~ tasa *f* de mortalidad; **unemployment** ~ índice *m* de desempleo 3. (*price*) precio *m*; ~ **of exchange** cambio *m*; **interest** ~ tipo *m* de interés ▶**at any** ~ de todos modos II. *vt* calificar; **to** ~ **sb/sth as sth** considerar algo/a alguien como algo III. *vi* **to** ~ **as** ser considerado como

rather ['ræð·ər] I. *adv* 1. (*somewhat*) ~ **sleepy** medio dormido 2. (*more exactly*) más bien 3. (*on the contrary*) más bien 4. (*very*) bastante 5. (*in preference to*) I **would** ~ **stay here** preferiría quedarme aquí; ~ **you than me!** ¡no quisiera estar en tu lugar! II. *interj* por supuesto

ratification [ˌræt·ə·fɪ·'keɪ·ʃən] *n* ratificación *f*

ratify ['ræt·ə·faɪ] *vt* ratificar

rating ['reɪ·tɪɳ] *n* 1. (*estimation*) evaluación *f* 2. *pl* TV, RADIO índice *m* de audiencia

ratio ['reɪ·ʃi·oʊ] *n* proporción *f*

ration ['ræʃ·ən] I. *n* 1. (*fixed allowance*) ración *f* 2. ~ **s** (*total amount allowed*) raciones *fpl*; **food** ~ **s** víveres *mpl* II. *vt* racionar

rational ['ræʃ·ə·nəl] *adj* 1. (*able to reason*) racional 2. (*sensible*) razonable

rationale [ˌræʃ·ə·'næl] *n* razón *f* fundamental

rationalism ['ræʃ·ə·nə·lɪz·əm] *n* racionalismo *m*

rationalist ['ræʃ·ə·nə·lɪst] PHILOS I. *n* racionalista *mf* II. *adj* racionalista

rationalistic [ˌræʃ·ə·nə·'lɪs·tɪk] *adj* racionalista

rationality [ˌræʃ·ə·'næl·ə·ti] *n* racionalidad *f*

rationalization [ˌræʃ·ə·nə·lɪ·'zeɪ·ʃən] *n* racionalización *f*

rationalize ['ræʃ·ə·nə·laɪz] *vt* racionalizar

rationing *n* racionamiento *m*

rat poison *n* raticida *m*

rat race *n* **the** ~ la lucha para sobrevivir

rattle ['ræt·əl] I. *n* 1. (*noise*) ruido *m*; (*of carriage*) traqueteo *m* 2. (*for baby*) sonajero *m*, cascabel *m AmL* II. *vi* hacer ruido; (*carriage*) traquetear III. *vt* 1. (*making noise*) hacer sonar 2. (*make nervous*) poner nervioso, -a; (*shock*) desconcertar

rattlesnake ['ræt·əl·sneɪk] *n* serpiente *f* de cascabel, víbora *f* de cascabel *Méx*

rattling ['ræt·lɪɳ] *adj* 1. (*noisy*) ruidoso, -a 2. (*fast, brisk*) rápido, -a

raucous ['rɔ·kəs] *adj* (*shout*) estridente; (*crowd*) ruidoso, -a

raunchy ['rɔn·tʃi] <-ier, -iest> *adj* atrevido, -a

ravage ['ræv·ɪdʒ] *vt* hacer estragos en

rave [reɪv] I. *n* 1. *inf* (*enthusiastic review*) reseña *f* entusiasta 2. (*dance party*) fiesta *f* Rave (*evento bailable con música electrónica*) II. *adj inf* (*review*) elogioso, -a III. *vi* desvariar; **to** ~ **about sth/sb** poner algo/a alguien por las nubes; **to** ~ **against sb/sth** despotricar contra alguien/algo

ravel ['ræv·əl] <-ll-, -l-> *vt* enredar

raven ['reɪ·vən] I. *n* cuervo *m* II. *adj liter* negro azabache

ravenous ['ræv·ə·nəs] *adj* (*person, animal*) hambriento, -a; (*appetite*) voraz

ravine [rə·'vin] *n* barranco *m*

raving ['reɪ·vɪɳ] I. *adj* (*success*) total; **a** ~ **madman** un loco de remate II. *adv* **to be** ~ **mad** estar como una cabra III. *npl* desvaríos *mpl*

ravioli [ræv·i·'oʊ·li] *n* ravioles *mpl*

ravish ['ræv·ɪʃ] *vt liter* 1. (*please greatly*) cautivar 2. (*rape*) violar

ravishing *adj* encantador(a)

raw [rɔ] *adj* 1. (*uncooked*) crudo, -a 2. (*unprocessed: sewage*) sin tratar; (*silk*) crudo, -a; (*data*) en sucio [*o* bruto]; ~ **material** materia prima; **to get a** ~ **deal** sufrir un trato injusto, ser víctima de una jugarreta 3. (*sore*) en carne viva 4. (*inexperienced*) novato, -a 5. (*unre-*

R

strained) salvaje **6.** (*weather*) crudo, -a
raw bar *n* CULIN barra o bar con mariscos y otros frutos de mar crudos
rawhide ['rɔ·haɪd] *n* cuero *m* sin curtir
rawness ['rɔ·nɪs] *n* **1.** (*harshness*) crudeza *f* **2.** (*inexperience*) inexperiencia *f*
ray[1] [reɪ] *n* **1.** (*of light*) rayo *m* **2.** (*trace*) resquicio *m*
ray[2] [reɪ] *n* (*fish*) raya *f*
rayon ['reɪ·an] *n* rayón *m*
raze [reɪz] *vt* arrasar
razor ['reɪ·zər] **I.** *n* navaja *f* de afeitar, barbera *f* Col; **electric** ~ maquinilla *f* de afeitar, rasuradora *f* Méx **II.** *vt* afeitar
razorbill *n* alca *f*
razorblade *n* hoja *f* de afeitar
razor-sharp *adj* **1.** (*knife*) muy afilado, -a **2.** (*person*) agudo, -a
razor wire *n* alambrado *m* de púas
RC [‚ar·'si] **1.** *abbr of* **Red Cross** Cruz *f* Roja **2.** *abbr of* **Roman Catholic** católico, -a *m, f*
Rd. *abbr of* **road** c/
re[1] [ri] *prep* con relación a
re[2] [reɪ] *n* MUS re *m*
reach [riʧ] **I.** *n* **1.** (*range*) alcance *m*; **to be within** (**sb's**) ~ *a. fig* estar al alcance (de alguien); **to be out of** (**sb's**) ~ *a. fig* estar fuera del alcance (de alguien); **to have a long** ~ tener mucho alcance **2.** (*of river*) tramo *m*; **the upper/lower** ~**es of the Amazon** la parte alta/baja del Amazonas **II.** *vt* **1.** (*stretch out*) alargar, extender **2.** (*arrive at: city, country*) llegar a; (*land*) tocar; (*finish line*) alcanzar **3.** (*attain*) alcanzar; (*agreement*) llegar a; **to** ~ **80** cumplir (los) 80 (años) **4.** (*extend to*) llegar a **5.** (*communicate with*) ponerse en contacto con **III.** *vi* **to** ~ **for sth** alargar la mano para tomar algo
◆**reach down** *vi* **to** ~ **to** (*land*) extenderse hasta; (*clothes*) llegar hasta
◆**reach out** *vi* tender la(s) mano(s); **to** ~ **for sth** estirar la mano para agarrar algo
react [rɪ·'ækt] *vi* reaccionar; **to** ~ **to sth** reaccionar ante algo; MED reaccionar a algo; **to** ~ **against sth** reaccionar contra algo; **to** ~ **on sth** producir una reacción en algo
reaction [rɪ·'æk·ʃən] *n* **1.** *a.* CHEM reacción *f*; **chain** ~ reacción en cadena **2.** MED efecto *m*
reactionary [rɪ·'æk·ʃə·ner·i] **I.** *adj* reaccionario, -a **II.** <-ies> *n* reaccionario, -a *m, f*
reactivate [ri·'æk·tə·veɪt] **I.** *vt* reactivar **II.** *vi* reactivarse
reactive [ri·'æk·tɪv] *adj* reactivo, -a
reactor [rɪ·'æk·tər] *n* reactor *m*
read[1] [rid] **I.** *n* lectura *f* **II.** *vt* <read, read> **1.** leer; **to** ~ **sth aloud** leer algo en voz alta; **to** ~ **sb a story** leer un cuento a alguien **2.** (*decipher*) descifrar; **to** ~ **sb's mind** [*o* **thoughts**] adivinar los pensamientos de alguien; **to** ~ **sb's palm** leer la mano a alguien; **to** ~ **sb like a book** conocer a alguien como la palma de la mano; ~ **my lips!** ¡léeme los labios! **3.** (*interpret*) interpretar **4.** (*inspect*)

inspeccionar; (*meter*) leer **5.** (*understand*) entender; **I don't** ~ **you** no te sigo **III.** *vi* <read, read> (*person*) leer; (*book, magazine*) leerse
◆**read off** *vt* leer (de un tirón)
◆**read on** *vi* seguir leyendo
◆**read out** *vt* **1.** (*read aloud*) leer en voz alta **2.** COMPUT (*data*) sacar
◆**read over** *vt* releer
◆**read through** *vt* leer de principio a fin [*o* de cabo a rabo]
◆**read up on** *vt* estudiar
read[2] [red] *adj* leído, -a; **little/widely** ~ poco/muy leído
readability [‚ri·də·'bɪl·ə·ʈi] *n* legibilidad *f*
readable ['ri·də·bəl] *adj* **1.** (*legible*) legible **2.** (*easy to read*) ameno, -a
reader ['ri·dər] *n* **1.** (*person*) lector(a) *m(f)* **2.** (*book*) libro *m* de lectura **3.** TECH lector *m* **4.** PUBL corrector(a) *m(f)*
readership ['ri·dər·ʃɪp] *n* lectores *mpl*
readily ['red·ə·li] *adv* **1.** (*promptly*) de buena gana **2.** (*easily*) fácilmente; ~ **available** disponible enseguida
readiness ['red·i·nɪs] *n* **1.** (*willingness*) (buena) disposición *f* **2.** (*preparedness*) preparación *f*
reading ['ri·dɪŋ] **I.** *n* **1.** lectura *f* **2.** (*interpretation*) interpretación *f* **3.** TECH medición *f* **II.** *adj* de lectura; **to have a** ~ **age of seven** leer al nivel de un niño de siete años
reading glasses *npl* gafas *fpl* para leer
reading lamp *n* lámpara *f* portátil
reading list *n* lista *f* de lecturas
reading room *n* sala *f* de lectura
readjust [‚ri·ə·'dʒʌst] **I.** *vt a.* TECH reajustar **II.** *vi* (*objects*) reajustarse; (*people*) readaptarse
readjustment [‚ri·ə·'dʒʌst·mənt] *n* TECH reajuste *m*
read only memory *n* COMPUT memoria *f* ROM
ready ['red·i] **I.** *adj* <-ier, -iest> **1.** (*prepared*) listo, -a, pronto, -a *Urug;* **to be** ~ estar listo; **to get** ~ (**for sth**) prepararse (para algo); **to get sth** ~ preparar algo **2.** (*willing*) dispuesto, -a **3.** (*available*) disponible; ~ **cash** dinero *m* en efectivo; **to be a** ~ **source of sth** ser una fuente fácil de algo; ~ **at hand** a mano **4.** (*quick, prompt*) vivo, -a; (*mind*) agudo, -a; (*tongue*) afilado, -a; **to find** ~ **acceptance** tener inmediata aceptación ►~, **set, go!** SPORTS ¡preparados, listos, ya! **II.** *n* **at the** ~ a punto; (**with**) **his pencil at the** ~ (con) su lápiz a mano **III.** *vt* preparar
ready-made [‚red·i·'meɪd] *adj* hecho, -a; (*meal*) precocinado, -a; (*clothing*) de confección
ready-to-wear [‚red·i·tə·'wer] **I.** *adj* prêt-à-porter **II.** *n* prêt-à-porter *m*
reaffirm [‚ri·ə·'fɜrm] *vt* reafirmar
real [ril] **I.** *adj* **1.** (*actual*) real; (*threat, problem*) verdadero, -a; **for** ~ de verdad **2.** (*genuine*) auténtico, -a; **the** ~ **thing** [*o* **deal**] lo auténtico; **a** ~ **man** *iron* un hombre como Dios

manda ▸ **the ~ McCoy** *inf* lo realmente genuino **II.** *adv inf* muy

real estate *n* bienes *mpl* raíces

realignment [ˌri·ə·ˈlaɪn·mənt] *n* reordenamiento *m*; AUTO realineamiento *m*

realism [ˈri·lɪz·əm] *n* realismo *m*

realist [ˈri·lɪst] *n* realista *mf*

realistic [ˌri·ə·ˈlɪs·tɪk] *adj* realista

reality [rɪ·ˈæl·ə·t̬i] *n* realidad *f*; **to come back to ~** volver a la realidad; **to face ~** enfrentarse a la realidad; **to become a ~** hacerse realidad; **in (all) ~** en realidad

reality show *n* TV reality show *m*

reality television *n*, **reality TV** *programación televisiva basada en la vida real*

realizable [ˈri·ə·laɪ·zə·bəl] *adj a.* FIN realizable

realization [ˌri·ə·lɪ·ˈzeɪ·ʃən] *n* 1.(*awareness*) comprensión *f* 2. *a.* FIN realización *f*

realize [ˈri·ə·laɪz] **I.** *vt* 1.(*be aware of*) ser consciente de; (*become aware of*) darse cuenta de 2.(*achieve*) realizar 3.(*fulfill*) cumplir 4. FIN realizar; (*acquire*) liquidar **II.** *vi* (*notice*) darse cuenta; (*be aware of*) ser consciente

really [ˈri·ə·li] **I.** *adv* 1.(*genuinely*) de verdad 2.(*actually*) en realidad 3.(*very*) muy **II.** *interj* 1.(*surprise and interest*) ¿ah sí? 2.(*annoyance*) pero bueno 3.(*disbelief*) ¿de veras?

realm [relm] *n* 1.(*kingdom*) reino *m* 2.(*area of interest*) campo *m*

realtor [ˈri·əl·tər] *n* agente *mf* inmobiliario, -a, corredor(a) *m(f)* de propiedades *Chile*

realty [ˈri·əl·ti] *n* bienes *mpl* raíces

reanimate [ri·ˈæn·ɪ·meɪt] *vt* reanimar

reap [rip] *vi, vt* cosechar

reaper [ˈri·pər] *n* 1.(*person*) cosechador(a) *m(f)* 2.(*machine*) cosechadora *f*

reappear [ˌri·ə·ˈpɪr] *vi* reaparecer

reapply [ˌri·ə·ˈplaɪ] **I.** *vi* **to ~ for sth** volver a presentar una solicitud para algo **II.** *vt* (*paint*) dar otra capa de

reappoint [ˌri·ə·ˈpɔɪnt] *vt* volver a nombrar

reappraisal [ˌri·ə·ˈpreɪ·zəl] *n* FIN revaluación *f*

rear¹ [rɪr] **I.** *adj* (*light*) trasero, -a; (*leg, wheel*) posterior **II.** *n* 1.(*back part*) parte *f* trasera 2. *inf* (*buttocks*) trasero *m* 3. MIL retaguardia *f*; **to bring up the ~** cerrar la marcha, cubrir la retaguardia

rear² [rɪr] **I.** *vt* 1.(*bring up: child, animals*) criar 2.(*raise*) **to ~ one's head** levantar la cabeza **II.** *vi* (*horse*) encabritarse; **to ~ above sth** erguirse por encima de algo

rear admiral *n* MIL contraalmirante *mf*

rear guard [ˈrɪr·gard] *n* retaguardia *f*; **to fight a ~ action** resistir en lo posible

rearm [ˌri·ˈarm] **I.** *vi* rearmarse **II.** *vt* rearmar

rearmament [ri·ˈar·mə·mənt] *n* rearmamento *m*

rearmost [ˈrɪr·moʊst] *adj* último, -a

rearrange [ˌri·ə·ˈreɪndʒ] *vt* 1.(*system*) reorganizar 2.(*furniture*) colocar de otra manera 3.(*meeting*) volver a concertar

rearview mirror *n* retrovisor *m*

rear-wheel drive *n* tracción *f* trasera

reason [ˈri·zən] **I.** *n* 1.(*motive*) motivo *m*; **the ~ why...** el motivo por el que...; **for no particular ~** sin ningún motivo en concreto; **for some ~** por algún motivo 2.(*common sense*) sensatez *f*; **within ~** dentro de lo razonable; **to listen to ~** atender a razones; **to be beyond all ~** no tener ninguna lógica; **the Age of Reason** HIST el Siglo de las Luces 3.(*sanity*) razón *f*; **to lose one's ~** perder la razón **II.** *vt* razonar **III.** *vi* razonar; **to ~ from sth** discurrir partiendo de algo

reasonable [ˈri·zə·nə·bəl] *adj* 1.(*sensible*) sensato, -a; (*demand*) razonable 2.(*fair*) juicioso, -a 3.(*inexpensive*) moderado, -a

reasonably [ˈri·zə·nə·bli] *adv* 1.(*fairly*) razonablemente 2.(*acceptably*) bastante

reasoning [ˈri·zə·nɪŋ] *n* razonamiento *m*

reassemble [ˌri·ə·ˈsem·bəl] **I.** *vt* (*machine*) volver a montar; (*people*) volver a reunir **II.** *vi* volver a reunirse

reassess [ˌri·ə·ˈses] *vt* 1.(*situation*) volver a valorar [*o* considerar] 2. FIN (*taxes*) volver a fijar; (*damages*) volver a valorar

reassurance [ˌri·ə·ˈʃʊr·əns] *n* 1.(*comfort*) palabras *fpl* tranquilizadoras 2. FIN reaseguro *m*

reassure [ˌri·ə·ˈʃʊr] *vt* tranquilizar

reassuring [ˌri·ə·ˈʃʊr·ɪŋ] *adj* tranquilizador(a)

reawaken [ˌri·ə·ˈweɪ·kən] *vt* volver a despertar

rebate [ˈri·beɪt] *n* 1.(*refund*) reembolso *m*; **tax ~** devolución *f* de impuestos 2.(*discount*) rebaja *f*

rebel¹ [ˈreb·əl] **I.** *n* rebelde *mf* **II.** *adj* rebelde

rebel² [rɪ·ˈbel] <-ll-> *vi* rebelarse

rebellion [rɪ·ˈbel·jən] *n* rebelión *f*

rebellious [rɪ·ˈbel·jəs] *adj* rebelde; (*child*) revoltoso, -a

rebirth [ˌri·ˈbɜrθ] *n* renacimiento *m*

reboot [ˌri·ˈbut] COMPUT **I.** *vt* reiniciar **II.** *vi* recargarse

rebound [ri·ˈbaʊnd] **I.** *vi* 1.(*bounce back: ball*) rebotar 2.(*recover*) mejorarse; **to quickly ~ from an injury** curarse rápidamente de una lesión 3.(*in basketball*) rebotar **II.** *vt* rebotar **III.** *n* 1.(*basketball*) rebote 2. *fig* **to marry on the ~** casarse por despecho

rebounder *n* (*in basketball*) rebotero, -a *m, f*

rebuff [rɪ·ˈbʌf] **I.** *vt* rechazar **II.** *n* rechazo *m*; **to meet with a ~** ser rechazado, -a

rebuild [ˌri·ˈbɪld] *vt irr* 1.(*build again*) reconstruir; *fig* (*one's life*) rehacer; (*economy*) reactivar 2.(*restore*) restablecer 3.(*replenish: stock*) reponer

rebuke [rɪ·ˈbjuk] **I.** *vt* reprender **II.** *n* 1.(*reproof*) reprimenda *f* 2.(*censure*) represión *f*

rebut [rɪ·ˈbʌt] <-tt-> *vt* rebatir

rebuttal [rɪ·ˈbʌt̬·əl] *n* refutación *f*

recalcitrant [rɪ·ˈkæl·sɪ·trənt] *adj* recalcitrante

recall [rɪ·ˈkɔl] **I.** *vt* 1.(*remember*) recordar 2.(*call back: ambassador*) retirar; (*troops*) llamar 3. ECON retirar (del mercado) **II.** *vi* recordar **III.** *n* 1.(*memory*) memoria *f* 2. POL retirada *f* 3. ECON retirada *f* (del mercado) ▸ **to be lost**

beyond ~ estar completamente perdido
recant [rɪ'kænt] I. *vt* retractarse de; **to** ~ **one's faith/belief** abjurar de su fe/creencia II. *vi* retractarse
recap[1] ['ri·kæp] *abbr of* **recapitulate** I. <-pp-> *vi, vt inf* recapitular II. *n inf* recapitulación *f*
recap[2] [,ri·'kæp] <-pp-> *vt* AUTO recauch(ut)ar, reencauchar *AmC*
recapitulate [,ri·kə·'pɪtʃ·ə·leɪt] *vi, vt* recapitular
recapitulation [,ri·kə·,pɪtʃ·ə·'leɪ·ʃən] *n* **1.** (*summary*) resumen *m* **2.** MUS, THEAT, CINE recapitulación *f*
recapture [,ri·'kæp·tʃər] I. *vt* **1.** (*town*) volver a tomar; (*fugitive*) volver a capturar **2.** (*experience again*) recuperar; (*beauty, feeling*) recobrar II. *n* (*of town*) reconquista *f*
recast [,ri·'kæst] *vt* **1.** THEAT, CINE cambiar el reparto de **2.** TECH, LIT refundir
recede [rɪ'sid] *vi* **1.** (*move backward: sea*) retirarse; (*tide*) bajar; (*fog*) desvanecerse; **to** ~ **into the distance** perderse en la distancia **2.** (*diminish*) disminuir; (*prices*) bajar
receding chin *n* barbilla *f* hundida
receding hairline *n* entradas *fpl*
receipt [rɪ'sit] I. *n* **1.** (*document*) recibo *m* **2.** ~**s** COM ingresos *mpl* **3.** (*act of receiving*) recepción *f*; **payment on** ~ pago *m* al recibo; **on** ~ **of...** al recibo de...; **to acknowledge** ~ **of** acusar recibo de II. *vt* acusar recibo de
receipt book *n* libro *m* talonario
receivable *adj* COM por cobrar
receive [rɪ'siv] I. *vt* **1.** (*be given*) *a.* TEL, RADIO recibir; (*pension, salary*) percibir **2.** (*react to: proposal, suggestion*) acoger; **the book was well/badly** ~**d** el libro tuvo buena/mala acogida **3.** (*injury*) sufrir **4. to** ~ **sb into the Church** admitir a alguien en el seno de la Iglesia **5.** LAW **to** ~ **stolen goods** comerciar con bienes robados II. *vi* SPORTS recibir
received [rɪ'sivd] *adj* admitido, -a; ~ **wisdom** creencia *f* popular
receiver [rɪ'si·vər] *n* **1.** TEL auricular *m*, tubo *m* AmL, fono *m* Chile **2.** RADIO receptor *m* **3.** ECON **the official** ~ el síndico (de la quiebra) **4.** SPORTS receptor(a) *m(f)*; (*tennis*) recibidor(a) *m(f)*
recent ['ri·sənt] *adj* reciente; **in** ~ **times** en los últimos tiempos
recently *adv* recientemente
receptacle [rɪ'sep·tə·kəl] *n* receptáculo *m*
reception [rɪ'sep·ʃən] *n* **1.** (*welcome*) acogida *f* **2.** (*in hotel*) recepción *f*
reception area *n* (zona *f* de) recepción
reception desk *n* (mesa *f* de) recepción
receptionist [rɪ'sep·ʃə·nɪst] *n* recepcionista *mf*
receptive [rɪ'sep·tɪv] *adj* receptivo, -a
receptiveness *n*, **receptivity** [ri·,sep·'tɪv·ə·ti] *n* receptividad *f*
recess ['ri·ses] I. <-es> *n* **1.** POL suspensión *f* de actividades, receso *m* AmL **2.** SCHOOL recreo *m* **3.** ARCHIT hueco *m* **4.** MED fosa *f* **5.** *often pl*

(*place*) lugar *m* recóndito II. *vi* prorrogar; (*meeting, session*) suspender III. *vt* ARCHIT rebajar
recession [rɪ'seʃ·ən] *n* **1.** (*retreat*) retroceso *m* **2.** ECON recesión *f*
recessive [rɪ'ses·ɪv] *adj* BIO recesivo, -a
recharge [,ri·'tʃardʒ] I. *vt* recargar II. *vi* recargarse
rechargeable [,ri·'tʃar·dʒə·bəl] *adj* recargable
recidivism [rɪ'sɪd·ə·vɪz·əm] *n* reincidencia *f*
recidivist [rɪ'sɪd·ə·vɪst] *n* reincidente *mf*
recipe ['res·ə·pi] *n a. fig* receta *f*
recipient [rɪ'sɪp·i·ənt] *n* (*of letter*) destinatario, -a *m, f*; (*of transplant*) receptor(a) *m(f)*; (*of gift*) beneficiario, -a *m, f*
reciprocal [rɪ'sɪp·rə·kəl] I. *adj* **1.** *a.* LING, MATH recíproco, -a **2.** (*reverse*) mutuo, -a II. *n* MATH recíproco *m*
reciprocate [rɪ'sɪp·rə·keɪt] I. *vt* corresponder a, reciprocar *AmL* II. *vi* **1.** corresponder **2.** TECH alternar
reciprocity [,res·ɪ·'pras·ə·ti] *n* reciprocidad *f*
recital [rɪ'saɪ·təl] *n* **1.** MUS recital *m* **2.** (*description*) relación *f*
recitation [,res·ɪ·'teɪ·ʃən] *n* LIT recitación *f*
recitative [,res·ɪ·tə·'tiv] *n* MUS recitativo *m*
recite [rɪ'saɪt] I. *vt* **1.** (*repeat*) recitar **2.** (*list*) enumerar II. *vi* dar un recitado
reckless ['rek·lɪs] *adj* imprudente; LAW temerario, -a
recklessness *n* imprudencia *f*, temeridad *f*
reckon ['rek·ən] I. *vt* **1.** (*calculate*) calcular **2.** (*consider*) considerar; **to** ~ (**that**)... creer (que)...; **I** ~ **not** me parece que no; **what do you** ~? ¿qué opinas? **3.** (*judge*) estimar II. *vi inf* calcular
◆**reckon with** *vt insep* tener en cuenta; **she is a force to be reckoned with** es alguien a quien hay que tener muy en cuenta
◆**reckon without** *vt insep* no tener en cuenta
reckoning ['rek·ə·nɪŋ] *n* **1.** (*calculation*) cálculo *m*; **to be out in one's** ~ calcular mal **2.** (*settlement*) ajuste *m* de cuentas
reclaim [rɪ'kleɪm] *vt* **1.** (*claim back: title, rights*) reclamar **2.** (*reuse: land*) recuperar; (*material*) reciclar **3.** (*reform*) regenerar
reclamation [,rek·lə·'meɪ·ʃən] *n* **1.** (*of title, rights*) reclamación *f* **2.** (*of land*) recuperación *f*; (*of material*) reciclaje *m* **3.** (*reformation*) regeneración *f*
recline [rɪ'klaɪn] I. *vi* apoyarse; **to** ~ **on** reclinarse contra [*o* en] II. *vt* reclinar
recliner [rɪ'klaɪ·nər] *n* asiento *m* reclinable
reclining seat *n*, **reclining chair** *n* asiento *m* reclinable, silla *f* reclinomática *Col*
recluse ['rek·lus] *n* ermitaño, -a *m, f*
reclusive [rɪ'klu·sɪv] *adj* solitario, -a
recognition [,rek·əg·'nɪʃ·ən] *n a.* COMPUT reconocimiento *m*; **optical character** ~ reconocimiento óptico de caracteres; **voice** ~ reconocimiento de la voz; **in** ~ **of** en reconocimiento de
recognizable ['rek·əg·naɪ·zə·bəl] *adj* reconocible

recognizance [rɪ·ˈkag·nɪ·zəns] *n* fianza *f*

recognize [ˈrek·əg·naɪz] *vt* reconocer

recognized [ˈrek·əg·naɪzd] *adj* reconocido, -a

recoil[1] [rɪ·ˈkɔɪl] *vi* **1.** (*draw back*) echarse atrás; **to ~ in horror** retroceder de miedo; **to ~ at sth** sentir repugnancia hacia algo; **to ~ from doing sth** rehuir hacer algo **2.** (*gun*) retroceder

recoil[2] [ˈri·kɔɪl] *n* retroceso *m*

recollect [ˌrek·ə·ˈlekt] *vi, vt* recordar

recollection [ˌrek·ə·ˈlek·ʃən] *n* **1.** recuerdo *m*; **to have no ~ of sth** no recordar algo **2.** recogimiento (espiritual) *m*

recommend [ˌrek·ə·ˈmend] *vt* recomendar; **it is not ~ed** no es recomendable

recommendable *adj* recomendable

recommendation [ˌrek·ə·mən·ˈdeɪ·ʃən] *n* **1.** (*suggestion*) recomendación *f*; **on sb's ~** por recomendación de alguien **2.** (*advice*) consejo *m*

recompense [ˈrek·əm·ˌpens] **I.** *n* **1.** (*reward*) recompensa *f* **2.** (*compensation*) compensación *f* **II.** *vt* **1.** (*reward*) recompensar **2.** (*make amends*) compensar

reconcile [ˈrek·ən·saɪl] *vt* **1.** (*person*) reconciliar; **to become ~d with sb** reconciliarse con alguien **2.** (*difference, fact*) conciliar; **to be ~d to sth** aceptar algo; **to become ~d to sth** resignarse a algo

reconciliation [ˌrek·ən·ˌsɪl·i·ˈeɪ·ʃən] *n* **1.** (*restoration of good relations*) reconciliación *f* **2.** (*making compatible*) conciliación *f*

recondition [ˌri·kən·ˈdɪʃ·ən] *vt* reacondicionar

reconnaissance [rɪ·ˈkan·ə·səns] *n* reconocimiento *m*

reconnaissance flight *n* vuelo *m* de reconocimiento

reconnoiter, reconnoiter [ˌri·kə·ˈnɔɪ·ʈər] **I.** *vt* reconocer **II.** *vi* reconocer el terreno

reconsider [ˌri·kən·ˈsɪd·ər] **I.** *vt* reconsiderar **II.** *vi* recapacitar

reconstruct [ˌri·kən·ˈstrʌkt] *vt* **1.** (*building*) reconstruir **2.** (*life*) rehacer; (*crime, event*) reconstituir

reconstruction [ˌri·kən·ˈstrʌk·ʃən] *n* **1.** (*of building*) reconstrucción *f* **2.** (*of crime, event*) reconstitución *f*

record[1] [ˈrek·ərd] **I.** *n* **1.** (*account*) relación *m*; (*document*) documento *m;* **medical ~** historial *m* médico; **to say sth off the ~** decir algo extraoficialmente; **to put sth on the ~** dejar constancia de algo **2.** (*sb's past*) antecedentes *mpl;* **to have a good ~** tener un buen historial; **to have a clean ~** no tener antecedentes **3. ~s** archivos *mpl* **4.** MUS disco *m;* **to make a ~** grabar un disco **5.** SPORTS récord *m;* **to break a ~** batir un récord **6.** LAW acta *f* **7.** COMPUT juego *m* de datos **II.** *adj* récord; **to do sth in ~ time** hacer algo en un tiempo récord; **to reach a ~ high** alcanzar un máximo sin precedentes

record[2] [rɪ·ˈkɔrd] **I.** *vt* **1.** (*store*) archivar **2.** *a.* COMPUT registrar; MUS grabar **3.** LAW hacer constar en acta **II.** *vi* grabar

record-breaker [ˈrek·ərd·ˌbreɪ·kər] *n* SPORTS plusmarquista *mf*

record-breaking *adj* que bate todos los récords

recorded [rɪ·ˈkɔr·dɪd] *adj* registrado, -a; (*history*) documentado, -a; (*music*) grabado, -a

recorder [rɪ·ˈkɔr·dər] *n* **1.** (*tape recorder*) magnetofón *m*, grabadora *f AmS* **2.** MUS flauta *f* dulce

record holder *n* SPORTS plusmarquista *mf*

recording *n* (*of sound*) grabación *f*

recording session *n* sesión *f* de grabación

recording studio *n* estudio *m* de grabación

record label *n* sello *m* discográfico

record library *n* discoteca *f,* fonoteca *f AmS*

record player *n* tocadiscos *m inv*

recount[1] [rɪ·ˈkaʊnt] *vt* **1.** (*narrate*) contar **2.** (*count again*) volver a contar

recount[2] [ˈri·kaʊnt] *n* POL recuento *m*

recoup [rɪ·ˈkup] *vt* (*expenditure, energy*) recuperar; (*losses*) resarcirse de

recourse [ˈri·kɔrs] *n* recurso *m;* **to have ~ to** recurrir a

recover [rɪ·ˈkʌv·ər] **I.** *vt a.* COMPUT recuperar; **to ~ one's composure** recobrar su compostura **II.** *vi* **1.** (*regain health*) reponerse **2.** (*return to normal*) recuperarse

re-cover [ˌri·ˈkʌv·ər] *vt* retapizar

recoverable [rɪ·ˈkʌv·ər·ə·bəl] *adj* **1.** *a.* COMPUT recuperable **2.** *a.* FIN reactivable

recovery [rɪ·ˈkʌv·ə·ri] <-ies> *n* **1.** *a.* MED, ECON recuperación *f;* **to be beyond ~** ser irrecuperable **2.** COMPUT reactivación *f*

recovery room *n* MED sala *f* de recuperación

recovery ship *n* barco *m* de salvamento

recovery vehicle *n* vehículo *m* de salvamento

recreate [ˌri·kri·ˈeɪt] *vt* recrear

recreation[1] [ˌri·kri·ˈeɪ·ʃən] *n* (*of conditions, situation*) recreación *f*

recreation[2] [ˌrek·ri·ˈeɪ·ʃən] *n* **1.** *a.* SCHOOL recreo *m* **2.** (*pastime*) diversión *f*

recreational [ˌrek·ri·ˈeɪ·ʃə·nəl] *adj* recreativo, -a

recreational vehicle *n* roulotte *f,* casa-carro *m Col*

recreation center *n* centro *m* recreativo

recreation room *n* salón *m* recreativo

recreative [ˈrek·rɪ·ˌeɪ·ʈɪv] *adj* recreativo, -a

recriminate [rɪ·ˈkrɪm·ə·neɪt] *vi* recriminar

recrimination [rɪ·ˌkrɪm·ə·ˈneɪ·ʃən] *n* recriminación *f*

recruit [rɪ·ˈkrut] **I.** *vt* MIL reclutar; (*employee*) contratar **II.** *n* MIL recluta *mf*

recruiting I. *n* MIL reclutamiento *m;* ECON contratación *f* **II.** *adj* MIL de reclutamiento; ECON de contratación

recruiting office *n* MIL oficina *f* de reclutamiento

recruitment I. *n* MIL reclutamiento *m;* ECON contratación *f;* (*of members*) afiliación *f* **II.** *adj* de reclutamiento

recruitment agency *n* agencia *f* de selección

de personal

rectangle ['rek·tæŋ·gəl] *n* rectángulo *m*

rectangular [rek·'tæŋ·gjə·lər] *adj* rectangular

rectification [ˌrek·tə·fɪ·'keɪ·ʃən] *n* rectificación *f*

rectify ['rek·tə·faɪ] *vt* rectificar

rectilinear [ˌrek·tə·'lɪn·i·ər] *adj* rectilíneo, -a

rectitude ['rek·tə·tud] *n* rectitud *f*

rector ['rek·tər] *n* 1. REL ≈ párroco *m* 2. SCHOOL director(a) *m(f)* 3. UNIV rector(a) *m(f)*

rectory ['rek·tə·ri] <-ies> *n* rectoría *f*

rectum ['rek·təm] *n* ANAT recto *m*

recumbent [rɪ·'kʌm·bənt] *adj liter* recostado, -a

recuperate [rɪ·'ku·pə·reɪt] I. *vi* recuperarse II. *vt* recuperar

recuperation [rɪ·ˌku·pə·'reɪ·ʃən] *n* recuperación *f*

recur [rɪ·'kɜr] *vi* repetirse

recurrence [rɪ·'kɜr·əns] *n* repetición *f*

recurrent [rɪ·'kɜr·ənt] *adj* (*dream, motif*) recurrente; (*problem*) repetido, -a; (*costs, expenses*) constante

recurring *adj* recurrente

recycle [ˌri·'saɪ·kəl] *vt* reciclar

recycling I. *n* reciclaje *m* II. *adj* de reciclaje

recycling plant *n* planta *f* de reciclaje

red [red] I. <-dd-> *adj* rojo, -a; (*cheeks, face a.*) colorado, -a; (*hair a.*) pelirrojo, -a; (*wine*) tinto; **to be** [*o go*] ~ ruborizarse II. *n* rojo *m*; **to be in the** ~ FIN estar en números rojos ▶**to make sb see** ~ sacar a alguien de quicio; **to see** ~ salir de sus casillas

Red Army *n* Ejército *m* Rojo

red blood cell *n* glóbulo *m* rojo

red-blooded [ˌred·'blʌd·ɪd] *adj* fogoso, -a

red cabbage *n* repollo *m* morado

redcap ['red·kæp] *n* (*railway porter*) mozo *m* de estación

Red Crescent *n* **the** ~ la Media Luna Roja

Red Cross *n* **the** ~ la Cruz Roja

redcurrant *n* grosella *f*

red deer *n inv* ciervo *m*

redden ['red·ən] I. *vi* enrojecerse; (*person*) ruborizarse; **to** ~ **with embarrassment** ponerse colorado de vergüenza II. *vt* enrojecer

reddish ['red·ɪʃ] *adj* rojizo, -a

redecorate [ˌri·'dek·ə·reɪt] *vt* redecorar; (*paint*) volver a pintar; (*wallpaper*) volver a empapelar

redecoration [ˌri·dek·ə·'reɪ·ʃən] *n* (*repainting*) cambio *m* de pintura; (*re-papering*) cambio *m* de papel de colgadura

redeem [rɪ·'dim] *vt* 1. *a.* REL (*person, soul*) redimir; (*situation*) salvar; **to** ~ **oneself** redimirse 2. FIN (*policy, share*) liquidar; (*pawned item*) desempeñar; (*debt*) pagar; **to** ~ **a mortgage** amortizar una hipoteca 3. (*fulfill: promise*) cumplir

redeemable *adj* FIN reembolsable

Redeemer [rɪ·'di·mər] *n* REL **the** ~ el Redentor

redeeming [rɪ·'di·mɪŋ] *adj* redentor(a); **he has no** ~ **qualities** no tiene ningún punto a su favor

redefine [ˌri·dɪ·'faɪn] *vt* redefinir

redemption [rɪ·'demp·ʃən] *n* 1. *a.* REL redención *f* 2. FIN (*of policy, share*) liquidación *f*; (*of mortgage*) amortización *f*

redeploy [ˌri·dɪ·'plɔɪ] *vt* (*workers, staff*) reorganizar, reubicar *AmL*; (*soldiers, troops*) cambiar de frente

redeployment *n* (*of workers, staff*) reorganización *f*, reubicación *f AmL*; (*of soldiers, troops*) redistribución *f*

redevelop [ˌri·dɪ·'vel·əp] *vt* reurbanizar

redevelopment [ˌri·dɪ·'vel·əp·mənt] *n* reurbanización *f*

redeye [ˌred·ˌaɪ] *n sl:* avión que opera a altas horas de la noche o de un día a otro

red-haired [ˌred·'herd] *adj* pelirrojo, -a

red-handed [ˌred·'hæn·dɪd] *adj* **to catch sb** ~ pillar a alguien con las manos en la masa

redhead ['red·hed] *n* pelirrojo, -a *m, f*

red-headed *adj* pelirrojo, -a

red herring *n fig* pista *f* falsa

red-hot [ˌred·'hat] *adj* 1. (*extremely hot*) candente; **to be** ~ estar al rojo vivo 2. (*exciting*) apasionante 3. (*up-to-the-minute: information*) de última hora

redirect [ˌri·dɪ·'rekt] *vt* reorientar; (*letter*) reexpedir; (*traffic*) desviar

redistribute [ˌri·dɪ·'strɪb·jut] *vt* redistribuir

redistribution [ˌri·dɪs·trɪ·'bju·ʃən] *n* redistribución *f*

red-letter day [ˌred·'let·ər·ˌdeɪ] *n* día *m* memorable

red light *n* semáforo *m* en rojo

red-light district *n* barrio *m* de mala fama

red meat *n* carne *f* roja

redneck ['red·nek] *n* campesino blanco de la clase baja rural, de los estados del Sur

redness ['red·nɪs] *n* rojez *f*

redo [ˌri·'du] *vt irr* rehacer

redolent ['red·ə·lənt] *adj* 1. *form* fragante; (*smelling of*); ~ **of sth** con olor a algo 2. (*suggestive of*) **to be** ~ **of sth** hacer evocar algo

redouble [rɪ·'dʌb·əl] *vt* redoblar; **to** ~ **one's efforts** redoblar los esfuerzos

redoubtable [rɪ·'daʊ·tə·bəl] *adj* imponente, temible

redound [rɪ·'daʊnd] *vi form* **to** ~ **to sb's advantage** redundar en beneficio de alguien; **to** ~ **to sb's credit** aumentar el prestigio de alguien

red pepper *n* pimiento *m* rojo

redraft[1] [ˌri·'dræft] *vt* volver a redactar

redraft[2] ['ri·dræft] *n* nuevo borrador *m*

redress [rɪ·'dres] I. *vt* (*grievance*) reparar; (*fault*) remediar; (*imbalance*) rectificar II. *n* (*of grievance, imbalance*) reparación *f*; **to seek** ~ exigir reparación

Red Sea *n* **the** ~ el Mar Rojo

redskin *n offensive* piel *mf* roja

red tape *n* papeleo *m*

reduce [rɪ·'dus] I. *vt* 1. (*diminish*) reducir; (*price*) rebajar; (*wages*) recortar 2. MIL degradar **3. to ~ sb to tears** hacer llorar a alguien; **to ~ sth to rubble/ashes** reducir algo a escombros/cenizas; **to be ~d to doing sth** verse forzado a hacer algo **4.** MATH (*fraction*) simplificar **II.** *vi* adelgazar

reduced [rɪ·'dʌst] *adj* **1.** (*lower*) reducido, -a; (*price*) rebajado, -a **2.** (*impoverished*) **to be in ~ circumstances** estar pasando estrecheces

reduced-sugar *adj inv* bajo, -a en azúcar

reduction [rɪ·'dʌk·ʃən] *n* reducción *f;* (*in price*) rebaja *f*

redundancy [rɪ·'dʌn·dən·si] <-ies> *n* (*uselessness*) superfluidad *f;* LING redundancia *f*

redundant [rɪ·'dʌn·dənt] *adj* (*superfluous*) superfluo, -a; LING redundante

reduplicate [rɪ·'du·plə·keɪt] *vi* reduplicar

reduplication [rɪ·,du·plə·'keɪ·ʃən] *n* reduplicación *f*

red wine *n* vino *m* tinto

redwood ['red·wʊd] *n* secuoya *f*

re-echo [,ri·'ek·oʊ] **I.** *vt* repetir **II.** *vi* resonar

reed [rid] *n* **1.** (*plant*) junco *m,* totora *f AmS* **2.** (*straw*) caña *f* **3.** MUS lengüeta *f,* caramillo *m*

reed instrument *n* instrumento *m* de lengüeta

re-educate [,ri·'edʒ·ə·keɪt] *vt* reeducar

reedy ['ri·di] *adj* **1.** (*full of reeds*) poblado, -a de juncos **2.** MUS (*voice*) aflautado, -a

reef [rif] **I.** *n* **1.** (*ridge*) arrecife *m* **2.** (*part of sail*) rizo *m* **3.** (*mine*) filón *m* **II.** *vt* NAUT arrizar

reefer ['ri·fər] *n sl* porro *m,* cacho *m Col*

reek [rik] **I.** *vi* apestar; **to ~ of corruption** apestar a corrupción **II.** *n* hedor *m*

reel[1] [ril] *n* (*storage or winding device*) carrete *m;* (*for film, rope, tape*) bobina *f*

reel[2] [ril] **I.** *vi* **1.** (*move unsteadily*) tambalearse **2.** (*recoil*) retroceder **II.** *n* reel *m* (*baile escocés*)

re-elect [,ri·ɪ·'lekt] *vt* reelegir

re-election [,ri·ɪ·'lek·ʃən] *n* reelección *f*

re-employ [,ri·ɪm·'plɔɪ] *vt* volver a emplear

re-engage [,ri·ɪn·'geɪdʒ] *vt* volver a contratar

re-enter [,ri·'en·tər] **I.** *vt* **1.** (*go in again*) volver a entrar en **2.** COMPUT teclear de nuevo **II.** *vi* reingresar

re-entry [,ri·'en·tri] <-ies> *n* reingreso *m*

ref [ref] *n* **1.** *inf abbr of* **referee** árbitro, -a *m, f* **2.** *abbr of* **reference** referencia *f*

refectory [rɪ·'fek·tə·ri] <-ies> *n* refectorio *m*

refer [rɪ·'fɜr] <-rr-> *vt* **to refer sth to sb** (*article*) remitir algo a alguien; **to ~ a patient to a specialist** mandar a un paciente a un especialista; **to ~ a case to sb/sth** LAW remitir una causa a alguien/algo

◆ **refer back to** *vt* remitir a; **~ your notes** consultar los apuntes

◆ **refer to** *vt* **1.** (*mention, allude*) referirse a; **to never ~ sth** no mencionar nunca algo; **to ~ sb as sth** calificar a alguien de algo; **referring to your letter/phone call,...** con relación a su carta/llamada,... **2.** (*concern*) concernir; **does this information ~ me?** ¿esta información tiene algo que ver conmigo? **3.** (*consult, turn to*) consultar; **to ~ one's notes** con-

sultar sus apuntes; **~ page 70** ver página 70; **I ~ the facts** me remito a los hechos

referee [,ref·ə·'ri] **I.** *n* **1.** SPORTS árbitro, -a *m, f,* referí *m AmL* **2.** (*in dispute*) mediador(a) *m(f)* **II.** *vi, vt* arbitrar

reference ['ref·ər·əns] *n* **1.** (*consultation*) consulta *f;* **to make ~ to sth** hacer referencia a algo **2.** (*source*) referencia *f* **3.** (*allusion*) alusión *f;* **with ~ to what was said** en alusión a lo que se dijo **4.** ADMIN (*number*) número *m* de referencia **5.** (*for job application*) referencias *fpl;* **to take up ~s** pedir referencias

reference book *n* libro *m* de consulta

reference library *n* biblioteca *f* de consulta

reference number *n* **1.** (*in document, on book*) número *m* de referencia **2.** (*on product*) número *m* de serie

referendum [,ref·ə·'ren·dəm] <-s *o* -da> *n* referéndum *m*

referral [rɪ·'fɜr·əl] *n* remisión *f*

refill[1] [,ri·'fɪl] *vt* (*fill again*) rellenar

refill[2] ['ri·fɪl] *n* (*replacement*) recambio *m*

refine [rɪ·'faɪn] *vt* **1.** (*oil, sugar*) refinar **2.** (*technique*) perfeccionar

refined [rɪ·'faɪnd] *adj* **1.** (*oil, sugar*) refinado, -a **2.** (*sophisticated*) sofisticado, -a **3.** (*very polite*) fino, -a

refinement [rɪ·'faɪn·mənt] *n* **1.** (*improvement*) refinamiento *m* **2.** (*purification*) refinación *f* **3.** (*good manners*) finura *f*

refinery [rɪ·'faɪ·nə·ri] <-ies> *n* refinería *f*

refit[1] [,ri·'fɪt] <-tt-> *a.* NAUT **I.** *vi* repararse **II.** *vt* reparar

refit[2] ['ri·fɪt] *n a.* NAUT reparación *f*

reflate [ri·'fleɪt] *vt* reflacionar

reflation [,ri·'fleɪ·ʃən] *n* reflación *f*

reflect [rɪ·'flekt] **I.** *vt* reflejar **II.** *vi* **1.** (*cast back light*) reflejarse **2.** (*contemplate*) reflexionar **3. to ~ badly on sth** no decir mucho de algo

reflecting *adj* reflectante

reflecting telescope *n* telescopio *m* reflector

reflection [rɪ·'flek·ʃən] *n* **1.** (*image*) reflejo *m* **2.** (*thought*) reflexión *f;* **~ on sth** reflexión acerca de algo; **on ~** pensándolo bien **3.** *fig* **to be a fair ~ of sth** ser un fiel reflejo de algo; **to be a poor ~ on sth** no decir mucho de algo

reflective [rɪ·'flek·tɪv] *adj* **1.** (*surface*) reflector(a) *f* **2.** (*thoughtful*) reflexivo, -a

reflector [rɪ·'flek·tər] *n* (*mirror*) reflector *m;* (*of bicycle, car*) captafaros *m inv*

reflex ['ri·fleks] <-es> **I.** *n* reflejo *m* **II.** *adj* reflejo, -a

reflex action *n* acto *m* reflejo

reflex camera *n* cámara *f* réflex

reflexive [rɪ·'flek·sɪv] **I.** *adj* **1.** (*independent of will*) reflejo, -a **2.** LING reflexivo, -a **II.** *n* LING reflexivo *m*

reflexology [,ri·flek·'sal·ə·dʒi] *n* reflexología *f*

reflux [,ri·'flʌks] *n* reflujo *m*

reforest [,ri·'fɔr·ɪst] *vt* reforestar

reform [rɪ·'fɔrm] **I.** *vt* reformar **II.** *vi* reformarse **III.** *n* reforma *f*

re-form [,ri·'fɔrm] **I.** *vt* formar de nuevo **II.** *vi* formarse de nuevo

reformation [ˌref·ər·ˈmeɪ·ʃən] *n* reforma *f;* **the Reformation** la Reforma

reformatory [rɪ·ˈfɔr·mə·tɔr·i] <-ies> *n* reformatorio *m*

reformer *n* reformador(a) *m(f)*

reform school *n* reformatorio *m*

refract [rɪ·ˈfrækt] *vt* PHYS refractar

refraction [rɪ·ˈfræk·ʃən] *n* refracción *f*

refractory [rɪ·ˈfræk·tə·ri] *adj* refractario, -a

refrain¹ [rɪ·ˈfreɪn] *vi form* abstenerse; **to ~ from doing sth** abstenerse de hacer algo

refrain² [rɪ·ˈfreɪn] *n* MUS estribillo *m*

refresh [rɪ·ˈfreʃ] *vt* refrescar; **to ~ oneself** refrescarse

refresher *n* refresco *m; ~* **course** cursillo *m* de perfeccionamiento [o de repaso]

refreshing *adj* **1.** (*drink*) refrescante **2.** (*change, difference*) reconfortante

refreshment [rɪ·ˈfreʃ·mənt] *n* **1.** (*drink*) refresco *m* **2.** (*food*) refrigerio *m*

refrigerant [rɪ·ˈfrɪdʒ·ər·ənt] *n* refrigerante *m*

refrigerate [rɪ·ˈfrɪdʒ·ə·reɪt] *vt* refrigerar

refrigeration [rɪ·ˌfrɪdʒ·ə·ˈreɪ·ʃən] *n* refrigeración *f*

refrigerator [rɪ·ˈfrɪdʒ·ə·reɪ·tər] *n* nevera *f,* refrigerador *m AmL,* frigider *m Chile*

refuel [ˌri·ˈfju·əl] <-ll-, -l-> I. *vi* repostar combustible II. *vt* reabastecer de combustible; *fig* renovar

refuge [ˈref·judʒ] *n* refugio *m;* **to take ~ in sth** refugiarse en algo

refugee [ˌref·ju·ˈdʒi] *n* refugiado, -a *m, f*

refugee camp *n* campo *m* de refugiados

refund¹ [ˌri·ˈfʌnd] *vt* reembolsar

refund² [ˈri·fʌnd] *n* reembolso *m*

refurbish [ˌri·ˈfɜr·bɪʃ] *vt* restaurar, refaccionar *AmL*

refusal [rɪ·ˈfju·zəl] *n* negativa *f*

refuse [rɪ·ˈfjuz] I. *vi* negarse II. *vt* (*request, gift*) rechazar; (*permission, entry*) denegar; **to ~ sb sth** negar algo a alguien

refusenik [re·ˈfjuz·nɪk] *n* POL objetor *m*

refutation [ˌref·ju·ˈteɪ·ʃən] *n* refutación *f*

refute [rɪ·ˈfjut] *vt* refutar

regain [rɪ·ˈgeɪn] *vt* (*freedom, possession*) recuperar; (*consciousness, health*) recobrar

regal [ˈri·gəl] *adj* regio, -a

regale [rɪ·ˈgeɪl] *vt iron* agasajar

regalia [rɪ·ˈgeɪ·li·ə] *n* **1.** (*clothes*) traje *m* de gala **2.** (*insignia*) insignias *fpl*

regard [rɪ·ˈgard] I. *vt* **1.** (*consider*) considerar; **to ~ sb highly** tener muy buena opinión de alguien **2.** *form* (*watch*) contemplar **3.** (*concerning*) **as ~s...** respecto a... II. *n form* **1.** (*consideration*) consideración *f;* **to pay no ~ to sth** no prestar atención a algo; **with ~ to...** en cuanto a... **2.** (*respect*) respeto *m,* estima *f;* **to hold sb/sth in high ~** tener una alta estima por alguien/algo **3.** (*point*) respecto *m;* **in this ~** con respecto a esto **4. ~s** (*in messages*) recuerdos *mpl;* **with kind ~s** muchos saludos

regardful [rɪ·ˈgard·fəl] *adj* atento, -a

regarding *prep* en cuanto a

regardless [rɪ·ˈgard·lɪs] I. *adv* a pesar de todo; **to press on ~** seguir cueste lo que cueste II. *adj* indiferente; **~ of...** sin tener en cuenta...

regatta [rɪ·ˈga·t̬ə] *n* regata *f*

regency [ˈri·dʒen·si] *n* regencia *f*

regenerate [rɪ·ˈdʒen·ə·reɪt] I. *vt* regenerar II. *vi* regenerarse

regeneration [rɪ·ˌdʒen·ə·ˈreɪ·ʃən] *n* regeneración *f*

reggae [ˈreg·eɪ] *n* reggae *m*

regime [rə·ˈʒim] *n* régimen *m*

regimen [ˈredʒ·ə·men] *n form* régimen *m*

regiment [ˈredʒ·ə·mənt] I. *n* **1.** MIL regimiento *m* **2.** *fig* multitud *f* II. *vt* reglamentar

regimentation [ˌredʒ·əm·ən·ˈteɪ·ʃən] *n* reglamentación *f*

region [ˈri·dʒən] *n* **1.** GEO, ANAT región *f;* **in the ~ of** 30 alrededor de 30 **2.** (*administrative area*) provincia *f*

regional [ˈri·dʒə·nəl] *adj* regional

regionalism [ˈri·dʒə·nə·ˌlɪz·əm] *n* regionalismo *m*

register [ˈredʒ·ɪ·stər] I. *n* registro *m;* **class ~** lista *f* de la clase II. *vt* registrar; (*car*) matricular; (*voter*) inscribir; (*letter, package*) certificar III. *vi* **1.** (*record*) inscribirse; UNIV matricularse, inscribirse *AmL* **2.** (*be understood*) **the information didn't ~ with him** no registró la información

registered [ˈredʒ·ɪ·stərd] *adj* registrado, -a; (*nurse*) diplomado, -a; (*student*) matriculado, -a; (*letter, package*) certificado, -a

registrar [ˈredʒ·ɪ·strar] *n* **1.** ADMIN secretario, -a *m, f* del registro civil **2.** UNIV secretario, -a *m, f* general **3.** MED médico *mf* asistente

registration [ˌredʒ·ɪ·ˈstreɪ·ʃən] *n* **1.** (*act*) inscripción *f;* **voter ~** registro de votantes **2.** AUTO matrícula *f,* placa *f Col* **3.** UNIV matriculación *f*

registration fee *n* cuota *f* de inscripción; UNIV matrícula *f*

registration number *n* matrícula *f*

registry [ˈredʒ·ɪ·stri] *n* registro *m;* **bridal ~** registro *m* de matrimonio

regress [rɪ·ˈgres] *vi* retroceder

regression [rɪ·ˈgreʃ·ən] *n* regresión *f*

regressive [rɪ·ˈgres·ɪv] *adj* regresivo, -a

regret [rɪ·ˈgret] I. <-tt-> *vt* lamentar; **to ~ doing sth** arrepentirse de haber hecho algo; **we ~ any inconvenience to passengers** lamentamos las molestias para los pasajeros II. *n* arrepentimiento *m;* **to have ~s** tener remordimientos; **to have no ~s about sth** no arrepentirse de algo; **much to my ~** muy a mi pesar; **to send one's ~s** enviar sus condolencias

regretful [rɪ·ˈgret·fəl] *adj* arrepentido, -a

regretfully *adv* lamentablemente

regrettable [rɪ·ˈgret·ə·bəl] *adj* lamentable

regroup [ˌri·ˈgrup] I. *vt* reagrupar II. *vi* reagruparse

regular [ˈreg·jə·lər] I. *adj* **1.** (*pattern*) regular;

(*appearance, customer*) habitual; (*procedure*) normal; **to have ~ meetings** tener reuniones periódicas **2.** (*gas*) normal **3.** LING regular **4.** *inf* (*real*) verdadero, -a **II.** *n* **1.** (*customer*) asiduo, -a *m, f* **2.** MIL soldado *m* regular
regularity [ˌreg·jʊ·ˈler·ə·ṭi] *n* regularidad *f*
regularize [ˈreg·jʊ·lə·raɪz] *vt* **1.** (*standardize*) normalizar **2.** (*normalize*) regularizar
regularly *adv* con regularidad
regulate [ˈreg·jʊ·leɪt] *vt* **1.** (*supervise*) reglamentar **2.** (*adjust*) regular
regulation [ˌreg·jʊ·ˈleɪ·ʃən] **I.** *n* **1.** (*rule*) regla *f*; **safety ~s** reglamento *m* de seguridad; **in accordance with** (**the**) **~s** de acuerdo con el reglamento **2.** (*adjustment*) regulación *f* **II.** *adj* reglamentario, -a
regulator [ˈreg·jʊ·leɪ·ṭər] *n* regulador *m*
regulatory [ˈreg·jə·lə·tɔr·i] *adj* regulador(a)
regurgitate [ri·ˈgɜr·dʒə·teɪt] *vt* **1.** (*food*) regurgitar **2.** (*ideas, facts*) repetir maquinalmente
rehab [ˈri·hæb] *n inf abbr of* **rehabilitation** rehabilitación *f*
rehabilitate [ˌri·hə·ˈbɪl·ə·teɪt] *vt* rehabilitar
rehabilitation [ˌri·hə·ˌbɪl·ə·ˈteɪ·ʃən] *n* rehabilitación *f*
rehabilitation center *n* centro *m* de rehabilitación
rehash[1] [ˌri·ˈhæʃ] *vt* hacer un refrito de
rehash[2] [ˈri·hæʃ] *n* (*new discussion*) refrito *m*, machaqueo *Col*
rehearsal [ri·ˈhɜr·səl] *n* ensayo *m*
rehearse [ri·ˈhɜrs] *vt, vi* ensayar
reign [reɪn] **I.** *vi* **1.** (*be monarch*) reinar **2.** *fig* (*be dominant*) imperar **II.** *n* **1.** (*sovereignty*) reinado *m* **2.** (*rule*) régimen *m*
reimburse [ˌri·ɪm·ˈbɜrs] *vt* reembolsar
reimbursement *n* reembolso *m*
rein [reɪn] *n* rienda *f* ▶ **to give free ~ to sb** dar rienda suelta a alguien; **to keep sb on a tight ~** atar corto a alguien, tener a alguien controlado; **to hold the ~s** sujetar las riendas
reincarnation [ˌri·ɪn·kar·ˈneɪ·ʃən] *n* reencarnación *f*
reindeer [ˈreɪn·dɪr] *n inv* reno *m*
reinforce [ˌri·ɪn·ˈfɔrs] *vt a.* MIL reforzar; (*argument*) fortalecer
reinforcement *n* refuerzo *m*
reinstate [ˌri·ɪn·ˈsteɪt] *vt form* restituir
reinsure [ˌri·ɪn·ˈʃʊr] *vt* reasegurar
reintegrate [ri·ˈɪn·tə·greɪt] *vt* reintegrar; (*criminal*) reinsertar
reintegration [ˈri·ˌɪn·tə·ˈgreɪ·ʃən] *n* reintegración *f*; (*of criminal*) reinserción *f*
reintroduce [ˌri·ɪn·trə·ˈdus] *vt* reintroducir
reissue [ˌri·ˈɪʃ·ju] **I.** *vt* volver a emitir **II.** *n* reexpedición *f*
reiterate [ri·ˈɪṭ·ə·reɪt] *vt* reiterar
reiteration [ri·ˌɪṭ·ə·ˈreɪ·ʃən] *n* reiteración *f*
reject[1] [ri·ˈdʒekt] *vt a.* MED, TECH rechazar; (*application, request*) desestimar; (*accusation*) negar; (*bill, motion*) impugnar; (*proposal*) descartar
reject[2] [ˈri·dʒekt] *n* **1.** (*cast-off*) artículo *m*

defectuoso **2.** (*person*) persona *f* rechazada
rejection [ri·ˈdʒek·ʃən] *n* rechazo *m*
rejoice [ri·ˈdʒɔɪs] *vi* regocijarse; **to ~ in doing sth** regocijarse haciendo algo; **I ~d to see that...** me alegré al ver que...
rejoicing *n* regocijo *m*
rejoin[1] [ri·ˈdʒɔɪn] **I.** *vt* (*join again*) volver a unirse con; (*regiment*) reincorporarse a; (*political party*) reintegrarse a **II.** *vi* reunirse
rejoin[2] [ri·ˈdʒɔɪn] *vt* (*reply*) replicar
rejoinder [ri·ˈdʒɔɪn·dər] *n* réplica *f*
rejuvenate [ri·ˈdʒu·və·neɪt] *vt* rejuvenecer
rekindle [ri·ˈkɪn·dəl] *vt a. fig* reavivar
relapse [ri·ˈlæps] **I.** *n* MED recaída *f* **II.** *vi a.* MED recaer
relate [ri·ˈleɪt] **I.** *vt* **1.** (*establish connection*) relacionar **2.** (*tell*) contar **II.** *vi* **1.** (*be connected with*) **to ~ to sb/sth** estar relacionado con alguien/algo **2.** (*understand*) **to ~ to sth/sb** comprender algo/a alguien
related *adj* **1.** (*linked*) relacionado, -a **2.** (*in same family*) emparentado, -a; **to be ~ to sb** estar emparentado con alguien; **to be closely/distantly ~** tener parentesco cercano/lejano
relating to *prep* acerca de
relation [ri·ˈleɪ·ʃən] *n* **1.** (*link*) relación *f*; **in ~ to** en relación a; **to bear no ~ to sb/sth** no tener relación con alguien/algo **2.** (*relative*) pariente *mf* **3. ~s** (*contact*) relaciones *fpl*
relationship [ri·ˈleɪ·ʃən·ʃɪp] *n* **1.** (*link*) relación *f* **2.** (*family connection*) parentesco *m* **3.** (*between two people*) relaciones *fpl*; **to be in a ~ with sb** tener una relación con alguien; **business ~s** relaciones comerciales
relative [ˈrel·ə·ṭɪv] **I.** *adj* relativo, -a **II.** *n* pariente *mf*
relative clause *n* oración *f* relativa
relatively *adv* relativamente
relativity [ˌrel·ə·ˈtɪv·ə·ṭi] *n* relatividad *f*
relaunch[1] [ˌri·ˈlɔntʃ] *vt* relanzar
relaunch[2] [ˈri·ˌlɔntʃ] *n* relanzamiento *m*
relax [ri·ˈlæks] **I.** *vi* relajarse; (*restrictions*) mitigarse, (*rules*) suavizarse; (*security*) debilitarse; **relax!** ¡cálmate! **II.** *vt* relajar; (*restrictions*) mitigar; (*rules*) suavizar; (*security*) debilitar; **to ~ one's efforts** disminuir sus esfuerzos; **to ~ one's hold on sth** dejar de agarrarse a algo *fig*
relaxation [ˌri·læk·ˈseɪ·ʃən] *n* relajación *f*
relaxed *adj* relajado, -a
relay [ˈri·leɪ] **I.** *vt* (*information*) pasar; TV retransmitir **II.** *n* **1.** (*group*) turno *m;* **to work in ~s** trabajar por turnos **2.** SPORTS carrera *f* de relevos **3.** ELEC relé *m*
re-lay [ˌri·ˈleɪ] *vt* volver a colocar
release [ri·ˈlis] **I.** *vt* **1.** (*set free*) poner en libertad **2.** (*cease to hold*) soltar; PHOT disparar **3.** (*allow to escape: gas*) emitir; (*steam*) desprender **4.** (*weaken: pressure*) aliviar **5.** (*make public: information*) anunciar; (*book*) publicar; (*film*) estrenar; (*CD*) poner a la venta **II.** *n* **1.** (*of prisoner*) excarcelación *f*; (*of hostage*) liberación *f* **2.** PHOT disparador *m* **3.** (*relax-*

ation) aflojamiento *m* **4.** (*escape*) escape *m* **5.** (*publication*) publicación *f;* (*of film*) estreno *m;* (*of CD*) puesta *f* a la venta; **press ~** comunicado *m* de prensa

relegate ['rel·ə·geɪt] *vt* relegar

relent [rɪ·'lent] *vi* (*person*) ceder; (*wind, rain*) amainar

relentless [rɪ·'lent·lɪs] *adj* (*pursuit, opposition*) implacable; (*pressure*) incesante; (*criticism*) despiadado, -a

relevance ['rel·ə·vəns] *n,* **relevancy** *n* pertinencia

relevant ['rel·ə·vənt] *adj* pertinente

reliability [rɪ·ˌlaɪ·ə·'bɪl·ə·ti] *n* **1.** (*dependability*) seguridad *f* **2.** (*trustworthiness*) fiabilidad *f*

reliable [rɪ·'laɪ·ə·bəl] (*credible*) fidedigno, -a; (*authority*) serio, -a; (*evidence*) fehaciente; (*statistics*) auténtico, -a; (*testimony*) verídico, -a **2.** (*trustworthy*) de confianza

reliance [rɪ·'laɪ·əns] *n* **1.** (*dependence*) dependencia *f* **2.** (*belief*) confianza *f*

reliant [rɪ·'laɪ·ənt] *adj* **to be ~ on sb/sth** depender de alguien/algo

relic ['rel·ɪk] *n a. fig* reliquia *f*

relief [rɪ·'lif] I. *n* **1.** (*relaxation*) alivio *m;* **it's a ~ that** es un alivio que +*subj;* **what a ~!** ¡menos mal! **2.** (*aid*) socorro *m* **3.** (*replacement*) relevo *m* **4.** MIL descerco *m* **5.** *a.* GEO relieve *m;* **to throw sth into ~** hacer resaltar algo **6. tax ~** desgravación *f* fiscal II. *adj* **1.** de relevo; (*driver*) suplente **2.** GEO en relieve

relief supplies *npl* provisiones *fpl* de socorro

relief worker *n* trabajador (a) *m(f)* de una organización humanitaria

relieve [rɪ·'liv] *vt* **1.** (*assist*) socorrer **2.** (*alleviate: pain*) aliviar; (*suffering*) mitigar; (*feelings*) desahogar; (*one's mind*) tranquilizar **3.** MIL descercar **4.** (*urinate, defecate*) **to ~ oneself** hacer sus necesidades

relieved *adj* aliviado, -a

religion [rɪ·'lɪdʒ·ən] *n* religión *f*

religious [rɪ·'lɪdʒ·əs] *adj* religioso, -a

relinquish [rɪ·'lɪŋ·kwɪʃ] *vt* (*claim, title*) renunciar a; (*control*) ceder; **to ~ one's grip on sth** soltar algo

relish ['rel·ɪʃ] I. *n* **1.** (*enjoyment*) gusto *m;* **with ~** con gusto **2.** (*enthusiasm*) entusiasmo *m* **3.** CULIN condimento *m* II. *vt* deleitarse en; I don't ~ ... no me entusiasma...

reload [ˌri·'loʊd] I. *vt* recargar II. *vi* recargarse

relocate [ri·'loʊ·keɪt] I. *vi* trasladarse II. *vt* trasladar

relocation [ˌri·loʊ·'keɪ·ʃən] *n* (*of company*) reubicación *f;* (*of person*) traslado *m*

reluctance [rɪ·'lʌk·təns] *n* desgana *f* [*o* desgano] *m;* **with ~** de mala gana

reluctant [rɪ·'lʌk·tənt] *adj* reacio, -a; **to be ~ to do sth** tener pocas ganas de hacer algo, ser reacio a hacer algo

rely [rɪ·'laɪ] *vi* **to ~ on** [*o* **upon**] (*trust*) confiar en; (*depend on*) depender de; **to ~ on** [*o* **upon**] **sb to do sth** contar con alguien para hacer algo

REM [rem] *abbr of* **Rapid Eye Movement** movimiento *m* rápido del ojo

remain [rɪ·'meɪn] *vi* **1.** (*stay*) quedar(se) **2.** (*continue*) permanecer; **to ~ aloof** mantenerse apartado; **to ~ seated** quedarse sentado; **to ~ unsolved** seguir sin solucionarse; **to ~ to be done** estar por hacer; **much ~s to be done** queda mucho por hacer; **the fact ~s that...** sigue siendo un hecho que...; **it** (**only**) **~s for me to...** sólo me resta...; **it ~s to be seen** (**who/what/how**) está por ver (quién/qué/cómo)

remainder [rɪ·'meɪn·dər] I. *n a.* MATH resto *m;* **the ~ of sb's life** lo que queda de la vida de alguien II. *vt* saldar

remaining [rɪ·'meɪ·nɪŋ] *adj* restante

remains [rɪ·'meɪnz] *npl* restos *mpl*

remake¹ [ˌri·'meɪk] <remade> *vt* volver a hacer

remake² ['ri·meɪk] *n* nueva versión *f*

remand [rɪ·'mænd] I. *vt* **to ~ sb to prison** [*o* **in custody**] poner a alguien en prisión preventiva; **to ~ sb on bail** poner a alguien en libertad bajo fianza II. *n* **to be on ~** estar en prisión preventiva

remark [rɪ·'mark] I. *vi* **to ~ on sth** hacer observaciones sobre algo II. *n* observación *f;* **to make ~s about sb/sth** hacer comentarios sobre alguien/algo

remarkable [rɪ·'mar·kə·bəl] *adj* extraordinario, -a; (*coincidence*) singular; **to be ~ for sth** ser notable por algo

remarkably *adv* extraordinariamente

remarry [ˌri·'mær·i] <-ie-> *vi* volver a casarse

remedial [rɪ·'mi·di·əl] *adj* (*action*) remediador(a); SCHOOL recuperativo, -a; MED terapéutico, -a

remedy ['rem·ə·di] I. <-ies> *n* **1.** remedio *m;* **to be beyond ~** no tener remedio **2.** LAW (**legal**) **~** recurso *m* (legal) II. *vt* remediar; (*mistake*) corregir

remember [rɪ·'mem·bər] I. *vt* **1.** (*recall*) recordar; **I can't ~ his name** no recuerdo su nombre **2.** (*commemorate*) conmemorar II. *vi* acordarse de

remembrance [rɪ·'mem·brəns] *n* (*act of remembering*) recuerdo *m;* **in ~ of** en conmemoración de

remind [rɪ·'maɪnd] *vt* recordar; **to ~ sb to do sth** recordar a alguien que haga algo; **he ~s me of you** me recuerda a ti; **that ~s me,...** por cierto,...

reminder [rɪ·'maɪn·dər] *n* **1.** (*note*) recordatorio *m* **2.** (*warning*) advertencia *f;* **to give sb a gentle ~** dar a alguien una advertencia amistosa **3.** (*memento*) recuerdo *m*

reminisce [ˌrem·ə·'nɪs] *vi* rememorar

reminiscence [ˌrem·ə·'nɪs·əns] *n* reminiscencia *f*

reminiscent [ˌrem·ə·'nɪs·ənt] *adj* **to be ~ of sb/sth** hacer pensar en alguien/algo

remiss [rɪ·'mɪs] *adj* negligente

remission [rɪ·'mɪʃ·ən] *n* remisión *f*

remit¹ [rɪ·'mɪt] <-tt-> *vt form* **1.** (*send*) remitir; (*money*) enviar **2.** LAW perdonar, condonar

remit² ['ri·mɪt] *n* competencia *f*

remittance [rɪ·'mɪt·əns] *n* giro *m*

remix I. ['ri·miks] *n* <-es> MUS mezcla *f* II. [ri·'miks] *vt* mezclar

remnant ['rem·nənt] *n* resto *m*

remodel [ˌri·'mad·əl] <-ll-, -l-> *vt* remodelar

remold ['ri·moʊld] I. *vt* recauchutar, refundir II. *n* recauchutado *m*

remonstrance [rɪ·'man·strəns] *n form* protesta *f*

remonstrate [rɪ·'man·streɪt] *vi* protestar

remorse [rɪ·'mɔrs] *n* remordimiento *m;* **without ~** sin remordimientos

remorseful [rɪ·'mɔrs·fəl] *adj* arrepentido, -a

remorseless [rɪ·'mɔrs·lɪs] *adj* (*merciless*) despiadado, -a; (*attack*) implacable

remote [rɪ·'moʊt] *adj* <-er, -est> (*place, possibility*) remoto, -a

remote control *n* mando *m* a distancia, control remoto *m Col*

remote-controlled *adj* teledirigido, -a

remoteness *n* alejamiento *m*, improbabilidad *f*

remount [ˌri·'maʊnt] I. *vt* subir de nuevo a II. *vi* volverse a montar en

removable [rɪ·'mu·və·bəl] *adj* **1.** (*stain*) que se puede quitar **2.** (*easy to take off*) desmontable; (*sleeves*) de quita y pon

removal [rɪ·'mu·vəl] *n* **1.** (*of stain, problem*) eliminación *f* **2.** (*extraction*) extracción *f*

remove [rɪ·'muv] *vt* **1.** (*take away*) quitar; (*clothes*) quitarse **2.** (*get rid of*) eliminar; (*cork, dent*) sacar; (*entry, name*) borrar; (*doubts, fears*) disipar; (*problem*) solucionar; **to ~ one's hair** depilarse **3.** (*dismiss from job*) destituir

remover [rɪ·'mu·vər] *n* **1.** agente *mf* de mudanzas **2. stain ~** quitamanchas *m inv* **3. nail polish ~** quitaesmalte

remunerate [rɪ·'mju·nə·reɪt] *vt form* remunerar

remuneration [rɪ·ˌmju·nə·'reɪ·ʃən] *n form* remuneración *f*

remunerative [rɪ·'mju·nə·reɪ·t̬ɪv] *adj form* lucrativo, -a

Renaissance [ˌren·ə·'sans] *n* **the ~** el Renacimiento

renal ['ri·nəl] *adj* renal

rename [ˌri·'neɪm] *vt* poner un nuevo nombre a

rend [rend] <rent *o* rended> *vt liter* desgarrar

render ['ren·dər] *vt form* **1.** (*make*) hacer; **to ~ sb speechless** dejar a alguien mudo **2.** (*perform*) representar; MUS interpretar **3.** (*give: thanks*) ofrecer; (*aid, service*) prestar; (*judgment*) emitir **4.** (*translate*) traducir **5.** ARCHIT enlucir, frisar *And* **6.** (*homage*) rendir

rendering ['ren·dər·ɪŋ] *n* **1.** (*performance*) representación *f;* MUS interpretación *f* **2.** (*translation*) traducción *f*

rendezvous ['ran·deɪ·vu] I. *n inv* **1.** (*meeting*) cita *f* **2.** (*place*) lugar *m* de reunión II. *vi* reu-

nirse

rendition [ren·'dɪʃ·ən] *n* **1.** (*performance*) interpretación *f* **2.** (*translation*) traducción *f*

renegade ['ren·ə·geɪd] I. *n* renegado, -a *m, f* II. *adj* renegado, -a

renege [rɪ·'nɪg] *vi form* **to ~ on sth** incumplir algo

renew [rɪ·'nu] *vt* **1.** (*begin again: membership, passport*) renovar; (*relationship*) reanudar; **to ~ one's efforts to do sth** recobrar fuerzas para hacer algo **2.** (*mend*) recuperar

renewable [rɪ·'nu·ə·bəl] *adj* renovable

renewal [rɪ·'nu·əl] *n* renovación *f*

renewed [rɪ·'nud] *adj* renovado, -a

rennet ['ren·ɪt] *n* cuajo *m*

renounce [rɪ·'naʊns] *vt* renunciar a

renovate ['ren·ə·veɪt] *vt* restaurar, renovar, refaccionar *Ven, Col*

renovation [ˌren·ə·'veɪ·ʃən] *n* renovación *f*

renown [rɪ·'naʊn] *n* renombre *m*

renowned [rɪ·'naʊnd] *adj* renombrado, -a

rent¹ [rent] I. *n* (*rip*) rasgadura *f* II. *pt, pp of* **rend**

rent² [rent] I. *vt* (*apartment, car, video*) alquilar; (*land*) arrendar II. *vi* alquilarse III. *n* alquiler *m;* **for ~** se alquila

rent-a-car *n* (*car*) coche *m* de alquiler; (*agency*) agencia *f* de alquiler de coches

rental ['ren·təl] I. *n* alquiler *m* II. *adj* de alquiler

rent control *n* control *m* de rentas

rent-free *adj* exento, -a de alquiler

renunciation [rɪ·ˌnʌn·si·'eɪ·ʃən] *n* renuncia *f*

reopen [ri·'oʊ·pən] I. *vt* reabrir II. *vi* reabrirse

reorder [ˌri·'ɔr·dər] I. *n* nuevo pedido *m* II. *vt* **1.** (*reorganize*) reordenar **2.** COM hacer un nuevo pedido de

reorganize [ri·'ɔr·gə·naɪz] I. *vt* reorganizar II. *vi* reorganizarse

rep [rep] *n inf* **1.** *abbr of* **representative** representante *mf* de ventas **2.** THEAT *abbr of* **repertory** repertorio *m*

Rep. 1. *abbr of* **Republic** Rep. **2.** *abbr of* **Republican** republicano, -a

repaint [ri·'peɪnt] *vt* repintar

repair [ri·'per] I. *vt* **1.** (*machine*) reparar; (*clothes*) arreglar **2.** (*set right: damage*) enmendar; (*friendship*) reestablecer II. *n* **1.** (*mending: of machine*) reparación *f;* (*of clothes*) arreglo *m;* **to be beyond ~** no tener arreglo; **to be under ~** estar en reparación **2.** (*state*) **to be in good/bad ~** estar en buen/mal estado

repairable [rɪ·'per·ə·bəl] *adj* reparable

repair kit *n* caja *f* de herramientas

repairman <-men> *n* (*for cars*) mecánico *m;* (*for television*) técnico *m*

repairperson *n* reparador(a) *m(f)*

repair shop *n* taller *m* de reparaciones

repaper [ri·'peɪ·pər] *vt* empapelar de nuevo

reparable ['rep·ər·ə·bəl] *adj* reparable

reparation [ˌrep·ə·'reɪ·ʃən] *n* **1.** (*setting right*) reparación *f* **2. ~s** FIN indemnización *f*

R

repartee [ˌrep·ar·'ti] *n* réplica *f*
repatriate [ri·'peɪ·tri·eɪt] *vt* repatriar
repatriation [ri·ˌpeɪ·tri·'eɪ·ʃən] *n* repatriación *f*
repay [ri·'peɪ] <repaid> *vt* (*money*) devolver; (*debts*) liquidar; (*person*) pagar; **to ~ money to sb** reintegrar dinero a alguien; **to ~ sb for sth** premiar a alguien por algo; **to ~ a debt** pagar una deuda
repayable [ri·'peɪ·ə·bəl] *adj* reembolsable
repayment [ri·'peɪ·mənt] *n* reembolso *m*
repeal [ri·'pil] I. *vt* revocar II. *n* revocatoria *f*
repeat [ri·'pit] I. *vt* 1. (*say or do again*) repetir 2. (*recite*) recitar II. *vi* (*happen again*) repetirse; (*taste*) repetir III. *n* 1. repetición *f* 2. TV retransmisión *f*
repeated *adj* repetido, -a
repeatedly *adv* repetidas veces
repeating decimal *n* decimal *m* periódico
repeat offender *n* reincidente *mf*
repeat performance *n* repetición *f*
repel [ri·'pel] <-ll-> *vt* 1. (*ward off*) rechazar 2. MIL, PHYS repeler 3. (*disgust*) repugnar
repellent [ri·'pel·ənt] I. *n* repelente *m* II. *adj* repugnante
repent [ri·'pent] I. *vi form* arrepentirse II. *vt* arrepentirse de
repentance [ri·'pen·təns] *n* arrepentimiento *m*
repentant [rə·'pen·tənt] *adj* arrepentido, -a
repercussion [ˌri·pər·'kʌʃ·ən] *n* repercusión *f*
repertoire ['rep·ər·ˌtwar] *n* repertorio *m*
repertory company ['rep·ər·tɔr·i] *n* compañía *f* de repertorio
repertory theater *n* teatro *m* de repertorio
repetition [ˌrep·ə·'tɪʃ·ən] *n* repetición *f*
repetitious [ˌrep·ə·'tɪʃ·əs] *adj*, **repetitive** [ri·'peɪ·ə·tɪv] *adj* repetitivo, -a
replace [ri·'pleɪs] *vt* 1. (*take the place of*) reemplazar; (*person*) sustituir 2. (*put back*) reponer
replaceable [ri·'pleɪ·sə·bəl] *adj* reemplazable
replacement [ri·'pleɪs·mənt] I. *n* 1. (*person*) sustituto, -a *m, f;* (*part*) recambio *m* 2. MIL reemplazo *m* 3. (*act of substituting*) sustitución *f* II. *adj* de repuesto
replay¹ [ˌri·'pleɪ] *vt* 1. SPORTS volver a jugar 2. MUS volver a tocar 3. TV repetir
replay² ['ri·pleɪ] *n* 1. SPORTS, TV repetición; **instant ~** repetición *f* instantánea 2. MUS reproducción *f*
replenish [ri·'plen·ɪʃ] *vt* rellenar; (*supplies*) abastecer de nuevo; (*stocks*) reponer
replete [ri·'plit] *adj* repleto, -a
replica ['rep·lɪ·kə] *n* réplica *f*
replicate ['rep·lɪ·keɪt] *vt* replicar
reply [ri·'plaɪ] I. <-ied> *vt* contestar II. <-ied> *vi* 1. (*verbally*) contestar 2. (*react*) responder III. <-ies> *n* respuesta *f*
report [ri·'pɔrt] I. *n* 1. (*account*) informe *m;* PUBL noticia *f;* (*longer*) reportaje *m;* **to give a ~** presentar un informe 2. (*unproven claim*) rumor *m* 3. (*explosion*) estallido *m* II. *vt* 1. (*recount*) relatar; (*discovery*) anunciar; **to ~**

that... informar que...; **nothing to ~** sin novedades 2. (*denounce*) denunciar III. *vi* 1. (*make results public*) presentar un informe 2. (*arrive at work*) presentarse; **to ~ sick** dar parte de enfermedad
◆ **report back** I. *vt* **to report sth back to sb** relatar algo a alguien II. *vi* presentar un informe
report card *n* cartilla *f* escolar
reporter [ri·'pɔr· țər] *n* reportero, -a *m, f*
repose [ri·'poʊz] I. *vi* 1. (*rest*) reposar 2. (*lie*) descansar II. *vt* 1. (*rest*) reposar 2. *fig* (*confidence*) depositar III. *n* reposo *m;* **in ~** de reposo
repository [ri·'paz·ɪ·tɔr·i] <-ies> *n* 1. (*store*) depósito *m* 2. (*person*) depositario, -a *m, f*
repossess [ˌri·pə·'zes] *vt* recobrar
repossession [ˌri·pə·'zeʃ·ən] *n* recuperación *f*
reprehensible [ˌrep·ri·'hen·sə·bəl] *adj* censurable
represent [ˌrep·ri·'zent] *vt* 1. (*act for, depict*) representar 2. (*state*) declarar
representation [ˌrep·ri·zen·'teɪ·ʃən] *n* 1. (*acting for, depiction*) representación *f* 2. (*statement*) declaración *f*
representative [ˌrep·ri·'zen·tə·țɪv] I. *adj* 1. *a.* POL representativo, -a 2. (*typical*) típico, -a II. *n* 1. *a.* COM representante *mf*, agenciero, -a *m, f* Arg 2. LAW apoderado, -a *m, f* 3. POL diputado, -a *m, f*
repress [ri·'pres] *vt* reprimir
repressed [ri·'prest] *adj* reprimido, -a
repression [ri·'preʃ·ən] *n* represión *f*
repressive [ri·'pres·ɪv] *adj* represivo, -a
reprieve [ri·'priv] I. *vt* indultar II. *n* indulto *m*
reprimand ['rep·rə·mænd] I. *vt* reprender II. *n* reprimenda *f*
reprint¹ [ˌri·'prɪnt] *vt* reimprimir
reprint² ['ri·prɪnt] *n* reimpresión *f*
reprisal [ri·'praɪ·zəl] *n* represalia *f;* **to take ~s** tomar represalias
reproach [ri·'proʊtʃ] I. *vt* reprochar II. *n* reproche *m;* **beyond ~** intachable; **to be a ~ to sb** ser una vergüenza para alguien
reproachful [ri·'proʊtʃ·fəl] *adj* acusador(a)
reprobate ['rep·rə·beɪt] I. *n a.* REL réprobo, -a *m, f* II. *adj* 1. (*wicked*) malvado, -a 2. REL réprobo, -a
reprocess [ˌri·'pras·es] *vt* reprocesar
reprocessing *n* reprocesamiento *m*
reprocessing plant *n* ECOL, TECH planta *f* reprocesadora
reproduce [ˌri·prə·'dus] I. *vi* reproducirse II. *vt* reproducir
reproduction [ˌri·prə·'dʌk·ʃən] *n* reproducción *f*
reproductive [ˌri·prə·'dʌk·tɪv] *adj* reproductor(a)
reproof [ri·'pruf] I. *n* reprensión *f* II. *vt* reprender
reprove [ri·'pruv] *vt* reprender
reproving [ri·'pru·vɪŋ] *adj* reprobatorio, -a
reptile ['rep·taɪl] *n* reptil *m*

reptilian [rep·'tɪl·i·ən] *adj* reptil
republic [rɪ·'pʌb·lɪk] *n* república *f*
republican [rɪ·'pʌb·lɪ·kən] **I.** *n* republicano, -a *m, f* **II.** *adj* republicano, -a
republication [,ri·,pʌb·lɪ·'keɪ·ʃən] *n* reedición *f*
repudiate [rɪ·'pju·di·eɪt] *vt* (*person*) repudiar; (*accusation*) negar; (*suggestion*) rechazar
repugnance [rɪ·'pʌg·nəns] *n* repugnancia *f*
repugnant [rɪ·'pʌg·nənt] *adj* repugnante
repulse [rɪ·'pʌls] **I.** *vt* **1.** (*disgust*) repulsar **2.** (*ward off*) rechazar **3.** MIL repeler **II.** *n* repulsa *f*
repulsion [rɪ·'pʌl·ʃən] *n* repulsión *f*
repulsive [rɪ·'pʌl·sɪv] *adj* repulsivo, -a
repurchase [,ri·'pɜr·tʃəs] **I.** *vt* readquirir **II.** *n* readquisición *f*
reputable ['rep·jə·ţə·bəl] *adj* acreditado, -a
reputation [,rep·jʊ·'teɪ·ʃən] *n* reputación *f*; **to have a good/bad ~** tener buena/mala fama; **to know sb by ~** conocer a alguien de oídas
repute [rɪ·'pjut] *n* reputación *f*
reputed [rɪ·'pju·ţɪd] *adj* supuesto, -a; **she is ~ to be rich** tiene fama de rica
request [rɪ·'kwest] **I.** *n* petición *f*; ADMIN solicitud *f*; **on ~** a petición; **to make a ~ for sth** pedir algo **II.** *vt* pedir; ADMIN solicitar
requiem ['rek·wi·əm] *n*, **requiem mass** *n* réquiem *m*
require [rɪ·'kwaɪr] *vt* **1.** (*need*) necesitar **2.** (*demand*) exigir; **to ~ sb to do sth** exigir a alguien que haga algo
requirement [rɪ·'kwaɪr·mənt] *n* requisito *m*
requisite ['rek·wɪ·zɪt] **I.** *adj* indispensable **II.** *n* requisito *m*
requisition [,rek·wɪ·'zɪʃ·ən] **I.** *vt* requisar **II.** *n* **1.** (*act of requesting*) requisición *f*; (*written request*) solicitud *f* **2.** MIL requisa *f*
reroute [,ri·'rut] *vt* desviar
rerun¹ [,rɪ·'rʌn] *vt irr* CINE, TV repetir; THEAT reestrenar
rerun² ['ri·rʌn] *n* CINE, TV repetición *f*; THEAT reestreno *m*
resale ['ri·seɪl] *n* reventa *m*
reschedule [,ri·'skedʒ·ul] *vt* reprogramar
rescind [rɪ·'sɪnd] *vt* rescindir
rescue ['res·kju] **I.** *vt* (*save*) rescatar; (*hostage*) liberar **II.** *n* rescate *m*; **to come to sb's ~** rescatar a alguien
rescuer ['res·kju·ər] *n* salvador(a) *m(f)*
research ['ri·sɜrtʃ] **I.** *n* investigación *f* **II.** *vi, vt* investigar
researcher *n* investigador(a) *m(f)*
research work *n* trabajos *mpl* de investigación
research worker *n* investigador(a) *m(f)*
resemblance [rɪ·'zem·bləns] *n* parecido *m*
resemble [rɪ·'zem·bəl] *vt* parecerse a
resent [rɪ·'zent] *vt* **to ~ sth** sentirse molesto por algo
resentful [rɪ·'zent·fəl] *adj* (*person*) resentido, -a; (*expression*) de resentimiento
resentment [rɪ·'zent·mənt] *n* resentimiento *m*
reservation [,rez·ər·'veɪ·ʃən] *n* **1.** (*booking*) reserva *f* (anticipada) **2.** (*doubt*) reserva *f*; **to**

have ~s about sth tener ciertas dudas sobre algo
reserve [rɪ·'zɜrv] **I.** *n* **1.** reserva *f*; **to have sth in ~** tener algo en reserva **2.** SPORTS suplente *mf* **3.** MIL **the ~** la reserva **II.** *vt* reservar
reserve currency *n* divisa *f* de reserva
reserved [rɪ·'zɜrvd] *adj* reservado, -a
reserve price *n* precio *m* mínimo
reservist [rɪ·'zɜr·vɪst] *n* MIL reservista *mf*
reservoir ['rez·ər·vwar] *n* **1.** (*tank*) depósito *m* **2.** (*lake*) embalse *m*
reset [,ri·'set] *vt irr* **1.** (*machine*) reajustar; COMPUT reiniciar **2.** (*jewel*) reengastar
reset button *n* COMPUT, ELEC tecla *f* de reinicio
resettle [,ri·'set·əl] **I.** *vi* reasentarse **II.** *vt* (*person*) asentar; (*area*) repoblar
reshuffle [,ri·'ʃʌf·əl] **I.** *vt* (*a government*) reorganizar; (*cards*) volver a barajar **II.** *n* reorganización *f*
reside [rɪ·'zaɪd] *vi form* residir
residence ['rez·ɪ·dəns] *n* **1.** (*home*) domicilio *m* **2.** (*act*) residencia *f*
residence permit *n* permiso *m* de residencia
resident ['rez·ɪ·dənt] **I.** *n* residente *mf* **II.** *adj* residente
resident alien *n* extranjero , -a *m, f* con residencia
residential [,rez·ɪ·'den·ʃəl] *adj* residencial
residual [rɪ·'zɪdʒ·u·əl] *adj* residual
residue ['rez·ə·du] *n* residuo *m*
resign [rɪ·'zaɪn] **I.** *vi* **1.** (*leave job*) renunciar; POL dimitir **2.** GAMES abandonar **II.** *vt* (*leave: job*) renunciar a; POL dimitir de; **to ~ oneself to sth** resignarse a algo
resignation [,rez·ɪg·'neɪ·ʃən] *n* **1.** (*from job*) renuncia *f*; POL dimisión *f* **2.** (*conformity*) resignación *f*
resigned [rɪ·'zaɪnd] *adj* resignado, -a, botado, -a *Ecua*
resilience [rɪ·'zɪl·jəns] *n* (*of material*) elasticidad *f*; (*of person*) resistencia *f*
resilient [rɪ·'zɪl·jənt] *adj* (*material*) elástico, -a; (*person*) resistente
resin ['rez·ɪn] *n* resina *f*
resinous ['rez·ɪ·nəs] *adj* resinoso, -a
resist [rɪ·'zɪst] **I.** *vt* resistir; **to ~ doing sth** resistirse a hacer algo **II.** *vi* resistir
resistance [rɪ·'zɪs·təns] *n* resistencia *f*
resistance fighter *n* miembro *mf* de la resistencia
resistant [rɪ·'zɪs·tənt] *adj* resistente
resistor [rɪ·'zɪs·tər] *n* resistencia *f*
resolute ['rez·ə·lut] *adj* resuelto, -a
resolution [,rez·ə·'lu·ʃən] *n a.* COMPUT, PHOT, TV resolución *f*
resolvable [rɪ·'zal·və·bəl] *adj* solucionable
resolve [rɪ·'zalv] **I.** *vt* **1.** (*solve*) resolver **2.** (*settle*) acordar; **to ~ that...** acordar que... +*subj* **II.** *n* resolución *f*
resolved [rɪ·'zalvd] *adj* resuelto, -a
resonance ['rez·ə·nəns] *n* resonancia *f*
resonant ['rez·ə·nənt] *adj* resonante
resonate ['rez·ə·neɪt] *vi* resonar

R

resort [rı·'zɔrt] *n* **1.** (*use*) recurso *m;* **without ~ing to sth** sin recurrir a algo; **as a last ~** como último recurso **2.** (*for holidays*) lugar *m* de veraneo; **ski ~** estación *f* de esquí
◆**resort to** *vt* recurrir a; **to ~ violence** recurrir a la violencia
resound [rı·'zaʊnd] *vi* resonar
resounding *adj* **1.** (*noise*) resonante **2.** (*failure, success*) rotundo, -a
resource ['ri·sɔrs] **I.** *n* **1.** (*asset*) recurso *m* **2. ~s, natural ~s** recursos *mpl* naturales **3.** (*resourcefulness*) inventiva *f* ▶**to be thrown back on one's own ~s** tener que apañárselas con sus propios recursos **II.** *vt* financiar
resourceful [rı·'sɔrs·fəl] *adj* ingenioso, -a
respect [rı·'spekt] **I.** *n* **1.** (*relation*) respeto *m* **2.** (*esteem*) estima *f;* **with all due ~** con el debido respeto **3.** (*point*) respecto *m;* **in all/many/some ~s** desde todos/muchos/algunos puntos de vista; **in every ~** en todos los sentidos; **in ~ of** respecto a; **in this ~** a este respecto; **with ~ to** con respecto a **II.** *vt* respetar
respectable [rı·'spek·tə·bəl] *adj* **1.** (*person*) respetable **2.** (*behavior*) decente **3.** (*performance, result*) aceptable
respected [rı·'spek·təd] *adj* respetado, -a
respectful [rı·'spekt·fəl] *adj* respetuoso, -a
respectfully [rı·'spekt·fə·li] *adv* respetuosamente
respecting [rı·'spek·tıŋ] *prep* respecto a
respective [rı·'spek·tıv] *adj* respectivo, -a
respectively *adv* respectivamente
respiration [res·pə·'reı·ʃən] *n* respiración *f*
respirator ['res·pə·reı·t̬ər] *n* respirador *m*
respiratory ['res·pər·ə·tɔr·i] *adj* respiratorio, -a
respiratory system *n* ANAT sistema *m* respiratorio
respite ['res·pıt] *n* **1.** (*pause*) pausa *f* **2.** (*delay*) prórroga *f*
resplendent [rı·'splen·dənt] *adj* resplandeciente
respond [rı·'spand] *vi* **1.** (*answer*) contestar **2.** (*react*) responder
respondent [rı·'span·dənt] *n* **1.** (*to questionnaire*) encuestado, -a *m, f* **2.** LAW demandado, -a *m, f*
response [rı·'spans] *n* **1.** (*answer*) respuesta *f* **2.** (*reaction*) reacción *f* **3.** REL responso *m*
responsibility [rı·span·sə·'bıl·ə· t̬i] *n* responsabilidad *f*
responsible [rı·'span·sə·bəl] *adj* responsable; **to be ~ for sth/to sb** ser responsable de algo/ante alguien
responsive [rı·'span·sıv] *adj* (*person*) receptivo, -a; (*mechanism*) sensible; **to be ~ to sth** MED responder a algo
rest¹ [rest] **I.** *vt* **1.** (*cause to repose*) descansar **2.** (*support*) apoyar **3.** LAW **to ~ one's case** terminar la presentación de su alegato **II.** *vi* **1.** (*cease activity*) reposar, descansar **2.** (*remain*) quedar **3.** (*be supported*) apoyarse; **to ~ on sth** (*theory*) basarse en algo **4.** LAW concluir ▶**you can ~ assured that...** esté seguro de que... **III.** *n* **1.** (*period of repose*) descanso *m;* **to come to ~** detenerse; **at ~** (*not moving*) en reposo; (*dead*) en paz **2.** MUS pausa *f* **3.** (*support*) apoyo *m*
rest² [rest] *n* resto *m;* **the ~** (*the other people*) los demás; (*the other things*) lo demás; **for the ~** por lo demás
rest area *n* (*on highway*) parador *m*
restate [ˌri·'steıt] *vt* exponer de nuevo
restaurant ['res·tər·ant] *n* restaurante *m*
restaurateur [ˌres·tər·ə·'t̬ɜr] *n* restaurador(a) *m(f)*
rest cure *n* cura *f* de reposo
restful ['rest·fəl] *adj* tranquilo, -a, relajante
rest home *n* residencia *f* de ancianos
resting place *n* morada *f*
restitution [ˌres·tı·'tu·ʃən] *n* **1.** (*return*) restitución *f* **2.** LAW indemnización *f*
restive ['res·tıv] *adj* inquieto, -a
restless ['rest·lıs] *adj* **1.** (*agitated*) inquieto, -a **2.** (*impatient*) impaciente **3.** (*wakeful: night*) en blanco
restock [ˌri·'stak] **I.** *vt* reabastecer; (*with animals, plants*) repoblar **II.** *vi* reponer existencias
restoration [ˌres·tə·'reı·ʃən] *n* **1.** (*act of restoring: of building, painting*) restauración *f;* (*of communication, peace*) restablecimiento *m* **2.** (*return to owner*) restitución *f;* (*of stolen goods*) devolución *f*
restorative [rı·'stɔr·ə·tıv] *adj* reconstituyente
restore [rı·'stɔr] *vt* **1.** (*reestablish: building, painting*) restaurar; (*communication, peace*) restablecer; **to ~ sb's sight** hacer que alguien recobre la vista; **to ~ sb's faith in sth** hacer que alguien recupere la fe en algo; **to ~ sb to health** devolver la salud a alguien; **to ~ sb to power** volver a colocar a alguien en el poder **2.** *form* (*return to owner*) restituir
restorer [rı·'stɔr·ər] *n* restaurador(a) *m(f)*
restrain [rı·'streın] *vt* (*person, animal*) contener; (*ambition*) dominar; (*trade*) restringir; (*inflation*) frenar; **to ~ sb from doing sth** impedir que alguien haga algo; **to ~ oneself** contenerse
restrained [rı·'streınd] *adj* (*person*) comedido, -a; (*style*) sobrio, -a; (*criticism, policy*) moderado, -a
restraint [rı·'streınt] *n* **1.** (*self-control*) dominio *m* de sí mismo; **to exercise ~** form mostrarse comedido **2.** (*restriction*) restricción *f*
restrict [rı·'strıkt] *vt* (*limit*) restringir; **to ~ oneself** limitarse
restricted *adj* **1.** (*limited*) restringido, -a; (*document*) confidencial; (*parking*) limitado, -a; **entry is ~ to...** sólo se permite la entrada a... **2.** (*small: space*) reducido, -a; (*existence, horizon*) limitado, -a
restricted area *n* MIL zona *f* restringida
restriction [rı·'strık·ʃən] *n* restricción *f;* **speed ~** límite *m* de velocidad; **to impose ~s on sth**

imponer restricciones a algo
restrictive [rɪ·'strɪk·tɪv] *adj* restrictivo, -a
restring [ˌri·'strɪŋ] *irr vt* (*instrument, tennis racket*) volver a encordar; (*necklace*) reensartar
rest room *n* aseos *mpl*, baños *mpl* Col
restructure [ˌri·'strʌk·tʃər] *vt* reestructurar
restructuring *n* reestructuración *f*
rest stop *n* (*on highway*) parada *f*
result [rɪ·'zʌlt] I. *n a.* MATH, SPORTS, POL resultado *m*; (*of exam*) nota *f*; **to get ~ s** obtener buenos resultados; **with no ~** sin resultado; **as a ~ of** a consecuencia de; **as a ~** por consiguiente II. *vi* **to ~ from** ser consecuencia de; **to ~ in** ocasionar
resultant [rɪ·'zʌl·tənt] *adj* resultante
resume [rɪ·'zum] I. *vt* **1.** (*start again: work, journey*) reanudar; (*speech*) proseguir con **2.** *form* (*reoccupy: place*) volver a ocupar; (*duties*) volver a asumir II. *vi form* proseguir
résumé ['rez·u·meɪ] *n* **1.** (*summary*) resumen *m* **2.** (*for jobs*) currículum *m* (vitae), hoja de vida *f Col*
resumption [rɪ·'zʌmp·ʃən] *n* **1.** (*of journey, work*) reanudación *f* **2.** (*of power, duties*) reasunción *f*
resurface [ˌri·'sɜr·fɪs] I. *vi* volver a salir a la superficie; *fig* resurgir II. *vt* repavimentar
resurgence [rɪ·'sɜr·dʒəns] *n form* resurgimiento *m*
resurgent [rɪ·'sɜr·dʒənt] *adj form* renaciente
resurrect [ˌrez·ə·'rekt] *vt a. fig* resucitar
resurrection [ˌrez·ə·'rek·ʃən] *n* resurrección *f*
resuscitate [rɪ·'sʌs·ə·teɪt] *vt* resucitar
retail ['ri·teɪl] COM I. *n* venta *f* al detalle, venta al por menor *f Col* II. *vt* vender al detalle III. *vi* venderse al detalle; **this product ~s at $5** el precio de venta al público de este producto es 5 dólares IV. *adv* al detalle
retail business *n* comercio *m* minorista
retailer *n* minorista *mf*, menorista *mf Chile, Méx*
retailing *n* venta *f* al detalle, venta al por menor *f Col*
retail outlet *n* COM punto *m* de venta
retail price *n* COM precio *m* de venta al público
retail price index *n* ECON índice *m* de precios al consumo
retail trade *n* ECON comercio *m* minorista
retain [rɪ·'teɪn] *vt* **1.** *form* (*keep: power*) retener; (*property*) quedarse con; (*right*) reservarse; (*title*) revalidar **2.** (*not lose: dignity*) mantener; (*color*) conservar **3.** (*hold in place: water*) contener **4.** (*remember*) retener **5.** (*employ*) contratar
retainer *n* **1.** ECON iguala *f* **2.** (*servant*) criado, -a *m, f*
retaining wall *n* muro *m* de contención
retake[1] [ˌri·'teɪk] *vt irr* **1.** (*recapture: town*) volver a tomar; (*person*) volver a capturar; **to ~ the lead** recuperar el liderazgo **2.** SCHOOL, UNIV (*exam*) volver a presentarse a **3.** CINE volver a rodar; PHOT volver a hacer

retake[2] ['ri·teɪk] *n* CINE toma *f* repetida
retaliate [rɪ·'tæl·i·eɪt] *vi* tomar represalias
retaliation [rɪ·ˌtæl·i·'eɪ·ʃən] *n* represalias *fpl*
retaliatory [rɪ·'tæl·i·ə·tɔr·i] *adj* vengativo, -a; **~ measures** represalias *fpl*
retard [rɪ·'tard] *vt form* (*growth, development*) retardar; (*journey*) retrasar; **mentally ~ed person** retrasado , -a *m, f* mental
retardation [ˌri·tar·'deɪ·ʃən] *n form* retraso *m*
retarded *adj* **1.** *offensive* (*mentally ill*) retardado mental **2.** *sl* (*very stupid*) retardado
retch [retʃ] *vi* tener arcadas [*o* náuseas]
retention [rɪ·'ten·ʃən] *n* **1.** *form* (*keeping: of properties, heat*) retención *f*; (*of rules, laws*) mantenimiento *m* **2.** *form* (*memory*) retentiva *f* **3.** (*of lawyer, consultant*) contratación *f*
retentive [rɪ·'ten·tɪv] *adj* retentivo, -a; **he's very ~** tiene muy buena memoria
rethink[1] [ˌri·'θɪŋk] *vt irr* replantearse
rethink[2] ['ri·θɪŋk] *n* replanteamiento *m*
reticent ['ret·ə·sənt] *adj* reticente
retina ['ret·nə] <-s *o* -nae> *n* retina *f*
retinue ['ret·ən·u] *n inv* séquito *m*
retire [rɪ·'taɪr] I. *vi* **1.** (*stop working*) jubilarse; (*soldier, athlete*) retirarse **2.** *form* (*withdraw*) retirarse; **to ~ to the drawing room** pasar al salón **3.** MIL replegarse **4.** SPORTS (*from a race*) abandonar II. *vt* **1.** (*stop working*) jubilar **2.** MIL (*soldier*) retirar **3.** FIN (*bond*) redimir
retired *adj* jubilado, -a; (*soldier, athlete*) retirado, -a
retirement [rɪ·'taɪr·mənt] *n* **1.** (*act of retiring*) retiro *m*; (*from race*) abandono *m* **2.** (*after working*) jubilación *f*; (*of soldier, athlete*) retiro *m*; **to be in ~** estar jubilado; **to come out of ~** salir de su retiro **3.** MIL retirada *f*
retirement age *n* edad *f* de jubilarse
retirement pay *n*, **retirement pension** *n* pensión *f* de jubilación
retiring *adj* **1.** (*reserved*) reservado, -a **2.** (*worker, official*) saliente
retort [rɪ·'tɔrt] I. *vt* replicar II. *vi* replicar III. *n* **1.** (*reply*) réplica *f* **2.** CHEM retorta *f*
retouch [ˌri·'tʌtʃ] *vt a.* ART, PHOT retocar
retrace [ri·'treɪs] *vt* repasar; **to ~ one's steps** volver sobre sus pasos
retract [rɪ·'trækt] I. *vt* **1.** (*statement, offer*) retirar **2.** (*claws*) retraer; (*wheels*) replegar II. *vi* **1.** (*withdraw statement, offer*) retractarse **2.** (*be withdrawn: claws*) retraerse; (*wheels*) replegarse
retractable [rɪ·'træk·tə·bəl] *adj* retráctil
retraction [rɪ·'træk·ʃən] *n* (*of statement, offer*) retractación *f*
retrain [ri·'treɪn] I. *vt* reconvertir II. *vi* hacer un curso de perfeccionamiento
retread[1] [ri·'tred] *vt* (*a tire*) recauchutar, reencauchar *Col, Perú*
retread[2] ['ri·tred] *n* neumático *m* recauchutado [*o* reencauchado]
retreat [rɪ·'trit] I. *vi* retroceder; MIL batirse en retirada II. *n* **1.** (*withdrawal*) *a.* MIL retirada *f*; (*signal*) retreta *f*; **to sound the ~** dar el toque

de retreta **2.**(*safe place*) refugio *m* **3.**(*seclusion*) retiro *m;* **to go on a** ~ hacer un retiro espiritual

retrench [rɪ'trentʃ] **I.** *vi* reducir costes **II.** *vt* (*reduce: personnel, expenses*) reducir; (*soldiers*) atrincherar

retrenchment *n* **1.**(*spending cut*) reducción *f* de gastos **2.**(*cutting down*) supresión *f* **3.**(*entrenchment*) atrincheramiento *m*

retrial ['ri·traɪl] *n* nuevo juicio *m*

retribution [ˌret·rə·'bju·ʃən] *n form* castigo *m* justo; **divine** ~ justicia *f* divina

retributive [rɪ'trɪb·jə·t̬ɪv] *adj form* punitivo, -a

retrieval [rɪ'tri·vəl] *n* (*finding*) a. COMPUT recuperación *f*; **on-line information** ~ recuperación de información en línea

retrieve [rɪ'triv] **I.** *vt* **1.**(*get back*) a. COMPUT recuperar **2.**(*make amends for: error*) enmendar **3.**(*repair: loss*) reparar; (*situation*) salvar **4.** SPORTS (*game*) cobrar; (*in tennis*) devolver **II.** *vi* SPORTS cobrar

retriever [rɪ'tri·vər] *n* perro *m* cobrador

retroactive [ˌret·rou·'æk·t̬ɪv] *adj* retroactivo, -a

retrograde ['ret·rə·greɪd] *adj* retrógrado, -a

retrospect ['ret·rə·spekt] *n* **in** ~ mirando hacia atrás

retrospective [ˌret·rə·'spek·t̬ɪv] **I.** *adj* **1.**(*looking back*) retrospectivo, -a **2.** LAW retroactivo, -a **II.** *n* ART exposición *f* retrospectiva

return [rɪ'tɜrn] **I.** *n* **1.**(*going back*) regreso *m;* (*home, to work, to school*) vuelta *f;* **on his** ~ a su regreso **2.**(*to previous situation*) retorno *m;* **a** ~ **to sth** un restablecimiento de algo **3.** MED (*of illness*) recaída *f* **4.**(*giving back*) devolución *f* **5.**(*recompense*) recompensa *f* **6.** FIN (*proceeds*) ganancia *f;* (*interest*) rédito *m;* ~ **on capital** interés *m* del capital **7.** ~ **s** POL resultados *mpl* de las elecciones **8.** COMPUT (tecla *f* de) retorno *m* **9.**(*report*) informe *m* **10.** FIN declaración *f* ▶ **many happy** ~**s!** ¡feliz cumpleaños!; **by** ~ **mail** a vuelta de correo; **in** ~ **for sth** a cambio de algo **II.** *adj* **1.**(*coming back*): *flight, journey*) de vuelta **2.** THEAT (*performance*) segundo, -a **III.** *vi* **1.**(*come back*) volver; (*home*) regresar a; (*to task*) reanudar **2.**(*reappear*) volver a aparecer **IV.** *vt* **1.**(*give back*) devolver **2.**(*reciprocate*) corresponder a; (*compliment, favor, ball*) devolver; **to** ~ **sb's call** devolver la llamada a alguien; **to** ~ **good for evil** devolver bien por mal **3.**(*send back*) volver a colocar; ~ **to sender** devuélvase al remitente **4.** FIN (*yield*) dar; (*profit*) proporcionar **5.** LAW (*pronounce: verdict*) emitir; (*judgment*) dictar **6.** POL (*elect*) elegir; (*re-elect*) reelegir **7.** ECON (*income*) declarar

returnable [rɪ'tɜr·nə·bəl] *adj* (*fee*) reembolsable; (*bottle*) retornable

return flight *n* viaje *m* de vuelta

return journey *n* viaje *m* de vuelta

return key *n* COMPUT tecla *f* de retorno

return ticket *n* billete *m* de vuelta

reunification [ri·ju·nə·fɪ·'keɪ·ʃən] *n* reunificación *f*

reunion [ˌri·'jun·jən] *n* **1.**(*meeting*) reunión *f* **2.**(*after separation*) reencuentro *m*

reunite [ˌri·ju·'naɪt] **I.** *vt* **1.**(*bring together*) volver a unir **2.**(*friends*) reconciliar **II.** *vi* reunirse

reusable [ˌri·'ju·zə·bəl] *adj* reutilizable

reuse [ˌri·'juz] *vt* volver a usar

rev. [rev] *n* AUTO revolution *f*

Rev. *abbr of* **Reverend** Rev.

◆**rev up** AUTO **I.** *vt* <-vv-> acelerar **II.** *vi* embalarse

revaluation [ri·væl·ju·'eɪ·ʃən] *n* revaluación *f*

revalue [ri·'væl·ju] *vt* revaluar

revamp [ˌri·'væmp] *vt inf* modernizar

reveal [rɪ'vil] *vt* **1.**(*divulge: secret, identity*) revelar; **he** ~ **d his identity** desveló su identidad; **to** ~ **how/why...** manifestar cómo/el porqué... **2.**(*uncover*) descubrir

revealing [rɪ'vi·lɪŋ] *adj* revelador(a)

reveille ['rev·ə·li] *n* MIL diana *f*

revel ['rev·əl] <-ll-, -l-> *vi* ir de juerga

◆**revel in** <-ll-, -l-> *vi* **to** ~ **sth** deleitarse con algo

revelation [ˌrev·ə·'leɪ·ʃən] *n* revelación *f;* **the Book of Revelations** el Apocalipsis

reveler *n,* **reveller** *n* juerguista *mf*

revelry ['rev·əl·ri] <-ies> *n* jolgorio *m*

revenge [rɪ'vendʒ] **I.** *n* **1.**(*retaliation*) venganza *f;* **in** ~ (**for sth**) como venganza (por algo); **to take** ~ (**on sb**) **for sth** tomar venganza (en [*o* de] alguien) de [*o* por] algo **2.** SPORTS revancha *f* **II.** *vt* vengar; **to** ~ **oneself** vengarse de alguien

revenue ['rev·ə·nu] *n* **1.**(*income*) ingresos *mpl* **2.**(*of government*) rentas *fpl* públicas; **tax** ~ declaración *f* de renta

reverberate [rɪ'vɜr·bə·reɪt] *vi* **1.**(*sound, light, heat*) reverberar **2.** *fig* tener gran repercusión

reverberation [rɪ·vɜr·bə·'reɪ·ʃən] *n* **1.**(*of sound, heat, light*) reverberación *f* **2.** *fig* repercusión *f*

revere [rɪ'vɪr] *vt* venerar

reverence ['rev·ər·əns] *n* veneración *f;* **to pay** ~ **to sth/sb** rendir homenaje a algo/alguien

reverend ['rev·ər·ənd] *adj* reverendo, -a

Reverend ['rev·ər·ənd] REL **I.** *adj* **the Most** ~ reverendísimo; **the Right** ~ el obispo; **the Most** ~ el arzobispo **II.** *n* (*Protestant*) pastor *m;* (*Catholic*) sacerdote *m*

reverent ['rev·ər·ənt] *adj* reverente

reverential [ˌrev·ə·'ren·ʃəl] *adj* reverencial

reverie ['rev·ə·ri] *n liter* ensueño *m;* **to be** (**lost**) **in** ~ estar absorto

reversal [rɪ'vɜr·səl] *n* **1.**(*change: of order, opinion*) inversión *f;* (*of policy*) cambio *m* completo; LAW (*of decision*) revocación *f* **2.**(*setback*) revés *m*

reverse [rɪ'vɜrs] **I.** *vt* (*turn other way*) volver al revés; (*order*) invertir; (*policy, situation*) cambiar radicalmente; (*judgment*) revocar; **to** ~ **the charges** TEL llamar a cobro revertido **II.** *vi* (*order, situation*) invertirse **III.** *n* **1.** **the** ~ lo contrario; **in** ~ a la inversa **2.** AUTO (*gear*) marcha *f* atrás; **to go into** ~ dar marcha atrás **3.** (*setback*) revés *m* **4.** (*the back*) reverso *m;* (*of cloth*) revés *m;* (*of document*) dorso *m* **IV.** *adj* **1.** (*inverse*) inverso, -a **2.** (*opposite: direction*) contrario, -a

reverse gear *n* AUTO marcha *f* atrás, reversa *f* Col

reversible [rɪ·ˈvɜr·sə·bəl] *adj* **1.** (*jacket*) reversible **2.** (*decision*) revocable

reversion [rɪ·ˈvɜr·ʒən] *n* reversión *f*

revert [rɪ·ˈvɜrt] *vi* volver; **to ~ to type** *fig* volver a ser el mismo de siempre

review [rɪ·ˈvju] **I.** *vt* **1.** (*consider*) analizar **2.** (*reconsider*) reexaminar; (*salary*) reajustar **3.** (*look over: notes*) revisar **4.** (*criticize: book, play, film*) hacer una crítica [*o* reseña] de **5.** MIL (*inspect*) pasar revista a **6.** (*study again*) repasar **II.** *n* **1.** (*examination*) análisis *m inv;* **to come under ~** ser examinado; **to hold a ~** MIL pasar revista **2.** (*reconsideration*) revisión *f;* **to come up for ~** estar pendiente de revisión **3.** (*summary*) resumen *m* **4.** (*criticism: of book, play, film*) crítica *f,* reseña *f* **5.** (*magazine*) revista *f* **6.** THEAT revista *f*

reviewer [rɪ·ˈvju·ər] *n* crítico, -a *m, f*

revise [rɪ·ˈvaɪz] *vt* (*alter: text, law*) revisar; (*proofs*) corregir; (*opinion*) cambiar de

revision [rɪ·ˈvɪʒ·ən] *n* **1.** (*of text, law*) revisión *f;* (*of proofs*) corrección *f;* (*of policy*) modificación *f* **2.** (*book*) edición *f* corregida

revisionist [rɪ·ˈvɪʒ·ə·nɪst] *n* revisionista *mf*

revitalize [ri·ˈvaɪ·tə·laɪz] *vt* revitalizar; (*trade*) reactivar

revival [rɪ·ˈvaɪ·vəl] *n* **1.** MED reanimación *f* **2.** (*rebirth: of interest*) renacimiento *m;* (*of idea, custom*) restablecimiento *m;* (*of economy*) reactivación *f;* (*of country*) resurgimiento *m* **3.** CINE, THEAT reestreno *m* **4.** REL despertar *m* religioso

revive [rɪ·ˈvaɪv] **I.** *vt* **1.** MED reanimar **2.** (*resurrect: interest*) hacer renacer; (*idea, custom*) restablecer; (*economy*) reactivar; (*conversation*) reanimar **3.** CINE, THEAT reestrenar **II.** *vi* **1.** (*be restored to life*) volver en sí **2.** (*be restored: country, interest*) resurgir; (*tradition*) restablecerse; (*style*) volver a estar de moda; (*trade, economy*) reactivarse

revocation [rev·ə·ˈkeɪ·ʃən] *n* **1.** (*of license*) suspensión *f* **2.** (*of law, decision*) revocación *f*

revoke [rɪ·ˈvoʊk] **I.** *vt* **1.** (*cancel: decision, order*) revocar **2.** (*license*) suspender **II.** *vi* GAMES renunciar

revolt [rɪ·ˈvoʊlt] POL **I.** *vi* rebelarse, alzarse *AmL;* **to ~ against sb/sth** sublevarse contra alguien/algo **II.** *vt* repugnar a; **it ~s me** me da asco **III.** *n* **1.** (*uprising*) revuelta *f;* **to rise in ~ against sb/sth** alzarse contra alguien/algo **2.** (*rebelliousness*) rebeldía *f*

revolting [rɪ·ˈvoʊl·tɪŋ] *adj* (*disgusting*) repugnante; **to look ~** tener un aspecto horrible

revolution [rev·ə·ˈlu·ʃən] *n a.* POL revolución *f*

revolutionary [rev·ə·ˈlu·ʃə·ner·i] **I.** <-ies> *n* revolucionario, -a *m, f* **II.** *adj* revolucionario, -a

revolutionize [rev·ə·ˈlu·ʃə·naɪz] *vt* revolucionar

revolve [rɪ·ˈvalv] *vi* girar; **to ~ on an axis** girar en torno a un eje; **that problem was revolving in his mind** aquel problema le daba vueltas en la cabeza

◆**revolve around** *vi a. fig* girar alrededor

revolver [rɪ·ˈval·vər] *n* revólver *m*

revolving *adj* giratorio, -a

revolving door *n* puerta *f* giratoria

revue [rɪ·ˈvju] *n* THEAT revista *f*

revulsion [rɪ·ˈvʌl·ʃən] *n* repulsión *f*

reward [rɪ·ˈwɔrd] **I.** *n* recompensa *f* **II.** *vt* recompensar

rewarding *adj* gratificante

rewind [ri·ˈwaɪnd] *irr* **I.** *vt* (*tape*) rebobinar; (*clock, watch*) dar cuerda a **II.** *vi* rebobinarse

rewire [ri·ˈwaɪr] *vt* renovar la instalación eléctrica de

reword [ri·ˈwɜrd] *vt* **1.** (*rewrite*) volver a redactar **2.** (*say again*) expresar de otra manera

rework [ri·ˈwɜk] *vt* revisar; (*theme*) adaptar

rewound [ri·ˈwaʊnd] *pt of* **rewind**

rewrite[1] [ri·ˈraɪt] *irr vt* volver a redactar

rewrite[2] [ˈri·raɪt] *n* nueva versión *f*

Rh *abbr of* **rhesus** Rh

rhapsody [ˈræp·sə·di] <-ies> *n* **1.** MUS rapsodia *f* **2.** (*enthusiasm*) éxtasis *m inv*

rhesus factor [ˈri·səs·fæk·tər] *n* MED factor *m* Rhesus

rhetoric [ˈret·ər·ɪk] *n* retórica *f*

rhetorical [rɪ·ˈtɔr·ɪ·kəl] *adj* retórico, -a

rhetorical question *n* pregunta *f* retórica

rheumatic [ru·ˈmæt̬·ɪk] *adj* reumático, -a

rheumatism [ˈru·mə·tɪz·əm] *n* reumatismo *m*

rheumatoid arthritis [ru·mə·tɔɪd·ˌar·ˈθraɪ·tɪs] *n* MED artritis *f inv* reumatoidea

rhinestone [ˈraɪn·stoʊn] *n* diamante *m* falso

rhino [ˈraɪ·noʊ] *n inf abbr of* **rhinoceros** rinoceronte *m*

R

rhinoceros [raɪˈnas·ər·əs] <-(es)> *n* rinoceronte *m*
rhinoplasty [ˈraɪ·noʊˌplæs·ti] *n* rinoplastia *f*
Rhode Island [ˌroʊdˈaɪ·ləd] *n* Rhode Island *m*
rhododendron [ˌroʊ·dəˈden·drən] *n* rododendro *m*
rhombus [ˈram·bəs] <-es *o* -i> *n* rombo *m*
rhubarb [ˈru·barb] *n* ruibarbo *m*
rhyme [raɪm] I. *n* 1. (*similar sound*) rima *f;* in ~ en verso 2. (*poem*) poesía *f* ▶ without ~ or reason sin ton ni son II. *vi* rimar
rhyming couplet [ˌraɪ·mɪŋˈkʌp·lɪt] *n* pareado *m*
rhythm [ˈrɪð·əm] *n* ritmo *m*
rhythmic [ˈrɪð·mɪk] *adj*, **rhythmical** *adj* rítmico, -a
RI *n abbr of* **Rhode Island** Rhode Island *m*
rib [rɪb] I. *n* 1. (*bone*) costilla *f;* to dig sb in the ~s dar a alguien un codazo en el costado 2. NAUT cuaderna *f* 3. FASHION canalé *m* II. <-bb-> *vt inf* tomar el pelo a
ribald [ˈrɪb·əld] *adj* picaresco, -a
ribbon [ˈrɪb·ən] *n* (*long strip*) cinta *f;* (*on medal*) galón *m;* to be cut to ~s estar hecho jirones
rib cage *n* tórax *m*
ribonucleic acid [ˌraɪ·boʊ·nu·kleɪ·ɪkˈæs·ɪd] *n* ácido *m* ribonucleico
rice [raɪs] I. *n* arroz *m* II. *vt* (*potatoes*) pasar
rice field *n* arrozal *m*
rice-growing *n* arrozal *m*
rice paddy *n* arrozal *m*
rice paper *n* papel *m* de arroz
rice pudding *n* arroz *m* con leche
rich [rɪtʃ] I. <-er, -est> *adj* 1. (*person*) rico, -a; (*soil*) fértil; (*furnishings*) opulento, -a; ~ pickings ganancias *fpl;* to become ~ enriquecerse; to be ~ in sth abundar en algo 2. (*stimulating: life, experience, history*) rico, -a 3. (*food*) pesado, -a 4. (*intense: color*) brillante; (*flavor*) intenso, -a; (*tone*) profundo, -a II. *n* the ~ los ricos
richness *n* 1. (*affluence*) riqueza *f;* (*of soil*) fertilidad *f* 2. (*of food*) pesadez *f* 3. (*intensity: of color*) brillantez *f;* (*of flavor*) intensidad *f*
rickets [ˈrɪk·ɪts] *n* raquitismo *m*
rickety [ˈrɪk·ə·ṭi] *adj* (*car*) desvencijado, -a; (*steps*) tambaleante; (*person*) raquítico, -a
rickshaw [ˈrɪk·ʃɔ] *n* carro *m* de culi
ricochet [ˈrɪk·ə·ʃeɪ] I. *vi* rebotar II. *n* rebote *m*
ricotta cheese [rɪˈka·ṭəˈtʃiz] *n* requesón *m*
rid [rɪd] <rid *o* ridded, rid> *vt* to ~ sth/sb of sth librar algo/a alguien de algo; to ~ oneself of sth librarse de algo; to be ~ of sth/sb estar libre de algo/alguien; to get ~ of sb/sth deshacerse de alguien/algo
riddance [ˈrɪd·əns] *n inf* good ~! ¡vete con viento fresco!; to bid sb good ~ desear a alguien un adiós y hasta nunca
ridden [ˈrɪd·ən] *pp of* **ride**
riddle¹ [ˈrɪd·əl] *n* 1. (*conundrum*) adivinanza *f* 2. *fig* (*mystery*) misterio *m;* to speak in ~s hablar en clave

riddle² [ˈrɪd·əl] *vt* acribillar; to be ~d with mistakes estar plagado, -a de errores
ride [raɪd] I. *n* (*on horse, motorcycle, car*) paseo *m;* to give sb a ~ llevar a alguien ▶ to take sb for a ~ *sl* tomar el pelo a alguien II. <rode, ridden> *vt* 1. (*sit on*) to ~ a bike en bici, montar en bicicleta *Col;* to ~ a horse montar a caballo; can you ~ a bike? ¿sabes montar en bici?; to ~ the waves surcar las olas 2. *inf* (*tease*) meterse con; to ~ sb about sth meterse con alguien por [*o* acerca de] algo III. <rode, ridden> *vi* 1. (*on horse, motorcycle*) montar; to ~ on a horse montar a caballo; to ~ by bicycle ir en bicicleta 2. (*do well*) to ~ high alcanzar popularidad 3. *inf* (*take no action*) to let sth ~ dejar pasar algo
♦ **ride down** *vt* atropellar
♦ **ride out** *vt a. fig* aguantar
♦ **ride up** *vi* (*person*) acercarse; (*dress*) subirse
rider [ˈraɪ·dər] *n* 1. (*on horse*) jinete *m*, amazona *f;* (*on bicycle*) ciclista *mf;* (*on motorcycle*) motociclista *mf* 2. LAW cláusula *f* adicional
ridge [rɪdʒ] *n* 1. GEO cresta *f* 2. METEO sistema *m* de altas presiones 3. (*of roof*) caballete *m*
ridgepole [ˈrɪdʒ·poʊl] *n* parhilera *f*
ridgeway [ˈrɪdʒ·weɪ] *n* ruta *f* de las crestas
ridicule [ˈrɪd·ɪ·kjul] I. *n* burlas *fpl;* to be an object of ~ ser el hazmerreír; to hold sb/sth up to ~ ridiculizar a alguien/algo II. *vt* ridiculizar
ridiculous [rɪˈdɪk·ju·ləs] *adj* ridículo, -a
riding *n* equitación *f*
riding breeches *n* pantalones *mpl* de montar
riding crop *n* fusta *f*
riding school *n* escuela *f* de equitación
riding whip *n s.* **riding crop**
rife [raɪf] *adj* extendido, -a; to be ~ with sth estar plagado, -a de algo
riffle [ˈrɪf·əl] *vt* (*cards*) barajar; (*pages*) volver; (*book*) hojear
riffraff [ˈrɪf·ræf] *n* chusma *f*
rifle¹ [ˈraɪ·fəl] *n* fusil *m*, rifle *m*
rifle² [ˈraɪ·fəl] I. *vt* 1. (*plunder*) saquear 2. (*steal*) robar II. *vt* revolver III. *vi* to ~ through sth rebuscar en algo
rifle butt *n* culata *f* de rifle
rifleman <-men> *n* fusilero *m*
rifle range *n* campo *m* de tiro
rifle shot *n* tiro *m* de fusil
rift [rɪft] *n* 1. (*in earth*) fisura *f* 2. *fig* ruptura *f;* to heal the ~ cerrar la brecha
rift zone *n* GEO falla *f*
rig [rɪg] <-gg-> I. *vt* 1. (*falsify*) amañar 2. NAUT aparejar II. *n* 1. TECH (*oil*) ~ plataforma *f* petrolífera 2. (*truck*) camión *m* 3. NAUT aparejo *m* 4. *inf* (*clothing*) atuendo *m*
rigger [ˈrɪg·ər] *n* NAUT aparejador(a) *m(f)*
rigging [ˈrɪg·ɪŋ] *n* 1. (*of result*) pucherazo *m;* ballot ~ fraude *m* electoral 2. NAUT jarcia *f*
right [raɪt] I. *adj* 1. (*correct*) correcto, -a; (*ethical*) justo, -a; (*change*) oportuno, -a; it is ~

that... es justo que...; **to be ~ (about sth)** tener razón (en algo), estar en lo cierto (sobre algo) *AmL;* **to do sth the ~ way** hacer algo correctamente; **to do the ~ thing** hacer lo que se debe hacer; **to be in the ~ place at the ~ time** estar en el lugar indicado en el momento indicado; **to be on the ~ side of forty** tener menos de cuarenta años **2.** (*direction*) derecho, -a; **a ~ hook** SPORTS un gancho de derecha **3.** POL de derechas **4.** (*well*) bueno, -a; **to be not (quite) ~ in the head** *inf* no estar muy bien de la cabeza **II.** *n* **1.** (*entitlement*) derecho *m;* **to have the ~ to do sth** tener el derecho de hacer algo **2.** (*morality*) **to be in the ~** tener razón **3.** (*right side*) derecha *f;* SPORTS derechazo *m* **4.** POL **the Right** la derecha **III.** *adv* **1.** (*correctly*) correctamente; **to do ~** obrar bien **2.** (*straight*) directamente; **~ away** inmediatamente **3.** (*to the right*) hacia la derecha **4.** (*precisely*) precisamente; **~ here** justo aquí; **to be ~ behind sb** estar inmediatamente detrás de alguien **IV.** *vt* **1.** (*rectify*) rectificar; (*mistake*) enmendar **2.** (*straighten*) enderezar **V.** *interj* de acuerdo, órale *Méx*

right angle *n* ángulo *m* recto

right-angled ['raɪt·ˌæŋ·gəld] *adj* en ángulo recto

righteous ['raɪ·tʃəs] **I.** *adj form* **1.** (*person*) virtuoso, -a **2.** (*indignation*) justificado, -a; (*tone*) de superioridad moral **II.** *n* **the ~** los justos

rightful ['raɪt·fəl] *adj* legítimo, -a

right-hand [ˌraɪt·'hænd] *adj* **on the ~ side** a la derecha

right-handed [ˌraɪt·'hæn·dɪd] *adj* diestro, -a

right-hander *n* **1.** (*person*) diestro, -a *m, f* **2.** (*punch*) derechazo *m*

rightist ['raɪ·tɪst] POL **I.** *n* derechista *mf* **II.** *adj* de derechas

rightly *adv* **1.** (*correctly*) correctamente; **if I remember ~** si recuerdo bien **2.** (*justifiably*) con razón; (*whether*) **~ or wrongly** con razón o sin ella

right-minded [ˌraɪt·'maɪn·dɪd] *adj* sensato, -a

right of way <-rights> *n* **1.** (*over private land*) servidumbre *f* de paso **2.** (*on road*) preferencia *f*

right-wing [ˌraɪt·'wɪŋ] *adj* POL de derechas; **to be ~** ser de derechas

right-winger *n* POL derechista *mf*

rigid ['rɪdʒ·ɪd] *adj* **1.** (*stiff*) rígido, -a; **to be ~ with fear/pain** estar paralizado, -a de miedo/ dolor **2.** (*inflexible*) inflexible; (*censorship*) estricto, -a **3.** (*intransigent*) intransigente

rigidity [rɪ·'dʒɪd·ə·ţi] *n* **1.** (*hardness*) rigidez *f* **2.** (*inflexibility*) inflexibilidad *f* **3.** (*intransigence*) intransigencia *f*

rigmarole ['rɪg·mə·roʊl] *n* galimatías *m inv*

rigor ['rɪg·ər] *n* (*severity*) rigor *m;* (*hardship*) desdicha *f*

rigor mortis [ˌrɪg·ər·'mɔr·ţɪs] *n* MED rigidez *f* cadavérica

rigorous ['rɪg·ər·əs] *adj* riguroso, -a

rile [raɪl] *vt inf* irritar

rim [rɪm] **I.** *n* **1.** (*of cup, bowl*) canto *m* **2.** (*frame for eyeglasses*) montura *f* **3.** GEO borde *m;* **the Pacific ~** los países de la costa del Pacífico **4.** (*dirty mark*) redondel *m* **II.** <-mm-> *vt* **1.** (*surround*) bordear **2.** (*frame*) enmarcar

rimless ['rɪm·lɪs] *adj* (*eyeglasses*) sin montura

rind [raɪnd] *n* (*of fruit*) cáscara *f;* (*of bacon, cheese*) corteza *f*

ring¹ [rɪŋ] **I.** *n* **1.** (*small circle*) círculo *m;* (*of people*) corro *m;* (*around eyes*) ojera *f* **2.** (*jewelry*) anillo *m* **3.** (*arena*) ruedo *m;* (*in boxing*) cuadrilátero *m;* (*in circus*) pista *f* **II.** *vt* **1.** (*surround*) rodear; **to be ~ed by sth** estar cercado, -a con algo **2.** (*bird*) anillar

ring² [rɪŋ] **I.** *n* **1.** (*metallic sound*) sonido *m* metálico; (*of bell*) toque *m* **2.** (*telephone call*) llamada *f;* **to give sb a ~** llamar a alguien (por teléfono) **II.** <rang, rung> *vt* (*bell*) tocar; (*alarm*) hacer sonar **III.** <rang, rung> *vi* (*telephone, bell*) sonar; **to ~ false/true** sonar falso/convincente

♦**ring in** *vt* **to ~ the New Year** recibir el Año Nuevo

♦**ring out** *vi* resonar

♦**ring up** *vt* COM (*at cash register*) **to ~ sb up** registrar la compra de alguien en la registradora

ringer ['rɪŋ·ər] *n* **to be a dead ~ (for sb)** *sl* ser el vivo retrato (de alguien)

ring finger *n* dedo *m* anular

ringing ['rɪŋ·ɪŋ] **I.** *n* repique *m* **II.** *adj* sonoro, -a

ringleader ['rɪŋ·ˌli·dər] *n* cabecilla *mf*

ringlet ['rɪŋ·lɪt] *n* tirabuzón *m,* crespo *m Col, Cuba*

ringside ['rɪŋ·saɪd] **I.** *n* **to be at the ~** estar junto al cuadrilátero **II.** *adj* (*seats*) de primera fila

ringtone *n* TEL ringtone *m* (*tono de repique que advierte una llamada en el celular*)

ringworm ['rɪŋ·wɜrm] *n* tiña *f*

rink [rɪŋk] *n* pista *f* de patinaje

rinse [rɪns] **I.** *vt* (*dishes, clothes*) enjuagar; (*hands*) lavar **II.** *n* **1.** (*wash*) enjuague *m;* **cold/hot ~** aclarado *m* frío/caliente **2.** (*hair coloring*) reflejos *mpl,* rayitos *mpl Col*

riot ['raɪ·ət] **I.** *n* **1.** disturbio *m;* **a ~ of color** un derroche de color; **to be a ~** *sl* ser la monda **II.** *vi* causar disturbios **III.** *adv* **to run ~** *fig* desmandarse; **to let one's imagination run ~** dar rienda suelta a su imaginación

rioter *n* alborotador(a) *m(f)*

riot gear *n* uniforme *m* antidisturbios

rioting *n* disturbios *mpl*

riotous ['raɪ·ə·ţəs] *adj* **1.** (*rebellious*) descontrolado, -a **2.** (*uproarious*) escandaloso, -a; (*party*) desenfrenado, -a

riot police *n* policía *f* antidisturbios

rip [rɪp] **I.** <-pp-> *vi* rasgarse **II.** <-pp-> *vt* rasgar; **to ~ sth open** abrir algo de un rasgón **III.** *n* rasgón *m,* rajo *m AmC*

♦**rip down** *vt* arrancar

♦**rip off** *vt* **1.** (*remove*) arrancar **2.** *sl*

R

(*swindle*) timar
♦**rip out** *vt* arrancar
♦**rip up** *vt* romper
RIP [ˌɑr·ɑɪ·ˈpi] *abbr of* **rest in peace** E.P.D., D.E.P
ripcord [ˈrɪp·kɔrd] *n* cordón *m* de apertura
ripe [raɪp] *adj* **1.** (*fruit*) maduro, -a; **at the ~ old age of 80** a la avanzada edad de 80 **2.** (*ready*) **the time is ~ for...** es el momento oportuno de... **3.** (*language*) atrevido, -a
ripen [ˈrɑɪ·pən] **I.** *vt* hacer madurar **II.** *vi* madurar
ripeness [ˈrɑɪp·nɪs] *n* madurez *f*
rip-off [ˈrɪp·ɔf] *n sl* timo *m*, vacilada *f Méx, inf*
ripple [ˈrɪp·əl] **I.** *n* onda *f*; ~ **of applause** unos cuantos aplausos *m* **II.** *vt* rizar **III.** *vi* rizarse
rip-roaring [ˌrɪp·ˈrɔr·ɪŋ] *adj inf* animadísimo, -a; **a ~ success** un éxito clamoroso
riptide [ˈrɪp·taɪd] *n* corriente *f* de resaca
rise [raɪz] **I.** *n* **1.** (*increase*) subida *f*; **to be on the ~** ir en aumento; **to give ~ to sth** dar lugar a algo; **to get** [*o* **take**] **a ~ out of sb** burlarse de alguien **2.** (*incline*) cuesta *f* **II.** <rose, risen> *vi* **1.** (*arise*) levantarse **2.** (*become higher: ground*) subir (en pendiente); (*temperature*) aumentar; (*river*) crecer **3.** (*go up: smoke*) subir; (*moon, sun*) salir; (*building*) elevarse **4.** (*improve socially*) ascender; (*in the ranks*) ganar; **to ~ to fame** alcanzar la fama **5.** (*be reborn*) resucitar **6.** (*rebel*) sublevarse
♦**rise above** *vt insep* **1.** (*be higher than*) estar por encima de **2.** (*problem, opposition*) superar
♦**rise up** *vi* **1.** (*arise*) levantarse **2.** (*rebel*) alzarse
risen [ˈrɪz·ən] *pp of* **rise**
riser [ˈraɪ·zər] *n* **1.** (*person*) **early ~** madrugador(a) *m(f);* **late ~** dormilón, -ona *m, f* **2.** (*part of step*) contrahuella *f*
risible [ˈrɪz·ə·bəl] *adj* risible
rising [ˈrɑɪ·zɪŋ] **I.** *n* levantamiento *m* **II.** *adj* (*in number*) creciente; (*in status*) ascendente; (*floodwaters*) en aumento; (*sun*) naciente
risk [rɪsk] **I.** *n* **1.** (*chance*) riesgo *m;* **to run the ~ of sth** correr el riesgo de algo **2.** (*danger*) peligro *m;* **at one's own ~** bajo su propia responsabilidad; **to be at ~** correr peligro **II.** *vt* arriesgar; **to ~ doing sth** arriesgarse a hacer algo; **to ~ one's life** poner la propia vida en peligro
risk capital *n* ECON capital *m* de riesgo
risk factor *n* factor *m* de riesgo
risk-free *adj*, **riskless** *adj* sin riesgo
risk liability *n* responsabilidad *f* sobre riesgos
risky [ˈrɪs·ki] <-ier, -iest> *adj* arriesgado, -a, riesgoso, -a *AmL*
risqué [rɪ·ˈskeɪ] *adj* atrevido, -a
rissole [ˈrɪs·oʊl] *n* croqueta *f*
rite [raɪt] *n* rito *m;* **last ~s** extremaunción *f*; **~ of passage** rito de paso
ritual [ˈrɪtʃ·u·əl] **I.** *n* ritual *m* **II.** *adj* ritual
ritzy [ˈrɪt·si] <-ier, -iest> *adj inf* lujoso, -a
rival [ˈrɑɪ·vəl] **I.** *n* rival *mf* **II.** *adj* competi-

dor(a); **a ~ brand** una marca rival **III.** <-ll-, -l-> *vt* competir con
rivalry [ˈrɑɪ·vəl·ri] *n* rivalidad *f*
river [ˈrɪv·ər] *n* río *m*
river basin *n* cuenca *f* de río
river bed *n* lecho *m* de un río
riverside [ˈrɪv·ər·saɪd] *n* ribera *f*
rivet [ˈrɪv·ɪt] **I.** *n* remache *m* **II.** *vt* **1.** (*join*) remachar **2.** (*interest*) **to be ~ed by sth** quedar absorto, -a con algo
riveting [ˈrɪv·ɪ·t̬ɪŋ] *adj inf* fascinante
rivulet [ˈrɪv·jʊ·lɪt] *n* **1.** *liter* (*stream*) arroyo *m* **2.** (*of sweat, blood*) gotas *fpl*
RN [ˌɑr·ˈen] *n abbr of* **registered nurse** enfermera *f* titulada
RNA [ˌɑr·en·ˈeɪ] *n abbr of* **ribonucleic acid** ARN *m*
roach[1] [roʊtʃ] <roach *o* -es> *n* (*fish*) rubio *m*
roach[2] [roʊtʃ] <-es> *n* **1.** *inf* (*cockroach*) cucaracha *f* **2.** *sl* (*marijuana*) cacho *m Col*
road [roʊd] *n* **1.** (*between towns*) carretera *f*; (*in town*) calle *f*; (*route*) camino *m;* **by ~** por carretera; **to be on the ~** (*fit for driving*) estar en circulación; (*traveling by road*) estar en camino; (*performing on tour*) estar de gira **2.** *fig* sendero *m;* **to be on the ~ to recovery** estar reponiéndose ►**all ~s lead to Rome** *prov* todos los caminos llevan a Roma *prov;* **let's hit the ~!** *inf* ¡vamos a ponernos en marcha!; **to get sth on the ~** *inf* empezar (con) algo
road accident *n* accidente *m* de circulación
roadblock *n* control *m* de carretera
road hog *n inf* loco, -a *m, f* del volante
roadhouse [ˈroʊd·haʊs] <-houses> *n* motel *m*
roadie [ˈroʊ·di] *n* persona encargada de transportar y montar el equipo de un grupo musical
roadkill *n* animal atropellado en la carretera
road map *n* mapa *m* de carreteras
road rage *n* furia *f* al volante
roadrunner *n* ZOOL correcaminos *m*
road safety *n* seguridad *f* vial
road show [ˈroʊd·ʃoʊ] *n* gira *f*
roadside [ˈroʊd·saɪd] **I.** *n* borde *m* de la carretera **II.** *adj* de carretera
road sign *n* señal *f* de tráfico
road surface *n* pavimento *m*
road-test *vt* **to ~ a car** someter un coche a una prueba de carretera
road traffic *n* tráfico *m* vial
road transportation *n* transporte *m* por carretera
road warrior *n inf: persona que viaja constantemente, especialmente en viajes de negocios*
roadway [ˈroʊd·weɪ] *n* calzada *f*
roadwork [ˈroʊd·wɜrk] *n* obras *fpl* de carretera
roam [roʊm] **I.** *vi* vagar **II.** *vt* vagar por
roan [roʊn] *n* ruano *m*
roar [rɔr] **I.** *vi* (*lion, person*) rugir; (*cannon*) tronar; **to ~ with laughter** reírse a carcajadas **II.** *vt* vociferar **III.** *n* (*of lion, person*) rugido

m; (*of engine*) estruendo *m*

roaring I. *adj* rugiente; (*thunder*) estruendoso, -a; (*fire*) furioso, -a; (*success*) clamoroso, -a; (*trade*) tremendo, -a **II.** *adv* completamente

roast [roʊst] **I.** *vt* **1.** (*food*) asar; (*coffee*) tostar **2.** (*poke fun at*) burlarse de **II.** *vi* (*food*) asarse; (*person*) achicharrarse **III.** *n* **1.** (*meat*) asado *m* **2.** (*party*) asado *m* **IV.** *adj* (*meat*) asado, -a; (*coffee*) tostado, -a

roaster ['roʊs·tər] *n* asador *m*

roasting ['roʊs·tɪŋ] **I.** *n* **1.** (*baking*) asado *m* **2.** *inf* (*telling off*) **to give sb a ~** echar una bronca a alguien **II.** *adj* abrasador(a) **III.** *adv* **~ hot** abrasador(a)

rob [rab] <-bb-> *vt* **1.** (*person, house*) robar; (*bank*) asaltar; **to ~ sb of sth** robar algo a alguien **2.** (*deprive*) **to ~ sb of sth** privar a alguien de algo

robber ['rab·ər] *n* ladrón, -ona *m, f;* **bank ~** atracador (a) *m(f)* de bancos

robbery ['rab·ə·ri] <-ies> *n* robo *m*

robe [roʊb] *n* (*formal*) toga *f;* (*dressing gown*) traje *m;* (*after bath*) albornoz *m;* (*of a priest*) sotana *f*

robin ['rab·ɪn] *n* ZOOL petirrojo *m;* (*songbird*) tordo *m* norteamericano

robot ['roʊ·bat] *n* (*machine*) robot *m;* (*person*) autómata *m*

robotics [roʊ·'baṭ·ɪks] *npl* robótica *f*

robust [roʊ·'bʌst] *adj* **1.** (*person*) robusto, -a; (*health*) de hierro; (*currency*) fuerte **2.** (*statement*) enérgico, -a

robustness *n* **1.** (*vitality*) robustez *f;* (*long-term strength*) solidez *f* **2.** (*frankness*) vigor *m*

rock¹ [rak] *n* **1.** GEO roca *f;* (*in sea*) escollo *m* **2.** (*music*) rock *m* ▶ **to be stuck between a ~ and hard place** estar entre la espada y la pared; **as solid as a ~** duro como una piedra; **to be on the ~s** estar sin blanca, estar pelado *Col;* **whisky on the ~s** whisky con hielo

rock² [rak] **I.** *vt* **1.** (*swing*) mecer **2.** (*shock*) sacudir **II.** *vi* balancearse

rock-and-roll [ˌrak·ənd·'roʊl] *n* rock and roll *m*

rock band *n* grupo *m* de rock

rock bottom *n* fondo *m;* **to hit ~** tocar fondo; **to be at ~** estar por los suelos

rock climber *n* escalador(a) *m(f)*

rock climbing *n* escalada *f* en roca

rocker ['rak·ər] *n* **1.** (*chair*) mecedora *f* **2.** *inf* (*musician, fan*) roquero, -a *m, f* ▶ **to be off one's ~** *inf* estar chiflado

rockery ['rak·ə·ri] <-ies> *n* jardín *m* rocoso

rocket ['rak·ɪt] **I.** *n* **1.** (*weapon*) misil *m* **2.** (*vehicle for space travel*) cohete *m* espacial **3.** (*firework*) cohete *m* **II.** *vi* (*costs, prices*) dispararse; **to ~ up** dispararse

rocket launcher *n* lanzacohetes *m inv*

rock face *n* pared *f* rocosa

rock festival *n* festival *m* de rock

rock garden *n* jardín *m* rocoso

Rockies ['rak·iz] *n* **the ~** las Rocosas

rocking chair ['rak·ɪŋ] *n* mecedora *f,* columpio

m AmL

rocking horse *n* caballito *m* mecedor

rock music *n* música *f* rock

rock 'n' roll *n* rock and roll *m*

rock salt *n* sal *f* gema

rock star *n* estrella *f* del rock

rocky¹ ['rak·i] <-ier, -iest> *adj* rocoso, -a; (*ground*) pedregoso, -a

rocky² ['rak·i] <-ier, -iest> *adj* (*unstable*) inestable

Rocky Mountains *n* Montañas *fpl* Rocosas

> **i** Las Montañas Rocosas (**Rocky Mountains**), también conocidas como "the Rockies" (las Rocosas), son una cadena montañosa en el oeste norteamericano que se extiende a lo largo de más de 3.000 millas (4.800 km) desde Columbia Británica, en Canadá, hasta Nuevo México, en Estados Unidos. Aunque desde el punto de vista geológico son mucho más jóvenes que los Montes Apalaches en el este norteamericano, los picos de las Rocosas tienden a ser más altos y más irregulares que los picos de los Apalaches. El pico más alto es Monte Elbert, en Colorado, con 14.440 pies (4.401 metros) sobre el nivel del mar. La Divisoria Continental (the **Continental Divide**), un filo de un lado del cual todo el agua fluye hacia el Océano Atlántico mientras que del otro lado fluye hacia el Océano Pacífico, se encuentra en las Montañas Rocosas.

rococo [rə·'koʊ·koʊ] **I.** *n* rococó *m* **II.** *adj* rococó

rod [rad] *n* (*stick*) varilla *f;* (*fishing rod*) caña *f* de pescar

rode [roʊd] *pt of* **ride**

rodent ['roʊ·dənt] *n* roedor *m*

rodeo ['roʊ·di·oʊ] <-s> *n* rodeo *m*

roe¹ [roʊ] *n* (*fish eggs*) hueva *f*

roe² [roʊ] <-(s)> *n* (*deer*) corzo, -a *m, f*

roebuck ['roʊ·bʌk] *n* corzo *m*

roger ['radʒ·ər] *interj* RADIO recibido

rogue [roʊg] **I.** *n* **1.** (*rascal*) pícaro, -a *m, f* **2.** (*villain*) bribón, -ona *m, f* **II.** *adj* (*animal*) solitario, -a; (*trader, company*) deshonesto, -a

roguery ['roʊ·gə·ri] <-ies> *n* (*of child*) pillería *f;* (*of adult*) truhanería *f*

roguish ['roʊ·gɪʃ] *adj* pícaro, -a

ROI [ˌar·oʊ·'aɪ] *n abbr of* **return on investment** rendimiento *m* de las inversiones

role *n,* **rôle** [roʊl] *n a.* THEAT papel *m;* **to play a ~** THEAT hacer un papel; *fig* desempeñar un papel

role model *n* modelo *m* a imitar

role play *n* juego *m* de imitación

role reversal *n* inversión *m* de papeles

roll [roʊl] **I.** *n* **1.** (*turning over*) voltereta *f*

2. (*swaying movement*) balanceo *m;* **to be on a ~** *fig* tener buena suerte **3.** (*cylinder: of cloth, paper*) rollo *m;* (*film*) carrete *m* **4.** (*noise: of drum*) redoble *m;* (*of thunder*) retumbo *m* **5.** (*catalog of names*) padrón *m;* (*for elections*) censo *m;* **to call the ~** pasar lista **6.** (*bread*) panecillo *m* **II.** *vt* **1.** (*push: ball, barrel*) hacer rodar; (*dice*) tirar; **to ~ one's eyes** poner los ojos en blanco **2.** (*form into cylindrical shape*) **to ~ sth into sth** enrollar algo en algo; **all ~ed into one** todo unido en uno **3.** (*make: cigarette*) liar **4.** (*flatten: grass*) allanar **III.** *vi* **1.** (*move*) rodar; (*with undulating motion*) ondular **2.** (*be in operation*) funcionar

◆ **roll back** *vt* **1.** (*cause to retreat*) hacer retroceder **2.** ECON reducir **3.** (*return to previous state*) hacer recular

◆ **roll by** *vi* (*vehicle, clouds*) avanzar; (*time, years*) pasar

◆ **roll down** **I.** *vt* (*sleeve*) desenrollar; (*window*) bajar **II.** *vi* rodar por

◆ **roll in** *vi* **1.** llegar en abundancia **2. to be rolling in money** *inf* nadar en dinero

◆ **roll off** *vi* caer rodando

◆ **roll on** *vi* seguir rodando; (*time*) pasar

◆ **roll out** **I.** *vt* **1.** (*flatten*) estirar; (*pastry*) extender **2.** (*unroll*) desenrollar **3.** COM (*new product*) lanzar **II.** *vi* (*wake up*) despertarse

◆ **roll over** *vi* (*movement*) dar vueltas

◆ **roll up** **I.** *vi* *inf* aparecer **II.** *vt* enrollar; (*sleeves*) arremangarse

roll bar *n* AUTO barra *f* protectora antivuelco
roll call *n* lista *f*
roller ['rou·lər] *n* **1.** TECH rodillo *m* **2.** (*wave*) ola *f* grande **3.** (*for hair*) rulo *m*
roller bearing *n* TECH cojinete *m* de rodillos
Rollerblade® **I.** *n* patín *m* en línea **II.** *vi* patinar en línea
roller coaster *n* montaña *f* rusa
roller skate **I.** *n* patín *m* de ruedas **II.** *vi* patinar
rollicking ['ral·ɪk·ɪŋ] *adj* (*amusing*) alegre; (*party*) divertido, -a
rolling *adj* rodante; (*hills*) ondulado, -a; (*program*) continuo, -a
rolling mill *n* **1.** (*machine*) tren *m* de laminación **2.** (*factory*) taller *m* de laminación
rolling pin *n* rodillo *m*
rolling stock *n* AUTO material *m* rodante
roll-on ['roul·an] *adj* (*deodorant*) de bola
roly-poly [,rou·li·'pou·li] *adj* *inf* regordete, -a
ROM [ram] *n* COMPUT *abbr of* **Read Only Memory** ROM *f*
Roman ['rou·mən] **I.** *adj* romano, -a; (*alphabet*) latino, -a; (*religion*) católico, -a **II.** *n* romano, -a *m, f*
Roman Catholic **I.** *n* católico, -a *m, f* **II.** *adj* católico, -a; **the ~ Church** la Iglesia católica romana
romance [rou·'mæns] **I.** *n* **1.** (*love affair*) romance *m* **2.** (*novel*) novela *f* rosa; (*film*) película *f* de amor **3.** (*glamour*) romanticismo *m* **II.** *vi* fantasear

Romanesque [,rou·mə·'nesk] *adj* románico, -a
Romania [rou·'meɪ·ni·ə] *n* Rumanía *f* [*o* Rumania] *f*
Romanian [rou·'meɪ·ni·ən] **I.** *adj* rumano, -a **II.** *n* **1.** (*person*) rumano, -a *m, f* **2.** LING rumano *m*
Roman numeral *n* número *m* romano
romantic [rou·'mæn·tɪk] **I.** *adj* *a.* LIT, ART romántico, -a **II.** *n* romántico, -a *m, f*
romanticism [rou·'mæn·tə·sɪz·əm] *n* romanticismo *m*
Rome [roum] *n* Roma *f* ► **~ was not built in a day** *prov* no se ganó Zamora en una hora *prov;* **when in ~** (**do as the Romans**) *prov* allí donde fueres haz lo que vieres *prov*
romp [ramp] **I.** *vi* juguetear; **to ~ home** ganar fácilmente **II.** *n* retozo *m*
roof [ruf] <-s> **I.** *n* (*of house*) tejado *m;* (*of car*) techo *m;* (*of tree*) copa *f;* (*of mouth*) paladar *m* ► **to go through the ~** (*prices*) estar por las nubes; (*person*) subirse por las paredes; **to hit the ~** subirse por las paredes; **to raise the ~** *inf* armar jaleo **II.** *vt* techar
roofer ['ru·fər] *n* techador *m*
roof garden *n* azotea *f* con flores y plantas
roofing *n* techumbre *f*
rooftop ['ruf·tap] *n* techo *m*
rook [rʊk] **I.** *n* **1.** (*bird*) grajo *m* **2.** (*in chess*) torre *f* **II.** *vt* *inf* estafar
rookery ['rʊk·ə·ri] *n* colonia *f* de grajos
rookie ['rʊk·i] *n sl* novato, -a *m, f*
room [rum] **I.** *n* **1.** (*in house*) habitación *m,* pieza *f* AmL, ambiente *m* CSur; **~ and board** pensión *f* completa **2.** (*space*) espacio *m;* **to make ~ for sb/sth** hacer sitio para alguien/algo; **there's no more ~ for anything else** ya no cabe nada más; **~ for improvement** posibilidad *f* de mejorar; **there is no ~ for doubt** no cabe duda **II.** *vi* **to ~ with sb** compartir alojamiento con alguien
roomie *n* *inf* compañero, -a *m, f* de habitación
roommate ['rum·meɪt] *n* compañero, -a *m, f* de habitación
room service *n* servicio *m* de habitaciones
room temperature *n* temperatura *f* ambiente
roomy ['ru·mi] <-ier, -iest> *adj* amplio, -a
roost [rust] **I.** *n* percha *f* ► **to rule the ~** llevar la voz cantante **II.** *vi* (*bird*) posarse para dormir; *fig* pasar la noche
rooster ['ru·stər] *n* gallo *m*
root [rut] *n* **1.** *a.* BOT, LING, MATH raíz *f;* **to take ~** *a. fig* arraigar **2.** (*source*) causa *f;* **the ~ of all evil** la esencia de todos los males; **the ~ of the problem is that...** el problema radica en que...

◆ **root about** *vi,* **root around** *vi* hozar; **to ~ for sth** buscar algo

◆ **root out** *vt* arrancar

ℹ️ Como **root beer** se conoce en EE.UU. un tipo de limonada a base de extractos de raíces. Con ella se puede preparar un **root beer**

float: se mezcla helado de leche con root beer y se bebe con una pajita.

---

root canal *n* **1.** (*part of tooth*) conducto *m* **2.** MED (*treatment*) tratamiento de conductos

root cause *n* causa *f* primordial

rootless *adj* desarraigado, -a

root sign *n* MATH raíz *f*

root vegetable *n* tubérculo *m*

rope [roʊp] I. *n* **1.** (*cord*) cuerda *f*; (*of garlic*) ristra *m*; (*of pearls*) sarta *f* **2.** ~**s** (*in boxing*) cuerdas *fpl* **3.** (*for capital punishment*) soga *f* ▸**to know the ~s** estar al tanto de todo; **to learn the ~s** aprender el oficio; **to show sb the ~s** enseñar el oficio a alguien; **to have sb on the ~s** tener a alguien contra las cuerdas II. *vt* atar con una cuerda
◆**rope in** *vt* **to rope sb in** (**to doing sth**) agarrar a alguien (para que haga algo)
◆**rope off** *vt* acordonar
◆**rope up** *vi* encordarse

rope ladder *n* escalera *f* de cuerda

rosary ['roʊ·zə·ri] <-ies> *n* rosario *m*

rose¹ [roʊz] I. *n* **1.** (*flower, color*) rosa *f* **2.** (*on watering can*) roseta *f* **3.** ARCHIT rosetón *m* ▸**to come up smelling of ~s** aparecer contento; **coming up ~s** a pedir de boca II. *adj* rosa

rose² [roʊz] *pt of* **rise**

rosebud ['roʊz·bʌd] *n* capullo *m*

rosebush *n* rosal *m*

rose garden *n* rosaleda *f*

rosehip ['roʊz·hɪp] *n* escaramujo *m*

rosemary ['roʊz·mer·i] *n* romero *m*

rosette [roʊ·'zet] *n* ARCHIT rosetón *m*; (*badge*) escarapela *f*

rose water *n* agua *f* de rosas

rose window *n* ARCHIT rosetón *m*

rosin ['raz·ən] *n* colofonia *f*

roster ['ras·tər] *n* lista *f*

rostrum ['ras·trəm] <-s *o* rostra> *n* (*for conductor*) estrado *m*; (*for public speaker*) tribuna *f*

rosy ['roʊ·zi] <-ier, -iest> *adj* **1.** (*rose-colored*) rosado, -a; (*cheek*) sonrosado, -a **2.** (*optimistic: viewpoint*) optimista; (*future*) prometedor(a)

rot [rat] I. *n* putrefacción *f* II. <-tt-> *vi* pudrirse [*o* podrirse] III. *vt* pudrir [*o* podrirse]
◆**rot away** I. *vt* pudrir II. *vi* pudrirse

rotary ['roʊ·t̬ə·ri] *adj* rotatorio, -a; (*pump*) giratorio, -a

rotate ['roʊ·teɪt] I. *vt* **1.** (*turn around*) dar vueltas a **2.** (*alternate*) alternar; (*duties*) turnarse en; AGR cultivar en rotación II. *vi* girar; **to ~ around sth** girar alrededor de algo

rotation [roʊ·'teɪ·ʃən] *n* **1.** *a.* ASTR, AGR rotación *f* **2.** (*alternation*) alternación *f*; **in ~** por turno

rotatory ['roʊ·tə·tɔr·i] *adj* rotativo, -a

rote [roʊt] *n* **by ~** de memoria

rotor ['roʊ·t̬ər] *n* rotor *m*

rotten ['rat·ən] *adj* **1.** (*food*) podrido, -a; **to go ~** pudrirse [*o* podrirse] **2.** *inf* (*nasty: behavior*) despreciable **3.** *inf* (*performance, book*) ma-

lísimo, -a

rotund [roʊ·'tʌnd] *adj* redondeado, -a

rotunda [roʊ·'tʌn·də] *n* ARCHIT rotonda *f*

rouble ['ru·bəl] *n s.* **ruble**

rouge [ruʒ] *n* colorete *m*, rouge *m* Arg, Chile, rubor *m* Col

rough [rʌf] I. *adj* **1.** (*uneven: road*) desigual; (*surface*) áspero, -a **2.** (*poorly made: work*) chapucero, -a **3.** (*harsh: voice*) bronco, -a **4.** (*imprecise*) aproximado, -a; (*idea*) impreciso, -a; ~ **work** borrador *m* **5.** (*unrefined: person, manner*) tosco, -a **6.** (*stormy: sea*) agitado, -a; (*weather*) tempestuoso, -a **7.** (*difficult*) difícil; (*treatment*) duro, -a; **to be ~ on sb** *inf* ser injusto con alguien II. *n* **1.** (*sketch*) borrador *m* **2.** SPORTS **the ~** el rough ▸**to take the ~ with the smooth** estar a las duras y a las maduras III. *vt* **to ~ it** *inf* pasar sin comodidades IV. *adv* **to play ~** jugar duro; **to live ~** vivir a la intemperie

roughage ['rʌf·ɪdʒ] *n* fibra *f* (de los alimentos)

rough-and-ready [,rʌf·ənd·'red·i] *adj* (*primitive*) tosco pero eficaz

rough-and-tumble *n* riña *f*; *fig* juegos *m pl* bruscos

roughen ['rʌf·ən] *vt* poner áspero

rough-hewn *adj* **1.** (*wood*) desbastado, -a **2.** (*features*) tosco, -a

roughhouse ['rʌf·haʊs] I. *vi* armar jaleo II. *n* *inf* jaleo *m*

roughly *adv* **1.** (*approximately*) aproximadamente; ~ **speaking** por así decirlo **2.** (*aggressively*) bruscamente

roughneck ['rʌf·nek] *n* **1.** *inf* (*violent man*) matón *m* **2.** *sl* (*oil rig worker*) trabajador *m* de un pozo petrolífero

roughness ['rʌf·nɪs] *n* **1.** (*of surface*) aspereza *f*; (*of ground*) desigualdad *f* **2.** (*unfairness*) dureza *f*

roughshod ['rʌf·ʃad] *adv* **to ride ~ over sb** no tener la menor consideración con alguien

rough-spoken [,rʌf·'spoʊ·kən] *adj* malhablado, -a

roulette [ru·'let] *n* ruleta *f*

round [raʊnd] I. <-er, -est> *adj* **1.** (*circular: object, number*) redondo, -a; (*arch*) de medio punto **2.** (*not angular*) arqueado, -a **3.** (*sonorous*) sonoro, -a II. *n* **1.** (*circle*) círculo *m* **2.** (*series*) serie *f*; (*of applause*) salva *f*; (*of shots*) descarga *f* **3.** ~**s** (*route*) recorrido *m*; MIL ronda *f*; MED visita *f* **4.** (*routine*) rutina *f* **5.** (*time period: of elections*) vuelta *f*; (*in card games*) mano *f*; SPORTS eliminatoria *f*; (*in boxing*) asalto *m* **6.** (*of drinks*) ronda *f*; **this ~ is on me** esta ronda la pago yo **7.** (*of ammunition*) bala *f* **8.** MUS canon *m* III. *vt* **1.** (*movement*) redondear; (*corner*) doblar **2.** MATH aproximar; **to ~ an amount to the nearest dollar** aproximar una cifra al siguiente valor
◆**round down** *vt* MATH redondear por defecto
◆**round off** *vt* **1.** (*finish*) rematar **2.** (*smooth*) pulir **3.** MATH redondear
◆**round out** *vt* acabar; **to ~ a list** completar

R

una lista

◆**round up** *vt* **1.** MATH redondear por exceso **2.** (*gather*) reunir; (*cattle*) rodear

roundabout ['raʊnd·ə·baʊt] *adj* indirecto, -a; **to take a ~ route** ir dando un rodeo

rounded *adj* redondeado, -a

roundly *adv* (*assert, deny*) categóricamente, rotundamente; **to defeat sb ~** derrotar de forma aplastante a alguien

round robin *n* **1.** (*letter*) carta *f* colectiva **2.** (*competition*) torneo *m* (*en el que cada participante se enfrenta con cada uno de los demás*)

round-shouldered [ˌraʊnd·'ʃoʊl·dərd] *adj* encorvado, -a; **to be ~** ser cargado de espaldas

round-table discussion *n* mesa *f* redonda

round-the-clock I. *adj* (*surveillance*) de veinticuatro horas; II. *adv* las veinticuatro horas; **to work ~** trabajar día y noche

round trip *n* viaje *m* de ida y vuelta; **~ ticket** billete *m* de ida y vuelta

roundup ['raʊnd·ʌp] *n* **1.** AGR rodeo *m* **2.** (*by police*) redada *f*

rouse [raʊz] *vt* **1.** (*awaken*) despertar **2.** (*activate*) provocar; **to ~ sb to do sth** animar a alguien a hacer algo; **to ~ sb to action** mover a alguien a la acción

rousing ['raʊ·zɪŋ] *adj* (*welcome*) caluroso, -a; (*speech*) vehemente

roustabout ['raʊst·ə·baʊt] *n* (*laborer*) peón *m*

rout [raʊt] I. *vt* **1.** (*defeat*) derrotar **2.** (*put to flight*) poner en fuga II. *n* **1.** (*defeat*) derrota *f* aplastante **2.** (*flight*) huida *f* en desbandada

◆**rout out** *vt* **1.** (*make come out*) hacer salir **2.** (*find*) encontrar

route [raʊt] I. *n* **1.** (*way*) ruta *f*; (*of parade, bus*) recorrido *m*; NAUT rumbo *m*; (*to success*) camino *m* **2.** (*delivery path*) recorrido *m*; **to have a paper ~** hacer un reparto de periódicos **3.** (*road*) carretera *f* II. *vt* **to ~ sth via New York** mandar algo vía Nueva York

---

ℹ️ La **Route 66** es una famosa carretera que une Chicago con Los Angeles. Durante la crisis económica de los años treinta, muchas personas recorrieron la Route 66 para mudarse a California. Atraviesa ocho estados de EE.UU.

---

routine [ru·'tin] I. *n* **1.** *a.* COMPUT rutina *f*; **he went into his usual ~** *inf* me vino con la misma cantinela de siempre **2.** (*of dancer*) número *m* II. *adj* **1.** (*regular*) habitual; (*inspection*) de rutina; (*medical case*) común **2.** (*uninspiring*) rutinario, -a

routinely *adv* habitualmente

roux [ru] *n* mezcla *f de mantequilla y harina para espesar las salsas*

rove [roʊv] I. *vi* **to ~ over sth** recorrer algo II. *vt* recorrer

rover ['roʊ·vər] *n* trotamundos *m inv*

roving ['roʊ·vɪŋ] *adj* (*animal, thieves*) errante;

(*ambassador*) itinerante; (*instructor*) ambulante

row[1] [roʊ] *n* **1.** (*line: of houses, cars*) hilera *f*; (*of people, of seats*) fila *f*; **to stand in a ~** estar en la fila **2.** (*succession*) sucesión *f*; **three times in a ~** tres veces consecutivas

row[2] [roʊ] I. *vi* remar II. *vt* (*boat*) llevar; **to ~ sb across the lake** llevar a alguien en bote al otro lado del lago III. *n* paseo *m* en bote; **to go for a ~** ir a dar un paseo en bote

rowboat ['roʊ·boʊt] *n* bote *m* de remos

rowdy ['raʊ·di] <-ier, -iest> *adj* **1.** (*noisy*) alborotador(a) **2.** (*quarrelsome*) pendenciero, -a

rower ['roʊ·ər] *n* remero, -a *m, f*

rowing *n* SPORTS remo *m*

rowing club *n* club *m* de remo

royal ['rɔɪ·əl] I. *adj* **1.** (*of monarch*) real; **the ~ we** el plural mayestático **2.** *fig* regio, -a; (*welcome*) espléndido, -a **3.** *inf* (*big*) soberano, -a; **a ~ pain in the ass** *vulg* un soberano dolor de cabeza *argot* II. *n inf* miembro *m* de la familia real

royal flush *n* (*in cards*) escalera *f* real

royal jelly *n* jalea *f* real

royalty ['rɔɪ·əl·ti] <-ies> *n* **1.** (*sovereignty*) realeza *f*; **to treat sb like ~** tratar a alguien a cuerpo de rey **2. royalties** (*payment*) derechos *mpl* de autor

rpm [ˌar·pi·'em] *n abbr of* **revolutions per minute** rpm

RR [ˌar·'ar] *n abbr of* **Railroad** F.C. *m*

RSI [ˌar·es·'aɪ] *n abbr of* **repetitive strain injury** lesión [*o* movimiento] por esfuerzo repetido *f*

RSVP [ˌar·es·vi·'pi] *vi abbr of* **répondez s'il vous plait** (= **please reply**) s.r.c.

rub [rʌb] I. *n* **1.** (*act of rubbing*) frotamiento *m*; **to give sth a ~** frotar algo **2.** *liter* (*difficulty*) dificultad *f*; **there's the ~** ahí está el quid de la cuestión II. <-bb-> *vt* frotar; (*one's eyes*) restregarse; (*one's hands*) frotarse; **to ~ sth clean** lustrar algo III. <-bb-> *vi* frotar

◆**rub against** *vi* **to ~ sth** rozar con algo; (*cat*) restregarse contra algo

◆**rub down** *vt* **1.** (*smooth*) pulir; (*horse*) almohazar **2.** (*dry*) secar frotando

◆**rub in** *vt* **1.** (*spread on skin*) aplicar frotando **2.** *inf* (*keep reminding*) reiterar; *pej* insistir en

◆**rub off** I. *vi* **1.** (*become clean: stain*) irse **2. to ~ on sb** (*affect*) pegarse a alguien II. *vt* (*dirt*) quitar frotando

◆**rub out** *vt* **1.** (*remove: writing*) borrar; (*dirt*) quitar **2.** *sl* (*murder*) liquidar

rubber ['rʌb·ər] *n* **1.** (*material*) goma *f*, hule *m* Méx **2.** *sl* (*condom*) goma *f*, forro *m* RíoPl **3.** (*game*) serie *f de tres o cinco partidos*; (*in bridge*) rubber *m*

rubber band *n* goma *f* (elástica), caucho *m* Col

rubber boots *npl* botas *fpl* de goma

rubber check *n sl* cheque *m* sin fondos, cheque *m* chimbo Col

rubber gloves *npl* guantes *mpl* de goma

rubberneck ['rʌb·ər·nek] I. *n sl* (*tourist*) tu-

rista *mf;* (*at accident*) mirón, -ona *m, f* **II.** *vi sl* (*sightsee*) hacer turismo; (*be nosy*) curiosear
rubbernecker *n sl* mirón, -ona *m, f*
rubber plant *n* planta *f* del caucho
rubber-stamp **I.** *vt* (*decision*) dar el visto bueno a **II.** *n* (*device*) sello *m* de goma
rubber tree *n* árbol *m* del caucho
rubbery <-ier, -iest> *adj* (*texture*) parecido a la goma; (*food*) correoso, -a
rubbing *n* frotamiento *m*
rubbing alcohol *n mezcla de alcohol etílico e isopropílico usada para frotar articulaciones o refrescar*
rubbish ['rʌb·ɪʃ] *n inf* tonterías *fpl*
rubble ['rʌb·əl] *n* escombros *mpl*
rubdown ['rʌb·daʊn] *n* fricción *f*
rubella [ru·'bel·ə] *n* MED rubéola *f*
rubicund ['ru·bə·kənd] *adj liter* rubicundo, -a
ruble ['ru·bəl] *n* rublo *m*
rubric ['ru·brɪk] *n* **1.** (*heading*) epígrafe *m* **2.** (*instructions*) normas *fpl* **3.** REL rúbrica *f*
ruby ['ru·bi] **I.** <-ies> *n* rubí *m* **II.** *adj* de color rubí
ruck [rʌk] **I.** *n* **1.** (*crowd*) melé *f* **2.** (*fold*) arruga *f* **II.** *vt* **to** ~ **up** (*clothes*) arrugar
ruckus ['rʌk·əs] *n inf* jaleo *m*, toletole *m CSur*
rudder ['rʌd·ər] *n* AVIAT, NAUT timón *m*
rudderless *adj a. fig* sin timón
ruddy ['rʌd·i] <-ier, -iest> *adj* **1.** *liter* (*cheeks*) rubicundo, -a **2.** (*light*) rojizo, -a
rude [rud] *adj* **1.** (*impolite*) grosero, -a, meco, -a *Méx* **2.** (*vulgar*) vulgar; (*joke*) verde **3.** (*sudden*) brusco, -a; (*surprise*) desagradable **4.** *liter* (*unrefined*) tosco, -a
rudimentary [,ru·də·'men·tə·ri] *adj* rudimentario, -a
rudiments ['ru·də·mənt] *npl* rudimentos *mpl*
rue [ru] *vt liter* lamentar
rueful ['ru·fəl] *adj* **1.** (*repentant*) arrepentido, -a **2.** (*sad*) triste
ruff [rʌf] *n* (*collar*) gorguera *f;* (*of an animal*) collar *m*
ruffian ['rʌf·i·ən] *n iron* canalla *mf*
ruffle ['rʌf·əl] **I.** *vt* **1.** (*agitate: hair*) alborotar; (*clothes*) fruncir; (*feathers*) erizar **2.** (*upset*) alterar **II.** *n* volante *m*
rug [rʌg] *n* (*small carpet*) alfombra *f*
rugby ['rʌg·bi] *n* rugby *m*
rugged ['rʌg·ɪd] *adj* **1.** (*uneven: cliff, mountains*) escarpado, -a; (*landscape, country*) accidentado, -a; (*ground*) desigual **2.** (*tough: face*) de facciones duras; (*construction, vehicle*) resistente
ruin ['ru·ɪn] **I.** *vt* **1.** (*bankrupt*) arruinar **2.** (*destroy: city, building*) destruir **3.** (*spoil: dress, surprise*) estropear; (*child*) malcriar **II.** *n* **1.** (*bankruptcy, downfall*) ruina *f;* **drugs will be his** ~ las drogas serán su ruina **2.** *pl* (*remains*) ruinas *fpl*
ruination [,ru·ə·'neɪ·ʃən] *n* ruina *f*
ruinous ['ru·ə·nəs] *adj* ruinoso, -a
rule [rul] **I.** *n* **1.** (*law*) regla *f;* (*principle*) norma *f;* ~**s and regulations** reglamento *m;* ~**s of**

the road normas *fpl* de tráfico; **to be the** ~ ser la norma; **to break a** ~ infringir una norma; **to play (it) by the** ~**s** obedecer las reglas; **it is against the** ~**s** va contra las normas; **as a** ~ por lo general **2.** (*control*) gobierno *m* **3.** (*measuring device*) regla *f* ▶ **a** ~ **of thumb** una regla general; ~**s are made to be** broken las normas están para desobedecerlas **II.** *vt* **1.** (*govern: country*) gobernar; (*company*) dirigir **2.** (*control*) dominar **3.** (*draw*) trazar con una regla; (*paper*) pautar **4.** LAW (*decide*) dictaminar, fallar **III.** *vi* **1.** (*control*) gobernar; (*monarch*) reinar **2.** (*predominate*) imperar **3.** LAW **to** ~ **for/against sb/sth** fallar a favor/en contra de alguien/algo
◆ **rule out** *vt* descartar
rule book *n* reglamento *m*
ruler *n* **1.** (*governor*) gobernante *mf;* (*sovereign*) soberano, -a *m, f* **2.** (*measuring device*) regla *f*
ruling ['ru·lɪŋ] **I.** *adj* **1.** (*governing*) gobernante; (*class*) dirigente; (*monarch*) reinante **2.** (*primary*) dominante **II.** *n* fallo *m;* **the final** ~ la sentencia definitiva
rum [rʌm] *n* ron *m*
Rumania [roʊ·'meɪ·ni·ə] *n s.* **Romania**
Rumanian [roʊ·'meɪ·ni·ən] *s.* **Romanian**
rumba ['rʌm·bə] *n* rumba *f*
rumble ['rʌm·bəl] **I.** *n* **1.** (*sound*) ruido *m* sordo; (*of thunder*) estruendo *m;* (*of stomach*) borborigmo *m* **2.** *sl* (*fight*) pelea *f* **II.** *vi* hacer un ruido sordo; (*thunder*) retumbar; **my stomach is** ~**ing** me suenan las tripas
rumbling **I.** *n* (*sound*) ruido *m* sordo; (*of thunder*) estruendo *m;* **there were** ~**s of war** se hablaba de una posible guerra **II.** *adj* retumbante
ruminant ['ru·mə·nənt] ZOOL **I.** *n* rumiante *mf* **II.** *adj* rumiante
ruminate ['ru·mə·neɪt] *vi* rumiar
ruminative ['ru·mə·,neɪ·t̬ɪv] *adj form* meditabundo, -a
rummage ['rʌm·ɪdʒ] **I.** *vi* hurgar; (*in drawer*) revolver **II.** *n* (*search*) **to have a** ~ **around for sth** buscar algo
rummage sale *n mercadillo donde se venden objetos usados*
rummy ['rʌm·i] *n* GAMES rummy *m*
rumor ['ru·mər] **I.** *n* rumor *m* **II.** *vt* **it is** ~**ed that...** se rumorea que...
rump [rʌmp] *n* **1.** (*back end: of horse*) grupa *f;* (*of bird*) rabadilla *f* **2.** (*cut of beef*) cuarto *m* trasero **3.** *iron* (*buttocks*) trasero *m*
rumple ['rʌm·pəl] *vt* arrugar; **to** ~ **sb's hair** despeinar a alguien
rump steak *n* filete *m* de lomo de ternera, bife *m* de chorizo *Arg, Col*
run [rʌn] **I.** *n* **1.** (*jog*) **to break into a** ~ echar a correr; **to go for a** ~ salir a correr **2.** (*trip*) viaje *m;* (*of train*) trayecto *m;* **to go for a** ~ **in the car** ir a dar una vuelta en el coche **3.** (*series*) racha *f;* (*of books*) tirada *f* **4.** (*demand*) demanda *f;* **a sudden** ~ **on the dollar** una

R

súbita presión sobre el dólar; **a ~ on the banks** un pánico bancario **5.** (*type*) categoría *f* **6.** (*direction, tendency*) dirección *f;* (*of opinion*) corriente *f;* **the ~ of events** el curso de los acontecimientos **7.** (*enclosure for animals*) corral *m* **8.** (*hole in tights*) carrera *f* **9.** SPORTS (*in baseball, cricket*) carrera *f;* (*ski slope*) pista *f* de esquí **10.** CINE, THEAT permanencia *f* en cartel **11.** MUS carrerilla *f* **12.** MIL **bombing ~** bombardeo *m* ▶ **to give sb a ~ for their money** hacer sudar tinta a alguien; **to have a (good) ~ for one's money** no poder quejarse; **in the long ~** a la larga; **in the short ~** a corto plazo; **on the ~** deprisa y corriendo; **to be on the ~** huir de la justicia **II.** *vi* <ran, run> **1.** (*move fast*) correr; **to ~ for the bus** correr para no perder el autobús; **to ~ for help** correr en busca de ayuda; **~ for your lives!** ¡sálvese quien pueda! **2.** (*operate*) funcionar; **to ~ smoothly** ir sobre ruedas *fig* **3.** (*go, travel*) ir; **to ~ off the road** salirse de la carretera; **to ~ ashore/onto the rocks** NAUT embarrancar **4.** (*extend*) extenderse; **the road ~s along the coast** la carretera bordea la costa **5.** (*last*) **to ~ for two hours** durar dos horas; **to ~ and ~** ser el cuento de nunca acabar *inf* **6.** (*be*) existir **7.** (*flow: river*) fluir; (*make-up*) correrse; (*nose*) gotear *inf* **8.** (*enter election*) presentarse, postularse *AmL;* **to ~ for election/President** presentarse a las elecciones/como candidato a presidente **9.** + *adj* (*be*) **to ~ dry** (*river*) secarse; **to ~ short** (*water*) escasear **10.** (*say*) decir **III.** *vt* <ran, run> **1.** (*move fast*) **to ~ a race** participar en una carrera **2.** (*enter in race: candidate, horse*) presentar **3.** (*drive*) llevar; **to ~ sb home** llevar a alguien a casa; **to ~ a truck into a tree** chocar contra un árbol con un camión; **to ~ a ship ashore** hacer encallar un barco **4.** (*pass*) pasar **5.** (*operate*) poner en marcha; (*car*) llevar; (*computer program*) ejecutar; (*engine*) hacer funcionar; **to ~ a washing machine** poner una lavadora **6.** (*manage, govern*) dirigir, pilotear *AmL;* **to ~ a farm** tener una granja; **to ~ a government** estar al frente de un gobierno; **to ~ a household** llevar una casa **7.** (*conduct*) realizar; (*experiment, test*) llevar a cabo **8.** (*provide: course*) organizar **9.** (*let flow*) dejar correr; (*bath*) preparar **10.** (*show: article*) publicar; (*series*) emitir **11.** (*smuggle*) pasar de contrabando **12.** (*not heed: blockade*) romper; (*red light*) saltar(se) (en rojo) **13.** (*incur*) exponerse a; (*risk*) correr **14.** (*perform tasks*) **to ~ errands** hacer recados
◆**run about** *vi* andar de un lado para otro
◆**run across I.** *vi* cruzar corriendo **II.** *vt* toparse con
◆**run after** *vt* correr tras
◆**run against** *vt* POL ir contra
◆**run along** *vi* marcharse
◆**run away** *vi* escaparse; (*water*) derramarse
◆**run away with** *vt* apoderarse de
◆**run back** *vi* volver corriendo

◆**run down I.** *vi* (*clock*) parar; (*battery*) gastarse **II.** *vt* **1.** (*run over*) atropellar **2.** (*disparage*) hablar mal de **3.** (*capture*) capturar
◆**run in I.** *vi* entrar corriendo **II.** *vt* **1.** AUTO rodar **2.** *sl* (*capture*) detener
◆**run into** *vt* dar con; AUTO chocar con
◆**run off I.** *vi* escaparse; (*water*) derramarse **II.** *vt* **1.** (*water*) dejar correr **2.** TYPO tirar **3.** (*make quickly*) hacer deprisa; (*letter*) escribir deprisa
◆**run on** *vi* **1.** (*continue to run*) seguir corriendo **2.** (*conversation*) continuar; (*words*) estar escritos sin dejar espacio
◆**run out of** *vi* quedarse sin
◆**run over I.** *vi* (*person*) irse; (*fluid*) rebosar **II.** *vt* AUTO atropellar a
◆**run through** *vt* **1.** (*station*) pasar sin parar por **2.** (*money*) derrochar
◆**run up I.** *vi* **1.** subir corriendo **2. to ~ against difficulties** tropezar con dificultades **II.** *vt* **1.** (*flag*) izar **2.** (*make quickly*) hacer deprisa **3.** (*debt*) contraer; **to ~ debts** endeudarse
runaround ['rʌn·ə·'raʊnd] *n* **to give sb the ~** traer a alguien al retortero
runaway ['rʌn·ə·weɪ] **I.** *adj* **1.** (*train*) fuera de control; (*person*) fugitivo, -a; (*horse*) desbocado, -a **2.** (*enormous: success*) arrollador(a) **II.** *n* fugitivo, -a *m, f*
rundown [rʌn·'daʊn] **I.** *n* **1.** (*report*) resumen *m;* **to give sb the ~ on sth** poner a alguien al tanto de algo **2.** (*reduction*) disminución *f;* (*of staff*) reducción *f* **II.** *adj* **1.** (*building, town*) mal conservado, -a **2.** (*person*) debilitado, -a
rune [run] *n* runa *f*
rung¹ [rʌŋ] *n* **1.** (*ladder*) peldaño *m* **2.** (*level*) nivel *m*
rung² [rʌŋ] *pp of* **ring²**
run-in ['rʌn·ɪn] *n* **1.** *inf* (*argument*) altercado *m* **2.** (*prelude*) etapa *f* previa
runner ['rʌn·ər] *n* **1.** SPORTS (*person*) corredor(a) *m(f);* (*horse*) caballo *m* de carreras **2.** (*messenger*) mensajero, -a *m, f* **3.** (*smuggler*) contrabandista *mf;* **drug ~** camello *m* **4.** (*rail*) riel *m;* (*on sledge*) patín *m* **5.** (*stem*) tallo *m* rastrero **6.** (*long rug*) alfombrilla *f* estrecha
runner-up [rʌn·ər·'ʌp] *n* subcampeón, -ona *m, f*
running I. *n* **1.** (*action of a runner*) carrera *f* **2.** (*operation*) acción *f;* (*of a machine*) funcionamiento *m;* **the day-to-day ~ of the business** el día a día del negocio ▶ **to be in/out of the ~** tener/no tener posibilidades de ganar **II.** *adj* **1.** (*consecutive*) sucesivo, -a; (*day*) consecutivo, -a **2.** (*ongoing*) continuado, -a **3.** (*operating*) que está funcionando **4.** (*flowing*) que fluye
running back *n* SPORTS running back *m*
runny ['rʌn·i] <-ier, -iest> *adj* líquido, -a; (*sauce*) acuoso, -a
run-off ['rʌn·ɔf] *n* **1.** POL desempate *m* **2.** SPORTS segunda vuelta *f* **3.** (*rainfall*) escorrentía *f*

run-of-the-mill [ˌrʌn·əv·ðə·ˈmɪl] *adj* corriente y moliente

runt [rʌnt] *n* ZOOL enano *m*

run-through [ˈrʌn·θru] *n* THEAT, MUS ensayo *m* (rápido); **to have a ~ of sth** ensayar algo

run-up [ˈrʌn·ʌp] *n* **1.** SPORTS carrerilla *f* **2.** (*prelude*) período *m* previo; **the ~ to sth** el preludio de algo

runway [ˈrʌn·weɪ] *n* pista *f*

rupee [ˈru·pi] *n* rupia *f*

rupture [ˈrʌp·tʃər] I. *vi* romperse II. *vt* romper; **to ~ oneself** herniarse III. *n* **1.** (*act of bursting*) ruptura *f* **2.** (*hernia*) hernia *f*, relajadura *f Méx*

rural [ˈrʊr·əl] *adj* rural

ruse [ruz] *n* treta *f*

rush¹ [rʌʃ] *n* BOT junco *m*

rush² [rʌʃ] I. *n* **1.** (*hurry*) prisa *f*; **to be in a ~** tener prisa; **to leave in a ~** salir corriendo **2.** (*charge, attack*) ataque *m*; (*surge*) ola *f*; (*of air*) corriente *f*; (*of customers*) oleada *f*; **there's been a ~ on oil** ha habido una fuerte demanda de aceite; **gold ~** fiebre *f* del oro **3.** (*dizziness*) mareo *m* II. *vi* ir deprisa III. *vt* **1.** (*do quickly*) hacer precipitadamente **2.** (*hurry*) apresurar **3.** (*attack*) asaltar

◆ **rush about** *vi* correr de acá para allá

◆ **rush at** *vt* precipitarse hacia

◆ **rush into** *vt* **1.** **to ~ sth** precipitarse en algo **2. to rush sb into doing sth** presionar a alguien para que haga algo

◆ **rush out** I. *vi* (*leave*) salir precipitadamente II. *vt* (*publish*) publicar con urgencia

◆ **rush through** *vt* aprobar urgentemente

rush hour *n* hora *f* punta

ℹ️ Esculpidos en las paredes de granito del **Mount Rushmore** (Monte Rushmore), en Dakota del Sur, entre 1927 y 1941, los bustos de los presidentes George Washington, Thomas Jefferson, Theodore Roosevelt y Abraham Lincoln, de 60 pies (18 metros) de altura, representan los primeros 150 años de la historia estadounidense y simbolizan el nacimiento, crecimiento, desarrollo y preservación de los Estados Unidos de América.

---

rush order *n* pedido *m* urgente

rusk [rʌsk] *n* bizcocho *m*

russet [ˈrʌs·ɪt] *liter* I. *adj* bermejo, -a II. *n* color *m* bermejo

russet potato *n* papa *f* colorada

Russia [ˈrʌʃ·ə] *n* Rusia *f*

Russian [ˈrʌʃ·ən] I. *adj* ruso, -a II. *n* **1.** (*person*) ruso, -a *m, f* **2.** (*language*) ruso *m*

rust [rʌst] I. *n* **1.** (*decay*) oxidación *f* **2.** (*substance*) herrumbre *f* **3.** (*color*) color *m* herrumbre II. *vi* oxidarse III. *vt* oxidar

rust-colored *adj* de color herrumbre

rustic [ˈrʌs·tɪk] *adj* **1.** (*rural*) rústico, -a **2.** (*simple, plain*) sencillo, -a

rustle [ˈrʌs·əl] I. *vi* (*leaves*) susurrar; (*paper*) crujir II. *vt* **1.** (*leaves*) hacer susurrar; (*paper*) hacer crujir **2.** (*steal: cattle*) robar III. *n* (*of leaves*) susurro *m*; (*of paper*) crujido *m*

rustler [ˈrʌs·lər] *n* ladrón , -ona *m, f* de ganado

rustproof [ˈrʌst·pruf] *adj* inoxidable

rusty [ˈrʌs·ti] <-ier, -iest> *adj* **1.** (*metal*) oxidado, -a **2.** (*in skill*) falto, -a de práctica; **my Spanish is a bit ~** tengo bastante olvidado el castellano

rut¹ [rʌt] *n* bache *m* ▶ **to be stuck in a ~** estar metido en la rutina

rut² [rʌt] *n* ZOOL celo *m*

rutabaga [ˌru·tə·ˈbeɪ·gə] *n* nabo *m* sueco

ruthless [ˈruθ·lɪs] *adj* (*person*) despiadado, -a; (*ambition*) implacable; **to be ~ in doing sth** hacer algo sin piedad; **to be ~ in enforcing the law** hacer cumplir la ley a raja tabla

ruthlessness *n* crueldad *f*

RV [ˌar·ˈvi] *abbr of* **recreational vehicle** caravana *f* pequeña, casa-carro *m Col*

Rwanda [ru·ˈan·də] *n* Ruanda *f*

Rwandan I. *adj* ruandés, -esa II. *n* ruandés, -esa *m, f*

rye [raɪ] *n* centeno *m*

S

S [es], **s** *n* S, s; **~ as in Sierra** S de Soria

s [es] *abbr of* **second** s *m*

S [es] *n* **1.** *abbr of* **south** S *m* **2.** *abbr of* **satisfactory** suficiente *m*

SA **1.** *abbr of* **South Africa** Sudáfrica *f* **2.** *abbr of* **South America** Sudamérica *f*

Sabbath [ˈsæb·əθ] *n* sabbat *m*

sabbatical [sə·ˈbæt̬·ɪ·kəl] UNIV I. *n* año *m* de permiso II. *adj* sabático, -a

saber [ˈseɪ·bər] *n* sable *m*

saber rattling [ˈseɪ·bər·ˌræt̬·lɪŋ] *n pej* belicosidad *f*

sable [ˈseɪ·bəl] *n* (*fur*) marta *f*

sabotage [ˈsæb·ə·taʒ] I. *vt* sabotear II. *n* sabotaje *m*

saboteur [ˌsæb·ə·ˈtɜr] *n* saboteador(a) *m(f)*

sac [sæk] *n* BIO, ANAT saco *m*

saccharin [ˈsæk·ər·ɪn] *n* sacarina *f*

saccharine [ˈsæk·ər·ɪn] *adj pej* empalagoso, -a

sachet [sæ·ˈʃeɪ] *n* bolsita *f*

sack¹ [sæk] I. *n* **1.** (*large bag*) saco *m*; (*paper or plastic bag*) bolsa *f* **2.** (*amount in bag*) **a ~ of potatoes** un saco de patatas **3.** *sl* (*bed*) **to hit the ~** irse al catre *inf* **4.** *sl* (*dismissal*) **to get the ~** ser despedido; **to give sb the ~** despedir a alguien II. *vt* despedir

sack² [sæk] I. *n* (*plundering*) saqueo *m* II. *vt* (*plunder*) saquear

sackcloth [ˈsæk·klɔθ] *n* arpillera *f*

sackful [ˈsæk·fʊl] *n* (*amount in bag*) saco *m*

sacking[1] ['sæk·ɪŋ] *n* **1.** (*sackcloth*) arpillera *f* **2.** *sl* (*dismissal*) despido *m*

sacking[2] ['sæk·ɪŋ] *n* (*plundering*) saqueo *m*

sacrament ['sæk·rə·mənt] *n* (*ceremony*) sacramento *m;* **the ~** (*consecrated bread and wine*) la Eucaristía

sacramental [,sæk·rə·'men·təl] *adj* sacramental

sacred ['seɪ·krɪd] *adj* sagrado, -a; **to be ~ to sb** estar consagrado a alguien; **is nothing ~ to you?** ¿no tienes respeto por nada?

sacrifice ['sæk·rə·faɪs] **I.** *vt* **1.** *a.* REL sacrificar **2.** (*give up: time, money*) renunciar a; **to ~ one's free time** privarse de tiempo libre **II.** *vi* **to ~ to the gods** hacer sacrificios a los dioses **III.** *n* sacrificio *m;* **at the ~ of sth** en detrimento de algo

sacrilege ['sæk·rə·lɪdʒ] *n* sacrilegio *m*

sacrilegious [,sæk·rə·'lɪdʒ·əs] *adj* sacrílego, -a

sacristan ['sæk·rɪ·stən] *n* sacristán *m*

sacristy ['sæk·rɪ·sti] *n* REL sacristía *f*

sacrosanct ['sæk·roʊ·sæŋkt] *adj* sacrosanto, -a

sacrum ['seɪ·krəm] <-a> *n* sacro *m*

SAD [,es·eɪ·'di] *n abbr of* **seasonal affective disorder** trastorno *m* afectivo estacional

sad [sæd] <-dd-> *adj* **1.** (*unhappy*) triste; **it is ~ that** es una pena que +*subj;* **to make sb ~** poner triste a alguien; **to become ~** entristecerse **2.** (*pathetic*) patético, -a **3.** (*deplorable, shameful*) lamentable; **~ to say...** lamentablemente...

sadden ['sæd·ən] *vt* entristecer; **to be deeply ~ed** estar muy afligido

saddle ['sæd·əl] **I.** *n* **1.** (*seat*) silla *f* de montar **2.** CULIN cuarto *m* trasero ▶ **to be in the ~** llevar las riendas **II.** *vt* **1.** (*horse*) ensillar **2.** *inf* (*burden*) **to ~ sb with sth** encajar algo a alguien

saddlebag ['sæd·əl·bæg] *n* alforja *f*

saddler ['sæd·lər] *n* talabartero, -a *m, f*

saddle sore ['sæd·əl·sɔr] *adj* dolorido, -a en las posaderas; **he's ~** le duelen las posaderas de montar

sadism ['seɪ·dɪz·əm] *n* sadismo *m*

sadist ['seɪ·dɪst] *n* sádico, -a *m, f*

sadistic [sə·'dɪs·tɪk] *adj* sádico, -a

sadly *adv* **1.** (*unhappily*) tristemente **2.** (*regrettably*) desgraciadamente; **to be ~ mistaken** estar muy equivocado

sadness ['sæd·nɪs] *n* tristeza *f*

safari [sə·'far·i] *n* safari *m;* **to go on ~** irse de safari

safari park *n* safari-park *m*

safe [seɪf] **I.** *adj* **1.** (*free of danger*) seguro, -a; (*driver*) prudente; **at a ~ distance** a una distancia prudencial; **it is not ~ to...** es peligroso... +*infin;* **just to be ~** por precaución; **have a ~ trip!** ¡buen viaje! **2.** (*secure*) salvo, -a; **to feel ~** sentirse a salvo; **to keep sth in a ~ place** guardar algo en (un) lugar seguro; **to put sth somewhere ~** poner algo a buen recaudo; **to win by a ~ margin** ganar con un

amplio margen **3.** (*certain*) seguro, -a; **a ~ bet** una apuesta segura **4.** (*trustworthy*) de fiar; **to be in ~ hands** estar en buenas manos **5.** (*not out in baseball*) a salvo ▶ **to be on the ~ side...** para mayor seguridad...; **it is better to be ~ than sorry** *prov* más vale prevenir que curar *prov;* **~ and sound** sano y salvo **II.** *n* caja *f* fuerte

safecracker *n* ladrón, -ona *m, f* de cajas fuertes

safe-deposit box *n* caja *f* de seguridad

safeguard ['seɪf·gard] **I.** *vt* salvaguardar **II.** *vi* protegerse; **to ~ against sth** protegerse contra algo **III.** *n* salvaguardia *f;* **as a ~ against sth** para evitar algo

safekeeping [,seɪf·'ki·pɪŋ] *n* custodia *f;* **to be in sb's ~** estar bajo la custodia de alguien

safely *adv* sin riesgos; **I can ~ say...** puedo decir sin temor a equivocarme que...

safe sex [seɪf·'seks] *n* sexo *m* seguro

safety ['seɪf·ti] *n* **1.** (*being safe*) seguridad *f;* **a place of ~** un lugar seguro; **for sb's ~** para la seguridad de alguien **2.** (*on gun*) seguro *m* **3.** (*football player*) defensor *m* ▶ **there's ~ in numbers** *prov* cuantos más, menos peligro

safety belt *n* cinturón *m* de seguridad

safety curtain *n* THEAT telón *m* de seguridad

safety glass *n* vidrio *m* inastillable

safety margin *n* margen *m* de seguridad

safety measures *npl* medidas *fpl* de seguridad

safety net *n* **1.** red *f* (de seguridad) **2.** *fig* protección *f*

safety pin *n* imperdible *m*

safety razor *n* maquinilla *f* (de afeitar)

safety regulations *npl* normas *fpl* de seguridad

safety valve *n* válvula *f* de seguridad

saffron ['sæf·rən] *n* azafrán *m*

sag [sæg] **I.** <-gg-> *vi* **1.** (*droop*) combarse, achiguarse *Arg, Chile* **2.** (*sink*) hundirse; (*spirit*) decaer; (*interest*) decrecer **II.** *n* **1.** (*drooping condition*) bajada *f* **2.** (*fall*) caída *f*

saga ['sɑ·gə] *n* saga *f*

sagacious [sə·'geɪ·[əs] *adj form* sagaz

sagacity [sə·'gæs·ə·t̬i] *n form* sagacidad *f*

sage[1] [seɪdʒ] *liter* **I.** *adj* (*wise*) sabio, -a **II.** *n* (*wise man*) sabio *m*

sage[2] [seɪdʒ] *n* (*herb*) salvia *f*

Sagittarius [,sædʒ·ə·'ter·i·əs] *n* Sagitario *m*

Sahara [sə·'her·ə] *n* **the ~** (**Desert**) el (desierto del) Sáhara

said [sed] **I.** *pp, pt of* **say II.** *adj* dicho, -a

sail [seɪl] **I.** *n* **1.** (*on boat*) vela *f* **2.** (*windmill blade*) aspa *f* ▶ **to set ~** (**for a place**) zarpar (hacia un lugar); **under full ~** a toda vela **II.** *vi* **1.** (*travel*) navegar; **to ~ around the world** dar la vuelta al mundo en barco **2.** (*start voyage*) zarpar **3.** (*move smoothly*) deslizarse **4.** *fig* (*do easily*) **to ~ through sth** hacer algo con facilidad ▶ **to ~ against the wind** nadar a contracorriente; **to ~ close to the wind** pisar terreno peligroso **III.** *vt* **1.** (*manage: boat,* *ship*) gobernar **2.**(*navigate*) cruzar; **to ~ the seas** surcar los mares

sailboard ['seɪl·bɔrd] *n* tabla *f* de windsurf

sailboarding *n* windsurf *m*

sailboat ['seɪl·boʊt] *n* barco *m* de vela

sailing *n* **1.** NAUT navegación *f* **2.** SPORTS vela *f* **3.**(*departure*) salida *f*

sailing ship *n*, **sailing vessel** *n* velero *m*

sailor ['seɪ·lər] *n* **1.**(*seaman*) marinero, -a *m, f* **2.** SPORTS navegante *mf*

sailor suit *n* traje *m* de marinero

saint [seɪnt, sənt] *n* santo, -a *m, f*

sainted *adj* santo, -a; **my ~ aunt!** *fig* ¡caray!

saintliness *n* santidad *f*

saintly ['seɪnt·li] *adj* santo, -a; (*life*) ejemplar

> ℹ️ El día de San Patricio (**Saint Patrick's Day**) se celebra el 17 de marzo y es la fiesta del santo patrono de Irlanda. En EE.UU. no es fiesta oficial, pero muchas personas se visten de verde y organizan fiestas. En algunas ciudades hay también desfiles, de los cuales el mayor y más famoso tiene lugar en Nueva York.

saint's day *n* (día *m* del) santo *m*

sake¹ [seɪk] *n* **1.**(*purpose*) **for the ~ of sth** por algo **2.**(*benefit*) **for the ~ of sb** por alguien ▶ **for Christ's ~**! *pej* ¡por Dios!; **for goodness ~**! ¡por el amor de Dios!; **for old times' ~** por los viejos tiempos

sake² *n*, **saki** ['sɑ·ki] *n* sake *m*

salable ['seɪ·lə·bəl] *adj* vendible

salacious [sə·'leɪ·ʃəs] *adj pej* salaz

salad ['sæl·əd] *n* ensalada *f*, verde *m CSur*

salad bowl *n* ensaladera *f*

salad days *npl* años *mpl* mozos

salad dressing *n* aliño *m*

salami [sə·'lɑ·mi] *n* salami *m*, salame *m CSur*

sal ammoniac [ˌsæl·ə·'moʊ·ni·æk] *n* sal *f* amoniacal

salaried ['sæl·ə·rid] *adj* (*employee, staff*) asalariado, -a

salary ['sæl·ə·ri] *n* sueldo *m*

salary cap *n* SPORTS cantidad máxima de dinero que un equipo se puede gastar en los sueldos de sus jugadores

sale [seɪl] *n* **1.**(*act of selling*) venta *f* **2.**(*reduced prices*) saldo *m*; **the ~s** las rebajas; **benefit ~** venta *f* benéfica; **end-of-season ~** liquidación *f* de final de temporada **3.**(*auction*) subasta *f* **4.** *pl* (*department that sells*) (departamento *m* de) ventas *fpl* ▶ **to put sth up for ~** poner algo en venta; **for ~** se vende; **on ~** en venta

saleable ['seɪ·lə·bəl] *adj s.* **salable**

sales associate *n* socio , -am, *f* de ventas

sales check *n* ticket *m* (de compra)

salesclerk *n* dependiente, -a *m, f*

sales executive *n* ejecutivo, -a *m, f* de ventas

sales force *n* personal *m* de ventas

salesman *n* (*in shop*) dependiente *m*; (*for company*) representante *m;* **door-to-door ~** vendedor a domicilio

salesmanship *n* habilidad *f* para vender

salesperson *n* vendedor(a) *m(f)*

sales pitch *n* rollo *m* publicitario

sales rep *n inf*, **sales representative** *n* agente *mf* de ventas

sales revenue *n* facturación *f*

sales tax *n* FIN impuesto *m* sobre las ventas

saleswoman *n* (*in a shop*) dependienta *f*; (*for company*) representante *f*; **door-to-door ~** vendedora a domicilio

salient ['seɪl·jənt] *adj* **1.**(*angle, structure*) saliente **2.** *fig* destacado, -a

saline ['seɪ·lin] **I.** *adj* salino, -a; **~ drip** gota a gota *m* **II.** *n* solución *f* salina

saliva [sə·'laɪ·və] *n* saliva *f*

salivate ['sæl·ə·veɪt] *vi* salivar

sallow ['sæl·oʊ] *adj* <-er, -est> (*skin, complexion*) cetrino, -a

salmon ['sæm·ən] *n* salmón *m;* **smoked ~** salmón ahumado

salmonella [ˌsæl·mə·'nel·ə] *n* **1.**(*bacteria*) salmonella *f* **2.**(*illness*) salmonelosis *f*

salmon farm *n* piscifactoría *f* de salmón

salmon ladder *n* paso *m* salmonero

salmon trout *n* trucha *f* asalmonada

salon [sə·'lɑn] *n* **1.**(*beauty establishment*) **beauty ~** salón *m* de belleza **2.**(*reception room*) recibidor *m*

saloon [sə·'lun] *n* bar *m*

salsify ['sæl·sə·faɪ] *n* BOT salsifí *m*

salt [sɔlt] **I.** *n* sal *f*; **bath ~s** sales de baño; **smelling ~s** sales aromáticas ▶ **~ of the earth** sal de la tierra; **to take sth with a grain of ~** creerse la mitad de la mitad de algo; **to rub ~ in a wound** hurgar en una herida; **to be worth** one's **~** merecer el pan que se come **II.** *vt* **1.**(*add salt to*) poner sal **2.**(*preserve in salt*) salar **3.**(*sprinkle with salt*) sazonar con sal **III.** *adj* salado, -a

salt-and-pepper *adj* (*hair*) entrecano, -a

salt mine *n* mina *f* de sal

saltpeter ['sɔlt·pi·tər] *n* salitre *m*

saltshaker *n* salero *m*

salt water *n* **1.**(*sea water*) agua *f* de mar **2.**(*water with salt*) agua *f* salada

saltwater ['sɔlt·wɔ·tər] *adj* de agua salada

salty ['sɔl·ti] *adj* (*taste*) salado, -a

salubrious [sə·'lu·bri·əs] *adj form* salubre

salutary ['sæl·jə·ter·i] *adj* saludable

salutation [ˌsæl·jə·'teɪ·ʃən] *n* saludo *m*

salute [sə·'lut] **I.** *vt* **1.** a. MIL saludar **2.** *fig* (*honor*) **to ~ sb** rendir homenaje a alguien **II.** *vi a.* MIL saludar **III.** *n* MIL **1.**(*hand gesture*) saludo *m* **2.**(*ceremonial firing of guns*) salva *f*

Salvadorian [ˌsæl·və·'dɔr·i·ən] **I.** *adj* salvadoreño, -a **II.** *n* salvadoreño, -a *m, f*

salvage ['sæl·vɪdʒ] **I.** *vt* salvar **II.** *n* **1.**(*retrieval*) salvamento *m* **2.**(*things saved*) objetos *mpl* salvados

salvage operation *n* operación *f* de salva-

S

mento

salvage vessel *n* buque *m* de salvamento

salvation [sæl·'veɪ·ʃən] *n* salvación *f*

Salvation Army *n* Ejército *m* de Salvación

salve [sæv] I. *n* 1.(*ointment*) ungüento *m* 2.*fig* bálsamo *m* II. *vt* curar; *fig* (*conscience*) tranquilizar

salvo ['sæl·voʊ] <-(e)s> *n* salva *f*; **to fire a ~** disparar una salva; **~ of applause** salva de aplausos

sal volatile [ˌsæl·voʊ·'læt̬·əl·i] *n* sal *f* de amonio

SAM [sæm] *n abbr of* **surface-to-air missile** misil *m* tierra-aire

same [seɪm] I. *adj* 1.(*identical*) igual; **the ~ (as sb/sth)** igual (que alguien/algo); **to go the ~ way (as sb)** llevar el mismo camino (que alguien) 2.(*not another*) mismo, -a; **the ~** el mismo; **at the ~ time** al mismo tiempo 3.(*unvarying*) idéntico, -a ▶ **to be one and the ~** ser lo mismo; **by the ~ token** del mismo modo II. *pron* 1.(*nominal*) **the ~** el mismo, la misma, lo mismo; **she's much the ~** sigue igual; **it's always the ~** siempre es lo mismo 2.(*adverbial*) **it's all the ~ to me** me da igual; **it's not the ~ as before** ya no es lo mismo; **all the ~** de todas formas; **~ to you** igualmente III. *adv* igual; **the two words are spelled the ~** las dos palabras se deletrean igual

sameness *n* 1.(*similarity*) igualdad *f* 2.(*monotony*) monotonía *f*

Samoa [sə·'moʊ·ə] *n* Samoa *f*

Samoan I. *adj* samoano, -a II. *n* samoano, -a *m, f*

sample ['sæm·pəl] I. *n* muestra *f*; **free ~** muestra gratuita; **urine ~** muestra de orina II. *vt* 1.(*try*) probar 2.(*survey*) tomar muestras

sampler ['sæm·plər] *n* 1.(*person*) catador(a) *m(f)* 2.(*device*) tomador *m* de muestras 3.(*embroidery*) dechado *m* 4.(*collection*) muestra *f* 5.*mus* sampler *m*

sampling ['sæm·plɪŋ] *n* muestreo *m*

sanatorium [ˌsæn·ə·'tɔr·i·əm] <-s *o* -ria> *n* sanatorio *m*

sanctify ['sæŋk·tɪ·faɪ] <-ie-> *vt* 1.*REL* santificar 2.*fig* (*legitimize*) avalar

sanctimonious [ˌsæŋk·tɪ·'moʊ·ni·əs] *adj pej* mojigato, -a

sanction ['sæŋk·ʃən] I. *n* 1.(*approval*) autorización *f*; **to give one's ~ to sth** dar su aprobación a algo 2.*LAW, POL* sanción *f* II. *vt* 1.(*authorize*) autorizar 2.(*approve*) aprobar 3.(*penalize*) sancionar

sanctity ['sæŋk·tə·t̬i] *n* 1.*REL* (*holiness*) santidad *f* 2.(*sacredness*) inviolabilidad *f*

sanctuary ['sæŋk·tʃu·er·i] *n* <-ies> 1.*REL* (*holy place*) santuario *m* 2.(*area around altar*) sagrario *m* 3.(*place of refuge*) refugio *m*; **to seek ~ in sth** refugiarse en algo 4.(*area for animals*) reserva *f*; **wildlife ~** reserva natural

sand [sænd] I. *n* arena *f*; **fine/coarse ~** arena fina/gruesa; **grains of ~** granos *mpl* de arena

▶ **the ~s of time are running out** el tiempo se agota II. *vt* 1.(*make smooth*) lijar; (*floor*) pulir 2.(*cover with sand*) enarenar

sandal ['sæn·dəl] *n* sandalia *f*, quimba *f AmL*

sandalwood ['sæn·dəl·wʊd] *n BOT* sándalo *m*

sandbag ['sænd·bæg] I. *n* saco *m* de arena II. <-gg-> *vt* proteger con sacos de arena

sandbank ['sænd·bæŋk] *n*, **sandbar** ['sænd·bar] *n* banco *m* de arena

sandblast ['sænd·blæst] *vt* pulir con chorro de arena

sandbox *n* cajón *m* de arena (*donde juegan los niños*)

sandcastle *n* castillo *m* de arena

sand dune *n* duna *f*

sand flea *n* pulga *f* de mar

sandpaper ['sænd·peɪ·pər] I. *n* papel *m* de lija II. *vt* lijar

sandpiper ['sænd·ˌpaɪ·pər] *n* (*bird*) andarríos *m inv*

sandstone *n* (*piedra f*) arenisca *f*

sandstorm *n* tormenta *f* de arena

sandwich ['sænd·wɪtʃ] I. <-es> *n* bocadillo *m*; (*made with sliced bread*) sándwich *m* II. *vt* intercalar

sandwich board *n* cartelón *m*

sandwich man <- -men> *n* hombre-anuncio *m*

sandy ['sæn·di] *adj* <-ier, -iest> arenoso, -a; (*hair*) rubio, -a rojizo, -a

sane [seɪn] *adj* 1.(*of sound mind*) cuerdo, -a 2.(*sensible*) sensato, -a

sang [sæŋ] *pt of* **sing**

sanguine ['sæŋ·gwɪn] *adj form* optimista

sanitarium [ˌsæn·ɪ·'ter·i·əm] <-s *o* -ria> *n* clínica *f*

sanitary ['sæn·ɪ·ter·i] *adj* 1.(*relating to hygiene*) sanitario, -a 2.(*clean*) higiénico, -a

sanitary napkin *n*, **sanitary pad** *n* compresa *f* (higiénica)

sanitation [ˌsæn·ɪ·'teɪ·ʃən] *n* saneamiento *m*

sanity ['sæn·ə·t̬i] *n* 1.(*of person*) cordura *f* 2.(*of decision*) sensatez *f*

sank [sæŋk] *pt of* **sink**

Santa (**Claus**) ['sæn·tə·(ˌklɔz)] *n* Papá *m* Noel

sap[1] [sæp] *n* 1.*BOT* savia *f* 2.(*vitality*) vitalidad *f*

sap[2] [sæp] <-pp-> *vt* 1.(*weaken*) socavar 2.*MIL* zapar

sap[3] [sæp] *n sl* (*fool*) papanatas *mf*

sapling ['sæp·lɪŋ] *n* (*young tree*) pimpollo *m*

sapper ['sæp·ər] *n* zapador(a) *m(f)*

sapphire ['sæf·aɪr] I. *n* 1.(*stone*) zafiro *m* 2.(*color*) azul *m* zafiro II. *adj* 1.(*necklace, ring*) de zafiro 2.(*color*) azul zafiro

sarcasm ['sar·kæz·əm] *n* sarcasmo *m*

sarcastic [sar·'kæs·tɪk] *adj* sarcástico, -a

sarcophagus [sar·'kaf·ə·gəs] <-es *o* -gi> *n* sarcófago *m*

sardine [sar·'din] *n* sardina *f* ▶ **to be packed (in) like ~s** estar como sardinas en lata

Sardinia [sar·'dɪn·i·ə] *n* Cerdeña *f*

Sardinian I. *n* sardo, -a *m, f f* II. *adj* sardo, -a

sardonic [sar·'dan·ɪk] *adj* sardónico, -a
sari ['sa·ri] *n* sari *m*
SARS [sarz] *n* MED *abbr of* **severe acute respiratory syndrome** SRAS *m*
sartorial [sar·'tɔr·i·əl] *adj* (*elegance*) en el vestir
SASE [ˌes·eɪ·es·'i] *n* *abbr of* **self-addressed stamped envelope** *sobre con las señas de uno y con sello*
sash¹ [sæʃ] <-es> *n* faja *f*
sash² [sæʃ] <-es> *n* ARCHIT marco *m* corredizo de ventana
sash window *n* ARCHIT ventana *f* de guillotina
Sat. *n* *abbr of* **Saturday** sáb.
sat [sæt] *pt, pp of* **sit**
Satan ['seɪ·tən] *n* Satanás *m*
satanic [sə·'tæn·ɪk] *adj* **1.** (*evil*) demoníaco, -a **2.** (*relating to Satanism*) satánico, -a
Satanism *n* satanismo *m*
satchel ['sætʃ·əl] *n* cartera *f* (de los libros), busaca *f* Col, Ven
sate [seɪt] *vt form* saciar; **to ~ sb** (**with sth**) hartar a alguien (con algo); **to be ~d** (**with sth**) estar saciado (de algo)
satellite ['sæt̬·ə·laɪt] **I.** *n* **1.** ASTR, TECH satélite *m* **2.** (*country*) satélite *m* **II.** *adj* TECH por satélite
satellite broadcasting *n* transmisión *f* por satélite
satellite dish *n* antena *f* parabólica
satellite state *n* estado *m* satélite
satellite television *n* televisión *f* por satélite
satiate ['seɪ·ʃi·eɪt] *vt* saciar
satiety [sə·'taɪ·ə·t̬i] *n form* saciedad *f*
satin ['sæt·ən] **I.** *n* raso *m*, satén *m* **II.** *adj* (*finish, paper*) satinado, -a
satire ['sæt·aɪr] *n* LIT sátira *f*
satirical [sə·'tɪr·ɪ·kəl] *adj* satírico, -a
satirist ['sæt̬·ər·ɪst] *n* escritor(a) *m(f)* satírico, -a
satirize ['sæt̬·ə·raɪz] *vt* satirizar
satisfaction [ˌsæt̬·ɪs·'fæk·ʃən] *n* **1.** satisfacción *f*; **to derive ~ from sth** conseguir satisfacción de algo; **to do sth to sb's ~** hacer algo para la satisfacción de alguien; **to be a ~** (**to sb**) ser una satisfacción (para alguien) **2.** (*compensation*) compensación *f*
satisfactory [ˌsæt̬·ɪs·'fæk·tə·ri] *adj* satisfactorio, -a; SCHOOL suficiente
satisfy ['sæt̬·əs·faɪ] <-ie-> *vt* **1.** (*person, desire*) satisfacer **2.** (*condition*) cumplir **3.** (*convince*) convencer; **to ~ sb that...** convencer a alguien de que... **4.** (*debt*) saldar
satisfying *adj* satisfactorio, -a
saturate ['sætʃ·ə·reɪt] *vt* **1.** (*soak*) empapar; **to be ~d in tradition** estar empapado en la tradición **2.** (*fill to capacity*) saturar; **to ~ the market** saturar el mercado
saturation [ˌsætʃ·ə·'reɪ·ʃən] *n* saturación *f*
saturation point *n* punto *m* de saturación; **to reach ~** alcanzar el punto de saturación
Saturday ['sæt̬·ər·deɪ] *n* sábado *m*; *s.a.* **Friday**
Saturn ['sæt̬·ərn] *n* Saturno *m*

satyr ['seɪ·t̬ər] *n* sátiro *m*
sauce [sɔs] *n* **1.** salsa *f*; **tomato ~** salsa de tomate **2.** (*impertinence*) frescura *f*
sauceboat *n* salsera *f*
saucepan ['sɔs·pæn] *n* cacerola *f*
saucer ['sɔ·sər] *n* platillo *m*
saucily ['sɔ·sɪ·li] *adv* con frescura
sauciness ['sɔ·sɪ·nɪs] *n* desfachatez *f*
saucy ['sɔ·si] *adj* <-ier, -iest> descarado, -a
Saudi Arabia [ˌsaʊ·di·ə·'reɪ·bi·ə] *n* Arabia *f* Saudí [*o* Saudita]
Saudi Arabian [ˌsaʊ·di·ə·'reɪ·bi·ən] **I.** *n* saudí *mf*, saudita *mf* **II.** *adj* saudí, saudita
sauerkraut ['saʊ·ər·kraʊt] *n* chucrut *f*
sauna ['sɔ·nə] *n* sauna *f*
saunter ['sɔn·tər] **I.** *vi* pasear **II.** *n* paseo *m*
sausage ['sɔ·sɪdʒ] *n* salchicha *f*; (*cured*) salchichón *m*
sausage meat *n* carne *f* de salchicha
sauté [sɔ·'teɪ] *vt* CULIN saltear
savage ['sæv·ɪdʒ] **I.** *adj* **1.** (*fierce*) salvaje, feroz **2.** *inf* (*bad-tempered*) de mal carácter **II.** *n pej* salvaje *mf* **III.** *vt* **1.** (*attack*) atacar salvajemente **2.** (*criticize*) criticar con saña
savagely *adv* **1.** (*attack*) salvajemente **2.** (*criticize*) con saña
savagery *n* ferocidad *f*
savanna(h) [sə·'væn·ə] *n* sabana *f*
save¹ [seɪv] **I.** *vt* **1.** (*rescue*) salvar; **to ~ sb's life** salvar la vida a alguien; **to ~ one's soul** salvarse; **to ~ face** salvar las apariencias; **to ~ one's own skin** salvar el pellejo **2.** (*keep for future use*) guardar **3.** (*collect*) coleccionar **4.** (*avoid wasting*) ahorrar **5.** (*reserve*) reservar **6.** (*prevent from doing*) impedir **7.** COMPUT guardar **8.** SPORTS parar **II.** *vi* **1.** (*keep for the future*) ahorrar; **to ~ for sth** ahorrar para algo **2.** (*conserve*) **to ~ on sth** guardar algo **III.** *n* SPORTS parada *f*
save² [seɪv] *prep* **~** (**for**) salvo; **all ~ the youngest** todos salvo los más jóvenes
saver ['seɪ·vər] *n* ahorrador(a) *m(f)*
saving ['seɪ·vɪŋ] **I.** *n* **1.** *pl* (*money*) ahorros *mpl* **2.** (*economy*) ahorro *m* **3.** (*rescue*) rescate *m* **II.** *adj* **his ~ grace** lo único que lo salva **III.** *prep* excepto
savings account ['seɪ·vɪŋz·ə·ˌkaʊnt] *n* cuenta *f* de ahorros
savings bank *n* caja *f* de ahorros
savior ['seɪv·jər] *n* salvador(a) *m(f)*
savor ['seɪ·vər] **I.** *n* **1.** (*taste*) sabor *m* **2.** (*pleasure*) gusto *m* **II.** *vt* saborear
savory ['seɪ·və·ri] *adj* **1.** (*salty*) salado, -a **2.** (*appetizing*) sabroso, -a; (*smell, taste*) apetitoso, -a **3.** (*socially acceptable*) respetable
Savoy [sə·'vɔɪ] *n* Saboya *f*
savvy ['sæv·i] *inf* **I.** *adj* <-ier, -iest> espabilado, -a **II.** *n* inteligencia *f*
saw¹ [sɔ] *pt of* **see**
saw² [sɔ] **I.** *n* sierra *f*; **power ~** sierra eléctrica **II.** <sawed, sawed *o* sawn> *vt* serrar
saw³ [sɔ] *n* dicho *m*
sawdust ['sɔ·dʌst] *n* serrín *m*

S

sawed-off shotgun *n* escopeta *f* de cañones recortados
sawmill ['sɔ·mɪl] *n* aserradero *m*
sawn [sɔn] *pp of* **saw**
Saxon ['sæk·sən] I. *n* sajón, -ona *m, f* II. *adj* sajón, -ona
Saxony ['sæk·sə·ni] *n* Sajonia *f*
saxophone ['sæk·sə·foʊn] *n* saxofón *m*
saxophonist ['sæk·sə·foʊ·nɪst] *n* saxofonista *mf*
say [seɪ] I.<said, said> *vt* **1.**(*speak*) decir; **to ~ sth to sb's face** decir algo a alguien a la cara; **~ no more!** ¡no diga(s) más! **2.**(*state information*) **to ~** (**that**)... decir (que)...; **to have something/nothing to ~** (**to sb**) tener algo/no tener nada que decir (a alguien); **to ~ goodbye to sb** decirle adiós a alguien **3.**(*express*) expresar **4.**(*think*) opinar; **people ~ that...** se dice que...; **to ~ to oneself** decirse a sí mismo **5.**(*recite*) recitar; (*prayer*) rezar **6.**(*indicate*) indicar; **to ~ sth about sb/sth** expresar algo sobre alguien/algo; **the said sb/sth...** *form* dicha persona/cosa... **7.**(*convey meaning*) significar **8.** *inf* (*suggest*) sugerir **9.**(*tell*) explicar; **to ~ where/when** explicar dónde/cuándo; **it's not for me to ~...** no me corresponde decir... **10.**(*for instance*) (**let's**) **~...** digamos...; ▶ **when all is said and done** a fin de cuentas; **having said that,...** una vez dicho eso,...; **to ~ when** decir basta; **you don't ~** (**so**)! ¡no me digas!; **you said it!** *inf* ¡dímelo a mí! II.<said, said> *vi* **I'll ~!** *inf* ¡ya lo creo!; **I must ~...** debo admitir...; **not to ~...** incluso...; **that is to ~...** es decir... III. *n* parecer *m;* **to have one's ~** expresar su propia opinión; **to have a ~ in sth** tener voz y voto en algo IV. *interj* (*positive reaction*) caramba; **~, that's a great idea!** ¡perfecto, es una gran idea!
saying ['seɪ·ɪŋ] *n* **1.**(*proverb*) dicho *m;* **as the ~ goes** como dice el refrán **2. it goes without ~** ni qué decir tiene
say-so ['seɪ·soʊ] *n inf* **1.**(*authority*) autoridad *f;* **to have the ~** tener la última palabra **2.**(*approval*) visto bueno *m;* **to get the ~** obtener el visto bueno **3.**(*assertion*) afirmación *f;* **don't just believe it on my ~** no te lo creas porque yo lo diga
SC [ˌsaʊθˌkær·ə·ˈlaɪ·nə] *n abbr of* **South Carolina** Carolina *f* del Sur
scab [skæb] *n* **1.**(*over wound*) costra *f* **2.** *pej, sl* (*strikebreaker*) esquirol *mf* **3.** BOT, ZOOL roña *f*
scabbard ['skæb·ərd] *n* vaina *f*
scabby ['skæb·i] *adj* <-ier, -iest> **1.**(*having scabs*) con costras **2.** ZOOL roñoso, -a **3.** *pej, sl* (*disgusting*) horrible
scabies ['skeɪ·biz] *n* MED sarna *f*, zarate *m* Hond
scabrous ['skæb·rəs] *adj* escabroso, -a
scaffold ['skæf·əld] *n* **1.**(*for execution*) patíbulo *m* **2.**(*for building*) andamio *m*
scaffolding ['skæf·əl·dɪŋ] *n* andamiaje *m*

scald [skɔld] I. *vt* **1.**(*burn*) escaldar **2.**(*clean*) esterilizar con agua hirviendo **3.**(*heat: milk*) calentar II. *n* MED escaldadura *f*
scalding ['skɔl·dɪŋ] *adj* que escalda; **~ hot** hirviendo
scale[1] [skeɪl] I. *n* **1.** ZOOL escama *f* **2.** TECH, MED sarro *m* II. *vt* **1.**(*remove scales*) escamar **2.** TECH, MED quitar el sarro de
scale[2] [skeɪl] *n* (*weighing device*) platillo *m;* **~s** balanza *f;* (*bigger*) báscula *f* ▶ **to tip the ~s** inclinar la balanza
scale[3] [skeɪl] I. *n* (*range, magnitude, proportion*) *a.* MUS escala *f;* **a sliding ~** ECON una banda fluctuante; **on a large/small ~** a gran/pequeña escala; **to draw sth to ~** dibujar algo a escala II. *vt* **1.**(*climb*) escalar; **to ~ the heights** (**of sth**) trepar a las alturas (de algo) **2.** TECH, ARCHIT reducir a escala
◆ **scale down** *vt* (*demand, expectations*) reducir
scale drawing *n* TECH, ARCHIT dibujo *m* a escala
scale model *n* modelo *m* a escala
scallop ['skal·əp] *n* ZOOL vieira *f;* **~** (**shell**) venera *f*
scalp [skælp] I. *n* **1.**(*head skin*) cuero *m* cabelludo **2.**(*war trophy*) cabellera *f;* **to be out after sb's ~** querer acabar con alguien II. *vt* **1.** *inf* (*resell*) revender **2.**(*in war*) **to ~ sb** arrancar la cabellera a alguien; *iron* cortar el pelo a alguien
scalpel ['skæl·pəl] *n* MED escalpelo *m*
scalper ['skæl·pər] *n* (*reseller of tickets, etc.*) reventa *mf inf*
scaly ['skeɪ·li] *adj* <-ier, -iest> **1.** ZOOL escamoso, -a **2.** MED (*skin*) reseco, -a
scam [skæm] *n sl* timo *m*
scamper ['skæm·pər] *vi* corretear
scampi ['skæm·pi] *npl* gambas *fpl* rebozadas
scan [skæn] I.<-nn-> *vt* **1.**(*scrutinize*) escudriñar **2.**(*look through quickly*) dar un vistazo; (*newspaper*) hojear **3.** MED explorar; (*brain*) hacer un escáner de **4.** LIT medir **5.** COMPUT escanear II.<-nn-> *vi* medir(se) III. *n* COMPUT escaneado *m;* MED escáner *m*
scandal ['skæn·dəl] *n* **1.**(*public outrage*) escándalo *m;* **to uncover** [*o* **expose**] **a ~** sacar a la luz un escándalo; **to cover up a ~** tapar un escándalo **2.**(*sth bad*) **what a ~!** ¡qué vergüenza! **3.**(*gossip*) chismorreo *m;* **to spread ~** difundir habladurías
scandalize ['skæn·də·laɪz] *vt* escandalizar
scandalmonger ['skæn·dəl·ˌmaŋ·gər] *n pej* chismoso, -a *m, f*
scandalous ['skæn·də·ləs] *adj* **1.**(*spreading scandal*) escandaloso, -a **2.**(*disgraceful*) vergonzoso, -a; **it is ~ that...** resulta vergonzoso que... +*subj*
Scandinavia [ˌskæn·dɪ·ˈneɪ·vi·ə] *n* Escandinavia *f*
Scandinavian I. *adj* escandinavo, -a II. *n* escandinavo, -a *m, f*
scanner ['skæn·ər] *n* COMPUT, MED escáner *m*
scanning *n* COMPUT, MED escaneo *m*

scant [skænt] *adj* escaso, -a; ~ **attention** poca atención

scantily *adv* insuficientemente; ~ **dressed** [*o* **clad**] ligero de ropa

scanty ['skæn·ti] *adj* 1. (*very small*) corto, -a; (*clothing*) ligero, -a 2. (*insufficient*) insuficiente

scapegoat ['skeɪp·goʊt] *n* cabeza *mf* de turco; **to be a ~ for sb/sth** ser un chivo expiatorio para alguien/algo

scapula ['skæp·jʊ·lə] <-s *o* -lae> *pl n* omóplato *m*

scar [skar] I. *n* 1. MED (*on skin*) cicatriz *f*; **to leave a ~** dejar cicatriz 2. (*mark of damage*) señal *f* 3. PSYCH trauma *m* 4. GEO paraje *m* rocoso II. <-rr-> *vt* marcar con cicatriz; **to be ~red (by sth)** tener una cicatriz (hecha por algo); **to be ~red for life** quedar marcado de por vida III. <-rr-> *vi* to ~ (**over**) cicatrizar(se)

scarab ['sker·əb] *n* escarabajo *m*

scarce [skers] *adj* escaso, -a; **to make oneself ~** *inf* desaparecer

scarcely ['skers·li] *adv* 1. (*barely*) apenas 2. (*certainly not*) ni mucho menos

scarcity ['sker·sə·t̬i] *n* escasez *f*

scare [sker] I. *vt* asustar, julepear *Arg, Par, Urug,* acholar *Chile, Perú;* **to ~ sb into/out of doing sth** espantar a alguien para que haga/no haga algo; **to be ~d stiff** estar muerto de miedo; **to ~ sb shitless** *vulg* acojonar a alguien II. *vi* asustarse; **to (not) ~ easily** (no) asustarse fácilmente III. *n* 1. (*fright*) susto *m,* julepe *m AmL;* **to have a ~** llevarse un sobresalto; **to give sb a ~** dar un susto a alguien 2. (*panic*) pánico *m*

♦ **scare away** *vt,* **scare off** *vt* ahuyentar

scarecrow ['sker·kroʊ] *n* espantapájaros *m inv*

scaremonger ['sker·ˌmaŋ·gər] *n pej* alarmista *mf*

scarf [skarf, *pl* skarvz] <-ves *o* -s> *n* (*around neck*) bufanda *f;* (*around head*) pañuelo *m*

♦ **scarf down** *vt sl* engullir

scarlet ['skar·lət] I. *n* escarlata *f* II. *adj* de color escarlata; **to turn ~** ponerse rojo

scarlet fever *n* MED escarlatina *f*

scarp [skarp] *n* GEO escarpe *m*

scary ['sker·i] *adj* <-ier, -iest> que da miedo; ~ **movie** película *f* de miedo

scat [skæt] *interj inf* fuera

scathing ['skeɪ·ðɪŋ] *adj* mordaz

scatological [ˌskæt̬·ə·'ladʒ·ɪ·kəl] *adj form* escatológico, -a

scatter ['skæt̬·ər] I. *vt* esparcir; **to ~ sth with sth** salpicar algo con algo; **to ~ sth to the four winds** esparcir algo a los cuatro vientos II. *vi* dispersarse; **to ~ in all directions** desparramarse en todas direcciones

scatterbrain ['skæt̬·ər·breɪn] *n pej* cabeza *mf* de chorlito

scatterbrained *adj* atolondrado, -a

scattered *adj* 1. disperso, -a 2. (*widely separated*) separado, -a 3. (*sporadic*) esporádico, -a

scavenge ['skæv·ɪndʒ] *vi* 1. (*search*) buscar cosas en la basura, pepenar *AmC, Méx* 2. ZOOL buscar comida

scavenger ['skæv·ɪn·dʒər] *n* 1. ZOOL animal *m* carroñero 2. (*person*) persona que hurga en la basura en busca de comida, etc.

scenario [sə·'ner·i·oʊ] *n* 1. (*situation*) marco *m* hipotético, escenario *m* 2. THEAT, LIT guión *m*

scene [sin] *n* 1. THEAT, CINE (*unit of drama*) escena *f;* (*setting*) escenario *m;* **nude ~** escena *f* de desnudo; **behind the ~s** *a. fig* entre bastidores 2. (*locality*) lugar *m;* **the ~ of the crime** la escena del crimen 3. (*view*) vista *f* 4. (*milieu*) mundo *m;* **the art/drugs ~** el mundo del arte/de las drogas; **this is/isn't my ~** *inf* esto es/no es lo mío; **to appear on the ~** presentarse; **to depart from the political ~** desaparecer del escenario político; **to set the ~** crear un ambiente 5. (*embarrassing incident*) escándalo *m;* **to make a ~** montar un número

scenery ['si·nə·ri] *n* 1. (*landscape*) paisaje *m* 2. THEAT, CINE decorado *m;* **to blend into the ~** conseguir pasar inadvertido

scenic ['si·nɪk] *adj* 1. THEAT escénico, -a 2. (*of beautiful scenery*) pintoresco, -a; ~ **road** ruta *f* turística

scent [sent] I. *n* 1. (*aroma*) aroma *m* 2. (*in hunting*) rastro *m;* **to be on the ~ of sth/sb** estar sobre la pista de algo/alguien; **to put [***o* **throw] sb off the ~** despistar a alguien 3. (*perfume*) perfume *m* II. *vt* 1. (*smell*) oler 2. (*sense, detect*) intuir; **to ~ that...** sospechar que... 3. (*apply perfume*) perfumar

scent bottle *n* frasco *m* de perfume

scentless *adj* inodoro, -a

scepter ['sep·tər] *n* cetro *m*

sceptic ['skep·tɪk] *n s.* skeptic

sceptical *adj s.* skeptical

scepticism ['skep·tɪ·sɪz·əm] *n s.* skepticism

schedule ['skedʒ·ul] I. *n* 1. (*timetable*) horario *m;* **bus ~** horario de autobuses; **flight ~** horario de vuelos; **to stick to a ~** seguir un horario; **everything went according to ~** todo fue según lo previsto 2. (*plan of work*) programa *m* 3. FIN inventario *m* II. *vt* 1. (*plan*) programar 2. (*list*) hacer una lista

scheduled *adj* programado, -a; ~ **flight** vuelo *m* regular

schematic [ski·'mæt̬·ɪk] *adj* esquemático, -a

scheme [skim] I. *n* 1. (*structure*) esquema *m* 2. (*plot*) treta *f* II. *vi pej* intrigar; **to ~ to do sth** intrigar para hacer algo

schemer ['ski·mər] *n* intrigante *mf*

scheming ['ski·mɪŋ] *adj* intrigante

schism ['skɪz·əm] *n* cisma *m*

schismatic [sɪz·'mæt̬·ɪk] REL I. *adj* cismático, -a II. *n* cismático, -a *m, f*

schist [ʃɪst] *n* GEO esquisto *m*

schizophrenia [ˌskɪt·sə·'fri·ni·ə] *n* esquizofrenia *f*

schizophrenic [ˌskɪt·sə·'fren·ɪk] I. *adj* esquizofrénico, -a II. *n* esquizofrénico, -a *m, f*

scholar ['skal·ər] *n* 1. (*learned person*) erudito, -a *m, f* 2. (*student*) estudiante *mf*

S

3. (*scholarship holder*) becario, -a *m, f*
scholarly *adj* erudito, -a
scholarship ['skal·ər·ʃɪp] *n* **1.** (*learning*) erudición *f* **2.** (*grant*) beca *f*
scholastic [skə·'læs·tɪk] *adj* académico, -a; PHILOS escolástico, -a
school[1] [skul] **I.** *n* **1.** (*institution*) escuela *f*, colegio *m;* **primary** ~ escuela *f* primaria; **secondary** ~ instituto *m* (de enseñanza secundaria), liceo *m Chile, Méx;* **public** ~ escuela pública; **dancing** ~ escuela de baile; **driving** ~ autoescuela; **to be in** ~ estar en edad escolar; **to go to** ~ ir al colegio; **to start** ~ empezar la escuela; **to leave** ~ terminar el colegio **2.** (*buildings*) colegio *m* **3.** (*classes*) clases *fpl* **4.** (*university division*) facultad *f* **5.** PHILOS escuela *f* **6.** (*university*) universidad *f* **II.** *vt* enseñar **III.** *adj* escolar
school[2] [skul] *n* ZOOL banco *m* (de peces)
school board *n* ADMIN consejo *m* escolar
school bus *n* autobús *m* escolar
school day *n* **1.** (*day*) día *m* de colegio **2.** (*part of day*) horas *f* de clase *pl*
school district *n* distrito *m* escolar
schooling *n* enseñanza *f*
schoolmate *n* compañero, -a *m, f* de clase
school nurse *n* enfermera *f* de escuela
school system *n* sistema *m* escolar

---

i El sistema escolar (**school system**) estadounidense comienza con la **elementary school,** que abarca desde el curso primero hasta el sexto u octavo. En algunos lugares, después del **sixth grade** (sexto grado) los alumnos pasan a otra escuela, la **junior high school,** donde cursan los grados séptimo, octavo y noveno. Posteriormente, ingresan en la **high school,** donde permanecen por espacio de tres años. En aquellos lugares donde no existe la **junior high school,** los alumnos pasan directamente de la **elementary school** (donde han permanecido durante ocho años) a la **high school,** que en este caso comienza con el **ninth grade** (noveno grado). Los alumnos finalizan su itinerario escolar al terminar el **twelfth grade** (décimosegundo grado).

---

schoolteacher *n* profesor(a) *m(f)*
schoolwork *n* trabajo *m* escolar
schoolyard *n* patio *m* del colegio
schooner ['sku·nər] *n* **1.** NAUT goleta *f* **2.** (*tall glass*) jarra *f*
sciatic [saɪ·'æt̬·ɪk] *adj* ciático, -a
sciatica [saɪ·'æt̬·ɪ·kə] *n* MED ciática *f*
science ['saɪ·əns] **I.** *n* ciencia *f;* **pure/applied** ~ ciencias *fpl* puras/aplicadas; **the wonders of modern** ~ las maravillas de la ciencia moderna **II.** *adj* de ciencias
science fiction I. *n* ciencia ficción *f* **II.** *adj* de

ciencia ficción
scientific [ˌsaɪ·ən·'tɪf·ɪk] *adj* científico, -a
scientist ['saɪ·ən·tɪst] *n* científico, -a *m, f*
sci-fi ['saɪ·faɪ] *n abbr of* **science fiction** ciencia *f* ficción
scintillating ['sɪn·tə·leɪ·t̬ɪŋ] *adj* (*performance*) brillante; (*wit*) chispeante
scion ['saɪ·ən] *n form* **1.** (*descendant*) descendiente *mf* **2.** BOT injerto *m*, esqueje *m*
scissors ['sɪz·ərz] *npl* tijeras *fpl;* **a pair of** ~ unas tijeras
sclerosis [sklɪ·'roʊ·sɪs] *n* MED esclerosis *f*
scoff [skaf] *vi* (*mock*) burlarse; **to** ~ **at sth/sb** reírse de algo/alguien
scold [skoʊld] *vt* regañar
scolding ['skoʊl·dɪŋ] *n* reprimenda *f*, raspada *f Méx, PRico,* trepe *m CRi*
scone [skoʊn] *n* bollo *m*
scoop [skup] **I.** *n* **1.** (*utensil*) cucharón *m;* **ice cream** ~ cuchara *f* de helado; **measuring** ~ cuchara de medición **2.** (*amount*) cucharada *f* **3.** PUBL primicia *f* informativa **II.** *vt* **1.** (*shovel*) sacar (con una pala) **2.** *inf* PUBL adelantarse con una exclusiva
◆ **scoop up** *vt* recoger
scoot [skut] *vi inf* largarse; **to** ~ **over** escabullirse
scooter ['sku·t̬ər] *n* **1.** (*toy*) patinete *m* **2.** (*vehicle*) (**motor**) ~ scooter *m*, Vespa® *f*
scope [skoʊp] *n* **1.** (*range*) alcance *m* **2.** (*possibilities*) posibilidades *fpl;* **limited/considerable** ~ campo *m* de acción limitado/considerable
scorch [skɔrtʃ] **I.** *vt* chamuscar **II.** *vi* chamuscarse **III.** *n* <-es> quemadura *f*
scorcher *n inf* día *m* de mucho calor
scorching *adj* abrasador(a); **it's** ~ **hot** hace un calor abrasador
score [skɔr] **I.** *n* **1.** SPORTS (*number of points*) puntuación *f;* **to keep** (**the**) ~ llevar la cuenta **2.** SPORTS (*goal, point*) tanto *m* **3.** SCHOOL nota *f* **4.** (*twenty*) veintena *f;* ~**s of people** mucha gente **5.** (*dispute*) rencilla *f;* **to settle a** ~ ajustar cuentas **6.** MUS partitura *f* **7.** (*line*) muesca *f* **II.** *vt* **1.** (*goal, point*) marcar; (*triumph, victory*) obtener **2.** (*cut*) cortar **3.** *sl* (*buy: drugs*) conseguir **4.** MUS (*arrange*) instrumentar **III.** *vi* **1.** SPORTS (*make a point*) marcar un tanto **2.** *sl* (*succeed*) triunfar **3.** *sl* (*make sexual conquest*) echar un polvo **4.** *sl* (*buy drugs*) comprar droga
scoreboard ['skɔr·bɔrd] *n* marcador *m*
scorecard *n* tarjeta *f* de registro de la puntuación
scorekeeper *n* encargado , -a*m, f* del marcador
scorer *n* **1.** (*player: in soccer*) goleador(a) *m(f);* (*in basketball*) jugador que marca uno o más tantos **2.** (*scorekeeper*) encargado , -a*m, f* del marcador
scoring *n* puntuación *f*
scorn [skɔrn] **I.** *n* desprecio *m;* **to be the** ~ **of sb/sth** ser despreciado por alguien/algo; **to**

pour ~ on sb/sth ridiculizar a alguien/algo
II. *vt* **1.** (*disdain*) despreciar, ajotar *Cuba*
2. (*refuse*) rechazar (por orgullo); **to ~ to do
sth** no dignarse a hacer algo
scornful ['skɔrn·fəl] *adj* desdeñoso, -a
Scorpio ['skɔr·pi·ou] *n* Escorpio *m*
scorpion ['skɔr·pi·ən] *n* escorpión *m*
Scot [skat] *n* escocés, -esa *m, f*
Scotch [skatʃ] **I.** *n* whisky *m* (escocés); **a ~ on
the rocks** un whisky con hielo, un whisky en
las rocas *Méx* **II.** *adj* escocés, -esa
Scotch tape® ['skatʃ·teɪp] *n* celo *m*, cinta *f*
adhesiva
scot-free [ˌskat·'fri] *adv* **1.** (*without punishment*) impunemente; **to get away** [*o* **off**] **~**
librarse del castigo **2.** (*unharmed*) sin un rasguño
Scotland ['skat·lənd] *n* Escocia *f*
Scots [skats] *adj s.* **Scottish**
Scotsman ['skats·mən] <-men> *n* escocés *m*
Scotswoman ['skats·ˌwʊm·ən] <-women> *n*
escocesa *f*
Scottish ['skat·ɪʃ] *adj* escocés, -esa
scoundrel ['skaʊn·drəl] *n pej* sinvergüenza *mf*
scour ['skaʊ·ər] **I.** *vt* **1.** (*scrub*) fregar
2. (*search*) recorrer; **the police are ~ing the
neighborhood** la policía esta haciendo una
batida en el vecindario **II.** *n* fregado, -a *m, f;* **to
give sth a ~** fregar algo
scourer *n* estropajo *m*
scourge [skɜrdʒ] **I.** *n a. fig* azote *m* **II.** *vt*
1. (*inflict suffering*) azotar **2.** (*whip*) flagelar
scouring pad *n* estropajo *m*
scout [skaʊt] **I.** *n* explorador(a) *m(f),* scout *mf
Méx;* **talent ~** cazatalentos *mf inv* **II.** *vi* **to ~
ahead** reconocer el terreno; **to ~ around for
sth** buscar algo
scoutmaster *n* jefe *m* de exploradores, akela
m Méx
scowl [skaʊl] **I.** *n* ceño *m* fruncido **II.** *vi* fruncir
el ceño
scrabble ['skræb·əl] *vi* **1.** (*grope*) hurgar
2. (*claw for grip*) escarbar
scraggly *adj* descuidado, -a
scraggy ['skræg·i] <-ier, -iest> *adj* flaco, -a
scram [skræm] **I.** <-mm-> *vi sl* largarse, rajarse
AmC **II.** *interj sl* **~!** ¡largo!
scramble ['skræm·bəl] **I.** *vi* **1.** (*move hastily*)
moverse apresuradamente **2.** (*try to get first*)
luchar; **to ~ for sth** esforzarse por algo **3.** AVIAT
(*take off quickly*) despegar rápidamente **II.** *vt*
1. (*mix together*) revolver; **~d eggs** huevos
revueltos **2.** (*encrypt*) codificar **3.** AVIAT (*launch
quickly*) hacer despegar rápidamente **III.** *n*
1. (*rush*) carrera *f;* (*chase*) persecución *f*
2. (*struggle*) pelea *f,* rebatinga *f Méx* **3.** (*aircraft launch*) despegue de emergencia para
interceptar un avión enemigo o desconocido
scrambler ['skræm·blər] *n* codificador *m* de
señales
scrap¹ [skræp] **I.** *n* **1.** (*small piece*) trozo *m;*
(*of paper, cloth*) pedazo *m* **2.** (*small amount*)
pizca *f;* (*of information*) retazo *m;* **not a ~ of**

truth ni un ápice de verdad **3.** *pl* (*leftover
food*) sobras *fpl* **4.** (*old metal*) chatarra *f*
II. <-pp-> *vt* **1.** (*get rid of*) desechar; (*abandon*) descartar; (*abolish*) abolir **2.** (*use for
scrap metal*) desguazar, deshuesar *Méx*
scrap² [skræp] **I.** *n inf* (*fight*) pelea *f,* agarrón
m Méx **II.** <-pp-> *vi* pelearse
scrapbook ['skræp·bʊk] *n* álbum *m* de
recortes
scrap dealer *n* chatarrero, -a *m, f*
scrape [skreɪp] **I.** *vt* **1.** (*remove layer*) raspar, rasquetear *Arg;* (*remove: dirt*) limpiar
2. (*graze*) rozar; (*scratch*) rascar **3.** (*rub
against*) rozar **II.** *vi* **1.** (*rub against*) rozar
2. (*make unpleasant noise*) chirriar **3.** (*economize*) ahorrar **III.** *n* **1.** (*act of scraping*) raspado, -a *m, f* **2.** (*graze on skin*) raspadura *f*
3. (*sound*) chirrido *m* **4.** *inf* (*situation*) lío *m;*
to get into a ~ meterse en un lío
◆**scrape along** *vi s.* **scrape by**
◆**scrape away** *vt* raspar
◆**scrape by** *vi* apañárselas
◆**scrape through I.** *vt* aprobar por los pelos
II. *vi* pasar por los pelos
scraper ['skreɪ·pər] *n* (*tool*) raspador *m;* (*for
cleaning shoes*) limpiabarros *m inv*
scrapheap ['skræp·hip] *n* montón *m* de
basura; **to end up in** [*o* **on**] **the ~** quedarse sin
futuro laboral
scrapings *npl* **1.** (*leftovers*) sobras *fpl* **2.** TECH
limaduras *fpl*
scrap iron *n* chatarra *f*
scrappy¹ ['skræp·i] <-ier, -iest> *adj* **1.** (*knowledge*) superficial **2.** (*performance, game*)
irregular
scrappy² ['skræp·i] <-ier, -iest> *adj* (*ready to
fight*) pendenciero, -a, peleonero, -a *Méx*
scratch [skrætʃ] **I.** *n* **1.** (*cut on skin*) rasguño
m, rayón *m AmL* **2.** (*mark*) raya *f* **3.** (*act of
scratching*) arañamiento *m* **4.** (*start*) principio
m; **from ~** desde cero **II.** *vt* **1.** (*cut slightly*)
arañar **2.** (*mark*) rayar **3.** (*relieve itch*) rascar
4. (*erase*) tachar **5.** (*exclude*) retirar **6.** *sl* (*cancel*) cancelar **7.** (*write*) garabatear **III.** *vi*
1. (*use claws: cat*) arañar **2.** (*relieve itch*) rascarse **IV.** *adj* improvisado, -a
◆**scratch out** *vt* **1.** (*with claws*) arañar; **to
scratch sb's eyes out** *fig* sacar los ojos a alguien **2.** (*line, word*) tachar
scratch card ['skrætʃ·kard] *n* tarjeta *f* rasca,
raspadita *f Arg*
scratch paper *n* papel *m* de borrador
scratchy ['skrætʃ·i] <-ier, -iest> *adj* **1.** (*record,
voice*) rayado, -a **2.** (*irritating*) áspero, -a
scrawl [skrɔl] **I.** *vt* garabatear **II.** *n* garabato *m*
scrawny ['skrɔ·ni] <-ier, -iest> *adj* escuálido,
-a, silgado, -a *Ecua*
scream [skrim] **I.** *n* **1.** (*cry*) grito *m;* (*shrill cry*)
chillido *m;* (*shout*) alarido *m* **2.** (*of animal*)
chillido *m* ▶ **to be a ~** *inf* ser la monda **II.** *vi*
(*shout*) gritar; (*cry shrilly*) chillar; **to ~ with
laughter** reír a carcajadas **III.** *vt* (*shout*) gritar;
(*abuse, obscenities*) lanzar; **to ~ oneself**

S

hoarse gritar hasta quedarse afónico
screech [skritʃ] **I.** *n* chillido *m* **II.** *vi* chillar; **to ~ with pain** lanzar gritos de dolor
screech owl *n* lechuza *f*
screen [skrin] **I.** *n* **1.** *a.* TV, CINE, COMPUT pantalla *f;* **split/touch ~** pantalla dividida/táctil **2.** (*framed panel*) biombo *m;* (*for protection*) cortina *f;* (*in front of fire*) pantalla *f;* **glass ~** vitral *m* **3.** (*thing that conceals*) cortina *f* **II.** *vt* **1.** (*conceal*) ocultar **2.** (*shield*) proteger **3.** (*examine*) examinar; (*revise*) revisar **4.** TV emitir; CINE proyectar **5.** (*put through a sieve*) cribar
♦**screen off** *vt* separar con un biombo
screening *n* **1.** (*showing: in cinema*) proyección *f;* (*on television*) emisión *f* **2.** (*testing*) prueba *f* **3.** MED (*examination*) chequeo *m*
screenplay ['skrin·pleɪ] *n* guión *m*
screen saver *n* COMPUT salvapantallas *m inv*
screen shot *n* COMPUT captura *f* de pantalla
screen test *n* prueba *f*
screenwriter *n* guionista *mf*
screw [skru] **I.** *n* **1.** (*small metal fastener*) tornillo *m;* **to tighten** (**up**)**/loosen a ~** apretar/aflojar un tornillo **2.** (*turn*) vuelta *f* **3.** (*propeller*) hélice *f* **4.** (*spin*) efecto *m*, chanfle *m* *Méx* **5.** (*twisted piece*) rosca *f* **6.** *vulg* (*sexual intercourse*) **I had a good ~ last night** anoche eché un buen polvo **7.** *vulg* (*sexual partner*) **she's a great ~** tiene un buen polvo ▶**he's got a ~** [*o* **a few ~s**] loose *inf* le falta (más de) un tornillo; **to** put **the ~s on sb** *sl* apretar las tuercas a alguien **II.** *vt* **1.** (*with a screw*) atornillar **2.** (*by twisting*) enroscar **3.** *sl* (*cheat*) timar **4.** *vulg* (*have sex with*) follar con, coger *AmL* **5.** *sl* **~ you!** ¡vete a la mierda! **III.** *vi* **1.** (*turn like a screw*) enroscarse **2.** (*become attached*) atornillarse **3.** *vulg* (*have sex*) echar un polvo, echarse un palo *Méx*
♦**screw around** *vi* **1.** *sl* (*act stupidly*) hacer el payaso **2.** *vulg* (*be sexually promiscuous*) ser un putón verbenero
♦**screw up** **I.** *vt* **1.** *sl* (*make a mess of*) joder **2.** *sl* (*injure*) fastidiar **3.** *inf* (*make anxious*) poner neurótico **II.** *vi* cagarla
screwball ['skru·bɔl] *n* **1.** *sl* (*odd person*) chiflado, -a *m, f* **2.** (*in baseball*) tirabuzón *m*
screwdriver ['skru·draɪ·vər] *n* **1.** (*tool*) destornillador *m*, desarmador *m AmL* **2.** (*drink*) destornillador *m*
screwed *adj sl* jodido, -a *vulg*
screw top *n* tapón *m* de rosca
screwy ['skru·i] <-ier, iest> *adj sl* chalado, -a
scribble ['skrɪb·əl] **I.** *vt* garabatear **II.** *vi* hacer garabatos **III.** *n* garabatos *mpl*
scrimmage ['skrɪm·ɪdʒ] *n* **1.** SPORTS (*practice game*) pachanga *f* **2.** (*fight*) escaramuza *f*
scrimp [skrɪmp] *vi* **to ~ on sth** escatimar en algo; **to ~ and save** apretarse el cinturón *fig*
script [skrɪpt] **I.** *n* **1.** CINE guión *m;* TV, THEAT argumento *m* **2.** (*writing*) escritura *f;* **Arabic ~** escritura árabe **II.** *vt* escribir el guión de
scriptural ['skrɪp·tʃər·əl] *adj* bíblico, -a

Scripture *n*, **scripture** ['skrɪp·tʃər] *n* Sagrada Escritura *f*
scriptwriter ['skrɪpt·raɪ·ţər] *n* guionista *mf*
scroll [skroʊl] **I.** *n* **1.** (*roll*) rollo *m* (de papel) **2.** ARCHIT voluta *f* **II.** *vi* COMPUT desplazarse; **to ~** (**to the**) **right/left** desplazarse a la derecha/izquierda; **to ~ down/up** bajar/subir
scrooge [skrudʒ] *n* tacaño, -a *m, f*
scrotum ['skroʊ·ţəm] <-tums *o* -ta> *n* escroto *m*
scrounge [skraʊndʒ] **I.** *vt sl* conseguir gorroneando, manguear *Arg;* **to ~ sth off** [*o* **from**] **sb** sacar algo de gorra a alguien **II.** *vi sl* gorronear
scrounger ['skraʊn·dʒər] *n pej, sl* gorrón, -ona *m, f*, pedinche *mf Méx*
scrub¹ [skrʌb] <-bb-> **I.** *vt* **1.** (*clean*) fregar **2.** (*cancel*) cancelar **II.** *vi* fregar; **to ~ at sth** restregar algo **III.** *n* **1.** (*act of scrubbing*) fregado *m;* **to give sth a** (**good**) **~** fregar algo vigorosamente **2.** *pl* (*clothing*) ropa *f* de uso hospitalario **3.** SPORTS (*reserve player*) reserva *m*, *que sólo juega en momentos intrascendentes*
scrub² [skrʌb] *n* matorral *m*
scrubber ['skrʌb·ər] *n* fregón, -ona *m, f*
scruff [skrʌf] *n* cogote *m;* **to grab sb by the ~ of the neck** coger a alguien por el cogote
scruffy ['skrʌf·i] <-ier, -iest> *adj* (*clothes*) deshilachado, -a; (*person*) desaliñado, -a, fachoso, -a *Méx*
scrum [skrʌm] *n* SPORTS melé *f*
scrummage ['skrʌm·ɪdʒ] *n* SPORTS *s.* **scrum**
scrumptious ['skrʌmp·ʃəs] *adj inf* de rechupete
scrunch [skrʌntʃ] **I.** *vi* crujir **II.** *vt* hacer crujir **III.** *n* crujido *m*
scruple ['skru·pəl] **I.** *n* escrúpulo *m;* **to have no ~s** (*about doing sth*) no tener escrúpulos (en hacer algo) **II.** *vi* tener escrúpulos
scrupulous ['skrup·jʊ·ləs] *adj* escrupuloso, -a
scrutinize ['skru·tə·naɪz] *vt* (*examine*) escudriñar; (*votes*) escrutar; (*text*) revisar
scrutiny ['skru·tə·ni] *n* escrutinio *m*
scuba diving ['sku·bə·ˌdaɪ·vɪŋ] *n* submarinismo *m*
scuff [skʌf] **I.** *vt* **1.** (*roughen surface*) raspar **2.** (*drag along ground*) arrastrar **II.** *n* rozadura *f*
scuffle ['skʌf·əl] **I.** *n* refriega *f* **II.** *vi* pelearse
scull [skʌl] **I.** *vi* remar **II.** *n* espadilla *f*
scullery ['skʌl·ə·ri] *n* antecocina *f*
sculpt [skʌlpt] *vt* esculpir
sculptor ['skʌlp·tər] *n* escultor *m*
sculptural ['skʌlp·tʃər·əl] *adj* escultórico, -a, escultural
sculpture ['skʌlp·tʃər] **I.** *n* escultura *f* **II.** *vt* esculpir
scum [skʌm] *n* **1.** (*foam*) capa *f* de impurezas *que se forma en la superficie de un líquido* **2.** (*evil people*) escoria *f*
scumbag ['skʌm·bæg] *n pej* cerdo, -a *m, f*
scurrilous ['skɜr·ɪ·ləs] *adj pej* (*damaging*) difamatorio, -a; (*insulting*) calumnioso, -a

scurry ['skɜr·i] <-ie-> *vi* corretear
scurvy ['skɜr·vi] **I.** *n* escorbuto *m,* berbén *m*
Méx **II.** *adj* vil; **a ~ trick** un truco ruin
scuttle¹ ['skʌt̯·əl] *vi* (*run*) corretear
scuttle away *vi,,* **scuttle off** *vi* (*run*) escabullirse
scuttle² ['skʌt̯·əl] *vt* **1.** (*sink*) hundir **2.** (*plan*)
echar por tierra
scuttle³ ['skʌt̯·əl] *n* (*for coal*) cajón *m* para el
carbón
scythe [saɪð] **I.** *n* guadaña *f* **II.** *vt* (*with a
scythe*) guadañar; (*with swinging blow*) segar
SD [ˌsɑʊθ·dəˈkoʊ·t̯ə] *n abbr of* **South Dakota**
Dakota *f* del Sur
SDI [ˌes·diˈaɪ] *n abbr of* **Strategic Defense
Initiative** IDE *f*
SE [ˌesˈi] *n abbr of* **southeast** SE *m*
sea [si] *n* **1.** mar *m o f;* **at the bottom of the ~**
en el fondo del mar; **by ~** por mar; **by the ~**
junto al mar; **out at ~** en alta mar; **to put** (**out**)
to ~ hacerse a la mar; **the open ~, the high
~s** el mar abierto **2.** (*wide expanse*) **a ~ of
people** un mar de gente ► **to sail the** seven
~s surcar los siete mares
sea anemone *n* anémona *f* de mar
seaboard ['si·bɔrd] *n* litoral *m*
seaborne ['si·bɔrn] *adj* transportado, -a por
mar
sea change *n* cambio *m* profundo
sea dog *n* lobo *m* de mar
seafarer ['si·ˌfer·ər] *n liter* marinero, -a *m, f*
seafaring *adj liter* marinero, -a
seafood ['si·fud] *n* marisco *m*
seafront ['si·frʌnt] *n* **1.** (*promenade*) paseo *m*
marítimo, malecón *m Méx* **2.** (*beach*) playa *f*
seagoing ['si·ˌɡoʊ·ɪŋ] *adj* (*ship*) de altura
seagull ['si·ɡʌl] *n* gaviota *f*
sea horse *n* caballito *m* de mar
seal¹ [sil] *n* ZOOL foca *f*
seal² [sil] **I.** *n* **1.** (*wax mark, stamp*) sello *m;*
given under my hand and ~ sellado y fir-
mado de mi puño y letra **2.** (*to prevent opening: on letter*) sello *m;* (*on goods*) precinto *m;*
(*on door*) precintado *m* ► **~ of** approval
aprobación *f* **II.** *vt* **1.** (*put a seal on*) sellar
2. (*prevent opening*) precintar **3.** (*block
access*) acordonar; (*border, port*) cerrar
◆ **seal up** *vt* precintar
sealant ['si·lənt] *n* silicona *f* selladora
sea legs *npl inf* equilibrio *m* (en un barco); **to
get one's ~** acostumbrarse a mantener el equilibrio (en barco)
sea level *n* nivel *m* del mar
sealing wax *n* lacre *m*
sea lion *n* ZOOL león *m* marino
sealskin ['sil·skɪn] *n* piel *f* de foca
seam [sim] **I.** *n* **1.** (*stitching*) costura *f;* **to
come** [*o* **fall**] **apart at the ~s** descoserse; *fig*
rebosar de gente **2.** (*junction*) juntura *f*
3. (*wrinkle*) arruga *f* **4.** MIN veta *f,* filón *m* **II.** *vt*
(*sew*) coser
seaman ['si·mən] <-men> *n* (*sailor*) marinero *m*

sea mile *n* milla *f* marina
seamless *adj* **1.** (*without seam*) sin costuras
2. (*transition*) perfecto, -a
seamstress ['sim·strɪs] *n* costurera *f*
seamy ['si·mi] <-ier, -iest> *adj* sórdido, -a
séance ['seɪ·ɑns] *n* sesión *f* de espiritismo
seaplane ['si·pleɪn] *n* AVIAT hidroavión *m*
seaport *n* puerto *m* marítimo
sea power *n* **1.** (*naval strength*) fuerza *f* naval
2. (*state*) potencia *f* naval
sear [sɪr] *vt* **1.** (*scorch*) quemar; (*into memory*) grabar a fuego **2.** (*wither*) secar, marchitar
3. CULIN brasar (a fuego vivo) **4.** MED cauterizar
5. (*make numb*) volver insensible
search [sɜrtʃ] **I.** *n a.* COMPUT búsqueda *f;* (*of
building*) registro *m,* cateo *m Méx,* esculco *m
Col, Méx;* (*of person*) cacheo *m;* **to go in ~ of
sth** ir en busca de algo **II.** *vi a.* COMPUT buscar;
to ~ for sth buscar algo; **to ~ high and low**
(**for sth**) buscar (algo) por todas partes; **~ and
replace** COMPUT buscar y reemplazar **III.** *vt*
1. *a.* COMPUT buscar en; (*building, baggage*)
registrar, catear *Méx,* escular *Col, Méx;* (*person*) cachear **2.** (*examine*) examinar; **to ~
one's memory** hacer memoria; **to ~ one's
conscience** hacer examen de conciencia ► **~
me!** *sl* ¡yo qué sé!
◆ **search out** *vt* (*people*) encontrar;
(*information*) averiguar
search engine *n* COMPUT motor *m* de búsqueda
searcher *n* miembro *m* de un equipo de salvamento
search function *n* COMPUT función *f* de
búsqueda
searching *adj* **1.** (*penetrating*) inquisitivo, -a;
(*look*) penetrante **2.** (*exhaustive*) minucioso, -a
searchlight ['sɜrtʃ·laɪt] *n* reflector *m*
search party <-ies> *n* equipo *m* de salvamento
search warrant *n* orden *f* de registro [*o* de allanamiento *AmL*]
searing *adj* **1.** (*heat*) abrasador(a) **2.** (*pain*)
punzante **3.** (*criticism*) virulento, -a
sea salt *n* sal *f* marina
seascape ['si·skeɪp] *n* **1.** (*picture*) marina *f*
2. (*view*) vista *f* marina
seashell ['si·ʃel] *n* concha *f* (marina)
seashore ['si·ʃɔr] *n* **1.** (*beach*) playa *f* **2.** (*near
sea*) costa *f*
seasick ['si·sɪk] *adj* mareado, -a; **to get ~**
marearse (*al viajar por mar*)
seasickness ['si·sɪk·nɪs] *n* mareo *m* (*al viajar
por mar*)
seaside ['si·saɪd] **I.** *n* **1.** (*beach*) playa *f*
2. (*coast*) costa *f* **II.** *adj* costero, -a; **a ~ resort**
un lugar de veraneo costero, un balneario *AmL*
season ['si·zən] **I.** *n* **1.** (*period of year*) estación *f* **2.** (*epoch*) época *f;* **the Christmas ~** las
Navidades; **Season's Greetings** Felices Fiestas; **the** (**fishing/hunting**) **~** la temporada (de
pesca/de caza); **the strawberry/apple ~** la
temporada de las fresas/manzanas; **to be in ~**

estar en sazón; **to be out of** ~ estar fuera de temporada; **high/low** ~ temporada alta/baja; **the concert/ballet/opera** ~ la temporada de conciertos/ballet/ópera **3.** SPORTS temporada *f* **4.** ZOOL **to be in** ~ estar en celo; **the mating** ~ la época de celo **II.** *vt* **1.** CULIN sazonar; (*add salt and pepper*) salpimentar **2.** (*dry out*) secar **III.** *vi* **1.** (*dry out*) secarse **2.** *fig* **to become** ~**ed to sth** acostumbrarse a algo

seasonable ['si·zə·nə·bəl] *adj* **1.** (*expected*) propio, -a de la estación **2.** *liter* (*appropriate*) oportuno, -a

seasonal ['si·zə·nəl] *adj* **1.** (*connected with time of year*) estacional **2.** (*temporary*) temporal; ~ **worker** temporero, -a *m, f* **3.** (*grown in a season: fruits, vegetables*) del tiempo

seasoned *adj* **1.** (*experienced*) experimentado, -a **2.** (*dried: wood*) secado, -a **3.** (*spiced*) sazonado, -a

seasoning ['si·zə·nɪŋ] *n* **1.** (*salt and pepper*) condimento *m* **2.** (*herb or spice*) sazón *f,* yuyos *mpl Ecua, Perú*

season ticket *n* abono *m* (de temporada)

season ticket holder *n* RAIL persona *f* en posesión de un abono; SPORTS, THEAT abonado, -a *m, f*

seat [sit] **I.** *n* **1.** (*furniture*) asiento *m;* (*on a bicycle*) sillín *m;* (*in theater*) butaca *f;* (*in a car, bus*) plaza *f;* **back** ~ asiento trasero; **is this** ~ **free/taken?** ¿está libre/ocupado este asiento?; **to hold a** ~ **for sb** guardar el sitio a alguien; **to take one's** ~ sentarse **2.** (*ticket*) entrada *f;* **to book a** ~ reservar una entrada **3.** (*part: of chair*) asiento *m;* (*of pants*) fondillos *mpl* **4.** (*buttocks*) trasero *m inf* **5.** POL escaño *m,* banca *f Arg, Par, Urug;* **to win/lose a** ~ ganar/perder un escaño **6.** (*center*) sede *f;* ~ **of learning** centro *m* de enseñanza **7.** (*country residence*) casa *f* solariega **8.** (*riding style*) **to have a good** ~ montar bien ▸ **to fly by the** ~ **of one's pants** dejarse guiar por el instinto **II.** *vt* **1.** (*place on a seat*) sentar; **to** ~ **oneself** *form* tomar asiento; (*offer a seat to*) colocar **2.** (*have enough seats for*) tener cabida para; **the bus** ~**s 20** el autobús tiene 20 plazas **3.** ARCHIT, TECH asentar

seat belt *n* cinturón *m* (de seguridad); **to fasten one's** ~ abrocharse el cinturón (de seguridad)

seating *n* **1.** (*seats*) asientos *mpl* **2.** (*number*) número *m* de asientos; ~ **capacity** número de plazas; ~ **for two thousand** aforo de dos mil personas **3.** (*arrangement*) distribución *f* de los asientos

SEATO ['si·ţoʊ] *n abbr of* **Southeast Asia Treaty Organization** Organización *f* del Tratado del Sudeste Asiático

sea urchin *n* erizo *m* de mar

seaward ['si·wərd] **I.** *adv* hacia el mar **II.** *adj* **1.** (*facing sea*) que da al mar **2.** (*moving towards sea*) que va hacia el mar

seawater ['si·ˌwɔ·ţər] *n* agua *f* de mar

seaway ['si·weɪ] *n* **1.** (*channel*) canal *m* marítimo **2.** (*route*) ruta *f* marítima

seaweed ['si·wid] *n* algas *fpl,* huiro *m Chile*

seaworthy ['si·ˌwɜr·ði] *adj* en condiciones de navegar

sebaceous gland [sə·'beɪ·ʃəs·ˌglænd] *n* glándula *f* sebácea

sec [sek] *n s.* **second** seg. *m;* **hang on just a** ~ espera un segundo

sec [sek] *adj* seco

SEC [ˌes·i·'si] *n abbr of* **Securities and Exchange Commission** ≈ Comisión Nacional del Mercado de Valores

secede [sɪ·'sid] *vi* separarse

secession [sɪ·'seʃ·ən] *n* secesión *f;* **War of Secession** Guerra *f* de Secesión

seclude [sɪ·'klud] *vt liter* recluir

secluded [sɪ·'klu·dɪd] *adj* (*place*) aislado, -a; (*life*) solitario, -a

seclusion [sɪ·'klu·ʒən] *n* aislamiento *m;* **to live in** ~ vivir aislado

second[1] ['sek·ənd] **I.** *adj* **1.** (*after first*) segundo, -a; **every** ~ **boy/girl** uno de cada dos chicos/una de cada dos chicas; **every** ~ **year** cada dos años; **every** ~ **week** una semana sí y otra no; **to be** ~ ser el segundo; **the** ~ **biggest town** la segunda ciudad más grande; **to be** ~ **only to sb/sth** ser superado únicamente por alguien/algo; **to be** ~ **to none** no ser inferior a nadie **2.** (*another*) otro, -a; **to be a** ~ **Mozart** ser otro Mozart; **to give sb a** ~ **chance** dar a alguien una segunda oportunidad; **to have** ~ **thoughts about sb/sth** tener dudas acerca de alguien/algo; **on** ~ **thought** pensándolo bien; **to do sth a** ~ **time** volver a hacer algo; **to get one's** ~ **wind** recobrar el aliento; **to have a** ~ **helping** repetir **3.** **the** ~ **floor** el primer piso, el segundo piso *AmL* **II.** *n* **1.** (*second gear*) segunda *f* **2.** *pl* (*extra helping*) **may I have** ~**s?** ¿puedo repetir? **3.** COM (*imperfect item*) artículo *m* con defectos de fábrica **4.** (*in duel*) padrino *m* **5.** MUS segunda *f* **6.** (*seconder*) persona *f* que secunda una propuesta **III.** *adv* en segundo lugar **IV.** *vt* **1.** (*support in debate*) secundar **2.** *form* (*back up*) apoyar

second[2] ['sek·ənd] *n* (*unit of time*) segundo *m;* **per** ~ por segundo; **at that very** ~ en ese preciso instante; **just a** ~! ¡un segundo!; **it won't take (but) a** ~! ¡sólo será un momento!

secondary ['sek·ən·der·i] **I.** *adj* **1.** (*not main*) secundario, -a; **to be** ~ **to sth** ser de menor importancia que algo **2.** (*school*) de enseñanza secundaria **3.** (*industry*) derivado, -a **II.** <-ies> *n* subalterno, -a *m, f*

secondary school *n* **1.** (*school*) instituto *m* de enseñanza secundaria, liceo *m Chile, Méx* **2.** (*education*) enseñanza *f* secundaria

second best *n* segundo, -a *m, f*

second-best I. *adj* **to be** ~ (*person*) ser un segundón; (*option*) ser una segunda alternativa **II.** *adv* **to come off** ~ (**to sb**) perder (contra alguien)

second class *n* segunda *f* (clase)

second-class I. *adj* **1.** (*in second class*) de

segunda clase; ~ **mail** correo *m* regular **2.** *pej* (*inferior: hotel, service*) de segunda categoría; (*goods*) de calidad inferior **II.** *adv* **1.** RAIL (*in the second class*) en segunda (clase) **2.** (*by second-class mail*) por correo regular

second cousin *n* primo, -a *m, f* segundo, -a

second-degree burn *n* quemadura *f* de segundo grado

second-guess [ˌsek·ənd·ˈges] *vt* anticiparse a

secondhand [ˌsek·ənd·ˈhænd] **I.** *adj* (*clothing, information*) de segunda mano; (*bookstore*) de viejo **II.** *adv* **1.** (*used*) de segunda mano **2.** (*from third party*) por terceros

second hand *n* (*on watch*) segundero *m*

second lieutenant *n* MIL alférez *mf*

secondly *adv* en segundo lugar

second-rate [ˌsek·ənd·ˈreɪt] *adj* mediocre

secrecy [ˈsi·krə·si] *n* **1.** (*confidentiality*) secreto *m;* **in** ~ en secreto; **to swear sb to** ~ hacer que alguien jure no revelar algo **2.** (*secretiveness*) secretismo *m*

secret [ˈsi·krɪt] **I.** *n* **1.** (*information*) secreto *m;* **an open** ~ un secreto a voces; **to let sb in on a** ~ revelar un secreto a alguien **2.** (*knack*) truco *m;* (*of success*) secreto *m* **3.** (*mystery*) misterio *m* **II.** *adj* (*known to few*) secreto, -a; **to keep sth** ~ (**from sb**) ocultar algo (a alguien)

secret agent *n* agente *mf* secreto, -a

secretarial [ˌsek·rə·ˈter·i·əl] *adj* administrativo, -a

secretary [ˈsek·rə·ter·i] <-ies> *n* **1.** (*in office*) secretario, -a *m, f* **2.** POL ministro, -a *m, f,* secretario, -a *m, f Méx*

secretary-general [ˌsek·rə·ter·i·ˈdʒen·ər·əl] <secretaries-general> *n* secretario, -a *m, f* general

Secretary of the Interior *n* ministro , -a *m, f* del Interior; **Secretary of the Treasury** ≈ Ministro de Hacienda; **Secretary of State** secretario de Estado

secrete¹ [sɪ·ˈkrit] *vt* (*discharge*) segregar, secretar

secrete² [sɪ·ˈkrit] *vt form* (*hide*) ocultar

secretion [sɪ·ˈkri·ʃən] *n* (*discharge*) secreción *f*

secretive [ˈsi·krɪ·t̬ɪv] *adj* reservado, -a

sect [sekt] *n* secta *f*

sectarian [sek·ˈter·i·ən] **I.** *adj* **1.** (*ideology*) sectario, -a **2.** (*schooling*) confesional **II.** *n* sectario, -a *m, f*

section [ˈsek·ʃən] **I.** *n* **1.** (*part*) *a.* MIL, MUS, PUBL sección *f;* (*of object*) parte *f* **2.** (*group*) sector *m* **3.** (*of area*) zona *f;* (*of city*) distrito *m* **4.** (*of document*) párrafo *m;* LAW artículo *m* **5.** (*of road*) tramo *m* **6.** (*cut*) corte *m* **II.** *vt* **1.** (*cut*) seccionar **2.** (*divide*) dividir

◆ **section off** *vt* acordonar

sectional [ˈsek·ʃə·nəl] *adj* **1.** (*limited to a group: interests*) particular; (*differences*) entre facciones **2.** (*done in section: design, view*) en sección **3.** (*made in sections: furniture, sofa*) modular

sector [ˈsek·tər] *n* sector *m;* **public/private** ~

sector público/privado

secular [ˈsek·jʊ·lər] *adj* **1.** (*non-religious*) secular; (*education*) laico, -a; (*art*) profano, -a **2.** REL seglar **3.** (*centuries-old*) secular

secularize [ˈsek·jʊ·lə·raɪz] *vt* secularizar

secure [sɪ·ˈkjʊr] **I.** *adj* <-rer, -est> **1.** (*safe*) seguro, -a; **to be** ~ **from sth** estar protegido contra algo; **to make sth** ~ **against attack** proteger algo contra los ataques **2.** (*confident*) **to feel** ~ **about sth** sentirse seguro respecto a algo; **to be** ~ **in the knowledge that...** tener la certeza de que...; **to feel emotionally** ~ tener estabilidad emocional **3.** (*guarantee*) **to be financially** ~ tener estabilidad económica **4.** (*fixed*) firme; (*foundation*) sólido, -a **II.** *vt* **1.** (*obtain*) obtener **2.** (*make firm*) asegurar; *fig* afianzar; (*door*) cerrar firmemente; (*boat*) amarrar; (*position*) consolidar **3.** (*make safe*) proteger **4.** (*put in safe place*) poner a buen recaudo **5.** (*guarantee repayment*) garantizar; **a** ~**d loan** un préstamo con garantía

securities market *n* mercado *m* de valores

security [sɪ·ˈkjʊr·ə·t̬i] <-ies> *n* **1.** (*safety*) seguridad *f;* ~ **risk** peligro *m* para la seguridad **2.** (*stability*) estabilidad *f;* ~ **of employment** estabilidad laboral **3.** (*safeguard*) salvaguardia *f* **4.** (*payment guarantee*) fianza *f;* **to stand** ~ **for sb** salir fiador de alguien **5.** *pl* FIN títulos *mpl*

Security Council *n* Consejo *m* de Seguridad (de las Naciones Unidas)

security guard *n* guarda *mf* jurado, -a

sedan [sɪ·ˈdæn] *n* AUTO sedán *m*

sedan chair *n* silla *f* de manos

sedate [sɪ·ˈdeɪt] **I.** *adj* (*lifestyle, person*) tranquilo, -a; (*color, style*) sobrio, -a **II.** *vt* MED sedar

sedation [sɪ·ˈdeɪ·ʃən] *n* MED sedación *f;* **under** ~ sedado

sedative [ˈsed·ə·t̬ɪv] **I.** *adj* sedante **II.** *n* sedante *m*

sedentary [ˈsed·ən·ter·i] *adj* sedentario, -a

sediment [ˈsed·ə·mənt] *n* sedimento *m;* (*in wine, coffee*) poso *m*

sedimentary [ˌsed·ɪ·ˈmen·tri] *adj* sedimentario, -a

sedition [sɪ·ˈdɪʃ·ən] *n form* sedición *f*

seditious [sɪ·ˈdɪʃ·əs] *adj form* sedicioso, -a

seduce [sɪ·ˈdus] *vt* seducir; **to** ~ **sb into doing sth** inducir a alguien a hacer algo

seducer [sɪ·ˈdu·sər] *n* seductor(a) *m(f)*

seduction [sɪ·ˈdʌk·ʃən] *n* **1.** (*act*) seducción *f* **2.** *pl* (*seductive quality*) atractivo *m*

seductive [sɪ·ˈdʌk·tɪv] *adj* **1.** (*sexy*) seductor(a) **2.** (*attractive*) atrayente; (*offer*) tentador(a)

see¹ [si] <saw, seen> **I.** *vt* **1.** (*perceive*) ver; **to** ~ **that...** ver que...; **to** ~ **sth with one's own eyes** ver algo con sus propios ojos; **it is worth** ~**ing** vale [*o* merece] la pena verlo **2.** (*watch*) ver; **you were** ~**n entering the building** se os vio entrar en el edificio **3.** (*inspect*) ver; **may I** ~ **your driver's license?** ¿me permite (ver) su permiso de conducir? **4.** (*visit*) visitar;

to ~ **a little/a lot of sb** ver a alguien poco/a menudo; ~ **you around!** ¡nos vemos!; ~ **you (later)**! *inf* ¡hasta luego! **5.** (*have relationship*) **to be** ~**ing sb** salir con alguien **6.** (*have meeting*) tener una entrevista con **7.** (*talk to*) **I would like to** ~ **you about that matter** me gustaría hablar contigo sobre ese asunto; **Mr. Brown will** ~ **you now** el Sr. Brown le recibirá ahora **8.** (*accompany*) acompañar a **9.** (*perceive*) darse cuenta de; (*understand*) comprender; **I don't** ~ **what you mean** no entiendo lo que quieres decir; **to make sb** ~ **reason** hacer entrar en razón a alguien; **to** ~ **sth in a new light** cambiar de opinión respecto a algo **10.** (*envisage*) creer; **as I** ~ **it...** a mi modo de ver...; **I don't** ~ **him doing that** no le creo capaz de hacer eso; **I could** ~ **it coming** lo veía venir **11.** (*investigate*) **to** ~ **how/what/if...** averiguar cómo/qué/si... **12.** (*ensure*) ~ **that you are ready when we come** procura estar listo cuando vengamos **II.** *vi* **1.** (*use eyes*) ver; **as far as the eye can** ~ hasta donde alcanza la vista **2.** (*find out*) descubrir; ~ **for yourself!** ¡compruébelo usted mismo!, ¡compruébalo tú mismo!; **let me** ~ ¿a ver?; **let's** ~ vamos a ver; **we'll/I'll** (**have to**) ~ ya lo veremos/veré; **you'll** ~ ya verás **3.** (*understand*) comprender; **I** ~ ya veo; **you** ~? ¿entiendes?; **as far as I can** ~ por lo que yo veo ▶ **he can't** ~ **further than the end of his nose** no puede ver más allá de sus narices
◆ **see about** *vt inf* encargarse de; (*consider*) pensarse ▶ **we'll soon** ~ **that!** *inf* ¡eso ya lo veremos!
◆ **see in** *vt* (*welcome*) hacer pasar; **to see the New Year in** celebrar el año nuevo
◆ **see off** *vt* despedir
◆ **see out** *vt* **1.** (*escort to door*) acompañar hasta la puerta **2.** (*continue to end*) seguir hasta el final de; (*project*) llevar a término **3.** (*last until end*) durar hasta el final de; **to see the winter out** resistir el invierno
◆ **see through** *vt* **1.** (*not be deceived by*) calar a *inf*; (*mystery*) penetrar en **2.** (*sustain*) **to see sb through** (**a difficult time**) mantener a alguien a flote (en tiempos difíciles) **3.** (*continue to end*) llevar a buen término *elev*
◆ **see to** *vt* **1.** (*attend to*) encargarse de **2.** (*ensure*) **to** ~ **it that...** asegurarse de que...
see² [si] *n* REL sede *f*; **the Holy See** la Santa Sede
seed [sid] **I.** *n* **1.** BOT (*source*) semilla *f*; (*of fruit*) pepita *f*, pepa *f* AmL **2.** (*seeds*) simiente *f* **3.** (*beginning*) germen *m*; (*of revolution*) semilla *f*; **to sow the** ~**s of doubt/discord** sembrar la duda/la discordia **4.** ANAT semen *m* **II.** *vt* **1.** AGR sembrar; **to** ~ **itself** (*a plant*) desgranarse **2.** (*help start*) contribuir a la puesta en marcha; **to** ~ **a project with money** aportar capital a un proyecto **3.** (*remove seeds*) despepitar **4.** SPORTS *en rondas eliminatorias, colocar a los competidores por orden de fuerza de tal forma que los mejores se*

enfrenten en las últimas rondas **III.** *vi* granar
seedbed *n* **1.** AGR semillero *m* **2.** *fig* foco *m*
seedless ['sid·lɪs] *adj* sin pepitas
seedling ['sid·lɪŋ] *n* planta *f* de semillero
seed money *n* capital *m* simiente
seedy ['si·di] <-ier, -iest> *adj* **1.** (*dubious*) sórdido, -a; (*place*) de mala muerte; (*clothing*) raído, -a **2.** (*unwell*) pachucho, -a *inf*; **to feel** ~ encontrarse mal
seeing I. *conj* ~ (**that**) en vista de (que) **II.** *n* visión *f*; ~ **is believing** ver para creer
seek [sik] <sought> **I.** *vt* **1.** (*look for*) buscar; **to** ~ **one's fortune** probar suerte **2.** (*try to obtain*) procurar obtener; (*solution*) tratar de encontrar; (*shelter*) buscar; (*damages*) reclamar **3.** (*ask for: help, approval*) pedir; (*job*) solicitar **4.** (*attempt*) tratar de **II.** *vi* (*search*) buscar
◆ **seek out** *vt* (*person*) ir a buscar; (*information*) averiguar
seeker *n* buscador(a) *m(f)*
seem [sim] *vi* **1.** (*appear to be*) parecer; **they** ~**ed to like the idea** parecía que les gustaba la idea; **to** ~ **as if...** parecer como si... +*subj*; **it is not all that it** ~**s** no es lo que parece; **things aren't always what they** ~ las apariencias engañan **2.** (*appear*) **it** ~**s that...** parece que...; **so it** ~**s, so it would** ~ eso parece
seeming *adj form* aparente
seemingly *adv* aparentemente
seemly ['sim·li] <-ier, -iest> *adj* apropiado, -a
seen [sin] *pp of* **see**
seep [sip] *vi* filtrarse
◆ **seep away** *vi* escurrirse
seepage ['si·pɪdʒ] *n* (*of water*) filtración *f*; (*of gas*) fuga *f*
seer [sɪr] *n liter* adivino, -a *m, f*
seersucker ['sɪr·ˌsʌk·ər] *n* (*fabric*) sirsaca *f*
seesaw ['si·sɔ] **I.** *n* **1.** (*in playground*) balancín *m* **2.** *fig* vaivén *m* **II.** *vi* **1.** (*play*) columpiarse **2.** *fig* oscilar **III.** *adj* ~ **motion** movimiento *m* oscilante
seethe [sið] *vi* **1.** *fig* (*be angry*) estar furioso, -a; **to** ~ **with anger** hervir de cólera **2.** *fig* (*be busy*) bullir; **to** ~ **with tourists** estar plagado de turistas
see-through ['si·θru] *adj* transparente
segment ['seg·mənt] **I.** *n* **1.** MATH, ZOOL segmento *m*; (*of orange*) gajo *m* **2.** (*of society*) sector *m* **II.** *vt* segmentar; (*orange*) dividir en gajos **III.** *vi* segmentarse
segmentation [ˌseg·mən·'teɪ·ʃən] *n* segmentación *f*
segregate ['seg·rə·ɡeɪt] *vt* (*races*) segregar; (*girls and boys*) separar
segregation [ˌseg·rə·'ɡeɪ·ʃən] *n* segregación *f*
seismic ['saɪz·mɪk] *adj* GEO sísmico, -a
seismograph ['saɪz·mə·ɡræf] *n* sismógrafo *m*
seismologist [saɪz·'mɑl·ə·dʒɪst] *n* sismólogo, -a *m, f*
seismology [saɪz·'mɑl·ə·dʒi] *n* sismología *f*
seize [siz] *vt* **1.** (*grasp*) asir *elev*, cachar *Arg*,

Nic, Urug, acapillar *Méx;* **to ~ sb by the arm/
by the throat** agarrar a alguien del brazo/por
el cuello **2.** (*take: opportunity*) no dejar escapar; (*initiative, power*) tomar **3.** (*overcome*)
he was ~ d by fear/desire el miedo/el deseo
se apoderó de él; **I was ~d with panic** estaba
sobrecogido por el pánico **4.** (*capture: criminal*) detener; (*fortress, town*) tomar **5.** (*confiscate: property*) confiscar; (*drugs, weapons*)
incautarse de **6.** (*understand*) captar **7.** (*kidnap*) secuestrar
◆ **seize on** *vt* aprovecharse de
◆ **seize up** *vi* (*stop*) paralizarse; (*engine,
muscles*) agarrotarse; COMPUT colgarse *inf*
seizure ['si·ʒər] *n* **1.** (*seizing*) asimiento *m*
2. (*taking possession: of town*) toma *f;* (*of
drugs*) incautación *f;* (*of property, contraband*) confiscación *f* **3.** MED (*stroke*) ataque *m*
4. (*seizing up*) agarrotamiento *m*
seldom ['sel·dəm] *adv* rara vez
select [sə·'lekt] **I.** *vt* (*candidate, player,
information*) seleccionar; (*gift, wine*) escoger;
~ ed works obras *fpl* escogidas **II.** *adj* **1.** (*high-
class*) selecto, -a; (*club, restaurant*) exclusivo,
-a; (*school, university*) elitista; (*product*) de
primera calidad **2.** (*exclusive*) **the ~ few** los
escogidos
select committee *n* POL comisión *f* investiga-
dora
selection [sə·'lek·ʃən] *n* **1.** (*act of choosing*)
selección *f* **2.** (*range*) gama *f;* (*of food, drinks*)
surtido *m* **3.** (*thing chosen*) selección *f;* (*person chosen*) persona *f* seleccionada; **he was a
last-minute ~ for the team** fue seleccionado
a última hora para el equipo
selective [sə·'lek·tɪv] *adj* selectivo, -a
selectivity [ˌsə·lek·'tɪv·ə·t̬i] *n* selectividad *f*
selector [sə·'lek·tər] *n* **1.** (*person*) seleccio-
nador(a) *m(f)* **2.** TECH selector *m*
selenium [sɪ·'li·ni·əm] *n* selenio *m*
self [self] *n* <selves> uno mismo, una misma;
his better ~ su mejor parte; **one's other ~** su
alter ego; **the ~** PSYCH el yo
self-abasement *n* rebajamiento *m* de sí mismo
self-absorbed *adj* absorto, -a en sí mismo, -a
self-addressed *adj* **~ envelope** sobre *m* con
la dirección de uno mismo
self-adhesive *adj* autoadhesivo, -a
self-analysis *n* autoanálisis *m inv*
self-appointed *adj pej* autoproclamado, -a
self-assurance *n* seguridad *f* en uno mismo;
to possess ~ tener confianza en uno mismo
self-assured *adj* seguro, -a de sí mismo, -a
self-centered *adj* egocéntrico, -a
self-colored *adj* **1.** (*natural*) de color natural
2. (*one color*) unicolor
self-complacent *adj pej* engreído, -a
self-composed *adj* dueño, -a de sí mismo, -a;
to remain ~ no perder la serenidad
self-confessed *adj* confeso, -a; **she's a ~
coward** se confiesa cobarde
self-confidence *n* seguridad *f* en uno mismo;
to have ~ confiar en sí mismo

self-conscious *adj* **1.** (*shy*) tímido, -a; **to feel
~** sentirse cohibido **2.** *pej* (*unnatural*) afectado, -a
self-contained *adj* **1.** (*self-sufficient: community, village*) autosuficiente; (*apartment*) con
cocina y cuarto de baño **2.** *pej* (*reserved*) reservado, -a
self-control *n* dominio *m* de sí mismo
self-critical *adj* autocrítico, -a
self-criticism *n* autocrítica *f*
self-deception *n* engaño *m* de uno mismo
self-defeating *adj* contraproducente
self-defense *n* **1.** (*protection*) defensa *f* personal **2.** LAW legítima defensa *f*
self-denial *n* abnegación *f*
self-destruct *vi* autodestruirse
self-determination *n* POL autodeterminación *f*
self-discipline *n* autodisciplina *f*
self-educated *adj* autodidacta
self-effacing *adj* humilde
self-employed **I.** *adj* **to be ~** trabajar por
cuenta propia **II.** *n* **the ~** los trabajadores por
cuenta propia
self-esteem *n* amor *m* propio
self-evident *adj* evidente
self-explanatory *adj* que se explica por sí
mismo
self-expression *n* expresión *f* de la propia personalidad
self-fulfilling *adj* (*prediction*) que tiene como
consecuencia su propio cumplimiento
self-governing *adj* autónomo, -a
self-government *n* autonomía *f*
self-help *n* autoayuda *f;* **~ group** grupo *m* de
apoyo mutuo
self-importance *n pej* presunción *f*
self-important *adj pej* presuntuoso, -a
self-imposed *adj* (*deadline*) autoimpuesto, -a;
(*exile*) voluntario, -a
self-indulgence *n* indulgencia *f* con uno
mismo
self-indulgent *adj* indulgente consigo mismo,
-a
self-inflicted *adj* autoinfligido, -a
self-interest *n* interés *m* propio; **to be moti-
vated by ~** estar motivado por el interés personal
selfish ['sel·fɪʃ] *adj pej* egoísta
selfishness *n pej* egoísmo *m*
self-justification *n* autojustificación *f*
selfless ['self·lɪs] *adj* desinteresado, -a
self-made [ˌself·'meɪd] *adj* que se ha hecho a
sí mismo, -a
self-opinionated *adj pej* testarudo, -a
self-pity *n* lástima *f* de sí mismo
self-portrait *n* ART autorretrato *m*
self-possessed *adj* dueño, -a de sí mismo, -a
self-preservation *n* instinto *m* de conservación
self-reliance *n* independencia *f*
self-reliant *adj* independiente
self-respect *n* amor *m* propio; **to lose all ~**
perder la dignidad

S

self-respecting *adj* con amor propio; **every ~ man...** todo hombre que se precie...

self-righteous *adj pej* farisaico, -a; (*tone*) de superioridad moral

self-rising flour *n* harina *f* con levadura incorporada

self-sacrifice *n* abnegación *f*

self-sacrificing *adj* sacrificado, -a

self-satisfaction *n pej* satisfacción *f* de sí mismo

self-satisfied *adj pej* satisfecho, -a de sí mismo, -a

self-seeking *adj form* egoísta

self-service I. *n* autoservicio *m* **II.** *adj* ~ **store** autoservicio *m*; ~ **restaurant** self-service *m*

self-sufficiency *n* autosuficiencia *f*

self-sufficient *adj* **1.** independiente **2.** ECON autosuficiente; ~ **economy** autarquía *f*

self-taught *adj* autodidacta; **to be ~ in sth** haber aprendido algo por su cuenta

self-willed *adj* obstinado, -a, voltario, -a *Chile*

self-winding watch *n* reloj *m* de cuerda automática

sell [sel] **I.** *vt* <sold, sold> **1.** (*exchange for money*) vender; **to ~ sth for $100** vender algo por [o en] 100$; **to ~ sth at half price** vender algo a mitad de precio; **to ~ sth at a loss** vender algo perdiendo dinero **2.** *fig* (*make accepted*) hacer aceptar; **I'm sold on your plan** tu plan me ha convencido ▸ **to ~ oneself short** no hacerse valer **II.** *vi* <sold, sold> **1.** (*be exchanged for money: product*) venderse; **to ~ at** [o for] **$5** venderse a 5$; (*company, shop*) estar en venta **2.** (*be accepted*) tener aceptación **III.** *n* **1.** *a.* FIN (*thing to sell*) venta *f* **2.** *sl* (*deception*) estafa *f*
  ◆ **sell off** *vt* (*shares, property*) liquidar; (*industry*) privatizar
  ◆ **sell out I.** *vi* **1.** COM, FIN agotarse **2.** *fig* venderse **II.** *vt* liquidar

sellable *adj* vendible

sell-by date ['sel·baɪ·ˌdeɪt] *n* COM fecha *f* límite de venta

seller *n* **1.** (*person*) vendedor(a) *m(f)*; **~'s market** mercado *m* de vendedores **2.** (*product*) **good/poor ~** artículo *m* que tiene mucha/poca demanda

selling point *n* atractivo *m* para el consumidor

sellout ['sel·aʊt] *n* **1.** THEAT, CINE éxito *f* de taquilla **2.** *sl* (*betrayal*) traición *f*

selves [selvz] *n pl of* **self**

semantic [sə·ˈmæn·tɪk] *adj* LING semántico, -a

semantics [sə·ˈmæn·tɪks] *npl* LING semántica *f*

semaphore ['sem·ə·fɔr] **I.** *n* semáforo *m* **II.** *vt* transmitir por semáforo **III.** *vi* hacer señales con semáforo

semblance ['sem·bləns] *n form* apariencia *f*

semen ['si·mən] *n* semen *m*

semester [sə·ˈmes·tər] *n* UNIV semestre *m* (académico)

semi ['sem·i] *n* **1.** *inf* (*truck*) trailer *m* **2.** *pl, inf* SPORTS semifinal *f*; **we lost in the ~s** caímos en semifinales

semiautomatic [ˌsem·i·ɔ·ˌtə·ˈmæt·ɪk] *adj* semiautomático, -a

semicircle ['sem·ɪ·ˌsɜr·kəl] *n* MATH semicírculo *m*

semicircular [ˌsem·ɪ·ˈsɜr·kjə·lər] *adj* semicircular

semicolon ['sem·ɪ·ˌkoʊ·lən] *n* punto *m* y coma

semiconductor [ˌsem·ɪ·kən·ˈdʌk·tər] *n* ELEC semiconductor *m*

semiconscious [ˌsem·ɪ·ˈkan·tʃəs] *adj* semiconsciente

semidetached [ˌsem·ɪ·dɪ·ˈtætʃt] *adj* ~ **house** casa *f* pareada

semifinal [ˌsem·ɪ·ˈfaɪ·nəl] *n* SPORTS semifinal *f*

semifinalist [ˌsem·ɪ·ˈfaɪ·nə·lɪst] *n* SPORTS semifinalista *mf*

seminal ['sem·ə·nəl] *adj* (*important*) fundamental

seminar ['sem·ə·nar] *n* UNIV seminario *m*

seminary ['sem·ɪ·ner·i] *n* REL seminario *m*

semiofficial *adj* semioficial

semiotics [ˌsi·mi·ˈaʈ·ɪks] *n* semiótica *f*

semiprecious [ˌsem·ɪ·ˈpreʃ·əs] *adj* semiprecioso, -a

semiskilled [ˌsem·ɪ·ˈskɪld] *adj* semicualificado, -a

Semite ['sem·aɪt] *n* semita *mf*

Semitic [sə·ˈmɪʈ·ɪk] *adj* semítico, -a

semitone ['sem·ɪ·toʊn] *n* MUS semitono *m*

semitrailer ['sem·ɪ·ˌtreɪ·lər] *n* tráiler *m*

semitropical [ˌsem·ɪ·ˈtrap·ɪ·kəl] *adj* subtropical

semivowel ['sem·ɪ·ˌvaʊ·əl] *n* LING semivocal *f*

semiyearly I. *adj* semestral **II.** *adv* semestralmente

semolina [ˌsem·ə·ˈli·nə] *n* sémola *f*

Sen. *n Am abbr of* **Senator** senador(a) *m(f)*

senate ['sen·ɪt] *n* **1.** POL senado *m* **2.** UNIV consejo *m*

senator ['sen·ə·tər] *n* POL senador(a) *m(f)*

senatorial [ˌsen·ə·ˈtɔr·i·əl] *adj* senatorial

send [send] **I.** *vt* <sent, sent> **1.** (*message, letter, flowers*) enviar, mandar; (*telegram*) poner; **to ~ sth by mail** enviar algo por correo; **to ~ sb to prison** mandar a alguien a la cárcel; **to ~ one's love to sb** mandar saludos cariñosos a alguien; ~ **her my regards** dale recuerdos de mi parte; **John ~s his apologies** John pide que lo disculpen; **to ~ word** (**to sb**) *form* informar (a alguien) **2.** (*propel*) lanzar; **to ~ sth flying** hacer saltar algo por los aires **3.** RADIO transmitir **4.** *inf* (*cause*) **to ~ sb to sleep** hacer que alguien se duerma ▸ **to ~ sb packing** *inf* mandar a alguien a freír espárragos **II.** *vi* <sent, sent> mandar a alguien
  ◆ **send away I.** *vi* **to ~ for sth** pedir algo (por correo) **II.** *vt* **1.** (*dismiss*) despedir **2.** (*send to another place*) enviar
  ◆ **send back** *vt* devolver; (*person*) hacer volver
  ◆ **send for** *vt* (*person*) llamar; (*assistance*) pedir; (*goods*) encargar

◆**send forth** *vt* **1.** *liter* (*make go*) enviar **2.** (*emit*) emitir; (*smell, heat*) despedir

◆**send in** *vt* **1.** (*application, report*) enviar; (*reinforcements*) mandar **2.** (*let in*) hacer pasar

◆**send off** I. *vt* (*cause to depart*) mandar; (*by mail*) enviar por correo II. *vi* to ~ **for sth** pedir algo (por correo)

◆**send on** *vt* **1.** (*send in advance*) mandar por adelantado **2.** (*forward: mail*) remitir; (*order*) transmitir

◆**send out** I. *vt* **1.** (*ask to leave*) echar **2.** (*send on errand*) mandar **3.** (*dispatch*) enviar **4.** (*emit: signal, rays*) emitir; (*smell, heat*) despedir II. *vi* to ~ **for sth** pedir que traigan algo

◆**send up** *vt* **1.** (*drive up: prices, temperature*) hacer subir **2.** *inf* (*mock*) parodiar **3.** *inf* (*put in prison*) meter preso

sender *n* remitente *mf;* '**return to ~**' 'devuélvase al remitente'

sendoff ['send·ɔf] *n* despedida *f;* **to give sb a good ~** dar una buena despedida a alguien

sendup *n,* **send-up** ['send·ʌp] *n inf* parodia *f*

Senegal [ˌsen·ɪ·'gɔl] *n* Senegal *m*

Senegalese [ˌsen·ɪ·gə·'liz] I. *adj* senegalés, -esa II. *n* senegalés, -esa *m, f*

senile ['si·naɪl] *adj* senil; **to become ~** chochear

senile dementia *n* demencia *f* senil

senility [sə·'nɪl·ə·ti] *n* senilidad *f*

senior ['sin·jər] I. *adj* **1.** *form* (*older*) mayor; **James Smith, Senior** James Smith, padre **2.** (*higher in rank*) superior; **to be ~ to sb** estar por encima de alguien **3.** (*of earlier appointment*) más antiguo, -a **4.** SCHOOL de los cursos superiores; (*pupil*) de último curso II. *n* **1.** (*older person*) mayor *mf;* **she is two years my ~** me lleva dos años **2.** (*of higher rank*) superior *mf* **3.** SCHOOL estudiante *mf* de último curso

senior citizen *n* jubilado, -a *m, f*

senior high school *n* instituto *m* de bachillerato

seniority [sin·'jɔr·ə·ti] *n* antigüedad *f*

senior officer *n* oficial *mf* de alto rango

senior partner *n* socio, -a *m, f* mayoritario, -a

sensation [sen·'seɪ·ʃən] *n* sensación *f;* **to be a ~** ser un éxito, ser una sensación; **to cause a ~** hacer furor

sensational [sen·'seɪ·ʃə·nəl] *adj* **1.** (*fabulous*) sensacional **2.** *pej* (*newspaper, disclosure*) sensacionalista

sense [sens] I. *n* **1.** (*faculty*) sentido *m;* **~ of hearing** oído *m;* **~ of sight** vista *f;* **~ of smell** olfato *m;* **~ of taste** gusto *m;* **~ of touch** tacto *m* **2.** (*ability*) sentido *m;* **to have no ~ of occasion** ser inoportuno; **to lose all ~ of time** perder la noción del tiempo **3.** (*way*) sentido *m;* **in every ~** en todos los sentidos; **in a ~** en cierto modo; **in no ~** de ninguna manera **4.** (*sensation*) sensación *f* **5.** *pl* (*clear mental faculties*) juicio *m;* **to come to one's**

~**s** (*see reason*) entrar en razón; (*recover consciousness*) recobrar el conocimiento; **to bring sb to his/her ~s** hacer entrar en razón a alguien; **to take leave of one's ~s** perder la razón **6.** (*good judgment*) (**common**) ~ sentido *m* común; **to have enough** [*o* **the good**] ~ **to...** tener la sensatez de...; **to talk ~** decir cosas sensatas **7.** (*feeling*) impresión *f;* **to feel a ~ of belonging** sentirse aceptado **8.** (*meaning*) significado *m,* sentido *m;* **to make ~** tener sentido; **in the full ~ of the word** en el sentido amplio de la palabra; **there's no ~ in doing...** no tiene sentido hacer...; **what's the ~ in doing...?** ¿qué sentido tiene hacer...? **9.** (*opinion*) opinión *f* (general) II. *vt* sentir; **to ~ that...** darse cuenta de que...

senseless ['sens·lɪs] *adj* **1.** (*pointless*) sin sentido; (*remark*) insensato, -a **2.** MED inconsciente; **to beat sb ~** dar una paliza a alguien hasta dejarlo inconsciente

sense organ *n* órgano *m* sensorial

sensibility [ˌsen·sə·'bɪl·ə·ti] *n* sensibilidad *f;* **to offend sb's sensibilities** herir la sensibilidad de alguien

sensible ['sen·sə·bəl] *adj* **1.** (*having good judgment: person, decision*) sensato, -a **2.** (*suitable: clothing, shoes*) práctico, -a **3.** (*noticeable*) notable **4.** *form* (*aware*) consciente

sensibly *adv* **1.** (*wisely*) sensatamente; (*behave*) prudentemente; (*decide*) acertadamente **2.** (*dress*) con ropa cómoda

sensitive ['sen·sɪ·tɪv] *adj* **1.** (*sympathetic*) sensible; **to be ~ to sb's needs** ser consciente de las necesidades de alguien **2.** (*touchy*) susceptible; **to be ~ about sth** ser susceptible a algo **3.** (*delicate: subject, moment*) delicado, -a; (*age*) conflictivo, -a **4.** (*classified: documents, work*) confidencial

sensitiveness *n,* **sensitivity** [ˌsen·sə·'tɪv·ə·ti] *n* **1.** (*touchiness*) susceptibilidad *f* **2.** (*understanding*) sensibilidad *f,* delicadeza *f* **3.** (*classified nature*) confidencialidad *f*

sensitize ['sen·sə·taɪz] *vt* sensibilizar; **to ~ sb to a problem** concienciar a alguien de un problema

sensor ['sen·sər] *n* TECH, ELEC sensor *m*

sensory ['sen·sə·ri] *adj* sensorial

sensual ['sen·ʃu·əl] *adj* sensual

sensuality [ˌsen·ʃu·'æl·ə·ti] *n* sensualidad *f*

sensuous ['sen·ʃu·əs] *adj* sensual

sent [sent] *pp, pt of* **send**

sentence ['sen·təns] I. *n* **1.** (*court decision*) sentencia *f;* (*punishment*) condena *f;* **jail ~** condena de encarcelamiento; **life ~** cadena perpetua; **to receive a ~** ser condenado; **to serve a ~** cumplir una condena **2.** LING frase *f* II. *vt* condenar

sententious [sen·'ten·ʃəs] *adj form* sentencioso, -a

sentient ['sen·ʃənt] *adj form* sensible

sentiment ['sen·tə·mənt] *n form* **1.** (*opinion*)

opinión *f;* **public/popular** ~ opinión pública/ popular; **to echo a** ~ hacerse eco de una opinión; **to share sb's** ~ compartir la opinión de alguien **2.** (*emotion*) sentimiento *m*

sentimental [,sen·tə·'men·təl] *adj* **1.** (*emotional*) sentimental; **to be** ~ **about sth** ser sentimental con algo **2.** *pej* (*mawkish*) sensiblero, -a

sentimentality [,sen·tə·men·'tæl·ə·ţi] *n pej* sentimentalismo *m*

sentimentalize [,sen·tə·'men·təl·aɪz] *vt pej* dar una visión sentimental de

sentry ['sen·tri] *n* centinela *m;* **to be on** ~ **duty** estar de guardia

sentry box *n* garita *f* de centinela

separable ['sep·ər·ə·bəl] *adj form* separable

separate¹ ['sep·ər·ɪt] I. *adj* separado, -a; **to remain a** ~ **entity** ser una entidad independiente; **a** ~ **piece of paper** una hoja de papel aparte; **to go one's** ~ **ways** ir por caminos distintos; **to keep sth** ~ mantener algo aparte II. *n pl* piezas *fpl* sueltas de ropa

separate² ['sep·ə·reɪt] I. *vt* separar; **to** ~ **two people** separar a dos personas; **to** ~ **egg whites from yolks** separar las claras de las yemas II. *vi* separarse

separated *adj* separado, -a

separation [,sep·ə·'reɪ·ʃən] *n* separación *f;* (*division*) división *f*

separatism ['sep·ər·ə·tɪz·əm] *n* separatismo *m*

separatist ['sep·ər·ə·tɪst] I. *n* separatista *mf* II. *adj* separatista

separator ['sep·ə·reɪ·ţər] *n* separador *m*

sepia ['si·pi·ə] I. *n* sepia *f* II. *adj* de color sepia

sepsis ['sep·sɪs] *n* MED sepsis *f*

Sept. *n abbr of* **September** sept.

September [sep·'tem·bər] *n* septiembre *m; s.a.* **April**

septic ['sep·tɪk] *adj* séptico, -a; **to go** [*o* **turn**] ~ infectarse

septicemia [,sep·tə·'si·mi·ə] *n* MED septicemia *f*

septic tank *n* pozo *m* séptico

septuagenarian [,sep·tu·ə·dʒə·'ner·i·ən] I. *n* septuagenario, -a *m, f* II. *adj* septuagenario, -a

sepulcher *n* sepulcro *m*

sepulchral [sə·'pʌl·krəl] *adj liter* **1.** (*silence*) sepulcral **2.** (*gloomy*) lóbrego, -a

sequel ['si·kwəl] *n* **1.** secuela *f;* **the** ~ **to an earlier success** la secuela de un éxito temprano **2.** (*follow-up*) continuación *f*

sequence ['si·kwəns] *n* **1.** (*order*) secuencia *f,* orden *m;* (*of events*) sucesión *f* **2.** (*part of film*) secuencia *f*

sequential [sɪ·'kwen·ʃəl] *adj form* secuencial

sequin ['si·kwɪn] *n* lentejuela *f*

sequoia [sɪ·'kwɔɪ·ə] *n* secuoya *f*

Serb [sɜrb] I. *adj* serbio, -a II. *n* serbio, -a *m, f*

Serbia ['sɜr·bi·ə] *n* Serbia *f*

Serbian ['sɜr·bi·ən] *n s.* **Serb**

Serbo-Croat [,sɜr·boʊ·kroʊ·'æt] *n* LING serbo-croata *m*

serenade [,ser·ə·'neɪd] I. *vt* **1.** (*sing to*) cantar una serenata a **2.** (*play music for*) dar una serenata a II. *n* serenata *f,* mañanita *f Méx*

serene [sə·'rin] *adj* **1.** (*calm*) sereno, -a; (*sea*) calmado, -a **2.** (*tranquil*) tranquilo, -a **3.** (*cheerful*) feliz

serenity [sə·'ren·ə·ţi] *n* **1.** (*calmness*) serenidad *f* **2.** (*tranquility*) tranquilidad *f* **3.** (*cheerfulness*) felicidad *f*

serf [sɜrf] *n* HIST siervo, -a *m, f*

serfdom *n* HIST servidumbre *f*

sergeant ['sar·dʒənt] *n* sargento *mf;* ~ **at arms** ujier *m*

sergeant major *n* brigada *mf*

serial ['sɪr·i·əl] I. *n* serial *m;* TV ~ serie *f* (de televisión) II. *adj* **1.** (*in series*) consecutivo, -a **2.** (*shown in parts*) por entregas

serialize ['sɪr·i·ə·laɪz] *vt* (*in newspaper, magazine*) publicar por entregas; TV, RADIO presentar por capítulos

serial killer *n* asesino, -a *m, f* en serie

serial number *n* número *m* de serie

serial port *n* COMPUT puerto *m* en serie

series ['sɪr·iz] *n inv* **1.** (*sequence*) serie *f* **2.** (*succession*) sucesión *f;* **in** ~ ELEC en serie **3.** (*set of broadcasts*) ciclo *m*

serious ['sɪr·i·əs] *adj* **1.** (*earnest, solemn*) serio, -a **2.** (*problem, injury*) grave **3.** (*not slight*) de consideración; (*argument*) importante **4.** (*determined*) firme; **to be** ~ **about sb** ir en serio con alguien **5.** *inf* (*significant*) significativo, -a; ~ **money** mucho dinero **6.** (*large: debt, amount*) considerable

seriously *adv* **1.** (*in earnest*) seriamente, en serio; **to** ~ **expect sb to do sth** esperar de verdad que alguien haga algo; **no,** ~... no, en serio...; **it would be** ~ **wrong of him if...** sería un gran error por su parte si... **2.** (*ill, damaged*) gravemente **3.** *inf* (*very*) extremadamente; **she was** ~ **drunk** estaba borracha a más no poder

seriousness *n* **1.** (*truthfulness*) seriedad *f;* **in all** ~ en serio **2.** (*serious nature*) gravedad *f*

sermon ['sɜr·mən] *n a. fig* sermón *m;* **to deliver a** ~ dar un sermón

serpent ['sɜr·pənt] *n* serpiente *f*

serpentine ['sɜr·pən·taɪn] *adj liter* **1.** (*snakelike*) serpentino, -a **2.** (*twisting*) serpenteante **3.** (*complicated*) complicado, -a **4.** (*sly*) ingenioso, -a; (*explanation*) artificioso, -a

serrated [sə·'reɪ·ţɪd] *adj* serrado, -a; ~ **knife** cuchillo *m* de sierra

serum ['sɪr·əm] <-s *o* sera> *n* suero *m*

servant ['sɜr·vənt] *n* criado, -a *m, f,* mucamo, -a *m, f AmL*

serve [sɜrv] I. *n* SPORTS saque *m,* servicio *m* II. *vt* **1.** (*attend*) atender **2.** (*provide*) servir; **to** ~ **alcohol** servir bebidas alcohólicas **3.** (*be enough for*) servir para **4.** (*work for*) estar al servicio de; **to** ~ **sb's interests** servir a los intereses de alguien **5.** (*complete: sentence, mandate*) cumplir; **to** ~ **time** (**for sth**) *inf* cumplir condena (por algo) **6.** (*help achieve*) ser útil a; **if my memory ~s me right** si la memoria no me falla **7.** SPORTS sacar **8.** (*deliver*) entregar; **to ~ sb with papers** proporcionar papeles a alguien ▸ **it ~s him/her right!** ¡se lo merece! III. *vi* **1.** (*put food on plates*) servir **2.** (*be useful*) servir; **to ~ as sth** servir de algo **3.** (*work for*) prestar servicio; **to ~ in the army** servir en el ejército **4.** (*be acceptable*) ser aceptable; (*suffice*) ser suficiente **5.** SPORTS sacar

◆ **serve out** *vt* (*sentence, mandate*) cumplir

◆ **serve up** *vt* CULIN servir; *fig* ofrecer

server ['sɜr·vər] *n* **1.** (*spoon*) cuchara *f* de servir; **salad ~s** cubiertos *mpl* para servir ensalada **2.** (*tray*) bandeja *f*; (*dish*) fuente *f* **3.** (*waiter*) camarero, -a *m, f* **4.** COMPUT servidor *m* **5.** SPORTS *jugador que tiene el saque*

service ['sɜr·vɪs] I. *n* **1.** (*in shop, restaurant*) servicio *m* **2.** (*help, assistance*) asistencia *f*, servicio *m*; **bus/train ~** servicio de autobuses/trenes; **to be of ~** (**to sb**) ser de utilidad (a alguien); **to operate a ~** llevar a cabo un servicio; **to press sth into ~** recurrir a algo **3.** (*department*) servicio *m*; **the Service** MIL el ejército; NAUT la marina; AVIAT la aviación; **to be fit/unfit for ~** ser apto/no ser apto para el servicio **4.** SPORTS saque *m*, servicio *m* **5.** REL oficio *m*; **morning ~** misa matinal; **to hold a ~** celebrar una misa **6.** TECH mantenimiento *m*; AUTO revisión *f* **7.** (*set*) vajilla *f*; **tea ~** juego *m* de té ▸ **to be at sb's ~** *iron* estar al servicio de alguien; **to be in ~** estar en uso II. *vt* **1.** (*car, TV*) revisar **2.** FIN **to ~ a loan** pagar el interés de un préstamo

serviceable ['sɜr·vɪ·sə·bəl] *adj* servible

service area *n* área *f* de servicio

service center *n* (*for repairs*) centro *m* de reparaciones; (*garage*) garaje *m*

service charge *n* gastos *mpl* de servicio

service industry *n* sector *m* servicios

servicemember *n* militar *mf*

service road *n* vía *f* de acceso

service station *n* estación *f* de servicio

servile ['sɜr·vəl] *adj pej* servil

servility [sɜr·'vɪl·ə·ti] *n pej* servilismo *m*

serving ['sɜr·vɪŋ] I. *n* (*portion*) ración *f* II. *adj* activo, -a

serving spoon *n* cuchara *f* de servir

servitude ['sɜr·və·tud] *n form* servidumbre *f*

servo ['sɜr·voʊ] *n* TECH servo *m*

sesame ['ses·ə·mi] *n* sésamo *m* ▸ **open ~!** ¡ábrete, sésamo!

session ['seʃ·ən] *n* **1.** (*meeting*) sesión *f*; **to be in ~** estar reunido; **a drinking ~** *inf* una borrachera **2.** SCHOOL **morning/afternoon ~** sesión de mañana/tarde; **spring/summer/fall/winter ~** temporada de primavera/verano/otoño/invierno

set [set] I. *adj* **1.** (*ready*) listo, -a; **to get ~** (**to do sth**) prepararse (para hacer algo) **2.** (*fixed*) fijo, -a; **to be ~ in one's ways** tener costumbres profundamente arraigadas **3.** (*assigned*) asignado, -a II. *n* **1.** (*group: of*

people*) grupo *m*; (*of cups, chess*) juego *m*; (*of kitchen utensils*) batería *f*; (*of stamps*) serie *f*; (*of tools*) set *m*; **~ of glasses** cristalería *f*; **~ of teeth** dentadura *f* **2.** (*collection*) colección *f*; **a complete ~** un juego completo **3.** CINE plató *m* **4.** (*television*) televisor *m* **5.** (*in tennis*) set *m* **6.** (*musical performance*) actuación *f*; **to play a long/short ~** tocar durante mucho/poco tiempo III. *vt* <set, set> **1.** (*place*) poner, colocar; **a house that is ~ on a hill** una casa situada sobre una colina; **to ~ a broken bone** colocar bien un hueso roto **2.** (*give: example*) dar; (*task*) imponer; (*problem*) plantear **3.** (*start*) **to ~ a boat afloat** poner una barca a flote; **to ~ sth on fire** prender fuego a algo; **to ~ sth in motion** poner algo en movimiento; **to ~ the country on the road to economic recovery** encaminar el país hacia la recuperación económica; **to set a dog on sb** hacer que un perro ataque a alguien **4.** (*adjust*) ajustar; (*prepare*) preparar; **to ~ the table** poner la mesa **5.** (*fix*) fijar; (*record*) establecer; (*date, price*) determinar; **to ~ oneself a goal** marcarse un objetivo **6.** (*arrange*) acordar **7.** (*encrust*) adornar; (*insert*) introducir; **to ~ a watch with sapphires** engastar zafiros en un reloj **8.** (*provide*) poner; **to ~ sth to music** poner música a algo IV. *vi* **1.** MED soldarse **2.** (*become firm: cement*) endurecerse; (*Jell-O, cheese*) cuajar **3.** (*sink*) hundirse **4.** (*sun*) ponerse

◆ **set about** *vt* emprender; **to ~ doing sth** comenzar a hacer algo

◆ **set against** *vt* **1.** (*compare*) comparar; **to set the advantages against the disadvantages** sopesar las ventajas y los inconvenientes **2.** (*make oppose*) **to set sb against sb/sth** poner a alguien en contra de alguien/algo

◆ **set apart** *vt* **1.** (*distinguish*) diferenciar **2.** (*reserve*) reservar

◆ **set aside** *vt* **1.** (*save*) reservar; (*time*) guardar; (*money*) ahorrar **2.** (*ignore*) ignorar; **to set one's differences aside** dejar a un lado sus diferencias **3.** (*overturn*) desechar **4.** (*put to side*) dejar de lado

◆ **set back** *vt* **1.** (*delay*) retrasar **2.** (*place away from*) apartar **3.** *inf* (*cost*) costar

◆ **set down** *vt* **1.** (*place on surface*) posar **2.** (*land*) poner en tierra; (*airplane*) hacer aterrizar **3.** (*write*) poner por escrito; (*record*) registrar

◆ **set forth** I. *vt form s.* **set out** II. *vi liter* partir

◆ **set off** I. *vi* partir; **to ~** (**for a place**) ponerse en camino (hacia un lugar) II. *vt* **1.** (*detonate*) hacer explotar; (*explosive*) detonar **2.** (*make sb do sth*) **to set sb off** (**doing sth**) hacer [*o* provocar] que alguien (haga algo) **3.** (*start*) causar **4.** (*enhance*) resaltar

◆ **set on** *vt* atacar

◆ **set out** I. *vi* **1.** *s.* **set off 2.** (*intend*) **to ~ to do sth** tener la intención de hacer algo II. *vt* **1.** (*display, arrange*) disponer, colocar **2.** (*explain*) exponer; **to set it out for sb**

S

exponer algo a alguien

◆**set to** *vi* **1.** (*begin working*) ponerse manos a la obra **2.** (*begin fighting*) llegar a las manos

◆**set up** *vt* **1.** (*prepare*) poner, construir **2.** (*establish*) establecer; (*arrange*) disponer; (*cause*) causar; (*committee*) constituir; (*corporation*) crear; (*dictatorship*) instaurar **3.** (*claim*) **to set oneself up as sth** dárselas de algo **4.** (*make healthy*) fortalecer **5.** (*provide*) proveer **6.** *inf* (*deceive*) defraudar

setback ['set·bæk] *n* revés *m;* **to experience a ~** tener un contratiempo

settee [se·'ti] *n* sofá *m*

setter ['set·ər] *n* (*dog*) setter *mf*

setting ['set·ɪŋ] *n* **1.** (*of sun*) puesta *f* **2.** (*scenery*) escenario *m;* (*surroundings*) entorno *m;* (*landscape*) marco *m* **3.** TECH ajuste *m* **4.** (*frame for jewel*) engaste *m* **5.** MUS arreglo *m*

settle ['set·əl] **I.** *vi* **1.** (*take up residence*) instalarse **2.** (*get comfortable*) ponerse cómodo, -a **3.** (*calm down*) calmarse; (*weather*) serenarse; (*situation*) normalizarse, aconcharse *Chile* **4.** (*reach an agreement*) llegar a un acuerdo **5.** *form* (*pay*) pagar; **to ~ with sb** saldar las cuentas con alguien **6.** (*accumulate*) acumularse; (*snow*) cuajar **7.** (*land*) asentarse; (*bird*) posarse **8.** (*sink*) hundirse **9.** (*food*) asentarse en el estómago **II.** *vt* **1.** (*calm down: stomach*) calmar **2.** (*decide*) acordar; **it's been ~d that...** se ha acordado que... **3.** (*conclude*) finalizar; (*resolve*) resolver; (*problem*) solucionar; (*affairs*) arreglar; **to ~ a lawsuit** poner fin a un litigio **4.** (*pay*) pagar; (*an account*) liquidar **5.** (*colonize*) colonizar ▶ **that ~s it!** ¡ya no hay más que decir!

◆**settle down I.** *vi* **1.** (*calm down*) calmarse **2.** (*take up residence*) instalarse **II.** *vt* **to set oneself down to sth** acostumbrarse a algo

◆**settle for** *vt* contentarse con

◆**settle in** *vi* acostumbrarse

◆**settle on** *vt* **1.** (*decide on*) decidir **2.** (*agree on*) acordar

◆**settle up** *vi* ajustar cuentas

◆**settle upon** *vt form s.* **settle on**

settled ['set·əld] *adj* **1.** (*established*) establecido, -a; (*in a regular way of life*) instalado, -a; **to feel ~** sentirse cómodo **2.** (*calm*) calmado, -a **3.** (*fixed*) fijo, -a

settlement ['set·əl·mənt] *n* **1.** (*resolution*) resolución *f;* (*of strike*) finalización *f* **2.** (*agreement*) acuerdo *m;* **to negotiate a ~** (**with sb**) negociar un acuerdo (con alguien) **3.** FIN, ECON liquidación *f,* pago *m;* **in ~ of sth** para liquidar algo **4.** (*village, town*) asentamiento *m;* (*act of colonization*) colonización *f* **5.** (*subsidence*) hundimiento *m*

settler ['set·lər] *n* colono, -a *m, f*

set-to ['set·tu] *n inf* bronca *f;* **to have a ~** (**with sb**) tener una bronca (con alguien)

setup ['set·ʌp] *n* **1.** (*way things are arranged*) estructura *f;* (*arrangement*) organización *f* **2.** *inf* (*trick*) trampa *f*

seven ['sev·ən] **I.** *adj* siete *inv* **II.** *n* siete *m; s.a.* **eight**

sevenfold ['sev·ən·foʊld] **I.** *adj* séptuplo, -a **II.** *adv* **to increase ~** aumentar en siete veces

seventeen [ˌsev·ən·'tin] **I.** *adj* diecisiete *inv* **II.** *n* diecisiete *m; s.a.* **eight**

seventeenth [ˌsev·ən·'tinθ] **I.** *adj* decimoséptimo, -a **II.** *n* **1.** (*order*) decimoséptimo, -a *m, f* **2.** (*date*) diecisiete *m* **3.** (*fraction*) diecisieteavo *m;* (*part*) diecisieteava parte *f; s.a.* **eighth**

seventh ['sev·ənθ] **I.** *adj* séptimo, -a **II.** *n* **1.** (*order*) séptimo, -a *m, f* **2.** (*date*) siete *m* **3.** (*fraction*) séptimo *m;* (*part*) séptima parte *f; s.a.* **eighth**

seventieth ['sev·ən·ti·əθ] **I.** *adj* septuagésimo, -a **II.** *n* (*order*) septuagésimo, -a *m, f;* (*fraction*) septuagésimo *m,* setentavo *m;* (*part*) septuagésima parte *f,* setentava parte *f; s.a.* **eighth**

seventy ['sev·ən·ti] **I.** *adj* setenta *inv* **II.** *n* <-ies> setenta *m; s.a.* **eighty**

sever ['sev·ər] *vt* (*limb, branch*) cortar; (*relationship*) romper

several ['sev·ər·əl] **I.** *adj* **1.** (*some*) varios, -as; (*reasons*) diversos, -as; **~ times** varias veces; (*distinct*) distintos, -as **2.** (*individual*) respectivos, -as **II.** *pron* (*some*) algunos, -as; (*different*) varios, -as; **~ of us** algunos de nosotros; **we've got ~** tenemos varios

severally *adv* **1.** (*individually*) respectivamente **2.** (*separately*) por separado

severance ['sev·ər·əns] *n form* ruptura *f*

severance pay *n* indemnización *f* por despido

severe [sə·'vɪr] *adj* **1.** (*problem, illness*) grave; (*pain*) fuerte; **to be under ~ strain** estar bajo una gran tensión **2.** (*criticism, punishment, person*) severo, -a; (*strict*) estricto, -a; (*rough*) duro, -a **3.** (*weather*) riguroso, -a; **~ frost** fuerte helada *f* **4.** (*austere*) austero, -a

severely *adv* **1.** (*harshly*) con severidad **2.** (*damaged*) seriamente; (*ill*) gravemente

severity [sə·'ver·ə·ti] *n* **1.** (*of illness, problem*) gravedad *f* **2.** (*of criticism, punishment, person*) severidad *f* **3.** (*austerity*) austeridad *f*

sew [soʊ] <sewed, sewn *o* sewed> **I.** *vt* coser; **hand ~n** cosido a mano **II.** *vi* coser

◆**sew on** *vt* coser

◆**sew up** *vt* **1.** (*repair*) coser, zurcir **2.** MED suturar **3.** *inf* (*arrange*) arreglar; **to ~ a deal** cerrar un trato

sewage ['su·ɪdʒ] *n* aguas *fpl* residuales

sewage plant *n* ECOL planta *f* de tratamiento de aguas residuales

sewer ['su·ər] *n* alcantarilla *f*

sewerage ['su·ər·ɪdʒ] *n* alcantarillado *m,* drenaje *m Méx*

sewing ['soʊ·ɪŋ] **I.** *n* costura *f* **II.** *adj* de costura

sewing machine *n* máquina *f* de coser

sewn [soʊn] *pp of* **sew**

sex [seks] **I.** <-es> *n* (*gender, intercourse*) sexo *m;* **to have ~** tener relaciones sexuales **II.** *vt* determinar el sexo de

sex appeal *n* sex-appeal *m*
sex discrimination *n* discriminación *f* sexual
sex education *n* educación *f* sexual
sexism ['sek·sɪz·əm] *n* sexismo *m*
sexist I. *adj* sexista II. *n* sexista *mf*
sexless ['seks·lɪs] *adj* asexual
sex life *n* vida *f* sexual
sex symbol *n* sex-symbol *mf*
sextant ['seks·tənt] *n* sextante *m*
sextet [sek·'stet] *n* sexteto *m*
sexual ['sek·ʃu·əl] *adj* sexual
sexual harassment *n* acoso *m* sexual
sexual intercourse *n* relaciones *fpl* sexuales
sexuality [,sek·ʃu·'æl·ə·ti] *n* sexualidad *f*
sexually *adv* sexualmente; **to be ~ abused** ser víctima de abusos sexuales
sexy ['sek·si] <-ier, -iest> *adj inf* 1. (*physically appealing*) sexy 2. (*exciting*) excitante
SGML *n* COMPUT *abbr of* **Standard Generalized Markup Language** SGML *m*
Sgt. *n abbr of* **sergeant** Sgto. *m*
shabby ['ʃæb·i] <-ier, -iest> *adj* 1. (*badly maintained*) deteriorado, -a 2. (*poorly dressed*) desharrapado, -a, encuerado, -a *Méx, Cuba* 3. (*substandard*) de poca calidad
shack [ʃæk] *n* choza *f*, ruca *f Arg, Chile*, jacal *m Méx*
◆**shack up** *vi* irse a vivir juntos, arrejuntarse *Méx*
shackle ['ʃæk·əl] I. *vt* poner grilletes a, encadenar II. *n pl* grilletes *mpl*
shade [ʃeɪd] I. *n* 1. (*shadow*) sombra *f*; (*of a painting*) sombreado *m*; **in the ~ of** a [*o* en] la sombra de 2. (*covering*) pantalla *f* 3. *pl* (*window blind*) persiana *f* 4. (*variation*) matiz *m*; (*of color*) tono *m*; **pastel ~s** tonos pastel 5. (*small amount*) pizca *f* 6. *pl, inf* (*sunglasses*) gafas *fpl* de sol 7. *pl, inf* (*reminder*) **~s of Nixon/1989** esto recuerda a Nixon/1989 II. *vt* 1. (*cast shadow on*) dar sombra a; (*protect*) resguardar (de la luz) 2. ART sombrear III. *vi* (*colors*) fundirse
shading *n* sombreado *m*
shadow ['ʃæd·oʊ] I. *n* 1. (*shade*) a. *fig* sombra *f*; **the ~s** las tinieblas 2. (*smallest trace*) pizca *f*; **without a ~ of a doubt** sin sombra de duda ▶**to have ~s under one's eyes** tener ojeras; **to be a ~ of one's former self** no ser ni la sombra de lo que se era; **to be afraid of one's own ~** tener miedo de la propia sombra; **to cast a ~ over sth** ensombrecer algo; **to be under sb's ~** estar a la sombra de alguien II. *vt* 1. ART sombrear 2. (*darken*) ensombrecer 3. (*follow*) seguir
shadowboxing ['ʃæd·oʊ·bak·sɪŋ] *n* boxeo con un adversario imaginario
shadowy <-ier, -iest> *adj* 1. (*containing darker spaces*) oscuro, -a; (*photograph*) oscuro, -a 2. (*vague*) impreciso, -a 3. (*suspicious*) sombrío, -a
shady ['ʃeɪ·di] <-ier, -iest> *adj* 1. (*protected from light*) sombreado, -a 2. *inf* (*dubious*) turbio, -a; (*character*) sospechoso, -a

shaft [ʃæft] I. *n* 1. (*of tool*) mango *m*; (*of weapon*) asta *f*; (*of arrow*) astil *m* 2. TECH eje *m* 3. (*ray*) rayo *m* 4. (*for elevator*) hueco *m*; (*of mine*) pozo *m*; **well ~** pozo 5. (*of penis*) verga *f* ▶**to give sb the ~** *sl* joder a alguien II. *vt sl* (*treat unfairly*) **I got ~ed at the meeting** me jodieron bien en la reunión
shag¹ [ʃæg] *n* 1. (*rug*) alfombra *f* 2. (*haircut*) greñas *fpl*
shag² [ʃæg] *vt* SPORTS **to ~ balls** (**in the outfield**) entrenarse cogiendo bolas bombeadas (bateadas a los jardines)
shag³ [ʃæg] I. *n* (*dance*) shag *m* (*paso de baile de los años 30, que consiste en ir saltando de un pie a otro*) II. *vi* (*dance*) bailar shag
shaggy ['ʃæg·i] <-ier, -iest> *adj* peludo, -a; (*coat*) lanudo, -a
shah [ʃa] *n* (*Persian king*) sah *m*
shake [ʃeɪk] I. *n* 1. (*wobble*) sacudida *f*; (*vibration*) vibración *f*; (*quiver*) temblor *m*; **to give sth a good ~** dar una buena sacudida a algo 2. *inf* (*milk shake*) batido *m*, malteada *f AmL* 3. (*handshake*) apretón *m* (de manos) 4. (*chance*) oportunidad *f*; **I don't think you've given him a fair ~** creo que no le has tratado con justicia 5. *inf* (*earthquake*) tembleque *m*, temblorina *f Méx* 6. *pl* (*sudden trembling*) tembleque *m*; **to get the ~s** *inf* entrarle el tembleque a uno 7. *inf* **in two ~s of a lamb's tail** en un santiamén II. <shook, shaken> *vt* 1. (*joggle*) agitar; (*person*) sacudir; (*house*) hacer temblar; **to ~ one's fist (at sb)** amenazar con el puño (a alguien); **to ~ hands** darse la mano; **to ~ sb by the hand** estrechar la mano de alguien; **to ~ one's head** negar con la cabeza; **to ~ one's hips** mover las caderas 2. (*unsettle*) debilitar 3. (*make worried*) desconcertar ▶**~ a leg** *inf* mover el culo III. <shook, shaken> *vi* 1. (*tremble*) temblar; '**~ well before opening**' 'agitar bien antes de abrir' 2. (*clasp hands*) **let's ~ on it** chócala *inf*
◆**shake down** *vt sl* 1. (*extort money from*) sablar 2. (*search*) registrar
◆**shake off** *vt* librarse de
◆**shake out** *vt* sacudir
◆**shake up** *vt* 1. (*reorganize*) reorganizar 2. (*upset*) desconcertar 3. (*jumble*) sacudir, zamarronear *Chile*
shakedown ['ʃeɪk·daʊn] *n inf* 1. (*extortion*) sablazo *m* 2. (*search*) redada *f*, arreada *f Arg*
shaken ['ʃeɪ·kən] *vi, vt pp of* **shake**
shaker ['ʃeɪ·kər] *n* (*for cocktails*) coctelera *f*; **salt ~** salero *m*
shakeup ['ʃeɪk·ʌp] *n* reorganización *f*
shakily ['ʃeɪ·kɪ·li] *adv* 1. (*physically weak*) de modo inestable 2. (*in an uncertain manner*) con poca firmeza
shaking ['ʃeɪ·kɪŋ] I. *n* temblor *m* II. *adj* tembloroso, -a
shaky ['ʃeɪ·ki] <-ier, -iest> *adj* 1. (*jerky*) tembloroso, -a; **to be ~ on one's feet** estar inseguro al andar 2. (*wavering*) inseguro, -a 3. (*unstable*) inestable; (*economy*) débil

shale [ʃeɪl] *n* esquisto *m*

shall [ʃæl] *aux* **1.** (*future*) I ~ **give back the money** devolveré el dinero; **we** ~ **win the match** ganaremos el partido **2.** (*ought to*) **he** ~ **call his mother** debería llamar a su madre; **we** ~ **overcome!** ¡nos sobrepondremos! **3.** (*expresses what is mandatory*) **that** ~ **be unlawful** eso es ilegal

shallot [ʃæl·ət] *n* chalote *m*, cebolleta *f AmL*

shallow [ʃæl·oʊ] **I.** *adj* **1.** (*not deep*) poco profundo, -a **2.** (*only light*) débil **3.** (*superficial*) superficial **II.** *npl* bajío *m*

shallowness *n* **1.** (*lack of depth*) poca profundidad *f* **2.** (*superficiality*) superficialidad *f*

sham [ʃæm] *pej* **I.** *n* **1.** (*fake*) fraude *m;* (*imposture*) impostura *f* **2.** (*impostor*) impostor(a) *m(f)* **3.** (*cover*) **a pillow** ~ una funda de almohada **II.** *adj* (*document, trial*) falso, -a; (*deal*) fraudulento, -a; (*sympathy*) hipócrita; (*marriage*) simulado, -a **III.** <-mm-> *vt* fingir **IV.** *vi* fingir

shambles [ʃæm·bəlz] *n inf* (*place*) escombrera *f;* (*situation*) confusión *f;* **to leave sth in** ~ dejar algo patas arriba

shame [ʃeɪm] **I.** *n* **1.** (*humiliation*) vergüenza *f*, pena *f AmL;* **to die of** ~ morirse de vergüenza; **to feel no** ~ no sentir vergüenza; **to put sb to** ~ avergonzar a alguien; ~ **on you!** *a. iron* ¡debería darte vergüenza! **2.** (*discredit*) deshonra *f;* **to bring** ~ **on sb** deshonrar a alguien **3.** (*pity*) pena *f;* **what a** ~! ¡qué pena!; **what a** ~ **that...** qué lástima que... +*subj;* **it's a** ~ **to have to...** +*infin* es una pena tener que... +*infin;* **it's a** ~ **that...** es una pena que... +*subj;* **it's a crying** ~ es una verdadera lástima **II.** *vt* **1.** (*mortify*) avergonzar **2.** (*discredit*) deshonrar

shamefaced [ˈʃeɪm·ˈfeɪst] *adj* abochornado, -a, apenado, -a *AmC*

shameful [ˈʃeɪm·fəl] *adj pej* **1.** (*causing disgrace*) vergonzoso, -a, penoso, -a *AmC* **2.** (*outrageous*) bochornoso, -a; **it's** ~ **that...** es vergonzoso que... +*subj*

shameless [ˈʃeɪm·lɪs] *adj pej* descarado, -a, conchudo, -a *AmL*, pechugón, -ona *AmL*, vaquetón, -ona *Méx*

shammy [ˈʃæm·i] <-ies> *n inf, inf* gamuza *f*

shampoo [ʃæm·ˈpu] **I.** *n* champú *m* **II.** *vt* lavar con champú; ~ **and set** lavar y peinar

shamrock [ˈʃæm·rak] *n* trébol *m*

shank [ʃæŋk] *n* **1.** (*leg*) pata *f;* (*of bird*) zanca *f* **2.** TECH mango *m* ▶ **to go on** ~'**s pony** ir en el coche de San Fernando, ir a pata *Méx*

shanty [ˈʃæn·ti] <-ies> *n* (*shack*) chabola *f*, favela *f AmL*, choza *f Méx*

shantytown *n* chabolas *fpl*, favelas *fpl AmL*, barriada *f Perú*, ciudad *f* perdida *Méx*, villa *f* miseria *RíoPl*

shape [ʃeɪp] **I.** *n* **1.** (*form*) forma *f;* **to get out of** ~ perder la forma; **to take** ~ adquirir forma; **in the** ~ **of sth** en forma de algo; **the** ~ **of things to come** lo que nos espera **2.** (*condition*) condición *f;* **in bad/good** ~ en malas/

buenas condiciones; **to get sth into** ~ acondicionar algo; **to get into** ~ ponerse en forma; **to knock sth/sb into** ~ poner algo/a alguien a punto **II.** *vt* **1.** (*form*) **to** ~ **sth into sth** dar a algo la forma de algo **2.** (*influence*) influenciar **3.** (*determine*) condicionar

shapeless [ˈʃeɪp·lɪs] *adj* **1.** (*without definite shape*) informe, amorfo, -a **2.** (*not shapely*) deforme

shapely [ˈʃeɪp·li] <-ier, -iest> *adj* bien proporcionado, -a; **she has a rather** ~ **figure** tiene una figura muy esbelta

shard [ʃard] *n* casco *m*, tepalcate *m Guat, Méx*

share [ʃer] **I.** *n* **1.** (*part*) parte *f*, porción *f;* **the lion's** ~ la parte del león **2.** (*portion*) parte *f;* **to do one's** ~ **of sth** hacer su parte de algo **3.** FIN acción *f;* **stocks and** ~**s** acciones y participaciones **II.** *vi* **1.** (*divide*) repartir **2.** (*allow others to use*) compartir ▶ **to** ~ **and** ~ **alike** compartir las cosas **III.** *vt* **1.** (*divide*) dividir **2.** (*allow others to use*) compartir **3.** (*have in common*) compartir; **to** ~ **sb's view** compartir las opiniones de alguien; **to want to** ~ **one's life with sb** querer compartir la vida con alguien

◆**share out** *vt* dividir

sharecropper [ˈʃer·ˌkrap·ər] *n* aparcero, -a *m, f*

shareholder [ˈʃer·ˌhoʊl·dər] *n* accionista *mf*

shareholding *n* participación *f* accionaria

shareware [ˈʃer·wer] *n* COMPUT shareware *m*, programa *m* compartido

shark [ʃark] <-(s)> *n* **1.** (*fish*) tiburón *m* **2.** *pej, inf* (*person*) estafador(a) *m(f)*

sharp [ʃarp] **I.** *adj* **1.** (*cutting*) afilado, -a; (*pointed*) puntiagudo, -a **2.** (*angular: feature*) anguloso, -a; (*corner, edge, angle*) agudo, -a; (*curve*) cerrado, -a **3.** (*severe*) severo, -a; (*pain*) agudo, -a, intenso, -a; (*look*) penetrante; (*reprimand*) violento, -a; **to have a** ~ **tongue** tener una lengua afilada [*o* viperina]; **to be** ~ **with sb** ser mordaz con alguien **4.** (*astute*) astuto, -a; (*perceptive*) perspicaz, alicuz *Hond;* (*mind*) vivo, -a **5.** (*pungent*) acre; (*wine*) ácido, -a; (*cheese*) muy curado, -a **6.** (*sudden*) súbito, -a; (*abrupt*) abrupto, -a; (*marked*) pronunciado, -a **7.** (*penetrating*) penetrante; (*cry*) agudo, -a **8.** (*distinct*) nítido, -a **9.** MUS sostenido, -a; **C** ~ do sostenido **II.** *adv* **1.** (*exactly*) en punto; **at ten o'clock** ~ a las diez en punto **2.** (*suddenly*) de repente; **to pull up** ~ frenar en seco **3.** MUS por encima del tono correcto **III.** *n* MUS sostenido *m*

sharpen [ˈʃar·pən] *vt* **1.** (*blade*) afilar; (*pencil*) sacar punta a **2.** (*intensify*) agudizar; (*mind*) aguzar; (*appetite*) abrir

sharpener [ˈʃar·pən·ər] *n* afilador *m*, afiladora *f Méx;* **pencil** ~ sacapuntas *m inv*

sharp-eyed [ˈʃarp·ˈaɪd] *adj* observador(a)

sharpness *n* **1.** (*of blade*) filo *m;* (*of pencil*) punta *f* **2.** (*of pain*) agudeza *f* **3.** (*of comment*) mordacidad *f* **4.** (*suddenness: of curve*) brusquedad *f* **5.** (*intensity*) intensidad *f;* (*of blow*) violencia *f* **6.** (*clarity*) nitidez *f* **7.** (*per-*

ceptiveness) perspicacia *f;* (*intelligence*) astucia *f* **8.** (*chic*) elegancia *f*

sharpshooter ['ʃarp·ʃu·tər] *n* tirador(a) *m(f)* de primera

sharp-sighted ['ʃarp·saɪ·tɪd] *adj* **1.** (*very observant*) de vista aguda **2.** (*alert*) sagaz

sharp-tongued *adj* mordaz

sharp-witted *adj* agudo, -a

shat [ʃæt] *pt, pp of* **shit**

shatter ['ʃæt·ər] **I.** *vi* hacerse añicos **II.** *vt* **1.** (*smash*) hacer añicos, destrozar; (*one's hopes, one's dreams*) destruir **2.** (*disturb*) perturbar; (*unity*) destruir

shattering *adj* tremendo, -a

shatterproof ['ʃæt·ər·pruf] *adj* inastillable

shave [ʃeɪv] **I.** *n* afeitado *m,* rasurada *f Méx;* **to give oneself a ~** afeitarse ▶ **to have a close ~** librarse por los pelos **II.** *vi* afeitarse **III.** *vt* **1.** (*remove body hair*) afeitar, rasurar *Méx* **2.** (*decrease: budget*) recortar; **he ~d three seconds off the world record** mejoró el récord mundial en tres segundos **3.** (*brush past*) rozar

shaven ['ʃeɪ·vən] *adj* (*face, legs*) afeitado, -a; (*head*) rapado, -a

shaver ['ʃeɪ·vər] *n* maquinilla *f* de afeitar, rasuradora *f Méx*

shaving cream *n* crema *f* de afeitar

shaving gel *n* gel *m* de afeitar

shawl [ʃɔl] *n* chal *m*

she [ʃi] **I.** *pron ers* (*female person or animal*) ella; **~'s my mother** (ella) es mi madre; **~'s gone away, but ~'ll be back soon** se ha ido pero regresará pronto; **here ~ comes** ahí viene; **~ who...** *form* aquella quien... **II.** *n* (*person*) fémina *f;* (*baby*) **it's a ~** es (una) niña; (*animal*) hembra *f*

sheaf [ʃif, *pl* ʃivz] <sheaves> *n* (*of wheat*) gavilla *f;* (*of documents*) fajo *m*

shear [ʃɪr] <sheared, sheared *o* shorn> *vt* **1.** (*sheep*) esquilar **2.** (*person*) rapar; **to be shorn of sth** *fig* ser despojado de algo ◆ **shear off** *vi* romperse

shears [ʃɪrz] *npl* (*for sheep*) tijeras *f* de esquilar *pl;* (*for plants*) tijeras *f* de podar *pl;* (*for metal*) cizalla *f*

sheath [ʃiθ] *n* **1.** (*covering*) funda *f;* (*for knife*) vaina *f,* funda *f AmL* **2.** (*dress*) vestido *m* de tubo

sheathe [ʃið] *vt* **1.** (*knife*) envainar, enfundar *AmL* **2.** (*cover*) revestir

shebang [ʃɪ·'bæŋ] *n sl* **the whole ~** todo el asunto

shed¹ [ʃed] *n* cobertizo *m,* galera *f AmL,* galpón *m AmC,* galerón *m CRi, ElSal*

shed² [ʃed] <shed, shed> **I.** *vt* **1.** (*cast off*) quitarse; (*clothes*) despojarse de; (*hair, weight*) perder; **to ~ one's skin** mudar la piel **2.** (*blood, tears*) derramar; (*light*) emitir **II.** *vi* (*snake*) mudar de piel; (*cat*) pelechar

sheen [ʃin] *n* brillo *m*

sheep [ʃip] *n* oveja *f;* (*ram*) carnero *m* ▶ **to separate the ~ from the goats** separar el

grano de la paja; **black ~** oveja negra

sheepdog ['ʃip·dɔg] *n* perro *m* pastor

sheepfold ['ʃip·foʊld] *n* redil *m,* majada *f CSur*

sheepish ['ʃi·pɪʃ] *adj* tímido, -a

sheepskin ['ʃip·skɪn] *n* piel *f* de borrego

sheer¹ [ʃɪr] **I.** *adj* **1.** (*unmitigated*) puro, -a; (*bliss*) completo, -a; (*agony, boredom, lunacy*) total; **~ coincidence** pura coincidencia **2.** (*vertical*) escarpado, -a; **~ drop** caída *f* en picado **3.** (*thin*) fino, -a; (*transparent*) transparente **II.** *adv liter* absolutamente

sheer² [ʃɪr] *vi* NAUT desviarse

sheer curtain(s) *n(pl)* visillo(s) *m(pl)*

sheet [ʃit] *n* **1.** (*for bed*) sábana *f* **2.** (*of paper*) hoja *f* **3.** (*plate of material*) placa *f;* (*of glass*) lámina *f* **4.** (*perforated set of stamps*) plancha *f* **5.** (*paper with information*) folleto *m* **6.** (*layer*) capa *f* **7.** (*broad mass*) cortina *f;* **~ of flame** cortina de llamas; **the rain was coming down in ~s** llovía a cántaros

sheet lightning *n* fucilazo *m*

sheet metal *n* metal *m* en planchas

sheet music *n* partituras *fpl*

sheik(h) [ʃik] *n* jeque *m*

shelf [ʃelf, *pl* ʃelvz] <shelves> *n* **1.** (*for storage*) estante *m;* **to buy sth off the ~** comprar algo hecho; **to put sth on the ~** *fig* arrinconar algo **2.** GEO arrecife *m*

shelf life *n* tiempo *m* de conservación

shell [ʃel] **I.** *n* **1.** (*of nut, egg*) cáscara *f;* (*of shellfish, snail*) concha *f;* (*of crab, tortoise*) caparazón *m* **2.** TECH armazón *m;* (*of house*) estructura *f;* (*of ship*) casco *m* **3.** (*projectile*) proyectil *m,* cartucho *m AmL* ▶ **to come** [*o* **bust**] **out of one's ~** salir del cascarón; **to crawl into one's ~** meterse en su cascarón **II.** *vt* **1.** (*remove shell*) pelar **2.** MIL bombardear **III.** *vi* bombardear

◆ **shell out** *inf* **I.** *vt* (*pay*) soltar **II.** *vi* aflojar; **to ~ for sth** apoquinar para algo

shellac [ʃə·'læk] *n* laca *f*

shellfish ['ʃel·fɪʃ] *n* **1.** CULIN marisco *m* **2.** ZOOL (*crustacean*) crustáceo *m;* (*mollusk*) molusco *m*

shelling *n* bombardeo *m*

shell shock *n* neurosis *f* de guerra

shell-shocked *adj* que padece neurosis de guerra; *fig* traumatizado, -a

shelter ['ʃel·tər] **I.** *n* refugio *m;* **to take ~** refugiarse **II.** *vt* resguardar **III.** *vi* refugiarse

sheltered *adj* **1.** (*protected against weather*) abrigado, -a **2.** *pej* (*overprotected*) sobreprotegido, -a **3.** (*tax-protected*) protegido, -a

shelve [ʃelv] **I.** *vt* **1.** (*delay, postpone*) posponer; POL postergar **2.** (*erect shelves in*) poner estantes en **II.** *vi* descender

shelving *n* estantería *f*

shenanigans [ʃɪ·'næn·ɪ·gənz] *npl* chanchullos *mpl*

shepherd ['ʃep·ərd] **I.** *n* pastor *m* **II.** *vt* (*sheep*) guiar; (*people*) dirigir

shepherd's pie *n* pastel *m* de carne

sherbet ['ʃɜr·bət] *n,* **sherbert** ['ʃɜr·bɜrt] *n*

sorbete *m*
sheriff ['ʃer·ɪf] *n* sheriff *mf*
sherry ['ʃer·i] <-ies> *n* jerez *m*
shield [ʃild] I. *n* 1.(*armor*) escudo *m* 2.(*protective layer*) revestimiento *m; fig* caparazón *m* 3.(*logo*) insignia *f* 4.(*badge*) placa *f* (de policía) II. *vt* proteger
shift [ʃɪft] I. *vt* 1.(*change, rearrange*) mover; (*reposition*) cambiar de sitio; **to ~ the blame onto sb** echar la culpa a alguien; **to ~ one's ground** cambiar de opinión 2.(*in mechanics: gears, lanes*) cambiar II. *vi* 1.(*change, rearrange position*) moverse; (*wind*) cambiar 2. *inf*(*move over*) correrse III. *n* 1.(*alteration, change*) cambio *m;* (*of power*) giro *m* 2.(*period of work*) turno *m;* **to work in ~s** trabajar por turnos 3.(*linguistic change*) mutación *f*
shifting *adj* movedizo, -a; (*values*) cambiante
shift key *n* tecla *f* de las mayúsculas
shiftless ['ʃɪft·lɪs] *adj pej*(*idle*) holgazán, -ana; (*lacking purpose*) haragán, -ana
shift work ['ʃɪft·wɜrk] *n* trabajo *m* por turnos
shift worker *n* trabajador(a) *m(f)* por turnos
shifty ['ʃɪf·ti] <-ier, -iest> *adj* sospechoso, -a; (*eyes*) furtivo, -a
Shiite ['ʃi·aɪt] I. *adj* chiíta II. *n* chiíta *mf*
shilling ['ʃɪl·ɪŋ] *n* HIST chelín *m*
shimmer ['ʃɪm·ər] I. *vi* brillar II. *n* resplandor *m*
shin [ʃɪn] *n* 1.(*leg below knee*) espinilla *f* 2.(*lower leg of beef*) jarrete *m*
shindig ['ʃɪn·dɪg] *n inf*juerga *f*
shine [ʃaɪn] I. *n* brillo *m* ▸ **to take a ~ to sb** sentir simpatía por alguien II. <shone *o* shined, shone *o* shined> *vi* 1.(*moon, sun, stars*) brillar; (*gold, metal*) relucir; (*light*) alumbrar; (*eyes*) resplandecer 2.(*be gifted*) destacar III. <shone *o* shined, shone *o* shined> *vt* 1.(*point light*) **to ~ a light at sth/sb** alumbrar algo/a alguien con una luz; **to ~ a flashlight onto sth** iluminar algo con una linterna 2.(*brighten by polishing*) sacar brillo a; (*shoes*) lustrar
shiner ['ʃaɪ·nər] *n inf*ojo *m* morado
shingle ['ʃɪn·gəl] *n* 1.(*roof tile*) teja *f* (de madera) 2.(*pebble mass alongside water*) guijarros *mpl*
shining ['ʃaɪ·nɪŋ] *adj* 1.(*gleaming*) reluciente, abrillantado, -a *AmL;* (*eyes*) brillante 2.(*outstanding*) magnífico, -a; **a ~ example** un ejemplo perfecto
shin splints ['ʃɪn·splɪnts] *npl* periostitis *f* tibial (*dolores en las espinillas por inflamación de los músculos circundantes*)
shiny ['ʃaɪ·ni] <-ier, -iest> *adj* brillante
ship [ʃɪp] I. *n* barco *m;* **passenger ~** buque *m* de pasajeros; **sailing ~** velero *m;* **to board a ~** subir a una embarcación, embarcar II. *vt* <-pp-> 1.(*send by boat*) mandar por barco; **to ~ freight** enviar mercancías por barco 2.(*transport*) transportar
◆**ship off** *vt* (*goods*) expedir; (*person*) enviar

◆**ship out** *vi* embarcarse
shipboard ['ʃɪp·bɔrd] I. *adj* de abordo II. *n* **on ~** a bordo
shipbuilder ['ʃɪp·ˌbɪl·dər] *n* constructor(a) *m(f)* naval
shipbuilding *n* construcción *f* naval
shipload ['ʃɪp·loʊd] *n* cargamento *m*
shipmate *n* camarada *mf* de a bordo
shipment ['ʃɪp·mənt] *n* 1.(*quantity*) remesa *f* 2.(*action*) envío *m*
shipowner *n* 1.(*person*) armador(a) *m(f)* 2.(*company*) naviera *f*
shipper *n* consignador(a) *m(f);* **wine ~** (*company*) exportadora *f* de vinos
shipping ['ʃɪp·ɪŋ] *n* 1.(*ships*) embarcaciones *fpl* 2.(*freight dispatch*) transporte *m*
shipping agent *n* consignatario, -a *m, f*
shipping lane *n* ruta *f* de navegación
shipshape ['ʃɪp·ʃeɪp] *adj inf* limpio y ordenado; **to get sth ~** tener algo en orden
shipway ['ʃɪp·weɪ] *n* canal *m* (navegable)
shipwreck I. *n* 1.(*accident*) naufragio *m* 2.(*remains of ship*) restos *mpl* de un naufragio II. *vt* hacer naufragar; **to be ~ed** naufragar; *fig* estar hundido
shipwright *n* carpintero *m* de navío
shipyard *n* astillero *m*
shirk [ʃɜrk] *pej* I. *vt* eludir II. *vi* escaquearse; **to ~ (away) from sth** escaquearse de algo
shirker ['ʃɜr·kər] *n pej*vago, -a *m, f*
shirt [ʃɜrt] *n* (*man's, woman's*) camisa *f;* (*woman's*) blusa *f* ▸ **to give sb the ~ off one's back** dar hasta la camiseta a alguien; **to have the ~ off sb's back** dejar a alguien sin camisa; **to lose one's ~** *inf* perder hasta la camisa; **keep your ~ on!** *inf* ¡no te sulfures!
shirtsleeve ['ʃɜrt·sliv] *n* manga *f* de camisa; **to be in ~s** estar en mangas de camisa
shit [ʃɪt] *inf* I. *n* 1.(*feces*) mierda *f* 2. *pej* (*nonsense*) gilipolleces *fpl*, pendejadas *fpl AmL* 3.(*nothing*) nada; **he doesn't know ~ about computers** no tiene ni zorra idea de ordenadores 4.(*as intensifier*) **I don't give a ~!** ¡me importa un carajo! ▸ **to beat the ~ out of sb** moler a alguien a palos; **to frighten the ~ out of sb** hacer que alguien se cague de miedo; **to be in deep ~** estar muy jodido; **when the ~ hits the fan** cuando la mierda empieza a salpicar; **no ~!** ¡no jodas! II. *interj* mierda III. <shit, shit> *vi* cagar IV. <shit, shit> *vt* cagar; **to ~ oneself** [*o* **one's pants**] cagarse (encima); *fig* cagarse de miedo; **to ~ bricks** [*o* **a brick**] acojonarse
shitty ['ʃɪt·i] <-ier, -iest> *adj pej, inf* 1.(*unfair, unpleasant*) asqueroso, -a 2.(*sick, ill*) jodido, -a; **to feel ~** sentirse fatal
shiver ['ʃɪv·ər] I. *vi* temblar; **to ~ with cold** tiritar de frío II. *n* estremecimiento *m;* **to feel a ~** tener un escalofrío; **to give sb the ~s** *inf* dar miedo a alguien
shoal¹ [ʃoʊl] *n* (*of fish*) banco *m*
shoal² [ʃoʊl] *n* 1.(*area of shallow water*) bajío *m* 2.(*sand bank*) banco *m* de arena

shock¹ [ʃak] I. *n* 1.(*unpleasant surprise*) conmoción *f*; batata *f CSur;* **the ~ of my life** *inf* el susto de mi vida; **look of ~** mirada *f* de asombro; **to give sb a ~** dar un disgusto a alguien 2. *inf* (*electric shock*) descarga *f* 3. MED shock *m;* **to die from ~** morir de la impresión 4. (*impact: of explosion, earthquake*) sacudida *f* II. *vt* 1.(*appall*) horrorizar 2.(*scare*) asustar III. *vi* impactar

shock² [ʃak] *n* (*of hair*) mata *f*

shock absorber ['ʃak·əb·ˌsɔr·bər] *n* amortiguador *m*

shocker ['ʃak·ər] *n inf* (*unpleasant news*) noticia *f* desagradable; (*surprising news*) bombazo *m*

shocking ['ʃak·ɪŋ] *adj* 1.(*causing indignation, distress*) espantoso, -a; (*news*) horrible 2.(*surprising*) chocante 3.(*offensive*) escandaloso, -a; (*crime*) espantoso, -a

shockproof ['ʃak·pruf] *adj* 1.(*mechanism*) a prueba de choques 2.(*person*) imperturbable

shock therapy *n,* **shock treatment** *n* terapia *f* de choque

shock troops *npl* tropas *fpl* de asalto

shock wave *n* 1. PHYS onda *f* expansiva 2. *fig* conmoción *f*

shod [ʃad] *pt, pp of* **shoe**

shoddy ['ʃad·i] <-ier, -iest> *adj pej* 1.(*goods*) de muy mala calidad 2.(*treatment*) mezquino, -a

shoe [ʃu] I. *n* (*for person*) zapato *m;* (*for horse*) herradura *f;* **high-heeled ~s** zapatos *mpl* de tacón alto; **athletic ~s** zapatillas *fpl* de deporte, playeras *fpl* ▶ **the ~'s on the other foot** se ha vuelto la tortilla, se volteó la torta; **to fill sb's ~s** pasar a ocupar el puesto de alguien; **if I were in your ~s** *inf* si estuviera en tu lugar II.<shod, shod *o* shodden> *vt* (*person*) calzar; (*horse*) herrar, encasquillar *AmL*

shoehorn ['ʃu·hɔrn] *n* calzador *m*

shoelace *n* cordón *m* (de zapato), pasador *m Perú;* **to tie one's ~s** atarse los cordones

shoemaker *n* zapatero, -a *m, f*

shoe polish *n* betún *m,* lustrina *f Chile*

shoeshine ['ʃu·ʃaɪn] *n* limpieza *f* de zapatos

shoestring ['ʃu·strɪŋ] I. *adj* 1.(*long and narrow*) largo, -a y delgado, -a; **~ potatoes** patatas fritas alargadas 2.(*monetarily limited*) **to do sth on a ~ budget** hacer algo con un presupuesto muy limitado II. *n* cordón *m* (de zapato) ▶ **to do sth on a ~** *inf* hacer algo con poquísimo dinero; **to start on a ~** comenzar con aprietos

shoetree *n* horma *f*

shone [ʃoʊn] *pt, pp of* **shine**

shoo [ʃu] I. *interj inf* fuera II. *vt inf* ahuyentar

shook [ʃʊk] *n pt of* **shake**

shoot [ʃut] I.<shot, shot> *vi* 1.(*fire weapon*) disparar; **to ~ to kill** tirar a matar; **to ~ at sth/ sb** disparar a algo/alguien 2.(*aim*) **to ~ for sth** intentar conseguir algo 3. SPORTS chutar, disparar 4. CINE rodar; PHOT disparar 5.(*move rapidly*) volar; **to ~ to fame** hacerse famoso de

repente; **to ~ past** (*car*) pasar como un rayo ▶ **to ~ for the moon** [*o* **the stars**] ir a por todas II.<shot, shot> *vt* 1.(*bullet*) disparar; (*missile, arrow*) lanzar 2.(*person*) disparar, abalear *AmS,* balear *AmC,* balacear *Méx;* **to ~ sb dead** matar a alguien a tiros 3. CINE (*film*) rodar; (*a scene*) filmar; PHOT tomar, sacar 4.(*direct*) **to ~ questions at sb** acribillar a alguien a preguntas; **to ~ a glance at sb** lanzar una mirada a alguien 5. *inf* **to ~ a goal/basket** meter un gol/una canasta 6. *inf* (*drugs*) **to ~ heroin** chutarse heroína ▶ **to ~ the breeze** *sl* cotillear, dar a la sinhueso; **to ~ darts at sb** *inf* lanzar miradas asesinas a alguien; **to ~ the works** *inf* tirar la casa por la ventana III. *n* 1.(*hunt*) cacería *f;* **to go on a ~** ir de caza 2. CINE rodaje *m;* PHOT sesión *f* 3. BOT retoño *m* IV. *interj euph* (*shit*) mecachis, miércoles

♦ **shoot ahead** *vi* tomar la delantera rápidamente

♦ **shoot down** *vt* (*aircraft*) derribar; *inf* (*proposal*) rebatir

♦ **shoot off** I. *vt* arrancar de un sitio ▶ **to shoot one's mouth off** *sl* cotorrear II. *vi* (*vehicle*) salir como un bólido

♦ **shoot out** *vi* salir disparado

♦ **shoot past** *vi* pasar como una bala

♦ **shoot up** *vi* 1.(*expand, increase rapidly*) crecer mucho; (*skyscraper*) aparecer (de la nada); *inf* (*child*) pegar un estirón 2. *inf* (*inject drugs*) chutarse

shooting ['ʃu·tɪŋ] I. *n* 1.(*killing*) asesinato *m* 2.(*firing of gun*) tiroteo *m* 3.(*hunting*) caza *f;* **to go ~** ir de caza 4. SPORTS tiro *m* al blanco II. *adj* (*pain*) punzante

shooting gallery *n* barraca *f* de tiro al blanco

shooting star *n* estrella *f* fugaz

shootout ['ʃut·aʊt] *n* tiroteo *m*

shop [ʃap] I. *n* 1.(*for sale of goods*) tienda *f;* **book ~** librería *f* 2.(*for manufacture*) taller *m* ▶ **to set up ~** (**as sth**) establecerse (como algo); **to talk ~** hablar de trabajo II.<-pp-> *vi* hacer compras

shopaholic [ʃap·ə·'hɔ·lɪk] *n inf* adicto, -a *m, f* a las compras

shopkeeper *n* comerciante *mf,* despachero, -a *m, f Chile*

shopkeeping *n* comercio *m*

shoplifter ['ʃap·ˌlɪf·tər] *n* ladrón, -ona *m, f* (*que roba en tiendas*)

shoplifting *n* robo *m* (en tiendas)

shopper *n* comprador(a) *m(f)*

shopping ['ʃap·ɪŋ] *n* 1.(*activity*) compra *f;* **to go ~** ir de tiendas 2.(*purchases*) compras *fpl*

shopping bag *n* bolsa *f* de la compra, jaba *f Cuba*

shopping basket *n* cesta *f* de la compra

shopping cart *n a.* COMPUT carrito *m* de la compra

shopping center *n* centro *m* comercial

shopping list *n* lista *f* de la compra

shopping mall *n* centro *m* comercial

shop steward *n* enlace *mf* sindical

shoptalk *n* conversación *f* sobre el trabajo
shopworn ['ʃap·wɔrn] *adj* 1. (*goods*) deteriorado, -a 2. (*cliché*) gastado, -a
shore [ʃɔr] *n* 1. (*coast*) costa *f* 2. (*beach*) orilla *f*; **on** ~ a tierra 3. *pl, liter* (*a country*) **these** ~ **s** estas tierras 4. ARCHIT puntal *m*
◆ **shore up** *vt a. fig* apuntalar
shore leave *n* permiso *m* para ir a tierra
shoreline *n* orilla *f*
shorn [ʃɔrn] *pp of* **shear**
short [ʃɔrt] I. *adj* 1. (*not long*) corto, -a 2. (*not tall*) bajo, -a, petizo, -a *CSur, Bol* 3. (*brief*) breve; (*memory*) malo, -a 4. (*not enough*) escaso, -a; **to be** [*o* **run**] ~ **on sth** andar escaso de algo; **to be** ~ **on brains** *inf* ser algo corto; **to be** ~ **of breath** quedarse sin aliento; **to be in** ~ **supply** escasear 5. LING (*vowel*) breve 6. (*brusque*) brusco, -a; **to be** ~ **with sb** tratar a alguien con sequedad II. *n* 1. CINE cortometraje *m* 2. *inf* ELEC cortocircuito *m* III. *adv* 1. (*abruptly*) **to cut** ~ interrumpir bruscamente; **to stop sth/sb** ~ parar algo/a alguien en seco 2. (*below the standard*) **to fall** ~ quedarse corto; **to fall** ~ **of sth** no alcanzar algo
shortage ['ʃɔr·tɪdʒ] *n* falta *f*; (*water*) escasez *f*
shortbread ['ʃɔrt·bred] *n* galleta *f* dulce de mantequilla
shortcake *n* pastel *m* relleno; **strawberry** ~ pastel de fresa
shortchange [ʃɔrt·'tʃeɪndʒ] *vt* dar mal el cambio; *fig* timar
short circuit *n* cortocircuito *m*
short-circuit [ʃɔrt·'sɜr·kɪt] I. *vi* producirse un cortocircuito II. *vt* 1. ELEC cortocircuitar 2. (*bypass*) saltarse
shortcoming ['ʃɔrt·kʌm·ɪŋ] *n* defecto *m*
shortcut *n* atajo *m*; *fig* fórmula *f* mágica; **keyboard** ~ COMPUT tecla *f* rápida
shortcut key *n* COMPUT tecla *f* rápida
shorten ['ʃɔr·tən] I. *vt* acortar; (*name, title*) abreviar II. *vi* acortarse
shortening ['ʃɔr·tən·ɪŋ] *n* 1. CULIN manteca *f* 2. (*reduction*) reducción *f*
shortfall ['ʃɔrt·fɔl] *n* deficiencia *f*; ECON déficit *m*
short fuse *n* *inf* mal genio *m*
shorthand ['ʃɔrt·hænd] *n* taquigrafía *f*
short-handed [ʃɔrt·'hæn·dɪd] *adj* falto, -a de mano de obra; **a** ~ **goal** un gol en inferioridad numérica
short-haul ['ʃɔrt·hɔl] *adj* de corto recorrido
short-list *vt* preseleccionar
shortlist *n* lista *f* de candidatos preseleccionados
short-lived *adj* efímero, -a; (*happiness*) pasajero, -a
shortly ['ʃɔrt·li] *adv* dentro de poco; ~ **after...** poco después...
shortness ['ʃɔrt·nɪs] *n* 1. (*condition of being short*) cortedad *f* 2. (*brevity*) brevedad *f* 3. (*insufficiency*) escasez *f*; ~ **of breath** falta *f* de aliento 4. (*brusqueness*) sequedad *f*
short order *n* comida *f* rápida; (*order*) pedido

m de comida rápida
short-order *adj* ~ **cook** cocinero *que prepara platos sencillos y rápidos*
short-range *adj* MIL de corto alcance
shorts [ʃɔrts] *npl* 1. (*short pants*) pantalones *mpl* cortos; **a pair of** ~ unos pantalones cortos 2. (*underpants*) calzoncillos *mpl*; **boxer** ~ gallumbos *mpl inf*, boxers *mpl*
short shrift [ʃɔrt·'ʃrɪft] *n* **to get** ~ **from sb** recibir cajas destempladas de alguien; **to give** ~ **to sb** echar a alguien con cajas destempladas; **to give** ~ **to sth** despachar algo
short-sleeved *adj* de manga corta
short-staffed *adj* falto, -a de personal
shortstop *n* 1. SPORTS (*position*) posición *entre la segunda y la tercera base* 2. SPORTS (*player*) jugador *que se coloca entre la segunda y la tercera base*
short story *n* narración *m* corta
short-tempered *adj* irascible
short-term *adj* a corto plazo
shortwave I. *n* onda *f* corta II. *adj* de onda corta
shot¹ [ʃat] I. *n* 1. (*act of firing weapon*) tiro *m*, disparo *m*, baleo *m* AmC; **to fire a** ~ disparar un tiro 2. (*shotgun pellets*) perdigones *mpl* 3. (*person*) tirador(a) *m(f)*; **to be a good/ poor** ~ ser un buen/mal tirador 4. SPORTS (*soccer*) tiro *m*, disparo *m*; (*tennis*) golpe *m*; (*basketball*) tiro *m* 5. (*photograph*) foto *f*; CINE toma *f* 6. *inf* (*injection*) inyección *f* 7. *inf* (*try, stab*) intento *m*; **to have** [*o* **take**] **a** ~ **at sth** probar suerte con algo; **to give sth one's best** ~ hacerlo lo mejor que se pueda 8. (*small amount of alcohol*) chupito *m* ▶ **a** ~ **in the arm** un estímulo *m*; **a** ~ **in the dark** *inf* un palo de ciego; **not by a long** ~ ni por asomo; **to call (all) the** ~ **s** cortar el bacalao *fig* II. *pp, pt of* **shoot**
shot² [ʃat] *adj* 1. *inf* (*worn out*) hecho, -a polvo 2. (*woven*) tornasolado, -a
shotgun ['ʃat·gʌn] *n* escopeta *f*
shot put *n* SPORTS lanzamiento *m* de peso
shot-putter *n* lanzador(a) *m(f)* de peso
should [ʃʊd] *aux* 1. (*expression of advisability*) **to insist that sb** ~ **do sth** insistir en que alguien debería hacer algo 2. (*asking for advice*) ~ **I/we...?** ¿debería/deberíamos...? 3. (*expression of expectation*) **I** ~ **be so lucky!** *inf* ¡ojalá! 4. *form* (*expressing a condition*) **I** ~ **like to see her** me gustaría verla 5. (*rhetorical expression*) **why** ~ **I/you...?** ¿por qué debería/deberías...? 6. *form* (*would*) **we** ~ **like to invite you** nos gustaría invitarte/invitaros
shoulder ['ʃoʊl·dər] I. *n* 1. ANAT hombro *m*; ~ **to** ~ hombro con hombro; **to glance over one's** ~ mirar por encima del hombro; **to sling sth over one's** ~ echarse algo al hombro; **to be sb's** ~ **to cry on** ser el paño de lágrimas de alguien; **to lift a burden off one's** ~ **s** *fig* quitarse un peso de encima 2. (*piece of meat*) paletilla *f*; (*of beef*) paleta *f* 3. (*side of road*)

arcén *m,* banquina *f Arg, Urug,* berma *f Col*
4. (*shoulder-like part of sth*) lomo *m* ▶ **to rub**
~s with sb codearse con alguien; **to stand ~**
to ~ with sb apoyar a alguien **II.** *vt* **1.** empujar; **to ~ one's way** abrirse paso a empujones;
to ~ sb aside empujar a alguien a un lado
2. (*place on one's shoulders*) llevar en los
hombros **3.** (*accept: responsibility*) cargar con
shoulder bag *n* bolso *m* de bandolera
shoulder blade *n* omóplato *m*
shoulder pad *n* hombrera *f*
shoulder strap *n* tirante *m*
shout [ʃaʊt] **I.** *n* grito *m* ▶ **to give sb a ~** *inf*
dar un toque a alguien **II.** *vi* gritar; **to ~ at sb**
gritar a alguien; **to ~ for help** pedir auxilio a
gritos ▶ **to give sb sth to ~ about** dar una
gran alegría a alguien **III.** *vt* gritar; (*slogans*)
corear
◆ **shout down** *vt* hacer callar a gritos
◆ **shout out** *vt* gritar
shouting *n* griterío *m*
shouting distance *n* **within ~** al alcance de la
voz
shouting match *n* pelea *f* de gallos *fig*
shove [ʃʌv] **I.** *n* empujón *m,* pechada *f Arg,*
Chile; **to give sth a ~** dar un empujón a algo
II. *vt* **1.** (*push*) empujar; **to ~ one's way**
through abrirse paso a empujones; **to ~ sb**
about [*o* **around**] *fig* abusar de alguien **2.** *vulg*
~ it (**up your ass**)! ¡métetelo por el culo!
III. *vi* empujar; **to ~ along** *inf* largarse
◆ **shove off** *vi* **1.** *inf* (*go away*) largarse
2. (*launch by foot*) desatracar
shovel [ˈʃʌv·əl] **I.** *n* **1.** (*tool*) pala *f;* **a ~ of sth**
una palada de algo **2.** (*machine*) excavadora *f*
II. <-ll-, -l-> *vt* palear; **to ~ food into one's**
mouth engullir comida **III.** <-ll-, -l-> *vi* palear
show [ʃoʊ] **I.** *n* **1.** (*expression*) demostración *f;*
~ of solidarity muestra *f* de solidaridad
2. (*exhibition*) exposición *f;* **dog ~** exposición
f canina; **fashion ~** desfile *m* de modelos;
slide ~ pase *m* de diapositivas; **to be on ~**
estar expuesto **3.** (*play*) espectáculo *m,* show
m; TV programa *m;* THEAT representación *f;* **quiz**
~ concurso *m* **4.** *inf* (*venture*) asunto *m* ▶ **- of**
hands voto a mano alzada; **let's get the ~ on**
the road *inf* vamos a ponernos manos a la
obra; **to put on a good ~** hacer un buen papel;
the ~ must go on *prov* el show debe continuar; **to run the ~** llevar la voz cantante
II. <showed, shown> *vt* **1.** (*display*) mostrar;
(*slides*) pasar; ART exponer **2.** (*express*)
demostrar; (*enthusiasm*) expresar **3.** (*expose*)
exponer **4.** (*point out, record*) señalar; (*sta-*
tistics) indicar **5.** (*prove*) probar; **to ~ sb**
that... demostrar a alguien que... **6.** (*escort*)
guiar; **to ~ sb to the door** acompañar a alguien hasta la puerta **7.** (*project*) proyectar;
(*on television*) poner **III.** *vi* <showed,
shown> **1.** (*be visible*) verse **2.** (*exhibit: film*)
proyectarse; (*artist*) exponer; (*work of art*)
estar expuesto, -a **3.** *inf* (*arrive*) aparecer
◆ **show around** *vt* guiar

◆ **show in** *vt* hacer pasar
◆ **show off I.** *vt* lucir **II.** *vi* alardear, compadrear *Arg, Urug*
◆ **show out** *vt* acompañar hasta la puerta
◆ **show up I.** *vi* **1.** *inf* (*arrive*) aparecer
2. (*be apparent*) ponerse de manifiesto **II.** *vt*
1. (*expose*) descubrir; **to show sb up as**
(**being**) **sth** demostrar que alguien es algo
2. (*embarrass*) poner en evidencia
show biz *n inf s.* **show business** mundo *m* del
espectáculo
showboat *n* **1.** (*boat*) barco-teatro *m* **2.** (*per-*
son) fanfarrón, -ona *m, f*
show business *n* mundo *m* del espectáculo
showcase I. *n* escaparate *m* **II.** *vt* exhibir
showdown [ˈʃoʊ·daʊn] *n* enfrentamiento *m*
shower [ˈʃaʊ·ər] **I.** *n* **1.** (*for washing*) ducha *f,*
lluvia *f Arg, Chile, Nic* **2.** (*of rain*) chaparrón
m; (*of sparks, insults*) lluvia *f* **3. bridal ~** fiesta
f (*con motivo de un matrimonio*); **baby ~**
fiesta *f* (*con motivo de un nacimiento*) **II.** *vi*
1. (*take a shower*) ducharse **2.** (*spray*) regar
III. *vt* **1.** (*spray*) derramar; **to ~ sb with water**
regar a alguien de agua **2.** (*bestow*) colmar; **to**
~ compliments on sb colmar de cumplidos a
alguien; **to ~ sb with gifts** colmar de regalos a
alguien
shower curtain *n* cortina *f* de ducha
shower gel *n* gel *m* de ducha
showery [ˈʃaʊ·ə·ri] *adj* lluvioso, -a
showgirl *n* corista *f*
showground *n* recinto *m* ferial
showing *n* **1.** (*exhibition*) exposición *f*
2. (*broadcasting*) proyección *f* **3.** (*perform-*
ance) actuación *f*
show jumping [ˈʃoʊ·dʒʌm·pɪŋ] *n* concurso *m*
hípico
showman [ˈʃoʊ·mən] *n* artista *m,* showman *m*
showmanship [ˈʃoʊ·mən·ʃɪp] *n* sentido *m* de
la teatralidad
shown [ʃoʊn] *pp of* **show**
showoff [ˈʃoʊ·ɔf] *n* fanfarrón, -ona *m, f*
showpiece [ˈʃoʊ·pis] **I.** *n* joya *f* **II.** *adj* excepcional
show room [ˈʃoʊ·rum] *n* salón *m* de exposición
showy [ˈʃoʊ·i] <-ier, -iest> *adj* llamativo, -a
shrank [ʃræŋk] *vt, vi pt of* **shrink**
shrapnel [ˈʃræp·nəl] *n* metralla *f*
shred [ʃred] **I.** <-dd-> *vt* (*cut into shreds*) cortar en tiras; (*document*) triturar **II.** *n* **1.** (*strip*)
tira *f;* **to be in ~s** estar hecho jirones; **to tear**
sb/sth to ~s hacer trizas a alguien/algo **2.** *fig*
(*of hope, truth, evidence*) pizca *f*
shredder [ˈʃred·ər] *n* trituradora *f*
shrew [ʃru] *n* **1.** (*animal*) musaraña *f* **2.** *pej*
(*bad-tempered woman*) arpía *f*
shrewd [ʃrud] *adj* (*person*) astuto, -a, habiloso,
-a *Chile,* lépero, -a *Cuba;* (*comment*) hábil;
(*decision*) inteligente; (*eye*) agudo, -a
shriek [ʃrik] **I.** *n* chillido *m* **II.** *vi* chillar; **to ~**
with laughter reírse a carcajadas **III.** *vt* chillar
shrill [ʃrɪl] *adj* agudo, -a

shrimp [ʃrɪmp] *n* <-(s)> **1.**ZOOL gamba *f* **2.** *inf* (*person*) renacuajo, -a *m*, *f*
shrimp cocktail *n* cóctel *m* de gambas
shrine [ʃraɪn] *n* **1.** (*tomb*) sepulcro *m* **2.** (*site of worship*) santuario *m*; **a ~ for sb** un altar en honor a alguien
shrink [ʃrɪŋk] **I.** *n* *inf* loquero, -a *m*, *f* **II.** <shrank *o* shrunk, shrunk *o* shrunken> *vt* **1.** (*make smaller*) encoger **2.** (*reduce: costs*) reducir **III.**<shrank *o* shrunk, shrunk *o* shrunken> *vi* **1.** (*become smaller: clothes*) encoger **2.** (*become reduced*) disminuir **3.** *liter* (*cower*) retroceder (por miedo); **to ~ away from sb/sth** encogerse ante alguien/algo **4.** (*be reluctant to*) **to ~ from** (**doing**) **sth** rehuir (hacer) algo
shrinkage ['ʃrɪŋ·kɪdʒ] *n* **1.** (*of clothes*) encogimiento *m* **2.** (*of costs*) reducción *m*
shrink-wrap ['ʃrɪŋk·ræp] **I.** *n* envoltura *f* de plástico **II.** *vt* (*food*) empaquetar en plástico
shrivel ['ʃrɪv·əl] <-ll-, -l-> **I.** *vi* (*fruit*) secarse; (*plant*) marchitarse; (*skin*) arrugarse; (*person*) consumirse **II.** *vt* (*fruit*) secar; (*skin*) arrugar
♦**shrivel up** *vi* (*fruit*) secarse; (*plant*) marchitarse; (*person*) consumirse
shroud [ʃraʊd] **I.** *n* (*covering*) velo *m*; (*for burial*) sudario *m*; (*of dust, fog*) capa *f* **II.** *vt* envolver; **to ~ sth in sth** envolver algo con algo; **~ed in mystery** envuelto en un halo de misterio
Shrove Tuesday [ʃroʊv·'tuz·deɪ] *n* martes *m* *inv* de Carnaval
shrub [ʃrʌb] *n* arbusto *m*
shrubbery ['ʃrʌb·ə·ri] *n* arbustos *mpl*
shrug [ʃrʌg] **I.** *n* encogimiento *m* de hombros **II.**<-gg-> *vt* **to ~ one's shoulders** encogerse de hombros **III.**<-gg-> *vi* encogerse de hombros
♦**shrug off** *vt* **1.** (*ignore*) negar importancia a **2.** (*overcome*) superar
shrunk [ʃrʌŋk] *pp*, *pt of* **shrink**
shrunken ['ʃrʌŋ·kən] **I.** *pp of* **shrink II.** *adj* encogido, -a
shuck [ʃʌk] *vt* **1.** (*oysters*) abrir; (*corn*) pelar **2.** (*get rid of: clothes*) quitarse
shucks [ʃʌks] *interj* *inf* caray
shudder ['ʃʌd·ər] **I.** *vi* (*person*) estremecerse; (*ground, machine*) vibrar; **to ~ at the memory of sth** temblar al recordar algo **II.** *n* (*of person*) estremecimiento *m*; (*of ground, machine*) vibración *f*; **it sent a ~ down my spine** hizo que me estremeciera
shuffle ['ʃʌf·əl] **I.** *n* **1.** (*of cards*) **to give the cards a ~** barajar las cartas **2.** (*of cabinet, management*) reestructuración *f* **3. with a ~** arrastrando los pies **II.** *vt* **1.** (*papers*) revolver; (*cards*) barajar **2.** (*cabinet, management*) reestructurar **3.** (*feet*) arrastrar **III.** *vi* **1.** (*mix cards*) barajar **2.** (*drag feet*) arrastrar los pies
♦**shuffle off** *vi* alejarse arrastrando los pies
shun [ʃʌn] <-nn-> *vt* rehuir
shunt [ʃʌnt] **I.** *vt* **1.** RAIL cambiar de vía **2.** *fig* **to ~ sb/sth aside** relegar a alguien/algo **II.** *n*

RAIL empujón *m*
shush [ʃʊʃ] **I.** *interj* silencio **II.** *vt* *inf* hacer callar **III.** *vi* *inf* callarse
shut [ʃʌt] **I.** <shut, shut> *vt* cerrar; **to ~ one's ears to sth** hacer oídos sordos a algo; **to ~ one's finger in the door** pillarse el dedo con la puerta **II.** <shut, shut> *vi* **1.** (*door, window*) cerrarse **2.** (*shop, factory*) cerrar **III.** *adj* cerrado, -a; **to slam a door ~** cerrar la puerta de un portazo
♦**shut away** *vt* encerrar; **to shut oneself away** recluirse
♦**shut down I.** *vt* **1.** (*shop, factory*) cerrar; (*airport*) paralizar **2.** (*turn off*) desconectar, apagar **II.** *vi* (*shop, factory*) cerrar; (*engine*) apagarse
♦**shut in** *vt* encerrar
♦**shut off** *vt* **1.** (*turn off*) desconectar, apagar **2.** (*isolate*) aislar
♦**shut out** *vt* **1.** (*block out*) ahuyentar; (*thoughts*) borrar de la memoria **2.** (*exclude*) dejar fuera; **to shut sb out** no dejar entrar a alguien **3.** SPORTS dejar a cero
♦**shut up I.** *vt* **1.** (*confine*) encerrar **2.** *inf* (*cause to stop talking*) hacer callar; **to shut sb up for good** *fig* hacer callar a alguien para siempre **II.** *vi* *inf* (*stop talking*) callarse
shutdown ['ʃʌt·daʊn] *n* cierre *m*
shuteye ['ʃʌt·aɪ] *n* *inf* sueñecito *m*; **to get some ~** echarse un sueñecito
shutoff **I.** *n* suspensión *f* **II.** *adj* (*valve*) de cierre
shutout ['ʃʌt·aʊt] *n* victoria *f* abrumadora (*sin que marque el adversario*)
shutter ['ʃʌt·ər] *n* **1.** PHOT obturador *m* **2.** (*of window*) contraventana *f*; (*of shop*) persiana *f*; **to put up the ~s** cerrar el negocio
shuttle ['ʃʌt·əl] **I.** *n* **1.** (*bus*) enlace *m*; (*train*) enlace *m*; (*plane*) puente *m* aéreo; (*space*) transbordador *m* espacial **2.** (*sewing-machine bobbin*) lanzadera *f* **II.** *vt* transportar **III.** *vi* AVIAT volar (regularmente); (*travel regularly*) ir y venir
shuttlecock ['ʃʌt·əl·kak] *n* volante *m*
shuttle flight *n* puente *m* aéreo
shuttle service *n* servicio *m* de enlace
shy [ʃaɪ] **I.** <-er, -est> *adj* **1.** (*timid*) tímido, -a **2.** (*lacking*) escaso, -a; **we're still a few hundred dollars ~ of our goal** todavía nos faltan unos cuantos dólares para alcanzar nuestro objetivo **II.** <-ie-> *vi* (*horse*) respingar, bellaquear *Arg, Bol, Urug*
♦**shy away from** *vi* **to ~ sth** asustarse de algo; **to ~ doing sth** evitar hacer algo
shyly *adv* tímidamente
shyness *n* timidez *f*
Siamese [ˌsaɪ·ə·'miz] **I.** *n* *inv* **1.** (*person*) siamés, -esa *m*, *f* **2.** (*language*) siamés *m* **II.** *adj* **1.** GEO, HIST siamés, -esa **2.** (*conjoined*) **~ twins** siameses *mpl*
Siberia [saɪ·'bɪr·i·ə] *n* Siberia *f*
sibling ['sɪb·lɪŋ] *n* *form* hermano, -a *m*, *f*
Sicilian [sɪ·'sɪl·jən] **I.** *adj* siciliano, -a **II.** *n* (*per-*

son) siciliano, -a *m, f*

Sicily ['sɪs·ɪ·li] *n* Sicilia *f*

sick [sɪk] **I.** <-er, -est> *adj* **1.** (*ill*) enfermo, -a; **to feel ~** sentirse mal; **to get ~** caer enfermo; **to be off ~** estar de baja (por enfermedad); **to be ~ at heart** *liter* estar muy deprimido **2.** (*about to vomit*) mareado, -a; **to be ~** (*nauseated*) tener náuseas; (*vomit*) vomitar; **to get ~** vomitar; **to feel ~ to one's stomach** tener el estómago revuelto; **too much alcohol makes me ~** beber demasiado alcohol me sienta fatal **3.** *inf* (*disgusted*) asqueado, -a; **to be ~ about sth** estar asqueado de algo **4.** (*angry*) furioso, -a; **to be ~ and tired of sth** estar (más que) harto de algo **5.** *inf* (*cruel*) cruel; (*joke*) de mal gusto **6.** *inf* (*car*) averiado, -a **II.** *n* **the ~** los enfermos

sickbag *n inf* bolsa *f* para vomitar

sickbay *n* enfermería *f*

sickbed *n* lecho *m* de enfermo

sicken ['sɪk·ən] **I.** *vi* (*become sick*) enfermar **II.** *vt* (*upset*) molestar, estar asqueado de algo; **so much violence in films ~s me** me pone enfermo tanta violencia en las películas

sickening ['sɪk·ən·ɪŋ] *adj* **1.** (*repulsive*) repugnante **2.** (*annoying*) ofensivo, -a

sickle ['sɪk·əl] *n* hoz *f*

sick leave ['sɪk·liv] *n* baja *f* por enfermedad; **to be on ~** estar de baja por enfermedad

sickly ['sɪk·li] <-ier, -iest> *adj* **1.** (*not healthy*) enfermizo, -a, apolismado, -a *Col, Méx, PRico,* telenque *Chile* **2.** (*pale*) pálido, -a **3.** (*disgusting*) empalagoso, -a

sickness ['sɪk·nɪs] *n* **1.** (*illness*) enfermedad *f* **2.** (*nausea*) mareo *m*

sick pay *n* subsidio *m* de enfermedad

sickroom ['sɪk·rum] *n* cuarto *m* del enfermo

side [saɪd] *n* **1.** (*vertical surface*) lado *m;* **at the ~ of sth** en el lado de algo; **at sb's ~** al lado de alguien; **~ by ~** uno al lado de otro **2.** (*flat surface*) superficie *f,* lado *m;* (*of page*) cara *f* **3.** (*edge*) límite *m;* (*of river*) ribera *f;* (*of road*) arcén *m;* **on all ~(s)** por todas partes **4.** (*half*) parte *f;* **I like to sleep on the right ~ of the bed** me gusta dormir en el lado derecho de la cama; **in Great Britain, cars drive on the left ~ of the road** en Gran Bretaña se conduce por la izquierda **5.** (*cut of meat*) costado *m* **6.** (*direction*) **from all ~(s)** de todas partes; **from ~ to ~** de lado a lado **7.** (*party in dispute*) bando *m;* (*team*) equipo *m;* **to take ~s** tomar partido; **to take sb's ~** ponerse de parte de alguien; **to be on the ~ of sb/sth** ser partidario de alguien/algo; **to have sth on one's ~** tener algo a su favor; **on my father's ~** por parte de mi padre **8.** (*aspect*) aspecto *m;* (*of story*) versión *f* **9.** (*aside*) **on the ~** aparte; **to leave sth on one ~** dejar algo a un lado ▸ **the other ~ of the coin** la otra cara de la moneda; **to come down on one ~ of the fence or other** tomar partido por una postura o por la otra; **to be on the right/wrong ~ of the law** estar dentro/fuera de la ley; **to get on the**

right/wrong ~ of sb congraciarse/ponerse a malas con alguien; **to be on the right/wrong ~ of 40** no llegar a/pasar de 40 años; **to be on the safe ~ ...** para mayor seguridad...

side arm *n* pistola *f* (*que se lleva en un costado del cuerpo*)

sideboard ['saɪd·bɔrd] *n* aparador *m,* bufet *m AmL*

sideburns ['saɪd·bɜrnz] *npl* patillas *fpl*

sidecar ['saɪd·kar] *n* sidecar *m*

side dish *n* acompañamiento *m*

side effect *n* efecto *m* secundario

sidekick *n* subordinado, -a *m, f*

sideline ['saɪd·laɪn] **I.** *n* **1.** SPORTS (*line*) línea *f* de banda; (*area*) banda *f;* **on the ~s** *fig* al margen; **from the ~s** desde fuera **2.** (*secondary activity*) actividad *f* secundaria **II.** *vt* SPORTS (*keep from playing*) dejar sin jugar

sidelong ['saɪd·lɔŋ] *adj* (*glance*) de soslayo

side road *n* carretera *f* secundaria

sidesaddle ['saɪd·sæd·əl] **I.** *n* silla *f* de amazona **II.** *adv* **to ride ~** montar a asentadillas

sideshow *n* caseta *f;* **to be a ~ of sth** *fig* tener una función secundaria respecto a algo

sideslip *n* AVIAT deslizamiento *m* lateral

sidestep ['saɪd·step] <-pp-> **I.** *vt a. fig* esquivar **II.** *vi* dar un paso hacia un lado

side street *n* calle *f* lateral

sidetrack ['saɪd·træk] **I.** *vt* apartar de su propósito, distraer **II.** *n* vía *f* muerta; *fig* cuestión *f* secundaria

side view *n* perfil *m*

sidewalk ['saɪd·wɔk] *n* acera *f,* vereda *f AmL,* banqueta *f Guat, Méx*

sideward ['saɪd·wərd], **sideways** ['saɪd·weɪz] **I.** *adv* **1.** (*to/from a side*) de lado; (*glance*) de reojo; **to look ~ to the left and right** mirar hacia la izquierda y hacia la derecha **2.** (*facing a side*) hacia un lado **II.** *adj* lateral; (*glance*) de reojo

sidewinder ['saɪd·waɪn·dər] *n* **1.** ZOOL crótalo *m* **2.** (*punch*) gancho *m* oblicuo

siding ['saɪ·dɪŋ] *n* **1.** (*wall*) recubrimiento *m* aislante **2.** RAIL vía *f* muerta

sidle ['saɪ·dəl] *vi* **to ~ up to sb** acercarse sigilosamente a alguien

siege [sidʒ] *n* MIL sitio *m,* asedio *m;* **to lay ~ to sth** sitiar algo; **to be under ~** estar sitiado

Sierra Leone [sɪ·er·ə·li·'oʊn] *n* Sierra *f* Leona

Sierra Leonean [sɪ·ˌerəli·'oʊnɪən] **I.** *adj* sierraleonés, -esa **II.** *n* sierraleonés, -esa *m, f*

sieve [sɪv] **I.** *n* (*for flour*) tamiz *m;* (*for liquid*) colador *m;* **to put sth through a ~** pasar algo por una criba ▸ **to have a memory like a ~** tener la cabeza como un colador **II.** *vt* (*flour*) tamizar; (*liquid*) colar

sift [sɪft] *vt* **1.** (*pass through sieve*) tamizar **2.** (*examine closely*) escudriñar

sigh [saɪ] **I.** *n* suspiro *m;* **to let out a ~** (*of relief*) dejar escapar un suspiro de alivio **II.** *vi* suspirar; **to ~ with relief** suspirar aliviado; **to ~ for sb** *form* suspirar por alguien

sight [saɪt] **I.** *n* **1.** (*view, faculty*) vista *f;* **to be**

out of (one's) ~ no estar a la vista (de uno); **to come into** ~ aparecer; **to catch** ~ **of sth** vislumbrar algo; **to hate the** ~ **of sth/sb** no poder ver algo/a alguien; **to know sb by** ~ conocer a alguien de vista; **to lose** ~ **of sth** perder algo de vista; *(to forget)* no tener presente algo; **at first** ~ a primera vista; **within** ~ **of sth** a la vista de algo; **I can't bear the** ~ **of him!** ¡no lo puedo ni ver!; **get out of my** ~! *inf* ¡fuera de mi vista!; **at the** ~ **of...** al ver... **2.** *pl (attractions)* lugares *mpl* de interés **3.** *(on gun)* mira *f;* **to line up the** ~**s** alinear las miras; **to lower one's** ~**s** *fig* apuntar más bajo (en cuanto a sus ambiciones); **to set one's** ~**s on sth** *fig* poner la mira en algo ▶ **to be a** ~ **for sore eyes** *inf* ser una alegría para los ojos; **out of** ~, **out of mind** *prov* ojos que no ven, corazón que no siente *prov;* ~ **unseen** sin haber visto; **I never buy anything** ~ **unseen** nunca compro nada sin verlo bien antes; **out of** ~! *inf* ¡fabuloso! II. *vt* ver
sighted *adj* vidente
sightless *adj* invidente
sightly ['saɪt·li] *adj* agradable a la vista
sight-read ['saɪt·riːd] MUS I. *vi* interpretar a primera vista II. *vt* ejecutar a primera vista
sightseeing ['saɪt·ˌsiː·ɪŋ] *n* turismo *m;* **to go** ~ visitar los lugares de interés
sightseeing tour *n* visita *f* a los lugares de interés
sightseer ['saɪt·ˌsiː·ər] *n* turista *mf*
sign [saɪn] I. *n* **1.** *(gesture)* señal *f;* **to make a** ~ **(to sb)** hacer un gesto (a alguien); **to make the** ~ **of the cross** hacer la señal de la cruz; **as a** ~ **that...** como señal de que... **2.** *(signpost)* indicador *m;* *(signboard)* letrero *m* **3.** *(symbol)* símbolo *m* **4.** *a.* MATH, ASTR, MUS signo *m;* **a** ~ **that...** un signo de que... **5.** *(trace)* rastro *m;* **they could not find any** ~ **of them** no pudieron encontrar ni rastro de ellos; **it's a** ~ **of the times** así son los tiempos actuales II. *vt* **1.** *(write signature on)* firmar; **he** ~**ed himself 'Mark Taylor'** firmó con el nombre de 'Mark Taylor' **2.** *(employ under contract)* contratar; SPORTS fichar **3.** *(gesticulate)* indicar; **to** ~ **sb to do sth** indicar a alguien que haga algo **4.** *(say in sign language)* decir por señas III. *vi* **1.** *(write signature)* firmar; ~ **here, please** firme aquí, por favor; **to** ~ **for sth** firmar el recibo de algo; **to** ~ **with a team** fichar por un equipo **2.** *(use sign language)* comunicarse por señas **3.** *(gesticulate)* gesticular; **to** ~ **to sb to do sth** hacer señas a alguien para que haga algo; **to** ~ **to sb that...** indicar con señas a alguien que...
◆**sign away** *vt* firmar la cesión de; *(land)* abandonar; *(rights)* ceder
◆**sign in** I. *vi* firmar en el registro de entrada II. *vt* **to sign sb in** firmar por alguien
◆**sign off** *vi inf* **1.** RADIO, TV terminar la emisión **2.** *(end)* terminar; **I think I'll** ~ **early today** creo que hoy acabaré pronto de trabajar
◆**sign on** I. *vi* firmar un contrato; **to sign on**

as a soldier enrolarse como soldado; **to** ~ **for sth** inscribirse en algo; **he has signed on for courses in Japanese** se ha apuntado a clases de japonés II. *vt* contratar
◆**sign out** I. *vi* firmar en el registro de salida II. *vt* **to** ~ **sth** firmar para retirar algo; **you must sign all books out** tienes que firmar para sacar libros prestados; **she signed out a company car** firmó para tomar prestado un coche de la empresa
◆**sign over** *vt* firmar un traspaso; **to sign property over to sb** poner algo a nombre de alguien
◆**sign up** I. *vi* apuntarse II. *vt* contratar
signal ['sɪɡ·nəl] I. *n* **1.** *(particular gesture)* seña *f;* **to give (sb) a** ~ **(to do sth)** hacer una señal (a alguien) (para que haga algo) **2.** *(indication)* signo *m;* **to be a** ~ **that...** ser signo de que... **3.** AUTO, RAIL, COMPUT señal *f* **4.** ELEC, RADIO transmisión *f;* *(reception)* recepción *f* II.<-ll-, -l-> *vt* **1.** *(indicate)* indicar; **to** ~ **that...** señalar que... **2.** *(gesticulate)* hacer señas; **he** ~**ed them to be quiet** les hizo señas para que se callaran III.<-ll-, -l-> *vi* hacer una señal; **the teacher** ~**ed for the examination to begin** el profesor señaló el comienzo del examen; **he was** ~**ed to stop** AUTO le hicieron señas de que parara IV. *adj form* notable
signally *adv* notablemente
signalman ['sɪɡ·nəl·mən] <-men> *n* RAIL guardavía *m*
signatory ['sɪɡ·nə·tɔr·i] *n* signatario, -a *m, f*
signature ['sɪɡ·nə·tʃər] *n* firma *f*
signboard ['saɪn·bɔrd] *n* letrero *m*
signet ring ['sɪɡ·nɪt·ˌrɪŋ] *n* (anillo *m* de) sello *m*
significance [sɪɡ·'nɪf·ə·kəns] *n* **1.** *(importance)* importancia *f* **2.** *(meaning)* significado *m*
significant [sɪɡ·'nɪf·ə·kənt] *adj* **1.** *(important)* importante; *(improvement)* significativo, -a; *(increase)* considerable; *(difference)* notable **2.** *(meaningful)* significativo, -a, con significado
signify ['sɪɡ·nə·faɪ] I. <-ie-> *vt* **1.** *form (mean)* significar; **to** ~ **that...** significar que... **2.** *(indicate)* indicar II. <-ie-> *vi form (matter)* tener importancia
sign language ['saɪn·ˌlæŋ·ɡwɪdʒ] *n* *(for the deaf)* lenguaje *m* de signos; *(between different languages)* lenguaje *m* por señas
signpost I. *n a. fig* señal *f* II. *vt* señalizar
Sikh [siːk] *n* REL sij *mf*
silage ['saɪ·lɪdʒ] *n* AGR ensilaje *m*
silence ['saɪ·ləns] I. *n* silencio *m* ▶ ~ **is golden** *prov* el silencio es oro II. *vt* *(machine, bells)* silenciar; *(person)* hacer callar
silencer ['saɪ·lən·sər] *n* silenciador *m*
silent ['saɪ·lənt] *adj* silencioso, -a; LING mudo, -a; ~ **film** película *f* muda; **the** ~ **majority** la mayoría silenciosa; ~ **partner** ECON socio *m* comanditario; **to be** ~ **on sth** no decir nada

sobre algo; **to fall** ~ callarse

silently *adv* silenciosamente, en silencio

silhouette [ˌsɪl·u·'et] **I.** *n* silueta *f* **II.** *vt* destacar; **to be ~d against sth** perfilarse sobre algo

silica ['sɪl·ɪ·kə] *n* sílice *f*

silicate ['sɪl·ɪ·keɪt] *n* silicato *m*

silicon ['sɪl·ɪ·kən] *n* silicio *m*

silicon chip *n* COMPUT, ELEC chip *m* de silicio

silicone ['sɪl·ɪ·koʊn] *n* silicona *f*

silk [sɪlk] *n* seda *f;* ~ **dress** vestido *m* de seda; ~ **scarf** pañuelo *m* de seda

silken ['sɪl·kən] *adj* (*clothing*) de seda; (*hair*) sedoso, -a; (*voice*) suave

silk-screen printing *n* serigrafía *f*

silkworm *n* gusano *m* de seda

silky ['sɪl·ki] <-ier, -iest> *adj* sedoso, -a; (*fur, voice*) suave

sill [sɪl] *n* (*of door*) umbral *m;* (*of window*) alféizar *m*

silly ['sɪl·i] <-ier, -iest> *adj* (*person*) tonto, -a, dundo, -a *AmC, Col,* baboso, -a *AmC;* (*idea*) estúpido, -a; ~ **season** período de verano en que los periódicos llenan sus páginas con noticias triviales.; **it was ~ of her to...** fue una estupidez por su parte...; **to look ~** parecer ridículo; **to laugh oneself ~** desternillarse de risa; **to knock sb ~** *inf* dejar a alguien atontado de una paliza

silo ['saɪ·loʊ] *n* silo *m*

silt [sɪlt] *n* sedimento *m*

◆ **silt up** *vi* encenagarse

silver ['sɪl·vər] **I.** *n* **1.** (*metal*) plata *f* **2.** (*coins*) monedas *fpl* de plata **3.** (*cutlery*) cubertería *f* de plata **4.** (*dishes, trays*) vajilla *f* de plata **II.** *adj* **1.** (*made of silver*) de plata **2.** (*silver-colored*) plateado, -a

silver anniversary *n* bodas *f* de plata *pl*

silver bullet *n* **1.** (*weapon*) arma *f* infalible **2.** (*remedy*) panacea *f*

silver dollar *n* **1.** (*coin*) dólar *m* de plata **2.** BOT kabuto *m*

silverfish ['sɪl·vər·fɪʃ] *n* **1.** (*fish*) pez *m* plateado **2.** (*insect*) lepisma *m*

silver lining *n* resquicio *m* de esperanza

silver plate *n* **1.** (*dishes, trays*) vajilla *f* de plata **2.** (*coating*) baño *m* de plata

silver-plate *vt* platear

silver screen *n* CINE **the ~** la pantalla cinematográfica

silversmith ['sɪl·vər·smɪθ] *n* platero, -a *m, f*

silverware ['sɪl·vər·wer] *n* **1.** (*cutlery*) cubertería *f* de plata **2.** (*dishes, trays*) vajilla *f* de plata

silvery <-ier, -iest> *adj* plateado, -a

simian ['sɪm·i·ən] **I.** *n* simio *m* **II.** *adj* simiesco, -a

similar ['sɪm·ə·lər] *adj* similar

similarity [ˌsɪm·ə·'ler·ə·t̬i] *n* similitud *f,* semejanza *f*

simile ['sɪm·ə·li] *n* LIT, LING símil *m*

similitude [sə·'mɪl·ə·tud] *n* **1.** (*quality of being similar*) similitud *f* **2.** (*comparison*) comparación *f*

simmer ['sɪm·ər] **I.** *vi* **1.** CULIN hervir a fuego

lento **2.** *fig* estar a punto de estallar **II.** *vt* cocer a fuego lento **III.** *n* ebullición *f* lenta; **to bring sth to a ~** poner algo a hervir; **to keep sth at a ~** mantener algo hirviendo a fuego lento

◆ **simmer down** *vi inf* tranquilizarse

simple ['sɪm·pəl] *adj* **1.** (*not difficult*) fácil **2.** (*not elaborate*) sencillo, -a **3.** (*honest*) honesto, -a **4.** (*ordinary*) normal **5.** (*foolish*) simple

simple-minded [ˌsɪm·pəl·'maɪn·dɪd] *adj inf* **1.** (*dumb*) tonto, -a **2.** (*naive*) ingenuo, -a

simpleton ['sɪm·pəl·tən] *n inf* simple *mf,* guanaco, -a *AmL*

simplicity [sɪm·'plɪs·ə·t̬i] *n* **1.** (*plainness*) sencillez *f* **2.** (*ease*) simplicidad *f*

simplification [ˌsɪm·plə·fɪ·'keɪ·ʃən] *n* simplificación *f*

simplify ['sɪm·plə·faɪ] *vt* simplificar

simplistic [sɪm·'plɪs·tɪk] *adj pej* simplista

simply ['sɪm·pli] *adv* **1.** (*not elaborately*) sencillamente **2.** (*just*) simplemente **3.** (*absolutely*) completamente **4.** (*naturally*) de forma natural

simulate ['sɪm·jʊ·leɪt] *vt* **1.** (*resemble*) simular **2.** (*feign*) fingir

simulation [ˌsɪm·jʊ·'leɪ·ʃən] *n* (*imitation*) simulación *f;* (*of feeling*) fingimiento *m*

simulator ['sɪm·jʊ·leɪ·t̬ər] *n* COMPUT, TECH simulador *m*

simultaneous [ˌsaɪ·məl·'teɪ·ni·əs] *adj* simultáneo, -a; ~ **broadcast** retransmisión *f* simultánea

sin [sɪn] **I.** *n* pecado *m;* **to confess a ~** confesar un pecado ► **to be as ugly as ~** ser más feo que Picio **II.** *vi* <-nn-> pecar

since [sɪns] **I.** *adv* **1.** (*from then on*) desde entonces; **ever ~** desde entonces **2.** (*ago*) **long ~** hace mucho (tiempo); **not long ~** hace poco (tiempo) **II.** *prep* desde; **how long has it been ~ the crime took place?** ¿cuánto tiempo ha pasado desde el crimen? **III.** *conj* **1.** (*because*) ya que, puesto que **2.** (*from the time that*) desde que; **it's been a week now ~ I came back** ya ha pasado una semana desde que llegué

sincere [sɪn·'sɪr] *adj* sincero, -a

sincerely *adv* sinceramente

sincerity [sɪn·'ser·ə·t̬i] *n* sinceridad *f;* **in all ~** con toda franqueza

sine [saɪn] *n* MATH seno *m*

sine qua non ['sɪn·ɪ·kwa·'noʊn] *n form* condición *f* sine qua non

sinew ['sɪn·ju] *n* tendón *m*

sinewy *adj* **1.** (*muscular*) nervudo, -a **2.** (*meat*) con nervios

sinful ['sɪn·fəl] *adj* (*person*) pecador(a); (*thought, act*) pecaminoso, -a; (*waste*) inmoral

sing [sɪŋ] <sang, sung> **I.** *vi* cantar; **to ~ to sb** cantar para alguien **II.** *vt* cantar; **to ~ sb to sleep** arrullar a alguien

◆ **sing out I.** *vi* (*sing*) cantar fuerte **II.** *vt inf* (*call*) **to ~ sb's name** llamar a alguien a voces

sing-along ['sɪŋ·ə·ˌlɔŋ] *n* canto *m* a coro

Singapore ['sɪŋ·ə·pɔr] *n* Singapur *m*

S

Singaporean ['sɪŋ·ə·pɔr·i·ən] **I.** *adj* de Singapur **II.** *n* habitante *mf* de Singapur

singe [sɪndʒ] **I.** *vt* chamuscar; (*hair*) quemar las puntas de **II.** *n* quemadura *f* superficial

singer ['sɪŋ·ər] *n* cantante *mf*

singer-songwriter *n* cantautor(a) *m(f)*

singing *n* canto *m*

singing telegram *n* telegrama que el mensajero canta al destinatario

single ['sɪŋ·gəl] **I.** *adj* **1.** (*one only*) único, -a; (*blow*) solo, -a; **not a ~ person/thing** nadie/nada; **not a ~ soul** ni un alma; **every ~ thing** cada cosa; **in ~ figures** en cifras de un solo dígito **2.** (*unmarried*) soltero, -a **3.** (*bed, room*) individual **4.** (*with one part*) simple **II.** *n* **1.** (*one-dollar bill*) billete *m* de un dólar **2.** (*record*) single *m* **3.** (*in baseball*) sencillo *m* **4.** (*single room*) habitación *f* individual

◆**single out** *vt* señalar; **to single sb out for criticism** criticar a alguien en particular

single-breasted *adj* (*suit*) recto, -a, sin cruzar

single-family house *n* chalet *m*

single-handedly *adv* sin ayuda de nadie

single-lens reflex *n* cámara *f* réflex (monoobjetivo)

single-minded *adj* resuelto, -a

single-mindedness *n* firmeza *f*

single mother *n* madre *f* soltera

single parent *n* (*father*) padre *m* soltero; (*mother*) madre *f* soltera

single-parent family <-ies> *n* familia *f* monoparental

singles bar *n* bar *m* de encuentros

single-seater *n* monoplaza *m*

singleton ['sɪŋ·gəl·tən] *n* persona *f* soltera

singly ['sɪŋ·gli] *adv* uno por uno

singsong ['sɪŋ·ˌsɔŋ] **I.** *n* sonsonete *m* **II.** *adj* **to speak in a ~ voice** hablar cantando

singular ['sɪŋ·gjə·lər] **I.** *adj* **1.** LING singular; **~ form** forma *f* de singular; **the third person ~** la tercera persona del singular **2.** (*notable*) singular; **of ~ beauty** de belleza sin par; **a ~ lack of tact** una increíble falta de tacto **II.** *n* LING singular *m;* **in the ~** en singular

singularity [ˌsɪŋ·gjə·'ler·ə·t̬i] *n form* singularidad *f*

singularly *adv form* singularmente

Sinhalese [ˌsɪn·hə·'liz] **I.** *n* **1.** (*person*) cingalés, -esa *m, f* **2.** (*language*) cingalés *m* **II.** *adj* cingalés, -esa

sinister ['sɪn·ɪ·stər] *adj* siniestro, -a

sink [sɪŋk] <sank *o* sunk, sunk> **I.** *n* (*in kitchen*) fregadero *m;* (*in bathroom*) lavabo *m* **II.** *vi* **1.** (*in water*) hundirse; **to ~ to the bottom** hundirse hasta el fondo **2.** (*price, level*) bajar **3.** (*drop down*) caer; **to ~ to the ground** caer al suelo; **to ~ to one's knees** hincarse de rodillas **4.** (*decline*) bajar; **to ~ in sb's estimation** perder la estima de alguien; **to ~ into depression** sumirse en la depresión; **to ~ into oblivion** caer en el olvido; **to be ~ing** (*fast*) (*in health*) estar empeorando (rápidamente) ►**to ~ or swim** a su suerte **III.** *vt* **1.** (*cause to*

submerge) hundir **2.** (*ruin*) destruir **3.** MIN excavar **4.** (*invest*) invertir; **to ~ money into a project** invertir dinero en un proyecto **5.** (*plant, bury: teeth*) hincar; **to ~ one's teeth into sth** hincar los dientes en algo **6.** SPORTS (*ball*) meter; **to ~ the winning basket** meter la canasta de la victoria

◆**sink back** *vi* (*lean back*) repantigarse

◆**sink in** *vi* **1.** (*go into surface*) penetrar **2.** (*be absorbed: liquid*) calar **3.** (*be understood*) entenderse

sinker ['sɪŋ·kər] *n* (*for fishing*) plomo *m*

sinkhole *n* dolina *f*

sinking ['sɪŋ·kɪŋ] **I.** *n* hundimiento *m* **II.** *adj* **a ~ feeling** una sensación de que todo se va a pique; **with a ~ heart** con el alma encogida

sinner ['sɪn·ər] *n* pecador(a) *m(f)*

sinuous ['sɪn·ju·əs] *adj* sinuoso, -a

sinus ['saɪ·nəs] *n* ANAT (*cavity*) seno *m*

sinusitis [ˌsaɪ·nə·'saɪ·t̬ɪs] *n* MED sinusitis *f*

Sioux [su] **I.** *adj* sioux **II.** *n* **1.** (*person*) sioux *mf* **2.** (*language*) sioux *m*

sip [sɪp] **I.** <-pp-> *vt* sorber **II.** <-pp-> *vi* sorber **III.** *n* sorbo *m;* **to have a ~** dar un sorbo

siphon ['saɪ·fən] **I.** *n* sifón *m* **II.** *vt* sacar con sifón

◆**siphon off** *vt* **1.** (*liquid*) sacar con sifón **2.** (*money*) malversar

sir [sɜr] *n* señor *m*

siren ['saɪ·rən] *n* sirena *f*

sirloin ['sɜr·lɔɪn] *n* solomillo *m,* diezmillo *m Méx*

sirocco [sə·'rak·oʊ] *n* METEO siroco *m*

sis [sɪs] *n inf abbr of* **sister** hermana *f*

sisal ['saɪ·səl] *n* **1.** (*plant*) pita *f* **2.** (*fiber*) sisal *m*

sissy ['sɪs·i] **I.** <-ies> *n inf* mariquita *m* **II.** <-ier, -iest> *adj inf* mariquita

sister ['sɪs·tər] *n a.* REL hermana *f*; **Sister Catherine** Sor Catherine; **~ company** empresa *f* asociada; **~ ship** barco *m* gemelo

sisterhood ['sɪs·tər·hʊd] *n* hermandad *f* de mujeres

sister-in-law ['sɪs·tər·ɪn·ˌlɔ] <sisters-in-law> *n* cuñada *f,* concuña *f AmL*

sisterly *adj* de hermana

sit [sɪt] <sat, sat> **I.** *vi* **1.** sentarse; (*be in seated position*) estar sentado, -a; **~!** (*to dog*) ¡siéntate! **2.** ART posar; **to ~ for one's portrait** hacerse retratar **3.** *inf* (*babysit*) **to ~ for sb** cuidar a alguien **4.** (*perch*) posarse; (*incubate eggs*) empollar **5.** (*be placed*) yacer; (*rest unmoved*) permanecer quieto, estar; **to ~ on the shelf** estar en el estante **6.** (*be in session*) celebrar sesión **7.** POL (*be in office*) **to ~ in Congress** ser diputado **8.** (*fit*) **to ~ well/badly** caer [*o* sentar] bien/mal **9.** (*be agreeable*) **the idea doesn't ~ well with any of them** la idea no les convence a ninguno ►**to be ~ting pretty** estar bien situado; **to ~ tight** (*not move*) no moverse; (*not change opinion*) no dar el brazo a torcer **II.** *vt* sentar

sit around *vi* estar sin hacer nada; **to ~ the**

house vagar por la casa

◆ **sit back** *vi* 1. (*in chair*) sentarse cómodamente, ponerse cómodo 2. (*do nothing*) cruzarse de brazos

◆ **sit down** I. *vi* 1. (*take a seat*) sentarse 2. (*be sitting*) estar sentado II. *vt* sentar; **to sit oneself down** sentarse

◆ **sit in** *vi* 1. (*attend*) asistir como oyente 2. (*represent*) **to ~ for sb** sustituir a alguien 3. (*hold sit-in*) hacer una sentada

◆ **sit on** *vt inf* 1. (*withhold: information*) guardar para sí; (*secret*) no revelar 2. (*suppress: idea, plan*) acabar con

◆ **sit out** *vt* 1. (*not take part in*) no tomar parte en; **to ~ a dance** no bailar 2. (*remain until the end of*) aguantar hasta el final

◆ **sit through** *vt* aguantar hasta el final

◆ **sit up** I. *vi* 1. (*sit erect*) sentarse derecho; **~!** ¡siéntate derecho! 2. *inf* (*pay attention*) prestar atención II. *vt* incorporar

sitcom ['sɪt·kam] *n inf* TV *abbr of* **situation comedy** comedia *f* de situación

site [saɪt] I. *n* 1. (*place*) sitio *m*; (*of battle*) lugar *m* 2. (*vacant land for building*) solar *m*; **building** ~ obra *f* 3. GEO, HIST yacimiento *m* 4. COMPUT página *f*, sitio *m*; **Web** ~ página *f* web, sitio *m* web II. *vt* situar

sit-in ['sɪt·ɪn] *n* sentada *f*; **to hold a** ~ hacer una sentada

siting *n* situación *f*

sitter *n* 1. (*babysitter*) canguro *mf* 2. ART modelo *mf*

sitting *n* (*session*) sesión *f*; (*for meal*) turno *m*

sitting duck *n inf* blanco *m* fácil

sitting room *n* salón *m*

situate ['sɪtʃ·u·eɪt] *vt form* 1. (*locate*) colocar, ubicar *Arg* 2. (*in context*) situar

situated ['sɪtʃ·u·eɪ·t̬ɪd] *adj* 1. (*located*) situado, -a; **to be ~ near the train station** estar ubicado cerca de la estación 2. (*in a state*) **to be well/badly** ~ estar bien/mal situado; **to be well ~ to do sth** estar en una buena situación para hacer algo

situation [ˌsɪtʃ·u·eɪ·ʃən] *n* 1. (*circumstances*) situación *f*; ECON, POL coyuntura *f*; **according to the** ~ conforme a la situación 2. (*location*) colocación *f*

sit-up ['sɪt·ʌp] *n* **to do ~s** hacer abdominales

six [sɪks] I. *n* seis *m*; **in** ~ **figures** por encima de cien mil ►**~ of one and half a dozen of the other** los dos tienen la misma culpa II. *adj* seis *inv*

six-footer [ˌsɪks·'fʊt·ər] *n inf*: persona que mide 1,83 metros o más

six-pack ['sɪks·pæk] *n* 1. (*of beer/soda*) paquete *m* de seis cervezas/refrescos 2. ANAT tableta *f* de chocolate *inf*

sixteen [sɪk·'stin] I. *adj* dieciséis *inv* II. *n* dieciséis *m*; *s.a.* **eight**

sixteenth [ˌsɪk·'stinθ] I. *adj* decimosexto, -a II. *n* 1. (*order*) decimosexto, -a *m, f* 2. (*date*) dieciséis *m* 3. (*fraction*) dieciseisavo *m*; (*part*) dieciseisava parte *f*; *s.a.* **eighth**

sixth [sɪksθ] I. *adj* sexto, -a II. *n* 1. (*order*) sexto, -a *m, f* 2. (*date*) seis *m* 3. (*fraction*) sexto *m*; (*part*) sexta parte *f*; *s.a.* **eighth**

sixtieth ['sɪk·sti·əθ] I. *adj* sexagésimo, -a II. *n* (*order*) sexagésimo, -a *m, f*; (*fraction*) sexagésimo *m*, sesentavo *m*; (*part*) sexagésima parte *f*, sesentava parte *f*; *s.a.* **eighth**

sixty ['sɪk·sti] I. *adj* sesenta *inv* II. *n* <-ies> sesenta *m*; *s.a.* **eighty**

size[1] [saɪz] I. *n* 1. (*of person, thing, space*) tamaño *m*; (*of problem, operation*) magnitud *f*; **a company of that** ~ una empresa de tal envergadura; **to be the same ~ as...** ser de las mismas dimensiones que...; **to increase/decrease in** ~ aumentar/disminuir de tamaño; **to double in** ~ doblar en tamaño; **of any** ~ de cualquier tamaño; **the ~ of a thumbnail** la medida de una uña 2. (*of clothes*) talla *f*; (*of shoes*) número *m*; **collar** ~ talla *f* de cuello 3. (*of bill, debt*) importe *m* II. *vt* 1. (*sort*) ordenar por talla 2. (*make*) hacer a la medida; (*clothes*) clasificar según la talla

◆ **size up** *vt* evaluar

size[2] [saɪz] *n* cola *f*; (*for cloth*) apresto *m*

siz(e)able ['saɪ·zə·bəl] *adj* bastante grande; (*sum*) considerable

sizzle ['sɪz·əl] I. *vi* chisporrotear II. *n* chisporroteo *m*

sizzler ['sɪz·lər] *n inf* (*day*) día *m* caluroso

skate[1] [skeɪt] I. *n* patín *m* II. *vi* patinar; **to ~ over an issue** tocar un tema muy por encima; **to ~ through a course** patinar por un circuito

skate[2] [skeɪt] *n* (*fish*) raya *f*

skateboard ['skeɪt·bɔrd] *n* monopatín *m*

skateboarder *n* skater *mf inf*

skater *n* patinador(a) *m(f)*, skater *mf*; **figure** ~ patinador(a) *m(f)* artístico, -a

skating *n* patinaje *m*

skating rink *n* pista *f* de patinaje

skedaddle [skɪ·'dæd·əl] *vi inf* escabullirse

skein [skeɪn] *n* 1. (*of wool*) madeja *f* 2. (*of geese, swans*) bandada *f*

skeleton ['skel·ɪ·tən] *n* 1. ANAT esqueleto *m*, cacastle *m AmC, Méx*; **to be reduced to a** ~ (*be very skinny*) quedarse en los huesos 2. (*framework: of boat, plane*) armazón *m*; (*of building*) estructura *f* 3. (*outline: of book, report*) esquema *m* ►**to have ~s in one's closet** tener un secreto vergonzoso

skeleton key *n* llave *f* maestra

skeptic ['skep·tɪk] *n* escéptico, -a *m, f*

skeptical *adj* escéptico, -a

skepticism ['skep·tɪ·sɪz·əm] *n* escepticismo *m*

sketch [sketʃ] I. *n* 1. ART boceto *m*; **to make a ~ of sb/sth** hacer un croquis de alguien/algo 2. (*rough draft*) borrador *m* 3. (*outline*) esquema *m* 4. THEAT, TV sketch *m* II. *vt* 1. ART hacer un boceto de 2. (*write draft of*) hacer un borrador de III. *vi* ART dibujar

◆ **sketch in** *vt* (*details*) resumir

◆ **sketch out** *vt* 1. ART bosquejar 2. (*describe*) esbozar

sketchbook ['sketʃ·bʊk] *n* cuaderno *m* de

S

dibujo

sketchy ['sketʃ·i] <-ier, -iest> *adj* (*vague*) impreciso, -a; (*incomplete*) incompleto, -a

skew [skju] *vt* (*distort*) distorsionar

skewbald ['skju·bɔld] **I.** *n* caballo *m* pío **II.** *adj* pío

skewed [skjud] *adj* sesgado, -a

skewer ['skju·ər] **I.** *n* pincho *m*, brocheta *f* **II.** *vt* ensartar

ski [ski] **I.** *n* esquí *m;* **on ~s** con esquís **II.** *vi* esquiar; **to ~ down a slope** bajar una pista esquiando

ski boot *n* bota *f* de esquí

skid [skɪd] **I.** <-dd-> *vi* **1.** (*on ice*) patinar, colear *AmC, Ant;* **to ~ to a halt** resbalar hasta detenerse; (*while driving*) derrapar; **to ~ off the road** derrapar y salirse de la carretera **2.** (*slide over*) **to ~ along** [*o* **across**] **sth** deslizarse sobre algo **II.** *n* **1.** (*while driving*) derrape *m;* **to go into a ~** empezar a resbalar **2.** AVIAT patín *m* ▶ **to be on the ~s** *inf* andar de capa caída

skid mark *n* AUTO huella *f* de un patinazo

skid row *n sl* barrio *m* bajo; **to be on ~** pordiosear

skier ['ski·ər] *n* esquiador(a) *m(f)*

skiff [skɪf] *n* esquife *m*

skiing *n* esquí *m; ~* **equipment** equipo *m* de esquiar; **~ lesson** lección *f* de esquí

ski instructor *n* monitor *m* de esquí

ski jump *n* **1.** (*jump*) salto *m* de esquí **2.** (*runway*) pista *f* para saltos de esquí

ski lift *n* telesquí *m;* (*with chairs*) telesilla *m*

skill [skɪl] *n* **1.** (*ability*) habilidad *f;* **to involve some ~** requerir cierta destreza **2.** (*technique*) técnica *f;* **communication ~s** facilidad *f* de comunicación; **language ~s** habilidad *f* para los idiomas; **negotiating ~s** artes *fpl* de negociación

skilled *adj* **1.** (*trained*) preparado, -a; (*skillful*) hábil, habiloso, -a *Chile, Perú* **2.** (*requiring skill*) cualificado, -a; **~ labor** mano de obra *f* cualificada

skillet ['skɪl·ɪt] *n* sartén *f*

skillful ['skɪl·fəl] *adj* hábil, tinoso, -a *Col, Ven*

skillfully *adv* hábilmente

skim [skɪm] <-mm-> **I.** *vt* **1.** CULIN espumar; (*milk*) desnatar **2.** (*move above*) rozar **II.** *vi* to **~ over sth** pasar rozando algo; **to ~ through sth** *fig* hojear algo

ski mask *n* pasamontañas *m inv*

skim milk *n* leche *f* desnatada

skimp [skɪmp] *vi* escatimar gastos; **to ~ (on sth)** escatimar (algo)

skimpy ['skɪm·pi] <-ier, -iest> *adj* **1.** (*clothing*) corto, -a y estrecho, -a **2.** (*meal*) escaso, -a; (*knowledge*) superficial

skin [skɪn] **I.** *n* **1.** (*of person*) piel *f;* (*of animal*) pellejo *m*, piel *f;* **to be soaked to the ~** estar calado hasta los huesos **2.** (*of apple, potato, tomato*) piel *f;* (*of melon*) corteza *f;* (*of banana*) cáscara *f* **3.** TECH revestimiento *m* **4.** (*on milk*) nata *f* ▶ **to be all ~ and bone(s)**

no ser más que piel y huesos; **it's no ~ off his/her** <u>back</u> *inf* ni le va ni le viene; **by the ~ of one's** <u>teeth</u> *inf* por los pelos; **to have a thick ~** ser insensible a las críticas; **to jump out of one's ~** *inf* llevarse un susto tremendo; **to get under sb's ~** (*affect*) afectar a alguien **II.** <-nn-> *vt* **1.** (*remove skin from: animal*) despellejar; **to ~ sb alive** *iron* desollar vivo a alguien **2.** (*graze*) despellejar

skin cancer *n* cáncer *m* de piel

skincare *n* cuidado *m* de la piel

skin-colored *adj* de color carne

skin-deep *adj* epidérmico, -a; (*beauty*) superficial

skin diver *n* submarinista *mf*

skin diving *n* submarinismo *m*

skin flick *n sl* película *f* porno

skinflint ['skɪn·flɪnt] *n* tacaño, -a *m, f*

skin graft *n* MED **1.** (*transplant*) injerto *m* de piel **2.** (*section*) trozo *m* de piel

skinhead ['skɪn·hed] *n sl* cabeza *mf* rapada

skinny ['skɪn·i] **I.** <-ier, -iest> *adj* flaco, -a, charcón, -ona *Arg, Bol, Urug* **II.** *n sl* verdad *f;* **to give sb the ~ on sth** contar a alguien la verdad sobre algo

skinny-dip ['skɪn·i·dɪp] <-pp-> *vi inf* bañarse en cueros

skintight [skɪn·'taɪt] *adj* muy ceñido, -a

skip [skɪp] **I.** <-pp-> *vi* **1.** (*take light steps*) brincar; **to ~ from one subject to another** saltar de un tema a otro; **to ~ out of town** hacer una escapadita fuera de la ciudad **2.** (*with rope*) saltar a la comba **3.** MUS (*not play properly: CD*) saltarse **II.** <-pp-> *vt* **1.** (*leave out*) omitir **2.** *inf* (*not participate in*) saltarse; **to ~ class** faltar a clase **3.** *inf* (*leave*) **to ~ town** salir de la ciudad apresuradamente **4.** (*hop with rope*) **to ~ rope** saltar a la comba **5.** SCHOOL **to ~ a grade** saltarse un curso **III.** *n* brinco *m;* **with a hop, a ~, and a jump** a un paso

ski pants *npl* pantalones *mpl* de esquí

ski pass *n* forfait *m*

ski plane *n* avión *m* que puede aterrizar sobre la nieve

ski pole *n* palo *m* de esquí

skipper ['skɪp·ər] **I.** *n* NAUT patrón, -ona *m, f;* (*captain*) capitán, -ana *m, f; inf* (*form of address*) jefe *m* **II.** *vt* (*ship*) patronear; (*aircraft*) pilotar; (*team*) capitanear

ski rack *n* portaesquís *m*

ski resort *n* estación *f* de esquí

skirmish ['skɜr·mɪʃ] **I.** *n* **1.** MIL escaramuza *f*, entrevero *m Arg, Chile, Urug* **2.** (*argument*) roce *m* **II.** *vi* **1.** MIL tener una escaramuza **2.** (*argue*) discutir

skirt [skɜrt] **I.** *n* (*garment*) falda *f*, pollera *f AmL;* (*lower part of coat*) faldón *m* **II.** *vt* **1.** (*path, road*) rodear **2.** (*avoid*) evitar

ski slope *n* pista *f* de esquí

skit [skɪt] *n* sátira *f;* **a ~ about sb/sth** una parodia sobre alguien/algo

skittish ['skɪt̬·ɪʃ] *adj* **1.** (*nervous: horse, per-*

son) nervioso, -a, pajarero, -a *AmL* **2.** (*fickle*) caprichoso, -a

skivvies ['skɪv·iz] *n pl, inf* ropa *f* interior

skulduggery [skʌl·'dʌg·ə·ri] *n s.* **skullduggery**

skulk [skʌlk] *vi* **1.** (*hide*) esconderse **2.** (*move furtively*) merodear

skull [skʌl] *n* calavera *f;* ANAT cráneo *m* ▶ **to be bored out of one's ~** *inf* estar aburrido como una ostra

skull and crossbones *npl* bandera *f* pirata

skullcap ['skʌl·kæp] *n* (*small cap*) casquete *m;* REL solideo *m*

skullduggery [skʌl·'dʌg·ə·ri] *n* trampas *fpl*

skunk [skʌŋk] *n* **1.** (*animal*) mofeta *f,* zorrino *m CSur,* mapurite *m AmC,* mapuro *m Col, Ven* **2.** *inf* (*person*) canalla *mf*

sky [skaɪ] <-ies> *n* cielo *m;* **the sunny skies of California** el soleado cielo de California; **under blue skies** bajo el cielo azul ▶ **the ~ 's the** limit todo es posible; **to praise sth/sb to the skies** poner algo/a alguien por las nubes

sky-blue [ˌskaɪ·blu] *adj* azul celeste *inv*

sky blue *n* azul *m* celeste, azul *m* cielo

skybox ['skaɪˌbaks] *n* SPORTS palco privado *en un estadio*

skydiving ['skaɪˌdaɪ·vɪŋ] *n* caída *m* libre (*en paracaídas*)

sky-high [ˌskaɪ·'haɪ] **I.** *adv a. fig* por las nubes; **to go ~** (*prices*) dispararse **II.** *adj* (*prices*) astronómico, -a

skyjack ['skaɪ·dʒæk] *vt* (*plane*) secuestrar

skylark ['skaɪ·lark] **I.** *n* alondra *f* **II.** *vi* juguetear

skylight ['skaɪ·laɪt] *n* tragaluz *m,* aojada *f Col*

skyline ['skaɪ·laɪn] *n* **1.** (*city rooftops*) perfil *m* **2.** (*horizon*) horizonte *m*

skyrocket ['skaɪˌrak·ɪt] *vi* subir (como un cohete); (*price*) dispararse

skyscraper ['skaɪ·skreɪ·pər] *n* rascacielos *m inv*

slab [slæb] *n* **1.** (*flat piece: of stone*) losa *f;* (*of marble*) placa *f;* (*of concrete*) bloque *m;* (*of wood*) tabla *f* **2.** (*slice: of cake, of cheese*) trozo *m;* (*of chocolate*) tableta *f* **3.** (*in mortuary*) mesa *f* de amortajamiento

slack [slæk] **I.** *adj* **1.** (*loose: rope*) flojo, -a; (*muscle*) flácido, -a **2.** *pej* (*lazy: student*) vago, -a; (*piece of work*) flojo, -a; (*writing style*) descuidado, -a; (*discipline*) laxo, -a; (*in paying*) negligente **3.** (*not busy*) de poca actividad; **~ period/season** período/temporada de poca actividad **II.** *n* **1.** (*looseness*) flojedad; **to take up the ~** (*of rope*) tensar la cuerda **2.** COM período *m* de inactividad ▶ **to** cut **sb some ~** *sl* dar más tiempo a alguien **III.** *vi* hacer el vago

slacken ['slæk·ən] **I.** *vt* **1.** (*loosen*) aflojar **2.** (*reduce: speed, vigilance*) reducir; (*pace*) aflojar **II.** *vi* **1.** (*loosen*) aflojarse, petaquearse *Col* **2.** (*diminish: demand, intensity*) disminuir

♦ **slack off** *vi,* **slacken off I.** *vi* **1.** (*make less effort*) hacer menos esfuerzo **2.** (*go more*

slowly) aflojar el paso **3.** (*diminish: demand, intensity*) disminuir **II.** *vt* reducir

slackening ['slæk·ən·ɪŋ] *n* **1.** (*loosening*) aflojamiento *m* **2.** (*of speed, intensity*) disminución *f*

slacker ['slæk·ər] *n inf* vago, -a *m, f*

slackness ['slæk·nɪs] *n* **1.** (*looseness*) falta *f* de tensión **2.** (*of discipline*) relajamiento *m;* (*negligence*) negligencia *f* **3.** COM inactividad *f* **4.** (*laziness*) pereza *f*

slacks [slæks] *npl* pantalones *mpl* (de sport)

slain [sleɪn] **I.** *pp of* **slay II.** *n* **the ~** los caídos

slake [sleɪk] *vt liter* aplacar; **to ~ one's thirst** apagar la sed

slalom ['slal·əm] *n* eslalon *m*

slam [slæm] **I.** <-mm-> *vt* **1.** (*strike*) golpear; **to ~ the door** dar un portazo; **to ~ a window/book shut** cerrar una ventana/un libro de un golpe; **to ~ the ball into the net** disparar la pelota a la red; **to ~ the phone down on sb** colgar el teléfono a alguien bruscamente **2.** *inf* (*criticize*) poner por los suelos **II.** <-mm-> *vi* **1.** (*close noisily*) cerrarse de golpe **2.** (*hit hard*) **to ~ against sth** chocar contra algo; **to ~ into sth** chocar con algo **III.** *n* (*of door*) portazo *m;* **to close a book with a ~** cerrar un libro de un golpe

slammer ['slæm·ər] *n inf* chirona *f,* cana *f AmS,* bote *m Méx,* guandoca *f Col*

slander ['slæn·dər] **I.** *n* LAW calumnia *f* **II.** *vt* calumniar

slanderer ['slæn·dər·ər] *n* calumniador(a) *m(f)*

slanderous ['slæn·dər·əs] *adj* calumnioso, -a

slang [slæŋ] **I.** *n* argot *m* **II.** *adj* de argot

slangy <-ier, -iest> *adj inf* argótico, -a

slant [slænt] **I.** *vi* inclinarse **II.** *vt* **1.** (*make diagonal*) inclinar **2.** (*give bias to*) presentar tendenciosamente **III.** *n* **1.** (*slope*) inclinación *f;* **to be built on a ~** estar construido en pendiente **2.** (*perspective*) perspectiva *f;* **to put a favorable ~ on sth** dar un sesgo favorable a algo

slanting *adj* (*roof*) inclinado, -a; (*eyes*) rasgado, -a

slap [slæp] **I.** *n* palmada *f;* **a ~ in the face** una bofetada, una biaba *Arg, Urug,* un bife *Arg, Urug, fig* un insulto; **the ~ of the waves** el rugir de las olas **II.** <-pp-> *vt* **1.** (*hit*) dar una palmada, guantear *AmL* **2.** (*put*) **to ~ the book onto the table** tirar el libro en la mesa; **to ~ paint onto the wall** pintar la pared rápidamente **3.** LAW *inf* **to ~ sb with a lawsuit** meter un juicio a alguien **III.** *adv inf* directamente, de lleno; **to drive ~ into sth** chocar de lleno contra algo; **to leave ~ in the middle of a meeting** marcharse justo en plena reunión

♦ **slap down** *vt* **1.** (*put down with slap*) tirar **2.** (*silence rudely*) hacer callar

slapdash ['slæp·dæʃ] *adj pej, inf* chapucero, -a

slapjack ['slæp·dʒæk] *n* crepe *m*

slapstick ['slæp·stɪk] *n* payasadas *fpl*

slash [slæʃ] **I.** *vt* **1.** (*cut deeply*) rajar; **to ~**

S

one's wrists cortarse las venas **2.** (*reduce: prices, spending*) rebajar (drásticamente); (*budget*) recortar (drásticamente) **II.** *n* **1.** (*cut*) corte *m* **2.** (*swinging blow*) latigazo *m* **3.** FASHION raja *f* **4.** TYPO barra *f*

slat [slæt] *n* (*of wood*) listón *m*, tablilla *f*; (*of plastic*) tira *f*

slate [sleɪt] **I.** *n* **1.** (*for roof, writing*) pizarra *f* **2.** POL lista *f* de candidatos ▶ **to have a <u>clean</u> ~** *inf* no tener borrones en la hoja de servicios; **to wipe the ~ <u>clean</u>** *inf* hacer borrón y cuenta nueva **II.** *vt* **1.** (*cover with slates*) empizarrar **2.** (*schedule*) programar; POL poner en la lista de candidatos

slather ['slæð·ər] **I.** *vt inf* extender una cantidad generosa de **II.** *n* sí **~s of sth** un montón de algo

slaughter ['slɔ·ţər] **I.** *vt* **1.** (*kill: animal*) matar, beneficiar *AmL*, carnear *CSur;* (*person*) masacrar **2.** *inf* (*defeat*) dar una paliza a **II.** *n* **1.** (*killing: of animal*) matanza *f,* beneficio *AmL,* carneada *f Arg, Chile, Par, Urug;* (*of person*) masacre *f* **2.** *inf* (*defeat*) paliza *f*

slaughterhouse ['slɔ·ţər·haʊs] *n* matadero *m,* tablada *f Par*

Slav [slav] **I.** *n* eslavo, -a *m, f* **II.** *adj* eslavo, -a

slave [sleɪv] **I.** *n* esclavo, -a *m, f* ▶ **to be a ~ to <u>fashion</u>** ser un esclavo de la moda **II.** *vi* trabajar como un burro

slave driver *n iron, inf* negrero, -a *m, f*

slaver ['sleɪ·vər] *n* HIST **1.** (*ship*) barco *m* que trafica con esclavos **2.** (*slave trader*) traficante *mf* de esclavos

slavery ['sleɪ·və·ri] *n* esclavitud *f*

slave trade *n* HIST trata *f* de esclavos

Slavic ['sla·vɪk] **I.** *n* eslavo, -a *m, f* **II.** *adj* eslavo, -a

slavish ['sleɪ·vɪʃ] *adj* **1.** (*servile*) servil **2.** (*unoriginal*) poco original

Slavonic [slə·'van·ɪk] **I.** *n* eslavo, -a *m, f* **II.** *adj* eslavo, -a

slay [sleɪ] <slew, slain> *vt* LIT matar

sleaze [sliz] *n* sordidez *f;* POL corrupción *f*

sleazy ['sli·zi] <-ier, -iest> *adj* (*area, bar, affair*) sórdido, -a; (*person*) con mala pinta; POL corrupto, -a

sled [sled] **I.** *n* trineo *m* **II.** <-dd-> *vi* ir en trineo

sledge [sledʒ] *n s.* **sledgehammer**

sledgehammer ['sledʒ·hæm·ər] *n* almádena *f*

sleek [slik] *adj* (*fur, hair*) lacio, -a y brillante; (*car*) de líneas elegantes; (*person*) muy aseado, -a

◆ **sleek down** *vt* alisar

sleep [slip] **I.** *n* **1.** (*resting state*) sueño *m;* **to go** [*o* **get**] **to ~** dormirse; **to fall into a deep ~** caer en un sueño profundo; **to not lose ~ over sth** no perder el sueño por algo; **to put sb to ~** dormir a alguien; **to put an animal to ~** (*kill*) sacrificar un animal; **go back to ~!** *iron* ¡sigue durmiendo! **2.** *inf* (*substance*) legañas *fpl;* **to rub the ~ from one's eyes** quitarse las legañas **II.** <slept, slept> *vi* dormir; **to**

~ <u>sound</u>(ly) dormir profundamente; **~ <u>tight</u>!** ¡que duermas bien! ▶ **to ~ <u>on</u> it** consultarlo con la almohada **III.** *vt* alojar

◆ **sleep around** *vi pej, inf* acostarse con cualquiera

◆ **sleep in** *vi* dormir hasta tarde

◆ **sleep off** *vt* **to sleep it off** dormir la mona, dormir la cruda *AmL*

◆ **sleep out** *vi* dormir al aire libre

◆ **sleep through** *vt* **to ~ noise** no despertarse con el ruido; **to ~ the entire trip** dormir durante todo el viaje

◆ **sleep together** *vi* **1.** (*have sex*) acostarse juntos **2.** (*share bed*) dormir juntos

◆ **sleep with** *vt* **1.** (*have sex with*) acostarse con **2.** (*share bed with*) dormir con

sleeper ['sli·pər] *n* **1.** (*person*) persona *f* dormida; **to be a heavy/light ~** tener el sueño profundo/ligero **2.** RAIL (*carriage*) coche *m* cama

sleeper cell *n* (*terrorists*) célula *f* durmiente

sleepiness *n* somnolencia *f*

sleeping bag *n* saco *m* de dormir

Sleeping Beauty *n* la Bella Durmiente

sleeping car *n* coche *m* cama

sleeping pill *n* somnífero *m*

sleeping sickness *n* enfermedad *f* del sueño

sleepless ['slip·lɪs] *adj* (*person*) insomne; (*night*) en vela

sleepwalk ['slip·wɔk] *vi* caminar dormido, -a; **he ~s** es sonámbulo

sleepwalker ['slip·wɔ·kər] *n* sonámbulo, -a *m, f*

sleepy ['sli·pi] <-ier, -iest> *adj* **1.** (*drowsy*) somnoliento, -a **2.** (*quiet: village*) aletargado, -a

sleepyhead ['sli·pi·hed] *n inf* dormilón, -ona *m, f*

sleet [slit] **I.** *n* aguanieve *f* **II.** *vi* **it is ~ing** cae aguanieve

sleeve [sliv] *n* **1.** (*of shirt*) manga *f;* **to roll up one's ~s** arremangarse **2.** (*cover*) manguito *m* **3.** (*for record*) funda *f* ▶ **to <u>have</u> sth up one's ~** tener algo en la manga

sleeveless ['sliv·lɪs] *adj* sin mangas

sleigh [sleɪ] *n* trineo *m*

sleight of hand [ˌslaɪt·əf·'hænd] *n* prestidigitación *f,* juego *m* de manos

slender ['slen·dər] *adj* **1.** (*person*) delgado, -a, silgado, -a *Ecua;* (*rod, branch*) fino, -a **2.** (*majority, resources*) escaso, -a; (*chance*) remoto, -a

slenderize ['slen·də·raɪz] *vi, vt inf* adelgazar

slept [slept] *pt, pp of* **sleep**

slew [slu] *pt of* **slay**

slice [slaɪs] **I.** *n* **1.** CULIN (*of bread*) rebanada *f;* (*of ham*) loncha *f;* (*of meat*) tajada *f;* (*of cake, pizza*) trozo *m;* (*of cucumber, lemon*) rodaja *f* **2.** (*share: of credit, profits*) parte *f* **3.** (*tennis*) golpe *m* cortado; (*golf*) slice *m* ▶ **to get a ~ of the <u>pie</u>** sacar tajada; **~ of <u>life</u>** estampa *f* realista **II.** *vt* **1.** (*bread*) cortar (en rebanadas); (*ham*) cortar (en lonchas); (*meat*) cortar (en tajadas); (*cake*) cortar (en trozos); (*cucumber,* *lemon*) cortar en (rodajas) **2.** sports **to ~ the ball** (*in tennis*) cortar la pelota; (*in golf*) golpear la bola de slice ▸ **any way you ~ it** lo mires por donde lo mires **III.** *vi* **to ~ easily** ser fácil de cortar

◆ **slice off** *vt* **1.** (*bread*) cortar (en rebanadas); (*ham*) cortar (en lonchas); (*meat*) cortar (en tajadas); (*cake*) cortar (en trozos); (*cucumber, lemon*) cortar (en rodajas) **2.** (*reduce by*) reducir en

◆ **slice up** *vt* (*bread*) cortar en rebanadas; (*ham*) cortar en lonchas; (*meat*) cortar en tajadas; (*cake*) cortar en trozos; (*cucumber*) cortar en rodajas

sliced *adj* (*bread*) cortado, -a en rebanadas; (*ham*) cortado, -a en lonchas; (*meat*) cortado, -a en tajadas; (*cake*) cortado, -a en trozos; (*cucumber, lemon*) cortado, -a en rodajas

sliced bread *n* pan *m* de molde ▸ **it's the best thing since ~** es lo mejor del mundo

slicer *n* (*for bread*) (máquina *f*) rebanadora *f* de pan; (*for meat*) máquina *f* de cortar fiambre

slick [slɪk] **I.** <-er, -est> *adj* **1.** (*performance*) pulido, -a **2.** (*person*) hábil; *pej* astuto **II.** *n* **1.** (*oil*) marea *f* negra **2.** (*racing tire*) neumático *m* liso

◆ **slick back** *vt*, **slick down** *vt* (*hair*) alisar

slide [slaɪd] **I.** <slid, slid> *vi* **1.** (*glide smoothly*) deslizarse; **the door ~s open/shut** la puerta se abre/se cierra corriéndola; **to ~ back into one's old habits** volver a las viejas costumbres **2.** (*slip*) resbalar **II.** <slid, slid> *vt* deslizar; **to ~ the door open/shut** correr la puerta; **to ~ sth across the floor** pasar algo deslizándolo por el suelo **III.** *n* **1.** (*act of sliding*) deslizamiento *m* **2.** (*incline*) rampa *f*; **a water ~** un tobogán acuático **3.** (*playground structure*) tobogán *m* **4.** phot diapositiva *f* **5.** (*for microscope*) portaobjetos *m inv* **6.** geo desprendimiento *m* **7.** fin caída *f* **8.** mus vara *f* corredera

slide projector *n* proyector *m* de diapositivas

slide rule *n* regla *f* de cálculo

sliding *adj* (*sunroof*) corredizo, -a; (*door*) corredero, -a

sliding scale *n* escala *f* móvil

slight [slaɪt] **I.** <-er, -est> *adj* **1.** (*small: chance*) escaso, -a; (*error*) pequeño, -a; **the ~est thing** la menor tontería; **not in the ~est** en absoluto; **not to have the ~est** (**idea**) no tener ni la menor idea **2.** (*slim: person*) delgado, -a **II.** *n* desaire *m* **III.** *vt* despreciar

slightly *adv* un poco; **to be ~ familiar with sth** conocer algo muy poco

slim [slɪm] **I.** <slimmer, slimmest> *adj* **1.** (*slender: person*) delgado, -a **2.** (*not as wide as tall: cigarette, book*) fino, -a **3.** (*slight: chance*) escaso, -a **II.** <-mm-> *vi* (*become slim*) adelgazar; (*try to get thinner*) hacer régimen

◆ **slim down** *vi* adelgazar

slime [slaɪm] *n* **1.** (*mud*) cieno *m* **2.** (*of fish, slug*) baba *f*

slimebag *n*, **slimeball** *n sl* asqueroso, -a *m*, *f*

slimy ['slaɪ·mi] <-ier, -iest> *adj* **1.** (*covered in slime*) viscoso, -a **2.** *pej* (*person*) asqueroso, -a

sling [slɪŋ] <slung, slung> **I.** *n* **1.** (*bandage*) cabestrillo *m* **2.** (*for carrying baby*) canguro *m*; (*for carrying rifle*) portafusil *m* **3.** (*for lifting*) eslinga *f* **4.** (*weapon*) honda *f* **II.** *vt* **1.** (*fling*) lanzar, aventar *Méx* **2.** (*hang*) colgar

slingshot ['slɪŋ·ʃat] *n* tirachinas *m inv*, honda *f CSur, Perú*, resortera *f Méx*

slink [slɪŋk] <slunk> *vi* **to ~ away** [*o* **off**] escabullirse

slinky ['slɪŋ·ki] <-ier, iest> *adj* (*gait*) furtivo, -a; (*outfit*) ceñido, -a

slip [slɪp] <-pp-> **I.** *n* **1.** (*slipping*) resbalón *m* **2.** (*mistake*) error *m*; **~ of the pen** lapsus *m* cálami; **~ of the tongue** lapsus (línguae) **3.** com resguardo *m*; **a ~ of paper** un trozo de papel **4.** (*women's underwear*) combinación *f* **5.** bot esqueje *m* **6.** naut (*place to dock*) grada *f* ▸ **to give sb the ~** darle el esquinazo a alguien **II.** *vi* **1.** (*slide*) resbalarse **2.** (*move quietly*) deslizarse; **to ~ into a pub** colarse en un bar; **to ~ into/out of one's pajamas** ponerse/quitarse el pijama **3.** (*decline*) decaer; **to ~ into a depression** caer en una depresión **III.** *vt* **1.** (*put smoothly*) deslizar; **to ~ sb a note** pasar una nota a alguien disimuladamente; **to ~ in a comment** dejar caer un comentario; **to ~ some money to sb** pasar dinero a alguien disimuladamente **2.** (*escape from*) escabullirse de; **to ~ sb's attention** pasar desapercibido por alguien; **it ~ped my mind** se me olvidó **3.** naut (*anchor*) soltar

◆ **slip away** *vi* **1.** (*leave unnoticed*) escabullirse; **to ~** (*from sb/sth*) escaparse (de alguien/algo) **2.** (*pass swiftly*) pasar rápidamente **3.** (*be dying*) morirse

◆ **slip by** *vi* **1.** (*pass quickly: time*) pasar rápidamente **2.** (*pass unnoticed*) pasar inadvertido, -a

◆ **slip down** *vi* dejarse caer

◆ **slip in** *vi* colarse

◆ **slip off I.** *vi* **1.** (*leave unnoticed*) escabullirse **2.** (*fall off*) caerse **II.** *vt* (*clothes*) quitarse

◆ **slip on** *vt* (*clothes*) ponerse

◆ **slip out** *vi* **1.** (*leave unobtrusively*) escabullirse **2.** (*be spoken accidentally*) escaparse; **the name slipped out** se me escapó el nombre

◆ **slip up** *vi* equivocarse

slipcase ['slɪp·keɪs] *n* estuche *m*

slipknot ['slɪp·nat] *n* nudo *m* corredizo

slip-on ['slɪp·an] **I.** *adj* (*shoes*) sin cordones **II.** *n pl* zapatos *mpl* sin cordones

slippage ['slɪp·ɪdʒ] *n* (*in value, standards*) disminución *f*

slipper ['slɪp·ər] *n* zapatilla *f*, pantufla *f AmL*

slippery ['slɪp·ə·ri] <-ier, -iest> *adj* **1.** (*not giving firm hold: surface*) resbaladizo, -a; (*soap*) escurridizo, -a **2.** (*untrustworthy: character*) que no es de fiar ▸ **to be a ~ customer** ser un pájaro de cuenta; **to be as ~ as an eel** ser

S

escurridizo como una anguila; **(to be on) the ~ slope** encontrarse en un terreno resbaladizo

slipshod ['slɪp·ʃad] *adj* chapucero, -a

slipstream ['slɪp·strim] *n* estela *f*

slip-up ['slɪp·ʌp] *n* desliz *m*

slipway ['slɪp·weɪ] *n* NAUT grada *f*

slit [slɪt] I.<slit, slit> *vt* cortar; **to ~ sb's throat** cortar el cuello a alguien; **to ~ one's wrists** cortarse las venas II. *n* 1.(*narrow opening*) rendija *f* 2.(*tear*) raja *f*

slither ['slɪð·ər] *vi* deslizarse; **to ~ down the slope** deslizarse por la pendiente; **to ~ on the ice** patinar sobre el hielo

sliver ['slɪv·ər] *n* (*of lemon*) rodaja *f* fina; (*of cake*) trocito *m*; (*of glass, wood*) astilla *f*

slob [slab] *n pej, inf* dejado, -a *m, f*

slobber ['slab·ər] *vi* babear, babosear

slog [slag] *inf* I.<-gg-> *vi* (*walk*) caminar con gran esfuerzo II.<-gg-> *vt* 1.(*move*) abrirse camino con gran esfuerzo 2.(*hit*) golpear III. *n* esfuerzo *m*

slogan ['slou·gən] *n* eslogan *m*

sloop [slup] *n* NAUT balandro *m*

slop [slap] <-pp-> I. *n* 1. *inf* (*watery food*) aguachirle *f* 2. *pl* (*waste liquid*) líquido *m* de desecho II. *vi inf* derramarse; **to ~ about** [*o* around] salpicarlo todo III. *vt inf* derramar

slope [sloup] I. *n* inclinación *f*; (*up*) cuesta *f*; (*down*) declive *m*; (*for skiing*) pista *f* II. *vi* inclinarse; **to ~ down** descender, bajar; **to ~ up** ascender, subir III. *vt* inclinar

sloping *adj* (*roof*) inclinado, -a; (*shoulders*) caído, -a

sloppiness *n* falta *f* de cuidado

sloppy ['slap·i] <-ier, -iest> *adj* 1.(*messy*) descuidado, -a 2.(*slipshod: language*) pobre 3.(*too wet: kiss*) baboso, -a

slosh [slaʃ] I. *vi* 1.(*splash*) chapotear 2.(*water*) agitarse II. *vt inf* (*liquid*) echar salpicando

◆**slosh about** *vi*, **slosh around** *vi* echar salpicando

sloshed *adj inf* borracho, -a; **to get ~** tajarse

slot [slat] I. *n* 1.(*narrow opening*) ranura *f* 2. TV espacio *m* 3. AVIAT slot *m* II.<-tt-> *vt* **to ~ sb/sth in** hacer encajar a alguien/algo

sloth [slɔθ] *n* 1. ZOOL perezoso *m* 2.(*laziness*) pereza *f*

slothful ['slaθ·fəl] *adj* perezoso, -a

slot machine ['slat·mə·ʃin] *n* máquina *f* tragaperras

slouch [slautʃ] I. *vi* 1.(*have shoulders bent*) encorvarse 2.(*walk*) caminar arrastrando los pies II. *n* postura *f* encorvada ▸ **to be no ~** no ser manco

slough[1] [slʌf] *n* 1.(*bog*) ciénaga *f* 2. *liter* (*depressed state*) abismo *m*

slough[2] [slu] *vt* ZOOL (*skin*) mudar de

Slovak ['slou·vak] I. *adj* eslovaco, -a II. *n* 1.(*person*) eslovaco, -a *m, f* 2. LING eslovaco *m*

Slovakia [slou·'va·ki·ə] *n* Eslovaquia *f*

Slovakian *n s.* **Slovak**

sloven ['slʌv·ən] *n* persona *f* dejada

Slovene ['slou·vin] I. *adj* esloveno, -a II. *n* 1.(*person*) esloveno, -a *m, f* 2. LING esloveno *m*

Slovenia [slou·'vi·ni·ə] *n* Eslovenia *f*

Slovenian *n s.* **Slovene**

slovenly ['slʌv·ən·li] *adj* descuidado, -a

slow [slou] I. *adj* 1.(*not fast*) lento, -a; (*poison*) de efectos retardados; **to be ~ to do sth** tardar en hacer algo; **to be (10 minutes) ~** ir (10 minutos) retrasado 2.(*stupid*) torpe, guanaco, -a *AmL* II. *vi* ir más despacio; **to ~ to a halt** detenerse gradualmente III. *vt* frenar; (*development*) retardar

◆**slow down** I. *vi* 1.(*reduce speed*) reducir la velocidad 2.(*be less active*) moderar el ritmo de vida II. *vt* ralentizar

slowdown ['slou·daun] *n* ECON ralentización *f*; **economic ~** reducción *f* de la actividad económica

slowly *adv* lentamente; **~ but surely** lento pero seguro

slow motion I. *n* cámara *f* lenta; **in ~** a cámara lenta II. *adj* a cámara lenta

slowness *n* 1.(*lack of speed*) lentitud *f* 2.(*stupidity*) torpeza *f*

slowpoke ['slou·pouk] *n inf* tortuga *f*

slow-witted *adj* lerdo, -a

SLR *n abbr of* **single-lens reflex** cámara *f* réflex (monoobjetivo)

sludge [slʌdʒ] *n* lodo *m*

slug[1] [slʌg] *n* ZOOL babosa *f*

slug[2] [slʌg] I. *n inf* 1.(*bullet*) bala *f* 2.(*coin*) ficha *f* 3. *inf* (*swig*) trago *m* II. *vi* <-gg-> *inf* (*hit*) aporrear; **to ~ it out** pegarse

sluggish ['slʌg·ɪʃ] *adj* (*person*) perezoso, -a, conchudo, -a *Méx;* (*progress, pace*) lento, -a; (*market*) flojo, -a

sluice [slus] I. *n* (*gate*) compuerta *f* II. *vt* regar; **to ~ sth down** enjuagar algo

sluicegate *n* compuerta *f*

sluiceway *n* canal *m* de desagüe

slum [slʌm] *n* (*area*) barrio *m* pobre; (*on outskirts*) suburbio *m*

slumber ['slʌm·bər] I. *vi liter* 1.(*sleep*) dormir 2.(*be dormant*) estar aletargado, -a II. *n liter* 1.(*sleep*) sueño *m* ligero 2.(*inactive state*) marasmo *m elev*

slump [slʌmp] I. *n* ECON 1.(*decline*) depresión *f;* **~ in prices** caída (repentina) de los precios *f* 2.(*recession*) recesión *f* II. *vi* desplomarse; (*prices*) caer

slung [slʌŋ] *pt, pp of* **sling**

slunk [slʌŋk] *pt, pp of* **slink**

slur [slɜr] <-rr-> I. *vt* pronunciar con dificultad; **to ~ one's words** arrastrar las palabras II. *n* 1.(*insult*) calumnia *f* 2.(*in speech*) pronunciación *f* incomprensible

slurp [slɜrp] *inf* I. *vt, vi* sorber (ruidosamente) II. *n* sorbo *m* (ruidoso)

slush [slʌʃ] *n* 1.(*snow*) nieve *f* medio derretida 2.(*sentimentality*) sentimentalismo *m*

slush fund *n pej* fondos *mpl* para sobornar

slushy *adj* <-ier, -iest> 1.(*snow*) a medio de-

rretir 2. (*sentimental*) sentimentaloide
slut [slʌt] *n pej* puta *f*
sly [slaɪ] *adj* 1. (*secretive*) sigiloso, -a; (*smile*) sutil; **on the ~** a hurtadillas 2. (*crafty*) astuto, -a, songo, -a *Col, Méx*
slyly *adv* 1. (*secretively*) sigilosamente 2. (*craftily*) con astucia
smack [smæk] I. *vt* 1. (*slap*) dar un manotazo a 2. (*hit noisily*) golpear; **to ~ one's lips** relamerse los labios II. *n* 1. *inf* (*slap*) bofetada *f;* (*soft blow*) palmada *f* 2. *inf* (*kiss*) besazo *m* 3. (*loud noise*) ruido *m* fuerte III. *adv* 1. (*with a loud noise*) haciendo un fuerte ruido 2. (*directly*) justamente; **~ in the middle** justo en el medio
◆**smack of** *vi* oler a
smacker ['smæk·ər] *n inf* beso *m* sonoro
small [smɔl] I. *adj* 1. (*not large*) pequeño, -a; (*person*) bajo, -a, petizo, -a *CSur, Bol* 2. (*young*) joven 3. (*insignificant*) insignificante; **on a ~ scale** a pequeña escala; **in his/her own ~ way** a pequeña escala; **with a ~ 'c'** con 'c' minúscula ▶**it's a ~ world** *prov* el mundo es un pañuelo *prov* II. *n* **the ~ of the back** la región lumbar
small arms *npl* armas *fpl* de bajo calibre
small change *n* calderilla *f,* (dinero *m*) suelto *m,* chaucha *f Bol, Chile, Perú,* chirolas *fpl Arg*
small-claims court *n* tribunal *m* de primera instancia que se ocupa de delitos menores
small fry *n inf* (*unimportant person*) don nadie *mf;* (*young person*) renacuajo, -a *m, f inf*
small intestine *n* intestino *m* delgado
smallish ['smɔ·lɪʃ] *adj* más bien pequeño, -a
small-minded [ˌsmɔl·'maɪn·dɪd] *adj pej* estrecho, -a de miras
smallness ['smɔl·nɪs] *n* pequeñez *f*
smallpox ['smɔl·paks] *n* viruela *f*
small-scale *adj* en [*o* a] pequeña escala
small talk *n* conversación *f* sin trascendencia; **to make ~** hablar de cosas sin importancia
smalltime *adj* de poca monta
smart [smart] I. *adj* 1. (*clever*) inteligente; **to make a ~ move** dar un paso inteligente; **to be too ~ for sb** ser demasiado listo para alguien 2. (*elegant*) elegante 3. (*quick*) rápido, -a; **to do sth at a ~ pace** hacer algo de forma rápida II. *vi* escocer; **my eyes ~** me pican los ojos III. *n* escozor *m*
smart-aleck [ˌsmart·'æl·ɪk] *n pej, inf* sabelotodo *mf*
smart-ass ['smart·æs] *n pej, inf* listillo, -a *m, f*
smart bomb *n* bomba *f* teledirigida
smart card *n* COMPUT tarjeta *f* electrónica
smarten ['smar·tən] I. *vt* **to ~ sth up** arreglar algo II. *vi* **to ~ up** arreglarse
smartness ['smart·nɪs] *n* 1. (*elegance*) elegancia *f* 2. (*intelligence*) inteligencia *f*
smash [smæʃ] I. *vt* 1. (*break*) romper, quebrar *AmL;* (*glass*) hacer pedazos 2. (*crush*) destruir; **to ~ a rebellion** acabar con una revuelta 3. SPORTS (*record*) pulverizar II. *vi* 1. (*break*

into pieces) romperse, quebrarse *AmL;* (*glass*) hacerse pedazos 2. (*strike against*) chocar; **to ~ into sth** chocar contra algo III. *n* 1. (*sound*) estruendo *m* 2. (*accident*) colisión *f* 3. SPORTS smash *m*
◆**smash in** *vt* forzar; **to smash sb's face in** *inf* romperle la cara a alguien
◆**smash up** *vt* hacer pedazos; (*car*) destrozar
smashed *adj inf* borracho, -a; **to get ~** emborracharse
smash (hit) *n* éxito *m*
smashup *n* choque *m* violento
smattering ['smæt̬·ər·ɪŋ] *n* nociones *fpl*
smear [smɪr] I. *vt* 1. (*spread*) untar 2. (*attack*) desprestigiar; **to ~ sb's good name** manchar el buen nombre de alguien II. *n* 1. (*blotch*) mancha *f* 2. (*accusation*) calumnia *f* 3. MED frotis *m;* **pap ~** prueba de Papanicolau
smear campaign *n* campaña *f* de desprestigio
smear tactics *n* tácticas *f* difamatorias *pl*
smell [smel] <smelled *o* smelt, smelled *o* smelt> I. *vi* 1. (*use sense of smell*) olfatear 2. (*give off odor*) oler 3. (*have unpleasant smell*) apestar II. *vt* (*person*) oler; (*animal*) olfatear III. *n* 1. (*sense of smelling*) olfato *m* 2. (*odor*) olor *m;* (*stink*) hedor *m* 3. (*sniff*) inhalación *f* 4. (*trace*) sabor *m;* **the ~ of victory** el sabor del triunfo
smelling salts ['smel·ɪŋ·sɔlts] *npl* MED sales *fpl* aromáticas
smelly ['smel·i] *adj* <-ier, -iest> apestoso, -a, que huele mal, foche *Chile*
smelt[1] [smelt] *vt* MIN fundir
smelt[2] [smelt] <-(s)> *n* (*fish*) eperlano *m*
smelt[3] [smelt] *pt, pp of* **smell**
smidgen ['smɪdʒ·ən] *n inf* pizca *f*
smile [smaɪl] I. *n* sonrisa *f;* **to be all ~s** ser todo sonrisas; **to give sb a ~** sonreír a alguien II. *vi* sonreír; **to ~ at** [*o* about] sth reírse de algo; **to ~ on sb/sth** mirar con buenos ojos a alguien/algo
smiley ['smaɪ·li] *n* COMPUT emoticón *m,* emoticono *m*
smiling *adj* sonriente
smirch [smɜrtʃ] *vt liter* mancillar
smirk [smɜrk] I. *vi* sonreír afectadamente II. *n* sonrisa *f* afectada
smite [smaɪt] <smote, smitten> *vt liter* golpear
smith [smɪθ] *n* herrero, -a *m, f*
smithereens [ˌsmɪð·ə·'rinz] *npl* añicos *mpl;* **to smash sth to ~** hacer algo añicos
smithy ['smɪθ·i] <-ies> *n* herrería *f*
smitten ['smɪt·ən] *adj* **to be ~ with sb/sth** estar loco por alguien/algo; **to be ~ by sb** estar enamorado de alguien; **she was ~ by remorse** le remordía la conciencia
smock [smak] *n* bata *f* corta
smocking *n* nido *m* de abeja
smog [smag] *n* niebla *f* con humo
smoke [smoʊk] I. *n* 1. (*from fire*) humo *m* 2. *inf* (*cigarette*) cigarrillo *m* ▶ **where there's ~, there's fire** *prov* cuando el río suena, agua

S

lleva *prov;* **to go up in** ~ quedarse en agua de borrajas **II.** *vt* **1.** (*cigarette, tobacco*) fumar, pitar *AmS;* **to** ~ **a pipe** fumar en pipa **2.** CULIN ahumar ▶ **to** ~ **the peace pipe** fumar la pipa de la paz; **put that in your pipe and** ~ **it!** ¡métetelo (por) donde te quepa! **III.** *vi* **1.** (*produce smoke*) echar humo **2.** (*smoke tobacco*) fumar, pitar *AmS*

♦ **smoke out** *vt* (*rats, insects*) hacer salir con humo; (*a scandal*) destapar

smoke bomb *n* bomba *f* de humo

smoked *adj* ahumado, -a; ~ **salmon** salmón ahumado

smoke detector *n* detector *m* de humo(s)

smokeless ['smoʊk·lɪs] *adj* sin humo; ~ **tobacco** tabaco de mascar

smoker *n* fumador(a) *m(f);* **to be a heavy** ~ fumar como un carretero

smoke screen *n a. fig* cortina *f* de humo

smoke signal *n* señal *f* de humo

smokestack ['smoʊk·stæk] *n* chimenea *f*

smoking *n* el fumar; **to give up** ~ dejar de fumar; ~ **ban** prohibición *f* de fumar

smoky ['smoʊ·ki] *adj* <-ier, -iest> **1.** (*filled with smoke*) lleno, -a de humo **2.** (*producing smoke*) humeante; (*fire*) que humea **3.** (*tasting of smoke*) ahumado, -a

smolder ['smoʊl·dər] *vi* **1.** (*burn slowly*) arder sin llama; (*cigarette*) consumirse lentamente **2.** *fig* arder

smooch [smutʃ] **I.** *vi* (*kiss*) besuquearse **II.** *n* (*kiss*) **to have a** ~ besuquearse

smooth [smuð] **I.** *adj* **1.** (*not rough*) liso, -a; (*surface*) llano, -a; (*skin, texture*) suave; (*sauce*) sin grumos; (*sea*) tranquilo, -a; **as** ~ **as silk** suave como la seda **2.** (*uninterrupted*) sin dificultades; (*flight*) tranquilo, -a; (*landing*) suave **3.** (*mild: wine, whiskey*) suave **4.** (*suave*) zalamero, -a; **to be a** ~ **talker** tener un pico de oro **II.** *vt* allanar

♦ **smooth down** *vt* alisar

♦ **smooth over** *vt* (*difficulty*) solucionar

smoothie *n,* **smoothy** ['smu·ði] *n inf* zalamero, -a *m, f*

smoothly *adv* **to go** ~ ir bien

smoothness *n* **1.** (*evenness*) lisura *f* **2.** (*lack of difficulty*) fluidez *f* **3.** (*mild taste or texture*) suavidad *f*

smooth-shaven *adj* bien afeitado, -a

smote [smoʊt] *pt of* **smite**

smother ['smʌð·ər] *vt* **1.** (*suffocate*) ahogar **2.** (*suppress*) contener **3.** (*cover*) **to be** ~**ed in sth** estar cubierto de algo

smudge [smʌdʒ] **I.** *vt* **1.** (*smear*) hacer borroso **2.** (*make dirty*) manchar; (*reputation*) destruir **II.** *vi* mancharse; (*make-up*) correrse **III.** *n* mancha *f*

smudgy ['smʌdʒ·i] *adj* <-ier, -iest> manchado, -a

smug [smʌg] *adj* <-gg-> presumido, -a; **to be** ~ **about sth** presumir de algo

smuggle ['smʌg·əl] *vt* LAW pasar de contrabando

smuggler ['smʌg·lər] *n* contrabandista *mf*

smuggling ['smʌg·lɪŋ] *n* contrabando *m*

smut [smʌt] *n* **1.** (*obscenity*) obscenidades *fpl* **2.** (*soot*) tizne *m*

smutty ['smʌt̬·i] *adj* <-ier, -iest> obsceno, -a; (*joke*) verde

snack [snæk] **I.** *n* refrigerio *m,* puntal *m AmL;* **to have a** ~ tomarse un tentempié **II.** *vi* picar

snack bar *n* cafetería *f*

snag [snæg] **I.** *n* **1.** (*problem*) dificultad *f;* **to hit a** ~ tropezar con una dificultad **2.** (*in clothing*) enganchón *m* **II.** <-gg-> *vt* **1.** (*catch and pull*) enganchar **2.** (*cause problems*) causar problemas a **III.** <-gg-> *vi* **to** ~ **on sth** engancharse en algo

snail [sneɪl] *n* caracol *m* ▶ **at a** ~**'s pace** a paso de tortuga

snail mail *n* COMPUT correo *m* ordinario

snake [sneɪk] **I.** *n* (*small*) culebra *f;* (*large*) serpiente *f* **II.** *vi* serpentear, viborear *Arg, Urug*

snake charmer *n* encantador(a) *m(f)* de serpientes

snakeskin *n* piel *f* de serpiente

snap [snæp] <-pp-> **I.** *n* **1.** (*sound*) chasquido *m* **2.** (*fastener*) (cierre *m*) automático *m* **3.** METEO **a cold** ~ una ola de frío **4.** CULIN **a ginger** ~ una galleta de jengibre **5.** (*photograph*) foto *f* **6.** (*in football*) snap *m* (*pase al quarterback con el que se inicia cada jugada*) **II.** *adj* repentino, -a; ~ **decision** decisión *f* repentina **III.** *vi* **1.** (*break*) romperse **2.** (*move*) **to** ~ **back** recolocarse; **to** ~ **shut** cerrarse de golpe **3.** (*make snapping sound*) hacer un chasquido **4.** (*bite*) **to** ~ **at sb** intentar morder a alguien **5.** (*speak sharply*) contestar con brusquedad; **to** ~ **at sb** contestar a alguien de forma brusca **IV.** *vt* **1.** (*break*) romper; **to** ~ **sth shut** cerrar algo de golpe **2.** (*make snapping sound*) chasquear; **to** ~ **a whip** sacudir un látigo; **to** ~ **one's fingers** chasquear los dedos **3.** PHOT tomar una fotografía de **4.** (*in football*) **to** ~ **the ball** pasar el balón al quarterback, al inicio de cada jugada

♦ **snap out** *vi* **to** ~ **of sth** quitarse algo de encima; ~ **of it!** ¡anímate!

♦ **snap up** *vt* lanzarse sobre

snapdragon ['snæp·dræg·ən] *n* BOT boca *f* de dragón

snappy ['ʃnæp·i] *adj* <-ier, -iest> **1.** *inf* FASHION de lo más elegante; **to be a** ~ **dresser** vestir con elegancia **2.** (*quick*) rápido, -a; **make it** ~**!** ¡date prisa!

snapshot ['snæp·ʃat] *n* (foto *f*) instantánea *f*

snare [sner] **I.** *n* trampa *f* **II.** *vt* (*catch: animal*) cazar (con trampa); (*person*) atrapar

snare drum *n* tambor *m*

snarl¹ [snarl] **I.** *vi* gruñir **II.** *n* gruñido *m*

snarl² [snarl] *n* **1.** (*tangle*) enredo *m* **2.** (*traffic jam*) atasco *m*

♦ **snarl up** *vi* enmarañarse

snarl-up ['snarl·ʌp] *n* atasco *m*

snatch [snætʃ] **I.** *vt* **1.** (*grab*) agarrar; **to** ~ **sth (away) from sb** arrebatar algo de alguien

2. (*steal*) *a. fig* robar; **to ~ victory** hacerse con el triunfo **3.** (*kidnap*) secuestrar **II.** *vi* quitar algo de las manos; **to ~ at sth** tratar de arrebatar algo **III.** <-es> *n* **1.** (*sudden grab*) arrebatamiento *m;* **to make a ~ at sth** intentar arrebatar algo **2.** (*kidnapping*) secuestro *m* **3.** *vulg* (*female genitals*) coño *m*

◆ **snatch up** *vt* agarrar

snazzy ['snæz·i] *adj* <-ier, -iest> *inf* de lo más elegante

sneak [snik] **I.** *vi* moverse furtivamente; **to ~ in/out** entrar/salir a hurtadillas; **to ~ away** [*o* **off**] escabullirse **II.** *vt* hacer furtivamente; **to ~ a look at sth/sb** mirar algo/a alguien con disimulo; **to ~ sb/sth in/out** lograr introducir/sacar algo/a alguien **III.** *n* persona *f* cobarde que no es de fiar

sneaker ['sni·kər] *n pl* zapatillas *fpl* de deporte, playeras *fpl*

sneaking *adj* **1.** (*slight*) **a ~ suspicion** una ligera sospecha **2.** (*secret*) secreto, -a

sneak preview *n* CINE preestreno *m*

sneaky ['sni·ki] *adj* <-ier, -iest> furtivo, -a

sneer [snɪr] **I.** *vi* hacer un gesto de burla y desprecio; (*mock*) mofarse; **to ~ at sth/sb** mofarse de algo/alguien **II.** *n* expresión *f* desdeñosa

sneering ['snɪr·ɪŋ] *adj* burlón, -ona

sneeze [sniz] **I.** *vi* estornudar ▶ **that's not something to be ~d at** no es de despreciar **II.** *n* estornudo *m*

snicker ['snɪk·ər] **I.** *vi* reírse con disimulo; **to ~ at sth** reírse de algo con disimulo **II.** *n* risa *f* disimulada

snide [snaɪd] *adj pej* vil

sniff [snɪf] **I.** *vi* **1.** (*inhale*) sorber; **to ~ at sth** oler algo **2.** (*show disdain*) despreciar algo **3.** (*snoop*) **to go ~ing around for sth** husmear en busca de algo ▶ **not to be ~ed at** no ser de despreciar **II.** *vt* (*animal esp.*) olfatear; (*person*) oler **III.** *n* **1.** (*smell*) husmeo *m;* **to have a ~** oler; **to catch a ~ of sth** captar el olor de algo **2.** (*expression of disdain*) expresión *f* de desdén

◆ **sniff out** *vt* (*locate by smelling*) encontrar olfateando; (*discover*) descubrir

sniffer dog ['snɪf·ər·ˌdɔg] *n* perro *m* rastreador

sniffle ['snɪf·əl] **I.** *vi* **1.** (*sniff*) sorberse los mocos; (*breath*) respirar haciendo ruido por la nariz **2.** (*cry*) lloriquear **II.** *npl* **to have the ~s** estar acatarrado

snifter ['snɪf·tər] *n* **1.** (*glass*) **a brandy ~** copa *f* de coñac **2.** *inf* (*small drink*) trago *m*

snip [snɪp] **I.** *vt* cortar (con tijeras) **II.** *n* **1.** (*cut*) tijeretazo *m* **2.** (*piece of cloth*) recorte *m*

snipe [snaɪp] *vi* **1.** MIL disparar (desde un escondite) **2.** *fig* **to ~ at sb** criticar a alguien

sniper ['snaɪ·pər] *n* francotirador(a) *m(f)*

snippet ['snɪp·ɪt] *n* (*small piece: of information*) retazo *m;* (*of conversation, text*) fragmento *m;* (*of cloth*) retal *m;* (*of paper*) pedazo *m;* (*of cardboard*) trozo *m*

snitch [snɪtʃ] *inf* **I.** *vi pej* chivarse; **to ~ on sb**

chivarse de alguien **II.** *vt* (*steal*) birlar **III.** <-es> *n* **1.** (*thief*) caco *mf* **2.** (*tattletale*) soplón, -ona *m, f*

snivel ['snɪv·əl] **I.** <-ll-, -l-> *vi* (*cry*) lloriquear **II.** *n* lloriqueo *m*

snivel(l)ing **I.** *n* lloriqueo *m* **II.** *adj* llorón, -ona

snob [snab] *n* esnob *mf*, pituco, -a *m AmS*

snobbery ['snab·ə·ri] *n* esnobismo *m*

snobbish ['snab·ɪʃ] <more, most> *adj* esnob

snooker ['snʊk·ər] **I.** *vt* **1.** *inf* (*trick*) poner en un aprieto **2.** GAMES (*block*) bloquear; **to be ~ed** *fig, inf* fastidiársele a uno el plan **II.** *n* (*billiards*) snooker *m*

snoop [snup] *pej, inf* **I.** *n* fisgón, -ona *m, f* **II.** *vi* fisgonear; **to ~ around** husmear

snooty ['snu·ṭi] <-ier, -iest> *adj* presumido, -a, pituco, -a *AmS*

snooze [snuz] *inf* **I.** *vi* (*nap*) echar una cabezada; (*nap lightly*) dormitar **II.** *n* cabezada *f*

snooze button *n* botón *m* de alarma de un despertador

snore [snɔr] MED **I.** *vi* roncar **II.** *n* ronquido *m*

snorkel ['snɔr·kəl] SPORTS **I.** *n* tubo *m* snorkel (de respiración) **II.** <-ll-, -l-> *vi* bucear con tubo

snorkeling *n* SPORTS **to go ~** bucear con tubo

snort [snɔrt] **I.** *vi* bufar, resoplar **II.** *vt* **1.** *inf* (*inhale*) inhalar; (*cocaine*) esnifar **2.** (*say with disapproval*) decir bufando **III.** *n* bufido *m*

snot [snat] *n inf* moco *m*

snotrag ['snat·ræg] *n sl* pañuelo *m*

snotty ['snaṭ·i] <-ier, -iest> *adj inf* **1.** (*full of mucus*) lleno, -a de mocos **2.** (*rude*) petulante

snout [snaʊt] *n* **1.** ZOOL hocico *m;* (*of pig*) morro *m* **2.** *inf* (*of person*) napia *f*

snow [snoʊ] **I.** *n* **1.** METEO nieve *f;* **a blanket of ~** un manto de nieve **2.** *inf* (*cocaine*) nieve *f* **II.** *vi* nevar

◆ **snow in** *vt* **to be snowed in** estar aprisionado por la nieve

◆ **snow under** *vt* **to be snowed under (with sth)** estar desbordado (de algo)

snowball ['snoʊ·bɔl] **I.** *n* bola *f* de nieve ▶ **to not have a ~'s** chance **in hell (of doing sth)** no tener ni la más remota posibilidad (de hacer algo) **II.** *vi fig* aumentar progresivamente

snowball effect *n* efecto *m* de bola de nieve

snowbank *n* banco *m* de nieve

snowboard *n* snowboard *m*

snowboarding *n* **to go ~** hacer snowboard

snowbound ['snoʊ·baʊnd] *adj* (*vehicle*) embarrancado, -a en la nieve; (*person*) aprisionado, -a por la nieve

snowcapped ['snoʊ·kæpt] *adj* cubierto, -a de nieve

snow chain *n* AUTO cadena *f* (para la nieve)

snow cone *n* calippo® *m*

snowfall *n* METEO **1.** (*amount snowed*) nevada *f* **2.** (*snowstorm*) tormenta *f* de nieve, nevazón *m* Arg, Chile, Ecua

snowflake *n* copo *m* de nieve

snowman *n* muñeco *m* de nieve

snowmobile *n* moto *f* de nieve

snowplow *n* **1.**(*snow mover*) quitanieves *m inv* **2.**SPORTS (*stop*) cuña *f*
snowshoe *n* raqueta *f* (de nieve)
snowstorm *n* tormenta *f* de nieve
snowsuit *n* mono *m* acolchado (para la nieve)
snow tire *n* AUTO neumático *m* de nieve
snow-white *adj* blanco, -a como la nieve
Snow White *n* ~ **and the Seven Dwarfs** LIT Blancanieves y los siete enanitos
snowy ['snoʊ·i] *adj* **1.**METEO (*region, season*) de mucha nieve; (*street, field*) cubierto, -a de nieve **2.**(*clouds*) níveo, -a *elev;* (*pure white: hair, flowers*) blanco, -a como la nieve
snub [snʌb] **I.**<-bb-> *vt* **to ~ sb** hacer el vacío a alguien **II.** *n* desaire *m*
snub nose *n* nariz *f* respingona
snub-nosed *adj* **1.**(*pliers*) de dientes cortos; (*gun*) de cañón corto **2.**(*person*) de nariz respingona
snuff [snʌf] **I.** *vt* **1.**(*put out*) apagar **2.** *inf*(*end*) acabar con **II.** *n* rapé *m*
◆**snuff out** *vt* **1.**(*candle*) apagar **2.** *sl*(*opposition*) sofocar; (*person*) liquidar
snuffbox *n* tabaquera *f*
snug [snʌg] *adj* **1.**(*cozy*) acogedor(a); (*warm*) cómodo, -a y bien caliente **2.**(*tight: dress*) ajustado, -a
snuggle ['snʌg·əl] *vi* acurrucarse; **to ~ up to sb** acurrucarse contra alguien
so [soʊ] **I.** *adv* **1.**(*in the same way*) tan, tanto; **~ did/do I** yo también; **~ to speak** por así decir **2.**(*like that*) así; **~ they say** así dicen; **is that ~?** ¿de verdad?; **I hope/think ~** así lo espero/pienso **3.**(*to such a degree*) tan, tanto; **I ~ love him** lo amo tanto; **~ late** tan tarde; **~ many books** tantos libros; **not ~ ugly as that** no tan feo como eso; **would you be ~ kind as to...?** ¿sería usted tan amable de...? **4.**(*in order that*) para; **I bought the book ~ that he would read it** compré el libro para que (él) lo leyera **5.**(*as a result*) así; **and ~ she won** y así ganó ▶ **and ~ on** [*o* **forth**] etcétera; **or ~** más o menos **II.** *conj* **1.**(*therefore*) por (lo) tanto **2.** *inf*(*and afterwards*) **~** (**then**) **he told me...** y entonces me dijo... **3.**(*summing up*) así que; **~ what?** ¿y qué?; **~ now,...** entonces...; **~, as I was saying...** entonces, como iba diciendo... **III.** *interj* **~ that's why!** ¡es por eso!
soak [soʊk] **I.** *vt* remojar, ensopar *AmS;* **to ~ sth in liquid** poner algo en remojo **II.** *vi* (*lie in liquid*) estar en remojo **III.** *n* remojo *m*
◆**soak in** *vi* penetrar
◆**soak up** *vt* **1.**(*absorb*) absorber; (*money, resources*) agotar **2.**(*take in: people*) embelesar; (*information*) absorber **3.**(*bask in: sun*) tomar; (*atmosphere*) disfrutar de
soaked *adj* empapado, -a
soaking I. *n* remojo *m;* **to get a good ~** calarse hasta los huesos **II.** *adj* ~ (**wet**) empapado, -a, calado, -a
so-and-so ['soʊ·ən·soʊ] *n inf* (*person*) fulano *m;* (*thing*) cosa *f* cualquiera

soap [soʊp] **I.** *n* **1.**(*for washing*) jabón *m* **2.** TV (*soap opera*) telenovela *f* ▶ **soft** ~ **coba** *f* **II.** *vt* enjabonar
soapbox ['soʊp·baks] *n* **1.**(*container*) caja *f* de jabón **2.**(*pedestal*) caja *f* vacía empleada como tribuna ▶ **to get on one's** ~ echar un discurso
soapbox derby *n* carrera en la que los participantes descienden una pendiente en vehículos fabricados por ellos mismos
soap bubble *n* burbuja *f* de jabón
soap opera *n* telenovela *f*
soapsuds *npl* espuma *f* de jabón
soapy ['soʊ·pi] <-ier, -iest> *adj* **1.**(*full of lather*) lleno, -a de jabón **2.**(*like soap*) jabonoso, -a; **to taste** ~ saber a jabón **3.**(*flattering*) zalamero, -a
soar [sɔr] *vi* **1.**(*rise*) subir muy alto; (*house*) elevarse mucho **2.**(*increase: temperature*) aumentar bruscamente; (*prices*) ponerse por las nubes; (*awareness*) crecer sensiblemente; (*hopes*) renacer **3.**(*bird, plane*) remontar el vuelo; (*glide*) planear **4.**(*excel*) llegar muy alto
soaring *adj* **1.**(*increasing*) en aumento; (*very high*) altísimo, -a **2.**(*gliding*) planeador, -a
sob [sab] **I.**<-bb-> *vi* sollozar **II.**<-bb-> *vt* decir sollozando **III.** *n* sollozo *m*
sober ['soʊ·bər] *adj* **1.**(*not drunk*) sobrio, -a **2.**(*serious: mood, atmosphere, expression*) serio, -a **3.**(*plain: attire*) sencillo, -a; (*colors*) discreto, -a **4.**(*straightforward: assessment*) sensato, -a
◆**sober up I.** *vi* **1.**(*become less drunk*) espabilar la borrachera **2.**(*become serious*) ponerse serio **II.** *vt* **to sober sb up** (*make less drunk*) quitar la borrachera a alguien; (*make serious*) poner serio a alguien
sobering *adj* que hace pensar
soberness *n* **1.**(*not drunkenness*) sobriedad *f* **2.**(*seriousness*) seriedad *f* **3.**(*plainness*) sencillez *f*
sobriety [sə·'braɪ·ə·t̬i] *n form* **1.**(*not drunkenness*) sobriedad *f* **2.**(*seriousness*) seriedad *f*
sobriety checkpoint *n* (puesto *m* de) control *m* de alcoholemia
sobriquet ['soʊ·brɪ·keɪ] *n* apodo *m*
sob story *n pej* dramón *m*
so-called [ˌsoʊ·'kɔld] *adj* así llamado, -a, presunto, -a
soccer ['sak·ər] *n* fútbol *m*
soccer player *n* futbolista *mf*
sociability [ˌsoʊ·ʃə·'bɪl·ə·t̬i] *n* sociabilidad *f*
sociable ['soʊ·ʃə·bəl] *adj* sociable
social ['soʊ·ʃəl] *adj* social; ~ **drinker** *persona que no bebe a solas, sino en compañía;* **to climb up the** ~ **ladder** trepar en la escalera social
socialism ['soʊ·ʃə·lɪz·əm] *n* socialismo *m*
socialist *n* socialista *mf*
socialite ['soʊ·ʃə·laɪt] *n* persona *f* con mucha vida social
socialize ['soʊ·ʃə·laɪz] **I.** *vi* alternar con la gente **II.** *vt* **1.**PSYCH socializar **2.**POL, ECON

nacionalizar
socially *adv* socialmente
social science *n* ciencia *f* social
social security *n* (subsidio *m* de la) seguridad social *f*
social service *n* **1.** (*community help*) servicio *m* social **2.** *pl* (*welfare*) servicios *mpl* sociales
social studies *n* SCHOOL estudios *mpl* sociales
social work *n* asistencia *f* social
social worker *n* asistente *mf* social
societal [sə·'saɪ·ə·ṭəl] *adj* social
society [sə·'saɪ·ə·ṭi] *n* **1.** (*all people*) sociedad *f*; (**high**) ~ alta sociedad; **to be a menace to ~** ser una amenaza para la sociedad **2.** (*organization*) asociación *f*
sociocultural [,sou·si·ou·'kʌl·tʃər·əl] *adj* sociocultural
socioeconomic [,sou·si·ou,ek·ə·'nam·ɪk] *adj* socioeconómico, -a
sociolinguistics [,sou·si·ou·lɪŋ·'gwɪs·tɪks] *n* sociolingüística *f*
sociological [,sou·si·ə·'ladʒ·ɪ·kəl] *adj* sociológico, -a
sociologist [,sou·si·'al·ə·dʒɪst] *n* sociólogo, -a *m, f*
sociology [,sou·si·'al·ə·dʒi] *n* sociología *f*
sociopolitical [,sou·si·ou·pə·'lɪṭ·ɪ·kəl] *adj* sociopolítico, -a
sock[1] [sak] *n* calcetín *m,* media *f AmL;* **knee-high** ~ calcetín *m* largo ▶ **to knock sb's ~s off** *inf* dejar a alguien fascinado
sock[2] [sak] **I.** *vt inf* (*hit*) pegar; **to ~ sb in the eye** dar un golpe a alguien en el ojo ▶ ~ **it to 'em!** ¡a por ellos! **II.** *n inf* tortazo *m*
socket ['sak·ɪt] *n* **1.** ELEC enchufe *m,* tomacorriente *m Arg, Perú;* **double/triple** ~ enchufe de dos/tres entradas **2.** (*of eye*) cuenca *f,* órbita *f;* (*of tooth*) alvéolo *m;* (*of shoulder, hip*) fosa *f*
sod [sad] *n* césped *m*
soda ['sou·də] *n* **1.** (*drink*) refresco *m* **2.** CHEM sosa *f* **3.** (*water*) soda *f*
soda fountain *n* (*pouring device*) surtidor *m* de refrescos
soda water *n* soda *f*
sodden ['sad·ən] *adj* empapado, -a
sodium ['sou·di·əm] *n* sodio *m*
sodium bicarbonate *n* bicarbonato *m* sódico
sodium carbonate *n* carbonato *m* sódico
sodium chloride *n* cloruro *m* sódico
sodomize ['sad·ə·maɪz] *vt* sodomizar
sodomy ['sad·ə·mi] *n form* sodomía *f*
sofa ['sou·fə] *n* sofá *m*
sofa bed *n* sofá cama *m*
soft [sɔft] *adj* **1.** (*not hard: ground, sand, contact lenses*) blando, -a; (*pillow, sofa*) mullido, -a; (*metal*) dúctil; ~ **tissue** MED tejido *m* blando **2.** (*smooth: cheeks, skin, landing*) suave; (*hair*) fino, -a; ~ **as silk** suave como la seda **3.** (*mild*) ligero, -a; (*drug*) blando, -a **4.** (*not bright: colors*) delicado, -a; (*glow*) suave; (*lighting, light*) tenue **5.** (*quiet: sound, music*) agradable; (*voice*) dulce **6.** (*lenient*)

indulgente; **to go ~ on sb** ser demasiado tolerante con alguien **7.** (*easy*) fácil; **a ~ target** un blanco fácil **8.** FIN (*currency*) débil
softball ['sɔft·bɔl] *n deporte similar al béisbol, sobre un terreno más pequeño y con pelota más grande que se lanza sin levantar el brazo por encima del hombro*
soft-boiled [,sɔft·'bɔɪld] *adj* pasado, -a por agua
soften ['sɔ·fən] **I.** *vi* **1.** (*get soft: butter, ground*) reblandecerse, amelcochar *Méx* **2.** (*become lenient*) ablandarse **II.** *vt* **1.** (*make soft: butter*) reblandecer; (*skin*) suavizar **2.** (*color, voice*) suavizar **3.** (*make easier to bear: effect*) mitigar; (*opinion, words*) suavizar; (*blow*) amortiguar
♦ **soften up** *vt* ablandar; MIL debilitar
softener ['sɔ·fə·nər] *n* **1.** (*for clothes*) suavizante *m* **2.** (*for water*) descalcificador *m*
softening **I.** *n* **1.** (*reduction of hardness*) reblandecimiento *m;* (*of voice*) suavización *f* **2.** (*of light*) debilitamiento *m* **II.** *adj* reblandecedor(a); (*agent*) suavizante
soft goods *npl* productos *m* textiles y de vestir *pl*
soft-headed *adj pej* bobo, -a
soft-hearted ['sɔft,har·ṭɪd] *adj* bondadoso, -a
softie ['sɔf·ti] *n inf* blandengue *mf*
softly *adv* **1.** (*not roughly*) suavemente **2.** (*quietly*) silenciosamente **3.** (*to shine*) tenuemente
softness ['sɔft·nɪs] *n* **1.** (*not hardness*) blandura *f* **2.** (*smoothness*) suavidad *f;* (*of hair*) finura *f* **3.** (*of light*) debilidad *f*
soft-spoken *adj* de voz suave
software ['sɔft·wer] *n* software *m;* **accounting** ~ programa *m* de contabilidad
software engineer *n* ingeniero, -a *m, f* de software
software piracy *n* piratería *f* de software
softy ['sɔf·ti] *n inf* blandengue *mf*
soggy ['sag·i] <-ier, -iest> *adj* empapado, -a
soil[1] [sɔɪl] *n* AGR suelo *m;* **fertile** ~ tierra *f* fértil; **foreign** ~ tierras *fpl* extranjeras
soil[2] [sɔɪl] **I.** *vt form* (*make dirty*) manchar; (*clothing, shoes*) ensuciar; **to ~ sb's reputation** manchar la reputación de alguien **II.** *vi* ensuciarse
soirée *n,* **soiree** [swa·'reɪ] *n form* velada *f*
sojourn ['sou·dʒɜrn] *n* estancia *f*
sol [soul] *n* MUS sol *m*
solace ['sal·ɪs] **I.** *n* consuelo *m* **II.** *vt* consolar
solar ['sou·lər] *adj* solar
solar battery *n* pila *f* solar
solar cell *n* célula *f* solar
solar eclipse *n* eclipse *m* de sol
solar energy *n* energía *f* solar
solarium [sou·'ler·i·əm] <-s *o* solaria> *n* solárium *m*
solar panel *n* placa *f* solar
solar plexus *n* plexo *m* solar
solar power *n* energía *f* solar
solar radiation *n* radiación *f* solar

S

solar system *n* sistema *m* solar
sold [soʊld] *pt, pp of* **sell**
solder ['sad·ər] I. *vt* soldar II. *n* soldadura *f*
soldering iron ['sad·ər·ɪŋ·ˌaɪ·ərn] *n* (*tool*) soldador *m*
soldier ['soʊl·dʒər] I. *n* 1. MIL (*military person*) militar *mf*; **old ~** veterano *m* 2. (*non officer*) soldado *mf* II. *vi* servir como soldado
 ◆ **soldier on** *vi* seguir adelante
sold-out [ˌsoʊld·'aʊt] *adj* vendido, -a; **the tickets are sold out** las entradas se han agotado
sole¹ [soʊl] *adj* (*unique*) único, -a; (*exclusive*) exclusivo, -a; **~ right** derecho *m* en exclusiva
sole² [soʊl] *n* (*of foot*) planta *f*; (*of shoe*) suela *f*
sole³ [soʊl] <-(s)> *n* (*fish*) lenguado *m*; **filet of ~** filete de lenguado
solecism ['sal·ə·sɪz·əm] *n form* 1. LING solecismo *m* 2. (*breach of good manners*) incorrección *f*
solely ['soʊl·li] *adv* únicamente
solemn ['sal·əm] *adj* (*occasion, promise*) solemne; (*person, appearance*) serio, -a
solemnity [sə·'lem·nə·t̬i] *n* solemnidad *f*
solemnize ['sal·əm·naɪz] *vt form* solemnizar
solenoid ['soʊ·lə·nɔɪd] *n* ELEC solenoide *m*
solicit [sə·'lɪs·ɪt] I. *vt* 1. (*ask for*) solicitar 2. (*offer sex*) abordar (a alguien) para ofrecerle servicios sexuales II. *vi* (*offer sex*) abordar a posibles clientes para ofrecerles servicios sexuales
solicitation *n* LAW ejercicio *m* de la prostitución
solicitous [sə·'lɪs·ɪ·t̬əs] *adj* solícito, -a
solicitude [sə·'lɪs·ɪ·tud] *n form* atención *f*
solid ['sal·ɪd] I. *adj* 1. (*hard*) sólido, -a; (*rock, metal, wood*) macizo, -a; (*table, door, wall*) robusto, -a; (*meal*) pesado, -a; **to be (as) ~ as a rock** ser duro como una piedra 2. (*not hollow*) macizo, -a 3. (*true*) real; (*facts*) verídico, -a; (*evidence*) sustancial; (*argument*) sólido, -a; (*reasons*) de peso; (*conviction*) firme; (*agreement*) concreto, -a 4. (*uninterrupted: wall, line*) ininterrumpido, -a; (*hour, day, week*) entero, -a 5. (*three-dimensional*) tridimensional 6. (*good: work, picture*) excelente II. *adv* **to be packed ~** estar lleno hasta los topes; **to be frozen ~** estar completamente helado III. *n* 1. (*shape*) sólido *m* 2. *pl* CULIN alimentos *mpl* sólidos
solidarity [ˌsal·ə·'der·ə·t̬i] *n* solidaridad *f*
solid fuel *n* combustible *m* sólido
solidify [sə·'lɪd·ə·faɪ] <-ie-, -ying> I. *vi* solidificarse; (*plans, project, idea*) concretarse II. *vt* 1. (*make hard*) solidificar 2. (*reinforce*) reforzar
solidity [sə·'lɪd·ə·t̬i] *n* solidez *f*
solidly *adv* 1. (*robustly*) sólidamente 2. (*without interruption*) ininterrumpidamente 3. (*in strong manner*) fuertemente 4. (*unanimously*) unánimemente
solid-state [ˌsal·ɪd·'steɪt] *adj* de estado sólido
soliloquy [sə·'lɪl·ə·kwi] *n* soliloquio *m*

solitaire ['sal·ə·ter] *n* solitario *m*
solitary ['sal·ə·ter·i] I. *adj* 1. (*alone, single*) solitario, -a 2. (*isolated*) solo, -a, íngrimo, -a *AmL*; (*unvisited*) apartado, -a; **to go for a ~ walk** ir a pasear solo II. *n inf* (*isolation*) incomunicación *f*
solitary confinement *n* aislamiento *m*
solitude ['sal·ə·tud] *n* 1. (*loneliness*) soledad *f* 2. (*isolation*) aislamiento *m*
solo ['soʊ·loʊ] I. *adj* solo, -a; **~ flight** vuelo *m* en solitario II. *adv* a solas; MUS solo; **to go ~** lanzarse como solista; **to fly ~** AVIAT volar en solitario III. *n* MUS solo *m*
soloist ['soʊ·loʊ·ɪst] *n* solista *mf*
Solomon Islands ['sal·ə·mən·ˌaɪ·ləndz] *n* Islas *fpl* Salomón
solstice ['sal·stɪs] *n* solsticio *m*
soluble ['sal·jə·bəl] *adj* (*substance, problem*) soluble
solution [sə·'lu·ʃən] *n* solución *f*
solve [salv] *vt* resolver
solvency ['sal·vən·si] *n* solvencia *f*
solvent ['sal·vənt] I. *n* disolvente *m* II. *adj* 1. FIN solvente 2. CHEM disolvente
Somali [soʊ·'ma·li] I. <-(s)> *n* 1. (*person*) somalí *mf* 2. (*language*) somalí *m* II. *adj* somalí
Somalia [soʊ·'mal·i·ə] *n* Somalia *f*
somber ['sam·bər] *adj* (*mood*) sombrío, -a; (*color*) oscuro, -a
some [sʌm] I. *adj indef* 1. *pl* (*several*) algunos, -as; **~ apples** algunas manzanas; **~ people think...** algunos piensan... 2. (*imprecise*) algún, alguna; (**at**) **~ place** (en) algún lugar; **~ day** algún día; (**at**) **~ time** (en) algún momento; **for ~ time** durante cierto tiempo; **~ other time** en algún otro momento; **~ time ago** hace algún tiempo; **in ~ way or another** de alguna u otra manera; **to have ~ idea of sth** tener alguna idea de algo 3. (*amount*) un poco de, algo de; **~ more tea** un poco más de té; **to have ~ money** tener algo de dinero; **to ~ extent** hasta cierto punto II. *pron indef* 1. *pl* (*several*) algunos; **I would like ~** quisiera algunos; **~ like it, others don't** a algunos les gusta, a otros no 2. (*part of it*) algo; **I would like ~** quisiera algo III. *adv* (*about*) unos, unas; **~ more apples** unas manzanas más; **~ more wine** un poco más de vino
somebody ['sʌm·ˌbad·i] *pron indef* alguien; **~ else** otra persona, (algún) otro; **~ or other** alguien; **there is ~ Spanish on the phone** hay alguien español al teléfono
somehow ['sʌm·haʊ] *adv* 1. (*through unknown methods*) de alguna manera 2. (*for an unclear reason*) por algún motivo 3. (*come what may*) de un modo u otro
someone ['sʌm·wʌn] *pron s.* **somebody**
someplace ['sʌm·pleɪs] *adv* en algún lugar
somersault ['sʌm·ər·sɔlt] I. *n* salto *m* mortal; **to do a ~** dar un salto mortal II. *vi* (*person*) dar un salto mortal; (*vehicle*) dar una vuelta de campana

something ['sʌm·θɪŋ] I. *pron indef, sing* 1.(*some object or concept*) algo; ~ **else/nice** algo más/bonito; ~ **or other** alguna cosa; **one can't have** ~ **for nothing** quien algo quiere, algo le cuesta 2.(*about*) ...**or** ~ *inf*...o algo así; **six-foot** ~ dos metros y pico; **his name is Paul** ~ su nombre es Paul no sé qué II. *n a little* ~ una cosita; **a certain** ~ cierta cosa ▶**that is** really ~! ¡ésa sí que es buena! III. *adv* ~ **around $10** alrededor de 10$; ~ **over/under $100** algo más/menos de 100$

sometime ['sʌm·taɪm] I. *adv* en algún momento; ~ **soon** pronto II. *adj form* antiguo, -a

sometimes ['sʌm·taɪmz] *adv* a veces

somewhat ['sʌm·hwat] *adv* algo; **to feel** ~ **better** sentirse un poco mejor

somewhere ['sʌm·hwer] *adv* 1.(*be*) en alguna parte; (*go*) a alguna parte; **to be** ~ **else** estar en otra parte; **to go** ~ **else** ir a otra parte; **to get** ~ *fig* progresar; **or** ~ *inf* o así 2.(*roughly*) alrededor de; **she is** ~ **around 40** tiene alrededor de 40 años; **he earns** ~ **around $40,000** gana alrededor de 40.000$

somnambulism [sam·'næm·bjə·lɪz·əm] *n* sonambulismo *m*

somnolent ['sam·nə·lənt] *adj* (*sleepy*) soñoliento, -a

son [sʌn] *n* hijo *m*

sonar ['soʊ·nar] *n* sónar *m*

sonata [sə·'na·t̬ə] *n* sonata *f*; **piano** ~ sonata para piano

song [sɔŋ] *n* 1.MUS (*piece of music*) canción *f* 2.(*action of singing*) canto *m* ▶~ **and** dance *inf* (*untrue justification*) rollo *m*; (**to go**) for a ~ venderse a precio de saldo

songbird ['sɔŋ·bɜrd] *n* pájaro *m* cantor

songbook *n* cancionero *m*

songwriter *n* compositor(a) *m(f)*

sonic ['san·ɪk] *adj* 1.(*relating to sound*) acústico, -a 2.(*at the speed of sound*) sónico, -a

sonic boom *n* AVIAT explosión *f* ultrasónica

son-in-law ['sʌn·ɪn·lɔ] <sons-in-law> *n* yerno *m*

sonnet ['san·ɪt] *n* soneto *m*

sonny (**boy**) ['sʌn·i] *n inf* hijito *m*; (*aggressive*) majo *m*

son of a bitch I. <sons of bitches> *n* 1.*vulg* (*jerk*) hijo *m* de puta 2.(*person*) **he's a real lucky** ~ es un cabrón con suerte II. *interj vulg* (*as insult*) hijo de puta; (*expressing annoyance*) joder

son of a gun I. <sons of guns> *n* tío *m* II. *interj* qué tío

sonorous [sə·'nɔr·əs] *adj* sonoro, -a

soon [sun] *adv* pronto, mero *AmC, Méx*; ~ **after...** poco después de...; **how** ~...? ¿para cuándo...?; **as** ~ **as possible** tan pronto como sea posible [*o* lo más pronto posible]; **I would just as** ~... preferiría...

sooner ['su·nər] *adv comp of* **soon** más temprano; ~ **or later** tarde o temprano; **no** ~... than apenas... cuando; **no** ~ **said than done** dicho y hecho; **the** ~ **the better** cuanto antes mejor

soot [sʊt] *n* hollín *m*

soothe [suð] *vt* 1.(*make calm*) calmar 2.(*reduce: pain*) aliviar

soothing *adj* 1.(*calming*) tranquilizador(a) 2.(*pain-relieving*) analgésico, -a; (*balsamic: ointment, balm, massage*) reparador(a)

soothsayer ['suθ·ˌseɪ·ər] *n* adivino, -a *m, f*

sooty ['sʊt̬·i] <-ier, -iest> *adj* lleno, -a de hollín

sophisticated [sə·'fɪs·tə·keɪ·t̬ɪd] *adj* 1.(*refined*) sofisticado, -a 2.(*cultured*) culto, -a 3.(*highly developed*) refinado, -a; (*method*) sofisticado, -a

sophistication [sə·ˌfɪs·tə·'keɪ·ʃən] *n* 1.(*refinement*) sofisticación *f* 2.(*complexity*) complejidad *f*

sophistry ['saf·ɪ·stri] *n* sofistería *f*

sophomore ['saf·ə·mɔr] *n* estudiante *mf* de segundo año

soporific [ˌsap·ə·'rɪf·ɪk] *adj* soporífero, -a

sopping ['sap·ɪŋ] *inf* I. *adj* empapado, -a II. *adv* ~ **wet** empapado

soppy ['sap·i] <-ier, -iest> *adj inf* sensiblero, -a

soprano [sə·'præn·oʊ] *n* 1.(*vocal range*) soprano *m* 2.(*singer*) soprano *f*

sorbet ['sɔr·beɪ] *n* sorbete *m*

sorcerer ['sɔr·sər·ər] *n liter* hechicero *m*

sorceress ['sɔr·sər·ɪs] *n liter* hechicera *f*

sorcery ['sɔr·sə·ri] *n liter* hechicería *f*

sordid ['sɔr·dɪd] *adj* 1.(*unclean*) sórdido, -a, miserable 2.*pej* (*base*) sórdido, -a; **all the** ~ **details** todos los detalles escabrosos

sore [sɔr] I. *adj* 1.(*aching*) dolorido, -a; **to be in** ~ **need of sth** necesitar algo a toda costa; **a** ~ **point** *fig* un punto delicado 2.*inf* (*offended*) ofendido, -a; (*aggrieved*) resentido, -a; ~ **loser** mal perdedor II. *n* MED llaga *f*; *fig* recuerdo *m* doloroso; **to open an old** ~ abrir una vieja herida

sorely ['sɔr·li] *adv form* muy; **he will be** ~ **missed** lo echarán mucho de menos; **to be** ~ **tempted to do sth** estar casi por hacer algo

sorority [sə·'rɔr·ə·t̬i] *n* UNIV club *m* femenino

sorrow ['sar·oʊ] *n* pena *f*; **to feel** ~ **over sth** sentirse apenado por algo; **to my** ~ *form* a mi pesar

sorrowful ['sar·ə·fəl] *adj* apenado, -a; **with a** ~ **sigh** con un suspiro de aflicción

sorry ['sar·i] I. <-ier, -iest> *adj* 1.triste, apenado, -a; **to be** ~ (**that**) sentir (que) +*subj*; **to feel** ~ **for oneself** compadecerse de sí mismo; **to feel** ~ **for sb** tener lástima de alguien 2.(*regretful*) arrepentido, -a; **to be** ~ **about sth** estar arrepentido por algo; **to say** ~ pedir perdón 3.(*said before refusing*) **I'm** ~, **but I don't agree** lo siento, pero no estoy de acuerdo 4.(*wretched, pitiful*) desgraciado, -a; (*choice*) desafortunado, -a; (*figure*) lastimoso, -a II. *interj* 1.(*expressing apology*) ~! ¡perdón! 2.(*requesting repetition*) ~? ¿cómo dice?; ~, **but before continuing...** disculpen, pero antes de continuar...

sort [sɔrt] I. *n* 1. (*type*) tipo *m;* (*kind*) especie *f;* (*variety*) clase *f;* **flowers of all ~s** toda clase de flores; **something/nothing of the ~** algo/ nada por el estilo 2. COMPUT ordenación *f* 3. (*expressing uncertainty*) **he was a friend of ~s** se le podía considerar amigo 4. *inf* (*to some extent*) **~ of** en cierto modo; **I ~ of feel that...** en cierto modo pienso que...; **that's ~ of difficult to explain** es algo difícil de explicar 5. (*not exactly*) **~ of** más o menos 6. (*person*) **to not be the ~ to do sth** no ser de los que hacen algo; **I know your ~!** ¡sé de qué pie calzas! ▶ **it takes all ~s to make a** <u>world</u> *prov* hay de todo en la viña del Señor *prov;* **to be/feel** <u>out</u> **of ~s** estar/encontrarse pachucho II. *vt* 1. (*arrange*) clasificar 2. COMPUT ordenar; **to ~ in ascending/descending order** poner en orden ascendente/descendente III. *vi* **to ~ through sth** revisar algo
◆ **sort out** *vt* 1. (*resolve*) solucionar; (*details*) aclarar 2. (*arrange*) clasificar; (*choose*) separar 3. (*tidy up*) arreglar

sorter *n* 1. (*postal employee sorting mail*) clasificador(a) *m(f)* 2. (*machine*) clasificadora *f*

sortie ['sɔr·ti] *n* MIL incursión

SOS [ˌes·ouˈes] *n* SOS *m*

so-so ['sou·sou] *inf* I. *adj* regular II. *adv* ni fu ni fa, así así

soufflé [suˈfleɪ] *n* suflé *m*

sought [sɔt] *pt, pp of* **seek**

sought-after ['sɔt·ˌæf·tər] *adj* solicitado, -a

soul [soul] *n* 1. (*spirit*) alma *f;* **to pray for sb's ~** rezar por el alma de alguien; **bless his/her ~** que en paz descanse 2. (*person*) alma *f;* **not a ~** ni un alma 3. MUS (*música f*) soul *m* 4. (*essence*) **to be the ~ of discretion** ser la discreción en persona

soul food *n* comida tradicional de los negros del Sur de los Estados Unidos

soulful ['soul·fəl] *adj* conmovedor(a)

soulless ['soul·lɪs] *adj pej* (*person*) desalmado, -a; (*building, town*) impersonal; (*work*) mecánico, -a

soul mate *n* amigo, -a *m, f* del alma

soul music *n* (música *f*) soul *m*

soul-searching *n* examen *m* de conciencia; **after much ~** después de mucha reflexión

sound[1] [saund] I. *n* 1. (*noise*) ruido *m;* **there wasn't a ~ to be heard** no se oía nada 2. LING, PHYS sonido *m* 3. (*radio, TV*) volumen *m;* **to turn the ~ down/up** bajar/subir el volumen 4. (*idea expressed in words*) **by the ~ of it** según parece; **I don't like the ~ of that** no me huele nada bien II. *vi* 1. (*make noise*) sonar 2. (*seem*) parecer III. *vt* (*alarm*) hacer sonar; (*bell, car horn*) tocar; **to ~ the retreat** MIL tocar (a) retirada

sound[2] [saund] I. *adj* 1. (*healthy*) sano, -a; (*robust*) fuerte; **to be of ~ mind** estar en su sano juicio; **to be safe and ~** estar sano y salvo 2. (*good: character, health*) bueno, -a; (*basis*) sólido, -a 3. (*trustworthy*) digno, -a de confianza; (*competent*) competente 4. (*thorough*) profundo, -a 5. (*undisturbed: sleep*) profundo, -a; **to be a ~ sleeper** tener el sueño profundo II. *adv* **to be ~ asleep** estar profundamente dormido

sound[3] [saund] *vt* 1. NAUT sondear 2. MED auscultar

sound[4] [saund] *n* (*channel*) estrecho *m;* (*inlet*) brazo *m* de mar
◆ **sound off** *vi inf* **to ~ about sb/sth** sentar cátedra sobre alguien/algo
◆ **sound out** *vt* tantear

sound barrier *n* barrera *f* del sonido

sound bite *n* (*in the media*) pequeño extracto de un discurso que reproduce el contenido más importante de unas declaraciones

soundboard *n* MUS s. **sounding board**

sound card *n* COMPUT tarjeta *f* de sonido

sound effects *n* efectos *mpl* de sonido

sound engineer *n* técnico *m* de sonido

sounding board *n* MUS tabla *f* armónica

soundless ['saund·lɪs] *adj* silencioso, -a

soundly *adv* 1. (*completely*) **to sleep ~** dormir profundamente 2. (*strongly*) **to thrash sb ~** dar una buena paliza a alguien

soundness *n* 1. (*firmness*) firmeza *f* 2. (*good sense*) sensatez *f*

soundproof ['saund·pruf] I. *vt* insonorizar II. *adj* insonorizado, -a

sound system *n* equipo *m* de sonido

soundtrack *n* CINE banda *f* sonora

sound wave *n* onda *f* sonora

soup [sup] *n* sopa *f;* (*clear*) caldo *m;* **homemade ~** sopa casera; **instant ~** sopa instantánea

soup bowl *n* plato *m* sopero

soupçon [supˈsɔn] *n* pizca *f*

souped-up *adj* AUTO trucado, -a

soup kitchen *n* comedor *m* de beneficencia

soupspoon *n* cuchara *f* sopera

sour ['sau·ər] *adj* 1. (*fruit, wine*) agrio, -a; (*milk*) cortado, -a; **to go ~** agriarse; (*milk*) cortarse 2. (*character, person*) agrio, -a II. *n* **whiskey ~** combinado de whisky, zumo de limón y azúcar III. *vt* agriar; *fig* amargar IV. *vi* agriarse; (*milk*) cortarse; *fig* (*person*) amargarse

source [sɔrs] I. *n* 1. (*information giver*) a. *fig* fuente *f;* **according to government ~s** según fuentes gubernamentales; **from a reliable ~** de una fuente fiable; **to list one's ~s** hacer la bibliografía 2. (*origin*) origen *m;* **a ~ of inspiration** una fuente de inspiración; **~ text** texto *m* original II. *vt* seleccionar

sourpuss ['sau·ər·pus] *n inf* amargado, -a *m, f*

souse [saus] *vt* (*food*) macerar

south [sauθ] I. *n* sur *m;* **to lie 5 miles to the ~ of sth** quedar a 8 km al sur de algo; **to go/ drive to the ~** ir hacia el sur; **further ~** más al sur; **in the ~ of France** en el sur de Francia II. *adj* del sur, meridional; **~ wind** viento *m* del sur; **~ coast** costa *f* sur

South Africa *n* Sudáfrica *f*
South African I. *adj* sudafricano, -a **II.** *n* sudafricano, -a *m, f*
South America *n* América *f* del Sur
South American I. *adj* sudamericano, -a **II.** *n* sudamericano, -a *m, f*
southbound ['saυθ·baυnd] *adj* hacia el sur
South Carolina [ˌsaυθ·ˌkær·ə·'laɪ·nə] *n* Carolina *f* del Sur
South Dakota [ˌsaυθ·ˌdə·'koυ·t̬ə] *n* Dakota *f* del Sur
southeast [ˌsaυθ·'ist] **I.** *n* sureste *m,* sudeste *m* **II.** *adj* del sureste; **Southeast Asia** el sureste asiático **III.** *adv* al sureste
southeasterly I. *adj* **in a ~ direction** hacia el sureste **II.** *n* (*wind*) viento *m* del sureste
southeastern *adj* (del) sureste
southeastward(s) *adv* hacia el sureste
southerly ['sʌð·ər·li] **I.** *adj* (*location*) en el sur; **in a ~ direction** en dirección sur; **~ wind** viento *m* meridional [*o* sur] **II.** *n* viento *m* meridional
southern ['sʌð·ərn] *adj* del sur; **the ~ part of the country** la parte sur del país
southerner ['sʌð·ər·nər] *n* sureño, -a *m, f*
southern hemisphere *n* hemisferio *m* sur
southern lights *npl* aurora *f* austral
southernmost *adj* más al sur
south-facing *adj* orientado, -a al sur
South Korea *n* Corea *f* del Sur
South Korean I. *adj* surcoreano, -a **II.** *n* surcoreano, -a *m, f*
southpaw ['saυθ·pɔ] *n* zurdo, -a *m, f*
South Pole *n* Polo *m* Sur
southward(s) ['saυθ·wərd(z)] *adv* hacia el sur
southwest [ˌsaυθ·'west] **I.** *n* suroeste *m* **II.** *adj* del suroeste **III.** *adv* al suroeste
southwesterly I. *adj* **in a ~ direction** hacia el suroeste **II.** *n* (*wind*) viento *m* del suroeste
southwestern *adj* del suroeste
southwestward(s) *adv* hacia el suroeste
souvenir [ˌsu·və·'nɪr] *n* recuerdo *m*
sou'wester [ˌsaυ·'wes·tər] *n* sueste *m*
sovereign ['sav·rən] **I.** *n* soberano, -a *m, f* **II.** *adj* (*self-governing*) soberano, -a; **~ state** estado *m* soberano
sovereignty ['sav·rən·ti] *n* soberanía *f*
soviet ['soυ·vi·et] **I.** *n* soviet *m* **II.** *adj* soviético, -a
Soviet Union *n* HIST Unión *f* Soviética
sow[1] [soυ] <sowed, sown *o* sowed> **I.** *vt* sembrar **II.** *vi* sembrar ►**as you ~, so shall you reap** lo que siembres cosecharás
sow[2] [saυ] *n* (*pig*) cerda *f* ►**you can't make a silk purse out of a ~'s ear** *prov* no se le puede pedir peras al olmo
sown [soυn] *pp of* **sow**
sox [saks] *npl* calcetines *mpl*
soy [sɔɪ] *n* soja *f*
soybean *n* soja *f*
soymilk *n* leche *f* de soja
soy sauce *n* salsa *f* de soja
spa [spa] *n* **1.** (*mineral spring*) manantial *m* de

agua mineral **2.** (*town*) ciudad *f* balnearia **3.** *Am* (*health center*) balneario *m*
space [speɪs] **I.** *n* espacio *m;* **parking ~** plaza *f* de aparcamiento; **in a short ~ of time** en un breve espacio de tiempo; **leave some ~ for dessert** deja hueco para el postre **II.** *vt* espaciar
♦**space out I.** *vt* espaciar **II.** *vi sl* **I was spaced out** se me fue la onda
space age *n* era *f* espacial
space bar *n* barra *f* espaciadora
space cadet *n sl* persona *f* en babia
space heater *n* calentador *m*
space probe *n* sonda *f* espacial
spacer *n* espaciador *m*
space-saving *adj* que ocupa poco espacio
spaceship ['speɪs·ʃɪp] *n* nave *f* espacial, astronave *f*
space shuttle *n* transbordador *m* espacial
space station *n* estación *f* espacial
spacing ['speɪ·sɪŋ] *n* **1.** (*arrangement*) espaciamiento *m* **2.** TYPO espacio *m;* **double ~** doble espacio
spacious ['speɪ·ʃəs] *adj* espacioso, -a
spade [speɪd] *n* **1.** (*tool*) pala *f* **2.** (*playing card*) pica *f* ► **to call a ~ a ~** llamar al pan, pan y al vino, vino
spaghetti [spə·'get̬·i] *n* espaguetis *mpl*
spaghetti Western *n* CINE spaghetti western *m*
Spain [speɪn] *n* España *f*
spam [spæm] **I.** *n* COMPUT spam *m* **II.** *vt* COMPUT enviar mensajes de correo no deseados
Spam® [spæm] *n fiambre enlatado hecho con carne de cerdo*
spambot ['spæmbɑt] *n* COMPUT spambot *m*
span[1] [spæn] *pt of* **spin**
span[2] [spæn] **I.** *n* **1.** (*of time*) lapso *m,* espacio *m;* (*of project*) duración *f* **2.** ARCHIT (*of bridge, arch*) luz *f* **3.** AVIAT, NAUT (*of wing, sail*) envergadura *f* **II.** <-nn-> *vt* **1.** (*cross*) atravesar **2.** (*include*) abarcar
spangle ['spæŋ·gəl] *n* lentejuela *f*
spangled *adj* con lentejuelas; **to be ~ with sth** *fig* estar salpicado de algo
Spanglish ['spæŋ·glɪʃ] *n* spanglish *m,* espanglis *m*
Spaniard ['spæn·jərd] *n* español(a) *m(f)*
spaniel ['spæn·jəl] *n* perro *m* de aguas
Spanish ['spæn·ɪʃ] **I.** *adj* español(a); **~ speaker** hispanohablante *mf* **II.** *n* **1.** (*people*) español(a) *m(f);* **the ~** los españoles **2.** LING español *m*
spank [spæŋk] *vt* dar unos azotes (en el trasero)
spanking ['spæŋ·kɪŋ] **I.** *n* zurra *f,* fleta *f AmC;* **to give sb a ~** zurrar a alguien **II.** *adj inf* (**brand**) **~ new** nuevo y flamante
spar[1] [spar] *n* <-rr-> **1.** (*in boxing*) entrenarse **2.** (*argue*) discutir
spar[2] [spar] *n* NAUT palo *m*
spar[3] [spar] *n* MIN espato *m*
spare [sper] **I.** *vt* **1.** (*pardon*) perdonar; **to ~ sb sth** ahorrar algo a alguien; **to ~ no effort** no

escatimar esfuerzos; **to ~ sb's feelings** no herir los sentimientos de alguien **2.** (*do without*) prescindir de; (*time*) disponer de **II.** *adj* **1.** (*additional: key*) de repuesto; (*room, minute*) libre **2.** (*remaining*) sobrante **3.** *liter* (*gaunt: build*) enjuto, -a; (*meal*) frugal, austero, -a **III.** *n* **1.** (*part*) repuesto *m* **2.** AUTO rueda *f* de recambio, rueda *f* de repueto **3.** (*in bowling*) semipleno *m*

spare part *n* repuesto *m,* recambio *m*

spareribs *n pl* costillas *fpl* (de cerdo)

spare time *n* tiempo *m* libre

spare tire *n* **1.** AUTO rueda *f* de recambio, rueda *f* de repuesto **2.** *iron* michelín *m*

sparing ['sper·ɪŋ] *adj* moderado, -a; **to be ~ with one's praise** escatimar los elogios

sparingly *adv* con moderación

spark [spark] **I.** *n* **1.** (*from fire, electrical*) chispa *f* **2.** (*small amount*) pizca *f;* **not even a ~ of interest/intelligence** ni una pizca de interés/inteligencia **II.** *vt* (*debate, protest, problems*) desencadenar; (*interest*) despertar, suscitar; (*riot*) hacer estallar; **to ~ sb into action** hacer que alguien se mueva

sparkle ['spar·kəl] **I.** *n* destello *m,* brillo *m* **II.** *vi* (*eyes*) brillar; (*fire*) chispear; (*sea*) destellar, centellear

sparkler ['spark·lər] *n* **1.** (*firework*) bengala *f* **2.** *inf* (*diamond*) diamante *m*

sparkling ['spark·lɪŋ] *adj* **1.** (*light, diamond*) brillante **2.** (*conversation, wit*) chispeante

spark plug ['spark·plʌg] *n* bujía *f*

sparring match ['spar·ɪŋ] *n* combate *m* de entrenamiento

sparring partner *n* **1.** SPORTS sparring *mf* **2.** *fig* antagonista *mf*

sparrow ['sper·oʊ] *n* gorrión *m*

sparrow hawk ['sper·oʊ·hɔk] *n* gavilán *m*

sparse [spars] *adj* escaso, -a

sparsely *adv* escasamente

Spartan *adj,* **spartan** ['spar·tən] *adj* espartano, -a

spasm ['spæz·əm] *n* MED espasmo *m;* (*of coughing, pain*) ataque *m;* (*of anger*) arrebato *m;* **to have ~s** contraerse espasmódicamente

spasmodic [spæz·'mad·ɪk] *adj* **1.** (*interest*) ocasional; (*activity*) irregular **2.** MED espasmódico, -a

spastic ['spæs·tɪk] *n pej* espástico, -a *m, f*

spat¹ [spæt] *pt, pp of* **spit**

spat² [spæt] **I.** *n inf* (*quarrel*) rencilla *f* **II.** <-tt-> *vi* (*quarrel*) reñir

spate [speɪt] *n* (*of burglaries*) racha *f,* serie *f;* (*of letters, inquiries*) aluvión *m*

spatial ['speɪ·ʃəl] *adj* espacial

spatter ['spæt̬·ər] **I.** *vt* salpicar; **to ~ sb with mud/water** salpicar de barro/agua a alguien **II.** *vi* salpicar **III.** *n* salpicadura *f,* salpicada *f Méx;* **~ of rain** cuatro gotas *fpl*

spatula ['spæt͡ʃ·ə·lə] *n* espátula *f*

spawn [spɔn] **I.** *n* **1.** ZOOL hueva(s) *f(pl)* **2.** *pej* (*offspring*) prole *f* **II.** *vt* generar, producir **III.** *vi* desovar

spay [speɪ] *vt* (*animal*) esterilizar (*extirpando los ovarios*)

speak [spik] <spoke, spoken> **I.** *vi* **1.** hablar; **to ~ to sb** hablar con alguien; **to ~ in riddles** hablar en clave; **to ~ on behalf of sb** hablar por alguien; **so to ~** por así decir; **~ when you're spoken to** contesta cuando te pregunten **2.** + *adv* **generally ~ing** en términos generales; **scientifically ~ing** desde el punto de vista científico; **strictly ~ing** en realidad **II.** *vt* decir, hablar; **to ~ dialect/a foreign language** hablar dialecto/un idioma extranjero; **to ~ one's mind** hablar claro [*o* con franqueza]; **to ~ the truth** decir la verdad; **to not ~ a word** no decir ni una palabra

◆**speak for** *vi* **1.** (*represent*) hablar por; **speaking for myself...** en cuanto a mí...; **it speaks for itself** habla por sí solo; **to be old enough to ~ oneself** ser lo bastante mayorcito para defenderse **2.** (*advocate, support*) hablar en favor de

◆**speak out** *vi* expresarse; **to ~ against sth** denunciar algo

◆**speak up** *vi* **1.** (*state views*) decir lo que se piensa; **to ~ for sth** hablar a favor de algo **2.** (*talk more loudly*) hablar más alto

speaker *n* **1.** (*person speaking*) hablante *mf* **2.** (*orator*) orador(a) *m(f)* **3.** (*loudspeaker*) altavoz *m*

speaking I. *n* **1.** (*action*) habla *f* **2.** (*public speaking*) oratoria *f* **II.** *adj* hablante; (*tour*) comentado, -a; **to be on ~ terms with sb** estar en buenas relaciones con alguien; **to not be on ~ terms** no hablarse, no dirigirse la palabra

speaking part *n* THEAT, CINE papel *m* hablado

spear [spɪr] **I.** *n* lanza *f;* (*for throwing*) jabalina *f;* (*for fishing*) arpón *m* **II.** *vt* atravesar (con una lanza); (*with fork*) pinchar

spearhead ['spɪr·hed] **I.** *vt* encabezar **II.** *n a. fig* punta *f* de lanza

spearmint ['spɪr·mɪnt] *n* menta *f* verde

special ['speʃ·əl] **I.** *adj* (*attention, case, diet*) especial; (*aptitude, character*) excepcional; **nothing ~** *inf* nada en particular **II.** *n* **1.** TV programa *m* especial **2.** CULIN especialidad *f* del día **3.** *pl* COM ofertas *fpl* especiales

special delivery *n* correo *m* urgente

special edition *n* edición *f* especial

special effects *n* efectos *mpl* especiales

specialist ['speʃ·ə·lɪst] *n* especialista *mf*

specialization [ˌspeʃ·ə·lɪ·'zeɪ·ʃən] *n* especialización *f*

specialize ['speʃ·ə·laɪz] **I.** *vi* especializarse; **to ~ in sth** especializarse en algo **II.** *vt* especializar

specialized *adj* especializado, -a

specially *adv* especialmente; **a ~ good wine** un vino especialmente bueno

special offer *n* oferta *f* especial

specialty ['speʃ·əl·ti] *n* <-ies> especialidad *f*

species ['spi·ʃiz] *n inv* especie *f*

specific [spə·'sɪf·ɪk] **I.** *adj* específico, -a; **to be**

~ dar detalles; **to be ~ to sth** ser propio de algo **II.** *npl* datos *mpl* específicos

specifically *adv* **1.** (*expressly*) expresamente; (*ask, mention*) explícitamente **2.** (*particularly*) específicamente

specification [ˌspes·ə·fɪ·'keɪ·ʃən] *n* especificación *f*

specify ['spes·ə·faɪ] <-ie-> *vt* especificar

specimen ['spes·ə·mən] *n* **1.** (*of blood, urine*) muestra *f;* (*of plant, animal, product*) espécimen *m;* (*example*) ejemplar *m;* **a ~ copy** un ejemplar de muestra **2.** *inf* (*person*) espécimen *m*

specious ['spi·ʃəs] *adj form* engañoso, -a

speck [spek] *n* punto *m;* (*of paint*) manchita *f;* (*of dust*) mota *f;* **not a ~ of sth** ni pizca de algo

speckle ['spek·əl] *n* motita *f*

speckled *adj* con motitas, moteado, -a

specs [speks] *npl* **1.** *inf abbr of* **spectacles** gafas *fpl* **2.** *inf abbr of* **specifications** especificaciones *fpl*

spectacle ['spek·tə·kəl] *n* **1.** espectáculo *m;* **to make a real ~ of oneself** dar el espectáculo **2.** *pl* (*glasses*) gafas *fpl,* anteojos *mpl AmL,* lentes *fpl AmL;* **a pair of ~** unas gafas

spectacled *adj* con gafas

spectacular [spek·'tæk·ju·lər] **I.** *adj* espectacular **II.** *n* programa *m* especial

spectator [spek·'teɪ·t̬ər] *n* espectador(a) *m(f)*

specter ['spek·tər] *n* espectro *m,* fantasma *m*

spectral ['spek·trəl] *adj* espectral

spectroscope ['spek·trou·skoup] *n* PHYS espectroscopio *m*

spectrum ['spek·trəm] <-ra *o* -s> *n* **1.** PHYS espectro *m* **2.** (*range*) gama *f;* **the political ~** el espectro político

speculate ['spek·ju·leɪt] *vi* **1. to ~ about sth** (*hypothesize*) especular acerca de algo; (*conjecture*) hacer conjeturas acerca de algo **2.** (*buy and sell*) especular

speculation [ˌspek·ju·'leɪ·ʃən] *n* especulación *f,* conjetura *f;* **stock-market ~** especulación bursátil

speculative ['spek·jə·lə·t̬ɪv] *adj* especulativo, -a

speculator ['spek·ju·leɪ·t̬ər] *n* especulador(a) *m(f);* **property ~** especulador en bienes raíces

sped [sped] *pt, pp* of **speed**

speech [spitʃ] <-es> *n* **1.** (*capacity to speak*) habla *f;* **to lose/regain the power of ~** perder/recobrar el habla **2.** (*words*) palabras *fpl* **3.** (*public talk*) discurso *m;* **to make** [*o* **give**] **a ~** pronunciar un discurso

speech defect *n* defecto *m* del habla

speechify ['spi·tʃə·faɪ] *vi* perorar

speech impediment *n* defecto *m* del habla

speechless ['spitʃ·lɪs] *adj* mudo, -a; **to leave sb ~** dejar a alguien sin palabras

speech recognition *n* COMPUT, LING reconocimiento *m* de voz

speech therapist *n* logopeda *mf*

speech therapy *n* logopedia *f*

speechwriter *n persona que escribe discursos*

para políticos

speed [spid] **I.** *n* **1.** (*velocity*) velocidad *f;* **at a ~ of...** a una velocidad de... **2.** (*quickness*) rapidez *f* **3.** (*gear*) marcha *f* **4.** PHOT sensibilidad *f* **5.** *inf* (*amphetamine*) anfetas *fpl* **II.** *vi* <sped *o* speeded, sped *o* speeded> **1.** (*go fast*) ir de prisa; **to ~ by** pasar volando **2.** (*hasten*) apresurarse **3.** (*exceed speed restrictions*) ir a exceso de velocidad **III.** *vt* <sped *o* speeded, sped *o* speeded> acelerar; **to ~ sb on their way** despedir a alguien

◆ **speed off** <sped *o* speeded, sped *o* speeded> *vi* salir disparado

◆ **speed up** <sped *o* speeded, sped *o* speeded> **I.** *vi* (*car*) acelerar; (*process*) acelerarse; (*person*) darse prisa, apurarse *AmL* **II.** *vt* (*process*) acelerar, expeditar *AmL;* (*person*) apresurar

speedboat ['spid·bout] *n* lancha *f* motora

speed bump *n* banda *f* rugosa

speed dating *n forma de conseguir citas amorosas en poco tiempo para encontrar pareja, organizada por miembros de minorías étnicas, religiosas, sociales, etc.*

speed demon *n persona que conduce por encima de la velocidad máxima permitida*

speed dial *n* marcación *f* rápida; **on ~** de marcación rápida

speeding *n* exceso *m* de velocidad

speed limit *n* velocidad *f* máxima permitida

speedometer [spi·'dam·ə·t̬ər] *n* velocímetro *m*

speed skater *n* patinador(a) *m(f)* de velocidad

speed skating *n* patinaje *m* de velocidad

speed trap *n* control *m* de velocidad

speedway ['spid·weɪ] *n* **1.** (*racetrack*) pista *f* de carreras **2.** (*expressway*) autopista *f*

speedy ['spi·di] <-ier, -iest> *adj* veloz

speleologist [ˌspi·li·'al·ə·dʒɪst] *n* espeleólogo, -a

speleology [ˌspi·li·'al·ə·dʒi] *n* espeleología *f*

spell¹ [spel] <spelled *o* spelt, spelled *o* spelt> **I.** *vt* **1.** (*form using letters*) deletrear; **how do you ~ it?** ¿cómo se deletrea? **2.** (*signify*) significar; **this ~s trouble** esto significa problemas **II.** *vi* escribir; **to ~ well** escribir sin faltas de ortografía

spell² [spel] *n a. fig* encanto *m;* **to be under a ~** estar hechizado

spell³ [spel] **I.** *n* **1.** (*period*) temporada *f* **2.** (*turn*) turno *m* **II.** *vt* relevar

◆ **spell out** *vt* deletrear; **to spell sth out for sb** *fig* explicar algo a alguien de un modo sencillo

spellbinding ['spel·baɪn·dɪŋ] *adj* cautivador(a)

spellbound ['spel·baund] *adj* hechizado, -a; *fig* fascinado, -a

spell checker *n* COMPUT corrector *m* ortográfico

speller *n* **to be a good/poor ~** tener buena/mala ortografía

spelling *n* ortografía *f;* **~ mistake** falta *f* de

S

ortografía

spelling bee *n* concurso *m* de ortografía

spelt [spelt] *pp, pt of* **spell**

spend [spend] <spent, spent> **I.** *vt* **1.** (*money*) gastar **2.** (*time*) pasar; **to ~ time (doing sth**) dedicar tiempo (a hacer algo) **3.** (*use up*) agotar **II.** *vi* gastar

spending *n* gasto *m*; **public ~** el gasto público

spending cut *n* FIN recorte *m* presupuestario

spending money *n* dinero *m* para gastos personales

spending power *n* ECON poder *m* adquisitivo

spending spree *n* derroche *m* de dinero; **to go on a ~** gastar dinero a lo loco

spendthrift ['spend·θrɪft] *inf* **I.** *adj* derrochador(a), botado, -a *AmC* **II.** *n* derrochador(a) *m(f)*, botador(a) *m(f) AmL*

spent [spent] **I.** *pp, pt of* **spend II.** *adj* **1.** (*used*) gastado, -a; **to be a ~ force** haber perdido su vigor **2.** *liter* (*very tired*) agotado, -a

sperm [spɜrm] <-(s)> *n* esperma *m o f*

sperm count *n* recuento *m* de espermatozoides

sperm donor *n* donante *m* de esperma

spermicide ['spɜr·mə·saɪd] *n* espermicida *m*

sperm whale ['spɜrm·weɪl] *n* cachalote *m*

spew [spju] *vi, vt* vomitar

SPF [ˌes·pi·'ef] *n abbr of* **sun protection factor** factor *m* de protección solar

sphere [sfɪr] *n* esfera *f*; **~ of influence** ámbito *m* de influencia

spherical ['sfɪr·ɪ·kəl] *adj* esférico, -a

spice [spaɪs] **I.** *n* **1.** CULIN especia *f*, olor *m* Chile **2.** (*excitement*) picante *m*; **to give ~ to sth** dar sabor a algo; **the ~ of life** la sal de la vida **II.** *vt* condimentar

spic(k)-and-span [ˌspɪk·ən·'spæn] *adj inf* impecable

spicy ['spaɪ·si] <-ier, -iest> *adj* **1.** (*seasoned*) condimentado, -a **2.** (*sensational*) picante

spider ['spaɪ·dər] *n* araña *f*

spiderweb ['spaɪ·dər·web] *n* telaraña *f*

spidery *adj* delgado, -a; **~ handwriting** letra *f* de trazos largos e inseguros

spiel [ʃpil] *n inf* (*talk*) rollo *m*

spiffy ['spɪf·i] *adj inf* con estilo

spigot ['spɪg·ət] *n* **1.** (*stopper*) espita *f* **2.** (*tap*) grifo *m*

spike [spaɪk] **I.** *n* **1.** (*pointed object*) pincho *m* **2.** (*on shoes*) clavo *m* **3.** *pl* (*running shoes*) zapatillas *fpl* con clavos **4.** (*increase*) pico *m* **5.** SPORTS (*in volleyball*) remate *m* **II.** *vt* **1.** *inf* **to ~ a drink** echarle alcohol a una bebida **2.** (*injure*) pinchar **3.** (*secure*) clavar **4.** **to ~ the ball** (*in volleyball*) rematar; (*in football*) lanzar el balón contra el suelo, *después de conseguir un touchdown* **III.** *vi* experimentar un fuerte aumento

spiky ['spaɪ·ki] <-ier, -iest> *adj* **1.** (*sharp*) puntiagudo, -a; (*hair*) de punta **2.** *inf* (*irritable*) susceptible

spill [spɪl] **I.** *n* **1.** (*act of spilling*) derrame *m*; **oil ~** vertido *m* de petróleo **2.** *inf* (*fall*) caída *f*;

to take a ~ tener un accidente **II.** *vt* <spilled *o* spilt, spilled *o* spilt> derramar **III.** *vi* derramarse

♦ **spill over** *vi* derramarse

spillage ['spɪl·ɪdʒ] *n* derrame *m*

spilt [spɪlt] *pp, pt of* **spill**

spin [spɪn] **I.** *n* **1.** (*rotation*) vuelta *f* **2.** (*drive*) **to go** [*o* **take the car**] **for a ~** dar un paseo (en coche) **3.** (*in washing machine*) revolución *f* **II.** *vt* <spun, spun> **1.** (*rotate*) girar; (*clothes*) centrifugar; **to ~ a ball** dar efecto a una pelota **2.** (*make thread out of*) hilar **3.** (*tell: story, tale*) contar **III.** *vi* <spun, spun> **1.** (*rotate*) girar **2.** (*make thread*) hilar

♦ **spin around** *vi* girar

♦ **spin out I.** *vi* (*car*) perder el control y salirse de la trazada **II.** *vt* (*car*) hacer perder el control y salirse de la trazada

spina bifida [ˌspaɪ·nə·'bɪf·ɪ·də] *n* MED espina *f* bífida

spinach ['spɪn·ɪtʃ] *n* BOT espinaca *f*; CULIN espinacas *fpl*

spinal ['spaɪ·nəl] *adj* espinal

spinal column *n* columna *f* vertebral

spinal cord *n* médula *f* espinal

spinal tap *n* punción *f* lumbar

spindle ['spɪn·dəl] *n* huso *m*

spindly <-ier, -iest> *adj* larguirucho, -a

spin doctor *n* POL asesor(a) *m(f)* (*encargado, -a de garantizar que su candidato recibe la mejor publicidad posible*)

spin-drier *n s.* **spin-dryer**

spin-dry ['spɪn·draɪ] *vt* centrifugar

spin-dryer *n* centrifugadora *f*

spine [spaɪn] *n* **1.** (*spinal column*) columna *f* vertebral **2.** (*spike*) púa *f* **3.** (*of book*) lomo *m* **4.** BOT espina *f*

spine-chilling ['spaɪn·ˌtʃɪl·ɪŋ] *adj* escalofriante

spineless ['spaɪn·lɪs] *adj* (*weak*) blando, -a

spinner *n* **1.** (*person*) hilandero, -a *m, f* **2.** (*machine*) máquina *f* de hilar

spinning *n* **1.** (*turning*) rotación *f* **2.** SPORTS spinning *m*

spinning top *n* peonza *f*

spinning wheel *n* rueca *f*

spinoff *n*, **spin-off** ['spɪn·ɔf] *n* **1.** (*byproduct*) subproducto *m* **2.** (*consequence*) efecto *m* indirecto

spinster ['spɪn·stər] *n pej* (*old maid*) solterona *f*

spiny ['spaɪ·ni] <-ier, -iest> *adj a. fig* espinoso, -a

spiny lobster *n* langosta *f*

spiral ['spaɪ·rəl] **I.** *n* espiral *f* **II.** *adj* de [*o* en] espiral; **~ staircase** escalera *f* de caracol **III.** *vi* <-ll-, -l-> **1.** (*travel in a spiral*) dar vueltas en espiral; **to ~ downwards** bajar en espiral **2.** (*increase*) aumentar (a un ritmo cada vez mayor); (*decrease*) disminuir (a un ritmo cada vez mayor); **to ~ out of control** descontrolarse

spire [spaɪr] *n* ARCHIT aguja *f*

spirit ['spɪr·ɪt] *n* **1.** (*soul*) espíritu *m* **2.** (*ghost*)

espíritu *m* **3.** *pl* (*mood*) ánimo *mpl;* **to be in high/low ~s** estar animado/desanimado **4.** (*character*) carácter *m* **5.** *pl* (*alcoholic drink*) licor *m* **6.** (*attitude or principle*) **the ~ of the age** el espíritu de la época; **that's the ~!** ¡muy bien!
◆**spirit away** *vt* hacer desaparecer
spirited *adj* (*energetic*) enérgico, -a; (*discussion*) animado, -a; (*person*) animoso, -a, entrador(a) *AmS*
spiritless ['spɪr·ɪt·lɪs] *adj pej* **1.** (*downhearted*) desanimado, -a **2.** (*irresolute*) indeciso, -a
spiritual ['spɪr·ɪ·tʃu·əl] **I.** *adj* espiritual **II.** *n* MUS espiritual *m* negro
spiritualism ['spɪr·ɪ·tʃu·ə·lɪz·əm] *n* espiritismo *m*
spit¹ [spɪt] **I.** *n inf* saliva *f* **II.** *vi* <spat, spat> **1.** (*expel saliva*) escupir **2.** (*crackle*) chisporrotear **III.** *vt* escupir
◆**spit out** *vt* **1.** (*expel from mouth*) escupir **2.** (*say angrily*) soltar; **spit it out!** *inf* ¡desembucha!
spit² [spɪt] *n* **1.** CULIN asador *m* **2.** (*sandbar*) banco *m* de arena
spite [spaɪt] **I.** *n* rencor *m;* **to do sth out of ~** hacer algo por despecho; **in ~ of** a pesar de; **in ~ of everyone/everything** a despecho de todos/todo; **in ~ of the fact that he is rich** a pesar (del hecho) de que sea rico **II.** *vt* fastidiar
spiteful ['spaɪt·fəl] *adj pej* rencoroso, -a
spitting image *n* vivo *m* retrato
spittle ['spɪt̬·əl] *n* escupitajo *m*, desgarro *m AmL*
spittoon [spɪ·'tun] *n* escupidera *f*, salivadera *f Arg, Urug*
splash [splæʃ] **I.** *n* **1.** (*sound*) chapoteo *m* **2.** (*small drops*) salpicadura *f*; **a ~ of color** una mancha de color ▶**to make a** (**big**) **~** causar sensación **II.** *vt* salpicar; **to ~ across the front page** poner algo en primera plana **III.** *vi* salpicar
◆**splash down** *vi* amerizar
splashboard ['splæʃ·bɔrd] *n* (*on vehicle*) guardabarros *m inv*; (*on boat, in kitchen*) alero *m*
splashdown ['splæʃ·daʊn] *n* amerizaje *m*
splash-resistant *adj* resistente al agua
splat [splæt] *n inf* plaf *m*
splatter ['splæt̬·ər] *vi, vt* salpicar
splay [spleɪ] **I.** *vt* extender **II.** *vi* extenderse
spleen [splin] *n* **1.** ANAT bazo *m* **2.** (*anger*) mal humor *m;* **to vent one's ~** descargar la rabia de uno
splendid ['splen·dɪd] *adj* espléndido, -a
splendiferous [splen·'dɪf·ər·əs] *adj inf* espléndido, -a
splendor ['splen·dər] *n* **1.** (*grandness*) esplendor *m* **2.** *pl* (*beautiful things*) maravillas *fpl*
splice [splaɪs] *vt* (*join*) juntar; **to get ~d** *inf* pasar por la vicaría
splint [splɪnt] **I.** *n* tablilla *f* **II.** *vt* entablillar
splinter ['splɪn·tər] **I.** *n* astilla *f* **II.** *vi* astillarse

splinter group *n* POL grupo *m* disidente
split [splɪt] **I.** *n* **1.** (*crack*) grieta **2.** (*in clothes*) desgarrón **3.** (*division*) división *f* **II.** *vt* <split, split> **1.** (*divide*) dividir; (*atom*) desintegrar; **to ~ sth between two people** repartir algo entre dos personas **2.** (*crack*) agrietar; **to ~ one's head open** abrirse la cabeza ▶**to ~ one's sides laughing** partirse de risa; **to ~ hairs** buscarle tres pies al gato **III.** *vi* <split, split> **1.** (*divide*) dividirse **2.** (*form cracks*) agrietarse **3.** *inf* (*leave*) largarse
◆**split off I.** *vt* separar **II.** *vi* separarse
◆**split up I.** *vt* partir **II.** *vi* **to ~ with sb** separarse de alguien
split infinitive *n* LING *infinitivo con un complemento adverbial intercalado entre la partícula 'to' y el verbo*
split-level *adj* de varios niveles
split pea *n* guisante *m* seco
split personality *n* PSYCH doble personalidad *f*
split screen *n* pantalla *f* dividida
split second *n* instante *m*
splitting headache *n inf* dolor *m* de cabeza atroz
split-up ['splɪt·ʌp] *n* ruptura *m*
splotch [splatʃ] *n* mancha *f*
splurge [splɜrdʒ] *inf* **I.** *vi* derrochar dinero **II.** *vt* derrochar **III.** *n* derroche *m*
splutter ['splʌt̬·ər] **I.** *vi* (*person*) farfullar; (*candle, engine*) chisporrotear **II.** *n* (*of person*) farfulla *f*; (*of candle, engine*) chisporroteo *m*
spoil [spɔɪl] **I.** *vt* <spoiled *o* spoilt, spoiled *o* spoilt> **1.** (*ruin*) estropear, salar *AmL;* (*party*) aguar **2.** (*child*) mimar demasiado, engreír *AmL*, papachar *Méx* **II.** *vi* <spoiled *o* spoilt, spoiled *o* spoilt> estropearse **III.** *n* **1.** *pl* (*profits*) botín *m* **2.** (*debris*) escombros *mpl*
spoiler *n* AUTO alerón *m*
spoilsport ['spɔɪl·spɔrt] *n inf* aguafiestas *mf inv*
spoilt [spɔɪlt] **I.** *pp, pt of* **spoil II.** *adj* mimado, -a, engreído, -a *AmL*
spoke¹ [spoʊk] *pt of* **speak**
spoke² [spoʊk] *n* (*of wheel*) radio *m;* **to put a ~ in sb's wheel** *fig* poner trabas a alguien
spoken [spoʊkn] *pp of* **speak**
spokesman ['spoʊks·mən] *n* portavoz *m*, vocero *m AmL*
spokesperson ['spoʊks·ˌpɜr·sən] *n* portavoz *mf*, vocero, -a *m, f AmL*
spokeswoman ['spoʊks·ˌwʊm·ən] *n* portavoz *f*, vocera *f AmL*
sponge [spʌndʒ] **I.** *n* **1.** (*animal*) esponja *f* **2.** (*absorbent*) esponja *f* **3.** (*person*) gorrón, -ona *m, f* **II.** *vt* limpiar con una esponja **III.** *vi inf* gorronear
◆**sponge down** *vt* limpiar con una esponja
◆**sponge off** *vt* **1.** (*clean*) limpiar con una esponja **2.** *inf* vivir a costa de
◆**sponge up** *vt* limpiar con una esponja
sponge bath *n* baño *m* con esponja
sponge cake *n* bizcocho *m*

S

sponger *n pej* gorrón, -ona *m, f*, sablero, -a *m, f* Chile

spongy ['spʌn·dʒi] <-ier, -iest> *adj* esponjoso, -a

sponsor ['span·sər] I. *vt* patrocinar II. *n* patrocinador(a) *m(f)*, propiciador(a) *m(f)* AmL

sponsorship *n* patrocinio *m*

spontaneity [ˌspan·tə·'neɪ·ə·t̪i] *n* espontaneidad *f*

spontaneous [span·'teɪ·ni·əs] *adj* espontáneo, -a

spoof [spuf] *n* parodia *f;* to do a ~ on sth parodiar algo

spook [spuk] I. *n* 1. *inf* (ghost) espectro *m* 2. *sl* (spy) espía *mf* II. *vt* asustar

spooky ['spu·ki] <-ier, -iest> *adj inf* que da miedo

spool [spul] *n* (of thread) bobina *f;* (of film) carrete *m*

spoon [spun] I. *n* 1. (utensil) cuchara *f* 2. (amount) cucharada *f* II. *vt* servir con cuchara

spoonbill ['spun·bɪl] *n* espátula *f*

spoon-feed ['spun·fid] *vt* 1. (feed) dar de comer con cuchara 2. *pej* to ~ sb dar todo masticado a alguien

spoonful ['spun·fʊl] <-s *o* spoonsful> *n* cucharada *f*

sporadic [spə·'ræd·ɪk] *adj* esporádico, -a

spore [spɔr] *n* espora *f*

sport [spɔrt] I. *n* 1. (activity) deporte *m* 2. *inf* (person) to be a good/poor ~ ser buena/mala gente; (in games, sports) ser un buen/mal perdedor II. *vt* llevar

sport coat *n* americana *f*

sporting *adj* deportivo, -a, esportivo, -a AmL

sports car *n* (coche *m*) deportivo *m*

sportscast ['spɔrts·kæst] *n* retransmisión *f* deportiva

sportscaster *n* locutor(a) *m(f)* deportivo, -a

sportsman ['spɔrts·mən] *n* deportista *m*

sportsmanlike ['spɔrts·mən·laɪk] *adj* de espíritu deportivo

sportsmanship *n* deportividad *f*

sports page *n* página *f* de deportes

sportswear *n* ropa *f* de deporte

sportswoman ['spɔrts·ˌwʊm·ən] *n* deportista *f*

sportswriter *n* cronista *mf* deportivo, -a

sporty ['spɔr·t̪i] <-ier, -iest> *adj* deportivo, -a

spot [spat] I. *n* 1. (mark) mancha *f* 2. (pattern) lunar *m* 3. (on skin) grano *m* 4. (place) lugar *m;* on the ~ (at the very place) in situ; (at once) en el acto 5. (part of TV, radio show) espacio *m* 6. *inf* foco *m* ▶ to really hit the ~ venir de perlas; to have a **soft** ~ for sb tener debilidad por alguien; to **put** sb on the ~ poner a alguien en un aprieto II. <-tt-> *vt* 1. (see) divisar 2. (speckle) manchar

spot check *n* control *m* al azar

spotless ['spat·lɪs] *adj* 1. (very clean) sin manchas, inmaculado, -a 2. (unblemished) sin mancha

spotlight ['spat·laɪt] I. *n* foco *m* ▶ to **be in the** ~ ser el centro de atención II. <spotlighted *o* spotlit, spotlighted *o* spotlit> *vt* iluminar

spot market *n* FIN mercado *m* al contado

spot price *n* precio *m* al contado

spotted *adj* manchado, -a; a ~ dress un vestido de lunares

spotter *n* SPORTS, AVIAT observador(a) *m(f)*

spotty ['spat·i] <-ier, -iest> *adj* 1. (having blemished skin) con granos 2. (inconsistent) irregular

spouse [spaʊs] *n form* cónyuge *mf*

spout [spaʊt] I. *n* 1. (of kettle) pitorro *m;* (of jar) pico *m;* (tube) caño *m* 2. (jet) chorro *m* II. *vt* 1. (send out: flames, water) echar 2. *pej* to ~ sth perorar sobre algo; to ~ facts and figures soltar una retahíla de datos y cifras III. *vi* 1. (gush) chorrear 2. *pej* (speechify) perorar

sprain [spreɪn] I. *vt* torcer II. *n* torcedura *f*

sprang [spræŋ] *vi, vt pt of* spring

sprat [spræt] *n* (fish) espadín *m*

sprawl [sprɔl] *pej* I. *vi* 1. (spread out) tumbarse; to send sb ~ing derribar a alguien 2. (town) extenderse II. *n* (of town) extensión *f;* urban ~ expansión urbana descontrolada

sprawling *adj pej* 1. (town) de crecimiento descontrolado 2. (handwriting) irregular

spray[1] [spreɪ] I. *n* 1. (mist) rocío *m* 2. (device) spray *m* II. *vt* (cover in a spray) rociar III. *vi* (gush) chorrear

spray[2] [spreɪ] *n* rama *f;* a ~ of flowers un ramo de flores

spray gun *n* pistola *f* pulverizadora

spread [spred] I. *n* 1. (act of spreading) propagación *f* 2. (range) gama *f* 3. (article) a fullpage ~ reportaje *m* a toda página 4. CULIN pasta *f* (para untar en pan o galletas) 5. (ranch) hacienda *f*, rancho *m* AmL 6. *inf* (meal) comilona *f* 7. SPORTS (number of points) point ~ diferencia por la que se espera que un equipo gane a otro al final del partido II. <spread, spread> *vt* 1. (news) difundir; (disease) propagar 2. (butter) untar 3. (payments, work) distribuir 4. (unfold: map, blanket) extender III. <spread, spread> *vi* (news) difundirse; (disease) propagarse; (liquid) extenderse

spread-eagled ['spred·'i·gəld] *adj* despatarrado, -a

spreadsheet ['spred·ʃit] *n* COMPUT hoja *f* de cálculo

spree [spri] *n* parranda *f*, tambarria *f* AmC; to go (out) on a drinking ~ ir de juerga; to go on a shopping ~ irse de compras a gastar mucho dinero

sprig [sprɪg] *n* ramita *f*

sprightly ['spraɪt·li] <-ier, -iest> *adj* vivaz

spring [sprɪŋ] I. *n* 1. (season) primavera *f* 2. (jump) salto *m* 3. (metal coil) muelle *m;* (in watch, toy) resorte *m* 4. (elasticity) elasticidad *f* 5. (source of water) manantial *m*, yurro *m* CRi II. <sprang, sprung> *vi* saltar; to ~ to one's feet levantarse de un salto; to ~ shut/open cerrarse/abrirse de golpe III. <sprang, sprung> *vt* to ~ sth on sb soltar algo a alguien

♦ **spring back** *vi* saltar para atrás

springboard ['sprɪŋ·bɔrd] *n* trampolín *m*

spring break *n* vacaciones *fpl* de primavera (*semana de vacaciones durante la evaluación de primavera en Estados Unidos*)

spring chicken *n* **to not be a ~** ya no ser ningún crío

spring-clean [,sprɪŋ·'klin] *vt* limpiar a fondo

spring-cleaning *n* limpieza *f* a fondo

spring roll *n* rollito *m* de primavera

springtime ['sprɪŋ·taɪm] *n* primavera *f*

springy ['sprɪŋ·i] <-ier, -iest> *adj* elástico, -a

sprinkle ['sprɪŋ·kəl] I. *vt* salpicar II. *n* salpicadura *f*

sprinkler ['sprɪŋ·klər] *n* aspersor *m*

sprinkling ['sprɪŋ·klɪŋ] *n* **a ~ of sth** unas gotas de algo

sprint [sprɪnt] SPORTS I. *vi* esprintar II. *n* **1.** (*race*) esprint *m* **2.** (*burst of speed*) carrera *f* corta

sprinter ['sprɪn·tər] *n* velocista *mf*

sprite [spraɪt] *n liter* duende *m*

sprocket ['sprak·ɪt] *n*, **sprocket wheel** *n* rueda *f* dentada

sprout [spraʊt] I. *n* **1.** (*of plant*) brote *m* **2.** *pl* (*Brussels sprouts*) coles *mpl* de Bruselas II. *vi* (*begin to grow*) brotar III. *vt* (*grow: leaves*) echar

♦ **sprout up** *vi* (*plant, child*) crecer rápidamente; (*building*) aparecer

spruce[1] [sprus] *n* BOT picea *f*

spruce[2] [sprus] *adj* aseado, -a

♦ **spruce up** *vt* **to spruce oneself up** arreglarse

sprung [sprʌŋ] *pp, Am: pt of* **spring**

spry [spraɪ] *adj* ágil

spud [spʌd] *n inf* patata *f*, papa *f AmL*

spun [spʌn] *pp, pt of* **spin**

spunk [spʌŋk] *n inf* agallas *fpl*, coraje *m*

spunky ['spʌŋ·ki] *adj* con arrojo

spur [spɜr] I. <-rr-> *vt* (*horse*) espolear, talonear *Arg; fig* estimular II. *n* **1.** (*device*) espuela *f* **2.** GEO espolón *m* **3.** (*encouragement*) estímulo *m* ▶ **on the ~ of the moment** *inf* sin pensarlo

spurious ['spjʊr·i·əs] *adj* falso, -a

spurn [spɜrn] *vt form* desdeñar

spurt [spɜrt] I. *n* **1.** (*jet*) chorro *m* **2.** (*burst*) esfuerzo *m* supremo; **a growth ~** un crecimiento repentino II. *vi* **1.** (*gush*) salir a chorros **2.** (*accelerate*) acelerar III. *vt* (*liquid*) echar

sputter ['spʌt·ər] I. *vi* (*person*) farfullar; (*candle, engine*) chisporrotear II. *n* (*of person*) farfulla *f;* (*of candle, engine*) chisporroteo *m*

sputum ['spju·țəm] *n* esputo *m*

spy [spaɪ] I. *n* espía *mf* II. *vi* espiar; **to ~ on sb** espiar a alguien III. *vt* divisar

spyglass ['spaɪ·glæs] *n* catalejo *m*

spyhole ['spaɪ·hoʊl] *n* mirilla *f*

spy satellite *n* satélite *m* espía

spyware ['spaɪ·wer] *n* COMPUT software *m*

espía

Sq. *abbr of* **square** Pza.

squabble ['skwab·əl] I. *n* riña *f* II. *vi* reñir

squad [skwad] *n* **1.** (*group*) pelotón *m; (of police*) brigada *f;* **anti-terrorist ~** brigada anti-terrorista **2.** (*sports team*) equipo *m*

squad car *n* coche *m* patrulla

squadron ['skwad·rən] *n* escuadrón *m*

squalid ['skwal·ɪd] *adj* **1.** *pej* (*dirty*) asqueroso, -a **2.** (*sordid*) sórdido, -a

squall [skwɔl] I. *n* ráfaga *f* II. *vi* chillar

squally ['skwɔ·li] *adj* turbulento, -a

squalor ['skwal·ər] *n* miseria *f*

squander ['skwan·dər] *vt* malgastar, botar *AmL;* **to ~ an opportunity** desperdiciar una oportunidad; **to ~ the lead** dilapidar la ventaja

square [skwer] I. *n* **1.** (*shape*) cuadrado *m* **2.** (*in town*) plaza *f* **3.** (*on chessboard*) casilla *f* **4.** (*tool*) escuadra *f* **5.** MATH cuadrado *m* ▶ **to go back to ~ one** volver al punto de partida II. *adj* **1.** (*square-shaped*) cuadrado, -a; **forty-three ~ feet** cuatro metros cuadrados **2.** (*fair*) **a ~ deal** un trato justo **3.** (*not owing anything*) en paz **4.** *sl* (*boring*) **be there or be ~** si no lo haces, eres un muermo III. *vt* **1.** (*make square*) cuadrar **2.** (*settle*) acomodar; **to ~ one's accounts** saldar sus cuentas **3.** MATH elevar al cuadrado IV. *vi* **to ~ with the facts** concordar con los hechos V. *adv* justamente; **to run** [*o* **drive**] **~ into sth** chocar de lleno contra algo

♦ **square up** *vi* **to ~ with sb** ajustar cuentas con alguien

square bracket *n* corchete *m*

square dance *n* baile *m* de figuras

> ℹ️ **Square dance** es el nombre de un tradicional estilo de baile norteamericano. Grupos de cuatro parejas bailan en círculo, en cuadro o formando dos líneas. Todos llevan a cabo los movimientos indicados por un **caller**. Éste puede dar las indicaciones cantando o dando voces. Los bailarines suelen bailar con acompañamiento de violín, bajo y banjo.

---

squarely *adv* directamente

square root *n* raíz *f* cuadrada

squash[1] [skwaʃ] *n* (*vegetable*) calabaza *f*

squash[2] [skwaʃ] I. *n* **1.** SPORTS squash *m* **2.** (*dense pack*) apiñamiento *m* II. *vt* aplastar

squash court *n* pista *f* de squash

squash racket *n*, **squash racquet** *n* raqueta *f* de squash

squashy ['skwaʃ·i] <-ier, -iest> *adj* blando, -a

squat [skwat] I. <-tt-> *vi* **1.** (*crouch down*) agacharse, ñangotarse *PRico, RDom* **2.** (*in property*) ocupar una vivienda sin permiso II. *n* **1.** (*exercise*) sentadilla *f* **2.** *sl* (*nothing*) **to not know ~** no tener ni idea III. <-tt-> *adj*

(*person*) rechoncho, -a
squatter ['skwaţ·ər] *n* okupa *mf*
squaw [skwɔ] *n a. pej: mujer india norteameri-cana*
squawk [skwɔk] **I.** *vi* graznar **II.** *n* graznido *m*
squeak [skwik] **I.** *n* chirrido *m* **II.** *vi* chirriar
squeaky ['skwi·ki] <-ier, -iest> *adj* chirriante
squeaky-clean [ˌskwi·ki·'klin] *adj* requetelim-pio, -a
squeal [skwil] **I.** *n* chillido *m* **II.** *vi* **1.** (*person, animal*) chillar; (*brakes, car*) chirriar **2.** *sl* (*inform on sb*) chivarse
◆ **squeal on** *vt sl* **to ~ sb** delatar a alguien
squeamish ['skwi·mɪʃ] *adj* remilgado, -a; **to feel ~** sentir náuseas
squeegee ['skwi·dʒi] *n* escobilla *f* de goma
squeeze [skwiz] **I.** *n* **1.** (*pressing action*) estru-jón *m* **2.** ECON (*limit*) restricción *f* **3.** (*pressure*) **to put the ~ on sb** apretar a alguien a **4.** *fig, sl* mi cariñito **II.** *vt* **1.** (*press together*) estrujar; **freshly ~d orange juice** zumo de naranja recién exprimido **2.** (*force*) presionar; **to ~ sth out of sb** sacarle algo a alguien
squeezer ['skwi·zər] *n* exprimidor *m*
squelch [skweltʃ] **I.** *vi* chapotear **II.** *vt* aplastar **III.** *n* chapoteo *m*
squid [skwɪd] <-(s)> *n* calamar *m*
squiggle ['skwɪg·əl] **I.** *n* garabato *m* **II.** *vi* gara-batear
squint [skwɪnt] **I.** *vi* **1.** (*be cross-eyed*) biz-quear **2.** (*look from corner of eye*) mirar de reojo; (*with eyes partly closed*) mirar con los ojos entrecerrados **II.** *n* **1.** (*eye condition*) estrabismo *m*, bizquera *f AmL* **2.** (*quick look*) mirada *f* furtiva
squire [skwaɪr] *n* HIST escudero *m*
squirm [skwɜrm] *vi* retorcerse; **to ~ with embarrassment** avergonzarse mucho
squirrel ['skwɜr·əl] *n* ardilla *f*
squirt [skwɜrt] **I.** *vt* (*liquid*) echar un chorro de; **to ~ sb with sth** echar un chorro de algo a alguien **II.** *vi* salir a chorros **III.** *n* **1.** (*small quantity*) chorrito *m* **2.** *pej* (*person*) farsante *mf*
Sr. *n abbr of* **senior** padre; **Henry Smith, Sr.** Henry Smith, padre
Sri Lanka [ˌsri·'laŋ·kə] *n* Sri Lanka *m*
Sri Lankan [ˌsri·'laŋ·kən] **I.** *adj* esrilanqués, -esa **II.** *n* esrilanqués, -esa *m, f*
SRO [ˌes·ar·'ou] *abbr of* **standing room only ~ tickets** entradas *fpl* de pie
SSE [ˌes·es·'i] *abbr of* **south-southeast** SSE *m*
SSgt. *n abbr of* **staff sergeant** sargento *mf* tercero
SSW [ˌes·es·'dʌb·əl·ju] *abbr of* **south-south-west** SSO
St. *n* **1.** *abbr of* **saint** S.; **~ Thomas** Sto. Tomás **2.** *abbr of* **street** c/
stab [stæb] **I.** <-bb-> *vt* apuñalar, achurar *CSur;* carnear *Méx;* **to ~ sb to death** matar a alguien de una puñalada; **to ~ sb in the back** *fig* dar a alguien una puñalada trapera **II.** <-bb-> *vi* señalar **III.** *n* **1.** (*blow*) puñalada

f **2.** (*sudden pain*) punzada *f* **3.** (*attempt*) **to take a ~ at** (**doing**) **sth** intentar (hacer) algo
stabbing **I.** *n* apuñalamiento *m* **II.** *adj* pun-zante
stability [stə·'bɪl·ə·ţi] *n* estabilidad *f*
stabilization [ˌster·bə·lɪ·'zeɪ·ʃən] *n* estabiliza-ción *f*
stabilize ['ster·bə·laɪz] **I.** *vt* estabilizar **II.** *vi* estabilizarse
stabilizer ['ster·bə·laɪ·zər] *n* **1.** (*on ship, bicycle*) estabilizador *m* **2.** CHEM estabili-zante *m*
stable¹ ['ster·bəl] *adj* **1.** *a.* ECON estable **2.** (*structure*) firme **3.** MED estacionario, -a
stable² ['ster·bəl] **I.** *n* cuadra *f* **II.** *vt* guardar en la cuadra
stack [stæk] **I.** *vt* **1.** (*arrange in a pile*) apilar **2.** (*fill: shelves*) llenar ▶ **the cards are ~ed against us** la suerte está en contra de nosotros **II.** *n* **1.** (*pile*) pila *f* **2.** *inf* (*large amount*) mon-tón *m*, ponchada *f CSur* **3.** *pl* (*bookcase*) estantería *f*
stadium ['ster·di·əm] <-s *o* -dia> *n* estadio *m*
staff [stæf] **I.** *n* **1.** (*employees*) personal *m*, elenco *m AmL;* **the editorial ~** la redacción; **the teaching ~** el claustro (de profesores) **2.** MIL Estado *m* Mayor **3.** (*stick*) bastón *m;* **~ of office** bastón de mando **4.** (*flagpole*) asta *f* **5.** <staves> MUS pentagrama *m* **II.** *vt* dotar de personal
staff sergeant *n* sargento *mf* tercero
stag [stæg] *n* **1.** ZOOL ciervo *m* **2.** (*unaccom-panied male*) hombre *m* solo (*en una fiesta o reunión social*)
stag beetle *n* ciervo *m* volante
stage [steɪdʒ] **I.** *n* **1.** (*period*) etapa *f*, pascana *f AmS;* **at this ~ in my life** en esta etapa de mi vida; **to do sth in ~s** hacer algo por etapas **2.** THEAT escena *f;* **the ~** el teatro; **to be on the ~** ser actor/actriz; **to go on the ~** hacerse actor/actriz; **to hold the ~** tener al público pendiente de su palabra **II.** *vt* **1.** (*produce on stage*) representar **2.** (*organize*) organizar
stagecoach ['steɪdʒ·koutʃ] *n* diligencia *f*
stage door *n* entrada *f* de artistas
stage fright *n* miedo *m* escénico
stagehand ['steɪdʒ·hænd] *n* THEAT tramoyista *mf*
stage-manage ['steɪdʒ·ˌmæn·ɪdʒ] *vt* **1.** THEAT dirigir la tramoya de **2.** *fig* orquestar
stage manager *n* THEAT director(a) *m(f)* de escena; CINE director(a) *m(f)* de producción
stage name *n* nombre *m* artístico
stage whisper *n* THEAT aparte *m*
stagflation [ˌstæg·'fleɪ·ʃən] *n* ECON estagfla-ción *f*
stagger ['stæg·ər] **I.** *vi* tambalearse **II.** *vt* **1.** (*amaze*) asombrar **2.** (*work, payments*) escalonar **III.** *n* tambaleo *m*
staggering *adj* (*amazing*) sorprendente
staging ['steɪ·dʒɪŋ] *n* THEAT puesta *f* en escena
stagnant ['stæg·nənt] *adj a. fig* estancado, -a
stagnate ['stæg·neɪt] *vi* estancarse

stagnation [stæg·'neɪ·ʃən] *n* estancamiento *m*
stag party *n* despedida *f* de soltero
stagy ['steɪ·dʒi] *adj pej* teatral
staid [steɪd] *adj* serio, -a
stain [steɪn] I. *vt* 1. (*mark*) manchar 2. (*dye*) teñir II. *vi* (*become marked*) mancharse III. *n* 1. (*mark*) mancha *f;* **blood/grease/red wine** ~ mancha *f* de sangre/grasa/vino tinto 2. (*dye*) tinte *m*
stained *adj* (*marked*) manchado, -a
stained glass *n* vidrio *m* de colores
stained-glass window *n* vidriera *f* (de colores)
stainless ['steɪn·lɪs] I. *adj* (*immaculate*) inmaculado, -a; (*that cannot be stained*) que no se mancha II. *n* acero *m* inoxidable
stainless steel *n* acero *m* inoxidable
stain remover *n* quitamanchas *m inv*
stair [ster] *n* 1. (*rung*) peldaño *m* 2. *pl* (*set of steps*) escalera *f*
staircase ['ster·keɪs] *n*, **stairway** ['ster·weɪ] *n* escalera *f*
stairwell ['ster·wel] *n* hueco *m* de la escalera
stake [steɪk] I. *n* 1. (*stick*) estaca *f;* **to be burnt at the** ~ HIST morir en la hoguera 2. (*share*) participación *f;* **to have a** ~ **in sth** tener interés en algo 3. (*bet*) apuesta *f;* **to play for high** ~s arriesgar mucho; **to be at** ~ estar en juego II. *vt* 1. (*mark with stakes*) marcar con estacas 2. (*bet*) apostar; **to** ~ **one's life on sth** poner la mano en el fuego por algo; **to** ~ **a claim to sth** reivindicar algo
◆ **stake out** *vt inf* poner bajo vigilancia
stakeholder ['steɪk·ˌhoʊl·dər] *n* tenedor(a) *m(f)* de apuestas
stakeout ['steɪk·ˌaʊt] *n* operación *f* de vigilancia
stalactite [stə·'læk·taɪt] *n* estalactita *f*
stalagmite [stə·'læg·maɪt] *n* estalagmita *f*
stale [steɪl] *adj* 1. (*not fresh*) pasado, -a; (*bread*) duro, -a; (*air*) viciado, -a; (*joke*) viejo, -a 2. (*tired*) cansado, -a
stalemate ['steɪl·meɪt] *n* 1. (*deadlock*) punto *m* muerto 2. GAMES tablas *fpl*
stalk[1] [stɔk] *n* (*of plant*) tallo *m;* **her eyes were out on** ~s se le salían los ojos de las órbitas
stalk[2] [stɔk] I. *vt* (*follow*) acechar II. *vi* **to** ~ **off** marcharse airadamente
stalker *n persona que sigue obsesivamente a otra*
stalking-horse *n* POL *candidato que se presenta para favorecer a otro*
stall [stɔl] I. *n* 1. (*for animal*) establo *m* 2. (*in market*) puesto *m*, tarantín *m Ven* 3. AUTO (*engine trouble*) calado *m* 4. (*compartment*) **shower** ~ cabina para ducharse; **toilet** ~ urinario II. *vi* 1. (*stop running: engine, vehicle*) calarse 2. *fig, inf* (*delay*) ir con rodeos; **to** ~ **for time** intentar ganar tiempo III. *vt* 1. (*engine, vehicle*) calar 2. *fig, inf* (*keep waiting*) retener
stallion ['stæl·jən] *n* semental *m*, padrón *m AmL*, padrote *m AmC, Méx*

stalwart ['stɔl·wərt] *form* I. *adj* 1. (*strong*) fornido, -a 2. (*loyal*) leal II. *n* partidario, -a *m, f* leal
stamen ['steɪ·men] <-s *o* -mina> *n* estambre *m*
stamina ['stæm·ə·nə] *n* resistencia *f*
stammer ['stæm·ər] I. *vi* tartamudear II. *vt* decir tartamudeando III. *n* tartamudeo *m*
stamp [stæmp] I. *n* 1. (*postage stamp*) sello *m*, estampilla *f AmL;* (*device*) tampón *m;* (*mark*) sello *m* 2. (*characteristic quality*) impronta *f* 3. (*with foot*) pisotón *m* II. *vt* 1. (*place postage stamp on*) pegar un sello en 2. (*impress a mark on*) estampar 3. **to** ~ **one's foot** patear (contra el suelo) III. *vi* patalear (contra el suelo)
◆ **stamp out** *vt* (*fire*) extinguir (con los pies)
stamp album *n* álbum *m* de sellos
stamp collector *n* coleccionista *mf* de sellos
stampede [stæm·'pid] I. *n* (*of animals*) estampida *f;* (*of people*) desbandada *f* II. *vi* huir en desbandada III. *vt* 1. (*cause to stampede*) provocar la desbandada de 2. (*force*) empujar; **to** ~ **sb into** (**doing**) **sth** empujar a alguien a (hacer) algo
stamping ground *n s.* **stomping ground**
stance [stæns] *n* postura *f*
stanch[1] [stɔntʃ] *adj s.* **staunch**
stanch[2] [stɔntʃ] *vt* restañar
stand [stænd] I. *n* 1. (*position*) posición *f;* **to take a** ~ **on** (**doing**) **sth** adoptar una postura con respecto a (hacer) algo; **to make a** ~ **against sth** oponer resistencia a algo 2. *pl* (*in stadium*) tribuna *f* 3. (*support, frame*) soporte *m;* **music** ~ atril *m* 4. (*market stall*) puesto *m*, trucha *f AmC* 5. (*for vehicles*) parada *f;* **taxi** ~ parada de taxis 6. LAW **witness** ~ estrado *m;* **to take the** ~ subir al estrado 7. (*group*) **a** ~ **of trees** un grupo de árboles II. <stood, stood> *vi* 1. (*be upright*) estar de pie; **to** ~ **6 feet tall** medir dos metros; **to** ~ **still** estarse quieto 2. (*be located*) encontrarse 3. (*remain unchanged: decision, law*) mantenerse en vigor III. <stood, stood> *vt* 1. (*place*) poner (de pie), colocar 2. (*bear*) aguantar; **I can't** ~ **her** no la soporto 3. LAW **to** ~ **trial** ser juzgado
◆ **stand about** *vi*, **stand around** *vi* esperar
◆ **stand aside** *vi* 1. (*move*) apartarse 2. (*stay*) mantenerse aparte
◆ **stand back** *vi* 1. (*move backwards*) retroceder 2. (*be objective*) distanciarse
◆ **stand by** I. *vi* 1. (*observe*) quedarse sin hacer nada 2. (*be ready to take action*) estar alerta II. *vt* (*support*) apoyar
◆ **stand down** *vi* renunciar
◆ **stand for** *vt* 1. (*represent*) representar; (*mean*) significar 2. (*believe in*) creer en 3. (*tolerate*) aguantar
◆ **stand in** *vi* **to** ~ **for sb** suplir a alguien
◆ **stand out** *vi* destacar
◆ **stand over** *vt* vigilar
◆ **stand up** I. *vi* 1. (*be upright*) levantarse, arriscarse *Col* 2. (*evidence, argument*) ser con-

S

vincente; **to ~ in court** sostenerse en el juicio ▶**to ~ and be** counted declararse abiertamente **II.** *vt* **to stand sb up** dar un plantón a alguien

standalone *n*, **stand-alone** ['stænd·ə·ˌloʊn] *adj* COMPUT **~ computer network** red *f* de ordenadores autónoma

standard ['stæn·dərd] **I.** *n* **1.** (*level*) nivel *m;* (*quality*) clase *f* **2.** (*norm*) norma *f* **3.** (*flag*) estandarte *m* **4.** MUS clásico *m* **II.** *adj* **1.** (*normal*) normal; (*procedure*) habitual **2.** LING estándar

standard-bearer ['stæn·dərd·ˌber·ər] *n* abanderado, -a *m, f*

standardization [ˌstæn·dər·dɪ·'zeɪ·ʃən] *n* estandarización *f;* TECH normalización *f*

standardize ['stæn·dər·daɪz] *vt* estandarizar; TECH normalizar

standard size *n* talla *f* estándar

standby ['stænd·baɪ] **I.** *n* **1.** (*of money, food*) reserva *f* **2.** AVIAT lista *f* de espera; **to be** (**put**) **on ~** estar sobre aviso; **to be on 24-hour ~** estar listo para partir dentro de 24 horas **II.** *adj* de reserva

stand-in ['stænd·ɪn] *n* suplente *mf;* CINE doble *mf*

standing ['stæn·dɪŋ] **I.** *n* **1.** (*status*) posición *f* **2.** (*duration*) duración *f;* **of long ~** desde hace mucho tiempo **II.** *adj* **1.** (*upright*) vertical **2.** (*permanent*) permanente **3.** (*water*) estancado, -a

standing order *n* pedido *m* regular

standing ovation *n* ovación *f* en pie

standing room *n* sitio *m* de pie

standing start *n* **to do sth from a ~** hacer algo partiendo de cero

standoffish [ˌstænd·'ɔ·fɪʃ] *adj pej, inf* distante, estirado, -a

standpipe ['stænd·paɪp] *n* fuente *f* provisional

standpoint ['stænd·pɔɪnt] *n* punto *m* de vista

standstill ['stænd·stɪl] *n* paralización *f;* **to be at a ~** estar parado

standup ['stænd·ˌʌp] *adj* **1.** (*cabaret*) **~ comedy** monólogo *m* humorístico; **~ comedian** cómico, -a *m, f* de micrófono **2.** (*upright*) **~ buffet** comida *f* tomada de pie **3.** FASHION **a ~ collar** un cuello alto **4.** *sl* (*honest*) legal

stank [stæŋk] *pt of* **stink**

stanza ['stæn·zə] *n* LIT estrofa *f*

staple¹ ['steɪ·pəl] **I.** *n* **1.** (*product, article*) producto *m* principal **2.** (*basic food*) alimento *m* de primera necesidad **3.** (*important component*) elemento *m* esencial **II.** *adj* **1.** (*principal*) principal **2.** (*standard*) corriente

staple² ['steɪ·pəl] **I.** *n* (*fastener*) grapa *f* **II.** *vt* grapar

staple gun *n* grapadora *f* industrial

stapler ['steɪp·lər] *n* grapadora *f*

star [star] **I.** *n* **1.** (*heavenly body*) estrella *f* **2.** (*asterisk*) asterisco *m* **3.** (*popular person*) famoso, -a *m, f;* **a movie ~** una estrella de cine ▶**to thank one's** lucky **~s** dar las gracias a Dios; **to be** written **in the ~s** estar escrito en

las estrellas; **to** reach **for the ~s** apuntar a lo más alto; **to** see **~s** ver las estrellas **II.** *vt* <-rr-> **1.** THEAT, CINE tener como protagonista **2.** (*mark with asterisk*) señalar con un asterisco

star billing [ˌstar·'bɪl·ɪŋ] *n* **to get ~** aparecer con letras grandes en los carteles

starboard ['star·bərd] **I.** *n* NAUT estribor *m* **II.** *adj* de estribor

starch [startʃ] **I.** *n* **1.** (*stiffening agent*) almidón *m* **2.** CULIN fécula *f* **II.** *vt* almidonar

starchy ['star·tʃi] <-ier, -iest> *adj* **1.** (*food*) que contiene fécula **2.** *pej, inf* (*person*) estirado, -a

stardom ['star·dəm] *n* estrellato *m,* estelaridad *f Chile*

stare [ster] **I.** *vi* mirar fijamente **II.** *vt* mirar fijamente; **to ~ sb in the face** *fig* saltar a la vista; **the answer was staring us in the face** la respuesta era evidente **III.** *n* mirada *f* fija

◆**stare down** *vt* mirar fijamente (*a alguien*) hasta que aparte la vista

starfish ['star·fɪʃ] <-(es)> *n* estrella *f* de mar

stargazer ['star·ˌgeɪ·zər] *n* (*astronomer*) astrónomo, -a *m, f;* (*astrologer*) astrólogo, -a *m, f*

staring ['ster·ɪŋ] *adj* que mira fijamente; **~ eyes** ojos desorbitados

stark [stark] **I.** *adj* **1.** (*desolate*) severo, -a; **a ~ landscape** un paisaje inhóspito **2.** (*austere*) austero, -a **3.** (*complete*) completo, -a; **a ~ contrast** un fuerte contraste **II.** *adv* **~ naked** en cueros, empelotado, -a *AmL;* **~ raving mad** loco de atar

starless ['star·lɪs] *adj* sin estrellas

starlet ['star·lɪt] *n* actriz *f* que aspira al estrellato

starlight ['star·laɪt] *n* luz *f* de las estrellas

starling ['star·lɪŋ] *n* estornino *m*

starlit ['star·ˌlɪt] *adj* iluminado, -a por las estrellas

starry ['star·i] <-ier, -iest> *adj* estrellado, -a

starry-eyed ['star·i·ˌaɪd] *adj* soñador(a)

Stars and Stripes *n* **the ~** la bandera de las barras y las estrellas

star sign *n* signo *m* del zodiaco

Star-Spangled Banner *n* (*flag*) bandera *f* de las barras y las estrellas; (*anthem*) himno *m* nacional de EE.UU.

star-studded *adj* **1.** (*sky*) estrellado, -a **2.** (*film*) lleno, -a de estrellas; **a ~ cast** un reparto estelar

start [start] **I.** *vi* **1.** (*begin*) comenzar; **to ~ to do sth** empezar a hacer algo **2.** (*begin journey*) salir; **the bus ~s from the main square** el autobús sale de la plaza principal **3.** (*begin to operate: vehicle, motor*) arrancar **4.** SPORTS (*play at beginning*) salir de titular **5.** (*begin at level*) empezar; **ticket prices ~ as low as $10** las entradas más baratas cuestan 10$ **6.** (*make sudden movement*) sobresaltarse; **to ~ at sb/sth** sobresaltarse con alguien/algo **II.** *vt* **1.** (*begin*) comenzar; **we ~ work at 6:30 every morning** entramos a trabajar a las 6:30 cada mañana **2.** (*set in operation*) poner en marcha; (*car*) arrancar **3.** COM (*establish:*

business) abrir **4.** SPORTS (*let play at beginning*) poner de titular ▶to ~ **something** *inf* crear problemas **III.** *n* **1.** (*beginning*) principio *m;* **to make an early/a late** ~ empezar temprano/tarde; **to make a fresh** ~ comenzar de nuevo; **to have a good** ~ **in life** tener una infancia fácil **2.** SPORTS (*beginning place*) salida *f;* (*beginning time*) inicio *m;* **false** ~ salida nula **3.** (*sudden movement*) sobresalto *m;* **to give a** ~ dar un respingo; **to give sb a** ~ dar un susto a alguien **4.** SPORTS (*action of playing at beginning*) titularidad *f;* **he will be making his third** ~ **of the year** saldrá de titular por tercera vez en este año
◆**start back** *vi* **1.** (*jump back suddenly*) retroceder **2.** (*begin return journey*) emprender el regreso
◆**start in on** *vt* empezar
◆**start off I.** *vi* **1.** (*begin*) empezar **2.** (*begin journey*) partir; (*train, plane*) salir **II.** *vt* empezar; **to start sb off** (**on sth**) ayudar a alguien (a empezar algo)
◆**start out** *vi* **1.** (*begin*) empezar; **to** ~ **to do sth** ponerse a hacer algo **2.** (*begin journey*) partir; (*train, plane*) salir
◆**start up I.** *vt* **1.** (*organization, business*) fundar **2.** (*vehicle, motor*) arrancar **II.** *vi* **1.** (*begin running: vehicle, motor*) arrancar **2.** (*open*) abrir **3.** (*jump up*) incorporarse bruscamente
starter *n* **1.** AUTO estárter *m* **2.** *inf* CULIN entrante *m* **3.** SPORTS (*player at beginning*) titular *mf* ▶**for** ~ **s** *inf* para empezar
starting *adj* de comienzo
starting line *n* línea *m* de salida
starting point *n* punto *m* de partida
startle ['star·ţəl] *vt* sobresaltar
startling *adj* (*surprising*) asombroso, -a; (*alarming*) alarmante
startup ['start·ʌp] *n* puesta *f* en marcha
start-up capital *n* capital *m* inicial
start-up costs *n* gastos *mpl* de puesta en marcha
starvation [star·'veɪ·ʃən] *n* hambre *m o f,* inanición *f;* **to die of** ~ morir de hambre
starvation diet *n* régimen *m* de hambre
starve [starv] **I.** *vi* **1.** pasar hambre, hambrear *AmL;* (*die of hunger*) morir(se) de hambre; **to** ~ **to death** morir(se) de hambre **2.** *inf* (*be very hungry*) morirse de hambre **II.** *vt* **1.** (*deprive: of food*) privar de alimentos; **to** ~ **sb to death** matar a alguien de inanición **2.** (*deprive: of love, support*) privar
starving *adj* hambriento, -a
stash [stæʃ] **I.** *vt* ocultar **II.** *n* <-es> *inf* **1.** (*hiding place*) escondite *m* **2.** (*cache*) alijo *m*
state [steɪt] **I.** *n* **1.** (*condition*) estado *m;* ~ **of siege/war** estado de sitio/guerra; **solid/liquid** ~ estado sólido/líquido; ~ **of mind** estado de ánimo **2.** (*nation*) estado *m* **3.** *pl, inf* (*USA*) **the States** los Estados Unidos **4.** (*pomp*) **to lie in** ~ yacer en la capilla ardiente **II.** *adj* (*pertaining to a nation*) esta-

tal; ~ **secret** secreto *m* de Estado **III.** *vt* **1.** (*express*) declarar **2.** LAW (*specify*) exponer
state-controlled *adj* controlado, -a por el Estado; (*business*) estatal
stated *adj* (*specified*) indicado, -a
State Department *n* Departamento *m* de Estado, ≈ Ministerio *m* de Asuntos Exteriores
stateless ['steɪt·lɪs] *adj* apátrida
stately ['steɪt·li] *adj* majestuoso, -a; ~ **home** casa *f* solariega
statement ['steɪt·mənt] *n* **1.** (*declaration*) declaración *f;* **to make a** ~ LAW prestar declaración **2.** (*from bank*) extracto *m* de cuenta
state of the art [ˌsteɪt·əv·ðiˈart] *adj* moderno, -a; ~ **technology** tecnología punta
state-owned *adj* nacional
state prison *n* prisión *f* estatal
stateroom ['steɪt·rum] *n* **1.** (*in palace, hotel*) salón *m* principal **2.** NAUT camarote *m*
stateside ['steɪt·saɪd] *adv* *inf* en los Estados Unidos
statesman ['steɪts·mən] <-men> *n* estadista *m*
statesmanship *n* arte *m* de gobernar
stateswoman ['steɪts·ˌwʊm·ən] <-men> *n* estadista *f*
state visit *n* visita *f* oficial
static ['stæt·ɪk] **I.** *adj* estático, -a; **to remain** ~ permanecer inmóvil **II.** *n* PHYS electricidad *f* estática
static electricity *n* electricidad *f* estática
station ['steɪ·ʃən] **I.** *n* **1.** RAIL estación *f* **2.** (*place*) sitio *m;* **police** ~ comisaría *f* (de policía); **gas** ~ gasolinera *f;* **research** ~ centro *m* de investigación **3.** RADIO emisora *f;* TV canal *m* **4.** (*position*) puesto *m;* **action** ~ **s!** MIL ¡a sus puestos! **II.** *vt* **1.** (*place*) colocar **2.** MIL destinar
stationary ['steɪ·ʃə·ner·i] *adj* (*not moving*) inmóvil
stationery ['steɪ·ʃə·ner·i] *n* artículos *mpl* de papelería
station house *n* comisaría *f*
stationmaster *n* jefe, -a *m, f* de estación
station wagon *n* monovolumen *m*
statistical [stə·'tɪs·tɪ·kəl] *adj* estadístico, -a
statistician [ˌstæt·ɪ·'stɪʃ·ən] *n* estadístico, -a *m, f*
statistics [stə·'tɪs·tɪks] *n* **1.** (*science*) estadística *f* **2.** *pl* (*data*) estadísticas *fpl*
statuary ['stætʃ·u·er·i] *n form* (*statues*) estatuas *fpl*
statue ['stætʃ·u] *n* estatua *f*
Statue of Liberty *n* **the** ~ la Estatua de la Libertad
statuesque [ˌstætʃ·u·'esk] *adj form* escultural
statuette [ˌstætʃ·u·'et] *n* estatuilla *f*
stature ['stætʃ·ər] *n* **1.** (*height*) estatura *f* **2.** (*reputation*) talla *f*
status ['steɪ·təs] *n* **1.** (*official position*) estatus *m* **2.** (*prestige*) prestigio *m*
status bar *n,* **status line** *n* COMPUT barra *f* de estado
status quo *n* statu quo *m*

S

status report *n* COMPUT informe *m* de situación

status symbol *n* signo *m* de prestigio social

statute ['stætʃ·ut] *n* LAW ley *f;* **by ~** de acuerdo con la ley

statute law *n* derecho *m* escrito

statute of limitations *n* ley *f* de prescripción

statutory ['stætʃ·ə·tɔr·i] *adj* legal; **~ rape** relaciones sexuales con un menor

staunch¹ [stɔntʃ] *adj* incondicional; **a ~ supporter** un seguidor incondicional

staunch² [stɔntʃ] *vt s.* **stanch**

stave [steɪv] *n* **1.** MUS pentagrama *m* **2.** (*piece of wood*) duela *f*

◆**stave off** <staved off, staved off> *vt* (*postpone*) aplazar; (*prevent*) evitar

staves *n* **1.** *pl of* **staff** I.6. **2.** *pl of* **stave**

stay [steɪ] **I.** *vi* **1.** (*remain present*) quedarse; **to ~ in bed** guardar cama **2.** (*reside temporarily*) alojarse **3.** (*remain*) permanecer; **to ~ friends** seguir siendo amigos **II.** *vt* **1.** (*endure*) resistir; **to ~ the course** [*o* **distance**] aguantar hasta el final **2.** (*assuage: hunger, thirst*) aplacar **3.** LAW (*suspend*) **to ~ an execution** posponer [*o* suspender] una ejecución **III.** *n* estancia *f,* estada *f* AmL

◆**stay away** *vi* ausentarse; **to ~ from sb/sth** mantenerse alejado de alguien/algo

◆**stay behind** *vi* quedarse

◆**stay in** *vi* quedarse en casa

◆**stay out** *vi* no volver a casa; **to ~ all night** pasar toda la noche fuera

◆**stay up** *vi* no acostarse; **to ~ late** acostarse tarde

stay-at-home ['steɪ·ət·hoʊm] **I.** *n* persona *f* hogareña [*o* casera] **II.** *adj* hogareño, -a

staying power *n* resistencia *f*

STD [ˌes·ti·'di] *n* MED *abbr of* **sexually transmitted disease** ETS *f*

Ste. *n abbr of* **saint** Sta.

stead [sted] *n* lugar *m;* **in his/her ~** en su lugar ▶ **to stand sb in good ~ (for sth)** ser útil a alguien (para algo)

steadfast ['sted·fæst] *adj* firme; **a ~ denial** una negativa rotunda

steady ['sted·i] **I.** <-ier, -iest> *adj* **1.** (*stable*) estable; (*job, employment*) fijo, -a; (*temperature*) constante **2.** (*regular*) regular; (*speed*) constante **3.** (*not wavering: hand*) firme **4.** (*calm*) sereno, -a **5.** (*regular: boyfriend*) formal **II.** *vt* **1.** (*stabilize*) estabilizar **2.** (*make calm*) calmar **III.** *adv* **to be going ~** ser novios formales **IV.** *interj* cuidado

steak [steɪk] *n* **1.** (*for frying, grilling*) bistec *m,* bife *m* AmL; (*for stew, mince*) carne *f* de ternera **2.** (*of lamb, fish*) filete *m*

steal [stil] **I.** <stole, stolen> *vt* robar, cachar AmC, apachar *Perú;* **to ~ sb's heart** robar el corazón a alguien; **to ~ a glance (at sb/sth)** echar una mirada furtiva (a alguien/algo) ▶ **to ~ the show** llevarse todos los aplausos; **to ~ someone's thunder** quitarle la primicia a alguien **II.** <stole, stolen> *vi* **1.** (*take things illegally*) robar **2.** (*move surreptitiously*) **to ~**

in entrar a hurtadillas; **to ~ away** escabullirse **III.** *n inf* ganga *f;* **to be a ~** ser una ganga

stealth [stelθ] *n* sigilo *m;* **by ~** con sigilo

stealthy ['stel·θi] *adj* sigiloso, -a

steam [stim] **I.** *n* (*water vapor*) vapor *m;* **full ~ ahead!** ¡a todo vapor!; **to run out of ~** *fig* perder fuerza ▶ **to let off ~** desahogarse **II.** *adj* de vapor **III.** *vi* (*produce steam*) echar vapor **IV.** *vt* cocer al vapor

◆**steam up** *vi* **1.** (*become steamy*) empañarse **2.** *inf* **to get steamed up (about sth)** acalorarse (por algo)

steam bath *n* baño *m* turco

steamboat *n* (barco *m* de) vapor *m*

steam engine *n* máquina *f* de vapor

steamer ['sti·mər] *n* **1.** (*boat*) (barco *m* de) vapor *m* **2.** CULIN vaporera *f*

steam iron *n* plancha *f* de vapor

steamroll ['stim·roʊl] *vt, vi s.* **steamroller**

steamroller¹ *n* apisonadora *f*

steamroller² **I.** *vt a. fig* aplastar **II.** *vi* ser una apisonadora

steamship **I.** *n* (barco *m* de) vapor *m* **II.** *adj* **~ line** compañía *f* naviera

steamy ['sti·mi] <-ier, -iest> *adj* **1.** (*full of steam*) lleno, -a de vapor **2.** (*very humid*) húmedo, -a **3.** *inf* (*sexy*) erótico, -a

steed [stid] *n liter* corcel *m*

steel [stil] **I.** *n* (*metal*) acero *m;* **nerves of ~** nervios *mpl* de acero **II.** *adj* de acero **III.** *vt* **to ~ oneself for sth** armarse de valor para algo

steel band *n* banda *f* de percusión típica del Caribe

steel industry *n* industria *f* siderúrgica

steel mill *n* planta *f* de laminación de acero

steel wool *n* lana *f* de acero

steelworker ['stil·wɜr·kər] *n* obrero, -a *m, f* siderúrgico, -a

steelworks ['stil·wɜrks] *n inv* planta *f* siderúrgica

steely ['sti·li] <-ier, -iest> *adj* (*determination*) férreo, -a; (*gaze*) duro, -a

steep¹ [stip] *adj* **1.** (*sharply sloping*) empinado, -a **2.** (*dramatic: increase, fall*) pronunciado, -a; **that's a bit ~!** ¡no hay derecho! +*subj* **3.** (*expensive*) exorbitante

steep² [stip] **I.** *vt* (*soak*) remojar; **to ~ tea** poner una bolsita de té en remojo **2.** *fig* **to be ~ed in tradition/history** tener mucha tradición/historia **II.** *vi* **to leave sth to ~** dejar algo en remojo

steepen ['sti·pən] *vi* **1.** (*become steeper*) empinarse **2.** *inf* (*become more expensive*) aumentar

steeple ['sti·pəl] *n* ARCHIT torre *f;* **church ~** campanario de una iglesia

steeplechase ['sti·pəl·tʃeɪs] *n* carrera *f* de obstáculos

steeplejack ['sti·pəl·dʒæk] *n* reparador(a) *m(f)* de torres

steer¹ [stɪr] **I.** *vt* **1.** (*direct*) dirigir; (*car*) conducir, manejar AmL **2.** (*guide*) guiar **II.** *vi* (*person*) conducir, manejar AmL; (*vehicle*) mane-

jarse; **to ~ clear of sth/sb** evitar algo/a alguien; **to ~ for sth** NAUT poner rumbo a algo
steer² [stɪr] *n* (*young bull*) novillo *m;* (*castrated bull*) buey *m*
steering committee *n inv* comité *m* directivo
steering wheel *n* (*of car*) volante *m,* guía *f* PRico; (*of ship*) timón *m*
stellar ['stel·ər] *adj* estelar; **a ~ performance** una actuación brillante
stem [stem] I. *n* 1.(*of plant*) tallo *m;* (*of leaf*) peciolo *m* 2.(*part of glass*) pie *m* 3. LING raíz *f* II.<-mm-> *vt* (*stop*) detener; (*bleeding*) restañar III.<-mm-> *vi* **to ~ from** resultar de
stench [stentʃ] *n* hedor *m*
stencil ['sten·səl] I. *n* 1.(*cut-out pattern*) plantilla *f* 2.(*picture drawn*) patrón *m* II. *vt* dibujar utilizando una plantilla
stenographer [stə·'nag·rə·fər] *n* estenógrafo, -a *m, f*
stenography [stə·'nag·rə·fi] *n* estenografía *f*
step [step] I. *n* 1.(*foot movement*) paso *m;* (*footprint*) huella *f;* **to take a ~** dar un paso; **~ by ~** paso a paso; **to take a ~ towards sth** *fig* dirigirse hacia algo; **to be in/out of ~** llevar/no llevar el paso; *fig* estar/no estar al tanto; **to watch one's ~** andar con cuidado; **watch your ~!** ¡mira por dónde pisas! 2.(*of stair, ladder*) peldaño *m* 3.(*measure*) medida *f;* **to take ~s** (**to do sth**) tomar medidas (para hacer algo) 4. MUS **whole ~** tono *m;* **half ~** semitono *m* II.<-pp-> *vi* 1.(*tread*) pisar 2.(*walk*) caminar
♦ **step aside** *vi* hacerse a un lado
♦ **step back** *vi* 1.(*move back*) retroceder 2.(*gain new perspective*) distanciarse
♦ **step down** I. *vi* (*resign*) dimitir; **to ~ from sth** renunciar a algo II. *vt* (*reduce*) reducir
♦ **step in** *vi* intervenir
♦ **step up** I. *vt* aumentar II. *vi* dar la cara (en caso de necesidad)
stepbrother *n* hermanastro *m*
stepchild *n* hijastro, -a *m, f*
stepdaughter *n* hijastra *f*
stepfather *n* padrastro *m*
stepladder ['step·læd·ər] *n* escalera *f* de mano
stepmother ['step·mʌð·ər] *n* madrastra *f*
steppe [step] *n* estepa *f*
stepping stone ['step·ɪŋ·stoʊn] *n* 1.(*stone*) pasadera *f* 2. *fig* trampolín *m*
stepsister ['step·sɪs·tər] *n* hermanastra *f*
stepson ['step·sʌn] *n* hijastro *m*
stereo ['ster·i·oʊ] I. *n* 1.(*hi-fi system*) (equipo *m*) estéreo *m* 2. **in ~** en estéreo II. *adj* estéreo
stereophonic [ˌster·i·ə·'fan·ɪk] *adj* MUS estereofónico, -a
stereoscopic [ˌster·i·ə·'skap·ɪk] *adj* estereoscópico, -a
stereotype ['ster·i·ə·taɪp] I. *n pej* estereotipo *m* II. *vt pej* estereotipar
sterile ['ster·əl] *adj* estéril
sterility [stə·'rɪl·ə·t̬i] *n* esterilidad *f*
sterilization [ˌster·ə·lɪ·'zeɪ·ʃən] *n* esteriliza-

ción *f*
sterilize ['ster·ə·laɪz] *vt* esterilizar
sterling ['stɜr·lɪŋ] I. *n* 1.(*metal*) plata *f* de ley 2. FIN libra *f* esterlina II. *adj* 1. FIN **pound ~** libra esterlina 2.(*of high standard*) excelente
stern¹ [stɜrn] *adj* 1.(*severe*) severo, -a; (*warning*) terminante 2.(*strict*) estricto, -a
stern² [stɜrn] *n* NAUT popa *f*
sternness ['stɜrn·nɪs] *n* severidad *f*
sternum ['stɜr·nəm] <-s *o* -na> *n* esternón *m*
steroid ['ster·ɔɪd] *n* esteroide *m*
stethoscope ['steθ·ə·skoʊp] *n* MED estetoscopio *m*
stevedore ['sti·və·dɔr] *n* estibador(a) *m(f)*
stew [stu] I. *n* estofado *m,* hervido *m AmS* ▶ **to be in a ~** *inf* sudar la gota gorda II. *vt* (*meat*) estofar; (*fruit*) hacer compota de III. *vi* cocer
steward ['stu·ərd] *n* 1. AVIAT auxiliar *m* de vuelo 2.(*at concert, demonstration*) auxiliar *mf* 3.(*estate administrator*) administrador(a) *m(f)* 4.(*representative*) **shop ~** representante *mf*
stewardess ['stu·ər·dɪs] <-es> *n* azafata *f,* aeromoza *f Méx, AmS*
stick¹ [stɪk] *n* 1.(*of wood*) vara *f,* palo *m;* (*of celery, rhubarb*) tallo *f;* (*of dynamite*) cartucho *m;* (*of deodorant, glue*) barra *f;* (*of chalk*) tiza *f* 2. *a.* SPORTS (*for hockey*) palo *m;* **walking ~** bastón *m* 3. MUS batuta *f* 4. *inf* (*remote area*) **in the ~s** en el quinto pino ▶ **to get the wrong end of the ~** coger el rábano por las hojas; **~s and stones may break my bones, but words can never hurt me** *prov* a palabras necias, oídos sordos *prov*
stick² [stɪk] <stuck, stuck> I. *vi* 1.(*adhere*) pegarse 2.(*be unmovable: person*) quedarse parado; (*door, window*) atascarse; (*mechanism*) bloquearse 3.(*endure*) **to ~ in sb's mind** grabarse a alguien (en la mente) II. *vt* 1.(*affix*) pegar 2. *inf* (*put*) poner; **to ~ one's head out the window** asomar la cabeza por la ventana
♦ **stick around** *vi inf* quedarse
♦ **stick at** *vt* seguir con
♦ **stick by** *vt* 1.(*continue to support: friend*) no abandonar 2.(*not change: opinion*) mantener 3.(*comply with: rules*) respetar
♦ **stick in** *vt* 1.(*knife, needle*) clavar 2.(*put*) poner, meter
♦ **stick on** *vt* 1.(*affix: stamp, label*) pegar 2. *inf* **to be stuck on sb** estar loco por alguien
♦ **stick out** I. *vt* asomar; **to stick one's tongue out at sb** sacar la lengua a alguien ▶ **to stick one's neck out** arriesgarse II. *vi* 1.(*protrude: nail, ears*) sobresalir 2.(*be obvious*) ser evidente; **to ~ a mile** verse [*o* notarse] a la legua, saltar a la vista; **to ~ like a sore thumb** saltar a la vista 3.(*endure*) **to stick it out** aguantar
♦ **stick to** *vt* 1.(*adhere to: rules*) ceñirse a; (*plan, idea*) seguir con; (*promise*) cumplir; (*principles, beliefs*) mantener 2.(*restrict oneself to*) limitarse a
♦ **stick together** I. *vi* 1.(*remain loyal*) mante-

S

nerse unidos **2.**(*not separate*) no separarse **3.**(*adhere*) juntarse **II.** *vt* juntar
♦**stick up I.** *vt inf* **1.**(*rob*) atracar **2.**(*raise*) **stick 'em up!** ¡manos arriba! **II.** *vi* sobresalir; (*hair*) estar de punta
♦**stick up for** *vt* defender
♦**stick with** *vt* **1.**(*not give up on*) seguir con; (*thought, idea, memory*) no abandonar **2.**(*persevere in*) seguir adelante con **3.**(*stay near*) no separarse de
stickball ['stɪk·bɔl] *n juego similar al béisbol que se juega con un palo y una pelota de goma*
sticker ['stɪk·ər] *n* pegatina *f*
sticker price *n* precio *m* de lista (de un vehículo)
sticker shock *n inf: sorpresa al ver el elevado precio de un artículo que se pretendía comprar*
stick figure *n* monigote *m*
stick-in-the-mud *n inf: persona rutinaria e inflexible*
stickler ['stɪk·lər] *n* **to be a ~ for sth** insistir mucho en algo
stick-on ['stɪk·an] *adj* adhesivo, -a
stickpin *n*, **stick pin** ['stɪk·ˌpɪn] *n* alfiler *m* de corbata
stick shift *n* AUTO transmisión *f* estándar
stickup ['stɪk·ʌp] *n sl* atraco *m*
sticky ['stɪk·i] <-ier, -iest> *adj* **1.**(*label*) adhesivo, -a; (*surface, hands*) pegajoso, -a **2.**(*weather*) bochornoso, -a
stiff [stɪf] **I.** *n inf* (*corpse*) fiambre *m* **II.** *adj* **1.**(*rigid: paper*) rígido, -a; (*brush*) duro, -a; (*shirt*) tieso, -a; (*paste, dough*) consistente; **to be (as) ~ as a board** estar más tieso que un palo **2.**(*not supple: joints*) entumecido, -a **3.**(*difficult to move: muscles*) agarrotado, -a; **to have a ~ neck** tener tortícolis **4.**(*very formal: manner*) encorsetado, -a **5.**(*strong: competition*) duro, -a; (*opposition, drink, breeze*) fuerte; (*resistance*) férreo, -a, tenaz; (*punishment, criticism, penalty*) fuerte, severo, -a **6.**(*strenuous: climb, hike*) agotador(a) **7.**(*very expensive: price*) exorbitante **III.** *adv* **to be bored ~** estar aburrido como una ostra; **to be scared ~** estar muerto de miedo
stiffen ['stɪf·ən] **I.** *vi* **1.**(*become tense: person*) ponerse tenso; (*muscles*) agarrotarse **2.**(*become dense*) espesarse **3.**(*become stronger: competition*) hacerse más duro **II.** *vt* **1.**(*make more difficult, severe: penalties*) endurecer; (*competition*) hacer más difícil **2.**(*make rigid: collar, cuff*) almidonar **3.**(*strengthen: morals*) fortalecer
stiff-necked ['stɪf·nekt] *adj* **1.**(*stubborn: person*) terco, -a; (*resistance*) obstinado, -a **2.**(*proud*) estirado, -a
stifle ['staɪ·fəl] **I.** *vt* **1.**(*suffocate*) sofocar **2.**(*suppress: yawn, scream, desire*) contener; (*initiative, opposition*) reprimir **II.** *vi* **1.**(*suffocate*) sofocarse **2.**(*suffer lack of air*) ahogarse
stifling ['staɪ·flɪŋ] *adj* (*heat, temperatures*) sofocante; (*room*) agobiante

stigma ['stɪg·mə] *n* estigma *m*
stigmatize ['stɪg·mə·taɪz] *vt* estigmatizar
stiletto [stɪ·'leʈ·oʊ] <-s> *n* **1.**(*dagger*) estilete *m* **2.** *pl* (*shoes*) zapatos *mpl* de tacón de aguja
stiletto heel *n* tacón *m* de aguja
still[1] [stɪl] **I.** *adj* **1.**(*calm*) tranquilo, -a **2.**(*peaceful*) quieto, -a; (*wind, waters*) en calma; **to keep ~** quedarse quieto **3.** PHOT **~ photography** fotografía *f* **II.** *n* **1.** *liter* (*peace*) quietud *f;* **the ~ of the night** la quietud de la noche **2.** CINE, PHOT fotograma *m* **III.** *vt* **1.**(*calm*) calmar **2.** *liter* (*quieten*) acallar
still[2] [stɪl] *adv* **1.** aún, todavía; **to be ~ alive** seguir vivo; **to want ~ more** querer todavía [*o* aún] más; **better ~** todavía mejor **2.**(*nevertheless*) sin embargo
still[3] [stɪl] *n* (*distillery*) destilería *f*
stillbirth ['stɪl·bɜrθ] *n* parto *m* de un bebé muerto
stillborn ['stɪl·bɔrn] *adj* **1.**(*born dead*) nacido, -a muerto, -a **2.**(*unsuccessful*) malogrado, -a
still life *n* ART naturaleza *f* muerta, bodegón *m*
stillness *n* **1.**(*tranquility*) tranquilidad *f* **2.**(*lack of movement*) quietud *f* **3.**(*calm*) calma *f*
stilt [stɪlt] *n pl* zanco *m*
stilted ['stɪl·tɪd] *adj* (*manner, style*) forzado, -a
stimulant ['stɪm·jə·lənt] *n* **1.**(*boost*) estímulo *m* **2.** MED estimulante *m*
stimulate ['stɪm·jə·leɪt] *vt* **1.**(*encourage*) estimular; (*economy*) potenciar, estimular; (*discussion*) fomentar **2.** MED estimular
stimulating *adj* estimulante
stimulation [ˌstɪm·jə·'leɪ·ʃən] *n* **1.**(*boost*) estimulación *f* **2.**(*thought, reaction*) estímulo *m*
stimulus ['stɪm·jə·ləs] <-li> *n* estímulo *m*
sting [stɪŋ] **I.** *vt* **1.**(*inject with poison*) picar **2.**(*cause pain: eyes*) hacer escocer; (*criticism*) herir profundamente **3.**(*goad*) incitar **II.** <stung, stung> *vi* **1.**(*injure with poison: insect*) picar **2.**(*be painful: cut*) arder; (*eyes*) escocer; (*criticism*) herir **III.** *n* **1.**(*injury*) picada *f* **2.**(*pain*) escozor *m; ~* **of remorse** remordimientos *mpl* de conciencia **3.** BOT pelo *m* urticante **4.** *sl police operation* operación *f* trampa para sorprender a delincuentes en un acto delictivo; **to conduct a ~** tender una trampa (a un delincuente)
stinginess ['stɪn·dʒɪ·nɪs] *n* tacañería *f*
stingray ['stɪn·reɪ] *n* (*fish*) raya *f* venenosa
stingy ['stɪn·dʒi] <-ier, -iest> *adj inf* (*person*) tacaño, -a, pijotero, -a *AmL*, amarrado, -a *Arg, Par, PRico, Urug*, coñete *Chile, Perú;* (*amount*) mísero, -a
stink [stɪŋk] **I.** *n* **1.**(*smell*) mal olor *m* **2.** *fig* escándalo *m;* **to create a ~** montar un escándalo **II.** <stank *o* stunk, stunk> *vi* **1.**(*smell*) apestar, bufar *AmL;* **to ~ of money** *inf* estar podrido de dinero **2.** *inf* (*be very bad*) ser pésimo, -a **3.** *inf* (*be suspicious: business, situation*) oler mal
stink bomb *n* bomba *f* fétida

stinker ['stɪŋ·kər] *n inf* **1.** (*bad person*) canalla *mf* **2.** (*unpleasant thing*) asco *m*

stint [stɪnt] *n* período *m*

stipulate ['stɪp·jə·leɪt] *vt* estipular

stipulation [ˌstɪp·jə·'leɪ·ʃən] *n* estipulación *f*; **with the ~ that** con la condición de que +*subj*

stir [stɜr] **I.** <-ring, -red> *vt* **1.** (*mix: coffee, sauce, mixture*) remover; (*fire*) atizar, avivar **2.** (*move*) mover **3.** (*stimulate: imagination*) estimular; **to ~ sb into action** incitar a alguien a la acción; **to ~ trouble** provocar problemas **II.** *vi* **1.** (*able to be agitated*) mezclarse; **these ingredients really ~ well** estos ingredientes se mezclan muy bien **2.** (*move*) moverse, agitarse **3.** (*rouse*) despertarse **III.** *n* **1.** (*agitation*) **to give sth a ~** remover algo **2.** (*excitement*) conmoción *f*; **to cause a ~** causar revuelo

stir-fry ['stɜr·fraɪ] <-ied, -ies> *vt* freír en poco aceite y removiendo constantemente

stirring I. *adj* conmovedor(a) **II.** *n* (*of envy*) principio *m*; (*of interest*) primeros indicios *mpl*

stirrup ['stɜr·əp] *n* estribo *m*

stitch [stɪtʃ] **I.** <-es> *n* **1.** (*in knitting*) punto *m*; (*in sewing*) puntada *f*; **cross ~** punto de cruz **2.** MED punto *m* (de sutura) ▸ **to leave sb in ~es** *inf* hacer que alguien se tronche de risa; **a ~ in time saves nine** *prov* una puntada a tiempo ahorra ciento *prov* **II.** *vi* coser **III.** *vt* coser

stock [stak] **I.** *n* **1.** (*reserves*) reserva *f* **2.** COM, ECON existencias *fpl*; **to have sth in ~** tener algo en stock; **to be out of ~** estar agotado; **to take ~** hacer el inventario; *fig* hacer un balance **3.** (*share*) FIN acción *f* **4.** AGR, ZOOL ganado *m* **5.** (*line of descent*) linaje *m*; ZOOL, BIO raza *f* **6.** (*popularity*) prestigio *m*; **her ~ had fallen/risen** *inf* había perdido/ganado prestigio **7.** (*belief*) **to put (no) ~ in sth** (no) dar crédito a algo **8.** CULIN (*broth*) caldo *m* **II.** *adj* (*model*) estándar; (*response*) típico, -a **III.** *vt* **1.** (*keep in supply: goods*) vender **2.** (*supply goods to: shop*) suministrar **3.** (*fill: shelves*) llenar

stockade [sta·'keɪd] *n* **1.** (*wooden fence*) empalizada *f* **2.** (*prison*) prisión *f* militar

stockbroker ['stak·ˌbroʊ·kər] *n* corredor(a) *m(f)* de bolsa

stockbroking *n* correduría *f* de bolsa

stock car *n* **1.** AUTO *coche de serie modificado para competir en carreras* **2.** RAIL vagón *m* para el ganado

stock exchange *n* bolsa *f*

stockholder ['stak·ˌhoʊl·dər] *n* accionista *mf*

stocking ['stak·ɪŋ] *n* media *f*

stock market *n* mercado *m* bursátil

stockpile ['stak·paɪl] **I.** *n* reservas *fpl*; (*of weapons, ammunition*) arsenal *m* **II.** *vt* almacenar

stockroom ['stak·rum] *n* almacén *m*, bodega *f Méx*

stocktaking ['stak·teɪ·kɪŋ] *n* inventario *m*

stocky ['stak·i] <-ier, -iest> *adj* bajo, -a y fornido, -a

stockyard ['stak·jard] *n* corral *m*

stodgy ['stadʒ·i] <-ier, -iest> *adj* **1.** (*food*) pesado, -a **2.** (*person, book*) aburrido, -a

stoic ['stoʊ·ɪk] *n* estoico, -a *m, f*

stoical ['stoʊ·ɪ·kəl] *adj* estoico, -a

stoicism ['stoʊ·ɪ·sɪz·əm] *n* estoicismo *m*

stoke [stoʊk] *vt* (*fire*) atizar; (*furnace*) echar carbón [*o* leña] a; *fig* avivar

stoker ['stoʊ·kər] *n* RAIL, NAUT fogonero, -a *m, f*

stole[1] [stoʊl] *pt of* **steal**

stole[2] [stoʊl] *n* FASHION estola *f*

stolid ['stal·ɪd] *adj* impasible

stomach ['stʌm·ək] **I.** *n* **1.** (*internal organ*) estómago *m*; **to have an upset ~** tener mal el estómago; **to have a strong ~** tener estómago **2.** (*belly*) barriga *f* **II.** *vt inf* (*drink, food*) tolerar; **to be hard to ~** (*person, insult*) ser difícil de soportar

stomachache *n* dolor *m* de estómago

stomp [stamp] *vi* pisar fuerte

stomping ground *n* lugar *m* predilecto

stone [stoʊn] **I.** *n* **1.** GEO piedra *f*; **to be a ~'s throw (away)** estar a tiro de piedra **2.** MED cálculo *m* **3.** (*jewel*) piedra *f* preciosa **4.** (*of fruit*) hueso *m*, carozo *m CSur* ▸ **a rolling ~ gathers no moss** *prov* piedra movediza nunca moho la cobija *prov*; **to cast the first ~** tirar la primera piedra; **to leave no ~ unturned** no dejar piedra por mover; **to be carved** [*o* **set**] **in ~** estar grabado en piedra **II.** *adv* **1.** (*like a stone*) **~ hard** duro, -a como una piedra **2.** *inf* (*completely*) **~ crazy** de remate **III.** *vt* **1.** (*throw stones at*) apedrear **2.** (*fruit, olives*) deshuesar

Stone Age *n* Edad *f* de Piedra

stone-broke *adj inf* sin blanca

stone-cold I. *adj* helado, -a **II.** *adv inf* **to knock sb out** ~ dejar helado [*o* de piedra]; **to be ~ sober** no haber bebido ni una gota (de alcohol)

stoned *adj inf* colocado, -a, fumado, -a

stone-deaf [ˌstoʊn·'def] *adj* sordo, -a como una tapia

stonemason ['stoʊn·ˌmeɪ·sən] *n* cantero, -a *m, f*

stonewall ['stoʊn·ˌwɔl] *fig* **I.** *vi* andarse con evasivas **II.** *vt* bloquear

stonewashed ['stoʊn·waʃt] *adj* lavado, -a a la piedra; **~ jeans** vaqueros deslavados

stony ['stoʊ·ni] <-ier, -iest> *adj* **1.** (*beach, ground*) pedregoso, -a **2.** (*expression*) frío, -a; (*silence*) sepulcral; (*feelings*) de piedra

stood [stʊd] *pt, pp of* **stand**

stooge [studʒ] *n* **1.** THEAT *personaje que sufre las bromas de los demás* **2.** *fig* (*puppet*) títere *m* **3.** *inf* (*informer*) soplón, -ona *m, f*

stool [stul] *n* **1.** (*seat*) taburete *m* **2.** *pl* MED deposición *f*

stool pigeon *n inf* soplón, -ona *m, f*

stoop[1] [stup] *vi* inclinarse; **to ~ to sth** *pej* rebajarse a algo; **to ~ low** caer (muy) bajo

stoop[2] [stup] *n* pórtico *m*

stop [stap] **I.** *n* **1.** (*break in activity*) pausa *f*; **to come to a ~** detenerse; **to put a ~ to sth**

S

poner fin a algo **2.** (*halting place*) parada *f*
3. MUS registro *m* ▶**to pull out** (**all**) **the ~s**
desplegar todos los recursos **II.** <- ping, -ped>
vt **1.** (*cause to cease*) parar **2.** (*refuse payment: payment*) suspender; **to ~ payment on
a check** dar orden de no pagar un cheque
3. (*switch off*) apagar **4.** (*block*) rellenar; (*hole,
one's ears*) tapar **III.** <- ping, -ped> *vi*
1. (*cease moving*) pararse; (*car*) detenerse
2. (*cease an activity*) **to ~ doing sth** dejar de
hacer algo **3.** (*pause*) **to ~ and think about
sth** pararse a pensar algo
◆**stop by** *vi* pasar por
◆**stop in** *vi* quedarse en casa
◆**stop off** *vi* detenerse un rato
◆**stop over** *vi* pasarse por
◆**stop up** *vt* (*block*) atascar; (*hole*) tapar;
(*gap*) rellenar
stopcock ['stap·ˌkak] *n* llave *f* de paso
stopgap ['stap·ˌgæp] **I.** *n* medida *f* provisional
II. *adj* provisional
stoplight ['stap·ˌlaɪt] *n* semáforo *m* en rojo
stopover ['stap·oʊ·ˌvər] *n* (*on journey*) parada
f; AVIAT escala *f*
stoppage ['stap·ɪdʒ] *n* **1.** (*cessation of work*)
interrupción *f* **2.** FIN, ECON retención *f* **3.** MED
oclusión *f*
stopper ['stap·ər] **I.** *n* **1.** (*plug*) tapón *m* **2.** (*in
baseball*) cerrador *m* **II.** *vt* taponar
stop sign *n* AUTO, LAW (señal *f* de) stop *m*
stopwatch *n* cronómetro *m*
storage ['stɔr·ɪdʒ] *n* **1.** (*of goods, possessions*)
almacenaje *m;* **to put sth in ~** almacenar algo
2. COMPUT almacenamiento *m*
storage battery *n* acumulador *m*
storage device *n* COMPUT dispositivo *m* de
almacenamiento
store [stɔr] **I.** *n* **1.** (*shop*) tienda *f;* **department
~** grandes almacenes *mpl*, emporio *m* AmC
2. (*supply: of food*) provisión *f;* (*of wine*)
reserva *f* **3.** (*place for keeping supplies*)
almacén *m*, depósito *m;* (*for weapons*) arsenal
m ▶**to be in ~ what is in ~ for us?** ¿qué nos
deparará el futuro? **II.** *vt* **1.** (*put into storage*)
almacenar **2.** (*keep for future use*) guardar
3. COMPUT (*file*) guardar; (*data*) almacenar
store detective *n* guarda *mf* de seguridad de
una tienda
storefront ['stɔr·frʌnt] *n* escaparate *m*
storehouse ['stɔr·haʊs] *n* almacén *m; fig*
mina *f*
storekeeper ['stɔr·ˌki·pər] *n* tendero, -a *m, f*,
comerciante *mf*
storeroom ['stɔr·rum] *n* depósito *m*, bodega *f*
Méx; (*for food*) despensa *f*
storied *adj* **two/three-~** de dos/tres pisos
stork [stɔrk] *n* cigüeña *f*
storm [stɔrm] **I.** *n* **1.** METEO tormenta *f* **2.** *fig*
(*argument*) trifulca *f;* (*of protest*) ola *f;* (*of criticism*) vendaval *f;* (*of applause*) salva *f;* **political ~** revuelo *m* político **3.** **to take sth by ~**
asaltar algo; **to take sb by ~** cautivar a alguien
▶**to ride out** [*o* **weather**] **the ~** capear el

temporal **II.** *vi* **1.** METEO haber tormenta;
(*winds*) soplar con fuerza **2.** (*speak angrily*)
bramar **III.** *vt* (*town, castle*) asaltar; (*house*)
irrumpir en
◆**storm into** *vi* irrumpir en
◆**storm out** *vi* salir airadamente
storm cloud *n* nubarrón *m*
storm door *n* contrapuerta *f*
storm-tossed *adj* (*boat*) sacudido, -a por la
tormenta
stormy ['stɔr·mi] <-ier, -iest> *adj* (*weather*)
tormentoso, -a; (*sea, relationship*) tempestuoso, -a; (*argument*) violento, -a
story[1] ['stɔr·i] <-ies> *n* **1.** (*account*) historia *f;*
(*fictional*) cuento *m;* **to tell a ~** contar un
cuento; **to tell stories** (*lie*) contar cuentos
(chinos); **so the ~ goes** eso dicen **2.** (*news
report*) artículo *m* ▶**that's another ~** eso es
harina de otro costal; **it's the same old ~** es la
misma historia de siempre; **a tall ~** un cuento
chino
story[2] ['stɔr·i] *n* piso *m*
storybook ['stɔr·i·bʊk] **I.** *n* libro *m* de cuentos
II. *adj* **a ~ romance** un romance de cuento de
hadas
story line *n* (*plot*) argumento *m*
storyteller *n* narrador(a) *m(f)*
stout [staʊt] **I.** *adj* (*person*) robusto, -a; (*shoes,
boots*) fuerte; (*defender*) firme; (*resistance*)
tenaz **II.** *n* (*beer*) cerveza *f* negra
stouthearted [ˌstaʊtˈhar·tɪd] *adj* (*support*)
incondicional; (*defender*) acérrimo, -a; (*resistance*) firme
stoutly ['staʊt·li] *adv* **1.** (*strongly*) sólidamente
2. (*firmly*) con firmeza
stove [stoʊv] *n* **1.** (*range*) cocina *f* **2.** (*heater*)
estufa *f*
stovepipe ['stoʊv·paɪp] *n* conducto *m* de
estufa
stow [stoʊ] *vt* guardar
◆**stow away I.** *vt* esconder **II.** *vi* viajar de
polizón
stowage ['stoʊ·ɪdʒ] *n* NAUT estiba *f*
stowaway ['stoʊ·ə·weɪ] *n* polizón *m*
straddle ['stræd·əl] *vt* (*horse*) sentarse a horcajadas sobre
straggle ['stræg·əl] *vi* **1.** (*lag behind*) rezagarse
2. (*come in small numbers*) llegar poco a poco;
(*move in a disorganized group*) avanzar desordenadamente **3.** (*hang untidily: hair*) caer en
desorden
straggler ['stræg·lər] *n* rezagado, -a *m, f*
straggly ['stræg·li] <-ier, -iest> *adj* (*hair*)
desordenado, -a
straight [streɪt] **I.** *adj* **1.** (*not bent*) recto, -a
2. (*honest*) honrado, -a; (*answer*) franco, -a; **to
be ~ with sb** ser sincero con alguien **3.** (*plain*)
sencillo, -a; (*undiluted: gin, vodka*) solo, -a
4. (*consecutive*) seguido, -a; **she won in ~
sets** ganó sin perder ningún set **5.** THEAT (*not
comic*) serio, -a **6.** (*traditional*) convencional
7. *inf* (*heterosexual*) hetero **II.** *adv* **1.** (*in a
direct line*) en línea recta; **to go ~ ahead** ir

todo recto; **to come ~ at sb** ir derecho a alguien; **to head ~ for sth** ir derecho a algo **2.** (*at once*) **to get ~ to the point** ir directo al grano **3.** *inf* (*honestly*) honestamente; **to give it to sb ~** ser franco con alguien **4.** (*clearly: see, think*) con claridad **III.** *n* (*straight line*) recta *f;* **the finishing ~** la recta final
straightaway [ˌstreɪt̬·ə·'weɪ] **I.** *adv* enseguida **II.** *n* sports recta *f*
straighten ['streɪ·t̬ən] *vt* **1.** (*make straight: hair*) alisar; (*wires*) enderezar **2.** (*unbend: arm, body, leg*) estirar **3.** (*make level: hem*) igualar
◆ **straighten out I.** *vt* **1.** (*make straight*) estirar **2.** (*make level*) igualar **3.** (*solve: situation*) arreglar; (*problem*) resolver **4.** (*clarify*) aclarar; **to straighten sb out** aclarar algo a alguien **II.** *vi* (*road*) hacerse recto, -a
◆ **straighten up I.** *vi* (*stand upright*) ponerse derecho, arriscarse *Col* **II.** *vt* **1.** (*make tidy*) ordenar **2.** (*make level*) igualar
straightforward [ˌstreɪt·'fɔr·wərd] *adj* **1.** (*honest*) honesto, -a **2.** (*easy*) sencillo, -a
straight-laced ['streɪt·leɪst] *adj s.* **strait-laced**
straight-out [ˌstreɪt·'aʊt] *adj inf* (*outright*) redomado, -a, consumado, -a; (*refusal*) tajante
strain¹ [streɪn] **I.** *n* **1.** (*pressure*) presión *f;* **to be under a lot of ~** tener mucho estrés; **to put a ~ on a relationship** crear tensiones en una relación **2.** phys deformación *f* **3.** med torcedura *f* **II.** *vi* (*try hard*) esforzarse; **to ~ for effect** utilizar recursos efectistas **III.** *vt* **1.** (*overexert*) **to ~ one's eyes** forzar la vista; **to ~ one's ears** aguzar el oído **2.** (*put stress on: relationship*) crear tensiones en; (*credulity*) poner a prueba **3.** culin (*coffee*) filtrar; (*vegetables*) escurrir
strain² [streɪn] *n* **1.** (*variety: of virus*) cepa *f;* (*of species*) raza *f* **2.** (*tendency or trait*) **~ of eccentricity** vena *f* excéntrica; **~ of puritanism** nota *f* de puritanismo **3.** mus tono *m*
strained [streɪnd] *adj* (*relations*) tenso, -a; (*smile*) forzado, -a
strainer *n* colador *m*
strait [streɪt] *n* **1.** geo estrecho *m;* **the Bering Strait** el estrecho de Bering **2.** (*bad situation*) apuro *m;* **to be in dire ~s** estar en grandes apuros
straitjacket ['streɪt·ˌdʒæk·ɪt] *n* psych, med camisa *f* de fuerza
strait-laced ['streɪt·leɪst] *adj* mojigato, -a
strand¹ [strænd] *n* **1.** (*thread: of wool*) hebra *f;* (*of rope, string*) ramal *m;* **a ~ of hair** un mechón de pelo **2.** (*string: of pearls*) sarta *f;* (*of plot*) hilo *m*
strand² [strænd] **I.** *n liter* (*shore*) ribera *f* **II.** *vt* varar; **to be ~ed** quedarse desamparado
strange [streɪndʒ] *adj* **1.** (*peculiar*) extraño, -a, raro, -a; **I felt ~** me sentía raro; **it's ~ that** es raro que +*subj;* **~r things have happened** cosas más raras han pasado; **~ to say** aunque parezca mentira **2.** (*unfamiliar: face*) desconocido, -a; (*bed*) ajeno, -a

strangely *adv* (*behave, dress*) de una manera rara; **~ enough...** aunque parazca mentira...
stranger ['streɪn·dʒər] *n* desconocido, -a *m, f;* **he is no ~ to controversy** la polémica no le es ajena
strangle ['stræŋ·gəl] *vt* (*person*) estrangular; (*cry*) ahogar
stranglehold ['stræŋ·gəl·hoʊld] *n* (*control*) dominio *m* total; (*on market*) monopolio *m;* **to have sb in a ~** tener a alguien dominado
strangulation [ˌstræŋ·gjʊ·'leɪ·ʃən] *n* estrangulación *f*
strap [stræp] **I.** *n* (*of bag*) correa *f;* (*of dress*) tirante *m* **II.** <-pp-> *vt* atar [*o* sujetar] con una correa
strapless ['stræp·lɪs] *adj* sin tirantes
strapping ['stræp·ɪŋ] **I.** *adj inf* robusto, -a **II.** *n* (*bandage*) esparadrapo *m*
stratagem ['stræt̬·ə·dʒəm] *n* estratagema *f*
strategic [strə·'ti·dʒɪk] *adj* estratégico, -a
strategist ['stræt̬·ə·dʒɪst] *n* estratega *mf*
strategy ['stræt̬·ə·dʒi] <-ies> *n* estrategia *f*
stratify ['stræt̬·ə·faɪ] *vt* estratificar
stratosphere ['stræt̬·əs·fɪr] *n* estratosfera *f;* **to go into the ~** (*prices*) irse por las nubes
stratum ['streɪ·t̬əm] <strata> *n* estrato *m*
straw [strɔ] *n* **1.** (*dry stems*) paja *f* **2.** (*for drinking*) pajita *f,* popote *m Méx,* pitillo *m And* ▶ **to be the last ~** ser el colmo; **to draw the short ~** tocarle a uno la china; **to clutch at ~s** agarrarse a un clavo ardiendo
strawberry ['strɔ·ˌber·i] <-ies> *n* **1.** (*fruit*) fresa *f,* frutilla *f AmL* **2.** *sl* (*scrape*) magullar
straw-colored ['strɔ·kʌl·əd] *adj* pajizo, -a
straw man *n* hombre *m* de paja
straw poll *n* sondeo *m* informal
stray [streɪ] **I.** *adj* **1.** (*homeless: dog, cat*) callejero, -a, realengo, -a *Méx, PRico* **2.** (*loose: hair*) suelto, -a; (*bullet*) perdido, -a **II.** *vi* (*wander*) errar; (*become lost*) perderse; **to ~ from** alejarse de; **to ~ off course** apartarse del camino; **they were warned not to stray beyond the border** se les advirtió que no se salieran del borde; **to ~ from the point** divagar **III.** *n* (*dog*) perro *m* callejero; (*cat*) gato *m* callejero
streak [strik] **I.** *n* **1.** (*stripe*) raya *f;* (*in hair*) mechón *m;* (*of light*) rayo *m;* (*of lightning*) relámpago *m* **2.** (*tendency*) vena *f;* **an aggressive ~** una vena agresiva; **to have a ~ of cowardice** tener algo de cobarde **3.** (*spell*) racha *f;* **to be on a winning ~** tener una buena racha; **a 20-game hitting ~** una racha de bateo de 20 partidos ▶ **like a ~ of lightning** como un rayo; **to talk a blue ~** *inf* hablar más que un loro **II.** *vt* rayar; **to have one's hair ~ed** hacerse mechas; **to be ~ed with sth** estar manchado de algo **III.** *vi* **1.** (*move very fast*) ir rápido **2.** (*run naked in public*) correr desnudo en un lugar público
streaker *n* persona que corre desnuda en un lugar público
streaky ['stri·ki] <-ier, -iest> *adj* rayado, -a

stream [strim] I. *n* **1.** (*small river*) arroyo *m*, estero *m Chile, Ecua* **2.** (*current*) corriente *f;* **to go against the ~** *fig* ir a contracorriente **3.** (*flow: of oil, water*) chorrito *m;* (*of people*) torrente *m;* (*of insults*) sarta *f* II. *vi* **1.** (*flow*) fluir; (*water*) chorrear; (*blood*) manar; (*tears*) caer; **tears ~ed down her face** lloraba a lágrima viva; **blood ~ed from his head** le chorreaba sangre de la cabeza **2.** (*move in numbers*) afluir en masa **3.** (*shine: sunlight*) entrar a raudales **4.** (*run: nose*) gotear; (*eyes*) llorar

streamer ['stri·mər] *n* serpentina *f*

streamline ['strim·laɪn] *vt* (*vehicle*) aerodinamizar; (*method*) racionalizar

streamlined *adj* (*vehicle*) aerodinámico, -a; (*method*) racionalizado, -a

street [strit] *n* (*road*) calle *f;* **in** [*o* **on**] **the ~** en la calle ▸ **to be out on the ~** no tener hogar; **to walk the ~s** (*wander*) deambular por las calles; (*be a prostitute*) hacer la calle

streetcar *n* tranvía *m*

streetcar line *n* **1.** (*track*) vía *f* del tranvía; (*route*) línea *f* de tranvía **2. ~s** (*in tennis*) líneas *fpl* laterales

street hockey *n* hockey *m* callejero

streetlamp *n*, **streetlight** *n* farola *f*

street lighting *n* alumbrado *m* (público)

street value *n* valor *m* de reventa

streetwalker *n* prostituta *f* que hace la calle

streetwise ['strit·waɪz] *adj* (*person*) espabilado, -a; (*politician*) astuto, -a

strength [streŋkθ] *n* **1.** (*power*) fuerza *f*, ñeque *m Chile, Ecua, Perú;* (*of feeling, light*) intensidad *f;* (*of alcohol*) graduación *f;* (*of economy*) solidez *f;* (*mental firmness*) fortaleza *f* **2.** (*number of members*) número *m;* **to be at full ~** tener el cupo completo; **to be below ~** (*office*) estar corto de personal **3.** (*strong point*) punto *m* fuerte; **one's ~s and weaknesses** sus virtudes y defectos

strengthen ['streŋk·θən] I. *vt* **1.** (*make stronger: muscles*) fortalecer; (*wall*) reforzar; (*financial position*) consolidar **2.** (*increase: chances*) aumentar **3.** (*intensify: relations*) intensificar; (*links*) estrechar II. *vi* fortalecerse

strenuous ['stren·ju·əs] *adj* (*activity, exercise, sport*) agotador(a); (*supporter*) acérrimo, -a; (*denial*) rotundo, -a

streptococcus [ˌstrep·tə·'kak·əs] <-ci> *n* estreptococo *m*

stress [stres] I. *n* **1.** (*mental strain*) estrés *m* **2.** (*emphasis*) énfasis *m inv* **3.** LING acento *m* **4.** PHYS tensión *f* II. *vt* **1.** (*emphasize*) recalcar **2.** LING acentuar

stressed *adj*, **stressed out** *adj inf* estresado, -a

stress fracture *n* fractura *f* de fatiga

stress-free *adj* sin estrés

stressful ['stres·fʊl] *adj* estresante

stress mark *n* LING acento *m*

stretch [stretʃ] I. <-es> *n* **1.** SPORTS estiramiento *m* **2.** (*elasticity*) elasticidad *f* **3.** GEO tre-

cho *m* **4.** (*piece*) trozo *m;* (*of road*) tramo *m;* (*of time*) período *m* **5.** (*stage of a race*) recta *f;* **the home ~** la recta final **6.** (*exertion*) **at full ~** a todo gas; **to work at full ~** trabajar al máximo de su capacidad; **not by any ~ of the imagination** ni por. asomo II. *vi* **1.** (*become bigger*) estirarse; (*clothes*) dar de sí **2.** (*extend muscles*) estirarse **3.** (*in time*) **to ~** (**all the way**) **back to...** remontarse a... **4.** (*cover an area: sea, influence*) extenderse III. *vt* **1.** (*extend: muscles*) estirar; **to ~ one's legs** estirar las piernas **2.** (*make go further*) estirar; **to ~ the limit** estirar el límite **3.** (*demand a lot of*) **to ~ sb's patience** poner a prueba la paciencia de alguien; **my present job doesn't ~ me** mi trabajo actual no me exige lo suficiente; **his nerves are ~ed to the breaking point** tiene los nervios a punto de estallar **4.** (*go beyond*) **to ~ a point** hacer una excepción; **now you're really ~ing it** ahora sí que estás exagerando **5.** LAW sobrepasar los límites de IV. *adj* elástico, -a

stretcher ['stretʃ·ər] *n* camilla *f*

stretcher bearer *n* camillero, -a *m, f*

strew [stru] <strewed, strewn *o* strewed> *vt* esparcir

stricken ['strɪk·ən] *adj* **1.** (*distressed*) afligido, -a **2.** (*wounded*) herido, -a **3.** (*afflicted*) **to be stricken with illness** estar enfermo; **she was stricken with remorse** le remordía la conciencia **4.** (*damaged: tanker*) siniestrado, -a

strict [strɪkt] *adj* (*person*) severo, -a, fregado, -a *AmC;* (*control, orders, sense*) estricto, -a; (*deadline*) inamovible; (*neutrality*) total; (*secrecy*) completo, -a; (*confidence*) absoluto, -a; **to be ~ with sb** ser severo con alguien

strictly ['strɪkt·li] *adv* **1.** (*exactly*) estrictamente; **not ~ comparable** no del todo comparable; **~ speaking** en rigor **2.** (*harshly*) severamente; **~ forbidden** terminantemente prohibido

stride [straɪd] I. <strode> *vi* andar a trancos; **to ~ ahead** andar dando zancadas; **to ~ across sth** cruzar algo de una zancada II. *n* **1.** (*long step*) zancada *f* **2.** (*progress*) progreso *m;* **to make (positive) ~s forward** hacer grandes progresos; **to make ~s towards sth** acercarse a algo ▸ **to get into** [*o* **hit**] **one's ~** coger el ritmo; **to take sth in ~** tomarse algo con calma

strident ['straɪ·dənt] *adj* estridente

strife [straɪf] *n* lucha *f;* (*verbal*) disputa *f;* **domestic ~** riñas *fpl* domésticas

strike [straɪk] I. *n* **1.** (*military attack*) ataque *m* **2.** (*withdrawal of labor*) huelga *f* **3.** (*discovery*) descubrimiento *m* **4.** (*in baseball*) strike *m* **5.** LAW fallo *m* de culpabilidad II. <struck, struck *o* stricken> *vt* **1.** (*collide with*) golpear; **to ~ a match** encender una cerilla; **to be struck by lightning** ser alcanzado por un rayo; **to ~ a blow against sb** asestar un golpe a alguien **2.** (*achieve*) conseguir; **to ~ a balance** encontrar un equilibrio; **to ~ a bar-**

gain with sb hacer un trato con alguien **3.** (*seem*) parecer; **it ~s me that...** se me ocurre que... **4.** (*impress*) impresionar; **I was struck by the news** la noticia me impactó **5.** (*engender*) **to ~ fear into sb** infundir miedo a alguien **6.** (*discover*) descubrir; (*find*) encontrar; **to ~ gold** (*have financial fortune*) descubrir un filón; (*win gold medal*) ganar el oro **7.** (*adopt*) **to ~ an attitude** adoptar una actitud **8.** (*sound the time: clock*) marcar; **the clock struck three** el reloj dio las tres **9.** (*manufacture: coin*) acuñar **10.** (*delete*) borrar, tachar ▶ **to ~ a chord with sb** llegar a entenderse con alguien; **to ~ the right note** dar con el tono justo; **to ~ sb dumb** dejar a alguien sin habla; **to ~ it rich** *inf* hacer fortuna **III.** <struck, struck *o* stricken> *vi* **1.** (*hit hard*) golpear; (*attack*) atacar; **to ~ at sth** asestar un golpe contra algo; **to ~ at the heart of sth** atacar directamente a algo; **to ~ home** dar en el blanco **2.** (*withdraw labor*) declararse en huelga; **the right to ~** el derecho a la huelga; **to ~ for sth** hacer una huelga para conseguir algo

♦**strike back** *vi* contraatacar; **to ~ at sb** tomar represalias contra alguien

♦**strike down** *vt* **1.** **she was struck down by cancer** fue abatida por el cáncer **2.** LAW revocar

♦**strike off** *vt* **to strike sb/sth off a list** tachar a alguien/algo de una lista

♦**strike out I.** *vt* **1.** (*in baseball*) eliminar (por strikes) **2.** (*delete*) borrar **II.** *vi* **1.** (*in baseball*) ser eliminado (por strikes); *fig* fallar **2.** (*move off*) andar resueltamente; **to ~ on one's own** hacerse independiente **3.** (*hit out*) empezar a repartir golpes

♦**strike up** *vt* (*conversation*) entablar; (*friendship*) trabar; (*relationship*) iniciar

strikebreaker ['straɪk·ˌbreɪ·kər] *n* esquirol *mf*

strikeout ['straɪk·ˌaʊt] *n* eliminación *f* (por strikes)

striker ['straɪ·kər] *n* **1.** (*strike participant*) huelguista *mf* **2.** SPORTS delantero, -a *m, f*

strike zone *n* zona *f* de strike

striking ['straɪ·kɪŋ] *adj* notable; (*result, beauty*) impresionante; (*resemblance*) sorprendente; (*contrast*) acusado, -a; (*change*) considerable; (*difference*) gran; **visually ~** llamativo

string [strɪŋ] **I.** *n* **1.** (*twine*) *a.* MUS cuerda *f;* (*on puppet*) hilo *m;* **to pull ~s** *fig* mover hilos; **with no ~s attached** sin compromiso alguno **2.** *pl* MUS (*section*) (instrumentos *mpl* de) cuerda *f;* (*players*) (instrumentistas *mpl* de) cuerda *f* **3.** (*chain*) cadena *f;* (*of pearls*) collar *m* **4.** (*sequence: of scandals*) serie *f;* (*of lies*) sarta *f;* (*of people*) hilera *f;* (*of oaths*) retahíla *f* **5.** COMPUT secuencia *f* **II.** <strung, strung> *vt* poner una cuerda a; (*instrument*) encordar; (*tennis racket*) encordar; (*beads*) ensartar

♦**string along** *inf* **I.** *vi* ir/venir también **II.** *vt* **to string sb along** embaucar a alguien

♦**string out** *vt* **1.** (*protract: activity*) prolongar **2.** (*extend*) espaciar

♦**string together** *vt* hilar

♦**string up** *vt inf* colgar

string band *n* banda *f* de cuerda

string bean *n* habichuela *f*

stringed instrument *n* instrumento *m* de cuerda

stringency ['strɪn·dʒən·si] *n* **1.** (*of measure*) severidad *f;* (*of test*) rigor *m* **2.** FIN dificultad *f*

stringent ['strɪn·dʒənt] *adj* **1.** (*measure*) severo, -a; (*rigorous: test*) riguroso, -a; (*law, requirement*) estricto, -a **2.** FIN restrictivo, -a

stringy ['strɪŋ·i] *adj* (*meat*) correoso, -a; (*person*) delgado, -a pero fuerte

strip [strɪp] **I.** *vt* **1.** (*lay bare*) dejar sin cubierta; **to ~ sb of sth** quitarle algo a alguien **2.** (*unclothe*) desnudar **3.** (*dismantle*) desmontar **II.** *vi* desnudarse **III.** *n* **1.** (*ribbon*) tira *f;* (*of metal*) lámina *f;* (*of land*) franja *f* **2.** (*striptease*) striptease *m* **3.** (*landing area*) **landing ~** pista *f* de aterrizaje

stripe [straɪp] *n* **1.** (*colored band*) raya *f* **2.** (*type*) **of every ~** de todo tipo; **governments of every ~** gobiernos de todos los colores **3.** MIL galón *m*

striped *adj* rayado, -a; (*shirt*) a rayas

strip mall *n* complejo comercial formado por una línea de varios establecimientos y restaurantes que van a dar a un párking común

strip mining *n* minería *f* a cielo abierto

stripper ['strɪp·ər] *n* **1.** (*person*) stripper *mf* **2.** (*solvent*) líquido *m* quitaesmaltes; (*for wallpaper*) líquido *m* quitapapeles

strip-search ['strɪp·ˌsɜrtʃ] *vt* **to ~ sb** hacer desnudar a alguien para registrarle

strip search *n* registro *m* en el que la persona tiene que desnudarse

striptease ['strɪp·tiz] *n* striptease *m*

stripy ['straɪ·pi] *adj* rayado, -a; (*shirt*) a rayas

strive [straɪv] <strove, striven *o* strived> *vi* esforzarse; **to ~ to do sth** esmerarse en hacer algo; **to ~ after sth** luchar por conseguir algo; **to ~ for sth** afanarse para conseguir algo

strobe [stroʊb] *n inf* luz *f* estroboscópica

strobe light *n* luz *f* estroboscópica

stroboscope ['stroʊ·bə·skoʊp] *n* estroboscopio *m*

strode [stroʊd] *pt of* **stride**

stroke [stroʊk] **I.** *vt* **1.** (*caress*) acariciar **2.** SPORTS (*hit smoothly*) golpear suavemente **II.** *n* **1.** (*caress*) caricia *f* **2.** MED derrame *m* cerebral; **to suffer a ~** tener una apoplejía **3.** (*of pencil*) trazo *m;* (*of brush*) pincelada *f* **4.** (*style of hitting ball*) golpe *m;* (*billiards*) tacada *f* **5.** *form* (*lash with whip*) latigazo *m* **6.** (*in swimming: style*) estilo *m;* (*single movement*) brazada *f* **7.** (*bit*) **by a ~ of fate** por cosas del destino; **a ~ of genius** una genialidad; **a ~ of luck** un golpe de suerte **8.** (*of clock*) campanada *f*

stroll [stroʊl] **I.** *n* paseo *m;* **to go for a ~** ir a dar una vuelta **II.** *vi* dar un paseo; **to ~ along**

S

the riverbank pasear por la orilla del río
stroller ['strou·lər] *n* **1.**(*pushchair*) cochecito *m* **2.**(*person*) paseante *mf*
strong [strɔŋ] **I.** *adj* **1.**(*powerful*) fuerte; (*coffee*) cargado, -a; (*competition*) duro, -a; (*condemnation*) severo, -a; (*doubt, incentive, influence*) gran, grande; (*protest, measure*) enérgico, -a; (*reason*) de peso; (*wind*) recio, -a; **to produce ~ memories** traer muchos recuerdos **2.**(*capable*) competente **3.**(*physically powerful*) robusto, -a; **as ~ as an ox** ser tan fuerte como un toro **4.**(*fit*) sano, -a; (*constitution*) fuerte **5.**(*durable*) sólido, -a; (*will, conviction*) firme; (*nerves*) de acero **6.**(*staunch*) arraigado, -a; (*antipathy*) gran; (*believer*) fervoroso, -a; (*bond*) fuerte; (*character*) enérgico, -a; (*emotion*) intenso, -a; (*friendship*) estrecho, -a; (*objection, opponent*) duro, -a; (*supporter*) acérrimo, -a **7.**(*tough*) resistente **8.**(*very likely*) muy probable; **~ chance of success** muchas posibilidades de éxito **9.**(*marked*) marcado, -a; (*color*) llamativo, -a; (*light, flavor*) intenso, -a; (*fragrance*) penetrante; (*language*) vulgar **10.**(*bright*) brillante **11.**(*having high value*) de gran valor **II.** *adv inf* **to come on ~ to sb** (*show sexual interest in*) ir por alguien; **to be still going ~** ir todavía bien
strong-arm ['strɔŋ·arm] **I.** *adj* (*methods*) de mano dura **II.** *vt* utilizar la fuerza física con
strongbox ['strɔŋ·baks] *n* caja *f* fuerte
stronghold ['strɔŋ·hould] *n* (*fortified place*) fortaleza *f; fig* baluarte *m*
strongly *adv* **1.**(*powerfully*) fuertemente; (*advise*) fervorosamente; (*condemn*) con dureza; (*criticize, force*) enérgicamente; **to smell ~ of sth** tener un fuerte olor a algo; **to be ~ opposed to sb/sth** estar muy en contra de alguien/algo; **to be ~ biased against sb/sth** tener una fuerte predisposición contra alguien/algo **2.**(*sturdily*) sólidamente
strong-minded [,strɔŋ·'main·dɪd] *adj* resuelto, -a
strong room ['strɔŋ·rum] *n* cámara *f* acorazada
strong-willed [,strɔŋ·'wɪld] *adj* resuelto, -a
strove [strouv] *pt of* **strive**
struck [strʌk] *pt, pp of* **strike**
structural ['strʌk·tʃər·əl] *adj* estructural
structure ['strʌk·tʃər] **I.** *n* estructura *f;* (*building*) construcción *f* **II.** *vt* estructurar
struggle ['strʌg·əl] **I.** *n* **1.**(*effort*) esfuerzo *m;* **to be a real ~** suponer un gran esfuerzo; **to give up the ~ to do sth** dejar de esmerarse en hacer algo **2.**(*skirmish*) lucha *f;* **to put up a ~** oponer resistencia **II.** *vi* **1.**(*make an effort*) esforzarse **2.**(*fight*) luchar
strum [strʌm] <-mm-> *vt* MUS rasguear
strung [strʌŋ] *pt, pp of* **string**
strut¹ [strʌt] **I.** <-tt-> *vi* **to ~ about** pavonearse **II.** *vt inf* **to ~ one's stuff** *iron* (*dance*) contonearse
strut² [strʌt] *n* (*in building, plane*) puntal *m;*

(*in plane*) riostra *f*
strychnine ['strɪk·naɪn] *n* CHEM estricnina *f*
stub [stʌb] **I.** *n* (*of check*) talón *m;* (*of cigarette*) colilla *f;* (*of pencil*) cabo *m* **II.** <-bb-> *vt* **to ~ one's toe against sth** tropezar con algo
stubble ['stʌb·əl] *n* **1.**(*beard growth*) barba *f* de varios días **2.** AGR rastrojo *m*
stubbly ['stʌb·li] *adj* (*bristly*) con barba de varios días
stubborn ['stʌb·ərn] *adj* (*person, animal*) terco, -a; **as a ~ as a mule** más terco que una mula; (*insistence*) tenaz; (*problem*) persistente; (*refusal*) rotundo, -a; (*resistance*) inquebrantable
stubby ['stʌb·i] *adj* (*fingers*) corto, -a y grueso, -a; (*person*) achaparrado, -a
stucco ['stʌk·ou] *n* estuco *m*
stuck [stʌk] **I.** *pt, pp of* **stick** **II.** *adj* **1.**(*jammed*) atascado, -a **2.** *inf* (*crazy about*) **to be ~ on sb** estar loco por alguien
stuck-up [,stʌk·'ʌp] *adj inf* engreído, -a
stud¹ [stʌd] *n* **1.**(*horse*) semental *m*, garañón *m AmL* **2.** *inf* (*good-looking guy*) semental *m;* (*clutch performer*) jugador *m* que no se arruga (en los momentos difíciles)
stud² [stʌd] *n* **1.**(*small metal item*) tachón *m;* (*decorative nail*) clavo *m* **2.**(*on shirt*) **collar ~** gemelo *m* **3.**(*on tire*) taco *m* **4.**(*earring*) pendiente *m*
student ['stu·dənt] *n* estudiante *mf;* **the ~ body** el alumnado
student teacher *n* profesor(a) *m(f)* en prácticas
student union *n* (*organization*) asociación *f* de estudiantes; (*meeting place*) club *m* de estudiantes universitarios
studhorse *n*, **stud horse** *n* semental *m*, garañón *m AmL*
studied ['stʌd·id] *adj* estudiado, -a; (*answer*) pensado, -a; (*insult*) premeditado, -a
studio ['stu·di·ou] <-s> *n* **1.**(*of artist*) taller *m* **2.** CINE estudio *m* **3.**(*apartment*) estudio *m*
studio apartment *n* estudio *m*
studio audience *n* público *m* en estudio
studious ['stu·di·əs] *adj* estudioso, -a
study ['stʌd·i] **I.** *vt* (*subject*) estudiar; (*evidence*) examinar **II.** *vi* estudiar **III.** <-ies> *n* **1.**(*of subject*) estudio *m;* (*of evidence*) investigación *f* **2.**(*room*) despacho *m*
study group *n* grupo *m* de estudio
stuff [stʌf] **I.** *n* **1.** *inf* (*things*) materia *f;* **to know one's ~** conocer su oficio **2.**(*belongings*) cosas *fpl* **3.**(*material*) material *m;* (*cloth*) tela *f;* **to be the ~ of which heroes are made** tener madera de héroe; **the (very) ~ of sth** la esencia de algo **II.** *vt* **1.**(*fill*) llenar; **to ~ sth into sth** meter algo en algo; **to ~ sb's head with sth** llenarle a alguien la cabeza de algo; **to ~ oneself** *inf* darse un atracón **2.**(*preserve: animal*) disecar
stuffed shirt *n inf* persona *f* estirada
stuffing ['stʌf·ɪŋ] *n* relleno *m*
stuffy ['stʌf·i] *adj pej* **1.**(*room*) mal ventilado,

-a; (*atmosphere*) cargado, -a **2.**(*blocked: nose*) taponado, -a **3.**(*person*) tieso, -a

stumble ['stʌm·bəl] *vi* **1.**(*trip*) tropezar; **to ~ on sth** tropezar con algo **2.**(*while talking*) balbucear; **to ~ over sth** tropezar en algo

stumbling block *n* obstáculo *m*

stump [stʌmp] **I.** *n* (*of plant*) tocón *m;* (*of arm*) muñón *m;* (*of tooth*) raigón *m* **II.** *vt inf* desconcertar **III.** *vi* **to ~ about** andar pisando fuerte

stumpy ['stʌm·pi] *adj inf* achaparrado, -a; (*tail*) corto, -a

stun [stʌn] <-nn-> *vt* **1.**(*stupefy*) dejar pasmado **2.**(*render unconscious*) dejar sin sentido

stung [stʌŋ] *pp, pt of* **sting**

stun grenade *n* MIL granada *f* detonadora

stunk [stʌŋk] *pt, pp of* **stink**

stunned *adj* aturdido, -a

stunner ['stʌn·ər] *n inf* **1.**(*surprise*) sorpresa *f* **2.**(*person*) **she's a ~** es un bombón

stunning ['stʌn·ɪŋ] *adj* **1.**(*surprising*) aturdidor(a) **2.**(*impressive*) maravilloso, -a; (*view*) espléndido, -a; (*dress*) estupendo, -a

stunt¹ [stʌnt] *n* **1.**(*acrobatics*) acrobacia *f* **2.**(*feat*) hazaña *f;* **to pull a ~** *inf* hacer una proeza **3.**(*publicity action*) truco *m* publicitario; **advertising ~** treta *f* publicitaria **4.** CINE toma *f* peligrosa

stunt² [stʌnt] *vt* (*plant*) atrofiar; (*growth*) impedir

stunted *adj* enano, -a; (*child*) poco desarrollado, -a; **emotionally ~** poco maduro emocionalmente

stuntman ['stʌnt·mæn] *n* especialista *m*

stuntwoman *adj* especialista *f*

stupefaction [ˌstu·pə·'fæk·ʃən] *n form* estupefacción *f*

stupefy ['stu·pə·faɪ] <-ie-> *vt* atontar; *fig* dejar estupefacto

stupendous [stu·'pen·dəs] *adj* estupendo, -a

stupid ['stu·pɪd] *adj* estúpido, -a, cojudo, -a *AmL,* zonzo, -a *AmL;* (*mistake*) tonto, -a

stupidity [stu·'pɪd·ə·t̬i] *n* estupidez *f,* dundera *f AmL*

stupor ['stu·pər] *n* estupor *m*

sturdy ['stɜr·di] *adj* **1.**(*robust*) robusto, -a; (*person*) fuerte **2.**(*resolute*) decidido, -a; **a ~ defender of sth** un defensor acérrimo de algo

sturgeon ['stɜr·dʒən] *n* esturión *m*

stutter ['stʌt̬·ər] **I.** *vi* (*stammer*) tartamudear, cancanear, *AmL* **II.** *vt* decir algo tartamudeando **III.** *n* tartamudeo *m;* **to have a ~** tartamudear

stutterer ['stʌt̬·ər·ər] *n* tartamudo, -a *m, f*

sty [staɪ] *n* (*pigsty*) pocilga *f*

style [staɪl] **I.** *n* **1.** *a.* ART, ARCHIT estilo *m;* (*of management*) modo *f;* (*of teaching*) forma *f* **2.**(*elegance*) elegancia *f;* **to have no ~** no ser elegante; **with ~** con estilo; **to do things with ~** hacer las cosas con estilo; **to live in (grand) ~** vivir a lo grande; **to travel in ~** viajar con todo el confort **3.**(*fashion*) moda *f;* **in ~** de

moda **4.**(*type*) normas *fpl* de estilo **II.** *vt* **1.**(*design*) diseñar; (*hair*) peinar **2.**(*label*) **to ~ oneself as...** hacerse llamar...

styling *n* estilización *f*

stylish ['staɪ·lɪʃ] *adj* **1.**(*fashionable*) a la moda **2.**(*elegant*) garboso, -a

stylist ['staɪ·lɪst] *n* estilista *mf*

stylistic [staɪ·'lɪs·tɪk] *adj* estilístico, -a

stylize ['staɪ·laɪz] *vt* estilizar

stylus ['staɪ·ləs] <-es *o* -li> *n* estilete *m*

stymie ['staɪ·mi] <-(y)ing> *vt inf* (*person, the opposition*) poner obstáculos infranqueables ante; (*project*) bloquear

Styrofoam® ['staɪ·rə·ˌfoʊm] *n* (espuma *f* de) poliestireno *m*

suave [swav] *adj* cortés; *pej* zalamero, -a

sub¹ [sʌb] *n* **1.** *inf abbr of* **substitute** sustituto, -a *m, f* **2.** *inf abbr of* **submarine** submarino *m* **3.** *inf abbr of* **sandwich** sándwich *m* mixto

sub² [sʌb] <-bb-> *vi abbr of* **substitute** sustituir

subatomic [ˌsʌb·ə·'tam·ɪk] *adj* PHYS subatómico, -a

subclass ['sʌb·klæs] *n* BIO subclase *f*

subcommittee [ˌsʌb·kə·'mɪt̬·i] *n* subcomisión *f*

subconscious [ˌsʌb·'kan·ʃəs] **I.** *n* subconsciente *m* **II.** *adj* subconsciente

subcontinent ['sʌb·ˌkan·tə·nənt] *n* GEO subcontinente *m;* **the ~** el subcontinente indio

subcontract ['sʌb·ˌkan·trækt] *vt* subcontratar

subcontractor [ˌsʌb·kən·'træk·tər] *n* subcontratista *mf*

subculture ['sʌb·ˌkʌl·tʃər] *n* subcultura *f*

subcutaneous [ˌsʌb·kju·'teɪ·ni·əs] *adj* subcutáneo, -a

subdivide [ˌsʌb·dɪ·'vaɪd] *vt* subdividir

subdivision [ˌsʌb·dɪ·'vɪʒ·ən] *n* **1.**(*division*) subdivisión *f* **2.**(*housing estate*) urbanización *f*

subdue [səb·'du] *vt* (*tame*) someter; (*repress*) reprimir

subdued *adj* (*color*) suave; (*person*) apagado, -a

subgroup ['sʌb·grup] *n* subgrupo *m*

subheading ['sʌb·ˌhed·ɪŋ] *n* subtítulo *m*

subject¹ ['sʌb·dʒɪkt] **I.** *n* **1.**(*theme*) tema *m;* **to change the ~** cambiar de tema; **to wander off the ~** salirse del tema; **on the ~ of sb/sth** a propósito de alguien/algo **2.** SCHOOL, UNIV asignatura *f;* (*research area*) ámbito *m* **3.** POL súbdito, -a *m, f;* (*citizen*) ciudadano, -a *m, f* **4.** LING sujeto *m* **5.**(*in experiment*) sujeto *m* (de experimentación) **II.** *adj* **1.** POL (*nation*) subyugado, -a **2.**(*exposed to*) **to be ~ to sth** estar sujeto a algo; **to be ~ to colds** ser propenso a acatarrarse; **to be ~ to many dangers** estar expuesto a muchos peligros; **to be ~ to high taxes** estar sujeto a impuestos elevados; **~ to prosecution** sujeto a persecución **3.**(*contingent on*) **~ to approval** pendiente de aprobación

subject² [səb·'dʒekt] *vt* dominar

subjection [səb·'dʒek·ʃən] *n* POL someti- miento *m*

subjective [səb·'dʒek·tɪv] *adj* subjetivo, -a

subject matter *n* (*of meeting, book*) tema *m;* (*of letter*) contenido *m*

sub judice [ˌsʌb·'dʒu·də·si] *adj* LAW sub júdice

subjugate ['sʌb·dʒə·geɪt] *vt form* **1.** (*control*) subyugar **2.** (*make submissive*) someter; **to ~ sb/sth to sb/sth** supeditar alguien/algo a al- guien/algo

subjugation [ˌsʌb·dʒə·'geɪ·ʃən] *n form* subyu- gación

subjunctive [səb·'dʒʌŋk·tɪv] *n* LING sub- juntivo *m*

sublease [ˌsʌb·'lis] *vt* subarrendar

sublet [sʌb·'let] <sublet, sublet> *vt* subarren- dar

sublimate ['sʌb·lɪ·meɪt] *vt* PSYCH sublimar

sublime [sə·'blaɪm] *adj* **1.** (*glorious*) sublime **2.** *iron* (*absolute*) absoluto, -a; **~ ignorance** ignorancia *f* supina

subliminal [ˌsʌb·'lɪm·ə·nəl] *adj* PSYCH subli- minal

submachine gun [ˌsʌb·mə·'ʃin·ˌɡʌn] *n* metra- lleta *f*

submarine ['sʌb·mə·rin] I. *n* **1.** NAUT, MIL sub- marino *m inv* **2.** *inf* (*sandwich*) sándwich *m* mixto II. *adj* submarino, -a

submenu [ˌsʌb·'men·ju] *n* COMPUT submenú *m*

submerge [səb·'mɜrdʒ] I. *vt* sumergir; **to ~ oneself in sth** *fig* dedicarse de lleno a algo II. *vi* sumergirse

submersible [səb·'mɜr·sə·bəl] *n* sumer- gible *m*

submersion [səb·'mɜr·ʒən] *n* sumersión *f*

submission [səb·'mɪʃ·ən] *n* **1.** (*acquiescence*) sumisión *f* **2.** (*of proposal*) presentación *f;* (*of document*) entrega *f*

submissive [səb·'mɪs·ɪv] *adj* sumiso, -a

submit [səb·'mɪt] <-tt-> I. *vt* **1.** (*hand in: pro- posal*) presentar; (*document*) entregar **2.** *form* (*propose*) proponer II. *vi* (*yield*) someterse

subordinate¹ [sə·'bɔr·dən·ɪt] I. *n* subordi- nado, -a *m, f* II. *adj* (*secondary*) secundario, -a; (*lower in rank*) subordinado, -a

subordinate² [sə·'bɔr·də·neɪt] *vt* subordinar

subordinate clause *n* LING frase *f* subordinada

subordination [sə·ˌbɔr·dən·'eɪ·ʃən] *n* subordi- nación *f*

subplot ['sʌb·plat] *n* argumento *m* secundario

subpoena [sə·'pi·nə] LAW I. *vt* citar; **to ~ sb to testify** mandar comparecer a alguien para tes- tificar II. *n* citación *f* (judicial)

subscribe [səb·'skraɪb] I. *vi* **1.** (*order*) suscri- birse **2.** (*agree with*) **to ~ to sth** suscribir algo II. *vt* **1.** (*contribute*) donar **2.** *form* (*sign*) firmar

subscriber [səb·'skraɪ·bər] *n* (*to magazine*) suscriptor(a) *m(f);* (*to phone service*) abo- nado, -a *m, f*

subscript [sʌb·'skrɪpt] *n* TYPO subíndice *m*

subscription [səb·'skrɪp·ʃən] *n* suscripción *f;* **to order a ~ to sth** suscribirse a algo

subsection ['sʌb·ˌsek·ʃən] *n* **1.** (*part*) subdivi- sión *f* **2.** LAW apartado *m*

subsequent ['sʌb·sɪ·kwənt] *adj* posterior; **~ to...** después de...

subsequently *adv* después; **~ to...** después de...

subservient [səb·'sɜr·vi·ənt] *adj* **1.** *pej* (*ser- vile*) servil **2.** (*secondary*) subordinado, -a

subset ['sʌb·set] *n* MATH subconjunto *m*

subside [səb·'saɪd] *vi* **1.** (*lessen*) disminuir **2.** (*sink: water*) bajar; (*ground*) hundirse

subsidiary [səb·'sɪd·i·er·i] I. *adj* subsidiario, -a; (*reason*) secundario, -a; ECON filial II. <-ies> *n* ECON filial *f*

subsidize ['sʌb·sə·daɪz] *vt* subvencionar

subsidy ['sʌb·sə·di] <-ies> *n* subvención *f,* subsidio *m;* **unemployment ~** subsidio de desempleo

subsist [səb·'sɪst] *vi form* subsistir; **to ~ on sth** sustentarse con [*o* a base de] algo

subsistence [səb·'sɪs·təns] *n* subsistencia *f;* **means of ~** medios *mpl* de subsistencia; **enough for a bare ~** suficiente para subsistir

substance ['sʌb·stəns] *n* **1.** (*matter*) sustancia *f* **2.** (*essence*) esencia *f* **3.** (*significance*) valor *m;* **a film of real ~** una película de gran valor *f* **4.** (*main point*) punto *m* más importante; **the ~ of the conversation** el punto esencial de la conversación; **in ~** en esencia **5.** (*possessions*) riqueza *f;* **a man of ~** un hombre acaudalado

substandard [ˌsʌb·'stæn·dərd] *adj* inferior

substantial [səb·'stæn·ʃəl] *adj* **1.** (*important*) sustancial; (*difference, improvement*) notable; **to be in ~ agreement** estar de acuerdo en gran parte **2.** (*large*) grande; (*meal*) copioso, -a; (*sum, damage*) considerable **3.** (*sturdy*) sólido, -a

substantially [səb·'stæn·ʃə·li] *adv* **1.** (*signifi- cantly*) considerablemente **2.** (*in the main*) esencialmente

substantiate [səb·'stæn·ʃi·eɪt] *vt* corroborar

substantive ['sʌb·stən·tɪv] I. *n* LING sustantivo *m* II. *adj form* de peso

substation ['sʌb·ˌsteɪ·ʃən] *n* **1.** ELEC subesta- ción *f* **2.** ADMIN subdelegación *f;* **police ~** comisaría *f* (de policía)

substitute ['sʌb·stə·tut] I. *vt* sustituir; **to ~ sb for sb** *inf* reemplazar a alguien por alguien; **to ~ margarine for butter, to ~ butter with margarine** sustituir la mantequilla por la mar- garina II. *vi* **to ~ for sb** suplir a alguien III. *n* **1.** (*equivalent*) sustituto *m;* (*alternative: for milk, coffee*) sucedáneo *m;* **there's no ~ for him** no hay nadie como él **2.** *a.* SPORTS suplente *mf;* **to come on as a ~** sustituir a alguien **3.** SCHOOL (*teacher*) suplente *mf*

substitute teacher *n* profesor , -a *m, f* suplente

substitution [ˌsʌb·stə·'tu·ʃən] *n* sustitución *f*

substratum ['sʌb·ˌstreɪ·təm] <-ta> *n* sus- trato *m*

subsume [səb·'sum] *vt form* subsumir; **to ~ sth under a category** subsumir algo dentro de una categoría

subtenant ['sʌb·ˌten·ənt] *n* subarrendatario, -a *m, f*

subterfuge ['sʌb·tər·fjudʒ] *n* subterfugio *m;* **by ~** por subterfugio

subterranean [ˌsʌb·tə·'reɪ·ni·ən] *adj* subterráneo, -a

subtext ['sʌb·tekst] *n* subtexto *m*

subtitle ['sʌb·ˌtaɪ·ṭəl] **I.** *vt* subtitular **II.** *n* subtítulo *m*

subtle ['sʌṭ·əl] *adj* **1.** (*delicate*) sutil; (*flavor*) suave; (*nuance*) tenue **2.** (*slight: difference*) sutil **3.** (*astute: person*) astuto, -a; (*question, suggestion*) inteligente; (*humor*) fino, -a

subtlety ['sʌt·əl·ti] <-ies> *n* **1.** (*delicacy: of flavor, smell*) delicadeza *f* **2.** (*of person, argument*) sutileza *f*

subtotal ['sʌb·ˌtoʊ·ṭəl] *n* subtotal *m*

subtract [səb·'trækt] *vt* sustraer; **to ~ 3 from 5** restar 3 a 5

subtraction [səb·'træk·ʃən] *n* resta *f,* sustracción *f*

subtropical [ˌsʌb·'trap·ɪ·kəl] *adj* subtropical

suburb ['sʌb·ɜrb] *n* barrio *m* periférico; **the ~s** la periferia; **to live in the ~s** vivir en las afueras

suburban [sə·'bɜr·bən] *adj* **1.** (*area*) periférico, -a; (*train*) de cercanías **2.** (*lifestyle*) aburguesado, -a

suburbia [sə·'bɜr·bi·ə] *n* barrios *mpl* periféricos

subvention [səb·'ven·ʃən] *n form* subvención *f*

subversion [səb·'vɜr·ʒən] *n form* subversión *f*

subversive [səb·'vɜr·sɪv] *form* **I.** *adj* subversivo, -a **II.** *n* persona *f* subversiva

subvert [sʌb·'vɜrt] *vt* (*authority*) minar; (*principle*) debilitar

subway ['sʌb·weɪ] *n* metro *m,* subte *m Arg*

sub-zero [ˌsʌb·'zɪr·oʊ] *adj* bajo cero

succeed [sək·'sid] **I.** *vi* **1.** (*be successful*) tener éxito; **to ~ in doing sth** lograr hacer algo; **the plan ~ed** el plan salió bien **2.** (*follow*) suceder ▶ **if at first you don't ~,** **try, try again** *prov* si no lo consigues a la primera, vuelve a intentarlo una y otra vez **II.** *vt* (*follow*) suceder a

succeeding *adj* **1.** (*next in line*) sucesor(a) **2.** (*following*) siguiente; (*generation*) venidero, -a; **in the ~ weeks** en las próximas semanas

success [sək·'ses] *n* **1.** (*outcome*) éxito *m;* **to meet with ~** tener éxito; **to be a big ~ with sb/sth** tener gran éxito con alguien/algo; **to have ~ in doing sth** conseguir hacer algo; **to make a ~ of sth** tener éxito en algo; **to wish sb ~ with sth** desear a alguien que le vaya bien algo; **to be a great ~** ser un gran éxito; **to enjoy ~** tener éxito; **~ story** éxito *m* **2.** (*successful person, thing*) éxito *m;* **he was a ~ with my children** les cayó muy bien a mis hijos

successful [sək·'ses·fəl] *adj* exitoso, -a; (*business*) próspero, -a; (*candidate*) electo, -a; (*solution*) eficaz; **to be ~** (*person*) tener éxito;

(*business*) prosperar; **commercially ~** con éxito comercial

succession [sək·'seʃ·ən] *n* sucesión *f;* **~ rights** derechos *mpl* de sucesión; **in ~** sucesivamente; **a ~ of** una serie de; **an endless ~ of** un sinfín de

successive [sək·'ses·ɪv] *adj* sucesivo, -a; **on ~ occasions** varias veces seguidas

successor [sək·'ses·ər] *n* sucesor(a) *m(f)*

succinct [sək·'sɪŋkt] *adj* sucinto, -a

succor ['sʌk·ər] **I.** *n* socorro *m;* **to give ~ to sb** socorrer a alguien **II.** *vt* socorrer

succulent ['sʌk·jʊ·lənt] **I.** *adj* (*steak, fruit*) suculento, -a; (*plant*) carnoso, -a **II.** *n* planta *f* carnosa

succumb [sə·'kʌm] *vi form* **1.** (*surrender*) sucumbir; **to ~ to pressure/temptation** sucumbir ante la presión/a la tentación **2.** (*die*) morir; **to ~ to one's injuries** morir a causa de las heridas

such [sʌtʃ] **I.** *adj* tal, semejante; **~ great weather/a good book** un tiempo/un libro tan bueno; **~ an honor** tanto honor; **to earn a lot of money** ganar tanto dinero; **or some ~ remark** o un comentario por el estilo; **to buy some fruit ~ as apples** comprar fruta como manzanas **II.** *pron* **~ is life** así es la vida; **people ~ as him** las personas que son como él; **~ as it is** tal como es; **as ~** propiamente dicho

such and such ['sʌtʃ·ən·ˌsʌtʃ] *adj inf* tal o cual; **to arrive at ~ a time** llegar a tal o cual hora; **to meet sb in ~ a place** encontrarse con alguien en tal o cual lugar

suck [sʌk] **I.** *vt* succionar; (*with straw*) sorber; (*air*) aspirar; (*breast*) mamar; (*sweets*) chupar; **to ~ one's thumb** chuparse el dedo **II.** *vi* **1.** (*with mouth*) chupar **2.** *inf* **this ~s!** ¡esto es una mierda! **III.** *n* chupada *f;* (*with straw*) sorbo *m*

◆ **suck up to** *vt* dar coba a

sucker ['sʌk·ər] **I.** *n* **1.** *pej* (*stupid person*) imbécil *mf* **2.** *sl* (*thing*) mierda *f* **3.** (*device*) a. ZOOL ventosa *f* **II.** *vt inf* timar; **to ~ sb into sth** timar a alguien en algo; **to ~ sb into/out of doing sth** engañar a alguien para que haga/no haga algo

suckle ['sʌk·əl] **I.** *vt* amamantar **II.** *vi* mamar

suckling pig ['sʌk·lɪŋ·ˌpɪg] *n* lechón *m*

sucrose ['su·kroʊs] *n* sacarosa *f*

suction ['sʌk·ʃən] *n* succión *f*

suction pump *n* bomba *f* de succión

Sudan [su·'dæn] *n* Sudán *m*

Sudanese [ˌsu·də·'niz] **I.** *n* sudanés, -esa *m, f* **II.** *adj* sudanés, -esa

sudden ['sʌd·ən] *adj* (*immediate*) repentino, -a, sorpresivo, -a *AmL;* (*death*) súbito, -a; (*departure*) imprevisto, -a; (*movement, drop*) brusco, -a; **to put a ~ stop to sth** detener algo de forma repentina; **all of a ~** *inf* de repente

suddenly *adv* de repente

suds [sʌdz] *npl* **1.** jabonaduras *fpl* **2.** cerveza *f*

sue [su] <suing> **I.** *vt* demandar; **to ~ sb for**

S

damages demandar a alguien por daños y perjuicios; **to ~ sb for divorce** ponerle a alguien una demanda de divorcio **II.** *vi* presentar demanda; **to ~ for peace** pedir la paz

suede [sweɪd] *n* ante *m*

suet ['suːɪt] *n* sebo *m*

suffer ['sʌf·ər] **I.** *vi* **1.** (*be in distress*) sufrir; **the economy is ~ing from...** la economía se está viendo afectada por...; **to ~ for sth** ser castigado por algo **2.** (*seem worse*) **to ~ in** [*o* **by**] **comparison** salir perdiendo en comparación con alguien/algo **II.** *vt* **1.** (*undergo: defeat, setback*) sufrir; **to ~ the consequences** sufrir las consecuencias; **to ~ the misfortune of...** tener mala suerte de... **2.** MED padecer de

sufferance ['sʌf·ər·əns] *n* tolerancia *f*; **on ~ de** mala gana

sufferer ['sʌf·ər·ər] *n* enfermo, -a *m, f*; **AIDS ~** enfermo de SIDA

suffering ['sʌf·ər·ɪŋ] *n* sufrimiento *m*; **years of ~** años de penurias

suffice [sə·'faɪs] *vi* bastar; **~ (it) to say that...** basta decir que...

sufficiency [sə·'fɪʃ·ən·si] *n* cantidad *f* suficiente

sufficient [sə·'fɪʃ·ənt] *adj* suficiente; **to have ~** tener bastante; **to be ~ for sth** ser suficiente para algo

suffix ['sʌf·ɪks] *n* LING sufijo *m*

suffocate ['sʌf·ə·keɪt] **I.** *vi* asfixiarse **II.** *vt* **1.** (*asphyxiate*) asfixiar **2.** *fig* sofocar

suffocating *adj* **1.** (*heat, fumes*) asfixiante **2.** *fig* sofocante

suffrage ['sʌf·rɪdʒ] *n* sufragio *m*; **universal ~** sufragio universal

suffragette [ˌsʌf·rə·'dʒet] *n* POL, HIST sufragista *f*

sugar ['ʃʊg·ər] **I.** *n* **1.** CULIN azúcar *m* **2.** *inf* (*term of affection*) cariño **II.** *vt* echar azúcar a

sugar beet *n* remolacha *f* azucarera

sugar cane *n* caña *f* de azúcar

sugarcoated [ˌsʊg·ər·'koʊ·tɪd] *adj* cubierto, -a de azúcar

sugar cube *n* terrón *m* de azúcar

sugar daddy *n hombre rico y mayor que da regalos o dinero a una mujer con el objetivo de tener relaciones sexuales con ella*

sugarless *adj* sin azúcar

sugary ['ʃʊg·ə·ri] *adj* **1.** (*sweet*) azucarado, -a **2.** *fig, pej* (*insincere*) meloso, -a

suggest [səg·'dʒest] *vt* **1.** (*propose*) proponer, sugerir; **to ~ (to sb) that...** sugerirle a alguien que... +*subj*; **to ~ doing sth** sugerir hacer algo; **an idea ~ed itself (to him)** se le ocurrió una idea **2.** (*indicate*) indicar **3.** (*hint*) insinuar; **what are you trying to ~?** ¿qué insinúas?

suggestible [səg·'dʒes·tə·bəl] *adj pej, form* sugestionable; **highly ~** muy influenciable

suggestion [səg·'dʒes·tʃən] *n* **1.** (*proposed idea*) sugerencia *f*; **to make the ~ that...** sugerir que... +*subj*; **to be open to new ~s** estar abierto a nuevas sugerencias; **at Ann's ~** a petición de Ann **2.** (*very small amount*) pizca

f; **there was a ~ of a smile on his face** esbozó una sonrisa **3.** (*insinuation*) insinuación *f*

suggestion box *n* buzón *m* de sugerencias

suggestive [səg·'dʒes·tɪv] *adj* **1.** (*lewd*) indecente **2.** (*evocative*) sugestivo, -a

suicidal [ˌsu·ə·'saɪ·dəl] *adj* suicida; **to feel ~** tener ganas de suicidarse; *fig* tener el ánimo por los suelos

suicide ['su·ə·saɪd] *n* **1.** (*act*) suicidio *m*; **to commit ~** suicidarse **2.** *form* (*person*) suicida *mf*

suit [sut] **I.** *vt* **1.** (*be convenient*) convenir; **to ~ sb** convenirle a alguien; **that ~s me fine** eso me viene bien **2.** (*be right*) ir [*o* sentar] bien; **they are well ~ed (to** [*o* **for**] **each other)** hacen (una) buena pareja; **this lifestyle seems to ~ her** parece ser que esta clase de vida le sienta bien **3.** (*look attractive with*) quedar bien; **this dress ~s you** este vestido te sienta bien **4.** (*choose at will*) **to ~ oneself** hacer lo que uno quiere; **~ yourself!** ¡haz lo que quieras! **II.** *n* **1.** (*jacket and pants*) traje *m*, terno *m Chile*, flus *m Ant, Col, Ven*; (*jacket and skirt*) traje *m* de chaqueta; **bathing** [*o* **swim**] **~** traje *m* de baño **2.** LAW pleito *m*; **to bring** [*o* **file**] **a ~** entablar un pleito **3.** GAMES palo *m*; **to follow ~** seguir el palo; *fig* seguir el ejemplo

suitable ['su·tə·bəl] *adj* apropiado, -a; **to be ~ for sb** ser apropiado [*o* adecuado] para alguien; **not ~ for children under 14** no apto para niños menores de 14 años

suitcase ['sut·keɪs] *n* maleta *f*, valija *f RíoPl*, petaca *f Méx*

suite [swit] *n* **1.** (*set of rooms*) suite *f*; **bridal ~** suite nupcial **2.** (*set of furniture*) juego *m* **3.** MUS suite *f*

suitor ['su·tər] *n* **1.** *a. iron* (*potential husband*) pretendiente *m* **2.** LAW demandante *mf*

sulfate ['sʌl·feɪt] *n* sulfato *m*

sulfide ['sʌl·faɪd] *n* sulfuro *m*

sulfur ['sʌl·fər] *n* azufre *m*

sulfur dioxide ['sʌl·fər·daɪ·'ak·saɪd] *n* dióxido *m* de azufre

sulfuric [sʌl·'fjʊr·ɪk] *adj* sulfúrico, -a

sulfuric acid *n* ácido *m* sulfúrico

sulfurous ['sʌl·fər·əs] *adj* (*solution*) de azufre; (*smell*) a azufre

sulk [sʌlk] **I.** *vi* enfurruñarse, alunarse *RíoPl*, amurrarse *Chile* **II.** *n* mal humor *m*; **to be in a ~** estar enfurruñado, -a, estar alunado, -a *RíoPl*, estar amurrado, -a *Chile*

sulky ['sʌl·ki] <-ier, -iest> *adj* enfurruñado, -a

sullen ['sʌl·ən] *adj* **1.** *pej* (*person*) malhumorado, -a **2.** *liter* (*sky*) sombrío, -a

sully ['sʌl·i] <-ied, -ied> *vt* mancillar, manchar

sultan ['sʌl·tən] *n* sultán *m*

sultana [sʌl·'tæn·ə] *n* pasa *f* de Esmirna

sultry ['sʌl·tri] <-ier, -iest> *adj* **1.** (*weather*) bochornoso, -a **2.** (*sensual*) sensual

sum [sʌm] *n* **1.** (*amount of money*) cantidad *f* (de dinero) **2.** (*total*) total *m*; **in ~** en resumen

3. (*calculation*) cuenta *f*
summarize ['sʌm·ə·raɪz] *vt* resumir
summary ['sʌm·ə·ri] **I.** *n* resumen *m* **II.** *adj* (*dismissal, execution*) inmediato, -a; LAW sumario, -a
summation [sə·'meɪ·ʃən] *n* **1.** MATH suma *f* **2.** LAW escrito *m* de conclusiones
summer ['sʌm·ər] **I.** *n* verano *m;* **a ~'s day** un día de verano, un día veraniego **II.** *adj* de verano, veraniego, -a **III.** *vi* veranear, pasar el verano
summer camp *n* campamento *m* de verano
summertime ['sʌm·ər·taɪm] *n* (*season*) verano *m;* **in the ~** en verano
summer vacation *n* vacaciones *fpl* de verano [*o* estivales]

> **i** Las vacaciones de verano (**summer vacation**) duran en EE.UU. tres meses — de mediados de junio a mediados de septiembre. Originalmente, su duración era tan larga para permitir a los niños trabajar en una granja o un rancho. Entre los siglos XIX y XX, cuando se produjeron importantes movimientos de población hacia las zonas urbanas, fueron ganando popularidad los campamentos de verano (**summer camps**), que ofrecían a los niños de las ciudades la oportunidad de experimentar la naturaleza de cerca. Hoy día existen campamentos de música, béisbol, equitación, etc.

summery ['sʌm·ə·ri] *adj* veraniego, -a
summing-up [,sʌm·ɪŋ·'ʌp] <summings-up> *n* LAW recapitulación *f*
summit ['sʌm·ɪt] *n* **1.** (*top of mountain*) cima *f* **2.** *fig* (*of career, power*) cumbre *f* **3.** POL cumbre *f;* **to hold a ~** celebrar una cumbre; **~ conference** (conferencia *f*) cumbre
summon ['sʌm·ən] *vt* (*people*) llamar; (*meeting*) convocar; LAW citar
◆**summon up** *vt* (*countable*) reunir; **to ~ the courage/strength to do sth** armarse de valor/fuerzas para hacer algo
summons ['sʌm·ənz] *n* llamamiento *m;* LAW citación *f;* **to issue a ~** despachar una citación; **to serve sb with a ~** entregarle una citación a alguien
sump [sʌmp] *n* **1.** (*cesspit*) pozo *m* negro **2.** MIN sumidero *m*
sumptuous ['sʌmp·tʃʊ·əs] *adj* suntuoso, -a
sun [sʌn] **I.** *n* sol *m;* **the ~'s rays** los rayos del sol; **the rising/setting ~** el sol naciente/poniente; **to sit in the ~** sentarse al sol ▶**to call sb every name under the ~** decir a alguien de todo; **to do/try everything under the ~** hacer/probar de todo **II.** <-nn-> *vt* **to ~ oneself** tomar el sol
Sun. *n abbr of* **Sunday** dom.
sunbaked ['sʌn·beɪkt] *adj* secado, -a al sol;

(*earth, street*) calcinado, -a
sunbath ['sʌn·bæθ] *n* baño *m* de sol
sunbathe ['sʌn·beɪð] *vi* tomar el sol
sunbeam ['sʌn·bim] *n* rayo *m* de sol
sunblock ['sʌn·blak] *n* filtro *m* solar
sunburn ['sʌn·bɜrn] *n* quemadura *f* de sol
sunburned *adj*, **sunburnt** *adj* quemado, -a (por el sol)
sundae ['sʌn·di] *n* helado con trozos de fruta, frutos secos, crema, etc.
Sunday ['sʌn·deɪ] *n* domingo *m;* **Palm/ Easter ~** domingo de Ramos/de Resurrección; *s.a.* **Friday**
Sunday best *n*, **Sunday clothes** *npl* vestido *m* de los domingos
Sunday school *n* REL ≈ catequesis *f inv*
sundial *n* reloj *m* de sol
sundown *n s.* **sunset**
sun-dried *adj* secado, -a al sol
sundry ['sʌn·dri] *adj* varios, -as; **~ items** objetos varios
sunflower ['sʌn·ˌflaʊ·ər] *n* girasol *m,* maravilla *f Chile*
sunflower oil *n* aceite *m* de girasol
sunflower seed *n* pipa *f*
sung [sʌŋ] *pp of* **sing**
sunglasses ['sʌn·ˌglæs·ɪs] *npl* gafas *fpl* de sol
sunhat *n* pamela *f*
sunk [sʌŋk] *pp of* **sink**
sunken ['sʌŋ·kən] *adj* **1.** (*ship, treasure*) sumergido, -a **2.** (*cheeks, eyes*) hundido, -a
sunlight ['sʌn·laɪt] *n* luz *f* del sol
sunlit ['sʌn·lɪt] *adj* soleado, -a
sunny ['sʌn·i] <-ier, -iest> *adj* **1.** (*day*) soleado, -a **2.** (*personality*) alegre
sunny-side up *adj* **she likes her eggs ~** le gustan los huevos fritos
sun protection factor *n* factor *m* de protección solar
sunrise ['sʌn·raɪz] *n* amanecer *m;* **at ~** al amanecer, al alba
sunrise industry *n* industria *f* del porvenir
sunroof ['sʌn·ruf] *n* techo *m* corredizo
sunroom *n habitación acristalada para que entre la luz del sol*
sunscreen *n* filtro *m* solar
sunset ['sʌn·set] *n* puesta *f* de sol; **at ~** al atardecer
sunshade ['sʌn·ʃeɪd] *n* **1.** (*umbrella*) sombrilla *f* **2.** (*awning*) toldo *m*
sunshine ['sʌn·ʃaɪn] *n* sol *m;* **in the ~** al sol
sunspot ['sʌn·spat] *n* mancha *f* solar
sunstroke *n* insolación *f,* asoleada *f Col, Chile, Guat;* **to have ~** tener una insolación
suntan ['sʌn·tæn] *n* bronceado *m;* **to get a ~** broncearse
suntan lotion *n* crema *f* bronceadora
suntanned *adj* bronceado, -a
suntan oil *n* aceite *m* bronceador
sunup ['sʌn·ʌp] *n s.* **sunrise**
sun visor *n* AUTO visera *f*
super ['su·pər] **I.** *adj inf* genial **II.** *adv inf* súper **III.** *n* **1.** *inf s.* **supervisor** súper *mf* **2.** AUTO

(gasolina *f*) súper *f*

superabundant [ˌsu·pər·ə·'bʌn·dənt] *adj* superabundante, sobreabundante

superb [sə·'pɜrb] *adj* magnífico, -a

> **i** En el fútbol americano profesional, el **Super Bowl** es el partido que se disputa cada año para definir el campeonato de la Liga Nacional de Fútbol (**NFL**). Iniciado en 1967, el partido se juega entre los dos mejores equipos de la NFL el "Domingo del Super Bowl", cuando concluye la temporada regular, y se ha convertido en uno de los eventos con mayor audiencia televisiva en Estados Unidos.

supercharged [ˈsu·pər·ˌtʃɑrdʒd] *adj* **1.**(*engine*) sobrealimentado, -a **2.**(*atmosphere*) cargado, -a de emotividad

supercharger [ˈsu·pər·ˌtʃɑr·dʒər] *n* TECH sobrealimentador *m*

supercilious [ˌsu·pər·'sɪl·i·əs] *adj pej* altanero, -a

superego [ˌsu·pər·'i·gou] *n* PSYCH superego *m*

superficial [ˌsu·pər·'fɪʃ·əl] *adj* superficial

superficiality [ˌsu·pər·ˌfɪʃ·i·'æl·ə·t̪i] *n* superficialidad *f*

superfluous [su·'pɜr·flu·əs] *adj* superfluo, -a; **to be ~** estar de más

superglue® [ˈsu·pər·glu] *n* superglue® *m*

superhero [ˈsu·pər·ˌhɪr·ou] <-heroes> *n inf* superhéroe *m*

superhighway [ˈsu·pər·ˈhaɪ·weɪ] *n* autopista *f* (de varios carriles); **information ~** autopista de la información

superhuman [ˌsu·pər·'hju·mən] *adj* sobrehumano, -a

superimpose [ˌsu·pər·ɪm·'pouz] *vt* PHOT superponer

superintend [ˌsu·pər·ɪn·'tend] *vt* supervisar

superintendent [ˌsu·pər·ɪn·'ten·dənt] *n* **1.**(*person in charge: of department, school district*) director(a) *m(f)*; (*of building*) portero, -a *m, f* **2.** LAW (*police officer*) superintendente *mf*

superior [sə·'pɪr·i·ər] **I.** *adj* **1.**(*better, senior*) superior; **to be ~** (**to sb/sth**) estar por encima de alguien/algo **2.**(*greater in amount*) **a ~ number of sth** un número mayor de algo **II.** *n* superior *mf*

superiority [sə·ˌpɪr·i·'ɔr·ə·t̪i] *n* superioridad *f*

superiority complex *n inf* complejo *m* de superioridad

superlative [su·'pɜr·lə·t̪ɪv] **I.** *adj* **1.**(*best*) excepcional **2.** LING superlativo, -a **II.** *n* LING superlativo *m*

superman [ˈsu·pər·mæn] *n* superhombre *m*; CINE Supermán *m*

supermarket [ˈsu·pər·ˌmar·kɪt] *n* supermercado *m*

supermodel [ˈsu·pər·ˌmad·əl] *n* super-

modelo *f*

supernatural [ˌsu·pər·'nætʃ·ər·əl] **I.** *adj* sobrenatural **II.** *n* the ~ lo sobrenatural

supernumerary [ˌsu·pər·'nu·mə·rer·i] **I.** *adj form* supernumerario, -a **II.**<-ies> *n form* supernumerario, -a *m, f*; THEAT figurante *mf*

superpower [ˈsu·pər·ˌpau·ər] *n* POL superpotencia *f*

superscript [ˈsu·pər·skrɪpt] *n* TYPO superíndice *m*

supersede [ˌsu·pər·'sid] *vt* sustituir

supersonic [ˌsu·pər·'san·ɪk] *adj* AVIAT supersónico, -a

superstar [ˈsu·pər·star] *n* superestrella *f*

superstition [ˌsu·pər·'stɪʃ·ən] *n* superstición *f*

superstitious [ˌsu·pər·'stɪʃ·əs] *adj* supersticioso, -a

superstore [ˈsu·pər·stɔr] *n* hipermercado *m*

superstructure [ˈsu·pər·ˌstrʌk·tʃər] *n* superestructura *f*

supertanker [ˈsu·pər·ˌtæŋ·kər] *n* superpetrolero *m*

supervise [ˈsu·pər·vaɪz] *vt* (*watch over*) supervisar; (*thesis*) dirigir

supervision [ˌsu·pər·'vɪʒ·ən] *n* supervisión *f*; **under the ~ of sb** bajo la supervisión de alguien

supervisor [ˈsu·pər·vaɪ·zər] *n* **1.**(*person in charge*) supervisor(a) *m(f)* **2.** POL alcalde, -esa *m, f*

supervisory [ˌsu·pər·'vaɪ·zə·ri] *adj* de supervisor

supine [su·'paɪn] **I.** *adj* supino, -a; **to be ~** estar tumbado de espaldas **II.** *adv* **to lie ~** estar tumbado de espaldas

supper [ˈsʌp·ər] *n* cena *f*; **to have ~** cenar

suppertime *n* hora *f* de cenar

supplant [sə·'plænt] *vt* sustituir

supple [ˈsʌp·əl] *adj* (*leather, skin*) flexible; (*person*) ágil

supplement [ˈsʌp·lə·mənt] **I.** *n* **1.**(*something extra*) complemento *m* **2.**(*part of newspaper*) suplemento *m* **3.**(*of book*) apéndice *m* **II.** *vt* complementar

supplementary [ˌsʌp·lə·'men·tə·ri] *adj* adicional, suplementario, -a

suppleness [ˈsʌp·əl·nɪs] *n* (*of leather, skin*) flexibilidad *f*; (*of person*) agilidad *f*

supplicant [ˈsʌp·lə·kənt] *n* suplicante *mf*

supplication [ˌsʌp·lə·'keɪ·ʃən] *n* súplica *f*

supplier [sə·'plaɪ·ər] *n* proveedor(a) *m(f)*

supply [sə·'plaɪ] **I.**<-ie-> *vt* **1.**(*provide: electricity, food, money*) suministrar; (*information*) proporcionar, facilitar; **to be accused of ~ing drugs** ser acusado de tráfico de drogas **2.** COM proveer **II.** *n* **1.**(*act of providing: of electricity, water*) suministro *m* **2.** ECON oferta *f*; **~ and demand** oferta y demanda; **to be in short ~** escasear

supply-side economics [sə·'plaɪ·saɪd·i·kə·'nam·ɪks] *npl* economía *f* de la oferta

support [sə·'pɔrt] **I.** *vt* **1.**(*hold up: roof*) sostener; (*weight*) aguantar, resistir; **to ~ oneself**

on sth apoyarse en algo **2.** (*provide for*) mantener; **to ~ four children** mantener a cuatro hijos; **to ~ oneself** ganarse la vida **3.** (*provide with money*) financiar **4.** (*encourage*) apoyar **5.** (*show to be true*) confirmar **II.** *n* **1.** (*backing, help*) apoyo *m;* **to give sb moral ~** darle apoyo moral a alguien **2.** (*structure*) soporte *m; fig* (*person*) sostén *m* **3.** FIN ayuda económica **4.** (*confirmation*) confirmación *f;* **to lend ~ to sth** respaldar algo; **in ~ of sth** en apoyo de algo

supporter *n* **1.** (*of cause, candidate*) partidario, -a *m, f* **2.** SPORTS (*fan*) seguidor(a) *m(f)* **3.** SPORTS (*protector for genitals*) suspensorio *m*

supporting *adj* (*film, role, actor*) secundario, -a

supportive [sə·'pɔr·ţɪv] *adj* comprensivo, -a; **to be ~ of sth/sb** apoyar algo/a alguien

suppose [sə·'poʊz] *vt* **1.** suponer; **to ~** (**that**)... suponer que...; **I ~ not/so** supongo que no/que sí; **I don't ~ so** supongo que no; **let's ~ that** supongamos que **2.** (*believe, think*) creer **3.** (*obligation*) **to be ~d to do sth** tener que hacer algo; **he was ~d to collect the money** tenía que ir a recoger el dinero; **you are not ~d to know that** no deberías saber eso **4.** (*opinion*) **the book is ~d to be very good** dicen que el libro es muy bueno; **she is ~d to be intelligent** dicen que es inteligente

supposed *adj* (*killer*) presunto, -a; (*date*) supuesto, -a

supposedly [sə·'poʊ·zɪd·li] *adv* supuestamente

supposing *conj* **~ that**... suponiendo que...

supposition [ˌsʌp·ə·'zɪʃ·ən] *n* suposición *f*

suppository [sə·'paz·ə·tɔr·i] <-ies> *n* supositorio *m*

suppress [sə·'pres] *vt* **1.** (*criticism, revolt, terrorism*) reprimir, sofocar **2.** (*sneeze, yawn, emotion*) reprimir; (*evidence, information*) ocultar **3.** MED inhibir

suppression [sə·'preʃ·ən] *n* **1.** (*of criticism, revolt*) represión *f* **2.** (*of anger, emotion*) represión *f;* (*of evidence*) ocultación *f* **3.** MED inhibición *f* **4.** PSYCH (*of memories*) represión *f*

supremacy [sə·'prem·ə·si] *n* supremacía *f*

supreme [sə·'prim] **I.** *adj* **1.** (*authority*) supremo, -a; (*commander*) en jefe; **Supreme Court** Tribunal Supremo **2.** (*achievement, sacrifice*) mayor; **to show ~ courage** mostrar una gran valentía **II.** *adv* **to reign ~** estar en la cumbre, no tener ningún rival

surcharge ['sɜr·tʃardʒ] **I.** *n* recargo *m* **II.** *vt* aplicar un recargo a

sure [ʃʊr] **I.** *adj* **1.** (*certain*) seguro, -a; **to be ~ of sth** estar seguro de algo; **to be ~** (**that**)... estar seguro de que...; **to make ~** (**that**)... asegurarse de que...; **to** (**not**) **be ~ if...** (no) estar seguro de si...; **she is ~ to come** vendrá seguro; **are you ~ you won't come?** ¿estás seguro de que no vendrás?; **I'm not ~ why/how** no sé muy bien por qué/cómo; **~ thing!**

¡claro!; **for ~** seguro **2.** (*confident*) **to be ~ of oneself** estar seguro de sí mismo **II.** *adv* seguro; **~ I will!** *inf* ¡seguro!; **for ~** a ciencia cierta; **~ enough** en efecto ▸ **as ~ as I'm standing here** como me llamo...

sure-footed [ʃʊr·'fʊţ·ɪd] *adj* **1.** (*when walking, climbing*) de pie firme **2.** (*confident*) seguro, -a de sí mismo, -a

surely ['ʃʊr·li] *adv* **1.** (*certainly*) sin duda **2.** (*to show astonishment*) por supuesto; **~ you don't expect me to believe that?** ¿no esperarás que me lo crea? **3.** (*yes, certainly*) ¡claro!

surety ['ʃʊr·ə·ţi] <-ies> *n* LAW **1.** (*person*) fiador(a) *m(f);* **to stand ~** (**for sb**) ser fiador de alguien **2.** (*guarantee*) fianza *f*

surf [sɜrf] **I.** *n* olas *fpl* **II.** *vi* SPORTS hacer surf **III.** *vt* COMPUT **to ~ the Internet** navegar por internet

surface ['sɜr·fɪs] **I.** *n* superficie *f;* **on the ~** *fig* a primera vista; **to scratch the ~ of sth** tratar algo superficialmente [*o por encima*] **II.** *vi* salir a la superficie **III.** *vt* (*road, wall*) revestir; (*with asphalt*) asfaltar

surface mail *n* **by ~** (*land*) por vía terrestre; (*sea*) por vía marítima

surface tension *n* PHYS tensión *f* superficial

surface-to-air missile *n* MIL misil *m* tierra-aire

surfboard ['sɜrf·bɔrd] *n* tabla *f* de surf

surfeit ['sɜr·fɪt] *n form* exceso *m*

surfer ['sɜr·fər] *n* **1.** surfista *mf* **2.** COMPUT internauta *mf*

surfing ['sɜr·fɪŋ] *n* surf *m*

surge [sɜrdʒ] **I.** *vi* **1.** (*move forward*) abalanzarse; (*waves*) levantarse **2.** (*increase*) aumentar vertiginosamente **II.** *n* (*of waves*) oleaje *m;* (*of anger*) arranque *m;* (*of indignation*) ola *f;* (*of prices, support*) aumento *m* repentino; **power ~** sobrecarga *f*

surgeon ['sɜr·dʒən] *n* cirujano, -a *m, f*

surgery ['sɜr·dʒə·ri] *n* cirugía *f;* **to perform ~** practicar una intervención quirúrgica; **to undergo ~** ser operado, someterse a una intervención quirúrgica

surgical ['sɜr·dʒɪ·kəl] *adj* (*procedure*) quirúrgico, -a; (*collar, gloves*) ortopédico, -a

Surinam(e) [ˌsʊr·ɪ·'nam] *n* Surinam *m*

Surinamese [ˌsʊr·ə·na·'miz] **I.** *adj* surinamés, -esa **II.** *n* surinamés, -esa *m, f*

surly ['sɜr·li] <-ier, -iest> *adj* hosco, -a

surmise [sər·'maɪz] *vt form* conjeturar

surmount [sər·'maʊnt] *vt* **1.** (*overcome*) superar **2.** *form* (*be on top of*) coronar

surname ['sɜr·neɪm] *n* apellido *m*

surpass [sər·'pæs] *vt* sobrepasar; **to ~ oneself** superarse

surplus ['sɜr·pləs] **I.** *n* (*of product*) excedente *m;* FIN superávit *m* **II.** *adj* sobrante

surprise [sər·'praɪz] **I.** *n* sorpresa *f;* **in a ~** con sorpresa; **to sb's ~** para sorpresa de alguien **II.** *vt* sorprender; **it ~d her that...** le sorprendió que... *+subj;* **to ~ sb doing sth** sorprender a alguien haciendo algo

surprised *adj* sorprendido, -a

S

surprising *adj* sorprendente, sorpresivo, -a *AmL*

surprisingly *adv* sorprendentemente

surreal [sə·'ri·əl] *adj* surrealista

surrealism [sə·'ri·ə·lɪz·əm] *n* ART surrealismo *m*

surrealist [sə·'ri·ə·lɪst] ART I. *n* surrealista *mf* II. *adj* surrealista

surrender [sə·'ren·dər] I. *vi* rendirse; **to ~ to sb** entregarse a alguien II. *vt form* entregar III. *n* 1.(*giving up*) rendición *f* 2.*form (of document)* entrega *f*

surreptitious [ˌsɜr·əp·'tɪʃ·əs] *adj* subrepticio, -a, furtivo, -a

surrogacy ['sʌr·ə·gə·si] *n* alquiler *m* de madres

surrogate ['sɜr·ə·gɪt] I. *adj* (*substitute*) sucedáneo, -a II. *n* sustituto, -a *m, f*

surrogate mother *n* madre *f* de alquiler

surround [sə·'raʊnd] I. *vt* rodear II. *n* (*frame*) marco *m*

surrounding *adj* de alrededor

surroundings *npl* alrededores *mpl*

surtax ['sɜr·tæks] *n* FIN, POL sobretasa *f*

surveillance [sər·'veɪ·ləns] *n* vigilancia *f;* **to be under ~** estar bajo vigilancia

survey¹ [sər·'veɪ] *vt* 1.(*poll*) encuestar 2. GEO medir 3.(*research*) investigar 4.(*look at carefully*) contemplar

survey² ['sɜr·veɪ] *n* 1.(*poll*) encuesta *f* 2. GEO medición *f* 3.(*report*) informe *m* 4.(*examination*) examen *m*

surveyor [sər·'veɪ·ər] *n* GEO topógrafo, -a *m, f*

survival [sər·'vaɪ·vəl] *n* 1.supervivencia *f* 2.(*relic*) reliquia *f* ► **the ~ of the fittest** la ley del más fuerte

survive [sər·'vaɪv] I. *vi* (*stay alive: person*) sobrevivir; (*book*) conservarse; **to ~ on sth** *inf* vivir [*o* alimentarse] a base de algo II. *vt* sobrevivir a; **to ~ an accident** salir con vida de un accidente

surviving *adj* superviviente

survivor [sər·'vaɪ·vər] *n* superviviente *mf*

susceptible [sə·'sep·tə·bəl] *adj* susceptible; MED propenso, -a

suspect¹ [sə·'spekt] *vt* 1.(*think likely*) sospechar, imaginar; **to ~ sth** sospechar [*o* imaginarse] algo 2.(*consider guilty*) sospechar de, cachar *Chile;* **to ~ sb's motives** dudar de los motivos de alguien

suspect² ['sʌs·pekt] I. *n* sospechoso, -a *m, f* II. *adj* sospechoso, -a

suspend [sə·'spend] *vt* 1.(*stop temporarily*) suspender; (*judgment, proceedings*) posponer 2. SCHOOL, UNIV expulsar temporalmente 3.(*hang*) colgar

suspender [sə·'spen·dər] *n pl* tirantes *mpl,* suspensores *mpl AmL,* calzonarias *fpl Col*

suspense [sə·'spens] *n* 1.(*uncertainty*) incertidumbre *f;* **to keep sb in ~** mantener a alguien sobre ascuas [*o* en vilo] 2. CINE suspense *m*

suspension [sə·'spen·ʃən] *n* 1.(*stop*) suspen-

sión *f* 2. SCHOOL, UNIV expulsión *f* temporal

suspension bridge *n* puente *m* colgante

suspicion [sə·'spɪʃ·ən] *n* 1.(*belief*) sospecha *f;* **to arrest sb on ~ of sth** arrestar a alguien como sospechoso de algo; **to be above ~** estar por encima de toda sospecha 2.(*mistrust*) recelo *m,* desconfianza *f* 3.(*small amount*) atisbo *m*

suspicious [sə·'spɪʃ·əs] *adj* 1.(*arousing suspicion*) sospechoso, -a, emponchado, -a *Arg, Bol, Perú* 2.(*lacking trust*) desconfiado, -a

sustain [sə·'steɪn] *vt* 1.(*maintain*) sostener 2.(*withstand*) aguantar 3.(*uphold: conviction*) confirmar; (*objection*) admitir

sustainable [sə·'steɪ·nə·bəl] *adj* ECOL (*resources*) sostenible; **~ development** desarrollo *m* sostenible

sustained [sə·'steɪnd] *adj* continuo, -a; (*applause*) prolongado, -a

sustenance ['sʌs·tə·nəns] *n* sustento *m;* **to give sb ~** sustentar a alguien

suture ['su·tʃər] MED I. *n* (*stitch*) sutura *f;* (*thread*) hilo *m* de sutura II. *vt* suturar

svelte [svelt] *adj* esbelto, -a

SW [ˌes·'dʌb·əl·ju] *abbr of* **southwest** SO

swab [swab] I. *n* 1. MED (*pad*) tapón *m;* (*for examination*) frotis *m inv* 2. NAUT fregona *f* II.<-bb-> *vt* 1. MED limpiar (con algodón) 2.(*wash*) fregar

swagger ['swæg·ər] I. *n* arrogancia *f* II. *vi* pavonearse

swallow¹ ['swal·oʊ] I. *vt* tragar, engullir, tambar *Ecua, inf* II. *vi* tragar saliva III. *n* trago *m*

♦ **swallow down** *vt* tragar

♦ **swallow up** *vt* (*absorb*) tragar

swallow² ['swal·oʊ] *n* ZOOL golondrina *f* ► **one ~ doesn't make a summer** *prov* una golondrina no hace verano *prov*

swam [swæm] *vi pt of* **swim**

swamp [swamp] I. *n* pantano *m,* suampo *m AmC,* wampa *f Méx* II. *vt* (*flood*) inundar; **to ~ sb** (**with sth**) abrumar a alguien (con algo); **to be ~ed with sth** estar agobiado de algo

swamp fever *n* MED paludismo *m,* fiebre *f* palúdica

swampland ['swamp·lænd] *n* pantano *m*

swampy ['swam·pi] <-ier, -iest> *adj* pantanoso, -a

swan [swan] *n* cisne *m*

swan dive *n* salto *m* del ángel

swank [swæŋk] I. *adj* 1.(*grand*) espléndido, -a 2.(*pretentious*) fanfarrón, -ona II. *n* gran elegancia *f*

swanky ['swæŋ·ki] *adj* pijo, -a

swan song *n* canto *m* del cisne

swap [swap] I.<-pp-> *vt* cambiar; **to ~ sth (for sth)** cambiar algo (por algo); **to ~ sth with sb** cambiarle algo a alguien II.<-pp-> *vi* cambiar III. *n* cambio *m*

swarm [swɔrm] I. *vi* 1. ZOOL, BIO (*bees*) enjambrar 2.(*move in large group*) aglomerarse 3.(*be full*) **to be ~ing with sth** estar plagado [*o* atestado] de algo II. *n* 1.(*of bees*) enjambre *m* **2.** *fig* (*of people*) multitud *f*

swarthy ['swɔr·ði] <-ier, -iest> *adj* moreno, -a

swashbuckling ['swaʃ·ˌbʌk·lɪŋ] *adj* de capa y espada

swastika ['swas·tɪ·kə] *n* cruz *f* gamada

swat [swat] <-tt-> *vt* (*insect*) matar (con un matamoscas)

swatch [swatʃ] *n* (*sample*) muestra *f;* (*sample book*) muestrario *m*

swath [swaθ] *n* **1.** (*long strip*) ringlera *f* **2.** (*space*) extensión *f* ▶ **to cut a ~ across** [*o* **through**] **sth** abrirse camino a través de algo

swathe [sweɪð] **I.** *vt* (*wrap around*) envolver; (*with bandages*) vendar **II.** *n* (*wrapping*) envoltura *f;* (*bandage*) vendaje *m*

sway [sweɪ] **I.** *vi* balancearse **II.** *vt* **1.** (*move from side to side*) balancear **2.** (*persuade*) persuadir **III.** *n* **1.** (*influence*) influencia *f;* **under the ~ of sb/sth** bajo el influjo de alguien/algo **2.** *form* (*control*) control *m;* **to hold ~ over sth/sb** dominar algo/a alguien

Swazi ['swa·zi] **I.** *adj* swazilandés, -esa **II.** *n* swazilandés, -esa *m, f*

Swaziland ['swa·zi·lænd] *n* Swazilandia *f*

swear [swer] <swore, sworn> **I.** *vi* **1.** (*take oath*) jurar; **to ~ on the Bible** jurar sobre la Biblia; **I couldn't ~ to it** *inf* no pondría la mano en el fuego **2.** (*curse*) decir palabrotas **II.** *vt* jurar; **to ~ blind allegiance to sb/sth** jurar lealtad ciega a alguien/algo; **to ~ sb to secrecy** hacer que alguien jure no revelar algo
◆ **swear by** *vt* **to ~ sth** tener una fe ciega en algo
◆ **swear in** *vt* LAW **to ~ sb** tomar juramento a alguien
◆ **swear off** *vt* **to ~ sth** renunciar a algo

swearing *n* palabrotas *mpl*

swearword ['swer·wɜrd] *n* taco *m,* palabrota *f,* brulote *m AmS,* garabato *m Chile*

sweat [swet] **I.** *n* **1.** (*perspiration*) sudor *m;* **to break into a ~** romper a sudar **2.** (*effort*) esfuerzo *m;* **no ~** *inf* ningún problema **3.** *pl inf* (*sweatsuit*) chándal *m* ▶ **it makes me break out in a cold ~** me hace correr un sudor frío por la espalda; **to work oneself into a ~** [*about sth*] preocuparse mucho [por algo] **II.** *vi* (*perspire*) sudar; **to ~ with sth** sudar de algo **III.** *vt* sudar; **to ~ bullets** *inf* sudar la gota gorda
◆ **sweat out** *vt* **1.** *inf* (*endure*) **to sweat it out** soportar (algo difícil) **2.** *sl* (*await*) **to sweat it out** esperar algo con gran impaciencia

sweatband *n* (*for head*) cinta *f;* (*for wrists*) muñequera *f*

sweater ['swet̬·ər] *n* jersey *m*

sweatshirt ['swet·ʃɜrt] *n* sudadera *f*

sweatshop ['swet·ʃap] *n pej:* fábrica donde se explota a los trabajadores

sweatsuit ['swet·sut] *n,* **sweat suit** *n* chándal *m*

sweaty ['swet̬·i] <-ier, -iest> *adj* sudado, -a

Swede [swid] *n* sueco, -a *m, f*

Sweden ['swi·dən] *n* Suecia *f*

Swedish ['swi·dɪʃ] **I.** *adj* sueco, -a **II.** *n* **1.** (*person*) sueco, -a *m, f* LING sueco *m*

sweep [swip] <swept, swept> **I.** *n* **1.** (*cleaning action*) barrido *m;* **to give sth a ~** barrer algo **2.** (*movement*) **with a ~ of her arm** con un amplio movimiento del brazo **3.** (*search*) **to make a ~ of an area** rastrear una zona **4.** SPORTS (*series of wins*) **a three-game ~** una serie de tres partidos ganados **5.** (*chimney cleaner*) **chimney ~** deshollinador(a) *m(f)* ▶ **to make a clean ~** hacer tabla rasa **II.** *vt* **1.** (*clean with broom: floor*) barrer; (*chimney*) deshollinar **2.** (*remove*) quitar **3.** (*search*) rastrear **4.** (*win*) ganar de manera aplastante; **to ~ a series** arrasar en una serie ▶ **to ~ sb off his/ her feet** enamorar a alguien **III.** *vi* **1.** (*clean with broom*) barrer **2.** (*move*) **to ~ into power** llegar al poder fácilmente; **to ~ into a room** entrar en una habitación majestuosamente **3.** (*follow path*) **the road ~s around the lake** la carretera rodea el lago **4.** (*extend*) extenderse
◆ **sweep aside** *vt* **1.** (*cause to move*) apartar **2.** (*dismiss*) desechar
◆ **sweep away** *vt* (*remove*) erradicar
◆ **sweep out** *vt* barrer
◆ **sweep up** *vt* **1.** (*brush*) barrer **2.** (*gather*) recoger

sweeper *n* **1.** (*device*) cepillo *m* **2.** (*person*) barrendero, -a *m, f*

sweeping **I.** *adj* **1.** (*broad: gesture*) amplio, -a **2.** (*overwhelming: victory*) aplastante **II.** *npl* basura *f;* **the ~s of society** la escoria de la sociedad

sweepstakes ['swip·steɪks] *n* apuesta, especialmente en carreras de caballos, en la que la persona que gana se lleva el dinero apostado por todos los demás

sweet [swit] **I.** <-er, -est> *adj* **1.** (*like sugar*) dulce **2.** (*pleasant*) agradable; (*sound*) melodioso -a; **to go one's own ~ way** hacer lo que a uno le da la gana **3.** (*cute*) mono, -a **4.** (*kind: smile*) encantador(a); (*person*) amable; **to be ~ on sb** estar enamorado de alguien **II.** *n pl* (*candy*) caramelo *m,* dulce *m Chile*

sweet-and-sour [ˌswit·ən·ˈsaʊ·ər] *adj* agridulce

sweetbread ['swit·bred] *n pl* CULIN lechecillas *fpl*

sweet corn ['swit·kɔrn] *n* maíz *m* (tierno)

sweeten ['swi·tən] *vt* endulzar; **to ~ sb up** ablandar a alguien

sweetener *n* **1.** CULIN edulcorante *m* **2.** *inf* (*incentive*) incentivo *m*

sweetheart ['swit·hart] *n* **1.** (*kind person*) encanto *m* **2.** (*term of endearment*) cariño *m* **3.** (*boyfriend, girlfriend*) novio, -a *m, f*

sweetie ['swi·t̬i] *n inf* cariño *m*

sweetness *n* dulzor *m;* **to be all ~ and light** *fig* estar de lo más amable

sweet pea *n* guisante *m* de olor

sweet potato *n* boniato *m*

sweet spot *n* SPORTS *inf* (*on bat, golf club,*

racket) punto *m* [*o* lugar *m*] ideal
sweet-talk *vt* camelar
sweet tooth *n* **to have a ~** ser goloso,-a
swell [swel] <swelled, swelled *o* swollen>
I. *vi* 1.(*get bigger*) hincharse 2.(*get louder: sound*) subir 3.(*increase*) aumentar II. *vt*
1.(*in size*) hinchar 2.(*in number*) engrosar
III. *n* (*of sea*) oleaje *m;* **a heavy ~** un fuerte
oleaje IV. <-er, -est> *adj inf* genial
swelling *n* hinchazón *f*
swelter ['swel·tər] *vi* morirse de calor
sweltering *adj* (*heat, temperatures*) sofocante
swept [swept] *vt, vi pt of* **sweep**
swerve [swɜrv] I. *vi* 1.(*car*) virar bruscamente;
(*person*) fintar 2.(*not uphold*) **to ~ from sth**
desviarse de algo II. *n* (*of car*) viraje *m* brusco;
(*of person*) finta *f*
swift[1] [swɪft] *adj* (*fast-moving*) rápido, -a;
(*occurring quickly*) súbito, -a
swift[2] [swɪft] *n* ZOOL vencejo *m*
swiftly *adv* rápidamente
swiftness *n* rapidez *f*
swig [swɪg] I. <-gg-> *vt inf* beber a tragos II. *n*
inf trago *m;* **to take a ~** tomar un trago
swill [swɪl] I. *n* 1.(*pig feed*) comida *f* para cerdos; *fig, iron* bazofia *f* 2.(*garbage*) basura *f*
II. *vt* 1.(*swirl: liquid*) remover 2.(*drink*) beber
a tragos 3.(*rinse*) baldear
◆ **swill down** *vt inf* **to swill sth down** beber
algo a tragos
swim [swɪm] I. <swam, swum> *vi* 1.(*in water*) *a. fig* nadar; **the French fries were ~ming in grease** las patatas fritas estaban
cubiertas de grasa 2.(*whirl*) **her head was ~ming** la cabeza le daba vueltas 3.(*be full of water*) estar inundado, -a; **to ~ with tears** deshacerse en un mar de lágrimas II. <swam, swum> *vt* 1.(*cross*) cruzar a nado 2.(*do*) **to ~ a few strokes** dar cuatro brazadas III. *n*
nado *m;* **I'm going to take a ~** voy a nadar
swimmer ['swɪm·ər] *n* nadador(a) *m(f)*
swimming *n* natación *f*
swimmingly *adv inf* **to go** ir sobre ruedas
swimming pool *n* piscina *f,* alberca *f Méx,*
pileta *f Arg*
swimming trunks *npl* traje *m* de baño (de
caballero)
swimsuit ['swɪm·sut] *n* bañador *m*
swindle ['swɪn·dəl] I. *vt* estafar II. *n* estafa *f*
swindler ['swɪnd·lər] *n pej* timador(a) *m(f)*
swine [swaɪn] *n* 1.*liter* (*pig*) cerdo *m*
2.<-(s)> *pej, inf* (*mean person*) cabrón, -ona
m, f
swing [swɪŋ] I. *n* 1.(*movement*) vaivén *m*
2.(*punch*) golpe *m;* **to take a ~ at sb** (intentar) pegar a alguien 3.(*hanging seat*) columpio
m, burro *m AmC* 4.(*sharp change*) cambio *m*
en redondo; **a mood ~** cambio en el estado de
ánimo; POL viraje *m* 5.(*quick trip*) viaje *m*
6.MUS swing *m* ► **to get** (**back**) **into the ~ of
things** *inf* cogerle el tranquillo a algo
II. <swung, swung> *vi* 1.(*move back and
forth*) oscilar; (*move circularly*) dar vueltas

2.(*hit*) **to ~ at sb** (intentar) dar un golpe a
alguien 3.(*on hanging seat*) columpiarse
4.(*alter*) cambiar; **to ~ between two things**
oscilar entre dos cosas 5.(*be exciting*) ser animado III. <swung, swung> *vt* 1.(*move back
and forth*) balancear, chilinguear *Col* 2.*inf*
(*influence*) influir
◆ **swing around** *vi* dar un giro
swing bridge *n* puente *m* giratorio
swing shift *n* turno *m* de tarde
swipe [swaɪp] I. *vt* 1.*inf* (*steal*) robar 2.(*pass: card*) pasar 3.(*graze: car*) dar un golpe a II. *n*
(*blow*) golpe *m; fig* (*criticism*) crítica *f;* **to take
a ~ at sb/sth** (*hit*) (intentar) pegar a alguien/
algo; (*criticize*) criticar a alguien
swirl [swɜrl] I. *vi* arremolinarse II. *vt* arremolinar III. *n* remolino *m*
swish [swɪʃ] I. *vi* (*cane*) silbar; (*dress*) hacer
frufrú; (*water*) borbotear II. *vt* (*cane*) hacer silbar III. *n* (*of cane*) silbido *m;* (*of dress*) frufrú *m*
Swiss [swɪs] I. *adj* suizo, -a; **~ German/
French** alemán/francés suizo II. *n* suizo, -a
m, f
Swiss ball *n* pelota *f* suiza
switch [swɪtʃ] I. <-es> *n* 1.ELEC interruptor *m,*
suiche *m Méx* 2.(*substitution*) reemplazamiento *m* 3.(*change*) cambio *m* 4.RAIL
(*device*) agujas *fpl* II. *vi* cambiar; **to ~ with sb**
cambiarse con alguien; **to ~ from sth to sth**
cambiar de algo a algo III. *vt* cambiar; **to ~ sth
for sth** cambiar algo por algo
◆ **switch around** *vt* cambiar
◆ **switch off** I. *vt* (*machine, engine*) apagar;
(*water, electricity*) cortar II. *vi* 1.(*machine,
engine*) apagarse 2.(*lose attention*) desconectar
◆ **switch on** I. *vt* (*machine, engine*)
encender; **to ~ the charm** ponerse encantador
II. *vi* encenderse
◆ **switch over** *vi* cambiar; **to ~ to another
channel** poner otro canal
switchback ['swɪtʃ·bæk] *n* carretera *f* en zigzag
switchblade ['swɪtʃ·bleɪd] *n* navaja *f* automática
switchboard ['swɪtʃ·bɔrd] *n* 1.ELEC conmutador *m* 2.TEL centralita *f*
switchboard operator *n* telefonista *mf*
switchman <-men> *n* guardagujas *m inv*
switchyard *n* patio *m* de maniobras
Switzerland ['swɪt·sər·lənd] *n* Suiza *f*
swivel ['swɪv·əl] I. *n* plataforma *f* giratoria
II. <-ll-, -l-> *vt* girar
swivel chair *n* silla *f* giratoria
swizzle stick ['swɪz·əl·ˌstɪk] *n* agitador *m*
swollen ['swoʊ·lən] I. *pp of* **swell** II. *adj* hinchado, -a
swoon [swun] I. *vi* 1.(*be in state of ecstasy*)
estar embelesado; **to ~ over sb** derretirse por
alguien 2.*liter* (*faint*) desvanecerse II. *n liter*
desvanecimiento *m*
swoop [swup] I. *n* 1.(*dive*) caída *f* en picado

2. *inf*(*surprise attack*) redada *f* ▶ **in one fell ~** de una sola vez **II.** *vi* **1.** (*dive*) *a.* *fig* bajar en picado; **to ~ that low** caer tan bajo **2.** *inf* **to ~ down on sb** (*make sudden attack*) abatirse sobre alguien; (*police*) hacer una redada

sword [sɔrd] *n* espada *f;* **to draw a ~** desenfundar una espada ▶ **to cross ~s with sb** cruzar espadas con alguien

swordfish <-(es)> *n* pez *m* espada

swordplay *n* esgrima *f;* **verbal ~** enfrentamiento *m* dialéctico

swordsman ['sɔrdz·mən] <-men> *n* **1.** HIST espadachín *m* **2.** (*fencer*) esgrimidor *m*

swordsmanship *n* destreza *f* en el manejo de la espada

swore [swɔr] *pt of* **swear**

sworn [swɔrn] **I.** *pp of* **swear II.** *adj* jurado, -a

swum [swʌm] *pp of* **swim**

swung [swʌŋ] *pt, pp of* **swing**

sycamore ['sɪk·ə·mɔr] *n* (*tree*) plátano *m*

sycophant ['sɪk·ə·fənt] *n pej* adulador(a) *m(f)*

syllable ['sɪl·ə·bəl] *n* sílaba *f;* **stressed/unstressed ~** sílaba tónica/átona; **not a ~** *fig* ni media palabra

syllabus ['sɪl·ə·bəs] <-es, *form:* syllabi> *n* (*in general*) plan *m* de estudios; (*for specific subject*) programa *m*

symbiosis [ˌsɪm·bɪ·'oʊ·sɪs] *n* simbiosis *f*

symbiotic [ˌsɪm·bɪ·'ɑt̬·ɪk] *adj* BIO simbiótico, -a

symbol ['sɪm·bəl] *n* símbolo *m*

symbolic [sɪm·'bɑl·ɪk] *adj,* **symbolical** [sɪm·'bɑl·ɪ·kəl] *adj* simbólico, -a

symbolism ['sɪmbəlɪz·əm] *n* simbolismo *m*

symbolize ['sɪm·bə·laɪz] *vt* simbolizar

symmetric [sɪ·'met·rɪk] *adj,* **symmetrical** [sɪ·'met·rɪ·kəl] *adj* simétrico, -a

symmetry ['sɪm·ə·tri] *n* simetría *f*

sympathetic [ˌsɪm·pə·'θet̬·ɪk] *adj* **1.** (*understanding*) comprensivo, -a; (*sympathizing*) receptivo, -a; **to lend a ~ ear to sb** estar dispuesto a escuchar a alguien **2.** POL simpatizante; **to be ~ towards sb/sth** apoyar a alguien/algo

sympathize ['sɪm·pə·θaɪz] *vi* **1.** (*understand*) mostrar comprensión; (*feel compassion for*) compadecerse de **2.** (*agree*) estar de acuerdo; **to ~ with sb/sth** simpatizar con alguien/algo

sympathizer *n* simpatizante *mf*

sympathy ['sɪm·pə·θi] *n* **1.** (*compassion*) compasión *f;* (*understanding*) comprensión *f;* **you have my deepest ~** le acompaño en el sentimiento **2.** (*solidarity*) solidaridad *f*

symphonic [sɪm·'fɑn·ɪk] *adj* sinfónico, -a

symphony ['sɪm·fə·ni] *n* **1.** (*piece of music*) sinfonía *f* **2.** (*orchestra*) orquesta *f* sinfónica

symphony orchestra *n* orquesta *f* sinfónica

symposium [sɪm·'poʊ·zi·əm] <-s *o* -sia> *n form* simposio *m*

symptom ['sɪmp·təm] *n* síntoma *m*

symptomatic [ˌsɪmp·tə·'mæt̬·ɪk] *adj* sintomático, -a

synagogue ['sɪn·ə·gɑg] *n* sinagoga *f*

synchronize ['sɪŋ·krə·naɪz] **I.** *vt* sincronizar

II. *vi* sincronizarse

synchronous ['sɪŋ·krə·nəs] *adj* sincrónico, -a

syndicate¹ ['sɪn·də·kɪt] *n* **1.** ECON consorcio *m* **2.** PUBL agencia *f* de noticias

syndicate² ['sɪn·də·keɪt] *vt* **1.** ECON agrupar **2.** PUBL vender

syndication [ˌsɪn·də·'keɪ·ʃən] *n* **1.** ECON agrupación *f* **2.** PUBL venta *f*

syndrome ['sɪn·droʊm] *n* síndrome *m;* **acquired immune deficiency ~** síndrome de la inmunodeficiencia adquirida

synergy ['sɪn·ər·dʒi] *n* sinergia *f*

synod ['sɪn·əd] *n* sínodo *m*

synonym ['sɪn·ə·nɪm] *n* sinónimo *m*

synonymous [sɪ·'nɑn·ɪ·məs] *adj* sinónimo, -a

synopsis [sɪ·'næp·sɪs] <-es> *n* sinopsis *f inv*

syntactic [sɪn·'tæk·tɪk] *adj,* **syntactical** [sɪn·'tæk·tɪ·kəl] *adj* sintáctico, -a

syntax ['sɪn·tæks] *n* sintaxis *f inv*

synthesis ['sɪn·θə·sɪs] <-es> *n* síntesis *f inv*

synthesize ['sɪn·θə·saɪz] *vt* sintetizar

synthesizer *n* sintetizador *m*

synthetic [sɪn·'θet̬·ɪk] *adj* **1.** (*man-made*) sintético, -a **2.** *pej* (*fake*) artificial

syphilis ['sɪf·ə·lɪs] *n* sífilis *f inv*

syphon ['saɪ·fən] *n s.* **siphon**

Syria ['sɪr·i·ə] *n* Siria *f*

Syrian ['sɪr·i·ən] **I.** *adj* sirio, -a **II.** *n* sirio, -a *m, f*

syringe [sə·'rɪndʒ] **I.** *n* jeringuilla *f* **II.** *vt* **to ~ sb's ears** destaponarle los oídos a alguien

syrup ['sɪr·əp] *n* **1.** CULIN almíbar *m,* sirope *m AmC, Col* **2.** MED jarabe *m;* **cough ~** jarabe para la tos

syrupy ['sɪr·ə·pi] *adj pej* empalagoso, -a

system ['sɪs·təm] *n* **1.** (*set*) sistema *m;* **music ~** equipo *m* de música **2.** (*method of organization*) método *m;* POL sistema *m* **3.** (*order*) método *m* ▶ **to get something out of one's ~** *inf* quitarse algo de encima

systematic [ˌsɪs·tə·'mæt̬·ɪk] *adj* sistemático, -a

systematize ['sɪs·tə·mə·taɪz] *vt* sistematizar

system check *n* verificación *f* del sistema

system crash <-es> *n* fallo *m* en el sistema

system disk *n* disco *m* de sistema

system error *n* error *m* en el sistema

system registry *n* registro *m* del sistema

systems analysis *n* análisis *m inv* de sistemas

systems analyst *n* analista *mf* de sistemas

system software *n* software *m* de sistemas

T

T, t [ti] *n* T, t *f;* **~ as in Tango** T de Tarragona ▶ **to a ~** *inf* **the description fits him to a ~** la descripción le va perfecta

t. *abbr of* **ton** t

TA *n abbr of* **teaching assistant** *ayudante de un profesor de universidad*

tab 1048 take

tab [tæb] *n* **1.** (*flap*) solapa *f;* (*on file*) lengüeta *f;* **write-protect** ~ COMPUT lengüeta protectora **2.** (*label*) etiqueta *f* **3.** *inf* (*bill*) cuenta *f;* **to put sth on the** ~ cargar algo a la cuenta **4.** (*ring-pull*) anilla *f* **5.** MED **a** ~ **of acid** una pastilla de LSD ▶ **to keep** ~**s on sth/sb** no perder de vista algo/a alguien

tabby ['tæb·i] I. *adj* atigrado, -a II. *n* gato *m* atigrado

tab key *n* tabulador *m*

table ['teɪ·bəl] I. *n* **1.** mesa *f;* **to clear/set the** ~ recoger/poner la mesa **2.** MATH tabla *f;* **multiplication** ~ tabla de multiplicar **3.** (*list*) lista *f;* ~ **of contents** índice *m* ▶ **the** ~**s have turned** han cambiado las tornas II. *vt* (*postpone discussion of*) posponer

tablecloth ['teɪ·bəl·klɒθ] *n* mantel *m*

tableland *n* meseta *f*

table linen *n* mantelería *f*

table manners *npl* modales *mpl* en la mesa

table mat *n* salvamanteles *m inv*

tablespoon *n* **1.** (*spoon*) cucharón *m* **2.** (*amount*) cucharada *f* (*con el cucharón*)

tablet ['tæb·lɪt] *n* **1.** (*pill*) pastilla *f,* comprimido *m* **2.** (*of stone*) lápida *f*

table tennis *n* ping-pong *m*

tableware *n form* servicio *m* de mesa

table wine *n* vino *m* de mesa

tabloid ['tæb·lɔɪd] *n* periódico *m* sensacionalista; **the** ~ **press** la prensa amarilla

taboo, tabu [tə·'bu] I. *n* tabú *m* II. *adj* tabú *inv*

tabular ['tæb·jʊ·lər] *adj form* tabular

tabulate ['tæb·jʊ·leɪt] *vt* disponer en tablas; COMPUT tabular

tabulator ['tæb·jʊ·leɪ·tər] *n form* tabulador *m*

tacit ['tæs·ɪt] *adj* tácito, -a

taciturn ['tæs·ə·tɜrn] *adj* taciturno, -a, soturno, -a *Ven*

tack [tæk] I. *n* **1.** (*short nail*) tachuela *f* **2.** (*riding gear*) montura *f* **3.** NAUT amura *f* **4.** (*approach*) política *f;* **to try a different** ~ intentar un enfoque distinto II. *vt* **1.** (*nail down*) clavar con tachuelas **2.** (*sew loosely*) hilvanar III. *vi* NAUT virar

tackle ['tæk·əl] I. *vt* **1.** (*in soccer*) entrar; (*in rugby, US football*) placar **2.** (*deal with: issue*) abordar; (*job*) emprender; (*problem*) atacar II. *n* **1.** (*in soccer*) entrada *f;* (*in rugby, US football*) placaje *m* **2.** (*line position*) atajo *m* **3.** (*equipment*) equipo *m* **4.** NAUT aparejo *m*

tacky ['tæk·i] <-ier, -iest> *adj* **1.** (*sticky*) pegajoso, -a **2.** *inf* (*showy*) hortera; (*shoddy*) de pacotilla

tact [tækt] *n* tacto *m*

tactful ['tækt·fəl] *adj* discreto, -a

tactic ['tæk·tɪk] *n* ~(**s**) táctica *f*

tactical ['tæk·tɪ·kəl] *adj* táctico, -a

tactician [tæk·'tɪʃ·ən] *n* táctico, -a *m, f*

tactile ['tæk·təl] *adj form* táctil

tactless ['tækt·lɪs] *adj* falto, -a de tacto

tactlessness *n* falta *f* de tacto

tad [tæd] *n* **a** ~ un poquitín

tadpole ['tæd·poʊl] *n* renacuajo *m*

taffeta ['tæf·ɪ·tə] *n* tafetán *m*

tag [tæg] I. *n* **1. a.** COMPUT (*label*) etiqueta *f;* (*metal*) herrete *m* **2.** (*game*) **to play** ~ jugar al pillapilla **3.** LING **question** ~ cláusula *f* final interrogativa II. <-gg-> *vt* (*label*) etiquetar; **to** ~ **sth onto sth** añadir algo a algo
◆ **tag along** *vi inf* seguir; **to** ~ **with sb** ir detrás de alguien

tail [teɪl] I. *n* **1.** ANAT, AVIAT cola *f;* (*of dog, bull*) rabo *m* **2.** ~**s** *inf* (*tail coat*) frac *m* **3.** ~**s** (*side of coin*) cruz *f* **4.** *inf* (*person*) perseguidor(a) *m(f)* **5.** *sl* (*bottom*) trasero *m* ▶ **to chase one's** ~ pillarse los dedos *fig;* **to turn** ~ **and run** salir por pies II. *vt* seguir
◆ **tail away** *vi* ir disminuyendo; (*get worse*) ir empeorando
◆ **tail off** *vi* disminuir; (*sound*) desvanecerse

tail end *n* extremo *m*

tailgate I. *n* (*of car*) puerta *f* de atrás; (*of truck*) compuerta *f* II. *vt* AUTO perseguir demasiado cerca

tailless *adj* sin cola

taillight *n* AUTO luz *f* trasera

tailor ['teɪ·lər] I. *n* sastre *m* II. *vt* **1.** (*clothes*) confeccionar **2.** (*adapt*) adaptar

tailor-made [ˌteɪ·lər·'meɪd] *adj* **1.** (*custom-made*) hecho, -a a medida **2.** (*perfect*) perfecto, -a

tailpiece ['teɪl·pis] *n* **1.** (*part added*) añadidura *f* **2.** AVIAT cola *f* **3.** TYPO viñeta *f*

tailpipe *n* tubo *m* de escape

tailspin *n* barrena *f* picada; **to go into a** ~ caer en picado

tail wind *n* viento *m* de cola

taint [teɪnt] I. *vt* (*food*) contaminar; (*reputation*) manchar II. *n* mancha *f*

Taiwan [ˌtaɪ·'wan] *n* Taiwán *m*

Taiwanese [ˌtaɪ·wə·'niz] I. *adj* taiwanés, -esa II. *n* taiwanés, -esa *m, f*

Tajikistan [ta·'dʒi·kɪ·ˌstan] *n* Tayikistán *m*

take [teɪk] I. *n* **1.** (*receipts*) ingresos *mpl* **2.** PHOT, CINE toma *f* ▶ **to be on the** ~ *inf* dejarse sobornar II. <took, taken> *vt* **1.** (*accept*) aceptar; (*advice*) seguir; (*criticism*) soportar; (*responsibility*) asumir; **to** ~ **sth seriously** tomar algo en serio; **to** ~ **one's time** tomarse su tiempo; **to** ~ **sth as it comes** aceptar algo tal y como es **2.** (*hold*) coger, agarrar *AmL* **3.** (*eat*) comer; (*medicine, drugs*) tomar **4.** (*use*) necesitar **5.** (*receive*) recibir **6.** (*capture: prisoners*) prender; (*city*) conquistar; (*power*) tomar **7.** (*assume*) **to** ~ **office** entrar en funciones **8.** (*bring*) llevar **9.** (*require*) exigir, requerir; **this shirt** ~**s a lot of ironing** hay que planchar mucho esta camisa **10.** (*do*) REL oficiar; UNIV cursar **11.** (*have: decision, bath, holiday*) tomar; (*walk*) dar; (*trip*) hacer; (*ticket*) sacar; (*census*) levantar; (*rest*) tomarse **12.** (*feel, assume*) **to** ~ (**an**) **interest in sb/sth** interesarse por alguien/algo; **to** ~ **offense** ofenderse; **to** ~ **pity on sb/sth** apiadarse de alguien/algo; **to** ~ **the view that...** adoptar la opinión de que... **13.**(*make money*) ganar **14.**(*photograph*) sacar **15.**(*use for travel: bus, train*) coger, tomar *AmL* **16.**(*regard as*) tener; **to ~ sb for sth** tener a alguien por algo ▶ **~ it or leave it** ¡tómalo o déjalo!; **what do you ~ me for?** ¿por quién me has tomado?; **~ it from me** puedes creerme; **I ~ it that...** supongo que...; **~ that!** ¡toma! **III.**<took, taken> *vi* tener efecto; (*plant*) prender; (*dye*) agarrar

◆**take aback** *vt* (*surprise*) sorprender; (*shock*) abatir

◆**take after** *vt* parecerse a

◆**take along** *vt* (*take*) llevar (consigo); (*bring*) traer (consigo)

◆**take apart I.** *vt* **1.**(*disassemble*) desmontar **2.**(*analyze*) reseñar **3.**(*destroy*) despedazar **II.** *vi* desmontarse

◆**take away I.** *vt* **1.**(*remove*) quitar **2.**(*go away with*) llevar(se) **3.**(*lessen*) disminuir **4.**(*subtract from*) restar **II.** *vi* quitarse; **to ~ from the importance/worth of sth** restar importancia/mérito a algo

◆**take back** *vt* **1.**(*return*) devolver **2.**(*accept back*) aceptar; (*employee*) volver a emplear; (*spouse*) reconciliarse con **3.**(*repossess*) recobrar **4.**(*retract*) retractar **5.**(*carry to past time*) evocar **6.**(*remind*) recordar

◆**take down** *vt* **1.**(*remove*) quitar; (*from high place*) bajar **2.**(*disassemble*) desmontar **3.**(*write down*) apuntar **4.** *inf* (*diminish the pride of*) **to take sb down** bajar los humos a alguien; (*humble*) humillar a alguien

◆**take in** *vt* **1.**(*bring inside*) recoger, acoger (en casa); (*admit*) aceptar **2.**(*hold*) **to take sb in one's arms** sostener a alguien entre sus brazos; **to take sth in hand** *fig* hacerse cargo de algo **3.**(*accommodate*) alojar; (*for rent*) hospedar **4.**(*bring to police*) entregar **5.**(*deceive*) estafar; **to be taken in** (**by sb/sth**) ser engañado (por alguien/algo) **6.**(*go to see*) ir a ver **7.**(*understand*) comprender; **to take sth in at a glance** asimilar algo en un abrir y cerrar de ojos **8.**(*include*) incluir **9.** FASHION estrechar

◆**take off I.** *vt* **1.**(*remove from*) retirar; **to take sb off a list** tachar a alguien de una lista **2.**(*clothes*) quitarse **3.**(*bring away*) llevarse **4.**(*subtract*) descontar **5.**(*stop showing*) quitar **II.** *vi* **1.** AVIAT despegar **2.** *sl* (*leave*) largarse; *sl* (*flee*) salir por pies **3.**(*have success*) empezar a tener éxito

◆**take on I.** *vt* **1.**(*agree to try*) aceptar **2.**(*acquire*) adoptar **3.**(*hire*) contratar **4.**(*fight*) enfrentarse a **5.**(*stop for loading: passengers*) recoger; (*fuel*) abastecerse de; (*goods*) cargar **II.** *vi* apurarse

◆**take out** *vt* **1.**(*remove*) quitar; (*extract*) extraer; (*withdraw*) retirar **2.**(*bring outside*) llevar fuera; (*garbage*) sacar, botar *Col, Ven* **3.**(*for walk: person*) llevar de paseo; (*dog*) sacar (de paseo) **4.** *sl* (*kill*) cargarse a; (*destroy*) cargarse **5.**(*arrange to get: license*) obtener **6.**(*borrow*) coger prestado **7.**(*vent anger*) **to take sth out on sb** desahogarse riñendo a al-

guien **8.** *sl* (*tire*) **to take it out of sb** dejar reventado a alguien *fig*

◆**take over I.** *vt* **1.**(*buy out*) comprar **2.**(*seize control*) tomar el control de **3.**(*assume*) asumir **4.**(*possess*) tomar posesión de; **to be taken over by one's work** estar dominado por su trabajo **5.**(*start using*) comenzar a usar **II.** *vi* tomar posesión

◆**take to** *vt* **1.**(*start to like*) encariñarse con **2.**(*begin as a habit*) **to ~ doing sth** aficionarse a hacer algo; **to ~ drink/drugs** darse a la bebida/las drogas **3.**(*go to*) dirigirse a; **to ~ the streets** (**in protest**) tomar las calles (para protestar); **to ~ one's bed** meterse en la cama

◆**take up I.** *vt* **1.**(*bring up*) subir **2. to ~ arms** (**against sth**) levantarse en armas (contra algo) **3.**(*start doing*) comenzar; (*job*) empezar; (*piano*) iniciarse en; (*fishing*) dedicarse a **4.**(*discuss*) tratar **5.**(*accept*) aceptar **6.**(*adopt*) adoptar **7.**(*continue doing*) proseguir **8.**(*join in*) participar **9.**(*occupy*) ocupar **10.**(*pull up*) alzar **11.**(*shorten*) acortar **12.**(*patronize*) patrocinar **13.**(*absorb*) absorber **II.** *vi* **to ~ with sb** relacionarse con alguien; **to ~ with sth** familiarizarse con algo

take-home pay ['teɪk·hoʊm·ˌpeɪ] *n* salario *m* neto

taken ['teɪ·kən] *vi, vt pp of* **take**

takeoff ['teɪk·ɔf] *n* AVIAT despegue *m*

takeout ['teɪk·aʊt] *n* comida *f* para llevar

takeover ['teɪk·ˌoʊ·vər] *n* POL toma *f* del poder; ECON adquisición *f*

takeover bid *n* oferta *f* pública de adquisición de acciones

taker ['teɪ·kər] *n* **the suggestion had no ~s** nadie aceptó la propuesta

take-up ['teɪk·ʌp] *n* **1.** TECH compensación *f* **2.**(*of scheme, suggestion*) aceptación *f*

taking ['teɪ·kɪŋ] **I.** *n* **1.**(*capture*) toma *f*; **it's yours for the ~** es tuyo si lo quieres **2. ~s** (*receipts*) ingresos *mpl* **II.** *adj* atractivo, -a

talc [tælk] *n*, **talcum** (**powder**) ['tæl·kəm·ˌpaʊ·dər] *n* **1.** CHEM talco *m* **2.** MED polvos *mpl* de talco

tale [teɪl] *n* **1.**(*story*) historia *f*; LIT cuento *m* **2.**(*lie*) mentira *f*; **dead men tell no ~s** los muertos no mienten ▶ **to tell ~s** chivarse

talent ['tæl·ənt] *n* (*ability*) talento *m*

talented *adj* talentoso, -a

Taliban ['tæ·lɪ·bæn] *n* talibán *m,f*

talisman ['tæl·ɪs·mən] *n* talismán *m*

talk [tɔk] **I.** *n* **1.**(*conversation*) conversación *f*, plática *f* Méx **2.**(*lecture*) charla *f* **3.**(*things said*) chisme *m;* **big ~** jactancia *f* **4. ~s** (*formal discussions*) negociaciones *fpl* ▶ **to be the ~ of the town** andar de boca en boca; **to be all ~** (**and no action**) hablar mucho (y no hacer nada), mucho ruido y pocas nueces *prov* **II.** *vi* (*speak*) hablar; **to ~ about sb behind their back** murmurar de alguien a sus espaldas; **to give sb something to ~ about** dar a alguien de qué hablar ▶ **to ~ dirty** decir obscenidades; **look who's ~ing** *inf* ¡mira quién habla! **III.** *vt*

1. (*utter*) decir **2.** (*discuss*) hablar de
◆ **talk around I.** *vt* **to talk sb around** convencer a alguien **II.** *vi* (*avoid*) **to ~ sth** dar vueltas a algo
◆ **talk back** *vi* replicar
◆ **talk down I.** *vt* (*speak louder than*) apabullar **II.** *vi pej* **to ~ to sb** hablar a alguien con condescendencia
◆ **talk out** *vt* **1.** (*discuss*) discutir **2.** (*convince not to*) **to talk sb out of sth** disuadir a alguien de algo
◆ **talk over** *vt* **to talk sth over** (**with sb**) hablar algo (con alguien)
◆ **talk through** *vt* **1.** (*discuss*) discutir **2.** (*explain*) explicar
talkative ['tɒk·ə·t̬ɪv] *adj* hablador(a), locuaz
talker *n* hablador(a) *m(f)*
talking I. *adj* parlante **II.** *n* habla *f;* **"no ~"** "silencio"
talking-to ['tɒ·kɪŋ·tu] *n* sermón *m;* **to give sb a ~** echar un sermón a alguien
talk show *n* programa *m* de entrevistas
talk time *n* TEL (*on cell phone*) minutos *m* libres, saldo *m*
tall [tɒl] *adj* alto, -a; **to grow ~(er)** crecer
tallow ['tæl·oʊ] *n* sebo *m*
tally[1] ['tæl·i] <-ie-> *vi* concordar; **to ~ with sth** coincidir con algo
tally[2] ['tæl·i] <-ies> **I.** *n* cuenta *f;* **to keep a ~** (**of sth**) llevar la cuenta (de algo) **II.** *vt* llevar la cuenta de
◆ **tally up** *vt* llevar la cuenta de
talon ['tæl·ən] *n* garra *f*
tamarind ['tæm·ə·rɪnd] *n* tamarindo *m*
tamarisk ['tæm·ə·rɪsk] *n* tamarisco *m*
tambour ['tæm·bʊr] *n* tambor *m*
tambourine [ˌtæm·bə·'rin] *n* pandereta *f*
tame [teɪm] **I.** *adj* **1.** (*domesticated*) doméstico, -a; (*not savage*) manso, -a **2.** (*unexciting*) soso, -a **II.** *vt* (*feelings*) dominar; (*animal*) domesticar, aguachar *Chile*
tamer ['teɪ·mər] *n* domador(a) *m(f)*
tamper ['tæm·pər] *vi* entrometerse
◆ **tamper with** *vt* manosear; (*document*) falsificar; (*witness*) sobornar; (*lock*) tratar de forzar
tamperproof ['tæm·pər·pruf] *adj*, **tamper-resistant** *adj* no manipulable
tampon ['tæm·pan] *n* MED tapón *m;* (*for absorbing menstrual blood*) tampón *m*
tan[1] [tæn] **I.** <-nn-> *vi* broncearse **II.** <-nn-> *vt* **1.** (*make brown*) broncear; **to be ~ned** estar moreno **2.** (*leather*) curtir ▶ **to ~ sb's hide** *inf* dar una paliza a alguien **III.** *n* bronceado *m;* **to get a ~** ponerse moreno **IV.** *adj* marrón claro
tan[2] MATH *abbr of* **tangent** tg
tandem ['tæn·dəm] **I.** *n* tándem *m;* **to work in ~** trabajar conjuntamente **II.** *adv* en tándem; **to ride ~** montar en tándem
tang [tæŋ] *n* olor *m* penetrante
tangent ['tæn·dʒənt] *n* tangente *f;* **to go off on a ~** salirse por la tangente

tangential [tæn·'dʒen·ʃəl] *adj* tangencial
tangerine [ˌtæn·dʒə·'rin] *n* mandarina *f*
tangible ['tæn·dʒə·bəl] *adj* tangible; (*benefit*) palpable; **~ asset** bien *m* material
Tangier [tæn·'dʒɪr] *n* Tánger *m*
tangle ['tæŋ·gəl] **I.** *n* **1.** (*in hair, string*) maraña *f* **2.** *fig* (*confusion*) enredo *m* **II.** *vt* enredar **III.** *vi* enredarse
◆ **tangle with** *vi* (*quarrel*) meterse con
tango ['tæŋ·goʊ] **I.** *n* tango *m* ▶ **it takes two to ~** *prov* es cosa de dos **II.** *vi* bailar un tango
tangy ['tæŋ·i] <-ier, -iest> *adj* fuerte
tank [tæŋk] *n* **1.** (*container*) depósito *m* **2.** (*aquarium*) acuario *m* **3.** MIL tanque *m*
tanked up *adj* **to be ~** ir como una cuba
tankard ['tæŋ·kərd] *n* jarra *f*
tanker ['tæŋ·kər] *n* **1.** (*truck*) camión *m* cisterna **2.** (*ship*) buque *m* cisterna; **oil ~** petrolero *m* **3.** (*aircraft*) avión *m* cisterna
tanned [tænd] *adj* bronceado, -a
tanner ['tæn·ər] *n* curtidor(a) *m(f)*
tannery ['tæn·ə·ri] *n* curtiduría *f*
tannic acid [ˌtæn·ɪk·'æs·ɪd] *n* ácido *m* tánico
tannin ['tæn·ɪn] *n* tanino *m*
tanning ['tæn·ɪŋ] *n* **1.** (*of leather*) curtido *m* **2.** *inf* (*beating*) paliza *f*
tanning bed *n* banco *m* solar
tantalize ['tæn·t̬ə·laɪz] *vt* **1.** (*torment*) atormentar **2.** (*tempt*) tentar
tantalizing *adj* tentador(a); (*smile*) seductor(a)
tantamount ['tæn·tə·maʊnt] *adj* equivalente; **to be ~ to sth** equivaler a algo
tantrum ['tæn·trəm] *n* berrinche *m,* dengue *m Méx;* **to have** [*o* **throw**] **a ~** coger [*o* agarrar *AmL*] una rabieta
Tanzania [ˌtæn·zə·'ni·ə] *n* Tanzania *f*
Tanzanian [ˌtæn·zə·'ni·ən] **I.** *adj* tanzano, -a **II.** *n* tanzano, -a *m, f*
tap[1] [tæp] **I.** *n* **1.** (*for water*) grifo *m,* canilla *f Arg, Par, Urug;* **beer on ~** cerveza *f* de barril; **to turn the ~ on/off** abrir/cerrar el grifo; **on ~** *fig* al alcance de la mano **2.** TEL micrófono *m* de escucha **II.** <-pp-> *vt* **1.** TEL intervenir; (*conversation*) interceptar; (*phone*) pinchar *inf* **2.** (*make use of*) utilizar; (*sources*) explotar **3.** (*let out*) espitar
tap[2] [tæp] **I.** *n* **1.** (*light knock*) golpecito *m* **2.** (*tap dancing*) claqué *m* **II.** <-pp-> *vt* golpear suavemente; **to ~ one's fingers on the table** tamborilear con los dedos sobre la mesa **III.** <-pp-> *vi* dar golpecitos
tap dance ['tæp·ˌdæns] *n* claqué *m*
tape [teɪp] **I.** *n* **1.** (*adhesive strip*) cinta *f* adhesiva; MED esparadrapo *m;* **masking ~** cinta adhesiva protectora; **Scotch ~** ® celo *m,* durex *m AmL* **2.** (*measure*) cinta métrica **3.** SPORTS cinta de llegada **4.** (*cassette*) cinta, tape *m RíoPl;* **to get sth on ~** grabar algo **II.** *vt* **1.** (*fasten with tape*) poner una cinta a **2.** (*record*) grabar
tape cassette *n* casete *m o f*
tape deck *n* platina *f*
tape measure *n* metro *m*

taper ['teɪ·pər] I. *n* (*slim candle*) candela *f*; (*wax-coated wick*) cerilla *f* II. *vt* afilar III. *vi* afilarse

♦**taper off** *vi* disminuir

tape-record *vt* grabar (en cinta)

tape recorder *n* grabadora *f*

tape recording *n* grabación *f* (en cinta)

tapestry ['tæp·əs·tri] *n* 1.(*art form*) tapicería *f* 2.(*object*) tapiz *m* 3.*fig* collage *m*

tapeworm ['teɪp·wɜrm] *n* tenia *f*, solitaria *f*

tapioca [ˌtæp·ɪ·'oʊ·kə] *n* tapioca *f*

tapir ['teɪ·pər] *n* tapir *m*

tappet ['tæp·ət] *n* alzaválvulas *m inv*

taproom ['tæp·rum] *n* cervecería *f*

tap water *n* agua *f* corriente

tar [tar] I. *n* alquitrán *m* II.<-rr-> *vt* alquitranar; **to ~ and feather sb** emplumar a alguien

tarantula [tə·'ræn·tʃə·lə] *n* tarántula *f*

tardy ['tar·di] <-ier, -iest> *adj liter* tardío, -a; *pej* (*sluggish*) lento, -a

tare [ter] *n* ECON tara *f*

target ['tar·gɪt] I. *n* 1.(*mark aimed at*) objetivo *m*; **to hit the ~** dar en el blanco 2. ECON objetivo; **to be on ~** ir de acuerdo con lo previsto II. *vt* centrarse en; **to ~ sth on sth** (*missile*) apuntar algo a algo; (*campaign*) destinar algo a algo

target date *n* fecha *f* límite

targeted ['tar·gɪ·ţɪd] *adj* elegido, -a como objetivo

target language *n* LING lengua *f* de destino; COMPUT lenguaje *m* objeto

target practice *n* prácticas *fpl* de tiro

target price *n* precio *m* indicativo

tariff ['tær·ɪf] *n* (*customs duty*) arancel *m*

tariff barrier *n* ECON barrera *f* arancelaria

tarmac® ['tar·mæk], **tarmacadam**® [ˌtar·mə·'kæd·əm] *n* 1.(*paving material*) asfalto *m* 2. AVIAT pista *f* de despegue

tarn [tarn] *n* lago *m* de montaña

tarnish ['tar·nɪʃ] I. *vi* deslustrarse II. *vt* deslustrar; (*reputation*) manchar III. *n* mancha *f*

tarpaulin [tar·'pɔ·lɪn] *n* lona *f* impermeabilizada

tarragon ['tær·ə·gan] *n* estragón *m*

tarsus ['tar·səs] *n* ANAT tarso *m*

tart[1] [tart] *adj* 1.(*sharp*) agrio, -a; (*acid*) ácido, -a 2.(*caustic*) cortante

tart[2] [tart] *n* CULIN tarta *f*

tartan ['tar·tən] *n* 1.(*cloth*) tela *f* de cuadros escoceses 2.(*design*) tartán *m*

Tartar ['tar·ţər] *n* (*bad-tempered person*) persona *f* intratable

tartar ['tar·ţər] *n* 1. MED sarro *m* 2. CHEM tártaro *m*

tartar(e) sauce *n* salsa *f* tártara

tartaric [tar·'tær·ɪk] *n* ácido *m* tartárico

task [tæsk] I. *n* tarea *f*, tonga *f Col*; **to take sb to ~** llamar la atención a alguien II. *vt* imponer una tarea; **to be ~ed with sth** estar encargado de algo

task force *n* MIL destacamento *m*; (*team*) equipo *m* de trabajo

taskmaster *n* capataz(a) *m(f)*; **to be a hard ~** ser un tirano

Tasmania [tæz·'meɪ·ni·ə] *n* Tasmania *f*

Tasmanian [tæz·'meɪ·ni·ən] I. *adj* tasmano, -a II. *n* tasmano, -a *m, f*

tassel ['tæs·əl] *n* borla *f*

taste [teɪst] I. *n* 1. sabor *m*; **sense of ~** sentido *m* del gusto 2.(*small portion*) bocado *m*; **to have a ~ of sth** probar algo 3.(*liking*) gusto *m*; **to lose the ~ for sth** perder el gusto por algo; **to have different ~s** tener gustos distintos [*o* diferentes]; **to get a ~ for sth** tomar el gusto a algo 4.(*experience*) experiencia *f* ▶ **to leave a bad ~** (**in one's mouth**) dejar un mal sabor de boca II. *vt* 1.(*food, drink*) saborear 2.(*experience*) experimentar; (*luxury*) probar III. *vi* saber; **to ~ bitter/sweet** tener un sabor amargo/dulce; **to ~ of** [*o* **like**] **sth** saber a algo

taste bud ['teɪst·bʌd] *n* papila *f* gustativa

tasteful ['teɪst·fəl] *adj* con gusto; (*decorous*) con delicadeza

tasteless ['teɪst·lɪs] *adj* 1.(*without flavor*) soso, -a 2.(*clothes, remark*) de mal gusto

taster ['teɪ·stər] *n* (*person*) catador(a) *m(f)*

tasty ['teɪ·sti] *adj* (*tasting good*) sabroso, -a

tattered ['tæţ·ərd] *adj* (*clothes*) hecho, -a jirones; (*person*) harapiento, -a; (*reputation*) destrozado, -a

tatters ['tæţ·ərz] *npl* jirones *fpl*; **to be in ~** estar hecho jirones

tattle ['tæţ·əl] *n* chismorreo *m*

tattler ['tæţ·lər] *n* cotilla *mf*

tattoo [tæ·'tu] I. *n* 1. MIL espectáculo *m* militar 2.(*marking on skin*) tatuaje *m* II. *vt* tatuar

tatty ['tæţ·i] <-ier, -iest> *adj pej* estropeado, -a

taught [tɔt] *pt, pp of* **teach**

taunt [tɔnt] I. *vt* burlarse de II. *n* insulto *m*

Taurus ['tɔr·əs] *n* Tauro *m*

taut [tɔt] *adj* (*wire, string*) tensado, -a; (*skin*) terso, -a; (*nerves*) tenso, -a

tautological [ˌtɔ·ţə·'lɑdʒ·ɪ·kəl] *adj* tautológico, -a

tautology [tɔ·'tal·ə·dʒi] <-ies> *n* tautología *f*

tavern ['tæv·ərn] *n* taberna *f*, estanquillo *m Ecua*

tawdry ['tɔ·dri] <-ier, -iest> *adj pej* (*vulgar*) hortera; (*pompous*) de relumbrón

tawny ['tɔ·ni] <-ier, -iest> *adj* de color ámbar oscuro

tax [tæks] I.<-es> *n* 1. FIN impuesto *m*; **hidden ~es** impuestos encubiertos; **to collect ~es** recaudar impuestos; **to increase ~es** subir los impuestos; **to put a ~ on sth** gravar algo con un impuesto; **free of ~** exento de impuestos 2. *fig* (*burden*) carga *f*; **to be a ~ on sb** ser una carga para alguien II. *vt* 1. FIN gravar con un impuesto 2.(*accuse*) acusar 3. *fig* (*need effort*) exigir un esfuerzo

taxable ['tæk·sə·bəl] *adj* imponible

tax allowance *n* desgravación *f* fiscal

taxation [tæk·'seɪ·ʃən] *n* (*taxes*) impuestos *mpl*; (*system*) sistema *m* impositivo

tax avoidance *n* evasión *f* de impuestos

T

tax base *n* base *f* imponible

tax bracket *n* categoría *f* impositiva

tax collector *n* recaudador(a) *m(f)* de impuestos

tax consultant *n* asesor(a) *m(f)* fiscal

tax-deductible *adj* deducible (a efectos impositivos)

tax dodger *n*, **tax evader** *n* evasor(a) *m(f)* de impuestos

tax evasion *n* evasión *f* de impuestos

tax exemption *n* exención *f* fiscal

tax-free *adj* libre de impuestos

tax haven *n* paraíso *m* fiscal

taxi ['tæk·si] I. *n* taxi *m* II. *vi* ir en taxi; AVIAT rodar

taxicab *n* taxi *m*

taxidermist ['tæk·sɪ·dɜr·mɪst] *n* taxidermista *mf*

taxidermy ['tæk·sɪ·dɜr·mi] *n* taxidermia *f*

taxi driver *n* taxista *mf*, ruletero, -a *m, f AmC, Méx*

taximeter ['tæk·si·mi·ţər] *n* taxímetro *m*

taxing *adj* difícil

taxi stand *n* parada *f* de taxis

taxman ['tæks·mæn] *n* recaudador(a) *m(f)* de impuestos; **the ~** Hacienda *f*

taxonomy [tæk·'san·ə·mi] *n* taxonomía *f*

taxpayer ['tæks·peɪ·ər] *n* contribuyente *mf*

tax rebate *n* devolución *f* de impuestos

tax relief *n* exención *f* de impuestos

tax return *n* declaración *f* de la renta

tax revenues *n* ingresos *mpl* fiscales

tax system *n* sistema *m* impositivo

tax year *n* año *m* fiscal

TB [ˌti·'bi] *n* abbr of **tuberculosis** tuberculosis *f* inv

T-bar ['ti·bar] *n*, **T-bar lift** *n* barra *f* en forma de T

tbs., tbsp. *abbr of* **tablespoonful** cucharada *f* (con el cucharón)

tea [ti] *n* (*plant, drink*) té *m;* **a cup of ~** una taza de té; **strong/weak ~** té fuerte/flojo; **chamomile ~** (*infusión f* de) manzanilla *f* ▶ **not for all the ~ in China** ni por todo el oro del mundo

tea bag *n* bolsita *f* de té

tea break *n* descanso *m* (para el té)

tea caddy *n* bote *m* para té

teacake ['ti·keɪk] *n* bollito *m* con pasas

teach [titʃ] <taught, taught> I. *vt* enseñar; **to ~ oneself sth** aprender algo por su propia cuenta; **to ~ sb a lesson** *fig* dar una lección a alguien II. *vi* dar clase(s)

teacher ['ti·tʃər] *n* profesor(a) *m(f)*

teacher training *n* formación *f* de profesorado

tea chest *n* caja *f* para transportar el té

teaching I. *n* 1. (*profession*) docencia *f* 2. ~**s** (*doctrine*) enseñanza *f* II. *adj* didáctico, -a

teaching staff *n* profesorado *m*

teacup *n* taza *f* de té

teahouse *n* salón *m* de té

teak [tik] *n* teca *f*

tea leaves *npl* hojas *fpl* de té

team [tim] I. *n* (*group*) equipo *m;* (*of oxen*) yunta *f;* (*of horses*) tiro *m;* (*of dogs*) traílla *f* II. *adj* de equipo III. *vt* asociar; (*match*) combinar

◆**team up** *vi* agruparse; **to ~ with** asociarse con

team captain *n* capitán, -ana *m, f* de equipo

team effort *n* esfuerzo *m* conjunto

teammate *n* compañero, -a *m, f*

team play *n* juego *m* de equipo

team spirit *n* espíritu *m* de equipo

teamwork *n* trabajo *m* en equipo

teapot ['ti·pat] *n* tetera *f*

tear¹ [tɪr] I. *n* lágrima *f;* **to bring ~s to sb's eyes** hacer que a alguien se le salten las lágrimas; **to burst into ~s** echarse a llorar; **to have ~s in one's eyes** tener los ojos llenos de lágrimas; **to not shed (any) ~s** no derramar una (sola) lágrima II. *vi* llorar

tear² [ter] I. *n* rotura *f* II.<tore, torn> *vt* 1. (*rip*) rasgar; (*ruin*) romper; **to ~ a hole in sth** hacer un agujero en algo; **to be torn between two possibilities** no saber qué opción elegir 2. (*strain: muscle*) distender III.<tore, torn> *vi* 1. (*rip*) rasgarse 2. (*rush wildly*) lanzarse; **to ~ down the stairs** precipitarse escaleras abajo

◆**tear apart** *vt* destrozar; *fig* dividir

◆**tear at** *vt* quitar precipitadamente

◆**tear away** I. *vi* salir disparado II. *vt* 1. (*make depart*) **to tear sb away** sacar a alguien; **to tear oneself away** irse de mala gana 2. (*pull*) arrancar

◆**tear down** *vt* derribar

◆**tear into** *vt* (*verbally*) arremeter contra; (*physically*) lanzarse sobre

◆**tear off** I. *vt* (*remove*) arrancar; **to ~ one's clothes** quitarse la ropa de un tirón II. *vi* (*leave quickly*) salir disparado

◆**tear out** *vt* arrancar de cuajo; **to tear one's hair out over sth** *fig* subirse por las paredes por algo

◆**tear up** *vt* despedazar; *fig* (*agreement*) anular

teardrop ['tɪr·drap] *n* lágrima *f*

tearful ['tɪr·fəl] *adj* lloroso, -a

tear gas *n* gas *m* lacrimógeno

tearjerker *n sl* (*film*) película *f* lacrimógena; (*song*) canción *f* lacrimógena

tearoom *n* salón *m* de té

tease [tiz] I. *vt* 1. (*make fun of*) tomar el pelo a; **to ~ sb about sth** tomar el pelo a alguien por algo 2. (*provoke*) provocar; (*sexually*) tentar 3. TECH cardar II. *n* bromista *mf;* (*sexually*) provocador(a) *m(f)*

teaser ['ti·zər] *n* rompecabezas *m inv*

tea service *n*, **tea set** *n* juego *m* de té

teashop *n* salón *m* de té

teaspoon *n* 1. (*spoon*) cucharilla *f* [o cucharita] *f* 2. (*amount*) cucharadita *f*

teaspoonful ['ti·spun·fʊl] *n* cucharadita *f*

tea strainer ['ti·streɪ·nər] *n* colador *m* para el té

teat [tit] *n* (*nipple: of animal*) teta *f*; (*of bottle*) tetina *f*

teatime ['ti·taɪm] *n* hora *f* del té

tea towel *n* paño *m* de cocina

technical ['tek·nɪ·kəl] *adj* técnico, -a; ~ **term** tecnicismo *m*

technical college *n* HIST escuela *f* politécnica

technicality [ˌtek·nə·'kæl·ə·t̬i] <-ies> *n* **1.** (*detail*) detalle *m* técnico; **to be acquitted on a** ~ ser absuelto por un defecto de forma **2.** (*technical matter*) carácter *m* técnico

technical school *n* escuela *f* de artes y oficios

technician [tek·'nɪʃ·ən] *n* técnico, -a *m, f*

technique [tek·'nik] *n* técnica *f*

technological [ˌtek·nə·'ladʒ·ɪ·kəl] *adj* tecnológico, -a

technology [tek·'nal·ə·dʒi] *n* tecnología *f*

technophile [ˌtek·noʊ·'faɪl] *n* tecnófilo, -a *m, f*

technophobe [ˌtek·nə·'foʊb] *n* tecnófobo, -a *m, f*

tectonics [tek·'tan·ɪks] *n* tectónica *f*

teddy¹ ['ted·i] *n* (*underwear*) camiseta *f* interior

teddy² ['ted·i] <-ies> *n*, **teddy bear** *n* osito *m* de peluche

tedious ['ti·di·əs] *adj* aburrido, -a, tedioso, -a *elev*

tediousness *n* pesadez *f*

tedium ['ti·di·əm] *n* tedio *m*

tee [ti] *n* SPORTS tee *m*

◆**tee off I.** *vi* **1.** SPORTS dar el primer golpe **2.** *sl* (*start*) arrancar(se) *fig* **II.** *vt sl* (*anger*) **to tee sb off** cabrear a alguien

teem [tim] *vi* rebosar; **to** ~ **with sth** estar repleto de algo; **to be** ~**ing with wildlife** estar repleto de flora y fauna

teeming *adj* muy numeroso, -a

teen [tin] *n* adolescente *mf*

teenage(d) ['tin·eɪdʒ(d)] *adj* adolescente

teenager ['tin·eɪ·dʒər] *n* adolescente *mf*

teens [tinz] *npl* adolescencia *f*; **to be in one's** ~ no haber aún cumplido los veinte

teensy ['tin·si] *adj*, **teensy-weensy** *adj*, **teeny** ['ti·ni] *adj* chiquitín, -ina

teenybopper ['ti·ni·ˌbap·ər] *n sl* quinceañero, -a *m, f*

teeny-weeny [ˌti·ni·'wi·ni] *adj inf s.* **teensy**

tee shirt ['ti·ʃɜrt] *n* camiseta *f*

teeter ['ti·t̬ər] *vi* **to** ~ (**around**) tambalearse; **to** ~ **on the brink of sth** estar a punto de algo

teeth [tiθ] *pl of* **tooth**

teethe [tið] *vi* echar los dientes

teething troubles *n fig* problemas *mpl* de partida

teetotal [ˌti·'toʊ·t̬əl] *adj* abstemio, -a

teetotaler [ˌti·'toʊ·t̬əl·ər] *n* abstemio, -a *m, f*

tel. *abbr of* **telephone** tel.

telecast ['tel·ɪ·kæst] *n* retransmisión *f* por televisión

telecommunications ['tel·ɪ·kə·ˌmju·nɪ·'keɪ·ʃənz] *npl* telecomunicaciones *fpl*

telecommuting ['tel·ɪ·kə·ˌmju·t̬ɪŋ] *n* COMPUT teletrabajo *m*

teleconference ['tel·ɪ·ˌkan·fər·əns] *n* teleconferencia *f*

Telecopier® ['tel·ɪ·ˌkap·i·ər] *n* (máquina *f* de) fax *m*

telecopy ['tel·ɪ·kap·i] *n* fotocopia *f*

telefax® ['tel·ɪ·fæks] *n* telefax *m*

telegenic [ˌtel·ə·'dʒen·ɪk] *adj* telegénico, -a

telegram ['tel·ɪ·græm] *n* telegrama *m*

telegraph ['tel·ɪ·græf] **I.** *n* telégrafo *m* **II.** *vt* telegrafiar; **to** ~ **sb** mandar un telegrama a alguien **III.** *adj* telegráfico, -a

telegraphese [ˌtel·ɪ·græ·'fiz] *n* estilo *m* telegráfico

telegraphic [ˌtel·ɪ·'græf·ɪk] *adj* telegráfico, -a

telegraph pole *n* poste *m* telegráfico

telegraphy [tə·'leg·rə·fi] *n* telegrafía *f*

telepathic [ˌtel·ə·'pæθ·ɪk] *adj* telepático, -a; **to be** ~ tener telepatía

telepathy [tə·'lep·ə·θi] *n* telepatía *f*

telephone ['tel·ə·foʊn] **I.** *n* teléfono *m*; **mobile** ~ (teléfono *m*) móvil *m* **II.** *vt* llamar por teléfono **III.** *vi* llamar por teléfono; **to** ~ **long-distance** hacer una llamada de larga distancia **IV.** *adj* telefónico, -a; (*booking*) por teléfono

telephone book *n* guía *f* telefónica

telephone booth *n* cabina *f* telefónica

telephone call *n* llamada *f* telefónica; **to make a** ~ hacer una llamada

telephone connection *n* conexión *f* telefónica

telephone conversation *n* conversación *f* telefónica

telephone directory *n* guía *f* telefónica

telephone exchange *n* central *f* telefónica

telephone information service *n form* servicio *m* de información telefónica

telephone message *n form* mensaje *m* telefónico

telephone number *n* número *m* de teléfono

telephone operator *n* operador(a) *m(f)* telefónico, -a

telephone rates *n* tarifa *f* telefónica

telephony [tə·'lef·ə·ni] *n* telefonía *f*; **digital mobile** ~ telefonía móvil digital

telephoto lens ['tel·ə·foʊ·t̬oʊ·'lens] *n* teleobjetivo *m*

teleprinter ['tel·ə·ˌprɪn·tər] *n* teletipo *m*

teleprocessing ['tel·ɪ·pra·ˌses·ɪŋ] *n* COMPUT teleproceso *m*

TelePrompter® ['tel·ə·ˌpramp·tər] *n* teleprompter® *m*

telescope ['tel·ə·skoʊp] **I.** *n* telescopio *m* **II.** *vi* plegarse

telescopic [ˌtel·ə·'skap·ɪk] *adj* **1.** (*vision, sight*) telescópico, -a **2.** (*folding*) plegable

teleshopping ['tel·ə·ʃap·ɪŋ] *n* telecompra *f*; (*shop*) teletienda *f*

Teletype® *n*, **Teletype®** ['tel·ə·taɪp] *n* teletipo *m*

teletypewriter [ˌtel·ɪ·'taɪp·raɪ·t̬ər] *n* teletipo *m*

televangelist [ˌtel·ɪ·'væn·dʒə·lɪst] *n* predicador(a) *m(f)* de la tele

T

televiewer ['tel·ə·ˌvju·ər] *n* telespectador(a) *m(f)*

televise ['tel·ə·vaɪz] *vt* televisar; **to ~ sth live** retransmitir algo en directo

television ['tel·ə·vɪʒ·ən] *n* televisión *f*; (*television set*) televisor *m*; **to watch ~** ver la televisión; **to turn the ~ on/off** encender/apagar el televisor

television announcer *n* locutor(a) *m(f)* de televisión

television camera *n* cámara *f* de televisión

television program *n* programa *m* de televisión

television set *n* televisor *m*

television studio *n* estudio *m* de televisión

telex ['tel·eks] **I.** *n* <-es> télex *m* **II.** *adj* por télex **III.** *vt* enviar por télex; **to ~ sb sth** comunicar algo por télex a alguien

tell [tel] **I.** <told, told> *vt* **1.** (*say*) decir; **to ~ sb of sth** comunicar algo a alguien; **to ~ sb whether...** informar a alguien de si...; **I told you so** te avisé **2.** (*narrate*) contar; **~ me another (one)** *inf* cuéntame otra **3.** (*command*) mandar; **to ~ sb to do sth** ordenar a alguien hacer algo; **do as you're told** *inf* haz lo que te mandan **4.** (*make out*) reconocer **5.** (*distinguish*) distinguir; **to ~ sth from sth** distinguir algo de algo **6.** (*know*) saber; **there is no ~ing** no hay manera de saberlo **7.** (*count*) contar; (*add up*) sumar; **all told** en total ▶ **to ~ it like it is** *inf* decir las cosas claras; **that would be ~ing** eso podría ser cierto; **you're ~ing me!** *inf* ¡a mí me lo vas a contar! **II.** <told, told> *vi* **1.** hablar; **to ~ of sth/sb** hablar de algo/alguien **2.** (*know*) saber; **you never can ~** nunca se sabe; **how can I ~?** ¡yo qué sé!; **who can ~?** ¿quién sabe? **3.** (*have an effect*) tener efecto

◆ **tell apart** *vt* distinguir

◆ **tell off** *vt* regañar; **to tell sb off for sth** regañar [*o* reñir] a alguien por algo

◆ **tell on** *vt* **to ~ sb** chivarse de alguien

teller ['tel·ər] *n* **1.** (*bank employee*) cajero, -a *m, f* **2.** (*vote counter*) escrutador(a) *m(f)*

telling ['tel·ɪŋ] **I.** *adj* **1.** (*revealing*) revelador(a) **2.** (*significant*) contundente **II.** *n* narración *f*

telling-off [ˌtel·ɪŋ·ˈɔf] <tellings-off> *n Can* bronca *f*; **to give sb a ~ for (doing) sth** echar una bronca a alguien por (hacer) algo

telltale ['tel·teɪl] **I.** *n pej* chivato, -a *m, f* **II.** *adj* revelador(a)

temerity [tə·ˈmer·ə· t̬i] *n form* temeridad *f*; **to have the ~ to do sth** atreverse a hacer algo

temp [temp] **I.** *vi* trabajar temporalmente **II.** *n* trabajador(a) *m(f)* temporal

temp. *abbr of* **temperature** temperatura

temper ['tem·pər] **I.** *n* (*temperament*) temperamento *m*; (*mood*) humor *m*; (*tendency to become angry*) genio *m*; **good ~** buen humor; **bad ~** mal genio; **to keep one's ~** no perder la calma; **to lose one's ~** perder los estribos; **~s were getting (rather) frayed** el ambiente se estaba cargando **II.** *vt* **1.** (*mitigate*) mitigar, ate-

nuar; **to ~ one's criticism** suavizar sus críticas **2.** (*make hard*) templar

temperament ['tem·prə·mənt] *n* (*character*) temperamento *m*; (*moodiness*) genio *m*; **a fit of ~** un ataque de furia

temperamental [ˌtem·prə·ˈmen·təl] *adj* **1.** (*relating to mood*) temperamental **2.** (*unpredictable*) caprichoso, -a

temperance ['tem·pər·əns] *n form* (*moderation*) moderación *f*; (*abstinence*) abstinencia *f*

temperate ['tem·pər·ət] *adj* (*moderate*) moderado, -a; (*climate*) templado, -a

temperature ['tem·pər·ə·t̬ər] *n* temperatura *f*; MED fiebre *f*; **to run a ~** tener fiebre

tempest ['tem·pɪst] *n liter* tempestad *f*

tempestuous [tem·ˈpes·tʃu·əs] *adj* tempestuoso, -a

template ['tem·plɪt] *n* plantilla *f*

temple¹ ['tem·pəl] *n* REL templo *m*

temple² ['tem·pəl] *n* ANAT sien *f*

tempo ['tem·poʊ] <-s *o* -pi> *n* **1.** MUS tempo *m* **2.** (*pace*) ritmo *m*

temporal ['tem·pər·əl] *adj form* temporal

temporarily ['tem·pə·rer·ə·li] *adv* temporalmente

temporary ['tem·pə·rer·i] *adj* (*improvement*) pasajero, -a; (*staff, accommodation*) temporal; (*relief*) momentáneo, -a

temporize ['tem·pə·raɪz] *vi* tratar de ganar tiempo

tempt [tempt] *vt* **1.** tentar; **to ~ sb into doing sth** tentar a alguien a hacer algo **2.** (*persuade*) convencer; **to ~ sb into doing sth** incitar a alguien a hacer algo

temptation [temp·ˈteɪ·ʃən] *n* **1.** (*attraction*) tentación *f*; **to resist ~ (to do sth)** resistir la tentación (de hacer algo); **to succumb to ~** caer en [*o* ceder a] la tentación **2.** (*tempting thing*) aliciente *m*

tempting ['temp·tɪŋ] *adj* atractivo, -a; (*offer*) tentador(a)

temptress ['temp·trɪs] <-es> *n* tentadora *f*

ten [ten] **I.** *adj* diez *inv* **II.** *n* diez *m*; **~ to one he comes** seguro que viene; **~s of thousands** decenas *fpl* de miles; *s.a.* **eight**

tenable ['ten·ə·bəl] *adj* defendible

tenacious [tə·ˈneɪ·ʃəs] *adj* (*belief*) firme; (*person*) tenaz

tenacity [tə·ˈnæs·ə·t̬i] *n* tenacidad *f*

tenancy ['ten·ən·si] <-ies> *n* **1.** (*status*) inquilinato *m* **2.** (*right*) arrendamiento *m*

tenant ['ten·ənt] *n* (*of land*) arrendatario, -a *m, f*; (*of house*) inquilino, -a *m, f*

tenant farmer *n* (*of land*) agricultor(a) *m(f)* arrendatario, -a

tend¹ [tend] *vi* **1.** (*have tendency*) tender; **to ~ to do sth** tender a hacer algo; **I ~ to disagree** no comparto completamente su opinión **2.** (*usually do*) soler

tend² [tend] *vt* (*look after*) ocuparse de; (*a person*) cuidar de

◆ **tend to** *vt* (*look after*) ocuparse de

tendency ['ten·dən·si] <-ies> *n* tendencia *f;* MED propensión *f*
tendentious [ten·'den·ʃəs] *adj* tendencioso, -a
tender¹ ['ten·dər] *adj* **1.**(*not tough*) vulnerable **2.**(*easily damaged*) débil **3.** *liter* (*youthful: age*) tierno, -a **4.**(*painful*) doloroso, -a; (*part of the body*) sensible; (*subject*) delicado, -a **5.**(*affectionate*) cariñoso, -a; **to have a ~ heart** tener buen corazón
tender² ['ten·dər] **I.** *n* COM oferta *f;* **to put in a ~** hacer una oferta; **to put sth out for ~** sacar algo a concurso **II.** *vt* (*offer*) ofrecer; (*apology*) presentar **III.** *vi* **to ~ for sth** hacer una oferta para algo
tender³ ['ten·dər] *n* RAIL ténder *m;* NAUT gabarra *f*
tenderfoot ['ten·dər·fʊt] <-s *o* -feet> *n* principiante *mf*
tenderhearted ['ten·dər·ˌhar·tɪd] *adj* bondadoso, -a; **to be ~** tener buen corazón
tenderize ['ten·də·raɪz] *vt* ablandar
tenderizer *n* ablandador *m* de carne
tenderloin ['ten·dər·lɔɪn] *n* lomo *m*
tenderly *adv* cariñosamente
tenderness ['ten·dər·nɪs] *n* **1.**(*softness*) blandura *f* **2.**(*affection*) ternura *f* **3.**(*sensitivity*) sensibilidad *f*
tendon ['ten·dən] *n* tendón *m*
tendril ['ten·drəl] *n* zarcillo *m*
tenement ['ten·ə·mənt] *n* bloque *m* de pisos
Tenerife [ˌten·ə·'rɪf] *n* Tenerife *m*
tenet ['ten·ɪt] *n* principio *m*
tenfold ['ten·foʊld] **I.** *adj* décuplo, -a **II.** *adv* diez veces
Tenn. *abbr of* **Tennessee** Tennessee *m*
Tennessee *n* Tennessee *m*
tennis ['ten·ɪs] *n* tenis *m inv*
tennis ball *n* pelota *f* de tenis
tennis court *n* pista *f* de tenis
tennis elbow *n* codo *m* de tenista
tennis player *n* tenista *mf*
tennis racket *n* raqueta *f* de tenis
tennis shoe *n* zapato *m* de tenis
tenon ['ten·ən] *n* espaldón *m*
tenor ['ten·ər] **I.** *n* **1.** *a.* MUS tenor *m* **2.**(*character*) tono *m;* (*of events*) curso *m* **II.** *adj* MUS de tenor
tenpins [ˌten·pɪn·'boʊ·lɪŋ] *npl* bolos *mpl*
tense¹ [tens] *n* LING tiempo *m*
tense² [tens] **I.** *adj* (*wire, person, atmosphere*) tenso, -a **II.** *vt* tensar **III.** *vi* ponerse tenso
◆**tense up** *vi* ponerse tenso
tension ['ten·ʃən] *n* tensión *f*
tent [tent] *n* (*for camping*) tienda *f* de campaña, carpa *f AmL;* (*in circus*) carpa
tentacle ['ten·tə·kəl] *n* tentáculo *m*
tentative ['ten·tə·tɪv] *adj* **1.**(*person*) vacilante **2.**(*decision*) provisional
tentatively *adv* **1.**(*suggest*) con vacilación **2.**(*decide*) provisionalmente
tenterhooks ['ten·tər·hʊks] *npl* **to be on ~** tener el alma en vilo; **to keep sb on ~** tener a alguien en ascuas

tenth [tenθ] **I.** *adj* décimo, -a **II.** *n* **1.**(*order*) décimo, -a *m, f* **2.**(*date*) diez *m* **3.**(*fraction*) décimo *m;* (*part*) décima parte *f; s.a.* **eighth**
tent peg *n* estaquilla *f* de tienda
tent pole *n* mástil *m* de tienda
tenuous ['ten·ju·əs] *adj* tenue; (*connection*) indirecto, -a; (*argument*) poco sólido, -a
tenure ['ten·jər] *n* **1.**(*possession*) posesión *f,* tenencia *f* **2.**(*period of holding sth*) ejercicio *m*
tepee ['ti·pi] *n* tipi *m*
tepid ['tep·ɪd] *adj* tibio, -a
terabyte ['ter·ə·baɪt] *n* COMPUT terabyte *m*
term [tɜrm] **I.** *n* **1.**(*label, word*) término *m;* **~ of abuse** insulto *m;* **~ of endearment** expresión *f* afectuosa; **in glowing ~s** con gran admiración; **in no uncertain ~s** en términos claros; **in simple ~s** en palabras sencillas **2.** **~s** (*conditions*) condiciones *fpl;* **to offer easy ~s** ofrecer facilidades de pago **3.**(*limit*) límite *m;* COM plazo *m;* **~ of delivery** plazo de entrega; **~ of notice** plazo de despido **4.**(*period*) período *m;* (*duration*) duración *f;* (*of contract*) vigencia *f;* (*of office*) mandato *m;* **prison ~** sentencia *f* de prisión; **in the short/long ~** a corto/largo plazo **5.**(*category*) término *m;* **to think in ~s of sth** pensar en términos de algo **6.** UNIV, SCHOOL trimestre *m* **7.** **~s** relaciones *fpl;* **to be on good/bad ~s with sb** llevarse bien/mal con alguien **II.** *vt* llamar; (*label*) calificar de
terminal ['tɜr·mɪ·nəl] **I.** *adj* terminal; (*extreme*) absoluto, -a; (*boredom*) mortal **II.** *n* **1.** RAIL, AVIAT, COMPUT terminal *f* **2.** ELEC polo *m*
terminate ['tɜr·mɪ·neɪt] *form* **I.** *vt* (*finish*) poner fin a; (*contract*) rescindir; (*pregnancy*) interrumpir **II.** *vi* terminarse
termination [ˌtɜr·mɪ·'neɪ·ʃən] *n* (*ending*) fin *m;* (*of contract*) rescisión *f;* (*of pregnancy*) interrupción *f*
terminological [ˌtɜr·mɪ·nə·'ladʒ·ɪ·kəl] *adj* terminológico, -a
terminology [ˌtɜr·mɪ·'nal·ə·dʒi] *n* terminología *f*
terminus ['tɜr·mɪ·nəs] <-es *o* -i> *n* (*station*) última estación *f;* (*bus stop*) última parada *f*
termite ['tɜr·maɪt] *n* termita *f*
tern [tɜrn] *n* golondrina *f* de mar
terrace ['ter·əs] **I.** *n a.* AGR terraza *f* **II.** *vt* formar terrazas en **III.** *adj* en terrazas
terraced house *n* casa *f* adosada
terrain [te·'reɪn] *n* terreno *m*
terrapin ['ter·ə·pɪn] <-(s)> *n* galápago *m*
terrestrial [tə·'res·tri·əl] *adj form* terrestre
terrible ['ter·ə·bəl] *adj* **1.**(*shocking*) terrible **2.**(*very bad*) espantoso, -a **3.** *inf* (*as intensifier*) fatal
terribly ['ter·ə·bli] *adv* **1.**(*very badly*) terriblemente **2.**(*very*) tremendamente
terrier ['ter·i·ər] *n* terrier *m*
terrific [tə·'rɪf·ɪk] *adj* **1.**(*terrifying*) terrorífico, -a **2.**(*excellent*) estupendo, -a **3.** *as intensifier* (*very great*) tremendo, -a

T

terrified *adj* aterrorizado, -a
terrify ['ter·ə·faɪ] <-ie-> *vt* aterrar
terrifying *adj* aterrador(a)
territorial [ˌter·ə·'tɔr·i·əl] I. *n* MIL reservista *m* II. *adj* territorial
territory ['ter·ə·tɔr·i] <-ies> *n* 1. (*area of land*) territorio *m;* **forbidden ~** zona *f* prohibida 2. (*activity*) terreno *m*
terror ['ter·ər] *n* terror *m;* **to have a ~ of sth** tener terror a algo; **to strike ~** infundir terror; **a little ~** *inf* un demonio de niño
terrorism ['ter·ə·rɪz·əm] *n* terrorismo *m*
terrorist ['ter·ə·rɪst] I. *n* terrorista *mf* II. *adj* terrorista
terrorize ['ter·ə·raɪz] *vt* aterrorizar
terror-stricken ['ter·ər·ˌstrɪk·ən] *adj,* **terror-struck** ['ter·ər·strʌk] *adj* aterrorizado, -a
terry cloth [ˌter·i·'klɔθ] *n* felpa *f*
terse [tɜrs] *adj* lacónico, -a
tertiary ['tɜr·ʃi·er·i] I. *adj form* terciario, -a II. <-ies> *n* **the Tertiary** GEO el Terciario
tessellated ['tes·ə·leɪ·tɪd] *adj* teselado, -a
test [test] I. *n* 1. SCHOOL, UNIV examen *m;* **to pass/fail a ~** aprobar/suspender un examen; **driving ~** examen de conducir 2. MED prueba *f;* **blood ~** análisis *m inv* de sangre 3. (*trial*) **to be a ~ of endurance** ser una prueba de resistencia; **to put sth to the ~** poner algo a prueba II. *vt* 1. (*examine*) examinar 2. MED analizar; (*hearing*) examinar; **to ~ sb for sth** hacer a alguien una prueba de algo 3. (*measure*) comprobar 4. (*try to prove*) someter a prueba 5. (*try with senses*) tocar; (*by tasting*) probar
testament ['tes·tə·mənt] *n* 1. *form* (*will*) testamento *m;* **last will and ~** última voluntad y testamento 2. *form* (*evidence*) testimonio *m* 3. REL **the Old/New Testament** el Antiguo/Nuevo Testamento
test ban *n* prohibición *f* de ensayos nucleares
test bench *n* banco *m* de pruebas
test card *n* carta *f* de ajuste
test case *n* causa *f* que sienta jurisprudencia
test drive *n* vuelta *f* de prueba
tester ['tes·tər] *n* 1. (*person*) examinador(a) *m(f)* 2. (*sample*) frasco *m* de muestra
test flight *n* vuelo *m* de prueba
testicle ['tes·tɪ·kəl] *n* testículo *m*
testify ['tes·tɪ·faɪ] <-ie-> I. *vi* 1. (*give evidence*) testificar 2. *form* (*prove*) **to ~ to sth** atestiguar algo II. *vt* 1. (*bear witness to*) demostrar 2. (*declare under oath*) testificar; **to ~ that...** declarar que...
testimonial [ˌtes·tɪ·'mou·ni·əl] *n form* 1. (*character reference*) referencias *fpl* 2. (*tribute*) homenaje *m*
testimony ['tes·tɪ·mou·ni] <-ies> *n* testimonio *m;* **to give ~** dar testimonio
testing I. *n* experiencia *f* II. *adj* duro, -a
testing ground *n* zona *f* de pruebas
test piece *n* MUS obra *f* elegida para un certamen
test pilot *n* piloto *mf* de pruebas
test stage *n* período *m* de pruebas

test tube *n* probeta *f*
test-tube baby *n* bebé *m* probeta
testy ['tes·ti] <-ier, -iest> *adj* irritable
tetanus ['tet·ə·nəs] *n* tétanos *m inv,* tétano *m;* **~ injection** vacuna *f* antitetánica
tetchy ['tetʃ·i] <-ier, -iest> *adj* irritable
tether ['teð·ər] I. *n* cuerda *f* ▶ **to be at the end of one's ~** no aguantar más II. *vt* amarrar; **to be ~ed to sth** *fig* estar atado a algo
Teutonic [tu·'tan·ɪk] *adj* teutónico, -a
Tex. *abbr of* **Texas** Tejas *m*
Texan ['tek·sən] I. *n* tejano, -a *m, f* II. *adj* tejano, -a
Texas ['tek·səs] *n* Tejas *m*
text [tekst] *n* texto *m*
textbook ['tekst·bʊk] I. *n* libro *m* de texto II. *adj* de manual
text editor *n* COMPUT editor *m* de textos
textile ['teks·taɪl] I. *n pl* tejidos *mpl* II. *adj* textil
textile mill *n* fábrica *f* de tejidos
text processing *n* COMPUT procesamiento *m* de textos
textual ['teks·tʃu·əl] *adj* textual
texture ['teks·tʃər] *n* 1. (*feel*) textura *f* 2. (*consistency*) consistencia *f*
Thai [taɪ] I. *adj* tailandés, -esa II. *n* 1. (*person*) tailandés, -esa *m, f* 2. LING tailandés *m*
Thailand ['taɪ·lənd] *n* Tailandia *m*
thalidomide [θə·'lɪd·oʊ·maɪd] *n* talidomida *f*
than [ðən, ðæn] *conj* que; **you are taller ~ she (is)** eres más alto que ella; **more ~ 60** más de 60; **more ~ once** más de una vez; **nothing else ~...** nada más que...; **no other ~ you** nadie más que tú; **no sooner had she told him, ~...** en cuanto se lo dijo...
thank [θæŋk] *vt* agradecer; **to ~ sb (for sth)** dar las gracias a alguien (por algo); **~ you** gracias; **~ you very much!** ¡muchas gracias!; **no, ~ you** no, gracias
thankful ['θæŋk·fəl] *adj* 1. (*pleased*) satisfecho, -a; **to be ~ that...** alegrarse de que... +*subj* 2. (*grateful*) agradecido, -a
thankfully *adv* afortunadamente
thankless ['θæŋk·lɪs] *adj* desagradecido, -a; (*task*) ingrato, -a
thanks [θæŋks] *npl* gracias *fpl;* **~ very much** muchísimas gracias; **~ to** gracias a; **in ~ for...** en recompensa por...; **no ~ to him** no fue gracias a él
thanksgiving [ˌθæŋks·'gɪv·ɪŋ] *n* acción *f* de gracias
Thanksgiving (Day) *n* Día *m* de Acción de Gracias

ℹ Thanksgiving (Día de Acción de Gracias) es una de las fiestas más importantes de EE.UU., que se celebra el cuarto jueves del mes de noviembre (en Canadá el segundo lunes de octubre). El primer **Thanksgiving Day** fue celebrado en 1621 por colonos ingleses **(Pilgrims)** en **Plymouth.** Habiendo sobrevivido con grandes dificultades a su primer invierno en Nueva Inglaterra, querían agradecer a Dios. En EE.UU., es costumbre que las familias se reúnan para celebrar este día. La comida tradicional en esta fecha consta de pavo relleno (**stuffed turkey**), que se sirve con salsa de arándanos (**cranberry sauce**), batatas (**yams, sweet potatoes**) y maíz (**corn**). El postre tradicional es la tarta de calabaza (**pumpkin pie**).

that [ðət, ðæt] **I.** *adj dem* <those> ese/esos, esa(s); (*more remote*) aquel/aquellos, aquella(s); ~ **table** esa/aquella mesa; ~ **book** ese/aquel libro **II.** *pron* **1.** *rel* que; **the woman** ~ **told me...** la mujer que me dijo...; **all** ~ **I have** todo lo que tengo **2.** *dem* ése/ésos, ésa(s), eso(s); **what is** ~? ¿eso qué es?; **who is** ~? ¿ése/ésa quién es?; **like** ~ así; **after** ~ después de eso; ~'**s it!** ¡eso es! **III.** *adv* tan; **it was** ~ **hot** hacía tanto calor **IV.** *conj* **1.** que; **I told you** ~ **I couldn't come** te dije que no podía ir; ~ **I should live to see this!** ¡que tenga que vivir para ver algo así! **2.** (*in order that*) para que +*subj*

thatch [θætʃ] **I.** *n* **1.** (*roof*) techo *m* de paja **2.** (*hair*) mata *f* (de pelo) **II.** *vt* poner un techo de paja a

thatched roof *n* techo de paja

thaw [θɔ] **I.** *n* **1.** (*weather*) deshielo *m* **2.** (*in relations*) distensión *f* **II.** *vi* **1.** (*weather*) deshelar; (*food*) descongelarse **2.** (*relations*) volverse más cordial **III.** *vt* derretir

the [ðə, *stressed, before vowel* ði] **I.** *def art* el *m*, la *f*, los *mpl*, las *fpl*; **from** ~ **garden** del jardín; **at** ~ **hotel** en el hotel; **at** ~ **door** a la puerta; **to** ~ **garden** al jardín; **in** ~ **winter** en invierno **II.** *adv* (*in comparison*) ~ **more one tries**, ~ **less one succeeds** cuanto más se esfuerza uno, menos lo logra; ~ **sooner** ~ **better** cuanto antes mejor

theater ['θi·ə·tər] *n* **1.** THEAT (*place, art*) teatro *m*; (*company*) compañía *f* de teatro **2.** CINE cine *m* **3.** UNIV auditorio *m* **4.** *fig* (*scene*) escenario *m*

theater company *n* compañía *f* de teatro

theater critic *n* crítica *f* teatral

theatergoer *n* aficionado, -a *m, f* al teatro

theatrical [θi·'æt·rɪ·kəl] *adj* teatral; **don't be so** ~ **about it** no hagas tanto teatro por eso

thee [ði] *pron pers* HIST te; **with** ~ contigo

theft [θeft] *n* robo *m;* **petty** ~ hurto *m*

their [ðer] *adj pos* su(s); ~ **house** su casa; ~ **children** sus hijos

theirs [ðerz] *pron pos* (el) suyo *m*, (la) suya *f*, (los) suyos *mpl*, (las) suyas *fpl;* **this house is** ~ esta casa es suya; **they aren't our bags, they are** ~ no son nuestras bolsas, son las suyas; **a book of** ~ un libro suyo

theism ['θi·ɪz·əm] *n* teísmo *m*

them [ðem, ðəm] *pron pers pl* **1.** *inf* (*they*) ellos, -as; **older than** ~ mayor que ellos; **if I were** ~ si yo fuera [*o* fuese] ellos **2.** *direct object* los, las; *indirect object* les; **look at** ~ míralos; **I saw** ~ yo los vi; **he gave** ~ **the pencil** les dio el lápiz **3.** *after prep* ellos, -as; **it's from/for** ~ es de/para ellos

thematic [θi·'mæ̱·ɪk] *adj* temático, -a

theme [θim] *n a.* MUS tema *m;* **on the** ~ **of** sobre el tema de

theme music *n* sintonía *f*

theme park *n* parque *m* temático

theme song *n*, **theme tune** *n* sintonía *f*

themselves [ðəm·'selvz] *pron* **1.** *subject* ellos mismos, ellas mismas **2.** *object, reflexive* se; **the children behaved** ~ los niños se portaron bien **3.** *after prep* sí mismos, sí mismas; **by** ~ solos, -as

then [ðen] **I.** *adj form* (de) entonces; **the** ~ **chairman** el entonces presidente **II.** *adv* **1.** (*at aforementioned time*) entonces; **before** ~ hasta entonces; **from** ~ **on(ward)** a partir de entonces; **since** ~ desde entonces; **until** ~ hasta aquel momento; (**every**) **now and** ~ de vez en cuando **2.** (*after that*) después; **what** ~? ¿y entonces qué? **3.** (*additionally*) además; **but** ~ (**again**) pero también, y además **4.** (*as a result*) por tanto, así pues; ~ **he must be there** entonces debe estar allí **5.** (*that being the case*) en ese caso **6.** (*agreement*) **all right** ~ de acuerdo pues

thence [ðens] *adv form* de ahí

thenceforth [,ðens·'fɔrθ] *adv form*, **thenceforward** [,ðens·'fɔr·wərd] *adv form* a partir de entonces

theocracy [θi·'ak·rə·si] *n* teocracia *f*

theodolite [θi·'ad·ə·laɪt] *n* teodolito *m*

theologian [θi·ə·'loʊ·dʒən] *n* teólogo, -a *m, f*

theological [θi·ə·'ladʒ·ɪ·kəl] *adj* teológico, -a

theology [θi·'al·ə·dʒi] <-ies> *n* teología *f*

theorem ['θi·ər·əm] *n* MATH teorema *m;* **Pythagoras's** ~ el teorema de Pitágoras

theoretical [θi·ə·'ret·ɪ·kəl] *adj* teórico, -a

theoretically *adv* teóricamente

theorist ['θi·ər·ɪst] *n* teórico, -a *m, f*

theorize ['θi·ə·raɪz] *vi* teorizar

theory ['θi·ə·ri] <-ies> *n* teoría *f;* **in** ~ en teoría

therapeutic [θer·ə·'pju·tɪk] *adj*, **therapeutical** [θer·ə·'pju·tɪ·kəl] *adj* terapéutico, -a

therapeutics [θer·ə·'pju·tɪks] *n* terapéutica *f*

therapist ['θer·ə·pɪst] *n* terapeuta *mf*

therapy ['θer·ə·pi] <-ies> *n* terapia *f*

there [ðer] **I.** *adv* allí [*o* allá]; **here and** ~ aquí y allá; ~ **is/are** hay; ~ **will be** habrá; ~ **you are!** ¡ahí lo tienes!; ~'**s the train** ahí está el tren; ~ **is no one** no hay nadie; ~ **and then** en el acto **II.** *interj* ¡vaya!; ~, **take this** toma esto; ~, **that's enough!** ¡bueno, basta ya!

thereabouts ['ðer·ə·baʊts] *adv* (*approximately*) más o menos; (*near*) por ahí

thereafter [ðer·'æf·tər] *adv* a partir de entonces

thereby [ðer·'baɪ] *adv form* por eso ▶ ~ **hangs**

a tale *iron* es una larga historia

therefore ['ðer·fɔr] *adv* por (lo) tanto; **to decide ~ to do sth** decidir, por consiguiente, hacer algo

therein [ðer·'ɪn] *adv form* ahí dentro; *fig* en eso

thereof [ðer·'ʌv] *adv form* de eso

thereupon [ˌðer·ə·'pan] *adv* acto seguido

therm [θɜrm] *n* (*unit of heat*) termia *f*

thermal ['θɜr·məl] **I.** *n* **1.** (*air current*) corriente *f* térmica **2.** **~s** (*underwear*) ropa *f* interior térmica **II.** *adj* PHYS, COMPUT térmico, -a; (*water*) termal

thermal underwear *n* ropa *f* interior térmica

thermodynamic [ˌθɜr·moʊ·daɪ·'næm·ɪk] *adj* termodinámico, -a

thermoelectric [ˌθɜr·moʊ·ɪ·'lek·trɪk] *adj* termoeléctrico, -a

thermometer [θər·'mam·ə·t̬ər] *n* termómetro *m*

thermonuclear [ˌθɜr·moʊ·'nu·kli·ər] *adj* termonuclear

thermos ['θɜr·məs] *n* (*bottle*) termo *m*

thermostat ['θɜr·mə·stæt] *n* termostato *m*

thermostatic [ˌθɜr·mə·'stæt̬·ɪk] *adj* termostático, -a

thesaurus [θɪ·'sɔr·əs] <-es *o* -ri> *n* diccionario *m* de sinónimos y antónimos

these [ðiz] *pl of* **this**

thesis ['θi·sɪs] <-ses> *n* tesis *f inv*

they [ðeɪ] *pron pers* **1.** (*3rd person pl*) ellos, -as; **~ are my parents/sisters** (ellos/ellas) son mis padres/hermanas **2.** (*people in general*) **~ say that...** dicen que...

they'll [ðeɪl] = **they will** *s.* **will**

they're [ðer] = **they are** *s.* **be**

they've [ðeɪv] = **they have** *s.* **have**

thick [θɪk] **I.** *adj* **1.** (*not thin: wall*) grueso, -a; (*coat*) gordo, -a **2.** (*dense: hair*) abundante; (*forest*) denso, -a; (*liquid*) espeso, -a **3.** (*extreme: darkness*) profundo, -a; (*accent*) marcado, -a **4.** (*stupid*) corto, -a; **to be a bit ~** ser un poco tonto; **to be as ~ as two short planks** *inf* no tener dos dedos de frente **5.** (*very friendly*) **to be ~ with sb** ser muy amigo de alguien ▶ **through ~ and thin** a las duras y a las maduras **II.** *n inf* **to be in the ~ of sth** estar de lleno en algo

thicken ['θɪk·ən] **I.** *vt* espesar **II.** *vi* espesarse

thickener *n*, **thickening** *n* espesante *m*

thicket ['θɪk·ɪt] *n* matorral *m*

thickheaded ['θɪk·ˌhed·ɪd] *adj* ceporro, -a

thickness ['θɪk·nɪs] *n* **1.** (*size*) grosor *m* **2.** (*of hair*) abundancia *f*; (*of sauce*) consistencia *f*

thickset ['θɪk·set] *adj* rechoncho, -a

thick-skinned ['θɪk·skɪnd] *adj* insensible; **he is ~** todo le resbala

thief [θif, θivz] <thieves> *n* ladrón, -ona *m, f*

thieve [θiv] *vi, vt liter* hurtar

thieving ['θi·vɪŋ] **I.** *n liter* hurto *m* **II.** *adj* de dedos largos

thigh [θaɪ] *n* muslo *m*

thighbone *n* fémur *m*

thimble ['θɪm·bəl] *n* dedal *m*

thin [θɪn] <-nn-> **I.** *adj* **1.** (*not thick: clothes*) fino, -a; (*person*) delgado, -a; (*very slim*) flaco, -a **2.** (*soup, sauce*) claro, -a; (*wine*) aguado, -a **3.** (*sparse: hair*) ralo, -a; **to be ~ on top** ser calvo **4.** (*voice*) débil; (*excuse*) poco convincente **II.** <-nn-> *vt* (*dilute*) aclarar

◆**thin down I.** *vi* adelgazar **II.** *vt* aclarar

◆**thin out I.** *vt* hacer menos denso; (*plants*) entresacar **II.** *vi* disminuir

thine [ðaɪn] *pron pos* HIST (el) tuyo *m*, (la) tuya *f*, (lo) tuyo *neuter*; (los) tuyos *mpl*, (las) tuyas *fpl*

thing [θɪŋ] *n* **1.** (*object, action*) cosa *f*; **the lucky/best/main ~** lo bueno/mejor/principal; **sweet ~s** pasteles *mpl*; **one ~ after another** una cosa después de (la) otra; **to be a ~ of the past** ser algo del pasado; **the last ~ she wants to do is...** lo último que quiere hacer es... **2.** (*matter*) **to know a ~ or two** saber algo; **above all ~s** por encima de todo; **another ~** otra cosa; **and another ~,...** y por otra parte,...; **if it's not one ~, it's another** cuando no es una cosa es otra **3.** (*social behavior*) **it's the in ~** es lo que hay que hacer **4.** (*fashion*) **the latest ~ in shoes** el último grito en zapatos **5.** *inf* (*the important point*) **the real ~** lo auténtico; **the very ~** lo importante **6.** **~s** (*possessions*) pertenencias *fpl*; **all his ~s** todas sus cosas **7.** **~s** (*the situation*), **as ~s stand, the way ~s are** tal (y) como están las cosas; **the shape of ~s to come** lo que se avecina **8.** *inf* (*term of affection*) **the poor ~!** ¡el pobre!; (*children, animals*) ¡pobrecito!; **you lucky ~!** ¡qué suerte tienes!; **lazy ~!** ¡vago!; **stupid ~!** ¡imbécil! ▶ **to be all ~s to all men** actuar según sopla el viento; **it's just one of those ~s** es una de esas cosas que pasan; **he won but it was a close ~** ganó por un pelo; **all ~s being equal** si no sale ningún imprevisto; **first ~s first** lo primero es lo primero; **to not know the first ~ about sth** no tener ni la más remota idea de algo; **to be onto a good ~** *inf* tener un chollo; **to do one's own ~** hacer la suya; **to have a ~ about sth** *inf* tener asco a algo; **to be hearing ~s** oír campanas; **to make a (big) ~ out of sth** armar un escándalo por algo

thingamabob ['θɪŋ·ə·mə·ˌbab] *n*, **thingamajig** ['θɪŋ·ə·mə·ˌdʒɪg] *n*, **thingy** ['θɪŋ·i] *n* (*object*) cosa *f*; (*person*) ése, ésa

think [θɪŋk] <thought, thought> **I.** *n* **to have a ~ about sth** pensarse algo **II.** *vt* **1.** (*believe*) pensar, creer; **who would have thought it!** ¡quien lo hubiese pensado! **2.** (*consider*) considerar; **to ~ sb (to be) sth** considerar a alguien (como) algo; **to ~ nothing of sb** no tener ninguna fe en alguien; **~ nothing of it!** no merece la pena mencionarlo **III.** *vi* pensar; **to ~ aloud** pensar en voz alta; **to ~ for oneself** pensar por sí mismo; **to ~ to oneself** pensar para sí mismo; **to ~ of doing sth** pensar en hacer algo; **to ~ about/of sb/sth** pensar en alguien/algo

◆**think ahead** *vi* pensar de cara al futuro
◆**think back** *vi* **to ~ to sth** recordar algo; **to ~ over sth** hacer memoria de algo
◆**think of** *vi* pensar en
◆**think out** *vt* **1.**(*consider*) pensar muy bien **2.**(*plan*) planear cuidadosamente
◆**think over** *vt* reflexionar sobre
◆**think through** *vt* estudiar detenidamente
◆**think up** *vt* inventar
thinker *n* pensador(a) *m(f)*
thinking I. *n* **1.**(*thought process*) pensamiento *m* **2.**(*reasoning*) razonamiento *m* **3.**(*opinion*) opinión *f* II. *adj* inteligente
think tank *n* gabinete *m* estratégico
thinner *n* disolvente *m*
thinness *n* delgadez *f*
thin-skinned ['θɪn·skɪnd] *adj* sensible
third [θɜrd] I. *adj* tercero, -a II. *n* **1.**(*order*) tercero, -a *m, f* **2.**(*date*) tres *m* **3.**(*fraction*) tercio *m* **4.** MUS, AUTO tercera *f; s.a.* **eighth**
third degree *n* **to give sb the ~** someter a alguien al tercer grado
third-degree burns *npl* quemaduras *fpl* de tercer grado
thirdly *adv* en tercer lugar
third party *n* tercero *m*
third-party insurance *n*, **third-party liability** *n* seguro *m* a terceros
third person *n* LING tercera persona *f*
third-rate *adj* de baja categoría
Third World *n* **the ~** el Tercer Mundo
thirst [θɜrst] *n* sed *f;* **to die of ~** morir de sed; **to quench one's ~** apagar la sed; **~ for power** ansias *fpl* de poder
thirsty ['θɜr·sti] <-ier, -iest> *adj* sediento, -a; **to be ~** tener sed; **to be ~ for sth** *fig* estar ansioso por algo
thirteen [θɜr·'tin] I. *adj* trece II. *n* trece *m; s.a.* **eight**
thirteenth [θɜr·'tinθ] I. *adj* decimotercero, -a II. *n* **1.**(*order*) decimotercero, -a *m, f* **2.**(*date*) trece *m* **3.**(*fraction*) decimotercero *m;* (*part*) decimotercera parte *f; s.a.* **eighth**
thirtieth ['θɜrt̪·i·əθ] I. *adj* trigésimo, -a II. *n* **1.**(*order*) trigésimo, -a *m, f* **2.**(*date*) treinta *m* **3.**(*fraction*) trigésimo *m;* (*part*) trigésima parte *f; s.a.* **eighth**
thirty ['θɜr·t̪i] <-ies> I. *adj* treinta II. *n* treinta *m; s.a.* **eighty**
this [ðɪs] I. <these> *adj det* este, -a; **~ car** este coche; **~ house** esta casa; **~ one** éste, -a; **~ day** hoy; **~ morning/evening** esta mañana/tarde; **~ time** esta vez; **~ time last month** hoy hace un mes; **these days** hoy en día II. <these> *pron dem* éste *m,* ésta *f,* esto *neuter;* **what is ~?** ¿esto qué es?; **who is ~?** ¿éste/ésta quién es?; **~ and that** esto y aquello; **~ is Ana (speaking)** (*on the phone*) soy Ana III. *adv* así; **~ late** tan tarde; **~ much** tanto; **~ big** así de grande
thistle ['θɪs·əl] *n* cardo *m*
tho [ðoʊ] *conj s.* **though**
thong [θɑŋ] *n* **1.**(*strip of leather*) correa *f*

2.(*G-string*) tanga *m* **3.** **~ s** (*sandals*) chanclas *fpl*
thorax ['θɔr·æks] <-es *o* -aces> *n* tórax *m inv*
thorn [θɔrn] *n* espina *f* ▶ **that's a ~ in my side** es una espina que tengo clavada
thorny ['θɔr·ni] <-ier, -iest> *adj* espinoso, -a, espinudo, -a *AmC, CSur;* (*issue*) peliagudo, -a
thorough ['θɜr·oʊ] *adj* **1.**(*complete*) absoluto, -a **2.**(*detailed*) exhaustivo, -a **3.**(*careful*) minucioso, -a
thoroughbred ['θɜr·oʊ·bred] I. *n* pura sangre *mf* II. *adj* de pura sangre
thoroughfare ['θɜr·oʊ·fer] *n form* vía *f* pública
thoroughgoing [ˌθɜr·oʊ·'goʊ·ɪŋ] *adj form* **1.**(*conscientious: analysis*) riguroso, -a **2.**(*complete: reform*) profundo, -a
thoroughly *adv* **1.**(*in detail*) a fondo **2.**(*completely*) completamente
thoroughness *n* meticulosidad *f*
those [ðoʊz] *pl of* **that**
thou¹ [ðaʊ] *pron pers, liter* tú
thou² [θaʊ] *abbr of* **thousand** mil
though [ðoʊ] I. *conj* aunque; **as ~** como si **+subj; even ~** aunque; **even ~ it's cold** aunque hace frío II. *adv* sin embargo; **he did do it, ~** sin embargo, él sí lo hizo
thought [θɔt] *n* **1.**(*process*) reflexión *f;* **on second ~** tras madura reflexión; **without ~** sin pensar; **after much ~** tras mucha reflexionar; **to be deep in ~** estar ensimismado; **lost in ~** absorto [*o* sumido] en sus pensamientos **2.**(*idea, opinion*) pensamiento *m;* **that's a ~** es posible ▶ **a penny for your ~ s** *prov* ¿en qué piensas?
thoughtful ['θɔt·fəl] *adj* **1.**(*pensive*) pensativo, -a **2.**(*careful*) cuidadoso, -a **3.**(*considerate*) atento, -a
thoughtless ['θɔt·lɪs] *adj* (*not thinking enough*) irreflexivo, -a; (*tactless*) desconsiderado, -a; (*careless*) descuidado, -a
thought-out [ˌθɔt·'aʊt] *adj* planeado, -a
thought-provoking *adj* que hace pensar
thousand ['θaʊ·zənd] I. *adj* mil II. *n* mil *m*
thousandth ['θaʊ·zəntθ] I. *n* milésimo *m* II. *adj* **1.**(*being one of a thousand*) milésimo, -a **2.**(*in a series*) **the ~** el número mil
thrash [θræʃ] *vt* **1.**(*beat*) apalear **2.** *inf*(*defeat*) dar una paliza a
◆**thrash out** *vt inf*(*problem*) discutir; (*agreement*) llegar a
thrashing *n* paliza *f,* batida *f AmL*
thread [θred] I. *n* **1.**(*for sewing*) hilo *m* **2.**(*of screw*) rosca *f* ▶ **to hang by a ~** pender de un hilo II. *vt* (*needle*) enhebrar; **to ~ sth through sth** pasar algo por algo; **to ~ sth onto sth** ensartar algo en algo
threadbare ['θred·ber] *adj* **1.**(*worn*) raído, -a **2.**(*argument, excuse*) trillado, -a
threat [θret] *n* amenaza *f*
threaten ['θret·ən] I. *vt* amenazar; **to ~ to do sth** amenazar con hacer algo II. *vi* amenazar
threatening *adj* amenazador(a)

T

three [θri] I. *adj* tres II. *n* tres *m; s.a.* **eight**
three-cornered [ˌθri·ˈkɔr·nərd] *adj* triangular; **~ hat** tricornio *m*
three-D [ˌθri·ˈdi] *adj inf abbr of* **three-dimensional** en tres D
three-dimensional *adj* tridimensional
threefold [ˈθri·foʊld] I. *adj* triple II. *adv* por triplicado
three-part *adj* de tres partes
three-piece [ˌθri·ˈpis] *adj* de tres piezas
three-piece suit *n* terno *m*
three-ply [ˈθri·plaɪ] *adj* de tres capas; (*wood*) contrachapado, -a; (*wool*) de tres hebras
three-quarter (**length**) *adj* tres cuartos
threesome [ˈθri·səm] *n* trío *m*
three-wheeler [θrɪ·ˈhwi·lər] *n* vehículo *m* de tres ruedas
thresh [θreʃ] *vt* trillar
threshing machine [ˈθreʃ·ɪŋ·mə·ˈʃin] *n* trilladora *f*
threshold [ˈθreʃ·hoʊld] *n* 1. (*doorway*) umbral *m* 2. (*limit*) límite *m*; **pain ~** umbral de dolor; **tax ~** nivel *m* mínimo de tributación
threw [θru] *pt of* **throw**
thrice [θraɪs] *adv* tres veces
thrift [θrɪft] *n* ahorro *m*
thrifty [ˈθrɪf·ti] <-ier, -iest> *adj* ahorrador(a) [*o* ahorrativo, -a]
thrill [θrɪl] I. *n* estremecimiento *m* II. *vt* estremecer, emocionar III. *vi* estremecerse
thriller [ˈθrɪl·ər] *n* (*book*) novela *f* de suspense; (*film*) película *f* de suspense
thrilling [ˈθrɪl·ɪŋ] *adj* emocionante
thrive [θraɪv] <thrived *o* throve, thrived *o* thriven> *vi* (*person, plant*) crecer mucho; (*business*) prosperar
thriving [ˈθraɪvɪŋ] *adj* próspero, -a
throat [θroʊt] *n* 1. (*internal*) garganta *f*; **sore ~** dolor *m* de garganta 2. (*external*) cuello *m*; **to grab sb by the ~** agarrar a alguien por el cuello ▶ **to stick in sb's ~** (*proposal*) no ser aceptable para alguien; (*words*) quedársele atragantado a alguien; **to be at each other's ~s** ser como el perro y el gato
throaty [ˈθroʊ·t̬i] <-ier, -iest> *adj* (*voice*) ronco, -a; (*laugh*) gutural
throb [θrab] I. *n* (*of engine*) vibración *f*; (*of heart*) palpitación *f* II. <-bb-> *vi* (*engine*) vibrar; (*heart*) palpitar
throes [θroʊz] *npl* angustia *f*; (*of death*) agonía *f*; **to be in the ~ of sth** estar de lleno en algo
thrombosis [θram·ˈboʊ·sɪs] <-es> *n* trombosis *f inv*
throne [θroʊn] *n* trono *m*
throng [θraŋ] I. *n* multitud *f* II. *vt* atestar; **to be ~ed** estar abarrotado III. *vi* ir en tropel; **~ to do sth** acudir en masa a hacer algo
throttle [ˈθrat̬·əl] I. *n* acelerador *m;* **to open the ~** acelerar; **at full ~** a todo gas *inf* II. <-ll-> *vt* estrangular
♦ **throttle back** *vi* reducir (la velocidad)
through [θru] I. *prep* 1. (*spatial*) a través de, por; **to go right ~ sth** traspasar algo; **to go ~**

the door entrar por la puerta; **to walk ~ a room** atravesar una habitación; **to walk ~ a village** caminar por un pueblo 2. (*temporal*) durante; **all ~ my life** durante toda mi vida; **to be ~ sth** acabar de (hacer) algo 3. (*until*) hasta; **open Monday ~ Friday** abierto de lunes a viernes 4. (*by means of*) por (medio de) II. *adv* 1. (*of place*) de un lado a otro; **I read the book ~** leí el libro entero; **to go ~ to sth** ir directo a algo 2. (*of time*) **all day ~** de la mañana a la noche; **halfway ~** a medio camino 3. TEL **to put sb ~ to sb** poner a alguien con alguien 4. (*completely*) completamente; **to think sth ~** pensarse algo detenidamente ▶ **~ and ~** de cabo a rabo III. *adj* 1. (*finished*) terminado, -a; **we are ~** hemos terminado 2. (*direct*) directo, -a 3. SCHOOL **to get ~** aprobar
through flight *n* vuelo *m* directo
throughout [θru·ˈaʊt] I. *prep* 1. (*spatial*) por todas partes de; **~ the town** por toda la ciudad 2. (*temporal*) a lo largo de; **~ his stay** durante toda su estancia II. *adv* 1. (*spatial*) por [*o* en] todas partes 2. (*temporal*) todo el tiempo
throughput [ˈθru·pʊt] *n* producción *f;* COMPUT procesamiento *m*
through traffic *n* (tráfico *m* de) tránsito *m*
through train *n* tren *m* directo
throughway [ˈθru·weɪ] *n* autopista *f* de peaje
throve [θroʊv] *pt of* **thrive**
throw [θroʊ] I. *n* 1. (*act of throwing*) lanzamiento *m* 2. SPORTS derribo *m* 3. *inf* (*chance*) oportunidad *f;* **his last ~** su última oportunidad II. <threw, thrown> *vi* lanzar III. <threw, thrown> *vt* 1. (*propel*) tirar; (*ball, javelin*) lanzar; **to ~ oneself into sb's arms** echarse a los brazos de alguien; **to ~ oneself at sb** tirar los tejos a alguien 2. (*cause to fall: rider*) desmontar; (*opponent*) derribar 3. (*dedicate*) **to ~ oneself into sth** entregarse de lleno a algo 4. (*direct: glance*) echar; (*remark*) dejar caer; (*kiss*) lanzar 5. *inf* (*confuse*) desconcertar 6. TECH tornear 7. (*turn on*) dar a; **to ~ the switch** pulsar el interruptor 8. (*have*) **to ~ a tantrum** coger [*o* agarrar *AmL*] una rabieta 9. (*give*) **to ~ a party** dar una fiesta 10. (*cast off*) soltar
♦ **throw away** *vt* 1. (*discard*) tirar 2. (*waste*) malgastar; **to throw money away on sth** despilfarrar (el) dinero en algo; **to throw oneself away** sacrificarse inútilmente 3. (*speak casually*) soltar
♦ **throw back** *vt* 1. (*return*) devolver 2. (*open: curtains*) correr; (*blanket*) apartar 3. (*remind unkindly*) echar en cara; **to throw sth back in sb's face** echar algo en cara a alguien; (*retort angrily*) replicar
♦ **throw down** *vt* 1. (*throw from above*) tirar 2. (*deposit forcefully*) dejar; (*weapons*) abandonar 3. (*drink quickly*) engullir
♦ **throw in** I. *vt* 1. (*put into*) arrojar 2. (*include*) agregar; (*comment*) soltar II. *vi* (*propel*) lanzar

◆**throw off** vt 1. (*remove*) quitarse 2. (*escape from*) despistar 3. (*rid oneself of*) deshacerse de 4. (*write quickly*) improvisar

◆**throw on** vt 1. (*clothes*) ponerse 2. (*pounce upon*) **to throw oneself on sb** abalanzarse sobre alguien

◆**throw out** vt 1. (*eject: person*) echar; (*thing*) tirar; (*case*) rechazar; (*suggestion*) despreciar 2. (*emit: heat, light*) despedir

◆**throw over** vt (*lover*) abandonar

◆**throw together** vt 1. inf (*make quickly*) hacer en un periquete 2. (*cause to meet*) juntar

◆**throw up** I. vt 1. (*project upwards*) lanzar al aire 2. (*bring to light*) revelar 3. (*build quickly*) levantar 4. inf (*give up*) dejar 5. inf (*vomit*) potar, buitrear *CSur;* revulsar *Méx* II. vi inf potar, buitrear *CSur,* revulsar *Méx*

throwaway ['θrou·ə·weɪ] adj desechable; ~ **razor** maquinilla f de usar y tirar; ~ **remark** comentario m hecho de paso

throwback ['θrou·bæk] n vuelta f; BIO atavismo m

thrower n lanzador(a) m(f)

throw-in ['θrou·ɪn] n (*in soccer*) saque m de banda; (*in baseball*) lanzamiento m

throwing n lanzamiento m

thrown pp of **throw**

thru [θru] prep, adj s. **through**

thrum [θrʌm] I. <-mm-> vt (*guitar*) rasguear II. vi (*engine*) vibrar III. n (*of engine*) vibración f

thrush¹ [θrʌʃ] n tordo m

thrush² [θrʌʃ] n MED afta f

thrust [θrʌst] I. <-, -> vi 1. (*shove*) empujar; **to ~ at sb with sth** asestar un golpe a alguien con algo 2. (*force one's way*) abrirse paso II. <-, -> vt (*push*) empujar; (*insert*) clavar; **to ~ one's hands into one's pockets** meterse las manos en los bolsillos III. n 1. (*shove*) empujón m; **sword ~** estocada f 2. (*impetus*) empuje m; **the main ~ of an argument** la idea central de una discusión 3. TECH (*propulsion*) propulsión f

thrusting ['θrʌs·tɪŋ] adj arribista

thruway ['θru·weɪ] n autopista f de peaje

thud [θʌd] I. <-dd-> vi dar un golpe sordo; **to ~ on the table with one's fist** pegar un puñetazo encima de la mesa II. n golpe m sordo

thug [θʌg] n matón, -ona m, f

thumb [θʌm] I. n pulgar m ▶ **to be all fingers and ~s, to be all ~s** ser un manazas; **to stand out like a sore ~** cantar como una almeja; **to be under sb's ~** estar dominado por alguien II. vt 1. (*hitchhike*) **to ~ a lift** hacer dedo 2. (*soil with the thumbs*) manosear 3. (*glance through: book*) hojear

thumb index n índice m recortado

thumbnail ['θʌm·neɪl] n uña f del pulgar

thumbnail sketch n pequeña reseña f

thumbscrew ['θʌm·skru] n empulgueras fpl

thumbtack n tachuela f

thump [θʌmp] I. vt golpear; **to ~ sth down** bajar ruidosamente II. vi 1. (*heart*) latir con

fuerza 2. (*beat*) **to ~ on sth** aporrear algo III. n 1. (*blow*) porrazo m; **to give sb a ~** dar un mamporro a alguien 2. (*noise*) golpe m sordo

thumping adj inf descomunal; **I've got a ~ headache** me va a estallar la cabeza

thunder ['θʌn·dər] I. n 1. METEO trueno m, pillán m *Chile;* **a clap of ~** un trueno 2. (*sound*) estruendo m ▶ **to steal sb's ~** quitar las primicias a alguien II. vi hacer gran estruendo; (*shout*) gritar III. vt bramar

thunderbolt ['θʌn·dər·boult] n 1. METEO rayo m 2. fig bomba f ▶ **to drop a ~ on sb** dejar a alguien fulminado

thunderclap n trueno m

thundercloud n nubarrón m

thundering ['θʌn·dər·ɪŋ] I. n estruendo m II. adj inf (*very noisy*) escandaloso, -a; fig (*very great*) enorme

thunderous ['θʌn·dər·əs] adj estruendoso, -a

thunderstorm ['θʌn·dər·stɔrm] n tormenta f

thunderstruck ['θʌn·dər·strʌk] adj form estupefacto, -a

Thurs. n abbr of **Thursday** juev.

Thursday ['θɜrz·deɪ] n jueves m inv; **Maundy** [o **Holy**] ~ Jueves Santo; s.a. **Friday**

thus [ðʌs] adv form 1. (*therefore*) por lo tanto 2. (*like this*) de este modo; ~ **far** hasta aquí

thwart [θwɔrt] vt frustrar; (*plan*) desbaratar

thy [ðaɪ] pron pos, liter tu(s)

thyme [taɪm] n tomillo m

thyroid ['θaɪ·rɔɪd] adj tiroides f inv

tiara [tɪ·'ær·ə] n diadema f

tibia ['tɪb·i·ə] <-iae> n tibia f

tic [tɪk] n tic m

tick¹ [tɪk] n garrapata f

tick² [tɪk] I. n 1. (*sound*) tic-tac m 2. (*mark*) visto m II. vi hacer tic-tac; **I don't know what makes her ~** no acabo de entender su manera de ser III. vt marcar (*con un visto*)

◆**tick off** vt 1. (*mark off*) marcar (*con un visto*) 2. inf (*exasperate*) dar la lata a

◆**tick over** vi 1. TECH ir al ralentí 2. fig ir tirando

ticker ['tɪk·ər] n 1. TEL teletipo m 2. (*watch*) reloj m 3. sl (*heart*) corazón m

ticker tape n cinta f de teletipo

ticker-tape parade n desfile m triunfal

ticket ['tɪk·ɪt] n 1. (*for bus, train*) billete m, boleto m AmL; (*for cinema, concert*) entrada f; (*for cloakroom*) ticket m; (*for lottery*) boleto; **return ~** billete m de ida y vuelta 2. (*price, information tag*) etiqueta f 3. AUTO multa f 4. POL programa m electoral ▶ **just the ~** justo lo que hacía falta

ticket agency n taquilla f

ticket collector n revisor(a) m(f)

ticket counter n mostrador m de venta de entradas o billetes

ticket holder n persona f que tiene entrada o billete

ticket machine n dispensador m de billetes

ticket office n RAIL ventanilla f de venta de billetes; THEAT taquilla *f*

ticking[1] ['tɪk·ɪŋ] *n* (*sound*) tic-tac *m*

ticking[2] ['tɪk·ɪŋ] *n* (*textile*) terliz *m*

tickle ['tɪk·əl] I. *vi* hacer cosquillas; (*clothes*) picar II. *vt* 1. hacer cosquillas 2. (*amuse*) hacer gracia ▸**to be ~d pink** *inf* estar encantado III. *n* cosquilleo *m;* (*tingling*) picor *m*

ticklish ['tɪk·lɪʃ] *adj* cosquilloso, -a; (*delicate*) delicado, -a

tidal ['taɪ·dəl] *adj* de la marea

tidal wave *n* sunami *m*

tidbit ['tɪd·bɪt] *n* 1. (*delicacy*) golosina *f* 2. (*piece: of information*) noticia *f;* (*of gossip*) cotilleo *m*

tiddlywink ['tɪd·li·wɪŋk] *n* pulga *f;* **~ s** juego *m* de las pulgas

tide [taɪd] *n* 1. (*of sea*) marea *f;* **high ~** plea-mar *f;* **low ~** bajamar *f* 2. (*of opinion*) co-rriente *f;* **to go against the ~** ir contraco-rriente; **to swim with the ~** seguir la co-rriente

◆**tide over** *vt always sep* **to tide sb over** sacar a alguien de un apuro

tideland ['taɪd·lænd] *n* marisma *f*

tidemark *n* (*mark left by high tide*) marca *f* que deja la marea

tidiness ['taɪ·dɪ·nɪs] *n* orden *m*

tidy ['taɪ·di] I. *adj* <-ier, -iest> 1. (*orderly*) ordenado, -a; **to have a ~ mind** ser metódico 2. *inf* (*considerable*) suculento, -a II. *vt* orde-nar

tie [taɪ] I. *n* 1. (*necktie*) corbata *f* 2. (*cord*) ata-dura *f* 3. **~ s** (*bonds*) lazos *mpl;* (*diplomatic*) relaciones *fpl* 4. (*equal ranking*) empate *m* II. *vi* 1. (*fasten*) atarse 2. SPORTS empatar III. *vt* 1. (*fasten*) atar; (*knot*) hacer 2. (*restrict*) limi-tar; **to be ~d by/to sth** estar limitado por/ limitarse a algo

◆**tie back** *vt* atar

◆**tie down** *vt* atar; **to tie sb down to sth** *inf* comprometer a alguien a algo

◆**tie in** I. *vt* relacionar II. *vi* coincidir

◆**tie up** *vt* 1. (*bind*) atar; (*hair*) recogerse; **to ~ some loose ends** *fig* atar cabos sueltos 2. (*delay*) bloquear 3. (*be busy*) **to be tied up** estar ocupado 4. FIN, ECON (*capital*) inmovi-lizar; **to be tied up in sth** estar invertido en algo

tiebreak ['taɪ·breɪk] *n,* **tiebreaker** *n* desem-pate *m*

tie clasp *n* aguja *f* [*o* alfiler] *m* de corbata

tie-in ['taɪ·ɪn] *n* 1. (*agreement*) acuerdo *m* 2. (*connection*) relación *f*

tie-on *adj* para atar

tier [tɪr] *n* (*row*) hilera *f;* (*level*) grada *f;* (*in a hierarchy*) nivel *m*

tie tack ['taɪ·tæk] *n* aguja *f* [*o* alfiler] *m* de cor-bata

tie-up ['taɪ·ʌp] *n* conexión *f*

tiff [tɪf] *n inf* pelea *f;* **to have a ~** tener un alter-cado

tiger ['taɪ·gər] *n* tigre *m* ▸**to have a ~ by the tail** tener el toro por los cuernos

tight [taɪt] I. *adj* 1. (*screw, knot*) apretado, -a, duro, -a; (*clothing*) ceñido, -a 2. (*rope*) tirante; (*skin*) terso, -a 3. (*condition, discipline*) estricto, -a, riguroso, -a; (*budget*) restringido, -a; (*situation*) difícil; (*schedule*) apretado, -a; **to keep a ~ hold on sth** mantener un control riguroso de [*o* sobre] algo; **to be ~ for money/time** ir escaso de dinero/tiempo 4. (*bend*) cerrado, -a 5. (*hard-fought*) reñido, -a 6. *sl* (*drunk*) como una cuba II. *adv* fuerte; **to close sth ~** cerrar bien algo; **sleep ~!** ¡que duermas bien!

tighten ['taɪ·ten] I. *vt* 1. (*make tight*) apretar; (*rope*) tensar 2. (*restrictions*) intensificar II. *vi* apretarse; (*restrictions*) intensificarse

tightfisted [ˌtaɪt·'fɪs·tɪd] *adj inf* agarrado, -a

tight-fitting *adj* ajustado, -a

tightlipped [ˌtaɪt·'lɪpt] *adj* callado, -a; **to be ~ about sth** no abrir boca sobre algo

tightness *n* 1. (*of clothing*) lo ajustado 2. (*of discipline*) lo estricto; (*of budget*) lo restrin-gido; (*of schedule*) lo apretado 3. PSYCH ten-sión *f*

tightrope ['taɪt·roʊp] *n* cuerda *f* floja; **to walk a ~** *fig* caminar en [*o* por] la cuerda floja

tightrope walker *n* funámbulo, -a *m, f*

tights [taɪts] *npl* 1. (*leggings*) medias *fpl* 2. (*for dancing*) mallas *fpl*

tightwad ['taɪt·wad] *n sl* tacaño, -a *m, f*

tigress ['taɪ·grɪs] *n* tigresa *f*

tike [taɪk] *n s.* **tyke**

tile [taɪl] I. *n* (*for roof*) teja *f;* (*for walls, floors*) azulejo *m* II. *vt* (*roof*) tejar; (*wall*) poner azule-jos a, alicatar; (*floor*) embaldosar

tiler ['taɪ·lər] *n* albañil *mf* (especializado en recubrimientos)

till[1] [tɪl] I. *prep* hasta II. *conj* hasta que

till[2] [tɪl] *n* caja *f* (registradora) ▸**he was caught with his hand in the ~** lo pillaron con las manos en la masa (*robando en el trabajo*)

till[3] [tɪl] *vt* cultivar

tiller ['tɪl·ər] *n* barra *f* del timón; **at the ~** al timón

tilt [tɪlt] I. *n* inclinación *f* ▸(at) **full ~** a toda máquina II. *vt* inclinar; **to ~ sth back** inclinar algo hacia atrás III. *vi* inclinarse; **to ~ back** inclinarse hacia atrás; **to ~ over** volcarse

timber ['tɪm·bər] *n* 1. (*wood*) madera *f* 2. (*beam*) viga *f,* madero *m* 3. (*trees*) árboles *mpl;* **~!** ¡árbol va!

timbered *adj* de madera

timberline ['tɪm·bər·laɪn] *n* límite *m* forestal

time [taɪm] I. *n* 1. tiempo *m;* **to kill ~** matar el tiempo; **to make ~** hacer tiempo; **to spend ~** pasar el tiempo; (**how**) **~ flies** el tiempo vuela; **~ passes** el tiempo apremia; **as ~ goes by** con el paso del tiempo; **in the course of ~** con el paso del tiempo; **to be a matter of ~** ser cues-tión de tiempo; (**only**) **~ can tell** (sólo) el tiempo lo dirá; **of all ~** de todos los tiempos; **in ~** a tiempo; **over ~** con el tiempo 2. (*period*) período *m; access* COMPUT tiempo de acceso; **extra ~** SPORTS prórroga *f;* **free ~** tiempo libre;

after a ~ al cabo de un tiempo; **all the** ~ continuamente; **a long** ~ **ago** hace mucho tiempo; **some** ~ **ago** hace algún tiempo; **for the** ~ **being** por ahora; **given** ~ con el tiempo; **to have a good** ~ pasárselo bien; **to have all the** ~ **in the world** tener todo el tiempo del mundo; **to run out of** ~, **to be (all) out of** ~ *inf* acabársele el tiempo (a alguien); **to save** ~ ganar tiempo; **to waste** ~ perder el tiempo; **most of the** ~ la mayor parte del tiempo; **in one week's** ~ dentro de una semana; **for a short/long period of** ~ durante un corto/largo período de tiempo; **there's no** ~ **to lose** no hay tiempo que perder; **can I have** ~ **off to go to the dentist?** ¿puedo salir (del trabajo) para ir al dentista?; **to take one's** ~ **in doing sth** tomarse su tiempo para hacer algo; **it takes a long/short** ~ se tarda mucho/poco; **to give sb a hard** ~ *inf* hacerlas pasar canutas a alguien; **I (don't) have a lot of** ~ **for him** (no) me cae bien **3.**(*clock*) hora *f;* **arrival/departure** ~ hora *f* de llegada/salida; **bus/train** ~**s** horario *m* de autobús/tren; **to have the** ~ tener hora exacta **4.**(*moment*) momento *m;* **the best** ~ **of day** el mejor momento del día; **this** ~ **tomorrow** mañana a esta hora; **at all** ~**s** a todas horas; **at a different** ~ en otro momento; **each** ~ cada vez; **the right** ~ el momento oportuno **5.**(*specific point in time*) hora *f;* **at any** ~ a cualquier hora; **at any given** ~, **at (any) one** ~ en un momento dado; **the last/next** ~ la última/próxima vez; **at other** ~**s** en otros tiempos; **at the present** ~ actualmente; **it is about** ~ **that...** ya es hora de que... +*subj;* ~ **and (**~**) again** una y otra vez; **ahead of** ~ con antelación; **to know at the** ~ saber en su momento; **to remember the** ~**...** recordar cuando... **6.**(*occasion*) vez *f;* **three** ~ **champion** tricampeón, -ona *m, f;* **lots of** ~**s** muchas veces; **for the hundredth** ~ por centésima vez; **from** ~ **to** ~ de vez en cuando **7.**(*right moment*) hora *f;* **breakfast** ~ hora de desayunar; **it's high** ~ **that...** ya es hora de que... +*subj;* **ahead of** ~ antes de tiempo; **to do sth right on** ~ hacer algo en el momento preciso; **the** ~ **comes** llega el momento **8.**(*epoch*) época *f;* **at one** ~ en una época; **from** [*o* **since**] ~ **immemorial** desde tiempos inmemoriales; **to be behind the** ~**s** estar anclado en el pasado; **in** ~**s gone by** en tiempos pasados; **to keep up with the** ~**s** estar al día **9.** SPORTS tiempo *m;* **record** ~ tiempo récord **10.** MUS tiempo **11.** ECON horas *fpl* de trabajo; **to work full/part** ~ trabajar a jornada completa/tiempo parcial; **to be on short** ~ estar en jornada reducida ▶ ~ **is of the essence** no hay tiempo que perder; **to have** ~ **on one's hands** tener tiempo de sobra; ~ **is a great healer** *prov* el tiempo lo cura todo; ~ **is money** *prov* el tiempo es oro; *prov;* **there's a** ~ **and a place (for everything)** *prov* todo a su debido tiempo; **a week is a long** ~ **in politics** *prov*

aún puede pasar de todo; **there's no** ~ **like the present** *prov* no dejes para mañana lo que puedas hacer hoy *prov;* ~ **and tide wait for no man** *prov* el tiempo no perdona; ~ **heals all wounds** *prov* el tiempo lo cura todo; **in less than no** ~ en menos (de lo) que canta un gallo; **to buy** ~ ganar tiempo; ~**s are changing** los tiempos cambian; **to do** ~ *sl* estar a la sombra; ~ **moves on** la vida sigue **II.** *vt* **1.** SPORTS cronometrar, relojear *Arg* **2.**(*choose best moment for*) elegir el momento para **III.** *adj* SPORTS ~ **trial** prueba *f* contrarreloj

time and motion study *n* COM estudio *m* de la racionalización del trabajo

time bomb *n* bomba *f* de relojería

timecard *n* tarjeta *f* de registro horario

time clock *n* reloj *m* de control de asistencia

time-consuming ['taɪm·kən·ˌsu·mɪŋ] *adj* que exige mucho tiempo

time difference *n* diferencia *f* horaria

timekeeper *n* **1.**(*device*) cronómetro *m* **2.**(*person*) cronometrista *mf;* **to be a poor** ~ no ser muy puntual

time lag *n* retraso *m*

time-lapse photography *n* fotografía *f* con disparos prefijados

timeless ['taɪm·lɪs] *adj* eterno, -a

time limit *n* límite *m* de tiempo

time lock *n* cerradura *f* de tiempo

timely ['taɪm·li] *adj* <-ier, -iest> oportuno, -a; **in a** ~ **fashion** a tiempo

time-out [ˌtaɪm·'aʊt] *n* **1.** SPORTS tiempo *m* muerto **2.**(*rest*) descanso *m*

timer ['taɪ·mər] *n* temporizador *m;* CULIN reloj *m* avisador

timesaving ['taɪm·ˌseɪ·vɪŋ] *adj* que ahorra tiempo

timescale ['taɪm·skeɪl] *n* escala *f* de tiempo

time-share *n* multipropiedad *f*

time-sharing *n* **1.**(*on holiday*) multipropiedad *f* **2.** COMPUT tiempo *m* compartido

time sheet *n* hoja *f* de asistencia

timetable I. *n* (*for bus, train*) horario *m;* (*for project, events*) programa *m* **II.** *vt* programar

timeworn ['taɪm·wɔrn] *adj* desgastado, -a; (*not original*) muy visto, -a; (*excuse*) trillado, -a

time zone *n* huso *m* horario

timid ['tɪm·ɪd] *adj* <-er, -est> tímido, -a

timidity [tɪ·'mɪd·ə·t̬i] *n* timidez *f*

timing ['taɪ·mɪŋ] *n* **1.** cronometraje *m;* **that was perfect** ~ ha sido el momento oportuno **2.**(*rhythm*) compás *m*

timpani ['tɪm·pə·ni] *npl* MUS tímpanos *mpl*

tin [tɪn] **I.** *n* **1.**(*metal*) estaño *m;* (*tinplate*) hojalata *f* **2.**(*container*) lata *f* **3.**(*for baking*) molde *m* **II.** *vt* enlatar

tin can *n* lata *f*

tincture ['tɪŋk·tʃər] *n* tintura *f*

tinder ['tɪn·dər] *n* yesca *f*

tinfoil *n* papel *m* de aluminio

ting [tɪŋ] *n* tilín *m*

tinge [tɪndʒ] **I.** *n* **1.**(*of color*) tinte *m* **2.**(*of emotion*) dejo *m* **II.** *vt* **1.**(*dye*) teñir **2.** *fig*

matizar
tingle ['tɪŋ·gəl] **I.** *vi* estremecerse **II.** *n* estremecimiento *m*
tin hat *n* casco *m* de acero
tinhorn *n inf* creído, -a *m, f*
tinker ['tɪŋ·kər] **I.** *n* **1.** HIST hojalatero, -a *m, f* **2.** gitano, -a *m, f* **II.** *vi* **to ~ with sth** tratar de reparar algo
tinkle ['tɪŋ·kəl] **I.** *vi* tintinear **II.** *vt* hacer tintinear
tinny ['tɪn·i] *adj* <-ier, -iest> (*sound*) metálico, -a; (*taste*) que sabe a lata
tin-pot ['tɪn·pat] *adj pej, inf* de pacotilla
tinsel ['tɪn·səl] *n* oropel *m*
tint [tɪnt] **I.** *n* (*color*) tono *m*; (*for hair*) tinte *m* **II.** *vt* teñir
tiny ['taɪ·ni] *adj* <-ier, -iest> menudo, -a, chiquito, -a, chingo, -a *Col, Cuba*
tip¹ [tɪp] **I.** <-pp-> *vt* cubrir **II.** *n* punta *f*; **from ~ to toe** de pies a cabeza; **the southern ~ of Florida** el cabo sur de Florida; **it's on the ~ of my tongue** lo tengo en la punta de la lengua
tip² [tɪp] **I.** <-pp-> *vt* (*incline*) inclinar; **to ~ the balance against/in favor of sb** inclinar la balanza en contra/a favor de alguien **II.** *vi* inclinarse
tip³ [tɪp] **I.** *n* **1.** (*for service*) propina *f*, yapa *f Méx;* **10 per cent ~** el diez por ciento de propina **2.** (*hint*) aviso *m*; **to give sb a ~** dar a alguien un consejo; **to take a ~ from sb** seguir el consejo de alguien **II.** <-pp-> *vt* (*give money*) dar una propina a **III.** <-pp-> *vi* dejar propina
◆**tip off** *vt* avisar
◆**tip over I.** *vt* volcar **II.** *vi* volcarse
◆**tip up I.** *vt* inclinar **II.** *vi* inclinarse
tip-off ['tɪp·ɔf] *n inf* soplo *m*
tipple ['tɪp·əl] **I.** *vi* (*drink*) beber **II.** *vt* beber(se) **III.** *n inf* bebida *f*, priva *f argot;* **favorite ~** trago *m* favorito
tipster ['tɪp·stər] *n* SPORTS pronosticador(a) *m(f)*
tipsy ['tɪp·si] *adj* <-ier, -iest> bebido, -a, achispado, -a *AmL*
tiptoe ['tɪp·toʊ] **I.** *n* punta *f* del pie; **on ~(s)** de puntillas **II.** *vi* ponerse de puntillas
tiptop ['tɪp·tap] *adj inf* de primera
tirade ['taɪ·reɪd] *n* diatriba *f*
tire¹ [taɪr] *n* neumático *m*, llanta *f Méx*, caucho *m Col, Ven;* **spare ~** neumático de repuesto
tire² [taɪr] **I.** *vt* cansar **II.** *vi* cansarse
tired ['taɪrd] *adj* <-er, -est> (*person*) cansado, -a; (*excuse*) trillado, -a; **to be sick and ~ of sth** estar aburrido de algo; **the same ~ old faces** las mismas caras de siempre
tiredness *n* cansancio *m*
tire gauge *n* medidor *m* de presión
tireless ['taɪr·lɪs] *adj* incansable
tire pressure *n* presión *f* del neumático
tiresome ['taɪr·səm] *adj* molesto, -a; (*person*) pesado, -a, molón, -ona *Guat, Ecua, Méx*
tiring ['taɪ·rɪŋ] *adj* agotador(a), cansador(a) *Arg*
'tis [tɪz] = **it is** *s.* **be**

tissue ['tɪʃ·u] *n* **1.** (*paper*) papel *m* de seda **2.** (*handkerchief*) pañuelo *m* de papel **3.** ANAT, BIO tejido *m*
tissue paper *n* papel *m* de seda
tit¹ [tɪt] *n* paro *m*; **blue ~** herrerillo *m*; **coal ~** carbonero *m*
tit² [tɪt] *n vulg* teta *f*
titanic [taɪ·'tæn·ɪk] *adj* titánico, -a
titanium [taɪ·'teɪ·ni·əm] *n* titanio *m*
titbit *n s.* **tidbit**
titillate ['tɪt·ə·leɪt] *vt* excitar
titillation [ˌtɪt·əl·'eɪ·ʃən] *n* excitación *f*
titivate ['tɪt̬·ə·veɪt] *vt* adornar; **to ~ oneself** arreglarse
title ['taɪt̬·əl] **I.** *n* **1.** (*name*) título *m* **2.** (*championship*) campeonato *m* **3.** LAW derecho *m* **II.** *vt* titular
title deed *n* título de propiedad
titleholder *n* titular *mf*
title page *n* portada *f*
title role *n* papel *m* principal
title track *n* canción *f* que da nombre al álbum
titter ['tɪt̬·ər] **I.** *vi* reírse disimuladamente **II.** *n* risa *f* disimulada
tittle-tattle ['tɪt̬·əl·ˌtæt̬·əl] *n inf* chismorreo *m*
tizzy ['tɪz·i] *n sl* agitación *f*; **to be in a ~** estar muy agitado
TN *abbr of* **Tennessee** Tennessee *m*
TNT [ˌti·en·'ti] *n abbr of* **trinitrotoluene** TNT *m*
to [tu] **I.** *prep* **1.** (*in direction of*) a; **to go ~ Mexico/New York** ir a México/Nueva York; **to go ~ town** ir a la ciudad; **to go ~ the dentist('s)** ir al dentista; **to go ~ the cinema/theater** ir al cine/teatro; **to go ~ bed** irse a la cama; **to go ~ the south** ir al [o hacia el] sur; **~ the left/right** a la izquierda/derecha; **to fall ~ the ground** caerse al suelo; **the path ~ the lake** el camino que lleva al lago **2.** (*before*) **a quarter ~ five** las cinco menos cuarto **3.** (*until*) hasta; **to count up ~ 10** contar hasta 10; **~ this day** hasta el día de hoy; **frightened ~ death** muerto de miedo; **done ~ perfection** hecho a la perfección; **~ some extent** hasta cierto punto **4.** *with indirect object* **to talk ~ sb** hablar con alguien; **to show sth ~ sb** mostrar algo a alguien; **I said ~ myself...** me dije a mí mismo...; **this belongs ~ me** esto es mío **5.** (*towards*) con; **to be kind/rude ~ sb** ser amable/grosero con alguien **6.** (*against*) contra; **elbow ~ elbow** codo con codo; **close ~ sth** cerca de algo; **to clasp sb ~ one's bosom** estrechar a alguien contra su pecho; **to fix sth ~ the wall** fijar algo en la pared; **5 added ~ 10 equals 15** 5 más 10 son 15 **7.** (*in comparison*) a; **3 (goals) ~ 1** 3 (goles) a 1; **superior ~ sth/sb** superior a algo/alguien **8.** (*from opinion of*) **to sound strange ~ sb** sonar extraño [o raro] a alguien; **it doesn't make any sense ~ me** eso para mí no tiene sentido; **what's it ~ them?** *inf* ¿qué les importa a ellos?; **~ all appearances** al parecer **9.** (*proportion*) **one liter ~ one person** un

litro por persona; **by a majority of 5 ~ 1** por una mayoría de 5 a 1; **the odds are 3 ~ 1** las probabilidades son de 3 contra 1 **10.** (*causing*) **much ~ my surprise** para mi sorpresa **11.** (*by*) por; **known ~ sb** conocido de [*o* por] alguien **12.** (*matching*) de; **the top ~ this jar** la tapa de este tarro **13.** (*of*) de; **the secretary ~ the boss** la secretaria del jefe **14.** (*for purpose of*) para ▶ **that's all there is ~ it** eso es todo **II.** *infinitive particle* **1.** (*infinitive: not translated*) **~ do/walk/put** hacer/andar/poner **2.** (*in command*) **I told him ~ eat** le dije que comiera **3.** (*after interrogative words*) **I know what ~ do** sé qué hacer; **she didn't know how ~ say it** no sabía cómo decirlo **4.** (*wishes*) **he wants ~ listen** quiere escuchar; **she wants ~ go** quiere irse **5.** (*purpose*) **he comes ~ see me** viene a verme; **to phone ~ ask sth** llamar para preguntar algo **6.** (*attitude*) **she seems ~ enjoy it** parece que disfruta; **~ be honest...** (dicho) sinceramente... **7.** (*future intention*) **the work ~ be done** el trabajo que hay que hacer; **sth ~ buy** algo que hay que comprar **8.** (*in consecutive acts*) para; **I came back ~ find she had left Madrid** volví para descubrir que se había ido de Madrid **9.** (*introducing a complement*) **he wants me ~ tell him a story** quiere que le cuente un cuento; **to be too tired ~ do sth** estar demasiado cansado para hacer algo **10.** (*in general statements*) **it is easy ~ do it** es fácil hacerlo **11.** (*in ellipsis*) **he doesn't want ~ eat, but I want ~** él no quiere comer, pero yo sí **III.** *adv* **to push the door ~** cerrar la puerta empujándola

toad [toʊd] *n* **1.** (*animal*) sapo *m* **2.** (*person*) mamarracho, -a *m, f*

toadstool ['toʊd·stul] *n* seta *f* venenosa

toady ['toʊ·di] **I.** <-ies> *n* adulador(a) *m(f)*, jalamecate *mf Ven* **II.** *vi* adular, jalar mecate *Ven*

to and fro *adv* de un lado a otro

toast [toʊst] **I.** *n* **1.** (*bread*) tostada *f*; **a piece of ~** una tostada **2.** (*drink*) brindis *m inv* **II.** *vt* **1.** (*cook*) tostar **2.** (*drink*) brindar **III.** *vi* tostarse

toaster *n* tostadora *f* [*o* tostador] *m*

toastmaster ['toʊst·ˌmæs·tər] *n* maestro, -a *m, f* de ceremonias

tobacco [tə·'bæk·oʊ] *n* tabaco *m*

tobacconist [tə·'bæk·ə·nɪst] *n* estanquero, -a *m, f*

to-be [tə·'bi] *adj* futuro, -a

toboggan [tə·'bag·ən] **I.** *n* trineo *m* **II.** *vi* deslizarse en trineo

toboggan run *n*, **toboggan slide** *n* pista *f* de trineos

today [tə·'deɪ] **I.** *adv* **1.** (*this day*) hoy **2.** (*nowadays*) hoy día **II.** *n* **1.** (*this day*) hoy *m* **2.** (*nowadays*) actualidad *f*

toddle ['tad·əl] *vi* **1.** (*walk*) andar tambaleándose; (*child*) dar los primeros pasos **2.** *inf* (*go*) **to ~** (**off**) largarse

toddler ['tad·lər] *n* niño, -a *m, f* que empieza a caminar

toddy ['tad·i] <-ies> *n* (*hot*) ~ ponche *m*

to-do [tə·'du] *n inf* lío *m*

toe [toʊ] **I.** *n* **1.** ANAT dedo *m* del pie; **on one's ~s** de puntillas **2.** (*of sock*) punta *f*; (*of shoe*) puntera *f* ▶ **to keep sb on their ~s** mantener a alguien en estado de alerta; **to step on sb's ~s** pisotear a alguien *fig* **II.** *vt* **to ~ the line** conformarse

toecap *n* puntera *f*

toehold *n* **1.** (*when climbing*) punto *m* de apoyo (para el pie) **2.** *fig* trampolín *m*

toenail *n* uña *f* del pie

toffee ['tɔ·fi] *n* toffee *m*

together [tə·'geð·ər] **I.** *adv* **1.** (*jointly*) juntos, juntas; **all ~** todos juntos, todas juntas; **~ with sb/sth** junto con alguien/algo; **to live ~** vivir juntos; **to get ~** juntarse; **to get it ~** *sl* organizarse **2.** (*at the same time*) a la vez **II.** *adj sl* equilibrado, -a

togetherness *n* compañerismo *m*

toggle ['tag·əl] **I.** *n* **1.** COMPUT tecla *f* de conmutación **2.** TECH palanca *f* acodada **II.** *vt* pulsar

toggle switch *n* interruptor *m* de palanca

Togo ['toʊ·goʊ] *n* Togo *m*

Togolese [ˌtoʊ·goʊ·'liz] **I.** *adj* togolés, -esa **II.** *n* togolés, -esa *m, f*

toil [tɔɪl] **I.** *n* labor *f* **II.** *vi* **1.** (*work hard*) afanarse **2.** (*move*) moverse con gran dificultad

toilet ['tɔɪ·lɪt] *n* **1.** (*room*) cuarto *m* de baño **2.** (*appliance*) váter *m*, inodoro *m* **3.** *form* (*process*) aseo *m*

toilet paper *n* papel *m* higiénico

toiletries ['tɔɪ·lɪ·triz] *npl* artículos *mpl* de tocador

toiletries bag *n* neceser *m*

toilet roll *n* rollo *m* de papel higiénico

toilet seat *n* taza *f* del váter

toilet soap *n* jabón *m* de tocador, jabón *m* de olor *Col, Ven*

toilet water *n* colonia *f*

token ['toʊ·kən] **I.** *n* **1.** (*sign*) señal *f*; (*of affection*) muestra *f*; **by the same ~** por la misma razón; **in ~ of** *form* en señal de **2.** (*for machines*) ficha *f* **II.** *adj* (*symbolic*) simbólico, -a

told [toʊld] *pt, pp of* **tell**

tolerable ['tal·ər·ə·bəl] *adj* soportable, tolerable

tolerably ['tal·ər·ə·bli] *adv form* pasablemente

tolerance ['tal·ər·əns] *n* tolerancia *f*

tolerant ['tal·ər·ənt] *adj* tolerante

tolerate ['tal·ə·reɪt] *vt* **1.** (*accept*) *a.* MED tolerar **2.** (*endure*) soportar

toleration [ˌtal·ə·'reɪ·ʃən] *n* tolerancia *f*

toll[1] [toʊl] *n* **1.** AUTO peaje *m* **2.** TEL tarifa *f* **3.** (*damage*) número *m* de víctimas

toll[2] [toʊl] **I.** *vt* tañer; **to ~ the knell** *fig* doblar las campanas por un difunto **II.** *vi* doblar

toll bridge *n* puente *m* de peaje

toll call *n* conferencia *f*

toll-free *adv* gratis

T

tollhouse *n* HIST cabina *f* de peaje
toll road *n* autopista *f* de peaje
tom [tam] *n* (*cat*) gato *m* (macho)
tomato [tə·'meɪ·t̮oʊ] <-es> *n* tomate *m*
tomato ketchup *n* ketchup *m*
tomb [tum] *n* tumba *f*, guaca *f* AmL
tomboy ['tam·bɔɪ] *n* marimacho *m*, marimacha *f* Ven
tombstone ['tum·stoʊn] *n* lápida *f* sepulcral
tomcat ['tam·kæt] *n* gato *m* (macho)
tome [toʊm] *n* librote *m*
tomfoolery [ˌtam·'fu·lə·ri] *n* tontería *f*
Tommy gun ['tam·i·gʌn] *n* metralleta *f*
tomograph ['tam·ə·græf] *n* MED tomógrafo *m*
tomography [toʊ·'mag·rə·fi] *n* MED tomografía *f*
tomorrow [tə·'mar·oʊ] I. *adv* mañana; **the day after ~** pasado mañana; **all** (**day**) **~** todo el día de mañana; **a week from ~** de mañana en una semana; **~ morning/evening** mañana por la mañana/tarde; **see you ~!** ¡hasta mañana! II. *n* mañana *m* ▸ **~ is another day** *prov* mañana será otro día; **never put off until ~ what you can do today** *prov* no dejes para mañana lo que puedas hacer hoy *prov;* **who knows what ~ will bring?** ¿quién sabe qué nos deparará el futuro?
tom-tom ['tam·tam] *n* tantán *m*
ton [tʌn] *n* tonelada *f; ~s of* *inf* montones de
tone [toʊn] I. *n* **1.** (*sound*) tono *m*; (*of instrument*) tonalidad *f*; (*of voice*) timbre *m* **2.** (*style*) clase *f* **3.** (*of color*) matiz *f*, tono **4.** (*condition*) tono II. *vt* (*muscles, skin*) tonificar
◆**tone down** *vt* moderar
◆**tone in** *vi* armonizar
◆**tone up** *vt* poner en forma
tone control *n* control *m* de tonalidad
tone-deaf ['toʊn·'def] *adj* falto, ·a de oído musical
toneless ['toʊn·lɪs] *adj* monótono, ·a
tone poem *n* poema *m* sinfónico
toner ['toʊ·nər] *n* **1.** (*for skin*) tonificante *m* **2.** (*for printer*) tóner *m;* PHOT virador *m*
Tonga ['taŋ·gə] *n* Tonga *f*
Tongan I. *adj* tongano, ·a II. *n* **1.** (*person*) tongano, ·a *m*, *f* **2.** LING tongano *m*
tongs [taŋz] *npl* tenazas *fpl*
tongue [tʌŋ] I. *n* **1.** ANAT lengua *f;* **to bite one's ~** morderse la lengua; **to find one's ~** recobrar el habla; **to hold one's ~** contenerse (*para no decir algo*)*;* **to stick one's ~ out** (**at sb**) sacar la lengua (a alguien); **to get one's ~ around a word** pronunciar una palabra **2.** (*language*) idioma *m;* **to speak in ~s** hablar en lenguas desconocidas **3.** (*expressive style*) expresión *f;* **to have a sharp ~** tener una lengua afilada ▸ **to say sth ~ in cheek** decir algo irónicamente; **to give sb the rough side of one's ~** *inf,* **to speak with a forked ~** hablar con lengua bífida, criticar a alguien severamente; **have you lost your ~?** ¿se te ha comido la lengua el gato?; **to set ~s wagging** dar (de)

qué hablar II. *vt* MUS tocar
tongue-tied ['tʌŋ·taɪd] *adj fig* **to be ~** cortarse
tongue twister *n* trabalenguas *m inv*
tonic¹ ['tan·ɪk] *n* (*stimulant*) tónico *m*, estimulante *m*
tonic² ['tan·ɪk] *n* MUS tónica *f*
tonic³ ['tan·ɪk] *n*, **tonic water** *n* tónica *f*
tonight [tə·'naɪt] *adv* (*evening*) esta tarde; (*night*) esta noche
tonnage ['tʌn·ɪdʒ] *n* tonelaje *m*
tonne [tʌn] *n* tonelada *f* (métrica)
tonsil ['tan·səl] *n* MED amígdala *f*
tonsillitis [ˌtan·sə·'laɪ·t̮ɪs] *n* amigdalitis *f inv*
too [tu] *adv* **1.** (*overly*) demasiado; **that's ~ much!** ¡es demasiado! **2.** (*very*) muy **3.** (*also*) también; **me ~!** *inf* ¡y yo! **4.** (*moreover*) además **5.** *inf* (*for emphasis*) ya lo creo
took [tʊk] *vt, vi pt of* **take**
tool [tul] I. *n* **1.** (*implement*) herramienta *f*, implemento *m* AmL **2.** (*instrument*) instrumento *m* II. *vt* (*shape with a tool*) trabajar
tool bag *n* bolsa *f* de herramientas
toolbar *n* COMPUT barra *f* de herramientas
toolbox *n*, **tool chest** *n* caja *f* de herramientas
toolkit *n* juego *m* de herramientas
toolmaker *n* fabricante *mf* de herramientas
toolshed *n* cobertizo *m* para herramientas
toot [tut] I. *n* toque *m* suave (de bocina); **to give a ~** tocar el claxon II. *vt* (*sound*) sonar III. *vi* pitar
tooth [tuθ] <teeth> *n* **1.** ANAT (*of person, animal*) diente *m*; (*molar*) muela *f;* **to bare one's teeth** enseñar los dientes; **he's cutting a ~** está saliendo un diente **2.** (*of comb*) púa *f;* (*of saw*) diente *m* ▸ **to set sb's teeth on edge** dar dentera a alguien; **to fight ~ and nail** (**to do sth**) luchar a brazo partido (para hacer algo); **to be long in the ~** ser entrado en años; **to have a sweet ~** ser goloso; **to cut one's teeth on sth** adquirir experiencia en algo; **to get one's teeth into sth** hincar el diente a algo; **to give sth teeth** dar efectividad a algo; **to grit one's teeth** aguantarse, apretar los dientes; **to lie through one's teeth** mentir descaradamente; **in the ~ of sth** (*straight into*) en medio de algo; (*despite*) a pesar de algo
toothache ['tuθ·eɪk] *n* dolor *m* de muelas
toothbrush ['tuθ·brʌʃ] *n* cepillo *m* de dientes
toothed *adj* dentado, ·a
toothpaste ['tuθ·peɪst] *n* pasta *f* dentífrica [o de dientes]
toothpick *n* palillo *m* (de dientes), pajuela *f* Bol, Col
toothsome ['tuθ·səm] *adj* sabroso, ·a
toothy ['tu·θi] <-ier, -iest> *adj* dentudo, ·a; **to give a ~ smile** sonreír enseñando los dientes
tootle ['tu·t̮əl] *vi inf* **to ~ along** ir sin prisas
toots [tʊts] *n sl* nena *f*
top¹ [tap] *n* (*spinning top*) peonza *f*
top² [tap] I. *n* **1.** (*highest part*) parte *f* superior; (*of mountain*) cima *f;* (*of tree*) copa *f;* (*of head*) coronilla *f;* **to get on ~ of sth** a. *fig* lle-

gar a lo más alto de algo; **from ~ to bottom** de arriba a abajo; **from ~ to toe** de pies a cabeza; **to feel on ~ of the world** estar loco de contento **2.** (*surface*) superficie *f;* **on ~ of** encima de **3.** (*highest rank*) lo mejor; **to be at the ~** estar en la cima; **to be at the ~ of the class** ser el primero de la clase; **to go to the ~** ir a la cima **4.** (*clothing*) top *m* **5.** (*end*) punta *f* superior; (*of street*) final *m;* (*of table, list*) cabeza *f* **6.** (*lid: of bottle*) tapón *m* ▸ **at the ~ of one's voice** a grito pelado; **to go over the ~** exagerar **II.** *adj* **1.** (*highest, upper*) de arriba **2.** (*best*) de primera (calidad) **3.** (*most successful*) exitoso, -a **4.** (*most important*) mejor **5.** (*maximum*) máximo, -a **III.** <-pp-> *vt* **1.** (*be at top of*) encabezar **2.** (*provide topping*) coronar **3.** (*surpass*) superar

◆**top off** *vt* **1.** CULIN coronar **2.** (*conclude*) rematar

◆**top up** *vt* **1.** (*fill up again*) rellenar; **to top sb up with sth** *inf* servir algo más a alguien **2.** (*add to*) completar

topaz ['toʊ·pæz] *n* topacio *m*

topcoat ['tap·koʊt] *n* sobretodo *m*

top copy *n* original *m*

top dog *n* *sl* **1.** (*boss*) mandamás *mf* **2.** (*victor*) ganador(a) *m(f)*

top-drawer *adj* de alta sociedad

top executive *n* ejecutivo, -a *m, f* superior

topflight *adj* de primera (clase)

top hat *n* sombrero *m* de copa, galera *f* AmL

top-heavy *adj* inestable

topic ['tap·ɪk] *n* tema *m*

topical ['tap·ɪ·kəl] *adj* de interés actual

topicality [ˌtap·ɪ·'kæl·ə·t̬i] *n* actualidad *f*

topless ['tap·lɪs] **I.** *adj* (*person*) en topless; (*clothes*) sin parte de arriba **II.** *adv* **to go ~** ir en topless

top-level ['tap·ˌlev·əl] *adj* **1.** (*of highest rank*) de alto nivel **2.** (*of highest importance*) de primera categoría

top loader *n* lavadora *f* de carga superior

top management *n* altos cargos *mpl*

topmost ['tap·moʊst] *adj* más alto, -a

top-notch [ˌtap·'natʃ] *adj* *inf* de primera

topographer [tə·'pag·rə·fər] *n* topógrafo, -a *m, f*

topographical [ˌtap·ə·'græf·ɪ·kəl] *adj* topográfico, -a

topography [tə·'pag·rə·fi] *n* topografía *f*

topping ['tap·ɪŋ] *n* CULIN cobertura *f*

topple ['tap·əl] **I.** *vt a.* POL derrocar **II.** *vi* **to ~ (down)** caerse

◆**topple over** *vi* volcarse

top price *n* precio *m* máximo

top priority *n* prioridad *f* máxima

top quality *n* máxima calidad *f*

top-ranking *adj* importante; (*university*) de alto nivel

topsail *n* gavia *f*

top salary *n* salario *m* máximo

top-secret *adj* confidencial

top-selling *adj* de mayor venta

topsoil *n* capa *f* superior del suelo

top speed *n* velocidad *f* máxima

topspin *n* SPORTS efecto *m* topspin

topsy-turvy [ˌtap·sɪ·'tɜr·vi] *inf* **I.** *adj* desordenado, -a **II.** *adv* patas arriba

torch [tɔrtʃ] <-es> *n* (*burning stick*) antorcha *f;* **to carry a ~ for sb** beber los vientos por alguien; **to put sth to the ~** prender fuego a algo

torchlight procession *n* desfile *m* con antorchas

tore [tɔr] *vi, vt pt of* **tear**

torment ['tɔr·ment] **I.** *n* **1.** (*suffering*) tormento *m;* **to be in ~** sufrir mucho; **to go through ~** sufrir lo indecible **2.** (*physical pain*) suplicio *m* **3.** (*torture*) tortura *f* **4.** (*annoying thing*) suplicio **II.** *vt* atormentar

tormentor [tɔr·'men·tər] *n* torturador(a) *m(f)*

torn [tɔrn] *vi, vt pp of* **tear**

tornado [tɔr·'neɪ·doʊ] *n* <-(e)s> tornado *m*

torpedo [tɔr·'pi·doʊ] MIL, NAUT **I.** <-es> *n* torpedo *m* **II.** *vt* torpedear

torpid ['tɔr·pɪd] *adj form* aletargado, -a

torpor ['tɔr·pər] *n form* sopor *m,* letargo *m*

torque [tɔrk] *n* PHYS par *m* de torsión

torrent ['tɔr·ənt] *n* **1.** (*large amount of water*) torrente *m;* **to rain in ~s** llover a cántaros **2.** (*of complaints, abuse*) torrente

torrential [tɔ·'ren·ʃəl] *adj* torrencial, torrentoso, -a AmL

torsion ['tɔr·ʃən] *n* TECH, MED torsión *f*

torso ['tɔr·soʊ] *n* torso *m*

tortoise ['tɔr·t̬əs] *n* tortuga *f*

tortoiseshell ['tɔr·t̬əs·ʃel] *n* concha *f*

tortuous ['tɔr·tʃu·əs] *adj* (*complicated, indirect*) tortuoso, -a; (*reasoning*) enrevesado, -a

torture ['tɔr·tʃər] **I.** *n* **1.** (*cruelty*) tortura *f;* (*mental*) tormento *m* **2.** (*suffering*) suplicio *m* **II.** *vt* **1.** (*cause suffering to*) torturar **2.** (*disturb*) atormentar; **to ~ oneself with sth** martirizarse con algo

torturer ['tɔr·tʃər·ər] *n* torturador(a) *m(f)*

toss [tɔs] **I.** *n* **1.** (*throw*) lanzamiento *m;* (*of head*) movimiento *m* brusco **2.** (*throwing of a coin*) sorteo *m* a cara o cruz; **to win/lose the ~** ganar/perder a cara o cruz **II.** *vt* **1.** (*throw*) lanzar; (*pancake*) dar la vuelta; **to ~ a coin** echar una moneda a cara o cruz **2.** (*shake: head*) sacudir **III.** *vi* **to ~ for sth** echar algo a cara o cruz ▸ **to ~ and turn** dar vueltas en la cama

◆**toss about** *vt*, **toss around** *vt* **1.** (*move roughly*) zarandear; (*head, hair*) agitar **2.** (*consider*) considerar

◆**toss away** *vt* tirar

◆**toss off** *vt* **1.** *inf* (*do quickly*) hacer rápidamente, currarse en un momento *argot;* (*write*) escribir rápidamente **2.** (*drink quickly*) beber de un trago

◆**toss out** *vt* tirar

◆**toss up** *vi* **to ~ for sth** echar algo a cara o cruz

toss-up ['tɔs·ʌp] *n* **it's a ~ between...** la cosa está entre...

T

tot [tat] *n inf* (*child*) niño, -a *m, f* chico, -a
◆**tot up** *vt inf* sumar
total ['toʊ·t̬əl] **I.** *n* (*sum, cost*) total *m* **II.** *adj*
1. (*entire: sum, cost*) total **2.** (*absolute*) total,
absoluto, -a; **a ~ failure** un fracaso total **III.** *vt*
1. (*count*) sumar **2.** (*amount to*) ascender a
totalitarian [toʊ·ˌtæl·ə·'ter·i·ən] *adj* POL totalitario, -a
totalitarianism *n* POL totalitarismo *m*
totality [toʊ·'tæl·ə·t̬i] *n* totalidad *f;* **in its ~** en
total
totally ['toʊ·t̬ə·li] *adv* totalmente
tote[1] [toʊt] *n* SPORTS totalizador *m*
tote[2] [toʊt] *vt inf* llevar consigo [*o* a cuestas]
tote bag *n* bolsa *f* grande
totem (**pole**) ['toʊ·t̬əm·(ˌpoʊl)] *n* tótem *m*
totter ['tat̬·ər] *vi* tambalearse
tottery ['tat̬·ə·ri] *adj* tambaleante
toucan ['tu·kæn] *n* tucán *m*
touch [tʌtʃ] <-es> **I.** *n* **1.** (*sensation*) tacto *m*
2. (*act of touching*) toque *m* **3.** (*communication*) **to be/get/keep in ~** (**with sb/sth**)
estar/ponerse/mantenerse en contacto (con
alguien/algo); **to be out of ~ with sb** no tener
contacto con alguien; **to lose ~ with sb**
perder el contacto con alguien **4.** (*skill*) habilidad *f;* **to lose one's ~** perder la destreza
5. (*small amount*) poquito *m;* (*of bitterness,
irony*) pizca *f;* **a ~ of genius** un punto de
genialidad **6.** (*detail*) toque; **the human ~** el
toque humano ▶**to be a soft ~** *inf* ser demasiado blando; (*person*) ser un blandengue **II.** *vt*
1. (*feel*) tocar; **to ~ the brake** pisar el freno
2. (*brush against*) rozar **3.** (*reach*) alcanzar
4. (*eat, drink*) probar; **he didn't ~ it** no lo
probó **5.** (*move emotionally*) conmover, enternecer **6.** (*equal*) **there's no painter to ~ him**
no existe pintor que le iguale **III.** *vi* **don't ~!**
¡no toques!; **for a moment our hands ~ed**
por un instante, nuestras manos se tocaron
◆**touch at** *vi* NAUT hacer escala en
◆**touch down** *vi* AVIAT aterrizar
◆**touch in** *vt* ART esbozar
◆**touch off** *vt* hacer estallar; (*protest*) provocar
◆**touch on** *vt* tocar
◆**touch up** *vt* (*improve*) mejorar; PHOT retocar
◆**touch upon** *vt* tocar
touch-and-go *adj* **to be ~ whether...** no estar
claro si...
touchdown ['tʌtʃ·daʊn] *n* **1.** AVIAT aterrizaje *m*
2. SPORTS (*American football*) touchdown *m;*
(*rugby*) ensayo *m*
touched [tʌtʃt] *adj* **1.** (*moved*) conmovido, -a
2. *inf* (*crazy*) chiflado, -a
touchiness ['tʌtʃ·ɪ·nɪs] *n inf* **1.** (*of person*)
malhumor *m* **2.** (*of issue*) delicadeza *f*
touching ['tʌtʃ·ɪŋ] *adj* conmovedor(a)
touch-sensitive *adj* COMPUT sensible al tacto
touchstone ['tʌtʃ·stoʊn] *n* piedra *f* de toque
touch-type ['tʌtʃ·taɪp] *vi* mecanografiar al
tacto
touchy ['tʌtʃ·i] <-ier, -iest> *adj* **1.** (*person*) sus-

ceptible; **she's very ~ about her work** es
muy susceptible cuando se trata de su trabajo
2. (*issue*) delicado, -a
tough [tʌf] **I.** *adj* **1.** (*fabric, substance*) fuerte;
(*meat, skin*) duro, -a; **to be ~ as old boots**
(*meat*) estar más duro que una suela **2.** (*hardy:
person*) duro, -a, resistente **3.** (*strict*) estricto,
-a; (*negotiator*) implacable; **to be ~ on sb** ser
severo con alguien **4.** (*difficult*) difícil; (*exam,
question*) peliagudo, -a **5.** (*violent*) violento,
-a; (*neighborhood*) peligroso, -a **6.** *sl* (*unlucky*)
~ luck mala suerte **II.** *n inf* matón, -ona *m, f*
◆**tough out** *vt* **to tough it out** (*endure*) no
ceder; (*face up to*) afrontar
toughen ['tʌf·ən] **I.** *vt* endurecer **II.** *vi* endurecerse
toughness *n* **1.** (*strength*) resistencia *f*
2. (*hardness: of meat*) dureza *f* **3.** (*difficulty*)
dificultad *f*
toupee [tu·'peɪ] *n* peluquín *m*
tour [tʊr] **I.** *n* **1.** (*journey*) viaje *m;* **guided ~**
excursión *f* guiada; **sightseeing ~** paseo *m*
por los lugares de interés **2.** (*of factory*) visita *f*
3. MUS gira *f;* **to be/go on ~** estar/ir de gira
II. *vt* **1.** (*travel around*) recorrer **2.** (*visit professionally*) visitar **3.** (*perform*) ir de gira por
III. *vi* ir de viaje
touring company *n* compañía *f* teatral itinerante
tourism ['tʊr·ɪz·əm] *n* turismo *m*
tourist ['tʊr·ɪst] *n* (*traveler*) turista *mf*
tourist agency *n* agencia *f* de viajes
tourist bureau *n* oficina *f* de turismo
tourist class *n* clase *f* turista
tourist guide *n* **1.** (*book*) guía *f* turística
2. (*person*) guía *mf*
tourist industry *n* industria *f* turística
tourist information office *n* oficina *f* de
información y turismo
tourist season *n* temporada *f* turística
tourist ticket *n* pasaje *m* de turista
tourist visa *n* visado *m* turístico
tournament ['tɜr·nə·mənt] *n* SPORTS torneo *m*
tour operator *n* operador *m* turístico
tousle ['taʊ·zəl] *vt* despeinar
tousled ['taʊ·zəlt] *adj* despeinado, -a
tout [taʊt] **I.** *n* revendedor(a) *m(f)* **II.** *vt* (*try to
sell*) tratar de vender **III.** *vi* **to ~ for customers** buscar clientes
tow [toʊ] **I.** *n* remolque *m;* **to give sth/sb a ~**
remolcar algo/a alguien; **to have sb in ~** *fig*
llevar a alguien a cuestas **II.** *vt* remolcar; **to ~ a
vehicle** llevarse un coche a remolque
toward(s) [tɔrd(z)] *prep* **1.** (*in direction of*)
hacia; (*of time*) hacia, cerca de **2.** (*for*) para
3. (*in respect of*) respecto a; **to feel sth ~ sb**
sentir algo por alguien
tow bar *n* barra *f* de tracción
towboat *n* NAUT remolcador *m*
towel ['taʊ·əl] **I.** *n* toalla *f* ▶**to throw in the ~**
tirar la toalla **II.** *vt* <-ll-> **to ~ sth dry** secar
algo (*con una toalla*)
towel(l)ing *n* felpa *f*

towel rack *n* toallero *m*

tower ['taʊ·ər] *n* torre *f* ▸ **a ~ of strength** un gran apoyo

◆ **tower above** *vi*, **tower over** *vi* **to ~ sth/sb** ser mucho más alto que algo/alguien

towering *adj* **1.** (*very high*) altísimo, -a **2.** (*very large*) inmenso, -a; (*temper*) intenso, -a

town [taʊn] *n* (*large*) ciudad *f*; (*small*) pueblo *m*; **the ~** el centro ▸ **to go out** on **the ~** salir de juerga; **to paint the ~ red** irse de juerga

town center *n* centro *m* urbano

town clerk *n* secretario, -a *m*, *f* del ayuntamiento

town council *n* ayuntamiento *m*

town councilor *n* concejal(a) *m(f)*

town hall *n* POL ayuntamiento *m*

townhouse *n* **1.** (*residence in town*) casa *f* de la ciudad **2.** (*part of terrace*) casa unifamiliar

town planning *n* urbanismo *m*

townscape ['taʊn·skeɪp] *n* paisaje *m* urbano

townsfolk ['taʊnz·foʊk] *npl* ciudadanos *mpl*

township ['taʊn·ʃɪp] *n* **1.** municipio *m* **2.** (*in South Africa*) distrito *m* segregado

townspeople ['taʊnz·ˌpi·pəl] *npl* ciudadanos *mpl*

tow truck *n* grúa *f*

toxemia *n*, **toxemia** [tak·'si·mi·ə] *n* toxemia *f*

toxic ['tak·sɪk] *adj* tóxico, -a

toxicology [ˌtak·sɪ·'kal·ə·dʒi] *n* toxicología *f*

toxic waste *n* residuos *mpl* tóxicos

toxin ['tak·sɪn] *n* toxina *f*

toy [tɔɪ] *n* juguete *m*; **cuddly ~** muñeco *m* de peluche

◆ **toy with** *vt* jugar con; **to ~ an idea** dar vueltas a una idea; **to ~ sb's affections** jugar con los sentimientos de alguien

toy car *n* coche *m* de juguete

toy dog *n* perro *m* faldero

toyshop *n* juguetería *f*

trace[1] [treɪs] *n* (*for horse*) correa *f*; **to kick over the ~s** sacar los pies del plato

trace[2] [treɪs] I. *n* **1.** (*sign*) rastro *m*; **to leave a ~ of sth** dejar indicios de algo; **to disappear without a ~** desaparecer sin dejar rastro **2.** (*slight amount*) pizca *f*; **~s of a drug/poison** rastros de droga/veneno; **without any ~ of sarcasm/humor** sin pizca de sarcasmo/humor II. *vt* **1.** (*locate*) localizar; **to ~ sb to somewhere** localizar a alguien en algún sitio; **it can be ~d back to the Middle Ages** se remonta a la Edad Media **2.** (*draw outline of*) trazar; (*with tracing paper*) calcar

traceable ['treɪ·sə·bəl] *adj* rastreable; **an easily ~ reference** una referencia fácil de encontrar

trace element *n* oligoelemento *m*

tracer ['treɪ·sər] *n* MIL bala *m* trazadora

tracery ['treɪ·sə·ri] *n* tracería *f*

trachea ['treɪ·ki·ə] <-s *o* -chae> *n* tráquea *f*

tracing *n* calco *m*

tracing paper *n* papel *m* de calco

track [træk] I. *n* **1.** (*path*) senda *f* **2.** (*rails*) vía *f* **3.** (*in station*) andén *m* **4.** (*mark*) pista *f*; (*of*

animal) huella *f*; (*of bullet*) trayectoria *f*; **to cover one's ~s** borrar sus huellas; **to leave ~s** dejar huellas; **to be on the ~ of sb** seguir la pista a alguien **5.** (*path*) camino *m*; **to be on the right/wrong ~** *a. fig* ir por buen/mal camino **6.** (*logical course*) curso *m*; **the ~ of an argument** el hilo; **to get off the ~** salirse del tema; **to be on ~ (to do sth)** estar en camino (de hacer algo) **7.** (*career path*) rumbo *m* (profesional); **to change ~** cambiar de rumbo **8.** SPORTS pista *f* **9.** (*song*) pista *f* ▸ **to live on the wrong side of the ~s** vivir en los barrios pobres; **to keep ~ (of sth/sb)** no perder (algo/a alguien) de vista; **to lose ~ (of sth/sb)** perder (algo/a alguien) de vista; **to make ~s** *inf* largarse; **to stop sb (dead) in his ~s** parar los pies a alguien; **to throw sb off the ~** despistar a alguien II. *vt* **1.** (*pursue*) seguir la pista de; **to ~ sth/sb** seguir algo/a alguien **2.** (*trace*) trazar III. *vi* CINE avanzar

◆ **track down** *vt* localizar

track and field *n* atletismo *m*

trackball *n* COMPUT trackball *m*

track event *n* SPORTS carrera *f* de atletismo

tracking station ['træk·ɪŋ·ˌsteɪ·ʃən] *n* AVIAT, TECH centro *m* de seguimiento

track record *n* historial *m*

track shoe *n* zapatilla *f* de atletismo

tracksuit *n* chándal *m*

tract[1] [trækt] *n* (*leaflet*) folleto *m*

tract[2] [trækt] *n* **1.** (*of land*) tramo *m* **2.** ANAT, MED tracto *m*; **digestive/respiratory ~** tracto digestivo/respiratorio

tractable ['træk·tə·bəl] *adj* (*person, animal*) dócil; (*problem*) soluble

traction ['træk·ʃən] *n* **1.** (*grip*) adherencia *f* **2.** MED tracción *f*

tractor ['træk·tər] *n* tractor *m*

tractor trailer *n* camión *m* articulado

trade [treɪd] I. *n* **1.** (*buying and selling*) comercio *m*; **~ in sth** comercio de algo **2.** (*business activity*) actividad *f* económica **3.** (*type of business*) industria *f*; **building ~** (sector *m* de la) construcción *f*; **fur ~** industria peletera **4.** (*profession*) oficio *m*; **to learn a ~** aprender un oficio; **to be a baker by ~** ser panadero de profesión **5.** (*swap*) intercambio *m* II. *vi* COM comerciar; **to ~ with sb** tener relaciones comerciales con alguien; **to ~ in sth** comerciar en algo III. *vt* **1.** (*swap, exchange*) intercambiar; **to ~ sth for sth** cambiar algo por algo **2.** (*sell*) vender

◆ **trade in** *vt* aportar como parte del pago

◆ **trade on** *vt* aprovecharse de

trade agreement *n* acuerdo *m* comercial

trade association *n* asociación *f* mercantil

trade balance *n* balanza *f* comercial

trade barrier *n* barrera *f* arancelaria

trade cycle *n* ciclo *m* mercantil

trade directory *n* guía *f* mercantil

trade discount *n* descuento *m* comercial

trade fair *n* COM feria *f* de muestras

trade gap *n* déficit *m pl* déficit(s) de la balanza

comercial

trade-in ['treɪd·ˌɪn] n COM permuta f
trade-in value n valor m de un artículo usado (*descontado al comprar uno nuevo*)
trade journal n periódico m gremial
trademark n 1.COM marca f; **registered ~** marca f registrada 2.fig distintivo m
trade name n (*of a firm*) razón f social; (*trademark*) marca f
tradeoff ['treɪd·ˌɔf] n 1.(*exchange*) intercambio m; **to make a ~ between things** hacer un intercambio de cosas 2.fig (*inconvenience*) precio m
trade policy n política f comercial
trade press n prensa f especializada
trader ['treɪ·dər] n comerciante mf
trade register n registro m mercantil
trade route n ruta f comercial
trade secret n secreto m profesional
tradesman ['treɪdz·mən] <-men> n tendero m
tradespeople ['treɪdz·ˌpi·pəl] npl comerciantes mfpl
trade surplus n excedente m comercial
trade union n sindicato m
trade unionism n sindicalismo m
trade unionist n sindicalista mf
trade war n guerra f comercial
trade wind n viento m alisio
trading ['treɪ·dɪŋ] n comercio m; **insider ~** uso m de información confidencial
trading area n zona f comercial
trading license n licencia f comercial
trading volume n volumen m comercial
tradition [trə·'dɪʃ·ən] n tradición f; **by ~** por tradición; **to be in the ~ of sb/sth** ser del estilo de alguien/algo
traditional [trə·'dɪʃ·ə·nəl] adj 1.(*customary*) tradicional 2.(*conventional*) clásico, -a
traditionalism [trə·'dɪʃ·ə·nə·lɪz·əm] n tradicionalismo m
traditionalist [trə·'dɪʃ·ə·nə·lɪst] n tradicionalista mf
traffic ['træf·ɪk] I. n 1.(*vehicles*) tráfico m; **heavy ~** tráfico denso; **air/rail ~** tráfico aéreo/ferroviario; **commercial ~** tráfico comercial; **passenger ~** tráfico de pasajeros; **to get stuck in ~** quedarse atrapado en un atasco 2.(*movement: of goods, passengers*) tránsito m; **drug ~** tráfico de drogas 3.form (*dealings*) **to have ~ with sb** tener relaciones comerciales con alguien II.<trafficked, trafficked> vi pej **to ~ in sth** traficar con algo
traffic accident n accidente m de tráfico
traffic circle n rotonda f
traffic island n isleta f
traffic jam n atasco m
trafficker ['træf·ɪk·ər] n pej traficante mf; **drug/arms ~** traficante de drogas/armas
traffic light n semáforo m
traffic regulation n normas fpl de circulación
traffic sign n señal f de tráfico
tragedy ['trædʒ·ə·di] <-ies> n tragedia f

tragic ['trædʒ·ɪk] adj trágico, -a
tragicomedy [ˌtrædʒ·ɪ·'kam·ə·di] <-ies> n tragicomedia f
trail [treɪl] I. n 1.(*path*) camino m 2.(*track*) pista f; (*of airplane*) estela f; **a ~ of destruction** una estela de destrucción; **to be on the ~ of sth/sb** seguir la pista de algo/alguien; **to be hot on the ~ of sb** estar muy cerca de encontrar a alguien; **to follow a ~** (*in hunting*) seguir un rastro II. vt 1.(*follow*) seguir la pista de; **to ~ an animal** seguir el rastro de un animal 2.(*drag*) arrastrar 3.(*be losing to*) **to ~ sb/sth** ir perdiendo ante [o contra] alguien/algo III. vi 1.(*drag*) **to ~ (somewhere)** arrastrarse (a algún sitio) 2.SPORTS ir perdiendo; **to ~ by 6 points** ir perdiendo por 6 puntos; **to ~ behind sth/sb** ir por detrás de algo/alguien
◆**trail along** I. vi arrastrarse II. vt arrastrar
◆**trail away** vi esfumarse
◆**trail behind** vi ir detrás
◆**trail off** vi esfumarse
trailblazer ['treɪl·ˌbleɪ·zər] n pionero, -a m, f
trailblazing ['treɪlˌbleɪzɪŋ] adj pionero, -a
trailer n 1.(*wheeled container*) remolque m 2.(*mobile home*) caravana f 3.(*advertisement*) avance m publicitario; CINE tráiler m
trailer park n cámping m de caravanas
train [treɪn] I. n 1.(*railway*) tren m; **to travel by ~** viajar en tren 2.(*series*) serie f; **~ of thought** hilo m de(l) pensamiento; **to put sth in ~** poner algo en movimiento 3.(*retinue*) séquito m 4.(*procession: of animals, things*) recua f 5.(*of dress*) cola f II. vi entrenarse; **to ~ to be sth** prepararse para ser algo III. vt formar; (*animal*) amaestrar; **to ~ sb in the use of sth** adiestrar a alguien en el uso de algo; **to ~ sb for sth** entrenar a alguien para algo
train accident n accidente m ferroviario
train connection n conexión f ferroviaria
trained [treɪnd] adj 1.(*educated*) formado, -a; (*animal*) amaestrado, -a; **to be ~ in sth** estar formado en algo 2.(*expert*) cualificado, -a
trainee [treɪ·'ni] n aprendiz(a) m(f)
trainer ['treɪ·nər] n (*person*) entrenador(a) m(f)
training n 1.(*education*) formación f; **~ on-the-job** formación f laboral 2.SPORTS entrenamiento m; **to be in ~ for sth** estar entrenando para algo; **to be good ~ for sth** ser un buen entrenamiento para algo
training camp n SPORTS campamento m de instrucción
training course n curso m de formación
training program n programa m de entrenamiento
train schedule n horario m de trenes
train service n servicio m de trenes
traipse [treɪps] vi pej andar sin ganas; **to ~ around the shops** patearse las tiendas
trait [treɪt] n rasgo m
traitor ['treɪ·tər] n traidor(a) m(f); **to turn ~** volver la casaca
traitorous ['treɪ·tər·əs] adj pej, form traicionero, -a

trajectory [trə·'dʒek·tə·ri] *n* 1. PHYS trayectoria *f* 2. *fig* (*path*) camino *m;* **to be on a downward/an upward ~** ir descendiendo/ascendiendo

tram [træm] *n* tranvía *m;* **to go by ~** viajar en tranvía

trammel ['træm·əl] *liter* I. *n* ~**s** trabas *fpl* II. *vt* <-ll-> poner trabas a

tramp [træmp] I. *vi* 1. (*walk heavily*) andar con pasos pesados 2. (*go on foot*) ir a pie II. *vt* pisar con fuerza; (*town, miles*) patearse *inf* III. *n* 1. (*sound*) ruido *m* de pasos 2. (*walk*) caminata *f;* **to go for a ~** ir de caminata 3. (*down-and-out*) vagabundo, -a *m, f* 4. *pej* (*woman*) fulana *f*

trample ['træm·pəl] I. *vt* pisar; **to ~ sb's foot** pisar el pie a alguien; **to be ~d to death** ser pisoteado hasta la muerte; **to ~ sth underfoot** pisotear algo II. *vi* **to ~ on sth** pisar algo

trampoline ['træm·pə·lin] *n* trampolín *m*

trance [træns] *n* trance *m;* **to be in a ~** estar en trance

tranquil ['træŋ·kwɪl] *adj* tranquilo, -a

tranquility [træŋ·'kwɪl·ə·ti] *n* tranquilidad *f*

tranquilize ['træŋ·kwɪ·laɪz] *vt* MED tranquilizar

tranquilizer *n* tranquilizante *m;* **to be on ~s** estar tomando tranquilizantes

transact [træn·'zækt] *vt* tramitar

transaction [træn·'zæk·ʃən] *n* COM transacción *f*, transa *f RíoPl;* **business ~** transacción comercial

transalpine [trænz·'æl·ˌpaɪn] *adj* transalpino, -a

transatlantic *adj*, **trans-Atlantic** [ˌtræns·ət·'læn·tɪk] *adj* transatlántico, -a

transceiver [træn·'si·vər] *n* transmisor-receptor *m*

transcend [træn·'send] *vt* 1. (*go beyond*) trascender; **to ~ barriers/limitations** superar las barreras/las limitaciones 2. (*surpass*) superar

transcendent [træn·'sen·dənt] *adj* trascendente; (*superior*) supremo, -a

transcendental [ˌtræn·sen·'den·təl] *adj* trascendental

transcontinental [ˌtræns·ˌkan·tə·'nen·təl] *adj* transcontinental

transcribe [træn·'skraɪb] *vt* transcribir

transcript ['træn·skrɪpt] *n* transcripción *f*

transcription [træn·'skrɪp·ʃən] *n* transcripción

transducer [træns·'du·sər] *n* ELEC transductor *m*

transept ['træn·sept] *n* ARCHIT crucero *m*

transfer¹ [træns·'fɜr] I. <-rr-> *vt* 1. (*move*) trasladar 2. (*reassign: power*) transferir 3. COM (*shop*) traspasar 4. SPORTS (*sell*) traspasar II. <-rr-> *vi* 1. (*move*) trasladarse 2. (*change train, plane*) hacer transbordo

transfer² ['træns·fər] *n* 1. (*process of moving*) traslado *m; ~* **of information** transmisión *f* de información 2. (*reassignment*) transferencia *f* 3. COM (*of a shop*) traspaso *m* 4. SPORTS traspaso 5. (*ticket*) billete *m* de transbordo 6. (*picture*) cromo *m*

transferable [træns·'fɜr·ə·bəl] *adj* transferible

transference ['træns·fɜr·əns] *n form a.* PSYCH transferencia *f*

transfigure [træns·'fɪg·jər] *vt* transfigurar

transfix [træns·'fɪks] *vt form* traspasar; **to be ~ed by sb/sth** estar totalmente paralizado por alguien/algo

transform [træns·'fɔrm] *vt* transformar

transformation [ˌtræns·fər·'meɪ·ʃən] *n* transformación *f*

transformer *n* ELEC transformador *m*

transfuse [træns·'fjuz] *vt* MED hacer una transfusión de

transfusion [træns·'fju·ʒən] *n* transfusión *f;* **blood ~** transfusión de sangre; **to give sb a ~** hacer a alguien una transfusión de sangre

transgress [træns·'gres] *form* I. *vt* transgredir; **to ~ a law** infringir una ley II. *vi* cometer una transgresión

transgression [træns·'greʃ·ən] *n form* transgresión *f*

transgressor *n* transgresor(a) *m(f);* REL pecador(a) *m(f)*

transient ['træn·zi·ənt] *form* I. *adj* pasajero, -a II. *n* residente *mf* temporal

transistor [træn·'zɪs·tər] *n* ELEC transistor *m*

transistorize [træn·'zɪs·tə·raɪz] *vt* transistorizar

transit ['træn·zɪt] *n* tránsito *m;* **in ~** de paso

transit business *n* negocio *m* de tránsito

transition [træn·'zɪʃ·ən] *n* transición *f*

transitional [træn·'zɪʃ·ə·nəl] *adj* (*period*) transitorio, -a; (*government*) de transición

transitive ['træn·sɪ·ˌtɪv] *adj* LING transitivo, -a

transitory ['træn·sə·ˌtɔr·i] *adj* pasajero, -a

transit passenger *n* pasajero, -a *m, f* de tránsito

transit visa *n* visado *m* de tránsito

translatable *adj* traducible

translate [træns·'leɪt] I. *vt* 1. LING traducir; **to ~ sth from English into Spanish** traducir algo del inglés al español 2. (*adapt*) adaptar; **to ~ a play for the cinema** adaptar una obra de teatro para el cine 3. (*transform*) **to ~ a plan into action** llevar a cabo un plan II. *vi* LING traducir; **to ~ from English into Spanish** traducir del inglés al español

translation [træns·'leɪ·ʃən] *n* traducción *f*

translator *n* traductor(a) *m(f)*

transliterate [træns·'lɪt·ə·reɪt] *vt* transliterar

transliteration [træns·ˌlɪt·ə·'reɪ·ʃən] *n* LING transliteración *f*

translucent [træns·'lu·sənt] *adj*, **translucid** *adj* translúcido, -a

transmigration [ˌtræns·maɪ·'greɪ·ʃən] *n* transmigración *f*

transmissible [træns·'mɪs·ə·bəl] *adj* transmisible

transmission [træns·'mɪʃ·ən] *n* transmisión *f;* **data ~** COMPUT transmisión de datos

transmission speed *n* COMPUT velocidad *f* de transmisión

transmit [træns·'mɪt] <-tt-> *vt* transmitir

T

transmitter *n* **1.** (*apparatus*) transmisor *m* **2.** (*station*) emisora *f*

transmitting station *n* emisora

transmogrify [træns·'mɑg·rə·faɪ] *vt* transformar completamente

transmutation [ˌtræns·mju·'teɪ·ʃən] *n form* transmutación *f*

transmute [ˌtræns·'mjut] *form* I. *vt* transmutar; **to ~ sth into sth** transmutar algo en algo II. *vi* **to ~ into sth** transmutarse en algo

transoceanic [ˌtræns·oʊ·ʃi·'æn·ɪk] *adj* transoceánico, -a

transom ['træn·səm] *n* **1.** (*horizontal bar*) travesaño *m* **2.** (*window*) montante *m*

transparency [træns·'per·ən·si] *n* <-ies> transparencia *f*

transparent [træns·'per·ənt] *adj* transparente

transpiration [ˌtræn·spɪ·'reɪ·ʃən] *n* transpiración *f*

transpire [træn·'spaɪ·ər] *vi* **1.** (*happen*) tener lugar; **it ~d that...** ocurrió que... **2.** (*come to be known*) saberse **3.** (*emit water vapor*) transpirar

transplant¹ [træns·'plænt] *vt* **1.** MED, BOT trasplantar **2.** (*relocate*) trasladar

transplant² ['træns·plænt] *n* trasplante *m*

transplantation [ˌtræns·plæn·'teɪ·ʃən] *n* trasplante

transport¹ [træns·'pɔrt] *vt* **1.** (*people, goods*) transportar **2.** *liter* (*fill with emotion*) arrebatar; **to be ~ed with joy** estar flotando de alegría; **to be ~ed with grief** estar sobrecogido de [*o* por la] pena

transport² ['træns·pɔrt] *n* **1.** (*means of conveyance*) transporte *m;* **public ~** transporte público; **~ costs** gastos *mpl* de transporte **2.** (*plane*) avión *m* de transporte; (*ship*) buque *m* de transporte **3.** *form* (*strong emotion*) arrebato *m;* **to be in ~s of joy** estar flotando de alegría

transportable *adj* transportable

transportation [ˌtræns·pər·'teɪ·ʃən] *n* **1.** (*of people, goods*) transporte *m* **2.** (*of a convict*) deportación *f*

transportation waiting area *n* sala *f* de tránsito

transporter [træns·'pɔr·ʈər] *n* transportador *m*

transpose [træns·'poʊz] *vt* **1.** (*reverse position of*) transponer **2.** (*change location*) trasladar **3.** MUS, MATH transportar

transsexual [træns·'sek·ʃu·əl] I. *n* transexual *mf* II. *adj* transexual

transverse ['træns·vɜs] *adj* transversal

transvestite ['træns·'ves·taɪt] *n* travesti *mf*

trap [træp] I. *n* **1.** (*device*) trampa *f;* **to set a ~** poner una trampa **2.** (*dangerous situation*) encerrona *f;* (*ambush*) emboscada *f;* **to fall into a ~** caer en una emboscada **3.** *sl* (*mouth*) pico *m;* **to shut one's ~** cerrar el pico; **to keep one's ~ shut** tener el pico cerrado **4.** (*curve in pipe*) sifón *m* **5.** HIST (*carriage*) tartana *f* **6.** (*for clay pigeons*) lanzaplatos *m inv* II. *vt* <-pp-> atrapar; **to feel ~ped** sentirse atrapado

trapdoor ['træp·dɔr] *n* escotillón *m*

trapeze [træ·'piz] *n* trapecio *m*

trapezoid ['træp·ɪ·zɔɪd] *n* MATH trapecio *m*

trapper ['træp·ər] *n* trampero, -a *m, f;* **fur ~** cazador(a) *m(f)* de pieles

trappings ['træp·ɪŋz] *npl* arreos *mpl;* **the ~ of power** el boato del poder

Trappist ['træp·ɪst] I. *adj* trapense II. *n* trapense *m*

trapshooting *n* tiro *m* al plato

trash [træʃ] I. *n* **1.** (*rubbish*) basura *f;* **to take the ~ out** sacar la basura **2.** *sl* (*people*) gentuza *f;* (*book, film*) basura **3.** *inf* (*nonsense*) chorradas *fpl;* **to talk ~** decir chorradas II. *vt sl* **1.** (*wreck*) hacer polvo **2.** (*criticize*) poner por los suelos

trash can ['træʃ·kæn] *n* cubo *m* de la basura

trashy ['træʃ·i] *adj inf* cutrísimo, -a

trauma ['trɔ·mə] *n* PSYCH, MED trauma *m*

traumatic [trɔ·'mæʈ·ɪk] *adj* traumático, -a

traumatize ['trɔ·mə·taɪz] *vt* traumatizar; **to be ~d by sth** estar traumatizado por algo

travel ['træv·əl] I. *vi* **1.** (*make journey*) viajar; **to ~ by air/car/train** viajar en avión/coche/tren; **to ~ first-class** viajar en primera clase; **to ~ light** viajar ligero de equipaje **2.** (*light, sound*) propagarse **3.** (*be away*) estar de viaje **4.** *inf* (*go fast*) ir como una bala II. *vt* viajar por; **to ~ a country/the world** viajar por un país/el mundo; **to ~ the length and breadth of a country** viajar a lo largo y ancho de un país III. *npl* viajes *mpl*

travel agency *n* agencia *f* de viajes

travel agent *n* agente *mf* de viajes

travel bureau *n* agencia de viajes

travel card *n* bono *m* de transporte

traveled *adj* que ha viajado

traveler ['træv·ə·lər] *n* viajero, -a *m, f;* **commercial ~** viajante *mf* de comercio

traveler's check *n* cheque *m* de viaje

travel expenses *n* gastos *mpl* de viaje

travel guide *n* (*person*) guía *mf* turístico, -a; (*book*) guía *f* turística

traveling *n* viajar *m*

traveling allowance *n* dietas *fpl*

traveling circus *n* circo *m* ambulante

traveling exhibition *n* exposición *f* ambulante

traveling salesman *n* viajante *mf* de comercio

travel insurance *n* seguro *m* de viaje

travelogue ['træv·əl·ɔg] *n* TV documental *m* de interés turístico; CINE película *f* de viajes

travel sickness *n* mareo *m*

traverse [trə·'vɜrs] *vt* **1.** (*cross*) atravesar **2.** (*move along*) recorrer

travesty ['træv·ɪ·sti] <-ies> *n pej* farsa *f*

trawl [trɔl] I. *vi* **1.** (*fish*) pescar al arrastre **2.** (*search*) **to ~ through sth** rastrear algo II. *vt* (*fish: sea*) hacer pesca al arrastre en III. *n* **1.** (*net*) red *f* barredera **2.** (*search*) rastreo *m*

trawler ['trɔ·lər] *n* pesquero *m* de arrastre

tray [treɪ] *n* bandeja *f,* charola *f AmS*

treacherous ['tretʃ·ər·əs] *adj* **1.** (*disloyal*) traicionero, -a **2.** (*dangerous: road, weather*) peligroso, -a

treachery ['tretʃ·ə·ri] *n* traición *f*

treacly ['tri·kli] *adj* **1.** (*thick and sticky*) meloso, -a **2.** (*sentimental*) empalagoso, -a

tread [tred] **I.** <trod, trodden *o* trod> *vi* pisar; **to ~ on** [*o* **in**] **sth** pisar algo **II.** *vt* pisar; **to ~ one's weary way** andar a paso cansino **III.** *n* **1.** (*manner of walking*) paso *m;* **a heavy ~** un paso fuerte **2.** (*step*) escalón *m* **3.** AUTO banda *f* de rodamiento [*o* rodadura]

treadle ['tred·əl] *n* pedal *m*

treadmill ['tred·mɪl] *n* **1.** (*wheel, exercise machine*) rueda *f* de andar **2.** *fig* rutina *f*

treason ['tri·zən] *n* traición *f; ***high ~ form** alta traición

treasonable ['tri·zə·nə·bəl] *adj*, **treasonous** ['tri·zə·nəs] *adj* traidor(a)

treasure ['treʒ·ər] **I.** *n* **1.** (*precious items*) tesoro *m* **2.** (*highly valued thing, person*) joya *f;* **my assistant is a ~** mi ayudante es una joya **II.** *vt* atesorar; **to ~ the memories of sb** guardar los recuerdos de alguien como un tesoro

treasure house *n* sala *f* del tesoro

treasure hunt *n* caza *f* del tesoro

treasurer ['treʒ·ər·ər] *n* tesorero, -a *m, f*

treasure trove *n* tesoro *m* hallado

treasury ['treʒ·ə·ri] <-ies> *n* tesorería *f;* **the Treasury** Hacienda *f*

Treasury bill *n* letra *f* del Tesoro

Treasury bond *n* bono *m* del Tesoro

Treasury note *n* pagaré *m* del Tesoro

Treasury Secretary *n* ≈ Ministro, -a *m, f* de Hacienda

treat [trit] **I.** *vt* **1.** (*deal with, handle*) *a.* MED tratar; **to ~ sth/sb badly** tratar mal algo/a alguien; **to ~ sth/sb as if...** tratar algo/a alguien como si... +*subj* **2.** (*process*) tratar; **to ~ a substance with acid** tratar una sustancia con ácido **3.** (*discuss*) tratar **4.** (*pay for*) invitar; **to ~ sb to an ice cream** invitar a alguien a un helado **II.** *vi* **to ~ with sb** negociar con alguien **III.** *n* **1.** (*pleasurable event*) convite *m;* (*present*) regalo *m;* **it's my ~** invito yo **2.** (*pleasure*) placer *m;* **it was a real ~** ha sido un auténtico placer

treatise ['tri·ţɪs] *n* tratado *m*

treatment ['trit·mənt] *n* **1.** trato *m;* **to get rough ~ from sb** recibir un mal trato de alguien; **to give sb the ~** *inf* hacerlas pasar canutas a alguien; **special ~** trato especial **2.** MED tratamiento *m;* **to respond to ~** responder al tratamiento

treaty ['tri·ţi] <-ies> *n* tratado *m;* **peace ~** tratado de paz

treble ['treb·əl] **I.** *adj* **1.** (*three times greater*) triple **2.** MUS de tiple **II.** *n* MUS tiple *mf* **III.** *vt* triplicar **IV.** *vi* triplicarse

treble clef *n* clave *f* de sol

tree [tri] **I.** *n* árbol *m;* **to climb a ~** trepar a un árbol; **the Tree of Knowledge** el árbol de la ciencia ▸ **you can't see the** forest **for the ~s** los árboles no te dejan ver el bosque; **to bark up the** wrong **~** *inf* tomar el rábano por las hojas; **to** grow **on ~s** caer del cielo; **money doesn't grow on ~s** el dinero no cae del cielo; **that doesn't grow on ~s** eso no se encuentra a la vuelta de la esquina **II.** *vt* (*animal*) hacer refugiarse en un árbol

tree frog *n* rana *f* de San Antonio

tree house *n* cabaña *f* en un árbol

treeless *adj* sin árboles

tree line *n* límite *m* forestal

tree-lined ['tri·laɪnd] *adj* arbolado, -a; **a ~ street** una calle bordeada de árboles

tree surgeon *n* arboricultor(a) *m(f)*

treetop *n* copa *f* del árbol; **in the ~s** en lo alto de los árboles

tree trunk *n* tronco *m* del árbol

trefoil ['tri·fɔɪl] *n* trébol *m*

trek [trek] **I.** <-kk-> *vi* caminar **II.** *n* **1.** (*walk*) caminata *f* (larga) **2.** (*migration*) migración *f*

trekking ['trek·ɪŋ] *n* senderismo *m;* **to go ~** hacer senderismo

trellis ['trel·ɪs] <-es> *n* espaldera *f;* (*for plants*) enrejado *m*

tremble ['trem·bəl] *vi* temblar; **to ~ with cold** tiritar de frío; **to ~ like a leaf** temblar como un flan

tremendous [trɪ·'men·dəs] *adj* **1.** (*enormous*) enorme, tremendo, -a; (*crowd, scope*) inmenso, -a; (*help*) inestimable; (*success*) tremendo, -a **2.** *inf* (*extremely good*) estupendo, -a

tremolo ['trem·ə·loʊ] *n* MUS trémolo *m*

tremor ['trem·ər] *n* **1.** (*shake*) vibración *f;* (*earthquake*) temblor *m* **2.** (*of fear, excitement*) estremecimiento *m*

tremulous ['trem·ju·ləs] *adj* trémulo, -a

trench [trentʃ] <-es> *n* zanja *f;* MIL trinchera *f*

trenchant ['tren·tʃənt] *adj* mordaz

trench coat *n* FASHION trinchera

trench warfare *n* guerra *f* de trincheras

trend [trend] **I.** *n* **1.** (*tendency*) tendencia *f;* **downward/upward ~** tendencia a la baja/al alza; **a ~ toward(s)...** una tendencia hacia... **2.** (*fashion*) moda *f;* **the latest ~** las últimas tendencias; **to set a new ~** fijar una nueva moda **II.** *vi* tender; **to ~ to sth** tender a algo

trendsetter ['trend·ˌseţ·ər] *n* persona *f* que inicia una moda

trendy ['tren·di] **I.** <-ier, -iest> *adj* (*clothes, bar*) de moda; (*person*) moderno, -a **II.** <-ies> *n* modernillo, -a *m, f inf*

trepidation [ˌtrep·ɪ·'deɪ·ʃən] *n* ansiedad *f;* **to do sth with ~** hacer algo inquietamente

trespass ['tres·pəs] *vi* **1.** LAW entrar ilegalmente **2.** REL pecar

trespasser ['tres·pæs·ər] *n* intruso, -a *m, f*

trestle ['tres·əl] *n* caballete *m*

trestle table *n* mesa *f* de caballete

triad ['traɪ·æd] *n* tríada *f*

trial ['traɪ·əl] *n* **1.** LAW proceso *m;* **~ by jury** juicio *m* con jurado; **to stand ~** ser procesado; **to**

be on ~ for one's life ser acusado de un crimen capital **2.** (*test*) prueba *f;* **clinical ~s** ensayos *mpl* clínicos; **~ of strength** prueba de fuerza; **to give sb a ~** poner a alguien a prueba; **to have sth on ~** tener algo a prueba **3.** (*source of problems*) suplicio *m;* **~s and tribulations** tribulaciones *fpl* **4.** (*competition*) competición *f*

trial period *n* período *m* de prueba

trial separation *n* separación *f* de prueba

triangle ['traɪ·æŋ·gəl] *n* triángulo *m*

triangular [traɪ·'æŋ·gjʊ·lər] *adj* triangular

tribal ['traɪ·bəl] *adj* tribal

tribalism ['traɪ·bə·lɪz·əm] *n* tribalismo *m*

tribe [traɪb] *n* tribu *f;* **the twelve ~s of Israel** HIST las doce tribus de Israel

tribesman ['traɪbz·mən] <-men> *n* miembro *m* de una tribu

tribulation [ˌtrɪb·jə·'leɪ·ʃən] *n form* tribulación *f*

tribunal [traɪ·'bju·nəl] *n* tribunal *m; (investigative body)* comisión *f* de investigación

tribune¹ ['trɪb·jun] *n* HIST tribuno *m*

tribune² ['trɪb·jun] *n* ARCHIT tribuna *f*

tributary ['trɪb·jə·ter·i] I.<-ies> *n* **1.** (*river*) afluente *m* **2.** HIST (*person*) contribuyente *mf; (state)* estado *m* tributario II. *adj form* **1.** (*river*) afluyente **2.** HIST (*state*) tributario, -a

tribute ['trɪb·jut] *n* **1.** (*token of respect*) homenaje *m;* **to pay ~ to sb/sth** rendir tributo a alguien/algo; **floral ~** *form* ofrenda *f* floral **2.** (*sign of sth positive*) elogio *m;* **to be a ~ to sth/sb** hacer honor a algo/alguien **3.** HIST (*money paid to a superior power*) tributo *m*

trice [traɪs] *n inf* **in a ~** en un santiamén

trick [trɪk] I. *n* **1.** (*ruse*) truco *m*, trampa *f;* **a dirty ~** *inf* una mala pasada; **to play a ~ on sb** tender una trampa a alguien; **to be up to one's (old) ~s again** volver a hacer de las suyas **2.** (*of magician*) truco **3.** (*technique*) truquillo *m* **4.** (*illusion*) ilusión *f;* **a ~ of the light** una ilusión óptica; **his eyes are playing ~s on him** ve visiones ▶ **to try every ~ in the book** intentar todos los trucos habidos y por haber; **the ~s of the trade** los trucos del oficio; **that'll do the ~** con eso solucionamos el tema; **to not miss a ~** no perder ripio II. *adj* **1.** (*deceptive*) **a ~ question** una pregunta con trampa **2.** *inf* (*weak*) débil III. *vt* (*deceive*) engañar; (*fool*) burlar; (*swindle*) timar

trickery ['trɪk·ə·ri] *n* artimañas *fpl;* **to resort to ~** recurrir a engaños

trickle ['trɪk·əl] I. *vi* **1.** (*flow slowly*) salir en un chorro fino; (*in drops*) gotear **2.** *fig* (*people*) **to ~ in/out** entrar/salir poco a poco; **to ~ out** (*information*) difundirse poco a poco II. *n* **1.** (*of liquid*) hilo *m;* (*drops*) goteo *m* **2.** (*of people, information*) goteo

◆**trickle away** *vi* consumirse poco a poco

trickster ['trɪk·stər] *n pej* estafador(a) *m(f)*, trácala *f Méx*

tricksy ['trɪk·si] *adj* (*playful*) juguetón, -ona

tricky ['trɪk·i] <-ier, -iest> *adj* **1.** (*crafty*)

astuto, -a **2.** (*difficult*) complicado, -a; (*situation*) delicado, -a; **to be ~ to do** ser difícil de hacer

tricycle ['traɪ·sɪ·kəl] *n* triciclo *m*

trident ['traɪ·dənt] *n* tridente *m*

tried [traɪd] I. *vi, vt pt, pp of* **try** II. *adj* probado, -a; **~ and tested** probado con toda garantía

triennial [traɪ·'en·i·əl] *adj* trienal

trier ['traɪ·ər] *n inf* persona *f* que se esfuerza mucho

trifle ['traɪ·fəl] *n* **1.** (*insignificant thing*) bagatela *f* **2.** (*small amount*) insignificancia *f;* **a ~** un poquito **3.** (*dessert*) dulce *m* de bizcocho borracho

◆**trifle away** *vt* malgastar; **to trifle one's time away** perder el tiempo

◆**trifle with** *vt* jugar con; **to ~ sb's affections** jugar con los sentimientos de alguien

trifling *adj* insignificante

trig. *abbr of* **trigonometry** trigonometría *f*

trigger ['trɪg·ər] I. *n* **1.** (*of gun*) gatillo *m;* **to pull the ~** apretar el gatillo; **~ mechanism** mecanismo *m* disparador **2.** *fig* detonante *m* II. *vt* **1.** (*reaction*) provocar; (*revolt*) hacer estallar **2.** (*start*) accionar; **to ~ an alarm** disparar una alarma

trigger-happy ['trɪg·ər·ˌhæp·i] *adj* de gatillo fácil

trigonometry [ˌtrɪg·ə·'nam·ə·tri] *n* MATH trigonometría *f*

trike [traɪk] *n inf abbr of* **tricycle** triciclo *m*

trilateral [traɪ·'læt̬·ər·əl] *adj* **1.** (*involving three parties*) trilateral **2.** MATH trilátero, -a

trilingual [ˌtraɪ·'lɪŋ·gwəl] *adj* trilingüe

trill [trɪl] I. *n* **1.** (*birdsong*) trino *m* **2.** (*quavering note*) trino *m* II. *vi* **1.** (*bird*) trinar **2.** (*speak*) hablar de forma afectada III. *vt* **to ~ one's r's** pronunciar la r con vibración

trillion ['trɪl·jən] *n* billón *m*

trilogy ['trɪl·ə·dʒi] <-ies> *n* trilogía *f*

trim [trɪm] I. *n* **1.** (*state*) (buen) estado *m;* **to be in ~** (for sth) estar listo (para algo); **to be in fighting ~** estar listo para entrar en combate **2.** (*hair*) **to give sb a ~** cortar las puntas a alguien; **to give sth a ~** dar un recorte a algo **3.** (*decorative edge*) borde *m* II. *adj* **1.** (*attractively thin, compact*) esbelto, -a **2.** (*neat*) aseado, -a; (*lawn*) cuidado, -a III.<-mm-> *vt* **1.** (*cut*) cortar; **to ~ one's beard** recortarse la barba **2.** (*reduce*) reducir

◆**trim down** *vt* recortar

◆**trim off** *vt* cortar

trimming *n* **1.** (*decoration*) adorno *m* **2.** **~s** CULIN guarnición *f*

Trinidad ['trɪn·ɪ·dæd] *n* Trinidad *f;* **~ and Tobago** Trinidad y Tobago

Trinidadian ['trɪn·ɪ·dæd·i·ən] I. *adj* de Trinidad II. *n* habitante *mf* de Trinidad

Trinity ['trɪn·ə·t̬i] *n* Trinidad *f;* **the (Holy) ~** la (Santísima) Trinidad

trinket ['trɪŋ·kɪt] *n* baratija *f*

trio ['tri·oʊ] *n a.* MUS trío *m;* **string ~** trío de cuerda

trip [trɪp] I. *n* 1. (*journey*) viaje *m;* (*shorter*) excursión *f;* **business** ~ viaje de negocios; **to go on a** ~ irse de viaje 2. *sl* (*effect of drugs*) viaje 3. (*fall*) tropezón *m* II. <-pp-> *vi* 1. (*stumble*) tropezar; **to** ~ **on sth** tropezar con algo 2. (*move lightly*) andar con paso ligero III. <-pp-> *vt* 1. (*cause to stumble*) **to** ~ **sb** (**up**) hacer tropezar a alguien 2. (*switch on*) encender
◆**trip over** *vi* dar un tropezón
◆**trip up** I. *vi* 1. (*stumble*) tropezar 2. (*verbally*) equivocarse II. *vt* 1. (*cause to stumble*) hacer tropezar 2. (*cause to fail*) confundir
tripartite [ˌtraɪˈpar·taɪt] *adj* tripartito, -a
tripe [traɪp] *n* 1. CULIN callos *mpl*, guata *f Méx* 2. *pej, inf* (*nonsense, rubbish*) chorradas *fpl;* **to talk** ~ decir chorradas
triple [ˈtrɪp·əl] I. *adj* triple II. *vt* triplicar III. *vi* triplicarse
triple jump *n* triple salto *m*
triplet [ˈtrɪp·lɪt] *n* 1. (*baby*) trillizo, -a *m, f;* **to have** ~**s** tener trillizos 2. MUS tresillo *m*
triplicate [ˈtrɪp·lɪ·kɪt] *adj* triplicado, -a; **in** ~ por triplicado
tripod [ˈtraɪ·pad] *n* trípode *m*
tripping [ˈtrɪp·ɪŋ] *adj* ligero, -a
trisect [traɪˈsekt] *vt* trisecar
trite [traɪt] *adj* tópico, -a
triumph [ˈtraɪ·ʌmf] I. *n* 1. (*success*) triunfo *m;* **a** ~ **over sth/sb** un triunfo sobre alguien; **to do sth in** ~ hacer algo triunfalmente; **to hail sth as a** ~ clamar algo como un triunfo 2. (*supreme example*) éxito *m;* **a** ~ **of engineering/medicine** un éxito de la ingeniería/medicina II. *vi* 1. (*achieve success*) triunfar; **to** ~ **over sth/sb** triunfar sobre algo/alguien 2. (*exult excessively*) mostrarse triunfante
triumphal [traɪˈʌm·fəl] *adj* triunfal
triumphant [traɪˈʌm·fənt] *adj* 1. (*victorious*) triunfante; (*return*) triunfal; **to emerge** ~ **from sth** salir triunfante de algo 2. (*successful*) exitoso, -a
trivia [ˈtrɪv·i·ə] *npl* trivialidades *fpl*
trivial [ˈtrɪv·i·əl] *adj* 1. (*unimportant*) irrelevante; (*dispute, matter*) trivial 2. (*insignificant*) insignificante
triviality [ˌtrɪv·iˈæl·ə· t̬i] *n* <-ies> 1. (*unimportance*) trivialidad *f* 2. (*unimportant thing*) nimiedad *f*
trivialize [ˈtrɪv·i·ə·laɪz] *vt* trivializar
trod [trad] *pt, pp of* **tread**
trodden [ˈtrad·ən] *pp of* **tread**
troglodyte [ˈtrag·lə·daɪt] *n* troglodita *mf*
Trojan [ˈtroʊ·dʒən] I. *n* troyano, -a *m, f* ▶ **to work** like a ~ trabajar como un esclavo II. *adj* troyano, -a; **the** ~ **Horse/War** el caballo/la guerra de Troya
trolley [ˈtral·i] *n* (*trolley car*) tranvía *m*
trolley bus [ˈtral·i·bʌs] *n* trolebús *m*
trolley car *n* tranvía
trollop [ˈtral·əp] *n pej, inf* zorra *f*, tusa *f Cuba*
trombone [tramˈboʊn] *n* trombón *m*

trombonist [tramˈboʊ·nɪst] *n* trombón *mf*
troop [trup] I. *n* 1. ~ **s** MIL tropas *fpl;* **cavalry** ~ escuadrón *m* de caballería 2. (*of people*) grupo *m* II. *vi* **to** ~ **in/out** entrar/salir en tropel
troop carrier *n* avión *m* de transporte de tropas
trooper [ˈtru·pər] *n* 1. MIL soldado *m* de caballería 2. (*state police officer*) policía *mf;* **state** ~ policía estatal ▶ **to swear like a** ~ soltar tacos como un carretero
trophy [ˈtroʊ·fi] *n* <-ies> trofeo *m*
tropic [ˈtrap·ɪk] *n* (*latitude*) trópico *m;* **the** ~ **s** los trópicos; **tropic of Cancer/Capricorn** Trópico de Cáncer/Capricornio
tropical [ˈtrap·ɪ·kəl] *adj* tropical
troposphere [ˈtroʊ·pə·sfɪr] *n* troposfera *f*
trot [trat] I. *n* 1. (*of horse*) trote *m* 2. ~ **s** *inf* (*diarrhea*), **to have the** ~**s** tener cagalera, tener obradera *Col, Guat, Pan* ▶ **on the** ~ sin parar II. *vi* 1. (*horse*) trotar; (*person*) andar trotando 2. (*run at moderate pace*) ir al trote 3. (*go busily*) ir apresurado III. <-tt-> *vt* (*horse*) hacer trotar
◆**trot off** *vi* marcharse
◆**trot out** *vt* (*excuse, explanation*) soltar; **to** ~ **arguments** sacar a relucir argumentos
trotter [ˈtra t̬·ər] *n* manita *f* de cerdo
trouble [ˈtrʌb·əl] I. *n* 1. (*difficulty*) dificultad *f*, problema *m;* **to have** ~ tener dificultades; **to ask for** ~ buscarse problemas; *inf;* **to spell** ~ traer problemas; **to store up** ~ hacer que el problema vaya a peor; **to be in/get into** ~ estar/meterse en un lío; **to be in serious** ~ estar metido en serios problemas; **to be in** ~ **with sb** tener problemas con alguien; **to land sb in** ~ meter en un lío a alguien; **to stay out of** ~ mantenerse al margen de los problemas 2. ~ **s** (*series of difficulties*) problemas *mpl;* **to be the least of sb's** ~**s** ser el menor de los males de alguien 3. (*inconvenience*) molestia *f;* **to go to the** ~ (*of doing sth*) tomarse la molestia (de hacer algo); **to go to a lot of** ~ **for sb** tomarse muchas molestias por alguien; **to put sb to the** ~ **of doing sth** comprometer a alguien para que haga algo; **to be** (**not**) **worth the** ~ (*of doing sth*) (no) merecer la pena (hacer algo) 4. (*physical ailment*) enfermedad *f;* **stomach** ~ dolor *m* de estómago 5. (*malfunction*) avería *f;* **engine** ~ avería del motor 6. (*strife*) conflictos *mpl;* **to stir up** ~ crear conflictos II. *vt* 1. *form* (*cause inconvenience*) molestar; **to** ~ **sb for sth** molestar a alguien con algo; **to** ~ **sb to do sth** molestar a alguien para que haga algo 2. (*make an effort*) **to** ~ **oneself about sth** esforzarse en algo 3. (*cause worry*) preocupar; (*cause pain*) afligir; **to be** ~ **d by sth** verse en problemas por algo III. *vi* esforzarse; **to** ~ **to do sth** molestarse en hacer algo
troubled *adj* 1. (*period*) turbulento, -a; (*water*) revuelto, -a 2. (*worried*) preocupado, -a; (*look*) de preocupación
trouble-free [ˌtrʌb·əlˈfri] *adj* sin problemas
troublemaker [ˈtrʌb·əlˌmeɪ·kər] *n* alborota-

dor(a) *m(f)*

troubleshooting ['trʌb·əl·ʃu·tɪŋ] *n* localización *f* de problemas

troublesome ['trʌb·əl·səm] *adj* molesto, -a

trouble spot *n* centro *m* de fricción

trough [trɔf] *n* **1.** (*receptacle*) abrevadero *m;* **feeding ~** comedero *m;* **to feed at the public ~** *fig* malversar los fondos públicos **2.** (*low point*) depresión *f* **3.** METEO zona *f* de bajas presiones

troupe [trup] *n* THEAT compañía *f*

trouper ['tru·pər] *n* artista *mf* veterano, -a

trouser clip *n* pinza *f* (para ir en bicicleta)

trouser leg *n* pernera *f*

trousers ['trau·zərz] *n pl* pantalones *mpl;* **a pair of ~** unos pantalones ▸ **to wear the ~** llevar los pantalones

trousseau ['tru·sou] *n* ajuar *m*

trout [traut] *n* <-(s)> (*fish*) trucha *f*

trowel ['trau·əl] *n* (*for building*) llana *f;* (*for gardening*) desplantador *m*

Troy [trɔɪ] *n* HIST Troya *f*

troy ounce *n* onza *f* troy

truancy ['tru·ən·si] *n* falta *f* injustificada (a clase)

truant ['tru·ənt] **I.** *n* persona *f* que hace novillos; **to be a ~** hacer novillos **II.** *vi* hacer novillos

truce [trus] *n* tregua *f;* **to call a ~** acordar una tregua

truck[1] [trʌk] **I.** *n* camión *m;* **pickup ~** camioneta *f* de plataforma **II.** *vt* transportar

truck[2] [trʌk] *n inf* (*dealings*) trato *m;* **to have no ~ with sb/sth** no tratar con alguien/algo

truck driver *n* camionero, -a *m, f*

trucker *n* camionero, -a *m, f*

truck farming *n* horticultura *f*

trucking *n* transporte *m* por carretera

trucking company *n* empresa *f* transportista

truculence ['trʌk·ju·ləns] *n* agresividad *f;* (*rebelliousness*) rebeldía *f*

truculent ['trʌk·ju·lənt] *adj* agresivo, -a; (*rebellious*) rebelde

trudge [trʌdʒ] **I.** *vi* caminar penosamente **II.** *vt* recorrer penosamente **III.** *n* caminata *f* penosa

true [tru] **I.** *adj* **1.** (*not false*) cierto, -a; **to be ~ (that...)** ser verdad [*o* cierto] (que...); **to hold sth to be ~** creer que algo es verdad; **to ring ~** sonar convincente **2.** (*genuine, real*) auténtico, -a; **~ love** amor *m* verdadero; **the ~ faith** la fe verdadera; **sb's ~ self** la verdadera personalidad de alguien; **to come ~** hacerse realidad; **in the ~ sense of the word** en el sentido real de la palabra **3.** (*faithful, loyal*) fiel; **to be/remain ~ to sth/sb** ser/mantenerse fiel a algo/alguien; **to be ~ to one's word** mantener su palabra; **to be ~ to oneself** ser fiel a sí mismo **4.** (*accurate*) exacto, -a **II.** *adv* **1.** (*truly*) verdaderamente **2.** (*accurately*) de forma precisa; **to aim ~** apuntar bien **III.** *n* **to be out of ~** no estar a nivel

◆**true up** *vt* corregir

true-blue [ˌtru·'blu] *adj inf* leal

trueborn ['tru·bɔrn] *adj form* legítimo, -a

true-hearted ['tru·ˌhar·tɪd] *adj form* fiel

true-life [ˌtru·'laɪf] *adj* real; (*story*) verídico, -a

truelove ['tru·lʌv] *n liter* gran amor *mf*

truffle ['trʌf·əl] *n* trufa *f*

truism ['tru·ɪz·əm] *n* (*obviously true*) perogrullada *f;* (*cliché*) tópico *m*

truly ['tru·li] *adv* **1.** (*accurately*) verdaderamente **2.** (*sincerely*) sinceramente **3.** (*as intensifier*) realmente ▸ **yours ~** (*at end of letter*) atentamente; (*the speaker*) su seguro servidor *elev*

trump [trʌmp] **I.** *n* (*in cards*) triunfo *m* **II.** *vt* **1.** (*in cards*) fallar **2.** (*surpass*) superar

◆**trump up** *vt* falsificar; **to ~ an accusation** inventar una acusación

trumpet ['trʌm·pət] **I.** *n* trompeta *f* ▸ **to blow one's own ~** *inf* echarse [*o* tirarse] flores **II.** *vi* (*elephant*) barritar **III.** *vt* (*news, success*) proclamar

trumpeter ['trʌm·pə·t̬ər] *n* trompetista *mf*

truncate [trʌŋ·'keɪt] *vt* truncar

truncheon ['trʌn·tʃən] *n* porra *f*, macana *f AmL*

trundle ['trʌn·dəl] **I.** *vi* rodar **II.** *vt* hacer rodar

trunk [trʌŋk] *n* **1.** ANAT, BOT tronco *m* **2.** (*of elephant*) trompa *f* **3.** (*for storage*) baúl *m* **4.** (*of car*) maletero *f*, baúl *m AmL* **5.** **~s** bañador *m;* **a pair of swimming ~s** un bañador (de hombre)

truss [trʌs] **I.** *n* **1.** (*bundle*) lío *m;* (*of hay*) haz *m* **2.** MED braguero *m* **II.** *vt* atar

◆**truss up** *vt* atar

trust [trʌst] **I.** *n* **1.** (*belief*) confianza *f;* **to gain sb's ~** ganarse la confianza de alguien; **to place one's ~ in sb/sth** depositar su confianza en alguien/algo; **to take sth on ~** aceptar algo con los ojos cerrados; **to betray sb's ~** traicionar la confianza de alguien **2.** (*responsibility*) responsabilidad *f;* **a position of ~** un puesto de responsabilidad **3.** FIN, COM consorcio *m;* **investment ~** grupo *m* de inversión **4.** LAW **to hold sth in ~** tener algo en fideicomiso **5.** (*association*) asociación *f* **II.** *vt* **1.** (*place trust in*) confiar en; **to ~ sb to do sth** confiar a alguien (el) hacer algo **2.** (*rely on*) dar responsabilidad a; **to ~ sb with sth** confiar la responsabilidad de algo a alguien **3.** (*hope*) **to ~ that...** esperar que... +*subj* **III.** *vi* confiar; **to ~ in sth/sb** confiar en algo/alguien

trusted ['trʌs·tɪd] *adj* (*friend, servant*) leal; (*method, remedy*) fiable

trustee [trʌs·'ti] *n* fideicomisario, -a *m, f;* **board of ~s** consejo *m* de administración

trustful ['trʌst·fəl] *adj* confiado, -a

trust fund *n* FIN fondo *m* de fideicomiso

trusting *adj* confiado, -a

trustworthiness ['trʌst·ˌwɜr·ðɪ·nɪs] *n* (*of person*) honradez *f;* (*of data*) fiabilidad *f*

trustworthy ['trʌst·ˌwɜr·ði] *adj* (*person*) honrado, -a; (*data*) fiable

trusty ['trʌs·ti] <-ier, -iest> *adj* leal

truth [truθ] *n* verdad *f;* **a grain of ~** una pizca de verdad; **in ~** en realidad; **to tell the ~**

(**about sth/sb**) decir la verdad (sobre algo/alguien); **to tell the ~,...** a decir verdad,...

truthful ['truθ·fəl] *adj* **1.**(*true*) veraz; (*sincere*) sincero, -a; **to be ~ with sb** ser sincero con alguien **2.**(*accurate*) preciso, -a

truthfulness *n* **1.**(*veracity*) veracidad *f;* (*sincerity*) sinceridad *f* **2.**(*accuracy*) exactitud *f*

try [traɪ] **I.** *n* **1.**(*attempt*) intento *m;* **to give sth a ~** intentar algo **2.**(*in rugby*) ensayo *m* **II.**<-ie-> *vi* esforzarse; **to ~ and do sth** *inf* intentar hacer algo **III.**<-ie-> *vt* **1.**(*attempt*) intentar; **to ~ one's best** esforzarse al máximo; **to ~ one's luck** probar suerte **2.**(*test*) probar **3.**(*sample*) probar, degustar **4.**(*annoy*) cansar; **his demands would ~ the patience of a saint** sus peticiones acabarían con la paciencia de un santo **5.** LAW juzgar

◆**try for** *vt insep* tratar de obtener

◆**try on** *vt* (*put on*) probarse; **to try sth on for size** probarse algo para ver la talla

◆**try out** *vt* probar; **to try sth out on sb** dar a probar algo a alguien

trying *adj* (*exasperating*) irritante; (*difficult*) difícil

tryout ['traɪ·aʊt] *n* prueba *f*

tsar *n s.* **tzar**

tsarina *n* zarina *f*

tsarist *adj, n s.* **tzarist**

tsetse fly ['tse·tsi·ˌflaɪ] *n* mosca *f* tse-tse

T-shirt ['ti·ʃɜrt] *n* camiseta *f,* playera *f Guat, Méx,* polera *f Chile*

tsp. *abbr of* **teaspoon** (*amount*) cucharadita *f*

T-square ['ti·skwer] *n* TECH regla *f* T

tub [tʌb] *n* **1.**(*container*) cubo *m* **2.**(*bathtub*) bañera *f* **3.**(*carton*) tarrina *f;* **a ~ of ice cream** una tarrina de helado

tuba ['tu·bə] *n* tuba *f*

tubby ['tʌb·i] <-ier, -iest> *adj inf* rechoncho, -a, requenete *Ven*

tube [tub] *n* **1.**(*hollow cylinder*) tubo *m* **2.** ANAT trompa *f;* **Fallopian ~** trompa de Falopio **3.** *inf* TV tele *f* ▶ **to go down the ~s** irse al traste

tuber ['tu·bər] *n* tubérculo *m*

tubercular [tu·ˈbɜr·kjə·lər] *adj* MED tuberculoso, -a

tuberculosis [tu·ˌbɜr·kjə·ˈloʊ·sɪs] *n* tuberculosis *f inv*

tuberculous [tu·ˈbɜr·kjʊ·ləs] *adj* tuberculoso, -a

tub-thumper ['tʌb·ˌθʌm·pər] *n pej, sl* arengador(a) *m(f)*

tuck [tʌk] **I.** *n* (*fold*) pliegue *m* **II.** *vt* (*fold*) plegar

◆**tuck away I.** *vt* (*hide*) poner a buen recaudo; **to be tucked away** estar en un sitio seguro **II.** *vi* comer con apetito

◆**tuck in** *vt* **1.**(*push into position*) colocar en su sitio; **to tuck one's shirt in** meterse la camisa **2.**(*settle in bed*) arropar

tucker ['tʌk·ər] *vt inf* hacer polvo

Tues. *n abbr of* **Tuesday** mart.

Tuesday ['tuz·deɪ] *n* martes *m inv;* **Shrove ~**

martes de carnaval; *s.a.* **Friday**

tuft [tʌft] *n* (*of hair*) mechón *m;* (*of feathers*) penacho *m;* (*of grass*) mata *f*

tug [tʌg] **I.** *n* **1.**(*pull*) tirón *m;* **to give sth a ~** dar un tirón a algo **2.** NAUT remolcador *m* **II.**<-gg-> *vt* **1.**(*pull*) tirar de **2.** NAUT remolcar

tuition [tu·ˈɪʃ·ən] *n* **1.**(*fee*) tasas *fpl* **2.**(*teaching*) enseñanza *f*

tuition fees *n* tasas

tulip ['tu·lɪp] *n* tulipán *m*

tumble ['tʌm·bəl] **I.** *n* caída *f;* **to take a ~** caerse **II.** *vi* **1.**(*fall*) caerse **2.** *fig* (*decline*) caer

◆**tumble down** *vi* desplomarse

◆**tumble over** *vi* caerse

tumbledown ['tʌm·bəl·ˌdaʊn] *adj* en ruinas

tumble dryer *n* secadora *f*

tumbler ['tʌm·blər] *n* vaso *m*

tumbleweed ['tʌm·bəl·wid] *n* planta *f* rodadora

tumescent [tu·ˈmes·ənt] *adj* tumescente

tummy ['tʌm·i] <-ies> *n childspeak* barriguita *f*

tummy ache *n childspeak* dolor *m* de tripita

tumor ['tu·mər] *n* tumor *m;* **brain/malignant ~** tumor cerebral/maligno

tumult ['tu·mʌlt] *n* **1.**(*uproar*) tumulto *m* **2.**(*emotional confusion*) agitación *f*

tumultuous [tu·ˈmʌl·tʃu·əs] *adj* **1.**(*uproariously noisy*) tumultuoso, -a; (*applause*) apoteósico, -a **2.**(*disorderly*) agitado, -a

tun [tʌn] *n* (*large vat*) tonel *m;* (*in brewery*) barril *m*

tuna ['tu·nə] *n* <-(s)> atún *m*

tundra ['tʌn·drə] *n* tundra *f*

tune [tun] **I.** *n* **1.** MUS melodía *f;* **a catchy ~** una tonada pegajosa **2.**(*pitch*) **to be in/out of ~** estar afinado/desafinado; **to be in/out of ~ with sth** *fig* armonizar/desentonar con algo ▶ **to change one's ~** cambiar de parecer; **to sing another ~** cambiar de parecer; **to the ~ of $100** por valor de 100 dólares **II.** *vt* **1.** MUS afinar **2.** AUTO poner a punto

◆**tune in I.** *vi* **1.** RADIO **to ~ to a station** sintonizar una emisora; TV sintonizar un canal **2.** *fig, sl* sintonizar con **II.** *vt* RADIO, TV sintonizar

◆**tune up** *vt* AUTO poner a punto

tuneful ['tun·fəl] *adj* MUS melódico, -a

tuneless ['tun·lɪs] *adj* MUS disonante

tuner *n* **1.** MUS (*person*) afinador(a) *m(f)* **2.**(*radio*) sintonizador *m*

tune-up ['tun·ʌp] *n* **1.** MUS afinado *m* **2.** AUTO puesta *f* a punto

tungsten ['tʌŋ·stən] *n* tungsteno *m*

tunic ['tu·nɪk] *n* FASHION casaca *f;* HIST túnica *f*

tuning *n* **1.** MUS afinación *f* **2.** RADIO sintonización *f* **3.** AUTO puesta *f* a punto

tuning fork *n* MUS diapasón *m*

Tunisia [tu·ˈni·ʒə] *n* Túnez *m*

Tunisian [tu·ˈni·ʒən] **I.** *n* tunecino, -a *m, f* **II.** *adj* tunecino, -a

tunnel ['tʌn·əl] **I.** *n* **1.** ARCHIT túnel *m* **2.** MIN galería *f* **II.** *vi* construir un túnel **III.** *vt* cavar; **to ~ one's way out** escapar haciendo un túnel

T

turban ['tɜr·bən] *n* turbante *m*
turbid ['tɜr·bɪd] *adj* (*water*) turbio, -a
turbine ['tɜr·bɪn] *n* turbina *f*
turbocharged ['tɜr·boʊ·ˌtʃɑrdʒd] *adj* ELEC, TECH turboalimentado, -a
turbocharger ['tɜr·boʊ·ˌtʃɑr·dʒər] *n* ELEC, TECH turbocompresor *m*
turbo engine *n* motor *m* turbo
turbojet *n* turborreactor *m*
turbot ['tɜr·bət] *n* <-(s)> rodaballo *m*
turbulence ['tɜr·bjʊ·ləns] *n* turbulencia *f*
turbulent ['tɜr·bjʊ·lənt] *adj* turbulento, -a
turd [tɜrd] *n vulg* **1.** (*excrement*) zurullo *m* **2.** (*person*) guarro, -a *m, f*
tureen [tʊ·'rin] *n* sopera *f*
turf [tɜrf] <-s *o* -ves> *n* **1.** BOT césped *m;* **a (piece of)** ~ un tepe; **the** ~ (*horse racing*) las carreras de caballos **2.** (*territory*) territorio *m*
turgid ['tɜr·dʒɪd] *adj form* **1.** *pej* (*style*) ampuloso, -a **2.** (*swollen*) hinchado, -a
Turk [tɜrk] *n* turco, -a *m, f*
turkey ['tɜr·ki] *n* **1.** ZOOL pavo *m* **2.** *sl* THEAT fiasco *m* **3.** *sl* (*stupid person*) papanatas *mf inv*
▶ **to talk** ~ *inf* hablar claro
Turkey ['tɜr·ki] *n* Turquía *f*
Turkish ['tɜr·kɪʃ] **I.** *adj* turco, -a **II.** *n* **1.** (*person*) turco, -a *m, f* **2.** LING turco *m*
turmoil ['tɜr·mɔɪl] *n* **1.** (*state of chaos*) caos *m inv;* **to be thrown into** ~ estar sumido en el caos **2.** (*of mind*) trastorno *m;* **to be in a** ~ estar desconcertado
turn [tɜrn] **I.** *vi* **1.** (*rotate*) girar, dar vueltas; **to** ~ **on sth** girar sobre algo **2.** (*switch direction*) volver; (*tide*) cambiar; (*car*) girar; **to** ~ **around** dar media vuelta, voltearse *AmL;* **to** ~ **right/left** torcer a la derecha/izquierda **3.** (*change*) cambiar, transformarse; (*for worse*) volverse; **to** ~ **traitor** volver la casaca; **to** ~ **gray (overnight)** encanecer (de la noche a la mañana) **4.** (*change color: leaves*) cambiar de color **5.** (*feel nauseous: stomach*) retorcerse **6.** (*spoil: cream, milk*) agriarse **II.** *vt* **1.** (*rotate*) (hacer) girar; (*key*) girar; (*screw on*) atornillar; (*unscrew*) desatornillar **2.** (*switch direction*) volver, voltear *AmL;* **to** ~ **one's head** volver la cabeza; **to** ~ **a page** pasar una página; **to** ~ **the coat inside out** volver el abrigo del revés **3.** (*attain a particular age*) cumplir **4.** (*pass a particular hour*) dar; **it has ~ed three o'clock** dieron las tres **5.** (*cause to feel nauseated*) **it ~ed my stomach** me revolvió el estómago ▶ **to** ~ **sth upside down** dejar algo patas arriba **III.** *n* **1.** (*change in direction*) cambio *m* de dirección; **to make a** ~ **to the right** girar a la derecha; **to take a** ~ **for the worse/better** empeorar/mejorar **2.** (*changing point*) giro *m;* **the** ~ **of the century** el cambio de siglo **3.** (*period of duty*) turno *m;* **to be sb's** ~ **to do sth** tocar a alguien hacer algo; **it's your** ~ te toca; **to do sth in** ~ hacer algo por turnos; **to miss a** ~ estar una vuelta sin jugar; **to speak out of** ~ hablar fuera de lugar **4.** (*rotation, twist*) rotación *f* **5.** (*service*) favor

m, servicio *m;* **to do sb a good** ~ hacer un favor a alguien; **one good** ~ **deserves another** *prov* favor con favor se paga *prov*
◆ **turn against** *vt* volverse en contra de
◆ **turn away I.** *vi* apartarse; **to** ~ **from sb/sth** alejarse de alguien/algo **II.** *vt* **1.** (*refuse entry*) no dejar entrar **2.** (*deny help*) rechazar
◆ **turn back I.** *vi* (*return to starting point*) retroceder **II.** *vt* **1.** (*send back*) hacer regresar **2.** (*bedcover, cuffs, corner of paper*) doblar
◆ **turn down** *vt* **1.** (*reject*) rechazar **2.** (*reduce volume*) bajar **3.** (*fold*) doblar
◆ **turn in I.** *vt* (*hand over*) entregar **II.** *vi inf* (*go to bed*) meterse en la cama
◆ **turn into** *vt* transformar en
◆ **turn off I.** *vt* **1.** ELEC, TECH desconectar; (*light*) apagar; (*motor*) parar; (*gas, faucet*) cerrar **2.** *sl* (*be unappealing*) dar asco **II.** *vi* (*leave path*) desviarse
◆ **turn on** *vt* **1.** ELEC, TECH conectar; (*light*) encender, prender *AmL;* (*gas, faucet*) abrir **2.** (*excite*) excitar; (*attract*) gustar **3.** (*show, demonstrate*) poner en juego; **to** ~ **the charm** desplegar el encanto **4.** (*attack*) atacar
◆ **turn out I.** *vi* **1.** (*end up, work out*) salir **2.** (*be revealed*) **it turned out to be true** resultó ser cierto **II.** *vt* **1.** (*light*) apagar **2.** (*kick out*) echar; **to turn sb out on the street** echar a alguien a la calle **3.** (*empty*) vaciar
◆ **turn over I.** *vi* (*start, operate: engine*) encender **II.** *vt* **1.** (*change the side*) dar la vuelta a **2.** (*criminal*) entregar **3.** (*control*) ceder; (*possession*) traspasar **4.** (*facts*) meditar; **to** ~ **an idea** dar vueltas a una idea **5.** COM, FIN mover, facturar **6.** *inf* (*search*) revolver buscando
◆ **turn around I.** *vi* volverse **II.** *vt* **1.** (*move*) girar **2.** (*change*) cambiar, transformar; (*reform*) reformar
◆ **turn to** *vt* **1.** (*face*) volverse hacia **2.** (*request aid*) **to** ~ **sb (for sth)** recurrir a alguien (para algo)
◆ **turn up I.** *vi* **1.** (*arrive*) llegar **2.** (*become available*) aparecer **3.** (*point upwards*) doblarse hacia arriba **II.** *vt* **1.** (*volume*) subir **2.** (*shorten*) acortar **3.** (*point upwards*) doblar hacia arriba **4.** (*find*) encontrar; (*locate*) localizar
turnabout ['tɜrn·ə·ˌbaʊt] *n*, **turnaround** ['tɜrn·ə·ˌraʊnd] *n* **1.** (*change*) giro *m* en redondo **2.** (*improvement*) mejora *f* **3.** COM procesamiento *m*
turnaround time *n* AVIAT, NAUT tiempo *m* en puerto; (*of project*) tiempo de respuesta
turncoat ['tɜrn·koʊt] *n* chaquetero, -a *m, f*
turner ['tɜr·nər] *n inf* tornero, -a *m, f*
turning ['tɜr·nɪŋ] *n* **1.** (*road*) bocacalle *f* **2.** (*act of changing direction*) giro *m*
turning point *n* momento *m* decisivo; **a** ~ **in one's career** un cambio decisivo en su carrera
turnip ['tɜr·nɪp] *n* nabo *m*
turnkey operation [ˌtɜrn·ki·ˌap·ə·'reɪ·ʃən] *n* operación *f* llave en mano

turnoff ['tɜrn·ɔf] *n* **1.** AUTO salida *f* **2.** *sl* (*something unappealing*) **to be a real ~** quitar las ganas

turnout ['tɜrn·aʊt] *n* **1.** (*attendance*) número *m* de asistentes **2.** POL número de votantes **3.** ECON producción *f* **4.** FASHION atuendo *m*

turnover ['tɜrn· oʊ·vər] *n* **1.** COM, FIN volumen *m* de negocios; (*sales*) facturación *f* **2.** (*in staff*) rotación *f* **3.** CULIN empanada *f*

turnpike ['tɜrn·paɪk] *n* AUTO autopista *f* de peaje

turnstile ['tɜrn·staɪl] *n* SPORTS torniquete *m*

turntable ['tɜrn·teɪ·bəl] *n* **1.** MUS (*record player*) plato *m* giratorio **2.** RAIL plataforma *f* giratoria

turpentine ['tɜr·pən·taɪn] *n* trementina *f*

turpitude ['tɜr·pɪ·tud] *n form* vileza *f*; **moral ~** inmoralidad *f*

turquoise ['tɜr·kwɔɪz] *n* **1.** (*stone*) turquesa *f* **2.** (*color*) azul *m* turquesa

turret ['tɜr·ɪt] *n* **1.** (*tower*) torreón *m* **2.** (*of tank, ship*) torreta *f*

turtle ['tɜr·ṭəl] <-(s)> *n* tortuga *f*

turtledove ['tɜr·ṭəl·dʌv] *n* tórtola *f*

turtleneck ['tɜr·ṭəl·nek] *n* cuello *m* de cisne

tusk [tʌsk] *n* colmillo *m*

tussle ['tʌs·əl] **I.** *vi* pelearse **II.** *n* (*physical struggle*) pelea *f*; (*quarrel*) riña *f*

tussock ['tʌs·ək] *n* mata *f* de hierba

tut [tʌt] *interj* **~ ~!** ¡vaya, vaya!

tutelage ['tu·ṭə·lɪdʒ] *n* tutela *f*

tutor ['tu·ṭər] **I.** *n* SCHOOL, UNIV (*private teacher*) profesor(a) *m(f)* particular; (*at home*) preceptor(a) *m(f)* **II.** *vt* SCHOOL, UNIV **to ~ sb (in sth)** dar clases particulares a alguien (de algo)

tutorial [tu·'bor·i·əl] *n* COMPUT tutorial *m*

tux [tʌks] *abbr of* **tuxedo** *inf* esmoquin *m*

tuxedo [tʌk·'si·doʊ] *n* esmoquin *m*

TV [ˌti·'vi] *n abbr of* **television** TV *f*

twaddle ['twad·əl] *n inf* chorradas *fpl*; **to talk ~** decir chorradas

twang [twæŋ] **I.** *n* **1.** MUS tañido *m* **2.** LING gangueo *m* **II.** *vt* hacer vibrar; (*strings*) puntear; **to ~ someone's nerves** crispar los nervios a alguien **III.** *vi* vibrar

tweak [twik] **I.** *vt* pellizcar **II.** *n* pellizco *m*

tweed [twid] *n* **1.** (*textile*) tweed *m* **2. ~ s** (*suit*) traje *m* de tweed

tweedy ['twi·di] *adj* <-ier, -iest> *fig* de clase alta rural

tweet [twit] **I.** *n* pío *m* **II.** *vi* piar

tweeter ['twi·ṭər] *n* tweeter *m*

tweezers ['twi·zərz] *npl* (**a pair of**) ~ (unas) pinzas

twelfth [twelfθ] **I.** *adj* duodécimo, -a **II.** *n* **1.** (*order*) duodécimo, -a *m, f* **2.** (*date*) doce *m* **3.** (*fraction*) duodécimo *m*; (*part*) duodécima parte *f*; *s.a.* **eighth**

twelve [twelv] **I.** *adj* doce **II.** *n* doce *m*; *s.a.* **eight**

twentieth ['twen·ti·əθ] **I.** *adj* vigésimo, -a **II.** *n* **1.** (*order*) vigésimo, -a *m, f* **2.** (*date*) veinte *m* **3.** (*fraction*) vigésimo *m*; (*part*) vigésima parte

f; *s.a.* **eighth**

twenty ['twen·ti] <-ies> **I.** *adj* veinte **II.** *n* veinte *m*; *s.a.* **eighty**

twerp [twɜrp] *n sl* capullo, -a *m, f*

twice [twaɪs] *adv* dos veces

twiddle ['twɪd·əl] **I.** *vt a.* TECH, ELEC (hacer) girar ▶ **to ~ one's thumbs** estar mano sobre mano **II.** *vi* **to ~ with sth** juguetear con algo **III.** *n* giro *m*

twig [twɪg] *n* ramita *f*

twilight ['twaɪ·laɪt] *n* crepúsculo *m*

twin [twɪn] **I.** *n* mellizo, -a *m, f*; **identical ~s** gemelos **II.** *adj* gemelo, -a **III.** *vt* <-nn-> hermanar **IV.** *vi* <-nn-> hermanarse

twin bed *n* cama *f* gemela

twin brother *n* hermano *m* gemelo

twine [twaɪn] **I.** *vt* **1.** (*wind up*) enrollar **2.** (*encircle*) rodear **II.** *n* cordel *m*

twinge [twɪndʒ] *n* **1.** MED punzada *f* **2.** *fig* arrebato *m*; **a ~ of conscience** un remordimiento de conciencia

twinkle ['twɪŋ·kəl] **I.** *vi* (*diamond, eyes*) brillar; (*star*) centellear **II.** *n* (*of stars*) centelleo *m*; (*of jewels, light, eye*) brillo *m* ▶ **to be just a ~ in sb's father's eye** no haber nacido todavía; **to do sth in a ~** hacer algo en un abrir y cerrar de ojos

twinkling ['twɪŋ·klɪŋ] **I.** *adj* (*diamond, eyes*) brillante; (*star*) centelleante **II.** *n* parpadeo *m*; **in the ~ of an eye** en un abrir y cerrar de ojos

twinning ['twɪn·ɪŋ] *n* hermanamiento *m* de dos ciudades

twin sister *n* hermana *f* gemela

twirl [twɜrl] **I.** *vi* girar; **to ~ around sth** dar vueltas alrededor de algo **II.** *vt* (*whirl*) dar vueltas a; (*moustache*) retorcer **III.** *n* pirueta *f*

twist [twɪst] **I.** *vt* **1.** (*turn*) dar vueltas a, girar **2.** (*wind around*) enroscar; **to ~ sth around sth** enrollar algo alrededor de algo **3.** MED torcer **4.** (*distort: truth*) tergiversar ▶ **to ~ sb's arm** presionar a alguien; **to ~ sb round one's little finger** manejar a alguien a su antojo **II.** *vi* **1.** (*squirm around*) (re)torcerse **2.** (*curve: path, road*) serpentear; **to ~ and turn** dar vueltas **3.** (*dance*) bailar el twist **III.** *n* **1.** (*turn*) vuelta *f*; **to give sth a ~** dar un giro a algo **2.** (*unexpected change*) giro *m* **3.** (*curl: of hair*) mecha *f*; (*of lemon*) rodajita *f*; (*of paper*) cucurucho *m*; (*of coil*) vuelta **4.** (*dance*) twist *m*

◆**twist off** *vt* desenroscar

twisted ['twɪs·tɪd] *adj* **1.** (*cable, metal*) retorcido, -a; (*ankle*) torcido, -a **2.** (*perverted*) pervertido, -a; (*logic, humor*) retorcido, -a

twister ['twɪs·tər] *n* METEO *inf* tornado *m*

twisty ['twɪs·ti] *adj* <-ier, -iest> *inf* (*road*) serpenteante

twit [twɪt] *n sl* capullo, -a *m, f*

twitch [twɪtʃ] **I.** *vi* ANAT, MED temblar; (*face*) contraerse **II.** *vt* **1.** ANAT, MED temblar **2.** (*pull*) tirar de **III.** *n* <-es> **1.** ANAT, MED movimiento *m* espasmódico, tic *m*; **to have a** (**nervous**) **~** tener un tic (nervioso) **2.** (*pull*) tirón *m*

twitter ['twɪt̬·ər] I. *vi* **1.** ZOOL gorjear **2.** (*talk*) parlotear II. *n* gorjeo *m*

two [tu] I. *adj* dos II. *n* dos *m* ▸ **that** makes ~ **of us** *inf* ya somos dos; **to** put ~ **and** ~ **together** *inf* sacar conclusiones; *s.a.* **eight**

two-bit [tu·'bɪt] *adj sl* de tres al cuarto

two-dimensional [,tu·dɪ·'men·ʃə·nəl] *adj* **1.** bidimensional **2.** *fig* superficial

two-door *adj* AUTO de dos puertas

two-edged *adj* de doble filo

two-faced *adj pej* falso, -a, falluto, -a *RíoPl*

twofold ['tu·foʊld] I. *adv* dos veces II. *adj* doble

two-part *adj* de dos partes

two-party system *n* sistema *f* bipartidista

two-phase *adj* ELEC bifásico, -a

two-piece *n* **1.** (*suit*) conjunto *m* de dos piezas **2.** (*bikini*) bikini *m*

two-seater AUTO I. *n* biplaza *m* II. *adj* de dos plazas

twosome ['tu·səm] *n* (*duo*) dúo *m;* (*couple*) pareja *f*

two-stroke AUTO I. *n* motor *m* de dos tiempos II. *adj* de dos tiempos

two-tiered *adj* de dos pisos

two-time *vt sl* poner los cuernos a

two-way ['tu·'weɪ] *adj* de doble sentido; (*tunnel, bridge*) de doble sentido; (*process*) recíproco, -a; (*conversation*) bilateral; (*switch*) de dos direcciones

two-way radio *n* transmisor *m* receptor

TX *abbr of* **Texas** Tejas *m*

tycoon [taɪ·'kun] *n* FIN magnate *mf*

tyke [taɪk] *n* **1.** (*child*) chiquillo, -a *m, f* travieso, -a **2.** (*dog*) perro *m* callejero

tympanum ['tɪm·pə·nəm] *n* tímpano *m*

type [taɪp] I. *n* **1.** (*sort, kind: style, print, language*) tipo *m;* (*of machine*) modelo *m* **2.** (*class: animal, person*) clase *f;* (*skin*) tipo **3.** *inf* (*person*) tipo, -a *m, f;* **he's not her** ~ no es su tipo **4.** TYPO tipo *m* (de letra) II. *vt* **1.** (*write with machine*) escribir a máquina; (*on computer*) escribir con el ordenador **2.** (*categorize*) clasificar III. *vi* escribir a máquina; (*on computer*) escribir con el ordenador

◆**type out** *vt* escribir a máquina; (*on computer*) escribir con el ordenador

◆**type up** *vt* pasar a máquina; (*on computer*) pasar a(l) ordenador

typecast ['taɪp·kæst] <typecast, typecast> *vt* encasillar

typeface ['taɪp·feɪs] *n* tipografía *f*

typescript ['taɪp·skrɪpt] *n* texto *m* mecanografiado

typesetter *n* **1.** (*machine*) máquina *f* de componer **2.** (*person*) tipógrafo, -a *m, f*

typesetting ['taɪp·,set̬·ɪŋ] *n* composición *f* tipográfica

typewrite ['taɪp·raɪt] *irr vt* mecanografiar

typewriter ['taɪp·,raɪ·t̬ər] *n* máquina *f* de escribir

typewriter ribbon *n* cinta *f* para máquina de escribir

typewritten *adj* mecanografiado, -a

typhoid ['taɪ·fɔɪd] *n*, **typhoid fever** *n* fiebre *f* tifoidea

typhoon [taɪ·'fun] *n* METEO tifón *m*

typhus ['taɪ·fəs] *n* tifus *m inv*

typical ['tɪp·ɪ·kəl] *adj* típico, -a; (*symptom*) característico, -a; **to be ~ of sb to do sth** ser típico de alguien (el) hacer algo

typically *adv* típicamente

typify ['tɪp·ɪ·faɪ] <-ie-> *vt* simbolizar

typing ['taɪ·pɪŋ] *n* mecanografía *f*

typist ['taɪ·pɪst] *n* mecanógrafo, -a *m, f*

typographer [taɪ·'pag·rə·fər] *n* tipógrafo, -a *m, f*

typographic [,taɪ·pə·'græf·ɪk] *adj,* **typographical** [,taɪ·pə·'græf·ɪ·kəl] *adj* tipográfico, -a

typographic(al) error *n* errata *f* de imprenta

typography [taɪ·'pag·rə·fi] *n* tipografía *f*

tyrannical [tɪ·'ræn·ɪ·kəl] *adj pej* tiránico, -a

tyrannize ['tɪr·ə·naɪz] *vt* tiranizar

tyranny ['tɪr·ə·ni] *n* tiranía *f*

tyrant ['taɪ·rənt] *n* tirano, -a *m, f*

tzar [zar] *n* zar *m*

tzarist ['zar·ɪst] I. *adj* zarista II. *n* zarista *mf*

tzetze fly ['te·tsi·,flaɪ] *n* mosca *f* tse-tse

U

U, u [ju] *n* U, u *f;* ~ **as in Uniform** U de Uruguay

U[1] *abbr of* **uranium** uranio *m*

U[2] *inf abbr of* **university** universidad *f*

UAE [,ju·eɪ·'i] *npl abbr of* **United Arab Emirates** EAU *mpl*

ubiquitous [ju·'bɪk·wə·t̬əs] *adj* omnipresente, ubicuo, -a

ubiquity [ju·'bɪk·wə·t̬i] *n* ubicuidad *f,* omnipresencia *f*

U-boat ['ju·boʊt] *n* submarino *m* alemán

udder ['ʌd·ər] *n* ubre *f*

UFO [ju·ef·'oʊ] *n abbr of* **unidentified flying object** OVNI *m*

Uganda [ju·'gæn·də] *n* Uganda *f*

Ugandan I. *adj* ugandés, -esa II. *n* ugandés, -esa *m, f*

ugh [ʒh] *interj inf* uf

ugliness ['ʌg·lɪ·nɪs] *n* **1.** (*unattractiveness*) fealdad *f* **2.** (*nastiness*) repugnancia *f*

ugly ['ʌg·li] <-ier, iest> *adj* **1.** (*not attractive*) feo, -a, macaco, -a *Arg, Méx, Cuba, Chile;* **to be ~ as sin** ser más feo que Picio **2.** (*angry: mood*) peligroso, -a; (*look*) repugnante **3.** (*violent*) violento, -a; **to turn ~** ponerse violento **4.** (*harsh*) desagradable; (*story*) fastidioso, -a; (*truth*) terrible; (*weather*) horroroso, -a; (*clouds*) amenazante; ~ **rumors** calumnias *fpl*

ugly duckling *n* patito *m* feo
UHF [ˌjuˈeɪtʃˈef] *n abbr of* **ultrahigh frequency** UHF *f*
UK [ˌjuˈkeɪ] *n abbr of* **United Kingdom** RU *m*
ukelele [ˌjuˈkəˈleɪˈli] *n s.* **ukulele**
Ukraine [juˈkreɪn] *n* Ucrania *f*
Ukrainian I. *adj* ucraniano, -a **II.** *n* **1.** (*person*) ucraniano, -a *m, f* **2.** LING ucraniano *m*
ukulele [ˌjuˈkəˈleɪˈli] *n* ukelele *m*
ulcer [ˈʌlˈsər] *n* **1.** MED úlcera *f*, chácara *f Col* **2.** *fig* llaga *f*
ulcerate [ˈʌlˈsəˈreɪt] *vi* ulcerarse
ulcerous [ˈʌlˈsərˈəs] *adj* ulceroso, -a
ulna [ˈʌlˈnə] <ulnae *o s*> *n* ANAT cúbito *m*
ulterior [ʌlˈtɪrˈiˈər] *adj* **1.** (*secret*) secreto, -a; (*motive*) oculto, -a **2.** (*beyond scope*) ulterior
ultimate [ˈʌlˈtəˈmɪt] **I.** *adj* **1.** (*best*) máximo, -a; (*experience, feeling*) extremo, -a **2.** (*highest degree of*) máximo, -a; (*accolade, praise*) supremo, -a; (*honor, sacrifice*) altísimo, -a **3.** (*maximum: authority*) máximo, -a **4.** (*final*) final; (*cost, consequences, effect*) definitivo, -a **5.** (*fundamental*) fundamental; (*cause, goal, responsibility*) primordial **II.** *n* (*the best*) **the ~** lo último; (*bad taste, vulgarity*) el colmo; **the ~ in fashion** el último grito en moda; **the ~ in stupidity** el colmo de la estupidez
ultimately [ˈʌlˈtəˈmɪtˈli] *adv* **1.** (*in the end*) finalmente **2.** (*fundamentally*) fundamentalmente
ultimatum [ˌʌlˈtəˈmeɪˈt̮əm] <ultimata *o* -tums> *n* ultimátum *m*
ultimo [ˈʌlˈtɪˈmoʊ] *adv* ECON, COM del mes pasado
ultrahigh frequency [ˌʌlˈtrəˌhaɪˈfriˈkwənˈsi] *n* frecuencia *f* ultraalta
ultramarine [ˌʌlˈtrəˈməˈrin] **I.** *adj* ultramarino, -a **II.** *n* azul *m* de ultramar
ultramodern [ˌʌlˈtrəˈmadˈərn] *adj* ultramoderno, -a
ultrashort wave [ˌʌlˈtrəˈʃɔrtˈweɪv] *n* onda *f* ultracorta
ultrasonic [ˌʌlˈtrəˈsanˈɪk] *adj* ultrasónico, -a
ultrasound [ˈʌlˈtrəˈsaʊnd] *n* ultrasonido *m*
ultraviolet [ˌʌlˈtrəˈvaɪˈəˈlɪt] *adj* ultravioleta
Ulysses [juˈlɪsˈiz] *n* Ulises *m*
umber [ˈʌmˈbər] **I.** *adj* de color ocre oscuro **II.** *n* ocre *m* oscuro
umbilical [ʌmˈbɪlˈɪˈkəl] *adj* umbilical
umbilical cord *n* cordón *m* umbilical
umbrage [ˈʌmˈbrɪdʒ] *n form* resentimiento *m;* **to take ~ at sth** ofenderse por algo
umbrella [ʌmˈbrelˈə] *n* **1.** (*rain*) paraguas *m inv;* (*sun*) sombrilla *f;* **beach ~** sombrilla *f,* parasol *m* **2.** (*protection*) cobertura *f;* MIL cortina *f* de fuego antiaéreo; **to do sth under the ~ of sth** hacer algo bajo el amparo de algo
umbrella organization *n* POL, ADMIN organización *f* paraguas, organización *f* sombrilla
umpire [ˈʌmˈpaɪr] SPORTS **I.** *n* árbitro *mf* **II.** *vt* arbitrar **III.** *vi* arbitrar
umpteen [ˈʌmpˈtin] *adj inf* incontable; **~ reasons** múltiples razones *fpl;* **to do sth ~ times**

hacer algo innumerables veces
umpteenth [ˈʌmpˈtinθ] *adj* enésimo, -a *elev*
UN [ˌjuˈen] *n abbr of* **United Nations** ONU *f*
unabashed [ˌʌnˈəˈbæʃt] *adj* desenvuelto, -a; (*behavior*) atrevido, -a
unabated [ˌʌnˈəˈbeɪˈt̮ɪd] *adj* continuado, -a; (*winds, storm*) persistente; (*fighting, rioting, energy*) constante; (*interest, enthusiasm*) vivo, -a; (*curiosity*) incesante
unable [ʌnˈeɪˈbəl] *adj* incapaz
unabridged [ˌʌnˈəˈbrɪdʒd] *adj* **1.** LIT, PUBL no abreviado, -a **2.** (*whole*) íntegro, -a
unacceptable [ˌʌnˈəkˈsepˈtəˈbəl] *adj* **1.** (*not good enough*) inaceptable; (*conditions*) inadmisible **2.** (*intolerable*) intolerable
unaccompanied [ˌʌnˈəˈkʌmˈpəˈnid] *adj* **1.** (*without companion*) solo, -a, sin compañía **2.** MUS sin acompañamiento
unaccountable [ˌʌnˈəˈkaʊnˈtəˈbəl] *adj* **1.** (*not responsible*) que no puede ser considerado, -a responsable **2.** (*inexplicable*) inexplicable
unaccounted-for [ˌʌnˈəˈkaʊnˈtɪdˌfɔr] *adj* **1.** (*unexplained*) inexplicado, -a **2.** (*not included in count*) sin contar
unaccustomed [ˌʌnˈəˈkʌsˈtəmd] *adj* **1.** (*seldom seen*) raro, -a **2.** (*something new*) inusual; **to be ~ to doing sth** no tener la costumbre de hacer algo
unacknowledged [ˌʌnˈəkˈnalˈɪdʒd] *adj* ignorado, -a; (*author, scientist*) no reconocido, -a; **to remain ~** permanecer en el anonimato
unaddressed [ˌʌnˈəˈdrest] *adj* sin señas
unadorned [ˌʌnˈəˈdɔrnd] *adj* **1.** (*plain*) sin adorno(s); (*story*) simple; (*fashion, style*) sencillo, -a **2.** (*pure*) puro, -a; **the ~ truth** la pura verdad
unadulterated [ˌʌnˈəˈdʌlˈtəˈreɪˈt̮ɪd] *adj* **1.** (*not changed*) sin mezcla **2.** (*pure: substance*) puro, -a; (*alcohol, wine*) no adulterado, -a; **~ nonsense** completo disparate *m*
unadventurous [ˌʌnˈədˈvenˈtʃərˈəs] *adj* poco atrevido, -a; (*style*) poco llamativo, -a
unaffected [ˌʌnˈəˈfekˈtɪd] *adj* **1.** (*not changed*) inalterado, -a **2.** (*not influenced*) espontáneo, -a **3.** (*down to earth*) sencillo, -a; (*manner, speech*) natural
unafraid [ˌʌnˈəˈfreɪd] *adj* sin temor; **to be ~ of sb/sth** no tener miedo de alguien/algo
unaided [ʌnˈeɪˈdɪd] *adj* sin ayuda; **to do sth ~** hacer algo por sí solo
unalloyed [ˌʌnˈəˈlɔɪd] *adj liter* puro, -a; (*happiness, pleasure*) absoluto, -a
unaltered [ʌnˈɔlˈtərd] *adj* inalterado, -a; **to leave sth ~** dejar algo tal como estaba
unambiguous [ˌʌnˈæmˈbɪgˈjuˈəs] *adj* inequívoco, -a; (*statement*) incuestionable; (*language, terms*) unívoco, -a
un-American [ˌʌnˈəˈmerˈɪˈkən] *adj* antiamericano, -a (*término empleado por los propios estadounidenses*)
unanimity [ˌjuˈnəˈnɪmˈəˈt̮i] *n form* unanimidad *f*

U

unanimous [juˈnæn·ə·məs] *adj* unánime; (*support*) total

unannounced [ˌʌn·əˈnaʊnst] I. *adj* 1.(*without warning*) sin aviso; (*arrival, appearance*) imprevisto, -a; (*visitor, guest*) inesperado, -a 2.(*not made known*) fortuito, -a; (*act*) repentino, -a II. *adv* de repente; (*arrive, visit*) sin aviso

unanswerable [ʌnˈæn·sər·ə·bəl] *adj* 1.(*without an answer*) que no se puede responder 2. *form* (*irrefutable*) irrefutable, incontestable; (*proof*) irrebatible

unanswered [ʌnˈæn·sərd] *adj* sin contestar

unappealing [ˌʌn·əˈpi·lɪŋ] *adj* poco atrayente

unappetizing [ʌnˈæp·əˌtaɪ·zɪŋ] *adj* poco apetitoso, -a

unapproachable [ʌn·əˈproʊ·tʃə·bəl] *adj* 1.(*person*) intratable 2.(*building*) inaccesible

unarmed [ʌnˈarmd] *adj* desarmado, -a

unashamed [ˌʌn·əˈʃeɪmd] *adj* desvergonzado, -a; (*greed, hypocrisy, selfishness*) descarado, -a; **to be ~ of sth** (*guilt*) no tener remordimientos por algo; (*shame*) no avergonzarse por algo

unasked [ˌʌnˈæskt] *adj* 1.(*not questioned*) no solicitado, -a 2.(*spontaneous*) espontáneo, -a

unassignable [ʌn·əˈsaɪ·nə·bəl] *adj* LAW intrasferible

unassuming [ˌʌn·əˈsu·mɪŋ] *adj* modesto, -a

unattached [ˌʌn·əˈtætʃt] *adj* 1.(*not connected*) suelto, -a; (*part*) separable 2.(*independent*) libre 3.(*unmarried*) soltero, -a

unattainable [ˌʌn·əˈteɪ·nə·bəl] *adj* inasequible; (*goal, ideal*) inalcanzable

unattended [ˌʌn·əˈten·dɪd] *adj* 1.(*alone*) sin compañía; **to leave the children ~** dejar a los niños sin vigilancia 2.(*unmanned*) desatendido, -a 3.(*not taken care of*) descuidado, -a

unattractive [ˌʌn·əˈtræk·tɪv] *adj* 1.(*not good-looking*) poco atractivo, -a; (*place, town*) poco atractivo, -a 2.(*unpleasant*) desagradable; (*personality, character*) antipático, -a

unauthorized [ʌnˈɔ·θə·raɪzd] *adj* no autorizado, -a

unavailable [ˌʌn·əˈveɪ·lə·bəl] *adj* inasequible; (*article*) agotado, -a; (*man, woman*) ocupado, -a

unavailing [ˌʌn·əˈveɪ·lɪŋ] *adj form* (*denial*) inútil; (*effort, attempt*) vano, -a

unavoidable [ˌʌn·əˈvɔɪ·də·bəl] *adj* ineludible; (*accident, fate*) inevitable

unaware [ˌʌn·əˈwer] *adj* **to be ~ of sth** ignorar algo

unawares [ˌʌn·əˈwerz] *adv* **to catch sb ~** coger a alguien desprevenido

unbalanced [ʌnˈbæl·ənst] *adj* 1.(*uneven*) desnivelado, -a; (*account*) desequilibrado, -a 2.(*mental state*) trastornado, -a

unbearable [ˌʌnˈber·ə·bəl] *adj* 1.(*painful*) insoportable, inaguantable 2.(*person*) insufrible

unbeatable [ʌnˈbi·t̬ə·bəl] *adj* 1.(*record, team*) imbatible; (*army*) invencible 2.(*value, quality*) inmejorable; (*pizza, meal*) insuperable

unbeaten [ʌnˈbi·t̬ən] *adj* (*team, player*) invicto, -a; (*record*) insuperado, -a

unbecoming [ˌʌn·bɪˈkʌm·ɪŋ] *adj* 1.(*dress, suit*) que sienta mal 2.(*attitude, manner*) impropio, -a

unbeknownst [ˌʌn·bɪˈnoʊnst] *adv form* **~ to her** sin saberlo ella

unbelievable [ˌʌn·bɪˈli·və·bəl] *adj* increíble

unbeliever [ˌʌn·bɪˈli·vər] *n* REL no creyente *mf*

unbelieving [ˌʌn·bɪˈli·vɪŋ] *adj* incrédulo, -a

unbend [ʌnˈbend] I. *vt* enderezar; (*wire*) desdoblar II. *vi irr* 1.(*straighten out*) enderezarse 2.(*relax*) relajarse

unbending *adj* firme; (*will, determination*) inquebrantable; (*attitude*) rígido, -a

unbiased [ʌnˈbaɪ·əst] *adj* imparcial; (*judge*) justo, -a; (*opinion, report, advice*) objetivo, -a

unbidden [ʌnˈbɪd·ən] *liter* I. *adv* espontáneamente, sin ser llamado, -a II. *adj* espontáneo, -a

unbind [ʌnˈbaɪnd] *irr vt* desatar

unbleached [ʌnˈblitʃt] *adj* sin blanquear; **~ flour** harina *f* integral

unblinking [ʌnˈblɪŋ·kɪŋ] *adj* 1.(*without blinking: gaze, look*) imperturbable 2.(*without doubt: devotion, help*) resuelto, -a

unblushing [ʌnˈblʌʃ·ɪŋ] *adj* desvergonzado, -a

unbolt [ʌnˈboʊlt] *vt* desatrancar

unborn [ʌnˈbɔrn] *adj* 1.(*not yet born: baby*) que aún no nacido, -a; (*fetus*) nonato, -a 2.*liter* (*future*) venidero, -a, por venir

unbosom [ʌnˈbʊz·əm] *vt form* 1.(*reveal*) revelar 2.(*confide in*) **to ~ oneself to sb** abrirse a alguien

unbounded [ʌnˈbaʊn·dɪd] *adj* (*optimism, enthusiasm, passion*) ilimitado, -a; (*hope*) infinito, -a; (*love, desire, joy*) inmenso, -a; (*ambition*) desmedido, -a

unbowed [ʌnˈbaʊd] *adj* 1.(*erect*) erguido, -a 2.(*not submitting*) orgulloso, -a

unbreakable [ʌnˈbreɪ·kə·bəl] *adj* (*material*) irrompible, indestructible; (*rule, promise, faith*) inquebrantable; (*record*) imbatible

unbridled [ʌnˈbraɪ·dəld] *adj* desenfrenado, -a

unbroken [ʌnˈbroʊ·kən] *adj* 1.(*not broken*) no roto, -a; **an ~ promise** una promesa no rota 2.(*uncrushed*) intacto, -a 3.(*continuous, without a break*) ininterrumpido, -a 4.(*unsurpassed: record*) no superado, -a 5.(*not tamed*) no domesticado, -a; **an ~ horse** un caballo salvaje

unbuckle [ʌnˈbʌk·əl] *vt* deshebillar; **to ~ a seatbelt** desabrochar el cinturón de seguridad

unburden [ʌnˈbɜr·dən] *vt* 1.(*unload*) aliviar 2.(*relieve oneself*) **to ~ oneself (of sth)** desahogarse (de algo); **to ~ oneself (to sb)** deshogarse (con alguien); **to ~ one's sorrows** contar las penas

unbusinesslike [ʌnˈbɪz·nɪsˌlaɪk] *adj* poco profesional

unbutton [ʌnˈbʌt·ən] I. *vt* desabrochar II. *vi* desabrocharse

uncalled-for [ʌn·'kɔld·fɔr] *adj* gratuito, -a, impropio, -a; **an ~ remark** un comentario fuera de lugar; **to be ~ to do sth** ser gratuito el hacer algo

uncanny [ʌn·'kæn·i] *adj* <-ier, -iest> **1.** (*mysterious*) misterioso, -a **2.** (*remarkable*) extraordinario, -a; **to be ~ how...** ser sorprendente cómo...; **an ~ knack** una destreza extraordinaria

uncared-for [ʌn·'kerd·fɔr] *adj* descuidado, -a

unceasing [ʌn·'si·sɪŋ] *adj form* incesante; **~ support** apoyo *m* incondicional

unceremonious [ʌn·ˌser·ɪ·'mou·ni·əs] *adj* **1.** (*abrupt*) brusco, -a **2.** (*informal*) informal

unceremoniously *adv* **1.** (*abruptly*) bruscamente **2.** (*informally*) de modo informal

uncertain [ʌn·'sɜr·tən] *adj* **1.** (*unsure*) dudoso, -a; **to be ~ of sth** no estar seguro de algo; **to be ~ whether/when...** no estar seguro de si/cuándo...; **in no ~ terms** claramente **2.** (*unpredictable, chancy*) incierto, -a; **an ~ future** un futuro incierto **3.** (*volatile*) volátil; **an ~ temper** un temperamento volátil

uncertainty [ʌn·'sɜr·tən·ti] <-ies> *n* **1.** (*unpredictability*) incertidumbre *f* **2.** (*unsettled state*) incertidumbre *f*; **~ about sth/sb** incertidumbre sobre algo/alguien **3.** (*hesitancy*) indecisión *f*

unchallenged [ʌn·'tʃæl·ɪndʒd] *adj* **1.** (*not questioned or doubted*) incontestado, -a **2.** (*not opposed*) no protestado, -a; **to go ~** pasar sin protesta

unchanged [ʌn·'tʃeɪndʒd] *adj* **1.** (*unaltered*) inalterado, -a **2.** (*not replaced*) no sustituido, -a

uncharacteristic [ʌn·ˌkær·ɪk·tə·'rɪs·tɪk] *adj* poco característico, -a; **to be ~ of sb/sth** no ser típico de alguien/algo

uncharitable [ʌn·'tʃær·ɪ·tə·bəl] *adj* **1.** (*severe*) duro, -a; **to be ~ in sth** ser severo en algo; **to be ~ (of sb) to do sth** ser duro (por parte de alguien) el hacer algo **2.** (*ungenerous*) poco caritativo, -a

unchecked [ʌn·'tʃekt] *adj* **1.** (*unrestrained*) desenfrenado, -a; **~ passion/violence** pasión *f*/violencia *f* desenfrenada **2.** (*not examined or verified*) sin examinar **3.** (*not checked*) sin comprobar

unchristian [ʌn·'krɪs·tʃən] *adj* indigno, -a de un cristiano

uncivil [ʌn·'sɪv·əl] *adj form* grosero, -a; **to be ~ to sb** ser grosero con alguien

unclad [ʌn·'klæd] *adj form* desnudo, -a

unclaimed [ʌn·'kleɪmd] *adj* **1.** (*not claimed*) sin reclamar **2.** (*not reclaimed*) no reclamado, -a

unclassified [ʌn·'klæs·ɪ·faɪd] *adj* ADMIN sin clasificar

uncle ['ʌŋ·kəl] *n* tío *m* ▶ **to say ~** *childspeak* rendirse

unclean [ʌn·'klin] *adj* **1.** (*unhygienic*) sucio, -a **2.** *form* (*taboo*) tabú **3.** (*soiled, impure*) impuro, -a

unclear [ʌn·'klɪr] *adj* **1.** (*not certain*) nada

claro, -a; **to be ~ about sth** no estar seguro de algo **2.** (*vague*) vago, -a; **an ~ statement** una afirmación vaga

uncluttered [ˌʌn·'klʌt·ərd] *adj* **1.** (*not messily crowded*) no muy concurrido, -a **2.** (*simple*) simple; **an ~ mind** una mente sencilla

uncollected [ˌʌn·kə·'lek·tɪd] *adj* **1.** (*not reclaimed*) no reclamado, -a **2.** (*missing in collected works*) no incluido, -a

uncolored [ʌn·'kʌl·ərd] *adj* **1.** (*having no color*) incoloro, -a **2.** (*impartial*) imparcial

uncomfortable [ʌn·'kʌm·fər·tə·bəl] *adj* **1.** (*situation*) incómodo, -a; **an ~ silence** un silencio incómodo **2.** (*person ill at ease*) incómodo, -a; **it makes sb ~ to do sth** le hace sentir incómodo a alguien el hacer algo

uncommitted [ˌʌn·kə·'mɪt·ɪd] *adj* **1.** (*nonaligned*) no alineado, -a **2.** (*not committed*) no comprometido, -a; **to be ~ to sth** no estar comprometido con algo

uncommon [ʌn·'kam·ən] *adj* **1.** (*rare*) poco común, extraño, -a; **to be not ~ for sb/sth** no ser raro para alguien/algo **2.** *form* (*exceptional*) extraordinario, -a; **with ~ interest** con un especial interés

uncommonly *adv* **1.** (*unusually*) raramente **2.** *form* (*extremely*) excepcionalmente

uncommunicative [ˌʌn·kə·'mju·nɪ·kə·tɪv] *adj* poco comunicativo, -a; **to be ~ about sth/sb** ser reservado respecto a algo/alguien

uncompromising [ʌn·'kam·prə·maɪ·zɪŋ] *adj* intransigente; **to take an ~ stand** adoptar una postura intransigente

unconcerned [ˌʌn·kən·'sɜrnd] *adj* **1.** (*not worried*) despreocupado, -a; **to be ~ about sth/sb** no preocuparse por algo/alguien **2.** (*indifferent*) indiferente; **to be ~ with sth/sb** ser indiferente con respecto a algo/alguien

unconditional [ˌʌn·kən·'dɪʃ·ə·nəl] *adj* incondicional; **~ love** amor *m* incondicional

unconfirmed [ˌʌn·kən·'fɜrmd] *adj* no confirmado, -a

uncongenial [ˌʌn·kən·'dʒi·ni·əl] *adj* **1.** (*unfriendly*) antipático, -a **2.** (*not pleasant*) desfavorable; **~ conditions** condiciones *fpl* adversas

unconnected [ˌʌn·kə·'nek·tɪd] *adj* desconectado, -a; **to be ~ to sth** estar desconectado de algo

unconscionable [ʌn·'kan·tʃə·nə·bəl] *adj form* desmedido, -a

unconscious [ʌn·'kan·tʃəs] **I.** *adj* **1.** (*not conscious*) inconsciente; **to knock sb ~** dejar a alguien inconsciente; **~ state** estado *m* de inconsciencia **2.** PSYCH (*subconscious*) subconsciente **3.** (*unaware*) no intencional; **to be ~ of sth** *form* no ser consciente de algo **II.** *n* PSYCH **the ~** el inconsciente

unconsciously *adv* inconscientemente

unconsciousness *n* **1.** (*loss of consciousness*) pérdida *f* de conocimiento **2.** *form* (*unawareness*) inconsciencia *f*

unconsidered [ˌʌn·kən·'sɪd·ərd] *adj form* irre-

flexivo, -a
unconstitutional [ˌʌn·kan·stə·'tu·ʃə·nəl] *adj* inconstitucional
unconsummated [ʌn·'kan·sə·meɪ·t̬ɪd] *adj* no consumado, -a
uncontested [ˌʌn·kən·'tes·t̬ɪd] *adj* 1.(*unquestioned*) incontestable 2.LAW (*not disputed*) sin oposición; **an ~ divorce** un divorcio sin oposición de ninguna de las partes
uncontrollable [ˌʌn·kən·'troʊ·lə·bəl] *adj* 1.(*irresistible*) irrefrenable 2.(*frenzied*) incontrolable; **an ~ child** un niño ingobernable
uncontrolled [ˌʌn·kən·'troʊld] *adj* descontrolado, -a
uncontroversial [ˌʌn·kan·trə·'vɜr·ʃəl] *adj* no controvertido, -a
unconvinced [ˌʌn·kən·'vɪnst] *adj* **to be ~ of sth** no estar convencido de algo
unconvincing [ˌʌn·kən·'vɪn·sɪŋ] *adj* 1.(*not persuasive*) nada convincente; **rather ~** poco convincente 2.(*not credible*) nada creíble
uncooked [ʌn·'kʊkt] *adj* crudo, -a
uncooperative [ˌʌn·koʊ·'ap·ər·ə·t̬ɪv] *adj* poco cooperativo, -a
uncork [ʌn·'kɔrk] *vt* 1.(*extract cork from bottle*) descorchar 2.*inf* (*let out sth repressed*) **to ~ one's feelings** dejar aflorar los sentimientos; **to ~ a surprise** destapar una sorpresa
uncorroborated [ˌʌn·kə·'rab·ə·reɪ·t̬ɪd] *adj* no corroborado, -a
uncountable noun [ʌn·'kaʊn·tə·bəl·naʊn] *n* LING substantivo *m* incontable
uncouple [ʌn·'kʌp·əl] *vt* **to ~ sth (from sth)** 1.TECH desacoplar algo (de algo) 2.(*separate*) separar algo (de algo)
uncouth [ʌn·'kuθ] *adj* basto, -a
uncover [ʌn·'kʌv·ər] *vt* destapar, desvelar; **to ~ a wound** *a. fig* dejar descubierta una herida; **to ~ a secret/the truth** desvelar un secreto/la verdad
uncritical [ʌn·'krɪt̬·ɪ·kəl] *adj* falto, -a de sentido crítico; **to be ~ of sth/sb** no criticar algo/a alguien
uncrowned [ʌn·'kraʊnd] *adj* sin corona
uncut [ʌn·'kʌt] *adj* 1.(*not cut*) sin cortar; **an ~ diamond** un diamante en bruto 2.(*not shortened*) sin cortes
undated [ʌn·'deɪ·t̬ɪd] *adj* sin fecha
undaunted [ʌn·'dɔn·tɪd] *adj form* impertérrito, -a; **to be ~ by sth** quedarse impávido ante algo
undeceive [ˌʌn·dɪ·'siv] *vt liter* **to ~ sb (of sth)** desengañar a alguien (de algo)
undecided [ˌʌn·dɪ·'saɪ·dɪd] *adj* 1.(*unresolved*) indeciso, -a; **to be ~ about sth** estar indeciso ante algo; **to be ~ as to what to do** no saber qué hacer 2.(*not settled*) no decidido, -a; **an ~ vote** un voto indeciso
undeclared [ˌʌn·dɪ·'klerd] *adj* 1.FIN (*kept secret*) no declarado, -a; **~ income** ingresos *mpl* no declarados; **~ goods** bienes *mpl* no

declarados 2.(*not official*) no oficial; **an ~ war** *a. fig* una guerra no declarada
undefined [ˌʌn·dɪ·'faɪnd] *adj* 1.(*not defined*) indefinido, -a 2.(*lacking clarity*) no claro, -a
undeliverable [ˌʌn·dɪ·'lɪv·rə·bəl] *adj* que no puede ser entregado, -a
undelivered [ˌʌn·dɪ·'lɪv·ərd] *adj* sin entregar
undemanding [ˌʌn·dɪ·'man·dɪŋ] *adj* 1.(*requiring little effort*) que exige poco esfuerzo 2.(*easy-going*) **to be rather ~** ser poco exigente
undemocratic [ˌʌn·dem·ə·'kræt̬·ɪk] *adj* antidemocrático, -a
undemonstrative [ˌʌn·dɪ·'man·strə·t̬ɪv] *adj form* reservado, -a
undeniable [ˌʌn·dɪ·'naɪ·ə·bəl] *adj* innegable; **~ evidence** prueba *f* irrefutable
undeniably *adv* indudablemente
under ['ʌn·dər] I. *prep* 1.(*below*) debajo de; **~ the bed** debajo de la cama; **~ there** ahí debajo 2.(*supporting*) bajo; **to break ~ the weight** romperse bajo el peso 3.(*less than*) **to cost ~ $10** costar menos de 10$; **those ~ the age of 30** aquellos con menos de 30 años de edad 4.(*governed by*) **~ Napoleon** bajo Napoleón; **to be ~ sb's influence** estar bajo la influencia de alguien 5.(*in state of*) **~ the circumstances** dadas las circumstancias; **~ repair** en reparación 6.(*in category of*) **to classify the books ~ fiction** clasificar los libros por ficción 7.LAW **~ the treaty** conforme al tratado II. *adv* 1.(*fewer*) menos 2.(*below*) **to crawl/go ~** meterse debajo de 3.*inf* (*unconscious*) **to go ~** quedar inconsciente
underachiever [ˌʌn·dər·ə·'tʃivər] *n* persona que rinde por debajo de lo esperado
underage [ˌʌn·dər·'eɪdʒ] *adj* menor de edad
underbid [ˌʌn·dər·'bɪd] *irr* I. *vi* declarar menos de lo que uno tiene II. *vt* **to ~ sb/sth** ofrecer un precio más bajo que alguien/algo
undercapitalized [ˌʌn·dər·'kæp·ɪ·t̬ə·laɪzd] *adj* subcapitalizado, -a; **to be ~** estar descapitalizado
undercarriage ['ʌn·dər·ˌkær·ɪdʒ] *n* AVIAT tren *m* de aterrizaje
undercharge [ˌʌn·dər·'tʃardʒ] I. *vt* **to ~ sb** cobrar de menos a alguien II. *vi* cobrar menos; **to ~ for sth** cobrar por algo menos de lo que es
underclothes ['ʌn·dər·kloʊz] *npl*, **underclothing** ['ʌn·dər·ˌkloʊ·ðɪŋ] *n* ropa *f* interior
undercoat ['ʌn·dər·koʊt] *n* primera capa *f* de pintura
undercover [ˌʌn·dər·'kʌv·ər] I. *adj* secreto, -a; **~ agent** agente *mf* secreto II. *adv* clandestinamente
undercurrent ['ʌn·dər·kɜr·ənt] *n* 1.(*undertow*) corriente *f* submarina 2.(*underlying influence*) trasfondo *m*
undercut [ˌʌn·dər·'kʌt] *irr vt* 1.(*charge less than competitors*) vender más barato 2.(*undermine*) socavar
underdeveloped [ˌʌn·dər·dɪ·'vel·əpt] *adj* 1.(*below its economic potential*) subdesarro-

llado, -a; **an ~ country** un país *m* subdesarrollado; **an ~ resource** un recurso infradesarrollado **2.** PHOT insuficientemente revelado, -a **3.** (*insufficiently mature*) inmaduro, -a

underdog ['ʌn·dər·dɔg] *n* desvalido, -a *m, f;* **to side with the ~** estar del lado de los perdedores

underdone [ˌʌn·dər·'dʌn] *adj* (*cooked less than necessary*) poco hecho, -a

underemployed [ˌʌn·dər·ɪm·'plɔɪd] *adj* **1.** (*having too little work*) subempleado, -a **2.** ECON (*insufficiently used*) **to be ~** ser poco utilizado, -a

underequipped [ˌʌn·dər·ɪ·'kwɪpt] *adj* mal equipado, -a; **an ~ expedition** una expedición con un equipamiento insuficiente

underestimate [ˌʌn·dər·'es·tə·meɪt] **I.** *vt* **to ~ sth/sb** subestimar algo/a alguien **II.** *n* infravaloración *f*

underexpose [ˌʌn·dər·ɪk·'spoʊz] *vt* PHOT **to ~ film/a photograph** subexponer una película/ fotografía

underexposure [ˌʌn·dər·ɪk·'spoʊ·ʒər] *n* PHOT subexposición *f*

underfed [ˌʌn·dər·'fed] *n* desnutrido, -a *m, f*

underfoot [ˌʌn·dər·'fʊt] *adv* (*below one's feet*) debajo de los pies; **to trample sb/sth ~** *a. fig* pisar a alguien/algo

underfund [ˌʌn·dər·'fʌnd] *vt* **to ~ sth** infradotar algo

underfunding [ˌʌn·dər·'fʌn·dɪŋ] *n* infradotación *f*

undergarment ['ʌn·dər·gar·mənt] *n form* prenda *f* de ropa interior

undergo [ˌʌn·dər·'goʊ] *irr vt* **to ~ sth** experimentar algo; **to ~ a change** sufrir un cambio; **to ~ surgery** ser operado

undergraduate [ˌʌn·dər·'grædʒ·u·ət] *n* estudiante *mf* no licenciado, -a; **~ program** programa *m* para no licenciados

underground ['ʌn·dər·graʊnd] **I.** *adj* **1.** (*below earth surface*) subterráneo, -a **2.** (*clandestinely anti-government*) clandestino, -a; **~ movement** movimiento *m* clandestino **II.** *adv* **1.** (*below earth surface*) bajo tierra **2.** **to go ~** pasar a la clandestinidad; **to drive sb ~** meter a alguien en la clandestinidad **III.** *n* **the ~** POL la resistencia; (*lifestyle*) el underground

undergrowth ['ʌn·dər·groʊθ] *n* maleza *f;* **dense ~** maleza espesa

underhand [ˌʌn·dər·'hænd], **underhanded** [ˌʌn·dər·'hæn·dɪd] **I.** *adj* **1.** (*secret*) subrepticio, -a **2.** (*with arm below shoulder*) por debajo del hombro **II.** *adv* **1.** (*secretly*) subrepticiamente **2.** (*below shoulder*) por debajo del hombro

underinsure [ˌʌn·dər·ɪn·'ʃʊr] *vt* **to ~ sth** asegurar algo por debajo del valor real

underlay [ˌʌn·dər·'leɪ] *vt pt of* **underlie**

underlie [ˌʌn·dər·'laɪ] *irr vt* **to ~ sth** subyacer a algo

underline [ˌʌn·dər·'laɪn] *vt* **1.** (*draw a line*

beneath) subrayar; **to ~ sth in red** subrayar algo en rojo **2.** (*emphasize*) enfatizar; **to ~ that...** subrayar que...

underling ['ʌn·dər·lɪŋ] *n pej* subordinado, -a

underlying [ˌʌn·dər·'laɪ·ɪŋ] *adj* subyacente; **the ~ reason for sth** la razón que subyace a algo

undermanned [ˌʌn·dər·'mænd] *adj* sin plantilla suficiente

undermanning [ˌʌn·dər·'mæn·ɪŋ] *n* escasez *f* de personal

undermine [ˌʌn·dər·'maɪn] *vt* **1.** (*damage, sap, weaken*) minar; **to ~ hopes** desalentar; **to ~ a currency** debilitar una divisa; **to ~ sb's confidence** hacer perder la confianza de alguien; **to ~ sb's health** perjudicar a la salud de alguien **2.** (*tunnel under*) socavar; **to ~ a river bank** socavar la orilla de un río

undermost ['ʌn·dər·moʊst] *adj* **the ~...** el más bajo...

underneath [ˌʌn·dər·'niθ] **I.** *prep* debajo de **II.** *adv* por debajo **III.** *n* **the ~** la superficie inferior **IV.** *adj* inferior

undernourished [ˌʌn·dər·'nɜr·ɪʃt] *adj* desnutrido, -a

underpaid [ˌʌn·dər·'peɪd] *adj* mal pagado, -a

underpants ['ʌn·dər·pænts] *npl* calzoncillos *mpl*

underpass ['ʌn·dər·pæs] <-es> *n* paso *m* subterráneo

underpay [ˌʌn·dər·'peɪ] *irr vt* pagar un sueldo insuficiente

underperform [ˌʌn·dər·pər·'fɔrm] *vi* rendir por debajo de lo suficiente

underplay [ˌʌn·dər·'pleɪ] **I.** *vt* **1.** (*play down*) subestimar; **to ~ the importance/seriousness of sth** subestimar la importancia/gravedad de algo **2.** (*act with restraint*) actuar con contención **II.** *vi* no actuar demasiado en un papel

underpopulated [ˌʌn·dər·'pap·jə·leɪ·tɪd] *adj* poco poblado, -a

underprivileged [ˌʌn·dər·'prɪv·ə·lɪdʒd] **I.** *adj* sin privilegios; **the ~ class** la clase no privilegiada **II.** *n* **the ~** *pl* los no privilegiados

underrate [ˌʌn·dər·'reɪt] *vt* **to ~ sth/sb** subestimar algo/a alguien; **to ~ the difficulty/ importance of sth** infravalorar la dificultad/ importancia de algo

underrepresented [ˌʌn·dər·rep·rɪ·'zen·tɪd] *adj* con mala representación

underscore [ˌʌn·dər·'skɔr] *vt* **1.** (*put a line under*) subrayar **2.** (*emphasize*) recalcar; **to ~ a point** recalcar un punto

undersea ['ʌn·dər·si] *adj* submarino, -a

undersecretary [ˌʌn·dər·'sek·rə·ter·i] *n* subsecretario, -a *m, f*

undersell [ˌʌn·dər·'sel] *irr vt* **1.** (*offer goods cheaper*) **to ~ goods** vender mercancías a un precio más bajo; **to ~ the competition** vender a precios más bajos que la competencia **2.** (*undervalue*) **to ~ sth/sb** no hacer la suficiente publicidad de algo/alguien; **to ~ one-**

U

self no saber venderse uno mismo

undershirt ['ʌn·dər·ʃɜrt] *n* camiseta *f* (interior)

underside ['ʌn·dər·saɪd] *n* superficie *f* inferior

undersigned ['ʌn·dər·saɪnd] *n form* the ~ el/ la abajo firmante

undersize *adj*, **undersized** ['ʌn·dər·saɪzd] *adj* de tamaño insuficiente

underskirt ['ʌn·dər·skɜrt] *n* enaguas *fpl*

understaffed [ˌʌn·dər·'stæft] *adj* falto, -a de personal

understand [ˌʌn·dər·'stænd] *irr* I. *vt* 1. (*perceive meaning*) **to ~ sth/sb** comprender [o entender] algo/a alguien; **to make oneself understood** hacerse entender; **to not ~ a word** no entender ni una palabra; **to ~ that...** entender que... 2. (*sympathize with*) **to ~ sb's doing sth** entender que alguien haga algo 3. (*feel empathetic insight*) **to ~ sb/an animal** ponerse en la piel de alguien/de un animal 4. *form* (*be informed*) **to ~ that...** quedar informado de que...; **to ~ from sb that...** saber por alguien que... 5. (*believe*) creer; (*infer*) sobreentender; **to ~ that...** sobreentender que...; **as I ~ it** según tengo entendido; **it is understood that...** se sobreentiende que... 6. (*interpret*) interpretar; **to ~ from sth that...** inferir a partir de algo que... II. *vi* entender; **to ~ about sth** entender de algo

understandable [ˌʌn·dər·'stæn·də·bəl] *adj* comprensible; **to be ~ that ...** ser comprensible que...

understanding I. *n* 1. (*comprehension, grasp*) entendimiento *m;* **to not have any ~ of sth** no tener ni idea de algo *inf;* **to come to an ~** llegar a entender; **sb's ~ of sth** la interpretación de alguien de algo 2. (*entente, agreement*) acuerdo *m;* **to come to an ~** llegar a un acuerdo; **a tacit ~** un acuerdo tácito 3. (*harmony, rapport*) comprensión *f;* **a spirit of ~** un espíritu de comprensión 4. (*condition*) condición *f;* **to do sth on the ~ that ...** hacer algo a condición de que... 5. *form* (*intellectual ability*) inteligencia *f* II. *adj* comprensivo, -a

understate [ˌʌn·dər·'steɪt] *vt* minimizar; **to ~ sb's viewpoint** quitar importancia a la opinión de alguien

understated *adj* sencillo, -a

understatement [ˌʌn·dər·'steɪt·mənt] *n* atenuación *f;* **to be the ~ of the year** *fig, iron* el eufemismo del año

understocked [ˌʌn·dər·'stakt] *adj* con pocas existencias; **~ shelves** estanterías *fpl* con pocas existencias

understood [ˌʌn·dər·'stʊd] *vt, vi pt, pp of* **understand**

understudy ['ʌn·dər·ˌstʌd·i] THEAT I.<-ies> *n* suplente *mf;* **to be the ~ for sb/sth** ser el suplente de alguien/algo II.<-ie-> *vt* **to ~ sb** estudiarse un papel para poder sustituir a un actor en caso necesario

undertake [ˌʌn·dər·'teɪk] *irr vt* 1. (*set about, take on*) emprender; **to ~ a journey** emprender un viaje 2. *form* (*commit oneself*

to) **to ~ to do sth** comprometerse a hacer algo; **to ~ (that)...** comprometerse a (que)...

undertaker ['ʌn·dər·ˌteɪ·kər] *n* director(a) *m(f)* de una funeraria

undertaking [ˌʌn·dər·'teɪ·kɪŋ] *n* 1. (*professional project*) empresa *f;* **noble ~** noble empresa 2. *form* (*pledge*) promesa *f;* **an ~ to do sth** una promesa de hacer algo

under-the-counter [ˌʌn·dər·ðə·'kaʊn·tər] I. *adj* (*deal*) poco limpio, -a II. *adv* ilícitamente

undertone [ˌʌn·dər·toʊn] *n* 1. (*low voice*) voz *f* baja; **to say sth in an ~** decir algo en voz baja 2. (*undercurrent, insinuation*) insinuación *f*

underused [ˌʌn·dər·'juzd] *adj*, **underutilized** [ˌʌn·dər·'ju·tə·laɪzd] *adj* infrautilizado, -a

undervalue [ˌʌn·dər·'væl·ju] *vt* infravalorar

underwater [ˌʌn·dər·'wɔ·tər] I. *adj* submarino, -a II. *adv* por debajo del agua

underwear ['ʌn·dər·wer] *n* ropa *f* interior

underweight [ˌʌn·dər·'weɪt] *adj* de peso insuficiente

underwhelming *adj inf inv* decepcionante

underworked *adj* 1. (*insufficiently used*) poco utilizado, -a 2. (*insufficiently challenged*) sin dificultades

underworld ['ʌn·dər·wɜrld] *n* 1. (*criminal milieu*) hampa *m* 2. ART, LIT (*afterworld*) **the Underworld** el inframundo

underwrite ['ʌn·dər·raɪt] *irr vt* 1. (*sign*) firmar; **to ~ a contract** firmar un contrato 2. FIN, ECON (*guarantee share issues*) garantizar una emisión de acciones 3. (*provide insurance for*) asegurar

underwriter ['ʌn·dər·ˌraɪ·tər] *n* asegurador(a) *m(f)*

undesirable [ˌʌn·dɪ·'zaɪ·rə·bəl] I. *adj* indeseable; **to be ~ that...** no ser recomendable que...; **an ~ character** un carácter difícil II. *n* indeseable *mf*

undetected [ˌʌn·dɪ·'tek·tɪd] *adj* no descubierto, -a; **to go ~** pasar inadvertido, -a

undeveloped [ˌʌn·dɪ·'vel·əpt] *adj* 1. POL, ECON subdesarrollado, -a 2. (*not built on or used*) poco utilizado, -a 3. PHOT no revelado, -a 4. BIO, PSYCH no desarrollado, -a

undid [ʌn·'dɪd] *vt, vi pt of* **undo**

undies ['ʌn·diz] *npl inf* paños *mpl* menores

undisclosed [ˌʌn·dɪs·'kloʊzd] *adj* no revelado, -a; **an ~ amount** una cantidad no desvelada; **an ~ location** una ubicación sin desvelar; **an ~ source** una fuente no revelada

undiscovered [ˌʌn·dɪs·'kʌv·ərd] *adj* no descubierto, -a; **to go ~** ir de incógnito

undisputed [ˌʌn·dɪ·'spju·tɪd] *adj* incontestable

undistinguished [ˌʌn·dɪ·'stɪŋ·gwɪʃt] *adj* mediocre

undisturbed [ʌn·dɪ·'stɜrbd] *adj* **they were ~ by the noise** el ruido no les molestaba

undivided [ˌʌn·dɪ·'vaɪ·dɪd] *adj* 1. (*not split*) íntegro, -a 2. (*intense*) intenso, -a; **sb's ~ attention** toda la atención de alguien

undo [ʌn·'du] *irr vt* **1.**(*unfasten*) soltar; **to ~ buttons** desabrochar botones; **to ~ a zipper** bajar una cremallera **2.**(*cancel*) anular; **to ~ the damage** reparar el daño; **to ~ the good work** deshacer el trabajo bueno **3.**(*cause ruin*) arruinar; **to ~ sb's good name** perjudicar el buen nombre de alguien ▶ **what's done cannot be undone** *prov* lo hecho, hecho está *prov*

undoing *n form* ruina *f*

undone [ʌn·'dʌn] **I.** *vt pp of* **undo** **II.** *adj* **1.**(*not fastened*) desatado, -a; **to come ~** deshacerse, desatarse **2.**(*uncompleted*) por hacer; **to leave sth ~** dejar algo sin hacer

undoubted [ʌn·'daʊ·t̬ɪd] *adj* indudable

undoubtedly *adv* indudablemente, sin duda

undreamed-of [ʌn·'drimd·ˌʌv] *adj*, **undreamt-of** [ʌn·'dremt·ˌav] *adj* inimaginable

undress [ʌn·'dres] **I.** *vt* desnudar, desvestir *AmL;* **to ~ sb with one's eyes** *fig* desnudar a alguien con la mirada **II.** *vi* desvestirse **III.** *n* **1.**(*informal clothing*) ropa *f* informal **2.** **to be in a state of ~** estar desnudo

undressed *adj* desvestido, -a; **to get ~** desnudarse

undue [ʌn·'du] *adj form* indebido, -a; **~ pressure** presión *f* excesiva

undulate ['ʌn·dʒə·leɪt] *vi form* ondular

undulating *adj form* **1.**(*moving like a wave*) ondulante **2.**(*shaped like waves*) ondulado, -a

unduly [ʌn·'du·li] *adv* indebidamente

undying [ʌn·'daɪ·ɪŋ] *adj liter* imperecedero, -a; **~ love** amor *m* eterno

unearned [ʌn·'ɜrnd] *adj* **1.**(*undeserved*) inmerecido, -a **2.**(*not worked for*) no ganado, -a

unearth [ʌn·'ɜrθ] *vt* **1.**(*dig up*) desenterrar **2.**(*discover with difficulty*) sacar a la luz; **to ~ the truth** descubrir la verdad

unearthly [ʌn·'ɜrθ·li] *adj* **1.**(*unsettling*) sobrenatural; **~ noise/scream** ruido *m*/grito *m* aterrador **2.** *inf* (*inconvenient*) intempestivo, -a **3.**(*not from the earth*) sobrenatural

unease [ʌn·'iz] *n* malestar *m;* **with growing ~** con creciente inquietud

uneasiness *n* inquietud *f*

uneasy [ʌn·'i·zi] *adj* <-ier, -iest> **1.**(*uncertain*) intranquilo, -a; **to be/feel ~ about sth/sb** estar/sentirse inquieto por algo/alguien **2.**(*causing anxiety*) ansioso, -a; (*suspicion*) inquietante; (*relationship*) inestable **3.**(*insecure*) dudoso, -a

uneconomic [ʌn·ˌek·ə·'nam·ɪk] *adj* poco lucrativo, -a

uneducated [ʌn·'edʒ·ə·keɪ·t̬ɪd] **I.** *adj* inculto, -a **II.** *n the ~* los ignorantes

unemotional [ʌn·ɪ·'moʊ·ʃə·nəl] *adj* **1.**(*not feeling emotions*) impasible **2.**(*not revealing emotions*) reservado, -a

unemployable [ʌn·ɪm·'plɔɪ·ə·bəl] *adj* incapacitado, -a para trabajar

unemployed [ʌn·ɪm·'plɔɪd] **I.** *n pl the ~* los

desempleados **II.** *adj* parado, -a

unemployment [ʌn·ɪm·'plɔɪ·mənt] *n* **1.**(*condition of lacking work*) desempleo *m* **2.**(*rate of joblessness*) desocupación *f,* paro *m*

unemployment benefit *n* subsidio *m* de desempleo

unending [ʌn·'en·dɪŋ] *adj* interminable

unenlightened [ʌn·ɪn·'laɪ·tənd] *adj* **1.**(*not wise or insightful*) poco instruido, -a **2.**(*lack of insight*) ignorante **3.** *a. iron* (*not informed*) desinformado, -a

unenviable [ʌn·'en·vi·ə·bəl] *adj* poco envidiable

unequal [ʌn·'i·kwəl] *adj* **1.** *form* (*different*) diferente; **~ triangle** triángulo *m* escaleno **2.**(*unjust, inequitable*) desigual **3.**(*unable*) **to be ~ to sth** no estar a la altura de algo; **to be ~ to a task** ser incapaz de realizar una tarea

unequaled *adj*, **unequalled** *adj* sin igual

unequivocal [ʌn·ɪ·'kwɪv·ə·kəl] *adj* inequívoco, -a; **an ~ success** un éxito indudable; **to be ~ in sth** ser claro en algo

unerring [ʌn·'ɜr·ɪŋ] *adj* infalible

UNESCO *n,* **Unesco** [ju·'nes·koʊ] *n abbr of* **United Nations Educational, Scientific, and Cultural Organization** UNESCO *f*

unethical [ʌn·'eθ·ɪ·kəl] *adj* poco ético, -a

uneven [ʌn·'i·vən] *adj* **1.**(*not flat or level*) desnivelado, -a **2.**(*unequal*) desigual **3.**(*different*) distinto, -a **4.**(*of inadequate quality*) irregular **5.**(*erratic, fluctuating*) cambiante **6.** MED anormal

uneventful [ʌn·ɪ·'vent·fəl] *adj* sin acontecimientos; (*unexciting*) tranquilo, -a

unexceptionable [ʌn·ɪk·'sep·ʃə·nə·bəl] *adj form* intachable

unexceptional [ʌn·ɪk·'sep·ʃə·nəl] *adj* corriente

unexciting *adj* **1.**(*commonplace*) trivial **2.**(*uneventful*) aburrido, -a

unexpected [ʌn·ɪk·'spek·tɪd] **I.** *adj* inesperado, -a **II.** *n the ~* lo inesperado

unexplained [ʌn·ɪk·'spleɪnd] *adj* inexplicado, -a; **her absence was ~** su ausencia era inexplicable

unexploded [ʌn·ɪk·'sploʊ·dɪd] *adj* sin explotar; **~ ordinance** *bombas que no explotaron durante la guerra en la que se utilizaron y cuya posible detonación sigue suponiendo un riesgo*

unexploited *adj* inexplotado, -a

unexpressed *adj* sobreentendido, -a

unexpressive [ʌn·ɪk·'spres·ɪv] *adj* inexpresivo, -a

unfailing [ʌn·'feɪ·lɪŋ] *adj* **1.**(*always present when needed*) indefectible *elev* **2.**(*not running out*) incansable

unfair [ʌn·'fer] *adj* injusto, -a; (*advantage, disadvantage*) injusto, -a

unfaithful [ʌn·'feɪθ·fʊl] *adj* **1.**(*adulterous*) infiel **2.**(*disloyal*) desleal **3.** *form* (*not accurate*) inexacto, -a

unfaltering [ʌn·'fal·tər·ɪŋ] *adj* **1.**(*without*

U

hesitation) resuelto, -a; **with ~ steps** con pasos firmes **2.** (*decided*) decidido, -a
unfamiliar [ˌʌn·fə·ˈmɪl·jər] *adj* **1.** (*new, not familiar*) desconocido, -a; **to be ~ to sb** no ser familiar a alguien **2.** (*unacquainted*) ajeno, -a
unfashionable [ʌn·ˈfæʃ·ə·nə·bəl] *adj* pasado, -a de moda
unfasten [ˌʌn·ˈfæs·ən] **I.** *vt* desatar; (*seat belt, zipper*) desabrochar **II.** *vi* soltarse
unfathomable [ʌn·ˈfæð·ə·mə·bəl] *adj* **1.** *a. fig* (*too deep to measure*) insondable **2.** (*inexplicable*) inexplicable
unfavorable [ˌʌn·ˈfeɪ·vər·ə·bəl] *adj* **1.** (*adverse*) adverso, -a **2.** (*disadvantageous*) desfavorable
unfeeling [ʌn·ˈfi·lɪŋ] *adj* insensible
unfeigned [ʌn·ˈfeɪnd] *adj* verdadero, -a
unfettered [ʌn·ˈfet̬·ərd] *adj* sin ataduras
unfilled *adj* sin llenar [o ocupar]
unfinished [ʌn·ˈfɪn·ɪʃt] *adj* inacabado, -a
unfit [ʌn·ˈfɪt] **I.** *adj* **1.** (*unhealthy*) **I'm ~** no estoy en forma; **to be ~ for sth** no estar en condiciones para algo **2.** (*incompetent*) incapaz **3.** (*unsuitable*) no apto, -a; **to be ~ for sth** ser no apto para algo; **to be ~ for** (**human**) **habitation** ser inhabitable (para el ser humano) **II.** *vt* <-tt-> *form* inhabilitar
unflagging [ʌn·ˈflæg·ɪŋ] *adj* incansable
unflappable [ʌn·ˈflæp·ə·bəl] *adj inf* imperturbable
unflinching [ʌn·ˈflɪn·tʃɪŋ] *adj* intrépido, -a; (*report*) atrevido, -a; (*support, honesty*) resuelto, -a
unfold [ʌn·ˈfoʊld] **I.** *vt* **1.** (*open out sth folded*) desdoblar; **to ~ one's arms** descruzar sus brazos **2.** *form* (*make known*) **to ~ one's ideas/plans** exponer sus ideas/planes **II.** *vi* **1.** (*develop, evolve*) desarrollarse **2.** (*become revealed*) revelarse **3.** (*become unfolded*) extenderse
unforeseeable [ˌʌn·fɔr·ˈsi·ə·bəl] *adj* imprevisible
unforeseen [ˌʌn·fɔr·ˈsin] *adj* imprevisto, -a
unforgettable [ˌʌn·fər·ˈget̬·ə·bəl] *adj* inolvidable
unforgivable [ˌʌn·fər·ˈgɪv·ə·bəl] *adj* imperdonable
unfortunate [ʌn·ˈfɔr·tʃə·nɪt] **I.** *adj* **1.** (*luckless*) desafortunado, -a; **to be ~ that...** ser lamentable que... **+subj 2.** *form* (*regrettable*) deplorable **3.** (*inopportune*) inoportuno, -a **4.** (*adverse*) funesto, -a **II.** *n* desgraciado, -a *m, f*
unfortunately *adv* por desgracia
unfounded [ʌn·ˈfaʊn·dɪd] *adj* infundado, -a
unfrequented [ʌn·ˈfri·kwen·tɪd] *adj* poco frecuentado, -a
unfriendly [ʌn·ˈfrend·li] *adj* <-ier, -iest> **1.** (*unsociable*) insociable **2.** *fig* (*hard to use*) complicado, -a **3.** (*inhospitable*) hostil
unfulfilled [ʌn·fʊl·ˈfild] *adj* **1.** (*not carried out*) incumplido, -a **2.** (*unsatisfied*) insatisfecho, -a **3.** (*frustrated*) frustrado, -a

unfurl [ʌn·ˈfɜrl] **I.** *vt* desplegar; **to ~ an umbrella** abrir un paraguas; **to ~ a sail** largar una vela; **to ~ a flag** desplegar una bandera **II.** *vi* desplegarse
unfurnished [ˌʌn·ˈfɜr·nɪʃt] *adj* desamueblado, -a
ungainly [ʌn·ˈgeɪn·li] *adj* <-ier, -iest> torpe
ungodly [ʌn·ˈgad·li] *adj* <-ier, -iest> **1.** *inf* (*unreasonable*) atroz; **at this ~ hour** a esta hora intempestiva **2.** (*impious*) impío, -a
ungovernable [ʌn·ˈgʌv·ər·nə·bəl] *adj* ingobernable
ungraceful [ʌn·ˈgreɪs·fəl] *adj* chabacano, -a
ungracious [ˌʌn·ˈgreɪ·ʃəs] *adj form* descortés
ungrateful [ʌn·ˈgreɪt·fəl] *adj* ingrato, -a
ungrudging [ʌn·ˈgrʌdʒ·ɪŋ] *adj* **1.** (*without reservation*) generoso, -a **2.** (*not resentful or envious*) incondicional
ungrudgingly *adv* de buena gana
unguarded [ʌn·ˈgar·dɪd] *adj* **1.** (*not defended or watched*) sin vigilancia **2.** (*careless*) desprevenido, -a; **in an ~ moment** en un momento de descuido
unhallowed [ʌn·ˈhæl·oʊd] *adj* **1.** (*not consecrated*) profano, -a **2.** (*unholy*) sacrílego, -a
unhappy [ʌn·ˈhæp·i] *adj* <-ier, -iest> **1.** (*sad*) infeliz; **to make sb ~** hacer desdichado a alguien **2.** (*unfortunate*) desafortunado, -a
unharmed [ʌn·ˈharmd] *adj* ileso, -a
UNHCR [ju·en·eɪtʃ·si·ˈar] *n abbr of* **United Nations High Commission for Refugees** ACNUR *m*
unhealthy [ʌn·ˈhel·θi] *adj* <-ier, -iest> **1.** (*sick*) enfermizo, -a **2.** (*unwholesome*) nocivo, -a **3.** *inf* (*dangerous*) arriesgado, -a **4.** PSYCH (*morbid*) morboso, -a
unheard [ʌn·ˈhɜrd] *adj* **1.** (*not heard*) desoído, -a **2.** (*ignored*) desatendido, -a
unheard-of [ʌn·ˈhɜrd·ˌʌv] *adj* **1.** (*incredible*) sin precedentes **2.** (*impossible*) inaudito, -a
unhelpful [ʌn·ˈhelp·fʊl] *adj* de poca ayuda
unhinge [ʌn·ˈhɪndʒ] *vt* **1.** (*take off hinges*) desgoznar **2.** (*make crazy*) desquiciar
unholy [ʌn·ˈhoʊ·li] *adj* <-ier, -iest> **1.** (*wicked*) impío, -a **2.** REL (*profane*) profano, -a **3.** (*outrageous*) atroz; **to get up at some ~ hour** levantarse a una hora infame
unhook [ʌn·ˈhʊk] *vt* **1.** (*remove hooks*) desenganchar **2.** (*unfasten*) soltar
unhoped-for [ʌn·ˈhoʊpt·ˌfɔr] *adj* inesperado, -a
unhurt [ʌn·ˈhɜrt] *adj* ileso, -a
UNICEF *n*, **Unicef** [ˈju·nɪ·sef] *n abbr of* **United Nations International Children's Emergency Fund** UNICEF *f*
unicorn [ˈju·nɪ·kɔrn] *n* unicornio *m*
unidentified [ˌʌn·aɪ·ˈden·tə·faɪd] *n* **1.** (*unknown*) no identificado, -a **2.** (*not yet made public*) no identificado, -a
unification [ju·nɪ·fɪ·ˈkeɪ·ʃən] *n* unificación *f*
uniform [ˈju·nə·fɔrm] **I.** *n* uniforme *m* **II.** *adj* **1.** (*same or similar*) uniforme **2.** (*constant*) constante

uniformity [ˌju·nə·ˈfɔr·mə·t̬i] *n* uniformidad *f*

unify [ˈju·nə·faɪ] *vt* unificar

unilateral [ˌju·nə·ˈlæt̬·ər·əl] *adj* unilateral

unimaginable [ˌʌn·ɪ·ˈmædʒ·nə·bəl] *adj* inimaginable

unimpeachable [ˌʌn·ɪm·ˈpi·tʃə·bəl] *adj form* intachable; **an ~ source** una fuente fidedigna

unimportant [ˌʌn·ɪm·ˈpɔr·tənt] *adj* sin importancia

uninformed [ˌʌn·ɪn·ˈfɔrmd] *adj* desinformado, -a

uninhabitable [ˌʌn·ɪn·ˈhæb·ɪ·t̬ə·bəl] *adj* inhabitable

uninhabited [ˌʌn·ɪn·ˈhæb·ɪt̬ɪd] *adj* **1.** (*not lived in*) deshabitado, -a **2.** (*deserted*) desierto, -a

uninhibited [ˌʌn·ɪn·ˈhɪb·ɪ·t̬ɪd] *adj* desinhibido, -a

uninjured [ʌn·ˈɪn·dʒərd] *adj* ileso, -a

uninsured [ˌʌn·ɪn·ˈʃʊrd] *adj* no asegurado, -a, sin seguro

unintelligent [ˌʌn·ɪn·ˈtel·ɪ·dʒənt] *adj* poco inteligente

unintelligible [ˌʌn·ɪn·ˈtel·ɪ·dʒə·bəl] *adj* **1.** (*not comprehensible*) incomprensible **2.** (*unreadable*) ininteligible

unintentional [ˌʌn·ɪn·ˈten·ʃə·nəl] *adj* involuntario, -a

unintentionally *adv* sin intención

uninterested [ʌn·ˈɪn·trə·stɪd] *adj* indiferente

uninteresting *adj* aburrido, -a

uninterrupted [ˌʌn·ˌɪn·tər·ˈʌp·tɪd] *adj* ininterrumpido, -a

union [ˈjun·jən] *n* **1.** (*act of becoming united*) unión *f* **2.** (*instance of becoming united*) asociación *f* **3.** + *sing/pl vb* (*organization representing employees*) sindicato *m;* **the ~ demands** las exigencias gremiales **4.** *form* (*marriage*) enlace *m*, unión *f* **5.** (*harmony, concord*) **to live in perfect ~** vivir en perfecta armonía

unionist [ˈjun·jə·nɪst] *n* unionista *mf*

unionize [ˈjun·jə·naɪz] **I.** *vt* agremiar **II.** *vi* agremiarse

Union Jack *n* (*British national flag*) bandera del Reino Unido

unique [ju·ˈnik] *adj* **1.** (*only one*) único, -a; **a ~ characteristic** una característica exclusiva **2.** (*exceptional*) excepcional

uniqueness *n* unicidad *f*

unisex [ˈju·nə·seks] *adj* unisex

unison [ˈju·nə·sən] **I.** *n* **1.** MUS **to sing in ~** cantar al unísono **2.** (*in agreement*) **to act in ~ with sb** obrar de acuerdo con alguien **II.** *adj* MUS unísono, -a

unit [ˈju·nɪt] *n* **1.** *a.* COMPUT, COM unidad *f;* **central processing ~** unidad central de proceso; **~ of currency** unidad monetaria **2.** + *sing/pl vb* (*organized group of people*) brigada *f* **3.** (*element of furniture*) elemento *m*

unit cost *n* COM coste *m* unitario

unite [ju·ˈnaɪt] **I.** *vt* **1.** (*join together*) juntar; (*bring together*) unir **2.** LAW (*join in marriage*)

unir (en matrimonio) **II.** *vi* **1.** POL, SOCIOL (*join in common cause*) **to ~ against sb** unirse para hacer frente a alguien **2.** (*join together*) juntarse

united *adj* unido, -a

United Arab Emirates *npl* **the ~** los Emiratos Árabes Unidos

United Kingdom *n* **the ~** el Reino Unido

United Nations *n* **the ~** las Naciones Unidas

United States *n* + *sing vb* Estados *mpl* Unidos; **the ~ of America** los Estados Unidos de América

unit price *n* COM precio *m* por unidad

unity [ˈju·nə·t̬i] *n* **1.** (*oneness*) unidad *f* **2.** (*harmony, consensus*) consenso *m*

univ. *abbr of* **university** univ.

universal [ˌju·nə·ˈvɜr·səl] **I.** *adj* universal; **~ agreement** acuerdo *m* global **II.** *n* universal *m*

universe [ˈju·nə·vɜrs] *n* **the ~** el universo

university [ˌju·nə·ˈvɜr·sə·t̬i] <-ies> *n* universidad *f;* **the ~ community** la comunidad universitaria

unjust [ʌn·ˈdʒʌst] *adj* injusto, -a

unjustifiable [ʌn·ˌdʒʌs·tɪ·ˈfaɪ·ə·bəl] *adj* injustificable

unjustified [ʌn·ˈdʒʌs·tɪ·faɪd] *adj* injustificado, -a; (*complaint*) no justificado, -a

unjustly *adv* **1.** (*in an unjust manner*) inmerecidamente **2.** (*wrongfully*) injustamente

unkempt [ʌn·ˈkempt] *adj* descuidado, -a; (*appearance*) desarreglado, -a; (*hair*) despeinado, -a

unkind [ʌn·ˈkaɪnd] *adj* **1.** (*not kind*) desagradable; **to be ~ to sb** tratar mal a alguien; **to be ~ to animals** ser cruel con los animales **2.** (*not gentle*) **to be ~ to hair/hands/skin** estropear el pelo/las manos/la piel

unkindly *adv* cruelmente; **to take sth ~** tomarse algo mal

unknowing [ʌn·ˈnoʊ·ɪŋ] *adj* no consciente

unknown [ʌn·ˈnoʊn] **I.** *adj* **1.** (*not known*) desconocido, -a; **~ to me...** sin saberlo yo... **2.** (*not widely familiar*) ignorado, -a **II.** *n* **1.** (*thing*) **the ~** lo desconocido; MATH la incógnita **2.** (*person*) desconocido, -a *m, f*

unlawful [ʌn·ˈlɔ·fəl] *adj* ilegal; (*possession, association*) ilícito, -a

unleaded [ʌn·ˈled·ɪd] *adj* sin plomo

unleash [ʌn·ˈliʃ] *vt* (*a dog*) soltar; *fig* (*passions*) desatar; (*a war*) desencadenar

unleavened [ʌn·ˈlev·ənd] *adj* (*bread*) sin levadura

unless [ən·ˈles] *conj* a no ser que +*subj*, a menos que +*subj;* **he'll buy it ~ she already has it** lo comprará a menos que ella ya lo tenga; **I don't say anything ~ I'm sure** yo no digo nada a menos que esté seguro; **he won't come ~ he has time** no vendrá a menos que tenga tiempo; **~ I'm mistaken** si no me equivoco

unlike [ʌn·ˈlaɪk] **I.** *adj* diferente, distinto, -a **II.** *prep* **1.** (*different from*) diferente; **to be ~**

U

sth/sb ser distinto de algo/alguien **2.** (*in contrast to*) a diferencia de **3.** (*not characteristic of*) **it's ~ sb/sth** no es característico de alguien/algo

unlikely [ʌn·'laɪk·li] <-ier, -iest> *adj* **1.** (*improbable*) improbable; (**sth**) **seems ~** (algo) parece poco probable; **it's ~ that...** es difícil que... **2.** (*unconvincing*) inverosímil

unlimited [ʌn·'lɪm·ɪ·t̬ɪd] *adj* **1.** (*not limited*) ilimitado, -a; (*access, visibility*) sin límite(s) **2.** (*very great*) impresionante

unlisted [ʌn·'lɪs·t̬ɪd] *adj* **1.** (*not in the phone book*) no incluido, -a en la guía telefónica **2.** FIN (*stock market*) no cotizado, -a; **~ securities** valores *mpl* no inscritos en bolsa

unload [ʌn·'loʊd] I. *vt* **1.** (*remove the contents*) **to ~ sth** descargar algo **2.** (*remove film: a camera*) vaciar **3.** *inf* (*get rid of*) **to ~ sth** deshacerse de algo **4.** (*express*) desahogarse; **to ~ one's worries on sb** vaciar las preocupaciones con alguien II. *vi* **1.** AUTO (*remove the contents*) descargar **2.** (*be emptied*) vaciarse; (*empty*) vaciar **3.** *inf* (*relieve stress*) tranquilizarse **4.** (*hit*) **to ~ on sb/sth** descargar un golpe sobre alguien/algo

unlock [ʌn·'lak] *vt* **1.** (*release a lock*) abrir (*con llave*) **2.** (*release*) liberar **3.** (*solve*) solucionar; (*mystery, riddle*) resolver

unlocked *adj* abierto, -a; *fig* resuelto, -a

unlucky [ʌn·'lʌk·i] *adj* **1.** (*unfortunate*) desgraciado, -a; (*at cards, in love*) desafortunado, -a; **to be ~ enough to get a cold** tener la mala suerte de coger un resfriado **2.** *form* (*bringing bad luck*) **to be ~** ser nefasto, -a; (*day*) ser funesto, -a

unmanageable [ʌn·'mæn·ɪ·dʒə·bəl] *adj* **1.** (*unwieldy: vehicle, boat*) difícil de manejar, ingobernable **2.** (*incontrollable: person, situation*) incontrolable

unmanned [ʌn·'mænd] *adj* AVIAT, TECH no tripulado, -a

unmarked [ʌn·'markt] *adj* **1.** SCHOOL, UNIV (*exam*) sin corregir **2.** (*without mark, stain*) sin marcas; **$10,000 in ~ bills** 10.000$ en billetes sin marcar

unmarried [ʌn·'mær·ɪd] *adj* soltero, -a; **~ mother** madre *f* soltera

unmask [ʌn·'mæsk] *vt* **to ~ sb/sth** (**as sb/ sth**) *a. fig* desenmascarar a alguien/algo (como alguien/algo)

unmatched [ʌn·'mætʃt] *adj* **1.** (*unequalled*) inigualable; **to be ~ by sb** no ser igualado por alguien **2.** (*extremely great*) sin par

unmentionable [ʌn·'men·ʃə·nə·bəl] *adj* inmencionable; (*disease*) tabú

unmentioned [ʌn·'men·ʃənd] *adj* indecible

unmindful [ʌn·'maɪnd·fəl] *adj* **to be ~ of sth** hacer caso omiso de algo

unmistakable [ʌn·mɪ·'steɪ·kə·bəl] *adj* inconfundible; (*symptom*) inequívoco, -a

unmitigated [ʌn·'mɪt̬·ɪ·geɪ·t̬ɪd] *adj* (*total*) absoluto, -a; (*disaster*) total; (*contempt*) rotundo, -a; (*evil*) implacable

unmoved [ʌn·'muvd] *adj* impasible

unnamed [ʌn·'neɪmd] *adj* no nombrado, -a

unnatural [ʌn·'nætʃ·ər·əl] *adj* **1.** (*contrary to nature*) poco natural; (*affected*) afectado, -a; (*sexual practices*) perverso, -a **2.** (*not normal*) anormal

unnecessarily [ʌn·ˌnes·ə·'ser·ə·li] *adv* innecesariamente

unnecessary [ʌn·'nes·ə·ser·i] *adj* **1.** (*not necessary*) innecesario, -a **2.** (*uncalled for*) superfluo, -a

unnerve [ʌn·'nɜrv] *vt* **to ~ sb** enervar a alguien

unnerving *adj* enervante

unnoticed [ʌn·'noʊ·t̬ɪst] *adj* desapercibido, -a; **to go ~ that...** pasar inadvertido que...

unnumbered [ʌn·'nʌm·bərd] *adj* **1.** (*not marked with a number: house, page*) sin numerar **2.** *form* (*too many to be counted*) innumerable

unobtainable [ʌn·əb·'teɪ·nə·bəl] *adj* inalcanzable

unobtrusive [ʌn·əb·'tru·sɪv] *adj* (*people*) modesto, -a; (*things*) discreto, -a

unoccupied [ʌn·'ak·jə·paɪd] *adj* **1.** (*uninhabited*) deshabitado, -a **2.** MIL desocupado, -a **3.** (*chair, table*) libre

unofficial [ʌn·ə·'fɪʃ·əl] *adj* no oficial; (*figures*) oficioso, -a; (*capacity*) extraoficial

unorganized [ʌn·'ɔr·gə·naɪzd] *adj* desorganizado, -a

unorthodox [ʌn·'ɔr·θə·daks] *adj* poco ortodoxo, -a; (*approach*) poco convencional

unpack [ʌn·'pæk] I. *vt* (*a car*) descargar; **to ~ sth** sacar lo que hay dentro de algo II. *vi* deshacer el equipaje

unpaid [ʌn·'peɪd] *adj* **1.** (*not remunerated*) no remunerado, -a; (*services*) sin sueldo **2.** (*not paid*) pendiente

unpalatable [ʌn·'pæl·ə·tə·bəl] *adj a. fig* desagradable

unparalleled [ʌn·'pær·ə·leld] *adj form* sin precedentes

unperturbed [ʌn·pər·'tɜrbd] *adj* impasible; **to be ~ by sth** quedarse impertérrito ante algo

unplanned [ʌn·'plænd] *adj* espontáneo, -a

unpleasant [ʌn·'plez·ənt] *adj* **1.** (*not pleasing*) desagradable; (*sensation*) repugnante **2.** (*unfriendly*) antipático, -a

unpleasantness *n* **1.** (*quality of being unpleasant*) **the ~** lo desagradable **2.** (*unfriendly feelings*) antipatía *f*

unplug [ʌn·'plʊg] <-gg-> *vt* **1.** (*disconnect an electric plug*) desenchufar **2.** (*unstop: drain, pipe*) destapar

unpolished [ʌn·'pal·ɪʃt] *adj* **1.** (*not polished*) sin pulir **2.** (*not refined*) poco refinado, -a

unpolluted [ʌn·pə·'lu·t̬ɪd] *adj* impoluto, -a; (*water*) no contaminado, -a

unpopular [ʌn·'pap·jə·lər] *adj* **1.** (*not liked*) impopular, que gusta poco **2.** (*not widely accepted*) que cae mal; **to be ~ with sb** caer mal a alguien

unpopularity [ʌn·ˌpap·jə·'ler·ə·t̬i] *n* impopularidad *f*

unpractical [ʌn·'præk·tɪ·kəl] *adj* **1.**(*impractical*) poco práctico, -a **2.**(*lacking skill in practical matters*) desmañado, -a

unpracticed [ʌn·'præk·tɪst] *adj form* inexperto, -a; **to be ~ in sth** no tener práctica en algo

unprecedented [ʌn·'pres·ə·den·tɪd] *adj* sin precedentes; (*action*) inaudito, -a

unpredictable [ʌn·prɪ·'dɪk·tə·bəl] *adj* **1.**(*not predictable*) imprevisible **2.**(*moody*) temperamental

unprejudiced [ʌn·'predʒ·ə·dɪst] *adj* **1.**(*not prejudiced*) imparcial; (*opinion*) objetivo, -a **2.**(*not prejudiced against race*) sin prejuicios

unpremeditated [ʌn·pri·'med·ɪ·tei·tɪd] *adj* no planeado, -a; LAW (*crime, murder*) no premeditado, -a

unpretentious [ʌn·prɪ·'ten·tʃəs] *adj* sin pretensiones

unprincipled [ʌn·'prɪn·sə·pəld] *adj* sin principios; (*person*) sin escrúpulos

unproductive [ʌn·prə·'dʌk·tɪv] *adj* (*business, land*) improductivo, -a; (*negotiations*) infructuoso, -a

unprofessional [ʌn·prə·'feʃ·ə·nəl] *adj* **1.**(*not meeting professional standards*) indigno, -a de su profesión **2.**(*not to be taken seriously*) poco profesional **3.**(*not conforming to professional ethics*) contrario, -a a la ética profesional; (*conduct*) inexperto, -a

unprofitable [ʌn·'praf·ɪ·ţə·bəl] *adj* **1.**(*not making a profit*) no rentable; (*investment*) infructuoso, -a **2.**(*unproductive*) inútil; (*day*) improductivo, -a

unprompted [ʌn·'pramp·tɪd] *adj* espontáneo, -a

unprovided for [ʌn·prə·'vai·dɪd·ˌfɔr] *adj* sin medios de subsistencia; **to leave sb ~** dejar a alguien desamparado

unprovoked [ʌn·prə·'voʊkt] *adj* no provocado, -a

unpublished [ʌn·'pʌb·lɪʃt] *adj* inédito, -a

unqualified [ʌn·'kwal·ə·faɪd] *adj* **1.**(*without qualifications*) sin título; **to be ~ for sth** no estar cualificado para algo **2.**(*unlimited, unreserved*) incondicional; (*denial*) sin restricciones; (*disaster*) absoluto, -a; (*success*) rotundo, -a; (*support*) total

unquestionable [ʌn·'kwes·tʃə·nə·bəl] *adj* incuestionable; (*evidence*) inapelable; (*fact*) innegable

unquestionably *adv* indudablemente, sin duda

unquestioning [ʌn·'kwes·tʃə·nɪŋ] *adj* incondicional; (*obedience*) ciego, -a

unquoted [ʌn·'kwoʊ·ţɪd] *adj* FIN que no cotiza en bolsa

unravel [ʌn·'ræv·əl] <-ll-, -l-> I. *vt* **1.**(*unknit, undo*) deshacer; (*a knot*) desenredar **2.**(*solve: a mystery, secret*) aclarar II. *vi* deshacerse

unreadable [ʌn·'ri·də·bəl] *adj* **1.**(*illegible*) ininteligible **2.**LIT (*badly written*) ilegible

3.(*hard to interpret: expression, face*) inescrutable

unreal [ʌn·'ril] *adj* **1.**(*not real*) irreal **2.** *sl* (*astonishingly good*) impresionante

unrealistic [ʌn·ri·ə·'lɪs·tɪk] *adj* **1.**(*not realistic*) poco realista **2.**LIT, THEAT, CINE (*not appearing convincingly real*) inverosímil

unrealized *adj* **1.**(*not realized*) sin explotar **2.** FIN (*not turned into money*) no realizado, -a

unreasonable [ʌn·'ri·zə·nə·bəl] *adj* **1.**(*not showing reason*) poco razonable **2.**(*unfair*) injusto, -a; (*demands*) excesivo, -a

unrecognized [ʌn·'rek·əg·naɪzd] *adj* no reconocido, -a; **to go ~** no obtener reconocimiento

unredeemed [ʌn·rɪ·'dimd] *adj* absoluto, -a; REL irredento, -a

unrefined [ʌn·rɪ·'faɪnd] *adj* **1.**(*not refined: sugar, oil*) sin refinar **2.**(*not socially polished*) poco refinado, -a

unregistered [ʌn·'redʒ·ɪ·stərd] *adj* (*birth, person*) no registrado, -a; (*mail*) sin certificar

unrelated [ʌn·rɪ·'lei·ţɪd] *adj* no relacionado, -a

unrelenting [ʌn·rɪ·'len·tɪŋ] *adj* **1.**(*not yielding*) implacable; **to be ~ in sth** ser inexorable en algo **2.**(*incessant, not easing: pain, pressure*) incesante; (*rain*) imparable **3.** *form* (*unmerciful*) despiadado, -a

unreliable [ʌn·rɪ·'lai·ə·bəl] *adj* informal, (*algo/alguien*) en lo que/quien no se puede confiar

unrelieved [ʌn·rɪ·'livd] *adj* total; (*poverty*) absoluto, -a; (*pressure, stress*) sin alivio; (*tedium*) monótono, -a

unremarkable [ʌn·rɪ·'mar·kə·bəl] *adj* normal

unremitting [ʌn·rɪ·'mɪţ·ɪŋ] *adj form* sin tregua; (*determination*) incesante; **to be ~ in sth** ser infatigable en algo

unrepeatable [ʌn·rɪ·'pi·ţə·bəl] *adj* (*shocking*) irrepetible; (*sale price*) inmejorable

unrepentant [ʌn·rɪ·'pen·tənt] *adj* impenitente

unrequited [ʌn·rɪ·'kwai·ţɪd] *adj* (*love*) no correspondido, -a

unreserved [ʌn·rɪ·'zɜrvd] *adj* **1.**(*not having been reserved: tickets, seats*) no reservado, -a **2.**(*absolute*) incondicional; (*support*) sin reservas **3.**(*not aloof*) abierto, -a; (*friendliness*) franco, -a

unresolved [ʌn·rɪ·'zalvd] *adj* sin resolver

unrest [ʌn·'rest] *n* descontento *m;* (*ethnic, social*) malestar *m*

unrestrained [ʌn·rɪ·'streind] *adj* incontrolado, -a; (*criticism, consumerism*) desenfrenado, -a; (*laughter*) desmedido, -a

unrestricted [ʌn·rɪ·'strɪk·tɪd] *adj* ilimitado, -a; (*access*) libre

unripe [ʌn·'raip] *adj* **1.**(*not ripe*) verde; **to pick sth ~** recoger algo que no está en su punto **2.** *form* (*immature*) inmaduro, -a

unrivaled *adj*, **unrivalled** [ʌn·'rai·vəld] *adj* incomparable

unroll [ʌn·'roʊl] I. *vt* **to ~ sth** desenrollar algo

U

II. *vi* desenrollarse

unruffled [ʌn·'rʌf·əld] *adj* 1.(*not nervous, disturbed*) sereno, -a; **to be ~ by sb/sth** no inmutarse ante alguien/algo 2.(*not ruffled up: feathers, fur, hair*) liso, -a

unruly [ʌn·'ru·li] <-ier, -iest> *adj* 1.(*disorderly*) indisciplinado, -a; (*crowd*) difícil de controlar 2.(*difficult to control: hair*) rebelde; (*children*) revoltoso, -a

unsaddle [ʌn·'sæd·əl] *vt* 1.(*remove a saddle: a horse*) desensillar 2.(*unseat: a rider*) derribar

unsafe [ʌn·'seɪf] *adj* inseguro, -a; (*animal*) peligroso, -a; **to declare sth ~** declarar algo arriesgado

unsaid [ʌn·'sed] I. *vt pt, pp of* **unsay** II. *adj form* sin decir; **to leave sth ~** callarse algo; **to be better left ~** mejor no hablar

unsatisfactory [ʌn·ˌsæt·ɪs·'fæk·tə·ri] *adj* 1.(*not satisfactory*) insatisfactorio, -a; (*answer*) poco convincente; (*service*) poco satisfactorio, -a 2.SCHOOL (*grade*) insuficiente

unsatisfied [ʌn·'sæt·ɪs·faɪd] *adj* 1.(*not content*) insatisfecho, -a 2.(*not convinced*) no convencido, -a; **sth leaves sb ~** algo deja a alguien descontento 3.(*not sated*) no saciado, -a

unsaturated [ʌn·'sætʃ·ə·ˌreɪ·ʈɪd] *adj* CULIN no saturado, -a

unsavory [ʌn·'seɪ·və·ri] *adj* 1.(*unpleasant to the taste, smell*) desagradable 2.(*disgusting*) repugnante 3.(*socially offensive*) repulsivo, -a; (*reputation*) indeseable

unsay [ʌn·'seɪ] *irr vt* **to ~ sth** desdecirse de algo ▶ what's <u>said</u> cannot be unsaid *prov* lo dicho, dicho está *prov*

unscathed [ʌn·'skeɪðd] *adj* ileso, -a; **to escape ~** escapar ileso

unscheduled [ʌn·'skedʒ·ʊld] *adj* no programado, -a; (*train, landing*) no previsto, -a

unscientific [ʌn·ˌsaɪ·ən·'tɪf·ɪk] *adj* 1.(*not scientific*) no científico, -a 2.(*not knowledgeable*) sin rigor científico

unscramble [ʌn·'skræm·bəld] *vt* 1.(*straighten out*) ordenar 2.(*make intelligible*) descifrar

unscrew [ʌn·'skru] I. *vt* 1.(*screw*) des(a)tornillar 2.(*lid*) desenroscar II. *vi* (*screw*) des(a)tornillarse

unscripted [ʌn·'skrɪp·ʈɪd] *adj* espontáneo, -a; (*speech*) improvisado, -a

unscrupulous [ʌn·'skru·pjə·ləs] *adj* sin escrúpulos; (*dealings, methods*) poco honesto, -a

unseal [ʌn·'sil] *vt* 1.(*open: a letter*) abrir 2.(*tell: a secret*) desvelar

unseat [ʌn·'sit] *vt* 1.(*remove from power*) derrocar 2.(*throw: a rider*) derribar

unsecured [ˌʌn·sɪ·'kjʊrd] *adj* 1.FIN (*stock, funds*) no garantizado, -a; (*loan*) sin aval 2.(*unfastened*) no sujeto, -a

unseemly [ʌn·'sim·li] *adj form* impropio, -a; (*behavior*) indecoroso, -a

unseen [ʌn·'sin] *adj* (*not seen by sb*) sin ser

visto, -a; **to do sth ~** hacer algo inadvertidamente; **sight ~** a ciegas

unselfish [ʌn·'sel·fɪʃ] *adj* generoso, -a

unserviceable [ʌn·'sɜr·vɪ·sə·bəl] *adj* inservible; (*appliances*) inutilizable

unsettle [ʌn·'set·əl] *vt* 1.(*make nervous*) **to ~ sb** alterar a alguien 2.COM (*make unstable: the market*) desestabilizar

unsettled [ʌn·'set·əld] *adj* 1.(*changeable*) cambiante; (*period*) agitado, -a; (*weather*) inestable 2.(*troubled*) inquieto, -a 3.(*unresolved: issue, question*) no resuelto, -a 4.(*without settlers*) no colonizado, -a

unsettling [ʌn·'set·əl·ɪŋ] *adj* 1.(*causing nervousness*) inquietante; CINE (*image*) desestabilizador(a) 2.(*causing disruption*) perturbador(a); COM variable

unshakable [ʌn·'ʃeɪ·kə·bəl] *adj* inquebrantable

unshaved *adj*, **unshaven** [ʌn·'ʃeɪ·vən] *adj* sin afeitar

unshrinkable [ʌn·'ʃrɪŋ·kə·bəl] *adj* que no encoge

unshrinking [ʌn·'ʃrɪŋ·kɪŋ] *adj fig* impávido, -a; **~ courage** valor *m* impávido; **to be ~ in the face of sth** quedarse impávido ante algo

unsightly [ʌn·'saɪt·li] <-ier, -iest> *adj* feo, -a

unsigned [ʌn·'saɪnd] *adj* sin firmar

unskilled [ʌn·'skɪld] *adj* 1.(*not skilled*) no cualificado, -a; **to be ~ at (doing) sth** no estar cualificado para (hacer) algo 2.(*not requiring skill*) no especializado, -a; **~ job** puesto *m* de trabajo no especializado

unsociable [ʌn·'soʊ·ʃə·bəl] *adj* insociable

unsocial [ʌn·'soʊ·ʃəl] *adj* insociable

unsold [ʌn·'soʊld] *adj* sin vender

unsolicited [ˌʌn·sə·'lɪs·ɪ·ʈɪd] *adj* no solicitado, -a

unsolved [ʌn·'salvd] *adj* sin resolver

unsophisticated [ˌʌn·sə·'fɪs·tə·keɪ·ʈɪd] *adj* 1.(*simple*) sencillo, -a; **~ pleasure** placer *m* sencillo 2.(*simple: person*) ingenuo, -a; (*taste*) cándido, -a 3.(*uncomplicated: machine*) simple

unsound [ʌn·'saʊnd] *adj* 1.(*weak, unstable*) débil 2.(*unreliable*) no de fiar; **to be ~ on sth** no ser de fiar en algo 3.(*not financially stable*) inestable 4.(*not valid*) erróneo, -a; **~ argument** argumento *m* no válido; **~ judgment** juicio *m* equivocado; **~ police evidence** prueba *f* policial falsa 5.(*unhealthy*) no sano, -a; **to be of ~ mind** ser un enfermo mental

unsparing [ʌn·'sper·ɪŋ] *adj* 1.(*merciless*) despiadado, -a 2.*form* (*lavish*) pródigo, -a; **to be ~ in one's efforts** no escatimar esfuerzos

unspeakable [ʌn·'spi·kə·bəl] *adj* indecible; **~ atrocities** atrocidades *fpl* incalificables

unspecified [ʌn·'spes·ɪ·faɪd] *adj* 1.(*not specified*) no especificado, -a 2.(*not named*) sin nombre

unspoiled [ʌn·'spɔɪld] *adj* (*countryside*) no estropeado, -a; (*child*) no mimado, -a

unspoken [ʌn·'spoʊ·kən] *adj* tácito, -a

unstable [ʌn·'steɪ·bəl] *adj* **1.**(*not stable*) inestable; *fig* voluble **2.**(*not emotionally stable*) volátil; **emotionally** ~ emocionalmente inestable

unsteady [ʌn·'sted·i] *adj* (*chair*) poco firme; (*hand*) tembloroso, -a

unstressed [ʌn·'strest] *adj* LING átono, -a

unstuck [ʌn·'stʌk] *adj* **to come** [*o* **become**] ~ (*be no longer stuck*) despegarse; *inf* (*fail*) fracasar

unsubscribe [ˌʌn·səb·'skraɪb] *vi* cancelar la subscripción (a algo)

unsubstantial [ˌʌn·səb·'stæn·tʃəl] *adj* **1.**(*not substantial*) insustancial; ~ **improvements** mejoras *fpl* no sustanciales **2.**(*not significant*) insignificante

unsubstantiated [ˌʌn·səb·'stæn·tʃi·eɪ·t̬ɪd] *adj* no probado, -a

unsuccessful [ˌʌn·sək·'ses·fəl] *adj* sin éxito, fracasado, -a; ~ **candidate** candidato, -a *m, f* fracasado, -a; **to be** ~ **in** (**doing**) **sth** fracasar en algo [*o* no lograr hacer algo]

unsuitable [ʌn·'su·t̬ə·bəl] *adj* inapropiado, -a; ~ **clothes** ropa *f* inapropiada; ~ **moment** momento *m* inoportuno; **to be** ~ **for sth** ser inapropiado para algo; **to be** ~ **to the occasion** no ajustarse a la ocasión

unsuited [ʌn·'su·t̬ɪd] *adj* inapropriado, -a; **to be** ~ **to** [*o* **for**] **sth** no ser apropiado para algo; **to be** ~ **to each other** ser incompatibles

unsullied [ʌn·'sʌl·id] *adj form* inmaculado, -a; **to be** ~ **by sth** no estar corrompido por algo

unsung [ʌn·'sʌŋ] *adj* olvidado, -a; **the** ~ **hero** el héroe desconocido

unsure [ʌn·'ʃʊr] *adj* inseguro, -a; **to be** ~ **how/what ...** no ser seguro cómo/qué...; **to be** ~ **about sth** no estar seguro de algo; **to be** ~ **of oneself** no estar seguro de uno mismo

unsuspecting [ˌʌn·sə·'spek·t̬ɪŋ] *adj* confiado, -a; **all** ~ nada suspicaz

unsustainable [ˌʌn·sə·'steɪ·nə·bəl] *adj* insostenible

unswerving [ʌn·'swɜr·vɪŋ] *adj* (*unshakable*) inquebrantable; **to be** ~ **in sth** ser firme en algo

unsympathetic [ˌʌn·sɪm·pə·'θet̬·ɪk] *adj* poco comprensivo, -a

untangle [ʌn·'tæŋ·gəl] *vt* **1.**(*hair*) desenredar **2.**(*mystery*) desentrañar

untapped [ˌʌn·'tæpt] *adj* **1.**(*not yet utilized*) sin explotar **2.**(*not bugged: line, telephone*) no intervenido, -a **3.**(*not tapped: a keg*) sin abrir

untaxed [ˌʌn·'tækst] *adj* libre de impuestos; ~ **income** FIN ingresos *mpl* no sujetos a contribuciones

untenable [ʌn·'ten·ə·bəl] *adj* insostenible

untested [ʌn·'tes·tɪd] *adj* no probado, -a

unthinkable [ʌn·'θɪŋ·kə·bəl] **I.** *adj* **1.**(*unimaginable*) inconcebible **2.**(*shocking*) impensable **II.** *n* **the** ~ lo inconcebible

unthinking [ʌn·'θɪŋ·kɪŋ] *adj* **1.**(*thoughtless*) irreflexivo, -a **2.**(*unintentional*) no intencio-

nado, -a

unthought-of [ʌn·'θɔt·əv] *adj* inimaginable

untidy [ʌn·'taɪ·di] <-ier, -iest> *adj* **1.**(*not neat*) desaseado, -a; (*room*) desordenado, -a; (*appearance*) desaliñado, -a **2.**(*not orderly*) sin método; **to have an** ~ **mind** tener una mente caótica

untie [ˌʌn·'taɪ] <-y-> *vt* desatar; **to** ~ **a boat** desamarrar un bote; **to** ~ **a knot** deshacer un nudo; **to** ~ **one's shoelaces** desatarse los cordones

until [ən·'tɪl] **I.** *adv temporal* hasta; ~ **then** hasta entonces; ~ **such time as sb does sth** hasta el momento en que alguien haga algo **II.** *conj* hasta que +*subj*; ~ **he comes** hasta que venga; **not** ~ **sb does sth** no hasta que alguien haga algo; **not** ~ **he's here** no antes de que él esté aquí

untimely [ʌn·'taɪm·li] *adj* **1.**(*premature*) prematuro, -a; **sb's** ~ **death** la muerte prematura de alguien **2.**(*inopportune*) inoportuno, -a

unto ['ʌn·tu] *prep* HIST *s.* **to**

untold [ˌʌn·'toʊld] *adj* **1.**(*immense*) incalculable; ~ **damage** daños *mpl* incalculables; **in** ~ **misery** en la más pura miseria **2.**(*not told*) inédito, -a, nunca contado, -a

untouched [ˌʌn·'tʌtʃt] *adj* **1.**(*not affected*) intacto, -a; **to leave sth** ~ dejar algo intacto **2.**(*not touched*) no tocado, -a; ~ **by human hands** no manipulado **3.**(*not eaten*) no comido, -a; **to leave a meal** ~ dejar una comida sin tocar **4.**(*not emotionally moved*) insensible

untoward [ʌn·'tɔrd] *adj form* desfavorable; ~ **side effects** efectos *mpl* secundarios adversos

untrained [ʌn·'treɪnd] *adj* **1.**(*skill*) no formado, -a; **to the** ~ **eye** para el ojo inexperto **2.**(*animals*) no adiestrado, -a

untransferable [ˌʌn·træns·'fɜr·ə·bəl] *adj* LAW intransferible

untreated [ʌn·'tri·t̬ɪd] *adj* no tratado, -a; ~ **sewage** aguas *fpl* residuales no tratadas; **to remain** ~ MED seguir sin estar tratado

untried [ʌn·'traɪd] *adj* **1.**(*not tested*) no probado, -a **2.** LAW no procesado, -a

untroubled [ʌn·'trʌb·əld] *adj* tranquilo, -a; **they seemed** ~ **about her decision** su decisión no parecía preocuparles

untrue [ʌn·'tru] *adj* **1.**(*not true*) falso, -a **2.**(*not faithful*) infiel; **to be** ~ **to sb/sth** ser infiel a alguien/a algo

untrustworthy [ʌn·'trʌst·wɜr·ði] *adj* indigno, -a de confianza

untruth [ʌn·'truθ] *n* **1.**(*lie*) mentira *f*; **to tell an** ~ contar una mentira **2.**(*quality of being untrue*) falsedad *f*

untruthful [ʌn·'truθ·fəl] *adj* **1.**(*not truthful*) falso, -a **2.**(*tending to tell lies*) mentiroso, -a

unturned [ˌʌn·'tɜrnd] *adj* inamovible; (*soil*) inclinado, -a

untutored [ˌʌn·'tu·t̬ərd] *adj form* indocto, -a; **to be** ~ **in sth** estar poco instruido en algo

U

unused [ʌn·'juzd] *adj* **1.** (*not in use*) no usado, -a; (*talent, energy*) malgastado, -a; ~ **good** bien *m* sin estrenar **2.** (*never having been used: clothing*) nuevo, -a

unused to [ʌn·'jus·tʊ] *adj* (*not accustomed*) **to be** ~ **sth** no estar acostumbrado a algo; **to be** ~ **sb doing sth** no estar acostumbrado a que alguien haga algo

unusual [ʌn·'ju·ʒu·əl] *adj* **1.** (*atypically positive*) inusitado, -a **2.** (*not usual*) inusual; **to be** ~ **for sb** ser poco usual en alguien **3.** (*atypically negative*) insólito, -a; ~ **taste** gusto *m* extraño

unutterable [ʌn·'ʌt̬·ər·ə·bəl] *adj form* indecible; ~ **suffering** sufrimento *m* indecible

unvarnished [ʌn·'var·nɪʃt] *adj* sin barnizar; ~ **furniture** muebles *mpl* sin barnizar; **the** ~ **truth** *fig* la pura verdad

unveil [ʌn·'veɪl] **I.** *vt fig* **1.** (*expose*) quitar el velo **2.** (*present to the public*) presentar **II.** *vi* quitarse el velo

unversed [ʌn·'vɜrst] *adj* **to be** ~ **in sth** ser poco versado en algo

unwanted [ʌn·'wan·tɪd] *adj* no deseado, -a

unwarranted [ʌn·'wɔr·ən·tɪd] *adj* **1.** (*not justified*) injustificado, -a; ~ **criticism** crítica *f* injustificada **2.** (*not authorized*) no autorizado, -a

unwavering [ʌn·'weɪ·vər·ɪŋ] *adj* inquebrantable; **to be** ~ **in one's support for sb** dar apoyo incondicional a alguien

unwed [ʌn·'wed] *adj form* soltero, -a

unwelcome [ʌn·'wel·kəm] *adj* (*guest*) inoportuno, -a; (*visit*) inoportuno, -a; (*information*) desagradable; **we were made to feel rather** ~ nos hicieron sentir que molestábamos

unwell [ʌn·'wel] *adj* indispuesto, -a; **to feel** ~ sentirse mal

unwieldy [ʌn·'wil·di] *adj* **1.** (*cumbersome*) abultado, -a **2.** (*difficult to manage*) difícil de manejar; ~ **system** sistema *m* difícil de manejar

unwilling [ʌn·'wɪl·ɪŋ] *adj* no dispuesto, -a; **to be** ~ **to do sth** no estar dispuesto a hacer algo; **to be** ~ **for sb to do sth** no querer que alguien haga algo

unwillingly *adv* de mala gana

unwind [ʌn·'waɪnd] *irr* **I.** *vt* desenrollar **II.** *vi* **1.** (*unroll*) desenrollarse **2.** *fig* (*relax*) relajarse

unwise [ʌn·'waɪz] *adj* imprudente, insensato, -a

unwitting [ʌn·'wɪt̬·ɪŋ] *adj* **1.** (*unaware*) inconsciente **2.** (*unintentional*) involuntario, -a, no intencional

unwittingly *adv* **1.** (*without realizing*) inconscientemente **2.** (*unintentionally*) de forma no intencionada

unwonted [ʌn·'wɔn·tɪd] *adj form* insólito, -a

unworkable [ʌn·'wɜr·kə·bəl] *adj* impracticable

unworldly [ʌn·'wɜrld·li] *adj* **1.** (*spiritual*) espiritual **2.** (*naive*) ingenuo, -a **3.** (*unearthly*) poco mundano, -a

unworthy [ʌn·'wɜr·ði] <-ier, -iest> *adj* **1.** (*not worthy*) que no merece la pena; **to be** ~ **of interest** no ser merecedor de la mínima atención **2.** (*discreditable, contemptible*) indigno, -a

unwrap [ʌn·'ræp] <-pp-> *vt* **1.** (*remove wrapping*) desenvolver **2.** *fig* (*open, reveal*) sacar a la luz

unwritten [ʌn·'rɪt̬·ən] *adj* **1.** (*not official*) ~ **agreement** pacto *m* verbal; ~ **law** LAW ley *f* basada en el derecho consuetudinario; **the** ~ **rules** el código no escrito **2.** (*not written down*) no escrito, -a; ~ **traditions** tradiciones *fpl* no escritas

unyielding [ʌn·'jil·dɪŋ] *adj* **1.** (*stubborn, obstinate*) inflexible; ~ **opposition/support** oposición *f*/apoyo *m* firme; **to be** ~ **in sth** ser inflexible en algo **2.** (*physically hard, firm*) ~ **ground** terreno *m* firme; **to be** ~ ser duro

unzip [ʌn·'zɪp] <-pp-> *vt* abrir la cremallera de

up [ʌp] **I.** *adv* **1.** (*movement*) (hacia) arriba; ~ **here/there** aquí/allí arriba; **to look** ~ mirar (hacia) arriba; **to stand/get** ~ ponerse de pie/levantarse; **to go** ~ subir; **to throw sth** ~ lanzar algo hacia arriba; **to jump** ~ saltar hacia arriba; (**stand**) ~! ¡levántate!/¡levantaos!; **on the way** ~ de subida **2.** (*to another point*) ~ **in Seattle** allá en Seattle; **to go** ~ **to Maine** irse a Maine **3.** (*position*) **to be** ~ **all night** no dormir en toda la noche; **to jump** ~ **on sth** saltar sobre algo; **with one's head** ~ con la cabeza en alto **4.** (*limit*) **time's** ~ se acabó el tiempo; **when 5 hours were** ~ cuando pasaron 5 horas; **from the age of 18** ~ a partir de los 18 años (de edad); **to have it** ~ **to one's ears** (**with sb/sth**) *fig* estar hasta la coronilla (de alguien/algo) **5.** SPORTS (*ahead*) **to be 7 points** ~ **at halftime** ir ganando por 7 puntos en el descanso **6.** COMPUT, TECH en función ▸ ~ **and down** arriba y abajo; **to walk** **and down** caminar de arriba a abajo; **what's** ~? ¿qué hay de nuevo?; **what's** ~ **with him?** ¿qué le pasa? **II.** *prep* **1.** (*at top of*) encima de; **to climb** ~ **a tree** subirse a un árbol **2.** (*higher*) **to go** ~ **the stairs** subir los escaleras; **to run** ~ **the slope** correr cuesta arriba; **to row** ~ **the river** remar río arriba; **to go** ~ **and down sth** ir de arriba a abajo de algo **3.** (*along*) **to go** ~ **the street** ir por la calle **III.** *n* ~ **s and downs** altibajos *mpl;* **to be on the** ~ **and** ~ *inf* estar cada vez mejor **IV.** <-pp-> *vi inf* **to** ~ **and do sth** +*infin* ponerse de repente a hacer algo **V.** <-pp-> *vt* subir **VI.** *adj* **1.** (*position: building*) levantado, -a; (*tent*) montado, -a; (*flag*) izado, -a; (*curtains, picture*) colgado, -a; (*hand*) alzado, -a; (*blinds*) subido, -a; (*person*) levantado, -a, a pie **2.** (*healthy*) bien; **to be** ~ **and about** [*o* **around**] estar en buena forma **3.** (*ready*) **to be** ~ **for** (**doing**) **sth** estar listo para (hacer) algo; ~ **for sale/discussion/trial** a la venta/a discusión/en juicio

◆ **up against** *vt* **to be** ~ **sth/sb** habérselas con algo/alguien

◆**up to** *vt* **1.**(*capable of*) **to feel ~ sth** sentirse capaz de algo **2.**(*limit*) hasta; **~ here** hasta aquí; **~ now** hasta ahora; **~ $100** hasta 100$ **3.**(*responsibility of*) **it's ~ you** tú decides; **it's ~ me to decide** me toca a mí decidir

up-and-coming [ˈʌp·ən·ˈkʌm·ɪŋ] *adj* joven y prometedor(a)

upbeat [ˈʌp·bit] **I.** *n* MUS tiempo *m* débil **II.** *adj inf* optimista; **to be ~ about sth** ser optimista respecto a algo

upbringing [ˈʌp·brɪŋ·ɪŋ] *n* educación *f*; **to have a good ~** tener una buena educación

upcoming [ˈʌp·ˌkʌm·ɪŋ] *adj* venidero, -a

upcountry [ˈʌp·kʌn·tri] **I.** *adv* tierra adentro **II.** *adj* del interior; **~ tribesmen** tribus *fpl* del interior **III.** *n* interior *m*

update [ˈʌp·deɪt] **I.** *vt* (*bring up to date*) poner al día; COMPUT actualizar **II.** *n* (*instance of updating*) puesta *f* al día; COMPUT actualización *f*; **to give sb an ~ (on sth)** poner a alguien al día (de algo)

updating *n* actualización *f*

updraft [ˈʌp·dræft] *n* corriente *f* ascendiente

upend [ʌp·ˈend] *vt* **to ~ sb** tumbar a alguien; **to ~ sth** poner vertical algo

up-front [ˌʌp·ˈfrʌnt] *adj inf* **1.**(*open, frank*) abierto, -a; **to be ~ and honest** ser franco y sincero; **to be ~ about sth** ser franco sobre algo **2.**(*advance*) por adelantado; **~ payment** pago *m* por adelantado

upgradable *adj* modernizable

upgrade [ˈʌp·greɪd] **I.** *vt* **1.**(*improve quality*) mejorar la calidad de; COMPUT mejorar; (*hardware, software*) modernizar **2.**(*raise in rank*) **to ~ sb (to sth)** ascender a alguien (a algo); **to ~ sth** valorar en más algo; **to ~ a job** asignar un grado más alto a un puesto de trabajo **3.** AVIAT (*move to better class*) **they ~ed him to first class** le cambiaron a primera clase **II.** *vi* **1.** COMPUT, TECH, COM (*improve quality*) mejorar **2.** AVIAT (*move to better class*) cambiar a una clase mejor **III.** *n* **1.** COMPUT, TECH, COM (*instance of upgrading*) mejora *f*; **a software ~** una modernización del software **2.**(*slope*) cuesta *f* **3.** AVIAT (*move to better class*) cambiar a una clase mejor **4.**(*be improving*) **to be on the ~** estar progresando; (*business, sales*) ir mejorando; MED ir recuperándose

upgrading *n* **1.**(*act of improvement*) mejoramiento *m*; COMPUT modernización *f* **2.**(*raising of rank*) subida *f* de rango

upheaval [ʌp·ˈhi·vəl] *n* **1.**(*condition of violent change*) sacudida *f*; **political ~** convulsión *f* política **2.**(*instance of violent change*) cataclismo *m* **3.** GEO (*violent upward push*) solevamiento *m*; **~ of the earth's crust** solevamiento *m* de la corteza terrestre

uphill [ʌp·ˈhɪl] **I.** *adv* (*in an ascending direction*) cuesta arriba; **to run/walk ~** correr/caminar cuesta arriba **II.** *adj* **1.**(*sloping upward*) ascendente **2.**(*difficult*) difícil; **~ battle** *fig* batalla *f* ardua

uphold [ʌp·ˈhoʊld] *irr vt* **1.**(*support, maintain*) sostener; **to ~ the law** defender la ley; **to ~ the principle that...** defender el principio de que...; **to ~ traditions** apoyar las tradiciones **2.** LAW (*confirm*) **to ~ a verdict** confirmar un veredicto

upholster [ʌp·ˈhoʊl·stər] *vt* **to ~ sth (in sth)** tapizar algo (de algo)

upholsterer *n* tapicero, -a *m, f*

upholstery *n* **1.**(*covering for furniture*) tapizado *m*; **leather ~** tapizado de piel **2.**(*act of upholstering*) tapicería *f*

UPI [juˈpiˈaɪ] *n abbr of* **United Press International** UPI *f*

upkeep [ˈʌp·kip] *n* **1.**(*maintenance*) mantenimiento *m* **2.**(*cost*) gastos *mpl* de mantenimiento

upland [ˈʌp·lənd] **I.** *adj* de la meseta; **~ plain** llanura *f* de la meseta; **~ village** pueblo *m* de la meseta **II.** *n* the **~s** las tierras altas

uplift[1] [ʌp·ˈlɪft] *vt* **1.**(*raise up*) elevar **2.**(*inspire*) inspirar; **to ~ sb's heart** edificar el alma de uno

uplift[2] [ˈʌp·lɪft] *n* **1.** GEO (*raising*) sustentación *f* **2.**(*spiritual/mental elevation, inspiration*) inspiración *f*; **moral ~** edificación *f* moral; **to give moral ~ to sb** edificar moralmente a alguien

uplifting [ʌp·ˈlɪf·tɪŋ] *adj* positivo, -a

upload [ˈʌp·loʊd] *vt* COMPUT subir

upmarket [ˈʌp·ˌmar·kɪt] **I.** *adj* (*goods*) superior; **~ consumers** consumidores *mpl* con poder adquisitivo; **~ products** productos *mpl* de categoría **II.** *adv* en la selección superior; **to go ~** buscar clientela de poder adquisitivo

upon [əˈpan] *prep form* **1.**(*on top of*) sobre, encima de **2.**(*around*) en; **a ring ~ the finger** un anillo en el dedo **3.**(*hanging on*) **to hang ~ the wall** colgar en la pared **4.**(*at time of*) **~ her arrival** a su llegada; **~ this** a continuación, acto seguido **5.**(*long ago*) **once ~ a time** érase una vez

upper [ˈʌp·ər] **I.** *adj* **1.**(*further up*) superior; **~ management** altos cargos *mpl* **2.** GEO (*northern*) **the ~ Northeast** el alto nordeste **II.** *n* **1.**(*of shoe*) pala *f*; **leather ~s** palas *fpl* de piel **2.** *sl* (*drug*) anfeta *f inf*, estimulante *m*

uppercase *n* TYPO (letra *f*) mayúscula *f*

upper class <-es> *n* clase *f* alta

upper-class *adj* de clase alta; **in ~ circles** en círculos de la alta sociedad

uppercut *n* SPORTS gancho *m*

upper deck *n* (*of ship*) cubierta *f* superior; (*of bus*) piso *m* superior; (*of stadium*) nivel *m* superior

uppermost I. *adj* (*highest*) más alto, -a; **to be ~ in one's mind** ocupar el primer lugar en sus pensamientos **II.** *adv* boca arriba; **to put sth ~** poner algo cara arriba

uppish [ˈʌp·ɪʃ] *adj inf*, **uppity** [ˈʌp·ə·t̬i] *adj inf* chulo, -a; **to get ~** ponerse chulo

upright [ˈʌp·raɪt] **I.** *adj* **1.**(*post, rod*) vertical

2. (*upstanding*) recto, -a; (*citizen*) honrado, -a **II.** *adv* verticalmente; **to stand ~** permanecer erguido; **to sit bolt ~** estar muy derecho en la silla **III.** *n* **1.** (*upright piano*) piano *m* vertical **2.** TECH montante *m* **3.** SPORTS poste *m*

uprising ['ʌp·raɪ·zɪŋ] *n* alzamiento *m;* **to crush an ~** aplastar una sublevación

uproar ['ʌp·rɔr] *n* alboroto *m,* batifondo *m CSur,* tinga *f Méx;* **to cause an ~** provocar un escándalo

uproarious [ʌp·'rɔr·i·əs] *adj* tumultoso, -a; (*joke*) divertidísimo, -a

uproot [ʌp·'rut] *vt* **1.** (*extract from ground*) arrancar de raíz **2.** (*remove from one's home*) desarraigar; **to ~ oneself** perder las raíces

upset¹ [ʌp·'set] **I.** *vt irr* **1.** (*unsettle*) trastornar; (*distress*) afligir; **to ~ oneself** afligirse **2.** (*throw into disorder*) alborotar **3.** (*overturn*) derrumbar; (*boat, canoe*) volcar **4.** (*cause pain*) hacer daño a, trastornar **II.** *adj* **1.** (*disquieted*) perturbado, -a; (*distressed*) acongojado, -a; (*sad*) apenado, -a; **to get ~ about sth** enfadarse por algo; **to be ~ (that)...** estar enfadado (porque)...; **don't be ~** no te enfades **2.** (*nauseated*) **to have an ~ stomach** tener el estómago revuelto **3.** (*overturned, upended*) trastornado, -a

upset² ['ʌp·set] *n* **1.** (*great surprise*) gran sorpresa *f* **2.** (*illness*) **stomach ~** trastorno *m* estomacal **3.** (*bad experience*) disgusto *m*

upset price *n* COM precio *m* mínimo

upsetting *adj* triste; **an ~ piece of news** una noticia desagradable

upshot ['ʌp·ʃat] *n* resultado *m;* **the ~ (of it all) is that...** el resultado (de todo ello) es que...

upside down [ʌp·saɪd·'daʊn] *adv* al revés; **to turn sth ~** poner algo del revés

upside-down [ʌp·saɪd·'daʊn] *adj* **1.** (*reversed in vertical axis*) al revés; **to be ~** (*pictures*) estar al revés **2.** (*confused*) muy confuso, -a; **an ~ world** un mundo al revés; **the house was ~** la casa estaba patas arriba

upstage¹ ['ʌp·steɪdʒ] **I.** *adj* THEAT del fondo de la escena; **~ position** posición *f* al fondo de la escena **II.** *adv* en el fondo de la escena; **to go ~** ir hacia el fondo de la escena **III.** *vt* **to ~ sb** robarle el protagonismo a alguien

upstage² [ʌp·'steɪdʒ] *vt* eclipsar

upstairs [ʌp·'sterz] **I.** *adj* de arriba; **the ~ rooms** las habitaciones del piso de arriba; **the ~ windows** las ventanas de arriba **II.** *adv* arriba; **to go ~** ir arriba; **the people who live ~** la gente que vive en el piso de arriba **III.** *n* (**the**) **~** el piso de arriba

upstanding [ʌp·'stæn·dɪŋ] *adj form* **1.** (*honest*) íntegro, -a **2.** (*strong*) **a fine ~ young woman** una mujer de buena apariencia

upstart ['ʌp·start] *n* arribista *mf*

upstate ['ʌp·steɪt] **I.** *adj* del norte; **in ~ New York** en el norte de Nueva York **II.** *adv* en el norte

upstream [ʌp·'strim] **I.** *adj* de las aguas de arriba; **~ pollution** contaminación *f* de las

aguas de la zona alta de un río **II.** *adv* aguas arriba; **to swim ~** nadar contra la corriente

upsurge ['ʌp·sɜrdʒ] *n* aumento *m; an ~ in sth* un aumento de algo; **the ~ of violence** el resurgir de la violencia; **the ~ of attention** el aumento de la atención

upswing ['ʌp·swɪŋ] *n* movimiento *m* hacia arriba; **an ~ in sth** un auge en algo; **an ~ in the economy** una mejora en la economía; **an ~ in exports** un aumento de las exportaciones; **to be on the ~** ir al alza; (*crime, violence*) ir en aumento

uptake ['ʌp·teɪk] *n* **1.** (*level of absorption*) absorción *f* **2.** (*vent*) salida *f* de humos ▸ **to be quick on the ~** *inf* cogerlas al vuelo; **to be slow on the ~** *inf* ser algo corto

uptight [ʌp·'taɪt] *adj sl* tenso, -a; **to be/get ~ (about sth)** estar/ponerse nervioso (por algo)

up-to-date [ʌp·tə·'deɪt] *adj* **1.** (*contemporary*) moderno, -a; (*book*) actualizado, -a **2.** (*informed*) al día; **the ~ news** las noticias del día; **to bring sb ~** poner a alguien al corriente

up-to-the-minute [ʌp·tə·ðə·'mɪn·ɪt] *adj* de última hora

uptown ['ʌp·taʊn] **I.** *adj* (*suburbs: north*) del norte; (*suburbs: general*) residencial; **in ~ Manhattan** en los barrios del norte de Manhattan; **an ~ shop** una tienda en los barrios periféricos de la ciudad **II.** *adv* hacia el norte/ los barrios periféricos

uptrend ['ʌp·trend] *n* tendencia *f* al alza; **an ~ in sth** una tendencia alcista en algo

upturn ['ʌp·tɜrn] *n* mejora *f;* **the ~ in consumer confidence** ECON el aumento de la confianza de los consumidores; **an ~ in the economy** ECON un repunte en la economía

upturned [ʌp·'tɜrnd] *adj* vuelto, -a hacia arriba; **~ nose** nariz *f* respingona; **with ~ palms** con las palmas hacia arriba

upward ['ʌp·wərd] **I.** *adj* ascendente; **~ movement** movimiento *m* ascendente; **~ trend** tendencia *f* alcista **II.** *adv* **1.** (*toward higher level*) (hacia) arriba **2.** (*going higher in number*) al alza; **to go ~** ir en aumento

upwards *adv* (hacia) arriba; **and ~** y más

uranium [ju·'reɪ·ni·əm] *n* uranio *m*

Uranus [ju·'reɪ·nəs] *n* Urano *m*

urban ['ɜr·bən] *adj* urbano, -a; **~ area** zona *f* urbana; **~ sprawl** urbanización *f* caótica; **~ decay** deterioro *m* urbano

urbane [ɜr·'beɪn] *adj* fino, -a

urbanity [ɜr·'bæn·ə· t̬i] *n* cortesía *f*

urbanization [ɜr·bə·nɪ·'zeɪ·ʃən] *n* urbanización *f*

urbanize ['ɜr·bə·naɪz] *vt* urbanizar

urchin ['ɜr·tʃɪn] *n iron* pilluelo, -a *m, f;* **street ~** golfillo, -a *m, f* callejero, -a

urethra [ju·'ri·θrə] <-s *o* -e> *n* uretra *f*

urge [ɜrdʒ] **I.** *n* (*strong desire*) ansia *f;* (*compulsion*) impulso *m;* PSYCH instinto *m; an ~ to do sth* un impulso de hacer algo; **the ~ to express oneself** el deseo de expresarse; **an ~**

for power/recognition un afán de poder/ reconocimiento; **an instinctive/irresistible** ~ un impulso instintivo/irresistible; **to feel an irresistible** ~ **to do sth** sentir un deseo irrefrenable de hacer algo; **an uncontrollable** ~ un deseo incontrolable; **to control/repress an** ~ controlar/reprimir un impulso; **a sexual** ~ un deseo *m* sexual **II.** *vt* **1.** (*strongly encourage*) fomentar; **to** ~ **sb to do sth** instar a alguien a hacer algo; **to** ~ **sb into sth** incitar a alguien a algo **2.** (*recommend*) recomendar; **to** ~ **caution upon sb** recomendar precaución a alguien

◆**urge on** *vt* **to urge sb on** (**to do sth**) animar a alguien (a hacer algo)

◆**urge upon** *vt form* **to** ~ **sb to do sth** apremiar a alguien para que haga algo

urgency ['ɜr·dʒən·si] *n* **1.** (*top priority, imperativeness*) urgencia *f;* **to be a matter of** (**great**) ~ ser un asunto de (gran) urgencia; **to realize/stress the** ~ **of sth** darse cuenta de/remarcar la urgencia de algo; **to show a sense of** ~ mostrar un sentido de perentoriedad *elev* **2.** (*insistence, clamorousness*) insistencia *f*

urgent ['ɜr·dʒənt] *adj* **1.** (*imperative, crucial: appeal, plea*) urgente; ~ **need** necesidad *f* perentoria *elev;* **to be in** ~ **need of sth** necesitar algo urgentemente; **an** ~ **request** una petición urgente **2.** *form* (*insistent, pleading*) insistente

urgently *adv* **1.** (*immediately*) urgentemente **2.** (*earnestly*) insistentemente

urinal ['jʊr·ə·nəl] *n* **1.** urinario *m* **2.** (*vessel*) orinal *m*

urinary ['jʊr·ə·ner·i] *adj* urinario, -a; ~ **diseases** enfermedades *fpl* urinarias; ~ **incontinence** incontinencia *f* urinaria

urinate ['jʊr·ə·neɪt] *vi* orinar(se)

urine ['jʊr·ɪn] *n* orina *f*

URL [ju·ar·'el] *n* COMPUT *abbr of* **universal resource locator** URL *f*

urn [ɜrn] *n* **1.** urna *f* **2.** (*for tea*) tetera *f*

Uruguay ['jʊr·ə·gwaɪ] *n* Uruguay *m*

Uruguayan [jʊr·ə·'gwaɪ·ən] **I.** *adj* uruguayo, -a **II.** *n* uruguayo, -a *m, f*

us [əs, *stressed:* ʌs] *pron pers* nos; *after prep* nosotros, -as; **it's** ~ somos nosotros; **older than** ~ mayores que nosotros; **look at** ~ míranos; **he saw** ~ (él) nos vio; **he gave the pencil to** ~ nos dio el lápiz; **it's for/from** ~ es para/de nosotros

US *n*, **U.S.** [ju·'es] *n abbr of* **United States** EE.UU. *mpl*

USA [ju·es·'eɪ] *n* **1.** *abbr of* **United States of America** EE.UU. *mpl* **2.** *abbr of* **United States Army** Ejército de los EE.UU.

USAF [ju·es·er·'ef] *n abbr of* **United States Air Force** Fuerza Aérea de los EE.UU.

usage ['ju·sɪdʒ] *n* **1.** (*how sth is used*) uso *m;* **in common** ~ de uso común; **in general** ~ de uso general **2.** *form* (*treatment*) tratamiento *m* **3.** LING uso *m;* **the earliest recorded** ~ **of the word 'X'** el primer uso documentado de la palabra 'X'

use¹ [jus] *n* **1.** (*practical application*) uso *m* **2.** (*possibility of applying*) empleo *m;* **in** ~ en uso; **to be of** ~ **to sb** ser de utilidad para alguien; **a ban on the** ~ **of chemical weapons** una prohibición sobre el uso de armas químicas; **the** ~ **of drugs** el consumo de drogas; **the correct** ~ (**of language**) el uso correcto (de la lengua); **to make** ~ **of sth** utilizar algo; **to put sth to** ~ poner algo en servicio; **to be out of** ~ estar fuera de servicio; **to come into** ~ empezar a utilizarse; **to go out of** ~ quedar en desuso **3.** (*purpose*) **to be no** ~ no ser de utilidad; **there's no** ~ **doing sth** no sirve de nada hacer algo; **it's no** ~ es inútil; **what's the** ~ **of doing sth?** ¿de qué sirve hacer algo?; **what** ~ **is doing sth?** ¿de qué sirve hacer algo? **4.** (*consumption*) consumo *m*

use² [juz] **I.** *vt* **1.** (*make use of*) usar; (*one's skills, training*) hacer uso de; **to** ~ **logic** emplear la lógica; **to** ~ **a name/pseudonym** utilizar un nombre/pseudónimo; **to** ~ **sth to do sth** utilizar algo para hacer algo; **to** ~ **sth against sb/sth** utilizar algo en contra de alguien/algo; **to** ~ **drugs** consumir drogas; **I could** ~ **some help** *inf* no me vendría mal algo de ayuda **2.** (*employ*) emplear; **to** ~ **common sense** emplear el sentido común; **to** ~ **discretion** ser discreto; ~ **your head** utiliza la cabeza **3.** (*consume*) utilizar, consumir; **to** ~ **energy** consumir energía **4.** (*manipulate*) utilizar; (*exploit*) explotar **5.** *form* (*treat in stated way*) **to** ~ **sb badly/well** tratar mal/bien a alguien **II.** *vi* **he** ~**d to be/do...** solía ser/hacer...; **they** ~**d not to enjoy horror films** no les gustaba ver películas de terror; **did you** ~ **to work in banking?** ¿trabajabas en banca?

◆**use up** *vt* agotar

used [juzd] *adj* (*second-hand*) usado, -a; (*clothing*) de segunda mano; ~ **car** coche usado [*o* de segunda mano]

used to *adj* (*familiar with*) acostumbrado, -a; **to be** ~ **sth** estar acostumbrado a algo; **to become** ~ **sth** acostumbrarse a algo; **to be** ~ **the cold/heat** estar acostumbrado al frío/calor; **to be** ~ **doing sth** tener la costumbre de hacer algo

useful ['jus·fəl] *adj* **1.** (*convenient*) útil; **a** ~ **thing** una cosa útil; **to be** ~ (**for sth**) ser útil (para algo) **2.** (*beneficial*) beneficioso, -a; **a** ~ **experience** una experiencia útil **3.** (*effective*) eficaz; (*competent*) competente; **to be** ~ **with sth** *inf* ser competente en algo; **to do sth** ~ hacer algo útil

usefulness *n* utilidad *f;* (*applicability*) aplicabilidad *f;* (*relevance*) relevancia *f;* **to outlive one's** ~ dejar de tener utilidad

useless ['jus·lɪs] *adj* **1.** (*in vain*) inútil; (*unusable*) inservible; **to be** ~ **doing sth** ser inútil hacer algo; **to be** ~ **for sb/sth** no ser de utilidad para alguien/algo; **to become** ~ **for sb/sth** dejar de ser útil para alguien/algo; **to be** ~ **to do sth** no servir de nada el hacer algo; ~ **details** detalles *mpl* sin importancia;

U

~ information información *f* inútil **2.** *inf* (*incompetent*) incompetente; **to be worse than ~** *inf* no servir para nada

user *n* usuario, -a *m, f;* (*of gas, electricity*) consumidor(a) *m(f);* (*of computer*) usuario, -a *m, f;* **drug ~** drogadicto, -a *m, f*

user-friendly *adj* COMPUT fácil de utilizar

user interface *n* COMPUT interfaz *f* de usuario

username *n* COMPUT nombre *m* de usuario

usher ['ʌʃ·ər] **I.** *n* ujier *m;* CINE acomodador(a) *m(f)* **II.** *vt* **to ~ sb into the office** hacer pasar a alguien a la oficina; **to ~ sb out** acompañar a alguien a la puerta

USMA [ˌju·es·em·'pi] *n abbr of* **United States Military Academy** Academia *f* Militar de Estados Unidos

USMC [ˌju·es·em·'si] *n abbr of* **United States Marine Corps** Cuerpo *m* de Infantería de Marina de Estados Unidos

USN [ˌju·es·'en] *n abbr of* **United States Navy** Marina *f* de Estados Unidos

USNA [ˌju·es·en·'eɪ] *n abbr of* **United States Naval Academy** Academia *f* Naval de Estados Unidos

USO [ˌju·es·'oʊ] *n abbr of* **United Service Organizations** Organizaciones *f* de Servicios Unidos *pl*

USPS [ˌju·es·pi·'es] *n abbr of* **United States Postal Service** Servicio *m* Postal de Estados Unidos

USS [ˌju·es·'es] *n* **1.** *abbr of* **United States Ship** *barco de los EE.UU.* **2.** *abbr of* **United States Senate** *Senado de los EE.UU.*

usual ['ju·ʒu·əl] **I.** *adj* usual; **(the) ~ problems** los problemas corrientes; **to find sth in its ~ place** hallar algo en el lugar en que acostumbra a estar; **as ~** como de costumbre; **to be ~ for sb** ser habitual para alguien; **to be ~ for sb to do sth** ser habitual para alguien hacer algo **II.** *n* **the ~** *inf* (*regular drink/food*) lo de siempre

usually *adv* normalmente

usufruct ['ju·zə·frʌkt] *n form* LAW usufructo *m*

usurer ['ju·ʒər·ər] *n* LAW usurero, -a *m, f*

usurious [ju·'ʒʊr·i·əs] *adj form* LAW usurario, -a

usurp [ju·'sɜrp] *vt* usurpar

usurper [ju·'sɜr·pər] *n* usurpador(a) *m(f)*

usury ['ju·ʒə·ri] *n* LAW usura *f*

UT *n abbr of* **Utah** Utah

Ut. *n abbr of* **Utah** Utah

Utah ['ju·tɔ] *n* Utah

utensil [ju·'ten·səl] *n* utensilio *m;* **kitchen ~s** utensilios *mpl* de cocina

uterine ['ju·tər·ɪn] *adj* uterino, -a

uterus ['ju·tər·əs] <-ri *o* -es> *n* útero *m*

utilitarian [ju·ˌtɪl·ə·'ter·i·ən] *adj* utilitario, -a

utility [ju·'tɪl·ə·t̬i] <-ies> *n* **1.** *form* (*usefulness*) utilidad *f* **2.** (*public service*) empresa *f* de servicio público **3.** COMPUT herramienta *f*

utilization [ju·t̬ə·lɪ·'zeɪ·ʃən] *n* utilización *f*

utilize ['ju·t̬ə·laɪz] *vt* utilizar

utmost ['ʌt·moʊst] **I.** *adj* mayor; **of the ~ brilliance** (*person, mind*) de una inteligencia sup-

rema; **with the ~ care** con sumo cuidado; **with the ~ caution** con toda precaución; **the ~ difficulty** la máxima dificultad; **a matter of ~ importance** un asunto de primerísima importancia **II.** *n* **the ~** lo máximo; **to offer the ~ in power** otorgar el máximo poder; **to be the ~** ser lo máximo; **to the ~** al máximo; **to try sb's patience to the ~** poner a prueba la paciencia de alguien al máximo; **to live life to the ~** vivir la vida al máximo; **to try one's ~** hacer todo lo que se puede

utopia [ju·'toʊ·pi·ə] *n* utopía *f*

utopian *adj* utópico, -a

utter¹ ['ʌt̬·ər] *adj* completo, -a; **in ~ despair** en la más absoluta desesperación; **~ nonsense** completa estupidez *f;* **an ~ fool** un completo idiota

utter² ['ʌt̬·ər] *vt* **1.** (*emit noise orally*) proferir; **without ~ing a word** sin mediar palabra **2.** (*express*) pronunciar; **to ~ blasphemy against sb/sth** proferir una blasfemia contra alguien/algo; **to ~ a threat** amenazar; **to ~ an oath** hacer un juramento; **to ~ a prayer** decir una oración; **to ~ a warning** dar un aviso

utterance ['ʌt̬·ər·əns] *n* **1.** (*speech act*) enunciado *m* **2.** (*style of delivery*) expresión *f;* **to give ~ to sth** expresar algo; **to give ~ to a feeling** manifestar un sentimiento

utterly *adv* completamente; **to be ~ convinced that...** estar completamente convencido de que...; **to ~ despise/hate sb** despreciar/odiar profundamente a alguien; **~ irresistible** totalmente irresistible

uttermost ['ʌt̬·ər·moʊst] *adj, n s.* **utmost**

U-turn ['ju·tɜrn] *n* **1.** AUTO cambio *m* de sentido **2.** giro *m* de ciento ochenta grados; **to do a ~** hacer un giro completo; **to make a ~** realizar un giro de 180 grados

UV [ju·'vi] *abbr of* **ultraviolet** UV

uvula ['ju·vjə·lə] *n* úvula *f*

Uzbek ['uz·bək] **I.** *adj* uzbeko, -a **II.** *n* uzbeko, -a *m, f*

Uzbekistan [uz·ˌbek·ɪ·'stæn] *n* Uzbekistán *m*

V

V, v [vi] *n* **1.** (*letter*) V, v *f;* **~ as in Victor** V de Valencia **2.** (*Roman numeral five*) V *m*

V 1. *abbr of* **velocity** V **2.** *abbr of* **volt** V **3.** *abbr of* **volume** vol.

VA [vər·'dʒɪn·jə] *n abbr of* **Virginia** Virginia *f*

vac [væk] **I.** *n inf* **1.** *abbr of* **vacuum cleaner** aspirador *m*, aspiradora *f;* **to give sth a quick ~** limpiar algo rápidamente con el aspirador **2.** *abbr of* **vacuum** vacío *m* **II.** <-cc-> *vt inf abbr of* **vacuum clean** pasar el aspirador a **III.** *vi abbr of* **vacuum clean** pasar el aspirador a

vacancy ['veɪ·kən·si] <-ies> *n* **1.** (*room*)

cuarto *m* vacío; '**~**' 'habitaciones *fpl* libres'; '**no ~**' 'no quedan habitaciones disponibles' **2.** (*employment opportunity*) vacante *f;* **to fill a ~** ocupar una vacante; **to have a ~** ofrecer un puesto de trabajo **3.** (*lack of expression*) vacuidad *f*

vacant ['veɪ·kənt] *adj* **1.** (*empty, void, not filled*) vacío, -a; (*seat*) libre; **~ lot** solar *m* libre; **to leave sth ~** dejar algo vacante; '**~**' '*libre*' **2.** (*unoccupied job situation*) vacante; **to become ~** quedarse vacante; **to fill a ~ position** ocupar una vacante **3.** (*expressionless, deadpan*) inexpresivo, -a

vacate ['veɪ·keɪt] *vt form* (*place, seat*) dejar libre; (*a room, offices, house, building*) desocupar; (*a job, position, post*) dejar vacante

vacation [veɪ·'keɪ·ʃən] **I.** *n* vacaciones *fpl;* **to take a ~** tomarse unas vacaciones; **on ~** de vacaciones; **paid ~** vacaciones *fpl* pagadas **II.** *vi* estar de vacaciones

vacationer *n* veraneante *mf*

vacation house *n* casa *f* de veraneo

vaccinate ['væk·sə·neɪt] *vt* MED vacunar; **to be ~ d against measles** estar vacunado contra el sarampión

vaccination [,væk·sə·'neɪ·ʃən] *n* MED vacunación *f;* **a ~ against measles** una vacuna contra el sarampión; **oral ~** vacunación *f* oral

vaccine [væk·'sin] *n* MED vacuna *f*

vacillate ['væs·ə·leɪt] *vi* dudar; **to ~ between... and...** dudar entre... y...; **to ~ between hope and despair** oscilar entre la esperanza y la desesperación

vacillation [,væs·ə·'leɪ·ʃən] *n* vacilación *f;* (*indecisiveness*) indecisión *f*

vacuous ['væk·ju·əs] *adj* bobo, -a; **a ~ remark** un comentario necio

vacuum ['væk·jum] **I.** *n* **1.** PHYS (*area without gas, air*) vacío *m;* **perfect ~** vacío *m* perfecto **2.** (*absence of direction*) **to fill/leave a ~** llenar/dejar un vacío **3.** (*isolated from influences, people*) **to live in a ~** vivir en una burbuja **4.** (*vacuum cleaner*) aspiradora *f* **II.** *vt* limpiar con la aspiradora; **to ~ sth up** pasar la aspiradora a algo

vacuum cleaner *n* aspiradora *f*

vacuum-packaged *adj,* **vacuum-packed** [,væk·jum·'pækt] *adj* envasado, -a al vacío

vagabond ['væg·ə·band] **I.** *n* vagabundo, -a *m, f* **II.** *adj* vagabundo, -a

vagary ['veɪ·gə·ri] <-ies> *n* **1.** (*caprice, whimsy*) capricho *m* **2.** **vagaries** (*unpredictable whimsical developments*) caprichos *mpl;* **the vagaries of the weather/of fashion** los caprichos del tiempo/de la moda

vagina [və·'dʒaɪ·nə] *n* vagina *f*

vagrancy ['veɪ·grən·si] *n* vagabundeo *m*

vagrant ['veɪ·grənt] **I.** *n* vagabundo, -a *m, f* **II.** *adj* **1.** vagabundo, -a **2.** *fig* errabundo, -a

vague [veɪg] *adj* **1.** (*imprecise: promise, pain*) vago, -a; (*word*) impreciso, -a; (*outline*) borroso, -a; **I haven't the ~st idea** no tengo la más mínima idea **2.** (*absent-minded:*

expression) distraído, -a; (*person*) despistado, -a

vagueness *n* **1.** (*imprecision*) vaguedad *f* **2.** (*absent-mindedness*) distracción *f*

vain [veɪn] *adj* **1.** (*conceited, self-admiring*) vanidoso, -a **2.** (*fruitless: attempt, hope*) vano, -a; **it is ~ to...** +*infin* es inútil... +*infin* **3. in ~** en vano; **it was all in ~** todo fue en vano

vainglorious [,veɪn·'glɔr·i·əs] *adj form* vanaglorioso, -a, jactancioso, -a

vale *n,* **Vale** [veɪl] *n liter* (*valley*) valle *m;* **this ~ of tears** *fig* este valle de lágrimas

valediction [,væl·ə·'dɪk·ʃən] *n form* **1.** (*farewell*) adiós *m* **2.** (*speech given when taking leave*) discurso *m* de despedida

valedictorian [,væl·ə·dɪk·'tɔr·i·ən] *n* universitario a cargo del discurso de despedida

valedictory [,væl·ə·'dɪk·tə·ri] *adj* de despedida; **~** (**address**) discurso *m* de despedida

valence ['veɪ·ləns], **valency** ['veɪ·lən·si] <-ies> *n* valencia *f*

valentine ['væl·ən·taɪn] *n* **1.** (*card*) tarjeta que se manda el día de los enamorados **2.** (*sweetheart*) enamorado, -a *m, f;* **be my ~!** ¿quieres ser mi novio?

Valentine's Day *n* día *m* de los enamorados, día *m* de San Valentín

valerian [və·'lɪr·i·ən] *n* valeriana *f*

valet [væ·'leɪ] *n* **1.** (*car parker*) aparcacoches *mf inv* **2.** (*in a hotel*) mozo *m* de hotel **3.** HIST (*male's private servant*) ayuda *m* de cámara

valet parking *n* servicio *m* de aparcacoches

valiant ['væl·jənt] *adj* valiente

valid ['væl·ɪd] *adj* **1.** (*worthwhile, weighty*) válido, -a; **no longer ~** caducado, -a **2.** (*reasonable because well-founded*) legítimo, -a **3.** LAW (*still in force*) vigente; (*contractually binding*) vinculante

validate ['væl·ə·deɪt] *vt* **1.** (*ratify, officially approve*) dar validez a **2.** *a.* COMPUT (*verify, authenticate: document*) validar; (*ticket*) sellar, picar

validity [və·'lɪd·ə·ţi] *n* **1.** (*soundness, weight*) legitimidad *f* **2.** (*legal force*) validez *f;* (*of a law*) vigencia *f*

Valium® ['væl·i·əm] *n* Valium® *m*

valley ['væl·i] *n* valle *m*

valor ['væl·ər] *n form* bravura *m*

valuable ['væl·ju·ə·bəl] **I.** *adj* (*help, information*) valioso, -a; (*time*) precioso, -a; **this ring is very ~** este anillo tiene mucho valor **II.** *n* **~s** objetos *mpl* de valor

valuation [,væl·ju·'er·ʃən] *n* **1.** (*estimation of financial value*) tasación *f* **2.** (*estimated value*) valor *m* **3.** (*acknowledgement of the excellence of sth*) valoración *f*

valuator *n* FIN tasador(a) *m(f)*

value ['væl·ju] **I.** *n* **1.** *a.* MATH, MUS (*worth, significance*) valor *m;* **~ judgment** juicio *m* de valor; **to be of ~ to sb** ser valioso para alguien; **to be of little ~** ser de poco valor; **to place a high ~ on sth** dar mucha importancia a algo; **to be a good ~** (**for one's money**) estar bien

V

de precio; **to be of great ~** ser muy valioso; **to increase (in)** ~ aumentar de valor; **to lose (in)** ~ depreciarse; **market** ~ valor de mercado; **to put a ~ on sth** poner precio a algo **2.** ~**s** (*moral ethics, standards*) valores *mpl;* **set of** ~**s** escala *f* de valores **II.** *vt* **1.** (*think to be significant*) apreciar; **to** ~ **sb as a friend** valorar a alguien como amigo **2.** (*estimate financial worth*) tasar; **to** ~ **sth at sth** valorar algo en algo

valued *adj form* apreciado, -a; ~ **customer** cliente *mf* valioso, -a

valueless ['væl·ju·lɪs] *adj* sin valor

valve [vælv] *n* **1.** AUTO, ANAT válvula *f;* **inlet** ~ válvula de admisión **2.** ELEC lámpara *f* **3.** MUS pistón *m*

vamp¹ [væmp] **I.** *n* **1.** (*of a shoe*) empeine *m* **2.** MUS acompañamiento *m* improvisado **II.** *vt* **1.** (*shoe*) poner el empeine a **2.** MUS improvisar un acompañamiento para **III.** *vi* MUS improvisar un acompañamiento

vamp² [væmp] *n* vampiresa *f*

vampire ['væm·paɪr] *n* vampiro *m*

van¹ [væn] *n* furgoneta *f;* **delivery** ~ furgoneta de reparto; **moving** ~ camión *m* de mudanzas

van² [væn] *n inf abbr of* **vanguard** vanguardia *f*

vandal ['væn·dəl] *n* gamberro, -a *m, f*

vandalism ['væn·də·lɪz·əm] *n* vandalismo *m*

vandalize ['væn·də·laɪz] *vt* destrozar

vane [veɪn] *n* **1.** (*weathercock*) veleta *f* **2.** (*of windmill*) aspa *f* **3.** (*of propeller*) paleta *f*

vanguard ['væn·gard] *n* vanguardia *f*

vanilla [və·'nɪl·ə] *n* vainilla *f*

vanish ['væn·ɪʃ] *vi* **to** ~ **(from sth)** desaparecer (de algo); **to** ~ **into thin air** *fig* esfumarse; (*fear, hopes*) desvanecerse; (*cease to exist: era, race*) extinguirse

vanishing point *n* punto *m* de fuga

vanity ['væn·ə·ti] <-ies> *n* **1.** (*self-satisfaction*) vanidad *f* **2.** (*dressing table*) tocador *m* **3.** (*bathroom cabinet*) mueble *m* de baño (*con lavabo empotrado*)

vanity bag *n,* **vanity case** *n* neceser *m*

vanity plate *n* AUTO matrícula *f* personalizada (*en vehículo*)

vanquish ['væn·kwɪʃ] *vt* derrotar

vantage ['væn·tɪdʒ] *n* ventaja *f*

vantage point *n* **1.** (*place with good view*) mirador *m* **2.** (*position which gives an advantage*) posición *f* de ventaja

Vanuatu [væ·'nu·a·tu] *n* Vanuatu *m*

vapid ['væp·ɪd] *adj* insulso, -a

vapor ['veɪ·pər] *n* **1.** (*steam*) vapor *m;* **water** ~ vapor de agua **2.** (*on glass*) vaho *m,* vaporizo *m Méx, PRico*

vaporization [ˌveɪ·pər·ɪ·'zeɪ·ʃən] *n* vaporización *f*

vaporize ['veɪ·pə·raɪz] **I.** *vt* vaporizar **II.** *vi* vaporizarse

vaporizer *n* vaporizador *m*

vapor pressure *n* presión *f* del vapor

vapor trail *n* AVIAT estela *f*

variability [ˌvær·i·ə·'bɪl·ə·ti] *n* variabilidad *f*

variable ['vær·i·ə·bəl] **I.** *n* MATH variable *f* **II.** *adj* variable

variance ['vær·i·əns] *n* **1.** (*disagreement, difference*) discrepancia *f;* **at** ~ en contradicción; **to be at** ~ **with sth** discrepar en algo; **to set two people at** ~ sembrar la discordia entre dos personas **2.** (*variation*) variación *f* **3.** (*in statistics*) variancia *f*

variant ['vær·i·ənt] **I.** *n* variante *f* **II.** *adj* **1.** (*different*) divergente; ~ **spelling** variante *f* ortográfica **2.** (*tending to change*) variable

variation [ˌvær·i·'eɪ·ʃən] *n* **1.** *a.* BIO, MUS variación *f;* **a** ~ **on sth** una variación de algo **2.** (*varying, difference, dissimilarity*) diferencia *f;* **wide** ~**s in sth** grandes diferencias de algo

varicose ['vær·ə·koʊs] *adj* MED varicoso, -a; ~ **veins** varices *fpl*

varied ['vær·id] *adj* **1.** (*altered, diverse*) variado, -a **2.** (*having different colors*) multicolor

variegated ['vær·i·ə·geɪ·t̬ɪd] *adj* multicolor

variety [və·'raɪ·ə·ti] <-ies> *n* **1.** (*diversity*) variedad *f;* **to lend** ~ **to sth** variar algo **2.** (*assortment*) surtido *m;* **for a** ~ **of reasons** por varias razones; **in a** ~ **of ways** de diversas formas **3.** (*sort, category*) tipo *m;* **a new** ~ **of tulip** una nueva variedad de tulipán; **a** ~ **of communism** una forma de comunismo **4.** THEAT variedades *fpl* ▶ ~ **is the spice of life** *prov* en la variedad está el gusto *prov*

variety show *n* **1.** THEAT espectáculo *m* de variedades **2.** RADIO, TV programa *m* de variedades

various ['vær·i·əs] *adj* **1.** (*numerous*) varios, -as; **for** ~ **reasons** por diversas razones **2.** (*diverse*) diferentes

varmint ['var·mɪnt] *n* **1.** ZOOL alimaña *f* **2.** (*person*) sinvergüenza *mf*

varnish ['var·nɪʃ] **I.** *n* barniz *m* **II.** *vt* barnizar

varsity ['var·sə·ti] <-ies> *n* equipo principal de un instituto o universidad

vary ['vær·i] <-ie-> **I.** *vi* **1.** (*change, be different*) variar; **opinions** ~ hay diversidad de opiniones; **to** ~ **between... and...** oscilar entre... y...; **to** ~ **from...** diferenciarse de... **2.** (*diverge*) desviarse; **to** ~ **from sth** apartarse de algo **II.** *vt* **1.** (*change*) variar **2.** (*diversify*) diversificar

varying *adj* variable

vascular ['væs·kjə·lər] *adj* vascular

vase [veɪs] *n* **1.** (*for flowers*) florero *m* **2.** (*ornamental*) jarrón *m* **3.** (*receptacle*) vasija *f*

vassal ['væs·əl] *n* HIST vasallo, -a *m, f*

vast [væst] *adj* **1.** (*of great extent: area, region*) vasto, -a; **a** ~ **country** un extenso país **2.** (*of great size*) enorme; **the** ~ **majority** la gran mayoría; **a** ~ **amount of money** una considerable suma de dinero **3.** (*great in degree: importance*) considerable; **his** ~ **knowledge of...** sus amplios conocimientos en el campo de...

vastly *adv* (*very*) sumamente; ~ **superior**

infinitamente superior

vastness *n* inmensidad *f*

vat [væt] *n* tanque *m;* (*for wine or oil*) cuba *f*

Vatican ['væt·ɪ·kən] **I.** *n* **the** ~ el Vaticano **II.** *adj* vaticano, -a

Vatican City *n* Ciudad *f* del Vaticano

vaudeville ['vɔd·vɪl] *n* vodevil *m*

vault[1] [vɔlt] *n* **1.** ARCHIT (*arched structure*) bóveda *f;* (*under churches*) cripta *f;* (*at cemeteries*) panteón *m;* **family** ~ panteón familiar **2.** (*underground chamber*) sótano *m;* (*secure repository*) cámara *f;* (*in a bank*) cámara acorazada

vault[2] [vɔlt] **I.** *n* salto *m* **II.** *vi, vt* saltar

vaulted *adj* ARCHIT abovedado, -a

vaulting I. *n* ARCHIT bóveda *f* **II.** *adj* (*exaggerated*) desmesurado, -a; (*ambition*) desmedido, -a

vaulting horse *n* potro *m*

vaunt [vɔnt] *vt* jactarse de

VC [ˌviˈsi] *n abbr of* **Vietcong** Vietcong *m*

VCR [ˌvi·siˈar] *n abbr of* **videocassette recorder** vídeo *m*

VD [ˌviˈdi] *n* MED *abbr of* **venereal disease** ETS *f*

veal [vil] *n* ternera *f*

veal cutlet *n* chuleta *f* de ternera

vector ['vek·tər] **I.** *n* **1.** MATH vector *m* **2.** BIO, MED portador(a) *m(f)* **II.** *adj* MATH vectorial

V-E Day [ˌviˈiˌdeɪ] *abbr of* **Victory in Europe Day** día de la victoria aliada en Europa en la Segunda Guerra Mundial

veer [vɪr] **I.** *vi* **1.** (*alter course: vehicle*) virar; (*wind*) cambiar de dirección; (*road, way*) torcer **2.** (*alter attitude, goal*) cambiar bruscamente; **to** ~ **from sb's usual opinions** desviarse de las opiniones habituales de alguien; **to** ~ **towards sth** dar un giro hacia algo **II.** *n* (*character, plan*) viraje *m;* (*movement*) cambio *m* de dirección

veg (**out**) [vedʒ] *vi inf* estar tirado sin hacer nada

vegan ['vi·gən] *n* vegetariano que no come ni huevos ni productos lácteos

vegetable ['vedʒ·tə·bəl] *n* **1.** (*plant*) vegetal *m* **2.** (*edible plant*) hortaliza *f;* (**green**) ~ verdura *f;* ~ **soup** sopa *f* de verduras; **root** ~ tubérculo *m;* **seasonal** ~ verdura del tiempo **3.** *offensive, sl* MED vegetal *m*

vegetable butter *n*, **vegetable fat** *n* margarina *f*

vegetable garden *n* huerto *m*

vegetable kingdom *n* reino *m* vegetal

vegetable oil *n* aceite *m* vegetal

vegetarian [ˌvedʒ·əˈter·i·ən] **I.** *n* vegetariano, -a *m, f* **II.** *adj* vegetariano, -a; **to go** ~ hacerse vegetariano

vegetate ['vedʒ·ə·teɪt] *vi a. fig* vegetar

vegetation [ˌvedʒ·əˈteɪ·ʃən] *n* vegetación *f*

veggie *n*, **vegie** ['vedʒ·i] *n* **1.** *inf* vegetariano, -a *m, f* **2.** ~ **s** (*vegetables*) hortalizas *fpl*

veggieburger *n* hamburguesa *f* vegetariana

vehemence ['vi·ə·məns] *n* vehemencia *f*

vehement ['vi·ə·mənt] *adj* vehemente

vehicle ['vi·ə·kəl] *n* **1.** (*method of transport*) vehículo *m;* **motor** ~ vehículo motorizado **2.** (*channel, means of expression*) medio *m;* **to be a** ~ **for sth** servir de vehículo para algo

vehicular [vi·ˈhɪk·jə·lər] *adj form* de vehículos; (*accident*) de circulación; ~ **traffic** tráfico *m* rodado; ~ **manslaughter** muerte por atropello

veil [veɪl] **I.** *n* velo *m;* (*of smoke*) cortina *f;* **bridal** ~ velo de novia; **a** ~ **of secrecy** un halo de misterio; **under the** ~ **of sth** *fig* con el pretexto de algo; **to draw a** ~ **over sth** *fig* correr un tupido velo sobre algo **II.** *vt* velar; (*disguise*) disimular; **to** ~ **one's face** taparse con un velo; **to be** ~**ed** estar cubierto con un velo; **to be** ~**ed in secrecy** estar rodeado de un halo de misterio; **the mist** ~**ed the mountains** *fig, liter* la bruma envolvía las montañas

veiled *adj* **1.** (*wearing a veil*) cubierto, -a con velo **2.** (*indirect, masked, concealed: criticism*) velado, -a; **thinly** ~ apenas disimulado

vein [veɪn] *n* **1.** ANAT, BOT vena *f* **2.** GEO veta *f,* sirca *f Chile;* **a quartz** ~ una veta de cuarzo **3.** (*trait, element of stated feeling*) disposición *f;* **a** ~ **of madness** una vena de loco; **to talk in a more serious** ~ hablar más en serio **4.** (*frame of mind, temperament*) estilo *m;* **in** (**a**) **similar** ~ del mismo estilo; **in the** ~ **of sth** a la manera de algo

veined *adj* **1.** (*stone, wood*) veteado, -a **2.** (*hand, leaf*) nervado, -a

velar ['vi·lər] **I.** *adj* LING velar **II.** *n* LING sonido *m* velar

Velcro® ['vel·kroʊ] *n* velcro® *m*

veld *n*, **veldt** [velt] *n* veld *m* (*meseta seca característica de Sudáfrica*)

velocity [və·ˈlɑs·ə·ţi] <-ies> *n form* velocidad *f;* **at the** ~ **of** a la velocidad de; **sound/light** ~ velocidad del sonido/de la luz

velvet ['vel·vɪt] **I.** *n* terciopelo *m* **II.** *adj* **1.** (*made of velvet*) de terciopelo **2.** *fig* (*smooth: voice*) aterciopelado, -a

velveteen [ˌvel·vɪ·ˈtin] *n* velvetón *m*

velvety ['vel·və·ţi] *adj fig* aterciopelado, -a

venal ['vi·nəl] *adj* **1.** (*corrupt: regime, ruler*) corrupto, -a **2.** (*that can be purchased*) venal

venality [vɪ·ˈnæl·ə·ţi] *n* **1.** (*corruptibility*) venalidad *f* **2.** (*corruption*) corrupción *f*

vend [vend] *vt* vender

vendetta [ven·ˈdeţ·ə] *n* vendetta *f*

vending machine *n* máquina *f* expendedora

vendor ['ven·dər] *n* vendedor(a) *m(f)*

veneer [və·ˈnɪr] **I.** *n* **1.** chapado *m* **2.** *fig* apariencia *f* **II.** *vt* chapar

venerable ['ven·ər·ə·bəl] *adj* **1.** (*person, position*) venerable **2.** (*tradition*) ancestral; (*building, tree*) centenario, -a; ~ **ruins** ruinas *fpl* milenarias

venerate ['ven·ə·reɪt] *vt* venerar

veneration [ˌven·ə·ˈreɪ·ʃən] *n* veneración *f;* **to hold sb in** ~ venerar a alguien

venereal [və·ˈnɪr·i·əl] *adj* MED venéreo, -a; ~ **disease** enfermedad *f* venérea

V

venetian blind [və·ˌni·ʃən·ˈblaɪnd] *n* persiana *f* veneciana

Venezuela [ˌven·ə·ˈzweɪ·lə] *n* Venezuela *f*

Venezuelan I. *adj* venezolano, -a II. *n* venezolano, -a *m, f*

vengeance [ˈven·dʒəns] *n* venganza *f;* **to take ~ (up)on sb** vengarse de alguien; **with a ~** con ganas

venial [ˈvi·ni·əl] *adj form* venial; (*offense*) leve; (*error*) sin importancia

venial sin *n* pecado *m* venial

venison [ˈven·ɪ·sən] *n* (carne *f* de) venado *m*

venom [ˈven·əm] *n* veneno *m; fig* malevolencia *f*

venomous [ˈven·ə·məs] *adj* venenoso, -a; (*malicious*) maligno, -a; (*tongue*) viperino, -a

venous [ˈvi·nəs] *adj* venoso, -a

vent[1] [vent] I. *n* **1.** (*small outlet for gas: of a building*) conducto *m* de ventilación; (*of a volcano*) chimenea *f;* **air ~** respiradero *m* **2.** (*release of feelings*) **to give ~ to sth** dar rienda suelta a algo; **to give ~ to one's feelings** desahogarse II. *vt* (*feelings*) dar rienda suelta a; (*opinion*) expresar; **to ~ one's anger on sb** descargar su ira contra alguien

vent[2] [vent] *n* FASHION abertura *f*

ventilate [ˈven·tə·leɪt] *vt* **1.** (*oxygenate a space*) ventilar; **artificially ~d** MED con respiración asistida **2.** (*give utterance to, verbalize*) expresar

ventilation [ˌven·tə·ˈleɪ·ʃən] *n* ventilación *f*

ventilation duct *n* conducto *m* de ventilación

ventilator [ˈven·tə·leɪ·tər] *n* **1.** (*device*) ventilador *m* **2.** MED respirador *m*

ventricle [ˈven·trɪ·kəl] *n* ventrículo *m*

ventriloquist [ven·ˈtrɪl·ə·kwɪst] *n* ventrílocuo, -a *m, f*

venture [ˈven·tʃər] I. *n* **1.** (*endeavor*) aventura *f* **2.** COM empresa *f;* **joint ~** empresa conjunta II. *vt* **1.** (*dare*) **to ~ to do sth** atreverse a hacer algo; **may I ~ a suggestion?** ¿me permite hacer una sugerencia? **2.** (*dare to express: an opinion*) aventurar **3.** (*put at risk, endanger*) **to ~ sth (on sth)** arriesgar algo (en algo) ▶ **nothing ~d, nothing gained** *prov* quien no se arriesga, no pasa la mar *prov* III. *vi* aventurarse ◆ **venture out** *vi* atreverse a salir

venture capital *n* FIN capital *m* de riesgo

venturesome [ˈven·tʃər·səm] *adj form* **1.** (*adventurous: person*) atrevido, -a; (*enterprising*) emprendedor(a) **2.** (*risky, not safe*) arriesgado, -a

venue [ˈven·ju] *n* (*for meeting*) lugar *m* (de reunión); (*for concert*) lugar (de celebración); (*of sporting event*) campo *m*

Venus [ˈvi·nəs] *n* Venus *m*

veracious [və·ˈreɪ·ʃəs] *adj form* **1.** (*honest*) honesto, -a **2.** (*accurate and precise*) veraz

veracity [və·ˈræs·ə·ti] *n* **1.** (*truthfulness*) honestidad *f* **2.** (*accuracy*) veracidad *f*

veranda *n*, **verandah** [və·ˈræn·də] *n* porche *m*

verb [vɜrb] *n* verbo *m;* **intransitive/transitive**

~ verbo intransitivo/transitivo

verbal [ˈvɜr·bəl] *adj* **1.** (*oral, unwritten*) verbal; **~ agreement** acuerdo *m* verbal; **~ facility** facilidad *f* de palabra **2.** (*word for word: translation*) literal

verbalize [ˈvɜr·bə·laɪz] *vt* expresar con palabras, verbalizar

verbally *adv* verbalmente

verbatim [vər·ˈbeɪ·t̬ɪm] I. *adj* literal II. *adv* literalmente

verbiage [ˈvɜr·bi·ɪdʒ] *n* verborrea *f*

verbose [vər·ˈboʊs] *adj* verboso, -a; (*speech*) prolijo, -a

verbosity [vər·ˈbas·ə·t̬i] *n* verbosidad *f*

verdant [ˈvɜr·dənt] *adj liter* verde

verdict [ˈvɜr·dɪkt] *n* **1.** LAW (*by jury*) veredicto *m;* (*by judge, magistrate*) fallo *m;* **~ of guilty/ not guilty** veredicto de culpabilidad/inocencia; **to bring in** [*o* **to return**] **a ~** (*jury*) emitir un veredicto; (*judge, magistrate*) dictar sentencia **2.** (*opinion after consideration, conclusion*) juicio *m;* **to give a ~ on sth/sb** dar una opinión sobre algo/alguien; **what is your ~?** ¿qué opinas?

verdigris [ˈvɜr·dɪ·grɪs] *n* verdín *m*

verge [vɜrdʒ] *n* **1.** (*physical edge, margin*) margen *m* **2.** *fig* (*brink*) borde *m;* **to be on the ~ of...** estar al borde de...; **to be on the ~ of a solution** estar a punto de encontrar una solución; **to be on the ~ of doing sth** estar a punto de hacer algo; **to be on the ~ of tears** estar a punto de llorar ◆ **verge on** *vt* rayar en; **to ~ the ridiculous** rayar en lo ridículo; **she is verging on fifty** ronda los cincuenta (años)

verger [ˈvɜr·dʒər] *n* sacristán *m*

verification [ˌver·ə·fɪ·ˈkeɪ·ʃən] *n* **1.** (*checking*) verificación *f* **2.** (*confirmation*) confirmación *f*

verify [ˈver·ə·faɪ] <-ie-> *vt* **1.** (*corroborate*) confirmar; (*suspicions, theory*) corroborar **2.** (*authenticate*) verificar

verisimilitude [ˌver·ə·sə·ˈmɪl·ə·tud] *n* verosimilitud *f*

veritable [ˈver·ə·t̬ə·bəl] *adj* auténtico, -a

vermicelli [ˌvɜr·mə·ˈtʃel·i] *n* fideos *mpl* finos

vermicide [ˈvɜr·mə·saɪd] *n* vermicida *m*

vermiform [ˈvɜr·mə·fɔrm] *adj* vermiforme

vermilion [vər·ˈmɪl·jən], **vermillion** I. *n* bermellón *m* II. *adj* bermellón *inv*

vermin [ˈvɜr·mɪn] *n* **1.** *pl* (*animals*) alimañas *fpl;* (*insects*) bichos *mpl* **2.** *pej* (*people*) gentuza *f*

verminous *adj* **1.** (*dog*) pulgoso, -a; (*person*) piojoso, -a **2.** (*disease*) verminoso, -a

Vermont [vər·ˈmant] *n* Vermont *m*

vermouth [vər·ˈmuθ] *n* vermut *m*, vermú *m*

vernacular [vər·ˈnæk·jə·lər] *n* **1.** (*local language*) lengua *f* vernácula **2.** (*everyday language*) lengua *f* coloquial

vernal equinox [ˌvɜr·nəl·ˈi·kwɪ·naks] <-es> *n* equinoccio *m* vernal

versatile [ˈvɜr·sə·t̬əl] *adj* **1.** (*flexible*) versátil; (*mind*) ágil **2.** (*multifaceted*) polifacético, -a

3. (*multipurpose: material*) polivalente

versatility [ˌvɜr·sə·'tɪl·ə·t̬i] *n* (*flexibility*) versatilidad *f*; (*of mind*) agilidad *f*

verse [vɜrs] *n* 1. LIT verso *m* 2. MUS estrofa *f* 3. REL versículo *m*

versed *adj* to be (well) ~ in sth estar (muy) versado en algo

versify ['vɜr·sə·faɪ] <-ie-> I. *vi* versificar II. *vt* poner en verso

version ['vɜr·ʒən] *n* versión *f*

verso ['vɜr·soʊ] *n* form 1. (*of printed page*) dorso *m* 2. (*of a coin, medal*) reverso *m*

versus ['vɜr·səs] *prep* 1. (*in comparison*) frente a 2. SPORTS, LAW contra

vertebra ['vɜr·t̬ə·brə] <-ae> *n* vértebra *f*

vertebral ['vɜr·t̬ə·brəl] *adj* vertebral

vertebrate ['vɜr·t̬ə·brɪt] I. *n* vertebrado *m* II. *adj* vertebrado, -a

vertex ['vɜr·teks] <-es *o* -tices> *n* vértice *m*

vertical ['vɜr·t̬ə·kəl] *adj* vertical; ~ **drop** caída *f* en picado

vertiginous [vər·'tɪdʒ·ə·nəs] *adj form* vertiginoso, -a

vertigo ['vɜr·t̬ə·goʊ] *n* vértigo *m*

verve [vɜrv] *n* ímpetu *m;* **with** ~ con brío; **to give sth** (**added**) ~ dar/añadir un toque a algo

very ['ver·i] I. *adv* 1. (*extremely*) muy; ~ **much** mucho; **not** ~ **much** no mucho; **to feel** ~ **much at home** sentirse como en casa; **I am** ~**,** ~ **sorry** de veras lo siento 2. (*expression of emphasis*) **the** ~ **best** lo mejor de lo mejor; **the** ~ **first** el primerísimo; **at the** ~ **most** como mucho; **at the** ~ **least** por lo menos; **the** ~ **next day** justo al día siguiente; **the** ~ **same** justo lo mismo ▶ ~ **well** muy bien; **to be all** ~ **fine, but...** estar muy bien y tal, pero... II. *adj* **at the** ~ **bottom** al final del todo; **the** ~ **fact** el mero hecho; **the** ~ **man** el mismísimo

Very light *n* bengala *f*

Very pistol *n* pistola *f* para disparar bengalas

vespers ['ves·pərz] *npl* REL (*evensong*) vísperas *fpl*

vessel ['ves·əl] *n* 1. (*any kind of boat*) embarcación *f*; (*large boat*) navío *m* 2. (*container*) recipiente *m* 3. ANAT, BOT vaso *m* 4. *liter* (*person*) baza *f*

vest¹ [vest] *n* chaleco *m;* **bullet-proof** ~ chaleco antibalas

vest² [vest] *vt* **to** ~ **sb with sth** investir a alguien de [*o* con] algo; **to** ~ **sth in sb** conferir algo a alguien; **to** ~ **one's hopes in sb/sth** depositar sus esperanzas en alguien/algo; ~**ed interests** intereses *mpl* creados

vestibule ['ves·tə·bjul] *n* vestíbulo *m*

vestige ['ves·tɪdʒ] *n* vestigio *m;* **a** ~ **of truth** un asomo de verdad; **to show a** ~ **of sth** mostrar un resquicio de algo

vestments ['vest·mənts] *npl* vestiduras *fpl*

vestry ['ves·tri] <-ies> *n* sacristía *f*

vet¹ [vet] *inf* I. *n* (*animal doctor*) veterinario, -a *m, f* II. *vt* <-tt-> 1. (*examine carefully*) examinar 2. (*screen*) someter a investigación

vet² [vet] *n inf, a. fig* MIL veterano, -a *m, f*

vetch [vetʃ] <-es> *n* algarroba *f*

veteran ['vet̬·ər·ən] I. *n a. fig* MIL veterano, -a *m, f* II. *adj a. fig* MIL veterano, -a

Veterans Day *n* día *m* de los Veteranos

ℹ️ La fiesta de **Veterans Day,** que se celebra el 11 de noviembre, fue creada inicialmente para conmemorar el armisticio firmado entre Alemania y los aliados en 1918, con el que se puso fin a la I Guerra Mundial. Hoy en día, en esta fecha se honra a los veteranos de todas las guerras estadounidenses.

veterinarian [ˌvet̬·ər·ə·'ner·i·ən] *n* veterinario, -a *m, f*

veterinary ['vet̬·ər·ə·ner·i] *adj* veterinario, -a; ~ **surgeon** veterinario, -a *m, f*

veto ['vi·t̬oʊ] I. *n* <-es> veto *m;* **to have a** ~ **over sth** tener derecho a veto en algo II. *vt* <-vetoed> 1. (*exercise a veto against*) vetar 2. (*forbid*) prohibir

vex [veks] *vt* 1. (*cause trouble for*) importunar 2. (*upset*) enfadar; **he is** ~**ed by computer problems** los problemas informáticos lo sacan de quicio

vexation [vek·'seɪ·ʃən] *n* disgusto *m;* **to be a** ~ **to sb** ser una irritación para alguien

vexatious [vek·'seɪ·ʃəs] *adj* fastidioso, -a; ~ **child** niño, -a *m, f* irritante; ~ **problem** problema *m* engorroso

VFW [ˌvi·ef·'dʌb·əl·ju] *abbr of* **Veterans of Foreign Wars** Veteranos *mpl* de Guerras Extranjeras

VHF [ˌvi·eɪtʃ·'ef] *abbr of* **very high frequency** VHF

VI *n abbr of* **Virgin Islands** Islas Vírgenes *fpl*

via ['vaɪ·ə] *prep* por; ~ **Denver/the bridge** por Denver/el puente

viability [ˌvaɪ·ə·'bɪl·ə·t̬i] *n* viabilidad *f*

viable ['vaɪ·ə·bəl] *adj* viable

viaduct ['vaɪ·ə·dʌkt] *n* viaducto *m*

vial ['vaɪ·əl] *n* ampolla *f*

vibe [vaɪb] *n sl* rollo *m;* **good/bad** ~**s** buen/mal rollo

vibrant ['vaɪ·brənt] *adj* 1. (*lively: personality*) enérgico, -a; (*music*) vibrante; ~ **performance** espectáculo *m* contundente 2. (*bustling*) efervescente; (*economy*) en ebullición 3. (*bright and strong: color, light*) radiante

vibrate ['vaɪ·breɪt] I. *vi* 1. (*shake quickly, oscillate*) vibrar; **to** ~ **with enthusiasm** estremecerse de entusiasmo 2. (*continue to be heard: sound*) vibrar II. *vt* hacer vibrar

vibration [vaɪ·'breɪ·ʃən] *n* vibración *f*

vibrator [vaɪ·breɪ·t̬ər] *n* TECH vibrador *m;* (*for sexual stimulation*) vibrador

vicar ['vɪk·ər] *n* vicario *m*

vicarage ['vɪk·ər·ɪdʒ] *n* vicaría *f*

vicarious [vɪ·'ker·i·əs] *adj* (*thrill*) indirecto, -a; (*authority*) delegado, -a

vice [vaɪs] *n* vicio *m;* ~ **squad** brigada *f* antivicio

V

vice chairman [ˌvaɪs·ˈtʃer·mən] <-men> *n* vicepresidente, -a *m, f*

vice chancellor *n* UNIV vicerrector(a) *m(f)*

vice president *n* **1.** (*deputy president*) presidente, -a *m, f* en funciones **2.** (*title*) vicepresidente, -a *m, f*

vice versa [ˌvaɪ·sə·ˈvɜr·sə] *adv* viceversa

vicinity [və·ˈsɪn·ə·t̬i] <-ies> *n* inmediaciones *fpl;* **in the ~ of...** en los alrededores de...

vicious [ˈvɪʃ·əs] *adj* **1.** (*malicious*) malo, -a; (*fighting*) salvaje; (*gossip*) malicioso, -a **2.** (*cruel, violent*) despiadado, -a **3.** (*able to cause pain: animal*) feroz **4.** (*extremely powerful: pain*) atroz; (*wind*) devastador(a)

vicious circle *n* círculo *m* vicioso

vicissitudes [vɪ·ˈsɪs·ə·tudz] *n form pl* vicisitudes *fpl;* **the ~s of life** los avatares de la vida

victim [ˈvɪk·tɪm] *n* víctima *f;* **to be the ~ of sth** ser víctima de algo ▶**to fall ~ to sb/sth** sucumbir a alguien/algo

victimize [ˈvɪk·tə·maɪz] *vt* discriminar; **to be ~d by law** ser víctima de la ley

victor [ˈvɪk·tər] *n* vencedor(a) *m(f);* **to emerge (as) the ~** salir victorioso

Victorian [vɪk·ˈtɔr·i·ən] **I.** *adj* victoriano, -a **II.** *n* victoriano, -a *m, f*

victorious [vɪk·ˈtɔr·i·əs] *adj* victorioso, -a; **~ team** equipo *m* ganador

victory [ˈvɪk·tə·ri] <-ies> *n* victoria *f;* **to clinch a ~ (over sb)** conseguir una victoria (sobre alguien); **to win a ~ (in sth)** obtener una victoria (en algo)

victuals [ˈvɪt̬·əlz] *n pl, a. iron* vituallas *fpl*

videlicet [vɪ·ˈdel·ə·set] *adv form* a saber

video [ˈvɪd·i·oʊ] **I.** *n* **1.** vídeo *m;* **to come out on ~** salir en vídeo **2.** (*tape*) cinta *f* de vídeo; **blank ~** cinta de vídeo virgen **II.** *vt* grabar en vídeo

video camera *n* videocámara *f*

videocassette *n* videocasete *m*

videoconference *n* videoconferencia *f*

video game *n* videojuego *m*

videophile *n* aficionado , -a a los vídeos o dvd *m*

videophone *n* videoteléfono *m*

video recorder *n* magnetoscopio *m*

video surveillance *n* vigilancia *f* con cámaras de vídeo

videotape **I.** *n* cinta *f* de vídeo **II.** *vt* grabar en vídeo

vie [vaɪ] <vying> *vi* **to ~ (with sb) for sth** competir (con alguien) por algo

Vienna [vi·ˈen·ə] *n* Viena *f*

Viennese [ˌvi·ə·ˈniz] **I.** *n inv* vienés, -esa *m, f* **II.** *adj* vienés, -esa

Vietcong [ˌvi·et·ˈkaŋ] *n inv* Vietcong *m*

Vietnam [ˌvi·et·ˈnam] *n* Vietnam *m*

Vietnamese [vi·ˌet·nə·ˈmiz] **I.** *adj* vietnamita **II.** *n* **1.** (*person*) vietnamita *mf* **2.** LING vietnamita *m*

view [vju] **I.** *n* **1.** (*opinion*) punto *m* de vista; **exchange of ~s** intercambio *m* de opiniones; **conflicting ~s** opiniones *fpl* contrapuestas;

the prevailing ~ la opinión *f* dominante; **to express a ~** expresar un parecer; **to have an optimistic ~ of life** ver la vida con optimismo; **to hold strong ~s about sth** mantener una postura fuerte sobre algo; **to share a ~** compartir un punto de vista; **in her ~...** a su modo de ver... **2.** (*perspective*) perspectiva *f;* **long-term ~** perspectiva a largo plazo; **to take the long ~ of sth** considerar algo a largo plazo **3.** (*sight*) vista *f;* **to afford a panoramic ~** permitir una vista panorámica; **to block sb's ~** estar tapando a alguien (la vista); **to come into ~** aparecer ante la vista; **to disappear from ~** perderse de vista; **to keep sb/sth in ~** mantener a alguien/algo en el punto de mira **4.** (*opportunity to observe*) panorama *m* ▶**to take a dim ~ of sth** ver algo con malos ojos; **to have sth in ~** tener algo en mente; **in ~ of sth** en vista de algo; **to be on ~** estar expuesto; **to be on ~ to the public** estar abierto al público; **with a ~ to sth** con vistas a algo; **with this in ~** con este fin **II.** *vt* **1.** (*consider*) considerar; **to ~ sth from a different angle** enfocar algo desde un ángulo distinto; **to ~ sth with reluctance** tomarse algo con reticencia **2.** (*watch*) ver **3.** (*take a look at*) mirar

viewer *n* **1.** (*person*) telespectador(a) *m(f)* **2.** (*device*) proyector *m* de diapositivas **3.** COMPUT visor *m*, visualizador *m*

viewfinder [ˈvju·ˌfaɪn·dər] *n* visor *m*

viewing *n* visita *f;* **a second ~ of the film is also frightening** ver la película por segunda vez también da miedo; **~ figures** índice *m* de audiencia

viewpoint [ˈvju·pɔɪnt] *n* **1.** (*point of view*) punto *m* de vista **2.** (*vista point*) mirador *m*

vigil [ˈvɪdʒ·əl] *n* vela *f;* **to keep ~** mantenerse alerta; **to hold a ~** velar

vigilance [ˈvɪdʒ·ɪ·ləns] *n* vigilancia *f;* **to relax ~** bajar la guardia

vigilant [ˈvɪdʒ·ɪ·lənt] *adj* vigilante; **to be ~ in doing sth** estar atento al hacer algo

vignette [vɪ·ˈnjet] *n* estampa *f*

vigor [ˈvɪg·ər] *n* vigor *m;* (*energy*) energía *f;* **to do sth with ~** hacer algo con energía

vigorous [ˈvɪg·ər·əs] *adj* **1.** (*energetic*) enérgico, -a; (*protest*) rotundo, -a **2.** (*flourishing: growth*) pujante

vile [vaɪl] *adj* **1.** (*disgusting, shameful*) vil **2.** *inf* (*very bad*) vomitivo, -a; (*weather*) asqueroso, -a; **~ mood** humor *m* de perros; **to be ~ to sb** portarse como un cerdo con alguien; **to smell ~** apestar

vilify [ˈvɪl·ə·faɪ] <-ie-> *vt form* envilecer

village [ˈvɪl·ɪdʒ] **I.** *n* **1.** (*small settlement*) aldea *f.* **+** *pl/sing vb* (*populace*) pueblo *m* **II.** *adj* de pueblo

village idiot *n* tonto, -a *m, f* del pueblo

villager [ˈvɪl·ə·dʒər] *n* aldeano, -a *m, f*

villain [ˈvɪl·ən] *n* **1.** (*evil person*) villano, -a *m, f;* **small-time ~** maleante *mf;* **to cast sb as a ~** quedar alguien como el malo **2.** (*bad guy*) granuja *mf* ▶**the ~ of the piece** *inf* el malo/la

mala de la obra
villainous ['vɪl·ə·nəs] *adj* infame
villainy ['vɪl·ə·ni] *n* vileza *f*
vim [vɪm] *n* brío *m*
VIN [vɪn] *n abbr of* **vehicle identification number** NIV *m*
vinaigrette [ˌvɪn·ə·'gret] *n* vinagreta *f*
vindicate ['vɪn·də·keɪt] *vt* 1. (*justify*) justificar 2. (*support*) reivindicar 3. (*clear of blame, suspicion*) vindicar
vindication [ˌvɪn·də·'keɪ·ʃən] *n* 1. (*justification*) justificación *f* 2. (*act of clearing blame*) vindicación *f*
vindictive [vɪn·'dɪk·tɪv] *adj* vengativo, -a
vine [vaɪn] *n* 1. (*grape plant*) vid *f* 2. (*climbing type*) parra *f*
vinegar ['vɪn·ə·gər] *n* vinagre *m*
vineyard ['vɪn·jərd] *n* viñedo *m*
vintage ['vɪn·tɪdʒ] I. *n* 1. (*wine from a particular year*) cosecha *f* 2. (*harvest season*) vendimia *f* II. *adj* 1. CULIN añejo, -a 2. (*high and classic quality*) excelente; ~ **music of the sixties** clásicos *mpl* de la música de los sesenta 3. AUTO antiguo, -a; ~ **car** coche *m* de época
vintner ['vɪnt·nər] *n* vinatero, -a *m, f*
vinyl ['vaɪ·nəl] I. *n* vinilo *m* II. *adj* de vinilo
viola[1] [vi·'ou·lə] *n* MUS viola *f*
viola[2] ['vi·ə·lə] *n* BOT viola *f*
violate ['vaɪ·ə·leɪt] *vt* 1. (*break, not comply with*) violar; **to ~ a cease-fire agreement** romper un acuerdo de alto al fuego 2. (*disturb*) perturbar; (*tomb*) profanar; **to ~ sb's privacy** violar la intimidad de alguien
violation [ˌvaɪ·ə·'leɪ·ʃən] *n* violación *f*; **traffic ~** infracción *f* de tráfico
violence ['vaɪ·ə·ləns] *n* violencia *f*
violent ['vaɪ·ə·lənt] *adj* 1. (*cruel*) violento, -a 2. (*very powerful*) fuerte; (*argument, objections*) duro, -a
violet ['vaɪ·ə·lɪt] I. *n* 1. BOT violeta *f* 2. (*color*) violeta *m* II. *adj* violeta
violin [ˌvaɪ·ə·'lɪn] *n* MUS violín *m*
violinist [ˌvaɪ·ə·'lɪn·ɪst] *n* MUS violinista *mf*
violoncellist [ˌvi·ə·lən·'tʃel·ɪst] *n* MUS violoncelista *mf*
violoncello [ˌvi·ə·lən·'tʃel·ou] *n* violoncelo *m*
VIP [ˌvi·aɪ·'pi] *s.* **very important person** VIP *mf*
viper ['vaɪ·pər] *n a. fig* víbora *f*
virgin ['vɜr·dʒɪn] *n* virgen *f*; **the Blessed Virgin** la Santísima Virgen
virginal ['vɜr·dʒɪ·nəl] *n* virginal
virgin forest *n* selva *f* virgen
Virginia [vər·'dʒɪn·jə] *n* Virginia *f*
Virgin Islands *n* Islas *fpl* Vírgenes
virginity [vər·'dʒɪn·ə·ti] *n* virginidad *f*; **to lose one's ~** perder la virginidad
Virgo ['vɜr·gou] *n* virgo *mf*
virile ['vɪr·əl] *adj* viril
virility [və·'rɪl·ə·ti] *n* 1. (*sexual vigor*) virilidad *f* 2. (*forcefulness*) fuerza *f*
virology [vaɪ·'ral·ə·dʒi] *n* virología *f*
virtual ['vɜr·tʃu·əl] *adj* virtual; **to be a ~**

unknown ser en efecto un desconocido; **to provoke a ~ collapse of the economy** provocar prácticamente un colapso de la economía
virtually *adv* prácticamente
virtual reality *n* realidad *f* virtual
virtue ['vɜr·tʃu] *n* 1. (*good moral quality*) virtud *f* 2. (*advantage, benefit*) ventaja *f* ▶ **to make a ~ of necessity** hacer de la necesidad virtud; **to make a ~ (out) of sth** convertir algo en virtud; **by ~ of** *form* en virtud de
virtuosity [ˌvɜr·tʃu·'as·ə·ti] *n form* virtuosidad *f*
virtuoso [ˌvɜr·tʃu·'ou·sou] <-s *o* -osi> I. *n* virtuoso, -a *m, f* II. *adj* virtuoso, -a; **a ~ display of diplomacy** un magnífico despliegue de habilidad diplomática
virtuous ['vɜr·tʃu·əs] *adj* 1. (*morally good*) virtuoso, -a 2. (*chaste*) casto, -a
virulence ['vɪr·jə·ləns] *n* virulencia *f*
virulent ['vɪr·jə·lənt] *adj* 1. MED virulento, -a 2. *form* (*hateful and fierce*) violento, -a
virus ['vaɪ·rəs] <-es> *n* COMPUT, MED virus *m inv*
visa ['vi·zə] I. *n* visado *m* II. *adj* de visado
vis-à-vis [ˌvi·zə·'vi] I. *prep* con relación a; (*compared to*) en comparación con II. *n* cara a cara *m*
viscera ['vɪs·ər·ə] *npl* vísceras *fpl*
viscose ['vɪs·kous] *n* viscosa *f*
viscosity [vɪ·'skas·ə·ti] *n* viscosidad *f*
viscount ['vaɪ·kaunt] *n* vizconde *m*
viscountess ['vaɪ·kaun·tɪs] *n* vizcondesa *f*
viscous ['vɪs·kəs] *adj* viscoso, -a
vise [vaɪs] *n* torno *m* de banco
visibility [ˌvɪz·ə·'bɪl·ə·ti] *n* 1. (*clearness of view*) visibilidad *f*; **poor ~** poca visibilidad 2. (*public awareness*) notoriedad *f*
visible ['vɪz·ə·bəl] *adj* 1. (*able to be seen, noticeable*) visible; **to be barely ~** ser a penas perceptible 2. (*in the public eye*) notorio, -a
vision ['vɪʒ·ən] *n* 1. (*sight*) vista *f*; **blurred ~** visión *f* borrosa 2. (*mental image*) *a.* REL visión 3. *fig* (*beautiful sight*) imagen *f*; **to have ~s of fame** soñar con ser famoso
visionary ['vɪʒ·ə·ner·i] I. *n* visionario, -a *m, f* II. *adj* 1. (*hallucinatory*) utópico, -a 2. (*future-orientated*) con visión de futuro
visit ['vɪz·ɪt] I. *n* visita *f*; **to have a ~ from sb** recibir una visita de alguien; **to pay a ~ to sb** ir a ver a alguien II. *vt* visitar III. *vi* ir de visita
visitation [ˌvɪz·ə·'teɪ·ʃən] *n* 1. (*act of visiting*) visita *f* 2. *iron* (*official visit*) inspección *f* 3. LAW (*parent's right*) derecho *m* de visita 4. REL visión *f*
visiting hours *npl* horario *m* de visita
visiting professor *n* profesor(a) *m(f)* visitante
visitor ['vɪz·ɪ·tər] *n* visitante *mf*; **~s' book** libro *m* de visitas
visor ['vaɪ·zər] *n* visera *f*
vista ['vɪs·tə] *n* 1. (*splendid view*) panorama *m* 2. *fig* perspectiva *f*; **to open up a ~** abrir una perspectiva; **to raise a ~** levantar perspectivas
visual ['vɪʒ·u·əl] *adj* visual; **~ sense** sentido *m* estético; **~ aid** soporte *m* visual

V

visualize ['vɪʒ·u·ə·laɪz] *vt* visualizar
vital ['vaɪ·ţəl] *adj* vital; ~ **ingredient** ingrediente *m* esencial; ~ **organs** órganos *mpl* vitales; ~ **part** parte *f* crucial; ~ **statistics** estadísticas *fpl* demográficas; **it is ~ to do...** es fundamental hacer...
vitality [vaɪ·'tæl·ə·ţi] *n* vitalidad *f*
vitalize ['vaɪ·ţə·laɪz] *vt* **1.** (*give life to*) vivificar **2.** (*animate*) dar vida; *fig* vitalizar
vitamin ['vaɪ·ţə·mɪn] *n* vitamina *f*
vitamin deficiency *n* avitaminosis *f inv*
vitreous ['vɪt·ri·əs] *adj* vítreo, -a
vitrify ['vɪt·rə·faɪ] <-ie-> I. *vt* vitrificar II. *vi* vitrificarse
vitriol ['vɪt·ri·əl] *n* vitriolo *m*
vitriolic [ˌvɪt·ri·'al·ɪk] *adj* vitriólico, -a
vituperate [vaɪ·'tu·pə·reɪt] *form* I. *vt* vituperar II. *vi* vituperarse
vituperation [vaɪ·ˌtu·pə·'reɪ·ʃən] *n form* vituperio *m*
vivacious [vɪ·'veɪ·ʃəs] *adj* vivaz; **a ~ blonde** una rubia llena de vida; **a ~ life** una vida animada
vivacity [vɪ·'væs·ə·ţi] *n* vivacidad *f*
vivarium [vaɪ·'ver·i·əm] <-s *o* vivaria> *n* vivero *m*
viva voce [ˌvaɪ·və·'voʊ·si] I. *n* examen *m* oral II. *adj* oral III. *adv* a viva voz
vivid ['vɪv·ɪd] *adj* (*color*) vivo, -a; (*language*) vívido, -a; (*imagination*) fértil
viviparous [vaɪ·'vɪp·ər·əs] *adj* vivíparo, -a
vivisect ['vɪv·ə·sekt] *vt* viviseccionar
vivisection [ˌvɪv·ə·'sek·ʃən] *n* vivisección *f*
vixen ['vɪk·sən] *n* **1.** ZOOL zorra *f* **2.** *pej* (*woman*) arpía *f*
viz. [vɪz] *adv abbr of* **videlicet** (**namely**) a saber
vocabulary [voʊ·'kæb·jə·ler·i] *n* vocabulario *m;* **limited ~** vocabulario limitado; **to widen one's ~** ampliar vocabulario; **the word 'politeness' isn't in his ~** *iron* la palabra 'modales' no entra en su vocabulario
vocal ['voʊ·kəl] I. *adj* **1.** (*of the voice*) oral; ~ **communication** comunicación *f* oral **2.** (*outspoken*) vehemente; **a ~ minority** una minoría que se hace oír; **to be ~ (about sth)** armar revuelo (acerca de algo) II. *n* voz *f,* vocalista *mf;* **lead ~** voz principal; **to be on ~s** cantar
vocal cords *n pl* cuerdas *fpl* vocales
vocalist ['voʊ·kə·lɪst] *n* vocalista *mf*
vocalize ['voʊ·kə·laɪz] I. *vi* vocalizar II. *vt* vocalizar
vocation [voʊ·'keɪ·ʃən] *n* vocación *f;* **to miss one's ~** equivocarse de carrera
vocational [voʊ·'keɪ·ʃə·nəl] *adj* vocacional; ~ **counseling** orientación *f* profesional; ~ **training** formación *f* profesional
vociferate [voʊ·'sɪf·ə·reɪt] I. *vi* vociferar II. *vt* vociferar
vociferation [voʊ·ˌsɪf·ə·'reɪ·ʃən] *n form* vocerío *m*
vociferous [voʊ·'sɪf·ər·əs] *adj* vociferante

vodka ['vad·kə] *n* vodka *f*
vogue [voʊg] *n* moda *f* ▶ **in ~** de moda; **to be back in ~** ponerse de moda de nuevo; **out of ~** pasado de moda
voice [vɔɪs] I. *n* voz *f;* **in a loud ~** en voz alta; **to raise/lower one's ~** levantar/bajar la voz; **to lose one's ~** quedarse afónico; **to listen to the ~ of reason** atender a razones; **to make one's ~ heard** hacerse escuchar; **with one ~** a coro; **to give ~ to sth** expresar algo; **the ~ within sb** la voz de la conciencia de alguien II. *vt* expresar
voice box <-es> *n inf* laringe *f*
voiced *adj* sonoro, -a
voiceless ['vɔɪs·lɪs] *adj* **1.** LING sordo, -a **2.** *liter* sin voz
voice mail *n* TEL correo *m* de voz
voice-over *n* TV, CINE voz *f* en off
void [vɔɪd] I. *n* **1.** (*empty space*) hueco *m* **2.** (*feeling of emptiness*) vacío *m* II. *adj* inválido, -a; **to be ~ of sth** estar falto de algo III. *vt* anular
vol. *abbr of* **volume** vol.
volatile ['val·ə·ţəl] *adj* volátil; (*situation*) inestable; (*person*) voluble
volcanic [val·'kæn·ɪk] *adj* volcánico, -a
volcano [val·'keɪ·noʊ] <-(e)s> *n* volcán *m*
vole [voʊl] *n* ratón *m* de campo
volition [voʊ·'lɪʃ·ən] *n form* voluntad *f;* **to do sth (out) of one's own ~** hacer algo por voluntad propia
volley ['val·i] I. *n* **1.** (*salvo*) descarga *f;* **to discharge ~s** descargar salvas **2.** (*onslaught*) llovia *f;* **a ~ of enquiries** una retahíla de preguntas; **a ~ of insults** una sarta de insultos **3.** SPORTS volea *f* II. *vi* SPORTS volear III. *vt* **to ~ a ball** sacar una pelota
volleyball ['val·i·bɔl] *n* voleibol *m*
volt [voʊlt] *n* voltio *m*
voltage ['voʊl·tɪdʒ] *n* voltaje *m*
voltage detector *n* ELEC voltímetro *m*
voltage drop *n* ELEC caída *f* de tensión
volte-face [ˌvɔlt·'fas] *n* cambio *m* radical (de opinión)
voluble ['val·jə·bəl] *adj form* **1.** (*loquacious*) locuaz **2.** (*wordy*) extenso, -a
volume ['val·jum] *n* (*all senses*) volumen *m;* ~ **of sales** COM volumen de ventas; **to turn the ~ up/down** subir/bajar el volumen ▶ **to speak ~s for sth** ser muy indicativo de algo
volume control, **volume regulator** *n* control *m* del volumen
volume discount *n* rappel *m*
voluminous [və·'lu·mə·nəs] *adj form* **1.** (*extensive*) exhaustivo, -a **2.** (*very large*) voluminoso, -a; (*trunk*) voluminoso, -a
voluntary ['val·ən·ter·i] *adj* voluntario, -a
volunteer [ˌval·ən·'tɪr] I. *n* voluntario, -a *m, f* II. *vt* **to ~ oneself for sth** ofrecerse (voluntario) para algo; **to ~ information** dar información por iniciativa propia III. *vi* ofrecerse; (*willingly join*) presentarse voluntario IV. *adj* de voluntarios; ~ **army** ejército *m* de volunta-

rios

voluptuous [və·'lʌp·tʃu·əs] *adj* **1.** (*sexually appealing*) voluptuoso, -a **2.** (*epicurean*) epicúreo, -a

volute [və·'lut] *n* **1.** ARCHIT voluta *f* **2.** ZOOL (*marine gastropod*) concha *f;* (*snail's shell*) caparazón *m*

vomit ['vam·ɪt] **I.** *vi* vomitar; **it makes me want to** ~ *a. fig* me produce náuseas **II.** *vt* vomitar **III.** *n* vómito *m*

voodoo ['vu·du] *n* **1.** (*black magic*) vudú *m* **2.** *inf* (*jinx*) maldición *f*

voracious [vɔ·'reɪ·ʃəs] *adj* voraz

voracity [vɔ·'ræs·ə·t̬i] *n* voracidad *f*

vortex ['vɔr·teks] <-es *o* vortices> *n* vórtice *m;* ~ **of emotion** torbellino *m* de emociones

vote [voʊt] **I.** *vi* **1.** (*elect*) votar; **to** ~ **for/ against sb/sth** votar a favor/en contra de alguien/algo **2.** (*formally decide*) **to** ~ **on sth** someter algo a votación **II.** *vt* **1.** (*elect*) elegir por votación **2.** (*propose*) **to** ~ **that...** votar que... +*subj* **3.** (*declare*) considerar **III.** *n* **1.** (*formally made choice*) voto *m* **2.** (*election*) votación *f;* **to put sth to the** ~ someter algo a votación **3.** (*right to elect*) **to have the** ~ tener derecho al voto

◆ **vote down** *vt* rechazar (por votación)

◆ **vote in** *vt* elegir (por votación)

◆ **vote on** *vt* aprobar (por votación)

◆ **vote out** *vt* **to vote sb out** (**of sth**) no reelegir a alguien (en algo)

voter *n* votante *mf*

voter's registration (**card**) *n* papeleta *f* electoral

voting I. *adj* de votos **II.** *n* votación *f*

voting booth <-es> *n* cabina *f* de votación

voting day *n* no *art* día *m* de elecciones

voting machine *n* máquina *f* de recuento de votos

vouch [vaʊtʃ] **I.** *vi* **to** ~ **for sth/sb** responder de algo/por alguien **II.** *vt* **to** ~ **that...** confirmar que...

voucher ['vaʊ·tʃər] *n* **1.** (*coupon*) vale *m* **2.** (*receipt*) comprobante *m*

vouchsafe [ˌvaʊtʃ·'seɪf] *vt form* **to** ~ (**sb**) **sth** dignarse a dar algo (a alguien); **to** ~ **to do sth** dignarse a hacer algo

vow [vaʊ] **I.** *vt* jurar; **to** ~ **chastity** hacer voto de castidad **II.** *n* **to take a** ~ hacer los votos

vowel ['vaʊ·əl] *n* vocal *f*

voyage ['vɔɪ·ɪdʒ] **I.** *n* viaje *m* **II.** *vi* viajar; **to** ~ **across sth** viajar por algo

voyager ['vɔɪ·ɪ·dʒər] *n* navegante *mf*

voyeur [vɔɪ·'jɜr] *n* mirón, -ona *m, f*

vroom I. *vi inf* hacer rugir el motor del coche **II.** *interj inf* brum

VT *n abbr of* **Vermont** Vermont *m*

Vt. *n abbr of* **Vermont** Vermont *m*

VTOL ['vi·tɔl] AVIAT *abbr of* **vertical take-off and landing** despegue *m* y aterrizaje *m* vertical

vulcanite ['vʌl·kə·naɪt] *n* vulcanita *f*

vulcanization [ˌvʌl·kə·nɪ·'zeɪ·ʃən] *n* vulcaniza-

ción *f*

vulcanize ['vʌl·kə·naɪz] *vt* vulcanizar

vulgar ['vʌl·gər] *adj* **1.** (*crude*) ordinario, -a **2.** (*commonplace*) vulgar; ~ **accent** acento *m* vulgar

vulgarity [vʌl·'gær·ə·t̬i] *n* **1.** (*crudeness*) grosería *f* **2.** (*ordinariness*) vulgaridad *f*

vulgarize ['vʌl·gə·raɪz] *vt* vulgarizar

vulnerable ['vʌl·nər·ə·bəl] *adj* vulnerable

vulture ['vʌl·tʃər] *n a. fig* buitre *m*

vulva ['vʌl·və] <-s *o* -e> *n* vulva *f*

vying ['vaɪ·ɪŋ] *pres p of* **vie**

W

W, w ['dʌb·əl·ju] *n* W, w *f;* ~ **as in Whiskey** W de Washington

W *n* **1.** *abbr of* **watt** W **2.** *abbr of* **west** O

WA ['waʃ·ɪŋ·tən] *n abbr of* **Washington** Washington *m*

wack [wæk] *adj sl* cutre

wacko ['wæk·oʊ] *n sl* bicho *m* raro

wacky ['wæk·i] <-ier, -iest> *adj sl* (*person*) chiflado, -a; (*thing*) estrambótico, -a

wad [wad] *n* (*of banknotes*) fajo *m;* (*of cotton*) bola *f;* (*of straw*) manojo *m;* (*of chewing tobacco*) pellizco *m* de tabaco de mascar; (*of forms*) montón *m*

wadding ['wad·ɪŋ] *n* relleno *m*

waddle ['wad·əl] **I.** *vi* anadear **II.** *n* andares *mpl* de pato

wade [weɪd] **I.** *vi* caminar por el agua; **to** ~ **across** vadear; **to** ~ **into sth** adentrarse en algo caminando; **to** ~ **into sb** *inf* tomarla con alguien; **to** ~ **through a book** leerse un libro con dificultad **II.** *vt* vadear **III.** *n* chapoteo *m*

wader ['weɪ·dər] *n* **1.** (*bird*) ave *m* zancuda **2.** ~ **s** (*boots*) botas *fpl* de pescador

wafer ['weɪ·fər] *n* **1.** (*biscuit*) galleta *f* de barquillo; (*for ice cream*) barquillo *m* **2.** REL hostia *f*

wafer-thin [ˌweɪ·fər·'θɪn] *adj* finísimo, -a

waffle[1] ['waf·əl] *n* CULIN gofre *m,* waffle *m AmL*

waffle[2] ['waf·əl] *inf* **I.** *vi* (*to talk*) **to** ~ (**on**) parlotear; (*in an essay*) meter paja *fig* **II.** *n* palabrería *f;* (*in an essay*) paja *f fig*

waffle iron *n* plancha *f* para gofres [*o* waffles *AmL*]

waft [waft] *liter* **I.** *vi* (*scent, sound*) llegar (flotando); **a delicious smell** ~**ed in from the kitchen** un delicioso aroma llegaba (flotando) de la cocina **II.** *vt* llevar por el aire

wag[1] [wæg] **I.** <-gg-> *vt* menear; **the dog** ~**ged its tail** el perro meneaba el rabo; **to** ~ **one's finger at sb/sth** apuntar a alguien/algo agitando el dedo **II.** <-gg-> *vi* menearse **III.** *n* meneo *m*

wag[2] [wæg] *n inf* bromista *mf*

wage [weɪdʒ] **I.** *vt* (*war*) hacer; **to ~ war against sth/sb** librar una batalla contra algo/alguien; **to ~ a campaign for/against sth** emprender una campaña por/contra algo **II.** *n* sueldo *m;* **living ~** salario de subsistencia; **minimum ~** salario mínimo; **real ~s** salario real; **to earn a ~** percibir un salario; **to get a good ~** tener un buen sueldo

wage earner *n* asalariado, -a *m, f*

wage freeze *n* congelación *f* salarial

wage increase *n* aumento *m* salarial

wager ['weɪ·dʒər] **I.** *n* apuesta *f;* **to place a ~** hacer una apuesta **II.** *vt* apostar; **to ~ one's reputation/life** jugarse su reputación/la vida

wage scale *n* escala *f* salarial

wageworker *n* asalariado, -a *m, f*

waggish ['wæg·ɪʃ] *adj inf* bromista

waggle ['wæg·əl] **I.** *vt* mover **II.** *vi* moverse

waggly ['wæg·li] <-ier, -iest> *adj* tambaleante

wagon ['wæg·ən] *n* **1.** (*horse-drawn*) carro *m* **2.** (*truck*) camión *m* ▶ **to be on the ~** *sl* no beber; **to fall off the ~** *sl* volver a darse a la bebida; **to go on the ~** *sl* dejar la bebida

waif [weɪf] *n liter* **1.** (*child*) niño, -a *m, f* sin techo **2.** (*animal*) animal *m* callejero

wail [weɪl] **I.** *vi* gemir; (*wind*) silbar; (*siren*) gemir **II.** *vt* lamentar **III.** *n* lamento *m*

wailing *n* gemidos *mpl*

Wailing Wall *n* Muro *m* de las Lamentaciones

waist [weɪst] *n* cintura *f*

waistband ['weɪst·bænd] *n* cinturilla *f*

waist-deep [ˌweɪst·'dip] *adj* hasta la cintura

waistline ['weɪst·laɪn] *n* cintura *f;* **to watch one's ~** guardar la línea

wait [weɪt] **I.** *vi* esperar; **to ~ for sth/sb** esperar algo/a alguien; **to keep sb ~ing** hacer esperar a alguien; **he cannot ~ to see her** está ansioso por verla; **~ and see** espera y verás; **(just) you ~!** ¡vas a ver! **II.** *vt* esperar; **to ~ one's turn** esperar su turno **III.** *n* espera *f;* **to lie in ~ for sb** estar al acecho de alguien

♦ **wait about** *vi*, **wait around** *vi* **to ~ for sth** estar a la espera de algo

♦ **wait behind** *vi* esperarse

♦ **wait on** *vt* **1.** (*serve*) servir **2.** *form* (*expect*) **to ~ sth** estar a la espera de algo

♦ **wait up** *vi* **to ~ for sb** esperar a alguien levantado

waiter ['weɪ·tər] *n* camarero *m*, garzón *m* *AmL*, mesero *m Méx*

waiting *n* **the ~** la espera

waiting game *n* **to play the ~** dejar pasar el tiempo

waiting list *n* lista *f* de espera

waiting room *n* sala *f* de espera

waitress ['weɪ·trɪs] *n* camarera *f*, garzona *f* *AmL*, mesera *f Méx*

waive [weɪv] *vt form* (*right*) renunciar a; (*rule*) no aplicar; (*charge*) cancelar

waiver ['weɪ·vər] *n* renuncia *f*

wake¹ [weɪk] *n* NAUT estela *f;* **in the ~ of sth** tras [*o* después de] algo

wake² [weɪk] *n* velatorio *m*

wake³ [weɪk] <woke *o* waked, woken *o* waked> **I.** *vi* despertarse **II.** *vt* despertar

♦ **wake up** *vi, vt* despertar

wakeful ['weɪk·fəl] *adj form* **1.** (*sleepless*) desvelado, -a; **~ night** noche *f* en vela **2.** (*vigilant, alert*) alerta; **to feel ~** sentirse despierto

waken ['weɪ·kən] *vt form* despertar

walk [wɔk] **I.** *n* **1.** (*stroll*) paseo *m;* **to take a ~** ir a dar un paseo; **to take sb out for a ~** sacar a alguien a pasear; **it's a five minute ~** está a cinco minutos a pie **2.** (*gait*) andar *m* **3.** (*walking pace*) paso *m* **4.** (*sth easy*) pan *m* comido; **to do sth in a ~** hacer algo con los ojos cerrados *fig;* **they won in a ~** ganaron de calle **5.** (*in baseball*) base *f* por bolas **6.** (*in basketball*) pasos *mpl* ▶ **~ of life** condición *f;* **people from all** (**different**) **~s of life** gente de todas las profesiones y condiciones sociales **II.** *vt* **1.** (*go on foot*) andar; (*distance*) recorrer a pie **2.** (*accompany*) **to ~ sb home** acompañar a alguien a su casa **3.** (*take for a walk*) **to ~ the dog** sacar a pasear al perro **4.** (*in baseball*) **to ~ a batter** otorgar al bateador una base por bolas **III.** *vi* **1.** (*go on foot*) andar, caminar; (*stroll*) pasear **2.** (*in baseball*) **he ~ed four times in the game** hizo cuatro bases por bolas a lo largo del partido **3.** (*in basketball*) hizo pasos cuatro veces a lo largo del partido ▶ **to ~ on air** no caber en sí de gozo

♦ **walk about** *vi*, **walk around** *vi* dar una vuelta

♦ **walk away** *vi form* irse; **to ~ from sb** alejarse de alguien; **to ~ from sth** desentenderse de algo; **to ~ from an accident without a scratch** salir ileso de un accidente

♦ **walk back** *vi* volver a pie

♦ **walk in** *vi* entrar

♦ **walk in on** *vt* **to ~ sb** (**doing sth**) sorprender a alguien (haciendo algo) al entrar

♦ **walk off I.** *vt* **to ~ the meal** dar un paseo para bajar la comida **II.** *vi* marcharse

♦ **walk on** *vi* seguir andando

♦ **walk out** *vi* **1.** (*leave*) salir **2.** (*go on strike*) ir a la huelga

♦ **walk out on** *vt inf* **to ~ sb** dejar a alguien

♦ **walk over** *vt* (*rights*) pisotear; **to walk (all) over sb** machacar a alguien

♦ **walk through** *vt insep* (*part*) ensayar

♦ **walk up I.** *vi* **1.** (*go up*) subir **2.** (*approach*) **to ~ to sb** acercarse a alguien **II.** *vt* **to ~ sth** subir algo

walkaway ['wɔk·ə·weɪ] *n* victoria *f* fácil, pan *m* comido *inf;* **to win in a ~** ganar sin problemas

walker ['wɔ·kər] *n* **1.** (*stroller*) paseante *mf* **2.** SPORTS marchista *mf* **3.** (*sb whose hobby is walking*) senderista *mf*

walkie-talkie [ˌwɔ·ki·'tɔ·ki] *n* walkie-talkie *m*

walk-in ['wɔk·ɪn] *adj* **1.** (*big*) empotrado, -a; **~ closet** vestidor *m* **2.** (*on street*) **~ apartment** apartamento con acceso directo desde la calle

walking I. *n* paseo *m;* SPORTS marcha *f* atlética;

to do a lot of ~ andar mucho II. *adj* **1. it is within ~ distance** se puede ir a pie **2.** (*human*) ambulante; **to be a ~ encyclopedia** ser una enciclopedia con patas

walking papers *npl sl* despido *m*, pasaporte *m inf;* **to give sb his/her ~** poner a alguien de patitas en la calle

walking stick *n* **1.** (*cane*) bastón *m* **2.** (*insect*) insecto *m* palo

walking wounded *npl* heridos *mpl* que aún pueden andar

Walkman® ['wɔk·mən] <-s> *n* walkman® *m*

walk-on ['wɔk·an] I. *adj* ~ **part** THEAT papel *m* de figurante; CINE papel *m* de extra II. *n* **1.** THEAT figurante *mf;* CINE extra *mf* **2.** SPORTS cedido, -a *m, f*

walkout ['wɔk·aʊt] *n* salida *f;* (*strike*) huelga *f;* **to stage a ~** salir

walkover ['wɔk·ˌoʊ·vər] *n inf* victoria *f* fácil; **it was a ~** fue pan comido

walkthrough ['wɔk·ˌθru] *n* ensayo *m*

walkway ['wɔk·weɪ] *n* pasarela *f*

wall [wɔl] I. *n* **1.** muro; (*in the interior*) *a.* ANAT pared *f;* (*enclosing town*) muralla *f;* (*enclosing house*) tapia *f;* **the city ~s** las murallas de la ciudad; **the Great Wall of China** la Gran Muralla China; **artery ~** pared arterial **2.** (*barrier*) barrera *f;* **a ~ of silence** un muro de silencio; **a ~ of water** una cortina de agua ► **to have one's back to** [*o* **up against**] **the ~** estar entre la espada y la pared; **to drive sb up the ~** *sl* sacar a alguien de quicio; **to hit the ~** *sl* quedarse sin fuerzas, venirse abajo *fig;* **to hit a brick ~** haber llegado a un callejón sin salida; **to be off the wall** *sl* ser un freaky; **the writing** [*o* **handwriting**] **is on the ~** tiene los días contados II. *vt* (*garden*) cercar con un muro; (*town*) amurallar

◆ **wall in** *vt* **1.** (*garden*) cercar con un muro; (*town*) amurallar **2.** *fig* encerrar

◆ **wall off** *vt* separar con un muro; **to wall oneself off** *fig* encerrarse en uno mismo

◆ **wall up** *vt* (*person*) emparedar; (*opening*) tapiar

wall chart *n* gráfico *m* de pared

wallet ['wal·ɪt] *n* cartera *f*, billetera *f AmL*

wallflower ['wɔl·ˌflaʊ·ər] *n* **1.** BOT al(h)elí *m* **2.** *fig* ≈ patito *m* feo

wall hanging *n* tapiz *m*

wallop ['wal·əp] I. *vt inf* **1.** (*hit hard*) dar un golpetazo **2.** (*punish*) dar una paliza, zurrar II. *n inf* **1.** (*hit*) golpetazo *f;* **to give sb a ~** dar a alguien un guantazo **2.** (*power*) **to pack a ~** causar (una) gran impresión

walloping I. *adj inf* **1.** (*very big*) enorme **2.** (*very good*) estupendo II. *n inf* zurra *f;* **to give sb a ~** dar una zurra a alguien

wallow ['wal·oʊ] I. *n* revolcón *m* II. *vi* **1.** (*lie in earth*) revolcarse **2.** (*remain in negative state*) sumirse; **to ~ in self-pity** sumirse en la autocompasión **3.** (*revel*) regodearse; **to ~ in wealth** nadar en la abundancia

wallpaper ['wɔl·ˌpeɪ·pər] I. *n* papel *m* pintado;

a roll of ~ un rollo de papel pintado; **to hang ~** empapelar II. *vt* empapelar

Wall Street *n* **1.** (*street*) calle bursátil y financiera en Nueva York **2.** *fig* mundo *m* bursátil

wall-to-wall ['wɔl·tə·ˈwɔl] *adj* ~ **carpeting** moqueta *f*

walnut ['wɔl·nʌt] *n* **1.** (*nut*) nuez *f* **2.** (*tree*) nogal *m*

walrus ['wɔl·rəs] <walruses *o* walrus> *n* morsa *f*

waltz [wɔlts] <-es> I. *n* vals *m* II. *vi* **1.** (*dance*) valsar **2.** *sl* (*walk confidently*) ir tan fresco III. *vt* **to ~ sb** bailar un vals con alguien

◆ **waltz about** *vi,* **waltz around** *vi* dar vueltas despreocupado

◆ **waltz in** *vi sl* entrar como si nada

◆ **waltz off** *vi sl* **to ~ with sth** birlar algo

◆ **waltz out** *vi sl* salir como si nada

wan [wan] <-nn-> *adj liter* macilento, -a

wand [wand] *n* (*conjuror's stick*) varita *f* mágica; **to wave one's magic ~** agitar la varita mágica

wander ['wan·dər] I. *vt* vagar por; **to ~ the streets** deambular por las calles, callejear II. *vi* (*roam*) vagar; (*stroll*) pasearse; **to let one's thoughts ~** dejar volar la imaginación III. *n inf* paseo *m;* **to go for a ~ around the city** dar una vuelta por la ciudad

wanderer ['wan·dər·ər] *n* hombre *m* errante, mujer *f* errante; *pej* vagabundo, -a *m, f*

wandering ['wan·dər·ɪŋ] *adj* **1.** (*nomadic*) errante; (*salesman*) ambulante; ~ **tribe** tribu nómada **2.** (*not concentrating*) divagante

wanderings ['wan·dər·ɪŋz] *n* andanzas *fpl; pej* vagabundeo *m*

wane [weɪn] I. *vi* menguar; **to wax and ~** crecer y menguar; *fig* tener altibajos II. *n* mengua *f;* **to be on the ~** menguar

wangle ['wæŋ·gəl] *vt inf* conseguir; **to ~ one's way into sth** arreglárselas para entrar en algo

want [want] I. *vt* **1.** (*wish*) querer; **to ~ to do sth** querer hacer algo; **to ~ sb to do sth** querer que alguien haga algo; **to ~ sth done** querer que se haga algo; **you're ~ed on the phone** te llaman por teléfono; **I was ~ing to leave** estaba deseando macharme **2.** (*need*) necesitar; **he is ~ed by the police** lo busca la policía; **'~ed'** 'se busca' II. *n* **1.** (*need*) necesidad *f;* **to be in ~ of sth** necesitar algo **2.** (*lack*) falta *f;* **for ~ of sth** por falta de algo; **to live in ~** *form* vivir necesitado

◆ **want in** *vi* **1.** (*want to take part*) **do you ~?** ¿te apuntas? **2.** (*want to enter*) querer entrar

◆ **want out** *vi* **1.** (*not want to take part*) **to ~** (**of sth**) querer salirse (de algo) **2.** (*want to exit*) querer salir

want ad *n inf* aviso *m*, anuncio *m* (*en periódico*)

wanting *adj* deficiente; **to be ~ in sth** estar falto de algo; **there is sth ~** falta algo

wanton ['wan·tən] *adj* **1.** (*extreme*) desenfrenado, -a **2.** (*mindless*) sin razón; ~ **destruction** destrucción sin sentido; ~ **disregard**

W

desatención injustificada; ~ **waste** dispendio gratuito **3.**(*licentious*) lascivo, -a **4.**(*capricious*) caprichoso, -a; (*playful*) juguetón, -ona
wapiti ['wɑp·ə·ṭi] *n inv* wapití *m*
war [wɔr] *n* guerra *f*; civil ~ guerra civil; **the Great War** la Primera Guerra Mundial; **the Second World War** la Segunda Guerra Mundial; **a holy** ~ una guerra santa; **the horrors of** ~ los horrores de la guerra; **in time of** ~ en tiempo(s) de guerra; **to be at** ~ estar en guerra; **to declare** ~ **on sb** declarar la guerra a alguien; *fig* hacer la vida imposible a alguien; **to go to** ~ entrar en guerra; **to make** ~ **on sb** hacer la guerra a alguien
war baby *n* niño, -a *m, f* nacido, -a durante la guerra
warble ['wɔr·bəl] *vi* (*bird*) trinar; (*lark*) gorjear; *iron* (*person*) hacer gorgoritos
warbler ['wɔr·blər] *n* curruca *f*
war bond *n* bono *m* de guerra
war correspondent *n* corresponsal *mf* de guerra
war crime *n* crimen *m* de guerra
war criminal *n* criminal *mf* de guerra
war cry *n* grito *m* de guerra
ward [wɔrd] *n* **1.**(*wardship*) tutela *f*; **in** ~ bajo tutela **2.**(*person*) pupilo, -a *m, f* **3.**(*in a hospital*) sala *f*; **geriatric/psychiatric** ~ pabellón *m* geriátrico/psiquiátrico; **maternity** ~ sala *f* de maternidad
◆**ward off** *vt* evitar
warden ['wɔr·dən] *n* guardián, -ana *m, f*; (*of a prison*) alcaide(sa) *m(f)*; **game** ~ guardabosque *mf*
wardrobe ['wɔrd·roʊb] *n* **1.**(*closet*) (armario *m*) ropero *m* **2.**(*clothes*) vestuario *m*
wardrobe malfunction *n sl:* desliz en el vestuario que deja ver más del cuerpo de una persona de lo que se supone que debería estar cubierto o tapado
wardrobe trunk *n* baúl *m* ropero
wardship ['wɔrd·ʃɪp] *n* tutela *f*
warehouse ['wer·əhaʊs] *n* almacén *m*
wares [werz] *npl inf* mercancías *fpl*
warfare ['wɔr·fer] *n* guerra *f*
war game *n* juego *m* de guerra
warhead ['wɔr·hed] *n* (*of rocket*) ojiva *f*
warily ['wer·ɪ·li] *adv* (*expecting danger*) cautamente; (*suspiciously*) recelosamente
warlike ['wɔr·laɪk] *adj* **1.**(*of war*) bélico, -a **2.**(*belligerent*) belicoso, -a; ~ **speech** discurso beligerante
warlord ['wɔr·lɔrd] *n* jefe *m* militar
warm [wɔrm] **I.** *adj* **1.**(*comfortably hot*) caliente; (*clothes*) de abrigo; **nice and** ~ a gusto y calentito; **as** ~ **as toast** *inf* bien calentito; **to be** ~ (*person*) tener calor; (*thing*) estar caliente; (*weather*) hacer calor **2.**(*affectionate*) afectuoso; ~ **welcome** calurosa bienvenida; **to be** ~ ser [o estar] efusivo **3.**(*day*) caluroso, -a; (*climate, wind*) cálido, -a **4.**(*fresh*) fresco, -a; ~ **tracks** huellas frescas
▶**you're getting** ~ ¡caliente, caliente! **II.** *n*

the ~ el calor **III.** *vt* calentar; **to** ~ **one's feet** calentarse los pies; **to** ~ **the soup** calentar la sopa; **to** ~ **sb's heart** reconfortar a alguien
◆**warm up I.** *vi* calentarse **II.** *vt* **1.**(*make hot*) calentar; **to warm sb up** hacer entrar en calor a alguien **2.**(*food*) recalentar
warm-blooded [ˌwɔrm·'blʌd·ɪd] *adj* de sangre caliente
warm front *n* frente *m* cálido
warm-hearted [ˌwɔrm·'har·ṭɪd] *adj* bondadoso, -a; (*affectionate*) cariñoso, -a
warmly *adv* **1.**(*of heat*) **wrap yourself up** ~! ¡abrígate bien! **2.**(*enthusiasm*) calurosamente; **she shook my hand** ~ me estrechó la mano afectuosamente
warmth [wɔrmθ] *n* **1.**(*heat*) calor *m* **2.**(*affection*) calidez *f*
warm-up, warmup ['wɔrm·ʌp] *n* SPORTS (pre)calentamiento *m*
warn [wɔrn] *vt* **1.**(*make aware*) avisar, advertir; **to** ~ **sb not to do sth** advertir a alguien que no haga algo; **to** ~ **sb of a danger** prevenir a alguien de un peligro **2.** LAW poner sobre aviso
◆**warn off** *vt* **to warn sb off sth** apercibir a alguien de algo; **to warn sb off doing sth** advertir a alguien que no haga algo
warning ['wɔr·nɪŋ] **I.** *n* aviso *m,* advertencia *f*; **a word of** ~ una advertencia; **to give sb a** ~ advertir a alguien; **to issue a** ~ (**about sth**) dar una advertencia (acerca de algo); **without** ~ sin previo aviso; ~! ¡atención! **II.** *adj* de advertencia
warning shot *n* disparo *m* de advertencia; **to fire a** ~ hacer un disparo de advertencia
warp [wɔrp] **I.** *vi* torcerse, deformarse **II.** *vt* **1.**(*wood*) torcer, deformar **2.**(*mind*) pervertir; **to** ~ **sb's mind/judgment** (re)torcer la mente/opinión de alguien **III.** *n* deformación *f*
war paint ['wɔr·peɪnt] *n* pintura *f* de guerra
warpath ['wɔr·pæθ] *n* **to be on the** ~ *inf* estar en pie de guerra; *fig* tener ganas de pelea
warped *adj* deformado, -a; (*mind*) pervertido, -a; **to have a** ~ **way of looking at things** tener una manera retorcida de ver las cosas
warrant ['wɔr·ənt] **I.** *n* **1.** LAW orden *f*; **arrest** ~ orden de detención; **search** ~ orden de registro; **to execute a** ~ ejecutar una orden judicial **2.**(*justification*) justificación *f* **3.** COM garantía *f* **II.** *vt* **1.**(*promise*) garantizar **2.**(*justify*) justificar
warrantee [ˌwɔr·ən·'ti] *n* beneficiario, -a *m, f* de una garantía
warrant officer *n* MIL brigada *mf*
warrantor ['wɔr·ən·tɔr] *n* garante *mf*
warranty ['wɔr·ən·ti] <-ies> *n* garantía *f*
warren ['wɔr·ən] *n* **1.** ZOOL conejera *f* **2.** *fig* laberinto *m*
warring *adj* en guerra; ~ **factions** facciones beligerantes
warrior ['wɔr·i·ər] *n* guerrero, -a *m, f*
Warsaw ['wɔr·sɔ] *n* Varsovia *f*
Warsaw Pact *n,* **Warsaw Treaty** *n* HIST Pacto

m de Varsovia

warship ['wɔr·ʃɪp] *n* barco *m* de guerra

wart [wɔrt] *n* verruga *f;* ~s **and all** *sl* (*description, portrait*) con sus virtudes y defectos

wart hog ['wɔrt·hɔg] *n* jabalí *m* verrugoso

wartime ['wɔr·taɪm] *n* tiempo *m* de guerra; **in** ~ en tiempos de guerra

war-torn ['wɔr·tɔrn] *adj* destrozado, -a por la guerra

war-weary ['wɔr·wɪr·i] *adj* cansado, -a de la guerra

wary ['wer·i] <-ier, -iest> *adj* (*not trusting*) receloso, -a; (*watchful*) cauteloso, -a; **to be** ~ **of sth/sb** recelar de algo/alguien; **to be** ~ **about** (**doing**) **sth** dudar sobre (si hacer) algo; **with a** ~ **note in one's voice** con una nota de alerta en la voz

war zone ['wɔr·zoʊn] *n* zona *f* de guerra

was [waz] *pt of* be

wash [waʃ] **I.** *vt* **1.** (*clean*) lavar; (*dishes*) fregar; **to** ~ **one's hair/hands** lavarse el pelo/las manos; **to** ~ **the floor** fregar el suelo **2.** (*waves*) bañar **3.** (*river, sea*) llevar, arrastrar; **to** ~ **sb overboard** arrojar a alguien por la borda **II.** *vi* **1.** (*person*) lavarse; (*cloth*) poderse lavar; **that excuse won't** ~ **with me** *inf* esa excusa conmigo no cuela **2.** (*do the laundry*) lavar la ropa **3.** (*sea*) chapotear **III.** *n* **1.** (*cleaning with water*) lavado *m;* **to have a** ~ darse un baño **2.** (*clothes for cleaning*) **the** ~ la ropa para lavar; **to be in the** ~ estar en la lavandería **3.** *liter* (*sound of water*) chapoteo *m* **4.** NAUT remolinos *mpl;* AVIAT disturbios *mpl* aerodinámicos **5.** (*thin layer*) capa *f,* baño *m;* (*painting*) mano *f* **6.** (*even situation*) empate *m* ▶ **to come out in the** ~ *prov* arreglarse todo

◆**wash away** *vt* **1.** (*clean*) quitar **2.** (*carry elsewhere*) llevar, arrastrar

◆**wash down** *vt* **1.** (*clean*) lavar **2.** (*carry elsewhere*) llevar, arrastrar **3.** *fig* (*drink*) **to** ~ **sth with sth** tragarse algo con algo

◆**wash out I.** *vi* quitarse **II.** *vt* **1.** (*clean*) lavar; (*remove*) quitar **2.** *fig* **our party was washed out** la fiesta fue cancelada

◆**wash over** *vt* **1.** (*flow over*) pasar por encima de **2.** (*have no effect on*) no afectar

◆**wash up I.** *vt* **1.** (*bring via water*) **the sea washed it up** el mar lo arrojó sobre la playa **2.** (*clean*) lavar **II.** *vi* **1.** (*wash*) lavarse (las manos y la cara) **2.** (*arrive*) ser traído por la corriente

Wash. *abbr of* Washington

washable *adj* lavable

wash-and-wear *adj* de lava y pon

washbasin *n* (*basin*) lavabo *m;* (*bowl*) palangana *m*

washboard *n* tabla *f* de lavar

washbowl *n s.* **washbasin**

washcloth *n* manopla *f*

washed-out [ˌwaʃt·'aʊt] *adj* **1.** (*faded*) desteñido, -a; ~ **jeans** vaqueros descoloridos; (*pale*) demacrado, -a **2.** (*tired*) cansado, -a

washer ['waʃ·ər] *n* **1.** (*washing machine*) lava-

dora *f* **2.** (*plastic ring*) arandela *f*

washing ['waʃ·ɪŋ] *n* **1.** (*clothes for cleaning*) ropa *f* sucia **2.** (*act*) lavado *f;* (*of clothes*) colada *f;* **to do the** ~ hacer la colada

washing machine *n* lavadora *f,* lavarropas *f* *inv Arg*

Washington ['waʃ·ɪŋ·tən] *n* Washington *m*

Washington D.C. *n* Washington D.C. *m*

washout ['waʃ·aʊt] *n inf* desastre *m;* **a complete** ~ un desatre total

wasn't ['wʌz·ənt] = **was not** *s.* **be**

wasp [wasp] *n* avispa *f*

WASP [wasp] *n pej, inf abbr of* White Anglo-Saxon Protestant *persona de la clase privilegiada de los EE.UU., blanca, anglosajona y protestante*

waste [weɪst] **I.** *n* **1.** (*misuse*) derroche *m;* **it's a** ~ **of energy/money** es un derroche de energía/dinero; **it's a** ~ **of time** es una pérdida de tiempo; **to lay** ~ **to the land** devastar la tierra; **to go to** ~ echarse a perder; **what a** ~! ¡qué pena! **2.** (*unwanted matter*) desechos *mpl;* **household/industrial/nuclear/toxic** ~ residuos *mpl* domésticos/industriales/nucleares/tóxicos; **to recycle** ~ reciclar la basura **II.** *vt* malgastar; (*time*) perder; (*an opportunity*) desaprovechar; **to** ~ **one's breath** *fig* gastar saliva; **to** ~ **no time in doing sth** apresurarse a hacer algo; **to not** ~ **words** no gastar saliva inútilmente **III.** *vi* agotarse ▶ ~ **not,** want **not** *prov* quien guarda, halla *prov* **IV.** *adj* sobrante; (*material*) de desecho; (*land*) yermo, -a

◆**waste away** *vi* consumirse

wastebasket ['weɪst·bæs·kət] *n* papelera *m*

wasteful ['weɪst·fəl] *adj* derrochador(a); **to be** ~ **with electricity** gastar mucha electricidad

waste heat *n* calor *m* residual

wasteland *n* yermo *m*

waste management *n* gestión *f* de residuos

wastepaper *n* papel *m* usado; (*recyclable*) papel *m* para reciclar

wastepaper basket *n* papelera *f*

waste pipe *n* tubo *m* de desagüe

waste product *n* residuos *mpl*

waster *n* **1.** (*person*) derrochador(a) *m(f);* **a money** ~ un manirroto **2.** (*good-for-nothing*) perdido, -a *m, f*

wastewater *n* aguas *fpl* residuales

wasting ['weɪ·stɪŋ] *adj* (*disease*) debilitante

wastrel ['weɪ·strəl] *n* **1.** (*wasteful person*) derrochador(a) *m(f)* **2.** (*good-for-nothing*) perdido, -a *m, f*

W

watch [watʃ] I. *n* 1. (*clock on wrist*) reloj *m* de pulsera; (*clock on chain*) reloj de bolsillo 2. (*act of observation*) vigilancia *f;* **to keep a close ~ on sb/sth** vigilar a alguien/algo con mucho cuidado; **to be on the ~ for sth/sb** estar pendiente de algo/alguien; **to put a ~ on sth/sb** poner algo/a alguien bajo vigilancia; **to be under ~** estar bajo vigilancia 3. (*group of guards*) guardia *f;* HIST ronda *f* 4. (*period of duty*) guardia *f;* **to keep** [*o* **be on**] **~** estar de guardia 5. (*alert*) METEO **a tornado/hurricane ~** una alerta de tornado/huracán II. *vt* 1. (*observe*) mirar; **to ~ the clock** mirar el reloj; **to ~ a film** ver una película; **to ~ TV** ver la televisión; **to ~ the world go by** mirar cómo pasa la gente; **to ~ sb/sth do sth** mirar a alguien/algo hacer algo; **to ~ how sb does sth** mirar cómo alguien hace algo 2. (*keep vigil*) vigilar; **to ~ sth/sb like a hawk** vigilar algo/a alguien como un perro guardián; **to ~ the kids** echar un ojo a los niños 3. (*mind*) fijarse en; **to ~ every penny** (**one spends**) estar pendiente de cada céntimo (que se gasta); **to ~ one's weight** cuidar la línea; **~ it!** ¡cuidado!, ¡aguas! *Méx;* **to ~ it** (**with sb**) tener cuidado (con alguien); **~ yourself** cuídate III. *vi* fijarse; **to ~ as sb/sth does sth** fijarse en cómo alguien/algo hace algo
◆**watch out** *vi* tener cuidado; **~!** ¡cuidado!
watchband ['watʃ,bænd] *n* correa *f* de reloj
watchdog ['watʃ·dɔg] *n* 1. (*dog*) perro *m* guardián 2. (*keeper of standards*) guardián, -ana *m, f;* (*official organization*) organismo *m* de vigilancia; **a ~ of sth** un guardián de algo
watcher ['watʃ·ər] *n* observador(a) *m(f)*
watchful ['watʃ·fəl] *adj* vigilante; **to keep a ~ eye on sb/sth** estar pendiente de alguien/algo; **under the ~ eye of sb** bajo la atenta mirada de alguien
watchmaker ['watʃ·,meɪ·kər] *n* relojero, -a *m, f*
watchman ['watʃ·mən] <-men> *n* guardián *m;* **night ~** vigilante *m* nocturno
watchtower ['watʃ·,taʊ·ər] *n* atalaya *f*
watchword ['watʃ·,wɜrd] *n* 1. (*symbol*) consigna *f* 2. (*password*) contraseña *f*
water ['wɔ·t̬ər] I. *n* 1. (*liquid*) agua *f;* **bottled ~** agua embotellada; **a bottle of ~** una botella de agua; **a drink/a glass of ~** un trago/un vaso de agua; **hot and cold running ~** agua corriente caliente y fría 2. (*area of water*) **the ~s of the Mississippi** las aguas del Misisipi; **coastal ~s** aguas costeras; **territorial ~s** aguas jurisdiccionales; **uncharted ~s** *fig* territorio *m* desconocido; **by ~** por mar 3. MED ~ **on the brain** hidrocefalia *f;* ~ **on the knee** derrame *m* sinovial ▶**to be ~ under the bridge** ser agua pasada; **like ~ off a duck's back** como si oyera llover; **to spend money like ~** gastar el dinero como si creciera en los árboles; **to pour cold ~ on sth** poner trabas a algo; **to be in deep ~** estar metido en un lío; **still ~s run deep** *prov* no te fíes del agua mansa *prov;* **to get into hot ~** meterse en hon-

duras; **to fish in troubled ~s** pescar en río revuelto; **to hold ~** (*explanation*) ser consistente; **to muddy the ~s** enmarañar las cosas II. *vt* (*plants*) regar; (*livestock*) dar de beber a III. *vi* 1. (*produce tears*) lagrimear 2. (*salivate*) salivar; **it makes my mouth ~** se me hace la boca agua
waterborne ['wɔ·t̬ər·bɔrn] *adj* por mar; **a ~ disease** enfermedad propagada por el agua; ~ **attack** ataque por agua
water bottle *n* botellín *m* de agua; (*for soldiers, travelers*) cantimplora *f*
water cannon *n inv* cañón *m* de agua
watercolor I. *n* acuarela *f* II. *adj* de [*o* en] acuarela
water-cooled ['wɔ·t̬ər·kuld] *adj* refrigerado, -a por agua
watercraft *n liter* embarcación *f*
watercress *n* berro *m*
waterfall *n* cascada *f*
waterfowl *n inv* ave *f* acuática
waterfront *n* (*harbor*) puerto *m*
water heater *n* calentador *m* de agua
water hose *n* manguera *f*
watering can ['wɔ·t̬ər·ɪŋ,kæn] *n* regadera *f*
watering hole *n* abrevadero *m*
watering place *n* abrevadero *m*
waterless ['wɔ·t̬ər·lɪs] *adj* árido, -a; ~ **desert/wasteland** desierto/páramo árido
water level *n* nivel *m* del agua
water lily <-ies> *n* nenúfar *m*
water line *n* línea *f* de flotación
waterlogged ['wɔ·t̬ər·lɔgd] *adj* anegado, -a
Waterloo ['wɔ·t̬ər·'lu] *n* **to meet one's ~** llegar a algo/alguien su San Martín
water main *n* cañería *f* principal
waterman <-men> *n* barquero *m*
watermark *n* 1. (*river or tide level*) línea *f* del agua 2. (*on paper*) filigrana *f*
watermelon *n* sandía *f*
water meter *n* contador *m* de agua
water pipe *n* 1. (*for transporting water*) cañería *f* 2. (*hookah*) pipa *f* de agua
water pistol *n* pistola *f* de agua
water pollution *n* contaminación *f* del agua
water polo *n* waterpolo *m*
water pressure *n* presión *f* del agua
waterproof ['wɔ·t̬ər·pruf] I. *adj* impermeable II. *vt* impermeabilizar
water-repellent *adj* hidrófugo, -a
water-resistant *adj* resistente al agua
watershed ['wɔ·t̬ər·ʃed] *n* 1. (*high ground*) divisoria *f* de aguas 2. *fig* (*great change*) punto *m* de inflexión; **to mark a ~** marcar un punto decisivo
waterside *n* orilla *f*, ribera *f*
water ski ['wɔ·t̬ər·ski] <-s> *n* esquí *m* acuático
water-ski ['wɔ·t̬ər·,ski] *vi* esquiar en el agua; **to go ~ing** hacer esquí acuático
water-skiing *n* esquí *m* acuático
water softener *n* ablandador *m* de agua
water-soluble *adj* soluble en agua

waterspout *n* METEO tromba *f*

water supply *n* suministro *m* de agua

water table *n* capa *f* freática

water tank *n* cisterna *f;* (*smaller one*) aljibe *m*

watertight ['wɔ·ţər·ˌtaɪt] *adj* **1.** (*not allowing water in/out*) hermético, -a **2.** *fig* (*not allowing doubt*) irrecusable; **a ~ alibi** una coartada a toda prueba

water tower *n* depósito *f* elevado de agua

water vapor *n* vapor *m* de agua

waterway *n* canal *m*

water wings *npl* flotadores *mpl;* **to wear ~** usar flotadores

waterworks *n pl* (*where public water is stored*) reserva *f* de abastecimiento de agua ▶**to turn on the ~** echar a llorar

watery ['wɔ·ţə·ri] <-ier, -iest> *adj* **1.** (*bland*) aguado, -a; **a ~ soup** una sopa aguada **2.** (*weak in color*) deslavado, -a; (*weak in strength*) diluido, -a; **a ~ sun** un sol pálido

watt [wat] *n* ELEC vatio *m*

wattage ['waţ·ɪdʒ] *n* ELEC vatiaje *m*

wave [weɪv] **I.** *n* **1.** (*of water*) ola *f;* (*on surface, of hair*) ondulación *f;* **to be on the crest of the ~** *fig* estar en la cumbre **2.** PHYS onda *f* **3.** (*hand movement*) **to give sb a ~** saludar a alguien con la mano ▶**to make ~s** causar problemas **II.** *vi* **1.** (*make hand movement*) **to ~ at** [*o* **to**] **sb** saludar a alguien con la mano **2.** (*move from side to side: field of corn*) mecerse con el viento; (*flag*) ondear **III.** *vt* **1.** (*signal*) **to ~ goodbye** decir adiós con la mano; **to ~ sb away** rechazar con la mano **2.** (*move from side to side*) agitar **3.** (*hair*) ondular; **to ~ one's hair** ondularse el pelo

◆**wave down** *vt* **to wave sb/sth down** hacer señales a alguien/algo para que pare

◆**wave on** *vt* **to wave sb/sth on** hacer señales a alguien/algo para que siga adelante

◆**wave through** *vt* hacer señales para dejar pasar

waveband *n* RADIO banda *f* de frecuencias

wavelength *n* longitud *f* de onda; **on a ~** en una onda; **to be on the same ~** *fig* estar en la misma onda

waver ['weɪ·vər] *vi* **1.** (*lose determination*) vacilar **2.** (*be unable to decide*) titubear; **to ~ between... and...** dudar entre... y...; **to ~ over sth** titubear acerca de algo **3.** (*lose strength*) desfallecer

waverer ['weɪ·vər·ər] *n* indeciso, -a *m, f*

wavering *adj* vacilante; (*between two options*) titubeante

wavy ['weɪ·vi] <-ier, -iest> *adj* (*hair*) ondulado, -a; (*pattern*) ondulante

wax¹ [wæks] **I.** *n* **1.** (*fatty substance*) cera *f;* **candle ~** cera de vela; (*for polishing*) cera lustradora **2.** (*inside ear*) cera, cerumen *m* **II.** *vt* **1.** (*polish: floor, furniture, car*) encerar; (*shoes*) lustrar **2.** (*remove hair from*) depilar con cera

wax² [wæks] *vi liter* **1.** (*moon*) crecer; **to ~ and wane** crecer y menguar; *fig* tener altibajos

2. (*become*) ponerse

wax(ed) paper *n* papel *m* encerado

waxy ['wæk·si] <-ier, -iest> *adj* **1.** (*oily, shiny*) lustroso, -a **2.** (*apparently of wax*) ceroso, -a

way [weɪ] **I.** *n* **1.** (*route*) camino *m;* **to be (well) on the ~ to doing sth** *fig* ir camino de hacer algo; **to be on the ~** estar en camino; **to be out of the ~** estar en un lugar remoto; **to be under ~** estar en curso; **on the ~ to sth** de camino a algo; **to elbow one's ~ somewhere** abrirse camino (a codazos) hasta algún lugar; **to find one's ~ around sth** encontrar el camino alrededor de algo; *fig* encontrar una manera de evitar algo; **to find one's ~ into/out of sth** encontrar la manera de entrar/salir trar el camino a través de algo; **to go out of one's ~ to do sth** *fig* tomarse la molestia de hacer algo; **to go one's own ~** *fig* irse por su lado; (**to go) by ~ of sth** (ir) vía algo; **to know one's ~ around sth** saber cómo moverse en algo; **to know one's ~ around the town** conocer el pueblo; **to lead the ~** mostrar el camino; **to lose one's ~** perderse; **to make one's ~** (*make progress*) progresar; (*move*) abrirse camino; **to make one's ~ through the crowd** abrirse camino a través de la muchedumbre; **to pay one's ~** *fig* ser solvente; **to talk one's ~ out of sth** *fig* salvarse de algo con labia; **to see the error of one's ~s** darse cuenta de sus errores; **to work one's ~ up the ladder** *fig* ascender por mérito propio **2.** (*road*) camino *m;* (*small one*) sendero *m;* **Way** (*name of road*) Vía *f* **3.** (*facing direction*) dirección *f;* **the right/wrong ~ around** del derecho/del revés; **to show the ~ forward** señalar el camino **4.** (*distance*) trayecto *m;* **all the ~** (*the whole distance*) todo el trayecto; (*completely*) completamente; **to be a long ~ off** estar muy lejos; **to have a (long) ~ to go** tener aún un (largo) camino por recorrer; **to have come a long ~** *fig* haber llegado lejos; **to go a long ~** *fig* llegar lejos **5.** (*fashion*) manera *f;* **in many ~s** de muchas maneras; **in some ~s** en cierto modo; **there are no two ~s about it** no tiene vuelta de hoja; **the ~ to do sth** la manera de hacer algo; **by ~ of a** modo de **6.** (*manner*) modo *m;* (*customs*) costumbres *fpl;* **sb's ~ of life** el estilo de vida de alguien; **to my ~ of thinking** tal como lo veo yo; **she wouldn't have it any other ~** no lo aceptaría de ninguna otra manera; **in a big ~ a** gran escala; **either ~** de cualquier forma; **no ~! ** *inf* (*impossible*) ¡de ninguna manera!; *inf* (*definitely no!*) ¡ni hablar!; **in no ~** ¡para nada!; **to get one's own ~** salirse con la suya; **in a ~** en cierto modo **7.** (*free space*) paso *m;* **to be in sb's ~** estorbar a alguien; **to stand in sb's ~** ir contra los deseos de alguien; **in the ~** en medio; **to get out of sth's/sb's ~** dejar el camino libre a algo/alguien; **to give ~** dar paso; *fig* dejar hacer; **to give ~ to sth** dar paso a algo; **to make ~ (for sth/sb)** abrir paso (a algo/alguien) **8.** (*condition*) estado *m;* **to be in a bad ~** estar en mala forma; **to be in a terrible ~** estar fatal; **to be in the family ~** *inf* estar embarazada ▶ **to go the ~ of all flesh** sucumbir a la inevitable muerte; **the ~ to a man's heart is through his stomach** *prov* el camino al corazón de un hombre pasa por el estómago *prov;* **to want things both ~s** querer estar en misa y repicando; **to see/find out which ~ the wind blows** ver/descubrir por donde van los tiros; **to rub sb the wrong ~** caer mal a alguien; **by the ~** por cierto **II.** *adv* **1.** *sl* mucho; **to be ~ past sb's bedtime** haber pasado con mucho de la hora de dormir **2.** *sl* (*very*) mogollón de; **that's ~ cool!** ¡mola mazo!

waybill ['weɪ·bɪl] *n* hoja *f* de ruta

waylay ['weɪ·leɪ] <waylaid, waylaid> *vt* acechar

way-out [ˌweɪ·'aʊt] *adj sl* (*very modern*) ultramoderno, -a; (*unusual or amazing*) fuera de serie

ways and means *npl* **the ~ of doing/to do sth** los medios (y arbitrios) para hacer algo

wayside ['weɪ·saɪd] **I.** *n* borde *m* del camino; **to fall by the ~** *fig* quedarse en aguas de borraja; (*person*) quedarse a mitad de camino **II.** *adj* al borde del camino; **~ inn** parador *m* de carretera

wayward ['weɪ·wərd] *adj* rebelde

wazoo [wa·'zu] *n* **up** [*o* **out**] **the ~** *inf* más que de sobra

we [wi] *pron pers* nosotros, -as; **~'re on our way to Philadelphia, but ~'ll be back tomorrow** vamos de camino a Filadelfia, pero volveremos mañana; **as ~ say** como decimos nosotros

weak [wik] *adj* **1.** (*not strong*) débil; (*coffee, tea*) claro, -a; **to be ~ with desire/love** languidecer de deseo/amor; **to be ~ with hunger/thirst** estar sin fuerzas por el hambre/la sed; **to be ~ at the knees** temblarle a uno las piernas; **the ~ link** *fig* el punto débil; **~ spot** *fig* flaqueza *f* **2.** (*below standard*) flojo, -a; **to be ~ (at sth)** estar flojo (en algo)

weaken ['wi·kən] **I.** *vi* (*become less strong*) debilitarse; (*diminish*) disminuir **II.** *vt* (*make less strong*) debilitar; (*diminish*) disminuir

weakling ['wik·lɪŋ] *n* enclenque *mf*

weakly ['wik·li] *adv* **1.** (*without strength*) débilmente **2.** (*unconvincingly*) sin convicción

weak-minded [ˌwik·'maɪn·dɪd] *adj* **1.** (*lacking determination*) indeciso, -a; (*weak-willed*) pusilánime **2.** *offensive* (*stupid*) tonto, -a

weakness ['wik·nɪs] <-es> *n* **1.** (*lack of strength*) debilidad *f* **2.** (*area of vulnerability*) punto *m* débil; (*flaw in artistic work*) imperfección *f;* (*flaw in character*) flaqueza *f* **3.** (*fondness*) **to have a ~ for sth** tener debilidad por algo

weal [wil] *n* cardenal *m*

wealth [welθ] *n* **1.** (*money*) riqueza *f;* (*for-*

tune) fortuna *f* **2.** (*large amount*) abundancia *f*

wealthy ['wel·θi] **I.** <-ier, -iest> *adj* rico, -a **II.** *n* **the ~** los ricos

wean [win] *vt* (*animal, baby*) destetar; **to ~ sb (off sth)** *fig* desenganchar a alguien (de algo), quitar a alguien la costumbre (de algo)

weapon ['wep·ən] *n* arma *f*

weaponry ['wep·ən·ri] *n* armamento *m*

wear [wer] <wore, worn> **I.** *vt* **1.** (*have on body: clothes, jewelry*) llevar; **to ~ one's hair loose/tied back** llevar el pelo suelto/recogido **2.** (*deteriorate*) desgastar **II.** *vi* (*spoil: clothes, machine parts*) desgastarse; **to ~ thin** raerse; *fig* desgastarse **III.** *n* **1.** (*clothing*) ropa *f;* **casual/sports ~** ropa informal/deportiva **2.** (*amount of use*) desgaste *m;* **to be the worse for ~** (*person*) estar desmejorado; (*thing*) estar desgastado

◆ **wear away I.** *vt* desgastar **II.** *vi* desgastarse; (*person*) consumirse

◆ **wear down** *vt* **1.** (*reduce*) gastar; *fig* (*tire*) desgastar; **to ~ sb's resistance** desgastar la resistencia de alguien **2.** (*make weak and useless*) agotar

◆ **wear off** *vi* desaparecer

◆ **wear on** *vi* (*time*) pasar lentamente

◆ **wear out I.** *vi* gastarse **II.** *vt* gastar; (*patience*) agotar

wearable ['wer·ə·bəl] *adj* que se puede llevar

wear and tear *n* deterioro *m* [*o* desgaste] *m* (natural); **to take some/a lot of ~** soportar algo de/mucho desgaste

wearing ['wer·ɪŋ] *adj* agotador(a)

wearisome ['wɪr·ɪ·səm] *adj form* (*causing boredom*) aburrido, -a; (*causing tiredness*) extenuante

weary ['wɪr·i] **I.** <-ier, -iest> *adj* **1.** (*very tired*) extenuado, -a **2.** (*tiring*) agotador(a) **3.** (*bored*) aburrido, -a; (*unenthusiastic*) desanimado, -a; **to be ~ of sth** estar harto de algo; **a ~ joke** un chiste viejo **II.** *vt* (*make tired*) **to ~ sb with sth** fatigar a alguien con algo; (*make bored*) aburrir a alguien con algo **III.** *vi* (*become tired*) cansarse; (*become bored*) aburrirse

weasel ['wi·zəl] *n* comadreja *f*

weather ['weð·ər] **I.** *n* tiempo *m;* (*climate*) clima *m;* **~ permitting** si lo permite el tiempo ▶ **to make heavy ~ of sth** complicar algo; **to be under the ~** estar indispuesto **II.** *vi* aguantar **III.** *vt* **1.** (*wear*) desgastar **2.** (*endure*) resistir; **to ~ sth** hacer frente a algo; **to ~ the storm** *fig* capear el temporal

weather-beaten ['weð·ər·ˌbi·tən] *adj* deteriorado, -a por la intemperie; **~ face** cara *f* curtida

weather-bound *adj* bloqueado, -a por el mal tiempo

weather bureau <-s *o* -x> *n* servicio *m* meteorológico

weather chart *n* mapa *m* meteorológico

weather forecast *n* previsión *f* meteorológica

weathering ['weð·ər·ɪŋ] *n* erosión *f*

weatherman ['weð·ər·mæn] *n* hombre *m* del tiempo

weatherproof ['weð·ər·ˌpruf] *adj* impermeabilizado, -a

weathervane ['weð·ər·ˌveɪn] *n* veleta *f*

weave [wiv] **I.**<wove *o* weaved, woven *o* weaved> *vt* **1.** (*produce cloth*) tejer; **to ~ sth into sth** tejer algo con algo *fig,* entretejer algo en algo **2.** (*intertwine things*) entretejer; *fig* tramar; **to ~ sth together** entrelazar algo **3.** (*move back and forth*) **to ~ one's way through sth** abrirse paso entre algo **II.**<wove *o* weaved, woven *o* weaved> *vi* **1.** (*produce cloth*) tejer **2.** (*move by twisting and turning*) serpentear **III.** *n* tejido *m;* **striped ~** tejido a rayas; **loose/tight ~** tejido amplio/ajustado

weaver ['wi·vər] *n* tejedor(a) *m(f);* **basket ~** canastero, -a *m, f*

web¹ [web] *n* **1.** (*woven net*) tela *f;* **spider('s) ~** telaraña *f;* **to spin a ~** tejer una telaraña **2.** *fig* (*complex network*) trama *f;* **a ~ of intrigue** una trama de intrigas; **a ~ of lies** una sarta de mentiras **3.** *fig* (*trap*) trampa *f* **4.** (*connective tissue*) membrana *f*

web² [web] **I.** *n* COMPUT red *f;* **on the ~** en la red **II.** *adj inv* COMPUT de internet

Web browser *n* COMPUT navegador *m* (de internet)

webcam ['web·ˌkæm] *n* webcam *f*

web-footed ['web·ˌfʊt·ɪd] *adj* palmípedo, -a

weblog ['web·ˌlɔg] *n* blog *m*

webmaster *n* COMPUT administrador(a) *m(f)* de sitio web

webpage *n* COMPUT página *f* web

web server *n* COMPUT servidor *m*

website *n* COMPUT sitio *m* web; **to visit a ~** visitar un sitio web

webzine *n* COMPUT revista *f* electrónica

wed [wed] <wedded *o* wed, wedded *o* wed> *form* **I.** *vt* **1.** (*marry*) **to ~ sb** casarse con alguien **2.** *fig* (*join closely*) casar; **to ~ sth and sth** unir algo a algo **II.** *vi* casarse

Wed. *n abbr of* **Wednesday** miérc.

we'd [wid] **1.** = **we had** *s.* **have 2.** = **we would** *s.* **would**

wedded ['wed·ɪd] *adj* **1.** (*married*) casado, -a; **lawfully ~ wife** *form* legítima esposa **2.** (*united*) **to be ~ to sth** estar unido a algo; **to be ~ to a habit** tener una costumbre; **to be ~ to an opinion** aferrarse a una opinión

wedding ['wed·ɪŋ] *n* boda *f*

wedding anniversary <-ies> *n* aniversario *m* de bodas

wedding cake *n* tarta *f* nupcial

wedding day *n* día *m* de la boda

wedding dress *n* traje *m* de novia

wedding night *n* noche *f* de bodas

wedding present *n* regalo *m* de boda

wedding ring *n* alianza *f*

wedge [wedʒ] **I.** *n* **1.** (*tapered block*) cuña *f* **2.** *fig* (*triangular piece*) porción; **a ~ of cake/pie** un trozo de pastel/tarta **II.** *vt* poner una cuña a; **to ~ the door open** mantener la puerta abierta (con una cuña); **to be ~d between sth** (*people*) estar apretado entre

algo; (*object*) quedar encajado entre algo

wedlock ['wed·lak] *n* matrimonio *m;* **out of ~** fuera del matrimonio; **sex out of ~** sexo *m* extraconyugal; **to be born in/out of ~** nacer dentro/fuera del matrimonio

Wednesday ['wenz·deɪ] *n* miércoles *m inv;* **Ash ~** Miércoles de Ceniza; *s.a.* **Friday**

wee [wi] *adj* **1.** (*tiny*) pequeñito, -a; **a ~ bit** un poquitín **2.** (*early*) **in the ~ hours of the morning** a altas horas de la madrugada

weed [wid] **I.** *n* **1.** (*plant*) mala hierba *f* **2.** *sl* (*marijuana*) maría *f* ▶ **to grow like a ~** crecer como la mala hierba **II.** *vt* desherbar **III.** *vi* arrancar las malas hierbas

◆ **weed out** *vt* arrancar *fig,* eliminar

weedkiller ['wid·ˌkɪl·ər] *n* herbicida *m*

weedy ['wi·di] *adj* <-ier, iest> **1.** (*full of weeds*) lleno, -a de malas hierbas **2.** *pej* (*very thin*) flaco, -a; (*underdeveloped*) canijo, -a

week [wik] *n* **1.** (*seven days*) semana *f;* **it'll be ~s before...** pasarán semanas antes de que... **+subj; a few ~s ago** hace pocas semanas; **last ~** la semana pasada; **once a ~** una vez por semana; **during the ~** durante la semana; **~ after ~** semana tras semana; **~ by ~** semana a semana **2.** (*work period, working days*) semana *f* laboral; **a forty hour ~** una semana laboral de cuarenta horas

weekday ['wik·deɪ] *n* día *m* laborable; **on ~s** en días laborables

weekend ['wik·end] *n* fin *m* de semana; **on the ~** el fin de semana; **over the ~** (durante) el fin de semana

weekender ['wik·ˌen·dər] *n persona que pasa fuera el fin de semana*

weekly ['wik·li] **I.** *adj* semanal; **~ magazine** revista *f* semanal **II.** *adv* semanalmente; **to meet/publish ~** reunirse/publicar semanalmente **III.** *n* <-ies> semanario *m*

weenie ['wi·ni] *n* **1.** *inf* (*a hot dog*) salchicha *f* (frankfurt) **2.** *vulg sl* (*penis*) nabo *m*

weeny ['wi·ni] *adj,* **weensy** ['win·si] *adj* <-ier, -iest> *inf* chiquitito, -a; **a ~ bit** un poquitín

weep [wip] **I.** *vi* <wept, wept> **1.** (*cry*) llorar; **to ~ like a baby** lloriquear como un bebé; **to ~ with joy/rage** llorar de alegría/rabia; **to ~ inconsolably** llorar desconsoladamente **2.** (*secrete liquid*) supurar **II.** *vt* <wept, wept> (*tears*) derramar; **to ~ tears of joy/rage** (over sb/sth) llorar de alegría/rabia (por alguien/algo) **III.** *n* llanto *m;* **to have a (good) ~** desahogarse llorando

weeping **I.** *adj* lloroso, -a **II.** *n* llanto *m*

weeping willow *n* sauce *m* llorón

weigh [weɪ] **I.** *vi* pesar **II.** *vt* **1.** (*measure weight*) pesar; **to ~ oneself** pesarse **2.** (*consider carefully*) sopesar; **to ~ one's words** medir sus palabras; **to ~ sth against sth** contraponer algo a algo; **to ~ one's options** sopesar sus opciones **3.** NAUT (*pull up*) **to ~ anchor** levar el ancla

◆ **weigh down** *vt* **1.** (*cause to bend*) doblar (*bajo un peso*)**;** **to weigh sb down with sth**

cargar a alguien con algo **2.** *fig* (*depress*) abrumar
◆**weigh in** *vi* **1.** (*be weighed*) pesarse; **to ~ at 176 pounds** pesar 80 kilos **2.** *inf* (*enter into, take part*) intervenir; **to ~** (**to sth**) **with sth** intervenir (en algo) afirmando algo; **to ~ to a discussion with one's opinion** intervenir en una discusión dando su opinión
weigh-in ['weɪ·ɪn] *n* pesaje *m*
weight [weɪt] **I.** *n* **1.** (*amount weighed*) peso *m;* **a decrease/an increase in ~** una disminución/un aumento de peso; **to lift a heavy ~** levantar algo pesado; **to put on ~** engordar **2.** (*metal specific weight*) pesa *f;* **to lift ~s** levantar pesas **3.** (*value, importance*) valor *m;* **to attach ~ to sth** dar importancia a algo; **to carry ~** tener mucho peso ▶ **to take the ~ off one's feet** sentarse y descansar; **to be a ~ off sb's mind** ser un alivio para alguien; **it's a great ~ off my mind** es un peso que me quito de encima; **to pull one's** (**own**) **~** *inf* poner de su parte **II.** *vt* cargar; **to ~ sth with stones** cargar algo de piedras
◆**weight down** *vt* **1.** (*overload*) sobrecargar **2.** (*make heavy*) sujetar con un peso **3.** *fig* (*strain*) apretar
weightless ['weɪt·lɪs] *adj* ingrávido, -a
weightlessness *n* ingravidez *f*
weightlifter *n* levantador(a) *m(f)* de pesas
weightlifting ['weɪt·ˌlɪf·tɪŋ] *n* levantamiento *m* de pesas; **to do ~** hacer pesas
weighty ['weɪ·t̬i] *adj* <-ier, -iest> **1.** (*heavy*) pesado, -a **2.** (*important*) importante; **~ matters** asuntos *mpl* de peso
weir [wɪr] *n* presa *f*
weird [wɪrd] *adj* misterioso, -a; **how ~** ¡qué raro!; **~ and wonderful** extraordinario
weirdie ['wɪr·di] *n*, **weirdo** ['wɪr·doʊ] *n sl* bicho *m* raro
welcome ['wel·kəm] **I.** *vt* **1.** (*greet kindly*) dar la bienvenida a; **to ~ sb warmly** recibir a alguien con los brazos abiertos **2.** (*support*) aprobar **II.** *n* **1.** (*friendly reception*) bienvenida *f;* **to give sb a warm ~** recibir a alguien con los brazos abiertos **2.** (*period of being wanted*) aceptación *f;* **to wear out one's ~** quedarse más tiempo de lo prudente **3.** (*expression of approval*) aprobación *f;* **to give sth a cautious ~** dar una acogida contenida a algo **III.** *adj* **1.** (*gladly received*) grato, -a; **a ~ guest** un invitado bienvenido; **to be ~** ser bienvenido **2.** (*greatly anticipated*) deseado, -a; **a ~ break** una ruptura deseada; **a ~ change** un cambio esperado ▶ **you are ~** de nada; **you're very ~** no hay de qué; **to be ~ to do sth** *inf* poder hacer algo; **you are ~ to use it** está a su disposición **IV.** *interj* ¡bienvenido!; **~ aboard** NAUT bienvenidos a bordo
welcoming *adj* acogedor(a); **~ arms** brazos abiertos; **a ~ smile** una sonrisa agradable
weld [weld] **I.** *vt* **1.** (*join metal*) soldar; **to ~ sth** (**together**) soldar algo **2.** (*unite*) unir; **to ~ players into a team** unir a jugadores en un

equipo **II.** *n* soldadura *f*
welder *n* soldador(a) *m(f)*
welding *n* soldadura *f*
welfare ['wel·fer] *n* **1.** (*health, happiness*) bienestar *m* **2.** (*state aid*) asistencia *f* social; **social ~** asistencia *f* social; **to be on ~** vivir a cargo de la asistencia social
welfare state *n* estado *m* del bienestar
welfare work *n* trabajos *mpl* de asistencia social
welfare worker *n* trabajador(a) *m(f)* social
we'll [wil] = **we will** *s.* **will**
well[1] [wel] **I.** *adj* <better, best> bien; **to feel ~** sentirse bien; **to get ~** recuperarse; **to look ~** tener buen aspecto **II.** <better, best> *adv* **1.** (*in a satisfactory manner*) bien; **~ enough** suficientemente bien; **~ done** bien hecho; **to do sth as ~ as...** hacer algo tan bien como...; **~ put** bien expresado; (**time/money**) **~ spent** (tiempo/dinero) bien empleado **2.** (*thoroughly, fully, extensively*) completamente; **that's ~ east/west of here** está muy al este/oeste; **~ enough** suficiente; **pretty ~** bastante a fondo; **to know sb pretty ~** conocer a alguien bastante bien; **~ and truly** de verdad; **it costs ~ over...** cuesta tranquilamente más de... **3.** (*very, completely*) muy; **to be ~ pleased with sth** estar muy satisfecho con algo **4.** (*fairly, reasonably*) justamente; **he couldn't very ~ refuse their kind offer** no podía rechazar su amable oferta; **you may ~ think it was his fault** bien podrías pensar que tiene la culpa; **he might ~ be the best person to ask** puede que sea la persona idónea a quien preguntar; **you might** (**just**) **as ~ tell her the truth** más valdría que le dijeras la verdad ▶ **all ~ and good** muy bien; **that's all very ~, but...** todo eso está muy bien, pero...; **as ~** (*also*) también; **as ~ as** así como; **just as ~** menos mal; **to be in ~ with sb** *inf* estar bien con alguien; **to be in ~ with sth** *inf* estar metido en algo **III.** *interj* (*exclamation*) vaya; **~, ~** ¡vaya, vaya!; **very ~!** ¡muy bien!
well[2] [wel] **I.** *n* (*hole for water etc.*) pozo *m;* **water ~** manantial *m* de agua; **to drill a ~** perforar un pozo **II.** *vi* (*flow*) manar; **to ~ up in sth** brotar en algo; **to ~** (**up**) **out of sth** (*water*) emanar de algo
◆**well up** *vi a. fig* (*rise*) brotar
well-advised [ˌwel·əd·ˈvaɪzd] *adj form* bien asesorado, -a; **he would be ~ to stay at home** haría bien en quedarse en casa
well-appointed [ˌwel·ə·ˈpɔɪn·tɪd] *adj form* bien amueblado, -a
well-balanced [ˌwel·ˈbæl·ənst] *adj* **1.** (*balanced*) equilibrado, -a; **~ diet** dieta equilibrada **2.** (*emotionally stable*) **~ children** niños equilibrados
well-behaved [ˌwel·bɪ·ˈheɪvd] *adj* bien educado, -a; (*child, dog*) obediente
well-being ['wel·bi·ɪŋ] *n* bienestar *m;* **a feeling of ~** una sensación de bienestar
well-bred [ˌwel·ˈbred] *adj* (*well brought up*)

bien educado, -a; (*classy, refined*) refinado, -a
well-chosen [ˌwelˈtʃoʊˌzən] *adj* elegido, -a
cuidadosamente; **to say a few ~ words** decir
unas palabras acertadas
well-connected [ˌwelˌkəˈnekˌtɪd] *adj* **to be ~**
tener contactos; **a ~ family** una familia
influyente
well-deserved [ˌwelˌdɪˈzɜvd] *adj* merecido, -a
well-developed [ˌwelˌdɪˈvelˌəpt] *adj* bien
desarrollado, -a; **~ area** zona desarrollada;
physically ~ físicamente desarrollado; **a ~
sense of humor** un agudo sentido del humor
well-disposed [ˌwelˌdɪˈspoʊzd] *adj* favorable; **to be ~ towards sth** ser favorable a
algo; **to feel ~ towards sb** tener una disposición favorable hacia alguien
well-done [ˌwelˈdʌn] *adj* **1.** (*task*) bien hecho,
-a **2.** (*meat*) muy hecho, -a
well-dressed [ˌwelˈdrest] *adj* bien vestido, -a
well-educated [ˌwelˈedʒˌʊˈkeɪˌtɪd] *adj* culto,
-a
well-fed [ˌwelˈfed] *adj* (*full of food*) lleno, -a;
(*from good feeding*) bien alimentado, -a
well-founded [ˌwelˈfaʊnˌdɪd] *adj* fundado, -a;
~ suspicions sospechas bien fundadas
well-heeled [ˌwelˈhild] **I.** *adj* inf ricachón, -ona
II. *npl* **the ~** los ricos
well-informed [ˌwelˌɪnˈfɔrmd] *adj* enterado,
-a; **to be ~ about sb/sth** estar bien informado
sobre alguien/algo; **to be ~ on a particular
topic** conocer a fondo un tema concreto
well-intentioned [ˌwelˌɪnˈtenˌʃənd] *adj* bienintencionado, -a
well-kept [ˌwelˈkept] *adj* (muy) cuidado, -a
well-knit [ˌwelˈnɪt] *adj* (*body*) robusto, -a; *fig*
(*scheme, idea*) lógico, -a; (*family*) muy unido,
-a; **a ~ plot/story** una trama/historia bien
construida
well-known [ˌwelˈnoʊn] *adj* conocido, -a; **to
be ~ for sth** ser conocido por algo; **it is ~
that...** es bien sabido que...
well-mannered [ˌwelˈmænˌərd] *adj* con buenos modales; **a ~ child** un niño educado
well-meaning [ˌwelˈmiˌnɪŋ] *adj* bienintencionado, -a; **~ comments** comentarios *mpl* sin
malicia
well-meant [ˌwelˈment] *adj* bienintencionado, -a
well-nigh [ˈwelˌnaɪ] *adv* casi; **to be ~ impossible** ser casi imposible
well-off [ˌwelˈɔf] **I.** *adj* **1.** (*wealthy*) acomodado, -a **2.** (*having a lot*) que tiene mucho; **the
city is ~ for parks** la ciudad tiene muchos parques; **to not know when one is ~** no saber la
suerte que tiene **II.** *npl* **the ~** los ricos
well-oiled [ˌwelˈɔɪld] *adj* **1.** (*functioning
smoothly*) eficaz **2.** *sl* (*drunk*) como una cuba
well-organized [ˌwelˈɔrˌgəˌnaɪzd] *adj* bien
organizado, -a
well-paid [ˌwelˈpeɪd] *adj* bien pagado, -a
well-placed [ˌwelˈpleɪst] *adj* bien situado, -a
well-proportioned [ˌwelˌprəˈpɔrˌʃənd] *adj*
bien proporcionado, -a

well-read [ˌwelˈred] *adj* **1.** (*knowledgeable*)
instruido, -a **2.** (*read frequently*) muy leído, -a
well-spoken [ˌwelˈspoʊˌkən] *adj* **1.** (*polite*)
bienhablado, -a **2.** (*refined*) con acento culto
well-thought-of [ˌwelˈθɔtˌəv] *adj* (*person*) de
buena reputación; (*school*) de prestigio
well-timed [ˌwelˈtaɪmd] *adj* oportuno, -a
well-to-do [ˌwelˌtəˈdu] *inf* **I.** *adj* de pelas **II.** *n*
the ~ la gente de pelas
well-turned [ˌwelˈtɜrnd] *adj* **1.** (*gracefully
shaped*) elegante **2.** (*cleverly expressed:
phrase*) bien construido, -a
well-wisher [ˈwelˌwɪʃˌər] *n* simpatizante *mf*
well-worn [ˌwelˈwɔrn] *adj* **1.** (*damaged by
wear*) raído, -a **2.** *fig* (*over-used*) trillado, -a
welt [welt] *n* **1.** (*from blow*) cardenal *m* **2.** (*in
shoe*) vira *f*
welterweight [ˈwelˌtərˌweɪt] *n* welter *m*
went [went] *pt of* **go**
wept [wept] *pt, pp of* **weep**
were [wɜr] *pt of* **be**
we're [wɪr] = **we are** *s.* **be**
weren't [wɜrnt] = **were not** *s.* **be**
west [west] **I.** *n* **1.** (*cardinal point*) oeste *m;* **in
the ~ of Mexico** en el oeste de México; **to lie
5 miles to the ~ of...** quedar a 8 km al oeste
de...; **to go/drive to the ~** ir/conducir hacia
el oeste **2.** (*part of the world*) the West el
mundo occidental **3.** (*part of the US*) **the Far
West** el lejano oeste; **the Wild West** el viejo
oeste **II.** *adj* occidental; **~ wind** viento *m* del
oeste; **~ coast** costa *f* oeste; **West African** de
África Occidental; **West Berlin** Berlín Occidental; **West Indies** Antillas *fpl* **III.** *adv* al
oeste; **further ~** más al oeste ▶ **to go ~** (*thing*)
estropearse; (*person*) irse al otro mundo
westbound [ˈwestˌbaʊnd] *adj* que va hacia el
oeste
westerly [ˈwesˌtərˌli] *adj* (del) oeste; **the ~
part of the site** la zona oeste del lugar;
~ winds vientos *mpl* del oeste
western [ˈwesˌtərn] **I.** *adj* del oeste, occidental; **the ~ part of the country** la parte occidental del país **II.** *n* CINE western *m*
westerner *n* **1.** (*person from the west*) occidental *mf* **2.** (*person from the western US*)
norteamericano, -a *m, f* del oeste
westernize [ˈwesˌtərˌnaɪz] *vt* occidentalizar
Western Samoa *n* Samoa *f* Occidental
West Germany *n* HIST Alemania *f* Occidental
West Virginia *n* Virginia *f* Occidental
westward [ˈwestˌwərd] *adj* occidental, del
oeste
westwards [ˈwestˌwərdz] *adv* hacia el oeste
wet [wet] **I.** *adj* <-tt-> **1.** (*soaked*) mojado, -a;
to get ~ mojarse; **to get sth ~** mojar algo;
~ through calado hasta los huesos **2.** (*not yet
dried*) húmedo, -a; **~ paint** pintura fresca
3. (*rainy*) lluvioso, -a; **~ weather** tiempo lluvioso ▶ **to be ~ behind the ears** estar con la
miel en los labios; **to be all ~** *sl* estar en la
parra **II.** <wet, wet> *vt* **1.** (*make damp*) humedecer **2.** (*urinate on*) **to ~ oneself** orinarse; **to**

W

~ **the bed** mojar la cama; **to** ~ **one's pants** mearse *inf* III. *n* 1. **the** ~ (*rain*) la lluvia 2. POL *inf* antiprohibicionista *mf*

wet nurse *n* HIST nodriza *f*

wetsuit *n* traje *m* de neopreno

we've [wiv] = **we have** *s.* **have**

whack [hwæk] I. *vt* golpear II. *n* (*blow*) golpe *m;* **to give sth** (**a good**) ~ golpear algo ruidosamente ▶ **to be** <u>out</u> **of** ~ estar fastidiado; **to** <u>have</u> **a** ~ **at sth** *inf* intentar algo

whacking *n* zurra *f;* **to give sb a** (**real**) ~ dar a alguien una (verdadera) tunda; **to take a** (**real**) ~ recibir una (verdadera) tunda

whale [hweɪl] *n* ballena *f;* **a beached** ~ una ballena varada ▶ **to have a** ~ **of a** <u>time</u> pasarlo bomba; **a** ~ <u>of</u> **a...** un(a) enorme...; **a** ~ **of a difference** una diferencia abismal

whaling *n* pesca *f* de ballenas

wham [hwæm] *interj inf* 1. (*sound-effect for blow*) ¡zas! 2. (*describes action*) y ¡zas!

wharf [hwɔrf] <-ves> *n* muelle *m;* **price ex** ~ precio *m* franco de muelle

what [hwʌt] I. *adj interrog* qué; ~ **kind of book?** ¿qué tipo de libro?; ~ **time is it?** ¿qué hora es?; ~ **men is he talking about?** ¿de qué hombres está hablando?; ~ **an idiot!** ¡qué idiota!; ~ **a fool I am!** ¡qué tonto soy! II. *pron* 1. *interrog* qué; ~ **can I do?** ¿qué puedo hacer?; ~ **does it matter?** ¿qué importa?; ~ '**s on for tonight?** ¿qué ponen esta noche?; ~ '**s up?** ¿qué hay?; ~ **for?** ¿para qué?; ~ **is he like?** ¿cómo es (él)?; ~ '**s his name?** ¿cómo se llama?; ~ '**s it called?** ¿cómo se llama?; ~ **about Paul?** ¿y Paul?; ~ **about a walk?** ¿te va a un paseo?; ~ **if it snows?** *inf* ¿y si nieva? 2. *rel* lo que; ~ **I like is** ~ **he says/is talking about** lo que me gusta es lo que dice/de lo que está hablando; ~ **is more** lo que es más; **he knows** ~ '**s** ~! sabe cuántas son cinco III. *interj* ~? ¡qué!; **so** ~? ¿y qué?; **is he coming, or** ~? ¿viene, o qué?

whatever [hwʌt·'ev·ər] I. *pron* 1. (*anything*) (todo) lo que; ~ **happens, happens** pasará lo que tenga que pasar 2. (*any of them*) cualquier(a); ~ **you pick is fine** cualquiera que elijas está bien II. *adj* 1. (*being what it may be*) cualquiera que; ~ **the reason** sea cual sea la razón 2. (*of any kind*) de ningún tipo; **there is no doubt** ~ no hay ningún tipo de duda

whatnot ['hwʌt·nat] *n* chisme *m;* **and** ~ *inf* y demás

whatsoever [ˌhwʌt·sou·'ev·ər] *adv* sea cual sea; **to have no interest** ~ **in sth** no tener interés alguno en algo; **nothing** ~ nada de nada

wheat [hwit] *n* trigo *m* ▶ **to separate the** ~ **from the** <u>chaff</u> separar la cizaña del buen grano

wheat belt *n* zona *f* de cultivo de trigo

wheat germ *n* germen *m* de trigo

wheel [hwil] I. *n* 1. (*of vehicle*) rueda *f;* **alloy** ~**s** llantas *fpl* de aleación; **front/rear** ~ rueda delantera/trasera; **big** ~ noria *f;* **to be on** ~**s** ir

sobre ruedas 2. TECH torno *m;* **spinning** ~ rueca *f* 3. AUTO volante *m;* **to be at the** ~ ir al volante; **to take the** ~ tomar el volante; **to get behind the** ~ ponerse al volante 4. ~**s** *sl* (*vehicle, car*) carro *m* 5. NAUT timón *m* ▶ **to be** <u>hell</u> **on** ~**s** *sl* ser un peligro (al volante) II. *vt* hacer girar; **to** ~ **a bicycle up the street** empujar una bicicleta calle arriba III. *vi* girar ▶ **to** ~ **and** <u>deal</u> *inf* trapichear

♦ **wheel around** *vi* dar media vuelta

wheelbarrow ['hwil·ˌbær·ou] *n* carretilla *f*

wheelchair *n* silla *f* de ruedas

wheeler-dealer [ˌhwi·lər·'di·lər] *n pej, inf* trapichero, -a *m, f*

wheelhouse ['hwil·haus] *n* timonera *f*

wheeze [hwiz] I. <-zing> *vi* resollar II. *n* (*of breath*) resuello *m*

wheezy *adj* <-ier, -iest> jadeante

whelp [hwelp] I. *n* cachorro *m* II. *vt* parir

when [hwen] I. *adv* cuándo; **since** ~? ¿desde cuándo?; **I'll tell him** ~ **to go** yo le diré cuándo ir II. *conj* 1. (*at which time*) en que; **at the moment** ~ **he arrived** en el momento en que vino 2. (*during the time that*) ~ **singing that song** cuando cantaba esa canción 3. (*every time that*) ~ **it snows** cuando nieva 4. (*although*) **he buys it** ~ **he could** (*just as easily*) **borrow it** lo compra cuando podría pedirlo prestado (con la misma facilidad) 5. (*considering that*) si; **how can I listen** ~ **I can't hear?** ¿cómo puedo escuchar si no puedo oír?

whence [hwens] *adv form* por lo cual; (*interrogative*) ¿de dónde?

whenever [hwen·'ev·ər] I. *conj* 1. (*every time that*) siempre que; ~ **I can** siempre que puedo 2. (*at any time that*) **he can come** ~ **he likes** puede venir cuando quiera II. *adv* ~ **did I say that?** ¿cuándo fue que dije yo eso?; **I can do it tomorrow or** ~ puedo hacerlo mañana o un día de estos

where [hwer] *adv* 1. *interrog* dónde; ~ **does he come from?** ¿de dónde es?; ~ **does he live?** ¿dónde vive?; ~ **is he going** (**to**)? ¿adónde va? 2. *rel* donde; **I'll tell him** ~ **to go** yo le diré adónde ir; **the box** ~ **he puts his things** la caja donde pone sus cosas; **this is** ~ **my horse was found** aquí es donde encontraron mi caballo; **Minnesota,** ~ **Paul comes from, is...** Minnesota, de donde viene Paul, es...

whereabouts ['hwer·ə·bauts] I. *n* + *sing/pl vb* paradero *m;* **do you know the** ~ **of my book?** *form* ¿sabes dónde se encuentra mi libro? II. *adv inf* dónde; ~ **in San Francisco do you live?** ¿en qué zona de San Francisco vives?

whereas [hwer·'æz] *conj* 1. (*while*) mientras que 2. LAW considerando que

whereby [hwer·'baɪ] *conj form* por lo cual

wherein [hwer·'ɪn] *conj form* en donde

wheresoever [ˌhwer·sou·ev·ər] *adv, conj form s.* **wherever**

whereupon ['hwer·ə·ˌpan] *conj form* con lo cual

wherever [ˌhwer·'ev·ər] **I.** *conj* dondequiera que; **~ I am/I go** dondequiera que esté/vaya; **~ there is sth** dondequiera que haya algo; **~ he likes** donde le plazca **II.** *adv* **~ did she find that?** ¿dónde demonios encontró eso?; **...or ~** ...o donde sea

wherewithal ['hwer·wɪð·ɔl] *n liter* recursos *mpl;* **to lack the ~** (**to do sth**) no tener los medios (para hacer algo)

whet [hwet] <-tt-> *vt* **1.** (*sharpen*) afilar **2.** *fig* (*increase, stimulate*) estimular; **to ~ sb's appetite** (**for sth**) aguzar el deseo de alguien (por algo)

whether ['hweð·ər] *conj* **1.** (*if*) si; **to tell/ask ~ it's true** (**or not**) decir/preguntar si es verdad (o no); **she doesn't know ~ to buy it or not** no sabe si comprarlo o no; **I doubt ~ he'll come** dudo que venga **2.** (*all the same*) sea; **~ rich or poor...** sean ricos o pobres...; **~ it rains or thunders...** aunque llueva o truene...; **~ I go by bus or bike...** vaya en autobús o en bici...

whetstone ['hwet·stoʊn] *n* piedra *f* de afilar

whew [hwu, fju] *interj inf* ¡uf!

whey [hweɪ] *n* suero *m*

which [hwɪtʃ] **I.** *adj interrog* qué; **~ one/ones?** ¿cuál/cuáles? **II.** *pron* **1.** *interrog* cuál, qué; **~ is his?** ¿cuál es el suyo? **2.** *rel* que, el que, la que, lo que, los que, las que; **the book ~ I read/of ~ I'm speaking** el libro que leí/ del que estoy hablando; **he said he was there, ~ I believed** dijo que estaba ahí, lo cual creí

whichever [hwɪtʃ·'ev·ər] **I.** *pron* cualquiera que; **you can choose ~ you like** puedes escoger el que quieras **II.** *adj* cualquier, el , la que; **you can take ~ book you like** puedes coger el libro que quieras

whiff [hwɪf] **I.** *n* **1.** (*quick smell*) olorcillo *m;* **to catch a ~ of sth** percibir un olorcillo a algo **2.** *fig* (*slight trace*) indicio *m;* **a ~ of corruption** una sospecha de corrupción **3.** SPORTS (*swing and miss: baseball*) strike *m;* (*with foot*) patada *m* al aire; (*strikeout*) ponche *m* **II.** *vi* SPORTS (*swing and miss: baseball*) hacer strike; (*with foot*) dar una patada al aire; (*strike out*) ponchar **III.** *vt* (*strike out*) ponchar

while [hwaɪl] **I.** *n* rato *m;* **a short ~** un ratito; **quite a ~** bastante tiempo; **after a ~** después de un tiempo; **for a ~** durante un rato; **once in a ~** de vez en cuando **II.** *conj* **1.** (*during which time*) mientras; **I did it ~ he was sleeping** lo hice mientras él dormía; **~ I'm alive** mientras (que yo) viva **2.** (*although*) aunque; **~ I like it, I won't buy it** aunque me guste, no lo compraré; **~ I know it's true...** a pesar de que sé que es verdad...

◆ **while away** *vt* pasar; **to ~ the time** hacer tiempo

whim [hwɪm] *n* capricho *m;* **to do sth on a ~** hacer algo por capricho; **as the ~ takes him** según se le antoja

whimper ['hwɪm·pər] **I.** *vi* quejarse; (*child*) lloriquear; (*dog*) gemir **II.** *n* quejido *m;* **a ~ of protest** un gemido de protesta; **to give a ~** dar un gemido

whimsical ['hwɪm·zɪ·kəl] *adj* **1.** (*odd*) peregrino, -a **2.** (*capricious*) caprichoso, -a

whimsicality [ˌhwɪm·zɪ·'kæl·ə·t̬i] *n* **1.** (*odd character*) extravagancia *f* **2.** (*caprice*) capricho *m*

whimsy ['hwɪm·zi] <-ies> *n pej* **1.** (*odd fancifulness*) extravagancia *f* **2.** (*odd, fanciful thing or work*) fantasía *f* **3.** (*whim*) capricho *m*

whine [hwaɪn] **I.** <-ning> *vi* **1.** (*complaining noise*) gemir; (*cry*) lloriquear **2.** (*engine*) zumbar **II.** *n* (*of a person or animal*) quejido *m;* (*of an engine*) zumbido *m*

whinny ['hwɪn·i] **I.** <-ied, -ing> *vi* relinchar **II.** *n* <-ies> relincho *m*

whip [hwɪp] **I.** *n* **1.** (*lash*) látigo *m*, chicote *m AmL,* fuete *m AmL;* **to crack a ~** hacer restallar un látigo **2.** (*person*) *persona encargada de la disciplina de partido;* **chief ~** diputado, -a *m, f* jefe encargado de la disciplina de partido **II.** <-pp-> *vt* **1.** (*strike with whip*) azotar **2.** (*strike*) fustigar **3.** *fig, inf* (*defeat*) **to ~ sb at** [*o* **in**] **sth** dar una paliza a alguien en algo **4.** CULIN batir **III.** <-pp-> *vi* **1.** (*strike*) restallar **2.** (*move fast*) volverse de repente; **to ~ around the corner** (*car*) doblar la esquina a toda velocidad

◆ **whip back** *vi* **1.** (*bounce back*) rebotar bruscamente hacia atrás **2.** *fig* (*return*) volverse de golpe

◆ **whip off** *vt* (*one's clothes*) quitarse con un movimiento brusco; (*tablecloth*) sacar de un tirón

◆ **whip on** *vt* **1.** (*urge on*) animar **2.** (*put on quickly*) ponerse rápidamente

◆ **whip out** *vt* **1.** (*take out*) sacar de repente **2.** (*produce*) hacer rápidamente

◆ **whip up** *vt* **1.** (*encourage*) avivar; **to ~ support** conseguir apoyo **2.** *inf* (*prepare quickly*) preparar rápidamente **3.** CULIN **to ~ eggs** batir huevos

whipcord ['hwɪp·kɔrd] *n* tralla *f*

whip hand *n* **the ~** el mando; **to hold the ~** llevar la batuta

whiplash *n* <-es> **1.** (*whip part*) tralla *f* **2.** (*blow from whip*) latigazo *m* **3.** (*injury*) traumatismo *m* cervical

whipped cream *n* nata *f* para montar

whippersnapper ['hwɪp·ər·ˌsnæp·ər] *n iron* mequetrefe *m*

whippet ['hwɪp·ɪt] *n* lebrel *m*

whipping **I.** *n* **1.** (*punishment*) azotaina *f;* **to be given a** (**good**) **~** dar una (buena) azotaina a alguien **2.** (*physical beating*) paliza *f;* **to give/get a ~** dar/llevarse una paliza **3.** (*gusting*) azote *m;* **the ~ of the wind** el azote del viento **II.** *adj* (*gusty*) racheado, -a; **a ~ wind** un golpe de viento

whipping boy ['hwɪp·ɪŋ·bɔɪ] *n* cabeza de

turco *f*

whipping cream *n* nata *f* para montar

whir [hwɜr] <-rr-> I. *vi* hacer ruido II. *n* ruido *m;* (*of bird's wings*) aleteo *m*

whirl [hwɜrl] I. *vi* girar rápidamente; **my head ~s** *fig* la cabeza me da vueltas II. *vt* hacer girar; **to ~ sb around** dar vueltas a alguien III. *n* torbellino *m;* **a ~ of dust** una polvareda ▶ **to give** sth a ~ probar algo

whirligig ['hwɜr·lɪ·gɪg] *n* 1. (*toy*) molinete *m* 2. *fig* vicisitudes *fpl*

whirlpool ['hwɜrl·pul] *n* remolino *m*

whirlwind *n* torbellino *m;* **a ~ romance** un idilio relámpago

whirlybird ['hwɜr·lɪ·ˌbɜrd] *n* *inf* (*helicopter*) helicóptero *m*

whisk [hwɪsk] I. *vt* 1. CULIN batir 2. (*take quickly*) llevar rápidamente; **to ~ sb off somewhere** llevar a alguien a toda prisa a algún sitio 3. (*with sweeping movement: tail*) sacudir II. *n* 1. (*kitchen tool*) batidora *f;* **electric ~** batidora eléctrica; **hand-held ~** batidora de mano 2. (*sweeping motion*) sacudida *f*

whisker ['hwɪs·kər] *n* 1. **~s** (*facial hair*) pelo *m* de la barba 2. **~s** (*of animal*) bigotes *mpl* ▶ **by a ~** por un pelo; **within a ~ (of doing sth**) a punto (de hacer algo)

whiskey *n,* **whisky** ['hwɪs·ki] *n* <-ies> whisky *m*

whisper ['hwɪs·pər] I. *vi* cuchichear II. *vt* 1. (*speak softly*) susurrar; **to ~ sth in sb's ear** decir algo al oído a alguien 2. *fig* (*gossip, speak privately*) rumorear; **it is ~ed that...** se rumorea que... III. *n* 1. (*soft sound or speech*) cuchicheo *m;* **to lower one's voice to a ~** bajar la voz y hablar en un susurro; **to speak in a ~** hablar en voz baja 2. *fig* (*rumor*) rumor *m* 3. *fig, liter* (*soft rustle*) susurro *m;* **the ~ of the leaves** el rumor de las hojas

whispering *n* 1. (*talking very softly*) susurro *m* 2. *fig* (*gossiping*) chismes *mpl*

whispering campaign *n* campaña *f* de rumores

whist [hwɪst] *n* whist *m;* **a game of ~** una partida de whist

whistle ['hwɪs·əl] I. <-ling> *vi* 1. (*of person*) silbar; **to ~ at sb/sth** silbar a alguien/algo; **to ~ in admiration** silbar de admiración 2. (*of bird*) trinar II. <-ling> *vt* silbar III. *n* 1. (*blowing sound*) silbido *m;* **the ~ of the wind** el silbido del viento 2. (*musical device*) pito *m;* **referee's ~** silbato *m* del árbitro; **to blow a ~** pitar ▶ **to blow the ~ on sb** llamar al orden a alguien; **to wet one's ~** remojar el gaznate

white [hwaɪt] I. *adj* blanco, -a; **~ sauce** bechamel *f;* **~ wedding** boda *f* tradicional; **to turn** [*o* **go**] **~ with fear** palidecer de miedo ▶ **to fly into a ~ rage** ponerse lívido de rabia II. *n* 1. (*color*) blanco *m;* **the ~ of an egg** la clara del huevo; **the ~ of sb's eyes** el blanco de los ojos de alguien 2. (*person*) blanco, -a *m, f*

white-collar [ˌhwaɪt·'kal·ər] *adj* **~ worker** oficinista *mf*

white elephant *n* armatoste *m*

white flag *n* bandera *f* blanca; **to fly** [*o* **raise**] **a ~** alzar una bandera blanca

white goods *npl* 1. (*major household appliances*) electrodomésticos *mpl* 2. (*household linen*) ropa *f* blanca

white hat *n* COMPUT sombrero *m* blanco, *hacker que entra en sistemas para comprobar su vulnerabilidad, pero que no persigue fines ilegales*

white heat *n* 1. (*of metal*) candencia *f* 2. *fig* (*passion*) apasionamiento *m*

White House *n* **the ~** la Casa Blanca

> **i** La Casa Blanca (**White House**), ubicada en 1600 Pennsylvania Avenue en Washington, D.C., es la residencia oficial del presidente de Estados Unidos, y su **Oval Office** (Oficina Oval) es su principal lugar de trabajo. La construcción del edificio neoclásico de piedra arenisca pintado de blanco se inició en 1792 y se terminó en 1800. Durante la guerra de 1812, la Casa Blanca fue saqueada y quemada por tropas británicas invasoras, pero la mansión de seis pisos, 55.000 pies cuadrados (5.100 m^2) y 132 habitaciones fue reconstruida y se puede visitar en internet en http://www.whitehouse.gov.

white lie *n* mentira *f* piadosa

white man <-men> *n* hombre *m* blanco

white meat *n* carne *f* blanca

whiten ['hwaɪ·tən] I. *vt* blanquear II. *vi* blanquear; (*go pale*) palidecer

whitener ['hwaɪt·nər] *n* blanqueador *m*

whiteness *n* blancura *f*

whiteout *n* 1. (*dense blizzard*) ventisca *f* 2. TYPO líquido *m* corrector

white sale *n* rebajas *f* en ropa blanca *pl*

white-tie I. *adj* **~ dinner** cena de etiqueta II. *n* pajarita *f*

whitewash ['hwaɪt·waʃ] I. <-es> *n* 1. (*for whitening walls*) cal *f* 2. (*coverup*) blanqueo *m* 3. *inf* (*overwhelming victory*) paliza *f* II. *vt* 1. (*cover in white solution*) encalar 2. (*conceal negative side of*) blanquear 3. *inf* SPORTS (*defeat completely*) dar un baño a

white-water rafting [ˌhwaɪt·wɔ·tər·'ræf·tɪŋ] *n* rafting *m* en aguas bravas

white wine *n* vino *m* blanco

whither ['hwɪð·ər] *adv form* adónde

whiting[1] ['hwaɪ·tɪŋ] *n* (*fish*) pescadilla *f*

whiting[2] ['hwaɪ·tɪŋ] *n* (*white substance*) tiza *f*

Whitmonday [ˌhwɪt·'mʌn·deɪ] *n* lunes *m inv* de Pentecostés

Whitsun ['hwɪt·sən] I. *n* Pentecostés *m;* **at ~** en Pentecostés II. *adj* de Pentecostés

Whitsunday [ˌhwɪt·'sʌn·deɪ] *n* domingo *m* de Pentecostés

Whitsuntide ['hwɪt·sən·taɪd] *n s.* **Whitsun**

whittle ['hwɪt̬·əl] <-ling> vt tallar
◆**whittle away at** vt **1.** (take little bits off) ir raspando **2.** fig (decrease) reducir poco a poco
◆**whittle down** vt reducir gradualmente
whiz [hwɪz] I. n **1.** inf (brilliant person) hacha m **2.** (noise) silbido m **3.** sl (act of urinating) **to take a** ~ echar un meo II. vi **1.** (move fast) ir a gran velocidad; **to** ~ **along** inf ir a toda pastilla; **to** ~ **by** inf pasar como una bala **2.** vulg sl **to take a** ~ (urinate) echar un cañete
whiz kid n inf joven prodigio m
whizz [hwɪz] n, vi s. **whiz**
who [hu] pron **1.** interrog quién, quiénes; ~ **broke the window?** ¿quién rompió la ventana?; ~ **were they?** ¿quiénes eran? **2.** rel que; **they have a daughter** ~ **works in Alaska** tienen una hija que trabaja en Alaska; **the people** ~ **work here** la gente que trabaja aquí; **all those** ~ **know her** todos los que la conozcan; **it was your sister** ~ **did it** fue tu hermana quien lo hizo
WHO [ˌdʌb·əl·ju·ˌeɪtʃ·'oʊ] n abbr of **World Health Organization** OMS f
whoa [hwoʊ] interj **1.** (command to stop a horse) ¡so! **2.** fig, inf (to stop something) ¡para el carro!
whodunit n, **whodunnit** [ˌhu·'dʌn·ɪt] n inf novela f policíaca
whoever [hu·'ev·ər] pron **1.** rel (who) quien, quienes, quienquiera que, quienesquiera que; **they didn't write to me,** ~ **they were** no me escribieron, quienesquiera que fuesen; ~ **said that doesn't know me** el que dijo eso no me conoce **2.** interrog, inf (angry) quién diablos; ~ **said that?** ¿quién diablos dijo eso?
whole [hoʊl] I. adj **1.** (entire) todo, -a; **the** ~ **world** el mundo entero **2.** (in one piece) entero, -a; **to swallow sth** ~ tragarse algo entero **3.** (intact: thing) intacto, -a; (person) ileso, -a II. n **1.** (a complete thing) todo m; **as a** ~ (concept) en su totalidad; **taken as a** ~ en conjunto; **on the** ~ en general **2.** (entirety) totalidad f; **the** ~ la totalidad; **the** ~ **of Los Angeles** toda Los Ángeles; **the** ~ **of next week** toda la semana que viene III. adv inf (completely) completamente; ~ **new** completamente nuevo; (great); **a** ~ **lot of people** un mogollón de gente; **to be a** ~ **lot faster** ser mucho más rápido
whole food n **1.** (unprocessed food) comida f naturista; ~ **diet** alimentación f naturista **2.** ~**s** (unprocessed food products) alimentos mpl ecológicos
wholegrain ['hoʊl·greɪn] adj integral; ~ **bread** pan m integral; ~ **food products** productos mpl integrales
wholehearted [ˌhoʊl·'har·t̬ɪd] adj entusiasta; (completely sincere) completamente sincero, -a; ~ **thanks** agradecimiento m de todo corazón
wholesale ['hoʊl·seɪl] I. n venta f al por mayor II. adj **1.** al por mayor; ~ **business** negocio m mayorista; ~ **prices** precios mpl al por mayor;

~ **supplier** proveedor m mayorista **2.** (on a large scale) a gran escala; ~ **reform** reforma f a gran escala III. adv **1.** COM al por mayor **2.** (in bulk) en masa
wholesaler ['hoʊl·seɪ·lər] n mayorista mf; **furniture** ~ mayorista de muebles
wholesome ['hoʊl·səm] adj sano, -a; **the** ~ **outdoor life** la vida sana al aire libre; (good) ~ **fun** diversión f sana; (good) ~ **food** comida f sana
whole-wheat adj de trigo integral
who'll [hul] = **who will** s. **will**
wholly ['hoʊ·li] adv enteramente; **to be** ~ **aware of sth** ser totalmente consciente de algo; ~ **different** completamente diferente
whom [hum] pron **1.** interrog a quién, a quiénes; after prep quién, quiénes; ~ **did he see?** ¿a quién ha visto?; **to** ~ **did he talk?** ¿con quién ha hablado? **2.** rel a quien, que; after prep quien, que; **those** ~ **I love** aquellos a quienes amo; **with** ~ con quien
whoop [hup] I. vi gritar II. vt **to** ~ **it up** echar una cana al aire III. n grito m; **a** ~ **of triumph** un grito de victoria; **to give a loud** ~ dar un grito muy fuerte
whoopee ['hwu·pi] I. interj estupendo II. n juerga f; **to make** ~ sl (have sex) echar un polvo; (celebrate) pasárselo de puta madre
whooping cough ['hu·pɪŋ·ˌkɔf] n tos f ferina
whoops [hwʊps] interj inf epa
whop [hwap] inf I. <-pp-> vt **1.** (strike) pegar **2.** (in competition) derrotar II. n zurra f
whopper ['hwap·ər] n iron **1.** (huge thing) cosa f muy grande; **a** ~ **of a fish** un pez enorme **2.** (lie) embuste m; **to tell a** ~ contar una mentira como una casa
whopping ['hwap·ɪŋ] adj sl enorme; **a** ~ **lie** una mentira como una casa
whore [hɔr] n pej puta f
whorl [hwɜrl] n liter espira f
who's [huz] **1.** = **who is** s. **is 2.** = **who has** s. **has**
whose [huz] I. adj **1.** interrog de quién, de quiénes; ~ **book is this?** ¿de quién es este libro?; ~ **son is he?** ¿de quién es hijo? **2.** rel cuyo, cuya, cuyos, cuyas; **the girl** ~ **brother I saw** la chica cuyo hermano vi II. pron de quién, de quiénes; ~ **is this pen?** ¿de quién es esta pluma?; **I know** ~ **this is** sé de quién es esto
why [hwaɪ] I. adv por qué; ~ **didn't you tell me about that?** ¿por qué no me dijiste nada sobre eso?; **that's** ~ **I didn't tell you** por eso no te dije nada; **I want to know** ~ **you came late** quiero saber por qué llegaste tarde; ~ **not?** ¿por qué no?; ~**'s that?** ¿y eso por qué? II. n porqué m; **the** ~**s and wherefores of sth** las razones [o el porqué] de algo III. interj ¡cómo!
WI [wɪs·'kan·sɪn] n abbr of **Wisconsin** Wisconsin m
wick [wɪk] n mecha f
wicked ['wɪk·ɪd] I. adj **1.** (evil) malvado, -a **2.** (playfully malicious) retorcido, -a; **a** ~ **sense**

W

of humor un sentido del humor mordaz 3. (*likely to cause pain*) inicuo, -a 4. *sl* (*very good*) de puta madre II. *n* the ~ los malos

wicker ['wɪk·ər] *n* mimbre *m*

wickerwork *n* 1. (*material*) artículo *m* de mimbre 2. (*art*) cestería *f*

wicket ['wɪk·ɪt] *n* 1. (*cricket target*) palos *mpl* 2. (*ground*) área *f*; to be in a sticky ~ estar en un apuro

wide [waɪd] I. *adj* 1. (*broad*) extenso, -a; (*as a measurement*) ancho, -a; it is 3 feet ~ mide 1 m de ancho; the (great) ~ world el ancho mundo; to search (for sb/sth) the ~ world over buscar (a alguien/algo) por todo el mundo 2. (*very open*) vasto, -a; eyes ~ with fear/surprise ojos *mpl* como platos de miedo/sorpresa 3. (*varied*) amplio, -a; a ~ range una amplia gama; to have ~ experience in (doing) sth tener una amplia experiencia haciendo algo/en algo 4. (*extensive*) grande; ~ support gran apoyo *m* ▶ to be ~ of the mark fallar por mucho II. *adv* extensamente; to be ~ apart estar muy lejos (el uno del otro); to open ~ abrir mucho; ~ open (*eyes*) abierto, -a como platos; (*door*) abierto, -a de par en par

wide-angle [ˌwaɪd·'æŋ·gəl] *adj* (*lens*) gran angular

wide-awake [ˌwaɪd·ə·'weɪk] *adj* completamente despierto, -a

wide-eyed ['waɪd·aɪd] *adj fig* inocente

widely *adv* 1. (*broadly*) extensamente; to gesture ~ gesticular mucho; to smile ~ at sb sonreír ampliamente a alguien 2. (*extensively*) ampliamente; ~ accepted/admired muy aceptado/admirado 3. (*to a large degree*) considerablemente; ~ differing aims objetivos *mpl* muy diferentes

widen ['waɪ·dən] I. *vt* extender; (*discussion*) ampliar II. *vi* ensancharse

wide-open ['waɪd·ˌoʊ·pən] *adj* 1. (*undecided*) abierto, -a 2. (*vulnerable, exposed*) expuesto, -a; to be ~ to comments estar expuesto a comentarios

widespread ['waɪd·spred] *adj* extendido, -a; *fig* general; ~ speculation especulación difundida; there is ~ speculation that... se especula mucho que...

widow ['wɪd·oʊ] I. *n* viuda *f*; to be left a ~ enviudar II. *vt* to ~ sb dejar viuda a alguien; to be ~ed enviudar

widowed *adj* viudo, -a

widower ['wɪd·oʊ·ər] *n* viudo *m*; to be left a ~ enviudar

widowhood ['wɪd·oʊ·hʊd] *n* viudez *f*

widow's peak *n* pico *m* las entradas del pelo

width [wɪdθ] *n* 1. (*distance across*) extensión *f*; (*of wallpaper*) anchura *f*; to be 4 inches in ~ medir 10 cm de ancho 2. (*full extent of sth: of clothes*) ancho *m*; to swim two ~s nadar dos anchos 3. (*amount, size*) amplitud *f*

wield [wild] *vt* 1. (*hold*) manejar 2. (*weapon*) empuñar 3. (*power*) ejercer

wife [waɪf] <wives> *n* mujer *f*, esposa *f*; my ~ mi mujer

wifely ['waɪf·li] *adj* de esposa; (*duties*) conyugal

wig [wɪg] *n* peluca *f*

wiggle ['wɪg·əl] I. *vt* menear; (*toes*) mover; (*one's hips*) contonear II. *vi* contonearse III. *n* (*movement*) meneo *m*; (*when walking*) contoneo *m*

wigwam ['wɪg·wam] *n* wigwam *m*

wild [waɪld] I. *adj* 1. (*not domesticated: animal, man*) salvaje; (*flower*) silvestre; (*horse*) no domesticado, -a 2. (*uncultivated: country, landscape*) agreste 3. (*undisciplined*) indisciplinado, -a; (*party*) loco, -a 4. (*not sensible*) insensato, -a; (*plan*) descabellado, -a; (*behavior, remarks*) delirante 5. (*not accurate: blow, punch, shot*) errado, -a, al aire; (*estimate, guess*) disparatado, -a 6. (*extreme*) absurdo, -a 7. (*stormy*) tormentoso, -a; (*wind, weather*) furioso, -a 8. *inf* (*angry*) hecho, -a una fiera; to drive sb ~ sacar de quicio a alguien; to go ~ ponerse (como) loco 9. *inf* (*very enthusiastic*) loquito, -a; (*applause*) entusiasta 10. (*untidy: hair*) descuidado, -a 11. GAMES, COMPUT (*substitutable*) comodín 12. *sl* (*wonderful*) genial II. *adv* silvestre; to grow ~ crecer libre ▶ to run ~ (*child*) crecer como un salvaje; (*horse*) desbocarse; to let one's imagination run ~ dejar volar la imaginación III. *n* 1. the ~ (*natural environment*) la naturaleza; to survive in the ~ (*animals*) sobrevivir en libertad 2. *pl* the ~s la tierra virgen; (out) in the ~s en el quinto pino *inf*

wild card *n* 1. *a.* COMPUT comodín *m* 2. SPORTS (*extra team or player*) wild card *m*

wildcat I. *n* 1. ZOOL (*wild cat*) gato *m* montés 2. *fig* (*fierce woman*) fiera *f* II. *adj* 1. (*very risky*) arriesgado, -a 2. (*unofficial: strike*) salvaje 3. (*exploratory: drilling, well*) exploratorio, -a

wilderness ['wɪl·dər·nɪs] *n* 1. (*desert tract*) páramo *m* 2. (*unspoiled land*) tierra *f* virgen 3. *fig* (*uncultivated garden*) selva *f* irón

wildfire ['waɪld·ˌfaɪr] *n* fuego *m* incontrolado ▶ to spread like ~ extenderse como un reguero de pólvora

wildfowl ['waɪld·faʊl] *inv n* ave *f* de caza

wild goose <- geese> *n* ganso *m* salvaje

wild-goose chase *n* empresa *f* desatinada; (*hopeless search*) búsqueda *f* inútil; to send sb (off) on a ~ mandar a alguien a buscar una aguja en un pajar

wildlife *n* fauna *f* y flora *f*

wildly *adv* 1. (*in an uncontrolled way*) como loco; (*to gesticulate*) con furia, violentamente; to behave ~ portarse como un salvaje; to talk ~ hablar sin ton ni son 2. (*haphazardly*) a lo loco; (*shoot, guess*) a tontas y a locas 3. *inf* (*very*) muy; ~ exaggerated superexagerado; ~ expensive carísimo; ~ improbable totalmente improbable

wildness *n* 1. (*natural state*) estado *m* salvaje;

(*of a country*) estado *m* agreste **2.**(*uncontrolled behavior*) desenfreno *m* **3.**(*haphazardness*) insensatez *f*

wiles [waɪlz] *npl* artimañas *fpl;* **to use all one's ~** usar todas sus tretas

wilful ['wɪl·fəl] *adj s.* willful

wiliness ['waɪ·lɪ·nɪs] *n* astucia *f*

will[1] [wɪl] <would, would> I. *aux* **1.**(*to form future tense*) **they'll be delighted** estarán encantados; **I'll be with you in a minute** estaré contigo en un minuto; **I expect they'll come by car** supongo que vendrán en coche; **I'll answer the telephone** contesto yo el teléfono; **she ~ have received the letter by now** ya debe haber recibido la carta **2.**(*with tag question*) **you won't forget to tell him, ~ you?** no se te olvidará decírselo, ¿verdad?; **they ~ accept this credit card in the pizzeria, won't they?** aceptarán esta tarjeta de crédito en la pizzería, ¿no? **3.**(*to express immediate future*) **we'll be off now** ya nos vamos; **I'll be going then** me voy entonces; **there's someone at the door — I'll go** llaman a la puerta — voy yo **4.**(*to express an intention*) **sb ~ do that** alguien lo hará; **I'll not be spoken to like that!** ¡no consiento que se me hable así! **5.**(*in requests and instructions*) **~ you let me speak!?** ¡déjame hablar!; **just pass me that knife, ~ you?** pásame ese cuchillo, ¿quieres?; **give me a hand, ~ you?** échame una mano, ¿quieres? **6.**(*in polite requests*) **~ you sit down?** ¿pueden hacer el favor de sentarse?; **~ you be having a slice of cake?** ¿quiere un trozo de tarta? **7.**(*used to express willingness*) **who'll mail this letter for me?** — lo ~ ¿quién me echa esta carta al buzón? — lo haré yo; **~ you do that for me?** — of course I ~ ¿harás eso por mí? — claro que sí **8.**(*used to express a fact*) **eat it now, it won't keep** cómetelo ya, antes de que se ponga malo; **the car won't run without gasoline** el coche no funciona sin gasolina **9.**(*to express persistence*) **he ~ keep doing that** se empeña en hacer eso; **they ~ keep sending me those brochures** no dejan de mandarme estos folletos; **the door won't open** no hay manera de que se abra esta puerta **10.**(*to express likelihood*) **they'll be tired** estarán cansados; **as you ~ all probably know already...** como todos sabrán... II. *vi form* disponer; **as you ~** como quieras

will[2] [wɪl] I. *n* **1.**(*faculty*) voluntad *f;* (*desire*) deseo *m;* **the ~ of the people** la voluntad del pueblo; **to have the ~ to do sth** tener la voluntad de hacer algo; **to lose the ~ to live** perder las ganas de vivir; **at ~** a voluntad **2.**(*testament*) testamento *m* ▸ **where there's a ~, there's a way** *prov* querer es poder *prov;* **with the best ~ in the world** con la mejor voluntad del mundo; **to have a ~ of one's own** ser cabezón II. *vt* **1.**(*try to cause by willpower*) sugestionar; **to ~ sb to do sth** sugestionar a alguien para que haga algo **2.** *form*

(*ordain*) ordenar; **God ~ed it and it was so** Dios así lo quiso **3.**(*bequeath*) legar

willful ['wɪl·fəl] *adj* **1.**(*deliberate*) deliberado, -a; (*disobedience of orders*) intencionado, -a; (*murder*) premeditado, -a **2.**(*self-willed*) testarudo, -a; (*obstinate*) obstinado, -a

willies ['wɪl·iz] *npl sl* **to have the ~** ponérsele los pelos de punta; **to give sb the ~** poner los pelos de punta a alguien

willing ['wɪl·ɪŋ] *adj* **1.**(*not opposed*) dispuesto, -a; **to be ~ to do sth** estar dispuesto a hacer algo; **to lend a ~ hand** echar una mano; **God ~** si Dios quiere **2.**(*compliant*) servicial

willingness *n* **1.**(*readiness*) disposición *f;* **to show a ~ to do sth** mostrar buena voluntad para hacer algo **2.**(*enthusiasm*) entusiasmo *m;* **lack of ~** falta *f* de ánimo

will-o'-the-wisp [ˌwɪl·ə·ðə·'wɪsp] *n* **1.**(*ghostly light*) fuego *m* fatuo **2.** *fig* (*elusive thing*) quimera *f*

willow ['wɪl·oʊ] *n* sauce *m*

willowy ['wɪl·oʊ·i] *adj* esbelto, -a

willpower ['wɪl·pau·ər] *n* fuerza *f* de voluntad

willy-nilly [ˌwɪl·i·'nɪl·i] *adv* **1.**(*like it or not*) sea como sea **2.**(*in disorder*) de cualquier manera

wilt [wɪlt] *vi* **1.**(*droop: plants*) marchitarse **2.**(*feel weak: person*) languidecer; (*lose confidence*) desanimarse

wily ['waɪ·li] <-ier, -iest> *adj* astuto, -a

wimp [wɪmp] *n sl* endeble *mf*

win [wɪn] I. *n* victoria *f* II. <won, won> *vt* **1.**(*be victorious in: lawsuit, competition*) ganar; MIL vencer; **to ~ first prize** llevarse el primer premio **2.**(*obtain*) obtener; (*promotion, contract*) conseguir; (*recognition, popularity*) ganarse; **to ~ a reputation as a writer** lograr ser reconocido como escritor; **to ~ sb's heart** conquistar el corazón de alguien ▸ **to ~ the day** prevalecer; **you can't ~ them all** no se puede pretender ganarlas todas; **you ~ some, you lose some** no se puede ganar todo III. <won, won> *vi* ganar; **to ~ easily** ganar con facilidad ▸ **to ~ hands down** ganar con mucha facilidad; **you (just) can't ~ with him/her** con él/ella, siempre llevas las de perder, ¡no hay caso!; **you ~!** ¡como tú digas!

◆ **win back** *vt* recuperar

◆ **win over** *vt* **to win sb over to sth** (*persuade to change mind*) convencer a alguien para algo; (*persuade to transfer allegiance*) ganarse a alguien para algo

wince [wɪns] I. *vi* **1.**(*with pain*) hacer un gesto de dolor **2.**(*with embarrassment*) estremecerse II. *n* mueca *f* de dolor; **to give a ~** hacer una mueca de dolor

winch [wɪntʃ] I. <-es> *n* torno *m* II. *vt* levantar con un torno

wind[1] [wɪnd] I. *n* **1.**(*current of air*) viento *m;* **a breath of ~** un poco de aire; **gust of ~** ráfaga *f* **2.**(*breath*) aliento *m;* **to get** [*o* **catch**] **one's ~** recobrar el aliento; **to have the ~ knocked out of sb** parar a alguien los pies **3.** MED ventosidad *f;* **to break ~** ventosear ▶**to take the ~ out of sb's** <u>sails</u> desanimar a alguien; **he who sows the ~ shall reap the** <u>whirlwind</u> *prov* quien siembra vientos recoge tempestades *prov;* **to sail** <u>close</u> **to the ~** estar a punto de pasarse de la raya; **to** <u>get</u> **~ of sth** enterarse de algo; **to go** [*o* <u>run</u>] **like the ~** correr como el viento; **there's sth** <u>in</u> **the ~** se está tramando algo **II.** *vt* dejar sin aliento

wind² [waɪnd] <wound, wound> **I.** *vt* **1.** (*coil*) enrollar; (*wool*) ovillar; **to ~ sth around sth** enrollar algo alrededor de algo **2.** (*wrap*) envolver **3.** (*turn: handle*) hacer girar; (*clock, watch*) dar cuerda a **4.** (*film*) hacer correr **II.** *vi* serpentear

◆**wind down I.** *vt* **1.** (*gradually reduce*) disminuir progresivamente; (*activities, operations, production*) reducir; (*business*) limitar **2.** (*relax*) relajarse **II.** *vi* **1.** (*become less active*) limitarse; (*business*) tocar a su fin **2.** (*relax after stress*) desconectar

◆**wind up I.** *vt* **1.** (*finish*) acabar; (*debate, meeting, speech*) concluir **2.** *sl* (*make tense*) dar cuerda a **II.** *vi* **1.** *inf* (*end up*) **to ~ in prison** ir a parar a la cárcel **2.** (*in baseball*) impulsarse

windbag ['wɪnd·bæg] *n sl* charlatán, -ana *m, f*
windbreaker ['wɪnd·ˌbreɪ·kər] *n* cortavientos *m inv*
winder ['waɪn·dər] *n* **1.** (*on watch*) cuerda *f* **2.** (*on toy*) manivela *f*
windfall ['wɪnd·fɔl] *n* **1.** *fig* (*money*) ganancia *f* imprevista **2.** (*fruit*) fruta *f* caída
wind farm *n* ECOL granja *f* con energía eólica
winding ['waɪn·dɪŋ] *adj* sinuoso, -a
wind instrument *n* instrumento *m* de viento
windjammer *n* NAUT velero *m* grande
windlass *n* torno *m*
windmill *n* **1.** (*wind-powered mill*) molino *m* de viento **2.** (*toy*) molinete *m*
window ['wɪn·doʊ] *n* **1.** (*in building*) ventana *f;* (*bedroom*) vitrina *f;* **~ ledge** alféizar *m;* **a ~ on the world** *fig* una ventana abierta al mundo **2.** (*of shop*) escaparate *m;* (*window display*) escaparate **3.** (*side windows*) ventanilla *f;* (*of vehicle*) ventanilla; **rear ~** ventanilla *f* trasera **4.** COMPUT ventana; **pop-up ~** ventana emergente **5.** (*in envelope*) ventanilla **6.** *fig* (*time period*) ocasión *f;* **a ~ of opportunity** una oportunidad ▶**to go** <u>out</u> **(of) the ~** *inf* (*plan*) venirse abajo
window box <-es> *n* jardinera *f*
window-dressing *n* **1.** (*in shop*) escaparatismo *m* **2.** *fig* fachada *f;* (*effort*) esfuerzo *m* por aparentar
window envelope *n* sobre *m* de ventanilla
window-shopping *n* **to go ~** ir a mirar escaparates
windowsill *n* repisa *f* de la ventana
windpipe ['wɪnd·paɪp] *n* tráquea *f*
windshield ['wɪnd·ʃild] *n* parabrisas *m inv*
windshield wiper *n* limpiaparabrisas *m inv*

windsock *n* manga *f* de viento
windsurfer ['wɪnd·ˌsɜr·fər] *n* windsurfista *mf*
windsurfing ['wɪnd·ˌsɜr·fɪŋ] *n* windsurf *m*
windswept ['wɪnd·swept] *adj* **1.** (*exposed to wind*) azotado, -a por el viento **2.** (*looking wind-blown*) despeinado, -a
wind tunnel *n* TECH túnel *m* aerodinámico
windward ['wɪnd·wərd] NAUT **I.** *adj* de barlovento **II.** *n* barlovento *m;* (**to**) **~** a barlovento
windy¹ ['wɪn·di] <-ier, -iest> *adj* ventoso, -a
windy² ['waɪn·di] <-ier, -iest> *adj* sinuoso, -a
wine [waɪn] **I.** *n* vino *m* **II.** *vt* **to ~ and dine sb** dar a alguien muy bien de comer y de beber
wine cooler *n* **1.** (*drink*) ≈ sangría *f* **2.** (*container*) recipiente *m* para mantener fresco el vino
wineglass <-es> *n* copa *f* de vino
winegrower *n* viticultor(a) *m(f)*
wine list *n* carta *f* de vinos
wine merchant *n* **1.** (*seller of wines*) vinatero, -a *m, f* **2.** (*shop*) vinatería *f*
winepress ['waɪn·pres] <-es> *n* prensa *f* de uvas
winery ['waɪ·nə·ri] <-ies> *n* bodega *f*
winetasting *n* **1.** (*activity*) cata *f* de vinos **2.** (*event*) degustación *f* de vinos
wing [wɪŋ] **I.** *n* **1.** ZOOL, AVIAT ala *f;* **to take ~** *liter* alzar el vuelo **2.** ARCHIT ala; **the west ~ of the house** el ala oeste de la casa **3.** SPORTS (*side of field: left, right*) ala exterior; (*player*) extremo, -a *m, f* **4.** POL ala; **left/right ~** ala izquierda/derecha **5.** ~**s** THEAT bastidores *mpl;* **to be waiting in the ~s** *fig* estar esperando su oportunidad **6.** ~**s** MIL (*pilot's badge*) insignia *f* ▶**to** <u>spread</u> [*o* <u>stretch</u>] **one's ~s** desplegar [*o* extender] las alas; **to** <u>take</u> **sb under one's ~** hacerse cargo de alguien **II.** *vt* **1.** (*wound: bird*) herir en el ala; (*person*) herir superficialmente **2.** (*fly*) volar ▶**to ~** <u>it</u> *inf* arreglárselas sobre la marcha **III.** *vi* volar
wing chair *n* sillón *m* de orejas
winged [wɪŋd] *adj* alado, -a; (*seed*) con alas
winger ['wɪŋ·ər] *n* SPORTS extremo, -a *m, f;* **left/right ~** extremo izquierdo/derecho
wing nut *n* TECH palomilla *f*
wingspan ['wɪŋ·spæn] *n,* **wingspread** ['wɪŋ·spred] *n* envergadura *f*
wink [wɪŋk] **I.** *n* guiño *m;* **to give sb a ~** guiñar el ojo a alguien ▶**to have** <u>forty</u> **~s** *inf* echarse una siestecita; **to not** <u>sleep</u> **a ~** no pegar ojo; **in a ~** en un abrir y cerrar de ojos **II.** *vi* **1.** (*close one eye*) guiñar el ojo; **to ~ at sb** guiñar el ojo a alguien **2.** (*flash: a light*) parpadear
winner ['wɪn·ər] *n* **1.** (*person*) ganador(a) *m(f)* **2.** *inf* SPORTS **the game ~** el tanto decisivo **3.** *inf* (*success*) éxito *m;* (*book*) obra *f* premiada; **to be on to a ~ with sth** tener mucho éxito con algo
winning ['wɪn·ɪŋ] **I.** *adj* **1.** (*that wins*) ganador(a); (*ticket*) premiado, -a; (*point*) decisivo, -a; (*team*) vencedor(a) **2.** (*charming*) encantador(a) **II.** *n* **1.** (*act of achieving victory*) triunfo *m* **2.** ~**s** (*money*) ganancias *fpl*

winnow ['wɪn·oʊ] *vt* **1.**(*grain*) aventar **2.**(*select*) seleccionar; **to ~ the list down to 8** seleccionar 8 de la lista

winsome ['wɪn·səm] *adj liter* atractivo, -a; (*charm, smile*) encantador(a)

winter ['wɪn·tər] **I.** *n* invierno *m* **II.** *vi* (*animals*) invernar, hibernar; (*person*) pasar el invierno

winter coat *n* chaqueta *f* de invierno; (*of animal*) pelaje *m* de invierno

winterize ['wɪn·tə·raɪz] *vt* preparar para el invierno

winter solstice *n* solsticio *m* de invierno

winter sports *npl* deportes *mpl* de invierno

wintertime *n* invierno *m;* **in** (**the**) **~** en invierno

wint(e)ry ['wɪn·tri] *adj* **1.**(*typical of winter*) invernal **2.** *fig* (*cold, unfriendly*) frío, -a

wipe [waɪp] **I.** *n* **1.**(*act of wiping*) limpieza *f;* **to give sth a ~** pasar un trapo a algo, limpiar algo; **to give the floor a ~** limpiar el suelo **2.**(*tissue*) toallita *f* **II.** *vt* **1.**(*remove dirt*) limpiar; (*floor*) fregar; (*one's nose*) sonarse; (*dishes*) secar; **to ~ sth dry** secar algo **2.**(*erase material from: disk, a tape*) borrar **III.** *vi* secar

◆**wipe down** *vt* pasar un trapo a; (*floor*) limpiar

◆**wipe off** *vt* **1.**(*remove by wiping*) quitar con un trapo **2.**(*erase: data, program*) borrar **3.** ECON reducir ▶**to wipe the smile off sb's** <u>face</u> borrar la sonrisa de la cara

◆**wipe out** **I.** *vt* **1.**(*destroy: population, village*) exterminar; (*sb's profits*) acabar con **2.**(*cancel: debt*) liquidar **3.** *inf*(*tire out*) dejar hecho polvo **4.** *inf* (*economically*) arruinar **5.** *sl* (*murder*) liquidar **II.** *vi inf* (*driving, skiing*) perder el control

◆**wipe up** **I.** *vt* limpiar **II.** *vi* secar

wire ['waɪr] **I.** *n* **1.**(*metal thread*) alambre *m* **2.** ELEC cable *m* **3.**(*telegram*) telegrama *m* **4.**(*hidden microphone*) micro *m* (oculto) **5.**(*prison camp fence*) alambrada *f* ▶**to get one's ~s** <u>crossed</u> *inf* tener un malentendido; **to** <u>get</u> (**sth**) **in under the ~** *inf* conseguir algo justo a tiempo; **to go** (**down**) **to the ~** *inf* no decidirse hasta el último momento **II.** *vt* **1.**(*fasten with wire*) sujetar con alambre; **to ~ sth to the door** sujetar algo a la puerta con alambre **2.** ELEC conectar; **to be ~d for cable TV** tener instalación de televisión por cable **3.**(*fit with concealed microphone*) poner un micro oculto a; **to be ~d** (*person*) llevar un micro oculto **4.**(*send telegram to*) **to ~ sb** mandar un telegrama a alguien; **to ~ sb money** enviar un giro telegráfico a alguien

wirehaired terrier [ˌwaɪr·herd·'ter·i·ər] *n* terrier *m* de pelo duro

wireless ['waɪr·lɪs] *adj* **1.**(*having no wires*) inalámbrico, -a **2.** TEL (*using cell phone applications*) inalámbrico, -a

wiretapping ['waɪr·ˌtæp·ɪŋ] *n* escuchas *fpl* telefónicas

wire transfer *n* transferencia *f* por cable

wiring ['waɪ·rɪŋ] *n* ELEC **1.**(*system of wires*) cableado *m* **2.**(*electrical installation*) instalación *f* eléctrica

wiry ['waɪ·ri] <-ier, -iest> *adj* **1.**(*course: hair*) áspero, -a, tieso, -a **2.**(*lean and strong: build, person*) enjuto, -a y fuerte

Wisconsin [wɪs·'kan·sɪn] *n* Wisconsin *m*

wisdom ['wɪz·dəm] *n* **1.**(*state of being wise*) sabiduría *f;* **with the ~ of hindsight** con la sabiduría que da la experiencia; **~ comes with age** más sabe el diablo por viejo que por diablo *prov* **2.**(*sensibleness*) prudencia *f*

wisdom tooth <- teeth> *n* muela *f* del juicio

wise [waɪz] *adj* **1.**(*having knowledge and sagacity*) sabio, -a; **the Three Wise Men** los Reyes Magos; **it's easy to be ~ after the fact** es muy fácil criticar a posteriori **2.**(*showing sagacity*) acertado, -a; (*advice, saying*) adecuado, -a; (*words*) juicioso, -a **3.**(*sensible*) sensato, -a; (*decision, choice*) inteligente **4.** *inf* (*aware*) consciente; **to be ~ to sb** tener calado a alguien; **to be ~ to sth** estar al tanto de algo; **to get ~ to sth** caer en la cuenta de algo; **to get ~ to sb's game** enterarse del juego de alguien; **to be none the ~r for sth** seguir sin enterarse de algo **5.** *sl* (*cheeky*) pícaro, -a; **to get ~ with sb** ponerse borde con alguien

◆**wise up** *sl* **I.** *vi* **to ~ to sth** ponerse al tanto de algo **II.** *vt* **to wise sb up about sth** poner a alguien al tanto de algo

wiseacre ['waɪz·ˌeɪ·kər] *n sl* sabelotodo *mf*

wisecrack ['waɪz·kræk] *sl* **I.** *n* broma *f;* **to make a ~ about sth** hacer un chiste sobre algo **II.** *vi* bromear

wise guy *n sl* gracioso, -a *m, f*

wish [wɪʃ] **I.** <-es> *n* **1.**(*desire*) deseo *m;* **against my ~es** en contra de mi voluntad; **to express the ~ that...** rogar que... +*subj;* **to have no ~ to do sth** no tener ganas de hacer algo; **to make a ~** expresar un deseo **2.~s** (*friendly greetings*) recuerdos *mpl;* **give him my best ~es** dale muchos recuerdos de mi parte; (**with**) **best ~es** (*at end of letter*) un abrazo **II.** *vt* **1.**(*feel a desire*) desear; **I ~ he hadn't come** ojalá no hubiera venido; **I ~ you'd told me** (*expressing annoyance*) me lo podrías haber dicho **2.** *form* (*want*) **to ~ to do sth** querer hacer algo; **I ~ to be alone** prefiero estar solo **3.**(*hope*) **to ~ sb luck** desear suerte a alguien; **to ~ sb happy birthday** felicitar a alguien por su cumpleaños; **to ~ sb good night** dar las buenas noches a alguien **III.** *vi* **1.**(*want*) desear; **as you ~** como usted mande; **if you ~** como quieras; **to ~ for sth** anhelar algo **2.**(*make a wish*) **to ~ for sth** desear algo; **everything one could ~ for** todo lo que uno podría desear

wishbone ['wɪʃ·boʊn] *n* espoleta *f*

wishful thinking *n* ilusión *f*

wishy-washy ['wɪʃ·i·ˌwaʃ·i] *adj pej* **1.**(*indeterminate and insipid*) insípido, -a; (*argument*) flojo, -a **2.**(*weak and watery: coffee, drink,*

W

soup) aguado, -a; (*food*) soso, -a

wisp [wɪsp] *n* (*of hair*) mechón *m;* (*of straw*) brizna *f;* (*of smoke*) voluta *f;* (*of clouds*) jirón *m;* **a little ~ of a boy** un chico menudito

wispy ['wɪs·pi] <-ier, -iest> *adj* (*hair*) ralo, -a; (*person*) menudo, -a; (*clouds*) tenue

wisteria [wɪ·'stɪr·i·ə] *n* glicina *f*

wistful ['wɪst·fəl] *adj* (*melancholy, nostalgic*) nostálgico, -a; (*longing*) añorante

wit [wɪt] **I.** *n* **1.** (*clever humor*) ingenio *m;* **to have a dry ~** ser mordaz **2.** (*practical intelligence*) inteligencia *f;* **to be at one's ~s' end** estar para volverse loco; **to gather one's ~s** poner las ideas en orden; **to frighten sb out of his/her ~s** dar a alguien un susto de muerte; **to have/keep one's ~s about one** andar con mucho ojo; **to live off one's ~s** vivir del cuento **3.** (*witty person*) chistoso, -a *m, f;* (*quick-witted person*) persona *f* ocurrente **II.** *vi form* **to ~** a saber

witch [wɪtʃ] <-es> *n* **1.** (*woman with magic powers*) bruja *f* **2.** *pej, inf* (*hag*) arpía *f*

witchcraft ['wɪtʃ·kræft] *n* brujería *f*, payé *m CSur*

witch doctor *n* curandero, -a *m, f*, payé *m CSur*

witch-hunt ['wɪtʃ·hʌnt] *n pej* caza *f* de brujas

witching hour ['wɪtʃ·ɪŋ.aʊr] *n liter* medianoche *f*

with [wɪð, wɪθ] *prep* **1.** (*accompanied by*) con; (**together**) **~ sb** (junto) con alguien **2.** (*by means of*) con; **to take sth ~ one's fingers/both hands** tomar algo con los dedos/las dos manos; **to replace sth ~ something else** reemplazar algo por otra cosa **3.** (*having*) **the man ~ the umbrella** el hombre del paraguas; **~ no hesitation at all** sin ningún titubeo **4.** (*on one's person*) **he took it ~ him** se lo llevó **5.** (*manner*) **~ all speed** a toda velocidad; **~ one's whole heart** de todo corazón **6.** (*in addition to*) **and ~ that he went out** y a continuación salió **7.** (*despite*) **~ all his faults** a pesar de todos sus defectos **8.** (*caused by*) **to cry ~ rage** llorar de rabia; **to turn red ~ anger** ponerse rojo de cólera **9.** (*full of*) **black ~ flies** cubierto de moscas; **to fill up ~ fuel** llenar de gasolina **10.** (*opposing*) **a war ~ Italy** una guerra contra Italia; **to be angry ~ sb** estar enfadado con alguien **11.** (*supporting*) **to be ~ sb/sth** estar de acuerdo con alguien/algo; **popular ~ young people** popular entre los jóvenes **12.** (*concerning*) **to be pleased ~ sth** estar satisfecho con algo; **what's up** [*o* **what's the matter**] **~ him?** ¿qué le pasa? **13.** (*understanding*) **I'm not ~ you** *inf* no te sigo; **to be ~ it** *inf* estar al tanto; **to get ~ it** ponerse al día ▶ **away ~ him!** ¡llévenselo!

withdraw [wɪð·'drɔ] *irr* **I.** *vt* **1.** (*take out*) quitar; (*money*) sacar **2.** (*take back*) retirar **3.** (*cancel*) cancelar; (*motion, action*) anular; (*charge*) apartar **II.** *vi* **1.** *form a.* MIL (*leave*) retirarse; **to ~ from public life** retirarse de la vida pública; SPORTS abandonar **2.** *fig* (*become*

quiet and unsociable) recluirse; (*into silence*) retraerse

withdrawal [wɪð·'drɔ·əl] *n* **1.** *a.* MIL retirada *f;* **to make a ~** FIN sacar dinero **2.** LAW retracto *m;* (*of consent, support*) supresión *f* **3.** (*sports*) abandono *m* **4.** (*distancing from others*) retraimiento *m* **5.** MED abstinencia *f;* **to go through ~** estar con el mono *inf*

wither ['wɪð·ər] **I.** *vi* **1.** (*plants*) marchitarse **2.** *fig* (*lose vitality*) debilitarse; **to allow sth to ~** dejar que algo pierda vida ▶ **to ~ on the vine** desaparecer poco a poco **II.** *vt* **1.** (*plant*) marchitar **2.** *fig* (*strength*) mermar

withering ['wɪð·ər·ɪŋ] *adj* **1.** (*fierce and destructive*) destructivo, -a; (*heat, fire*) abrasador(a) **2.** (*contemptuous: criticism*) hiriente

withhold [wɪð·'hoʊld] *irr vt* **1.** (*not give*) **to ~ sth (from sb)** ocultar algo (a alguien); (*one's support*) negar; (*evidence, information*) ocultar **2.** (*not pay: benefits, rent*) retener

within [wɪð·'ɪn] **I.** *prep* **1.** *form* (*inside of*) dentro de, en; **~ the country/town** dentro del país/de la ciudad **2.** (*in limit of*) **~ sight/hearing** al alcance de la vista/del oído; **~ easy reach** al alcance de la mano **3.** (*in less than*) en (el transcurso de); **~ one hour** en una hora; **~ 3 days** en (el plazo de) tres días; **~ 5 miles of the town** a menos de 8 km de la ciudad **4.** (*in accordance to*) de acuerdo a; **~ the law** dentro de la legalidad **II.** *adv* dentro; **from ~** desde dentro

without [wɪð·'aʊt] **I.** *prep* sin; **~ warning** sin previo aviso; **to be ~ relatives** no tener parientes; **to do ~ sth** apañárselas sin algo **II.** *adv liter* fuera; **from ~** desde fuera

withstand [wɪð·'stænd] *irr vt* resistir; (*heat, pressure*) soportar

witness ['wɪt·nɪs] **I.** *n* **1.** *a.* LAW testigo *mf;* **~ for the defense** testigo de descargo; **according to ~es** según testigos; **to be (a) ~ to sth** ser testigo de algo **2.** *form* (*testimony*) testimonio *m;* **to bear ~ to sth** dar fe de algo **II.** *vt* **1.** (*see*) ser testigo de; **to ~ sb doing sth** observar a alguien haciendo algo **2.** (*be there during*) vivir; (*changes*) presenciar **3.** (*attest authenticity of*) dar fe de

witness stand *n* tribuna *f* (de los testigos)

witty ['wɪt̬·i] <-ier, -iest> *adj* (*possessing or showing wit*) ingenioso, -a; (*funny*) gracioso, -a

wizard ['wɪz·ərd] *n* **1.** (*magician*) mago, -a *m, f* **2.** (*expert*) genio *mf;* **to be a ~ at sth** ser un genio haciendo algo

wizardry ['wɪz·ər·dri] *n* magia *f*

wizened ['wɪz·ənd] *adj* marchito, -a; (*face, skin*) arrugado, -a

wk. *n abbr of* **week** semana *f*

WNBA [,dʌb·əl·ju,en·bi·'eɪ] *n abbr of* **Women's National Basketball Association** WNBA *f*

WNW *abbr of* **west-northwest** ONO

w/o *prep abbr of* **without** sin

wobble ['wab·əl] **I.** *vi* **1.** (*move unsteadily*) tambalearse; (*wheel*) bailar; (*jelly, fat*) temblar;

(*rock*) balancearse **2.**(*tremble: voice*) temblar **3.** *fig* (*fluctuate: prices, shares*) fluctuar **II.** *vt* hacer tambalearse; (*camera*) mover **III.** *n* **1.**(*wobbling movement*) tambaleo *m* **2.**(*quavering sound*) temblor *m* **3.** ECON fluctuación *f*

wobbly ['wɑb·li] <-ier, -iest> *adj* **1.**(*unsteady*) tambaleante; (*line*) zigzagueante; (*chair*) cojo, -a **2.**(*wavering: a note, a voice*) tembloroso, -a

woe [woʊ] *n* **1.** *liter*(*unhappiness*) desgracia *f;* **a tale of** ~ una tragedia **2.** ~ **s** *form* (*misfortunes*) males *mpl;* **to pour out one's** ~ **s** contar a alguien sus penas ▶ ~ **betide you!** ¡maldito seas!; **woe is me!** ¡pobre de mí!

woebegone ['woʊ·bɪ·gɑn] *adj liter* angustiado, -a

woeful ['woʊ·fəl] *adj* **1.**(*deplorable*) deplorable; (*ignorance, incompetence*) lamentable **2.** *liter*(*sad*) afligido, -a

wok [wɑk] *n* wok *m* (*puchero chino de metal*)

woke [woʊk] *vt, vi pt of* **wake**

woken ['woʊ·kən] *vt, vi pp of* **wake**

wolf [wʊlf] **I.**<wolves> *n* **1.**(*animal*) lobo *m* **2.** *sl* (*seducer*) donjuán *m* ▶ **to keep the** ~ **from the door** mantenerse a flote; **a** ~ **in sheep's clothing** un lobo disfrazado de cordero; **to cry** ~ dar una falsa alarma; **to throw sb to the wolves** arrojar a alguien a los lobos **II.** *vt inf* engullir

wolfhound *n* perro *m* lobo

wolf whistle *n* silbido *m* de admiración

woman ['wʊm·ən] *n* **1.**(*female human*) mujer *f;* **the other** ~ la amante; ~ **candidate** candidata *f;* ~ **president** presidenta *f;* **women's libber** defensor(a) *m(f)* de los derechos de la mujer **2.** *inf* (*man's female partner*) parienta *f*

womanhood ['wʊm·ən·hʊd] *n* **1.**(*female adulthood*) condición *f* de mujer; **to reach** ~ hacerse adulta **2.**(*women as a group*) mujeres *fpl*

womanish ['wʊm·ən·ɪʃ] *adj pej* afeminado

womanize ['wʊm·ə·naɪz] *vi inf* andar detrás de las faldas

womanizer *n* mujeriego *m*

womankind ['wʊm·ən·kaɪnd] *n form* sexo *m* femenino; **all** ~ todas las mujeres

womanly ['wʊm·ən·li] *adj* **1.**(*not manly*) femenino, -a; (*wiles*) de mujer **2.**(*not girlish*) de mujer adulta

womb [wum] *n* útero *m; in the* ~ en el seno materno

women's center *n* centro *m* para mujeres

women's lib *n inf abbr of* **women's liberation** liberación *f* de la mujer

women's shelter *n* centro *m* de acogida para mujeres

won [wʌn] *vt, vi pt, pp of* **win**

wonder ['wʌn·dər] **I.** *vt* **1.**(*ask oneself*) preguntarse; **to make sb** ~ hacer pensar a alguien **2.**(*feel surprise*) **I** ~ **why he said that** me extraña que dijera eso **II.** *vi* **1.**(*ask oneself*) preguntarse; **to** ~ **about sth** preguntarse algo; **to** ~ **about doing sth** pensar si hacer algo

2.(*feel surprise*) sorprenderse; **to** ~ **at sth/sb** maravillarse de algo/alguien; **I don't** ~ (**at it**) no me extraña **III.** *n* **1.**(*marvel*) maravilla *f;* **to do** [*o* **work**] ~ **s** hacer maravillas; **the** ~ **s of modern technology** los prodigios de la tecnología moderna; **it's a** ~ (**that**)... es un milagro que... +*subj;* ~ **s** (**will**) **never cease!** *iron* ¡eso sí es increíble! **2.**(*feeling*) asombro *m; in* ~ con estupefacción; **to listen in** ~ escuchar estupefacto

wonder drug *n* remedio *m* milagroso

wonderful ['wʌn·dər·fəl] *adj* maravilloso, -a

wonderland ['wʌn·dər·lænd] *n* país *m* de las maravillas

wonderment *n* admiración *f*

wont [wɑnt] **I.** *adj form* acostumbrado, -a; **to be** ~ **to do sth** soler hacer algo **II.** *n form* costumbre *f;* **as is her** ~ como suele hacer

won't [woʊnt] = **will not** *s.* **will**

woo [wu] *vt* **1.**(*try to attract*) **to** ~ **sb** (*customers, investors*) atraer a alguien; (*voters*) buscar el apoyo de alguien **2.**(*court*) cortejar

wood [wʊd] *n* **1.**(*material*) madera *f;* (*for a fire*) leña *f* **2.** ~ **s** (*group of trees*) bosque *m* **3.** SPORTS (*golf*) palo *m* de madera ▶ (**to**) **touch** [*o* **knock on**] ~ tocar madera; **to be out of the** ~ **s** *inf* estar a salvo

wood alcohol *n* metanol *m*

woodcraft *n* **1.**(*outdoor skills*) conocimientos *mpl* de supervivencia **2.**(*artistic skill*) artesanía *f* en madera

woodcut *n* ART grabado *f* en madera

woodcutter *n* leñador(a) *m(f)*

wooded ['wʊd·ɪd] *adj* boscoso, -a

wooden ['wʊd·ən] *adj* **1.**(*made of wood*) de madera; ~ **leg** pata *f* de palo **2.**(*awkward*) rígido, -a; (*smile*) inexpresivo, -a

woodland ['wʊd·lənd] **I.** *n* bosque *m* **II.** *adj* de los bosques

woodpecker *n* pájaro *m* carpintero

woodpile *n* montón *m* de leña

wood pulp *n* TECH pulpa *f* de madera

woodshed ['wʊd·ʃed] **I.** *n* leñera *f* **II.**<-dd-> *vi sl* tocar (*un instrumento musical*)

woodwind ['wʊd·wɪnd] MUS **I.** *n* instrumentos *mpl* de viento (de madera) **II.** *adj* de viento

woodwork ['wʊd·wɜrk] *n* (*wooden parts of building*) maderamiento *m* ▶ **to come out of the** ~ *sl* salir de quién sabe dónde

woodworking *n* (*carpentry*) ebanistería *f;* (*craftsmanship*) artesanía *f* en madera

woodworm *n inv* **1.**(*larva that attacks wood*) carcoma *f* **2.**(*damage*) madera *f* carcomida

woody ['wʊd·i] **I.**<-ier, -iest> *adj* **1.**(*tough like wood: plant, stem, tissue*) leñoso, -a **2.**(*like wood: flavor*) amaderado, -a **3.**(*wooded*) boscoso, -a **II.** *n vulg* (*erection*) empalmada *f*

woof [wʊf] **I.** *n* (*dog*) ladrido *m;* **to give a loud** ~ ladrar **II.** *vi* ladrar; **to** ~ **at sb** gritar a alguien

woofer ['wʊf·ər] *n* bafle *m*

wool [wʊl] *n* lana *f* ▶ **to pull the** ~ **over sb's eyes** dar a alguien gato por liebre

woolen *adj*, **woollen** ['wʊl·ən] *adj* de lana
woolly *n*, **wooly** ['wʊl·i] <-ier, -iest> *adj*
1.(*made of wool*) de lana 2.(*wool-like*)
lanoso, -a 3.(*vague*) vago, -a; (*ideas, thinking*)
impreciso, -a
woozy ['wu·zi] <-ier, -iest> *adj inf* grogui
word [wɜrd] **I.** *n* 1.(*unit of language*) palabra *f;*
a ~ of Hebrew origin una voz de origen
hebreo; **to be a man/woman of few ~s** ser
hombre/mujer de pocas palabras; **to not
breathe a ~ of sth** no decir ni pío de algo; **to
be too ridiculous for ~s** ser tremendamente
ridículo; **in other ~s** en otros términos; **~ for
~** palabra por palabra 2.(*news*) noticia *f;*
(*message*) mensaje *m;* **to get ~ of sth** enterarse de algo; **to have ~ from sb** tener un
recado de alguien; **to have ~ that...** tener
conocimiento de que... 3.(*order*) orden *f;* **a ~
of advice** un consejo; **a ~ of warning/caution** una advertencia; **to say the ~** dar la
orden; **just say the ~** sólo tienes que pedirlo
4.(*promise*) palabra *f* (de honor); **to be a
man/woman of one's ~** ser un hombre/una
mujer de palabra; **to keep one's ~** cumplir su
promesa; **take my ~ for it!** ¡acepta mi palabra!
5.(*statement of facts*) explicación *f* 6.~s MUS
(*lyrics*) letra *f* 7. REL **the Word of God** la palabra de Dios ▶**to have a quick ~ with sb**
hablar en privado con alguien; **by ~ of mouth**
de viva voz; **to put ~s in(to) sb's mouth** atribuir a alguien algo que no dijo; **to take the ~s
(right) out of sb's mouth** quitar la palabra de
la boca a alguien; **to not have a good ~ to say
about sb/sth** no poder decir nada bueno
sobre alguien/algo; **to put in a good ~ for sb**
interceder por alguien; **~s fail me!** ¡no tengo
palabras!; **from the ~ go** desde el primer
momento; **mark my ~s!** ¡toma nota!; **to
mince one's ~s** medir sus palabras; **to not
mince one's ~s** no tener pelos en la lengua;
my ~! ¡caramba! **II.** *vt* expresar
wording *n* 1.(*words used*) términos *mpl*
2.(*style*) estilo *m*
wordless ['wɜrd·lɪs] *adj* mudo, -a
word order *n* LING orden *m* de las palabras
wordplay ['wɜrd·pleɪ] *n* juego *m* de palabras
word processing *n* COMPUT tratamiento *m* de
textos
word processor *n* COMPUT procesador *m* de
textos
word wrap *n* COMPUT salto *m* de línea automático
wordy ['wɜr·di] <-ier, iest> *adj pej* farragoso, -a
wore [wɔr] *vt*, *vi pt of* **wear**
work [wɜrk] **I.** *n* 1.(*useful activity*) trabajo *m;*
to be hard ~ (doing sth) (*strenuous*) costar
un gran esfuerzo (hacer algo); (*difficult*) ser
una tarea difícil (hacer algo); **to set sb to ~**
poner a trabajar a alguien; **good ~!** ¡bien
hecho! 2.(*employment*) empleo *m;* **to be out
of ~** estar en paro 3.(*place of employment*)
(lugar *m* de) trabajo *m* 4.(*product*) *a.* ART, MUS
obra *f;* **reference ~** obra *m* de consulta 5.~s

+ *sing/pl vb* (*factory*) fábrica *f;* **steel ~s** fundición *f* de acero 6.~s TECH (*of a clock*) mecanismo *m* 7. PHYS trabajo *m* ▶**to have one's ~
cut out to do sth** costarle trabajo a uno hacer
algo; **to make short ~ of sb** hacer trizas a alguien; **to make short ~ of sth** despachar algo
rápidamente; **to get to ~ on sb** *inf* ponerse a
convencer a alguien; **to get to ~ on sth** *inf*
ponerse manos a la obra con algo; **the ~s** *sl*
toda la historia [*o* pesca]; **give me a pizza
with the ~s** dame una pizza con todo lo que
haya; **to give sb the ~s** *sl* tratar a alguien
como a un perro **II.** *vi* 1.(*do job*) trabajar; **to ~
abroad** trabajar en el extranjero; **to ~ as sth**
trabajar de algo 2.(*be busy*) estar ocupado; **to
get ~ing** poner manos a la obra; **to ~ hard** ser
aplicado; **to ~ to do sth** dedicarse a hacer algo
3. TECH funcionar; **to get sth to ~** conseguir
que algo funcione 4.(*be successful*) salir adelante; (*plan, tactics*) dar resultado 5. MED hacer
efecto 6.(*have an effect*) obrar; **to ~ against sb/sth**
obrar en contra de alguien/algo; **to ~ against
a candidate** resultar negativo para un candidato; **to ~ for sb** ser eficaz para alguien; **to ~
both ways** ser un arma de doble filo 7.(*move*)
to ~ (somewhere) moverse (hacia algún sitio)
8. + *adj* (*become*) **to ~ free** soltarse; **to
~ loose** desprenderse 9. *liter* (*change
expression: sb's face*) cambiar; (*contort*) contraerse; (*twitch*) temblar ▶**to ~ like a charm**
funcionar de maravilla; **to ~ like a dog, to ~
like a slave** trabajar como un esclavo; **to ~
around to sth** prepararse con tranquilidad
para algo **III.** *vt* 1.(*make sb work*) **to ~ sb
hard** hacer trabajar duro a alguien; **to ~ oneself to death** matarse trabajando; **to ~ a fortyhour week** tener una semana laboral de cuarenta horas 2. TECH (*operate*) hacer funcionar;
to be ~ed by sth ser accionado por algo
3.(*move back and forward*) mover; **to ~ sth
backwards and forwards** tirar algo hacia
adelante y hacia atrás; **to ~ sth free** liberar
algo; **to ~ sth loose** desprender algo; **to ~
one's way along sth** abrirse camino por algo
4.(*bring about*) producir; (*a cure*) efectuar; (*a
miracle*) lograr; **to ~ it** [*o* things] **so that...**
arreglárselas para que... + *subj* 5.(*shape*) tallar;
(*bronze, iron*) trabajar 6. FASHION (*embroider*)
bordar 7. MIN explotar; AGR cultivar 8.(*pay for
by working*) **to ~ one's way through college**
pagarse la universidad trabajando
◆**work away** *vi* trabajar sin parar
◆**work in** *vt* 1.(*mix in:: into a dough*) añadir;
(*on one's skin*) penetrar poco a poco
2.(*include*) introducir; (*fit in*) colocar
◆**work off I.** *vt* 1.(*counter effects of*) contrarrestar; (*one's anger, frustration*) desahogar;
(*stress*) aliviar 2.(*pay by working*) pagar con
el trabajo; (*a debt, loan*) amortizar **II.** *vi* TECH
separarse
◆**work on** *vt* (*a car, project*) trabajar en;
(*accent, fitness, skills*) esforzarse para mejorar; (*assumption, hypothesis*) partir de; (*per-

son) intentar persuadir a

◆**work out** I. *vt* 1. (*solve*) resolver; **to work things out** arreglárselas 2. (*calculate*) calcular 3. (*develop*) desarrollar; (*a settlement*) llegar; (*a solution*) encontrar; (*decide*) determinar 4. (*understand*) darse cuenta, comprender 5. (*complete*) completar; (*one's contract*) cumplir con 6. **to be worked out** (*lode, mine, quarry*) estar agotado II. *vi* 1. (*give a result: a calculation, sum*) resultar; (*cheaper, more expensive*) salir 2. (*be resolved*) resolverse 3. (*be successful*) acabar bien; **to ~ for the best** salir perfectamente 4. (*do exercise*) entrenarse

◆**work over** *vt sl* dar una paliza a

◆**work up** *vt* 1. (*generate: courage, energy, enthusiasm*) estimular 2. (*arouse strong feelings*) sacar; **to work oneself up** emocionarse; **to ~ into a frenzy** emocionarse hasta el frenesí; **to work sb up into a rage** sacar a alguien de quicio 3. (*develop*) desarrollar; (*idea, plan, sketch*) llevar a cabo; (*business*) fomentar; **to work one's way up through the company** ir ascendiendo en la empresa

workable ['wɜrk·ə·bəl] *adj* 1. (*feasible*) factible; (*compromise, plan*) viable 2. (*able to be manipulated*) que se puede trabajar; AGR (*ground, land*) explotable

workaday ['wɜrk·ə·deɪ] *adj* de todos los días

workaholic ['wɜrk·ə·hɒ·lɪk] *n* trabajador (a) *m(f)* compulsivo

workaround *n* solución *f* de emergencia; (*temporary*) solución *f* provisional (hasta encontrar una mejor)

workbench <-es> *n* mesa *f* de trabajo

workbook *n* cuaderno *m* de ejercicios

workday *n* (*weekday*) día *m* laborable; (*time*) jornada *f* laboral

worker ['wɜr·kər] *n* trabajador(a) *m(f)*; (*in factory*) obrero, -a *m, f*

work force *n* + *sing/pl vb* población *f* activa

workhorse *n* bestia *f* de carga

working I. *adj* 1. (*employed*) empleado, -a; (*population*) activo, -a 2. (*pertaining to work*) de trabajo; (*control*) efectivo, -a; (*day, hour, week*) laboral 3. (*functioning*) que funciona; (*moving: model*) móvil; (*part of a machine*) operativo, -a 4. (*used as basis: theory, hypothesis*) de base; **to have a ~ knowledge of sth** tener conocimientos básicos de algo II. *n* 1. (*activity*) actividad *f* 2. (*employment*) trabajo *m*

working class ['wɜr·kɪŋ·klæs] <-es> *n* **the ~** la clase obrera

working-class *adj* obrero, -a; (*background*) humilde

workload ['wɜrk·loʊd] *n* (volumen *m* de) trabajo *m*; **to have a heavy/light/unbearable ~** tener mucho/poco/demasiado trabajo

workman ['wɜrk·mən] <-men> *n* obrero *m*

workmanlike ['wɜrk·mən·laɪk] *adj* 1. (*showing skill: performance, job*) profesional 2. (*technically sufficient: performance*) co-

rrecto, -a

workmanship ['wɜrk·mən·ʃɪp] *n* 1. (*skill in working*) destreza *f* 2. (*work executed*) trabajo *m* 3. (*quality of work*) confección *f*; **shoddy ~** mala calidad; **of fine ~** de excelente factura

work of art *n* obra *f* de arte

workout ['wɜrk·aʊt] *n* SPORTS entrenamiento *m*

work permit *n* permiso *m* de trabajo

workplace *n* COM (lugar *m* de) trabajo *m*; **safety in the ~** seguridad *f* en el trabajo

work-sharing ['wɜrk·ʃer·ɪŋ] *n* sistema en el cual dos personas comparten un puesto de trabajo

worksheet ['wɜrk·ʃit] *n* hoja *f* de trabajo

workshop ['wɜrk·ʃap] *n* 1. (*repair place*) taller *m* 2. (*meeting for learning*) seminario *m*; **drama ~** taller de arte dramático

workspace ['wɜrk·speɪs] *n* COMPUT área *f* de trabajo

workstation *n* COMPUT estación *f* de trabajo

work-study program *n* SCHOOL, UNIV, COM programa *m* de becas que exigen que el estudiante trabaje dentro de la universidad

worktable ['wɜrk·teɪ·bəl] *n* mesa *f* de trabajo

workweek ['wɜrk·wik] *n* semana *f* laborable

world [wɜrld] *n* 1. GEO mundo *m*; **the ~'s population** la población mundial; **a ~ authority** una autoridad mundial; **the ~ champion** el campeón del mundo; **the best/worst in the ~** el mejor/peor del mundo; **the tallest man in the ~** el hombre más alto del mundo; **the (whole) ~ over** en el mundo entero; **to see the ~** ver mundo; **to travel all over the ~** viajar por todo el mundo 2. (*defined group*) **the ~ of dogs/horses** el mundo del perro/caballo; **the animal ~** el mundo animal; **the Christian/Muslim ~** el mundo cristiano/musulmán; **the New/Old/Third ~** el Nuevo/Viejo/Tercer Mundo ▸ **to be a ~ of difference between...** haber un abismo entre...; **to have the ~ at one's feet** tener el mundo a sus pies; **the ~ at large** el mundo en general; **the ~ is his/her oyster** tiene el mundo a sus pies; **to feel on top of the ~** estar en el séptimo cielo; **that's the way of the ~** ¡así es la vida!; **to be for all the ~ like...** ser exactamente como...; **to be ~s apart** ser como la noche y el día; **to have the best of both ~s** nadar y guardar la ropa; **to be dead to the ~** dormir como un tronco; **to be out of this ~** *inf* ser algo nunca visto; **it's a small ~!** ¡el mundo es un pañuelo!; **I wouldn't do that for (all) the (money in the) ~** no haría algo así por nada/ni por todo el oro del mundo; **to move up in the ~** *inf* prosperar; **to move down in the ~** *inf* venir a menos; **to live in a ~ of one's own** vivir en su mundo; **to mean (all) the ~ to sb** serlo todo para alguien; **to think the ~ of sb/sth** tener un alto concepto de alguien/algo; **what/who/how in the ~...?** ¿qué/quién/cómo demonios...?

World Bank *n* **the ~** el Banco Mundial

W

world-class *adj* reconocido, -a mundialmente

World Cup *n* SPORTS **the** ~ la Copa del Mundo; **the ~ Finals** la final de la Copa del Mundo

world-famous ['wɜrld·ˌfeɪ·məs] *adj* de fama mundial

world language *n* lengua *f* universal

worldly ['wɜrld·li] *adj* **1.** (*of physical, practical matters*) material; ~ **goods** bienes materiales **2.** (*having experience*) mundano, -a; (*manner*) sofisticado, -a; ~ **wise** (*person*) cosmopolita

world power *n* potencia *f* mundial

world record *n* SPORTS récord *m* mundial

World Series *n* (*world baseball championship*) Serie *f* Mundial

---

i La **World Series** (Serie Mundial) es la serie de siete partidos de desempate entre los campeones de la Liga Americana y los campeones de la Liga Nacional para definir los "Campeones Mundiales" del Béisbol de Grandes Ligas en Estados Unidos y Canadá. Esta serie de partidos, un evento anual desde 1903, se realiza en octubre y es visto por millones de hinchas del béisbol en Estados Unidos y Canadá.

World's Fair *n* feria *f* mundial

world-shaking *adj*, **world-shattering** *adj* a ~ **piece of news** una noticia que ha conmocionado al mundo

world war *n* HIST guerra *f* mundial

world-weary ['wɜrld·ˌwɪr·i] *adj* hastiado, -a; **to be** [*o* feel] ~ estar hastiado

worldwide ['wɜrld·ˌwaɪd] **I.** *adj* mundial **II.** *adv* por todo el mundo

World Wide Web *n* COMPUT Red *f* Mundial

worm [wɜrm] **I.** *n* **1.** gusano *m*; (*insect larva*) oruga *f*; **earth** ~ lombriz *f* **2.** COMPUT gusano **II.** *vt* **1.** (*treat for worms*) desparasitar **2.** (*squeeze slowly through*) **to** ~ **one's way through people** colarse entre la gente; **to** ~ **oneself under sth** deslizarse por debajo de algo **3.** (*gain trust dishonestly*) **to** ~ **oneself into someone's trust** ganarse la confianza de alguien con artimañas **4.** (*obtain dishonestly*) **to** ~ **a secret out of sb** sonsacar un secreto a alguien **III.** *vi* **to** ~ **through the crowd** colarse entre el gentío

worm-eaten ['wɜrm·ˌi·tən] *adj* (*beam, table, wood*) carcomido, -a; (*fruit*) picado, -a; (*cloth*) apolillado, -a

wormhole ['wɜrm·hoʊl] *n* agujero *m* de lombriz; **the cupboard was full of ~s** el armario estaba todo carcomido

wormy ['wɜr·mi] <-ier, -iest> *adj* (*full of worms: fruit*) agusanado, -a; (*wood*) carcomido, -a

worn [wɔrn] **I.** *vt*, *vi* *pp of* **wear II.** *adj* **1.** (*shabby, deteriorated*) desgastado, -a; (*clothing*) raído, -a **2.** (*exhausted: person*) ojeroso, -a **3.** (*overused: expression, news, story*) tópico, -a

worn-out [ˌwɔrn·'aʊt] *adj* **1.** (*exhausted: person, animal*) rendido, -a **2.** (*used up: clothing*) raído, -a; (*wheel bearings*) desgastado, -a

worried *adj* preocupado, -a; **to be** ~ **about** [*o* by] **sth** estar preocupado por algo; **I am** ~ **that he may be angry** tengo miedo de que esté enfadado; **to be** ~ **sick about sb/sth** estar preocupadísimo por alguien/algo; **with a** ~ **expression** con semblante preocupado

worrisome ['wɜr·i·səm] *adj* preocupante

worry ['wɜr·i] **I.** <-ies> *n* **1.** (*anxiety, concern*) preocupación *f*; **to be a cause of** ~ **to sb** dar problemas a alguien; **to have a** ~ (*about sth*) estar preocupado (por algo); **do you really have no ~s about the future?** ¿no te preocupa el futuro de verdad? **2.** (*trouble*) problema *m*; **financial worries** problemas *fpl* económicos; **it is a great** ~ **to me** me preocupa mucho **II.** *vt* <-ie-, -ing> **1.** (*preoccupy, concern*) preocupar; **she is worried that she might not be able to find another job** tiene miedo de no encontrar otro trabajo; **that doesn't** ~ **me** eso me tiene sin cuidado **2.** (*bother*) molestar **3.** (*pursue and scare*) perseguir; **to** ~ **an animal** correr tras un animal **4.** (*shake around*) **to** ~ **sth** juguetear con algo; **the dog worries the bone** el perro mordisquea el hueso **III.** <-ie-, -ing> *vi* (*be preoccupied, concerned*) **to** ~ (*about sth*) preocuparse (por algo); **don't** ~! ¡no te preocupes!; **not to** ~! *inf* ¡no pasa nada!

worrying *adj* preocupante

worse [wɜrs] **I.** *adj comp of* **bad** peor; **to be** ~ **than...** ser peor que...; **to be even/much** ~ ser aún [*o* todavía]/mucho peor; **he was none the** ~ **for it** no le había pasado nada; **from bad to** ~ de mal en peor; **to get** ~ **and** ~ ser cada vez peor; **it could have been** ~ podría haber sido peor; **to make matters** ~... por si fuera poco...; **so much the** ~ **for her!** ¡tanto peor para ella!; ~ **luck** *inf* (por) mala suerte; **to get** ~ empeorar; **if he gets any** ~... si se pone peor... **II.** *n* **the** ~ el/la peor; **to change for the** ~ cambiar para mal; **to have seen** ~ haber visto cosas peores; **I don't think any the** ~ **of her** mi opinión sobre ella no ha cambiado; ~ **was to follow** lo peor estaba por llegar **III.** *adv comp of* **badly** peor; **to do sth** ~ **than...** hacer algo peor que...; **he did** ~ **than he was expecting in the exams** los exámenes le fueron peor de lo que esperaba; **to be** ~ (off) estar peor

worsen ['wɜr·sən] *vi*, *vt* empeorar

worship ['wɜr·ʃɪp] **I.** *vt* <-pp-, -p-> **1.** *a.* REL adorar; **to** ~ **God** rendir culto a Dios; **to** ~ **money/sex** tener obsesión por el dinero/sexo **2.** (*feel great admiration for*) idolatrar ▶ **to** ~ **the ground sb walks on** besar el suelo que alguien pisa **II.** *vi* <-pp-, -p-> REL hacer sus devociones **III.** *n* **1.** (*adoration*) adoración *f*; (*reverence*) veneración *f* **2.** *a.* REL culto *m*; (*religious service*) oficio *m*

worshipper *n* REL fiel *mf;* **hundreds of ~s attended the ceremony** cientos de fieles asistieron a la ceremonia; **devil ~** satanista *mf*

worst [wɜrst] **I.** *adj superl of* **bad the ~** el/la peor; **the ~ soup I've ever eaten** la peor sopa que he comido (nunca); **the ~ mistake** el error más grave **II.** *adv superl of* **badly** peor; **to be ~ hit/affected by sth** ser los más azotados/afectados por algo **III.** *n* (*most terrible one, time, thing*) **the ~** lo peor; **the ~ of it is that…** lo peor de todo es que…; **the ~ is over now** ya ha pasado lo peor; **at ~** en el peor de los casos; **at her ~** en su peor momento; **this problem has shown him at his ~** este problema ha sacado a relucir lo peor de él; **to fear the ~** temerse lo peor; **~ of all** lo peor de todo ▶ **if (the) ~ comes to (the) ~** en el peor de los casos; **to get the ~ of it** (*suffer the worst*) llevarse la peor parte

worsted ['wʊs·tɪd] *n* (*fabric*) estambre *m*

worth [wɜrθ] **I.** *n* 1. (*excellence, importance: of a person*) valía *f;* (*of a thing*) valor *m;* **to prove one's ~** demostrar su valía; **to be of great/little ~ to sb** tener gran/poco valor para alguien 2. (*monetary value*) **4 thousand dollars ~ of gift items** objetos de regalo por valor de 4.000 dólares; **to get one's money's ~ from sth** sacar partido a algo; **of comparable ~** de precio similar; **a month's/three hour's ~ of work** un mes/tres horas de trabajo 3. (*wealth*) fortuna *f* **II.** *adj* 1. *a.* COM, FIN, ECON **to be ~…** valer…; **it is ~ about $200 000** está valorado en unos 200.000 dólares; **it's ~ a lot to me** tiene mucho valor para mí; **to be ~ millions** *inf* ser millonario 2. (*significant enough, useful*) **to be ~…** merecer…; **to be ~ a mention** ser digno de mención; **it's not ~ arguing about!** ¡no vale la pena discutir por eso!; **it is ~ seeing** es digno de ver; **it's ~ remembering that…** conviene recordar que…; **it is (well) ~ a listen/visit** merece la pena escucharlo/visitarlo; **it's ~ a try** vale la pena intentarlo ▶ **to be ~ sb's <u>while</u> it isn't ~ my while** no me compensa; **to make sth ~ sb's <u>while</u>** compensar a alguien por algo; **if a thing is ~ <u>doing</u>, it's ~ doing well** *prov* lo que se hace hay que hacerlo bien *prov;* **to do sth <u>for</u> all one's ~** hacer algo con todas sus fuerzas; **<u>for</u> what it's ~** *inf* por si sirve de algo; **to be (well) ~ it** valer la pena

worthless ['wɜrθ·lɪs] *adj* 1. (*of no monetary value*) sin ningún valor 2. (*of no significance, use*) inútil

worthwhile [ˌwɜrθ·'hwaɪl] *adj* 1. (*profitable, beneficial*) que vale la pena; **it's not ~ making such an effort** no merece la pena esforzarse tanto; **it isn't financially ~ for me** no me compensa económicamente 2. (*useful*) útil

worthy ['wɜr·ði] **I.** <-ier, -iest> *adj* 1. *form* (*admirable*) encomiable; (*principles*) loable; **a ~ cause** una noble causa 2. (*appropriate for, to*) digno, -a; **to be ~ of sth** ser merecedor de algo; **to be ~ of attention** merecer atención **II.** <-ies> *n iron* (*important person*) personaje *m* ilustre; **the local worthies** las personalidades más destacadas del lugar

would [wʊd] *aux pt of* **will** 1. (*future in the past*) **he said he ~ do it later on** dijo que lo haría más tarde 2. (*future seeing past in the past*) **we thought they ~ have done it before** pensamos que lo habrían hecho antes 3. (*intention in the past*) **he said he ~ always love her** dijo que siempre la querría 4. (*shows possibility*) **I'd go myself, but I'm too busy** iría yo mismo, pero estoy demasiado ocupado; **it ~ have been very boring to do that** habría sido muy aburrido hacer eso 5. (*conditional*) **what ~ you do if you lost your job?** ¿qué harías si te quedaras sin trabajo?; **I ~ have done it if you had asked** lo habría hecho si me lo hubieras pedido 6. (*polite request*) **if you ~ just wait a moment, I'll see if I can find her** espere un momento, por favor, que voy a buscarla; **~ you phone him, please?** ¿me harías el favor de llamarlo?; **~ you mind saying that again?** ¿te importaría repetir eso?; **~ you like…?** ¿te gustaría…?; **~ you like me to come with you?** ¿quieres que vaya contigo? 7. (*regularity in past*) **they ~ help each other with their homework** solían ayudarse con los deberes 8. (*stresses as being typical*) **of course the bus ~ be late when I'm in a hurry** por supuesto, el autobús siempre llega tarde cuando tengo prisa; **he ~ say that, wouldn't he?** era de esperar que lo dijera, ¿no? 9. (*courteous opinion*) **I ~ imagine that…** me imagino que…; **I ~n't have thought that…** nunca habría pensado que… 10. (*probably*) **the guy on the phone had an Australian accent — that ~ be Tom, I expect** el chico con quien hablé por teléfono tenía acento australiano — debía de ser Tom 11. (*shows preference*) **I ~ rather have water** prefiero beber agua; **I ~ rather die than do that** antes morir que hacer eso 12. (*offering polite advice*) **I ~n't worry, if I were you** yo que tú no me preocuparía 13. (*asking motives*) **why ~ anyone want to do something like that?** ¿por qué nadie querría hacer algo así? 14. (*shows a wish*) **ah, ~ I were richer and younger!** ¡ojalá fuera más rico y más joven!; **~ that he were here!** ¡ojalá estuviera aquí!

would-be ['wʊd·bi] *adj* 1. (*wishing to be*) aspirante a; **a ~ politician** un aspirante a político 2. (*pretending to be*) supuesto, -a

wouldn't ['wʊd·ənt] = **would not** *s.* **would**

wound¹ [waʊnd] *vi, vt pt, pp of* **wind²**

wound² [wund] **I.** *n* herida *f;* **a gunshot/war ~** una herida de bala/guerra; **a leg ~** una herida en la pierna **II.** *vt a. fig* herir

wounded ['wun·dɪd] **I.** *adj a. fig* herido, -a **II.** *npl* **the ~** los heridos

wove [woʊv] *vt, vi pt of* **weave**

woven ['woʊ·vən] **I.** *vt, vi pp of* **weave II.** *adj* (*made by weaving*) tejido, -a

W

wow [waʊ] *inf* **I.** *interj* (*demonstrates surprise, excitement*) ¡caray! **II.** *n* (*hit, popular item*) exitazo *m;* **to be a ~ with the public** ser un exitazo entre el público; **I had a ~ of a time** me lo pasé en grande **III.** *vt* (*delight*) **to ~ sb** volver loco a alguien

wpm, w.p.m. *abbr of* **words per minute** ppm

wraith [reɪθ] *n liter* espectro *m*

wrangle ['ræŋ·gəl] **I.** <-ling> *vi* **1.** (*argue, debate angrily*) discutir; **to ~ (with sb) about sth** discutir (con alguien) por algo **2.** (*round up cattle*) arrear ganado **II.** *vt* **1.** (*win by arguing*) conseguir discutiendo **2.** (*round up: horses, cattle*) arrear, rodear *CSur, Cuba, Nic, Col, Perú* **III.** *n* (*intricate argument*) riña *f;* **a ~ about sth** una disputa sobre algo

wrap [ræp] **I.** *n* **1.** (*robe-like covering*) bata *f* **2.** (*shawl*) chal *m* **3.** (*protective covering material*) envoltorio *m;* **foil ~** papel *m* de aluminio ▸ **to keep sth under ~s** mantener algo en secreto; **to take the ~s off (of) sth** sacar algo a la luz **II.** *vt* <-pp-> **to ~ sth (up) (in a blanket)** envolver algo (con una manta); **~ the glasses in plenty of paper** envuelve bien los vasos con mucho papel; **to ~ sth around sth/sb** envolver algo/a alguien con algo; **he ~ped a scarf around his neck** se puso una bufanda; **to ~ one's fingers around sth** agarrar algo con las manos; **to ~ one's arms around sb** estrechar a alguien entre sus brazos; **a matter ~ped in secrecy** un asunto rodeado de misterio

◆ **wrap up I.** *vt* <-pp-> **1.** (*completely cover*) envolver; **to wrap oneself/sb up (against the cold)** (*dress warmly*) abrigarse **2.** *inf* (*finish well*) poner fin a; (*deal*) cerrar; (*problem*) acabar con; **that wraps it up for today** eso es todo por hoy **II.** *vi* **1.** (*dress warmly*) abrigarse; **to ~ well/warm** abrigarse bien **2.** (*be absorbed in*) **to be wrapped up in sth** estar absorto en algo; **to be wrapped up in one's work** vivir para el trabajo **3.** (*finish*) terminar

wraparound ['ræp·ə‚raʊnd] *adj* (*skirt, dress*) cruzado, -a; (*sunglasses*) envolvente

wrapper ['ræp·ər] *n* **1.** (*packaging*) envoltorio *m;* (*for a book*) sobrecubierta *f* **2.** (*robe-like covering*) bata *f*

wrapping paper *n* (*plain*) papel *m* de embalar; (*for presents*) papel de regalo

wrath [ræθ] *n liter* (*fury, anger*) ira *f*

wrathful ['ræθ·fəl] *adj liter* iracundo, -a

wreak [rik] <-ed, -ed *o* wrought, wrought> *vt form* **1.** (*forcefully cause*) causar; **to ~ damage/havoc (on sth)** causar estragos (en algo) **2.** (*anger*) descargar; **to ~ vengeance on sb** vengarse de alguien

wreath [riθ] <wreaths> *n* (*of flowers, greenery*) corona *f;* (*of smoke*) espiral *f*

wreathe [rið] *vt liter* **1.** (*gather around*) **to be ~d in sth** estar rodeado de algo; **~d in clouds** envuelto en nubes; **to be ~d in melancholy** estar sumido en la melancolía; **to be ~d in smiles** ser todo sonrisas **2.** (*crown as with a*

wreath) coronar (*de flores, laurel…*) **3.** (*intertwine*) entretejer

wreck [rek] **I.** *vt* **1.** (*damage*) destrozar; (*ship*) hundir; (*train*) hacer descarrilar **2.** (*demolish*) derribar **3.** (*hopes, plan*) arruinar; (*chances*) echar por tierra; **to ~ sb's life** arruinar la vida de [*o a*] alguien **II.** *n* **1.** NAUT naufragio *m;* AUTO accidente *m;* *fig* hundimiento *m* **2.** (*ship*) restos *mpl* del naufragio; **a ~ of a car/plane** un coche/avión siniestrado; **an old ~** un cacharro **3.** *inf* (*any derelict thing*) ruina *f;* (*mess*) caos *m;* **to feel like a complete ~** estar hecho polvo; **to be a nervous ~** tener los nervios destrozados

wreckage ['rek·ɪdʒ] *n* (*of ship, car, plane*) restos *mpl;* (*of building*) escombros *mpl*

wrecker ['rek·ər] *n* **1.** (*tow truck*) camión-grúa *m* **2.** (*worker who demolishes houses*) obrero, -a *m, f* de demolición; (*worker who demolishes cars*) desguazador(a) *m(f)* **3.** (*person who causes shipwrecks*) provocador(a) *m(f)* de naufragios **4.** (*hooligan*) gamberro, -a *m, f*

wren [ren] *n* chochín *m*

wrench [rentʃ] **I.** *vt* **1.** (*jerk and twist out*) arrancar; **to ~ sth from sb** arrancar algo a alguien; **to ~ oneself away** soltarse de un tirón **2.** (*injure*) **to ~ one's ankle** torcerse el tobillo; **to ~ one's shoulder** dislocarse el hombro **3.** *fig* (*forcefully take from*) separar; **to ~ sth/sb from sth/sb** separar algo/a alguien de algo/alguien **II.** *n* **1.** TECH (*tool*) llave *f* inglesa **2.** (*twisting jerk*) tirón *m,* jalón *m CSur;* **to give sb a ~** dar un tirón a alguien **3.** (*injury*) torcedura *f;* **to give one's ankle a ~** torcerse el tobillo **4.** (*pain caused by a departure*) dolor *m* (*por una separación*)*;* **what a ~, seeing you board the plane!** ¡qué doloroso verte subir al avión!

wrestle ['res·əl] SPORTS **I.** <-ling> *vt* **1.** *a.* SPORTS luchar; **to ~ sb** forcejear con alguien; **to ~ sb to the ground** luchar con [*o contra*] alguien hasta derribarlo **2.** *fig* lidiar con **II.** <-ling> *vi* luchar; **to ~ professionally** ser luchador profesional **III.** *n* lucha *f*

wrestler *n* luchador(a) *m(f)*

wrestling *n* SPORTS lucha *f;* **freestyle ~** lucha libre

wrestling match *n* SPORTS combate *m* de lucha

wretch [retʃ] <-es> *n* **1.** (*unfortunate person*) infeliz *mf;* **a poor ~** un pobre diablo **2.** (*mean person*) miserable *mf;* (*mischievous person*) sinvergüenza *mf inf*

wretched ['retʃ·ɪd] *adj* **1.** (*miserable, pitiable: life, person*) desdichado, -a; **to be in a ~ state** estar en un estado lamentable; (*house, conditions*) miserable **2.** (*despicable*) despreciable **3.** (*very bad, awful: weather*) horrible; **to feel ~** (*sick*) estar muy mal; (*depressed*) estar muy abatido **4.** (*expressing annoyance*) **my ~ car's broken down again!** ¡este maldito coche se me ha vuelto a estropear!

wriggle ['rɪg·əl] **I.** <-ling> *vi* **1.** (*squirm around*) retorcerse **2.** (*move forward by twist-*

ing) serpentear; **to ~ through sth** deslizarse por algo; **to ~ out of sth** *fig, inf* escapar de un apuro **II.** <-ling> *vt* (*jiggle back and forth*) menear; (*body, hand, toes*) mover; **to ~ one's way along** avanzar serpenteando; **to ~ one-self into sth** introducirse con dificultad en algo; **to ~ (one's way) out of sth** escaquearse de algo *inf* **III.** *n* meneo *m;* **with a ~, she managed to crawl through the gap** logró deslizarse por el agujero serpenteando

wring [rɪŋ] <wrung, wrung> *vt* **1.** (*twist forcibly*) retorcer; **to ~ one's hands** retorcerse las manos; **to ~ sb's neck** *inf* retorcer el cuello a alguien **2.** (*twist to squeeze out*) escurrir; **to ~ water out of sth** escurrir algo [*o a*] **3.** (*extract forcibly*) **to ~ the truth out of sb** sonsacar la verdad a alguien **4.** (*cause pain to*) **to ~ sb's heart** partir el corazón a alguien

wringer ['rɪŋ·ər] *n* rodillo *m* para escurrir la ropa ▸ **to put sb through the ~** *sl* someter a alguien al tercer grado

wrinkle ['rɪŋ·kəl] **I.** *n* (*fold, crease*) arruga *f* ▸ **to iron the ~s out** limar asperezas **II.** <-ling> *vi* (*form folds, creases*) arrugarse; (*apple, fruit*) pasarse **III.** <-ling> *vt* (*make have folds, creases*) arrugar ▸ **to ~ one's brow** fruncir el ceño

wrinkled *adj,* **wrinkly** ['rɪŋ·kli] *adj* (*clothes, face, skin*) arrugado, -a; (*apple, fruit*) pasado, -a

wrist [rɪst] *n* **1.** ANAT muñeca *f;* **to slash one's ~s** cortarse las venas **2.** (*of a garment*) puño *m*

wristband ['rɪst·bænd] *n* **1.** (*end of sleeve*) puño *m* **2.** (*strap*) correa *f* **3.** (*sweatband*) muñequera *f*

wristlet *n* muñequera

wristwatch <-es> *n* reloj *m* de pulsera

writ [rɪt] *n* orden *f* judicial; **~ of summons** notificación *f* de emplazamiento; **to issue a ~ against sb** expedir un mandato judicial contra alguien; **to serve a ~ on sb** notificar un mandato judicial a alguien

write [raɪt] <wrote, written, writing> **I.** *vt* **1.** escribir; **to ~ sth in capital letters** escribir algo con mayúsculas; **to ~ a book/a thesis** escribir un libro/una tesis; **he wrote me a poem** me dedicó un poema; **to ~ sb** escribir a alguien; **to ~ sb a check** extender un cheque a alguien **2.** MUS componer; **to ~ a song** escribir una canción **3.** COMPUT (*save*) guardar; **to ~ sth to a disk** grabar algo en un disco ▸ **to be nothing to ~ home about** no ser nada del otro mundo **II.** *vi* **1.** escribir; **to ~ clearly/legibly** escribir con letra clara/legible; **to ~ to sb** escribir a alguien; **to ~ about sth** escribir sobre algo; **to ~ for a newspaper** escribir en un periódico **2.** COMPUT (*save*) **to ~ to sth** grabar en algo

♦**write away** *vi* **to ~ for sth** (*brochures, information*) solicitar algo por escrito

♦**write back I.** *vt* **to write (sth/sb) back** contestar (algo/a alguien) **II.** *vi* contestar

♦**write down** *vt* apuntar

♦**write in I.** *vi* (*send a letter to*) escribir **II.** *vt* **1.** (*insert*) escribir; **to write sth in a space** escribir algo en un espacio; **just write your name in, you can fill the rest of the form in later** escriba sólo su nombre, después podrá rellenar el resto del formulario **2.** LAW (*put in: clause*) incluir **3.** TV, CINE (*character*) añadir

♦**write off I.** *vi* (*send away to ask for*) **to ~ for** (*brochures, information*) solicitar por escrito **II.** *vt* **1.** (*give up doing: attempt*) abandonar; (*project*) dar por perdido **2.** (*abandon as no good*) **to write sth/sb off as useless** descartar algo como/a alguien por inútil **3.** FIN (*debt*) cancelar

♦**write out** *vt* **1.** (*put into writing*) escribir **2.** (*copy*) copiar **3.** (*fill in*) rellenar; **to write a check out to sb** extender un cheque a alguien **4.** (*remove from*) suprimir; **to write sb out of a will** desheredar a alguien

♦**write up** *vt* poner por escrito; (*article, report, thesis*) redactar; **to ~ a concert** escribir una crítica sobre un concierto

write-in ['raɪt·ɪn] *adj* POL **a ~ candidate** un candidato cuyo nombre debe añadir el votante en la papeleta

write-off ['raɪt·ɔf] *n* **1.** FIN (*cancellation*) cancelación *f* (de una deuda incobrable) **2.** (*sth reduced in value*) siniestro *m* total; **the camera was a complete ~** la cámara estaba hecha trizas

write-protected ['raɪt·prə·'tek·təd] *adj* COMPUT protegido, -a contra escritura

writer ['raɪ·tər] *n* **1.** (*person*) escritor(a) *m(f);* **~ of children's books** autor(a) *m(f)* de libros infantiles **2.** COMPUT **CD-ROM/DVD ~** grabador *m* de CD-ROM/DVD

write-up ['raɪt·ʌp] *n* ART, THEAT, MUS crítica *f*

writhe [raɪð] <writhing> *vi* **1.** (*squirm and twist around*) retorcerse; **to ~ (around) in pain** retorcerse de dolor **2.** (*be uncomfortable: with horror*) estremecerse; (*with embarrassment*) sentirse violento

writing ['raɪ·tɪŋ] *n* **1.** (*handwriting*) letra *f;* **in ~** por escrito; **to put sth in ~** poner algo por escrito; **there was some ~ in the margin of the page** había algo escrito en el margen de la página **2.** *a.* LIT escribir *m;* **she likes ~** le encanta escribir **3.** LIT, THEAT (*process*) redacción *f;* **creative ~** escritura *f* creativa **4.** LIT, THEAT (*written work*) obra *f;* **women's ~** literatura *f* escrita por mujeres **5.** LIT (*style*) estilo *m* ▸ **the ~ is on the wall** tiene los días contados

writing desk *n* escritorio *m*

writing pad *n* libreta *f*

writing paper *n* papel *m* de carta

written ['rɪt·ən] **I.** *vt, vi pp of* **write II.** *adj* (*recorded in writing*) escrito, -a ▸ **to have guilt ~ all over one's face** llevar la culpa escrita en la cara; **the ~ word** la palabra escrita

wrong [rɔŋ] **I.** *adj* **1.** (*not right: answer*) incorrecto, -a; **to be ~ about sth** equivocarse en algo; **to be ~ about sb** juzgar mal a alguien; **he is ~ in thinking that...** se equivoca si piensa que...; **to be in the ~ place** estar mal colocado; **to be plainly ~** estar completamente equivocado; **to get the ~ number** equivocarse de número; **sorry, ~ number!** lo siento, se ha equivocado (de número); **to go the ~ direction** tomar el camino equivocado; **to prove sb ~** demostrar que alguien se equivoca **2.** (*not appropriate*) inoportuno, -a; **to do/say the ~ thing** hacer/decir lo que no se debe; **she's the ~ person for the job** no es la persona adecuada para el trabajo; **this is the ~ time to...** no es el momento oportuno para...; **the ~ side of town** una mala zona de la ciudad; **she got in with the ~ crowd** se juntó con quien no le convenía **3.** (*bad*) **is there anything ~?** ¿te pasa algo?; **what's ~ with you today?** ¿qué te pasa hoy?; **there's nothing ~ with your stomach** su estómago está perfectamente; **something's ~ with the television** el televisor no funciona bien **4.** LAW, REL mal; **it is ~ to do that** está mal hacer eso; **it was ~ of him (to do that)** ha hecho muy mal (en hacer eso); **what's ~ with that?** ¿qué hay de malo en ello? ► **to fall into the ~ hands** caer en manos equivocadas; **to go down the ~ way** (*food, drink*) bajar por mal sitio **II.** *adv* **1.** (*incorrectly*) incorrectamente; **to do sth ~** hacer algo mal; **to get sth ~** equivocarse en algo; **to get it ~** entender mal; **you got it ~**, **it's Maria who's coming, not Marina** no lo has entendido, es María quien viene, no Marina; **don't get me ~** no me malinterpretes; **to go ~** equivocarse; (*stop working*) estropearse, descomponerse *Méx;* (*fail*) salir mal; **after 300 feet turn to the left, you can't go ~** siga recto 100 m y gire a la izquierda, no tiene pérdida **2.** (*in a morally reprehensible way*) mal; **to do sth ~** hacer algo mal **III.** *n* **1.** *a.* LAW, REL mal *m;* (**to know**) **right from ~** saber distinguir entre lo que está bien y lo que está mal; **to put sb in the ~** echar la culpa a alguien; **to do sb no ~** no hacer nada malo a alguien **2.** (*unjust action*) injusticia *f;* **to do sb (a) ~ (in doing sth)** portarse mal con alguien (al hacer algo); **to right a ~** enderezar un entuerto; **to suffer a ~** sufrir una injusticia ► **to do ~** obrar mal; **he can do no ~** es incapaz de hacer nada malo; **to be in the ~** (*not right, mistaken*) estar equivocado; (*do something bad*) actuar mal **IV.** *vt form* **to ~ sb** (*treat unjustly*) ser injusto con alguien; (*judge unjustly*) juzgar mal a alguien

wrongdoer ['rɔŋ·duː·ər] *n* malhechor(a) *m(f)*

wrongdoing *n* maldad *f;* LAW delito *m;* **to accuse sb of ~** acusar a alguien de comportamiento ilícito

wrongful *adj* **1.** (*unfair*) injusto, -a **2.** LAW (*unlawful: arrest*) ilegal; (*dismissal*) improcedente

wrong-headed *adj pej* (*person*) cerril; (*concept, idea, plan*) desatinado, -a

wrongly *adv* mal; (*spell*) incorrectamente; (*believe, state*) erróneamente; (*accuse, con-*

vict) injustamente

wrote [roʊt] *vi, vt pt of* **write**

wrought [rɔt] **I.** *vt pt, pp of* **work** III.4., 5., **wreak** **II.** *adj form* (*crafted*) trabajado, -a; (*metal*) labrado, -a

wrought iron *n* hierro *m* forjado

wrought-up [rɔt·'ʌp] *adj* nervioso, -a; **to be/get ~ (about sth/sb)** estar/ponerse nervioso (por algo/alguien)

wrung [rʌŋ] *vt pt, pp of* **wring**

wry [raɪ] <wrier, wriest *o* wryer, wryest> *adj* **1.** (*dry and ironic: comments, humor*) cáustico, -a; **a ~ smile** una sonrisa irónica **2.** (*showing dislike*) **to make a ~ face** torcer el gesto

WSW *abbr of* **west-southwest** OSO

wt. *n abbr of* **weight** peso *m*

WV [ˌwest·vər·'dʒɪn·jə] *n abbr of* **West Virginia** Virginia *f* Occidental

WWI *n abbr of* **World War I** Primera Guerra *f* Mundial

WWII *n abbr of* **World War II** Segunda Guerra *f* Mundial

WWW *n abbr of* **World Wide Web** COMPUT WWW *f*

WY [waɪ·'oʊ·mɪŋ] *n*, **Wyo.** *n abbr of* **Wyoming** Wyoming *m*

Wyoming [waɪ·'oʊ·mɪŋ] *n* Wyoming

X

X, x [eks] **I.** *n* **1.** X, x *f;* **~ as in X-ray** X de xilófono **2.** MATH (*unknown number*) x **3.** (*used in place of name*) **Mr./Mrs./Ms. ~** el Sr./la Sra. X **4.** (*symbol for kiss*) un beso; **all my love, Katy ~~~** besos, Katy **5.** (*cross symbol*) aspa *f;* **~ marks the spot** el punto está marcado con una cruz **II.** *vt* (*delete*) **to ~ (out) sth** tachar algo

X-chromosome ['eks·ˌkroʊ·mə·soʊm] *n* cromosoma *m* X

xenophobia [ˌzen·ə·'foʊ·bi·ə] *n* xenofobia *f*

xenophobic [ˌzen·ə·'foʊ·bɪk] *adj* xenófobo, -a

Xerox®, xerox ['zɪr·aks] **I.** *n* (*photocopy*) fotocopia *f* **II.** *vt* (*photocopy*) fotocopiar; **a ~ed copy of the document** una fotocopia del documento

XL *adj abbr of* **extra large** XL

Xmas ['krɪs·məs] *n abbr of* **Christmas** Navidad *f*

X-rated ['eks·ˌreɪ·tɪd] *adj* **an ~ film** una película X

X-ray ['eks·reɪ] **I.** *n* **1.** (*photo*) radiografía *f;* **~s** rayos *mpl* X **2.** (*hospital department*) radiología *f* **II.** *vt* radiografiar; **to ~ sth/sb** hacer una radiografía de algo/a alguien

xylophone ['zaɪ·lə·foʊn] *n* MUS xilófono *m*

Y

Y, y [waɪ] *n* **1.** Y, y *f;* ~ **as in Yankee** Y de yema **2.** MATH (*unknown quantity*) y

yacht [jat] **I.** *n* **1.** (*for pleasure*) yate *m* **2.** (*for racing*) velero *m;* ~ **club** club *m* náutico; ~ **race** regata *f* **II.** *vi* **1.** (*sail in a yacht*) navegar **2.** (*race in a yacht*) participar en una regata

yachting *n* **1.** (*sailing in yachts*) navegación *f* de recreo **2.** (*racing in yachts*) navegación *f* a vela; **to go** ~ navegar

yachtsman ['jats·mən] <-men> *n* (*yacht owner*) dueño *m* de un yate; (*yacht sailor*) regatista *m*

yack [jæk] **I.** *n sl* cháchara *f* **II.** *vi sl* rajar

yam [jæm] *n* **1.** (*plant, vegetable*) ñame *m* **2.** (*sweet potato*) batata *f,* camote *m AmL*

yank [jæŋk] **I.** *vt sl* **to** ~ **sth** tirar de algo, jalar de algo *AmL* **II.** *vi inf* **to** ~ (**on sth**) tirar (de algo), jalar (de algo); **she** ~**ed at his hair** le tiró del pelo **III.** *n inf* tirón *m,* jalón *m AmL;* **to give sth a** (**good**) ~ dar un (buen) tirón [*o* jalón] a algo

◆**yank out** *vt* (*remove forcefully*) sacar de un tirón; **to** ~ **a tooth** arrancar un diente

Yank [jæŋk] *n,* **Yankee** ['jæn·ki] *n pej, inf* yanqui *mf,* gringo, -a *m, f AmL*

yap [jæp] **I.** <-pp-> *vi* **1.** (*bark*) ladrar **2.** *sl* (*talk continuously*) cotorrear **II.** *n* **1.** (*bark*) ladrido *m* **2.** *pej, sl* (*foolish talk*) cotorreo *m*

yard¹ [jard] *n* **1.** (*3 feet*) yarda *f* (*0'91 m*); **square** ~ yarda cuadrada; **it's about a hundred** ~**s down the road** está a unas cien yardas de aquí **2.** NAUT verga *f*

yard² [jard] *n* **1.** (*enclosed paved area: of a house, school, prison*) patio *m* **2.** (*land next to house*) jardín *m* **3.** (*work area*) taller *m;* **shipbuilding** ~ astillero *m* **4.** (*outside area used for storage*) almacén *m;* **wood** ~ depósito *m* de madera **5.** (*enclosure for livestock*) corral *m*

yardstick ['jard·stɪk] *n* **1.** (*measuring tool*) vara *f* de una yarda **2.** (*standard*) criterio *m*

yarn [jarn] **I.** *n* **1.** (*thread*) hilo *m* **2.** *inf* (*story*) trola *f;* **to spin a** ~ inventarse una trola **II.** *vi inf* inventar trolas

yaw [jɔ] AVIAT, NAUT, TECH **I.** *vi* (*move sideways: car*) dar bandazos; (*boat*) guiñar **II.** *n* (*sideways movement: of a car*) bandazo *m;* (*of a boat*) guiñada *f*

yawl [jɔl] *n* yola *f*

yawn [jɔn] **I.** *vi* **1.** (*show tiredness*) bostezar **2.** *fig, liter* (*open wide*) abrirse **II.** *n* **1.** (*sign of tiredness*) bostezo *m* **2.** *inf* (*boring thing*) plomo *m fig;* **it was a** ~ fue un rollo

yawning *adj* **1.** (*bored: audience*) que bosteza **2.** (*wide and deep: chasm, crater*) enorme; **there's a** ~ **gap between... and...** hay un abismo entre... y...

Y-chromosome ['waɪ·kroʊ·mə·soʊm] *n* cromosoma *m* Y

yd. *abbr of* **yard**(**s**) yarda *f*

yea [jeɪ] **I.** *adv* HIST (*yes*) sí **II.** *n* voto *m* a favor; **the** ~**s and the nays** los votos a favor y los votos en contra

yeah [jeə] *adv inf* (*yes*) sí; **oh** ~! *iron* (*indicating disbelief*) ¡no me digas!; ~, ~, **we've heard that one before** ¡sí, sí, eso ya lo hemos oído otras veces!

year [jɪr] *n* **1.** (*twelve months*) año *m;* ~ **of birth** año de nacimiento; ~ **in,** ~ **out** año tras año; **fiscal** ~ FIN ejercicio *f* fiscal; **leap** ~ año bisiesto; **all** (**the**) ~ **round** (durante) todo el año; **every other** ~ cada dos años; **happy new** ~! ¡feliz año nuevo!; **last/next** ~ el año pasado/que viene; **$5000 a** ~ 5.000 dólares al año; **the** ~ **when...** el año en que...; **this** ~ este año; **I'm eight** ~**s old** tengo ocho años; ~**s ago** hace años; **I haven't seen her for** ~**s** hace muchísimo que no la veo; **it's taken me** ~**s to...** he tardado años en...; **it's been** ~**s since we had a summer as good as this one** hacía años que no teníamos tan buen tiempo en verano; **it'll be** ~**s before...** pasarán años hasta que...; **over the** ~**s** con el tiempo **2.** SCHOOL, UNIV curso *m;* **the academic** ~ el año académico; **she was in my** ~ **at college** estaba en mi promoción en la universidad ▶ **to put** ~**s on sb** avejentar a alguien; **to take** ~**s off** (**of**) **sb** quitar años (de encima) a alguien

yearbook ['jɪr·bʊk] *n* anuario *m*

yearling ['jɪr·lɪŋ] **I.** *adj* (*colt*) de un año; (*calf, goat, sheep*) añal **II.** *n* (*colt*) potro *m* de un año; (*year-old calf, goat, sheep*) añal *m*

yearlong ['jɪr·lɔŋ] *adj* que dura un año

yearly I. *adj* (*happening every year*) anual; **on a** ~ **basis** cada año **II.** *adv* (*every year*) anualmente; **to take place** ~ tener lugar cada año; **twice** ~ dos veces al año

yearn [jɜrn] *vi* (*long*) **to** ~ **to do sth** ansiar hacer algo; **to** ~ **after sth** anhelar algo; **to** ~ **for sth/sb** añorar algo/a alguien

yearning *n* anhelo *m;* ~ **for sth** anhelo de algo; **to have a** ~ **to do sth** tener ansias de hacer algo

yeast [jist] *n* levadura *f*

yeasty <-ier, -iest> *adj* de levadura

yell [jel] **I.** *n* **1.** (*loud shout*) chillido *m;* **to give a** ~ dar un grito; **a** ~ **of laughter** una carcajada **2.** (*chant*) grito para animar a un equipo **II.** *vi* (*shout loudly*) chillar; **to** ~ **at sb** (**to do sth**) gritar a alguien (que haga algo); **to** ~ **for sb** llamar a alguien a gritos; **to** ~ **for help** pedir ayuda a gritos **III.** *vt* (*shout loudly*) gritar

yellow ['jel·oʊ] **I.** *adj* **1.** (*color*) amarillo, -a; **golden** ~ amarillo canario; **to turn** [*o* **go**] ~ ponerse amarillo **2.** *pej, sl* (*cowardly*) gallina **II.** *n* amarillo *m;* ~ **of an egg** yema *f* de huevo **III.** *vi, vt* amarillear(se)

yellow-bellied ['jel·oʊ·ˌbel·id] <-ies> *n pej, sl* gallina

yellow fever *n* MED fiebre *f* amarilla

yellowish ['jel·oʊ·ɪʃ] *adj* amarillento, -a

yellowness ['jel·oʊ·nɪs] *n* amarillez *f*

Yellow Pages® *npl* the ~ las páginas amarillas
yellowy *adj* amarillento, -a
yelp [jelp] **I.** *vi* (*cry: a dog*) aullar; (*a person*) gritar; **to** ~ **with pain** gritar de dolor **II.** *n* (*cry: of animal*) aullido *m;* (*of person*) grito *m*
Yemen ['jem·ən] *n* Yemen *m*
Yemeni ['jem·ə·ni] **I.** *adj* yemení **II.** *n* yemení *mf*
yen[1] [jen] *inv n* FIN yen *m*
yen[2] [jen] *n inf* (*strong desire*) deseo *m;* (**to have**) **a** ~ **for sth/sb** morirse por algo/alguien; (**to have**) **a** ~ **to do sth** tener unas ganas locas de hacer algo
yeoman ['jou·mən] <-men> *n* **1.** (*in the Navy*) oficial *m* subalterno en la naval **2.** (*freeholder*) pequeño terrateniente *m* ▶ **to do** ~('**s**) **service** prestar valiosos servicios
yep [jep] *adv inf* (*yes*) sí
yes [jes] **I.** *adv* **1.** (*affirmative answer*) sí; ~, **sir/ma'am** sí, señor/señora; ~**, please** sí, por favor; **to answer** ~ **to sth** contestar que sí a algo; **I'm not a very good cook** — ~ **you are** no soy muy buen cocinero — sí que lo eres; ~ **indeed** por supuesto que sí; ~**, of course!** ¡claro que sí! **2.** (*as question*) ~? TEL ¿sí?; **Johnny?** — **yes?** — **can I have a word?** Johnny — ¿qué? — ¿puedo hablar contigo? **3.** (*indicating doubt*) **oh** ~**?** ¿de verdad? **II.** <yeses> *n* (*statement in favor*) sí *m*
yes man ['jes·mæn] <-men> *n pej* servil *m inf*
yesterday ['jes·tər·dei] **I.** *adv* ayer; ~ **morning** ayer por la mañana, ayer en la mañana *AmL,* ayer a la mañana *CSur;* **the day before** ~ anteayer, antes de ayer **II.** *n* el día de ayer
yet [jet] **I.** *adv* **1.** (*up to a particular time*) todavía; **it's too early** ~ **to...** aún es muy pronto para...; **not** ~ aún no; **she hasn't told him** ~ todavía no se lo ha contado; **as** ~ hasta ahora; **the issue is as** ~ **undecided** todavía no se ha decidido la cuestión; **her best/worst film** ~ la mejor/peor película que ha dirigido hasta ahora; **have you finished** ~**?** ¿ya has terminado?; **isn't supper ready** ~**?** ¿aún no está lista la cena?; **can you see the lighthouse** ~**?** ¿ya ves el faro?; **the best is** ~ **to come** aún queda lo mejor; **there's a great deal of work** ~ **to be done** todavía queda mucho por hacer **2.** (*in addition*) ~ **again** otra vez más; ~ **more food** todavía más comida **3.** + *comp* (*even*) ~ **bigger/more beautiful** aún más grande/bonito **4.** (*despite that*) sin embargo **5.** (*in spite of everything*) a pesar de todo; **you wait, I'll get you** ~**, you jerk!** ¡ya te pillaré, so gilipollas!; **you'll do it** ~ algún día lo conseguirás; **we're not giving up, we'll get there** ~ no nos hemos rendido, llegaremos allí a pesar de todo **II.** *conj* con todo, a pesar de todo
yew [ju] *n* (*tree and wood*) tejo *m*
YHA *n abbr of* **Youth Hostel Association** asociación de albergues juveniles
Yiddish ['jɪd·ɪʃ] **I.** *adj* yiddish **II.** *n* yiddish *m*
yield [jild] **I.** *n* **1.** (*amount produced*) rendimiento *m;* AGR producción *f* **2.** COM, FIN

(*profits*) beneficio *m;* (*interest*) interés *m;* **fixed/variable** ~ renta *f* fija/variable **II.** *vt* **1.** (*provide: results*) dar; (*information*) proporcionar **2.** AGR (*produce*) producir **3.** COM, FIN (*profit*) proporcionar; (*interest*) devengar *elev;* **to** ~ **8%** (**interest**) dar un (interés del) 8% **4.** (*give up*) **to** ~ **ground** ceder terreno; **to** ~ **responsibility** delegar responsabilidades; **to** ~ **sth to the enemy** entregar algo al enemigo **III.** *vi* **1.** AGR, COM, FIN ser productivo **2.** (*give way*) **to** ~ **to sth/sb** ceder ante algo/alguien; **to** ~ **to temptation** ceder a la tentación **3.** (*surrender*) rendirse **4.** (*give priority*) **to** ~ **to sth/sb** dar prioridad a algo/alguien **5.** AUTO ceder el paso
yielding *adj* **1.** (*pliable: a material, a substance*) flexible; (*soft*) blando, -a **2.** *fig* (*compliant*) complaciente
yippee ['jɪp·i] *interj inf* ¡yupi!
YMCA [ˌwai·em·si·'ei] *abbr of* **Young Men's Christian Association** YMCA *f*
yodel ['jou·dəl] MUS **I.** <-ll-, -l-> *vi, vt* (*sing*) cantar al estilo tirolés **II.** *n* (*yodeled song*) canción *f* tirolesa
yoga ['jou·gə] *n* yoga *m*
yoghourt *n*, **yoghurt** ['jou·gərt] *n s.* **yogurt**
yogi ['jou·gi] *n* yogui *mf*
yogurt ['jou·gərt] *n* yogur *m*
yoke [jouk] **I.** *n* **1.** *a. fig* AGR yugo *m;* **to throw off the** ~ liberarse del yugo **2.** FASHION canesú *m* **II.** *vt* **1.** AGR (*fit with yoke*) uncir; **to** ~ **an animal** (**to sth**) enyuntar un animal (a algo) **2.** *fig* (*combine*) **to** ~ **two things together** ligar una cosa a otra
yokel ['jou·kəl] *n iron, pej* (*country person*) paleto, -a *m, f,* pajuerano, -a *m, f* Arg, Bol, Urug
yolk [jouk] *n* yema *f* (de huevo)
Yom Kippur [ˌjam·'kɪp·ər] *n* Yom Kip(p)ur *m*
yonder ['jan·dər] *reg: esp. Southern* **I.** *adv* (*over there*) allá **II.** *adj* (*situated over there*) aquel, aquella; *pl:* aquellos, -as
yore [jɔr] *n liter* **in** (**the**) **days of** ~ antaño
you [ju] *pron pers* **1.** *2nd pers sing* tú, vos *CSur; pl:* vosotros, -as, ustedes *AmL;* **I see** ~ te/os veo; **do** ~ **see me?** ¿me ves/veis?; **I love** ~ te/os quiero; **it is for** ~ es para ti/vosotros; **older than** ~ mayor que tú/vosotros; **if I were** ~ si yo fuera tú/vosotros; ~'**re my brother** tú eres mi hermano **2.** (*2nd person sing, polite form*) usted; *pl:* ustedes; ~ **have a car** usted tiene/ustedes tienen un coche; ~'**re going to Toronto** va/van a Toronto
you'd [jud] = **you would** *s.* **would**
you'll [jul] = **you will** *s.* **will**
young [jʌŋ] **I.** *adj* **1.** *a.* GEO (*not old*) joven; ~ **children** niños *mpl* pequeños; **a** ~ **man** un joven; ~ **people/persons** los jóvenes *pl;* **sb's** ~ **er brother/son** el hermano/hijo menor de alguien; **the** ~ **er generation** la nueva generación; **the night is still** ~ la noche es joven **2.** (*junior*) **old Mr. Brown and** ~ **Mr. Brown** el Sr. Brown padre y el Sr. Brown hijo

3. (*young-seeming: appearance, clothes*) juvenil; **to be ~ at heart** ser joven de espíritu; **she is ~ for her age** parece más joven de lo que es; **to be ~ looking** tener un aspecto juvenil **4.** (*pertaining to youth: love*) de juventud; **in my ~(er) days** cuando era joven ▶ **you're only ~ once!** ¡sólo se es joven una vez! **II.** *n pl* **1.** (*young people*) **the ~** los jóvenes **2.** ZOOL (*offspring*) crías *fpl;* **with ~** preñada

youngster ['jʌŋ·stər] *n* joven *mf*

your [jʊr] *adj pos* **1.** *2nd pers sing* tu(s); *pl:* vuestro(s), vuestra(s) **2.** (*2nd pers sing and pl: polite form*) su(s)

you're [jʊr] = **you are** *s.* **be**

yours [jʊrz] *pron pos* **1.** *sing:* (el) tuyo, (la) tuya, (los) tuyos, (las) tuyas; *pl:* (el) vuestro, (la) vuestra, (los) vuestros, (las) vuestras, el/la de ustedes *AmL;* **this glass is ~** este vaso es tuyo/vuestro **2.** *polite form* (el) suyo, (la) suya, (los) suyos, (las) suyas; **~ truly** le saluda atentamente

yourself [jʊr·'self] *pron reflexive* **1.** *sing:* te; *emphatic:* tú (mismo, misma); *after prep:* ti (mismo, misma) **2.** *polite form:* se; *emphatic:* usted (mismo, misma); *after prep:* sí (mismo, misma)

yourselves *pron reflexive* **1.** os, se *AmL; emphatic, after prep:* vosotros (mismos), vosotras (mismas), ustedes (mismos, mismas) *AmL* **2.** *polite form:* se; *emphatic:* ustedes (mismos, mismas); *after prep:* sí (mismos, mismas)

youth [juθ] *n* **1.** (*period when young*) juventud *f;* **during her** (**early**) **~** en su (primera) juventud; **he is a friend from my ~** es un amigo de juventud **2.** (*young man*) joven *m* **3.** (*young people*) jóvenes *mpl;* **the ~** la juventud; **~ culture** cultura *f* juvenil

youth center *n*, **youth club** *n* club *m* juvenil

youthful ['juθ·fəl] *adj* **1.** (*young-looking*) juvenil; **~ appearance** aspecto *m* juvenil **2.** (*typical of the young*) de la juventud **3.** (*young*) joven

youth hostel *n* albergue *m* juvenil

you've [juv] = **you have** *s.* **have**

yowl [jaʊl] **I.** *vi* (*howl: dog*) aullar; (*cat*) maullar; (*person*) dar alaridos **II.** *n* (*howl: of a dog*) aullido *m;* (*of a cat*) maullido *m;* (*of a person*) alarido *m*

yo-yo ['jou·jou] *n* (*toy*) yo-yo *m*

yr. *abbr of* **year** año *m*

yuan [ju·'æn] *n* FIN yuan *m*

yucky ['jʌk·i] *adj sl* asqueroso, -a

Yugoslav ['ju·gou·slav] *adj, n s.* **Yugoslavian**

Yugoslavia ['ju·gou·'slav·i·ə] *n* HIST Yugoslavia *f*

Yugoslavian I. *adj* yugoslavo, -a **II.** *n* yugoslavo, -a *m, f*

yukky ['jʌk·i] <-ier, -iest> *adj s.* **yucky**

Yukon Territory ['ju·kan] *n* Territorio *m* del Yukón

yule log ['jul·lɒg] *n* **1.** (*log*) nochebueno *m* **2.** CULIN tronco *m* de Navidad

Yuletide ['jul·taɪd] *n liter* Navidades *fpl*

yummy ['jʌm·i] *adj* de rechupete

yuppie ['jʌp·i] *n* yuppy *mf*

YWCA [ˌwaɪ·dʌb·əl·ju·si·'eɪ] *abbr of* **Young Women's Christian Association** YWCA *f*

Z

Z, z [zi] *n* Z, z *f;* **~ as in Zulu** Z de Zaragoza ▶ **to catch some ~'s** *sl* echar una cabezada, apolillar un poco *RíoPl*

Zaire [zaɪ·'ɪr] *n* Zaire *m*

Zairean [zaɪ·'ɪr·i·ən] **I.** *adj* zaireño, -a **II.** *n* zaireño, -a *m, f*

Zambia ['zæm·bi·ə] *n* Zambia *f*

Zambian ['zæm·bi·ən] **I.** *adj* zambiano, -a **II.** *n* zambiano, -a *m, f*

zany ['zeɪ·ni] <-ier, -iest> *adj inf* (*person*) chiflado, -a; (*idea*) disparatado, -a; (*clothing*) estrafalario, -a

zap [zæp] **I.** <-pp-> *vt* **1.** *sl* (*destroy*) liquidar **2.** *sl* (*send fast*) mandar echando leches **3.** *sl* CULIN (*microwave*) hacer en el microondas **II.** <-pp-> *vi sl* **1.** TV **to ~ through the channels** hacer zapping **2.** (*move fast*) **to ~ somewhere** ir a un sitio echando leches; **to ~ through sth** despachar algo **III.** *interj sl* ¡zas!

zapping ['zæp·ɪŋ] *n inf* zapping *m*

zeal [zil] *n* celo *m;* **religious ~** fervor *m* religioso; **reforming ~** afán *m* reformista

zealot ['zel·ət] *n* fanático, -a *m, f*

zealous ['zel·əs] *adj* ferviente; **to be ~ in** (**doing**) **sth** poner gran celo en hacer algo

zebra ['zi·brə] *n* cebra *f*

zenith ['zi·nɪθ] <-es> *n* **1.** ASTR (*highest point*) cenit *m* **2.** (*most successful point*) apogeo *m;* **to be at the ~ of sth** estar en el apogeo de algo

zero ['zɪr·ou] **I.** <-s *o* -es> *n* cero *m;* **below ~** METEO bajo cero; **to be a ~** ser un cero a la izquierda **II.** *adj* cero *inv;* **~ growth** crecimiento *m* cero; **~ hour** hora *f* cero; **~ visibility** visibilidad *f* nula; **my chances are ~** no tengo ninguna posibilidad **III.** *vt* (*return to zero: device*) poner a cero

◆ **zero in on** *vi* **1.** (*aim precisely*) apuntar a **2.** (*focus on*) **to ~ sth** centrarse en algo

zero tolerance *n* **policy of ~** política *f* de mano dura

zest [zest] *n* **1.** (*enthusiastic energy*) entusiasmo *m;* **to do sth with ~** hacer algo con brío; **~ for life** ganas *fpl* de vivir **2.** (*charm, interest*) gracia *f;* **the story lacks ~** a la historia le falta garra **3.** (*rind*) corteza *f;* **lemon/ orange ~** corteza de limón/naranja; **grated lemon ~** raspadura *f* de limón

zigzag ['zɪg·zæg] **I.** *n* (*crooked line*) zigzag *m* **II.** *adj* (*crooked*) zigzagueante; (*pattern*) en

zigzag **III.** <-gg-> *vi* zigzaguear
zillionaire *n inf* archimillonario, -a *m, f*
Zimbabwe [zɪm·'bab·weɪ] *n* Zimbabue *m*
Zimbabwean [zɪm·'bab·wi·ən] **I.** *adj* zimbabuense **II.** *n* zimbabuense *mf*
zinc [zɪŋk] *n* cinc *m* [o zinc] *m*
zip [zɪp] **I.** *n* **1.** (*ZIP code*) código *m* postal
2. (*whistle*) silbido *m* **3.** *inf* (*vigor*) garra *f* **4.** *sl*
(*nothing*) nada; **I know ~ about that** no
tengo ni idea de eso **II.** <-pp-> *vt* **to ~ a bag**
cerrar la cremallera de un bolso; **to ~ a dress**
subir la cremallera de un vestido; **to ~ sth**
open/shut/up abrir/cerrar/subir la cremallera de algo; **will you ~ me up?** ¿me subes la
cremallera? **III.** <-pp-> *vi* **to ~ in/past**
entrar/pasar volando; **the days ~ped by** los
días pasaron volando
ZIP code *n* código *m* postal
zipper ['zɪp·ər] *n* cremallera *f*, cierre *m* relámpago *Arg*
zippy ['zɪp·i] <-ier, -iest> *adj inf* (*fast: car*)
veloz; (*energetic*) enérgico, -a
zither ['zɪð·ər] *n* cítara *f*
zloty ['zlɔ·t̬i] *n* zloty *m*
zodiac ['zou·di·æk] *n* zodíaco *m*
zombie ['zam·bi] *n* zombi *mf*
zonal ['zou·nəl] *adj* zonal; **a ~ division** una
división en zonas

zone [zoun] **I.** *n* zona *f;* **nuclear-free ~** zona
desnuclearizada; **time ~** zona horaria; **frigid/**
temperate/torrid ~ METEO zona glacial/tem-
plada/tórrida **II.** *vt* **1.** (*divide*) dividir en zonas
2. ADMIN, LAW (*designate*) **to ~ an area for**
residential use declarar un lugar zona residencial
zoning *n* ADMIN, LAW zonificación *f*
zoo [zu] *n* zoo *m*
zoological [,zou·ə·'ladʒ·ɪ·kəl] *adj* zoológico,
-a; **~ garden** (parque *m*) zoológico *m*
zoologist [zou·'al·ə·dʒɪst] *n* zoólogo, -a *m, f*
zoology [zou·'al·ə·dʒi] *n* zoología *f*
zoom [zum] **I.** *n* **1.** PHOT zoom *m* **2.** AVIAT subida
f vertical **3.** (*buzz*) zumbido *m* **II.** *vt* **1.** AVIAT
(*plane*) hacer subir verticalmente **2.** PHOT enfocar con el zoom **III.** *vi* **1.** *inf* (*move very fast*) ir
zumbando; **to ~ away** salir pitando; **to ~ past**
pasar volando **2.** (*plane*) elevarse abrup-
tamente; (*costs, sales*) dispararse *inf*
◆**zoom in** *vi* PHOT enfocar en primer plano; **to**
~ on sth/sb enfocar algo/a alguien en primer
plano
◆**zoom out** *vi* PHOT cambiar a un plano general
zoom lens *n* zoom *m*
zucchini [zu·'ki·ni] <-(s)> *n inv* calabacín *m*,
calabacita *f AmL*

Concise Spanish Grammar
Breve gramática de la lengua española

I. Articles

Spanish has both definite and indefinite articles.

		Definite article	Indefinite article
Singular	Masculine	**el** amigo	**un** amigo
	Feminine	**la** rosa	**una** rosa
Plural	Masculine	**los** amigos	**unos** amigos
	Feminine	**las** rosas	**unas** rosas

Feminine nouns beginning with a stressed *a* or *ha* take the masculine article *el* in the singular and the feminine article *las* in the plural.

el alma	**las** almas

The neutral article *lo* is used when forming nouns from adjectives, participles, possessive pronouns, and adverbial expressions.

lo bueno	**lo** hablado	**lo** mío	**lo** maravillosamente

II. Nouns
Singular and plural

The plural of nouns ending in a consonant or a stressed *í* or *ú* is formed by adding -*es*. The plural of nouns ending in an unstressed vowel or a stressed *é* or *ó* is formed by adding -*s*. Singular nouns ending in an -*s* that is preceded by an unstressed vowel remain unchanged in the plural. Masculine and feminine nouns that are stressed on the last syllable in the singular are stressed on the next-to-last syllable in the plural.

Masculine

Singular	Plural	Singular	Plural
el libro	los libros	el poeta	los poetas
el coche	los coches	el café	los cafés
el dominó	los dominós	el rubí	los rubíes
el tabú	los tabúes	el mensaje	los mensajes
el árbol	los árboles	el pastor	los pastores
el bastón	los bastones	el corazón	los corazones
el galán	los galanes	el parlanchín	los parlanchines
el martes	los martes	el turista	los turistas
el arroz	los arroces	el fiambre	los fiambres
el actor	los actores	el avión	los aviones

Feminine

Singular	Plural	Singular	Plural
la radio	las radios	la mesa	las mesas
la lente	las lentes	la nación	las naciones
la verdad	las verdades	la libertad	las libertades
la multitud	las multitudes	la especie	las especies
la actriz	las actrices	la certidumbre	las certidumbres
la parlanchina	las parlanchinas	la burlona	las burlonas
la trabajdora	las trabajdoras	la crisis	las crisis
la turista	las turistas	la canción	las canciones
la luz	las luces	la razón	las razones

Exceptions

The meaning of some nouns changes in the plural.

Meaning in the singular	Meaning in the plural
el padre – the father	los padres – the parents
la letra – the letter	las letras – the humanities

Other nouns can be both masculine and feminine but have different meanings depending on their gender.

Masculine meaning	Feminine meaning
el capital – the capital *(wealth)*	la capital – the capital city
el cura – the priest	la cura – the cure

The preposition *a*

The preposition *a* precedes direct objects that refer to people or animals, except when the verbs *tener, necesitar, buscar,* and *encontrar* are used.

Acompaño **a** Pilar.	¿Entiendes **al** profesor?
Tengo muchos amigos.	Necesitamos un médico.

The preposition *a* combines with the masculine singular definite article *el* to form the contraction *al* (*a* + *el*).

Voy **al** cine.

The preposition *de*

The preposition *de*
• is used to show what things are made of and what they are used for;

mesa **de** mármol	máquina **de** escribir

• comes after nouns of quantity, measure, or number;

dos kilos **de** manzanas	un litro **de** leche

• and indicates origin, possession, or an adverbial phrase.

| Soy **de** Valencia. | María tiembla **de** miedo. |

The preposition *de* combines with the masculine singular definite article *el* to form the contractions *del* (*de* + *el*).

| Viene **del** jardín. |

Diminutives and augmentatives

The endings *-ito, -cito, -ico,* and *-illo* form diminutives as demonstrated below with the words *pajaro* and *coche.*

| pajar**ito** | coche**cito** |
| pajar**ico** | pajar**illo** |

These endings can also indicate tenderness or sympathy.

| ¡Hola, Pedr**ito**! |

The endings *-ón, -tón, -azo,* and *–ote* form augmentatives as demonstrated below with the word *hombre.*

| hombr**ón** | hombr**ote** |

The endings *-aco, -acho,* and *-ucho* indicate contempt as demonstrated below with the words *libro* and *amigo* .

| libr**aco** | amig**acho** |

III. Adjectives

Adjectives provide information about the noun they modify. They qualify or classify the noun (e.g., un día *soleado*, problemas *económicos*,), give information about color (una camiseta *roja*) or emphasize (un fracaso *total* y *absoluto*).

1. Demonstrative Adjectives

Demonstrative adjectives (so-called *determinantes demostrativos*) refer to nouns in a definite way. For nouns that are so close to the speaker that he or she can touch them, *este, esta, estos, estas* are used.

ese, esa, esos, esas, and *eso* indicate things that are near the speaker but not close enough to be touched.

aquel, aquella, aquellos, aquellas, and *aquello* indicate things that are not near the speaker or the person being spoken to.

este	ese	aquel	libro
esta	esa	aquella	silla
estos	esos	aquellos	libros
estas	esas	aquellas	sillas

| **Aquel** día ocurrió el accidente. | Me gusta **esa** flor. |
| **Este** libro es caro. | **Aquellas** casas son caras. |

2. Possessive Adjectives

Possessive adjectives (so-called *determinantes posesivos*) indicate possession or the connection that the noun that they modify has with someone. Spanish has unstressed and stressed forms.

Unstressed forms		Stressed forms
mi	trabajo	mío(s), mía(s)
tu	amigo	tuyo(s), tuya(s)
su	jardín	suyo(s), suya(s)
nuestro	padre	nuestro(s), nuestra(s)
vuestro	tren	vuestro(s), vuestra(s)
su	coche	suyo(s), suya(s)

The stressed forms of possessive adjectives are used after nouns, the verb *ser,* and definite articles.

Tengo unas cartas **tuyas.**	Ese diccionario es **mío.**
Estas son las **suyas.**	Los libros son **nuestros.**

3. Gender and number of adjectives

Adjectives in Spanish must agree with nouns in **gender** and **number.**

el muchach**o** hermos**o**	la muchach**a** hermos**a**
los muchach**os** rubi**os**	las muchach**as** rubi**as**

Masculine adjectives ending in *-or, -án, -ín,* and *-ón* add *-a* to express the feminine form. Masculine adjectives that are stressed on the last syllable are stressed on the next-to-last syllable in the feminine form.

trabajad**or**	trabajad**ora**	harag**án**	harag**ana**
parlanch**ín**	parlanch**ina**	burl**ón**	burl**ona**

Feminine adjectives of nationality are formed by adding *-a* to the masculine form, unless the masculine form ends in *-i* or *-e.* In such cases, the adjectives are the same in both the masculine and feminine form.

españ**ol**	españ**ola**	alem**án**	alem**ana**
árabe	árabe	marroqu**í**	marroqu**í**

Most other adjectives have the same ending in both the masculine and feminine forms.

el tiempo/la vida brev**e**	el traje/la camisa gris

The rules for forming the plural of adjectives are the same as those for pluralizing nouns *(see p. 637–638).*

4. Placement of adjectives

In general, adjectives follow the nouns that they modify.

el traje **negro/azul/gris**	un abrigo **alemán/inglés**

The meaning of an adjective may change depending on its position in a sentence. In general, adjectives that follow nouns give objective or logical descriptions, whereas adjectives that precede nouns give subjective or affective descriptions.

un hombre **pobre**	as opposed to	un **pobre** hombre
a poor man *(without money)*		*a poor man* *(one to pity)*

When the adjectives *bueno* and *malo* precede a noun, they drop the *-o* ending in the masculine singular.

un **buen** comienzo	as opposed to	un comienzo **bueno**
un **mal** día	as opposed to	un día **malo**

When the adjective *grande* precedes a noun, it drops the *-de* ending in both the masculine and feminine singular.

un **gran** hombre	as opposed to	un hombre **grande**
una **gran** mujer	as opposed to	una mujer **grande**

The adjectives *mucho, poco,* and *otro* always precede nouns.

mucha suerte	**poca** paciencia
otro vaso	

IV. Adverbs

Adverbs are invariable and modify adjectives, verbs, and adverbs.

There are primary adverbs such as *bien, mal, pronto,* and *aquí,* as well as adverbial expressions such as *sin embargo* and *de repente.*

Juan llegará **pronto**.	**De repente** Juan se cayó.

Adverbs can also be derived from adjectives by adding the ending *-mente* to the feminine singular form of the adjective.

Lo he hecho **rápidamente**.	Hace un día **terriblemente** frío.

Whereas the adverb *muy* always precedes an adjective or adverb, *mucho* and *poco* can stand alone with a verb.

Es un vino **muy** bueno.	Hemos llegado **muy** tarde.
Juan escribe **muy** lentamente.	Los camareros ganan **poco**.
Esta película es **mucho** más interesante.	Marisa escribe **mucho**.

V. Comparisons
Regular forms of comparison
Here is an example of the regular adjective forms of comparison.

caro	1. Las rosas son **caras**. (positive)
	2. Esas rosas son **más caras** que los claveles. (comparative)
	3. Aquellas rosas son **las más caras**. (relative superlative)
	4. Estas rosas son **carísimas**. (absolute superlative)

Here is an example of the regular adverb forms of comparison.

maravillosamente	1. María canta **maravillosamente**. (positive)
	2. María canta **más maravillosamente** que Juana. (comparative)
	3. María es **la que** canta **más maravillosamente**. (relative superlative)
	4. María canta **lo más maravillosamente posible**. (absolute superlative)

Irregular forms of comparison
Note the irregular forms of comparison for the adjectives *bueno, malo, grande,* and *pequeño.*

bueno	mejor/más bueno	el mejor	(*absolute supert.* buenísimo)
malo	peor/más malo	el peor	(*absolute supert.* malísimo)
grande	mayor/más grande	el mayor	(*absolute supert.* grandísimo)
pequeño	menor/más pequeño	el menor	(*absolute supert.* pequeñísimo)

Note the irregular forms of comparison for the adverbs *bien* and *mal.*

bien	mejor	el mejor
mal	peor	el peor

Adjectives that end in *-ble, -co, -guo,* and *-go* may change orthographically and phonetically in the superlative.

amable	más amable	el más amble	(*absolute supert.* amabilísimo)
rico	más rico	el más rico	(*absolute supert.* riquísimo)
antiguo	más antiguo	el más antiguo	(*absolute supert.* antiquísimo)
amargo	más amargo	el más amargo	(*absolute supert.* amarguísimo)

Comparisons of equality
The adjectival and adverbial constructions *tan ... como, tanto ... como,* and *tanto/tanta/tantos/tantas ... como* are used to form comparisons.

Cose **tan** bien **como** tú.	Es **tan** alta **como** Juan.
¿Quién tiene **tantos** amigos **como** Julia?	Gana **tanto como** él.

Negative and positive comparisons
Negative comparisons are formed using *menos ... que* and positive comparisons are formed using *más ... que.*

menos tiempo **que** ayer	una casa **más** grande **que** la tuya

VI. Verbs

Regular verbs

Verbs conjugate differently in the indicative and the subjunctive. Parts 1–5 below present verb conjugations in various tenses in the indicative.

In general, there are three types of verbs: those that end in -ar (1st conjugation), those that end in -er (2nd conjugation), and those that end in -ir (3rd conjugation).

Verbs that, when conjugated, undergo vowel changes, orthographic changes, or changes in stress, or which omit the unstressed i are listed separately in the conjugation tables following this grammar section (see p. 653 and following). The entries for these verbs in the Spanish–English part of the dictionary refer directly to the model translation in the conjugation tables (e.g., c → qu).

Irregular verbs

Comprehensive conjugation tables of irregular verbs follow this grammar section (see p. 661 and following). The marker irr in the dictionary entries of the English–Spanish section refers to the conjugations in these tables.

1. Present Tense

	-ar	-er	-ir
	hablar	**comprender**	**recibir**
yo	hablo	comprendo	recibo
tú	hablas	comprendes	recibes
él/ella/usted	habla	comprende	recibe
nosotros/nosotras	hablamos	comprendemos	recibimos
vosotros/vosotras	habláis	comprendéis	recibís
ellos/ellas/ustedes	hablan	comprenden	reciben

The present tense is used to express actions and processes that are occurring at the present time, as well as common facts.

En este momento **leo** un libro.	En julio **hace** mucho calor.

2. Imperfect – Preterite – Perfect Tenses

Imperfect tense

	hablar	**comprender**	**recibir**
yo	hablaba	comprendía	recibía
tú	hablabas	comprendías	recibías
él/ellla/usted	hablaba	comprendía	recibía
nosotros/nosotras	hablábamos	comprendíamos	recibíamos
vosotros/vosotras	hablabais	comprendíais	recibíais
ellos/ellas/ustedes	hablaban	comprendían	recibían

Preterite tense

	hablar	comprender	recibir
yo	hablé	comprendí	recibí
tú	hablaste	comprendiste	recibiste
él/ella/usted	habló	comprendió	recibió
nosotros/nosotras	hablamos	comprendimos	recibimos
vosotros/vosotras	hablasteis	comprendisteis	recibisteis
ellos/ellas/ustedes	hablaron	comprendieron	recibieron

Perfect tense

	hablar	comprender	recibir
yo	he hablado	he comprendido	he recibido

Comparison of preterite and imperfect

The **imperfect** is primarily used to describe conditions, but is also used to describe habitual past occurrences or actions that were repeated an unspecified number of times.

The **preterite** is used with completed actions that occurred at a definite time or within a definite time period.

Imperfect	Preterite
Cuando **iba** a dormirme …	… **sonó** el teléfono.
Quería ser medico …	… pero no **terminó** la carrera.
Sabías mis señas …	… pero no **escribiste**.
Cuando **estábamos** durmiendo …	… **llamó** por teléfono.

Comparison of preterite and perfect

The **perfect** (always formed with the helping verb *haber*) is used for completed actions that occurred in the past and have a connection with the present.

The **preterite** is used for such actions that have a connection with the past.

The **perfect** is always used in connection with the following temporal expressions: *hoy, esta semana/este mes/este año, nunca*, etc. The **preterite** is used with: *ayer, anoche, la semana pasada, el mes pasado, el año pasado*, etc.

Perfect	Preterite
Este año **he tenido** suerte.	Ayer **vi** a Juan en el concierto.
Nunca **he estado** en tu casa.	El sábado pasado **dormimos** hasta las 10.

3. Future Tense

	hablar	comprender	recibir
yo	hablaré	comprenderé	recibiré
tú	hablarás	comprenderás	recibirás
él/ella/usted	hablará	comprenderá	recibirá
nosotros/nosotras	hablaremos	comprenderemos	recibiremos
vosotros/vosotras	hablaréis	comprenderéis	recibiréis
ellos/ellas/ustedes	hablarán	comprenderán	recibirán

Instead of using the future tense for expressions of the near future, the present tense form of *ir* + *a* + infinitive is often used.

Voy a hablar con Pedro.	¿**Vas a leer** pronto el libro?

4. Conditional Mood

	hablar	comprender	recibir
yo	hablaría	comprendería	recibiría
tú	hablarías	comprenderías	recibirías
él/ella/usted	hablaría	comprendería	recibiría
nosotros/nosotras	hablaríamos	comprenderíamos	recibiríamos
vosotros/vosotras	hablaríais	comprenderíais	recibiríais
ellos/ellas/ustedes	hablarían	comprenderían	recibirían

The conditional is often used in polite expressions.

¿**Podría** usted ayudarme?	**Querría** pedirle algo.
Si lo tuviera, te lo **daría**.	

5. Imperative
Affirmative forms

	hablar	comprender	recibir
tú	habla	comprende	recibe
él/ella/usted	hable	comprenda	reciba
nosotros/nosotras	hablemos	comprendamos	recibamos
vosotros/vosotras	hablad	comprended	recibid
ellos/ellas/ustedes	hablen	comprendan	reciban

In Latin America, *ustedes* and its corresponding verb form is usually used in place of *vosotros*.

No **hablen** tan alto, niños.

Negative forms

	hablar	comprender	recibir
tú	no hables	no comprendas	no recibas
él/ella/usted	no hable	no comprenda	no reciba
nosotros/nosotras	hablemos	no comprendamos	no recibamos
vosotros/vosotras	no habléis	no comprendáis	no recibáis
ellos/ellas/ustedes	no hablen	no comprendan	no reciban

6. Subjunctive Mood

The subjunctive is used to express possible happenings. As with the indicative, the subjunctive can be formed in several tenses.

Present subjunctive

	hablar	comprender	recibir
yo	hable	comprenda	reciba
tu	hables	comprendas	recibas
él/ella/usted	hable	comprenda	reciba
nosotros/nosotras	hablemos	comprendamos	recibamos
vosotros/vosotras	habléis	comprendáis	recibáis
ellos/ellas/ustedes	hablen	comprendan	reciban

Imperfect subjunctive

The imperfect subjunctive can have two separate forms. The one represented here is the most common form. For both forms see the verb tables beginning on p. 652.

	hablar	comprender	recibir
yo	hablara	comprendiera	recibiera
tu	hablaras	comprendieras	recibieras
él/ella/usted	hablara	comprendiera	recibiera
nosotros/nosotras	habláramos	comprendiéramos	recibiéramos
vosotros/vosotras	hablarais	comprendierais	recibierais
ellos/ellas/ustedes	hablaran	comprendieran	recibieran

The perfect subjunctive and pluperfect subjunctive are formed by using the corresponding form of the helping verb *haber* together with the respective participle.

perfect	haya	hayamos	hablado
	hayas	hayáis	comprendido
	haya	hayan	recibido
pluperfect	hubiera	hubiéramos	hablado
	hubieras	hubierais	comprendido
	hubiera	hubieran	recibido

The subjunctive is used in main clauses that express a wish or a probability.

Ojalá **llueva** pronto.	Quizás **venga** mañana mi abuela.

The subjunctive is also used in relative clauses that express a wish or a condition.

Busco una casa que **tenga** un jardín grande.

A dependent clause that follows **que** takes the subjunctive if the main clause expresses:

1. A desire or a wish	Quiero que **salga** el sol.
2. Advice	Te aconsejo que **escribas** la carta.
3. Doubt or negation	Dudo que **haya dicho** la verdad.
4. An impersonal evaluative statement	Es necesario que **comprenda** esto.

7. *Ser* and *Estar*

The verb *ser*

- describes fundamental, permanent, and characteristic qualities;
- is used before nouns;
- and is used in connection with time, days, professions, familial relationships, nationality, and religion.

Juan **es inteligente.**	La puerta **es de madera.**
Vámonos, ya **es la una.**	Mañana **es domingo,** ¡qué bien!
Carmen **es médica.**	¿Tú **eres español** o argentino?

The verb *estar*

- means "to be somewhere," "to lie," or "to stand;"
- expresses the meaning "to find oneself" and "to feel;"
- and, when used in front of an adjective or a participle expresses a temporary quality, condition, or a change that has already taken place.

Fernando **está en Nueva York.**	Segovia **está en España.**
Marisa **está** hoy **mejor.**	¿Por qué **está** Luisa **triste?**
La puerta **está abierta.**	La sopa **está** muy **salada.**

Comparison of ser and estar

ser = to be	**estar** = to temporarily be, to appear
Luis **es un hombre enfermo.** *Luis is a sick person.*	Maria **está enferma.** *Maria is sick (right now).*
Luis **es generoso.** *Luis is a generous person.*	María **está** muy **generosa.** *Maria is being very generous (today).*
Luis **es joven.** *Luis is young.*	María **está joven.** *Maria looks young.*

8. Participles

Participles are invariable.

habl**ar**	comprend**er**	recib**ir**
habl**ado**	comprend**ido**	recib**ido**

The participle is used with the verbs *ser* and *estar* to form the passive.

La carta fue **escrita** por mi padre.	Soy **invitado** por mi novia.
La carta está **escrita** por mi padre.	Estoy **invitado** por mi novia.

The participle is used with the helping verb *haber* to form the compound tenses.

El estreno no me ha **gustado.**	**Había llovido** mucho.

A participle that follows *estar* refers to an action that is complete with reference to the present.

Concha está **sentada** en una butaca.	El reloj está **roto.**

9. Gerunds

cantar – cant**ando**	comer – com**iendo**	escribir – escrib**iendo**
reír – r**iendo**	leer – le**yendo**	oír – o**yendo**
pedir – p**idiendo**	sentir – s**intiendo**	dormir – d**urmiendo**

The gerund is formed with the verbs *estar, ir,* and *seguir* and is used for actions that are currently happening.

Siempre **está cantando.**	¿Todavía **estás comiendo?**
Voy organizando mi viaje a Sudamérica.	**¡Siga usted leyendo!**
Seguimos preparando la comida.	**Leyendo** se aprende mucho.

VII. Pronouns

1. Personal Pronouns

Indirect object	Direct object	After prepositions
me	me	sobre **mí**
te	te	sobre **ti**
le	le, la, lo	sobre **él/ella/usted**
nos	nos	sobre **nosotros**
os	os	sobre **vosotros**
les	les, las, los	sobre **ellos/ellas/ustedes**

Indirect object and direct object pronouns without prepositions always immediately precede the verb, and direct object pronouns always follow indirect object pronouns.

¿Quién **me** llama?	Siempre **me lo** dice.

When a noun that is a direct or indirect object precedes a verb, the corresponding pronoun must also be used.

La maleta **la** lleva Pedro.	A Juan no **le** he dado dinero.

Personal pronouns can precede or be added to an infinitive or gerund. Personal pronouns must always be added to the end of affirmative imperatives.

¿Quieres ver**lo**?	**¿Lo** quieres ver?
Está haciéndo**lo.**	**Lo** está haciendo.
¡Dáme**lo**, por favor!	

The indirect object pronouns *le* and *les* change to *se* if they precede the direct object pronouns *lo, los, la,* and *las.*

¿La llave? **Se** la he dado a tu hermano.	¿El libro? Mañana **se** lo doy.

2. Reflexive Pronouns and Reflexive Verbs

		acostumbrarse
yo	me	acostumbro
tú	te	acostumbras
él/ella/usted	se	acostumbra
nosotros/nosotras	nos	acostumbramos
vosotros/vosotras	os	acostumbráis
ellos/ellas/ustedes	se	acostumbran

Reflexive pronouns precede main or helping verbs and follow negation. They can also precede or be added to the end of infinitives and gerunds. Reflexive pronouns must always be added to the end of affirmative imperatives.

Pedro no **se** quiere peinar.	¿**Se** ha levantado ya Luis?
¿No quieres afeitar**te**?	¿No **te** quieres afeitar?
Isabel está levantándo**se**.	Isabel **se** está levantando.
¡Tranquilíza**te**, hombre!	

With reflexive verbs, the *-d* is eliminated in the second person plural of affirmative imperatives.

¡March**ad**!	**as opposed to**	¡March**aos**!

The impersonal of non-reflexive verbs is formed in the third person with *se*, whereas the impersonal of reflexive verbs is formed in the third person with *uno se*. This is a way to avoid using the passive.

Aquí **se respira** mucho mejor.	**Uno se siente** cansado.
Se alquilan coches.	

Some verbs can be both **reflexive** and **non-reflexive**. With some of them, the reflexive form is used to express stronger emotions of the speaker.

El general **murió** en 1975. *The general died in 1975.*	Esta mañana **se ha muerto**. *He/she passed away today.*

Other verbs have different meanings, depending on whether they are reflexive or not.

cambiar	*to change*	cambiarse	*to change clothes*
dormir	*to sleep*	dormirse	*to fall asleep*
ir	*to go, to drive*	irse	*to leave*
parecer	*to appear*	parecerse	*to resemble*
quedar	*to remain*	quedarse	*to stay*

3. Relative Pronouns

Que, the most common relative pronoun, is invariable. After a preposition, the definite article often precedes *que*.

Tengo el libro **que** buscas.
El diccionario **con el que** traduzco.

quien and *quienes* are only used to refer to people and almost always follow a preposition. *El cual, la cual, los cuales,* and *las cuales* refer to people or things and are not used as often.

| El amigo **con quien** viajo. |
| Tengo la cadena **la cual** me regalaste. |

cuyo, cuya, cuyos, and *cuyas,* can be used to refer to people or things and agree in gender and number with the noun that follows.

| La escritora **cuyo libro** apareció ayer es muy famosa. |
| El escritor **cuya novela** apareció el año pasado no es famoso. |

The preposition that complements the verb always precedes the relative pronoun.

| Mi amigo, **en cuya casa** estuve ayer, es médico. |
| La señora, **a cuyos padres** te presenté, es la mujer de Juan. |

The adverbs *donde, como, cuando,* and *cuanto* can replace relative pronouns.

| La casa **en la que/en la cual/donde** vivo. |
| No me gusta el modo **con que/como** te mira. |
| Todo **lo que/cuanto** decía era divertido. |
| Recordaba los años **en que/cuando** íbamos juntos a la escuela. |

4. Demonstrative Pronouns

Demonstrative pronouns are the same as their corresponding demonstrative adjectives (see p. 639) except that they carry an accent.

éste	ése	aquél
ésta	ésa	aquélla
éstos	ésos	aquéllos
éstas	ésas	aquéllas
esto	eso	aquello

éste, ésta, éstos, éstas, and *esto* indicate things that are close to and can be touched by the speaker. *ése, ésa, ésos, ésas,* and *eso* indicate things that are near the speaker but not close enough to be touched.
aquél, aquélla, aquéllos, aquéllas, and *aquello* indicate things that are not near the speaker or the person being spoken to.

| **Ésta** es una silla nueva. | ¿Cuándo dijiste **aquello**? |
| ¿Son **ésos** los señores que llamaron? | ¿Qué es **eso**? |

5. Interrogative Pronouns and Question Words

All interrogative pronouns, question words, and interjections have accents.

quién	¿Quién ha llamado? ¿A quién esperas?	qué	¿Qué has dicho? ¿De qué se trata?
cuánto	¿Cuánto dinero necesitas? ¿Cuántas chaquetas tienes?	dónde	¿Dónde estudias español? ¿Dónde está la parada?
adónde	¿Adónde quieren ir ustedes? ¿Adónde vas tan pronto?	de dónde	¿De dónde vienes? ¿De dónde es esa muchacha?
cuál	¿Cuál es la capital? ¿Cuál de las dos quieres?	cómo	¿Cómo te llamas? ¿Cómo está su señora?
por qué	¿Por qué os vais ya? No sé por qué está tan triste.		

7. Indefinite Pronouns

The indefinite pronouns *alguno* and *ninguno* change to *algún* and *ningún* when they precede masculine nouns in the singular.

When *todo* precedes a noun, the definite article usually has to come between *todo* and the noun. The article can be left out in generalizations.

The placement in sentences with *nada, nadie,* and *ninguno* (and with *nunca*), is shown in Section VIII.

algo	Mejor es algo que nada.	nada	¿Por qué no dices nada?
alguien	¿Ha llamado alguien?	nadie	No ha llamdo nadie.
alguno	¿Alguno de vosotros lo sabe? ¿Vive aquí algún médico?	ninguno	No he visto ninguno. Aquí no hay ningún libro.
todo	Aquí todo está limpio. Inés limpia toda la casa. Todo hombre es mortal.		

VIII. Negation

No precedes verbs and any personal and reflexive pronouns that are connected with them.
Nada generally follows verbs, whereas *nadie, ninguno,* and *nunca* can precede or follow verbs.
No must also precede verbs when negation is expressed using *nada, nadie, ninguno,* or *nunca*.

Pablo no volverá hoy.	Este chico no aprende nada.
Laura no volverá nunca más.	Nunca más volverá Laura.
Mi hija no me lo ha dado.	¿No tienes ninguna foto de él?

Los verbos regulares e irregulares españoles
Spanish regular and irregular verbs

Abreviaturas:

pret. ind.	pretérito indefinido
subj. fut.	subjuntivo futuro
subj. imp.	subjuntivo imperfecto
subj. pres.	subjuntivo presente

Verbos regulares que terminan en -*ar*, -*er* e -*ir*

1.ª conjugación

hablar

presente	imperfecto	pret. ind.	futuro	
hablo	hablaba	hablé	hablaré	**gerundio**
hablas	hablabas	hablaste	hablarás	hablando
habla	hablaba	habló	hablará	
hablamos	hablábamos	hablamos	hablaremos	**participio**
habláis	hablabais	hablasteis	hablaréis	hablado
hablan	hablaban	hablaron	hablarán	

condicional	subj. pres.	subj. imp.	subj. fut.	imperativo
hablaría	hable	hablara/-ase	hablare	
hablarías	hables	hablaras/-ases	hablares	habla
hablaría	hable	hablara/-ase	hablare	hable
hablaríamos	hablemos	habláramos/-ásemos	habláremos	hablemos
hablaríais	habléis	hablarais/-aseis	hablareis	hablad
hablarían	hablen	hablaran/-asen	hablaren	hablen

2.ª conjugación

comprender

presente	imperfecto	pret. ind.	futuro	
comprendo	comprendía	comprendí	comprenderé	**gerundio**
comprendes	comprendías	comprendiste	comprenderás	comprendiendo
comprende	comprendía	comprendió	comprenderá	
comprendemos	comprendíamos	comprendimos	comprenderemos	**participio**
comprendéis	comprendíais	comprendisteis	comprenderéis	comprendido
comprenden	comprendían	comprendieron	comprenderán	

condicional	subj. pres.	subj. imp.	subj. fut.	imperativo
comprendería	comprenda	comprendiera/ -iese	comprendiere	
comprenderías	comprendas	comprendieras/ -ieses	comprendieres	comprende
comprendería	comprenda	comprendiera/ -iese	comprendiere	comprenda
comprenderíamos	comprendamos	comprendiéra- mos/-iésemos	comprendiéremos	comprendamos
comprenderíais	comprendáis	comprendierais/ -ieseis	comprendiereis	comprended
comprenderían	comprendan	comprendieran/ -iesen	comprendieren	comprendan

3.ª conjugación

recibir

presente	imperfecto	pret. ind.	futuro	
recibo	recibía	recibí	recibiré	**gerundio**
recibes	recibías	recibiste	recibirás	recibiendo
recibe	recibía	recibió	recibirá	
recibimos	recibíamos	recibimos	recibiremos	**participio**
recibís	recibíais	recibisteis	recibiréis	recibido
reciben	recibían	recibieron	recibirán	

condicional	subj. pres.	subj. imp.	subj. fut.	imperativo
recibiría	reciba	recibiera/-iese	recibiere	
recibirías	recibas	recibieras/-ieses	recibieres	recibe
recibiría	reciba	recibiera/-iese	recibiere	reciba
recibiríamos	recibamos	recibiéramos/ -iésemos	recibiéremos	recibamos
recibiríais	recibáis	reciebierais/ -ieseis	recibiereis	recibid
recibirían	reciban	recibieran/-iesen	recibieren	reciban

Verbos con cambios vocálicos

<e → ie>   pensar

presente	imperfecto	pret. ind.	futuro	
pienso	pensaba	pensé	pensaré	**gerundio**
piensas	pensabas	pensaste	pensarás	pensando
piensa	pensaba	pensó	pensará	
pensamos	pensábamos	pensamos	pensaremos	**participio**
pensáis	pensabais	pensasteis	pensaréis	pensado
piensan	pensaban	pensaron	pensarán	

condicional	subj. pres.	subj. imp.	subj. fut.	imperativo
pensaría	piense	pensara/-ase	pensare	
pensarías	pienses	pensaras/-ases	pensares	piensa
pensaría	piense	pensara/-ase	pensare	piense
pensaríamos	pensemos	pensáramos/-ásemos	pensáremos	pensemos
pensaríais	penséis	pensarais/-aseis	pensareis	pensad
pensarían	piensen	pensaran/-asen	pensaren	piensen

\<o → ue\>   contar

presente	imperfecto	pret. ind.	futuro	
cuento	contaba	conté	contaré	**gerundio**
cuentas	contabas	contaste	contarás	contando
cuenta	contaba	contó	contará	
contamos	contábamos	contamos	contaremos	**participio**
contáis	contabais	contasteis	contaréis	contado
cuentan	contaban	contaron	contaron	

condicional	subj. pres.	subj. imp.	subj. fut.	imperativo
contaría	cuente	contara/-ase	contare	
contarías	cuentes	contaras/-ases	contares	cuenta
contaría	cuente	contara/-ase	contare	cuente
contaríamos	contemos	contáramos/-ásemos	contáremos	contemos
contaríais	contéis	contarais/-aseis	contareis	contad
contarían	cuenten	contaran	contaren	cuenten

\<e → i\>   pedir

presente	imperfecto	pret. ind.	futuro	
pido	pedía	pedí	pediré	**gerundio**
pides	pedías	pediste	pedirás	pidiendo
pide	pedía	pidió	pedirá	
pedimos	pedíamos	pedimos	pediremos	**participio**
pedís	pedíais	pedisteis	pediréis	pedido
piden	pedían	pidieron	pedirán	

condicional	subj. pres.	subj. imp.	subj. fut.	imperativo
pediría	pida	pidiera/-iese	pidiere	
pedirías	pidas	pidieras/-ieses	pidieres	pide
pediría	pida	pidiera/-iese	pidiere	pida
pediríamos	pidamos	pidiéramos/-iésemos	pidiéremos	pidamos
pediríais	pidáis	pidierais/-ieseis	pidiereis	pedid
pedirían	pidan	pidieran/-iesen	pidieren	pidan

Verbos con cambios ortográficos

<c → qu> atacar

presente	imperfecto	pret. ind.	futuro	
ataco	atacaba	ataqué	atacaré	**gerundio**
atacas	atacabas	atacaste	atacarás	atacando
ataca	atacaba	atacó	atacará	
atacamos	atacábamos	atacamos	atacaremos	**participio**
atacáis	atacabais	atacasteis	atacaréis	atacado
atacan	atacaban	atacaron	atacarán	

condicional	subj. pres.	subj. imp.	subj. fut.	imperativo
atacaría	ataque	atacara/-ase	atacare	
atacarías	ataques	atacaras/-ases	atacares	ataca
atacaría	ataque	atacara/-ase	atacare	ataque
atacaríamos	ataquemos	atacáramos/-ásemos	atacáremos	ataquemos
atacaríais	ataquéis	atacarais/-aseis	atacareis	atacad
atacarían	ataquen	atacaran/-asen	atacaren	ataquen

<g → gu> pagar

presente	imperfecto	pret. ind.	futuro	
pago	pagaba	pagué	pagaré	**gerundio**
pagas	pagabas	pagaste	pagarás	pagando
paga	pagaba	pagó	pagará	
pagamos	pagábamos	pagamos	pagaremos	**participio**
pagáis	pagabais	pagasteis	pagaréis	pagado
pagan	pagaban	pagaron	pagarán	

condicional	subj. pres.	subj. imp.	subj. fut.	imperativo
pagaría	pague	pagara/-ase	pagare	
pagarías	pagues	pagaras/-ases	pagares	paga
pagaría	pague	pagara/-ase	pagare	pague
pagaríamos	paguemos	pagáramos/-ásemos	pagáremos	paguemos
pagaríais	paguéis	pagarais/-aseis	pagareis	pagad
pagarían	paguen	pagaran/-asen	pagaren	paguen

<z → c>   **cazar**

presente	imperfecto	pret. ind.	futuro	
cazo	cazaba	cacé	cazaré	**gerundio**
cazas	cazabas	cazaste	cazarás	cazando
caza	cazaba	cazó	cazará	
cazamos	cazábamos	cazamos	cazaremos	**participio**
cazáis	cazabais	cazasteis	cazaréis	cazado
cazan	cazaban	cazaron	cazarán	

condicional	subj. pres.	subj. imp.	subj. fut.	imperativo
cazaría	cace	cazara/-ase	cazare	
cazarías	caces	cazaras/-ases	cazares	caza
cazaría	cace	cazara/-ase	cazare	cace
cazaríamos	cacemos	cazáramos/-ásemos	cazáremos	cacemos
cazaríais	cacéis	cazarais/-aseis	cazareis	cazad
cazarían	cacen	cazaran/-asen	cazaren	cacen

<gu → gü>   **averiguar**

presente	imperfecto	pret. ind.	futuro	
averiguo	averiguaba	averigüé	averiguaré	**gerundio**
averiguas	averiguabas	averiguaste	averiguarás	averiguando
averigua	averiguaba	averiguó	averiguará	
averiguamos	averiguábamos	averiguamos	averiguaremos	**participio**
averiguáis	averiguabais	averiguasteis	averiguaréis	averiguado
averiguan	averiguaban	averiguaron	averiguarán	

condicional	subj. pres.	subj. imp.	subj. fut.	imperativo
averiguaría	averigüe	averiguara/-ase	averiguare	
averiguarías	averigües	averiguaras/-ases	averiguares	averigua
averiguaría	averigüe	averiguara/-ase	averiguare	averigüe
averiguaríamos	averigüemos	averiguáramos/-ásemos	averiguáremos	averigüemos
averiguaríais	averigüéis	averiguarais/-aseis	averiguareis	averiguad
averiguarían	averigüen	averiguaran/-asen	averiguaren	averigüen

<c → z>   **vencer**

presente	imperfecto	pret. ind.	futuro	
venzo	vencía	vencí	venceré	**gerundio**
vences	vencías	venciste	vencerás	venciendo
vence	vencía	venció	vencerá	
vencemos	vencíamos	vencimos	venceremos	**participio**
vencéis	vencíais	vencisteis	venceréis	vencido
vencen	vencían	vencieron	vencerán	

condicional	subj. pres.	subj. imp.	subj. fut.	imperativo
vencería	venza	venciera/-iese	venciere	
vencerías	venzas	vencieras/-ieses	vencieres	vence
vencería	venza	venciera/-iese	venciere	venza
venceríamos	venzamos	venciéramos/-iésemos	venciéremos	venzamos
venceríais	venzáis	vencierais/-ieseis	venciereis	venced
vencerían	venzan	vencieran/-iesen	vencieren	venzan

\<g → j\>   coger

presente	imperfecto	pret. ind.	futuro	
cojo	cogía	cogí	cogeré	**gerundio**
coges	cogías	cogiste	cogerás	cogiendo
coge	cogía	cogió	cogerá	
cogemos	cogíamos	cogimos	cogeremos	**participio**
cogéis	cogíais	cogisteis	cogeréis	cogido
cogen	cogían	cogieron	cogerán	

condicional	subj. pres.	subj. imp.	subj. fut.	imperativo
cogería	coja	cogiera/-iese	cogiere	
cogerías	cojas	cogieras/-ieses	cogieres	coge
cogería	coja	cogiera/-iese	cogiere	coja
cogeríamos	cojamos	cogiéramos/-iésemos	cogiéremos	cojamos
cogeríais	cojáis	cogierais/-ieseis	cogiereis	coged
cogerían	cojan	cogieran/-iesen	cogieren	cojan

\<gu → g\>   distinguir

presente	imperfecto	pret. ind.	futuro	
distingo	distinguía	distinguí	distinguiré	**gerundio**
distingues	distinguías	distinguiste	distinguirás	distinguiendo
distingue	distinguía	distinguió	distinguirá	
distinguimos	distinguíamos	distinguimos	distinguiremos	**participio**
distinguís	distinguíais	distinguisteis	distinguiréis	distinguido
distinguen	distinguían	distinguieron	distinguirán	

condicional	subj. pres.	subj. imp.	subj. fut.	imperativo
distinguiría	distinga	distinguiera/-iese	distinguiere	
distinguirías	distingas	distinguieras/-ieses	distinguieres	distingue
distinguiría	distinga	distinguiera/-iese	distinguiere	distinga
distinguiríamos	distingamos	distinguiéramos/iésemos	distinguiéremos	distingamos
distinguiríais	distingáis	distinguierais/-ieseis	distinguiereis	distinguid
distinguirían	distingan	distinguieran/-iesen	distinguieren	distingan

\<qu → c\> delinquir

presente	imperfecto	pret. ind.	futuro	
delinco	delinquía	delinquí	delinquiré	**gerundio**
delinques	delinquías	delinquiste	delinquirás	delinquiendo
delinque	delinquía	delinquió	delinquirá	
delinquimos	delinquíamos	delinquimos	delinquiremos	**participio**
delinquís	delinquíais	delinquisteis	delinquiréis	delinquido
delinquen	delinquían	delinquieron	delinquirán	

condicional	subj. pres.	subj. imp.	subj. fut.	imperativo
delinquiría	delinca	delinquiera/-iese	delinquiere	
delinquirías	delincas	delinquieras/-ieses	delinquieres	delinque
delinquiría	delinca	delinquiera/-iese	delinquiere	delinca
delinquiríamos	delincamos	delinquiéramos/-iésemos	delinquiéremos	delincamos
delinquiríais	delincáis	delinquierais/-ieseis	delinquiereis	delinquid
delinquirían	delincan	delinquieran/-iesen	delinquieren	delincan

Verbos con desplazamiento en la acentuación

\<1. pres: envío\> enviar

presente	imperfecto	pret. ind.	futuro	
envío	enviaba	envié	enviaré	**gerundio**
envías	enviabas	enviaste	enviarás	enviando
envía	enviaba	envió	enviará	
enviamos	enviábamos	enviamos	enviaremos	**participio**
enviáis	enviabais	enviasteis	enviaréis	enviado
envían	enviaban	enviaron	enviarán	

condicional	subj. pres.	subj. imp.	subj. fut.	imperativo
enviaría	envíe	enviara/-iase	enviare	
enviarías	envíes	enviaras/-iases	enviares	envía
enviaría	envíe	enviara/-iase	enviare	envíe
enviaríamos	enviemos	enviáramos/-iásemos	enviáremos	enviemos
enviaríais	enviéis	enviarais/-iaseis	enviareis	enviad
enviarían	envíen	enviaran/-iasen	enviaren	envíen

<1. pres: continúo>   continuar

presente	imperfecto	pret. ind.	futuro	
continúo	continuaba	continué	continuaré	**gerundio**
continúas	continuabas	continuaste	continuarás	continuando
continúa	continuaba	continuó	continuará	
continuamos	continuábamos	continuamos	continuaremos	**participio**
continuáis	continuabais	continuasteis	continuaréis	continuado
continúan	continuaban	continuaron	continuarán	

condicional	subj. pres.	subj. imp.	subj. fut.	imperativo
continuaría	continúe	continuara/-ase	continuare	
continuarías	continúes	continuaras/-ases	continuares	continúa
continuaría	continúe	continuara/-ase	continuare	continúe
continuaríamos	continuemos	continuáramos/-ásemos	continuáremos	continuemos
continuaríais	continuéis	continuarais/-aseis	continuareis	continuad
continuarían	continúen	continuaran/-asen	continuaren	continúen

Verbos que pierden la i átona

<3. pret: tañó>   tañer

presente	imperfecto	pret. ind.	futuro	
taño	tañía	tañí	tañeré	**gerundio**
tañes	tañías	tañiste	tañerás	tañendo
tañe	tañía	tañó	tañerá	
tañemos	tañíamos	tañimos	tañeremos	**participio**
tañéis	tañíais	tañisteis	tañeréis	tañido
tañen	tañían	tañeron	tañerán	

condicional	subj. pres.	subj. imp.	subj. fut.	imperativo
tañería	taña	tañera/-ese	tañere	
tañerías	tañas	tañeras/-eses	tañeres	tañe
tañería	taña	tañera/-ese	tañere	taña
tañeríamos	tañamos	tañéramos/-ésemos	tañéremos	tañamos
tañeríais	tañáis	tañerais/-eseis	tañereis	tañed
tañerían	tañan	tañeran/-esen	tañeren	tañan

<3. pret: gruñó> gruñir

presente	imperfecto	pret. ind.	futuro	
gruño	gruñía	gruñí	gruñiré	**gerundio**
gruñes	gruñías	gruñiste	gruñirás	gruñendo
gruñe	gruñía	gruñó	gruñirá	
gruñimos	gruñíamos	gruñimos	gruñiremos	**participio**
gruñís	gruñíais	gruñisteis	gruñiréis	gruñido
gruñen	gruñían	gruñeron	gruñirán	

condicional	subj. pres.	subj. imp.	subj. fut.	imperativo
gruñiría	gruña	gruñera/-ese	gruñere	
gruñirías	gruñas	gruñeras/-eses	gruñeres	gruñe
gruñiría	gruña	gruñera/-ese	gruñere	gruña
gruñiríamos	gruñamos	gruñéramos/-ésemos	gruñéremos	gruñamos
gruñiríais	gruñáis	gruñerais/-eseis	gruñereis	gruñid
gruñirían	gruñan	gruñeran/-esen	gruñeren	gruñan

Los verbos irregulares

abolir

presente	subj. pres.	imperativo	
–	–		gerundio
–	–	–	aboliendo
–	–	–	
abolimos	–	–	participio
abolís	–	abolid	abolido
–	–	–	

abrir

participio:	abierto

adquirir

presente	imperativo	
adquiero		gerundio
adquieres	adquiere	adquiriendo
adquiere	adquiera	
adquirimos	adquiramos	participio
adquirís	adquirid	adquirido
adquieren	adquieran	

airar

presente		
aíro	gerundio	
aíras	airando	
aíra		
airamos	participio	
airáis	airado	
aíran		

andar

presente	pret. ind.	
ando	anduve	gerundio
andas	anduviste	andando
anda	anduvo	
andamos	anduvimos	participio
andáis	anduvisteis	andado
andan	anduvieron	

asir

presente	imperativo	
asgo		**gerundio**
ases	ase	asiendo
ase	asga	
asimos	asgamos	**participio**
asís	asid	asido
asen	asgan	

aullar

presente	imperativo	
aúllo		**gerundio**
aúllas	aúlla	aullando
aúlla	aúlle	
aullamos	aullemos	**participio**
aulláis	aullad	aullado
aúllan	aúllen	

avergonzar

presente	pret. ind.	imperativo	
avergüenzo	avergoncé		**gerundio**
avergüenzas	avergonzaste	avergüenza	avergonzando
avergüenza	avergonzó	avergüence	
avergonzamos	avergonzamos	avergoncemos	**participio**
avergonzáis	avergonzasteis	avergonzad	avergonzado
avergüenzan	avergonzaron	avergüencen	

caber

presente	pret. ind.	futuro	condicional	
quepo	cupe	cabré	cabría	**gerundio**
cabes	cupiste	cabrás	cabrías	cabiendo
cabe	cupo	cabrá	cabría	
cabemos	cupimos	cabremos	cabríamos	**participio**
cabéis	cupisteis	cabréis	cabríais	cabido
caben	cupieron	cabrán	cabrían	

caer

presente	pret. ind.		
caigo	caí	**gerundio**	
caes	caíste	cayendo	
cae	cayó		
caemos	caímos	**participio**	
caéis	caísteis	caído	
caen	cayeron		

ceñir

presente	pret. ind.	imperativo	
ciño	ceñí		**gerundio**
ciñes	ceñiste	ciñe	ciñendo
ciñe	ciñó	ciña	
ceñimos	ceñimos	ciñamos	**participio**
ceñís	ceñisteis	ceñid	ceñido
ciñen	ciñeron	ciñan	

cernir

presente	imperativo	
cierno		**gerundio**
ciernes	cierne	cerniendo
cierne	cierna	
cernimos	cernamos	**participio**
cernís	cernid	cernido
ciernen	ciernan	

cocer

presente	imperativo	
cuezo		**gerundio**
cueces	cuece	cociendo
cuece	cueza	
cocemos	cozamos	**participio**
cocéis	coced	cocido
cuecen	cuezan	

colgar

presente	pret. ind.	imperativo	
cuelgo	colgué		**gerundio**
cuelgas	colgaste	cuelga	colgando
cuelga	colgó	cuelgue	
colgamos	colgamos	colgamos	**participio**
colgáis	colgasteis	colgad	colgado
cuelgan	colgaron	cuelguen	

crecer

presente	imperativo	
crezco		**gerundio**
creces	crece	creciendo
crece	crezca	
crecemos	crezcamos	**participio**
crecéis	creced	crecido
crecen	crezcan	

dar

presente	pret. ind.	subj. pres.	subj. imp.	subj. fut.
doy	di	dé	diera/-ese	diere
das	diste	des	dieras/-eses	dieres
da	dio	dé	diera/-ese	diere
damos	dimos	demos	diéramos/-ésemos	diéremos
dais	disteis	deis	dierais/-eseis	diereis
dan	dieron	den	dieran/-esen	dieren

imperativo	
da	**gerundio**
dé	dando
demos	
dad	**participio**
den	dado

decir

presente	imperfecto	pret. ind.	futuro	
digo	decía	dije	diré	**gerundio**
dices	decías	dijiste	dirás	diciendo
dice	decía	dijo	dirá	
decimos	decíamos	dijimos	diremos	**participio**
decís	decíais	dijisteis	diréis	dicho
dicen	decían	dijeron	dirán	

condicional	subj. pres.	subj. imp.	subj. fut.	imperativo
diría	diga	dijera/-ese	dijere	
dirías	digas	dijeras/-eses	dijeres	di
diría	diga	dijera/-ese	dijere	diga
diríamos	digamos	dijéramos/-ésemos	dijéremos	digamos
diríais	digáis	dijerais/-eseis	dijereis	decid
dirían	digan	dijeran/-esen	dijeren	digan

dormir

presente	pret. ind.	imperativo	
duermo	dormí		**gerundio**
duermes	dormiste	duerme	durmiendo
duerme	durmió	duerma	
dormimos	dormimos	durmamos	**participio**
dormís	dormisteis	dormid	dormido
duermen	durmieron	duerman	

elegir

presente	pret. ind.	imperativo	
elijo	elegí		**gerundio**
eliges	elegiste	elige	eligiendo
elige	eligió	elija	
elegimos	elegimos	elijamos	**participio**
elegís	elegisteis	elegid	elegido
eligen	eligieron	elijan	

empezar

presente	pret. ind.	imperativo	
empiezo	empecé		**gerundio**
empiezas	empezaste	empieza	empezando
empieza	empezó	empiece	
empezamos	empezamos	empecemos	**participio**
empezáis	empezasteis	empezad	empezado
empiezan	empezaron	empiecen	

enraizar

presente	pret. ind.	imperativo	
enraízo	enraicé		**gerundio**
enraízas	enraizaste	enraíza	enraizando
enraíza	enraizó	enraíce	
enraizamos	enraizamos	enraicemos	**participio**
enraizáis	enraizasteis	enraizad	enraizado
enraízan	enraizaron	enraícen	

erguir

presente	pret. ind.	subj. pres	subj. imp.	subj. fut.
yergo	erguí	irga	irguiera/-ese	irguiere
yergues	erguiste	irgas	irguieras/-eses	irguieres
yergue	irguió	irga	irguiera/-ese	irguiere
erguimos	erguimos	irgamos	irgiéramos/-ésemos	irguiéremos
erguís	erguisteis	irgáis	irguierais/-eseis	irguiereis
yerguen	irguieron	irgan	irguieran/-esen	irguieren

imperativo		
yergue	**gerundio**	
yerga	irguiendo	
yergamos		
erguid	**participio**	
yergan	erguido	

errar

presente	pret. ind.	imperativo	
yerro	erré		**gerundio**
yerras	erraste	yerra	errando
yerra	erró	yerre	
erramos	erramos	erremos	**participio**
erráis	errasteis	errad	errado
yerran	erraron	yerren	

escribir

participio:	escrito

estar

presente	imperfecto	pret. ind.	futuro	
estoy	estaba	estuve	estaré	**gerundio**
estás	estabas	estuviste	estarás	estando
está	estaba	estuvo	estará	
estamos	estábamos	estuvimos	estaremos	**participio**
estáis	estabais	estuvisteis	estaréis	estado
están	estaban	estuvieron	estarán	

condicional	subj. pres.	subj. imp.	subj. fut.	imperativo
estaría	esté	estuviera/-ese	estuviere	
estarías	estés	estuvieras/-eses	estuvieres	está
estaría	esté	estuviera/-ese	estuviere	esté
estaríamos	estemos	estuviéramos/-ésemos	estuviéremos	estemos
estaríais	estéis	estuvierais/-eseis	estuviereis	estad
estarían	estén	estuvieran/-esen	estuvieren	estén

forzar

presente	pret. ind.	imperativo	
fuerzo	forcé		**gerundio**
fuerzas	forzaste	fuerza	forzando
fuerza	forzó	fuerce	
forzamos	forzamos	forcemos	**participio**
forzáis	forzasteis	forzad	forzado
fuerzan	forzaron	fuercen	

fregar

presente	pret. ind.	imperativo	
friego	fregué		**gerundio**
friegas	fregaste	friega	fregando
friega	fregó	friegue	
fregamos	fregamos	freguemos	**participio**
fregáis	fregasteis	fregad	fregado
friegan	fregaron	frieguen	

freír

presente	pret. ind.	imperativo	
frío	freí		**gerundio**
fríes	freíste	fríe	friendo
fríe	frió	fría	
freímos	freímos	friamos	**participio**
freís	freísteis	freíd	frito
fríen	frieron	frían	

haber

presente	imperfecto	pret. ind.	futuro	
he	había	hube	habré	**gerundio**
has	habías	hubiste	habrás	habiendo
ha	había	hubo	habrá	
hemos	habíamos	hubimos	habremos	**participio**
habéis	habíais	hubisteis	habréis	habido
han	habían	hubieron	habrán	

condicional	subj. pres.	subj. imp.	subj. fut.	imperativo
habría	haya	hubiera/-iese	hubiere	
habrías	hayas	hubieras/-ieses	hubieres	he
habría	haya	hubiera/-iese	hubiere	haya
habríamos	hayamos	hubiéramos/-iésemos	hubiéremos	hayamos
habríais	hayáis	hubierais/-ieseis	hubiereis	habed
habrían	hayan	hubieran/-iesen	hubieren	hayan

hacer

presente	imperfecto	pret. ind.	futuro	
hago	hacía	hice	haré	**gerundio**
haces	hacías	hiciste	harás	haciendo
hace	hacía	hizo	hará	
hacemos	hacíamos	hicimos	haremos	**participio**
hacéis	hacíais	hicisteis	haréis	hecho
hacen	hacían	hicieron	harán	

condicional	subj. pres.	subj. imp.	subj. fut.	imperativo
haría	haga	hiciera/-iese	hiciere	
harías	hagas	hicieras/-ieses	hicieres	haz
haría	haga	hiciera/-iese	hiciere	haga
haríamos	hagamos	hiciéramos/-iésemos	hiciéremos	hagamos
haríais	hagáis	hicierais/-ieseis	hiciereis	haced
harían	hagan	hicieran/-iesen	hicieren	hagan

hartar

participio:	hartado – *saturated*
	harto (*only as attribute*): estoy harto – *I've had enough*

huir

presente	pret. ind.	imperativo	
huyo	huí		**gerundio**
huyes	huiste	huye	huyendo
huye	huyó	huya	
huimos	huimos	huyamos	**participio**
huís	huisteis	huid	huido
huyen	huyeron	huyan	

imprimir

participio:	impreso

ir

presente	imperfecto	pret. ind.	subj. pres.	subj. imp.
voy	iba	fui	vaya	fuera/-ese
vas	ibas	fuiste	vayas	fueras/-eses
va	iba	fue	vaya	fuera/-ese
vamos	íbamos	fuimos	vayamos	fuéramos/-ésemos
vais	ibais	fuisteis	vayáis	fuerais/-eseis
van	iban	fueron	vayan	fueran/-esen

subj. fut.	imperativo		
fuere		**gerundio**	
fueres	ve	yendo	
fuere	vaya		
fuéremos	vayamos	**participio**	
fuereis	id	ido	
fueren	vayan		

jugar

presente	pret. ind.	subj. pres.	imperativo	
juego	jugué	juegue		**gerundio**
juegas	jugaste	juegues	juega	jugando
juega	jugó	juegue	juegue	
jugamos	jugamos	juguemos	juguemos	**participio**
jugáis	jugasteis	juguéis	jugad	jugado
juegan	jugaron	jueguen	jueguen	

leer

presente	pret. ind.		
leo	leí	**gerundio**	
lees	leíste	leyendo	
lee	leyó		
leemos	leímos	**participio**	
leéis	leísteis	leído	
leen	leyeron		

lucir

presente	imperativo		
luzco		**gerundio**	
luces	luce	luciendo	
luce	luzca		
lucimos	luzcamos	**participio**	
lucís	lucid	lucido	
lucen	luzcan		

maldecir

presente	pret. ind.	imperativo		
maldigo	maldije		**gerundio**	
maldices	maldijiste	maldice	maldiciendo	
maldice	maldijo	maldiga		
maldecimos	maldijimos	maldigamos	**participio**	
maldecís	maldijisteis	maldecid	maldecido	*cursed*
maldicen	maldijeron	maldigan	maldito	*noun, adjective*

morir

presente	pret. ind.	imperativo		
muero	morí		**gerundio**	
mueres	moriste	muere	muriendo	
muere	murió	muera		
morimos	morimos	muramos	**participio**	
morís	moristeis	morid	muerto	
mueren	murieron	mueran		

oir, oír

presente	pret. ind.	imperativo	subj. imp.	subj. fut.
oigo	oí		oyera/-ese	oyere
oyes	oiste	oye	oyeras/-eses	oyeres
oye	oyó	oiga	oyera/-ese	oyere
oímos	oímos	oigamos	oyéramos/-ésemos	oyéremos
oís	oísteis	oid	oyerais/-eseis	oyereis
oyen	oyeron	oigan	oyeran/-esen	oyeren

gerundio	participio
oyendo	oído

oler

presente	imperativo
huelo	
hueles	huele
huele	huela
olemos	olamos
oléis	oled
huelen	huelan

gerundio
oliendo

participio
olido

pedir

presente	pret. ind.	imperativo
pido	pedí	
pides	pediste	pide
pide	pidió	pidas
pedimos	pedimos	pidamos
pedís	pedisteis	pedid
piden	pidieron	pidan

gerundio
pidiendo

participio
pedido

poder

presente	pret. ind.	futuro	condicional
puedo	pude	podré	podría
puedes	pudiste	podrás	podrías
puede	pudo	podrá	podría
podemos	pudimos	podremos	podríamos
podéis	pudisteis	podréis	podríais
pueden	pudieron	podrán	podrían

gerundio
pudiendo

participio
podido

podrir, pudrir

presente	imperfecto	pret. ind.	futuro	condicional
pudro	pudría	pudrí	pudriré	pudriría
pudres	pudrías	pudriste	pudrirás	pudrirías
pudre	pudría	pudrió	pudrirá	pudriría
pudrimos	pudríamos	pudrimos	pudriremos	pudriríamos
pudrís	pudríais	pudristeis	pudriréis	pudriríais
pudren	pudrían	pudrieron	pudrirán	pudrirían

imperativo

	gerundio
pudre	pudriendo
pudra	
pudramos	**participio**
pudrid	podrido
pudran	

poner

presente	pret. ind.	futuro	condicional	imperativo
pongo	puse	pondré	pondría	
pones	pusiste	pondrás	pondrías	pon
pone	puso	pondrá	pondría	ponga
ponemos	pusimos	pondremos	pondríamos	pongamos
ponéis	pusisteis	pondréis	pondríais	poned
ponen	pusieron	pondrán	pondrían	pongan

gerundio	participio
poniendo	puesto

prohibir

presente	imperativo	
prohíbo		**gerundio**
prohíbes	prohíbe	prohibiendo
prohíbe	prohíba	
prohibimos	prohibamos	**participio**
prohibís	prohibid	prohibido
prohíben	prohíban	

proveer

presente	pret. ind.	
proveo	proveí	**gerundio**
provees	proveíste	proveyendo
provee	proveyó	
proveemos	proveímos	**participio**
proveéis	proveísteis	provisto
proveen	proveyeron	

pudrir *see* **podrir**

querer

presente	pret. ind.	futuro	condicional	imperativo
quiero	quise	querré	querría	
quieres	quisiste	querrás	querrías	quiere
quiere	quiso	querrá	querría	quiera
queremos	quisimos	querremos	querríamos	queramos
queréis	quisisteis	querréis	querríais	quered
quieren	quisieron	querrán	querrían	quieran

gerundio	participio
queriendo	querido

raer

presente	pret. ind.	
raigo/rao	raí	**gerundio**
raes	raíste	rayendo
rae	rayó	
raemos	raímos	**participio**
raéis	raísteis	raído
raen	rayeron	

reír

presente	pret. ind.	imperativo	
río	reí		**gerundio**
ríes	reíste	ríe	riendo
ríe	rió	ría	
reímos	reímos	riamos	**participio**
reís	reísteis	reíd	reído
ríen	rieron	rían	

reunir

presente	imperativo	
reúno		**gerundio**
reúnes	reúne	reuniendo
reúne	reúna	
reunimos	reunamos	**participio**
reunís	reunid	reunido
reúnen	reúnan	

roer

presente	pret. ind.	subj. pres.	subj. imp.	subj. fut.
roo/roigo	roí	roa/roiga	royera/-ese	royere
roes	roíste	roas/roigas	royeras/-eses	royeres
roe	royó	roa/roiga	royera/-ese	royere
roemos	roímos	roamos/roiga-mos/royamos	royéramos/-ésemos	royéremos
roéis	roísteis	roáis/roigáis/royáis	royerais/-eseis	royereis
roen	royeron	roan/roigan	royeran/-esen	royeren

imperativo

	gerundio
roe	royendo
roa/roiga	
roamos/roigamos	**participio**
roed	roído
roan/roigan	

saber

presente	pret. ind.	futuro	condicional	subj. pres.
sé	supe	sabré	sabría	sepa
sabes	supiste	sabrás	sabrías	sepas
sabe	supo	sabrá	sabría	sepa
sabemos	supimos	sabremos	sabríamos	sepamos
sabéis	supisteis	sabréis	sabríais	sepáis
saben	supieron	sabrán	sabrían	sepan

imperativo

	gerundio
sabe	sabiendo
sepa	
sepamos	**participio**
sabed	sabido
sepan	

salir

presente	futuro	condicional	imperativo	
salgo	saldré	saldría		**gerundio**
sales	saldrás	saldrías	sal	saliendo
sale	saldrá	saldría	salga	
salimos	saldremos	saldríamos	salgamos	**participio**
salís	saldréis	saldríais	salid	salido
salen	saldrán	saldrían	salgan	

seguir

presente	pret. ind.	subj. pres.	subj. imp.	subj. fut.
sigo	seguí	siga	siguiera/-ese	siguiere
sigues	seguiste	sigas	siguieras/-eses	siguieres
sigue	siguió	siga	siguiera/-ese	siguiere
seguimos	seguimos	sigamos	siguéramos/-ésemos	siguiéremos
seguís	seguisteis	sigáis	siguierais/-eseis	siguiereis
siguen	siguieron	sigan	siguieran/-esen	siguieren

imperativo

	gerundio
sigue	siguiendo
siga	
sigamos	**participio**
seguid	seguido
sigan	

sentir

presente	pret. ind.	subj. pres.	subj. imp.	subj. fut.
siento	sentí	sienta	sintiera/-ese	sintiere
sientes	sentiste	sientas	sintieras/-eses	sintieres
siente	sintió	sienta	sintiera/-ese	sintiere
sentimos	sentimos	sintamos	sintiéramos/-ésemos	sintiéremos
sentís	sentisteis	sintáis	sintierais/-eseis	sintiereis
sienten	sintieron	sientan	sintieran/-esen	sintieren

imperativo

	gerundio
siente	sintiendo
sienta	
sintamos	**participio**
sentid	sentido
sientan	

ser

presente	imperfecto	pret. ind.	futuro	
soy	era	fui	seré	**gerundio**
eres	eras	fuiste	serás	siendo
es	era	fue	será	
somos	éramos	fuimos	seremos	**participio**
sois	erais	fuisteis	seréis	sido
son	eran	fueron	serán	

condicional	subj. pres.	subj. imp.	subj. fut.	imperativo
sería	sea	fuera/-ese	fuere	
serías	seas	fueras/-eses	fueres	sé
sería	sea	fuera/-ese	fuere	sea
seríamos	seamos	fuéramos/-ésemos	fuéremos	seamos
seríais	seáis	fuerais/-eseis	fuereis	sed
serían	sean	fueran/-esen	fueren	sean

soltar

presente	imperativo	
suelto		**gerundio**
sueltas	suelta	soltando
suelta	suelte	
soltamos	soltemos	**participio**
soltáis	soltad	soltado
sueltan	suelten	

tener

presente	pret. ind.	futuro	condicional	imperativo
tengo	tuve	tendré	tendría	
tienes	tuviste	tendrás	tendrías	ten
tiene	tuvo	tendrá	tendría	tenga
tenemos	tuvimos	tendremos	tendríamos	tengamos
tenéis	tuvisteis	tendréis	tendríais	tened
tienen	tuvieron	tendrán	tendrían	tengan

gerundio	participio
teniendo	tenido

traducir

presente	pret. ind.	imperativo	
traduzco	traduje		**gerundio**
traduces	tradujiste	traduce	traduciendo
traduce	tradujo	traduzca	
traducimos	tradujimos	traduzcamos	**participio**
traducís	tradujisteis	traducid	traducido
traducen	tradujeron	traduzcan	

traer

presente	pret. ind.	imperativo	
traigo	traje		**gerundio**
traes	trajiste	trae	trayendo
trae	trajo	traiga	
traemos	trajimos	traigamos	**participio**
traéis	trajisteis	traed	traído
traen	trajeron	traigan	

valer

presente	futuro	imperativo	
valgo	valdré		**gerundio**
vales	valdrás	vale	valiendo
vale	valdrá	valga	
valemos	valdremos	valgamos	**participio**
valéis	valdréis	valed	valido
valen	valdrán	valgan	

venir

presente	pret. ind.	futuro	condicional	imperativo
vengo	vine	vendré	vendría	
vienes	viniste	vendrás	vendrías	ven
viene	vino	vendrá	vendría	venga
venimos	vinimos	vendremos	vendríamos	vengamos
venís	vinisteis	vendréis	vendríais	venid
vienen	vinieron	vendrán	vendrían	vengan

gerundio	participio
viniendo	venido

ver

presente	imperfecto	pret. ind.	subj. imp.	subj. fut.
veo	veía	vi	viera/-ese	viere
ves	veías	viste	vieras/-eses	vieres
ve	veía	vio	viera/-ese	viere
vemos	veíamos	vimos	viéramos/-ésemos	viéremos
veis	veíais	visteis	vierais/-eseis	viereis
ven	veían	vieron	vieran/-esen	vieren

gerundio	participio
viendo	visto

volcar

presente	pret. ind.	imperativo	
vuelco	volqué		**gerundio**
vuelcas	volcaste	vuelca	volcando
vuelca	volcó	vuelque	
volcamos	volcamos	volquemos	**participio**
volcáis	volcasteis	volcad	volcado
vuelcan	volcaron	vuelquen	

volver

presente	imperativo	
vuelvo		**gerundio**
vuelves	vuelve	volviendo
vuelve	vuelva	
volvemos	volvamos	**participio**
volvéis	volved	vuelto
vuelven	vuelvan	

yacer

presente	subj. pres.	imperativo	
yazco/yazgo/yago	yazca/yazga/yaga		**gerundio** yaciendo
yaces	yazcas/yazgas/yagas	yace/yaz	
yace	yazca/yazga/yaga	yazca/yazga/yaga	
yacemos	yazcamos/yazgamos/yagamos	yazcamos/yazgamos/yagamos	**participio** yacido
yacéis	yazcáis/yazgáis/yagáis	yaced	
yacen	yazcan/yazgan/yagan	yazcan/yazgan/yagan	

Breve gramática de la lengua inglesa
Concise English Grammar

I. Sustantivos

En inglés, el **género** del sustantivo coincide con el género natural. Esto sólo puede apreciarse en los pronombres personales, ya que el artículo que acompaña al sustantivo es siempre el mismo.

the boy	**he**	él
the girl	**she**	ella
the book	**it**	ello

Por lo general, los nombres de barcos son femeninos. También suelen recibir un pronombre femenino los países, coches y aviones.

Para formar el **plural** se añade una **-s** al sustantivo en singular. Esta **s** es sonora [z] si aparece después de vocales y consonantes sonoras:

day**s**	días
dog**s**	perros
boy**s**	chicos

Y sorda [s], después de consonantes sordas:

book**s**	libros
hat**s**	sombreros

En las palabras que terminan en **-ce, -ge, -se, -ze**, la **-e**, que en singular es muda, pasa a pronunciarse como una [i]:

pie**ces**	pedazos
si**zes**	tamaños

Las palabras que terminan en sonido sibilante (**s, ss, sh, ch, x, z**) añaden **-es** [iz] para formar el plural:

bo**xes**	cajas
bo**sses**	jefes

Las palabras terminadas en **y** precedidas por una consonante cambian la **y** a **i** para formar el plural en **-ies** [iz]:

lady	lad**ies**	señoras
body	bod**ies**	cuerpos

También suelen añadir **-es** para formar el plural las palabras terminadas en **-o** precedida de una consonante:

tomat**oes**	tomates
her**oes**	héroes

Algunas palabras terminadas en *-f* o *-fe* forman el plural con la terminación *-ves*:

Singular	Plural	
half	hal**ves**	mitades
knife	kni**ves**	cuchillos
leaf	lea**ves**	hojas
wife	wi**ves**	esposas

Otras palabras cambian de vocal o vocales:

Singular	Plural	
foot	f**ee**t	pies
man	m**e**n	hombres
woman	wom**e**n	mujeres

En la parte del inglés al español del diccionario se incluye la formación de los plurales irregulares, así como los terminados en *-ves, -oes, -os*.

Nominativo/complemento directo/complemento indirecto/genitivo

El nominativo y el complemento directo tienen la misma forma. El genitivo se construye generalmente con la preposición *of* y el objeto indirecto, con la preposición *to*.

- El **objeto indirecto** también puede formarse sin *to*, cuando no es necesario resaltarlo. En este caso, el objeto indirecto se coloca inmediatamente después del verbo:

	She gave the man the ticket.
en lugar de:	She gave the ticket **to** the man.

- El **genitivo sajón**, de uso frecuente para determinar la posesión de personas y conceptos personificados, es la otra variante para formar el genitivo en inglés. Se construye anteponiendo el poseedor al sustantivo definido. En singular se añade un **apóstrofo** y una *s* al poseedor:

my sister**'s** room	la habitación de mi hermana

Y en **plural**, únicamente el **apóstrofo**:

my sister**s'** room	la habitación de mis hermanas

Las palabras del tipo: *shop, church, cathedral*, etc., suelen omitirse tras el genitivo sajón:

at the butcher's	*en lugar de:*	at the butcher's shop	en la carnicería
St. Paul's	*en lugar de:*	St. Paul's Cathedral	la catedral de Saint Paul

II. Adjetivos

Los adjetivos aportan información sobre el sustantivo al que acompañan. Califican o clasifican el sustantivo (p. ej. a *sunny* day, *financial* problems), informan del color (a *blue* shirt) o enfatizan (an *utter* flop).

1. Determinantes demostrativos

Los determinantes demostrativos se refieren al sustantivo de manera determinada. Para sustantivos cercanos al hablante, ya sea en el tiempo o en el espacio, se usan *this* y *these*.

| **this** hat | **this** year | este sombrero | este año |
| **these** pants | **these** days | estos pantalones | estos días |

Para sustantivos que se hallan más lejanos en el tiempo o en el espacio se usan *that* y *those*.

| that man | that party | ese hombre | esa fiesta |
| those children | those celebrations | esos niños | esas festividades |

2. Determinantes posesivos

Existen además los determinantes posesivos, que expresan pertenencia, o bien la relación entre el sustantivo y alguien.

my	book	mi libro	**my**	books	mis libros
your	book	tu libro; su libro	**your**	books	tus/sus libros
his	book	su libro	**his**	books	sus libros
her	book	su libro	**her**	books	sus libros
its	application	su aplicación	**its**	applications	sus aplicación
our	car	nuestro coche	**our**	cars	nuestros coches
your	car	vuestro coche; su coche	**your**	cars	vuestros coches; sus coches
their	car	su coche	**their**	cars	sus coches

En inglés la terminación del adjetivo no varía aunque cambie de género o de número.

3. Los grados del adjetivo

Los adjetivos regulares de una sílaba añaden la terminación -*er* para formar el comparativo, y -*est* para formar el superlativo.

| small | small**er** (than) | (the) small**est** |
| pequeño | más pequeño, -a (que) | (el/la/lo) más pequeño, -a |

- Los adjetivos terminados en -*e*, añaden solamente -*r*, -*st*, sin la *e:* fin**e**, fin**er**, fin**est**.
- Las consonantes finales *d, g, n, t* se duplican al añadir -*er*, -*est* cuando van precedidas de las vocales cortas y acentuadas *a, e, i, o:* big, bi**gger**, bi**ggest**.

Los adjetivos de dos o más sílabas forman el comparativo anteponiendo la palabra *more* (más), y el superlativo añadiendo *most* (más).

| difficult | **more** difficult (than) | (the) **most** difficult |
| difícil | más difícil (que) | (el/la/lo) más difícil |

4. Adjetivos irregulares

good	better (than)	(the) best
bueno	mejor (que)	(el/la/lo) mejor

bad	worse (than)	(the) worst
malo	peor (que)	(el/la/lo) peor

much/many	more (than)	(the) most
mucho/muchos	más (que)	(el/la/lo) más

little	less (than)	(the) least
poco	menos (que)	(el/la/lo) menos

Los adjetivos con formas comparativas o superlativas irregulares aparecen en la parte del inglés al español del diccionario.

III. Adverbios

Los adverbios se forman añadiendo -*ly* a un adjetivo.

slow	slowly	He speaks slowly.	Habla despacio.
quick	quickly	He runs quickly.	Corre deprisa.

• Una excepción es **well**, el adverbio de **good** (bueno).

He speaks English well.	Habla bien inglés.

• Los adverbios terminados en -*ly* forman el comparativo con **more** y el superlativo con **most**.

slowly	more slowly	most slowly
despacio	más despacio	lo más despacio

IV. Verbos

1. Presente

Infinitivo: (base)		to talk	to call	to go	to wash	to study
		hablar	llamar	ir	lavar	estudiar
I	(yo)	talk	call	go	wash	study
you	(tú, usted)	talk	call	go	wash	study
he	(él)					
she	(ella)	talks	calls	goes	washes	studies
it	(ello)					
we	(nosotros, -as)	talk	call	go	wash	study
you	(vosotros, -as, ustedes)	talk	call	go	wash	study
they	(ellos, ellas)	talk	call	go	wash	study

Sólo cambia la tercera persona del singular.

La -s es sorda tras consonantes sordas *(he talks)* y sonora si va precedida de vocales *(he goes)* o de consonantes sonoras *(he calls)*.

2. Pasado y participio perfecto

El pasado se forma añadiendo -ed a la base del verbo.

Infinitivo: (base)	to open	to arrive	to stop	to carry
	abrir	llegar	parar	llevar
I, you, he, she, it, we, you, they	opened	arrived	stopped	carried

- Los verbos terminados en -e añaden -d solamente: agreed, arrived.
- La -y se transforma en -ied: tried, carried.
- Las consonantes finales b, d, g, m, n, p, s, t se duplican si van precedidas de vocal corta acentuada: fitted, stopped.
- En inglés británico, los verbos de más de una sílaba terminados en l suelen duplicar la consonante final: travel, travelled.
- El participio perfecto se forma añadiendo la misma terminación que en el pasado:

opened	arrived	stopped	carried
abierto	llegado	parado	llevado

Las formas de los **verbos irregulares** se incluyen en una lista aparte (v. pág. 691–695).

V. Los verbos auxiliares

1. Presente y participio de presente (gerundio)

Infinitivo: (base)	to be	to have	to do
	ser, estar	tener	hacer
I	am	have	do
	yo soy, estoy	yo tengo	yo hago
you	are	have	do
	tú eres, estás usted es, está	tú tienes usted tiene	tú haces usted hace
he/she/it	is	has	does
	él/ella/ello es, está	él/ella/ello tiene	él/ella/ello hace
we	are	have	do
	nosotros, -as somos, estamos	nosotros, -as tenemos	nosotros, -as hacemos
you	are	have	do
	vosotros, -as sois, estáis ustedes son, están	vosotros, -as tenéis ustedes tienen	vosotros, -as hacéis ustedes hacen
they	are	have	do
	ellos/ellas son, están	ellos/ellas tienen	ellos/ellas hacen
	being	having	doing
Gerundio:	siendo	teniendo	haciendo

En inglés hablado se suelen utilizar formas abreviadas:

am	→ 'm	I'm
are	→ 're	you're
is	→ 's	he's
have	→ 've	I've
has	→ 's	he's

Negación	Forma abreviada
are not	aren't
is not	isn't
have not	haven't
has not	hasn't
do not	don't
does not	doesn't

2. Pasado y participio perfecto

Infinitivo: (base)	to be / ser, estar	to have / tener	to do / hacer
I	was / yo fui, era, estuve, estaba	had / yo tuve, tenía	did / yo hice, hacía
you	were / tú fuiste, eras, estuviste, estabas; usted fue, era, usted estuvo, estaba	had / tú tuviste, tenías; usted tuvo, tenía	did / tú hiciste, hacías; usted hizo, hacía
he/she/it	was / él/ella/ello fue, era, estuvo, estaba	had / él/ella/ello tuvo, tenía	did / él/ella/ello hizo, hacía
we	were / nosotros, -as fuimos, éramos, estuvimos, estábamos	had / nosotros, -as tuvimos teníamos	did / nosotros, -as hicimos, hacíamos
you	were / vosotros, -as fuisteis, erais, estuvisteis, estabais; ustedes fueron, eran, estuvieron, estaban	had / vosotros, -as tuvisteis, teníais; ustedes tuvieron, tenían	did / vosotros, -as hicisteis, hacíais; ustedes hicieron, hacían
they	were / ellos/ellas fueron, eran, estuvieron, estaban	had / ellos/ellas tuvieron, tenían	did / ellos/ellas hicieron, hacían
Participio:	been / sido, estado	had / tenido	done / hecho
Forma abreviada:		'd	
Negación:	wasn't / weren't	hadn't	didn't

3. Presente perfecto

El presente perfecto se forma con el verbo auxiliar *have* (haber) + participio perfecto.

I **have** had	yo he tenido
I **have** been	yo he sido, yo he estado
I **have** done	yo he hecho
I **have** called	yo he llamado
I **have** arrived	yo he llegado
I **have** gone	yo he ido

4. Pluscuamperfecto

El pluscuamperfecto se construye con *had* (forma de pasado de *have*) + participio perfecto.

I **had** had	yo había tenido
I **had** been	yo había sido, yo había estado
I **had** done	yo había hecho
I **had** called	yo había llamado
I **had** arrived	yo había llegado
I **had** gone	yo había ido

5. Verbos auxiliares

Son verbos que no pueden funcionar de forma independiente, sino que acompañan siempre a otro verbo (en infinitivo sin *to*).

I, you, he, she, it, we, you, they	can	may	shall	will	must
	poder (capacidad)	poder (permiso)	deber, forma de futuro	querer, forma de futuro	deber
Negación:	**cannot**	**must not**	**shall not**	**will not**	**need not**
Forma abreviada:	**can't**	**mustn't**	**shan't**	**won't**	**needn't**

Estos verbos son iguales en todas las personas: la tercera persona del singular **no añade -s**.

Pasado		Alternativa	
could	pudo, podía	to be able (to)	ser capaz (de)
might	podría	to be allowed (to)	tener permiso (para)
would	forma de condicional	to want, to wish (to)	querer, desear
should	debería	to be obliged (to)	verse obligado (a)

Negación:	**could not**	**might not**	**would not**	**should not**
Forma abreviada:	**couldn't**	**mightn't**	**wouldn't**	**shouldn't**

- Las formas de pasado, idénticas a las del condicional, se utilizan en tono formal:

Could you give me...?	¿Me podría dar...?
Would you..., please.	Por favor, le ruego que...
Would you like...?	¿Desearía...?
I **should** like...	Me gustaría...

6. Futuro y condicional

El futuro se forma con **_shall/will_** (primera persona del singular y del plural) y **_will_** para el resto de personas. Para el condicional se emplean **_should/would_** (primera persona del singular y del plural) y **_would_** para el resto. En el lenguaje oral se utiliza casi únicamente la forma abreviada.

Futuro		Condicional	
I **shall/will** go	yo iré	I **should/would** go	yo iría
you **will** go	tú irás; usted irá	you **would** go	tú irías; usted iría
he/she/it **will** go	él/ella/ello irá	he/she/it **would** go	él/ella/ello iría
we **shall/will** go	nosotros, -as iremos	we **should/would** go	nosotros, -as iríamos
you **will** go	vosotros, -as iréis; ustedes irán	you **would** go	vosotros, -as iríais; ustedes irían
they **will** go	ellos/ellas irán	they **would** go	ellos/ellas irían
Forma abreviada:	I'**ll** go, you'**ll** go, he'**ll** go ... I'**d** go, you'**d** go, he'**d** go ...		

7. Pregunta y negación con *do*

El verbo auxiliar **_do_** se utiliza para la creación de las formas interrogativa y negativa (en la que se añade **_not_**) de los verbos principales.

Do you speak Spanish? **Does** he know? **Did** you call?	¿Hablas español?, ¿Habla usted español? ¿Lo sabe? ¿Has llamado?, ¿Ha llamado usted?
I **do not (don't)** speak Spanish. He **does not (doesn't)** know. I **did not (didn't)** call.	No hablo español. No lo sabe. No he llamado.
Didn't he come? **Didn't** she call?	¿No ha venido él? ¿No ha llamado ella?

- **_do_** no se utiliza para las preguntas en las que la partícula interrogativa es el propio sujeto de la oración:

Who wrote the letter?	¿Quién escribió la carta?
Which of these trains goes to Chicago?	¿Cuál de estos trenes va a Chicago?

Tampoco se utiliza en las oraciones que contienen los verbos auxiliares:

am, are, is, was, were, can, could, may, might, must, shall, should, will, would

8. Presente continuo

Este tiempo verbal se forma con el verbo auxiliar **_be_** y el participio de presente (**_-ing_**). El presente continuo sirve para expresar una acción que transcurre en este momento, que todavía se está produciendo o que no ha/había/habrá concluido.

I **am** work**ing**.	Estoy trabajando.
I **was** work**ing**.	Estaba trabajando.
I **shall** be work**ing**.	Estaré trabajando.
It **is** rain**ing**.	Está lloviendo.

- Los verbos terminados en -*e* pierden esta vocal: arrive, arriv**ing**.
- Los verbos terminados en -*ie* cambian esta terminación a *y:* lie, l**ying**.
- Para la duplicación de consonantes finales se aplican las mismas reglas que para la formación del pasado: stop, sto**pping**; tug, tu**gging**.
- La forma *be going to* designa una certeza en el presente acerca de una acción prevista que se va a producir en el futuro.

I **am going to** go to New York next week.	Voy a ir a Nueva York la semana que viene.
She **is going to** buy a new dress.	Se va a comprar un vestido nuevo.

9. Gerundio

El gerundio (verbo + -*ing*) es la forma sustantivada del infinitivo.
En español se utiliza el infinitivo para estos casos.

Smoking is dangerous.	Fumar es peligroso.

10. Voz pasiva

Para construir la voz pasiva se utiliza el auxiliar *be* y el participio perfecto.
La voz pasiva es más frecuente en inglés que en español.

The doctor examines Peter.	Peter **is examined** (by the doctor).
El doctor examina a Peter.	Peter es examinado (por el doctor).
Somebody stole my bike.	My bike **was stolen**.
Alguien ha robado mi bicicleta.	Mi bicicleta ha sido robada.

VI. Pronombres

1. Pronombres personales

Sujeto		Objeto	
I	yo	**me**	me/mí
you	tú; usted	**you**	te/ti; le
he	él	**him**	le/lo
she	ella	**her**	le/la
it	ello	**it**	le/lo
we	nosotros, nosotras	**us**	nos/nosotros, nosotras
you	vosotros, vosotras; ustedes	**you**	os/vosotros, vosotras; les
they	ellos, ellas	**them**	les

- *to* se puede añadir al complemento indirecto cuando se desee resaltar el pronombre:

I gave the book **to** him.	Le di el libro a él.
en lugar de: I gave him the book.	Le di el libro.

2. Pronombres Posesivos

Los pronombres posesivos toman las mismas formas tanto para el singular como para el plural.

mine	mío, mía, míos, mías
yours	tuyo, tuya, tuyos, tuyas; suyo, suya, suyos, suyas
his	suyo, suya, suyos, suyas
hers	suyo,suya, suyos, suyas
ours	nuestro, nuestra, nuestros, nuestras
yours	vuestro, vuestra, vuestros, vuestras; suyo, suya, suyos, suyas
theirs	suyo, suya, suyos, suyas

It's not my book. It's **yours**.	No es mi libro. Es tuyo.

3. Pronombres Demostrativos

En inglés, a diferencia del español, las formas de los demostrativos para las funciones adjetival y pronominal son las mismas.

Singular:	**this**	Plural:	**these**
Adj.:	este, esta		estos, estas
Pron.:	éste, ésta, esto		éstos, éstas
	that		**those**
Adj.:	ese, esa		esos, esas
	aquel, aquella		aquellos, aquellas
Pron.:	ése, ésa, eso		ésos, ésas
	aquél, aquélla, aquello		aquéllos, aquéllas

This is an English book and **that** is a Spanish book.
Éste es un libro inglés y ése es un libro español.

These pictures are nicer than **those**.
Estas fotos son más bonitas que aquéllas.

4. Pronombres reflexivos

myself	me	ourselves	nos
yourself	te; se	yourselves	os; se
himself	se	themselves	se
herself	se		
itself	se		
I enjoy **myself**.	Yo me divierto.		
You enjoy **yourself**.	Tú te diviertes; usted se divierte.		
He enjoys **himself**.	Él se divierte.		
She enjoys **herself**.	Ella se divierte.		
We enjoy **ourselves**.	Nosotros, -as nos divertimos.		
You enjoy **yourselves**.	Vosotros, -as os divertís; ustedes se divierten.		
They enjoy **themselves**.	Ellos/ellas se divierten.		

5. Pronombres relativos

	Personas	Cosas	Personas o cosas
Nominativo (¿Quién? ¿Qué?)	who	which	that
Genitivo (¿De quién?)	whose	of which	
Complemento indirecto (¿A quién?)	to whom	to which	
Complemento directo (¿A quién? ¿Qué?)	whom/who	which	that

El pronombre relativo tiene la misma forma en singular y en plural.
* El complemento directo *that* puede omitirse:

This is the strangest book (**that**) I have ever read.
Este es el libro más extraño que he leído nunca.

6. Partículas interrogativas
Función pronominal (independientes)

who?	¿quién?	**Who** are you?	¿Quién es usted?
whose?	¿de quién?	**Whose** car is this?	¿De quién es este coche?
whom?/who?	¿a quién?	**Who(m)** did you help?	¿A quién has ayudado?
		Who(m) did you see?	¿A quién has visto?
what?	¿qué?	**What** is that?	¿Qué es eso?
which?	¿cuál?	**Which** is the quickest way?	¿Cuál es el camino más rápido?

who/whose/whom se utilizan para preguntar por personas, *what* pregunta por cosas y *which*, por personas o cosas de un grupo determinado.

• Las preposiciones se colocan al final de la pregunta:

Where do you come **from**?	¿De dónde eres?
What are you looking **for**?	¿Qué buscas?
What do you want this **for**?	¿Para qué quieres esto?
What are you laughing **at**?	¿De qué te ríes?
Who are you speaking **to**?	¿Con quién hablas?

Función adjetival (unidas a un sustantivo)

What book?	¿Qué libro?
What English songs?	¿Qué canciones inglesas?
Which book?	¿Qué libro? (¿cuál de ellos?)

Los pronombres indefinidos: *some* y *any*
some/somebody/someone/something

some y sus compuestos aparecen:
1. en oraciones afirmativas,
2. en oraciones interrogativas para las que se espera una respuesta afirmativa.

1.	I'd like **some** strawberry jam.
	Me gustaría tomar mermelada de fresa.
	Give me **some** stamps, please.
	Déme unos sellos, por favor.
	Somebody/Someone has stolen my wallet.
	Alguien me ha robado la cartera.
	I'd like **something** to drink.
	Me gustaría tomar algo.
2.	May I have **some** more tea, please? – Yes, of course.
	¿Podría tomar otro poco de té, por favor? – Por supuesto.

any/anybody/anyone/anything

any y sus compuestos se emplean en:
1. oraciones negativas,
2. oraciones interrogativas para las que la respuesta es incierta,
3. oraciones condicionales.

1.	I haven't got **any** friends in Chicago.
	No tengo amigos en Chicago.
2.	Is there **anybody/anyone** here who speaks Spanish?
	¿Hay alguien aquí que hable español?
	Have you got **any** stamps?
	¿Tiene usted sellos?
	Can I do **anything** for you?
	¿Puedo ayudarle en algo?
3.	If I had **any** stamps I would mail the letter.
	Si tuviera sellos, enviaría la carta.

Los verbos irregulares ingleses
English irregular verbs

Infinitive	Past	Past Participle
abide	abode, abided	abode, abided
arise	arose	arisen
awake	awoke	awaked, awoken
be	was *sing*, were *pl*	been
bear	bore	borne, born
beat	beat	beaten
become	became	become
beget	begot	begotten
begin	began	begun
behold	beheld	beheld
bend	bent	bent
beseech	besought, beseeched	besought
beset	beset	beset
bet	bet, betted	bet, betted
bid	bade, bid	bid, bidden
bind	bound	bound
bite	bit	bitten
bleed	bled	bled
blow	blew	blown
break	broke	broken
breed	bred	bred
bring	brought	brought
build	built	built
burn	burned, burnt	burned, burnt
burst	burst	burst
buy	bought	bought
can	could	-
cast	cast	cast
catch	caught	caught
choose	chose	chosen
cleave *(cut)*	cleft, cleaved, clove	cleft, cleaved, cloven
cling	clung	clung
come	came	come
cost	cost, costed	cost, costed
creep	crept	crept
cut	cut	cut
deal	dealt	dealt
dig	dug	dug
dive	dived, dove	dived

Infinitive	Past	Past Participle
do	did	done
draw	drew	drawn
dream	dreamed, dreamt	dreamed, dreamt
drink	drank	drunk
drive	drove	driven
dwell	dwelt, dwelled	dwelt, dwelled
eat	ate	eaten
fall	fell	fallen
feed	fed	fed
feel	felt	felt
fight	fought	fought
find	found	found
flee	fled	fled
fling	flung	flung
fly	flew	flown
forbid	forbade, forbad	forbidden, forbid
forget	forgot	forgotten
forsake	forsook	forsaken
freeze	froze	frozen
get	got	gotten, got
gild	gilded, gilt	gilded, gilt
gird	girded, girt	girded, girt
give	gave	given
go	went	gone
grind	ground	ground
grow	grew	grown
hang	hung, LAW hanged	hung, LAW hanged
have	had	had
hear	heard	heard
heave	heaved, hove	heaved, hove
hew	hewed	hewn, hewed
hide	hid	hidden
hit	hit	hit
hold	held	held
hurt	hurt	hurt
keep	kept	kept
kneel	knelt, kneeled	knelt, kneeled
know	knew	known
lade	laded	laden, laded
lay	laid	laid
lead	led	led
leap	leaped, leapt	leaped, leapt

Infinitive	Past	Past Participle
learn	learned, learnt	learned, learnt
leave	left	left
lend	lent	lent
let	let	let
lie	lay	lain
light	lighted, lit	lighted, lit
lose	lost	lost
make	made	made
may	might	-
mean	meant	meant
meet	met	met
mistake	mistook	mistaken
mow	mowed	mown, mowed
pay	paid	paid
put	put	put
quit	quit, quitted	quit, quitted
read [rid]	read [red]	read [red]
rend	rent, rended	rent, rended
rid	rid, ridded	rid, ridded
ride	rode	ridden
ring	rang	rung
rise	rose	risen
run	ran	run
saw	sawed	sawed, sawn
say	said	said
see	saw	seen
seek	sought	sought
sell	sold	sold
send	sent	sent
set	set	set
sew	sewed	sewn, sewed
shake	shook	shaken
shave	shaved	shaved, shaven
shear	sheared	sheared, shorn
shed	shed	shed
shine	shone, shined	shone, shined
shit	shit, *iron* shat	shit, *iron* shat
shoe	shod	shod, shodden
shoot	shot	shot
show	showed	shown, showed
shrink	shrank, shrunk	shrunk, shrunken
shut	shut	shut

Infinitive	Past	Past Participle
sing	sang, sung	sung
sink	sank, sunk	sunk
sit	sat	sat
sleep	slept	slept
slide	slid	slid
sling	slung	slung
slink	slunk	slunk
slit	slit	slit
smell	smelled, smelt	smelled, smelt
smite	smote	smitten, smote
sow	sowed	sown, sowed
speak	spoke	spoken
speed	sped, speeded	sped, speeded
spell	spelled, spelt	spelled, spelt
spend	spent	spent
spill	spilled, spilt	spilled, spilt
spin	spun	spun
spit	spat, spit	spat, spit
split	split	split
spoil	spoiled, spoilt	spoiled, spoilt
spread	spread	spread
spring	sprang, sprung	sprung
stand	stood	stood
steal	stole	stolen
stick	stuck	stuck
sting	stung	stung
stink	stank, stunk	stunk
strew	strewed	strewn, strewed
stride	strode	stridden
strike	struck	struck
string	strung	strung
strive	strove	striven, strived
swear	swore	sworn
sweep	swept	swept
swell	swelled	swollen, swelled
swim	swam	swum
swing	swung	swung
take	took	taken
teach	taught	taught
tear	tore	torn
tell	told	told
think	thought	thought

Infinitive	Past	Past Participle
thrive	thrived, throve	thrived, thriven
throw	threw	thrown
thrust	thrust	thrust
tread	trod	trodden, trod
wake	woke, waked	waked, woken
wear	wore	worn
weave	wove	woven
weep	wept	wept
win	won	won
wind	wound	wound
wring	wrung	wrung
write	wrote	written

Prefixes and Suffixes: Spanish-English
Prefijos y Sufijos: Español – Inglés

Spanish Prefixes and Combining Forms
Prefijos y Elementos de Compuestos españoles

Prefix	English Equivalents	Meanings and Uses	Examples	English equivalents
a-[1]	a-	lack of; negation	ateísmo	atheism
a-[2]	a-	var. of ad-	afirmar	to afirm
a-[3]	–	to make, cause to become	abaratar, ablandar	to make cheaper, to soften
ab-	ab-	away from	abjurar	to renounce, abjure
abs-	abs-	variant of ab- before c, t	abstraer	to abstract
ac-	ac-	variant of ad- before c	acceso	access
acro-	acro-	1) hight 2) extreme	1) acróbata 2) acrónimo	1) acrobat 2) acronym
ad-	ad-	indicates direction; tendency; proximity, contact	adosar admirar adjunto	to put or place against to admire enclosed
aero-	air-	air	aerolínea	airline
afro-	Afro-	related to Africa	afrocaribeño	Afro-Caribbean
agri-, agro-	agri-, agro-	field	agricultura agronomía	agriculture agronomy
alti-, alto-	alti-, alto-	high	altitud altoparlante	altitude loudspeaker
ambi-	ambi-	1) two, both 2) around	1) ambivalente 2) ambiente	1) ambivalent 2) surroundings, environment
an-	an-	1) without; var. of a- before vowels 2) variant of ana- before vowels	1) anarquía 2) ánodo	1) anarchy 2) anode
ana-	ana-	1) up 2) in accordance	1) anatema 2) analogía	1) anathema 2) analogy
andro-	andro-	male, man	androfobia	androphobia
anfi-	amphi-	1) around 2) double, of both kinds	1) anfiteatro 2) anfibio	1) amphitheater 2) amphibian
anglo-	Anglo-	of English, England	angloamericano	Anglo-American
ant-	ant-	variant of anti-	antagonista	antagonist m antagonistic adj
ante-	–	indicates anteriority 1) in time: prior to 2) in space: in front of	1) anteanoche antecedente 2) antebrazo	1) the night before last antecedent 2) forearm

Prefix	English Equivalents	Meanings and Uses	Examples	English equivalents
anti-	anti-	1) opposed 2) not 3) protection against 4) MED prevention of 5) fight against	1) antisocial 2) antinatural 3) anticongelante 4) antiinflamatorio 5) antiterrorista	1) antisocial 2) unnatural 3) antifreeze 4) anti-inflammatory 5) antiterrorist
antropo-	anthropo-	man, human being	antropología antropófago	anthropology cannibal
apo-	apo-	outside of, far from	apogeo	apogee
archi-	arch- very, super	Indicates: 1) superiority, preeminence 2) very	1) arzobispo 2) archisabido	1) archbishop 2) very well-known
arque-	arche-	var. of archi-	arquetipo	archetype
arqueo-	archeo-	ancient	arqueólogo	archeologist
arqui-	archi-	var. of archi-	arquitectura	architecture
artro-	arthro-, arthr-	joint	artrosis artritis	arthrosis arthritis
aster-	aster-	var. of astro-	asteroide	asteroid
astro-	astro-	1) star 2) outer space	1) astrología 2) astronauta	1) astrology 2) astronaut
atto-	atto-	10^{-18}, one quintillionth	attogramo	attogramm
audi(o)-	audi(o)-	sound, hearing	audífono auditorio	hearing aid audience
auto-[1]	auto-, self-	1) self 2) on its own	1) autobiografía autocensura 2) autómata	1) autobiography self-censorship 2) automatic device
auto-[2]	driving	pertaining to driving	autoescuela	driving school
ben(e)-	bene-	well, good	beneficioso	beneficial
bi-	two-, bi- semi-, twice bi-	1) two 2) twice 3) every two	1) bicolor, bípedo 2) bimensual 3) biennal	1) two-color, biped 2) semi-monthly, twice monthly 3) biennial
biblio-	biblio-, libr-	referring to books	bibliografía, biblioteca	bibliography library
bio-	bio-	relating to life	biología	biology
bis-	great-	var. of bi-	bisabuelo	great-grandfather,
biz-	great-	var. of bi-	biznieto	great-grandson
caco-	caco-	bad	cacofonía	cacophony
cardi(o)-	cardi(o)-	relating to the heart	cardiaco cardiovascular	cardiac cardiovascular
cata-	cata-	down downwards	catalogar catarata	to catalog waterfall
cefalo-	cephalo-	head	cefalópodo	cephalopod
cent(i)-	cent(i)-	1) hundredth 2) one hundred	1) centímetro 2) centenario	1) centimeter 2) centennial
centri-	centri-	var. of centro-	centrifugar	to centrifuge
centro-	central	referring to the center	centroamericano	Central American

Prefix	English Equivalents	Meanings and Uses	Examples	English equivalents
cicl(o)-	cyclo	circle, cycle	ciclón cicloturismo	cyclone bicycle touring
circun-, circum-	circum-	around	circunferencia	circumference
cito-	cyto-	cell	citoplasma	cytoplasm
clepto-	klepto-	relating to stealing	cleptómano	kleptomaniac
cloro-	chloro-	green	clorofila	chlorophyll
co-	co-	var. of con-	coexistir	to coexist
com-	com-	var. of con- before b and p	compañero compartir	companion to share
con-	co(n)-	together, cooperation, company	concordar confluir	to coincide to meet
contra-	counter-	1) opposite, against, return 2) support	1) contracorriente contraataque 2) contrafuerte	1) crosscurrent counterattack 2) buttress
cosmo-	cosmo-	1) cosmos 2) world	1) cosmonauta 2) cosmopolita	1) cosmonaut 2) cosmopolitan
cripto-	crypto-	hidden, secret	criptografía	cryptography
crom(o)-	chrom(o)-	color	cromático	chromatic
crono-	chrono-	relating to time	cronológico cronometrar	chronological to time
cuadri-, cuatri-, cuadru-, cuatro	quadr(i)-, quadru-	four	cuadrilátero cuatrimestre cuadrúpedo	quadrilateral four-month period quadruped
dactilo-	–	dedo	dactilógrafo	typist
de-	de-	indicates: 1) direction downwards 2) away, off 3) origin 4) privation, opposite action 5) intensifier	1) decaer 2) defender 3) derivar 4) decrecer deforestación 5) denegar	1) to decline 2) to defend 3) to derive 4) to decrease deforestation 5) to deny
dei-	dei-	god	deificar	to deify
deca-	deca-	ten	decálogo	Decalogue
deci-	deci-	1) tenth (fraction) 2) ten	1) decilitro 2) decimal	1) deciliter 2) decimal
demo-	demo-	people	democracia	democracy
derma-, derm(o)-	derma-, derm(o)-,	skin	dermatólogo	dermatologist
des-	dis-	indicates: 1) opposite action 2) privation 3) excess 4) past, beyond	1) desmontar 2) desacuerdo 3) deslenguado 4) destiempo	1) to disassemble 2) disagreement 3) gossipy 4) wrong moment
di-[1]	di-	twice, double	dicromático	dichromatic

Prefix	English Equivalents	Meanings and Uses	Examples	English equivalents
di-[2]	de-	indicates: opposition, contrariness origin propagation	difamar dimanar difundir	to defame to emanate to spread
dia-	dia-	1) between 2) across, through	1) diálogo 2) diámetro	1) conversation; dialog 2) diameter
dina-	dyna-	power, energy	dinamismo	dynamism
diplo-	diplo-	double	diploide	diploid
dis-	dis-	indicates: 1) anomaly, difficulty 2) opposite 3) separation	1) disfunción 2) discontinuo 3) distender	1) disfunction 2) discontinuous 3) to stretch
e-	e-	1) away from 2) indicates origin	1) eliminar 2) emigración	1) eliminate 2) emigration
eco-	eco-	home, environment ecological	ecosistema ecoturismo	ecosystem agritourism
ecto-	ecto-	outer, external	ectoplasma	ectoplasm
ecue-	eque-	relating to horses	ecuestre	equestrian
ecua-	equa-	even, equal	ecuador ecuación	equator equation
ego-	ego-, self-	I, me	egocéntrico	egocentric, self-centered
electri-, electro-	electri-, electro-	electricity, electrical	electricista electrocardiograma	electrician electrocardiogram
em-	em-, im-	variant of en- before b, p	empobrecer	impoverish
en-	en-	1) in, into 2) on 3) used to form verbs from adjectives and nouns: to become/make	1) encerrar 2) engomar 3) engrasar, ennoblecer	1) to lock in, to enclose 2) to put glue/gel on 3) to grease, to ennoble
endo-	endo-	within, internal	endocalidad endocarpio	inner worth endocarp
entre-	inter-	1) intermediate state, limits the sense of an action 2) between	1) entreabierto entresacar 2) entretiempo, entreacto	ajar, partially open to pick out 2) between season, intermission
epi-	epi-	1) over, above 2) around, outer 3) after	1) epicentro 2) epidermis 3) epílogo	1) epicenter 2) epidermis 3) epilogue
equi-[1]	equi-	equal	equilátero	equilateral
equi-[2]	equi-	horse	equino	equine
esclero-	sclero-	hard	esclerosis	sclerosis
esquizo-	schizo-	split	esquizofrenia	schizophrenia
estereo-	stereo-	1) solid 2) three-dimensional	1) TYPO esteriotipo 2) estereofónico	1) stereotype 2) stereophonic

Prefix	English Equivalents	Meanings and Uses	Examples	English equivalents
etimo-	etymo-	origin	etimología	etymology
etno-	ethno-	people, race	etnología	ethnology
eu-	eu-	good, well	eufemismo	euphemism
ex-[1]	ex-	1) outside, outwards 2) beyond 3) removal	1) exportar 2) exorbitante 3) exfoliar excomulgar	1) to export 2) exorbitant 3) to exfoliate to excommunicate
ex-[2]	ex-	former	exalumno	ex-student
exa-	exa-	10^{18}, one quintillion	exabyte	exabyte
exo-	exo-	outside, external	exótico exoesqueleto	exotic exoskeleton
extra-	extra-	1) outside, in addition to 2) very, more than usual	extraescolar extraplano extraordinário	extracurricular superflat extraordinary
extro-	extro-	variant of extra-	extrovertido	extrovert, outgoing
fago-	phago-	eat	fagocitosis	phagocytosis
femto-	femto-	10^{-15}, one quadrillionth	femtogramo	femtogram
ferr-, ferro-	ferro-	iron	ferroso ferrocarril	ferrous railway
fil-	phil-	variant of filo-	filatelia	philately
filo-	philo-	1) friend of, loving 2) leaf	1) filosofía 2) filoxera	1) philosophy 2) phylloxera
fisio-	physio-	1) physical 2) nature	1) fisioterapia 2) fisiología	1) physiotherapy 2) physiology
fito-	phyto-	plant	fitocultura fitogenético	plant breeding phytogenetic
fono-	phono-	voice, sound	fonoteca fonología	sound archive phonology
fos-	phos-	light	fosforescente	phosphorescent
foto-	photo-	photography, light	fotocopia	photocopy
franco-	Franco-	French	francófilo	Francophile
gamo-	gamo-	joined	gamopétalo	gamopetalous
gastr(o)-	gastr(o)-	stomach	gastroenteritis gastritis	gastroenteritis gastritis
geo-	geo-	Earth	geopolítico	geopolitical
germano-	Germano-	German	germanófilo	Germanophile
geronto-	geronto-	old	gerontología	gerontology
giga-	giga-	10^9	gigabyte	gigabyte
gimno-	gymno-	naked	gimnosperma	gymnosperm
gin(o)-	gyn(o)-	woman, feminine	ginecólogo	gynecologist
gono-	gono-	relating to reproduction	gonorrea	gonorrhea
grafo-	grapho-	writing	grafólogo	graphologist
greco-	Greco-	Greek	grecolatino	Greco-Latin

Prefix	English Equivalents	Meanings and Uses	Examples	English equivalents
haplo-	haplo-	single	haploide	haploid
hecto-	hecto-	hundred	hectómetro	hectometer
helico-	helico-	1) helix, spiral 2) pertaining to helicopters	1) helicoidal 2) heliport	1) helicoid 2) helipuerto
helio-	helio-	sun	heliocéntrico	heliocentric
hema(to)-, hemo-	hema(to)-, hemo-	blood	hematoma hemoglobina	hematoma hemoglobin
hemi-	hemi-	half	hemipléjico	hemiplegic
hepat(o)-	hepat(o)-	liver	hepatitis	hepatitis
hepta-	hepta-	seven	heptágono	heptagon
hetero-	hetero-	1) other, different 2) varying, unequal	1) heterodoxo 2) heterogéneo	1) heterodox 2) heterogeneous
hex(a)-	hex(a)-	six	hexágono	hexagon
hidr(o)-	hydro-	water	hidrodinámico hidroavión	hydrodynamic seaplane (hydroplane)
hiper-	hyper- super- mega-	1) extreme, extremely 2) huge 3) *inf* very	1) hiperactivo 2) hipermercado 3) hiperlejos	1) hyperactive 2) superstore 3) mega-far
hipno-	hypno-	sleep	hipnotizar	to hypnotize
hipi-, hipo-	equ-	horse	hípico hipódromo	equestrian, horse *adj* racetrack
hipo-	hypo-	1) below, beneath 2) less than normal	1) hipodérmico 2) hipotensión	1) hypodermic 2) low blood pressure
hispano-	Spanish-, Hispano-	Spanish Hispanic	hispanohablante hispanista	Spanish-speaking Hispanist
histo-	histo-	body tissue	histocompatibilidad	histocompatibility
hol(o)-	hol(o)-	whole, entirely	holístico holograma	holistic hologram
homeo-	homeo-	similar, like	homeopático	homeopathic
homo-	homo-	same	homónimo	homonym
i-	i-	var. of in- before l	ilegítimo	illegitimate
icono-	icono-	image, icon	iconoclasta	iconoclast
ictio-	ichthyo-	fish	ictiología	ichthyology
ideo-	ideo-	idea	ideología	ideology
idio-	idio-	own, personal	idiosincrasia	idiosyncrasy
im-	im-	var. of in- before b, p	improbable	improbable
in-[1]	in-	in	inaugurar	inaugurate
in-[2]	in-	negation	intolerable	intolerable
Indo-	Indo-	India Indoeuropean	Indochina indoeuropeo	Indochina Indoeuropean
infra-	1) infra- 2) sub-	1) below 2) indicates a level below a determined limit	1) infraestructura 2) infrahumano	1) infrastructure 2) subhuman

Prefix	English Equivalents	Meanings and Uses	Examples	English equivalents
inter-	inter-	1) between 2) amongst many	1) intersección 2) intercambio, inter-comunicador	intersection exchange, intercom
intra-	intra-	within	intravenoso	intravenous
intro-	intro-	within	introvertido	introverted
iso-	iso-	equal, same	isotónico	isotonic
ítalo-	Ítalo-	Italian	ítalo-americano	Italian-American
kilo-	kilo-	thousand	kilogramo	kilogram
lacto-	lacto-	milk	lactosa	lactose
lito-	litho-	stone	litografía	lithography
logo-	logo-	word, speech	logotipo logopedia	logotype speech therapy
macro-	macro-	large, great	macroinstrucción	macro
magn(i)-	magni-	large	magnífico	magnificent
mal-	mal-, mis-	bad, badly	maltratar malacostumbrado	maltreat, mistreat spoiled, pampered
mani-	mani-	hand	manicura maniatar	manicure to tie sb's hands up
manu-	manu-	var. of mani-	manuscrito	manuscript
matri-	matri-	mother, maternal	matricidio matrilineal	matricide matrilineal
medio-	mid-	middle	mediodía	midday
media-	mid-	var. of medio-	medianoche	midnight
mega-	mega-	1) large 2) one million 3) *inf* extraordinary	1) megáfono 2) megabyte megalargo	1) megaphone 2) megabyte 3) megalong
megalo-	megalo-	very large	megalomanía	megalomania
melano-	melano-	black	melanoma	melanoma
melo-	melo-	singing	melodía melodrama	melody melodrama
meso-	meso-	in the middle of, intermediate	mesocarpio Mesolítico	mesocarp Mesolithic
meta-	meta-	1) together with, after, between 2) change 3) beyond	1) metafísica 2) metamorfosis 3) metalenguaje	1) metaphysics 2) metamorphosis 3) metalanguage
metro-	metro-	1) measure 2) city	1) metrónomo 2) metrópoli	1) metronome 2) metropolis
micro-	micro-, mini- micro-	1) very small, tiny 2) millionth	1) microonda microbús 2) microgramo	1) microwave minibus 2) microgram
mili-	mili-	thousandth	miligramo	milligram
mini-	mini-	small, brief, short	minifalda minigolf	miniskirt miniature golf
mio-	myo-	muscle	miocardio	myocardium
miria-	myria-	1) ten thousand 2) many	1) miriámetro 2) miriápodo	1) myriameter 2) myriapod

Prefix	English Equivalents	Meanings and Uses	Examples	English equivalents
miso-	miso-	dislike, hatred	misoginia	misogyny
mono-	mono-	only, one single	monogamia	monogamy
morfo-	morpho-	form	morfogénesis	morphogenesis
muco-	muco-	mucous	mucolítico	mucolytic
multi-	multi-	many	multiuso	multi-purpose
nano-	nano-	1) one billionth 2) extremely small	1) nanosegundo 2) nanotecnología	1) nanosecond 2) nanotechnology
necro-	necro-	dead, death	necrológico	necrological
nefr(o)-	nephr(o)-	kidney	nefritis	nephritis
neo-	neo-	new, recent	neocapitalismo	neocapitalism
neumo-	pneumo-	lung	neumonía	pneumonia
neur(o)-	neur(o)-	nerve, nervous system	neurología	neurology
o(b)-	o(b)-	resistance confrontation	ofender obstruir	to offend to obstruct
oct(o)-	oct(o)-	eight	octogésimo	eightieth
odonto-	odonto-, dent-	tooth	odontología	dentistry
olig(o)-	olig(o)	few, insufficient	oligarquía oligofrenia	oligarchy mental deficiency
omni-	omni-	totality	omnipresente	omnipresent
onoma-	onoma-	name	onomástica	onomastics
oo-	oo-	egg	oogénesis	oogenesis
orto-	ortho-	1) straight 2) correct	1) ortogonal 2) ortografía	1) right-angled 2) spelling
osteo-	osteo-	bone	osteoporosis	osteoporosis
ovi-, ovo-	ovi-	egg	ovíparo, ovoide	oviparous, oviform
ox(i)-	oxy-	oxygen	oxidar	to oxidize
paleo-	paleo-	1) ancient 2) primitive	1) paleontología 2) Paleozoico	1) paleontology 2) Paleozoic
palin-	palin-	again, same	palíndromo	palindrome
pan-	pan-	totality	panamericana	Panamerican
para-	para-	1) near to, next to 2) bordering on 3) against	1) paramilitar 2) paraestatal 3) paragolpes	1) paramilitary 2) semi-official 3) bumper
pato-	patho-	illness, affliction	patógeno	pathogen
patr(i)-	patr(i)-	father	patriarca	patriarch
pedi-[1]	pedi-	foot	pedicura	pedicure
pedi-[2]	pedi-	child	pediatría	pediatrics
pen-	pen-	almost	península penúltimo	peninsula penultimate
penta-	penta-	five	pentagrama	pentagram
per-	per-	1) bad 2) indicates intensity 3) totality	perjuicio perdurar perenne	damage to persist perennial

Prefix	English Equivalents	Meanings and Uses	Examples	English equivalents
peri-	peri-	around	periferia perífrasis	periphery circumlocution
peta-	peta-	10^{15}, one quadrillion	petabyte	petabyte
petri-, petro-	petri-, petro-	1) rock 2) petroleum	1) petrificar 2) petrodólar	1) to petrify 2) petrodollar
pico-	pico-	10^{-12}, one trillionth	picogramo	picogram
piro-	pyro-	fire	pirotecnia	pyrotechnics
pisci-	pisci-	fish	piscicultura	fish farming, pisciculture
pod(o)-	pod-	foot	podólogo	podiatrist
poli-	poly-	many	políglota polifacético	polyglot multifaceted
porta-	–	designates a person or object that supports or carries something	portaaviones portamaletas	aircraft carrier auto trunk
pos(t)-	post-	after, behind	posdata posterioridad	postscript posteriority
pre-	pre-	indicates anteriority in: 1) time 2) space	1) preaviso preestreno 2) prefijo	1) forewarning preview 2) prefix
pro-	pro-	1) for, in the place of 2) before, in front of 3) in favor of 4) indicates movement forward 5) indicates negation or contradiction	1) pronombre 2) prólogo 3) pro francés 4) promover 5) proscribir	1) pronoun 2) prologue, foreword 3) pro-French 4) cause, advance, promote 5) to ban
proto-	proto-	first, anterior	prototipo	prototype
pseudo-	pseudo-	false, fake	pseudónimo	pseudonym
psico-, sico-	psycho-	mind, soul, mental process	psicología psicofármaco	psychology psychotropic drug
quilo-	kilo-	var. of kilo-	quilogramo	kilogram
quinqu-	quinque	five	quinquenio	quinquennial
quir(o)-	chiro-	hand	quirófano quiropráctico	operating room chiropractic
radio-	radio-	1) radiation, radioactivity 2) indicates a relationship with broadcasting	1) radiografía 2) radioyente	1) radiography 2) listener (of radio)
re-	re-	1) repetition 2) reverse action 3) intensification 4) resistance, opposition	1) reabrir 2) reflujo 3) reforzar 4) rechazar	1) to reopen 2) ebb; reflux 3) to reinforce 4) to repel
requete-	–	*inf* very	requetebueno	really good
retro-	retro-	backwards	retrospectivo retrovisor	retrospective rearview mirror

Prefix	English Equivalents	Meanings and Uses	Examples	English equivalents
rino-	rhino-	nose	rinoplastia	rhinoplasty
rizo-	rhizo-	root	rizófago	rhizophagous
semi-	semi-	1) half 2) partially	1) semicírculo 2) semiautomático semifinal	1) semicircle 2) semiautomatic semifinal
sept(i)-	sept(i)-	seven	septillizos	septuplets
sero-	sero-	serum	serodiagnóstico	serodiagnostic
seudo-	pseudo-	var. of pseudo-	seudónimo	pseudonym
sico-	sycho-	var. of psico-	sicología	psychology
sim-	sym-	var. of sin- before p, b	simbiosis	symbiosis
sin-	sym-	1) union 2) lack of	1) sinfonía 2) sinsentido	1) symphony 2) absurdity
sino-	sino-	Chinese	sinologia	Sinology
so-	–	var. de sub-	soportar	support
sobre-	over-, super-	1) above, after 2) excess 3) intensifier 4) indicates sudden action	1) sobremesa 2) sobredosis 3) sobrehumano 4) sobrecoger	1) after-lunch conversation 2) overdose 3) superhuman 4) to take by surprise
sos-	sus-	var. of sub-	sostener	to sustain
su-	su-	var. of sub-	suplantar	to supplant
sub-	sub-	1) underneath, below 2) inferior 3) part of a subdivision 4) scarcity	1) subsuelo 2) subsecretario 3) subgrupo 4) subalimentación	1) subsoil 2) undersecretary 3) subgroup 4) undernourishment
super-	super- over-	1) above, over, upon 2) very 3) excessive 4) *inf* very	1) superponer 2) superdotado 3) superpoblación 4) supercontento	1) to superimpose 2) extremely gifted 3) overpopulation 4) really happy
supra-	supra-	1) over; above 2) transcending	1) suprarenal 2) supranacional	1) suprarenal 2) supranational
sus-	sus-	var. of sub- before c	susceptible	susceptible
taqui-	tachy-	rapid	taquicardia taquigrafía	tachycardia shorthand
taxi-, taxo-	taxi-, taxo-	order	taxidermia	taxidermy
tele-	tele- TV	1) distance 2) television 3) telephone	1) telecompra, 2) televidente telediario 3) teleconferencia	1) teleshopping 2) TV viewer TV news 3) teleconference
teo-	theo-	divinity	teología	theology
tera-	tera-	10^{12}, one trillion	teragramo	teragram
termo-	thermo-	heat, temperature	termómetro	thermometer
tetra-	tetra-	four	tetravalente	tetravalent
topo-	topo-	place	topografía	topography
toxic(o)-	toxic(o)-	toxic	toxicidad toxicómano	toxicity drug addict

Prefix	English Equivalents	Meanings and Uses	Examples	English equivalents
tra(n)s-	trans-	1) on the other side, across 2) through 3) change	1) tra(n)sbordar 2) transparencia 3) transformar	1) to ferry across, to transfer 2) transparency 3) to transform
tras-	trans-	1) behind, back 2) var. of trans-	1) trastienda 2) trasladar	1) back room 2) to transfer
tri-	three-, tri-	1) three 2) three times 3) every three	1) tridimensional 2) trimensual 3) trimestral	1) three-dimensional 2) three times a month 3) trimonthly
ultra-	ultra-	1) beyond, on the other side of 2) very, highly	1) ultramar 2) ultramoderno	1) overseas 2) ultramodern
un(i)-	un(i)-	one, as one	unánime unicelular	unanimous unicellular
vi-	vice-	var. of vice-	virrey	viceroy
vice-	vice-	deputy	vicerrector vicecónsul	vice president vice consul
viz-	vis-	var. of vice-	vizconde	viscount
xeno-	xeno-	foreign	xenofobia	xenophobia
xero-	xero-	dry	xerófilo	xerophilous
xilo-	xylo-	wood	xilófono	xylophone
yocto-	yocto-	10^{-24}, one septillionth	yoctogramo	yoctogram
yota-	yotta	10^{24}, one septillion	yotabyte	yottabyte
yuxta-	juxta-	near, next to	yuxtaponer	juxtapose
zecto-	zecto-	10^{-21}	zectogramo	zectogram
zeta-	zetta-	10^{21}, one sextillion	zetabyte	zettabyte
zoo-	zoo-	animal	zoológico	zoology

Spanish Suffixes and Combining Forms
Sufijos y Elementos de Compuestos españoles

Suffix	English Equivalents	Meanings and Uses	Examples	English Equivalents
-a	–	1) result of an action 2) used for feminine form	1) toma 2) bonita profesora Roberta	1) taking capture 2) pretty teacher Roberta
-able	-able	forms adjectives expressing ability	aceptable	acceptable
-able-mente	-ably	forms adverbs with the sense 'in such a way'	posiblemente extraordinariamente	possibly extraordinarily

Suffix	English Equivalents	Meanings and Uses	Examples	English Equivalents
-áceo, -a	-ish -acean -aceous	forms adjectives and nouns expressing: 1) pertaining to, similar to 2) member of a taxonomic group 3) characteristic of	1) violáceo 2) crustáceo 3) sebáceo herbáceo	1) purplish 2) crustacean 3) sebaceous herbaceous
-acho, -a	–	1) augmentative 2) pejorative forms adjectives and nouns	1) hombracho 2) hombracho el populacho	strong man brute the masses
-achón, -chona	–	variant of -ón, -ona	hombrachón	strong man; brute
-acia	-acy	forms nouns expressing quality of, condition	aristocracia	aristocracy
-acidad	-acity	forms nouns with the sense "full of, with the quality of"	veracidad capacidad	veracity capacity
-ación	-ation	var. of -ción; forms nouns	imaginación	imagination
-aco, -a	 -ac -ac	forms adjectives and nouns expressing: 1) nationality 2) relation 3) characteristic 4) afflicted by	1) polaco, austríaco 2) policiaco 3) afrodisíaco 4) hipocondríaco	1) Pole, Austrian 2) police 3) aphrodisiac 4) hypochondriac
-acón, -cona	–	forms adjectives with a pejorative connotation	machacón	annoyingly insistent
-ada	 -ful	forms nouns expressing: 1) group, set 2) blow, wound 3) abundance, excess 4) contents 5) action and result 6) time period	1) camada 2) palmada 3) riada 4) cucharada 5) barricada pelada 6) temporada jornada década	1) litter 2) pat 3) flood 4) spoonful 5) barricade haircut 6) season working day decade
-adero, -a	–	var. of -dero, -a forms adjectives and nouns	llevadero panadero	bearable baker
-adizo, -a	–	var. of -izo, -a; forms adjectives	olvidadizo	forgetful
-ado	–	forms nouns expressing: 1) time period 2) place, area 3) office, title 4) group, set 5) action and effect	1) reinado 2) ducado 3) rectorado 4) electorado 5) lavado	1) reign 2) duchy 3) rectorship 4) electorate 5) wash, washing

Suffix	English Equivalents	Meanings and Uses	Examples	English Equivalents
-ado,-a	–	forms adjectives expressing: 1) relationship, similarity 2) presence of	1) dorado 2) enamorado	1) golden 2) in love
-ador, -dora	-(a)tor	var. of -dor, -dora; forms adjectives and nouns	refrigerador	refrigerator
-adura	–	var. of -dura; forms nouns	soldadura	welding
-agogia, -agogía	-agogy	forms nouns referring to leading, guiding	demagogia	demagogy
-agogo, -a	–	forms nouns express-ing the sense "guide, leader"	pedagogo	educator, teacher
-aico, -a	–	forms adjectives expressing: belonging to, origin, relationship	pirenaico judaico	Pyrenean Jewish, Judaic
-aina	–	forms adjectives and nouns expressing: 1) collectivity 2) contempt	1) azotaina 2) tontaina	1) spanking 2) silly
-aje	-age -age	forms nouns express-ing: 1) action and result 2) sth given in exchange for pay-ment 3) group, set	1) aterrizaje homenage 2) hospedaje 3) plumaje foliage	1) landing homage 2) accommodations 3) plumage foliage
-ajo, -a	–	forms adjectives and nouns expressing: 1) diminutive 2) contempt	1) pequeñajo 2) migaja	1) kid 2) crumb, scrap
-al	 -al -al, -ar	forms adjectives and nouns expressing: 1) relation 2) relevance 3) place where some-thing is abundant	 individual racial lineal maizal	 individual racial linear cornfield
-ales	–	forms adjectives with a comic connotation	viejales mochales	old boy crazy
-algia	-algia	forms nouns express-ing pain	neuralgia lombalgia	neuralgia low back pain
-alla	–	forms collective nouns; can also express contempt	rondalla quincalla	group of street musi-cians scrap metal; trinkets
-ambre	–	forms nouns express-ing a group or abun-dance of something	pelambre	thick hair; fur

Suffix	English Equivalents	Meanings and Uses	Examples	English Equivalents
-ámbulo	-walker, -walking	forms adjectives and nouns expressing walk, gait	funámbulo sonámbulo	tightrope walker sleepwalker; sleep-walking
-amen	–	forms collective nouns	gravamen	burden
-amento	-ation	var. of -mento	salvamento	salvation
-amiento	-ment	var. of -miento; forms nouns	nombramiento	appointment; commission
-án, -ana	-an	forms adjectives and nouns denoting: 1) origin, nationality 2) relation	 1) alemán 2) haragán	 1) German 2) loafer
-ancia	-ance, -ancy	var. of -ncia when the adjective from which it derives ends in -ante; forms nouns	redundancia	redundancy
-anco, -a	–	expresses contempt; forms adjectives	zurumbanco *CRica, Méx*	very drunk
-ando	-ing	forms gerund, present participle	jugando	playing
-andria	-andry	forms nouns referring to men	poliandria	polyandry
-áneo, -a	-anean, -ary, -eous	forms adjectives expressing pertinence, condition, relationship	subterráneo comtemporáneo espontáneo	subterranean contemporary spontaneous
-ano	-ane	saturated hydrocarbon; forms nouns	metano	methane
-ano, -a	-an	forms adjectives and nouns referring to 1) pertinence, relationship 2) origin, nationality	 1) metropolitano 2) mexicano	 1) metropolitan 2) Mexican
-ante, -a	-ant, -ing	var. of -nte in the first conjugation; forms adjectives	causante militante	causing militant
-ántropo, -a	-anthropist *n*, -thropic *adj*	human being; forms adjectives and nouns	filántropo	philanthropist
-anza	–	forms nouns expressing: 1) action and result 2) quality 3) instrument, means	 1) enseñanza 2) alianza 3) libranza	 1) education; teaching 2) alliance 3) order of payment
-ar	–	forms adjectives and nouns expressing: 1) quality 2) relevance, relationship 3) place in which something abounds	 espectacular familiar *n* pinar	 spectacular relative *n* pine grove
-aracho, -a	–	var. of -acho, -a; forms adjectives	vivaracho	vivacious

Suffix	English Equivalents	Meanings and Uses	Examples	English Equivalents
-arca	-arch	forms nouns denoting the source of a power	patriarca	patriarch
-arada	–	var. of -ada; forms nouns	llamarada	blaze
-ardo, -a	–	forms adjectives and nouns expressing augmentation contempt	moscarda	ZOOL bluebottle
-ario	-arium	protected place from which to observe	acuario vivario	aquarium vivarium
-ario, -a	-ary	forms adjectives and nouns expressing: 1) relevance, relationship 2) place 3) profession, activity	1) disciplinario 2) balneario 3) empresario vegetariano	1) disciplinary 2) spa 3) businessman, -woman; THEAT impresario vegetarian
	-aire	4) person with a certain quality	4) millonario doctrinario	4) millionaire doctrinaire
	-arian	5) referring to age 6) referring to sign of the zodiac	5) octogenario 6) acuario, -a	5) octogenarian 6) Aquarian
-arquía	-archy	forms nouns denoting government, rule	monarquía	monarchy
-arraco, -a	–	forms nouns expressing contempt	pajarraco	rogue
-arro, -a	–	var. of -rro; forms adjectives and nouns	cacharro	gadget; piece of junk
-arrón, -ona	–	augmentative: var. of -ón, -ona; forms adjectives and nouns	nubarrón	storm cloud
-asa	-ase	forms nouns with the sense *enzyme*	oxidasa	oxidase
-asis	-asis	var. of -sis; forms nouns	psoriasis	psoriasis
-asta	-ast	1) agent 2) person with a certain quality forms nouns	1) gimnasta 2) entusiasta	1) gymnast 2) enthusiast
-astre	–	var. of -astro 1), -a; forms nouns	pillastre *inf*	rascal
-astro, -a	–	forms nouns expressing 1) contempt 2) member of stepfamily	1) camastro 2) hermanastro	1) hard, old bed 2) stepbrother/sister

Suffix	English Equivalents	Meanings and Uses	Examples	English Equivalents
-ata	–	forms nouns and adjectives expressing 1) action and result 2) native of 3) *inf* abbreviation	1) caminata 2) croata 3) bocata *inf* cubata *inf*	1) long walk 2) Croat(ian) 3) sandwich rum and coke
-atario,-a	-ee	forms nouns denoting the person in whose favor an action is carried out	consignatario	addressee
-ático, -a	-at, -atic	denotes relationship, pertinence; forms nouns and adjectives	diplomático	diplomat *n*; diplomatic *adj*
-ativo, -a	-ative	var. of -ivo, -a; forms adjectives and nouns	ahorrativo administrativo comparativo *n*	thrifty administrative comparative
-ato	–	forms nouns indicating: 1) dignity, charge 2) place, institution 3) action and result 4) animal young 5) time, period	1) virreinato 2) orfanato 3) desacato 4) lobato ballenato 5) incanato	1) viceroyalty 2) orphanage 3) disrespect 4) wolf cub young whale 5) Incan period
-ato, -a	–	forms adjectives expressing quality	novato	novice
-avo, -a	-th	partitive; forms adjectives and nouns	dieciseisavo	sixteenth
-az	-aceous	forms adjectives expressing quality, aptitude	veraz voraz locuaz	truthful voracious loquacious
-azgo	–	forms nouns indicating 1) dignity, charge 2) state, condition 3) action and result	1) almirantazgo 2) noviazgo 3) hallazgo	1) admiralty 2) engagement 3) discovery
-azo, -a	–	forms adjectives and nouns expressing: 1) augmentative 2) blow, hit 3) contempt	1) golazo DEP 2) cabezazo 3) pelmazo	1) great goal 2) blow on the head 3) bore
-azón	–	forms nouns expressing an action and result; can have an augmentative or contemptive connotation	matazón picazón	massacre itch
-bilidad	-bility	var. of -dad; forms nouns	probabilidad	probability
-bio	–	forms nouns referring to life	microbio	microbe
-ble	-ble	forms adjectives referring to capability, aptitude, attitude, quality	navegable	navigable

Suffix	English Equivalents	Meanings and Uses	Examples	English Equivalents
-bundo, -a	-bund	forms nouns and adjectives denoting tendency	vagabundo moribundo	wandering moribund, dying
-cardia	-cardia	forms nouns referring to the heart	taquicardia	tachycardia
-carpio	-carp	forms nouns referring to fruit	endocarpio	endocarp
-cefalia	-cephaly	forms nouns referring to a condition of the head	microcefalia	microcephaly
-céfalo, -a	-cephalous	forms nouns referring to the head	bicéfalo	bicephalous
-céntrico, -a	-centric	having something as the center	geocéntrico egocéntrico	geocentric egocentric
-cía	-cy	1) office 2) quality	1) presidencia 2) supremacía	1) presidency 2) supremacy
-ciclo	-cycle	forms nouns denoting a circle, wheel	triciclo	tricycle
-cico, -a	–	var. of -ico, -a; forms nouns	pececico	little fish
-cida	-cide	forms: 1) adjectives 2) nouns denoting that which kills, exterminates	1) homicida 2) insecticida	1) homicidal 2) insecticide
-cidio	-cide	forms nouns referring to killing	fratricidio	fratricide
-cillo,-a	–	var. of -illo, -a; forms adjectives and nouns	jaboncillo	bar of toilet soap
-ción	-tion	forms nouns referring to 1) action and result 2) place, object of	1) intervención 2) fortificación	1) intervention 2) fortification
-cioso, -a	-tious	forms adjectives from nouns ending in -ción	ambicioso	ambitious
-cista	-cian	having a skill	electricista	electrician
-cito	-cyte	forms nouns referring to cells	leucocito	leukocyte
-cito,-a	–	var. of -ito, -a, forming diminutives	jovencito	young boy
-cola	-dweller	forms adjectives denoting 1) inhabitant 2) cultivation	1) terrícola urbanícola 2) hortícola	1) earthling city dweller 2) horticultural
-cornio	-corn	horn	unicornio	unicorn
-cosmos	-cosm	referring to the cosmos	microcosmos	microcosm
-cracia	-cracy	forms nouns relating to government, control, power	aristocracia	aristocracy

Suffix	English Equivalents	Meanings and Uses	Examples	English Equivalents
-crata	-crat	forms nouns referring to the owner of power	burócrata	bureaucrat
-cromo, -a	-chrome	forms adjectives referring to color	monocromo	monochrome
-cula	-cle	diminutive	partícula	particle
-culo, -a	-cle	diminutive: very small	minúsculo	miniscule
-cultor, -ora	-culturalist	forms nouns referring to a person who cultivates, raises	apicultor floricultor	beekeeper floriculturalist
-cultura	–	cultivation, care, raising; forms nouns	fruticultura	fruit growing
-dáctilo	-dactyl	forms nouns referring to the finger	pterodáctilo	pterodactyl
-dad	-ness, -ty	forms nouns referring to quality, state, condition	maldad oportunidad falsedad	wickedness opportunity falsehood
-dera	–	forms nouns denoting 1) instrument, 2) reiterated action	1) podadera 2) tosedera	1) pruning shears 2) nagging cough
-dermia	-dermy	skin; forms nouns	taxidermia	taxidermy
-dermis, -dermo	-dermis -derm	skin; forms nouns	epidermis paquidermo	epidermis pachyderm
-dero, -a	–	forms adjectives and nouns denoting: 1) possibility 2) place 3) profession, activity	1) venidero 2) fondeadero 3) ganadero	1) future 2) anchorage 3) cattle farmer
-dimensional	-dimensional	referring to the number of dimensions	bidimensional	two-dimensional
-dino, -a	-dyne	strength	anodino	anodyne
-dizo, -a	–	var. of -izo, -a; forms adjectives	espantadizo	jittery
-dor, -dora	-er	forms adjectives and nouns denoting: 1) agent 2) instrument 3) place 4) profession, occupation 5) quality	1) bebedor 2) escurridor 3) comedor 4) enterrador 5) encantador	1) drinker 2) colander 3) dining room 4) gravedigger 5) charming
-dromo	–	forms nouns denoting place, track	hipódromo	racetrack, hippodrome
-dura	–	forms nouns denoting: 1) an action and result 2) an instrument	1) limadura 2) armadura	1) polishing, filings 2) armor; framework
-e	–	forms nouns denoting an action and result	aguante	patience, stamina

Suffix	English Equivalents	Meanings and Uses	Examples	English Equivalents
-ear	–	1) forms verbs also denoting: 2) frequency, repeated action 3) beginning of an action	1) telefonear 2) palmotear 3) amarillear	1) to phone 2) to clap 3) to turn yellow
-eciente	-escent	forms nouns and adjectives of verbs in -ecer	convaleciente	convalescent
-ecencia	-escence	forms nouns of verbs in -ecer	convalecencia	convalescence
-ecer	–	forms verbs denoting: beginning of an action, change of state	rejuvenecer reblandecer	to rejuvenate to soften
-ecillo, -a	–	var. of -illo; forms adjectives and nouns	panecillo	(bread) roll
-ecito, -a	–	var. of -ito, -a; forms adjectives and nouns	cochecito viejecito	little car little old man
-ectomía	-ectomy	forms nouns denoting removal by surgery	apendectomía	appendectomy
-edad	–	var. of -dad; forms nouns	soledad suciedad	solitude dirtiness
-edal	–	var. of -edo, -a; forms nouns	humedal	wetland
-edero, -a	–	var. of -dero, -a; forms adjectives and nouns	imperecedero	imperishable
-edizo,-a	–	var. of -izo, -a; forms adjectives	llovedizo	leaky *(of roof)*
-edo, -a	–	forms nouns denoting the place in which something abounds	viñedo	vineyard
-edor, -a	-er	var. of -dor, -dora; forms adjectives and nouns	perdedor	loser
-edro	-hedron	forms nouns denoting surfaces of a geometric figure	poliedro	polyhedron
-edura	–	var. of -dura; forms nouns	mordedura	bite
-ego, -a	-ian	forms adjectives and nouns denoting origin	gallego noruego	Galician Norwegian
-ejo, -a	–	forms adjectives and nouns expressing diminutive or contempt	pelleja	skinny bones
-ejón,-ona	–	var. of -ón,-ona; forms adjectives and nouns	callejón	alley
-ema	-eme	linguistic unit	morfema	morpheme
-emia	-emia	forms nouns referring to blood	anemia	anemia

Suffix	English Equivalents	Meanings and Uses	Examples	English Equivalents
-ena	–	forms collective numeral nouns	decena	group of 10
-encia	-ence, -ency	var. of -ncia when the adjective from which it derives ends in -ente, -iente	preferencia	preference
-enco, -a	–	forms adjectives and nouns denoting: 1) origin 2) relationship 3) similarity	1) ibicenco 2) azulenco 3) zopenco	1) Ibizan 2) bluish 3) oafish
-engo, -a	–	forms adjectives and nouns denoting relationship, pertinence, quality	realengo	Crown *adj*
-eno, -a	–	forms adjectives and nouns denoting 1) origin, nationality 2) ordinal numbers 3) similarity	1) chileno 2) noveno 3) moreno	1) Chilean 2) ninth 3) brown
-ense	–	forms adjectives and nouns denoting 1) origin 2) relationship, pertinence	1) cretense bonaerense 2) circense	1) Cretan from Buenos Aires province 2) circus
-ente, -a	–	variant of -nte in the 2nd and 3rd conjugation; forms adjectives and nouns	creyente	believer
-ento, -a	-ish	forms adjectives denoting quality	amarillento	yellowish
-eño,-a	–	forms adjectives and nouns denoting 1) similarity 2) origin 3) relationship	1) aguileño 2) madrileño 3) navideño	1) aquiline 2) from Madrid 3) Christmas, festive
-eo	–	forms nouns denoting action and result	gorjeo	twittering
-eo, -a	–	forms adjectives denoting quality, pertinence, relationship	férreo	iron
-ería	–	forms 1) collective nouns 2) usually negative quality 3) occupation 4) establishment, place of work	1) pradería 2) grosería 3) fontanería 4) ferretería	1) meadowlands 2) rudeness 3) plumbing 4) hardware store

Suffix	English Equivalents	Meanings and Uses	Examples	English Equivalents
-erio	–	forms nouns denoting: 1) action and result 2) situation, state 3) place	1) vituperio 2) cautiverio 3) presbiterio	1) criticism vituperation 2) captivity 3) presbytery
-ero	–	forms nouns denoting: 1) the place in which something abounds 2) fruit tree 3) utensil 4) piece of furniture	1) basurero 2) limonero 3) monedero 4) ropero	1) garbage dump 2) lemon tree 3) purse 4) wardrobe
-ero, -a	–	forms adjectives and nouns denoting: 1) position, post, occupation 2) relationship	1) pastelero cajero 2) pendenciero	1) pastry chef cashier 2) quarrelsome *adj*, troublemaker *n*
-erón	–	forms nouns indicating an augmentative	caserón	large house
-érrimo, -a	–	forms adjectives indicating the superlative	paupérrimo	very poor
-es	-(e)s	forms the plural of nouns	colores	colors
-és, -esa	-ese	forms adjectives and nouns denoting: 1) origin, nationality 2) relationship 3) language	1) pequinés 2) montañés 3) francés	1) Pekinese 2) Highlander 3) French
-esco, -a	–	var. of -sco, -a; forms adjectives expressing relationship, similarity to	caballeresco gigantesco funambulesco	chivalrous gigantic acrobatic
-ésimo, -a	–	forms adjectives 1) for ordinal numbers above 20 2) for fractions	octogésimo centésimo	eightieth hundredth
-esis	-esis	var. of -sis; forms nouns	diuresis	diuresis
-estre	–	forms adjectives denoting: pertinence, relationship	pedestre terrestre	pedestrian terrestrial
-ete, -a	–	forms adjectives and nouns denoting 1) diminutive 2) affective	1) barrilete 2) amiguete	1) small keg 2) buddy
-ez	–	forms nouns denoting a quality	invalidez brillantez	invalidity brilliance
-eza	–	forms nouns denoting a quality	grandeza	greatness
-ezno, -a	–	forms adjectives referring to animal young	lobezno	wolf cub

Suffix	English Equivalents	Meanings and Uses	Examples	English Equivalents
-fagia	-phagia, -phagy	forms nouns referring to eating, swallowing, digestion	aerofagia	aerophagia
-fago,- a	-phagous *adj* -phagus *n*	forms adjectives and nouns denoting an eater of	antropófago	anthropophagus
-fero, -a	-ferous	forms adjectives expressing that which carries, contains or produces	petrolífero fructífero conífero	oil-bearing fruitful coniferous
-ficar	-fy	to make	fortificar intensificar	to fortify to intensify
-fico, -a	-fic	forms adjectives expressing that which does, produces, converts to	catastrófico	catastrophic
-filia	-philia	forms nouns referring to affection, liking, love	anglofilia	Anglophilia
-filo, -a	-phile	forms adjectives referring to an enthusiast, friend, lover of	bibliófilo hispanófilo	bibliophile Hispanophile
-fito	-phyte	forms nouns referring to plants, vegetables	micrófito	microphyte
-floro, -a	-florous	forms nouns referring to flowers	multiflora	multiflorous
-fobia	-phobia	forms nouns referring to aversion, horror of	claustrofobia	claustrophobia
-fóbico, -a	-phobic	forms adjectives from nouns ending in -fobia	claustrofóbico	clastrophobic
-fobo, -a	-phobe	forms adjectives expressing horror, repulsion, hatred of something	xenófobo	xenophobe
-fono, -a	-phone	forms adjectives and nouns referring to 1) sound, voice 2) speaker of	1) xilófono interfono teléfono 2) francófono	1) xylophone intercom telephone 2) Francophone
-fonía	-phony	sound	cacofonía eufonía	cacophony euphony
-forme	-form	forms adjectives denoting the form of something	gaseiforme	gasiform
-fugo, -a	–	denotes thing or person which/who: 1) dispels 2) impedes 3) flees	1) centrífugo 2) ignífugo 3) prófugo	1) centrifugal 2) fireproof 3) mil deserter
-gamia	-gamy	forms nouns expressing union	monogamia	monogamy

Suffix	English Equivalents	Meanings and Uses	Examples	English Equivalents
-gamo	-gamous	forms adjectives denoting the people in a union	polígamo	polygamous
-genia	-geny	forms nouns denoting origin, the process of formation	orogenia	orogeny

-génico, -a	-genic	1) suited for
		
		2) causing, generating
			1) fotogénico
			   telegénico
			2) alergénico
				1) photogenic
				   telegenic
				2) allergenic

-génito, -a	–	forms adjectives referring to birth, conception	primogénito	first-born

-geno, -a	
	
	-genic
	
	-gen
		forms adjectives referring to
		1) that which generates or produces
		2) that which is produced
			
			1) cancerígeno
			   accidentógeno
			2) hidrógeno
				
				1) carcinogenic
				   accident-prone
				2) hydrogen

-gero, -a		var. of -fero, -a; forms adjectives	flamígero	blazing
-gino, -a	-gynist m -gynistic, -gynous adj	forms adjectives and nouns referring to women	misógino andrógino	misogynist n, misogynistic adj androgynous
-glota	-glot	forms adjectives referring to language, languages	políglota	polyglot
-gono, -a	-gon	forms nouns referring to the number of angles in a shape	hexágono	hexagon
-grado, -a	–	forms adjectives expressing movement	retrógrado	reactionary
-grafía	-graph, -graphy	forms nouns denoting: 1) description, treatise 2) writing 3) graphic representation 4) collectivity	 1) monografía 2) caligrafía 3) fotografía 4) filmografía	 1) monograph 2) calligraphy 3) photograph 4) movies
-grafo	-graph	forms nouns denoting writing	autógrafo	autograph
-grafo	-graph	forms nouns denoting a recording or writing tool	telégrafo bolígrafo cinematógrafo	telegraph ballpoint pen projector
-grafo, -a	-grapher	forms nouns denoting person or thing that/ which 1) describes 2) writes 3) practices a certain profession	 1) geógrafo 2) mecanógrafo 3) tipógrafo	 1) geographer 2) typist 3) printer
-grama	-gram	forms nouns denoting: 1) writing 2) chart 3) representation	 1) crucigrama 2) diagrama 3) electrocardiograma	 1) crossword (puzzle) 2) diagram 3) electrocardiogram

Suffix	English Equivalents	Meanings and Uses	Examples	English Equivalents
-gramo	-gram	referring to weight in metric system	kilogramo	kilogram
-í	-i	forms adjectives and nouns denoting origin, relationship	saudí	Saudi
-ia	-y -ia	forms: 1) abstract nouns 2) names of countries and regions 3) names of flowers	1) eficacia 2) Grecia, Galicia 3) fucsia	1) efficiency 2) Greece, Galicia 3) fuchsia
-ía	-y	forms: 1) collective nouns 2) abstract nouns 3) nouns referring to stores 4) office, profession 5) place, region, country	1) artesanía mantelería 2) cercanía armonía 3) panadería floristería 4) abogacía 5) abadía Andalucía Turquía	1) handicrafts table linen 2) proximity harmony 3) bakery flower shop 4) legal profession 5) abbey Andalusia Turkey
-íaco, -	-ac	characteristic; var. of -ico, -a	maníaco afrodisíaco	maniac aphrodisiac
-ial	-ial	forms adjectives with the sense "pertaining to"	ministerial gerencial	ministerial managerial
-iasis	-iasis	illness, condition	elefantiasis	elephantiasis
-iatra	-iatrician, -iatrist	forms nouns referring to medical specialists	pediatra psiquiatra	pediatrician psychiatrist
-iatría	-iatry, -iatrics	forms nouns referring to medical specialization	psiquiatría pediatría	psychiatry pediatrics
-ible	-ible	var. of -ble; forms adjectives	comprensible	comprehensible
-ica	–	forms derogatory adjectives denoting repeated action	llorica	crybaby
-icamente	-ically	forms adverbs of adjectives ending in -ico, -a	alfabéticamente heroicamente	alphabetically heroically
-icio, -a	-ice	forms adjectives and nouns expressing: 1) relationship 2) quality 3) intense action	1) natalicio 2) servicio 3) bullicio	1) birthday 2) service 3) uproar
-ición	-tion	var. of -ción; forms nouns	maldición medición nutrición	curse measurement nutrition
-ico, -a	–	forms adjectives expressing a diminutive form	pequeñico	tiny
-ico, -a	-ic, -ical	forms adjectives and nouns expressing relationship	céntrico heroico poético	central heroic poetic

Suffix	English Equivalents	Meanings and Uses	Examples	English Equivalents
-idad	-ity	var.of -dad; forms nouns	barbaridad	barbarity
-ido, -a	–	forms adjectives and nouns referring to 1) quality 2) sound	1) florido 2) mugido	1) flowery, flowering 2) moo
-idor, -dora	-er	variant of -dor, -dora; forms adjectives and nouns	fundidor	founder
-idura	–	variant of -dura; forms nouns	hendidura	split
-iego, -a	–	forms adjectives and nouns expressing: 1) pertinence, relationship 2) origin	1) palaciego 2) griego	1) *adj* palace, *n* courtier 2) Greek
-iendo	-ing	forms gerunds, present participles	diciendo	saying
-iense	-ian	var. of -ense; forms adjectives	parisiense, canadiense	Parisian, Canadian
-iente, -a	-ent	var. of -nte in the 2nd and 3rd conjugations; forms adjectives and nouns	dependiente	dependent
-iento, -a	–	var. of -ento, -a; forms adjectives	harapiento	ragged
-ificar	-ify	forms verbs denoting: making, producing, converting to	santificar	to sanctify
-iguar	–	forms verbs from adjectives and nouns	apaciguar	to pacify
-ijo, -a	–	forms adjectives and nouns expressing: 1) diminutive 2) contempt 3) action and result	1) escondrijo 2) canijo *AmL* 3) amasijo	1) hideout 2) sly 3) kneading; dough
-il	-il, -ile	forms adjectives denoting: 1) relationship, tendency 2) capability for	1) civil febril 2) portátil	1) civil feverish 2) portable
-ilidad	-ibility	forms nouns from adjectives ending in -ible	compatibilidad	compatibility
-illo, -a	–	forms adjectives expressing diminutive	cursillo	short course
-imento	-iment	var. of -mento; forms nouns	impedimento	impediment
-imiento	–	var. of -miento; forms nouns	ofrecimiento	offering

Suffix	English Equivalents	Meanings and Uses	Examples	English Equivalents
-ín, -ina	–	forms adjectives and nouns expressing: 1) diminutive 2) origin 3) agent	 1) chocolatina 2) mallorquín danzarín	 1) chocolate bar 2) of/from Majorca 3) dancer
-ina	-ine	forms nouns expressing: 1) sudden or violent action 2) fruit 3) chemical substance 4) forms abstract nouns	 1) regañina 2) mandarina 3) morfina vitamina 4) disciplina	 1) reprimand 2) mandarin, tangerine 3) morphine vitamin 4) discipline
-íneo, -a	–	forms adjectives designating similarity, relationship	sanguíneo	sanguineous
-ino, -a	-ine	forms adjectives and nouns denoting 1) origin 2) relationship, pertinence	 1) grecolatino 2) canino	 1) Greco-Latin 2) canine
-iño, -a	–	forms adjectives and nouns expressing: 1) diminutive 2) affective	 casiña	 small house
-ío, -a	–	forms adjectives and nouns expressing 1) relationship, pertinence 2) collective nouns	 1) sombrío 2) gentío	 1) shady 2) crowd
-ión	-ion	forms abstract nouns	opinión	opinion
-irucho, -a	–	var. of -ucho, -a; forms adjectives and nouns	larguirucho *inf*	lanky
-is	–	forms adjectives with a comic effect	finolis	la-di-da
-isco, -a	–	variant of -sco, -a; forms adjectives and nouns expressing a relationship	mordisco pedrisco marisco	bite hail seafood
-ísimo, -a	–	forms superlative adjectives	novísimo	brand new
-ismo	-ism	forms nouns expressing: 1) system, doctrine, movement 2) attitude, tendency 3) sports 4) profession 5) linguistic category pertaining to words	 1) socialismo 2) egoísmo 3) atletismo malabarismo montañismo 4) periodismo 5) anglicismo neologismo	 1) socialism 2) selfishness, egoism 3) athletics juggling mountaineering 4) journalism 5) anglicism neologism

Suffix	English Equivalents	Meanings and Uses	Examples	English Equivalents
-ista	-ist	forms adjectives and nouns expressing: 1) follower, member 2) quality, attitude 3) profession, occupation 4) inclination	1) marxista 2) materialista sexista 3) lingüista dentista 4) madridista	1) Marxist 2) materialistic sexist 3) linguist dentist 4) Real Madrid fan
-ística	-istics	forms nouns expressing branch, specialty	lingüística	linguistics
-ístico, -a	-istic	forms adjectives and nouns expressing relationship, pertinence to	estilístico	stylistic
-ita	–	forms adjectives and nouns expressing: 1) origin 2) relationship, pertinence 3) diminutive, feminine of -ito	1) vietnamita 2) jesuita 3) cajita	1) Vietnamese 2) Jesuit 3) small box
-itis	-itis	forms nouns denoting an infection, inflammation	laringitis	laryngitis
-itivo, -a	-itive	var. of -ivo, -a; forms nouns and adjectives	fugitivo	fugitive
-ito, -a	-ite	forms adjectives and nouns expressing: 1) diminutive 2) contempt 3) names of minerals	1) chiquito 2) garito 3) grafito	1) little boy 2) nightclub 3) graphite
-ivo, -a	-ive	forms adjectives and nouns expressing: 1) capacity for 2) inclination towards 3) profession, activity, charge	1) competitivo 2) administrativo 3) deportivo directivo	1) competitive 2) administrative 3) sports club director
-ización	-ization	forms nouns from verbs in -izar	centralización	centralization
-izante	-er	var. of -nte; forms adjectives and nouns	fertilizante suavizante	fertilizer conditioner
-izar	-ize	forms verbs expressing conversion, change of state	digitalizar popularizar	to digitalize to popularize
-izo, -a	–	forms adjectives and nouns expressing: 1) similarity, relationship 2) quality, predisposition	1) plomizo 2) enfermizo enamoradizo	1) leaden 2) sickly romantic, always falling in love
-landa, -landia	-land	forms names of countries	Irlanda Nueva Zelanda Islandia	Ireland New Zealand Iceland

Suffix	English Equivalents	Meanings and Uses	Examples	English Equivalents
-látero, -a	-lateral	side; forms adjectives and nouns	cuadrilátero	quadrilateral
-latra	-later, -lator	forms adjectives expressing adoration	idólatra	idolater, -tress
-latría	-latry	forms nouns expressing adoration	idolatría	idolatry
-lepsia	-lepsy	seizure	epilepsia narcolepsia	epilepsy narcolepsy
-lisis	-lysis	forms nouns expressing dissolving, decomposition	diálisis	hydrolysis
-lita	-lite	denoting minerals	criolita	cryolite
-lítico	-lithic	phases of archeology	Paleolítico	Paleolithic
-lito	-lith	forms nouns referring to stone, fossils	monolito	monolith
-logía	-logy	forms nouns expressing study, science, treatise	etimología biología	etymology biology
-logo, -a	-logist -logue, -log	forms nouns denoting 1) a scholar, specialist 2) speech	1) farmacólogo 2) monólogo	1) pharmacologist 2) monolog
-mancia, -mancía	-mancy	forms nouns pertaining to fortune-telling	quiromancia	palmistry
-manía	-mania	forms nouns expressing an obsession with something	megalomanía	megalomania
-mano, -a	-maniac	forms nouns denoting someone with an excessive affection, pathological habit	melómano megalómano morfinómano	music lover megalomaniac morphine addict
-menta	–	forms collective nouns	osamenta	skeleton; bones
-mente	-ly	forms adverbs describing mode or manner	soberanamente anteriormente	supremely previously
-mento	-ment	forms nouns denoting an action and result	argumento	argument
-metría	-metry	forms nouns referring to measurement	geometría	geometry
-metro	-meter	forms nouns referring to measurement, instrument for measurement	cronómetro parámetro	chronometer parameter
-miento	–	forms nouns denoting an action and result	pensamiento	thought
-morfo, -a	-morphous	forms adjectives denoting form	polimorfo	polymorphous
-motor, -ora	-motor, -motive	forms nouns denoting movement, propulsion	ciclomotor locomotora	moped; motorbike locomotive
-ncia	-ence	forms nouns denoting a quality	insolencia carencia	impertinence lack

Suffix	English Equivalents	Meanings and Uses	Examples	English Equivalents
-nomía	-nomy	Forms nouns denoting 1) a science 2) a set of norms or laws 3) control	1) astronomía 2) taxonomía 2) autonomía	1) astronomy 2) taxonomy 3) autonomy
-nomo, -a	-nome -nomer	forms nouns denoting a scholar or specialist	gastrónomo astrónomo	gastronome astronomer
-nte, -a	-nt	forms nouns and adjectives denoting: 1) agent 2) activity, profession 3) quality	1) habitante 2) cantante 3) grandilocuente	1) inhabitant 2) singer 3) grandiloquent
-o	–	forms nouns expressing and action and result	amago	threat
-o, -a	–	forms adjectives and nouns denoting origin	sueco	Swiss
-oico	-oic	forms adjectives denoting organic acids	benzoico	benzoic
-oidal	-oid	forms adjectives denoting relationship, similarity to	helicoidal	helicoid
-oide	-oid	forms adjectives and nouns denoting relationship, similarity to	humanoide	humanoid
-ol, -ola	-ol	forms adjectives and nouns denoting 1) origin 2) an alcohol	1) español 2) etanol	1) Spanish 2) ethanol
-ología	-ology	study of	biología geología	biology geology
-oma	-oma	forms nouns denoting a tumor	melanoma	melanoma
-ón	-on -on	forms nouns denoting: 1) violent action and its result 2) particles 3) noble gases	1) empujón 2) neutrón 3) xenón	1) shove 2) neutron 3) xenon
-ón, -ona		forms adjectives and nouns denoting: 1) augmentative, intensifier 2) reiteration (expresses contempt) 3) age (expresses contempt) 4) lack	1) lamparón 2) llorón 3) cuarentón 4) pelón inf	1) grease stain 2) crybaby 3) 40-year old 4) poor wretch
-onimia	-onymy	forms nouns from adjectives in -ónimo, -a	sinonimia	synonymy
-ónimo	-onym	forms adjectives and nouns referring to designation, name	acrónimo	acronym

Suffix	English Equivalents	Meanings and Uses	Examples	English Equivalents
-ónimo, -a	-onymous	forms adjectives from nouns in -ónimo	sinónimo	synonymous
-opía	-opia	referring to the eye	miopía	myopia
-opsia	-opsy	forms nouns denoting a view, examination	biopsia	biopsy
-or	-ness	forms nouns denoting a quality	frescor	coolness
-or, -ora	-or, -er	agent; forms adjectives and nouns	defensor profesor	defending *adj*, defendor *n* teacher
-orial	-orial	forms adjectives of nouns ending in -or, -orio	ecuatorial	equatorial
-orio, -a	-ory, -orious	forms adjectives expressing relationship, pertinence	directorio	directory
-orrio, -a	–	forms adjectives expressing contempt	villorrio	small village, dump
-orro, -a	–	var. of -rro, -a; forms adjectives and nouns	abejorro	bumblebee
-osis	-osis	var. of -sis; forms nouns	trombosis	thrombosis
-oso, -a	-ful -ous	forms adjectives denoting: 1) abundance of; having; causing 2) quality of, similarity to	1) rencoroso pantanoso numeroso pavoroso 2) verdoso	1) spiteful marshy numerous terrifying 2) greenish
-ote, -a	–	forms adjectives denoting augmentative or expressing contempt	machote	tough guy
-paro, -a	-parous	forms adjectives expressing the sense "that bears, brings forth"	ovíparo	oviparous
-pata	-path	forms adjectives and nouns denoting: 1) person afflicted by an illness 2) specialist doctor	1) psicópata 2) homeópata	1) psychopath 2) homeopath
-patía	-pathy	Forms nouns designating: 1) illness 2) medication, treatment 3) feeling, sentiment	1) ludopatía 2) homeopatía 3) simpatía	1) complusive gambling 2) homeopathy 3) liking, friendliness
-pático, -a	-pathic	forms adjectives of nouns ending in -patía	homeopático telepático	homeopathic telepathic

Suffix	English Equivalents	Meanings and Uses	Examples	English Equivalents
-peda	-pedist	forms nouns denoting an educator, specialist	ortopeda	orthopedist
-pedia	-pedia	forms nouns denoting education, instruction	enciclopedia logopedia	encyclopedia speech therapy
-pedo, -a	-ped, -footed	forms nouns and adjectives expressing the presence of the given number of feet	bípedo	biped, two-footed
-pepsia	-pepsia	having to do with digestion	dispepsia	dyspepsia
-plastia	-plasty	forms nouns expressing reconstruction of something	abdominoplastia	abdominoplasty
-plejía	-plexy	forms nouns expressing paralysis	apoplejía	apoplexy
-podo, -pode	-pod	forms adjectives and nouns in the sense "foot"	miriápodo trípode	myriapod tripod
-poli(s)	-polis	forms nouns with the sense "city"	metrópoli(s)	metropolis
-ptero, -a	-pter	forms adjectives and nouns referring to wings	helicóptero	helicopter
-rragia	-rrhage	forms nouns denoting flow, shedding of	hemorragia	hemorrhage
-rrea	-rrhea	forms nouns denoting outward flow	verborrea diarrea	verbosity diarrhea
-rro, -a	–	forms adjectives and nouns expressing diminutive or contempt	ceporro	dim-witted *adj* dimwit *n*
-s	-(e)s	forms the plural of nouns	iglesias	churches
-sco, -a	–	forms adjectives and nouns expressing: 1) relationship, pertinence 2) quality, similarity 3) augmentative 4) origin, nationality	1) novelesco 2) picaresco 3) peñasco 4) monegasco	1) novel, amazing 2) cunning, mischievous 3) boulder 4) of/from Monaco
-scopia	-scopy	forms nouns denoting examination, investigation	radioscopia	radioscopy
-scopio	-scope	forms nouns denoting an instrument for seeing, examining	telescopio	telescope
-seccionar	-sect	cut	diseccionar	to dissect
-sferio	-sphere	ball	hemisferio	hemisphere
-sión	-sion	var. of -ción; forms nouns	decisión	decision

Suffix	English Equivalents	Meanings and Uses	Examples	English Equivalents
-sis	-sis	forms nouns expressing an illness, anomaly	cirrosis	cirrhosis
-soma	-some	forms nouns referring to a body	cromosoma	chromosome
-stático, -a	-static	forms adjectives referring to: 1) balance, equilibrium 2) that which detains, retains	1) aerostático 2) hidrostático	1) aerostatic 2) hydrostatic
-stato	-stat	forms nouns expressing constance, balance, position of stability	termostato	thermostat
-tad	-ty	var. of -dad; forms nouns	libertad	liberty
-tear	–	var. of -ear; forms verbs	golpetear	to hammer
-teca	–	forms nouns referring to a collection	cinemateca pinacoteca	film library art gallery
-tecnia	-technics	forms nouns referring to a certain art, skill	pirotecnia	pyrotechnics
-terapia	-therapy	forms nouns referring to treatment	psicoterapia	psychotherapy
-termia	-thermia	forms nouns denoting heat, temperature	hipotermia	hypothermia
-termo, -a	-therm	forms adjectives and nouns denoting the presence of heat, temperature	isotermo	isotherm
-tipia	-typy, -type	forms nouns referring to printing, imprint	linotipia	Linotype
-tipo	-type	forms nouns designating a sample, example	prototipo	prototype
-tomía	-tomy	forms nouns expressing a cut, incision	anatomía lobotomía	anatomy lobotomy
-tomo, -a	-tom	forms nouns denoting that which cuts, divides	micrótomo átomo	microtome atom
-tor, -tora	-tor	forms adjectives and nouns denoting an agent	traductor	translator
-torio	–	forms nouns referring to a place where something is done	escritorio	desk
-torio, -a	-ory	forms adjectives designating a relationship to an action	oscilatorio	oscillatory

Suffix	English Equivalents	Meanings and Uses	Examples	English Equivalents
-triz	-tress	feminine form of -dor, -tor; forms adjectives and nouns	actriz	actress
-trofia	-trophy	forms nouns referring to food, nourishment, eating	hipertrofia	hypertrophy
-tud	-tude, -ness	forms nouns expressing a quality	ineptitud lentitud	ineptitude slowness
-ucho, -a	–	forms adjectives and nouns expressing a diminutive or contempt	feúcho	unattractive, plain
-uco, -a	–	forms adjectives and nouns expressing a diminutive or contempt	1) patuco 2) mameluco	1) bootee 2) idiot
-udo, - a	–	forms adjectives expressing an abundance of something	peludo	hairy
-uelo, -a	–	forms adjectives and nouns expressing a diminutive or contempt	polluelo	chick
-ujo, -a	–	forms adjectives and nouns expressing a diminutive or contempt	papelujo	insignificant paper
-ulento, -a	-ulent	forms adjectives expressing an abundance of something	turbulento suculento	turbulent tasty; juicy
-ulo, -a	-ulous / -ule	1) forms adjectives expressing an inclination, tendency 2) forms nouns expressing diminutive	1) incrédulo 2) gránulo	1) incredulous 2) granule
-umbre	–	forms 1) collective nouns 2) nouns expressing abundance, quality	1) muchedumbre 2) pesadumbre	1) crowd 2) affliction
-undo, -a	–	forms adjectives expressing a quality, tendency	iracundo	irate
-uno, -a	-ine	forms adjectives and nouns expressing relationship, pertinence	vacuno gatuno	bovine feline, catlike
-ura	-ness	forms nouns expressing a quality	frescura	freshness
-uro	-ide	forms nouns denoting a chemical salt	cianuro cloruro	cyanide chloride
-urro, -a	–	var. of -rro, -a; forms adjectives and nouns	cazurro	sullen, stubborn

Suffix	English Equivalents	Meanings and Uses	Examples	English Equivalents
-usco, -a	–	var. of -sco, -a; forms nouns and adjectives	pardusco	brownish-gray
-uzco, -a	-ish	var. of -sco, -a; forms adjectives and nouns	negruzco	blackish
-uzo, -a	–	forms adjectives and nouns expressing contempt	gentuza	rabble
-voro, -a	-vorous	forms adjectives referring to eating, subsisting on	carnívoro	carnivorous
-zoo	-zoan	forms nouns denoting taxonomic groups of animals	protozoo	protozoan
-zuelo, -a	–	var. of -uelo, -a; forms adjectives and nouns	ladronzuelo	petty thief

Prefijos y Sufijos: Inglés–Español
Prefixes and Suffixes: English-Spanish

Prefijos y Elementos de Compuestos ingleses
English Prefixes and Combining Forms

Prefijo	Equiva-lentes en español	Significados y usos	Ejemplos	Equivalentes en español
a-[1]	–	de	anew	de nuevo
a-[2]	–	en	ashore	en tierra
a-[3]	a-	var. de ab-	aversion	aversión
a-[4]	a-	var. de ad-	aspect	aspecto
a-[5]	a-	var. de an-	asexual	asexual
ab-	ab-	separación	abdicate	abdicar
ac-	ac-	var. de ad-	access	acceso
acro-	acro-	1) altura 2) extremo	1) acrobat 2) acronym	1) acróbata 2) acrónimo
ad-	ad-	indica dirección	adapt	adaptar
af-	a-	var. de ad-	affable	afable
Afro-	afro-	relacionado con África	Afro-Caribbean	afrocaribeño
after-	pos(t)-	después de	after-hours	después de horas
ag-	a-	var. de ad-	aggravate	agravar
agora-	agora-	multitud o gran espacio público	agoraphobia	agorafobia
agri-, agro-	agri-, agro-	campo	agribusiness agronomy	industria agropecuaria agronomía
al-	a-	var. de ad-	alloy	aleación
all-	–	1) todo 2) completamente	1) all-night 2) all-around	1) que dura toda la noche 2) completo
alti-	alti-, alto-	alto; altura	altimeter	altímetro
ambi-	ambi-	1) ambos 2) alrededor de	1) ambidextrous 2) ambient	1) ambidextro 2) ambiental
amphi-	anfi-	1) a ambos lados 2) alrededor de	1) amphibian 2) amphitheater	1) anfibio 2) anfiteatro
an-[1]	a-	var. de ad-	annotate	anotar
an-[2]	an-	sin	anarchy	anarquía
ana-	ana-	1) sobre 2) según	1) anathema 2) analogy	1) anatema 2) analogía
andro-	andro-	masculino	androgynous	andrógino
Anglo-	anglo-	inglés	Anglophile	anglófilo
ante-	ante-	antes de	antecedent	antecedente
anthropo-	antropo-	ser humano	anthropology	antropología

Prefijo	Equiva-lentes en español	Significados y usos	Ejemplos	Equivalentes en español
anti-	anti-	1) opuesto a 2) no 3) situado enfrente de 4) preventivo	1) antiabortion 2) antisocial 3) antithesis 4) antifreeze	1) antiabortista 2) antisocial 3) antítesis 4) anticongelante
ap-	a-	var. de ad-	appear	aparecer
aqua-	acui-	sobre o en el agua	aquacize aquaculture	aeróbic en el agua acuicultura
aqui-	acui-	var. de aqua-	aquifer	acuífero
ar-	ar-	var. de ad-	arrogant	arrogante
arch-	archi-	1) de mayor autoridad 2) extremo	1) archbishop 2) archenemy	1) arzobispo 2) archienemigo
arthr(o)-	artro-	articulación	arthritis	artritis
as-	a-	var. de ad-	assail	atacar
astro-	astro-	relacionado con las estrellas o el espacio sideral	astronaut astronomy	astronauta astronomía
at-	a-	var. de ad-	attorney	abogado
audio-	audi(o)-	sonido o audición	audit	asistir de oyente
auto-	auto-	propio, por uno mismo	autobiography	autobiografía
avi-	– avi-	1) relacionado con las aves 2) relacionado con volar	1) aviary 2) aviation	1) pajarera 2) aviación
be-	– de-	1) forma verbos transitivos: convertirse en 2) separar, quitar	1) befriend 2) behead	1) hacerse amigo de 2) decapitar
bene-	ben(e)-	bien; bueno	beneficial	beneficioso
bi-	bi-	1) dos veces 2) dos	1) bimonthly 2) bilingual	1) quincenal 2) bilingüe
biblio-	biblio-	acerca de libros	bibliophile	bibliófilo
bin-	bin-	dos cada uno	binary	binario
bio-	bio-	vida	biography	biografía
brevi-	–	corto	brevity	brevedad
caco-	caco-	mal	cacophony	cacofonía
cardi(o)-	cardi(o)-	corazón	cardiogram	cardiograma
centi-	cent(i)-	1) cien 2) centésima parte	1) centipede 2) centimeter	1) ciempiés 2) centímetro
centri-	centri-	var. de centro-	to centrifuge	centrifugar
cephalo-	cefalo-	cabeza	cephalopod	cefalópodo
chiro-	quir(o)-	mano	chiropractor	quiropráctico
chloro-	cloro-	verde	chlorophyll	clorofila
chrom-	crom-	color	chromatic	cromático
chrono-	crono-	tiempo	chronology	cronología

Prefijo	Equivalentes en español	Significados y usos	Ejemplos	Equivalentes en español
circum-	circum-, circun-	alrededor de	circumference circumnavigate	circunferencia circunnavegar
co-	co-	con o junto a	coauthor	coautor
col-	co-	var. de co-	collaborate	colaborar
com-	com-	var. de co-	combat	combate
con-	con-	var. de co-	concave	cóncavo
contra-	contra-	contra	contradict contraception	contradecir contracepción
cor-	cor-	var. de co-	correct	correcto
cosmo-	cosmo-	1) espacio sideral 2) del mundo	cosmonaut cosmopolitan	cosmonauta cosmopolita
counter-	contra-	1) contra o enfrente de 2) paralelo 3) duplicar	1) counteractive 2) counterbalance 3) counterfeit	1) neutralizador 2) contrapeso 3) falsificado
cross-	–	de un lado a otro	crossfire	fuego cruzado
crypto-	cripto-	oculto	cryptic	críptico
custom-	–	especialmente	custom-built	hecho de encargo
cyber-	ciber-	ordenador	cybercafé	cibercafé
cyto-	cito-	célula	cytoplasm	citoplasma
de-	de-	1) disociación, separación 2) negación 3) de arriba abajo	1) deforest 2) decriminalize 3) decrepit	1) deforestar 2) despenalizar 3) decrépito
deca-	deca-	diez	decade	década
deci-	deci-	décima parte	deciliter	decilitro
dei-	dei-	dios	to deify	deificar
demi-	semi-	medio	demigod	semidiós
demo-	demo-	pueblo	democracy	democracia
derm-	derm(o)-, dermato-	piel	dermatology	dermatología
di(a)-	dia-	a través de	diameter	diámetro
di-[1]	di-	doble	dilemma	dilema
di-[2]	di-	var. de dis-	digress	hacer una digresión
dif-	di-	var. de dis-	difficult	difícil
diplo-	diplo-	doble	diploid	diploide
dis-	des-, dis-	1) negación 2) separación	1) disadvantage 2) disappear	1) desventaja 2) desaparecer
down-	–	más bajo	downcast	alicaído
duo-	duo-	dos	duodenum	duodeno
dyna-	dinam(o)-	fuerza	dynamic	dinámico
dys-	dis-	dificultad; anomalía	dysfunctional	disfuncional
e-[1]	–	electrónico	e-commerce	comercio electrónico
e-[2]	e-	var. de ex-[2]	ebullient	exaltado

Prefijo	Equivalentes en español	Significados y usos	Ejemplos	Equivalentes en español
eco-	eco-	medio ambiente o naturaleza	ecology	ecología
ecto-	ecto-	exterior, externo	ectoplasm	ectoplasma
ef-	e-	var. de ex-[2]	effusion	efusión
ego-	ego-	yo	egocentric	egocéntrico
electro-	electro-	electricidad	electromagnet	electroimán
em-[1]	em-	var. de en-[1]	emboss	grabar en relieve
em-[2]	em-	var. de en-[2]	embryo	embrión
en-[1]	en-	1) poner dentro de/sobre 2) hacer que esté en un lugar o que sea algo	1) encode 2) enact	1) codificar 2) embarcar; llevar a cabo
en-[2]	en-	en, dentro de	energy	energía
entomo-	entomo-	insecto	entomology	entomología
ep-	e-	var. de epi-	epoch	era
eph-	e-	var. de epi-	ephemeral	efímero
epi-	epi-	1) sobre, encima de 2) junto a 3) antes de 4) después de	1) epicenter 2) epitome 3) episode 4) epithet	1) epicentro 2) personificación 3) episodio 4) epíteto
eque-	ecue- hipi-, hipo-	relativo a los caballos	equestrian	ecuestre hípico
equa-, equi-	ecua-, equi-	igual	equator equation equinox	ecuador ecuación equinoccio
eso-	eso-	oculto, secreto	esoteric	esotérico
ethno-	etno-	pueblo, raza	ethnology	etnología
etymo-	etimo-	origen	etymology	etimología
eu-	eu-	bien, bueno	eulogy	elogio
Euro-	euro-	europeo (occidental)	Eurocrat	eurócrata
ever-	–	siempre	evergreen	de hoja perenne
ex-[1]	ex	antiguamente	ex-girlfriend	ex novia
ex-[2]	ex-	fuera de, de	excavate	excavar
exo-	exo-	fuera	exodus	éxodo
extra-	extra-	más allá de	extraordinary	extraordinario
extro-	extro-	var. de extra-	extrovert	extrovertido
fore-	ante-, pre-	1) antes de 2) parte delantera	1) forecast 2) forearm	1) predicción 2) antebrazo
Franco-	franco-	francés	francophone	francófono
fresh-	recién	nuevo, reciente	freshman fresh-baked	novato recién horneado
gastr(o)-	gastr(o)-	estómago	gastronomy	gastronomía
gamo-	gamo-	unido	gamopetalous	gamopétalo

Prefijo	Equiva-lentes en español	Significados y usos	Ejemplos	Equivalentes en español
gen-	gen-	generación	genealogy gene	genealogía gen
geno-	geno-	pueblo, raza	genocide	genocidio
geo-	geo-	tierra	geography	geografía
Germano-	germano-	alemán	Germanophile	germanófilo
geronto-	geronto-	viejo	gerontology	gerontología
giga-	giga-	billón	gigabyte	gigabyte
gono-	gono-	relativo a la reproducción	gonorrhea	gonorrea
grand-	–	saltando una gene-ración	grandmother grandfather	abuela abuelo
graph-	grafo-	escritura	graphology	grafología
great-	bis-, biz-	añadiendo una gene-ración	great-grandchild	bisnieto, -a
Greco-	greco-	greco	Greco-Latin	grecolatino
gymno-	gimno-	desnudo	gymnosperm	gimnosperma
gynec(o)-	ginec(ó)-	mujer	gynecologist	ginecólogo
gyr-	giro-	girar	gyroscope	giroscopio
haplo-	haplo-	simple	haploid	haploide
hect(o)-	hect(o)-	cien	hectare	hectárea
heli-	heli-	relacionado con los helicópteros	heliport	helipuerto
helio-	helio-	sol	heliocentric	heliocéntrico
hema-, hemo-	hem(ato)-, hemo-	sangre	hematoma hemoglobin	hematoma hemoglobina
hemi-	hemi-	medio	hemisphere	hemisferio
hepat(o)-	hepat(o)-	hígado	hepatitis	hepatitis
hepta-	hepta-	siete	heptathlon	heptatlón
heter(o)-	hetero-	1) diferente 2) variable	1) heterosexual 2) heterogeneous	1) heterosexual 2) heterogénico
hex(a)-	hex(a)-	seis	hexagon	hexágono
Hispano-	hispano-	Hispanic, Spanish	hispanophile	hispanófilo
histo-	histo-	relacionado con tejido orgánico	histology	histología
holo-	holo-	todo, completo	holocaust	holocausto
homeo-	homeo-	similar	homeopathy	homeopatía
homo-	homo-	igual	homograph	homógrafo
hydro-	hidr(o)-	agua	hydrophobia	hidrofobia
hyper-	hiper-	en exceso	hyperbole	hipérbole
hypno-	hipno-	sueño	hypnotherapy	hipnoterapia
hypo-	hipo-	1) debajo de 2) por debajo de lo normal	1) hypodermic 2) hypothermia	1) hipodérmico 2) hipotermia

Prefijo	Equivalentes en español	Significados y usos	Ejemplos	Equivalentes en español
hyster(o)-	hister-	1) útero 2) histeria	1) hysterectomy 2) hysterical	1) histerectomía 2) histérico
ichthyo-	ictio-	pez	ichthyology	ictiología
icono-	icono-	imagen, icono	iconoclast	iconoclasta
ideo-	ideo-	idea	ideology	ideología
idio-	idio-	propio, personal	idiosynchrasy	idiosincrasia
il-[1]	i-	var. de in-[1]	illuminate	iluminar
il-[2]	i-	var. de in-[2]	illiterate	inculto
im-[1]	im-, in-	var. de in-[1]	immense	inmenso
im-[2]	in-	var. de in-[2]	immobile	inmóvil
in-[1]	in-	en	inaugurate	inaugurar
in-[2]	in-	no	inapt	inadecuado
Indo-	indo-	India	Indonesia	Indonesia
infra-	infra-	debajo de	infrastructure	infraestructura
inter-	inter-	entre, entre varios	international	internacional
intra-	intra-	dentro de	intravenous	intravenoso
intro-	intro-	dentro de, en el interior	introvert	introvertido
ir-[1]	ir-	var. de in-[1]	irradiate	irradiar
ir-[2]	ir-	var. de in-[2]	irregular	irregular
iso-	iso-	igual	isotope	isótopo
Italo-	italo-	italiano	Italophile	italófilo
kilo-	kilo-	mil	kilometer	kilómetro
klepto-	clepto-	robar	kleptomaniac	cleptómano
lacto-	lacto-	leche	lactose	lactosa
litho-	lito-	piedra	lithography	litografía
logo-	logo-	palabra, habla	logotype	logotipo
macro-	macro-	grande, excesivo	macroeconomic	macroeconómico
magn(i)-	magn(i)-	grande	magnificent	magnífico
mal-	mal-	mal; malo	malice maltreat	malicia maltratar
mani-	mani-	mano	manicure	manicura
manu-	manu-	var. de mani-	manuscript	manuscrito
matri-	matri-	madre, maternal	matricide matrilineal	matricidio matrilineal
mega-	mega-	grande	megaphone	megáfono
megalo-	megalo-	muy grande	megalomania	megalomanía
melano-	melano-	negro	melanoma	melanoma
melo-	melo-	singing	melody melodrama	melodía melodrama
meso-	meso-	en medio de, intermedio	mesocarp Mesolithic	mesocarpio Mesolítico

Prefijo	Equiva-lentes en español	Significados y usos	Ejemplos	Equivalentes en español
meta-	meta-	1) cambio 2) detrás de, después de 3) sobre; referido a un orden superior, abstracto	1) metamorphosis 2) metacarpal metaphysics 3) metaphor	1) metamorfosis 2) metacarpal metafísica 3) metáfora
metro-	metro-	medida	metronome	metrónomo
micro-	micro-	1) diminuto 2) millonésima parte	1) microorganism 2) microgram	1) microorganismo 2) micrograma
mid-	medio-, media-	medio	midnight	medianoche
milli-	mil-, mili-	1) mil 2) millonésima parte	millipede millibar	milpiés milibar
mini-	mini-	pequeño	miniskirt minibus	minifalda microbús
mis-	–	de forma incorrecta	miscalculate	calcular mal
miso-	miso-	aversión, odio	misogyny	misoginia
mono-	mono-	único, uno solo	monopoly	monopolio
morph(o)-	morf(o)-	forma	morphology	morfología
muco-	muco-	mucosidad	mucolytic	mucolitico
multi-	multi-	muchos	multilingual multipurpose	multilingüe multiuso
must-	–	obligatoriedad	must-see	que hay que ver
myo-	mio-	músculo	myocardium	miocardio
myriad-	miria	1) diez mil 2) muchos	1) myriameter 2) myriapod	1) miriámetro 2) miriópodo
near-	–	cerca	near-sighted	miope
necro-	necro-	dead, death	necrological	necrológico
neo-	neo-	nuevo, reanimado	neoconservative	neoconservador
nephr-	nefr(o)-	riñón	nephritis	nefritis
neur(o)-	neur(o)-	nervio	neurosis	neurosis
new-	recién	recientemente	newfound	recién descubierto
non-	no	no	nonaggression	no agresión
o(b)-	o(b)-	resistencia, confront-ación	to offend to obstruct	ofender obstruir
octa-	oct(o)-	ocho	octagon	octágono
octo-	oct(o)-	ocho	octogenarian octopus	octogenario pulpo
odonto-	odonto-	diente	odontophore	odontóforo
olig(o)-	olig(o)-	poco, insuficiente	oligarchy	oligarquía
omni-	omni-	todo	omnipotent	omnipotente
onoma-	onoma-	nombre	onomastics	onomástica
oo-	oo-	huevo	oogenesis	oogénesis
ornitho-	ornito-	pájaro	ornithology	ornitología

Prefijo	Equiva-lentes en español	Significados y usos	Ejemplos	Equivalentes en español
ortho-	orto-	1) correcto 2) recto	1) orthography 2) orthodontist	1) ortografía 2) ortodoncista
osteo-	osteo-	hueso	osteoporosis	osteoporosis
out-	–	fuera de	outlaw	forajido
ov(i)-, -ovo	ov(i)-, ovo-	huevo	ovary	ovario
over-	sobre-, super-	demasiado	overbook overabundant overcautious	sobrecontratar superabundante demasiado cauto
oxy-	ox(i)-	relativo al oxígeno	to oxidize	oxidar
pale(o)-	paleo-	antiguo	paleontology	paleontología
pan-	pan-	todo	pantheon	panteón
para-	para-	1) junto a 2) secundario 3) más allá de	1) paragraph 2) paramilitary 3) paranormal	1) párrafo 2) paramilitar 3) paranormal
patho-	pato-	enfermedad	pathology	patología
patri-	patr(i)-	1) padre 2) país de origen	1) patriarchy 2) patriotism	1) patriarcado 2) patriotismo
ped(i)-	pedi-	pie	pedicure	pedicura
ped(o)-	pedi-, pedo-	niño	pediatrics	pediatría
pen-	pen-	quasi	peninsula penultimate	península penúltimo
penta-	penta-	cinco	pentagon pentathlon	pentágono pentatlón
per-	per-	1) a través de 2) muy; completa-mente	1) perennial 2) perfect	1) perenne 2) perfecto
peri-	peri-	alrededor de	periphery	periferia
petri-, petro-	petri-, petro-	1) rock 2) petróleo	1) to petrify 2) petrodollar	1) petrificar 2) petrodólar
phago-	fago-	comer	phagocytosis	fagocitosis
phil(o)-	fil-, filo-	amante de; amigo de	philanthropy philharmonic	filantropía filarmónica
phleb-	fleb-	vena	phlebitis	flebitis
phon(o)-	fono-	sonido	phonology	fonología
phos-	fos-	luz	phosphorescent	fosforescente
photo-	foto-	fotografía, luz	photosensitive photocopy	fotosensible fotocopia
physio-	fisio-	cuerpo	physiognomy	fisonomía
pisci-	pisci-	pez	pisciculture	piscicultura
plur-	plur-	muchos, variado	pluralistic	pluralista
pneum-	neum-	aire	pneumatic	neumático
pneumo-	neumo-	respirar, pulmones	pneumonia	neumonía
pod-, pedo-	pod(o)-	pie	podiatrist	podólogo
poly-	poli-	muchos	polytheism	politeísmo

Prefijo	Equiva-lentes en español	Significados y usos	Ejemplos	Equivalentes en español
post-	pos(t)-	después de, detrás de	postwar	de la posguerra
pre-	pre-	antes de	prewar	de preguerra
pro-[1]	pro-	en favor de	proactive	con iniciativa
prot(o)-	proto-	primero	prototype	prototipo
pseud(o)-	(p)seudo-	falso	pseudonym	seudónimo
psych(o)-	(p)sico-	alma o mente	psychosis	psicosis
pyro-	piro-	fuego	pyrotechnic	pirotécnico
quadri-, quadru-	cuadr(i)-, cuatri-, cuatro-	cuatro	quadrilateral quadruped	cuadrilátero cuadrúpedo
quasi-	cuasi	casi	quasigovernmental	cuasi gubernamental
quinqe-	quinqu-	cinco	quinquennium	quinquenio
radio-	radio-	1) comunicación por ondas 2) radiactivo	1) radiotelegraphy 2) radiotherapy	1) radiotelegrafía 2) radioterapia
re-	re-	repetición	rearrange	reorganizar
rect(i)-	rect-	derecho	rectify	rectificar
rent-a-	–	de alquiler	rent-a-car	coche de alquiler
retro-	retro-	hacia atrás	retroactive	retroactivo
rhino-	rino-	nariz	rhinoplasty	rinoplastia
rhizo-	rizo-	raíz	rhizophagous	rizófago
schizo-	esquizo-	escindir	schizophrenia	esquizofrenia
sclero-	esclero-	duro	sclerosis	esclerosis
seismo-	sismo-	terremoto	seismograph	sismógrafo
self-	auto-	independiente(mente)	self-help	autoayuda
semi-	semi-	medio o parcial	semifinal	semifinal
sept(i)-	sept(i)-	siete	septet	septeto
sero-	sero-	suero	serodiagnostic	serodiagnóstico
sex-	sex-	seis	sextet	sexteto
short-	–	corto; demasiado bajo	shortfall	deficiencia
sino-	Sino-	Chinese	Sinology	sinología
soli-	soli-	solo	soliloquy, solitaire	soliloquio, solitario
step-	–	relación familiar debida a un nuevo matrimonio	stepmother	madrastra
stereo-	estereo-	1) sólido 2) tridimensional	1) TYPO stereotype 2) stereophonic	1) estereotipo 2) estereofónico
strato-	estrato-	capa, estrato	stratosphere	estratosfera
sub-	sub-	debajo de	submarine	submarino
suc-	su-	var. de sub-	succumb	sucumbir
suf-	su-	var. de sub-	suffix	sufijo
sup-	su-	var. de sub-	suppress	suprimir
super-	sobre-, super-	encima de	superimpose	superponer

Prefijo	Equiva-lentes en español	Significados y usos	Ejemplos	Equivalentes en español
supra-	supra-	1) arriba, encima de 2) más allá de	1) suprarenal 2) supranational	1) suprarrenal 2) supranacional
sur-	su-	var. de sub-	surreptitious	subrepticio
sus-	sus-	var. de sub-	susceptible	susceptible
syl-	si-	var. de syn-	syllable	sílaba
sym-	sim-	var. de syn-	symbiosis	simbiosis
syn-	sin-	juntos	synergy	sinergia
tachy-	taqui-	rápido	tachycardia	taquicardia
taxi-, taxo-	taxi-, taxo-	orden	taxidermy	taxidermia
tele-	tele-	a distancia	television	televisión
tetra-	tetra-	cuatro	tetrahedron	tetraedro
theo-	teo-	dios, de los dioses	theology	teología
therm(o)-	termo-	calor, caliente	thermostat	termostato
top(o)-	topo-	lugar	topical	tópico
toxic(o)-	toxic(o)-	tóxico	toxicology	toxicología
trans-	tra(n)s-	al otro lado de a través de	transact	tramitar
tri-	tri-	tres	triangle	triángulo
tropo-	tropo-	vuelta, respuesta	troposphere	troposfera
typo-	tipo-	tipo	typography	tipografía
ultra-	ultra-	más allá de, extremo	ultrasound	ultrasonido
un-	in-, des-	1) no 2) deshacer	1) undoubted 2) undo	1) indudable 2) desatar
under-	sub-	debajo de	underscore	subrayar
uni-	un(i)-	uno	unilateral	unilateral
up-	–	arriba	uptown	del norte
vermi-	vermi-	gusano	vermicide	vermicida
vice-	vice-	asistente o sustituto de	vice-chairman	vicepresidente
vis-	viz-	var. de vice-	viscount	vizconde
with-	–	1) contra 2) atrás	1) withstand 2) withdraw	1) resistir 2) quitar
xeno-	xeno-	extranjero, extraño	xenophobia	xenofobia
xero-	xero-	seco-, árido	xerophilous	xerófilo
xylo-	xilo-	madera	xylophone	xilófono
zoo-	zoo-	animal	zoology	zoología

Sufijos y Elementos de Compuestos ingleses
English Sufffixes and Combining Forms

Suffix	Spanish Equivalents	Meanings and Uses	Examples	Spanish
-a	-a	1) forma el plural de nombres proce- dentes del griego o del latín 2) empleado para la forma femenina	1) criteria 2) Roberta	1) criterios 2) Roberta
-ability	-abilidad	forma nombres a partir de adjetivos termina- dos en -able o -ible	reliability stability	fiabilidad estabilidad
-able, -ble, -ible	-able, -ble, -ible	forma adjetivos a partir de verbos con el sig- nificado: "algo que puede ser"	reliable acceptable edible	de confianza aceptable comestible
-ably	-ablemente	forma adverbios con el significado: "de esta forma"	reliably remarkably arguably	de confianza extraordinariamente
-ac	-aco, -a	1) característica; var. de -ic 2) que padece	1) maniac aphrodisiac cardiac 2) hypochondriac	1) maníaco afrodisíaco cardíaco 2) hipocondríaco
-acean	-áceo, -a	perteneciente a un grupo taxonómico	crustacean	crustáceo
-aceous	-áceo, -a	forma adjetivos con el significado: "caracter- ístico de"	sebaceous herbaceous	sebáceo herbáceo
-acious	-az, -ioso, -a	var. de -aceous	efficacious loquacious rapacious	eficaz locuaz codicioso
-acity	-acidad	forma nombres con el significado: "lleno de, con la cualidad de"	veracity capacity sagacity	veracidad capacidad sagacidad
-acy	-idad -acia	forma nombres con el significado "cualidad de'"	accuracy intimacy aristocracy bureaucracy	precisión intimidad aristocracia burocracia
-ade	-ada	indica el resultado de una acción	barricade crusade	barricada cruzada
-age	 -aje -aje	forma nombres con los significados: 1) acción de, efecto de 2) estado 3) lugar 4) grupo, conjunto	 1) blockage drainage foliage 2) marriage shortage 3) orphanage 4) plumage, foliage	 1) obstrucción drenaje follaje 2) matrimonio escasez 3) orfanato 4) plumaje, follage
-agog(ue)	-agogo, -a	líder	pedagogue demagogue	pedagogo demagogo

Suffix	Spanish Equivalents	Meanings and Uses	Examples	Spanish
-aholic, -oholic	-ólico, -a	adicto a	alcoholic workaholic chocoholic	alcohólico trabajador compulsivo adicto al chocolate
-aire	-ario, -a	persona con una cierta cualidad	millionaire doctrinaire	millonario doctrinario
-al	-al	forma adjetivos abstractos con el significado "relacionado con"	cultural national	cultural nacional
-algia, -algy	-algia	dolor	neuralgia	neuralgia
-ally	-mente	forma adverbios	occasionally officially	ocasionalmente oficialmente
-an, -ian	-ense -iense -án, -ana -ano, -ana	1) natural de; origen 2) involucrado en o perteneciente a	1) American Canadian German Mexican 2) optician geriatrician	1) estadounidense canadiense alemán, -ana mexicano 2) óptico geriatra
-ana	–	colección de	Americana	aspectos característicos de Estados Unidos
-ance, -ancy -ence, -ency	-ancia, -encia -ncia	forma adjetivos y nombres con los significados: 1) acción de; cualidad 2) proceso	1) intolerance guidance 2) ignorance infancy assistance	1) intolerancia orientación 2) ignorancia infancia, asistencia
-andry	-andria	forma nombres referidos a hombres	polyandry	poliandria
-ane	-ano	designa hidrocarburos saturados	methane	metano
-anean	-áneo, -a	forma adjetivos que expresan pertinencia, condición o relación	subterranean	subterráneo
-ant	-ante, -ente, -iente, -nte	agente	inhabitant accountant disinfectant	habitante contable desinfectante
-ar	-al	1) var. de -al 2) agente	1) jocular linear 2) beggar liar	1) jocoso lineal 2) mendigo mentiroso
-arch	-arca	gobernante	monarch	monarca
-archy	-arquía	gobierno	monarchy	monarquía
-arian	-ario, -a	forma adjetivos referidos a personas: 1) edad 2) doctrina, creencia 3) de un signo del zodiaco	1) octogenarian 2) totalitarian vegetarian 3) Aquarian	1) octogenario 2) totalitario vegetariano 3) acuario

Suffix	Spanish Equivalents	Meanings and Uses	Examples	Spanish
-armed	–	que tiene un determinado número de brazos	one-armed	manco
-arium	-ario	lugar protegido desde el que se puede observar	aquarium planetarium solarium	acuario planetario solárium
-ary, -ery	-ía	1) acción de 2) lugar de una acción 3) cualidad 4) relevancia, relación	1) burglary 2) bakery 3) bravery 4) disciplinary	1) robo 2) panadería 3) valentía 4) disciplinario
-asis	-asis	var. de -sis	psoriasis	psoriasis
-ast	-asta	persona con una cierta habilidad	enthusiast gymnast	entusiasta gimnasta
-at	-ático	forma nombres que demotan pertinencia o relación	diplomat	diplomático
-ate	–	forma verbos con el significado "causar, hacer"	gyrate habituate hallucinate humiliate	girar habituar alucinar humillar
-athon	–	acontecimiento similar a una maratón	walkathon talkathon	marcha benéfica larga discusión
-atic	-ático, -a	estado, relación	problematic rheumatic schematic symptomatic	problemático reumático esquemático sintomático
-ation	-ación	var. de -tion	celebration	celebración
-atious	–	forma adjetivos a partir de nombres terminados en -ation	flirtatious ostentatious	coqueto ostentoso
-ative	-ativo, -a	var. de -tive	administrative	administrativo
-backed	–	respaldado por	US-backed	respaldado por Estados Unidos
-based	–	1) con el centro principal en 2) con un ingrediente principal	1) community-based US-based 2) wine-based punch	1) basado en la comunidad con sede en Estados Unidos 2) ponche de vino
-bedroom	–	que cuenta con el número de dormitorios especificado	a three-bedroom house	una casa de tres dormitorios
-behaved	–	describe el comportamiento de alguien	well-/badly-behaved	que se comporta bien/mal
-bodied	–	indica un determinado tipo de complexión	strong-bodied weak-bodied	de complexión fuerte de complexión débil
-born	–	modo, lugar de nacimiento	newborn firstborn American-born	recién nacido primogénito nacido en Estados Unidos

Suffix	Spanish Equivalents	Meanings and Uses	Examples	Spanish
-borne	–	transportado por	airborne	aerotransportado
-bound	–	1) forma adverbios con el significado: "que va hacia algún lugar"	1) westbound	1) que va hacia el oeste
		2) detenido	2) housebound wheelchairbound	2) confinado en casa confinado a una silla de ruedas
		3) forma adjetivos que hacen referencia al material con el que un libro está encuadernado	leather-bound	encuadernado en cuero
-brained	–	indica la capacidad intelectual u organizativa de alguien	bird-brained scatterbrained	estúpido atolondrado
-bund	-bundo	forma nombres y adjetivos que indican tendencia	moribund	moribundo
-burger	–	referido a un bocadillo similar a una hamburguesa	veggieburger	hamburguesa vegetariana
-cardia	-cardia	forma nombres referidos al corazón	tachycardia	taquicardia
-carp	-carpio	forma nombres referidos a fruta	endocarp	endocarpio
-centric	-céntrico, -a	que tiene algo como centro	geocentric egocentric	geocéntrico egocéntrico
-cephalous	-céfalo, -a	forma nombres referidos a la cabeza	bicephalous	bicéfalo
-cephaly	-cefalia	forma nombres referidos a las características de cabeza	microcephaly	microcefalia
-chrome	-cromo, -a	color	monochrome	monocromo
-cidal	-cida	forma adjetivos a partir de nombres terminados en -cide	homicidal	homicida
-cide	-cida, cidio	1) que mata	1) homicide insecticide fratricide	1) homicida insecticida fratricidio
		2) acción y efecto de matar	2) homicide fratricide	2) homicidio fratricidio
-cian	-cista	que tiene una habilidad	electrician mathematician	electricista matemático
-cide	-cidio	acción y efecto de matar	homicide	homicidio
-cle	-cula	var. de -cule	particle	partícula
-clud, -clus	–	cerrar	exclude seclusion	excluir aislamiento
-conscious	–	consciente de algo	self-conscious class-conscious	tímido con conciencia de clase

Suffix	Spanish Equivalents	Meanings and Uses	Examples	Spanish
-corn	-cornio	cuerno	unicorn	unicornio
-cosm	-cosmos	referido al cosmos	microcosm	microcosmos

-cracy	-cracia	1) gobierno, autoridad
		2) clase gobernante
			1) democracy
			   meritocracy
			2) aristocracy
				1) democracia
				   meritocracia
				2) aristocracia

-crat	-crata	miembro de una entidad política	democrat aristocrat	demócrata aristócrata
-cule, -cle	-culo, -a	muy pequeño	miniscule molecule particle	minúsculo molécula partícula

-cy	-cia	1) estado
		2) cargo
		3) cualidad
			1) pregnancy
			2) presidency
			3) proficiency
			   secrecy
				1) embarazo
				2) presidencia
				3) competencia
				   secreto

-cycle	-ciclo	forma nombres que denotan: 1) un proceso circular 2) ruedas	 1) to recycle 2) tricycle	 1) reciclar 2) triciclo
-cyte	-cito	célula	leucocyte	leucocito
-derm, -dermis	-dermo, -dermis	piel	pachyderm epidermis	paquidermo epidermis
-dermy	-dermia	piel	taxidermy	taxidermia
-dimensional	-dimensional	indica el número de dimensiones	two-dimensional three-dimensional	bidimensional tridimensional
-dom	–	1) estado 2) reino	1) boredom 2) kingdom	1) aburrimiento 2) reino

-driven	–	1) accionado
		
		2) estimulado por
			1) menu-driven
			   software
			2) export-driven
			   economy
				1) software guiado
				   por menús
				2) economía cuyo
				   motor son las
				   exportaciones

-drome	-dromo	pista	hippodrome	hipódromo
-dweller	-cola	alude al que vive en un lugar	city-dweller	urbanícola
-dyne	-dino, -a	fuerza	anodyne	anodino
-ean	–	natural de, perteneciente a	Belizean Andean	beliceño andino
-ectomy	-ectomía	escisión quirúrgica	appendectomy	apendectomía

-ed	–	1) forma el pasado y el parcticipio de los verbos
		2) forma adjetivos que indican cualidad
		3) posesión
			1) talked
			
			2) midpriced
			
			3) moneyed
			   bearded
				1) hablado
				
				2) de gama media
				
				3) adinerado
				   barbudo

-ee	–	1) beneficiario de una acción
		2) condición
			1) devotee
			   employee
			2) refugee
				1) devoto
				   empleado
				2) refugiado

-eer	–	1) agente 2) forma verbos	1) auctioneer 2) electioneer	1) subastador 2) hacer campaña electoral

Suffix	Spanish Equivalents	Meanings and Uses	Examples	Spanish
-ella	–	enfermedad	rubella salmonella	rubéola salmonela
-eme	-ema	unidad	morpheme	morfema
-emia	-emia	de la sangre	leukemia anemia	leucemia anemia
-en	– -ecer	1) hecho de 2) forma verbos a partir de adjetivos con el significado: "hacer"	1) woolen 2) toughen, soften	1) de lana 2) endurecer, reblandecer
-enabled	–	1) equipado con una tecnología determinada 2) activado por algo	1) WAP-enabled (cell phone) 2) voice-enabled (software)	1) con tecnología WAP (móvil) 2) (software) activado por voz
-ence, -ency	-encia	forma nombres a partir de adjetivos terminados en -ent	turbulence vehemence clemency	turbulencia vehemencia clemencia
-enne	-a	forma el femenino	comedienne	cómica
-ent	-ente, -a	1) nombres abstractos 2) nombres que indican un agente 3) adjetivos que provocan una determinada acción o que designan un estado	1) alignment agreement nourishment 2) opponent 3) absorbent obedient	1) alineación acuerdo alimento 2) oponente 3) absorbente obediente
-eous	-oso, -a	forma adjetivos a partir de nombres con el significado: "abundancia de", "calidad de"	courageous courteous advantageous	valiente cortés ventajoso
-er	-ero, -or, -(e)dor	1) agente: profesiones y acciones 2) origen	1) baker teacher driver drinker conditioner 2) foreigner New Yorker	1) panadero profesor conductor bebedor suavizante 2) extranjero neoyorquino
-ern	–	forma adjetivos que indican procedencia	northern southern	del norte del sur
-ery, -ry	-ería	1) grupo de objetos 2) actividad 3) lugar donde se realiza algo 4) estado, condición	1) jewelry pottery 2) chemistry industry cookery 3) bakery 4) slavery	1) joyas cerámica 2) química industria cocina 3) panadería 4) esclavitud
-es	-s	1) forma el plural de nombres 2) forma la 3ª persona del singular de verbos	1) churches 2) watches	1) iglesias 2) (él/ella) mira

Suffix	Spanish Equivalents	Meanings and Uses	Examples	Spanish
-escence	-ecencia	forma nombres a partir de verbos terminados en -esce	convalescence	convalecencia
-escent	-eciente	forma nombres y adjetivos a partir de verbos terminados en -esce	convalescent	convaleciente
-ese	-és, -esa	origen, idioma	Japanese officialese	japonés jerga burocrática
-esis	-esis	var. de -sis	diuresis	diuresis
-esque	-esco, -a	referido a la apariencia, al estilo	picturesque picaresque	pintoresco picaresco
-ess	-esa	forma el femenino de nombres	princess	princesa
-est	–	forma el superlativo de adjetivos	softest	el más suave
-et	-ero, -a	forma diminutivos	wristlet cutlet anklet	muñequera chuleta pulsera tobillera
-eth	-ésimo, -a	forma: 1) números ordinales 2) fracciones	1) thirtieth 2) thirtieth	1) trigésimo 2) treintavo
-etic	-ético, -a	forma adjetivos a partir de verbos y nombres	apathetic apologetic pathetic	apático de disculpa patético
-ette	-ito, -a	1) forma diminutivos 2) imitación 3) forma femeninos	1) kitchenette launderette novelette statuette 2) leatherette 3) usherette	1) cocinita lavandería novela rosa estatuilla 2) imitación de cuero 3) acomodadora
-eur	–	profesión	masseur restaurateur entrepreneur	masajista restaurador empresario
-euse	–	forma femenina de -eur	masseuse	masajista
-ey	–	var. de -y	New-Agey	de la Nueva Era
-ferous	-fero, -a	que contiene, produce	coniferous pestiferous	conífero pestilente
-fest	–	ocasión especial	music fest chilifest	festival de música fiesta del chili
-fic	-fero, -a, -fico, -a	que causa	soporific	soporífero
-fication	-ficación	forma nombres a partir de verbos terminados en -fy	specification	especificación
-filled	–	lleno de	fun-filled smoke-filled	muy divertido lleno de humo
-flavored	–	con un sabor determinado	lemon-flavored	con sabor a limón

Suffix	Spanish Equivalents	Meanings and Uses	Examples	Spanish
-footed	-pedo, -a	referido a los pies	four-footed	cuadrúpedo
-form	-forme	con forma de	vermiform	vermiforme
-free	–	1) exento de 2) sin	1) interest-free 2) lead-free trouble-free	1) sin intereses 2) sin plomo sin problemas
-friendly	–	1) inofensivo para 2) apropiado para	1) environmentally-friendly 2) family-friendly	1) ecológico 2) para toda la familia
-fugal	-fugo, -a	forma adjetivos a partir de nombres terminados en -fuge	centrifugal	centrífugo
-fuge	–	que huye	subterfuge centrifuge	subterfugio centrifugadora
-ful	-oso, -a, -ada, -o	1) lleno de 2) característica 3) contenido de	1) doubtful spiteful 2) careful 3) cupful spoonful mouthful	1) indeciso rencoroso 2) cuidadoso 3) taza cucharada bocado
-fy	-ficar	hacer	fortify intensify	fortificar intensificar
-gamous	-gamo, -a	forma adjetivos que indican unión	monogamous	monógamo
-gamy	-gamia	forma nombres que indican unión	monogamy	monogamia
-gen	-geno	forma nombres a partir de lo que éstos generan	allergen	alérgeno
-genic	-génico, -a -geno, -a	1) apropiado para 2) que causa, que genera	1) photogenic telegenic 2) hallucinogenic allergenic	1) fotogénico telegénico 2) alucinógeno alergénico
-geny	-genia	forma nombres a partir del origen o proceso de formación de éstos	orogeny	orogenia
-gnosis	–	conocimiento	prognosis diagnosis	pronóstico' diagnosis
-gnostic	–	forma adjetivos a partir de nombres terminados en -gnosis	diagnostic	diagnóstico
-goer	–	referido a alguien que frecuenta algo	moviegoer	cinéfilo
-gon	-gono	angular	hexagon	hexágono
-grade	-grado, -a	que se mueve	retrograde upgrade	retrógrado mejorar
-grader	–	referido a alguien de un determinado curso en la escuela	second-grader	estudiante de segundo curso
-gram	-grama -gramo	1) escrito 2) peso del sistema métrico	1) diagram 2) kilogram	1) diagrama 2) kilogramo

Suffix	Spanish Equivalents	Meanings and Uses	Examples	Spanish
-graph	-grafiar -grafo -grafía	1) forma verbos con el significado: "escribir" 2) forma nombres con el significado: "escrito, grabado"	1) choreograph 2) autograph photograph	1) coreografiar 2) autógrafo fotografía
-grapher	-grafo, -a	forma nombres referidos a alguien que describe algo	geographer lexicographer	geógrafo lexicógrafo
-graphy	-grafía	1) ciencia, arte de 2) relacionado con la escritura 3) escrito, grabación de	1) oceanography lexicography 2) stenography 3) orthography	1) oceanografía lexicografía 2) estenografía 3) ortografía
-gynist **-gynistic**	-gino, -a	forma nombres y adjetivos referidos a mujeres	misogynist n, adj misogynistic	misógino misógino
-gynous	-gino, -a	de las mujeres	androgynous	andrógino
-haired	–	referido al pelo	long-haired dark-haired	de pelo largo de pelo moreno
-hater	–	que odia	woman-hater	misógino
-head	–	1) relacionado con la cabeza 2) referido a la estupidez 3) parte superior de	1) redhead 2) knucklehead fathead hammerhead 3) letterhead	1) pelirrojo, 2) cabeza de chorlito imbécil cabeza de martillo 3) membrete
-hearted	–	forma adjetivos referidos a ciertas características	wholehearted broken-hearted	entusiasta destrozado
-oholic	-ólico, -a	var. de -aholic	alcoholic	alcohólico
-hood	-dad	1) estado o condición 2) grupo de personas	1) falsehood fatherhood childhood 2) brotherhood	1) falsedad paternidad infancia 2) hermandad
-hungry	–	con un fuerte deseo de algo	power-hungry	hambriento de poder
-hunter	–	alguien que busca algo	job-hunter house-hunter fortune hunter	persona que busca trabajo persona que busca una vivienda cazafortunas
-ia	-ia –	1) países y regiones 2) forma plurales de palabras procedentes del latín	1) Australia Andalusia 2) bacteria	1) Australia Andalucía 2) bacteria
-ial	-ial	forma adjetivos con el significado: "perteneciente a"	ministerial industrial managerial	ministerial industrial gerencial
-ian	–	var. de -an	Canadian optician	canadiense óptico

Suffix	Spanish Equivalents	Meanings and Uses	Examples	Spanish
-iana	–	var. de -ana	Canadiana	aspectos característicos de Canadá
-iasis	-iasis	enfermedad, condición	elephantiasis amebiasis	elefantiasis amebiasis
-iatrician, -iatrist	-iatra	forms nouns referring to medical specialists	pediatrician psychiatrist	pediatra psiquiatra
-iatrics, -iatry	-iatría	referido a una especialidad médica	geriatrics psychiatry	geriatría psiquiatría
-ibility	-ilidad	var. de -ability	compatibility	compatibilidad
-ible	-ible	var. de -able	edible	comestible
-ibly	-iblemente	var. de -ably	audibly terribly	de forma audible terriblemente

-ic, -ical	-ico, -a	1) similar a
		
		2) relacionado con
			1) acidic
			   heroic
			2) poetic
			   mathematic
				1) ácido
				   heroico
				2) poético
				   matemático

-ically	-icamente	forma adverbios a partir de adjetivos terminados en -ic, -ical	alphabetically heroically	alfabéticamente heroicamente
-ice	–	estado, condición	cowardice service	cobardía servicio
-ics	-ica	forma nombres que indican un campo de actividad	ceramics cybernetics economics	cerámica cibernética economía
-id	-ido, -a	indica pertenencia a una familia zoológica	arachnid	arácnido
-ie	-ito, -a	*inf* var. de -y como diminutivo	birdie	pajarito
-ier	-ero, -a –	1) forma nombres referidos a profesiones 2) forma el comparativo de adjetivos terminados en -y	1) cashier 2) happier	1) cajero 2) más feliz
-ify	-ificar	forma verbos a partir de adjetivos con el significado: "hacer"	clarify glorify	aclarar glorificar
-ile	-il	1) relacionado con 2) capaz de	1) infantile 2) mobile	1) infantil 2) móvil
-ility	-ilidad	forma nombres referidos a la capacidad de ser o hacer algo	versatility visibility	versatilidad visibilidad
-iment	-imento	var. de -mento	impediment	impedimento
-in	-ina	referido a sustancias químicas	vitamin gelatin lanolin toxin	vitamina gelatina lanolina toxina
-ina	-ina	forma femeninos	tsarina, ballerina	zarina, bailarina

Suffix	Spanish Equivalents	Meanings and Uses	Examples	Spanish
-induced	-	se une al agente de la acción	self-induced work-induced	autoinducido provocado por el trabajo

-ine	-ino, -a	1) con un carácter determinado
		2) forma nombres abstractos
		3) origen, procedencia
		4) sustancias químicas
			1) crystalline
			   feminine
			2) medicine
			
			3) Argentine
			4) antihistamine
			   caffeine
				1) cristalino
				   femenino
				2) medicina
				
				3) Argentina
				4) antihistamínico
				   cafeína

-ing	-ando, -iendo
	-
		1) forma gerundios
		2) forma el participio de presente que puede utilizarse de forma adjetival
			1) playing
			2) they are playing
			   playing children
				1) jugando
				2) están jugando
				   niños que juegan

-ious	-oso, -a	forma adjetivos con el significado: "con la cualidad de"	capricious cautious	caprichoso cuidadoso

-ish	-áceo, -a;
	ento,-a;
	-uzco
		1) naturaleza
		2) origen; de un idioma
		3) similar a
		
		4) bastante, un tanto
			1) childish
			2) British, English
			
			3) piggish
			   nightmarish
			   puplish
			   yellowish
			   blackish
			4) newish
				1) infantil
				2) británico, inglés
				
				3) puerco
				   espeluznante
				   violáceo
				   amarillento
				   negruzco
				4) bastante nuevo

-ism	-ismo	forma nombres referidos a un sistema, doctrina, modo o condición	totalitarianism cynicism tourism	totalitarismo cinismo turismo
-ist	-ista	agente, alguien que realiza una actividad o profesión determinada	artist dentist plagiarist realist tourist	artista dentista plagiario realista turista
-istic	-ista	forma adjetivos a partir de nombres terminados en -ist	realistic	realista
-istics	-ística	ciencia, práctica	linguistics statistics logistics	lingüística estadística logística

-ite	-ita	1) natural de
		2) creyente en
			1) Wisconsinite
			2) Shiite
			   socialite
				1) wisconsinita
				2) chiíta
				   persona con mucha vida social

-itis	-itis	referido a una infección	conjunctivitis cystitis	conjuntivitis cistitis
-itive	-itivo, -a	que tiene tal tendencia, que causa	inquisitive repetitive	curioso repetitivo
-ity	-idad	estado de, cualidad	absurdity captivity clarity complexity	absurdo cautiverio claridad complejidad

Suffix	Spanish Equivalents	Meanings and Uses	Examples	Spanish
-ive	-ivo, -a	1) tendencia hacia 2) que causa 3) capacidad para	1) appreciative 2) digestive 3) competitive	1) agradecido 2) digestivo 3) competitivo
-ization	-ización	forma nombres de verbos terminados en -ize	familiarization centralization	familiarización centralización
-ize	-izar	hacer, realizar una acción	familiarize centralize computerize	familiarizar centralizar informatizar
-ject	–	lanzar	eject inject reject	expulsar inyectar rechazar
-kin	–	diminutivo	bumpkin manikin napkin	paleto maniquí servilleta
-land	-landa, -landia	forma nombres de países, regiones y nombres de tipos de campo	Switzerland Newfoundland Finnland swampland	Suiza Terranova Finlandia pantano
-lateral	-látero, -a	significa "lado" y forma adjectivos y nombres	quadrilateral	cuadrilátero
-legged	–	referido a las piernas o patas	six-legged	de six patas
-length	–	forma adverbios que indican una longitud	knee-length shoulder-length	hasta la rodilla hasta los hombros
-lepsy	-lepsia	ataque	epilepsy narcolepsy	epilepsia narcolepsia
-less	–	sin	effortless careless homeless	sin esfuerzo distraído sin hogar
-let	–	diminutivo	leaflet piglet quintuplet rivulet	folleto cochinillo quintillizo arroyo
-like	–	similar, parecido a	sportsmanlike businesslike childlike	de espíritu deportivo formal infantil
-ling	–	1) diminutivo 2) despectivo	1) duckling fledgling 2) underling hireling	1) patito polluelo 2) subordinado mercenario
-lite	-lita -litis	1) referido a minerales 2) var. de -itis, referido a una condición	1) cryolite 2) cellulite	1) criolita 2) celulitis
-lith	-lito	piedra	monolith	monolito
-lithic	-lítico, -a	periodos en arqueología	paleolithic	paleolítico
-load	–	carga, que va muy cargado	busloads truckload	autobuses llenos carga de un camión
-log, -logue	-logo	referido a palabras	monolog epilog	monólogo epílogo

Suffix	Spanish Equivalents	Meanings and Uses	Examples	Spanish
-logist	-logo	forma nombres de especialistas en algún campo	pharmacologist	farmacólogo, -a
-logic, -logy	-logía	estudio de	anthropology dermatology	antropología dermatología
-ly	-mente	1) forma adverbios de modo 2) forma adjetivos y adverbios que indican intervalos de tiempo	1) madly carelessly 2) weekly monthly	1) frenéticamente de forma imprudente 2) semanal(mente), mensual(mente)
-lysis	-lisis	forma nombres que expresan "disolución", "descomposición"	hydrolysis	diálisis
-maker	–	persona o máquina que hace algo	dressmaker watchmaker coffeemaker icemaker	modisto relojero máquina de café máquina de hielo
-man	–	1) referido a un hombre con una determinada característica, actividad o profesión 2) indica el número de personas en un grupo	1) linesman madman mailman 2) a four-man team	1) juez de línea loco cartero 2) un equipo de cuatro
-mania	-manía	indica una obsesión	pyromania megalomania kleptomania	piromanía megalomanía cleptomanía
-mannered	–	significa "educado" y forma adjetivos	ill-mannered mild-mannered	mal educado educado
-manship	–	indica una habilidad	swordsmanship workmanship marksmanship	destreza en el manejo de la espada destreza puntería
-meister	–	referido a una persona considerada habilidosa en algo	spinmeister	*persona que difunde información positiva acerca de un político*
-ment	-mento, -miento	forma nombres con los significados: 1) estado de 2) resultado de	1) contentment excitement 2) alignment	1) satisfacción emoción 2) alineación
-meter	-metro	medida	chronometer speedometer	cronómetro velocímetro
-minded	–	referido a un tipo de mentalidad	narrow-minded strong-minded	de mentalidad cerrada/resuelto
-morphous	-morfo, -a	referido a forma, a apariencia	amorphous polymorphous	amorfo polimorfo
-most	–	forma superlativos	outermost rearmost southernmost	más exterior último más al sur

Suffix	Spanish Equivalents	Meanings and Uses	Examples	Spanish
-motive	–	movimiento, propulsión	automotive locomotive	automovilístico locomotora
-mouthed	–	referido a la forma de hablar de alguien	loudmouthed foulmouthed	gritón malhablado
-natured	–	que tiene una cierta cualidad esencial	good-natured	bondadoso por naturaleza
-ness, -iness	–	estado o cualidad de	hopelessness carelessness bitterness sleepiness	desamparo despreocupación amargura somnolencia
-nik	–	alguien asociado a algo	beatnik peacenik	beatnik persona que prefiere la negociación en lugar de recurrir a la fuerza
-nome	-nomo	especialistas en algún campo	gastronome	gastrónomo
-nomy	-nomía	1) ley o estructura de 2) estudio de	1) taxonomy economy autonomy 2) astronomy	2) taxonomía economía autonomía 2) astronomía
-o	–	forma designaciones jergales de personas con determinados hábitos o características	wino weirdo dumbo	borrachín bicho raro tonto
-ock	–	diminutivo	bullock hillock	novillo montículo
-oholic	-ólico, -a	adicto a	alcoholic	alcohólico
-oid	-oide	parecido a	spheroid	esferoide
-ology	-ología	estudio de	biology geology	biología geología
-oma	-oma	tumor	carcinoma melanoma	carcinoma melanoma
-onym	-ónimo	referido a un nombre	synonym pseudonym	sinónimo seudónimo
-onymous	-ónimo, -a	forma adjetivos a partir de nombres terminados en -onym	synonymous	sinónimo
-onymy	-onimia	forma nombres a partir de adjetivos terminados en -onymous	synonymy	sinonimia
-opia	-opía	referido al ojo	myopia	miopía
-opsy	-opsia	da lugar a nombres que denotan "análisis" o "estudio"	biopsy	biopsia
-or	-or	agente	actor exhibitor agitator processor	actor expositor agitador procesador

Suffix	Spanish Equivalents	Meanings and Uses	Examples	Spanish
-orial	-orial	forma adjetivos a partir de nombres terminados en -or, -ory	senatorial dictatorial territorial	senatorial dictatorial territorial
-oriented	-	referido al objetivo de algo	profit-oriented	orientado a la obtención de beneficios
-orium	-orio	indica un lugar	crematorium emporium sanatorium	crematorio emporio sanatorio
-ory	-orio, -a	relacionado con, con un determinado carácter	circulatory transitory contradictory contributory	circulatorio transitorio contradictorio contributivo
-ose	-oso, -a	lleno de, que se caracteriza por	verbose	verboso
-osis	-osis	1) enfermedad 2) proceso	1) psychosis neurosis 2) hypnosis narcosis	1) psicosis neurosis 2) hipnosis narcosis
-ous	-oso, -a	1) lleno de 2) que tiene	1) mysterious nervous acrimonious 2) voluminous cancerous	1) misterioso nervioso mordaz 2) voluminoso canceroso
-owned	–	denota propiedad	family-owned state-owned	propiedad de la familia propiedad del estado
-packed	–	lleno de	action-packed	lleno de acción
-path	-pata	1) referido a alguien que cura de un determinado modo 2) referido a alguien que padece una determinada enfermedad	1) homeopath naturopath 2) psychopath	1) homeópata naturópata 2) psicópata
-pathic	-pático, -a	forma adjetivos a partir de nombres terminados en -pathy	homeopathic telepathic	homeopático telepático
-pathy	-patía	1) que siente 2) relacionado con un tratamiento médico	1) empathy sympathy telepathy 2) homeopathy	1) empatía compasión telepatía 2) homeopatía
-ped	-pedo, -a	que tiene un determinado número de pies	biped quadruped	bípedo cuadrúpedo
-pedia	-pedia	forma nombres que denotan educación, instrucción	encyclopedia	enciclopedia
-pepsia	-pepsia	relacionado con la digestión	dyspepsia	dispepsia

Suffix	Spanish Equivalents	Meanings and Uses	Examples	Spanish
-person	–	forma designaciones de género neutro a partir de palabras terminadas en -man para designar profesiones o cargos	spokesperson chairperson	portavoz presidente
-phagia, phagy	-fagia	alimentación, digestión	aerophagia	aerofagia
-phagous	-fago, -a	designa al que come	anthropophagus	antropófago
-phile	-filo, -a	amigo de, amante de	technophile bibliophile Anglophile	tecnófilo bibliófilo anglófilo
-philia	-filia	denota un gusto o una inclinación por algo	Anglophilia	anglofilia
-phobe	-fobo, -a	referido a alguien que siente aversión a algo/ alguien	technophobe Anglophobe	tecnófobo anglófobo
-phobia	-fobia	aversión	claustrophobia xenophobia hydrophobia	claustrofobia xenofobia hidrofobia
-phobic	-fóbico, -a	forma adjetivos a partir de nombres terminados en -phobia	xenophobic claustrophobic	xenófobo claustrofóbico
-phone	-fón, -fono -fono, -a	1) instrumentos que emplean o producen sonido 2) hablante de un idioma	1) saxophone megaphone microphone telephone xylophone 2) Anglophone Francophone	1) saxofón megáfono micrófono teléfono xilófono 2) anglófono francófono
-phony	-fonía	sonido	cacophony euphony	cacofonía eufonía
-phyte	-fito	planta, vegetal	microphyte	micrófito
-plane	–	avión	seaplane biplane	hidroavión biplano
-plasty	-plastia	forma nombres que expresan una reconstrucción	abdominoplasty	abdominoplástia
-plex	–	formado por un determinado número de unidades	duplex multiplex	casa adosada multicines
-plexy	-plejía	indica una parálisis	apoplexy	apoplejía
-pod	-pode	pie	tripod	trípode
-polis	-poli(s)	ciudad	metropolis	metrópoli
-powered	–	referido a cómo funciona una máquina	battery-powered nuclear-powered	que funciona con pilas que utiliza energía nuclear

Suffix	Spanish Equivalents	Meanings and Uses	Examples	Spanish
-proof	–	que es resistente a	ovenproof rustproof shatterproof soundproof bulletproof	refractario inoxidable inastillable insonorizado a prueba de balas
-prone	–	al que le suele ocurrir algo	accident-prone	propenso a tener accidentes
-red	–	condición de	hatred sacred	odio sagrado
-ria	-ria	1) designa nombres de enfermedades y nombres científicos 2) designa nombres de lugares	1) diphtheria malaria wisteria 2) Bulgaria	1) difteria malaria glicina 2) Bulgaria
-rrhage	-rragia	flujo anómalo de	hemorrhage	hemorragia
-ridden	–	lleno de	guilt-ridden	atormentado por un sentido de culpabilidad
-ry	–	var. de -ery	chemistry	química
's	–	indica posesión	Mark's car	el coche de Mark
-s	-s	1) forma el plural de nombres 2) forma la 3ª persona del singular del presente de los verbos	1) cats 2) she lives	1) gatos 2) ella vive
-scape	-	designa un determinado tipo de vista	landscape seascape townscape	paisaje vista marina paisaje urbano
-scope	-scopio	instrumento que permite ver	microscope gyroscope hygroscope	microscopio giroscopio higroscopio
-scopy	-scopia	examen realizado con un instrumento	gastroscopy	endoscopia
-sect	-seccionar	cortar	dissect	diseccionar
-ship	-	1) estado 2) cargo 3) habilidad	1) friendship 2) championship dictatorship 3) horsemanship marksmanship	1) amistad 2) campeonato dictadura 3) equitación puntería
-sion	-sión	1) acción 2) resultado 3) condición	1) emission inclusion 2) emulsion explosion 3) tension	1) emisión inclusión 2) emulsión explosión 3) tensión
-some	–	1) propenso a 2) un grupo de (cuando se añade a numerales)	1) quarrelsome tiresome troublesome 2) twosome foursome	1) pendenciero pesado molesto 2) dúo grupo de cuatro personas

Suffix	Spanish Equivalents	Meanings and Uses	Examples	Spanish
-speak	–	designa el idioma de un determinado grupo, jerga	doublespeak netspeak technospeak	palabras ambiguas lenguaje de la red lenguaje tecnológico
-sphere	-sferio	esfera	hemisphere	hemisferio
-ster	–	designa a una persona con una cualidad determinada, o a quien lleva a cabo una determinada acción	youngster, mobster pollster tipster trickster	joven gángster encuestador pronosticador estafador
-stress	–	forma femeninos	seamstress	costurera
-sy	–	forma adjetivos y nombres; suele tener una connotación negativa	tipsy tricksy whimsy artsy	bebido juguetón capricho pseudoartístico
-technics	-tecnia	forma nombres referidos a algún arte o habilidad	pyrotechnics	pirotecnia
-teen	–	1) forma los números entre el 13 y el 19 2) parecido a	1) nineteen 2) velveteen	1) diecinueve 2) velvetón
-th	–	1) estado de; acción 2) números ordinales	1) youth death; growth 2) thirteenth	1) juventud muerte; crecimiento 2) decimotercero
-therapy	-terapia	tratamientos médicos	psychotherapy	psicoterapia
-therm	-termo, -a	significa "calor" y forma nombres y adjetivos	isotherm	isotermo
-thermia	-termia	forma nombres y denota calor	hypothermia	hipotermia
-tion	-ción	1) resultado 2) estado	1) inflation reflection salvation 2) infection inhibition	1) inflación reflexión salvamento 2) infección inhibición
-tious	-cioso, -a	forma adjetivos a partir de nombres terminados en -tion	ambitious cautious	ambicioso cauto
-tomy	-tomía	operación, escisión	appendectomy	apendectomía
-tor	-ador, -dora	agente	arbitrator collaborator calculator	árbitro colaborador calculador
-tory	–	agente	anticipatory accusatory	previsor acusador
-trophy	-trofia	forms nouns referring to food, nourishment	hypertrophy	hipertrofia
-tude	-tud	estado de	gratitude solitude	gratitud soledad

Suffix	Spanish Equivalents	Meanings and Uses	Examples	Spanish
-ty	-dad	1) cualidad, estado 2) forma las decenas de los numerales	1) royalty safety 2) seventy	1) realeza seguridad 2) setenta
-ule	-ulo, -a	diminutivo	granule	gránulo
-ulent	-ulento, -a	con abundancia de	fraudulent	fraudulento
-ulous	-oso, -a	propenso a, que tiende a	miraculous nebulous	milagroso nebuloso
-ure	-	1) indica el resultado de algo 2) condición	1) mixture exposure 2) moisture pleasure	1) mezcla exposición 2) humedad placer
-ville	-	1) indica el nombre de un lugar 2) *sl* denomina un lugar, cosa o condición que tiene una determinada cualidad	1) Jacksonville 2) dullsville	1) Jacksonville 2) lugar aburrido
-vore,	-voro, -a	relacionado con comer	carnivore herbivore	carnívoro herbívoro
-vorous	-voro, -a	forma adjetivos a partir de palabras terminadas en -vore	carnivorous herbivorous omnivorous	carnívoro herbívoro omnívoro
-walker, -walking	-ámbulo	forma adjetivos y nombres con relación al caminar	sleepwalker tightrope walker	sonámbulo funámbulo
-ward(s)	–	hacia	backward(s) inwards outwards upwards	hacia atrás hacia dentro hacia fuera hacia arriba
-ways	–	dirección	lengthways	a lo largo
-wide	–	en todo un lugar	worldwide nationwide	mundial a nivel nacional
-wise	–	forma adverbios que indican dirección	clockwise	en el sentido de las agujas del reloj
-woman	–	equivalente femenino de -man	chairwoman	presidenta
-worthy	–	1) que merece 2) apropiado para algo	1) trustworthy newsworthy 2) roadworthy	1) honrado de interés periodístico 2) apto para circular
-y, -ey	–	1) forma nombres que designan un estado o acción 2) diminutivo informal (ver -ie) 3) forma adjetivos con los significados: "con abundancia de", "que tiende a ser"	1) captivity 2) puppy 3) bumpy faulty bubbly creamy clingy	1) cautiverio 2) cachorro 3) desigual defectuoso burbujeante cremoso pegajoso
-yer	–	var. de -er	lawyer	abogado

Falsos amigos

Para más información el usuario debe consultar la entrada en el diccionario. En los casos en los que la palabra inglesa está fuera del orden alfabético, ésta aparece en *cursiva*.

False friends

Readers should consult the main section of the dictionary for more complete translation information. When the English term appears out of alphabetical order, it is shown in *italics*.

Meaning(s) of the Spanish word:	falso amigo false friend		Significado(s) de la palabra inglesa:
	español	English	
1) enormous	abismal	abysmal	pésimo
1) present 2) current	actual	actual	verdadero
at the moment	actualmente	actually	en realidad
1) appropriate 2) fitting, suitable	adecuado, -a	adequate	1) suficiente 2) adecuado
1) engagement calendar 2) agenda	agenda	agenda	orden del día
bedroom	alcoba	alcove	nicho
1) entertainment 2) enjoyment	amenidad	amenities	comodidades
1) to attend (*vi*) 2) to help (*vt*)	asistir	to assist	ayudar
1) audience 2) (JUR) hearing; courtroom	audiencia	audience	1) público 2) audiencia
1) to notify 2) to warn 3) to call	avisar	*to advise*	aconsejar, asesorar
1) (10^{12}) trillion 2) (10^9 *esp AmL*) billion	billón	billion	1) (10^9) mil millones, millardo 2) (10^{12}, *esp Brit*) billón
1) white 2) pale	blanco, -a	blank	1) en blanco 2) vacío, sin expresión 3) absoluto, completo
1) soft 2) mild 3) cowardly	blando, -a	bland	1) suave, 2) soso
1) (*interj*) well done 2) brave 3) wild 4) hot	bravo, -a	brave	valiente
1) countryside 2) field 3) camp	campo	camp	1) campamento 2) grupo
1) understanding 2) tolerant 3) comprehensive	comprensivo, -a	comprehensive	exhaustivo, completo
1) commitment 2) promise 3) agreement 4) awkward situation	compromiso	compromise	1) transigencia 2) arreglo

Meaning(s) of the Spanish word:	falso amigo false friend		Significado(s) de la palabra inglesa:
	español	English	
1) leader 2) driver	conductor(a)	conductor	1) (MUS) director 2) (PHYS, ELEC) conductor 3) cobrador, (RAIL) revisor
1) lecture 2) conference 3) call	conferencia	conference	congreso, conferencia
estar constipado: to have a cold	constipado, -a	constipated	estreñido, -a
1) to build 2) to construe	construir	to construe	interpretar
1) to check 2) to control	controlar	to control	1) dominar 2) controlar
1) habit 2) custom	costumbre	costume	1) traje 2) disfraz
disappointment	decepción	deception	1) engaño 2) fraude
to disappoint	decepcionar	to deceive	engañar
1) request 2) (COM) demand 3) (JUR) action	demanda	demand	1) exigencia 2) (COM)demanda
1) to ask for 2) (JUR) to sue	demandar	to demand	1) reclamar 2) requerir
1) to displease 2) to anger, to offend	disgustar	to disgust	1) dar asco 2) repugnar
1) displeasure 2) suffering 3) quarrel	disgusto	disgust	1) repugnancia, asco 2) indignación
1) to divert 2) to entertain 3) to embezzle	distraer	to distract	distraer
1) pregnancy 2) awkwardness	embarazo	embarrassment	1) vergüenza 2) molestia
1) escape 2) excursion	escapada	escapade	aventura
1) stage 2) scene	escenario	scenery	1) paisaje 2) (THEAT, CINE) decorado
1) possible 2) extra	eventual	eventual	final
fortuitously, possibly	eventualmente	eventually	1) finalmente 2) con el tiempo
1) to incite 2) to irritate 3) to arouse	excitar	to excite	1) emocionar 2) estimular
success	éxito	exit	1) salida 2) (AUTO) desvío
1) strangeness 2) eccentricity	extravagancia	extravagance	1) derroche 2) lujo 3) extravagancia

Meaning(s) of the Spanish word:	falso amigo false friend		Significado(s) de la palabra inglesa:
	español	English	
1) odd 2) eccentric	extravagante	extravagant	1) despilfarrador 2) lujoso 3) excesivo 4) extravagante
1) factory 2) masonry 3) building	fábrica	fabric	1) tejido 2) estructura
1) to manufacture 2) to build 3) to fabricate	fabricar	to fabricate	1) inventar 2) fabricar 3) falsificar
crème caramel	flan	flan	1) tarta 2) flan
1) sentence 2) expression, saying 3) style 4) (MÚS) phrase	frase	*phrase*	1) locución 2) expresión
1) study 2) dressing room 3) office 4) (POL) cabinet	gabinete	*cabinet*	1) armario, vitrina 2) (POL) gabinete de ministros
1) brilliant 2) funny 3) great	genial	genial	afable
1) genius 2) stroke of genius	genialidad	geniality	afabilidad
1) pagan 2) dashing, elegant 3) considerate	gentil (*adj*)	genteel	distinguido
1) to be ignorant of 2) to ignore	ignorar	to ignore	no hacer caso de
uninhabitable	inhabitable	inhabitable	habitable
uninhabited	inhabitado, -a	inhabited	habitado
insult, harm	injuria	injury	1) lesión 2) herida
to insult, to injure	injuriar	*to injure*	1) herir 2) estropear 3) perjudicar
poisoning	intoxicación	intoxication	1) embriaguez 2) (MED) intoxicación
to poison	intoxicar	*to intoxicate*	1) embriagar 2) (MED) intoxicar
1) to insert 2) to put in	introducir	to introduce	1) presentar 2) iniciar 3) abordar 4) introducir
long	largo, -a	large	grande
1) reading 2) reading material	lectura	lecture	1) discurso, conferencia 2) sermón 3) consejo

Meaning(s) of the Spanish word:	falso amigo false friend		Significado(s) de la palabra inglesa:
	español	English	
1) bookshop 2) stationer's 3) library 4) bookcase	librería	library	1) biblioteca 2) colección
mask	máscara	mascara	rímel
1) poverty 2) pittance 3) stinginess 4) misfortune	miseria	misery	1) infelicidad 2) sufrimiento 3) miseria, lipidia *AmC*
to inconvenience, to annoy	molestar	to molest	1) importunar 2) abusar (sexualmente) de
piece of news	noticia	notice	1) interés 2) letrero, anuncio 3) aviso
1) well-known 2) obvious	notorio, -a	notorious	de mala reputación
obvious	ostensible	ostensible	aparente
relative	pariente	parent	padre, madre
newspaper	periódico	periodical	1) publicación periodica 2) boletín
1) arrogant 2) insolent	petulante	petulant	enfurruñado
condom	preservativo	preservative	conservante
conceited	presuntuoso, -a	presumptuous	1) impertinente 2) osado
1) to aspire to 2) to expect 3) to mean to 4) to try to	pretender	to pretend	1) fingir 2) pretender
teacher	profesor	professor	profesor de universidad
1) to carry out, to make 2) to make real, to fulfil 3) (ECON) to realize 4) (CINE, TV) to produce	realizar	to realize	1) ser consciente de 2) realizar 3) cumplir
container, vessel	recipiente	recipient	destinatario
1) to remember 2) to remind	recordar	to record	1) archivar 2) registrar, grabar
saying, proverb	refrán	refrain	estribillo
importance	relevancia	relevance	pertinencia
1) important 2) outstanding	relevante	relevant	pertinente
to summarize	resumir	to resume	1) reanudar, proseguir con 2) volver a ocupar
1) insinuating 2) reluctant	reticente	reticent	reticente
reward, remuneration	retribución	retribution	castigo justo
health	sanidad	sanity	cordura

Meaning(s) of the Spanish word:	falso amigo false friend		Significado(s) de la palabra inglesa:
	español	English	
1) healthy 2) intact	sano, -a	*sane*	1) cuerdo 2) sensato
sensitive, impressionable	sensible	sensible	1) sensato, prudente 2) práctico 3) notable 4) consciente
1) liking 2) friendliness	simpatía	sympathy	1) compasión, comprensión 2) solidaridad
friendly	simpático, -a	*sympathetic*	1) comprensivo, receptivo 2) simpatizante
1) to support 2) to stand	soportar	*to support*	1) sostener, aguantar 2) mantener 3) financiar
1) smooth 2) soft 3) gentle 4) mild	suave	suave	afable, cortés
1) poor suburb 2) slum area	suburbio	suburb	barrio periférico
1) to succeed (*vi*) 2) to happen (*vi*) 3) to follow on (*vi*) 4) to inherit (*vt*)	suceder	to succeed	1) tener éxito, lograr hacer algo 2) suceder
1) event, incident 2) outcome	suceso	success	éxito
1) hypnotic power 2) suggestion 3) inspiration	sugestión	suggestion	1) sugerencia 2) insinuación
1) commonplace 2) cliché	tópico	topic	tema
1) (10^{18}) quintillion	trillón	trillion	1) (10^{12}) billón 2) (10^{18}, *esp Brit*) trillón
2) dissolute 3) habit-forming 4) defective 5) spoiled	vicioso, -a	vicious	1) malo, salvaje 2) despiadado 3) feroz 4) atroz

Los numerales

Numerals

Los numerales cardinales

Cardinal numbers

cero	0	zero
uno (*apócope* un), una	1	one
dos	2	two
tres	3	three
cuatro	4	four
cinco	5	five
seis	6	six
siete	7	seven
ocho	8	eight
nueve	9	nine
diez	10	ten
once	11	eleven
doce	12	twelve
trece	13	thirteen
catorce	14	fourteen
quince	15	fifteen
dieciséis	16	sixteen
diecisiete	17	seventeen
dieciocho	18	eighteen
diecinueve	19	nineteen
veinte	20	twenty
veintiuno (*apócope* veintiún), -a	21	twenty-one
veintidós	22	twenty-two
veintitrés	23	twenty-three
veinticuatro	24	twenty-four
veinticinco	25	twenty-five
treinta	30	thirty
treinta y uno (*apócope* treinta y un) -a	31	thirty-one
treinta y dos	32	thirty-two
treinta y tres	33	thirty-three
cuarenta	40	forty
cuarenta y uno (*apócope* cuarenta y un) -a	41	forty-one
cuarenta y dos	42	forty-two
cincuenta	50	fifty
cincuenta y uno (*apócope* cincuenta y un) -a	51	fifty-one
cincuenta y dos	52	fifty-two
sesenta	60	sixty

sesenta y uno (*apócope* sesenta y un) –a	61	sixty-one
sesenta y dos	62	sixty-two
setenta	70	seventy
setenta y uno (*apócope* setenta y un) –a	71	seventy-one
setenta y dos	72	seventy-two
setenta y cinco	75	seventy-five
setenta y nueve	79	seventy-nine
ochenta	80	eighty
ochenta y uno (*apócope* ochenta y un) –a	81	eighty-one
ochenta y dos	82	eighty-two
ochenta y cinco	85	eighty-five
noventa	90	ninety
noventa y uno (*apócope* noventa y un) –a	91	ninety-one
noventa y dos	92	ninety-two
noventa y nueve	99	ninety-nine
cien	100	one hundred
ciento uno (*apócope* ciento un) -a	101	one hundred and one
ciento dos	102	one hundred and two
ciento diez	110	one hundred and ten
ciento veinte	120	one hundred and twenty
ciento noventa y nueve	199	one hundred and ninety-nine
dos cientos, -as	200	two hundred
dos cientos uno (*apócope* doscientos un) –a	201	two hundred and one
dos cientos veintidós	222	two hundred and twenty-two
tres cientos, -as	300	three hundred
cuatro cientos, -as	400	four hundred
quinientos, -as	500	five hundred
seiscientos, -as	600	six hundred
setecientos, -as	700	seven hundred
ochocientos, -as	800	eight hundred
nuevecientos, -as	900	nine hundred
mil	1 000	one thousand
mil uno (*apócope* mil un) -a	1 001	one thousand and one
mil diez	1 010	one thousand and ten
mil cien	1 100	one thousand one hundred
dos mil	2 000	two thousand
diez mil	10 000	ten thousand
cien mil	100 000	one hundred thousand
un millón	1 000 000	one million
dos millones	2 000 000	two million

dos millones quinientos, -as mil	2 500 000	two million, five hundred thousand
mil millones, un millardo	1 000 000 000	one billion
un billón	1 000 000 000 000	one trillion
mil billones	1 000 000 000 000 000	one quadrillion
un trillón	1 000 000 000 000 000 000	one quintillion

Los numerales ordinales   Ordinal numbers

primero (*apócope* primer), -a	1°, 1ª	1st	first
segundo, -a	2°, 2ª	2nd	second
tercero (*apócope* tercer), -a	3°, 3ª	3rd	third
cuarto, -a	4°, 4ª	4th	fourth
quinto, -a	5°, 5ª	5th	fifth
sexto, -a	6°, 6ª	6th	sixth
séptimo, -a	7°, 7ª	7th	seventh
octavo, -a	8°, 8ª	8th	eighth
noveno, -a	9°, 9ª	9th	ninth
décimo, -a	10°, 10ª	10th	tenth
undécimo, -a	11°, 11ª	11th	eleventh
duodécimo, -a	12°, 12ª	12th	twelfth
decimotercero, -a	13°, 13ª	13th	thirteenth
decimocuarto, -a	14°, 14ª	14th	fourteenth
decimoquinto, -a	15°, 15ª	15th	fifteenth
decimosexto, -a	16°, 16ª	16th	sixteenth
decimoséptimo, -a	17°, 17ª	17th	seventeenth
decimoctavo, -a	18°, 18ª	18th	eighteenth
decimonoveno, -a	19°, 19ª	19th	nineteenth
vigésimo, -a	20°, 20ª	20th	twentieth
vigésimo, -a primero, -a (o vigesimoprimero, -a)	21°, 21ª	21st	twenty-first
vigésimo, -a segundo, -a (o vigesimosegundo, -a)	22°, 22ª	22nd	twenty-second
vigésimo, -a tercero, -a (o vigesimotercero, -a)	23°, 23ª	23rd	twenty-third
trigésimo, -a	30°, 30ª	30th	thirtieth
trigésimo, -a primero, -a	31°, 31ª	31st	thirty-first
trigésimo, -a segundo, -a	32°, 32ª	32nd	thirty-second
cuadragésimo, -a	40°, 40ª	40th	fortieth
quincuagésimo, -a	50°, 50ª	50th	fiftieth
sexagésimo, -a	60°, 60ª	60th	sixtieth
septuagésimo, -a	70°, 70ª	70th	seventieth
septuagésimo, -a primero, -a	71°, 71ª	71st	seventy-first

septuagésimo, -a segundo, -a	72°, 72ª	72nd	seventy-second
septuagésimo, -a noveno, -a	79°, 79ª	79th	seventy-ninth
octogésimo, -a	80°, 80ª	80th	eightieth
octogésimo, -a primero, -a	81°, 81ª	81st	eighty-first
octogésimo, -a segundo, -a	82°, 82ª	82nd	eighty-second
nonagésimo, -a	90°, 90ª	90th	ninetieth
nonagésimo, -a primero, -a	91°, 91ª	91st	ninety-first
nonagésimo, -a noveno, -a	99°, 99ª	99th	ninety-ninth
centésimo, -a	100°, 100ª	100th	one hundredth
centésimo, -a primero, -a	101°, 101ª	101st	one hundred and first
centésimo, -a décimo, -a	110°, 110ª	110th	one hundred and tenth
centésimo, -a nonagésimo, -a quinto, -a	195°, 195ª	195th	one hundred and ninety-fifth
ducentésimo, -a	200°, 200ª	200th	two hundredth
tricentésimo, -a	300°, 300ª	300th	three hundredth
quingentésimo, -a	500°, 500ª	500th	five hundredth
milésimo, -a	1 000°, 1 000ª	1 000th	one thousandth
dosmilésimo, -a	2 000°, 2 000ª	2 000th	two thousandth
millonésimo, -a	1 000 000°, 1 000 000ª	1 000 000th	one millionth
diezmillonésimo, -a	10 000 000°, 10 000 000ª	10 000 000th	ten millionth

Numeros fraccionarios (o quebrados)   Fractional numbers

mitad; medio, -a	$^1/_2$	one half
un tercio	$^1/_3$	one third
un cuarto	$^1/_4$	one quarter
un quinto	$^1/_5$	one fifth
un décimo	$^1/_{10}$	one tenth
un céntesimo	$^1/_{100}$	one hundredth
un milésimo	$^1/_{1000}$	one thousandth
un millonésimo	$^1/_{1\,000\,000}$	one millionth
dos tercios	$^2/_3$	two thirds
tres cuartos	$^3/_4$	three quarters
dos quintos	$^2/_5$	two fifths
tres décimos	$^3/_{10}$	three tenths
uno y medio	$1\,^1/_2$	one and a half
dos y medio	$2\,^1/_2$	two and a half
cinco tres octavos	$5\,^3/_8$	five and three eighths
uno coma uno	1,1	one point one

Medidas, pesos y temperaturas

Weights, measures and temperatures

Sistema (de numeración) decimal

Decimal system

giga-	1 000 000 000	G	giga-
mega-	1 000 000	M	mega-
hectokilo-	100 000	hk	hectokilo-
miria-	10 000	ma	myria-
kilo-	1 000	k	kilo-
hecto-	100	h	hecto-
deca- (o decá-)	10	da	deca-
deci- (o decí-)	0,1	d	deci-
centi- (o centí-)	0,01	c	centi-
mili-	0,001	m	milli-
decimili-	0,000 1	dm	decimilli-
centimili-	0,000 01	cm	centimilli-
micro-	0,000 001	µ	micro-

Tablas de equivalencia

Damos el llamado **imperial system** solamente en los casos en los que en el lenguaje cotidiano éste todavía se sigue usando en los EEUU. Para convertir una medida métrica en la imperial estadounidense, se debe multiplicar por el factor en **negrita**. Asimismo, dividiendo la medida imperial estadounidense por ese mismo factor, se obtiene el equivalente métrico.

Conversion tables

Only U.S. Customary units still in common use are given here. To convert a metric measurement to U.S. Customary measures, multiply by the conversion factor in **bold**. Likewise dividing a U.S. Customary measurement by the same factor will give the metric equivalent.

Sistema métrico
Metric measurement

Sistema imperial
U.S. Customary System

Medidas de longitud

Length measure

milla marina	1 852 m	–	nautical mile			
kilómetro	1 000 m	km	kilometer	**0,62**	mile (=1 760 yards)	m, mi
hectómetro	100 m	hm	hectometer			
decámetro	10 m	dam	decameter			
metro	1 m	m	meter	**1,09** **3,28**	yard (= 3 feet) foot (= 12 inches)	yd ft
decímetro	0,1 m	dm	decimeter			
centímetro	0,01 m	cm	centimeter	**0,39**	inch	in
milímetro	0,001 m	mm	millimeter			
micrón, micra	0,000 001 m	µ	micron			
milimicrón	0,000 000 001 m	mµ	millimicron			
ángstrom	0,000 000 000 1 m	Å	angstrom			

Medidas de superficie   Surface measure

kilómetro cuadrado	1 000 000 m²	km²	square kilometer	**0,386**	square mile (= 640 acres)	sq. m., sq. mi.
hectómetro cuadrado	10 000 m²	hm²	square hecto-meter	**2,47**	acre (= 4 840 square yards)	a.
hectárea		ha	hectare			
decámetro cuadrado	100 m²	dam²	square deca-meter			
área		a	are			
metro cua-drado	1 m²	m²	square meter	**1.196** **10,76**	square yard (9 square feet) square feet (= 144 square inches)	sq. yd sq. ft
decímetro cuadrado	0,01 m²	dm²	square deci-meter			
centímetro cuadrado	0,000 1 m²	cm²	square cen-timeter	**0,155**	square inch	sq. in.
milímetro cuadrado	0,000001 m²	mm²	square milli-meter			

Medidas de volumen y capacidad   Volume and capacity

kilómetro cúbico	1 000 000 000 m³	km³	cubic kilometer			
metro cúbico	1 m³	m³	cubic meter	**1,308**	cubic yard (= 27 cubic feet)	cu. yd
estéreo		st	stere	**35,32**	cubic foot (= 1 728 cubic inches)	cu. ft
hectolitro	0,1 m³	hl	hectoliter			
decalitro	0,01 m³	dal	decaliter			
decímetro cúbico	0,001 m³	dm³	cubic decimeter	**0,26**	US gallon	gal.
litro		l	liter	**2,1**	US pint	pt
decilitro	0,000 1 m³	dl	deciliter			
centilitro	0,00001 m³	cl	centiliter	**0,338**	US fluid ounce	fl. oz
centímetro cúbico	0,000001 m³	cm³	cubic centimeter	**0,061**	cubic inch	cu. in.
mililitro	0,000001 m³	ml	milliliter			
milímetro cúbico	0,000000001 m³	mm³	cubic millimeter			

Pesos   **Weight**

tonelada	1 000 kg	t	ton	**1,1**	[short] ton *Am* (= 2000 pounds)	t.
quintal métrico	100 kg	q	quintal			
kilogramo	1 000 g	kg	kilogram	**2,2**	pound (= 16 ounces)	lb
hectogramo	100 g	hg	hectogram			
decagramo	10 g	dag	decagram			
gramo	1 g	g	gram	**0,035**	ounce	oz
quilate	0,2 g	–	carat			
decigramo (o decagramo)	0,1 g	dg	decigram			
centigramo	0,01 g	cg	centigram			
miligramo	0,001 g	mg	milligram			
microgramo	0,000 001 g	µg, g	microgram			

Temperatura

Para convertir una temperatura indicada en grados centígrados a Fahrenheit se debe multiplicar por 1,8 y restar 32. Para convertir una temperatura indicada en Fahrenheit a centígrados se deben restar 32 y dividir por 1,8.

Temperature

To convert a temperature in degrees Celsius to Fahrenheit, multiply by 1.8 and deduct 32. To convert Fahrenheit to Celsius, deduct 32 and divide by 1.8.

Nombres geográficos: Español-Inglés
Geographical names: Spanish-English

Países, derivados, capitales, monedas –
Countries, Derivatives, Capitals, Currencies

Los países están ordenados alfabéticamente según su denominación en español.
Countries are arranged in alphabetical order by their Spanish names.

País Country	Derivados Derivates	Capital Capital	Moneda Currency
Afganistán (el) *Afghanistan*	afgano (-a) *Afghan*	Kabul *Kabul*	afgani *afghani*
Albania *Albania*	albanés (-esa) *Albanian*	Tirana *Tiranë*	lek *lek*
Alemania *Germany*	alemán (-ana) *German*	Berlín *Berlin*	euro (antiguamente: marco alemán) *euro (formerly deutschmark)*
Andorra *Andorra*	andorrano (-a) *Andorran*	Andorra la Vella *Andorra la Vella*	euro (antiguamente: franco francés y peseta) *euro (formerly French franc and peseta)*
Angola *Angola*	angoleño (-a)/angolano (-a) *Angolan*	Luanda *Luanda*	nuevo kwanza *new kwanza*
Antigua y Barbuda *Antigua and Barbuda*	antiguano (-a) *Antiguan, Barbudan*	Saint John *St. John's*	dólar del Caribe Oriental *East Caribbean dollar*
Arabia Saudí/Arabia Saudita *Saudi Arabia*	saudí/saudita *Saudi Arabian*	Riad *Riyadh*	riyal saudí *Saudi riyal*
Argelia *Algeria*	argelino (-a) *Algerian*	Argel *Algiers*	dinar argelino *Algerian dinar*
Argentina (la) *Argentina*	argentino (-a) *Argentine, Argenti- nean*	Buenos Aires *Buenos Aires*	nuevo peso argentino *Argentine peso*
Armenia *Armenia*	armenio (-a) *Armenian*	Ereván *Yerevan*	dram *dram*
Australia *Australia*	australiano (-a) *Australian*	Canberra/Camberra *Canberra*	dólar australiano *Australian dollar*
Austria *Austria*	austriaco (-a)/austríaco (-a) *Austrian*	Viena *Vienna*	euro (antiguamente: chelín austriaco) *euro (formerly schilling)*
Azerbaiyán *Azerbaijan*	ayerbaiyano (-a) *Azerbaijani*	Bakú *Baku*	manat *manat*
Bahamas (las) *Bahamas*	bahameño (-a) *Bahamian*	Nassau *Nassau*	dólar de las bahamas *Bahamian dollar*
Bahréin *Bahrain*	bahreiní *Bahraini*	Manama *Al Manama*	dinar bahreiní *Bahrainian dinar*
Bangladés *Bangladesh*	bangladesí *Bangladeshi*	Dacca *Dhaka*	taka *taka*

País Country	Derivados Derivates	Capital Capital	Moneda Currency
Barbados *Barbados*	barbadense *Barbadian*	Bridgetown *Bridgetown*	dólar de Barbados *Barbadian dollar*
Bélgica *Belgium*	belga *Belgian*	Bruselas *Brussels*	euro (antiguamente: franco belga) *euro (formerly Belgian franc)*
Belice *Belize*	beliceño (-a) *Belizean*	Belmopán *Belmopan*	dólar beliceño *Belizean dollar*
Benin *Benin*	beninés (-esa) *Beninese*	Porto Novo *Porto Novo*	franco CFA *CFA franc*
Bielorrusia *Belarus*	bielorruso (-a) *Belarusian*	Minsk *Minsk*	rublo bielorruso *Belarusian ruble*
Birmania/Myanmar *Burma/Myanmar*	birmano (-a) *Burmese*	Rangún/Yangon *Rangoon/Yangon*	kyat *kyat*
Bolivia *Bolivia*	boliviano (-a) *Bolivian*	Sucre *Sucre*	boliviano *Boliviano*
Bosnia-Herzegovina *Bosnia-Herzegovina*	bosnio (-a)/bosnioher- zegovino (-a) *Bosnian*	Sarajevo *Sarajevo*	marco convertible *convertible mark*
Botsuana *Botswana*	botsuano (-a) *Botswanan*	Gaborone *Gaborone*	pula *pula*
Brasil *Brazil*	brasileño (-a) *Brazilian*	Brasilia *Brasilia*	real *real*
Brunéi Darussalam *Brunei*	bruneano (-a) *Bruneian*	Bandar Seri Begawan *Bandar Seri Begawan*	dólar de Brunei *Brunei dollar*
Bulgaria *Bulgaria*	búlgaro (-a) *Bulgarian*	Sofía *Sofia*	lev *lev*
Burkina Faso *Burkina Faso*	burkinés (-esa) *Burkinese*	Uagadugú *Ouagadougou*	franco CFA *CFA franc*
Burundi *Burundi*	burundés (-esa) *Burundian*	Buyumbura *Bujumbura*	franco de Burundi *Burundi franc*
Bután *Bhutan*	butanés (-esa) *Bhutanese*	Timbu *Thimphu*	ngultrum *ngultrum*
Cabo Verde *Cape Verde*	caboverdiano (-a) *Cape Verdean*	Praia *Praia*	escudo de Cabo Verde *Cape Verde escudo*
Camboya *Cambodia*	camboyano (-a) *Cambodian*	Phnom Penh *Phnom Penh*	riel *riel*
Camerún (el) *Cameroon*	camerunés (-esa) *Cameroonian*	Yaundé *Yaoundé*	franco CFA *CFA franc*
Canadá (el) *Canada*	canadiense *Canadian*	Ottawa *Ottawa*	dólar canadiense *Canadian dollar*
Chad (el) *Chad*	chadiano (-a) *Chadian*	Yamena *N'Djamena*	franco CFA *CFA franc*
Chile *Chile*	chileno (-a) *Chilean*	Santiago de Chile *Santiago de Chile*	peso chileno *Chilean peso*
China *China*	chino (-a) *Chinese*	Pekín *Beijing/Peking*	yuan *yuan*
Chipre *Cyprus*	chipriota *Cypriot*	Nicosia *Nicosia*	libra chipriota *Cypriot pound*

País Country	Derivados Derivates	Capital Capital	Moneda Currency
Ciudad del Vaticano *Vatican City*	vaticano (-a) *Vatican*		euro (antiguamente: lira) *euro (formerly lira)*
Colombia *Colombia*	colombiano *Colombian*	Bogotá *Bogota*	peso colombiano *Colombian peso*
Comores (las) *Comoros*	comorano (-a) *Comoran*	Moroni *Moroni*	franco comorano *Comoran franc*
Congo (República del Congo) *Congo (Republic of the Congo)*	congoleño (-a) *Congolese*	Brazzaville *Brazzaville*	franco CFA *CFA franc*
Congo (República Democrática del Congo) *Congo (Democratic Republic of the Congo)*	congoleño (-a) *Congolese*	Kinshasa *Kinshasa*	franco congoleño *Congolese franc*
Corea del Norte *North Korea*	norcoreano (-a) *North Korean*	Pyongyang *Pyongyang*	won *won*
Corea del Sur *South Korea*	surcoreano (-a) *South Korean*	Seúl *Seoul*	won *won*
Costa de Marfil *Ivory Coast/Côte d'Ivoire*	marfileño (-a) *Ivoirian*	Yamusukro *Yamoussoukro*	franco CFA *CFA franc*
Costa Rica *Costa Rica*	costarricense *Costa Rican*	San José *San José*	colón costarricense *Costa Rican colón*
Croacia *Croatia*	croata *Croatian*	Zagreb *Zagreb*	kuna *kuna*
Cuba *Cuba*	cubano (-a) *Cuban*	La Habana *Havana*	peso cubano *Cuban peso*
Dinamarca *Denmark*	danés (-esa) *Danish*	Copenhague *Kopenhagen*	corona danesa *Danish krone*
Dominica *Dominica*	dominiqués (-esa) *Dominican*	Roseau *Roseau*	dólar del Caribe Oriental *East Caribbean dollar*
Ecuador (el) *Ecuador*	ecuatoriano (-a) *Ecuadorian*	Quito *Quito*	dólar estadounidense *US dollar*
EE. UU. *USA*	estadounidense *American*	Washington D. C. *Washington D. C.*	dólar estadounidense *US dollar*
Egipto *Egypt*	egipcio (-a) *Egyptian*	El Cairo *Cairo*	libra egipcia *Egyptian pound*
El Salvador *El Salvador*	salvadoreño (-a) *Salvadoran*	San Salvador *San Salvador*	dólar estadounidense *US dollar*
Emiratos Árabes Unidos (los) *United Arab Emirates*	emiratense *(United Arab) Emiratian*	Abu Dhabi *Abu Dhabi*	dirhan emiral *dirham*
Eritrea *Eritrea*	eritreo (-a) *Eritrean*	Asmara *Asmara*	nafka *nafka*
Escocia *Scotland (GB)*	escocés (-esa) *Scottish*	Edimburgo *Edinburgh*	libra esterlina *pound sterling*

País / Country	Derivados / Derivates	Capital / Capital	Moneda / Currency
Eslovaquia *Slovakia/Slovak Republic*	eslovaco (-a) *Slovak*	Bratislava *Bratislava*	corona eslovaca *Slovak koruna*
Eslovenia *Slovenia*	esloveno (-a) *Slovene, Slovenian*	Liubliana *Ljubljana*	tolar *tolar*
España *Spain*	español (a) *Spanish*	Madrid *Madrid*	euro (antiguamente: peseta) *euro (formerly peseta)*
Estados Unidos de América (los) *United States of America/USA*	estadounidense *American*	*Washington D. C.* *Washington D. C.*	dólar estadounidense *US dollar*
Estonia *Estonia*	estonio (-a) *Estonian*	Tallin *Tallinn*	corona estonia *Estonian kroon*
Etiopía *Ethiopia*	etíope *Ethiopian*	Adís Abeba *Addis Abeba*	birr *birr*
Filipinas (las) *Philippines*	filipino (-a) *Philippine, Filipino*	Manila *Manila*	peso filipino *Philippines peso*
Finlandia *Finland*	finlandés (-esa) *finés (-esa) [idioma]* Finnish	Helsinki *Helsinki*	euro (antiguamente: marco finlandés) *euro* *(formerly Finnish markka)*
Francia *France*	francés (-esa) *French*	París *Paris*	euro (antiguamente: franco francés) *euro (formerly French franc)*
Gabón (el) *Gabon*	gabonés (-esa) *Gabonese*	Libreville *Libreville*	franco CFA *CFA franc*
Gambia *Gambia*	gambiano (-a) *Gambian*	Banjul *Banjul*	dalasi *dalasi*
Georgia *Georgia*	georgiano (-a) *Georgian*	Tbilisi/Tiflis *Tbilisi/Tiflis*	lari georgiano *lari*
Ghana *Ghana*	ghanés (-esa) *Ghanaian*	Accra *Accra*	cedi *cedi*
Gran Bretaña (la) *Great Britain*	británico (-a) *British*	Londres *London*	libra esterlina *pound sterling*
Granada *Grenada*	granadino (-a) *Grenadian*	Saint George *St. George's*	dólar del Caribe Oriental *East Caribbean dollar*
Grecia *Greece*	griego (-a) *Greek*	Atenas *Athens*	euro (antiguamente: dracma) *euro (formerly drachma)*
Guatemala *Guatemala*	guatemalteco (-a) *Guatemalan*	Guatemala *Guatemala*	quetzal *quetzal*
Guinea (la) *Guinea*	guineano (-a) *Guinean*	Conakry *Conakry*	franco guineano *Guinean franc*
Guinea Ecuatorial (la) *Equatorial Guinea*	ecuatoguineano (-a) *Equatorial Guinean*	Malabo *Malab*	franco CFA *CFA franc*

País Country	Derivados Derivates	Capital Capital	Moneda Currency
Guinea-Bissau *Guinea-Bissau*	guineano (-a) *Guinean*	Bissau *Bissau*	franco CFA *CFA franc*
Guyana *Guyana*	guyanés (-esa) *Guyanese*	Georgetown *Georgetown*	dólar guyanés *Guyanese dollar*
Haití *Haiti*	haitiano (-a) *Haitian*	Puerto Príncipe *Port-au-Prince*	gourde *gourde*
Honduras *Honduras*	hondureño (-a) *Honduran*	Tegucigalpa *Tegucigalpa*	lempira *lempira*
Hungría *Hungary*	húngaro (-a) *Hungarian*	Budapest *Budapest*	forint *forint*
India (la) *India*	indio (-a) *Indian*	Nueva Delhi *New Delhi*	rupia india *rupee*
Indonesia *Indonesia*	indonesio (-a) *Indonesian*	Yakarta *Jakarta*	rupia indonesia *rupiah*
Inglaterra *England (UK)*	inglés (-esa) *English*	Londres *London*	libra esterlina *pound sterling*
Irán *Iran*	iraní *Iranian*	Teherán *Tehran*	rial iraní *rial*
Iraq/Irak *Iraq*	iraquí *Iraqi*	Bagdad *Baghdad*	dinar iraquí *Iraqi dinar*
Irlanda *Ireland*	irlandés (-esa) *Irish*	Dublín *Dublin*	euro (antiguamente: libra irlandesa) *euro (formerly Irish pound)*
Irlanda del Norte *Northern Ireland (UK)*	norirlandés (-esa) *Northern Irish*	Belfast *Belfast*	libra esterlina *pound sterling*
Islandia *Iceland*	islandés (-esa) *Icelandic*	Reykjavik *Reykjavik*	corona islandesa *Icelandic krona*
Islas Cook (las) *Cook Islands*	Cookiano, -a *Cook Islander*	Avarua *Avarua*	dólar neozelandés *New Zealand dollar*
Islas Fiji (las) *Fiji*	fijiano (-a) *Fijian*	Suva *Suva*	dólar de Fiji *Fijian dollar*
Islas Marshall (las) *Marshall Islands*	marshalés (-esa) *Marshall Islander*	Majuro *Majuro*	dólar estadounidense *US dollar*
Islas Salomón (las) *Solomon Islands*	salomonense *Solomon Islander*	Honiara *Honiara*	dólar de las Islas Salomón *Salomon dollar*
Israel *Israel*	israelí *Israeli*	Jerusalén *Jerusalem*	nuevo shekel *new shekel*
Italia *Italy*	italiano (-a) *Italian*	Roma *Rome*	euro (antiguamente: lira) *euro (formerly lira)*
Jamaica *Jamaica*	jamaicano (-a) *Jamaican*	Kingston *Kingston*	dólar jamaicano *Jamaican dollar*
Japón *Japan*	japonés (-esa) *Japanese*	Tokio *Tokyo*	yen *yen*
Jordania *Jordan*	jordano (-a) *Jordanian*	Ammán *Amman*	dinar jordano *Jordanian dinar*
Kazajstán *Kazakhstan*	kazajo (-a) *Kazakh*	Astana *Astana*	tenge *tenge*

País Country	Derivados Derivates	Capital Capital	Moneda Currency
Kenia *Kenya*	keniano (-a)/keniata *Kenyan*	Nairobi *Nairobi*	chelín de Kenia *Kenyan shilling*
Kirguizistán *Kyrgyzstan*	kirguiso (-a)/kirguís *Kyrgyz*	Bishkek *Bishkek*	som *Kyrgystani som*
Kiribati *Kiribati*	kiribatiano (-a) *I-Kiribati*	Bairiki *Bairiki*	dólar australiano *Australian dollar*
Kuwait *Kuwait*	kuwaití *Kuwaiti*	Kuwait *Kuwait City*	dinar kuwaití *Kuwaiti dinar*
Laos *Laos*	laosiano (-a) *Laotian*	Vientián *Vientiane*	kip *kip*
Lesoto *Lesotho*	lesotense *Sotho*	Maseru *Maseru*	loti *loti*
Letonia *Latvia*	letón (-ona) *Latvian*	Riga *Riga*	lats *Lats*
Líbano (el) *Lebanon*	libanés (-esa) *Lebanese*	Beirut *Beirut*	libra libanesa *Lebanese pound*
Liberia *Liberia*	liberiano (-a) *Liberian*	Monrovia *Monrovia*	dólar liberiano *Liberian dollar*
Libia *Libya*	libio (-a) *Libyan*	Trípoli *Tripoli*	dinar libio *Libyan dinar*
Liechtenstein *Liechtenstein*	liechtensteiniano (-a) *Liechtensteiner*	Vaduz *Vaduz*	franco suizo *Swiss franc*
Lituania *Lithuania*	lituano (-a) *Lithuanian*	Vilna *Vilnius*	litas *litas*
Luxemburgo *Luxembourg*	luxemburgués (-esa) *Luxembourg*	Luxemburgo *Luxembourg*	euro (antiguamente: franco luxemburgués) *euro (formerly Luxembourg franc)*
Macedonia (Ex-República Yugoslava de Macedonia) *Macedonia (Former Yugoslav Republic of Macedonia)*	macedonio (-a) *Macedonian*	Skopje *Skopje*	denar macedonio *Macedonian denar*
Madagascar *Madagascar*	malgache *Madagascan*	Antananarivo *Antananarivo*	franco malgache *Madagascan franc*
Malasia *Malaysia*	malayo (-a) *Malaysian*	Kuala Lumpur *Kuala Lumpur*	ringgit *Malaysian ringgit*
Malawi *Malawi*	malawí *Malawian*	Lilongwe *Lilongwe*	kwacha de Malawi *Malawian kwacha*
Maldivas (las) *Maldives*	maldivo (-a) *Maldivian*	Malé *Malé*	rufiyaa *rufiyaa*
Mali/Malí *Mali*	malí *Malian*	Bamako *Bamako*	franco CFA *CFA franc*
Malta *Malta*	maltés (-esa) *Maltese*	La Valeta *Valletta*	lira maltesa *Maltese lira*
Marruecos *Morocco*	marroquí *Moroccan*	Rabat *Rabat*	dirham marroquí *dirham*
Mauricio *Mauritius*	mauriciano (-a) *Mauritian*	Port Louis *Port Louis*	rupia mauriciana *Mauritian rupee*

País Country	Derivados Derivates	Capital Capital	Moneda Currency
Mauritania *Mauritania*	mauritano (-a) *Mauritanian*	Nuakchot *Nouakchott*	ouguiya *ouguiya*
México *Mexico*	mexicano (-a) *Mexican*	Mexico D. F. *Mexico City*	peso mexicano *Mexican peso*
Micronesia (la) *Micronesia (Federated States of Micronesia)*	micronesio (-a) *Micronesian*	Palikir *Palikir*	dólar estadounidense *US dollar*
Moldavia *Moldavia*	moldavo (-a) *Moldavian*	Chisinau *Chişinău*	leu *Moldavian leu*
Mónaco *Monaco*	monegasco (-a) *Monegasque*	Mónaco *Monaco-Ville*	euro (antiguamente: franco francés) *euro (formerly French franc)*
Mongolia *Mongolia*	mongol (-a) *Mongolian*	Ulán-Bator *Ulaanbaatar*	tugrik *tugrik*
Mozambique *Mozambique*	mozambiqueño (-a) *Mozambican*	Maputo *Maputo*	metical *metical*
Myanmar/Birmania *Myanmar/Burma*	birmano (-a) *Burmese*	Rangún/Yangon *Rangoon/Yangon*	kyat *kyat*
Namibia *Namibia*	namibio (-a) *Namibian*	Windhoek *Windhoek*	dólar namibio *Namibian dollar*
Nauru *Nauru*	nauruano (-a) *Nauruan*	Yaren *Yaren*	dólar australiano *Australian dollar*
Nepal (el) *Nepal*	nepalés (-esa)/nepalí *Nepalese*	Katmandú *Kathmandu*	rupia nepalí *Nepalese rupee*
Nicaragua *Nicaragua*	nicaragüense *Nicaraguan*	Managua *Managua*	córdoba oro *córdoba*
Níger *Niger*	nigerino (-a) *Nigerois*	Niamey *Niamey*	franco CFA *CFA franc*
Nigeria *Nigeria*	nigeriano (-a) *Nigerian*	Abuja *Abuja*	naira *naira*
Noruega *Norway*	noruego (-a) *Norwegian*	Oslo *Oslo*	corona noruega *Norwegian krone*
Nueva Zelanda *New Zealand*	neozelandés (-esa) *New Zealander*	Wellington *Wellington*	dólar neozelandés *New Zealand dollar*
Omán *Oman*	omaní *Omani*	Mascate *Muscat*	rial omaní *Omani rial*
País de Gales (el) *Wales (GB)*	galés (-esa) *Welsh*	Cardiff *Cardiff*	libra esterlina *pound sterling*
Países Bajos (los) *Netherlands*	neerlandés (-esa) *Dutch*	Amsterdam *Amsterdam*	euro (antiguamente: florín neerlandés) *euro (formerly gulden)*
Pakistán *Pakistan*	pakistaní *Pakistani*	Islamabad *Islamabad*	rupia pakistaní *Pakistani rupee*
Palau *Palau*	palauano (-a) *Palauan*	Koror *Koror*	dólar estadounidense *US dollar*
Panamá *Panama*	panameño (-a) *Panamanian*	Panamá *Panama City*	balboa *balboa*
Papúa Nueva Guinea *Papua New Guinea*	papú *Papuan*	Port Moresby *Port Moresby*	kina *kina*

País Country	Derivados Derivates	Capital Capital	Moneda Currency
Paraguay (el) *Paraguay*	paraguayo (-a) *Paraguayan*	Asunción *Asunción*	guaraní *guaraní*
Perú (el) *Peru*	peruano (-a) *Peruvian*	Lima *Lima*	nuevo sol *nuevo sol*
Polonia *Poland*	polaco (-a) *Polish*	Varsovia *Warsaw*	zloty *zloty*
Portugal *Portugal*	portugués (-esa) *Portuguese*	Lisboa *Lisbon*	euro (antiguamente: escudo) *euro (formerly escudo)*
Puerto Rico (EE.UU.) *Puerto Rico (USA)*	puertorriqueño (-a) *Puerto Rican*	San Juan *San Juan*	dólar estadounidense *US dollar*
Qatar *Qatar*	qatarí *Qatari*	Doha *Doha*	rial de Qatar *Qatari riyal*
Reino Unido (el) *United Kingdom*	británico (-a) *UK/British*	Londres *London*	libra esterlina *pound sterling*
República Centro-africana (la) *Central African Republic*	centroafricano (-a) *Central African*	Bangui *Bangui*	franco CFA *CFA franc*
República Checa (la) *Czech Republic*	checo (-a) *Czech*	Praga *Prague*	corona checa *Czech koruna*
República Dominicana (la) *Dominican Republic*	dominicano (-a) *Dominican*	Santo Domingo *Santo Domingo*	peso dominicano *Dominican peso*
Ruanda *Rwanda*	ruandés (-esa) *Rwandan*	Kigali *Kigali*	franco ruandés *Rwandan franc*
Rumanía *Romania*	rumano (-a) *Romanian*	Bucarest *Bucharest*	leu *leu (pl. lei)*
Rusia *Russia (Russian Federation)*	ruso (-a) *Russian*	Moscú *Moscow*	rublo *ruble*
Samoa *Samoa*	samoano (-a) *Samoan*	Apia *Apia*	tala *tala*
San Cristóbal y Nieves *St. Kitts and Nevis*	sancristobaleño (-a) *Kittsian, Nevisian*	Basseterre *Basseterre*	dólar del Caribe Oriental *East Caribbean dollar*
San Marino *San Marino*	sanmarinense *San Marinese*	San Marino *San Marino*	euro (antiguamente: lira) *euro (formerly lira)*
San Vicente y las Granadinas *St. Vincent and the Grenadines*	sanvicentino (-a) *Saint Vincentian*	Kingstown *Kingstown*	dólar del Caribe Oriental *East Caribbean dollar*
Santa Lucía *St. Lucia*	santalucense *St. Lucian*	Castries *Castries*	dólar del Caribe Oriental *East Caribbean dollar*
Santo Tomé y Príncipe *Sao Tomé and Príncipe*	santotomense *Sao Tomean*	Santo Tomé *São Tomé*	dobra *dobra*
Senegal (el) *Senegal*	senegalés (-esa) *Senegalese*	Dakar *Dakar*	franco CFA *CFA franc*

País Country	Derivados Derivates	Capital Capital	Moneda Currency
Serbia y Montenegro *Serbia and Montene-* *gro*	serbiomontenegrino (-a) *Serbian-Montenegran*	Belgrado *Belgrade*	dinar serbio, euro Serbian *dinar, Euro*
Seychelles (las) *Seychelles*	seychelense *Seychellois*	Victoria *Victoria*	rupia de Seychelles *Seychelles rupee*
Sierra Leona *Sierra Leone*	sierraleonés *Sierra Leonean*	Freetown *Freetown*	leone *leone*
Singapur *Singapore*	singapurense *Singaporean*	Singapur *Singapore*	dólar de Singapur *Singapore dollar*
Siria *Syria*	sirio (-a) *Syrian*	Damasco *Damaskus*	libra siria *Syrian pound*
Somalia *Somalia*	somalí *Somali*	Mogadiscio *Mogadishu*	chelín somalí *Somalian shilling*
Sri Lanka *Sri Lanka*	esrilanqués (-esa) ceilandés (-esa) *Sri Lankan*	Colombo *Colombo*	rupia de Sri Lanka *Sri Lankan rupee*
Suazilandia *Swaziland*	suazi *Swazi*	Mbabane *Mbabane*	lilangeni *lilangeni*
Sudáfrica *South Africa*	sudafricano (-a) *South African*	Pretoria *Pretoria*	rand *rand*
Sudán (el) *Sudan*	sudanés (-esa) *Sudanese*	Jartum *Khartoum*	libra sudanesa *Sudanese pound*
Suecia *Sweden*	sueco (-a) *Swedish*	Estocolmo *Stockholm*	corona sueca *Swedish krone*
Suiza *Switzerland*	suizo (-a) *Swiss*	Berna *Berne*	franco suizo *Swiss franc*
Surinam *Suriname*	surinamés (-esa) *Surinamese*	Paramaribo *Paramaribo*	florín surinamés *Surinamese gulden*
Tailandia *Thailand*	tailandés (-esa) *Thai*	Bangkok *Bangkok*	baht *baht*
Taiwán *Taiwan*	taiwanés *Taiwanese*	Taipei *Taipei*	dólar de Taiwán *Taiwanese dollar*
Tanzania *Tanzania*	tanzano (-a) *Tanzanian*	Dodoma (Dar es Salaam) *Dodoma (Dar es* *Salaam)*	chelín tanzano *Tanzanian shilling*
Tayikistán *Tajikistan*	tayiko (-a) *Tajik*	Dusambé *Dushanbe*	rublo tayiko *ruble*
Togo (el) *Togo*	togolés (-esa) *Togolese*	Lomé *Lomé*	franco CFA *CFA franc*
Tonga *Tonga*	tongano (-a) *Tongan*	Nuku'alofa *Nuku'alofa*	pa'anga *pa'anga*
Trinidad y Tobago *Trinidad and Tobago*	trinitense, tobaguense *Trinidadian, Tobagan*	Puerto España *Port of Spain*	dólar de Trinidad y Tobago *Trinidad and Tobago* *dollar*
Túnez *Tunisia*	tunecino (-a) *Tunisian*	Túnez *Tunis*	dinar tunecino *Tunisian dinar*

País Country	Derivados Derivates	Capital Capital	Moneda Currency
Turkmenistán *Turkmenistan*	turkmeno (-a)/turcom- ano (-a) *Turkmen*	Ashjabad *Ashgabat*	manat turcomano *manat*
Turquía *Turkey*	turco (-a) *Turkish*	Ankara *Ankara*	lira turca *Turkish lira*
Tuvalu *Tuvalu*	tuvaluano (-a) *Tuvaluan*	Funafuti *Funafuti*	dólar australiano *Australian dollar*
Ucrania *Ukraine*	ucraniano (-a) *Ukrainian*	Kiev *Kiev*	hrivnia *hryvnia*
Uganda *Uganda*	ugandés (-esa) *Ugandan*	Kampala *Kampala*	chelín ugandés *Ugandan shilling*
Uruguay (el) *Uruguay*	uruguayo (-a) *Uruguayan*	Montevideo *Montevideo*	peso uruguayo *Uruguayan peso*
Uzbekistán *Uzbekistan*	uzbeko (-a) *Uzbek*	Tashkent *Tashkent*	sum *Uzbek sum*
Vanuatu *Vanuatu*	vanuatense *Vanuatian*	Port Vila *Port Vila*	vatu *vatu*
Venezuela *Venezuela*	venezolano (-a) *Venezuelan*	Caracas *Caracas*	bolívar *bolivar*
Vietnam *Vietnam*	vietnamita *Vietnamese*	Hanói *Hanoi*	dong *dong*
Yemen (el) *Yemen*	yemení *Yemeni*	Saná *Sanaa*	riyal *Yemeni rial*
Yibuti *Djibouti*	yibutiano (-a) *Djiboutian*	Yibuti *Djibouti*	franco yibutiano *Djiboutian franc*
Yugoslavia HIST *v. Serbia y Montenegro*	yugoslavo (-a) *Yugoslav*	Belgrado *Belgrade*	dinar yugoslavo *Yugoslav dinar*
Zambia *Zambia*	zambiano (-a) *Zambian*	Lusaka *Lusaka*	kwacha zambiano *kwacha*
Zimbabue *Zimbabwe*	zimbabuense *Zimbabwean*	Harare *Harare*	dólar de Zimbabue *Zimbabwean dollar*

* Franco CFA = Franco de la Comunidad Financiera Africana

Continentes, islas, océanos, mares, lagos, ríos, golfos y montañas – Continents, Islands, Oceans, Seas, Lakes, Rivers, Gulfs, and Mountains

Continentes
Continents

África *Africa*	Antártida (la) *Antarctica*
América *America*	Asia *Asia*
América Central *Central America*	Eurasia *Eurasia*
América del Norte *North America*	Europa *Europe*
América del Sur *South America*	

Islas
Islands

Antigua *Antigua*	Guadalcanal *Guadalcanal*
Antillas (las) *Antilles*	Guadalupe *Guadeloupe*
Antillas (las) *West Indies*	Guam *Guam*
Antillas Mayores (las) *Greater Antilles*	Hébridas (las) *Hebrides*
Antillas Menores (las) *Lesser Antilles*	Hokkaido *Hokkaido*
Aruba *Aruba*	Honshu *Honshu*
Azores (las) *Azores*	Indias Orientales (las) *East Indies*
Bali *Bali*	Isla de Man (la) *Isle of Man*
Bermudas (las) *Bermuda*	Isla de Pascua (la) *Easter Island*
Borneo *Borneo*	Isla del Príncipe Eduardo (la) *Prince Edward Island*
Célebes *Celebes*	Isla Victoria (la) *Victoria Island*
Comores (las) *Comoros*	Islandia *Iceland*
Corfú *Corfu*	Islas Aleutianas (las) *Aleutian Islands*
Creta *Crete*	Islas Baleares (las) *Balearic Islands*
Curaçao *Curaçao*	Islas Canarias (las) *Canary Islands*
Groenlandia *Greenland*	Islas Carolinas (las) *Caroline Islands*

Islas de Barlovento (las) *Windward Islands*	Madagascar *Madagascar*
Islas de Cabo Verde (las) *Cape Verde Islands*	Maldivas (las) *Maldive Islands*
Islas de Sotavento (las) *Leeward Islands*	Mallorca *Majorca*
Islas del Canal (las) *Channel Islands*	Martinica *Martinique*
Islas Feroe (las) *Faroe Islands*	Menorca *Minorca*
Islas Galápagos (las) *Galapagos Islands*	Mindanao *Mindanao*
Islas Madeira (las) *Madeira Islands*	Okinawa *Okinawa*
Islas Malvinas (las) *Falkland Islands*	Orcadas (las) *Orkney Islands*
Islas Marianas (las) *Mariana Islands*	Reunión *Réunion*
Islas Marquesas (las) *Marquesas Islands*	Rodas *Rhodes*
Islas Marshall (las) *Marshall Islands*	Ryukyu *Ryukyu Islands*
Islas Salomón (las) *Solomon Islands*	Sajalín *Sakhalin*
Islas Shetland (las) *Shetland Islands*	Shikoku *Shikoku*
Islas Vírgenes (las) *Virgin Islands*	Sumatra *Sumatra*
Iwo Jima *Iwo Jima*	Tahití *Tahiti*
Java *Java*	Tasmania *Tasmania*
Kyushu *Kyushu*	Tierra de Baffin (la) *Baffin Island*
La Española *Hispaniola*	Tierra del Fuego (la) *Tierra del Fuego*
Leyte *Leyte*	Timor *Timor*
Long Island *Long Island*	Vancouver *Vancouver Island*
Luzón *Luzon*	Zanzíbar *Zanzibar*

Océanos
Oceans

océano Atlántico (el) *Atlantic Ocean*	océano Índico (el) *Indian Ocean*
océano Glacial Antártico (el) *Southern Ocean, Antarctic Ocean*	océano Pacífico (el) *Pacific Ocean*
océano Glacial Ártico (el) *Arctic Ocean*	

Mares
Seas

mar Adriático (el) *Adriatic Sea*	mar de la China oriental (el) *East China Sea*
mar Amarillo (el) *Yellow Sea*	mar de los Sargazos (el) *Sargasso Sea*
mar Arábigo (el)/mar de Arabia (el) *Arabian Sea*	mar de Ojotsk (el) *Sea of Okhotsk*
mar Báltico (el) *Baltic Sea*	mar de Tasmania (el) *Tasman Sea*
mar Blanco (el) *White Sea*	mar del Japón (el)/mar Oriental (el) *Sea of Japan*
mar Caribe (el)/mar de las Antillas (el) *Caribbean Sea*	mar del Norte (el) *North Sea*
mar Caspio (el) *Caspian Sea*	mar Egeo (el) *Aegean Sea*
mar de Aral (el) *Aral Sea*	mar Mediterráneo (el) *Mediterranean Sea*
mar de Azov (el) *Sea of Azov*	mar Muerto (el) *Dead Sea*
mar de Bering (el) *Bering Sea*	mar Negro (el) *Black Sea*
mar de Irlanda (el) *Irish Sea*	mar Rojo (el) *Red Sea*
mar de la China meridional (el) *South China Sea*	

Lagos
Lakes

Gran Lago de los Esclavos (el) *Great Slave Lake*	lago Ladoga (el) *Lake Ladoga*
Gran Lago de los Osos (el) *Great Bear Lake*	lago Malawi (el) *Lake Nyasa, Lake Malawi*
Gran Lago Salado (el) *Great Salt Lake*	lago Michigan (el) *Lake Michigan*
Grandes Lagos (los) *Great Lakes*	lago Onega (el) *Lake Onega*
lago Alberto (el) *Lake Albert (Nyanza)*	lago Ontario (el) *Lake Ontario*
lago Baikal (el) *Lake Baikal*	lago Superior (el) *Lake Superior*
lago Chad (el) *Lake Chad*	lago Tanganica (el) *Lake Tanganyika*
lago Erie (el) *Lake Erie*	lago Titicaca (el) *Lake Titicaca*
lago Ginebra (el)/lago Léman (el) *Lake Geneva*	lago Victoria (el) *Lake Victoria*
lago Hurón (el) *Lake Huron*	

Ríos
Rivers

(río) Amarillo (el)/Huang Ho (el) *Yellow River/Huang Ho*	Missouri (el) *Missouri*
Amazonas (el) *Amazon*	Níger (el) *Niger*
Amur (el) *Amur*	Nilo (el) *Nile*
(Río) Bravo (el) *Rio Grande*	Obi (el) *Ob*
Columbia (el) *Columbia*	Oder (el) *Oder*
Congo (el) *Congo*	Ohio (el) *Ohio*
Danubio (el) *Danube*	Orinoco (el) *Orinoco*
Delaware (el) *Delaware*	Paraná (el) *Paraná*
Dniéper (el) *Dnieper*	Po (el) *Po*
Dniéster (el) *Dniester*	Potomac (el) *Potomac*
Don (el) *Don*	Rin (el) *Rhine*
Elba (el) *Elbe*	Ródano (el) *Rhône*
Éufrates (el) *Euphrates*	San Lorenzo (el) *St. Lawrence*
Ganges (el) *Ganges*	Sena (el) *Seine*
Huang Ho (el)/(río) Amarillo (el) *Huang Ho/Yellow River*	Susquehanna (el) *Susquehanna*
Hudson (el) *Hudson*	Támesis (el) *Thames*
Indo (el) *Indus*	Tigris (el) *Tigris*
Irrawaddy (el) *Irrawaddy*	Ural (el) *Ural*
Irtish (el) *Irtysh*	Vístula (el) *Vistula*
Jordán (el) *Jordan*	Volga (el) *Volga*
Lena (el) *Lena*	Volta (el) *Volta*
Loira (el) *Loire*	Yangtzé (el) *Yangtze*
Mackenzie (el) *Mackenzie*	Yeniséi (el) *Yenisei*
Mekong (el) *Mekong*	Yukón (el) *Yukon*
Mississippi (el) *Mississippi*	Zambeze (el) *Zambezi*

Golfos, Bahías, Estrechos, Canales
Gulfs, Bays, Straits, Canals

bahía de Hudson (la) *Hudson Bay*	estrecho de Magallanes (el) *Strait of Magellan*
Bósforo (el) *Bosporus*	golfo de Adén (el) *Gulf of Aden*
canal de la Mancha (el) *English Channel*	golfo de Bengala (el) *Bay of Bengal*
canal de Panamá (el) *Panama Canal*	golfo de California (el) *Gulf of California*
canal de San Lorenzo (el) *St. Lawrence Seaway*	golfo de México (el) *Gulf of Mexico*
canal de Suez (el) *Suez Canal*	golfo de San Lorenzo (el) *Gulf of St. Lawrence*
estrecho de Bering (el) *Bering Strait*	golfo Pérsico (el) *Persian Gulf*
estrecho de Florida (el) *Straits of Florida*	mar Cantábrico (el) *Bay of Biscay*
estrecho de Gibraltar (el) *Strait of Gibraltar*	

Montañas
Mountain Ranges

(montes) Apalaches (los) *Appalachian Mountains*	Cáucaso (el) *Caucasus*
Adirondack (las) *Adirondack Mountains*	cordillera de las Cascadas (la) *Cascade Range*
Allegheny (las) *Allegheny Mountains*	Himalaya (el) *Himalaya Mountains/Himalayas*
Alpes (los) *Alps*	Pirineos (los) *Pyrenees*
Andes (los) *Andes*	(montañas) Rocosas (las) *Rocky Mountains*
Balcanes (los) *Balkans*	(montes) San Elías (los) *St. Elias Mountains*
Cárpatos (los) *Carpathian Mountains*	Sierra Nevada *Sierra Nevada*
Catskill (los) *Catskill Mountains*	(montes) Urales (los) *Ural Mountains*

Picos
Mountain Peaks

Aconcagua (el) *Aconcagua (Andes)*	(monte) Kilimanjaro (el) *Kilimanjaro*
Elbrús (el) *Elbrus*	(monte) Logan (el) *Logan*
Etna (el) *Etna*	Matterhorn (el)/Cervino (el) *Matterhorn*
Everest (el) *Everest*	Mauna Loa (el) *Mauna Loa*

McKinley (el)	Pikes Peak (el)
McKinley	*Pike's Peak*
Mont Blanc (el)	Popocatépetl (el)
Mont Blanc	*Popocatepetl*
Monte Fuji (el)	(monte) Rosa (el)
Fujiyama	*Monte Rosa*
(pico de) Orizaba (el)	
Orizaba	

Geographical names: English-Spanish
Nombres geográficos: Inglés-Español

Countries, Derivatives, Capitals, Currencies –
Países, derivados, capitales, monedas

Countries are arranged in alphabetical order by their English names.
Los países están ordenados alfabéticamente según su denominación en inglés.

Country País	Derivates Derivados	Capital Capital	Currency Moneda
Afghanistan *Afganistán (el)*	Afghan *afgano (-a)*	Kabul *Kabul*	afghani *afgani*
Albania *Albania*	Albanian *albanés (-esa)*	Tiranë *Tirana*	lek *lek*
Algeria *Argelia*	Algerian *argelino (-a)*	Algiers *Argel*	Algerian dinar *dinar argelino*
Andorra *Andorra*	Andorran *andorrano (-a)*	Andorra la Vella *Andorra la Vella*	euro (formerly French franc and peseta) *euro (antiguamente: franco francés y peseta)*
Angola *Angola*	Angolan *angoleño (-a) / angolano (-a)*	Luanda *Luanda*	new kwanza *nuevo kwanza*
Antigua and Barbuda *Antigua y Barbuda*	Antiguan, Barbudan *antiguano (-a)*	St. John's *Saint John*	East Caribbean dollar *dólar del Caribe Oriental*
Argentina *Argentina (la)*	Argentine, Argentinean *argentino (-a)*	Buenos Aires *Buenos Aires*	Argentine peso *nuevo peso argentino*
Armenia *Armenia*	Armenian *armenio (-a)*	Yerevan *Ereván*	dram *dram*
Australia *Australia*	Australian *australiano (-a)*	Canberra *Canberra / Camberra*	Australian dollar *dólar australiano*
Austria *Austria*	Austrian *austriaco (-a) / austríaco (-a)*	Vienna *Viena*	euro (formerly schilling) *euro (antiguamente: chelín austriaco)*
Azerbaijan *Azerbaiyán*	Azerbaijani *ayerbaiyano (-a)*	Baku *Bakú*	manat *manat*
Bahamas *Bahamas (las)*	Bahamian *bahameño (-a)*	Nassau *Nassau*	Bahamian dollar *dólar de las bahamas*

Country País	Derivates Derivados	Capital Capital	Currency Moneda
Bahrain *Bahréin*	Bahraini *bahreiní*	Al Manama *Manama*	Bahrainian dinar *dinar bahreiní*
Bangladesh *Bangladés*	Bangladeshi *bangladesí*	Dhaka *Dacca*	taka *taka*
Barbados *Barbados*	Barbadian *barbadense*	Bridgetown *Bridgetown*	Barbadian dollar *dólar de Barbados*
Belarus *Bielorrusia*	Belarusian *bielorruso (-a)*	Minsk *Minsk*	Belarusian ruble *rublo bielorruso*
Belgium *Bélgica*	Belgian *belga*	Brussels *Bruselas*	euro (formerly Belgian franc) *euro (antiguamente: franco belga)*
Belize *Belice*	Belizean *beliceño (-a)*	Belmopan *Belmopán*	Belizean dollar *dólar beliceño*
Benin *Benin*	Beninese *beninés (-esa)*	Porto Novo *Porto Novo*	CFA franc *franco CFA*
Bhutan *Bután*	Bhutanese *butanés (-esa)*	Thimphu *Timbu*	ngultrum *ngultrum*
Bolivia *Bolivia*	Bolivian *boliviano (-a)*	Sucre *Sucre*	Boliviano *boliviano*
Bosnia-Herzegovina *Bosnia-Herzegovina*	Bosnian *bosnio (-a) / bosnioher- zegovino (-a)*	Sarajevo *Sarajevo*	convertible mark *marco convertible*
Botswana *Botsuana*	Botswanan *botsuano (-a)*	Gaborone *Gaborone*	pula *pula*
Brazil *Brasil*	Brazilian *brasileño (-a)*	Brasilia *Brasilia*	real *real*
Brunei *Brunéi Darussalam*	Bruneian *bruneano (-a)*	Bandar Seri Begawan *Bandar Seri Begawan*	Brunei dollar *dólar de Brunei*
Bulgaria *Bulgaria*	Bulgarian *búlgaro (-a)*	Sofia *Sofía*	lev *lev*
Burkina Faso *Burkina Faso*	Burkinese *burkinés (-esa)*	Ouagadougou *Uagadugú*	CFA franc *franco CFA*
Burma/Myanmar *Birmania/Myanmar*	Burmese *birmano (-a)*	Rangoon/Yangon *Rangún/Yangon*	kyat *kyat*
Burundi *Burundi*	Burundian *burundés (-esa)*	Bujumbura *Buyumbura*	Burundi franc *franco de Burundi*
Cambodia *Camboya*	Cambodian *camboyano (-a)*	Phnom Penh *Phnom Penh*	riel *riel*
Cameroon *Camerún (el)*	Cameroonian *camerunés (-esa)*	Yaoundé *Yaundé*	CFA franc *franco CFA*
Canada *Canadá (el)*	Canadian *canadiense*	Ottawa *Ottawa*	Canadian dollar *dólar canadiense*
Cape Verde *Cabo Verde*	Cape Verdean *caboverdiano (-a)*	Praia *Praia*	Cape Verde escudo *escudo de Cabo Verde*
Central African Republic *República Centroafricana (la)*	Central African *centroafricano (-a)*	Bangui *Bangui*	CFA franc *franco CFA*

Country País	Derivates Derivados	Capital Capital	Currency Moneda
Chad *Chad (el)*	Chadian *chadiano (-a)*	N'Djamena *Yamena*	CFA franc *franco CFA*
Chile *Chile*	Chilean *chileno (-a)*	Santiago de Chile *Santiago de Chile*	Chilean peso *peso chileno*
China *China*	Chinese *chino (-a)*	Beijing/Peking *Pekín*	yuan *yuan*
Colombia *Colombia*	Colombian *colombiano*	Bogota *Bogotá*	Colombian peso *peso colombiano*
Comoros *Comores (las)*	Comoran *comorano (-a)*	Moroni *Moroni*	Comoran franc *franco comorano*
Congo (Democratic Republic of the Congo) *Congo (República Democrática del Congo)*	Congolese *congoleño (-a)*	Kinshasa *Kinshasa*	Congolese franc *franco congoleño*
Congo (Republic of the Congo) *Congo (República del Congo)*	Congolese *congoleño (-a)*	Brazzaville *Brazzaville*	CFA franc *franco CFA*
Cook Islands *Islas Cook (las)*	Cook Islander *Cookiano (-a)*	Avarua *Avarua*	New Zealand dollar *dólar neozelandés*
Costa Rica *Costa Rica*	Costa Rican *costarricense*	San José *San José*	Costa Rican colón *colón costarricense*
Croatia *Croacia*	Croatian *croata*	Zagreb *Zagreb*	kuna *kuna*
Cuba *Cuba*	Cuban *cubano (-a)*	Havana *La Habana*	Cuban peso *peso cubano*
Cyprus *Chipre*	Cypriot *chipriota*	Nicosia *Nicosia*	Cypriot pound *libra chipriota*
Czech Republic *República Checa (la)*	Czech *checo (-a)*	Prague *Praga*	Czech koruna *corona checa*
Denmark *Dinamarca*	Danish *danés (-esa)*	Kopenhagen *Copenhague*	Danish krone *corona danesa*
Djibouti *Yibuti*	Djiboutian *yibutiano (-a)*	Djibouti *Yibuti*	Djiboutian franc *franco yibutiano*
Dominica *Dominica*	Dominican *dominiqués (-esa)*	Roseau *Roseau*	East Caribbean dollar *dólar del Caribe Oriental*
Dominican Republic *República Dominicana (la)*	Dominican *dominicano (-a)*	Santo Domingo *Santo Domingo*	Dominican peso *peso dominicano*
Ecuador *Ecuador (el)*	Ecuadorian *ecuatoriano (-a)*	Quito *Quito*	US dollar *dólar estadounidense*
Egypt *Egipto*	Egyptian *egipcio (-a)*	Cairo *El Cairo*	Egyptian pound *libra egipcia*
El Salvador *El Salvador*	Salvadoran *salvadoreño (-a)*	San Salvador *San Salvador*	US dollar *dólar estadounidense*
England (UK) *Inglaterra*	English *inglés (-esa)*	London *Londres*	pound sterling *libra esterlina*
Equatorial Guinea *Guinea Ecuatorial (la)*	Equatorial Guinean *ecuatoguineano (-a)*	Malab *Malabo*	CFA franc *franco CFA*

Country País	Derivates Derivados	Capital Capital	Currency Moneda
Eritrea *Eritrea*	Eritrean *eritreo (-a)*	Asmara *Asmara*	nafka *nafka*
Estonia *Estonia*	Estonian *estonio (-a)*	Tallinn *Tallin*	Estonian kroon *corona estonia*
Ethiopia *Etiopía*	Ethiopian *etíope*	Addis Abeba *Adís Abeba*	birr *birr*
Fiji *Islas Fiji (las)*	Fijian *fijiano (-a)*	Suva *Suva*	Fijian dollar *dólar de Fiji*
Finland *Finlandia*	Finnish *finlandés (-esa)* finés (-esa) [idioma]	Helsinki *Helsinki*	euro (formerly Finnish markka) *euro (antiguamente: marco finlandés)*
France *Francia*	French *francés (-esa)*	Paris *París*	euro (formerly French franc) *euro (antiguamente: franco francés)*
Gabon *Gabón (el)*	Gabonese *gabonés (-esa)*	Libreville *Libreville*	CFA franc *franco CFA*
Gambia *Gambia*	Gambian *gambiano (-a)*	Banjul *Banjul*	dalasi *dalasi*
Georgia *Georgia*	Georgian *georgiano (-a)*	Tbilisi/Tiflis *Tbilisi/Tiflis*	lari *lari georgiano*
Germany *Alemania*	German *alemán (-ana)*	Berlin *Berlín*	euro (formerly deutschmark) *euro (antiguamente: marco alemán)*
Ghana *Ghana*	Ghanaian *ghanés (-esa)*	Accra *Accra*	cedi *cedi*
Great Britain *Gran Bretaña (la)*	British *británico (-a)*	London *Londres*	pound sterling *libra esterlina*
Greece *Grecia*	Greek *griego (-a)*	Athens *Atenas*	euro (formerly drachma) *euro (antiguamente: dracma)*
Grenada *Granada*	Grenadian *granadino (-a)*	St. George's *Saint George*	East Caribbean dollar *dólar del Caribe Oriental*
Guatemala *Guatemala*	Guatemalan *guatemalteco (-a)*	Guatemala *Guatemala*	quetzal *quetzal*
Guinea *Guinea (la)*	Guinean *guineano (-a)*	Conakry *Conakry*	Guinean franc *franco guineano*
Guinea-Bissau *Guinea-Bissau*	guineano (-a) *Guinean*	Bissau *Bissau*	CFA franc *franco CFA*
Guyana *Guyana*	Guyanese *guyanés (-esa)*	Georgetown *Georgetown*	Guyanese dollar *dólar guyanés*
Haiti *Haití*	Haitian *haitiano (-a)*	Port-au-Prince *Puerto Príncipe*	gourde *gourde*
Honduras *Honduras*	Honduran *hondureño (-a)*	Tegucigalpa *Tegucigalpa*	lempira *lempira*

Country País	Derivates Derivados	Capital Capital	Currency Moneda
Hungary *Hungría*	Hungarian *húngaro (-a)*	Budapest *Budapest*	forint *forint*
Iceland *Islandia*	Icelandic *islandés (-esa)*	Reykjavik *Reykjavik*	Icelandic krona *corona islandesa*
India *India (la)*	Indian *indio (-a)*	New Delhi *Nueva Delhi*	rupee *rupia india*
Indonesia *Indonesia*	Indonesian *indonesio (-a)*	Jakarta *Yakarta*	rupiah *rupia indonesia*
Iran *Irán*	Iranian *iraní*	Tehran *Tehéran*	rial *rial iraní*
Iraq *Iraq/Irak*	Iraqi *iraquí*	Baghdad *Bagdad*	Iraqi dinar *dinar iraquí*
Ireland *Irlanda*	Irish *irlandés (-esa)*	Dublin *Dublín*	euro (formerly Irish pound) *euro (antiguamente: libra irlandesa)*
Israel *Israel*	Israeli *israelí*	Jerusalem *Jerusalén*	new shekel *nuevo shekel*
Italy *Italia*	Italian *italiano (-a)*	Rome *Roma*	euro (formerly lira) *euro (antiguamente: lira)*
Ivory Coast/ Côte d'Ivoire *Costa de Marfil*	Ivoirian *marfileño (-a)*	Yamoussoukro *Yamusukro*	CFA franc *franco CFA*
Jamaica *Jamaica*	Jamaican *jamaicano (-a)*	Kingston *Kingston*	Jamaican dollar *dólar jamaicano*
Japan *Japón*	Japanese *japonés (-esa)*	Tokyo *Tokio*	yen *yen*
Jordan *Jordania*	Jordanian *jordano (-a)*	Amman *Ammán*	Jordanian dinar *dinar jordano*
Kazakhstan *Kazajstán*	Kazakh *kazajo (-a)*	Astana *Astana*	tenge *tenge*
Kenya *Kenia*	Kenyan *keniano (-a)/keniata*	Nairobi *Nairobi*	Kenyan shilling *chelín de Kenia*
Kiribati *Kiribati*	*kiribatiano (-a)*	Bairiki *Bairiki*	Australian dollar *dólar australiano*
Kuwait *Kuwait*	Kuwaiti *kuwaití*	Kuwait City *Kuwait*	Kuwaiti dinar *dinar kuwaití*
Kyrgyzstan *Kirguizistán*	Kyrgyz *kirguiso (-a)/kirguís*	Bishkek *Bishkek*	Kyrgystani som *som*
Laos *Laos*	Laotian *laosiano (-a)*	Vientiane *Vientián*	kip *kip*
Latvia *Letonia*	Latvian *letón (-ona)*	Riga *Riga*	Lats *lats*
Lebanon *Líbano (el)*	Lebanese *libanés (-esa)*	Beirut *Beirut*	Lebanese pound *libra libanesa*
Lesotho *Lesoto*	Sotho *lesotense*	Maseru *Maseru*	loti *loti*
Liberia *Liberia*	Liberian *liberiano (-a)*	Monrovia *Monrovia*	Liberian dollar *dólar liberiano*

Country País	Derivates Derivados	Capital Capital	Currency Moneda
Libya *Libia*	Libyan *libio (-a)*	Tripoli *Trípoli*	Libyan dinar *dinar libio*
Liechtenstein *Liechtenstein*	Liechtensteiner *liechtensteiniano (-a)*	Vaduz *Vaduz*	Swiss franc *franco suizo*
Lithuania *Lituania*	Lithuanian *lituano (-a)*	Vilnius *Vilna*	litas *litas*
Luxembourg *Luxemburgo*	Luxembourg *luxemburgués (-esa)*	Luxembourg *Luxemburgo*	euro (formerly Luxembourg franc) *euro (antiguamente: franco luxemburgués)*
Macedonia (Former Yugoslav Republic of Macedonia) *Macedonia (Ex-República Yugoslava de Macedonia)*	Macedonian *macedonio (-a)*	Skopje *Skopje*	Macedonian denar *denar macedonio*
Madagascar *Madagascar*	Madagascan *malgache*	Antananarivo *Antananarivo*	Madagascan franc *franco malgache*
Malawi *Malawi*	Malawian *Malawí*	Lilongwe *Lilongwe*	Malawian kwacha *kwacha de Malawi*
Malaysia *Malasia*	Malaysian *malayo (-a)*	Kuala Lumpur *Kuala Lumpur*	Malaysian ringgit *ringgit*
Maldives *Maldivas (las)*	Maldivian *maldivo (-a)*	Malé *Malé*	rufiyaa *rufiyaa*
Mali *Mali/Malí*	Malian *malí*	Bamako *Bamako*	CFA franc *franco CFA*
Malta *Malta*	Maltese *maltés (-esa)*	Valletta *La Valeta*	Maltese lira *lira maltesa*
Marshall Islands *Islas Marshall (las)*	Marshall Islander *marshalés (-esa)*	Majuro *Majuro*	US dollar *dólar estadounidense*
Mauritania *Mauritania*	Mauritanian *mauritano (-a)*	Nouakchott *Nuakchot*	ouguiya *ouguiya*
Mauritius *Mauricio*	Mauritian *mauriciano (-a)*	Port Louis *Port Louis*	Mauritian rupee *rupia mauriciana*
Mexico *México*	Mexican *mexicano (-a)*	Mexico City *Mexico D. F.*	Mexican peso *peso mexicano*
Micronesia (Federated States of Micronesia) *Micronesia (la)*	Micronesian *micronesio (-a)*	Palikir *Palikir*	US dollar *dólar estadounidense*
Moldavia *Moldavia*	Moldavian *moldavo (-a)*	Chişinău *Chisinau*	Moldavian leu *leu*
Monaco *Mónaco*	Monegasque *monegasco (-a)*	Monaco-Ville *Mónaco*	euro (formerly French franc) *euro (antiguamente: franco francés)*
Mongolia *Mongolia*	Mongolian *mongol (-a)*	Ulaanbaatar *Ulán-Bator*	tugrik *tugrik*
Morocco *Marruecos*	Moroccan *marroquí*	Rabat *Rabat*	dirham *dirham marroquí*
Mozambique *Mozambique*	Mozambican *mozambiqueño (-a)*	Maputo *Maputo*	metical *metical*

Country País	Derivates Derivados	Capital Capital	Currency Moneda
Myanmar/Burma *Myanmar/Birmania*	Burmese *birmano (-a)*	Rangoon/Yangon *Rangún/Yangon*	kyat *kyat*
Namibia *Namibia*	Namibian *namibio (-a)*	Windhoek *Windhoek*	Namibian dollar *dólar namibio*
Nauru *Nauru*	Nauruan *nauruano (-a)*	Yaren *Yaren*	Australian dollar *dólar australiano*
Nepal *Nepal (el)*	Nepalese *nepalés (-esa)/nepalí*	Kathmandu *Katmandú*	Nepalese rupee *rupia nepalí*
Netherlands *Países Bajos (los)*	Dutch *neerlandés (-esa)*	Amsterdam *Amsterdam*	euro (formerly gulden) *euro (antiguamente: florín neerlandés)*
New Zealand *Nueva Zelanda*	New Zealander *neozelandés (-esa)*	Wellington *Wellington*	New Zealand dollar *dólar neozelandés*
Nicaragua *Nicaragua*	Nicaraguan *nicaragüense*	Managua *Managua*	córdoba *córdoba oro*
Niger *Níger*	Nigerois *nigerino (-a)*	Niamey *Niamey*	CFA franc *franco CFA*
Nigeria *Nigeria*	Nigerian *nigeriano (-a)*	Abuja *Abuja*	naira *naira*
North Korea *Corea del Norte*	North Korean *norcoreano (-a)*	Pyongyang *Pyongyang*	won *won*
Northern Ireland (UK) *Irlanda del Norte*	Northern Irish *norirlandés (-esa)*	Belfast *Belfast*	pound sterling *libra esterlina*
Norway *Noruega*	Norwegian *noruego (-a)*	Oslo *Oslo*	Norwegian krone *corona noruega*
Oman *Omán*	Omani *omaní*	Muscat *Mascate*	Omani rial *rial omaní*
Pakistan *Pakistán*	Pakistani *pakistaní*	Islamabad *Islamabad*	Pakistani rupee *rupia pakistaní*
Palau *Palau*	Palauan *palauano (-a)*	Koror *Koror*	US dollar *dólar estadounidense*
Panama *Panamá*	Panamanian *panameño (-a)*	Panama City *Panamá*	balboa *balboa*
Papua New Guinea *Papúa Nueva Guinea*	Papuan *papú*	Port Moresby *Port Moresby*	kina *kina*
Paraguay *Paraguay (el)*	Paraguayan *paraguayo (-a)*	Asunción *Asunción*	guaraní *guaraní*
Peru *Perú (el)*	Peruvian *peruano (-a)*	Lima *Lima*	nuevo sol *nuevo sol*
Philippines *Filipinas (las)*	Philippine, Filipino *filipino (-a)*	Manila *Manila*	Philippines peso *peso filipino*
Poland *Polonia*	Polish *polaco (-a)*	Warsaw *Varsovia*	zloty *zloty*
Portugal *Portugal*	Portuguese *portugués (-esa)*	Lisbon *Lisboa*	euro (formerly escudo) *euro (antiguamente: escudo)*
Puerto Rico (USA) *Puerto Rico (EE.UU.)*	Puerto Rican *puertorriqueño (-a)*	San Juan *San Juan*	US dollar *dólar estadounidense*
Qatar *Qatar*	Qatari *qatarí*	Doha *Doha*	Qatari riyal *rial de Qatar*

Country País	Derivates Derivados	Capital Capital	Currency Moneda
Romania *Rumanía*	Romanian *rumano (-a)*	Bucharest *Bucarest*	leu (pl. lei) *leu*
Russia (Russian Federation) *Rusia*	Russian *ruso (-a)*	Moscow *Moscú*	ruble *rublo*
Rwanda *Ruanda*	Rwandan *ruandés (-esa)*	Kigali *Kigali*	Rwandan franc *franco ruandés*
Samoa *Samoa*	Samoan *samoano (-a)*	Apia *Apia*	tala *tala*
San Marino *San Marino*	San Marinese *sanmarinense*	San Marino *San Marino*	euro (formerly lira) *euro (antiguamente: lira)*
Sao Tomé and Príncipe *Santo Tomé y Príncipe*	Sao Tomean *santotomense*	São Tomé *Santo Tomé*	dobra *dobra*
Saudi Arabia *Arabia Saudí/Arabia Saudita*	Saudi Arabian *saudí/saudita*	Riyadh *Riad*	Saudi riyal *riyal saudí*
Scotland (GB) *Escocia*	Scottish *escocés (-esa)*	Edinburgh *Edimburgo*	pound sterling *libra esterlina*
Senegal *Senegal (el)*	Senegalese *senegalés (-esa)*	Dakar *Dakar*	CFA franc *franco CFA*
Serbia and Montenegro *Serbia y Montenegro*	Serbian-Montenegran *serbiomontenegrino (-a)*	Belgrade *Belgrado*	Serbian dinar, Euro *dinar serbio, euro*
Seychelles *Seychelles (las)*	Seychellois *seychelense*	Victoria *Victoria*	Seychelles rupee *rupia de Seychelles*
Sierra Leone *Sierra Leona*	Sierra Leonean *sierraleonés*	Freetown *Freetown*	leone *leone*
Singapore *Singapur*	Singaporean *singapurense*	Singapore *Singapur*	Singapore dollar *dólar de Singapur*
Slovakia/Slovak Republic *Eslovaquia*	Slovak *eslovaco (-a)*	Bratislava *Bratislava*	Slovak koruna *corona eslovaca*
Slovenia *Eslovenia*	Slovene, Slovenian *esloveno (-a)*	Ljubljana *Liubliana*	tolar *tolar*
Solomon Islands *Islas Salomón (las)*	Solomon Islander *salomonense*	Honiara *Honiara*	Salomon dollar *dólar de las Islas Salomón*
Somalia *Somalia*	Somali *somalí*	Mogadishu *Mogadiscio*	Somalian shilling *chelín somalí*
South Africa *Sudáfrica*	South African *sudafricano (-a)*	Pretoria *Pretoria*	rand *rand*
South Korea *Corea del Sur*	South Korean *surcoreano (-a)*	Seoul *Seúl*	won *won*
Spain *España*	Spanish *español (a)*	Madrid *Madrid*	euro (formerly peseta) *euro (antiguamente: peseta)*
Sri Lanka *Sri Lanka*	Sri Lankan *esrilanqués (-esa)/ ceilandés (-esa)*	Colombo *Colombo*	Sri Lankan rupee *rupia de Sri Lanka*

Country País	Derivates Derivados	Capital Capital	Currency Moneda
St. Kitts and Nevis *San Cristóbal y Nieves*	Kittsian, Nevisian *sancristobaleño (-a)*	Basseterre *Basseterre*	East Caribbean dollar *dólar del Caribe Oriental*
St. Lucia *Santa Lucía*	St. Lucian *santalucense*	Castries *Castries*	East Caribbean dollar *dólar del Caribe Oriental*
St. Vincent and the Grenadines *San Vicente y las Granadinas*	Saint Vincentian *sanvicentino (-a)*	Kingstown *Kingstown*	East Caribbean dollar *dólar del Caribe Oriental*
Sudan *Sudán (el)*	Sudanese *sudanés (-esa)*	Khartoum *Jartum*	Sudanese pound *libra sudanesa*
Suriname *Surinam*	Surinamese *surinamés (-esa)*	Paramaribo *Paramaribo*	Surinamese gulden *florín surinamés*
Swaziland *Suazilandia*	Swazi *suazi*	Mbabane *Mbabane*	lilangeni *lilangeni*
Sweden *Suecia*	Swedish *sueco (-a)*	Stockholm *Estocolmo*	Swedish krone *corona sueca*
Switzerland *Suiza*	Swiss *suizo (-a)*	Berne *Berna*	Swiss franc *franco suizo*
Syria *Siria*	Syrian *sirio (-a)*	Damaskus *Damasco*	Syrian pound *libra siria*
Taiwan *Taiwán*	Taiwanese *taiwanés*	Taipei *Taipei*	Taiwanese dollar *dólar de Taiwán*
Tajikistan *Tayikistán*	Tajik *tayiko (-a)*	Dushanbe *Dusambé*	ruble *rublo tayiko*
Tanzania *Tanzania*	Tanzanian *tanzano (-a)*	Dodoma (Dar es Salaam) *Dodoma (Dar es Salaam)*	Tanzanian shilling *chelín tanzano*
Thailand *Tailandia*	Thai *tailandés (-esa)*	Bangkok *Bangkok*	baht *baht*
Togo *Togo (el)*	Togolese *togolés (-esa)*	Lomé *Lomé*	CFA franc *franco CFA*
Tonga *Tonga*	Tongan *tongano (-a)*	Nuku'alofa *Nuku'alofa*	pa'anga *pa'anga*
Trinidad and Tobago *Trinidad y Tobago*	Trinidadian, Tobagan *trinitense, tobaguense*	Port of Spain *Puerto España*	Trinidad and Tobago dollar *dólar de Trinidad y Tobago*
Tunisia *Túnez*	Tunisian *tunecino (-a)*	Tunis *Túnez*	Tunisian dinar *dinar tunecino*
Turkey *Turquía*	Turkish *turco (-a)*	Ankara *Ankara*	Turkish lira *lira turca*
Turkmenistan *Turkmenistán*	Turkmen *turkmeno (-a)/turcomano (-a)*	Ashgabat *Ashjabad*	manat *manat turcomano*
Tuvalu *Tuvalu*	Tuvaluan *tuvaluano (-a)*	Funafuti *Funafuti*	Australian dollar *dólar australiano*
Uganda *Uganda*	Ugandan *ugandés (-esa)*	Kampala *Kampala*	Ugandan shilling *chelín ugandés*

Country País	Derivates Derivados	Capital Capital	Currency Moneda
Ukraine *Ucrania*	Ukrainian *ucraniano (-a)*	Kiev *Kiev*	hryvnia *hrivnia*
United Arab Emirates *Emiratos Árabes Unidos (los)*	(United Arab) Emir-ation *emiratense*	Abu Dhabi *Abu Dhabi*	dirham *dirhan emiral*
United Kingdom *Reino Unido (el)*	UK/British *británico (-a)*	London *Londres*	pound sterling *libra esterlina*
United States of America/USA *Estados Unidos de América (los)*	American *estadounidense*	Washington D. C. *Washington D. C.*	US dollar *dólar estadounidense*
Uruguay *Uruguay (el)*	Uruguayan *uruguayo (-a)*	Montevideo *Montevideo*	Uruguayan peso *peso uruguayo*
USA *EE. UU.*	American *estadounidense*	Washington D. C. *Washington D. C.*	US dollar *dólar estadounidense*
Uzbekistan *Uzbekistán*	Uzbek *uzbeko (-a)*	Tashkent *Tashkent*	Uzbek sum *sum*
Vanuatu *Vanuatu*	Vanuatian *vanuatense*	Port Vila *Port Vila*	vatu *vatu*
Vatican City *Ciudad del Vaticano*	Vatican *vaticano (-a)*		euro (formerly lira) *euro (antiguamente: lira)*
Venezuela *Venezuela*	Venezuelan *venezolano (-a)*	Caracas *Caracas*	bolivar *bolívar*
Vietnam *Vietnam*	Vietnamese *vietnamita*	Hanoi *Hanói*	dong *dong*
Wales (GB) *País de Gales (el)*	Welsh *galés (-esa)*	Cardiff *Cardiff*	pound sterling *libra esterlina*
Yemen *Yemen (el)*	Yemeni *yemení*	Sanaa *Saná*	Yemeni rial *riyal*
Yugoslavia HIST *see Serbia and Montenegro*	Yugoslav *yugoslavo (-a)*	Belgrade *Belgrado*	Yugoslav dinar *dinar yugoslavo*
Zambia *Zambia*	Zambian *zambiano (-a)*	Lusaka *Lusaka*	kwacha *kwacha zambiano*
Zimbabwe *Zimbabue*	Zimbabwean *zimbabuense*	Harare *Harare*	Zimbabwean dollar *dólar de Zimbabue*

* Franco CFA = Franco de la Comunidad Financiera Africana

Continents, Islands, Oceans, Seas, Lakes, Rivers, Gulfs, and Mountains – Continentes, islas, océanos, mares, lagos, ríos, golfos y montañas

Continents
Continentes

Africa *África*	Eurasia *Eurasia*
America *América*	Europe *Europa*
Antarctica *Antártida (la)*	North America *América del Norte*
Asia *Asia*	South America *América del Sur*
Central America *América Central*	

Islands
Islas

Aleutian Islands *Islas Aleutianas (las)*	Corfu *Corfú*
Antigua *Antigua*	Crete *Creta*
Antilles *Antillas (las)*	Curaçao *Curaçao*
Aruba *Aruba*	East Indies *Indias Orientales (las)*
Azores *Azores (las)*	Easter Island *Isla de Pascua (la)*
Baffin Island *Tierra de Baffin (la)*	Falkland Islands *Islas Malvinas (las)*
Balearic Islands *Islas Baleares (las)*	Faroe Islands *Islas Feroe (las)*
Bali *Bali*	Galapagos Islands *Islas Galápagos (las)*
Bermuda *Bermudas (las)*	Greater Antilles *Antillas Mayores (las)*
Borneo *Borneo*	Greenland *Groenlandia*
Canary Islands *Islas Canarias (las)*	Guadalcanal *Guadalcanal*
Cape Verde Islands *Islas de Cabo Verde (las)*	Guadeloupe *Guadalupe*
Caroline Islands *Islas Carolinas (las)*	Guam *Guam*
Celebes *Célebes*	Hebrides *Hébridas (las)*
Channel Islands *Islas del Canal (las)*	Hispaniola *La Española*
Comoros *Comores (las)*	Hokkaido *Hokkaido*

Honshu *Honshu*	Okinawa *Okinawa*
Iceland *Islandia*	Orkney Islands *Orcadas (las)*
Iwo Jima *Iwo Jima*	Prince Edward Island *Isla del Príncipe Eduardo (la)*
Java *Java*	Réunion *Reunión*
Kyushu *Kyushu*	Rhodes *Rodas*
Leeward Islands *Islas de Sotavento (las)*	Ryukyu Islands *Ryukyu*
Lesser Antilles *Antillas Menores (las)*	Sakhalin *Sajalín*
Leyte *Leyte*	Shetland Islands *Islas Shetland (las)*
Long Island *Long Island*	Shikoku *Shikoku*
Luzon *Luzón*	Solomon Islands *Islas Salomón (las)*
Madagascar *Madagascar*	Sumatra *Sumatra*
Madeira Islands *Islas Madeira (las)*	Tahiti *Tahití*
Majorca *Mallorca*	Tasmania *Tasmania*
Maldive Islands *Maldivas (las)*	Tierra del Fuego *Tierra del Fuego (la)*
Isle of Man *Isla de Man (la)*	Timor *Timor*
Mariana Islands *Islas Marianas (las)*	Vancouver Island *Isla de Vancouver*
Marquesas Islands *Islas Marquesas (las)*	Victoria Island *Isla Victoria (la)*
Marshall Islands *Islas Marshall (las)*	Virgin Islands *Islas Vírgenes (las)*
Martinique *Martinica*	West Indies *Antillas (las)*
Mindanao *Mindanao*	Windward Islands *Islas de Barlovento (las)*
Minorca *Menorca*	Zanzibar *Zanzíbar*

Oceans
Océanos

Arctic Ocean *océano Glacial Ártico (el)*	Pacific Ocean *océano Pacífico (el)*
Atlantic Ocean *océano Atlántico (el)*	Southern Ocean, Antarctic Ocean *océano Glacial Antártico (el)*
Indian Ocean *océano Índico (el)*	

Seas
Mares

Adriatic Sea *mar Adriático (el)*	Irish Sea *mar de Irlanda (el)*
Aegean Sea *mar Egeo (el)*	Sea of Japan *mar del Japón (el)/mar Oriental (el)*
Arabian Sea *mar Arábigo (el)/mar de Arabia (el)*	Mediterranean Sea *mar Mediterráneo (el)*
Aral Sea *mar de Aral (el)*	North Sea *mar del Norte (el)*
Sea of Azov *mar de Azov (el)*	Sea of Okhotsk *mar de Ojotsk (el)*
Baltic Sea *mar Báltico (el)*	Red Sea *mar Rojo (el)*
Bering Sea *mar de Bering (el)*	Sargasso Sea *mar de los Sargazos (el)*
Black Sea *mar Negro (el)*	South China Sea *mar de la China meridional (el)*
Caribbean Sea *mar Caribe (el)/mar de las Antillas (el)*	Tasman Sea *mar de Tasmania (el)*
Caspian Sea *mar Caspio (el)*	White Sea *mar Blanco (el)*
Dead Sea *mar Muerto (el)*	Yellow Sea *mar Amarillo (el)*
East China Sea *mar de la China oriental (el)*	

Lakes
Lagos

Albert (Nyanza) *lago Alberto (el)*	Ladoga *lago Ladoga (el)*
Baikal *lago Baikal (el)*	Michigan *lago Michigan (el)*
Chad *lago Chad (el)*	Nyasa/Malawi *lago Malawi (el)*
Erie *lago Erie (el)*	Onega *lago Onega (el)*
Geneva *lago Ginebra (el)/lago Léman (el)*	Ontario *lago Ontario (el)*
Great Bear *Gran Lago de los Osos (el)*	Superior *lago Superior (el)*
Great Lakes *Grandes Lagos (los)*	Tanganyika *lago Tanganica (el)*
Great Salt *Gran Lago Salado (el)*	Titicaca *lago Titicaca (el)*
Great Slave *Gran Lago de los Esclavos (el)*	Victoria *lago Victoria (el)*
Huron *lago Hurón (el)*	

Rivers
Ríos

Amazon *Amazonas (el)*	Nile *Nilo (el)*
Amur *Amur (el)*	Ob *Obi (el)*
Columbia *Columbia (el)*	Oder *Oder (el)*
Congo *Congo (el)*	Ohio *Ohio (el)*
Danube *Danubio (el)*	Orinoco *Orinoco (el)*
Delaware *Delaware (el)*	Paraná *Paraná (el)*
Dnieper *Dniéper (el)*	Po *Po (el)*
Dniester *Dniéster (el)*	Potomac *Potomac (el)*
Don *Don (el)*	Rhine *Rin (el)*
Elbe *Elba (el)*	Rhône *Ródano (el)*
Euphrates *Éufrates (el)*	Rio Grande *(Río) Bravo (el)*
Ganges *Ganges (el)*	St. Lawrence *San Lorenzo (el)*
Huang Ho/Yellow River *Huang Ho (el)/(río) Amarillo (el)*	Seine *Sena (el)*
Hudson *Hudson (el)*	Susquehanna *Susquehanna (el)*
Indus *Indo (el)*	Thames *Támesis (el)*
Irrawaddy *Irrawaddy (el)*	Tigris *Tigris (el)*
Irtysh *Irtísh (el)*	Ural *Ural (el)*
Jordan *Jordán (el)*	Vistula *Vístula (el)*
Lena *Lena (el)*	Volga *Volga (el)*
Loire *Loira (el)*	Volta *Volta (el)*
Mackenzie *Mackenzie (el)*	Yangtze *Yangtzé (el)*
Mekong *Mekong (el)*	Yellow *(río) Amarillo (el)/Huang Ho (el)*
Mississippi *Mississippi (el)*	Yenisei *Yeniséi (el)*
Missouri *Missouri (el)*	Yukon *Yukón (el)*
Niger *Níger (el)*	Zambezi *Zambeze (el)*

Gulfs, Bays, Straits, Canals
Golfos, Bahías, Estrechos, Canales

Gulf of Aden *golfo de Adén (el)*	Hudson Bay *bahía de Hudson (la)*
Bay of Bengal *golfo de Bengala (el)*	Strait of Magellan *estrecho de Magallanes (el)*
Bering Strait *estrecho de Bering (el)*	Gulf of Mexico *golfo de México (el)*
Bay of Biscay *mar Cantábrico (el)*	Panama Canal *canal de Panamá (el)*
Bosporus *Bósforo (el)*	Persian Gulf *golfo Pérsico (el)*
Gulf of California *golfo de California (el)*	Gulf of St. Lawrence *golfo de San Lorenzo (el)*
English Channel *canal de la Mancha (el)*	St. Lawrence Seaway *canal de San Lorenzo (el)*
Straits of Florida *estrecho de Florida (el)*	Suez Canal *canal de Suez (el)*
Strait of Gibraltar *estrecho de Gibraltar (el)*	

Mountain Ranges
Montañas

Adirondack Mountains *Adirondack (las)*	Catskill Mountains *Catskill (los)*
Allegheny Mountains *Allegheny (las)*	Caucasus *Cáucaso (el)*
Alps *Alpes (los)*	Himalaya Mountains/Himalayas *Himalaya (el)*
Andes *Andes (los)*	Pyrenees *Pirineos (los)*
Appalachian Mountains *(montes) Apalaches (los)*	Rocky Mountains *(montañas) Rocosas (las)*
Balkans *Balcanes (los)*	Sierra Nevada *Sierra Nevada*
Carpathian Mountains *Cárpatos (los)*	St. Elias Mountains *(montes) San Elías (los)*
Cascade Range *cordillera de las Cascadas (la)*	Ural Mountains *(montes) Urales (los)*

Mountain Peaks
Picos

Aconcagua (Andes) *Aconcagua (el)*	Fujiyama *Monte Fuji (el)*
Elbrus *Elbrús (el)*	Kilimanjaro *(monte) Kilimanjaro (el)*
Etna *Etna (el)*	Logan *(monte) Logan (el)*
Everest *Everest (el)*	McKinley *McKinley (el)*

Mauna Loa *Mauna Loa (el)*	Orizaba *(pico de) Orizaba (el)*
Mont Blanc *Mont Blanc (el)*	Pike's Peak *Pikes Peak (el)*
Monte Rosa *(monte) Rosa (el)*	Popocatepetl *Popocatépetl (el)*
Matterhorn *Matterhorn (el)/Cervino (el)*	

España
Spain

Capital: Madrid

comunidad autónoma *autonomous region*	capital *capital city*
Andalucía *Andalusia*	Sevilla *Seville*
Aragón	Zaragoza
Asturias	Oviedo
Baleares *Balearic Islands*	Palma de Mallorca
Canarias *Canary Islands*	Santa Cruz de Tenerife
Cantabria	Santander
Castilla y León	Valladolid
Castilla-La Mancha	Toledo
Cataluña *Catalonia*	Barcelona
Extremadura	Mérida
Galicia	Santiago de Compostela
La Rioja	Logroño
Comunidad de Madrid	**Madrid**
Murcia	Murcia
Navarra	Pamplona
País Vasco *Basque Country*	Vitoria
Comunidad Valenciana	Valencia

Hispanoamérica
Spanish America

país *country*	capital *capital city*
Argentina	Buenos Aires
Bolivia	La Paz
Chile	Santiago
Colombia	Bogotá
Costa Rica	San José
Cuba	La Habana *Havana*
Ecuador	Quito
El Salvador	San Salvador
Guatemala	Guatemala *Guatemala City*
Honduras	Tegucigalpa

país *country*	capital *capital city*
México *Mexico*	Ciudad de México D.F. *Mexico City*
Nicaragua	Managua
Panamá *Panama*	Panamá *Panama City*
Paraguay	Asunción
Perú *Peru*	Lima
Puerto Rico	San Juan
República Dominicana *Dominican Republic*	Santo Domingo
Uruguay	Montevideo
Venezuela	Caracas

The United States of America – States, abbreviations, nicknames, inhabitants and capital cities
Estados Unidos de América – Estados, abreviaturas, apodos, habitantes y capitales

Capital: Washington, D.C.

state *estado*	abbreviation *abreviatura*	nickname *apodo*	inhabitant *habitante*	capital city *capital*
Alabama	Ala., AL	Yellow Hammer State Heart of Dixie	Alabamian *alabamiano, -a* *alabamiense*	Montgomery
Alaska	Alas., AK	The Last Frontier	Alaskan *alasqueño, -a* *alaskeño, -a* *alask(i)ano, -a* *alaskense*	Juneau
Arizona	Ariz., AZ	Grand Canyon State	Arizonan *arizoniano, -a* *arizonense*	Phoenix
Arkansas	Ark., AR	Land of Opportunity	Arkansan *arkansano, -a* *arkansino, -a*	Little Rock
California	Calif., CA	Golden State	Californian *californiano, -a*	Sacramento
Colorado	Colo., CO	Centennial State	Coloradoan Coloradan *coloradino, -a* *coloradense*	Denver
Connecticut	Conn., CT	Constitution State Nutmeg State	Nutmegger; (Connecticut) Yankee *conectiqués, -esa*	Hartford
Delaware	Del., DE	First State Diamond State	Delawarean *delawareño, -a*	Dover

state *estado*	abbreviation *abreviatura*	nickname *apodo*	inhabitant *habitante*	capital city *capital*
Florida	Fla., FL	Sunshine State	Floridian *floridano, -a*	Tallahassee
Georgia	Ga., GA	Empire State of the South Peach State	Georgian *georgiano, -a*	Atlanta
Hawaii *Hawái*	HI	Aloha State Paradise of the Pacific	Hawaiian *hawaiano, -a*	Honolulu *Honolulú*
Idaho	Id., ID	Gem State	Idahoan *idahoano, -a*	Boise
Illinois	Ill., IL	Prairie State	Illinoisan *ilinoisiano, -a*	Springfield
Indiana	Ind., IN	Hoosier State	Indianan Hoosier *indianense*	Indianapolis *Indianápolis*
Iowa	Ia., IA	Hawkeye State	Iowan *iowense* *iowano, -a*	Des Moines
Kansas	Kans., KS	Sunflower State	Kansan *kanseño, -a* *kansense*	Topeka
Kentucky	Ky., KY	Bluegrass State	Kentuckian *kentuckiano, -a*	Frankfort
Louisiana *Luisiana*	La., LA	Pelican State	Louisianan *luisiano, -a*	Baton Rouge
Maine	Me., ME	Pine Tree State	Mainer *mainés, -esa*	Augusta
Maryland	Md., MD	Old Line State	Marylander *marilandés, -esa*	Annapolis *Anápolis*
Massachusetts	Mass., MA	Bay State	New Englander Bay Stater *massachusetano, -a*	Boston
Michigan	Mich., MI	Wolverine State Lake State	Michiganian Michigander *michigano, -a* *michiganense*	Lansing
Minnesota	Minn., MN	Gopher State North Star State	Minnesotan *min(n)esotano, -a*	Saint Paul *San Pablo*
Mississippi *Misisipí*	Miss., MS	Magnolia State	Mississippian *misisipiano, -a* *misisipiense*	Jackson
Missouri *Misuri*	Mo., MO	Show Me State	Missourian *misuriano, -a*	Jefferson City
Montana	Mont., MT	Treasure State Big Sky Country	Montanan *montanés, -esa*	Helena
Nebraska	Nebr., NE	Corn Husker State	Nebraskan *nebrascano, -a* *nebraskano, -a* *nebraskeño, -a* *nebrasqueño, -a*	Lincoln

state *estado*	abbreviation *abreviatura*	nickname *apodo*	inhabitant *habitante*	capital city *capital*
Nevada	Nev., NV	Sagebrush State Silver State	Nevadan *nevadeño, -a* *nevadense*	Carson City
New Hampshire *Nueva Hampshire*	N.H., NH	Granite State	New Hampshirite *neohampshireño, -a*	Concord
New Jersey *Nueva Jersey*	N.J., NJ	Garden State	New Jerseyite New Jersian *neojerseíta*	Trenton
New Mexico *Nuevo México*	N.M., NM	Land of Enchant- ment	New Mexican *neomexicano, -a*	Santa Fe
New York *Nueva York*	N.Y., NY	Empire State	New Yorker *neoyorquino, -a*	Albany
North Carolina *Carolina del Norte*	N.C., NC	Tarheel State Old North State	North Carolinian *norcarolino, -a*	Raleigh
North Dakota *Dakota del Norte*	N.D., ND	Sioux State Peace Garden State Flickertail State	North Dakotan *nordakoteño, -a*	Bismarck
Ohio	O., OH	Buckeye State	Ohioan *ohioano, -a*	Columbus
Oklahoma	Okla., OK	Sooner State	Oklahoman *oklahomense* *oklahomeño, -a*	Oklahoma City
Oregon *Oregón*	Ore., OR	Beaver State	Oregonian *oregoniano, -a* *oregonés, -esa* *oregonense*	Salem
Pennsylvania *Pensilvania*	Pa., PA	Keystone State	Pennsylvanian *pensilvan(ian)o, -a* *pensilvaniense*	Harrisburg
Rhode Island	R.I., RI	Ocean State Little Rhody	Rhode Islander *rodislandés, -esa*	Providence
South Carolina *Carolina del Sur*	S.C., SC	Palmetto State	South Carolinian *surcarolino, -a*	Columbia
South Dakota *Dakota del Sur*	S.D., SD	Coyote State Sunshine State	South Dakotan *surdakoteño, -a*	Pierre
Tennessee	Tenn., TN	Volunteer State	Tennessean *tennesiano, -a*	Nashville
Texas *Texas/Tejas*	Tex., TX	Lone Star State	Texan *tejano, -a* *texano, -a*	Austin
Utah	Ut., UT	Beehive State Mormon State	Utahn, Utahan *Utaheño, -a*	Salt Lake City
Vermont	Vt., VT	Green Mountain State	Vermonter *vermontés, -esa*	Montpelier
Virginia	Va., VA	Old Dominion Mother of Presidents Mother of States	Virginian *virginiano, -a*	Richmond
Washington	Wash., WA	Evergreen State	Washingtonian *washingtoniano, -a*	Olympia

state estado	abbreviation abreviatura	nickname apodo	inhabitant habitante	capital city capital
West Virginia Virginia Occidental	W.V., WV	Mountain State	West Virginian virginiano, -a del oeste	Charleston
Wisconsin	Wis., WI	Badger State	Wisconsinite wisconsinita	Madison
Wyoming	Wyo., WY	Equality State	Wyomingite Wyominguita	Cheyenne

Territories and Districts
Territorios y distritos

Territory/District Territorio/Distrito	Abbreviation Abreviatura
American Samoa Samoa Americana	AS
District of Columbia Distrito de Columbia (asiento del Gobierno Federal)	DC
Guam	GU
Northern Mariana Islands Islas Marianas del Norte	MP
Puerto Rico	PR
United States Virgin Islands Islas Vírgenes de los Estados Unidos	VI

Nicknames of some of the cities in the US
Apodos de algunas ciudades estadounidenses

city ciudad	nickname apodo
Chicago	The Windy City
Denver	The Mile-High City
Detroit	Motor City
New York	The Big Apple, Gotham
Los Angeles	The City of the Angels, The Big Orange
Minneapolis and St. Paul	Twin Cities
New Orleans	The Big Easy
Philadelphia	The City of Brotherly Love

Canada
El Canadá

Capital: Ottawa

province *provincia*	abbreviation *abreviatura*	capital city *capital*
Alberta	Alta., AB	Edmonton
British Columbia *Columbia Británica*	B.C., BC	Victoria
Manitoba	Man., MB	Winnipeg
New Brunswick *Nuevo Brunswick*	N.B., NB	Fredericton
Newfoundland *Terranova*	Nfld., NF	St. John's *San Juan*
Nova Scotia *Nueva Escocia*	N.S., NS	Halifax
Ontario	Ont., ON	Toronto
Prince Edward Island *Isla del Príncipe Eduardo*	P.E.I., PE	Charlottetown
Québec *Quebec*	Que., PQ	Québec *Quebec*
Saskatchewan	Sask, SK	Regina

territory *territorio*	abbreviation *abreviatura*	capital city *capital*
North West Territories *Territorios del Noroeste*	N.W.T., NT	Yellowknife
Nunavut Territory (*since 1st April 1999*) *Territorio del Nunavut*	NU	Iqaluit
Yukon Territory *Territorio del Yukón*	Y.T., YT	Whitehorse

Símbolos y abreviaturas

Symbols and abbreviations

bloque fraseológico	▶	idiom block
contracción	=	contraction
corresponde a	≈	approximate equivalent
cambio de interlocutor	−	change of speaker
marca registrada	®	trademark
	◆	phrasal verb
	1st pers	1st person
	3rd pers	3rd person
	a.	also
abreviación de	*abr de, abbr of*	abbreviation of
adjetivo	*adj*	adjective
administración	ADMIN	administration
adverbio	*adv*	adverb
agricultura	AGR	agriculture
América Central	A*m*C	
América Latina	A*m*L	
América del Sur	AmS	
anatomía	ANAT	anatomy
Zona Andina	*And*	
Antillas	*Ant*	
argot	*argot*	
arquitectura	ARCHIT, ARQUIT	architecture
República Argentina	Arg	
artículo	*art*	article
arte	ART	art
astronomía, astrología	ASTR	astronomy, astrology
automóvil y tráfico	AUTO	automobile, transport
verbo auxiliar	*aux*	auxiliary verb
aviación, tecnología espacial	AVIAT	aviation, aerospace, space technology
biología	BIO	biology
Bolivia	*Bol*	
botánica	BOT	botany
	Can	Canadian English
	CHEM	chemistry
Chile	*Chile*	
cine	CINE	cinema
Colombia	*Col*	
comercio	COM	commerce
comparativo	*comp*	comparative
computadores	COMPUT	computing
conjunción	*conj*	conjunction
Costa Rica	*CRi*	

Cono Sur (República Argentina, Chile, Paraguay, Uruguay)	*CSur*	
Cuba	*Cuba*	
culinaria	CULIN	culinary
definido	*def*	definite
demostrativo	*dem*	demonstrative
deporte	DEP	
República Domenicana	*DomR*	
ecología	ECOL	ecology
economía	ECON	economics
Ecuador	*Ecua*	
electrotécnica, electrónica	ELEC	electricity, electronics
elevado, literario	*elev*	
El Salvador	*ElSal*	
enseñanza	ENS	
	EU	European Union
feminino	*f*	feminine
	FASHION	fashion and sewing
ferrocarril	FERRO	
figurativo	*fig*	figurative
Filipinas	*Fili*	
filosofía	FILOS	
finanzas, bolsa	FIN	finance, banking, stock exchange
física	FÍS	
	form	formal language
fotografía	FOTO	
	GAMES	games
geografía, geología	GEO	geography, geology
Guatemala	*Guat*	
Guayana	*Guay*	
Guinea Ecuatorial	*GuinEc*	
historia, histórico	HIST	history, historical
Honduras	*Hond*	
imperativo	*imper*	imperative
impersonal	*impers*	impersonal
indefinido	*indef*	indefinite
lenguaje informal	*inf*	informal language
infinitivo	*infin*	infinitive
	insep	inseparable
interjección	*interj*	interjection
interrogativo	*interrog*	interrogative
invariable	*inv*	invariable
irónico, humorístico	*iron, irón*	ironic, humorous
irregular	*irr*	irregular